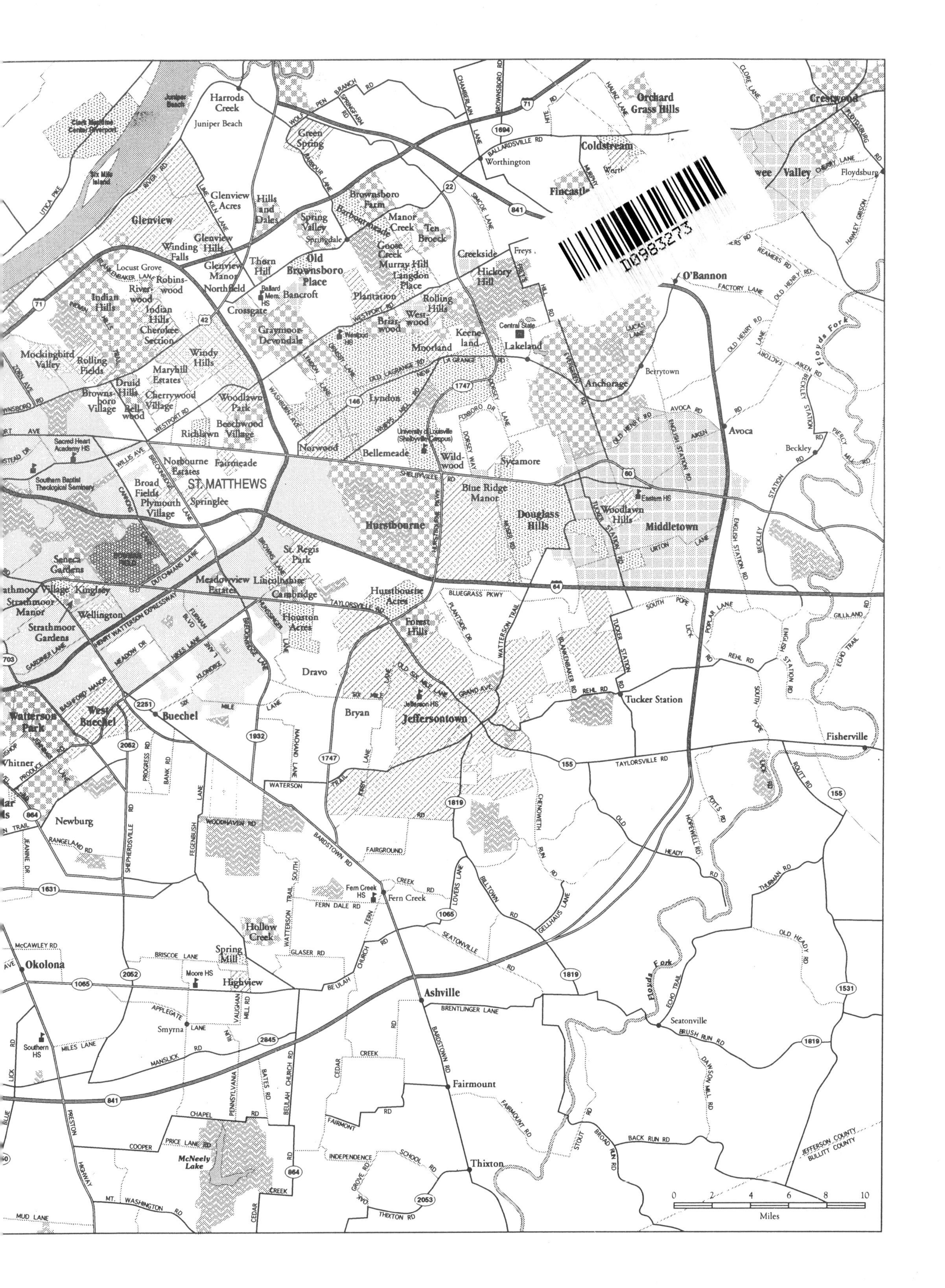
Harrods Creek
Juniper Beach
Clark Maritime Center Riverport
Six Mile Island
Glenview
Glenview Acres
Hills and Dales
Green Spring
Brownsboro Farm
Barbourmeade
Spring Valley
Springdale
Manor Creek
Ten Broeck
Goose Creek
Murray Hill
Lyndon Place
Glenview Hills
Winding Falls
Glenview Manor
Northfield
Thorn Hill
Old Brownsboro Place
Locust Grove
Robinswood
Riverwood
Indian Hills
Indian Hills Cherokee Section
Ballard Mem. HS
Bancroft
Crossgate
Plantation
Rolling Hills
Westwood
Briarwood
Graymoor-Devondale
Westport HS
Mockingbird Valley
Rolling Fields
Windy Hills
Maryhill Estates
Druid Hills
Brownsboro Village
Bellewood
Cherrywood Village
Woodlawn Park
Richlawn
Beechwood Village
Moorland
Keeneland
Lyndon
Norwood
Bellemeade
University of Louisville (Shelbyville Campus)
Wildwood
Sycamore
Creekside
Hickory Hill
Central State
Lakeland
Anchorage
Berrytown
O'Bannon
Avoca
Beckley
Orchard Grass Hills
Coldstream
Worthington
Crestwood
Floydsburg
Fincastle
Sacred Heart Academy HS
Southern Baptist Theological Seminary
Norbourne Estates
Fairmeade
Broad Fields
ST. MATTHEWS
Plymouth Village
Springlee
Hurstbourne
Blue Ridge Manor
Douglass Hills
Woodlawn Hills
Middletown
Eastern HS
Seneca Gardens
St. Regis Park
Strathmoor Village
Kingsley
Strathmoor Manor
Meadowview Estates
Lincolnshire
Cambridge
Hurstbourne Acres
Wellington
Strathmoor Gardens
Houston Acres
Forest Hills
Dravo
Tucker Station
Watterson Park
West Buechel
Buechel
Bryan
Jefferson HS
Jeffersontown
Fisherville
Whitner
Newburg
Fern Creek HS
Fern Creek
Hollow Creek
Okolona
Spring Mill
Moore HS
Highview
Ashville
Seatonville
Smyrna
Southern HS
Fairmount
McNeely Lake
Thixton
Floyds Fork
JEFFERSON COUNTY
BULLITT COUNTY
0 2 4 6 8 10
Miles

The Encyclopedia of Louisville

Dedicated to Wilson W. Wyatt

THE ENCYCLOPEDIA OF Louisville

JOHN E. KLEBER
Editor in Chief

MARY JEAN KINSMAN
Managing Editor

THOMAS D. CLARK
CLYDE F. CREWS
GEORGE H. YATER
Associate Editors

THE UNIVERSITY PRESS OF KENTUCKY

Scholarly publisher for the Commonwealth,
serving Bellarmine College, Berea College, Centre
College of Kentucky, Eastern Kentucky University,
The Filson Club Historical Society, Georgetown College,
Kentucky Historical Society, Kentucky State University,
Morehead State University, Transylvania University,
University of Kentucky, University of Louisville,
and Western Kentucky University.

Editorial and Sales Offices: The University Press of Kentucky
663 South Limestone Street, Lexington, Kentucky 40508-4008

04 03 02 01 00 5 4 3 2 1

Library of Congress Cataloging-in-Publication Data

The encyclopedia of Louisville / edited by John Kleber.
p. cm.
Includes bibliographical references and index.
ISBN 0-8131-2100-0 (acid-free paper)
1. Louisville (Ky.)—Civilization—Encyclopedias.
I. Kleber, John E., 1941-

F459.L85 E54 2000
976.9'44—dc21 99-053755

This book is printed on acid-free paper meeting
the requirements of the American National Standard
for Permanence in Paper for Printed Library Materials.

Manufactured in the United States of America.

Sponsors

James Graham Brown Foundation, Inc.
The Gheens Foundation, Inc.
Jefferson County
City of Louisville
The Filson Club Historical Society
PNC
Edith and Barry Bingham, Jr.
Lucille Caudill Little
Scripps Howard Foundation
Ashland, Inc.
Rotary Club of Louisville, Inc.
Brown-Forman Corporation
The Honorable Order of Kentucky Colonels
William T. Young Family Foundation
J.J.B Hilliard, W.L. Lyons, Inc.
Martin F. Schmidt/Kate Schmidt Moniger Fund
Churchill Downs, Inc.
W.L. Lyons Brown Foundation
The Courier-Journal/Gannett Foundation
Ford Motor Company
Thomas D. Clark
The Cralle Foundation, Inc.
Rudd Foundation, Inc.
Wyatt, Tarrant & Combs
Robert D. Bell
Charles McClure III
Donald B. Towles
Longview Foundation, Inc.
BellSouth
City of Jeffersontown
City of St. Matthews
Henry V. Heuser, Sr.
Brown & Williamson Tobacco Corporation
Mr. and Mrs. George Duthie
Louisville Historical Society
Merrily Orsini
Sutherland Foundation
Guthrie/Mayes Public Relations
Peter Bernard
Robin Bleakley
Thomas Brumley
Helen B. Chenery
Nancy Lampton
Henry Levy
Vince Noltemeyer
Charles Owen
T.E. Spragens, Jr.

Editorial Staff

Editor in Chief
John E. Kleber

Managing Editor
Mary Jean Kinsman

Associate Editors
Thomas D. Clark
Clyde F. Crews
George H. Yater

Authors

Rhonda Abner
Mary Milner Adelberg
Michelle Alford
Betty Lou Amster
James C. Anderson
Nathalie Taft Andrews
Lindsey Apple
Kristy M. Applegate
Thomas H. Appleton Jr.
Philip Ardery
David Armstrong
Charles W. Arrington
Jack Ashworth
D. Alexander Atty
W.F. Axton
Patricia Ayers
Anne Tobbe Bader
Nancy D. Baird
Yvonne Honeycutt Baldwin
Everett E. Ballard
Martha Stoll Ballard
Anita P. Barbee
James Houston Barr III
John Barrow Jr.
Alan L. Bates
James Bates
Doris J. Batliner
Donald Maclean Bell
Mary Margaret Bell
Mary Jane Benedict
Eric Benmour
James R. Bentley
Susan Crowell Berigan
Richard R. Bernier
Indu Bhatnager
Kunwar Bhatnagar
Harry Bickel
Martin E. Biemer
Chris Bingaman
Terry L. Birdwhistell
Graham C. Blankenbaker
Laurie A. Birnsteel
John H. Blunk
Donald Boarman
Mary Boewe
Brenda K. Bogert
Cornelius Bogert
Aaron J. Bohnert
James Duane Bolin
Rowena E. Bolin
Carol Bonura
Joy Bale Boone
Shirley J. Botkins
Anne Braden
Matthew J. Brandon
James F. Braun
Joseph E. Brent
Charles W. Brockwell Jr.
Carolyn Brooks
Sylvia Cardwell Bruton
Ron D. Bryant
Delinda Stephens Buie
Phyllis Glover Bunnell
Marlow G. Burt
Bruce Baird Butler
Robert A. Bylund
Ed Cahill
James M. Caldwell
Mary Caldwell
James Burnley Calvert
Robert S. Cameron
Clay W. Campbell
Lindsay Crawford Campbell
Lisa Grace Carpenter
William Pfingst Carrell II
Soni Castlebery
Charles B. Castner
Annette Chapman-Adisho
Morton O. Childress
Roosevelt Chin
Eric Howard Christianson
Patricia A. Clare
Susan Castleman Clare
Thomas D. Clark
Grady Clay
Kevin Collins
Barbara Conkin
James E. Conkin
Eugene H. Conner
Paul A. Coomes
Madeline C. Covi
Patrick Cowles
Dwayne Cox
Hubert Crawford
Clyde F. Crews
Steve Crews
Martha M. Cull
Donald R. Curtis
Robert I. Cusick
Dennis Cusick
Jack E. Custer
Sandra Miller Custer
Michael Daniel
Betty Rolwing Darnell
Barry Lee Daulton Jr.
Alice S. Davidson
Sean M. Davis
Nelson L. Dawson
David R. Deatrick Jr.
Ronald F. Deering
Kenneth Dennis
Diana DeVaughn
Garland R. Dever Jr.
Philip DiBlasi
Otis Amanda Dick
Thomas Diener
Allan E. Dittmer
Adron Doran
Melinda Dorris
Amy Drozt
Nancy S. Dysart
David Patrick Ecker
Bob Edwards
Andrew Eggers
William F. Ekstrom
William E. Ellis
Linda Raymond Ellison
T. Kyle Ellison
William L. Ellison Jr.
Sam O. English Jr.
Kadie Engstrom
John Ernst
Stan Esterle
Susan Buren Eubank
Tanya Evans
Mildred Long Ewen
Niels O. Ewing
David M. Fahey
Gary Falk
Edward A. Farris
Pamela Federspiel
Jay R. Ferguson
Jo M. Ferguson
Michael A. Flannery
Lee Fletcher
Kenneth W. Forcht
Gordon Ford
Catherine Fosl
Mary Anne Fowlkes
Olivia M. Frederick
Robert Bruce French
Jeanette H. Fridell
Roger H. Futrell
Frank M. Gaines
Harry C. Gans
Hoyt D. Gardner Jr.
W.H. Garnar
Mary Garry
James F. Gates
John Spalding Gatton
Kay Gill
John S. Gillig
Martha S. Gilliss
Alan Goldstein
C. Walker Gollar

Joseph E. Granger
David A. Graves
Karen R. Gray
William Crawford Green
Peter Richard Guetig
Blaine A. Guthrie Jr.
Erna O. Gwinn
Charline Judd Hall
Neal O. Hammon
Louis "Bud" Harbsmeier
Shirley M. Harmon
John A. Hardin
Nancy D. Harris
Robin R. Harris
Benjamin T. Harrison
Lowell H. Harrison
Richard L. Harrison Jr.
Warder Harrison
Ann S. Hassett
Melba Porter Hay
Marie A. Heckel
Donald Hellmann
Jack B. Helm
Ed Henson
Gail Ritchie Henson
Jacqueline M. Hersh
Craig M. Heuser
Henry V. Heuser
Schuyler N. Heuser
Bob Hill
Henning Hilliard
Philip T. Hines Jr.
Charles D. Hockensmith
Aaron Hoffman
Paul Wolf Holleman
Hope L. Hollenbeck
James J. Holmberg
Ruthe Pfisterer Holmberg
Shawn H. Howe
J. Blaine Hudson
Nickey Hughes
Marguerite Hume
Walter W. Hutchins
Robert M. Ireland
Jonathan Jeffrey
Christine Johnson
Katherine Burger Johnson
Matthew H. Johnson
Joellen Tyler Johnston
Kenneth Johnston
Ben Jones
Elizabeth Fitzpatrick "Penny" Jones
Helen Hammon Jones
Trish Pugh Jones
Jane Julian
Elsa Taylor Kalmbach
Katherine K. M. Kamin
Anne S. Karem
David K. Karem
Vivian Keinonen
Clifton Keller
Jane K. Keller
Arthur L. Kelly
James Dale Kendall
William D. Kenney
John Kielkopf
Thomas J. Kiffmeyer
George A. Kilcourse Jr.
Mary Jean Kinsman
Adam Kirby
James T. Kirkwood
John E. Kleber
John Klee
Gene Klein
James C. Klotter
Yvonne B. Knight
Claudia Knott
Barry Kornstein
Carl E. Kramer
Mary Kagin Kramer
Joe Krill
Arthur L. Kurk
Miguel Lagunas
Allen L. Lake
Herman Landau
Helen L. Lang
David Langdon
Margaret "Meg" Leibson
Bill J. Leonard
Frank R. Levstik
R. Kenneth Lile
Patti Linn
Mickey List Jr.
Becky Loechle
Rick Loechle
Zack H. Logan
Charles T. Long
Gary W. Luhr
Susan McNeese Lynch
Charles H. Mackay
Barbara Kuprion Mackovic
Mary Lou Smith Madigan
Alejandro Magallanez
Robert F. Magers
Margaret H. Mahoney
Michelle Mandro
John P. Marcum Jr.
Marilyn Markwell
William Marshall
John Franklin Martin
Joan C. Masters
Dominic Mattei
Henry C. Mayer
James R. McCabe
Mary Rush McCaulley
Karen C. McDaniel
Andrea McDowell
Maxine Crouch McEwen
S. Norman McKenna
Jean S. McVickar
Lorelei Meadows
Gail McGowan Mellor
Rosetta Stasel Melton
Joan H. Meriwether
Joseph T. Merkt
Margaret Merrick
Clara L. Metzmeier
Tamsie Meurer
Robert S. Michael
Lillian C. Milanof
Stevens Miles Jr.
Kenneth L. Miller
Louis A. "Lew" Miller
Rod A. Miller
Charles Michael Mills
Ronald L. Mitchelson
James H. Molloy
Robert T. Moore
William Mootz
David Morgan
William Morgan
William J. Morison
Peter Morrin
Ellen Birkett Morris
Michael Stoner Morris
Marilyn A. Mote-Yale
Bob Mueller
Larry Muhammad
John M. Mulder
John David Myles
Herman Naber
David A. Nakdimen
Francis M. Nash
Donna M. Neary
Bronislava Nedelin
Glenda S. Neely
Anthony Newberry
Rick L. Nutt
Mary Lawrence Bickett O'Brien
Mary E. O'Dell
Cynthia A. Odell
Joseph Woodson Oglesby
Nettie Oliver
Dana Olson
Lynn Olympia
Barbara S. Oremland
Virginia Leighton Orndorff
J.W. Ostertag
Tom Owen
Tom Pack
Brainard L. Palmer-Ball Jr.
Penelope Papangelis
Julia C. Parke

Frederick M. Parkins
Charles E. Parrish
Angela Partee
Christian V. Patterson
John Ed Pearce
Nancy Lee Pearcy
Ed Peck
Iris Biggs Peers
Gay Helen Perkins
Candace K. Perry
Donna L. Peterson
Shannon Phlegar
Tristan G. Pierce
Janie Pitcock
Suzanne Post
Charles B. Price Jr.
Charlotte Williams Price
Stephen R. Price Sr.
James M. Prichard
Jacil Puckett
Aaron D. Purcell
Susan M. Rademacher
James A. Ramage
Mark A. Ray
Sharon Receveur
James R. Recktenwald
Jennifer L. Recktenwald
Debbie Redmon
Susan H. Reigler
Mark Reilly
Joseph R. Reinhart
Lynn S. Renau
Robert M. Rennick
Jerry L. Rice
Joan Riehm
Louisa Riehm
Cassie R. Roberts
Joe Wayne Roberts
George Robinson
Jeffrey S. Rodgers
Eric Paul Roorda
George Rorrer
Keith L. Runyon
Meme Sweets Runyon
Alan S. Rupp
LaVern S. Rupp
Dorothy C. Rush
Steven Rush
Rusty Russell
Jane M. Sarles
Dona Schicker
Martin F. Schmidt
Shirley Schramm
William Joseph Schultz
Alana Cain Scott
James Seacat
Conrad Selle
Shirley Shields Settle
Nancy Niles Sexton
Bettie Shadburne
Allen J. Share
Ron Sheets
William Taylor Simpson
Billy Sue Smith
Donald R. Smith
Gerald L. Smith
Kim Lady Smith
Tamara Somerville
Thomas W. Spalding
Ruth Spangler
Deborah C. Spearing
Dennis L. Spetz
Stuart Sprague
Roland T. Stayton
Allan M. Steinberg
Forrest F. Steinlage
Marios Stephanides
Barbara H. Stephens
Thomas E. Stephens
Douglas L. Stern
John Joseph Sterne
Ann Hart Stewart
Sue Lynn Stone
M. Jay Stottman
J. Garrison Stradling
Ronald L. Street
Martin C. Striegel
Paul E. Stroble
James Strohmaier
William W. Struck
W. Daniel Sturgeon
Sung John Suh
Gregg Swem
Ibrahim B. Syed
Zach Tackett
Richard Taylor
Janna Tajibaeva
Paul A. Tenkotte
Azra K. Terzic
Charles H. Thomas
Joan E. Thomas
Samuel W. Thomas
Charles Thompson
Doris Metcalf Thompson
Michelle Thompson
Margaret Thomson
Gregory A. Thornbury
Joanne G. Tingley
Carol Brenner Tobe
Lou Torok
Donald B. Towles
John Trawick
Jeanine P. Triplett
Edwin A. Tuttle
Bruce M. Tyler
C. Robert Ullrich
Michael D. Unthank
Nanette M. Vale
Ronald R. Van Stockum Jr.
Ronald R. Van Stockum Sr.
Julian P. VanWinkle III
George T. Vaughn
Michael R. Veach
Jeannie Litterst Vezeau
Ronald K. Vogel
Anne Vouga
Evelyn L. Waldrop
M. Concetta Waller
Michael E. Walters
Joe Ward
Mike Ward
Teka Ward
Ross A. Webb
Paul J. Weber
Carl Wedekind
Dottie Weed
Joanne Weeter
Lee Shai Weissbach
Darlene Welch
Amy E. Wells
Joseph Rettner Wells
Paul Wesslund
Mark V. Wetherington
Lauren Whelan
Juanita Landers White
Clarita Whitney
S. Mont Whitson
Paul B. Whitty
Craig R. Wilkie
Bill Williams
David Williams
Jane-Rives Williams
Gregory A. Wills
Thomas G. Wills
Chris A. Wilson
Jack T. Wilson
David Winges
Stephen A. Wiser
David F. Withers
Timothy L. Wood
Frederick William Woolsey
John Yarmuth
George H. Yater
Sarah Yates
Kyle Yochum
Al Young
Mary Lawrence Young
Eric Yussman
Lorna Sprague Zeck
Charles E. Ziegler
Leo W. Zimmerman
Barbara G. Zingman

Contents

Preface

In the progression of American history, Louisville is an elderly city. Born in the battles of the American Revolutionary War, its roots lie in the 1778 invasion of the British territories north of the Ohio River, when it became a supply base for General George Rogers Clark's army. It was, however, the geography of the Falls, the only obstruction in the more than nine hundred-mile-long river, that explains Louisville's development. That geography also explains the dichotomy many people sense in the place. Located at the top of the South, it is separated by only one mile of water from the Midwest. Located in a slave state, it always faced south but it could never completely ignore the free territory at its back, although it did its best to do so. The dichotomy was intensified by the fact that the city is one of the very few urban areas in a state still known for its vast stretches of rural countryside and small town life. Those areas lack the religious and ethnic diversity of Louisville. Today it constitutes the left point of a designated "Golden Triangle" that contains the urban centers of Lexington and Covington-Newport. Perhaps these differences explain why Louisville has not been well understood, if not actually disliked, by many who live in the state's rural areas. Its power and wealth, forces it never hesitated to use for its aggrandizement in the General Assembly, often placed it at loggerheads with other communities.

During most of Kentucky's history, Louisville has been its largest city. Today it is the center of a metropolitan area of nearly one million people that straddles the Ohio River and stretches away into urban sprawl. A center of early trade and commerce, it developed into a place of banking and manufacturing, and more recently a medical and cultural center. Yet, despite its importance, Louisville has not done a good job remembering itself. Only one comprehensive history has been written of the city in the last century. While there certainly is a wealth of information available in bits and pieces, this is the first attempt to pull all of it together since the publication of George Yater's *Two Hundred Years at the Falls of the Ohio: A History of Louisville and Jefferson County* (1987).

The decision to rectify this situation through the publication of an encyclopedia was made by and undertaken with the guidance of The Thomas D. Clark Foundation. A charitable, nonprofit foundation established in 1994, its sole purpose is to provide financial support for The University Press of Kentucky. It is named in honor of Kentucky's historian laureate and the founder of The University Press of Kentucky, Dr. Thomas D. Clark. The Foundation and the Press both believed the heralding of a new millennium to be an auspicious time to celebrate Greater Louisville's past, present, and future by the publication of a comprehensive reference work devoted to the people, places, things, and events that have made metropolitan Louisville a proud and prosperous area. We undertook to preserve the city's rich intellectual history by delving into libraries, archives, rare books, documents, newspapers, and highly specialized collections, often not easily accessible to the public. The result is a single-volume research tool containing the latest research and information written by Kentucky scholars. In so doing, Louisville becomes one of a select group of cities to present its history in an encyclopedic format. It is intended for use by a wide variety of people: business and industrial leaders, governmental officials, city planners, teachers and scholars, the news media, librarians, and—most important—the students who will be the city's leaders in the twenty-first century. This will be a work for all natives, visitors, and the merely curious, for all library collections in the metropolitan area and the state, and for major research collections.

In 1992 *The Kentucky Encyclopedia* was published by The University Press of Kentucky. A comprehensive statewide work, it naturally included the city of Louisville. At first, it was thought that there would be much redundancy in an encyclopedia of the city, but such was not the case. This was partly because of the decision to include more than simply the city itself. Indeed, the work contains even more than the metropolitan counties of Bullitt, Jefferson, Oldham in Kentucky and Clark, Floyd, Scott, and Harrison in Indiana. Shelby and Spencer Counties, Kentucky, and Scott County, Indiana, were included as well in the belief that they are already tied closely to the city, and the next census may include them within the metropolitan area.

As with any major publication, the task has been daunting. Thanks to the diligence of many people, the four-year schedule was realized and the book published on schedule. It includes 1,799 entries, the work of more than five hundred writers. The identification of those entry titles and writers was the major responsibility of the associate and consulting editors; however, many other knowledgeable individuals came forward to assist. For much of the time, every day brought new suggestions, most of them excellent. One will find here a variety of topics from architecture to women that will, when combined, provide a comprehensive view of the community's development, both good and bad. Overviews provide in-depth study of such subjects as art, architecture, communications, etc. A chronological balance was one principle guiding the selection process. Beginning with the geology and geography of the region, the material follows settlement from prehistoric times in the Ohio River Valley up to the deaths of recently deceased notable individuals.

As noted, the encyclopedia is the work of hundreds of dedicated people. In every sense it is a community-wide project that bespeaks the nature of the community itself. The more than five hundred editors and writers, possessed of diverse backgrounds and experiences, represent every facet of the city's life. The sum of their contributions reflects the voice of Louisville, its strengths and weaknesses, at the beginning of the twentieth-first century.

The encyclopedia is a millennium gift, a permanent record if you will, prepared by the community of Louisville as a gift to itself and to its posterity.

No community the size of Louisville can be static. At the beginning of the new century, the city is debating its internal development and external national role in the new millennium. The result of those debates will doubtless produce a much different sort of place in the not-too-distant future. As is the nature of such projects, this book is already on its way to being outdated. The inherent value, however, remains because it provides knowledge of the foundation upon which Greater Louisville was built, a foundation for the future. As industrialist Henry Ford noted, "The farther one can look back, the farther one can look ahead." This book will prove the adage. It is only a beginning, because an encyclopedia cannot provide more than a sampling. What is here will answer many questions about Louisville, but if it does its job well, this book will generate even more questions, which will provide the incentive for more research in the new century. While questioning may not be the mode of conversation among gentlemen, as Dr. Johnson observed, it is the beginning of new knowledge, and, as Plato notes, "The beginning is the most important part of the work."

Acknowledgments

In every way, the *Encyclopedia of Louisville* is a cooperative venture. I have only coordinated the good work of hundreds of individuals. A few of them deserve special recognition. Mr. Robert Bell of The Thomas D. Clark Foundation approached me with the idea of editing the book. I am grateful to Mr. Bell and the members of the Foundation who initiated the idea, hired me, and then found the financial support.

The Foundation approached individuals, foundations, corporations, and families to acquire that financial support. In the beginning, Mr. Michael Harreld, President of PNC Bank, took an interest in the project and helped us to procure funds. Toward the end, he encouraged individuals and organizations to purchase the book.

At the start, I identified three associate editors. Dr. Thomas D. Clark continued to encourage me, just as he had done while I was editing *The Kentucky Encyclopedia*. He continually reviewed our entry list, read some of the entries, and wrote others. As with the earlier project, in this visible manner he generously donated his wonderful gift of knowledge of the commonwealth. Mr. George Yater is the author of *Two Hundred Years at the Falls of the Ohio: A History of Louisville and Jefferson County*. Rev. Clyde Crews is an authority on the religious and secular history of the Louisville area and author of several books, including *An American Holy Land: A History of the Archdiocese of Louisville* and *Spirited City*. Both gentlemen began by advising me about entry titles and prospective authors. Then they undertook the Herculean tasks of reading and revising every one of the entries for greater clarity and quality. Their diligence caught many errors and improved the style of the manuscript. In addition, both men wrote many entries. I am grateful to the three associate editors for their support as well as the good-natured comradeship they displayed as we struggled through those early days to get the project under way and then to wade through the masses of material.

Thanks to the advice of the three associate editors, I was able to identify men and women who possessed an expertise one of in the twenty categories of the book. They became the consulting editors. I utilized them to further help me identify entries and writers. They also read all the entries in their respective categories, and this additional check often enhanced accuracy and style. I am grateful to them all.

In the day-to-day operations of the office, the staff provided invaluable assistance in many ways. First and foremost, I am indebted to Joe W. Roberts who came with me from Morehead State University to set up and keep running the computers and other technological gadgets. He remained for three years as assistant editor, performing many jobs and all of them well. I respect his professionalism and cherish his friendship. I could not have completed this project without him. He was a tough act to follow, but Aaron J. Bohnert did a remarkable job as project assistant for the last year. A stroke of luck was finding Mary Jean Kinsman just as she was retiring from The Filson Club Historical Society and recruiting her to serve as managing editor. Her knowledge of Louisville and especially the city's photographic collections was invaluable. She brought good cheer to the workplace and was an able liaison between our office and The University Press of Kentucky offices in Lexington.

Part of the staff included student researchers, most of them from the University of Louisville or Bellarmine College, who undertook to write the entries for which we could find no one else. Sometimes a thankless task, but they did it well. In addition to researching and writing, they checked facts, and there were thousands of them. I came to consider them friends as well as colleagues. I trust that the research and writing experiences they gained will in some way compensate for the meager monetary rewards.

All of us worked on the campus of the University of Louisville in the archives and records division of the Ekstrom Library. Even before the project began, I visited my old friend Dr. William Morison, director of the archives. Without hesitation, he found a wonderful place to for us to work as well as the furniture we needed. Our large picture window, facing the skyline of downtown, kept us focused on what we were about. The archivists became friends and assisted us in every way. We thank Mary Margaret Bell, Katherine Burger Johnson, Margaret Merrick, and Thomas L. Owen. I am particularly grateful to Sherri Faye Pawson, who worked closely with us to facilitate our presence. She was always helpful in procuring the resources we needed and joined with the other archivists to make us feel genuinely welcomed.

From our offices we reached out into the community to tap the resources of many repositories. None was more helpful than The Filson Club Historical Society, which maintains the best collection of material related to Louisville and its history. Its staff was always available to assist. I am particularly grateful to Mark Wetherington, director, and to James J. Holmberg, Judith Partington, Rebecca Rice, Cassie Bratcher, Nettie Oliver, and Michael Veach.

Other photographs were provided through the generosity of the University of Louisville Photographic Archives. Its director, James C. "Andy" Anderson, was receptive to our needs from the start. He worked tirelessly to help identify and caption the photographs. He was assisted by William J. Carner and Susan Knoer. The *Courier-Journal*'s Sharon Bidwell also provided photographs.

Vivian Keinonen of the Louisville Free Public Library helped us to utilize that library's excellent Kentucky history collection. Sue Locke, who works there, assisted our researchers. In the beginning, John Meehan helped us to edit copy, and near the end Joan C. Rapp and Ethel S. White read nearly all the manuscript. Other people were there for me throughout the project and assisted in more ways than I can say.

John E. Kleber

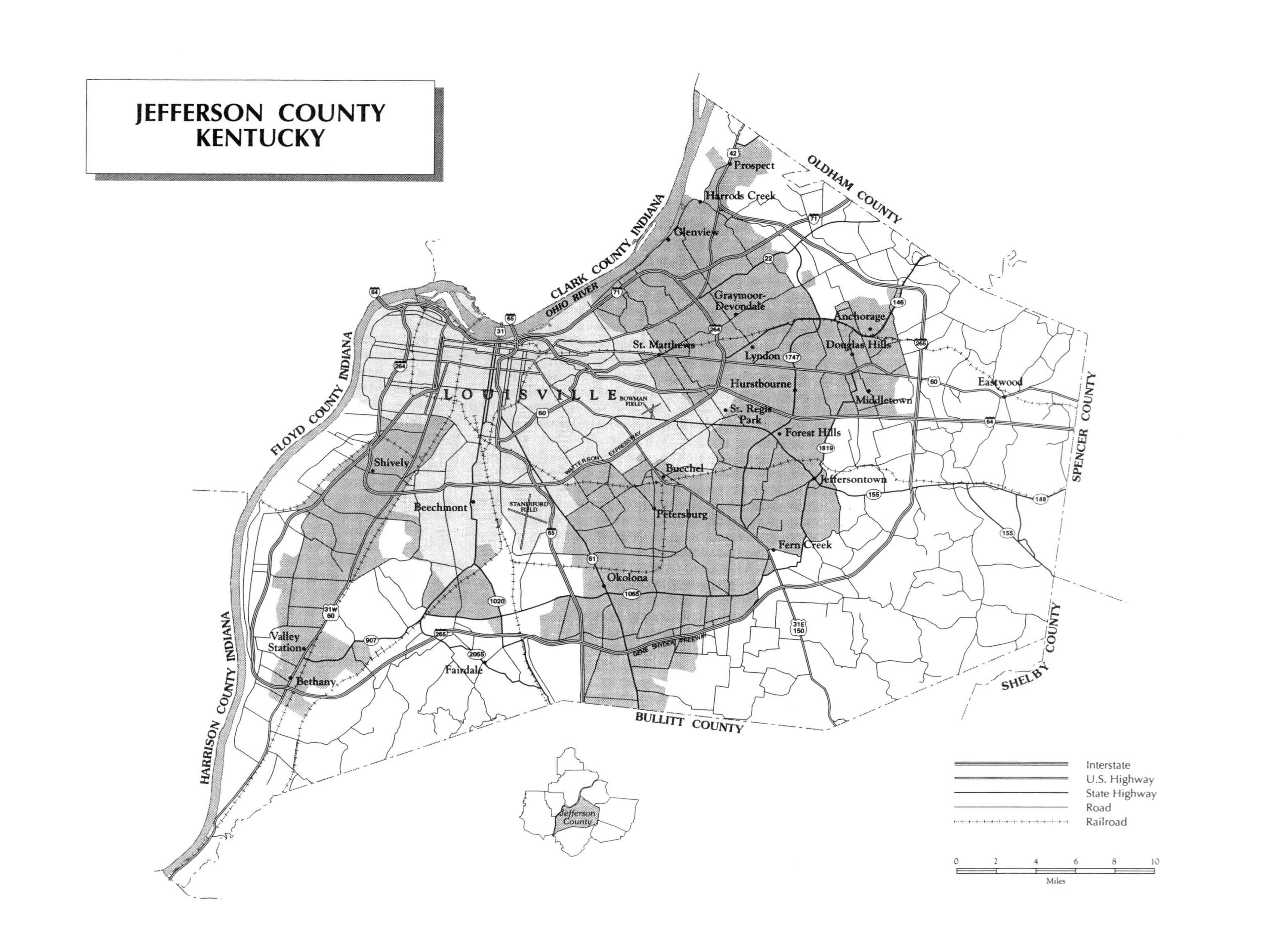
JEFFERSON COUNTY
KENTUCKY
OLDHAM COUNTY
SPENCER COUNTY
SHELBY COUNTY
BULLITT COUNTY
HARRISON COUNTY INDIANA
FLOYD COUNTY INDIANA
CLARK COUNTY INDIANA
OHIO RIVER
LOUISVILLE
Prospect
Harrods Creek
Glenview
Graymoor-Devondale
Anchorage
Douglas Hills
Middletown
Eastwood
St. Matthews
Lyndon
Hurstbourne
St. Regis Park
Forest Hills
Jeffersontown
Buechel
Petersburg
Fern Creek
Okolona
Shively
Beechmont
Valley Station
Bethany
Fairdale
BOWMAN FIELD
STANDIFORD FIELD
WATTERSON EXPRESSWAY
GENE SNYDER FREEWAY
Jefferson County
Interstate
U.S. Highway
State Highway
Road
Railroad
0 2 4 6 8 10
Miles

Louisville: A Historical Overview

George H. Yater

The Falls of the Ohio, created by an ancient and stubborn limestone ledge cutting across the Ohio River's course, marked the site of what would become Louisville long before George Rogers Clark and his mixed party of Virginia militiamen and settlers arrived in the spring of 1778. The Falls was well known to the French, who lost the Ohio Valley to the British in 1763 after their defeat in the French and Indian War. Beargrass Creek had been named before 1755 when it first appeared on a map. The first Anglo-Americans to pass over the rapids were five Virginians commissioned by that colony in 1742 to make "discoveries toward the Mississippi." They described the Falls as marked by "great Rocks and large Whirlpools." In 1766 the first detailed map of the Falls was made by a party of British army engineers reconnoitering England's new-won territory.

The first individual to see the Falls area as the site of a town was John Connolly, who was to become a Tory troublemaker during the American Revolution. Born in about 1744 in Pennsylvania, Connolly was the nephew of George Croghan of Pittsburgh, the British Indian agent and a well-to-do trader with the Indians. In the late 1760s Connolly toured the Ohio Valley and the Illinois country, perhaps accompanying his uncle on trading ventures. He was impressed with the potential of the Falls area for settlement. When George Washington visited Pittsburgh in the fall of 1770, Connolly took the opportunity to extol the Ohio Valley and in later correspondence with the future president attempted unsuccessfully in 1773 to recruit Washington's aid in securing "two thousand Acres from the Government of Virginia" (*Letters to Washington* IV:208).

Connolly, however, had also cultivated the friendship of Virginia's royal governor, Lord Dunmore, at a propitious time. King George III had issued a proclamation awarding land to Americans who had served as officers in the British forces during the French and Indian War, in which Connolly, trained in medicine, had served as a surgeon. Through Dunmore's aid he was able to gain title to his two thousand acres at the Falls in 1773 in a survey made by Captain Thomas Bullitt. At the same time a Charles DeWarrensdorff, also from Pennsylvania, was awarded two thousand acres that was to become Louisville's West End. Lying adjacent to Connolly's tract and extending south to what would become Broadway, as did Connolly's land, it stirred his interest. To purchase it, he enlisted the financial aid of John Campbell, an important Pittsburgh-based Indian trader associated with Connolly's uncle, George Croghan. In return for advancing Connolly's share of the purchase price in 1774, Campbell received a half-interest in Connolly's now four thousand acres, plus a mortgage note. In April 1774 they advertised in *The Virginia Gazette* their intention to "lay out a Town" at the Falls and were prepared to sell half-acre lots. But this ambitious plan was thwarted, first by the outbreak of Indian hostilities (often called Dunmore's War) along the upper reaches of the Ohio River in the fall of 1774, and then by the events at Boston in 1775 that led to the American Revolution.

Thus when George Rogers Clark and his company of militiamen and settlers arrived at the Falls in the spring of 1778 they were relative latecomers. Though Clark is enshrined as Louisville's founder, he had no intention of founding a town. His mission, unknown to his party until the arrival at the Falls, was to assert Virginia's claim to the Illinois country. The Spanish commandant in St. Louis noted that "Although his [Clark's] soldiers are bandits in appearance, he has them under the best of control" (*American Historical Review*, October 1935, 98). After Clark's easy success in Illinois, the sixty or so civilian settlers he had left on Corn Island at the Falls moved to the mainland in the autumn of 1778. There they erected what has come to be known as Fort on Shore in the vicinity of Twelfth Street and the river. Lots and streets were surveyed by visiting Baptist minister John Corbly in April 1779 in response to an order of the Kentucky County Court in Harrodsburgh to all Kentucky settlers that they "keep themselves as united and compact as possible, settling themselves in Towns and Forts. . .and choose three or more of the most judicious . . . as Trustees." Most remarkable is that Corbly's map was labeled "Plan of the Town of Louisville on the Ohio." The town was named even before it received a charter, though who chose the name is unknown. Corbly perhaps? Perhaps by majority vote? It obviously honors the French monarch Louis XVI. News of the French alliance with the Americans had been sent from Pittsburgh by John Campbell. The first lots in the newly named settlement were sold in April 1779.

The only eye-witness notice we have of Louisville in its birth pangs is a brief mention in the fall of 1779: ". . . there is a great number of Cabins here and a considerable number of inhabitants . . ." (Draper Mss 2ZZ75). But a new problem faced the settlers. The land they occupied was owned jointly by John Connolly and John Campbell. Since Connolly had joined the Tory side in the Revolution, his land was subject to seizure and sale by Virginia. It was seized on July 1, 1780. Campbell had been captured by an Indian party in 1779 as he was returning to Pittsburgh from his first visit to the Falls and was imprisoned by the British in Montreal. At about the same time, Connolly was imprisoned in Philadelphia.

The settlers, fearful that the lots they had purchased in "the Burrough of Lewisville" would be sold from under them, appealed to the Virginia General Assembly for a town charter and confirmation of ownership so they would not be "turned out of the houses we have built." The Assembly granted the request in May 1780 and appointed trustees to govern the town and sell the remaining lots. The original stockaded fort of 1778 had been replaced (or supplemented) in 1780 by the "upper garrison" somewhat upriver from its predecessor. But in 1781 Fort Nelson (named for Virginia Governor Thomas Nelson) was constructed.

Built according to George Rogers Clark's direction, this was undoubtedly the strongest fortification south of Pittsburgh. The precise location is uncertain, but it apparently extended from Main Street south toward Market Street, although the monument commemorating it is on the north side of Main at Seventh Street, where tradition holds that a gate was located. In 1832 and 1844 remains of the fort wall were uncovered during building excavations on the north side of Main between Sixth and Seventh Streets. The fort could not have extended north toward the river because of the steep slope of the riverbank, which would have made it indefensible. The moat surrounding the fort would have been impossible on the slope. The work was still standing in 1804 when a hat maker announced in Louisville's first newspaper that he had removed "to his new house in Main Street opposite the Old Fortgate" (*Farmer's Library*, February 25, 1804).

By early 1786 a total of three hundred lots had been sold, many apparently for speculative purposes. Erkuries Beatty, visiting Louisville that year, reported only fifty or sixty houses, "a good deal scattered, chiefly log, some frame." (*Magazine of American History*, April 1877, 239) Virginian Moses Austin, passing through in 1797, counted only about thirty houses. Austin was not complimentary of what he saw. Noting that the town was the landing place for all boats going beyond the Falls and thus attracted "a great resort of Company, yit there is not a Tavern in the place that deserves a better name than that of Grog Shop" (*American Historical Review*, 5, 1899-1900, 527).

Certainly Louisville's early growth was slow, and the federal census of 1800 found only 359 inhabitants, making it the fifth largest community in Kentucky, behind Lexington, Frankfort, Washington, and Paris. There were numerous reasons for this lag in development. In the early days Indian raids, mostly for stealing horses, had discouraged many. The uneven topography (downtown Louisville's present flat surface bears no resemblance to its original state) resulted in numerous mosquito-breeding ponds that caused malaria to be common; the town gained the reputation of "Graveyard of the West." The Ohio River and the Falls, which were to become its greatest assets, could not be fully exploited until the development of the steamboat and its widespread use by the 1820s and 1830s.

At the beginning of the nineteenth century flatboat traffic between Louisville and New Orleans averaged about sixty thousand tons per year, including tobacco, cured meat, and farm produce. Bringing imported luxuries upriver against the current of the Mississippi and Ohio Rivers was a different matter. It took three to four months to reach the Falls as long as human muscle was the only motive power. Upriver shipments averaged only about 6,500 tons annually. As late as 1806 eight keelboats sufficed to bring goods from New Orleans to the Falls.

River traffic was to change dramatically after 1811. On October 28, the little town, still largely huddled along the river, was awakened about midnight by a roaring and hissing sound. Alarmed residents gathered along the shore, where brilliant moonlight revealed a strange craft—the first steamboat to traverse the Ohio—making its landing. The *New Orleans* had come from Pittsburgh in only eight days. Built under Robert Fulton's patents, the vessel also sported sails in the event of machinery breakdown. The *New Orleans* was delayed at Louisville for some two months by low water that prevented passage over the Falls. To refute doubts that the vessel could go upstream against the current, Captain Nicholas Roosevelt ran a series of excursions to Six Mile Island and even a trip to Cincinnati. Finally it was able to cross the Falls in December and reached New Orleans in early January. Now quick navigation upstream was a reality.

The first steamboat to arrive at Louisville from New Orleans was the *Enterprize* on May 20, 1815, after a trip of twenty-five days, the final proof that steamboats could indeed stem the rivers' current. The ship's master, Henry M. Shreve, then added to his laurels by taking her *up* the Falls and on to Pittsburgh. The Ohio and Mississippi Rivers had been transformed into major arteries of commerce through what was then still regarded as the West. Two-way traffic, the missing element that would transform Louisville into a thriving city, had arrived.

In 1816 the first steamboat built at Louisville, the *Governor Shelby*, was launched at the mouth of Beargrass Creek, which then flowed into the Ohio between Third and Fourth Streets. Boats were also built in New Albany and Jeffersonville on the Indiana shore and in Shippingport (founded 1806) and Portland (founded 1814), communities a short distance below Louisville and the Falls. They could be called Louisville's first suburbs.

If the river made Louisville a town, the steamboat made Louisville a city. In a sudden spurt of growth the population tripled between 1810 and 1820 and by 1830 reached 11,345, including Portland and Shippingport, making it the largest urban area in Kentucky. In 1828 Louisville had achieved city status by act of the state legislature, the first Kentucky community to be granted this greater measure of home rule. Among other advantages Louisville was now able to establish its own court, which speeded criminal prosecutions through daily sessions. City status also conferred greater taxing power, which permitted a vigorous program of grading and paving streets with cobblestones and limestone quarried from Corn Island. The grading began to shape the irregular natural topography into the flat plain that is characteristic of older parts of the city.

Two-way traffic on the Ohio River and the break in navigation around the Falls made Louisville a lively place, and impressive buildings began rising, especially on Main Street, housing commission merchants, wholesalers, marine insurers, banks, importers, freight forwarders, and warehousers—all related to the mercantile trade. The leading hotels—the Galt House and the Louisville Hotel—were on Main Street, as well as others of lesser rank. Captain Basil Hall of the British Royal Navy, visiting Louisville in 1828, reported finding "excellent accommodations at a hotel in Louisville, the best ordered upon the whole, which we met with in all America, though the attendants were all slaves." Yet he could also characterize the city as "this most interesting station of all the backwoods" (*Travels in North America* (1829) 375).

The riverfront, rowdy at night, was full of commercial uproar and tumult during the day, as recorded by Edmund Flagg in The *Far West* in 1838. "Drays were rattling hither and thither over the rough pavement; Irish porters were cracking their whips and roaring forth alternate staves of blasphemy and song; clerks hurrying to and fro, with fluttering notebooks; hackney coaches dashing down to the water's edge, apparently with no motive to the nervous man but noise; while at intervals . . . some incontinent steamer would hurl forth from the valves of her overcharged boilers one of those deafening, terrible blasts, echoing and re-echoing along the river banks and streets, and among the lofty buildings, till the very welkin rang again."

Henry Huffner, visiting Louisville that same year, recalled that "Our boat landed about eleven o'clock at night, and lay till morning. When I got out and looked about, I found on the bank, the city of Louisville, and along the shore the greatest sight of steamboats that I ever beheld. They lay as thickly as they could crowd, with their noses to the land, for the space of half a mile, many of them vessels of large burden, giving evidence at once that here was the greatest commercial port on the Ohio" ("Notes on a Tour from Virginia to Tennessee," in *Southern Literary Messenger* 5 ([Jan.-Apr. 1839]).

The activity on the waterfront was indicative of Louisville's transition from frontier village to a center of mercantile capitalism in its first half-century. By the late 1820s it displayed what one visitor termed a "smile of wealth and grandeur" (Caleb Atwater, *Remarks Made on a Tour to Prairie du Chien . . . 1829*). This change resulted in a very different community than the one envisioned by its early settlers in 1779. At the first sale of lots that year it was stipulated that buyers could purchase only one of the half-acre lots and that it could be sold only to a person who did not own a lot. This democratic clause of equality was lost when Virginia granted town status and needed funding badly.

By the 1830s class differences were marked. When Hugh Hays, father of noted Louisville songwriter William S. Hays, arrived in Louisville in 1831 he found few manufacturing establishments: a cotton mill, a pottery, one or two flour mills, the giant Hope Distillery at the western edge of town, and a handful of foundries and machine shops. Hays intended to establish a plow manufactory and "applied to the richest landowner in the county for ground to erect a factory on. This worthy, venerable gentleman told me that this was no place for workingmen, but only a fit place for merchants and retired gentlemen to live in" (Hays's recollections in *The Courier-Journal*, July 2, 1882, 11.) Hays and a partner did secure a site at Hancock and Main Streets.

A major factor in the slow growth of manufacturing was the "peculiar institution" of slavery, an inheritance from the city's Virginia past. Many African Americans, both slave and free, worked in the few manufactories, often alongside whites. Both groups were poorly paid. Hand labor, even the most skilled, was seen as a menial occupation. Competent white mechanics often avoided Louisville, preferring the free soil of cities such as Cincinnati and Pittsburgh. Sir Charles Lyell, the eminent English geologist, visited Louisville in 1846 and noted that "Several merchants expressed to me their opinions that Cincinnati, founded at a later date, would not have outstripped her rival in the race, so as now to number a population of nearly 100,000 souls, more than double that of Louisville, but for the existence of slavery" (*A Second Visit to the United States* [1849], II:279-80).

Black workers, slave or free, had little opportunity to improve pay or working time, which could be as long as twelve hours or more a day. But white workers often formed associations (they could hardly yet be called unions) to improve conditions. By 1835 the tailors, leather workers, printers, coach makers, saddlers, cabinetmakers, and tin-plate workers had organized groups that were more benevolent societies than trade unions. But in 1844 the Journeymen Carpenters Association placed a notice in the newspapers advising "newcomers" that the ten-hour day was standard in Louisville. The warning was clear; do not endanger the gains we have won. The Working Men's Association, apparently a catch-all group, was in existence by the middle 1840s. By the 1850s the iron molders had formed a union and in July 1857 the tanners at W.H. Stokes's tanyard went on strike, perhaps the first strike in Louisville. The rift between capital and labor was plain as the city grew.

Political rifts, too, reflected economic changes. During these years the city shifted from strongly Jacksonian to strongly Whig, although the Jacksonians, headed by Worden Pope, dominated the county offices. The demise of the Democratic *Louisville Public Advertiser* in 1841, edited by Shadrack Penn, and the rise of *The Louisville Daily Journal*, founded in 1830 and edited by George D. Prentice, was one indicator of the change. The Whigs and their Kentucky champion, Henry Clay, opted for federal support of internal improvements, protective tariffs, and a national bank to provide stable currency and sound credit. This program suited mercantile Louisville's burgeoning commercial trade and its merchant princes, who also constituted its voters.

Since the ballot was restricted to property-owning white males, the majority of the working men, who tended to vote the Democratic ticket when they eventually won the ballot, were not voters in the 1830s and 1840s. This party division led in 1835 to an attempt to have Louisville secede from Jefferson County and become a county on its own. This plan was opposed by the Democrats, who controlled the county government through the votes of landowners outside Louisville. It was supported by the Whigs, who would have controlled the new county; however, the state legislature, by a narrow vote, failed to give permission for the split. Jeffersontown would likely have been the county seat of Jefferson County had the move succeeded.

The rapid change from sleepy village in 1800 to bustling city in the 1830s (total wholesale business in 1835 was estimated at $29 million, including $8 million handled by the twenty-eight commission houses) was also marked by new elements in local leadership. Town trustees had been predominantly of the merchant class, but in the 1820s non-mercantile professionals, especially attorneys, began sharing leadership roles. The most notable was attorney James Guthrie, principal mover toward incorporation as a city. Though he was a Democrat, his hard-driving persona kept him in a seat of power even during the Whig ascendancy. He used his post as chairman of the City Council's finance committee to inaugurate numerous improvement projects, including the new courthouse, begun in 1836 after a design by Gideon Shryock, gas street lighting, the University of Louisville, street grading and paving, public schools, and later the first bridge over the river at Louisville. He saw the courthouse as the future state capitol but was disappointed in that hope.

Guthrie was also a director (and later president) of the Louisville and Portland Canal Company that completed the bypass around the treacherous Falls of the Ohio in late 1830. Guthrie was instrumental in securing federal funding (through government purchase of stock) to begin construction. Numerous earlier attempts to build a canal—some on the Indiana side—had failed. The federal aid, based on statistics of the loss of boats and cargo on the Falls, got the project under way. But when Andrew Jackson became president in 1829, government aid ceased. Private capital, most from Philadelphia, anxious to protect its long-time trade relations with the Ohio and Mississippi Valleys, was provided. The two-mile-wide "ditch," only fifty feet wide, became within a few years more of an obstacle to navigation than an aid.

As steamboats grew larger, the canal proved too narrow and its locks too short for most and complaints were rife that tolls (average about $80) were exorbitant. The fear that the canal would end the profitable carrying trade around the Falls proved groundless in the long run, though the canal did have a short-term negative effect. *Haldeman's Picture of Louisville* (1844, 58) noted that "the trade and business of Louisville was doubtless greatly changed . . . by the opening of the canal. The 'Forwarding and Commission' houses were idle and deserted, hundreds of drays were thrown out of employment . . . and the most stable establishments quailed before the storm."

This was when steamboats were smaller and flatboats still carried a sizable part of the Ohio Valley's agricultural produce and manufactured products to New Orleans and other Mississippi River destinations. Both types of vessels fit the canal comfortably. As the number of larger steamboats increased, the carrying trade revived and with it the warehousing, commission, and forwarding business. In addition, the spread of the South's cotton culture westward to the Mississippi River and beyond created an expanding market for Ohio Valley production. River tonnage leaped upward by bounds, and the Louisville and Portland wharves remained as busy as ever despite the canal, through which 1,585 steamboats and 394 flatboats passed in 1845.

By that year the upriver boats were bringing another kind of cargo—Irish and German immigrants fleeing famine in the one country and a failed democratic revolution in the other. By 1850 there were 7,537 German-born immigrants in Louisville (including German-speaking Swiss) and 3,105 Irish. Newcomers of Germanic background had been in the Louisville area, along with the Scots-Irish and English, from the beginning of settlement. But they were relatively few in number and engaged mostly in farming near Jeffersontown. By the early 1850s the tide of Irish and German immigrants reached flood proportions. The Germans, mostly Catholic, numbered about five thousand in 1850, while the Irish were about three thousand. As with the Germans, the Irish had been migrating to America for years, but in earlier days little distinction was made between Scots-Irish (almost uniformly Presbyterian with a sprinkling of Anglicans) and the Irish (almost uniformly Catholic). The Potato Famine Irish, however, were a different economic group. They were mostly tenant farmers, almost penniless, and they flocked to the cities to take almost any kind of work that required only muscle power. They were at the bottom of the white social scale, saved from the lowest rung of the ladder only by free blacks and, in the South, slaves with whom they often competed in the labor market. This mass immigration upset both the political and religious balances in Louisville. The overwhelmingly Protestant city now had a strong Catholic presence. Moreover, the newcomers had a distressing tendency, in Whig thinking, of joining the Democratic party once they were naturalized. This was quickly accomplished in the Louisville City Court since there was no federal role in naturalization until 1906.

The Germans, who brought trade skills with them, gravitated easily to beer brewing and meat packing. The latter had been an important trade in Louisville from at least the 1830s. Cattle and hogs were driven on foot from the Bluegrass area to Louisville, where they were slaughtered and packed for local consumption and shipment by river to the South. The slaughtering and the related leather tanning and soap making trades had been banned from the core of the city at an early date. This activity shifted to the eastern edge of the city in an area that became known as Butchertown, where German names abounded. Louisville in the 1850s was the third-largest pork-packing center in the nation.

Louisville historian Ben Casseday did not feel the Irish (who lived mostly in Portland and the western edge of Louisville) worth mentioning in his 1852 *History of Louisville*, but he praised the Germans, whom he described as "careful, pains-taking and industrious people, of quiet, unobtrusive and inoffensive manners, and . . . in a majority of instances, men of some education and ability." Casseday was particularly pleased with the Germans' "enthusiastic love and reverence for the intellectual and the beautiful." There was no hint in Casseday's work of the anti-foreign, anti-Catholic spirit boiling through the nation that would give rise to the American (or Know-Nothing) Party even as his book was on the press.

Walter Haldeman, publisher of the *Louisville Courier*, had adopted this nativist stance in the 1840s. This irrational response was particularly strong among Whigs, dominant in Louisville for some twenty years, because most immigrants voted the Democratic ticket. By 1854 the Know-Nothings, aided by Whig votes, gained control of the county government in an election marred by disturbances, including fights between nativists and Germans.

The Whig party, meanwhile, crippled by the death of Henry Clay in 1852 and split into pro- and anti-slavery factions, was in its death throes. George D. Prentice of the *Louisville Journal* concluded on March 20, 1855, that it was useless for the party to make nominations for state offices in the forthcoming August elections but that each Whig should vote his conscience. A short time later Prentice's conscience made him a shrill voice for Know-Nothingism. His editorial effusions have caused him to be blamed (somewhat unfairly) for the Know-Nothing riots known as "Bloody Monday" that swept the city on August 6, 1855. Scare tactics won the day for the Know-Nothings. Walter Haldeman had abandoned his nativist stance earlier that year, just in time to save his reputation. The deaths, property destruction, and voting irregularities of that infamous day shocked the city. Bloody Monday was perhaps one factor in turning Louisville into a Democratic stronghold during the rest of the nineteenth century. In 1865, only ten years after Bloody Monday, Philip Tomppert, German-born and a Democrat, was elected mayor.

Despite Bloody Monday, August 1855 brought one cheery note to the city. On August 25 the first train to carry passengers on the Louisville & Nashville (L&N) Railroad steamed south from its Ninth and Broadway terminus. Though it was only a demonstration run that went eight miles to the end of track in a dismal, swampy area known as the Wet Woods, it was a significant occasion. The long-hoped-for railroad to Nashville was taking tangible form. On board the train were "railroad dignitaries, the Mayor of the city, municipal officers, Know-Nothing Councilmen, Paddies by the dozen, a half-score of Afric's tawny children, and private citizens in abundance" (*Louisville Courier*, August 27, 1855). At the Wet Woods Irish track gangs were laying rails southward toward Tennessee. Louisville, which grew with the river trade, was turning to a new technology to maintain its strong stake in the southern market. The advent of railroads had initiated a slow shift of the nation's major transportation routes from water to land, threatening the city's position as a trans-shipment point around the Falls.

Louisville had gained its first rail connection in 1851, reaching Frankfort and Lexington. New Albany had opened its first railroad, the New Albany and Salem, to Salem, Indiana, in the same year. In 1852 the Jeffersonville Railroad completed its line to Columbus, Indiana, where it made connection to Indianapolis. But Louisville needed a rail route south and in 1850 the L&N was chartered. Construction was financed by the city of Louisville through purchase of $1 million in stock, and by private investors. It was the largest construction project in Kentucky up to that time and had to traverse rough knob country between Louisville and Elizabethtown. But on November 1, 1859, the first through train to Nashville carried distinguished guests with appropriate ceremonies at towns along the way. The 509 miles to Nashville via the Ohio and Cumberland Rivers had been reduced to 180 land miles. At Nashville connection was made with a line on to Atlanta. No longer would Louisville merchants be stymied by low water on the Ohio River in summer or ice blockage in winter. Ironically, initial construction was slowed by low water that delayed arrival of rails being shipped by steamboat.

With the opening of the L&N's main stem to Nashville, plus branches to Lebanon, Kentucky, and Memphis, Tennessee, Louisville thought that its new railroad spelled expanded, prosperous, and uninterrupted trade with the South. Yet less than two years later the city faced a total cutoff from its traditional trade territory. The guns that roared at Charleston, South Carolina, in April 1861, put Louisville in an awkward position. As a border city in a slave state with commercial ties to the North as well as the South, Louisville attempted for a short while to adopt a neutral stance. The City Council created perhaps the only municipal generalship in American history, naming attorney Lovell H. Rousseau a brigadier general commanding local military companies. His orders were to repel invaders from the North or the South. Though the city was divided in sentiment, local recruits for the Union army outnumbered Confederate recruits by three to one. What the majority of Louisvillians wanted was maintenance of the status quo—the Union and slavery.

Even before the Confederate assault on Fort Sumter (commanded by Major Robert Anderson, born at the Soldiers' Retreat plantation in eastern Jefferson County), when southern states were seceding one by one, a Union rally was held in Louisville. After "the raising of the stars and stripes over our magnificent Court House," James Speed spoke to the crowd. "Let us . . . be on our guard how we rashly step from off the Constitution and from under that flag" (*Louisville Courier*, February 23, 1861). But it was Louisville attorney and radical Republican Joseph Holt, postmaster general in the James Buchanan administration, who met the issue head-on in a speech July 13, 1861, at the Masonic Temple. "There is not and there cannot be any neutral ground for loyal people between their own government and those who, at the head of armies, are menacing its destruction. Your action is not neutrality, though you may delude yourself with the belief that it is so," he asserted. Walter Haldeman of the *Courier* was also one of the few who recognized that neutrality was impossible. Haldeman, who espoused the southern cause, asserted of Kentucky that "She will not be permitted to be so. Her [geographic] position forbids it."

That position also brought a near total stoppage of commerce and industry, even when secession was still only a threat. In a letter dated December 21, 1860, a partner in Brinly, Dodge & Hardy (now Brinly-Hardy) reported that "We have stopped both our bell and plow factory and business through our entire city has almost come to a stand. All seem with great anxiety and uneasiness to await the impending storm" *(Louisville*, May 1961, 12.) The following spring, after the firing on Fort Sumter, Haldeman's *Courier* (May 21, 1861) noted that "Our trade is blocked and our shipyards deserted." On May 2, the Treasury Department had issued an order banning trade with the Confederacy, although the surveyor of customs at Louisville was Walter Haldeman, who failed to enforce the order. The Confederacy, stockpiling while it could, found Louisville merchants and the new L&N Railroad willing to oblige as long as possible. The *Louisville Daily Democrat* of September 1, 1861, described the lively scene at the L&N depot at Ninth and Broadway as jammed "with drays, black drivers with long whips, singing amidst the tumult, and laughing and pushing forward . . . Broadway between Ninth and Tenth perfectly blocked . . . shipments of bacon, coffee, pork, beef—everything possible and impossible, and unexpected—from lady's gloves to terra cotta for a church in Tennessee."

The unreal hopes of neutrality for Kentucky were blasted on September 13, 1861, when Unionists, who controlled the General Assembly after the summer elections, rejected Governor Beriah Magoffin's demand that Confederate and Union forces that had occupied far-western Kentucky be withdrawn. The legislators instead demanded only withdrawal of the Confederate forces. With Kentucky decisively in the Union, federal authorities quickly suppressed Haldeman's *Courier* as "an advocate of treason," and Haldeman fled south to avoid arrest. The southern blockade was enforced, and the Confederates, in a quick move, seized Bowling Green on September 1 and sent an advance force to occupy Munfordville. Half of Louisville's new railroad to Nashville was in Confederate hands.

The situation was bleak for Louisville and remained so for the next two years. In addition to loss of trade, most merchants were unable to collect debts owed by southern customers for earlier purchases. The troubled economy was reflected in tax valuations for real estate, personal property, and merchandise. Real estate, valued at $27.2 million in 1860, reached a low of $19.8 million in 1862. Personal property sank from $462,243 in 1860 to a low of $281,454 in 1863. Merchandise on hand, valued at $5.2 million in 1860, reached a low of $2.9 million in 1862. Research by Stuart Seely Sprague of Morehead State University on the incomes of the wealthiest Louisvillians during the war years shows that most suffered drastic declines because of loss of trade. Though Louisville became a beehive of military activity, Sprague's research shows that military contracts with local businesses were minimal. Only the L&N Railroad, vital lifeline to the theater of war in Tennessee, Georgia, and Alabama, profited greatly.

One reason for the paucity of quartermaster contracts for food, clothing, and other military supplies may have been the bias of quartermaster officers from the North that Louisvillians were politically untrustworthy, harboring southern sympathies. Certainly that seems to have been the reason for the formation in March 1862 of the Louisville Board of Trade by more than one hundred merchants and manufacturers. Membership required a pledge of loyalty to the Union. The economic picture brightened somewhat in 1863 when Union forces controlled the Ohio and Mississippi Rivers from Louisville to New Orleans. The fall of Vicksburg was followed shortly by a note in the *Louisville Daily Democrat* that "A boat is loading for New Orleans." And on Christmas Eve 1863 a cargo of sugar and molasses arrived by river from New Orleans. Too, as Union forces occupied Nashville and other parts of Tennessee, restrictions on trade were eased and the L&N Railroad, now in Union hands, carried Louisville trade goods, as well as military materiel, south. The city's economic pinch was easing somewhat.

Only once was Louisville seriously threatened by Confederate forces. In the late summer of 1862 two Confederate armies, one commanded by General Edmund Kirby Smith, the other by General Braxton Bragg, moved into Kentucky. One objective was Louisville. Kirby Smith's forces entered Lexington on September 2. The state General Assembly, in session at Frankfort, fled to Louisville and resumed business in the Jefferson County Courthouse. While a ring of entrenchments was hastily dug around the city and pontoon bridges were constructed across the river to Indiana, women and children were ordered to evacuate to the Hoosier state. Bragg's troops approached Louisville, engaging in skirmishes at Middletown and, in some places, entering such suburban locations as California, where they could see the city's church spires in the distance. But the Confederate effort failed and southern troops fell back under Union pressure. The two forces finally met in combat at the bloody battle of Perryville. Louisville came out of this close call unscathed and was never threatened again.

Louisville's black population at the beginning of hostilities seemed to regard the conflict as a white man's war, even though the extension of slavery to new western states was the root cause. An Ohio officer's most vivid memory of Louisville in 1861 was "a sign bearing the inscription, in large black letters, NEGROES BOUGHT AND SOLD" (John Beatty, *The Citizen Soldier, or Memoirs of a Volunteer, 1861-1863*, Cincinnati 1879, 69-70). Though President Abraham Lincoln's Emancipation Proclamation did not apply to Kentucky as a Union state, slavery was dying slowly at the Falls of the Ohio. In the 1849 election for delegates to the convention to revise the state constitution 46 percent of Louisville voters cast ballots for the emancipation slate.

In 1860 African Americans, slave and free, were only 10 percent of the city's population and only 11.5 percent of Jefferson County's as a whole. Slaves made up only 7.5 percent of the city's population, but 25 percent of the county outside Louisville, where agriculture was dominant. Yet even this was down from the 32 percent recorded in 1850. Part of the reason for the relative decline in the city and county was the huge immigration of Germans and Irish in the 1850s that had increased the city's white population to 61,213 in 1860, an increase of nearly 60 percent over 1850. Some immigrants, especially Germans, took up farming in the county but used no slave labor. The decline in slavery was not only relative but also real. In Louisville the number of slaves dropped from 5,432 to 4,903 between 1850 and 1860. In the county outside Louisville the drop was from 5,479 to 5,402.

The coup de grace to Kentucky slavery was the decision of the Union army to recruit blacks beginning in March 1864. When a runaway slave enlisted he automatically became a free man and his owner was compensated at $300. By July 1864 an average of one hundred slaves a day were enlisting across the state. The Taylor Barracks in Louisville at Third and Oak Streets, then the outskirts of the city, was the induction point for area African Americans. The leader of one group of runaways from Shelby County, who came to Louisville under cover of darkness, recalled that "by twelve o'clock noon the owner of every man of us was in the city hunting his slaves but we had all enlisted save one boy, who was considered too young" *(Life and History of the Rev. Elijah P. Marrs,* Louisville 1885, 20).

With the end of the war and Confederate defeat in April 1865, Louisville relaxed somewhat. Unionists had celebrated the fall of Richmond, the Confederate capital, joined by other Louisvillians who, regardless of sympathies, celebrated the end of the four-year national convulsion. An official observance was proclaimed by Mayor Kaye for April 14, with parades, fireworks, and band concerts. Illuminated transparencies shone forth at night. One on a military headquarters building bore the welcome news of "No More Draft." A householder at Fifth and Broadway proclaimed his sentiments with a huge transparency reading "The Republic Triumphs Over Traitors at Home and Abroad."

Whatever the negative impact the hostilities had on Louisville, the end of the war found the city unscathed by battle and apparently in good economic shape. The tax valuations, which had plunged during the early stages of the conflict, were substantially higher in 1865 than they had been in 1860. Real estate was valued at $36 million, personal property at more than $503,000, and merchandise on hand at $9.1 million. Only five months after Lee's surrender at Appomattox Court house the *Democrat* observed that "Every carpenter, brick layer, and plasterer in the city is kept busy." The task now was to chart the city's course in a changed world.

It would take some time for Louisville to realize how much had changed. The first reaction was to resume the antebellum status quo. The *Courier* on July 12, 1866 (Walter Haldeman had returned), declared that "The merchants and business men of Louisville are now reaching out for the Southern trade. If Louisville is to grow and increase in prosperity and greatness it must be through the influence of the Southern trade." But the South, Louisville's traditional market area, was economically demoralized by the loss of the war and of a slave labor force.

Louisville's growth and prosperity had depended on its "middleman" role in supplying the prewar southern market through wholesalers and commission merchants, who lined Main Street That role was made possible by the Falls of the Ohio, which dictated that most goods had to be transported by land around the break in navigation. Those goods were stored in Louisville warehouses, handled by Louisville forwarders, insured by Louisville insurers, and the costs financed by Louisville banks. Now the expanding railroad network was changing that profitable pattern and undercutting the major role of the Ohio-Mississippi Rivers system. Merchandise could be shipped directly to the South from northern urban areas by rail, as northern capital took advantage of southern distress to finance and control new enterprises such as cotton mills and railroads. The Louisville wharf became a much quieter place as river traffic declined.

The L&N Railroad connected Louisville to Nashville, Memphis, and to the deeper South. One historian has described the L&N, in which city government had a heavy investment, as "Louisville's imperial weapon" (Leonard P. Curry, *Rail Routes South* Lexington, Kentucky, 1969). The city by the Falls took full advantage of the L&N and adopted new strategies for the changed southern market. The end of slavery and the rise of tenant farming meant the plantation owner was no longer the major customer, buying for his plantation operation. The crossroads store catering to tenant farmers, black and white, was now the sales target. Louisville merchants now had to employ traveling salesmen to reach this market. These drummers were almost all former Confederate officers, welcome in the South. Louisville also took pains to point out that rival Cincinnati was on the north side of the Ohio River.

But the major shift in postwar Louisville was the changed attitude toward manufacturing. It was noted in 1837 that "The spirit of manufactures is not manifested to a great extent" (*The Western Address Directory*, Baltimore 1837, 361-62). Yet an 1844 publication reported of Louisville: "Whilst it continued merely a commercial town, the increase in population was slow; but when, about four years ago, an impetus was given to manufactures, population commenced increasing rapidly" (*Kimball & James' Business Directory for the Mississippi Valley*, 345.) (This reference is apparently to foundries and machine shops.) A poll of factory owners in 1856 by the Louisville *Commercial Review* found that manufacturers' greatest complaint was that banks gave credit preference to merchants, thus slowing industrial growth.

With the change in the southern market and the shift in trade patterns from north-south to east-west with the populating of the western states, the city's financial institutions were apparently more willing to lend money for industrial enterprises, and manufacturing was a theme that rang through discussions of the city's future.

Newspapers were peppered with stories of new industrial undertakings. Some of the important products were listed in the Minute Book of the Louisville Board of Trade: agricultural implements, cement, furniture, iron work, oil, leather, wagons, whiskey, white lead, and woolen goods (minutes of October 24 and November 23, 1868, meetings). Among new enterprises and products were hydraulic elevators, paper, glass, oil refineries, edge-tool works, furniture factories, and others. The number of manufactories jumped from 436 in 1860 to 651 in 1870, and to 1,108 in 1880. Capitalization was $5 million in 1860, $10.7 million in 1870, and $21.6 million in 1880.

By 1870 the Louisville Cement Company, tapping its raw material from the limestone ledge that created the Falls of the Ohio and processing it in the old Tarascon Mill in Shippingport, was shipping an average of five rail carloads per day to Chicago. Louisville woolens found a ready market in St. Louis. Bremaker-Moore Paper Company, founded in May 1864 at the very dawning of the postwar era, sold its product in all parts of the nation.

Manufacturing provided new muscle for the city's economy, utilizing large forces of workers from laborers to highly skilled mechanics. The city never surpassed Cincinnati or St. Louis in output, but industrial employment climbed from 7,396 in 1860 to 10,315 in 1870, and to 21,937 in 1880. Manufacturing also disbursed its wages more widely than did the mercantile trade. Industrial gross profits in 1880 were $14.2 million, of which $5.8 million was paid in wages. Wholesalers had a small labor force, mostly unskilled, so that wages paid would have been much lower than for manufacturing.

No wonder that a writer in 1875 praised the promise of the "little forest of smokestacks that adorns our city" and chided the mercantile establishment: "By mere trading among ourselves the community can never be enriched . . . the secret of substantial and steady growth is found in workshops teeming with laborers and mechanics who are earning money from those living in distant parts of the country" (*Louisville Past and Present*, Louisville, 1875).

The rise of manufacturing also spurred the rise of street railways for public transit. *The Louisville Industrial and Commercial Gazette* pointed out that they not only spelled an end to "omnibuses with their rattling, rumbling motion and always "room for one more" but were essential to industrialization. "If we would have cheap labor, we must have cheap living. No city can . . . push forward her mechanical and manufacturing interests without providing ample and cheap accommodations for the operatives upon whom we are mainly dependent for our resources." The cheap accommodations were the shotgun cottages that were built in the thousands during the rest of the nineteenth century on the outskirts of the city. (The elite still lived close to the center of town on such streets as Broadway and Chestnut.) The shotgun cottage, probably originating in New Orleans, had reached Louisville by the 1850s and probably earlier. The street railways were necessary for workers to reach the rising factories. Soon the gaudily painted streetcars, drawn by mules with tinkling bells on their collars, trundled along all the main thoroughfares and many secondary streets.

The city's long-distance railway connections also proliferated. A route to Paducah, tapping the western Kentucky coal fields, lessened Louisville's dependence on river-borne Pennsylvania coal for its burgeoning industries. A line to Cincinnati, pushed by James Guthrie, opened in 1869. A route across Indiana and Illinois linked Louisville to St. Louis by 1890. Another route to western Kentucky paralleled the Ohio River, passing through Owensboro and Henderson and linking Louisville to Evansville, Indiana. But the most impressive local accomplishment was the building of the first bridge across the Ohio River at Louisville, linking the railroads of the South and North. At one mile in length, it was the longest iron bridge in the world when it was completed in 1870 according to Albert Fink's design. The moving spirit behind the construction was James Guthrie, who first broached the project in 1837.

Fink, who had completed Gideon Shryock's unfinished Jefferson County Courthouse in 1859, joined in the industrial surge as the founder of the Louisville Bridge and Iron Company in the early 1870s. With a large plant erected on Oak Street near Tenth, it garnered contracts for many bridges, especially for railroads. The iron work was produced by Louisville's two rolling mills along the riverfront.

To promote its new industrial stance, the Louisville business community sponsored a showcase for the city's manufacturers to display their products to potential buyers. The Louisville Industrial Exposition opened on September 3, 1872, in a specially constructed building on the northeast corner of Fourth and Chestnut Streets. With working machinery and displays of local products as chief attractions, the exposition was an annual event for several years. The annual expositions also offered band concerts, an art gallery, an aquarium, a natural history display, and other educational exhibits.

An even more elaborate display of the city's productions was the Southern Exposition, also privately financed and which opened August 1, 1883, in a huge building on a site between Hill Street and Magnolia Avenue and Fourth and Sixth Streets. The du Pont estate, later Central Park, immediately to the north, was also called into service as a promenade, picnic ground, and site of an art gallery. The most spectacular attraction was the electric lights—Thomas Edison's newly developed incandescent bulb. It was the largest installation yet of this new light source—4,600 bulbs. Although Edison himself did not attend the exposition, as Louisville myth holds, his invention was a nightly phenomenon. Another Edison development, an electric engine pulling a train of cars, was also part of the exposition. Running through the grounds of the du Pont estate, it was a marvel that foreshadowed the electric streetcars that would come to Louisville in 1889 and soon banish the mule-drawn cars to oblivion.

Both expositions were among Louisville's first serious efforts to market itself, its industrial production, and its commercial position to the world at large. The Southern Exposition was so popular that its projected single season was continued annually through 1887, receiving national attention each year. *Harper's Weekly* of August 4, 1883, for instance, commented that "The Great Southern Exposition . . . is an undertaking of the utmost importance, not only to the South, but to the entire Union, and the promoters of it are entitled to the highest credit . . . Unlike the Atlanta Cotton Exposition . . . the Louisville Exposition will not be confined to a single industry . . . The arrangements have been perfected in Louisville and all the money required has been obtained from those immediately interested. This fact, of itself, speaks volumes for the energy and self-respect of the community, for the Exposition is the most ambitious that has been undertaken in this country, with the exception of the Centennial."

The Courier-Journal, looking at Louisville as the exposition closed, catalogued $10 million in new construction in 1887 alone. With hometown pride it called Louisville "A New Gotham." By 1887 the area surrounding the exposition, later called Old Louisville, was becoming an elite neighborhood filled with substantial homes in the latest architectural styles, and Third Street was the city's choicest address.

As the nineteenth century neared its end, Louisvillians found new technologies entering their everyday lives. By 1900 the electric streetcar, at first greeted with some reservation because electricity was such a mysterious and dangerous force, had taken over all public transit except for three lightly used lines: one to Crescent Hill; another, known as the Beargrass line, from Bonnycastle Avenue out Bardstown and Taylorsville roads to Breckinridge Station, now Bowman Field; and a line along Greenwood Avenue to Riverview Park (later Chickasaw Park). All got electric cars in 1901, first year of the new century. Electric street lights began replacing the gas lights that had provided night-time illumination since 1837. The telephone, by the 1890s, was becoming common among businesses and the well-to-do.

The electric streetcar, far faster and more comfortable (it had heat) than its mule-drawn predecessor, had an unexpected effect. Suburban developments served by the electric car began springing up beyond the city limits. The eastern Highlands and the South End particularly were scenes of rapid development advertised heavily in the newspapers. Also adding incentive to this outward growth was the public parks system launched in the early 1890s and designed by the firm of Frederick Law Olmsted, the father of landscape architecture in America. Increasing air pollution from coal smoke was one incentive to create the parks as a place of clean air and recreation. *The Courier-Journal* as early as July 8, 1883, had noted that "Louisville is not a clean city, and since we have become a manufacturing town . . . we get blacker and blacker each year."

Developers in the Highlands capitalized on the creation of Cherokee Park as a lure to home buyers. Iroquois Park, south of the city limits, led to the development of Beechmont, Oakdale, Wilder Park, and other suburban enclaves. The West End, somewhat slower to respond to the real-estate boom, nevertheless benefited from Shawnee Park. Fontaine Ferry, a picnic ground boasting a riverside hotel as a retreat from summer heat, was served by the electric car and soon after the turn of the twentieth century was turned into an amusement park that was a summer destination of several generations of fun-seeking Louisvillians.

The tall office building also appeared in downtown Louisville for the first time. The best known was the Columbia Building (originally the Commercial Club Building), opened on January 1, 1891, on the northwest corner of Fourth and Main Streets. At ten stories, it was Louisville's tallest building for several years. The first "skyscraper" was the Kenyon Building of 1885. At six stories, it was the first in the city to exceed five stories. Later two additional stories were added. These early tall structures were supported by load-bearing walls. Later and taller ones were constructed of steel framing, much of which was supplied by Louisville's Grainger and Company.

As the century drew to a close Louisville could count three bridges across the Ohio River to Indiana, all railroad bridges. The Kentucky & Indiana Bridge, connecting Portland and New Albany, was opened in 1886. The Big Four Bridge (named for the Cleveland, Cincinnati, Chicago, and St. Louis Railroad, reaching all four big cities) opened in 1895. Nationwide economic depression had marked part of the decade, but Louisville struggled through and gained population. The 161,129 residents of 1890 had grown to 204,000 in 1900. *The Courier-Journal* was optimistic. On January 1, 1901, the first day of the twentieth century, the newspaper admonished its readers: "So, as the bells which ring out the old century still sound in our ears, let us thrill with exultation in the race which we know [mankind] is to run in the century that is to come."

The century that came proved a mixed bag in its first decade, with good news and bad. Industrial employment had increased from 17,921 in 1890 to 29,926 at the turn of the century. On January 4, 1901, James Ross Todd announced plans for the city's second ten-story office building, following the Columbia

Building of 1891. The Todd Building was erected on the northeast corner of Fourth and Market Streets. Other building projects followed: the elegant new Seelbach Hotel at Fourth and Walnut (Muhammad Ali Blvd.) in 1905, replacing the original Seelbach at Sixth and Main Streets; the Paul Jones Building of 1906 (later the Marion E. Taylor Building) on Fourth Street between Jefferson and Liberty Streets on the site of the fire-destroyed Masonic Temple; the Washington Building on the northwest corner of Fourth and Market Streets (1906) reaching fourteen stories; Stewart's Dry Goods Company (1907), at Fourth and Walnut across from the Seelbach; the Louisville & Nashville Railroad office building at Ninth and Broadway (1907), an early example of the elongated slab-shaped office structure; the Electric Building (1912), home of the Louisville Lighting Company, on Fourth Street south of Chestnut Street. The Starks Building (1912), on the northeast corner of Fourth and Walnut rose to an amazing sixteen stories.

All of this building was related to the spread of the central business district, especially south on Fourth Street toward Broadway, and the simultaneous decline of Market Street as the principal shopping thoroughfare. The southward push on Fourth Street replaced the substantial residences of the well-to-do that still lined Fourth south of Walnut Street, as well as the original St. Joseph's Infirmary, predecessor of Audubon Hospital. Jeweler William C. Kendrick, who lived on Fourth near Broadway at the turn of the century, recalled, "How often, when sitting on our front porch, watching the passing throng and looking at the few electric lights . . . I asked my wife if she thought business would sufficiently encroach upon this block during our lifetime to make it unpleasant as a residence" (Kendrick, *Reminiscences of Old Louisville*, 1937:47). It did.

At the same time once-prestigious residential addresses such as Walnut and Chestnut Streets and Broadway were beginning to fade, losing their residents especially to the rapidly developing areas east of downtown, known collectively as the Highlands. There, Cherokee Park had gained the reputation as the finest of Frederick Law Olmsted's three major public parks of the 1890s. The South and West Ends also witnessed substantial growth, but neither matched the Highlands in prestige.

A new residential form, the apartment building, also blossomed during the decade. Louisville's first apartment complex, the Rossmore (later the Berkeley Hotel) had been erected in 1893-94 on Fourth Street a bit north of Broadway. It was slow, however, to be emulated. Only the five-story St. James Flats (1897) on prestigious St. James Court followed the Rossmore in that decade. But by 1912 there were 138 apartment buildings, most in or near downtown. The most impressive was the Weissinger-Gaulbert (1903, 1912) at Third and Broadway with spacious apartment units boasting all the latest advances in plumbing, heating, lighting, and other residential creature comforts.

The turn of the century also brought a new entertainment medium—the motion picture—that was to largely change the function of the theater from live actors on stage to projected images on a silver screen. Louisville's first movie theater—the Dreamland—opened in 1904 in a remodeled storefront on Market Street near Fifth. Admission to see a short one-reel film was a nickel. Other "nickelodeons" soon appeared. In 1909 the Hopkins Theater (formerly Liederkranz Hall) switched to motion pictures, and in 1912 Hollywood's increasingly sophisticated products prompted construction of the Majestic Theater on Fourth Street near Guthrie. It was the first theater in Louisville built especially for movies and in subsequent years was joined by many others, both downtown and in the neighborhoods. By 1913 the Mary Anderson, named for Louisville's own renowned actress, admitted the motion picture. Even the venerable Macauley's Theatre screened an occasional outstanding film, such as one-time Louisvillian David Wark Griffith's *Birth of a Nation* in 1916 and *Intolerance* in 1917.

Yet, despite all these new trappings and the ascendancy of Fourth Street (called Fourth Avenue to give it more panache), the city was in for a shock when the results of the 1910 census were released. Louisville had continued to gain during the decade but added only 19,197 new residents for a total of 223,928. It was the slowest rate of growth since Louisville's founding—only 9.4 percent. Even worse, industrial employment had decreased to 28,716 from the 1900 total of 29,926. Clearly something was amiss. At the same time population in the county beyond the city had increased by thirteen thousand, or 42.4 percent. In previous decades county population had increased very slowly—by only 349, for example, during the 1890s.

The reasons for the shift in statistics were easily identified. The spread of population to new suburban areas was made possible by the network of electric interurban railways that spread out from the city, reaching such points as Prospect, Anchorage, Jeffersontown, St. Matthews, Middletown, Fern Creek, Okolona, Pleasure Ridge Park, and many others. Each route became a corridor of urban development with frequent service, allowing employment in the city and residence in semirural areas. Still, political power remained in the city since the county's 39,000 residents were no match for Louisville's nearly 224,000.

The decline in industrial employment was another matter. Many of the city's smaller manufacturers had ceased operations, unable to compete on price with mass production by the large national corporations that were emerging. These corporations were able to ship their output nationwide because of the virtual completion of the railroad network. Other local manufacturers had shifted operations beyond the city limits where land costs were cheaper. The incorporated town of Highland Park, south of the city, was especially favored. Workers tended to follow their employers out of the city.

The answer to population spillage beyond the city limits was annexation, although court challenges delayed the huge expansion of the city boundaries until 1922, when eleven square miles and some forty thousand residents were added. The answer to the decline in manufacturing was long debated in the business community, which came up with a plan in 1916. That year the Board of Trade launched what was called the Million Dollar Factory Fund, raising private funding to make loans to promising enterprises that might have trouble securing bank credit. The nonprofit Louisville Industrial Foundation was created in which some 540 local businesses and individuals participated in raising $1 million. The funds were used to make the loans, on which interest was charged. Through the years numerous small enterprises with potential were attracted to Louisville. Most were successful, especially a small cleaning-powder manufacturer owned by three Reynolds brothers who moved the operation from Virginia. It evolved into Reynolds Metals. The foundation continued its operation into the 1950s though its basic purpose was diminished by Roosevelt-era federal agencies such as the Small Business Administration. (The foundation was closed in December 1986 after a long period of inactivity.)

The new apartment buildings and suburban developments were populated exclusively by whites. African Americans could not afford to reside in such quarters, and even if they had been economically able to do so they were barred by custom. The black community, growing in numbers, was restricted to its traditional neighborhoods created by the influx of former slaves after the Civil War. Smoketown, east of the central city, along with California and Little Parkland (sometimes called Little Africa) on the west were the principal African American enclaves. There was also Fort Hill to the south and even farther south in the incorporated community of Highland Park was Bucktown. To the east was Clifton Heights north of Crescent Hill on the rising ground along Brownsboro Road.

This informal (and thus incomplete) pattern of segregation, with areas where blacks had established their own institutions and social groups, was well understood by both races. Relations between blacks and whites had deteriorated during the latter years of the nineteenth century, as they had throughout the South, and in 1914 an attempt was made to turn the informal boundaries into rigid, legal ones. This move was kindled by the growing black population and "the gradual influx of the Negro into blocks or squares where none but whites reside" (The *Courier-Journal*, Nov. 15, 1913, quoting a speech before the Louisville Real Estate Exchange). The ordinance, prohibiting blacks from buying property on blocks where whites resided and whites from buying on blocks where blacks resided, was adopted unanimously by the City Council and the Board of Aldermen (Louisville had a bicameral legislative system at the time) and signed by Mayor John Buschemeyer on May 11, 1914. Among newspapers, only the Republican-oriented *Louisville Herald* exhibited opposition, but only mildly. A two-paragraph article on page five of the May 12, 1914, issue observed that the ordinance would "colonize the white and Negro races in Louisville."

African-American reaction to the law was immediate. The Louisville Chapter of the National Association for the Advancement of Colored People (NAACP) was formed and moved quickly to set up a test case with the help of a white real-estate agent who opposed the law. After the legislation was upheld by both the Jefferson Circuit Court (December 24, 1914) and the Kentucky Court of Appeals (June 18, 1915), the NAACP took the case to the United States Supreme Court. In a unanimous decision on November 5, 1917, the court declared the law unconstitutional, not because it discriminated but because it interfered with the right of a property owner to dispose of property as he or she pleased. One of the justices was Louisvillian Louis D. Brandeis, the first Jewish member of the high court.

By the time the Supreme Court ruled on the housing issue a larger development was engaging Louisville. The United States entered World War I in April 1917, and the fact that Louisville possessed some political clout in Washington was demonstrated by the announcement that one of the military training camps to be established Camp Zachary Taylor, would be just south of the city, named for the only United States president to come from Jefferson County. The Board of Trade was instrumental in securing the post that by the end of November 1917 housed twenty-eight thousand recruits learning the trade of war and spending money in Louisville. It was a mixed blessing, however, when the worst influenza epidemic the nation has known spread to Camp Taylor and then to the civilian population in the fall of 1918. Soldiers returned from France were the likely source of the epidemic that earned the name of "the Spanish Lady." Altogether more than eleven thousand soldiers became ill and fifteen hundred died. Louisville civilian deaths from the flu in 1918 totaled 879 compared to 41 in 1917. In the spring of 1921 the federal government sold Camp Taylor's nearly three thousand acres in bits and pieces at auction. Through the 1920s the site developed into a lower-middle-class enclave, its winding streets designed for a military camp serving a rather hodgepodge residential area still called Camp Taylor.

On January 16, 1920, the United States went officially dry. The sale or use of alcoholic beverages was prohibited except for "near beer," a product with only 0.5 percent alcohol. That loophole permitted Louisville brewers to survive the ultimately failed "noble experiment." Oertel's Brewery developed a cereal beverage with the legal limit of alcohol and advertised it as "a pleasant memory." The whiskey distillers were left without a market, however, except for sales of "medicinal" whiskey through pharmacies by a physician's prescription. The loss of jobs by the distilleries and related businesses (such as barrel makers) was estimated at between six and eight thousand.

But other segments of the Louisville economy boomed along with the wave of prosperity that swept across the nation. The decline in industrial employment, a worry earlier, was dramatically reversed. It climbed from 29,902 in 1919 to 36,860 by the end of the decade. From 1923 to 1927 alone the city gained 153 new manufacturing plants, many through the efforts of the Louisville Industrial Foundation. As in earlier periods, the new industries were a diversified group, including the production of scales for food markets, trailers for the new trucking industry, components for automobile bodies, and gasoline refineries to feed the voracious appetite of the flood of automobiles.

If the decade was the Jazz Age as described by novelist F. Scott Fitzgerald, who spent time at Camp Taylor as a second lieutenant during World War I (and time drinking at the Seelbach Hotel), it was also the flowering of the automobile age. The number of motor vehicles in Jefferson County doubled during the 1920s, reaching 54,524 by 1930. Traffic jams developed downtown. It was seriously planned to widen Fourth Street between York and Chestnut, and J. Graham Brown, who had made a fortune from lumbering operations in the South had his fifteen-story Brown Hotel, opened in 1923 at Fourth and Broadway, built so as to allow the widening that never was accomplished. The onslaught of automobiles required that police direct traffic at downtown intersections and finally led to the use of traffic lights. The proliferation of automobiles also resulted in a new bridge across the Ohio River to Indiana. The ferries between Louisville and Jeffersonville had long carried horse-drawn wagons and carriages, but the sheer number of autos swamped this transportation mode and caused irritating delays. The first move for a new bridge began in 1923, but financing was a problem. That was finally solved by building a toll bridge and using the tolls to pay off the construction bonds. The Municipal Bridge (later the George Rogers Clark Bridge) at Second Street opened November 1, 1929. During its first hour of business seventy-two cars paid the thirty-five-cent toll to cross. On December 31, the Jeffersonville ferries made their last runs. Many of the cars crossing the bridge were Fords assembled at the plant opened in 1925 on Southwestern Parkway, replacing the assembly plant built only a decade earlier at Third Street and Eastern Parkway. In that short period its output capacity fell short of meeting demand.

The automobile brought with it a new and uncontrolled mobility. Suburban developments, once dependent on the controlled mobility (a defined corridor) of the electric streetcar and interurban, could now spring up almost anywhere. It was the beginning of sprawl (halted only temporarily by the Depression and World War II) that was to change the landscape of Jefferson County as farms were turned into housing tracts. The automobile was bad news for public transit. Louisville Railway Company officials, with an air of naive optimism, declared in 1924 that "The increasing difficulties of finding suitable parking space . . . together with the cost of operation, we believe, are gradually discouraging the use of automobiles by private owners." The company did begin using a few buses in 1923 to reach the new suburban developments beyond the end of streetcar routes and even established an east-west cross-town bus route on Hill Street.

The automobile was a major factor in another development of the 1920s—the introduction of planning and zoning in Louisville. Previously the city had developed willy-nilly. There was no attempt to designate specific uses for private land, except in the early days when butchering and leather tanning were barred from the heart of the community. A patchwork pattern of usage developed, with industrial plants, housing, retail stores, and other uses sometimes side by side. Suggestions for zoning certain areas for specific uses began as early as 1901, but the automobile brought the issue to the fore. Motorists caught at long waits at railroad crossings, gasoline stations on residential streets, the need to control on-street parking and to provide more direct auto routes through the metropolitan area caused civic leaders to seek state authority to enact planning and zoning regulations. The General Assembly was, at best, lukewarm to such a proposal and several efforts to gain approval were rebuffed, but in 1930 the authority was granted. The first priority was a planning blueprint for street improvements to speed traffic flow. Zoning was tackled later. Louisville became the first Kentucky city with a planning and zoning agency. It later became a joint city/county agency.

Another form of transportation came to the community in the form of an airfield along Taylorsville Road in 1919. It was created by A.H. Bowman, owner of a local truck-delivery firm and an aviation enthusiast. He leased the land from the federal government and in 1922 his lease was taken over by the U.S. Army as a pilot training center. In 1923 the Army gave it the name Bowman Field. Seeing the possibilities of commercial aviation, the Board of Trade pushed for municipal ownership and succeeded in this goal in 1927. The following year Continental Air Lines, predecessor of American Airlines, began Cleveland-Louisville service. A passenger terminal in the fashionable art deco style followed in 1929, along with paved runways.

The African-American community, which had won a Supreme Court victory in the segregated housing case, confronted another issue in 1920 and won the day. The University of Louisville, which for years consisted only of the medical and law schools, had added an academic department in 1907 providing classes in the sciences and liberal arts. It was housed in a former residence on Broadway and by 1920, with an enrollment of 615, was pressed for space. The university had been given a campus site in the Highlands by the Belknap family in 1916 but had no building funds. In 1920 a $1 million city bond issue for construction of a modern education plant was defeated at the polls. It was the black voters who made the difference. They saw no reason to tax themselves to help finance an institution from which they were barred by law and custom. In 1924 university trustees saw an opportunity to expand by purchasing the vacated grounds of the Industrial School of Reform, which had moved from Third Street to eastern Jefferson County. Here was a campus setting with buildings that could be adapted to educational use. The purchase was financed largely by selling the Highlands property, and the name Belknap Campus was given the new site to honor the Belknap gift. Again a $1 million bond issue was put on the ballot, but this time $100,000 would be put aside to provide higher education facilities for blacks. On November 4, 1925, the bond issue was approved overwhelmingly. More Speed gifts were also forthcoming: one for the J.B. Speed Art Museum on the north end of the campus; another for the Speed Scientific School to train engineers. In 1931 the Louisville Municipal College at Seventh and Kentucky Streets was opened for African Americans.

Another development in higher education was the opening, in 1920, of Spalding (originally Nazareth College), a Catholic school for women, in the former Tompkins/Buchanan mansion on Fourth Street near Breckinridge Street. Founded by the Sisters of Charity of Nazareth, its goal was to prepare women for their expanding role "in social, public, and political life." In that year women had at last won the right to vote. Presumably in Louisville most voted Republican. That party controlled city and county government all through the 1920s.

Meanwhile, despite the spreading automobile suburbs, downtown Louisville thrived with the prosperity of the Twenties. By 1923 plans for new office building expenditures totaled $15 million. It was the place for serious shopping, though each neighborhood was served by a small collection of grocery, hardware, and drug stores (most of the latter with soda fountains), barber shops, and the like. *Forbes Magazine* in 1927 reported "an awful lot of riveting" downtown, and property values escalated. The Starks Building at Fourth and Walnut (Muhammad Ali Boulevard) was enlarged to the east along Walnut in 1925, taking over the site of Macauley's Theatre in the process. At the same time J. Graham Brown was erecting the Brown Medical Building next to his hotel. He added the Brown Theatre to his plans so that traveling stage troupes would still have a performance site. By 1930, motion pictures had been added. In 1926 Brown erected the Martin Brown Building on the northwest corner of Fourth and Broadway. The following year William Heyburn, president of the Belknap Hardware empire, began construction of the Heyburn Building on the southeast corner. It seemed that Fourth and Broadway might replace Fourth and Walnut as the heart of downtown. The *Herald-Post* was moved on January 27, 1927, to call it "the Magic Corner."

Sumptuous new cinemas also appeared on Fourth Street: the

Rialto, with marble splendor, in 1921; and Loew's State, the most elaborate of all, in 1928. Out at Churchill Downs the Kentucky Derby, under the tutelage of Matt Winn, was achieving its rank as America's premier Thoroughbred racing event. The city was prospering and the population at the end of the decade had reached a satisfying 307,745, a gain of nearly seventy-three thousand over 1920.

President Herbert Hoover was still in his first year in office when he arrived in Louisville by river from Cincinnati on October 23, 1929, the first president to come to the city by boat in decades. The occasion was the completion of the Ohio River canalization project, funded by federal appropriations. It provided a minimum nine-foot depth of water year-round. It had taken years to complete the series of locks and dams that made it possible. It was expected to give a shot in the arm to the ailing river trade that in the 1820s had transformed Louisville from a slowly growing town to the largest city in Kentucky. After a speech at the new Memorial Auditorium at Fourth and Kentucky Streets, the president spent the night at the Brown Hotel and departed the next day by train for Washington.

The weather in Louisville during the president's visit was damp and chilly, a seeming omen of what happened a week later. On October 29, the stock market crashed, leading *Variety*, the theatrical publication, to coin its famous headline "Wall Street lays an Egg." It was the beginning of the Great Depression that was to last a decade and its impact was soon felt in Louisville. The riveting stopped on Fourth Street Construction employment in March 1930 was down 50 percent from a year earlier. Overall unemployment in April was 9 percent and rising. By fall, city government was forced to launch an aid program, providing employment at odd jobs three days a week for thirty cents an hour. More than eleven thousand registered for work, more than could be handled. Two years later only twenty-two hundred make-work jobs could be provided.

The most spectacular effect of the sudden change in the economy was the failure of the National Bank of Kentucky on November 17, 1930. Headed by the flamboyant James B. Brown, the bank had engaged for some time in questionable loan practices and had withdrawn from the Federal Reserve Bank system. In its plunge Brown's bank took with it the Louisville Trust Company, the Security Bank, the Bank of St. Helens, and two African-American institutions, First Standard and American Mutual Savings Banks. All had used National of Kentucky as a depository. By 1932 Louisville unemployment was an estimated 23.5 percent among whites and 37.2 percent among blacks. Retail sales that year were 60 percent below 1929.

Fortunately Louisville had some depression-proof industries. Demand was high for inexpensive clothing like that turned out by Enro Shirt Company. The Kentucky Macaroni Company's product price suited depression-era budgets, while demand for tobacco products boomed. Louisville's production of ten-cents-a-pack cigarettes increased every year of the Depression, reaching literally in the billions annually. Brown & Williamson Tobacco Corporation, a 1929 newcomer to Louisville, averaged three thousand production workers throughout the Thirties. Axton-Fisher Tobacco Company constructed a seven-story addition to its plant in 1932 to keep up with demand. (The company was later taken over by Philip Morris Tobacco Company.)

Another bright spot was the resumption of beer brewing in 1933, providing more jobs. The new Congress, elected with the Franklin D. Roosevelt landslide in 1932, quickly amended Prohibition to permit brewing of beer with a 3.2 percent alcohol content. The new product went on sale in Louisville on April 6, 1933, labeled by the press as "Foamy Friday." The repeal of Prohibition also brought new jobs. Brown-Forman Distillers, anticipating approval of repeal, began construction of a new distillery in the summer of 1933 and began mashing operations on November 11, later hiring a thousand women to operate the bottling line. Other distilleries were also reopened or built anew. In 1935 Joseph E. Seagram & Sons chose Louisville as the site of the world's largest distillery, completed in 1937 on Seventh Street Road.

Though employment remained below normal all through the Thirties, the darkest days were behind by 1934. In the fall of that year The *Board of Trade Journal* happily reported that all "For Rent" signs had vanished from downtown Fourth Street between Main and Broadway. By 1937 the city had entered a period of mild boom compared to 1932-33. The value of industrial output in 1937 was $294 million, higher than the 1929 figure of $271 million. Only two other cities, Detroit and Atlanta, showed such a result.

Federal job-creation programs also provided employment to some six thousand Louisvillians and left some permanent monuments in the city: a new home on Belknap Campus for the University of Louisville School of Law, branch libraries, newly paved streets, sewer lines, and other urban improvements, including construction of subsidized housing projects. During the 1930s it was first recognized that government had a major role to play during times of economic distress.

And it was during this decade that African-Americans achieved significant political breakthroughs. An attempt in the 1920s to elect black candidates for city and state offices through the Independent Lincoln Party had failed. But with shifting political alliances in the 1930s both the Democrat and Republican parties were willing to sponsor black candidates in areas with a heavy black vote. In 1933 C. Eubank Tucker, an attorney and a bishop of the AME Zion church, became a candidate for state representative as an independent with Democratic backing. He was defeated by his white Republican opponent but attracted enough black votes for the overall Democratic slate that Neville Miller was elected mayor, ending Republican control of City Hall that dated from World War I.

In 1937, when the Great Depression was in slow retreat, a natural disaster of unprecedented dimensions brought Louisville—and the whole Ohio Valley—to a temporary standstill. The greatest flood the valley had ever known began on January 6 with an inch of rain, followed shortly by day after day of rain from Pittsburgh to Cairo. Nearly half the rainfall for the year fell in the month of January. By January 20, the river had risen eighteen feet. On January 23, the rise was thirty feet, equaling the highest flood ever recorded, and it continued rising. The next day electric power failed, and tap water was available only two hours each day. The crest was reached on January 27 at nearly eleven feet over the 1884 record. Three-quarters of the city had been inundated, affecting 250,000 residents, most of whom had to be moved to places of refuge. There were ninety flood-related deaths and some

$50 million in property damage. The river was not back to normal until mid-February. WPA workers scraped tons of mud from streets and sidewalks. By the running of the sixty-third Kentucky Derby on the first Saturday in May there were few physical reminders of the great flood. Billboards throughout the city had been transformed into exhortations in giant letters: "San Francisco Did It; Chicago Did It; Louisville Can Do It!"

As the troubled decade ended there were some hopeful signs. Jefferson County in 1940 showed an overall population increase of more than thirty thousand, and also the beginning of a trend that would reshape the dynamics of city and county. The county outside Louisville increased by 18,710, more than the city's increase of 11,332. Although the city population was larger than the rest of the county (319,077 to 66,315), it was the first time that the non-city area had increased more than the city. It was a trend that would accelerate in the future. On the cultural front, the decade ended with a symphony orchestra led by a professional, salaried conductor, Robert Whitney, who came to Louisville in 1937 to lead the Louisville Civic Orchestra, which soon changed its name to the Louisville Philharmonic Orchestra and then simply the Louisville Orchestra. That same year, *Harper's Monthly Magazine* ran an article on Louisville that referred to the city as "an American museum piece," largely because it boasted no national manufacturing names except Ford Motor Company in its industrial economy. It was a city of home-owned industry. That would soon change.

World War II probably had more impact on Louisville than any previous conflict, perhaps even more than the Civil War, though, unlike that struggle, it was far from the scenes of battle. When the nation adopted a stance of "defense preparedness" after the outbreak of war in Europe in 1939, it was to have an immediate economic impact on the greater Louisville area and would erase the last vestiges of Depression-era unemployment.

The first inkling of what was to come made news in early 1940 when E.I. du Pont de Nemours & Company took options on six thousand acres of prime Indiana farmland near the small community of Charlestown (population 750) in Clark County. Though the company refused to comment, the local guess was that Du Pont would build a plant to manufacture its new synthetic fabric, nylon. Not until July 1940 was it revealed that the $30-million facility would produce smokeless powder for artillery shells. It was officially the Indiana Ordnance Works, but in popular parlance it was "the powder plant." Predictions were that it would employ some four thousand workers. By the summer of 1941 there were thirty-two thousand.

The powder plant was only the first in a series of defense-related industrial operations that came to Louisville and southern Indiana. In late 1940 the city was selected as the site for a $26-million naval ordnance station to turn out heavy guns for battleships. In southern Indiana an installation to prepare bagged powder charges for artillery was built adjacent to the powder plant. It was officially the Hoosier Ordnance Works, but in common usage "the bag plant." Then in early 1941 the Louisville Industrial Foundation announced that the city was in the running for a plant to make synthetic rubber. In March it was confirmed that the plant, to be operated by Du Pont, would come to Louisville. A month earlier it had been announced that National Carbide Company would build a plant in the Bell's Lane area to make acetylene, an essential ingredient in Du Pont's synthetic rubber formula. Before the year was over two more synthetic rubber plants were in the works, operated by Goodrich and National Synthetic Rubber. Their formula was different from Du Pont's, but Louisville distilleries turned to wartime production of industrial alcohol, essential to butadiene used in the formula. Louisville, almost overnight, became the world's largest producer of synthetic rubber, turning out 195,000 tons in the peak production year of 1944. The Bell's Lane area was soon dubbed Rubbertown.

Another wartime newcomer was the Curtiss-Wright Corporation facility designed to turn out a largely wooden experimental cargo plane, the C-76. When the first plane crashed on a test flight in May 1943, the plant turned to production of conventional C-46 cargo carriers. The plant was located at Louisville's second airport, with the prosaic name of Municipal Airport Number Two, renamed Standiford Field in July 1941. In April 1942 it was announced that Nichols General Hospital would be erected at Berry Boulevard and Manslick Road. The $318 million facility with a thousand beds was by far the largest medical institution in Louisville. At the same time the huge Louisville Medical Depot was built south of Louisville along the Louisville & Nashville Railroad. In Jeffersonville the preparedness program brought the venerable Howard Shipyard & Dry Dock operation back to life. The Navy contracted with the adjoining Jeffersonville Boat & Machine Company to operate the yard, which turned out submarine chasers and specialized craft used for assault landings on beaches in Normandy and the Pacific Islands. The craft were small enough to navigate the Ohio/Mississippi Rivers system to the sea.

Other long-established industries also turned to war production: Tube Turns and Henry Vogt Machine Company made artillery shells; Hillerich & Bradsby turned out rifle stocks; Ford Motor Company produced nearly one hundred thousand jeeps at the Louisville plant on Southwestern Parkway. There was hardly an industrial operation in Louisville that was not engaged in war production in some way. The distilleries not only produced alcohol for use in making synthetic rubber, but also for smokeless-powder manufacture and for general industrial use. Defense employment in the area reached a peak of eighty thousand in 1944, many of them women, black and white, while older black males found good paying jobs as well.

There was concern that at war's end the civilian economy would not be able to keep the industrial bonanza in operation since demand for much of the output would drop drastically. As early as January 1, 1942, shortly after the United States entered the war, a *Courier-Journal* editorial asked "What is to happen when the war is over? Can the powder plant and the naval gun plant and the other war materials plants be readily converted? If so, will there be tenants willing to convert them?"

The answer was a resounding yes. The Curtiss-Wright plant was taken over by International Harvester for tractor production. Synthetic rubber had become a staple, and Louisville remained the largest center of production. Some of the plants were taken over by plastics producers. Reynolds Metals expanded its Louisville operations. It was, for Louisville, an industrial revolution.

Downtown Louisville at the end of the war was still the area of serious shopping, although plans for the first suburban shopping center were announced in December 1945. The center was in St. Matthews, still an unincorporated community, in the triangular space where Frankfort Avenue and Lexington Road join to form Shelbyville Road. It included a movie theater as well as shops. No planner seems to have realized that with the end of the war all restraints on an outward flow from the city had been removed. The age of sprawl had arrived. Thousands of acres of farmland were transformed into subdivisions in the postwar years, and the transformation continued at the end of the twentieth century.

Accelerating this momentum, curbed by fifteen years of depression and war, were two other developments. Louisville, which had expanded its boundaries through the years by annexation, found itself severely restricted in continuing this process. In addition, the expressway system, seen as a way to easily reach the heart of the city, turned out to also make suburbia easily accessible.

The annexation problem arose, oddly enough, from the repeal of Prohibition. Many of the new distilleries were near the unincorporated community of Shively, commonly known as St. Helens. In order to prevent annexation by Louisville and the higher taxes that would follow, the distilleries in 1938 encouraged Shively to incorporate. During most of its history Jefferson County was home to only three municipalities: Louisville (1780), Jeffersontown (1797), and Anchorage (1878). Strathmoor Village and Strathmoor Manor followed in 1928 and 1931. Shortly before Shively's sixth-class city status was approved, a bill passed the state General Assembly requiring a first-class city (thus only Louisville) to receive approval of at least 50 percent of the citizens of an incorporated community before it could be annexed. Seven of the eight Louisville representatives, including future Mayor Charles Farnsley, voted for it, as did all three Louisville senators. The bill had been introduced by a legislator from western Kentucky, obviously acting on behalf of other interests. Farnsley himself is suspected of originating the bill. His family had long-time Shively connections.

Soon other communities outside Louisville such as Audubon Park and Indian Hills incorporated as cities. In the past Louisville had annexed neighboring incorporated communities, beginning with Portland in 1852, and later Crescent Hill, Parkland, Oakdale, South Louisville, and many others. Some asked to be annexed; others objected. The latter often sued to annul the action, but the courts invariably held that the annexation would provide better services and upheld the action. Because of the 1938 legislation, Louisville could annex only unincorporated county territory. The result after World War II was a spate of small cities throughout Jefferson County. At the end of the twentieth century there were ninety-three incorporated communities, not including Louisville. This wholesale small city creation was one of the problems with which Farnsley had to deal as mayor from 1948 to 1953.

His answer was the occupational license tax—an income tax on the wages of every person who worked in Louisville. Since most suburbanites worked in the city, it meant they had to pay a tax to the city. The additional revenue—$3 million the first year—eased Louisville's financial stringency and allowed Farnsley to pursue badly needed street paving projects, additional police, more playgrounds, new schools, better public-health services, and more funds for the public library system. Jefferson County government, impressed with the results of the tax, later adopted a similar system. With Louisville's geographical expansion severely restricted Farnsley concluded by late 1948 that consolidation of city and county was the only solution and was an early voice advocating such a move. But several attempts in later years to get voters to approve a merger were defeated. Suburban voters, especially, were opposed.

Farnsley, a fountain of innovative ideas himself, also had the assistance of the Louisville Area Development Association (LADA), that had been formed in 1943 under the aegis of Mayor Wilson W. Wyatt. Looking to postwar readjustment and planning, LADA was a private, non-partisan group funded by businesses to correct problems created by past haphazard growth, to create an orderly framework for future growth, and—especially—to see that the great growth in industrial capacity during the war years would continue in operation. During the next few years LADA was active in numerous fields: planning an expressway system long before the Interstate highway system was conceived, school planning, the arts, health, housing, consolidation of certain city and county governmental functions, parks and recreation, to name a few. The Watterson Expressway is a direct descendant of LADA planning. In a further move to centralize planning and development, LADA in 1950 became the chief organization merged into the new Louisville Chamber of Commerce (later Greater Louisville, Inc.). The new organizations also absorbed the Board of Trade and a few smaller groups concerned with conventions and tourism. While Chamber planners were wooing industry, the biggest postwar development of all came out of the blue.

In the spring of 1951 the giant General Electric Corporation announced that it would consolidate all its home-appliance manufacturing in a huge plant, to be called Appliance Park, on a one-thousand-acre site near the small community of Buechel, southeast of Louisville. It came as a surprise to everyone, even to the Chamber of Commerce. General Electric had scouted several cities in profound secrecy before choosing Louisville as central to its market. Rail and road transport provided the network to reach all areas of that market; electric power costs were below the national average; the Louisville Water Company could supply more than enough of its commodity; the labor force was adequate. Appliance Park was to become the area's largest employer, each of its five divisions providing an average of five thousand jobs.

General Electric, along with the war-born industrial plants, looked to a national market for their products. This was a profound shift for Louisville, where the South had been the primary market since before the Civil War. It was also these national corporations, whose headquarters tended to be on the East Coast, who lent their muscle to the effort to have Louisville put on Eastern Standard Time, a goal accomplished in July 1961.

Another significant development in the postwar years was the slow erosion of the color bar that had kept African Americans from most public facilities, restaurants, and the leading downtown department stores. Black employment in war industries and service in the armed forces had created rising expectations and a new activism in seeking equal opportunities with whites. In 1948, at Mayor Farnsley's urging, the main public library was opened to blacks, with all branch libraries following suit in 1952. Also in 1948 two Catholic hospitals began admitting African Americans, whose only choice had been the Red Cross Hospital or the basement wards of the Louisville General Hospital. Other hospitals soon changed their admission policies.

The most publicized change, however, was initiated by Louisvillian Lyman T. Johnson, who went to court when the University of Kentucky refused him admission to its graduate school. The case, which went to the United States Supreme Court, was a victory for Johnson and led the state General Assembly in 1950 to repeal the infamous Day Law of 1904 that prohibited integration of institutions of higher education. (The law was directed at Berea College.) All Louisville colleges and seminaries opened their doors to African Americans shortly after. Sit-ins at lunch counters and picketing at downtown stores in the 1950s and 1960s led to their opening to all regardless of race.

Then in 1954 a decision of the United States Supreme Court in the landmark *Brown vs.* the *Topeka Board of Education* case reversed the 1896 "separate but equal" doctrine of that court. A strong dissenter from the latter decision had been Justice John Marshall Harlan, who had practiced law in Louisville after the Civil War. Governor Lawrence W. Wetherby, a native of Jefferson County, announced that Kentucky would obey the law. The Louisville School Board set the fall of 1956 as the date for full integration. Superintendent Omer Carmichael presided over a system with more than forty-five thousand students, one of the nation's largest to integrate in 1956. Carmichael had initiated a detailed, patient preparation for the event. Twenty-seven percent of the students were black, the highest in any system integrating that year. Schools opened on September 10, without incident. It was the quiet heard throughout the nation. Louisville received good press from coast to coast. (That was not the case when school busing was initiated in September 1975 and was followed by an outburst of violence, though there were no problems at most schools.)

The Chamber of Commerce continued its efforts at development, including a push for facilities to lure large trade shows. Success was achieved when the state agreed to construct the Kentucky Fair & Exposition Center adjacent to Standiford Field (later Louisville International Airport). Opened in 1956, the facility provided not only space for trade shows but musical events, a stadium, and a new home for the Kentucky State Fair that moved from its long-time home in the West End. In the city itself the new Chamber of Commerce originated a plan to rehabilitate housing in the central core, especially west of downtown. The plan also called for demolition of deteriorated housing east of downtown and its replacement with a Medical Center that would bring hospitals and physicians' offices together. The western project resulted in the construction of Village West, a private housing project. On the east the Medical Center became a reality after voters approved a $5 million city bond issue for redevelopment, including the center. It was hoped that clearing blight from east and west of downtown would encourage private renewal efforts to enhance the central business district's attractiveness. These measures led to full-scale urban renewal that extended to such residential neighborhoods as Old Louisville, and, in the West End, Little Africa, which was renamed Southwick.

But the outward flow from the almost static city boundaries continued unabated. Industry, too, made moves beyond the city limits, a trend set by General Electric. Ford Motor Company, for example, opened a new assembly plant in 1955 on Grade Lane far from its Southwestern Parkway plant of 1925. When Ford chose the Louisville area in 1968 for its heavy truck plant the site chosen was far eastern Jefferson County—almost in Oldham County. In 1963 the Mall Street Matthews had opened on Shelbyville Road, the first of the enclosed shopping malls in the area and precursor of others that followed, such as Oxmoor in 1971. The population shift was transforming once tranquil eastern Jefferson County into a high-traffic area of sixth-class cities, shopping centers, freeway interchanges, restaurants, and motels. The effect on downtown was catastrophic. Fourth Street, the once-premier shopping thoroughfare, assumed a bedraggled air in the next two decades as Stewarts and Kaufman–Straus, the two leading department stores, closed, along with the Brown and Seelbach Hotels, the once-posh movie palaces, and numerous shops.

As suburbia sprawled, the city—for the first time in its history—lost population. The 1970 census revealed a decline of nearly thirty thousand residents during the 1960s. The move to the suburbs began to include office buildings, such as the fifteen-story Lincoln Income Life Insurance Company headquarters along the Watterson Expressway at Breckenridge Lane. Designed by William Wesley Peters of Taliesin Associated Architects (successor to the practice of Frank Lloyd Wright) and completed in 1965, the innovative structure later became the Kaden Tower.

The downtown decline was a worry for businesses headquartered there, especially the banks. "Gray and growing grayer" is the way that Maurice Johnson, head of Citizens Fidelity Bank & Trust Company, described downtown at the end of the 1960s. The Chamber of Commerce had recognized the problem as early as 1958 and formed a committee to recommend ways of reversing the trend. That committee in 1959 became Louisville Central Area, Inc., which served, in effect, as the planning agency for downtown redevelopment. Its first success was fostering construction of The 800 apartment building at Fourth and York Streets. It was opened in 1963, and its twenty-nine stories made it Louisville's tallest building at the time. Meanwhile the Medical Center was progressing, and by the 1980s was home to five hospitals: Norton, Kosair Children's, Jewish, University of Louisville, and Alliant Medical Pavilion (formerly Methodist Evangelical), as well as the University of Louisville medical and dental schools.

The 1970s proved to be the decade during which center city revitalization shifted into high gear. Interestingly, it started at the riverfront where Louisville had begun to take shape some two hundred years earlier. Called the Riverfront Project, it was a public-private partnership involving the city of Louisville, federal urban renewal funding, and private developers. Though the Columbia Building of 1891, often called the city's first skyscraper, was demolished as part of the project, the result was an underground garage topped by a public open space, the Plaza/Belvedere, and a hotel, the Galt House (third of that name), built by developer Al J. Schneider. A twenty-four story office building built by the Louisville Trust Company occupied the site of the Columbia Building. The project was completed in 1973.

Other banks, too, joined in downtown renewal by erecting new headquarters buildings, of which some were high-rise towers. To keep downtown shopping viable a bold move led to the construction of the $143.5 million Galleria, opened on Fourth Street between Liberty Street and Muhammad Ali Blvd. in September 1982. With its glass structure covering most of the block, it is a kind of suburban shopping center in downtown Louisville, flanked at each end by an office tower. State funding had earlier made possible a convention center on Fourth Street between Market and Jefferson Streets. Completed in 1977 (and expanded in 1999), the center made Louisville competitive in attracting large conventions and replaced the inadequate Armory (Gardens of Louisville) for such events. The adjacent Hyatt Regency Hotel, with a skywalk to the center, followed soon after. The momentum continued with the reopening of the Brown and Seelbach Hotels and the creation of Theater Square at Fourth and Broadway in the late 1970s and early 1980s. Two distinguished high-rises in the 1980s and 1990s were the Humana Building at Fifth and Main Streets in 1985 and the Aegon Center (1993) with its lighted dome at Fourth and Market.

Although the central business district is not the retail powerhouse it once was, it remains the governmental, financial, and legal affairs center and has acquired new sheen as the performing arts center. It had been home to numerous legitimate theaters and performance halls in the nineteenth and early twentieth centuries, including the beloved Macauley's, but the advent of the motion picture doomed them all. The Brown Theater of 1925, designed for stage productions, soon switched to movies. Live theater returned in a small way in the 1950s with the group that became Actors Theatre of Louisville (ATL), presenting live drama upstairs in a Fourth Street building. By the 1960s the Louisville Theatrical Association (LTA) had been formed to bring Broadway road shows to Louisville with performances at the Brown Theater. The arts were in the first flowering of their phenomenal success.

But then J. Graham Brown asked LTA to surrender its lease so that he could demolish the Brown and erect a garage to bolster sagging hotel use, suffering from motel competition. As a result performance groups began to think of building a hall larger than the Brown that could be used by all: orchestra, ballet, opera, and road shows. A complicated series of events followed, but in the mid-1970s state funding was promised by Governor Julian Carroll, provided Louisville sources, public and private, made a substantial financial commitment. The center, on Main Street between Fifth and Sixth Streets was opened on November 19, 1983. It has brought a new dimension to the arts in Louisville.

Meanwhile, Actors Theatre had graduated to the former railroad station at Seventh Street and the river but had to move when Riverside Expressway construction doomed the structure. ATL found a new home in the 1837 Greek Revival bank building at 316 W Main Street and an adjacent Victorian commercial building. ATL has achieved national and even international fame for its innovative productions. The Brown Theater (for a short time called The Macauley) continues as a performing venue and was completely renovated in 1999. The former Loew's State cinema, renovated in the 1990s and renamed The Palace, presents visiting troupes and musical groups.

Not in the arts, but definitely in the entertainment category, are other developments in the area. Slugger Field, the home of the Louisville Riverbats, opened in the spring of 2000 at Preston and Main Streets. At the other end of Main Street the Hillerich & Bradsby Company plant, where Louisville Slugger bats are manufactured, opened in 1996 after a move from New Albany, Indiana. It offers visitors both a baseball museum and plant tours. Between is the Louisville Science Center (originally the Museum of History and Science in 1977), where lessons in science are specially geared to children.

These developments spurred further interest in the nineteenth-century buildings on Main Street. With both federal and local tax incentives available, private rehabilitation of many structures became a viable option. Real-estate values rose as offices and restaurants moved to the street and the thoroughfare breathed with new life. The momentum continued at the twentieth century's end. In July 1999, the first phase of the Waterfront Park was completed, transforming much of the old wharf area into a landscaped area with "water features," including fountains and waterfalls.

At the beginning of the twenty-first century Louisville and its metropolitan area remains in a process of change, as it has since its beginnings in 1778. The expressways, originally thought of as strengthening center city (the area of first settlement), have proven to create an outward flow of business, industry, and population from the city into what were once considered the hinterlands. The flow goes even beyond Jefferson County.

Louisville's estimated mid-1998 population declined to 255,045 from 269,555 in 1990, according to the U.S. Census Bureau, reducing it in rank to the sixty-fourth largest city in the nation. Yet Jefferson County, including Louisville, grew in population from 665,480 in 1990 to an estimated 672,100 in the mid-1998, reflecting the suburbanization surge. All seven counties in the Standard Metropolitan Statistical Area (SMSA) gained population with a mid-1998 population of 999,267. This inflow of residents has created some fiscal problems for outlying counties in both Kentucky and southern Indiana, which must increase expenditures for schools, sewers, drainage, water supply, roads, and other amenities.

Yet Louisville and Jefferson County remain the powerhouse in the SMSA, providing the lion's share of employment. In addition, job opportunities in Louisville/Jefferson County continued to increase at the twentieth century's end, particularly in the non-manufacturing sectors. The total number of new jobs increased by nearly 1,900 between 1997 and1998, and by 89,000 jobs between 1989 and 1999. Manufacturing, on the contrary, fell from 122,166 in 1970 to 88,900 in 1998. But services jobs rose from 75,554 in 1970 to 292,380 in 1998. All non-manufacturing jobs rose from 292,562 in 1970 to 488,800 in 1998. These figures represent such developments as the rise of Humana, founded in 1962 as Extendicare; the move of the headquarters of the Presbyterian Church (USA) headquarters to Louisville in 1987; the national sorting center of United Parcel Service opened in 1981 and in 1999 became the largest employer, at 18,600, (replacing General Electric in that category).

Jefferson County, including Louisville, is the single largest contributor to Kentucky's state tax revenue: $750 million in fiscal year 1997, up from $591 million in fiscal year 1991.

The job opportunities in Louisville/Jefferson County attract a huge volume of workers commuting from Kentucky and southern Indiana counties. In 1990 (latest figures available) 32,466 came from Indiana and 38,187 from Kentucky counties. No doubt the figures were higher at the end of the twentieth century. More than twenty thousand workers from Jefferson County commute outward. These commuters contribute to heavy traffic on main thoroughfares and the incoming workers to occupational license revenues that reached nearly $98 million in Louisville in 1998, and more than $71 million in Jefferson County that year. Obviously the SMSA is a single economic unit even though it is divided among seven counties and two states.

As the twentieth century ends, the Louisville metro area is performing well economically, but there remain problems that must be addressed. Louisville and Jefferson County will likely be merged in the future, although there are strong objections from certain groups. African Americans, for instance, feel it would dilute the political gains they have made in the city. Small incorporated cities point to better services and government closer to the people. Suburban sprawl is coming to the fore as something to be tamed.

The problem of divided governmental authority and its drawbacks was tackled in 1985 by newly elected Mayor Jerry Abramson and former Mayor Harvey I. Sloane who had been elected county judge/executive. They devised the city/county "compact," approved by the state legislature in 1986 and effective January 1, 1987. It was to be effective for twelve years, until 1999 but was extended in that year. It freezes Louisville boundaries, alleviating suburban fears of annexation of unincorporated county land. The two governments also share occupational tax revenues under a complex formula, as a step in ending competition for new jobs. A single economic development office replaced the two former competing offices, and the county increased its share of funding for joint city/county agencies such as health, parks, and planning and zoning.

Building new roads to alleviate traffic congestion seems only to attract more cars and more sprawl. Efficient and rapid public transportation is a problem that must be addressed. Local financial support will be needed to realize the full potential of the University of Louisville and other local institutions of higher education as strong research centers and part of the area's economic underpinning. The city's emergence as a nationally known medical center is a promising area of development.

The twenty first century will undoubtedly bring its own problems unforeseen at the end of the twentieth. But Louisville has had more than two hundred years of experience at problem solving, sometimes failing but more often succeeding. The twenty-first century will offer us new opportunities to use our accumulated wisdom.

Guide for Readers

In order to assist the user, the following explanations are provided on type of entries, scope, bibliographic citations, indices and cross-referencing, bibliographic essay, and photographs.

Types of Entries

The encyclopedia contains four types of entries—people, places, things, events—falling within twenty categories: architecture, art, communications, communities, culture, economics, education, ethnology, geography, geology, government and law, literature, medicine, pioneer and military, politics, recreation, religion, sports, transportation, and women.

Scope

The encyclopedia encompasses the Louisville metropolitan statistical area and more. In Kentucky the counties of inclusion are Bullitt, Jefferson, Oldham, Shelby, and Spencer. In Indiana the counties include Clark, Floyd, Harrison, and Scott. Until recently, the vast majority of the people of Jefferson County resided within Louisville's city limits. In its more than two hundred years of existence, it has dominated and continues to dominate Jefferson County; therefore, most of the entries are tied directly to the city. Jefferson and other Kentucky counties are included only because they are in some way associated with the city. The counties of Indiana are included for the same reason, but their number of entries is smaller. The one mile of river separating Louisville from southern Indiana has been a gap that more often than not divided the two areas and minimized their interaction. Nevertheless, an effort was made to determine just where they significantly connect and to document that with entries.

All entries contain information important in the history of Greater Louisville. They were written during the period 1996 through November 1999. Unsigned entries were written by the staff and comprise nearly one third of the total.

Biographical sketches of people who died prior to December 1999 constitute a large percentage of the total entries. Sketches include date and place of birth, parent's names, educational background, accomplishments, marriage and children, date and place of death, and site of burial. Biographical information on living people is contained in other entries, and names of these individuals can be found by using the index. Some exceptions were to the rule that no sketches of living people would be included. We felt that Muhammad Ali is so important that he must have this recognition. Some are included by virtue of the office they hold. For example, Louisville mayors, Jefferson county judge/executives, U.S. senators and representatives fall into that category. A concerted effort was made to identify minorities and women although many times, it was difficult to find the information. The editor is not satisfied with the number of these biographical sketches. It reflects an America that far too often denied opportunities to many, rather than an America one wishes would have been true to the original principles of the Declaration of Independence. Louisville, a segregated city for much of its history, was an enclave of white male leadership. It is to be hoped that an encyclopedia heralding the beginning of the twenty-second century will reflect a correction of the past's problem.

In the matter of "things," a criterion of longevity was used, usually one hundred years, and with the additional criterion of significance. If a thing has ceased to exist, such as a church, school, or restaurant, and it was important or well known, it is contained here. In the case of businesses, the most important criterion was that they are recognized as centennial businesses by the Kentucky Historical Society. Since this list is in constant revision, some business may be excluded since they were not so recognized at the time of our research. Once again, many businesses no longer in existence are included. Newer businesses that have a great impact on the area's economy are included also. In determining entries of things, selection is highly selective.

Places include cities. No Kentucky city below the fourth class was given an individual entry. Indiana cities include the county seats, with a couple of additions deemed significant, such as Utica. In the matter of cities and counties, population figures for 1980, 1990, and 1996 were used. All Louisville neighborhoods were included. Neighborhood names and boundaries were taken from a map of the city published by the Department of Public Works and dated 1975.

In order to acquaint the user with the history of the metropolitan area, an Overview has been included. By reading this overview, the reader can gain a timeline of the community's development from prehistoric settlements to the present.

Although an attempt was made to establish and stick with criteria for inclusion and exclusion of entries, as Ralph Waldo Emerson said, "A foolish constancy is the hobgoblin of little minds." Some selectivity was necessary, and certainly anyone can raise questions with what appears or fails to appear here. That is to be expected. The exceptions are solely the decision of the editor, who assumes full responsibility.

Bibliographic Citations

Many entries are followed by bibliographic citations. These do not necessarily reflect the author's sources: Their purpose is to direct the user to additional information on the specific topic of the entry. The number of references that could be cited in individual entries was strictly limited, and we attempted to cite those that would be most readily available to the user. For that reason we have included few unpublished works, works available in only one repository, or primary source materials other than newspapers.

Indices and Cross-Referencing

Many topics not treated in separate entries are included in more general articles and can be located by means of the index. Within certain entries, the name of a person, place, thing, or event in small capitals indicates that the reader may consult that other entry in the book for more detail.

The Encyclopedia of Louisville

ABELL, HELEN (b Louisville, June 16, 1914; d Louisville, January 24, 1996). Historic preservationist. Helen Abell was the second of six children born to Judge James Percival and Margaret (Wathen) Edwards. She grew up on Fourth St. and graduated from the University of Louisville and the Kent School of Social Work. She married physician Irvin Abell Jr. on December 28, 1940. Before she began preservation work, she served in a number of community and civic organizations, including the Community Chest, the Cerebral Palsy School, and the Tuberculosis Association.

In 1961 when Locust Grove, the final home of George Rogers Clark, opened as a house museum, she was asked to join its acquisitions committee. This position educated her on historic preservation and on running a historic house. She served on the board of advisors of the National Trust for Historic Preservation from 1967 to 1970 and was vice chairwoman in 1970–71. She also served on the board of trustees for nine years and was vice chairwoman for three years.

Abell was appointed to the Louisville Landmarks Commission when it was formed in 1973 and became chairwoman in 1978. As chairwoman she was instrumental in saving and restoring a number of buildings. In one of the most celebrated preservation cases in the city, Abell and the commission took on the Woman's Club of Louisville to save two Richardsonian Romanesque mansions. The two historic mansions and a third building, all located on Fourth St. and Park Ave., were threatened with demolition by the Woman's Club, which wanted to create a parking lot adjacent to its Fourth St. site. Abell, who was a former member of the Woman's Club, led a bitter but successful court battle against the organization, resulting in the buildings being saved. She was also among those who unsuccessfully took on the developers of the downtown Galleria over the proposed demolition of the Atherton, Will Sales, and Watterson Hotel buildings.

In 1982 she received the National Trust for Historic Preservation's highest honor, the Louise du Pont Crowninshield Award, for her achievements in historic preservation. A founder and board member of the Preservation Alliance of Louisville and Jefferson County, she was presented its annual award in 1986 for outstanding achievement. This award now bears her name. In 1986 she also received the Founders Award from the Junior League of Louisville, of which she was a sustaining member. She was a founding member of the Commonwealth Preservation Advocates; a charter member of the Louisville Historical League, serving on its board of directors; and president of the Cerebral Palsy School. She also served on the Save the Mansion Committee, which supported the restoration of the governor's mansion in Frankfort.

She was survived by two children: Irvin and Helen. She is buried in Calvary Cemetery.

See *Voice Tribune*, Jan. 31, 1996; Jim Oppel, "Grande Dame of Preservation," *Louisville* (Sept. 1982): 52–59.

ABELL, IRVIN (b Lebanon, Kentucky, September 13, 1876; d Kamp Kaintuck, Ontario, Canada, August 28, 1949). Surgeon. Born to William Irvin and Sarah Silesia (Rogers) Abell, Irvin attended St. Augustine's Parochial School in Lebanon (1882–89) and worked at Mackin and Kennedy's Drug Store, where he got his first taste for medicine. He graduated from St. Mary's College in St. Mary, Kentucky, in 1894 with a master of arts and went on to receive a degree from the Louisville Medical College in 1897. Abell left Kentucky for two years to study in New York, and in Germany at the University of Marburg and the University of Berlin, before returning to Louisville in 1899.

A year later, Abell joined the Louisville Medical College faculty and became a professor of surgery when the school merged with the University of Louisville in 1908. In 1923, he became clinical professor of surgery, where he remained until his retirement from active teaching in 1947. Abell's professional affiliations included the American Medical Association, of which he was president in 1938–39, the Southern Medical Association (president, 1933), the American College of Surgeons (president, 1946–47), the Association of Military Surgeons of the United States (president, 1944–45), the American College of Surgeons (president, 1944), the Southeastern Surgical Congress (president, 1937), and the Kentucky State Medical Association (president, 1927). Additionally, Abell sat on the board of trustees at the University of Louisville from 1935 until 1950 and headed the national committee that consulted with the Defense Commission on matters of public health at the onset of World War II. World-renowned for his abilities and his attempts to improve medical and health education, he was awarded one of fifty honorary fellowships at the Royal College of Surgeons in London in 1947. Author of approximately seventy-five published articles, Abell also penned a book, *Retrospect of Surgery in Kentucky* (1926).

Abell married Carrie C. Harting of Lexington, Kentucky, on October 19, 1907; they had four sons: Irvin Junior, William Harting, Jonathon Rogers, and Joseph Spalding. Abell died suddenly of a heart attack while on a fishing trip with friends in Canada and is buried in Cave Hill Cemetery.

See *Courier-Journal Magazine*, Nov. 23, 1941.

ABRAMSON, JERRY EDWIN (b Louisville, September 12, 1946). Mayor. He is the son of Roy and Shirley Botwick Abramson. He graduated from Seneca High School in 1964, and from Indiana University in 1968. He served in the United States Army from 1969 to 1971 and was awarded the Army Commendation Medal for meritorious service. In 1973 he graduated from the Georgetown University School of Law, where he was a member of the editorial board of the law journal. Upon his return to Louisville in 1973, Abramson joined the law firm of Greenebaum, Doll, and McDonald. He was twice elected Third Ward alderman, serving from 1975 through 1978. From 1979 to 1981 he was general counsel to Kentucky governor John Y. Brown Jr.

Abramson was elected mayor of Louisville in November 1985, garnering a record 73 percent of the vote over his Republican opponent, Robert Heleringer. Abramson had won a hard-fought Democratic primary that spring over William Ryan Sr. He was reelected in 1989, defeating Frank Stanley in the primary and unknown independent Erin Lee Stewart in a landslide in the November election. Abramson was matched against Stewart because his Republican opponent, perennial candidate Tommy Klein, was declared ineligible because he also signed up to run for county judge. In 1993 Abramson was elected to a record third term, beating Helen Combs and Darryl Owens in the primary, and Klein, his Republican opponent, in the November election. He also was the city's first Jewish mayor. On June 24, 1989, he married Mary Madeline Malley (1955–). The couple had one son, Sidney Robert Abramson. During all three of his mayoral terms, the Abramsons lived on Eastover Court in Crescent Hill.

Abramson provided leadership to many community projects and programs such as Operation Brightside, an environmental campaign that resulted in the removal of tons of trash and litter, the planting of over a million flowers, and an ongoing community-wide school program to educate youth about the need for environmental stewardship; the development of more than three thousand units of inner-city affordable housing; the implementation of volunteer curbside recycling; and the creation of initiatives to benefit at-risk young people.

Abramson's administration also saw such capital projects as the $500 million airport expansion that significantly improved the Louisville International Airport; a commitment from business and civic leaders to construct a Triple-A baseball park; the expansion of the Kentucky International Convention Center; the revitalization of Louisville's downtown waterfront through the design of the Waterfront Master Plan to include park, festival, and residential spaces alongside the community's riverside; the development of the Riverwalk, designed to entice the residents of the community back to the shores of the Ohio; the expansion of Louisville's Enterprise Zone, the nation's most successful, with over $1 billion in investments; the creation of the Main Street Cultural Arts District, with its renovation of Main Street's cast-iron buildings, land- and streetscaping, and the location of the headquarters of Hillerich and Bradsby and the Louisville Slugger Museum on Main St. Abramson also created the Olmsted Conservancy, a public-private partnership that has as its mission the restoration of Louisville parks and parkways that had been designed by the famous nineteenth-century landscape architect, Frederick Law Olmsted.

Throughout his mayoral terms, Abramson encouraged and supported public-private economic development initiatives. He implemented the Empowerment Zone initiative to encourage investment in the city's most disinvested neighborhoods. The initiative included raising the equity for the creation of a community development bank, bringing $51 million in federal funding to the community for the development of mixed-income housing, and creating a job skills training center, a business incubator, and a neighborhood travel center to provide transportation to outlying job sites.

Although Abramson helped bring many businesses to the city, others closed or moved out of Louisville. Some of these included the Louisville Forge and Gear Works, Bremner Biscuit, and Brinly-Hardy. As mayor, Abramson was also instrumental in pushing the expansion of Louisville International Airport, a controversial issue because the Highland Park neighborhood had to be razed to make way for the project. Since the mid-1980s when Abramson was elected, the city's population has continued to decline, although the rate has slowed from the double-digit highs of the 1960s and 1970s when there was mass migration to the suburbs.

In 1993 Abramson was elected by his fellow mayors to serve as the president of the U.S. Conference of Mayors. That same year Abramson received the U.S. Conference of Mayors' Michael A. diNunzio Special Award in recognition of his outstanding leadership in mobilizing the private sector to address the needs of inner-city youth. In 1996 *Newsweek* magazine named him as one of the nation's "Top 25 Most Dynamic Mayors."

Abramson was also active in local and national Democratic politics. He gave speeches at both the 1992 and 1996 Democratic national conventions, co-chaired the Bill Clinton for President campaigns in Kentucky in 1992 and 1996, was a member of the Democratic National Committee from 1987 to 1994, and was an officer of the Democrat Mayors of America from 1988 to 1994.

Sharon Receveur

ACCOUNTING. Accounting has made possible the building of a productive industrial system. Among the contributions of certified public accountants (CPAs) are research concerning accounting principles and practices and cooperation with the stock exchanges, the Securities and Exchange Commission, and other public and governmental bodies. CPAs also consult with industry and government concerning innumerable problems of mergers, taxation, regulation, financing, creditor and stockholder relationships, and, as independent auditors, add credibility to financial statements for all purposes.

The accounting profession in the United States is relatively new. The first CPA law was enacted in New York in 1896. The law resulted from a demand for audits that developed in the latter part of the nineteenth century as individuals sought more information about their investments. Investors from England and Scotland were sending their auditors to the United States to check on these investments. The Society of Accountants in Edinburgh was started on October 23, 1854, and on May 11, 1880, the Institute of Chartered Accountants in England and Wales was organized.

Auditing developed rapidly in the early 1900s. The prosperity of the early 1890s; the passage of the Sherman Anti-Trust Act (1890); and the Federal Reserve Act (1913) created a growing demand by large businesses for accountants and contributed greatly to their professional status. During this period, J.P. Morgan and Co. engaged Price Waterhouse to audit U.S. Steel, the largest U.S. corporation. This action was a milestone in the profession.

George B. Ewing was the first accountant in Louisville and Kentucky. In 1875 Ewing lost his job as bookkeeper at Casseday and Hopkins, a chinaware shop on Jefferson St., and thereafter established himself as an accountant.

It was not until 1916 that the Kentucky General Assembly enacted the CPA law. The Kentucky Society of CPAs was not organized until 1924. The period prior to the passage of the law was one of "expert accountants," the terminology used for accountants before the occupation was recognized as professional. There were several expert accountants during these years; some were accountants out of a regular job. Among those who lasted throughout this era were James S. Escott (1869–1933), Charles G. Harris (1869–1945), and Overton S. Meldrum (1859–1933). Charles G. Harris & Co., the first accounting firm in Louisville (ca. 1912), continued until it merged with Yeager, Ford, & Warren (which later merged with Coopers & Lybrand, now known as Pricewater-house Coopers).

Humphrey Robinson made a great contribution to the future development of accountancy in Kentucky. Robinson (1869–1931) was a native of Louisville and a graduate of Louisville Male High School. In 1900 he became a clerk at the American National Bank. In 1914 Robinson became the examiner for the Louisville Clearing House Association. For their mutual protection, banks were to be examined and reports made to the Clearing House. Clerks recruited from the various banks assisted the examiner because it was not required that he carry a full staff. Eventually, it developed that the amount of work did not even require the permanent organization. Robinson, realizing the need of the banks and their customers for audits designed to meet credit requirements, agreed with member banks that he would organize a public accounting firm and continue to serve the banks. The firm of Humphrey Robinson & Co. was organized in 1919 and performed audit work for the banks' customers and the public as well.

A force in the development of professional accounting in Louisville was the firm of Cotton & Eskew. Natives of Nelson County, Sam W. Eskew and William Cotton were brothers-in-law. Both Cotton and Eskew made substantial contributions to the accounting profession in Kentucky in the development of the demands for audits of public funds. Their firm has continued as two firms, Cotton & Allen and Eskew & Gresham. Cotton & Allen audited the accounts of many cities and counties and occasionally most departments of state government. The firm's work can be traced to regulations and statutes on the books today. So far as is known, no accountant or group of accountants has ever attempted to influence any legislation affecting accountancy.

An unusual person during this period of development was L.C.J. Yeager. Keen and brilliant, he had a great ability to get things done. Although making money was not his principal goal, he was one of the top earners in the profession. His primary goal was to build a quality firm and the largest one in Kentucky. Born near Danville, Kentucky, on May 26, 1902, Yeager graduated from Centre College, receiving an A.B. degree in history. He started his career as a schoolteacher. In 1927 he became associated with the Louisville office of Ernst & Ernst. He left the firm and on September 1, 1933, established the firm of Yeager, Ford, & Warren, having been joined by Gordon Ford and James C. Warren. Ford and Warren were graduates of Bowling Green College of Commerce, now a division of Western Kentucky University. The firm adopted the policy of restricting admission to college graduates, which was unusual at the time. Yeager served a three-year term as a member of the council of the American Institute of Certified Public Accountants. He was also a member and past president of the Kentucky Society of Certified Public Accountants. He was a past president and served on the State Board of Accountancy from 1948 through 1954.

There are now many Louisville-area firms that serve local clients. The larger companies have merged with and are served by the larger international firms as a result of needing that expertise to service their clients. Business has become global and is continuing to expand. Some examples are Yeager, Ford, & Warren, Kentucky's largest accounting firm, merging with Coopers & Lybrand, now PricewaterhouseCoopers; Humphrey Robinson & Co., a firm that began in 1919, merging with Deloitte & Touche; and Escott & Grogan, which was started in 1909 by James S. Escott, merging with Peat Marwick.

There have been many changes in accounting in the past few decades. Since the early 1970s computers have become a mainstay of the practice. At first, only a few women were in public accounting; now almost half of new CPAs are women. CPAs are becoming better educated, with new CPAs often having masters' and doctoral degrees. The Kentucky CPA law requires a candidate to have 150 college credit hours to sit for the CPA examination. As a result, professional accounting is becoming an increasingly challenging occupation. Growth is limited only by the CPA's ability to solve problems and create confidence in his or her judgment, as the U.S. economy continues to expand and creates greater competition in the business and financial worlds.

Largest Area Accounting Firms (1998)

PricewaterhouseCoopers LLP (Louisville) 55 CPAs
Ernst & Young LLP (Louisville) 48 CPAs
KPMG Peat Marwick (Louisville) 44 CPAs
Deming, Malone, Livesay & Ostroff (Louisville) 41 CPAs
Arthur Anderson LLP (Louisville) 35 CPAs
Deloitte & Touche LLP (Louisville) 29 CPAs
Carpenter, Mountjoy & Bressler PSC (Louisville) 28 CPAs
Cotton & Allen PSC (Louisville) 28 CPAs
Crowe, Chizek, & Co. LLP (Louisville) 26 CPAs
McCauley, Nicolas, & Co. LLC (New Albany, Indiana) 26 CPAs

See L.C.J. Yeager and Gordon Ford, *History of Professional Practice of Accounting in Kentucky* (Louisville 1968); *Business First Book of Lists* (Louisville, Oct. 26, 1998).

Gordon Ford

ACT OF INCORPORATION (LOUISVILLE). On April 7, 1779, the members of the Kentucky County (Virginia) Court at Harrodstown ordered the inhabitants to "keep themselves as united and compact as possible" and to draw up plans for towns and forts. They were to choose from the intended citizens three or more trustees from the "most judicious of their body." The trustees were charged to "lay off such town with regularity" and "to prescribe the terms of residence and building therein." At a public meeting on April 10, the inhabitants of Louisville appointed seven trustees—William Harrod, Richard Chenoweth, Edward Bulgar, James Patten, Henry French, Marsham Brashears, and Simeon Moore. On April 17 the trustees met and agreed upon the location and the plan of the town, commissioned John Corbly to draw up a map, and adopted rules for its government. The new town was to be named Louisville, in honor of King Louis XVI of France for his assistance to the United States during the War of Independence. This plan, accepted by the court on April 24, is seen as the first official act in the genesis of the city of Louisville.

Under Virginia law the land and property of those found to be Tories (British sympathizers during the War of Independence) could be seized and sold by the state. Residents suspected that this might happen because John Connolly, a land speculator from Pittsburgh who had been given a land grant of a thousand acres at the present site of downtown Louisville in 1773, had been in prison since 1775 for attempting to organize a regiment of Indians against the colonists. In April 1780, they petitioned the Virginia legislature for a confirmation of what they had already done (issued titles on Connolly's land) under the orders of the Kentucky County Court a year earlier and asked that Connolly's land be forfeited and appropriated to the new town while confirming the ownership of their respective properties. In May 1780, the Virginia legislature responded with a charter (although it was not signed by the speaker of the House of Delegates until July 1, 1780, after the conviction of Connolly by a jury in Lexington), and the town of Louisville was formally recognized in the following act:

> Whereas sundry inhabitants of the County of Kentucky have, at great expense and hazard, settled themselves upon certain lands at the Falls of Ohio, said to be the property of John Connolly, and have laid off a considerable part thereof into half-acre lots for a town, and having settled thereon, have preferred petitions to this general assembly to establish the said town.
>
> Be it therefore enacted, that one thousand acres of land, being the forfeited property of the said John Connolly, adjoining to the lands of John Campbell and Taylor, be and the same is hereby vested in John Todd, Jr., Stephen Trigg, George Slaughter, John Floyd, William Pope, George Meriwether, Andrew Hines, James Sullivan, and Marsham Brashears, Gentlemen, trustees, to be by them, or any four of them, laid off into lots of an half acre each, with convenient streets and public lots, which shall be and the same is hereby established a town by the name of Louisville. And be it further enacted, that after the said lands shall be laid off into lots and streets, the said trustees, or any four of them, shall proceed to sell the said lots, or so many as they shall judge expedient, at public auction, for the best price that can be had, the time and place of sale being previously advertised two months, at the court-houses of the adjacent counties, the purchasers respectively to hold their said lots subject to the condition of building on each a dwelling-house, sixteen feet by twenty at least, with a brick or stone chimney, to be finished within two years from the day of sale. And the said trustees, or any four of them, shall and they are hereby empowered to convey the said lots to the purchasers thereof in fee simple, subject to the condition aforesaid, on payment of the money arising from such sale to the said trustees for the uses hereafter mentioned, that is to say: If the money arising from such sale shall amount to thirty dollars per acre, the whole shall be paid by the said trustees into the treasury of this commonwealth, and the overplus, if any, shall be lodged with the court of the county of Jefferson, to enable them to defray the expenses of erecting the publick buildings of the said county. Provided, that the owners of lots already drawn shall be entitled to the preference therein upon paying to the said trustees the sum of thirty dollars for such half-acre lot, and shall be thereafter subject to the same obligations of feeing as other lot-holders within the said town. And be it further enacted, that the said trustees, or the major part of them, shall have power from time to time to settle and determine all disputes concerning the bounds of the said lots, and to settle such rules and orders for the regular building thereon as to them shall seem best and most convenient. And in case of death or removal from the county of any of the said trustees, the remaining trustees shall supply such vacancies by electing of others, from time to time, who shall be vested with the same powers as those already mentioned. And be it further enacted, that the purchasers of the lots in the said town, so soon as they shall have saved the same according to their respective deeds of conveyance, shall have and enjoy all the rights, privileges, and immunities which the freeholders and inhabitants of other towns in this State not incorporated by charter have, hold, and enjoy. And be it farther enacted, that, if the purchaser of any lot shall fail to build thereon within the time before limited, the said trustees, or a major part of them, may thereupon enter into such lot, and may either sell the same again, and apply the money towards repairing the streets, or in any other way for the benefit of the said town, or appropriate such lot to publick uses for the benefit of the inhabitants of the said town. Provided, that nothing herein contained shall extend to affect

or injure the title of lands claimed by John Campbell, Gentleman, or those persons whose lots have been laid off on his lands, but that their titles be and remain suspended until the said John Campbell shall be relieved from his captivity.

a True Copy May, 1780
Th. Jefferson
[Governor]

The original charter for Louisville disappeared in the mid-1850s, not to be rediscovered for over seventy years. The document was entrusted to a city official by the name of Mr. Price. Price kept the charter in his home for safekeeping; however, following his death, the charter, along with the rest of his papers, was moved to Nicholasville, Kentucky. Several years later, a member of the United States Senate from Mississippi and friend of the late Price, Clarence Andrew Cannon, found the charter while sifting through Price's old papers. Cannon gave the charter to his friend, Civil War hero Gen. Bennett Young. Young kept the charter until his death in 1916. The general's personal collection of antique documents was sold, and among them was the charter. Several years later, in the early 1930s, the charter resurfaced in New York City and was purchased by W.K. Stewart, a Louisville book merchant and collector. The charter was later purchased by the Bingham family and donated to the city. Presently it is housed in the rare books collection of the University of Louisville's Ekstrom Library.

See George H. Yater, *Two Hundred Years at the Falls of the Ohio* (Louisville 1987); *Louisville Herald-Post*, Nov. 6, 1931.

ACTORS THEATRE OF LOUISVILLE.

Actors Theatre of Louisville (ATL), founded in 1964 and designated in 1974 the State Theatre of Kentucky, has emerged as one of America's most innovative professional theater companies. It has been a major force in revitalizing American playwriting, and its unique approach to the presentation of the classical dramatic repertoire is well known.

The nonprofit organization began when a pair of theater companies, Actors Inc. and Theatre of Louisville, merged under the title Actors Theatre of Louisville. It was housed in a tiny second-floor loft, formerly the Gypsy Tea Room, at 617 S Fourth St. The founding directors were Richard Block and Ewel Cornett. Quickly outgrowing its hundred-seat domicile, the fledgling troupe moved to an abandoned Illinois Central Railroad station at Seventh St. and the Ohio River. Louisville architect Jasper D. Ward converted the building into a 350-seat theater, preserving most of the station's interior structure.

Due to demolition of the station to make way for Interstate Highway 64, the company's final production at the station was Arthur Miller's *Death of a Salesman* in May 1972. The station had been a good home—a place where

Actors Theatre buildings, south side of Main Street between Third and Fourth Streets.

ATL had grown from several hundred season subscribers to over nine thousand, and where more than sixty-five productions had been staged.

ATL established a new complex in the old Bank of Louisville building and the adjacent Myers-Thompson Display Co. Building on Main St. between Third and Fourth Streets. Erected in 1837 and designated a National Historic Landmark, the bank was designed by prominent nineteenth-century architect James H. Dakin and is a fine example of small-scale Greek Revival architecture. The Chicago-based architectural firm of Harry Weese and Associates melded the two diverse structures and constructed at the rear of the two buildings the 637-seat Pamela Brown Auditorium, with a modified thrust proscenium stage. It was built in part with a gift from businessman John Y. Brown Jr., the brother of Pamela, after she was lost at sea in a failed balloon attempt to cross the Atlantic Ocean. It opened in October 1972. The 159-seat Victor Jory Theatre, a three-quarter arena performance space, opened in April 1973.

In March 1969 Jon Jory was appointed the theater's new producing director. His October 1969 directing debut with Dylan Thomas's *Under Milkwood* marked a renaissance for the organization. Jory's partner was Alexander Speer, later the theater's executive director, who began his tenure with ATL in 1965. The innovative style of Jory include the introduction of new plays and the development of fledgling playwrights. This created outstanding regional theater and contributed to making him a well-known and powerful force in contemporary theater. Jory arrived in Louisville after several years as a freelance director following a stint as one of the founding directors of Long Wharf Theatre in New Haven, Connecticut. Jory's first season included an appearance by Jon Jory's father, film and stage actor Victor Jory, in Tennessee Williams's *Cat on a Hot Tin Roof.* The elder Jory became a vital asset in ATL's success, appearing at least once each season until his death in 1982.

Jon Victor Jory was born June 1, 1938, in Pasadena, California, to Victor and Jean (Innes) Jory. He was educated at the University of Utah and Yale University.

In 1976 Jon Jory started the internationally celebrated Humana Festival of New American Plays, an annual showcase of new theatrical work, underwritten since 1979 by The Humana Foundation. It draws theater-lovers, critics, producers, and playwrights from around the world. Many of the Humana Festival plays have been published. The theater's New Play Program also includes a national Ten-Minute Play Contest, started in 1989. It evolved from the National One-Act Contest (1979–89).

Parallel to the growth of the New Play Program, attention was focused on the one-act play form. Shorts became ATL's festival of one-act plays. In the 1980–85 seasons the Shorts Festival introduced nearly a hundred new short plays. These mini-plays became part of the Humana Festival.

The Humana Festival has premiered the Pulitzer Prize–winning plays *The Gin Game* (D.L. Coburn) and *Crimes of the Heart* (Beth Henley) as well as *Getting Out* (Marsha Norman), *Agnes of God* (John Pielmeier), *Lone Star* (James McLure), *Extremities* (William Mastrosimone), *My Sister in This House* (Wendy Kesselman), *Tales of the Lost Formicans* (Constance Congdon), *Danny and the Deep Blue Sea* (John Patrick Shanley), *Marisol* (Jose Rivera), *Slavs!* (Tony Kushner), and *Talking With* and *Keely and Du* (Jane Martin).

ATL has received the three most prestigious

awards given to regional theaters: in March 1979 the Margo Jones Award, presented for the encouragement of new playwrights; in May 1979 the Schubert Foundation's James N. Vaughan Memorial Award for exceptional achievement and contribution to the development of professional theater; and in June 1980 a Special Tony Award as an outstanding non-profit resident theater.

In the fall of 1980 the theater launched an overseas tour to Yugoslavia, Ireland, and Israel. Since then, the international touring program has included invitational performances in over twenty-nine cities in fifteen foreign countries.

The Brown-Forman Classics in Context Festival, an annual event through 1997, was a multi-disciplinary arts and cultural event started in 1985 and underwritten by Brown-Forman Corporation. It documents dramatic literature's masterworks for today's audiences by examining the social, political, and aesthetic influences surrounding the creation of the plays.

Complementing the classics festival is the biennial Bingham Signature Shakespeare, launched in May 1989. The Mary and Barry Bingham Sr. Fund makes it possible for the theater to produce Shakespeare without compromise. Avant-garde solo and small-ensemble performances were featured in the Flying Solo & Friends Festival, featured each September from 1993 through 1997.

In the fall of 1994, a $12.5 million expansion and renovation project included the new 318-seat Bingham Theatre and a flexible arena theater. The Pamela Brown Auditorium and Victor Jory Theatre stage were enlarged and enhanced. Also included in the expansion were lobbies, ticket sales areas, restroom facilities, and seating in the theater's restaurant. A nine-level parking garage became part of the complex. Harry Weese and Associates and Theatre Projects Consultants handled the project, blending historic Main St. architecture with modern facilities. In 1998 restoration of the theater's main lobby refurbished the original colors and gold leaf accents of the decor and allowed for new lighting arrangements.

Jon Jory resigned in Janurary 2000 to accept a tenured professorship at the University of Washington School of Drama in Seattle.

James Seacat

ADAMS, HENRY (b Franklin County, Georgia, 1803; d Louisville, November 3, 1872). Baptist minister and dominant religious figure in the African American community. In 1839 Adams came to Louisville to become pastor of a small black Baptist congregation that worshiped in a house on Market St. between Seventh and Eighth Streets. He established a school in the church, and the congregation grew dramatically under his leadership. In April 1842 Adams led the congregation out of the white First Baptist Church and organized the First Colored Baptist Church of Louisville. Under Adams's vigorous leadership, the church established itself by 1848 on Fifth St. south of Walnut (now Muhammad Ali). Ten years later the original structure was replaced by a handsome building designed by famed Louisville architect Gideon Shryock. It later became known as the Fifth Street Baptist Church. Adams remained as pastor of the church until his death.

See H.C. Weeden, *Weeden's History of the Colored People of Louisville* (Louisville 1897); Marion B. Lucas, *A History of Blacks in Kentucky, vol. 1, From Slavery to Segregation, 1760–1891* (Frankfort 1992).

Cornelius Bogert

ADATH JESHURUN. Congregation Adath Jeshurun started in 1894, having absorbed Beth Israel, Louisville's second congregation, established in 1851 at 127 W Green St. (now Liberty). Adath Jeshurun's first home was on the southwest corner of Floyd and Chestnut Streets. On July 5, 1919, it held its first service in a new domed building (now Unity Temple) at Brook and College Streets, designed by architect James J. Gaffney. Four years later an auditorium and classroom building were added.

As the congregation continued to grow after World War II and until it erected its present building at 2401 Woodbourne, High Holy Day services were held in Louisville Memorial Auditorium. In the 1950s, growth and shifting population led the congregation to seek its present site in the Highlands. The synagogue, designed by Braverman and Halperin of Cleveland, was completed in 1957. The sanctuary seats 445, with 750 more seats made possible by a movable partition. A religious-school building was dedicated in February 1966. It was named the J.J. Gittleman Educational Center in honor of the rabbi emeritus who had served the congregation since 1917. In 1993 the main building was given a complete renovation, including a remodeling of the Switow Chapel, where weekday services are held. The chapel contains a wall simulating the Western Wall in Jerusalem.

At the turn of the century, the spiritual leader was Dr. Simon F. Solinger, who had come to Louisville as rabbi of Beth Israel. In 1891 he went to Pittsburgh to study medicine and then returned to the pulpit at Adath Jeshurun, practicing medicine at the same time. Dr. Solinger, a man of liberal bent, introduced mixed seating of men and women. Since then the congregation has been part of the Conservative movement. In April 1908 Rabbi Herman H. Rubenowitz took over the pulpit, and in 1912 he was succeeded by Rabbi Abraham Nowak. Rabbi J.J. Gittleman came in 1917 and became rabbi emeritus in 1965. Under his administration, Adath Jeshurun became a real force in the community, growing from some fifty families when he arrived to some six hundred by the time of his death in 1971. His successor was Rabbi Simcha Kling, a scholar, author, and translator who emphasized adult education and promoted women's participation. He was a founder of Mercaz, the Conservative Zionist movement, and wrote biographies of several Zionist pioneers. Rabbi Robert Slosberg arrived in 1981 to be assistant to Rabbi Kling. When ill health curbed Kling's activities, Rabbi Slosberg became senior rabbi in 1988.

See Herman Landau, *Adath Louisville: The Story of a Jewish Community* (Louisville 1981).

Herman Landau

ADVERTISING. Local advertising is nearly as old as the first settlement at the Falls of the

Temple Adath Jeshurun, northeast corner of Brook at College, 1921.

Ohio. In the nineteenth century, the earliest examples can be found in Louisville newspapers. Samuel Vail's *Farmer's Library, or Ohio Intelligencer*, later shortened to the *Farmer's Library*, appeared weekly in early 1801 as the city's first newspaper and occasionally contained ads from merchants, book publishers, slave owners searching for runaways, and tavern proprietors.

More often, there were private advertisements from persons settling disputes, announcing land sales, or giving pedigrees of horses that were at stud. For the high cost of one dollar, ads "of no more length than breadth" could be placed for three weeks, with each additional week costing seventy-five cents. The only illustrations, created by woodcuts, were of horses. However, upside-down script was also used to catch the reader's eye.

Advertising played an increasingly important role in the newspapers after Shadrack Penn Jr. upgraded his paper, the *Louisville Public Advertiser*, to the city's first daily in 1826. Merchants and professionals utilized the forum to peddle their wares and services—Snead and Anderson announced their goods for sale in 1827, while Henry W. Fontaine publicized his new law office on Jefferson St. Newspaper advertising has remained the most consistent and unchanging form of local presentation of goods and services.

In 1832 Richard Otis published the city's first directory. Aside from names of residents and information on the city, it contained over forty pages of advertisements ranging from sign painter L.S. Wicker's simple ad to the elaborate, full-page woodcut for stonecutter Patrick Garvey. Such advertisements became more intricate and detailed as other directories, such as Henry Tanner's *The Louisville Directory and Business Advertiser for 1859–60* appeared. By the time of the Civil War, advertising constituted a large part of the directories and included a modern version of the Yellow Pages as well as an index to advertisers.

A prevalent form of advertising during the mid-1800s was the use of storefront signs. In addition to signaling location, the advertisements gave the name of the shop. Signs originally flush with the building were eventually hung to be visible and attract the attention of sidewalk strollers. One prominent sign marked George Blanchard's clothing shop at Fifth and Main Streets. With its fingers pointing toward the door, the "Sign of the Golden Hand" attempted to entice prospective patrons. By the 1880s the practice of dangling signs from storefronts had become common.

While most early advertisements were done by individual establishments, advertising agents, who were frequently involved in some way with the newspapers or directories, first appeared in *Edwards' Annual Directory* of 1866–67. With offices on the northeast corner of Main and Eighth Streets, Lucius Walker proclaimed himself to be a newspaper advertising agent. By 1871 Walker had joined the F.I. Dibble and Co. agency as one of the four listed advertising firms in town, along with McGill and Lucas; Perrin, Nicholson, and Co.; and Abraham Tomlinson. Turnover was rapid in the early years, and, by 1876, only one of the firms from five years earlier still existed. The A.E. McBee Co. specialized in streetcar advertising, informing its customers that "Your car advertising problem will be permanently solved if you turn all your space over to us." Such advertising was important at least from the 1880s. In the 1990s some buses were entirely covered in advertisements, using special paint so that passengers could see out. It reflected the difficulty in the late twentieth century to find any public place devoid of advertisements.

During the Gilded Age the increasing importance of the profession and of print publications such as magazines was reflected by the listing of two advertising writers and ten agencies in the 1901 city directory. While many were a single person, the Standard Advertising Co. of Coshocton, Ohio, was a larger establishment that handled streetcar advertising as well as signs and novelties. Evident as well was the increased number of sign and ornamental painters, as agencies increasingly hired painters such as the Falls City Sign Co. or the 2–Jakes Sign Co. At this point, the practice of advertising became one of art, as clients sought eye-catching posters and handbills to alert customers about their products or services.

Perhaps the city's greatest contribution to the advertising profession occurred in the early 1900s. After discussing the need for truth in advertising for several years, the Associated Advertising Clubs of America, the forerunner of the Advertising Federation of America, came to Louisville for its fifth annual convention in 1909. Headed by Samuel C. Dobbs of Coca-Cola Co., the organization took its first united stand against false advertising in its meetings at the Galt House. This movement led to the concept of the Better Business Bureau, and Louisville established the nation's third chapter in 1918.

By the 1910s larger billboard signs had begun to appear throughout the city, such as the Coca-Cola sign on the southeast corner of Market and Sixth Streets and the sign atop the National Vaudeville Theatre at Fifth and Walnut (Muhammad Ali Blvd.) advertising ten- and twenty-cent shows. With the coming of the automobile and a concomitant move to the suburbs, street-side billboards also began to appear, prompting the establishment of companies such as the General Outdoor Advertising Co. in the mid-1920s. Advertisements were painted on the sides of buildings, sometimes high up in order to be unobstructed. Posters were put on fences and anywhere there was a vacant space. They often advertised circuses but advertised other activities as well.

Following World War II, agencies found new ways to promote their clients: space on city-leased trash cans throughout the city was used, advertising posters on the sides of buses became more common, and by 1948 the Robinson Flying Service flew aerial signs attached to planes and sent up skywriters from Bowman Field. After its introduction, television competed for radio advertising dollars.

Since the 1960s, computers; the specialization of the industry into different roles such as graphic design, copywriting, media, production, and public relations; and the added importance of advertising have prompted many new agencies to appear and others to disappear. In 1960 the city directory listed twenty-six advertising agencies. By 1997 only 3 of the 26 remained, and the overall number of agencies had skyrocketed to 116. By the end of 1998 the three top agencies in town, in terms of gross income, were Creative Alliance Inc., founded in 1987; Power Creative, founded in 1976; and Doe-Anderson Advertising and Public Relations, founded in 1915 and the seventh-oldest ad agency in the nation in 1998.

Louisville is also served by two advertising associations for area professionals. The Advertising Club of Louisville was organized as the Ad Writers League of Louisville in 1906. Holding their meetings in the former Columbia Building at the corner of Fourth and Main Streets, the membership was initially restricted to males of good moral standing who worked in an agency or as a buyer, manager, writer, or illustrator. Later it was opened to everyone associated with the business. It sponsors luncheons and speakers and annually hands out the Louie awards to recognize excellence in local advertising. As a junior advertising club, Ad2 Louisville was founded in 1978 and is open to professionals and students under the age of thirty-one with an interest in the field.

See Samuel W. Thomas, *Views of Louisville since 1766* (Louisville 1971); Mary Verhoeff, "Louisville's First Newspaper, The Farmer's Library," *Filson Club History Quarterly* 21 (Oct. 1947): 278–79.

AEGON CENTER. The AEGON Center is Louisville's, and the state of Kentucky's, tallest building. Located at 400 W Market St., it occupies the block bounded by Fourth, Fifth, Market, and Jefferson Streets. The building has 35 stories and is 538 feet in height. It contains 640,000 square feet and was built at a total development cost of $100 million. The groundbreaking ceremony was held in July 1991, with initial occupancy in October 1992 and final completion in April 1993. To reflect changes in the company name, the structure was originally called the Capital Holding Building and then the Providian Center until it became part of AEGON USA in June 1997.

The concrete-framed structure is clad in gray Italian granite with polished black granite and stainless steel trim accentuating the base. There are two street-level lobbies containing cherry and walnut woods and rich marbles and granites. An 80-foot-high, 105-foot-diameter Romanesque-style dome tops the AEGON Center. This elegant dome is an open-air, metal-framed structure that is not occupied. At night it is dramatically lit from the interior, providing a shining beacon over the city. In December the dome glows with green lights and the tower below is illuminated with red lights, giving a holiday-season appearance.

A variety of office tenants occupy the building, including AEGON USA (an insurance company), numerous law firms such as Stites & Harbison and Brown, Todd, & Heyburn, as well as financial investment firms. Several retail businesses are located in the street-level spaces. A one-acre public plaza, on the south side, contains impressive water fountains and unique art-glass light fixtures. A five-hundred–car, five-level parking garage also adjoins the structure.

John Burgee Architects, of New York City, was the design architect; and Hines Interests Limited Partnership, of Houston, was the developer. Mr. Burgee (b 1934) is best known for his association with the acclaimed architect Philip Johnson (b 1906). During their partnership (1969 to 1991) they produced several landmark architectural buildings: AT&T Headquarters Building in New York City and the Pittsburgh Plate Glass Headquarters Building in Pittsburgh, among many other notable achievements.

Stephen A. Wiser

AEGON USA. In December 1996 Providian Corp. boasted $29 billion in assets and nine thousand employees across its consumer lending, home service insurance, direct response, and capital management businesses and corporate staff. The corporation's mission was to assist individuals and families in achieving their financial objectives with its product and service offerings. These included life insurance, consumer credit, auto insurance, and retirement and savings products. These are available through a variety of distribution channels, including agents, direct marketing media, and investment professionals. At least one of the corporation's broad range of financial products and services is sold in all fifty states. It was headquartered in the tallest building in downtown Louisville, variously called the Capital Holding Building, the Providian Building, and the AEGON CENTER. Its post-modern architecture and lighted dome were visible from many parts of the city.

Providian Corporation's history dates back to 1904, when Commonwealth Life Insurance Co. was founded in Louisville, taking its name from the Commonwealth of Kentucky and adopting the state's seal and motto, "United we stand, divided we fall." Commonwealth has remained a home service company, marketing traditional life and health insurance and related products to individuals and families throughout the Southeast and the Mid-Atlantic states. The home service distribution system allows Commonwealth Insurance to emphasize two basic strengths: face-to-face contact with the customer and the matching of financial products and services to people's needs. Commonwealth agents concentrate on conserving existing business while also increasing business in existing homes and adding new customers. Commonwealth products also are offered through partnerships with third-party insurance and marketing organizations.

Commonwealth's first president was western Kentucky businessman Col. Joshua D. Powers. Along with Darwin W. Johnson, Powers directed the firm and served as secretary-treasurer. Under their guidance, the company enjoyed immediate success, although initially profit was not always measured in dollars. In the beginning, policyholders sometimes used nonmonetary means such as chickens, eggs, or vegetables to pay their premiums.

The early years of the GREAT DEPRESSION brought major losses. In what would turn out to be a successful effort to turn the company around, Commonwealth president Homer Ward Batson took extreme measures by reducing all officers' salaries—beginning with his own—from $22,000 to $15,000. Employees were asked to turn off unnecessary lights and to use pencils until they were worn to their nubs. Field offices were consolidated, and problem debits were eliminated. Morton Boyd succeeded Batson as president and achieved the company's greatest growth up to that point.

In 1969 Capital Holding Corp. was created by Commonwealth in order for the company to expand through acquisitions while allowing the acquired companies to retain their names and identities. It acquired mostly debit insurance companies located throughout the southeastern United States. Debit insurance means that premiums are automatically withdrawn without checks being utilized. Over the years, Capital Holding expanded its reach to include direct insurance, retirement and savings, and consumer lending, thereby outgrowing its designation as a holding company. In 1994 Capital Holding's name was changed to Providian Corp. in order to reflect the holistic focus of the financial services company, yet Commonwealth Insurance retained its brand name and remained a community supporter.

Although the insurance niche was initially profitable to Capital Holding, the company's home service business was in need of a facelift by the late 1970s. In 1978 TOM SIMONS arrived to take over as chairman, president, and CEO, with a mandate from the board of directors to turn the company around. Under Simons, Capital Holding became one of the first companies to offer new insurance/investment combinations. For example, in 1982 Capital Holding announced an agreement to sell insurance and other financial products in Kroger grocery stores. Simons also led Capital Holding into the credit card business by acquiring First Deposit Corp., a small New Hampshire bank, in 1981. Simons retired in 1988 after fulfilling the goal given him by the board ten years before. He was succeeded by the corporation's chief investment officer, Irving W. Bailey II, who set increasing shareholder wealth as his goal.

As Capital Holding grew and prospered, its name became less synonymous with its diverse businesses. On May 11, 1994, Capital Holding Corp. became Providian Corp. by an overwhelming shareholder vote. By 1994 four businesses had evolved to share the Providian name:

Providian Bancorp (now Providian Financial Services), based in San Francisco, offers consumer credit, loans, deposit products, and other banking services nationwide. Qualified, active credit users are then offered an array of products to meet their needs, including secured and unsecured credit cards, revolving lines of credit, home equity loans, and VISA and MasterCard credit cards.

Providian Direct Insurance, headquartered in Frasier, Pennsylvania, specializes in life, supplemental health, and automobile insurance, offered primarily by telephone, television, and direct mail. Target marketing offers tailored products and services to specific customer segments such as military veterans and active duty personnel.

Providian Agency Group, based in Louisville, markets traditional life insurance, health insurance, and related products through its 2,800–member field force working throughout the Southeast and Mid-Atlantic. It also joined with third-party insurance and marketing organizations to provide product development and administration and/or licensing agreements.

Providian Capital Management focuses on the retirement savings marketplace by offering investment products to individual and group customers and managing the insurance assets. Its goal is financial security for customers and a profitable return for the corporation.

To further realize the goal of increasing shareholder value, Providian's insurance operations became part of the AEGON Insurance Group on June 10, 1997. AEGON USA is the United States arm of AEGON N.V., an international insurance group headquartered in the Netherlands. The acquisition created the fifth-largest life insurance group in the nation. Providian and AEGON USA's combined assets of $105.2 billion created the seventeenth-largest insurance group in the world when it was merged.

As part of the merger agreement, Providian Bancorp was spun off to create Providian Financial Corp., headquartered in San Francisco. The direct insurance, home service, and retirement savings businesses were retained by AEGON. AEGON retained diversified financial products (formed from the capital management business), marketing partnerships, and shared services (a technology function) in Louisville.

Michelle Alford

AERONAUTICS. From the early days of powered flight to the present time, the Louisville area has been in the forefront of aviation progress. While early powered flight elsewhere received much newspaper coverage here, the first flight by a powered heavier-than-air machine occurred here in 1910. Because of the scarcity and fragility of early airplanes, flying was left to exhibition fliers and record-seekers. It was not until 1919 and the availability of numerous surplus WORLD WAR I military aircraft that flying began to contribute to the nation's commerce and require established airfields with supporting services.

The first actual flight in Louisville occurred on July 31, 1837, when a gas balloon named Star of the West lifted from the center of the city and landed at what is now CHURCHILL DOWNS. It was piloted by Richard Clayton of Cincinnati. An event that produced equal interest in the local population was when Horace B. Wild, in his elongated dirigible balloon, set an American endurance record in Louisville on August 30, 1906, by steering his airship up and down the OHIO RIVER for five hours and twenty minutes, landing in NEW ALBANY when his fuel ran out.

One of America's earliest aviation supply and manufacturing companies was established in Louisville by Robert Owen Rubel Jr. The Aero Supply House of America was initially located at 132 N Fourth St. and did much business by catalog. Rubel was agent for all types of aeronautical supplies and built some dozen airplanes. He also maintained flying fields at Doup's Point and elsewhere. The business closed in 1912.

In the early days of aviation, thousands of spectators turned out to view air shows. One occurred on June 18 and 19, 1910, in a widely publicized aviation meet sponsored by the *LOUISVILLE TIMES*. Held at Churchill Downs, it featured world-famous aviator Glenn Curtiss, who was joined by Bud Mars in a flying exhibition before large audiences. The event was the first demonstration of an airplane in Louisville. The Kentucky State Fair Grounds, then located on Woodland Ave., was the site of airplane flights by Phil Parmelee and Clifford Turpin on November 2, 1911. What is said to be the first airmail service in Kentucky was offered here when, in all probability, mail was carried aloft and returned to the same location for the usual forwarding. Yet the novelty of it made this a popular event.

Military aviation activity was carried out at CAMP ZACHARY TAYLOR in 1918 during World War I. There was apparently no airfield identified as such, and it is believed that operations took place from the parade or maneuver grounds. The next year the first civilian airfield in Kentucky was established in September 1919 along Taylorsville Rd. Louisville's airport was officially named BOWMAN FIELD for businessman ABRAM HITE BOWMAN in 1923. Although not a pilot, Bowman was a strong supporter of aviation in Louisville. ROBERT H. GAST and W. Sidney Park are also considered cofounders of the airport. The operator of the field in 1919 was Stanley Hubbard, who also headed the Kentucky Aeroplane Supply Co. in Louisville, which specialized in rebuilding and selling war-surplus training planes.

Not the airport but the river was the site of the landing of the Curtiss NC-4, a U.S. Navy flying boat and the first to fly across the Atlantic Ocean. It visited Louisville on November 11 and 12, 1919, during a goodwill tour.

Flight came to southern Indiana when an unnamed airfield in the vicinity of today's 2549 Charlestown Rd. in New Albany was established in 1921 by Ernest Dixon. Dixon operated the Mason-Dixon Air Line, a sight-seeing and charter service, until accidents closed operations in 1923.

During 1925, in an effort to promote and develop aviation in Louisville, the Aero Club of Kentucky was organized and played a leading role in the early management of Bowman Field. Shortly after WORLD WAR II the club was renamed the Aero Club of Louisville. On a more serious note, the 465th Pursuit Squadron, U.S. Army Reserve, was authorized for Bowman Field in late 1922. It not only trained many pilots and ground personnel in this area but made the first real improvements to the airfield. In 1928 it became the 325th Observation Squadron and existed until the onset of World War II.

In 1925, W. Russell Beeler of New Albany opened an airport with flying service in CLARKSVILLE in the area of Carter Ave. and Highway 62. Around 1928 he moved to the opposite end of Carter Ave. at Eastern Blvd., and, in 1929, a third move was to land that is now a shopping center across from Carter Ave. Beeler's Airport remained active until 1941. After World War II, it was taken over by Charles Bush and known as Bush Field. It operated until 1954.

Around 1927 a second Louisville Airport opened in the area of today's LaGrange Rd. and Shelbyville Rd. Operated by Carlton M. Cruger, it was a distributor for Swallow biplanes. With one hangar, the airport closed in 1931 upon Cruger's death.

On August 12, 1928, Watterson Airport opened at what is now the northwest corner of GENERAL ELECTRIC'S APPLIANCE PARK. The airport had one hangar and was managed by W.S. Rinehart. It is believed that operations were continuous into the years after World War II.

Charles Lindbergh, the first to fly across the Atlantic Ocean nonstop and alone in May 1927, stopped at Bowman Field on August 8 and 9 during a national goodwill tour. His trip across country was to stimulate interest in flying. His arrival was the beginning of a triumphant visit that took the "Lone Eagle" down FOURTH ST. in a tickertape parade. The next year the General Assembly authorized the formation of local airport governing authorities, and the first to be organized was the Louisville and Jefferson County Air Board.

While many recognized that flight was important in military use and for novelty performances, others saw the potential in the commercial use of airlines. The first regularly scheduled commercial airline service to Kentucky was inaugurated by Continental Air Lines (today's American Airlines) between Cleveland and Louisville's Bowman Field on August 1, 1928. At first only air mail was carried, but the following year passenger service was added. The city of Louisville then issued revenue bonds that allowed it to purchase Bowman Field, thus making it the first municipal airport in Kentucky.

For many years Bowman Field remained most important, and, during the Ohio River flood of 1937, it provided valuable services to the city. Many special flights were operated into the airport delivering medicine, food, and other urgent shipments. Additional land adjoining Bowman Field's east side was purchased for the construction of a new air base for the Army Air Forces. During World War II this facility was used chiefly to train combat glider pilots and cargo transport crews. In addition, the only SCHOOL OF AIR EVACUATION in the Army Air Forces from 1942 to 1944 operated here to train flight nurses, doctors, and medical technicians in air evacuation skills. An auxiliary field was established in OLDHAM COUNTY during the war years. In 1960, because of the training of many student pilots, Bowman Field became the busiest local-traffic airport in the nation.

A short-lived airport known as Riverside operated on Utica Pike near Allison Ln. in JEFFERSONVILLE during 1947. Also in southern Indiana, William E. Happel opened Hap's Airport with flight service on Potters Ln. (now Progress Way) in 1953. Other airfields and landing strips in Jefferson County have been known to exist before and after World War II. They include Shawnee Airport on Millers Ln., two airports on Lees Ln., and one on or near Ash Bottom Rd. in the vicinity of today's Ford Motor Fern Valley Rd. assembly plant. Following World War II, a floatplane base was established on the Ohio River east of Second St. Perhaps the earliest of these was an airfield that existed for a brief time during the 1920s where Goldsmith Ln. intersects Bardstown Rd.

With the need for a larger airport in Louisville, development of Standiford Field began on the city's south side. Until after World War II, this facility was used almost entirely for C-76 and C-46 transport aircraft production by the CURTISS-WRIGHT CORP. in a plant that later became INTERNATIONAL HARVESTER. Additionally, Consolidated-Vultee modified nearly two thousand B-24 bombers in a building later owned by Bremner Biscuit. On February 16, 1947, federal recognition was extended to the newly formed KENTUCKY AIR NATIONAL GUARD for operation at Standiford Field. The 123rd Wing, 165th Squadron, now occupies its third location at the airport. In November 1947 all airline operations through Louisville moved from Bowman Field to Standiford Field. Operations were located in the cafeteria of the former World War II Consolidated-Vultee Modification Center on the east side of the field. On May 25, 1950, the 42,400-square-foot terminal, named for longtime chairman of the Louisville and Jefferson County Air Board Addison W. Lee Jr., opened on the north side of Standiford Field for airline service. This facility would be enlarged numerous times during the next thirty-five years.

During the Korean War the Air Force's 436th Troop Carrier Group operated from Standiford Field from October 20, 1950, to April 16, 1951. The first serious crash occurred on September 28, 1953, when a Resort Airlines C-46 on a nonscheduled charter flight from Philadelphia crashed at Standiford Field while landing. There were twenty-five fatalities among the forty-one on board.

Radio station WHAS began SkyWatch 84 for daily helicopter traffic reports above Louisville in 1970. On April 3, 1974, pilot/reporter Dick Gilbert broadcast from SkyWatch 84 dramatic details of a tornado that devastated much of the city. In later years other Louisville radio stations would use airborne traffic reports. Television coverage from helicopter "Sky 11" was started by WHAS-TV in 1978. It is predominantly used by the news department, and improvements in picture quality have been added over the years. By 1998 four Louisville television stations had helicopters.

Another practical use of flight began during 1972 when a helicopter unit was inaugurated by the Jefferson County Police. In addition to police work, the unit performs search-and-rescue and assists other law enforcement organizations. In 1999 it had two helicopters and nine officers assigned.

On September 1, 1975, the U.S. Army Reserve's 412th Medical Detachment Helicopter Ambulance Squadron was established at Bowman Field. Although it had a primary military medical evacuation mission, it was also tasked to assist civilian medical emergencies. It was transferred to Georgia on August 13, 1989. Before it moved in 1978, Kosair Children's Hospital began a high-risk neonatal care flight using fixed-winged aircraft. It was transferred to Bowman Field in 1987 and currently utilizes two aircraft. During 1982 University Hospital established Stat Flight using a helicopter for rapid movement of patients. A year later Jewish Hospital followed with its own Sky Care helicopter service. Both were consolidated under the name Stat Care in 1998.

In 1981 United Parcel Service established its national air distribution center at Standiford Field. Phenomenal growth at this center was highlighted by a 1998 announcement of a new $860–million automated sorting facility scheduled for completion in 2001. Operating its own fleet of airplanes, UPS also has maintenance and pilot training here. It has become Louisville's largest employer and the airport's major tenant. Growth of UPS and commercial service required the expansion of the airport. Controversy often characterized the acquisition of adjacent land, while the noise generated by increased flights was a widely debated community problem.

In Indiana the current Clark County, Indiana, Airport was opened in 1981 on Highway 31. At that time William E. Happel moved his operations there. Clark County Airport is a fast-growing, modern airport serving both the pleasure and corporate pilot.

In 1985 a new 183,000-square-foot Landside Terminal opened at Standiford Field, replacing the outgrown Lee Terminal. This was followed in 1989 with the opening of a new 225,000-square-foot, 2-concourse Airside Terminal. This project was completed in 1997 with an adjacent multilevel parking garage. In a name change, Standiford Field became Louisville International Airport at Standiford Field on April 3, 1995.

An ambitious ten-year program to expand Louisville International Airport came to an end on October 11, 1998, with the dedication of a new twenty-four–story air traffic control tower. This $700–million project closed an existing runway and added two new north-south parallel runways. The first, an eastside runway, opened in 1995; and the second, a westside runway, opened in 1998.

See David Carter, Joe Bates, Valerie Sexton, and Teresa Andrews, *Louisville International Airport: Serving the City that Delivers,* 50th Anniversary Yearbook (Liverpool, U.K., 1998); Charles A. Ravenstein, *Air Force Combat Wings: Lineage and Honors Histories 1947–1977* (Washington, D.C., 1984); George H. Yater, *Two Hundred Years at the Falls of the Ohio* (Louisville 1979); *Courier-Journal Magazine,* April 22, 1979; *Arrivals,* Regional Airport Authority of Louisville and Jefferson County (various issues).

Charles W. Arrington

AFRICAN AMERICAN BASEBALL.

Louisville has contributed significantly to the African American legacy in baseball. Blacks were playing baseball throughout the 1800s in the United States. By the 1860s notable black teams were developing in New York City and Philadelphia. In 1867 baseball made its first attempt to ban blacks by not allowing an all-black team from Philadelphia to join the National Association of Baseball Players, later to become the National League.

All-black professional baseball teams began developing in the 1880s. Moses Fleetwood "Fleet" Walker, a well-known black catcher from Ohio, even made it to the big leagues briefly, and he did it in Louisville. Walker was a catcher with the Toledo Blue Stockings, and when they became a major-league team in 1884 by joining the American Association, their season opener was in Louisville.

Walker had almost played in Louisville in 1881 as a catcher for the White Sewing Machine Co. of Cleveland, which played the Eclipse team. Articles in the Courier-Journal on August 22, 1881, said a mulatto baseball player would be a fine specimen for studying the race question. Some of the Eclipse Club players walked off the field when Walker arrived, and he was not permitted to play.

But in the May 1, 1884, season opener for the Toledo Blue Stockings against Louisville, Walker became the first African American to play major-league baseball when he walked onto the field for the first time in Louisville. There was concern that Walker might not be able to

Louisville Black Colonels at Parkway Field in the 1940s.

play in Louisville because of its southern inclination and the incident in 1881. The *Louisville Commercial* wrote that, since other cities had accepted Walker, Louisville should have no objection to his playing. Also, a refusal to play would mean forfeiture and a five-hundred-dollar fine for the Louisville Club. The crowd's behavior took a toll on Walker's performance. The *Toledo Blade* commented: "Walker is one of the most reliable men in the club, but his poor playing in a city where the color line is closely drawn as it is in Louisville, should not be counted against him. Many a good player under less aggravating circumstances than this has become rattled and unable to play. It is not creditable to the Louisville management that it should permit such outrageous behavior to occur on the grounds."

When the integrated Toledo Blue Stockings came to play the Louisville Eclipse Club, an all-black Louisville team known as the Falls Citys was in its second year. In 1887 it became part of one of the first Negro leagues, the League of Colored Base Ball Players (also known as the League of Colored Base Ball Clubs). This included the Cincinnati Browns, the Washington Capital Citys, the Keystones of Pittsburgh, Lord Baltimores of Baltimore, Boston Resolutes, Pythians of Philadelphia, and the Gothams of New York. This league existed for only a week (some sources say two weeks), but it was a strong indication that there were many black baseball players and there was a need for a league. The Falls Citys began in 1883, playing at Falls Citys Park at Sixteenth and Magnolia Streets.

Louisville soon developed a reputation as a source of great black teams and some extraordinary players. Napoleon Ricks, who played with the Fall Citys, was a shortstop with a startling batting average of .529. There were many other black teams to follow the Fall Citys, and some entered the Negro leagues. Louisville was represented by the Louisville White Sox in 1914 and the Louisville Sox in 1915. In 1930 the Louisville White Sox (also known as the White Caps) played in the Negro National League (NNL), and finished ninth in the league with a 14–27 won-lost record. In 1931 the Louisville White Sox played in the NNL.

In 1932 the Louisville Black Caps played in the Negro Southern League. Two outstanding players were associated with this team. Sammy Hughes, who later played with the Baltimore Elite Giants, started with the Black Caps in 1930. Jimmie Lyons, considered one of the greatest all-around ball players, played with the Chicago American Giants during the early twenties. In 1932, his last year in baseball, he managed the Louisville Black Caps.

Other Louisville black teams included the 1933 Red Caps, the 1938 Black Colonels, and the 1949 Buckeyes of the Negro American League (NAL). In 1954, the Black Colonels of the NAL took Louisville through the end of the Negro League era. The only Louisville Negro League player to make it to the major leagues was Dave Hoskins of the Louisville Buckeyes, who pitched for the Cleveland Indians in April 1953.

The 1931 Louisville White Sox, the 1932 Black Caps, and the 1949 Buckeyes all played at PARKWAY FIELD on Eastern Pkwy. just east of Third St. Parkway Field was segregated in seating, drinking fountains, and restrooms. It was the first concrete-and-steel stadium in Louisville, built in 1923 as the main Louisville ballpark and dismantled in 1961.

In 1946 PARKWAY FIELD was the scene of an important event in African American baseball history. When Jackie Robinson signed with the Brooklyn Dodgers in 1946, he was the first black in the twentieth century to play major-league baseball, breaking the gentleman's agreement of the late 1800s to ban blacks. Robinson was first sent to a Dodger farm team, the Montreal Royals, which won the International League pennant in 1946. They played the American Association pennant winner, the LOUISVILLE COLONELS, in the Little World Series. The first three games were in Louisville, and Robinson played his first professional playoff game in September 1946.

There was speculation that Robinson might not be able to play in Louisville, as had been the case for Walker in 1881, because of the city's racial atmosphere. Bruce Dudley, the Colonels' president, had opposed the signing of Robinson the year before. But he said that, as long as baseball accepted Robinson, Robinson could play at Parkway Field. Also, the players were warned not to harass Robinson.

In a stadium that could seat over 14,000, only 466 tickets were allotted for the colored section for the 3 games. Thousands of blacks were turned away even though there were empty seats in the bleachers being held for white patrons. Many blacks worked around these obstacles by paying high prices to whites for their tickets or by climbing on telephone poles or sitting on shacks along the LOUISVILLE & NASHVILLE RAILROAD tracks that ran behind the park.

Black writer Sam Lacy said he knew when Robinson entered the field because of the chorus of boos that came from the crowd. John Welaj, a Colonels player, recalled some of the names tossed out to Robinson—watermelon eater, nigger, chicken thief. Tommy Fitzgerald, a *Courier-Journal* sportswriter, wrote that Robinson "took it most gracefully and conducted himself in his every move as a gentleman." Letters in the *Courier-Journal* reflected what many felt about the reaction to Robinson. One chastised the white spectators referring to the "petty prejudice of witch hunting bigots"; a group of FORT KNOX soldiers said the behavior caused them to change their opinion of Louisville, which they now viewed as "a city of obnoxious futility."

Another important Louisville link to Jackie Robinson was the friendship between native son and famed Dodger PEE WEE REESE and Robinson when they were teammates in Brooklyn. Robinson developed his closest friendship with Reese, the team's captain. Reese's refusal to sign a petition to prevent Robinson's coming to the Dodgers was instrumental in killing the petition. His support and gestures towards Robinson became a model for others to follow. Reese's friendship with Robinson made a significant contribution to baseball and the way the nation viewed integration. It was considered to be a contributing factor in Reese's election to the Baseball Hall of Fame in 1984.

Black promotion teams, some of which developed in the 1930s, used gimmicks as well as great baseball to draw crowds. With the decline of the Negro leagues as a result of baseball integration, these teams were an option for talented black players from Louisville in the 1940s. Many of the players on these teams were Black Colonels. Barnstorming was a way of life for the Louisville Black Zulus, also known as Zulu Cannibals. These teams were on the road regularly. When in Louisville, they played at Parkway Field.

The Zulus played a very high level of baseball and also added a gimmick to increase gate receipts. They would dress up in grass skirts and face paint. They played other promotion teams such as the House of David, who were dressed as orthodox rabbis with long beards. Both whites and blacks came in the thousands to see the Zulus play because it was fun and they had a chance to see an outstanding level of baseball.

The last year of the Black Colonels was 1954, which took Louisville to the end of the Negro league era. Cardinal Stadium was built in 1957 to host the LOUISVILLE COLONELS and in 1982 became home to the Class AAA Louisville Redbirds of the American Association, and in 1999 the LOUISVILLE RIVERBATS of the Class AAA International League. Cardinal Stadium is not segregated, but its original 1948 plans show segregated restrooms.

Another important Louisville connection to African American baseball is the HILLERICH & BRADSBY CO., manufacturers of the famous LOUISVILLE SLUGGER baseball bat. Hillerich & Bradsby made bats for many Negro league teams, including many legends of the game from teams such as the Kansas City Monarchs and the Homestead Grays of Pittsburgh, where Josh Gibson, considered one of the best long-ball hitters of all time, played. Hillerich & Bradsby also made bats for many black players who were able to merge their Negro-League careers into the major league, such as Satchel Paige, Willie Mays, and Ernie Banks. Hillerich & Bradsby also made bats for Jackie Robinson, who was honored in 1949 along with George Kell of the Detroit Tigers with the company's first Silver Bat Awards for outstanding hitting. Hillerich & Bradsby had bestowed a similar award to minor-league batting champions since 1934, but this was the first to go to major-league players.

Louisville has contributed a great deal to African American baseball history. The legacy continues with the RiverBats, top farm club of the Milwaukee Brewers of the National League, until they signed a five-year contract in September 1999 with the Cincinnati Reds. From 1982 to 1997 as the Louisville Redbirds, the franchise sent many African Americans to the major leagues. Among them were Willie McGee, Ray Lankford, Brian Jordan, Bernard Gilkey, Terry Pendleton, and Lance Johnson.

See Dick Clark and Larry Lester, eds., *The Negro Leagues Book* (Cleveland 1994); Robert Peterson, *Only the Ball Was White* (New York 1970); Mark Ribowsky, *A Complete History of the Negro Leagues 1884–1955* (Secaucus, N.J., 1995); Jules Tygiel, *Baseball's Great Experiment* (New York 1983); Philip Von Borries, *Louisville Diamonds* (Paducah, Ky., 1996); David Zang, *Fleet Walker's Divided Heart* (Lincoln, Neb., 1995); Walter Barney, ed., *A Celebration of Louisville Baseball in the Major and Minor Leagues* (Cleveland 1997).

Barbara S. Oremland

AFRICAN AMERICAN BUSINESSES. Businesses owned by African Americans were in existence and flourishing in Louisville by the nineteenth century. The *Weekly Planet,* an African American newspaper, was publishing by 1874; and blacks operated other businesses, a number of them in the service industries. On September 12, 1901, the Louisville Negro Business League was organized to foster and encourage African American businesses in the city. The organizers were W.T. Garnett, owner of Garnett Feed and Transfer Co.; D.L. Knight, a mover; and William H. Brown, an owner of a dray and transfer company. By 1909, when the National Negro Business League met in Louisville, a large number and variety of African American businesses were in existence.

The Louisville city directories through the years listed a wide variety of African American professions and businesses, including physicians, dentists, real estate agents, moving companies, beauticians, hairdressers, chiropodists, and photographers. The program for the national league's meeting also documented the wide variety of African American businesses. Watson's Undertaking Establishment was described as an old and large funeral business owned and operated by African Americans. Ridley Undertakers, J.B. Cooper, A.D. Porter and Sons, and G.C. Williams later joined them as prominent funeral home owners in Louisville. Another business listed was the Louisville Cemetery Association, organized and incorporated in 1886. The association, owned and controlled by African Americans from its inception, employed a white man as sexton in its early years. C.B. Clay, a tailor, had owned his business for twenty-nine years, according to the 1909 Business Directory.

The former Walnut St. (now Muhammad Ali Blvd.) was home to a number of African American commercial and social operations. The district offered stores, theaters, clubs, and restaurants to black patrons, who were denied entrance to white establishments in the segregated city. By 1950, businesses such as the Rufus Beason Grocery, Hodge's Florist, Page's Ice Cream, Bright's Pharmacy, the Allen Hotel, the College Court Inn, and Taylor's Filling Station all operated in the West End. The Top Hat Club, owned by Robert Williams and managed by Frankie Maxwell until 1961, was a popular nightclub on Walnut St. with a curved glass bar. It regularly showcased out-of-town jazz artists for its patrons, both black and white.

One of the most famous local businesses was Joe's Palm Room. The Palm Room was at Thirteenth and Magazine Streets until 1967, when it moved to 1821 W Jefferson St. The club, owned by Joseph Hammond from the early 1960s until he sold it in 1979, was famous for its live jazz. Notable local musicians who performed at the Palm Room included Hazel Miller, Bobby Ledford, and Pete Peterson. Hammond also owned and operated the Hammond Realty Co. and a dry-cleaning store, and he was the first African American salesperson for the Falls City Brewing Co.

Bowman's Apothecary was another longstanding black business and operated for over forty years in the Walnut St. district. The Grand, the Lincoln, and the Lyric movie theaters for black patrons also provided shows with performers that included Louis Armstrong, Redd Foxx, Dinah Washington, and Sarah Vaughn.

White Printing and News Service on W Walnut was owned by Larry F. White Sr. and operated as a family-owned business from the 1950s into the 1990s. News media owned by blacks included the *Louisville Leader,* published by I. Willis Cole, and Frank Stanley's *Louisville Defender.* Both of the newspapers provided national and local news relevant to the black community and championed civil rights issues. The *Leader* began circulation in 1917 and ceased publication in 1950. The *Defender,* founded in 1933, is still in publication. Two other newspapers, the *Kentucky Reporter* and the *American Baptist,* were also published by African Americans.

The Urban Renewal process in the late 1950s and the 1960s took nine blocks of the Walnut St. district. Because of the destruction of the area, the number and vibrancy of black-owned businesses declined.

African American businesses, however, were not confined to retail or service industries. Samuel Plato, a building contractor, was one of the most successful African American builders in Louisville. During World War II he was one of only a few contractors who won contracts to build housing for defense workers. Plato was the first African American awarded a federal contract to build post offices. He also built churches, apartment buildings, office buildings, banks, and houses.

One of Kentucky's largest black-owned businesses was Mammoth Life and Accident Insurance Co. Founded in 1915 by W.H. Wright, Rochelle I. Smith, B.O. Wilderson, and H.E. Hall, the company was located on Sixth and Walnut in the old Walnut St. (now Muhammad Ali Blvd.) business district and operated until its merger with Atlanta Life Insurance Co. in 1992. The First Standard Bank, at Sixth and Walnut Streets, thrived through the 1920s only to collapse during the Great Depression. American Mutual Savings Bank and Louisville Bank opened in 1922. Continental National Bank was opened in 1975.

African American businesses in Louisville include the longstanding Mr. Klean's Janitor and Maintenance Service organized in 1964 by George King. WLOU, a radio station that was one of seven black-formatted stations of Rounsaville Radio, was purchased by local businessman William Summers III in 1971. WLOU was the first such station in Kentucky owned and operated by an African American. Liberty Cab Co. also was an African American–owned company. Active Transportation Co. was founded in 1987 by Charlie Johnson and remains as one of the largest minority-owned businesses in Louisville. Alice and Wade Houston are also presidents of transportation companies, Dallas Mavis Specialized Carrier and Automotive Carrier Service, respectively.

The first African American in Kentucky to own an automobile dealership was Robert W. Smith. He bought the Universal Chevrolet dealership on W Broadway in 1971 and renamed it Bob Smith Chevrolet. Smith later built another dealership on Westport Rd. Another black-owned dealership, Cardinal Dodge, with CEO Winston Pittman Sr., was listed in *Black Enterprise* in 1998 as a prominent black-owned company. Lenny Lyles, one of the first African Americans to play regularly on the University of Louisville's football team, developed a shopping mall in West Louisville as well as a shopping center of retail stores and offices. Niche Marketing Inc. was founded by Rohena Miller, a native of Louisville who started her first agency while a student at the University of Louisville. Other black-owned businesses include: architectural firms Anderson Design Group and Brazely & Brazely Inc.; the travel agency TravelPlex; accounting firm Ollie Green and Co.; dry cleaners Superb Cleaners and Laundry and Pressed4Time; tool and die company Magnafac Inc., owned by Frank Shields; and mapping company Spatial Data Integrations Inc., founded by Audwin Helton. These businesses are part of the trend from small businesses toward the corporate world.

In 1998–99 the seventh edition of the *Louisville Black Pages* noted that there were 621,000 businesses in the United States owned by African Americans. That was an increase of 46 percent over 1987. The top one hundred Black Businesses generated annual sales of more than $12 billion.

See "Official Souvenir Program of the National Negro Business League, Louisville, Ky.,

Thirteenth and Liberty (S. Coleridge Taylor) School, 1921.

Aug. 18, 19, and 20, 1909," University of Louisville Archives and Records Center; Kentucky Commission on Human Rights. *Kentucky's Black Heritage* 1971; H.C. Weeden, *History of the Colored People of Louisville* 1897 (typed transcript, reprint 1984); "Minority Enterprise," *Business First*, Feb. 8, 1999; Reference and Biographical Files, University of Louisville Archives and Records Center; *Courier-Journal*, Feb. 7, 1998; *Louisville Defender*, May 23, 1996; George Yater, *Two Hundred Years at the Falls of the Ohio* (Louisville 1987).

Margaret Merrick

AFRICAN AMERICAN CATHOLIC MINISTRIES. The Office of African American Catholic Ministries (OAACM) was established August 1, 1988. Archbishop Thomas C. Kelly acted on the advice of the African American Catholic community and the committee for African American Catholic planning. With the establishment of the office of multicultural ministry in 1997, the OAACM was referred to as African American Ministries. AAM works in collaboration with all offices and agencies in implementing the Archdiocesan strategic plan and the national black Catholic pastoral plan through the following:

Serves as a vehicle to provide spiritual, cultural, educational, and social nourishment for African American Catholics.

Provides a voice and representation at the decision-making level within the archdiocesan structure.

Assists archdiocesan agencies in the development, coordination, and implementation of programs and activities that involve the African American community.

Identifies African American leadership within the Archdiocese of Louisville.

Encourages archdiocesan participation with African American organizations.

Provides opportunities, through programs, to address racism.

Represents the Archdiocese of Louisville at state and national African American Catholic conferences and other functions.

Angela Partee

AFRICAN AMERICAN EDUCATION. Unlike the Deep South, there was no law in antebellum Kentucky prohibiting slaves' learning to read and write, although public sentiment was against educating slaves. An early school for African Americans in Kentucky was started in Louisville in 1827 by three white northern Presbyterian teachers. It was forced to close by whites. In 1833 a white man named Thomas Cook started another school, and in 1834 a Mr. and Mrs. Culture made an attempt, but both schools were forced to close.

Several white religious denominations facilitated the work of black churches by advocating education of slaves for religious and humanitarian purposes. Though some masters taught their slaves, most education came from ministers who felt that slaves should also receive the gospel. The religious nature of the information taught lessened the hostility of many whites. Henry Adams, an African American Baptist preacher, started a school for blacks in December 1841, located in Woods Alley between Walnut (Muhammad Ali Blvd.) and Madison Streets between Ninth and Tenth Streets. This school lasted for a number of years and was transferred to the Fifth Street Baptist Church in 1864, where it continued to operate until the first public schools for blacks opened in 1870. William H. Gibson Sr. opened a school at the Fourth Street Methodist Church at the corner of Fourth and Green (Liberty) Streets in 1847 and opened another for a short time in the early 1850s on Seventh Street between Green and Jefferson Streets. In 1859 he opened a school at Quinn Chapel AME Church on Walnut Street (Muhammad Ali Blvd.) between Eighth and Ninth Streets. This closed during the war but reopened in 1866 and was in operation until 1870.

After the Civil War a number of other private schools opened. The Jackson Street Methodist Episcopal Church opened a school in 1865 between Jefferson and Green Streets. As early as 1865 a school was taught by D.A. Straker at St. Marks Episcopal Church on Green Street between Ninth and Tenth Streets. This moved to Madison Street between Ninth and Tenth Streets and was taught by the Rozborough Sisters. In 1868 it was incorporated as St. Marks High School for Negroes.

There were other schools established soon after, including one by Henry Henderson in the Center Baptist Church and one by Aunt Pendy, Reverend Brooks, and Jessie Davis on Baptist Row (now Madison St.) between Floyd and Shelby Streets. Belle Gains taught in a private school in 1868–69 on Center St. north of Walnut St. She moved several times, including one location at Magazine and Eighteenth Streets and then again at the rear of Daney Pawe's home on Magazine, west of Thirteenth St. She had several students who later became teachers in the public schools. In 1869 the Reverend W.W. Taylor conducted an elementary school in his home at Baptist Row. That same year the Ely Normal School was opened under the auspices of the Freedman's Bureau and the American Missionary Association under the direction of Professor Pope. In 1869 the Roman Catholic church established St. Augustine's Church and School for Negroes, taught by the Sisters of Charity. By 1870 there were at least fifteen schools in Louisville providing education for about fifteen hundred African Americans.

As a result of petitions from Louisville African Americans, in 1866 the Kentucky General Assembly adopted a tax that charged blacks five cents per hundred dollars of property value to pay for black schools, since the tax from property owned by whites went only to white schools. Because African Americans owned little property, the tax did not generate enough money. Changes in the law in 1870 that equalized the distribution of tax money allowed for the first schools to be started that year. The first one opened in the Fifth Street Baptist Church, and the second opened in the Center Street Methodist Church. In 1873 the Central Colored School, an elementary school, opened at the corner of Kentucky and Sixth Streets. This was the first new facility built for the education of African American children by the city. In 1894 it was turned into an all-white school, and the children were sent to other "colored" schools. Known for a while as the Sixth Street School, the name was changed to Mary D. Hill School in 1917 in honor of the supervisor of public schools who had died the previous year. Other early schools in the mid-1870s were Western Colored School, Eastern Colored School, Portland Colored School, and the Fulton Street Colored School. Others later included Benjamin Banneker School in Butchertown and one in Highland Park (Bucktown).

Until 1975 Louisville and Jefferson County had separate school districts. The earliest records of the county school district show that there were ten public schools in the county outside the city in 1875 for African Americans, although many were one-room, part-time operations. By 1900 the county had twenty black schools.

In 1882 Central Colored High School opened in the same building as Central Elementary. It was little more than a middle school until 1893, when it was able to offer four-year study. In 1895 it moved to its own building at Ninth and Magazine Streets and again to Ninth and Chestnut Streets in 1912. It was not until 1951 that Central received its first new building at Chestnut and Twelfth Streets. Until 1907 the school was exclusively an academic institution, but, under the prodding of Booker T. Washington, a case was made for manual training. Since then the school has been geared toward academics and useful skills in a large number of fields. CENTRAL HIGH SCHOOL became a beacon of black pride in the city, excelling at academics and athletics. Basketball is particularly important, as Central has won several state and national championships. The school's most notable student was Cassius Clay (Muhammad Ali), class of 1960, who went on to win the heavyweight boxing championship three times.

White and black schools were not funded equally. Black schools were often located in older buildings, supplies were scarce, and teachers were paid less. African American teachers were also required to sign contracts containing morality clauses. Black leaders, realizing that any questionable action on their part could lead to dismissal, remained aloof from controversial issues. Only ALBERT E. MEYZEEK was bold enough to consistently, over his fifty years of service, denounce discrimination and become involved in racial uplift movements. However, it is believed that he was disciplined as well. Despite the fact that he was one of the most qualified principals in the system, he spent most of his career as an elementary school principal rather than in the coveted Central High position, which he held for only three years.

To help mitigate the discrepancy between funding, in 1917 Julius Rosenwald, president of Sears, Roebuck, & Co., established the Julius Rosenwald Fund, which became the largest African American school-construction project since Reconstruction. Rosenwald believed that better vocational training for Southern blacks would boost the national economy. He provided matching money to the amount of $4.4 million and built in the rural areas. By the program's end in 1932, it had helped build 4,977 schools. According to the fund's records, 5 of the 155 schools constructed in Kentucky under the Rosenwald program were located in Jefferson County. The Jefferson Jacobs School on Jacobs School Rd. in PROSPECT was built first, in 1916. The Harrison Kennedy School was built in 1923–24 in the area known as THE POINT on River Road. In 1928–29 South Park School was built on the old National Turnpike northeast of FAIRDALE. The last two schools were built in 1929–30, Jefferson Colored School on Shelby St. in JEFFERSONTOWN and Newburg School located between the Southern Railroad tracks and Indian Trail.

SIMMONS UNIVERSITY, originally called State University, was founded in 1869 when the Kentucky legislature granted the General Association of Colored Baptists authorization to establish a school. It was opened in 1879 at Seventh and Kentucky Streets by two brothers, E.P. and H.C. MARRS. Dr. C.H. PARRISH SR., president from 1918 to 1931, was responsible for having the name changed to Simmons University in honor of WILLIAM J. SIMMONS, an early president. Kentucky State University in Frankfort, established in 1886, was the first state-supported college for blacks in Kentucky. It was first called the State Normal School for the training of teachers to work in black schools.

In 1891 a provision was written into the state constitution clearly stating that white and black children must attend different public schools. This did not apply to Berea and other private colleges. Visiting Berea in 1904, state representative Carl Day was shocked by the sight of white and black students mingling as equals. He returned to Frankfort and pushed for the Day Law, which enforced segregation in all schools in the state. Having lost a long court battle, trustees of Berea along with Dr. JAMES BOND and Kirke Smith, two African American Berea alumni, organized the LINCOLN INSTITUTE in Simpsonville in 1912. Primarily a high school, it offered a small number of college-level courses and had a strong emphasis on vocational training. The institute closed in 1966.

LOUISVILLE MUNICIPAL COLLEGE opened in 1931 as a result of demands of black leaders that the city make provisions for the higher education of blacks, since they were not allowed into the UNIVERSITY OF LOUISVILLE. Located on the former site of Simmons University, which closed because of financial problems in 1930, it was a liberal arts college and a division of the University of Louisville. It closed in 1951 when the University of Louisville desegregated.

The desegregation of higher education began in 1948 when black representative CHARLES A. ANDERSON placed a bill before the General Assembly that provided for both races to attend nursing schools. The bill passed and included postgraduate courses for doctors in hospitals so that black physicians could take residencies at white hospitals in Kentucky. In 1948 Central High School teacher LYMAN T. JOHNSON applied to the University of Kentucky graduate school. When he was denied admission due to his race, he took his case to federal court, where, in 1949, Judge H. Church Ford ordered the university to accept African Americans to the College of Engineering, Pharmacy, and the Graduate School, since Kentucky State did not offer those programs. In 1950 the General Assembly further amended the Day Law to permit students of both races to attend the same institution of higher education, provided that the governing institutions approved and that a comparable course was not offered at Kentucky State. Immediately, BELLARMINE COLLEGE, Nazareth College (later SPALDING), URSULINE COLLEGE, the SOUTHERN BAPTIST THEOLOGICAL SEMINARY, and the LOUISVILLE PRESBYTERIAN SEMINARY opened their doors to black students. When the University of Louisville attempted to delay desegregation, the NAACP prepared to file suit. The lawsuit was not necessary because the university trustees voted to open the graduate and professional schools that coming year and the rest of the university beginning the 1951–52 school year.

In May 1954, the historic *Brown v. Board of Education of Topeka* decision was rendered by the Supreme Court. Shortly after the decision, school superintendent OMER CARMICHAEL and Gov. LAWRENCE W. WETHERBY announced that Louisville and the state of Kentucky would do whatever was necessary to comply with the law of the land. These statements had the effect of eliminating school desegregation as a political issue. Thus Louisville avoided anything that resembled the ugly debacle that took place at Little Rock, Arkansas. The Louisville plan, which was implemented in 1956, redistricted the entire school district to serve all children as conveniently as possible regardless of race. All parents were allowed to request a transfer to another school district, provided that school was not at capacity with students from its own district. In almost all cases, parents were granted the transfer of their first choice. In the end there was 100 percent integration as far as the principle was concerned, but because of the transfers there was very little actual integration. Throughout the sixties and seventies, whites left the city for the suburbs in large numbers, many to escape integration. This made the schools even more segregated.

In 1966 Dr. James S. Coleman, a renowned University of Chicago sociologist, submitted a report to Congress based on an extensive study of the performance of students in public schools. Coleman concluded that disadvantaged African American children learned better in integrated classes. His findings became the manual for political and court action and were used to support busing to achieve racial balance in the schools. In 1973 a suit was brought against the public schools by a coalition of civil rights groups in an effort to take positive action to integrate schools. The suit was dismissed by Judge JAMES F. GORDON, but the decision was reversed by the United States Circuit Court in the summer of 1975, which ordered Gordon to implement a desegregation plan by the fall term. Gordon worked with school officials to impose a plan that integrated the communities' public schools through the busing of students. BUSING caused enormous resistance, leading to school boycotts and violent demonstrations in the southern and southwest parts of the county.

In the early 1990s Supreme Court rulings loosened restrictions over the busing process, leading to new plans for mixing of the races. In December 1991 the Jefferson County School Board allowed parents to enroll their children in the school of their choice. The plan expanded the magnet programs to encourage students to attend different schools. Only students within certain clusters of schools that did not meet a required 15 to 50 percent black student body in each school would be assigned and bused involuntarily to a school.

One of the biggest challenges was to convince white families to send their children to inner-city schools. Many urban schools at the elementary and middle school level closed because of low attendance. As a result, busing has become somewhat of a one-way trip as more students are bused out of the inner city than are bused into the city. Some African American parents complain that they are unable to monitor their children's education miles from their homes and that children still feel isolated in unfriendly school settings. Some longtime teachers said that, after busing, resources were distributed more equally and that inner-city children were exposed to new and enlightening experiences.

Since busing was implemented in 1975, the debate over its effectiveness in improving education for black children has continued. In early 1997 the federal Department of Education released state-by-state standardized test scores, concluding that the gap between white and black achievement is growing throughout the nation. Kentucky Education Reform Act (KERA) test scores for nonwhite 11th graders dropped from 27.7 in 1993–94 to 24.6 in 1994–95, while remaining virtually the same for whites, 43.2 and 43.1. This represents a widening of the achievement gap by nearly 5 percent, leading some to ask if the new integration plan is working as well for black students as it is for whites.

Central High School has become a center of controversy in Louisville African American education. Historically an all-black institution with a long and illustrious record of offering a superior education to the black community, Central's student population was mandated to be 50 percent white in 1975. The 50 percent African American limit and its strong identity as a black school lessened white student enrollment. Out of a total capacity of 1,400, only 823 students were enrolled in the 1996–97 school year. Central offered special programs in business law, government, computer technology, and health care; but, unlike plans in many school districts, Jefferson County's student assignment plan did not exclude special magnet programs.

A combination of its historical significance to the black community and the fact that black students were being turned away from specialized magnet programs while enrollment was low served as an impetus for the formation of CEASE (Citizens for Equitable Assignment to School Environment), a small organization whose members asked the school board to forgo its racial guidelines for Central High School. CEASE asked that Central's African American student body ratio be permitted to be as high as 80 percent so that black students could enroll in the special programs offered at the school. The Jefferson County School Board refused this request, saying that once an exception was made, others would have to follow. Therefore, although Jefferson County was considered one of the most integrated school systems in the nation, six parents filed a federal lawsuit in April 1998 against the Jefferson County Public Schools that challenged limits on black enrollment at Central.

In 1998 there were nine schools that were named for various black educators and leaders. These include Carter Traditional Elementary, named for Jessie R. Carter; Johnson Middle School, named for Lyman T. Johnson; King Elementary, named for Martin Luther King Jr.; Maupin Elementary, named for Milburn T. Maupin; Meyzeek Middle, named for Albert E. Meyzeek; Roosevelt-Perry Elementary, named in part for William H. Perry; Price Elementary, named for Sarah J. Price; Young Elementary, named for WHITNEY M. YOUNG JR.; and Wheatley Elementary, named for Phillis Wheatley.

See Alice Allison Dunnigan, *The Fascinating Story of Black Kentuckians: Their Heritage and Traditions* (Washington, D.C., 1982); *Kentucky's Black Heritage* (Frankfort 1971); George D. Wilson, *A Century of Negro Education in Louisville, Kentucky* (Louisville 1986); Bruce Allar, "Central to the Debate," *Louisville* (Aug. 1997): 36–43, 63; Omer Carmichael and Weldon Janes, *The Louisville Story* (New York 1957); *Courier-Journal*, Nov. 13, 1998.

AFRICAN AMERICAN JOCKEYS. Unlike the Inner Bluegrass Region, nineteenth-century Louisville had neither the natural resources nor a population sufficiently interested in Thoroughbred racing to sustain an agricultural complex that nurtured the development of first-class horses or riders. However, without Louisville's racetracks and sports writers, Bluegrass-based African American jockeys would not have gained lasting fame. Throughout the 1800s black jockeys dominated Southern racing, capping their accomplishments by winning sixteen of the KENTUCKY DERBY's first twenty-eight runnings. CHURCHILL DOWNS, with its well-publicized semiannual meets, also enhanced the fortunes of black jockeys-turned-trainers and owners, especially when they raced Derby-caliber horses.

Prior to the 1870s, riders were randomly named in press accounts of racing results. An exception was Cato (?-?) (pronounced Cate-o), a slave who rode Virginia-bred Wagner against Kentucky's standard bearer, Grey Eagle, in the 1839 "match race of the century" at Louisville's OAKLAND COURSE. Cato was freed and accorded celebrity status after his victory.

Talented black youngsters started riding professionally around age ten, when they weighed between fifty-five and seventy-five pounds. Injury, death, and adolescent growth spurts took a heavy toll on these boys; few competed beyond age sixteen. A black jockey cemetery located on the outskirts of the WOODLAWN RACE COURSE (1858–75) site in eastern Jefferson County gave credence to reports that virtually all successful antebellum riders were African Americans.

Woodlawn's successor, the Louisville Jockey Club and Driving Park Association (Churchill Downs), opened in 1875. Thirteen of the fifteen first Derby jockeys, including winning rider Oliver Lewis (?-?), were black. The winning trainer was Ansel Williamson (1810–81). By 1875 this Virginia-born former slave was one of the top-ranked trainers in America. Fourth-place finisher William Walker (1860–1933) won the Derby in 1877 and then rode, among other greats, Ten Broeck for successful black Derby jockey-turned-trainer "Rolly" Colston Jr. (?-1928). By the 1890s, Walker, who settled in Louisville, had become a consultant on Thoroughbred pedigrees, a profession that made him one of the wealthiest blacks in Kentucky.

Finishing "up the track" (dead last) in an 1875 Spring Meet race was Lexington-born Isaac Burns (1860–96), who took his maternal grandfather's name, Murphy; won three Kentucky Derbies; and became American racing's hero—his 44 percent win record has never been equaled—before he succumbed to pneumonia.

The legacy of black horsemen had been forgotten when Keeneland librarian Amelia Buckley asked Frank Borries, grandson of Louisville's post–Civil War German ambassador, to locate ISAAC MURPHY's grave. The search required two years. Murphy was reinterred, first at Faraway Farm in 1967 and then at the Kentucky Horse Park, next to Man o' War.

See Lynn S. Renau, *Racing around Kentucky* (Louisville 1995); Alexander Mackay-Smith, *The Race Horses of America 1832–1872: Portraits and Other Paintings by Edward Troye* (Saratoga Springs, N.Y., 1981).

Lynn S. Renau

AFRICAN AMERICANS. African Americans have been a vital, although often unacknowledged, presence in Louisville and Jefferson County since the earliest days of settlement. At least one African American, CATO WATTS, was with the group accompanying GEORGE ROGERS CLARK on the expedition that landed on CORN ISLAND in May 1778. At least one other, CAESAR, served in Clark's military campaigns in the Old Northwest during the American Revolution. However, the lives of African Americans in early Louisville were shaped and constrained both by the institution of slavery and by a culture that accepted and justified human bondage.

Louisville remained a small village until the appearance of steamboats on the OHIO RIVER (1811) and the completion of the LOUISVILLE AND PORTLAND CANAL in 1830. But it grew rapidly thereafter. Of the 1,357 Louisville residents in 1810, 495 (36.5 percent) were African Americans, 484 of whom were enslaved. By 1830 the city population had grown to 10,341, with an African American population of 2,638 (25.5 percent), 2,406 of whom were enslaved.

Throughout the antebellum period, African Americans represented roughly one-third of the county population, and virtually all African Americans living in the county were slaves. However, the conditions of slavery in the region were unusual. For example, large-scale cotton cultivation was precluded by Kentucky's climate, and, thus, most whites (approximately 70 percent) did not own slaves. Those who did owned comparatively few (approximately five slaves per slave-owning household). Still, there was a surplus, and slave-hiring became common in Louisville and Jefferson County, allowing businesses and less-affluent whites to rent slaves for varying periods. Domestic slave trade, which shifted slaves from the upper South to the cotton-growing regions of the lower South, became common as well, and, by 1860, there were various domestic slave trade businesses in Louisville, with slave pens located in the downtown area.

Still, beyond impersonal statistics, few enslaved African Americans stand out as individuals in the early historical record. The most significant exception to this general anonymity is YORK, the slave who accompanied WILLIAM CLARK on the famed LEWIS AND CLARK EXPEDITION (1803–6) to the Pacific shore. York came to be known as the Big Medicine to the Indians of the Great Plains.

Between 1830 and 1860, the number of free people of color living in Louisville increased by 726.3 percent, from 232 to 1,917. Growing numbers brought a degree of residential segregation, and, as a result, between 1830 and 1860 the African American presence underwent a fundamental transformation into an African American community located immediately west and east of downtown. Enslaved African Americans who lived on their owner's property were concentrated most heavily in the affluent sections of the Third, Fourth, and Fifth Wards of the city; i.e., between Second and Eighth Streets north of Walnut (Muhammad Ali Blvd.).

The growing population of free people of color, the only significant concentration of free blacks in Kentucky, along with slaves who hired their time and "lived out," could also be found largely in the same wards but closer to the southern limit of the city (then Prather St., or Broadway), with growing numbers west of Sixth St. This community developed an institutional and leadership infrastructure, patterns of relations with whites, and a reputation for being helpful to fugitive slaves. By 1860 there were eight independent African American churches in Louisville, with the First African Baptist Church (now FIFTH STREET BAPTIST CHURCH) tracing its origins to 1829. Along with churches, fraternal organizations were established by the 1850s; e.g., MASONS and Odd Fellows. Furthermore, the first school for African Americans opened in the basement of the First African Baptist Church in December 1841, and several others were sponsored by local black churches in later years.

Free people of color were limited to the same occupations practiced by urban slaves but could on rare occasions establish businesses that were generally an extension of these occupations. For example, in the 1830s SHELTON MORRIS operated a barbershop and bathhouse under a local hotel. Other free people of color owned barbershops, did hauling, and had related businesses. One African American, WASHINGTON SPRADLING, owned a barbershop, speculated in real estate, and, by the 1860s, was worth over a hundred thousand dollars. He used his wealth to help more than thirty enslaved African Americans purchase their freedom. However, free African Americans were "more black than free," were prevented from voting, and had little real freedom to compete in the free market economy. City ordinances were enacted, particularly after 1830, that prohibited them from obtaining licenses to engage in certain businesses; e.g., to own confectioneries, retail groceries, restaurants, or fruit stores. Opportunities to own property or businesses were even more circumscribed for the few free people of color in antebellum Jefferson County. The most notable exceptions were Henry and ELIZA TEVIS, free people of color who in February 1851 purchased forty acres in southeastern Jefferson County on which the NEWBURG/Petersburg community later developed.

Although slavery was driven principally by economic motives, an elaborate cultural mythology evolved to rationalize the inherent evils of the institution. Despite the popular belief that Kentucky slavery was "mild" and relations between blacks and whites were "good," antebellum newspapers, official records, and the testimony of slaves themselves suggest otherwise. For example, the lash was applied liberally in Louisville and Jefferson County. Slaves were sometimes executed for stealing a few dollars' worth of goods, while only beaten for murdering other slaves. A slave named Reuben was executed in 1812 for conspiring to rebel.

Even in early January 1861, as the CIVIL WAR approached, throngs of whites gathered to enjoy the carnival atmosphere of the public hanging of David Caution, a black man. Notwithstanding the risks, there was a steady trickle of runaway slaves, an average of one per day by the 1850s, and fugitive slave ads suggested that physical and/or sexual mistreatment often precipitated slave escapes. Beyond these facts, there was the specter of domestic slave trade, which attenuated and severed family and other personal relations among slaves. In essence, slavery in Kentucky differed in some respects from slavery in other regions but was certainly no better.

Kentucky was deeply divided during the Civil War but remained nominally loyal to the Union. In essence, both Louisville and Kentucky wanted "Union with slavery," a position that became increasingly untenable as the war unfolded. However, Kentucky African Americans were not divided in their sympathies, and 23,703 served in the Union army. Louisville became one of the state's primary induction centers for U.S. Colored Troops. Black soldiers were concentrated in barracks at Third and Oak Streets, and a ten-acre refugee camp for their families was located at Eighteenth and Broadway, then the outskirts of town. Local African Americans organized aid societies through their churches to provide food, clothing, and medical care to black refugees. Mary Lewis of the GREEN STREET BAPTIST CHURCH Soldiers Aid Society even presented a battle flag to the 123rd Regiment of the U.S. Colored Infantry in January 1865.

Since the Emancipation Proclamation applied only to enslaved African Americans in Confederate territory and Kentucky refused to enact emancipatory legislation, slavery did not end in Kentucky until December 18, 1865, with the ratification of the Thirteenth Amendment. With the end of slavery, differences in legal status between African Americans and whites disappeared literally overnight. However, racial attitudes and the determination to maintain the subordination of African Americans did not change. In the crucible of RECONSTRUCTION, racial segregation evolved as a means of ensuring a safe status difference between the races; i.e., any condition or interaction that implied white subordination to or equality with African Americans was proscribed. Discrimination, poverty, poor housing, crime, and police brutality became commonplace. Separate was seldom, if ever, equal; and African Americans found themselves, in the words of President James A. Garfield, on the "middle ground between slavery and freedom." The local African American community continued to develop despite, but also within, these limitations.

Through an influx of rural African Americans, Louisville's black population increased by 120 percent, to 14,956 in 1870, and continued to grow. Postwar commercial growth, manufacturing expansion, and railroad construction provided job opportunities for many new arrivals, and some achieved limited success in the city's thriving economy. However the informal economies of Louisville's households and streets absorbed most of the growing population of African American immigrants but often permitted only bare subsistence because of low wages and frequent unemployment. Limitations increased the resourcefulness of many marginalized blacks in postbellum Louisville and encouraged the use of a wide range of casual income opportunities. Women often took in washing and ironing. Boarders also supplemented limited family wages and provided income during times of unemployment. Men entered into a variety of informal economic pursuits such as barter, peddling, gleaning, day labor, and carrying parcels.

By 1900 Louisville ranked seventh among all United States cities in African American population, at 39,139 (19.1 percent). Population growth prompted overcrowding and the emergence of new black neighborhoods—SMOKETOWN, CALIFORNIA, LITTLE AFRICA (western Parkland)—and also stimulated the development of black settlements in Jefferson County, the rural communities of BERRYTOWN and GRIFFYTOWN near ANCHORAGE. With leaders such as the Reverend HENRY ADAMS, HORACE MORRIS, A.E. MEYZEEK, WILLIAM J. SIMMONS, WILLIAM STEWARD, and the Reverend C.H. PARRISH SR., African Americans pressed for economic opportunities, political rights, and access to quality education and achieved several limited but noteworthy successes.

Local African Americans spearheaded successful statewide efforts to secure voting rights, the right to testify in court (against whites), and the right to serve on juries but failed to prevent the segregation of railroad cars and facilities in the 1890s. Freedom rides organized through QUINN CHAPEL AME CHURCH challenged segregation on local streetcars in 1870. Public schools were also established for African Americans in October 1870, and CENTRAL COLORED HIGH SCHOOL opened in October 1873 at Sixth and Kentucky Streets.

In November 1879, State (later Simmons) University was founded at Seventh and Kentucky Streets, with theological and liberal arts programs. In the early 1890s local whites began agitating for a library that would be open, at no cost, to all citizens. Because no mention was made of library access for African Americans, A.E. MEYZEEK organized an African American library committee, and, after several years of discussions, city leaders agreed to establish a separate branch library for African Americans. The Western Branch Library opened in 1905 and moved to its own building at Tenth and Chestnut Streets in 1908.

From the perspective of African Americans, several factors combined to make Louisville a unique and important city at the beginning of this century. The combination of a tradition of African American self-help, community activism along politically moderate lines, the concentration of black population, and the retention of the franchise gave African Americans—despite the racial antagonism or, at best, paternalism ("polite racism," in the words of historian George Wright) of Louisville's white leaders—sufficient bargaining power to force concessions and compromises. Thus, although separate and unequal, Louisville's African American community was nonetheless reasonably well organized and comparatively stable. For example, by 1900 the percentage of African American homeowners was higher in Louisville than in any other U.S. city. There were sixty-six churches, sixty-seven fraternal organizations boasting seventy-five hundred total members, twelve black women's clubs, thirteen physicians, eight attorneys, fifty-nine ministers, an orphans home (founded 1878), an old folks home (founded 1888), a YMCA (founded 1892), and more than one hundred teachers in the city. There were also 2 tailor shops, 20 restaurants, 10 saloons, 3 newspapers, 20 barbershops, a hospital (RED CROSS, founded 1899), numerous groceries, several funeral parlors, and 1,272 African Americans in the skilled trades, many of whom operated their own businesses.

After World War I, local African Americans became more assertive in politics and more ambitious in entrepreneurship. Local chapters of the National Association for the Advancement of Colored People (NAACP), the National Urban League, and the more conservative Commission on Interracial Cooperation, headed by the Reverend JAMES M. BOND (grandfather of former Georgia legislator Julian Bond), were organized during this period. By 1914 fear of black encroachment into white neighborhoods prompted the passage of a residential segregation ordinance. However, the Louisville NAACP challenged this ordinance in the *BUCHANAN V. WARLEY* case and succeeded in having it ruled unconstitutional in 1917, after which the eastern section of the RUSSELL neighborhood soon became all-black and African Americans began moving west of Twenty-first St.

In 1920 African American voters, with white allies, defeated a UNIVERSITY OF LOUISVILLE bond issue because the university refused to admit or make provision for African Americans. In addition, frustration with the insensitivity of both the REPUBLICAN and DEMOCRATIC Parties led local African Americans to organize the LINCOLN INDEPENDENT PARTY (LIP) in 1921, running A.D. PORTER for mayor, along with a full slate of candidates for other local and state offices. No LIP candidates were elected, but the increased political leverage that resulted brought the appointment of the first African Americans to the police (1923) and fire (1925) departments, although they could exercise authority only in black neighborhoods.

A second generation of African American businesses emerged as well, led by the MAMMOTH LIFE AND ACCIDENT INSURANCE CO., the largest African American business in Kentucky, founded in July 1915. Domestic Life and Accident Insurance Co. was established in June 1920, and the FIRST STANDARD BANK of Louisville—the first African American bank in Kentucky—opened in December 1920. SAMUEL PLATO operated an architectural and building firm and built numerous local houses and thirty-seven post offices (under government contract) between 1925 and 1941. He constructed a complex of eighty-eight co-op housing units in the Camp Taylor neighborhood beginning in 1941.

According to the *LOUISVILLE LEADER,* by the mid-1920s there were two other insurance companies, another African American bank, two hotels, two building and loan associations, six real estate firms, three drugstores, eight undertakers, two photographers, fifteen grocery stores, four newspapers, two other architectural firms, and three movie houses in Louisville. Despite the nostalgia often attached to Old Walnut St. of the 1940s and 1950s, the true golden age of African American businesses occurred between 1900 and 1930, when the center of business activity was actually closer to the Pythian Building at Tenth and Chestnut.

The GREAT DEPRESSION brought massive economic dislocation as local African American unemployment rose from 12.1 percent in 1930 to 37.2 percent in 1932. African Americans lost their limited capacity to support businesses in their own neighborhoods, and these businesses failed in droves. However, some of the older businesses survived and new ones appeared, notably the *LOUISVILLE DEFENDER* newspaper (founded in 1933; FRANK STANLEY SR. became publisher in 1936) and Frank Moorman's gas station (1937). In the political arena, local attorney CHARLES W. ANDERSON was elected to the Kentucky General Assembly in 1935, the first African American so chosen.

Led by the efforts of LYMAN T. JOHNSON, the local NAACP, and many liberal whites, the structure of legal segregation collapsed after World War II. In 1948 the main LOUISVILLE FREE PUBLIC LIBRARY was desegregated, followed by the desegregation of all neighborhood branches in 1952. Also in 1948, the desegregation of local hospitals began with the admission of African American patients to St. Joseph Infirmary. In 1952 local golf courses were desegregated by court order, and, in 1955, Mayor ANDREW BROADDUS issued an executive order desegregating all local parks. Under threat of a lawsuit against the University of Louisville, the Kentucky General Assembly in March 1950 revoked the Day Law, Kentucky's educational segregation statute, and all Louisville colleges and universities desegregated by 1951. Unfortunately, the desegregation of the University of Louisville brought the closing of Louisville Municipal College, and, after a bitter controversy, only one LMC faculty member, Dr. C.H. PARRISH JR., joined the University of Louisville faculty. However, the desegregation of higher education paved the way for desegregation of Louisville's PUBLIC SCHOOLS in 1956.

In 1945 Eugene S. Clayton became the first African American elected to the BOARD OF ALDERMEN, followed by many others such as LOUISE REYNOLDS, LOIS MORRIS, and the Reverend W.J. Hodge. In the 1960s and 1970s, local leaders such as Georgia Davis Powers and MAE STREET KIDD played important roles in the Kentucky Senate and House, respectively.

Georgia (Montgomery) Davis Powers was born October 29, 1923, in Springfield, Kentucky. She was the only female of the nine children of Ben and Frances (Walker) Montgomery. In Louisville she graduated from CENTRAL HIGH SCHOOL and from LOUISVILLE MUNICIPAL COLLEGE in 1942. From 1962 to 1967 Powers (as she has been known since her second marriage) served as campaign chairperson for candidates running for a variety of offices, including mayor of Louisville, governor of Kentucky, and the U.S. Congress. She was Kentucky chairperson for the Jesse L. Jackson presidential campaigns in 1984 and 1988 and the first African American woman to serve on the Jefferson County Democratic executive committee, beginning in 1964. Powers was one of the organizers of the Allied Organization for Civil Rights, which worked for passage of the statewide Public Accommodations and Fair Employment Law of 1964. She was the first woman and the first African American to be elected to the Kentucky Senate, serving from January 1968 to January 1989 as a Democrat. As senator, she chaired two legislative committees: Health and Welfare and Labor and Industry. She sponsored or co-sponsored an open housing law; a low-cost housing bill; a law to eliminate the identification of race from Kentucky operator's licenses; an amendment to the Kentucky Civil Rights Act to eliminate discrimination based on race, gender, or age; an equal opportunity law; the Equal Rights Amendment resolution; the Displaced Homemaker's Law; and a law to increase the minimum wage in Kentucky. In 1995 her memoir *I Shared the Dream* was published. Powers was married to Norman F. Davis from 1943 to 1968. She married James L. Powers in 1973.

Economic conditions improved for many African Americans as a result of the political struggle for racial justice. Local African American unemployment declined to 6.9 percent in 1970, and median African American income rose from 55 percent of the white family median in 1959 to 61 percent in 1969. By 1969 African Americans owned 490 businesses in Louisville and Jefferson County, or 4.6 percent of all businesses in the region; and several local African American business leaders such as Woodford Porter Sr., WILLIAM E. SUMMERS III, and Joseph Hammond became prominent in the affairs of the larger community.

Over the course of its history, the local African American community also produced a number of artists, entertainers, and athletes of national consequence, although many found it necessary to leave Kentucky to pursue their careers. Among the most noteworthy were opera singer Todd Duncan (1903–98), the first Porgy in Gershwin's *Porgy and Bess;* jazz vocalist HELEN HUMES; and Ford Lee Washington (1906–55) and John William Sublett (1902–84), who, as Buck and Bubbles, became the nation's leading vaudeville song, dance, and comedy team in the 1920s and 1930s. In the late 1800s and early 1900s, JOSEPH S. COTTER SR. and Joseph S. Cotter Jr. became well-known poets. Other important contemporary figures include painter Sam Gilliam and sculptor Edward Hamilton. Along with the many African American jockeys and trainers who worked at CHURCHILL DOWNS through the early 1900s, Louisville also fielded an African American baseball team, the Louisville Giants, in 1887. The football and basketball teams of Central High School were national powers in the 1940s and 1950s, and state powers in the 1960s and 1970s. African Americans such as Leonard Lyles, Westley Unseld, and Darryl Griffith brought national stature to University of Louisville football and basketball. And Louisville produced perhaps the best-known and most influential athlete in U.S. history—MUHAMMAD ALI.

While the end of legal segregation brought African Americans closer to the goal of racial equality, it still failed to achieve it. Louisville remained two communities divided by race. The struggle for public accommodations was long and difficult, prompting the Nothing-New-for-Easter boycott of downtown Louisville businesses in 1961 and culminating in the passage of a public accommodations ordinance in 1963. URBAN RENEWAL in the late 1950s and early 1960s leveled black residential areas both east and west of downtown Louisville, including the Old Walnut St. business corridor. Residential segregation persisted and only after repeated demonstrations—often enlisting the assistance of national leaders such as Dr. Martin Luther King Jr.—was an open-housing ordinance passed in 1967. Many African Americans failed to benefit from these grudging reforms, and festering racial tensions erupted in a race riot in West Louisville following an incident in which police overreacted in May 1968. In 1969 and 1970, African American student unrest at the University of Louisville led to the creation of the Office of Black Affairs, special scholarship programs, and the Department of Pan-African Studies. Merger of the Louisville and Jefferson County school systems (1975), and district-wide busing mandated by the U.S. 6th Circuit Court of Appeals (decision of December 28, 1973) caused civil unrest in southwestern Jefferson County. Ironically, in 1982 and 1983 city-county merger referenda were defeated by a coalition of African Americans from the West End and whites from southwest Jefferson County, where the most intense opposition to busing was centered.

In recent years, there have been notable successes in the establishment of profitable janitorial service and transportation firms, in addition to the founding of (Leonard) Lyle's Mall in West Louisville, the unfortunately short-lived Continental National Bank of Kentucky, and even a fledgling television station (WYCS). Since the 1980s African Americans have occupied roughly one-third of all seats on the Board of Aldermen and one seat on the local board of education. One county commissioner has been an African American. Although no Kentucky African Americans have been elected to national political office, Gerald A. Neal of Louisville succeeded Georgia Davis Powers in the Kentucky Senate, and several local African Americans continue to serve in the lower house of the General Assembly. Moreover, in the civil rights arena, local leaders such as the Reverend Louis Coleman of the Justice Resource Center have kept alive the tradition of community activism born in the streetcar demonstrations of 1870.

Louis Henry Coleman Jr. was born in Louisville November 21, 1943, to Louis H. and Dorothy (Figg) Coleman. He is a graduate of Kentucky State University and the recipient of two master's degrees, one from U of L and one from the LOUISVILLE PRESBYTERIAN THEOLOGICAL SEMINARY. Pastor of the First Congregational Methodist Church, he has also served as pastor of Shelbyville Congregational Methodist. Coleman has worked as director of Housing and Urban Development for Louisville, executive director of the PRESBYTERIAN COMMUNITY CENTER, and director of Recreation and Social Services for the Shelby Community Center. He founded the Justice Resource Center in 1975. In 1998 he established the Louisville Black Chamber of Commerce. Coleman is married to Carolyn (Martin); they have two daughters and one son.

By 1990 the city's 79,783 African American residents were concentrated primarily in the West End; another 44,978 were scattered throughout the metropolitan area. Local African American unemployment stood at 21.7 percent in 1987 and, by 1989, median African American family income had dropped to only 52 percent of the white median in Louisville and only 43 percent in Jefferson County. Violent crime had become endemic in the most segregated and impoverished African American neighborhoods despite efforts launched by local government and financial institutions to build low-cost housing and stimulate economic development. Mandatory BUSING gave way in the 1990s to a school-district-wide student assignment plan featuring magnet and optional school programs operating within specific racial enrollment parameters. Despite this change and the reforms engendered by the Kentucky Education Reform Act (1990), African American students remained largely segregated within local schools (by tracking and program assignment) and continued to achieve decidedly unequal educational outcomes.

Responding to such conditions, a broadly representative group of local African Americans, convened by County Commissioner Darryl T. Owens, developed an "African American Strategic Plan" between September 1996 and January 1998 identifying dramatic inequalities between whites and African Americans in education, economic development and wealth-building, and health and social wellness as key problem areas requiring immediate and sustained attention. A similar plan could have been written a century ago; thus, despite a rich history of African American achievement, the struggle to make Louisville one community remains unfinished.

Population, City of Louisville

Year	*Total Population*	*African American Population*	*Percentage*
1850	43,194	6,970	16.1
1860	68,033	6,820	10.0
1870	100,753	14,956	14.8
1880	123,758	20,905	16.8
1890	161,129	28,651	17.7
1900	204,731	39,139	19.1
1910	223,928	40,522	18.0
1920	234,891	40,087	17.0
1930	307,745	47,354	15.3
1940	319,077	47,158	14.8
1950	369,129	57,657	15.6
1960	390,639	70,075	17.9
1970	361,472	86,040	23.8
1980	298,451	84,080	28.2
1990	269,555	79,783	29.5
1996	260,689	83,420	32.0

See S. Cummings and M. Price, *Race Relations in Louisville: Southern Racial Traditions and Northern Class Dynamics* (Louisville 1990); A.A. Dunningan, *The Fascinating Story of Black Kentuckians: Their Heritage and Traditions* (Washington, D.C., 1982); W.H. Gibson, *Historical Sketch of the Progress of the Colored Race in Louisville, Ky.* (Louisville 1983); J.H. Kerns, *A Survey of the Economic and Cultural Conditions of the Negro Population of Louisville, Kentucky* (New York 1948); C.B. Lewis, "Louisville and its Afro- American Citizens," *Colored American Magazine* 10 (April 1906): 259–64; M. O'Brien, *Slavery in Louisville during the Antebellum Period,* M.A. thesis, University of Louisville, 1979; H.D. Stafford, *Slavery in a Border City: Louisville, 1790–1860,* Ph.D. dissertation, University of Kentucky, 1982; H.C. Weeden, *Weeden's History of the Colored People of Louisville* (Louisville 1898); George C. Wright, *Life Behind a Veil: Blacks in Louisville, Kentucky, 1865–1930* (Baton Rouge, La., 1985); "'Living by Means Unknown to Their Neighbors,'" *Filson Club History Quarterly* 72 (Oct. 1998): 357–78; Wade Hall, *Passing for Black: The Life and Careers of Mae Street Kidd* (Lexington 1997).

J. Blaine Hudson

AGRICULTURE. Since 1820 and the emergence of the steamboat trade, Jefferson County has been Kentucky's largest urban center. This almost obscures the county's importance in the field of agriculture. It was not until 1850, under the superintendency of J.B.D. DeBow, that the United States Census began including county statistics. Thus the history of agriculture of Jefferson County has to be drawn from a multiplicity of sources. At an early date, the land about the FALLS OF THE OHIO attracted land surveyors and speculators. For instance, the 1773 account of the region by THOMAS BULLITT and the subsequent land surveys reflect the attraction of the county as both a potentially rich agricultural land and a promising commercial site.

Like Kentucky itself, Jefferson County is highly sectional, with the more fertile agricultural lands located in the Ohio River flood plain. The eastern section, where many of the big plantations were located, also possessed desirable farmland. Though Jefferson County at the time of its formation was encapsulated in a much larger area loosely bounded by stream courses, it is possible to identify within its present 375–square-mile area several original land-grant farmsteads.

At an unspecified date a crop of wheat was grown at the Falls and ground into flour. Almost assuredly Indian corn was grown at the same time, because there is a note of the corn trade in the disastrous winter blizzard of 1780–81. From the outset, small grains and Indian corn were mainstay field crops. Hogs, sheep, and cattle were the chief livestock; horse and mule production in the county never equaled that of the east-central Bluegrass counties.

The history of agriculture and boating on the OHIO RIVER is closely linked. Once settlement was made in the county and boat traffic downriver to the emerging Old Southwest increased, local agrarian fortunes were largely tied to the river. This became a cardinal fact after 1820 and the emergence of the steamboat trade.

Agricultural and commercial development in Jefferson County quickly became codependent. For example, in 1819 the HOPE DISTILLERY on W Main St. was a major processor of grain. The distillery was said to have produced twelve hundred gallons of whiskey a day, and the slop was fed to twelve hundred hogs. The hogs reflect that Louisville was an early packinghouse town depending on local farms for hogs and beef cattle. Louisville and SHIPPINGPORT, located slightly downriver, became important milling centers, producing at one time five hundred or more barrels of flour and corn meal per day. Aside from this, Louisville became a central market for agricultural products gathered from a large area.

By one standard, Jefferson County at mid-nineteenth century was still, landwise, underdeveloped agriculturally. Only 70,720 acres out of 295,161 were classed as improved. There were 877 farms that produced 39,522 hogs, 10,790 sheep, and 8,135 cattle. The two major field crops were still small grains and Indian corn. From 1780 to 1980 this pattern held, with a new crop, soybeans, now in ascendancy.

In terms of human occupation of the land, there were 10,911 slaves out of a total population of 59,831 in 1850. There was, however, a sharp imbalance between rural and urban dwellers of 16,637 rural to 43,194 urban. In contrast, a century later out of a population of 684,615, 86.9 percent were classed as urban. This population was spread over 375 square miles, and in 1950 there were 1,743 relatively small farms, averaging 68 acres and yielding a combined income from all farm products sold of $5,545,000.

The agricultural and historical significance of Jefferson County and Louisville does not rest on locally produced field crops and livestock. Situated adjacent to the Ohio River, from the outset of settlement farmers have had access to transportation facilities. First there were the flatboats, then STEAMBOATS, railways, highways, and, later, airways. Louisville has always been more or less an agricultural market town where grains, meat, hemp, and TOBACCO were sold. In the same measure it has been a supply town, manufacturing and selling farm implements, harness, blacksmith and hand tools, field crop and garden seeds, and agricultural chemicals.

The manufacture of agricultural implements was one of the oldest and largest industries in nineteenth-century Louisville. By 1880, Louisville was considered to be the largest producer of implements in the world with $2 million in capital investments and over nine hundred employees. Its seven factories supplied southern states with one hundred thousand plows and cultivators per year.

The names of agricultural suppliers are written indelibly in the history of Louisville and Jefferson County, among them AVERY, BRINLY, McCormack, KENTUCKY WAGON WORKS, Harbison and Gathright, BELKNAP, BROWN AND WILLIAMSON, Ballard and Ballard, and scores of distilleries, breweries, and packinghouses. All of these reflect the importance of Louisville and Jefferson County to the rest of Kentucky, to southern Indiana, and to the Lower South.

Time has brought changes in Jefferson County agriculture. The family farm has become all but a time-encrusted artifact. Since 1920 its farms have become mechanized. The advent of rural electrification and the extension of urban services have wrought deep changes in the way of agrarian life in the county. There are a few surviving eighteenth-century landholds, such as OXMOOR, Mill Stream, Spring Lake, and Clearwater farms. Their horizons, however, have been encroached upon by the expansion of urban residential communities, factories, warehouses, offices, shopping malls, and other commercial establishments. The span of time in Jefferson County's agrarian history may well be measured on two chronological scales. On one hand, the span of time was remarkably short from the moment of settlement to the present sprawling urban occupation of the land. On the other, the rise of the present urban-industrial presence took longer.

Louisville had a long history as an important agricultural market center and as a major source for agricultural supplies. Since the loss of the large INTERNATIONAL HARVESTER plant in the 1980s, Louisville has not been a major center for the production of farm machinery, and only minor amounts of fertilizer are produced in the area. In the field of agricultural production, however, the Jefferson County farms have been reduced in both numbers and size, farming has become highly mechanized, and the agrarian way of life has all but become absorbed in that of the urban way.

Since 1925 Jefferson County has consistently slipped downward in the Kentucky agricultural tables to a middle position of the lower third of the state's counties. Major crops in the county include corn, soybeans, wheat, hay, and tobacco, which traditionally have been the backbone of farming in the region. Burley tobacco is the variety grown, and it is predominantly used in the manufacturing of cigarettes. Minor crops include fruits and vegetables, nursery stock, and hardwood timber. Farmers in the Louisville area raise cattle, hogs, and horses. Although the hog production is significant, it is still not sufficient to meet local pork processors' demand. Horse-breeding operations, primarily in OLDHAM COUNTY, have become a major source of farm income since the 1980s. Thoroughbred, Arabian, Saddlebred, and Quarter horses are raised on a number of breeding farms.

Agricultural services, landscaping, greenhouses, and nurseries together account for more area jobs than traditional farming activities. However, livestock and crop production generate more sales and income for farm owners and workers than the more urban horticultural activities. Above all, agricultural business in the Louisville area directly accounts for more than thirty-five thousand jobs in 1996, nearly 8 percent of all jobs. Louisville's meat-processing industry is the largest single employment category in the food-and-beverage sector, but, in terms of the value of shipments, alcoholic beverages is the largest category.

Since the early times, Louisville has had a tradition of markets where fresh fruits and vegetables are sold directly to consumers by local farmers. One of these places was the HAYMARKET, opened in downtown Louisville in 1891 and popular among residents for many years before the start of the URBAN RENEWAL program in the 1960s. Today there are many smaller markets dispersed within the city that offer a variety of fresh agricultural produce to consumers.

By 1998 there was spread across the face of Jefferson County a growing rural nonfarm population that lived on limited landholds but that extracted little, if any, of its livelihood from the land. The core population of Louisville and its satellite urban incorporations has grown too numerous to subsist to any degree on locally grown farm products. The bulk of produce consumed in the community is brought in from other parts of Kentucky and Indiana, from other areas of the United States, or from Mexico and Central America.

See J.B.D. DeBow, *Statistical View of the United States, Being a Compendium of the Seventh Census* (Washington, D.C., 1854); *The Census of the United States, Taken in the Year, 1920* (Agriculture), vol. 15 (Washington, D.C., 1922); *A Statistical Abstract (Supplement), County and City*, Data Book, 1956 (Washington, D.C., 1957); *Kentucky Agricultural Statistics, 1996–1997* (Frankfort 1997); *Seventeenth Biennial Bureau of Agriculture* (Frankfort 1908); Ben Casseday, *The History of Louisville from Its Earliest Settlement Till the Year 1852* (Louisville 1852); *Kentucky's Historic Farms* (Paducah, Ky., 1994); Paul Coomes, *Agribusiness in the Louisville Area Economy* (a report for the Agribusiness Committee, Louisville Area Chamber of Commerce) (Louisville 1996); *Courier-Journal*, Feb. 23, 1997.

Thomas D. Clark

AHRENS, THEODORE JACOB, JR. (b Baltimore, Maryland, September 21, 1859; d Louisville, June 12, 1938). Business leader and philanthropist. Ahrens was the son of German immigrants Georg Andreas Theodor and Maria Christine (Lohmann) Ahrens, who came to Louisville shortly after his birth. Although he attended public schools as a youngster, at the age of thirteen he went to work in his father's brass foundry, where he remained for the next five years.

After working on the East Coast, Ahrens returned to Louisville in 1880 and opened his own plumbing business on MARKET ST. Six years later he bought an interest in his father's company, Ahrens and Ott, which produced plumbing supplies. As the popularity of in-home bathrooms grew, Ahrens's business interests thrived.

Around the turn of the century, Ahrens spearheaded the effort to consolidate nine other companies with his own, resulting in the organization of the Standard Sanitary Manufacturing Co. Ahrens was elected its president. After WORLD WAR I, the company merged with the American Radiator Co., making it one of America's major industrial firms. Its branches spread across the nation and Canada, and its sales were worldwide. Ahrens remained at the helm until he retired in 1934.

Ahrens's days as an unskilled laborer in his father's factory had taught him the value of skilled labor. He believed well-trained workers were an asset to both themselves and their employers. Consequently he was intensely interested in the city's new vocational school project. In a joint effort with ETHEL LOVELL, the vocational school principal, plans for a new and innovative approach to teaching trade skills to students was developed. Through his efforts, the city's first vocational school, established in 1913, became a model facility for teaching skilled trades. As the school grew, so did Ahrens's contributions. In 1925 Ahrens contributed $300,000 for the new building—$250,000 for the construction of the building, and $50,000 for a gymnasium, with the provision that the school board contribute land and equipment. In 1926 the new facility, at 546 S First St., was dedicated and the name changed from Louisville Vocational School to Theodore Ahrens Trade School in honor of his unparalleled interest and generosity. During his lifetime, Ahrens donated over $1 million to the school. Although the school closed in 1980, the building continues to be used as the home of the Brown School and the Ahrens Educational Resource Center.

Theodore Ahrens married Elizabeth Pfiester on April 30, 1885, and they had two daughters. He is buried in Cave Hill Cemetery.

See *Courier-Journal*, May 17, 1930, June 13, 1938, Nov. 23, 1995; Margaret M. Bridwell, *The Ahrens Story* (Louisville 1954).

AHRENS VOCATIONAL CENTER. The response to turn-of-the-century progressive ideals is illustrated in the rich history of Louisville's only school exclusively dedicated to vocational training. In 1911, at the prompting of ETHEL LOVELL, a teacher at the MONSARRAT SCHOOL at Fifth and York Streets, the Consumers' League of Kentucky made a survey of trade and vocational schools from New York to Wisconsin. This resulted in a 1913 plan for vocational training by the Louisville Board of Education. The idea was conceived in response to the urgent need for specific training for young people entering the workforce. Echoing the goals of the great American philosopher and educator William James, introduction of vocational education was seen as a step forward for the school system because it would develop a child's intellectual, moral, and physical faculties and give added value not only to industry but also to society and themselves.

The Louisville BOARD OF EDUCATION hired Ethel Lovell and Lewis Bacon as the first teachers and provided the Consumers' League Committee with the names of children who had expressed a desire to leave school and go to work. After home visits and careful consideration, sixteen boys and sixteen girls were selected to participate in the first class of the experimental Prevocational School. Lovell was then sent to the Industrial Education Department of the University of Chicago for training. Her advisor there, Frank Leavitt, was invited to Louisville to survey the community's needs and make recommendations for instruction. Under his direction, printing was the first course offered, because it afforded excellent opportunities. Cabinetmaking and dressmaking were added to the curriculum, followed by bookbinding, electrical wiring, and concrete construction. The cabinetmaking course taught skills in woodworking both by hand and machines in order to develop a well-rounded knowledge of furniture construction and design. The dressmaking class was an instant success. One small class quickly grew to four classes and two teachers. Instruction focused on children's clothing, both by order and for stock in the student-run store at the school.

After two years of demonstrated success, the board of education incorporated the vocational school into its public school system as a partnership of private and public funding. A building at 546 S First St., owned by the board for seventy years and vacated by MALE HIGH SCHOOL in 1915, and several surrounding lots were selected for the new school's location.

The board encouraged the school to begin a two-year program and placement services. The board also supported steady growth by adding instruction in new areas, while Lovell, by now the principal, added after-hours extracurricular activities such as a chorus and folk dancing and piano lessons to help the students become well-rounded citizens. A commercial course including shorthand, typing, bookkeeping, and filing was added. Related academic subjects such as English and economics were incorporated to offer a balance for training office workers.

In February 1917 Congress passed the Smith-Hughes Act to provide for the promotion of vocational education in agriculture, trades, and industry and to appropriate money and regulate how it was spent in schools below college level. The qualifications for funding required lengthening the new school's day to six and one-half hours. Half of that time was devoted to academic classes and the other half to trade instruction. The school's name was officially changed from the Prevocational School to Louisville Vocational School as the enrollment quickly grew.

THEODORE AHRENS, president of the Standard Sanitary Manufacturing Co., became intensely interested in the project. A manufacturer who had started as an unskilled laborer, he understood the value of a skilled workforce. In 1925 he donated $250,000 for a new building at the old location. Ahrens and Ethel Lovell, the newly appointed principal, worked together to develop innovative classrooms and curriculum for the program. Ahrens later added $50,000 for a gymnasium and in 1930 gave the Louisville Board of Education an additional gift of $350,000. In all, Ahrens donated roughly $1 million to the enterprise, with the stipulation that the board of education provide suitable property and equipment. The new building, dedicated in 1926, was built to resemble a school without and a factory within. The name was changed to Theodore Ahrens Trade School. Other community leaders, such as ROBERT WORTH BINGHAM, publisher of the *COURIER-JOURNAL*, funded linotype machines and donated to the project. To target trades in need of skilled workers, the BOARD OF TRADE (predecessor of GREATER LOUISVILLE, INC.), the Associated Industries of Kentucky, and individual manufacturers of Louisville helped determine courses offered by keeping track of employee supply-and-demand.

The name was changed to Theodore Ahrens Trade High School in 1939 when the facility was enlarged. Beginning in the fall of 1956, Ahrens's 750 night students were, for the first time, charged $20 a semester. LABOR unions paid half the cost for their apprentices, and some businesses paid the entire charge for employees who wanted to improve themselves after working hours.

In October 1962 an expansion plan to increase the school size to two and one-half acres began. In 1975 changes were made in response to the merger of the Jefferson County and Louisville school districts. An opportunity was provided for students to come in on a half-day basis from their home high school for technical training. In 1976 two educational concepts were incorporated—Ahrens High School, which operated as a district school, and Ahrens Vocational Center, which functioned as a center for half-day vocational instruction. In an effort to keep pace with expanding technology, nineteen different areas of training were offered, from auto body repair to upholstery.

May 1980 witnessed the last graduating class of 130 from Ahrens High School. Eventually the vocational school's classes were distributed throughout the Jefferson County Public School System's high schools to allow students easier access. In the 1990s it operated as Ahrens Educational Resource Center. Rooms that once housed vocational classes became offices for various educational programs and a day-care center. The Ahrens name was still prominently displayed on the front of the building in 2000.

See *Louisville Times*, May 17, 1930; *Courier-Journal*, Sept. 20, 1956, May 15, 1980; Open Files, Jefferson County Public School Archives and Records Center.

Jane-Rives Williams

AIR DEVILS INN. Air Devils Inn, located across the street from BOWMAN FIELD at 2802 Taylorsville Rd., opened for business in 1934, in the days when the airport still had dirt runways. The local bar, now a neighborhood landmark, occupies a building originally built as a schoolhouse—Maple Grove School, number 57. The school was listed in the report of the Commission of Common Schools of Jefferson County in 1876–77. It was described as a frame structure with a seating capacity of forty-six. By 1926 it was referred to as Breckinridge or Maple Grove School. It was consolidated with Melbourne Heights and Alex R. Kennedy Schools in 1926 and was sold the next year to George Hartman for eighty-five hundred dollars.

In the 1930s Bowman Field was—in addition to being an Army Air Corps depot, an airmail terminal, and a commercial passenger airport—home to the Aero Club of Kentucky and aerial exhibitions. Barnstorming air shows, with stunt flying, parachute jumping, air races, and skywriting, would attract thousands. These air shows provided the bar with its name and many of its customers, who would cross the road for refreshments. Like many watering holes in pre–air-conditioning days, Air Devils Inn had a beer garden.

In the late 1990s the bar is known locally for its musical acts and, since 1986, as a meeting place for motorcycle enthusiasts. On any given Thursday night, beginning about 7:00 p.m., Air Devils Inn can host a gathering of several hundred bikers, a cross-section of Louisville that will include stockbrokers, mechanics, doctors, local businessmen, the occasional nurse, the moneyed, and the tattooed. By 8:30 p.m. the unconventional convention is on the road, happily Harleying down the highway to some predetermined destination.

See George H. Yater, "Mr. Bowman's Cow Pasture," *Louisville* (Oct. 1968): 26–29; *Courier-Journal*, Sept. 30, 1995.

Barry L. Daulton Jr.

ALBERT E. MEYZEEK MIDDLE SCHOOL. Named after a noted African American educator, the school is located at 828 S Jackson St. It has a long and varied history in Louisville's SMOKETOWN neighborhood. It began in 1874 when the Eastern Colored School relocated to the 800 block of S Jackson. That school was renamed Booker T. Washington Elementary in 1915. In 1929 Jackson Junior High was completed and opened next door.

In 1966 the two schools were combined into one facility when a new Booker T. Washington Elementary was constructed and joined to the existing junior high. The following year the school was renamed for Meyzeek. In 1975 the elementary section closed, allowing for the expansion of the junior high.

In 1986 Meyzeek launched Jefferson County's first magnet program for middle school students. The program offers intensive course work in the areas of mathematics, science, and technology.

ALBERTS, JOHN BERNARD, JR. (b Louisville, July 9, 1886; d Louisville, April 24, 1931). Artist. The son of J. Bernard Alberts Sr. and Clara (Burnam) Alberts, he attended Louisville public schools and then entered the Cincinnati Art Academy, where he studied under Frank Duveneck for three years. An additional three years were spent at the school of the Boston Museum of Fine Arts as a pupil of Frank Benson and Edward Tarbell. He then spent a year in New York before going to Europe in 1913 to study art. Alberts was a versatile artist who worked as a painter, book illustrator, and designer of stained-glass windows in his father's glass shop on First St. between Green (Liberty) and Walnut (Muhammad Ali Blvd.) Streets.

He chiefly painted allegorical works and portraits, two of his most noted being of MADISON CAWEIN and OTTO ROTHERT. Alberts enlisted in the army at CAMP ZACHARY TAYLOR in 1917. He contracted multiple sclerosis in 1918, just as he was beginning to receive recognition for his work. Leaving his room very few times after 1918, Alberts died at the home of his brother on Westport Rd. He is buried in Cave Hill Cemetery.

See *Courier-Journal,* Aug. 25, 1931, Oct. 4, 1931; *Exhibition of Paintings and Drawings of J.B. Alberts, Jr.* (Louisville 1931); Bettie M. Henry, *Biographical Extracts Relating to Prominent Artists of Louisville and Kentucky* (Louisville 1939); Arthur F. Jones and Bruce Weber, *The Kentucky Painter from the Frontier Era to the Great War* (Lexington 1981).

Candace K. Perry

ALCOHOLICS ANONYMOUS. Alcoholism has been a problem throughout history. Attempts to control this disease have, in the past, embraced everything from astronomy to voodoo. Today's modern resources include social agencies, self-help organizations, and medical help, both chemical and psychological. Of these methods, each of which has known some degree of success, Alcoholics Anonymous appears to be the most effective. Media, medical societies, and church and business leaders have all praised this program.

The origin of the AA program is recognized as June 10, 1935, in Akron, Ohio. A stockbroker, Bill W., on a business trip to Akron, Ohio, met a medical doctor, Bob S.. Both men were chronic alcoholics and veterans of several failed treatment methods. From their fruitful association came both sobriety for themselves and the formation of the Fellowship of Alcoholics Anonymous. The nucleus of the Alcoholics Anonymous program is the twelve steps, which were not assembled until the program was in effect for several years. The members wanted to tell others how they reached sobriety and serenity. June 10, 1999, marked the sixty-fourth anniversary of AA as an organization. In that time, in the United States, Canada, and other countries, it had grown to more than 95,000 groups consisting of more than 2,000,000 alcoholics in recovery. These men and women meet in local groups ranging in size from a handful in some locations to hundreds in larger communities.

Early in 1941 a member of the Indianapolis AA group, Jim M., was transferred to Louisville. As a means to effect his continuing sobriety, he sought to establish a group of fellow alcoholics, and by June the first Louisville Fellowship was formed. The first meeting was held at the YMCA at Third St. and Broadway. The initial group varied from five to ten people. In September the Sunday *Courier-Journal* featured a story, "So You Think Drunks Can't Be Cured," which undoubtedly helped increase membership. In November the Kentucky Dairies, on Third and Kentucky Streets, offered the group use of a meeting room on the third floor, where they met until 1946.

In 1943, Bill W., one of the founders, visited Louisville. This visit stimulated the growth of the local AA, so that by November 1946 a larger meeting place was necessary. Meetings were moved to the Columbia Auditorium, now part of Spalding University. In the same year, local members also formed their first social club, the Token Club, named after the local custom of marking each year of a member's sobriety with a token. While Token Clubs are separate from Alcoholics Anonymous, they are available for use by the AA membership. By 1947 AA had grown large enough to hire a full-time secretary and to establish a phone-answering system for anyone seeking its assistance.

By 1954 there were approximately twenty groups comprising the Louisville Fellowship. They met in churches, libraries, restaurants, and public halls. Groups for families of alcoholics, called Al-Anon and Al-Ateen, grew along with AA and generally met in the same facilities.

Through the recommendation of doctors, treatment centers, and religious and industrial leaders, Alcoholics Anonymous has flourished. The number of involved recovering alcoholics in the Louisville and southern Indiana areas is difficult to estimate, but as of January 1, 1999, there were about 340 local meetings each week. There are two types of meetings, open and closed. Open meetings welcome alcoholics, their families, and anyone else interested in solving a drinking problem. Closed meetings are limited to alcoholics only. Generally, the meetings last about an hour. Some meetings have a speaker for the hour, while other meetings encourage member dialogue within the group.

The AA program remains simple and flexible. It has few guidelines and limited organizational controls. There are no dues or fees, no regulations, and no governing offices. AA is self-supporting through member contributions and accepts no outside funding. Much of the success in Louisville and throughout the world may be attributed to members' continuous support of each other and to their commitment to maintaining anonymity.

Jack B. Helm

ALEXANDER, GROSS (b Scottsville, Kentucky, June 1, 1852; d Los Angeles, September 6, 1915). Methodist theologian. He was the son of Charles Holliday and Eliza (Drane) Alexander. In 1867, the family moved to Louisville, where Alexander attended Male High School, graduating in 1871. Following his graduation, he taught at Male for two years. From the fall of 1873 to the spring of 1875, he taught Latin and Greek at Warren College in Bowling Green, Kentucky. In 1875 Alexander entered the Drew Theological Seminary at Madison, New Jersey, receiving his bachelor of divinity degree in June 1877. As a minister in the Methodist Episcopal Church, South, he served in the Louisville Conference in the Portland and Middletown churches during 1877–79.

After a year spent touring Europe, Alexander became chaplain at Vanderbilt University in Nashville in September 1884. In June 1885 he became an instructor in New Testament Greek at Vanderbilt and taught there as a professor until 1902. Returning to Louisville that year, Alexander served as presiding elder to the Louisville Conference of the Methodist Church until 1906, when he was elected editor of the *Methodist Quarterly Review.* He held that position until his death. Alexander translated from the Greek *Chrysostom's Homilies on Galatians and Ephesians* (1889) and *The Son of Man* (1889); edited *The Doctrines and Disciplines of the Methodist Episcopal Church* (1914); and was a member of the commission that prepared the 1911 *Authorized Version of the English Bible,* a commemorative tercentenary edition. Alexander's other works include *The Son of Man: Studies of His Life and Teaching* (1900), *Steve P. Holcombe, the Converted Gambler: His Life and Work* (1888), and *Discussions in Theology, Doctrinal and Practical* (1890).

Alexander married Helen M. Watts of Louisville in August 1875; they had two children, Edith and Clay. Helen died in November 1885. Alexander married Arabel Wilbur of Chicago in 1887; they had two children, Gross Junior and Ruth. Alexander died on September 6, 1915, while on a trip to Long Beach, California. He is buried in Cave Hill Cemetery.

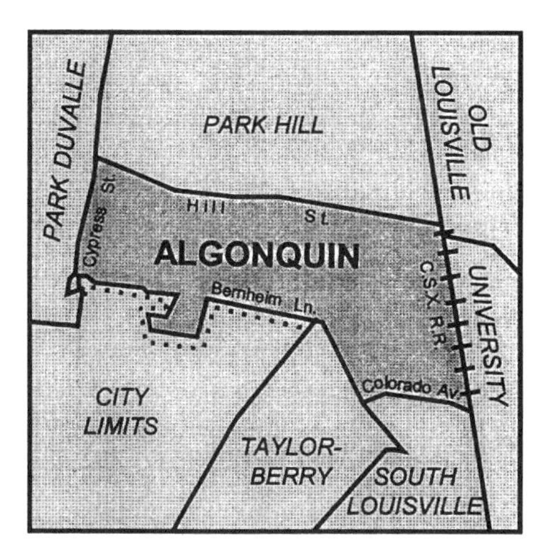

ALGONQUIN. The Algonquin neighborhood was established in the 1920s. It is bounded by Hill St. to the north, Cypress St. to the west, the CSX railroad tracks to the east, and a combination of Bernheim Ln., Colorado Ave., and Algonquin Pkwy. to the south. It derived its name from nearby Algonquin Park and Algonquin Pkwy. An important facility in the residential neighborhood is the Samuel D. Jones Park located on Thirteenth and Brashear Streets.

ALI, MUHAMMAD (b Louisville, January 17, 1942). Kentucky Athlete of the Century and arguably the most-recognized person in the contemporary world, Ali was born Cassius Marcellus Clay Jr. to Cassius Marcellus Clay Sr. and Odessa (Grady) Clay of Louisville. The Clay family lived at 3302 Grand Ave. in what was then the African American section of the Parkland neighborhood.

Louisville during and immediately after World War II, in which Ali came of age, was a rigidly segregated city with African Americans concentrated in a few neighborhoods in its western and eastern sections. The African American community had a long history, dating to the 1820s, and a long record of moderate, but effective, political activism. However, limited gains in education and politics over time had neither blurred the local "color-line" nor translated into significant economic opportunities, as most black adults worked as industrial, service, or domestic laborers—with a small contingent of professionals and small-business owners. Although spared the blatantly overt racism and endemic racial violence that typified the social dynamics in the Deep South, Louisville African Americans were nonetheless expected to keep to their separate and unequal place. As a nuclear, working-class family, Ali, his brother, Rudolph (now Rahaman Ali), and their parents were, perhaps, far more representative of African Americans in Louisville than were the better-known black leaders of the period.

Muhammad Ali and his mother, Odessa Grady Clay, in her home in Louisville. 1963.

Muhammad Ali's boxing career began inauspiciously in October 1954 when the theft of his bicycle prompted him to seek boxing instruction from Joe Martin, an Irish American Louisville policeman. Ali trained at Columbia Gym, developed under Martin's tutelage, and soon began appearing on *Tomorrow's Champions,* a local television program featuring amateur boxing. His extraordinary talent became increasingly apparent, and by 1960 Ali had fought in 167 bouts, winning 161, including 6 Kentucky and 2 National Golden Glove tournaments and 2 national AAU titles.

In 1960, Ali graduated from Louisville Central High School and, later that summer, defeated Zbiebniew Pietrzykowski to win the Olympic gold medal as a light heavyweight. By the time he turned professional, Ali had become well known as a brash, cocky, and extremely vocal fighter. No other African American athlete since the legendary Jack Johnson had been so outspoken, and, against the backdrop of the civil rights era, the impact of Ali's words, actions, and choices would extend far beyond the bounds of his profession. However, although race relations in the United States were changing, Ali discovered that his achievements and celebrity did not insulate him from discrimination. In his own memorable account, he threw his Olympic gold medal into the Ohio River after receiving such treatment following his return to Louisville. Still, race was not always a barrier—or not always the same barrier in all situations. Thus, as controversial as the "Louisville Lip" was becoming, black attorney Alberta Jones arranged for a group of prominent white Louisville businessmen to form a syndicate to promote Ali's professional career in return for 50 percent of his earnings. The "Sponsoring Group" included Archibald M. Foster, Patrick Calhoun Jr., Gordon Davidson, William S. Cutchins, J.D. Stetson Coleman, William Faversham Jr., James R. Todd, Vertner D. Smith Sr., George W. Norton IV, William Lee Lyons Brown, E. Gary Sutcliffe, and Robert Worth Bingham III. Ali's relationship with this group would last until 1966.

Ali won his first professional fight on October 29, 1960, defeating Tunney Hunsaker in a six-round decision. After hiring Angelo Dundee as his trainer, Ali began predicting the round in which he would knock out his opponents. Although his cocky flamboyance infuriated many, Ali's flair for self-promotion was exceeded only by his talent. His knockout predictions were correct in thirteen of seventeen fights—and his drawing power grew as increasing numbers of boxing fans were willing to pay in hopes of witnessing his defeat. Victory followed victory as Ali moved ever higher in the rankings. Still, although Ali was not a power puncher in the mold of Joe Louis, his unique combination of heavyweight size and middleweight speed, and the cumulative effect of his lethal left jab and flurries of combinations took a heavy toll on fighters who underestimated him. This unusual ability to "float like a butterfly, sting like a bee" stunned the nation when, on February 25, 1964, Ali won the heavyweight championship by defeating the heavily favored Charles "Sonny" Liston in Miami, Florida.

In a press conference the next morning, Ali announced that he was a member of the Nation of Islam, commonly known as the "Black Muslims," and, on March 6, 1964, changed his name officially from Cassius Clay to Muhammad Ali as decreed by Elijah Muhammad, then leader of the Nation. While the announcement of Ali's conversion surprised many, his actual association with the Nation dated to 1961, and, through relationships with Muslim ministers such as Jeremiah Shabbazz and Malcolm X, his actual conversion had occurred in 1962. Ali's relationship with Malcolm X has been the subject of considerable speculation and analysis, but Elijah Muhammad himself was the strongest influence on Ali at this time, and Ali remained loyal to Elijah Muhammad after Malcolm X left the Nation in 1964. Perhaps, more than anything, the Nation offered a strong and spiritual basis for racial and gender identity that was profoundly appealing to many young African Americans—including Muhammad Ali. After the death of Elijah Muhammad in 1975, his son, Wallace, directed the Nation and Ali away from its image as an "anti-white" sect and along the path of Islamic orthodoxy, with its emphasis on universal justice and peace.

Had Ali declared himself a Muslim before 1964, he might never have been permitted to contend for the heavyweight championship. As champion, the racial and religious controversy surrounding his public declaration could not derail his career, particularly since so many "fans" were still willing to pay in hopes of seeing him lose. Denying them their wish, Ali defeated Liston again on May 25, 1965, and easily bested his other challengers. However, while he could not be defeated in the ring, he could be driven from it, and his next and perhaps his most difficult challenge was unrelated to boxing. After his requests for a military draft deferment and exemption from service as a conscientious objector were denied in 1966, Ali refused to "take one step forward" at the Houston induction center on April 28, 1967. This stand was entirely consistent with the Muslim emphasis on uprightness, spirituality, and strong black manhood. It was complemented by a commitment to pacifism—as exemplified by Elijah Muhammad's imprisonment for being a conscientious objector during World War II. The New York Athletic Committee promptly suspended his boxing license and stripped him of his title and awarded it to Joe Frazier. The following week, a federal grand jury in Houston indicted him for resisting the draft. Ali was tried and found guilty on June 20, 1967, and was sentenced to five years in prison and a ten-thousand-dollar fine. Ali posted bail and subsequently appealed.

Ali's principled opposition to war, at a time when U.S. involvement in Vietnam was deepening daily, aroused both hatred and admiration, but he rose in stature as a man as he drifted into limbo as an athlete. Many prominent African American athletes rallied to his defense, including Lew Alcindor (soon to become Kareem Abdul-Jabbar) of UCLA, Bill Russell of the Boston Celtics, and Gale Sayers of the Chicago Bears. Furthermore, although he was barred from boxing, antiwar groups across the nation clamored for Ali's services as a speaker. His college lectures and his brief movie and theatrical career—Ali even starred in a Broadway musical, "Big Time Buck White"—provided a livelihood during his twenty-nine-month exile from the ring. Finally, on June 28, 1970, the United States Supreme Court reversed Ali's conviction after learning that the FBI had tapped Ali's telephone illegally. Ali regained his boxing license and, on October 26, 1970, defeated Jerry Quarry in his first return bout. On March 8, 1971, he fought to regain his title from "Smokin'" Joe Frazier in the first of their three titanic battles but lost a fifteen-round decision for his first defeat as a professional. Ali suffered his second defeat and a broken jaw on March 31, 1973, in a bout with Ken Norton. As a thirty-two-year-old fighter, Ali could easily have retired, but he persevered and scored two of his most memorable victories late in his career.

By 1974, George Foreman was world champion, and, after Ali defeated Joe Frazier on January 28, 1974, rising fight-promoter Don King arranged for Ali to fight Foreman for a purse of $5 million for each boxer. Then, on October 30, 1974, in Kinshasa, Zaire, in the "Rumble in the Jungle," Ali abandoned his customary dancing style and allowed the heavily favored Foreman to punch himself out in the early rounds. Ali knocked out the weary and confused Foreman in the eighth round and re-

Overview of Fights

Date	*Opponent*	*Location*	*Result*
10/29/60	Tunney Hunsaker	Louisville	W (6 pts)
12/27/60	Herb Siler	Miami Beach	W (4 KO)
1/17/61	Tony Esperti	Miami Beach	W (3 KO)
2/7/61	Jim Robinson	Miami Beach	W (1 KO)
2/21/61	Donnie Fleeman	Miami Beach	W (7 KO)
4/19/61	Lamar Clark	Louisville	W (2 KO)
6/26/61	Duke Sabedong	Las Vegas	W (10 pts)
7/22/61	Alonzo Johnson	Louisville	W (10 pts)
10/7/61	Alex Miteff	Louisville	W (6 KO)
11/29/61	Willie Besmanoff	Louisville	W (7 KO)
2/11/62	Sonny Banks	New York	W (4 KO)
2/28/62	Don Warner	Miami Beach	W (4 KO)
4/23/62	George Logan	Los Angeles	W (4 KO)
5/19/62	Billy Daniels	New York	W (7 KO)
7/20/62	Alejandro Lavorante	Los Angeles	W (5 KO)
11/15/62	Archie Moore	Los Angeles	W (4 KO)
1/24/63	Charlie Powell	Pittsburgh	W (3 KO)
3/13/63	Doug Jones	New York	W (10 pts)
6/18/63	Henry Cooper	London	W (5 KO)
2/25/64	Sonny Liston	Miami Beach	W (7 KO)
5/25/65	Sonny Liston	Lewiston	W (1 KO)
11/22/65	Floyd Patterson	Las Vegas	W (12 KO)
3/29/66	George Chuvalo	Toronto	W (15 pts)
5/21/66	Henry Cooper	London	W (6 KO)
8/6/66	Brian London	London	W (3 KO)
9/10/66	Karl Mildenberger	Frankfurt	W (12 KO)
11/14/66	Cleveland Williams	Houston	W (3 KO)
2/6/67	Ernie Terrell	Houston	W (15 pts)
3/22/67	Zora Folley	New York	W (7 KO)
10/26/70	Jerry Quarry	Atlanta	W (3 KO)
12/7/70	Oscar Bonavena	New York	W (15 KO)
3/8/71	Joe Frazier	New York	L (15 pts)
7/26/71	Jimmy Ellis	Houston	W (12 KO)
11/17/71	Buster Mathis	Houston	W (12 pts)
12/26/71	Jürgen Blin	Zurich	W (7 KO)
4/1/72	Mac Foster	Tokyo	W (15pts)
5/1/72	George Chuvalo	Vancouver	W (12 pts)
6/27/72	Jerry Quarry	Las Vegas	W (7 KO)
7/19/72	Al Lewis	Dublin	W (11 KO)
9/20/72	Floyd Patterson	New York	W (7 KO)
11/21/72	Bob Foster	Stateline	W (8 KO)
2/14/73	Joe Bugner	Las Vegas	W (12 pts)
3/31/73	Ken Norton	San Diego	L (12 pts)
9/10/73	Ken Norton	Los Angeles	W (12 pts)
10/21/73	Rudi Lubbers	Djakarta	W (12 pts)
1/28/74	Joe Frazier	New York	W (12 pts)
10/30/74	George Foreman	Kinshasa	W (8 KO)
3/24/75	Chuck Wepner	Cleveland	W (15 KO)
5/16/75	Ron Lyle	Las Vegas	W (11 KO)
6/30/75	Joe Bugner	Malaysia	W (15 pts)
10/1/75	Joe Frazier	Manila	W (14 KO)
2/20/76	J.P. Coopman	San Juan	W (5 KO)
4/30/76	Jimmy Young	Landover	W (15 pts)
5/24/76	Richard Dunn	Munich	W (5 KO)
9/28/76	Ken Norton	New York	W (15 KO)
5/16/77	Alfredo Evangelista	Landover	W (15 pts)
9/29/77	Earnie Shavers	New York	W (15 pts)
2/15/78	Leon Spinks	Las Vegas	L (15 pts)
9/15/78	Leon Spinks	New Orleans	W (15 pts)
10/2/80	Larry Holmes	Las Vegas	L (10 KO)
12/11/81	Trevor Berbick	Nassau	L (10 pts)

claimed his championship after nearly eight years. Joe Frazier challenged Ali one last time in what many boxing aficionados consider to be the greatest heavyweight fight in history, the "Thrilla in Manila" on September 30, 1975. Ali won again and defended his title until losing to Leon Spinks on February 15, 1978. Then, at thirty-six years old, Ali became world champion for the third time by defeating Spinks on September 15, 1978. He lost his championship to Larry Holmes, a former sparring partner, on October 2, 1980, and retired in 1981 with a 56–5 record and thirty-seven knockouts.

The last great challenge of Muhammad Ali's life followed his boxing career. Ali developed Parkinson's syndrome, a condition that left his mental faculties intact but slurred his speech and slowed his movements. As a Muslim committed to peace and harmony and as perhaps the best-known person in the world, Ali overcame his physical limitations and became a global ambassador in the 1980s. His international stature was never more obvious than when he lit the flame for the 1996 Summer Olympic Games and was greeted with a thunderous and sustained ovation.

An assessment of the life of any living person, particularly someone as vital and engaged in life as Muhammad Ali, is impossible, since so many important chapters in his personal history may remain unwritten. Still, much can be said of the meaning and impact of his life in the last half of the twentieth century. In this context, Muhammad Ali rose to prominence as a boxer during an era that witnessed the transformation of the sport. The Olympic Games (in 1952, 1956, and 1960) became an international arena in which many athletes achieved celebrity through the new medium of television and through which many lucrative professional careers were launched. Congressional probes into the involvement of organized crime and, as colonialism ended, the emergence of numerous boxers of color in "Third World" nations forced far-reaching changes both in how the sport was governed and in its racial demography. The World Boxing Association (WBA) and the World Boxing Council (WBC), both formed in the early 1960s, were far more representative internationally—and African American fighters became major figures in the heavier weight classes regulated by each organization.

Transcending his celebrity as a boxer, Muhammad Ali achieved international recognition as a symbol of black masculinity, pride, and racial consciousness against the backdrop of social revolution in the 1960s and the beginnings of the decolonialization of Africa and other regions of the non-European world. Beyond the practiced theatrics of his youth, the mature Ali forced the boxing establishment and the American and global public to respect him on his own terms. In so doing, he not only insisted upon and preserved his own dignity, but he epitomized the courage to stand on principle and defy injustice. Ali became a hero to millions throughout the world. As Arthur Ashe concluded, "In retrospect, one must agree with Ali's self-assessment: He was 'The Greatest.'"

Ali married four times, first to model Sonji Roi in 1964. After his divorce from Roi in 1966, he married Kalilah Tolona (formerly Belinda Boyd) in April 1967, with whom he had three daughters and a son. In June 1977, Ali married Veronica Porshe, and, in November 1986, he married Yolanda "Lonnie" Williams of Louisville. On October 7, 1998, Ali and his wife announced plans to build "The Muhammad Ali Center" near the downtown Louisville waterfront. The center will chronicle Ali's career, emphasize the value of a healthy lifestyle, and promote his vision of global tolerance and peace. Fittingly, on September 13, 1999, the Kentucky Athletic Hall of Fame recognized Ali as "Kentucky Athlete of the Century."

See Muhammad Ali, *The Greatest* (New York 1975); Arthur R. Ashe Jr., *A Hard Road to Glory: A History of the African American Athlete since 1946* (New York 1988); E. Franklin Frazier, *Negro Youth at the Crossways* (1939); Elliott J. Gorn, ed., *Muhammad Ali: The People's Champ* (Urbana, Ill., 1995); Thomas Hauser, *Muhammad Ali: His Life and Times* (New York 1991); George C. Wright, *Life behind a Veil: Blacks in Louisville, Kentucky, 1865-1935* (Baton Rouge, La., 1985); Jan Philipp Reemtsma, *More Than a Champion: The Style of Muhammad Ali* (New York 1998).

J. Blaine Hudson

ALLEN DALE FARM. In 1795 Robert Polk Allen, arriving in Shelby County the year after the death of his father, John Allen of Frederick County, Virginia, founded Allen Dale, now a historic 473–acre farm about 4 miles south of Shelbyville, Kentucky, on the Zaring Mill Rd. Robert and his widowed mother, Ann Polk Allen, are buried on the property. John Allen's descendants have owned Allen Dale continuously since its establishment, aided by several court decisions favorable to the family.

The first legal test, in the form of an ejectment action filed in 1815 because of overlapping and interfering patents, was settled nearly ten years later. In 1889 Bettie Allen Meriwether was successful in a suit against her brother, George Baylor Allen, who then had title to the farm, to forestall his plans to mortgage the farm outside the family.

The Allen Dale residence, built in 1904 on the lines of an old English manor house, replaced a nineteenth-century house that had burned. Constructed of limestone quarried on the farm, it has as a distinguishing feature a porte cochere that leads through the body of the house to the gardens and service area. The Allen Dale farmstead tract of 13.4 acres, including the main residence and two large barns, is listed on the National Register of Historic Places.

During the period 1907–28, Sue Thornton Meriwether Henning, wife of James W. Henning Jr. of Louisville and a direct descendant of John and Ann Allen, was owner and breeder of a prizewinning herd of registered Jersey cattle at Allen Dale. In 1914 the farm produced the national grand champion Jersey bull. Under the direction of Henning, who became the first woman to serve on the board of the American Jersey Cattle Club, Allen Dale Farm became nationally and internationally renowned. Sue Henning, although winning many prizes in state and national competition, possessed insufficient capital to continue this expensive operation. The failure of her husband on Wall Street in 1911 and the death in 1921 of her supporter, C.I. Hudson, New York City financier and owner of a prize Jersey herd himself, hastened the farm down the road toward insolvency.

In 1923 she mortgaged the life interest in the farm left by her mother Bettie Allen Meriwether; and in 1924, following a decision of the Shelby Circuit Court that awarded her a fee simple title, she mortgaged that interest also. Then in 1926, in a decision that obliterated all hope for Henning, the Court of Appeals of Kentucky, in a landmark decision, overruled the lower court. Thus the farm itself, as opposed to the life interest, was protected from creditors and preserved for the heirs. Henning was required by her creditors to leave Allen Dale in 1930 and vowed until her death in 1933 that she was "going back to Allen Dale."

Upon her mother's death, Susanne Henning, Marquise de Charette, acquired life interest in the 406–acre main tract of Allen Dale Farm and title in fee simple to the adjoining 67 1/2–acre Meriwether tract. Returning from France, she lived for several months at Allen Dale, subsequently leasing a Park Avenue apartment in New York, where she lived with her lifelong supporter and benefactor, Lulie Henning, her aunt. In January 1964 she deeded the acreage that she owned outright to her daughter, also named Susanne and married to Brig. Gen. Ronald R. Van Stockum, U.S. Marine Corps. On her mother's death later that year, Susanne Van Stockum acquired title in fee simple to the rest of the farm and in 1970 took up residence at Allen Dale with her husband. In 1993 she deeded the main house to their son, Ronald R. Van Stockum Jr.

See R.R. Van Stockum, *Kentucky and the Bourbons: The Story of Allen Dale Farm* (Louisville 1991).

Ronald R. Van Stockum Sr.

ALLEN R. HITE INSTITUTE. The Allen R. Hite Art Institute, the Fine Arts Department of the University of Louisville on Belknap Campus, is named for the Louisville financier who donated more than $1 million to fund art education at U of L in 1942. Hite, a law school alumnus and university trustee, was heir to a river trade fortune. His wife, Marcia, a local arts patron, encouraged Hite to make the bequest; it became effective after her death in 1946. Over the next fifty years, the Hite Institute earned a solid reputation by offering a full complement of courses in creative art and art history. In the late 1990s, the Hite Institute remained the only fine arts department in Kentucky to offer a Ph.D. in art history.

See Kentucky Writers Project, *A Centennial History of the University of Louisville* (Louisville 1939); Dario A. Covi, "History of the Allen R. Hite Art Institute," Margaret M. Bridwell Art Library Archival Papers, 1963.

Jennifer L. Rectenwald

Alley south of Main Street between 11th and 12th, 1920.

ALLEYS. To skulk and prowl through the American alley has been to step backward in time, downward on the social ladder, and quickly to confront the world of trash collectors, garbage-pickers, weekend car mechanics, and children. Refugees, all of them, from the wide-open world Out Front: the big street, the Main Drag. Even during the half-century since automobiles invaded the American city, bringing "progress" in their wake, this has been the history of alleys in Louisville and elsewhere. Only in the 1960s and again in the 1990s did there appear signs of a reversal.

Historically, the alley has been the outback world of the unmentionable, if not the unwanted: displaced persons, places, things. A few glaring exceptions include unpaved greenways through old bucolic suburbs such as Louisville's Crescent Hill and remodeled garages and stables in Old Louisville and the Cherokee Triangle.

Alleys penetrated and reinforced the structure of nineteenth-century Louisville. They were part and parcel of the city's original gridiron pattern. Alleys were carved out to serve the rear of street-fronting properties, and in so doing set up a second and inferior class of locations. Typical of nineteenth-century commentary was that of Utopian reformer Frances Wright, 1821, on New York City's "dark alleys, whose confined and noisome atmosphere marks the presence of a dense and suffering population." Thus alleys were feared for the criminals and prospective muggers-rapists lurking, most vividly among the mental images of suburbanites who had moved away from older parts of the city.

Closer to home, it has pleased most proper Louisvillians in the past to leave alleys to the general poor, to the domestic poor (i.e., mostly black servants) and to others with little choice in housing. The latter-day exceptions stood out: refurbished carriage houses and servant quarters in the Cherokee Triangle and Old Louisville and a few scattered elsewhere.

But back in 1909, social worker Janet E. Kemp of Baltimore was commissioned to study five districts for the former Louisville Tenement House Commission. She concluded that no study of congestion and unsanitary conditions could be complete if it neglected alleys, which she called "horizontal tenements." She found Louisville's tenements to be widely scattered but "somewhat more thickly in the heart of the city," including "in the alleys and small side streets."

The turnaround in Louisville probably dates to the 1960s with the onset of urban renewal and its practice of "superblocking." Large projects such as Louisville's Downtown, its Medical Center and civic center, were reorganized into large blocks; scores of old alleys were either abandoned or reconfigured to serve large structures or form new plazas. "Closing an alley" became almost routine, as aldermen placated petitioning business property owners.

On occasions, old alleys were added to new neighborhood parks, as at Rubel Park in Phoenix Hill in 1982 and to form a "green strip" from Ninth to Eleventh Streets between Chestnut and Magazine in 1953. In 1994 the new Louisville Ballet headquarters on E Main St. had an alley closed for its construction. In the process, Louisville's downtown alley system was much changed; the Board of Aldermen had voted $250,000 in 1971 for "improvements" that included alley-widening from twelve to twenty-nine feet wide on either side of Fourth St., making truck deliveries easier for shops on the new Fourth Street Mall.

Renaming alleys in 1958 was a favorite project of then-Mayor Charles P. Farnsley, who supported street-lighting and street signs giving a dozen or so old alleys new designations such as Court or Place. One memorable revival was Billy Goat Strut east of Preston Street, with "Alley" added onto its end. Farnsley's official chauffeur, Anderson Izzard, gave many a visitor the "Alley Tour."

By 1977 many alleys Miss Kemp had photographed in 1909 had been wiped out in central Louisville by expanding businesses, parking lots, and the North-South Expressway. One noxious tenement cluster Miss Kemp photographed in 1909, along the west side of Preston St. in the eastern portion of the Haymarket district, was razed for the north-south Interstate 65.

In some nineteenth-century commuting suburbs, alleys were built cheaply and without paving; a few paved with limestone block or brick in Louisville have been protected by history buffs and a helpful city works director. Along many a steep and rolling hillside, as in Louisville's Crescent Hill, the alleys were never "made" at all. Some were left as open grassy easements to be maintained and enjoyed by residents, and sometimes to puzzle later generations of title lawyers and property owners.

Alleys offer clear historical evidence that property owners who developed them, and officials who sanctioned them, conceived of access to land in hierarchical terms: out front there was the respectable world that paid taxes; out back were servants and riffraff to do the dirty work. Expensive materials went into the front of the houses, cheaper stuff on the sides and back. Most alleys, therefore, became a second city (and second-class city) within the framework of houses and buildings out front. Alleys proved to be a handy "Siberia" into which powerful local interests could relegate those persons or activities offensive to proper viewers.

But alleys do not stand alone; they are parts of a larger system. The generations that produced nineteenth-century alleys looked upon the city as a mechanism that needed mass-produced services, water, police, gas, and electricity. It also needed mass-produced access, so streets, alleys, sidewalks, and easements were viewed as elements of a single system, and systems-thinking was an important civic discovery of that century. Streets and alleys also reveal that the landscape, which later was to be viewed romantically for its aesthetic potential, was seen in the nineteenth century merely as a set of physical conditions needing revision and improvement—by whatever means.

By World War I, the fad for curvilinear suburbs popularized by Frederick Law Olmsted was on the rise, and these new windblown and winding layouts left little room for alleys. In the wild boom of the 1920s, thousands of lots were laid out around Louisville in the cheapest, most easily platted form. The no-alley trend was reinforced by the 1930s Great Depression and was further reinforced by the Federal Housing Administration, which carried the no-alley pattern into the suburban housing boom after World War II.

Furthermore, the quick jump in national automobile ownership from 2,490,932 in 1915 to 9,239,161 in 1925 meant that alleys were no longer required as access for horses, barns, and stables, with their manure, smells, and animal noises. The auto speeded up what the trolley had begun, spreading out the old walk-in city. Another blow to alleys came in the 1950s when automakers lengthened new models, making obsolete old garages and narrow alleys—many still weedy and neglected in the 1990s. This in turn shifted cars for display out front—paving the way for suburban front-yard garages of the 1990s.

For all these reasons, alleys by the late 1940s had become distinctively old hat. By 1955 the American Society of Planning officials published a report that alleys were vanishing. Urban redevelopment in the 1960s consolidated many blocks, getting rid of alleys. There is some reason, however, to suspect that growing affection for alleys can be found among many disillusioned suburbanites as well as among confirmed city-dwellers. One account of Parisian alleys observes that they were "laden with mystery and almost erotic meaning." Some of the old-time mystery and small-scale charm that the nineteenth-century city possessed are today most highly visible in refurbished alleys and courts.

Thus, the historical denigration of the alley may be ending. As energy costs go up, traffic jams lengthen, and commuting costs increase, the value of older city blocks has begun to stabilize or even to rise in select locations. And the value of land inside those blocks—which often means land accessible only via alleys—has shown signs of increase.

A trend in urban design called "New Urbanism" in the 1990s also favored the return of alleys in sometimes modified forms and name (Laneways, Courts) along with nostalgic house design: front porches, white picket fences. As they show in their new guise, alleys offer an urban rather than suburban or rural "retreat," a quiet enclave just off the busy street, a step away from the hurly-burly. It is precisely these just-off locations that American tourists seek in Europe. It is just this sort of intimacy that, when well designed, can be offered in the interior of thousands of city blocks. When such sites are redesigned—especially when controlled by local residents—they provide land already served by utilities and close to jobs, schools, churches—all such reinforcements that city families need.

Toward this end, Louisville cautiously began to revise rules to make it easier to resubdivide city land into more effective layouts that could reduce lot sizes and include alleys and courts. The "2020" revisions to the Comprehensive Plan were expected in 1997 to make this more feasible. A handful of Louisville builders in the 1990s "discovered" selected alleys in the Lower and Upper Highlands, Smoketown, and Clifton for their potentials as good places to build and sell small houses fitted to narrow nineteenth-century lots—including the ubiquitous "shotgun" and its "camelback" variations. Although most new houses were in suburbia, the promise of redesigned city blocks and alleys offered new appeal to more central locations.

See Ellen Beasley, *The Alleys and Back Buildings of Galveston (Tex.)* (Houston 1997); James Borchert, *Alley Life in Washington* (Urbana, Ill., 1980); Grady Clay, *Alleys: A Hidden Resource* (Louisville 1978); Michael Martin, "Learning from Alleys," M.A. thesis, University of Oregon, 1995.

Grady Clay

ALLISON, YOUNG EWING (b Henderson, Kentucky, December 23, 1853; d Louisville, July 7, 1932). Writer and editor. He was the son of Young Ewing and Susan Speed (Wilson) Allison. His father served Henderson County as both county judge executive and county clerk. Allison's partial deafness limited his formal education to less than three years, for which he compensated by extensive reading. By age fourteen, he was setting type for the *Henderson News* and a year later became its editor. At nineteen, he and his older brother established Henderson's first daily newspaper, the *Chronicle*, an enterprise that failed. Between 1873 and 1880, Allison was the city editor of the *Evansville (Indiana) Journal*, and he returned to Kentucky in 1880 to become city editor of the *Courier-Journal*. In 1888 he founded and edited an insurance trade newspaper called the *Insurance Herald*, which he sold in 1899. That same year, he and Louis T. Davidson started the *Insurance Field*, of which he was editor, a position he held until his death.

Allison, an omnivorous reader of literature, wrote novels, stories, poems, and essays, many of which found wide reception. Allison is remembered for his epic poem *On Board the Derelict* (1891). The poem is a favorite of readers of pirate lore. Fond of novels, he wrote two series of essays on reading novels, each entitled *The Delicious Vice* (1907 and 1909).

Although he was not a professional musician, Allison wrote much about music and music publications. In cooperation with Henry Waller, Allison wrote many songs and four operas. *The Ogaliallos* (1893) was performed by the Bostonians, a leading opera company of the time. The piece was a romantic opera comique, but the music demands were too great for a light opera company and they used it only once. *Brother Francisco* (1893), a one-act tragic opera, was produced at the Royal Opera House in Berlin, Germany, in 1895. Its production was ordered by Kaiser Wilhelm II. Two other operas, *The Scout* (1891) and *The Mouse and the Garter* (n.d.), were never performed.

Allison was among a group of early preservationists who were instrumental in saving Federal Hill at Bardstown, the Rowan family home alleged to be the inspiration for Stephen Foster's *My Old Kentucky Home*. He was a frequent contributor to the state's historical journals and wrote for many literary periodicals. From 1886 to 1889 he was secretary of the Board of Trade committee, organized to boost Louisville business. He was also instrumental in organizing the Commercial Club and was elected its second honorary life member.

Allison married Maggie Yeiser on March 27, 1883; they had two children, George S. and Young Ewing III. Allison died in his home at 4601 S Third St. after suffering two heart attacks within the last three weeks of his life. He is buried in Cave Hill Cemetery. Many of his writings and private papers were donated to The Filson Club Historical Society in Louisville.

See *Courier-Journal*, July 8, 1932.

ALTENHEIM. The Louisville Protestant Altenheim, later simply the Altenheim, is a retirement home for the elderly at 936 Barret Ave. The idea for such a facility was conceived in December 1905 by the Good Will Circle, a women's group at St. John's Evangelical Church at Clay and Market Streets. Early minutes record that the group wished "to serve their Master in serving old and homeless men and women." In January 1906 the circle formally organized the Protestant Altenheim Society and purchased a forty-six-year-old home on Barret Ave. for twelve thousand dollars. The house was renovated, and the first residents were admitted in 1907.

Although founded by a women's group from a single Evangelical church, the Altenheim did not remain their project alone. The home gained support from both men and women and from numerous other Evangelical congregations. The vast majority of the twenty-one-member board of directors were males who were active members of Louisville's German-American business community. The first president of the board was H.F. Frigge, who served until 1913. Meanwhile, the need for the Altenheim's services had grown to the point that several rooms were added in 1910.

Within a decade after its first residents moved in, the Altenheim had developed a substantial governance and support structure. The board of directors set up standing committees on application, finance, membership, house, grievance, and auditing. A ladies' aid society mobilized volunteers from Evangelical churchwomen. A medical staff of seven local physicians looked after the residents' health, and the University of Louisville College of Dentistry provided dental care. More than twenty local ministers from the Evangelical and Reformed churches, as well as other denominations, provided for the residents' spiritual needs.

Membership fees and funds raised by the ladies' aid society, as well as admission fees, legacies, and interest, provided most of the funding. Still, President Fred J. Drexler in 1916 urged members "to start an endowment fund in connection with this Home." Whatever the response to Drexler's appeal, the Altenheim continued to draw sufficient patronage and financial support to warrant another expansion in 1925.

In October 1955 the Altenheim dedicated its most extensive addition yet. The $170,000 fireproof brick structure included nineteen bedrooms, a large dormitory for the ill, and a large kitchen and dining room in the basement. The addition increased the home's capacity to fifty-one. Another project in 1961 included adding a memorial chapel and renovating the office and living room areas. During the early 1970s the original structure was restored over a three-year period. In 1989 the home opened a new intermediate care wing for persons requiring a higher level of care and assistance. The new wing increased the Altenheim's capacity by twenty-four beds. In 1991 the Stitzel Wing was renovated.

As with many other hospitals, children's homes, and human services facilities in cities with a strong German Protestant heritage, the Altenheim remains a continuing symbol of the tendency of Louisville's German immigrants and their descendants to create and support institutions to minister to the needs of children, the elderly, and the sick and dying.

Carl E. Kramer

ALTSHELER, JOSEPH ALEXANDER (b Three Springs, Kentucky, April 29, 1862; d New York City, June 5, 1919). Author. His father, Joseph, came to Three Springs, Kentucky, from Bergen on the Rhine, Germany, in 1849 and married Lucy Curd Snoddy of Glasgow, Kentucky, in 1853. They built a home and general store in what is now Metcalfe County. Altsheler and his brothers helped in the store as well as with crops, but young Altsheler was more interested in books and tales of travels. He graduated from Liberty College in Glasgow in 1880 and entered Vanderbilt University in Tennessee. His father's death forced him to leave college and seek employment in Louisville in 1882.

He worked briefly as a clerk at John P. Morton Book Shop, then joined the *Louisville* *COURIER-JOURNAL* as a reporter, city editor, and editorial writer. He left in 1892 to become a feature writer for the *New York World.* In 1900 Altsheler was named editor of the *World's* magazine section, a position he held until his death.

Most of Alshelter's books were fiction for teenage boys. He wrote novels of adventure and mystery that were predecessors of the Hardy Boys and Nancy Drew. He was voted most-popular writer of boys' stories in the nation according to a poll taken of libraries in 1918, and, during the bicentennial in 1976, the Lighthouse Press reissued four of his junior novels as a tribute to his genuine interest in American history. Three of these were part of an eight-volume series called *The Young Trailers* (1907–17), which included *The Young Trailers* (1907), *The Forest Runners* (1909), and *The Border Watch* (1912). The series deals with the fortunes of two young boys, Henry Ware and Paul Cotter, and their friends who, with their families, had come to Kentucky at about the time of the Revolutionary War. The novels depict frontier life, the taming of the wilderness, conflict with the Native Americans, and the rigors and dangers the settlers faced.

Taking a strong interest in the CIVIL WAR, Altsheler wrote a seven-volume series of historic novels on the subject, among them *The Guns of Bull Run* (1914), *The Scouts of Stonewall* (1915), and *Shades of the Wilderness: A Story of Lee's Great Stand* (1916). He also wrote a series on the West including *Last of the Chiefs* (1909) and *Horsemen of the Plains* (1911). Altsheler tried his hand at nonhistorical adult fiction. Among them were *The Candidate* (1905) and *Guthrie of the Times* (1905), a novel on contemporary journalism and politics. Neither, however, succeeded as did his series of historical novels for boys.

In 1888 Altsheler married Sallie Boles of Glasgow; they had one son, Sydney. After several years of poor health, Altsheler died of a heart attack and is buried in Louisville's CAVE HILL CEMETERY.

See Ora Belle Demaree, "Joseph A. Altsheler: His Contribution to American History for Boys," M.A. thesis, University of Louisville, 1938; William S. Ward, *A Literary History of Kentucky* (Knoxville, Tenn., 1988).

AMERICAN AIR FILTER COMPANY (AAF INTERNATIONAL). For many years, American Air Filter Co. was recognized as a world leader in the manufacture and sale of industrial and commercial air filtration, ventilation, and air-handling equipment. It held many patents for air filtration and air movement products and processes.

Shortly after WORLD WAR I, William M. Reed, a Louisville engineer working at Louisville Auto and Trim Co., was bothered that dust and dirt settled on the freshly painted vehicles. Founding the Reed Engineering Co., he began experimenting with what are now called air-filter devices. The company name was changed in 1922 to Reed Air Filter Co. American Air Filter Co. was incorporated in 1925 as a patent-holding firm. In 1929 it reorganized to include manufacturing. William Reed was its president, and its plants and headquarters were in Louisville. During the great FLOOD OF 1937 it built skiffs to assist in the rescue and evacuation of stranded residents. During WORLD WAR II, AAF made boat hulls for navy ships and hulls for army pontoon bridges. In 1940 it was almost sold to Westinghouse, but the deal was never consummated.

Following the war, AAF began to expand. It played an important role in the rebuilding of the industrial segments of Europe and the Pacific area. AAF purchased several firms that made related products. The Herman Nelson Co., of Moline, Illinois, which was purchased in 1950, manufactured heating, ventilating, air-handling, and air-conditioning products for schools, hospitals, and auditoriums. In 1952 it acquired Illinois Engineering Co. of Chicago, a producer of steam traps and valves. In 1958 the St. Louis–based Kennard Corp., whose primary products were heating coils, was added. Along the way the defense products division grew, with its heating and air-handling products sold to the military, especially for in-ground sites at ICBM missile installations. AAF also developed a line of disposable glass fiber air filtering products for residential and commercial applications. In 1965 the common stock of AAF began being traded on the New York Stock Exchange.

AAF was acquired by the Allis-Chalmers Corp. in 1978, but in 1987 Allis-Chalmers put the AAF part of its business up for sale as part of its efforts to work itself out of bankruptcy. The next year AAF was sold to Snyder General Co. of Dallas. Then in 1994 it was sold to a Malaysian consortium that owns and operates many businesses. OYL Industries BHD is part of the Hong Leong Group and is privately owned. AAF is a division of AAF McQuay Inc., which, in turn, is wholly owned by OYL Industries BHD, which sells its products both in the United States and internationally. Thereafter known as AAF International, the Louisville site, which specialized in industrial air-filter systems, became part of the company's Environmental Products Division. After a three-month strike and poor economic performance, the Louisville manufacturing site was closed in June 1998 and two hundred employees were released. In 2000 AAF International headquarters and its American parent moved to Forest Green on Hurstbourne Parkway.

William M. Reed was president from 1922 until December 1955. He was succeeded by William G. Frank, who was succeeded by Jesse M. Shaver. Richard O. Buese became the last CEO.

See *American Air Facts* (Dec. 1955, Feb. 1956, April 1968); *Courier-Journal*, Sept. 27, 1978, April 25, 1988.

Harry C. Gans

AMERICAN BAPTIST, THE. Following the CIVIL WAR, in 1865 Kentucky's African American Baptists formed the Colored Baptist

State Convention. In 1869 the official name of this organization was changed, for unknown reasons, to the General Association of Kentucky Baptists. The official periodical of that association, published in Paducah, was the *Baptist Herald,* with Rev. George W. Dupee as managing editor and owner. The General Association recommended this publication when it said "the truths contained in this paper faithfully studied and well understood will enable our ministers and Sunday School teachers to preach and teach the word of God intelligently." In 1879, by declaration of the General Association, the *Baptist Herald* was renamed the *American Baptist.* The paper carried personal news columns, news of interest to citizens in Paducah, and the news sent from out-of-city correspondents. While not confined to Baptist news, it was highly race conscious. The paper had a high standard of ethical and journalistic conduct. It was strictly civic, religious, and educational in tone and content.

The same year that its name was changed, editorship and ownership of the paper was transferred from Rev. G.W. Dupee to Bro. W.H. Steward, secretary of the General Association. Steward resided in Louisville and had the offices moved there from Paducah. Historians of the paper credit Steward with the continuance of the paper through its early years. Although the paper was an organ of the General Association, it was owned and operated by Steward. He was aided in his work by his daughter, Carolyn Blanton, who did much of the office work.

Under Steward's leadership, the paper acquired its own press, printing not only the paper but also many other publications, announcements, and private materials for the community. Its influence was not localized. Because it was the largest African American Baptist journal, it was for a time the official organ of the National Baptist Convention. However, the paper never made a profit and was always subsidized by the General Association.

In 1935 Steward transferred ownership to the General Assembly. Dr. W.H. Ballew, who had been groomed by Steward, took over the paper while also serving as moderator of the association. During the Great Depression the paper faced financial difficulty but was kept solvent through the generosity of I. Willis Cole, editor of the *Louisville Leader.* The paper was moved to the I. Willis Cole printing plant, where it was published for about six years.

After Dr. Ballew retired as secretary/treasurer of the paper, Henrietta Butler took over its management when she was convinced to give up her job as a teacher. After forty years of service to the paper she retired. During her tenure several people served as editor, an elected position in those years.

In 1943 the paper bought the building at 1715 W Chestnut St. In the early 1960s the building was renovated. Since Butler's retirement in 1971, Dr. Victor McKinney has served as manager and editor of the paper. McKinney is also moderator of the General Association of Baptists in Kentucky.

See *American Baptist Newspaper Centennial Volume 1878–1978* (Louisville 1978).

AMERICAN CAR AND FOUNDRY COMPANY. Located in Clarksville, Indiana, the company was originally organized in June of 1864 as the Ohio Falls Car and Locomotive Co. With the Jeffersonville city limits located directly to the east of the factory and the Ohio River only five hundred feet away, it was in an ideal location for cheap transportation of iron, coal, and other supplies. Although locomotive-building was never undertaken, the company did build rail cars and rail car supplies for over sixty-five years. Getting off to a shaky start with its stock low and credit questionable, the company did not prosper until Joseph W. Sprague became president and manager in 1866. In 1872 the works caught fire and burned. The factory was rebuilt, but the Panic of 1873 paralyzed the business, causing it to suspend operations and ultimately offer its property for sale to cover indebtedness. In 1876 the Ohio Falls Car Co. was formed with virtually all the same officers and stockholders and with Sprague as president and general manager. The company purchased the lands, buildings, machinery, and tools of the old company. By 1893 there were as many as twenty-three hundred workers when another panic swept the country and the company suspended work in the fall and did not resume until the beginning of 1895. However it was not until 1898 that the company would begin to prosper. In 1899 the company merged with twelve other firms around the country to form the American Car and Foundry Co., becoming one of the most prosperous companies. It became the giant of the railcar building industry, providing passenger and freight equipment for the steam railroads as well as rolling stock for electric streetcars, interurban lines, and subway and elevated systems. Many of its cars were used on Louisville metropolitan lines. The plant in Clarksville closed in the early 1930s, and the factory was used as a warehouse. During World War II caterpillar tracks were manufactured there for the navy.

See Lewis C. Baird, *Baird's History of Clark County* (Indianapolis 1909).

American Car and Foundry, immediately west of the George Rogers Clark Bridge in Clarksville, Indiana, 1944.

AMERICAN CIVIL LIBERTIES UNION OF KENTUCKY. The American Civil Liberties Union of Kentucky was founded in 1955 as an affiliate of the national ACLU, and was at first called the Kentucky Civil Liberties Union. The mission of the ACLU of Kentucky is specifically to protect and defend the Bill of Rights of the United States Constitution. The principal organizers were Patrick Kirwan, Arthur Kling, and Louis Kesselman. They and a few others were responding to a move by the commonwealth's attorney's office in Louisville against feared Communist influence, and specifically the criminal trial of Carl Braden, charged with sedition against the commonwealth of Kentucky.

The Braden case raised basic issues of freedom of speech and assembly, freedom of the press, and freedom from unreasonable search and seizure, all freedoms guaranteed by the Bill of Rights. Since its founding the ACLU of Kentucky has played a role in practically every major civil rights issue arising in Kentucky. Some of the principal volunteer attorneys have been Grover Sales, Louis Lusky, Bob Sedler, Thomas Hogan, Robert Delahanty, Edward Post, William Stone, Joseph Freeland, and David Friedman. They and many others have participated in numerous lawsuits defending individual rights. Most of the ACLU court cases have gone to the Kentucky Supreme Court, and five have gone to the United States Supreme Court, where four were won.

The ACLU of Kentucky is frequently involved in controversy because of its willingness to defend those individuals most likely to be involved in unpopular causes. It believes that every defendant, no matter the charge, must receive due process, adequate counsel, and a jury of his or her peers. The ACLU of Kentucky holds that the lessening of a fundamental right for any individual is the lessening of freedom for all.

For these reasons the ACLU of Kentucky led the struggle for the integration of the Kentucky public schools, was the major defender of objectors to the war in Vietnam, is a leading advocate of reproductive freedom and gay and lesbian rights, and is involved on almost a continuous basis in issues regarding separation of church and state. It objects to government-sponsored prayer in public schools and to government-sponsored religious displays and ceremonies. Issues of equal protection of the law, and due process, police brutality, prison conditions, and capital punishment are major concerns of the ACLU of Kentucky, both in court and in the state legislature.

In 1992, Everett Hoffman, an attorney, was appointed executive director for ACLU of Kentucky. Jeffrey E. Vessels, an Owensboro native with a background in social work, was hired in April 1999 to replace Hoffman, who returned to the private practice of law.

See ACLU of Kentucky, *A Celebration, 1955 to l995* (Madison, Ind., 1995); Ann Braden, *The Wall Between* (New York 1958); Jeffery Davis, "A Kentucky Response: The Founding of the Kentucky Civil Liberties Union, 1955–1960," M.A. thesis, University of Washington, 1981; *Courier-Journal*, April 14, 1999.

Carl Wedekind

AMERICAN LIFE AND ACCIDENT INSURANCE COMPANY BUILDING. The structure, located at Fifth and Main Streets, was built as headquarters of the Kentucky-based insurance company. In 1969 Dinwiddie Lampton Jr. commissioned the eminent architect Ludwig Mies van der Rohe to design the building. The structure of the building is a simple yet perfectly proportioned box, with a Cor-ten steel exterior pierced by bronze-tinted windows. Defined by twelve supporting columns, the upper stories are situated above a glass-enclosed ground floor. Completed in 1973, four years after Mies's death, the building is a legacy of Mies's style and is his only building in Kentucky.

American Printing House for the Blind, 1839 Frankfort Avenue, 1922.

Dinwiddie Lampton Jr., president and chief operating officer of the company since the early forties, joined the family firm in 1935. Lampton was born to Johanna and Dinwiddie Lampton Sr. March 18, 1914. The elder Lampton founded the company in 1906. The younger Lampton had a passion for steeplechase and polo, which found expression in his Hardscuffle Farm near Prospect, where from 1974 to 1996 he hosted the Bolla Hardscuffle Steeple Chase with the proceeds going to support the Kentucky Opera. The eight-race event was considered one of the nation's most prestigious steeplechases. Lampton was most familiar to metropolitan citizens from his television insurance ads featuring him as a carriage driver advising people to "Be wise, be insured." Lampton was educated at Culver Military Academy, graduating in 1934, and St. John's College, Annapolis, Maryland. He married Nancy Houghland May 24, 1941. She died in 1991. They had one daughter, Nancy "Nana" Lampton, and two sons, Dinwiddie III and Mason Houghland.

See *Louisville* (Feb. 1972); William Morgan, *Architecture and the Urban Environment* (Dublin, N.H., 1979); Werner Blaser, *After Mies: Mies van der Rohe—Teaching and Principles* (New York 1977).

Cynthia A. Odell

AMERICAN PRINTING HOUSE FOR THE BLIND. The American Printing House for the Blind (APH) is a private, not-for-profit corporation. It is the oldest publishing house for visually impaired people in the United States and the largest in the world. The mission of the printing house is to promote independence of blind and visually impaired persons by providing special media, tools, and materials needed for education and life.

In 1858 APH was established in response to the growing need for books for blind students. Dempsey Sherrod, a blind man from Mississippi, promoted the idea of a central printing house for books for blind people and raised funds for the enterprise. In 1857 Sherrod obtained a charter in Mississippi to establish a publishing house to print books in raised letters. Then, since Louisville had been chosen as a central location, Sherrod obtained a charter from the Kentucky legislature in 1858.

James Guthrie was the first president of APH, with other prominent Louisvillians serving on the board. Bryce Patten, superintendent of the Kentucky School for the Blind, was the first executive director and provided space at the school for the printing operation. When funding became available in 1860, a specially designed press was ordered from Boston. The disruption of the Civil War prevented its operation until 1866, when the first book, *Fables and Tales for Children*, was produced.

The country's leaders in education of the blind realized that printing books in raised letters could never be commercially successful and that federal support was essential to assure a permanent printing fund. In 1876 a committee of these educators, led by B.B. Huntoon, superintendent of APH and the Kentucky School for the Blind, drew up a bill to provide funding for literature and educational aids for blind students.

The bill was presented to the United States Congress by local representative Albert Shelby Willis (1843–97). An Act to Promote the Education of the Blind became law on March 3,

1879. The American Printing House for the Blind was designated as the official source of educational texts and aids for legally blind students throughout the United States—a mandate that continues.

Trustees of APH purchased land adjacent to the Kentucky School for the Blind, where, in 1883, a building was erected to house the growing operations of APH. Still on the same site, the current APH facility occupies nearly a city block and has more than three hundred employees.

APH established a "talking book" recording studio and production facility in 1936. In the late 1990s the studio was recording about five hundred books for the National Library Service and producing over three million cassette tapes each year.

In 1959, APH completed the largest braille project ever undertaken—the braille edition of the *World Book Encyclopedia,* produced in 145 braille volumes. The first recorded encyclopedia was the 1981 APH cassette edition of the *World Book Encyclopedia.*

In addition to millions of braille pages printed each year, APH produces books and periodicals in large type and in recorded and electronic formats. Other products include a wide range of educational and daily living aids. Free magazines, a database of accessible materials, and referral and consulting services are among APH services to people who are blind or visually impaired.

See Annual Reports 1866–1996, American Printing House for the Blind (Louisville); *First Report of the American Printing House for the Blind,* published by order of the Mississippi Board (Louisville 1860); B.B. Huntoon, "Printing for the Blind as Developed by the American Printing House for the Blind, Louisville, Ky.," *Outlook for the Blind* 3 (Winter 1913): 97–104.

Carol Brenner Tobe

AMERICAN PROTECTIVE ASSOCIATION. A secret anti-Catholic, nativistic organization founded in Clinton, Iowa, in 1887 and established in Louisville by 1890, the organization carried on the virulent hatred reminiscent of the KNOW-NOTHING PARTY of the 1850s.

In 1891 the APA dominated the City Council and tried to rename all city streets that had been named after saints. The group had an APA doctor and head nurse appointed to the city hospital at a time when it was staffed by volunteer Sisters of Charity nurses; the sisters resigned and left the facility seriously shorthanded. The organization even went so far as to demand that all Catholic gravediggers at CAVE HILL CEMETERY be fired, as it was "unbecoming and indecent, an unbearable outrage on propriety indeed, that papistical gravediggers should be allowed to handle . . . the interment of those who had not professed their faith in Catholic teaching when living." The cemetery board refused, and the issue died.

By 1894 the APA claimed thirty thousand members in Kentucky, although the figure is speculative. The organization was most active in Louisville, though chapters existed in Lexington, Paducah, Ashland, and various small towns throughout the state. In 1895 Covington's *Kentucky Post* reported there were fourteen thousand members in Louisville, where two APA newspapers circulated: *Freedom's Banner* and *Justice.* During congressional elections in 1894, the APA was instrumental in defeating Irish-Catholic contender EDWARD J. MCDERMOTT with APA-backed candidate WALTER EVANS.

On August 26, 1895, the Republican city and county convention held at the Louisville Music Hall (MUSIC HALL CONVENTION) was hijacked by APA members who strong-armed the organization into fielding a platform and candidates to their liking. The greatest effect of this move was to drive the city's rising Catholic populace strongly to the Democratic camp.

The APA's political influence waned after the election of President William McKinley in 1896, when internecine fighting broke out among pro- and anti-McKinley factions. When state APA president Charles Sapp was appointed by McKinley as collector of internal revenue for the Louisville district, many feared the APA was being repaid for campaign work done for McKinley, though there is no evidence McKinley ever rewarded or acknowledged APA work on his behalf. The death of the organization's last national president in 1911 ended APA's influence on Louisville politics, but the reemergence of the Ku Klux Klan continued fueling the xenophobic fires.

See John Wiltz, "APA-ism in Kentucky and Elsewhere," *Register of the Kentucky State Historical Society* 56 (April 1958): 143–55; James Klotter, *Kentucky: Decades of Discord 1865–1900* (Frankfort 1977).

AMERICAN RED CROSS, LOUISVILLE CHAPTER. In the spring of 1917, as it became clear that the United States would enter WORLD WAR I, twenty-six Louisvillians petitioned the national American Red Cross for authority to organize a chapter. On March 29 the Louisville Chapter came into being. A charter was granted on April 3, and three days later war was declared. Relief committees were immediately formed to help local servicemen and their dependents. Large numbers of volunteers sewed and knitted hospital garments, collected clothing, provided medical supplies, and took the classes offered in first aid, home care of the sick, and making surgical dressings.

By the time of the first annual meeting in October 1917, the chapter had 71 units and 3,252 volunteers. A Red Cross War Fund Committee was formed; the Gray Ladies, a volunteer group, brought personal support and encouragement to wounded servicemen at CAMP ZACHARY TAYLOR; and a Motor Car Committee was activated. Returning veterans were supplied with food, clothing, counseling, and other necessities. The first volunteer board of directors was formed, and volunteers have continued to guide the chapter.

Meanwhile the Junior Red Cross became active in helping disadvantaged youth locally and sending clothing and other supplies to help the children of war-torn Europe. About 1921 a disaster preparedness program began, providing emergency relief to fire victims. In 1927 the Red Cross lifesaving course became a requirement for swimming pool lifeguards.

In the early 1930s a local drought, combined with the nationwide economic depression, caused an emergency situation. The Louisville Chapter, working with the federal government, distributed food, clothing, and supplies to affected families throughout the state and contributed funds to provide seed and livestock feed. Then, in 1937 came the worst Ohio Valley flood in history. The chapter provided shelters and first aid stations and coordinated health programs; more than 33,000 families in Jefferson County were helped, at a cost of $4,937,630.

A move to a new chapter house at 1355 S Third St. in 1938 was followed quickly by the beginning of WORLD WAR II in Europe. As part of a nationwide effort by the American Red Cross, more than eight thousand local volunteers served during World War II, and surgical dressings and knitted garments were made in volume and shipped to hospitals near the front. Nurses were recruited and nurses' aides trained. The Home Service department was moved to 307 S Fifth St. in order to meet hundreds of requests from families of service men and women at times of war-related imprisonment, hospitalization, or death, and to fill urgent needs for service personnel to return home to help families deal with emergencies.

Blood plasma, for the first time pooled and processed by the Red Cross, was used to meet the astonishing demands of the battlefield. The Louisville Chapter's blood program was born in May 1943; by V-E Day two years later, volunteer donors had made it possible for the center to give two hundred thousand pints to the war effort, in addition to supplying whole blood for FORT KNOX.

In 1945 another flood visited the city, making it necessary to combine flood relief with the war effort. The Farnsley home next to the chapter house was acquired to house Home Service and the Regional Blood Center, which covered sixty counties in Kentucky and southern Indiana and opened in 1949. The KOREAN WAR, which began in 1950, caused another military buildup. During three years of fighting, 1,648 pints of whole blood and 56,716 units of blood fractions were supplied to the armed forces. The Home Service caseload mounted again as casualties increased and veterans' services climbed.

In 1958 the Junior Red Cross moved into the carriage house behind the chapter. The first

Foundry workers at the Standard Sanitary Manufacturing Co. (later American Standard Co.) 1920s.

annual Youth Leadership Training Center was held at Camp Crescendo in BULLITT COUNTY in 1960. In 1964 Red Cross services in Jefferson and Bullitt Counties merged; two years later Oldham County Red Cross joined them to become the Louisville Area Chapter. Fund-raising had become a difficult and very time-consuming year-round operation when, in 1961, Red Cross and the Community Chest formed a fund-raising partnership called the United Appeal, which has continued successfully.

In 1963 and for the decade following, the VIETNAM WAR again caused a sharply rising demand for services to military personnel and their families. Counseling and support were offered to several groups. An Overseas Wives Club was formed, a group for relatives of prisoners of war, and, eventually, a support group for widows. Again caseloads soared. In 1971 the chapter moved into a new and larger building in the downtown MEDICAL CENTER. In 1972, all states, including Kentucky, were named divisions of the national Red Cross, and Louisville chapter personnel became responsible for training and otherwise assisting the smaller units in the state. (In 1983, however, the national organization returned to a field service concept, employing specialists for this purpose.)

Various innovative programs have been developed by the chapter especially to meet local needs. The WHEELS program has provided transportation to the elderly and handicapped since 1975. In the same year, the WSYL (We Speak Your Language) program began to provide free emergency translation services to Louisville's increasingly diverse population. Community WINTERHELP is a program born of a 1983 agreement between the Louisville Area Red Cross and LOUISVILLE GAS AND ELECTRIC to assist families unable to cover the cost of utilities in the cold winter months. It continues with involvement of urban ministries. A newer program, PALS (Partners in Advancing Life Skills), serves disabled adults with day care.

In 1989 the national Red Cross decided to separate the management of blood services from chapter operations nationwide. The Louisville Area Chapter and blood services continue to share the same building, however, and to cooperate in many other ways.

The area covered directly by the chapter has gradually enlarged, now encompassing six counties and Fort Knox in Kentucky and three counties in southern Indiana. There are now six sub-offices of the chapter, including one in southern Jefferson County, that exist to bring services more quickly to nearby residents. Each has its own corps of loyal volunteers. Currently the Louisville Area Chapter is in the Midwest region of the national organization and is the coordinating chapter for the state of Kentucky. In 1997, eighty eventful years after its founding, the Louisville Area Chapter hosted the annual convention of the national Red Cross.

See Marjorie Jordan Boylan, "It's a Long Way from Tipperary to Vietnam . . ." (Red Cross Archives [private papers] 1967); "Whatever It Takes," *1995–96 Annual Report*, Louisville Area Chapter, American Red Cross.

Marguerite Hume

AMERICAN STANDARD COMPANY.

Although it grew to become the world's largest manufacturer of bathroom and kitchen fixtures and fittings, American Standard could trace its beginnings to a humble little shop in downtown Louisville. In 1858 Georg Andreas Theodor Ahrens, a native of Hamburg, Germany, moved to Louisville from Baltimore, Maryland, in search of employment, which he found at the foundry of Barbaroux and Snaden. A year later, he brought his family to Louisville and opened his own brass molding works on E Market St. between Preston and Jackson.

The little business prospered, and in 1865 Ahrens decided to broaden his services to include plumbing and pipe fitting. At this time he took on a partner, Henry Ott, a plumber, and the newly christened firm of Ahrens and Ott flourished. However, it was under the direction of Ahrens's son, Theodore Junior, that the company achieved national prominence. In 1899 he led the merger of his father's business with eight other companies to form the Standard Sanitary Manufacturing Co., a producer of plumbing fixtures and enameled, cast-iron tubs and sinks. Ahrens Junior became president of the new firm, whose headquarters were first in Pittsburgh, then New York City. The Louisville offices were located on W Main, with a factory at Seventh St. and Shipp Ave.

In 1929 Standard Sanitary, the pioneer of such plumbing improvements as the one-piece toilet, combination faucets, and tarnish-proof finishes for brass fittings, merged with the American Radiator Co., a producer of heating equipment. The resulting company was dubbed the American Radiator and Standard Sanitary Corp. Its name was shortened in 1967 to American Standard.

The Louisville plant was situated on fifty-three acres and included more than sixty buildings. Employment peaked in 1956 at fifty-six hundred workers. LABOR unions organized at the local factory in 1941, uniting in the Allied Trades Council. Relations between management and labor were sometimes rocky. From 1959 to 1978 the unions went on strike each time their contracts were up for renewal.

With the onset of the 1980s, the plant began to lose money. Consumers no longer preferred the heavy cast-iron bathroom fixtures but instead began to choose those made with plastic or other lighter and cheaper materials. At one point in the 1960s, cast iron accounted for 60 percent of the tub market, but by the 1990s it had fallen to under 10 percent. American Standard developed an alternative in 1988 known as Americast tubs. These had porcelain-enamel surfaces and were half the weight of their cast-iron counterparts. Unfortunately for the Louisville plant, Americast tubs were already being produced at American Standard's Salem, Ohio, plant. As a result, American Standard decided to close its operations in Louisville in 1992.

See *Courier-Journal*, June 1, 1992; Margaret M. Bridwell, *The Ahrens Story* (Louisville 1954).

AMPHITHEATRE AUDITORIUM.

Known simply as "The Auditorium," the theater boasted the second-largest stage in America (after that of New York's original Metropolitan Opera House) upon its opening at the southwest corner of Fourth Ave. and Hill St. on September 23, 1889. The large wooden Auditorium, with thousands of electric lights inside and out, seated 3,072 people, with additional space in the aisles. Its stage, ninety feet across and sixty feet deep, stood behind a proscenium opening fifty feet wide and twenty-seven feet high. Confirming the theater's motto—"Only for Great Attractions"—were performances by the day's outstanding actors, musicians, singers, and orators, including Helena Modjeska, Sarah Bernhardt, Sir Henry Irving, Ellen Terry, John Philip Sousa, Victor Herbert, Nellie Melba, the Metropolitan Opera Co., Theodore Roosevelt, and Booker T. Washington. Part of a large entertainment complex bounded by Fourth Ave., Fifth, Hill, and A (now Gaulbert) Streets, the site also contained a man-made lagoon, a deer park, a bicycle track, a promenade, and a ten-thousand–seat open-air Fireworks Amphitheatre, which hosted such pyrotechnic extravaganzas as *The Last Days of Pompeii* and *Americus*.

Its proprietor and manager for most of its fifteen-year existence was the eccentric philanthropist, "Captain" William F. Norton Jr. (1849–1903), who conducted business as "Daniel Quilp," after Charles Dickens's villain in *The Old Curiosity Shop*. After presenting a profitable production in Louisville's former Southern Exposition building in 1888, the Paducah, Kentucky, native erected the ten-thousand-dollar structure and opened with a production of *The Merchant of Venice* starring Edwin Booth, brother of John Wilkes Booth, and Lawrence Barrett. By 1892 the amphitheater's summer series was so popular that eighteen thousand citizens flocked to shows that included *The Mikado*, *Patience*, and *H.M.S. Pinafore*, which was performed in the lagoon. Aside from his numerous presentations, Norton, who was considered generous and public-spirited although he dubbed Louisville "Deadtown" and "Calamity Gulch," earning him the nickname "The Duke of Deadville," used the Auditorium one morning a week to hand out money to needy persons.

After Norton's death, no buyers could be found for the Auditorium; the last event, "The Children's Floral Ball," was held on April 30, 1904. Following an auction of its contents on May 5 and 6, the building was purchased for nine hundred dollars by real estate agent Bruce Hoblitzell, who razed it and used the lumber for other projects.

See John Spalding Gatton, *"Only for Great Attractions"—The Amphitheatre Auditorium, Louisville, Kentucky: A Brief History and a Checklist of Performances*, 1889–1904 (Louisville 1977); *Courier-Journal & Times Magazine*, June 13, 1965; *Courier-Journal*, Jan. 2, 1916; Raymond J. Randles, "A Biography of the Norton Family," M.A. thesis, University of Louisville, 1961; Samuel W. Thomas and William Morgan, *Old Louisville: The Victorian Era* (Louisville 1975); *Courier-Journal*, June 10, 1979.

John Spalding Gatton

AMUSEMENT PARKS. Louisville's increasing use of electric power following the 1880s revolutionized not only the city's homes but also its places of amusement. By 1910 numerous tranquil riverside picnic groves, bandstands, and swimming and boating spots were transformed into beckoning destinations of thrilling rides and innovative incandescent lighting, often powered by the excess direct current of trolley lines terminating at park entrances.

The Amphitheater Auditorium on the south west corner of Fourth Street at Hill in the 1890s. Much of the building material was salvaged from the Southern Exhibition building.

The region's most popular and longest-operating place of amusement, Fontaine Ferry Park, 230 South Western Pkwy., enthralled both young and old from 1905 to its closing in 1969. Subsequent reopenings under the names of Ghost Town on the River and River Glen Park from 1972 to 1975 were unsuccessful, and the original sixty-four-acre property is today a city-owned park and sports field, plus private town homes. The site was commonly called "Fountain Ferry" throughout its history.

A short distance downriver was White City, located at the western end of Greenwood Ave. Opened in 1907 but ill-fated because of fire, White City's operations assumed the name of surrounding parkland, Riverview Park, in 1911. By 1913, the venture was failing; by 1922, the entire property had succumbed to spreading residential development.

During the first half of the twentieth century, smaller and often short-lived amusement parks such as Sugar Grove, downstream from New Albany on the Ohio River's Indiana shore, and Glenwood Park, at the eastern end of Spring St. in New Albany, welcomed Indiana and Kentucky visitors alike. Farther upriver, on the Indiana shore, Rose Island, opened in 1928, carved a Roaring Twenties business out of the former Fern Grove picnic and campgrounds. Situated at the mouth of Clark County's Fourteen Mile Creek, Rose Island was actually bordered by water on only two sides. The recreational complex drew huge crowds by steamboat before its demise as a result of the 1937 flood.

Though devoid of thrill rides, many past amusement spots, such as Shippingport Island's Elm Tree Garden or Louisville's Senning's Park and Zoo on New Cut Road, repeated a popular beer garden, games, and entertainment theme. The huge, rambling Auditorium and outdoor Amphitheatre, at the southwest corner of Fourth and Hill Streets, had already set the standard for lavish variety, including fireworks spectaculars, from 1889 to 1904.

Post–World War II amusement ventures concentrated on scaled-down rides for a booming generation of youngsters. Shively's Kiddieland, plus many area drive-in theaters, successfully catered to this trend. Following the final closure of the former Fontaine Ferry Park property in 1975, primarily due to racial strife, Louisville had no major amusement park for more than a decade. However, the 1987 opening of Kentucky Kingdom on leased property at the Kentucky Fair and Exposition Center spelled promise. The initial seventeen-acre park, owned by out-of-state investors, failed after its inaugural season; nevertheless, new Louisville-based ownership brought increasing success and stability to Kentucky Kingdom since its reopening in 1990. The entire operation, valued at $64 million, was sold in November 1997 to Oklahoma-based Premier Parks Inc. Featuring world-class thrill rides and expanded to twenty-eight acres, Six Flags Kentucky Kingdom (renamed in June 1998) is now the state's largest amusement park.

See Jerry L. Rice, "Fontaine Ferry Park, A Time of Innocence" video (Louisville 1992); George H. Yater, *Two Hundred Years at the Falls of the Ohio* (Louisville 1979); R.C. Riebel, *Louisville Panorama* (Louisville 1960).

Jerry L. Rice

ANCHORAGE. Of all the outlying villages that developed in the two-hundred-year history of Jefferson County, Anchorage has most nearly retained its character in the path of the suburban growth of Louisville. Located in eastern Jefferson County along LaGrange Rd., it is a park-like community of some seven hundred and fifty residences, a school, churches, and a few businesses located in the wooded hills and valleys adjoining branches of BEARGRASS and Goose Creeks.

The northwestern boundary is formed by land claimed in 1773 by Isaac Hite and identified on John Filson's first map of Kentucky as Hite's Mill, later part of the grounds of CENTRAL STATE HOSPITAL and the E.P. SAWYER STATE PARK. The connecting roads to the OHIO RIVER at HARRODS CREEK and to MIDDLETOWN on the south were early transportation routes along which the farms of the first settlers were located.

Most influential among the early landowners was EDWARD DORSEY HOBBS, whose family was in business in Middletown. As a surveyor, he had drawn some of the earlier maps of Louisville as well as Anchorage and planned for the orderly growth of the area. He was involved with the establishment of the LOUISVILLE AND FRANKFORT RAILROAD (later purchased by LOUISVILLE & NASHVILLE RAILROAD) through Anchorage in 1849. For several years the crossroads was known as Hobbs's Station. Although the Ohio River is twelve miles away, the nautical name of the retirement home of riverboat captain James W. Goslee was adopted when the town was incorporated in 1878, three years after his death at a railroad crossing. Tradition has it that the anchor that hangs inside the rim of a locomotive wheel in the center of town is the one that Captain Goslee removed from his ship, the *Matamora,* and put on his lawn at "The Anchorage" in 1869. It is a monument to the river and the railroad and those who shaped the town's growth.

With train service available, including the Louisville, Anchorage, and PEWEE VALLEY interurban line starting in 1901, students seeking a high school education could attend the local boarding schools: Bellewood Female Seminary, Pine Hill Academy, and Forest Military Academy. Construction of the Citizens National Life Insurance Co. building in 1911 generated enough tax base to allow the community to create Anchorage Graded and High School.

The chapel at the Bellewood Seminary had become the meeting place of a Presbyterian congregation organized in Middletown in 1799. In 1869 the Gothic Revival–style sanctuary of the ANCHORAGE PRESBYTERIAN CHURCH was built. St. Luke's Episcopal Church was built in 1908, and the Catholic Church of the Epiphany was constructed in 1975.

ISAAC W. BERNHEIM, a Louisville distiller and the benefactor of BERNHEIM FOREST, was among those prominent citizens who acquired a summer house in Anchorage. Through his influence, the Frederick Law OLMSTED firm of Brookline, Massachusetts, was commissioned in 1914 to design a plan for the growth of Anchorage. The plan incorporated the stone bridges and triangle intersections that were features of the Louisville park system, also designed by the firm. Bernheim was the first president of the Anchorage Civic League, formed in 1914. The league has worked closely with the town board on issues of public concern. With growth stimulated by the rail lines, the town board acted in 1901 to confine commercial growth to a limited district, thus beginning the zoning and land use planning that protected the town from incompatible development.

Between 1878 and 1978, many of the large estates were subdivided into smaller building sites. The number of houses nearly doubled between 1977 and 1997. To preserve the rural character of the town, an Anchorage Historic District was created, with listing on the NATIONAL REGISTER OF HISTORIC PLACES in 1982. Ten years later, the boundaries of the district were extended to include most of the town. The town became a fifth-class city in 1966 and moved to a fourth-class city in 1984.

The population of Anchorage was 1,477 in 1970 and 1,726 in 1980. By 1990 it had increased to 2,082 and in 1996 the population was 2,058.

See Edith Woods, *Middletown Days and Deeds* (Louisville 1946); Leone W. Hallenberg, *Anchorage* (Anchorage 1959); Mildred Ewen, *Anchorage Revisited* (Louisville 1976).

Mildred Long Ewen

ANCHORAGE PRESBYTERIAN CHURCH. Believed to be the first Presbyterian congregation in the area, the church is now located at 11403 Park Rd. in ANCHORAGE. The Anchorage Presbyterian Church actually started in MIDDLETOWN in 1799. Prior to 1799 several Presbyterian families from Pennsylvania had settled in Middletown and the area known as Pennsylvania Run in southern Jefferson County. The families and the town had grown large enough that by 1799 the Presbytery deemed it necessary that a pastor be called. James Vance, who had opened a classical school in the area, was called in November 1799 to pastor both the Middletown and the Pennsylvania Run churches. In 1800 the Presbytery called Vance to pastor the congregation at Louisville as well. Services at the Middletown church were first held in a small log building on Old Main St. Following Vance's death in 1829 there was a period of instability as a series of pastors came and went. It is not known why a pastor could not be kept. From 1830 to 1853 three different pastors served, and for several years no pastor was installed.

In 1853 William Wallace Hill, whose daughter Patty composed the "Happy Birthday" song, was called as pastor. In 1869 the church moved from Middletown to Anchorage. A brick building, which seated three hundred, was erected at the cost of twelve thousand dollars, an enormous sum at that time. It was designed by Louisville architect WILLIAM HENRY REDIN. It was not recorded why the church moved, although there is speculation it was due to Hill's work with Bellewood Seminary, which he established in Anchorage in 1860. However, for a while church services alternated weekly between the Middletown and the Anchorage churches, and the church was known as the Middletown and Anchorage Presbyterian Church. In 1877 the Middletown property was sold. After the move to Anchorage the church shared buildings with the seminary. Bellewood and the church were practically a merged institution until the school closed in 1916. All the pupils attended the church, and the elders were members of the school's board of trustees.

The church used ecclesiastical trials to deal with the immoral behavior of the members, including profanity, anger at a neighbor, intoxication, desecration of the Sabbath, dancing, and divorce. There was even conflict over the use of musical instruments during church services. In 1869 the church's first committee made up entirely of women was organized. By 1878, when Everett W. Bedinger became pastor, the church was rapidly expanding. In 1882 the church helped organize the Springdale Presbyterian Church. After Bedinger left in 1889, the church was led by three interim pastors for the next decade. From 1898 to 1905 F.R. Beattle pastored the church, but from 1905 to 1924 there were seven different pastors, most of whom served for only a year and then resigned. In fact from 1920 to 1924 there was no minister installed. The church was reprimanded by the Presbytery for their inability to keep a pastor. The next pastor, Duke T. Williams, stayed for four years, but it was the following pastor who would hold the position for the longest in the church's history.

Edgar E. Houghton was pastor for thirty-seven years, beginning in 1929, and provided the stability the church so desperately needed. By 1945 membership had risen to 280. Extensive renovation began in the 1950s, and the church was active in local, national, and international missions. By 1966, when Houghton retired, membership had reached 380.

From 1966 to 1973 Robert Lawrence led the church through the CIVIL RIGHTS era and the VIETNAM WAR. In this period, transportation was provided for those patients and staff of the nearby CENTRAL STATE HOSPITAL who wanted to attend worship, and a class for prisoners at the Correctional Institute for Women in Pewee Valley was organized.

Following Reverend Lawrence's pastorate, John Turner Ames served the church from 1974 until 1995. During this time, the church established a formal "covenant" relationship with the Catholic community of the Church of the Epiphany in 1986. St. Luke's Episcopal Church of Anchorage joined this covenant in 1987.

In 1997 Dee Hamilton Wade began his call to serve Anchorage Presbyterian Church. Mary Doyle Morgan was named the first associate pastor of the church in 1981. After her departure, the Reverend Larry Ann Bridgman was called in 1989, followed by Barbara Evans Tesorero, who served from 1993 to 1996.

See Isabelle Andersen, *From Haystack to Covenant, 1869–1974* (Louisville); Rev. Edward L. Warren, D.D. *The Presbyterian Church in Louisville* (Chicago 1896).

ANDERSON, BARBARA (TUNNELL) (b Mansfield, Massachusetts, 1894; d Richmond, Virginia, October 27, 1974). Writer, poet. Anderson graduated from Smith College and moved to Louisville in 1926, where she wrote advertising copy for the Chambers Agency, with offices in the Starks Building. In 1931 she married Dwight Anderson, dean of the University of Louisville School of Music. By the summer of 1933 Anderson had assumed editorship of *Kentucky Progress Magazine*, the official publication of the Kentucky Progress Commission. The state publication attempted to stimulate economic development during the Great Depression.

She was born Barbara Madison Tunnell, the daughter of a minister who moved frequently. The years she and her family spent in small towns of the Deep South became the basis for her fictionalized accounts of race relations and tolerance. Her antebellum theme underscored her love of the region's people and places. Her best-known novel, *The Days Grow Cold,* was a Literary Guild selection in 1941 and was followed by *Southbound*, which was published in England in 1949. Anderson also wrote articles on historic homes and composed poetry, both of which were published in popular magazines. The unique poetic style she employed lent itself to vivid descriptions of childhood innocence.

Anderson's only play, *The Tall Kentuckian*, portrayed Abraham Lincoln's close ties to Louisville, especially to his friend Joshua Speed, whose family owned the Farmington plantation. Lincoln visited there for several weeks in 1841. The two-act musical, with an original score by Norman Dello Joio, was first performed in Louisville in June 1953. The play was produced for the city's 175th anniversary, and African Americans were admitted to Iroquois Amphitheater for the first time so that they could attend performances.

Anderson moved to Richmond, Virginia, in 1973.

See *Courier-Journal*, Oct. 28, 1974; William S. Ward, *A Literary History of Kentucky* (Knoxville 1988).

ANDERSON, BENJAMIN M. (b 1836?; d Cincinnati, February 21, 1865). Soldier. Born about 1836, this ill-fated adventurer and Confederate officer was the son of James Anderson and Mary Wrigglesworth of Louisville. In the spring of 1856, young Anderson joined a band of Kentucky volunteers that set out to join Gen. William Walker's "Filibusters" in Nicaragua. As a captain in Col. Jack Allen's Kentucky Rifles, the Louisville youth was gravely wounded at the Siege of Granada (November 24–December 11, 1856).

One of the most ardent "Southern Rights" men in Louisville, Anderson journeyed to the temporary capital in Montgomery and offered the services of a regiment of Kentuckians to the Confederate government in March of 1861. He subsequently returned to Louisville and organized a company of volunteers known as the "Davis Guards." Departing the city on April 17, 1861, Anderson led his men to New Orleans, where they were initially assigned to the First Louisiana Infantry. Transferred to the Virginia front, Anderson was promoted major of the First Kentucky Infantry on July 19, 1861. He was subsequently ordered to the western theater, where he became lieutenant-colonel of the Third Kentucky Infantry on October 25, 1861. Wounded at Shiloh on April 6, 1862, he was forced to resign on May 24.

Hoping to raise an independent command for partisan service, Anderson apparently received authority to organize his own regiment. However, after serving as a staff officer, he despaired of the Confederate cause and returned to Louisville. Anderson reported to Brig. Gen. Jeremiah T. Boyle, Union commander of the District of Kentucky, and took the Oath of Allegiance. Literally a man without a country, Anderson afterwards found himself shadowed by Union detectives and shunned by Southern sympathizers. According to one source, he joined the secret, pro-Confederate "Sons of Liberty" in the summer of 1864 and made his way to Canada. Recruited by the Confederate secret service, Colonel Anderson was involved in the initial phase of the "Northwest Conspiracy," a plot to liberate Confederate prisoners at Camp Douglas in Chicago and spark a "Copperhead" revolt in Illinois and Indiana.

Led by Capt. Thomas Hines, one of John Hunt Morgan's bold raiders, the conspirators left Toronto on or about August 25, 1864. Anderson was among several rebel agents who arrived in Chicago on the eve of the Democratic National Convention. The discovery of the plot by federal authorities and the reluctance of the "Copperheads" to take arms forced Hines to temporarily abandon his plans on August 30. However, Anderson may have already disassociated himself from the conspiracy. Suspected as a "double agent" by several of Hines's followers, the proud soldier left Chicago in disgust and returned to Kentucky. It should be noted however that captured letters indicate that, despite his withdrawal from the Camp Douglas plot, Anderson was still willing to serve Hines in another capacity.

Scheduled to take place during the November 1864 presidential election, Hines's second attempt to liberate the Camp Douglas prisoners was foiled and many of those involved were rounded up in Chicago. According to standard accounts, Anderson, who was ordered to arm the Missouri guerrillas expected to support the liberated POWs, was among those taken prisoner. In reality, Anderson joined Jeremiah T. Boyle, Kentucky's former Union commander, in the oil business shortly after he returned to Louisville in September. Arrested in Louisville on December 18, 1864, Anderson was taken to Cincinnati under guard and confined in McLean Barracks.

At the conspiracy trial that began in Cincinnati on January 11, 1865, Anderson claimed that he had disassociated himself from the conspiracy during the initial phase and returned home. Accounts that he appeared as a government witness against his codefendants are not supported by the trial records. On February 19, 1865, the Kentuckian wrested a pistol from his guard and shot himself. Anderson lingered in great agony until his death in St. John's Hospital on February 21, 1865. During his final hours he reportedly repented his association with the Confederate cause, adding that while he "did not fear death" he "would prefer being dead than disgraced." The brief association with Hines's followers proved that he had not only violated his oath but betrayed Boyle's trust as well—a disgrace Anderson was apparently unwilling to bear.

Tragically, even though he was one of the first men to raise Confederate volunteers in Kentucky, Anderson was remembered by many former comrades as a traitor to the "Lost Cause." A victim of his own strict code of personal honor, he is buried in the family plot in Cave Hill Cemetery.

See obituary, *Louisville Daily Democrat*, Feb. 23, 1865; House of Representatives Executive Documents, 39th Congress, 2d Session, vol. 8, No. 50 (Serial 1290); John B. Castleman, *Active Service* (Louisville 1917); James D. Horan, *Confederate Agent* (New York 1954); Stephen Z. Starr, *Colonel Grenfell's Wars* (Baton Rouge, La., 1971).

James M. Prichard

ANDERSON, CHARLES W., JR. (b Louisville, May 26, 1907; d Louisville, June 14, 1960). Attorney, legislator, United Nations delegate. Anderson was the son of Dr. Charles W. and Tabatha Murphy Anderson. He attended Kentucky State College (now University) (1925), and received a bachelor's degree from Wilberforce University (1927) and the LL.B. from Howard University (1930). He was also awarded an honorary LL.D. from Wilberforce

(1936). Anderson was admitted to the Kentucky bar in 1933 and began practicing law with Willie C. Fleming, Harry S. McAlpin, O.B. Hinnant, and J. Earl Dearing in Louisville. Anderson was an excellent trial attorney and served as a mentor and trainer to new attorneys in the firm.

In November 1935 Anderson became the first African American to be elected to the Kentucky House of Representatives and the first African American legislator in the South after Reconstruction. A Republican, he was reelected and served from 1936–46. During his legislative career, Anderson was instrumental in seeing that issues relative to African Americans remained before the Kentucky legislature. As a representative, he successfully helped to defeat the Senate's resolution that opposed a federal anti-lynching law (1938) and also succeeded in making electrocution mandatory in all Kentucky death cases. The Anderson-Mayer Act provided funds for African Americans to attend graduate school outside of Kentucky and included a bill that allowed married women to teach, thereby providing extra income for many families, and the legislation that provided minimum wages and improved working conditions for domestic servants in the state.

Anderson was a strong advocate for education and supported better educational opportunities for all Kentuckians. He enhanced rural high school educational facilities for all students through his legislative action, led the fight for the integration of the state universities in Kentucky, and introduced legislation to integrate the nursing schools and postgraduate hospital training and residency programs in the state. These pieces of legislation improved the economic and educational conditions for poor whites as well as for blacks. He also fought and defeated a bill to segregate people by race on Kentucky buses, in schools, libraries, trains, and other public places.

Anderson resigned from the General Assembly to become assistant commonwealth's attorney for Jefferson County in May 1946. This was another first for Kentucky and for the South. He served in this capacity until 1952. Anderson received the GOP nomination for judge in the Louisville Third District municipal court in 1949 but was defeated in the election.

President Dwight D. Eisenhower appointed Anderson as an alternate United States delegate to the United Nations' fourteenth general assembly in 1959. As a member he helped draft documents that protected the rights of children against abuse, exploitation, and neglect. Other documents prohibited any practices that allowed discrimination based on race, religion, or other criteria.

Anderson married Victoria McCall of Detroit November 30, 1948. They had two children, Charles III and Victoria. He was killed when his car was struck by an Ashland-bound Chesapeake & Ohio passenger train. He is buried in Louisville's Eastern Cemetery.

Anderson was the recipient of numerous awards and honors for his achievements in government and public service. In 1940 he received the Lincoln Institute Award for outstanding service to blacks. In 1945 he was awarded the Howard University Alumni Award for distinction in law and government. He was the first black to receive a Kentucky Colonel's commission. In 1971 the Kentucky Human Rights Commission honored Anderson in its poster series of Kentucky's Outstanding African Americans. On June 14, 1997, the thirty-seventh anniversary of his death, a historical marker honoring Anderson's distinguished career was unveiled in Louisville in front of the Jefferson County Hall of Justice. Another lasting tribute to Anderson is the Anderson Medal. Gov. Wallace Wilkinson's Equal Employment Opportunity Conference and the Department of Personnel created the Anderson Medal in 1989 as a perpetual memorial prize to be given to a Kentuckian who has "enhanced the opportunity for equality" in the workplace, classroom, or marketplace. The medal is given to individuals only.

See Jessie C. Smith, ed., *Notable Black American Men* (Detroit 1998).

Karen C. McDaniel

ANDERSON, DWIGHT (b Chicago, June 3, 1896; d Louisville, December 25, 1962). Music educator. The son of Francis Wayland and Annie Hill Anderson, Dwight was reared in Pensacola, Florida. He was awarded a scholarship at the age of seventeen to the Cincinnati Conservatory of Music to study piano. He graduated in 1918 and served one year as a medical corpsman in France during World War I. At the war's end he returned to Cincinnati, where he taught at the Conservatory before going to New York City for further study in 1921. In 1923–24 he studied in Paris under the famed piano pedagogue Isador Philipp.

Anderson came to Louisville in 1926 to join the piano faculty of the old Louisville Conservatory of Music. In 1931 he married Barbara Tunnell, a poet who, as Barbara Anderson, later published two novels. When the University of Louisville formed a School of Music in 1932, Anderson served on its faculty before accepting the position of dean. Under his leadership, the school moved in 1948 from its small quarters on the Belknap Campus to Gardencourt, the estate of Mattie Norton.

From 1944 to 1952, he was chief music critic for the *Courier-Journal*, where his gracefully written, enlightened reviews reflected his passionate commitment to the highest ideals of his profession. In 1953, Anderson and his wife visited seven South American countries as a goodwill ambassador for the United States State Department. During the tour, he lectured, in both Spanish and Portuguese, on American music.

Dwight Anderson served as dean of the University of Louisville School of Music from 1937 to 1955. During that time, he not only made the School of Music a vital part of Louisville's musical life but was instrumental in the formation of other institutions that have since enriched Louisville's artistic scene. He was instrumental in bringing Robert Whitney to Louisville to found the Louisville Orchestra in 1937. He was a founder and early director of the Louisville Chamber Music Society, which celebrated its fiftieth anniversary during the 1997–98 season. In 1949, he established an opera department at the School of Music under the leadership of German-born Moritz Bomhard, who organized the Kentucky Opera in 1952. Anderson retired as dean in 1955 but continued to teach piano at the school until his death.

In 1926, when Anderson chose to make Louisville his home, most musicians aspired to live in cities with a long musical tradition, such as New York, Boston, Philadelphia, or Cincinnati. But Anderson, as he explained in a 1944 interview, always had what he called "the decentralization bug. I have never seen any sense in musicians ganging up in the congested areas. They should get out to where they are needed, and build more discriminating performers and audiences in smaller cities." Because Anderson practiced what he preached, he established standards that continue to bear fruit in Louisville's arts life. Louisville's musical and theatrical organizations flourish because they attract artists who have left the congested areas to work where they are needed.

William Mootz

ANDERSON, MARY (b Sacramento, California, July 28, 1859; d Worcestershire, England, May 29, 1940). Leading actress of the theater. Mary was born to Charles Henry and Marie Antoinette (Leugers) Anderson. The family moved to Louisville the following year. Anderson's father, who was born in England, enlisted in the Confederate army at the outbreak of the Civil War and died in 1863.

In 1867, her mother married Dr. Hamilton Griffin, who strongly encouraged Mary's dramatic efforts. She was educated at St. Michael's School, Ursuline Academy, and Presentation Academy, but at age fourteen was allowed to leave school and study at home.

On November 27, 1875, at the age of sixteen, Anderson made her stage debut, appearing as Juliet in a benefit performance of Shakespeare's *Romeo and Juliet* at Louisville's original Macauley's Theatre. This launched a career that was to be spectacular and, by theatrical standards, brief. For fourteen years Anderson performed around the United States and abroad in roles both classical and contemporary. She first appeared on the New York stage as Pauline in the 1877 production of *The Lady of Lyons*. One of her favorite roles was that of Galatea in *Pygmalion and Galatea*, which she played for the first time in 1881. Success fol-

Mary Anderson as photographed by Edward Klauber.

lowed success.

In 1883 Anderson made her London stage debut, captivating audiences as Parthenia in *Ingomar*. Her triumph, professionally and socially, was unprecedented. As a result, she spent most of the next five years in England. Finally returning to the United States in 1888, Anderson performed as Perdita in *A Winter's Tale*. On March 7, 1889, she collapsed on stage, ill and exhausted, and shortly thereafter retired from performing. She was not yet thirty years old.

In June 1890, Anderson married lawyer Antonio de Navarro, and the couple settled in the English countryside. They had two children, Elena and Jose. Anderson wrote her memoirs, *A Few Memories*, in 1896 and collaborated with Robert S. Hichens in the dramatization of his novel, *The Garden of Allah*, which was produced in New York in 1911. She maintained close ties with Louisville through the years, donating property she owned near Floyds Knobs, Indiana, to the Franciscan Order for the Mount St. Francis Seminary. She was an honorary life member of Louisville's ARTS CLUB, which received annual Christmas greetings from her until her death. The Mary Anderson Theater, on the west side of FOURTH ST. between BROADWAY and Chestnut St., was named in her honor.

See Mary Anderson, *A Few Memories* (New York 1896); John E. Kleber, ed., *The Kentucky Encyclopedia* (Lexington 1992); J. Stoddard Johnston, ed., *Memorial History of Louisville* (Chicago 1896).

Kenneth Dennis

ANDERSON, OLOF, JR. (b Louisville, December 1899; d Louisville, April 14, 1987). Presbyterian leader. Anderson was the son of Olof A. and Carrie L. (Johnson) Anderson. At the University of Virginia, where he earned a B.A. degree, he studied architecture and then worked four years in his family's lumber business before attending LOUISVILLE PRESBYTERIAN THEOLOGICAL SEMINARY. In 1927 he was awarded a B.D. degree from the seminary. In 1927 and 1928 he did postgraduate work at Oxford and Edinburgh Universities.

One of Louisville's best-known Presbyterian ministers, Anderson served as pastor of the Harvey Browne Memorial Presbyterian Church for eleven years, from 1949 to 1960. Under his pastorate the congregation grew from a small ST. MATTHEWS neighborhood church to the largest congregation in the state. Prior to that post he was pastor at Kentucky churches in JEFFERSONTOWN, Frankfort, Lebanon, and Richmond.

In 1960 Anderson became executive secretary of the Louisville Presbytery of the Presbyterian Church in the United States (Southern). The second executive secretary in the presbytery's history, he was elected without opposition in 1959 and served nine years until his retirement in 1969. He was moderator of the Kentucky Synod and Transylvania Presbytery, and chairman of the synod's education committee for three years.

Anderson played a major role in both the CIVIL RIGHTS and peace movements in Kentucky. From 1964 to 1965 he was chairman of the Allied Organizations for Civil Rights in Kentucky, a group that worked for the passage of a public accommodations law in the 1964 General Assembly and sponsored a civil rights march of ten thousand on Frankfort in March 1964. He also served as chairman of the Louisville Peace Council, a nonsectarian organization of various peace groups; was a member of the Louisville Area Council on Religion and Race; and was a board member of the Kentucky Council on Human Relations. In 1950 he received an honorary doctor of divinity degree from Centre College, where he had been a frequent guest speaker.

Anderson married Martha Ward Jones, a native of Monticello, Kentucky. They had three daughters: Mary, Lanier, and Ann Stewart. After his death, his body was donated to the University of Louisville School of Medicine.

See *Courier-Journal*, April 15, 1987; Louis B. Weeks, *Kentucky Presbyterians* (Atlanta 1983).

ANDERSON, RICHARD CLOUGH, JR. (b Louisville, August 4, 1788; d Turbaco, Panama, July 24, 1826). Politician and diplomat. Anderson was the first child of RICHARD CLOUGH and ELIZABETH (CLARK) ANDERSON. In 1789 the Andersons settled on an estate some seven miles east of Louisville that Richard Senior christened SOLDIER'S RETREAT. A tutor taught Richard Junior and his sisters, and in 1800 he was sent to Albemarle and King William Counties in Virginia, where he attended a private school. In 1802 he entered the College of William and Mary. After graduating in 1804 he read law in Williamsburg, Virginia, and Frankfort, Kentucky, before returning to William and Mary to complete his legal studies. In 1809 he returned to Louisville, practicing law and speculating in land. He also became involved in politics and served in the state legislature in 1812–16 and 1821–22, and in the United States House of Representatives from March 4, 1817, to March 3, 1821. While in Congress he chaired the committee on public lands. He was chosen speaker of the house for the 1822 session of the state legislature. He made his mark at both the state and national levels, especially being noted for his debates and speeches. On January 27, 1823, he was appointed minister plenipotentiary to Colombia (at that time a union of New Granada (Colombia), Ecuador, and Venezuela known as *La Gran Colombia*), in the administration of President James Monroe and Secretary of State John Quincy Adams, both friends of Anderson. The new minister and his family arrived in Colombia in July 1823 and slowly traveled to the capital of Bogotá, arriving there in December. In October 1824 he negotiated the United States' first treaty with a Latin American republic. Anderson was appointed one of the American delegates to the Panama Congress of Nations in 1826. While on his way to the meeting in Cartagena, he died of yellow fever. His remains were returned to Kentucky, and he was buried in the family cemetery at Soldier's Retreat.

Anderson married his first cousin, Elizabeth Clark Gwathmey, daughter of Owen and Ann Clark Gwathmey, on December 1, 1810, in Jefferson County. They had eight children, but only three—Elizabeth, Arthur, and Anita—survived their father. Elizabeth Gwathmey Anderson died in January 1825 in Colombia. After her death, Anderson briefly returned to the United States to place his children in school and under the care of the Gwathmey family in Louisville.

A diary Anderson kept sporadically from 1814 to 1826 is an informative and sometimes insightful account of life in Kentucky, Washington, and Colombia in the early 1800s. He is generally recognized as a man of great promise and character who may have risen to greater office in the service of his state and country had he not died prematurely.

See Alfred Tischendorf and E. Taylor Parks, eds., *The Diary and Journal of Richard Clough Anderson, Jr., 1814–1826* (Durham, N.C., 1964); Ellis Merton Coulter, "Richard Clough Anderson," *Dictionary of American Biography* (New York 1928).

James J. Holmberg

ANDERSON, RICHARD CLOUGH, SR. (b Hanover County, Virginia, January 12, 1750; d Jefferson County, Kentucky, October 16, 1826). Soldier, farmer, and businessman. Anderson was born at his family's estate,

Goldmine (also appears as Goldmines). He was the son of Robert and Elizabeth (Clough) Anderson. The family was of English, Welsh, and perhaps Scottish heritage. He received a sound education but reportedly loved the outdoors, preferring to hunt, follow the hounds, and ride rather than concentrate on his studies. A wealthy merchant named Patrick Coots reportedly was impressed with Anderson's outdoor abilities and offered him a position with his firm. Anderson accepted, against his father's will, and from the age of sixteen until the outbreak of the Revolutionary War he served as supercargo on merchantmen traveling from the American colonies to the Caribbean and England.

When hostilities erupted between Great Britain and her North American colonies in 1775, Anderson sided with the patriots and joined the Hanover County militia, serving as quartermaster. On January 26, 1776, he received his commission as captain of the company of Hanover County regulars, and on March 7 he entered the continental line as a captain in the Fifth Virginia Regiment. Over the next five years Anderson served in the Fifth, Sixth, First, and Ninth Virginia Regiments, respectively, and rose to the rank of lieutenant colonel. He served in both the mid-Atlantic and Southern theaters of the war and participated in the battles of Trenton, Brandywine, Germantown, Monmouth, Savannah, and Charleston. He was wounded at Trenton on January 2, 1777, and while recuperating in a Philadelphia hospital contracted smallpox. On October 9, 1779, during the American assault on the British line at Savannah, Anderson was again wounded and, in falling from a parapet, received a rupture that bothered him for the rest of his life. In May 1780 the American army at Charleston surrendered, and Anderson spent the next nine months as a prisoner of war. He was paroled in February 1781. From this point accounts of his military service differ. Records state that he retired from the army in February 1781, but various accounts, too numerous to ignore and seemingly supported by reliable information, state that he joined the staff of the Marquis de Lafayette upon being exchanged and then assisted Gov. Thomas Nelson of Virginia in organizing the militia during the siege of Yorktown. He was one of the charter members of the Society of the Cincinnati in 1783, and in that same year was appointed surveyor general of Virginia military lands in Kentucky and Ohio, a position he would hold until his death.

Anderson moved to Kentucky in 1783 or 1784 and established his office in Louisville. In 1789 he moved to a tract of land he had purchased some seven miles east of Louisville. He christened the estate Soldier's Retreat. The original log cabin was replaced in the early 1790s by a stone mansion, and Soldier's Retreat became well known for hospitality and hosting famous guests such as James Monroe and Andrew Jackson. Anderson was an early leader in the county and state but did not seek office himself. He represented Jefferson County as a delegate to the 1788 Kentucky statehood convention, as an elector for state senators in 1792, as a presidential elector in 1793, and as a justice of the peace. His duties as surveyor general and personal business, including building a seagoing ship named *Caroline*, demanded much of his time. The merchant ship venture failed when the *Caroline* was lost at sea after only one voyage, and land speculation caused Anderson financial problems. He died at Soldier's Retreat and is buried in the family cemetery there.

Anderson had served in the army with several of George Rogers Clark's brothers, and when he moved to Louisville he and Clark became friends. The relationship with the Clark brothers became even stronger on November 24, 1787, when Anderson married their sister Elizabeth Clark (1768–95). Richard and Elizabeth Anderson had four children: Richard Junior, Ann, Cecilia, and Elizabeth. On January 15, 1795, Elizabeth died, never having recovered from giving birth to their fourth child the month before. Anderson married Sarah Marshall (1779–1854) on September 17, 1797. They had twelve children: Frances, Maria, Larz, Robert, William, Mary Louise, John Roy, Hugh Roy, Charles, Lucelia Poindexter, Matthew, and Sarah. Four of his sons—Richard Junior, Larz, Robert, and Charles—achieved national recognition.

See Ellis Merton Coulter, "Richard Clough Anderson," *Dictionary of American Biography* (New York 1928): 270–71; Edward Lowell Anderson, *Soldier and Pioneer: A Biographical Sketch of Lt. Col. Richard C. Anderson of the Continental Army* (New York 1879); Lawrence L. Barr, *A New Look at the History of Soldier's Retreat* (Louisville 1979).

James J. Holmberg

ANDERSON, ROBERT (b Jefferson County, Kentucky, June 14, 1805; d Nice, France, October 26, 1871). Military officer. Anderson was born at his family's plantation, Soldier's Retreat. His parents were Richard Clough Anderson, a Revolutionary War officer, and Sarah (Marshall) Anderson. An 1825 graduate of the United States Military Academy at West Point, Anderson served in the Black Hawk War (1832), and in 1837–38 during the Second Seminole War (1835–42). In the Mexican War (1846–48) he was wounded and breveted major.

In December 1860, when South Carolina seceded from the Union, Major Anderson was sent to Charleston to command the island forts in the harbor. Anticipating attack, he moved his seventy-man unit on December 26 from Fort Moultrie to the more-defensible Fort Sumter. There they held out for nearly four months without supply shipments from the North. On April 11, 1861, on word that the newly installed Lincoln administration was

Robert Anderson, from a Matthew Brady negative.

sending a shipload of provisions, the Confederate forces in Charleston demanded Anderson's surrender. He refused, and the bombardment of Fort Sumter began on April 12.

After thirty-four hours of almost continuous shelling—when food supplies had reached the vanishing point—Anderson surrendered. His command was evacuated by ship to New York. Anderson immediately became a hero in the North. Commissioned a brigadier general by President Lincoln, he was placed in charge of recruiting Union troops in Kentucky and later headed the Union army's Department of the Cumberland. Ill health, however, forced him to retire from active duty. At the end of the conflict Anderson was selected to hoist the United States flag over the ruins of Fort Sumter.

He married Eliza (Bayard) Clark of Georgia in 1845; they had four children: Robert, Eba, Maria, and Sophie. Seeking better health, Anderson went to the south of France in 1870, where he died. He is buried at West Point Military Academy.

See Eba (Anderson) Lawton, *An Artillery Officer in the Mexican War, 1846–47: Letters of Robert Anderson* (New York 1911); Thomas McArthur Anderson, *Monograph of the Anderson, Clark, Marshall and McArthur Connection* (n.p., 1908).

George H. Yater

ANDREWARTHA, JOHN (b Falmouth, England, August 25, 1839; d Austin Texas, November 7, 1916). Architect. Andrewartha came to Louisville in 1865. There he married Louise Oakshott and had four sons, John, Lewis, William, and Ernest, and one daughter, Florence. He moved to Austin, Texas, in 1881 and was one of eight architects in the Texas State Capi-

Life Saving Station (with observation tower) of the United States Coast Guard. Louisville Wharf at the foot of Second Street, 1921.

tol competition.

While in Louisville, Andrewartha designed residential, commercial, and civic buildings. He is best known for his Italianate CITY HALL on the northwest corner of Jefferson and Sixth Streets, completed in 1873 and reflecting a dramatic example of the sense of dynamic growth that was infusing postwar Louisville. He won a contest to be the City Hall's designer for which he received five hundred dollars.

Andrewartha designed the 1874 Alms House, Female High School, the National Hotel, the 1872–73 Elliott residence (later the Louisville Military Academy), the Jockey Club House at the Louisville Jockey Club (later CHURCHILL DOWNS) in 1875, and the 1876 Courier-Journal building, all demolished. In addition, he designed several "commercial palaces" on Main St. and numerous residences.

He is buried in Oakwood Cemetery in Austin.

See William Elton Green, "'A Question of Great Delicacy': The Texas Capitol Competition, 1881," *Southwestern Historical Quarterly* 92 (Oct. 1988): 245–70; Samuel W. Thomas, *Views of Louisville since 1766* (Louisville 1971); Robert J. Elliott papers, Filson Club Historical Society, Manuscripts Division, Louisville, Kentucky.

Elizabeth Fitzpatrick "Penny" Jones

ANDREW BROADDUS WHARF BOAT/LOUISVILLE LIFE SAVING STATION. The United States Life Saving Service was established in 1848 to provide aid and rescue to shipwrecked mariners; the first stations were located along coastal waters. The Steamboat Inspection Act of 1852, enacted in response to the occurrence of many boat wrecks and deadly explosions, set standards for boat construction and their operators and created a federal system of inspection, with an inspection point at Louisville. Later, in response to advocacy for lifesaving stations on the western rivers, the first was established at Louisville due to the great danger in navigating the FALLS OF THE OHIO. The floating station was built at JEFFERSONVILLE, INDIANA, and placed in operation on November 4, 1881, at the foot of Second St. Known as Life Saving Station No. 10, its crew performed rescue duties by rowing out in skiffs to save passengers and cargo stranded on the Falls. The station crew provided valuable services to the Falls Cities well into the twentieth century, assisting stranded vessels, rescuing recreational boaters, grappling for bodies of drowned swimmers, fighting fires, aiding towboats, and retrieving cars that had skidded into the river from the wharf.

In 1902 the first station was replaced by another wooden-hulled vessel. The Life Saving Station and the Revenue Cutter Service were combined in 1915 to become the United States Coast Guard. Operations of the stations were expanded, and Louisville was made a Group Headquarters in the Coast Guard. The second Louisville station was replaced by the existing station vessel, a steel-hulled design similar in appearance to the one it replaced, with double-deck superstructure and lookout tower. It was built at Dubuque, Iowa, towed to Louisville, and commissioned in 1928.

During the PROHIBITION era of the 1920s, the Coast Guard was given enforcement responsibilities under the Volstead Act, and the crew of the Louisville Station transported agents to remote islands on the OHIO RIVER to search for and destroy illicit operations. In 1929, a Coast Guard report noted that, in the forty-eight years since the station began operations, "property valued at $6,500,000 has been saved, and more 7,000 men, women, and children have been rescued from watery graves. More than seven hundred bodies have been recovered by this little band of men, always alert and ready for the unexpected." The location of the station remained at the foot of Second St. from 1881 until construction began in the 1920s on the Clark Memorial Bridge and it was relocated to the foot of FOURTH ST. As requirements for Coast Guard assistance at the Falls diminished after construction of MCALPINE LOCKS AND DAM and due to personnel and budget cuts, the Louisville Station was "disestablished" on October 1, 1972. The station was declared surplus and transferred to the City of Louisville; it was renamed *Andrew Broaddus* in honor of a former mayor. Since the 1960s the *Broaddus* has served as wharf boat and offices for the operations of the *BELLE OF LOUISVILLE*, both of which are National Historic Landmarks.

A noted member of the station crew was Capt. JOHN "JACK" GILLOOLY, who, in a long career in the Life Saving Service, rescued more than six thousand people, earning him the title "Hero of the Falls." He entered the service around 1870, retired in 1917, and died in 1926. In his career he was awarded medals by the United States Congress and the Kentucky Legislature.

See Historical Files Louisville District, U.S. Army Corps of Engineers, Louisville.

Charles E. Parrish

ANGELA MERICI HIGH SCHOOL. Angela Merici High School, 1935 Lewiston Place, was a Catholic high school (grades 9–12) established by the Ursuline Sisters of Louisville in 1959 in southwest Jefferson County for the education of young women.

It was named for the foundress of the Ursuline Sisters, Saint Angela Merici, a prophet and reconciler. Angela Merici High School strove to be a community of faith founded on the values of freedom and responsibility, respect, and love for oneself and others. The first classes began in September 1959 with 135 students (90 freshmen and 45 sophomores) and 8 faculty members (7 sisters and 1 lay teacher). Sister Marjorie Burge was the first principal. The school was dedicated in 1960.

In 1962 Sister Carmel Price became principal and remained at Angela Merici High until 1968. In 1963–64 the school reached its highest enrollment with 653 students. Other principals were Sister Eileen Carney (1968–71), Sister Louise Willenbrink (1971–78), and Sister Paula-Klein-Kracht (1978–84).

In response to the 1980 recommendation of the Louisville Archdiocesan Task Force, Angela Merici and Bishop David High Schools began a cooperative study of the two schools, with the goal the merger of the two schools.

Voting machines were set up to determine a name for the new school. Care was taken to include all involved in the Angela Merici and Bishop David High Schools: administrators, faculties, other staff members, students, alumni/ae, parents, and the wider community. Rev. Thomas Duerr, head of the Catholic School Office, was involved from the beginning. The culmination of the efforts was Holy Cross High School, at 5144 Dixie Hwy., in September 1984. The old property at 1935 Lewiston Place currently houses the Flaget Center.

M. Concetta Waller

A.N. ROTH COMPANY. A.N. Roth Co., one of Louisville's oldest businesses, is located at 749 E Jefferson St. It has been operated continuously by four generations of the same family. Jacob Roth opened a tin shop at 1403 Story Ave. in 1866. He specialized in installing tin roofs and setting up and disassembling coal- and wood-burning stoves. At his death in 1897 his son Alfred N. Roth took over and expanded the business to include hardware items.

In 1945 Alfred's three sons, Karl P., Alfred J., and Frederick W. Roth, assumed control. They phased out the hardware business and expanded by adding commercial and industrial heating and sheet metal clients to the existing residential heating service. From 1945 to 1955 the company handled such jobs as the architectural metal installation at Ireland Army Hospital, Fort Knox, Kentucky, and the installation of duct work at the French Lick Sheraton Hotel in Indiana. Karl P. Roth participated in designing the first blower on the forced-air gas furnace manufactured by Bryant.

In 1971 Karl Phillip Roth Jr. took over operations and continues to be president and general manager. In 1978 he was joined in the business by his sister, Rose Mary Roth-Beckwith, as comptroller.

A.N. Roth Co. serves many residential, commercial, and industrial clients. The company has been recognized by awards from governors Bert Combs and Martha Layne Collins.

Audrea McDowell

APARTMENT BUILDINGS. Apartment dwelling in urban America by the nation's wealthier citizens is a phenomenon that dates back to the 1860s. While the urban poor had earlier been crowded into multistory tenements, competing demands on larger cities' limited space generated new proposals for upper-class living following the Civil War. However, smaller cities such as Indianapolis and Louisville had plenty of land for expansion and did not see their first apartment buildings for several more decades.

Louisville's first apartment building was the Rossmore, (later the Berkeley Hotel and demolished in the early 1980s) erected on Fourth St. just north of Broadway in 1893–94. The Rossmore was a five-story, twelve-unit block of flats constructed of masonry brick with stone and rusticated brick trim. The structure contained commercial space and a lobby on the ground floor, three floors of flats with adjoining servants' quarters for each, and storage space for the units on the top floor. The Rossmore was fully occupied almost immediately, inducing the owners to build an addition in 1899.

The Rossmore was quickly followed in 1897 by the St. James, another five-story block of flats located on St. James Court. Built by prominent local businessmen Theophilus Conrad, the St. James towered over the two- and three-story residences of the area until the two top floors were removed following a fire in 1912.

By 1905 the city could boast of more than ten apartment buildings; within another five years, seventy-five complexes existed in Louisville. Some of the most significant structures were the four-story Belvoir (1903) on Cherokee Pkwy., St. Charles Place (1901–02) on Second St., and the impressive eight-story Weissinger-Gaulbert Apartments (1903) at Third St. and Broadway. By 1912, 138 apartment buildings were listed in *Who's Who in Louisville*. The number increased, reaching 303 by 1928, when the onset of the Great Depression would end most apartment construction.

Examples completed before the end of the 1920s included the Thierman Apartments (1913) on W Breckinridge St.; the Puritan (1913) at S Fourth and W Ormsby; the Willow Terrace (1924) and the Dartmouth (1928), both on Willow Ave.; the Commodore (1929) on Bonnycastle Ave.; Hampton Hall (1925) on York St.; Tudor Terrace (1927–28) on Spring Dr.; and the nine-story Mayflower (1925) on W Ormsby Ave. The final high-rise erected before the Depression was the Cumberland, a nine-story complex built at Second and York Streets in 1930.

St. Charles Apartments, Second Street at Guthrie, 1919.

While the apartment was viewed as a solution to the problem of increasingly scarce housing near the city's business district, many of the multifamily residences were being constructed outside of the downtown area. Of the complexes listed in 1912, only about thirty had downtown addresses, while a majority were in Old Louisville and the Highlands. While almost no additional buildings were erected downtown before 1928, the western reaches of the city boasted of more than forty complexes, and the South End had about ten.

The Depression ended much of the middle- and upper-class apartment construction throughout the nation. However, the creation of the Public Works Administration's (PWA) emergency housing project in 1933 brought a new kind of complex to the Louisville area. Public housing projects soon began to dot the city's landscape and included Clarksdale, encompassed by Muhammad Ali Blvd., Liberty, Shelby, and Clay Streets; College Court at Seventh and Kentucky Streets; LaSalle Place at Seventh St. and Algonquin Pkwy.; and Beecher Terrace along Muhammad Ali Blvd. between Roy Wilkins Ave. and Thirteenth St. This trend continued through the 1940s and 1950s with the addition of several other projects such as Park DuValle's Cotter and Southwick homes, Sheppard Square in the Smoketown neighborhood, and Parkway Place in the Algonquin neighborhood.

To meet the post–World War II housing shortage, during the late 1940s and 1950s privately funded apartment construction resumed, although at a slower pace than during the boom years of the 1910s and 1920s. It would not be until the 1960s that apartment construction would once again accelerate. In 1956 only 196 units were built in the Louisville area. This figure would climb to 3,245 units by 1965, when two of every five new dwelling units being erected were in apartment complexes. Propelled by easily obtained financing for builders and the increased need for housing as the baby-boomer generation matured, apartment construction was concentrated on cheap land at the fringe of the city mainly along the Watterson Expressway between Newburg and Taylorsville Roads, the Brownsboro Rd.–Zorn Ave. area, the Highlands–Cherokee Triangle area, along Preston Hwy., and on Dixie Hwy. north of Valley Station. These were mainly middle-class dwellings.

By 1969 the percentage of apartments increased to 66 percent of new housing starts, and complexes popped up all over the county, not staying concentrated in any particular areas. While much of this new construction was between two and four stories high, Brown's Apartments (1962) on Bardstown Rd. stood high above the nearby Watterson Expressway. Erected by J. Graham Brown next to his Brown Suburban Hotel, the twelve-story apartment building was the first balconied skyscraper in the suburbs and beaconed to drivers for years with its well-known neon "Brown's" sign on top.

While a majority of the new complexes were being built in the suburbs, some of the most impressive examples in the 1960s were once again erected downtown. Completed in 1963 at Fourth and York Streets, The 800, a twenty-nine-story balconied skyscraper, was the city's tallest building upon completion. With an exterior of glass panels, white marble, and porcelainized aluminum panels tinted an eye-catching aqua, the owners hoped that the structure would attract residents back to the downtown corridor. In 1997 a $15-million renovation plan was proposed to convert The 800 into luxury condominiums. Trinity Towers (1962) was a seventeen-story steel-and-brick complex at Third and Guthrie Streets. Representing a new experiment in living, the Trinity Temple Methodist Church had undertaken the project and placed its church facilities in the structure along with its residential units.

Other significant projects during this time included the twelve-story Glenview on Brownsboro Rd. at Lime Kiln Ln., the Mallgate Apartments located on Sherburn Ln. behind the Mall St. Matthews, as well as the conversion of the Kentucky Hotel at Fifth St. and Muhammad Ali Blvd. into the Kentucky Towers apartments. The Treyton Oak Towers, at Oak between Second and Third Streets, was one of many retirement and life-care communities that began to proliferate in the 1980s.

Although the boom slowed by the mid-1970s, apartment construction began to pick up again by the early 1980s, propelled both by a resurgence in downtown living and additional suburban complexes. One of the most ambitious downtown projects was the 209–unit Crescent Centre, located between Second and Third Streets between Broadway and Chestnut St. and funded with a $24.5-million financial package consisting of loans from the state, city, and county. Although many of the living units were eventually rented, the complex also contained commercial space at the street level that failed to attract any businesses. Because of this, the property was foreclosed upon in 1990, leaving the state, city, and county with a $7.5-million loss. A much greater success was the up-scale, twenty-story 1400 Willow (1980), located just to the east of downtown in the Cherokee Triangle next to the Dartmouth and the Willow Terrace.

Several other Louisville area projects during this time involved the transformation of older commercial structures into new dwellings. Examples of this included the Billy Goat Strut Apartments at Main and Hancock Streets. By 1998 the number of rental units in the Louisville area numbered over a hundred thousand. All of them are governed by city and county housing codes.

See "Apartment Development: Louisville's Catching Up," *Louisville* 14 (Jan. 1963): 13–14; *Courier-Journal,* Oct. 9, 1966, Jan. 18, 1970; George H. Yater, *Two Hundred Years at the Falls of the Ohio* (Louisville 1987).

Carolyn Brooks

APPEL'S. In 1883 Appel's Menswear began in its original location at 440 W Market St. The locally owned and operated business was founded by Louis Appel, who died in 1936. By that time his three sons, Louis, Joe, and Sidney, were deeply involved in the store's affairs. The store, which in 1960 continued to identify itself as a haberdasher, occupied a four-floor structure at 425–27 S Fourth St. Beginning in 1929, the business brought into its product assortment various lines of women's sportswear. Appel's closed in late 1963. Sidney Appel completed his career in menswear as a salesman at Rodes-Rapier.

Kenneth L. Miller

ARCHAEOLOGY. Prior to 1967, little historical archaeology was accomplished in the city, but in the years from 1967 through 1997 archaeological knowledge of historic sites, both as standing structures and as former structure locations, has increased dramatically through investigations mandated by development projects.

Few excavated data are available for the period from 1777 to circa 1850, and the Civil War military presence remains relatively unexplored. On the periphery of the city, in urbanized Jefferson County, restoration of early-nineteenth-century Upland South plantation houses at Farmington, Locust Grove, and Riverside, and their dependencies, has generated much plantation or African American slave archaeology.

Outside Jefferson County, in city-owned Otter Creek Park, the "plain folks" Hoover log cabin was excavated. Here a simpler and traditional middle-class farming lifestyle was recovered in 1981 by University of Louisville (U of L) archaeologists. Post–Civil War transformations and developments from 1865 to 1930 have only recently been investigated, as represented by literature studies, oral-history interviewing, and archaeological survey in several urban neighborhoods.

Urban archaeology in the city of Louisville has grown together with U of L's legally required urban emphasis and the University of Kentucky's (UK) statewide mandate. Early urban archaeology within the city proper was generally fortuitous and unsuccessful and from 1967 to 1978 mainly recorded disturbance and loss. Today, questions of occupation patterns and consumer choice, as well as ethnic and status differentiation, dominate urban archaeological research and have been explored by the "neighborhood approach."

In 1782 Fort Nelson, Louisville's earliest settlement, was situated on the mainland east of Corn Island, but this waterfront was greatly altered by 1830. In 1978 a fortuitous but systematic exploration of the small Fort Nelson park at Seventh and Main Streets by U of L confirmed this loss. The park yielded no archaeological deposits. However, three 1870s brick cisterns were found on the site where Carter Dry Goods building was erected, now the Louisville Science Center. These structures lay twelve feet below the surface of Main St. Old building plans showed their existence, but they were cemented over in a basement renovation of ca. 1900. Transfer-print whiteware ceramics, patent medicine bottles, and a moderate-sized sample of butchered pig and cow bones were recovered during testing in 1979, and the cisterns were recorded and resealed.

Archaeology of the central business district has been variable, with several archaeological monitoring projects producing limited results. In the central downtown area, 1880s to 1920s construction impact of up to sixteen feet or more is not unusual. Very little of old Fourth Ave. was found by the U of L archaeologists beyond a residual arch, a wall fragment, and several acontextual artifacts dated 1864 to 1956, leaving no possibility for interpretation. The Galleria in downtown has a twenty-six–foot foundation and basement; this depth is enough to encounter Pleistocene sands anywhere in Louisville. Renovations in 1982 of the Jefferson County Fiscal Court Building ground floor yielded subfloor midden-filled trash pits (ca. 1830) and a possible cache of a handgun. Similar excavations in the basement of the Cathedral of the Assumption (1989-90) revealed a suite of artifacts and structures related to the daily life of religious leaders in the early nineteenth century. Later monitoring at One Commonwealth Place (1994) resulted in a mere handful of artifacts, with no data on archaeological or systemic context, where houses of the 1840s adjacent to the historic Brennan House (1868) on Fifth St. were removed.

Recently, however, 1995 excavations by UK archaeologists at the Kentucky International Convention Center expansion site (bounded by Jefferson, Market, Second, and Third Streets) recovered material from three nineteenth-century commercial building privies dating back to the 1850s. These privies produced a wide range of artifacts such as whole wine and whiskey bottles, sets of transfer-printed china, and food remains that revealed much about the consumer habits of people living and working in the heart of Louisville's commercial district from the 1840s through the 1880s. Combined with earlier work in Parkland, Russell, and Highland Park, the research conducted on nearly thirty privies revealed much about the importance and slow development of quality sanitation in Louisville from the early 1800s to the mid-1900s. In addition to providing a useful chronological baseline for further work, it demonstrated that politics and poor understanding of sanitation relegated Louisville to a dangerously poor health state.

City administrators were reluctant to allow

streets, parking lots, basements, and backyards to be torn up for archaeological exploration in historic areas. In 1983 a strategy was developed by U of L to overcome problems of loss and arbitrary urban excavation. Intensive archival searches and a survey of urban open spaces (vacant city tracts and parks), together with clearly threatened private historic sites, were conducted in a one-year project. Open localities of one acre to thousands of acres were investigated, with emphasis on historic archaeological sites in a broad range of city neighborhoods. Over twenty historic urban locations were initially surveyed or tested. In addition to some described below, these included several other privately owned historic sites and publicly acquired properties, such as the site of the 1780s to 1917 log cabin home of George Rogers Clark's parents (Mulberry Hill) and an 1840–1900 convent in the Russell neighborhood. Today a destroyed Mulberry Hill is included inside the boundaries of George Rogers Clark Park.

Archaeology in 1983 at the site of the transshipment village of (pre-canal) old Portland by U of L discovered the entire 1840s to 1880s waterfront residential/commercial area from the old cobblestone 1840 wharf to warehouses and residences for several blocks inland. The area had been preserved by flood alluviation (1937) and lack of development in this flood-prone area outside the Louisville flood wall. Here also was the 1840s house of Paul Villier's, an upper-class resident of the town, with the hewn-cedar log floor joists of the cellar floor intact, with many wine bottles scattered about one corner.

Commercial residence was observed archaeologically at the St. Charles Hotel (1850s), where the glazed tiles known to have been on the floors of the public rooms were in evidence, along with institutional-grade white ceramic dinnerware. The Portland Museum accomplished an archival study that identified houses, businesses, and street plans of this lively town just downriver from Louisville and the Falls of the Ohio River. The Portland wharf area is being actively curated as a major archaeological resource of nineteenth-century river life.

The Point neighborhood, a now extinct community, was formed on the point bar of Beargrass Creek's juncture with the Ohio River, east from the downtown area. Here in the 1820s to 1840s large, upper-class houses like the Paget House, whose environs were excavated in 1995–96, were followed by a series of lower economic class structures seen in residential and midden occurrences, which were sampled by U of L (1983), UK (1994), and other archaeologists in 1995 and 1996. Numerous artifacts reinforce the 1890s view of the area as a working-class neighborhood (1870s to 1914) built around river-associated enterprises. Cellars, house ghosts (packed floors under houses built on corner piers), trash pits, cisterns, and privy pits all produced an artifact inventory of cheap plain and transfer-print ceramics, wine and liquor bottles, a wide variety of patent medicine bottles, and artifacts ranging from doll parts to cut-glass droplets from bawdy-house chandeliers. The artifacts convey an impression of a lower economic type of residence and usage. Slightly to the east, on the main artery, River Rd., the Captain Bowles subdivision addition established in the 1870s was surveyed archaeologically and shown to have been lightly built before being abandoned in the 1937 and 1945 floods that caused the city to clear the Point. Farther along the road, the middle-class Thomas Jacobs farmstead (1880s) and an early tollhouse (1850s) at Zorn Ave. were explored archaeologically.

In 1979 it was learned from U of L's monitoring of urban renewal efforts in the Phoenix Hill neighborhood, directly adjacent and east of the central business district, that in the period of 1820–1900, eight-foot basements succeeded no basements or root cellars (1820–40s), and thence successively, twelve-foot (to 1865–70) and finally sixteen-foot basement depths for commercial buildings (post-1870). This depth succession often wiped out all prior indications of occupation. A series of middle- to lower-class residences was recorded in major portions of fifty-eight blocks of 1830–60s Phoenix Hill. Backyards retained trash pits, former privies, cisterns, and instances of horse or offal burial.

Industrial archaeology began in 1978 in the Butchertown neighborhood around Hadley Pottery. No pottery industry appurtenances were discovered, because the nineteenth-century building housed successive factories making candles, rope, mops, and, finally, saddles and girths. Later UK archaeologists discovered the Thomas Pottery (1850s-70s) in the Point. Findings included waste debris, rejects, and kiln furniture. Excavations conducted at the site of the downtown Lewis Pottery in 1997 uncovered the remains of a pottery kiln used in the manufacture of smoking pipes and stoneware during the 1840s. There was also evidence indicating that Louisville was the site of one of the first attempts in the United States to produce whiteware ceramics similar to English types. This was during the late 1820s.

Another historic industrial site, the 1809–17 Tarascon Mill on Shippingport Island, was destroyed by fire in 1898. Subsequent major land alterations (1948–56) took all but a corner wall fragment, identified by archaeologists in 1980. This grist-sawmill was replicated in Cherokee Park by the contemporary, but smaller, Ward's Grist Mill built in 1817 and operated for less than ten years. This Highlands neighborhood mill ended as a "cornhouse of low resort" (liquor still) in 1830, but the ruin was protected as a "picturesque folly" by Frederick Law Olmsted, designer of Louisville's parks, in 1908. Test excavations by U of L of thirty square meters, combined with a smaller test by the Louisville Archaeological Society in 1971, showed that the mill was thirty-two feet on a side, with a height of four to six feet of dressed limestone foundation walls and all corners still in situ. Traces of the dam upstream of Big Rock in Beargrass Creek, the millrace, and location of the south wall indicated that the wheel was overshot and powered by water funneled from the dam. About a hundred artifacts were found. These corroborated the mill's early date and also that mill traces were further leveled in 1914.

In a portion of the California neighborhood, an 1840s glassworks specializing in plate glass was discovered and tested in 1983. Numerous pieces of green-glass slag and brick were recovered from the fired oven area, and some structural details were recorded. Elsewhere, although Schroeder's Spice & Stomach Bitters bottles from the 1835–75 Louisville Glassworks are quite well known from historic sites, the search for their site of origin was frustrated by its probable location under the "Spaghetti Junction" of Interstates 65 and 64.

U of L investigations of Old Louisville's 2111 S First St. house and environs on the university's Belknap Campus in 1989–91 provided observation of the transformations of a large Italianate residence from an upper-middle-class railroad manager's home (1858–70), to rental apartments (1870–88), to boardinghouse (1888–98), to house of "ill repute" (1898–1932), to Art Center (1932–1970s), to derelict (1970–92), to Arts & Sciences honors program center (1993–). Examination of the extensive and rich exterior architectural detail and archaeological recovery of well-made and carefully laid walkways and patios create the impression of upper-middle-class ostentation, at least at time of construction. Based upon two 1900 photographs, later episodes of occupation apparently managed to preserve a tarnished gentility. Artifact recovery in excavations in 1989 generally corroborated dates in the chain-of-title search. This helped to understand transformations in the Old Louisville neighborhood and University of Louisville campus close to the center city.

However, often it is in the gray areas of lower- and middle-class residence and the uniformity of a simplicity of lifestyle in the city's semiperipheral neighborhoods that the anthropology of urban archaeology lies. In Iroquois Park, now on the residential suburban edge of the city, U of L discovered in 1983 an early farmstead (1840–70) known only as a ruin on an 1894 plat map. The survey found the house and a line of stone sill supports indicating a barn situated on a north-facing hogback. This farmstead, in contrast to the Hoover site at Otter Creek, gave insight into a lower-class urban peripheral ruralism in a refuge area generally considered useless to farming. Such conditions were rarely recorded in the nineteenth century. Archaeological investigation in 1992–93 of a tenant farmstead (Hall Site 1860–1913) within the agriculturally marginal former Wet Woods, or Standiford neighborhood (Louisville International Airport), allowed insight into the decline of this also peripheral area. Ultimately peripheral farmsteads gave way to a planned residential/industry community. Highland Park was a late-nineteenth-/early-twentieth-century suburban worker subdivision adjacent to the railroad yards. Documentary and archaeological investigation of seventeen house lots and associated privies and cisterns in this mostly lower- and middle-income working-class subdivision showed patterns of migration, ethnicity, local consumerism, and development of class structure.

In more inner-city neighborhoods, archaeology in the Parkland/Russell neighborhoods has yielded significant amounts of data. In Parkland, an excavation of privy and cistern provided a huge late-nineteenth-century assemblage from occupation of a large multiple-family house from 1897 through the 1950s. The house had a fairly rapid turnover of lower-class to middle-class, blue-collar tenants. In the Russell neighborhood, a research plan was constructed whereby a sample of nineteenth-century redevelopment properties could be stratified by ethnicity (black/white), residence/type (architecture), resident status (lower working class, middle working class, upper-middle-class white-collar), commercial/industrial sites, and public/administrative sites. Finally, fifty house (or structure) lots were culled to sixteen and ten, and then tested. In 1994 five lots or lot sections containing four residences and one drugstore and several features, including seven privies, were subjected to data recovery excavations. The area's diverse ethnic background from the 1850s to early 1900s was demonstrated, along with the quality of sanitation in Louisville in the same period. While the Parkland chronology and class divisions were replicated by the archaeology in Russell, much was learned about internal neighborhood population demographics heretofore encountered in Highland Park.

David Pollack (ed.), *The Archaeology of Kentucky: Past Accomplishments and Future Directions.* Vol. 2, Part Two Historical Period Context (W. Steven & Kim A. McBride, Frankfort, 1990; Symposium on Ohio Valley Urban and Historic Archaeology, *Proceedings of the Symposium on Ohio Valley Urban and Historic Archaeology* (Louisville 1983).

Joseph E. Granger

ARCHITECTURAL FIRMS. Architectural history professor Dr. John Coolidge, visiting Louisville from Harvard University in 1981, marveled at the "consistent character and flashes of excellence" exhibited by the city's architectural heritage. From the ornate mansions of Old Louisville and Cherokee Triangle to the diverse urban styles of Richardsonian Romanesque, Greek Revival, Art Deco, and Post-Modern, Louisville's built environment is a wonderful design mosaic created by the city's talented legacy of architects.

Over the past two hundred years, the practice of architecture in Louisville has evolved from simple shelters to elaborate, complex facilities. The city's architectural firms began as offices of one or two persons who used pen-and-ink sketches to illustrate their visions. Skilled carpenters and masons were relied upon to give depth to the details. Today, firms are technologically advanced, with computer-aided drafting (CAD) systems that produce numerous plots of documents at the push of a button. Most firms now average between ten and fifteen staff members, with some numbering close to forty, and one approaching a personnel level of two hundred (Luckett & Farley).

Prior to 1930 the title of architect was one of self-recognition. There was no regulatory license that limited the title's use. But it is clear that the vast majority who practiced this profession before 1930 did so with artistry and dedication toward improving the quality of life in Louisville through well-designed buildings.

The first substantial structure that established Louisville was the wilderness outpost known as Fort Nelson (1782) near Seventh and Main Streets. Richard Chenoweth built the fort, constructed under the command of Col. George Slaughter. After Fort Nelson, most buildings were strictly utilitarian for homes and for merchant purposes. A notable exception was the residence of John and Lucy Speed, known as Farmington (started in 1815), on Bardstown Rd. The house plan was possibly based on an unidentified drawing by Thomas Jefferson. Architectural similarities in the two plans and Lucy Speed's Virginia family connections to the Jefferson family give some support for this attribution.

The first chronicled resident architect was Hugh Roland (b 1795), who was listed in R.W. Otis's *The Louisville Directory* in 1832. Relocating to Louisville from Nashville, Roland designed the Catholic Chapel of St. Louis (1831) and the Louisville Hotel (1831), a Greek Revival design. In 1838 four architects were listed in *The Louisville Directory:* Roland, Gideon Shryock, J. Sterewalt *[sic]*, and Elias E. Williams (1791–1880), architect for the old U.S. Post Office and Custom House (1858), Third and Liberty Streets. Of this group, Gideon Shryock (1802–80) is the best-known early Louisville architect. Educated in Philadelphia, he studied in 1823 under William Strickland. Shryock rose to fame on his design for Kentucky's third state capitol (1830) in Frankfort. In attempting to relocate the state capital to Louisville, local officials commissioned him to create the Jefferson County Courthouse (1837–65). Shryock supervised construction of the acclaimed Greek Revival style for the Bank of Louisville (1836), now Actors Theatre, 320 W Main St., which was designed by architect James Dakin. A native of New York state, Dakin migrated south through Louisville before settling in New Orleans.

Henry Whitestone (1819–93) was Louisville's foremost architect in the nineteenth century; he founded a firm that continues today. Born in Ireland, Whitestone is credited with creating the "handsomest courthouse" in Ennis, County Clare, Ireland, which still stands today. He arrived in the United States in 1852 and collaborated in Louisville with Massachusetts-born architect Isaiah Rogers (1800–69). Rogers was known as the "father of American hotel design," and Whitestone supervised the construction of Frankfort's Capital Hotel for Rogers in 1853. Rogers was based in Cincinnati, while Whitestone lived in Louisville. They also teamed up on the expansion of the old Galt House and the renovation of the Louisville Hotel.

In 1857 Whitestone began his own firm, with offices located at Bullitt and Main Streets, near the current Riverfront Plaza-Belvedere. He was known for his residences such as the James C. Ford house (Second and Broadway, since demolished) and Landward house (1385 S Fourth St.). His best-known commercial work was the Louisville & Nashville Railroad office building (1877) at 131 W Main St. The Italian Renaissance style was his trademark. He also served as president of the Louisville Gas Co. from 1877 to 1885. Following his death, Whitestone's firm changed under the leadership of Dennis Xavier Murphy (1854–1933). In 1894 a twenty-four-year-old draftsman for the firm, Joseph D. Baldez, designed Louisville's world-famous symbol, the twin spires of Churchill Downs. Murphy changed the name of the firm to D.X. Murphy & Brother in 1890 and was joined in practice by brothers James Cornelius Murphy (1864–1935) and Pete W. Murphy (1868–1955). Two of their structures were the old Jefferson County Jail (1905) at 514 W Liberty St. and the former General Hospital on E Chestnut St. In 1962 the firm name changed once again to Luckett & Farley, named for then-owners Thomas Dade Luckett (1909–96) and Jean D. Farley (b 1927). This firm, now located at 737 S Third St., is believed to be one of the oldest architectural firms in the nation. Projects include the Kosair Pediatric Building (1994), Chestnut and Floyd Streets, and the Kentucky Farm Bureau headquarters (1988), Bunsen Pkwy.

Numerous architectural firms flourished in the late nineteenth century, providing the city a rich legacy of distinguished buildings. Many of these structures still stand, such as the former Louisville Medical School (1893), First and Chestnut Streets, and the former Carter Dry Goods Building (1878), now the Louisville Science Center, 727 W Main, both by architect Charles Julian Clarke (1836–1908). Mason Maury (1847–1919) created many fine residential structures as well as the Kaufman-Straus Building (1903), which is now part of the urban complex known as the Galleria. He also designed the city's first skyscraper, the Kenyon Building (1886), which rose a full six stories above Fifth St. near Main, and the former Louisville Trust Building (1891), Fifth and Market Streets. Brinton Beauregard Davis

(1862–1952) also built on a grand scale, with structures such as the Jefferson County Armory (1905), now the GARDENS OF LOUISVILLE, 525 W Muhammad Ali Blvd., and the Kentucky Home Life Building (1911), 239 S Fifth St.

In the early twentieth century a new generation of Louisville architects began to make its mark on the landscape. Thomas J. Nolan Sr. (1884–1969) founded his firm in 1911, concentrating initially on ecclesiastical, educational, and governmental facilities. Examples of early works include the Knights of Columbus building (1925), St. Francis of Rome (1929) on Payne St., and the Hardin County Courthouse (1933). The firm, now in its third generation, is continued by his grandsons, Thomas and Robert Jr. More recent projects include the former Life of Kentucky building (1970), Second and Main Streets; the Carmelite Monastery (1951), Newburg Rd.; Norton Hospital (1970), Chestnut and Brook Streets; and Kosair Children's Hospital (1986), Chestnut and Floyd Streets.

Alfred S. Joseph Sr. (1878–1973) and his brother, Oscar G. Joseph, began Joseph & Joseph in 1908, which produced projects such as the Rialto Theatre on S Fourth St. (demolished, 1969); the old Elks Club, Third and Chestnut Streets (later the Henry Clay Hotel); Republic Building at Fifth and Muhammad Ali Blvd.; Almsted Building, Market near Fourth; and the Joseph E. Seagram & Sons Distillery (1908) on Howard St. Oscar relocated to Los Angeles in the 1930s, along with his son, to start another firm named Joseph & Joseph. Recent projects include Brown-Forman's Forester Center (1989), 850 DIXIE HWY., which has received national preservation accolades.

Fred J. Hartstern (1903–84) worked in the architectural department of the old Louisville BOARD OF EDUCATION and became its chief architect in 1948. He was associated with another firm, Louis & Henry, for a brief period but had his own firm, Hartstern, Campbell, & Schadt (1964–78), which created over forty-five Jefferson County public school buildings such as Ballard High School and Moore High School in the 1960s and 1970s. SAMUEL M. PLATO (1882–1957) was an African American architect/builder who designed over forty U.S. post offices across the country. His Broadway Temple AME Zion Church, 662 S Thirteenth St., is a community landmark.

Beginning on August 28, 1930, the title *architect* became a licensed, regulated profession by the commonwealth of Kentucky. Louisville architects who were among the initial group of registered professionals include Ossian P. Ward (#2), W.S. ARRASMITH (#5), Hermann Wischmeyer (#6), Arthur Tafel (#7), Brinton B. Davis (#12), E.T. Hutchings (#16), and Thomas J. Nolan (#17). Louise Leland (#183) became the first registered female architect on January 4, 1938.

Frederick P. Louis (1910–92) and A. Read Henry (1911–94) formed Louis & Henry in 1939. Known for their modern approach to design, Louis & Henry quickly became a firm that gave many of Louisville's prominent businesses their signature appearance. The firm's projects include such notable structures as television studios for both WHAS and WAVE, PRESBYTERIAN THEOLOGICAL SEMINARY, South Central Bell, Kentucky Fried Chicken (KFC) headquarters, the new wing of the LOUISVILLE FREE PUBLIC LIBRARY, the LOUISVILLE WATER CO. headquarters (1998), and the new Jefferson County courts complex (1999). Principals Larry Leis and Rick Kremer continue the firm's mission.

The firm of Wischmeyer & Arrasmith was established in 1926 and, under the leadership of William Strudwick Arrasmith (1898–1965), and would evolve into one of Louisville's most recognized firms. Hermann Wischmeyer (1875–1945) opened the original practice in 1906, and it was renamed in 1937 to Wischmeyer, Arrasmith, and Elswick. W.S. Arrasmith was known nationally for his art deco–inspired Greyhound bus stations, which are now historic landmarks. He designed over a hundred terminals, including one in Louisville at Fifth and Broadway (now demolished). The firm is now known as Arrasmith, Judd, & Rapp. Focusing on healthcare and educational facilities, AJR projects include the Rudd Heart and Lung Tower (1995) of Jewish Hospital, Baptist East Hospital, and various contemporary parking garages, including two for the UNIVERSITY OF LOUISVILLE (Medical Center campus at Preston and Chestnut and on the Belknap campus on Floyd St.).

While most architects concentrate on commercial and institutional projects, one Louisville architect built his career solely on residential work. STRATTON HAMMON (1904–97) crafted stately classical homes, usually in the Georgian Revival style. His favorite design was a curved brick facade home on River Hill Rd. Other examples are located on Norbourne Blvd., Bow Ln., Orion Rd., and Lexington Rd. at Braeview.

The late twentieth century has continued to define Louisville's architectural heritage. Jasper Ward (b 1921) was a leading designer whose concrete-built structures were noted for their bold, sculptural forms. Ward's significant works included NEIGHBORHOOD HOUSE (1964), Portland school (1968), KENTUCKY SCHOOL FOR THE BLIND recital hall and music building (1977), and the City Blueprint building (1968). He collaborated on the University of Louisville Student Activities Center (1990) and the Sixth and Main parking garage (1990). Ward also was a strong advocate for comprehensive community planning and participated in various land-use planning efforts.

Founded in 1972 as Voight Chapman Martin and undergoing various name changes, the firm now known as Grossman Chapman Klarer gave contemporary flair to residences and ecclesiastical buildings, including the 1989 renovation of the FIRST UNITARIAN CHURCH (1871) at York and Fourth Streets and the BELLARMINE COLLEGE campus expansion (1985). The firm also won a local competition in 1984 for the construction of the Humana Conference and Fitness Center, Fifth and Market Streets. This competition resulted from the fact that no Louisville firms were involved in the national HUMANA TOWER competition. Stow Chapman's white modern townhouse (1978), 1444 Cherokee Rd., drew much attention in the historical context of the Cherokee Triangle neighborhood.

Carey Anderson opened the first African American registered architectural firm in 1980, and along with firms such as Potter & Cox (1977), Voelker Winn (1983), Tucker & Booker (1972), K. NORMAN BERRY (1971), Michael Koch (1983), Godsey & Associates (1967), and Bravura (1991) continue to create and expand Louisville's built environment. Projects such as the Ballet Building (Bravura, 1995, 315 E Main St.) and the Louisville Gas & Electric Corporate Tower (Tucker & Booker, 1989, Third and Main) represent the "consistent character and flashes of excellence" of today's Louisville architectural firms, founded upon their ancestry of Shryock and Whitestone.

Largest Area Architectural Firms (1999)

Luckett & Farley Architects, Engineers and Construction Managers Inc. (Louisville) nineteen architects
Nolan & Nolan Inc. (Louisville) fourteen architects
Arrasmith, Judd, Rapp Inc. (Louisville) ten architects
Tucker & Booker Inc. (Louisville) ten architects
Louis and Henry Group (Louisville) nine architects
The Estopinal Group Architects (Jeffersonville, Indiana) seven architects
Bravura (Louisville) six architects
META Associates (Louisville) six architects
Michell Timperman Ritz Architects (New Albany, Indiana) six architects

Kenyon building, 216 S. Fifth Street, 1927.

Bainbridge's Row, Jefferson Street, north side between Seventh and Eighth streets, 1940.

K. Norman Berry Associates Architects (Louisville) five architects
Godsey Associates Architects (Louisville) five architects
Potter & Cox Architects (Louisville) five architects
Scott/Klausing & Co. Inc. (La Grange, Kentucky) five architects
Voelker Winn Architects Inc. (Louisville) five architects

See *Business First Book of Lists* (Louisville, Oct. 26, 1998).

Stephen A. Wiser

ARCHITECTURE. Architecture in Louisville and the surrounding counties mirrors the pattern of building on the eastern coast of the United States in the late eighteenth and early nineteenth centuries. The late eighteenth century shows the influence brought by the early settlers, mainly French, Scottish, and English immigrants. As the nineteenth century progressed, the influence of the German immigrants, and to some extent of the Irish, and the Italian craftsmen became apparent. By the middle of the nineteenth century, Louisville's architects had embraced a variety of styles in keeping with the popular trends across the country.

In the latter part of the eighteenth century, settlers were coming to the Falls of the Ohio area from different parts of the East Coast and bringing architectural influences with them. For example, some settlers came down the Ohio River bringing influences from the German settlers in Pennsylvania, while transplants from Tidewater Virginia, many coming through Cumberland Gap, brought influences from England. French settlers came upriver and brought along their architectural influences. The building techniques and traditions of the time were influenced by the materials available and by the skilled labor that was available, be it free or slave. In addition, publications by English authors Stewart and Revett, *The Philadelphia Carpenter's Guide*, and later works by Asher Benjamin gave local owners and craftsmen examples and ideas to emulate and refine to their needs. With the many travelers coming down, as well as upriver, the area was never too far behind the architectural trends popular on the East Coast. For example, Locust Grove, ca. 1790, exhibits characteristics of Georgian architecture, although by then the East Coast had moved on to the Federal style.

Early architecture was simple, utilitarian, and often temporary until other buildings could be constructed. These early buildings were often built of logs or stone, which were readily available in the region. Brick structures were built early in the history of the area from brick fired on site with mortar made from the local limestone. Stone was plentiful, and limestone quarries were founded early.

A number of substantial houses, such as late-eighteenth-century Oxmoor, ca. 1784; Springfield, home of President Zachary Taylor, ca. 1795; Spring Station, ca. 1808; Ridgeway ca. 1817; and ca. 1815 Farmington with its Jeffersonian architectural roots, were built in the early period in the outlying county, while the core area of the city of Louisville took longer to develop in terms of substantial buildings. Early founding families, including the Hikes, Hite, and Herr families in Jefferson County, built a number of late-eighteenth- and early- and mid-nineteenth-century houses that still exist amid twentieth-century subdivisions. Various early utilitarian structures exist and show early building techniques such as the stone Wolf Pen Branch Mill and the stone Eight Mile house, probably built as a tollhouse, on Shelbyville Rd. Many early residences in the area have outbuildings such as smokehouses, springhouses, icehouses, slave cabins, barns, and kitchens built of stone, frame, and brick.

The river has always been a catalyst for building. The first structure in what is now downtown Louisville was Fort Nelson, built in 1781 in response to news of the planned British invasion of that same year. Some of the earliest buildings in the Louisville area were built in Shippingport, and, when the Louisville and Portland Canal was completed in 1830, many were destroyed. Other early stuctures were constructed in Portland, which had grown up below the Falls of the Ohio. Both Shippingport and Portland had early French influence in their buildings.

In Indiana early communities included Clarksville, chartered by George Rogers Clark in 1783; Jeffersonville, which began in 1802; and New Albany, dating from 1813. In these communities, the architectural trends followed the course of those in Louisville.

Settlements at Pond Creek, Mann's Lick, Shively's Mill, Flat Lick, Transylvania, Middletown, and Brunerstown (Jeffersontown) are shown on an 1819 map of Jefferson County. At the same time that Louisville was gaining residents, outlying communities such as Middletown and Jeffersontown were growing. Most of Middletown's early architecture is gone, but buildings such as the Federal-style stone house built ca. 1813 for Benjamin Head and the brick ca. 1804 Joseph Abell house retain the early character of the town, while other nineteenth-century buildings show the continuum of architecture, particularly in vernacular styles. Jeffersontown reflects its early history through a variety of structures.

The Louisville landing and riverfront area and Main St. once were the sites of log structures that gave way by the 1830s to substantial edifices on Main St., including the first Galt House and the late-Federal U.S. Branch Bank, both demolished, and the Bank of Louisville designed by James Dakin, ca. 1835, in the Greek Revival style. Main St. today has several blocks of cast-iron and other late-nineteenth-century buildings. Another Greek Revival building was the 1832 Louisville Hotel by architect Hugh Roland, who came to Louisville from Nashville. The former State Bank Building at E Main and Bank Streets in New Albany is a ca. 1837 Greek Revival-style structure with fluted Doric columns on the main facade and engaged pilasters on the side walls.

Early civic buildings included several different courthouses that were built and demolished. The extant ca. 1835 Greek Revival Jefferson County Courthouse, with its Doric portico, was designed by Gideon Shryock, who had trained with William Strickland in Philadelphia. It was completed about 1860 by ALBERT FINK and is the most imposing structure in downtown from the early period. Nearby, at Third and LIBERTY STREETS, is another pre-Civil War building, the Post Office and Custom House (known now as the LANDMARK BUILDING) completed in 1858 in the Tuscan-Italianate style under supervising architect of the treasury Ammi B. Young and local architect ELIAS E. WILLIAMS. Portland was the site of the elegant U.S. MARINE HOSPITAL, opened in 1852. The Greek Revival KENTUCKY SCHOOL FOR THE BLIND, now demolished, was completed by E.E. Williams in 1855.

Early homes in what became downtown Louisville were made of logs, but by 1810 at least one substantial two-and-one-half story brick house stood on Sixth near Cedar, the home of early innkeeper John Gwathmey. The townhouse on S Fifth St., built ca. 1829 by Rizon Butler and known for years as the OLD HOUSE RESTAURANT, is in the late Federal style. By the 1830s elegant three-and-one-half-story brick residences with Greek Revival details existed, such as E.T. Bainbridge's Row on Jefferson between Seventh and Eighth Streets. The unique ca. 1837 Grisamore-Tyler House in Jeffersonville exhibits both Federal and Greek Revival motifs. In Jefferson County many fine examples of Greek Revival residences exist such as Rosewell, designed by Isaiah Rogers and HENRY WHITESTONE in the 1850s, in the old Transylvania area near HARRODS CREEK.

Throughout the area are numerous examples of houses built in what cultural geographer Fred Kniffen calls the "I-style" house. These typically nineteenth-century houses are two-story, one-room-deep structures with interior or exterior chimneys, and were usually frame or brick, with an ell or wing added.

Churches were evident in the early period but the architecture was not very distinguished. In 1837 churches in a Gothic Revival mode were built for the PRESBYTERIANS (Sixth and Green, now Liberty St.), and EPISCOPALIANS (Sixth and Cedar). Churches for the METHODISTS, UNITARIANS, and CHRISTIANS graced downtown street corners, and Adath Israel synagogue, chartered in 1843, moved from its original location on Green St. to several sites in downtown. College Street Presbyterian Church, built by JOHN STIREWALT in 1867, unfortunately no longer stands.

CATHOLICS first worshiped in a church built in 1811 at Tenth and Main Streets. The Catholic CATHEDRAL OF THE ASSUMPTION on Fifth St. was built from 1849 to 1852 in the Gothic Revival mode by William Keely with a tower and spire completed by Henry Whitestone. Churches in the late nineteenth century followed the Gothic Revival mode, including the façade added to CHRIST CHURCH, CALVARY EPISCOPAL, and the UNITARIAN CHURCH at Fourth and York. Christ Church was renovated extensively in 1872 and still stands on its original 1824 location on Second St. Many fine church edifices exist throughout the area in a wide variety of styles. Early churches exist throughout Jefferson County, including the ca. 1845 LONG RUN BAPTIST, now in stabilized ruins in eastern Jefferson County near the SHELBY COUNTY line. On New Albany's E Main St., the Second Presbyterian Church with its classically inspired facade was built in 1852.

One of most significant industrial buildings in the area is the elegant, Corinthian-columned Louisville Water Works on River Rd., designed by engineer Theodore R. Scowden ca. 1858. The WATER TOWER with its zinc statues, all classical except for one of an Indian, was rebuilt after severe damage from the 1890 TORNADO. Other industrial structures such as the many distilleries, breweries, and cigarette manufacturing plants contribute to the architectural landscape. The ca. 1873 QUARTERMASTER DEPOT in Jeffersonville covers four city blocks and was designed by Montgomery C. Meigs, who is best known for his Pension Building in Washington.

In 1852 Louisville's best-known nineteenth-century architect, Henry Whitestone, came as the partner of Isaiah Rogers, known as the "Father of the American Hotel," to rebuild the Louisville Hotel in the 600 block of Main St. Whitestone, who had emigrated from Ireland where he had designed the Ennis Courthouse in County Clare, was a partner with Rogers on rebuilding the Galt House that burned in 1865, as well as the MONSARRAT SCHOOL at Fifth and York Streets. Whitestone was the architect of the opulent Galt House, completed in 1869 at First and Main Streets, known as Louisville's finest hotel for several decades. It was demolished in 1921 for expansion of the BELKNAP HARDWARE CO. Whitestone was the premier Louisville architect in the second half of the nineteenth century, designing Renaissance Revival and Italianate-style residences for James Coleman Ford, H.D. NEWCOMB, Silas Miller, Joseph Tompkins, and many others. The ca. 1868 BRENNAN HOUSE on Fifth St. is an excellent example of an Italianate-style townhouse.

In addition to his famous residences, Whitestone designed many commercial structures in downtown including the extant LOUISVILLE & NASHVILLE RAILROAD headquarters at Second and Main Streets, other Main St. warehouses, and the tower of CITY HALL. His designs were executed in the Renaissance Revival and Italianate modes with ventures in the 1870s into French Second Empire and Gothic-inspired designs. D.X. MURPHY, who started as a draftsman with Whitestone in the 1870s, took over the firm that continues today as Luckett and Farley Inc.

During the 1860s and throughout the nineteenth century, many other architects were also working in Louisville, such as JOHN ANDREWARTHA, from Wales, whose best-known structure is the 1873 Louisville City Hall with its sculptures of cows and pigs reflecting the importance of agriculture and the stockyards in the economy. Other architects included H.P. Bradshaw, Stancliff and Vodges, and McDONALD BROTHERS.

The three-story brick buildings, probably second- and third-generation structures, still standing on Main St. as shown on the birdseye view of 1855, were, with a few exceptions, replaced with "commercial palaces" designed in the 1860s, 1870s, 1880s, and 1890s by architects including Henry Whitestone, John Andrewartha, CHARLES J. CLARKE, Charles D. Meyer, W.H. REDIN, and MASON MAURY. These warehouse buildings of four and more stories, many of which had CAST-IRON fronts, or a combination of brick, stone, and cast iron, remain. The cast iron was manufactured at local foundries such as Snead & Co., and Barbaroux & Co. The pre–CIVIL WAR Pickett Tobacco Warehouse, which stood on the southwest corner of Eighth and Main Streets until 1996, had stylish brick pilasters. West of Ninth and Main Streets were the TOBACCO warehouses with their simple, low profiles and cavernous interiors.

An unfortunate architectural loss in 1979 was the 1876 *COURIER-JOURNAL* BUILDING, attributed to John Andrewartha and known later as the WILL SALES BUILDING, one of Louisville's few examples of the High Victorian Gothic style. It incorporated Second Empire features with its mansard roof and a highly detailed and contrasting brick-and-stone facade with iron embellishments.

Louisville has many small, vernacular cottages in brick and frame that are known as "SHOTGUN HOUSES." These narrow, long houses were built in the second half of the nineteenth century and the early twentieth century in many neighborhoods including BUTCHERTOWN, Portland, PHOENIX HILL, GERMANTOWN, PARKLAND, and the HIGHLANDS.

Some Louisville neighborhoods developed because of special economic reasons, such as Butchertown with the stockyards and meat-butchering. Other neighborhoods, such as CRESCENT HILL, formed around the 1853 Fair Grounds built specifically near the then-new railroad tracks. Architecture in Butchertown and Crescent Hill reflects vernacular structures of the nineteenth and early twentieth century including farmhouses, cottages, and shotguns in Butchertown, and bungalows in Crescent Hill. As in many early neighborhoods, residential and commercial structures stood side by side. The pumphouse and superintendent's residence at the Crescent Hill Reservoir, completed in 1879, are excellent examples of High Victorian Gothic architecture.

Communities beyond the city such as FERN CREEK and ANCHORAGE, incorporated in 1878, developed early along the turnpikes and later the railroad tracks, both of which brought people and goods to Louisville. Fern Creek and Anchorage each possess vernacular buildings of architectural interest from throughout the nineteenth and early twentieth centuries.

Although there had been expositions held

since 1872 in the Industrial Exposition Building at Fourth and Chestnut, nothing rivaled the inauguration of the Southern Exposition, opened by President Chester A. Arthur. In 1883 the Southern Exposition, celebrating Louisville's commercial vitality, began in the area that later became Belgravia and St. James Courts. The exposition building was a massive wooden structure with educational displays, and lighted with electricity. Visitors traveled there by railroad or mule car.

After the exposition closed in 1887, the site was a prime location for development. Residential development had been marching out Brook, First, Second, Third, and Fourth Streets for several decades, with substantial residences in Italianate, Renaissance Revival, Richardsonian Romanesque, Colonial Revival, Eastlake, Neo-Grec, and other styles popular across America at this time. St. James Ct., platted on part of the exposition site, was an elegant neighborhood with a large greensward in the center with a cast-iron fountain. One of the first houses was a limestone mansion designed ca. 1893 in the Richardsonian Romanesque style by Arthur Loomis for Theophilus Conrad. No expense was spared on the highly decorated interior and exterior. It later became the Rose Anna Hughes Home for elderly Presbyterian women. Other houses and several apartment houses followed in a variety of eclectic styles, but none matched the opulence of the Conrad house. In Jeffersonville the Richardsonian Romanesque style is represented with Victorian characteristics in the 1890s Howard house overlooking the Ohio River.

Listed on the National Register of Historic Places and protected by a local preservation ordinance, the area now known as Old Louisville, which includes St. James and Belgravia courts, exhibits some of the finest late-nineteenth-century eclectic architecture in the region. The edifices are mostly two- and three-story brick-and-stone residences set relatively close together with deep yards in the rear. Stained and leaded glass doors and windows are part of the ensemble, with interiors of finely carved woodwork, staircases, and mantels. The streetcars that brought visitors to the exposition transported people to Old Louisville, expediting its development. At mid-century at the southern end of Old Louisville were the grounds of the House of Refuge, now the Belknap Campus of the University of Louisville (U of L). Several of the former House of Refuge buildings remain, reused by U of L, including the Gothic Revival chapel, which has been moved to a new site and used as a theater. The Administration Building, completed in 1929, was based on the rotunda by Thomas Jefferson at the University of Virginia.

Late in the nineteenth century, architects began designing structures using full brick-and-stone facades in the style known as Richardsonian Romanesque (named after nationally known architect Henry Hobson Richardson) that had swept the nation. Commercial examples include the Kenyon Building (demolished); the former Louisville Trust Building of 1891 designed by Maury and Dodd; the 1893 Levy Brothers building at Third and Market by Clarke and Loomis; the Columbia Building at Fourth and Main (Louisville's first skyscraper) by Cornelius Curtin; the American National Bank (later the Vaughan Building) by H.P. McDonald at Third and Main St.; the former University of Louisville Medical School, completed in 1893 and designed by C.J. Clarke, at First and Chestnut; and the Chesapeake and Ohio freight terminal at Preston and Main Streets.

As the population of Louisville grew after the Civil War, residents began to move to the streetcar suburbs such as the Henning-Speed Subdivision now known as the Cherokee Triangle. The flood of 1884 also contributed to the migration to the hills on the eastern perimeter of the city. The eclecticism in architecture that was beginning to take hold across the United States was also quite prevalent in Louisville and was manifested in these new suburbs. Some of the new houses continued the use of the Italianate design, but classical and colonial details were also popular. Residential styles were influenced by the 1876 Centennial Exposition in Philadelphia when the Colonial Revival style was introduced. Its use became even more pronounced in Louisville and the surrounding area from the influence of the Columbian Exposition in Chicago in 1893 that utilized classical details. As the twentieth century dawned, houses incorporating details of the Arts and Crafts movement and the Prairie-School style were built in the Highlands and Cherokee Triangle neighborhoods and in St. James Ct.

New Albany's Main St. exhibits a fine panorama of early-, mid-, and late-nineteenth-century styles, including the ca. 1847 Stoy-Moody House with Greek Revival details, Gothic Revival and Italianate structures, and an excellent Second-Empire residence, the ca. 1868 Culbertson Mansion. E Main St. in New Albany presents a textbook case of nineteenth-century residential architectural styles in America.

The advent of the Louisville & Nashville Railroad in 1850 brought a new type of architecture to Louisville, the railroad station. Early stations have been demolished, although vernacular depots with new uses remain throughout the county in Anchorage, Buechel, and other communities. The Richardsonian Romanesque style L&N station, completed in 1893 and designed by F.J. Mowbray, still stands at Broadway and Tenth Streets and is now used as a transportation center by the Transit Authority of River City (TARC). The L&N shops and yards with their utilitarian buildings covered many acres south of the station and included a roundhouse.

Even before the twentieth century arrived, Louisville's architecture was on a par with cities throughout America. Local architects had access to national periodicals that influenced their work. The Kaufman-Straus building, designed by Mason Maury, was built in 1903 on the site of the first Louisville Free Public Library, and its facade is now part of the downtown Galleria. The striking design of Maury's building recalls the architecture of Chicago, which was then the arbiter of architectural taste, according to most critics. The former Jefferson County Jail, completed in 1905 by the firm of D.X. Murphy and Brothers and now housing Jefferson County offices and court facilities, is unique with its vertical emphasis. The Murphy firm also designed the famous twin spires grandstand at Churchill Downs in 1894, replacing John Andrewartha's Gothic Revival clubhouse and the original grandstand from the 1870s.

Downtown Louisville turned its back on the river as it grew and expanded south toward Broadway, with taller buildings dwarfing the earlier nineteenth-century structures. In 1905 the Seelbach Hotel, designed by Frank M. Andrews, with its Beaux Arts classical details and unique tiled Rathskeller by Cincinnati's Rookwood Pottery, opened its doors at Fourth and Walnut (now Muhammad Ali Blvd.). The new Louisville Free Public Library, with its Beaux Arts classical limestone facades and built with funding from the Carnegie Foundation, was designed by George Tachau and Lewis F. Pilcher on York St. and opened in 1908. A concrete addition in the "brutalism" style was added in 1969. Several Louisville neighborhood libraries such as the Western branch and the Highlands branch were built in the early twentieth century with classical exteriors. The Jeffersonville Public Library, endowed by the Carnegie Foundation, was completed in 1903 in a classical style by Arthur Loomis. The classically detailed New Albany Public Library, also a Carnegie library, was completed in 1904, according to plans signed by Clarke and Loomis.

By the 1920s the center of attention had turned to Broadway, where the Brown Hotel opened at Fourth St. in 1923. Other architecturally significant structures were the atmospheric Loew's Theatre (1928) on Fourth St. by John Eberson, the YMCA, the Weissinger-Gaulbert Apartments at Third and Broadway, and the Heyburn Building at Fourth and Broadway. Also in the area, at Fourth and Kentucky, is the 1929 Municipal Auditorium with its Beaux Arts classical design by the New York firm of Carrere and Hastings.

As Louisville's population grew in the twentieth century, classical revival residences and bungalows were designed for the Highlands, Southern Parkway neighborhoods, St. Matthews, Crescent Hill, and other neighborhoods across the area. Architects including Brinton B. Davis, D.X. Murphy, Joseph and Joseph, E.T. Hutchings, Fred Morgan, Arthur Smith, J.J. Gaffney, Thomas J. Nolan, Arthur Tafel, Ossian P. Ward, and Stratton Hammon designed these residences.

The best-known African American architect and builder in Louisville was SAMUEL PLATO, partly self-taught and partly trained through correspondence courses. He designed Steward Hall at SIMMONS UNIVERSITY Bible College (later the LOUISVILLE MUNICIPAL COLLEGE), numerous post office buildings, churches, and residences.

The J.B. Speed Art Museum was designed in a classical revival mode by Arthur Loomis and was built from 1925 to 1927, one of his last buildings. It has had numerous additions over the decades by architects such as Brenner, Danforth, and Rockwell of Chicago; Robert Geddes of Princeton, New Jersey; and Peter Rose.

In the 1930s a new type of transportation-related architecture, pioneered by a Louisville architect, was the intercity bus station. Greyhound Lines hired the Louisville firm of Wischmeyer, Arrasmith, and Elswick to design a modern, sleek station at Fifth and Broadway to help market bus travel. WILLIAM ARRASMITH then developed Art Deco–style trademark stations for Greyhound across the country. Although the 1937 Louisville station was demolished in 1970, some of these stations still stand in Washington, D.C., and Evansville, Indiana, adaptively used for other purposes. Art Moderne or Art Deco styling had been used earlier for the terminal at BOWMAN FIELD in the late 1920s. The Art Deco entrance to the George Rogers Clark Memorial Bridge at Second and Main Streets was designed in 1929 by Paul Cret. A late Art Deco structure was the COURIER-JOURNAL and Louisville Times building, completed in 1948 at Sixth and Broadway.

The old post office at Fourth and Chestnut, completed in 1893, was demolished in 1943. A new classically styled Post Office and Federal Building had been constructed in 1930 on Broadway at Sixth.

In 1963 the construction of the twenty-nine–story 800 Apartments at Fourth and York brought modern high-rise residential living to downtown. The suburban skyline was augmented in 1965 by the fifteen-story Lincoln Income Life Building designed by Frank Lloyd Wright's successor firm, Taliesin Associated Architects.

The Liberty Bank on Jefferson St. between Fourth and Fifth Streets exhibited the first curtain wall construction in Louisville in 1960. A return to the Ohio River waterfront was punctuated with the construction of the First National Tower in 1972 at Fifth and Main Streets, a forty-story glass-and-steel tower designed by Harrison and Abramowitz of New York. American Life and Accident Insurance chose Ludwig Mies Van der Rohe for a signature Cor-Ten steel structure completed in 1973 on the Riverfront Plaza. The RIVERFRONT PLAZA and the BELVEDERE had been built over the 1976 I-64 expressway to ameliorate the damage of cutting off the city from its original lifeblood, the Ohio River. The University of Louisville School of Medicine, designed by Smith, Hinchman, and Grylls of Chicago, was constructed of concrete in the style known as "brutalism" in 1968.

The cast-iron, brick-and-stone buildings and warehouses on Main St., composing the West Main Street Preservation District, achieved a renewed life in the 1970s with adaptive uses for the JUNIOR LEAGUE OF LOUISVILLE, the Museum of Natural History and Science (now LOUISVILLE SCIENCE CENTER), law and architecture offices, restaurants, and shops. The 1983 KENTUCKY CENTER FOR THE ARTS with its brick and mirrored façade is a sharp contrast to the earlier buildings.

The Postmodern age arrived in Louisville with the choice of architect Michael Graves in a 1982 competition for the HUMANA Building, completed in 1985, with its richly colored marble, gold-leaf details, and other sumptuous materials. Louisville's downtown skyline was augmented by the advent of the AEGON CENTER completed in 1992 by architect John Burgee.

Architecture in Louisville has for the most part followed the stylistic tendencies of architecture in America, and some of Louisville's buildings rank among the nation's finest.

See Theodore M. Brown, *Introduction to Louisville Architecture* (Louisville 1960); Elizabeth F. Jones and Mary Jean Kinsman, eds., *Jefferson County: Survey of Historic Sites in Jefferson County* (Louisville 1981); C. Julian Oberwarth and William B. Scott Jr., eds., *A History of the Profession of Architecture in Kentucky* (Frankfort 1987); Samuel W. Thomas, *Views of Louisville since 1766* (Louisville 1971); idem., *Louisville since the Twenties* (Louisville 1978).

Elizabeth Fitzpatrick "Penny" Jones

ARCHIVES. Many institutions and organizations in the Louisville area have established archives for the purpose of preserving their records and making them available to the public. Jefferson County created its archives in 1969 and in 1980 attached it to its historic preservation program to form an agency known as Jefferson County Historic Preservation and Archives (renamed the Jefferson County Department of Public History in 1999). The city of Louisville's archives was formed in 1978. Both of these important government repositories contain records dating from the town's frontier settlement in the late 1770s. The Jefferson County Public Schools also maintain an active archives and records management program, preserving records from the 1830s to the present. The LOUISVILLE FREE PUBLIC LIBRARY system maintains some historical manuscripts collections. A notable example is the Western Branch, which contains materials relating to Louisville AFRICAN AMERICAN history.

Colleges and universities in the vicinity have preserved their own records and, in most instances, have acquired other historical materials relating to their educational missions. The THOMAS MERTON Center, established in 1969 and located in the W.L. LYONS BROWN Library at BELLARMINE COLLEGE, contains the college archives and other special collections, most notably the personal papers, photographs, and other materials of Merton, Trappist monk and internationally known author. SPALDING UNIVERSITY maintains both an archives, begun in 1969, which includes college records and material relating to the Sisters of Charity of Nazareth, and the Edith Stein Center for Study and Research, which contains original manuscripts and first and special editions of the works of this renowned philosopher. The SOUTHERN BAPTIST THEOLOGICAL SEMINARY Archives, created in 1982, contains seminary records, papers of its founders, minutes of Baptist associations and conventions, and a Billy Graham collection. In 1950 the LOUISVILLE PRESBYTERIAN THEOLOGICAL SEMINARY Library began acquiring papers of its presidents and of selected faculty members, institutional records, area church records, and photographs.

The UNIVERSITY OF LOUISVILLE (U of L), which celebrated its bicentennial in 1998, established its principal archives and manuscripts repository in 1973. In addition to managing its parent institution's records, the University Archives and Records Center is known for its extensive Louisville urban history collections, nineteenth- and twentieth-century records of important businesses, cultural organizations, social service agencies, and churches, and the personal papers of political figures, scholars, women, and members of the Jewish and African American communities. The archives, part of the university libraries system, also administers the university's Oral History Center, preserving over thirteen hundred recollections of community leaders, members of ethnic communities, workers, business executives, and university students, faculty, and administrators.

Other U of L libraries maintain nationally significant historical collections as well. In the Ekstrom Library, the Photographic Archives contains the magnificent Roy Stryker collection of negative files and manuscripts of this noted photographer who documented American life in the 1930s, 1940s, and 1950s for the Farm Security Administration, Standard Oil of New Jersey, and Jones and Laughlin Steel. Many other collections document Louisville in the era of photography. Rare Books and Special Collections preserves papers of authors Edgar Rice Burroughs, Diane di Prima, Jesse Stuart, Hortense Flexner, and other literary figures.

The Margaret M. Bridwell Art Library contains papers of selected Kentucky artists. The Kornhauser Health Sciences Library contains records related to the early history of the U of L School of Medicine and the schools it absorbed, personal papers of area health professionals, and research materials gathered by the WORK PROJECTS ADMINISTRATION's Kentucky Medical Historical Research Project during the 1930s. The DWIGHT ANDERSON Memorial Music Library houses papers of Kentucky folklorist, ballad singer, and author Jean Thomas ("The

Traipsin' Woman") and those of several other musicians. The Law Library houses major collections of the papers of U.S. Supreme Court justices Louis Dembitz Brandeis (1856–1941) and John Marshall Harlan (1833–1911).

Chief among the area's private historical societies is the Filson Club Historical Society, established in 1884. It has built nationally renowned collections of maps, photographs, nineteenth-century Kentucky newspapers, artifacts, and genealogical materials. Its manuscript collections of Kentucky pioneer, antebellum, and Civil War–era materials are unparalleled. Of particular note are letters written by William Clark during the Lewis and Clark Expedition; the papers of the Bingham and Haldeman families, both of whom were associated with the *Courier-Journal;* and important collections relating to the upper South and the early Ohio Valley. Since 1926 it has published the *Filson Club History Quarterly.* Another area institution holding useful genealogical materials is the national headquarters of the Sons of the American Revolution, which encourages research on the era of the revolution. As is the case with the Filson Club, nonmembers are permitted access to its resources by paying a small fee.

Among the religious groups having archives in Louisville is the Ursuline Sisters of the Immaculate Conception, whose archive contains materials predating the congregation's arrival in Louisville in 1858. The Louisville Sisters of Mercy Archives, housed at St. Catherine Convent on E Broadway, contains records dating from the order's arrival in the city in 1869. The archives of the Archdiocese of Louisville was established in 1994, but its records date to 1808. The Kentucky Baptist Convention's archives in Middletown, established in 1987, contains administrative records and minutes of the state's Baptist associations. The Temple and other area synagogues preserve their minutes and related records, while both the Jewish Community Center's Israel Naamani Library and the University of Louisville Archives contain useful materials on the history of one of Louisville's most prominent and influential religious groups. The archives for the Sisters of Charity of Nazareth, located forty miles southeast of Louisville, contains records dating to 1812.

Some area companies and institutions maintain archival collections, usually in connection with their records management activities. Notable examples include the Brown-Forman Corp., Cave Hill Cemetery, Churchill Downs, the Kentucky Derby Museum, the J.B. Speed Art Museum, Papa John's International, Tricon Global Restaurants, and the Louisville Water Co.

At Fort Knox, thirty-seven miles southwest of Louisville, is the Patton Museum of Cavalry and Armor. It contains the personal papers of several U.S. Army generals and other soldiers, and photographs and other materials documenting the history of the fort, tank warfare, and the career of Gen. George S. Patton. Also at Fort Knox is the U.S. Armor School Library, which contains personal reports of military engagements and other materials.

Several important archival collections related to Louisville have found their way to repositories in other states. Among them is the outstanding collection compiled by Reuben T. Durrett, a founder of the Filson Club, which was sold to the University of Chicago after his death in 1913. Lyman C. Draper assembled a unique collection of materials related to Kentucky and the American frontier for the State Historical Society of Wisconsin, where they remained after his death in 1891.

Most Louisville-area archival repositories are staffed by professional archivists. They provide essential services to researchers from their metropolitan area and from around the nation and the world.

William J. Morison

ARISTIDES. The golden-red chestnut won the first Kentucky Derby, which was then one and one-half miles in length, on May 17, 1875, by one length over Volcano in a time of 2:37 3/4. It was the fastest time for a three-year-old to that date. Owned and bred by H. Price McGrath of the McGrathiana Stud Farm in Versailles, Kentucky, the offspring of Leamlington and Sarong defeated fourteen other horses, including his stablemate and the favorite, Chesapeake. In front of an estimated ten thousand spectators at the Louisville Jockey Club (now Churchill Downs), Aristides captured the lead at the half-mile marker and did not relinquish it to capture the $2,850 prize and the sterling-silver Derby trophy. The winner was ridden by African American jockey Oliver Lewis and trained by the famous African American trainer Ansel Williamson, who was the track's leading trainer for the spring meet. Williamson is believed to have started training about 1845, and he remained active until the late 1870s; he died in 1881. After establishing record times for the two-miles-and-a-furlong and two-and-a-half-mile distances, Aristides was retired at age six to an unsuccessful stud career. He died in St. Louis in 1893.

See Brownie Leach, *The Kentucky Derby Diamond Jubilee* (Louisville 1949); Lynn S. Renau, *Racing around Kentucky* (Louisville 1995); George H. Yater, "The First Kentucky Derby," *Louisville* 25 (April 1974), 57–58, 101–11.

ARMSTRONG, DAVID LOVE (b Hope, Arkansas, August 6, 1941). Jefferson County judge/executive, Louisville mayor. The son of Lyman Guy Armstrong Sr. and Elizabeth (Evans) Armstrong, he was reared in Madison, Indiana. He graduated from Madison High School in 1959. After attending Hanover College for three years, he transferred to Murray State University, where he received a B.S. degree in 1966. He earned his juris doctorate from the University of Louisville School of Law in 1969 and has done postgraduate work at the University of Nevada, Harvard Law School, and the National College of District Attorneys at University of Houston. He married Carol Smith Burress on November 29, 1963, and they have two children, Shannon and Bryce.

Armstrong's legal and public service career began in 1969 when he entered private practice in the Louisville firm of Frockt and Benovitz. In 1970 he formed his own firm, Turner, McDonald, & Armstrong, and accepted appointment as assistant prosecutor in the Louisville Police Court. In 1971 he became Jefferson County juvenile court judge, serving until 1973 when he was appointed administrative law judge for the Kentucky Department of Insurance and the Jefferson County Board of Health. In 1975 he was elected Jefferson County commonwealth's attorney on the Democratic ticket. After serving two terms, he was elected Kentucky attorney general in 1983. In 1987 he ran for lieutenant governor but lost. In 1989, after practicing for two years with the Louisville law firm of Wyatt, Tarrant, & Combs, he was elected Jefferson County judge/executive.

Upon taking office, Armstrong corrected a $15-million budgetary shortfall and a schedule of bonded indebtedness that threatened the county's long-term financial stability. He implemented a combination of spending cuts, fee increases, and personnel reductions that returned the county to a sound financial footing. He also initiated a broad range of innovations in virtually every sector of county government. These included establishment of the Office for Women; initiation of the Cornerstone 2020 comprehensive land use plan; creation of Victim Information and Notification Everyday (VINE), the nation's first automated, twenty-four–hour-a-day system to notify crime victims that perpetrators have been released from jail; and creation of more than forty-five hundred jobs at Jefferson Riverport International, making it the sixth-fastest-growing industrial park in the nation. He increased the land holdings of the Jefferson Memorial Forest. He also spearheaded efforts to preserve and restore the historic Farnsley-Moremen home (now Riverside, The Farnsley-Moremen Landing), which resulted in the designation of a three-hundred acre Jefferson County Historical Landmark District.

In December 1997 Armstrong announced his candidacy for the office of mayor. In the May 1998 Democratic primary he defeated alderman Tom Owen by the narrow margin of 1,504 votes out of more than 35,000 cast. He crushed Republican Bill Wilson and the other minor party candidates, receiving more than 75 percent of the popular vote. Armstrong took office on January 1, 1999, to serve a four-year term.

Armstrong was elected president of the National Council of Elected County Executives, 1997; vice chair of the National Association of Attorneys General, 1984; and president of the

Greyhound bus station, southeast corner Broadway at Fifth Street, 1928. William S. Arrasmith, architect.

National District Attorneys Association, 1982. He served on President Ronald Reagan's seven-member Task Force on Violent Crime, resulting in over fifty federal legislative changes to fight crime.

Carl E. Kramer

ARMSTRONG AGENCY INC. The Armstrong Agency Inc., presently located at 721 Main St., SHELBYVILLE, is an insurance company founded by George A. Armstrong in 1877. In those days, Armstrong serviced the insurance needs of SHELBY, SPENCER, OLDHAM, and parts of Jefferson Counties from a horse-drawn carriage. As the insurance business grew, he saw a need for a local insurance agents' association, and in 1890 he publicly advocated the idea. This was the progenitor of the present-day Independent Insurance Agents Association of Kentucky.

Armstrong stayed active in business until 1914, and at the time of his death the agency was acquired by his brother-in-law, S.B. Moxley. Moxley owned and operated the agency until 1932, at which time Lloyd Pollard purchased an interest in the firm. Later, in 1936, James J. Hackworth, who had worked for the firm as a solicitor, bookkeeper, and policy writer, also became a partner in the business. Still later, in 1942, Hackworth would serve as president of the Independent Insurance Agents Association of Kentucky.

Moxley retired in 1936. Hackworth and Pollard remained partners in the business until Hackworth eventually, bought out Pollard's interest. In 1982 Neil S. Hackworth, the son of James, became owner of the business. In 1986 the firm acquired the Taggert Insurance Agency. Then, on April 1, 1999, Hackworth sold the Armstrong Agency to Bates Insurance Agency Inc., whose main office is in Louisville.

ARRASMITH, WILLIAM STRUDWICK (b Hillsboro, North Carolina, July 15, 1898; d Louisville, November 30, 1965). Architect. Born to Thomas and Mary (Strudwick) Arrasmith, he had a brother, Thomas, and two sisters, Carol and Anne. Arrasmith attended the University of North Carolina and graduated from the University of Illinois in 1921 with a bachelor of science degree in architecture. That same year he married Elizabeth Beam. They had one child, Anne.

Arrasmith moved to Louisville in 1922 and worked for several architects before he formed a partnership with Herman Wischmeyer in 1929. That firm became Wischmeyer, Arrasmith, and Elswick and was responsible for the design of the Federal Land Bank, the Scottish Rite Temple, and the Bingham and Girdler residences.

Arrasmith served in the Army Reserves and commanded a company of the Civilian Conservation Corps. He entered WORLD WAR II in February 1942 as the commanding officer, area engineer, and contracting officer for the design and construction of Camp Atterbury near Columbus, Indiana. He was promoted to major in the Corps of Engineers and served in a combat engineer regiment in the Fifth Army in Italy and North Africa. He was a staff planner and mapper for the 1943 beachhead invasion of Salerno, Italy, followed by the battles of Anzio and Cassino. He won three battle stars and was discharged in November 1944 as a lieutenant colonel.

After the war he returned to Louisville and formed the Arrasmith and Tyler partnership but eventually went out on his own as W.S. Arrasmith. In 1963 he joined with Arnold M. Judd to form Arrasmith and Judd. In 1965 Graham W. Rapp joined the partnership, and it became Arrasmith Judd Rapp Inc.

Among his design projects in Louisville were the police department headquarters, the state highway department building located at the Fairgrounds, the Cotter-Duvalle School, the UNIVERSITY OF LOUISVILLE Science Building, the BOWMAN FIELD administration building, and the Greyhound Bus terminal on the southeast corner of Fifth St. and BROADWAY. He also collaborated with a Chicago firm on the design of the 800 Apartment Building. During the FLOOD OF 1937 he designed a PONTOON BRIDGE to connect the downtown area with the dry HIGHLANDS.

He became interested in Greyhound Bus terminals and invented a process for coloring the enamel with which they were covered. He designed more than sixty-five Greyhound terminal buildings including the terminal in Washington D.C., which was built in 1939 and called the "Grand Central Station of the motor bus world" by Jim Lehrer of the Public Broadcasting Service television network.

In 1964 Arrasmith joined the board of directors of the METROPOLITAN SEWER DISTRICT. He died at home in Louisville and is buried in Resthaven Memorial Park.

See Mary Caldwell, "Greyhound," *Louisville Eccentric Observer*, (Dec. 5–18, 1991); *Courier-Journal*, Dec. 1, 1965.

Hope L. Hollenbeck

ARTS CLUB OF LOUISVILLE. The club was founded in 1920 by a group of artists and civic leaders as an organization for all the arts. Its membership would include, as reported in a Louisville newspaper in December of that year, "Those who are interested in the arts, and those who have contributed to art interests." By January 1921 membership had reached 273. As membership continued to grow, it was limited to four hundred, with a waiting list.

Among charter members were poet CALE YOUNG RICE, who was the first president, and his wife, ALICE HEGAN RICE, author of *Mrs. Wiggs of the Cabbage Patch* (1901); artist CHARLES SNEED WILLIAMS; Mrs. J.B. SPEED, founder of the SPEED ART MUSEUM; and Mrs. MORRIS BELKNAP, of the hardware business family.

Although the visual arts, LITERATURE, and THEATER have been the strongest elements in the Arts Club; MUSIC, dance, PHOTOGRAPHY, ARCHITECTURE, and the culinary arts have also been included. For many years the club maintained an art gallery with rotating exhibits. It also sponsored the biennial Bluegrass Painting Exhibition, which drew works from professional and amateur artists in the region. The Corneille Overstreet Competition, a biennial music event open to students in area schools, was begun in the 1960s and continues to award prize money and a chance to perform at the UNIVERSITY OF LOUISVILLE School of Music.

Membership through the years has included Louisville mayor WILSON W. WYATT; pioneer radio station manager Credo Harris; bookstore owner W.K. Stewart; theatrical director BOYD MARTIN; musician Frederic Cowles; writers ELEANOR MERCEIN KELLY, Dorothy Park Clark, and Isabel McMeekin; artists NORMAN KOHLHEPP, Mary Spencer Nay, and Lennox Allen; and architect FREDERIC L. MORGAN.

The Arts Club's first headquarters was at 314 W Chestnut St. in the Flexner Building. It remained there until 1935 when it moved to the Hotel Henry Watterson on W Walnut (now

Muhammad Ali Blvd.), its home for some thirty years. Subsequent downtown quarters were in the Heyburn Building and Theater Square, both at Fourth and Broadway. In 1990 the Arts Club moved to the Water Tower on River Rd., home of the Louisville Visual Art Association. Club members have always met on Sunday nights for a meal and a program such as a Gilbert and Sullivan operetta or a poetry reading. For many years, programs were held every Sunday. With decreased membership in recent years, dinner meetings are held only on the second and fourth Sundays of each month.

In 1998 there were forty-two members in the Arts Club of Louisville. Although the decline in membership may be attributable to the growth of professional arts organizations in the city, from theater to dance, the Arts Club continues to be a viable force in Louisville's arts community.

See *The Arts Club*, 50th anniversary booklet (Louisville 1970); "The Arts Club Bulletin," May 1964 and Dec. 1968; "Bluegrass Painting Exhibition" booklet, 1982.

Gregg Swem

ARTS IN LOUISVILLE, THE SOCIETY FOR THE. The Society for the Arts was founded and chartered in September 1955 as a nonprofit organization for the promotion and stimulation of interest and participation in the various arts in Louisville. The founders were several first-chair solo players under the direction of Leo Zimmerman, a young painter recently returned to Louisville from five years in Paris. He had heard that Louisville was experiencing an "arts renaissance." Although burgeoning modestly, the renaissance seemed to him somewhat less than it might be encouraged to become.

A master plan for a stimulation of interest in Louisville's arts evolved. It was based on the publication of an informative and educational arts magazine with the subsequent organization of its subscribers into an association of active arts proselytizers. With the cooperation of numerous local arts organizations and arts-affiliated merchants offering special considerations to the membership at large, a varied group of some three thousand arts enthusiasts was enlisted within the first two years. An art gallery was opened in a historic carriage house near downtown Louisville. An art school for adults was established. A Linotype machine, foundry type, and a printing press were acquired.

An illustrated arts publication, the thirty-two-page monthly magazine of the arts, *Arts in Louisville Magazine,* began publication in October 1955 and was printed and distributed nationally through April 1958. Published were 237 major arts essays. Many local, regional, and national artists and writers contributed the many perceptive articles that appeared alongside editorials, arts calendars, previews, reviews, letters, and so forth. Being an all-volunteer mission, the magazine, later retitled the *Louisvillian,* was self- supporting through its advertising income and the modest membership dues.

The summer of 1958 saw the monthly magazine's replacement by the *Gazette of the Arts in Louisville*, a fortnightly six-page, tabloid-size newspaper that blazoned the arts news through 1959. Up-to-the-minute arts-publicizing graphic flyers were mailed to all members on a weekly basis after 1959.

December 1957 brought the opportunity to lease the historic Louisville Athletic Club building at Zane St. and Garvin Pl. Built in 1888 as Louisville's most fashionable club, it was a perfect setting for the society's purposes. There was space for a 132–seat intimate theater in which the "Arts in Louisville Players" would produce a smattering of exciting theater. Two spacious art galleries were lavished with continuing panoplies of the art creation of regional painters and sculptors.

The vast second floor, originally the gymnasium, was to become "The Great Hall." It was remodeled and equipped for seating and serving as many as 250 members at dinner. Evenings saw a variety of enterprises. There were local chamber-music nights, and numerous local groups played exciting weekend jazz. On occasion, big-name jazz weekends were staged with celebrities the likes of Dizzy Gillespie, Roy Eldridge, Coleman Hawkins, Ramsey Lewis, and Cannonball Adderley.

There were local poets' poetry-reading nights, in-the-round theater of the absurd, and occasional local ballet demonstrations. Then, there was the wine-cellar bar, down under, which featured folksingers, small music ensembles, and bunnies.

The society neither sought nor accepted handouts from government, business, or individuals. On principle, it paid its own way successfully through April 1963, when it was voluntarily closed down, citing staff cultural exhaustion.

The giant poplar-wood-frame building burned to the ground in May 1969.

Leo W. Zimmerman

ASBURY CHAPEL. Asbury Chapel is one of Louisville's oldest Methodist churches. Founded in 1845, it was named for prominent Methodist missionary Francis Asbury. Originally at the corner of Fourth and Green (Liberty) Streets, the church began as an African American congregation under the auspices of the Methodist Episcopal Church South. A second and entirely distinct congregation named Asbury Chapel, also associated with the Methodist Episcopal Church, South, worshiped at a one-room brick structure on Ohio St. from 1845 until 1936.

By the late 1840s, under the leadership of Rev. James Harper, the congregation had seceded from the Southern Methodists, affiliated themselves with the African Methodist Episcopal Church (AME), and moved to a new location at Ninth and Walnut (Muhammad Ali Blvd.) Streets. Harper was soon transferred to New Orleans by the AME hierarchy, and the church's leadership passed to Rev. Hiram R. Revels, who later moved to Mississippi and became the first African American to serve in the United States Senate.

Denominational membership, however, remained controversial. In 1851 a faction of the church, fearing the loss of church autonomy and property to the AME hierarchy, attempted to gain an independent status. Spearheading the effort was former pastor James Harper, who had since been dismissed from the AME denomination in New Orleans and had returned to Louisville to resume control of his old congregation. That dispute was taken to the Kentucky Court of Appeals, which decided in *Harper v. Straws* (1853) that the church facilities remained under the control of Revels, the recognized AME pastor.

Again in 1939 the church faced a similar controversy when a party under the leadership of Rev. W.E. Spillman attempted to withdraw Asbury Chapel from the AME denomination in order to assert greater control in the appointment of pastors. In *Clay v. Crawford* (1944), the Kentucky Court of Appeals reaffirmed the 1853 decision, granting the AME hierarchy the right to control church property and affairs (the dissenting faction later founded the Spillman Memorial Church). Since 1939 the church has been at its present site at 1801 W Chestnut St. In 1990 the chapel suffered damage in what police believed to be a racially motivated arson attempt.

See "Clay v. Crawford," *Reports of Civil and Criminal Cases Decided by the Court of Appeals of Kentucky,* vol. 298 (Lexington 1944); Ben Monroe, ed., "Harper v. Straws," *Reports of Cases at Common Law and in Equity Decided in the Court of Appeals of Kentucky*, vol. 14 (Frankfort 1854); *Courier-Journal,* Nov. 20, 1996.

Timothy L. Wood

ASHLAND INC. Ashland Inc. was founded in 1924 as Ashland Refining Co., the refining subsidiary of the Swiss Oil Corp. of Lexington, Kentucky. Ashland founder Paul G. Blazer was hired by Swiss Oil to find a refinery that would be able to process Swiss's Kentucky crude oil production. Blazer located a thousand–barrel-per-day refinery near Catlettsburg in eastern Kentucky and recommended its purchase to Swiss. After Swiss purchased the facility, Blazer was installed as general manager. After a few years of improving operations at the Catlettsburg refinery, Ashland Refining Co. purchased a second refinery along with an extensive Kentucky pipeline network. In 1936 Swiss merged into Ashland Refining Co., forming Ashland Oil and Refining Co. and offering stock to the public for the first time.

In 1998 Ashland merged its petroleum-refining and marketing operations with those of the USX-Marathon Group, creating a joint venture known as Marathon Ashland Petroleum LLC. Ashland owns 38 percent of the joint venture, which operates the Catlettsburg refinery; several terminals, including light products and asphalt terminals in Louisville; and numerous retail gasoline marketing outlets in Kentucky, including several in Louisville.

Ashland Inc. consists of four wholly owned businesses: Ashland Specialty Chemical Co. and Ashland Distribution Co., both headquartered in Columbus, Ohio; the Valvoline Co., based in Lexington, Kentucky; and APAC Inc. highway construction operations, headquartered in Atlanta, Georgia. In addition, Ashland has an ownership position in Arch Coal Inc., a publicly traded company that mines coal in Kentucky.

Ashland's involvement in Louisville dates to the company's rapid postwar growth era. The purchase of the Louisville Refining Co. in 1959 strengthened Ashland's presence in Louisville and brought facilities that would later prove invaluable in Ashland's development of the RCC® Process, patented refining technology that increases the yield of gasoline per barrel of crude oil refined. The RCC Process is being used by other oil companies, including Chevron Corp. and Statoil, the state oil company of Norway.

The Louisville refinery also served as a valuable fuel production site. When operating, the plant was the principal supplier of gasoline to the Louisville area. The refinery also supplied petroleum products to the greater Cincinnati area through a terminal in Covington, Kentucky. Economic considerations forced Ashland to halt crude oil processing at the Louisville refinery in 1983, and the plant was dismantled in a process concluding in 1996.

Ashland remains part of the Louisville economy. Ashland Distribution operates a major distribution center in Louisville, serving regional needs for industrial chemicals, solvents, and many products used in industrial production. Ashland serves retail customers through several Valvoline Instant Oil Change centers in Louisville and Jefferson County. Ashland also owns Equal Opportunity Finance, a minority enterprise small business investment company in Louisville.

See Ashland Inc. annual reports; Joseph L. Massie, *Blazer and Ashland Oil* (Lexington 1960); Otto J. Scott, *The Exception* (New York 1968).

ASSUMPTION GREEK ORTHODOX CHURCH. Eastern Orthodox churches are often identified by their national origin, such as Greek, Russian, or Antiochian, and are direct descendants of the early churches founded by the apostles of Christ in Jerusalem, Antioch, Rome, and Greece. All Orthodox churches are in communion with one another and consider themselves parts of the one true church. The first Orthodox church in Louisville (and Kentucky) was founded in 1925 by about twenty-five GREEK immigrant families. Assumption parish members initially worshiped in two small houses joined together at the current location on 932 S Fifth St. near Saint Catherine St. It was rebuilt in 1967 to seat 150, with walls graced by icons imported from Greece by the founding families, beneath an arched, wooden ceiling.

The Greek annual festival during the last weekend of June, one of the major outdoor festivals in Louisville, draws about twenty-five thousand visitors. In addition to church tours, it offers Greek food, drama, literature, folk dancing, and music. In March, many join the Greek community in a Glendi, a feast of food and dancing a week or two before Great Lent, a forty-day period in which the community concentrates on fasting and prayer in preparation for the great feast of Pascha (Easter).

Through intermarriage and the influence of converts, the church is moving away from a tight-knit, Greek-speaking community toward a more pan-Orthodox vision. In 1996 a mission church was established in Evansville, Indiana, formalizing a long-standing relationship with the Orthodox community there.

See Marios Stephanides, "The Greek Community of Louisville," *Filson Club History Quarterly* 55 (Jan. 1981): 5–26; Timothy Ware, *The Orthodox Church* (New York 1993).

Patrick Cowles

ASTRONOMY. A thousand years ago on a typical spring night, Native Americans looked out from the caves along the OHIO RIVER where Zorn Ave. is today to see the Great Bear rising in the sky over the forests of southern Indiana. Those frequent dark, crystal-clear night skies must also have greeted THOMAS EDISON as he left Louisville in 1866, fired for spilling battery acid at a Western Union telegraph office. When the SOUTHERN EXPOSITION opened in 1883, forty-six hundred of his glowing incandescent lamps suggested a brighter future for the city. First in the early 1890s with lamps supplied with gas piped from wells near Brandenburg and then in 1899 with brilliant electric arcs, lighting on the city streets soon obscured the Milky Way.

Yet as Louisville lost its night sky to growth and technology, its residents developed an interest in astronomy unusual for a city of its size. EDWIN HUBBLE, about to become the most famous astronomer of the twentieth century, moved to Louisville following the death of his father, John Hubble, in 1913. He lived with his mother, sisters, and brother at 1287 Everett Ave. in the HIGHLANDS and commuted to New Albany High School, where he taught Spanish, physics, and mathematics and coached basketball. Hubble did not remain in Louisville for long. He read astronomy while he monitored study halls and then escaped in 1914 to graduate school at Yerkes Observatory of the University of Chicago. During his time in Louisville he was seen looking at the stars with a small telescope and hiking the KNOBS of Indiana under the night sky.

Three years later the new hundred–inch telescope at Mount Wilson Observatory in California went into use. Hubble was soon there, and with it he discovered that other galaxies were moving away from our own, suggesting an expanding universe of which we were a small part. The announcement of his discovery came in 1931, and astronomy clubs formed in many large cities to promote the art and skill of telescope-making so that everyone could see galaxies for themselves. In Louisville small groups of amateurs were gathering at the UNIVERSITY OF LOUISVILLE, the YWCA, and the BOY SCOUTS of America utilizing telescopes they built themselves.

Under the influence of Dr. Walter Lee Moore (1898–1989), professor of mathematics at U of L, they joined together to form the Louisville Astronomical Society in 1933. The new organization set a goal to promote public interest and education in astronomy and soon decided that Louisville needed a public observatory with its own large telescope.

The unfinished mirror of the giant two-hundred–inch telescope destined for Mt. Palomar was successfully cast from Pyrex in late 1934. This new material would allow large telescopes to deliver images of high quality because their mirrors would not distort with small changes in temperature. Moore gave a series of public lectures to raise the money needed to purchase glass for Louisville's telescope. In 1936 the Astronomical Society ordered a twenty-one–inch-diameter Pyrex disk, to be made from the same formula as the two-hundred–inch. When it was delivered in 1937, society members built a machine to grind it to the proper shape just in time to be interrupted by the FLOOD OF 1937. What was expected to take three years, in the end took eighteen more years of dedicated effort and finished with Dr. Moore's careful work by hand to create a nearly perfect optical surface. Local companies including Schmutz Foundry, the LOUISVILLE & NASHVILLE RAILROAD, the Louisville Gas & Electric Co., and Murphy Elevator gave time and materials for the mechanical components needed to create a truly unique community telescope.

The Louisville Astronomical Society's telescope was placed on Moore's property at Finley Hill south of Iroquois Park in what was then a dark, remote part of the county, off the road known as Star Ln., which led to his home. When it made its debut, it was the largest telescope in the country open to the public for viewing, and about a thousand visitors attended an observation of Mars there in 1956. For fifteen years the Star Ln. telescope was operated by enthusiastic high school students, several of whom were to become professional scientists.

By the time Moore retired from his professorship in 1966, the area near Star Ln. was awash in lights from development. In 1972 the Astronomical Society closed Star Lane Observatory and donated their telescope to the University of Louisville. Given this remarkable asset, the University built a new facility at the Horner Wildlife Refuge in nearby Oldham County. It was dedicated in 1978 as Moore Observatory, and the rebuilt telescope was moved there to be used for instruction and research in astronomy. Moore Observatory now also houses a sixteen-inch robotic telescope that is remotely accessible to students taking classes on the campus in the city. The quest for dark skies continues today. The Louisville Astronomical Society is planning a new public observatory to be located in rural southern Indiana in the same area where Edwin Hubble took his outings years before. It is far enough from the city to be safe from its growth for a few more decades.

While the observatory provided hands-on experience for students and visitors, the Rauch Memorial Planetarium, which was added to the University's Belknap Campus in 1963, demonstrated the appearance of the night sky to many more, even in the daytime. Moore was the first director of the planetarium, and he helped establish it as a center for the education of school children about astronomy.

In 1997 growth of the J.B. Speed Art Museum adjacent to Belknap Campus necessitated razing the planetarium to make way for a parking garage. Strong support from the community for its contributions to educating young people encouraged a generous gift from the Gheens Foundation that made a replacement possible. The Gheens Science Center and Rauch Planetarium reopened in the fall of 2000 equipped with a new Spitz star projector and an electronic theater.

See Joel Gwinn, "Edwin Hubble in Louisville, 1913–1914," *Filson Club History Quarterly* 56 (Oct. 1982): 415–19; Donald Osterbrock, Ronald Brashear, and Joel Gwinn, "Young Edwin Hubble," *Mercury* 19 (1990): 2–15; Gale E. Christianson, *Edwin Hubble, Mariner of the Nebulae* (New York 1995).

John Kielkopf

ATHERTON, JOHN MCDOUGAL (b Larue County, Kentucky, April 1, 1841; d Louisville, June 5, 1932). Businessman and civic leader. Atherton was the son of Peter and Elizabeth (McDougal) Atherton. His father was a native of Virginia who came to Kentucky to take up a land grant in the 1790s. After attending public schools he was sent to Bardstown to school for a year. He attended Georgetown College in Kentucky but withdrew because of bad health. At the age of nineteen he read law in Louisville. Over the years he developed considerable business and political interests in the city. He served in the General Assembly from 1869 to 1871 and was Democratic state central committee chairman for several years.

Early in his career he became involved in the distilling business in Larue County. By 1882 he had acquired four distilleries that, when combined, were said to have had the largest capacity of any bourbon producer in the United States. In 1882 he moved the J.M. Atherton Co. business offices to 125 W Main St. in Louisville. He sold it in 1899 to devote his time to real estate and financial investments and invested in property at several key intersections in downtown, including Fourth and Chestnut Streets and Fourth and Walnut (Muhammad Ali Blvd.) Streets. The latter became the site of the Stewart Dry Goods Co. Because of Atherton's vast real estate holdings, he served on several boards of directors. In 1881 he was elected a member of the board of the Bank of Kentucky (later the National Bank of Kentucky) and continued in that position until 1928. He was made a director of the Louisville Gas Co. in 1884, and in 1898 was elected to the board of the Louisville & Nashville Railroad. Atherton also served as vice president, then president of the National Bank of Kentucky and was the first president of the Lincoln Bank & Trust Co.

Atherton was an ardent opponent of prohibition. He was a national founder and first president of the National Protective Association, organized in 1886 to oppose constitutional Prohibition. The great newspaper editor Henry Watterson declared that, through his involvement with the association, Atherton demonstrated the effectiveness of open-discussion campaigns in American politics. His interest in education resulted in changing Louisville's trustee system of school administration to that of a board of education. In appreciation of his efforts, the Louisville Board of Education named the J.M. Atherton High School for Girls on Morton Ave. in his honor in 1923.

He was married October 24, 1861, at Georgetown, Kentucky, to Maria B. Farnam, daughter of Johnathan E. Farnam, a professor at Georgetown College. They had one son, Peter Lee, born in 1862. Atherton is buried in Cave Hill Cemetery.

See *Courier-Journal*, June 6, 1932.

ATHERTON, PETER LEE (b Athertonville, Kentucky, October 7, 1862; d near San Antonio, Texas, January 13, 1939). Financier, real estate developer, and distiller. He was the son of John McDougal and Maria Butler Farnum Atherton. He was the namesake of his grandfather, who brought the family to Kentucky around 1790. His father, John M. Atherton, established a distillery and town for his workers near the Rolling Fork River in 1867, and in 1924 the Louisville Board of Education named a new school J.M. Atherton Girls High School to honor his work on the board in 1884.

Peter Atherton was a graduate of Louisville Male High School and, from 1883 to 1899, the vice president and general manager of the John M. Atherton Co., a chemical and distilling business. The company's distillery was one of the largest in the country.

Atherton was interested in both the civic and political affairs of the city. He was elected to the Kentucky General Assembly in 1912, where he was known for his interest in prison reform. His civic interests were quite varied. They included such diverse activities as trustee of the University of Louisville, 1908–12, where he was instrumental in buying the Louisville Medical College to ensure no rivalry with the University of Louisville's medical school; chairman of the Louisville Sewer Commission, 1906–13; member of the commission for revision of Kentucky's tax system, 1908–14. He also was instrumental in bringing the Kentucky State Fair to Louisville and was associated with the Lincoln Savings Bank.

Atherton married Cornelia S. Anderson of Louisville on May 23, 1914, in New York City. They were the parents of three children: Sarah Anderson, Cornelia E., and John McDougal Atherton. He is buried in Cave Hill Cemetery.

See Mary Southard, *Who's Who in Kentucky 1936* (Louisville 1936); Robert Rennick, *Kentucky Place Names* (Lexington 1984).

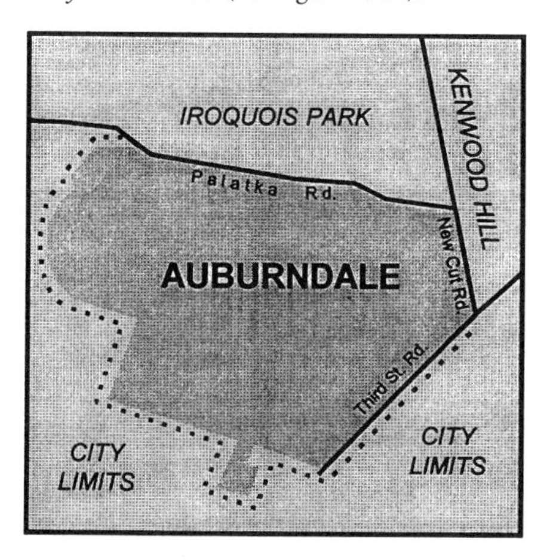

AUBURNDALE. Southernmost neighborhood in Louisville, located directly south of Iroquois Park and bounded by Palatka Rd. to the north, a combination of Third St. and New Cut Rd. to the east, and the city limits to the west and south. The area was once part of Isaac H. Fenley's farm, known as Hickory Grove, which covered eleven hundred acres by 1879. In 1907 engineer and developer W.E. Stonestreet acquired a parcel of land around New Cut Rd. and Third Street Rd. and began to subdivide the area for residential use. The community remained sparsely populated until the 1960s, when developers promoted its proximity to the park and the city annexed the area. The community remains mostly residential.

AUDUBON. Neighborhood bounded by Clarks Ln. to the north, Preston Hwy. to the west, Poplar Level Rd. to the east, and the fifth-class city of Audubon Park to the south, excluding the sixth-class city of Parkway Village. Developer Harold W. Miller attempted to capitalize on the popularity of neighboring Audubon Park by developing the Audubon neighborhood in the 1940s with inexpensive homes and small lots. Residents of Audubon

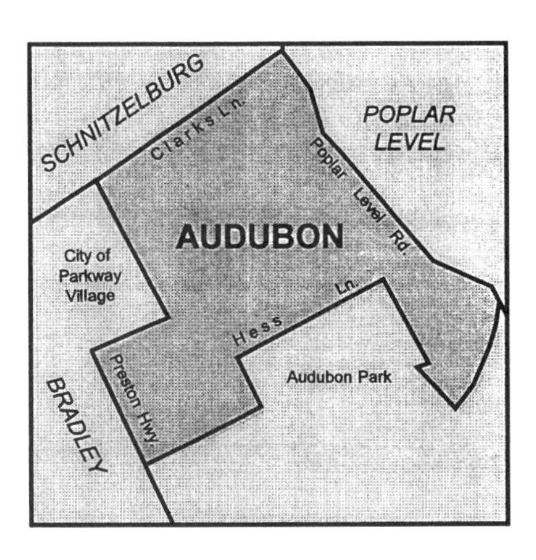

Park, hoping to maintain their community's unique character and status, unsuccessfully tried to block the creation of the new neighborhood. George Rogers Clark Park is an important landmark in the area. Once the site of Clark's parents' farm and cabin, the area was established as a public park in 1921.

AUDUBON, JOHN JAMES (b Les Cayes, Santo Domingo (now Haiti), April 26, 1785; d New York City, January 27, 1851). Painter, John James Audubon's father was Jean Jacques Audubon, a merchant seaman of Nantes, France. His mother, Jeanne Rabin, also from France, died six months following his birth. In 1789 Audubon was taken to the family home at Nantes and raised by his stepmother, Anne Moynet Audubon.

Audubon seldom attended school, preferring to spend his time observing nature, drawing, and collecting specimens. At age fourteen, he attended a military school in Rochefort, France. For the most part, he was self-educated and self-trained.

In 1803 Audubon came to America to oversee a family farm near Philadelphia. There, Audubon continued his passion of collecting and drawing portraits of birds. On an adjoining farm in 1804 he met LUCY GREEN BAKEWELL, his future wife.

Audubon and a partner, Ferdinand Rozier, moved to Louisville in September 1807 to operate a mercantile store. Audubon established friendships with Louisville residents Maj. WILLIAM CROGHAN, Dr. WILLIAM C. GALT, James Berthoud, the TARASCONS, GEORGE ROGERS CLARK, and others. On April 5, 1808, Audubon married Lucy, and they returned to Louisville and life at the Indian Queen Hotel at Fifth and MAIN STREETS, their home for more than two years. On June 12, 1809, the Audubons' first son, Victor Gifford, was born. While in Louisville, Audubon spent a great deal of his time in the woods, observing and drawing birds.

By 1810 competition from other stores forced Audubon west to Henderson, Kentucky. Audubon continued the mercantile business in Henderson for nine years. His son, John Woodhouse, was born on November 30, 1812, and daughter Lucy in 1815. The store prospered, and with land speculation Audubon became financially secure. He continued to develop his artistic skills and add to his portfolio of bird drawings. Daughter Lucy died in the winter of 1817. His construction of a steam-driven flour mill on the cusp of a severe economic depression spelled bankruptcy for Audubon by 1819.

Audubon returned to Louisville in the fall of 1819 to look for work. There he was arrested for debt and briefly imprisoned. His release was accomplished by filing a declaration of bankruptcy. Audubon then made a living by sketching charcoal portraits. Lucy's sister Eliza and her husband, Nicholas Berthoud, provided their lodging. While there a second daughter, Rosa, was born.

In early 1820 Audubon moved to Cincinnati to work as a taxidermist at the Western Museum. Following Rosa's death at seven months, Lucy and the two sons joined Audubon in Ohio. In October 1820 Audubon traveled to Louisiana to begin his great work, *The Birds of America.* In May 1826 Audubon sailed for England in search of a publisher. The publication was completed in 1838. Audubon's four-volume *The Birds of America* ensured his place in history. His artistic renderings of America's birds and animals are unsurpassed in their accuracy and beauty. The work was followed by the portfolios (1842-45), three-volume *The Viviparous Quadrupeds of America* (1846–54). Audubon also wrote *Ornithological Biography* (1831–39), the text of the fifth volume of *The Birds of America*, and *Synopsis of Birds of North America* (1839), which cataloged the birds. His portraits and descriptions of the birds and his later stories of the American frontier brought him world fame, respect, and financial success.

Upon returning to America, the Audubons settled in New York City, where the second edition of *The Birds of America* (1844) and *The Viviparous Quadrupeds of America* (1853), were published. Audubon died at his home at the age of sixty-five. He is buried in the Trinity Cemetery at 155th St. and Riverside Dr. in New York City.

See Francis Hobart Herrick, *Audubon the Naturalist* (New York 1938); Alice Ford, *John James Audubon: A Biography* (New York 1988); Mary Durant and Michael Harwood, *On the Road with John James Audubon* (New York 1980); Shirley Streshinsky, *Audubon: Life and Art in the American Wilderness* (New York 1993).

Don Boarman

AUDUBON, LUCY GREEN (BAKEWELL) (b Burton-on-Trent, England, January 18, 1787; d Shelbyville, Kentucky, June 18, 1874). Lucy Green (Bakewell) Audubon's father was William Bakewell of Derbyshire, England; her mother was Lucy Green of Burton-on-Trent, England. Lucy spent her childhood and early adolescence in England, where she attended boarding school and studied under private tutors.

In 1803 the family journeyed to America and settled on a farm near Philadelphia, Pennsylvania. There Lucy met and, on April 5, 1808, married JOHN JAMES AUDUBON. They settled in Louisville, where Audubon operated a mercantile store until the fall of 1810. The Audubons had four children. Victor Gifford was born in 1809, John Woodhouse was born in 1812, Lucy was born in 1815, and Rosa was born in 1819. Both daughters died in infancy. While Audubon worked on his publication, *The Birds of America* (1838), Lucy at times supported the family by teaching, and she often acted as saleswoman, editor, and business manager.

Following the deaths of Audubon in 1851 and her sons in 1860 and 1862, Lucy returned to teaching. In 1869 she wrote and published

Louisville Railway Company Car no. 572 at Audubon Park in 1912.

The Life of John James Audubon, the Naturalist. In her later years she lived in Louisville with her granddaughter Harriet. Lucy died at the home of a widowed sister-in-law in SHELBYVILLE, Kentucky. Her ashes were buried with Audubon in Trinity Cemetery in New York City.

See Carolyn E. Delatte, *Lucy Audubon* (Baton Rouge, La., 1982); Francis Hobart Herrick, *Audubon the Naturalist* (New York 1938); Mary Durant and Michael Harwood, *On the Road with John James Audubon* (New York 1980).

Don Boarman

AUDUBON PARK. An early twentieth-century residential suburban development located three miles south of downtown Louisville. The community was developed on approximately 230 acres of rolling pastureland once owned by Gen. William Preston. Preston had received the land in 1774 as part of a thousand-acre land grant from the British government as payment for services rendered during the French and Indian War.

A portion of the old Preston tract, which became more valuable after the opening of the OKOLONA line of the INTERURBAN in 1905, was sold to G. Robert Hunt of Hunt, Bridgeford, and Co. in 1906. The Audubon Park Country Club and golf course were developed by the firm, along with avid golfer Russell Houston, who co-owned the land through the Prestonia Land Co. Some of the remaining land from Preston's tract, which encompassed the area to Durrett Ln., was sold off during WORLD WAR I to construct CAMP ZACHARY TAYLOR, the military training site.

The Audubon Park Realty Co. purchased the land from Hunt, Bridgeford, and Co. in 1912. The developers named the neighborhood after famous American naturalist and wildlife painter JOHN JAMES AUDUBON, while naming many of the streets after birds, such as Cardinal, Oriole, and Crossbill. Developers sought to combine the best attributes of a pastoral country life while maintaining a close residence to downtown. They also promoted the high elevation of the new neighborhood as safe from floods. However, Audubon Park was largely ignored until the early 1920s when the Louisville Gas and Electric Co. laid mains and placed streetlights. By the late 1920s, it was estimated that a new home was begun every two weeks.

Reflecting the time's rough idea of a garden suburb, the most distinctive element is the manipulated grid pattern of tree-lined streets incorporating planned green spaces. The lack of natural obstacles makes the pattern possible with few exceptions. One exception, Cardinal Dr., winds a curvilinear path around the periphery of the golf course, marking the southern boundary of the residential district. The pattern was established from early development of the district by the firm Clifford B. Harmon and Co. This large New York suburban property firm had developed over a hundred pieces of property in the largest United States cities with much success.

Large stone gateways, which flank the entrances from Audubon Pkwy. at PRESTON ST., and Oriole Dr. at Hess Ln., date from the time of the subdivision's design by the Harmon Co. These "signature entrances," as they are referred to in modern suburban developments, emphasize the enclave. A similar gateway at Poplar Level Rd. was demolished during its widening in the 1960s. The remaining gates visually mark the boundaries of Audubon Park from Preston Hwy. and the surrounding Louisville area.

Audubon Park is noted for its massive trees, manicured lawns, and planned green spaces. Large oaks and flowering trees, such as magnolias and dogwoods, shade and line every street. There are as many as five planned green spaces and three special planting areas that contribute to the parklike atmosphere. The annual spring Audubon Park Dogwood Festival and the Arts and Crafts Festival during the fall season are traditions that take advantage of the beauty of the neighborhood.

The houses are primarily a revival of designs from earlier United States and English history, such as neo-colonial, Dutch colonial, neo-federal, and more prominently, neo-Tudor. Some houses are also examples of Craftsman-inspired bungalows and Prairie-influenced styles.

In the beginning of Audubon Park's development, five acres were planned as a nursery to start ten thousand young trees that could be transplanted permanently within the suburb to enhance landscaping. Five city parks contribute to the landscape. They are named Wren (renamed Henderson Park in 1996), Robin, Oriole, Crossbill, and Curlew. Three special shrub/floral areas are located at intersections of Crossbill and Audubon Pkwy., Oriole Dr. and Audubon Pkwy., and at a juncture of Robin, Wren, and Cardinal Dr. These are known as Crossbill Triangle, Oriole Circle, and Robin Triangle. Oriole Circle lies in the middle of the intersection of Audubon Pkwy. and Oriole Dr. The neighborhood also houses a bird sanctuary. Audubon Park, which became a sixth- class city in 1941 and a fifth-class city in 1954, was listed in the NATIONAL REGISTER OF HISTORIC PLACES as a historic district in 1996. The population was 1,571 in 1980, 1,520 in 1990, and 1,561 in 1996.

Donna M. Neary

AUTHORS CLUB. Founded by *COURIER-JOURNAL* literary critic Evelyn Snead Barnett in the late 1890s, the roster of the all-female Authors Club of Louisville boasted some of America's most popular writers at the turn of the century. Meeting at Barnett's apartment in the Weissinger-Gaulbert Apartments on W BROADWAY every Saturday morning for a number of years, the twelve members of the Authors Club provided each other with inspiration, editorial assistance, and "constructive and destructive" discussion of each others' work. Reflecting the individual talents of each writer, the group capably handled numerous forms of literary composition, including articles, novels, short stories, and poems. Furthermore, the Authors Club enlivened Louisville's literary community through its activities and assisted in achieving recognition for Kentucky authors on the nation's top-ten bestseller lists and in the 1909 *Who's Who in America.*

Besides assisting with individual projects, several collaborative pieces provide evidence of the group's friendship, energy, and creativity. One project, the then-provocatively entitled *A Young Lady Alone in a Barbershop at Midnight,* a thematic series of short stories, resulted in an exclusive issue of the popular magazine, *The Black Cat.* Another project resulting from each writer contributing one character's part as in a play, produced the novel, *A Comedy of Circumstances.*

In addition to Barnett (1861–1921), seven other "aspiring" women writers maintained their status as original club members, albeit with varying amounts of participation. Their literary contributions ranged from local-color fiction to children's literature and newspaper editorial writing. The first Authors Club members included Margaret Steel Anderson (1869–1921), ANNIE FELLOWS JOHNSTON (1863–1931), Mary Finley Leonard (1862–1948), Eva Madden (1863–1958), GEORGE MADDEN MARTIN (1866–1946), ALICE HEGAN RICE (1870–1942), and MARGARET WOMACK VANDERCOOK (1868–1936). They were later joined by Frances Caldwell Macaulay (1863–1941), who used the pseudonym Frances Little; Abby Meguire Roach (1876–1968); ELLEN CHURCHILL SEMPLE (1863–1932); and Venita Seibert White (1878–?). The full list of book publications for women writers associated with the Authors Club totals seventy. While the Authors Club thrived for many years, the association informally dissolved as members died, married and moved away, or advanced their careers in other locations.

See *Courier-Journal,* Dec. 22, 1946; William S. Ward, *A Literary History of Kentucky* (Knoxville, Tenn., 1988); Abby Meguire Roach, "The Authors Club of Louisville: An Inside Story—I Remember. . . ." *Filson Club History Quarterly* 31 (Jan. 1957): 28–37.

Amy E. Wells

AUTOMOBILE MANUFACTURERS. Predating automobiles, Louisville's location on the OHIO RIVER allowed cheap and easy access to materials for manufacturing horse-drawn carriages. Most factories were founded in the two decades preceding the CIVIL WAR and by 1880 had capital investments of over three hundred thousand dollars, with an average employment of five hundred. Carriage manufacturing remained a small but thriving industry in Louisville until the advent of the automobile at the turn of the century.

The automobile age dawned in Louisville on October 4, 1898, when the first self-propelled vehicle—electrically powered—arrived in

Dixie Flyer automobile, manufactured by the Kentucky Wagon Works, atop the lookout in Iroquois Park, 1919.

the city. It was a Waverly, made in Indianapolis and delivered by rail freight to John E. Roche, president of the Louisville Carriage Co. (predecessor of the YELLOW CAB CO.). He picked up the "machine" at the freight depot and drove it about the city, astonishing onlookers. Two years later he replaced it with a steam-powered car, followed in about 1903 with a gasoline-powered vehicle. By then Louisville counted thirty-six automobiles, and in 1908 the total had climbed to four hundred. That year the first of a long-running series of annual automobile shows was held in the armory.

As the American love affair with the car grew in intensity, numerous fledgling auto manufacturing plants appeared in cities across the nation, including Louisville and NEW ALBANY, Indiana. The first local one was the American Automobile Manufacturing Co., which had been founded in Kansas City, Missouri, about 1908. In 1910 its founders appeared in Louisville, setting up headquarters in the Lincoln Bank Building and declaring their intention to establish an auto plant. That happened in 1911, but the plant was in New Albany, at the former woolen mill buildings at Vincennes and Locust Streets. The mill had closed during the depression of the 1890s.

The promoters sought investors by wild claims of profits, calling auto manufacturing "a golden dream that would have crazed King Midas himself" and suggesting that dividends might range from 60 percent to 1,300 percent. No record of production survives, but some cars were produced. Marketed as the Jonz, the car took its name from the engine used. It had been developed by three Johns brothers in Kansas.

The Jonz was hand-assembled, with parts purchased from other manufacturers. The bodies were made by the Kahler Co., a New Albany woodworking and furniture factory. Despite the promises of impossibly high profits, the company soon went bankrupt. Fred Kahler purchased the company, largely to protect his investment in auto bodies. He formed the Ohio Falls Motor Co. and turned out a car called the Pilgrim, also hand-assembled, retailing at eighteen hundred dollars. Production was twenty or so completed cars. Discouraged by lack of sales, Kahler closed the plant but about 1914 found a purchaser. The Crown Motor Car Co., founded in Louisville, planned to build a car called the Crown but soon changed its name to the Hercules Motor Car Co. and produced the Hercules—perhaps only one. About 1915 the material on hand was sold to the KENTUCKY WAGON MANUFACTURING CO. of Louisville, which was planning to build a car called the Dixie Flyer. The Kahler Co. was able to capitalize on its early experience in bodybuilding and made hundreds of Ford Model T bodies until the advent of the Model A in the late 1920s.

In Louisville, the Kentucky Wagon Manufacturing Co., seeing the automotive revolution as a threat to its business, began building battery-powered delivery trucks about 1910, under the name Urban Electric. They seem to have been sold mainly, perhaps exclusively, in the Louisville area. The wagon company enlisted the aid of New Albanian Earl Walker in this venture. Walker had begun experiments with steam-powered cars in the late 1890s by mounting a small steam engine and boiler on a buckboard and driving long distances to such Indiana towns as Paoli and French Lick. Not satisfied with the kerosene burners then available to heat the boiler water, he designed his own. It was so successful that he built up a profitable business manufacturing them and gained a reputation as an authority on all types of self-propelled vehicles.

In 1912, with the backing of two Louisville partners, Walker formed the Transit Motor Truck Co. to manufacture chain-driven gasoline trucks. The plant was at Jackson and Lampton Streets in Louisville. A number of trucks were sold, the first to the Louisville Varnish Co. The Frank Fehr Brewery operated seven, and others were sold out of town. Sales, however, did not cover expenses, and operations ceased about 1916.

By that time the Kentucky Wagon Manufacturing Co. was producing the Dixie Flyer automobile at its plant on Third St. in South Louisville. This was the most successful of the locally owned auto manufacturing ventures. The four-cylinder cars were produced from about 1916 to about 1924. Production reached more than six thousand in two styles: the runabout and the larger touring car. Prices ranged from $850 to about $1,500. But in the long run this operation, like many others across the nation, could not compete against Detroit's assembly lines and nationwide system of dealerships.

Detroit came to Louisville in 1912 in the form of a FORD MOTOR CO. assembly operation in a small building at Third and Breckinridge Streets. Twelve Model T cars were turned out each day. In 1916 a large assembly plant was opened at Third St. and Eastern Pkwy., with a capacity of seven thousand Model T cars per year. Ironically, this plant was almost directly across the street from the Dixie Flyer plant. With the demise of the latter car, Ford Motor Co. is now the only producer of automobiles in the Falls Cities area. In 1925 the Third St. operation was succeeded by a larger assembly plant at 1400 South Western Pkwy., with a capacity of four hundred Model T cars per day. It later produced Model A cars and, during World War II, hundreds of Jeeps.

An even larger plant was opened on Fern Valley Rd. in 1955. This plant in 1981 ceased assembly of automobiles (LTDs) and shifted to light trucks (Rangers) and later to the Bronco II and the Explorer. The Kentucky Truck Plant opened in 1969 on Chamberlain Ln., producing Ford's medium- to extra-heavy-duty trucks, dubbed "The Louisville Line." In 1997 Ford sold its heavy truck line to Freightliner Corporation and shifted the Chamberlain plant to production of medium and light trucks.

See *Courier-Journal,* June 8, 1902, March 25, 1913, Oct. 25, 1997; *Courier-Journal Magazine,* March 1953; *New Albany Tribune,* Feb. 19, 1971; "Indiana-Built Automobiles," *Indiana History Bulletin,* Sept. 1961; George H. Yater, "Autos," in *Historical Series of New Albany,* no. 2 (New Albany 1957).

George H. Yater

AVERY, BENJAMIN FRANKLIN (b Aurora, New York, December 3, 1801; d Louisville, March 3, 1885). Businessman. Avery grew up on his father's farm in New York. He studied law at Union College in Schenectady, New York, where he graduated in 1822. Although admitted to the bar, he found the practice of law not to his liking. His decision to enter the plow-manufacturing business came from farmwork. He was certain that plows could be improved. He made several alterations, lightening it, deepening the furrow, and decreasing the draft. Avery moved to Clarksville, Virginia, where he opened his first foundry. He lived briefly in both North Carolina and Virginia.

On December 25, 1847, Avery moved to Louisville to help his nephew Daniel H. Avery start up an agricultural foundry at MAIN and PRESTON STREETS. The business was successful, supplying much of the South with farm equipment, including the so-called Avery plow. Before the CIVIL WAR, Avery established a large manufactory at the corner of Main and Fifteenth Streets. Operations were suspended during the Civil War when the Union army sought to halt the flow of supplies to the Confederacy and the foundry building was used as a military hospital. But soon he was back in business and making a great deal of money. In 1867 his taxable income was the second-greatest in the city, behind patent medicine manufacturer JOHN BULL, at $67,321. In 1868 Avery formed a new firm, B.F. Avery and Sons, with his two sons, Samuel and George, and his son-in-law, J.C. Coonley. The firm made many different kinds of CAST-IRON and steel plows and published a semimonthly paper called *Home and Farm*. B.F. Avery and Sons was among the city's largest industries. Avery, together with other agricultural manufacturers, made Louisville the world's largest producer of plows. Avery also served as director of the BANK OF LOUISVILLE and owned Tamadge Lake Ice Co. He married Susan H. Look, with whom he had six children: Lydia, Samuel, Gertrude, George, Nelly, and William. He is buried in CAVE HILL CEMETERY.

See *History of the Ohio Falls Cities and Their Counties*, (Cleveland 1882); George Yater, *Two Hundred Years at the Falls of the Ohio* (Louisville 1987); *Courier-Journal*, March 4, 1885.

AVERY, SUSAN HOWES (LOOK) (b Conway, Massachusetts, October 27, 1817; d Wyoming, New York, February 1, 1915). Civic leader. The daughter of Samuel and Polly Look, at the age of eighteen Susan attended Utica Female Seminary, where she later became a teacher. She married BENJAMIN AVERY on April 27, 1844. She lived quietly until her six children were old enough to do without her constant care.

In 1881, Avery met with the famous pioneer suffragist, Lucy Stone. Stone was in Louisville for the first meeting of the American Woman Suffrage Association held south of the Mason-Dixon Line. As a result, Susan became an ardent advocate of equal suffrage, temperance, municipal ownership of public utilities, the single tax—a 100 percent fee imposed on the annual economic rent of land designed to eliminate exploitation and rural income disparity—the rights of labor, and free trade. She was opposed to militarism and war, except in self-defense, and capital punishment.

On March 1, 1890, Avery gathered thirty-nine women into her parlor and began the WOMAN'S CLUB OF LOUISVILLE. For one year, she served as second vice president, the only office she would consent to hold. A firm believer in hard work, her favorite aphorism was, "It is bad for the ignorant and the vicious to do ill, but it is worse for the educated and honest to do nothing."

See *The Woman's Club Bulletin*, vol. 29, no. 7. March 1965; *Courier-Journal*, May 13, 1923, April 19, 1951, June 2, 1951.

Laurie A. Birnsteel

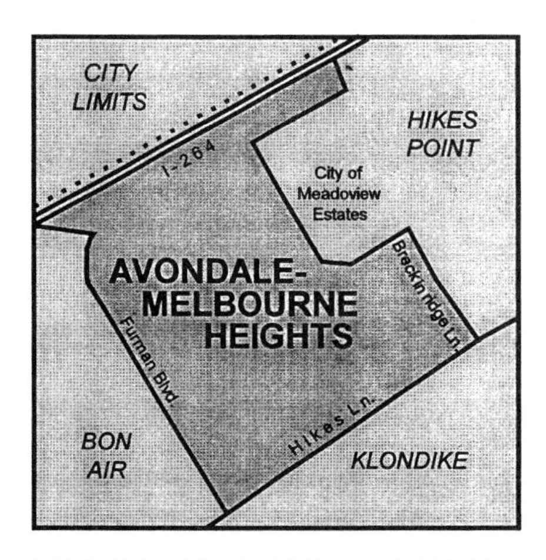

AVONDALE-MELBOURNE HEIGHTS. Neighborhood in eastern Louisville bounded by Breckenridge Ln. on the east, Hikes Ln. to the south, Furman Blvd. to the west, and the WATTERSON EXPRESSWAY on the north, excluding the sixth-class city of Meadowview Estates. The AVONDALE half of the neighborhood, lying to the north of Taylorsville Rd., which bisects the community, was initiated in 1914 by Crown Real Estate Co. This project failed. Developer Clarence C. Hieatt acquired the land in the 1920s and advertised the area as a suburban retreat with large lots and all of the comforts of city life. Although smaller additions were built after WORLD WAR II, much of the development in Avondale was completed before the 1940s. To the south of Taylorsville Rd. lies the MELBOURNE HEIGHTS half of the neighborhood. Originally known as Maywood, the development was started by H.G. Whittenberg in 1955.

AXTON-FISHER TOBACCO COMPANY. The Axton-Fisher Tobacco Co. (AFTC) began its corporate life in Louisville on January 2, 1905. It operated as a manufacturer of leaf products until its assets were sold in 1944 to PHILIP MORRIS, which continued to make cigarettes at the AFTC plant at Twentieth and Broadway. After twenty-five years as a corporation with growing regional sales—Old Hillside bagged tobacco; White Mule, Axton's Natural Leaf, 8 Hour, Booster, and Wage Scale chewing tobacco; and the Turkish cigarette, Clown—AFTC broke onto the national market when in May 1926 it introduced Spud, the first mentholated smoke, and followed that in June 1932 with the highly successful ten-cent Depression cigarette, Twenty Grand. By 1934 AFTC annual sales had reached $28 million, with profits of $1.4 million. Three shifts ran the greatly expanded plant, which employed twelve hundred workers. AFTC shares were trading on the New York Curb Exchange, and the company was selling 5 percent of all American cigarettes.

Woodford Fitch Axton, president of AFTC, and his brother, secretary-treasurer Edwin Dymond Axton, together directed the fortunes and controlled the voting stock of the company. Upon Woodford's death in 1935 and Edwin's retirement soon thereafter, the heirs were forced to sell the family shares to outside interests. The company languished until liquidation put it in capable, but not local, hands.

Under the Axton family aegis, AFTC gained a reputation as an outspoken advocate of union labor, union scale wages, and humane working conditions, including free meals on every shift, free milk for children of working mothers, special restrooms and attendants for female employees, showers for men, fifteen-minute breaks for shift workers on every shift, company-sponsored sports, recreational and social activities, a pioneering credit union, and other enlightened measures. Many company products were aimed at the workingman's market.

Defeated for mayor on the "Bull Moose" Progressive ticket in 1913, president Wood Axton, an ardent opponent of the Whallen political machine, lent his support to many liberal causes, including antitrust legislation, public ownership of utilities, LaFollette Progressivism, the Louisville Taxpayers League, the American Federation of Labor, the National Recovery Act, and the New Deal generally. He campaigned for lower executive salaries—he limited his stipend to ten thousand dollars a year—and encouraged leaf growers to participate in the Agricultural Adjustment Act crop support program, even though that meant higher prices for tobacco and narrowed profit margins for tobacco companies.

W.F. Axton

B

BABIES' MILK FUND ASSOCIATION. The Progressive movement of the early 1900s brought about tremendous changes in the national perception of people's responsibilities to one another and to society. Temperance and Prohibition, the more notable efforts of the age, proved that a community concerned about the behavior and lifestyle of its neighbors could interact on their behalf to save them from themselves. But the social reforms taking place at the time also included attention to the working conditions of the nation's poor, as well as to their health concerns. Issues of sanitation in the food industry and labor practices received national attention. One of the more successful and popular movements at the time was the Babies' Milk Fund, a nationwide movement that not only provided milk to babies whose mothers could not afford it but also tried to educate mothers about the importance of a proper diet and other childcare issues.

Louisville's efforts in the babies' milk movement began late in 1906. While helping to conduct the city of Louisville's health studies that year, Dr. Leichfield Smith discovered that the majority of milk in the city, especially in the poorer parts of town, was unsanitary by the time it was given to babies, mainly due to poor refrigeration. When a milk ordinance to ensure safe milk for babies seemed to have little chance of passing, Leichfield and some friends set up pure-milk supply stations in poor sections of the city to show the benefits of pure and clean milk.

The Babies' Milk Fund Association was organized out of this idea with the intention of reducing Louisville's infant mortality rate and increasing the health of surviving children by teaching the importance of proper diet and cleanliness to mothers. The association's primary method of education was through several nurses working at the milk stations throughout the city. The nurses would distribute milk to any mothers who came, selling the milk at a small loss to those who could afford to pay something and giving the milk to those who could not. While handing out the milk, the nurses would also instruct the mothers on the importance of having their babies examined regularly by a physician and monitoring the babies' diets, and would give other general child health-care information.

Early in 1908 one nurse worked at three distributing stations in the city, collecting seven hundred dollars and distributing twelve hundred bottles of milk. The following year there were 6 stations serving 284 registered children, with 6 graduate nurses and 4 assistants working at the stations. That same year Dr. Smith rented two rooms on Sixth St. and organized a milk-purifying laboratory to prepare milk for the entire city's baby population. The six stations were set up in areas of greatest need, determined by a map of the city indicating the deaths of children under one year old from intestinal diseases, and the laboratory was centrally located to serve them.

The site of each station was provided by the city school board, which decreed that the association could establish a depot in any school necessary. This helped to keep down the cost of providing the service. Each station was equipped with an icebox, a thermometer, scales and a weighing table, two chairs, and an index box to keep track of the patients. All of the furniture was painted white, to encourage the workers to keep them as clean as possible and to show visiting mothers a good example of cleanliness. Contributions from the city, county, and private donors were sufficient to keep the association in supplies and milk and to pay for the nurses. Consulting physicians offered their services free of charge to mothers whose children needed checkups.

The association also attempted to educate the mothers about proper care. Each year a number of mothers' meetings were held. Visiting mothers were served refreshments and given practical advice through lectures entitled "The Care of the Pregnant Mother," "Clean Milk," "Fresh Air, Bathing, and Clothing," and "Flies as Carriers of Disease." These lectures were organized by mothers themselves at stations where they received help, and lectures were made by volunteer doctors and nurses.

Dr. Smith died early in 1909, but his widow carried on much of his work. For the next two years, the Babies' Milk Fund Association increased its efforts to make the public aware of its work and importance. Dr. Henry Tuley became spokesman for the association and had to face accusations that the group was diluting milk with water to increase its profits. Dr. Tuley explained that very young babies required modified milk and pointed out that the organization, examined each year by a public accountant, had to rely on donations to pay its nurses, as no profits were made from the milk sales. The publicity of this argument hastened the sale of pasteurized milk citywide, as the public became more aware of the association's message and the need for properly treated milk. In 1910 the association became affiliated with the American Association for the Study of Infant Mortality, and Dr. Tuley prepared an exhibit of the work going on in Louisville, which was shown all over the country.

In 1911, 787 babies were registered with the project. They were primarily fed from pure-milk stations but were also breast-fed, with the mothers receiving guidance from the nurses or working their way up to mixed food and milk diets. As a result, compared to the city's death rate for children under the age of five of 14.1 percent, children under the care of the association suffered a death rate of only 3.1 percent. The association encouraged breast-feeding where possible and even provided whole milk to mothers who were not properly nourished.

In 1913 a Junior Department of the Babies' Milk Fund Association was organized to involve Louisville youth in the operation. Baby Week in March 1916 provided another opportunity for the organization to publicize its efforts. Staff nurses and volunteer doctors visited several settlement houses throughout the city and set up a free three-day clinic, during which they illustrated proper feeding and clothing. During lunch hours these same groups visited local factories, encouraging fathers to get involved in keeping their babies healthy.

With the advent of World War I, finances and manpower were diverted to other organizations, and the efforts of the association suffered, as did the health of its benefactors. To concentrate health-care efforts in the city, the Babies' Milk Fund Association was merged with the District Nurse Association in 1919, which had been providing general bedside care and working against tuberculosis in the city, to form the Visiting Nurse Association. This group proved more effective in increasing awareness of health needs for all ages, while at the same time providing the basic services that had been the basis of the Milk Fund's efforts.

See M.L. Spalding, "History of the Visiting Nurse Association of Louisville," *University of Louisville Local History Series,* vol. 17 (Louisville 1942).

BACON'S. Bacon Dry Goods, Louisville's oldest continuous department store, first appeared in the community in 1845. It was started by Jeremiah Bacon, who was born in Pennsylvania in 1811. Bacon moved to Kentucky in 1834 and traveled the state as a peddler and auction proprietor. Once in Louisville, he located his concern on Market St. (the retail hub) near Hancock St. By 1876 Bacon's business had expanded into a structure four times larger than the original one. Now assisting him were his three sons, Edwin, John, and Jeremiah Junior. In 1901 J. Bacon and Sons moved to a new building that had its main entrance on Market St. and another on Fourth St. This location, at 330–34 W Market, with its distinctive spiraling atrium, was to be Bacon's downtown presence until 1972. In 1903 Bacon's sons sold their interests in the store to H.B. Claflin who, in turn, passed on the business to the Mercantile Co. in 1914. Bacon's held the distinction of being the oldest store group in the Mercantile Stores Co., which controled 105 outlets, with names such as McAlpin's, Lion, and Root's.

In 1954 Bacon's opened its first suburban location in St. Matthews. Other outlets would appear in Shively; the Mall St. Matthews;

Bashford Manor Mall; Jeffersonville, Indiana; and Owensboro, Kentucky. In 1982 Bacon's resurrected its downtown Louisville presence by opening in the Galleria. In Louisville's retail history, Bacon's longevity as a department store is unprecedented. In 1945, as the company celebrated its centennial anniversary, its slogan was "More Merchandise for Less Money." As post–World War II Louisville began to expand farther outward to suburbia, Bacon's was able to promote an image that clearly fit the spending styles and tastes of the growing middle-class market. In 1998 the Mercantile Stores Co. was purchased for an estimated $3 million by Dillard's, a competitive chain that also caters to the middle- to upper-class market. At that time, Bacon's owned five department stores and three home stores in the Louisville metropolitan area, and one department store in Owensboro.

See James Speed, "J. Bacon and Sons: History of a Mercantile Firm in Louisville," (1945).

Kenneth L. Miller

BAHÁ'ÍS OF GREATER LOUISVILLE. The Bahá'í Faith originated in nineteenth-century Persia. Its founder, Bahá'u'lláh [Mirzá Husayn 'Alí of Nur (1817-1892)], was a follower of The Báb (Gate) [Sayyid 'Ali Muhammad (1819-1850)]. Bahá'ís believe The Báb to be a manifestation of God who also foretold of another manifestation who would soon come. Bahá'u'lláh, whose name translates to "Glory of God," announced in 1863 that He was the one promised by The Báb.

The Bahá'í Faith has no clergy or ritual, yet there are laws and obligations. Community members gather every nineteen days (on the first day of each Bahá'í month) to worship and consult. Administrative bodies, called spiritual assemblies, are formed in civil jurisdictions where nine or more adult Bahá'ís reside. Although the Bahá'í Faith has had a presence in the Louisville area since at least 1920, the Spiritual Assembly of the Bahá'í of Louisville was not formed until 1944 when the community reached that number. In 1971 a second assembly formed in the unincorporated area outside Louisville in Jefferson County.

A Bahá'í Center opened in Louisville in 1967 at 104 Forest Ct. in Crescent Hill and was sold in 1985 when the community outgrew its space. Community growth stemmed from people of various religious backgrounds joining the faith as well as from an influx of Iranian Bahá'í fleeing persecution in their native land after the revolution of 1979. In November 1998, property for a new Bahá'í Center was purchased at 3808 Bardstown Rd. in Buechel. The center is used by all Bahá'í in the greater Louisville area.

Since the Bahá'í teachings emphasize the unity of the peoples of the world and the creation of world peace, Bahá'ís are involved in various interfaith and multicultural organizations in the Louisville area. The local Bahá'í community has hosted local and national seminars, conferences, and award presentations focusing on such topics as racial harmony, gender equality, universal education, the arts, the environment, children, and families.

See William S. Hatcher and J. Douglas Martin, *The Bahá'í Faith: The Emerging Global Religion* (Wilmette, Ill., 1998); Bahá'u'lláh *Gleanings from the Writings of Bahá'u'lláh* (Wilmette, Ill., 1976); Hugh C. Adamson and Philip Hainsworth, *Historical Dictionary of the Bahá'í Faith* (Lanham, Md., 1998).

Nancy D. Harris

BALLARD, BLAND W. (b Spotsylvania County, Virginia, October 16, 1761; d Shelby County, Kentucky, September 5, 1853). Pioneer, soldier, legislator. Ballard was the third child and eldest son of Bland Ballard. Ballard and his father came to Kentucky in 1779. Ballard joined the militia that year and served in Col. John Bowman's expedition against the British and their Indian allies in the Revolutionary War. Ballard also accompanied George Rogers Clark against the Piqua towns in 1780 and 1782, spied for Clark in the 1786 Wabash expedition, and served with Gen. Anthony Wayne at the battle of Fallen Timbers on August 20, 1794. Ballard reached the rank of major during the War of 1812 and led the charge into Frenchtown, Michigan, where he was wounded and taken prisoner.

Ballard's family settled first in the Louisville area. In 1787 they moved to Shelby County's Tick Creek, where Ballard's father, stepmother, brothers John and Benjamin, and three younger children lived in a cabin located about a hundred yards from a fort known as Tyler Station. In spring 1788, a party of Delaware Indians shot and killed John at the woodpile, then surrounded the house. As Ballard rushed out to guard his father's front door, several Indians ran to the back of the house, broke out chinking, and shot and killed the elder Ballard, fourteen-year-old Benjamin, and one small daughter. Mrs. Ballard was tomahawked as she ran out the front door. Another little daughter, injured by a hatchet, recovered. A son, James, was not at home. It is said that Ballard fired six shots and killed six Indians. The enemy later admitted that they had lost seven. The attack became known as the Tick Creek Massacre.

In addition to his duties as soldier and scout, Ballard helped mark the best route from the site of Shelbyville to the Falls of the Ohio, served as a trustee of Shelby Academy, and represented Shelby County in the General Assembly (1800, 1803, 1805). He married Elizabeth Williamson. The couple had seven children: James, Mary, Dorothy, Susan, Sally, Martha "Patsy," and Nancy. His second wife was Diane Matthews; his third wife was Elizabeth Weaver Garrett. He was buried near his home but was reinterred two months later in the state cemetery at Frankfort. In 1842 Ballard County was named in his honor.

See Margaret Morris Bridwell, "Notes on One of the Early Ballard Families of Kentucky, Including the Ballard Massacre," *Filson Club History Quarterly* 13 (Jan. 1939): 1–20; Lewis and Richard H. Collins, *History of Kentucky*, vol. 2 (Frankfort 1966; orig. pub. 1874); G. Glenn Clift, *Remember the Raisin!* (Frankfort 1961); E.D. Shinnick, *Some Old Time History of Shelbyville and Shelby County* (Frankfort 1974).

Mary Lou(Smith)Madigan

BANCOKENTUCKY COMPANY. Chartered in Delaware in July 1929 as a holding company in control of the National Bank of Kentucky and the Louisville Trust Co., BancoKentucky was created in order to sell stock and raise the cash needed to replace the doubtful assets accumulated because of the unsound lending practices of the Louisville branch of the Bank of Kentucky. The company was headed by National Bank's president, the "colorful, careless, and reckless" gambler James B. Brown, and was run under the same management as the National Bank.

In 1908 Brown had become the head of the National Bank, which dated back to 1834. It was the South's largest bank by 1919, due to his ties with the Democratic Party and its leader, James Whallen. To much fanfare, Brown, who also owned the *Louisville Herald-Post,* announced Banco's creation and attempted to excite the public into funding his new venture. By April 1930, speculative fever prompted Louisvillians to drive the price of the stock up five dollars—to twenty-five dollars per share—in one week. However, after a brief optimistic turn in the stock market, the shares leveled off and saw only short gains throughout the summer, finally reaching a peak of thirty-four and a half by mid-October.

Earlier in 1930, Rogers C. Caldwell of Caldwell and Co., a well-respected Nashville securities and investment banking house, had contacted Brown about the possibility of a merger. While the BancoKentucky stock was still enjoying a moderate upswing, the questionable loans were starting to take their toll. However, the Nashville bank was in a much worse position. It was completely insolvent. After little negotiating and no exchange of balance sheets, Brown, who considered the merger a chance to market his stock, diversify his portfolio, and raise the capital he sought, recommended that his board accept the plan, which they did in May by a vote of 26 to 1.

Only then did Caldwell release the figures that showed Brown the dismal state of his new partner's holdings. Brown started to transfer money from the declining National Bank into Caldwell's company in an attempt to revive it. When the *Herald-Post* announced the merger on June 30, 1930, conservative residents and companies, including Standard Oil of Kentucky and the Louisville & Nashville Railroad, became concerned over the deal and began to pull their money out of the National Bank.

On November 6, Caldwell's problems were

disclosed to the public. Brown attempted to disassociate Banco from the Nashville company to allay the public's fears as he liquidated banks in Cincinnati and Northern Kentucky. The public realized the danger, and National Bank's withdrawals totaled $8.8 million by November 15, leaving the bank with only seventeen thousand dollars at the end of the day. To the surprise of many uninformed residents, National Bank did not open on Monday, November 17, by order of the directors. Louisville Trust Co. was found closed by anxious depositors as well, although after reorganization the bank reopened in 1931. Security Bank, a smaller institution owned by BancoKentucky, remained opened and was flooded with account holders, who withdrew their balances and caused its failure. Other banks that used the National Bank of Kentucky as a depository, including the Bank of St. Helens and the African American banks, First Standard and American Mutual Savings, collapsed as well.

While BancoKentucky folded soon after the panic in November, the shareholders continued to suffer. A court ruled that they should be liable for the losses of the depositors and assessed them approximately five dollars per share. To worsen matters in the depression-stricken town, the bank's receiver pressed for quick payments on loans and caused a rash of mortgage foreclosures. This forced many, including James B. Brown, to declare bankruptcy.

The effects on the city were dramatic as residents panicked about the possibility of other banks faltering. This induced the remaining depositories to take out advertisements in local newspapers to assuage these fears and to pledge their establishments' soundness. There is little doubt that the collapse of the city's largest bank stuck in the minds of future bankers and caused a prevalent conservative attitude in the city's banking industry, which remained into the 1970s.

See Robert Fugate, "The BancoKentucky Story," *Filson Club History Quarterly* 50 (Jan. 1976): 29–46; John Berry McFerrin, *Caldwell and Company* (Nashville 1969); George H. Yater, *Two Hundred Years at the Falls of the Ohio* (Louisville 1987).

Craig M. Heuser

BANKING. Banking in Louisville began in the early 1800s, at the same time as the industry was developing nationally. The First Bank of the United States, federally chartered in 1791, was the first attempt to establish central banking and to provide uniform currency. Its charter was not renewed in 1811, however. State-chartered banks and private banks issued their own notes and currencies, which had varying degrees of reliability of exchange value or conversion value to specie—gold and silver coins. Louisville's population in 1800 was only 359. By 1810 it had increased to 1,357 and by 1820 to 4,012. This growth warranted the development of local banking.

The first chartered bank in Kentucky was the Kentucky Insurance Co., chartered by the Kentucky legislature in 1802. In 1806 the state chartered the Bank of Kentucky. The Louisville branch of the Bank of Kentucky was one of nine branches opened in 1815 throughout the state to hold off potential competitors. The Bank of Kentucky, however, did not provide currency as plentifully as desired by the legislature. The state chartered forty more banks soon thereafter, but only sixteen were in operation in 1819. The Kentucky legislature chartered the Bank of the Commonwealth in 1820 with the intent of replacing the Bank of Kentucky and transferring the state's interest to the Bank of the Commonwealth by 1826. A branch of the Bank of the Commonwealth opened in Louisville in 1822.

In 1816 the Second Bank of the United States was granted a charter to extend until 1836. A branch of the Second Bank was established in Louisville in 1817, located on Main between Third and Second Streets. This bank was not well managed and was on the verge of bankruptcy during the panic of 1819. By 1821 general prosperity aided the bank's recovery. Nevertheless, the Second Bank did little business until 1826.

In December 1822 the state repealed the charter of the Bank of Kentucky, and its demise was finalized in 1823 when the Bank of the Commonwealth began the process of withdrawing and buying its paper. Between 1822 and the chartering of the Louisville Bank of Kentucky in 1833, the only active banks in Kentucky were the branches of the Second Bank of the United States in Louisville and Lexington.

In the legislative sessions of 1833 and 1834, the Kentucky General Assembly anticipated that the Second Bank of the United States would not be rechartered. Three state banks were chartered to provide banking in Kentucky: the Bank of Louisville in 1833, the Bank of Kentucky (the second one) in 1834, and the Northern Bank of Kentucky in 1835, with headquarters in Lexington and a branch in Louisville. The Bank of Kentucky, with headquarters in Louisville, purchased the building of the Louisville branch of the Second Bank of the United States.

The end of the Second Bank of the United States in 1836 left the United States in a free, or wildcat, banking era, with state-chartered banks operating under widely varying degrees of regulation. During the banking crisis in 1837, specie disappeared from circulation entirely, and the smaller coin was replaced by paper tickets issued by cities, towns, and individuals, creating a local currency that was worthless beyond the range of their immediate neighborhood.

Another banking crisis occurred in 1839 when banks again suspended payment in specie. Because of so many bankruptcies, Kentucky raised its direct taxes by 50 percent to achieve fiscal balance. In 1841, taxes were raised from ten cents to fifteen cents per hundred dollars. The tax hike was designed to increase the resources of the state sinking fund, as the revenue was applied to the principal and interest on debts owed by the state. The decline in economic activity lasted until 1844, after the passage of the banking act in 1843 allowing banks to legally suspend specie payment. The act released the same banks from penalties if they violated their own charters but only if they made loans within all ten congressional districts in the state.

The next panic revolving around the banking industry arose in 1857, but the Kentucky and Louisville economies were not severely impacted. The origin of Liberty National Bank (now Bank One) dates back to 1854 when the state chartered the German Insurance Co., incorporating it with banking powers. In 1872, because the state mandated the separation of banking and insurance, the banking portion of the original company became the German Insurance Bank.

In 1858 the Merchants Deposit Bank, the origin of Citizens Fidelity Bank & Trust (PNC), was chartered by the state. Its name changed to Citizens Bank in 1863.

Three national banking acts were passed in 1863, 1864, and 1865. These acts led to a more uniform currency throughout the United States when a 10 percent tax on state bank notes drove the notes from circulation. The chartering of national banks was expected to improve the standardization and quality of banks. To help finance the Civil War, national banks were required to keep a specified amount of their reserves in Treasury certificates.

Louisville responded immediately with the chartering of the First National Bank of Louisville in 1863, heralded as the oldest national bank south of the Ohio River. First National's original location was in the Hamilton Block at the corner of Sixth and Main Streets. Citizens Bank obtained a federal charter and became Citizens National Bank, located at Bullitt and Main Streets until 1919.

The advancement of banking in Louisville continued with the establishment of the Louisville Clearing House Association, with operations beginning January 3, 1876. Banking crises in 1877, 1884, and 1890 impacted Louisville, as many banks failed and closed. In 1890 the Louisville Clearing House developed a payment system among the member banks to aid each other in times of serious need and to also impose standards set by the association on banks using the Clearing House. The strategy was successful, for it helped soften Louisville's economic downturn. The Kentucky Bankers Association was organized in 1891 in response to the decline in public confidence in the banking system after the failures of several banks in 1890.

In 1889 Louisville was home to ten national banks and twelve state banks. These banks were key contributors to the financing and development of industry, especially railroads and the two bridges connecting Louisville with New Albany and Jeffersonville, Indiana. The recession in 1893, however, placed numerous projects and businesses into receivership, causing several Louisville banks to fail. By 1895 the number of banks in Louisville declined to sixteen—seven national banks and nine state banks—a composition similar to that of the rest of the United States at that time.

In 1904 Stock Yards Bank & Trust Co. was founded to serve the financial needs of Louisville's growing livestock business. Stock Yards' offices are at the corner of E Main and Johnson Streets, across from the former Bourbon Stock Yards. In 1913 the Federal Reserve Act was passed to develop a central monetary authority to protect the banking system and the rest of the economy from banking panics or crises. Also its purpose was to develop monetary tools to guide the growth and stability of the U.S. economy. This act directed an organizing committee to conduct hearings and to choose the number (from eight to twelve) of Federal Reserve Banks, their locations, and their district boundaries. The committee's selections were determined by city size, bankers' preferences, some banking realities, and a lot of politics. Louisville bankers wanted Cincinnati as a reserve bank and wanted Louisville to be included in the Cincinnati district. Cincinnati was not selected as one of the twelve reserve banks, however. St. Louis and Cleveland were two of the twelve cities chosen. Louisville, western Kentucky, and southern Indiana were included in the St. Louis district because St. Louis alone had insufficient capital. The rest of Kentucky was included in the Cleveland district. Louisville bankers felt slighted by having the state cut into two districts.

A member of the organizing committee of the St. Louis Federal Reserve Bank was from the National Bank of Kentucky, reflecting the local bank's importance. In addition, the president of the National Bank of Kentucky at Louisville, Oscar Fenley, was elected to be one of the first Class A directors of the Federal Reserve Bank of St. Louis.

On July 5, 1916, the member banks of Louisville sent a petition to the board of directors of the St. Louis Reserve Bank, asking for the establishment of a branch of the district bank at Louisville. The committee presenting the arguments to form a branch in Louisville was headed by Embry L. Swearingen, president of the First National Bank of Louisville. The Louisville petition was the first received by the Board of Governors in Washington. (New Orleans, however, had already become a branch city in the Atlanta district because the Atlanta Federal Reserve Bank had initiated the process itself.) No immediate action was taken on the request by the Louisville bankers because the board had not yet adopted a policy regarding branches of the twelve district banks.

The board of directors of the St. Louis Federal Reserve Bank opposed the Louisville branch. An agency of the St. Louis Bank had been opened in Memphis. Louisville bankers argued that their whiskey and tobacco paper was special and required a local board to pass on it for rediscounting. Furthermore, Louisville bankers believed bank balances were being diverted to St. Louis banks from Louisville banks because western Kentucky banks were pressured to place funds in St. Louis rather than Louisville. The Louisville bankers even offered to guarantee the expenses of the branch.

Not until July 3, 1917, after the Federal Reserve Act was amended that year to clarify the establishment of branches, was Louisville granted a branch. The initial board of the Louisville branch consisted of five directors, three elected by the St. Louis bank and two appointed by the Federal Reserve Board. The territory of the Louisville branch included all of Kentucky in the Eighth District and thirteen counties in Indiana. The branch bank opened for business on December 3, 1917. The branch's original office was the second floor of the Columbia Building at Fourth and Main Streets. In 1919 it moved into the Louisville National Bank Building at the corner of Fifth and Market Streets until operations were moved in 1958 to its current location at the southwest corner of Fifth and Liberty Streets.

The period of the 1920s was one of growth, consolidation, and new charters. In 1918 the German Insurance Bank, the first state bank in Kentucky to become a member bank of the Federal Reserve, changed its name to Liberty Insurance Bank to reflect patriotism. In 1919 James B. Brown orchestrated the merger of the National Bank of Commerce and American Southern Bank into the National Bank of Kentucky. Also in 1919, the forerunners of Citizens Fidelity Bank & Trust Co. took another step into the future when Union National Bank, chartered in 1889, and Citizens National Bank consolidated and became Citizens Union National Bank.

In 1921 Kentucky's Department of Banking, which was organized in 1912 and is now the Department of Financial Institutions, authorized the charter of First Standard Bank. Touted as the "million dollar bank," First Standard, at Sixth and Walnut (Muhammad Ali Blvd.), was the first African American bank in Kentucky. In 1926 the trustees of the New Trust of First National Bank of Louisville and Kentucky Title Savings Bank & Trust Co. established the First Kentucky Co. In 1926 and 1927, assets of Portland Bank and South Louisville Bank were sold to First National Bank. In 1926 the Morris Plan Industrial Bank opened. This was the origin of the current Bank of Louisville.

In 1929 BancoKentucky was chartered in Delaware as a holding company of the National Bank of Kentucky and Louisville Trust Co. The purpose of the holding company was to issue stock to obtain cash to replace the doubtful assets of the National Bank of Kentucky. BancoKentucky also controlled Security Bank.

Louisville banking suffered from 1929 to 1933, as did banking throughout the United States. The crash of 1929, however, did not lead to immediate failures in banking in Louisville. In fact, even though there were twenty bank failures around the state of Kentucky between July 1929 and June 1930, during those twelve months no banks failed in Louisville.

As of the end of June 1929 there were three national banks in Louisville with assets of about $119 million and seventeen state-chartered banks and trusts with assets totaling about $145 million. At the end of June 1933 the Louisville banking community included two federally chartered banks with assets totaling $57.9 million and thirteen state-chartered banks with assets of $88.5 million.

The big story in Louisville was the fall of the BancoKentucky Co., the holding company of National Bank of Kentucky, Louisville Trust Co., and Security Bank in Louisville and a number of banks throughout the state. Under the aggressive and colorful leadership of James B. Brown, the company believed a merger with Caldwell and Co. in Tennessee would stop its deteriorating financial situation. Once the hasty merger was agreed upon and publicly disclosed, Caldwell provided Brown with the financial truth that Caldwell and Co. was already insolvent. Corporate depositors immediately began to withdraw funds from National Bank of Kentucky. On November 17, 1930, National Bank of Kentucky closed its doors, leading to the closings of American Mutual Savings Bank and First Standard. The two merged and opened as Mutual Standard Bank but quickly went into liquidation in May 1931.

Security Bank closed only temporarily and reopened later in November. Other banks liquidating in the July 1930 to June 1931 year included Bankers Trust Co., Title Guarantee Trust Co., and Union Central Bank. In the July 1931 to June 1932 period, the following banks went into liquidation: Prestonia Bank, Okolona State Bank, Farmers Bank & Trust Co. (St. Matthews), and Jefferson County Bank (Jeffersontown). In the July 1932 to June 1933 period, the only area bank that went into liquidation was the Bank of Fern Creek. Farmers Bank in West Louisville closed but reopened in August 1932. From July 1933 through June 1934, there were no Louisville bank closings or new liquidations. Upon liquidation of Farmers Bank & Trust, depositors received 100 percent of their deposits. Depositors at Title Guarantee were not so lucky; they received only 7 percent.

The trust financing of First Kentucky Co., the stock owner of First National Bank of Louisville, provided capital funding for First National Bank to enter an agreement with the receiver of National Bank of Kentucky. First National purchased the assets of National Bank of Kentucky by accepting 100 percent of the debt owed to the bank's preferred creditors and 67 percent of the debt owed to creditors with

Main lobby of the Citizens Union National Bank, Fifth and Jefferson Streets, 1926.

nonsecured claims. Depositors were creditors with nonsecured claims.

Louisville Trust Co. also closed its doors on November 17, 1930. First National Bank of Louisville, through the receiver of Louisville Trust Co., acquired the already successful installment loan business developed by Louisville National Bank & Trust Co., which had been merged into Louisville Trust Co. in May 1929. Louisville Trust Co. reorganized and reopened in July 1931. To restore public confidence in the new Louisville Trust Co., many important community and financial leaders publicly supported the reorganization both verbally and financially.

The GREAT DEPRESSION was a blow to the Louisville banking community, but the impact was not evenly distributed. The liquidation of the largest Louisville bank, National Bank of Kentucky, hit hard and made news nationally. In retrospect, one might consider its demise the result of folly and greed. Other banks of historical interest fared somewhat better or even quite well given the circumstances. Liberty Bank & Trust Co., with assets of $33.5 million at the end of June 1929, had shrunk to $21.4 million four years later. In contrast, two forerunners of Citizens Fidelity Bank & Trust Co. fared better. Fidelity and Columbia Trust Co. increased its assets from $8.9 million to $10.5 million over the same four-year period, while assets of Citizens Union National Bank slid only $1 million, from $39.6 to $38.6 million. Assets of First National Bank of Louisville fell about $0.8 million, from $20.1 million to $19.3 million. Assets of Stock Yards Bank fell from $1.095 million to $1.004 million. The forerunner of the Bank of Louisville, Morris Plan Industrial Bank, increased in asset size from $697,000 to $847,000. In March 1936 Peoples Bank was given a new charter, with James B. Brown as president. In May 1939 Peoples Bank was placed in liquidation.

During the 1960s and 1970s, as market interest rates moved above regulated rates, banks' losses of deposits led to constraints on bank profitability and competitiveness. Upward adjustments of regulated rates that banks could pay on deposits helped but did not diminish their loss of competitiveness. Nonbank financial institutions continued to attract funds away from regulated banks. Money-market mutual funds became a popular substitute for savings accounts and banks' certificates of deposit. During this era, large banks pushed for both state and national reform to allow them to offer more services at more competitive rates in broader geographical markets.

Savings and loan associations were fearful of banks overtaking them, and small banks were fearful that they would be absorbed or unable to compete with large banks. State regulators began to allow banks to cross state borders in 1975. The economics of the combination of deregulation, gains from technology, and the national presence of nonbank competitors brought banking into a new era of consolidation and expansion that continues into the twenty-first century.

The lobbying for ease in regulation to allow expansion by large Louisville banks was strongly contested by the community banks throughout the state. Finally, as the economics and future structure of banking became more clear, Kentucky legislation was passed in 1984 to essentially rid the state of its limited branching law by permitting multibank holding companies to own banks in different counties. Furthermore, the state 1984 bank-holding company law allowed reciprocal interstate banking among banks in states contiguous to Kentucky for the first two years and then nationally in 1986. Acquisitions within the state were limited, however. No bank-holding company could hold more than 15 percent of total state deposits.

The move by Louisville banks to acquire other state banks was immediate, but the number of acquisitions was limited. The purchases had to make sense financially. First Kentucky National Corp. (First National Bank of Louisville) acquired banks in Ashland, Lexington, Bowling Green, and Owensboro. To broaden its regional presence, it also moved into southern Indiana.

Citizens Fidelity Corp. (Citizens Fidelity Bank & Trust Co.) acquired eight community banks across Kentucky in Lexington, Elizabethtown, Harrodsburg, LAGRANGE, Madison County, and in southern Indiana. In addition, in 1991 Citizens was the assignee of the failed Future Federal Savings Bank in Louisville.

Liberty National Bancorp (Liberty National Bank) had a jump on the merger movement, bringing United Kentucky Bank (Louisville) into its organization in 1982. From the passage of the 1984 act through 1990, Liberty acquired banks in Fort Thomas-Bellevue; Owensboro; Madisonville; CORYDON, Indiana; Elizabethtown; Charlestown, Indiana; Shelbyville; Jessamine County; Florence; Erlanger; Lexington; Hardin County; and Muhlenberg County.

Since the 1960s, Louisville banks have been most instrumental in the development of downtown Louisville. The city of Louisville was facing erosion of population, tax receipts, and businesses located in the central city. The heads of the banks, along with other community leaders, focused on changing attitudes about the downtown and the flow of financing. New banking structures included Liberty's new headquarters at 416 W Jefferson; Citizens Plaza, a structure at Fifth and Jefferson, built in 1971; and First National Tower at Fifth and Main in 1972. Not only did these banks redesign Louisville's skyline, but they provided support for renovation, the Riverfront Plaza/Belvedere, the Kentucky Center for the Arts, and development of the Broadway area, including new housing.

The competitive spirit was quite strong during this period, especially between First National and Citizens, as they continuously vied for being the largest bank in Kentucky. This period of deregulation, bank consolidation, and geographic expansion was not without problems, however. Throughout the nation during the 1980s and early 1990s, a banking and savings-and-loan crisis resulted from losses on bad loans, bad investments in junk bonds, fraud, and excessive rates paid on deposits to retain funds. During this time, several savings and loan associations and one bank in Louisville went out of business—Avery Federal Savings & Loan Association (1981), South East Federal Savings & Loan Association (1982), Continental National Bank of Kentucky (1986), Lincoln Federal Savings & Loan Association (1986), and Future Federal Savings Bank (1991). Because the size of these institutions in relation to the total financial community was small, the impact on the Louisville economy was negligible.

More recently in this era of merger and consolidation, out-of-state banks or holding companies became the buyers of the big local banks or holding companies. The period of expansion by the large, local banks was short-lived. The big fish, little fish scenario was also a cat-and-mouse type game of acquiring or being acquired. The game was in full progress. Louisville banks simply had not had the length of time other banks had throughout the country to expand beyond their county or state borders to make major purchases. Furthermore, their sizes limited the size of their acquisitions. And sometimes it is better for stockholders to be acquired than to be the buyer.

Acquisitions from outside the state were plentiful. PNC Financial Corp. acquired Citizens Fidelity Bank & Trust Co. (now PNC) in its purchase of Citizens Fidelity Corp. in 1987. National City Corp. acquired First National Bank of Louisville (now National City Bank of Kentucky) in its purchase of First Kentucky National Corp. in 1988. Bank One Corp. purchased Liberty National Bank (now Bank One Kentucky, NA) in its acquisition of Liberty National Bancorp Inc. in 1994.

Among contemporary Louisville bankers who have provided active leadership to the city during this period are Malcolm Chancey, J. David Grissom, Dan Ulmer, Michael Harreld, Steven Miles, Morton Boyd, Leonard Hardin, and Frank B. Hower Jr.

Malcolm B. Chancey Jr. was born December 2, 1931. He graduated from the University of Louisville with a bachelor's degree in business administration in 1954. He joined Liberty National Bank & Trust Co. as vice president of the computer department in 1968. In 1986 he was elected to the bank's board of directors. Chancey became president of the bank in 1990 and retired in December 1996 from what became Banc One Kentucky Corp. and Bank One Kentucky, NA. Chancey's greatest civic efforts were in education, with a particular interest in strengthening Jefferson County Public Schools and the University of Louisville. He personally contributed to the university's business school in 1997 to establish scholarships for business entrepreneurs interested in setting up technical firms. Between 1983 and 1986 Chancey also helped head up the University of Louisville's Quest for Excellence campaign that vastly increased its endowment.

J. David Grissom, CEO of Citizens Fidelity Bank & Trust Co. (now PNC) from 1979 to 1989, joined it in 1973. A native of Louisville and a Centre College and University of Louisville alumnus, Grissom received his law degree from U of L in 1962. Grissom teamed up with David A. Jones and Wendell Cherry to help start the company that ultimately became Humana. After Grissom left the bank, he and William Lomicka, Kentucky's secretary of economic development in 1987 and 1988, began running Louisville-based Mayfair Capital, a private investment company they founded as equal partners in 1989. Among civic organizations Grissom has served are the state Council of Higher Education, the Kentucky Independent College Foundation Inc., Louisville Central Area Inc., the Louisville Area Chamber of Commerce, the Kentucky Economic Development Committee, University of Louisville, and Metro United Way.

In 1989 Daniel C. Ulmer Jr. succeeded J. David Grissom as chairman and CEO of Citizens Fidelity Bank (PNC). Ulmer became Citizens Fidelity president in 1976, a bank he had gone to work for in 1957 following his graduation from the University of Louisville in 1955 with a marketing degree and two years of service in the U.S. Navy. After his retirement from banking in 1993, Ulmer continued as a civic booster and baseball fan. He orchestrated the installation of the Redbirds (renamed RiverBats) in 1981 and prevented a threatened move in 1986, becoming part-owner of the team and ultimately team chairman. A long list of Ulmer's leadership positions includes serving the State Fair Board, the University of Louisville, Louisville Central Area Inc., the Regional Airport Authority, Actors Theatre, the Fund for the Arts, the Louisville Orchestra, and Metro United Way.

Michael Neal Harreld received his degree in history and political science from the University of Louisville in 1966 and his J.D. degree from the University of Louisville Law School in 1969. That same year he joined Citizens Fidelity Bank in the trust division. Harreld was named president in 1989 and in 1993 CEO of PNC. Active in civic affairs and with a particular interest in higher education, Harreld has served as chair of the board of trustees for Bellarmine College and as a member of the board for Western Kentucky University, Murray State University, and the University of Louisville. He has also served as a member of the Prichard Committtee for Academic Excellence and chaired the Kentucky Council on Higher Education. Harreld has been a board member of a host of other civic activities, among them the J.B. Speed Art Museum, the Library Foundation, Greater Louisville Inc., the Filson Club Historical Society, the Kentucky Historical Society, and many others. Harreld was born October 14, 1944, in Louisville.

A. Stevens Miles joined First National Bank of Louisville in 1954 (later First Kentucky, now National City Bank of Kentucky), becoming an executive vice president in 1969 and the president and chief operating officer in 1973. Miles was named president and chief executive officer of First Kentucky National Corp. and its principal subsidiaries in 1974; in 1986 he was elected chairman. After the merger of First Kentucky National Corp. and National City Corp. in 1988 he was elected president of National City Corp. and continued as chairman of First Kentucky. He also continued as director of National City Corp. and First Kentucky National Corp. Miles retired from banking in 1989. Miles is a graduate of Washington & Lee University and the Stonier Graduate School of Banking at Rutgers University. In civic affairs he has served as chairman of the Louisville Waterfront Development Corp., the Museum of History and Science (now Louisville Science Center), and as vice chairman of the Kentucky Derby Museum. In addition he has served on the Campaign for Greater Louisville and Kentucky Economic Development Corp., the Louisville Fund for the Arts, and the Old Kentucky Home Council of the Boy Scouts of America.

Morton Boyd, retired chairman and chief executive officer of National City Bank, joined First National Bank of Louisville in 1959 as a management trainee. After serving in a variety of positions, he was named chief executive officer of First National's parent, First Kentucky National Corp., in 1989. He also served as executive vice president of National City Corp. Boyd retired in 1996 but continued as a board member. Boyd is a graduate of the University of Virginia and the Stonier Graduate School of

Banking. Public service includes the Kentucky Economic Development Corp., the GREATER LOUISVILLE ECONOMIC DEVELOPMENT PARTNERSHIP, the Fund for the Arts, the J.B. Speed Art Museum, the University of Louisville, and Bellarmine College.

Leonard V. Hardin began his banking career in 1953. He held various positions in First National Bank of Louisville, becoming executive vice president in 1976, president in 1987, and chief executive officer in 1988. After the bank assumed the name of National City Bank of Kentucky, also in 1988, Hardin served as president and director. In 1996 Hardin was named chairman, retiring in 1999. Hardin is a native of Brownsville, Kentucky, a graduate of the University of Louisville with a B.S. in commerce, banking, and finance, and a graduate of the Stonier Graduate School of Banking. Among institutions he has served are the Louisville Chamber of Commerce, LEADERSHIP LOUISVILLE, the Greater Louisville Economic Development Partnership, Metro United Way, the Fund for the Arts, the University of Louisville, the SOUTHERN BAPTIST THEOLOGICAL SEMINARY, Bellarmine College, and the Council on Postsecondary Education.

Frank B. Hower Jr., born November 26, 1928 in Louisville, was a graduate of LOUISVILLE MALE HIGH SCHOOL. After earning his B.A. degree from Centre College in 1950, he worked briefly for Liberty National Bank & Trust Co. (now Bank One Kentucky, NA) as a proof clerk, before enlisting in the Marines. After the KOREAN WAR he returned, in 1953, to Liberty as the first trainee in their first-ever trainee program. Before becoming CEO and chairman of the bank in 1973, Hower had spent the majority of his professional life as a commercial lending officer. During his seventeen years as chairman the bank increased its assets from $430 million to 43.2 billion, taking Liberty National Bancorp of Louisville from a community bank to the state's largest independent banking company at that time. In 1982 he oversaw the nation's first merger of competing banks, when Liberty merged with United Kentucky Bank. On February 1, 1990, after forty years, he retired. In addition to service on the boards of the James Graham Brown Foundation, Norton Health Systems, CHURCHILL DOWNS, AMERICAN LIFE & ACCIDENT CO., and Anthem Inc., Hower served as chairman of the United Way Campaign in 1969, president of the Chamber of Commerce in 1973, and chairman of the Regional Airport Authority from 1985 to 1993. He is also a former trustee of Centre College.

Deregulation and reregulation of the financial institutions did not stop with commercial banks. The powers of savings and loan associations became more like those of full-service banks. Commercial banks were allowed to acquire savings and loans. Savings and loans converted from mutual to stock ownership, posturing themselves to buy or to be acquired. Star Bank, NA from Cincinnati (now Firstar Bank, NA) acquired Great Financial Bank in 1998 (formerly Great Financial Federal Savings and Loan). Fifth Third Bancorp acquired the Cumberland Federal Bancorporation Inc. (the Cumberland Federal Savings Bank) in 1994. The loss of corporate headquarters of financial institutions in Louisville was not limited to depository institutions. Providian Corp. (formerly Capital Holding Corp.) was acquired in 1997 by Aegon N.V.

In spite of all of the acquisitions and consolidation, there continues to be room for the small and medium-size banks. Survivors include the Bank of Louisville and Stock Yards Bank & Trust Co., which continue to be successful in their respective areas of lending and trust services. Republic Bank & Trust, chartered in 1982, developed its niche and increased its deposits to nearly $400 million by 1998.

As of 1999, there were 15 banks in Louisville, 4 nationally chartered and 11 state-chartered, with 252 offices and deposits totaling $12.8 billion. The largest was National City Bank of Kentucky, with fifty-three offices and deposits of $3.8 billion. The smallest was the Louisville Community Development Bank with one office and $21.3 million in deposits.

The banking industry has become part of the new financial services industry in which the complex financial institution offers services ranging from accepting deposits and making loans to writing insurance policies and providing brokerage and trust services and financial advice. Further deregulation and technological advancement will support additional consolidation, more name changes, and a broadening of services offered by any one institution.

See Wilber Clarence Bothwell, "The Federal Reserve Bank of St. Louis," Ph.D. dissertation, Washington University, 1941; Department of Financial Institutions, State of Kentucky, *Annual Report,* selected years; Sarah A. Kelly, "History of the First National Group, Louisville, Kentucky, 1874–1974," Aug. 29, 1980, unpublished; Robert T. Fugate Jr., "The Banco Kentucky Company and the Depression in Louisville," M.A. thesis, University of Louisville, 1972; Capt. John H. Leathers, "Banks and Banking Institutions," in J. Stoddard Johnston, ed., *Memorial History of Louisville* (Chicago and New York 1896); *1998 Bank & Thrift Branch Office Data Book, Central Region* (Federal Deposit Insurance Corp., Washington, D.C.); James Neal Primm, *A Foregone Conclusion* (Federal Reserve Bank of St. Louis, 1989), Rand McNally *Bankers Directory,* selected Years; Dale Royalty, "Banking and the Commonwealth Ideal in Kentucky, 1806–1822," *Register of the Kentucky Historical Society* 77 (Spring 1979): 91–107.

James R. McCabe

BANK OF KENTUCKY. In the first years following statehood, it quickly became apparent that Kentucky's traditional frontier ECONOMY of personal loan and barter would no longer be sufficient. The rapid settlement of vacant lands, POPULATION growth, and the development of farms and industry required capital and, of course, banks. In response, the Kentucky General Assembly chartered the Bank of Kentucky in 1806 (it was in later years commonly called the "First" or "Old" Bank of Kentucky). With an authorized capital stock of $1 million (one-half of which was reserved for the state), the bank was immediately successful, and a period of overall prosperity and conservative management kept the bank sound. A branch of the Bank of Kentucky was established in Louisville in 1812, and a few years later the bank's authorized capital was increased to a total of $3 million.

The general collapse of the United States economy following the War of 1812 prompted the legislature to charter forty new banks (quickly dubbed the "forty thieves"). Soon creditors were presented with a flood of paper money worth only a fraction of its face value. An escalating spiral of speculation and paper money drove up prices and culminated in the panic of 1819. By 1820 the Bank of Kentucky was forced to suspend payments in hard currency, and two years later the legislature repealed the portions of its charter that allowed it to lend money, thus effectively ending BANKING operations. The branch banks, including the Louisville branch, were closed in 1824, but the final obligations of the first Bank of Kentucky were not settled until 1870.

The emergence of the second Bank of the United States, which had a branch in Louisville and had constructed a fine brick-and-stone building on MAIN between Second and Third Streets, had lessened the need for state banks, but it was opposed by President Andrew Jackson (1829–37), and its charter was not renewed. The Kentucky General Assembly had anticipated this, and in 1834 the legislature chartered a second Bank of Kentucky, headquartered in Louisville, with a capital stock of $5 million. The new Bank of Kentucky eventually purchased the building of the Louisville branch of the Bank of the United States and hired its former director, John J. Jacob, as its first president. Branches were thereafter established in Lexington, Frankfort, Maysville, Greensburg, Bowling Green, Hopkinsville, and Danville.

The Bank of Kentucky survived the financial storms of the late 1830s by suspending general payment of specie until 1842, when prosperity finally returned to the country. The bank participated in the financing of business and railroad construction, much of it in Louisville, with considerable success and weathered in large extent the difficulties caused by the CIVIL WAR. In 1866 the directors decided to close down the various branch banks, except at Frankfort. The Bank of Kentucky became a national bank in 1900, thus ending its existence as a state-created institution, but continued well into the century as the National Bank of Kentucky.

The Bank of Kentucky building, then 139 years old, was razed in 1971.

See Basil W. Duke, *History of the Bank of Kentucky* (Louisville 1895); *Courier-Journal*, Feb. 9, 1896, Feb. 22, 1920.

John S. Gillig

BANK OF LOUISVILLE. The first institution to operate under this name was started after President Andrew Jackson vetoed rechartering the second Bank of the United States in July 1832, prompting Louisville to charter its own bank. The first Bank of Louisville, which later became the Southern Bank of Louisville, was created on February 2, 1833. Its Greek Revival building, completed in 1837, was located at what is now 316 W MAIN ST. and today houses ACTORS THEATRE of Louisville.

On January 4, 1926, the current Bank of Louisville and Trust Co., which is not related to the first Bank of Louisville, was opened as a philanthropic enterprise by a LOUISVILLE BOARD OF TRADE committee to provide low-interest loans to working people. It was initially opened as the Morris Plan Industrial Bank by a group of Louisville businessmen led by Jesse F. Streng. He was referred to as the "the father of installment credit in Louisville" by local media and was connected with the bank until his death in 1973 at the age of ninety-two. It was the first city bank to use drive-in facilities and the first to offer a no-minimum-balance checking account. In 1946 the Morris Plan, which had its headquarters at 427 W MARKET ST., changed its name to Bank of Louisville, although there was no corresponding change in ownership, management, or services.

In 1963 Bank of Louisville merged with the larger Royal Bank and Trust Co. The new bank was named the Bank of Louisville-Royal Bank and Trust Co. and was headed by Royal Bank's president and chief stockholder, SAMUEL KLEIN. Klein remained president until he retired in 1985, handing control of the company over to his nephew, Bertram Klein.

The merger with Royal Bank followed two failed attempts to merge with Citizens Fidelity Bank and Trust Co. in 1960 and 1961. The Federal Reserve Board denied the mergers, stating it was not in the public interest. Board approval was necessary since Citizens was a member of the Federal Reserve System. The merger between Bank of Louisville and Royal Bank and Trust Co. needed only permission from the state's banking commissioner and the Federal Deposit Insurance Corp., because neither was a member of the Federal Reserve System.

In 1965 the bank's name was shortened to Bank of Louisville-Royal, and in 1967, just before the company moved to its new headquarters, the name became Bank of Louisville. The new eleven-story headquarters at BROADWAY and Fifth St. was built as part of a center-city development project. It was built by developer Al J. Schneider and was one of the first to add rental office space to the downtown inventory.

A downtown branch of Bank of Louisville was also the scene of one of the most dramatic bank robbery attempts in the city's history. In October 1984 a former prosecuting attorney from Arkansas and Tennessee, William Hightower, robbed a branch bank at 626 W Broadway and threatened to blow up the building. After taking five bank employees hostage, including the bank manager, Hightower was killed by police after attempting to escape by motorcycle.

In 1983 Bank of Louisville formed the Mid-America Bancorp as a holding company and to expand loan servicing offices in Kentucky, Ohio, and southern Indiana. Bank of Louisville, which in 1998 was only one of two locally owned and operated banks (the other being the STOCK YARDS BANK), is a primary subsidiary of Mid-America Bancorp. There are thirty-three banking centers in greater Louisville. Mid-America Savings Bank, FSB (federal savings bank), is also a subsidiary of Mid-America Bancorp. As of late 1997, the Bank of Louisville was the sixth-largest bank in Louisville and the largest independent, locally owned commercial bank in the city, with assets totaling more than $1.6 billion. It opened the Women's Banking Center, designed to serve women entrepreneurs. It is the only publicly traded local thrift or bank with assets over $1 billion.

On February 23, 1998, Mid-America Bancorp adopted a shareholders' rights plan to protect shareholder interests in the event of a hostile takeover attempt.

See George H. Yater, *Two Hundred Years at the Falls of the Ohio* (Louisville 1987); *Courier-Journal*, Feb. 27, 1988.

BANK ONE KENTUCKY, NA. The origin of Bank One Kentucky, NA, Louisville's oldest continuous financial institution, dates back to March 9, 1854, when the General Assembly of Kentucky approved the incorporation of the German Insurance Co., chartered not only to conduct insurance business but to conduct banking as well. The original organizers, primarily of German descent, were substantial merchants of the city. Interestingly, the first president of the company was Jacob Laval, who was of French descent.

The activities of the company in the early years were more in banking than in insurance. The original office was on the northeast corner of FOURTH and MARKET and then moved to Third St. between MAIN and Market STREETS. Business was good. A new bank building built in 1868 on the north side of Market between Second and Third was the home of the famous clock tower, which became a landmark for Louisville. Continuing to expand, the bank moved in 1887 to an even larger, new three-story building near Second and Market, the home of the bank until it moved to its new headquarters on Jefferson and Liberty between Fourth and Fifth Streets in 1960.

New state laws in 1872 made it mandatory to separate banking from insurance. Thus, a new charter was drawn to form the GERMAN INSURANCE BANK. The insurance company voted to keep all of its surplus funds at the newly formed bank as long as the bank agreed to pay 5 percent interest. Under the presidency of Joseph J. Fischer from 1889 to 1896, the bank grew, expanding beyond its German customer base and attracting not only the smaller merchants but also larger businesses because of its sound, conservative management practices.

The bank established a savings department in 1913 and continued to be a leader in savings deposits among all financial institutions in Kentucky. During WORLD WAR I the bank changed its name to Liberty Insurance Bank. Under the presidency of John E. Huhn, Liberty inaugurated a system of branch banks, a trust department, and a real estate loan department. A name change to Liberty Bank and Trust Co. came in 1928 along with the new trust department.

Liberty responded to the trials of the GREAT DEPRESSION in December 1933 by hiring thirty-three-year-old New York banker Merle E. Robertson to lead the bank. In 1935 Liberty reorganized and obtained a federal charter, changing its name to Liberty National Bank and Trust Co.

Expansion of the bank continued during the next three decades, primarily through the increase in branches within the city and Jefferson County, as the population increased more rapidly in the SUBURBS. Liberty Bank captured a number of firsts, including the first female correspondent bank officer in Kentucky (1970); the first four ATMs in Kentucky, including the first airport ATM in the country, and the first two drive-up ATMs in the country (February 1971); the first Louisville bank to go on-line with its network of ATMs (February 9, 1976); and the first bank in the Louisville area to offer brokerage services to customers and correspondent banks (April 25, 1983). Even as it made the nationally noticed advances, Liberty Bank maintained strong ties to the Louisville community, sponsoring *A Louisville Panorama,* a history of the city published in 1954 and again in 1960. To keep pace with the expansion of services offered and changes in regulations, Liberty National Bancorp, Inc. a one-bank holding company, was established in July 1980. On December 23, 1982, United Kentucky Bank merged into Liberty. This merger is historic in that it was the first cross-town merger approved by the U.S. Justice Department based upon the evidence that the banking competition not only included banks, themselves, but other financial institutions delivering similar services and products, as well.

In January 1984 LNB Life Insurance Co. was formed as a wholly owned subsidiary of the bank. Expansion of services and geographical area occurred even more rapidly after the passage of state legislation in 1984 allowing statewide acquisitions of other banks and interstate acquisitions in states with a reciprocal arrangement. Liberty National Mortgage Corp. began operations in 1984 as a subsidiary to originate, sell, and service single-family residential loans for other companies' portfolios and to service the bank's own mortgage portfolio.

In 1985 Liberty acquired Fort Thomas-Bellevue Bancorp in Northern Kentucky and Citizens First Bancorp in Owensboro. In 1986 Liberty purchased KBT Corp., a holding company for Kentucky Bank and Trust Co. of Madisonville, and Corydon State Bancorp of CORYDON, Indiana, Liberty's first out-of-state acquisition. Acquisitions continued with Indiana First National, First Indiana, the Bank of Shelbyville, the Bank of Elizabethtown, and the Bank of Jessamine in 1988. In 1990 Liberty continued its expansion with the acquisitions of Commbanc Shares Inc. to obtain the Community Bank in Erlanger and the Florence Deposit Bank. In 1991 Liberty purchased the Bank of Lexington and in 1993 Dominion Bancshares in Radcliff, Kentucky, for its banks in Radcliff and Brandenburg. Liberty Bank pioneered another trend for Louisville banks when in the late 1960s it built its headquarters on Jefferson St. in the first glass-curtain-wall building downtown. Following in the footsteps of Louisville-based Citizens Fidelity and First National of being acquired by out-of-state banks, Liberty National Bank was acquired and later became Bank One Kentucky, NA, in September 1995 after Bank One Corp. purchased Liberty National Bancorp Inc. on August 4, 1994.

See "Liberty National Bank: Historical Chronology and 'Firsts,'" Liberty National Bank Memorandum, Kentucky Bankers Association; "1854–Liberty National Bank and Trust Company, Louisville" *500th Edition of the Kentucky Bankers Magazine* (Feb. 1967); Charles Raymond Reibel, "The Story of Louisville's Oldest Financial Institution," in *Louisville Panorama: A Visual History of Louisville* (Louisville 1954).

James R. McCabe

BAPTISTS. The earliest Baptist presence in Kentucky was probably in 1776, with a sermon delivered by a Virginia itinerant preacher, William Hickman, in Harrodstown (Harrodsburg). By June 1781 the first Baptist church in Kentucky was founded at Severns Valley in what is now Elizabethtown. In 1784 the Beargrass (Baptist) Church became the first Baptist church to be established near Louisville. A building was constructed by 1798, but the site is now unknown. In 1792 the Chenoweth Run Church became the second congregation founded within the Jefferson County region. Churches came and went with the settlers, some appearing and disappearing with frequency. By October 1802, however, the LONG RUN BAPTIST Association of churches "on the North side of SALT RIVER" was established, incorporating Louisville and Jefferson County.

One Kentucky Baptist tradition also claims Daniel Boone's brother, Squire, "an occasional preacher in the Calvinistic Baptist Church," was one of the earliest preachers in Louisville (some say the earliest).

Although documentation is difficult, the tradition remains that the first Baptist church in Louisville was constituted by Henson Hobbs (1772–1821) in the home of Mark Lampton, located on Chestnut St. That church applied for admission to the Long Run Association in 1815 and claimed thirty-seven members in 1817 and seventy members at the death of pastor Hobbs in 1821. In 1815 the Baptist church established a mission for slaves that became the First African Baptist Church in 1829. In 1826 the First Baptist congregation joined with the local Masonic lodge (a controversial relationship for many anti-Mason Baptists) in constructing a three-story building used by both groups. Growth was significant. First Baptist Church baptized 637 people during the years 1838–44. Its membership included such well-known personages as architect GIDEON SHRYOCK (1802–80). In 1838 Louisville's SECOND BAPTIST CHURCH was constituted in a location on Third St. (Pearl). William C. Buck (1790–1842), Baptist preacher and editor, was instrumental in founding East Baptist Church on Green St. (LIBERTY) near PRESTON in 1842. Buck came to Louisville in 1836, serving four years as pastor of First Baptist Church and "general agency" (fund-raiser) for the General Association of Baptists in Kentucky. In 1841 he became editor of the *Baptist Banner and Western Pioneer*, one of the early Baptist periodicals in the state. Fourth Baptist was founded in 1845.

African American Baptists may have worshiped separately from whites by 1829. The Louisville directory for 1832 describes a "Baptist church, devoted to colored persons" that was located "on MARKET ST., between 7th and 8th." In 1844 the congregation bought facilities owned by FIRST CHRISTIAN CHURCH on Fifth St. HENRY ADAMS began pastoral work at the church by 1839. Although separate, the large congregation was connected to and counted among the membership of First Baptist Church, whose white members represented blacks at the Long Run Association meetings. Protests for their own representation were rejected, however, by the association.

The Baptist churches in and around Louisville experienced their first major controversy and resulting schism in the 1830s due to the influence of the theology of Alexander Campbell (1788–1866). Campbell visited the region in 1823, debating Presbyterian William McCalla not far from Washington, Kentucky. Campbell suggested that the New Testament church, lost since the Constantinian era (fourth century), had been "restored." Restorationists (Campbellites) eschewed denominational names, constituting communities of faith for "Christians only." They rejected human-made creeds or confessions, affirmed simple faith in Jesus as Messiah, practiced immersion baptism, and observed weekly communion on the Lord's Day. Numerous Baptist congregations, including segments of Louisville's First Baptist Church, "apostatized" to Campbellism.

During the late 1820s and early 1830s, Benjamin Allen and John Curl served as supply preachers for First Baptist Church. Their appreciation for Restorationism led to a schism (1831) in which all but 85 of the 245 members broke with the Baptists to form First Christian Church. As the majority, the Restorationists retained possession of the church property and records. The 1832 Louisville directory listed the "Old Baptist church" and the "Reformed Baptist Church," the latter the Restorationist congregation.

The Baptists recouped some of their losses, numbering almost 700 members in 1842, when some 279 African American members formed the African church into an autonomous congregation. That church was added to the Long Run Association in 1842. Thus by 1846 there were numerous Baptist churches in Louisville, including First, Second, East, Jefferson Street, and Fourth Baptist. In 1849 the First and Second Baptist Churches merged, taking the name of the WALNUT STREET BAPTIST CHURCH, the oldest continuous Baptist church in Louisville.

Louisville Baptist churches declared the gospel of Christ, gathered for worship, and practiced strict discipline of members. Records from First Baptist Church illustrate the tenor of disciplinary action. In 1848 "Sister Tumey" was charged with "fornication," and the investigating committee reported, "We have waited on our Sister Tumey by request and from appearance we would judge that reports are true. She positively denies it and says upon our peril we are not to exclude her from the church. But we believe from her general appearance that she is not worthy to be a member of this church any longer." The sister was thus excluded from church membership. Churches often appointed women and men to serve as collectors, visiting members to secure contributions and chastening those considered delinquent in their giving.

Other religious activities were evident in the practices of the Second Baptist Church, which in 1842 reported holding revival meetings, four weekly prayer meetings, a Sabbath school, and raising "nearly seventy dollars for Georgetown College" (founded in 1829). In 1844 First Baptist Church dedicated its new gothic sanctuary, with a seating capacity of eight hundred and an organ valued at ten thousand dollars. During the 1840s the church reported that "a maternal society has been formed, and the mothers belonging to it meet on the first Thursday in each month to pray for the salvation of their children. There are five weekly prayer meetings, one of which is the young converts' prayer meeting, and another the female prayer meeting."

When W.W. Everts (1814–90) accepted the pastorate of Walnut Street Baptist Church in 1853, John L. Waller wrote to him: "Louisville is the emporium of the greatest Baptist State in the World." He noted that "the great [Ohio] valley required 'a point of influence,' politically and religiously." Waller asked, "Where can this be done so well as in Louisville?"

In 1854 the small number of German Baptists in Louisville founded a congregation in the HAYMARKET district. In 1884 they called a student summer minister named Walter Rauschenbusch (1862–1918). Rauschenbusch became one of the chief proponents of the Social Gospel movement in America and a major influence on Baptist life worldwide. He wrote of his brief time in the Louisville church: "When I left I was as thin as a ghost, but I rejoiced in a number of conversions; I saw the members united by their common affection for their common Master. I saw them deeply affected when I said farewell."

The first African school was established in Louisville in 1841 by African American Baptist minister Henry Adams. It was moved to the First African Church (Fifth St.) in 1864 and remained there until PUBLIC SCHOOLS admitted blacks in 1870. In 1879 the Kentucky Normal and Theological Institute was founded in Louisville with ELIJAH MARRS as president. WILLIAM JAMES SIMMONS (1849–90) became the school's president in 1880. Born in slavery in South Carolina, he received both bachelor's and master's degrees from Howard University and came to Kentucky in 1879, first to Lexington and then Louisville.

While president of the Normal Institute, Simmons also organized the Colored Press Association in 1880 and founded a journal known as the *AMERICAN BAPTIST*. In 1884 the name of the school was changed to State University, offering the only advanced degrees for which blacks were able to study in Kentucky. It also was the only African American school offering undergraduate, medical, and law degrees. In 1918 the school was named SIMMONS UNIVERSITY. It remained a university until 1931, when financial difficulties of the GREAT DEPRESSION led to its demise. It continues to provide ministerial training as Simmons Bible College.

In 1845 the Southern Baptist Convention was formed in Augusta, Georgia, as a result of differences between Baptists north and south over slavery and the appointment of slave-holding missionaries. The southerners defended the practice, insisting that holding slaves should not be an issue in determining missionary service. When the Mission Society (triennial convention) rejected such an appointment, the southerners formed their own denomination. While no representatives from Kentucky Baptist churches attended the organizational meeting, Louisville churches soon affiliated with the new denomination. In 1857 the Southern Baptist Convention held its first annual meeting in Kentucky at the Walnut St. church.

In August 1865, delegates from twelve of the seventeen African American Baptist churches in Kentucky gathered in Louisville and organized the State Convention of Colored Baptists in Kentucky. In 1869 its name was changed to the General Association of Baptists in Kentucky, with some 55 churches and a membership of 12,620.

In 1869 the Louisville Baptist Orphans' Home was founded in a house on Walnut St. (Muhammad Ali Blvd.), with leadership from numerous Louisville Baptists, including George Lorimer, pastor of Walnut St. church. The charter was officially approved by the General Assembly in 1870. It remains the oldest continuously operating children's home in the south. Also in 1870, the location was moved to First and St. Catherine Streets. In 1947 the charter was amended and the name changed to the Spring Meadows Children's Home. In 1950 new facilities were opened in MIDDLETOWN.

In 1877 the SOUTHERN BAPTIST THEOLOGICAL SEMINARY was moved from Greenville, South Carolina, to Louisville. Founded in 1859, it was the first seminary sponsored by the Southern Baptist Convention and was originally on W BROADWAY. The school moved to its Lexington Rd. location in 1925. The Southern Baptist Seminary created a significant Baptist presence in Louisville through students, faculty, visiting lecturers, and almost unending controversy. For example, divisions over the Landmark controversy (the effort to establish Baptists as the only true church linked directly to the New Testament community) set T.T. Eaton, pastor of Walnut Street Baptist Church, against WILLIAM H. WHITSITT, seminary president. Whitsitt's claim that Baptists did not discover immersion until more than thirty years after their origins in England cast doubts on the faulty Landmark history. As a result, Whitsitt resigned in 1899, returning to his native Virginia. Later controversies involved charges that professors taught evolution, German theology, the Social Gospel, and various liberal ideas, and promoted the visit of such controversial speakers as Martin Luther King Jr., Philip Berrigan, Will Campbell, and W.A. Criswell. A controversy over issues of biblical inerrancy and institutional control during the 1980s and 1990s led to various faculty-trustee-administrative conflicts and ultimately the resignation or dismissal of more than 80 percent of the faculty and staff.

Philanthropy among Baptist laity in Louisville had significant impact on the churches in general and the theological seminary in particular. GEORGE W. NORTON (1814–99) and his family provided financial support for many Baptist causes, including BROADWAY BAPTIST CHURCH, founded in 1870, and the seminary's move from Greenville to Louisville. Norton was a charter member of Broadway church and a deacon and treasurer of the Southern Baptist Convention (1866–89). In the twentieth century, Baptists also benefited from the benevolence of automobile executive V.V. Cooke Sr. and businessman EDWIN GHEENS and his wife Mary Jo.

Broadway Baptist Church was the location for the inauguration of the Woman's Missionary Union Training School for Christian Workers on October 2, 1907. The school was established by the Woman's Missionary Union (WMU), auxiliary to the Southern Baptist Convention. Fannie E.S. Heck, president of the WMU, and William Owen Carver, professor at the Southern Baptist Theological Seminary, were leaders in the effort. The school provided education for women preparing for mission work and other areas of service. In 1953 it became the W.O. CARVER SCHOOL OF MISSIONS AND SOCIAL WORK, jointly sponsored by the seminary and WMU. In the 1980s it became the first theological seminary in the country to offer joint Master of Divinity and Master of Social Work degrees. By the 1990s controversy over the work of the school and its relationship to the fundamentalist leadership of the seminary and the Southern Baptist Convention brought about the end of the social work program.

In 1918 the Kentucky Baptist Hospital was chartered in Louisville by the General Association of Baptists in Kentucky. Its official opening occurred in 1924, the same year that a School of Nursing also began. An affiliation was also developed later between the hospitals and the School of Radiologic Technology at BELLARMINE COLLEGE. The hospital was subsequently divided between two locations: Highlands Baptist Hospital and Baptist East Hospital (opened in 1975). Highlands was closed in the 1980s.

In Louisville, Baptists were instrumental in the formation of a new educational institution, KENTUCKY SOUTHERN COLLEGE, in 1962. It was sponsored by the Long Run Baptist Association and later the Kentucky Baptist Convention. Rollin S. Burhans, pastor of CRESCENT HILL BAPTIST CHURCH, Louisville, was named the first president. Classes began on the campus of the Southern Baptist Theological Seminary and then moved to the Shelbyville Rd. location in 1963. The school offered creative teaching methods and curriculum but was unable to sustain financial support. In 1967 the trustees voted to merge the college with the UNIVERSITY OF LOUISVILLE, which in 1969 took over the campus facilities.

Baptist churches in Louisville cooperated in such common endeavors as the Dwight L. Moody revival campaign of 1888 and providing shelter for refugees after the 1937 FLOOD and the 1974 tornado. They divided over issues of race, theology, and denominational governance. During the 1960s and 1970s, African American Baptist leaders such as LYMAN JOHNSON and W.J. Hodge offered leadership in the CIVIL RIGHTS movement and went on to serve in political office. During the controversy over school BUSING for racial integration of the 1970s, some white Baptist clergy supported the plan, even riding the first buses in order to provide security for students. Others opposed the practice and worked to overturn the decision.

By the 1980s African American churches

such as St. Stephen's Baptist had developed programs urging Afrocentrism and stronger cultural and racial identities among black youth. White churches affiliated with the Southern Baptist Convention divided between fundamentalists and "moderates" over theological and political issues relative to funding and control of the denomination itself. In 1997 Louisville was the site of the annual meeting of the Cooperative Baptist Fellowship, an organization of moderate Baptists founded in 1991.

See Ira V. Birdwhistell, *Gathered at the River: A Narrative History of the Long Run Baptist Association* (Louisville 1978); *Encyclopedia of Southern Baptists*, vols. 1–4 (Nashville 1956); Samuel S. Hill, ed., *Religion in the Southern States* (Macon, Ga., 1983); Bill J. Leonard, *Community in Diversity: A History of the Walnut Street Baptist Church, 1815–1990* (Louisville 1990); *Dictionary of Baptists in America* (Downers Grove, Ill., 1994); *God's Last and Only Hope: The Fragmentation of the Southern Baptist Convention* (Grand Rapids, Mich., 1990); J.H. Spencer, *A History of Kentucky Baptists* (Louisville 1885); Lawrence H. Williams, *The History of Simmons University* (Louisville 1987).

Bill J. Leonard

BARBEE, JOHN (b Pewee Valley, Kentucky, September 16, 1815; d Pewee Valley, December 22, 1888). Mayor. John Barbee was the son of James Barbee and Jane Sherrard Barbee. Both of his parents had died by the time Barbee was eleven. At age fourteen he went to Louisville and took a position at Elisha Attry's dry goods store. In 1837 he was employed by J. & J.W. Anderson, operators of the largest wholesale dry goods house in Louisville.

In 1841 he was elected by the City Council to the post of collector of revenues for the Eastern District of Louisville. He left politics briefly in 1845 and established the wholesale dry goods house of Anderson, McLane, and Barbee. After several years he left the firm and established another dry goods business with A.O. Brannin. In 1849 and 1851 he was elected to the City Council. He remained a councilman until he was elected to another office.

In 1855 Barbee was elected MAYOR over incumbent James S. Speed, who did not declare his candidacy or run a campaign because of confusion about the expiration of his term of office. Speed, with legal support from Louisville's Chancery Court, contended that his term of office had not expired.

Barbee was a candidate of the KNOW-NOTHING, or American, Party, a vehemently anti-foreign and anti-Catholic political party that grew out of the old WHIG PARTY. Local NEWSPAPERS, such as WALTER N. HALDEMAN'S *LOUISVILLE DAILY COURIER*, waged a campaign against Speed, who had converted to Catholicism. After Barbee won, Speed filed a suit in Jefferson Circuit Court disputing the election results. The suit was eventually settled in the Know Nothing–dominated State Court of Appeals, where Barbee was declared the new mayor. Barbee was installed as mayor by a resolution of the general council on April 30, but he officially took office in June 1855. He served until April 6, 1857.

Barbee was mayor during "BLOODY MONDAY," the uprising in Louisville against IRISH and GERMAN immigrants on August 6, 1855. It was election day in Kentucky for governor and members of Congress. It was certain that riots would occur; nevertheless, neither Barbee nor any of the city government provided security at the voting booths. The riots broke out when Know-Nothings prevented naturalized Germans and Irish from voting. The riots erupted first in the streets of the East End and BUTCHERTOWN. Many Germans were beaten, and some were killed. The riots then moved down to the Eighth Ward, where most of the Irish lived. QUINN'S ROW, a housing complex, became the focus of the rioters. The row was set afire and many were burned to death, including Francis Quinn. Barbee did intercede and prevented the rioters from destroying the Catholic cathedral, but the day would forever be remembered for its brutality.

After serving as mayor, Barbee was elected to the City Council in 1858 and served until 1861. In 1860 he was president of the Board of Councilmen. After the CIVIL WAR Barbee became a Democrat and remained affiliated with the party until his death.

Barbee married Eliza Kane, daughter of Thomas Kane, in 1841. They had four children: Alice, Charlotte, Thomas, and John Junior. He died at the family home, within ten feet of the spot where he was born. He is buried in CAVE HILL CEMETERY.

See Josiah Stoddard Johnston, ed., *Memorial History of Louisville*, 2 vols., (Chicago and New York 1896); George H. Yater, *Two Hundred Years at the Falls of the Ohio* (Louisville 1987).

BARBERSHOP QUARTET SINGING. The distinctive sound of a cappella barbershop harmony singing is the result of bass, baritone, lead (melody), and tenor voices blending in a perfect pitch relationship. Louisville barbershop groups have excelled in achieving this sound for many years.

Organized barbershop singing in Louisville began in 1945 when Louisville businessman Fritz Drybrough organized a chapter of the Society for the Preservation and Encouragement of Barbershop Quartet Singing in America (SPEBSQSA). Until 1957 the chorus practiced in the old Henry Clay Hotel and presented only local chapter shows.

In 1957 a competitive chorus, the Thoroughbreds, was formed. This group won the district competition in 1958 and qualified for the international contest, where it finished eighth in 1959. The group placed sixth in 1960, second in 1961, and won the international contest in 1962. The Thoroughbreds also won the gold medal in 1966, 1969, 1974, 1978, 1981, and 1984.

The first women's barbershop chorus was the Bluegrass Chorus, formed in 1953 as a chapter of Sweet Adelines Inc. The group was dissolved in 1958 to be followed by the Kentuckiana Chorus in 1964. In 1972 a second chorus, Falls of the Ohio, was organized. In 1982 these two groups consolidated to form the Derby City Chorus. In 1984 several members of Derby City left to form yet another women's group, the Pride of Kentucky.

Another addition to Louisville barbershop singing organizations was the Louisville Times Chorus, chartered by the SPEBSQSA in 1994. While several Louisville barbershop choruses and quartets have won regional awards, three Louisville quartets have been named international champions: Bluegrass Student Union (1978), Interstate Rivals (1987), and Second Edition (1989).

Dennis L. Spetz

BARKER, HORACE M. (b Irvine, Kentucky, March 31, 1898; d Louisville, July 28, 1980). Jefferson County judge. Barker attended Kentucky Wesleyan College and received his law degree from Washington and Lee University. He was admitted to the Louisville bar in 1930.

Barker was Jefferson County judge from January 7, 1946, until January 1, 1950. He defeated Democrat Edwin C. Willis by 684 votes out of the more than 110,000 cast. The Republicans won nearly every city and county office in 1945, with the exception of the mayor's office, which was won by 204 votes by Democrat E. LELAND TAYLOR. Barker did not run for reelection in 1949.

In January 1946 Barker initiated an investigation of the county police department that eventually led to the dismissal of several officers, some of whom were eventually reinstated. Barker requested the help of the Federal Bureau of Investigation to reorganize the county police, and more stringent hiring criteria were adopted. The FBI also helped the county to start a training academy for new officers. Barker launched major road-improvement programs and acquired new park- and timberlands for public use. He also established a county fire department, but it was abandoned by subsequent administrations.

Barker married Edith Bealmear on July 2, 1932, in Louisville. The couple had three children: Patricia Ann, Lawrence B., and Bruce D. The family lived on Osage Rd. in ANCHORAGE. He died at Baptist East Hospital at the age of eighty-two and is buried in Calvary Cemetery.

See *Courier-Journal*, July 29, 1980.

BARRY, JOHN MICHAEL "MIKE" (b Louisville, August 6, 1909; d Louisville, January 10, 1992). Journalist. One of nine children of John J. and Winifred Hennessy Barry and a graduate of ST. XAVIER HIGH SCHOOL, Barry served in WORLD WAR II as a captain with the

292nd Joint Assault Signal Observation Corps in the Pacific. In 1946 he married Benjamina "Bennie" Lancaster, and eventually seven children would be born to the couple.

Mike Barry served as editor of the *Kentucky Irish American* from 1950 until the paper's demise in 1968. He then joined the *Courier-Journal* and the *Louisville Times* as a sportswriter. He also had been a sports broadcaster on Louisville radio stations and track announcer for Miles Park and Louisville Downs. As editor of the *Kentucky Irish American*, Barry became well known for his salty style and his outspoken editorials, especially for his barbed verbal assaults on Gov. A.B. "Happy" Chandler and the *Courier-Journal.* He also was an early supporter of civil rights legislation in the 1950s and 1960s.

Barry was perhaps best known popularly as a handicapper and commentator on horse racing. A famous photo of Barry (used for years in his column) shows him studying the *Racing Form,* while his crossed-leg posture reveals a large hole in the sole of his shoe. Barry is buried in St. Louis Cemetery.

See Clyde F. Crews, *Mike Barry and the Kentucky Irish American* (Lexington 1995).

Clyde F. Crews

The Jefferson Cafe, 238 West Jefferson Street, 1934

BARS, TAVERNS, AND SALOONS. The story of the American tavern is the evolution of a woodland refuge to a vital civic center and, finally, to a destination for entertainment. It is a development that would reflect the country's shifting social structures, sensibilities, and hunger for new modes of transportation.

Echoing this national history, Louisville's taverns began in the late 1770s as one-room cabins providing scant lodging for weary adventurers, many of whom found their way by foot and fortuity. Typical accommodations included a loaf of bread, a cup of hard "cyder," an open hearth, and a floor for sleeping. For those traveling by water, riverside taverns offered simple respite from long flatboat journeys. Harrod's Tavern, established in the late 1770s near a settlement on the present-day River and Guthrie Beach Roads, was a popular landing for tired boatmen.

The introduction of stagecoach travel to Kentucky at the end of the eighteenth century and the corresponding outgrowth of dirt trails inspired proprietors to situate taverns along newly formed crossroads. Sometimes the only public spaces for miles, these "ordinaries" or "tippling houses" provided local men access to news and information from the accounts of stagecoach passengers. One such tavern, built later in the 1840s, was Daniel Gilman's enterprise at the juncture of Shelbyville Rd., Westport Rd., and present-day Breckenridge Ln. This crossroads was the heart of the rural St. Matthews business district and a strategic location for a tavern.

Taverns became young Louisville's assembly houses, the more elaborate of which were equipped with taprooms for serving whiskey, rum, gin, and applejack; dining rooms for simple meals; and newsrooms for political debate and storytelling. These were also popular venues for lotteries, elections, musical acts, freak shows, and fortune-telling.

The dawning of the nineteenth century brought the Spanish emancipation of river commerce, the Louisiana Purchase, and the first successful steamboat trip up the Mississippi River, all of which ultimately encouraged travel to and past Louisville and patronage of its taverns. The city's prosperity and growth inspired specialization of drinking establishments, from luxurious to squalid, and redistributed the functions of the traditional tavern. Inns and hotels adopted the province of lodging travelers and were often equipped with barrooms of their own. The Indian Queen, located on the northeast corner of Fifth and Main, and Washington Hall, on the south side of Main near Third St., were two of Louisville's first inns complete with bars. Other inns and hotels would eventually follow their lead, bestowing on visitors and locals alike a posh version of the old, all-accommodating tavern. They included the Louisville Hotel (1833) on Main between Sixth and Seventh Streets, the first Galt House (1835) on the northeast corner of Main and Second Streets, the Wall Street House (by 1836) on Wall St., the Kentucky Inn (by 1836) on Fifth St.; the Seelbach Hotel (1905) at Fourth and Walnut (Muhammad Ali Blvd.), the Brown Hotel (1923) on Fourth and Broadway, and the Kentucky Hotel (1925) at Fifth and Walnut.

Whereas hotel barrooms steadily courted tourists and diners, saloons were distinct neighborhood fixtures for the local working man. Louisville's saloons, some no more than narrow, dimly-lit passageways, saw their greatest prosperity from the mid-1800s until 1920 and have been described as ubiquitous institutions. Their numbers increased from 56 in 1858 to 840 in 1895.

The large influx of German and Irish immigrants to Louisville in the 1840s and 1850s played a notable role in the ascendancy of the era's saloons. Bringing with them beer-making traditions of their homelands and memories of European drinking houses, these newcomers quickly established similar enterprises in working-class neighborhoods such as Germantown and Limerick. One such operation, begun by August 1852, was Metcalfe and Grainger's "Bierhaus" saloon on Fifth St. German (and lesser numbers of Swiss) immigrants were especially significant in popularizing beer production in Louisville.

Local breweries often operated adjoining saloons from which they could sell their beer exclusively and thus contributed to the saloon's role as neighborhood draft distributor. It was common practice, for instance, for Clifton saloons to serve only the local brewery's dusky concoction garnished with ice chunks taken from nearby Edward's Pond. When competition increased, independently owned saloons were courted by brewers with propositions of costly bar fixtures and emblazoned glasses on credit in exchange for exclusivity agreements. Beer consumption and saloon patronage were at times matters of fierce parochial and trademark loyalty. Some saloons, adhering to familiar tavern traditions, enticed pedestrians with the promise of nickel lunches and five-cent beers to wash them down.

"Rushing the growler" or "shooting the can"

was a tradition initiated in the mid-1800s and revived temporarily after PROHIBITION ended. Patrons would buy tin pails, or "growlers," of beer from local saloons and carry them home for residential consumption. Indeed, children were sent by their parents to fetch a pail of the afternoon's or evening's refreshment. This practice was profitable for saloons before the innovation of bottled beer and was particularly valuable for women, who, unless creatures of disrepute, were not found in such establishments.

The nineteenth-century drinking house was decidedly a man's world in which men made important social contacts. Taverns and saloons were hotbeds for political debate and the rallying of constituents. JOHN WHALLEN, an Irish Democrat who moved to Louisville in 1871, opened a saloon on Green St. (LIBERTY) and became known for both his five-cent schooners of beer and his political maneuverings. Along with debates and election handbills, saloons were also the consequent local points of party antagonism and demonstrations.

On Monday, August 6, 1855, a few German saloons in Louisville were among properties raided and vandalized during the BLOODY MONDAY anti-Catholic and anti-immigrant riot. One such establishment was C. Kiszier's beerhouse on the corner of Walnut and Shelby Streets. Armbruster's brewery and saloon, between Jefferson and Green St., was pillaged and later consumed in a mob-induced fire. The perpetrators of this devastating event later blamed their actions on the "Anti-American" threat initiated at the day's polling booths and coursing from immigrant-owned drinking and assembly houses.

Transportation developments in the mid to late 1800s altered the number and reach of the city's drinking houses. The advent of railroad travel brought more tourists and a corresponding call for additional saloons. Mule-powered STREETCARS eased access to Louisville's new suburban areas after the CIVIL WAR and generated demand for new drinking establishments in the city's urban fringes. Even towns beyond the streetcar's domain were influenced. As early as 1840 JEFFERSONTOWN's population of 350 was served by 12 churches and 20 taverns. Meanwhile, the PORTLAND wharf area was strung with saloons, some of them owned by the colorful "Big Jim" PORTER, alias "the Kentucky Giant."

By the close of the nineteenth century, the excess and disproportion of the Gilded Age were manifest in Louisville's saloon society. The city's grand hotels were famous for their extravagant barroom revelries. Opened in 1905, the Seelbach Hotel distinguished itself with the area's most opulent New Year's Eve celebration. Farther east, the PHOENIX HILL BREWERY boasted a 111–foot bar from which it could serve its Bohemian beer. Saloons in more squalid parts of town accommodated the destitute and were disparagingly referred to as "grog shops." O'Neal's Alley, situated on the riverfront, was one such operation noted for its debauchery.

Advocates of the long-budding TEMPERANCE movement did not distinguish grand hotel barrooms from grog shops. In their estimation, all drinking houses were centers of moral corruption, threatening family life. The Women's Christian Temperance Union, established in the 1880s, was soon joined in Louisville by the Anti-Saloon League (also known as the Dry League), in its push for prohibitionist action. The Anti-Saloon League, an interdenominational, apolitical reform movement, descended from Ohio in 1895 and would later become the Temperance League of America in 1948. In a mission statement, the Anti-Saloon League of Louisville stated that its "sole purpose was to destroy the beverage liquor traffic."

Temperance groups unwittingly promoted brewery control over corner saloons. When the city government responded to prohibitionist crusades for increased barroom license fees, permits became costly for many saloonkeepers. Breweries were then able to offer debt reparation in exchange for exclusivity agreements and saloon loyalty. Temperance groups impelled saloon inspections by the Liquor Board of Control and the enforcement of Kentucky's law prohibiting the sale of alcohol on Sundays. Police raids to check for the presence of prostitutes and minors in saloons and saloon license revocations became weekly events reported in the local NEWSPAPERS. Only after MAYOR and temperance sympathizer ROBERT WORTH BINGHAM took office in 1907 did most saloonkeepers observe the Sunday law they had for years ignored. When an outbreak of flu hit the city in 1918, all large gatherings were prohibited. For weeks patrons were denied access to their favorite saloons until the EPIDEMIC ran its course.

As a result of Prohibition's official enforcement on January 16, 1920, hundreds of Louisville and Jefferson County saloons ostensibly shut down, and first-floor hotel barrooms disappeared. These once-conspicuous operations yielded to the disbursement of liquor in homes, in "roadhouses," at newsstands, and in the thriving speakeasies of undercover Louisville. Private clubs, most notably the PENDENNIS CLUB, secretly catered to the now-outlawed thirst of the city's privileged set. After visiting the periodically raided Pendennis Club, one revenue agent commented that he had never seen such a variety of beverages. A few bars, however, lawfully continued operations by serving only "near-beer," an unpopular beverage containing a mere .5 percent alcohol. The Oertel Brewery offered its own "near-beer" under the enticing label, "Double Dark." Cunningham's, at Fifth and Breckinridge, likewise served the legal draft but was notorious for spiking its drinks with a more powerful brew.

The dusk of Prohibition arrived with the repeal of the Volstead Act and the legitimate vending of beer with a 3.2 percent alcohol content. On April 6, 1933, aptly named "Foamy Friday," 324 Louisville saloons began selling beer legally. When the city's distilleries resumed operation by the end of that year, whiskey assumed its rank as a local barroom staple.

The decade following Prohibition and leading up to WORLD WAR II was a time of liberation for saloon and tavern proprietors. Government regulation after 1933 prohibited the once-common brewery control of retail operations. In 1939 Louisville's Sunday Law was repealed, sanctioning the sale of beer on Sundays after l:00 P.M. Liquor licenses were granted more freely, resulting in the existence of at least 1,000 cocktail bars, taverns, and beer joints within the city limits by 1941. Procuring a saloon license that year cost local proprietors $1,852 each.

Colorful saloon reputations were born during this time of newfound freedom. The HAYMARKET area was infamous for its inebriated pedestrians and late-night merrymaking during the 1930s and 1940s. The now-demolished HIGHLAND PARK neighborhood, with several bars and pool halls on Louisville Ave., was home to the Bloody Bucket, a tavern remembered for its weekly knife fights and shootings. Patrons were often able to gamble at the corner saloon. Dice and the numbers game were popular, and bookies were known to set tables in back rooms or at the far end of the bar. The Arcade Nite Club on Taylor Blvd. was one such enterprise where wagering and beer consumption were considered complementary. Since drinking establishments were then segregated, AFRICAN AMERICANS patronized bars in the old Walnut St. business district. The Top Hat, a favorite Walnut St. haunt for nightclub entertainment, catered to a black and white clientele.

As the nation's mobility increased dramatically following the war, so too did the portability of alcohol consumption. Packaged beer and spirits were convenient for consumers to carry home and so directly competed with neighborhood saloons. New highways and the automobile encouraged the development of farther-reaching SUBURBS and created niches for additional drinking establishments.

The social revolutions of the 1960s and 1970s were mirrored in the changing face of Louisville bars. Although women and minorities were sometimes seen in predominantly white, male bars, the women's and CIVIL RIGHTS movements made these sightings common. It was because of this altered social morality that drinking houses became associated with dating and romantic encounters. Lococo's Bar and Lounge at Third and Liberty Streets was an enterprise known for its assignations and sultry atmosphere. Some proprietors saw this development as an opportunity to specialize, thus creating designated singles bars, gay bars, alternative clubs, and dance clubs.

In the last two decades of the twentieth century other specialized drinking establishments have developed. Sports bars, microbrewery pubs (including the Bluegrass Brewing Co. and the Silo Brewing Co.), gentrified bar and grill eateries (including the Bristol Bar & Grille, the Buckhead Mountain Grill, and Baxter Station), and singles and music spots (Phoenix Hill Tavern) are now popular Louisville haunts. Notable, too, is the resurrection of interest in Louisville's heritage as seen in patronage of long-standing neighborhood taverns (such as CHECK'S, operating since 1948), nostalgia-inspired bistros (including Brasserie Deitrich and Bobby J's), and pubs bespeaking the city's rich immigrant past (including the Irish Rover and Molly Malone's).

See J. Winston Coleman, *Stage-Coach Days in the Bluegrass* (Lexington 1935); George H. Yater, *Flappers, Prohibition and All That Jazz* (Louisville 1984); idem., *Two Hundred Years at the Falls of the Ohio* (Louisville 1987); Bruce M. Tyler, *African American Life in Louisville* (Charleston, S.C., 1998).

Susan Crowell Berigan

BARTH, PAUL C. (b Louisville, 1858; d Louisville, August 21, 1907). Mayor. He was the son of William Barth, a cabinetmaker who died when Barth was eleven years old. His mother had died several years earlier. As the oldest child, he took responsibility for the family and went to work at an early age doing odd jobs. At seventeen he was employed by the Utica Lime Co. as a porter and six years later was made city salesman. About 1897 he was made sales manager. In 1892 Barth, along with John Settle and several other business partners, started the Ohio River Sand Co.

Barth entered politics in 1890 when Fred Hoertz, a member of the BOARD OF ALDERMEN, decided to step down. At the time the old CITY CHARTER allowed for retiring aldermen to choose their successor. Hoertz chose Barth, who served on the board from 1891 through 1895. He was elected to the board in 1897 and served as president from November 1897 through November 1898. He was again elected to the board in 1902 and 1904. He also served as president of the board from November 1902 through November 1905.

Barth, a Democrat, served as MAYOR from November 14, 1905, until June 1907, when he was removed from office. Barth ran against JOSEPH T. O'NEAL. O'Neal was a candidate of the FUSIONISTS, a mixture of Republicans and Progressives who united against the WHALLEN brothers' Democratic machine. Barth defeated O'Neal by 4,826 votes in the election, but the result was contested by the Fusionists in the courts. The Fusionists, led by attorneys WILLIAM MARSHALL BULLITT, HELM BRUCE, and Alexander G. Barret, leveled charges of widespread ballot-box tampering and other strong-arm tactics on the part of the Democrats. The city police and fire departments were said to have played an active role in the fraud by intimidating voters and stuffing ballot boxes. The *Lexington Herald* ran strong editorials denouncing the "corrupt election officers and more corrupt policemen" and demanded these "outrages . . . be met only by force."

The Jefferson Circuit Court upheld the election results, but the Kentucky Court of Appeals eventually ruled the election invalid in May 1907. All Democratic officials elected in 1905 in Louisville and Jefferson County were thrown out of office, including Barth. Governor Beckham appointed ROBERT WORTH BINGHAM, a Democrat, to serve as mayor until the November 1907 special election.

During his tenure as mayor, Barth secured for the city a $4 million sewerage system. He helped to gain financing for an annex to CITY HALL and established a tuberculosis hospital. Barth also acquired land between Jackson and Clay Streets belonging to the Caldwell family for the purpose of creating a city park. The city was unable to purchase the land directly, so Barth put up fifty thousand dollars of his own funds. He eventually sold the land, which became Shelby Park, to the city for the same price.

Barth committed suicide over an incident involving an expensive saddle horse. While mayor, Barth purchased a horse with city funds to be used as special transportation for the mayor. Upon leaving office, he took the horse with him. Bingham made a formal inquiry into the matter, and the press publicized the event. Barth eventually paid for the horse, but his actions had already been ridiculed in the opposition press.

Barth, who was described by the COURIER-JOURNAL as a "sensitive man," shot himself in the head on August 21, 1907, with a 32-caliber revolver. He was in the lavatory next to his private office at the Utica Lime and Cement Co. on W MAIN St. The gun had been purchased the day before by a friend for an outing Barth was planning with his children.

Barth's funeral was one of the largest in Louisville at the time, according to a local newspaper. About thirty thousand people were reported to have attended the funeral procession and burial. Barth married Julia Small, who died in 1893. The couple had three sons: Frank, Paul, and Albert. He is buried in St. Louis Cemetery.

See *Courier-Journal*, Aug. 22, 1907; *Louisville Times*, Aug. 21, 1907; George H. Yater, *Two Hundred Years at the Falls of the Ohio* (Louisville 1979), 145–50; Thomas D. Clark, *Helm Bruce, Public Defender* (Louisville 1973).

BASEBALL, PROFESSIONAL. The first organized baseball team in Louisville, the Louisville Base Ball Club, began playing in 1858 in an open lot on the northwest corner of FOURTH and Breckinridge STREETS. An amateur team, it allowed spectators to watch for free. At the time Louisville was one of the twelve largest cities in the United States. The city had four daily NEWSPAPERS, five foreign consuls resided here, and slaves made up a quarter of the population. Indeed, "gentlemen" went to the practice grounds "attended" by slaves who carried "their bats and the accouterments of battle," according to a 1913 COURIER-JOURNAL article.

On July 15, 1858, the *Louisville Democrat* reported that the Louisville Base Ball Club played every Tuesday and Thursday afternoon in uniforms that consisted of blue cottonade pants, leather belts, white flannel shirts edged with blue, and dark-blue caps. A roster was also provided. By that year the game had become so popular that a second team, the Phoenix, was formed to provide "an opportunity to the young gentlemen to try their skill in a match between the two clubs" (*Louisville Journal*, Aug. 9, 1858.)

In 1865, after a disruption caused by the CIVIL WAR, several semipro and amateur clubs such as the Louisville Eagles and the LOUISVILLE ECLIPSE team were formed. Games were played at several sites, including a large, open field at Nineteenth and Duncan Streets. The Eagles team was good enough to play some of the best teams of the day, including the Cincinnati Red Stockings, America's first professional team (1869). The Red Stockings humbled them 94–7 on April 21, 1870. Another local team, the Olympic Club, established a park at Twenty-eighth and Elliott Streets by 1871. It was taken over by the Eclipse team in the late 1870s.

In December 1875 Louisville was the site of the initial organizational meetings for the National League, the first stable major league backed by businessmen. While local legend holds that the meetings were held in the back room of baseball enthusiast Larry Gatto's saloon on Green St. (LIBERTY), newspaper accounts indicate that the meetings took place in the LOUISVILLE HOTEL on MAIN ST. League members were the Chicago White Stockings, the Hartford Dark Blues, the Boston Red Stockings, the St. Louis Browns, the Mutuals (of New York), the Athletics (Philadelphia), the Cincinnati Reds, and the Louisville Grays.

The National League opened its season in Louisville on April 25, 1876, as six thousand people paid ten cents to see the Louisville Grays lose to the Chicago White Stockings 4–0 (the first shutout in the major leagues) at a facility on the site of present ST. JAMES and BELGRAVIA COURTS. The Grays, whose president was *Courier-Journal* founder and publisher WALTER HALDEMAN, finished next to last in 1876.

The 1877 Louisville Grays team was vastly improved over its 1876 counterpart. By August, with only fifteen of its sixty-two games remaining, it was in first place by five games. Then strange things began to happen. The Grays dropped seven games in a row, with several members seemingly playing in a careless manner. By September 8 they were firmly ensconced in second place. Suspicions raised by a series of articles written by John Haldeman, the son of Walter Haldeman, eventually led to lifetime bans for four players (pitcher James Devlin, left fielder George Hall, shortstop William Craver, and utility fielder Alfred Nichols), two of whom were found to have accepted hundred-dollar bribes from Eastern gamblers. It was the big leagues' first major scandal.

In a poignant scene star pitcher Jimmy Devlin got on his knees and pleaded his case

Louisville Baseball Club, 1888.

for the sake of his wife and child before league president William Ambrose Hulbert. Although the two had more than a passing friendship and both were moved to tears, Hulbert pressed fifty dollars into Devlin's hands and exclaimed, "That's what I think of you personally. But damn you, Devlin, you are dishonest. You have sold a game, and I can't trust you. Now go. And never let me see your face again, for your act will not be condoned so long as I live." Devlin, a broken man, died of consumption in 1883 at the age of thirty-four.

The scandal caused Louisville to lose its National League entry in l878. Another semi-pro and professional team, the Louisville Eclipse Club, played regional foes in the early 1880s. Many of the early games were played at the first Eclipse Park, located in West Louisville at Twenty-eighth and Elliott Streets. In 1882 a Louisville club joined with teams from Cincinnati, Philadelphia (the Athletics), Pittsburgh (the Alleghenies), St. Louis, and Baltimore to form the American Association, a league intended to rival the National League.

No one could agree on a nickname for the local team. In 1882 and 1883 the team, which was owned by W.L. Lyons, Zach Phelps, W.L. Jackson, and John Phelps, used the name Eclipse. Thereafter, it was sometimes called the Colonels, the Louisvilles, and sometimes just the Louisville Baseball Club. In 1890 it was nicknamed the Cyclones because a destructive tornado struck Louisville that year.

The American Association was nicknamed "the Beer and Whiskey League" or the "Beer Ball League" because it allowed the sale of alcoholic beverages at its parks and many team owners operated breweries and distilleries. Indeed, the Louisville team's star second baseman, Joe Gerhardt, received a one-third share of the bar concessions at the park to supplement his eighteen-hundred-dollar salary. Reputedly he would occasionally vend drinks himself while awaiting his turn at bat, to encourage business. Although the 1882 Louisville club placed third, it achieved little better than a .500 record through most of the 1880s.

Nevertheless, the team featured several outstanding players, including pitcher Guy Hecker and outfielder Pete "The Old Gladiator" Browning. Browning was the dominant hitter in the American Association, taking the league batting titles in 1882 and 1885. Tall and ungainly, this ultimate line-drive hitter finished with a lifetime average of .341. Browning's love of drink, his argumentative nature, his growing deafness, and other idiosyncrasies sometimes made him a manager's nightmare. He was also superstitious—refusing to slide into bases and always stepping on third base at the end of an inning. Even his long eyebrows, which drooped well over his eyes, caused problems. When ordered to cut them off, he replied, "No, the Lord put them there and so let 'em stay." Whenever he would bat, he would always take his right finger and plaster his hairs to his brow.

The Louisville American Association entry earned other distinctions. For instance in 1889 it became the first professional baseball team to stage a strike, when the team's new owner and self-appointed manager, Mordecai H. Davidson, levied excessive fines on two players who had made errors in the previous night's game. The strike lasted one day but eventually led to Davidson's ouster as both owner and manager. He eventually turned the club over to the American Association. The 1889 team also established a major-league record by losing twenty-six games in a row and compiling baseball's first 100–loss season (27–111).

The team bounced back from having finished 66 1/2 games behind Brooklyn in 1889 to win the American Association pennant in 1890. The cause of Louisville's good fortune was the formation of the Players League by John Montgomery Ward. Since the Players League was not interested in last-place teams, Louisville lost only Pete Browning off its 1889 team to the new league, leaving it the strongest team in the American Association.

Louisville, the 1890 champion of the American Association, played the National League champion Brooklyn Bridegrooms in a "world's championship" series that was never completed. The teams played only seven of the scheduled nine games. Each team won three games, and one was played to a tie. Louisville's victories were primarily the result of the superb pitching of ace Red Ehret, who won two games. The games, which were played in rainy and cold weather, were poorly attended. One game, played in Brooklyn, was completed in a blizzard. With predictions for more snow and freezing temperatures, the remaining games were scheduled to be played in the spring but never took place. Brooklyn and Louisville were 1890 co-champions by default.

When the American Association folded at the end of the 1891 season, the Louisville Colonels rejoined the revamped National League in 1892. The first Eclipse Park was destroyed by fire in 1892; another ballpark, also called Eclipse Park, was erected on the southwest corner of Twenty-eighth and Broadway. Initially, the park was located within the city limits of Parkland, a small community that strenuously enforced an ordinance prohibiting Sunday baseball. To solve the problem the city of Louisville simply annexed the park site. Although the team had terrible records through the 1890s, it boasted several outstanding players, including pitchers Nick Altrock (1898), Deacon Phillipe (1899), and Rube Waddell (1897, 1899); infielders Dan Brouthers (1895), Jimmy Collins (1895), Hugh Jennings (1892-93), Tommy Leach (1898–99), and Honus Wagner (1897–99); outfielder William "Dummy" Hoy (1898–99); and outfielder/manager Fred Clarke (1894–99).

The Colonels of the 1890s were presided over by Dr. T. Hunt Stuckey (1892–93), Fred Drexler (1894–96), and H.C. Pulliam (1897–98). They were followed by Barney Dreyfuss, a German immigrant who first came to Paducah in 1883 to join the Bernheim Brothers distillery as a bookkeeper. In 1890 he purchased stock in the Colonels. Eventually he became the team's treasurer and, when he gained control of the club in 1899, its president.

Late in the 1899 season a fire destroyed the team's grandstand. Already disenchanted with the team's attendance, Dreyfuss decided to leave Louisville. With a little over a month remaining in the season, he announced that there would be no more home games in the city. At season's end, with the National League reducing its number of teams from twelve to eight, Dreyfuss made a deal with the seventh-place Pittsburgh Pirates to merge the two teams. Dreyfuss moved to Pittsburgh and took Honus Wagner with him. As a result the Pirates won pennants in 1901, 1902, and 1903.

Twentieth-century baseball in Louisville has been a minor-league affair. In 1901 Louisville briefly fielded a team in the Western Association, but the team moved to Grand Rapids in July because of poor attendance. The following year, Louisville joined the newly formed Class AAA American Association. When George "White Wings" Tabeau (1901–9) started his team in what had become known as "the graveyard of baseball," he was not given much encouragement. Nevertheless, the team finished second, thanks to pitcher Ed Dunklein's thirty victories. The Louisville Colonels, who played at the third field to bear the name Eclipse Park, an eighty-five-hundred–seat wooden structure at Seventh and Kentucky Streets, thrived as a civic institution. In 1909 the Colonels captured the American Association pennant under owner William Grayson (1909–12) and again in 1916 under the ownership of distiller Otto Wathen (1912–19). During the 1915 season, pitcher Dan Danforth struck out eighteen Kansas City batters—a league record until 1938.

The most famous Colonels teams played in the 1920s during the ownership of William "Cap" Neal (1919–30) and William Knebelkamp (1919–39). Winning American Association pennants in 1921, 1925, 1926, and 1930, the team featured three future Hall-of-Famers: manager/infielder Joe McCarthy, infielder Billy HERMAN, and outfielder Earle Combs. Combs is perhaps the most famous Colonel of the century. He hit .344 and .380 in 1923 and 1924 before beginning his auspicious career with the New York Yankees in 1925.

Perhaps the most colorful Louisville player of the period was former major-leaguer Jay Kirke, a first baseman who had 286 hits and batted .386 in 1921 for the Colonels. Kirke was part of an infield combination that included third baseman Red Corriden, shortstop Roxie Roach, and second baseman Joe McCarthy, famous for playing an entire season without missing a game. McCarthy also managed the Colonels between 1919 and 1925 and later went on to fame by leading both the Chicago Cubs and New York Yankees to world championships. McCarthy, who managed some of the most famous Yankees teams of the 1920s and 1930s, is the winningest manager of all time.

In 1922 Eclipse Park burned to the ground, which allowed Knebelkamp to build a steel-and-concrete facility called PARKWAY FIELD near Eastern Pkwy. and Third St. Inspired by Chicago's Wrigley Field, it seated almost 16,500, cost $250,000 to build, and was one of the finest facilities of its day. While left field required a high fence because of its close proximity to home plate, balls hit to dead centerfield (which measured 507 feet to the fence) were almost sure outs.

Parkway Field was the site in 1938 of local star HAROLD "PEE WEE" REESE's rookie season. Reese (1918-1999) earned his nickname because he was Louisville's city marbles champion (like Pete Browning before him). The shortstop's great fielding skills quickly attracted the notice of major league scouts. In 1939 the Colonels were acquired by a group which included Frank McKinney, Donnie Bush, and Red Sox owner Tom Yawkey for $195,000 largely because they wanted Reese's contract. Later in 1939, Reese was sold to the Brooklyn Dodgers for $35,000 and four players–an almost unheard of sum at that time. Another member of the Hall of Fame, Reese went on to play in seven World Series with the Dodgers.

During WORLD WAR II the Colonels were one of only a handful of minor-league teams to play throughout the conflict. In spite of the reduced level of play, baseball was extremely popular during the war, as the Colonels won American Association crowns in both 1944 and 1945. The 1944 Junior World Series, between Louisville and Baltimore, attested to the popularity of the game, as 52,833 saw them play at Baltimore's Memorial Stadium—16,265 more than any single regular World Series game that year.

With the return of postwar baseball, the team established a single-season club attendance record in 1946 of 355,241 as well as a single-game record of 17,716. Nevertheless, 1946 was not Louisville's finest hour. The Colonels unwittingly participated in the integration of baseball in 1946. After winning the American Association pennant, the team faced Jackie Robinson and the Montreal Royals of the International League in the Junior World Series. Robinson's appearance at previously segregated Parkway Field brought out the worst in many fans, as he was greeted with catcalls, boos, and foul language. As Robinson recalled later, Louisville proved to be the most critical test of his ability to handle abuse. "The tension was terrible," he noted, "and I was greeted with some of the worst vituperation I had yet experienced."

Louisville baseball in the 1940s was dominated by executive Bruce Dudley, a former sports editor of the *Courier-Journal.* Named the minor-league executive of the year by the *Sporting News* in 1939, his imaginative promotions allowed the team to establish several attendance records. He also served as president of the American Association from 1948 to 1953. The Colonels were a Boston Red Sox farm club, so Colonels fans witnessed the early careers of some exciting players who later played in the big league. These included pitchers Harry Dorish (1946, 1949), Mel Parnell (1947), Maury McDermott (1947, 1949), and Willard Nixon (1949, 1950); infielders Walt Dropo (1950), Billy Goodman (1947), Frank Malzone (1954), and Johnny Pesky (1941); and outfielders Jimmy Piersall (1951) and Tommy Wright (1948–49).

Maury McDermott thrilled Colonels fans when he struck out a record twenty batters in a 1949 game. The Colonels appeared in the American Association playoffs in 1947, 1951, and 1953–56. The 1954 squad took the league

Jack Teigh (2nd from left) Joe McCarthy, Babe Ruth and Earl Combs at Parkway Field, 1932.

championship, defeating Columbus and Indianapolis. By the mid-1950s, however, TELEVISION and other leisure activities caused interest in Louisville baseball to wane. After drawing only 139,948 fans in 1955, the Red Sox moved its franchise to San Francisco for the 1956 season.

In 1956 a Cuban syndicate purchased the team and attempted to integrate it both on the field and in the stands. With players supplied by the Washington Senators and Max Carey as manager, attendance reached only seventy- eight thousand fans. A dismal failure, the team ended up in bankruptcy proceedings. In 1957, under community ownership, the Colonels moved to the new Fairgrounds Stadium. In 1959 the team became affiliated with the Milwaukee Braves and, with an infusion of new talent, drew 228,000 fans. Moreover, the Colonels made three trips to the Junior World Series, taking the championship in 1960. But in 1962 the American Association folded.

The city suffered through a six-year baseball hiatus until Walter J. Dilbeck purchased the Toronto Maple Leafs of the International League and moved them to Louisville in 1968. The following year the team was purchased by local attorney and businessman William Gardner. Charles O. Finley, the owner of the Kansas City Athletics (later the Oakland Athletics), briefly toyed with the idea of bringing his major-league team to Louisville in 1964, but he was blocked by American League owners.

The International League team was again affiliated with the Boston Red Sox and featured such players as Dwight Evans (1972), Carlton Fisk (1971), and Cecil Cooper (1972). It appeared in the International League playoffs in 1969 and 1972. In 1972 the Kentucky State Fair Board eliminated baseball at the Fairgrounds when it approved major renovations making FOOTBALL the stadium's prime function. The Red Sox moved its franchise to Pawtucket.

Louisville was again without a team until Louisville banker Dan Ulmer and Louisville businessman and former Jefferson County judge ARMIN WILLIG raised $4.1 million in 1981 to renovate the Fairgrounds Stadium for baseball. In 1982 Ulmer persuaded Texan A. Ray Smith to move his Springfield (Illinois) Redbirds to Louisville. The entrepreneurial Smith was an instant success. The Redbirds broke the minor-league attendance record (670,563 established by San Francisco in 1946) in 1982 when 868,418 fans streamed through the turnstiles. Smith's 1983 franchise became the first minor-league team to attract more than a million fans (1,052,438). They outdrew five major-league teams, including the Cincinnati Reds, in per-game attendance.

The Redbirds, an affiliate of the St. Louis Cardinals, made the final round of the league playoffs three years in a row and took titles in 1984 and 1985. The Redbirds also made the American Association playoffs in 1987 and 1994 and in 1995 defeated Indianapolis and Buffalo to take the league championship. Well-

J.W. Reccius advertisement, 1886.

known major-league players who appeared in a Redbirds uniform include Bernard Gilkey (1990–91, 1995), Jeff Fassero (1989), Ken Hill (1989–91), Lance Johnson (1987), Ray Lankford (1990), Joe Magrane (1986–88), Willie McGee (1982, 1989), Tom Pagnozzi (1985–87, 1993–96), Terry Pendleton (1984), Andy Van Slyke (1983), Todd Worrell (1983, 1985, 1989, 1991), and Todd Zeile (1989, 1992, 1995). Owned by a group headed by chairman Dan Ulmer, the team became affiliated with the Milwaukee Brewers following the 1997 season. After a contest to solicit names from fans, the team name was changed to LOUISVILLE RIVERBATS in 1998. Following the 1999 season the RiverBats joined the Cincinnati Reds farm system. The RiverBats moved to a new downtown stadium, Louisville Slugger Field, in April 2000.

The Louisville area has also produced a number of native sons who played in the major leagues. Some of the more famous players include Louis "Pete" Browning, Hubert "Hub" Collins, Philip "Red" Ehret, and William "Chicken" Wolf from the nineteenth century, and DAVID "GUS" BELL, Billy Herman (NEW ALBANY, Indiana), Homer "Dixie" Howell, Kenneth Kuhn, and Harold "Pee Wee" Reese (Ekron, Kentucky) from the twentieth. More recent players who were born in Louisville include David C. Anderson and Jay Buhner. While no well-known AFRICAN AMERICAN Louisvillians have reached the major leagues, the city had an original entry in the six-team League of Colored Baseball Players in 1887.

Unfortunately, this first black professional baseball league in the country collapsed after only a two-week existence. Nevertheless, Louisville African Americans participated in independent or semipro baseball throughout the first sixty years of the twentieth century and hosted a number of teams in various baseball leagues prior to the integration of baseball in the 1940s. Louisville has also sent a number of players to the Negro leagues, including slugger John Beckwith and infielder Bill Evans, both with the Homestead Grays, and infielder Sammy T. Hughes of the Baltimore Elite Giants.

See A.H. Tarvin, *Seventy-Five Years on Louisville Diamonds* (Louisville 1940); *The Voice*, April 14, 1982, B-17–20; Philip Von Borries, *Legends of Louisville: Major League Baseball in Louisville 1876–1899* (West Bloomfield, Mich., 1993); idem, *Louisville Diamonds: The Louisville Major-League Reader 1876–1899* (Paducah, Ky., 1996); George H. Yater, "Major League Memories," *Louisville* (May 1987), 31–32; Albert C. Spalding, *America's National Game: Historic Facts Concerning the Beginning, Evolution, Development, and Popularity of Baseball, with Personal Reminiscences of Its Vicissitudes, Its Victories, and Its Votaries* (New York 1911); Roger Kahn, *The Boys of Summer* (New York 1972).

William Marshall

BASE BALL ALLEY. Base Ball Alley runs on the north side of LOUISVILLE MEMORIAL AUDITORIUM, between Fourth and Fifth Streets. It was used as a shortcut to ECLIPSE PARK, the home of the LOUISVILLE COLONELS BASEBALL team from 1902 until 1922. Baseball fans would exit the Fourth Ave. trolley, cut through Base Ball Alley, and walk three blocks west to Eclipse Park, at Seventh and Kentucky Streets. After 1922, when Eclipse Park was destroyed by fire, Base Ball Alley remained quiet. However, the street still bears the name, a reminder of a past era.

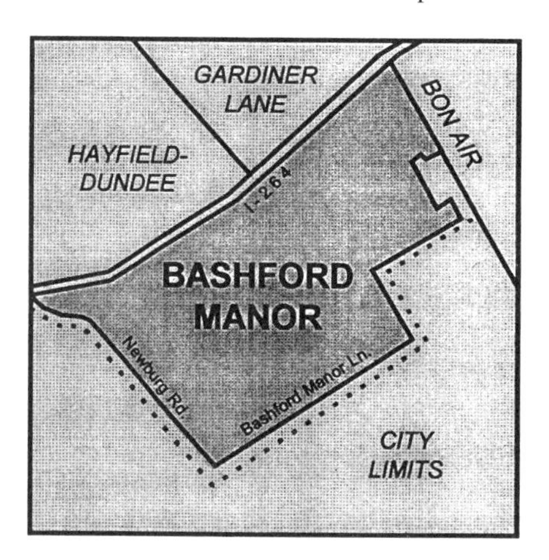

BASHFORD MANOR. This Louisville neighborhood is bounded by the WATTERSON EXPRESSWAY on the north, Bardstown Rd. on the east, Bashford Manor Ln. on the south, and Newburg Rd. on the west. The area was part of Thomas Byrd's thousand-acre tract he received from Virginia in 1787. James Bennett Wilder bought the land in 1870 and built a home that he named BASHFORD MANOR after his family's ancestral home in England. In 1888 George James Long bought the property and turned it into a horse farm, which produced three Kentucky Derby winners: Azra in 1892, Manuel in 1899, and Sir Huon in 1906. The home and land stayed in the Long family until it was sold in 1951. Development began in 1952, and the area was annexed by the city in 1953 and 1955.

The first stage of residential development began in 1952 north of Bashford Manor Ln. Developer Harold Miller laid out the first section of the neighborhood, called Bashford Manor Gardens, around an oval loop formed by Tyrone and Wexford Drives. The same year Henry Hayden, of Hayden's Manorview Corp., and Louis Arru, of Gerald Realty Corp., were developing the Manorview subdivision on the west end of Bashford Manor Ln. In 1954 Joshua Adams, of Martin L. Adams & Sons, platted one of the area's largest single subdivisions, Village Green, located just off Bardstown Rd. and bounded by Goldsmith Ln. and Summer Rd. In the late 1950s the development concentrated along Meadow Creek Dr. and Pemaquid Rd. off Newburg Rd.

In the 1960s most residential developments were in garden apartment complexes along Goldsmith and Peabody Lanes. In 1965 Kemmons Wilson, chairman of the board of Holiday Inn, began construction of a high-rise commercial, office, and residential complex called Watterson City on Bishop Ln. and just off the Watterson Expressway. As his development grew, Wilson sold parcels of land to other developers who erected HOTELS, RESTAURANTS, and condominiums. By the early 1970s Watterson City was Jefferson County's largest suburban commercial center. The Bashford Manor mansion, which was southeast of Bashford Manor Ln., was razed when the Bashford Manor Mall was built.

Bashford Manor was also the site of institutional development. The Louisville Protestant Orphans' Home began construction of a new facility at the intersection of Bardstown Rd. and Goldsmith Ln. in 1960. The facility changed its name to BROOKLAWN Children's Home in 1961 and remains in the Bashford Manor neighborhood.

See *Courier-Journal*, Dec. 13, 1964; Carl E. Kramer, *Louisville Survey East* (Louisville 1980).

BASHFORD MANOR ESTATE. Located along Bardstown Rd. in West Buechel. The initial survey for the Bashford Manor property was made in 1774. In 1787 this thousand–acre tract was granted to Thomas Byrd. After a succession of title transferals, James Bennett Wilder, a prominent area businessman who was coowner of a drug firm and a director of both the LOUISVILLE & NASHVILLE RAILROAD and the BANK OF LOUISVILLE, purchased the land from J.P.D. Craddock in 1870.

Wilder, who greatly disliked the previous owner, decided to tear down the home that existed and erect a new one on the original foundation. He commissioned HENRY WHITESTONE, a noted Louisville architect, to design the new mansion, a French Renaissance three-story brick manor house with a mansard roof and fifteen rooms. The home was built in 1871–72. Wilder named it Bashford Manor after both his ancestral home in Maryland and the English home of his ancestor, Lord Baltimore.

In 1888 Bashford Manor and the surrounding property was purchased by George James Long, who established a nationally renowned Thoroughbred farm. Long's Bashford Manor Farms produced three Kentucky Derby winners, Azra in 1892, Manuel in 1899, and Sir Huon in 1906. In 1902 CHURCHILL DOWNS launched the Bashford Manor Stakes.

In 1951 the Buechel Woman's Club bought the house and a portion of the land from Annie Long Peabody for approximately twenty-five thousand dollars. The club used the house for its meetings, but eventually the expense of maintaining it became too much. The club hoped to restore the home, but when its attempts to get aid from various historical societies and preservation organizations failed, the house and one acre around it were sold to the Louisville Trust Bank for $142,500 in early 1972. The club did keep possession of the household furnishings, which later were auctioned off.

The Louisville Trust Bank, which built a branch on the northeast corner of the property, unsuccessfully tried to find a buyer for the home. In the spring of 1973 the bank sold the manor house to attorney J. Royden Peabody Jr. and the Fourth Avenue Corp., headed by D. Irving Long. Both men were grandsons of George J. Long, a previous owner of Bashford Manor, and both Peabody and Long led the corporations that owned the adjacent Bashford Manor Mall, which had opened in 1973. After attempts to save the historic building by trying to sell it to two different restaurant chains failed, the Bashford Manor mansion was demolished in June 1973.

See *Courier Journal,* July 26, 1969, July 30, 1972, Feb. 26, 1973, April 10, 1973, May 25, 1973, May 27,1973; *A Place in Time: The Story of Louisville Neighborhoods* (Louisville 1989); Walter Langsom, *Preservation: Metropolitan Preservation Plan* (Louisville: Falls of the Ohio Metropolitan Council of Governments, 1973), 137.

BASKETBALL. Basketball has long been an important and proud part of Louisville's sporting tradition. The UNIVERSITY OF LOUISVILLE (U of L) Cardinals have had a long history of victory and success. Louisville even sported one of the most successful teams of the upstart American Basketball Association (ABA) in the 1960s and 1970s—the KENTUCKY COLONELS. Louisville has also taken pride in its intra-city and high school basketball programs.

The Cardinals' basketball program has been an integral part of national collegiate athletics since 1914. The Cardinals achieved an all-time record of a .656 winning percentage by 1997. This ranks them as the twenty-first-winningest team in collegiate history. The team has shown remarkable consistency over the years. Cardinal basketball ranks second all-time with forty-six consecutive winning seasons from 1944 to 1989, topped only by the University of California at Los Angeles (UCLA). As the times changed technologically, success has also been measured by exposure. For Cardinal basketball, TELEVISION success has also been a victory. At least 480 games had been televised locally and 120 games televised nationally as of 1997. Cardinal pride is also evident in game attendance, which has placed U of L in the top ten teams in average home attendance from 1977 to 1997.

During the early days of collegiate basketball the Cardinals saw the likes of Jack Coleman and John Turner. Coleman, a humble star-player, was exemplary of the good athletes the program has produced. Scoring 1,114 points during his college career, Coleman is thirty-seventh on U of L's all-time list, though he thought of himself as a defensive player. Coleman played on the 1947–48 team that won the national championship and went on to play professionally in the National Basketball Association (NBA). John Turner, forward on the impressive 1958–59 Cardinal roster, also went on to play professionally for both the NBA and the ABA. He helped to lead the Cards to two appearances in the tournament games.

Westley Unseld, born March 14, 1946, in Louisville, became an All-State player as he led Louisville's Seneca High School to two state championships in 1963 and 1964. He attended the University of Louisville from 1965 to 1968, where he was named All-Conference three times, All-American twice, and ranked among the national leaders in rebounding. He was selected in the first round of the 1968 NBA draft by the Washington Bullets and was named the NBA's Rookie of the Year and Most Valuable Player of the 1968–69 season. Unseld played until 1981 with the Bullets, when he retired. He was named to the NBA All-Star team five times and was the most valuable player of the 1978 NBA championship series. He retired as the Bullets' career leader in games, rebounds, minutes played, and assists. In 1988 he was elected to the Basketball Hall of Fame in Springfield, Massachusetts. He married Connie Martin; they had two children, Kimberly and Westley.

Allen Murphy scored a sixteenth-best 1,453 career points in the early 1970s before going on to play with the Kentucky Colonels in 1975. Junior Bridgeman, who ranks twenty-first on the all-time scoring list, also went on to play professionally for the NBA, eventually becoming the president of its players' association.

Darrell Anthony Griffith, college basketball's "Dr. Dunkinstein," was born on June 16, 1958, in Louisville, the son of Monroe and Maxine Griffith. As a youngster, he practiced with the Kentucky Colonels of the American Basketball Association. After leading LOUISVILLE'S MALE HIGH SCHOOL to the 1976 state basketball championship, he was named a high school All-American and later that year entered the University of Louisville, the only high school player invited to the 1976 Olympic trials. Following the 1977 World University Games, he was an All-American guard in 1979–80. Griffith led the "Doctors of Dunk" to the 1980 National Collegiate Athletic Association (NCAA) national championship and received the John Wooden Award as the nation's top player. He finished as the career leading scorer at U of L with 2,333 points. After graduating with a B.A. degree in mass communications, he was chosen in the first round of the National Basketball Association draft by the Utah Jazz. Following an outstanding first season, Griffith was named the NBA rookie of the year in 1980–81. Griffith left the Utah Jazz after the 1990–91 season.

Denzel "Denny" Edwin Crum, head basketball coach for the University of Louisville, was born March 2, 1937, in San Fernando, California, to Alwin Denzel and June (Turner) Crum. Crum received his B.A. from the University of California, Los Angeles, (UCLA) in 1958 and a secondary teaching certificate from San Fernando Valley State College in 1960. Crum spent the years 1967–70 as an assistant coach at UCLA under the legendary John Wooden. He became the head basketball coach at the University of Louisville in 1971 and led the Cardinals to two NCAA championships in 1980 and 1986. The 1997–98 season saw Crum reach a record six hundred wins, becoming one of twenty-eight coaches who had reached this mark. In 1994 Crum was inducted into the Naismith Memorial Hall of Fame, one of three active basketball coaches in the Hall of Fame. Crum married Joyce Ellaine Lunsford in 1951; they had two children, Cynthia and Stephen. In 1977 Crum married Joyce Phillips; they had one son, Robert Scott.

By making four Final Four appearances and winning two championships in the 1980s, Crum's Cardinals sported a record matched by no other team in the NCAA. The Cardinals are the only team to have taken the championship of three national tournaments: the 1948 NAIB; the 1956 NIT; and the 1980 and 1986 NCAA. Since the 1960s, the Cardinals have missed reaching the NCAA or NIT tournaments only three times.

In NCAA tournament games, the Cardinals have been extremely impressive. Only three teams count more appearances than the Cardinals: Kentucky, UCLA, and North Carolina. Denny Crum's record in NCAA tournament games is 42–21, with only three coaches having coached more Final Four teams. Only two collegiate teams have had more appearances in the Sweet 16 level of championship play than the U of L Cardinals.

Men's basketball is not the only success at the University of Louisville. By 1997 the Lady Cards were playing their own games on their own terms, with huge success and a lot of fans. The women's basketball program at University of Louisville began in 1910. By 1913 it was an impressive and competitive squad consisting of Charlotte Wimp, Florence McCallum, Peggy Mann, Grace Huber, Bess Hoskins, Effie Best, and Elviere Gaugh. Their first season produced a losing record, marred mostly by program size and inexperience. But by 1915 the Lady Cards were boasting impressive wins over the power teams of the University of Kentucky and Transylvania University. Unfortunately the early decades of the twentieth century were not as kind to women or women's sports. With very few women's programs around the nation, the Lady Cards often played against high school teams. And with few places to practice or play, they often found themselves seeking gymnasiums around Jefferson County to compete and learn.

By the mid-twenties the women's program at University of Louisville was gone, and it was not resurrected again until the 1975–76 season. By the end of coach Terry Hall's stay at Louisville, the Lady Cards had a 60 percent win ratio and were well on their way to a strong, impressive new program. Despite a 46 percent win ratio, coach Peggy Fiehrer would take the Lady Cards to four consecutive conference championships between 1980 and 1983. Their most impressive run came in the early 1990s with coach Bud Childers, whose star player Nell Knox (1989–93) led the Lady Cards to a conference title in 1993. Well regarded for his dedication to the team and his innovative coaching, Childers helped to make the Lady Cards a national powerhouse. He would also produce yet another star player in Kristin Mattox, who racked up several honors.

In 1996 husband-and-wife team Sarah White and Martin Clapp took the reins from Childers. Formerly assistant coaches to Childers, the new co-head coaches continued the innovative style used by their mentor. White and Clapp made the Lady Cards their family, fostering strong bonds with the players and promoting the healthy, wholesome values of the community.

The attention that Louisville has gained through athletics has not only helped to spotlight the university but the city as well. University merchandising, enrollment, and tourism have seen direct effects from the success of Louisville athletics over the years. More important is the effect on the community. With deep-rooted athletic traditions, the pride and support Louisville directs toward the university and the athletes have been phenomenal.

A negative aspect of Cardinal basketball occurred in the NCAA rulings of regulation violations in the early 1990s. During an excruciating investigation, the NCAA found several instances of rules violations in the Cardinal Athletics Department, including the basketball program. But with fines and punishments levied, U of L quickly rebounded.

Contrary to what could be considered overshadowing of the Cardinal basketball program, "Wildcat Fever" for the University of Kentucky's basketball program has helped to instill a proud rivalry between the two schools and inject hysteria into the fans of basketball in Kentucky. While a yearly match-up in regular-season play leaves even the weakest basketball fan in a frenzy, Cardinal and Wildcat fans alike continue to wish for that perfect championship match-up between the University of Louisville and the University of Kentucky in the NCAA tournament.

Until the creation of the Conference USA in the early 1990s, U of L athletics was one of the few independent programs nationally recognized and consistently involved in national tournaments.

The University of Louisville is not the only basketball program in town, however, to benefit from quite a bit of attention. Impressive as well have been BELLARMINE COLLEGE, SULLIVAN COLLEGE, and SPALDING UNIVERSITY. The Bellarmine College Knights, members of the NCAA Division II Great Lakes Valley Conference (GLVC), have repeatedly turned out winning seasons and numerous showings in the conference tournaments over the years with both their men's and women's programs. This is, in part, due to the quality of their head coaches and their staffs. This list is headlined by a former member of Adolph Rupp's "Fab Five" from the University of Kentucky, Alex Groza, who coached from 1959 through 1966. The GLVC, in fact, is a prime example of the influence of basketball on the communities of Kentucky. The GLVC includes Kentucky Wesleyan, INDIANA UNIVERSITY SOUTHEAST, and Northern Kentucky University. The women's program at Bellarmine, just as with U of L, has been impressive. The Lady Knights played in the NCAA tournament eight times between 1986 and 1997, with their best showing being a Final Four appearance in 1994. Bellarmine College has also hosted the NCAA Division II Elite Eight men's championship, held at the Commonwealth Convention Center every year since 1995.

Sullivan College is held in special regard by many because in 1996 the team, led by coach Gary Shourds, earned the National Junior Collegiate Athletic Association title championship with a 27–10 winning record. Sullivan College, as well as Bellarmine, has seen many conference honors and come out victorious in several classic tournaments in their division. The 1989 Elite Championship and the 1990 conference title are just a few of those honors. Spalding University put together a team in the early 1990s.

The success of the Cardinal program and the emergence of Louisville on the national scene helped to create an ABA team, the Kentucky Colonels. The Colonels boasted many achievements in professional basketball. Many of the former U of L stars went on to play for the Colonels or other ABA teams.

The Kentucky Colonels were one of the few ABA teams that existed during the entire nine-year history of that league, and they carried away the title of winningest team in the ABA. Dan Issel and Artis Gilmore, the two star Colonel players, boasted their own records in the league and helped to promote the wild and woolly play for which the ABA was famous. Another Colonel star, Louie Dampier, walked away with the title of most prolific scorer in the ABA after nine years.

Through seven coaches, nine seasons, record-breaking athletics, and consistent tournament showing, the Kentucky Colonels finally won the ABA Championship one year before the league was discontinued. Of those nine seasons, the Kentucky Colonels saw eight winning seasons. So successful were the Kentucky Colonels, many were shocked when they were not absorbed into the NBA in 1976. Owner John Y. Brown Jr. decided an NBA franchise would not be demographically feasible, especially under onerous financial terms laid down by the NBA. Brown sold the Colonels, bought the Syracuse Nats and traded the Nats for the San Diego Clippers, then swapped the Clippers for the Boston Celtics.

Collegiate and professional basketball are not the only programs of which Louisville has to be proud. Since the mid-1980s, intra-city athletic programs have been growing as well. A myriad of community programs offered by the city and Louisville social and religious organizations have provided children with sports leagues, including basketball. One of the most prominent is the Louisville Catholic Archdiocese Basketball Program, which consists of a network of regional teams of all ages. Louisville has also seen the growth of intra-city tournament programs and summer camps for basketball. Most notable is the Street Ball Showdown.

While basketball has not seen the same kind of popularity as football in Louisville high schools, the sport has seen its share of tradition among the young. Dating back to the early 1920s and with considerable resurgence in the 1950s, basketball programs have been prominent at Manual, Male, and Ballard High Schools as well as the inner-city Catholic schools. The women have seen incredible leaps and bounds in sports as well, most notably Holy Rosary Academy, which has boasted a formidable team through the century.

See Dave Kindred, *Basketball, The Dream Game in Kentucky* (Louisville 1975); Gary Tuell, *Above the Rim* (1988); Deborah Skaggs, "U of L Women Courted Basketball in 1908," *Potential* (Feb. 9, 1980); *Courier-Journal*, Oct. 4 and 10, 1988, Nov. 13 and 25, 1988, Dec. 14, 1988, June 25, 1989, Nov. 18, 1989, Dec. 17, 1989, Jan. 20 and 25, 1997, Feb. 8, 1997, May 7, 1997, June 29, 1997, July 19, 1997; May Charlotte Wimp Butler Collection and the Florence McCallum Collection, University of Louisville Archives and Records Center.

Paul Wolf Holleman

BATHHOUSES. Bathhouses, once an urban necessity, provided a convenient way to bathe before Louisville had a water system. Even after running water was introduced in 1860, many homes, even those of the affluent, were not connected to the water mains. It was many years before homes of lower-income residents boasted such a luxury. The earliest bathhouses were privately owned. The first, called the Louisville Bathing House, was opened in 1829 by Patrick Maxcy. But he gave up this pioneer venture in late 1830 because too few residents took advantage of his service. He sold his fixtures, including copper pipe and bathing tubs, and went into the pork-packing and lard-rendering business as being more lucrative.

Despite this inauspicious start, bathhouses eventually became part of the city scene. By the 1850s both the Louisville Hotel and the Galt House offered bathing facilities to the public at large. By 1870 there were three bathhouses, all operated in connection with barber shops. By 1880 the number had increased to six, including two Turkish baths. All of these were for white male clientele, but four were operated by African Americans. As bathrooms became common in homes during the 1890s, the bathhouses ceased operations.

Low-income Louisvillians, however, were often unable to afford the luxury of a bath in the house. In 1902 the city established four public, shower-equipped bathhouses that were free of charge and accommodated both sexes, with separate entrances for each. They were on Seventh St. south of Hill, on Preston St. near Market, at 128 N Eighteenth St., and for African Americans, on Eleventh St. Attendants handed out soap and rented towels. By 1954 usage had declined to only nine thousand bathers per year at a cost of seventeen thousand dollars, and the bathhouses were closed.

See *Louisville Public Advertiser,* Nov. 24, 1830; Louisville city directories for 1871 and 1881.

Herman Landau

BAXTER, JOHN GEORGE, JR. (b Lexington, December 12, 1826; d Hot Springs, Arkansas, March 30, 1885). Mayor. He was the son of John George Senior, and Elizabeth (Smith) Baxter. John G. Baxter Sr. immigrated to Philadelphia from Dundee, Scotland, where he had been a successful linen manufacturer. He went to Lexington to manufacture hemp bagging. His son was educated at local schools until he was fourteen, when he went to work as a clerk in a Lexington store. He worked there until he came to Louisville in 1847, where he became a successful stove and range manufacturer. His business expanded into several southern states.

Baxter was elected to the City Council in 1862 from the Seventh Ward. He was elected again in 1863, serving as president of the Board of Councilmen that year. In 1865 he was elected to the Board of Aldermen and served there until 1867. He was president of the Board of Aldermen in 1866 and 1867. In March 1870 he was elected mayor and served until 1872. Baxter also served as mayor from 1879 through 1881. He was elected both times as a Democrat.

During his administration, construction on the new city hall was started and was completed in June 1873, at a cost of $464,778. He also helped get a new city hospital and almshouse built and raised the city's bond rating. Baxter was going to run for mayor again in 1872 but withdrew from the race because the new city charter made it almost impossible for the incumbent mayor to serve a consecutive term.

Baxter ran again for mayor in 1875 against incumbent mayor Charles D. Jacob. Baxter lost by a small majority but was elected again in 1879. He was also a member of the board of managers for the House of Refuge, serving as president of that organization for six years. He was a director of the Louisville & Nashville Railroad and served many years as president of the Louisville Gas Co.

In 1852 he married Alicia Mary McCready, daughter of George W. and Mary McCready of Louisville. The couple had eight children—two sons and six daughters. Baxter Avenue was named in his honor. He is buried in Cave Hill Cemetery.

See Josiah Stoddard Johnston, ed., *Memorial History of Louisville*, vol. 1 (Chicago and New York 1896).

BEALL, NORBORNE BOOTH (b Williamsburg, Virginia, 1780; d Meade County, Kentucky, 1843). Pioneer and politician. Born to Samuel and Ann (Booth) Beall, his father was a successful Virginia merchant in Williamsburg. Samuel launched into a land speculation scheme with John May of Petersburg, Virginia, in 1779, and the two accumulated an interest in almost 750,000 acres of land throughout Kentucky. About 1784 Samuel Beall purchased Richard Southall's half of the six-thousand–acre Southall and Charlton tract lying east of Louisville. After the death of Samuel in 1793, Beall received half of his father's lands.

About 1802 Beall moved to Kentucky and settled at Spring Station, along Bealls (Beals) Branch of Beargrass Creek. Located on high land, the station was a small fort that sat near the later intersection of Lexington Rd. and Cannons Ln. Here Beall oversaw construction of his house, also known as Spring Station. He served in the Kentucky House of Representatives in 1810, 1811, and 1813. Through bad investments and extravagant living, Beall had lost most of his inheritance by 1825. After losing his home in 1826, Beall eventually moved to Big Bend in Meade County, where he lived with one of his daughters.

Beall married Ann Maupin in 1800; they had five children: Harriet, Louisa, Mary, Samuel, and William. He is buried in Meade County.

James T. Kirkwood

BEARD, ELEANOR (ROBERTSON) (b Covington, Kentucky, July 17, 1888; d Louisville, March 23, 1951). Entrepreneur. Eleanor Robertson was a daughter of Ben Robertson, a varnish manufacturer, and Anna (Collins) Robertson. In 1921 she started a quilting business, Eleanor Beard Inc., in a small clapboard studio in the backyard of her house in Hardinsburg, Kentucky. Bedspreads, robes, comforters, and other items for the home were designed, cut, and marked for quilting at the studio. Beard then employed nearby women to do the work in their homes. The business grew rapidly, and, in the 1930s and 1940s, Beard employed as many as a thousand women.

In her designs Beard used the quilting technique known as trapunto, raised quilted designs on one piece of cloth, rather than the more familiar pieced patchwork. By combining trapunto with more traditional quilting, she was able to develop a unique and popular combination.

In 1936 Beard moved to Louisville and managed her business from an office on Deerwood Ave. Beard's sales force was made up of women across the country who acted as representatives in retail outlets or through shows in their homes. Beard herself opened several quilt shops in a number of cities such as New York, Chicago, Pasadena, and Santa Barbara.

The ingredients for Beard's success were her good taste and executive ability combined with the formidable native talent in needlework among the women in Kentucky. The Metropolitan Museum of Art has included a bedspread designed by Eleanor Beard in its collection. After Beard's death, the business passed through several owners and continues to operate out of Hardinsburg, producing unique hand-quilted items.

Eleanor Robertson married Marvin Beard of Hardinsburg. They had one daughter, Barbara Beard Castleman. Eleanor Beard is buried in Cave Hill Cemetery.

See *Courier-Journal*, March 24, 1951; Amelia Peck, *American Quilts and Coverlets in the Metropolitan Museum of Art* (New York 1990).

Susan Castleman Clare

BEARGRASS CHRISTIAN CHURCH (DISCIPLES OF CHRIST). Beargrass Christian Church (Disciples of Christ) was constituted on December 24, 1842, as the result of a merger of segments of two other congregations—Beargrass Baptist Church and the Goose Creek Church of Christ. Beargrass Baptist Church had been founded in 1784, eight years before any other church made its appearance within a thirty-mile radius of Louisville. Early settlers of the region were members—the Arterburns, Cannons, Hites, Herrs, Hubbards, and Rudys.

In 1917 Beargrass Christian bought land at the corner of Shelbyville Rd. and Browns Ln. and built a new church, moving from its original location on Westport Rd. Between 1931 and 1993, the church had only two senior ministers, Walter E. Lawrenson and R. Willard Van Nostrand. The church celebrated its sesquicentennial in 1992 and was selected in 1996 to provide the national Christmas broadcast on television, the only Kentucky church ever so designated.

See Donald B. Towles and David B. Whitaker, *A History of Beargrass Christian Church 1842–1992* (1992).

Donald B. Towles

Beargrass Creek in Cherokee Park. c. 1900.

BEARGRASS CREEK. One of the first maps to show Beargrass Creek was the work of Lewis Evans, dated 1766. The creek is shown as entering the Ohio River just above the Falls, and it is labeled "Rotten C. or Bear Grass C."

Some have suggested that an early hunter saw or shot a bear in the grass alongside the creek and afterward it was called Bear Grass. Others assumed Beargrass was the nickname of the yucca plant because it was eaten by bears. Some think it was originally called Barre Gros by French traders. The word *barre* is translated as bar, a piece of wood such as would be placed behind a door to keep it secured; a more obscure definition is a barrier or obstruction in a river. The adverb *gros* attached to barre would mean large. Some speculate that since the creek entered the Ohio just above the Falls, it was named because of its position; that is, for being near a falls that was certainly a big obstruction in the river—the barre gros.

But from the earliest times, the English traders and settlers called the creek Beargrass, not Barre Gros. The first land grant west of the Appalachian Mountains mentions this creek as follows: "on the south side of the Ohio River opposite to the Falls, Beginning at a Box Elder & Hickory on the River Bank & runnith thence down the River S 83 W 35 poles to the mouth of Bear Grass Creek" (Fincastle County, Va. Survey Book, 167). This survey was the two thousand acres that was awarded to John Connolly in 1773. Six years later the land was escheated by Virginia and used to form the newly chartered town of Louisville.

Early settlements or stations were built along the course of the creek. When the settlers first arrived, beavers were plentiful in all the smaller streams, including Beargrass Creek. Author Henry McMurtrie noted in 1819 that a beaver dam located four miles up Beargrass Creek was fourteen feet high and fifteen hundred feet long. There were also buffaloes in the area. John Floyd's survey made on the Middle or Sinking Fork of Beargrass Creek began "on a hillside near the creek by a Buffalo Ford" (Fincastle County, Virginia, Survey Book, 58).

Originally the mouth of Beargrass Creek reached the Ohio River in what became downtown Louisville between Third and Fourth Streets. Before 1818 a bridge was constructed at the end of Second St., which crossed Beargrass Creek and connected to what was then called the Point. Fulton St., now River Rd., ran parallel to the river; and Water St. ran along the south side of Beargrass Creek as far east as Preston St.

Beargrass Creek has three main branches: the South Fork, the Middle or Sinking Fork, and Muddy Fork. Each of these forks separates near the headwaters.

The headwaters of the South Fork begin north of the headwaters of Fern Creek near the intersection of Taylorsville Rd. and Hurstbourne Pkwy. It is joined by several branches and runs through Calvary Cemetery on Newburg Rd., then in a concrete ditch past Eastern Pkwy., and then under E Broadway. The South Fork joins the Middle Fork on the east side of the old BOURBON STOCK YARDS near BUTCHERTOWN.

There are two main branches of the Middle Fork, called Weicher Creek and the Sinking Fork. Originally the entire Middle Fork was called by the latter name. Weicher Creek has its headwaters south of Interstate 64 in Hurstbourne Acres and joins the Sinking Fork near Breckenridge Ln. and WATTERSON EXPRESSWAY in ST. MATTHEWS. The Sinking Fork starts in ANCHORAGE. When combined, the Middle Fork flows westward through Cherokee and Seneca Parks and more or less follows between Lexington Rd. and Interstate 64 to its junction with the South Fork near the stockyards.

The Muddy Fork runs parallel to the Ohio, with branches originating in the higher land to the southeast. Its tributaries drain much of northeastern Jefferson County. Along the lowlands near the Ohio River, much of the Muddy Fork was relocated during the construction of Interstate 71, and some parts of the Middle Fork were relocated during construction of Interstate 64. It meets Beargrass Creek near Interstate 71.

The Beargrass "cut-off" was dug in the 1850s, with the idea of extending the Louisville wharf by diverting the creek before it reached the downtown. The cut-off diverted the waste from Butchertown into the Ohio above Louisville instead of its flowing through. The lower part of the creek eventually silted up, and in 1881 railroad tracks were moved from Jefferson St. onto the filled-in creek bed, where they have remained.

Beginning in 1948 a floodwall was constructed to protect downtown Louisville. Since Beargrass Creek flows through the city, a solid wall would have prevented it from flowing into the Ohio River, and a gap in the floodwall at the creek would have permitted flood waters of the Ohio River to flow into Louisville. Therefore, a pumping station was constructed on the creek so that water from Beargrass Creek can be pumped into the Ohio River when the latter is flooded. However, this pumping station does not help in getting rid of the excess water that reaches the creek after heavy rains and thunderstorms.

Beargrass Creek drains approximately seventy square miles of a rather densely populated area. It has flooded and will flood again, which is one good reason to avoid building habitable structures along the lowlying banks.

See Lloyd Brown, *Early Maps of the Ohio Valley* (Pittsburgh 1959).

Neal O. Hammon

BEARGRASS STATE NATURE PRESERVE. Owned by the Kentucky State Nature Preserve Commission and managed by the LOUISVILLE NATURE CENTER, the forty-one-acre preserve is located in the heart of Louisville, off of Trevilian Way. The preserve is, at different times, home to more than 150 species of BIRDS, including a host of various migratory songbirds and herons, as well as great horned owls and different species of woodpeckers.

With more than 180 species of plant life, this natural site is also characterized by its diverse vegetation. Its lush woodlands, ideal for hiking, are populated by sycamore, maple, walnut, and black cherry trees, among many other species.

See Carolyn Hughes Lynn, *Kentucky Wildlife Viewing Guide*, (Helena, Mont., 1994).

BEARGRASS STATIONS. The station, a type of defensible residential site, was common during Kentucky's early settlement in the last quarter of the eighteenth century. The layout owed much to the hostile relationship between the Euroamerican settlers and the Indians as well as to the physical environment, including access to water. BEARGRASS CREEK drains a large section of Jefferson County, and along it were built many early settlements. The first Beargrass station was begun on November 3, 1779, by JOHN FLOYD near the center of his two one thousand-acre military surveys. Floyd had led the first Fincastle County surveying party to the Louisville area in 1774. The inhabitants of the station were John Floyd and his wife, the former Jane Buchanan; his brother Isham; several friends, including William Breckinridge; and Floyd's slave, Bob. The cemetery and the remains of the stone springhouse still exist. This station was on the high ground on the north side of Beargrass Creek, southwest of the present Breckenridge Ln.

In the early spring of 1780 a number of people arrived at the FALLS OF THE OHIO to seek Kentucky land. Among the new arrivals were Dutch pioneers who had migrated from Adams County, Pennsylvania, under the leadership of Hendrick Banta. Other families connected with this group were the Van Arsdales, Shucks, Bergens, Coverts, Ruckers, Akers, Smocks, and Brewers. Floyd allowed these families to settle on his property, as did Col. WILLIAM CHRISTIAN. By April they had established three more stations on Beargrass Creek. One was Hogland's, or the Lower Dutch Station, constructed just two thousand feet down the creek from Floyd; it is likely that the clubhouse of the Big Spring Country Club now occupies the exact site.

In the other direction, near where Browns Ln. now crosses Beargrass Creek, a second station was built. It was called either the Dutch or the New Holland Station by contemporaries; this caused some historians to list them as two separate settlements. The site was later acquired by James Brown. Part of his western boundary ran along the present Browns Ln.

A'Sturgus, or Sturgus Station, was on the land of Col. William Christian. The founder was said to be Peter A'Sturgis. This settlement was located about two miles above Floyd's and a mile northeast of New Holland Station; it was about a thousand feet southwest of the present Oxmoor SHOPPING CENTER. There can be no doubt that it was built in the spring of 1780, as Peter Bellus Felt lived there that year. Several other pioneers stated that corn was raised at this location during that summer. Floyd noted, "I expect 200 acres will be tended in corn this year on my place but very little of it will come to my share" (Draper Mss., 17CC125).

Not far from Hogland's Station, and about a mile and a half west of Floyd's, is high land where a large spring is the source of Beals Branch of Beargrass Creek, where the Spring Station was constructed. This was a unique little fort with a stockade running from the main walls of the fort to the spring. The station was located about eight hundred feet south of the present Lexington Rd. near Cannons Ln. at the head of Beals Branch. It was constructed near the edge of a six-thousand-acre tract owned by James Southall and Richard Charlton. Samuel Beall purchased this station and Charlton's interest before February 1783.

The sixth and most eastward of the stations on the Sinking or Middle Fork of Beargrass Creek was known as Linns or Lynns. This settlement was approximately two miles east of A'Sturgus station on a tract of land owned by Henry Harrison. Capt. WILLIAM LINN, who had come to the Falls with GEORGE ROGERS CLARK's army in 1778, had staked off a settlement claim on this site and started construction in March 1780, not knowing that the land had been surveyed on a military warrant for Harrison by Floyd in 1774. Col. RICHARD ANDERSON purchased the Linn Station tract in 1787, where he built his home called SOLDIER'S RETREAT.

On the South Fork of Beargrass Creek, James Sullivan constructed a station in the spring of 1780. This station was built on land that he had supposedly purchased from RICHARD CHENOWETH but which was actually on the southern part of the six-thousand-acre military survey owned by James Southall and Richard Charlton. This station was located in the vicinity of the present Bardstown Rd. and Goldsmith Ln. In 1783, William Fleming referred to this settlement as Sullivan's Upper Station or Pope's Station, but it was generally called Sullivan's Old Station.

After Sullivan discovered he did not own the land where he had constructed his first station, he purchased 340 acres from Peyton Short, which was originally part of James McCorkle's military survey. Here he built what was called Sullivan's New Station. His tract of land was east of Norris Pl. and extended from about Eastern Pkwy. to Trevillian Way. The station is said to have been near Deerwood.

On May 5, 1780, John Floyd wrote, "We have six stations on Bear Grass with no less than six hundred men. You would be surprised to see ten or fifteen wagons at a time going to and from the Falls every day with families and corn" (Draper Mss., 17CC124). Soon after these stations were occupied, roads were established between them that were thereafter used by most people going from Louisville (and these stations) to the settlements around Lexington or Harrodsburg. One such road passed the four stations along the Middle Fork of Beargrass Creek and led to SQUIRE BOONE'S STATION at Painted Stone in the present SHELBY COUNTY. Another road led southward from Beargrass Creek to BULLITT'S LICK, more or less along what later became Shepherdsville Rd. Dutchmans Ln. appears to be a vestige of an old trail that led between Sullivan's and Hogland's Stations.

In 1782 Moses Kuykendall constructed another station on the South Fork of Beargrass Creek. Old deeds would indicate that it was just south of where the present Buechel Bank Rd. crosses the creek. By 1785 Kuykendall had built a mill at this site. The station was either on or immediately adjacent to a fourteen-hundred-acre settlement and preemption tract obtained by ABRAHAM HITE for William Linn, then deceased, the founder of Linn's Station. In 1787 Hite constructed his home nearby, after acquiring the tract.

See Neal O. Hammon, "Early Louisville and the Beargrass Stations," *Filson Club History Quarterly* 52 (April 1978): 147–65.

Neal O. Hammon

BEATTY, DAVID L. (b Bourbon County, Kentucky, December 3, 1798; d Louisville, February 21, 1881). Mayor. He was the son of John Beatty, who settled in Bourbon County in the late 1700s. His mother died when he was an infant, and he was raised by his grandparents on a farm in Jefferson County, where he attended country school.

At seventeen he left the farm to seek a career in Louisville as a machinist. He went to work for Joshua Headington, a successor of Paul Skidmore, the pioneer of the IRON-FOUNDRY business in Louisville. After three years as an apprentice, Beatty became a foreman.

In 1829 he started his own steam-engine-building business as Beatty, Curry, & Co., on Ninth St. The business was dissolved in 1837. After 1837 he became interested in the business potential of STEAMBOATS as well as in the public affairs of the city.

Beatty served as a city councilman in 1839 and 1840, and again in 1855. He was elected to the BOARD OF ALDERMEN in 1856 and 1857. In 1841 Beatty was elected mayor after a second election was called. Earlier in March, WILLIAM COCKE, a former mayor, and James Harrison ran against each other for mayor. Cocke won the election, but Harrison introduced reasons why Cocke should not take office. Cocke called for a new election, and Beatty emerged the winner with a plurality of the vote. Beatty served in office from May 17, 1841, until May 10, 1844. During his administration the State Institute for the Blind was established in Louisville, a waterworks was authorized for construction by the General Assembly, and the mercantile library began operating. He is buried in Cave Hill Cemetery.

See *Louisville Past and Present: Its Industrial History* (Louisville 1875); Josiah Stoddard Johnston, ed., *Memorial History of Louisville*, 2 vols. (Chicago and New York 1896).

BEAUCHAMP, JAMES MARK (b Taylorsville, Kentucky, January 22, 1883; d Louisville, January 2, 1966). Jefferson County judge. Beauchamp was the son of Isaac Dudley and Louisa Katherine (Alexander) Beauchamp. His father owned a flour mill, which he ran until his death in 1920. Beauchamp attended public and private schools in TAYLORSVILLE and at the age of eighteen went to Massey Business College in Louisville. He graduated from the college and went to work for the Louisville Car Wheel & Railway Supply Co. as a clerk for one year.

He then went to work for the *COURIER-JOURNAL* in the ADVERTISING department. He stayed with the newspaper for nine years, until 1912. During that time he earned a degree from the JEFFERSON SCHOOL OF LAW in 1907 and was admitted to the Louisville bar that same year. Beauchamp married Florence Caruthers, a native of Montgomery City, Missouri, on April 20, 1912. The couple had two children, Mark Junior and Jane C. Beauchamp.

Beauchamp, a Democrat, served two terms as Jefferson County judge, from January 1, 1938, until December 31, 1945. In the 1937 election he defeated Republican George J. Mayer by 15,200 votes out of the more than 123,000 cast. During his administration, Beauchamp was responsible for the development of a nationally recognized playground and recreation program in Jefferson County. As county judge he appointed the first Playground and Recreation Board in 1944.

Beauchamp ran for a third term in 1945 but was defeated by 924 votes in a hotly contested primary race by Democrat Edwin C. Willis, who was the local party organization's candidate. Beauchamp's campaign manager was Mrs. LENNIE W. MCLAUGHLIN, who later became secretary of the Democratic County Executive Committee and served as head of the party for many years. Beauchamp, alleging voter fraud, contested the nomination, but Circuit Judge Gilbert Burnett ruled that Willis had been nominated. During the two-week trial it was revealed that fraudulent votes had been cast for both candidates. Willis eventually lost the November election to Republican HORACE M. BARKER.

Beauchamp also served as judge pro tem of the Jefferson County court and was chairman of the Jefferson County DEMOCRATIC PARTY and a member of the Democratic State Committee. He was appointed to serve on the BOARD OF ALDERMEN in 1925 after the Kentucky Court of Appeals nullified the 1923 election. He also was elected aldermanic president during the term and served as MAYOR pro tem for one month before the November 1925 special election. Beauchamp was Louisville's director of LAW for four years before becoming county judge. He also served as county commissioner for eleven years, from 1950 until he retired from politics in 1961. He is buried in CAVE HILL CEMETERY.

See Mary Young Southard and Ernest C. Miller, eds., *Who's Who in Kentucky: A Biographical Assembly of Notable Kentuckians* (Louisville 1936); George Lee Willis Sr., *A History of Kentucky Democracy*, 3 vols. (Louisville 1935); Temple Bodley, *History of Kentucky*, 4 vols. (Chicago and Louisville 1928); *Courier-Journal*, Jan. 3, 1966.

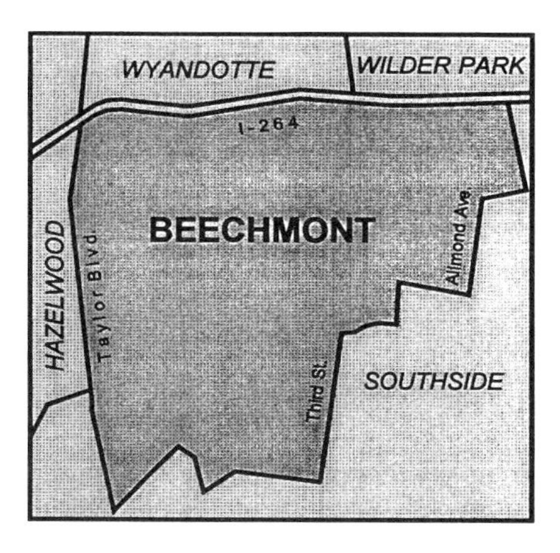

BEECHMONT. Neighborhood in southern Louisville bounded by the WATTERSON EXPRESSWAY to the north, Taylor Blvd. to the west, Southland Blvd. to the south, and a combination of the CSX Railroad tracks, Allmond Ave., Third St., and Southside Dr. to the east. The neighborhood was conceived in 1871 as a residential area for manufacturing employees and executives. However, it was not developed until the 1890s when the Coleman-Bush Co. subdivided the land, which included the HIGHLAND PARK neighborhood. The area was named for its many beech trees.

Beechmont was considered undesirable until the extension of the electric streetcar in 1892, the development of Iroquois Park and Grand Blvd. (now Southern Pkwy.), the opening of the LOUISVILLE & NASHVILLE RAILROAD'S south Louisville car shops, and the opening of the DOUGLAS PARK racetrack in 1895. Developers advertised the area as "Beechmont the Beautiful" and "The Grand Dame" and targeted wealthier citizens with enticements of larger lots, green medians, and easy access to downtown. Beechmont continued to grow after the completion of the Louisville & Nashville Railroad's nearby Strawberry Yards in the 1920s and was annexed by Louisville in 1922. The neighborhood maintained its large lot sizes until the 1940s, when the city sought increased affordable housing for returning servicemen and for Louisvillians from flood-prone areas who desired Beechmont's elevated land after the 1937 FLOOD.

The neighborhood is home to the Beechmont Women's Club and the Iroquois Branch of the LOUISVILLE FREE PUBLIC LIBRARY, a WPA project completed in 1938. The Beechmont

Woodlawn Avenue in Beechmont, looking east toward Southern Parkway, 1924.

Neighborhood Association is an organization that is very active in keeping the community clean and overseeing a community festival held every August.

See Carl Kramer, *Louisville Survey: Central and South Report* (Louisville 1978); *A Place in Time: The Story of Louisville's Neighborhoods* (Louisville 1989).

BEER GARDENS. Beer gardens played an important role in the social life of Louisville's large GERMAN-speaking immigrant community during the nineteenth and early twentieth centuries. During the warmer months, in a pre-air-conditioning age, there were a number of popular beer gardens operating in Louisville and the surrounding area. These establishments catered to families, not just male drinkers, and Sunday was by far their biggest business day, since it was the only day most people were off work. In the summer beer gardens sold two to five times as much beer on Sunday as the rest of the week put together. A variety of entertainment was offered, with concerts and religious music being the most popular. Various social organizations held their group picnics there, and they were favorite sites for political speeches and rallies.

Louisville already had two popular outdoor resorts answering to the description of beer gardens in 1832 when the first city directory was published. These were the Vaux-Hall Garden, on Fifth St. between Main and Water, and the WOODLAND GARDEN, at the head of MARKET ST., and later the site of the BOURBON STOCK YARDS. These halls were owned and frequented mostly by English-speaking residents at that time. Most of the German beer gardens opened after 1848, when large numbers of German immigrants arrived in the Louisville area. In the 1850s the Woodland Garden passed into the hands of German proprietors. It operated under a number of owners until it closed about 1880.

The ELM TREE GARDEN was located on the eastern end of SHIPPINGPORT Island, founded in 1829 by Frenchman Joseph L. Detiste as Elm Tree Pavilion. Centered around a giant elm tree, the outdoor tavern was actually suspended aboveground on a platform built in the branches. By the early 1830s, Detiste had added an amusement park ride, a China Pavilion, a pagoda, a tree arbor, and a dance pavilion. It was renamed the Louisville Garden by 1868 but was selling only about ten kegs of beer a week. It was closed by 1873.

The PHOENIX HILL PARK, covering two or three acres between Baxter and Rubel Avenues and Barret and Hull Streets, opened in 1865 and included two dance halls, two beer gardens, a skating rink, picnic grounds, and a bowling alley, as well as the Phoenix Brewery, the largest brewery in the state in 1877. Many bands and singing societies held concerts there. It was a popular site for political rallies and speeches. Among the speakers were Theodore Roosevelt, Charles Evans Hughes, and William Jennings Bryan. The bowling alley was the home of the Phoenix Kegel Club, formed in 1883. Above the bowling alley was a card room where high-stakes poker games were played, and pistols had to be checked at the bar. An indoor BASEBALL game was held in the dance hall on January 18, 1891, and ladies' six-day bicycle races were held in 1897. The park and brewery were closed by PROHIBITION.

Philip Eisenmenger opened his inn and beer garden on the southwest corner of Thirty-fourth and Market Streets soon after his arrival in Portland in 1851. The 1905 Sanborn Fire insurance map shows a saloon, bowling alley, dance hall, and beer garden on a one-acre site. The festivities at Eisenmenger's Garden were largely ended by the Sunday Closing Law in 1906, which prohibited the sale of alcoholic beverages on the Sabbath.

Many gardens in outlying areas took advantage of the improved transit system to attract visitors. Visitors to Henry Holms's Harrod's Creek Garden or Philip Heser's Shooting Park could take the narrow gauge railroad from downtown to PROSPECT. Additionally, the placement of a STREETCAR line down Bardstown Rd. in the early 1900s spurred visitors to Zehnder's Garden, a family-run establishment located at the modern-day intersection of Bardstown Rd. and Baxter Ave.

Those unfamiliar with the German custom of celebrating life, as well as those fundamentalists who viewed Sunday as a day for sedate worship, made beer gardens and entertainment halls a target of the new TEMPERANCE movement from the time of the first arrival of large numbers of immigrants in the 1840s. The Prohibitionists finally were able to impose their will in 1906, with a state Sunday closing law that put an end to public drinking on Sunday (and

Zehnder's Cherokee Park Tavern, on Bardstown Road at the intersection with Baxter Avenue, 1890s.

greatly increased the home consumption of bottled beer). All legal public drinking in Louisville and elsewhere ended with the enactment of the Eighteenth Amendment in 1920. When Prohibition was repealed in 1933, public drinking was resumed in a society that was much changed. German language and customs were far less prevalent then, and private drinking of bottled beer had become more prevalent. As a result, the number of saloons was much smaller. Saloons that opened following Prohibition often did not bother to add beer gardens. Then, too, movies were more popular than live entertainment, and automobiles were in widespread use, taking people to places once inaccessible. Air-conditioning made it unnecessary to move outside during the hot summer months. While outdoor entertainment was often held, the Sunday Closing Law and Prohibition insured the virtual extinction of the old-style beer gardens. Modern-day areas tend to be called patios and are generally associated with upper-scale watering holes, rather than the reverse of earlier days.

See Peter Guetig and Conrad Selle, *Louisville Breweries* (Louisville 1995).

Peter Richard Guetig
Conrad Selle

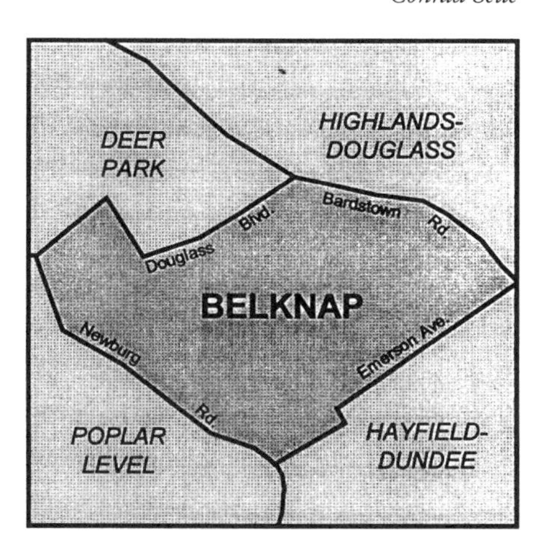

BELKNAP. Neighborhood in eastern Louisville bounded by Bardstown Rd. to the east, Strathmoor Manor to the south, Newburg Rd. to the west, and a combination of Richmond Dr. and Douglass Blvd. to the north. The community, located in the outer HIGHLANDS, has an abundance of historic buildings and landmarks, including the Belknap School, Jonathan Clark's home, the Zimlich stagecoach stop, and the Lakeside Swim Club.

In 1916, two years after the death of William R. Belknap, the civic-minded son of the hardware magnate, residents opened the William R. Belknap School on Sils Ave. in his honor. The neighborhood derived its name from this landmark, which also inspired the Belknap Neighborhood Association logo. The Belknap family donated a piece of land to the growing UNIVERSITY OF LOUISVILLE with hopes of building a new campus. In 1917, the area east of this land was developed as the University Park subdivision, named because it was intended to eventually adjoin the future campus. After a tax measure to underwrite the construction of the new campus was rejected by the voters in 1923, the land that the Belknaps had donated was sold to William F. Randolph for ninety-five thousand dollars. He developed the Aberdeen and Tecomah sections of the neighborhood.

After a period of inactivity, the Belknap Neighborhood Association was reorganized in 1992 in response to a controversial property zoning proposal that would have changed the status of the old Bonanza building, formerly a supermarket, to allow liquor sales in a dining establishment. Since that time, the organization has committed itself to beautification projects and the preservation of the residential character of the neighborhood. The Douglass Loop, which serves with Bardstown Rd. as the commercial hubs of the neighborhood, underwent a major facelift in the late 1990s. The Belknap Neighborhood Association holds a fall festival at the Douglass Loop on the second Saturday in October.

See George H. Yater, *Two Hundred Years at the Falls of the Ohio* (Louisville 1987); *Louisville Survey: East Report* (Louisville 1980).

Mary Garry

BELKNAP, MORRIS BURKE (b Louisville, June 7, 1856; d Louisville, April 13, 1910). Businessman, soldier, and civic leader. The youngest child of WILLIAM BURKE BELKNAP and Mary (Richardson) Belknap, he grew up in the family residence on Walnut St. (now Muhammad Ali Blvd.) and attended the private school of BENJAMIN B. HUNTOON on Breckinridge St. He entered the Sheffield Scientific School of Yale University in 1874, where he was a classmate of William Howard Taft. Graduating in 1877, Belknap remained at Yale as a graduate student for one year.

The young man returned to Louisville in 1879 and worked for a time in his father's business, W.B. Belknap & Co.—later BELKNAP INC., a hardware company. He also joined the First Regiment of the Kentucky State Guard, known as the LOUISVILLE LEGION. Shortly thereafter, Belknap became a partner (with Thomas Meikle and Barry Coleman) in Thomas Meikle & Co., which manufactured plows and elevators. In 1883 Belknap returned to his father's company, first as secretary, then as vice president—a position he held the rest of his life—and helped to promote the hardware wholesaler throughout the nation. A leading industrialist and civic leader, he served as chairman of the Board of Parks from 1907 to 1909 and as president of the LOUISVILLE BOARD OF TRADE for several years. Belknap also served on the staff of Gov. Simon Bolivar Buckner, his father-in-law, beginning in 1887.

With the start of the Spanish-American War, the Louisville Legion was activated by Gov. WILLIAM O'CONNELL BRADLEY as the First Regiment, Kentucky Volunteer Infantry. Belknap, by then lieutenant colonel of the Legion, assumed that rank in the volunteer unit. The regiment served in Puerto Rico, and Belknap became its commander upon the promotion of Col. JOHN B. CASTLEMAN to brigadier general. During his service, Belknap contracted a mysterious disease that was considered to be the cause of his death eleven years later. He was discharged on February 24, 1899.

He ran for governor as a Republican in 1903, losing to incumbent governor J.C.W. Beckham by 19,250 votes out of more than 400,000 cast. Belknap married Lily Buckner, only daughter of the governor—who had also been a Confederate general—on June 14, 1883, and had four children: Gertrude, Walter Kingsbury, Lily, and Morris Burke Junior. Following his wife's death on December 29, 1893, Belknap had a bridge in Cherokee Park erected in her memory. He married Marion Stewart Dumont of Plainfield, New Jersey, on July 16, 1900. Belknap died of "pernicious anemia" and is buried in the family's plot in CAVE HILL CEMETERY.

See *Courier-Journal*, April 14, 1910; William B. Belknap, *Memorandum of the Family of William Burke Belknap* (Louisville 1936); Charles Kerr, William Elsey Connelley, and E.M. Coulter, *History of Kentucky* 1 (Chicago, New York 1922); *Caron's Directory of the City of Louisville* (1881).

Thomas E. Stephens

BELKNAP, WILLIAM BURKE (b Brimfield, Massachusetts, May 17, 1811; d Louisville, February 24, 1889). Entrepreneur and philanthropist. William Burke Belknap was a son of Morris Burke Belknap and Phoebe Locke (Thompson) Belknap. The family moved in 1816 from Worcester, Massachusetts, to Pittsburgh, Pennsylvania, where Morris Belknap entered the furnace and rolling mill manufacturing business, becoming a pioneer in that city's burgeoning iron industry.

William attended a school in nearby Allegheny, Pennsylvania, operated by the Reverend Joseph Stockton. At sixteen William received a communication from his father, who had been exploring business opportunities in eastern Tennessee, ordering him to buy the necessary equipment to construct an iron furnace and to bring it, as well as the family and belongings, to him in Tennessee. Everything was loaded onto a steamboat, and the family journeyed down the OHIO and Cumberland RIVERS to the wilderness spot along the Cumberland that his father had designated.

After helping his father in the furnace business for two years, Belknap, at nineteen, left home to seek his own business opportunities. He started a merchandising business in Mill's Point, now Hickman, Kentucky, and later entered into a partnership with Elias J. Walton and Henry T. Lonsdale, two young Louisville businessmen. Despite being ill for much of this period, he successfully operated branches of the business in nearby Moscow, Kentucky, and in

Vicksburg, Mississippi, and was preparing to sell his interest in it when the financial collapse that accompanied the panic of 1837 bankrupted him and his partners.

After stops in Texas, St. Louis, and Cincinnati, among other places, Belknap settled in Louisville and, on April 1, 1840, started an iron nail business at Third and MAIN STREETS as an agent of Pittsburgh iron manufacturers and former schoolmates, George K. and John H. Shoenberger. Although Belknap said that that business ended in 1861, the 1840 date is considered the beginning of the later Belknap Hardware and Manufacturing Co.

By 1849 he had purchased and completed, in partnership with Thomas C. Coleman, Lewis Ruffner, and William Stewart, a partially constructed rolling mill, "the first mill of the kind at Louisville or in its vicinity." Operating as the Louisville Rolling Mill Co., the partners quickly built a reputation as a manufacturer of quality iron. Belknap also established a separate iron and hardware business—W.B. Belknap & Co.—with his brother Morris Locke Belknap, which later became Belknap Hardware and Manufacturing Co.

A supporter of the Union cause in the CIVIL WAR, Belknap often fed and entertained officers and their men in his home, including Ulysses S. Grant and William T. Sherman. He also supported the U.S. Sanitary Commission and the U.S. Refugee Commission and was an early advocate of a library in the city. He devoted his later years to charity work and philanthropy, often without seeking credit.

On May 30, 1843, in Louisville, Belknap married Mary Richardson, daughter of William Richardson, then president of the Northern Bank of Kentucky. They had five children: Frances "Fanny," Caroline, William Richardson, Lucy, and Morris Burke. Belknap is buried in CAVE HILL CEMETERY.

See William B. Belknap, *Memorandum of the Family of William Burke Belknap* (Louisville 1936); *History of the Ohio Falls Cities and their Counties* (Cleveland 1882); Charles Kerr, William Elsey Connelley, and E.M. Coulter, *History of Kentucky* (Chicago, New York 1922); *Courier-Journal*, Feb. 16, 1986.

Thomas E. Stephens

BELKNAP INC. A large wholesale hardware business, Belknap was officially founded on June 1, 1880, on Main St., by WILLIAM BURKE BELKNAP, an entrepreneur originally from Massachusetts. After a failed business venture in western Kentucky, Belknap settled in Louisville and, on April 1, 1840, started an iron nail and boiler plate business on the northeast corner of Third and MAIN STREETS. He was an agent of Pittsburgh iron manufacturers George K. and John H. Shoenberger, who had once been Belknap's schoolmates in Pennsylvania.

About 1849 Belknap purchased and completed, in partnership with Thomas C. Coleman, Lewis Ruffner, and William Stewart, a partially constructed rolling mill, "the first mill of the kind at Louisville or in its vicinity." Operating as the Louisville Rolling Mill Co., the partners quickly built a reputation as a manufacturer of quality iron. Likely soon afterward, Belknap established a separate iron and hardware business—W.B. Belknap & Co.—with his brother Morris Locke Belknap. It was this enterprise that became Belknap Hardware and Manufacturing Co., although company officials claimed the 1840 starting date of the earlier venture.

Tool and toy display in the sales room of Belknap Hardware & Manufacturing Co., 1926.

By 1865 the Belknaps' company was operating in two locations. The first, at 83 W Main, sold blacksmiths' tools, springs and axles, and several varieties of scales, among other things. The second, at Third and Main Streets, sold iron and steel items, nails, and horseshoes, in addition to scales. By 1874 the venture—which included William and Morris along with their brother-in-law Charles J.F. Allen and William's son, William Richardson Belknap—was located at 113 and 115 Main St.

The growing enterprise, incorporated on June 1, 1880, expanded along Main between First and Second Streets and assumed the form it would take for the next century: a wholesaler of hardware and other items. William R. Belknap assumed the presidency upon the death of his father in 1889, and the company expanded its line further, becoming a supply house to consumers and retailers throughout the region. It advertised everything from revolvers, rifles, ammunition, and hunter's clothing to church bells, "fine English" table knives, and croquet sets. Changing its name in 1903 to Belknap Hardware and Manufacturing Co. Inc., with "Manufacturing" added after the company began to produce horse collars, the company expanded through the years to about forty-two acres of warehouse and display space inside fourteen buildings on property bounded by Main St., the OHIO RIVER, and Second and Jackson Streets.

A selling strategy that made it easy for rural customers to find everything they might need in one place at a wholesale price was enormously successful. In 1960 it was announced that Belknap had become the largest hardware wholesaler in the world in sales, net worth, and floor space, selling to customers in thirty states. It boasted more than ninety thousand items in its inventory. The informal atmosphere also endeared the company to many of its employees, and some continued their employment for forty or fifty years. Assistant buyer Frank Strohm worked there for seventy years, from 1880 to 1950.

Belknap experienced LABOR problems, however, after employees sought union representation. It eliminated its catalog printing operation in 1947, claiming that the printing employees' union refused to negotiate. It sold its trucks after employees in that department organized. In October 1974 warehouse and maintenance workers joined Teamster's Local 89. The union called a strike against Belknap in 1978, and the company replaced striking workers. Union complaints led the company to rehire the former strikers and lay off their replacements. Those workers then sued, and Belknap settled the case for $625,000.

The company changed its name to Belknap Inc. on July 22, 1968, to conform to provisions of that year's Fair Packaging and Labeling Act. By the early 1980s, Belknap had weathered an increasingly competitive market that had seen many of its competitors go out of business. It posted $2.1 million in profits on $170.1 million in sales in 1983.

David A. Jones, chairman and chief executive officer of HUMANA INC., bought the company for $35 million in a leveraged buyout in 1984, hiring protégé Frank Lambert as president. Returning the company to private ownership, Lambert attempted to streamline Belknap operations and expand sales. He eliminated one-third of the company's workforce and cut product lines, while shifting distribution to the new LOUISVILLE AND JEFFERSON COUNTY RIVERPORT AUTHORITY site and sites in Dallas, Texas, and Charlotte, North Carolina.

The moves lowered Belknap's profits and reduced its cash flow. Unable to pay suppliers, the company filed for bankruptcy protection on December 4, 1985, and closed February 4, 1986. The decisions were blamed on increasing competition, a declining building market, and debt incurred in Jones's acquisition.

Jones donated two of the former Belknap buildings to the PRESBYTERIAN CHURCH (USA) when it moved its headquarters from New York City to Louisville in 1987. Humana uses one as its Waterside Building. Two others were imploded in 1993 during a production that aired on cable television's MTV. The remainder were demolished. The site is now a portion of the Waterfront Development Project.

See William B. Belknap, *Memorandum of the Family of William Burke Belknap* (Louisville 1936); *Caron's Annual Directory of the City of Louisville* (Louisville 1874): 100; *Courier-Journal*, Feb. 16, 1986, July 31, 1960, Dec. 5, 1985; *Louisville Times*, July 11, 1984.

Thomas E. Stephens

BELKNAP PLAYHOUSE. Designed by C.J. CLARKE and built in 1874, this Louisville landmark, which is listed on the NATIONAL REGISTER OF HISTORIC PLACES, was originally an interdenominational chapel on the grounds of the HOUSE OF REFUGE, a local orphanage and reform school. The board-and-batten chapel was a steeply gabled building, constructed in the Carpenter Gothic style. Enlargements were first made in 1894, when north and south wings were added. Two quarter-circle sections, one on each side of the chapel, were added later.

In 1923 the UNIVERSITY OF LOUISVILLE bought the former refuge property along Third St. and moved to the site in 1925, naming its new home the Belknap Campus (after the family that provided money to the school). Shortly thereafter the chapel was converted into the university theater. After a number of modifications had been made, including the addition of a lobby area and property room plus the installation of a stage, the Playhouse, as it was called, was formally opened on November 13, 1925, with a production of Ferenc Molnar's *The Swan*.

In 1977 the Playhouse, which was situated between the J.B. SPEED ART MUSEUM and the Law School, was dismantled and put into storage to make space for the construction of the Ekstrom Library. Two years later it was reassembled at a new location along Cardinal Blvd., between Second and Third Streets, at a cost of more than $1 million. The reopening of the theater was celebrated in November 1980 with another presentation of *The Swan*.

See Joan d'Antoni Harris, "The Reconstruction of the Playhouse," M.A. thesis, University of Louisville, 1984; Historic Landmarks and Preservation Districts Commission, City of Louisville, "The Belknap Playhouse Landmark and Landmark Site Designation Report," Aug. 1976.

BELL, DAVID RUSSELL "GUS" (b Louisville, November 15, 1928; d Montgomery, Ohio, May 7, 1995). Professional baseball player. Bell was educated at FLAGET HIGH SCHOOL where he was a star in FOOTBALL, BASKETBALL, and BASEBALL. He also played for a Louisville team that won the National Amateur Baseball Federation junior championship.

Between 1950 and 1964 Bell was an outfielder with the Pittsburgh Pirates, the first New York Mets expansion team, and the Milwaukee Braves; but he was best known for playing nine seasons with the Cincinnati Reds. He was the patriarch of the second family with three generations of professional baseball players. He was the father of "Buddy" Bell, a five-time All-Star third baseman who also played for Cincinnati and became manager of the Detroit Tigers in 1996. Gus Bell was also the grandfather of Cleveland Indians third baseman David Bell and Michael Bell of the Texas Rangers' farm system. The first family with three generations of professional baseball players was the Boones—Ray, Bob, Bret, and Aaron.

Gus Bell was a four-time National League All-Star with the Reds (1953–61) in 1953, 1954, 1956, and 1957. Commissioner Ford Frick prevented Bell from starting in the 1957 game when Cincinnati fans flooded the ballot box with votes for their players. Cincinnati elected seven players that year, but Frick had Bell and outfielder Wally Post benched in favor of future Hall-of-Famers Hank Aaron and Willie Mays. Bell had a .333 batting average in All-Star games, with one homer and four runs batted in.

Bell was a lifetime .281 hitter with 206 home runs and 942 runs batted in (RBIs). Gus and son Buddy hold the major-league record for most combined hits (4,337) by a father-son duo. His best seasons were 1953, his first with the Reds, when he hit .300 with 30 homers and 105 RBIs, and 1955 when he hit .308 with 27 home runs. Bell was on the Reds' 1961 World Series team that was defeated in five games by the New York Yankees. He was hitless in three at-bats. He was voted into the Cincinnati Reds Hall of Fame.

Bell was picked up by the New York Mets in the expansion draft before the 1962 season and got the team's first hit in an 11–4 loss to St. Louis. He finished his career with the Milwaukee Braves. After his baseball career he worked for an auto dealership in Cincinnati, ran a temporary employment agency, and worked as a scout for the Texas Rangers.

Bell and his wife Joyce were the parents of seven children and thirty-six grandchildren. He died of a heart attack and is buried in the Gate of Heaven Cemetery in Cincinnati.

See *Courier-Journal*, May 9, 1995.

BELL, JAMES FRANKLIN (b Shelby County, Kentucky, January 9, 1856; d New York City, January 8, 1919). Soldier and educator. James Franklin Bell, the son of John Wilson Bell and his first wife, Sarah Margaret Allen, was raised on a farm about three miles south of SHELBYVILLE, Kentucky, close to ALLEN DALE, the farm of his close friends and cousins Bettie Allen Meriwether and her daughter SUE THORNTON HENNING. After receiving his preparatory education in the public schools of SHELBY COUNTY and working as a bookkeeper, he attended the United States Military Academy at West Point between 1874 and 1878. Graduating thirty-eighth in a class of forty-three, Bell received his command as second lieutenant in the Ninth Cavalry, a black regiment. Due to his racist tendencies, he tried to resign this commission. Bell's attempts to resign failed, however, and he was transferred in August 1878 to the Seventh Cavalry at Fort Abraham Lincoln in the Dakota Territory.

From 1886 to 1889 Bell was an instructor in military science and tactics at Southern Illinois University at Carbondale, where he also taught mathematics. During his tenure, Bell read LAW and passed the Illinois bar examination. In 1889 Bell returned to the Seventh Cavalry. He was on personal leave when the regiment participated in the massacre of Indians at Wounded Knee, South Dakota, in December 1890. Bell was promoted to first lieutenant on December 29, 1890, and participated in the campaign on the Pine Ridge Sioux Reservation subsequent to Wounded Knee to quell unrest in 1891. When the Seventh Cavalry was posted to Fort Riley, Kansas, later that year, Bell joined the staff at the newly opened Cavalry and Light Artillery School and soon became adjutant, then secretary of the school. In November 1894 Bell became aide-de-camp to Gen. James Forsyth and was posted to the Department of California; then in July 1897 to Fort Apache, Arizona Territory; and to Vancouver Barracks, Washington, in February 1898.

With the outbreak of the Spanish-American War, Bell was made head of the Office of Military Information of the Philippine Expeditionary Force. He received a promotion to temporary major of the Engineers, U.S. Volunteers, on May 17, 1898, and to the rank of captain of the regular army in March 1899, following the outbreak of the Filipino Insurrection. On April 17, 1899, he became temporary major assistant adjutant general, U.S. Volunteers. On July 5, 1899, he was promoted to temporary colonel and assembled the 36th Regiment, which became known as the "Fighting 36th" and the "Suicide Club." Their duty was to prevent Filipino raids on work parties rebuilding the railroad between San Fernando and Calulut. Bell, who was a specialist in guerrilla warfare, received the CONGRESSIONAL MEDAL OF HONOR for "most distinguished gallantry in action" for his bravery while fighting to protect the American supply lines on the San Antonio-Porac road at Luzon on September 9, 1899. In December 1899 he was promoted to brigadier general in the volunteers while retaining his regular army rank of captain. He was given command of the Third Brigade. Among his duties in the Philippines were those of provost marshal general of Manila. In February 1901 when the regular army was reorganized, Bell was promoted to brigadier general.

In July 1903 Bell was transferred to Fort Leavenworth, Kansas, where he headed the Command and General Staff School until April 14, 1906. In his efforts to raise the professional standards of the army, Bell established the Staff College at Fort Leavenworth in 1905. In April 1906 Bell was appointed U.S. Army chief of staff and, unlike his predecessors, served his full four-year tour of duty. His subsequent post, 1911–14, was commanding general of the Philippine Department. During 1914–15 he commanded the Second (Tactical) Division, then the Western Department from 1915 to 1917. Bell was then put in command of the Eastern Department, with a brief training assignment to the newly formed Seventy-seventh Division in 1917.

The University of Kentucky conferred the degree of LL.D. upon him in 1907. Bell married Sarah Buford on January 5, 1881. Bell died while in command at New York City, and is buried in Arlington National Cemetery.

See Edgar F. Raines Jr., "Major General J. Franklin Bell, U.S.A.: The Education of a Soldier, 1856–1899," *Register of the Kentucky Historical Society* 83 (Aug. 1985): 315–46.

BELL, JESSE BURNETT (b Tallulah, Louisiana, April 20, 1904; d Louisville, November 27, 1998). Physician. Jesse Burnett Bell graduated from Morehouse College in Atlanta and then from Meharry Medical College in Nashville in 1931. The following year he moved to Frankfort, Kentucky, and began practicing MEDICINE.

In 1935 Bell moved to Louisville and worked at the WAVERLY HILLS SANATORIUM and then the city's health department. In 1946 he began his own practice. He became a member of the Mount Lebanon Baptist Church, where he would eventually serve on the board of trustees. He also served as vice chairman of the LOUISVILLE URBAN LEAGUE and was a member of the JEFFERSON COUNTY MEDICAL SOCIETY, Falls City Medical Association, American Heart Association, the Bureau of Health Services for Kentucky, and the Kentucky Commission on Higher Education.

In October 1965 Bell became the first African American to serve on the UNIVERSITY OF LOUISVILLE Board of Overseers, a board of fifty-one voting members elected by the board of trustees to advise the university's president.

Bell is buried in CAVE HILL CEMETERY.

See *Courier-Journal,* Nov. 29, 1998.

BELLARMINE COLLEGE. Bellarmine College, located on 120 acres along Newburg Rd. near BEARGRASS CREEK, is the largest private college in Kentucky. The college was named for Cardinal Robert Bellarmine, a seventeenth-century Italian Jesuit scholar, canonized in 1922. The college motto *In Veritatis Amore* (in the love of truth) was adopted from the prayer in the Mass on Bellarmine's feast day. Now coeducational, it was founded by Archbishop JOHN A. FLOERSH in 1950 with special assistance of the Conventual Franciscan Fathers, as an archdiocesan liberal arts college for men. At its inception, the school became one of the first in the commonwealth to be open to all races. The Reverend Alfred F. Horrigan served as first president, with the Reverend Raymond Treece as vice president and the Reverend John T. Loftus, O.F.M. Conventual, a Franciscan friar, as registrar and dean of students.

Horrigan was born in Wilmington, Delaware, December 9, 1914, to Anna (Kienle) and William James Horrigan II. He graduated with a B.A. from St. Meinrad's Seminary in 1940 and was ordained in 1940. Horrigan received his M.A. in 1942 and his Ph.D. in 1944 from the Catholic University of America. He was appointed the first president of Bellarmine in 1949 and served until 1973. Horrigan was well known for his community involvement and academic acuteness and was widely visible in civic circles. He was chairperson of the Louisville Human Relations Commission in the 1960s. He attended Vatican II as an observer. After his retirement from Bellarmine he continued in his peace and justice work and took on pastoral duties at St. James parish.

In 1968 Bellarmine merged with URSULINE COLLEGE, a Catholic college for women established by the Ursuline nuns of Louisville in 1938. For three years the merged institution was known as Bellarmine-Ursuline College. At the time of merger, the college's governing board of trustees became independent from the Archdiocese of Louisville and became self-perpetuating, although the archbishop remained the chancellor. In 1971 the name Bellarmine College was restored. In 1973, when Monsignor Horrigan retired, Dr. Eugene V. Petrik became president. Under Petrik's tenure, the first graduate program, the Master of Business Administration, was initiated in 1975. This was followed by graduate programs in education in 1981 and 1986 and the Master of Science in NURSING in 1984. In a reorganization in 1984, the College of Arts and Sciences was joined by the Allan and Donna Lansing School of Nursing and the W. Fielding Rubel School of Business.

In 1990 Joseph J. McGowan Jr. became president. Under his leadership, the W.L. Lyons Brown Library was constructed and opened in January 1997. It houses the Thomas Merton Studies Center, begun in 1963. There are more than twenty thousand items in this internationally significant archive. Other collections are the Harry T. Miles Collection of books and monographs on the American Civil War and the ELEANOR MERCEIN KELLY Collection of manuscripts, correspondence, and papers of that author.

Since 1955 Bellarmine College has presented the Bellarmine Medal to persons of civic and moral excellence on the national and international levels. Recipients have included Carlos P. Romulo, former president of the Philippines; Mother Teresa of Calcutta; Arthur Ashe; and Lech Walesa. In 1984 the Guarnaschelli Lecture Series was begun to bring noted speakers such as James Dickey, William L. Shirer, Ken Burns, Norman Mailer, and Irish poet Seamus Heaney to the campus annually in the arts and humanities. The Wilson and Ann Wyatt Annual Endowed Lectures, begun in 1989, bring outstanding national and international speakers in public service or public affairs to the college, such as former British Prime Minister, Sir Harold Wilson. The first lecture was given by former Senator and U.S. Ambassador to Japan Mike Mansfield.

Bellarmine grants the Bachelor of Arts degree, the Bachelor of Science degree, Master of Business Administration, Master of Arts in Education, Master of Arts in Teaching, and Master of Science in Nursing. Near the turn of the century, more than seventeen hundred undergraduate and more than four hundred graduate students were enrolled. More than twelve thousand alumni are counted worldwide. Accrediting agencies include the Southern Association of Colleges and Schools, National League for Nursing, Kentucky Board of Education, and the National Council for the Accreditation of Teacher Education. Dr. Wade Hall, professor emeritus, wrote the history of the first fifty years of Bellarmine College, entitled *High Upon a Hill: A History of Bellarmine College* (1999).

See *Bellarmine College Data Book,* 11th edition, 1997.

Margaret H. Mahoney

BELL AWARDS. Established in 1978, the Bell Awards are given annually in October by WLKY-TV Spirit of Louisville Foundation to a maximum of ten unpaid volunteers from Louisville, Jefferson County, and southern Indiana. The winners, who have demonstrated the "true spirit of Louisville through unselfish, humanitarian service," are presented with a miniature cast replica of the bell from the *BELLE OF LOUISVILLE* and are also awarded the Jefferson Medallion, a nationally recognized honor from the

American Institute of Public Service in Washington, D.C. In addition to the primary recipients, the foundation also recognizes two high school students and several "honored volunteers" from the community for their volunteer efforts.

BELLE OF LOUISVILLE. Launched on October 8, 1914, the ferry-excursion steamer *Idlewild* was delivered in January 1916 to the West Memphis Packet Co. by the James Rees and Sons Co. of Pittsburgh. Her hull was 157.5 feet long, 36 feet wide, and 5 feet deep, and she was allowed 1,600 passengers. During her first ten years, the *Idlewild* operated primarily as a ferry between Memphis, Tennessee, and Arkansas. After 1925 she served as a day packet carrying freight and passengers, then as an excursion boat carrying tourists, and during World War II towed barges filled with oil along the Mississippi and Ohio Rivers. She was renamed *Avalon* in 1948 and continued as an excursion boat on the western rivers system. In 1963 she was rechristened *Belle of Louisville*.

The *Belle* has been extensively altered since her inception. Today her dimensions, including the stage and paddlewheel, are 200 feet long, 46 feet wide, with a hull depth of 5.2 feet. Her fuel has been changed from coal to fuel oil. Her passenger allowance is now 1,353 persons, but the *Belle*'s operating board limits her to 800.

In May 1962 the boat was purchased at auction by Jefferson County judge Marlow Cook for thirty-four thousand dollars. She is a joint agency of Louisville and Jefferson County. Exclusively an excursion boat, she seldom leaves Louisville, serving there as a prime tourist attraction and drawing visitors from around the globe. Many conventions use her as a pleasant part of their stays in Louisville. The annual Great Steamboat Race with the *Delta Queen* began in 1963. With a rated horsepower of four hundred and a top speed of approximately eleven miles per hour, the *Belle of Louisville* is slightly faster than her rival but is often handicapped in the races by a huge load of passengers. On June 30, 1989, the *Belle* was named a National Historic Landmark by the National Park Service.

On August 24, 1997, as the result of a valve to a fresh water pipe being left open, the *Belle* filled with water and partially sank while docked. Seven days later, she was refloated and placed in drydock at Jeffboat for repairs. The *Belle* was placed back in service in the spring of 1998.

See Alan L. Bates, *Belle of Louisville* (Berkeley, Calif., 1965); Alan L. Bates and Clarke C. Hawley, *Moonlite at 8:30* (Louisville 1994); Frederick Way Jr., *Inland River Record 1965* (Pittsburgh 1965); *Way's Packet Directory* (Athens, Ohio, 1983).

Alan L. Bates

Steamer *Idlewild* (later *Belle of Louisville*) at Fontaine Ferry Park landing, 1934.

BENDL, GERTA (KOPEREK) (b New Kensington, Pennsylvania, July 5, 1931; d Louisville, June 25, 1987). Legislator. Bendl was the youngest of three children of Mary and Paul Koperek. She graduated from high school in New Kensington in 1949 and briefly attended the Pennsylvania College for Women (Chatham College) in Pittsburgh, studying music and art without graduating.

After moving to Louisville from Atlanta in late 1967 with her husband and three children, Bendl quickly got involved in a variety of local community causes. She helped start the "Dames of Dundee," a neighborhood group of mothers who successfully fought to change the city's school district boundaries to allow children living near Atherton High School to attend, rather than be bused to another school in the county. In 1970 she helped to establish the Dundee neighborhood area's Water Management Committee to address the flooding problems caused by Beargrass Creek's South Fork.

In May 1971 Bendl defeated incumbent Third Ward alderman Stanley Benovitz and two others in the Democratic primary. In November she was elected to the board, serving until 1975. Always with her trademark—exotic hats—Bendl was a fixture in Kentucky politics until her death.

In 1975 she was elected to the Kentucky House of Representatives to represent the Thirty-fourth District, serving in that position until her death. In 1980 she was tapped by the party leadership to head the Health and Welfare Committee, making her the first woman to head a standing committee in the General Assembly. She headed the committee until 1984.

In Frankfort she worked on behalf of women, the poor, and the elderly. She sponsored the Nursing Home Reform Bill, passed in 1982, which helped to protect the legal rights of people living in nursing homes. She also supported legislation to address the problem of domestic abuse.

In 1953 she married C. Richard Bendl, and the couple had three children: Paula, Kurt, and Eric. She died of a heart attack at the age of fifty-five. The body was cremated.

See Gerta Bendl papers, *Women's Manuscript Collection,* University of Louisville Archives and Records Center.

BENEDICT, JENNIE CARTER (b Louisville, March 25, 1860; d Louisville, July 24, 1928). Restaurateur/author. The daughter of John C. and Mary C. (Richards) Benedict, she is best known as the creator of Benedictine, a spread made of cucumbers and cream cheese.

Formally educated in Louisville's public schools, she studied at the Boston School of Cooking with Fannie Farmer. She began her career as a chef and caterer in 1893 after hiring a carpenter to build a small kitchen in her parents' backyard near Harrods Creek. The kitchen was built on credit, and much of her equipment was donated by her wealthy friends. Her catering service was an immediate success, and she was much in demand throughout Kentucky and adjoining states. Jennie became Louisville's first "businesswoman."

In 1894, Jennie became editor of the household department of the *Courier-Journal* and helped start the Louisville Businesswoman's

Interior of Jennie Benedict's restaurant at 554 South Fourth Street, 1922.

Club three years later. In 1900 she opened "Benedict's," a restaurant and tea room on S FOURTH St. In 1902, the first edition of her *Blue Ribbon Cookbook* was published. A year later she was invited to join the LOUISVILLE BOARD OF TRADE. She served as superintendent of the Training School for Nurses (1887–1912) and devoted time to the WOMAN'S CLUB OF LOUISVILLE and the King's Daughters' Home for Incurables.

Although she never married, Jennie was said to have loved children. She often hosted weekend costume parties for the offspring of the fortunate and less fortunate. Jennie sold her business in 1925 for fifty thousand dollars and retired to Dream Acre, her home east of Louisville overlooking the OHIO RIVER. She is buried in CAVE HILL CEMETERY.

See Jennie Benedict, *Road to Dream Acre* (Louisville 1928); *Courier- Journal*, May 12, 1949.

Laurie A. Birnsteel

BEN SNYDER'S DEPARTMENT STORE. Ben Snyder's Department Store, Louisville's last major locally owned retail chain, was founded in 1913 by Ben Snyder. A Jewish immigrant from Russia, Snyder arrived in Louisville in 1893 at the age of five. By 1913 he started his own business with three thousand dollars in capital and only one employee. His company made steady progress and in 1919 relocated to its permanent downtown location at 522 W MARKET.

Ben Snyder's was the first store in the city to offer "coupon days" and to give away automobiles as prizes each week. It had a cash-and-carry policy until 1959 when it established in-store charge accounts. Many of the store's employees were there more than twenty years.

At the time of his death in 1946, Snyder had turned one of Louisville's smallest DEPARTMENT STORES into one of its largest. His wife, Jessie, served as the store's president until her death in 1957. Then the Snyders' only son, Monty, became president. By this time, Snyder's had become a chain, with two stores in Louisville and one in Lexington.

By 1987, Snyder's had grown to eight stores, six in Louisville and two in Lexington. That year Snyder's was sold to the Hess's Department Store chain of Pennsylvania, and its name disappeared from the Louisville scene.

BERNHEIM, ISAAC WOLFE (b Schmieheim, Baden, Germany, November 4, 1848; d Santa Monica, California, April 1, 1945). The son of Leon and Fannie (Dreyfuss) Bernheim, young Bernheim came to the United States in 1867. He worked for a time as a peddler and then settled in Paducah, Kentucky. In 1872 he established a distillery in partnership with his younger brother, Bernard, and in 1874 he married Amanda Uri. In 1888 the Bernheim brothers moved their DISTILLING business to Louisville, where it continued to prosper. The firm was sold to the SCHENLEY DISTILLING CORP. in 1937.

Bernheim was active in several Jewish organizations. He was on the executive board of the Union of American Hebrew Congregations for more than forty years and was treasurer of the American Jewish Committee from 1907 to 1922. However, he opposed Zionism and favored Jewish acculturation. He advocated the adoption by JEWS of a Sunday sabbath and urged the formation of a "Reform Church of American Israelites."

A prominent philanthropist, Bernheim donated money for the first library at the Hebrew Union College in Cincinnati, statues of Henry Clay and Ephraim McDowell for Statuary Hall in the Capitol Building in Washington, and a waterworks for his native town in Germany. For the people of Louisville, Bernheim provided the first home of the Young Men's Hebrew Association (1889), Moses Ezekiel's statue of JEFFERSON at the county courthouse (1899), an addition to Jewish Hospital (1918), George Gray Barnard's statue of Lincoln at the LOUISVILLE FREE PUBLIC LIBRARY (1922), and the fourteen-thousand-acre BERNHEIM FOREST in BULLITT COUNTY (1929).

Bernheim published two autobiographical volumes, *The Story of the Bernheim Family* (1910) and *Closing Chapters of a Busy Life* (1929), as well as several other brief works. After the death of his first wife in 1922, Bernheim married Emma Uri in 1924. Toward the end of his life he moved to Denver, Colorado. He left four sons and three daughters.

See Frank H. Bunce, "Dreams from a Pack: Isaac Wolfe Bernheim and Bernheim Forest," *Filson Club History Quarterly* 47 (Oct. 1973): 323–32; Abraham I. Shinedling, "Bernheim, Isaac Wolfe," *Universal Jewish Encyclopedia,* vol. 2 (New York 1940).

Lee Shai Weissbach

BERNHEIM ARBORETUM AND RESEARCH FOREST. Located about twenty miles south of Louisville near Clermont, Kentucky, in BULLITT and Nelson Counties, the forest consists of approximately ten thousand acres of native Kentucky woodlands and park area created and maintained for the conservation of nature and enjoyment of the public. The original fourteen thousand acres of "knoblands" were purchased by Louisville distiller and philanthropist ISAAC WOLFE BERNHEIM in 1928 from the United States Trust Co., with the goal of fulfilling his dream of creating an area of natural beauty and recreation for all people.

The land was transferred to the private, not-for-profit Isaac W. Bernheim Foundation upon its creation on May 10, 1929. The Bernheim Trust simultaneously was created to manage the endowment Bernheim gave the foundation to develop and operate the forest. A board of directors and trustees, respectively, governs the foundation and trust. An executive director is in charge of daily operations. The foundation also owns an adjoining undeveloped four-thousand-acre tract called Knobs Forest.

The early years of the Bernheim Estate, as it was called, were devoted to returning the majority of the area to a natural state, implementing conservation measures, and developing the necessary projects for public use and enjoyment. The ten thousand acres open to the public were officially named Bernheim Forest on May 19, 1951, in honor of Isaac W. Bernheim. The forest has been open to the public from March to November of each year since 1950. An internationally recognized arboretum, a nature center, hiking trails, picnic areas, scenic drives, education programs, and other attractions annually draw hundreds of thousands of visitors.

See Bernheim Foundation records, University Archives and Records Center, University of Louisville; Bernheim Foundation and Forest oral history, University of Louisville Oral History Center, University Archives, University of Louisville; Frank H. Bunce, "Dreams from a Pack: Isaac Wolfe Bernheim and Bernheim Forest," *Filson Club History Quarterly* 47 (Oct. 1973): 323–32.

James J. Holmberg

BERNHEIM BROTHERS. Isaac Wolfe Bernheim and his brother, Bernhard, and a silent partner, Elbridge Palmer, created the firm of Bernheim Brothers in Paducah, Kentucky, in 1872. By 1888 the railroads and the Ohio River made Louisville a major center for the transportation of whiskey on its way to markets across the nation, and Louisville became the distillery's new home.

In Paducah, Bernheim Brothers was a rectifier that bought bulk whiskey and bottled their own brand names, such as I.W. Harper. The brothers wanted a brand name for their premium whiskey that reflected both family heritage and pride in their new homeland. They wanted it to sound "American" in origin. The "I.W." was Isaac Wolfe's initials. The name "Harper" comes from the last name of horse breeder F.B. Harper, who had horses in the first three Kentucky Derbies. In 1885 the whiskey won its first gold medal at the New Orleans Cotton Exposition.

In Louisville it invested into the distilling side of the business, buying into the Pleasure Ridge Park Distillery. That distillery had been established in 1881 by F.G. Paine & Co. near Mill Creek in the southwestern part of Jefferson County. It had a capacity of five hundred bushels of corn a day. Bernheim Brothers' office was located on the north side of Main near Second St., in the heart of Louisville's "Whiskey Row." In 1899, in need of more space, the company sold its old building to W.L. Weller and Sons and moved to a new building on the south side of Main near Seventh St.

In 1897 Bernheim Brothers started construction on their distillery. It was located on Bernheim Ln. at the Illinois Central railroad tracks. In 1903 Bernheim Brothers incorporated to form Bernheim Distilling Co. with a $2 million capital investment.

Isaac retired from the company in 1915. This led to the first of three sales of the company during the next two decades. Eventually Bernheim became a subsidiary of United Distillers Manufacturing Inc., a subsidiary of Guinness PLC. In 1928 Isaac bought fourteen thousand acres of "knobland" in Bullitt and Nelson Counties and developed part of it into the present Bernheim Forest and Arboretum.

Michael R. Veach

BERRYTOWN. The predominantly African American community known as Berrytown is located on the eastern boundary of the city of Anchorage. The community had its origins in the post–Civil War reconstruction era, when many new patterns of rural settlement developed in Jefferson County.

Several African Americans purchased land adjoining the Louisville, Cincinnati and Lexington Railroad at the Forest Station in the 1870s. This group began the subdivision of land that is the core of Berrytown, along the road running between LaGrange Rd. and English Station Rd. The trustees of the First Colored Baptist Church of Anchorage, also known as the Little Flock Church, also purchased land. These initial purchases created the nucleus for the community.

Berrytown was named for Alfred Berry, one of several African Americans who bought ten-acre parcels in 1874. Other original landowners were Kidd Williams, William Butler, and Sallie Carter. The land was purchased from Samuel L. and Mary E. Nock, who had acquired the land from the estate of John B. Heafer in 1868. Nock sold additional parcels throughout the 1890s.

The introduction of the interurban railroad at the turn of the century facilitated travel to Louisville and LaGrange. The neighborhood was enlarged in 1901 when the tract of land on the north side of Berrytown Rd. became the Marr's and Gaddie's Subdivision.

The community of Berrytown was expanded to the south as part of an urban renewal project in the 1960s. The plan, which called for the entire redevelopment of Berrytown, was resisted by residents. As a result, most of the original pattern of streets was preserved. In the late twentieth century new construction altered the rural village profile of the community to one more resembling the surrounding suburban development.

See Louisville and Jefferson County Planning Commission, *Berrytown Redevelopment Plan* (Louisville 1976).

Donna M. Neary

BETHEL–ST. PAUL UNITED CHURCH OF CHRIST. Bethel–St. Paul United Church of Christ was founded on December 10, 1995, by a merger between St. Paul Evangelical United Church of Christ and Bethel United Church of Christ. German immigrants had established St. Paul Evangelical in Louisville in 1836. It was the original congregation of the United Church of Christ in the Louisville area. After enjoying many fruitful years of ministry and mission, the church experienced several decades of declining membership. Demographically, a large number of whites moved from the inner city to the suburbs. In the early 1990s the congregation decided that merger with a sister church was the best way to continue its 159–year mission. Following a year of discussions beginning in January 1995, both congregations voted affirmation of a proposed plan of merger on October 8, 1995. The final worship service was held in the St. Paul facility on December 3 of that year, followed by merger on Sunday, December 10, 1995, at the Bethel St. Matthew's location.

Bethel Church was established on the eastern edge of Louisville in 1923 and built its current facilities in the 1930s. These buildings at 4004 Shelbyville Rd. house the merged congregation. Affectionately, Bethel has been known to the community as the "turtle soup church" by virtue of a tradition of preparing and serving turtle soup as an annual Saturday activity that began in 1929.

The St. Paul Evangelical Church of Christ brings a long history to the merged congregation. Founded as the earliest German Protestant church in Louisville, it offered services for many years in both English and German. It occupied locations first at Fourth and Green (Liberty) Streets, followed by a location on Hancock near Main St. In 1841 the church moved to Preston and Green Streets. A larger building was built at the same site in 1861–62. In 1906 a Gothic Revival church was built at 213 E Broadway and housed the congregation for ninety years until its merger. This church, designed by the Louisville architectural firm of Clarke and Loomis, was cited by the Historic Landmarks and Preservation Districts Commission in 1980 as aesthetically brilliant, with a unique interior space. The building narrowly escaped demolition in 1996 when it was slated to become a parking lot for Alliant Health Care Systems (later Norton Healthcare Systems); it was renovated for doctors' offices in 1998.

BETTER BUSINESS BUREAU INC. The Better Business Bureau (BBB) has a rich history in Louisville of promoting ethical business practices, excellence in customer service, and truth in advertising. Indeed, the national Better Business Bureau system has its roots in Louisville. In 1909 Samuel Dobbs, a sales manager with Coca-Cola who later became president of the company, addressed a meeting of the Associated Advertising Clubs of America at the Galt House (a historical marker noting this event rests at First and Main Streets in Louisville). Dobbs believed that, unless companies and advertising agencies adhered to truthful advertising, the public's trust would be lost and no advertisement would be effective. This speech laid the foundation for the Better Business Bureau.

Dobbs's concern over truth in advertising grew from a government lawsuit filed against Coca-Cola under the Federal Pure Food and Drug Act for false advertising. As disturbed as Dobbs was that his company was the target of a false-advertising lawsuit, he was utterly stunned by his own attorney's argument that "all advertising is exaggerated." Although the attorney did not realize the impact of his words at the time, his comments sparked the start of the Better Business Bureau movement.

The next step toward forming the Better Business Bureau was the establishment of vigilance committees sponsored by local advertising clubs. These vigilance committees exposed untruthful advertising while creating advertising codes and standards. Vigilance Committees set the pattern of business and consumer education and the promotion of voluntary efforts to stem abuses that formed the foundation of the Better Business Bureau. The standards have evolved into the BBB's Code of Advertising, which is a vital part of the bureau's work to promote ethics in business.

But for a brief closing during WORLD WAR II, the Better Business Bureau has been Kentucky's leading advocate of marketplace ethics and business and consumer education for over eighty years. Today the Better Business Bureau system reaches throughout the United States and Canada. The Louisville office is on S FOURTH ST. in the downtown area. It serves the city, western Kentucky, and southern Indiana.

See Charles Wansley, *History and Traditions* (Council of Better Business Bureaus Inc. 1973); H.J. Kenner, *The Fight for Truth in Advertising* (New York 1936).

Christian V. Patterson

BICYCLING. Bicycles have been widely used in the Louisville area for sport, exercise, recreation, transportation, and law enforcement for well over a century. At the end of 1997 the general-membership Louisville Bicycle Club had six hundred members. A smaller, more specialized mountain bike club—the Kentucky Mountain Bike Association—had about 175 Louisville members. Many cyclists ride without affiliating with either group. Police bicycle patrols, absent since automobiles became practical early in the century, appeared on the streets again in 1992 and soon proved effective for enlarging the area that could be covered by foot patrols, for making arrests in ALLEYS and parking garages, and for patrolling large crowds. More than fifty units were in use by police in 1998, and numerous others were used by private security forces.

But the heyday of cycling, for social status and visibility, was in the 1890s, when people from every social level in Louisville—as elsewhere in America and Europe—made it a fundamental of popular culture for several years. The annual convention and racing meeting of the League of American Wheelmen, a national cycling political and social organization, drew thirty thousand members to Louisville in 1896, according to Louisville newspapers. The gathering dominated the front pages of the *COURIER-JOURNAL* and the *LOUISVILLE TIMES* for three days. The next year, ten thousand cyclists—by a count reported in the *Louisville Times*—participated in a bicycle parade from BROADWAY down Third St. and out Southern Pkwy. to Iroquois Park. On a July day in 1897, a *Courier-Journal* reporter counted 2,836 people riding bicycles to work through the intersection of Fourth and Walnut (Muhammad Ali Blvd.) Streets in three hours commencing at 5:30 a.m.

The bicycle has its origins in France in the 1790s, in adult versions of the child's hobby horse—essentially the body of a horse with two wheels. Baron Karl von Drais improved on that *Celeriferes* in 1817 by making the front wheel steerable, though riders still propelled the *Draisienne* by pushing on the ground, first with one foot and then the other. Kirkpatrick Macmillan, working in Courthill, Scotland, between 1839 and 1842, added pedals and levers to drive the back wheel. But his idea did not catch on until the bicycle chain was invented in the 1870s.

Instead, a progression of heavy, wooden-spoked two-wheelers called "Boneshakers," driven by cranks on the front wheel like modern children's tricycles, sparked a cycling craze in Europe and America in the 1860s. English engineers looking for speed and comfort enlarged the front wheel—so that each revolution, and thus pedal stroke, would carry the rider farther—and traded wooden spokes and frame for lighter ones of metal, softening the ride. They produced what was later called the Penny-Farthing, or Ordinary bicycle, which could easily be ridden long distances, and sent cyclists through the countryside in the 1870s and 1880s. After engineering achieved the fine tolerances that made chains possible, gearing replaced the high front wheel and made bicycles safe enough for the masses, causing an explosion of sales in the 1890s. Except for gearing systems, the bicycle of that decade remained essentially unchanged into the 1980s, when new experimentation—much of it in connection with mountain bikes—led to suspension systems and some radical new frame and wheel designs.

Cycling was well established in Louisville by the time Karl Kron, a New York City cyclist at work on his *Ten Thousand Miles on a Bicycle,* visited in 1880 and reported on area roads in use by cyclists. A national cycling magazine called *Outing and the Wheelman*, in its February 1884 issue, gave two Louisvillians—Henry Schimpler and Orville M. Anderson—credit for the first United States century ride, or a hundred miles within twenty-four hours, riding to Frankfort and back in December 1880.

By 1890 bicycle stories were staples in the society and sports sections of the *Courier-Journal*, and at least one club—the Louisville Cycling Club—had its own clubhouse at 716 Second St., between Chestnut St. and Broadway. In 1897 there were many clubs, and the west side of FOURTH ST. between then Walnut and Chestnut Streets had so many bike shops it was called Bicycle Row. Women rode as well as men, and thousands cycled together in the evenings on the Southern Pkwy. The *Courier-Journal* reported a mysterious rider called Scorchy Kate who dressed in black and zipped up and down the streets anonymously.

CHARLES P. WEAVER, running for MAYOR in the fall of 1897, estimated there were twenty thousand cyclists in the city, and he courted their vote by promising to pave a section of Broadway. He won. The 1898 Kentucky General Assembly passed a law ordering that bicycles be carried on trains free as luggage. Gov. WILLIAM O. BRADLEY (1895–99), supporting the RAILROADS, vetoed it. Another law governing cyclists

Phil Laib posing with his velocipede near the Louisville Wheelmen's clubhouse on Southern Parkway, c. 1890.

in Louisville was passed in 1894. The ordinance was passed at the urging of the Board of Public Safety. Wishing to make sidewalks safer for pedestrians, the law compelled bicycle riders to use the STREETS and have bells and lanterns attached to the bikes.

Bicycle racing was a popular sport at the time. Organized and spontaneous races were held at fairgrounds, on trotting and dirt tracks, and occasionally indoors, where bicycle riders would race on the outside of a roller-skating rink. The first official bicycle race was held at Beacon Park in Boston on May 24, 1878. Louisville had its own bicycle races at the SOUTHERN EXPOSITION in the 1880s, and a one-third-mile racing track with twin-spired grandstand was at FONTAINE FERRY PARK in the 1890s.

Cycling activity dropped sharply after 1898 as the fad wore off. But Howard Jefferis, who had owned one of the bicycle row shops, told a young employee in the 1940s that a Louisville group—thirty or more—still did regular weekend rides as late as WORLD WAR I. That employee, Gil Morris, later bought Jefferis's shop and began leading new riders on some of the old routes in the 1950s. In 1957 he and others formed the Louisville Wheelmen, which changed its name to Louisville Bicycle Club in 1996. The club eventually developed a full riding schedule, with several rides each weekend and some on weekdays. Club members teach cycling skills, and the club's annual invitational ride to Bardstown and back in September—the Old Kentucky Home tour—draws seven hundred riders. The club helped city parks officials restore a stone bench at the head of Southern Pkwy. that had been built in 1897 in memory of A.D. Ruff, a noted cyclist who had left money to the Kentucky division of the League of American Wheelmen.

See Andrew Ritchie, *King of the Road: An Illustrated History of Cycling* (London 1975); James E. Starrs, ed., *The Literary Cyclist: Great Bicycling Scenes in Literature* (New York 1997); Karl Kron, *Ten Thousand Miles on a Bicycle* (New York 1887); Orville W. Lawson, "First Century Run," *Southern Cycler* (Oct. 10, 1896); the Louisville Free Public Library has daily articles about cycling from about 1885 through 1898).

Joe Ward

Ohio River, January, 1893 at Jeffersonville, Indiana, with partially completed Big Four Bridge.

BIG FOUR BRIDGE. The Cleveland, Cincinnati, Chicago, and St. Louis Railroad (known as the Big Four from the four major cities in its title) entered Louisville in 1895 over this bridge that crosses the river to JEFFERSONVILLE, Indiana. Althouth riverboat interests protested the location, urging that it be built farther upstream, the U.S. ARMY CORPS OF ENGINEERS approved the location after a hot fight. It is the only bridge in the Louisville area that suffered serious accidents during its construction; thirty-seven lives were lost.

The bridge was first proposed by Jeffersonville interests in 1885. The Louisville and Jeffersonville Bridge Co. was chartered in Indiana in 1887 and in Kentucky the following year. Construction began on October 10, 1888. A year later the first losses of life occurred when a caisson, holding water away from the work on a pier foundation on the riverbed, flooded and drowned twelve workers. A few months later another pier caisson section was being lowered when a wooden beam broke, killing four men. The most incredible event came on December 15, 1893, when a sharp wind gust dislodged the construction crane atop one span. In falling, the crane damaged the falsework supporting the truss, which fell into the river. It carried forty-one men with it; only twenty survived. The falling span narrowly missed a Louisville-Jeffersonville ferry.

Later on the same day, a completed span adjacent to the one that collapsed also fell into the river after a violent wind gust. It had apparently been knocked out of line by the fall of its neighboring truss. No one was on it, so no more lives were lost. These events ranked among the worst bridge disasters in the country, and the lessons learned changed bridge engineering practice. Henceforth, falsework was adequately braced in the longitudinal direction, wind-sway bracing was installed in the bottom frame as soon as a truss was completed, and it became the rule to "never trust a bolted joint any longer than is necessary to put a riveted one in place." The bridge was completed in September 1895, but the huge losses sustained in the collapse left it in a precarious financial situation. It was sold to the Big Four Railroad. That road had sought an entry to Louisville and would, no doubt, have been a tenant on the bridge in any event.

Increasing tonnage caused the original bridge to be replaced with a more massive one. The construction contracts were awarded in June 1928, and the new bridge was opened on June 25, 1929. This short construction time was achieved through a novel building process. The new span was erected within the old one, which acted as its support. No falsework was needed, and the original piers were used. The new bridge was single track, as was the first, and no trains were operated during the year-long building process. Big Four traffic was rerouted over the KENTUCKY AND INDIANA BRIDGE, while interurban electric cars from Indianapolis (which had used the bridge since 1905) shifted passengers to buses at Sellersburg, Indiana, for the trip on to Louisville.

The Big Four Railroad was a subsidiary of the New York Central. When that road merged with the Pennsylvania and became Penn-Central in 1968, all traffic was routed over the FOURTEENTH STREET BRIDGE. The Big Four Bridge thus became the first in the Louisville area to go out of use. The steel approaches on both sides of the river were taken down for scrap, but the bridge itself remained.

See David Plowden, *Bridges: The Spans of North America* (New York 1974); Carl W. Condit, *American Building Art: The Nineteenth Century* (New York 1960); Lewis C. Baird, *Baird's History of Clark County, Indiana* (Indianapolis 1909); J.H. Hunley, "Bridge of Unusual Design Replaces Crossing of Big Four at Louisville," *Engineering News-Record,* Sept. 5, 1929.

George H. Yater

Billy Goat Hill.

BILLY GOAT HILL. Area east of downtown Louisville along Payne St. in the 1700–1900 blocks. To honor the goat farm owned by Ed Whalen, which was situated on the jagged hillside just south of Payne St., a subdivision named Angora Heights was created in the late nineteenth century. Feeling that the name was too highbrow for their neighborhood, the residents changed the name to Billy Goat Hill. The goats, largely unrestrained and free to roam the streets and climb the rocky cliffs, inspired the street names of Angora Ct. and Angora Ave., along with the Billy Goat Hill Democratic Club. By the mid-twentieth century, most of the goats had either fled the area or been shot by hunters. The street names are the only reminders of the area's origins.

See *A Place in Time: The Story of Louisville's Neighborhoods* (Louisville 1989).

BINGHAM, GEORGE BARRY (b Louisville, February 10, 1906; d Louisville, August 15, 1988). Journalist, publisher, and civic leader. He was the son of ROBERT WORTH and Eleanor (Miller) BINGHAM. In 1913 young Barry survived a freakish automobile crash in which his mother was killed. He attended schools in Louisville and Asheville, North Carolina, where his grandfather operated the Bingham School. He went to boarding school at Middlesex School in Concord, Massachusetts and then to Harvard College, where he graduated magna cum laude in 1928. While at Harvard, he met MARY CLIFFORD CAPERTON, a Radcliffe student from Richmond, Virginia. They were married on June 9, 1931. The Binghams had five children: Robert Worth Bingham III (1932–66), George Barry Bingham Jr. (1933–) Sarah Montague Bingham (1937–), Jonathan Worth Bingham (1942–64) and Eleanor Miller Bingham (1946–).

In 1918 Bingham's father had purchased the *COURIER-JOURNAL* and the *LOUISVILLE TIMES* from the Haldeman family. Following his first job at the family-owned WHAS radio, Bingham began his newspaper career as a police reporter on the *Louisville Times*. In 1933 he joined the *Courier-Journal's* Washington bureau as a reporter and covered the early days of President Franklin D. Roosevelt's New Deal. In that same period, Bingham's father was named by Roosevelt to be ambassador to the Court of St. James's, where he served until shortly before his death in December 1937. Meanwhile, Barry returned to Louisville, where he took an active interest in the newspapers' editorial pages and assumed several managerial positions.

Following his father's death, Barry Bingham took more direct responsibility for the newspaper, especially for the editorial page, which gained attention for its progressive, internationalist views. On the advice of President Roosevelt, Bingham and his father had in 1935 hired MARK F. ETHRIDGE to run the *Courier-Journal* and *Louisville Times* news operations. They hired Lisle Baker Jr., a Frankfort banker, to run the business operations, and Barry Bingham directed the editorial page. It was a triumvirate that would dominate public affairs in the city and much of the commonwealth for the next three decades.

Bingham joined the U.S. Navy in 1941 and spent the early years of WORLD WAR II in New York and London. He served as PUBLIC RELATIONS director for American naval forces in Europe until 1945; after the victory in Europe he transferred to Asia, where he directed public relations for the Japanese surrender. Bingham received two Bronze Stars.

After the war, he returned to Louisville and his media business, which also included STANDARD GRAVURE CORP., one of America's leading rotogravure printing operations. In 1950 Bingham launched WHAS-TV, extending his family's interests into the emerging medium of TELEVISION. Over the years, WHAS garnered many awards, as did the NEWSPAPERS.

George Barry Bingham and Mary Clifford (Caperton) Bingham, 1986.

Bingham's leadership of the *Courier-Journal* was interrupted at various times by terms of public service. The defense department asked him to travel in Germany, Austria, and Italy in 1946 and 1947. In 1949 he was appointed chief of the Marshall Plan in France, and he continued in that post until 1950, when he resigned to return to Louisville. A friend and adviser to Gov. Adlai E. Stevenson of Illinois, Bingham was informally involved in the 1952 presidential campaign; in 1956, he was cochairman of the national Volunteers for Stevenson organization.

Beginning in 1964 the *Courier-Journal* was ranked among the nation's ten best newspapers by *Time* magazine. In Louisville, the newspaper played a crucial role in the various phases of the CIVIL RIGHTS struggle, including the peaceful integration of city schools in 1956 and the passage of an open-housing ordinance in the late 1960s.

A national reputation was enhanced by the *Courier-Journal's* vigorous opposition to Sen. Joseph McCarthy's anti-Communist witchhunts. The newspaper also served as a dogged advocate for better schools and LIBRARIES, improved MENTAL HEALTH services, and enhanced arts opportunities.

In the early 1960s, with the retirements of Ethridge and Baker, Bingham began to prepare his sons for leadership in the family businesses. Tragedy struck twice—in 1964 when his youngest son, Jonathan, was accidentally electrocuted, and in 1966 when his elder surviving son, Worth, was killed in an automobile accident. In 1971, his sole surviving son, Barry Bingham Jr., became editor and publisher of the newspapers.

Over the following fifteen years, Bingham remained active nationally in press organizations and was engaged in other forms of public service. He served on the board of the Pulitzer Prize, and he was president of the International Press Institute. He served as national president of the ENGLISH-SPEAKING UNION and was for many years involved with that organization's Kentucky branch. He was cochair of the endowment campaign for the KENTUCKY CENTER FOR THE ARTS. In 1955 he was a founder of the National Conference of Editorial Writers. Each year that organization gives an important award in his name to a leading journalism educator of minorities.

In 1986, following a period of dissension among his children, Bingham placed all of the family's media holdings on the market. A chief player in family dissension was Sarah "Sallie" Montague Bingham, author and philanthropist, who was born in Louisville January 22, 1937, during the great FLOOD. She graduated magna cum laude from Radcliffe College in 1958 with a B.A. in English. After the sale of the Bingham communications empire, Sallie Bingham devoted part of her share of the proceeds to establishing the Kentucky Foundation for Women, which supports original works and other programs by and for women, including publication of the *American Voice.* In 1999, Sallie Bingham granted a conservation easement on her historic eastern Jefferson County farm to RIVER FIELDS, INC., the river conservation organization. The easement, which protects the property from development, was believed to be one of the largest in the state, and reaffirmed her family's interest in conservation causes. Thrice married and divorced. Sallie Bingham had three sons, Barry Ellsworth and Will and Chris Iovenko.

Barry Bingham and his wife, Mary, gave away approximately $60 million to various causes through the Mary and Barry Bingham Sr. Fund. He was especially proud of the $2.4 million given to the city of Louisville for the construction of the Falls River Fountain, dedicated the week following his death from cancer. In 1998 the fountain was damaged by river debris, and its future funding became a subject of public debate.

After his death, numerous tributes followed. A street on Louisville's waterfront was named for him and his wife. A series of books about the newspapers confirmed his place in twentieth-century American journalism. In 1996 the National Portrait Gallery included a portrait of Barry Bingham in a gallery of key figures in the civil rights movement. He was the only newspaper publisher chosen for that honor.

See *Remembering Barry Bingham* (Louisville 1990); Susan F. Tifft and Alex S. Jones, *The Patriarch: The Rise and Fall of the Bingham Dynasty* (New York 1991); Samuel W. Thomas, ed., *Barry Bingham: A Man of His Word* (Lexington 1993).

Keith L. Runyon

BINGHAM, MARY CLIFFORD (CAPERTON) (b Richmond, Virginia, December 24, 1904; d Louisville, April 18, 1995). Journalist and philanthropist. Born to Clifford Randolph and Helena (Lefroy) Caperton, she graduated from Radcliffe College in 1928 with a major in classics. After graduation she won a scholarship to study in Athens, Greece.

From 1942 to 1985, Bingham was vice president and director of the Courier-Journal and Louisville Times Co., which owned WHAS radio and television, WAMZ radio, and the STANDARD GRAVURE CORP., as well as the two NEWSPAPERS. She became well known as the editor of the Sunday features page "World of Books," where she frequently encouraged the publication of quality children's literature. Her drive for improved education throughout the state was evidenced by her role in the Kentucky Bookmobile project, which extended library services into rural counties. She was the director and president of the Council for Basic Education, served on several national education councils, and was a trustee of Radcliffe College.

Bingham's philanthropic endeavors extended to environmental and humanitarian issues. She was a vocal opponent of strip-mining, fought for the preservation of the American elm tree and the Lilley Cornett Woods in Letcher County, and was an active member of the Garden Club of America, the Nature Conservancy, RIVER FIELDS INC., and the State Environmental Quality Commission.

Bingham was an energetic supporter of the Kentucky Arts and Bicentennial Commissions, the LOUISVILLE FREE PUBLIC LIBRARY, Shakertown, and the FILSON CLUB HISTORICAL SOCIETY. Toward the conclusion of WORLD WAR II, she supported the creation of the United Nations and headed drives after the war to send food and clothing to Europe.

She married GEORGE BARRY BINGHAM SR. on June 9, 1931. They had five children:Jonathan, Worth, Barry Junior, Sallie, and Eleanor. After the death of her husband in 1988, Bingham spent much of her time aiding the arts, the environment, the humanities, education, MEDICINE, religion, and HISTORIC PRESERVATION through the Mary and Barry Bingham Sr. Fund. The fund has given about $60 million to various projects throughout the city and state.

While speaking at a Rotary Club benefit dinner given in her honor, Bingham claimed she was so happy that the "the best thing would be for a big pink cloud to come down and take me away." At that moment, she collapsed and died of a heart attack. She is buried in CAVE HILL CEMETERY.

See David Leon Chandler, *The Binghams of Louisville: The Dark History behind One of America's Great Fortunes* (New York 1987); Marie Brenner, *House of Dreams: The Bingham family of Louisville* (New York 1988).

BINGHAM, MARY LILY (KENAN) FLAGLER (b Kenansville, North Carolina, June 14, 1867; d Louisville, July 27, 1917). Heiress. The daughter of William Rand and Mary (Hargrave) Kenan, Mary Lily was a member of one of the South's leading families. She was educated at Peace Institute, a two-year college in Raleigh, North Carolina, and Madame Roche's finishing school in New York City.

At about the age of twenty-four, she developed a friendship with Elizabeth Ashley, the niece of multimillionaire Henry M. Flagler. Flagler had been John D. Rockefeller's partner in the Standard Oil Co. and one of the company's principal stockholders. Flagler was also a major Florida land developer, creator and owner of the Florida East Coast Railway, and a hotel magnate. Through Ashley, Kenan was introduced to the married Flagler, whose wife, Ida Alice, went insane. Flagler, after the Florida legislature passed an act making certifiable dementia grounds for divorce, divorced his wife on August 14, 1901. Ten days later, Flagler and Kenan, who was almost forty years his junior, were married.

Flagler died in May 1913, leaving Mary Lily the bulk of his fortune, which was estimated at $60 to $100 million, and making her the wealthiest woman in the United States. In New York City on November 15, 1916, she wed ROBERT WORTH BINGHAM, a prominent Louisvillian and former MAYOR and judge of that city. The two had met in the late 1880s at a commencement dance at the University of North Carolina and had become reacquainted in 1915 following the death of their respective spouses. The newlyweds came to Louisville and lived at the SEELBACH HOTEL until January 1917 when they traveled to Florida, where they wintered. Upon their return in the spring, the Binghams moved into Lincliff, the former home of W.R. Belknap on River Rd.

Mary Lily was generous to her new husband. She reportedly paid off many of his debts, gave him thousands of dollars in cash as a wedding gift, and granted him a yearly allowance of fifty thousand dollars. Although Mary Lily named her niece, Louise Wise Lewis, as her principal heir and Bingham had agreed to relinquish his claim to her millions, a codicil leaving Bingham $5 million was signed by Mary Lily on June 19, 1917. Bingham used the money to purchase the Louisville *COURIER-JOURNAL.*

The circumstances surrounding Mary Lily Bingham's death on July 27, 1917, have long been a source of controversy. It was rumored that Mary Lily was poisoned or died from alcohol addiction. The official cause of death, however, was heart disease. At the insistence of her family, Mary Lily's body, which had been interred in Oakdale Cemetery in Wilmington, North Carolina, was exhumed on September 19, 1917, and an autopsy performed. No evidence of poison in her system was found. Her body was reburied in Oakdale Cemetery.

See *New York Times*, July 28, 1917; *Courier-Journal*, July 28, 1917; Marie Brenner, *House of Dreams: The Bingham Family of Louisville* (New York 1988); Samuel W. Thomas, "Let the Documents Speak," *Filson Club History Quarterly* 63 (July 1989): 307–61.

BINGHAM, ROBERT WORTH (b Orange County, North Carolina, November 8, 1871; d Baltimore, Maryland, December 18, 1937). Politician, journalist, and diplomat. Robert Worth Bingham lived a life that was full of power, controversy, and service to his adopted state and to the nation.

Bingham attended his father's school, the Bingham School in North Carolina, where he taught Latin and Greek from 1892 to 1896. Although he attended the University of North Carolina and the University of Virginia, he never graduated. After moving to Louisville in the mid-1890s, he did receive a law degree from the UNIVERSITY OF LOUISVILLE School of Law in

1897. He began practice with Pryor, O'Neal, and Pryor before forming a firm with W.W. Davies, an old friend.

Shortly before moving to Louisville, on May 20, 1896, Bingham married Eleanor Miller, a union that brought the transplanted North Carolinian into contact with the prominent Miller and Long families. They had three children: Robert, Henrietta, and George Barry. Only Barry would live up to his father's expectations, coming on board the family newspapers in the early 1930s.

Bingham soon became deeply involved in the political maelstrom that was Louisville and Kentucky. Though a registered Democrat, he began to develop a reputation as a political maverick. He became embroiled in Louisville politics at a crucial stage of the Progressive Era. Appointed interim MAYOR in June 1907 after disputed election results in Louisville, Bingham ran into opposition from the DEMOCRATIC PARTY machine that acted with all the abandon of most big-city political monopolies of the time. The young mayor was able to control the illegal political shenanigans of the police and fire departments and bring about a few other needed reforms, but the realities of the political situation finally set in, not allowing him to run for a full term in the special election of 1907.

Bingham ran unsuccessfully on the Republican ticket for the Kentucky Court of Appeals in 1910 and as a Democrat for JEFFERSON FISCAL COURT in 1917. He took solace in an appointment to the Jefferson Circuit Court in 1911, being known as "Judge Bingham" for the rest of his life by friend and foe alike. He had many of both varieties, particularly after the death of Eleanor in 1913 and his marriage in 1916 to Mary Lily (Kenan) Flagler, reputed to be the richest woman in America.

Mary Lily died within a year, touching off controversy that lives to the present day. Some old enemies and members of Mary Lily's family contended that, if he did not murder her, he did see that she did not receive proper medical care, which contributed to her death. In the 1980s, as the Bingham empire was collapsing, several biographers scurrilously charged that Robert Worth killed his second wife for her money. All of these charges are utterly false, but not a few Louisvillians still believe these jejune accusations.

Bingham took part of his $5 million bequest from Mary Lily's will and purchased the *COURIER-JOURNAL* and *LOUISVILLE TIMES* in 1918. He clashed immediately with HENRY WATTERSON at the *Courier-Journal* over WOMAN SUFFRAGE, PROHIBITION, and the impending League of Nations treaty. Watterson resigned, and Bingham's personality and political agenda soon dominated both papers. In the 1920s he pushed for farm cooperatives and generally challenged the local and state Democratic Party bosses, allying himself with kindred spirits Percy Haly and J.C.W. Beckham to form a strong faction. His papers became a voice for better public education and attention to the needs of AFRICAN AMERICANS and the rural poor.

Bingham married his third wife, Aleen Lithgow (Muldoon) Hilliard, widow of brokerage house owner J. Byron Hilliard, in London, England, on August 21, 1924.

One of the first people to support the presidential candidacy of Franklin D. Roosevelt, Bingham contributed substantially to the 1932 campaign. He was rewarded with the ambassadorship to Great Britain the following year. While at the Court of St. James's he pushed for closer ties between the United States and Britain. Bingham became a valuable conduit for information, diplomatic and otherwise, to the White House and the Department of State. He strongly opposed the rise of Fascism and Nazism in Europe and often spoke harshly in public about the rise of totalitarianism in the world. He took part in the London Economic Conference, chaired the International Wheat Advisory Committee, and participated in the Naval Arms Limitation Conferences and the preliminary discussions of the Anglo-American trade agreement. In effect, Bingham played a somewhat independent role in diplomacy, saying and doing things that Roosevelt could not do at the time.

Bingham was an avid hunter and fisherman and raised bird dogs. He bought a large house in GLENVIEW, just to the east of Louisville. When he died in late 1937, BARRY BINGHAM took over full control of the family enterprises. Both are buried in CAVE HILL CEMETERY.

See William E. Ellis, *Robert Worth Bingham and the Southern Mystique: From the Old South to the New South and Beyond* (Kent, Ohio, 1997); Samuel W. Thomas, ed., *Barry Bingham: A Man of His Word* (Lexington 1993); Samuel W. Thomas, "Let the Documents Speak: An Analysis of David Leon Chandler's Assessment of Robert Worth Bingham," *Filson Club History Quarterly* 63 (July 1989): 307–61.

William E. Ellis

BINGO. Numbers games have a long history in the United States, and in Louisville. In the late eighteenth century, the terms "bingo" and "lotto" (and "beano") were used interchangeably in reference to any form of wagering in which bettors received a series of numbers in advance of a drawing. Kentucky in general, and Louisville in particular, earned reputations as centers of GAMBLING. Certainly early teamsters hauling cargo around the FALLS OF THE OHIO bet on an early version of bingo in taverns along the wharf.

Gambling in all its forms thrived in the port cities of inland waterways such as the OHIO RIVER and on the hundreds of steamships on these rivers in the late eighteenth and early nineteenth centuries. Numbers games came under attack from the religiously inspired reform movements of the 1830s-40s and again from the Progressive reformers of the early twentieth century who believed that gambling, like alcohol, hurt families in particular and society in general.

Games of chance found refuge first in carnivals, which featured bingo for prizes, and then in the city's ROMAN CATHOLIC churches, which have been sponsoring bingo events since at least the turn of the twentieth century. The onset of the GREAT DEPRESSION spread the popularity of bingo, sponsored not only by churches but by service clubs, fraternal societies, and other nonprofit organizations. This form of gaming, taking place as a kind of charity, reduced the stigma attached to gambling, which was denounced by religious and social reformers alike. MOVIE THEATERS also scheduled bingo nights to attract audiences during the 1930s, connecting the game with the booming cinema industry.

WORLD WAR II ended the Depression, but bingo was here to stay. Although "numbers games" were illegal, charitable bingo nights were allowed to continue with neither regulation nor clear legality. Not only did the game survive in Louisville's neighborhoods, it became a regular feature on the social calendar of Veterans of Foreign Wars (VFW) halls, Catholic congregations, ethnic associations, and fraternal lodges; and it emerged as a business in its own right, housed in permanent bingo halls. Along the way, the particular game of "bingo" took shape, played on cards with twenty-five numbered squares that players mark with colored ink "daubers" as numbers are drawn and called, with the winning player yelling "Bingo!" when he or she completes a full row or column. Bingo attracted a subculture of enthusiasts who play a dizzying array of games on multiple cards. "Bingo centers" and large weekly games offer "jackpots" of several hundred dollars, ranging up to one thousand dollars for "triple" wins, though charitable gaming laws limit payouts to five thousand dollars per day.

Gaming laws have only recently come about; bingo for charitable purposes was formally legalized in 1992 with an amendment to the state constitution (when the state began its own numbers game, the lottery). The state began to regulate bingo with the Charitable Gaming Act of 1994, which set up the Department of Charitable Gaming and established licensing requirements for all games making more than five thousand dollars a year. Regulations stipulate that only nonprofit organizations with Internal Revenue Service "501C3" status for at least three years are eligible to run bingo games, although the rules permit a wide variety of venues to provide regular sessions, sometimes with only a thin veneer of nonprofit fundraising to qualify the operation as "charitable gaming."

The law requires the bingo sponsors to keep meticulous records on the fate of each bingo card (each with a serial number), the names and addresses of all players and winners of more than one dollar, all money taken in and paid out, and the eventual use of all profits. Furthermore, bingo workers are all supposed to be volunteers, barred from receiving wages or tips (rules that outlawed a preexisting class of "professional volunteers") or even to play bingo themselves.

As of 1998, there were 234 organizations licensed to conduct charitable gaming in Jefferson County, collecting gross receipts of nearly $200 million, of which almost $17 million was available to the organizations. Presently there are twenty-one "bingo centers" operating as businesses in Louisville, nine of them on Dixie Hwy. Nearly all of the 126 parishes in the Archdiocese of Louisville, 73 of them in Jefferson County, hold licenses to operate bingo games. At least eight of Jefferson County's thirteen VFW posts host at least one, and often two, weekly bingo nights. A wide variety of other nonprofit organizations, from Lions Clubs to patriotic societies to Bellarmine College, benefit from bingo games in Louisville today, with untold thousands of weekly participants.

Eric Paul Roorda

BIRDS. The Louisville metropolitan area supports a great variety of birdlife. Although not located along a major avian flyway, Jefferson and surrounding counties include portions of three physiographic regions: the Bluegrass, the Knobs, and the Highland Rim. This landscape diversity results in the presence of a relatively large variety of habitats. Moreover, the Ohio River adds immensely to the diversity of birdlife that can be encountered. Of the 350 bird species that have been reported from Kentucky, about 310 have been observed in the Louisville area. Most are species that are broadly distributed throughout the eastern United States, but Louisville's centralized location results in the presence of both northern and southern species.

Common permanent residents of the area include the red-tailed hawk, American kestrel, great horned owl, mourning dove, downy and red-bellied woodpeckers, blue jay, American crow, Carolina chickadee, tufted titmouse, Carolina wren, eastern bluebird, American robin, northern mockingbird, northern cardinal, song sparrow, and house finch. Widespread summer residents include the chimney swift, eastern kingbird, barn swallow, purple martin, wood thrush, red-eyed vireo, and indigo bunting. Species that appear commonly only during the winter include the ring-billed gull (mostly along the Ohio River), dark-eyed junco, and white-throated sparrow. A few species have been introduced from Europe. They include the rock dove (or domestic pigeon), European starling, and house (or English) sparrow. In addition, several vagrant species have been found nowhere else in the state, including the reddish egret, harlequin duck, Sabine's and black-headed gulls, and gull-billed tern.

Parks and woodlands in the area offer excellent opportunities to observe migrant songbirds, which peak in occurrence from mid-April to mid-May and again from early September to mid-October. During the peak of spring migration, it is not uncommon to find more than a hundred species of birds locally in a single day. Approximately 130 species have been reported nesting in the Louisville area (Palmer-Ball 1996), but some are quite rare and a few have disappeared from the region as it has become heavily settled. As a result, only seventy to eighty can be found regularly in summer. In winter only about sixty-five to seventy species can be found with relative ease, but the local Christmas count regularly tallies more than eighty-five species, with many birders combing a seven-and-one-half-mile radius area centered in the northeastern part of Jefferson County.

Perhaps the most interesting breeding species is the black-crowned night heron, a colony of which has nested in the area for many decades. Over the years the colony has occupied several locations, including Six Mile Island, Sand Island, and Shippingport Island, all in the river. Most recently the colony has moved to the Louisville Zoo. Only a few other nesting colonies are known statewide. In addition, the peregrine falcon, a federally endangered species that nearly became extinct in the late 1960s and early 1970s because of pesticide use, has staged a comeback. A pair of these majestic raptors has nested in downtown Louisville since 1997.

The Falls of the Ohio is the most interesting birding spot in the Louisville area. In addition to attracting many songbird migrants, the variety of waterbirds that stop to rest and feed on the exposed fossil beds and associated pools and riffles is unmatched across the state. In fact, more than 260 species of birds have been reported from the Falls area alone (Palmer-Ball and Hannan 1986). Other good birding areas in the local vicinity include Beargrass Creek State Nature Preserve (spring and fall periods for songbird migrants), Bernheim Forest (year-round for songbirds and locally the best place for the variety of nesting songbirds), Otter Creek Park (year-round for songbirds; best local location for spotting a bald eagle—along the Ohio River from November through March), Deam Lake in southern Indiana (early spring and late fall for waterbird migrants), Ohio River from downtown to Twelve Mile Island (early spring and late fall for waterbird migrants), and Cave Hill Cemetery (spring and fall for songbird migrants, winter for waterfowl and northern finches).

One of the more spectacular annual ornithological events in the Louisville area is the fall passage of sandhill cranes. Louisville lies along the center line of a narrow migration corridor between these birds' breeding grounds in south-central Canada and wintering grounds in the southeastern United States. Although flocks regularly pass through the area in early spring on their way north, it is the fall migration that is noticed by most people. From early November to late December, flocks of cranes pass through the area in large 'V' formations, typically on cool, sunny days with light breezes. Many people think these large flocks are migrating geese. However, the birds' long legs trailing behind; their rolling, guttural calls; and periodic circling of the large flocks all distinguish them from geese.

Bird study in the local area essentially commenced during John James Audubon's residence in Louisville from 1807–10. His writings provided the first real picture of the birdlife of the region, and it is from this era that we are provided local reports of now extinct or extirpated species such as the passenger pigeon, Carolina parakeet, swallow-tailed kite, and whooping crane. In addition, Audubon provided the original scientific descriptions of several species from observations made in the Louisville area. In the latter part of the nineteenth century, several ornithologists visited and resided in the area, contributing much to the knowledge of the local birdlife. Among these was Charles W. Beckham, who resided at Bardstown and documented the birdlife of the entire region. Contemporary ornithologists of the region include several local individuals who have contributed greatly to our knowledge of the area's birdlife: Burt L. Monroe Sr. (active during the mid-1930s to late 1960s), Robert M. Mengel (late 1930s to early 1950s), Harvey B. Lovell (1940s to 1950s), Leonard C. Brecher (late 1930s to early 1970s), Burt L. Monroe Jr. (1950s to early 1990s), and Anne L. Stramm (1950s to late 1990s). A summary listing of the area's birdlife, "Birds of the Louisville Region," was published by the Kentucky Ornithological Society in 1961 (Monroe and Monroe 1961) and updated in 1975 (Monroe 1975).

Many references to birds of the Louisville area also can be found in two works summarizing the birdlife of the entire state. Robert Mengel's *Birds of Kentucky* (1965) is the most complete reference to Kentucky's birds. The more recently published *Annotated Checklist of the Birds of Kentucky* (Monroe, Stamm, and Palmer-Ball 1988) does not match the level of detail found in Mengel's book but serves to update in an abbreviated fashion the information contained in *Birds of Kentucky*.

The Beckham Bird Club, Louisville chapter of the Kentucky Ornithological Society, was founded in 1935 and named for the aforementioned C.W. Beckham. The club sponsors the local Audubon Christmas bird count and the North American spring and full migration counts for Jefferson County and holds monthly meetings on a variety of birding topics.

Feeding birds in the Louisville area can be done year-round but is most popular during winter. Most local songbirds are attracted to sunflower seeds, although niger (thistle) seed attracts finches and a cracked corn/millet mix will attract cardinals, juncos, white-throated sparrows, song sparrows, and mourning doves. Ruby-throated hummingbirds can be attracted readily to most suburban and rural situations if a sugar-water feeder is kept out consistently and cleaned regularly. Hummingbirds are here from mid-April to early October but occur most frequently at feeders from mid-July to mid-September. Songbirds also can be attracted to local backyards when water and nest boxes are provided. Most common inhabitants of standard boxes with an entrance hole diameter of approximately one and one-quarter inches include the Carolina wren and house wren (suburban yards), eastern bluebirds (open areas, farmland), and Carolina chickadees (woodland edges).

See Robert M. Mengel, *The Birds of Kentucky* (Lawrence, Kan., 1965); Burt L. Monroe Jr., "Birds of the Louisville Region," *The Kentucky Warbler* 52 (1976): 39–64; Burt L. Monroe Sr. and Burt L. Monroe Jr. "Birds of the Louisville Region," *The Kentucky Warbler* 37 (1961): 23–42; Burt L. Monroe Jr., Anne L. Stamm, and Brainard L. Palmer-Ball Jr., *Annotated Checklist of the Birds of Kentucky* (Louisville 1988); Brainard L. Palmer-Ball Jr., *The Kentucky Breeding Bird Atlas* (Lexington 1996); and Brainard L. Palmer-Ball Jr. and Richard R. Hannan, *Resident and Migrant Bird Study, McAlpine Locks and Dam* (Louisville 1986).

Brainard L. Palmer-Ball

BISHOP, STEPHEN (b Glasgow, Kentucky, 1817; d Edmonson County, Kentucky, 1857). Cave guide and explorer. Bishop won lasting fame as one of the earliest and most widely known Mammoth Cave guides. Bishop was born enslaved. His owner, Frank Gorin, a Glasgow attorney, purchased Mammoth Cave in 1838 and moved Bishop there to work as a guide. Gorin, however, lacked sufficient capital to develop the cave as a profitable tourist attraction, and, in 1839, Dr. John Croghan of Locust Grove in Jefferson County bought the property and Bishop for ten thousand dollars. Croghan added tours, expanded the inn, and had roads built.

Only twenty miles of the cave had been explored when Bishop arrived. In 1838 he was the first person to cross the Bottomless Pit. He later discovered Mammoth Dome, the River Styx, Dismal Hollow, Bandits' Hall, the sightless creatures of the cave depths, and other famous and up-to-then-unknown sections of the cave. Bishop is still credited with exploring more of Mammoth Cave than any other individual. In 1842, while visiting Locust Grove, he drew from memory a remarkably accurate map of Mammoth Cave.

Along with being a first-rate and daring explorer, Bishop was an even more remarkable guide. Described as a short, wiry, "charismatic" and "incredibly handsome" mulatto, he led tours by lantern light and educated himself by watching, listening to, and discreetly questioning the many learned visitors who followed him into the subterranean darkness. In time he learned to speak some Latin and Greek and amazed visitors with his knowledge of history and geology. Although other black guides such as brothers Masterson and Nicholas Bransford were hired to assist him, Bishop himself became almost as great an attraction as Mammoth Cave itself by the mid 1840s. His fame was even more extraordinary given that his role as guide placed him in authority over whites, authority that could only be exercised safely with a mixture of deference and affability.

On his 1842 trip to Locust Grove, Bishop "married" Charlotte, another slave of John Croghan (under the Kentucky Constitution, slave marriage was not recognized by law). Charlotte returned with him to Mammoth Cave and worked as a maid at the nearby inn. When Croghan died in 1849, his will stipulated that Bishop and his family, including his son, Thomas, born in 1843, be emancipated in 1856 and assisted in emigrating to the west African nation of Liberia—which had been established in the early 1820s as an African site to which free blacks could be "returned." Instead, Bishop, who was officially emancipated in February 1856, saved his money and bought property near Mammoth Cave. Unfortunately, he was unable to enjoy his new freedom and died suddenly and mysteriously in the summer of 1857. Bishop is buried in the Guides' Cemetery near the Mammoth Cave entrance.

See Marianne Finch, *An Englishwoman's Experience in America* (London 1853); Jefferson County Will Book 4, 121; *Courier-Journal*, Feb. 22, 1996; Jeanne C. Schmitzer, "The Sable Guides of Mammoth Cave," *Filson Club History Quarterly* 67 (April 1993): 240–58; Samuel W. Thomas, Eugene H. Conner, Harold Meloy, "A History of Mammoth Cave, Emphasizing Tourist Development and Medical Experimentation under Dr. John Croghan," *Register of the Kentucky Historical Society* 64 (Oct. 1970): 319–41; Marion B. Lucas, *A History of Blacks in Kentucky, From Slavery to Segregation, 1760–1891, vol. 1* (Frankfort 1992).

J. Blaine Hudson

BITTNERS. Following his arrival in Louisville in the 1840s with his wife Magdalena, Gustav Bittner worked in several shops before opening his own cabinetmaking workshop in a small brick building on Brook St. in 1854. Bittner later expanded his talents to furniture, and his work became so well known that it was said that every wealthy family in Kentucky possessed at least one Bittner furnishing by the outbreak of the Civil War.

Bittner's son, William C. Bittner, joined the family business after completing his education. Upon the death of his father in 1895, he moved into a management position and became president when the company was incorporated as G. Bittner's Sons in 1909. During this time, the company was moved into a new facility on First St. and began selling antiques and other fine home furnishings.

In 1982 the founder's great-grandson, William Schneider, sold the company to Owsley Brown Frazier of the Brown-Forman Corp. After the sale, Bittners expanded its residential and commercial interior design group but continued to produce its renowned custom-made furniture as well. By 1998 the company had four locations: E Main St., Holiday Manor, and Mall St. Matthews in Louisville, and Kenwood Mall in Cincinnati.

See Temple Bodley and Samuel M. Wilson, *History of Kentucky* (Louisville 1928).

BLACKACRE STATE NATURE PRESERVE. Blackacre State Nature Preserve occupies more than 270 acres of the 600–acre Tyler Settlement Rural Historic District east of Jeffersontown. The land was donated to the Kentucky State Nature Preserves Commission in 1979 by Judge and Mrs. Macauley Smith and is managed by the Jefferson County Public Schools as a center for environmental education. Originally the Moses Tyler farm, the property includes a pre-1800 log barn and two-room stone cottage, an 1840s brick farmhouse, a reconstructed springhouse, a twentieth-century smokehouse, and other utility structures. About ten thousand students a year visit this outdoor classroom, where they get hands-on experience while learning about the past.

See *Courier-Journal,* April 4, 1990.

Joellen Tyler Johnston

BLACKBURN, LUKE PRYOR (b Spring Station, Woodford County, Kentucky, June 16, 1816; d Frankfort, September 14, 1887). Physician and governor. Luke Pryor Blackburn, the only physician to serve as governor of Kentucky (1879–83), received a medical degree from Transylvania University in 1835, practiced briefly in Frankfort and Versailles, and served an uneventful term in the 1843–44 Kentucky legislature. In 1846 he moved to Natchez, where he won acclaim during the 1848 and 1854 yellow fever epidemics by establishing the first effective quarantines in the Mississippi Valley.

During the Civil War Blackburn served as a civilian agent for the Confederate governors of Kentucky and Mississippi and instigated and apparently carried out an unsuccessful plot to infect northern metropolitan and military centers with yellow fever. The plot was revealed in April 1865, and the Bureau of Military Justice charged the doctor with conspiracy to commit murder. Living in Canada and beyond United States jurisdiction, Blackburn was tried and acquitted by a Toronto court for violating Canadian neutrality.

Blackburn moved to Louisville in 1872 and in subsequent years won fame for his humanitarian efforts during yellow fever outbreaks in Tennessee (1873) and Florida (1877). In the spring of 1878 he announced his desire to be governor, an idea that few Kentuckians took seriously. However, when officials in Hickman announced that yellow fever had reached epidemic proportions there, Blackburn hastened to western Kentucky, worked day and night caring for fever victims, and won the admiration of the electorate. The following spring, the "Hero of Hickman" received the Democratic convention's nomination. In September 1879, despite newspaper reports of his germ warfare activities, Kentuckians swept the physician into office on a wave of gratitude over Republican Walter Evans of Hopkinsville by a vote of 125,790 to 81,882.

Blackburn's administration accomplished the first important reforms of the postwar era. At his urging the legislature increased property taxes, revamped the district court system, established a superior court to hear some appeals cases, set salaries for judges and prosecuting attorneys, and reorganized the Agricultural and Mechanical College—and doing so created the University of Kentucky. The legislature also increased the powers of the state Board of Health. Blackburn appointed Joseph N. McCormack to the board; he would serve more than thirty years as its dynamic executive officer, drafting and enforcing legislation that advanced the course of public health.

Blackburn's major contribution, however, resulted from his crusade to improve conditions at the overcrowded and poorly administered Kentucky Penitentiary. Using the only means at his disposal—his executive pardon—Blackburn alleviated some of the prison's inhumane conditions by releasing the very young, the infirm, and those he believed were victims of injustice. He forced the General Assembly to institute a new governing system for "Kentucky's Black Hole of Calcutta" and set in motion plans for a new penal institution (Eddyville Reformatory). To address the immediate problem of overcrowding, the state hired out convicts to work on public projects, a program Blackburn abhorred. At the end of his administration, Blackburn returned to the Falls City and opened the Louisville Sanitarium, a hospital for "the treatment of lunatics and inebriates" near Cave Hill Cemetery. He is buried in the Frankfort Cemetery.

Blackburn married Ella Gist Boswell of Lexington in November 1835. Their only child, Cary Bell, practiced medicine in Louisville. In 1857 Blackburn married Julia Churchill of Louisville; the couple had no children.

See Nancy Disher Baird, *Luke Pryor Blackburn: Physician, Governor, Reformer* (Lexington 1979); "Luke Pryor Blackburn's Campaign for Governor," *Register of the Kentucky Historical Society* 74 (Oct. 1976): 300–13; "The Yellow Fever Plot," *Civil War Times, Illustrated* 13 (Nov. 1974): 16–23.

Nancy D. Baird

BLIGH, DELOS THURMAN "YANKEE" (b Franklin, New York, March 19, 1823; d Louisville, March 1, 1890). Lawman. D.T. "Yankee" Bligh left home at the age of nineteen to seek his fortune as a Rocky Mountain fur trader, only to find himself stranded in Louisville. Forced to find work as a bricklayer, he eventually abandoned his westward trek. He worked as a bricklayer on what is now the Landmark Building at Third and Liberty Streets, originally the U.S. Custom House and Post Office, which was completed in 1858. After serving with the Louisville Legion in the Mexican War (1846–48), he resumed his former occupation until 1856, when he was appointed one of the city's five supernumerary day watchmen.

Bligh's great physical strength, his bulldog tenacity, and his photographic memory soon made him a terror to Louisville's criminal element. Regarded as a formidable foe by pickpockets, thieves, and levee toughs, he successfully matched wits with international criminals, including some of the most notorious swindlers and counterfeiters of his day. His equally relentless pursuit of agents of the "Underground Railroad" is perhaps the only blight on his distinguished record.

Appointed to the police force in 1861, Bligh chose not to join the Secret Service during the Civil War but operated against Confederate agents and sympathizers in the city. He became a city detective in 1865 and five years later was promoted to chief of detectives, a position he held until his death.

Bligh's investigation of robberies committed by the notorious James-Younger Gang in Kentucky proved the most colorful episode in his career. The first professional detective to pursue the outlaws, Bligh was widely regarded as the nemesis of the gang. He personally assisted in the capture of one gang member after the gang robbed the Russellville bank in 1868, and he led the investigations of the bank robberies in Columbia, Kentucky (1872), and Huntington, West Virginia (1875). Published in Louisville, Nashville, and St. Louis newspapers in 1875, a letter signed by Jesse W. James bitterly denounced Bligh as one of the many lawmen who blamed him for every "bold robbery in the country."

The shooting of Sam Bing, a Chinese immigrant, on December 31, 1881, was perhaps the only questionable act of Bligh's career. Bing, who had just been assaulted by a citizen in his laundry, grabbed a hatchet and gave chase. The enraged youth, who barely understood English, began to swing the weapon wildly at a gathering crowd of onlookers, until Bligh brought him down with a single shot. Although cleared of all charges, Bligh, who maintained he acted in self-defense, regretted the killing for the rest of his life.

Regarded by many contemporaries as an equal to the great Allan Pinkerton, Bligh died of heart failure at his Louisville residence. He is buried in Cave Hill Cemetery.

See *Courier-Journal*, March 2, 1890, March 12, 1916; William C. Mallieu, "Exploits of Yankee Bligh," *Filson Club History Quarterly* 43 (Jan. 1969): 23–29; Bob Watson, "The Day Jesse Turned Yankee Bligh Around," *Real West* 28 (Jan. 1975): 26–30; William A. Settle Jr., *Jesse James Was His Name* (Lincoln, Neb., 1977); *Louisville Times*, Jan. 23, 1958.

James M. Prichard

BLINDNESS EDUCATION. The first known effort to aid blind people in Louisville occurred on June 29, 1839, when Bryce M. Patten began teaching a special class for blind children at the Louisville Collegiate Institute. Patten's pioneering effort led to presentations in 1841 by Samuel Gridley Howe, noted leader in the education of blind people, to the Kentucky General Assembly promoting the establishment of a state school for the blind. During the same year Louisville physician Daniel Drake gave a series of lectures on the education of blind children. W.F. Bullock, a member of the legislature, was so motivated by Drake's words that he sought his help in drafting legislation. Established in 1842, the Kentucky School for the Blind was the third state school for the blind in the United States.

Dr. Theodore Stout Bell was a founding member of the school's Board of Visitors. Bell served the school for forty-two years, from its founding until his death, both as a trustee and as an ophthalmologist and general physician to the students. Ophthalmology was practiced in Louisville along with general surgery, and there was strong interest in the subject in the Louisville medical community. The first volume of the *Western Journal of Medicine and Surgery* (1840) carried an ophthalmologic article by Louisville physician William Adair McDowell. The study of ophthalmology at the University of Louisville was developed by physicians who were national leaders in the field. The first ophthalmic lectures were given by James Morrison Bodine in 1872. Bodine bequeathed his extensive professional library to the University of Louisville Medical School, thereby furthering the ophthalmologic education of medical students.

In 1993 the University of Louisville Department of Ophthalmology created the world's first Ph.D. program in Visual Sciences. Faculty and students of the department staff the Kentucky Lions Eye Research Institute in downtown Louisville. The Kentucky Lions Eye Clinic, established at Louisville General Hospital in 1956; the Kentucky Lions Eye Bank, established in 1958; and the Kentucky Lions Eye Research Institute, opened in 1968, operate under the auspices of the Kentucky Lions Eye Foundation Inc. Finis E. Davis, president of the American Printing House for the Blind (1947-1976), served as president of the Lions International and headed the fund-raising for the Research Institute. When the building was expanded in 1997, it was dedicated to him.

Another aspect of Louisville's national leadership in blindness education was the establishment of the American Printing House for the Blind in 1858. With strong local support from leaders of the Kentucky School for the Blind, encouragement on the national level from leaders in the blindness field, and financial commitments from individuals and the state legislature, the Printing House began printing books in raised letters in 1866. In 1879 the Printing House received federal funding to provide educational materials to blind students nationwide—a mission that continues.

The need for vocational training and employment for adult blind people was recognized by the state legislature when, in 1913, it extended the scope of the Kentucky School for the Blind to include adult vocational education. A separate department, the Kentucky Workshop for the Adult Blind, was established. C.B. Martin, a teacher at the school, set up the workshop, beginning with two blind employees making mops.

In 1918 the need for expansion prompted the state to make an annual appropriation to the workshop, and by 1919 the workshop moved into several buildings on Frankfort Ave. In 1924 a new factory building was erected. The workshop eventually occupied the entire complex, and the buildings were united with a common facade. The new building stimulated mop and broom production and allowed for expanded mattress and rug production, crafts that employed women.

In 1956 the workshop was separated from the Kentucky School for the Blind and renamed Kentucky Industries for the Blind. Under the directorship of Ned Cox, subcontracting work was obtained. The first contract was for stuffing envelopes, then assembling whiskey bottle stoppers and chair swivels.

In 1970 a new building was erected at 1900 Brownsboro Rd., and the subcontracting work was expanded. In the late 1990s Kentucky Industries for the Blind made the transition to a private, not-for-profit organization.

Rehabilitation services for blind adults were originally provided by the state through the Division of Services for the Blind, located in Louisville. Offices and training centers were scattered throughout the city. When the Industries for the Blind building was built in 1970, the second floor became the first home of the Rehabilitation Center for the Blind, which had formerly sent clients out of state for mobility training. The Bureau for the Blind (now Department for the Blind) became a separate agency of state government in 1976. In 1994 the Charles W. McDowell Comprehensive Rehabilitation Center was built on Westport Rd. This allowed all the services of the department to be under one roof.

Blind and visually impaired adults are served by the Kentucky Department for the Blind. The department is nationally recognized for training programs that use assistive technology, a specialized technology that allows blind people to use computers. The department offers classes in basic education toward a GED, college preparation, and career exploration. There are also classes in mobility training, independent living, and Braille.

While the Kentucky School for the Blind educates children from kindergarten through grade twelve, preschool children are served by Visually Impaired Preschool Services. This not-for- profit organization, organized in 1985, assists families of children with visual impairments from the time the disability is detected until the child enters kindergarten.

In 1910 Kentucky was one of four states with the highest incidence of blindness in the country. The contagious disease trachoma, associated with poverty and lack of sanitation, was largely responsible for this statistic. In 1914 Louisville schoolchildren who were found to have trachoma were required to seek treatment. Indigent patients were sent to the eye clinic at the new City Hospital. Kentucky's "New Law for the Prevention of Blindness" (approved March 9, 1914) required reporting to the local board of health all cases of trachoma or opthalmia in infants.

Volunteer organizations such as the Kentucky Society for the Prevention of Blindness were organized in response to the trachoma epidemic. Volunteer efforts in prevention of blindness are carried out by the Kentucky division of the national organization Prevent Blindness America. Founded in 1951, the Kentucky organization conducts vision screening for preschool children and adults and sponsors public education programs on eye health and safety.

In addition to working for blindness prevention, Louisville volunteers have a history of responding to the needs of blind people. In 1952 several Louisville women became interested in the national organization, Recording for the Blind, and founded a Kentucky unit. Recording for the Blind and Dyslexic, the Kentucky unit, has studios on Haldeman Ave. and provides educational materials to people who cannot read standard print. The Audio Studio for the Reading Impaired is another local volunteer recording studio that records materials requested by individuals. Volunteer braillists have provided materials in Braille for individual blind people. The Adath Israel Sisterhood had a dedicated group of volunteer braillists who served for many years.

Probably the first opportunity given the Louisville Free Public Library to serve blind people was the donation, in about 1900, of the embossed book library of deaf-blind poet Morrison Heady. Unfortunately the collection was lost in the 1937 flood. Since 1976 the library has been a subregional talking book library of the National Library Service for the Blind and Physically Handicapped.

Several Louisville blind men are nationally known for their work as leaders in the field of adaptive technology. Tim Cranmer has a number of inventions for blind people to his credit, including the Cranmer Modified Perkins Braille Writer, the first electronic desktop Braille embosser. Emerson Foulke (1929-1977), a psychology professor at the University of Louisville, founded the Perceptual Alternatives Laboratory at the university in 1968. There he developed techniques to compress information from audio tapes. Foulke was one of the nation's most widely quoted and widely published authorities in the field of Braille research and tactile communications. In collaboration with Wayne Thompson, Fred Gissoni invented the Porta-braille, the first portable, battery-operated computer designed for blind people. An updated version of the device, known as the Braille 'N Speak is widely used.

Louisville has attained national stature in both historic and current contributions to the vision field. Leading pioneering institutions such as the Kentucky School for the Blind and the American Printing House for the Blind continue to expand their services. Later organizations—the University of Louisville School of Ophthalmology, the Lions Eye Research Institute—along with gifted individuals, both sighted and blind, perpetuate Louisville's contribution on a national level. State government, local affiliates of national organizations, and local not-for-profit and volunteer organizations serve blind people and work for the prevention of blindness in the community.

See "Report of the Kentucky Workshop for the Adult Blind," *Kentucky School for the Blind Annual Reports*, 1919, 1924, 1925; Ned Cox, *Ned Cox Remembers: An Autobiography* (Louisville 1996); "The Trachoma Problem," *Bulletin of the State Board of Health of Kentucky*, July 1915, reprinted in *Outlook for the Blind* 9 (Autumn 1915); The Kentucky Lions Eye Foundation Inc., annual report 1996–97; *Louisville Herald Post*, Oct. 4, 1932; Amy Board Higgs, "A New View of the World," *Health Care Quarterly, a supplement to Business First* 2 (Sept. 21, 1998); *Louisville Post*, Jan. 6, 1924.

Carol Brenner Tobe

BLIZZARD OF 1994. On January 16 and 17, 1994, a devastating snowfall covered the Louisville area, setting the record to that time exactly sixteen years after the previous record snowfall of 1978. In a twenty-four-hour period, 15.9 inches of snow blanketed the Falls City, thus closing highways, businesses, and schools; halting EMS vehicles; stopping mail service; slowing road crews; and resulting in massive power outages. Because of the hazardous conditions on January 18, Gov. Brereton Jones ordered that Kentucky's Interstate highways be closed indefinitely. For the next week temperatures in Louisville plunged as low as -22 degrees and kept the city at a complete standstill. By Saturday, January 20, roads had reopened and temperatures had returned to above-freezing marks, leaving behind a city that had been virtually shut down for an entire week. On February 4, 5, and 6, 1998, a deeper snow of 22.3 inches fell in the area, but warmer temperatures and better-prepared road crews kept incidents to a minimum.

See *Courier Journal,* Jan. 18–23, 1994.

Aaron D. Purcell

BLOEMER'S CHILI. Bloemer's Chili is the signature product of the Bloemer Food Sales Co. Inc., located at 925 S Seventh St. in Louisville. The company, founded by Frank B.

Bloemer Sr. in 1919, is a food production and distribution firm. Frank Senior, who started by running a corner grocery store at Second and Jefferson Streets, made a take-home chili base and sold it to customers at the grocery, who would use it to prepare chili at home. The chili was originally made in an iron pot about fourteen inches deep on a gas burner, hand-stirred and poured into one-pound and half-pound oblong tins. After being placed in a refrigerator to harden, it would be taken out and wrapped in parchment paper. Today the chili base in the original recipe is prepared in a 150-gallon kettle and put into eight-ounce plastic cups for sale in grocery stores.

In 1923 Frank Junior, after graduating from college, started working for the grocery store. In 1926 it moved to Second and LIBERTY STREETS, and the Bloemers started packaging chili under the Bloemer's Food Sales name. In 1937 the operation moved to the Seventh St. location. Frank Senior headed the company until he retired in 1941, and Frank Junior took over and served until 1957, when he retired. Frank Junior's brother, Lawrence A. "Larry," took over as president and headed the company until 1980, when Larry Junior became president.

Bloemer's started in the food distribution business in the early 1950s. It distributes to a variety of institutions such as RESTAURANTS, HOSPITALS, and schools. In 1954 Larry Senior and thirteen distributors across the South and Midwest founded the National Institutional Food Distributors Association (NIFDA) to distribute food to these institutions. The organization, providing a range of food products, is a member of UniPro, a cooperative of food service distributors with annual sales of $18 billion in the late 1990s.

Bloemer's is still recognized by the company's trademark red-and-white checkerboard, in use since it began. In addition to the chili base, the company manufactures a shredded beef with barbecue sauce, a shredded pork with barbecue sauce, an original chili powder, and a hot chili powder. They are primarily distributed in and around the Louisville area, carried in most local grocery stores.

See *Courier-Journal,* Aug. 21, 1951, Oct. 14, 1963.

BLOODY MONDAY. The anti-foreigner and anti-Catholic riot in Louisville on the election day of August 6, 1855, gave that day the name Bloody Monday. At least twenty-two persons were killed. The riot was an ugly manifestation of the national tensions arising from rapidly mounting IRISH and GERMAN immigration, the collapse of the WHIG PARTY, and the escalating debate over the extension of SLAVERY into territories such as Kansas and other areas west of the Mississippi River.

After 1848 the failed German democratic revolution and the Irish potato famine swelled the influx of immigrants to the United States. By 1850 these newcomers numbered nearly 11,000 out of Louisville's total white population of 36,224. They added a new and exotic element to the city, where the white population was predominantly Protestant and of English or Scots-Irish ancestry. Most of the Germans and Irish were Catholic.

The influx threatened the dominance of the Whigs in Louisville, since most of the newcomers, once naturalized, joined the DEMOCRATIC PARTY. At the same time the Whig Party was torn internally over the slavery-extension issue, and many Whigs joined the new American, or KNOW-NOTHING PARTY. Anti-foreigner and anti-Catholic, the party fanned the fear that immigrants threatened both Protestantism and democracy. By 1854 it claimed a million members nationwide and was well entrenched in the OHIO VALLEY. As early as the mid-1840s the *LOUISVILLE DAILY COURIER* began to comment on what its editor and publisher, Walter N. Haldeman, saw as the immigrant threat. By 1854, when the American Party gained control of the Jefferson County GOVERNMENT, Haldeman had abandoned the Whigs and openly supported the Know-Nothings.

At the same time the city's foremost editor, GEORGE D. PRENTICE of the *LOUISVILLE DAILY JOURNAL*, sadly watched his Whig Party disintegrate. On January 15, 1855, he wrote: "It is evident that this foreign question is to override all others, even the slavery question, as we see men of the most opposite views on slavery, forgetting their differences and acting together." By that summer he was lending his vitriolic pen to all-out support of the Know-Nothings. To Prentice this was apparently a way of defusing the slavery issue that threatened the Union.

The violence that had been sporadic in 1854 became frequent in 1855. The election for MAYOR and city councilmen on April 7 produced turbulence and a Know-Nothing victory. Mayor JAMES S. SPEED, a Whig and member of a pioneer Jefferson County family, was ousted by Know-Nothing JOHN BARBEE. Speed, a convert to Catholicism, moved his family to Chicago. Violence increased at the May 5 election of members of the county court, which resulted in another Know-Nothing victory. It was enough to shock even Haldeman, who soon abandoned the nativist cause and began to support the Democrats.

As the August 6 election for state officers and congressmen approached, the Know-Nothing rhetoric became ever more intense. The *Louisville Daily Democrat* of August 1 advised its readers to go to the polls with "unblanched cheek and unfaltering step, relying on no official protection." Those who followed the advice found that the American Party controlled the polls, admitting its members while keeping naturalized citizens waiting in long lines in sweltering heat. Fistfights broke out between waiting voters and taunting Know-Nothing bullies. By noon the Germans and Irish had given up trying to vote.

Precisely what spark set off the riots, arson, and murder during the afternoon and night of August 6 is impossible to determine. The disorder began east of downtown in the "uptown" area where most Germans lived. (More recently this area has been designated PHOENIX HILL.) Know-Nothing mobs howled through the streets, ransacking shops, taverns, and homes; beating hapless passersby; and setting fires on Shelby St. There were exchanges of gunfire, and the new ST. MARTIN'S CHURCH was saved only by the intercession of Know-Nothing mayor Barbee. The mayor also examined the cathedral on Fifth St. and verified that no munitions were stored within. The rioters burned the Armbruster brewery near BEARGRASS CREEK after helping themselves to the establishment's product.

The mob next turned its attention to the heavily Irish area west of downtown, setting fires and bludgeoning residents. QUINN'S ROW, a group of eleven buildings near Main and Eleventh Streets owned by, longtime Irish resident Patrick Quinn, went up in flames. As it burned, several Irish attempting to escape (including Quinn) were shot to death. Firemen were warned not to extinguish the blaze. The fires and rampages continued into the early hours of August 7, and ugly scenes continued for several more days. Needless to say, the Know-Nothing slate swept Louisville and Jefferson County. A year later the *Louisville Daily Times* of April 10, 1856, reported that foreign citizens were afraid to vote in the city elections of that month, and the American Party carried the polls.

The spasm passed relatively quickly, however, as a chastened city counted the toll in lives and property and the American Party itself foundered on the slavery issue. The former Know-Nothings drifted to the Democratic Party or the newly founded REPUBLICAN PARTY. As early as January 3, 1857, the *Louisville Daily Courier* reported that "the 'Know-Nothing' headquarters on Jefferson Street has been turned into a German theater." In 1865, ten years after Bloody Monday, PHILIP TOMPPERT, whose native language was German, was elected mayor.

See Agnes Geraldine McGann, *Nativism in Kentucky to 1860* (Washington, D.C., 1944); Charles E. Deusner, "The Know Nothing Riots in Louisville," *Register of the Kentucky Historical Society* 61 (April 1963): 122–47; Wallace S. Hutchson, "The Louisville Riots of August, 1855," *Register* 69 (April 1971): 150–72; Betty Carolyn Congleton, "George D. Prentice and Bloody Monday; A Reappraisal," *Register* 65 (July 1965): 220–39; George H. Yater, *Two Hundred Years at the Falls of the Ohio* (Louisville 1979 and 1987).

George H. Yater

BLUE, THOMAS FOUNTAIN, SR. (b Farmville, Virginia, 1866; d Louisville, November 10, 1935). Librarian. The son of former slaves, Blue distinguished himself as a leader in the field of library science training and service for AFRICAN AMERICANS. Educated at the Hampton Normal and Agricultural Institute in Virginia, from which he graduated in 1888, he went on to study at the Richmond Theological Seminary, earning a bachelor of divinity degree in 1898. A year later, Blue came to Louisville to work as the secretary of the YMCA, a position he held until 1905.

In 1905, the first CARNEGIE LIBRARY for blacks in the United States opened in Louisville. The Western Colored Branch of the LOUISVILLE FREE PUBLIC LIBRARY had its genesis in three rented rooms in a house at 1123 W Chestnut St., and Thomas Blue was appointed to be its head librarian. In 1908 the library moved to its permanent facility at 604 S Tenth St. Six years later, in 1914, the Eastern Colored Branch library was established at Hancock and Lampton Streets, and Blue was put in charge of it as well. By 1920 he had also been named director of the Louisville Free Public Library's new Colored Division, the first African American in the country to attain such a position. Blue had a substantial impact on library science training programs for blacks. Historian Cherye Knott Malone noted in her study of early black libraries and librarians that "most of the African American librarians who went to work for segregated branches in the South . . . received their training under Blue's tutelage."

Blue was also active in a number of professional organizations, including the American Library Association and the Negro Library Conference. He was an original member of the Louisville chapter of the Association for the Study of Negro Life and History and remained active in the ministry, sitting on the city's special committee of black ministers.

At the time of his death, Blue was survived by his wife and sons, Thomas F. and Charles J. He is buried at Eastern Cemetery.

See Cherye Knott Malone, "Louisville Free Public Library's Racially Segregated Branches, 1905–1935," *Register of the Kentucky State Historical Society* 93 (Spring 1995): 159–79.

BLUE BOAR CAFETERIA. Blue Boar Cafeteria, a name that comes from an English pub, was founded as Britling Cafeteria in Birmingham, Alabama, by A.W.B. Johnson in 1917. Johnson moved to Memphis, Tennessee, in the 1920s to open additional cafeterias under the same name. The successful business spread to several other locations, including Lexington, Nashville, Little Rock, Cleveland, and, by 1920, 410 W Walnut (now Muhammed Ali Blvd.) in Louisville.

Johnson's son, L. Eugene Johnson Sr., came to Louisville and opened the first Blue Boar Cafeteria at 644 S FOURTH ST. in 1931. The 1936 City Directory indicates a second Blue Boar on the site of the original Britling's Cafeteria. They were so busy that two serving lines were necessary, and both had balconies and basements where customers sat to eat. Other locations were established during the post–WORLD WAR II suburban building boom. L. Eugene Johnson Sr. died in 1982, and his two sons took over the business.

During Blue Boar's height of popularity in the mid-1980s, there were seventeen cafeterias in the Midwest, seven of which were in Louisville. Due to stiff competition, by the late 1990s most had closed. Blue Boar became associated with the Buckhead's restaurant chain in the mid-1990s.

See *Courier-Journal*, Jan, 15, 1999.

BLUEGRASS MUSIC. From the late 1960s through the mid-1970s, Louisville and Lexington were home to a particularly rich and intertwined bluegrass music environment because of two main factors: the presence of influential bands in both cities (The Bluegrass Alliance in Louisville and the various incarnations of the J.D. Crowe bands in Lexington), and the success of clubs in both cities that featured bluegrass several times a week.

One such Louisville establishment, on Bardstown Rd., changed names and/or proprietors several times during this period, but remained a magnet for bluegrass fans until it closed in the mid-seventies. The Storefront Congregation (the name which people seem to remember most) was home to both the Bluegrass Alliance and, later, the Newgrass Revival, but it also featured a good mix of local bands and occasional touring acts. A frequent sit-in performer was local fiddler Art Stamper, who had recorded with the Stanley Brothers in the 1940s and the Osborne Brothers in the 1950s.

The Great Midwestern Bluegrass Music Hall on Washington St. soon became the focal point of bluegrass in Louisville. Live MUSIC by both local and touring acts could be heard virtually every night of the week, and the place was often full to capacity. The Great Midwestern also offered a healthy smattering of folk, JAZZ, and BLUES. Lonnie Peerce's Bluegrass Alliance was the catalyst for much of the popularity of bluegrass in Louisville. Many superb musicians played with the band over the years, including Vince Gill, Tony Williamson, Dan Crary, Tony Rice, Sam Bush, and others.

J.D. Crowe and the New South also drew musicians such as Doyle Lawson, Ricky Skaggs, Tony Rice, and Jerry Douglas. Much bluegrass activity also centered around a house in Louisville's CHEROKEE TRIANGLE owned by Harry Bickel, a local musician. Beginning in 1975, it was home to dozens of local musicians and the stopping off place for so many touring bands that a critic for the *COURIER-JOURNAL* nicknamed it the Bluegrass Hotel.

In 1972 Bluegrass Alliance members Sam Bush, Curtis Burch, Courtney Johnson, and Ebo Walker quit to form the New Grass revival, a band which took bluegrass in a new direction and rankled many traditional bluegrass fans. In addition to using electric bass guitar and drums, New Grass Revival also grafted jazz and rock styling into its music, including long improvisational breaks. Members also dressed differently and wore their hair longer than traditional bands, facts that caused Bill Monroe to ban them from the Beanblossom Festival, but at the same time caused them to attract a younger crowd.

In 1967 many people began making what would become an annual two-hour trek to Beanblossom, Indiana, for Bill Monroe's bluegrass festival, a ritual that continued well into the 1970s. In 1973 LOUISVILLE CENTRAL AREA INC. developed the Bluegrass Music Festival of the United States in an effort to draw people to the RIVERFRONT PLAZA/BELVEDERE and the RIVER CITY MALL (Fourth St.). An estimated 40,000 people attended the three-day event that featured The Cumberlands, John Hartford, The Bluegrass Alliance, and the Juggernaut Jug Band. In 1974 PHILIP MORRIS contributed $9,000, and the LCA advertised the festival on radio stations in Indianapolis, Cincinnati, Dayton, Columbus, Nashville, Knoxville, and Chattanooga. By 1976 more than 100,000 bluegrass fans were being treated to national acts, such as Bill Monroe and His Blue Grass Boys, Ralph Stanley and the Clinch Mountain Boys, and the Goins Brothers.

By 1980 the festival started attracting larger named acts such as Emmy Lou Harris and Ricky Skaggs, both of whose careers were rooted in bluegrass despite their more country music sound. In 1982 the KENTUCKY FRIED CHICKEN CORP. (KFC) sponsored the festival, its budget grew to $150,000, and the event attracted 150,000 people. But support had evaporated by 1985, and Louisville was without a bluegrass festival until 1992 when local musician Gary Brewer organized the Strictly Bluegrass Festival, first in Central Park and later in the IROQUOIS AMPHITHEATRE.

The Kentuckiana Bluegrass Pickers Association was formed in March 1977, led by music store owner Bob Smith. Dues were $12 a year, and about seventy members met at the Sun Valley Community Center in southwest Jefferson County on the third Sunday of each month.

In 1983 BARRY BINGHAM SR. began pushing for a Bluegrass Music Center in downtown Louisville. Bill Monroe and Ricky Skaggs were invited to join a local board charged with raising money to establish a center, which would have included a museum, archives, recording studio, classrooms, and a performance hall. The center and the affiliation with Monroe and Skaggs never developed.

In the late 1990s local bluegrass bands included New Horizon, Gary Brewer and the Kentucky Ramblers, and the more eclectic, less traditional Galoots. Blue Moon Records, a mostly-bluegrass record store, closed after a few years, but bluegrass was heard live each week at the Hideaway Saloon, as well as on radio station WFPK-FM, which featured a two -and one-half-hour Sunday night bluegrass show hosted by Burke Bryant, himself a bluegrass musician.

Since it opened in 1983 the KENTUCKY CENTER FOR THE ARTS has been host to several touring bluegrass bands, many of whose performers cut their musical teeth in the bluegrass clubs of 1960s Louisville and Lexington. In 1997 the International Bluegrass Music Association moved its annual convention and fanfest from Owensboro, Kentucky, to downtown Louisville, an event that attracts musicians and fans from all over the world.

Traditional ("old time") music and western swing have also been found in Louisville since about 1930, such as in the bands of Clayton "Pappy" McMichen (Log Cabin Boys; Georgia Wildcats), who moved to the city in 1934 after a recording career with Gid Tanner's Skillet Lickers; Gene Autry, who sang with radio station WHAS briefly in the 1930s just before going to Hollywood, and Country Music Hall of Fame member PEE WEE KING, writer (with Redd Stewart) of *The Tennessee Waltz,* who worked with Autry and then formed the Golden West Cowboys in 1936. An important symbolic event in the city took place in 1932 when county music superstars Jimmie Rodgers and the Carter Family were brought together for the only recording session they did together. This took place in a warehouse near the site where the Kentucky Center for the Arts was later built. In the late seventies, the Buzzard Rock String Band became a popular group specializing in string band music from the twenties and thirties.

See Neil Rosenberg, *Bluegrass: A History* (Urbana, Illinois 1985).

Harry Bickel
Jack Ashworth
James T. Kirkwood

BLUES. There is considerable disagreement over when and where the blues developed into a separate musical style. It does seem clear that the blues, which began as a vocal tradition, has its roots in nineteenth-century African American work songs and other folk expressions, as well as in musical styles developed in the black churches. The characteristics of blues—vocal inflections, improvisation, repeated phrases, and personalized lyrics—seem to have been widespread by the late nineteenth century. JOHN JACOB NILES, the Kentucky folklorist, reported hearing his father talk of a Louisville "blues shouter" performing in a medicine show as early as 1898. Chester Mason, an AFRICAN AMERICAN guitarist, recalled hearing his brothers play blues on their ST. MATTHEWS farm as early as 1908.

The blues became popular through the commercial publication of W.C. Handy's *The Memphis Blues* (1912) and *The Saint Louis Blues* (1914). The first blues recording, "Crazy Blues," was made in 1920 by Mamie Smith, and it was an instant hit. From 1920 to 1927 blues recordings were dominated by the phenomenally successful blues queens, including Bessie Smith, Ethel Waters, and Louisville singers SARAH MARTIN, EDITH WILSON, and EDMONIA HENDERSON. Martin discovered Louisville guitarist SYLVESTER WEAVER, and he recorded the first blues guitar instrumental, "Guitar Rag," in 1923. In the 1930s popular Louisville blues singer and guitarist WILLIAM "BILL" GAITHER made more than a hundred records.

After WORLD WAR II, blues styles changed dramatically with the addition of amplified guitars and harmonicas. Artists such as Muddy Waters and B.B. King had a great influence on young blues singers. In the 1950s the Morgan Brothers Band and Mary Ann Fisher were popular at the Orchid Bar on Ninth St. Guitarist Foree Wells traveled to Memphis in the 1950s and played with B.B. King and others. He made many studio recordings and led an active blues band until his untimely death in 1997.

Blues music remains a vital part of Louisville's African American community. Older blues styles are preserved by harmonica player Fred Murphy, and more modern interpretations of blues forms are given by guitarists B.B. Taylor and George Brackens.

See Paul Oliver, *Songsters and Saints* (New York 1984); Lawrence Cohn, ed., *Nothing but the Blues* (New York 1993).

Cornelius Bogert

B'NAI B'RITH. Louisville Lodge No. 14 of this international Jewish order began February 22, 1904, with the merger of two older chapters, Har Moriah Lodge No. 14, organized in 1852, and Mendelssohn Lodge No. 40, organized in 1860. It moved from fraternal concerns into welfare and civic service activities and flourished as the national organization grew in importance.

Before the era of TELEVISION, the lodge conducted public forums on topics of the day. Currently Louisville Lodge helps provide support for four B'nai B'rith Youth Organization chapters at the JEWISH COMMUNITY CENTER and a Hillel chapter at the UNIVERSITY OF LOUISVILLE. Since 1956 the lodge has selected and honored a "Person of the Year," a significant honor in the Jewish community. It also conducts a Fresh Air Fund that provides camp scholarships for underprivileged Jewish children and lends support to the Anti-Defamation League of B'nai B'rith. At one time there was a local chapter of B'nai B'rith Women, but that group disbanded. Since 1992 women have been accepted as members of the older lodge. Although its membership has dwindled, its loyal followers continue to work toward the founders' original program of "benevolence, brotherly love, and harmony."

Herman Landau

BOARD OF ALDERMEN. The Board of Aldermen has been the sole legislative body for the city of Louisville since 1929. The story of law-making, however, reaches back much further, to 1779, before the town was chartered, when the pioneers at the FALLS OF THE OHIO selected five men to be trustees. The following year the Virginia legislature provided for local

Thomas Fountain Blue with staff of Western Colored Branch, Louisville Free Public Library, 1927. Rachel Davis Harris (see Harris entry) is 2nd from left in the front row.

government by naming nine "Trustees or Commissioners." When Kentucky became a state twelve years later, the new legislature continued to appoint trustees for the town, but in 1797 the citizens were again allowed the privilege of choosing their local leaders. In 1828 the General Assembly permitted greater local autonomy when a charter of incorporation was granted. Under this charter, a ten-member Common Council, working with a MAYOR, governed the growing city of almost 8,000.

In 1851 the CITY was given its second CHARTER, which established the Board of Aldermen. Under a two-house arrangement, the Board of Aldermen was the "upper house" and the Board of Common Council was a larger but less prestigious body. The two-house polity continued until 1929, when the Common Council was eliminated.

In the city's early decades, the Virginia and then the Kentucky legislature jealously guarded their power over the localities. As a result, Louisville's trustees were mostly administrators, rather than legislators. With each successive charter, however, Louisville officials were generally given greater latitude in conducting their affairs.

A superficial view of the alderman's job reveals a seemingly powerless routine of budget hearings, contract and policy- reviews, and ceremonial approval of the actions of the mayor or administrative agencies. More serious issues, however, have not been unusual on the aldermanic agenda. In the 1990s, for instance, mayoral proposals for closing Third St. for an expanded convention center and a garbage-to-steam incinerator were dropped due to a lack of legislative support. Further in the 1990s it was the Board that initiated a "Fairness Ordinance," prohibiting employment discrimination against homosexuals. These actions are much more weighty than some problems the aldermen dealt with which at a distance appear superficial. In 1828, the trustees tried to control Louisville's increasing rat population by offering a bounty of one-half cent for each rat scalp brought in.

The earliest trustees, who were appointed by the state legislatures, did not even have to live in Louisville. By 1795 residence in the city was required, and under the first charter, a council member had to live in the ward that he represented. Each councilman was chosen by the residents of his ward, until political reforms late in the nineteenth century changed that system. The architects of the reform of 1893 believed that the political machines that controlled the individual WARDS were corrupt, so they provided that each alderman be chosen by all the voters of the city and live in any part of Louisville. Members of the Common Council were chosen in the same manner, but continued to represent a specific ward and were required to reside there. This system of voting remained in place until the Common Council was deemed no longer necessary. At that time all aldermen were required to live in the ward they represented. The city-wide election essentially prevented the election of a black alderman until 1945, when Eugene S. Clayton joined the Board and W.J. Hodge became the Board's first black president in 1977. The voting practice also assured that the mayor-elect would carry a politically compatible slate of aldermen with him into office, with a few exceptions.

Women also were brought into the city's governance soon after WOMEN'S SUFFRAGE was instituted in this country in 1920. In just two years, EMMA E. RATTERMAN (later BRANCH) was elected to and eventually served as president of the Common Council (lower house). Hattie E. Hoffman became the first woman alderman in 1929 with Melissa Mershon serving as the Board's first female president beginning in 1990. In 1999 one woman elected to the board, Tina Ward-Pugh, insisted on being referred to as alderwoman, an unprecedented request but one to which all members of the board agreed.

The aldermen and alderwomen serve for a two-year term. They must be at least twenty-one years of age, residents and qualified voters of their ward, and not behind in paying any debts owed the city. They must disqualify themselves from voting or using their influence on contracts involving corporations in which they hold stock and must not seek a city contract while in office. Their salary is based on cost of living figures during each term that they serve, but their wages are not intended to be compensation for a full-time position. Adequate compensation for the aldermen has made it possible for persons to serve who might not otherwise have been able to afford the hours away from their jobs and allows some members to make it their sole income.

The aldermen have continued to gain influence in the city's GOVERNMENT. In 1978 the board moved to impeach then- Mayor WILLIAM STANSBURY, citing an incident in which Stansbury lied about his whereabouts during a firefighters strike. They intensified their efforts when federal investigators in a campaign fund-raising scandal involving another city official found evidence that Stansbury also profited from the extortion. The aldermen were forced to give up their impeachment proceedings when the state Court of Appeals denied them the power to subpoena witnesses including Stansbury. This move tested the power both of the mayor and the board, but demonstrated that the board would exercise greater scrutiny over the mayor. In 1981 the board's staff was expanded by six full-time aides, giving each of the board members his or her own full-time assistant, which allowed the board members opportunity to devote themselves more fully to thorough research and work in their committees. By 1994 the staff had expanded beyond a personal aide to each alderman to include a full time pool of nine other assistants. The year 1981 also brought about a change in the voting process, as more attention was focused on the wards by holding party primaries for aldermen to be nominated from each ward before entering the citywide general election.

Tom Owen

BOARD OF EDUCATION. The Louisville Board of Education dates to 1828 when the charter of the city of Louisville provided for the establishment of free schools for white children in each ward of the city. Management of the schools was vested in six trustees elected by the MAYOR and City Council. The first trustees included some of the luminaries of the city such as JAMES GUTHRIE, John P. Harrison, William Sale, James Overstreet, FORTUNATUS COSBY Jr., and Samuel Dickinson. During its first two decades, the selection of trustees boasted some of the most colorful figures in both Kentucky and national circles. Among the most prominent were Dr. LUNSFORD P. YANDELL, a charter member of the Kentucky Medical Association, founder of the LOUISVILLE MEDICAL INSTITUTE, and editor of several medical journals; Dr. Edward Jarvis, nationally recognized for his work in vital statistics and with the mentally ill; and HUMPHREY MARSHALL, Revolutionary War veteran, author of the early *History of Kentucky*, and a colorful political figure. The first three decades of board history profiled some of the most accomplished individuals in the Louisville business and medical communities.

In the spring of 1851 a change to the CITY CHARTER expanded school governance in several areas. First, governance increased to two trustees to be elected by voters in each of the city's twelve WARDS (later eight wards) for two-year terms. Additionally, these twenty-four individuals served as "Trustees of the University and Public Schools of Louisville." Such governance continued until 1860 when a charter change made elected officials "Trustees of the MALE HIGH SCHOOL, FEMALE HIGH SCHOOL, and PUBLIC SCHOOLS of the City of Louisville." Five years later, the trustees were given the power to fill vacancies due to death, resignation, or removal of a fellow trustee. Soon after the CIVIL WAR, trustees were given governing authority over the newly established separate schools for African American children in Louisville. To assist the trustees, a nine-member Board of Visitors, appointed annually from the African American community by the Committee on Colored Public Schools, performed in an auxiliary capacity.

By 1873 new charter amendments made trustee election subject to certain minimum qualifications. The change required trustees to be at least thirty years of age, owner of real estate or a householder, a United States citizen, a bona fide voter, and a resident of Kentucky for at least five years and Louisville for three years. In addition, the trustees could not have a contract with the schools or have a father, son, brother, wife, daughter, or sister employed as a teacher or professor.

Early in 1893 board composition was further modified when members came to be elected by legislative district rather than by ward. For education administration purposes, the city was divided into seven districts with two trustees from each district. The direct result was a board membership drop from a one-time high of twenty-four to fourteen. In 1910 the board underwent further changes, with five members to be elected at large for four-year terms. By 1921, with suffrage extended to women, Lelia C. Leidenger became the first female elected to the board. She was reelected and served until her resignation in 1932.

In 1908 Jefferson County was divided into eight districts, or educational divisions, with similar numbers of pupils and schools. Each district was further divided into subdivisions, each represented by a trustee. The trustees of each district then elected a chairman to act as representative on the Jefferson County Board of Education. Including the superintendent, the board numbered nine. Later the process of selecting members for the board was changed to the method of electing one member from each of the county's five political districts.

Beginning in late 1950 the city board passed a resolution "to determine the nature of educational and financial problems involved with a merger with Jefferson County Schools." For the next twenty years there were numerous studies and discussions on the subject without substantial progress on resolving the issue. During the 1956–57 school year under Superintendent Omer Carmichael, Louisville schools were integrated. Two years later, in 1959, Woodford Porter became the first African American elected to the board.

Following the passage of the Civil Rights Act in 1964, both the Louisville and the Jefferson County schools came under the scrutiny of the federal government on the subject of pupil enrollment and staff assignment by race. By the early 1970s issues of school finance, integration, and busing came to dominate public life in Louisville. After decades of discussion and a charged political climate, the Louisville public schools merged with those of Jefferson County in 1975. The Jefferson County Board of Education is made up of seven members elected by district. The term of office is for four years.

See J. Stoddard Johnston, ed., *Memorial History of Louisville* (Chicago 1896); "Minutes of the Louisville Board of Education" (Louisville 1834–1975); "Annual Reports of the Board of Education of Louisville" (Louisville 1894–1895, 1941–1942).

Frank R. Levstik

BOARD OF HEALTH. A city ordinance of 1823 authorized the first health officers of Louisville; they served gratuitously. Since that time many and varied groups have been appointed to preserve the health of the community. The mandates presented to these groups reflect the major threats to public health and changes in medical and scientific thought. Initially their major emphasis was upon maintaining clean premises and the draining of ponds and marshes.

The ordinance to establish a Board of Health was passed in 1865. It called for the General Council of the city to elect twenty-four well-informed physicians for two-year terms. An amendment in 1866 called for a health officer to be elected from the board with an annual salary of two thousand dollars.

A city ordinance of November 1853 represents the earliest effort to establish a death registry requiring all sextons to report name, age, residence, and cause of death of all persons interred. Registry of all births, marriages, and deaths in Jefferson County became law in 1898. A similar state law was passed in 1911.

Waterborne diseases such as typhoid fever continued to be a threat to the public health until well into the twentieth century, as many citizens still relied upon shallow, contaminated wells for their drinking water. Untreated river water was first distributed in Louisville in October 1860. Chemical analysis of drinking water by the Louisville Board of Health laboratories was instituted in 1902. Later, bacteriological study was added. In 1911, following the installation of a filter plant by the Louisville Water Co., the incidence of typhoid fever was reduced by 50 percent.

When the Louisville Marine Hospital became the City Hospital in 1836, health officials became responsible for its operation. In 1893 the Louisville Board of Health established a Division of Hospitals for operation of the City and St. John's Eruptive Hospitals. By 1910 general operation of the City Hospital was assigned to the Bureau of Public Safety, but the medical aspects remained with the Board of Health until 1979, when ownership of the hospital was transferred to the University of Louisville.

Tuberculosis was a major cause of death in the nineteenth and twentieth centuries. Waverly Hills Sanitorium for treatment of tubercular patients was opened in 1910 and soon received tuberculosis patients from the City Hospital. In 1945, 35–mm stereo-fluorographic x-ray units were acquired for screening citizens for the presence of tuberculosis.

The Board of Health often vaccinated against diseases. In 1831 vaccination against smallpox was offered free of charge by health officer John P. Declary, M.D. By September 1840, the physician to the Work House was vaccinating, free of charge, all unvaccinated school children. These were major steps in the control of smallpox, but compulsory vaccination was not made law until 1911. Vaccinations with Sabin oral polio vaccine were conducted throughout Jefferson County during October 1962 to March 1963 in a combined effort of public and private institutions—the Jefferson County Medical Society and the Junior Chamber of Commerce, coordinated by the Director of Health. As a result, about 96 percent of the population was vaccinated against poliomyelitis.

Efforts to provide unadulterated milk with a low bacterial count from tuberculosis-free cows finally met with success in 1909, although pasteurized milk (1905) and certified milk (1906) had already been produced in Jefferson County.

The Jefferson County Department of Health provided health care by its physicians in four health clinics and by financing the operation of the Louisville General Hospital. Its public health nurses conducted teaching clinics for the care of infants and children, staffed public school nurses' offices, and extended their teaching efforts to the Nurses Training Program at the Louisville General Hospital until 1970.

The Jefferson County Department of Health (1942) continues to be a valuable resource for educating the public about ways individuals can preserve their own health as well as that of their fellow citizens. Since World War II, prevention of heart disease, hypertension, and stroke has received much attention, but viral diseases such as hepatitis A, B, and C and AIDS continue to challenge the facilities and ingenuity of the staff of the Department of Health.

Eugene H. Conner

BOAT-BUILDING. The Louisville vicinity has been the site of boat-building activities from the earliest days of settlement. Indeed, evidence has been unearthed that dugouts and canoes were built here long before Columbus's voyages. Gen. George Rogers Clark had a galley built in 1782 at Louisville to use in restraining the Indians along the north side of the Ohio River, an idea that failed owing to the weight and clumsy construction of the boat, plus the reluctance of militia to serve on it. The U.S. Marine Corps claims it as the beginning of the corps.

The settlers in the new community needed means to travel up, down, and across the river, so flatboats, dugouts, and canoes were also built here. They were constructed directly along the riverbank from materials near at hand by the settlers, none of whom could be called professional boat-builders. By 1790 there were men who specialized in the building of skiffs, flatboats, and keelboats in this vicinity. Their building sites could not be dignified by the term boatyard, for almost any gently sloping shore with a nearby forest would serve. Even after the arrival of the first steamboat in 1811, boat-building in the vicinity of Louisville remained almost unchanged until 1819.

Throughout the wooden steamboat-building era, boat-building in Louisville remained a casually organized business run by highly individualistic and independent small contractors. Many were engaged to build one boat, then went on to other endeavors. The boatyards themselves were temporary. The physical plant usually was limited to a set of sloping timbers on which to build and launch the boat. They tended to cluster along the waterfront west of Sixth and east of Twelfth Streets, but a number

Partially completed steamboats on the ways at the Howard Shipyard and Dock Co. Jeffersonville, Indiana, c. 1910.

of boats were built above the city wharf in an area known as THE POINT (outcropping of land created by BEARGRASS CREEK at Third St.). There was virtually no building machinery such as cranes. Almost all work was done by hand-woodworking tools. Specialization was rare, and boat builders frequently contracted to build land-based structures. Boat owners often built boats for themselves. Machinery and cabins were often placed on the hulls after launching, and the hulls were towed to locations convenient to the contractors and suppliers who did that work.

Steamboats required an industrial base of foundries and mills and a cadre of experienced mechanics that did not exist here in that period. By 1819 Prentice and Bakewell were making steam engines in Louisville, and there was a foundry in NEW ALBANY, Indiana, as well. In 1819 the Philadelphia shipbuilding firm of Carter and Van Dusen sent forty ship carpenters to JEFFERSONVILLE, Indiana, to build the *United States*, perhaps the first large steamboat constructed here. Despite the crowing of NEWSPAPERS, these were not the floating palaces developed in the 1840s and perfected in the 1860s but were heavily timbered hulls with crude and boxy cabins.

Between 1820 and 1830 Louisville's population grew from 4,612 to 10,336. Her population doubled again by 1836. The towns in Indiana increased proportionately. During that decade Louisville gained the needed industrial capacity in the form of ship carpenters, foundries, machinists, boiler shops, and lumber mills whose output was largely used for riverboat construction and repairs. Workers were largely immigrants from both abroad and other parts of the United States.

Boatyards in the Falls Cities included the Carter and Van Dusen yard, the HOWARD SHIPYARD AND DOCK CO., the David Barmore Yard, the Sweeney Brothers Yard, the Robert C. Green Yard, and the William French Yard in Jeffersonville. Henry French and Peter Myers built boats on the site of the Barmore Yard in the early days. Dowerman and Humphreys and Hill Roberts and Co. were in New Albany. In Louisville a firm called Desmarie and McClary built steamboats at the mouth of Beargrass Creek. Richard P. Smith built a few boats in Louisville. Morton and Johnson built one boat at the mouth of Paddy's Run. Many other boat-builders came and went to and from Louisville. James Howard had yards in SHIPPINGPORT and on the Point before he settled in Jeffersonville.

Jeffersonville had some distinct advantages. The river level above the falls was far more stable than below. Delivery of log and lumber rafts was easy in Jeffersonville but was extremely difficult below the falls. There was less boat congestion than in Louisville, and land was cheaper. In addition, the slope of the bank was ideal and the water was deep close to shore.

Many other river-oriented firms in the Falls Cities worked as subcontractors or suppliers to the boat-builders. Few of those firms dealt with steamboats exclusively. There were many other smaller firms that supplied pipe, brass parts, glass, paint, and other necessary products. In 1860 it was estimated that 1,683 hands were directly employed in boatyards, foundries, and machine shops devoted to steamboat building. Several thousand other workmen were indirectly involved in products used in boat-building.

Boat-building continues today in the Louisville vicinity. JEFFBOAT INC., formed in 1933 in Jeffersonville, is a direct descendant of the French, Sweeney, Howard, and Barmore yards and maintains traditions dating back to 1834. Prospect Boat Works builds high-quality yachts and houseboats, renowned throughout America. The Kelly Shop also builds large pleasure boats. Marine Builders Inc. at UTICA, INDIANA, builds towboats and excursion boats. Jeffboat, Prospect Boat Works, the Kelly Shop, and Marine Builders Inc. continue to build commercial passenger, pleasure, and towing boats in the Louisville area.

See Charles Preston Fishbaugh, *From Paddlewheels to Propellers* (Indianapolis 1970); Charles H. Clarke, *J.M. White Descriptive Brochure* (1878); Louisville Directory, 1832; Louisville City Directory, 1836, 1867–68; Louis C. Hunter, *Steamboats on the Western Rivers* (Cambridge, Mass., 1949); Frederick Way Jr., *Way's Packet Directory, 1948–1993* (Columbus, Ohio, 1983).

Alan L. Bates

BODLEY, TEMPLE (b Louisville, August 5, 1852; d Louisville, November 23, 1940). Lawyer and historian. The ninth of eleven children and fifth son of William Stewart and Ellen (Pearce) Bodley, he was educated in Louisville and at the University of Virginia and graduated from the University of Louisville Law School in 1875. He practiced LAW in Louisville, and, although retiring from full-time practice in 1913, he apparently continued to handle some legal business until about 1930. He also was active in civic affairs, serving as Louisville's park commissioner, 1893–97, and as the first president of the Louisville Art Association. Bodley had a great interest in his family's history and the history of the early West, and beginning in 1903 he published a number of biographical and historical works. His better-known works include *George Rogers Clark: His Life and Public Services* (1926) (Clark was a forbear), volume one of a four-volume *History of Kentucky* (1928), and *Our First Great West* (1938), a history of the West during the Revolutionary War. Bodley married Jane Edith Fosdick (1866–1950) of Louisville on November 22, 1892. They had four children: William Fosdick, Ellen Pearce, Edith Fosdick, and Temple Junior. He is buried in CAVE HILL CEMETERY.

See John Frederick Dorman III, "Descendants of General Jonathan Clark, Jefferson County, Kentucky, 1750–1811," *Filson Club History Quarterly* 23 (April 1949): 129–32; Temple Bodley collection, Filson Club Historical Society, Louisville.

James J. Holmberg

BOLL, ROBERT HENRY (b Badenweiler, Germany, June 7, 1875; d Louisville, April 13, 1956). Editor and preacher. Boll immigrated to Zanesville, Ohio, with an aunt, and in 1895 enrolled in the Nashville Bible School, becoming a student of founders David Lipscomb and James Harding. After graduation he quickly rose to the upper echelon of the CHURCHES OF CHRIST, becoming front-page editor of the prestigious *Gospel Advocate*. Boll was dismissed from the staff in 1915. He soon became a pariah and eventually was disfellowed from the church. The dispute was over his "premillennial" views (belief in a thousand-year reign of Christ on earth and a return of JEWS to Palestine). This doctrine became the central focus of his preaching.

From 1904 until his death a half century

later, Boll lived in Louisville, where he preached for the Portland Avenue Church of Christ. He established the Portland Christian School and the Kentucky Bible College in Winchester, Kentucky, and became editor of the premillennial publication, *Word and Work.*

Boll's influence was felt and often opposed by churches in America and in the mission fields of Africa and Japan. Not until his death did premillennialism decline, with fewer than a hundred premillennial churches among the Churches of Christ in the late 1990s. He is buried in CAVE HILL CEMETERY.

See Earl Irvin West, *The Search for the Ancient Order*, vols. 3 and 4 (Germantown, Tenn., and Indianapolis, Ind., 1967 and 1978); Richard T. Hughes, *Reviving the Ancient Faith* (Grand Rapids, Mich., 1996); S. Mont Whitson, "Campbell's Concept of the Millennium," M.A. thesis, Butler University, 1951.

S. Mont Whitson

BOMHARD, HEINRICH HANS CLAUS MORITZ VON (b Munich, Germany, June 19, 1908; d Salzburg, Austria, July 23, 1996). Opera founder. He was the son of Ernst von Bomhard, an industrial engineer, and his wife, Jóhanna. They sent their son to the University of Leipzig, Germany, for a degree in law, but at the same time he got a diploma from the Leipzig Conservatory of Music. Bomhard came to the United States in 1935, had a graduate fellowship at the Juilliard School of Music, and joined the music staff of Princeton University. In 1942 he became a United States citizen and that year went into the U.S. Army Air Corps. His first wife, also a musician whom he had met in Germany, died in 1945, a victim of mental illness that led to her hospitalization.

In 1949 Bomhard came to Louisville to help the UNIVERSITY OF LOUISVILLE mount a production of Mozart's *The Marriage of Figaro.* The production attracted attention with two sold-out performances that showed off the local singers and instrumentalists of skill and polish. There were a few more of these once-a-year ventures and then a citizen group proposed to Bomhard that he leave his Princeton, New Jersey–New York City base and move permanently to Louisville to create the KENTUCKY OPERA. He agreed in 1952. Bomhard's backers ranged from the immensely rich who could give big sums to those of slender means who could, and did, give unstinting moral support. They all provided him with what he needed, namely their conviction that, through Bomhard, Kentucky Opera could be of great merit to the cultural climate of the community.

He and his board recognized that a lot of fans go to opera just to hear familiar arias and much-loved melodies. So he frequently put on three bread-and-butter lyric dramas (Puccini's *La Boheme,* Verdi's *Traviata,* and Bizet's *Carmen*). Until Kentucky Opera's fiscal backing became sturdy enough to hire help, Bomhard not only designed sets but painted them, too. When it was necessary, he made singable translations of librettos into English, for he was an advocate of opera in English. His composing talent was helpful when scores had to be edited to fit his slender budget for ORCHESTRAS. And he went to New York City to hear young singers before fame inflated their fees. Some of his finds went on to international careers, notably the great mezzo-soprano Tatyana Troyanos, who sang her first Carmen anywhere for Kentucky Opera. Professionals admired his skills because he not only staged twentieth-century works not often performed (he conducted a Janacek opera before the Metropolitan Opera got around to it) but also presented commissioned works by, among others, Nicolas Nabokov, Rolf Liebermann, and Lee Hoiby, and his opera company stayed afloat financially.

Louisville society has always cherished men of talent who enlivened the social scene; and at this Bomhard, impeccably attired for every occasion, was a master. He was erudite, witty, loved gossip, and enjoyed good food and wine. Bomhard taught frequently, most often at the University of Louisville School of Music, but also at Princeton and Columbia Universities. He retired in 1982.

In 1983 the KENTUCKY CENTER FOR THE ARTS was opened with a 622-seat theater named for Bomhard. He was present for the dedication of this facility that has been used for small operas, jazz performances, Stage One children's theater, fashion shows, business presentations, and the Lonesome Pine specials.

The death of his second wife, mezzo-soprano Charme Riesley, in 1984, was a blow from which he never really recovered. Had she lived he probably would not have left Louisville. Only two years before his death, he chose to go back to Europe and be with a niece and a nephew, who were all that were left of his family. He is buried in the Bomhard tomb in Munich.

See *Courier-Journal,* July 25, 1996, Sept. 15, 1996.

Frederick William Woolsey

BON AIR. Neighborhood in eastern Louisville bounded by the Watterson Expressway to the north, Bardstown Rd. to the west, Furman Blvd. to the east, and an irregular line along the city limits to the south. The community got its start in 1939 when Ralph Drake laid out the Wellingmoor subdivision, but growth was slow until after World War II. While construction of the Watterson Expressway in the late 1940s and early 1950s disrupted the expansion of the neighborhood, the improved access encouraged development in the area as well. Local landmarks include Farnsley Park and Father Maloney's Boys' Haven, established in 1950 as an education and treatment center for abused and neglected boys.

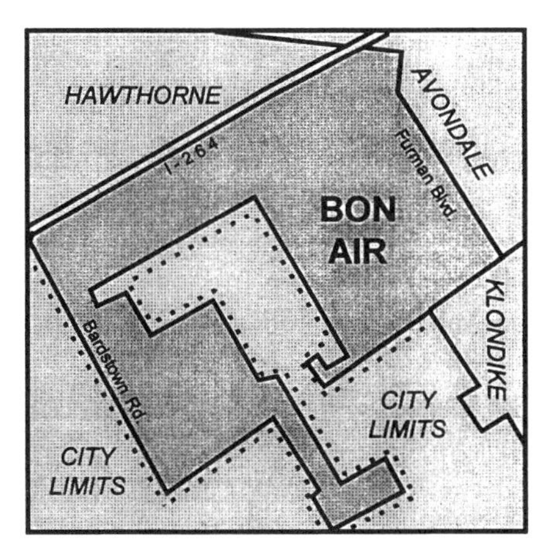

BOND, JAMES (b Lawrenceburg, Kentucky, September 5, 1863; d Louisville, January 15, 1929). Minister. Born into slavery to Jane Bond, he was freed at the age of two by the Thirteenth Amendment. His mother took him and his brother to Barbourville, Kentucky, where he was reared on the farm of Edward Arthur, son of Jane Bond's first master, Ambrose Arthur. In the early 1880s, Bond left home and walked seventy-five miles to Berea College to begin his education; he used a calf to pay his expenses. While at Berea, Bond worked as the chapel janitor and bellringer. At his graduation in 1892, he was one of about two thousand AFRICAN AMERICANS in the country to hold a college degree. Bond then went to Oberlin College in Ohio, where he received his divinity degree in 1895.

Bond spent much of his life outside Kentucky ministering to several churches. He moved first to Birmingham, Alabama, then to Nashville, where he was pastor of the Howard Congregational Church until 1906. He then returned to Kentucky at the request of Berea College. Kentucky's Day law of 1904, which outlawed biracial education, led Berea to establish a separate college for black youths called the LINCOLN INSTITUTE. Bond was asked to lead its fund-raising. The campaign, begun in 1907, was a success, and the institute opened near SIMPSONVILLE in 1912. Bond sat on the first board of the institute, but soon left for Atlanta.

WORLD WAR I marked Bond's return to Kentucky, this time to Louisville, where he volunteered for the army but was turned down because of his advanced age (fifty-five). Bond served from October 14, 1917, to November 17, 1918, as the YMCA camp service director at CAMP ZACHARY TAYLOR. After the war, Bond continued his work with the YMCA and was appointed Kentucky secretary for YMCAs for blacks. He also served as director to the newly formed Kentucky Commission on Interracial Cooperation, later known as the Kentucky Council on Human Relations. In both positions, Bond toured the state extensively, speaking out against SEGREGATION and urging interracial communication. In 1926 Bond was chosen as a delegate to the YMCA World Conference in Finland.

Bond met his wife, Jane Browne, at Oberlin. They had six children: Gilbert, James Palmer

Junior, Horace Mann, Max, Thomas, and Lucy. Horace Mann Bond became a noted educator; he was the father of civil rights activist Julian Bond.

Bond is buried in the Louisville Cemetery.

See Roger M. Williams, *The Bonds: An American Family* (New York 1971).

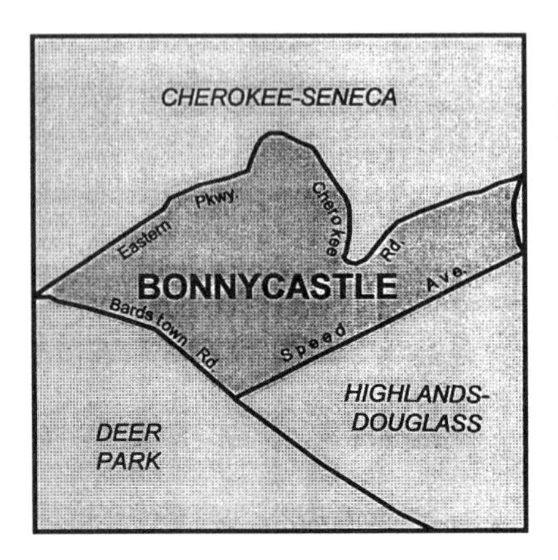

BONNYCASTLE. Neighborhood in eastern Louisville bounded by Speed Ave. to the south, Bardstown Rd. to the west, Eastern Pkwy. to the north, and Cherokee Park to the east. In 1848 Isaac Everett, a wholesale dry goods merchant and later a proprietor of the old Galt House, purchased 158 acres from Angereau and Myrah Gray and built Walnut Grove, near Cowling and Maryland Avenues, a family farm centered around a large mansion. Everett's daughter Harriet married Capt. John C. Bonnycastle, and the couple assumed control of the family land in the late 1860s. Area development began in 1872 with the plotting of the Sherwood Subdivision. While this community drew little interest at first, the area received a boost at the end of the century when Cherokee Park opened to the public and streetcar service was extended along Bardstown Rd. beyond Highland Ave.

Mrs. Bonnycastle, widowed in 1884, decided to capitalize on the area's new accessibility in 1900 by opening streets and subdividing large lots in a new neighborhood known as the "Bonnycastle Addition." Although subdivisions continued to be added until 1953, most of the growth in the area occurred before 1912, when the streetcar loop, which had been at Bonnycastle Ave., was extended out to Douglass Blvd. Local landmarks in the area include Cherokee Park and the Everett/Bonnycastle mansion. The neighborhood accommodates a mixture of commercial activity along Bardstown Rd. coupled with residences that dominate the remainder of the community.

See *A Place in Time: The Story of Louisville's Neighborhoods* (Louisville 1989).

BON TON. Bon Ton, which in French means good taste, appeared at 322 S Fourth St. in 1916. The name was selected by the specialty store's founder, Joseph H. Greenstein, because it was a commonly accepted colloquialism for a city business at that time. It occupied the same northwest corner at Fourth and Liberty Streets until it closed in December 1961. The one-floor concern, located at street level, was housed in the Marion E. Taylor Building. Bon Ton specialized in women's sportswear. Greenstein died in January 1935, and for the next twenty-six years this independently owned business was operated by his widow, Sara W. Greenstein. Though many of the family-owned businesses in the community had female members as active participants, in her day Mrs. Greenstein was the sole female owner-operator in the city.

Kenneth L. Miller

Bardstown Road in the Bonnycastle neighborhood, 1930s.

BOONE, SQUIRE (b Berks County, Pennsylvania, October 5, 1744; d Harrison County, Indiana, August 1815). Hunter, explorer, frontiersman. The tenth of eleven children of Squire Senior and Sarah (Morgan) Boone, Squire Boone in 1780 established the first settlement in Shelby County, Kentucky. Historians, including Willard Rouse Jillson, have concluded that, having been overshadowed by his older brother Daniel, he has not been accorded his proper place in history. He learned a great deal from his brother but was more active as an Indian fighter and did not possess the diplomatic talents of Daniel in dealing with the Indians.

In 1759 Squire was taken by his family—then settled at the Forks of the Yadkin in North Carolina—to Pennsylvania, where he served as an apprentice to his first-cousin Samuel Boone, an accomplished gunsmith. He developed skills in working with iron and displayed an inventiveness that later made him a valuable companion on the frontier. On August 8, 1765, soon after returning from his apprenticeship, Squire married Jane Van Cleve, not yet sixteen, whose father was of Amsterdam Dutch descent.

The Boone brothers hunted and explored the Kentucky wilderness in 1769–71. In March 1775 Squire accompanied Daniel, who had been employed by Judge Richard Henderson of the Transylvania Co., to lead a trail-blazing party into Kentucky. On April 1 the party arrived at the chosen site for a settlement subsequently called Boonesborough, near the confluence of Otter Creek and the Kentucky River, an area that he and Squire had explored during their long hunt of 1769–71. Daniel and Squire, once Boonesborough was thought to be secure, located land and brought out their families.

Squire participated with his brother in the great siege of Boonesborough in September 1778. In response to demands for surrender carried back into the fort by Daniel, Squire responded that he would fight to the death. The rest were of the same opinion. When negotiations outside the stockade were terminated by the threatening action of the Indians, the settlers ran for the fort. All except Squire Boone, who later had a rifle ball cut out of his shoulder by his brother, escaped without serious injury.

In the spring of 1779 Boone moved his family from Boonesborough to the Falls of the Ohio, where he purchased some lots and built a cabin. He signed the early petitions of 1779 and 1780 by the residents of Louisville to the legislature of Virginia asking for the official establishment of a town at the Falls.

In November 1779 Squire appeared before the Kentucky District Land Court, then sitting at the Falls, to obtain a certificate in the name of his brother-in-law, Benjamin Van Cleve, for a settlement and preemption of fourteen hundred acres for the "Painted Stone" tract. In the spring of 1780 he brought thirteen families to this tract, where he built a large station, the first settlement in present Shelby County. As a captain, he organized a small company of militia.

In April 1781 when the Indians attacked the Painted Stone Station, Squire received two gunshot wounds, one breaking his right arm just below the elbow and the other in his right side. Squire's right arm was shattered and when it healed was an inch and a half shorter than the other. The Painted Stone Station continued to be harassed. The hunters had to steal out at night, hunt by day, and return by night with their game. Squire Boone was confined all spring and summer as a result of his wounds.

It was decided to abandon the undermanned station and seek the relative safety of Linn's Station, the nearest settlement, about twenty-one miles to the west. Early in the morning of September 13, 1781, nearly all the families departed. Only Boone, so weak from his wounds that he could barely creep around, and his family, including his twelve-year-old son, Moses, remained with widow Hinton and her family to await the return of packhorses to evacuate them. At midday as the fleeing families approached the main ford at Long Run, about halfway to their destination, they were suddenly attacked in what has become known as the Long Run Massacre.

In 1782 Squire represented Jefferson County in the Virginia House of Delegates. Acting as a land locator for wealthy men who did not relish the hazards of the frontier, Squire became one of Shelby County's largest landowners. However, as a result of losses from conflicting and interfering land claims, he was compelled to sacrifice his property, including his station, which he left in 1786, settling elsewhere in Shelby County. His son Judge Moses Boone said later, "Boone did not go to law—yet felt not a little vexed that others who never settled the country nor aided in its defense should have ousted him."

While Squire Boone, like many other pioneers, was involved in securing land, he had to give first priority to hunting to feed his family and to defending them against the Indians. Further, he had little interest in administrative matters, little knowledge of the proper legal procedures, and little time for such mundane activities. Thus it can be argued that his financial and land problems could be attributed more to his inattention to administrative detail than to the actions of land speculators. In a deposition given in his own house in Shelby County in 1804, Squire testified that he was "principaled against going into the town of Shelbyville upon any business whatsoever." This lament of the old Indian fighter was caused by remembrance of the many suits brought against him in land disputes, one resulting in his being imprisoned for debts in Louisville for a time before his friends could secure his release.

Restless and discouraged by his land losses, Squire attempted unsuccessfully to establish a settlement at Chickasaw Bluffs near present Vicksburg, Mississippi, and visited St. Simon's Island in Georgia. He joined his brother Daniel in Missouri in 1799 for a year or two, returned to Shelby County, but left for the last time in 1806 to settle with his family in Harrison County, Indiana. Here, twenty-five miles west of Louisville, he built a small mill and again took up gunsmithing. He died in 1815 and at his request was buried in a cave on his property not far from Corydon.

See Willard Rouse Jillson, "Squire Boone," *Filson Club History Quarterly* 16 (July 1942): 141–71; Interviews with three of Squire Boone's sons, Draper Mss., 19C:1-155, Filson Club Historical Society; Ella Hazel (Atterbury) Spraker, *The Boone Family* (Rutland, Va., 1922); Squire Boone papers, manuscript department, Filson Club Historical Society.

Ronald R. Van Stockum Sr.

BOSNIANS. The first Bosnians arrived in the Louisville area in early 1993 as refugees driven out of Bosnia and Herzegovina by war tearing that nation apart. Bosnia and Herzegovina comprises an area of multiethnic character that existed as a state in various forms for almost a thousand years.

The first wave of Bosnians who arrived in Louisville were Bosnian Muslims, a group forced to leave their homes. The United States allowed three categories of Bosnian Muslims to enter the country—women who had been raped, individuals who had experienced concentration camps and had been captured as POWs by Serbs or Croats, and their families, and individuals who had a child or children born in the United States while visiting or studying here.

Bosnians speak the Bosnian language, which is written in the Latin alphabet. Before the war, all three nations—Bosnians, Croatians and Serbs—used the shared dialect and called it Serbo-Croatian. Many Bosnians had no knowledge of the English language before arriving in Louisville. However, well-educated people had a knowledge of at least one foreign language, and that gave them a better base with which to learn English quickly.

Bosnians traditionally value education. Many are well educated and willing to continue their education in the United States. Some already practice medicine, law, or work as educators or computer scientists. Those Bosnians who came to Louisville with little or no prior education were employed in many fields of Louisville's job market, including assembly line work, sewing, small metal production, hotel staffing, and stockyard work. Many Bosnians have found business success in Louisville, including Ermin's French Bakery and Cafe. Most Bosnians have found it difficult to find jobs equivalent to those they had in Bosnia partly because of the language problem. Most Bosnians living in Louisville are Muslims and belong to the Louisville Islamic Center.

In 1995 Bosnians organized Bosnian Community Inc., a nonprofit organization that gathers all people whose motherland is Bosnia, regardless of their national origin or religious affiliation. The organization has a youth group, "Golden Lilies," which practices Bosnian folk dance and traditional music. The intent is to maintain language, culture, and tradition, with all respect to the adjustment to American culture and lifestyle.

Azra K. Terzic

BOSSE FUNERAL HOME. For many years, this family-owned business was located at Hancock St. and Broadway, in the midst of the first German immigrant community. The funeral home was founded in 1865 by Henry Bosse Sr., a native of Hanover, Germany. He came to Louisville as a wood carver in the midst of the Civil War. He got many orders for coffins, and soon he was acting as mortician as well as manufacturer. The senior Bosse was active in nearby St. Boniface Parish and the St. Joseph Orphans Society. Family members soon were active in several professional, civic, fraternal, and religious organizations. These activities often put them in touch with German Americans from other parts of the city. A grandson, Robert Bosse, expanded the business to a second location with James Embry in 1950. In 1960, along with four other funeral directors, he opened the Highland Funeral Home. It was the first joint venture of its kind. By then, the firm had moved to Barret and Ellison. Some years previously, the Bosses had helped to launch a program that shares transportation service with other morticians.

See *Courier-Journal,* Oct. 6, 1943, July 25, 1979.

Henry C. Mayer

BOTTLE-MAKING. There is very little record of glass production in Louisville before 1850, though there may have been a glasshouse as early as 1814. Large-scale production of glass began at the Kentucky Glass Works in 1850. The operation was located on the southeast corner of Clay and Franklin Streets (marks on the bottom of bottles were Ky.G.W. and Ky G W). It was known as the Louisville Glass Works from 1855 to 1873 and operated at the same address. There were a number of owners, the most prominent being Dr. John A. Krack, a native of Baltimore who received his medical degree in Louisville in 1850.

He bought an interest in the glassworks in 1857 and was the principal in charge until 1873. Krack had operated a drugstore at the northwest corner of Shelby and Market Streets from 1852 to 1857, and it is likely that he ordered his pharmaceutical bottles and apothecary glass from the nearby works. During his leadership at the works, a wide variety of interesting glass was produced, including vials, ink bottles, pickle and sauce jars, demijohns, paperweights, commemorative flasks, pipes, canes, rolling pins, lamps and lamp chimneys, steamboat glass, doll's dishes, doorstops, whimseys, telegraph insulators, and other items.

From 1874 to 1878 the Louisville Glass Works was at Twenty-eighth and Montgomery Streets. In 1879 the location was listed as the north side of High St. (North Western Pkwy.) between Twenty-seventh and Twenty-eighth Streets. In 1880 the operation was purchased and operated by the DePauw American Plate Glass Works of New Albany, Indiana.

Other Louisville glassworks were the Southern Glass Works, at Eleventh and Monroe Streets from 1878 to 1889 (marks S.G.W. Lou. Ky. and S.G. Co.); the Kentucky Glass Works Co. at Fourth and C Streets from 1880 to 1890 (marks Ky. G. W. Co. and Ky G W Co); the Falls City Glass Co. on Bank St. from 1884 to 1890 and perhaps later (marks F.C.G.C., F.C.G. Co., F.C.G.CO.); and the Louisville Glass Works Co., also known as the Southern Glass Works Co., which operated about 1886 at 1101 Monroe St. (mark entwined LGWC logo).

One of the most important uses of glass was to contain drinks, both alcoholic and nonalcoholic, including water. Before 1870 whiskey purchasers brought their own bottles or jugs to be filled directly from the barrel. Apothecaries often dispensed alcohol. In 1870 George Garvin Brown, of J.T.S. Brown (later Brown-Forman) began to put whiskey in bottles with tamperproof seals. This protected customers from diluted or contaminated bottled whiskey. Whiskey bottled by the distilleries was such a success that in 1887 T.H. Sherley, who operated three Nelson County distilleries, leased the Kentucky Glass Works Co. and Southern Glass Works to supply bottles for his product.

Early Louisville glass bottles, as elsewhere, were mostly of the so-called "black glass," actually a nearly opaque dark olive green, though a wide variety of other colors were produced. Nineteenth-century glass bottles were handblown into molds, and embossed names and markings were common after 1850. This often makes very precise dating of the bottles easy by checking old city directories and other records. The top or crown of the bottle had to be applied to the neck of the blown bottle after it was removed from the blowpipe. This was done to all types of bottles until after the invention of the automatic bottle machine in 1904. Some applied tops are found on Louisville bottles as late as 1915. Applied top bottles can be recognized by the discontinuation of the bottle seam at the crown. With the advent of automatic bottle machines, the production of glass shifted to larger plants outside the Louisville area, marking the virtual end of local glass production.

Peter Richard Guetig
Conrad Selle

BOURBON STOCK YARDS. Bourbon Stock Yards, the oldest stockyard in the United States, originated at the Bourbon House, a hotel established in 1834. Situated between Washington St. and Story Ave. near Cabel St., the hotel operated as an inn for farmers and had pens to confine livestock bound for local slaughterhouses. By 1854 the hotel had become known as Bourbon House and Stock Yard and was owned by slaughterhouse operator Herman F. Vissman. He built a new facility at the southeast corner of Main and Johnson Streets close to the railroad in 1864; in 1875 it was incorporated as the Bourbon Stock Yard Co. During the last quarter of the nineteenth century, presidents John G. Barret and William R. Ray built a modern public market with offices for professional purchasing agents and commission firms, loading and unloading docks, and other essential facilities and services that allowed it to dominate the cattle market in Kentucky for more than a century.

Between 1900 and 1950, presidents Oscar Fenley and Ernest L. German extended the reach of the Louisville market and expanded the physical plant. Buyers from the eastern United States and as far away as Chicago came especially to purchase what were referred to as Kentucky Bluegrass milk-fed lambs. Beginning in 1950, presidents Louis Seelbach and George K. Tomes introduced numerous promotional programs to increase volume and initiated major physical improvements but could not overcome the decline caused by changes in modes of transportation from railroads to trucking.

In 1968 ownership passed to the Lincoln Finance Co. (later the Lincoln International Corp.), headed by DeCoursey Combs. To upgrade and better serve the local small farmer, the new owners built truck-loading docks, established a livestock auction program, and installed a computer system. Beginning in 1994 the stockyards were managed by Kentucky Livestock Exchange under contract with Lincoln International Corp. The yards served Kentucky and Indiana livestock producers until its last auction on March 29, 1999. On March 5, 1999, the Home of the Innocents purchased the 20.5 acre site for $3.4 million to build an expanded campus for needy and vulnerable children.

See Carl E. Kramer, *Drovers, Dealers and Dreamers: 150 Years at Bourbon Stock Yards, 1834–1984* (Louisville 1984); *Pride in the Past, Faith in the Future: A History of Michigan Livestock Exchange, 1922–1997* (Lansing, Mich., 1997); *Courier-Journal,* Nov. 12, 1998; March 30, 1999.

Carl E. Kramer

BOURGARD, CAROLINE B. (b Cannelton, Indiana, June 23, 1862; d Louisville, August 3, 1928). Educator. Upon graduation from Louisville Girls High School in 1879, Bourgard continued her studies at colleges of music in Louisville, Cincinnati, Chicago, and New York City.

Bourgard was connected to Louisville's public schools for nearly forty years. She started her career as a music teacher and later in 1892 became the first public school supervisor of music. In 1908 she founded the first Louisville Music Teacher's Association and in 1916 the State Music Teacher's Association. In 1921 Bourgard established the first Louisville Woman's Chorus and was a chairman of the Music Week programs held in Louisville under Mayor Huston Quin during 1921–25. In 1923 she was appointed state director of music and held the post until her resignation because of ill health. Bourgard initiated a bill through the General Assembly making singing a required subject in public schools.

In 1927 Bourgard helped found the first art college in Louisville for African American children at the Phillis Wheatley branch of the YWCA. She personally supervised the work there and secured good instructors for talented black students who were able to study various art disciplines. In 1928 that College of Music and Art, which bears Bourgard's name, moved to a new location at 2503 W Walnut St.(Muhammad Ali

Bourbon Stock Yards offices, southeast corner of Main and Johnson Streets, 1923.

Blvd.). She left the college an endowment.

Bourgard was an organist at Highland Presbyterian Church. She was the author of *Woman's Song Reader, Child's Song Reader No. 1, A Manual of Music and Outlines for Teachers*, and the *Book of Health Songs* that she dedicated to the children of Kentucky. Bourgard is buried in Cave Hill Cemetery.

See *Who's Who in Louisville* (Louisville 1926); *Louisville Library Collections,* vol. 3, (Louisville 1940); *Courier-Journal*, August 4, 5, 8, 1928.

BOUSMAN, LOU TATE (b Bowling Green, Kentucky, October 19, 1906; d Louisville, June 2, 1979). Master weaver, author, and weaving teacher. She was the only daughter of John Henry and Anne W. Bousman. The family moved from Bowling Green to Louisville and lived at 1725 S Third St. Lou Tate Bousman graduated from the Louisville Girls High School in 1924 and entered the University of Louisville, where she remained for one year. She then enrolled at Berea College and earned a B.A in 1927. Tate entered the University of Michigan and received an M.A. in art history in 1929. After she received her graduate degree, Tate worked for a time at the Dark Hollow School, which was located in the Blue Ridge Mountains of Virginia.

During her university career, she developed her love of weaving and weaving patterns. When she taught at the Dark Hollow School, she began collecting traditional coverlets and patterns from weavers in the mountains. The patterns and drafts became the basis of her extensive research work on the folk art of weaving. Known professionally as Lou Tate, she became a recognized authority on colonial and nineteenth-century handwoven textiles. Tate began her professional weaving career in 1933. Her exhibit "Folk Arts of Kentucky" opened on May 22, 1937, at the Folk Arts Center in New York City. This exhibit was followed by her exhibition of Kentucky handweavings at the J.B. Speed Art Museum during October 3–31, 1937.

Tate returned to Louisville and moved into one of three cabins located on Kenwood Hill at 328 Kenwood Hill Rd., in the southern edge of the city. The cabins, built in the late nineteenth century, became known as the Little Loomhouse. The property had been purchased by her mother for Lou Tate's use. The cabins and their setting won praise from Frank Lloyd Wright in 1948 during a visit to Louisville. The cabins, named Esta, Wisteria, and Tophouse, became Lou Tate's home and weaving workshop until her death.

Lou Tate Bousman was an acquaintance of several First Ladies. Herbert Hoover's wife, Lou Henry Hoover, persuaded Bousman to shorten her name to Lou Tate. Mrs. Hoover also is credited with helping Tate to develop a small portable table loom. This loom was sold for many years at the Loomhouse. It was also used in physical therapy exercises for injured World War II servicemen. Eleanor Roosevelt, during her tenure as First Lady, visited the Loomhouse to admire Tate's collections of coverlets. She purchased woven mats for the White House.

In 1945 Tate organized the Little Loomhouse Country Fair to showcase contemporary handwoven textiles. She also founded the Kentucky Weavers Guild on February 15, 1948, and was the longtime editor of the *Kentucky Weaver* magazine. Exhibitions of weaving and textiles curated by Lou Tate were held at the Little Loomhouse. She conducted weaving classes at the Loomhouse for generations of schoolchildren. She also helped organize the Midsummer Arts and Crafts Fairs, which were held on Kenwood Hill.

The Lou Tate Foundation now operates the Loomhouse as a nonprofit organization. The foundation continues the mission of weaving instruction and preserving the art of weaving. In July 1976 the Loomhouse cabins were placed on the National Register of Historic Places.

See Alice S. Davidson, *The Little Loomhouse, A Brief History* (Louisville 1997).

Alice S. Davidson

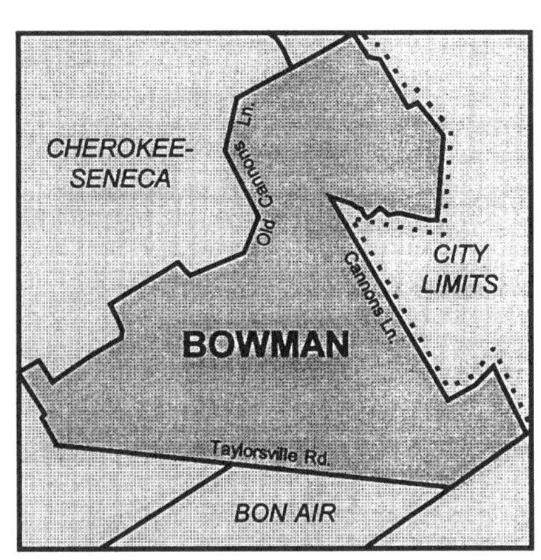

BOWMAN. A neighborhood in eastern Louisville comprising the area surrounding Bowman Field north of Taylorsville Rd., including that along Dutchmans Ln. and the area north of Interstate 64, south of Hycliffe Ave., and west of Cannons Ln. to the city limits. While scattered development occurred as far back as 1928, the increased use of the airport during World War II as a military installation induced soldiers and airport workers to move into the area. The area was annexed by the city in 1947. The neighborhood, adjacent to Seneca Park, is dominated by the airport and Big Spring Country Club, although residences exist around the Jewish Community Center on Dutchmans Ln. and in the area north of the Interstate.

BOWMAN, ABRAM HITE (b Bardstown Junction, Kentucky, March 13, 1875; d Louisville, July 19, 1943). Civic leader and aviation enthusiast. Known as the "father of Louisville aviation" in his later years, Abram was born to A.H. and Mary Pauline (Callahan) Bowman and moved to Louisville in 1903 after scaling Chilkoot Pass in Alaska and seeking gold in the Klondike. He set up a hay and grain business, which was later converted to a freight transfer business.

Abram Hite Bowman as photographed by the Herald Post, 1920s.

But within a few years he suffered pleurisy attacks that brought on tuberculosis. After receiving successful treatment in Saranac Lake, New York, Bowman returned home a vocal advocate for modern tuberculosis treatments and was instrumental in the establishment of Waverly Hills Sanatorium.

His interest in flying, heightened by tales of World War I pilots, led to his purchase of a surplus Canadian JN-4 "Jenny" plane in 1920. After forming a partnership with W. Sidney Park, who replaced Robert H. Gast after a brief association, the Bowman-Park Aero Co., a leader in aerial photography, was born. Understanding the future benefits, Bowman established an airfield on land he leased along Taylorsville Rd. In 1922 the Army Air Corps took over the lease and, in 1929, named the field Bowman Field. Because of his involvement throughout the city with flight, Waverly Hills, the board of trade, and the Morris Plan Bank, Bowman was selected as "Louisville's most useful citizen" in 1925 by the Kiwanis Club.

Bowman married Pauline Newman. They had three children: Abram Hite Junior, Josephine, and Pauline. He suffered a heart attack and is buried in Cave Hill Cemetery.

See *Courier-Journal*, July 20, 1943; George H. Yater, "Mr. Bowman's Cow Pasture," *Louisville* 19 (Oct. 20, 1968): 26–29.

BOWMAN FIELD. Bowman Field, Kentucky's oldest continuously operated public airport, is located in the eastern section of Louisville along Taylorsville Rd. The land had long been owned by the Breckinridge family, one of whose members, Mary Breckinridge Caldwell, married Baron Kurt Von Zedtwitz, a German nobleman. Their son, young Baron Waldemar Konrad Von Zedtwitz, inherited the property in 1918 when he turned twenty-one (both parents were deceased). But he was serv-

Main building and Curtis Flying Service Hangar at Bowman Field, 1931.

ing in the German army, and the federal Custodian of Alien Property Office immediately seized the property, since the United States was at war with Germany.

In 1919 Louisville aviation enthusiast ABRAM H. BOWMAN leased fifty acres of the six-hundred-acre tract, built a wooden hangar, and established an airfield. Daring Louisvillians took short flights in Bowman's secondhand Canadian JN-4 "Jenny" flown by a veteran pilot of the British Royal Corps of World War I, ROBERT GAST. In 1922 the Army Air Corps leased the field for five years at one dollar a year, and it became home to the Air Corps Reserve 456th Pursuit Squadron. On August 15, 1923, the field was officially dedicated and named Bowman Field.

As the potential of commercial aviation became apparent, the LOUISVILLE BOARD OF TRADE and the Aero Club of Kentucky—founded in 1922 to promote local aviation—pushed for municipal ownership. Passenger service was begun in 1924 by the Yellow Taxi Airline Co. In 1927 the entire Von Zedtwitz estate was purchased by the city for $750,000 (part became Seneca Park), and the Louisville and Jefferson County Air Board was created in 1928 to administer the airport. The initial attempt to provide passenger service between Louisville and Cleveland in 1927 proved premature, but the following year Continental Airlines (later American Airlines) established airmail service between the cities and in 1931 began carrying passengers. The terminal building was opened on August 1, 1929, and enlarged in 1937. In 1930 a weather station was installed along with six individual metal hangars. Eastern Airlines established service to Miami and Chicago in 1934. The airport was complete in 1938 with the construction of concrete runways.

Louisvillians felt a new appreciation for the airport during the FLOOD OF 1937. Bowman Field, because of its elevation, gave supply planes a place to land when the roads were washed out and the railways impassable.

During WORLD WAR II an Army Air Force facility occupied an eastern extension of the airport where thousands of troops were trained and the Glider Combat Training School was located. A second airport (Standiford Field, later to be named LOUISVILLE INTERNATIONAL AIRPORT) was constructed during the war to serve the CURTISS-WRIGHT and Vultee production facility built as a war measure. All commercial airline operations were transferred to Standiford Field on November 15, 1947.

Bowman Field became Louisville's general aviation airport serving private, corporate, and charter aircraft services, as well as flight instruction. In 1988 two original hangars and the Administration Building were entered in the NATIONAL REGISTER OF HISTORIC PLACES as the Bowman Field Historic District. It was the first such group of airport buildings so recognized.

See George H. Yater, "Mr. Bowman's Cow Pasture," *Louisville* (Oct. 1968): 26–29; idem., *Two Hundred Years at the Falls of the Ohio* (Louisville 1979 and 1987); Carl Kramer, *Louisville Survey East Report* (Louisville 1980).

Edward Peck

BOWYER, DAVID "KEN" (b Jeffersonville, Indiana, October 1, 1933; d Jeffersonville, March 11, 1994). Veteran, entrepreneur, and CIVIL RIGHTS activist. After Bowyer completed compulsory education, he finished a tour of duty in the United States Navy during the KOREAN WAR. He went on to own and operate a Gateway Supermarket in Louisville on Thirty-fourth St. Bowyer left the grocery business and became director of the Minority Small Business Development Center for the Hoosier Valley Economic Opportunity Development Corp. in JEFFERSONVILLE.

Throughout his professional career, he demonstrated a commitment to civic and civil rights causes, serving as president of the Jeffersonville/Clark County Chapter of the NAACP and area director consultant for the State Youth Coalition of the NAACP in southern Indiana. He also served as project director of the Stepping Stone Substance Abuse Prevention Program.

See *Louisville Times*, Sept. 15, 1980; *Courier-Journal*, Jan. 16, 1995.

Billy Sue Smith

BOXING. The history of boxing in Louisville can be divided into four time periods: the bare-fisted era (1780s-1889), the early gloved era (1889–1920), the "golden era" (1920–50), and the modern era (1950–present). During the first era, boxing was little more than an organized brawl. Rules of conduct were loose, and participants often brutalized each other. An example of bare-fisted fighting occurred in Louisville on election day, April 8, 1781. Noted by one source as the town's first fight, it involved two well-known citizens, Daniel Sullivan and John Carr, who fought near FORT NELSON at Seventh and MAIN STREETS. A large crowd of voters witnessed the evenly matched battle that ended with Sullivan having part of his ear bitten off.

Bare-knuckle fighting was the norm in the United States until the London Prize Ring Rules (later known as the Marquis of Queensberry Rules) were adopted. This 1838 code called for the use of gloves and the elimination of wrestling holds, and it designated ten seconds as the time of recovery for a floored fighter. However, their use did not become widespread in the United States until the late 1800s. In the interim, American boxing had mixed appeal; it attracted few wealthy spectators, and many fighters were actually criminals.

The career of the great John L. Sullivan was a turning point in boxing history. His popularity raised the sport to a new level and brought it much-needed patronage and respectability. Most importantly, his use of the Marquis of Queensberry rules led to widespread use of padded gloves and ushered in a new era of boxing. Sullivan's bout with Jake Kilrain on July 8, 1889, was the last bare-fisted championship match. The *COURIER-JOURNAL* provided extensive coverage of the fight "not only in recognition of the avowed general interest in it, but for the gratification of those estimable people who are loudest in condemnation of prize fights and hungriest for news concerning them." The July 9 headline proclaimed, "Boston Bruiser Wins . . . John L. Sullivan Once More the Champion of the World." The seventy-five-round, two-hour-and-eighteen-minute-long fight in Richburg, Mississippi, attracted three thousand spectators, including a sizable delegation from Louisville. Among them were an ex-police lieutenant, an alderman, and Chief of Police EDWARD HUGHES, who worked in the Sullivan corner during the bout.

In Louisville, where boxing was nominally illegal, the fight provoked intense interest and "scenes of universal jollification" when news of Sullivan's victory came over the telegraph. Thirty thousand copies of the *LOUISVILLE TIMES* sold on the afternoon of July 8. An Indianapolis merchant staying at the first SEELBACH HOTEL at Sixth and Main Streets described the pandemonium: "I never saw so much interest displayed over less than a presidential election. As I came down on the morning train, there were crowds of farmers and country people collected at every depot, anxiously awaiting word from the fight. They all seemed to be for Sullivan, and as the train pulled out from each stopping place, three cheers and a tiger went up from the excited rustics."

Although there seemed to be intense boxing interest in Louisville, there were mixed opinions of it. Boxing was made a state felony in 1896, but local officials often turned a blind eye as long as public decorum was maintained. In 1903 the Kentucky Court of Appeals clarified the illegality of boxing in the case of *Commonwealth v. McGovern.* The ruling specified that local COURTS had the duty to suppress and prevent boxing as a public nuisance. Talented local fighters such as Fern Creek's MARVIN HART were forced to seek fights elsewhere. In 1905 Hart defeated the famous African American boxer Jack Johnson in San Francisco and then won the heavyweight championship from Jack Root in Reno, Nevada.

Louisvillians had to look elsewhere to sate their boxing interest. The July 4, 1910, bout in Reno between Johnson and James Jeffries, an aging "white hope," was billed as the "fight of the century." Huge crowds gathered at ECLIPSE PARK, Fresh Air Park, and at the Courier-Journal building awaiting results. Johnson's stunning victory in a time of racial intolerance and SEGREGATION led to riots and assorted violence across the country. The *Courier-Journal* reported no local incidents and generally took a respectful tone in assessing Johnson's victory. The *Kentucky Reporter,* an African American paper published in Louisville from the late 1910s through the early 1930s, declared that the fight demonstrated what blacks could do if given a fair chance.

In 1918 city boxing fans found a source of entertainment at the new CAMP ZACHARY TAYLOR army post. On August 7, 1918, five thousand fans filled the Knights of Columbus Hall to view five fast matches involving soldiers. In response to reporter inquiries, the officer in charge of recreational activities at the post responded in regards to boxing: "This is perhaps now being indulged in as much as any other sport in the army today. It adds grace to the body, quickens the eye, trains the mind to quick thinking, but the greatest asset of all seems to be that the movement is very closely allied to those used in bayonet work and other hand-to-hand training."

Fight fans rejoiced on March 12, 1920, when the Bryson-Perry bill legalized twelve-round contests and set up a commission to issue permits. The bill was sponsored by Sen. William Perry of Louisville and Rep. Rodney Bryson of Covington.

Not all Louisvillians were pleased. On July 16, 1920, the City Council passed an ordinance that set up a license fee of five hundred dollars per contest. Boxing enthusiasts feared that anti-boxing politicians would effectively tax the sport out of existence. Mayor GEORGE W. SMITH, confident that the majority of citizens did not want the sport, signed the bill, saying, "Boxing is undesirable from a police standpoint because it draws some questionable persons and because of the aftermath. For twenty-five years the people of Louisville have fought the evilness of the game."

A political battle ensued when the Southern Athletic Club invited French war hero and heavyweight challenger Georges Carpentier to an exhibition bout in the Jefferson County Armory (THE GARDENS OF LOUISVILLE) on June 26, 1920. Carpentier ushered in the "golden age" of fighting with the return of legalized boxing to Louisville and impressed fans with his agility, footwork, and rapport. Fearing that opponents would block the exhibition, supporters rallied around Judge Harry Robinson, who issued an order restraining the MAYOR, the police, or anyone else from interfering with the fistic card at the Armory, which he "wouldn't have missed for a one hundred dollar note."

Opposition faded during the 1920s as the new boxing commission assumed control. On May 6, 1921, a forty-year tradition began of Derby Eve boxing matches at the Armory. Two noteworthy local fighters during the 1920s and 1930s were Cecil Payne and Jimmy Dell. Payne was a featherweight and lightweight who fought more than two hundred fights in fourteen years. He won more than 85 percent of his bouts, and it was said that "he never fought a bad fight." Never a champion himself, Payne fought against five world champions in eleven matches and won four of the bouts. Among his opponents were champions Tony Canzoneri, Freddy Miller, "Battling" Battalino, Bushy Graham, and Tod Morgan. Payne's style was unique and colorful, said a former promoter. "He was a master of deception with plenty of speed and body rhythm." Payne's last fight was in October 1937 at the Armory.

Jimmy Dell had been knocked down many times during his 303 fights but had the unusual record of never having suffered a "knock-out." During his last fight on August 25, 1925, Dell suffered a horrible beating during the middle and late rounds. More concerned with maintaining his record than his inevitable loss, Dell bravely stayed on his feet until the final bell sounded. Following his retirement, Dell became a promoter. In 1932 he brought his idol, heavyweight champion Jack Dempsey, to Louisville for a four-round exhibition with Frankie Wine. Although this was in the midst of the GREAT DEPRESSION, the bout was a huge success and took in fourteen thousand dollars.

Derby Eve 1940 saw Louisville's own Sammy Angott battle Chicago's Davey Day in a fifteen-round lightweight title bout. In a fight witnessed by 4,458 fans in the Armory, referee and ex-champ Jack Dempsey gave the Louisvillian a 2-point decision that was popular with the home crowd. The *Courier-Journal* noted that Louisville had "its first ring champion since Marvin Hart gained somewhat of a recognition as heavy king in the free lunch-with-a-beer days." Among the notables who witnessed the event were actors Al Jolson, Bing Crosby, Don Ameche, George Raft, and IRENE DUNNE, and U.S. senator A.B. "Happy" Chandler. But by then local boxing was in the doldrums.

Courier-Journal sports editor Earl Ruby proposed that integrated boxing matches should be given a trial. Kentucky state athletic commissioner Johnson S. Mattingly approved the move and noted that Kentucky was "one of only a few states that does not allow white-Negro fights."

On February 23, 1942, "fistic history" was made at the Columbia Gym as 1,388 customers saw the first "mixed" program in Louisville fight history. In the ten-round main event, FORT KNOX sergeant Mike Raffa outpointed Cleveland Brown, an African American from Cincinnati. Three of the five matches were black-white affairs, with white fighters scoring two wins and a draw. The *Courier-Journal* reported that the crowd was fair in its behavior.

WAVE-TV was the first station to bring televised network boxing to Louisville in 1949, and in 1950 WHAS-TV followed with a short-lived program that featured local amateur bouts from the Columbia Gym. TELEVISION was a mixed blessing for boxing. It exposed professional fighters to an increasingly larger fan base but encouraged people to view from the comforts of their own homes. As television viewers increased, attendance at local bouts declined.

Ironically, local boxing had much to offer during the 1950s. There were numerous venues where boxing could be enjoyed, including the Columbia Gym, the Armory, and the newly built FREEDOM HALL. Even outdoor boxing was popular at such sites as Preston Street Park, where a ring was built over a pitcher's mound and spectators included babes-in-arms and neighborhood dogs. The Louisville police were solid supporters of Golden Gloves boxing as a positive influence for inner-city youth. Politicians touted youth boxing as a proven and inexpensive way of decreasing juvenile delinquency. "Tomorrow's Champions," a WAVE-TV show produced by policeman and fight trainer JOE MARTIN and featuring young boxers, began a twelve-year run in 1954.

Most importantly, there were a number of talented young Louisvillians who rose to national prominence during the late 1950s and early 1960s. Among them were Rudell Stitch, Cassius Clay (MUHAMMAD ALI), and Jimmy Ellis.

Rudell Stitch was the number-ten-ranked welterweight in the nation when he performed a heroic rescue of a man drowning in the OHIO RIVER on September 16, 1959. A day later, he defeated Luther Rawlings on a technical knockout. The *Courier-Journal* called him "a stalking killer inside the ring, but a gentleman outside of it." By 1960 the popular Stitch was ranked number two and appeared to be in position to challenge for the world championship. Tragedy struck on June 5, 1960, as Stitch drowned in another Ohio River rescue attempt.

In 1954 a twelve-year-old Cassius Clay (Muhammad Ali) wandered into the Columbia Gym and met Joe Martin. Martin taught Cassius and his brother Rudolph discipline and boxing fundamentals. A high point in Louisville's boxing history occurred on February 4, 1960, at Freedom Hall. In the state Golden Gloves final, Rudolph won the light-heavyweight title, Cassius won the heavyweight title, and Jimmy Ellis won the middleweight crown. Later that year Cassius Clay won a gold medal at the Olympics in Rome.

Jimmy Ellis fought his first professional fight on April 19, 1961. Later he served as an Ali sparring partner for two years. After moving up to the heavyweight level, Ellis defeated Jerry Quarry on April 27, 1968, to become champion. He successfully defended his crown against Floyd Patterson but lost the title to Joe Frazier on February 16, 1970. Ellis retired with a record of forty wins, twelve losses, and one draw. Although he was often overshadowed in the national arena by Ali, Frazier, and George Foreman, it is noteworthy that Jimmy Ellis, who weighed 197 pounds, was the lightest man to win the heavyweight championship in 35 years.

As Louisville fighters gained recognition, interest in local boxing events waned. May 4, 1962, saw the last Derby Eve boxing matches. Even though the Jimmy Ellis–Holly Mims fight was the main event, fewer than six hundred fans showed up. A minor resurgence occurred as a new generation of local boxers challenged for national glory during the 1980s and 1990s. Greg Page briefly held the World Boxing Association (WBA) heavyweight championship, which he won in 1984 with a knockout of Gerry Coetzee. Mike Peak won the WBA light-heavyweight title in 1989 and held it until 1991. James Pritchard was a highly regarded heavyweight until his 1988 loss to Michael Dokes sent his career into a tailspin. Pritchard had the dubious honor of having been knocked out twenty-four seconds into a 1991 cruiserweight title fight. That is believed to be a record.

Louisville boxing fans cheered the arrival of the first Ali Cup amateur boxing tournament in September 1997. The five-day event held at the Kentucky International Convention Center was to honor Muhammad Ali and promote amateur boxing. Unfortunately, the event suffered low attendance, had organizational snags, and failed to earned any money for a planned Ali museum in Louisville.

See *Courier-Journal,* July 9, 1889, July 5, 1910, Aug. 8, 1918, May 7, 1921, May 4, 1940, Feb. 24, 1942, June 6, 1960, May 5, 1962, Sept. 14, 1997; Thomas Hauser, *Muhammad Ali: His Life and Times* (New York 1992); Louis Golding, *The Bare-knuckle Breed* (New York 1954).

David F. Withers

BOYD, EDWARD CLARENCE (b Ironton, Ohio, August 15, 1855; d Louisville, June 8, 1883). Artist. The son of a wealthy iron merchant, Boyd moved with the family business to Louisville when he was a boy. Boyd's artistic ability was recognized while he was attending public school in Louisville. In 1872 he entered the National Academy of Design in New York City. After two years, Boyd moved to Paris, where he entered the ateliers of Leon Bonnat (1833–1922) and Carolus-Duran (1837–1917). He returned to Louisville in 1876 upon the reversal of his father's fortunes and established a studio on the second floor of the Courier-Journal building at Fourth and Green (Liberty) Streets. There he created a number of ambitious landscape and figurative paintings whose subject matter frequently made allusion to scenes in famous literary works. His works were exhibited at the local Southern Exposition in 1886 and at the National Academy of Design. He was murdered in 1883 by his brother-in-law in a family quarrel over the latter's separation from Boyd's sister. Boyd is buried in Cave Hill Cemetery.

See Arthur F. Jones and Bruce Weber, *The Kentucky Painter from the Frontier Era to the Great War* (Lexington 1981).

BOY SCOUTS OF KENTUCKIANA. The Scouting movement was begun in 1910 by Sir Robert Baden Powell. The movement spread quickly among boys, and Louisville was no exception. According to the first Eagle Scouts in Louisville there were six or seven troops in 1910. In 1916 The Louisville Area Council, Boy Scouts of America was incorporated.

During the first World War Boy Scouts were very active in community service. Scouts sold Liberty Loan Bonds, collected scrap materials, planted war gardens, and distributed government materials in support of the war movement. Louisville Scouts conducted 60,000 hours of community service during the war. Scouts helped police during parades, and answered distress calls. Several Scoutmaster recruiting drives took place both to fill the need for leaders of the growing organization and to replace leaders who had been drafted for the war.

The first Eagle Scouts in Louisville received their badges in 1921. The recipients were Murray W. Phillips, Saul B. Ades, Richard Schulhafer, and Carl F. Barin. In 1998 there were 160 Eagle Scouts in the Lincoln Heritage Council.

Also in 1921 the Louisville Area Council bought its first property for camping. Before this scouts camped on private property. The property, located on Beargrass Creek in Oldham County, was called Camp Covered Bridge. This camp served as the primary camp for Scouts in Louisville until 1986. The Camp is now preserved as a neighborhood.

The Colored Division of Scouting used Camp Dan Beard which is now the location of Valhalla Golf Course. Separate from the main office, the colored division was housed by the Pythian Temple on Chestnut Street. Today this building is the Chestnut Street YMCA. Scouting followed the lead of the military, desegregating after 1949.

In 1956 the name was changed from Louisville Area Council to the Old Kentucky Home Council. The council office had long been located downtown, first at 424 W Jefferson Street and later at 431 W Liberty Street. The office moved to its current location at 824 Phillips Ln. in 1968.

After years of service to the area it was concluded that the still growing council had outgrown its facilities. It needed a new facility to replace the aging Camp Covered Bridge. The Council slowly sold and closed the other property holdings of Camp Covered Bridge, Rough River Reservation, and Horine Reservation consolidating resources into one facility. Now called the Old Kentucky Home Reservation, the nearly one thousand acre facility with a lake now serves the region as a premier camping facility for Scouts and other large groups. The camp is located adjacent to Bernheim Forest in Bullitt County. In 1997, a record 3,000 Scouts attended the summer camp program.

The Lincoln Heritage Council was formed in 1993, with the merger of the Old Kentucky Home Council and the George Rogers Clark Area Council which had served Southern Indiana since 1927. This strategic merger resulted in a unified scouting program available to all youth in the Greater Louisville Metropolitan region. On December 31, 1992, the combined council reached 25,238 young people, making it the largest youth organization in the area.

In 1997, scouting served more than 40,000 young people in the six Indiana counties of Washington, Clark, Floyd, Harrison, Scott, and Crawford, and the nineteen Kentucky counties of Adair, Breckinridge, Bullitt, Carroll, Grayson, Green, Hardin, Henry, Jefferson, Larue, Marion, Meade, Nelson, Oldham, Shelby, Spencer, Taylor, Trimble, and Washington.

The mission of the council today is to achieve excellence in fostering the character development, worldwide citizenship, and the moral, mental, and physical fitness of young people, and in other ways prepare them to make lifelong ethical choices by instilling the values found in the Scout Oath and Law.

In 1993, Operation First Class was launched as a program to bring scouting to urban youth. The Lincoln Heritage Council also began a Sports Club education program, which concentrates on at-risk middle school age youth. In 1997 all Jefferson County public middle schools had a Sports Club, with pilot programs in several fifth grades around the area. In 1997 more than 5,000 urban youth participated in a scouting program.

More than 350 chartering organizations work with scouting volunteers and staff to serve the nearly 770 packs, troops, and posts within the council. More than 7,000 adult volunteers help serve the scouting units. Today the camp has two properties, the new camp in Bullitt County, and Tunnel Mill Scout Camp near Charlestown, Indiana, which had long been a part of the George Rogers Clark Area Council.

The Scouting Program is conducted through several divisions to meet the needs of nearly all ages:

Tiger Cubs BSA

A school-year program for first-grade (or 7-year-old) boys and their adult partners that stresses simplicity, shared leadership, learning about the community, and family understanding. Each boy/adult team meets for family activities, then once or twice a month all the teams meet for Tiger Cub group activities.

Cub Scouting

A family- and home-centered program for boys in the second through fifth grade (or 8, 9, and 10 years old). Cub Scouting's emphasis is on a quality program at the local level, where the most boys and families are involved. Fourth- and fifth-grade (or 10-year-old) boys are called Webelos (WE'll BE LOyal Scouts) and participate in more advanced activities that begin to prepare them to become Boy Scouts.

Boy Scouting

A program for boys 11 through 17 designed to achieve the aims of Scouting through a vigorous outdoor program and peer group) leadership with the counsel of an adult Scoutmaster. (Boys also may become Boy Scouts if they have earned the Arrow of Light Award or have completed the fifth grade.)

Varsity Scouting

An active, exciting program for young men 14 through 17 built around five program fields of emphasis: advancement, high adventure, personal development, service, and special programs and events.

Venturing

Venturing is a new program of the Boy Scouts of America for young men and women who are 14 (and have completed the eighth grade) through 20 years of age.

National Eagle Scout Association

The National Eagle Scout Association (NESA) is a fellowship of men who have achieved the Eagle Scout rank and who desire to use their efforts and influence to form the kind of young men America needs for leadership.

Chris Bingaman

BRADEN, CARL JAMES (b New Albany, Indiana, June 27, 1914; d Louisville, February 18, 1975). Journalist, civil rights and civil liberties activist. Carl Braden was a white radical whose social and racial justice crusades made him a thorn in the side of Kentucky authorities and earned him two indictments for sedition against the commonwealth.

Braden was the oldest child of Mary Elizabeth (Kiefer), a German Catholic, and James Braden, a socialist trade unionist of IRISH descent. His hardscrabble upbringing in the working-class PORTLAND neighborhood and his father's views helped to shape his Marxist idealism. At sixteen, Braden left Mount St. Francis Preparatory Seminary in Indiana to become a newspaper reporter, working on papers in Louisville, Knoxville, Harlan County, and Cincinnati, where he became active in labor organizing for the Congress of Industrial Organizations (CIO). In 1948 Braden married Anne McCarty, a fellow reporter who shared his passion for social justice.

Anne (McCarty) Braden was born July 28, 1924, in Louisville—the child of Anita (Crabbe) and Gambrell McCarty, both of elite, longtime Kentucky families. On her mother's side, Anne's earliest known ancestor was Anne Poage McGinty, one of the first dozen white women to come into Kentucky with Daniel Boone. Anne Braden grew up in Anniston, Alabama, however, in a strictly segregated society that never quite fit with her social conscience. She graduated from Randolph-Macon Woman's College in Virginia in 1945 and wrote for newspapers in Anniston and Birmingham.

After she returned to Louisville in 1947 to join the staff of the *LOUISVILLE TIMES,* she rejected the culture of her upbringing and became Carl's coworker and partner in social reform. The two left mainstream journalism to work full-time in left-leaning desegregation and organized LABOR campaigns. They also became the parents of three children: James, Anita (d 1964), and Elizabeth.

In 1954 they made headlines when they bought a house on behalf of an AFRICAN AMERICAN couple in segregated SHIVELY, Kentucky. When the house was dynamited, the Bradens found themselves the objects of a local anti-Communist hysteria, labeled as "red," and indicted for sedition in what is known as the WADE-BRADEN AFFAIR. Carl's highly sensationalized trial and imprisonment made "the Bradens" the city's most infamous agitators, but they refused to be driven from Louisville. Instead they took jobs with the Southern Conference Educational Fund (SCEF), organizing whites throughout the South to work with African Americans for racial justice. Anne Braden also chronicled their sedition case in *The Wall Between,* a memoir highly critical of SEGREGATION and of the "Red Scare." The book became a nonfiction finalist for the 1958 National Book Award; it was republished in 1999.

Carl's refusal on First Amendment grounds to answer questions posed by the House Committee on Un-American Activities (HUAC) brought him a second prison term in 1961, increasing the couple's notoriety. Yet they also became mentors to a new generation of sixties activists to whom they imparted their media skills and social commitments. In 1967 the Bradens were indicted for sedition in Pike County, where SCEF was organizing against strip-mining. That case resulted in Kentucky's sedition law being declared unconstitutional. Although they remained pariahs in their hometown until well after Carl's death, Anne and Carl Braden participated in virtually every CIVIL RIGHTS, civil liberties, and social reform drive that swept Louisville and the South throughout the 1960s and beyond.

After 1975, Anne continued to be a constant presence in local and regional campaigns for racial justice. In 1984 and again in 1988 she was a central figure in Kentucky's Rainbow Coalition supporting Jesse Jackson's bids for the presidency. She has been a leading activist in the Kentucky Alliance against Racist and Political Repression, with its headquarters in the Braden Center, which was established as a memorial to Carl at 3208 W BROADWAY.

By the 1990s, Anne Braden found herself transformed from pariah to heroine. In 1990 she became the first recipient of the AMERICAN CIVIL LIBERTIES UNION's national award, the prestigious Roger Baldwin Medal of Liberty, for her contributions to civil liberties. In 1994 Randolph-Macon bestowed her with the college's Alumnae Achievement Award. In 2000 Anne still resided in the same West End home on which angry segregationists had marched forty-five years before.

Carl's ashes are buried in Eminence, Kentucky, alongside six earlier generations of Anne's family.

See Carl and Anne Braden papers, Manuscript 6, State Historical Society of Wisconsin.

Catherine Fosl

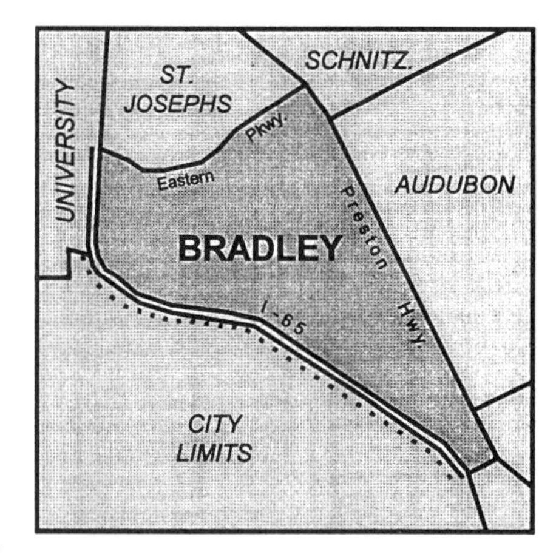

BRADLEY. Neighborhood south of downtown Louisville bounded by Eastern Pkwy. to the north, Preston Hwy. to the east, and a combination of Interstate 65 and the Norfolk Southern railroad tracks to the west and south. One of the three neighborhoods, including MERIWETHER (FORT HILL) and ST. JOSEPHS, known as "Greater SCHNITZELBURG." The community, adjacent to the KENTUCKY FAIR AND EXPOSITION CENTER, includes a mixture of residences and commercial establishments and the Jewish cemeteries along Preston Hwy.

BRADLEY, WILLIAM O'CONNELL (b Garrard County, Kentucky, March 18, 1847; d

Washington, D.C., May 23, 1914). Politician. The state's first Republican governor, William O'Connell was born to noted attorney Robert McAfee and Nancy Ellen (Totten) Bradley. The family moved to Somerset, where Bradley attended school. Age thwarted his attempt to enlist in the Union army at age fifteen. Bradley read LAW when Kentucky law required that one must be twenty-one to practice. Because he was only eighteen at the time, a special legislative act was required to let him be examined for the bar in 1865.

Bradley was elected Garrard County attorney in 1870, but, as a Republican, he suffered several defeats in elections for various offices. An excellent public speaker with an arresting appearance, "Billy O'B" became the leading Republican in the state, frequently attending national meetings. In 1887 he opposed Simon Bolivar Buckner for governor on a platform that emphasized improvements in education, a high protective tariff, development of MINERAL RESOURCES, and criticism of Democratic spending.

Bradley received strong support from African American voters, and, although he lost to Buckner 143,466 to 126,754, it was the best showing that had been made by a Republican candidate for governor. Nominated again in 1895, Bradley stressed the scandals and factionalism in the DEMOCRATIC PARTY. A number of Gold Democrats supported him as their party moved toward free silver, and the economic depression hurt the Democrats. Bradley was attacked for his party's alleged dominance by black voters, but he beat Democrat P. Wat Hardin 172,436 to 163,524.

During Bradley's term as governor (1895–99), the Democrats controlled the Senate, while the Republicans had a majority in the House; this deadlock, as well as infighting within the Democratic Party, contributed to the making of one of the weakest administrations of the century. In 1898 the Goebel Election Law was passed over Bradley's veto, giving control in disputed elections to a three-man commission. Bradley continued his effort to curb violence in the eastern part of the state, and he also had to contend with the tollgate wars to eliminate tolls that were especially prevalent in central Kentucky. An ineffective compulsory school law, the first of its kind in the South, was passed during his term, and two reform houses were established for minors. A pure food and drug act became law without the governor's signature. As his term ended, Bradley became an influential advisor to William S. Taylor in the gubernatorial election.

In 1900, following his unsuccessful bid for a seat in the U.S. Senate, Bradley returned to Garrard County briefly and then moved to Louisville in 1902. He opened a law office on Fifth St. where he worked until 1908, forming a brief partnership with H.W. Batson in 1903 and 1904. Legislators selected United States senators at the time, and he defeated J.C.W. Beckham, 64 to 60, with the vital aid of four "wet" Democratic votes in the General Assembly. Bradley maintained his residency and offices in Louisville during his term as senator (March 4, 1909, to May 23, 1914). In 1909 he moved his office to the Kentucky Title Building between Fifth St. and Court Pl., taking on a partner in Nathaniel C. Cureton until 1911, when he took on a new partner in Jason M. Chilton. He again moved in 1913 to open his own private practice in the Inter-Southern Life Building at the corner of Fifth and Jefferson Streets. Bradley changed location for the last time in 1914 when he formed a firm with MAURICE H. THATCHER and William G. Dearing in the Paul Jones Building. Bradley died in Washington of uremia before his term expired, and he was succeeded by Johnson N. Camden Jr.

Bradley married Margaret R. Duncan in 1867; they had a son and a daughter. He is buried in the Frankfort Cemetery.

See Hambleton Tapp and James C. Klotter, *Kentucky: Decades of Discord, 1865–1900* (Frankfort 1977); Maurice H. Thatcher, *Stories and Speeches of William O. Bradley* (Lexington 1916); Lowell H. Harrison, ed., *Kentucky's Governors 1792–1985* (Lexington 1985).

Lowell H. Harrison

BRAMLETTE, THOMAS ELLIOTT (b Cumberland [now Clinton] County, Kentucky, January 3, 1817; d Louisville, January 12, 1875). Kentucky governor. His parents, Ambrose S. and Sarah Bramlette, saw that he received a sound common school education. He studied LAW, was admitted to the bar in 1837, and was elected to the Kentucky House of Representatives in 1841. Appointed a commonwealth's attorney in 1848, he resigned in 1850 and moved to Columbia, Kentucky, where in 1856 he was elected judge of the Sixth Circuit Judicial District.

Commissioned colonel in the Union army in 1861, Bramlette raised the Third Kentucky Volunteer Infantry Regiment. He resigned in 1862 to accept President Abraham Lincoln's appointment as United States district attorney for Kentucky, at which time he moved to Louisville. Commissioned a major general in 1863, Bramlette resigned to accept the Union Democrats' nomination for governor. He defeated regular Democrat Charles A. Wickliffe by 62,422 votes to 17,503 and was inaugurated on September 1, 1863.

While governor, Bramlette declined nomination to the United States Congress and the offer of nomination as vice president on the National Democratic ticket in 1864. When he left office in September 1867 he returned to Louisville and established a law practice on Jefferson St. with his son. During his last years, he was a patron of numerous public organizations, especially the LOUISVILLE FREE PUBLIC LIBRARY.

Bramlette married Sallie Travis in 1837; they had two children, Eugene and James. After her death in 1872, he married Mary E. Graham Adams, a widow. Bramlette is buried in CAVE HILL CEMETERY.

An able politician, Bramlette provided strong leadership during one of the most traumatic periods in Kentucky's history. While devoted to preservation of the Union and the Constitution, he defended the state against what he saw as invasions of its rights. He responded angrily when the Union army began to enlist AFRICAN AMERICANS and when President Lincoln suspended the writ of habeas corpus in the state. Bramlette protested interference with elections by Gen. Stephen G. Burbridge and other military officers in the state but took strong action against guerrilla activities of Confederate sympathizers.

Under his leadership, the Democrats swept the 1865 elections, and President Andrew Johnson soon ended martial law and restored the writ of habeas corpus. Bramlette issued a general pardon to most ex-Confederates who had been indicted in the state, as he sought to restore harmony. The General Assembly conferred some CIVIL RIGHTS upon ex-slaves, but Bramlette and a majority of the legislators strongly opposed the Fourteenth and Fifteenth Amendments to the United States Constitution; the legislature had earlier refused to ratify the Thirteenth Amendment. The governor also protested when the Freedmen's Bureau was established in the state.

Not preoccupied solely with the CIVIL WAR and its aftermath, Bramlette took pride in the reduction of the state's debt, an apparent decline in crime, and the establishment of the Agricultural and Mechanical College, the predecessor of the University of Kentucky, in Lexington. He was a supporter of immigration to secure adequate LABOR, the development of natural resources, and the construction of turnpikes financed by bond issues.

See E. Merton Coulter, *The Civil War and Readjustment in Kentucky* (Chapel Hill, N.C., 1926); Lowell H. Harrison, ed., *Kentucky's Governors 1792–1985* (Lexington 1985).

Lowell H. Harrison

BRAMSON, STERN J. (b Louisville, January 30, 1912; d Louisville, December 24, 1989). Photographer. Stern J. Bramson was the only son of Louis and Bessie Bramson. Louis was a native German who immigrated to the United States with his family in 1883. After being trained in PHOTOGRAPHY in Chicago, Louis moved to Louisville where he opened the Royal Photographic View Co. (later known as just the Royal Photo Co.) in 1904 at 309 W MARKET ST. In 1911 he married Bessie, a native Louisvillian, and Stern was born the following year.

Bramson got his start in photography in 1922 by assisting his father on his commercial photographic jobs. He graduated from DU PONT MANUAL TRAINING HIGH SCHOOL in 1930 and went directly to work for his father. Throughout the 1930s Stern acted as commercial photographer for agencies such as baseball bat manufacturers Hillerich & Bradsby, law firms, insurance companies, distillers, and tobacco companies. Bramson was particularly busy in 1937 when he took photographs for businesses and insurance companies in order to assess the damage resulting from the Ohio River flood. Following the flood, Bramson moved his studio to 310 W Jefferson St.

In 1943 Bramson joined the U.S. Army Signal Corps and was assigned to the corps photo center housed in the old Paramount Studios property in Astoria, New York. Bramson's skill was immediately realized, and, after spending only four days in training, he was promoted from student to instructor. In 1945 he was assigned to the 288th Field Artillery Observation Battalion and sent to Germany. Following World War II, Bramson was reassigned to Blackpool, England, outside of Manchester, where he ran the public relations photographic section of the Wharton School, a vocational training center for veterans. He remained there until 1946 when he was discharged.

Upon his return to Louisville in 1946, Bramson married Dorothy Tyler. Bramson considered the 1950s and 1960s to be the peak years of the Royal Photo Co. This was in large part due to the construction of the General Electric and Ford truck plants, both of which contracted his services to photograph the progress of their construction.

Bessie Bramson, Stern's mother, died in 1962, and four years later, in 1966, Louis died. Following his father's death, Stern inherited the Royal Photo Co. and continued his work as a commercial photographer until his retirement in 1972. Bramson decided to retire because his office on Jefferson St. was to be torn down by the city of Louisville to make way for a new convention center. He did not relocate his studio because he was tired of the demands of business, and his children had no interest in taking it over. In 1973 Bramson sold the business, including his equipment and archives, to William Blackwell, an aspiring commercial photographer. Bramson took this opportunity to devote his time and attention to the Vinecrest Boarding Kennel that he and his wife had purchased in 1970.

Realizing the value of Bramson's work, Barry Bingham Jr., publisher of the *Courier-Journal*, purchased Bramson's collection of negative files, dating from as far back as 1937, from Blackwell Studios and donated it to the University of Louisville's photographic archives in 1982. Bramson sold his kennels soon after, in 1983, and helped the photographic archivists sort through his photos and identify their subjects. This led to a nationwide tour of his collection, which was shown in galleries from New York to San Francisco and places in between, including The Art Institute of Chicago.

The sudden fame perplexed Bramson. He had always thought of photography as a business and therefore considered himself to be a technician rather than an artist. He even described himself as a camera operator instead of a photographer. His photographs have since become quite popular, as they have been sold to major museums and private collectors as well as being replicated and sold as postcards. Some of his most popular photographs were "Testing Tracer Rounds for Machine Guns" (1942), "Blindfolded Girl and Plymouth" (1956), "Baron La Velle in his Home Theater" (1962), and "Bruised Face" (1963).

Amazingly, Bramson did not take several shots of the same subject. Once situated he snapped a single picture, and for this he was given the nickname "One Shot" Bramson. He also used frontal lighting and the central placement of his subject in his frame that gave his photographs great clarity, as they were clean, direct, and technically precise. Bramson used his approach quite effectively to capture the surreal aspects of everyday life in middle-class, post–World War II Louisville.

Bramson was survived by his second wife, Claire (Dinkelspiel) Bramson, his son, and two daughters.

See Bill Carner, "Stern Bramson and the Royal Photo Co., Louisville, Kentucky," *History of Photography: The American South* 19 (Spring 1995): 50–54.

BRANCH, EMMA (SMITH) RATTERMAN (b Boone County, Kentucky, March 20, 1894; d Louisville, November 20, 1987). Legislator. The daughter of William and Sally (Miller) Smith, Branch moved to Louisville with her family in the late 1890s, where she attended the city's public schools. Not long after graduating from Louisville Girls High School, she married Raymond G. Ratterman in 1915, with whom she later had one son, George. Branch, who as a youth had attended political rallies with her father, had long been attracted to the legislative world. In 1921, just one year after the passage of the Nineteenth Amendment to the U.S. Constitution, she became the first female to be elected to the city's now-defunct Common Council. She served as a Republican on the council, which, along with the Board of Aldermen, made up the city's old bicameral government, representing the First Ward until 1929. During her last term in office, in 1927, she became the first woman to be elected president of the Louisville Common Council.

Branch's first husband died in 1932, and she later married William Branch, who also preceded her in death. Emma Ratterman Branch is buried in Cave Hill Cemetery.

See *Courier-Journal*, Nov. 22, 1987.

BRANDEIS, ADELE (b Louisville, July 6, 1885; d Louisville, June 1, 1975). Civic leader. Adele, or Maidie, as she was called by her family, was the eldest daughter of Alfred and Jennie (Taussig) Brandeis and the niece of U.S. Supreme Court Justice Louis D. Brandeis. Upon graduation from Bryn Mawr, Brandeis became involved in different organizations promoting art and culture in Kentucky. She joined the Art Center Board in 1925 and lectured on art at the University of Louisville in the 1930s. From 1934 to 1940 Brandeis was director for the Works Progress Administration and Treasury art projects for Kentucky. In 1945 Brandeis joined the staff of the *Courier-Journal*, where she worked as an editorial researcher and writer until the early 1960s. She wrote editorials on art and history and did weekly book reviews for the paper. In 1949 Brandeis was appointed to the University of Louisville's Board of Trustees by Mayor Charles P. Farnsley. Brandeis was the first woman to sit on the university board, where she served for twenty years.

BRANDEIS, LOUIS D. (b Louisville, November 13, 1856; d Washington, D.C., October 5, 1941). Jurist. One of eleven Kentuckians who have served as justices of the Supreme Court of the United States, Brandeis was also a leader in American reform movements for social and economic betterment of the working class and leader of the American Zionist movement.

Louis D. Brandeis was the son of Adolph and Frederika (Dembitz) Brandeis. He attended Louisville Male High School. He graduated from the Harvard Law School in 1877 after compiling a near-perfect academic record. Brandeis rose rapidly in the legal profession, first in St. Louis (1878) and from 1879 on in Boston, Massachusetts. He and his first law partner, Samuel Warren, wrote "The Right to Privacy," published in the *Harvard Law Review* in 1890. This article is the cornerstone of the legal concept of the right to be let alone. By the 1890s Brandeis, already well on the way to affluence, became more deeply involved with various reforms, earning a growing reputation as the "People's Attorney."

Brandeis came into national prominence by means of his involvement in such dramatic events as the famous "Brandeis Brief" in the Supreme Court case of *Muller v. Oregon* (1908), a milestone in the emergence of sociological jurisprudence, and in the Ballinger-Pinchot controversy (1910-11) of the Taft administration. During this period he also became a leader in the American Zionist movement.

By 1912 Brandeis had become the articulate spokesman for a distinctive liberal social philosophy based on his conviction that freedom can flourish best when both government and business are small enough to be manageable. He distrusted bigness, believing that it constituted a threat to efficiency and, more ominously, to freedom. This philosophy led Brandeis to stress the importance of small business and local government.

Brandeis played a key role as an advisor to Woodrow Wilson during the presidential campaign of 1912, providing the basis of Wilson's

"New Freedom" program, which adopted Brandeis's view of the curse of bigness. By 1916 Brandeis had so risen in Wilson's esteem that he nominated him for the Supreme Court on January 28. He was confirmed on June 1 by a vote of forty-seven to twenty-two after a vigorous debate, tinged at times with anti-Semitism.

During his time on the Supreme Court, Brandeis emerged as a brilliant, innovative justice, constituting with Oliver Wendell Holmes Jr. the court's liberal bloc. Though usually outvoted, Brandeis eloquently championed liberal causes. The onset of the GREAT DEPRESSION in 1929 followed by the victory of Franklin D. Roosevelt over Herbert Hoover in 1932 changed the political landscape dramatically.

Always an activist, Brandeis sought to influence the course of the New Deal by continuing to advocate his social philosophy by direct contact with Roosevelt and by developing a network of reformers, led by Felix Frankfurter, to influence policy. In addition to his long-held social philosophy, Brandeis also advocated a specific program for economic recovery. It involved heavy taxation of those he called the super-rich to finance massive public-works projects, which, he hoped, could jump-start the languishing economy.

Although the Roosevelt administration did not adopt Brandeis's recovery program, certain policies did reflect elements of his social philosophy, and he remained an influential figure. His relationship with Roosevelt was strained at times, particularly when he voted with the Supreme Court majority to overturn key New Deal legislation in 1935 and 1936 and when he opposed Roosevelt's plan to reorganize the federal judiciary in 1937. Failing health forced Brandeis to retire on February 13, 1939.

Despite his national prominence and workaholic lifestyle, Brandeis maintained an interest in his family in Louisville by corresponding regularly with them, particularly his brother Adolph and his niece Fanny. He also maintained a deep interest in the UNIVERSITY OF LOUISVILLE and materially supported the law school, its law library, and the university library. Following his death his personal papers were given to the university.

Brandeis married Alice Goldmark of New York City on March 23, 1891. They had two daughters, Susan and Elizabeth. Brandeis died on October 5, 1941, and his wife died four years later, on October 12, 1945. Both were cremated and buried at the University of Louisville School of Law Building.

See Nelson L. Dawson, ed., *Brandeis and America* (Lexington 1989); Philippa Strum, *Louis D. Brandeis: Justice for the People* (Cambridge, Mass., 1984); Melvin I. Urofsky, *A Mind of One Piece: Brandeis and American Reform* (New York 1971).

Nelson L. Dawson

BRANHAM, WILLIAM MARRION (b Burksville, Kentucky, April 6, 1909; d Amarillo, Texas, December 24, 1965). Evangelist and faith healer. Born in a small mountain town, "Brother Billy" was the son of Charles and Ella Branham. Poverty kept the family in transit, and while William was still young they moved from Kentucky to the small river town of UTICA, INDIANA. From there, they soon relocated to nearby JEFFERSONVILLE, the community that Branham would consider home.

As a child Branham was exceptionally sensitive to spiritual matters and began to feel that God had set him aside for important work. About 1916, he experienced what he believed was the first of several divine encounters meant to prepare him for his future ministry. In this particular instance, while Branham was completing an errand for his parents, a mysterious and powerful voice commanded him to avoid worldliness and vice, for God had a special plan for him when he grew up.

Branham left home in September 1927 to work as a ranch hand in Arizona. About a year later, he experienced a religious conversion and felt a call into the ministry. About 1929 he returned to southern Indiana, where he became an ordained Baptist minister, began preaching, and worked as a local game warden.

In 1933 Branham's congregation built a facility on the corner of Eighth and Penn Streets in Jeffersonville. Known as the Branham Tabernacle, it was Branham's base of operations.

On June 22, 1934, Branham was married to Hope Brumback. Two children, Billy Paul and Sharon Rose, soon followed. However, in 1937 tragedy struck the Branham family with the deaths of both his wife Hope and daughter Sharon. In 1941 Branham married Meda Broy. Their union produced three children: Rebekah, Sarah, and Joseph.

By 1946 traveling evangelism had become a major part of Branham's ministry. Branham's followers believed that God had confirmed the uniqueness of his ministry in two ways: by the gift of divine healing and by the ability to see into the secret thoughts and sins of unbelievers. As Branham preached his message across the United States, accounts of miraculous healing, and even resurrections from the dead, abounded. Those for whom Branham claimed to have sought divine healing were U.S. representative William Upshaw of Georgia and King George VI of Great Britain.

By the 1960s, Branham's teachings had moved strongly in the direction of premillennial dispensationalism. Premillennial dispensationalists believe that the period of time between Christ's resurrection and His second coming has been divided into several distinct periods, or dispensations, in which God dealt with his church in a particular manner. Branham's followers equated those dispensations with the seven churches mentioned in the Book of Revelation. In Revelation 1–3, Jesus addressed seven first-century churches, assessing the strengths and weaknesses of each one. Branham perceived those descriptions to be a prophecy of the condition of the worldwide church through seven consecutive church ages. Furthermore, Branham believed that each church age had a prophet, a messenger of God commissioned explicitly to proclaim the Lord's will to the church of their generation. Branham's followers quickly embraced him as the prophet of the seventh and final church age and considered his message to the modern church definitive until the return of Christ.

On December 18, 1965, while driving through Texas, Branham's car collided with a drunk driver, injuring the evangelist. Almost a week later, on Christmas Eve, Branham died. His body was returned to Jeffersonville for burial in Eastern Cemetery. After his death a loose coalition of Branham's followers continued to keep his memory and message alive. A popular belief has persisted among his followers that he may be resurrected from the dead one Easter Sunday. Although it is not encouraged by any official organization, large crowds still gather at his grave every Easter, awaiting his return.

See *Courier-Journal,* April 12, 1982; Gordon Lindsay, *William Branham: A Man Sent from God* (Jeffersonville, Ind., 1950).

BRECKINRIDGE, ALEXANDER AND ROBERT (Alexander b near Staunton, Virginia, ca. 1752; d near Lexington, February 1801; Robert b near Staunton, Virginia, ca. 1754; d Louisville, September 10, 1833). Pioneer settlers and surveyors. Brothers Alexander and Robert Breckinridge (often misspelled Breckenridge), who gave their name to Breckenridge Ln. in eastern Jefferson County, were sons of Robert and Mary (Poage) Breckinridge, both natives of Ireland (probably Ulster) of Scots-Irish descent. Their mother died ca. 1757, and the father married Letitia Preston in July 1758. She was the sister of Col. William Preston, surveyor of Fincastle County, which included Kentucky. He authorized the first official surveys for LAND GRANTS in Kentucky in 1774 by JOHN FLOYD at the FALLS OF THE OHIO and in the Bluegrass area. It was from the elder Breckinridge's second marriage that the well-known Breckinridge clan of Fayette County had its origin.

Robert, nicknamed "Billy," and Alexander did not get along well with their stepmother; Colonel Preston about 1773 (the year their father died) arranged for both brothers to go to Hanover County, Virginia, as apprentices to a carpenter/builder. At the outbreak of the American Revolution, both brothers enlisted in the Virginia Continental Line and both attained officer rank, Robert as a first lieutenant and Alexander as a captain. The latter's unit spent the winter of 1777–78 at the Valley Forge, Pennsylvania, encampment. Both brothers were taken prisoner at the surrender of Charleston, South Carolina, to the British on May 12, 1780. Robert had just returned from his first visit to Kentucky at John FLOYD'S STATION in present ST. MATTHEWS. Both spent some time on British prison ships before being exchanged in the spring of 1781.

Nothing is known of their education, but some formal training is evident in their surviving letters. They also learned surveying, their profession in Kentucky, where both made their home in 1783 at or near Floyd's Station. Robert especially gained a reputation for particular knowledge of the 1774 Floyd surveys and later conflicting claims. He also speculated in land and acted as agent for many Piedmont Virginians in Kentucky land transactions, gaining a considerable fortune.

Little is known of Alexander's personality, but Robert was described as shy, compassionate, and quiet. Both became figures of importance in their new home and were recommended to the governor by the Jefferson County Court on April 6, 1785, as potential members of the court. They were named justices on August 2. On November 3, 1784, Alexander and his half-brother James were appointed deputy surveyors of Jefferson County, serving under William May. When May resigned the following year, he recommended Alexander for the post. Soon Robert was named a deputy surveyor.

In 1787 the Virginia General Assembly appointed Robert a trustee of the infant town of Louisville, a post he continued to hold from time to time well into the nineteenth century. His most important political activity, however, was in 1788 as a Jefferson County delegate to the Virginia Ratifying Convention, where he broke ranks with most of his fellow Kentuckians and voted in favor of the federal Constitution. This was also the time when Kentucky was debating the question of separation from Virginia. Both Breckinridge brothers were elected to the 1787 Danville convention on the issue, and Robert also to the 1789 meeting. Following Kentucky statehood, Robert was elected a member of the convention held April 2–19, 1792, to draft the first state Constitution, then was elected to the new House of Representatives. He was reelected to three successive terms, serving as speaker in each term.

Alexander, meanwhile, had married Jenny Buchanan Floyd, John Floyd's widow, in 1784. Family tradition holds that Jenny favored Robert, but that after a long absence on a trip to Virginia he was presumed slain by Indians. The marriage was reported to have been an unhappy one; Alexander was said to have learned "habits of intemperance" during his military career. Whatever the truth, Robert never married. One of Jenny and Alexander's three sons, James D., entered politics and was a Jefferson County representative in Congress, 1821–23. Louisville's Breckinridge St. is named for him.

Robert filled numerous public posts in subsequent years: a trustee of the JEFFERSON SEMINARY, a remote ancestor of the UNIVERSITY OF LOUISVILLE; an incorporator in 1817 and long-term president of the Louisville Marine Hospital (predecessor of the University of Louisville Hospital); designer in 1820 of the county clerk's office in Georgian style (similar to such structures in Virginia) on the northwest corner of Sixth and Jefferson Streets. This task perhaps reflects his carpenter/builder apprenticeship. In 1792 he was appointed brigadier general commanding the Kentucky Militia's First Brigade in Jefferson and surrounding counties.

Following the death of Alexander at John Breckinridge's home, Cabell's Dale in Fayette County, and of Alexander's widow on May 12, 1812, Robert eventually added much of the Floyd's Station tract to his extensive land holdings. He spent the years from about 1815 in Louisville and toward the end of his life became quite reclusive. He died September 10, 1833, and is buried in the Floyd-Breckinridge Cemetery on his own acreage. The cemetery, off Plymouth Rd. near now-misspelled Breckenridge Ln., is in the midst of suburban development.

See Breckinridge-Marshall papers, Filson Club Historical Society; James C. Klotter, *The Breckinridges of Kentucky 1760–1981* (Lexington 1981); Draper Mss., 13W25, 6J89, 3JJ364; James Breckinridge Letters, Manuscript Division, University of Virginia Library.

George H. Yater

BRECKINRIDGE, JAMES DOUGLAS

(b Woodville, Jefferson County, Kentucky, ?; d Jefferson County, May 6, 1849). Attorney and politician. While there were rumors about his paternity, Breckinridge was officially the son of ALEXANDER and Jane Floyd BRECKINRIDGE. He was the nephew of ROBERT BRECKINRIDGE, the state's first attorney general. His father's half-brother, John, served the commonwealth as U.S. senator and attorney general. James Breckinridge attended what is now Washington and Lee University from 1800 to 1803, and in 1806 was admitted to the bar as an attorney in Louisville. Within three years he successfully ran for a seat in the state House of Representatives, holding that post from 1809 to 1811. Elected to Congress to fill a vacancy, he served from November 21, 1821, through March 3, 1823. *Lawyers and Lawmakers* called him "a man of influence, wealth, and refinement." His daughter Mary Eliza married into the Caldwell family, and her two daughters became well-known benefactors, particularly to Catholic University in the District of Columbia. Breckinridge's second wife was Lucy Fry Speed, the daughter of John Speed of FARMINGTON. In 1848 Breckinridge's law office was on Jefferson near Fifth St. and his residence was in "the country." James Douglas Breckinridge was buried in Louisville's St. John's Cemetery; the body was reinterred in St. Louis Catholic Cemetery in 1867.

See *Biographical Directory of the American Congress 1774–1971* (Washington, D.C., 1971); H. Levin, *Lawyers and Lawmakers of Kentucky* (Chicago 1897).

James C. Klotter

BRENNAN, MICHAEL JOSEPH "MICKEY"

(b Louisville, February 19, 1877; d Hot Springs, Arkansas, November 25, 1938). Politician. Brennan was the son of Daniel and Lucy (Hyde) Brennan. He was educated at Sacred Heart Catholic School and in Louisville PUBLIC SCHOOLS. As a youth, Brennan became involved in politics in the PORTLAND area.

At an early age he was employed as a plasterer's apprentice and was involved later in contracting. He then operated two saloons on LIBERTY ST. at Eighth and Tenth Streets until the advent of PROHIBITION. His work in the Tenth Ward attracted the attention of Democratic boss JOHN WHALLEN and his brother JAMES. He soon became one of the Democratic stalwarts, known for his sharp wit and keen memory. After John Whallen's death in 1913, Brennan became closely associated with James and learned a great deal about politics from him. He carried on the social service functions of the Whallen machine by providing food, clothing, heaters, and money to the poor. He was known to withdraw from the bank and distribute between fifty and one hundred dollars a day to the poor. He was also known to have never turned down a request for aid. His generosity stemmed from numerous motivations, many of which were certainly political, but he was known to be a person interested in helping those who, like himself, had experienced hard times.

When the Republicans swept into office in the 1925, 1927, and 1929 elections, local Democrats were dismayed and demoralized, and closed the doors to their headquarters. Brennan raised money to pay the party's expenses and reopened the doors of the headquarters. He became chairman of the Louisville DEMOCRATIC PARTY in 1930 and built the machine that controlled the city for thirty years. This began with the election of JOSEPH D. SCHOLTZ as MAYOR in 1933. In 1931 he aligned his organization with the successful movement that placed Kentucky governor Ruby Laffoon (1931–35) in office. This led to his appointment in 1931 as state revenue agent, a position he retained until Gov. A.B. Chandler (1935–39) abolished the post in 1936. As state revenue agent he controlled considerable patronage in the state administration. In 1935 his organization supported Laffoon's candidate, Thomas Rhea, for the Democratic nomination for governor, but A.B. Chandler was nominated and later elected. In August 1936 he was appointed by the fiscal court as Jefferson County tax collector, a position he held until his death. Brennan never held an elected office.

He never married and lived in the HIGHLANDS with his two sisters, Mrs. Frank Knoll and Miss Elizabeth M. Brennan, at the time of his death. He died following an emergency operation for an intestinal obstruction. He is buried in St. Louis Cemetery. In 1951 the Louisville and Jefferson County Democratic Party moved its headquarters to a building at 133–35 S FOURTH ST. and named it the Brennan Building. The building, which at one time had been the OLD VIENNA BAKERY AND RESTAURANT, was razed in the mid-1980s to make way for a parking garage.

See *Courier Journal*, Nov. 26, 1938, Dec. 11, 1938; Carolyn Luckett Denning, "The Louisville Democratic Party: Political Times of 'Miss Lennie' McLaughlin," M.A. thesis, University of Louisville, 1981.

BRENNAN HOUSE. The Brennan House, a historic home at 631 S Fifth St., offers a unique glimpse inside the Victorian world. Now located among office buildings and parking lots, the Brennan House is what the *COURIER-JOURNAL* once described as "an echo of what Fifth Street once was, a choice residential neighborhood on the edge of downtown."

It was built in 1868 by tobacco wholesaler Francis Slaughter Jones Ronald. The architect is unknown, but the style of the house was reflective of those designed by Louisville architect HENRY WHITESTONE. In 1884 the house was purchased by Thomas Brennan for twelve thousand dollars and remained the family home until 1969. Brennan, a native of Ireland, was a Louisville farm equipment manufacturer and inventor. He and his wife, Anna (Bruce) Brennan, were the parents of eight children.

The three-story house is an example of a mid-nineteenth-century townhouse in the Italianate style. It was traditionally painted chocolate brown and featured stained-glass windows, a highly decorative cast-iron veranda, and an ornamental cast-iron fence separating it from the street. Inside were trappings of Victorian splendor. The most luxurious and ornate furnishings decorated the high-ceilinged rooms.

The Brennan House features such things as hand-carved marble and slate mantels, matching crystal chandeliers, gilt-framed mirrors, glass-doored bookcases, Tiffany table lamps, family portraits, and a ten-foot walnut hatrack. Although most of the decor had a Victorian flavor, it was sometimes described by admirers as eclectic in nature.

After the death of Dr. John Arvid Ouchterlony Brennan, one of the last surviving Brennan children, in 1963, the house was willed to the FILSON CLUB HISTORICAL SOCIETY. The Brennan family, whose members were all active in civic affairs, were longtime endowment supporters of the club. During the time the Filson Club owned it, the KENTUCKY OPERA office was housed on the third floor. The club managed the Brennan House until 1992, when it was sold to a private foundation. The foundation opened the historic home for weekday tours and agreed to house the office of the New Performing Arts group on the third floor.

See Helen Leopold, "Island of Elegance," *Courier-Journal Magazine* (Oct. 9, 1960); George H. Yater, "19th Century Louisville Lives! Out of Sight in the Brennan House," *Louisville* (Aug. 1974).

Brennan House, 631 South Fifth Street, c. 1920.

BRENNER, CARL CHRISTIAN (b Lauterecken, Germany, August 1, 1838; d Louisville, July 22, 1888). Landscape artist. Brenner showed an early talent for art and was admitted to the Royal Academy in Munich. However, his father, a glazier, refused art education for his son and trained young Carl in his own trade. The family immigrated to the United States in 1853. They settled in Louisville the next year.

After attending a private school in BUTCHERTOWN, Brenner went into business as a house painter and later a sign and ornamental painter and paint store proprietor. He became known for his artistic glass signs—one of which was exhibited at the 1869 Paris Exposition. His earliest major work was a thirty-five-thousand-square-foot panorama of scenes of the CIVIL WAR for Louisville's Masonic Hall, painted in 1863. In 1878 he was listed for the first time as a landscape painter in the Louisville City Directory. He also changed his name from "Charles" to "Carl" and exhibited his work for the first time at the National Academy of Design in New York City. It was in 1881 that Brenner's friend, Congressman (later governor) Proctor Knott, introduced Brenner's work to a curator of the Corcoran Art Gallery in Washington, D.C., who purchased a PAINTING for their collection.

The beech tree was the favorite subject of Brenner, and he adopted it as a sort of "trademark." He was quoted in the December 17, 1878, *COURIER-JOURNAL* as exclaiming, "The beech trees preach sermons, and your artist in the woods is a true worshipper."

Brenner hosted an annual sale at his studio during the Christmas season. He also held "Art Distributions," which were lotteries with his art works as prizes. He sold tickets for $5, names were drawn, and winners received a work of art. The smallest prizes were etchings, and the largest were major oil paintings. He was a prolific painter, exhibiting eighty-four paintings at his 1885 sale. Carl Brenner and his wife, Anna Glass, were married in 1864 and had six children.

See Justus Bier, "Carl C. Brenner, A German American Landscapist," *The German-American Review* (Aug. 1951): 20–33; *Courier-Journal,* July 22, 1888, Nov. 8, 1979, Feb. 3, 1985.

Carol Brenner Tobe

BREWING INDUSTRY. Like most large American cities, Louisville had an extensive brewing industry from the mid-nineteenth to late twentieth century, and its growth and development generally followed that of the industry as a whole.

Beer was mostly a local product in Louisville in the nineteenth century. A large number of neighborhood breweries operated in various parts of town, including CALIFORNIA, BUTCHERTOWN, Downtown, PORTLAND, PHOENIX HILL, GERMANTOWN, and CLIFTON. Breweries generally distributed their products in those surrounding neighborhoods. One reason was the limitation of horse-drawn wagons. Many brewing companies operated saloons adjacent to the brewery. Smaller breweries could often sell their entire production within three or four miles of the brewery. The proprietor, his family, and the brewery employees usually lived at the brewery.

The first recorded brewery in Kentucky, at Scott's Landing on the Kentucky River, was advertised in the *Kentucky Gazette* in 1789. The first brewery in Louisville of which there is any record was Elisha Applegate's in 1808, which closed within a few years. Dr. HENRY

City Brewery Advertisement. From Satellites of Mercury Program, 1889.

McMurtrie's *Sketches of Louisville* lists two breweries in 1817. The *Louisville Public Advertiser* carried advertisements for the Louisville Brewery in 1819 and for James Carroll's Harp Brewery in 1820, the latter selling "Ale, Beer, and Porter." Breweries of this period were small, most producing a few hundred barrels of beer annually. Whiskey, apple brandy, and cider were the principal alcoholic beverages of the period. Local demand for beer was largely supplied from breweries in Pennsylvania and Ohio and shipped down the Ohio River to the Falls.

The local brewing industry grew substantially after the arrival of English and Scotch immigrant brewers around 1830. In 1832 there were three brewers listed in Otis's first *Louisville City Directory*—John Nuttall, Hew Ainslie, and Joseph Metcalfe. Ainslie was from Scotland; Nuttall and Metcalfe were English. Metcalfe's Market Street Brewery grew to be the largest, producing about four to six thousand barrels annually by 1852. All beer produced was top-fermented, the principal products being ale, beer, porter, and brown stout.

In the 1840s German-speaking immigrants began to arrive in Louisville in substantial numbers and by 1855 accounted for about 30 percent of the local population of around fifty thousand. The immigrants were mainly from Bavaria and other petty states in southwestern Germany, Alsace-Lorraine, and Switzerland. They brought with them the brewing techniques of their homeland. The Spring Brewery, at Twelfth and Rowan Streets, was founded by George Barth in 1839. By 1852 five of the six local breweries were operated by German-speaking immigrants, including the William Tell Brewery, later site of the Frank Fehr Brewing Co. at Preston and Green (now Liberty) Streets. By 1852 Peter Noll was producing lager beer in Louisville, and by 1855 all the local breweries, including Metcalfe, produced lager beer in addition to ales.

At least one German-owned brewery was a target of Know-Nothing rioters in the Bloody Monday riot of August 6, 1855. William Ambruster's Washington Brewery in the triangle formed by the intersection of Liberty St. and Baxter Ave. was stormed by the mob despite rifle fire, and set ablaze. Ten persons inside were burned to death. The rioters helped themselves to copious drafts of the brewery's product. The establishment was rebuilt, and Ambruster eventually won some monetary compensation from the city after a lengthy court case.

After the Metcalfe Brewery closed in 1859, the local brewing industry was entirely in the hands of the Germans and Swiss. In 1850 the six local breweries employed 30 persons and produced $108,000 worth of beer, about 18,000 barrels. There were ten breweries operating in 1857, with a total of seventy-four employees. Immigrant breweries were mostly family-owned operations and usually operated a saloon on the property in addition to the brewery.

The local brewing industry expanded greatly in the late nineteenth century. Beer production in Kentucky, most of it in Louisville, increased from 52,111 barrels in 1863 to 534,750 in 1902. Beer quality improved as barley from the upper Midwest replaced locally grown barley for malting. Pure yeast cultures and pasteurization of bottled beer were introduced. The introduction of ice-making machines in the 1880s provided a cheap year-round supply of ice to refrigerate and age lager beer and ale. At least 85 percent of beer was sold as draft beer, even after crown-top bottles and modern bottling equipment were introduced during the 1890s (packaged beer did not outsell draft beer until about 1940). Several large breweries were established in Louisville during this period: the Phoenix Brewery in 1865, Frank Fehr in 1872, Senn and Ackerman in 1877, Schaefer-Meyer in 1890, Oertel's Butchertown Brewery in 1892, and Falls City in 1905. Many smaller breweries also thrived during this period, including the Clay St., Walnut St., Franklin St., Germantown, Clifton, Jackson St., Fifteenth St., Lexington St., and West Louisville. Beer production in Kentucky in 1907, at least two-thirds of it in Louisville, was 753,533 barrels. Ohio, Indiana, and many northern states produced more beer, but none of the southern states produced as much.

Before the Brewery Workers Union was organized, employees usually worked twelve to fourteen hours a day, six days a week, and often a half day on Sunday. As a result of union efforts the workweek was reduced to six 9-hour days. By 1903 most local breweries were unionized.

In the early twentieth century the Prohibition movement rapidly gained momentum. Local brewery sales declined after 1914. When the Eighteenth Amendment was ratified (1919), there were seven breweries remaining: Falls City, Fehr's, Oertel's, Phoenix, Lexington St., Clay St., and Clifton. Fehr's, Oertel's and Falls City survived Prohibition by selling beer of a low alcoholic content, ice, and soft drinks. When beer production resumed in 1933, all three prospered, and the brewery plants were expanded. The three breweries dominated the local market, and their products were widely distributed in neighboring states. Production of beer in Kentucky, located entirely in Louisville, Covington, and Newport, increased steadily during this period, peaking at 2,252,481 barrels in 1954. Listed capacities of the breweries in 1958 were Falls City, 750,000 barrels annually; Oertel's 500,000; and Fehr's 500,000. At least eight hundred people were employed at the breweries, and hundreds of other jobs were generated by them. In the late 1950s increased advertising and distribution of the national brands put production into a gradual decline. Fehr's filed for bankruptcy in 1957. The company was reorganized but was obliged to close in 1964. Oertel's was sold to Brown-Forman Distillers Corp. in June 1964 for about six hundred thousand dollars. In the face of widespread brewery closings throughout the country, the decision was made to close Oertel's in 1967. Falls City remained a profitable operation into the late 1970s but began to lose money about 1977. In 1978 the corporate officers decided to liquidate the brewery plant, and the last Louisville brewery closed.

Microbreweries became popular in many cities in the 1990s. Louisville had several, including the Bluegrass Brewing Co. (1993) on

Shelbyville Rd. in St. Matthews and the Oldenberg Brewing Co. (1997) on Dutchmans Ln. Production was quite small compared to the heyday of brewing.

The Frank Fehr Brewing Company

The Frank Fehr Brewing Co. was founded by Frank Fehr, an Alsatian immigrant, on Liberty St. (then Green St.) between Preston and Jackson, in 1872. The site had originally been the William Tell Brewery, first operated by Andrew Nicholas and Louis Weyd about 1848, and later by Gerhardt Otto. From 1872 to 1876 it was operated by Otto Brohm and Frank Fehr. In the years after Fehr became sole proprietor, the plant was repeatedly expanded and was soon the largest and most modern brewery in Kentucky. The F.F.X.L. brand of lager, a pale malt/rice beer, was introduced about 1883 with great success. Frank Fehr died in 1891, and Fred Kellner became president. In 1901 the Fehr Brewing Co. joined with Senn and Ackerman, the Phoenix Brewing Co., the Schaefer-Meyer Brewing Co., and the Nadorff Brewing Co. to form the Central Consumers Corp. It sought to dominate the local beer market by owning or otherwise controlling the saloons, which in those days were the principal retail outlets for beer. Saloons usually sold products from only one brewery. The Fehr Brewery was the only Central Consumers brewery to reopen after Prohibition. Under the direction of "Colonel" Frank Fehr, son of the founder, production peaked in 1949, but the company suffered a rapid decline in the following years and was bankrupt by 1958. The brewery continued to operate under new management, with M.R. Kopfmeyer as president. Faced with continued operating losses, the company was obliged to close in 1964. The last 7,663 barrels of Fehr's beer were poured into the sewers to save paying excise taxes and the expense of bottling and distribution. The Fehr Brewery site was later occupied by Dosker Manor, a low-rent housing facility for the elderly.

The Falls City Brewing Company

The Falls City Brewing Co. was founded by a group of local grocers and saloon keepers who were dissatisfied by the overly-controlling tactics of the Central Consumers Co. A corporation was formed in 1905, and a new modern seventy-five-thousand-barrel lager beer brewery was built at Thirtieth and Broadway. Sales of beer began on November 17, 1906. The original board of directors included Ben H. Schrader, Theodore Evers, Ben Fihe, Lawrence Huffman, E.R. Bathrick, F.C. Toelle, and M.J. Hickey. Otto Doerr, formerly of the Schaefer-Meyer Brewing Co., was the first brewmaster. After some tough early years, the company prospered. In 1919, just before the enforcement of Prohibition, the company was reorganized as the Falls City Ice and Beverage Co. During Prohibition the company survived and even operated at a profit, producing near beer, "cereal beverages," and a variety of soft drinks. The company resumed beer production and expanded after Repeal in 1933. In 1936 longtime president and guiding force Ben Schrader died and was succeeded as president by Charles W. Bornwasser. In 1951 Lillian "Miss Lillian" Madden became president. George Goetz became president in 1964. After 1967 Falls City was the last operating brewery in Louisville. The company continued to prosper and was profitable until 1977. The company was innovative in its products and packaging and kept its plant up to date. In 1940 it was the first local brewery to package beer in flat-top cans. Drummond Bros. beer, an early light-bodied beer, was introduced in 1973. The Billy Beer brand, introduced in 1977, proved to be a failure. In 1978, faced with increased mass-market advertising by national brands and declining sales, management elected to close down. The plant equipment was sold, and the brand name rights to Falls City and Drummond Bros. were sold to the Heileman Brewing Co. It continued to produce Falls City and Drummond Bros. beer brands at its Evansville, Indiana, plant.

The Oertel Brewing Company

Frank Rettig operated a brewery at the corner of Story and Webster by 1865. After a brief stint as a distillery the plant was acquired by the Hartmetz brothers in 1873 and was operated by Charles Hartmetz until his death in 1887. From 1887 to 1892 it was operated by his widow, Magdalena Hartmetz, in partnership with John F. Oertel, the former brewmaster of the Franklin Street Brewery. In 1892 J.F. Oertel bought out Magdalena Hartmetz and became sole proprietor of what was then called the Butchertown Brewery. Oertel bought an ice machine and expanded production to perhaps ten thousand barrels. In 1903 he built a large, modern brewery with an annual capacity of seventy-five thousand barrels. The only beer type produced was dark common or cream beer, a slightly sweet, highly drinkable ale of modest alcoholic content that was especially popular in the summertime. The Oertel Brewing Co. incorporated in December 1906, with Oertel as president, William Rueff vice president, and Louis Bauer secretary and treasurer. The three men also owned all two hundred shares of the original stock, valued at a hundred thousand dollars. The brewery burned down in a spectacular fire in March 1908. Oertel continued to produce beer at the Phoenix Brewery until a new brewery was built and opened in June 1909. Pale ale was added to the product line in 1913, and a new bottling plant was constructed. The first batch of lager beer was brewed on November 24, 1915. The brewery operated near full capacity until the Prohibition movement gained momentum in the World War I period, when sales declined sharply, as they did at other breweries. The Oertel Brewing Co. declared bankruptcy in 1919, at the eve of Prohibition, and was purchased by John F. Oertel for sixty-eight thousand dollars. During Prohibition the company survived by producing de-alcoholized beer, "cereal beverages," root beer, ginger ale, and other soft drinks. John F. Oertel died in 1929 and was succeeded as president by John F. Oertel Jr. The company expanded and thrived in the years following Repeal. The popular Oertel's '92 brand, a pale lager that eventually became nearly synonymous with the brewery, was introduced about 1935, along with Little Brown Jug Ale. The brewery continued to expand and thrive until the late 1950s, when sales began to decline as national brands claimed a larger share of the local beer market. John F. Oertel Jr. died in 1961, and in July 1964 the company was purchased by the Brown-Forman Distillers Corp., with the view to increase plant capacity from 450,000 to 1 million barrels annually. Oertel's Real Draft, an early microfiltered beer, was introduced in 1964, along with Thorobred Malt Liquor. Faced with the need to spend several million dollars to update the plant, especially the bottling and canning lines, and the widespread closing of regional breweries all over the United States, Brown-Forman attempted to sell the plant in 1967. Unable to find a buyer, the company closed the brewery in December 1967. The brewery was torn down and a medical center laundry was constructed at the site. In 1991 an attempt was made by longtime Oertel brewmaster Friedrich W. "Fritz" Finger Jr. and other partners to open a microbrewery in the old bottling shop building. The effort failed when adequate capital could not be raised.

The Phoenix Brewing Company

The Phoenix Brewery and Phoenix Hill Park were designed and built by Gottfried Miller on the hillside above Beargrass Creek, on the west side of Baxter Ave. between Barret and Hull. The original proprietors, Philip Zang, Philip Schillinger, and Gottfried Miller, opened the brewery in November 1865. The Phoenix Hill Park was soon one of the most popular beer gardens in the city and the site of many concerts and other events. The Phoenix Brewery was relatively large for its time and included four huge vaults, each a hundred feet long, deep underground for the beer to age. It was the largest brewery in Kentucky in 1877, producing 17,364 barrels. Gottfried Miller left the partnership in 1868. Philip Zang left in 1869 and operated a brewery in Denver, Colorado, that became the largest brewery in that state. Peter Weber, an Alsatian immigrant who already operated a brewery in Madison, Indiana, became a partner; and the company was known as Weber and Schillinger. In 1884 Weber bought out Schillinger, who moved to Mobile, Alabama, and founded the Philip Schillinger Brewing Co. After Peter Weber died in 1891, the name of the company was changed to the Phoenix Brewing Co. Charles A. Weber, son of Peter Weber, was president from 1892 until the brewery closed. By 1892 the brewery had a sixty-ton, a thirty-ton, and a fifteen-ton ice machine, and the brewery produced Bohemian, Wurzburger, and Lager beer. In 1901 the Phoenix Brewing Co. joined four other breweries to form the Central Consumers Corp., which dominated the local brewing industry. The Phoenix Brewery was especially noted for its common beer, one of the most popular examples of the ale type, around 1910–15. The Phoenix Hill Brewery and Park were closed by Prohibition, and most of the buildings became dilapidated. The buildings were demolished in 1938, and large amounts of earth removed from the hill were used for road fill. The excavations exposed parts of the two upper beer vaults.

The Senn and Ackerman Brewing Company
Frank Senn and Philip Ackerman opened a modern brewery on the south side of MAIN ST. between Seventeenth and Eighteenth Streets in 1877. The brewery was considerably enlarged in the following years, and by 1900 occupied virtually the whole block between Seventeenth and Eighteenth, from Main to Pirtle, and was second in size only to Fehr's Brewery. Senn and Ackerman joined the Central Consumers Corp. in 1901. The brewery closed in 1914, and the site is currently a scrapyard. The former stable building was later occupied by Production Heating and Cooling, at Eighteenth and Pirtle Streets.

The Schaefer-Meyer Brewing Company
John Zeller founded a brewery on the northwest corner of Shelby St. and Roselane in 1861. It was acquired by Charles A. Schaefer and Adolph Meyer in 1881. In 1889 the operation was incorporated as the Schaefer-Meyer Brewing Co., and in 1890 it was moved to a newly constructed modern brewing plant on the southwest corner of Logan and Lampton Streets. In 1901 it became part of the Central Consumers Corp., and in 1911 the plant became Frank Fehr Brewing Co. Plant #2. In 1919 the plant was converted to cold storage and later became the Merchants Ice and Cold Storage Co. Most of the original 1890 brewery buildings were incorporated in the plant, including the brewhouse and aboveground cellars.

The Clay Street Brewing Company
Conrad Walter founded a brewery on Clay St. near Madison in 1858. It was operated by the Walter family until it was closed by Prohibition. The brewery never bottled beer, and its principal product was the locally popular dark common beer.

The Paul Reising Brewing Company, New Albany
A brewery was operated on the south side of W Fourth St., between Spring and Market, by Bottomly and Ainslie in 1840. After several further changes of ownership, it was acquired by Paul Reising in 1861. Since 1857 Reising had operated the Metcalfe Brewery at Eighteenth and Main. He moved his operation to the larger brewery. By 1868 he employed four or five men, making thirty barrels of beer at each brewing. He made both lager and common beer. By 1891 capacity had been increased to twelve thousand barrels annually, and a fifteen-ton ice machine had been installed. Paul Reising died in 1897, but the company continued to be known as the Paul Reising Brewing Co. In 1913 the brewery had thirty employees and seven beer wagons and produced twenty-five thousand barrels of beer annually. The company went bankrupt in 1915 and was sold to Michael Schrick for thirty-four thousand dollars. The company name was changed to the Southern Indiana Brewing Co. Beer production was halted by Prohibition, and the company changed its name to the Southern Indiana Ice and Beverage Co. It produced soft drinks, as well a cereal beverage, Hop-O. In 1923 federal agents closed the plant after a shipment of Hop-O was found to contain several percent of alcohol, being in fact real beer instead of near beer. In 1927 it was acquired by Ernest Boone and became the Southern Indiana Ice Co. In 1933 the Southern Indiana Ice and Beverage Co. resumed operation and the production of beer. The brewery was known as the Ackerman Brewery after its brewmaster and superintendent, Philip Ackerman. For two years the company produced and bottled hundred–barrel batches of Vienna Select, Old Rip, Royal Munich, India Pale Ale, and Daniel Boone. Undercapitalized and unable to operate on a sufficiently large scale to compete with the larger Louisville breweries, the Ackerman Brewery closed at midnight November 15, 1935.

A large number of other breweries operated in Louisville, New Albany, and Jeffersonville at more than sixty sites in the nineteenth and twentieth centuries. Many breweries were operated by several different owners on the same sites over the years.

Louisville Brewery Sites

1. Elisha Applegate Brewery, street address unknown (1808–15?)
2. Louisville Brewery, near the courthouse (1819–?); may be same as 5
3. Harp Brewery, Market St. (1820–21); may be same as 5
4. Hew Ainslie Brewery, Seventh St. between Water and Main Streets (1829–32)
   Cowden and Co. (1836)
5. Joseph Metcalfe Brewery, S side of Market St. between Sixth and Seventh Streets (1832–44)
   Metcalfe and Grainger (1844–54)
   Joseph Metcalfe (1854–58)
   Henry Clay Metcalfe and Ben Franklin Metcalfe (1858–59)
   Philip Zang (1859–65)
   Leopold Stoll (1865–74)
6. John Nuttall, City Brewery, W side of Sixth St. between Water and Main (1832–41)
   Charles Thirlwell (1841–52)
   Peter Noll (1852–61)
   William Paddon (1861–65)
   William Paddon and Son (1865–68)
7. Zoeller Brothers, Bavaria Brewery, SE corner Seventeenth St. and Portland Ave. (1836–69)
   Nadorff and Bro. (1884–92)
   Nadorff Brewing Co. (1892–1901)
   Nadorff Brewing Co., branch Central Consumers Corp. (1901–3)
8. George W. Barth, Spring Brewery, SE corner of Twelfth and High Streets (1839–44)
   Jacob Fischer (1844–67)
   Kopf and Walter (1867–69)
   Franz Walter (1870)
   Jacob Fischer (1871, '75)
9. (Andrew) Nicholas and (Louis) Weyd, S side of Green between Preston and Jackson Streets (1848)
   Andrew Nicholas, William Tell Brewery, (1849–51)
   (Franz) Steinhauer and (Andrew) Nicholas, (1851–54)
   Gerhard H. Otto (1854–72)
   Brohm and Fehr (1872–76)
   Frank Fehr, City Brewery (1876–91)
   Frank Fehr Brewing Co. (1891–1901)
   Frank Fehr Brewing Co., branch of Central Consumers Corp.(1901–33)
   Frank Fehr Brewing Co. (1933–64)
10. Adolph Peter, Green Street Brewery, N side of Green St. E of Wenzel St. (1848–65)
   (Francis) Schad and Jaeger (1865)
   Dohn and Jaeger (1865–69)
   P. and M. Pfeiffer (1869)
   Martin Pfeiffer (1869–75)
   Stein and Doern, Salvator Brewery (1875–77)
   Joseph Stein and Co. (1875–91)
   Joseph Stein Brewing Co. (1891–1900)
   Stein Brewing Co., Columbia Finance and Trust owner, (1900–2)
11. William Ambruster, Washington Brewery, Baxter Ave. near Liberty St. (1848–65)
   Sophia Armbruster (1866–70)
   Yann and Mueller (1870–71)
   Nicholas Christ (1872–73)
   Michael Christ (1873–92)
   Christ and Son (1892–93)
   Christ and Sons (1893–96)
   George J. and John M. Christ (1893–1914)
   Christ Brewing Co. (1914–18)
12. Luetzelschwab and Co., Jackson Brewery, NW corner of Green and Jackson Streets (1849–63)
   John Luetzelschwab (1863–69)
13. Conrad Schuh, Kentucky Brewery, Fourteenth and High Streets (ca. 1853–56)
14. Peter Merkel, Market St. or U.S. Brewery, Market between Campbell and Wenzel Streets (1854–63)
   George G. Knapper (1863–66)
   Charles Dorsey (1869)
15. Peter Schmitt, Workhouse Rd. (later Hamilton Ave., now Lexington Rd.) (1856–65)
   A. Laval and Co. (1865–67)

John Dohn, Southern Brewery, N side of Hamilton Ave. near Beargrass bridge (1867–68)
John Engeln (1872–74)
Gebhard and Co. (Louisa Gebhard), Star Brewery (1874–78)
Julius Gebhard (1878–82)

16. Bernard Hillerich, New California Brewery (1858–67)
Frank Hillerich, Kentucky between Sixteenth and Seventeenth Streets (1867–73)
Peter Laux, 1627 Kentucky St. (1873–82)
John Nuneman (1882–85)
Schneider Bros. (1885)
(John) Beierle, (John) Schneider and Bro. (1885–89)
Peter Laux , Westview Brewery (1889–95)
Ben Laux, Westview Brewery, Kentucky Street Brewery (1895–99)
Laux and Rettner (1899–1901)
Nicholas Rettner (1901–3)

17. Conrad Walter, Clay Street Brewery, northwest corner Clay and Walnut Streets (1858–74)
Eva Walter (1874–91)
John E. and Frank Walter (1891–1908)
Walter Brewing Co., Mrs. John E. and Frank Walter (1908–19)

18. Adam Loeser, Walnut Street Brewery, Walnut between Shelby and Clay Streets (1858–59)
Loeser and (John) Zeller (1859–61)
Adam Loeser (1861–90)
John Loeser (1890–94)
Carle Bros. (1894–1900)

19. X. (Xavier) Joseph and Co., N side of Geiger between Campbell and Wenzel Streets (1859–65?)

20. Jacob Schanzenbacher, E Jefferson between Campbell and Shelby Streets (1859–69)

21. Heybach and Borst (Charles Heybach and Peter Borst), NE corner of Nineteenth St. and Portland Ave. (1859)
Charles Heybach (1859–61)
Kaelin and Eberle, Falls City Brewery, (1863–74)

22. John F. Franck and Charles Haungs, N side of Eighteenth and High Streets (1861) (on Shippingport Island, same as S2.)

23. John Zeller, NW corner of Shelby St. and Roselane (Shelby Street Brewery, 1861–81)
Kirchgessner and Co. (1881–82)
Schaefer-Meyer Brewing Co. (1882–90)

24. (Thomas) Goss and (Frank) Bentz, 514 E Jefferson St. (1864–65)
Yann and Christ, Jefferson Street Brewery, Jefferson and Baxter (1865–72)

25. Philip Zang and Co., Phoenix Brewery, SW corner Baxter and Barret Ave. (1865–68)
Zang, Vogt, and Schillinger (1868–69)
Weber and Schillinger (1869–84)
Phoenix Brewing Co. (1884–1901)
Phoenix Brewing Co., branch of Central Consumers Corp. (1901–16)

26. John Bauer, Franklin Street Brewery, NW corner of Franklin and Wenzel (1865–77)
Elizabeth Bauer (1877–88)
Union Brewing Co. (1898–1911)

27. Frank Rettig, Butchertown Brewery, SE corner of Story Ave. and Webster (1865–68)
Hartmetz and Bro. (Charles and John Hartmetz) (1873–77)
Charles Hartmetz (1877–88)
Hartmetz and Oertel (1888–92)
John F. Oertel (1892–1907)
John F. Oertel Co. (1907–19)
The Oertel Co., Inc.(1919–36)
Oertel Brewing Co. (1936–67)

28. Helt and Althaus, S side of Jefferson at Shelby St. (1865)
Althaus and Schenkel (1866)
Burge and Co. (Joseph Burge and Henry Althaus) (1866–67)

29. John Rapp, NE corner Shelby and Goss (1865–69)
Henry Althaus (1869–73)
William Rapp (1873–74)
Philip Ackerman (1874–76)
Henry Huber (1876)
Huber and Mueller (1876–79)
Henry Huber, Jefferson County Brewery (1879–98)
Huber and Redle (1898–1900)
Otto Redle, Germantown Brewery (1900–11)

30. (Michael) Thomas and (Gottlieb) Gentner, Washington, Campbell and Wenzel Streets (1865–66)

31. Jacob Steurer Brewery, S side Story Ave. between Webster and Cabel (1866–1905)

32. Andrew Mucklebauer, Jefferson Street Brewery, Jefferson between Hancock and Clay (1866–69)

33. (Franz) Walter and (Gustav) Reinhackel (1865–67) SE corner Market and Seventeenth Streets
Reinhackel and Senn, Boone Brewery, (1867–69)
Charles Haungs (1869–72)
William Thierman (1874–76)
Charles Haungs (1876–78)
Nadorff and Co. (1878–84)

34. Charles Hartmetz and Bro., Main between Campbell and Wenzel Streets (1866–73)

35. Michael Thomas, 164 Underhill St. (now Lexington Rd. near Baxter Ave.) (1867–70)
Kuipers and (Henry) Nadorff, 1336 Hamilton, near Beargrass Creek (1870–72)
Gerhard Kuipers (1876–81)
Kuipers and Son (1881–82)
Gerhard Kuipers (1882–83)
Jacob L. Abraham, Falls City Brewery (1884)
(Jacob) Niedenthal and (Albert) Schnaebel (1885)
Schnaebel and (Alois) Koebel (1886)
Herman Dolle (1887)
Jacob L. Abraham (1888–89)
M. Ladenburger (1890)

36. John Metz, N side of Market St. between Twenty-third and Twenty-fourth Streets (1867–69)
Mistler and Co. (1869–70)
Graf and Mistler (1870–71)
Martin Mistler (1871–72)

37. Joseph Stein, Jefferson County Brewery, W side Preston between Mechanic and Saluda (1859–70)

38. John Hald, 390 Eighth St. near Breckinridge (1869)
James McKiernan (1874)

39. Gabriel Schurch, N side Southgate between Seventeenth and Eighteenth Streets (1871–?)
Sebastian Bott, Lexington Street Brewery, SE corner Eighteenth and Breckinridge Streets (1880–93)
John Bott (1893–97)
Anna Bott (1897–98)
Lexington Street Brewing Co. (1898–1901)
Lexington Street Brewing Co., Theodore Menk, pres. (1901–19)
Theodore Menk Industrial Distillery (1920–23)
Theodore Menk Brewing Co. (1924–25)
Theodore Menk Ice Manufacturing Co. (1926–?)

40. Frank Senn Fifteenth Street Brewery, W side Fifteenth St. between Oak and Gallagher Streets (1871–76)
Frank Senn and Bros. (1876–77)
Martin Senn and Bro. (1877–88)
Wegenast and Huber (1888–92)
George F. Huber (1893–1908)

41. Alonzo Templeton, Gray Street Brewery (1872–84)

42. (Xavier) Schnabel and (Frank) Nadorff, 744 Baxter near Broadway (1873–74)
(Frank) Nadorff and (John) Bossemeier "Ale Depot" (1874–76)

43. Senn and Ackerman Brewing Co., Main Street Brewery, W Main between Seventeenth and Eighteenth Streets (1877–1901)
Senn and Ackerman Brewing Co., branch of Central Consumers Corp. (1901–16)

44. (Gottlieb) Lauffer and (Henry) Brands, SE corner Thirty-fourth and Market Streets (1878–80)
Gottlieb Lauffer, West Louisville Brewery, (1880–1903)
Gregory and Stuber (1903–4)
West Louisville Brewing Co. (1904–16)

45. Walter and Hittinger, Jackson Street Brewery, Jackson and Kentucky (1879–86)
Henry Walter (1886–97)
Martin Senn (1897)
Wegenast and Berger (1897–99)
Jackson Brewing Co. (1899–1900)
Martin Senn (1900)
Joseph Lehmann (1900–1)

46. William Palmer, Clifton Brewery, SW corner Brownsboro Rd. and Ewing Ave. (1880–1918)

47. J.T. Diersen, Otto Brewery, SE corner of Jackson and Green Streets (1881–95)
Catherine A.M. Diersen (1895–1900)
Diersen Bros. (Joseph T. and Henry W. Diersen) (1900–8)

Henry W. Diersen (1908–10)
48. Gerhard Kuipers, Kentucky Brewery, NW corner of Beargrass Creek bridge, Baxter Ave. (1883–86)
Gerhard Kuipers and Son, 934 Baxter Ave. (1886–89)
M. Kuipers and Son (H. Joseph Terstegge) (1889–90)
49. (John) Beierle and (John) Schneider, NE corner Seventeenth and Harney Streets (1888–94)
(Englebert) Beierle and (John) Schneider (1894–1902)
Engelbert Beierle (1902–3)
50. John Rohrman, northeast corner Seventh and Hill (1889–90)
Moritz Ladenburger, Falls City Brewery (1890–94)
51. Schaefer-Meyer Brewing Co., Logan and Lampton Streets, (1890–1901)
Schaefer-Meyer Brewing Co. branch of Central Consumers Co. (1901–11)
Frank Fehr Brewing Co. plant #2 (1911–18)
52. Falls City Brewing Co., Thirtieth and Broadway (1905–19)
Falls City Ice and Beverage Co. (1919–33)
Falls City Brewing Co. (1933–78)
53. Kentucky Brewing Co., 1445 S Fifteenth St. (1934–38)
Kentucky-Frankenmuth Brewing Co. (1939–42)
54. Alex Stegner Brewing Co., 317–19 Pearl St. (1938–40)
55. Silo Brewery, 630 Barret Ave. (1991–97)
56. Bluegrass Brewing Co., 3929 Shelbyville Rd. (1993–)
57. Oldenberg Brewery, Dutchmans Ln. (1997–)

Shippingport
S1. Ainslie Brewery, near Tarascon's mill, (ca. 1829)
S2. Elm Tree Brewery, at Elm Tree Garden, upper end of Shippingport near canal entrance (ca. 1859)

New Albany, Indiana
N1. Bottomly and Ainslie, Lower Fourth and Spring Streets (1840–?)
Joseph and George Kealchle (1848–?)
John Yaeger (1856–57)
Bath and Rickle (1859–60)
David Bath (1860–61)
Paul Reising, City Brewery (1861–84)
Paul Reising and Co. (1884–92)
Paul Reising Brewing Co. (1892–1915)
Southern Indiana Brewing Co. (1915–23)
Southern Indiana Ice and Beverage Co. (1933–35)
N2. Joseph Metcalfe, City Brewery, W side of Eighteenth between Main and Stone Streets (1847–55)
William Grainger, Upper High St. (now E Main St.) (1856)
Reising and Bros. (1857–61)
Martin Kaelin, Main Street Brewery (1862–72)
Louis Schmidt (1882)
Hornung and Atkins (1883–86)
Jacob Hornung (1886–89)
Indiana Brewing Co. (1889–95)
Pank-Weinmann Brewing Co. (1895–99)
N3. Peter Bucheit, Market Street Brewery, NW corner of Market and Upper Tenth Streets (1856–76)
Barbara Bucheit (1876–84)
Julius Gebhard and Co., Enterprise Brewery (1884–88)
Andres Schlosser, National Brewery (1888–91)
N4. Andrew Sohn, Spring Brewery, Upper Vincennes between Locust and Chartres Streets (1865–74)
Louisa Sohn (1874–77)
Frank Nadorff (1877–84)
Threcy Nadorff (1884–91)
Peter Engel (1891–1902)
Engel and Nadorff Bros. (1902–7)
N5. Terstegge and Co., State Street Brewery, W side State St. opposite Green (1888–90)
Frederick S. Ruoff (1890–93)
Bochardt and Birk (1898)
Edward Birk (1898–99)
Andres Schlosser (1899)
Veit Nirmaier (1899–1915)
State Street Brewery (1915–18)

Jeffersonville, Indiana
J1. Franz Rettig, street address unknown (?-1865); may be same as J2.
J2. Henry Lang, NW corner Graham and Maple Streets (1875–80)
Kirchgessner and Seng (1880–84)
John Kirchgessner and Co., City Brewing Co. (1884–97)
City Brewing Co. Inc. (1897–99)
See Peter R. Guetig and Conrad D. Selle, *Louisville Breweries: A History of the Brewing Industry in Louisville, Kentucky, New Albany and Jeffersonville, Indiana* (Louisville 1995).

Peter Richard Guetig
Conrad Selle

BRICK INDUSTRY. Bricks are the oldest continuously used manufactured building material known. In the Middle East sun-dried bricks were made as early as 6000 B.C. and were fire-made by about 3500 B.C. In North America, the Indians of the southwest built houses of adobe long before the arrival of European settlers.

Commercial production of bricks in America began in the 1600s. No one knows for certain when bricks were first made in Louisville or Jefferson County. Louisville's first brick house, erected in 1789 by Frederick Augustus Kaye, as well as brick houses built in what is now Jefferson County by John Floyd in 1783 and William Johnson in 1788, attest to the fact that bricks were used locally very early.

The abundance of both sedimentary and residual clays, as well as shale deposits, provided excellent and easily obtained raw materials for a thriving brick industry in and around Louisville. Thousands of brick buildings in Louisville still stand as monuments to the brickyards that produced their external fabric.

A letter in the possession of the Filson Club Historical Society dated April 23, 1816, to John Corlis, Esq., from his son, George, speaks to the early economics of brick-making in Kentucky. Two Negroes, hired at twelve dollars and ten dollars per month, respectively, could dig sufficient clay in one day to make eight thousand bricks. A third person, Charles, a slave, could mold two thousand bricks per day, having had seven years' previous experience as a molder in a brickyard. A young boy, hired at six dollars a month, completed the labor requirements. Under this arrangement bricks could be made for less than fifty cents per thousand.

Early brick-making was a transient operation. Clay was dug on or near the building site. Bricks were hand-molded, or struck, and then dried in the sun. Temporary kilns, improvised onsite, burned and hardened the sun-dried brick. Relocation to another developing area was very easy.

The early brick industry was such an ad hoc arrangement, in fact, that the April 16, 1806, *Minutes of the Trustees and Commissioners* of the city ordered "that all persons be prohibited from taking dirt or sand from or making bricks in the Streets under penalty of $3 for every offence to be recovered before any Justice of the Peace." Apparently the order was only minimally effective, and in 1841 the City Council passed another resolution to stop the mining of clay and sand from Prather St. (Broadway), and directed those responsible "to restore the street to its original grade."

Most early brickyards were listed under the owner's name. Henry McMurtrie, in *Sketches of Louisville*, listed six brickyards operating in Louisville in 1815. He noted that several million good bricks were being manufactured in the city by 1819.

Louisville's Smoketown neighborhood apparently gained its name from the large number of brick kilns in the area, which produced great volumes of smoke. In 1823, a newspaper advertisement claimed that many residents of the area were well skilled in the brick-making business.

Walter Haldeman, in *Haldeman's Picture of Louisville, Directory and Business Advertiser*, offers this glimpse of the city's brick industry in 1844–45: "There are eight brickyards within the city, doing an extensive business. Collectively, they will produce this season, 15,200,000 bricks; and this large quantity will have been laid in the various improvements made, and in progress, during the present year. General average price $4.25 per M (thousand)." These eight brickyards each produced, annually, between 1 and 2.5 million bricks and employed between ten and forty workers. The 1852 Louisville

Directory noted there were thirty-six brickmakers that employed 339 men and produced $224,000 worth of bricks in 1850. *Caron's Louisville City Directory* for 1871 lists nine of the twenty city brickyards as located in the Smoketown area. By 1880, however, most of the clay had been mined out, and the brickyards had vanished. Abandoned clay pits collected water and attracted frogs, and the Smoketown area around Lampton and Jackson Streets became known as Frogtown.

In the 1870s local clays and shales were used in the manufacture of paving bricks. The decade of the 1870s saw, at various times, a total of sixty brickyards in operation. During this decade the first company names, such as the Ohio Valley Press Brick Co., appeared. In 1875 the first dry-press bricks were made in Louisville. These were machine-manufactured bricks. Dry or damp brick mix was placed in a metal mold box and compressed under pressure by a hydraulic ram. The bricks, kiln-fired, were quite dense and made excellent paving material. By the 1890s vitrified bricks, made by the Louisville Vitrified Press Brick Works, the Kentucky Vitrified Paving Brick Co., or the Patton Vitrified Brick Co., among others, became a standard paving material for Louisville's STREETS. They were first used, in 1891, to pave Second St. between Broadway and Jacob St. Today, however, in 2000, PETERSON AVE. HILL is one of the last visible brick streets in the city, paving bricks having given way to ready-mix concrete and asphalt.

In the late nineteenth and early twentieth centuries, special fire clays were hauled by train from Carter, Rowan, and Boyd Counties in eastern Kentucky to Louisville. Here, the LOUISVILLE FIRE BRICK WORKS, the Louisville & Portsmouth Fire Brick Co., and later, in the 1940s, the CORHART REFRACTORIES Co., among others, made high-quality fire bricks, called refractories. Refractories, which can withstand temperatures between two thousand and four thousand degrees Fahrenheit, are highly resistant to chemical damage, physical wear, and rapid changes in temperature. As bricks, they are used to line blast furnaces, kilns, forges, soaking pits, steam-engine fireboxes, and the like. As thin tiles, they are used today on the outside of spacecraft to provide protection against high temperatures.

Since the 1820s at least 196 individuals, partnerships, and companies have made bricks commercially in Jefferson County. Among the earliest, in the 1820s to 1830s, was the Lampton family in Smoketown. Brickyards that spanned at least three decades of activity before 1900 include, among others, Hamilton Figg, William Planka, Henry Schoppenhorst, Frederick Perkins, James McCollum, Soloman McCollum, and Henry KRUPP. The oldest company, Louisville Fire Brick Works, built a plant in Louisville in 1890 that manufactured five thousand bricks a day. Important companies of the first fifty years of the twentieth century include, among others, Theophilus Bishop, Coral Ridge Brick & Tile, Progress Press Brick, Southern Brick and Tile, Louisville Brick and Tile, Corhart Refractories, and Kentucky Vitrified Paving Brick. The most unusual brick manufacturing concern was the city's WORKHOUSE brickyard. Here, in a QUARRY at the corner of Payne St. and Lexington Rd., bricks were made by men and women convicted of misdemeanors. They worked from sunup to sundown at a rate of about fifty cents a day. In the 1870s pressure from privately owned commercial brickyards closed the city workhouse brickyard.

Today, out of a long local tradition of brickmaking, only three companies remain active in Jefferson County. The Corhart Refractories Co. and the Louisville Fire Brick Works make refractory brick. The General Shale Products Corp. Coral Ridge Division manufactures paving and building brick.

See Heinrich Ries, "The Clay Deposits of Kentucky," *Kentucky Geological Survey* series 6, vol. 8 (Frankfort 1922); Charles Butts, "Geology and Mineral Resources of Jefferson County, Kentucky," *Kentucky Geological Survey* series 4, vol. 3, part 2 (Frankfort 1915); H. McMurtrie, *Sketches of Louisville and Its Environs* (Louisville 1819); Richard W. Otis, *The Louisville Directory, for the Year 1832* (Louisville 1832); Karl Gurcke, *Bricks and Brickmaking: A Handbook for Historical Archaeology* (Moscow, Idaho, 1987); The Filson Club Historical Society, Louisville, Ky., Corlis-Respess Family Papers, 23 April 1816.

Charles D. Hockensmith

BRIDGES, AUTOMOBILE. The advent of the automobile at the turn of the twentieth century radically changed the mode of travel across the OHIO RIVER between Louisville and the communities of southern Indiana. Early car owners depended upon ferryboats to transport them across the river. But as automobile ownership grew, drivers began demanding construction of bridges to handle highway traffic.

The first bridge capable of carrying automobiles was the second KENTUCKY & INDIANA TERMINAL BRIDGE between NEW ALBANY and Louisville's PORTLAND neighborhood. Construction on the new K&I Bridge began in August 1910 and was completed in November 1912. The new structure was built next to the old one, which was then dismantled. The new span cost just over $2 million. At the time of its completion, it was one of the heaviest and largest plain-truss bridges on earth. Like its predecessor, the new K&I was designed primarily to carry railroad traffic, and much of its seventy-foot width was devoted to two pairs of rail lines. However, it also followed the pattern of the old bridge by having wagonways on each side. These were paved with heavy, creosoted wood blocks and were intended primarily to accommodate horse-and-wagon traffic, which used the bridge on a toll basis. But within a few years cars and trucks replaced horse-drawn vehicles as the primary modes of personal and business transportation. The creosote paving blocks remained in service until 1952, when they were replaced by a steel gridwork. The K&I continued to serve automobile traffic until February 1979, when a section of roadbed broke under the weight of an overloaded gravel truck.

While the K&I Bridge served the needs of drivers between New Albany and Louisville, road travelers between JEFFERSONVILLE and Louisville still depended upon ferryboats to get them across the river. As automobile ownership mushroomed after WORLD WAR I, the need for an automobile bridge became increasingly evident. The first serious suggestion that Louisville undertake construction of such a span was offered by ROBERT WORTH BINGHAM, publisher of the *COURIER-JOURNAL* and *LOUISVILLE TIMES,* at the LOUISVILLE BOARD OF TRADE's 1919 New Year's Day reception. Bingham's remarks stimulated much discussion, but the matter did not begin to crystallize until mid-1923. In August the Board of Trade appointed a committee chaired by United States senator FREDERIC M. SACKETT to mobilize support for construction of a bridge. The Merchants and Manufacturers Association, the LOUISVILLE AUTOMOBILE CLUB, the Louisville Real Estate Board, and the Retail Merchants Association quickly endorsed the idea. The city governments of Louisville, Jeffersonville, and New Albany also lent their support, and the Bingham newspapers published favorable editorials. Meanwhile, bridge advocates began assembling technical and financial data to determine the feasibility of such a project. During the fall several bridge plan options were presented to Sackett's committee, but no decision was made.

In December 1923 a controversy erupted over whether the bridge should be funded entirely from tax levies and operated without tolls or financed with revenue bonds, which would be retired through toll collections. Fearing the controversy would jeopardize voter approval of a large public improvement bond issue already on the ballot, Mayor HUSTON QUIN postponed further consideration of the matter. But in April 1925, with the bond referendum behind him, Quin revived the bridge question and appointed a mayor's bridge committee to restudy the entire matter. The committee was composed of Sackett, William Heyburn, William Black, R.E. Filson, George W. Hubley, T.B. Wilson, and Alex Johnson, all of Louisville, and Charles T. Hertzsch and William Y. Fillebrown, both of Jeffersonville.

After studying numerous financial, engineering, and site proposals for seven months, the committee issued a report calling for construction of a highway toll bridge to be financed through a $5 million bond issue and managed by a five-member bridge commission. The report set off an eighteen-month period of public debate between backers of a toll bridge and those who favored a free bridge. In the winter of 1926 the Kentucky General Assembly en-

Municipal (now George Rogers Clark Memorial) bridge in 1931.

acted and Gov. William J. Fields signed legislation authorizing construction of a toll bridge and creating a Louisville Bridge Commission. But free-bridge forces, spearheaded by some of Louisville's most prominent business leaders, appeared to gain the upper hand when they persuaded the city's general council to submit the issue to the voters. However, on October 1926 the Kentucky attorney general announced that the Kentucky Highway Commission lacked authority to expend money to maintain a free bridge. On election day the voters decisively defeated the free bridge proposal.

In November 1927 the bridge commission presented a $5 million bond issue to the electorate. It won a substantial majority of the votes cast but fell short of the required two-thirds majority. Mayor William B. Harrison, determined that the bridge should be built, turned to private capital. In January 1928 the bridge commission contracted with the Toledo, Ohio, investment house of Stranahan, Harris, & Oatis to finance construction of the bridge, the bonds to be retired through toll receipts. Meanwhile, work proceeded apace on project engineering. In September 1926 the commission engaged architect Paul P. Cret and the Philadelphia engineering firm of Ralph Modjeski and Frank M. Masters to design the structure. In April 1928 the bridge commission approved the designers' recommendation for a four-lane bridge between Second and Main Streets in Louisville and Illinois Avenue in Jeffersonville. Construction began two months later by the American Bridge Co. of Pittsburgh, which submitted the low bid of $1.9 million for the base structure. The new span, known as the Municipal Bridge, opened in October 1929 and cost a total of $4.7 million. It operated as a toll facility until 1946, when the bonds were paid off several years early because of heavy wartime traffic to the Indiana Ordnance Works near Charlestown. It was renamed the George Rogers Clark Memorial Bridge in 1949 in honor of Louisville's founder.

Ironically, the combined effects of the postwar economic boom and the removal of the tolls created conditions that nearly made it necessary to reimpose them. By 1952 the Clark Memorial Bridge was approaching peak capacity, and traffic congestion was becoming unacceptable. Studies in 1952 and 1953 by Louisville attorney and state senator Arthur W. Grafton, who also served as counsel to the Louisville Bridge Commission, recommended that the tolls be reestablished in order to finance revenue bonds for two new bridges, one to Jeffersonville and another to New Albany. But most Indiana residents and many Louisvillians opposed new tolls. Anti-toll petitions circulated by the Jeffersonville Chamber of Commerce got signatures from commuters as far away as Scottsburg, thirty miles north of Louisville. The controversy held up progress for three more years, prompting the frustrated *Courier-Journal* to editorialize in May 1955, "The blunt fact is: no tolls on Clark Bridge, no new bridge."

The impasse was broken when the federal government agreed to incorporate a Louisville–to–New Albany bridge into the recently created interstate highway system to relieve congestion on the overcrowded K&I Bridge. Under the agreement, the federal government would pay 90 percent of the construction cost for the New Albany bridge, which would carry traffic via Interstate 64 into western Louisville, and the state of Indiana would supply the remaining 10 percent of the expense. Likewise, the federal government would pay 90 percent of the cost of a new bridge to Jeffersonville, with the commonwealth of Kentucky picking up the 10 percent state match.

Once the financing problem had been resolved, the New Albany project moved quickly. In 1956 the Louisville engineering firm of Hazelet and Erdal was chosen to design the span. The designers executed plans for a graceful twin-arch, double-deck span. With completion of right-of-way acquisition, construction began in June 1959 and was completed in August 1962. The cost totaled $14.8 million. Four months after it opened, Indiana governor Matthew E. Welsh announced that the new span would be named in honor of former United States senator and Supreme Court justice Sherman Minton of New Albany. In 1962 the American Institute of Steel Construction honored Hazelet & Erdal by declaring the Sherman Minton Bridge the nation's most beautiful long-span bridge for 1961.

While the Minton Bridge neared construction, planning for the new Louisville-Jeffersonville bridge gained momentum. When first proposed in 1951, many suggested that this facility be placed alongside the Clark Memorial Bridge. As late as April 1957, city engineer Wallace W. Sanders echoed this idea, with the qualification that the new span be built to carry traffic in one direction and that the Clark Bridge be relined to carry vehicles in the opposite direction. Meanwhile, some Kentucky highway engineers had concluded that it would be cheaper to route the North-South Expressway, a toll road that would become Interstate 65, eastward toward Campbell St., where it would be linked by a huge interchange to a proposed Riverside Expressway and a new bridge. Indiana opposed this proposal because it already had built expressway approaches to the Clark Bridge in anticipation of similar action by Kentucky. But the Campbell St. route gained momentum in May 1957 when the West Kentucky chapter of the American Institute of Architects wrote Louisville mayor Andrew Broaddus that routing an expressway through downtown to a new span next to the Clark Bridge would create the appearance of "a picket fence, crowding the east side of the business district, and would deter any redevelopment in adjacent areas." The logjam finally was broken in 1958 when Kentucky highway commissioner Henry J. Ward selected the Campbell St. route.

As with the Minton Bridge, Hazelet and Erdal won the design contract for the Louisville-Jeffersonville bridge. The firm initially proposed a double-deck span similar to the Minton Bridge. Federal highway officials favored this design because it would be cheaper than a wide, single-deck structure. But further studies indicated that any economies would be offset by traffic hazards and engineering problems that might be created in the effort to join a double-deck bridge and a complicated expressway interchange. Thus, the designers prepared a six-lane, single-deck cantilever plan that received federal approval.

Construction began in April 1961 and was nearing completion on November 16, 1963, when the *Courier-Journal* announced in a tongue-in-cheek headline that the "23,000–Ton Baby Needs Name." The matter came to a resolution ten days later when Gov. Bert T. Combs announced that Kentucky and Indiana officials agreed that the new span should be named the John Fitzgerald Kennedy Memorial Bridge, in memory of the president of the United States, who had been assassinated on November 22. The bridge was formally dedicated on December 6, opening a 135-mile stretch of I-65 for northbound traffic between Upton, Kentucky, and Taylorsville, Indiana. Southbound traffic opened a few weeks later.

In December 1996 the Transportation Policy Committee of the Kentuckiana Regional Planning and Development Agency approved recommendations by its Ohio River major investment study committee to build two new interstate highway bridges and to rebuild "Spaghetti Junction," the interchange that connects Interstates 64, 65, and 71 at the Kennedy Bridge. The recommendations, developed over a two-year period with assistance from a consulting team headed by JHK Associates of Alexandria, Virginia, resolved a decade-long controversy between proponents of an east-end bridge joining the Gene Snyder Freeway in Jefferson County and I-265 in Clark County, Indiana, and advocates of a second downtown bridge paralleling the Kennedy Bridge.

See Carl E. Kramer, "Bridging the Ohio," *Louisville* 30 (Aug. 1979): 46–47, 59–62; Carl E. Kramer, "Two Centuries of Urban Development in Central and South Louisville," *Louisville Survey: Central and South Report* (Louisville 1978).

Carl E. Kramer

BRIGHT, JEPTHA BARNARD "BARNEY" (b Shelbyville, Kentucky, July 8, 1927; d Louisville, July 23, 1997). Sculptor. Bright was born to Jeptha and Deanie (Wakefield) Bright of Shelby County, Kentucky. He attended Shelbyville High School and Davidson College in North Carolina. During World War II, he served in the navy and later attended the University of Louisville and the Art Center School. Bright was married twice. His second wife was Gayle Sandefur, with whom he had four children: Jeptha, Michael, Rebecca, and Leslie, and two stepchildren, Evylyn and Jack Royce.

In 1953 he began his career as an independent sculptor. At the time of his death, he had more outdoor sculptures in Kentucky than any other person, with an estimated twelve hundred in private collections and forty in public collections, the majority in the Louisville area. Bright is best known for the *Louisville Clock*, a large timepiece that charts the hours through a race that features caricatured historical figures such as Daniel Boone and Gen. George Rogers Clark. For a time the clock was displayed on the River City Mall (Fourth St.). Some of his other works include the *River Horse*, located outside the Romano Mazzoli Federal Building in Louisville; the *Winged Man*, at the WAVE-TV garden; and the *Firefighter Memorial*, at Jefferson Square. Bright left a lasting contribution to Cave Hill Cemetery through his bronze art. In contrast to the monotony of the granite headstones, he has a number of bronze memorials in the cemetery. In 1979 he completed a memorial for Jody White, a sixteen-year-old boy who had died in a car accident. The emotional work shows the nude figure who seems to leap from his pedestal with his arms reaching for the sky. A formation of geese flies overhead just touching the boy's fingertips. "God Always Seems to Pick His Prettiest Flower" is the inscription on the memorial for Saundra Twist. Created in 1981, it was criticized by some for its revealing long dress that clings to her form. Other life-size or nearly so sculptures include *Harry Collins* and *Sheri Lynn Applegate.*

Bright sculpted statues of people ranging from common citizens to United States senators such as Thruston B. Morton and Wendell Ford. Children and nude figures were major themes in his work. He taught sculpting, and among his protégés was Ed Hamilton, one of the nation's foremost African American sculptors. Bright died of lung cancer and is buried in Cave Hill Cemetery. Bright's last sculpture for the cemetery marks his resting place and that of his wife. The sculpture shows the two affectionately cuddling, reflecting the strength of their relationship. The two parts (man and woman) form a whole.

See *Courier-Journal*, July 25, 1997; *Courier-Journal Magazine*, Nov. 2, 1980.

BRINEY, MELVILLE (OTTER) (b Louisville, March 26, 1899; d Louisville, January 29, 1986). Newspaper columnist. Briney was the daughter of John D. Otter, the director of the Louisville Title Mortgage Co. for more than fifty years beginning in the late nineteenth century, and Mellie Carter of the Carter Dry Goods family. Otter was also appointed president of the Louisville Board of Aldermen by Gov. J.C.W. Beckham (1900–7) after the Kentucky Court of Appeals ruled that the November 1905 election was invalid because of instances of voter fraud. Otter served under Mayor Robert Worth Bingham, who in 1918 became the owner of the *Courier-Journal*. Briney graduated from Louisville Girls' High School in 1916 and Vassar College in 1921.

Briney worked for several years as a newspaper columnist for the *Louisville Times*. She wrote a weekly editorial page column from 1950 to 1962 entitled "Old Louisville" about colorful people and famous events from the city's past, particularly Louisville's early history. A compilation of her columns, called *Fond Recollections—Sketches of Old Louisville*, was published in 1955. She also coauthored a play, *A Portrait of Harry*, which was performed by the Carriage House Players in 1956. Briney was a strong preservationist. She assisted in the purchase and renovation of Farmington, the home of John Speed and the first museum house in the city. Briney was a member of the board of the Louisville Free Public Library and a member of The Filson Club Historical Society. She was married to Russell Briney, an editorial page editor for the *Courier-Journal* for ten years. The couple had a son, John O. Briney, who worked as a reporter for the *Courier-Journal*. She is buried in Cave Hill Cemetery.

See *Courier-Journal*, May 21, 1950, Jan. 30, 1986.

This freight station, c. 1910, later owned by the Brinly-Hardy Co., was incorporated into Louisville Slugger Field, home of the Louisville RiverBats baseball team.

BRINLY-HARDY COMPANY. A major supplier of tractor attachments, sold nationwide under the Brinly line, and custom-manufactured parts for tractor producers. The company traces its origins to "Little John" Brinly of Simpsonville, Kentucky, who began manufacturing plows around 1800. He also shod horses and mules for newly arrived settlers and those continuing the trek westward. A "Brinly" plow, with wooden moldboard, cast-iron front, point, and heel point, was a common sight in early Kentucky and was in use on many farms.

The son of Little John, Thomas Edward Cogland Brinly, forged a one-piece plow from a saw blade around 1837. He is considered the first manufacturer of steel plows in this region. Brinly continued to turn out plows for local farmers until demand outstripped supply. Brinly was forced to open manufacturing centers in other southern cities, though the main forge was still located in Simpsonville. Nearly the entire output of the Simpsonville shop was sold to the W.B. Belknap and Co. iron warehouse and merchants for shipment downriver to Memphis, Natchez, Vicksburg, and New Orleans. This earned the Brinly plow a strong reputation throughout the South.

In 1859 Brinly's business associate, MORRIS BELKNAP, persuaded him to move his operation to Louisville. Originally located at a site on MAIN ST. between Brook and Floyd, the factory and office later moved one block to PRESTON and Floyd. The company was known as Brinly-Dodge and Co. until 1863, when James Edward Hardy joined the firm and the company became Brinly, Dodge, and Hardy.

As a result of Brinly's strong southern sympathies (his son served as a soldier in the Confederate army), many of the branch shops were destroyed by federal troops. The company opted not to rebuild but concentrated operations at its Louisville plant. The company was incorporated as Brinly, Miles, and Hardy Co., with Brinly's brother-in-law, A.D. Miles, who is shown in the Louisville CITY DIRECTORIES to be a partner as early as 1869. In 1900, Miles sold his interest. Despite the death of the firm's last Brinly that same year, the name has remained unchanged. The business has remained in the hands of the Hardy family, with fifth-generation president Jane W. Hardy ascending in 1994.

A part of the company located at 324–32 E Main, known as the Brinly-Hardy Building, is a complex of four structures, some dating to 1867. These are Brinly-Hardy's original buildings, occupied by them perhaps since 1859.

In 1998 construction began at the shipping warehouse, located along E Main St. between Preston and Jackson Streets, to transform the structure into the primary entry for a new riverfront BASEBALL stadium. Louisville Slugger Field, completed spring 2000, will be the home of the Louisville minor-league baseball team. In the search for a new home, Brinly-Hardy decided to move its lawn-equipment operation across the river to JEFFERSONVILLE.

BRISTOW, BENJAMIN HELM (b Elkton, Kentucky, June 20, 1832; d New York City, June 22, 1896). Lawyer and statesman. Bristow was the eldest son of Francis Marion and Emily Edwards Helm Bristow. After graduating from Jefferson College in Pennsylvania, he studied LAW under his father and was admitted to the Kentucky bar in 1854. He married Abigail Slaughter in 1854; they had two children.

With the outbreak of the CIVIL WAR, because of their Union sentiment, the family fled to Indiana. Benjamin remained to help recruit the Twenty-fifth Kentucky Volunteer Regiment for the Union army. He saw service at the battles of Fort Donelson and Shiloh. He was wounded at Shiloh and resigned his commission, but when he recovered he helped organize the Eighth Kentucky Cavalry. He resigned as colonel in 1863 and returned to Hopkinsville to practice law. Without his knowledge he was elected to the state senate, where he served on the Military Affairs and the Federal Relations Committees.

Bristow was active in building support for the REPUBLICAN PARTY in Kentucky. Recognizing the importance of public support, he encouraged the establishment of the *Louisville Daily Commercial* as a voice for the party. He supported the unsuccessful bid by his former law partner, JOHN MARSHALL HARLAN, for the governorship of Kentucky in 1871.

In the fall of 1865, through the influence of his friend, Attorney General JAMES SPEED, Bristow was appointed assistant district U.S. attorney for Kentucky. This necessitated a move to Louisville, where he purchased property on Third St. In 1869 he built a house at a cost of twenty-three thousand dollars. The Bristow library became a leading salon of the city where politicians, lawyers, and writers gathered to discuss the affairs of the day. A friendship with John Marshall Harlan ensued, which resulted in Harlan joining the Republican Party and Bristow joining him in the famous "Presbyterian Church Case." This involved the controversy between pro-northern and pro-southern factions over the ownership of the Walnut Street Presbyterian Church of Louisville.

Since the district attorney was not well, Bristow assumed a leading role in prosecuting the government's cases. With the resignation of the district attorney in 1868, Bristow was appointed to that position. Kentucky was hostile to the federal government following the passage of the Thirteenth Amendment and the establishment of the Freedman's Bureau in the state. While the General Assembly had repealed the slave code, it continued to refuse the use of black testimony in cases involving whites. Following the passage of the Civil Rights Act (1866), white supremacy groups known as "Regulators" took the law into their own hands. Bristow was determined that the Civil Rights Act would be enforced. Two test cases emerged: the Rhodes, Stewart, Vickers case and the Blyew and Kennard case. Since black testimony was denied in state COURTS, writs of habeas corpus were issued transferring the cases to the federal court. Although guilty verdicts were rendered, appeals were made to the United States Supreme Court.

Meanwhile, because of his CIVIL RIGHTS record, Bristow was appointed the first solicitor general of the United States in 1870. In this post, he argued the government's cases before the Supreme Court. When the Blyew and Kennard case was reviewed by the Court, despite Bristow's efforts, the Supreme Court declared that it was not within its jurisdiction. This proved a serious blow to the right of black testimony.

With President Ulysses Grant's victory assured in 1872, Bristow resigned and returned to Louisville. When Grant nominated him as attorney general, Bristow asked that his name be withdrawn. But when scandals threatened the Grant administration, the president offered Bristow the post of secretary of the treasury, and he accepted. After establishing civil service rules for the office, Bristow took the lead in securing the resumption of specie payment and began the exposure of governmental fraud. He achieved national recognition for his exposure of the notorious Whiskey Ring, which defrauded the government of more than $300 million.

Initially Grant supported Bristow's investigation, but when his close friends and advisers became involved, the president lost confidence in Bristow, who had brought some 250 civil and criminal suits, resulting in 176 indictments and 110 fraud convictions. Bristow resigned in 1876 and immediately became a presidential nominee of the moderate faction of the Republican Party. Bristow Clubs were formed, and his name was placed in nomination at the Cincinnati convention by John Marshall Harlan. Unfortunately, as treasury secretary he had alienated too many of the party leaders to win the nomination. A compromise candidate, Rutherford B. Hayes, was nominated. Bristow campaigned on behalf of Hayes, claiming that the time had come to lay aside the animosities of the Civil War and to accept the challenge of rebuilding the nation.

Bristow became a successful corporation lawyer in New York City, representing such companies as the Atlantic and Pacific and LOUISVILLE & NASHVILLE RAILROADS, the Interstate Telephone Co., the American Rapid Telegraph Co., the Panama Railroad Co., Westinghouse Electric Co., and the Carnegie Steel Co. His ambition was to sit on the Supreme Court, but this was frustrated by the appointment of John Marshall Harlan to the court in 1877. He refused an appointment as minister to the Court of St. James's and declined to be a presidential candidate in 1880. He continued to be an outspoken advocate of civil service reform. Like many Republicans in 1884, he refused to accept James G. Blaine's presidential nomination and joined the "Mugwumps" who supported Grover Cleveland. At his home gathered the leading political figures of his day, including Presidents Cleveland and Benjamin Harrison. Suffering from an acute attack of appendicitis, he refused an operation and died. He is buried in Woodlawn Cemetery in New York City.

See Ross A. Webb, *Benjamin Helm Bristow: Border State Politician* (Lexington 1967).

Ross A. Webb

BROADCASTING. Louisville gave birth to the broadcasting industry in Kentucky. The first licensed radio station in the state was WHAS and the first TELEVISION station was WAVE-TV.

Early radio programs were heard from stations outside the state in late 1920. In 1921 William Virgil Jordan of Louisville installed receivers in the WAVERLY HILLS SANATORIUM for patients to hear the "radiocasts" over his amateur radio 9LK, which he operated from his Big Six Auto Repair Shop on W Breckinridge St. In September 1922 he received an official license for a station, with the call letters WLAP.

Prior to that, WHAS began operation on July 18, 1922, with regular programming from studios located at Third and LIBERTY STREETS. The station was adjacent to the headquarters building of the *COURIER-JOURNAL* and *LOUISVILLE TIMES*, which founded the station at the request of ROBERT W. BINGHAM, the newspapers' publisher. He had enlisted the aid of Credo Fitch Harris and J. Emmett Graft to purchase equipment and outline a plan of operation for a radio station. Bingham envisioned bringing the arts, music, and entertainment to the people of the Louisville area and the state. NEWSPAPERS supported many of the early radio stations in the country, since ADVERTISING revenue was not realized until the mid-1920s when the first radio commercials began airing.

WHAS broadcasts in the early years consisted of live evening musical performances as well as special events, sports, political speeches, and weather reports. There was little news, that being the domain of the newspaper staff. Network shows came to Louisville when WHAS joined the NBC-Red network in 1926. In 1929 the station began carrying live educational broadcasts from the University of Kentucky after donating and installing equipment on the Lexington campus.

WLAP radio was unable to sustain much regular programming, and, in 1926, Jordan sold the station to the Virginia Avenue Baptist Church, where broadcasting was limited mainly to the Sunday services. In 1928 Dinwiddie Lampton purchased the station and moved the studios to the Inter-Southern Building at Fifth and Jefferson Streets. He improved programming, hired new staff, and brought the CBS network to the station before selling out to Ralph Atlass of Chicago in 1931.

In 1932 Louisville radio became the focus of heated debate before the Federal Radio Commission after WFIW in Hopkinsville sought to move to Louisville. About that time, WLAP had been purchased by George Norton Jr., and CBS switched its programming to WHAS. Norton opposed the Hopkinsville move, seeking a better frequency and power allocation for his station. The FRC ruled in favor of WFIW, and WLAP appealed. The matter was resolved, however, when Norton simply purchased WFIW and moved its transmitter to the Brown Hotel, changing the call letters to WAVE at 940 kHz and affiliating with NBC. The station moved to 970 on the dial in 1941.

WAVE radio, with Nathan Lord as manager, began its operation with a gala opening on December 30, 1933. The Nortons would join the Binghams in becoming the city's two most influential broadcast families for the next fifty years. WLAP went off the air, with its assets eventually sold to Turner Rush and Alvin Witt, who moved the station to Lexington.

A third Louisville station went on the air in 1936 as WGRC, licensed to NEW ALBANY, Indiana. WGRC opened studios there and in downtown Louisville at the Kentucky Home Life Building. By this time, the government allowed selection of specific call signs for stations, and "GRC" commemorated GEORGE ROGERS CLARK, founder of Louisville. The station was built by Northside Broadcasting, with stockholders Arthur and Charles Harris, Robert McIntosh, and Adolph Zeller. WGRC joined the Mutual network, and J. Porter Smith began a long career in management.

In 1940 D.E. "Plug" Kendrick, who worked for WFIW and WAVE, broke away from the Nortons to start his own station, going on the air with WINN-1240 radio, with studios at the Tyler Hotel. WINN was the city's fourth station.

The golden age of radio spanned the period of the GREAT DEPRESSION and WORLD WAR II, when radio proved so valuable in communicating with an anxious nation during those troubled times. Listeners were also entertained by a variety of network soap operas, dramas, comedies, game shows, and musical shows. There was a dramatic increase in the number of homes with radios and improvement in the quality of receivers.

In 1933 WHAS received permission to advance power to 50,000 watts at 840 kHz, becoming the state's first and only clear-channel, full-power AM station.

News and on-the-spot reporting became an integral part of the daily schedule on stations. When the tragic FLOOD OF 1937 hit Louisville, radio was there to render emergency service. WHAS and WAVE cooperated to assure that the public was served during the disaster, and radio was credited with saving thousands of lives.

Radio and technological developments took a pause until 1945, when the end of the war marked the beginning of a new era of expansion in station numbers, the establishment of an FM radio band, and the coming of television. At that time, twelve radio stations were operating in Kentucky, with four in Louisville. Hugh Potter, of WOMI in Owensboro, called for a meeting of all broadcasters in the state to form an association to help meet the new challenges in the industry.

That meeting was held in Louisville in October 1945 at the WAVE studios in the Brown Hotel. A constitution was drafted establishing the Kentucky Broadcasters Association. Potter was named president, with Harry McTigue of WINN as vice president and J.H. Callaway of WHAS as secretary-treasurer. Kentucky was the fourteenth state to establish a radio trade organization. The national association had been active for several years, with MARK ETHRIDGE of WHAS as the first interim president, in 1938. NEVILLE MILLER, a former MAYOR of Louisville, was hired as a paid chief executive of the National Association of Broadcasters.

Three of the Louisville stations quickly obtained FM licenses once standards were established by the Federal Communications Commission (FCC). WHAS had joined in some government experiments of the high-fidelity signal in the early 1940s. WHAS, WAVE, and WGRC soon were broadcasting with new stations on the FM band. But there were few FM receivers among the public and not enough interest to make it a profitable venture. All the FM commercial stations were silent by 1952, and commercial FM remained dormant in the city until a revival in the 1960s.

Noncommercial stations on the FM band, supported by schools, LIBRARIES, and foundations, continued to function around the state and nation with mostly classical music and educational programs. The LOUISVILLE FREE PUBLIC LIBRARY started WFPL-89.3 in February 1950 and added WFPK-91.9 four years later when equipment was donated by WAVE from its defunct FM station.

WSDX at the SOUTHERN BAPTIST THEOLOGICAL SEMINARY was the first college station in the city. It was built in the 1950s, but it was unable to sustain operation. The UNIVERSITY OF LOUISVILLE's FM station, WUOL-90.5, grew out of gifts from the Bingham family in 1976 from the abandoned FM affiliate of WHAS. The oldest noncommercial FM station in the metropolitan area is at New Albany High School. WNAS went on the air in 1949 at 88.1 and is the nation's oldest high-school-owned and -operated station.

While FM did not attract many listeners in those early years, the AM band began a frenzied growth period during the late 1940s and early '50s. The number of Louisville stations doubled with the addition of WKYW, WLOU, WKLO, and WTMT.

WKYW signed on in 1946 at 900 kHz and was dubbed the Noah's Ark Station by the press. It received quite a bit of curious attention when Steve Cisler, the vice president, took army pontoon barges and set the transmitter building on them so that it would float in case of flood. The transmitter and tower were located in the flood-prone area of River Rd. near Zorn Ave.

WLOU was started in 1948 by Mrs. John Messervy. The station and tower were located near PARKWAY FIELD, the home of the LOUISVILLE COLONELS baseball team. It did not affiliate with any network and wanted to utilize local talent in programming. In 1951 the station suspended operation, was purchased by the Robert Rounsaville broadcasting group, and returned to the air with a format of BLUES and spirituals, calling itself the station for the Negro community. WLOU obtained 5,000 watts at 1350 kHz and was one of the first stations to focus on a specific segment of the population as a target audience. WILLIAM SUMMERS III started working at WLOU and eventually became general manager and part-owner. As president of the Kentucky Broadcasters Association in 1979, he became the first minority person in the nation to head up a state broadcast association.

In 1941 a permit was issued for a Louisville station at 1080 on the dial, with call letters WINK, but the war prevented its construction. In 1948, the station signed on as WKLO after being built by Mid-America Corp. James Brownlee was president, and Joe Eaton was general manager. It was purchased by Charles Sawyer's Great Trails Co. in 1955.

Another entry into the Louisville radio market was WTMT, going on the air at 620 kHz in 1958 as a daytime-only station playing country music, with studios on FOURTH ST. Earl Hash was president and Lee Stinson sales manager. Stinson purchased the company in 1974, with Lee Stinson Jr. succeeding his father as owner in 1995. It was one of the few facilities to remain locally owned.

Following the end of the war in 1945, radio stations quickly expanded their interests into the new field of television. WHAS and WAVE had obtained construction permits for TV, and the first broadcast in the state was on November 24, 1948, from the studios of WAVE's new location on E BROADWAY at PRESTON ST., which it had acquired in 1940. WAVE started on Channel 5, but five years later under government realignment was switched to Channel 3. The first show originated from a set designed to look like a Kentucky barn and featured a variety of performers. Burt Blackwell, who had brought WAVE radio on the air for the Norton family fifteen years earlier, served as host.

Meanwhile, the Binghams had planned their entrance into TV for some time, but several construction delays in the studios at Sixth and Broadway kept them from going on the air until March 27, 1950. Victor Sholis served as the master of ceremonies for the first evening broadcast. WHAS started on Channel 9 but moved to full power and Channel 11 in 1953. It was estimated that twenty-five thousand television sets were in use in Louisville at that time.

Other radio stations contemplated entering the new medium, but only two VHF channels were assigned to the city, in accordance with FCC guidelines. UHF-TV channel frequencies were available but less desirable, since they required a different antenna and special converters for station selection.

WKLO established the first such UHF station, signing on the air as Channel 21 on October 18, 1953. WKLO used the personnel and facilities of its radio station. Advertisers were reluctant to purchase commercials, and the station suspended operations in the spring of 1954 after just six months in business. WKLO saw a glimmer of hope for returning to TV when the government proposed moving a new VHF channel to the city. The plan was abandoned, however, and Channel 21 did not become a reality in the city until thirty years later, as WBNA.

The failure of WKLO-TV had the effect of discouraging other radio operators who had planned to invest in the TV field on the UHF band. WLOU was granted a permit for Channel 41 in 1953 but never commenced broadcasting. The license was sold several times before going on the air in 1971 as WDRB.

Kentucky's first noncommercial educational television station debuted in Louisville in September 1958, the twenty-eighth public station in the nation. WFPK-TV 15 was licensed to the Louisville Free Public Library. The tower and transmitter were located at the library, but the programming was actually under the auspices of the Jefferson County Board of Education. In the early years it was primarily a classroom educational resource and was supported by several foundation grants and help from the commercial stations. The licensee was officially changed to the school board in 1967, and the call letters became WKPC—"Kentuckiana's People's Choice." In 1969 the station affiliated with the new PBS network, and new studios were constructed on Bishop Ln. in 1973. The publicly supported station struggled financially, and in 1981 a community board began governing operations of Channel 15.

In 1970 viewers began receiving programming from the Kentucky Educational Television network (KET), with the initiation of service from WKMJ, Channel 68. All KET programming originated from headquarters in Lexington. After several years of discussion and negotiation, a merger was forged in 1997 between WKPC and KET-68.

The first successful UHF commercial venture was WLKY, licensed to a group of independent business people who had formed Kentuckiana Broadcasting with George Egger as president. The Channel 32 debut occurred on September 16, 1961. It was one of the first UHF stations in the nation to be able to compete in a VHF market. Part of the ability to succeed came from obtaining full ABC network affiliation and heavy promotion for all-channel sets capable of receiving the signal.

The early days of Louisville television allowed many of the voices associated with WAVE and WHAS radio to be seen on television, with a variety of talent shows, children's programs, music hours, and local news, sports, and weather. At WAVE, Livingston Gilbert became the state's first TV newscaster and was an anchor for thirty-two years. Gilbert, along with the quartet of voices—Bill Gladden, Ed Kallay, Ryan Halloran, and Bob Kay—served WAVE radio and TV for decades. At WHAS, there were enduring careers for, among others, Bud Abbott, Paul Clark, Sam Gifford, Milton Metz, Ken Meeker, Bill Small, and one of the first female reporters, Phyllis Knight. Jim Walton hosted many programs, including the annual WHAS fund-raiser, *CRUSADE FOR CHILDREN*. Long- time University of Kentucky sportscaster Cawood Ledford joined WHAS in 1956. Ken Rowland reported area news for more than thirty years on WLKY and WHAS. Network news correspondent and anchor Diane Sawyer began her career in Louisville as the Channel 32 weather forecaster, and network reporter David Dick started in news at WHAS.

As the national broadcasting networks gradually began moving their popular shows over to television, radio was forced to revise its philosophy. It returned to more local programming, centered around music and the so-called disc-jockey, who spun the records with hype and humor. This national transition was aided by the emergence of ROCK 'n' roll MUSIC as a cultural and entertainment trend in the mid-1950s.

The movement made its way to Louisville in 1958 when rock radio pioneer Gordon McLendon arrived to purchase the conservative WGRC-790 and convert it to WAKY, "wacky radio." With the birth of WAKY, the rock revolution hit Louisville. The station went on to become one of the most influential teen stations in the nation, guided by program director and announcer Johnny Randolph.

WKLO also changed formats to rock and, with morning personality Bill Bailey, who dubbed himself the "Duke of Louisville," challenged WAKY for listeners. In the mid-1960s the two stations together would often garner two-thirds of the city's total audience. Bailey left for Chicago but returned in 1970 to work for WAKY.

Other stations made adjustments in programming to feature pop music, country, religious, or a block format—mixing music styles to appeal to a broad audience. The city's two oldest stations, WHAS and WAVE, relied heavily on local news and information in addition to their variety of music. WKYW turned to religious programming and became WFIA in the mid-1960s. WINN was purchased by Bluegrass Broadcasting of Lexington in 1962, and Claude Sullivan became manager. It promoted a "country-politan" format for years, with program director Moon Mullins becoming widely respected in country music circles. The station was sold in 1979 to become WLLV, playing big band, then later gospel.

Other early AM stations in the Louisville area were officially licensed in Indiana, including New Albany's WLRP-1570 kHz in 1949. It became WHEL, a country music station, in the 1960s and later turned to gospel. New Albany's 1290 AM station went on the air in 1966 and eventually played urban contemporary music. JEFFERSONVILLE's WXVW-1450 was started by Clarence Henson and Keith Reising in 1961. Charlie Jenkins came in 1965, eventually bought into the station, and began a long career in broadcasting local sports.

The development of stereo broadcasting in the FM band and increased production of dual-band radios marked a major change in the industry. FM licenses again became popular, and audiences for those stations grew, starting in the late 1960s.

The first stereo signal heard in Louisville was WLRS, 102.3 MHz, going on the air in October 1964. The station's main purpose, at first, was as a training tool for students at the Louisville Radio School. The school was started in 1946 by Clarence Henson, Russell Warren, and Bob McGregor to train TV and radio technicians. Henson established a low-key, limited-commercial schedule for the station. In the early 1970s, Ed and Louisa Henson became more involved in the family business and took WLRS to a hit-rock format and eventually to the top of the ratings in 1978. It was the first time, nationally, that an FM station had won an audience survey in a major market. FM listenership was overtaking the AM band by larger and larger margins each year.

WKLO built the first FM companion station at 99.7 MHz in 1962 to simultaneously broadcast its AM programs. That signal later brought music to Louisville-area listeners for several years before becoming WDJX in the mid-1980s. It was a popular urban rock station.

In 1966, J.W. "Woody" Dunavent started WSTM-FM 103.1 in St. Matthews, playing everything from jazz to country to rock. After undergoing numerous ownership changes through the years, the station captured a good audience in the 1990s by playing the oldies music of the early days of rock. In 1967, WKRX, another stand-alone FM station, was built by Keith Reising at 106.9 MHz, later becoming the easy listening sound of WVEZ.

WFIA built a companion FM station—103.9 in 1974. Several stations in outlying communities began operation in the 1970s, including WQMF–95.7 in Jeffersonville, Indiana, and WZZX–101.7 in JEFFERSONTOWN, Kentucky.

One early attempt at bringing Louisville listeners quality music on the FM band started in 1959 when Steve Cisler and William F. Johnston received a license for 97.5 FM and operated WLVL for two years. It was not a commercial success, but five years later, when WHAS returned to the FM radio scene, it used that frequency to build one of the most successful stations in the country. After trying news and beautiful music formats, WHAS finally went all-country with WAMZ in 1977. It became the dominant FM station in the local market in the 1980s and 1990s.

WHAS made changes in the early 1970s, switching to a more personality-oriented format. The commitment of the management to news and public affairs kept WHAS near the top of the ratings heap and brought many state and national awards.

Both WHAS and WAVE ran combined radio and TV operations. WAVE-3 was the NBC-TV affiliate, and WHAS-11 brought CBS-TV programs to the area. Many local personalities did double duty as radio and TV stars.

Louisville's first three commercial television stations originated with local ownership, but by 1990 all had been sold to outside groups. The two families who brought Louisville the first taste of radio and TV relinquished control of their stations.

In June 1979 the Jefferson County government passed its ordinance concerning CABLE TELEVISION. In November Storer Communications of Jefferson County, a branch of the Storer Broadcasting Co. of Miami, was awarded the county franchise. By mid-1981 cable television had a firm grip in the Louisville area, as the entire city had been connected and outlying counties had selected their services as well.

WAVE-TV, under Norton family guidance, had acquired stations in four different states and in 1969 became Orion Broadcasting Co. After the deaths of George Norton III and his son, JANE MORTON NORTON sought to divest herself of company stock and sold Orion to Cosmos Corp. in 1981. The radio station went to Henson Broadcasting and became WAVG.

In 1986 BARRY BINGHAM SR. announced that the *Courier-Journal* and the broadcast properties would be sold. WHAS-TV was purchased by the Providence Journal Co. of Rhode Island, while Clear Channel Communications Inc. of San Antonio bought the radio station. Providence Journal Co. properties were sold to the A.H. Belo Corp. of Dallas in 1997.

WLKY-TV changed ownership and management several times. It has been controlled by major publishing corporations, including the Gannett Co.,the Pulitzer Broadcasting Co. and Hearst-Argyle.

WDRB-41 entered the TV picture in 1971, becoming the fourth commercial station in the market. It proved successful with its independent schedule of reruns, movies, and sports. The station was built by a group of stockholders, Consolidated Broadcasters, with Elmer Jaspan the local investor. In 1977, the station was purchased by the Minneapolis Star and Tribune Co., and it was acquired by the Toledo Blade Corp. in 1984.

Louisville got its fifth TV station in 1986 when Bob Rodgers and Word Broadcasting put Christian station WNBA-21 on the air.

The local network lineup for television shows had been stable for years when it was suddenly shaken in 1990 by the announcement that WHAS would end a forty-year affiliation with CBS and switch to ABC. WAVE remained with NBC, and WLKY signed an agreement with CBS, while WDRB had joined the new Fox network. WDRB began management and operation of a new independent station, WFTE-58 in Salem, Indiana, in 1994.

In the mid-1980s the broadcasting industry began undergoing dramatic changes. The federal government made allowances for many more FM radio stations to enter the marketplace, and the 1990s saw a relaxation of multiple-station ownership rules that would mean a tremendous flurry of buying, selling, and consolidation of stations, completely reshaping the Louisville radio landscape. Older stations were sold to outside interests, and stronger ones took over the weaker ones. Stations changed call letters, formats, and owners rapidly in order to compete, and the radio dial found room for a new AM station and nine new FM stations. A return to network radio marked the era, with satellite-delivered programming replacing the local "DJ" on many stations. The studio operation was transformed from tape and turntables to computers and digital audio.

The consolidation movement brought together media giants Clear Channel and Jacor Communications of Covington, Kentucky, in 1999 in a merger deal reportedly worth $14.4 million, that gave the combined group ten FM and four AM stations and the Kentucky News Network, making them the largest radio company in Louisville.

Kentucky group owner Jack Mortenson added two stations on his religious network in the city, while Cox and Blue Chip Broadcasting groups became multiple station owners in the market. Radio was again linked with a TV partner, as WLKY-TV purchased the AM 970 frequency.

In the public radio sector, the two library stations, WFPL, and WFPK, and WUOL at the University of Louisville, trimmed costs through merger. They formed the Public Radio Partnership in 1993 with Gerry Weston as president.

After fifty years of television, Louisville executives were looking at increased competition from hundreds of cable TV channels and satellite-delivered home systems, which reduced overall viewership of their network programs. More emphasis was placed on new technology to deliver local news, with four stations providing daily and nightly newscasts.

The Kentucky Journalism Hall of Fame includes Louisville air personalities and newspeople James Caldwell, David Dick, Livingston Gilbert, Phyllis Knight, Milton Metz, Ken Rowland, and Diane Sawyer. Along with them are sportscasters Cawood Ledford, farm broadcasters Barney Arnold and FRED WICHE, political analyst David Nakdimen, and media executives Barry Bingham Sr., Barry Bingham Jr., and Jane Morton Norton.

Other broadcast personalities with many years of tenure in Louisville have won recognition and awards for their work, including Coyote Calhoun, Jack Crowner, Bob Domine, Jim Mitchell, Terry Meiners, Wayne Perkey, and Van Vance.

Diane Sawyer, a Glasgow native, graduated from Louisville's Seneca High School and began her career at WLKY-TV. In 1970, she moved to Washington and began work in the press office of President Richard Nixon. She accompanied Nixon to San Clemente following his resignation to help research his memoirs. Returning to Washington in 1978, she became a reporter for CBS News. In 1984, she became the first female reporter for *60 Minutes* and in 1989 she moved to ABC to become co-anchor with Sam Donaldson on *Prime Time Live.* In 1999 she began work with Charles Gibson on the *Good Morning America Show* as well as working as a correspondent on *20/20.*

Bob Edwards, a Louisville native, graduated from St. Xavier High School and the University of Louisville. After beginning his career with work at WHEL in New Albany, he went on to produce programs for the Army and following his service, became news anchor at WTOP radio in Washington. In 1979 he began hosting the National Public Radio's *Morning Edition.* Edwards published *Fridays with Red: A Radio Friendship* (1993), a recollection of his interviews and friendship with broadcaster Red Barber.

Many other area broadcasters have been active in leadership positions in the Kentucky and National Broadcasters Association, including Chris Baker, Lee Browning, Jim Caldwell, Neil Cline, J.R. Curtin, John Dorkin, Joe Eaton, Mark Ethridge, Rodney Ford, Bob Gardner, Art Grunewald, Ed Henson, Charlie Jenkins, Nathan Lord, Harry McTigue, Bob Scherer, Ed Shadbourne, Victor Sholis, J. Porter Smith, William Summers, Charlotte Tharp, Mark Thomas, Jim Topmiller, and Donna Zapata.

Radio and television broadcasting played an important role in the growth of the Lousiville area in the twentieth century. The way of life and leisure, culture, the dynamics of politics and commercial development were dramatically impacted by the rise of radio and television communication. Through entertainment, information, advertising, and public service, Louisville broadcasters made a difference in individual lives and the quality of life within the community.

See Francis M. Nash. *Towers over Kentucky* (Lexington 1995); Richard Weston. "The Man Who Turned on WHAS," The Courier-Journal Magazine, November 22, 1959. *The Courier-Journal,* October 9, 1998.

Francis M. Nash

BROADDUS, ANDREW (b Louisville, May 15, 1900; d Louisville, September 7, 1972). Mayor. He was the son of Russell and Julia Duncan (Ely) Broaddus. His grandfather, Andrew Broaddus (1841–1929) was assistant general freight agent for the Louisville & Nashville Railroad for more than twenty-six years.

The younger Broaddus was educated in public schools in Louisville, graduating in 1918 from Louisville Boys High School. He joined the United States Navy, serving as a radio operator and apprentice seaman from 1918–19. He attended Centre College at Danville from September 1919 until February 1921. He became associated with the family laundry business in 1921 and by 1930 was its vice president and general manager. The company became known as Capital Laundry & Dry Cleaning Co. in 1935.

Broaddus was first elected to the Board of Aldermen in 1933, and served for ten years. He served as president of the board three times, from November 1937 until December 1, 1943. A Democrat, Broaddus was mayor of Louisville from 1953 to 1957. His administration is perhaps best known for the unsuccessful attempt by the city to annex large sections of contiguous land in Jefferson County. Known as the Mallon Plan, it was defeated by voters in 1956. The plan had been put together by a seven-member Local Government Improvement Committee appointed by Broaddus and County Judge Bertram Van Arsdale. The group was headed by John Mallon, an executive with the Louisville Cement Co. The plan offered county residents cheaper fire insurance and water rates, an extension of sewers, and other city services but was defeated 2 to 1 by suburban voters. City residents, however, voted in favor of the plan by a margin of fourteen thousand.

In 1955, Broaddus issued an executive order ending segregation in Louisville's public parks, swimming pools, and amphitheater. Some of the other accomplishments of his administration included the construction of the city's incinerator, construction of a sewage-treatment plant on South Western Parkway, and completion of the police headquarters at Seventh and Jefferson Streets.

During his term of office, a bond issue initiating urban renewal in the city was passed, with Broaddus later serving as chairman of the Urban Renewal Advisory Committee under Mayor Bruce Hoblitzell. With the election of Frank Burke as mayor in 1969, Broaddus was named city civil-defense director.

Broaddus returned to the family business after his tenure, but in 1969 Capital merged with Swiss Cleaners and Laundry and the family was no longer associated with the business.

Broaddus married Elizabeth Bland Robertson of Norfolk, Virginia, on September 24, 1924. The couple had three children: Elizabeth Bland, Julia Duncan, and Andrew III. Broaddus was also active in the Red Cross and the Community Chest charity drives in Louisville. He died of a heart attack at his apartment at 3621 Brownsboro Rd. He is buried in Cave Hill Cemetery.

See W.T. Owens, *Who's Who in Louisville: The Gateway to the South* (Louisville 1926); Citizens Historical Association, *Biographical Sketches* (Indianapolis 1950); *Louisville Times,* Sept. 8, 1972.

BROADUS, JOHN ALBERT (b Culpeper County, Virginia, January 21, 1827; d Louisville, March 16, 1895). Educator and clergyman. After a private elementary education, Broadus entered the University of Virginia in 1846 and received his M.A. in 1850. Considered an outstanding student of Greek, within two years after graduation he was offered and accepted a teaching position at the same school. At the same time Broadus also served as pastor of the Charlottesville Baptist Church. In 1857 he left the University of Virginia to become the church's full-time pastor. In that same year Broadus's first wife, Maria, daughter of his mentor, Gessner Harrison, died. In 1859 he married Charlotte E. Sinclair.

As a distinguished and admired Southern Baptist minister, Broadus was chosen to draft a plan of instruction for a proposed seminary. When the church convention of 1858 endorsed the seminary, they also invited Broadus to accept a professorship at the new institution to be located in Greenville, South Carolina. At first he declined, but in the following year he changed his mind and accepted. From that time until his death, his life was closely intertwined with the development of the seminary, both in South Carolina and at its new home in Louisville.

Broadus served the Southern Baptist Theological Seminary enthusiastically over the next thirty-six years, first as professor of New Testament and Homiletics and later, from 1889 to 1895, as its president. Although he published six books and about twenty pamphlets, his most influential was *On the Preparation and Delivery of Sermons* (1870). This book is still in use today. In 1889 Broadus gave an outstanding series of talks, the *Yale Lectures on Preaching,* which won him national fame.

Newspaper accounts of his death show that both his involvement with the seminary and his interest in civic affairs made him a greatly admired citizen of Louisville. He is buried in Cave Hill Cemetery.

See A.T. Robertson, *Life and Letters of John Albert Broadus* (Philadelphia 1901); *Courier-Journal,* March 15, 1895, March 16, 1895, March 17, 1895.

Ronald F. Deering

BROADWAY. Originally known as Dunkirk Rd. and later as Prather St., Broadway grew longer and broader as the city of Louisville expanded south from the Ohio River. In 1832, Broadway ended on the west end at Twelfth St. and on the east end at Shelby St. By 1856, it extended on the west to Shippingport Rd. (just beyond Twenty-sixth St.), at which point Broadway became Western Turnpike. The west end of Broadway joined with Dunkirk Rd. and extended to the Ohio River.

Broadway extended on the east end to the Louisville and Bardstown Turnpike (now Baxter Ave.). At that time the Presbyterian Orphans' Home and Louisville & Nashville train depot were located on Broadway. During the CIVIL WAR, Broadway was the site of the United States General Hospital and a Louisville schoolhouse. In 1870, when the Henrie Barret Montford Home was built on Broadway between FOURTH and Fifth STREETS, Broadway was considered a suburb.

Five years later, Broadway "had its building boom and became a highly fashionable street." By 1879 Broadway ran from the Ohio River on the west end to Baxter Ave. on the east, at that time the longest street in the city (a fraction over seven miles). It was straight except for a slight angle at Seventh St. and was 120 feet wide. As the city grew, Broadway became the southern terminus of the business district, which stretched along FOURTH ST.

By the mid-1950s Broadway was home to the Federal Building, the *COURIER-JOURNAL* and *LOUISVILLE TIMES*, the Commonwealth Building, the Brown Hotel, and the L&N RAILROAD headquarters. The intersection of Fourth St. and Broadway was known as "the magic corner," due to its importance in the commercial and entertainment life of the city.

The large residences had been gradually razed or converted into other uses as the street became a commercial thoroughfare. By 1966, the STREETCAR tracks had been removed and the number of traffic lanes on Broadway from Barret to Eighteenth St. was increased from six to seven to accommodate growing traffic demands. By the 1980s many of the businesses and churches had moved from the street so that in the 1990s the "Broadway Renaissance" was undertaken to return the luster to the corner. The renovations and refurbishments to the CAMBERLEY BROWN HOTEL and Theatre Square revitalized a section of Broadway having a number of significant buildings, many of which have been placed on the NATIONAL REGISTER OF HISTORIC PLACES. Ironically many of Louisville's commercial and entertainment sites had already moved back toward the river.

See Samuel Thomas, *Views of Louisville since 1766* (Louisville 1971); *Courier-Journal,* March 11, 1951, June 18, 1965.

Ellen Birkett Morris

BROADWAY BAPTIST CHURCH. Located at 4000 Brownsboro Rd., the church originated in the WALNUT STREET BAPTIST CHURCH lecture room on May 17, 1870, when a group of 110 people committed themselves to be the Broadway Baptist Church. The new congregation already had a recently built lecture room at the rear of a lot on E BROADWAY between First and Brook Streets. This building housed worship services while the sanctuary was being built on the property. Worship services in the new sanctuary were held for the first time in May 1872. The first pastor called was Dr. J.B. Hawthorne, a noted orator.

During the later part of the nineteenth and early twentieth century, the Broadway Baptist Church neighborhood exuded wealth and education. Several important educational and mission institutions with which Broadway Baptist had close connections grew and developed in the vicinity, including the SOUTHERN BAPTIST SEMINARY at Fifth and Broadway and the Louisville Baptist Orphans' Home at First and St. Catherine. A prominent Louisville family, the Nortons, were members of the church and contributed more than $250,000 to Southern Seminary. In addition, the LOUISVILLE PRESBYTERIAN THEOLOGICAL SEMINARY, located directly to the west of Broadway Baptist Church by the mid-1890s, began building its permanent Gothic-style buildings in 1902 (now home of JEFFERSON COMMUNITY COLLEGE).

In 1912 the church started planning for a Sunday school building, but WORLD WAR I interrupted and it was not completed until 1927. From 1941 to 1943 Dr. Duke K. McCall served as pastor of the church, leaving to become president of the Baptist Bible Institute (now New Orleans Baptist Theological Seminary) and returning to Louisville in 1951 to serve as president of Southern Baptist Theological Seminary and rejoining Broadway at that time. Under the leadership of the new pastor, Dr. James A. Stewart, 1944 to 1947, the church decided to move to its Brownsboro Rd. location. By 1948, after almost seventy-eight years at the same site, much of the congregation had moved to the eastern SUBURBS, and the condition of the buildings and the neighborhood had drastically changed. Southern Seminary's move to its current location on Lexington Rd. in the 1920s was one of the factors that caused a decline in the membership and influence of Broadway Baptist at its original location. On May 16, 1948, the church held its final service in the buildings. A lot on Brownsboro Rd. at the church's current location was purchased. The first building at the Brownsboro Rd. site was what is now the chapel and was first used for services in July 1950. The church began to grow rapidly. In 1959 it began building a new sanctuary as well as education facilities, a larger library, and more office space. During the period from 1970 to 1995, two major additions were added—a multipurpose unit and a family life center.

Dr. Edwin F. Perry, pastor from 1949 to 1980, oversaw the rebirth of Broadway Baptist as a large and influential church in its new location. Dr. Ronald W. Higdon, pastor since 1980, has led the development of facilities enhancing the opportunities for church fellowship and the establishment of a radio ministry.

From the beginning of its history, Broadway Baptist has been prominent in developing mission churches throughout the city, including Calvary Baptist in 1888, Immanuel Baptist in 1890, HIGHLAND BAPTIST in 1893, West Broadway Baptist in 1909, Highland Park First Baptist in 1916, Van Buren Baptist in 1924, and Green Hills Baptist Church in 1991.

BROOKLAWN. Brooklawn was founded in 1851 as the German Protestant Orphans' Asy-

Rush hour traffic on Broadway at Fourth, 1930.

lum by the Reverend Karl Daubert, pastor of St. Paul's Evangelical Church. The orphanage was originally located on W Jefferson St. between Nineteenth and Twentieth Streets. In 1902 it moved to a nine-acre campus on Bardstown Rd. in the HIGHLANDS where Mid-City Mall is now located. In 1962 it moved to its current twenty-five-acre campus on Goldsmith Ln. and changed its name to Brooklawn. In 1991 Brooklawn adopted a new mission to serve emotionally and behaviorally troubled youth and their families. Brooklawn operates as Brooklawn Youth Services and is a private nonprofit agency affiliated with the UNITED CHURCH OF CHRIST and METRO UNITED WAY.

Brooklawn offers a multiservice treatment program that serves youth ages six to eighteen years of age. A continuum of care that ranges from intensive psychiatric residential treatment to independent living is provided. Children referred to Brooklawn exhibit emotional disturbance and serious behavioral problems. Additionally, many have been abused, come from dysfunctional backgrounds, or have a history of multiple placement failures. The treatment approach is based on the principles of Reality Therapy. The focus is on creating a supportive and caring therapeutic environment and teaching procedures that lead to change.

David A. Graves

"Cactus" Tom Brooks (left) and Randy Atcher, stars of *T-Bar-V Ranch* and *Hayloft Hoedown* on WHAS-TV, 1951.

BROOKS, WILLIAM THOMAS "CACTUS" (b Louisville, March 4, 1910; d Louisville, December 14, 1997). Actor and radio announcer. Brooks was one of eight children of Edna (Megowan) and Pleasant M. Brooks. He got his start as Cactus on the WHAS radio show *Circle Star Ranch.* He was an early pioneer in local TELEVISION and was best known as Cactus, the cook on the WHAS children's show *T-Bar-V Ranch.* Cactus dressed in overalls and an old hat turned-up in the front and used face paint to appeal to children. He was a household name and usually appeared with Randy Atcher, his sidekick on the program, during a time when television stations competed for the children's audience.

The show was one of WHAS's most popular programs from 1950 to 1971. Brooks also appeared with Atcher in the shows *Ladies Day* and *Hayloft Hoedown,* which showcased local singers and dancers. In 1962 he received the Silver Horseshoe Award for volunteering time to better the community. He was also a staple on the annual *CRUSADE FOR CHILDREN.* Brooks was not only an entertainer, but a role model who admonished children to study hard, mind their parents, and to look both ways before crossing the street. Brooks is buried in Resthaven Memorial Cemetery.

The brother of Tom Brooks, Foster Brooks, comedian, radio, and television announcer, was born on May 11, 1912, in Louisville. At the age of thirteen he began his radio career at WHAS in Louisville, where his mother was a performer. During the 1937 Ohio River FLOOD. Brooks and two other WHAS announcers maintained a twenty-four-hour vigil to provide news of the disaster. Brooks later broadcast for WAVE and WKLO radio in Louisville and worked at stations in St. Louis and in Rochester and Buffalo, New York. In the 1950s he moved into television and worked for WAVE-TV in Louisville. Brooks left local BROADCASTING for a career as a comedian, and by the 1960s he was often seen in guest roles on television series. In the role of a "Lovable Lush, " he appeared frequently on stage in Las Vegas and Atlantic City. In the 1970s this character became a regular on television's "Dean Martin Show" and earned an Emmy nomination. Brooks was a regular on the television series "New Bill Cosby Show" and "Mork and Mindy." Brooks returned to Louisville annually for the Foster Brooks Pro-Am Golf Tournament which had a twenty-six year run from 1970 to 1996.

BROWN, GEORGE GARVIN (b Munfordville, Kentucky, September 2, 1846; d Louisville, January 24, 1917). Distiller. The son of J.T.S. Brown Sr. and Mary Garvin, Brown moved to Louisville in 1862, engaged for a time in the wholesale drug trade, and in 1870 began a modest whiskey business, catering mainly to doctors and pharmacists. Within a few months, however, he had expanded his marketing to clubs and the general public. The company was formed by incorporating the name of GEORGE FORMAN, his partner and bookkeeper, who died in 1901. The modest enterprise grew to become BROWN-FORMAN CORP., one of the largest wine and spirits companies in the world, and a diversified manufacturer of china, crystal, silver, and luggage.

At the time Brown began his DISTILLING enterprise, most whiskey was shipped in barrels to retailers, who could and often did mix or dilute it, leading consumers to complain that it was hard to find a whiskey with uniform taste and quality. Brown solved the problem when he began bottling and sealing his whiskey at the plant, assuring the buyer of the desired uniformity. He also put his signature on the bottle containing the company's premier bourbon, Old Forester, with his assurance that there was "Nothing better in the Market," an assurance the brand still carries. "I decided," he told his son Owsley, to whom he left major control of the firm upon his death, "that we would make quality whiskey for quality prices, from which we would make quality profits."

A conservative Democrat and staunch Presbyterian, Brown established a reputation for integrity and enterprise. He also became known for his stern opposition to PROHIBITION, which he saw coming and which he considered the work of the devil. He wrote a book against Prohibition: *The Holy Bible Repudiates Prohibition* (1910). He was the first president of the National Liquor Dealers' Association formed in St. Louis in 1894.

In 1876 Brown married Amelia Bryant Owsley; they had two sons, Owsley and Robinson, whom he persuaded to follow him in the company. Brown died in Louisville in 1917 and is buried in CAVE HILL CEMETERY.

See John Ed Pearce, *Nothing Better in the Market* (Louisville 1970).

John Ed Pearce

BROWN, JAMES BUCKNER (b Lawrenceburg, Kentucky, November 28, 1872; d Louisville, October 24, 1940). Banker and politician. The son of John Thornton and Paralee (McKee) Brown, he was educated in SHELBYVILLE, Kentucky, public schools. Brown worked as a bookkeeper for the Southern Railway News Co. in Louisville during 1889–97. He then became cashier in Louisville's tax receiver's office and in 1901 was elected tax receiver as a Democrat. After his four-year term, Brown became cashier at the First National Bank through his connections to city political boss JOHN H. WHALLEN.

By 1908 Brown was president of the bank, and by 1911 was president of the Bank of Commerce as well. In 1919 Brown oversaw the merger of three Louisville banks into the National Bank of Kentucky and was elected its president. This institution was to dominate Kentucky BANKING during the 1920s. However, by 1929 Brown's lenient banking policies had resulted in overextensions on loans. With the onset of the GREAT DEPRESSION, the bank failed, closing its doors on November 17, 1930, forcing the closure of other banks that had used the institution as depository including BANCO-KENTUCKY CO., the holding company of the National Bank of Kentucky and the Louisville Trust Co. Brown declared bankruptcy on December 12, 1930. On February 27, 1931, federal and state indictments were handed down against Brown, including charges of willful misappropriations; he was acquitted of the charges.

Brown's political influence came not through elected office but as a supporter of the city's Sinking Fund Commission during 1908–19. In 1924 he was appointed chairman of the state Tax Commission by Gov. William Fields (1923–27); he resigned in December 1924 after his appointment was questioned. Brown purchased the *Louisville Herald* and *Louisville Post* in January 1925 and merged them as the *Herald-Post*, his forum of political expression. His editorials opposed the anti-gambling views of fellow Democrat and newspaperman ROBERT W. BINGHAM. The consequent split in the Democratic Party caused it to lose the 1927 gubernatorial election.

Brown married Elizabeth Barclay Kennedy on September 9, 1901. He is buried in CAVE HILL CEMETERY.

See George H. Yater, *Two Hundred Years at the Falls of the Ohio* (Louisville 1979).

BROWN, JAMES GRAHAM (b Madison, Indiana, August 18, 1881; d Louisville, March 30, 1969). Lumberman, real estate developer, horse breeder, philanthropist. The son of William Pool and Mary Craig (Graham) Brown, he settled in Louisville in 1903. Brown began his business career with his father and brother when they opened the W.P. Brown and Sons Lumber Co., of which James became president in 1918 and the sole owner after his brother's death in 1920.

Brown began developing commercial buildings in Louisville, culminating with the construction of the Brown Hotel in 1923 (now the Camberly Brown Hotel), the Brown Building in 1925, and in 1926 the Brown Theater, all on the north side of BROADWAY between Third and Fourth. The Martin Brown Building (named after his late brother), later the Commonwealth Building, was constructed in 1928 across FOURTH ST. from the hotel and was home to retail stores and business offices. In 1929 he built the Brown Garage and the Greyhound bus terminal at Broadway and Fifth St.

In 1955 an additional nineteen stories were added to the Martin Brown Building, and the BROWN SUBURBAN HOTEL was built on Bardstown Rd. The latter began the transformation of the area from farmland into highly developed real estate. In 1960 Brown oversaw the construction of the twelve-story Brown's apartment building adjacent to the Suburban Motel. He also was publicly recognized for his outstanding contribution to community life, becoming the first honorary trustee of the Old Kentucky Home Council of the BOY SCOUTS OF AMERICA in recognition of "his help throughout fifty years of Scouting."

In 1962 Brown fulfilled a campaign promise to then-mayor WILLIAM COWGER to "do something nice for Louisville" and gave $1.5 million to underwrite the construction of the LOUISVILLE ZOO. Two years later he enriched his alma mater, Hanover College, with $1.5 million for a student center. In an example of his visionary investments, Brown earmarked $1.5 million for renovation of the Brown and Kentucky Hotels, claiming "downtown hotels are coming back and coming back strong."

In 1966 Brown developed ninety-seven acres of land on his farm in Louisville's East End, creating Breckinridge Square. This became the home of Baptist Hospital East and a variety of office buildings and retail outlets. A horse breeder, Brown owned stables in Nelson and Jefferson Counties, served as president of the Thoroughbred Breeders Association of Kentucky, and was a director of CHURCHILL DOWNS for thirty-two years.

Brown lived modestly, mostly in a small suite at the Brown Hotel, where for many years his French poodle "Woozum"—a gift from a professional magician who frequently played the Bluegrass Room at the Brown—was his constant companion. Brown gave generously to local charitable organizations, donating millions of dollars to the UNIVERSITY OF LOUISVILLE and other schools, as well as to various HOSPITALS and cultural programs. Many of his donations were anonymous. In 1943 his assets were incorporated into the James Graham Brown Foundation to benefit charities. Brown Park in ST. MATTHEWS, a historic site originally part of the JOHN FLOYD plantation and purchased by Brown in 1939, was given to the city of St. Matthews and turned into a park honoring Brown's enduring legacy. Upon his death his will bequeathed fifty thousand shares of Churchill Downs stock, valued at approximately $1 million, to fund and maintain the KENTUCKY DERBY MUSEUM. At his death, Brown's fortune was estimated to be upwards of $100 million. After his death, his foundation continued underwriting projects locally, statewide, and nationally.

While his generosity to his community made him adored by many, his rocky relations with LABOR unions made him less than endearing to others. A threat by Brown to sell the Brown Hotel outright if labor unions attempted to organize hotel employees created animosity, as did a strike that nearly caused a shutdown of the hotel during the 1951 Derby weekend.

He died at Norton Hospital of congestive heart failure and is buried in CAVE HILL CEMETERY.

See Dorothy Park Clark, *Louisville's Invisible Benefactor: The Life Story of James Graham Brown* (Louisville 1978); Kay Gill, *The Brown Hotel and Louisville's Magic Corner* (Louisville 1984); *Courier-Journal and Times Magazine*, Sept. 10, 1967.

BROWN, JOHN MASON (b Louisville, July 3, 1900; d New York City, March 16, 1969). Writer and drama critic. Brown, who grew up on Louisville's Park Ave., was the son of John Mason and Carrie (Ferguson) Brown. He represented the sixth generation of his family, descended from Sen. John Brown, one of Kentucky's first United States senators and builder of Liberty Hall in Frankfort. He began his writing career at age seventeen as a cub reporter for the *COURIER-JOURNAL*.

Brown left Louisville after his second year at LOUISVILLE MALE HIGH SCHOOL to attend a prep school in New Jersey. After receiving a bachelor's degree from Harvard in 1923, he became associate editor of the *Theatre Arts Monthly* from 1924 to 1928. He also worked for the *New York Post* (1929–41), the *World-Telegram* (1941–42), and the *Saturday Review* (1944–55). In 1955 he was named editor-at-large of the *Saturday Review*, resigning in 1963.

Brown was author of more than twenty books, including *The Modern Theatre in Revolt* (1929) and *To All Hands, an Amphibious Adventure* (1943). Most of his books dealt with the THEATER, but some were about his personal experiences or were reprints of his critical essays. For more than thirty years he was a versatile lecturer who was known to charm his audiences with a "rat-tat-tat conversational" speaking style, while flooding them with facts.

Between his writing and lecturing duties, he served as a regular panelist on the CBS television show, *The Last Word.* He was also a Book-of-the- Month-Club judge and a member of the Pulitzer Prize drama jury. During WORLD WAR II, Brown served as a lieutenant in the U.S. Navy and received a Bronze Star. He received a distinguished career award in 1965 from the South Eastern Theater Conference. In 1966, the University of Kentucky presented him an honorary doctorate.

In February 1933 he married Catherine Screvin Meredith, and they had two sons, Preston and Meredith. Brown died of emphysema and is buried in Stonington, Connecticut.

See George Stevens, *Speak for Yourself, John: The Life of John Mason Brown, with Some of His Letters and Many of His Opinions* (New York 1974); *Courier-Journal,* March 17, 1969.

BROWN, JOHN THOMAS (b Alamo, Tennessee, October 10, 1869; d Louisville, November 21 [?], 1926). Evangelist and author. Brown was the son of Susan and James T. Brown, who was a bricklayer by profession. After attending local PUBLIC SCHOOLS, Brown worked as a brick mason for several years. In 1890 he moved to Kentucky to continue his education, where in 1894 he graduated in elocution from the College of the Bible in Lexington. In addition Brown received a B.A. degree in 1896 and an M.A. in 1899 from Centre College in Danville.

While living in Lexington and Danville he became an active member of the CHURCH OF CHRIST and began to preach. In 1897 he was selected as editor of the *Christian Guide,* published in Louisville. During his ten-year tenure with that publication, Brown wrote several articles concerning biblical criticism, evolution, and the missionary organization in the Church of Christ. In 1902 he published a biography, *Bruce Norman,* and in 1904 he edited *Churches of Christ.* The latter was a historical, biographical, and pictorial study of the restoration movement in the United States, Australia, England, and Canada.

During his career as an editor and evangelist, Brown traveled and stayed in foreign mission stations in twenty-one different countries, where he lectured and held revivals. In 1907 he married Ida May Tyler. Brown is buried in CAVE HILL CEMETERY.

BROWN, WILLIAM LEE LYONS. (b Louisville, July 26, 1906; d Louisville, January 5, 1973). Entrepreneur. William Lee Lyons Brown was the son of Owsley Brown, chairman of BROWN-FORMAN CORP., and Laura Lee Lyons. Brown was educated at the University of Virginia and at the Naval Academy in Annapolis, Maryland. Upon graduation, Brown went to work as a stockbroker with the brokerage firm of W.L. Lyons and Co., and, temporarily, acted as tour director with the Dollar Steamship Lines. He entered the Brown-Forman Corp., begun in 1870 by his grandfather GEORGE GARVIN BROWN, as secretary in 1933. In 1941 he was named vice president and in 1945 he succeeded his father as president. Brown served as chairman of the board from 1951 to 1966 when he assumed the chairmanship of the board of Jack Daniels Distilleries. He reclaimed his position as chairman of the board at Brown-Forman in 1969 following the death of his brother Garvin, and retained it until his retirement in 1971. He also served as vice president of the Navy League, in addition to being a lifetime member. He was director of several other businesses, including Pennzoil United Inc., Atapaz Petroleum Inc., the Monon Railroad, and the Jefferson Island Salt Co. In addition, Brown served as the president of Ashbourne Realty and Land Development Corp.

Known as a big man with a big smile, Brown was a civic-minded individual, who sat on the board of THE FILSON CLUB HISTORICAL SOCIETY and supported higher education and the arts with generous donations, especially to the FUND FOR THE ARTS, ACTORS THEATRE, and the LOUISVILLE ORCHESTRA. An active farmer, he owned and maintained Ashbourne Farm. He raced thoroughbred horses and won more than 100 races.

Brown married Sara Shallenberger, and they had four children: W.L. Lyons Junior, Martin Shallenberger, Owsley II, and Ina Brown Bond. He is buried in CAVE HILL CEMETERY.

On March 9, 1995, ground was broken on a new $10 million library at BELLARMINE COLLEGE dedicated to Brown. The W.L. Lyons Brown Library is a seventy-two-thousand-square-foot state-of-the-art facility that was officially opened and dedicated on April 9, 1997. In addition to books, periodicals, and multimedia resources, the library also houses the Merton Center and the Merton Collection, the life works and personal effects of the noted Trappist monk from Gethsemani, THOMAS MERTON.

In 1925 JAMES GRAHAM BROWN built the Brown Theater on W BROADWAY near Fourth St. In 1972 the theater's name was changed to the Macauley Theatre. Over the years the condition of the theater deteriorated until a $4.2 million facelift was given to the fourteen-hundred-seat facility beginning in 1996. On October 29, 1998, it was reopened as the W.L. Lyons Brown Theatre, to rave reviews, and dedicated to the former chairman of Brown-Forman Corp.

BROWN & WILLIAMSON TOBACCO CORPORATION. The nation's third-largest tobacco manufacturer in 1998, Brown & Williamson (B&W) is a subsidiary of BAT Industries PLC, a London-based company with worldwide financial and TOBACCO holdings.

In 1893 George T. Brown and Robert F. Williamson, brothers-in-law from prominent North Carolina tobacco families, formed a partnership and took over Robert's father's business in Winston-Salem. To the existing Red Crow and Red Juice chewing tobacco and Golden Grain smoking tobacco, the partners added new products such as Bugler and Bloodhound. Operations continued to expand in the early 1900s after several small acquisitions, and the brothers finally incorporated as the Brown & Williamson Tobacco Co. in 1906.

Brown & Williamson entered the snuff market in 1907 with its Tube Rose, Granny, and Polly blends. However, its acquisition of the J.G. Flynt Tobacco Co. in 1925, along with the regionally popular Sir Walter Raleigh pipe tobacco, afforded the company its first opportunity to distribute a product nationally. It was also during this time that Brown & Williamson began to move into the cigarette market.

Before World War I, the company focused primarily on chewing tobacco, but as the demand for manufactured cigarettes increased following the war (they had been issued to soldiers), Brown & Williamson aggressively sought a new niche in the market for "tailor-mades." In 1927 the flourishing company's growth caught the eye of BAT Industries PLC, a British tobacco syndicate, which purchased B&W as one of its subsidiaries. Along with a new name (Brown & Williamson Tobacco Corp.), the acquisition gave the North Carolina company the financial resources to become a national competitor. Brown & Williamson had increased its production from 8 billion cigarettes per year in 1910 to 119 billion twenty years later.

In 1927 Brown & Williamson executives decided that, rather than expand the facilities at Winston-Salem, the company should search for a new location. Louisville was chosen as the site for the new manufacturing plant and headquarters because of its central location, transportation links, and proximity to the major burley markets. Construction at the site near Hill and Sixteenth Streets began later that year, and manufacturing started two years later. The executive offices formerly based in New York City moved to Louisville in 1931. By 1971 seven buildings and a headquarters building had been constructed on the seventy-two-acre site. To meet increased demand, another manufacturing facility was opened in a former CIVIL WAR hospital in Petersburg, Virginia, in 1932.

Several innovations in the 1930s allowed Brown & Williamson to continue its remarkable development during the GREAT DEPRESSION years. As the number of smokers continued to rise, the company began offering several long-cut, roll-your-own tobaccos for frugal consumers. Of the new blends, Bugler became the most successful with its Thrift Kit, which included two packages of tobacco, a rolling machine, and a carrying case for prepared cigarettes. The airtight cellophane wrapping on tobacco packs, now an industry standard, also appeared during this time. It was first featured in 1930 on the Wings brand, an economy blend that sold for ten cents per pack versus the normal fifteen cents. Another novelty arrived in 1933 when B&W released its Kool brand cigarette, the first nationally marketed menthol type. Advertised with a penguin emblem (later named Willie), the product became one of the company's best-sellers. Another strong seller, Viceroy, was introduced in 1936 with the tobacco industry's first cork-tipped filter constructed of paper. The paper filter was replaced with the first cellulose acetate filter in 1952. By the mid-1970s, brand introductions and increased productivity allowed B&W to capture 17 percent of the national cigarette market.

The Louisville manufacturing operation was closed in 1982, although the research and development department stayed in Louisville until 1994. In 1983 Brown & Williamson moved its headquarters to the twenty-six-story north tower of the downtown Fourth Street GALLERIA complex after having purchased it for $33.5 million the previous year in 1995. United Catalysts Inc. purchased the old headquarters site on Hill St. where most of the old manufacturing buildings had been imploded in 1986.

In the late 1960s Brown & Williamson determined that, in order to best utilize cash resources, it needed to diversify the company's holdings by targeting non-tobacco and service companies. A number of acquisitions started when the corporation purchased Vita Foods, a seafood company, in 1969. Between 1972 and 1988, Brown & Williamson acquired the Kohl Corp. (supermarkets and drug and department stores), Gimbel Brothers Inc. (department stores), Saks Fifth Avenue (department stores), Appleton Papers Inc. (manufacturer of carbonless copying paper), Marshall Field (department stores), the Export Leaf Tobacco Co., and the Farmers Group Insurance Co. In 1977 a central management unit was formed to oversee these holdings and was restructured as BATUS Inc. in 1980. As BAT Industries attempted to refocus itself in 1990, BATUS Inc. was dissolved, and its retail holdings were divested along with Appleton Papers. B&W and Farmers Group Insurance became the parent organization's principal operating companies.

Although the number of smokers declined during the 1960s and 1970s, the number of cigarettes sold continued to climb. Unfortunately, B&W failed to capitalize on this trend and actually lost ground to competitors. Analysts claimed the decline was caused by the company's failure to convert its TELEVISION ADVERTISING to print ads and the slowed growth of the Kool brand. By 1986 Brown & Williamson's share of the domestic market had dropped to 12 percent, down 5 percent from the previous decade. During the 1980s, the company attempted to regain a foothold in the market by introducing several value-priced brands such as GPC Approved and attempted to increase their presence in the growing international market. Both tactics had paid off by 1991 as B&W brands captured 21 percent of the value-oriented segment and the company's international brands accounted for 45 percent of its total sales. However, it would take the 1994 acquisition of the American Tobacco Co. and its popular brands such as Lucky Strike, Pall Mall, and Misty to push Brown & Williamson's percentage of the national market back over 17 percent.

In the 1990s Brown & Williamson faced other challenges as the entire industry came under attack from a number of sides. Between 1989 and 1992 Merrell Williams worked as a paralegal for the Wyatt, Tarrant, and Combs law firm classifying documents for Brown & Williamson in preparation for possible lawsuits. After being told that his job would end in 1992, Williams secretly copied approximately four thousand internal documents that suggested that B&W executives knew of nicotine's addictive nature in the 1960s and had performed numerous tests that linked smoking and cancer. Although B&W attempted to retrieve the papers after learning of their existence, Williams delivered the papers to Mississippi anti-smoking attorney Richard Scruggs, who turned copies over to U.S. Representative Henry Waxman of California and to the medical school of the University of California at San Francisco. The papers were eventually placed on the worldwide web for public use and became the focus of several lawsuits. States suing tobacco companies to recover medical costs incurred treating smokers' ills attempted to use the documents as evidence.

The tobacco industry received another blow the following year when former Brown & Williamson vice president Jeffrey Wigand publicly spoke out against his former employer. Serving in the research and development department from 1989 until he was fired in 1993, Wigand claimed to have been hired to work on a "safer" cigarette. After teaching for two years at DU PONT MANUAL HIGH SCHOOL, the "whistleblower" claimed in a condemnatory interview with CBS's "60 Minutes" that executives knowingly had allowed a harmful additive to be placed in cigarettes and had altered incriminating documents. After B&W threatened to sue, network executives delayed the segment until 1996, when most of the information had become public knowledge. Brown & Williamson later sued Wigand for violating his confidentiality agreements and for stealing company documents. The suit was dropped during the summer of 1997 (although Wigand was still bound to a confidentiality agreement), and Wigand moved to Charleston, South Carolina, later in the year to start an anti-smoking campaign. Both of these instances gave the federal Food and Drug Administration (FDA) enough information to have nicotine classified as a drug. In 1996 President Bill Clinton signed new guidelines allowing the FDA to regulate nicotine and target teen smoking, although they were later ruled unconstitutional by an appeals court.

By the end of 1997 the Macon, Georgia, facility, which could produce over 500 million cigarettes per day, had been joined by other production centers in Winston-Salem, North Carolina; Chester, Virginia; and Lancaster, Pennsylvania. Brown & Williamson also had leaf storage sites in Blacksburg, South Carolina, and Richmond, Virginia, and a leaf processing facility in Wilson, North Carolina. The Louisville area has benefited greatly from Brown & Williamson's ongoing support of the Metro UNITED WAY, the FUND FOR THE ARTS, DARE TO CARE, Clothe-A-Child, and Light Up Louisville.

Employing a local workforce of approximately five hundred and fifty, and a corporate worldwide workforce of fifty-eight hundred, the Brown & Williamson Tobacco Corp.'s sales exceeded $4.3 million in 1997. By that time, its cigarette brands included GPC Approved, Misty, Viceroy, Raleigh, Raleigh Extra, Richland, American Lights, Kool, Carlton, Capri, Lucky Strike, Barclay, Belair, Pall Mall, Tareyton, Silva Thins, Tall, Private Stock, Prime, Summit, Kent, and Finesse. Specialty tobacco products include Kite, Bugler, Sir Walter Raleigh, Bloodhound, Brown & Williamson's Sun Cured, Red Juice, and Tube Rose.

See David Mote, "Brown & Williamson Tobacco Corp.," in Gretchen Antelman et al., *International Directory of Company Histories* 14 (Detroit 1996): 77–79; *Brown & Williamson Tobacco Corporation: The First Hundred Years* (Louisville 1993); *Courier-Journal*, April 2, 1995, May 25, 1997, June 21, 1997, June 18, 1998.

BROWNE, JOHN ROSS (b Beggars Bush, Ireland, February 11, 1821; d Oakland, California, December 9, 1875). Writer and traveler. Browne was the third of seven children born to Thomas Egerton and Elizabeth (Buck) Browne. As a boy he lacked the means to attend school and had to rely on the instruction of his accomplished parents. He rebelled against the classics and preferred the more genial exploits of Gil Blas and Robinson Crusoe. The radical political views of his father, resulting in three months of incarceration, forced the family to emigrate to the United States. In 1833 they settled in Louisville, where Thomas Browne operated a private school for girls. When John Browne was eighteen, he attended Louisville Medical College for several months, just long enough to provide material for his first book, *Confessions of a Quack* (1841), a satire on the medical profession. Also in 1841, Browne wrote a satire of a contemporary proposal for aerial navigation, *The Great Steam Duck*, under the pseudonym of the Louisville Literary Brass Band. The lithograph, showing a large machine shaped like a goose with wings operated by steam power, was accompanied by a booklet on aviation, the second such book published west of the Alleghenies. When an airplane crossed the Atlantic in 1919, the editor of the *Magazine of History* decided that the pamphlet was sufficiently topical to be reprinted.

Browne began his adventures in 1838 when he hired out as a common hand on a flatboat trading between Louisville and New Orleans. By boat, horse, ship, stagecoach, train, and foot, Browne traveled over much of the world. He left Kentucky in 1841 and lived for a year in Washington, D.C., before departing on his great adventure aboard a whaling vessel. There he collected material for his first major work, *Etchings of a Whaling Cruise* (1846), which exposed the harsh conditions aboard the whaling ships. Browne's travels would be the inspiration for most of his writing. He wrote adventure tales that were published in the *Southern Literary Messenger* and *Graham's Magazine*. He wrote numerous sketches of Western life, originally published in *Harper's Magazine*. His books, thirteen volumes in all, can be divided into two categories—scientific and literary. The scientific works, nine in all, are official reports to the federal Treasury Department on various subjects. Among these were *Reports of the Debates of the California Constitutional Convention* (1850), *The Indian Wars in Oregon and Washington Territory* (1858), and *The Policy of Extending Local Aid to Railroads* (1870).

His best-known works, however, were his literary writings, which described his adventures and were autobiographical. *Crusoe's Island* (1864) gives an account of his trip around the Horn to California in 1849; it contains a chapter titled "The Indians in California" protesting the government's Indian policy. He also wrote a somewhat comedic work about a tour of Palestine entitled *Yusef* (1853). *Adventures of Apache Country* (1869) contains sketches of Arizona and Nevada. In addition to his writing, Browne worked as a customhouse inspector, clerk, sailor, and Indian agent. For sixteen months, he served as ambassador to China. In 1849 he made his first trip to California. Though he traveled to many different countries, he considered that state his home. Brown influenced two of the most important American authors in the nineteenth century, Herman Melville and Mark Twain.

Browne married Lucy Anne Mitchell in 1844. The couple had nine children.

See Lina Fergusson Browne, *J. Ross Browne: His Letters, Journals and Writings* (Albuquerque, N.Mex., 1969); Francis J. Rock, *J. Ross Browne, A Biography* (Washington, D.C., 1929); John Weisert, "John Ross Browne's Great Steam Duck," *Huntington Library Quarterly* 22 (May 1959): 251–54. (138)

BROWN-FORMAN CORPORATION. Brown-Forman Corp. was founded in Louisville in 1870 by George Garvin Brown, who came from Munfordville, Kentucky, after the Civil War. He worked in the wholesale drug trade for a while but soon turned to the somewhat turbulent whiskey business, eventually incorporating the name of his bookkeeper partner, George Forman, into the name of the new firm, Brown, Forman, & Co. Forman died in 1901, but his name was retained. What began as a small local distillery became in time one of the ten largest wine and spirits companies in the world and a diversified producer and marketer of fine American china, crystal, silver, and luggage.

At the time Brown began his enterprise, most whiskey was sold in barrels to retailers. Brown noted that saloon and club owners, who, along with doctors and pharmacists, were his chief customers, often blended straight whiskey with other alcohol or watered and thus diluted it. This caused consumers to complain that it was hard to find a whiskey that was uniform in taste from one barrel to another. Brown solved the problem by selling his Old Forester whiskey only in bottles that were sealed at the plant, preventing middlemen from diluting it. He later became a champion of the Bottled-in-Bond Act of 1897, which specified that bonded whiskey had to be distilled at one place all at the same time, aged for four years in a government-supervised warehouse, and bottled at one hundred proof. Bonded whiskey also had to identify the distiller.

Brown urged his son Owsley, in whose control he left the family business, to emphasize quality of product and sell at quality prices rather than sell greater volume of inferior whiskey at lower prices.

Owsley Brown, born in Louisville in 1879, assumed management duties in 1917 and directed the firm through the precarious years of Prohibition, the Great Depression, and two world wars. He was assisted by his brother, Robinson Swearingen Brown (1886–1968), who was a member of the board of directors from 1917 to 1951 and later served as both secretary and treasurer of the company. Owsley steered Brown-Forman through Prohibition by gaining government permission to use some of the corporation's considerable stores of bourbon for sale to doctors and pharmacists, who were permitted to prescribe and sell whiskey for ailments ranging from toothache to nervous disorders. This kept the company afloat and ready to resume production when Prohibition ended in 1933.

Under Owsley Brown's guidance, the company not only survived but flourished. This was markedly so after Owsley acquired Early Times whiskey, which with Old Forester became the company's most popular and profitable brands. He also acquired in 1940 the small but distinguished distilling firm of Labrot & Graham, which the company sold in 1973, then repurchased, refurbished, and returned to the production of super premium bourbon (Woodford Reserve) in 1996. Owsley demonstrated his concern for the nature and reputation of the entire distilling industry when he helped to found and became the first president of the organization known today as DISCUS, the Distilled Spirits Council of the United States, which sets and oversees standards of practice for the distilled spirits industry.

More outgoing than his reserved father, Owsley Brown was active in local civic and political affairs and served as county chairman of the Democratic Party. He was married to Laura Lee Lyons, and they became parents of W.L. Lyons Brown, George Garvin Brown II, and Amelia Brown. Owsley died in 1952 and is buried in Louisville's Cave Hill Cemetery.

Brown-Forman grew to national prominence during the tenure of W.L. Lyons Brown, board chairman from 1951 to 1966 and 1969 to 1971; George Garvin Brown II, president from 1951 to 1966, and chairman from 1966 to 1969; and Robinson S. Brown Jr., the firm's first executive director of sales and marketing, and chairman from 1971 to 1982. D.L. Street, president from 1966 to 1969, and William F. Lucas, president from 1969 to 1975, also played important roles. Beginning in the 1950s, the company expanded its brands beyond Kentucky bourbon to include Jack Daniel's Tennessee Whiskey, Usher's Scotch Whiskey, Bushmill's Irish Whiskey, Pepe Lopez Tequila, Korbel California Champagne and Brandy, Bolla Italian Wines, Canadian Mist, and Southern Comfort.

In 1983 William Lee Lyons "Lee" Brown Jr., chief executive officer from 1975 to 1993, led the company in its first acquisition outside the beverage alcohol industry. The company acquired Lenox Inc., the leading American manufacturer of fine china and crystal, and its subsidiary, Hartmann Luggage. Brown, who retired in 1995 as board chairman, was born in Louisville on August 22, 1936, to W.L. Lyons and Sara (Shallenberger) Brown. He attended private schools and graduated from the University of Virginia and the American Graduate School of International Management. In 1960 he joined Brown-Forman in its international division and advanced to executive vice president and executive director of marketing for all domestic, import, and export operations before being elected president and chief executive officer. Brown married Alice Cary Farmer of Louisville in 1962; they had three children.

Owsley Brown II was selected to succeed his older brother W.L. Lyons "Lee" in 1993. Born September 10, 1942, he joined the company in 1969 as an assistant treasurer and served as president from 1983 to 1993. A 1964 graduate of Yale University with a B.A. in history and a 1966 M.B.A. degree from Stanford University, Brown also served for two years in U.S. Army Intelligence from 1966–68. Besides his leadership in the business community, Brown has served as officer in many arts-oriented organizations including Actor's Theatre, the Fund for the Arts, The Filson Club Historical Society, the Louisville Orchestra, and the Government Commission for the Kentucky Center for the Arts. Brown and his wife, Christina Lee, had one son and two daughters.

In the 1990s the management team included Owsley Brown II, Owsley Brown Frazier, and William M. Street, a vice chairman of the corporation and president and chief executive officer of the company's wine and spirits subsidiary, Brown-Forman Beverages Worldwide.

Owsley Brown Frazier, vice chairman and member of the executive committee and board of directors, began his career at Brown-Forman in 1955. He became resident counsel in 1959 and in 1960 company attorney, joining the board of directors in 1964. Frazier is a graduate of the old Louisville Country Day School and attended Centre College (Danville), returning during his sophomore year to attend the University of Louisville. He has an undergraduate degree and a law degree from the University of Louisville. Frazier is a committed community fund-raiser, having headed up campaigns for Kentucky educational institutions including BELLARMINE COLLEGE and the Louisville Country Day School. Frazier has served on community development committees including Kentucky Economic Development, Louisville Housing Development Corp., the Campaign for Greater Louisville, Downtown Development Corp., and the Regional Cancer Center. He is the son of Amelia Brown and Harry Frazier, a physician. Owsley Brown Frazier was born in 1935; he and his first wife, Anne, had three daughters.

The company continued to expand its beverage product line with Jack Daniel's Country Cocktails, Fetzer Vineyards California Wines, and Finlandia Vodka, while embarking on a drive to open new global markets. The Lenox Inc. subsidiary acquired Dansk International Designs and Gorham silver, stainless, and crystal products.

Brown-Forman has been a major contributor to and participant in community arts and educational institutions, with major contributions to Bellarmine College, the University of Louisville, J.B. Speed Art Museum, Actors Theatre of Louisville, Kentucky Center for the Arts, and the Filson Club Historical Society. The company has also supported many social causes, particularly in the area of affordable housing.

See John Ed Pearce, *Nothing Better in the Market,* (Louisville 1970).

John Ed Pearce

BROWN-GORDON MURDERS. Two of the most sensational murders in Louisville's criminal history occurred on May 30, 1895. This double murder was to have political consequences well beyond the city's limits. Archibald Dixon Brown, son and personal secretary of Gov. John Young Brown Jr., had a somewhat extended illicit relationship with Mrs. Nellie Bush Gordon, the wife of Fulton Gordon. The latter was a Louisville-Frankfort businessman who had served as a clerk in the GALT HOUSE hotel and the Kenyon House and was at the time a clerk in the Merchant's Advice.

Arch Brown had gone to Louisville on several occasions to meet Mrs. Gordon in Lucy Smith's house of assignation at 1025 W Madison St. On the occasion of the murders, an anonymous informant in Frankfort sent Fulton Gordon a telegram suggesting that he might want to investigate his wife's activities. The informant even gave Gordon the suggestion that she might be found at Lucy Smith's house.

Gordon armed himself with a revolver and went there. He found Arch Brown and his wife in bed in a room on the second floor. There was a scuffle in which Gordon shot and killed both his wife and Brown. There followed a sensational trial and much publicity and a period when Fulton Gordon was so emotionally unstable his doctor would not let him appear in court.

Governor Brown sent Col. James Scott, a fiery Frankfort attorney, to Louisville to represent his slain son in the trial, which was held on May 9, 1895, in the Louisville Police Court. At 3:30 that afternoon Judge Thompson issued the opinion that Fulton Gordon, under the law, was not guilty, and that his actions would teach adulterers a lesson. The *COURIER-JOURNAL* reported, "The verdict was received with cheers in the courtroom, and was generally commended all over the city." Colonel Scott commented, "If the judge is to be swayed by public opinion and the newspapers I was not. While I think he was sincere in his verdict, I believe he misinterpreted the law."

Occurring during the closing months of the Brown administration, the incident had a thwarting effect on the governor's political ambition. He wrote Cassius M. Clay Jr. on July 1, 1895, that because of the tragedies in his family he was withdrawing his candidacy for nomination to be a United States senator.

See John Young Brown Jr. to Cassius M. Clay Jr., July 1, 1895, Cassius M. Clay Jr. papers, Special Collections, Margaret I. King Library, University of Kentucky; *Courier-Journal*, May 1–10, 1895.

Thomas D. Clark

BROWNING, CHARLES ALBERT "TOD" (b Louisville, July 12, 1881; d Los Angeles, California, October 6, 1962). Cinema actor, writer, and director. The so-called Edgar Allen Poe of the cinema was born to Charles and Lydia J. (Fitzgerald) Browning. His uncle was the famous Louisville BASEBALL player PETE BROWNING. After dropping out of Louisville Boys' High School and working for several years as a stockboy and clerk at a wholesale saddlery, he ran away from home in late 1899 or early 1900 to join a circus. Performing as a clown and contortionist, he later joined the World of Mirth vaudeville troupe and toured the nation.

While visiting New York City in 1913, Browning began his cinematic career after he was hired as an actor for a project of director DAVID W. GRIFFITH, a fellow Kentuckian. Later that year Browning followed Griffith to Hollywood, where he continued acting and began to write scripts and direct two-reelers. Aside from playing a crook in the "Modern Story" section of Griffith's *Intolerance* (1916), Browning was also one of Griffith's twelve assistant directors.

In 1919 Browning, as director and screenwriter, collaborated with actor Lon Chaney Sr. on *The Wicked Darling* for Universal Studios. For a number of years following this project, Browning made several romantic melodramas before Chaney, who worked with Browning on a total of ten films, convinced MGM Studios to hire the struggling director. It was during this period that Browning found his niche in atmospheric horror films for which he later became famous. After returning to Universal, Browning directed his two most famous movies, the classic horror film *Dracula* (1931), starring Bela Lugosi, and the ghoulish *Freaks* (1932). Now a cult classic, *Freaks* aroused such controversy after its original release that the studio withdrew it from general circulation. It was rarely seen until it was honored at the 1962 Venice Festival. After the commercial failure of *Freaks*, Browning made only four more films before he retired in 1939 after completing *Miracles for Sale*.

Browning married Alice Houghton in 1918. Following his wife's death in 1944, he lived alone in their Malibu Colony home. He is buried in Los Angeles.

See Rory Guy, "Horror: The Browning Version," *Cinema* (June/July 1963): 26–28; George Geltzer, "Tod Browning," *Films in Review* (Oct. 1953): 410–16.

BROWNING, LOUIS RODGERS "PETE" (b Louisville, June 17, 1861; d Louisville, September 10, 1905). Professional baseball player. He was the son of Samuel and Mary Jane (Sheppard) Browning and the youngest of eight children.

Browning was the original LOUISVILLE SLUGGER, playing professional BASEBALL from 1882 until 1894. He had a career .341 batting average, the eleventh-highest in baseball history. He was one of only three among the all-time top-twenty hitters not to be enshrined in the Baseball Hall of Fame. The others are "Shoeless" Joe Jackson, who was banned from baseball for the 1919 "Black Sox" World Series scandal, and still-active Tony Gwynn.

Browning, who was known as the "Gladiator" more for his frequent battles with the media than for his style of play, spent most of his career with the Louisville team of the major-league American Association, a league that arose in 1882 to compete with the National League. The American Association dissolved in 1891. Browning, who won three batting titles, led the league in hitting in both 1882, his rookie year, with a .378 average, and 1885, with a .362 average. He hit a career-best .402 in 1887 but was beaten out by Tip O'Neill, who hit .435, the second-highest mark for a single season.

Although Browning was one of the best natural hitters in the game, he was a poor fielder. He had a lifetime .880 fielding percentage, reaching a personal low of .791 in 1886. Originally an infielder, Browning was moved to the outfield in 1885, more than once finishing as the league's worst-fielding center fielder.

After his worst season, 1889, he left the Colonels for the Cleveland Infants of the new Players League. There he won a third batting title with a .387 average in 1890. The league folded after a year, and Browning finished his career splitting seasons with five other teams, including Louisville, in the National League. He retired from the major leagues in 1894 with career totals of 295 doubles, 85 triples, 46 home runs, and 659 runs batted in. He played two more seasons in the minor leagues, retiring from baseball permanently in 1896.

Browning is perhaps best known for an incident that occurred off the field. According to Hillerich & Bradsby company lore, the first Louisville Slugger bat was lathed for Browning in a local wood-turning shop by a young apprentice, John Andrew "Bud" Hillerich, son of company founder J. Fred Hillerich. According to legend, Browning broke a bat during a spring game in 1884, and Hillerich jumped out of the stands and offered to make a new bat for the local hero out of white ash. Browning accepted the offer, and, after Browning knocked out three hits with the custom-made bats in the following game, demand quickly spread. It helped launch the Hillerich & Bradsby Co. The bats became known as Louisville Sluggers. The story's veracity has been questioned, competing with several other versions of how the first bat was turned.

After baseball, Browning opened a saloon at the corner of Thirteenth and Market Streets, across from St. Patrick's Catholic Church. The business failed, and he became a cigar salesman briefly before he retired to care for his mother.

Browning, who was illiterate and partially deaf, battled alcoholism throughout his life, even spending time in the Lakeland (later Central State Hospital) insane asylum shortly before his death. Browning lived with his mother at 1427 W Jefferson St. his whole life.

Browning is buried in Cave Hill Cemetery. In 1984, to commemorate the hundredth anniversary of Hillerich & Bradsby, the company, along with the city of Louisville, donated a new headstone to mark Browning's grave. He was also the uncle of movie director Tod Browning, who made the 1931 Bela Lugosi classic *Dracula*.

See Philip Von Borries, *Legends of Louisville: Major League Baseball in Louisville 1876–1899* (West Bloomfield, Mich., 1993).

BROWN MEMORIAL CME CHURCH. The edifice housing the current church, located at 813 W Chestnut St., is the last known work of noted Louisville architect Gideon Shryock, who also designed the Jefferson County Courthouse and the Old Kentucky State Capitol. The church is a blend of two distinct nineteenth-century styles: Greek Revival and Romanesque Revival. It was built as the Chestnut Street Methodist Church. Construction began in 1863 and was completed in 1864, with the formal dedication on Sunday, September 17, 1865.

The building was purchased in 1907 by the Center Street CME Church, then located on Center St. (Armory Place) between Green (Liberty) and Walnut (Muhammad Ali Blvd.). The Christian Methodist Episcopal church grew out of the Methodist church South. The Center Street CME Church was the first church of its denomination to be organized in Louisville—in 1870. The third general conference of the CME church was held in Louisville at the Center Street Church in 1874. Later the congregation, under the leadership of Dr. L.H. Brown, became the first black church in Louisville to move from an undesirable location. The Jefferson County Jail was built in front of the Center Street Church on Green (Liberty) St. at Sixth. It was then that Dr. Brown purchased the Chestnut St. property and moved the congregation to the new location.

The first service in the renamed Chestnut Street CME Church was held the second Sunday in May 1907. In May 1954 the congregation changed the name to Brown Memorial as a tribute to Dr. Brown. Three of its pastors became bishops: W.H. Miles (the first bishop of the CME Church), C.H. Phillips, and C.L. Russell. The church was rededicated on Sunday, April 1, 1990, following extensive restoration. The church was listed on the National Register of Historic Places in July 1979.

Evelyn L. Waldrop

Pete Browning (back row, 2nd from left) with 1882 Louisville Eclipse team.

BROWNSBORO-ZORN. Neighborhood in northeastern Louisville bounded by Brownsboro Rd. to the south, Birchwood Ave. and the Veterans Affairs Hospital to the west, Mellwood Ave. to the north, and the city limits to the east. Development began in the area in 1911 between Birchwood Ave. and Zorn Ave., which bisects the community. Although much of the neighborhood comprises single-family homes and apartment complexes, the area along Brownsboro Rd. is developed commercially. Local landmarks include the Veterans Medical Center, which moved to its present forty-seven-acre site on Zorn Ave. in 1952, and Selema Hall, a nationally registered Greek Revival house from the mid-nineteenth century. The area was the scene of the 1835 marriage of Sarah Knox Taylor, daughter of Zachary Taylor, and Jefferson Davis, in a now-vanished home at Brownsboro Rd. and Zorn Ave.

See Samuel W. Thomas, *Crescent Hill Revisited* (Louisville 1987).

BROWNSTOWN. Brownstown, a little-known African American community in part of what is now Old Louisville, developed shortly after the Civil War with the influx of former slaves into Louisville. The community was centered around Second and Magnolia Streets when this area was some distance from the built-up parts of the city. It was named for a man named Brown. The *Globe*, a short- lived newspaper, noted on September 3, 1875, that "the original Brown, a brown-skinned, gray-haired old man, for whom this place is named, is still located out here. He is growing old now and looks very much as one would suppose that 'old black Joe' looks."

The person may have been Henry Brown, a laborer who lived on the west side of Third St. between Bloom St. and Cardinal Blvd., originally B and C Streets. He is the only Brown shown in that area in city directories of the period. By 1875 the Little Flock African (Baptist) Church had been established on Second St. near Shipp Ave., an area now within the Belknap Campus of the University of Louisville. By the early 1880s there were two additional black churches: Zion Methodist on Second St. near Magnolia, and Washington Chapel (Methodist) on Second near Shipp.

Apparently, as in Smoketown to the northeast, the residents built "shotgun" cottages on leased land. The cottages were still in place on Second in the early 1890s between Magnolia and Bloom Streets, but during the decade were replaced with substantial brick homes as middle-class white suburbanization spread to the area and property values rose.

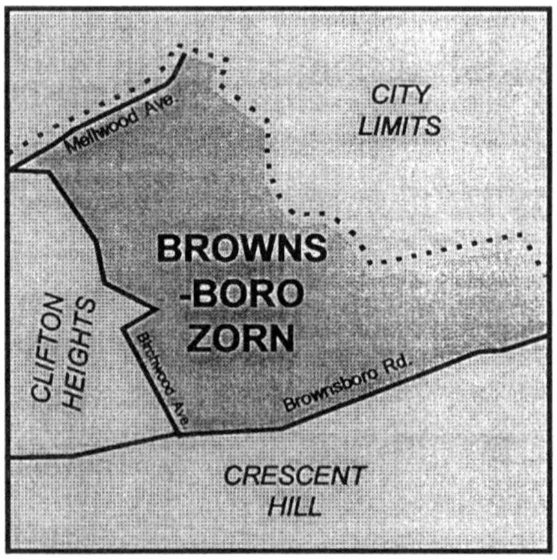

As old Brownstown vanished under the suburban tide, the black churches vanished too. The Little Flock Church had moved to E Broadway as early as 1886 and Zion Methodist to Fifteenth St. by 1893. Washington Chapel vanished from the record even earlier. The African American residents scattered to various parts of the city, some perhaps to the black community of Fort Hill directly to the east, which was named for a Civil War fort in the vicinity.

See *Caron's Louisville City Directories* for 1884–1892; *Sanborn Atlas: Louisville* (1892).

George H. Yater

BROWN SUBURBAN HOTEL. A large hotel, restaurant, and lounge complex built in the mid-1950s by Louisville real estate developer J. Graham Brown at 3300–4 Bardstown Rd. and Goldsmith Ln. It was the first major commercial complex constructed at the now-thriving Watterson Expressway interchange area and is an early example of motor lodges built near expressways. Brown said the complex was "designed to look like a Florida hotel."

Construction began on the initial 133 rooms and 400-seat restaurant in June 1955 at a cost of $2.5 million. Seventy-five rooms were added in 1957 at a cost of an additional $1 million. The expansion made the facility one of the largest of its kind south of the Ohio River. A twelve-story, eighty-six-unit apartment building was added in 1961. The apartments later were turned into condominiums.

Following Brown's death in 1969, the complex was sold in August 1971 for $3.1 million to a California real estate company that immediately turned the facility into a unit of the Motel 6 discount lodging chain and transformed the restaurant into a dinner theater. With a seating capacity of 312, the Showcase Playhouse opened in October 1971 with actress Imogene Coca and husband King Donovan starring in Neil Simon's *Plaza Suite.* By 1973 the restaurant had been reborn as the Toy Tiger bar and entertainment complex. The Motel 6 facilities became the Junction Inn in 1995, and the Toy Tiger was renamed Pharoah's in 1999.

See *Courier-Journal,* Aug. 2, 1971, June 24, 1955.

BRUCE, HELM (b Louisville, November 16, 1860; d Louisville, August 10, 1927). Attorney. Bruce was the son of Horatio Washington and Elizabeth Barbour (Helm) Bruce. His father was a prominent Louisville attorney who served in the Kentucky General Assembly, the Confederate Congress, and also as chancellor of one of the chancery divisions of the Jefferson (County) Circuit Court. His mother was the daughter of John L. Helm, a president of the Louisville & Nashville Railroad (L&N) and two-time governor of Kentucky. The elder Bruce was also general counsel for the L&N, a position his son would also hold.

Helm Bruce was educated at Louisville's public schools and graduated from Washington and Lee University in Lexington, Virginia, in 1880. He got his legal training at the University of Louisville, receiving his law degree in 1882. He began practicing law in April 1882 with Wilkins G. Anderson under the firm name Anderson and Bruce; the partnership lasted one year. In 1884 he re-formed the firm of Helm and Bruce with an uncle, James P. Helm, and it lasted until 1906. The original firm of Helm and Bruce had been formed before the Civil War by Bruce's father and uncle, Ben Hardin Helm, and was one of the most successful legal firms of its era. Ben Hardin Helm was married to Emily Todd, sister of Mary Todd Lincoln. After leaving the firm in 1906, Bruce practiced law without partners until 1910, when he teamed up with William Marshall Bullitt to form Bruce and Bullitt, which survived until Bruce's death.

Bruce was connected with some of the most celebrated legal cases of his day. As a leader of the fusionist movement (so named because it was a "fusion" of Republicans and Democratic reformers), Bruce, who led the legal team; his partner Bullitt; and another attorney, Alexander G. Barret, were responsible for bringing the case of fraud in the 1905 election to the Jefferson Circuit Court. The three attorneys, representing a group of business and community leaders calling themselves the Committee of One Hundred, alleged that the Democratic Party, led by the political machine of the brothers James and John Whallen, had stuffed or stolen ballot boxes and intimidated voters. The Kentucky Court of Appeals, then the highest court in the state, declared the election invalid in May 1907, and all the elected Democrats in both the city and county were removed from office. Gov. J.C.W. Beckham (1900–7) appointed individuals to fill the offices and serve out the remainder of the term.

Bruce also represented William Taylor, the Republican nominee for governor in the disputed 1899 election in which Democrat William Goebel was eventually declared the winner. Taylor initially won the election, but the results were overturned by the Democrat-led General Assembly, which ruled the results invalid due to fraud. Bruce represented Taylor in his case against Goebel and later in the case to determine who would succeed Goebel after his assassination—either Taylor or Goebel's lieutenant governor, J.C.W. Beckham. Taylor lost the case after the U.S. Supreme Court refused to hear it, letting stand the decision of the General Assembly to put Beckham in office.

Bruce also was involved in one of the most notorious civil cases in the city's history—the last will of Mary Lily Flagler Bingham, the wife of Robert Worth Bingham, patriarch of the famous newspaper publishing family. Mary Lily's immediate family, the Kenans, challenged a codicil to Mrs. Bingham's will, signed less than two months before her death, leaving $5 million to her husband. The Kenan family, led by her brother William, hired Bruce to represent the family in probate court. After a protracted court battle, the Kenans dropped their case against Bingham.

Bruce, an independent Democrat, was also active in state and national politics. He campaigned in favor of the National Prohibition (Volstead) Act and played an active role in the movement to repeal that portion of the anti-gambling act of 1886 that allowed pari-mutuel betting at Kentucky's racetracks, particularly through his leadership role in the Louisville Churchmen's Federation. The federation, a predecessor of the Louisville Area Council of Churches, was an organization of Protestant churches created in 1910 that helped launch the anti-gambling movement in the 1920s.

He also was active in business and civic affairs in the city, serving as director of the First National Bank, the Kentucky Title Trust Co., and the Fidelity and Columbia Trust Co. He was vice president of the Board of Trustees of the University of Louisville and served as director of the American Printing House for the Blind and the Louisville YMCA. He was also an elder in the Second Presbyterian Church from 1902 until his death.

In 1884 he married Sallie Hare White of Lexington. The couple had four children: James W., Elizabeth, Louise, and Helm Junior. Bruce died at St. Joseph's Infirmary after a brief illness. He is buried in Cave Hill Cemetery.

See Thomas D. Clark, *Helm Bruce, Public Defender: Breaking Louisville's Gothic Political Ring, 1905* (Louisville 1973); *Courier-Journal,* Aug. 11, 1927.

BRYANT, EDWIN (b near Pelham, Massachusetts, 1805; d Louisville, December 16, 1869). Journalist and diarist. He was the son of Silence and Ichabod Bryant. His father was a ne'er-do-well who spent some time in a debtors' prison, and he grew up at the home of his mother's brother in Bedford, New York. Bryant's academic record is unclear; he may have attended Brown University. In the mid-1820s he founded and edited the *Providence Literary Gazette* in Rhode Island and went on to edit the *New York Examiner* in Rochester.

While in Providence he became acquainted with George Prentice. Bryant arrived in Louisville in the fall of 1830, joining Prentice as co-editor of the newly established *Louisville Journal*. For a brief time he wrote editorials for the *Journal* under the signature "B." Bryant departed Louisville for Frankfort on January 27, 1831, to report on the doings of the General Assembly. When this fledgling newspaper failed to make enough money to support two editors, he went to Lexington in May to become editor of the *Lexington Observer*. In 1832 this paper was consolidated with the *Lexington Reporter*, which Bryant edited for two years. From 1834 to 1844 Bryant edited the *Lexington Intelligencer*.

Like Prentice, Bryant was a strong Henry Clay partisan. In 1844 Clay and Sen. John J. Crittenden persuaded Bryant to return to Louisville to establish a second Whig journal. Bryant then became associated with Walter N. Haldeman, who had acquired a failing newspaper called the *Daily Dime* that he was able to transform into the successful *Louisville Courier*.

On April 26, 1844, Haldeman announced that Bryant and a party of other young Louisville men had departed for California in search of better health, with Bryant expecting to write a book when he returned. In Independence, Missouri, the Bryant party joined that of Missouri governor Lillburn Boggs, a native of Lexington, and Gen. William "Owl" Russell of Fayette and Nicholas Counties. Between Independence and Fort Laramie, dissension caused Bryant's party, along with William Russell, to mount themselves on Missouri mules and set off over Hastings Cutoff to the Great Salt Lake, the Humboldt River, and the Johnson Ranch on the Sacramento River. The party arrived in San Francisco on September 21, 1846.

In California Bryant became involved in the fight to wrest the region from Mexican control. He was also a figure in the dispute between Gen. Stephen Watts Kearny and John C. Frémont, leader of volunteer troops, over the command of the Los Angeles post. Active in establishing American control of San Francisco and the bay area, Bryant was appointed alcalde (mayor) of the town, a position that favored his speculation in town lots on the bay front.

On June 2, 1847, Bryant joined General Kearny's party to return to Kentucky. In the return party was Frémont, a prisoner of General Kearny's command. Bryant's detailed overland journal, *What I Saw in California* (1848), quickly went through seven editions and then through eleven further editions. The book came from the press just in time to become the cardinal guide book for gold rushers to California in 1849.

After Bryant's visit to Washington, D.C., to testify in the Kearny-Frémont dispute, he returned to Kentucky and settled in the literary colony of Pewee Valley. Twice more he visited California, the last time making the journey by the just-opened transcontinental Union Pacific Railroad train in June 1869. The sale of the San Francisco lots yielded a happy financial return. In December 1869 Bryant became seriously ill and was moved to the Willard Hotel on W Jefferson St. in Louisville, where on December 16 he jumped to his death. He was buried in Cave Hill Cemetery and reburied in Spring Grove Cemetery in Cincinnati.

See Edwin Bryant, *What I Saw in California: Being the Journal of a Tour* (New York 1848); Thomas D. Clark, "Edwin Bryant and the Opening of the Road to California," *Essays in Western History in Honor of T.A. Larson* (Laramie, Wyo., 1979).

Thomas D. Clark

BUCHANAN V. WARLEY. A decision of the United States Supreme Court on November 5, 1917, that held unconstitutional a 1914 Louisville ordinance prohibiting a person from moving into a block where a majority of the residents were of another race. The housing ordinance, passed unanimously by the Louisville Board of Aldermen, stated that, once a house or an apartment became vacant after May 11, 1914, only members of the same race last living in the house could move into it. It also prohibited African Americans from building a home in areas that were designated for whites and vice versa. Violators would be fined no less than five dollars a day and no more than fifty dollars a day. By November of that year, the Louisville branch of the National Association for the Advancement of Colored People (the local branch grew out of opposition to the ordinance) had developed a test case to challenge the ordinance. William Warley, a member of the local NAACP, purchased a lot in the Portland neighborhood from Charles Buchanan, a white realtor opposed to the ordinance. In the sales agreement, it was stated by Warley: "It is understood that I am purchasing the above property for the purpose of having erected thereon a home which I propose to make my residence, it is a distinct part of this agreement that I shall not be required to accept a deed on the above property or to pay for the said property unless I have the right under state laws of the state of Kentucky and the city of Louisville to occupy said property as said residence."

Although the property was in a white area, Buchanan agreed to Warley's terms. On December 1, 1914, Buchanan's lawyer, Clayton Blakey, filed suit in Jefferson County Court to test the validity of the ordinance. To avoid collusion, Warley asked city attorney Pendleton Beckley to represent him. Here was an unusual case of a white man who called for the outlawing of the discriminatory ordinance, while a black man was fighting to uphold it.

The Jefferson Circuit Court upheld the constitutionality of the Louisville housing ordinance and dismissed Buchanan's suit in April 1915. That June the Kentucky Court of Appeals unanimously agreed with the ruling of the circuit court. On April 17, 1917, the Supreme Court (with Louisvillian Louis D. Brandeis a new member) heard the case of *Buchanan v. Warley*. Beckley and Stuart Chevalier, who represented Warley, argued that the ordinance applied equally to whites as well as to blacks and that failure to uphold the ordinance would spur racial antagonism and the destruction of white property values. Buchanan was represented by Moorfield Storey, president of the NAACP, and Clayton Blakey, who argued that the ordinance restricted the rights of citizens to buy and sell property, thereby depriving them of income without due process of law. They further argued that, even if the law was applied equally to both races, "the Constitution cannot be satisfied by any such offsetting of inequality and that inequality against one race is not [a] whit less a discrimination because in some other matter a discrimination is made against the other race."

The Supreme Court held that the ordinance denied members of both races the right to own and dispose of property as they saw fit and thus violated the due-process clause of the Constitution as well as the Civil Rights Act of 1866. States and municipalities, the Court conceded, should be accorded wide latitude in meeting the asserted objectives of the ordinance—protecting racial purity, preserving racial peace, and maintaining property values. However, such objectives could "not be promoted by depriving citizens of their constitutional rights and privileges." Nor, upon analysis, was the ordinance found to be reasonably related to the attainment of its stated objectives.

The Court distinguished the Buchanan case from precedents like *Plessy v. Ferguson* (1896) and *Berea College v. Kentucky* (1908) that had upheld state segregation laws. The laws upheld in these cases merely limited the enjoyment of a right by "reasonable rules in regard to the separation of races." By contrast, the Court asserted, the Louisville ordinance imposed absolute limitations on the disposal of property and thus amounted to an unconstitutional taking. Although the *Buchanan* case did not overturn the precedents, its affirmation of federal civil rights laws and amendments and its recognition of limits on segregation were one of the first judicial steps away from Jim Crow.

See Paul A. Freund and Stanley N. Katz, eds., *History of the Supreme Court of the United States* (New York 1984); George Wright, *Life Behind a Veil: Blacks in Louisville, Kentucky 1865–1930* (Baton Rouge, La., 1985); idem, "The NAACP and Residential Segregation in Louisville, Kentucky, 1914–1917," *Register of the Kentucky Historical Society* (Winter 1980): 39–54.

BUCKLIN, JOHN CARPENTER (b Providence, Rhode Island, 1773; d Louisville,

March 5, 1844). Louisville's first mayor. Bucklin was the son of Daniel and Elizabeth (Carpenter) Bucklin, the youngest of seven children. Daniel Bucklin was a mariner and merchant in Providence, Rhode Island. During the Revolutionary War he was a captain in the navy.

John Bucklin followed his father into the shipping and trading businesses. He was a captain and first lieutenant in the Rhode Island militia. He owned and captained several trade ships, some of which made excursions to South America. In 1803 he married Sarah Smith in Providence. She was the daughter of Capt. Simon Smith, a prosperous merchant and shipper. The couple had eight children.

For a time in the early 1800s, Bucklin and his family lived in New York City and Baltimore, at one time residing at the same New York boarding establishment as Washington Irving. The family moved to Louisville between 1819 and 1820. In 1823 Bucklin became secretary of the Louisville Insurance Co., the second INSURANCE company to be chartered in Kentucky. He was an active member of the UNITARIAN Church. He was also a merchant, selling a variety of goods such as Alabama cotton, green coffee, and stock in the Louisville and Shippingport Turnpike Road Co., according to advertisements of the day.

Bucklin became Louisville's first MAYOR on March 3, 1828, after the state legislature approved the new CITY CHARTER in February. Initially the mayor, who served a one-year term, was not directly selected by popular election. By terms of the charter, the top two vote-getters were presented after the March election to the governor, who then commissioned the mayor with the advice and consent of the state Senate. Between 1828 and 1836, when the City Council was briefly given authority to select the mayor, the top vote-getter was always selected to serve. In the first contest, Bucklin defeated William T. Tompkins by a mere 20 votes out of the close to 650 votes cast. Bucklin served six one-year terms of office from 1828 to 1834.

Under the city's first charter, the mayor was not allowed any judicial authority in civil matters but did have the power of justice of the peace over slaves and free blacks. The mayor also had no vote on the City Council, with the exception of breaking a deadlock.

During his second year in office, he urged the City Council to act on a provision of the city's first charter calling for the establishment of a free school. The first PUBLIC SCHOOL was opened in the upper story of the Baptist church on the southeast corner of Fifth and Green (LIBERTY) STREETS. It was the first public school in Kentucky and had 250 students. The first city school building was built on the southwest corner of Fifth and Walnut (Muhammad Ali Blvd.) Streets in 1830. The school averaged four hundred students, all of them white children between the ages of six and fourteen. They were under the care of three teachers.

Bucklin also had to deal with one of Louisville's most devastating FLOODS. On February 10, 1832, floodwater reached more than fifty-one feet above the low-water mark, causing major damage to homes and businesses in the city. Three miles of wagon road running between Louisville and PORTLAND was also built during Bucklin's tenure. Bucklin was instrumental in the drive to drain the city's numerous disease-infested ponds, which had earned the city the nickname "Pondtown."

He died suddenly at his home on Green St. (Liberty). His widow stayed in Louisville until her death in 1856. He is buried in Cave Hill Cemetery.

See *Louisville Times,* May 10, 1962; Josiah Stoddard Johnston, ed., *Memorial History of Louisville,* vol. 1 (Chicago and New York 1896); *Herald- Post,* Aug. 24, 1930; Attia Martha Bowmer, *The History of the Government of the City of Louisville 1780–1870,* M.A. thesis, University of Louisville, 1948.

BUECHEL. A mixed residential and commercial suburb in southeast Louisville, roughly bounded by Bashford Manor Ln. and Hikes Ln. to the north, Breckenridge Ln. to the east, Buechel Bank Rd. to the south, and Newburg Rd. to the west.

About 1791 George HIKES, whose family cemetery and a rebuilt version of his cabin still existed in the 1990s, migrated to the area from Pennsylvania and built a sawmill, gristmill, and wool-processing machine. The area along Bardstown Rd. may have been known as Two-Mile Town for its location in Two-Mile Precinct, so named due to its northern edge's distance from Louisville. Two-Mile Town's population slowly grew as vegetable farmers moved to the unspoiled pasture lands.

In 1883, John Buechel, a cabinetmaker from Switzerland, established a post office at the White Cottage, a tavern he had acquired in 1880 that soon became known as the Buechel Tavern. The saloon and hotel, situated just south of the Southern Railway tracks, became a popular stop for those who disembarked at Stine's Station after rail lines came through town in 1888. However, the area did not officially adopt its name until 1883 when John Buechel moved the POST OFFICE to a separate building near his tavern. The saloon was destroyed by fire in 1983.

Bank of Buechel.

Buechel Produce Exchange was built around 1900 by Charles Scoggans. The building was used by local farmers who were shipping their crops (apples, peaches, onions, and potatoes) via the Southern Railway. At the turn of the century, the area received increased attention because of the three Derby winners, Azra in 1892, Manuel in 1899, and Sir Huon 1906, produced by George Long's BASHFORD MANOR Farm, later the site of Bashford Manor Mall. This publicity prompted the establishment of the community's first bank in 1909, and a commercial strip along Bardstown Rd. that included a grocery store, a drugstore, a hardware store, and a barber shop.

The area, a popular distribution site for illegal whiskey during PROHIBITION, continued its steady growth until WORLD WAR II, as the farms gradually gave way to suburban development. Buechel received its most substantial boost in 1950 when the GENERAL ELECTRIC CO. revealed plans to purchase roughly seven hundred acres adjacent to the community and construct Appliance Park. The resulting influx of workers and their families created not only a housing boom but significant traffic problems. Buechel Bypass Rd. was built just to the west of the Bardstown Rd. and significantly improved traffic flow. A year after the GE announcement, Louisville officials declared their plans to annex the Buechel area. This prompted several residents to incorporate themselves as the sixth-class city of West Buechel in 1952. The remaining residents continually challenged the annexation proposal in court until 1955 when Louisville called off the attempt due to the bitterness the proposal had caused.

See *A Place in Time: The Story of Louisville's Neighborhoods* (Louisville 1989); *History of the Ohio Falls Cities and their Counties* (Cleveland 1882).

BUELL, DON CARLOS (b near Marietta, Ohio, March 23, 1818; d Muhlenberg County, Kentucky, November 19, 1898). CIVIL WAR general. Following the death of his father, the five-year-old Buell, son of Salmon D. and Eliza Buell, was sent to live with his uncle George P. Buell in Leavenworth, Indiana. He graduated from the U.S. Military Academy at West Point on July 1, 1841, and on June 18, 1846, was promoted to first lieutenant. Buell served in the MEXICAN WAR and was brevetted a captain for meritorious service during the Battle of Monterrey. After the war he became assistant adjutant general (1848–49), then served in the Washington military bureaucracy as chief of several departments. On May 11, 1861, Buell was promoted to lieutenant colonel and in July was made brigadier general in the United States Volunteers.

During the Civil War, Buell arrived in Louisville on November 15, 1861, and assumed command of the Department of the Ohio, which included Kentucky. His actions were instrumental in keeping Kentucky in the Union. On February 14, 1862, Buell entered and took control of Bowling Green as a Confederate force under Gen. Albert S. Johnston retreated toward Nashville. The following September, Buell was again in Louisville and prepared to repulse Gen. Braxton Bragg's Confederate invasion of Kentucky. Initially, Buell and most of his forces had to retreat into the defenses protecting Louisville, and many civilians were evacuated across the river. Then Buell's Federals surprised Bragg at Bardstown, forcing him to divide his army and withdraw south. Buell and others pursued and engaged the Confederates at Perryville on October 8, 1862. The following day, Bragg withdrew to Harrodsburg, while Buell moved to Danville, thus threatening Bragg's line of communication. With a superior cavalry force, Bragg completed his retreat from Kentucky through the Cumberland Gap.

Buell's failure to prevent Bragg's escape, along with his refusal to permit confiscation of property in Kentucky, Tennessee, and Alabama, precipitated questions about his loyalty; he was relieved of command on October 30, 1862, by Maj. Gen. William S. Rosecrans. On April 25, 1863, a commission hearing the allegations reported no serious misjudgments and recommended that Buell be returned to duty. The damage to Buell's reputation had been done, however, and his political enemies prevented his reassignment. He resigned his commission on June 1, 1864. Buell then moved to Kentucky, becoming president of the Green River Iron Co. in Muhlenberg County. In 1885 Buell returned to Louisville after receiving a presidential appointment as state pension agent. He held the position until 1890 and resided in the GALT HOUSE.

Buell married Margaret (Hunter) Mason of Mobile, Alabama, and adopted her daughter by a previous marriage. He died on November 19, 1898, at his Airdrie estate in Muhlenberg County and is buried in Bellefontaine Cemetery in St. Louis.

See Hobert L. Sanders, "The Military Career of Don Carlos Buell during the Civil War," M.A. thesis, University of Kentucky, 1937.

BULL, JOHN (b near Simpsonville, Kentucky, 1813; d Louisville, April 26, 1875). Patent medicine man. At the age of twelve, Bull moved to Louisville and became a porter in Hyers and Butler's drugstore. He studied medicine under a Dr. Shrock and later became J.B. Wilder & Co.'s prescription clerk. Bull concocted at home a sarsaparilla and soon went in business for himself.

By forty he was making "at least $20,000 by his nostrum." By 1854 the R.G. Dun and Co. credit agency reported that "Bull is rich and coining money by his preparation." Two years later he moved away but returned chastened after losing some ten thousand dollars and complaining that New Yorkers "are a sharp set of fellows."

Bull soon revived his operation "making sarsaparilla as fast as ever and shipping it off as fast as he makes it." By 1860 he employed fifteen men. Most of his raw material expenses were for sarsaparilla and bottles at a factory located on Fifth between MAIN and Water STREETS. Proceeds were equally divided among his pills, sarsaparilla concoction, and an anti-worm product. Profits were moderate. The CIVIL WAR came, and by mid-1861 he was "doing very little business." Nine months later the sheriff seized his factory and stock. He was in such straits that he was thankful to become federal provost marshal at seventy-five dollars monthly.

Nonetheless, by 1868 his taxable income was $132,963. In 1870 the figure was pared to $123,112, still $45,000 more than any other Louisvillian. By 1874 he was selling between four and five hundred thousand dollars' worth of his Bull's Worm Destroyer, Smith's Tonic Syrup, and Cedron Bitters, and employed fifty men. His office was located on Main beween Eighth and Ninth Streets, with another office near the Fifth St. factory. Patent medicines were heavily laced with alcohol, which proved as addictive to their consumers as the fifteen to twenty cigars Bull smoked daily. He reportedly died "of congestion of the brain" and is buried in CAVE HILL CEMETERY.

See *History of the Ohio Falls Cities and Their Counties* (Cleveland 1882); *Courier-Journal*, Feb. 22, 1874, April 27, May 4, 1875; R.G. Dun and Company Collection, Baker Library, Harvard University Graduate School of Business, Kentucky 24: 23.

Stuart S. Sprague

BULLITT, ALEXANDER SCOTT (b Dumfries, Virginia, 1762; d Louisville, April 13, 1816). Pioneer, political leader. Born in 1762 to Judge Cuthbert and Helen (Scott) Bullitt of Dumfries, Virginia, he was the nephew of THOMAS BULLITT, who had originally surveyed the site of the city of Louisville in 1773. Bullitt was elected to the Virginia House of Delegates at the age of twenty. After he was commissioned a major in the militia of Prince William County in 1785, he left for the Kentucky frontier, where he had visited prior to 1784, claiming that he wanted to make his fortune fighting Indians. He settled on Bull Skin Creek in SHELBY COUNTY for two years. However, Bullitt decided that not only was his land too far from the FALLS OF THE OHIO but that the Indians made life too difficult. He then moved to A'Sturgis Station in eastern Jefferson County where he purchased a thousand–acre tract of land adjoining the two-thousand–acre farm of Col. WILLIAM CHRISTIAN.

Bullitt married Colonel Christian's daughter, Priscilla, and the couple received a thousand acres on BEARGRASS CREEK and Goose Creek from Christian's holdings as a wedding present. The land became known as OXMOOR. Who named the tract is in dispute, but all agree the name Oxmoor came from the book *Tristram Shandy.* The following year, Bullitt was named lieutenant in the Jefferson County militia by Patrick Henry. He was also designated one of the trustees of Louisville by the Virginia legislature. In 1788 Bullitt was a delegate to the Kentucky convention in Danville, and, in 1792, he helped George Nicholas draft the state's first constitution. He was selected as one of the eleven original state senators and was elected speaker of the Senate, a position he held until 1804. During the state's second constitutional convention in 1799, Bullitt oversaw the drafting of a new constitution that remained in place until 1850. In 1800 he was elected as Kentucky's first lieutenant governor. Bullitt continued to serve in the Senate until his retirement in 1808. BULLITT COUNTY was named for him.

He married Priscilla Christian on January 31, 1786. They had four children: Cuthbert, Annie, Helen, and William Christian. Priscilla died on November 11, 1806. Bullitt married Mary (Churchill) Prather on July 31, 1807; they had three children: Thomas, James, and Mary. Bullitt is buried in the Oxmoor Cemetery.

See Thomas W. Bullitt, Oxmoor and the Bullitts: 1685–1980 (Louisville 1981); Thomas W. Bullitt, *My Life at Oxmoor: Life on a Farm in Kentucky before the War* (Louisville 1995).

BULLITT, HENRY MASSIE (b Shelby County, Kentucky, February 28, 1817; d Louisville, February 5, 1880). Physician and teacher. The son of Cuthbert and Harriet (Willett) Bullitt, Henry began studying medicine with Dr. Coleman Rogers Sr. of Louisville in 1834 and graduated with high honors from the medical school of the University of Pennsylvania in 1838. Bullitt set up a medical partnership with Dr. Joshua B. Flint in Louisville. In 1845 he went to Europe for further medical study and the next year began teaching medicine at St. Louis Medical College. He returned to Kentucky in 1848 and taught for a year at Transylvania University.

In 1850 Bullitt helped establish the Kentucky School of Medicine in Louisville, where he served as professor of physiology and pathology and dean of faculty until 1866. Bullitt then served as chair of theory and practice of MEDICINE (1866) and physiology (1867) at the UNIVERSITY OF LOUISVILLE. He left his chair in 1868 to help found the Louisville Medical College, where he remained until his death. The two private medical colleges that Bullitt helped establish later became part of the University of Louisville Medical School.

During his career, Bullitt served as associate editor of the medical journals of the various institutions where he taught: the *St. Louis Medical Journal*, the *Transylvania Journal of Medicine*, and the *Louisville Medical Record*, which he founded. Two of his best-known articles were "The Art of Observing in Medicine" in an 1847 issue of the *St. Louis Medical Journal* and "Medical Organization and Reform," which appeared in the *Transylvania Journal of Medicine*.

Bullitt married Julia Anderson on May 26, 1841; they had seven children, two of whom survived to adulthood. After he was widowed, he married Sarah Crow Paradise on September 14, 1854; they had six children, one son and five daughters. Bullitt, who suffered from Bright's disease, is buried in Cave Hill Cemetery.

See Howard A. Kelly and Walter L. Burrage, *American Medical Biographies* (Baltimore 1920).

BULLITT, THOMAS (b Prince William County, Virginia, 1730; d Fauquier County, Virginia, 1778). Surveyor, soldier, and explorer. One of five children of Benjamin and Elizabeth (Harrison) Bullitt, he entered the militia at an early age and achieved the rank of captain for his service in the Virginia regiment during the French and Indian War (1754–63).

He commanded companies under Col. George Washington between 1754 and 1758, and it was reported that Bullitt saved Washington's troops at the battle near Fort Duquesne (more commonly known as Braddock's Defeat) on July 9, 1755; however, a disagreement with the future president hampered Bullitt's chances for quick advancement. In the opening years of the American Revolution, Bullitt served as deputy adjutant general and adjutant general, 1776–77, and as a colonel, 1776–78, in the southern department of the Virginia militia.

In 1773 Bullitt was commissioned by Lord Dunmore, the governor of Virginia, to lead a group of approximately forty men into Kentucky to begin surveying land claims in the fertile Ohio River Valley for officers who had served in the French and Indian War. Bullitt undertook his expedition later that summer with additional support from William and Mary College.

After being joined by Isaac Hite's party along the way, the group extensively explored the Big Bone Lick in Boone County. By early July, Bullitt and his men reached the Falls of the Ohio and placed their camp just north of the mouth of Beargrass Creek.

The surveyors, wandering as far as what became known as Bullitt's Lick on the Salt River, surveyed the land that is now Louisville. They reportedly platted a town on the site of the future city, although the plan was never realized. Bullitt left Kentucky later in the year and did not return. He resigned his commission in 1776. He died in Virginia without marrying, leaving his entire estate to his brother, Judge Cuthbert Bullitt.

See Neal O. Hammon, "Pioneers in Kentucky, 1773–1775," *Filson Club History Quarterly* 55 (July 1981): 268–69; *History of the Ohio Falls Cities and Their Counties* (Cleveland, Ohio, 1882); Thomas W. Bullitt, *Oxmoor and the Bullitts (1685–1980)* (Louisville 1981); Thomas W. Bullitt, *My Life at Oxmoor: Life on a Farm in Kentucky before the War* (Louisville 1995).

BULLITT, WILLIAM MARSHALL (b Louisville, March 4, 1873; d Louisville, October 3, 1957). Attorney. William Marshall Bullitt was a descendant of one of Louisville's pioneer families. The son of Thomas and Annie (Logan) Bullitt, he received his early education in Louisville at Miss Sally Booth's School, the Rugby School, and Trinity Hall. In 1889 he attended prep school at the Lawrenceville School in New Jersey, and the following year he enrolled in Princeton University, where he graduated with a B.S. degree in 1894. Returning to Louisville, Bullitt earned his law degree from the University of Louisville in 1895.

Bullitt joined the law firm of Bullitt & Shield, in which his father and Charles A. Shield were partners. Through the years the firm became Bullitt & Bullitt; then Bruce & Bullitt; Bruce, Bullitt, & Gordon; Bruce, Bullitt, Gordon, & Laurent; Bruce & Bullitt again; and Bullitt & Middleton. At the time of his death, he was senior partner in the firm of Bullitt, Dawson, & Tarrant, which had been formed in 1948.

In 1912 President William Howard Taft appointed Bullitt solicitor general of the United States, a post he held for one year. The following year he was the unsuccessful Republican nominee for the U.S. Senate. The final year of World War I (1918) found Bullitt in Paris, representing the American Red Cross as deputy commissioner for France with the rank of major. In 1921 he became special counsel to the United States Shipping Board and in 1924 was named special assistant to the attorney general of the United States. Throughout his long career, Bullitt argued more than fifty cases before the Supreme Court.

During the first half of the twentieth century, Bullitt was regarded as one of Louisville's most influential figures. In law, banking, commerce, real estate, and politics his expertise was widely known and highly respected. He was a trustee of the Carnegie Endowment for International Peace, served as chairman of the Board of Public Safety of Louisville, sat on the boards of numerous banks and insurance companies, wrote a number of pamphlets, and was editor of *Bullitt's Civil and Criminal Codes of Kentucky, 1899–1902.* Among his varied interests and hobbies were early murder trials in Kentucky, mathematics, and the collection of first editions, especially publications of the great mathematicians.

Bullitt married Nora Iasigi of Boston, Massachusetts, on May 31, 1913. They had three children: Thomas, Nora, and Barbara. He is buried in the cemetery at Oxmoor, the Bullitt ancestral estate near Louisville.

See Mary Young Southard, ed., *Who's Who in Kentucky* (Louisville 1936); Winfield Scott Downs, ed., *The Encyclopedia of American Biography* (New York 1959).

Kenneth Dennis

BULLITT COUNTY. Named after Kentucky pioneer and politician Alexander Scott Bullitt, owner of the Oxmoor estate, Bullitt County, Kentucky, is located in north-central Kentucky immediately south of and adjacent to Jefferson County. Bullitt is bounded on the east by Spencer County, on the south by Nelson County, and on the west by Hardin County. It was created by an act of the Kentucky legislature on December 13, 1796. Bullitt County, taken from parts of Jefferson and Nelson Counties, was the twentieth county to be created. Nelson County had been created in 1784, being taken from Jefferson County. Salt River was the dividing line between the two counties.

Selected Statistic for Bullitt County, 1990

Population	47,567
Population per Square Mile	159
Percent African-American	0.4
Percent 0-17 Years	29.3
Percent 65 Years and Older	6.8
Percent 25 Years and Older with a High School Degree or Equivalency	64.7
Percent 25 Years and Older with a Bachelors Degree	6.3
Per Capita Income in 1989	$29,455
Unemployment Rate (%)	6.4
Married-Couple Families as a Percent of Total Households	71.7
Median Home Value	$51,000

At the time of its creation, all that part of Bullitt County that lies north of Salt River was taken from Jefferson County, and all that part of the county that lay south of Salt River was taken from Nelson County. In 1811 a small pie-shaped wedge of land was taken from Jefferson County and added to western Bullitt County. This addition extended the western boundary from the mouth of Brier Creek to Pond Creek, the present-day boundary between Bullitt and Jefferson. In 1824 a section of land was taken from eastern Bullitt County and added to land taken from other counties to create a new county called Spencer. Bullitt's present shape has remained the same since then.

Approximately 58 percent of Bullitt's land area is covered by the land formation called the Knobs. Salt River runs roughly through the middle of the county, entering from Spencer County to the east and exiting to the west between Jefferson and Hardin Counties. Floyd's Fork empties into Salt River from the north, a short distance from Shepherdsville. The Rolling Fork forms the southwest boundary of Bullitt County, joining the Salt at a place that was once the town of Pitts Point. The Salt continues from this point northwest to West Point, where it empties into the Ohio River. Other streams in the county include Knob Creek, Blue Lick Creek, Pennsylvania Run, Cedar Creek (north), Brooks Run, Mud Run, Brown's Run,

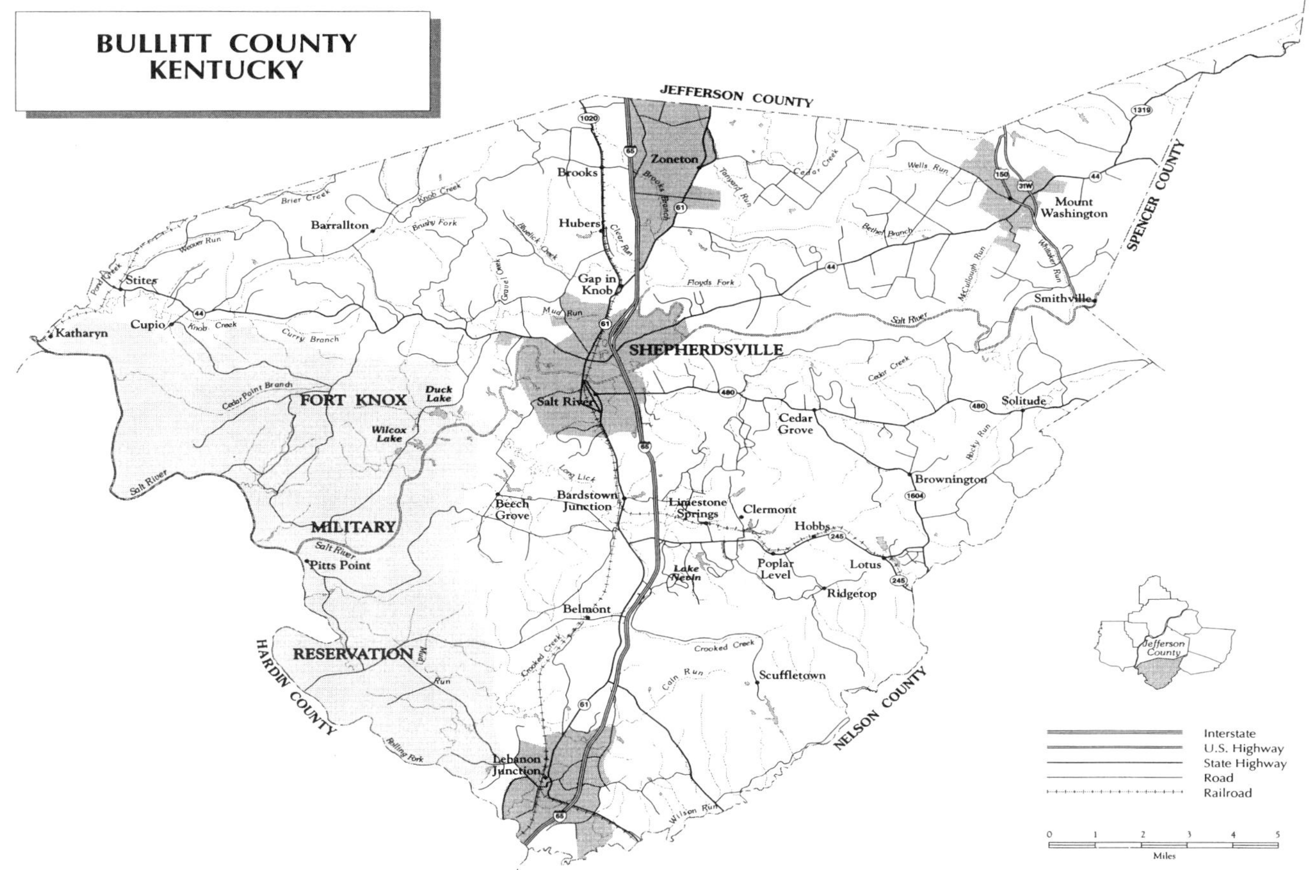

Long Lick Creek, Cedar Creek (south), Crooked Creek, Cane Run, Cox's Creek, East Fork and West Fork of Cox's Creek, Buffalo Run, Whitaker Run, Wilson Creek, Little Dutchman Creek, McCullough Run, and Weaver's Run, as well as numerous smaller streams.

The first fort constructed in Bullitt County was Brashear's Station, built in 1779. It was the first fort built on the road between the FALLS OF THE OHIO and Harrodsburg. Other forts built by the early settlers included Mud Garrison, Dowdall's Station, Clear's Cabins, and Fort Nonsense.

Early settlers needed SALT to preserve their food. Salt was brought from eastern settlements, if it could be had. Bullitt County contained a number of SALT LICKS from which salt could be produced so the production of salt was a drawing force for many settlers to come to Bullitt County. During the earliest pioneer days, salt was used in the place of money. The largest and most extensively developed salt lick was BULLITT'S LICK, discovered by Capt. THOMAS BULLITT in 1773 and opened by others for the production of salt in 1779. Other licks used for the production of salt included the Long Lick, Dry Lick, Iron's Lick, and Parakeet Lick.

Shepherdsville, the oldest city in Bullitt County, was established in 1793, just one year into Kentucky's statehood and three years before the county was created. The town is named for Adam Shepherd, who set aside fifty acres on the north bank of Salt River at the place known as the Falls of Salt River. Shepherd owned nine hundred acres on the north side and six hundred acres on the south side. Shepherd picked the site because it was the best crossing of Salt River. When Bullitt County was created, Shepherdsville became the county seat.

The second town to be established was MOUNT WASHINGTON, originally named Mount Vernon after the home of George Washington. Located on the Louisville-to-Bardstown turnpike, the town was referred to as Crossroads by the early nineteenth century and was an important stop on that road. It was chartered in 1822 on fifty acres of land that had been set aside from the lands of Joseph Hough, a county justice of the peace. Its name was changed to Mount Washington in 1830 when a post office was applied for; the Mount Vernon name had been preempted by the seat of Rockcastle County, Kentucky.

There are deposits of low-grade iron ore in various parts of the county. The discovery of this ore led to the development of an iron industry that lasted for several years. The manufacture of iron and iron products began as early as 1819, when John W. Beckwith began the construction of a forge, rolling mill, and grist mill on the Salt River just west of Shepherdsville. Two furnaces, the Salt River furnace and the Belmont Furnace, furnished the pig iron to be made into various products. Many people were employed in ironmaking: teamsters to drive the large ore wagons, woodcutters to cut the wood to be made into charcoal to fire the furnaces, hands at the furnaces, workers at the slitting mills, and even operators of the company store.

In 1837 the Shepherdsville Iron Manufacturing Co. was established at the site of Beckwith's works. Notable products included the Shaker stoves found at Shakertown at Pleasant Hill. The decline of the iron industry in Bullitt County was caused by larger and better-grade iron ore deposits being found elsewhere. The panic of 1837, a nationwide economic downturn, also contributed to the decline of Bullitt's iron industry.

Pitts Town, more commonly called Pitts Point, was the third city to be established in Bullitt County. In 1831 two brothers, James G. and John S. Pitts, purchased six hundred acres of land from Abraham Froman. This acreage included the land that bordered the junction of the Rolling Fork and Salt Rivers. Froman operated a ferry at the location. The Pitts brothers laid out twenty-eight lots to the town that bore their name. Buyers of lots were to pay their money to Froman. Pitts Point was important because of its location on the Salt River. Boats could travel up Salt River as far as Pitts Point anytime there was sufficient water to float a boat—usually at least six months of the year. The rivers beyond Pitts Point could be navigated only a limited distance unless the Rolling Fork and the Salt were in high water. Timber and farm products could be brought to Pitts Point and loaded on boats to be shipped to markets, particularly to Louisville. The town is no longer in existence; its demise was brought about by the expansion of FORT KNOX. The entire town was purchased and made a part of the military reservation. It was allowed to fall into decay until today there is very little trace of its existence.

In 1838 John D. Colmesnil opened what proved to be a popular and fashionable mineral spring called Paroquet Springs that was situated near Shepherdsville and was just nineteen miles southeast of Louisville. Originally a salt lick, the water contained minerals that made a poor-quality salt, but with the promotion of its medicinal qualities the lick blossomed into a very important spa. At its peak, the grounds contained one hundred acres.

The Louisville & Nashville Railroad (now csx Transportation) was constructed through Bullitt County in the mid-1850s. The railroad not only opened Bullitt to new markets but also gave rise to a number of small communities, some of which remain today. The railroad enters Bullitt from the north and exits to the south, covering almost twenty miles. Two branch lines, the Bardstown branch and the Lebanon branch, created railroad junctions. As the railroad prospered, so did Bullitt. In the early days the railroad relied on wood to fuel its engines. This necessitated frequent stops to take on water and a supply of wood. Trains also hauled passengers, so many stops were made. Some of these stops developed into communities, while others remained merely flag stops where the train was halted by waving your arms.

Communities that came into being because of the railroad include Brooks, Hubers, Gap-In-Knob, Salt River, Bardstown Junction, Belmont, Lebanon Junction, Chapeze, Clermont, and Hobbs. When the railroad switched to diesel engines, the need for frequent stops for fuel and water was eliminated. Eventually passenger service was also eliminated. These two events contributed to the decline of the railroad communities, Lebanon Junction being the exception. Passing through these communities today reveals little of their once-thriving existence.

One community that has survived the changes in the railroad is Lebanon Junction, the fourth major city in Bullitt County. The town came into being because of its location, the point on the main line of the Louisville & Nashville Railroad where the branch line from Lebanon intersects. By the time of the Civil War, a hotel had been constructed. Over the years others moved to the area, and roads were built from other parts of the county to the junction. The real impetus came when the railroad constructed a coaling station and a roundhouse at the junction, increasing employment and population. The town was incorporated in 1895. During the early part of the twentieth century, Lebanon Junction was the largest town in Bullitt County. The railroad is no longer the primary employer in Lebanon Junction. An event that should ensure its continued growth and importance was the reconstruction of Interstate 65. Previously there was only an exit and entrance to the north; now there is a full interchange.

Several Civil War skirmishes occurred in the county, as well as troop movements on both sides. The railroad was under constant attack by Confederate forces. Bridges and other important structures were guarded by federal troops. Nonetheless, the railroad bridges across Salt River and Rolling Fork were destroyed.

Two disasters that are burned into the fabric of the county were the train wreck at Shepherdsville on December 20, 1917, and the 1937 flood. The train wreck resulted in fifty-one deaths and almost as many injuries when an express passenger train composed of nine steel cars rammed the rear of the Bardstown Accommodation train of three wooden cars. The local was full of passengers, most of whom had been Christmas shopping in Louisville. The 1937 flood affected many parts of the county, especially Shepherdsville, plus Lebanon Junction, Bardstown Junction, and areas all along the Salt River and its tributaries. It was the worst flooding in Shepherdsville's history, as well as in the history of Bullitt County.

Bullitt County had an important educational institution for blacks, Eckstein Norton Institute, opened in 1890. It was created by William J. Simmons and Charles H. Parrish Sr. and was named after Eckstein Norton, president of the Louisville & Nashville Railroad, who helped to raise money for the institution. The university offered academic and vocational training to pursue either bachelor of arts or bachelor of science degrees. In 1912 the university was merged with the newly established Lincoln Institute at Simpsonville, Kentucky.

Agriculture formed the basis of early Bullitt County wealth. Livestock was raised and sold in the Louisville market. Crop production was varied, with tobacco an important product. Bullitt County was drawn out of the agricultural age into modern times with the construction of the Kentucky Turnpike from Louisville to Elizabethtown in the 1950s. This modern limited-access highway had a full interchange at Shepherdsville and a partial interchange at Lebanon Junction. Population figures reflect the growth brought about by this highway: 9,511 in 1940; 11,349 in 1950, and 15,726 in 1960. In the 1980s the turnpike became part of Interstate 65. The road was rebuilt, and full interchanges were constructed at Brook's Hill Rd., Cedar Grove Rd., and Bernheim Rd.

Since 1960 Bullitt's population has continued to increase. Four new incorporated cities have sprung up, primarily in the north section of the county: Hunters Hollow, Pioneer Village, Hebron Estates, and Hillview. Hillview has become Bullitt's largest city.

Printing, distilling, manufacturing, and quarrying are the major industries. Soybeans and tobacco are the major agricultural crops. Much of the county is wooded, with ten thousand acres in Bernheim Forest and approximately thirty-five thousand acres in the Fort Knox military reservation. Bullitt's land area covers three hundred square miles.

Among the important people in Bullitt's history are Henry Crist and James Turner Morehead. Crist represented Kentucky in the U.S. Congress (1809–11) and was made a general in the Kentucky militia in 1811. Morehead was born near Shepherdsville on May 24, 1797. He was elected lieutenant governor of Kentucky in 1832 and served as governor of Kentucky from l834 to 1836. Morehead was the first native-born governor of Kentucky.

The population of Bullitt County was 26,090 in l970, 43,346 in 1980, 47,567 in 1990, and 58,005 in 1997.

See Robert E. McDowell, "Bullitt's Lick: The Related Saltworks and Settlements," *Filson Club History Quarterly* 30 (July 1956): 241–69; Audrea McDowell, "The Pursuit of Health and Happiness at the Paroquet Springs in Kentucky, 1838 to 1888," *Filson Club History Quarterly* 69 (Oct. 1995): 390–420.

Tom Pack

BULLITT COUNTY BANK. The Bullitt County Bank was organized in 1889 in Shepherdsville, Kentucky, as E.W. Hall and Co. Bankers and is the oldest existing bank in Bullitt County. It occupied a building attached to the east side of Troutman's Store, selling general merchandise. E.W. Hall was president. Other stockholders were Frank Straus, Fletcher Combs, Dr. Leon Straus, H.F. Troutman, and C.F. Troutman. Each stockholder contributed twenty-five hundred dollars in capital.

In 1903, after the death of Hall, the bank's name was changed to the Bullitt County Bank. Harry Combs, an employee in the early years, divided his work between the bank and Troutman's Store. Through good management, the bank progressed during its first eleven years. It continued to grow despite a national panic in 1893 and the Spanish American War, and by 1912 had capital of twenty thousand dollars with a ten-thousand-dollar surplus. To better serve its customers and the community, a new building was completed in 1923 on the northeast corner of Second and Main Streets.

The 1929 stock market crash and the Great Depression closed many of the nation's banks, but the Bullitt County Bank remained open. It continued to grow and prosper through the recovery years of World War II. In 1948 the bank had fifty thousand dollars in capital funds, thirty-five thousand dollars surplus, and ten thousand dollars in undivided profits.

During the next thirty-seven years, the bank continued to prosper under the guidance of Roger Alford, the board of directors, and the employees. Alford turned the institution over to new ownership in 1985—J. Chester Porter, William G. Porter, and Maria L. Bouvette. The operations of the bank were changed over from the old manual methods to full computer automation.

In 1986 a branch of the People's Bank of Mt. Washington was acquired by Bullitt County Bank in the fast-growing area of north Bullitt County. A new modern branch building was built there and opened in 1998. Bullitt County Bank has assets in excess of $100 million.

BULLITT'S LICK. Bullitt's Lick is located in BULLITT COUNTY approximately three miles west of SHEPHERDSVILLE. Herds of buffalo and other wild animals frequented the area to obtain salt necessary to their survival. These animals would lick the ground, which had been impregnated by salt water that had flowed to the surface over a period of time. Animals going to the SALT LICKS would create paths that the early settlers called buffalo roads. Since Bullitt's Lick covered a wide area and the strength of the salt in the water was stronger than that of other licks in the area, many of these animal roads led to that lick.

The lick was discovered in 1773 by, and named for, Capt. THOMAS BULLITT, who was in the area surveying lands, including a thousand acres for Col. WILLIAM CHRISTIAN, who had received the land for services in the French and Indian War. The first owner of Bullitt's Lick was the Christian family. They did not operate the saltworks themselves but leased the lick to others. The rent was usually paid in salt. HENRY CRIST was one of the more prominent saltmakers.

The first saltworks were erected in 1779. Salt was in scarce supply and almost impossible to obtain elsewhere since transportation was costly and difficult. The works consisted of trenches lined with stone supporting iron kettles strung out along the top. The kettles were filled with salt water obtained from wells dug for that purpose. A fire was built in the trench, which heated the kettles until the salt water boiled. After a period of boiling the water evaporated, leaving salt crystals. A shed-style roof was usually erected over the furnace for protection against rain. The salt was shipped to all points of Kentucky, the Illinois country, and even New Orleans. The first commercial production of salt in Kentucky was carried out at Bullitt's Lick. The wells were at first dug by hand but later were bored by an auger. The first kettles weighed about a hundred pounds and later ones as much as two hundred pounds. An adequate supply of wood was necessary. After a period of time, all the timber was cut around the furnace. It was cheaper to move the furnace to the source of wood than to transport the wood to the furnace. As the wood source pushed farther from the furnace, the salt water was transported from the wells by means of wooden pipes. One string of pipes went from Bullitt's Lick to Shepherdsville, across SALT RIVER south to the source of wood.

Salt was made at Bullitt's Lick until the 1830s when cheaper salt was produced elsewhere, and the fires were allowed to burn out and salt was no longer produced commercially. Bullitt's Lick was one of Kentucky's first businesses and hired a large number of workers, in addition to slave labor.

See Robert E. McDowell, "Bullitt's Lick: The Related Saltworks and Settlements," *Filson Club History Quarterly* 30 (July 1956): 241–69.

Tom Pack

BULLOCK, RICE (b Louisa County, Virginia, December 17, 1755; d Cincinnati, Ohio, March 17?, 1800). Soldier and constitutional convention delegate. He was the eldest of ten children, six sons and four daughters, of John and Ann (Rice) Bullock. The family, of English descent and members of the Anglican Church, resided at "Whitehall" on Little River in Virginia. Nothing is known of Bullock's early life other than that he must have received an education, because he was literate. During the Revolutionary War he served at least three years, ca. 1779-82, as an ensign, lieutenant, and assistant quartermaster general in Joseph Crockett's Virginia regiment. He was with Crockett's regiment on the western frontier in 1781 and may have been absorbed by GEORGE ROGERS CLARK's garrison at the FALLS OF THE OHIO in 1782. Records indicate that he had earlier served as a volunteer militiaman in the company of James Dabney in Samuel Meredith's regiment in 1776. Bullock is listed as serving in both the Continental and Virginia State lines, and a Rice Bullock is listed as serving in the Fifteenth Virginia Regiment. His family received a half-pay pension for him posthumously under an invalid's claim retroactive to February 1781. He received LAND GRANTS totaling at least 2,666 2/3 acres for his service, but there is no evidence that he ever lived on the land. By April 1785, and probably earlier, Bullock had settled in Jefferson County, Kentucky, most likely living in Louisville. On March 4, 1788, Bullock was chosen as one of two Jefferson County delegates to the Virginia convention to ratify the United States Constitution. He attended the June convention and was one of only three Kentuckians to vote for ratification. Bullock disappears from Jefferson County records in 1791 and reappears in Hamilton County, Ohio, records in January 1795. He resided in Cincinnati until his death.

Rice Bullock's main importance was his military service during the Revolutionary War and tenure as a constitutional convention delegate. As one of only three Kentucky delegates to vote in favor of the new federal constitution, Bullock set himself apart from most of his fellow Kentuckians. Given Bullock's lack of political and governmental involvement both before and after the convention, a question arises as to why he was chosen. Bullock was at the courthouse in Louisville in early March 1788 serving on juries and tending to legal affairs when the electors met at the courthouse to select Jefferson County's two delegates to the convention. Bullock's service as an army officer, his literacy, and possibly his political beliefs and availability resulted in his selection. In voting for the federal constitution it is not known if he was influenced by fellow Jefferson County delegate ROBERT BRECKINRIDGE; but whatever his reasons, Rice Bullock secured his place in history by serving his young country and supporting the document that is the foundation of the United States federal government.

See Mary Bullock Aker, *Bullocks of Virginia and Kentucky and Their Descendants* (Parkville, Mo., 1952); John Frederick Dorman, *Virginia Revolutionary Pension Applications*, vols. 11–13, 26 (Washington, D.C., 1965–67, 1977); *Journal of the House of Delegates of the Commonwealth of Virginia* (Richmond 1833)

James J. Holmberg

BULLOCK, WILLIAM FONTAINE (b Fayette County, Kentucky, January 16, 1807; d near Shelbyville, Kentucky, August 9, 1889). Lawyer, politician, and civic leader. Born to Edmund and Elizabeth (Fontaine) Bullock, young Bullock attended Lexington public schools and graduated from Transylvania University in 1824. Four years later he moved to Louisville and established a LAW office at the corner of Fifth and Jefferson Streets.

In 1838, 1840, and 1841 he was elected to the state legislature by the citizens of Louisville. At that time, Bullock spearheaded the revision of the state's faltering public education system. In 1838 he drafted and secured passage of an act to establish a new system of common schools in Kentucky. Over the next twelve years Bullock fought to preserve the funding for the fledgling system. He helped ward off proposals to use the money for questionable internal improvements and saw the act solidified in the new state constitution of 1850. Bullock continued his work in education by helping to establish the Kentucky Institution for the Education of the Blind in 1842, sitting on the board of managers for the HOUSE OF REFUGE, drawing up the bill for the AMERICAN PRINTING HOUSE FOR THE BLIND in 1858, and unsuccessfully attempting to establish an AFRICAN AMERICAN school for the blind in the early 1880s. He also was a member of the UNIVERSITY OF LOUISVILLE law school faculty from 1849 until 1861.

In addition to his educational contributions, Bullock was active in establishing the Louisville and Portland Railway. He was one of eighteen incorporators who initiated the project. The three-mile railway, which at first proved unsuccessful, was to be operated for the financial benefit of the Kentucky Institution for the Education of the Blind. Bullock also was one of the citizens of Louisville who was most active in founding and building the LOUISVILLE & NASHVILLE RAILROAD. In 1846 he was appointed judge of the Fifth Judicial Circuit and served in that position until he retired in 1855 and resumed his private practice.

Bullock's first marriage, to the daughter of Jefferson County judge J.P. Oldham, produced one son, John. His second marriage, to Mary Pearce, produced three sons: William, Pearce, and Wallace. Bullock is buried in CAVE HILL CEMETERY.

See J. Stoddard Johnston, ed., *Memorial*

History of Louisville (Chicago 1896); *Courier-Journal*, Aug. 10, 1889.

BULLOCK, WINGFIELD (b Spotsylvania, Virginia, ?; d Shelbyville, Kentucky, October 13, 1821). United States representative. Wingfield received his education in Virginia. After completing his law studies, he moved to SHELBY COUNTY, Kentucky, and was elected to represent that area in the state senate from 1812 through 1814. On March 4, 1821, Bullock began his term in Congress, which was cut short by his death at home on October 13, 1821. He is buried near Shelbyville.

See *Biographical Directory of the American Congress 1776–1961* (Washington, D.C., 1961)

BUNCE, JOSEPH H. (b New York, 1825?; d. ?). Mayor. Bunce was MAYOR of Louisville for less than a year in 1869. He ran for mayor against fellow Democrats JOHN BAXTER and police chief Robert Gilchriest in 1869. Bunce led the party's "bolter" faction and defeated Baxter even though Baxter had won the party's nomination and had received the endorsement of the *COURIER JOURNAL*. Bunce received 4,266 votes in the April 3 contest to Baxter's 3,965 and Gilchriest's 2,340.

In 1870 the CITY'S CHARTER was amended by the state legislature, and the mayor's term of office was extended from two years to three. Bunce was given the option of serving out his two-year term or running for reelection to a three-year term in March. Bunce chose the latter and was defeated by 580 votes by Baxter, who had garnered the backing of influential politicians and business leaders.

Bunce was also elected to the City Council for the Twelfth Ward in 1866 and to the BOARD OF ALDERMEN in 1867 and 1868. He was Board of Aldermen president in 1868.

Bunce worked as a steamboat captain in Louisville in the late 1850s to the mid-1860s. He then joined Griffith & Co., a produce dealer and wholesale grocery. The firm then became Griffith, Bunce, & Co., located on MAIN between Third and FOURTH STREETS.

About 1870, Bunce went into the gate- and fence-manufacturing business with Alexander Hunter. The firm, Bunce & Hunter, was located on Third St. between Main St. and River Rd. In 1872 he became president of the Louisville Bromophyte Fertilizer Co. In 1873 Bunce & Hunter acquired the Kentucky Gate and Fence Co. in PORTLAND.

Bunce was married to Josephine Bunce from Kentucky. The couple had four children: Alice, Charles, Hattie, and Marshal. The family lived in PORTLAND.

See *Courier Journal*, Oct. 9, 1881, March 6, 1870, April 4 and 5, 1869.

BURKE, FRANK WELSH (b Louisville, June 1, 1920). United States representative and Louisville mayor. He is the son of Joseph M. and Ann (Welsh) Burke. Educated at parochial schools in Louisville and a 1938 St. Xavier High School graduate, Burke attended the University of Southern California before graduating from Xavier University, Cincinnati, Ohio, in 1942. He played FOOTBALL at both schools. He served in the United States Army from 1942 until 1946, then received a law degree from the UNIVERSITY OF LOUISVILLE in 1948. He was admitted to the bar that same year.

Burke, a Democrat, was elected MAYOR of Louisville in November 1969 and served until 1973. He defeated Republican John Porter Sawyer 48,337 to 40,810. The Democrats, including County Judge TODD HOLLENBACH, were swept back into most city and county offices after eight years of Republican rule.

As mayor, Burke pledged to make the city a safer, brighter, and cleaner place. The city installed more than forty-five hundred new street lights and increased the wattage of fifty-three hundred others. Crime declined during his term as a result of expanding the police force and improving law enforcement facilities. The city's garbage-collection and street-cleaning systems were also improved, including a yearly neighborhood-by-neighborhood pickup program to remove accumulated junk. Burke was a behind-the-scenes mayor known less for confrontation than for his ability to help the city through cooperative efforts with community leaders.

Burke also pushed development of the RIVERFRONT PLAZA/BELVEDERE, including the underground parking garage, the construction of the FOURTH ST. pedestrian mall and the new Federal Square, and the renovation of many downtown streets and sewers. He also was responsible for implementing the city's first retirement system covering all city employees.

Burke's administration witnessed a 1971 federal investigation into illegal GAMBLING and PROSTITUTION in the city that brought national publicity but had few results. The mayor was also at the center of a firemen's strike in June 1971 over a pay dispute. He got a court order to send the striking workers back to work just after the walkout.

Burke was a protégé of popular mayor CHARLES P. FARNSLEY. He was an administrative assistant and city attorney (1950–51) and director of public safety (1953) during Farnsley's tenure, and he was a lawyer in Farnsley's legal firm.

Burke was a member of the Kentucky House of Representatives in 1957 and 1958. He was elected to the Eighty-sixth and Eighty-seventh Congresses (January 3, 1959 through January 3, 1963), defeating three-term Republican incumbent JOHN M. ROBSION JR. in 1958 for the Third-District seat. As a congressman, Burke contributed technical amendments to the 1961 Federal Housing Act that helped to redefine government's role in URBAN RENEWAL. The amendments placed greater emphasis on neighborhood rehabilitation as opposed to slum clearance. In 1962 Burke was defeated by Republican MARION GENE SNYDER, who was then the First-District magistrate, by 2,565 votes (93,627–91,062).

Burke was married to Evalyne Hackett in 1943. The couple had four children.

See Lawrence F. Kennedy, *Biographical Directory of the American Congress, 1774–1971* (Washington, D.C., 1971); *Courier-Journal*, Nov. 30, 1973.

BURKE, ROBERT T., JR. (b Louisville, 1913; d Louisville, January 3, 1967). Jefferson County judge. He was the son of Robert T. and Marie M. Burke. His father was a well-known attorney, serving as legal counsel for the Catholic Archdiocese of Louisville. The younger Burke attended ST. XAVIER HIGH SCHOOL. He graduated from the University of Notre Dame in 1936 and received his law degree from the UNIVERSITY OF LOUISVILLE two years later. From 1942 to 1944, he was a special agent for the Federal Bureau of Investigation in Washington, D.C.; Boston; New York; and Providence, Rhode Island. He then joined the navy and served two years.

Burke, a Democrat, was assistant city attorney under Mayor CHARLES P. FARNSLEY from early 1948 until December 1949. He was Jefferson County judge from March 25, 1954, until June 7, 1954, having been appointed to the post by the governor after the incumbent died. Burke served as president of the LOUISVILLE BAR ASSOCIATION in 1957 and was a University of Louisville trustee from 1950 to 1962, serving as board secretary. He was also a long-standing member of the Democratic State Central Executive Committee. He also served as Jefferson County probate commissioner and as a member of the Commission on (Legislative) Reapportionment.

Burke, who was legally deaf but could hear with the use of a hearing aid, also worked as a music critic for the *KENTUCKY IRISH-AMERICAN*, a Louisville weekly newspaper. Burke married Frances Eady, and the couple had two daughters.

See "Atty. Robert T. Burke Dies of Heart Attack," *Courier-Journal*, Jan. 4, 1967.

BURLESQUE. Burlesque came to America in the late 1800s, riding the wave of increased interest in new forms of entertainment. Burlesque theater, like its cousin, literary burlesque, attempted to use or imitate "serious matter of manner, made amusing by the creation of an incongruity between style and subject," as defined by Richard P. Bond in *English Burlesque Poetry*. A companion to the burgeoning vaudeville genre of live entertainment, burlesque crossed the Atlantic from London to sweep the northeast. Lydia Thompson, an English actress, was the herald of this new form of entertainment, charming Americans with her beauty and grace. Thompson was just one of many acts that took America by storm.

As the popularity of burlesque grew, so did the need for better organization. Samuel A. Scribner created the Traveling Variety Managers' Association to handle booking and organization of both vaudeville and burlesque acts. This propelled the art of burlesque theater beyond the East Coast.

In Louisville, the Buckingham was the most prominent of these theaters. It was originally built as an add-on to a gentleman's clothier at the corner of Third and Jefferson Streets in 1880. After several name and location changes, it was billed as the Grand Opera House. Its architect and owner, D.X. MURPHY, planned it as a stage for dramatic fare. The *COURIER-JOURNAL* went so far as to describe its opulent decor on opening night, September 3, 1894. The management promised refined vaudeville and burlesque for men only.

By 1898 the building had been sold and reopened again as the Buckingham located at 223–27 W Jefferson. Owned and operated by then–DEMOCRATIC PARTY boss JOHN WHALLEN and his brother James, it welcomed such vaudeville acts as Jimmy Durante and W.C. Fields. It was not long before burlesque shows featuring the likes of Lydia Thompson were gracing the Buckingham as well. In 1919 it became the Jefferson.

During the early twentieth century, the Buckingham and its nearby rival, the Gayety (opened in 1909 and located on Jefferson between Third and FOURTH STREETS) experienced excellent business. The two were considered the premier show houses in Louisville. It was not uncommon for men to leave the cathedral on Sunday afternoons, dismiss their wives, and walk to the theaters for an afternoon of burlesque shows, according to local historian Gary Falk.

During the 1920s and 1930s, burlesque and vaudeville suffered at the hands of a new form of entertainment, talking movies. Many vaudeville acts transferred well to the big screen; but burlesque, with its bawdy and often risqué humor and antics, did not transfer as well. The Buckingham, which had also suffered from PROHIBITION, in 1922 had a new name—the Savoy—and soon had a movie screen.

In an effort to compete with Hollywood, many burlesque houses across the country took the art form to a new level in hopes of recouping its clientele. Burlesque queens were now full-fledged strippers. Even the Savoy attempted to utilize this new variety of an old theme, with a live burlesque-strip show in 1958. Before it closed, the Savoy offered both X-rated motion pictures and strip shows. Many historians see this move by the industry as the death knell for burlesque. By the 1960s hardly a trace of the once-lively art form of burlesque existed in theaters. Burlesque in the form of stripping continued to be found around the county, especially in clubs in the area of Seventh Street Rd. in SHIVELY.

See Robert C. Allen, *Horrible Prettiness* (Chapel Hill, N.C., 1991); John D. Jump, *The Critical Idiom: Burlesque* (London 1972); Bernard Sobel, *A Pictorial History of Burlesque* (Toronto 1956); K.L. Davis, "A Chronicle of the Savoy Theatre, Louisville, Kentucky," M.A. thesis, University of Louisville, 1980.

Paul Wolf Holleman

Savoy burlesque theater, 223-227 West Jefferson Street, 1941. Also known as the Buckingham Theater and Jefferson Theater.

BURWINKLE-HENDERSHOT. A wholesaler in plastic and paper products run by Dick and Cynthia Weller and family at 127 W MAIN ST. in downtown Louisville. Weller is a descendant of Herman Burwinkle, who arrived in Louisville from Dinklage, Germany, in 1854. At the end of the CIVIL WAR, Burwinkle was a boot and shoe dealer at 226 FOURTH ST. Some years later, Herman Burwinkle's son, William, ran a bar and grocery called Burwinkle's Station. It was located in the building that became the Sahara Club (razed in 1997) in BUECHEL at the juncture of Bardstown Rd. and Buechel Bypass. In 1912 William Burwinkle closed Burwinkle's Station and went into business with his son-in-law, Jerome Hendershot, selling non-food items wholesale to country stores. Burwinkle-Hendershot operated in two locations downtown before occupying its present site in 1944. For many years the company was run by David Weller, husband of Jerome Hendershot's daughter, Gertrude. David's son, Dick, is the fifth generation of his family to operate a business in downtown Louisville.

Bob Edwards

BUSCHEMEYER, JOHN HENRY (b Louisville, February 24, 1869; d Louisville, October 7, 1935). Mayor. The son of Henry and Helen (Bollinger) Buschemeyer, he was educated at LOUISVILLE'S MALE HIGH SCHOOL. He graduated from the Louisville College of PHARMACY in 1889 and earned an M.D. degree from the UNIVERSITY OF LOUISVILLE in 1892. He was also a graduate student at New York's Polyclinic from 1892 until 1893. He began practicing MEDICINE in Louisville in 1893.

Twice elected president of the BOARD OF ALDERMEN, he served from November 1909 to November 1913. Buschemeyer, a Democrat, served as MAYOR of Louisville from November 18, 1913, through November 20, 1917. He was the last Democratic mayor elected with the support of the WHALLEN political machine. Buschemeyer defeated Wood F. Axton, head of AXTON-FISHER TOBACCO CO. and a Progressive Party candidate, and Republican George T. Wood. The Progressives ran against the "invisible government" of the Whallen machine and its connection to such big corporations as the newly formed Louisville Gas & Electric Co. Buschemeyer defeated Axton 24,944 to 20,399. Wood, whose party lost votes to the Progressives, received only 1,388 votes.

Buschemeyer's administration was marred by growing antipathy toward Louisville's African American community. In 1914 the City Council passed an ordinance to keep blacks from moving into white neighborhoods. Conversely, whites were also forbidden from moving into black neighborhoods. Buschemeyer signed the ordinance into law on May 11, 1914. The ordinance was later challenged by the newly formed Louisville chapter of the NATIONAL ASSOCIATION FOR THE ADVANCEMENT OF COLORED PEOPLE (NAACP). The case reached the United States Supreme Court, which unanimously ruled that the ordinance was unconstitutional because it interfered with property rights. The decision was subsequently cited to overturn similar housing SEGREGATION ordinances in other cities.

Buschemeyer was also a prison physician for the United States government in Louisville from 1893 to 1897. He served as president of the board of the LOUISVILLE FREE PUBLIC LIBRARY and was a trustee of the University of Louisville and the New York Polyclinic.

Buschemeyer married Florence Byrne of Louisville in 1903. The couple had three sons: John, Charles, and William. The former mayor died at his home on River Park Dr. He is buried in St. Louis Cemetery.

See Mary Young Southard and Ernest C. Miller, eds., *Who's Who in Kentucky: A Biographical Assembly of Notable Kentuckians* (Louisville 1936); George H. Yater, *Two Hundred Years at the Falls of the Ohio* (Louisville 1987).

BUSINESS FIRST. *Business First* of Louisville began publication in August 1984. The weekly newspaper was started by two Kansas City entrepreneurs who started or acquired business NEWSPAPERS in other cities. In 1989, the businessmen sold *Business First* and other publications to Shaw Publishing of Charlotte, North Carolina. The company, known as American City Business Journals, was a publicly traded company until 1995 when the newspaper chain was sold to Advance Publications, a private company that owns magazines and daily newspapers. Advance is owned by Donald and S.I. Newhouse Jr.

Business First has had three addresses in its history: 607 W MAIN ST., 111 W Washington Street and 501 S FOURTH ST. Founding president and publisher Mike Kallay moved to a sister newspaper in Hawaii in 1995. Longtime editor Tom Monahan replaced him.

While *Business First's* primary mission is to cover business news in the metropolitan area, it also produces various special publications and supplements such as Breeders Cup and KENTUCKY DERBY magazines and First Honors, a special publication which focuses on the achievements of high school students. *Business First* has a staff of thirty-four, circulation of fifteen thousand, and weekly readership of about sixty thousand.

See "Sale of *Business First* Parent Likely Will Close in October," *Business First* (Aug. 14, 1995): 4; "Advance Completes Purchase of ACBJ," *Business First* (Oct. 23, 1995): 15; "Carol Timmons Named *Business First* Editor," *Business First* (Dec. 19, 1994): 1; Rachael Kamuf, "Giving 'em the Business," *Business First* (Aug. 8, 1994): B-4; Carolyn Tribble, "*Business First* Parent Owns 26 Other Business Journals," *Business First* (Aug. 8, 1994): B-5.

Eric Benmour

BUSING, PUBLIC SCHOOL. After the U.S. Supreme Court ruled in the 1954 *Brown v. Board of Education of Topeka* that SEGREGATION in PUBLIC SCHOOLS was unconstitutional, Gov. LAWRENCE W. WETHERBY announced that the state would abide by the law of the land. His statement differed from that of other southern governors and put Kentucky at the forefront of school integration. In Louisville, Supt. OMER CARMICHAEL and the Louisville school board began a two-year planning process for desegregation of the city's public schools. All grade levels were to be integrated and the entire school system completely redistricted regardless of race. An important aspect was what became a "safety valve" in order to lessen opposition to the plan. All students were allowed transfers to a school other than the one to which they were assigned, provided there was room in that school. Most parents received the transfers of their first choice for their children, resulting in virtually no integration.

During the 1960s many white families left the city for the SUBURBS, thus increasing segregation in Louisville's schools. By 1973 Louisville schools had about 49,800 students. That total was down from the 1968–69 high of 51,626, and the downward trend was expected to continue through 1981, when enrollment was estimated to be 38,109. The idea of merging the Louisville and Jefferson County school systems began in 1947, but legal questions and opposition from an organization called "Save Our Neighborhood Schools" prevented the plan from being implemented. By the early 1970s the idea of integrating schools through the busing of white and black students to different areas gained support from a number of local CIVIL RIGHTS groups.

In 1966 Dr. James S. Coleman, a renowned University of Chicago sociologist, submitted a report to Congress based upon an extensive study of the performance of students in public schools. Coleman concluded that disadvantaged African American children learned better in integrated classes. His findings became the manual for political and court actions and were used by Louisville groups to support busing to achieve a racial balance in the schools. These groups included West End and Mid-city Citizens for Desegregation, Kentucky Civil Liberties Union (KCLU), Kentucky Commission on Human Rights, National Association for the Advancement of Colored People (NAACP), and Louisville Legal Aid Society.

The issue of school desegregation was forced upon the community when in 1971 the U.S. Department of Health, Education, and Welfare ordered the Jefferson County BOARD OF EDUCATION to remove the "racial identity" of Newburg Elementary School. Newburg was an African American community lying along Newburg Rd. in the southeast part of the county.

The Jefferson County board did submit plans for integrating the Newburg school, but, when Jefferson Circuit Judge Marvin J. Sternberg ruled that the Louisville school system's minority transfer plan was unconstitutional and that the system was segregated, then the Jefferson County School Board missed the deadline for desegregating the school. The KCLU and the Legal Aid Society then filed suit in U.S. District Court asking for desegregation of the Jefferson County school system. The following year, the KCLU and NAACP filed suit asking for the desegregation of the Louisville schools. The Kentucky Commission on Human Rights noted that Louisville was then behind all major southern cities in both student and faculty desegregation. It stated that a merger of the city and county school systems was the necessary step that must be taken as a part of an overall desegregation plan. On September 6, 1972, U.S. District Judge JAMES F. GORDON ruled that he would not order merger or annexation as a method of desegregation. On March 8, 1973, Gordon dismissed the KCLU, Legal Aid Society, and NAACP suits. The civil rights groups appealed the decision, and it was reversed by the Sixth Circuit Court of Appeals on December 28, 1973, and a desegregation plan was ordered for the school districts. Although the districts appealed the case to the U.S. Supreme Court, ANCHORAGE and Jefferson County filed desegregation plans. Judge Gordon had hearings on various desegregation plans, and, on July 23, 1974, he adopted one that called for cross-district busing of more than thirty thousand students and declared the Louisville and Jefferson County systems merged, effective immediately. However, the U.S. Supreme Court sent the case back to the Sixth Circuit in a ruling banning most cross-district busing. On December 11, 1974, the circuit court reinstated its desegregation order, and the Jefferson County and Louisville school boards appealed to the U.S. Supreme Court. During the appeal process, Judge Gordon ordered the Jefferson County system to draw up a desegregation plan. On February 28, 1975, a significant event in the long process of desegregation occurred when the state Board of Education ordered the Louisville and Jefferson County school systems merged effective April 1, 1975. The city and county boards had little choice when on April 21 the U.S. Supreme Court denied their appeals against the Circuit Court of Appeals desegregation order. On July 17, 1975, the Court of Appeals, referring to the case *Newburg Area Council Inc. et al. v. Board of Education of Jefferson County, Kentucky*, ordered that a writ of mandamus issue directing a plan for the desegregation of the newly created Jefferson County school district "to the end that all remaining vestiges of the state imposed segregation shall be removed from the said school district." It was to take effect at the beginning of the 1975–76 school year.

The plan combined Louisville's 73 public schools with the 107 schools in the rest of the county. Of 130,000 students, 22,600 (11,300 white, 11,300 black) were bused that first year. School assignments were made according to the first letter of a child's last name. An exemption clause was built into the plan designed to prevent further "white flight." Any neighborhood could gain exemption from busing provided its racial makeup met the statistical goals established in the federal court order. It also provided that children of any family moving into a neighborhood where the other race predominated were exempted from busing. A black family moving into a white neighborhood increased the chances of eliminating busing for all families in that neighborhood. The LOUISVILLE TIMES printed a special section on July 31, 1975, giving maps of how busing would occur and telling who would be exempt. Twenty-eight schools were exempted from the plan, and another twelve were closed.

The plan met stiff resistance from a number of groups, including parents, unions, and the Ku Klux Klan. It was supported by some churches, government, and some citizen groups. When school started in September, more than half of the county's students were kept home by their parents as part of a school boycott. A number of demonstrations took place throughout the county on the first day; but it was at the end of the second day, Friday, that the situation grew ugly. At the end of the day students blocked the traffic driving to a football game at Valley High School on DIXIE HWY. The crowd eventually grew to ten thousand people and rioting began. Police were pelted with rocks and bottles, police cars were damaged, and a bonfire was started. The violence spread to other areas, including Southern High School, where the school's windows were smashed, school bus tires were slashed, and several other small bonfires were lit. At Fairdale High School, buses were attacked. Three hundred and fifty state troopers were called in to assist county and city police. The next day, a thousand state guardsmen were brought into the area to control the demonstrations and riots that continued throughout the weekend. By the end of September more than six hundred had been arrested and two hundred injured. The school board, refusing to give in to pressure, continued to roll the buses, each with an armed guard.

When the riots occurred, a group of people from the Kentucky Alliance against Racists and Political Oppression formed a group called Progress in Education. Led by veteran civil rights activist Anne Braden, the organization worked to counter the acts of the anti-busing forces. Working to encourage public support for desegregation, they held workshops, spoke at hearings, and attended school board meetings. Progress in Education lasted for four years and was instrumental in working to promote busing.

The efforts of the organization paled, however, in comparison to that of the anti-busing forces. A number of groups were formed in opposition to busing. The largest and most prominent was Concerned Citizens Inc. led by Susan Connor, the most vocal and well-known anti-busing leader. Connor organized a number of rallies and demonstrations, including one where eight thousand people marched on BROADWAY on September 28, 1975. Other groups included Save Our Community Schools led by Joyce Spond, Citizens against Busing led by Bill Kellerman, Union Labor against Busing led by Jim Luckett, and Restore Our Alienated Rights. The COURIER-JOURNAL and the *Louisville Times* were openly supportive of busing during these heated days. Publisher BARRY BINGHAM SR. later said that at no other time in the paper's history was it more hated than it was during the busing controversy and the open housing movement in 1967. Demonstrations continued throughout the school year almost on a daily basis. During the next school year many demonstrations took place but with less frequency and violence.

In the end, the law prevailed. However, this was at the cost of a drop in public school attendance. In September 1975 the private school population increased by 22 percent from the previous year. Under the leadership of Archbishop THOMAS MCDONOUGH, the CATHOLIC SCHOOLS formed a policy that worked to discourage the enrollment of students avoiding busing. The first adjustments to the 1975 plan were made by the school board on April 4, 1984. Under the old system, the schools were grouped into clusters (thirteen schools per cluster for the elementary level) each containing at least one African American neighborhood. Each school was required to have an African American student membership between 23 and 43 percent. In the early 1990s, Supreme Court rulings loosened restrictions over the busing process, leading to new plans for racial integration. As a result, Jefferson County reacted by developing a desegregation plan based on programmatic options, including magnet schools located in the inner city to give families choices regarding school attendance.

In December 1991, the Jefferson County School Board voted to adopt a new plan, Project Renaissance, that replaced mandatory busing. Under the new plan, the racial guidelines were changed to 15 to 50 for elementary, 16 to 46 for middle, and 12 to 42 percent for high schools. The elementary schools remain in clusters, but the percentage goal of each cluster is reached by voluntary transfers within the cluster. Magnet programs were expanded to attract transfers. Students are bused involuntarily only if they are in a cluster with too few voluntary transfers to keep all the schools within the new racial guidelines for two consecutive years or for three of any five years. If involuntary busing is necessary, the students are bused according to the first letter of their last name. At the middle and high school levels, students are placed in the geographic district of Jefferson County. They may request two school choices. In most cases they are granted one of those requests, providing it does not upset the racial balance or school capacity. If neither choice is granted, they are assigned a school in their district.

The debate over the academic effectiveness of busing continues. At the close of the twentieth century, there were suits pending that questioned busing for desegregation. The issue is the validity of any race-based school attendance plan.

See *Courier-Journal,* Sept. 14, 1975; Bruce Allar, "Central to the Debate," *Louisville* (Aug. 1997): 36–43.

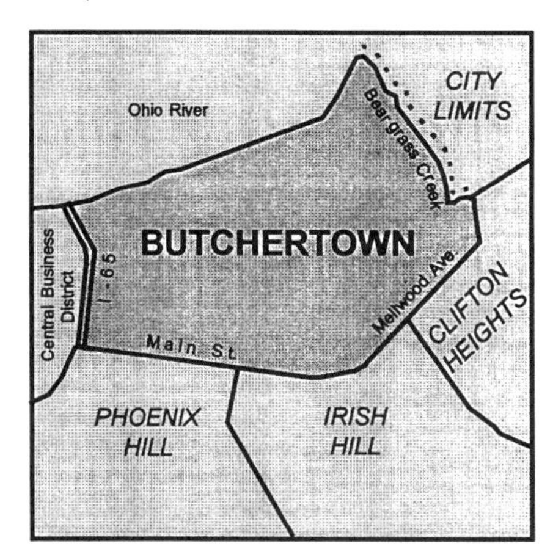

BUTCHERTOWN. A neighborhood located just east of the downtown area, bordered by the OHIO RIVER to the north, Interstate 65 to the west, MAIN ST. to the South, and Mellwood Ave. and BEARGRASS CREEK to the east. Butchertown's history can be traced to the year 1796 when Henry Fait established one of Jefferson County's first gristmills in the area. Later, Col. Frederick Geiger came into possession of the land and built a twenty-one-room farmhouse around 1815, opened a flour mill, and inaugurated ferry service to southern Indiana.

It was not until 1827 that Butchertown began taking on its present character. In that year, Louisville annexed parts of the area. Shortly thereafter, the first wave of GERMAN immigrants arrived and many became butchers. Butchering animals had been banned from the city core early on, but this did not present a problem because the city's eastern reaches were more practical for the task. The land sat astride a major turnpike from the east (now Frankfort and Story Avenues), and Beargrass Creek was useful for dumping animal wastes. To accommodate the growing industry, the BOURBON STOCK YARDS was established in 1834. Other related businesses such as tanneries, cooperages, soapmakers, agricultural supply dealers, and blacksmiths soon sprang up. Breweries and distilleries were built to satisfy German thirsts.

The neighborhood's present street system took shape on April 16, 1841, when city surveyor John Tunstall platted the area. Most of the present street names date from that time. For years, local historians have held that street names such as Washington, Adams, Franklin, and Webster were chosen out of patriotic fervor, but that is not quite so. Two early Butchertown landowners, George Buchanan (for whom Buchanan St. is named) and Isaac Stewart, were Whigs. When it came time to

Farmers waiting to deliver their hogs, sheep and cattle to the Bourbon Stock Yards in the Butchertown neighborhood, 1930s.

name streets on their land, Federalist or Whig names were chosen. Except for Calhoun (named for a renegade southern Democrat), no Democratic names were picked.

For most of the nineteenth century, Butchertown remained a thriving, petit bourgeois neighborhood, with a continental flavor still hinted at today. Other Louisvillians often professed shock at the Sunday gatherings at WOODLAND GARDEN, where beer-drinking and bowling took place without regard for the Sabbath.

The Butchertown culture began to fade as large MEAT-PACKING plants moved into the area toward the end of the nineteenth century. The next few decades witnessed even more dramatic changes. In 1931, the city's new zoning laws designated the entire neighborhood industrial. After the devastating FLOOD OF 1937, many homes were pulled down. Housing stock deteriorated as homeowners moved to the SUBURBS in the 1950s. The 1960s saw an interstate highway built through the area. Through it all, St. Joseph Roman Catholic Church and its impressive spires have been a center of much activity.

Faced with even further encroachment by industry, a few remaining homeowners finally banded together in the mid-1960s to fight for neighborhood preservation. Their first success came in 1966 when they persuaded the city to switch the neighborhood's zoning to partial residential. A new corporation, Butchertown Inc., began buying dilapidated structures to renovate for resale. The result was a more stabilized community that was quieter, yet energetic. Butchertown's remarkable preservation movement was inspired by the revitalization efforts of older neighborhoods such as OLD LOUISVILLE, and its success led to further renewal in other areas.

See *Courier-Journal,* Dec. 9, 1973; George Yater, *Two Hundred Years at the Falls of the Ohio* (Louisville 1979).

David Williams

BUTLER, EDWARD MANN (b Baltimore, Maryland, July 1784; d St. Louis, November 1, 1855). Educator. Butler was one of Louisville's most prominent educators in the early nineteenth century. At the age of three he moved to his grandfather's house in Chelsea, England, returning to the United States eleven years later. He earned degrees in medicine and law from St. Mary's College in the District of Columbia and, after briefly practicing law in Lexington, established an academy in Versailles, Kentucky in 1806. In August 1806 he married Martha Dedman, who bore him at least one child, a son. He moved to Maysville in 1810, where he taught until at least 1811.

After teaching in Frankfort and Lexington, Butler moved to Louisville about 1815, serving as a journalist and as first principal of the all-male JEFFERSON SEMINARY. In 1817 he moved to Frankfort, where he first wrote for the *Commentator* and then taught at the Kentucky Seminary. In 1822 he moved to Lexington, where he headed the grammar school at Transylvania University. Sometime thereafter he returned to Louisville and resumed his position as principal of the Jefferson Seminary until its closing in 1829. The city of Louisville was given authority to form a public school, supported by taxes, that same year. Butler became principal of the grammar department of this school. During his tenure there he worked on his history of Kentucky, considered to be one of the first reliable histories of the commonwealth, which was published in 1834. He resigned that same year as the result of a dispute over instructional methods. In 1844 he went to St. Louis, where he served as justice of the peace and notary public. He died of injuries sustained in a train wreck.

Butler helped establish a library in Washington (Mason County) and Louisville's Free Public Library. He was also a founder of the Kentucky Association of Professional Teachers and was elected its first president in 1833. He also aided in founding the UNIVERSITY OF LOUISVILLE. He was at work on a history of the Ohio Valley at the time of his death.

See G. Glenn Clift, "Preface," in Mann Butler, *Valley of the Ohio* (Frankfort 1971); Richard H. Collins, *History of Kentucky* 2 vols. (Frankfort 1966).

Robert M. Ireland

BUTT, ARCHIBALD WILLINGHAM DEGRAFFENRIED (b Augusta, Georgia, September 25, 1865; d aboard *Titanic* April 14, 1912). Military aide. After a tour of Europe in 1912, Maj. Archibald Butt was making the final leg of his journey home aboard the *Titanic* when it hit an iceberg and sank. Major Butt went down with the ship a hero, having assisted women and children aboard what lifeboats there were. He was last seen standing on the sinking deck with John Jacob Astor.

"Archie," as he was known to his friends, had been sent to Rome by President William Howard Taft to thank Pope Pius X for the appointment of three Americans as cardinals. After the sinking of the steamer, the White House claimed the trip was not an official diplomatic mission but a vacation.

Born near the end of the CIVIL WAR, Butt attended the University of the South in Sewanee, Tennessee, graduating in 1888. After graduation he came to Louisville to visit military hero JOHN BRECKINRIDGE CASTLEMAN and his family. HENRY WATTERSON, a friend of Castleman and editor of the *COURIER-JOURNAL*, offered Butt a job as a reporter, perhaps because of his connection to the Castleman family. Butt took the job as an opportunity to hone his writing skills. He stayed in Louisville for three years before moving to Macon, Georgia, and then to Washington, D.C., where he served as a correspondent for several southern newspapers.

His interests in writing started at Sewanee where he began the school newspaper, but he was destined to become a soldier. In 1898, at the outbreak of the Spanish-American War, Butt was commissioned as lieutenant and assistant quartermaster, United States Volunteers, and in 1900 received a regular army commission. His military service took him to the Philippines, where his superb work as quartermaster caught the eye of the governor-general, William H. Taft. Taft recommended Butt to President Theodore Roosevelt to be the president's military aide, which Roosevelt accepted. Butt stayed on as military aide once Taft became president in 1909. He was commissioned as major in 1911.

Butt was last in Louisville after he and President Taft had traveled to Hodgenville to dedicate the monument to President Lincoln's birthplace in November 1911. The Louisville Press Club used the occasion to hold its first public gala at the SEELBACH HOTEL and invited their former colleague to be their guest of honor; President Taft was his special guest. Most people were more interested in "Louisville's own Archie Butt" than they were in President Taft.

Writing to his sister-in-law, Clara Butt, as he did daily, he wrote, "There never has been a moment that I have not looked back upon my life in Louisville as one of its brightest epochs. The friendships which I formed then are my most intimate friendships of today. . . . The greatest compliment paid me is when I see myself mentioned as 'an old Louisville boy.'"

Of the people who died aboard the *Titanic,* Major Butt was among the more famous. Memorial services for those lost in the sinking took place around the country. In Louisville services for Butt were held at the church he once attended, ST. PAUL'S EPISCOPAL. He was also remembered at a large ecumenical service held at the Armory (GARDENS OF LOUISVILLE) for all the *Titanic* victims. Over ten thousand people attended, with many more being turned away at the door. In his hometown of Augusta, at another memorial service, President Taft said of him, "Major Archie Butt was my military aide. He was like a member of my family, and I feel his loss as if he had been a younger brother."

Monuments to Archibald Butt include a fountain in Washington near the White House, a memorial marker in Arlington National Cemetery, and a bridge in his hometown of Augusta, Georgia.

BYCK, DANN CONRAD. (b Atlanta, Georgia, Oct. 24, 1899; d Louisville, May 30, 1960). Clothier. Byck was the son of Louis S. and Carrie (Dann) Byck. The family moved to Louisville in 1902, where Louis Byck, in partnership with his brother Werner, opened BYCK BROTHERS & CO., a retail shoe store that eventually became a women's and children's clothing store, one of the largest locally owned clothing stores in the city.

Dann Byck was educated in the public grade schools and graduated from LOUISVILLE MALE HIGH SCHOOL in 1917. He attended the University of Pennsylvania and graduated from the university's Wharton School of Finance with a degree in economics in 1921.

Byck spent a year in New York City working with a retail firm before returning to Louisville in 1922 to work in the advertising department and later in various merchandising departments in his father's company. He became vice president and general manager of Byck Brothers & Co. in 1925 and president in 1930. He incorporated the company, which had a store on S FOURTH ST. in Louisville and another on Lexington Rd. in ST. MATTHEWS. Byck contributed much of his time to charities, particularly Jewish welfare relief programs. He was an active member of the Community Chest for years and a member of the board of the Adath Israel Temple.

Byck was elected to the Louisville BOARD OF ALDERMEN in 1947 and served as president of the board from 1947 until 1953, when he decided not to seek reelection. As an alderman, Byck led the way in Louisville's expressway program. Together with his wife, Mary Helen, he was a leader in establishing the LOUISVILLE ORCHESTRA. He also helped sponsor passage of the city's 1 percent occupational tax, which assisted in numerous civic improvements.

When Louisville mayor E. LELAND TAYLOR died suddenly in 1947, Byck was acting mayor for a month until the Board of Aldermen named CHARLES FARNSLEY to succeed Taylor. As acting mayor, Byck cast the deciding vote in favor of Farnsley serving the remainder of Taylor's term.

Byck also served on the city's BOARD OF EDUCATION from 1955 to 1959, during the execution of the city's desegregation plan. He was president of the board in 1958 and a strong advocate of the merger of city and county schools. He was also a member of the UNIVERSITY OF LOUISVILLE Board of Overseers.

A lover of the arts, Byck was a three-time president of the Louisville Philharmonic Society, which managed the orchestra. He was also a member of the Players Club—later the Little Theater Co.—a local production company for plays, frequently taking on leading roles in such productions as Sidney Howard's *Lucky Sam McCarver.*

Byck enlisted as a private in the army in 1918 to serve in WORLD WAR I and was honorably discharged that same year. He also served as an infantryman during WORLD WAR II, from 1942 until 1945, rising to the rank of major. He married Mary Helen Adler on June 27, 1931; they had three children: Lucy, Elizabeth, and Dann Junior. Byck died at his home after an eight-month illness; his body was cremated. Byck Elementary School on Cedar Street is named in his honor.

BYCK, MARY HELEN (ADLER) (b Louisville, June 28, 1907; d Louisville, July 24, 1991). Businesswoman and civic leader. The only daughter of Cyrus Adler, Mary Helen Byck was one of Louisville's most prominent and well-respected community leaders, whose interests ranged from the support of the arts to politics and social activism.

She graduated from Vassar College in 1928 and shortly thereafter, on June 27, 1931, married DANN C. BYCK, head of Byck's women's clothing stores of Louisville. She was president of the business for two and a half years during WORLD WAR II, while her husband was in the army. She became the head of Byck's again in 1960 after her husband's death.

Though Byck was an influential force in the city's business community, she also had numerous public interests, including a lengthy affiliation with the DEMOCRATIC PARTY. Her involvement in politics began in 1930 when she went to work for the national convention of the LEAGUE OF WOMEN VOTERS. For a number of years she was an active worker for the Democratic Party at the local level, and in 1964 she represented Kentucky as a Democratic national committeewoman.

Byck was involved in the CIVIL RIGHTS movement. She was a staunch supporter of open housing and was one of the first to serve on the Kentucky Human Rights Commission. She was also a member of the Louisville-Jefferson County Urban Renewal Commission, and, as a proponent of Planned Parenthood, she funded the first such center for blacks in Louisville.

Another outlet for Byck's social activism was the HEALTH field. Not only was she involved with the Louisville Medical Research Foundation, but she also served for a time as vice president of the Regional Cancer Center Corp. In addition, she played a significant role in the establishment of the J. Graham Brown Cancer Center and the Park DuValle Community Health Center.

In 1937 Byck, along with her husband, Dann, helped to establish the modern version of the LOUISVILLE ORCHESTRA. In the early 1980s she was an important player in the campaign to construct the KENTUCKY CENTER FOR THE ARTS. Byck sat for almost twenty-five years on the board of the GARDENS OF LOUISVILLE, and in 1986 the auditorium was renamed the Mary Helen Byck Arena. Byck also served on the UNIVERSITY OF LOUISVILLE's Board of Overseers and in 1979 was elected its chair. She was also an active member of Louisville's Jewish community, and in 1964 her civic contributions were recognized when she received the Ottenheimer Award.

Mary Helen Byck and her husband, Dann, had three children, two daughters and a son. Ironically, she succumbed to cancer just one day after the Byck's stores in Louisville closed. Her body was cremated.

See *Courier-Journal,* July 25, 1991.

BYCK BROTHERS & COMPANY. Byck's appeared in Louisville in 1902 at 416 FOURTH ST. The concern was brought to the community by Louis Byck and his brother Werner, both of whom came to Louisville from Georgia. After a couple of years, the store moved to 338 Fourth St. and, by 1910, was located at 434–38 S Fourth. By 1924 the business, which had begun as a shoe store, had broadened to include quality women's wear and had once again relocated to a three-story establishment at 532–34 S Fourth St. Louis's son, Dann Byck Senior, who had graduated from LOUISVILLE MALE HIGH SCHOOL in 1917 and the University of Pennsylvania in 1921, went to work in his father's company in 1922. In 1925 he was named vice president and general manager of the store and, five years later, became president.

Dann Senior and his wife Mary Helen, a graduate of Vassar College, combined their retailing skills with their many civic interests. Byck served as the president of the BOARD OF ALDERMEN from 1947 to 1953, sat on the city's BOARD OF EDUCATION from 1955–59 and was a president of the Louisville Philharmonic Society. He died in 1960. MARY HELEN BYCK, who took over the management of the store after her husband's death, was an outspoken proponent of open housing. She was one of the original members of the Kentucky Commission on Human Rights.

Byck's was the first major downtown retailer to open a suburban location. In 1946 a branch was opened in ST. MATTHEWS at 3738 Lexington Rd. Eventually other outlets were located at Oxmoor Mall, Bashford Manor Mall, and Lexington's Fayette Mall. In 1982 the downtown store moved to the new GALLERIA nearby. On July 23, 1991, all of the Byck stores closed. Mary Helen Byck, who had been ill for some time, passed away the following day.

Kenneth L. Miller

CABBAGE PATCH. The Cabbage Patch area of Louisville was well known throughout the English-speaking world at the beginning of the twentieth century, thanks to the best-selling book *Mrs. Wiggs of the Cabbage Patch* (1901) by Louisville author ALICE HEGAN RICE. The book, set at the turn of the century, is a simple and somewhat sentimental story of a poor but cheerful widow who lived with her five children in a small cottage adjacent to railroad tracks. The family overcame all sorts of hardships, aided by a wealthy young woman who spent much of her time helping the poor.

The setting was based on an area west of Seventh St. along Hill St. The actual location extended west from Seventh to Fourteenth Streets and south from Victoria Place (Magnolia) to A St. (Gaulbert Ave.), part of which had been the back side of the old OAKLAND RACE COURSE. Prior to the CIVIL WAR, the rural nature of the neighborhood was changed by a LOUISVILLE & NASHVILLE RAILROAD (L&N) track built through the farmland in 1855. By the 1880s factories began to spring up there.

There were about five hundred to six hundred residents by the time Rice wrote her novel. The majority was AFRICAN AMERICAN surrounded by IRISH and GERMAN immigrants. The roads were dirt, and most residences were small cottages with adjoining sheds. Almost every house had its own growth of sunflowers, grapevines, and hollyhocks and a collection of geese, ducks, dogs, and cats. Water came from public pumps, while outhouses set over privy vaults provided a crude method of sanitation.

It was there that Louise Marshall chose to open the Cabbage Patch Settlement House in 1910 that focused on the specific needs of the residents. The facility was first located at 1461 S Ninth St. Marshall described the surroundings as "a section where there were truck gardens and there were people from the L & N shops who lived around them. The truck gardeners raised cabbages." In truth, most shop people lived in LIMERICK, north of the Patch.

Rice's fictional description coincided with Marshall's: "It was not a real cabbage patch, but a queer neighborhood, where ramshackle cottages played hop-scotch over the railroad tracks. There were no streets, so when a new house was built the owner faced it any way his fancy prompted. Mr. Bagby's grocery, it is true, conformed to convention, and presented a solid front to the railroad track, but Miss Hazy's cottage shied off sidewise into the Wiggses' yard, as if it were afraid of the big freight-trains that went thundering past so many times a day."

The origin of the name *Cabbage Patch* is open to interpretation; however, the area was first developed as Burghardt's Addition, and the designation seems to have been used after the publication of Rice's novel. Today the area is included in the ALGONQUIN and PARK HILL NEIGHBORHOODS.

See Alice Hegan Rice, *Mrs. Wiggs of the Cabbage Patch* (New York 1901); *Courier-Journal*, Aug. 11, 1901; Martin E. Biemer, *The Story of the Cabbage Patch Settlement House As Told by Those Who Lived It* (Louisville 1993).

Jacqueline M. Hersh

CABLE TELEVISION. The beginnings of cable television are linked to the reception problems of the mountainous areas of Pennsylvania in the late 1940s. Shortly thereafter, entrepreneurs in the mountain towns of eastern Kentucky began setting up common antennas on mountaintops so that numerous families could receive clearer television signals from stations in Huntington, West Virginia, and Lexington. Due to technological improvements by 1971, Kentucky had eighty-eight small cable companies. Because of their proximity to the signal's origination, larger cities at first had little need for cable television. However, the prospect of piping in channels from other cities and an expanded capability of up to twenty channels prompted cable companies to enter larger markets in the 1970s.

In 1969 Cablecom Inc., a venture owned by several local and out-of-state businessmen, submitted a proposal to the BOARD OF ALDERMEN to establish a cable service franchise in Louisville. With the Federal Communications Commission (FCC) still determining rules and guidelines for the burgeoning cable market, the local government was cautious. The aldermen passed an ordinance late in 1969 detailing guidelines for the cable industry in Louisville, but, because of proposed FCC minimum requirements, it was repealed early in 1971 before a franchise was awarded.

While the Louisville side of the river argued over regulations, GRC TV Inc. began offering the area's first cable service to residents of JEFFERSONVILLE and CLARK COUNTY, INDIANA, in October 1971. A month later, the Louisville aldermen passed another cable television ordinance, and, by the following March, seventeen companies sought the nonexclusive franchise. In February 1972 the FCC passed its final regulations, which, among other things, opened up the top one hundred markets, including Louisville, to outside channel feeds.

Early in 1973 the aldermen began sifting through twelve formal proposals. In November they awarded the franchise to River City Cable Television Inc., a subsidiary of Communications Properties Inc. (CPI) of Austin, Texas (later purchased by Times Mirror Corp.). However, as southern Indiana continued to be hooked up, little work, outside of mapping wire locations, transpired in Louisville into 1978, prompting questions and complaints. Finally, in January 1979, the first fifty homes in the city were connected to cable.

In June 1979 the Jefferson County government passed its ordinance concerning cable television. In November Storer Communications of Jefferson County, a branch of the Storer Broadcasting Co. of Miami, was awarded the county franchise despite the objections of County Judge/Executive MITCH MCCONNELL, who wanted the same system as the city's. By mid-1981 cable television had a firm grip in the Louisville area, as the entire city had been connected and outlying counties had selected their services as well. In late 1982 CPI changed its name to Dimension Cable Services.

Cabbage Patch Settlement House, 1409-1413 S. Sixth Street, 1947.

With the two competing companies vying for the many suburban city franchises in Jefferson County, neither was able to get a dominant foothold in the area. In 1984 CPI and Storer's parent companies agreed to a deal in which Storer got the franchise to all of Jefferson County and Louisville along with two other cities in the Midwest. In 1985 the Board of Aldermen voted to extend a twenty-year contract to Storer.

After Storer's parent company sold off its cable television franchises in 1992, Louisville's cable company changed its name the following year to TCI/TKR Cable of Greater Louisville (commonly referred to as TKR) to reflect its new affiliation with TKR Cable of New Jersey. In 1994 TKR announced that it would spend more than $150 million over five years to upgrade the Louisville system to fiber-optic cable, enabling the system to carry up to five hundred channels. By the end of 1996 much of Jefferson County had been upgraded, but work was halted before entering the city limits because of a dispute over the extension of the franchise, set to expire in 2005. In April 1998, the Board of Aldermen agreed to extend the franchise until 2010. Promising to have the work completed by July 1999, TKR outlined a citywide installation schedule that prevented preferential treatment to higher-income neighborhoods. Later that spring, InterMedia Partners, a Nashville firm, purchased TCI's (now known as AT&T Broadband & Internet Services) majority ownership in TKR.

In 1999 Insight Communications Co. of New York purchased a 50 percent interest and management control of InterMedia Partners. AT&T Broadband & Internet Services will continue to own the other half of the stock in TKR. The acquisition makes Insight the tenth-largest cable company in the United States, with 780,000 customers in Kentucky and Indiana.

See *Courier-Journal,* Nov. 14, 1979, June 7, 1997.

CAESAR (b Chesterfield County, Virginia, ca. 1758; d Fayette County, Kentucky, 1836). Artificer. Caesar was born a slave on the plantation of William Robertson. In 1773 Robertson's son, James (1751–82), inherited Caesar and decided to migrate to the Natchez District on the Mississippi River. He took Caesar with him, and they arrived at the Holston River, where they and about 150 other settlers and their slaves built boats and embarked on a long and perilous voyage down the Tennessee, Ohio, and Mississippi Rivers to Natchez. After reaching the settlement that summer, Robertson, a carpenter, settled on 250 acres and made a living building houses for settlers and merchants in the area.

In the spring of 1778, Capt. James Willing led an expedition down the Mississippi River to raid British settlements in West Florida (which included Natchez) and to keep the river open as a supply route from New Orleans to CLARK'S forces in the Illinois country. When Willing secured Natchez for the Americans in March, Robertson joined his forces, under the command of Capt. Robert George, and sailed up the Mississippi River to Fort Clark (Kaskaskia, Illinois), taking Caesar with him. In March 1779 Robertson was commissioned a lieutenant, and Caesar was made an artificer in Captain George's artillery company.

Artificers were skilled carpenters, sawyers, coopers, and blacksmiths who constructed most of the forts, wagons, and boats that were used by the Americans in the Illinois country. Caesar, a carpenter, was one of the artificers who rebuilt Fort Clark in the spring of 1779. That summer Captain George's company was ordered to Louisville. After spending the bitterly cold winter of 1779–80 there, they went down the OHIO RIVER and built Fort Jefferson, just south of present-day Wickliffe, Kentucky. The artificers built the stockade fence, blockhouses, boats, gun carriages, and storehouses. Caesar was the only known AFRICAN AMERICAN who served as an artificer at Fort Jefferson, enduring Indian attacks and lack of food and other supplies until the fort was evacuated in June 1781.

Caesar and the rest of Captain George's company sailed up the Ohio River to FORT NELSON (Louisville), and Caesar spent the next two years repairing the fort and building boats, including a large armed galley that patrolled the Ohio River. In 1782 James Robertson, who had been on detached duty on the Mississippi River throughout the war, died in Natchez, and Caesar came into the possession of Philip Barbour, a Virginia merchant and trader. Barbour sold Caesar to JOHN CAMPBELL, whose slave he remained until Campbell's death in 1799. By 1807 Caesar had been taken to Lexington, Kentucky, by William Beard, one of Campbell's heirs. Caesar lived on the Beard farm for the rest of his life and died there.

See George Rogers Clark papers 1779–84, (photostats of original papers) Filson Club Historical Society, Special Collections Department; Jefferson County Order and Minute Book, July 1, 1782, Estate Inventory of James Robinson, 45; Old Chancery Court (Jefferson County) Case #1738, James Robinson Heirs v. Philip C.S. Barbour, 1818.

Cornelius Bogert

CAESARS INDIANA. In 1994 the voters of HARRISON COUNTY, INDIANA, approved a gaming referendum that opened the door for riverboat GAMBLING. After sifting through five proposals filed in January 1995 to develop a Harrison County–based casino, the Indiana Gaming Commission awarded a preliminary license to the partnership of Riverboat Development Inc. (RDI) and Caesars, a division of the ITT Corp., in May 1996. RDI/Caesars unveiled plans for a $228 million (a figure that had grown to $275 million by early 1998) complex near the unincorporated town of Bridgeport, located approximately fifteen miles southwest of Louisville near the FLOYD COUNTY line.

After Louisville officials, trying to protect the HORSE-RACING industry, and environmental groups raised concerns about the impact of the project on the local wildlife, waterways, and air quality, the U.S. ARMY CORPS OF ENGINEERS, responsible for issuing the work permit, began a preliminary study. In February 1998 the corps concluded that a full environmental evaluation, which would have delayed construction a year, would not be necessary. Along with the work permit, the corps specified restrictions on clearing trees, preservation of certain woods and wetlands, and the treatment of runoff water going into the river. By the time the permit was issued, RDI/Caesars had already begun $11 million in improvements at the site. Gambling was set to begin in late summer 1998. However, following heavy spring rains, questions from the Environmental Protection Agency concerning the corps' lack of a full environmental impact study, and a lawsuit filed by three Indiana environmental groups, Caesars officials pushed their projected opening to fall. Finally, on November 16, 1998, the casino opened for a VIP cruise followed by public cruises that began November 20, 1998.

The complex includes a $50 million, four-story vessel, *The Glory of Rome,* North America's largest riverboat. *The Glory of Rome* is 452 feet long and 100 feet wide, comprising 173,200 square feet excluding the hold spaces, and extends 8 feet below the waterline and 100 feet from the waterline to the top of the smokestacks. More than 140 gaming tables, 2,800 slot machines, and 3,600 gaming positions await up to 5,000 passengers in the 93,000-square-foot casino. Additions to the site include a five-hundred-room hotel and conference center, a sports and entertainment coliseum, four restaurants, a shopping center, a nature preserve, and an offsite golf course. These projects resulted in a total employment of twenty-four hundred people. Economic impact upon the metropolitan area was projected to be extensive, while critics pointed to the social problems it would create. It was estimated that the casino would take $12 million annually from the Kentucky lottery.

Starwood Hotels and Resorts Worldwide, Inc., acquired Caesars World, Inc. in 1998 as part of a $14.6 billion purchase of ITT Corp. In 1999 Starwood Hotels, which owns Sheraton and St. Regis/Luxury Collection hotels, sold Caesars World, Inc. to focus on its hotel business. Park Place Entertainment Corp., the world's largest gaming company, bought Caesars World Inc. (the parent company of Caesars Indiana) for $3 billion cash.

See *Courier-Journal,* Feb. 11, 1998, April 17, 1998, Nov. 15, 1998; April 28, 1999.

CALDWELL, CHARLES (b Caswell County, North Carolina, May 14, 1772; d Louisville, July 9, 1853). Physician and educator.

He was the son of Lt. Charles and Mrs. Murray Caldwell, both Irish immigrants from County Tyrone in Ulster. He earned an M.D. degree in 1796 from the University of Pennsylvania, where he studied under renowned physician Benjamin Rush. Caldwell then practiced medicine in Philadelphia, taught at his alma mater, and edited the magazine *Port Folio* (1814–16), a most influential literary journal of the early nineteenth century, to which he also contributed.

He moved to Lexington in 1819 at the invitation of the president of Transylvania University, where he developed the medical faculty into one of the nation's strongest, although his arrogance and quarrelsomeness made opponents of many. In 1821, with ten thousand dollars appropriated by the General Assembly and with other funds, Caldwell purchased in France a notable collection of rare scientific books, many of which are still at Transylvania.

Dismissed by the university's trustees in 1837, Caldwell helped to found the LOUISVILLE MEDICAL INSTITUTE, one of the two forerunners of the UNIVERSITY OF LOUISVILLE; its success was the downfall of Transylvania's medical program. He was elected professor of the institutes of medicine and clinical practice and medical jurisprudence at the school. In 1849 he was also dismissed from the Louisville medical department of the Institute. He is said to have gone to Nashville, Tennessee, to start another medical school, but no other information is available. Caldwell felt his dismissal from Louisville was engineered by his replacement, Dr. Lunsford P. Yandell, whom Caldwell felt harbored petty jealousies over his successes.

Author of more than two hundred publications, Caldwell was advanced for the time in his study of fevers and in his teaching that nature tends to restore health without the physician's intervention. He introduced clinical instruction in medicine at the Blockley Alms House (Philadelphia General Hospital) in 1802, gave one of the first courses in medical jurisprudence in the United States in 1812, and helped to define maritime quarantine procedures for many East Coast port cities such as New York and Boston. But Caldwell courted controversy in his defense of such pseudo-scientific medical theories as phrenology, or the study of the skull; mesmerism; and the outmoded concept of vitalism.

Caldwell married Eliza Leaming on January 3, 1799, and the couple had one son, Thomas Leaming Caldwell, before divorcing. He then married Mrs. Mary (Warner) Barton in 1842. After his death, a stepdaughter edited his autobiography, which remains the principal source of information on his life. He is buried in Cave Hill Cemetery.

See Charles Caldwell, *Autobiography of Charles Caldwell, M.D.* (Philadelphia 1855); Emmet Field Horine, *Biographical Sketch and Guide to the Writings of Charles Caldwell, M.D.* (Brooks, Ky., 1960).

CALDWELL, ISAAC (b near Columbia, Adair County, Kentucky, June 30, 1824; d Louisville, November 25, 1885). Attorney and educator. The son of William and Anne (Trabue) Caldwell, he attended Kentucky's Georgetown College, studied LAW, and was admitted to the bar in 1847. He practiced law in Columbia, first with Judge Zachariah Wheat, then with his brother, U.S. congressman George Alfred Caldwell.

In 1852 they moved their office to Louisville, where Caldwell became one of the city's most successful criminal lawyers. In 1870 Caldwell championed the LOUISVILLE AND NASHVILLE RAILROAD and its business interests when the Kentucky General Assembly considered granting a charter to the Cincinnati Southern Railroad, Cincinnati's challenge to the L&N in the southern trade. In 1872 Caldwell opposed the primacy of federal authority in Kentucky civil rights matters when he argued the case of *Blyew v. United States* before the U.S. Supreme Court.

He was the third president of the UNIVERSITY OF LOUISVILLE (1869–85). During those years the university's medical department joined the American Medical College Association (founded in 1876) and raised its standards for admission and graduation. As he was seriously ill in his last year, he called meetings of the board of trustees at his home.

Caldwell married Catherine Smith of Louisville on January 20, 1857. He is buried in Louisville's St. Louis Cemetery. An editorial in the *COURIER-JOURNAL* on the day after his death declared that Caldwell left "no equal behind him at the bar whose recognized head he was [for] so long."

See *A Centennial History of the University of Louisville* (Louisville 1939); Leonard P. Curry, *Rail Routes South: Louisville's Fight for the Southern Market* (Lexington 1969); J. Stoddard Johnston, ed., *Memorial History of Louisville,* (Chicago 1896).

William J. Morison

CALDWELL, MARY ELIZABETH BRECKINRIDGE (b Cincinnati, Ohio, December 26, 1865; d Thoune, Switzerland, December 16, 1910) and **MARY GUENDALINE BYRD** (b Cincinnati, Ohio, October 21, 1863; d on the North Atlantic, October 5, 1909). Philanthropists and property owners. Mary Elizabeth Breckinridge (Baroness von Zedtwitz) and Mary Guendaline (also spelled Gwendoline) Byrd (Marquise des Monstiers Merinville) Caldwell were the daughters of WILLIAM SHAKESPEARE CALDWELL (1821–74), one of Louisville's first multimillionaires.

Born in New Orleans and the son of an actor, William Shakespeare Caldwell had some success as a theatrical producer. He inherited some wealth and turned it into a vast fortune through various business ventures. He owned several extensive tracts of real estate in Louisville, including property at Brook and Breckinridge Streets, later the site of MALE HIGH SCHOOL. His estate included downtown Louisville property and land that became BOWMAN FIELD, Seneca Park, and part of Cherokee Park. He also had a mansion in New York City and another in Newport, Rhode Island.

After settling in Louisville, Caldwell married Mary Eliza Breckinridge, the daughter of JAMES D. BRECKINRIDGE, a former congressman and brigadier general in the War of 1812, and the niece of brothers JAMES and JOSHUA SPEED. Mary Eliza died in 1867. The Saints Mary and Elizabeth Hospital was financed by Caldwell to honor his wife. The hospital, which was opened may 18, 1874, was a four-story structure located at Twelfth St. and Magnolia Ave. built at a cost of eighty-four thousand dollars. Caldwell also contributed a fifty-thousand-dollar trust fund to help maintain the facility. Sadly, the elder Caldwell died only five days after the hospital's dedication.

Shakespeare Caldwell and his daughters often made trips to Europe. During one of those trips, Mary Guendaline was briefly engaged to Prince Murat, a grandson of the King of Naples, until the prince insisted that she give him half of her estate as part of the marriage settlement. Mary Guendaline finally wed the Marquis des Monstiers Merinville in October 1896 in Paris. Bishop JOHN LANCASTER SPALDING of Peoria, Illinois, and formerly of Louisville, performed the ceremony.

The marriage was unsuccessful, and she returned to New York City. She gave much of her fortune to Catholic charities and institutions, one of the largest being a gift of three hundred thousand dollars for the divinity school housed in the Caldwell Building of Washington's Catholic University of America. In 1904 she renounced her membership in the Catholic church. In a statement to the press she said, "My Protestant blood has asserted itself." Her younger sister also later left the Catholic church.

Mary Elizabeth followed in her older sister's footsteps by marrying a foreign noble, the Baron Kurt von Zedtwitz. He was a promising German diplomat who at one time held the post of minister to Mexico. He also served in the German missions at St. Petersburg, Tokyo, Stockholm, and in Washington, D.C., where he met Mary Elizabeth. It was in Washington that von Zedtwitz commissioned the famous naval designers, the Herreschoffs, to build him a yacht he later named the *Isolde*. On August 18, 1896, the baron was killed while taking part in the Royal Albert Regatta at Southsea, England. When the *Isolde* was rammed by Kaiser Wilhelm II's royal yacht, *Meteor*, the baron was thrown into the water and drowned in front of the Kaiser. The baron and Mary Elizabeth had one son, Waldemar Conrad von Zedtwitz.

Following his mother's death, Waldemar Conrad von Zedtwitz inherited the family fortune, including the substantial property holdings in Louisville. The young Zedtwitz became involved in litigation over the property because he was a German citizen and had served in the German army during WORLD WAR I. Believed to have been killed at the Battle of Verdun, he resurfaced in the 1920s to claim his mother's American estate. His property in Louisville, at the time valued at approximately $1 million, had been seized during the war by the custodian of the Alien Property Office. The courts eventually restored most of it to him. In 1928 the estate was purchased by the city, and the property became Bowman Field and Seneca Park.

The two sisters died within a year of each other. It was generally believed that the sisters had strong ties to Louisville because of their vast holdings here, yet the baroness is thought to have visited the city only once in her lifetime, in May 1906. However, both are buried in Louisville's CAVE HILL CEMETERY. Their grave site is marked by the Gilbert Bayes statue of the Two Sisters, a well-known cemetery landmark. There are also reminders of the family in addition to the monument, including streets named Baroness, Caldwell, and Gwendolyn.

The hospital moved from its initial location in January 1958 because of increasing industrialization in that neighborhood. The new structure, on Bluegrass Ave. in the South End, was renamed as a Caritas Hospital in April 1995. Following the dissolution of the Catholic Sisters of Charity health system, the 331-bed facility was renamed as part of the Catholic Health Initiative in September 1997.

See J. Stoddard Johnston, *A Memorial History of Louisville* (Chicago 1896); George H. Yater, *Two Hundred Years at the Falls of the Ohio* (Louisville 1987); *Herald Post*, May 8, 1928; *Courier-Journal*, June 15, 1928.

CALDWELL, WILLIAM SHAKESPEARE (b Fredricksburg, Virginia, February 11, 1821; d Richmond, Virginia, May 1874). Businessman. Caldwell was the son of an English-born actor, James H. Caldwell, and Maria Carter (Hall) Caldwell. He achieved early success as a theater manager and owner. However, it was not until Caldwell left the stage and moved from New Orleans to Louisville that he amassed his real fortune, establishing gas companies in such cities as Cincinnati, St. Louis, New Orleans, and Mobile, Alabama. This, along with his prosperous ventures in Louisville real estate, made Caldwell one of the city's first multimillionaires by the late 1850s.

Shortly before the Civil War, Caldwell and his wife, Mary Eliza Breckinridge, moved to Cincinnati, where their two daughters, MARY GUENDALINE BYRD and Mary Elizabeth Breckinridge, were born. The family traveled extensively along the East Coast and in Europe until Caldwell's wife died suddenly in January 1867. Overcome by grief, Caldwell moved to Richmond, Virginia, where he sought solace in Catholicism. Under the guidance of his spiritual advisor, Father JOHN LANCASTER SPALDING, Caldwell generously donated to various Catholic charities. In particular, he paid for the construction of the Saints Mary and Elizabeth Hospital at Twelfth and Magnolia Streets in Louisville. Managed by the Sisters of Charity of Nazareth, the hospital also received a fifty-thousand-dollar operating trust from Caldwell. At the time of his death in 1874, Caldwell's estate included holdings of land along Taylorsville Rd. and the site of MALE HIGH SCHOOL on Brook St.

See Carl E. Kramer, *The Strange Genealogy of Louisville's Bowman Field and Seneca Park* (Louisville 1986); *Herald Post*, May 8, 1928.

CALDWELL TANKS INC. Caldwell Tanks Inc., is the largest privately owned, elevated water-tank company in the United States. Founded in 1887 by William E. Caldwell and originally named W.E. Caldwell Co., the firm built tanks to supply water to railroad steam locomotives and also to towns, mills, and factories. The firm remained a family business until 1986, when it was purchased by industrialist James W. Robinson. He appointed former banker Bernard S. Fineman president. Caldwell Co., originally located at Brook and Brandeis Streets, is now situated at 4025 Tower Rd.

Barbara G. Zingman

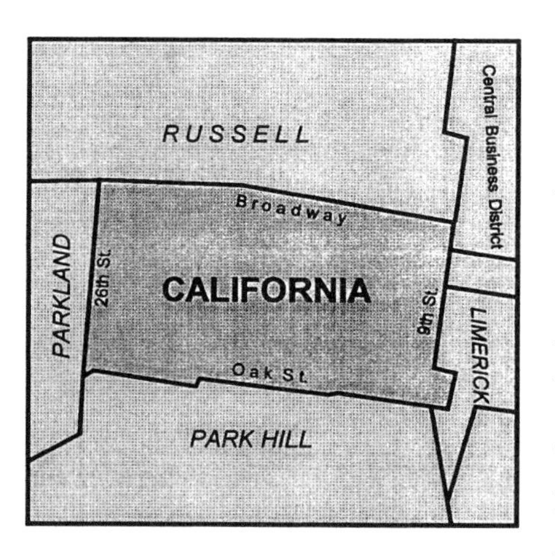

CALIFORNIA. While no written records are known to exist about the beginning of the California neighborhood (ringed by Ninth and Twenty-sixth Streets and BROADWAY and Oak St.), the area was settled by GERMANS around the time of the 1849 Gold Rush. Oral tradition holds that because the land, dubbed the Henderson subdivision, was the "far west" of the city, it was called California.

After the CIVIL WAR, many AFRICAN AMERICANS began settling in the area, which led to the establishment of the California Colored School and the local branch of the Freedman's Bureau. By the 1870s, California was a working-class neighborhood with a mixed population of whites and African Americans. Many of the white families began leaving the region for the SUBURBS around the turn of the century.

From 1950 to 1980, the area was plagued by crime and decaying property. It lost approximately 50 percent of its population and 40 percent of its single-family housing. URBAN RENEWAL programs unsuccessfully attempted to revitalize California in the 1960s. The BROWN-FORMAN CORP., whose headquarters and bottling supplies warehouse are in the neighborhood, began a program in 1989 that funded $250,000 in renovations and housing projects in the area.

See George Yater, *Two Hundred Years at the Falls of the Ohio* (Louisville 1979).

CALLAHAN, PATRICK HENRY (b Cleveland, Ohio, October 15, 1866; d Louisville, February 4, 1940). Businessman, progressive. The son of Irish Catholic immigrants Comac John and Mary Frances (Connolly) Callahan, Patrick came of age in a late-nineteenth-century melting pot. He attended SPENCERIAN BUSINESS COLLEGE in Louisville and went to work for the Glidden Paint Co. in Chicago. He prospered as a leader in the PAINT and varnish business in Louisville from the 1890s to his death.

A devout Catholic, he actively participated in the affairs of the church. During WORLD WAR I, he initiated a crusade against religious intolerance that consumed much of his time in the years ahead. He often personally confronted such organizations as the Ku Klux Klan. While Callahan adamantly defended the tenets of Catholicism, he often took his own co-religionists to task for not adhering to his ideals of American civil religion. As president of the Louisville Varnish Co., Callahan directly applied his religious beliefs to the workplace. With the collaboration of Monsignor John A. Ryan of the Catholic University of America, he designed a workable profit-sharing plan in 1912 that weathered the GREAT DEPRESSION.

After the turn of the century, Callahan became increasingly active in politics. He employed the "Callahan Correspondence," a widely distributed mimeographed series of communications with leading political, religious, and business figures, to influence public opinion. Using the honorary Kentucky title of "Colonel," he gained entry to political and religious circles in the South because of his unbending support of PROHIBITION. In 1928 he broke with the DEMOCRATIC PARTY for the only time and stoutly opposed the presidential candidacy of Gov. Al Smith, a wet.

Callahan's life served as a model of the archetypal progressive. A large, handsome man with a hail-fellow-well-met personality in the best sense, he counted among his friends such diverse personalities as William Jennings Bryan and H.L. Mencken.

Callahan married Julia Laure Cahill on January 20, 1891. They had three children: John, Robert, and Edith. Callahan is buried in Calvary Cemetery.

See William E. Ellis, *Patrick Henry Callahan:*

Progressive Catholic Layman in the American South (Lewiston, N.Y., 1989); idem, "Patrick Henry Callahan: A Kentucky Democrat in National Party Politics," *Filson Club History Quarterly* 39 (Jan.–March 1979): 51–61; idem, "Labor Management Relations in the Progressive Era: A Profit-Sharing Experience in Louisville," *Register of the Kentucky Historical Society* 78 (Spring 1980): 140–56; idem, "Kentucky Catholic and Maryland Skeptic: The Correspondence of Colonel Patrick Henry Callahan and H.L. Mencken," *Filson Club History Quarterly* 58 (July 1984), 336–48; idem, "Patrick Henry Callahan: A Maverick Catholic and the Prohibition Issue," *Register of the Kentucky Historical Society* 92 (Spring 1994): 175–99.

William E. Ellis

CALVARY EPISCOPAL CHURCH. Calvary Episcopal Church was founded on December 24, 1860, when members of the Sehon Methodist Church at Third and Guthrie Streets seceded from that denomination and united with the Episcopal church. The congregation worshiped in the former Sehon Chapel (later the site of Trinity Towers), until 1872 when construction was begun on a new church on FOURTH ST. between York and Breckinridge.

William H. Redin, a local architect with a reputation for ecclesiastical design, drew up the plans for the new structure. The work was completed in two phases: the sanctuary and part of the nave between 1872–75, and the remainder of the nave and the asymmetrical west front between 1885–89. The second phase, done by the firm of MCDONALD BROTHERS, relied heavily upon Redin's concepts.

Calvary Church is Victorian Gothic Revival in style. The main facade, constructed with two types of Indiana limestone, consists of a central gable with flanking spire and tower of differing heights. In designing the interior, Redin took into account the congregation's theological orientation. It was neither "high nor low," with equal emphasis on ritual and preaching. To accommodate this viewpoint, Redin combined a traditional Latin cross longitudinal form suited for liturgical processions, with a circular form suitable for preaching. The crossing between the narrow nave and flanking transepts at Calvary is unusual in its octagonal design. Other unusual characteristics include a ceiling patterned after Westminster Hall in London and a variety of stained glass windows, including early Victorian survivors of the Sehon Chapel, works of the Tiffany studios, and windows painted in a Renaissance style.

Two priests distinguished Calvary with long years of service. The Reverend James G. Minnegerode, serving from 1878–1913, guided the completion of the building, and the Reverend Frank William Charles Elliot-Baker officiated from 1926–57.

A devotion to excellence in MUSIC has been a hallmark of Calvary Church since the turn of the century.

See Walter E. Langsam, *Calvary Episcopal Church* (An Unofficial History) undated; *Cornerstone Centennial Celebration of Calvary Episcopal Church 1872–1972* (Louisville 1972); J. Stoddard Johnston, ed., *Memorial History of Louisville* (Chicago 1896).

Olivia M. Frederick

CAMBERLEY BROWN HOTEL. The fifteen-story, six-hundred-room Brown Hotel opened in October 1923 on the northeast corner of BROADWAY and FOURTH ST., ushering in a spate of development at that intersection that prompted the *Herald-Post* in 1927 to call it the "magic corner." The hotel, designed by St. Louis architect Preston I. Bradshaw, was the city's largest hostelry and vied with the SEELBACH HOTEL of 1905 as the finest. It took its name from builder JAMES GRAHAM BROWN, who had come to Louisville at the turn of the century, made a fortune in lumber, and developed a passion for improving his adopted city. The hotel's Crystal Ballroom, with its crystal chandeliers, became the scene of Louisville's most elaborate social events, and the English Grill its finest restaurant. In May 1928 the hotel's amenities were further enhanced with the Roof Garden. Much fanfare was made over former British Prime Minister David Lloyd George being the first to sign the guest register, but Lloyd George never stayed at the Brown; he was simply impressed with the ARCHITECTURE and asked to see it.

Then came the GREAT DEPRESSION of the 1930s. The hotel survived, although it was touch-and-go at times. It bounced back during WORLD WAR II and the immediate postwar years, but by the 1960s downtown was suffering body blows from spreading suburbia with its proliferation of shopping malls and motels. During its heyday, however, the Brown entertained the most fashionable and famous who passed through Louisville: Al Jolson got in a fight in the English Grill, Queen Marie of Romania sat in court in the Crystal Ballroom atop a gold throne; and Bing Crosby, Bob Hope, Liberace, Elizabeth Taylor, Mary Pickford, and Helen Hayes all took in the elegance of the Bluegrass Room. A sixty-two-year-old D.W. GRIFFITH married a twenty-two-year-old woman on the third-floor mezzanine, Gen. Dwight Eisenhower drank at the Bluegrass Room bar, and a young VICTOR MATURE even worked as a hotel elevator operator until his fixation with a young lady dancing in the Roof Garden cost him his job. Guests became fewer, and the hotel's spit and polish began to lose its gleam. When lifelong bachelor Brown died in 1969 at the age of eighty-seven, the hotel's death knell seemed to sound too. The bulk of his estate, including the Brown Hotel, went to the J. Graham Brown Foundation, which he had established in 1943 to make grants to causes that benefited Louisville.

The foundation determined to sell the hotel. It found a buyer in the Louisville BOARD OF EDUCATION, which turned the structure into administrative offices and the Brown Education Center. The hotel closed on March 1, 1971. It was little noted at the time, but a number of longtime residents were permitted to stay, paying rent to the board. The building remained, but its days as a top-notch hotel were over, or so it seemed.

Yet on January ll, 1985, a totally refurbished Brown opened its doors to the public. This transformation followed the merger of the Louisville public schools with the county system in 1975, plus the effort to revitalize downtown. The Broadway/Brown Partnership was formed to renew the business district's southern edge, with the restoration of the Brown Hotel the prime objective. Returned to its pristine beauty and with its 600 rooms reduced to 296—but each twice as large—the hotel has been operated by national hotel chains.

See Kay Gill and Mary Lou Northern, *The Brown Hotel* (Louisville 1985); and George H. Yater, *Flappers, Prohibition and All That Jazz: Louisville Remembers the Twenties* (Louisville 1984).

George H. Yater

CAMP, EDWARD FRANKLIN, JR. (b Trenton, Kentucky, December 23, 1905; d Louisville, January 26, 1986). Football coach. Camp graduated in 1930 from Transylvania University, where he was a quarterback on the football team. Following graduation he was a high school football coach at Hodgenville, Glasgow, and Henderson. In 1946 he was hired to restart the UNIVERSITY OF LOUISVILLE's (U of L) languishing football program, which had been dormant from 1943 to 1945 during WORLD WAR II.

Known as "The Little Man" because of his height, Frank Camp served as head coach of Cardinal football for twenty-three years (1946–69). During that time he coached such future professional football greats as Johnny Unitas, Lenny Lyles, Doug Buffone, and Ernie Green. Unitas played from 1951 to 1954 and was later a Hall of Fame quarterback with the Baltimore Colts. Lyles, who played at U of L from 1954 to 1957, enjoyed a twelve-year career in the National Football League. Buffone was an all-pro linebacker for the Chicago Bears. Green was Jim Brown's running mate in the backfield of the Cleveland Browns.

With a record of 118 wins, 95 losses, and 2 ties, Camp was U of L's winningest football coach. He retired in 1969 but continued as assistant director of athletics from 1969 to 1975.

Camp married Nancy Elmore in 1946. They had four daughters. Camp is buried in Resthaven Memorial Park.

See *Courier-Journal*, Jan. 27, 1986.

CAMPBELL, JOHN (b Strabane in Ulster, Northern Ireland, ca. 1735; d Frankfort, 1799). Entrepreneur and land speculator. John Campbell, who with Dr. JOHN CONNOLLY attempted to found a town at the FALLS OF THE

OHIO in 1774, was a frontier entrepreneur and civic leader. He may have come to Pennsylvania in 1755 with Gen. Edward Braddock's troops in the failed effort to wrest Fort Duquesne (Pittsburgh) from the French during the French and Indian War. In 1761, after the French were ousted, he was listed as a "trader" and owner of a house in Pittsburgh.

Campbell, with Philadelphia commercial connections, became one of the more successful Indian fur traders on the frontier. He was also a backer of Virginia's claim to the Pittsburgh area. This stance helped him gain a half-interest in a four-thousand-acre land grant at the Falls in 1773 made by Virginia governor Dunmore. The grant, shared with Dr. Connolly, encompassed much of present Louisville north of BROADWAY. Their attempt to found a town was thwarted by Dunmore's War in 1774 and then the outbreak of the American Revolution. Campbell, as a partner in and agent of a speculative venture to acquire vast tracts of land in the Illinois country, came to Louisville in 1779 and no doubt informed the settlers of his claim to the land. On his return river journey to Pittsburgh, the flotilla in which he traveled was attacked by Indians near present day Cincinnati. He was taken prisoner and held by the British in Montreal until late 1782.

On his release, Campbell resumed his mercantile career and speculation from his land (now Louisville's West End) at the Falls. He became a leading citizen: a justice of the Jefferson County Court, a delegate to two of the Danville statehood conventions (1784 and 1785), a Jefferson County representative in the Virginia legislature, a member of the convention that framed Kentucky's first constitution in 1792, and a state senator from Jefferson County that same year. In 1783 he was one of three commissioners (with GEORGE ROGERS CLARK and John Bailey) to pick the site of a town in the Illinois Grant made to Clark's troops. The town is CLARKSVILLE, INDIANA. In 1785 he founded Campbell Town (later SHIPPINGPORT) at the lower end of the Falls, built the area's first tobacco warehouse, and established a ferry to Clarksville.

About 1795 he moved to his extensive land holdings southeast of Lexington and in that year was elected chairman of the board of Transylvania University, succeeding John Bradford, publisher of the *Kentucky Gazette.* Philadelphian Dr. George Hunter, touring the West in the 1790s, recorded that Campbell kept "Bachelors Hall in a truly hospitable and genteel style—is very rich." Lexingtonian William A. Leavy recalled Campbell as "herculian[4] in form." He was elected to the state Senate from Fayette County in 1796 and died suddenly at his Senate seat in 1799. He is buried near the Nicholasville Pike on his own acreage. His grave is unmarked.

See William A. Leavy, "A Memoir of Lexington and its Vicinity," *Register of the Kentucky Historical Society* 40 (April 1942): 117; Thomas Clark, ed., *The Voice of the Frontier: John Bradford's Notes on Kentucky* (Lexington 1993).

George H. Yater

CAMPBELL, THOMAS (b Scotland, ca. 1810; d Louisville, September 17, 1847) Artist. The son of Thomas Frazer Campbell, the artist was first listed in an 1832 Baltimore newspaper as a "painter from Edinburgh." In 1834 he formed a partnership for a lithographic press in Baltimore with lithographer COLIN MILNE. To enhance his income during this period, Campbell also became a general agent for medicinal products, such as "Morison's Hygeian Medicine," and publications. After moving to Louisville in 1835, he convinced Milne to join him due to the abundant amount of work available here.

Milne sold the medicinal business, and the two resumed work in Louisville and outlying areas in 1836. He remained active in Louisville until his death, although he lived and worked in Cincinnati from 1840 to 1844. Most of Campbell's miniature portraits have been lost, but two of Samuel and Abigail Churchill have survived, along with several stone plates for the proposed *Kentucky Stock Book*, scenic covers for sheet music, and book illustrations. Some works are located in the Los Angeles County Museum of Art, while others are held in the FILSON CLUB HISTORICAL SOCIETY collection.

Campbell and his wife, Mary, who died on August 20, 1858, had six children: Thomas F., a stone engraver, carver, and sculptor; John Allan, a landscape painter and sculptor; Dougald, a sculptor who was killed during the Civil War battle at Chickamauga; Sarah McKee; Charlotte; and Margaret.

See Martin F. Schmidt, "The Artist and the Artisan: Two Men of Early Louisville," *Filson Club History Quarterly* 62 (Jan. 1988): 32–51.

Martin F. Schmidt

CAMP TAPAWINGO. Opened in the summer of 1924 by the Young Men's Hebrew Association (YMHA) and predecessor to the JEWISH COMMUNITY CENTER, Camp Tapawingo was eight miles east of Louisville, about one mile below HARRODS CREEK along the River Rd. The seventeen-acre facility served as a gathering place for Louisville Jews during the summer as well as a summer camp for both boys and girls.

Originally, the camp was a grouping of tents set up for temporary usage; however, in a fundraising endeavor, thirty-five permanent cottages were built along the gravel road that led to the OHIO RIVER. These cottages were rented out, and the proceeds went toward the development of the recreational complex.

Camp Tapawingo built boys' and girls' lodges complete with bathhouses. There were volleyball and handball courts on the property in addition to the BASEBALL diamond, TENNIS courts, and horseshoe pits. Campers seeking recreation could also take advantage of the Ohio River. There was boating and a barge docked near a sandy beach off of which campers could dive and swim. The camp also built a recreation center that doubled as a mess hall. Movies and shows were held there as well as Sunday evening dances. The mess hall served kosher food and became a favorite place for Louisville's Jewish community to go for Sunday dinner. The camp held an annual picnic and carnival each summer. The carnival, attended by thousands, marked the beginning of the boys' and girls' summer camp program.

The 1937 FLOOD completely destroyed the camp. Instead of rebuilding, the land was planted with corn. In 1939 the YMHA leased a plot of land at Otter Creek Park in Meade County from the federal government. It was here that they built Camp Tall Trees, later sold to the Archdiocese of Louisville. It continued operating until 2000.

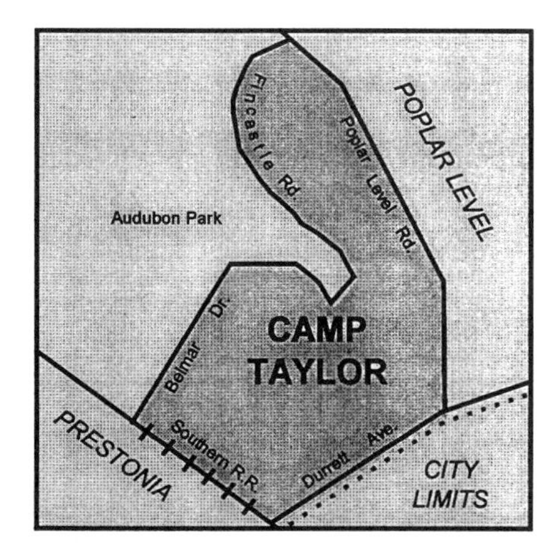

CAMP TAYLOR. Neighborhood in south Louisville and bounded by Poplar Level Rd. to the east and northeast, the Watterson Expressway (I-264) to the southeast, and the Southern Railroad to the southwest. Fincastle Rd. and Belmar Dr. create the northwestern and western borders, separating the subdivision from Audubon Country Club and Fincastle Park.

On July 11, 1917, the U.S. Army announced that Louisville had been selected as the site of CAMP ZACHARY TAYLOR, an officer training facility. The camp was constructed on open fields and farmlands six miles south of downtown Louisville between Preston Hwy. and Newburg Rd. The encampment generated local excitement when it was announced that it would be the largest in the United States to date.

Construction began in the summer of 1917 with the employment of ten thousand builders and carpenters. The facility, large enough to house 47,500 men (approximately one-fifth of Louisville's total population at the time), was completed in late August. The cost of the project, largely due to the 45.3 million feet of lumber used, totaled $7.2 million. Camp Taylor was opened on September 5, 1917, as the home of the 84th division and was immediately filled with aspiring soldiers from Indiana, Illinois, and Kentucky. After the war Camp

Taylor was closed and its activities taken over by Camp Henry Knox (now FORT KNOX).

In the 1920s the military divided the land upon which Camp Taylor sat into parcels and auctioned it off at a huge loss, receiving only $1.1 million. The land, because of its low price, was bought by many soldiers returning from the war as well as other working-class people. Vestiges of the camp remain today, as wood from the barracks and stables was reused to build the predominantly one-story, wood-framed homes in the new neighborhood. Many houses were built directly over the old bathrooms and showers of the barracks, as the concrete served as ready-made foundations for the homes. The former site of the camp's headquarters, on the northwest side of the I-264 interchange at Poplar Level Rd., is now Taylor Memorial Park. The area was annexed by the city of Louisville in 1950.

See *A Place in Time: The Story of Louisville's Neighborhoods* (Louisville 1989); George H. Yater, *Two Hundred Years at the Falls of the Ohio* (Louisville 1987).

Troops drilling at Camp Zachary Taylor, located in what is now the Camp Taylor neighborhood, 1920.

CAMP ZACHARY TAYLOR. Camp Zachary Taylor was created in June 1917 for the purpose of training American troops following the United States entry into WORLD WAR I in April of that year. The camp was located southeast and south of Louisville, with camp headquarters being north of the later Poplar Level Rd. and WATTERSON EXPRESSWAY interchange. The selected area was primarily farm and pasture land, and was quickly acquired. The camp was named in honor of general and president ZACHARY TAYLOR, who had been raised in Jefferson County. Louisville businessmen and leaders actively sought an army cantonment, and a committee from the LOUISVILLE BOARD OF TRADE and U.S. Representative SWAGER SHERLEY (the area's congressman) led the campaign.

Construction began in June and was basically finished by mid-August. The cantonment contained approximately twenty-seven hundred acres and two thousand buildings and cost about $10 million to build and maintain. As many as ten thousand civilians were hired in building and maintaining the facility. The first inductees arrived on September 5, 1917. The camp served as the home of the 84th or Lincoln Division (so known because its recruits came from the Abraham Lincoln–related states of Kentucky, Indiana, and Illinois), 159th Depot Brigade, the Field Artillery Central Officers Training School, and various other units. Its highest population was reached in the summer of 1918, when approximately sixty-four thousand soldiers were stationed there. In all, more than 150,000 men were trained, and some 250,000 were housed at Camp Zachary Taylor, among them novelist F. SCOTT FITZGERALD. Because of its designation in June 1918 as a field artillery replacement depot, the camp soon became the largest artillery training camp in the United States up to that time. National and local service organizations such as the YMCA and Knights of Columbus provided support for soldiers stationed there, many of whom were away from home for the first time. After the war the facility was used primarily as a demobilization center and HOSPITAL. During the fall of 1918 the camp was particularly hard hit by the Spanish influenza EPIDEMIC when approximately fifteen hundred died there. In September 1919 the House military affairs committee recommended abandoning the camp, citing insufficient acreage as the reason. On July 27, 1920, the order was given to begin closing the camp about September 1. All camp land, buildings, and equipment not removed by the army were to be sold at auction. The camp's artillery school and adjunct artillery range at West Point, Kentucky, already had been transferred to Camp Henry Knox (FORT KNOX). Camp Zachary Taylor was to be disposed of by June 30, 1921. The Louisville Real Estate and Development Company administered the auction, which began April 4 with the sale of the rifle range near SOUTH PARK Rd. and ended in June when the hospital land and buildings along PRESTON STREET Rd.(Highway) were sold. Approximately $1 million was realized from the sale. The former camp reverted to farm and pasture land but also became a residential area called CAMP TAYLOR where the main camp had been located. Some of the camp buildings were converted to houses and still existed at the end of the twentieth century.

See John P. Meyer, "History and Neighborhood Analysis of Camp Taylor," M.A. thesis, University of Louisville, 1981; Maurice Dunn, ed., *Camp Zachary Taylor Souvenir* (Louisville ca. 1917); Ledford H. Day, "Camp Taylor 20 Years After," *Courier- Journal Magazine,* June 20, 1937.

James J. Holmberg

CANAAN MISSIONARY BAPTIST CHURCH. This AFRICAN AMERICAN church is recognized as one of the fastest-growing religious congregations in Louisville. In January 1999 the Canaan Missionary Baptist Church moved its headquarters to the former SOUTHEAST CHRISTIAN CHURCH facility at 2840 Hikes Ln. With twenty-two hundred seats, the new home accommodated the sixteen-year-old congregation. The church moved from its previous location at 2203 DIXIE HWY., having grown to three thousand members.

Founded by the Reverend Walter Malone Jr. in March 1983 with ninety-seven charter members, the church worshiped at Magazine Street Seventh Day Adventist Church. One year later the DIXIE HWY. location, accommodating eight hundred, was purchased and became home to the church for fifteen years. After the move the Dixie Hwy. property became the Canaan Community Development Corp., a nonprofit organization that offered job training, substance abuse counseling, and parenting workshops.

Malone, the senior pastor, is a native of Nashville, Tennessee, and married Sandra K. (Fisher) Malone. They had one son. Malone graduated from American Baptist College and holds a masters from SOUTHERN BAPTIST THEOLOGICAL SEMINARY and a doctorate from United Theological Seminary in Dayton, Ohio.

CARITAS HEALTH SERVICES. Caritas Health Services can trace its beginnings to 1812, when three Sisters of Charity of Nazareth banded together in a log cabin in Bardstown, Kentucky, to care for the residents of the surrounding area. CATHERINE SPALDING, the mother superior, led the sisters to Louisville in 1832 to provide home nursing for victims of a cholera EPIDEMIC.

Upon their arrival, the Sisters established St. Joseph's Infirmary for the many cholera victims. The HOSPITAL was located on Fourth St. between Chestnut St. and BROADWAY. In 1913 St. Joseph's Infirmary was both the oldest and the largest private hospital in the state, accommodating several hundred patients. In the mid-1920s the infirmary moved to a new facility on Preston Hwy. and Eastern Pkwy. It closed in 1979.

Thanks to the generosity of philanthropist WILLIAM SHAKESPEARE CALDWELL, the Sisters of Charity opened Saints Mary and Elizabeth Hospital at Twelfth and Magnolia Streets. The hospital, built as a memorial to Caldwell's wife, Mary Eliza, was opened in 1872, dedicated in 1874, and remained on the southwest edge of the city until 1958.

In that year, with half of Louisville's population living in the south end of Louisville, the hospital relocated to a new building at 1850 Bluegrass Ave. Built at a cost of $4 million, the facility was state-of-the-art, offering a full range of care and medical services.

Across town, at 2020 Newburg Rd., the sisters opened Our Lady of Peace Hospital. The new facility replaced Mount St. Agnes Sanitarium, which operated from 1913 until 1951 as an infirmary for the care of convalescing, aged, and tubercular patients. Insufficient space, inadequate equipment, and a growing need for more facilities necessitated construction of the new hospital. Our Lady of Peace offered advanced psychological care for the mentally and emotionally disturbed and remains one of the premier psychiatric facilities in the nation.

While the sisters continued their sponsorship of the hospital, by the 1960s administration and nursing were in the hands of lay professionals. In 1971 the sisters identified a need for home nursing services, and, in a sense, returned to their roots when they established Nazareth Home Health in Bardstown, Kentucky.

The Sisters also operated other health-care institutions in Kentucky, Tennessee, and Arkansas. In 1971 they consolidated all their operations under a new corporation, the Sisters of Charity of Nazareth Health System (SCNHS).

By 1994 the sisters realized that Saints Mary and Elizabeth Hospital, Our Lady of Peace Hospital, and Nazareth Home Health could better complement each other if they were merged into a single SCNHS affiliate. The new affiliate, under the direction of president and CEO Peter J. Bernard, was officially named Caritas Health Services in 1995.

In September 1997 the Sisters of Charity of Nazareth Health System consolidated with Catholic Health Initiatives (CHI), one of the largest Catholic health organizations in the country. CHI has health care organizations in twenty-two states, including its southeastern region that serves Arkansas, Kentucky, and Tennessee.

Donna L. Peterson

CARMICHAEL, OMER (b Hollins, Alabama, March 7, 1893; d Louisville, January 9, 1960). Educator and school administrator. The oldest of eight children, he was the only son of William Colin and Lucy (Wilson) Carmichael. Educated at the University of Alabama, he graduated in 1913 with a degree in mathematics. He began his career in education as a teacher and coach at a secondary school in Selma, Alabama, in 1914.

Swiftly advancing through the ranks of Alabama's public education system, Carmichael became principal of Selma's high school in his third year and later served as superintendent of schools in both Selma and Talledega. After receiving a master's degree from Columbia University in 1924, he went on to become superintendent of schools in Tampa, Florida (1926–32), and Lynchburg, Virginia (1932–45), before accepting the same position in Louisville in 1945.

Carmichael's most celebrated accomplishment came in 1956 when he presided over the peaceful desegregation of Louisville's PUBLIC SCHOOLS. Two years earlier the Supreme Court had ruled in *Brown v. Board of Education of Topeka* that SEGREGATION in public education was unconstitutional. Almost immediately, Carmichael and the local school board began a two-year planning process for the integration of Louisville's public schools. The procedure devised called for the simultaneous integration of all grade levels, and the complete redistricting of the city's school system without regard to race. Another important aspect of the plan was the opportunity for "free-choice transfers." This feature, by which students could be granted transfers if a school had room, was considered a "safety valve" to lessen opposition to the plan and allay the concerns of both black and white parents.

When the integration program went into effect on September 10, 1956, Louisville, with a student population of over forty-five thousand, had the highest percentage (27 percent) of black students of any sizable city to desegregate that year. Many wondered if the city would experience the same outbreaks of racial violence that had plagued other southern cities' attempts at desegregation. However, Louisville's transition to integrated classrooms went smoothly, and its success gained national acclaim.

Carmichael received a number of honors, including a reception by President Dwight D. Eisenhower at the White House, honorary doctorate degrees from the University of Kentucky and Dartmouth College, and honorary masters' of science degrees from Harvard and Yale Universities. In addition, he often was asked to speak to national and area educational organizations.

Carmichael married Elnora Blanchard in 1926, and they had three children. He died in 1960 and is buried in Hatchett Creek Presbyterian Church Cemetery in Goodwater, Alabama.

See Omer Carmichael and Weldon James, *The Louisville Story* (New York 1957).

CARNEGIE LIBRARIES. The citizens of Louisville built nine free public library branches between 1906 and 1914, with the assistance of industrialist/philanthropist Andrew Carnegie. Designed by the city's best architects of the time, these gems are reminders of one of the century's greatest social movements.

As a poor boy working in Pittsburgh, Scottish-born Carnegie (1835–1919) grew to believe that a strong free public library system was a great leveler of classes. He later wrote, "I resolved, if ever wealth came to me, that it should be used to establish free libraries, that other poor boys might receive opportunities."

Abetted by the fortunes of Carnegie and other aging, late-nineteenth-century magnates, the establishment and construction of libraries and other cultural institutions became a test of civic virtue throughout the United States. Louisville's experience bears this out. Local communities would provide the land and the upkeep of the buildings once they were constructed. The city's nine library buildings endowed by Carnegie spanned the city and served poor and middle-class NEIGHBORHOODS alike:

Main Library, 301 York St. (1906–8)
Parkland, 2743 Virginia Ave.(1908)—Closed
Western Colored, 604 S Tenth St. (1908)
Highland, 1000 Cherokee Rd. (1908)—Closed
Crescent Hill, 2762 Frankfort Ave. (1908)
Shelby Park, 600 E Oak St. (1911)—Closed
Jefferson, 1718 W Jefferson St. (1912)—Closed
Portland, 3305 Northwestern Pkwy. (1913)
Eastern Colored, Hancock and Lampton (1914)—Closed

Each library was a neighborhood center as well, with meeting rooms hosting community activities meant to encourage the masses in their pursuit of happiness. The Carnegie branches also nurtured the city's architectural spirit, representing a Who's Who of Louisville ARCHITECTURE at the turn of the century. Parkland was designed by BRINTON B. DAVIS; Western Colored, MCDONALD and DODD; Highland, HUTCHINGS and Hawes; Crescent Hill, Thomas and Bohne; Shelby Park, Loomis and Hartman; Jefferson, D.X. MURPHY; Portland, Val P. Collins; and Eastern Colored, Brinton B. Davis. Arthur Loomis also designed the all-stone, domed, Carnegie-endowed branch in nearby JEFFERSONVILLE, INDIANA.

The main library, however, was a qualified exception. Its designers, Pilcher and Tachau, practiced out of New York City and Philadelphia, but partner George Tachau was a Louisville native. In addition, the grounds around the main library and Shelby Park branch were designed by the famed landscape architects, OLMSTED Brothers.

The neighborhood branches follow a coherent architectural program. The buildings are all one story in height, with a raised basement. Reading and stack rooms flank a central circulation space. Brick is the predominant material, often trimmed heavily with Indiana limestone. Shelby Park, with its great arched entrance, is all stone, as is the main library, a Beaux Arts masterpiece with smooth Indiana limestone wings flanking a colossal columned portico.

Carnegie libraries also were built in the surrounding metropolitan counties, including FLOYD and CLARK COUNTIES in Indiana and SHELBY COUNTY in Kentucky. In Clark County, the Jeffersonville Township Public Library was established in 1900. Until 1903 it shared space with the township trustees, when a Carnegie grant permitted the opening of the Jeffersonville Carnegie Library, which opened in 1904 in Warder Park. The present building housing the Jeffersonville Township Public Library on Court Ave. was completed in 1970. The Shelby County library was established in 1898 by the Women's Club with two hundred donated books. In 1902 Carnegie donated ten thousand dollars to build the new library. Located on land that had been the site of a Presbyterian church, the library was designed by Louisville architect Val P. Collins. It was completed in 1903. There have been three additions to the building, the latest in 1997. The New Albany–Floyd County Public Library was founded on May 9, 1884. It moved into the Carnegie building at 201 E Spring St. in March 1904. In 1969 a new library building was opened on W Spring St., while the Carnegie building housed the Floyd County Museum, a department of the library. After a $1 million renovation in 1998–99, the museum was renamed the Carnegie Center for Art and History.

Douglas L Stern
Pamela Federspiel
Lee Fletcher
Tamsie Meurer

CARTER DRY GOODS CO. This leading Louisville dry goods wholesaler traced its roots to 1854 when brothers John A. and James G. Carter from Simpson County, Kentucky, began their business careers in the partnership of Brannon, Smith, and Carters at Sixth and Main Streets. The firm soon became Smith and Carters when Stephen Brannon left the partnership. In 1859 the Carter brothers purchased George P. Smith's interest and the firm became Carter and Brother, with James as the senior partner.

In 1862 the fledgling enterprise was forced to suspend operations due to the CIVIL WAR and the closing of the southern market. Business was resumed in 1865 and four years later was expanded by the purchase of Garvin, Bell, and Co. after that firm's senior partner, WILLIAM GARVIN, was killed in a steamboat collision on the OHIO RIVER. John T. Fisher, a partner in Garvin's firm, joined the Carters to form Carters, Fisher, and Co. After Fisher's death in 1872 the firm became Carter Brothers and Co.

Prospering in the post–Civil War era, the firm moved in 1878 to a new four-story building on Main St. between Seventh and Eighth Streets. The structure was built for the Carters by entrepreneur Joseph Peterson. It was designed by Louisville architect CHARLES J. CLARKE and served as the firm's location for seventy-six years, having been expanded twice during that time.

Following the death of James Carter in 1889, the firm was incorporated in 1892 as the Carter Dry Goods Co. with John Carter as its first president. Much of the stock was distributed to the employees who had been with the firm for many years. When John Carter died in 1894, he was succeeded as president by Joseph Bethel, who had been a junior partner before incorporation.

After a hundred years of local ownership, Carter Dry Goods was sold in 1954 to the Nashville Industrial Corp. In the mid-1960s the company was sold again, this time to William R. Moore Inc. of Memphis, Tennessee, which changed the company's name to Carter Corp. In 1971 Carter Corp. moved to the Bluegrass Industrial Park and remained there until 1982, when it closed. Its former quarters on Main St. became the home of the Museum of History and Science, later renamed the LOUISVILLE SCIENCE CENTER.

See "Nashville Firm Buys Carter Dry Goods Co.," *Louisville* (Nov. 20, 1954).

Jay R. Ferguson

CARUTH, ASHER GRAHAM (b Scottsville, Kentucky, February 7, 1844; d Louisville, November 25, 1907). U.S. congressman. Caruth's early education was received in the public schools of Pennsylvania. He graduated from LOUISVILLE MALE HIGH SCHOOL in 1864, and he went on to study law at the UNIVERSITY OF LOUISVILLE, graduating in 1866. Caruth began his law career in Hopkinsville, where he established the *Kentucky Weekly New Era.* He moved to Louisville in 1871, continuing to practice law. Over the course of the next nine years he served as attorney for the board of trustees of the public schools of Louisville as well as being a presidential elector in 1876. In 1880 he was elected commonwealth's attorney for the Ninth Judicial District of Kentucky, resigning the office in 1887 despite being reelected, to serve in Congress as a Democrat. He served three terms there from March 4, 1887, through March 3, 1895, but failed to receive renomination in 1894. After leaving Congress he returned to practicing law in Louisville. He served as judge in Jefferson Circuit Court, Criminal Division, in 1902 and was commissioner of the Louisiana Exposition of 1904 in St. Louis. He is buried in CAVE HILL CEMETERY.

See *Biographical Directory of the American Congress 1776–1961.*

Western Branch, Louisville Free Public Library, southwest corner of Tenth Street at Chestnut, 1927.

Carter Dry Goods Co. building, north side of Main Street between Seventh and Eighth, now the Louisville Science Center, 1922.

CARVER SCHOOL OF CHURCH SOCIAL WORK. The women's suffrage movement, the concern for social injustice, and increased interest in foreign missions brought the need for theological training to prepare Southern Baptist women for Christian service. The Woman's Missionary Union Training School was established in Louisville (1907–52) because women were not allowed to enroll in seminary courses. Maude Reynolds McClure, the first principal, followed the social work education model of class study and field practice in settlement work. Curriculum changes responded to the development of social work education. As women began to be accepted in the seminary, the training school also began to recruit men. In 1953 the name was changed to the Carver School of Missions in Social Work (1953–62) in honor of Dr. William Owen Carver, a seminary faculty member, in recognition of his years of commitment to social work.

The development of accreditation standards for social work education meant that the Carver School could not be accredited as a freestanding school; it had to be part of an institution of higher education. Consequently, the Carver School was merged with the SOUTHERN BAPTIST THEOLOGICAL SEMINARY School of Religious Education in 1963. A dual degree was established: Master of Religious Education (MRE) from the seminary and a Master of Social Work (MSW) from the Raymond A. Kent School of Social Work, UNIVERSITY OF LOUISVILLE (1963–83), instead of developing the MSW program fully within the seminary. The social work program grew so fast that enrollment was capped to keep it from overwhelming the School of Religious Education in which it was housed.

Walter Delamarter was the first director of the social work program and full-time faculty member. In August 1970, with an increase in students and curriculum expansion, a second full-time person, C. Anne Davis, a Carver School graduate, was employed. Upon Delamarter's resignation, Davis became director. Her priorities (1973–77) were to stabilize the program, adapt to the seminary's imposed no-growth enrollment limit, and rebuild the faculty. Davis's request for a 1979 study confirmed the need for professionals educated in theology and social work. A Master of Social Work degree program was planned, the purpose for which the Carver School had been merged with the seminary.

The seminary established its fourth professional school—the Carver School of Church Social Work—on August 1, 1984, headed by Dean Davis. The Commission on Accreditation of the Council on Social Work Education (CSWE) granted accreditation on February 13, 1987, retroactive to 1982. Diana Garland became the second dean upon Davis's retirement in 1993.

With the appointment of R. Albert Mohler Jr. as seminary president in 1993, the goal became the reshaping of this moderate seminary and its faculty in the new direction of the 1980 fundamentalist takeover of the Southern Baptist Convention. When Garland found administrative restraints were jeopardizing accreditation standards, she protested and was terminated as dean in the spring of 1995. She remained as a faculty member for one additional year. Associate Dean Janet Spressart became acting dean. Garland and Spressart left in 1996; more than 80 percent of the faculty of the institution left during the first five years of Mohler's presidency. Paul Kim, on sabbatical from Louisiana State University, became dean for one year. To accommodate students in the program, CSWE extended accreditation for one year, until the school was closed in May 1997.

A seminary committee studied the Carver School and found that the theological positions of the administration and the accrediting standards for social work were not congruent. The committee's rationale was based on its review of the Code of Ethics by the National Association of Social Workers. Their recommendation was to transfer Carver to a Baptist university. The school has remained closed, although assets have been transferred to Campbellsville University in Campbellsville, Kentucky.

See Anne Minahan, ed., *Encyclopedia of Social Work* (Silver Spring, Maryland 1997); C. Anne Davis, "The History of the Carver School of Church Social Work," *Review and Expositor* 85 (Spring 1988): 209–20.

Lillian C. Milanof

CASSEDAY, JENNIE (b Louisville, June 9, 1840; d Louisville, February 8, 1893). Philanthropist/civic leader. She was the daughter of Samuel and Elizabeth (McFarland) Casseday. When a carriage accident in 1861 left her an invalid, she devoted the rest of her life to helping others, conducting affairs from her bed.

Casseday was instrumental in the 1878 creation of the Jennie Casseday Flower Mission, which distributed flowers and text of scriptures to the destitute and sick. Mission work also included distribution of clothing, fruits, fuel, and attending the sick, among other acts of charity. Her birthday, June 9, was designated Flower Mission's Prison Day, when volunteers would distribute flowers and scripture passages in prison houses nationwide. Four years after its inception, the mission became a department of the Women's Christian Temperance Union, and Casseday became its national superintendent. Flower Missions were established throughout North America with units as far away as Africa.

Casseday also helped organize the Louisville Order of the King's Daughters, which served the sick and the poor, and the Lying-In Hospital for Pregnant Women of Small Means, which opened on Sixth St. in 1882. She was the chief supporter and founder of the 1889 School for Training Nurses that began in the old City Hospital. In 1890, she started the Jennie Casseday Rest Cottage for Working Women in PEWEE VALLEY. Ten months before her death in 1893, the King's Daughters dedicated the Jennie Casseday Infirmary, located at 1912 Sixth St. She is buried in CAVE HILL CEMETERY.

Laurie A. Birnsteel

CAST-IRON ARCHITECTURE. Cast iron as a building product was developed in the mid-nineteenth century. The advantages of this inexpensive, high-carbon ferrous alloy were that it could be mass-produced, and it is lighter and stronger than brick. The load-bearing capacity gave builders the ability to make taller structures with wider openings for windows. The material made for a very flexible product. Buildings made of cast iron were considered to be the forerunners of skyscrapers.

Its use began in Great Britain toward the end of the eighteenth century. Americans saw the benefits to rapidly growing cities where land was expensive. Daniel D. Badger and James Bogardus were pioneers in developing cast iron as a building product, and they made New York City the center of cast-iron ARCHITECTURE. Louisville began using cast iron in the 1850s. A number of these buildings were designed by architects, but one of the advantages of cast iron was that a person could pick out designs from a catalogue and construct a building with a facade of his choosing. Construction did not take a lot of expertise.

Louisville has the second-largest assembly of cast-iron buildings in the United States (only New York City has more). It constitutes a fine architectural legacy. One of the finest cast-iron buildings was built for Hart Hardware Co. on Main between Seventh and Eighth Streets in 1884. Designed by local architect Charles D. Meyer, it is considered by the Friends of Cast Iron in New York to be one of the finest examples of cast-iron construction in the nation. The design includes cast-iron Corinthian columns and segmental arches, giving the building an airy and attractive facade.

MAIN ST. is also home to many other cast-iron buildings with interesting detail, from vines around the columns to lion heads in the cornice. One advantage over stone is that ornamental detail could be achieved in the casting process. Cast iron was used less for building purposes when steel beams became available in the mid-1880s, allowing steel framing. Still Louisville's numerous IRON FOUNDRIES turned out many products well into the twentieth century. As late as the 1920s simple, one-story storefronts continued to contain elements of iron. However, the use of iron did not survive the GREAT DEPRESSION.

Many cast-iron buildings served as warehouses until the turn of the century, when Louisville turned away from the waterfront to FOURTH ST. and BROADWAY. Out of the mainstream of commerce, much of Main St. was spared the ravages of URBAN RENEWAL. The cast-iron buildings remained, often vacant, until their architectural and commercial value was realized. Beginning in the 1970s some people saw the value in their preservation, since so much of early Louisville architecture had been razed. Since the 1980s many of Louisville's cast-iron structures have been renovated and are being used in many ways. The historic W Main St. Preservation District has many first-floor and full-building facades in cast iron. There are many new uses for these buildings: museums, law firms, RESTAURANTS, ARCHITECTURAL FIRMS, public relations firms, galleries, condominiums,

The Hart Block, Louisville's best example of cast-iron architecture, 1889.

and the LOUISVILLE SCIENCE CENTER (formerly the Museum of History and Science).

Main St. is the center of Louisville's cast-iron architecture. Presently there are many clues to the early residents and former uses of Main St. To identify cast iron, visitors may use a magnet to test the facade. In the renewal of Main St., the identity of cast-iron buildings was further facilitated by laying rows of bricks, flecked with iron, sideways from the cast-iron columns in the sidewalk. Ironwood trees are in front of the cast-iron buildings. Around the base of some of these trees, cast-iron replicas of walking sticks tell of some of the products that were in the original warehouses. Iron guards at the base of the trees are made with the design of former COAL HOLE COVERS found in front of each building for coal delivery. Other cast-iron buildings are found on E Main, E MARKET, Baxter Ave., and some on Bardstown Rd.

See William Morgan, *Louisville Architecture and the Urban Environment* (Dublin, N.H., 1979); Theodore M. Brown, *Introduction to Louisville Architecture* (Louisville 1960).

Martha M. Cull

CASTLEMAN, JOHN BRECKIN-RIDGE

CASTLEMAN, JOHN BRECKINRIDGE (b Lexington, June 30, 1841; d Louisville, May 23, 1918). Soldier, civic leader, and horseman. Born to David and Virginia (Harrison) Castleman, young Castleman received his early education at Fort Hill Academy in Lexington. He entered Transylvania University but left to join the Confederate army at the outbreak of the CIVIL WAR. In 1862, Castleman and forty-one men he had brought from Lexington became part of Gen. John Hunt Morgan's command at Knoxville, Tennessee, with Castleman being made captain of Company D of the Second Kentucky Cavalry. He eventually achieved the rank of major.

Castleman's best-known undertaking during the war was his involvement in the Northwestern Conspiracy, an ill-fated attempt to free Confederate prisoners of war in the old northwestern states. When this plan went awry at Camp Douglas near Chicago, Castleman proceeded with a band of guerrillas to St. Louis intending to burn Union supply boats at the wharf. This effort, however, was also unsuccessful, and Castleman was captured at Sullivan, Indiana, in October 1864. Charged with spying, he was held in solitary confinement for nine months in the federal prison at Indianapolis, Indiana.

Fearing his execution, Judge S.M. Breckinridge of St. Louis, Castleman's brother-in-law and a Union sympathizer, interceded in his behalf with President Abraham Lincoln and obtained a stay of execution should such sentence be passed. In July 1865 Castleman was released on parole, promising to leave the United States and never return. He went to Europe, remaining there until December 1866, at which time President Andrew Johnson allowed his return.

Castleman received his law degree from the UNIVERSITY OF LOUISVILLE in 1868 and married Alice Barbee on November 24 that same year. He entered the insurance business with his father-in-law, JOHN BARBEE, and their firm, Barbee & Castleman, became the southern representative for the Royal Insurance Co. of Liverpool. In 1878 Castleman was a leading figure in the reorganization of the First Regiment, Kentucky State Guard, more widely known as the LOUISVILLE LEGION. He was elected colonel of the legion in 1880 and remained in command for twenty years, making the militia unit one of the best-disciplined and best-known in the United States. In 1883 Gov. J. Proctor Knott appointed Castleman adjutant general of Kentucky.

When the Spanish-American War began in 1898, Castleman and the Louisville Legion volunteered for service. He was commissioned a colonel in the United States Army, and the legion became the First Kentucky Volunteers. The unit invaded and secured the island of Puerto Rico, where Castleman, by then a brigadier general, served as military governor. In 1900 Castleman was again called to duty as adjutant general, quelling the civil unrest in Frankfort, Kentucky, that resulted from the assassination of Gov. William Goebel.

A lifelong Democrat, Castleman was chairman of the Democratic State Central Committee of Kentucky in 1891 and 1892. In the latter year, he was a delegate from Kentucky to the Democratic National Convention in Chicago. During this time he also was instrumental in developing the city's park system, serving on the Board of Park Commissioners for over twenty-five years. Always an avid horseman, Castleman was one of the founders of the American Saddlebred Horse Association and was elected its first president in 1891. In 1893 Castleman rode his five-gaited mare Emily to win the grand championship at the Chicago Columbian Exposition World's Fair. An equestrian statue of Castleman and his American Saddlebred mare Carolina was created in 1913. It stands near the edge of Cherokee Park at the intersection of Cherokee Pkwy. and Cherokee Rd.

Castleman is buried in CAVE HILL CEMETERY. He was survived by his wife and three children, Kenneth, Elise, and Alice. He was predeceased by two sons, David and Breckinridge.

See John Breckinridge Castleman, *On Active Service* (Louisville 1917); J. Stoddard Johnston, ed., *Memorial History of Louisville* (Chicago 1896); E. Polk Johnson, *History of Kentucky and Kentuckians* (Chicago 1912).

Kenneth Dennis

CATHEDRAL HERITAGE FOUNDATION. The Cathedral Heritage Foundation is a nonprofit organization formed initially in 1985 to raise the funds for and oversee the restoration of the historic Roman Catholic CATHEDRAL OF THE ASSUMPTION in downtown Louisville. This cathedral, completed in 1852, is one of the oldest in the United States in continuous use and is among the oldest buildings in downtown Louisville.

Following the tenets of Vatican Council II, which acknowledged the values of other faiths and encouraged the spiritual growth of all people, the foundation rapidly dedicated itself to developing spiritual, educational, and cultural programming to inspire and foster individual growth while increasing understanding and harmony among diverse cultures and faiths. The foundation reaches out to the community through its Spiritual Life Lecture Series, a free Downtown Arts & Music Series, its Interfaith Spiritual Art Gallery, its spiritual gift shop "Inspirations," symposia, and other events.

In November 1996, the foundation held the country's first Festival of Faiths. This program brought together under one roof forty-six different faith groups having their genesis in downtown Louisville between 1800–70. The subsequent national attention to the festival later spawned similar events in other communities. Its innovative methods in demonstrating new community roles for urban cathedrals and other houses of worship also focused greater attention on the foundation itself. The major inspiration for the development of this unique venture was the vision of Father J. Ronald Knott, then the cathedral pastor, and foundation president Christina Lee Brown.

Among the many who have visited to learn about the work of the foundation are His Holiness the Dalai Lama, prominent Protestant historian Martin Marty, and the 102nd Archbishop of Canterbury, Lord Robert Runcie. Mrs. Brown also made a presentation to former Russian leader Mikhail Gorbachev during his visit to Louisville in 1995.

Trish Pugh Jones

Cathedral of the Assumption, 443 South Fifth Street, 1889.

CATHEDRAL OF THE ASSUMPTION. Designed by William Keeley, the Cathedral of the Assumption was constructed in American Gothic style between 1849 and 1852. It is the ecclesiastical seat of the Roman Catholic Archdiocese of Louisville, the oldest inland diocese in the United States. In the undercroft, beneath the altar, lie the remains of BENEDICT JOSEPH FLAGET, "first bishop of the West," and Peter Joseph Lavialle, Louisville's bishop from 1865 to 1867. The church contains several examples of historic and liturgical art. The tower, designed by HENRY WHITESTONE and Isaiah Rogers, was completed in the late 1850s.

The Cathedral parish began about 1805 when Stephen Badin, the first priest ordained in America, began making regular priestly visits to Louisville from the Bardstown area. The church attained its first building—named in honor of St. Louis—on Tenth St. between Main and the OHIO RIVER in 1811; several Protestant citizens contributed to this enterprise. A new St. Louis church was built on the site of the current cathedral (443 S Fifth St.) in 1830. On these grounds, CATHERINE SPALDING of the Sisters of Charity of Nazareth established a school, an orphanage, and an infirmary.

When the seat of the old Bardstown diocese was moved by Pope Gregory XVI to Louisville in 1841, St. Louis Church became its cathedral. When the new structure opened in 1852, the St. Louis title was dropped in favor of the one now in use.

At the time of the BLOODY MONDAY Riot of 1855, in the face of fears in the city, the mayor searched the cathedral for armed men and their munitions. Finding neither, he reassured the citizenry by an official notice in the newspapers.

In 1862 the cathedral hosted a memorial mass for the fallen of both North and South in the Civil War, led by Bishop MARTIN JOHN SPALDING. In the gaslight era, the cathedral became a major urban parish sponsoring civic and cultural events besides its usual worship work and service to the poor. The cathedral was of outstanding service to the community during the FLOOD OF 1937 and two world wars.

With the arrival of Rev. Ronald Knott as pastor in 1983 and the establishment of the CATHEDRAL HERITAGE FOUNDATION led by Christina Lee Brown in 1985, the cathedral grew in its scope. Advancing from a membership of one hundred to fourteen hundred, it also increasingly sought to maintain its Catholic core while serving those in physical need in its inner-city neighborhood; it also set out to serve the spiritual, civic, and cultural needs of the wider metropolitan interfaith community.

After major restoration, the main body of the church was reopened in November 1994 with great civic acclaim. Over the years, famous visitors have included Cardinal Joseph Bernardin, the Dalai Lama, Rose Kennedy, Martin Marty, Karl Rahner, Babe Ruth, Al Smith, and THOMAS MERTON.

See Clyde F. Crews, *Presence and Possibility: Louisville Catholicism and its Cathedral* (Louisville 1973).

Clyde F. Crews

CATHOLIC COLORED HIGH SCHOOL. Louisville's only Catholic high school exclusively for AFRICAN AMERICANS opened in 1921 when Saint Augustine Catholic Elementary School at 1310 W Broadway added high school classes. In 1929 the name was changed from Saint Augustine High School to Catholic Colored High School when the Archdiocese of Louisville took over the school and moved it to the Saint Mary's (Immaculate Conception) Catholic School building at 428 S Eighth St. near Cedar. By 1931 Sister Frances Louise was listed as the principal.

The black parish elementary schools in Louisville, Saint Augustine and Saint Peter Claver at 522 Lampton St., sent their graduates to Catholic Colored High School. However, because of the small number of black Catholics in Louisville, the classes at the high school remained small. The school's sense of community was heightened by kinship among the students, many of whom had come from Bardstown and nearby Springfield, Kentucky.

The size of the student population did not deter the Sisters of Charity of Nazareth from offering their pupils an education grounded in classical studies. The nuns taught classes in mathematics, chemistry, English, Latin, algebra, and economics, accompanied by strict discipline. Like other high schools, dances, plays, and sports were also a part of school life. The pastor of SAINT AUGUSTINE CHURCH drove the basketball team throughout the state to play other black schools. When integration made all-black schools no longer necessary, the archdiocese closed the facility in 1958.

See *Courier-Journal*, Feb. 28, 1999.

CATHOLIC SCHOOLS. The Catholic schools in Louisville have roots in central Kentucky, where the first Catholics settled. In 1775 several Catholic families settled at Harrods Station (later Harrodsburg) and founded a school. This school's founder, Jane Coomes, is arguably the commonwealth's first schoolteacher. Ten years later a group of twenty-five families led by Basil Hayden established the Pottinger Creek Catholic settlement a few miles from Bardstown. In 1792 they built the first Catholic church in Kentucky with the support of Father William de Rohan (who reportedly had served as a professor at the Sorbonne in Paris). By 1805 they were inviting newly arrived Trappist monks to help them found the first Catholic school of consequence.

In April 1808 Pope Pius VII created the diocese of Bardstown and appointed Father BENEDICT JOSEPH FLAGET, a professor from Georgetown College (Georgetown University) in Washington, D.C., as its first bishop. Flaget founded a Catholic seminary, St. Thomas, and appointed Father John B. David as rector. It trained Catholic clergy for leadership in such cities as Louisville, Charleston, Milwaukee, St. Louis, and New Orleans. Flaget moved to Louisville as Bishop of Louisville in 1841. He died in office in 1850.

In April 1812 three lay teachers in the school of the St. Charles congregation on Hardin's Creek (Lebanon, Kentucky), sought Father Charles Nerinckx's help in forming a religious community, the Sisters of Loretto. Within thirty years, some members of that congregation would settle in Louisville near Our Lady's parish in PORTLAND and would open CEDAR GROVE ACADEMY in 1842, which was to become LORETTO HIGH SCHOOL in 1926. On December 1, 1812, the Sisters of Charity of Nazareth were founded near Bardstown, Kentucky. Under their newly chosen leader, CATHERINE SPALDING, the sisters started a number of schools, including Louisville's oldest continuous Catholic school—PRESENTATION ACADEMY (1831). A third sisterhood was founded on February 28, 1822, when nine women united to live as Dominicans near Springfield, Kentucky. In Louisville, they founded an elementary school at ST. LOUIS BERTRAND (1866) and the academy that developed into HOLY ROSARY ACADEMY (1867).

When Bishop Flaget transferred the seat of the diocese from Bardstown to Louisville in 1841, there were three thriving parishes: St. Louis (English-speaking), Our Lady of Notre Dame du Port (French-speaking), and ST. BONIFACE (German-speaking). St. Louis had access to Presentation Academy, which charged tuition, or to the nearby free school sponsored by the academy that opened in 1843. Our Lady soon would rely on Cedar Grove. In 1836 St. Boniface founded the first truly parochial (parish) school. Its first faculty was lay, as had been the faculty at Holy Cross and Saint Charles and as would be the faculty at St. Mary's School, founded in 1849 on Eighth St., and at St. Peter's School, founded in 1860 at Seventeenth and Garland. The latter three schools were founded after the 1850 death of Bishop Flaget. His successor, Bishop MARTIN JOHN SPALDING (1850–1864), soon engaged several new teaching communities: Xaverian Brothers from Belgium in 1854, Ursuline Sisters from Bavaria in 1858, and Sisters of Mercy from St. Louis in 1869. Each staffed new elementary schools, and each established foundations for secondary schools: ST. XAVIER HIGH SCHOOL for boys in 1864, URSULINE ACADEMY for girls in 1858, and MERCY ACADEMY for girls in 1885. By 1863 Bishop Spalding reported twenty Catholic schools in Louisville, with sixteen serving the poor and the immigrants.

This building of schools was on the agenda of the Third Plenary Council of Baltimore (1884), which required each pastor in the United States to build his own parish school. Each Catholic school was virtually autonomous, raising its own money, collecting its own tuition, and administering its own instructional program. Schools maintained contact with each other through the religious communities that staffed them. To increase this communication, Bishop William McCloskey (1868–1909) established a Catholic school board of pastors in 1887. By 1892 Louisville's twenty-five parochial schools, five Catholic academies, and three Catholic ORPHANAGES had a total of seven thousand students.

In the 1920s and 1930s, states began regulating the proliferating nonpublic schools. Kentucky's legislature required the certification of all teachers in the state by 1926. One response was the establishment of Louisville's female Catholic liberal arts colleges that could prepare teachers for certification: Nazareth College, now SPALDING UNIVERSITY (1920–present); Sacred Heart Junior College and Normal School (1921–38); and URSULINE COLLEGE (1938–68 when it merged with all-male BELLARMINE COLLEGE). Finally the archdiocese founded all-male Bellarmine College (1950–present).

Bishop (later Archbishop) JOHN A. FLOERSH (1924–67) responded by reorganizing the Catholic School Board in 1925 and entrusting Father FELIX N. PITT with the title of executive secretary (1925–67). His role was that of a superintendent, and he quickly established diocesan-wide processes for teacher certification, textbook standardization, teacher in-service, academic and personnel recordkeeping, supervision of teachers, student assessment, and a league of Catholic parent/teacher associations (PTA). In 1946 he assisted the U.S. government in aiding Germany's postwar educational system. He was elected president of the National Catholic Education Association in 1947 and again in 1948. In 1950 he founded today's Cerebral Palsy School. In 1958 he won a Ford Foundation Grant of fifty-seven thousand dollars to help Louisville's Catholic elementary schools become the first in the nation to teach a Great Books program to challenge gifted students.

In the 1940s three elementary schools were built and one Archdiocesan high school, FLAGET HIGH SCHOOL (1942), which was staffed by Xaverian Brothers along with some diocesan priests. An important church and state issue was decided in 1946. The Kentucky Court of Appeals approved legislation allowing each county transport Catholic children on public school buses.

In 1950 the Kentucky General Assembly repealed the 1904 Day Law prohibiting racially integrated education. Immediately the Catholic colleges opened all their programs to all races. St. Xavier quickly added all-black CENTRAL HIGH SCHOOL to its athletic schedule. All Catholic high schools joined in reaching out to CATHOLIC COLORED HIGH SCHOOL (founded by the Sisters of Charity in 1929 with support from the diocese), so that its students could study in newly integrated institutions. Colored High would close in 1958.

In the 1950s baby boomers crowded into Catholic schools, bringing forty to seventy students to a classroom. Catholics were joining the move to the SUBURBS, and new schools were built as quickly as possible. Archbishop Floersh established an office for Catholic high schools in 1947 and appointed Father Alfred W. Steinhauser as director. In the 1950s six Catholic high schools were built: the Sisters of Mercy's Assumption High School in 1955, the Ursulines' ANGELA MERICI in 1959, the archdiocese's ST. THOMAS SEMINARY in 1952, Trinity High School in 1953, DeSales High School in 1956, and Bishop David High School in 1959.

Between 1950 and 1966, twenty-nine new parishes (most with new schools) were formed in Jefferson County. By 1966 there were 50,924 Catholic school students in the archdiocese. This record number doubled the enrollment of the early 1950s and made it possible for 95 percent of Catholic children to be in Catholic schools. The majority were in the seventy-two elementary schools and nine high schools located in Jefferson County. This success was not long-lived. There were not enough young sisters to replace the retiring sisters or those moving to other ministries. In 1966 only 50 percent of the Catholic schoolteachers were vowed religious. An additional one hundred religious retired at the end of that school year. By 1974, 72 percent of the Catholic school teachers were lay.

This transition was filled with challenges to

Catholic school identity, religious effectiveness, just wages, budget maintenance, and teacher recruitment. Most newly hired lay teachers had attended Catholic elementary or secondary schools and often had their own children in Catholic schools. They asked for assistance in teaching religion and negotiated their own salaries (until the 1960 archdiocesan salary scale tripled lay salaries over those of vowed religious, making some school budgets jump 400 percent). With lay salaries still remaining substantially lower than a comparable public school salary, much effort went into teacher recruitment and promotion of the non-monetary benefits of teaching in a Catholic school.

Escalating school costs triggered a number of difficult decisions. To raise income, new debt-ridden suburban parishes relied on tuition increases and sometimes on BINGO, while older inner-city parishes frequently began to use their limited savings and relied more heavily on bingo. To cut costs, some parishes dropped junior high grades. To raise funds, the archdiocese in 1968 started the annual Archdiocesan Fund Drive (later called the Catholic Service Appeal) and later dedicated its Easter collection to Catholic education. To cut costs, the archdiocese decided in 1967 that Catholic schools should drop their first grades. In 1969 Father Thomas Casper (superintendent 1967–74), who promoted individual parish school boards, modified this decision, giving parishes the option to keep or drop the first grade.

In the 1970s the Catholic schools experienced two additional traumas. In 1972 their hopes for financial relief were dashed by Gov. Wendell Ford, (1971-74) who vetoed long-sought legislation offering tax credits to private school parents. The year 1975 saw court-ordered BUSING to desegregate public schools in Jefferson County. Under the guidance of Archbishop THOMAS J. MCDONOUGH (1967–82) and Father Casper, the archdiocese established a "no haven" policy that severely restricted student transfers to Catholic schools from bused schools. This momentous decision was vigorously pursued by Casper's successor, Father Joseph McGee (1974–83). Because of these efforts, overall Catholic school enrollment increased only slightly in 1975, 1976, and 1977.

Decreasing family size and population shifts to the suburbs left a gap in Louisville's West End: enrollment dropped from 5,848 in 1958 to 3,745 in 1965 and to 2,078 in 1970. For example, the West End's Flaget High School's enrollment fell from 1,100 in 1950 to 375 in 1970. Some twenty-four elementary schools were closed or merged between 1970 and 1996: three in the suburbs, three in the South End, and eighteen in Louisville's center city and West End, leaving only the merged Community Catholic at St. Cecilia's on the edge of Portland. Five high schools were closed or merged. In the city, Ursuline Academy (1859–1972), Loretto High School (1842–1973), and Flaget High School (1942–74) closed. In southern Jefferson County, Angela Merici High School and Bishop David High School merged into Holy Cross High School (1984), thus becoming the first coed permanent Catholic secondary school in Jefferson County.

The 1980s and 1990s were years of consolidation. When Father Joseph McGee was superintendent (1974–83) there was special focus on inclusion—inclusion of students as active participants in conferences assessing academic progress along with parents and teachers; inclusion of teachers along with school administrators and school office consultants in the determination of academic policy; inclusion of counseling as integral to school services; inclusion of parishioners at large along with parents on parish school boards; and the inclusion of educators on the archdiocesan school board so that those who guided parishes in paying the bills (pastors), those who paid much of the money (parents), and those who lived on the salaries (educators) could work together.

When Father Thomas Duerr was superintendent (1983–91) there was a special focus on enrichment—in curriculum through technology, family life education, and drug-and-alcohol-prevention education; in student care through student assistance counseling; in religious instruction through catechetical in-service; in teacher salaries by new benefits; and in school viability by employing the first diocesan school development director to guide individual schools in strategic planning.

During the term of Michael Franken (1991–92), the focus was on consolidation of services to students, families, and parishes through merger of archdiocesean offices (Catholic schools, religious education, and youth ministry) into the Office of Life Long Formation and Education.

During the service of Sr. Amelia Stenger, OSU-MSJ, (1992–97) the focus was on restructuring in the light of the Kentucky Education Reform Act. This included increased decentralization of schools, promotion of a statewide organization of private schools to develop and implement a state-recognized accreditation of nonpublic schools process (with each school being assessed by a visiting team every five years), and preparation for her successor, the first lay woman superintendent, Leisa Speer, on January 1, 1998.

Some inner-city parishes and their schools closed in the 1990s. Only five new suburban parishes have been created in Jefferson County since 1976. Of those only St. Patrick Parish (1988) was conceived with a school as integral to its planning. St. Michael Parish (1976) began to add a school in 1997 in spite of costs that continued to rise. In the 1997–98 school year, tuition in some ELEMENTARY SCHOOLS reached $2,750, while in some high schools it went over $5,000.

In spite of limited school expansion and steadily rising tuition, there was a 5 percent enrollment increase between 1992 and 1997 in the county's Catholic schools, with two-thirds of the elementary schools and three-quarters of the high schools participating in that increase. The 1997–98 school year began with an enrollment of 20,238 students, with 14,422 in the 43 elementary schools and 5,816 in the 9 high schools.

See Clyde F. Crews, *An American Holy Land—A History of the Archdiocese of Louisville* (Wilmington, Del., 1987); idem, *Presence and Possibility: Louisville Catholicism and its Cathedral* (Louisville 1973); John R. Clancy, "Vital Administrative Problems of Catholic Schools in the Diocese of Louisville since the Third Plenary Council of Baltimore," Ph.D. dissertation, Fordham University, 1954; Miriam Corcoran, "An Overview of SCN Education" and "A Tale of Two Colleges" in *Survey of the Educational Ministry of the Sisters of Charity of Nazareth* (unpublished manuscript 1998); Paschala Noonan, *Signadu: History of the Kentucky Dominican Sisters* (New York 1997); Mary Prisca Pfeffer, *In Love and Mercy: A History of the Sisters of Mercy in Louisville, Kentucky, 1869–1989* (Louisville 1992); Archives of the Archdiocese of Louisville.

Joseph T. Merkt

CAVE HILL CEMETERY. Originally part of William Johnston's Cave Hill Farm, the cemetery is a landscaped burial ground east of downtown Louisville with its main entrance at the intersection of Baxter Ave., Cherokee Rd., and E BROADWAY. William Johnston, appointed the county's first clerk by the Virginia legislature in 1783, supposedly built the area's first brick house in 1788 on the land known for its stone QUARRIES and the spring that emanated from a hillside cave. After Johnston died in 1797 and his wife Elizabeth remarried some years later, Johnston's land was divided and sold according to his will.

In the mid-1830s, meetings about developing a railroad between Louisville and Frankfort prompted city officials to purchase part of the farm for the expected railroad path. Some of the land was also set aside for burial plots and a WORKHOUSE. After the track's final route bypassed the property, the fields were leased to local farmers, and the brick residence was turned into the city's pesthouse to accommodate people with contagious diseases.

In 1846 Mayor FREDERICK KAYE and the City Council appointed a committee consisting of LEVEN SHREVE, WILLIAM BELKNAP, and Dr. James C. Johnston, William Johnston's son, to investigate the possibility of developing the grounds as a garden-style cemetery, a concept that was gaining popularity at the time. The committee retained the services of Edmund Francis Lee, a civil engineer from Hartford, Connecticut, who convinced the city to build a cemetery using the area's natural rolling landscape instead of leveling the site for burials. Already present was the Methodist (later Eastern) Cemetery located along Baxter Ave. adjacent to Cave Hill, where burials had been made as early as 1844.

In February 1848 the General Assembly chartered the Cave Hill Cemetery Co., and shortly thereafter the city deeded approximately fifty acres to the corporation. However, the city retained the land containing the quarries, the pesthouse, and the right-of-way to each. This caused some friction between the city and cemetery company until the present Baxter Ave. entrance was opened. Later that year, on July 25, 1848, the manicured grounds were dedicated in a religious ceremony, with the Reverend Dr. E.P. Humphrey delivering the consecration address. With deadly contagious diseases wreaking havoc throughout the city at the time, the cemetery quickly began accepting its first interments. Increased burials continued into the Civil War, especially after the administrators sold several acres near the workhouse at twenty-five cents per square foot for the burial of fallen Union soldiers. In response to this, several local Confederate supporters, including Elijah L. Huffman and Samuel Hamilton, purchased land nearby for the burial of downed southerners.

By the end of the 1860s, burials had become so numerous that the cemetery hired local civil engineer Benjamin Grove to lay out newly acquired lands. He was called upon again in 1888 to remap the entire cemetery and plot further territories as additional property brought the cemetery grounds to nearly three hundred acres.

In 1880 the cemetery company chose a design for the main entrance at Baxter Ave. from Calvary Episcopal Church architect William H. Redin. Selected over proposals submitted by Henry Whitestone, Charles and Gideon Shryock, and John Stirewalt, the Corinthian-style entry includes a two-thousand-pound bell and a clock tower, both of which were added in 1892. Another entrance, originally the entryway to Beechhurst Sanitarium, which was located in the northeastern part of the grounds, was opened off Grinstead Dr. about 1913. The hospital's welcoming lodge at this gate, designed by Louisville architects Arthur Loomis and Julius Hartman, was retained by the cemetery company after Beechhurst was torn down in the 1930s.

The spring branch of Beargrass Creek divides the 296-acre cemetery into what is commonly referred to as the new (eastern) and old (western) parts. Through grading and the construction of dams, several lakes have been created along the ravine and are a feeding spot for waterfowl. Extensive planting started with the first superintendent, David Ross, and has created a collection of over five hundred species of trees and shrubs.

By 1998 the cemetery had interred approximately 118,000 people and one parrot named Pretty Polly, the only animal known to be buried at Cave Hill. In time it became the burial site of Louisville's older families. Some who are buried there include George Rogers Clark, editor Henry Watterson, author Alice Hegan Rice, and chicken entrepreneur Col. Harland Sanders. To mark these and other graves, the cemetery contains one of the city's finest collections of outdoor monumental sculptures, ranging from decorative tombstones to mausoleums.

See Samuel W. Thomas, *Cave Hill Cemetery: A Pictorial Guide and Its History* (Louisville 1985); J. Stoddard Johnston, ed., *Memorial History of Louisville* (Chicago 1896).

Watchman's shelter in Cave Hill Cemetery, 1895.

CAWEIN, MADISON JULIUS (b Louisville, March 23, 1865; d Louisville, December 8, 1914). Poet. Madison Julius Cawein had inherited from his father, "Dr." William Cawein, a successful herbalist, the scientist's eye that created his botanically rich nature poems. From his mother, Christiana Stelsly, a clairvoyant, he received the gift of "second-sight" that animates them.

Childhood years, spent around Brownsboro, Kentucky (1874–75), and near New Albany, Indiana (1876–79), permitted the boy to revel in unspoiled nature and to fantasize its stories.

An encounter at Louisville Male High School with the legendary teacher of literature and psychology, Reuben Post Halleck, awakened his call to be a poet. After graduation in 1886, he worked in a local poolroom. On Sundays he roamed neighboring hills and woods, taking in scenes he would transmute, in spare hours, to poetic landscapes.

Carefully saving and investing his money, he paid for the publication of his early books and by 1892 freed his whole time for writing. He married Gertrude Foster McKelvey in 1903 and fathered a son, Preston Hamilton, born in 1904—his name was changed to Madison Cawein II in 1917. Although he was a well-known poet, Cawein found himself in dire financial straits just prior to World War I. The responsibility of a family, the expenses of maintaining a lifestyle commensurate with his reputation (for example, traveling), the mortgage on his elegant house at 1436 St. James Ct., the failure to secure other gainful employment, and his own poor health culminated in his death from apoplexy.

Louisville, especially its parks, and the Indiana knobs, were the chief settings for his poems. *Blooms of the Berry* (1887), the first of his thirty- six books, won the enthusiasm of William Dean Howells. Fifteen years later, English critic Edmund Gosse volunteered to introduce *Kentucky Poems* (1902), giving him international prominence. Although his sudden death seemed to mirror his fame's swift eclipse, one piece, "The Wasteland" (*Minions of the Moon*, 1913), antedates and likely influenced T.S. Eliot's poem of the same name (1922), linking Cawein to the early modern tradition.

See Otto A. Rothert, *The Story of a Poet: Madison Cawein* (Louisville 1921); John Rutledge, "Madison Cawein as an Exponent of German Culture," *Filson Club History Quarterly* 51 (Jan. 1977): 5–16; Robert Ian Scott, "'The Waste Land' Eliot Didn't Write," *Times Literary Supplement* 4386 (Dec. 8, 1995): 14.

Madeline C. Covi

CEDAR CREEK BAPTIST CHURCH. Rich in history and tradition, Cedar Creek Baptist Church is a conservative Southern Baptist fellowship in Fern Creek. It is dedicated to missions, both home and foreign, and it has growing ministries to youth, children, seniors, and the hearing impaired.

Established June 16, 1792, just days after Kentucky became a state, it was first organized under the name of Chenoweth Run Baptist Church with a congregation of twenty members. From 1792 to 1806, seven lay preachers or traveling ministers served the church. Since 1806 there have been sixty-four pastors and interim pastors who have served.

The first church building was a log structure measuring thirty by forty feet. It was located south of JEFFERSONTOWN on a one-and-a-half-acre tract of land donated by William Fleming.

The second church building, at the corner of Cedar Creek and Bardstown Roads, was dedicated in 1850. This building was a frame structure, thirty-five by forty-five feet, with a tin roof. The name of the church was changed to Cedar Creek Church of Jesus Christ, but by 1892 the church was called Cedar Creek Baptist Church.

In 1905–6, the church decided to build a new larger building, completed on the same site early in 1908. The new building had an imposing steeple that housed two bells, one to call members to worship, and the other, of a different tone, tolled for deaths. On November 16, 1940, this building burned to the ground. Services were held in the Fern Creek Elementary School until the basement of a new church was completed June 3, 1945. The sanctuary was erected in 1952.

By 1957 the church purchased a thirteen-and-a-half-acre tract of land across Bardstown Rd. On September 30, 1962, the commodious new sanctuary was dedicated, and by 1968 the educational annex was added to provide rooms needed for the diverse age groups and church-wide activities. In the spring of 1992, the Christian Activities Center was completed.

During the bicentennial celebratory year of 1992, a historical marker was dedicated by former Kentucky governor MARTHA LAYNE COLLINS (1983–87), a previous member.

Janie Pitcock
Jacil Puckett

Cedar Grove Academy, 318 Thirty-fifth Street, c. 1925.

CEDAR GROVE ACADEMY. In 1812 three women lay teachers from the school of the Saint Charles Congregation in Lebanon, Kentucky, under the direction of Father Charles Nerinckx, founded the first American religious congregation with no foreign affiliation or connection at St. Charles Church near Bardstown, Kentucky. The order, named the Sisters of Loretto at the Foot of the Cross, spread throughout Kentucky and the Midwest, eventually reaching as far as New Mexico.

The principal missions of the congregation were the glory of God, the sanctification of their own souls, and the salvation of their neighbors through the education and instruction of young females. It was that responsibilility that led in 1842 to the founding of Cedar Grove Academy in the PORTLAND area of Louisville. The school was officially christened St. Michael's Academy and shortly thereafter renamed Mount St. Benedict's Academy. By 1860 the "young ladies' academy" at 318 Thirty-fifth St. was popularly known as Cedar Grove because of the numerous evergreens surrounding the property. Located on an elevated site, it was known for its healthy and pleasant situation. A low wall surrounded the buildings, and there was a graveyard for the teaching nuns. It expanded to include a three-story building housing classrooms and a dormitory for boarding students. It had a reputation for excellence; classes included rhetoric, composition, botany, natural philosophy, ASTRONOMY, and mythology. After WORLD WAR I the school suffered financial setbacks and was forced to close in 1925. The property was converted into a subdivision known as "Cedar Grove Beautiful," with the main building becoming an apartment complex.

In 1926 the academy reopened as LORETTO HIGH SCHOOL in the Basil Doerhoefer mansion at the corner of BROADWAY and Forty-fifth St. The institution closed in 1973 because of monetary difficulties. The remaining students were enrolled in FLAGET HIGH SCHOOL, until then a boys' school. Flaget closed a year later.

See Anna C. Minogue, *Loretto, Annals of the Century* (New York 1912); Benedict Joseph Webb, *The Centenary of Catholicity in Kentucky* (Louisville 1884).

CEMENT INDUSTRY. Cement manufacturing is one of the Louisville region's oldest basic industries. The roots of the industry go back to 1830 when builders of the Louisville and Portland Canal discovered huge deposits of natural cement stone in the Ohio River bedrock. Two Louisville businessmen, John Hulme and Francis McHarry, joined forces to take advantage of the discovery. They began grinding cement at the Tarascon Brothers' grist mill at Shippingport and selling it to the canal company.

Their company, J. Hulme & Co., bought the mill in 1845 and began selling cement beyond the Louisville market. In 1866 six Louisville businessmen purchased the firm and renamed it Louisville Cement and Waterpower Co. Three years later it became the Louisville Cement Co., and its traveling agent, James Breckinridge Speed, became the general manager.

Meanwhile, the cement industry had begun to expand into Clark County, Indiana. In 1832 Lawson Very established a gristmill in Clarksville that later became a cement mill owned by William D. Beach. It is considered Clark County's first cement mill. In 1866 the Falls City Cement Co. erected a mill about a mile south of Sellersburg. Later taken over by the Dexter Belknap Co., it remained one of the county's more successful firms into the early twentieth century. The Louisville Cement Co. moved into Clark County in 1869 when it purchased a large tract of land at Petersburg on the Muddy Fork of SILVER CREEK from Lewis Bottorff. There it built a mill capable of producing a hundred thousand barrels of cement annually. The success of the Louisville Cement Co. and Dexter Belknap operations encouraged other producers to join the competition, and by 1898 Clark County boasted seventeen mills that produced approximately 90 percent of the nation's cement.

Black Diamond Cement Mill at Cementville, Indiana, 1890s.

However, in addition to being highly competitive, the industry also experienced a technological revolution with the development of portland cement at the turn of the century. As opposed to natural cement, portland cement—a carefully proportioned combination made up mainly of calcium, silicon, aluminum, and iron—was of a higher quality and more predictable, and its setting time could be regulated. By far the leading producer, Louisville Cement Co. was the only firm with both the capital and natural resources necessary to make the conversion to this new cement. Its new portland plant opened in 1906, and within a few years all its local competitors were out of business.

But Louisville Cement Co.'s triumph over its Clark County competitors did not leave it a monopoly in the region. In 1904 the Horner family established the Kosmos Portland Cement Co. on the Ohio River about twenty miles southwest of Louisville. In addition to its new mill, which began shipping in late 1905, the company also created a company town called KOSMOSDALE. In September 1908 fire destroyed the plant, which was rebuilt and reopened in 1909. As business expanded, the firm opened terminals in Evansville in the late 1920s and in Cincinnati in 1935. In 1957 it merged with Flintkote Co. In 1960 the plant underwent extensive modernization and expansion; additional improvements occurred during the 1970s to comply with air-quality standards and to increase capacity. Kosmos changed ownership three times between 1980 and 1988, when it was purchased by Southdown Inc.

Meanwhile, the Louisville Cement Co. was purchased in October 1984 by Coplay Cement Co., a Pennsylvania-based subsidiary of Societe des Ciments Francais of Paris, France, for $112.5 million. Now known as Essroc Materials Inc., the firm's offices were subsequently consolidated at the Speed plant in Clark County, leaving Kosmos Cement Co. as the only cement firm with a physical presence in Jefferson County.

See C.E. Siebenthal, "The Silver Creek Hydraulic Limestone of Southeastern Indiana," *Indiana Department of Geology and Natural Resources Twenty-Fifth Annual Report* (Indianapolis 1901).

Carl E. Kramer

CEMETERIES. Throughout history, man has attempted to memorialize the dead in ways that the culture of the family and the community sees fit. In the culture in which we live the prevailing habit is burial, with fitting ceremony, in a cemetery and with an identifying gravestone or marker. Throughout Louisville and Jefferson County a great variety of final resting places exist. While some are elaborately designed and maintained, others are simple and suffer from neglect. While some display handsome and ornate monuments and markers, others are simple, deteriorated, or have no markers at all.

In the first half of the nineteenth century, family cemeteries were widely used for interments, and rural families reserved portions of their property for the burial of their dead. There are hundreds of these graveyards scattered throughout Jefferson County. Many are well marked and kept by the descendants of the families, while others, because of development and the ravages of time, are lost. By the middle of the century, with increasing population and urbanization, public burial grounds became a more fitting and popular place for burial.

The first public cemetery was located on JEFFERSON ST. between Eleventh and Twelfth and was used as early as 1786. This earliest burial ground is referred to as the Upper Jefferson St. cemetery. By 1820 this first cemetery was found to be filling so fast that a need for additional burial space was soon to come. The site was made into a city park in 1880 and named Baxter Square for the mayor at the time.

The second burial ground, Western, was established in 1830 between Fifteenth and Eighteenth Streets on Jefferson and referred to as the Lower Jefferson, or pioneer, cemetery. The first Louisville CITY DIRECTORY in 1832 includes a map by E.D. HOBBS that shows the "New burying ground." This second public burying ground officially closed in 1893, and many of those buried there were removed to other cemeteries. Today much of this cemetery lies in ruins, and only a few records remain. Many of the earliest citizens were laid to rest in this pioneer cemetery.

Some few years after the opening of Western, a need for a new burying ground in the east was realized. The Johnston family farm, called CAVE HILL, was purchased. The cemetery was dedicated on July 25, 1848. Cave Hill, located at 701 Baxter Ave., contains the largest number of burials to date.

The Portland Cemetery was located at Thirty-sixth and Pflanz. A deed to the city of PORTLAND was entered in 1847 by JOHN ROWAN for four acres of land to be used as a family graveyard. However, an early grave marked 1828 suggests that the graveyard may have existed prior to this 1847 date. The city of Louisville acquired possession of the cemetery in 1852 when Portland was annexed by Louisville. It contains the graves of many FRENCH families who were prominent in the early development of this area, as well as many other nationalities that played important roles.

The Schardein Cemetery, located on the east side of Seventh St., was opened as a family burial place and in 1878 became a public cemetery. It is presently owned by a private corporation.

Many communities such as MIDDLETOWN and JEFFERSONTOWN maintained burial grounds. After the turn of the century more cemeteries were opened to fill the needs of the expanding county and city. The South Jefferson Cemetery opened in 1902 on DIXIE HWY. near VALLEY STATION. Evergreen, located in south-central Jefferson County, opened in 1912, followed by Resthaven in 1926 on Bardstown Rd. The Louisville Memorial Gardens opened in 1936 and serves the SHIVELY area.

AFRICAN AMERICANS also have reserved areas for the burials of their communities. The Eastern Cemetery, located at 641 Baxter Ave., and Western Cemetery both had sections reserved for blacks in the early years. By 1886 the Louisville Cemetery opened on Poplar Level Rd. in what was then a rural setting and in 1903 the Greenwood Cemetery opened at Fortieth and Greenwood. Only African Americans are buried in these two cemeteries. Serving the NEWBURG area is the Forest Home Cemetery at 3650 Petersburg Rd., which opened in the

1940s. A much newer burial place is the Green Meadows at 3506 Shanks Ln.

At the beginning of the nineteenth century, different religious congregations felt the need for separate burial grounds. These became the preferred places of burial, as proper care became the responsibility of the church members.

The first Catholic cemetery was located at Tenth and Main Streets on the site of the first St. Louis Church. When the new St. Louis Church was built on Fifth St. in 1830, the graves were removed to the Catholic portion of the Western Cemetery on Jefferson. The present-day St. Louis Cemetery did not open until 1867, and it is believed that many of those who were re-interred in the Western Cemetery were again removed to the newer St. Louis Cemetery in 1880. A portion of the Portland Cemetery was also reserved for Catholic burials.

St. Mary's or St. John's Cemetery at Twenty-sixth and Duncan began in 1849 and was the burying ground for the German Catholic community near Portland. The property for the cemetery was conveyed by deed November 30, 1849, by the Sisters of Charity of Nazareth to the Diocese of Louisville. The first burial took place in 1851. Another German Catholic burial ground, St. Stephen's, located on S Preston and Rawling Streets, opened in 1851. Many German Catholics of the time were angered by the six-dollar fee charged for burial in the Portland Cemetery and were determined to keep the St. Stephen's ground separate from the church's holdings. A refusal to turn over the lot's deed led to heated exchanges and threats of banishment. Due to opposition from one of the local parishes and the Archdiocese, it is now cared for by a private organization.

St. Louis Cemetery, located on Barret Ave. and Ellison St., was incorporated on May 28, 1872, but interments were made as early as 1867. This Catholic cemetery was laid out by local designer Benjamin Grove. St. Michael's Cemetery, opened in 1851 on Texas Ave. near Goss, replaced St. Stephen's as a burial ground for the German Catholics. St. Andrew's Cemetery, located in southern Jefferson County near PLEASURE RIDGE PARK, adjoined the Church of St. Andrew's, which was completed in 1851. St. Edward's Cemetery, located in JEFFERSONTOWN, opened in 1903 and served the Catholic population of that area. Calvary, 1600 Newburg Rd., opened in 1921. This cemetery serves as the central repository for all Catholic burial records.

The earliest record of a Jewish burial site was ADATH ISRAEL, known as Hebrew Cementery, first described in 1859. It was located on the southwest corner of Preston and Woodbine. The cemetery was moved to its present location on PRESTON ST. south of Eastern Pkwy. when Interstate 65 was constructed. At one time there was a Hebrew cemetery on the south side of Wathen Ln., west of Seventh Street Rd., but about 1934 those buried there were removed to the cemetery on Preston.

Each of the Jewish congregations—The Temple (a merger of Adath Israel and Brith Shalom), Adath Jeshurun, Keneseth Israel, Anshei Sfard, and Temple Shalom—has its own burial site. All but Temple Shalom own land on Preston St.; Temple Shalom uses a consecrated site in Cave Hill Cemetery. Across Preston St. from the others is Agudath Achim Cemetery, which retains its name though the congregation merged with Adath Jeshurun.

Many early Protestant churches also had suitable burial places for their congregations. The early Baptists had graveyards at the Floyd's Fork Baptist Church near FISHERVILLE, Chenoweth Run near Jeffersontown, and LONG RUN in eastern Jefferson County. The Methodist, or as it is known today, the Eastern Cemetery, is located at 641 Baxter. It borders Payne St. and is next to Cave Hill on the southeast side. The land was purchased by the Fourth Street Methodist Episcopal Church South and the Brook Street Methodist Episcopal Church South as a burial place for their members. It was incorporated on March 4, 1854, but burials began as early as 1844. Also the Cane Run Methodist off Thurman Rd., Mt. Holly in FAIRDALE, Fairmount off Bardstown Rd,, Hobbs Chapel in ANCHORAGE on the site of the Anchorage Methodist Church, and the Eastwood Methodist Church all had cemeteries. The Presbyterians had burial grounds at the Cane Run Presbyterian Church near Fisherville, the German Reformed Presbyterian on the northeast corner of Shelby and Main in Jeffersontown, Bethlehem Presbyterian on the Old Taylorsville Rd. and at the early Pennsylvania Run Presbyterian Cemetery in southeast Jefferson County. A 1795 tombstone for William Cummins of Pennsylvania indicates that this is one of the oldest cemeteries in the county. The Lutheran Cemetery, located in Jeffersontown on Watterson Trail, opened in 1833, and the Mt. Zion Lutheran on Pope Lick Rd. in 1859. A Christian Church cemetery is on Poplar Level Rd. at the site of the Newburg Christian Church.

Some of the early cemeteries had reserved portions for the indigent, but by 1873 a burial site was chosen on Manslick Rd. It was known as the pauper's graveyard, or the Manslick Cemetery. In the last few years a newer site was chosen in southwestern Jefferson County and named Southwest Memorial Gardens.

Two important military cemeteries are also in the Louisville area. A portion of Cave Hill was set aside for the burial of Union soldiers. It is known as the Cave Hill National Cemetery and is maintained by federal contract with Cave Hill. An additional site in Cave Hill was purchased for the burial of Confederate soldiers. Another military cemetery is the ZACHARY TAYLOR NATIONAL CEMETERY, located on Brownsboro Rd. in eastern Jefferson County. This was once the private burying ground for the Taylor family and is the final resting place for the twelfth president, ZACHARY TAYLOR. The cemetery was officially made a national cemetery in May 1928.

While interment of the body remained the favorite practice, paying for burials became increasingly difficult during the GREAT DEPRESSION. This fact, coupled with potential land shortages within the city, inspired interest in an alternative means of disposing of the dead. In 1933 retired building inspector J.L. Obier embarked on a plan to build Louisville's first crematorium. Obier discussed his plans with several funeral home directors to discover if a crematorium would be suitable for the area and then took several trips to other crematoriums in Ohio and Indiana with the cemetery board. Louisville's Crematorium was a composite of the best features of these facilities.

In 1935 a site for the crematorium was chosen at 641 Baxter Ave. in the Eastern Cemetery. The building had two large furnaces into which the bodies could be lowered at temperatures approaching two thousand degrees Fahrenheit. The first official cremation in the state of Kentucky took place there on December 13, 1935, and the Louisville Crematorium officially opened for business as a nonprofit organization on December 24.

Cemeteries Represented in This Article

Adath Israel
Bethlehem Presbyterian
Calvary
Cane Run Methodist
Cave Hill
Chenoweth Run Baptist
Eastern or Methodist Cemetery
Eastwood Methodist
Evergreen
Fairmount
First Catholic or St. Louis
Floyd's Fork Baptist
Forest Home
German Reformed Presbyterian
Greenwood
Hebrew Cemetery
Hobbs Chapel
Jefferson Street Cemetery
Jeffersontown
Long Run Baptist
The Louisville Cemetery
Louisville Memorial Gardens
Lutheran Cemetery
Manslick Cemetery
Middletown
Mt. Holly
Mt. Zion Lutheran
Newburg Christian
Pennsylvania Run Presbyterian
Portland
Resthaven Memorial Gardens
St. Andrew's
St. Edward's
St. Mary's or St. John's
St. Michael's
St. Stephen's
Schardein
Second St. Louis
South Jefferson

Southwest Memorial Gardens
Western
Zachary Taylor National

See Samuel W. Thomas, *The History of Cave Hill Cemetery* (Louisville 1985); *Courier-Journal*, May 22, 1938, Feb. 21, 1954, July 20, 1987, July 23, 1990, Nov. 14, 1990; J. Stoddard Johnston, ed, *Memorial History of Louisville* (Chicago 1896); John B. Wuest, *One Hundred Years of St. Boniface Parish* (Louisville 1937); Warren Kellar Frederick, *A History of Some of the Churches and Cemeteries in Jefferson County, Kentucky* (Louisville 1932).

Nettie Oliver

CENTRAL COLORED/MARY D. HILL SCHOOL. Although public schools were first established in Louisville in 1829, African American students were not provided with a free education until after the CIVIL WAR. On October 7, 1873, the first public school building in Kentucky for those students was dedicated. The choir of FIFTH STREET BAPTIST CHURCH opened the program with a setting of Psalm 40, appropriately titled, "I Waited Patiently."

Central Colored (later Mary D. Hill) School, Sixth and Kentucky, 1930.

Built by the city for twenty-three thousand dollars, the Central Colored School was erected on the southeast corner of Sixth and Kentucky Streets. J.B. McElfatrick and Son, the architects of this Renaissance Revival building, also designed MACAULEY'S THEATRE, which opened six days later. Taxes from all black-owned property in Louisville were allocated for the support of the school. Within three years, more than one thousand children attended classes there, which significantly upgraded local AFRICAN AMERICAN education.

The school continued to teach grades one through eight until 1882, when junior and senior classes were added. Part of the building then became CENTRAL COLORED HIGH SCHOOL. In 1893 another year was added, making it a three-year high school. Due to overcrowding, Central moved to Ninth and Magazine Streets in 1894. The original building was then named Sixth Street School and was used as an elementary school for white children only. In 1917 the name was changed to Mary D. Hill School in honor of the supervisor of public school kindergartens who had died the previous year. The school closed in 1970 and became the Hill Adult Learning Laboratory. In 1981 the building was sold to a graphic design firm.

See *Louisville Commercial*, Oct. 8, 1873; *Courier-Journal*, Dec. 15, 1916, April 14, 1954, Dec. 6, 1982; *Louisville Herald*, April 17, 1921; *Mary D. Hill School: Landmark and Landmark Site Designation Report* (Louisville 1975).

Robert Bruce French

CENTRAL HIGH SCHOOL MAGNET CAREER ACADEMY. Originally called the Central Colored High School, it was Louisville's first AFRICAN AMERICAN high school. It was opened in September 1882 on the corner of Sixth and Kentucky Streets. The school began with twenty-seven students, a principal, and one teacher. In 1895 Central moved to Ninth and Magazine Streets.

Until 1907 the school was exclusively an academic institution. But under the prodding of Booker T. Washington and other black national leaders, a case was made for manual training. Central's curriculum was then geared toward both academic and useful skills, among the latter dressmaking, cosmetology, automobile mechanics, plumbing, electricity, home economics, blueprinting, and machine shop.

In 1912 Central moved to Ninth and Chestnut Streets. However, in order to accommodate the growing interest in vocational education, the manual training department remained at Ninth and Magazine Streets until 1952, when it also moved to Chestnut St.

By 1932 Central Colored High School had nine hundred students and thirty teachers, and was still expanding. The school improved both in size and quality so that in 1932 it was accredited by the Southern Association of Colleges and Secondary Schools. In 1945 the name was changed to Central High School in response to students' and parents' protests about the use of the word "colored." By 1950 the school had nearly thirteen hundred students and fifty-two teachers.

Because of rapid growth, Central High School moved to its fourth location at Twelfth and Chestnut Streets in September 1952. Its new facilities were unsurpassed in the Louisville school system.

At Central High School, athletics were important, especially BASKETBALL. Central won several state and national championships, most notably under the head coaching of WILLIAM L. KEAN (1923–58) and Robert Graves (1965–84). Although BOXING was not included in the school curriculum, a number of boys participated in it in private gymnasiums. Most notable was Cassius Clay (MUHAMMAD ALI), class of 1960, who won the world heavyweight championship three times.

In 1963 Atwood Wilson retired after serving twenty-nine years as principal. His retirement ushered in a period of many changes. In 1964 the Louisville BOARD OF EDUCATION initiated a plan of "token" integration by transferring a few of Central's teachers to East End schools and East End teachers to Central. Despite these efforts, Central remained Louisville's only predominantly African American high school until September 1975 when court-ordered BUSING began. This led to tension between old and new students. The desegregation of Central was met with protest from alumni, teachers, parents, and students who believed that the school would lose its tradition, spirit, and excellence. By 1982 what had once been Louisville's only all–African American high school was about 70 percent white.

In 1986 Central High School began offering magnet courses in order to draw the area's top African American students. In 1991 the Jefferson County School Board voted to adopt a new plan, Project Renaissance, which replaced the busing plan in which a student's school assignment was decided by the first letter of his or her last name. The plan required each school to be at least 15 but not more than 50 percent

Faculty of Central High School, July 1920. Educators Joseph Seamon Cotter (left) and Albert Meyzeek are seen standing in rear.

African American. Magnet career programs were used in schools throughout the county to encourage integration. That same year, Central became a countywide magnet with programs in law, medicine, and other areas. Its name was changed to Central High School Magnet Career Academy, and it offered a four-year precollegiate program, an advanced program, and an honors program. In 1997 a new issue arose over quotas. While the student body at Central was nearly 50 percent African American in the 1996–97 school year, there were at least six hundred vacancies in the school due to the inability to attract white students. At the same time, large numbers of African American students were turned away, and citizens asked that an exception be made at Central by increasing the 50 percent limit. The school board refused, saying that making an exception for Central would poke a hole in the desegregation dike.

In the late nineties Central students began receiving national attention as merit scholars, and the school has continued to develop its role as an important magnet school for the area.

See Bruce Allar, "Central to the Debate," *Louisville* (Aug. 1997): 36.

CENTRAL PRESBYTERIAN CHURCH. A long heritage of Presbyterian presence at Fourth and Kentucky Streets is being continued by Central Presbyterian Church. From the original McKee Mission Chapel in 1868, there has been a succession of mergers, consolidations, and new names for the churches on this site. The present congregation is a result of the 1957 merger of Fourth Avenue Presbyterian Church at that corner and Warren Memorial Presbyterian Church at Fourth and Broadway. The present building at Fourth and Kentucky was designed by Louisville architect E.T. Hutchings.

A decision was made to remain in the Old Louisville area to serve a widely diverse and inclusive group of people. The mission of each congregation emphasized service to the urban and Old Louisville areas as well as the entire community.

In recent years approximately $1 million has been spent renovating, modernizing, and improving the parish house (built in 1909) and the sanctuary (1930). Music is provided by Central's 1930 E.M. Skinner pipe organ that has been restored to its original brilliance.

Harry C. Gans

CENTRAL STATE HOSPITAL. Located at 10510 LaGrange Rd. in eastern Jefferson County, Central State Hospital (CSH) is a 192-bed acute-care, adult psychiatric hospital. Land was bought by the commonwealth from the Hite family in 1869 to build a state house of reform for juvenile delinquents. In 1873 the General Assembly authorized its conversion to the Fourth Kentucky Lunatic Asylum because of severe overcrowding at the Eastern Lunatic Asylum in Lexington and the Western Lunatic Asylum in Hopkinsville. (Another state institution in Frankfort for "feeble-minded" children was the Third Kentucky Lunatic Asylum.) By 1900 the hospital had been renamed the Central Kentucky Asylum for the Insane; it was also commonly known as Lakeland Hospital after Lakeland Rd., which borders the grounds, and for the lake that marks the entrance.

In the nineteenth century a secluded, pastoral environment was thought helpful in treating mental illness, and CSH was typical of the time in that it was located beyond the city. Not all patients had psychiatric illnesses. Many had neurological disorders; others were mentally retarded or simply elderly and poor. The growing demand for care and a persistent lack of funds eventually led to serious overcrowding. By 1940 there were twenty-four hundred patients in a facility built for sixteen hundred; many patients were hospitalized for years. The development of effective psychiatric medications in the 1950s, the emphasis in the state on Mental Health care with the creation of a department, and a growing societal belief that

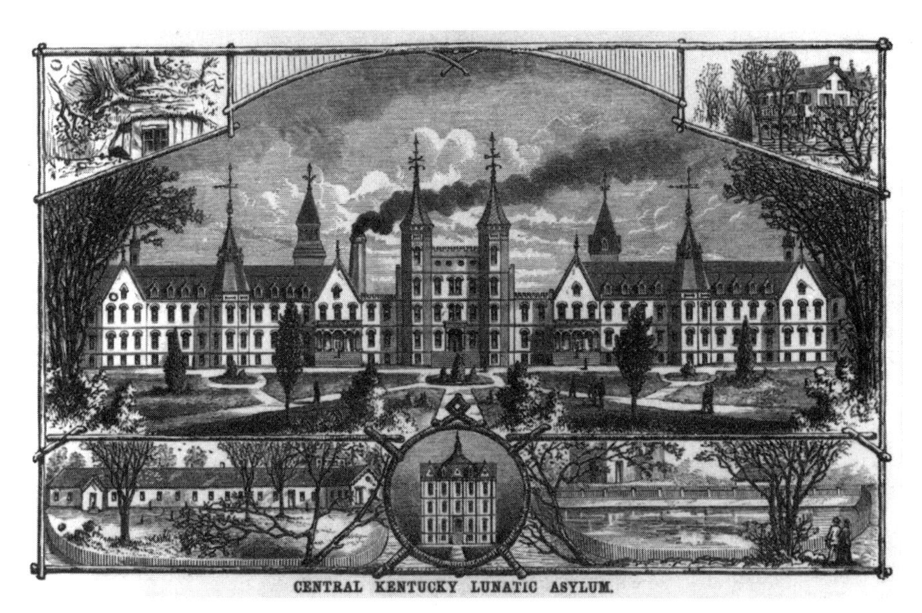

Central Kentucky Lunatic Asylum (now Central State Hospital) from the 1889 annual report.

people should, if possible, be treated in the community began the trend toward less use of institutions. Still, in the late 1990s more than nineteen hundred patients a year were treated at CSH, and the average length of stay was about two weeks.

From 1974 to 1977 the hospital was privatized under the River Region Mental Health–Mental Retardation Board, after which time the state resumed operation. In 1986 CSH moved to a new facility on the grounds, and the old hospital buildings were razed. In 1993 public officials began a long consideration of developing the old hospital site into a public park with lakes, trails, an amphitheater, and picnic areas.

See W.H. Perrin, J.H. Battle, and G.C. Kniffin, *Kentucky: A History of the State* (Louisville 1886); *Courier-Journal*, June 10, 1997; *Souvenir: Central Kentucky Asylum for the Insane, Lakeland, Kentucky* (Pittsburgh 1900).

Joan C. Masters

CERAMICS. Until recent years it was thought that shards found in the earth around Louisville had come from pottery transported west across the mountains from Pennsylvania and New Jersey. We know today it was the potters themselves who came west to fashion their wares in small manufactories close to where the shards were found.

Most early earthenwares were simple and unadorned, but the secret of coaxing common clay into shapes upon a potter's wheel was passed down from one generation of craftsmen to the next, often within families. So it was that Valentine and William Conrad brought the Germanic skill of slip-trailing to JEFFERSONTOWN early in the nineteenth century, the gaudy stripes found on remnants of their redware being exceptions to the general simplicity rule.

It was John, Abram, and Isaac Dover, three brothers from the vicinity of Wheeling, Virginia, who introduced stoneware to Louisville between 1815 and 1817 at the pottery of Jacob Lewis.

Lewis, who was originally from Pennsylvania, had 157 1/2 feet of frontage on MAIN ST. at the corner of Jackson, running back 204 feet to what would come many years later to be called "Billy Goat Strut Alley," which parallels Main. In front he built a brick residence for his family and opened a potter's store. Behind, and off Jackson St., was his pottery.

Despite difficulties suffered in the Panic of 1819, Lewis had lofty dreams. After locating kaolin near Commerce, Missouri, he brought the Staffordshire potters Jabez Vodrey and William Frost to Louisville to try to make white tableware. In December 1829 the Lewis Pottery for the manufacture of "queensware" was incorporated by an act of the Kentucky legislature. In March 1829, Isaac Dover, the youngest brother and last to work with Lewis, opened his own stoneware pottery across Main St. and a block to the east. Though shards from a 1997 archaeological dig revealed that the Lewis pottery made mocha-decorated whiteware earlier than any previously documented to an American manufactory, it was unable to produce tableware in sufficient quantity or cheaper than what was being imported from Staffordshire. But the products themselves were good enough to convince local businessmen to petition Congress in 1834 asking that a tract of government land along the Mississippi River be granted to a company headed by Jacob Lewis for the manufacture of whiteware. Their pleas were rejected.

In 1836, James Clews visited Louisville. The name "Clews" on tableware imported from the Staffordshire pottery he managed with his brother Ralph was familiar to most of the local merchants who had signed their names to the 1834 petition. Unaware that the brothers had just declared bankruptcy in England, they rushed to offer him almost unlimited backing if he would set up a fineware pottery somewhere nearby. Clews decided that suitable clay and coal were available at Troy, Indiana, several miles down the OHIO RIVER. So was born the Indiana Pottery Co., the leading stockholder being Samuel Casseday of the Louisville firm of Bull and Casseday, dealers in queensware, china, and glass.

Jacob Lewis threw in his lot with the new enterprise, so Jabez Vodrey and William Frost moved across the street to the pottery once run by Isaac Dover, who had gone to join his brothers in Orange County, Indiana. By 1838 Clews had spent fifty thousand dollars of his backers' money and had little to show for the effort, so once again Louisville merchants petitioned Congress to grant them land containing clay beds in Indiana, Illinois, or Missouri. Once again they were turned down.

Also in 1838, a stoneware pottery was begun by George Washington Doane at 728 Main St. on the northeast corner of PRESTON. He was joined by William Frost when Jabez Vodrey left for Troy in 1839 to manage what was left of the Indiana Pottery Co. In the same year, Jacob Lewis, whose fortunes had declined following the failure of Clews, retired from business at the age of sixty-eight and moved to Hickman, Kentucky, where he ended his days. But John Shallcross, a steamboat captain married to Lewis's eldest daughter, Mary, continued to lease the old pottery site to others. G.W. Doane had New England stoneware potters John and Frederick Hancock working there in 1840. Then there was a family of German immigrant stoneware potters named Melcher. Following 1848, however, when Anton Melcher and Martin Doll signed an agreement to work at Doane's pottery across the street, it is doubtful that kilns were ever again fired at the Lewis site. Soon afterwards, Anton Melcher moved to Fourteenth St. and Portland Ave., where the pottery impressed "A.Melcher" was probably made.

Louisville's potteries closed before the onset of the CIVIL WAR in 1861 and did not resume production for some years afterward. In the twentieth century, the tradition of pottery-making in Louisville continues with LOUISVILLE STONEWARE and HADLEY POTTERY, building on the foundations of the early artisans who crafted works of utility and beauty at the edge of the frontier.

J. Garrison Stradling

CHARLES DICKENS'S VISIT. During their first visit to the United States and Canada, between January and June 1842, Charles Dickens (1812–70), Victorian England's foremost novelist, and his wife, Catherine (1815–79), twice sampled Louisville. His travel book, *American Notes for General Circulation* (1842), records his impressions.

In chapter twelve, which he entitled, "From Cincinnati to Louisville in another Western Steamboat, and from Louisville to St. Louis in another," he recounts his brief stay. Upon arrival from Cincinnati late on April 6, they were "as handsomely lodged" at the original GALT HOUSE as though they "had been in Paris, rather than hundreds of miles beyond the Alleghenies." On a negative note, Louisville lacked "objects of sufficient interest" to detain them, but a morning ride on the seventh prior to their departure for St. Louis revealed the city as "regular and cheerful; the streets being laid out at right angles, and planted with young trees....There did not appear to be much business stirring; and some unfinished buildings and improvements seemed to intimate that the city had been over-built in the ardour of 'going ahead,' and was suffering under the reaction consequent upon such feverish forcing of its powers."

Dickens observed Louisville's coal-blackened buildings and noted: "but an Englishman is well used to that appearance, and indisposed to quarrel with it," and that "here, as elsewhere in these parts, the road was perfectly alive with pigs of all ages." He continued, "On our way to Portland we passed a 'Magistrate's office,' which amused me, as looking far more like a dame school than any police establishment: for this awful Institution was nothing but a little, lazy, good-for-nothing front parlour, open to the street; wherein two or three figures (I presume the magistrate and his myrmidons) were basking in the sunshine, the very effigies of languor and repose. It was a perfect picture of Justice retired from business for want of customers; her sword and scales sold off; napping comfortably with her legs upon the table."

Aboard their steamer in the PORTLAND CANAL, the Dickenses were called on by the "Kentucky Giant," JIM PORTER (1810–59). At "seven feet eight inches, in his stockings," he resembled "a lighthouse walking among lamp-posts."

Returning from St. Louis to Cincinnati, the couple again "gladly availed" themselves of Louisville's "excellent" Galt House on the night of April 17.

Charles "Charley" Dickens (1837–96), the author's son, arrived in Louisville on December 5, 1887, as part of a literary tour of America

Burnett Avenue at Hickory Street, showing Checks Café, 1952.

and read several chapters from *David Copperfield* and *Bob Sawyer's Party* at the Masonic Temple Theatre at Fourth and Jefferson Streets. The *Courier-Journal*, on December 6, 1887, described Dickens's reading as "inclined to the monotonous, yet there are frequent occasions on which he seems to catch the fire of inspiration from the author" and commented on his rather portly size, English waxed mustache, and his late arrival for the evening, claiming "his carriage driver had professed not to know the way."

See Charles Dickens, *American Notes for General Circulation* (1842); Charles Dickens, *The Letters of Charles Dickens: The Pilgrim Edition* (Oxford 1974); William Glyde Wilkins, *Charles Dickens in America* (New York 1970); Michael Slater, *Dickens on America and the Americans* (Austin, Tex., 1978); Jerome Meckier, *Innocent Abroad: Charles Dickens's American Engagements* (Lexington 1990).

John Spalding Gatton

CHECK'S CAFÉ. Check's Café is a Germantown neighborhood landmark at 1101 E Burnett Ave. at the corner of Hickory St. Joe Murrow opened the café in 1948 in a former Kroger grocery store. Check's is noted for hearty food at cheap, stable prices. It has served daily helpings of its well-known homemade soup, rolled oysters, fish sandwiches, fried chicken, and other favorites since the days of Harry Truman's presidency. No items on its board were priced over five dollars in 1999. The café is also known for having no printed menus and for its quirky ordering system. Customers make their selections at the bar without giving their names and wait for servers to call out the similar food orders. Diners have to determine if the latest bowl of soup emerging from the kitchen is theirs. Jimmy Carter and his brother, Billy, and basketball commentator Al McGuire are among notables who have enjoyed Check's down-home charm during Louisville visits.

See *Courier-Journal*, Jan. 16, 1993.

Mary Margaret Bell

CHEMICALS. The chemical industry has long been an important factor in the Louisville economy and includes the most important names in chemical engineering. The chemical industry in Louisville includes everything from compound and catalyst manufacturing to research.

The home ground of Louisville's chemical industry is Rubbertown, an industrial district on the southwest side of the city near Riverport. The majority of chemical facilities are located there, including industry giants Du Pont and Rohm & Haas. Downtown, however, is the site for German-owned catalyst leader United Catalyst Inc. (UCI).

The Du Pont company soared to industrial and economical heights previous to and during World War II with its line of synthetic products created through chemistry. Of particular note is the Du Pont discovery of nylon. As a result of this and other chemical wonders created and manufactured by the Du Pont company, Louisville maintained an important role in supporting military needs during World War II. The chemical industry, as well as other industries that were instrumental during the war, led Louisville into a prosperous future after the war. In the 1950s new techniques in chemistry allowed companies such as Du Pont and Rohm and Haas to expand operations, creating more opportunities and employment for Louisville.

One of the many reasons chemical companies chose Louisville is the Ohio River. Stretching from the Mississippi to the Pittsburgh basin, the Ohio River is one of the most important water trade routes in the eastern United States. Relatively nonvolatile and touching on several major riverports, the Ohio River provides a safe and efficient means of transportation.

The Ohio River also contributes to the Louisville aquifer, a natural, reservoir water table that extends into the floodplain of the region. Many chemical processes in manufacturing require a cooling technique that relies on immense amounts of water. By building in the Rubbertown area directly over the aquifer, many of these companies were able to tap wells right into the water table at low cost.

Railroads are another Louisville advantage for the chemical industry. From the beginning of the chemical industry in Louisville, the Louisville & Nashville Railroad (now csx Transportation) and other railroads were an important means for transporting chemical products. This was especially true during World War II.

With the growth of the chemical industry throughout the twentieth century, safety has become more of an issue for Louisville, and especially Rubbertown. As early as 1956 studies were conducted to ascertain the problems of pollution and chemical effects on the local environment. The studies were critical of the industry, its practices, and its effects. At that time, Louisville's West End was considered the most affected by pollution. Many of the problems in 1956 followed from factors that disappeared with time. Among them were the use of coal for heating, garbage-burning, and uncontrolled industrial emissions.

By the mid-1980s a bevy of local, state, and federal laws set strict guidelines for the emission and disposal of chemical and hazardous waste. With time Rubbertown has been subject to various regulations that are routinely monitored by local and federal authorities, including the Environmental Protection Agency (EPA). While many problems have been eradicated, the impressive growth of the chemical industry has created new problems.

Attention to such problems and effects has been created and encouraged by several notorious incidents. A particularly infamous incident surrounded an industrial waste dump at what became known as the Valley of the Drums in Bullitt County, where in 1976 the EPA found toxic chemicals being illegally disposed. As early as 1964 the Tri-Cities industrial waste dump had been disposing of questionable chemical waste. At the Smith Farm off Pryor Valley Rd., as many as a hundred thousand barrels of toxic chemicals had been dumped. By 1987 the EPA had found conclusively that the environment in this area had been tainted.

Smaller, less notorious problems have prompted local, state, and federal reaction as well. By the 1980s studies of Louisville air showed an increase in air pollution. While vehicle emissions are the major cause of poor air quality, the contributions of the chemical industry to the dilemma continued to be questioned and monitored. In the early 1990s the city of Louisville found itself left with the facility cleanup of the defunct Exmet Co. Sinkholes used as waste dumps and possible tainted water continue to be a problem.

The chemical industry in Louisville has worked with agencies and officials to better prepare for unexpected events. From local organized efforts such as the Rubbertown Environmental Group to involvement in the nationwide Chemical Manufacturers Association's responsible care program, the chemical industry strives to live by Du Pont's motto: Better living through chemistry.

In May 1997 the Louisville Du Pont plant suffered a chemical leak that prompted quick response. All safety and warning plans were carried out as planned, from evacuation to public relations to the reaction plan. As a result, disaster was averted. Regulations set by the federal Occupational Safety and Health Administration (OSHA) and the cooperation of Louisville's chemical industry have brought about progress,[6] as records indicate a dramatic drop in the type of incidents that shadowed the industry from the 1960s to the early 1980s.

Two fields of chemistry often overlooked are pharmaceuticals and research. Louisville's contributions to these fields have been notable. The UNIVERSITY OF LOUISVILLE has hosted such research projects as the Hein-Mervis Study of genetics in relation to cancer-causing chemicals. Because of the sustained growth of medical services in Louisville, pharmacology has played an important role in local economics, research, and development.

See Peter Galison, *Big Science: The Growth of Large-Scale Research* (Palo Alto, Calif., 1992); Joseph Frazier Wall, *Alfred I. du Pont: The Man and His Family* (New York 1990); John T. Williams and Daniel T. Muir, *Corporate Images* (Wilmington, Del., 1984); *Courier-Journal,* Jan. 26, 1997, May 21, 1997, May 27, 1997, July 7, 1997, Sept. 28, 1997.

Paul Wolf Holleman

CHENOWETH, MARGARET "PEGGY" MCCARTY (b Hampshire County, Virginia (now West Virginia), ca. 1751; d Shelby County, Kentucky, ca. 1825). Pioneer/settler. About 1769 Margaret married RICHARD CHENOWETH. They were among the first families to arrive with Maj. Gen. GEORGE ROGERS CLARK at the FALLS OF THE OHIO in 1778. The Chenoweths settled on a tract of land about two miles from Middletown, Kentucky.

On July 17, 1789, the Chenoweths were attacked by a party of sixteen Shawnee Indians. Peggy was shot between the shoulder blades with an arrow. The story goes that she was assumed dead, so a warrior pulled the arrow from her flesh and, with a jagged and dull knife, sliced a path around her hairline. Gripping the bloody knife between his teeth and placing a foot upon her back for balance, he stripped off her entire scalp. Before leaving, he hit her naked skull twice with the butt of his tomahawk.

Peggy Chenoweth endured the procedure in silence. She not only recovered her health and energy, she bore two more daughters before her husband died about 1802. To hide the absence of hair, she wore a skullcap. Peggy is buried in the Chenoweth family cemetery near present-day Middletown in Jefferson County.

See Blaine Guthrie Jr., "Captain Richard Chenoweth: A Founding Father of Louisville," *Filson Club History Quarterly* 46 (April 1972): 147–60.

Laurie A. Birnsteel

CHENOWETH, RICHARD (b near Gunpowder Creek, Baltimore County, Maryland, 1735; d Jefferson County, Kentucky, 1802). Pioneer. His parents, John Chenoweth Jr. and Mary Smith, had emigrated from St. Martin Island off the Cornwall coast shortly before Richard's birth. The family moved to Frederick County, Virginia (now West Virginia), prior to 1746. There Chenoweth married Margaret McCarty. His family came to Kentucky with GEORGE ROGERS CLARK's army in 1778 and helped establish Clark's base on CORN ISLAND at the FALLS OF THE OHIO. He helped build Fort-on-Shore the following year.

Chenoweth was one of seven elected in 1779 as trustees of the newly formed town of Louisville. He was a militia captain and commanded an artillery company for Clark's expeditions in 1780 and 1782 against Ohio Indian towns. Chenoweth was probably Jefferson County's first sheriff and a justice of the peace for the Jefferson County Court from 1783–85.

Chenoweth moved his family in 1784 to establish Chenoweth Station near MIDDLETOWN. Its exposed position was an invitation for raids by Indian parties, who attacked on at least three occasions, including the CHENOWETH MASSACRE in 1789. His greatest service occurred in 1781 when he contracted to build FORT NELSON in Louisville. Col. George Slaughter, who commanded the garrison, made a sworn statement that "Mr. Chenoweth at his own expense (which was very considerable) completed the Fortification in March 1781 in a proper manner." It was agreed that Virginia would pay Chenoweth twelve thousand pounds in paper currency. The commonwealth, however, failed to meet this obligation. As a result, Chenoweth was forced to sell his considerable land holdings to satisfy debts owed workmen and suppliers. This created severe financial distress for the balance of Chenoweth's life. He was declared insolvent by the Jefferson County Court following his death in 1802.

See Blaine A. Guthrie Jr., "Captain Richard Chenoweth: A Founding Father of Louisville," *Filson Club History Quarterly* 46 (April 1972): 147–60; Alfred Pirtle, *James Chenoweth: The Story of One of the Earliest Boys of Louisville and Where Louisville Started* (Louisville 1921).

Blaine A. Guthrie Jr.

CHENOWETH MASSACRE. The Chenoweth Massacre was the last major Indian raid in Jefferson County. Capt. RICHARD CHENOWETH established his station northeast of present-day MIDDLETOWN in 1784. The closest neighbors were at Linn's Station, approximately five miles from his exposed position. This proved to be an invitation for attacking Indians, who raided it in 1786–87.

The Chenoweth Massacre occurred on July 17, 1789. Evidently trouble was expected, as authorities sent a squad of soldiers from the garrison at the FALLS OF THE OHIO to aid in the station's defense. But before the soldiers could take their positions, a large Indian party attacked, killing three Chenoweth children and two guards. Captain Chenoweth and his son James were wounded. PEGGY CHENOWETH, the

Springhouse at Chenoweth massacre site, 1911.

captain's wife, was injured by an arrow. She fell to the ground and was scalped. She survived the ordeal and was found the next day by a rescue party led by Col. RICHARD C. ANDERSON. WILLIAM CLARK, future co-leader of the LEWIS AND CLARK EXPEDITION, was a member of that party.

See Blaine A. Guthrie Jr., "Captain Richard Chenoweth: A Founding Father of Louisville," *Filson Club History Quarterly* 46 (April 1972): 147–60; Alfred Pirtle, *James Chenoweth: The Story of One of the Earliest Boys of Louisville and Where Louisville Started* (Louisville 1921).

Blaine A. Guthrie Jr.

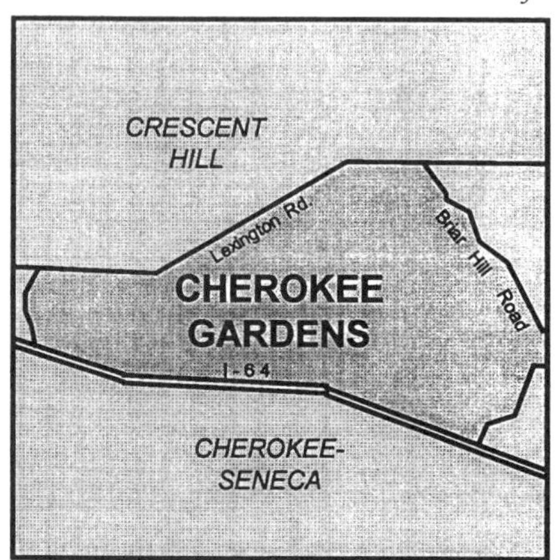

Advertisement for Seneca Gardens.

CHEROKEE GARDENS. Residential neighborhood in eastern Louisville bounded by Lexington Rd. to the north, Briar Hill Rd. to the east, Interstate 64 to the south, and the Cherokee Gardens West subdivision to the west. Part of the tract originally given to Richard Charlton and James Southall in 1774 for their service during the French and Indian War, the land remained relatively untouched until the middle of the nineteenth century. In 1849 the LOUISVILLE AND FRANKFORT RAILROAD Co. was granted permission to build its line nearby (adjacent to modern-day Frankfort Ave.). It prompted the Shelbyville and Louisville Turnpike Co. in 1851 to build a road known as the Shelbyville Branch (present-day Lexington Rd.) for those travelers who wished to avoid the railroad.

The newfound popularity of the area was shown by the creation of large family estates and the celebration of Kentucky's first state fair on the site of today's ST. JOSEPH CHILDREN'S HOME on Frankfort Ave. in 1853. The community got a boost with the development of Cherokee Park, beginning in the 1890s. By the 1920s, the large estates were becoming expensive to maintain, and the arrival of the automobile made the area a short commute to downtown. In 1925 OSCAR TURNER JR. and Mary Viglini sold their parcels of about seventy acres to Helm Bruce Jr. and Clarence C. Hieatt, who developed the Viglini Unit of the subdivision. In the same year, William S. Speed purchased the land between Fairfield Dr. and Primrose Way and began development of the Fairfield Unit. To maintain the rolling, wooded nature of the area, the developers hired OLMSTED Brothers, the firm responsible for planning nearby Cherokee Park, to lay out their units. The area collectively became known as Cherokee Gardens.

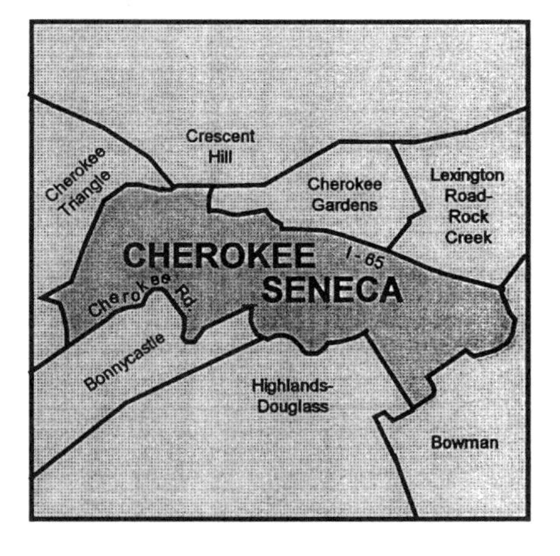

CHEROKEE-SENECA. Neighborhood in eastern Louisville comprising the homes that exist on the peripheries of Cherokee and Seneca Parks as well as the parks themselves. Its boundary roughly follows the outlines of the parks. A major landmark in the neighborhood is the PRESBYTERIAN THEOLOGICAL SEMINARY on Alta Vista Rd. and the mansion GARDENCOURT. The Seminary was built in 1963.

CHEROKEE TRIANGLE. The Cherokee Triangle is a National Register and Local Landmark District located in the HIGHLANDS area of Louisville. Its main boundaries are Bardstown Rd., Highland Ave., Eastern Pkwy., Cherokee Park, and CAVE HILL CEMETERY. It is known for its sense of history, tree-lined streets, "neighborhood feeling," and ARCHITECTURE. Cherokee Triangle is an example of Louisville's "post-bellum, pre–WORLD WAR I street car suburb."

Although there are several different sections of Cherokee Triangle, the largest and best-known was developed in the 1880s by two businessmen, JAMES W. HENNING and Josiah S. Speed. Three factors influenced the surge in population: a favorable topography, the perfection of rapid electric transport, and the establishment of Cherokee Park in the early 1890s. Baringer Farms subdivision and the remaining Slaughter-Longest land were soon developed.

However, due to the limited access to transportation, the neighborhood was originally inhabited only by affluent residents. The wealth in Cherokee Triangle was evident in its architecture. Homes were stately, spacious, and architecturally eclectic, reflecting the income, status, and power of many of the residents. Carriage houses, servants' quarters, and stables were common. In the late 1800s, a close proximity to the stockyards gave these wealthy residents a feel of rural life. A walkway known as "the enclosure" was a double row of fences be-

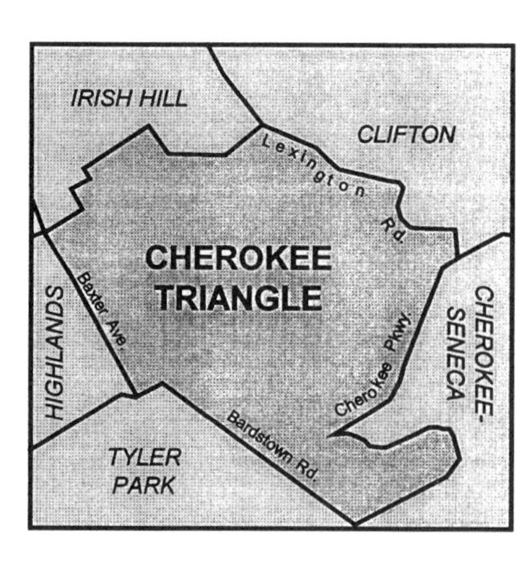

tween front yards and Cherokee Rd. curbsides. This protected yards and pedestrians from stray cattle and hogs that were driven down Bardstown turnpike.

One of the earliest residences was built at Grinstead Dr. and Cherokee Rd. by James Henning as a wedding gift for his daughter Maria and husband J.J.B. Hilliard. Other prominent residents were JOHN A. "BUD" HILLERICH, producer of the first LOUISVILLE SLUGGER, and J. Stoddard Johnston, historian and a Kentucky secretary of state (1875–79).

A little-known aspect of Cherokee Triangle was the town of Enterprise. Embracing most of the Longest family and Eastern Park Land Co. lands between Bardstown Rd. and Cherokee Pkwy., the town, which contained its own school on the corner of Bardstown Rd. and Cherokee Pkwy., incorporated in 1884 to keep taxes low and to exclude liquor. However, as the region grew following the establishment of Cherokee Park, Louisville officials began annexation proceedings in 1894. In 1896, Enterprise gave up its bid to stay independent and became part of the city. The white frame Enterprise School became the Enterprise Branch of the now Bloom Elementary on Lucia Ave.

In the early 1900s the trolley line spurred new businesses along Bardstown Rd., including Zehnder's Garden, a family beer garden. The Highland Public Library on Cherokee Rd. was also built. After WORLD WAR II, many families left for the suburbs. Multistory homes were split into apartments or fell into disrepair. In 1962 the Cherokee Triangle Association was founded by residents to stop the decline of their neighborhood. Down-zoning was implemented; multiple-family structures were no longer allowed on certain streets.

Cherokee Triangle's name reflects both its triangular shape and its identification with Cherokee Park. One distinguishing landmark is the Gen. JOHN BRECKINRIDGE CASTLEMAN monument, dedicated in 1913. The monument of Castleman astride his favorite mare, Caroline, is supposedly the only equestrian statue in the world for which the horse posed also. Castleman, a Confederate soldier, helped develop Cherokee Park, which lies adjacent to the Triangle.

See Anne S. Karem, *The Cherokee Area: A History* (Louisville 1971), M.A. Allgeier, *Highland Neighborhood History* (Louisville, 1978).

Anne S. Karem

CHERRY, WENDELL (b Hart County, Kentucky, September 25, 1935; d Louisville, July 16, 1991). Health-care executive. Wendell Cherry was born to Geneva (Spillman) and Layman S. Cherry in rural Hart County and reared in Horse Cave, Kentucky. In 1953 he graduated from that town's Caverna High School. Cherry attended the University of Kentucky, where he earned a B.A. degree in business in 1957. Two years later, Cherry received an LL.B. degree with distinction from the university's School of Law, graduating first in his class.

He moved to Louisville in 1959, where he practiced law and taught economics at the UNIVERSITY OF LOUISVILLE. In 1960 he met David A. Jones, who would be his partner in business and many civic activities throughout the remainder of his life. Cherry and Jones founded HUMANA, one of the nation's leading health-care companies, in 1961.

Soon after moving to Louisville, Cherry embarked on a long and fruitful series of personal commitments to the enhancement of athletics, the arts, and the quality of life in his adopted community. He was the attorney for a group of Louisvillians who sponsored Cassius Clay (MUHAMMAD ALI), the three-time heavyweight boxing champion. He was co-owner and president of the KENTUCKY COLONELS franchise in the American Basketball Association. In the late 1960s he headed Forward Thrust, a campaign to gain voter support for bond issues to finance several civic projects, including the rebuilding of Louisville General Hospital.

An art connoisseur, Cherry was the chief catalyst and first chairman of the board of the KENTUCKY CENTER FOR THE ARTS. In 1985 *Art & Antiques* magazine listed Cherry among the top one hundred American collectors. He was instrumental in using the indoor and outdoor venues around Fifth and MAIN STREETS to assemble and display an outstanding concentration of twentieth-century sculpture. He served as a member of the boards of Humana, the BANK OF LOUISVILLE, and the J.B. SPEED ART MUSEUM.

Cherry and his first wife, Mary Elizabeth Baird, were the parents of four children: Angela, Alison, Andrew, and Hagan. Cherry married Dorothy O'Connell, an interior designer, on June 12, 1977. Cherry is buried in CAVE HILL CEMETERY.

Kristy M. Applegate

CHESTNUT STREET YMCA/ KNIGHTS OF PYTHIAS. The six-story building at 930 W Chestnut St. has been the home to both the Pythian Temple and the YOUNG MEN'S CHRISTIAN ASSOCIATION, two organizations that have played an important role in Louisville's African American community.

The Order of the Knights of Pythias, originally a white organization only, was founded in 1864 in Washington, D.C., by Justice H. Rathbone. Its principles were friendship, charity, and benevolence. While the first white Pythian lodge was organized in Louisville in 1869, very little is known about the formation of black lodges. By 1893 two were listed in the Louisville city directory. By 1915 there were eleven African American Pythian lodges in the city, all meeting at 419 S Sixth St. In addition to charity work, the organization served as a source of social entertainment. Members were generally the better educated and most prominent and successful leaders of the black community, who served as role models for black youth. In 1925 the national convention for African American Pythians was held in Louisville and drew twenty-five thousand delegates.

In 1915 a new building was completed at 930 W Chestnut St. that served as the state headquarters for African American Pythian lodges. The architect was Henry Wolters (1845–1921), who was born in Germany and moved to Louisville in 1872. The six-story structure is built of buff brick with limestone trim and entrances. At one time the building housed a drugstore, a movie theater, a restaurant, a photography studio, an ice cream parlor, and doctors' offices. It also included hotel rooms for men, rooms for lodge meetings, and a ballroom on the sixth floor that led up to a roof garden. The Pythian lodge became inactive in the 1930s because of the GREAT DEPRESSION, but the building continued to be used for offices and apartments. During WORLD WAR II it was used as a USO for black soldiers, with dances held regularly. After the war a portion of it housed the Davis Trade School for AFRICAN AMERICANS.

One of the first YMCA branches in the city was the branch for African Americans. In 1885 Albert Mack began a one-man campaign to establish the organization. With the assistance of others such as THOMAS F. BLUE, first librarian of the Western Colored Branch of the LOUISVILLE FREE PUBLIC LIBRARY, the first facility opened in 1892 at 942 W Walnut St. (Muhammad Ali Blvd.). In 1906 the western branch bought the former John P. Byrne house at 920 W Chestnut St., adjacent to the site of the future Pythian building. At this point, the branch adopted the name of Chestnut Street Branch YMCA.

The YMCA served as an alternative to pool halls and other "hang-outs" of black youth. It served as a recreational center with reading rooms and Bible study classes. It also organized baseball and BASKETBALL teams. This branch closed in 1932, also because of the Depression, but was reorganized in 1946. In 1953 a citywide YMCA capital funds campaign goal of $1.5 million was completed. The Chestnut Street Branch's allocation was used to purchase and renovate the Pythian building at a cost of $550,000. The structure provided lodging for men, meeting and conference rooms, and space for various youth and adult activities. Another capital funds drive took place by the YMCA of Greater Louisville in 1976. Of the $5 million raised, the Chestnut Street Branch used five hundred thousand dollars for construction of a gymnasium at 920 Chestnut. An additional $150,000 in funds was made available through a grant from the City Community Development Fund to upgrade the facility in the Pythian building and the extension unit at Market and Thirty-eighth Streets. In 1978 another grant was secured to renovate the sixth floor for a teen center and ballroom.

See George C. Wright, *Life Behind a Veil: Blacks in Louisville, Kentucky 1865–1930* (Baton Rouge 1985).

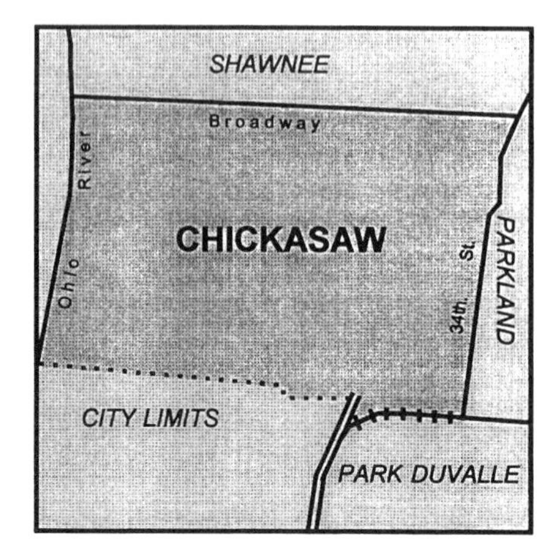

CHICKASAW. A primarily African American residential neighborhood in western Louisville bounded by the OHIO RIVER to the west, BROADWAY to the north, Thirty-fourth St. to the east, and a combination of Woodland Ave. and the city limits to the south. The land, which was part of Jacob Garr's fifteen-hundred-acre farm in the early nineteenth century, was first labeled the Chickasaw neighborhood in 1922 when the African American Chickasaw Park was established on the former estate of political boss JOHN WHALLEN. The area not only housed the first permanent state fairgrounds on Cecil Ave. and Gibson Ln. in 1908; it was also the site, from 1907 to 1910, of the short-lived WHITE CITY AMUSEMENT PARK near present-day Chickasaw Park. A FORD MOTOR CO. ASSEMBLY PLANT located in the area was reportedly the largest in the South when it opened in 1925. Greenwood Cemetery opened in 1903.

CHINESE. The first Chinese came to Louisville from Canton, China in the 1920s. Following a tradition of Chinese in America, most opened hand laundries. One family operated Louisville's first Chinese restaurant. Typical Chinese families in Louisville lived in apartments adjacent to their businesses. Only a few of the adults could speak broken English, but all of the children born in Louisville were bilingual. However, no formal Chinese education was available. The laundries and RESTAURANTS of the 1920s and 1930s included:

Chinese Laundries

Charles Woo Sang	801 W Walnut St. (Muhammad Ali Blvd.)
Joe Woo	205 W Chestnut St.
Charlie Woo	203 W Chestnut St.
Ah Pong	403 S Preston Hwy.
Chin Lee	218 W Jefferson St.
George Woo	306 S Third St.
Woo Young	916 S Third St.
Chin Pon	558 S Fifth St.
Chin Moy	1620 Bardstown Rd.

Chinese Restaurants

Liberty Inn	305 S Fourth St.
Loyang Tea Garden	645 S Fourth St.
Oriental Restaurant	637 S Fourth St.
Hong Kong Restaurant	234 W Jefferson St.
Canton Restaurant	450 S Fifth St.

Chin Ming and his wife, Chiu Beck, arrived in Chicago in 1920 from Canton, China. Chin's father was a Chicago Chinatown property owner and leader of the Tong Association (he was assassinated years later by rival gang leader Al Capone). In settling a business deal, he acquired property located in Louisville. It was this property, given as a wedding present, that brought Chin to Louisville.

Chin's first restaurant, Golden Hour, closed in 1928 after several cooks refused to work in a building they claimed was haunted. He opened the Liberty Inn that same year. The restaurant was located on the second floor and had ornate stained glass windows, two large dining rooms, and a dance floor. The family lived on the third floor, and the restaurant staff lived on the fourth floor.

During WORLD WAR II, Chin formed a Chinese-American organization to address homeland concerns and a growing anti-Asian atmosphere in the United States. By 1948 the Chin family had moved to S First St. After Chin's death in 1954, his oldest son, Richard, operated the family's only remaining restaurant, China Inn, which had opened in the 1940s and was located on Third St. near BROADWAY. He later relocated on DIXIE HWY. and renamed it Lotus. In 1968 he was elected a senator to the Kentucky General Assembly.

In the 1960s, many other Chinese restaurants opened as Louisville's taste in dining expanded beyond traditional American fare. George and Lolly (Woo Sang) Leong operated the Hoe Kow at BOWMAN FIELD. By the 1980s there were over seventy Chinese restaurants operated by Asian families. The influx of Asians included many who were involved with the UNIVERSITY OF LOUISVILLE and the medical community.

In the mid-1950s and through the 1960s, a number of Chinese university professors were appointed to the University of Louisville Medical School, Speed School, and Arts and Sciences. Trained elsewhere, they slowly immigrated to Louisville as positions opened up. Many of the new wave were students from Taiwan who came to the United States for doctoral degrees. After receiving their Ph.D.s or M.D.s, they would often apply for positions in Louisville, with a few going into PHARMACY. In the 1980s and 1990s, mainland China was sending graduate students to this country and a large number, after obtaining their graduate degrees, found positions in Louisville.

In the late 1990s the Chinese population numbered approximately two thousand in Louisville. To serve the community, the China Institute was founded in 1987 as the CRANE HOUSE, a Chinese cultural center. In 1996 it broadened its mission to become an Asian center, an organizations inclusive of other Asian countries for social interaction and the understanding of its people within the community in Louisville and the region.

Helen L. Lang
Roosevelt Chin

CHRIST CHURCH CATHEDRAL. The Episcopal Christ Church, which became a cathedral in 1894, was organized at a public meeting on May 31, 1822. During the following year, 182 subscribers pledged $6,354 toward the construction of the church. That first structure, completed in 1824, was brick and rectangular in the style of the early Federal meetinghouse. Several additions and modifications have been made to that early structure, which forms the central nave of the existing building, located on the east side of Second St. between Muhammad Ali and LIBERTY. In 1846 an addition, designed by architect JOHN STIREWALT, was made to the east end. The present chancel with its elaborate arches and foliated columns was added in 1859. Eleven years later the west front was extended to its present location. At that time a limestone facade with two asymmetrical towers and a central gable replaced an original central tower. WILLIAM H. REDIN, a local architect, designed both the 1859 and 1870 additions. The exterior modifications were completed during the 1890s with the installations of the existing stained-glass windows, some of which are Tiffany-designed. The cathedral complex was completed in 1911–12, with the Cathedral House constructed south of the sanctuary. That building was designed by JOHN BACON HUTCHINGS and Sons of Louisville. Christ Church Cathedral, the oldest church building in Louisville, is on the NATIONAL REGISTER OF HISTORIC PLACES and is a designated Louisville Landmark.

The historic ups and downs of the cathedral are reflected in the character of its spiritual leaders. The resignation of its first rector in "moral disgrace" and loss of most of the congregation, including the rector, to St. Paul's in 1839 highlighted the early troubled years of Christ Church. But the selection of JAMES CRAIK as rector in 1844 signaled the start of a long line of capable rectors and deans. Craik was a gifted person who guided Christ Church to a prominent position both in the diocese and in the national church. Through his strong stance, he played an instrumental part in keeping Kentucky in the Union during the CIVIL WAR and preventing the national church from dividing into northern and southern branches.

CHARLES EWELL CRAIK was appointed rector upon the death of his father in 1882. The parish was elevated to cathedral status in 1894. At Craik's death in 1917, Richard Lightburne McCready was selected as dean. In the twentieth century, the leadership qualities of the cathedral's deans, most notably Elwood L. Haines, Robert W. Estill, Alan L. Bartlett Jr., and Geralyn Wolf, elevated them to the office of bishop.

A sense of community service has distinguished the cathedral throughout its history. This was evidenced in the assistance rendered during numerous nineteenth-century EPIDEMICS; a night school for the poor established in 1867; services for the deaf organized in 1877; industrial classes conducted from 1872 until 1924; a Montessori school for children with learning problems, 1911–12; relief efforts during the GREAT DEPRESSION including creation of a welfare council and employment of a social worker; the support extended to service organizations during the two world wars; and recent endeavors to help homeless persons.

Numerous local institutions have roots in congregational support. These include the Protestant Episcopal Orphans' Asylum (for girls), 1835; Orphanage of the Good Shepherd (for boys), 1860; HOME OF THE INNOCENTS, 1879; John Norton Infirmary, 1881; the Church Home, 1881; and St. John Center, 1980s. Members of Christ Church also have given support to Louisville's other Episcopal parishes. Ten local Episcopal churches, starting with St. Paul's in 1839, were established with the assistance of Christ Church.

See Christ Church Cathedral Archives, Christ Church Cathedral, Louisville; James C. Craik Family Papers, Filson Club Historical Society, manuscript division; James C. Craik, *Historical Sketches of Christ Church* (Louisville 1862); G.L. Davenport, ed., *A History of Christ Church Cathedral Vol. 2 1938–1971* (Louisville 1972); Richard Lightburne McCready, *History of Christ Church Cathedral, 1822–1937* (Louisville 1937).

Olivia M. Frederick

CHRIST CHURCH UNITED METHODIST. The congregation of Christ Church United Methodist traces its history back to 1806, when the first Methodist congregation in Louisville was established in a log schoolhouse on the present site of the JEFFERSON COUNTY COURTHOUSE. The denomination was known then as the Methodist Episcopal Church. In 1816 the congregation built a church building where the KENTUCKY INTERNATIONAL CONVENTION CENTER stands.

In 1835, because of substantial growth, the Fourth Street Methodist Episcopal Church voted to divide into three congregations: Fourth Street Methodist Episcopal, Eighth Street Methodist Episcopal, and Brook Street Methodist Episcopal Churches. The Brook St. church, whose lineage is continued in Christ Church, built on the west side of Brook St. between MARKET and JEFFERSON. The FOURTH ST. and Eighth St. churches have long since lost their identities in a series of mergers.

In 1845 the denomination divided over the issue of SLAVERY and other concerns. The conference establishing the Methodist Episcopal Church, South, was held at the Fourth St. church building. The Brook Street Methodist Episcopal Church and its sister congregations then also took the name Methodist Episcopal Church, South.

In 1865, to be closer to the residential area, the Brook St. congregation sold its building and moved a few blocks away to E BROADWAY at Floyd and renamed itself Broadway Methodist Episcopal Church, South.

In 1939 three Methodist denominations—the Methodist Episcopal church; the Methodist Episcopal church, South; and the Methodist Protestant church—united to form the Methodist Church. The Broadway church was then renamed Broadway Methodist Church.

In 1955 the Broadway Methodist Church congregation voted to move to an area of growth in the county on Brownsboro Rd. A base congregation, Indian Hills Methodist, was established to facilitate the move. The same pastor led both congregations, and they chose the new name Christ Methodist Church. In 1956 ground was broken for the building at 4614 Brownsboro Rd.

In 1968 the Methodist denomination merged with the Evangelical United Brethren denomination to become the United Methodist church, and Christ Methodist Church was renamed CHRIST CHURCH UNITED METHODIST.

See Rev. John Cunningham, "Methodism: The Church in Louisville," in J. Stoddard Johnston, ed., *Memorial History of Louisville* (Chicago 1896), vol. 2, 204–25.

CHRISTIAN, WILLIAM (b Staunton, Virginia, 1743; d near JEFFERSONVILLE, INDIANA, April 9, 1786). Statesman, military officer, and early Jefferson County settler. Christian was the son of Israel and Elizabeth (Stark) Christian. While still in his late teens he commanded a company in William Byrd's regiment during the French and Indian War (1754–63). Later he studied law in the office of Patrick Henry and soon after married Henry's sister, Ann. From 1773 to 1775 he represented Fincastle County (which included part of West Virginia and all of present Kentucky) in the lower house of the Virginia legislature. When he moved to Botetourt County he represented both that county and Fincastle in the Virginia senate in 1776.

In 1774 during Lord Dunmore's War (so named for the royal governor of Virginia) he commanded a regiment of the Fincastle militia. In 1775 he became a member of the Fincastle Committee of Safety as American relations with Great Britain worsened. When the Revolution began he was appointed a lieutenant colonel of the First Virginia Regiment of the Continental Line, but soon resigned to accept a colonelcy in the Virginia militia. He led a successful expedition against the Over-Hill Cherokees in the Holston Valley, but the bulk of his service was keeping down "the *tory* spirit in his quarter of Virginia throughout the revolutionary struggle" (Richard H. Collins, *History of Kentucky*, vol. 2: 127).

Like many other Virginians, Christian was lured by the reputation of Kentucky as a land of milk and honey. In 1785 he brought his family from Virginia's Holston Valley to Jefferson County. He had acquired a two-thousand-acre tract that had been laid out in 1774 by JOHN FLOYD'S surveying party at the Falls of the Ohio. Christian had apparently purchased it from the original grantees. The tract was in the eastern part of the county, mostly north of later Shelbyville Rd. The WATTERSON EXPRESSWAY cuts through the acreage from north to south. A'Sturgus Station, one of the pioneer Beargrass fortified points, was on this land but south of Shelbyville Rd. It was at this station that the Christian family settled, arriving on August 17, 1785. Shortly after, he was named commanding officer of the Jefferson County militia.

Early in 1786 the Christians' daughter, Priscilla, married young ALEXANDER SCOTT BULLITT, who in 1787 bought the property known as OXMOOR south of Christian's land. But Christian himself was becoming disenchanted with Jefferson County. Frequent Indian incursions and the general primitiveness of the country led him to think of moving to the Danville area. But it was not to be. In April 1786 a group of Indians from the Wabash River towns made off with a number of horses from the BEARGRASS STATIONS. Christian, commanding the militia, quickly gathered a group of eight to ten men, including his son-in-law, to go in pursuit. The Indians were encountered some miles above present Jeffersonville, Indiana, and in the ensuing gunfire Christian was mortally wounded. He is buried on his own land at A'Sturgus Station, the first burial in what was to become the Bullitt family cemetery, the oldest in Jefferson County. Christian County, carved from Logan County in 1796, is named for him.

See *The Kentucky Encyclopedia* (Lexington 1992) 184–85; Neal O. Hammon, "The Fincastle Surveyors at the Falls of the Ohio, 1774," *Filson Club History Quarterly* 47 (Jan. 1973): 14–28; Blaine A. Guthrie Jr., "The Eight-Mile House—A Search for History," *Filson Club History Quarterly* 47 (Oct. 1973): 343–48; Neal O. Hammon, "Early Louisville and the Beargrass Stations," *Filson Club History Quarterly* 52 (April 1978): 147–65.

George H. Yater

CHRISTIAN SCIENCE. The Church of Christ, Scientist, was founded by Mary Baker Eddy in Boston, Massachusetts. In 1875 she published the first edition of her primary work, *Science and Health with Key to the Scriptures.* In 1879 the Church of Christ, Scientist, was organized "to commemorate the word and works of our Master [Christ Jesus], which should reinstate primitive Christianity and its lost element of healing" (Church Manual, p. 17). Christian Science teaches that sickness, relationship difficulties, inadequate supply of things and other problems can be healed through an understanding of God and humanity's relationship to God. This is part of working out one's salvation. Students of Christian Science are taught how to heal these problems through prayer and Christian Science practitioners are available to assist them and anyone who requests their help.

In 1895 Mrs. Eddy first published the *Manual of The Mother Church.* It contains the Tenets and By-Laws governing the church. Christian Science churches around the world are branches of The Mother Church, and each is governed democratically by its members under its own self-constituted set of bylaws.

In Louisville, the first Christian Science service was held in 1888 when a small group met at the home of Mrs. Virginia D. Allen, 107 College St. Services continued in various rented properties downtown, and on September 3, 1898, the group was incorporated as First Church of Christ, Scientist, Louisville, Kentucky, and then became a branch of The Mother Church The First Church of Christ Scientist, in Boston.

First Church, Louisville, was located at several places downtown until in 1908 it purchased property at 1142 S Third St. The cornerstone for the edifice at Third St. and Ormsby Ave. was laid in 1917, and the structure was finished in 1927. Built in a Grecian design with white stone and monolithic columns, the completed church property cost approximately five hundred thousand dollars and is one of the largest of its denomination in the country. It seats approximately twelve hundred people. It is a rule that Christian Science churches are not dedicated until they are free from debt. First Church was dedicated December 30, 1951.

A second Christian Science church was organized in 1916 when a group of members decided it would be good to have two meeting places. Interest in Christian Science was increasing, and meetings were overflowing. This group was recognized as Second Church of Christ, Scientist, Louisville, on June 29, 1916. It rented quarters in Elks Hall, 316 W Walnut St. (Muhammad Ali Blvd.), and in 1920 purchased a church building at 738 S FOURTH ST. In 1952 the congregation purchased property at 4125 Shelbyville Rd. A church was built on the property, and the first service was held there in 1957. All the property was paid for, and the church was dedicated on November 19, 1967.

Two other groups of Christian Scientists organized branches of The Mother Church in Louisville, one in 1940, the other in 1943. They were disbanded in 1986 and 1966 respectively. The members then joined the two existing churches.

Today the two Christian Science churches in Louisville conduct worship services and Sunday Schools on Sunday mornings and hold testimony meetings on Wednesday evenings. They also maintain Christian Science Reading Rooms and sponsor public lectures in which information about the religion and its founder is made available.

See Mary Baker Eddy, *Science and Health with Key to the Scriptures* (Boston 1934); Mary Baker Eddy, *Prose Works Other than Science and Health* (Boston 1925); Robert Peel, *Mary Baker Eddy, the Years of Discovery* (New York 1966); Robert Peel, *Mary Baker Eddy, the Years of Trial* (New York 1971); Robert Peel, *Mary Baker Eddy, the Years of Authority;* Robert Peel, *Spiritual Healing in a Scientific Age* (San Francisco 1987).

John H. Blunk

CHRISTIANS/DISCIPLES OF CHRIST. The Christian church (Disciples of Christ) is one of the Protestant Christian denominations in Louisville and across Kentucky. It is a church body that looks to Kentucky as one of its founding locations. The church has been active in Louisville at least since the 1820s.

The denomination began in Kentucky as a division within the Presbyterian church. Barton Warren Stone (1772–1844), a minister in Bourbon and Nicholas Counties, hosted a major revival in August 1801 at his Cane Ridge (Presbyterian) Church in Bourbon County, Kentucky. This was the largest of the camp-meeting revivals associated with the Great Awakening of early nineteenth-century America. The experience led Stone and several Presbyterian colleagues on June 28, 1804, to renounce the Presbyterian name and adopt the general name of Christian, thus beginning the Christian Church movement.

Meanwhile, another Presbyterian group in western Pennsylvania broke off from the Seceder Presbyterians to form what would later be called the Disciples of Christ. These were led by a father and son, Thomas and Alexander Campbell. Thomas Campbell (1763–1854) came to the United States from Northern Ireland in 1807. He was assigned pastoral responsibilities in the Allegheny valleys west of Pittsburgh. He became involved in a controversy over his offering the Lord's Supper to other branches of the PRESBYTERIANS. He withdrew from the Seceder Presbyterians and began working on plans to introduce nondenominational evangelism in the Northwest Territory (Ohio). Thomas Campbell received great assistance when his son, Alexander (1788–1866), joined him in the work.

Like Barton Stone's Christian movement, the Disciples movement was also formed out of a desire to overcome divisions among Christians. Its leaders believed that the only way for Christians to reunite was to accept a common denominator; namely, the teachings of the New Testament, with great tolerance for differences among members as to the meaning and interpretation of the Bible.

In 1819 Thomas Campbell came to Burlington, Kentucky, to open a school and to preach. However, he ran afoul of local opinion when he attempted to teach a Sunday school for slave children. He refused to remain in Kentucky with such limitations placed on his opportunity to teach the Christian faith.

Alexander Campbell came to Kentucky in 1823 to debate Presbyterian minister William L. Maccalla in Washington, near Maysville. The theme of the debate was Christian baptism. The event attracted large crowds, and Campbell's popularity soared. After the debate he preached in Baptist churches around the Bluegrass, including Lexington. He attracted strong Baptist preachers to his cause, including Philip Slater Fall (1798–1890), an English immigrant then serving as the minister of a Baptist church in Louisville. Fall began preaching on some of Campbell's themes.

It would appear that the first fully "Campbellite" church in Kentucky was Philip Slater Fall's Baptist church in Louisville. In 1825 the congregation rejected the Baptist creed known as the Philadelphia Confession of Faith, saying that henceforth only the Bible would be used to make decisions in the church.

Many BAPTISTS were not at all pleased with Campbell's influence, and in Kentucky (as well as in Virginia) opposition began to grow. By 1830 the Campbell churches were clearly being separated from the Baptists. The conflict was bitter and was largely fought out in congregational and Baptist association meetings and in the pages of Campbell's monthly magazine, the *Christian Baptist,* and in the Baptist periodical, the *Baptist Recorder.* By the time the division was final, an estimated one-fourth to one-third of Kentucky Baptist churches had gone with the Campbell movement, now being called "Disciples of Christ." As the division between the Disciples and the Baptists played itself out, conversations between Disciples and Barton Stone's Christian churches continued. In April 1831, a Disciples church and a Christian church in Millersburg, Kentucky, became one of the earliest united Christian-Disciple churches. A meeting over Christmas in Georgetown under the leadership of Stone and Campbell follower John T. Johnson (1788–1856) led to a union of two congregations in the Georgetown area. This meeting had significant consequences, as the participants in the discussions carried their conversations to Lexington.

There, in a meeting that concluded on January 1, 1832, representatives from the Disciples and Christians from all over Kentucky, and some from beyond Kentucky, agreed to unite. They sent out a team to preach, urge congregations to join together, and raise funds for evangelistic purposes. The convergence of the two religious movements resulted in a new denomination that was, ironically, opposed to denominationalism.

The first statewide meeting of the Christian churches was in May 1840 in Harrodsburg. This would lead to the formation of the Kentucky Christian Missionary Society, predecessor of the Christian church (Disciples of Christ) in Kentucky.

Disciples had African American members

from the beginning of the church, although most were slaves who belonged to their owner's church. The earliest black congregation of the Disciples for which there is clear evidence was probably in Lexington, founded in 1851. The earliest black Disciples congregation in Louisville was founded with the assistance of FIRST CHRISTIAN CHURCH. About 1860 a group of black Disciples who had been meeting in the church was given land on Hancock St., thus forming the Hancock Street Christian Church. One of their first converts in the church was Preston Taylor, who would go on to become the most prominent African American Disciple in the denomination's history.

Soon after the CIVIL WAR several attempts were made at establishing schools to educate black preachers. Among these were the Louisville Christian Bible School, founded in 1873, the Christian Bible College in New Castle, and the Louisville Bible School. The latter was established in 1892 and survived until 1914. Black Disciples founded a state missionary society in 1873, later known as the Kentucky Christian Missionary Convention. Black Disciples women organized the Kentucky Christian Woman's Board of Missions Convention in 1880. In the twentieth century the two organizations merged, along with a Sunday school society.

Disciples women organized nationally in 1874 with the establishment of the Christian Woman's Board of Missions. A year later a Kentucky Christian Woman's Board of Missions was established, followed by local organizations in individual congregations. By 1888 Disciples ordained their first woman as a minister. However, it was much later before a woman was ordained in Kentucky. Ellen Moore Warren graduated from the College of the Bible in 1916 and was ordained in 1923 at Morganfield.

In 1884, after twelve years of effort, the predecessor to the Christian Church Homes of Kentucky was established in Louisville. Initially developed to serve widows and orphans, the Christian Church Homes, headquartered in Louisville, eventually developed four locations for children across Kentucky. These serve children from abusive backgrounds. The Widows' Home has evolved into more than twelve locations across the state for care for the elderly, ranging from independent living to nursing home care.

In the years after the Civil War, the Disciples, one of the few denominations that did not formally divide during the war, began a process of division that was a result both of sectional differences related to the war and theological conflicts. Between 1865 and 1900, there emerged a separate group of conservative Disciples, generally calling themselves Churches of Christ, but with a radical congregational system that denied any legitimacy to organizations above the congregation. Because they rejected the use of instrumental music in worship, they have come to be referred to as the non-instrumental Churches of Christ. In the twentieth century the Disciples divided again. Again, the division was between those who maintained a strongly conservative view on the interpretation of scripture and those who were willing to accept broad differences in opinion. The conservative churches, called Christian Churches and Churches of Christ, are often identified by their national relationship to the annual North American Christian Convention. These churches are sometimes referred to as "Independents" because they reject the propriety of cooperative missionary societies. SOUTHEAST CHRISTIAN CHURCH in Louisville is one of their largest congregations in the United States at the start of the twenty-first century.

The Disciples, representing a broad conservative-to-liberal spectrum, have been active in the international ecumenical movement. They have participated in the founding of councils of churches, including the Kentucky Council of Churches. Theologically the Disciples are a part of the mainstream Reformed family of churches. Worship centers around a weekly observance of the Lord's Supper. BEARGRASS CHRISTIAN CHURCH in Louisville and Central Christian Church in Lexington are two of the largest Disciples congregations in the United States. In 1998 there were 60,000 baptized Disciples in Kentucky, and 250 congregations.

See Richard L. Harrison Jr., *From Camp Meeting to Church: A History of the Christian Church (Disciples of Christ) in Kentucky* (St. Louis 1992); Lester G. McAllister and William E. Tucker, *Journey in Faith: A History of the Christian Church (Disciples of Christ)* (St. Louis 1975); Mark G. Toulouse, *Joined in Discipleship: The Shaping of Contemporary Disciples Identity* Revised edition (St. Louis 1997).

Richard L. Harrison Jr.

CHURCHILL DOWNS. Churchill Downs, touted as America's most famous race track, was designated a National Historic Landmark in 1986. Located south of downtown Louisville at 700 Central Ave., since 1875 it has been the venue for the country's premier HORSE-RACING event, the KENTUCKY DERBY, a mile-and-a-quarter annual test for three-year-olds held on the first Saturday in May.

Horsemen and racing enthusiasts had been trying to reestablish a track in the state's principal city since the demise of the OAKLAND and WOODLAWN race courses. The Louisville Jockey Club and Driving Park Association was formed in 1874, and twenty-eight-year-old MERIWETHER LEWIS CLARK JR. became its president. When the grandson of explorer WILLIAM CLARK, named for the co-leader of the expedition to the Pacific Ocean, eloped with heiress Mary Martin Anderson in 1871, he was introduced to the racing world. She had been living with her aunt, Pattie Anderson Ten Broeck, and her husband on their farm, Hurstbourne, on Shelbyville Rd. east of Louisville.

Richard Ten Broeck had been this country's most accomplished horse breeder and trainer before being the first to take American horses to Europe to race. His celebrity was such that Lewis and Mary Clark were introduced to the racing establishment on the continent. They attended the English Derby at Epsom Downs outside London accompanied by John Churchill, one of the brothers of Lewis's mother, who had helped rear him. So, when land was needed for the new track, Churchill family property along the LOUISVILLE & NASHVILLE RAILROAD (used for transportation of the race-horses) was selected.

An entrance lodge, grandstand, clubhouse, and stables had been constructed when the opening day of the inaugural meeting of the Louisville Jockey Club on Monday, May 17, 1875, featured the running of the Kentucky Derby. Before the fourth Derby, the *COURIER-JOURNAL* remarked: "The field will present a sight never before witnessed in this country, for rich and poor, white and black, will be on the same footing there, and a general picnic and holiday is anticipated."

However, it was a match race held on July 4, 1878, that put Churchill Downs on the racing map. The horse Ten Broeck, which held record times for distances of one, two, three, and four miles, was pitted against the California mare, Mollie McCarthy, in a race of multiple heats, not uncommon for the time. Ten Broeck's winning time for the long race was 8:19 3/4—a far cry from the present day's greatest two minutes in sports. But there was spectacle, and the horse was still an integral part of everyday life. In 1882 the modest grandstand was enlarged and three towers were erected on top, connected by a promenade. Ladies were segregated at the end nearest the clubhouse and farthest from the betting shed that was strictly the gentlemen's domain.

By the time the first Kentucky Derby winner ARISTIDES died in 1893 at the age of twenty-one, distance racing at Churchill Downs was being criticized, in particular the mile-and-a-half length of the Derby. The old school and Clark considered the longer races to be better tests of Thoroughbreds, but, after the 1894 Derby, the *Louisville Commercial* railed: "Time for a Change . . . Men no longer race for glory in this country." Clark's will and resources had worn thin, so he sold the track to a syndicate with bookmaking interests controlled by William E. Applegate. The New Louisville Jockey Club was established. The architectural firm of D.X. MURPHY & Bro. designed a modern, brick-and-metal-girder grandstand with its signature twin towers, readied on the opposite side of the track for the 1895 Derby. A spacious betting shed was erected, but the clubhouse was dispensed with. A year later, the race was shortened to a mile and a quarter, and the winner was adorned with a garland of roses for the first time.

Applegate soon began to see waning spectator interest in his track geared to wagering. In a

Louisville Jockey Club (later Churchill Downs) c. 1895.

bold move, he turned over the entire operation in 1902 to CHARLES F. GRAINGER, the sitting mayor of Louisville, and a group of the mayor's prominent friends. A clubhouse was erected to attract the social element that had made racing successful in Meriwether Lewis Clark's day. To put on special events, Grainger brought in MATT J. WINN, a tailor who had seen every Derby. Steeplechases, automobile races, air shows, and band concerts were sponsored. Even two railroad locomotives were crashed head-on in the infield when the State Fair was held on the grounds. For the 1908 spring meet, pari-mutuel machines were introduced at Churchill Downs, and this system of betting was deemed fair and declared legal by the Kentucky Court of Appeals. Grainger, whose family fortune had been made in the foundry business, began to manufacture pari-mutuel machines for Churchill Downs and other tracks. Betting became respectable, and the country's racing industry was revived. Within several years, Matt Winn was a Kentucky Colonel and was building a racing empire around Churchill Downs.

The Louisville Racing Association was formed in 1907 and controlled both Churchill Downs and nearby competitor DOUGLAS PARK. By 1919, when the New Louisville Jockey Club was succeeded by the Kentucky Jockey Club, Winn was masterminding the organization centered at Churchill Downs that also owned or controlled Latonia; Douglas Park; the Kentucky Association (Lexington); Fairmount Park (East Saint Louis); Lincoln Fields (Crete, Illinois); and Washington Park (Chicago). Improvements were being made on a yearly basis at Churchill Downs. The Kentucky Derby was broadcast on radio and was shown on newsreels. Winn made it a place for celebrities to be seen. The American Turf Association was established in 1928 to better reflect the holdings in other states associated with Churchill Downs. Matt Winn was nearly seventy-six years old when he was pictured on the cover of *Time* on May 10, 1937. By WORLD WAR II, however, his empire had been reduced to only Churchill Downs.

Winn, unfortunately, had trained no one to take over the operation. His associates had long since retired or died, but Winn was determined to preserve his track. Late in 1948 a committee was appointed to study a proposal that a foundation purchase the track and provide the University of Louisville School of Medicine with future earnings. At the same time, board chairman Samuel A. Culbertson died at eighty-six, and Winn died in October 1949 at age eighty-eight. Columnist and radio commentator Bill Corum took his place, and the track's sale to a foundation was shelved. Corum died in late 1958 and was succeeded by Wathen R. Knebelkamp.

A one-story, concrete-block museum was opened adjacent to the track on Central Ave. in 1962. Knebelkamp's particular improvement was to build VIP sky boxes over the location where the clubhouse had been. An aggressive takeover attempt by National Industries was thwarted by a group including John Galbreath, A.B. Hancock, and WARNER L. JONES JR.; Knebelkamp retired, and resident manager Lynn Stone took over. When horse breeder Warner L. Jones Jr. became board chairman in 1984, local attorney Thomas H. Meeker was made track president and chief executive.

Together Jones and Meeker made Churchill Downs more aggressive and once more a model for the industry. A new $7.5 million museum opened in 1985 complete with a multi-projector slide program. In less than ten years, revenues were doubled and profits made respectable, even in the face of competing state lotteries. Still the full impact of riverboat GAMBLING is a growing concern.

In addition to the famous track, Churchill Downs Inc. owns Sports Spectrum (off-track betting parlor), EqulSource (a group-purchasing company for the thoroughbred racing industry), Tracknet (a telecommunications company), Ellis Park (racetrack in Henderson), Kentucky Horse Center (training center in Lexington), Kentucky Downs (racetrack in Franklin, Kentucky), off-track betting parlors (Pineville, Corbin, Maysville, and Jamestown, Kentucky, and Merrillville, Indianapolis, and Fort Wayne, Indiana), Charlson Broadcast Technologies (Erlanger), Hoosier Park (racetrack in Anderson, Indiana), and Calder Race Course (Miami, Florida).

In 2000 construction was completed on a new main entrance to Churchill Downs and a $10 million expansion and renovation of the KENTUCKY DERBY MUSEUM. Work also continued on a three-phase project to widen Central Ave. to four lanes.

See Samuel W. Thomas, *Churchill Downs: A Documentary History of America's Most Legendary Race Track* (Louisville 1995); *Courier-Journal*, Jan. 22, 1999.

Samuel W. Thomas

CHURCH OF CHRIST. A manifestation of the Second Great Awakening, the Restoration Movement of the early 1800s sought to return American religious life to a simple, New Testament Christianity. Its goal was to restore the Church of Christ that had been established in Jerusalem, basing its doctrine solely on the gospel of Jesus Christ, instead of relying on the human creeds and theological confessions of faith adopted by most denominations in the post-biblical era. The plea of the early restorers was to return to the Bible as the only rule of faith and practice.

The efforts to restore the ancient order of things were led by a trio of disenchanted PRESBYTERIANS: Barton Warren Stone (1772–1844) in Bourbon County, Kentucky, and Thomas Campbell (1763–1845) and his son, Alexander Campbell (1788–1866), in Pennsylvania and Virginia. Frustrated by the rapidly multiplying sects and creeds pouring into the frontier, Stone and the Campbells, acting independently of each other, all sought to bring a new unity to Christians through their simple Biblicism. Preachers representing the Stone-Campbell movement came to the Louisville area in the early 1820s. Philip Slater Fall, a minister with strong Campbellite leanings, moved to Louisville from Frankfort in 1823 and assumed the pastorate of the First Baptist Church in Louisville, also becoming head of the academy it sponsored.

Fall had come from England to America in 1817 with his parents and eleven siblings and settled in Logan County on a two-hundred-acre farm. Within a year his parents had both died and left the twenty-year-old Philip to take care of the family. Fall moved to Franklin County, where in 1821 he was married to Anne Apperson Bacon. Fall was licensed and ordained to preach by the Forks of the Elkhorn Baptist Church. He became head of an academy in Frankfort. Fall then moved to Louisville.

Fall soon became acquainted with the restoration plea as advocated by Alexander Campbell. He read Campbell's *Sermon on the Law*, the published debate between Campbell and John Walker, a seceded Presbyterian preacher in Mt. Pleasant, Ohio, in 1820 on the mode and design of baptism. He also read the *Christian Baptist*, published by Campbell from 1823 to 1830. Fall also heard about Campbell's position on the scriptures from Jeremiah Vardeman, who served as Campbell's moderator for the debate with W.L. Maccalla at Washington, Mason County, in 1823.

Vardeman described Campbell to Fall as "a man of earnest piety and wonderful scriptural attainment." It remained for Fall to meet Campbell and hear him preach when Campbell visited Louisville in 1824. Upon hearing Campbell, Fall saw and understood the difference between Baptist doctrine and the teaching of the New Testament as a "revelation from God." By the time Fall was ready to leave Louisville in 1825, he had converted a majority of the members of the Baptist church from the Philadelphia Confession of Faith to the concept of a church based on the New Testament.

Fall wrote to Jacob Creath, one of the early reformers, on December 15, 1825, and in describing the situation in Louisville he said, "There is no place in which there is a greater field of usefulness offered." The congregation in Louisville came to be known as the Baptist Church of Christ, under the leadership of Benjamin Allen, until it severed all connections with the Long Run Baptist Association.

In the early years of Philip Fall's ministry in Louisville the congregation met for worship and preaching in the courthouse. When Campbell came to Louisville in 1824 he spoke in a classroom at Fall's academy. When the division between the Campbellites and BAPTISTS came, the church was located on the corner of Fifth and Green (LIBERTY) STREETS. The Baptists then bought the property from the Church of Christ for $2,550. The Christians bought a small house on Second St. between MARKET and Jefferson. In 1836 they decided to purchase a lot and erect a building on Fifth St. between Walnut (Muhammad Ali Blvd.) and Chestnut.

During the early years of the Restoration Movement, the congregations used the names Churches of Christ and Christian Churches interchangeably. The congregation organized by Fall and Allen was also referred to by both names. Among the Christian preachers who followed Fall and Allen were George W. Elley, David S. Bumett, and Carroll Kendrick. The meeting house on Fifth St. was sold on June 30, 1845, to an African American Baptist church, and the Church of Christ/Christian Church purchased a lot at the corner of FOURTH and Walnut Streets. The basement of the building was constructed, and the congregation moved to the new location on March 17, 1861. An auditorium in a second story was finished and occupied on April 24, 1870, while Winthrop H. Hopson was serving as the preacher.

About this time, two controversial issues emerged within the Christian Church/ Churches of Christ. First, the use of musical instruments was being introduced into the public worship by a number of congregations in the Restoration Movement (expanding the limits of "New Testament simplicity"). Secondly, some congregations were affiliating themselves with the American Christian Missionary Society (challenging the traditional idea of congregational independence). The organ and the society issues divided the churches into Organ-Society Churches and Non-Organ Non-Society Churches. The congregations that introduced an organ into the worship and affiliated with the Missionary Society, in the main, came to be known as Christian Churches, and the congregations that rejected both as being unscriptural retained the name Churches of Christ.

Benjamin Franklin, editor of the *American Christian Review*, wrote that prior to 1870 there were no more than fifty restored churches that had introduced an organ into their public worship, to which estimate John William McGarvey, president of the Lexington College of the Bible, agreed.

While the congregation of disciples meeting at the corner of Fourth and Walnut Streets in Louisville became recognized as an Organ-Society Christian Church by 1871, many others continued to oppose the use of such instruments of music. Notable among them were the Campbell St., the Highland, and the Portland Avenue Churches of Christ.

M.C. Kurfees, of the Kurfees Paint Co. family, became the minister of the Campbell Street Church of Christ. A lot was purchased on Campbell St. between MAIN and Market STREETS in 1876, and a house of worship was erected and occupied on March 18, 1877. The dedicatory sermon was delivered by John William McGarvey, who was a strong opponent of instrumental music in worship. McGarvey took as his text Jeremiah 6:16 and stressed in his lecture the importance of walking in the "old paths" wherein is the good way.

The Campbell St. property was sold in 1920 to a manufacturing company, and a lot was bought at the corner of Frankfort and Haldeman Avenues in 1922. The Haldeman Avenue Church of Christ was organized and a seven-hundred-seat auditorium was erected and occupied on June 17, 1923. Kurfees, who had preached for the Campbell Street and Haldeman Churches of Christ for forty-five years, died on February 17, 1931.

More recent issues have divided many of the Churches of Christ in Louisville. Under the preaching of ROBERT H. BOLL (1875–1956) and associates, the Portland Avenue church accepted the doctrine of premillennialism, and soon other congregations followed. That doctrine states that after the second coming of Christ and before the final resurrection and judgment there will be an age or dispensation of one thousand years in which Christ will rule over the earth in perfect righteousness. Many people opposed that doctrine because of its implication that radical divine intervention (the Second Coming) was needed before humanity could rise to a higher moral and spiritual plateau. Consequently, hundreds of articles and thousands of sermons across the nation were preached and written against this view. Many were disfellowshipped or were examined for their soundness via this litmus test.

In the early 1950s, many of the Churches of Christ in Louisville became embroiled in a debate over the practice of institutionalism. The term refers to the practice of two or more local congregations cooperating with each other to support church missions and other work. Many congregations in the Louisville area accepted the doctrine; however, opposition remained.

In 1997 there were at least three diverse groups among the Churches of Christ in Louisville (sixteen were premillennial, twelve were anti-institutional, and eighteen were institutional). There is very little, if any, fellowship among these groups, who all claim to have roots in the Stone-Campbell movement.

See Vicky Fuqua, *Douglass Boulevard Christian Church: 150 Years of Building a Future* (Louisville 1997).

Adron Doran

CHURCH OF GOD. The Church of God reformation movement, headquartered in Anderson, Indiana, was a manifestation of the late-nineteenth-century holiness movement. Led by Daniel Sidney Warner, it stressed freedom from denominationalism or "sectism" and sanctification as a second work of grace (the complete dedication of your life to doing God's will and living a holier life.) The movement appeared in Louisville in 1894, followed by the organization of a congregation in 1895.

Known as First Church of God, it met at

several locations over the next twenty-five years. Contributing to its growth were revivals by evangelists H.M. Riggle and J. Grant Anderson. In 1920 the congregation purchased an existing church at Nineteenth and Jefferson Streets. Called as pastor was W.E. Monk, who was followed in 1923 by J.T. Wilson, previously the first principal of Anderson Bible and Training School, forerunner of Anderson University.

In 1938 First Church organized and built Larchmont Church of God at Larchmont Ave. and Taylor Blvd. Under the leadership of Pastor W.T. Wallace, most of the congregation left First Church for Larchmont, which was closer to their homes. First Church moved to Algonquin Pkwy. in 1949 and relocated to 4408 Taylorsville Rd. in 1969. Several pastors at both churches, including Lawrence Brooks, Denzel R. Lovely, Charles H. Joiner Jr., Forrest Carlson, Lawrence C. Reynolds, and Jack R. Anderson of First Church, and H. Ross Minkler and Ernest H. Gross Jr. of Larchmont have played leadership roles in the Church of God nationally. Other Louisville area congregations include POPLAR LEVEL, FERN CREEK, and PARKLAND. The movement also has congregations in NEW ALBANY, Georgetown, JEFFERSONVILLE, CLARKSVILLE, and CHARLESTOWN, INDIANA.

Carl E. Kramer

CHURCH OF JESUS CHRIST OF LATTER-DAY SAINTS. The earliest role Louisville played pertaining to the Church of Jesus Christ of Latter-day Saints (Mormon) was as a river city transportation center. Indeed, the first known member of the church to visit the city of Louisville was Joseph Smith Jr., founder and prophet of the Mormon church. On June 19, 1831, he and other early leaders of the church (including Sidney Rigdon, Martin Harris, Edward Partridge, and W.W. Phelps) traveled to the city on their way to the Midwest. However, there is no record of meetings being held or of proselytizing conducted as a part of that visit.

He visited the city several times, recording once that "when we arrived at Cincinnati, some of the mob which followed us, left us, and we arrived at Louisville the same night. Captain Brittle offered us protection on board of his boat, and gave us supper and breakfast gratuitously." (Smith, *History of the Church*) Samuel Smith, the brother of Joseph, and Reynolds Cahoon, early leaders of the church, also visited the city in 1831, traveling down the OHIO RIVER by steamer.

Mormon missionaries Wilford Woodruff and Warren Parish toured Kentucky in 1834 and spent a number of days in Louisville. Their journals contain records of street meetings being held in the city and indicate that they "preached on the gospel of Jesus Christ, the authenticity of the Book of Mormon and the scattering and gathering of the House of Israel." In July 1843 Brigham Young and Wilford Woodruff visited Kentucky to gather and baptize converts. The number of converts who joined the church as a result of these early efforts is not known. Records are incomplete from that era, as converts at the time were urged to gather (for strength and protection from persecution) with the main body of the church in Kirtland, Ohio, and later in Nauvoo, Illinois, and the Salt Lake Valley of Utah. Brigham Young wrote a letter to Gov. William Owsley in April 1845 requesting religious asylum for the Mormons. There is no record of a response.

The North Kentucky Conference (church administrative unit) was organized on May 6, 1899, and headquartered in Louisville, with Elder Albert Arrowsmith (a missionary at the time) as president. Other Kentucky cities included in the conference were Lexington, Newport, Covington, and Paris. The members met mostly in homes and rented buildings.

Benjamin E. Rich, president of the southern states mission (proselytizing administrative unit formed in 1876), which included Kentucky, visited the city on November 25, 1899, and held meetings with the missionaries and local members. He also visited the city in 1901, 1902, 1906, and 1907. His father, Charles C. Rich, was a native of Campbell County, Kentucky, and had assisted Brigham Young with the church's movement to the West. In 1906 Elder George Albert Smith, of the church Quorum of the Twelve Apostles, one of the governing bodies of the church, visited the city for a conference. Other members of the quorum who at various times visited the city included Heber J. Grant (1911), George F. Richards (1925), David O. McKay (1926), and Orson F. Whitney (1927).

The first recorded Sunday school was organized on January 31, 1915, with Elder John H. Ripplinger as superintendent. It was later discontinued, and on January 31, 1921, a Sunday school was organized for the second time with Elder J.G. Ecshler presiding.

Elder P. Skousen, president of the Kentucky Conference, organized the first branch of the church in Louisville on April 13, 1921, with various missionaries presiding. It was not until September 30, 1928, that the Louisville branch was presided over by a local member, Elder William M. Blake.

Louisville also played a significant role in Mormon church history during this time period relative to the church as a whole. George Albert Smith (president of the church) noted that the first printing of the *Book of Mormon* (considered by Latter-day Saints as companion scripture to the Bible) in Braille was done in Louisville in 1933. It was reported in a general conference address that "It was printed by the AMERICAN PRINTING HOUSE FOR THE BLIND, at Louisville, Kentucky, the same company that prints Bibles in Braille for the American Bible Society" (Smith, *Sharing the Gospel with Others*).

On November 28, 1928, the East Central States Mission was formed by a division from the Southern States Mission, with Louisville designated the mission headquarters. Kentucky, Tennessee, North Carolina, and West Virginia were the states within the new mission, with the headquarters at 927 S FOURTH ST. Later the offices were moved to Baxter Ave. In 1969 the mission was changed again to Kentucky-Tennessee Mission, then in 1975 became the Kentucky-Louisville Mission.

In 1950 the Louisville area became headquarters to the newly organized Kentucky Central District, with Elder William Wells of Lexington as president. Over the next nineteen years Elders Henry H. Griffith, Doyle Crenshaw, and Arnold Foster presided over the district. In 1969 there were three branches in the city, consisting of some eight hundred members.

On January 17, 1971, the Louisville Stake was organized (similar to a Catholic diocese), with Elder Henry H. Griffith as president and Lamont Wilson and Scott Bybee as counselors. Stakes are the unit of church organization and administration above the local level. The units of the new stake consisted of Louisville First, Second, and Third Wards; in Indiana, NEW ALBANY and Salem; and in Kentucky, Lebanon, FORT KNOX, Battletown, and Sulphur Well.

A new stake center was built and dedicated off Hurstbourne Ln. in 1975 for local members to meet and also for various stake offices. In recent years the Evansville, Indiana, and Madisonville, Kentucky, stakes were formed off of the strength of the Louisville area. Louisville has also served as the regional center for church gatherings. Approximately every four years members from the stakes in the region meet with members of the Quorum of the Twelve Apostles and other general authorities of the church. The first LDS temple to be built in Kentucky, The Kentucky Louisville Temple, was completed in the spring of 2000 (located at 7114 W. Hwy. 22, Pewee Valley) and serves ten stakes in Kentucky and Indiana

See Daniel Roth, *Kentuckians and Mormonism* (Lexington 1985); Andrew Jensen, *Encyclopedic History of the Church of Jesus Christ of Latter-day Saints* (Salt Lake City 1941); Joseph Smith, *History of the Church* (Salt Lake City 1980); B.H. Roberts, *A Comprehensive History of The Church of Jesus Christ of Latter-day Saints, Century I* (Salt Lake City 1930); George Albert Smith, *Sharing the Gospel with Others* (Salt Lake City 1948).

Donald R. Curtis
Robert A. Bylund

CHURCH OF OUR LADY IN PORTLAND–NOTRE DAME DU PORT. Founded in 1839, it was Louisville's third ROMAN CATHOLIC parish. Its first official name, Notre Dame du Port, indicates its earliest parishioners were FRENCH immigrants, or the children of French émigrés, as were its founder and earliest pastors. Religious services were held as early as 1806. Services were conducted by the

Reverend Stephen Badin, who later deeded the property to Bishop Benedict Flaget. The cornerstone of the original church was laid September 13, 1840, but the church as it stands today is the result of two reconstructions: the first increased its size, and the second, in 1873, corrected dangerous errors made in the first reconstruction. The steeple, however, remains from the original 1840 construction.

The Reverend Napoleon J. Perché was the first resident pastor. He raised much of the construction funding in New Orleans and in 1870 became archbishop of that archdiocese. It was under his direction that the church became the church of Catholics living in the two villages of Portland and Shippingport, later annexed by Louisville. The original parish boundaries ran from Eighteenth St. and the Ohio River south to the county line, approximately thirty miles.

The parish has always been a survivor and provider, serving as a place of refuge for the working-class parishioners. Located at 3515 Rudd Ave. near the Ohio River, church buildings and many parishioners' homes were inundated several times by river overflow and major floods. The January 1937 flood devastated the interior of the church, with water standing up to the stained-glass window sills. Restoration cost over eighteen thousand dollars in 1938. An ironic twist to the devastation was an improvement in the tone of the organ, believed to be the result of the dampness causing tiny cracks in the parts to swell shut.

Parishioners and parish alike also felt the impact of several severe economic depressions. All the while, the parish strove to provide religious services and education and to do what it could to alleviate human suffering. Parishioners have been generous, given the limitations of their resources. Several old French, German, and Irish family names can still be seen among the parish's membership, descendants of the first families who worshiped there. The parish school, staffed by Sisters of Loretto and Mercy, operated from 1857 to 1971.

See Clyde Crews, *An American Holy Land: A History of the Archdiocese of Louisville* (Louisville 1987); John Lyons and Henry C. Mayer, *Our Lady Notre Dame du Port: A History of the Parish 1839–1964* (Louisville 1964); *Church of our Lady: Centenary of the Parish, 1839–1839* (Louisville 1939)

Henry C. Mayer

CHURCH OF OUR MERCIFUL SAVIOUR. The oldest African American Episcopal church in Louisville, the Church of Our Merciful Saviour traces its origin to 1861. At that time, Rev. William I. Waller, a missionary, started St. Mark's Episcopal Mission as a "separate and distinct congregation" for Louisville blacks. It purchased the German Lutheran church building on Green (Liberty) and Preston Streets and by 1867 was led by the talented preacher Rev. Joseph Atwell. The church thrived under Atwell's leadership but ceased to exist after he left the state in 1868.

In 1870 a black Episcopal presence re-emerged in the form of a mission on Eighth near Cedar St. The church became an official mission of the Episcopal Diocese in May 1872 and was recognized as the Church of Our Merciful Saviour. In 1873 an endowment by the Reverend John Norton allowed the church to move to Grayson (Madison) and Ninth Streets. Rapid growth made it necessary to secure a larger sanctuary and, in April 1891 the church again moved to a ca.-1854 Gothic structure built by plow magnate B.F. Avery. The church on the site had been gutted by fire, but the congregation was able to preserve the structure until another fire leveled the building in January 1912. One of its influential pastors was Rev. LeRoy Ferguson. His close association with blacks and whites contributed to his high regard in philanthropic circles. His efforts resulted in several contributions from steel magnate Andrew Carnegie's foundation.

A new church was built in 1912 under the leadership of Bishop Charles Woodcock at the present site at Eleventh and Walnut (Muhammad Ali Blvd.) Streets. It was designed by Louisville architect George Herbert Gray. When the federal government completed the Beecher Terrace Housing Project in 1940, the church was allowed to remain, and the new development was built around it; it was reported that the church was so well-respected in the community that local gambling houses would not open their doors to customers until after church services were finished.

During World War II, the church worked in cooperation with other area churches to support United Services Organization (USO) clubs for GIs, with Dudley Hall of the church serving as an officer's lounge and the parish house serving as a military police battalion headquarters.

See Marion Lucas, *History of Blacks in Louisville* (Frankfort 1992).

CITIES AND TOWNS. Based on population figures, the Kentucky and Indiana governments have different legislation and classifications for their incorporated communities. For a Kentucky city to be incorporated, organized local residents must petition the General Assembly and have this minimum number of inhabitants: first-class—one hundred thousand; second-class—twenty thousand; third-class—eight thousand; fourth-class—three thousand; fifth-class—one thousand; and sixth-class—three hundred.

In order for a Kentucky city to move to a higher class, its population must increase beyond the designated minimum, and the City Council must submit an additional application to the legislature for reclassification. In first-, second-, and third-class cities, the mayor and legislative bodies are elected by all qualified voters. In the other three classes, the mayor and councils may either be elected or appointed, as designated by law.

In Indiana, upon petition from its inhabitants, cities and towns are incorporated by the state under an arrangement that is also based on population figures. These divisions are first-class—250,000 or more, second-class—from 35,000 to 249,999, third-class—fewer than 35,000, and towns—fewer than 2,000. A number of communities with populations greater than two thousand people have never sought incorporation and are governed by their counties, while others are permitted to be towns as well as cities. The legislative body of a city includes an elected mayor, an elected city clerk, and an elected common council. The legislative body of a town includes an elected board of town trustees, an elected town clerk, and, if desired by the trustees, a delegated town manager.

Kentucky Cities' Populations

Location	*1980*	*1990*	*1996*
Bullitt County			
First-Class			
None			
Second-Class			
None			
Third-Class			
None			
Fourth-Class			
Hillview	5,196	6,119	5,815
Mt. Washington	3,997	5,256	7,051
Shepherdsville ‡	4,454	4,805	4,667
Fifth-Class			
Lebanon Junction	1,581	1,741	2,253
Pioneer Village	637	1,130	1,456
Sixth-Class			
Fox Chase	275	528	678
Hebron Estates	433	930	1,197
Hunters Hollow	260	286	367
Jefferson County			
First-Class			
Louisville ‡	298,451*	269,555*	260,689*
Second-Class			
Jeffersontown	15,795	23,223	25,596
Third-Class			
Shively	16,819	15,535	14,899
Fourth-Class			
Anchorage	1,726	2,082	2,058
Douglass Hills	4,384	5,431	5,195
Graymoor-Devondale	3,191	2,911	3,074
Hurstbourne	3,530	4,420	4,698
Lyndon	1,553	8,037	7,675
Middletown	4,262	5,016	5,298
Prospect	1,981	2,788	2,963
St. Matthews	13,354	15,691	16,562
St. Regis Park	1,735	1,725	1,649
Fifth-Class			
Audubon Park	1,571	1,520	1,561
Barbourmeade	1,038	1,386	1,324
Beechwood Village	1,462	1,263	1,341
Hurstbourne Acres	386	1,072	1,140
Indian Hills	1,113	1,074	1,130
Indian Hills-Cherokee	585	1,005	1,066
Lynnview	1,157	1,017	1,080
Meadow Vale	1,008	798	849
Minor Lane Heights	1,882	1,675	1,781

Location	1980	1990	1996
Northfield	906	898	948
Plantation	969	830	882
Rolling Hills	1,067	1,135	1,206
Watterson Park	1,101	1,378	1,539
West Buechel	1,205	1,587	1,416
Windy Hills	2,214	2,452	2,370
Woodlawn Park	1,052	1,099	1,167
Sixth-Class			
Bancroft	725	582	618
Bellemeade	918	927	985
Bellewood	307	329	348
Blue Ridge Manor	465	565	930
Briarwood	374	658	699
Broadfields	311	273	290
Broeck Pointe	216	325	344
Brownsboro Farm	790	670	713
Brownsboro Village	410	361	361
Cambridge	193	193	205
Cherrywood Village	362	340	360
Coldstream	549	862	918
Creekside	419	323	345
Crossgate	292	261	277
Druid Hills	338	305	321
Fairmeade	272	280	298
Fincastle	804	838	892
Forest Hills	502	454	182
Glenview	511	653	686
Glenview Hills	433	353	375
Glenview Manor	212	197	210
Goose Creek	361	321	340
Green Spring	634	768	817
Hickory Hill	171	152	162
Hills and Dales	151	154	164
Hollow Creek	1,023	991	1,052
Hollyvilla	476	649	688
Houston Acres	N/A	496	528
Keeneland	432	393	417
Kingsley	464	399	411
Langdon Place	407	874	929
Lincolnshire	139	158	169
Manor Creek	241	179	190
Maryhill Estates	225	177	190
Meadowbrook Farm	203	163	172
Meadowview Estates	212	199	211
Mockingbird Valley	205	193	199
Moorland	513	467	448
Murray Hill	434	619	658
Norbourne Estates	446	461	483
Norwood	254	372	391
Old Brownsboro Place	358	348	371
Parkway Village	754	707	727
Plymouth Village	231	162	172
Poplar Hills	381	377	401
Richlawn	485	435	462
Riverwood	435	506	538
Robinswood	273	250	266
Rolling Fields	731	593	629
Seneca Gardens	748	684	702
South Park View	248	214	228
Spring Mill	426	342	365
Spring Valley	510	425	452
Springlee	498	451	479
Strathmoor Manor	368	391	399
Strathmoor Village	466	361	367
Sycamore	195	188	199
Ten Broeck	134	128	136
Thornhill	233	192	203
Wellington	653	593	620
Westwood	826	734	781
Whipps Millgate	548	454	482
Wildwood	309	266	282
Winding Falls	454	657	698
Woodland Hills	839	714	759
Worthington Hills	1,023	973	1,035
Oldham County			
First-Class			
None			
Second-Class			
None			
Third-Class			
None			
Fourth-Class			
La Grange ‡	2,971	3,853	5,040
Fifth-Class			
Orchard Grass Hills	1,047	1,058	1,354
Pewee Valley	982	1,283	1,631
Sixth-Class			
Crestwood	531	1,435	1,841
Goshen	N/A	903	1,155
Park Lake	291	263	336
River Bluff	283	452	579
Shelby County			
First-Class			
None			
Second-Class			
None			
Third-Class			
None			
Fourth-Class			
Shelbyville ‡	5,329	6,155	6,954
Fifth-Class			
None			
Sixth-Class			
Pleasureville	837	761	866
(also in Henry Co.)			
Simpsonville	642	907	1,042

Indiana Cities' and Towns' Populations

Location	1980	1990	1996
Clark County			
New Providence	384	270	524
Charlestown			
(also a third-class city)	5,596	5,889	6,022
Clarksville	15,164	19,784	19,749
Jeffersonville ‡			
(also a third-class city)	21,220	21,830	25,787
Sellersburg	3,209	5,745	6,028
Utica	501	411	398
Floyd County			
Georgetown	1,494	2,092	2,248
Greenville	537	508	585
New Albany ‡			
(also a second-class city)	37,103	36,322	38,224
Harrison County			
Crandall	176	147	159
Corydon ‡	2,724	2,661	2,652
Elizabeth	178	153	167
Laconia	58	75	80
Lanesville	570	512	559
Mauckport	109	95	107
Milltown			
(also in Crawford Co.)	1,006	917	916
New Amsterdam	31	30	33
New Middletown	115	82	89
Palmyra	692	621	682
Scott County			
Austin	4,857	4,310	4,371
Scottsburg ‡	5,068	5,334	5,708

‡ county seat
* metropolitan area

See John Clements, *Kentucky Facts* (Dallas 1990); Kentucky Cabinet for Economic Development, *Kentucky Deskbook of Economic Statistics* (Frankfort 1996); Courtney M. Slater and George E. Hall, eds., *1992 County and City Extra* (Lanham, Md., 1992); U.S. Department of Commerce, Bureau of the Census, *1990 Census of Population and Housing, Indiana* (Washington, D.C., 1990); U.S. Department of Commerce, Bureau of the Census, *1980 Census of Population and Housing, Indiana* (Washington, D.C., 1980); John Clements, *Indiana Facts* (Dallas 1995).

CITIZENS UNION BANK (SHELBYVILLE). The Citizens Union Bank was organized in Shelbyville, Kentucky, as the Citizens' Bank on January 21, 1888. Its first president was Prof. Charles Kinkel, formerly the principal of the music faculty at the local Science Hill Female Academy. Later that year the bank constructed a building at 527 Main St., where it remained until 1973 when it moved to a new and larger facility at 827 Main St.

For the first eighty years of its existence the bank grew steadily, relying on business generated by farmers and merchants. After 1960, with the movement of industry into the county, the bank began to grow more rapidly. On October 1, 1970, it merged with the Bank of Simpsonville and changed its name to Citizens Union Bank. The merged assets of the two banks were $7.3 million. In September 1982 Citizens Union Bancorp became the owner of all the shares of Citizens Union Bank. The majority of the present shareholders are residents of Shelby County. In 1986 the bank merged with the Farmers and Traders Bank that had operated in Shelbyville since 1871. The Citizens Union Bank moved its main office in April 1996 to a new banking center at 1854 Midland Trail. The bank presently operates branches in Shelbyville, Bagdad, and SIMPSONVILLE in Shelby County and in TAYLORSVILLE in SPENCER COUNTY. Total assets as of June 30, 1999, were $282 million.

See *Shelby Sentinel,* Jan. 5, 1888, June 28, 1888, July 5, 1888; *Sentinel-News,* April 19, 1996, May 17, 1996.

Charles T. Long

CITY CHARTERS. Louisville was founded May 1, 1778 on land owned by JOHN CONNOLLY, a British sympathizer and recently convicted traitor. The next year, the residents petitioned the Virginia House of Burgesses to confiscate his land and confirm their titles. The state legislature granted their request on May 1, 1778 by establishing a town GOVERNMENT for Louisville.

Louisville was a thriving commercial town by the mid-1820s, with a population of 7,063 but it was outgrowing its trustee government. The town's leading citizens, aware of the need to enlarge municipal powers, held a public meeting on November 3, 1827. Resolutions were adopted appointing a committee to draft an ACT OF INCORPORATION, appointing another committee to draft a charter, and requesting the General Assembly to pass an act incorporating Louisville. The proposed act of incorporation and charter were presented to the General Assembly and approved on February 13, 1828.

The 1828 charter replaced the board of trustees with a government composed of a MAYOR and city council. The charter divided the city into five WARDS and provided that property-owning voters would annually elect two council members from each ward. The charter did not, however, allow the local electorate alone to choose a mayor but provided that the governor would select the mayor from the two persons having the highest number of votes. An 1836 statute took the selection of the mayor away from the governor and granted it to the City Council. When this method proved unsatisfactory, an 1838 charter amendment provided for popular election of the mayor.

The 1828 charter vested the mayor and council with broader powers to pass bylaws than those delegated to the trustees. It expressly granted them the power to erect suitable buildings for a poorhouse and WORKHOUSE, establish free schools in each ward, and select subordinate officers. At the same time, the charter reflected a preference for a strong City Council with its limits on the mayor's executive and legislative powers. He had no power to appoint or dismiss, and he had no veto power. The charter also gave the council the power to set his salary. A charter amendment, in effect from 1836 to 1838, granted the council the power to select the mayor. His limited judicial power, derived from the trustee charter, made him a justice of the peace. The General Assembly broadened these powers in 1833 to authorize him, as a member of a mayor's court, to adjudicate cases involving state penal laws, but an 1836 charter amendment abolished the mayor's court, eliminated the mayor's judicial authority, and established a one-judge police court.

At first, the 1828 charter had only a five-year life span. Apparently the General Assembly viewed the city's charter as an experiment, but an 1833 statute extended its life indefinitely. Still, the General Assembly continued to change the charter by altering the qualifications for city offices, the methods of electing officials, the length of their terms of office, and the powers of their offices. Many changes were initiated by the City Council, which requested specific grants of authority to address needs of a growing city. Some changes, such as those governing the making of contracts and the conduct of fiscal affairs, reflected a legislative interest in limiting the opportunities for local government mismanagement. In all, this mass of piecemeal special legislation created a body of local law that was often ambiguous, contradictory, and obscure, and clearly in need of change.

Once again, Louisville had outgrown its charter and needed to have its governmental powers rationalized and enlarged. In 1831 the PORTLAND CANAL had been opened to trade. The city's first railroad had begun operation in 1838, and by 1850 the city's POPULATION had reached 43,194, the largest in the state. A new state constitution, ratified in 1850, also required changes in the city's charter. In July 1850 four delegates from each ward were elected to a charter convention, not by property-owning voters but by an expanded electorate composed of all free white male citizens. The convention met in September and wrote a new charter, which the voters approved and the General Assembly enacted into law on March 24, 1851.

The 1851 charter divided the city's government into three distinct departments composed of a mayor, a two-chamber general council, and a city court judge. They, along with other executive and judicial officials, would be chosen by a broadened electorate of all free white male citizens. The mayor, elected for two years, was granted only a little more power than he had under the 1828 charter. He had minimal control over the city's executive branch, which was composed of a city attorney, a treasurer, an auditor, a tax assessor, and two tax collectors, all elected by the voters. The mayor was head of a forty-eight-member police force, but it was elected by the City Council.

The charter created a two-chamber general council composed of a Board of Common Councilmen and a BOARD OF ALDERMEN and authorized it to exercise the city's legislative powers. Under the authority of the charter, the general council divided the city into eight wards and provided for the election of two councilmen and one alderman from each ward. The charter broadened the suffrage and permitted all free white male citizens to elect aldermen for two years and councilmen for one year, later extended to two years by an 1865 charter amendment.

The charter also limited the council's power by giving the voters a greater voice. More city offices were taken out of the council's hands and made elective. The charter did not permit the council to contract debts or liabilities beyond the revenues for the current fiscal year without voter approval. Nor did the charter permit the council to submit any charter amendments to the General Assembly unless they were approved by the voters at a general election. The charter also recognized that council committees could not administer the city's growing governmental responsibilities. Thus they created a health board chosen by the council, a popularly elected school board, and a board composed of the mayor, treasurer, and president of the Board of Aldermen that would manage a sinking fund to finance public projects.

The charter established the office of judge of the city court, also popularly elected, who was granted the powers of a justice of the peace in criminal and civil matters, the authority to decide criminal misdemeanor cases, and, sitting with another judge, the authority of a court examination and commitment in felony cases. The 1851 charter expanded the city's electorate and differentiated its governmental functions for the first time. But by 1870 Louisville's rapid population growth, more than double that of 1850, and the city's investments in private business and public construction made demands that the 1851 charter could not meet.

On April 5, 1868, the voters approved a charter convention and elected delegates from each ward. The delegates drew up a new charter that was approved first by the voters and then by the General Assembly. The framework of government provided by the 1870 charter was essentially the same as the 1851 charter and its amendments, but there were a few modifications, such as the extension of the mayor's term of office to three years. With the new charter came another expansion of the electorate. Negroes, forbidden to vote by the Kentucky Constitution in municipal elections, were granted that right with the passage of the Fifteenth Amendment to the U.S. Constitution on March 30, 1870.

The 1870 charter's chief reforms involved the reorganization and coordination of municipal police, fire, and welfare administration by the creation of public commissions and boards and the restructuring of others. The new charter reorganized the police force by establishing a board of police commissioners composed of the mayor, the presidents of the Board of Councilmen and the Board of Aldermen, and the chairmen of the police committees in each chamber of the general council. The mayor nominated the police chief, who was confirmed by the police board that each year elected the entire police force. The charter provided for a paid FIRE DEPARTMENT, first established in 1858, and for the popular election of the fire chief to a two-year term. Finally, the charter established a board of commissioners of public charities to coordinate the functions of the city almshouse, pesthouse, workhouse, and HOUSES OF REFUGE.

A new state constitution, ratified in 1891, made substantial changes in the government of Louisville. Prior to 1890, the city had operated under specific charters granted by the General Assembly. The new constitution abolished special legislation; revoked existing city charters; adopted a classified charter system that assigned cities to one of six classes, defined by population; and required the General Assembly to enact uniform legislation for each class. At the same time, the framers of the 1891 Constitution recognized Louisville's unique status as the state's largest city when they created the classification of cities of the first class. Since that class contained only one city, Louisville, all legislation for that class would be special legislation tailored to the specific needs of the city.

The current Louisville city charter, approved July 1, 1893, continued the division of the city government into three distinct branches. The mayor, now elected to a four-year term, had the power to appoint executive officials and to supervise all executive offices. Under the charter, the principal executive boards were the Board of Public Safety and Board of PUBLIC WORKS, consisting of three members each, who were appointed to four-year terms by the mayor subject to the approval of the Board of Aldermen. The General Council, now composed of twenty-four councilmen and twelve aldermen, represented the city's twelve wards. The councilmen, two from each ward, and the aldermen were elected by the voters of the city at large. A charter amendment in 1929 eliminated the Board of Common Councilmen and made the Board of Aldermen the city's legislative body. Finally, the charter provided for a judge of the police court elected by the voters.

The charter provided for the city's educational interests by creating a Board of School Trustees, which consisted of two members from each ward elected by the voters for two-year terms. The charter placed the control of the public PARKS under the authority of a six-member Board of Park Commissioners popularly elected by the voters for four-year terms. To manage the city's fiscal affairs, the charter provided for offices to collect and disburse revenue, including an assessor elected by the General Council for four years; a comptroller, appointed by the mayor to a four-year term with the approval of the Board of Aldermen; and a tax receiver and an auditor elected by the voters. To manage the city's bonded indebtedness, the charter also provided for the sinking fund commission first introduced by the 1851 charter.

In 1972 the General Assembly recognized the need to give Louisville greater local autonomy, by rewriting the statutory provisions governing cities of the first class to grant the city HOME RULE. House Bill 355 preserved statutes that established the basic structure of city government but repealed those that conferred its powers and duties. Then it substituted a broad home rule grant that permitted the city to enact "any ordinances or resolutions for municipal purposes not in conflict with the Constitution or the law of this state or the United States." In the preamble to House Bill 355, the General Assembly justified action by stating that "the conditions found in cities of the first class are sufficiently different from those found in other cities to necessitate this grant of authority and complete home rule."

Louisville's home rule statute created a very strong mayor who has the power to recommend legislation to the Board of Aldermen, to veto legislation subject to a two-thirds override, to make appointments to and remove persons from all executive offices, to supervise executive offices, to recommend the reorganization of executive agencies, and to enforce the ordinances of the city.

The City Charter Commission of 1868.

The Board of Aldermen, in addition to exercising any power not granted to the mayor and not prohibited to it by state law, has the power to impeach and remove any executive officer, to establish and reorganize executive departments, to approve the city's annual budget, to levy taxes, to approve contracts made by the city, and to consider and adopt legislation they believe is expedient or necessary to provide for the health, education, safety, and welfare of the city.

In sum, Louisville's growth from a frontier settlement to a major metropolitan center has been reflected in its governmental charters. The 1780 charter from the Virginia House of Burgesses granted the town only limited powers, which grew only marginally after Kentucky became a state. The General Assembly firmly controlled the powers it granted the city in its 1828 charter and in the charters that followed in 1851, 1870, and 1893, and in their numerous charter amendments. Those charters recognized Louisville's need to provide municipal functions created by the city's social and economic growth. Then in 1972 the General Assembly freed the city from legislative control over its affairs by granting it home rule.

See Attia Bowmer, "A History of the Government of the City of Louisville," M.A. thesis, University of Louisville, 1948; Charlie Bush, ed., *Citizen's Guide to the Kentucky Constitution,* Kentucky Legislative Research Commission Research Report No. 137 (Frankfort 1991); J. Stoddard Johnston, ed., *Memorial History of Louisville* (Chicago 1896); J. David Morris, *The New Municipal Law: Kentucky's Cities under Home Rule,* Kentucky Legislative Research Commission Informational Bulletin No. 138 (Frankfort 1981).

William Crawford Green

CITY DIRECTORIES. The first directory listing the inhabitants of an American city was the Baltimore broadside (1752). City and business directories served an important communication function for consumers and commercial establishments, especially before the advent of the TELEPHONE, and they remain valuable tools for research. They tell us of the most popular trades, and their advertisements allow us to follow popular styles of clothing and furniture. Unlike telephone books, such as those printed by BellSouth, city directories attempted to include a listing of all adults in the household and their occupations as well as people who do not own telephones.

Louisville's first city directory appeared in 1832. Published by Richard W. Otis, it included a listing of most non-slave Louisville residents, their occupations, and street addresses. Businesses were also included, as well as a map of the Louisville area. Toward the back of the directory, the publisher included an outline of the origin and settlement of Louisville and other information about the city including a listing of STEAMBOATS; religious and benevolent societies; military groups; state, county, and GOVERNMENT officers; post office regulations; whiskey inspections; and other useful facts. Forty-one pages out of the entire 198 pages of the directory consisted of advertisements. The next directory followed in 1836 and was published by Gabriel Collins, an engineer. The 1845 directory was the first to include information about adjacent SHIPPINGPORT and PORTLAND, and NEW ALBANY and JEFFERSONVILLE in Indiana.

Until 1866 Louisville directories were printed sporadically and by different publishers. From 1858 to 1859, they were published by Hurd and Burrows on Third St. between MARKET and JEFFERSON STREETS. The 1858 publication claimed to be the fifth edition of the *Louisville City Directory* and contained similar information as Otis's directories. Hurd and Burrows also included help on how to spot counterfeit money and an extensive listing of public organizations, agencies, companies, and city offices. Helpful facts about Louisville such as the present POPULATION, MAPS, and calendars gave the books the appearance of almanacs. Hurd and Burrows included one of the first renditions of the later telephone directory Yellow Pages by listing businesses in alphabetical order by subject, with proprietors' names. The 1858–59 issue was titled *Louisville City Directory and Business Mirror*. The publisher changed the name in the 1859–60 issue to *Louisville Directory and Business Advertiser.*

In 1864 Richard Edwards began directory publication under the title *Edwards' Annual Director.* Edwards printed advertisements in the front of the book, before the listing of residents and businesses. Like Hurd and Burrows, he also included a listing of businesses by type.

With the exception of *Williamson's Annual Directory* of 1865–66, Edwards was the only directory publisher until 1870, when competition appeared. Edwards's last directory was 1870. At the same time, *Louisville City Guide and Business Directory* for 1869–70 appeared. This book was published by German and Brothers. The directory, along with a listing of residents and businesses, contained lithograph maps and illustrations of the city of Louisville. Among them were sketches of the GALT HOUSE and the Louisville Water Works engine department. C.K. Caron was the compiler.

The German and Brothers directory lasted only one year. C.K. Caron established his own publishing company, Bradley and Gilbert, on Green (Liberty) St. on the northwest corner of Third St., and in 1871 *Caron's Louisville City Directory* claimed to be the "largest and most comprehensive directory ever published in this city." The directory enumerated fully the "colored" population of the city and all churches, chapels, and synagogues. It contained 34,446 names and reported that the next issue would be out no later than January 15, 1872. Until the mid-1920s, Caron's Directory Co. was the sole directory publisher.

The first and only *Louisville and New Albany Directory* was published in 1848 by Gabriel Collins. It did not include a commercial index but contained a listing of residents as well as steamboats manufactured in Louisville and the Indiana cities. In 1873 a directory was compiled for New Albany by A.E. Sholes called *Sholes' New Albany City Directory.* C.K. Caron was also involved in this project. In a tribute to Sholes inside the directory, Caron stated, "Mr. A.E. Sholes has had charge of this canvass, and as a partial recognition of his long and faithful services, the directory has been named *Sholes' New Albany Directory*, and will continue to be published in his name." However in 1877 Sholes's name disappears and C.K. Caron had taken over the entire operation, becoming publisher and compiler for the New Albany directory. In 1884 Caron included Jeffersonville in his directory, titled *Caron's New Albany and Jeffersonville Directory.*

R.L. Polk and Co. purchased Caron's Directory Co. in 1925. Because the Caron name was already well known in the community, that name was continued until the 1970s. Throughout the 1970s R.L. Polk and Co. gradually introduced the name *Polk's City Directory* for both Louisville and New Albany/Jeffersonville directories. The format remained identical to Caron's publication. R.L. Polk and Co. continued to print directories for areas throughout Kentucky, including Louisville and CLARK and FLOYD COUNTIES in Indiana. In 1957 R.L. Polk and Co.'s publication split into two versions for the Louisville area—the *Louisville Suburban Directory* and the *Louisville City Directory.* Both directories continue to be published annually. The *Louisville Suburban Directory* includes Eastern Jefferson County and SHELBY, OLDHAM, and BULLITT COUNTIES. The directory remains the sole source of easy reference for names and occupations.

See Dorothea N. Spear, *Bibliography of American Directories through 1860* (Worcester, Mass., 1961); J. Winston Coleman Jr., *Bibliography of Kentucky History* (Lexington 1949).

CITY HALL. Placed on the NATIONAL REGISTER OF HISTORIC PLACES in 1976, this Louisville landmark at 601 W Jefferson St. is an impressive piece of civic ARCHITECTURE and a metaphor for Louisville's post–CIVIL WAR optimism and can-do attitude. Its exuberance is a stylistic counterpoint to the far more austere, 1836 Greek Revival–style county courthouse across Sixth St.

Before city hall was built, there was no city GOVERNMENT building. City officials had shared space in the COUNTY COURTHOUSES. Plans for the city hall were initiated when a design competition was held with the winner receiving five hundred dollars. In April 1867 the winning design, created by Louisville architects JOHN ANDREWARTHA and C.S. Mergell, was chosen. By late summer 1870 the final plans of construction had been drawn by Andrewartha, in association with local architects C.L. Stancliff and Co. The existing government buildings on the site were demolished, and ground was broken for the building's foundation. The city engineer, I.M. St. John, had been chosen by Louisville's General Council to oversee the project, and Andrewartha was named the managing architect.

Built with stone from the White River quarries near Salem, Indiana, city hall's construction took place between 1870 and 1873 at a cost of $464,778. The city hall, with its three stories and raised basement, was a blend of Italianate motifs and the French Second Empire style that was prominent in civic buildings after the Civil War. The edifice is also characterized by prolific use of symbolic ornamentation. Louisville's trust in progress and RAILROADS is reflected in the building's upper carvings. For instance, the pediment over the main entrance displays a bas relief of the city seal represented by a train "plowing through the wilderness" past such Southern flora as a palm tree and bearing the slogan, "Progress, 1871." This not only indicated the direction of Louisville's principal trade but was also an apt symbol of the tremendous influence the railroads, especially the LOUISVILLE AND NASHVILLE line, had on the city's commercial development. Likewise, the stone livestock carvings along the sides of the building reflect the importance of Louisville's STOCKYARDS in her economic history.

Another prominent feature of the city hall is its 196-foot-high, four-faced clock tower with a mansard roof, built by HENRY WHITESTONE in 1876 after an 1875 fire had damaged the original. The original three-ton bell housed in the tower was made in a local foundry. The bell stopped ringing in 1964 when the clock broke, but it was repaired in 1968. It ceased ringing again in the 1970s and remained silent until 1991. Though the exterior of city hall has remained largely unchanged, several renovation and remodeling projects have left little of the original interior intact.

See Theodore M. Brown, *Introduction to Louisville Architecture* (Louisville 1960); William L. Lebovich, *America's City Halls* (Washington, D.C., 1984).

Douglas L Stern

CIVIL DISTURBANCES OF 1968. Generally racial, religious, or economic in origin, civil disturbances constitute a dark part of America's past. In the 1960s, unrest boiled just beneath the surface as the Vietnam War escalated and the civil rights crusade moved into high gear. Major disturbances erupted in a number of American cities, some in a partial response to the murder of Dr. Martin Luther King Jr. in 1968. Louisville was no exception. On Monday evening, May 27, 1968, approximately four hundred people, primarily African Americans, gathered at the intersection of Twenty-eighth St. and Greenwood Ave. in the Parkland neighborhood to protest the possible reinstatement of police officer Michael Clifford. Clifford, who admitted having hit and slapped African American Manfred Reid during an incident earlier in May, was serving a suspension but was awaiting a decision on his return to the force. After several African American leaders, including James Cortez of the Student Nonviolent Coordinating Committee and members of the Black Unity League of Kentucky (BULK), arrived and explained that no decision had been reached, the agitated crowd began to disperse.

However, rumors that whites were forbidding the arrival of militant SNCC speaker Stokely Carmichael by keeping his plane airborne—allegations that were denied by Eastern Airlines—coupled with the launching of several bottles by youths from the roof of House of Champs Poolroom caused the crowd to explode. The arrival of police, completely undermanned against the inflamed crowd, only exacerbated the situation, as groups of rioters began to move into the surrounding streets. By 11:00 p.m. the agitators had looted numerous shops as far east as Fourth St.; had overturned and ignited several automobiles, including one police car; and had vandalized the streets throughout the neighborhood. In an effort to restore peace, approximately seven hundred Kentucky National Guardsmen were sent in, and Mayor Kenneth Schmied established a citywide curfew from 11:00 p.m. until 5:30 a.m.

City Hall. Engraving from Atlas of the City of Louisville, 1876.

While things appeared calm the next morning, more trouble at the same intersection occurred the following day at 2:00 p.m., although scattered instances arose as far west as Cecil Ave. and as far east as Shelby St. Schmied summoned more guardsmen to the primary area and reinstituted the curfew, this time beginning at 8:00 p.m. After several discussions with West End leaders, Schmied agreed to remove the curfew as well as replace the guardsmen with thirty black marshals. As fewer incidents arose on the third day, business owners began to return to their shops, and the city began to total the damages, which were later estimated at four hundred thousand dollars. The violence had also caused 2 deaths, both African American teenage boys, and police reported 472 arrests. Six of the arrested were singled out as the plotters and charged with conspiracy to destroy private property. However, the "Black Six"—James Cortez, Manfred Reid, Samuel Hawkins, Robert Kuyu Sims, Ruth Bryant, and Walter T. "Pete" Cosby—were acquitted in July 1970. Louisville had escaped with much less serious violence than the major occurrences in Detroit, Washington, and other cities.

See Samuel W. Thomas, *Louisville since the Twenties* (Louisville 1978).

CIVIL RIGHTS. Civil rights activity in Louisville is a long history of struggle, with each step forward coming after an organized demand and usually an intense campaign.

The period called the Civil Rights Era of the twentieth century, the 1950s and 1960s, brought profound changes to the city's racial landscape. The AFRICAN AMERICAN community produced three major mass movements in those years.

The first was in 1961 when mass sit-ins by African American high school students at downtown RESTAURANTS and THEATERS brought arrests of more than seven hundred demonstrators and solid support from adult African Americans. The adults gave money, attended rallies, conducted a 98-percent-effective economic boycott of Louisville merchants, and organized a voter registration and electoral campaign. Within two months—two years before changes were written into law in a city public accommodations ordinance—two hundred business establishments opened their doors. Downtown Louisville, which had been rigidly segregated, was integrated.

The second mass action was a march of ten thousand people in Frankfort in 1964, demanding state civil rights legislation. The third mass campaign came in spring 1967. An Open Housing Movement challenged the system of unwritten laws that kept African Americans from renting or buying property in most of Louisville. There were nightly marches in the city's South End, violent attacks by opponents of the movement, an injunction, more than four hundred arrests, a mass sit-in at the intersection of FOURTH and BROADWAY to protest a negative vote on a proposed ordinance by the BOARD OF ALDERMEN, and a threat to disrupt the DERBY.

The activism of the 1960s did not spring from a vacuum. There had been a tradition of struggle for justice in Louisville's African American community since 1870. In that year, Louisville STREETCARS were integrated by African Americans employing the same tactics used eighty-five years later in the Montgomery, Alabama, bus protest that launched the modern civil rights movement. Three blacks took front seats; there followed arrests, court action, mass rallies, a boycott of the streetcars, and organization by churches of alternative transportation. In 1871, federal judge BLAND BALLARD ordered streetcars desegregated. Throughout the rest of the nineteenth century and the first half of the twentieth, African Americans formed a succession of organizations that fought discrimination in the RAILROADS, employment, and education, and organized to stop persistent police brutality against African Americans.

Nor did militant action end with the movements of the 1960s. Demonstrations and electoral campaigns continued until the end of the century around a multiplicity of specific issues of discrimination. During this 130 years of activism, Louisville African Americans combined the entire array of social change struggle methods: court action, rallies and demonstrations, economic boycotts, nonviolent direct action, political activity, and public education through churches, organizations, and the black press. (Louisville had eight black newspapers, one of which, the *DEFENDER,* continues to thrive at the start of the century. Its publisher for many years, FRANK STANLEY SR., carried on a steady crusade for civil rights. A similar role was played earlier in the century by William Warley, who published the *Louisville News,* and I. Willis Cole, publisher of the *Louisville Leader.*)

Political activity was key. Unlike the situation in the Deep South, after the Civil War African Americans in Louisville were never denied the right to vote. The city's black population was never higher than 20 percent until the latter half of the twentieth century when it grew to 30 percent, but black voters when they organized had leverage. For example, in 1920 black voters defeated a bond issue for the UNIVERSITY OF LOUISVILLE because it made no provision for education of African Americans. When the issue came up again later in the 1920s, its advocates promised benefits for African Americans, it passed, and LOUISVILLE MUNICIPAL COLLEGE for African Americans was established. Meantime, in 1921 some militant young African Americans—disgusted because the DEMOCRATIC PARTY ignored them, and the REPUBLICAN PARTY, still considered the "party of Lincoln," took them for granted—organized the LINCOLN INDEPENDENT PARTY and ran their own candidates. They did not elect anyone, but the threat won them some jobs in local GOVERNMENT, and by the end of the 1920s both parties knew they needed the black vote.

This became important in the struggles of the 1960s. The public accommodations ordinance was passed after the African American vote removed a Democratic Board of Aldermen that had rejected the LAW; they installed Louisville's first Republican MAYOR and aldermanic board in twenty-eight years. In 1967, the African American vote defeated a Republican administration that opposed an open housing ordinance and elected a Democratic one. The new Board of Aldermen passed the ordinance just a few weeks after it took office.

Many struggles of the late nineteenth and early twentieth centuries revolved around court challenges to discrimination. But these incorporated what can accurately be called direct action, because, when people came to meetings and rallies and gave money, they were taking courageous public stands. Often these gatherings were held at QUINN CHAPEL, which had been known in an earlier time as an "abolitionist" church and became known as Louisville's "civil rights" church. For example, it was the staging ground for a victorious campaign against a local residential SEGREGATION ordinance between 1914 and 1917. That battle, centered on the court case of *BUCHANAN V. WARLEY*, set national precedent and launched the local branch of the National Association for the Advancement of Colored People (NAACP), under the leadership of Dr. C.H. PARRISH SR.

Also, many struggles of the 1930s sought only more justice for African Americans within the segregated system, but blacks believed that with such pressure on the system, it would eventually fall of its own weight. For example, when attorney CHARLES ANDERSON of Louisville became the state's first African American legislator in 1936, he pushed through a bill requiring the state to pay for education out of state that it did not provide blacks within the state. Educator ALBERT MEYZEEK, who led challenges to the Louisville power structure from the early 1890s through the first five decades of the twentieth century and became known as the "Old War Horse," battled mainly for resources that would improve the lives of segregated African Americans—for example, branch LIBRARIES and a YMCA. (Meyzeek continued to speak out against discrimination almost until his death in 1963 at age 101.) Teacher LYMAN JOHNSON, who became the very personification of the community's struggle against segregation, began his battles in Louisville in a 1930s campaign to equalize salaries of black and white teachers.

By the mid-1940s, Louisville African Americans were demanding that segregation be dismantled. Black veterans came home from WORLD WAR II determined to have the democracy they had fought for. The Progressive Party, which ran Henry Wallace for president in 1948, became more than an electoral campaign; it attracted young blacks who, for example, challenged segregation by direct action in Louisville PARKS and on picket lines at the large hall then known as the Armory (GARDENS OF LOUISVILLE) at Sixth and Walnut Streets (Muhammad Ali Blvd.).

In the late 1940s, the Louisville LABOR movement became a center of action against racial discrimination. Local CIO director William Taylor announced that his organization would oppose all segregation laws. A militant group of four unions that shared a hall on S Seventh St. lifted up a banner of anti-racist unionism. One represented three thousand workers at the INTERNATIONAL HARVESTER plant, where Sterling Neal and other black workers were in leadership positions. The Seventh St. unions developed a branch of the national Negro Labor Council that agitated for fair hiring at the new GENERAL ELECTRIC plant and organized people to pay phone bills in pennies to pressure the phone company to hire more blacks.

Meantime, local NAACP lawyers—led by attorneys James Crumlin, EARL DEARING, Ben Shobe, and Harry McAlpin—constantly challenged segregated institutions in the courts. The most famous suit was Lyman Johnson's successful one to gain admission to the University of Kentucky graduate school. But because of suits and threats of suits, barriers also fell at Louisville libraries, on the GOLF courses, in the parks, and at the University of Louisville. NAACP leader Dr. Maurice Rabb led struggles to open the doors of medical facilities that were closed to African Americans.

In 1950, after three young African Americans injured in an auto accident were denied admission to a Hardinsburg, Kentucky, hospital and one died on the waiting room floor, ten thousand people in Louisville signed petitions and two hundred marched in Frankfort. They eventually won a state law that said HOSPITALS could not be licensed if they denied emergency treatment to anyone. This battle was coordinated by the Interracial Hospital Movement, initiated by a Progressive Party activist, Mary Agnes Barnett, and supported by the Militant Church Movement. That organization was led by Rev. J.C. Olden and included other African American ministers who continued on the front lines of struggle into the 1960s such as Rev. M.M.D. Perdue, Rev. Daniel Hughlett, Rev. W.F. Owens, and Rev. J.V. Bottoms. In 1953 this group launched a Committee for Democratic Schools, which circulated a petition asking repeal of the state's entire school segregation law, got a bill to do so introduced in the legislature, and, in March 1954, packed a Frankfort hearing chamber with citizens who supported integrated schools—thus helping create the atmosphere that enabled Gov. LAWRENCE WETHERBY to announce in May 1954 that Kentucky would comply with the U.S. Supreme Court decision outlawing school segregation. Louisville schools began peaceful, although token, desegregation in 1956, but there was a decade of struggle before faculties were fully desegregated, and ultimately the number of black teachers declined.

The direct action that blossomed in the 1960s began in the 1950s. The Greyhound bus station was integrated in 1953 by a one-man sit-in staged by Rev. C. EWBANK TUCKER, an African American minister and militant lawyer who continued as a crusader throughout the fifties and sixties. The NAACP Youth Council integrated dime-store lunch counters in the late 1950s through unpublicized sit-ins. In 1959, the council picketed the Brown Theater on Broadway when it refused to admit African Americans to see *Porgy and Bess*. The demonstrations that grew to mass proportions in 1961 were started by a small group of young people who formed a chapter of the Congress of Racial Equality (CORE) and began regular stand-ins at downtown facilities in 1960. Sometimes there were only three demonstrators, but they continued week after week. On February 18, 1961, ten demonstrators were at a department store tearoom. Police arrested them; the next day there were seventy-five, then a hundred, then twice that. The demonstrations spread throughout the downtown, and the rest became history.

The momentum of the 1961 demonstrations fed into a continuing movement that turned its eyes toward Frankfort. Louisville African American leaders called on Gov. BERT COMBS to add state civil rights legislation to the agenda for a special session of the General Assembly that he was calling in 1963. He refused, saying that adding this controversial issue could disrupt the bipartisan unity he hoped to achieve to prevent the closing of United Mine Workers hospitals in Eastern Kentucky. Instead, he issued an executive order mandating all state agencies to use their licensing powers and economic and political clout to advance integration of public facilities throughout the state. That action brought him vehement criticism from both sides. Opponents accused him of infringing on privacy and property rights. Louisville civil rights leaders called the order a "hoax." They began organizing to put pressure on the 1964 General Assembly for a law, and eventually fifty organizations statewide joined in supporting the ten-thousand-strong March on Frankfort while the General Assembly was in session in March 1964.

This event was joined by many national personalities, including Dr. Martin Luther King Jr., Jackie Robinson, Rev. Ralph Abernathy, James Farmer of CORE, Rev. Wyatt Tee Walker, singer Mahalia Jackson, and comedian Dick Gregory. Throughout the following week, thirty-two young hunger strikers sat in the General Assembly gallery. Frank Stanley Jr., who had emerged as leader of Louisville's youth movement, said, "If Gandhi—one man—by fasting could move the British Empire, then thirty-two ought to have some effect on the legislative process in Kentucky."

The General Assembly adjourned that year without acting. However, pressure in both Louisville and across the state continued for the next two years, and the 1966 session passed Kentucky's basic civil rights law, barring discrimination in public accommodations and employment and giving enforcement power to the Kentucky Commission on Human Rights that had been established in 1960. It was the first such law in the south and one of the strongest in the nation. In 1968, the General Assembly adopted a Fair Housing Act, also a first in the South.

Several organizations cooperated to solidify the movements of the 1960s. The Open Housing Movement was led jointly by three of them—the NAACP, a local branch of the

Southern Christian Leadership Conference (SCLC), and the West End Community Council, which had carried on an unsuccessful effort to keep the city's West End racially integrated. Leadership was provided by the Reverend W.J. Hodge, an African American minister who later served as president of the Louisville Board of Aldermen; Rev. Leo Lesser, who went on to mount a serious campaign for mayor; Rev. A.D. King, pastor of Zion Baptist Church and brother of Dr. Martin Luther King Jr., who visited Louisville often in that period; and Hulbert James, a young black organizer who turned the West End Community Council into a broad human-rights action group.

In the mid-1960s, an interracial regional organization, the Southern Conference Educational Fund (SCEF), moved its headquarters to Louisville and bought two buildings in the 3200 block of W Broadway. One of them, an educational center, became a meeting place and rallying point for local activists in several organizations. Later this building was renamed the Carl Braden Memorial Center, honoring a controversial Louisville civil rights advocate who died in 1975. This center continued throughout the rest of the century as a staging ground for a series of human rights movements and organizations and became the home of the Kentucky Alliance against Racist and Political Repression, which was in the forefront of continuing struggles for full human rights during the last three decades of the century.

After 1967 the African American movement changed. Young blacks, disillusioned that the end of segregation had brought no real changes in their lives, turned to new organizations. At the University of Louisville, African American students seized the Administration Building, seeking attention for black studies, more scholarship aid, and assistance to blacks inadequately prepared for college—changes ultimately achieved. In the community, young African Americans formed BULK (Black Unity League of Kentucky), a chapter of JOMO (Junta of Militant Organizations, based in Florida), and a local chapter of the Black Panthers. BULK organized against continuing police abuse of black citizens. The Panthers launched a campaign to drive out the drug dealers, who were just beginning to invade the African American community.

These endeavors brought repression and some criminal charges. New movements among African Americans often were successful efforts to turn defensive battles against these attacks into new offensives. For example in 1968, about two months after the murder of Dr. Martin Luther King Jr., Louisville's worst racial violence of the century occurred in a week of turmoil that started at Twenty-eighth and Greenwood Streets during a protest against police mistreatment of a black citizen. Eyewitnesses said the outbreak was precipitated when police jumped out of their cars with guns drawn. In the wake of the turmoil, six African Americans were charged with conspiring to blow up oil refineries along the Ohio River. They became known as the Black Six, and many African Americans believed they were scapegoats for deep problems the white power structure did not want to face. There followed two years of demonstrations and mass turnouts for court hearings; at one point hundreds of marchers took over Fourth St. downtown, proceeded to the courthouse, climbed the statue of Thomas Jefferson that stands in front of that building, and raised a black flag. In 1970, a judge ordered the charges against the Black Six dismissed for lack of evidence.

Throughout the 1970s, actions developed around a variety of issues—for example, pressure on employers and unions for justice on the job. These struggles, similar to those begun in the 1950s by the Negro Labor Council, were coordinated by the Black Workers Coalition, led by Roosevelt Roberts, an African American worker at Louisville's Ford plant. There were also many community struggles—for example, one organized by a group called the Dirty Dozen Demolition Crew, led by an African American Catholic nun, Pat Haley; they occupied dangerous dilapidated buildings in Louisville's West End to dramatize demands for rehabilitation of their neighborhoods. SCLC, under the leadership of Rev. Charles Kirby, kept up a steady pace of protest against police practices and job discrimination.

In 1975, Louisville faced a major racial crisis. In a suit filed by the American Civil Liberties Union and the NAACP, a federal court ordered merger of Louisville and Jefferson County school systems and a massive busing program to desegregate public schools, which had maintained only token desegregation since the process began in 1956. Anti-busing whites mobilized rallies of ten thousand, and the Ku Klux Klan reappeared. Black parents—believing that better educational opportunity awaited them—took their children to dark corners in the early morning hours and put them on the buses, knowing that there might be rock-throwing mobs at the end of the bus ride, as there sometimes were. A new organization, the United Black Protective Parents (UBPP), was formed to protect the black students both outside and inside the schools, and also, they said, to look out for white children entering schools in the black community. On Martin Luther King's birthday in January 1976, forty organizations came together to organize a march of three thousand people in downtown Louisville supporting school desegregation; the theme was "Make Real the Dream."

After two years, the hysteria over busing subsided, and the yellow buses rumbling through the streets became an accepted part of the Louisville scene. But black students encountered pronounced discrimination inside some of the schools, and UBPP continued to work as their advocate throughout the 1970s. The struggle for real equity in education went on for the next two decades and was still a major issue as the twentieth century drew to a close.

The reappearance of the Klan and other violent racist groups sparked continuing struggles by African Americans in the 1970s and 1980s, often campaigns to support black families who were harassed when they moved to white areas. One major victory of the 1980s came when the city administration finally settled a lawsuit that had been filed fourteen years earlier by the Louisville Black Police Officers Organization on behalf of ninety-one blacks who claimed they had been denied jobs and promotions by the police department. That settlement came after Rev. Louis Coleman, who emerged as a late-century spokesperson for human rights, threatened demonstrations during Derby Week—a tactic protesters had used several times since it was first tried during the Open Housing Movement. It was especially effective in the police case, since, at that time, the city was involved in an intensive (and ultimately successful) lobbying campaign to persuade the Presbyterian Church (USA) to move its headquarters to Louisville.

Some of the major struggles of African Americans in the late twentieth century came in the electoral arena. The ferment of the 1950s and 1960s propelled an increasing number of African Americans into public office. In 1958, Woodford Porter Sr. became the first black elected to the Louisville Board of Education. In 1961, Amelia Tucker, wife of Bishop C. Ewbank Tucker and a leader in her own right, became the first African American woman to serve in the General Assembly. She was followed in the late 1960s by Louisville state senator Georgia Powers and representative Mae Street Kidd, who led major human rights battles from their Frankfort base for twenty years. In the late 1960s and early 1970s, Lois Morris organized community campaigns from the vantage point of a seat on the Louisville Board of Aldermen.

In 1981, a small group of African American leaders came together to form PAC 10, a political action committee designed to organize the black vote, raise funds for election campaigns, and put its own candidates in office. The committee was the brainchild of Joe Hammond, a businessman and firm supporter of human rights who wielded major political power behind the scenes for several decades and whose Joe's Palm Room in the West End became a center of both political and social activity in the African American community. Among the most visible and steadfast leaders of PAC 10 were Dr. Joe McMillan, then a vice president of the University of Louisville, and real estate agent Frank Clay Jr. The committee worked with great skill to maximize the power of the black vote, which was still only a minority in the community. One of its most notable successes was in spearheading the campaigns that defeated proposed merger of city and county government, a step that many African Americans believed would strip them of political leverage. In this effort, African Americans united with some of their former foes in the anti-busing movement in predominantly white southwest Jefferson County. Meantime, PAC 10 began to put some of its own candidates on the Louisville Board of Aldermen and played a key role in the 1983 campaign that elected African American attorney Darryl Owens to represent the predominantly white C District on the JEFFERSON COUNTY FISCAL COURT, a post he continued to hold at the end of the century. PAC 10 also nurtured other African Americans who were later elected to city, county, and state office, including attorney Gerald Neal, who was a leader of the U of L student movement in the late 1960s and went on to begin a distinguished tenure in the state senate in 1988.

By the mid-1980s, however, PAC 10 began to fall apart, partly because some of its activists faded into the scenery of traditional political circles and, in the opinion of some observers, repression in the form of economic and political pressure was applied to others. Meantime, however, the committee's work provided local motor power for the two presidential campaigns of Rev. Jesse Jackson, which became more a people's movement than election campaigns, as Jackson carried the Third Congressional District twice, in a caucus system in 1984 and in a primary election in 1988.

In the 1990s, the major focus of civil rights activity in Louisville was the issue of economic justice, which here as throughout the country was the unfinished part of the civil rights revolution. In 1995, a coalition of people from fifty organizations who came together to defend affirmative action in Louisville publicized a census figure that revealed that median family income of African Americans in the Louisville area was just 43 percent of white. Fired by this dramatic disparity and the alarming phenomenon of jails and prisons bulging to overflowing with African American youth, the high unemployment rates among African Americans, and the sense of hopelessness that seemed to grip many young people and lure them into the drug culture, African American activists organized campaigns to win training, jobs, and opportunity, as well as better health care, education, and housing. A series of demonstrations that sometimes brought arrests, usually led by Rev. Louis Coleman, demanded not only more and better jobs for African Americans but contracts for African American companies in Louisville's booming construction upsurge. By the end of the decade, these campaigns were beginning to bring some results.

Throughout the long struggle of African Americans for equity in Louisville, there was always some activist white support. In general, white relationships to African Americans in Louisville have been characterized by paternalism and what historian George Wright called "polite racism." But some whites were on the front lines. Two white lawyers helped with legal action against the streetcar companies in 1870; a white man was key to the battle against the residential segregation ordinance in 1914. Some whites were active in all the campaigns that followed WORLD WAR II, and many were part of the Interracial Hospital Movement in the early 1950s, two of them joining African Americans in leadership roles—Rev. Albert Dalton, an Episcopal minister, and Allen Coones, a leader of the International Harvester union. White members of the Unitarian Social Action Committee joined the NAACP Youth Council on the Brown Theater picket lines in 1959. Two white students, Birdie McHugh and Lynn Pfuhl, were part of the original group that launched the downtown stand-ins in the 1960s. In the Open Housing Movement, 20 percent of the nightly demonstrators were white. In the 1950s and 1960s, Louisville state representatives THELMA STOVALL and Norbert Blume were staunch white allies in the General Assembly. Rev. Olof Anderson and BELLARMINE COLLEGE dean John Loftus were among white religious leaders who were on the front lines, and a Louisville Council on Religion and Race mobilized in white churches in support of the 1960s and 1970s civil rights struggles. In the mid-1970s, whites formed an organization, Progress in Education, to join black parents in countering terror imposed by the anti-busing movement; they organized a march of a thousand white supporters of desegregated schools. Rev. Charles Tachau, a white Episcopal minister, and his brother Eric Tachau both played consistent roles in civil rights struggles over several decades—the former as a community activist in the West End and the latter seeking to build support in the broader Louisville white community. In the 1980s, a significant number of whites were active in the Jesse Jackson campaigns, and some were on the picket lines for economic justice in the 1990s.

In the last two decades of the twentieth century, a new and different civil rights campaign developed, organized by LESBIANS and GAYS seeking full human rights and legal protections. Through fifteen years of patient educational work, they changed the minds of multitudes of citizens and won legislation in both city and county government barring discrimination on the basis of sexual orientation. Efforts of their opponents to divide the mostly white lesbian and gay Fairness Campaign from the African American community were countered by an independent poll that showed that 70 percent of African Americans favored such legislation. And the predominantly African American Kentucky Alliance, taking the position that "freedom is indivisible," worked effectively to build bridges between white lesbian and gay activists and black organizations. The lesbian and gay movement also produced a new army of active white supporters for anti-racist work, as the Fairness Campaign convinced its members that the struggle against racism was their battle too. This development resulted mainly from the dedicated work of Carla Wallace and Pam McMichael, two white Fairness leaders who had been active in anti-racist crusades long before they began organizing for lesbian and gay rights.

Throughout their long history of struggle, Louisville African Americans always welcomed the active support of white allies. But none of the civil rights campaigns of the nineteenth and twentieth centuries would have developed without the initiatives by African Americans, and they were always firmly in leadership. Whites who joined these movements recognized that leadership and respected it.

By the 1990s, a substantial black middle class had developed in Louisville. But for the majority of black citizens, the justice promised by the civil rights movement still remained illusory. Responding to this contradiction, in mid-decade County Commissioner Darryl Owens convened a broad array of African American citizens who formed an African American Strategic Planning Group, which developed a detailed plan designed to bring equity to African Americans in economics, education, and health care by the year 2010.

See George C. Wright, *Life Behind a Veil: Blacks in Louisville, Kentucky, 1865–1930* (Baton Rouge 1985); idem, *A History of Blacks in Kentucky, Volume 2, In Pursuit of Equality, 1890–1980* (Frankfort 1992); John Benjamin Horton, *Not without Struggle* (New York 1979); Wade Hall, *The Rest of the Dream: The Black Odyssey of Lyman Johnson* (Lexington 1988); Georgia Powers, *I Shared the Dream: The Pride, Passion and Politics of the First Black Woman Senator from Kentucky* (Far Hills, N.J., 1995); *Kentucky's Black Heritage: The Role of the Black People in the History of Kentucky from Pioneer Days to the Present,* Kentucky Commission on Human Rights (Frankfort 1971); *Lessons of Louisville; A White Community Response to Black Rebellion,* Southern Conference Educational Fund, (Louisville 1971); *Salute to the 1970s: A Decade of Struggle,* Kentucky Alliance against Racist and Political Repression (Louisville 1980); Richard R. Bernier, "White Activists and Support in the Louisville, Kentucky, Open Housing Movement, 1962–67," M.A. thesis, University of Louisville, 1998; *The Southern Patriot,* 1942–1973.

Anne Braden

CIVIL WAR. In 1861 Louisville was a neutral city in the only officially declared neutral state in the United States. Kentucky was the cradle of both President Abraham Lincoln of the United States and the president of the Confederacy, Jefferson Davis. Kentucky was a border state poised strategically between the lion of the northern states and the tiger of the southern states below the Mason-Dixon line. President Lincoln wrote his friend Orville H. Browning his view of the importance of Kentucky in maintaining the fragile Union: "I think to lose Kentucky is nearly the same as to lose the whole game. Kentucky gone, we can not hold Missouri, nor, as I think, Maryland. These all against us, and the job against us is too large

Encampment of the Kentucky State Guard at the agricultural fairgrounds on Frankfort Avenue in Crescent Hill, 1860.

for us" (Washington, September 22, 1861).

Louisville was a jewel in the western crown and a bustling mercantile and industrial mecca by 1861. Sturdy, burly, and bibulous wharfmen loaded and unloaded STEAMBOATS making regular runs north to Cincinnati and south to Nashville and New Orleans. Louisville had a growing ECONOMY. Wholesale grocers earned $12 million in annual profits, and dry goods firms and drug wholesalers did almost as well. In the West, Louisville was second only to Cincinnati in the production of pork products. The burgeoning city at the FALLS OF THE OHIO was famed for its burley TOBACCO markets. The Dennis Long Co. could boast of being the largest CAST-IRON pipe foundry in the West. Farm implements were manufactured in huge quantities. Fifteen thousand plows were made and sold by one firm in the immediate prewar period. Almost 10 percent of the POPULATION was involved in manufacturing and industry. The 1860 United States census listed the population of 68,033 as being made up of whites (61,213), slaves of African descent (4,903), and freed blacks (1,917). There were five hundred retail groceries, six public markets, eighty-seven BANKING firms, two hundred taverns or coffee houses, and four HOSPITALS. Louisville was the largest city in Kentucky and took civic pride in being the twelfth-largest city in the republic. By the end of the war in 1865, Louisville's population had risen to eighty thousand.

The political scene in Louisville during the period was volatile. Voters cast ballots in overwhelming numbers for pro-Union, anti-abolitionist John Bell of the Constitutional Union Party in the 1860 presidential election. By voting for Bell, Louisvillians showed their opposition to Lincoln's Republican position against the expansion of SLAVERY into territories and Kentuckian John C. Breckinridge's bid for the presidency as a candidate of the pro-slavery Democrats.

From 1850 to 1860 the number of slaves in Louisville decreased by 10 percent to 4,903, which was less than 10 percent of the city's population. Another contributing factor was the influx of immigrants to the city, namely IRISH, who sometimes competed with slaves for work. Slavery was dying a natural death in this urban area where it was unprofitable for slave owners.

The legendary editor GEORGE PRENTICE and his *LOUISVILLE DAILY JOURNAL* were strongly Union in sentiment, while WALTER N. HALDEMAN'S *LOUISVILLE MORNING COURIER* favored the Confederacy. Haldeman's paper was banned in September 1861, though it continued to be printed at various sites in the Confederacy. The majority of those who favored the Confederacy in Louisville came from the wealthy and professional classes. Their cause had difficulty in Louisville, which, as an industrial and commercial metropolis, was unsympathetic to the plantation aristocracy to be found in Dixie.

That Louisville was a Union city was manifested on February 21, 1861, when a huge American flag was raised to the top of the county courthouse. Louisville evinced a naive belief in the viability of Kentucky's neutrality policy promulgated by both houses of the General Assembly and the governor in May 1861. Kentucky and Louisville saw the end of neutrality when on September 13, 1861, the legislature demanded that all Confederate forces withdraw from the state, without demanding that Union forces leave. This followed the invasion of western Kentucky by both sides. Elections to the Kentucky House and Senate that year resulted in the selection of strongly pro-Union candidates opposed to pro-southern governor Beriah Magoffin, who resigned his post on August 28, 1862, and was succeeded by openly pro-Union James F. Robinson. JOHN M. DELPH, elected MAYOR in April 1861 on a neutrality platform, eventually became noted as a strong Union leader. Confederate sentiment in Louisville was not, however, without defenders. On April 20, 1861, two companies of Confederate volunteers left for New Orleans.

On June 24, 1861, the surveyor of the port of Louisville ordered that permits must be granted by his office for anyone wishing to do business with the South. This pro-Union action was meant to prevent traffic to the Confederacy. The order was opposed by many warehouse owners and merchants loyal to the Confederacy. Merchants Michael Brady and David Davis sought an injunction against this order. Judge George P. Muir heard the case and ruled that the federal government had a right to stop any traffic not deemed appropriate.

RAILROADS played a crucial role in Civil War battles, campaigns, and strategy. Without access to reliable rail transportation, the Northern victory would have been difficult to achieve.

The president of the L&N from 1860 to 1868 was JAMES GUTHRIE, a former secretary of the United States Treasury under the administration of President Franklin Pierce (1853–57). Guthrie was a staunch Union supporter who once declared, "I hate that word 'secession' because it is a cheat!"

As the war progressed, Louisville became the great Union supply base in the Western theater. Trains unloaded their materials in JEFFERSONVILLE, INDIANA, and they were transported across the OHIO RIVER to the Louisville wharf, where a track was built to connect to the L&N. The L&N made a profit of $6 million during the war. Despite raids on the railroad by Confederate raiders such as John Hunt Morgan and raids during Bragg's 1862 Kentucky campaign, the L&N functioned well during the war. It is doubtful if Sherman would have been successful in his Atlanta and march-to-the-sea expeditions without the L&N.

Well over a hundred thousand Union soldiers (many of them from the Army of the Cumberland) passed through Louisville during the war, and thousands more returning home after the war. On April 23, 1861, the Louisville City Council appropriated fifty thousand dollars to defend the city against attacks by Confederates. More than a year later eleven major earthen breastwork forts were built in a semicircle around the city from Paddy's Run to CLIFTON and on to Brownsboro Rd.

On October 16, 1861, Gen. William Tecumseh Sherman and other military and political figures met with Simon Cameron, the United States secretary of war, to discuss the conduct of military operations in Kentucky. Sherman would later be replaced by Gen. DON CARLOS BUELL, whose forces would oppose Braxton Bragg in the 1862 Confederate invasion of Kentucky. A contemporary report stated: "between Lincoln's election and his inauguration military companies raised for the South could be seen marching down one side of the street while Federal volunteers marched up the other" (*Southern Bivouac*, December 1882, 159).

In July 1861, Col. LOVELL H. ROUSSEAU opened a recruiting camp (Camp Joe HOLT) just west of Jeffersonville, Indiana, to recruit Kentuckians for the Union army. By early September, over two thousand men, mostly from Louisville, had enlisted there. Rousseau was a Louisville attorney and MEXICAN WAR veteran, and he initially led Louisville's Home Guards (militia). Colonel Rousseau commanded the famous LOUISVILLE LEGION (Fifth Kentucky Volunteer Infantry Regiment U.S.), which he organized at Camp Joe Holt. He became a brigadier general and then major general. Union historian Capt. Thomas Speed estimated that over six thousand men from Louisville served in the Union army. The city furnished over four hundred officers to the Union army. Accurate information is not available on how many Louisvillians served in the Confederate army.

A Confederate force under Gen. Simon Bolivar Buckner occupied Munfordville in September 1861, causing many Louisvillians to fear invasion. Mayor Delph and Generals Sherman and Rousseau reacted promptly to Buckner's threat. A Union force moved toward Lebanon Junction to clash with Buckner, only to discover that the Confederates had not planned to attack Louisville. Buckner had only sent a skirmishing force to destroy the L&N bridge over the Rolling Fork River.

Soon after this scare the cornucopia of Union military might began to pour into Louisville. Troops from as far away as Pennsylvania and Wisconsin arrived, along with men from Indiana and Ohio, as well as pro-Union troops from Kentucky. Besides bivouacking at the old OAKLAND racetrack (near Seventh and Magnolia Streets), many troops were quartered in today's OLD LOUISVILLE neighborhood. Training grounds were established in the PORTLAND area, at Eighteenth and BROADWAY, and along the Frankfort and Bardstown turnpikes. Louisville's economy received a shot in the arm from this quartering of such a huge Yankee army. Sometimes there was friction between soldiers and civilians due to drinking, GAMBLING, political arguments, and incidents of violence. PROSTITUTION was widespread.

Louisville was a city of HOSPITALS for the troops. Between September 1861 and June 1862, 930 soldiers died in the city's hospitals, and thousands more died in these hospitals as the war continued. Both Union and Confederate wounded would eventually be treated in the nineteen military hospitals established by 1863. A portion of CAVE HILL CEMETERY was designated in 1861 as a national cemetery for the Union dead. This action prompted Confederate supporters to purchase adjacent land for their fallen soldiers.

On September 17, 1862, Louisville began fortifying for an expected invasion by Gen. E. Kirby Smith's and Gen. Braxton Bragg's rebel forces. On September 25 General Buell's Union army beat Confederate general Bragg in the race to Louisville. It was from Louisville that Buell would launch his legions against Bragg. On October 8, 1862, Bragg would begin his retreat from Buell and Kentucky following the key battle of Perryville. Following the battle, Louisville mourned many of her native sons. Louisville's hospitals cared for both Confederate and Union troops transported from Perryville's bloody fields. The city also provided prison space for Confederates taken captive. The largest, with the capacity for three hundred prisoners, was located at Tenth and Broadway. Food became scarce and prices soared due to the need to feed many soldiers, prisoners, and civilians.

When the Emancipation Proclamation became law on January 1, 1863, many Louisvillians were angry and voiced opposition to Lincoln's government. (Lincoln would lose the presidential vote in Louisville to Gen. George McClellan in November 1864.) Secret FRATERNAL groups sprang up in the city with connections to the Copperhead movement in Ohio and Indiana. These groups opposed emancipation of slaves and were hostile to the Lincoln administration.

The Knights of the Golden Circle organized into chapters called "castles" and actively opposed the federal authority. Members were urged to resist the draft, engage in spying for the Confederacy, circulate anti-Lincoln printed material, cooperate with the enemy in raiding activities, and attack black troops in Louisville.

Gen. Jeremiah T. Boyle, since May 31, 1862, the military commandant of Kentucky, was headquartered in Louisville. This native Kentuckian's greatest military crisis came in July 1863 when John Hunt Morgan invaded Kentucky on his famed Indiana and Ohio raid. Fortunately for Boyle and Louisville Unionists, Morgan did not attack the city but instead moved westward, crossing the Ohio River at Brandenburg. The closest Morgan's men came to battle in Louisville occurred on July 11, 1863. About a hundred rebel troops tried to cross the Ohio River at Twelve Mile Island above the city but were repelled by the gunboat *Moose*.

Boyle was relieved of command on January 12, 1864; and on February 15, 1864, Gen. Stephen Burbridge succeeded Gen. Jacob Ammen (who served only one month) as commander of the military district of Kentucky. Burbridge was quite unpopular because of such actions as refusal of trade permits for southern-sympathizing businessmen, interference with the electoral process, gaining jobs for his friends and political cronies, arresting "perceived" enemies on slight evidence, and brutal suppression of guerrilla activities. (The most famous wartime execution of a guerrilla in Louisville occurred on March 15, 1865, when the notorious MARCELLUS JEROME CLARKE, alias "Sue Mundy," was hanged.)

Louisville had become a meeting place for high officers in federal service. On March 9, 1864, Generals Grant and Sherman met in the GALT HOUSE to plan the final campaigns of the war. The Galt House had won fame when, prior to the Perryville Campaign, Gen. Jefferson C. Davis had murdered Gen. WILLIAM "BULL" NELSON there on September 29, 1862.

Louisville was in a depressed condition as the war wound down. The economy was in shambles, and beggars wearily trod the city's streets. The city had moved from neutrality to Union advocacy to a dissatisfaction with the federal government. This change in attitude was due to war-weariness, the behavior of the Union soldiers stationed in the city, and the emancipation of slaves in those states in rebellion. In the years ahead Louisville would be a city with very strong pro-southern political views.

In many ways the war had not been kind to Louisville. No street or wharf repairs had occurred during the war. The city was in need of a facelift as building had been halted, PAINT peeled on businesses, and despair's virus dampened the city's businesses. Southern trade carried on rolling stock was restricted. No capital improvements occurred in Louisville during the war.

Mayor WILLIAM KAYE, elected in November 1863, set aside April 14, 1865, as an official day to celebrate the Union victory. On April 15, 1865, flags were flown at half-staff as the city and nation mourned the assassination of President Lincoln. The long trauma of the Civil War and Louisville's exciting and convoluted role in the struggle was over.

See Robert Emmett McDowell, *City of Conflict: Louisville in the Civil War 1861–1865* (Louisville 1962); Lowell H. Harrison and James C. Klotter, *A New History of Kentucky* (Lexington 1997); Lowell H. Harrison, *The Civil War in Kentucky* (Lexington 1975); George H. Yater, *Two Hundred Years at the Falls of the Ohio* (Louisville 1987); William McCready, "Louisville during the War" (Wilmington, N.C., 1992, a reprint of the original issue of *Southern Bivouac,* Louisville 1882); James A. Ramage, *Rebel Raider: The Life of General John Hunt Morgan* (Lexington 1986).

Charles Michael Mills

CIVIL WAR FORTIFICATIONS. In the summer of 1862 the Confederacy launched a bold offensive. Its armies were on the move in both the eastern and western theaters of the war. Kentucky was invaded by two armies. One came through the Cumberland Gap, and the second, larger force moved north from Tennessee through the central part of the state. A Union army raced to Louisville to head off the Confederate advances.

In Louisville, a former navy officer, Gen. WILLIAM "BULL" NELSON, ordered the construction of a defensive perimeter. In addition he had pontoon bridges constructed in the event of a Confederate siege, to insure that supplies from the north could reach the defenders from across the Ohio River or to facilitate their withdrawal if necessary. The southern forces never made it to Louisville. Their armies were stopped at Perryville in October 1862, forcing the Confederate troops to retreat back to Tennessee.

But the scare generated by the Confederate threat to the city caused federal authorities to take action to prepare Louisville in case the Confederates ever returned. The task of insuring the safety of the city and other strategic points in the Ohio Valley fell to Col. James H. Simpson, the chief engineer for the Department of the Ohio. Simpson assigned the actual construction of the fortifications to a civilian engineer, John R. Gilliss.

After an examination of the defensive works constructed by General Nelson, it was determined that they had been built too near the center of the city to be an effective deterrent to enemy artillery fire. Consequently, Gilliss had to begin from scratch. Construction began sometime in early 1863. It proceeded very slowly until the fall of 1864, when a Confederate army was once again moving north, this time toward Nashville. The Confederate threat was crushed in Tennessee, but the fortifications of Louisville were undertaken in earnest. By mid-October Gilliss reported that he had almost completed one fort and that construction was well under way on four others. He had at his disposal a labor force of some 450, including 30 prisoners sentenced to work on the fortifications.

The engineer's plans for the defensive works at Louisville were grand. They called for a line of eleven forts and twelve batteries stretching over a ten-and-one-quarter-mile arc around the city. The line anchored on the east at the Beargrass Creek cutoff and on the west at the mouth of Upper Paddy's Run. The forts were to mount four to six guns and have a minimum complement of 250 soldiers (200 infantry and 50 artillery). The forts or redoubts were to be 550 to 700 feet in length, with the smaller batteries placed between them. The walls of the forts were six to seven feet high and fifteen to thirty feet thick. Each was to have a magazine that could hold two hundred rounds for each gun. The batteries were to be similar but without magazines. The batteries were to be manned by a mobile force of field artillery and infantry that would move where it was needed in the event of an attack.

Fort McPherson was the exception. This fort was twice as large as the others; it was designed to be manned by five hundred infantry and one hundred artillery. It held a huge Parrott gun capable of firing a hundred-pound shell five miles. This fort was constructed to house government stores or other property in case of a raid or other attack. It was located south of the old city limits above Dry Run between the Shepherdsville Turnpike and the Louisville & Nashville Railroad.

The eleven forts were named after fallen Union officers, mostly from the Army of the Ohio and were:

Fort Elstner—named after Lt. Col. George R. Elstner, Fiftieth Ohio Infantry, who was killed in action near Utoy Creek, Georgia, August 8, 1864. It was located at approximately what is today Bellaire Ave., Vernon Ave., and Emerald Ave. between Frankfort Ave. and Brownsboro Rd., and anchored the defenses on the upper side of the city close to where the Beargrass Creek cutoff emptied into the river.

Fort Engle named after Capt. Archibald H. Engle, an aide-de-camp to the staff of Major General Schofield and member of the Thirteenth U.S. Infantry, killed in battle at Resaca, Georgia, May 14, 1864. The fort was located at what is now Spring St. and Arlington Ave., commanding at that time the Louisville and Lexington Railroad.

Fort Saunders—named after Capt. E.D. Saunders of the A.A.G. Volunteers, killed in action at Dallas, Georgia, June 2, 1864. Its site was on property since taken in by Cave Hill Cemetery.

Fort Hill—named after Capt. George W. Hill, Twelfth Kentucky Infantry, killed in action at Atlanta, Georgia, August 6, 1864. It was located on the hillside between Goddard Ave. and the St. Louis Cemetery above Barret Ave., commanding the Newburg Rd. The section of Newburg Rd. lying directly south of and in front of the fort is now Castlewood Ave.

Fort Horton—named after Capt. M.C. Horton, 104th Ohio Infantry, killed in action at Dallas, Georgia, May 28, 1864. It was situated at the approximate confluence of Shelby

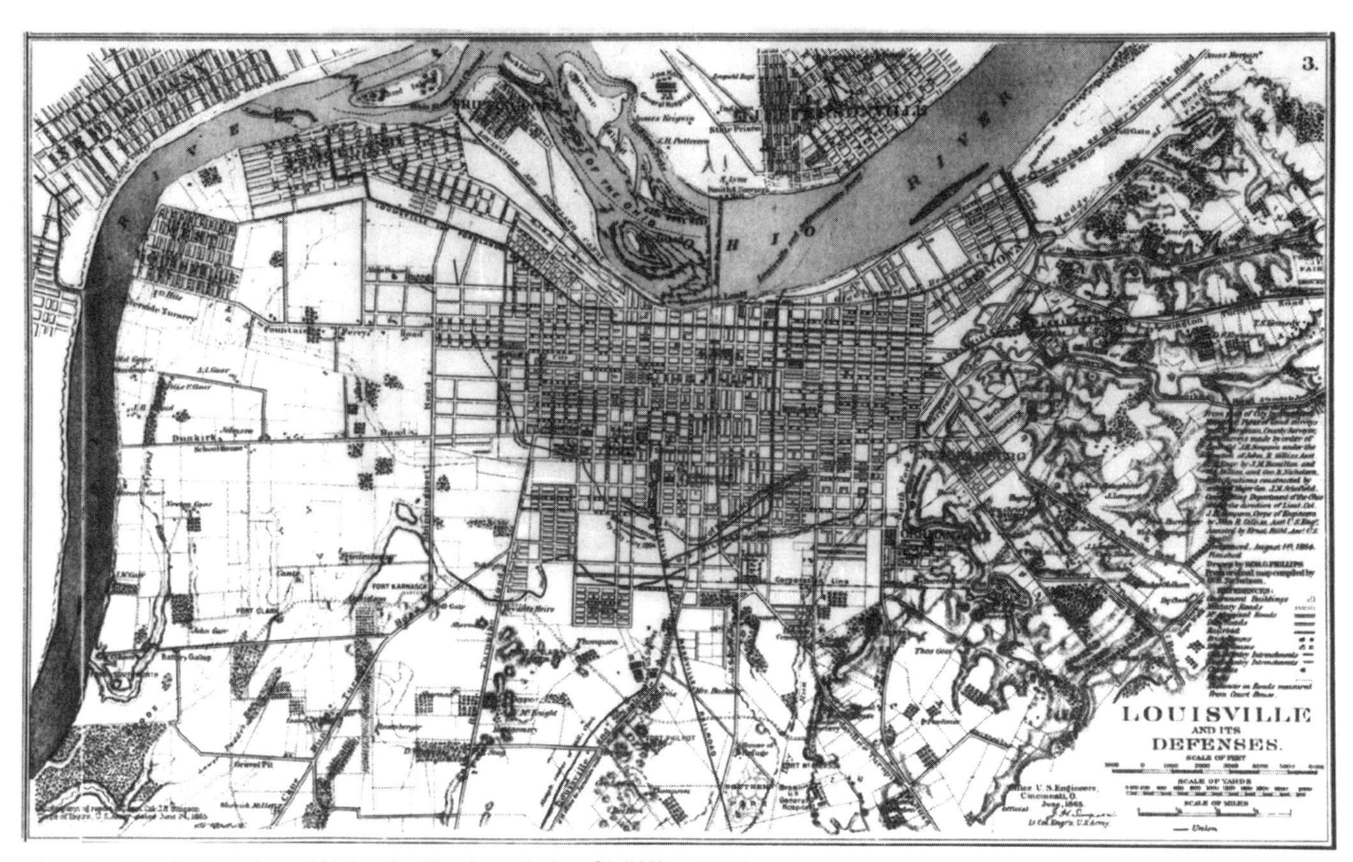

Map showing the location of Union fortifications during Civil War, 1865.

St. and Meriwether St.

Fort McPherson—this was the largest of the forts and sixth from the left in the ring of the city. It was named after Maj. Gen. James B. McPherson, who fell July 22, 1864, in fighting at Atlanta, Georgia. The fort was located just west of PRESTON ST. in the area bounded by Barbee, Brandeis, Hahn, and Fort Streets. This fort held the angle of the defense line and thus held eleven guns with a contingent of five hundred infantrymen and one hundred artillerymen.

Fort Philpot—named for Capt. J.D. Philpot, 103rd Ohio Infantry, killed in the battle of Resaca, Georgia, May 14, 1864. It was just east of Seventh Street Rd., then known as the LOUISVILLE AND NASHVILLE TURNPIKE Rd., and north of where Algonquin Pkwy. now crosses.

Fort Saint Clair Morton—named for Maj. James St. Clair Morton of the Corps of Engineers, who was killed June 17, 1864, during an assault on Petersburg, Virginia. It was built on a rise at what is now Sixteenth St. and Hill St. and commanded the SALT RIVER Turnpike Rd., now DIXIE HWY.

Fort Karnasch—named for 2d Lt. Julius E. Karnasch of the Thirty-Fifth Missouri Infantry, who was killed in action at Atlanta, Georgia, August 4, 1864. Fort Karnasch was located at what is now Wilson Ave. between Twenty-sixth and Twenty-eighth Streets but was then the junction of the SHIPPINGPORT Rd. and the Cane Run Turnpike Rd.

Fort Clark—named for Lt. Col. Merwin Clark, 183rd Ohio Infantry, killed in action in the Battle of Franklin, Tennessee, November 30, 1864. It stood at approximately Thirty-sixth St. and Magnolia St.

Fort Southworth—the most westerly of the forts, it was named for Capt. A.J. Southworth, killed August 16, 1864, at Atlanta. It was located on the north side of a bend of Upper Paddy's Run at about a quarter of a mile from the Ohio River below the city.

Of the proposed batteries, only two were completed, and they were:

Battery Camp—located between Fort Saunders and Fort Hill, it was named after Capt. Edgar Camp of the 107th Illinois Infantry who was killed at the Battle of Lost Mountain, Georgia. The battery was situated at what is now Baxter Ave. and Rufer Ave.

Battery Gallup—located between Fort Clark and Fort Southworth, it was named after Capt. A.G. Gallup of the Thirteenth Kentucky Infantry, who fell September 1, 1864, in action near Lovejoy's Station, Georgia. It was located on Gibson's Ln. at what is now Western Pkwy., at least part of it being on the old State Fairgrounds.

It is unlikely that the fortifications of the city were ever completed. A report of March 31, 1865, noted that the eleven named forts were mostly finished, but only two of the twelve batteries had been built. Of the forty-four to sixty-six guns that the forts were designed to house, only twenty-two had actually been placed in the fortifications. Federal authorities halted all construction on unfinished fortifications on May 1, 1865.

See Leland R. Johnson, *The Falls City Engineers: A History of the Louisville Corps of Engineers United States Army*, (Louisville 1974); *War of the Rebellion: A Compilation of the Official Records of the Union and Confederate Armies*, 129 vols. (Washington, D.C., 1880–1901); series 1, vol. 45, Part I Correspondence, Etc., Serial No. 9; series 1, vol. 49, Part I, Reports, Correspondence, Etc. Serial No. 103; and series 1, vol. 49, Part II, Correspondence, Etc. Serial No. 104; Robert E. McDowell, *City in Conflict: Louisville in the Civil War, 1861–1865* (Louisville 1962).

Joseph E. Brent

CLARK, GEORGE ROGERS (b near Charlottesville, Albemarle County, Virginia, November 19, 1752; d Jefferson County, February 13, 1818). Soldier and founder of Louisville. He was the second son and second-oldest of ten children of John and Ann (Rogers) Clark. While he was still a small child, the family moved from the Virginia frontier eastward to a plantation bequeathed to his father by an uncle in the southwestern corner of Caroline County, Virginia. It was here that Clark grew up. He attended the academy of well-known Virginia educator Donald Robertson in King and Queen County. Clark did best in mathematics, geography, history, and natural history. He then was tutored informally by family friend George Mason. Seeing an opportunity in surveying and being drawn to the frontier and wilderness, Clark in 1772 began exploring and surveying land on the OHIO RIVER as far downstream as the mouth of the Kanawha. The following year he returned to the Ohio, surveyed in the area of Fish Creek, 130 miles below Pittsburgh, and then explored down the river another 170 miles. That winter, instead of returning home as he had done the year before, he and a companion spent the winter on Fish Creek, improving his claim and surveying.

In 1774 Clark's life took a turn that forever changed it. Clark became actively engaged in military operations and made his first trip to Kentucky. Friction with the American Indian tribes of the area increased as the tide of white settlement pushed westward. Clark served in Cresap's War, McDonald's expedition against the Shawnee, and Lord Dunmore's War that year. He was commissioned a militia captain during Lord Dunmore's War. After the end of the war, Clark went to Kentucky and surveyed land along the Kentucky River for the Ohio Co. He returned the next year to survey but soon became active in the politics of the infant settlements. Clark quickly became one of the leaders of the pioneers. He was elected a delegate to go to Williamsburg, Virginia, to seek the creation of a new county called Kentucky from Fincastle County, and government assistance for the beleaguered forts. Clark succeeded in his mission. Kentucky County was created on December 31, 1776, and he returned with five hundred pounds of gunpowder to help with the defense of the settlements against Indian attack. He also was promoted to major in the Virginia militia and given command of the Kentucky militia.

The Revolutionary War was not going well for the Americans, and Clark saw an opportunity not only for a stunning victory to bolster the young country but also to gain immense territory for it. In 1777 he traveled to Williamsburg and met again with Virginia governor Patrick Henry and gained his support for an expedition against the British posts in the Illinois country. Promoted to lieutenant colonel in the Virginia militia, Clark began recruiting at Pittsburgh. He was disappointed in his efforts, raising only some 175 of a planned 350 men, but he was undaunted and set off down the Ohio River with his men and a group of settlers. The little flotilla reached the FALLS OF THE OHIO in late May 1778, possibly May 27, and built a fort on CORN ISLAND. This settlement became Louisville, and Clark the city's acknowledged founder. On June 24, Clark and his men left the Falls, sailed downriver to the ruins of Fort Massac in the Illinois country, and then traveled overland to Kaskaskia, which capitulated on July 4. Two days later Cahokia surrendered to Capt. Joseph Bowman. Vincennes, on hearing the news of Kaskaskia and Cahokia falling to the Americans and of America's alliance with France, voluntarily changed allegiance to the United States. Capt. Leonard Helm and one soldier took possession of the post for Virginia.

Using intelligence, daring, persuasion, psychology, and the new Franco-American alliance, Clark had seized the Illinois Territory for the United States and won the support of the French inhabitants. He then had to try to maintain possession of the posts against British counterattack. That attack was soon in coming. Upon hearing word of the posts' capture, Col. Henry Hamilton, lieutenant governor of Canada, set out from Detroit with a force to retake them and invade Kentucky. Vincennes fell to Hamilton in December 1778, and he decided to wait until spring before continuing his campaign. Clark, meanwhile, decided to attack Hamilton. Leaving Kaskaskia on February 5, 1779, Clark and his force of some 130 men (including 60 French) marched overland through often-flooded prairies. They surprised the British force at Fort Sackville in Vincennes, and after a short siege Hamilton surrendered on February 25. The way to Clark's main goal, Detroit, now lay open, but he was frustrated in pursuing it because of a lack of support from the Virginia government and Kentucky settlements. He also was heavily in debt, having pledged his own credit to prosecute the campaign, believing he would he reimbursed by

Virginia. Clark's victory in his Illinois campaign was the high point of his career and earned him the sobriquets "Hannibal of the West" and "Conqueror of the Northwest." It is one of the most daring and brilliant campaigns in American military history.

Returning to Kentucky, Clark led a force to the confluence of the Ohio and Mississippi Rivers in the spring of 1780. He began construction of the short-lived Fort Jefferson a short distance to the south of the confluence, near the mouth of Mayfield Creek. While this effort failed because of its isolation and lack of support, Clark and his men did succeed in possibly saving the Louisiana territory for Spain. That country also had gone to war with Great Britain, and St. Louis (and Cahokia) were being threatened by a force of British and Indians. Clark and his men helped turn back the attack. Clark then returned to Kentucky, which was under even more serious attack by the British and their Indian allies. He pursued a force of Shawnee and British across the Ohio and destroyed some of the Indians' towns and crops. On January 22, 1781, he was promoted to brigadier general. Clark maintained his headquarters at Louisville and had FORT NELSON built to bolster its defense. A planned campaign against Detroit failed to take place because of a lack of support from Kentucky counties. In the summer of 1782, the British and Indians invaded Kentucky yet again and dealt the Kentuckians a severe defeat at Blue Licks. Clark was asked to lead another campaign against the Shawnee towns in Ohio to try to end this threat to Kentucky's settlements. Under Clark's leadership the campaign destroyed Shawnee towns and crops. This ended the threat of further significant Shawnee invasions.

The official end of the Revolutionary War in 1783, with the Treaty of Paris and the ceding of the Northwest Territory to the United States, should have been a time of triumph and praise for Clark. Instead his reputation and fortunes began to decline. Clark had received more than eighteen thousand acres of land for his Revolutionary War service and more than two thousand pounds sterling in back pay for five years' service, but his debts incurred in supporting his western military campaigns exceeded twenty thousand dollars. The Virginia government refused to pay most of his claims; and he and his brothers, especially William, spent years settling his wrecked financial situation. In 1783 reports began to circulate that he was drinking too much and often was drunk. While it is true that Clark did become an apparent alcoholic, it is believed that the stress of his situation militarily, politically, and financially, as well as rheumatism, were major factors in his drinking. His political enemies, especially James Wilkinson, used the charges of his drunkenness to their particular advantage in undermining Clark with Virginia officials.

In the summer of 1786 an expedition led by Clark against the Wabash River tribes ended in failure following the mutiny of some of the Kentucky militia. The seizure by Clark of the goods of three Spanish merchants at Vincennes to feed and clothe his men further damaged his reputation. Clark's bitterness over his treatment led him to look to other governments for opportunities and the honor he believed he was due. Early in 1788 he proposed founding a colony in Spanish Louisiana across from the mouth of the Ohio, but his demand for political and religious freedom was unacceptable to the Spanish. In 1791 he agreed to lead a thousand-man force down the Mississippi. This was part of a private venture to seize land between the Yazoo River and Natchez that was disputed between the United States and Spain, but President Washington forbade allowing the plan to proceed. Two years later France accepted Clark's proposal that he lead an expedition to seize Louisiana for it from Spain and commissioned him major general of the Independent and Revolutionary Legion of the Mississippi. Washington again stepped in. He ordered the French minister, Edmund Genêt, to leave the country because of his intrigues and forbade any American citizen to participate in the scheme. In 1798 France again planned to retake Louisiana, and Clark again was willing to lend his services. The government still frowned on its citizens involving themselves with foreign governments in such a manner and ordered Clark to resign his French commission or face arrest. He initially refused and took refuge in St. Louis for a time before returning to Louisville.

George Rogers Clark portrait by John Wesley Jarvis.

Clark's involvement in these failed foreign schemes marked the end of his military activities. His health continued to decline, and he still battled alcoholism. He lived with his brother William at MULBERRY HILL, and in early 1803 he moved across the river to Point of Rocks, or Clark's Point, in CLARKSVILLE, INDIANA Territory. He had helped lay out the town of Clarksville in August 1784 and owned extensive property there. That same year he had been appointed chief surveyor of Virginia military lands in Kentucky, a post he held until 1789; and he served as one of the land commissioners for surveys and grants of land in the Illinois Grant, including Clarksville. In March 1809 he suffered a severe burn on his right leg when he fell in front of his fireplace. There are two versions as to how this happened. One states that, already hampered by the effects of a stroke, Clark accidentally fell. In avoiding having his upper body fall into the fire, his leg did instead. The other story is that he was drunk and passed out, and that his leg fell into the fire. Regardless of how the injury occurred, the leg could not be saved. It was amputated on March 25.

The loss of his leg and frail health necessitated constant care, and he consequently moved to LOCUST GROVE, the home of his sister Lucy and brother-in-law WILLIAM CROGHAN. There he spent the last nine years of his life. He suffered a stroke in 1813 that partially paralyzed him and affected his speech; and on February 13, 1818, he suffered a fatal stroke. He was buried in the Croghan family cemetery at Locust Grove and was reinterred at CAVE HILL CEMETERY in 1869. Clark never married and had no known offspring. A number of towns, counties, and schools are named in Clark's honor, especially in Kentucky, Indiana, and Illinois; and statues pay tribute to his accomplishments. The most significant memorial is the George Rogers Clark National Historic Site in Vincennes that commemorates his greatest victory.

See James Alton James, *The Life of George Rogers Clark* (Chicago 1929); John Bakeless, *Background to Glory: The Life of George Rogers Clark* (Philadelphia 1957); William H. English, *Conquest of the Country Northwest of the River Ohio, 1778–1783 and Life of George Rogers Clark* (Indianapolis 1896); Temple Bodley, *George Rogers Clark: His Life and Public Services* (Boston 1926).

James J. Holmberg

CLARK, MERIWETHER LEWIS, JR. (b Louisville, January 27, 1846; d Memphis, Tennessee, April 22, 1899). Horseman. Meriwether Lewis Clark Jr. was the fourth child and third son of Meriwether Lewis Clark and Abigail Prather Churchill. Clark's ancestral background was impressive. His paternal grandfather was WILLIAM CLARK of the LEWIS AND CLARK EXPEDITION; and his maternal ancestors, the Prathers and Churchills, were prominent members of the Louisville community. Clark was a West Point graduate who served in the Black Hawk War and the Confederate army. His mother died when he was only six, and his father divided the children among the relatives. Lutie, as he was nicknamed, went to live with his two bachelor uncles, John and Henry Churchill. The Churchill brothers owned a fair amount of property south of the city limits. They resided on Sixth St. between Walnut

(Muhammad Ali Blvd.) and Chestnut Streets. Not much is known about Clark's education. He attended St. Joseph's College in Bardstown and upon graduation took a job as a teller in Louisville's Second National Bank. After a few years he switched to the tobacco business. In 1871 he married Mary Martin Anderson of Jeffersonville, Indiana. They had three children, a son and two daughters.

In 1872 a group of horse breeders approached Clark to help resurrect the waning HORSE-RACING business in Louisville. The sport had diminished so that the breeders were almost ready to call it quits and leave the area. It was highly likely that they approached Clark because he was wealthy, but also because horse racing was a passion of his family. His grandfather Churchill was one of the founders and the first president of the OAKLAND RACE COURSE at Seventh and Hill Streets in the 1830s. Even though his family had ties to the sport, Clark had no background in racing or management. He went to Europe to study the race tracks of England and France. Upon his return in 1873 his plan was to establish a classic American race in the tradition of the Epsom Derby. Clark outlined the plan to the breeders, which was a permanent series of races with the greatest race being the KENTUCKY DERBY.

Clark was active in the committee of subscribers to form the Louisville Jockey Club and Driving Park Association in 1874. The long name provided for the fact that during nonracing times the property could be used for picnicking and carriage rides. After raising thirty-two thousand dollars, the committee began looking for the ideal property. A site a few miles south of downtown was selected. It belonged to Clark's uncle, who agreed to lease the property. However, after the land was cleared and the racing track and clubhouse were constructed, the funds were depleted before a grandstand could be built. W.H. Thomas, a local merchant, lent the track enough money to complete a small wooden grandstand. The year was 1875, and on May 17 the track opened for business and the first Kentucky Derby was run. Ten thousand spectators were present to see ARISTIDES win the race.

Clark's life revolved around the promotion and operation of the track. He worked on ways to attract ladies to the races. Although it was improper for them to bet, Clark believed that if he catered to the women he could get the patronage of their husbands. He was a gregarious man who hosted parties at the Jockey Club and lavish dinners after the Derby. Clark even resided in the clubhouse from time to time. As a result his family life suffered. In 1886 the couple separated, and in 1891 Mary moved to Paris, never to return to Louisville. Clark moved into the PENDENNIS CLUB, then a private bachelor's club, founded in 1881.

In 1878 Clark tried his hand in politics. He was elected councilman of the Fifth Ward. He served a little over a year and left politics to recuperate from an altercation at the GALT HOUSE with Capt. Thomas Moore in September of 1879. Apparently Moore believed Clark had insulted him the day before when he would not let Moore enter his horse in a race because he was behind on some registration payments. Moore demanded a public apology. When Clark did not oblige, Moore informed him he was going to shoot him. Clark drew his pistol, but Moore quickly fired, striking Clark in the chest. The wound was dangerous but not critical, and Clark recovered. Moore was ruled off the track but was reinstated just a year later by Clark himself because he found out that Moore's family was experiencing financial hardships.

In 1890 Clark was appointed park commissioner, a position created by Mayor CHARLES D. JACOB. Clark proposed that the city acquire the area known as Burnt Knob, now Iroquois Park, for park purposes. Undoubtedly Clark's interest was business for the track, because people would have to pass by it to get to the park.

As much as he loved running the track, it was a financial failure. Clark forfeited his salary for many years to keep the track operating. In 1894 stockholders decided to sell the track. A group headed by William Schulte, a racehorse owner and bookmaker, bought the track and immediately constructed a new fifteen-hundred-seat grandstand on the west side of the track. It was topped by the now famed twin spires. Clark remained presiding judge, having a great reputation for honesty, until his death.

After the sale of CHURCHILL DOWNS, Clark traveled around the South acting as presiding judge at various racetracks. He was the author of many turf rules. He was in demand and commanded high pay for his services. At Garfield Park in Chicago he once had a contract that included a hundred dollars a day, a personal servant in the judge's stand, a carriage to transport him to and from the track, and his living expenses. In 1899 Clark's health began to deteriorate. He was suffering from a nervous prostration and narcolepsy. Clark also feared he was becoming senile, even though he was only fifty-three. He committed suicide in the Gaston Hotel in Memphis, where he had gone to act as presiding judge at the track. Clark is buried in CAVE HILL CEMETERY.

See Joe Hirsch and Jim Bolus, *Kentucky Derby: A Great American Tradition* (New York 1988); Samuel Thomas, *Churchill Downs: A Documentary History of America's Most Legendary Race Track* (Louisville 1995); Jim Bolus, *Kentucky Derby Stories* (Gretna, La., 1993); "The Louisville Jockey Club," in *Louisville and a Glimpse of Kentucky* (Louisville 1887).

Jay R. Ferguson

CLARK, WILLIAM (b Caroline County, Virginia, August 1, 1770; d St. Louis, Missouri, September 1, 1838). Explorer, soldier, and government official. He was the ninth of ten children and youngest of six sons of John and Ann (Rogers) Clark. Clark received some formal schooling in Virginia. When he was fourteen the family moved to Jefferson County, Kentucky, settling at MULBERRY HILL, about three miles southeast of Louisville. The site is now George Rogers Clark Park along Poplar Level Rd.

William pursued a more practical education at this point, becoming proficient in surveying, cartography, wilderness living, and operating a plantation. By the time he reached twenty-one he was a planter, surveyor, frontiersman, and soldier. A military career seemed a natural occupation for Clark. All five of his older brothers had served in the Revolutionary War, including the "Hannibal of the West," GEORGE ROGERS CLARK. Two (John Junior and Richard) had died in the service of their country.

William grew up hearing tales of his brothers' and their contemporaries' military exploits. He might have served under his brother George in a 1786 militia expedition against the Wabash River Indians, but it is certain that he served in John Hardin's 1789 expedition against the White River Indian towns and Charles Scott's 1791 expedition against the Ouiatanon Indian towns. Clark also assisted with the defense of the settlements against Indian attack. His abilities were recognized and praised by his commanders.

On March 7, 1792, he received a second lieutenant's commission in the infantry of the regular army. Clark went on recruiting duty and in September was assigned to the Fourth Sub-legion of the United States Army.

Gen. Anthony Wayne was preparing for a campaign against the Northwestern Indians in Ohio and Indiana, and Clark served under his command for the next four years. In June 1793 Clark led a mission to the Chickasaw Bluffs (present Memphis, Tennessee) to take arms and ammunition to the Chickasaw in order to keep them allied to the United States, rather than defecting to the Spanish. In September 1793 Clark was placed in command of a rifle corps and during the winter of 1793–94 commanded a detachment at Vincennes.

In the spring and summer of 1794, Wayne launched his campaign against the Indians. Clark was placed in command of a supply train and successfully defended it against an Indian attack. He commanded a rifle company in the American victory at Fallen Timbers in August and was present at the Treaty of Greenville in 1795. It was in early 1796 that he met and became friends with Meriwether Lewis, a junior officer under his command.

The appeal of a military career had begun to fade for Clark, and he decided to resign in order to pursue business opportunities, assist his brother George with his tangled legal and financial affairs, and help run the family's plantation. Before resigning he went on one more mission southward, to New Madrid, where he protested to Spanish officials the fortification of Chickasaw Bluffs.

Clark resigned his commission as a first lieutenant of infantry on July 1, 1796, and returned home to Mulberry Hill. He was frustrated in his plans for a mercantile career, largely because of family responsibilities, and particularly because of his brother George's tangled affairs. For the next few years he traveled thousands of miles on business, especially on behalf of his brother, visiting New Orleans, Baltimore, Washington, and Virginia. Much of what George Rogers Clark retained was due largely to his brother's efforts, but William Clark impoverished himself in the effort. William Clark's own financial straits now forced him to sell Mulberry Hill and settle across the river in CLARKSVILLE in 1803. Clark continued to have an interest in military matters. On May 28, 1800, he was commissioned captain of a troop of cavalry in the Jefferson County militia, First Regiment of Kentucky militia.

In July 1803 Clark received an invitation that changed his life and secured his place in history. His friend and former subordinate, Capt. Meriwether Lewis, then private secretary to President THOMAS JEFFERSON, invited Clark to join him as co-commander of an expedition to the Pacific Ocean. Clark accepted in July and began recruiting men in Louisville and Clarksville. On October 14, Lewis reached Louisville, and, on October 26, the co-commanders and the nucleus of the Corps of Discovery set off down the OHIO on a journey that would last for three years. Clark and Lewis complemented each other's talents. Clark was an effective negotiator with the Indians encountered, faithfully kept a journal, and almost invariably his practical, gregarious temperament served the expedition well.

Following the expedition's September 1806 return to St. Louis, the captains continued on to Louisville, and eventually to Washington. They were met with praise—and often banquets and balls—from St. Louis to Washington. On February 27, 1807, his resignation as a first lieutenant in the artillery was accepted. He had been denied a promised captain's commission in the infantry and instead received a second lieutenancy in the artillery. In February 1806 he had been promoted to first lieutenant. Jefferson's proposal to secure a lieutenant colonel's commission in the army for him was denied by the U.S. Senate. Instead, as a reward for his services, he received a commission as brigadier general of the Louisiana Territory militia and was appointed Indian agent for the territory. Clark also received double pay for the period of the expedition and a sixteen-hundred-acre land grant. In September 1807 he supervised a fossil dig at Big Bone Lick in Boone County, Kentucky, for Thomas Jefferson.

Clark settled permanently in St. Louis in June 1808 and was an important figure in Missouri affairs for the next thirty years. Within a couple of months of arriving, he traveled up the Missouri River east of present-day Kansas City and established Fort Osage. Much of his time was occupied with government business, especially Indian affairs. He also acquired land and attempted to reap some of the benefits of commercial trade in the frontier town. Following the death of his close friend and partner in discovery, Meriwether Lewis, in October 1809, the task of publishing their expedition journals fell to him. Knowing that his strengths lay in other areas, he retained Nicholas Biddle to edit them. He answered extensive questions from Biddle and had expedition member George Shannon assist Biddle as necessary. The journals were published in 1814.

In 1813 Clark was appointed territorial governor of Missouri and retained the post until 1821. During the War of 1812 he organized the defense of Missouri and led an expedition up the Mississippi River to Prairie du Chien (Wisconsin), where he built a fort. With the expiration of the militia's enlistments he was forced to return to St. Louis, and the garrison left behind later surrendered to the British. Both as governor of Missouri Territory and as superintendent of Indian affairs (a position he assumed as governor and retained after leaving that office), he negotiated frequently with Indian delegations from various tribes. He was well respected and trusted by the Indians, who called him the Red Headed Chief. While doing what he could for the Indians' eventual acculturation and assimilation, he worked to extinguish their land claims and further open up the West for white settlement. Over the years he acquired a large collection of Indian and natural history artifacts that he displayed in his town home, his office, and his country estate, Minoma.

President Monroe appointed him surveyor general of Illinois, Missouri, and Arkansas, 1824–25, and he founded Paducah, Kentucky, in 1828. His later years were marked by some financial difficulties and physical and mental decline, but he continued his habit of hospitality until his death. Clark died in St. Louis on September 1, 1838, and was buried on his nephew John O'Fallon's estate, Athlone, in what his son, Meriwether Lewis Clark, identified as the Font Hill vault. His remains and those of other Clarks were reinterred in Bellefontaine Cemetery in St. Louis on October 23, 1860.

While in the East in 1807, Clark renewed his acquaintance with Judith (better known as Julia) Hancock (1791–1820) of Fincastle, Virginia. They married in Fincastle in January 1808. They had five children: Meriwether Lewis, William Preston, Mary Margaret, George Rogers Hancock, and John Julius. Julia Clark died at Fotheringay, the Hancock family estate in Montgomery County, Virginia, on June 27, 1820. Clark married her cousin, Harriet Kennerly Radford (1788–1831), the widow of Dr. John Radford, on November 28, 1821, in St. Louis. They had two children: Jefferson Kearny and Edmund.

See John Loos, "A Biography of William Clark, 1770–1813," Ph.D. dissertation, Washington University, 1953; Jerome O. Steffen, *William Clark: Jeffersonian Man on the Frontier* (Norman, Okla., 1977); James J. Holmberg, "William Clark," in Christy H. Bond, *Gateway Families* (Boston 1994); Louise Phelps Kellogg, "William Clark," in *Dictionary of American Biography* (New York 1930) 4:141–44.

James J. Holmberg

CLARK COUNTY, INDIANA. Clark County, Indiana's second-oldest county, was created February 3, 1801, by proclamation of Indiana territorial governor William Henry Harrison. It was carved from land formerly part of Knox County. At the time of its organization, it encompassed approximately the southeastern fifth of the present state of Indiana. During the years that followed, its area was successively reduced to form at least eighteen new counties. Bounded on the south by the OHIO RIVER, it is bordered today by FLOYD, Washington, SCOTT, and Jefferson Counties in Indiana. Its area now measures 384 square miles.

The county is named for Gen. GEORGE ROGERS CLARK, in honor of his capture of the British forts at Kaskaskia, Cahokia, and Vincennes in 1777–78. It includes most of CLARK'S GRANT, a 150,000-acre tract awarded to Clark and his regiment by the state of Virginia in 1783 in recognition of the triumphant Illinois campaign. The military grants surveyed from Clark's Grant remain the basis of most land titles in Clark County.

The county was formally organized on April 7, 1801, when the first session of the county court of general quarter sessions of the peace met at Springville, a tiny settlement of approximately one hundred residents near the intersection of High Jackson and Bethany Roads in present Charlestown Township. Springville was the site of a trading post owned by a man named Tully; consequently, the village was often referred to as Tullytown, especially by Native Americans who traded with the proprietor. The court's first action was to divide the county into three townships—CLARKSVILLE, Springville, and Spring Hill.

Clarksville Township included the town of Clarksville, a thousand-acre section of Clark's Grant overlooking the FALLS OF THE OHIO. Over the next half-century, as new counties were created, Clark County was gradually reorganized into its present twelve townships, beginning with SILVER CREEK in 1815; Wood, Bethlehem, and Washington in 1816; JEFFERSONVILLE and Charlestown, 1817; Monroe, 1827; Owen about 1830; UTICA, 1847; Oregon, 1852; Carr, 1854; and Union, 1858.

In mid-1802 the seat of county government moved to the newly organized town of Jeffersonville, located just across the Ohio River from Louisville on land owned by Isaac Bowman, one of George Rogers Clark's officers. Springville vanished a short time later. Jeffersonville served as county seat for nine years.

During this period, the county court was preoccupied with such tasks as licensing taverns and ferrying operations and building roads between Jeffersonville and neighboring villages. Its most ambitious project was construction of a jail in Jeffersonville in August 1802 at a cost of nine hundred dollars.

In 1808 the United States government established a land office in Jeffersonville, signifying the town's strategic position in the westward movement of settlement. The same year, Barzillai Baker and James McCampbell organized the town of Charlestown, about twelve miles upriver from Jeffersonville and about two miles from Springville. It was named for Charles Beggs, one of the surveyors. Four years after its founding, in response to growing sentiment that local government should be more centrally located, Charlestown became the Clark County seat. The county's first courthouse was erected on the town square the following year. One of Charlestown's most prominent citizens during its early years was JONATHAN JENNINGS, a young attorney whose leadership in the fight against the adoption of slavery during Indiana's Constitutional Convention in 1816 paved the way for his election as the state's first governor the same year.

Although Jeffersonville had lost its status as county seat, it was not without political significance. In December 1813 it became, for all practical purposes, Indiana's temporary territorial capital when Gov. Thomas Posey took up residence there. Posey did not like CORYDON, the territorial capital, as a place of residence. Moreover, he was in poor health, and his physician was in Louisville. The legislature resisted Posey's action to no avail. The governor remained in Jeffersonville until the end of his term in November 1816, making only occasional visits to Corydon.

The period from 1810 to the CIVIL WAR witnessed the proliferation of towns and villages throughout the county. Most served as market centers for surrounding farms, while others became commercial and manufacturing centers. Bethlehem, platted upstream from Charlestown in 1812, was for many years a center of ferrying operations between Clark County and OLDHAM and Trimble Counties in Kentucky. New Washington, laid out three years later, served as the marketing center for Washington Township. Utica, organized in 1816 and located on the Ohio between Jeffersonville and Charlestown, became a ferrying point between southern Clark County and eastern Jefferson County, Kentucky. As the county's population moved westward, New Providence (popularly known as Borden) was laid out in 1817. It served as a coach stop for traffic between Jeffersonville and Salem, the Washington County seat.

Town development waned during the 1820s, no doubt as a result of the economic depression that followed the panic of 1819. But as recovery set in, town platting resumed late in the decade. Germany, laid out in 1829, and Herculaneum, platted the following year, were located on the Ohio at the mouth of Bull Creek. Both were ferrying hamlets that disappeared when that mode of crossing became obsolete. However, nearby Hibernia, also established in 1830, became the locus of economic and social life in Owen Township. Seven years later, Abram Littell and Thomas Cunningham laid out Hamburg at the intersection of the NEW ALBANY and Charlestown Rd. and the Jeffersonville and Salem Rd. in Silver Creek Township. Situated on the Jeffersonville and Salem stagecoach line, it was for a time a communication and trade center for the central part of the county. Platted in 1839 by Robert Henthorn, New Market in Oregon Township provided postal and marketing services for farmers in the north-central region of the county.

In 1846 the Indiana General Assembly incorporated the Jeffersonville Railroad Co. and empowered it to build a line from Jeffersonville to Columbus, where it would connect with the Madison and Indianapolis Railroad and continue on to the state capital. Shortly thereafter, Moses Sellers and John Hill established SELLERSBURG at the intersection of the Utica and Salem Rd. and the New Albany and Charlestown Rd., near the Jeffersonville Railroad's right-of-way. With the railroad's completion about 1852, Sellersburg became a flourishing commercial center. The railroad also provided the impetus for Henryville in Monroe Township. Platted in 1850 as Morristown, it was renamed in 1853 in honor of its proprietor, Henry Ferguson. Meanwhile, Thompson McDeitz platted Memphis in Union Township, midway between Sellersburg and Henryville, in 1852. Two years later, Samuel Cowling laid out Otisco near the point where the Oregon, Monroe, and Charlestown Township boundaries intersect. The same year, Lewis Bottorff established Petersburg on the banks of Muddy Fork near Sellersburg. It was named for Peter Makowsky, a prominent local farmer.

The decades before the Civil War also witnessed the emergence of a substantial industrial economy in Clark County. As farms spread across the landscape, they created a demand for gristmills to grind their grain. Numerous entrepreneurs erected mills along Fourteen-Mile Creek, Bull Creek, Silver Creek, and other streams throughout the county. Particularly notable was John Work's Tunnel Mill on Fourteen-Mile Creek near Charlestown. Constructed between 1814 and 1817, this feat of pioneer engineering required blasting a three-hundred-foot tunnel through solid rock to take advantage of a twenty-four-foot drop in the creek's flow as it winds around a hill that rises to one hundred feet above water level. The tunnel served as the millrace that carried water to power an overshot wheel that measured twenty feet in diameter and operated two large buhrs. Tunnel Mill operated until the early twentieth century. The property is now part of Tunnel Mill Reservation, the oldest Boy Scout camp in Indiana.

Blessed with vast stands of virgin timber, the county also developed a large sawmill industry. Typical of these establishments was Redman's Mill. Erected on Silver Creek near Sellersburg in 1815, it passed through a succession of owners and was still operating as late as 1882. Among the major customers of Clark County sawmills were Jeffersonville's burgeoning shipbuilders. Jeffersonville entered the steamboat era in 1819 when several investors built the *United States*, a seven-hundred-ton vessel capable of carrying three thousand bales of cotton. Over the next few years, several local entrepreneurs established shipyards in Jeffersonville, including brothers William, George, and Henry French; Robert C. Green; Peter Meyers; and David S. Barmore. All had a degree of success, but the most successful was James Howard. The immigrant son of an English weaver, Howard launched his first steamboat, *Hyperion*, in 1834. Fourteen years later, after similar ventures in Louisville and Madison, he returned to Jeffersonville to open the HOWARD SHIP YARDS. For nearly a century, the Howard family turned out some of the finest craft on American rivers, including the *Glendy Burke*, *Robt. E. Lee II*, and *J.M. White*.

Another major industry was lime production. Lime-burning began in the Utica area about 1818. At first, lime was burned on brush and log fires; but as the product's profit potential became more apparent, producers began using kilns dug in the ground. In 1826 a man named Starkweathers built a coal-burning kiln that operated until 1847. Numerous technological improvements occurred during the 1830s and 1840s, and by the beginning of the Civil War producers in Utica were shipping lime upriver to Pittsburgh and downriver to New Orleans.

In 1821 Clark County became the site of Indiana's first state prison. Located at the corner of Ohio and Market Streets in Jeffersonville, it was financed by the people and built of logs at a cost of three thousand dollars. It had fifteen cells and made little provision for sanitation and health. The facility was leased by the state, which in turn leased it to Seymour Westover, a blacksmith who operated it on the state's behalf. In 1845 the prisoners were transferred to a new facility in nearby Clarksville. The following year prison reformer Dorothea Dix visited the structure and commented that the cells were too small and poorly ventilated.

In 1870 Clark County's population stood at 24,770, with settlement spread throughout the county. But, with nearly half the county's residents and a growing industrial and commercial economy, Jeffersonville was by far the county's leading urban center. This robust growth set off a movement to reclaim the city's former status as the county seat. In early 1876 the Jeffersonville City Council, at the urging of Mayor Luther F. Warder, inaugurated a cam-

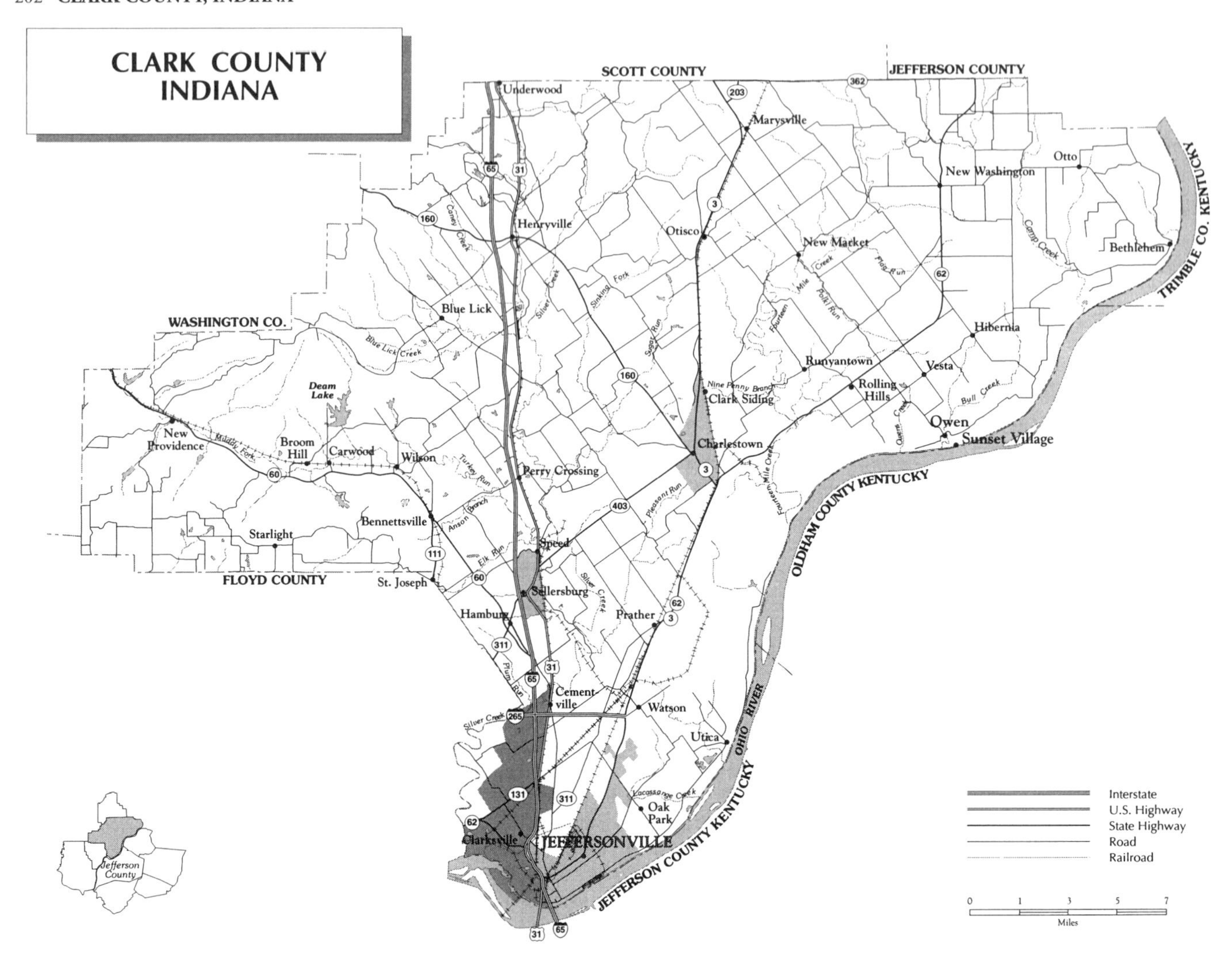

paign to finance construction of a new courthouse. In September 1878, after a bitter "county seat war," the county's records were transferred from Charlestown back to Jeffersonville.

As the twentieth century dawned, Clark County boasted a flourishing industrial economy. The Howard Ship Yards was one of the nation's leading producers of STEAMBOATS, barges, and other river craft. The QUARTERMASTER DEPOT, established at Jeffersonville in temporary quarters during the Civil War, moved into permanent facilities in 1874 and became a major producer of equipment for the United States Army. In neighboring Clarksville, the AMERICAN CAR AND FOUNDRY CO., which in 1899 absorbed the former Ohio Falls Car Manufacturing Co., employed some two thousand workers in the manufacture of railroad rolling stock.

One of the most important developments in the local industrial economy was the displacement of lime-burning by CEMENT production. The first cement mill in Clark County was established by William Beach in Clarksville. In 1866 the Falls City Cement Co. began manufacturing cement south of Sellersburg. Three years later the LOUISVILLE CEMENT CO. purchased a large tract at Petersburg on Muddy Fork near the Jeffersonville, Madison, and Indianapolis Railroad tracks. Numerous other producers entered the business over the next two decades, and by 1898 seventeen cement mills were operating in Clark County. Two years later, output was more than two million barrels. But this situation did not last long. As a result of intense competition, technological innovations, and a flurry of mergers, the LOUISVILLE CEMENT CO. at Speed (formerly Petersburg), triumphed over its rivals, and by 1905 it was one of the nation's leading cement producers.

Clark County also emerged as a regional recreation and entertainment center during the early twentieth century. In 1903 the state of Indiana established the CLARK STATE FOREST near Henryville—an area that would eventually grow to about twenty thousand acres. Two years later private entrepreneurs established Fern Grove at the base of the Devil's Backbone, a rugged peninsula at the mouth of Fourteen-Mile Creek near Charlestown. Equipped with picnic tables, benches, and other simple amenities, Fern Grove, later called ROSE ISLAND, was a popular destination for Ohio River excursionists for nearly two decades.

A form of recreation that survived both the GREAT DEPRESSION and the 1937 FLOOD was illegal GAMBLING. In 1927 Claude Williams built a casino known as the Log Cabin near the intersection of present State Roads 31 and 131. Two years later, Joe H. Adams, a Kentucky-born, Florida-based dog track promoter, opened a dog-racing track called the Jeffersonville Dog Mart near the intersection of Eastern Blvd. and State Rd. 131, in what is now Clarksville. The track operated until 1936. For most of the next two decades, Jeffersonville and the surrounding area hosted numerous establishments that offered every form of big-time gambling, along with fine dining; the bands of Lawrence Welk, Guy Lombardo, and the Dorsey Brothers; and entertainers such as Al Jolson, Helen Morgan, Wee Bonnie Baker, and the Andrews Sisters. Except for periodic crackdowns, illegal gambling flourished, with the support of corrupt local officials, until 1948, when Clark circuit judge James Bottorff and Indiana State Police superintendent Robert Rossow staged a surprise raid against five gambling establishments in downtown Jeffersonville.

A major force in fueling gambling during the 1940s was high wages at local war production plants like Jeffersonville Boat and Machine Co. (Jeffboat, Inc.), successor to the Howard Ship Yards; the Quartermaster Depot; the Louisville Cement Co.; and the INDIANA ARMY AMMUNITION PLANT. The latter facility, established in 1940, consisted of a huge smokeless powder plant and bag plant for the manufacture of ammunition for the United States Army. Encompassing approximately six thousand acres along State Rd. 62 and the Ohio River between Jeffersonville and Charlestown, the plant was the region's largest single employer for more than four decades and attracted approximately four thousand new residents to Charlestown during the early war years.

Clark County has grown and changed substantially since WORLD WAR II. The population grew from 31,020 in 1940 to 87,777 in 1990 and 92,530 in 1996 (in 1970 it was 75,876, and in 1980, 88,838). While Jeffersonville has experienced considerable growth as a result of suburbanization and annexation, the primary growth center has been Clarksville, which benefited from construction of Interstate 65, development of large regional SHOPPING CENTERS such as Green Tree Mall and River Falls Mall, and conversion of hundreds of acres of farmland into scores of residential subdivisions. Substantial growth also has occurred in and around Sellersburg, Charlestown, and Henryville.

Contributing to the county's long-term economic growth were construction of several industrial parks in the southern portion of the county during the 1970s and 1980s, along with completion of the Clark County Airport in 1981 and the CLARK MARITIME CENTRE in 1985.

See Lewis C. Baird, *Baird's History of Clark County* (Indianapolis 1909); Henry and Kate Ford, *History of the Falls Cities and Their Counties* (Cleveland 1882); Gerald O. Haffner, *A Brief, Informal History of Clark County, Indiana* (New Albany, Ind., 1985); Carl E. Kramer, *Sellersburg: A Century of Change* (Sellersburg, Ind., 1990).

Carl E. Kramer

CLARK COUNTY POOR FARM. The building housing the poor, aged, and infirm of CLARK COUNTY, INDIANA, in the late 1800s and early 1900s was described as disgraceful, and the care given as inferior to that given the animals on the surrounding farms. Public outcry led to the appropriation of twenty-five thousand dollars to build a new facility.

Clarence Howard of JEFFERSONVILLE was appointed as architect and builder, and Robert Plaskett of New Washington was superintendent of construction. The completed building was turned over to the county commissioners on November 20, 1907, with an actual cost of construction of $23,669.

The building accommodated sixty persons in a sanitary and comfortable environment. Men and women were housed in separate wings and ate in separate dining rooms. More elegant quarters were provided for the superintendent and his family. The residents farmed the sixty-seven acres of the farm.

Due to changing social conditions, the poor farm was abandoned prior to WORLD WAR II, with the last inmate enrolled on January 16, 1941. It was taken over by the United States Army Ordnance Field Office and operated in conjunction with the Indiana Arsenal. The building was renovated and converted into offices. Later the farm became available to other armed services first and to educational facilities second. With the help of political leaders, the 4-H Club was recognized as an educational institution, and a parcel was acquired for the use of the Clark County 4-H Club in 1962. In 1965 the building and eight to ten acres surrounding were leased for use as a nursing home. It continues to operate in that capacity.

The site of the former poor farm is on Highway 62 about eight miles north of Jeffersonville and about two miles south of Charlestown.

See Louis C. Baird, *Baird's History of Clark County* (Indianapolis 1909).

Charline Judd Hall

CLARKE, CHARLES JULIAN (b Franklin County, Kentucky, December 16, 1836; d Louisville, March 9, 1908). Architect. The son of Joseph and Harriett (Julian) Clarke, he was Kentucky's fourth native architect, behind the Shryock brothers and John McMurtry. He was educated in Kentucky. During the CIVIL WAR he worked in Louisville with HENRY WHITESTONE and afterward with the Bradshaw brothers, eventually becoming a partner. After Whitestone's retirement in 1881, some considered Clarke Louisville's premier designer. In 1882 he became Kentucky's first architect to join the Western Association of Architects.

ARTHUR LOOMIS, a native of Massachusetts, entered the Clarke office in 1876 and became Clarke's chief draftsman in 1885. In 1891 Clarke and Loomis established a partnership that was one of the leading ARCHITECTURAL FIRMS in Louisville for the rest of the century. The Theophilus CONRAD residence on ST. JAMES COURT and the George A. Robinson residence on FOURTH ST. between Kentucky and St. Catherine are their best residential works; the 1893 LEVY BROTHERS men's clothing store at Third and MARKET STREETS is their most noted commercial structure. The Chicago-style TODD BUILDING, at Fourth and Market Streets, was designed principally by Loomis and completed in 1902. It was demolished in 1983. They also designed the Louisville Medical College of 1893 and the 1893 Manual Training School, both notable institutional buildings. Their Louisville churches included St. Paul's German Evangelical Church on E Broadway, St. Matthew's German Evangelical Church on E St. Catherine St., and the demolished First Presbyterian Church on Fourth St. between York and BROADWAY. Clarke is buried in the Frankfort, Kentucky, Cemetery.

William B. Scott Jr.

CLARKE, MARCELLUS JEROME "SUE MUNDY" (b near Franklin, Simpson County, Kentucky, August 25, 1844 (1845?); d Louisville, March 15, 1865). CIVIL WAR guerrilla. Marcellus Jerome Clarke, who fought under the *nom de guerre* Sue Mundy, was the son of Brig. Gen. Hector M. and Mary (Hail) Clarke. Both parents died before he was ten, and Clarke was reared by relatives and received a common school education.

With his foster brother John Patterson, he enlisted in the Confederate army on July 4, 1861, and was mustered into Co. B, Fourth Kentucky Infantry, First Brigade, at Camp Burnett near Clarksville, Tennessee, on August 25, 1861. In February 1862 he was taken prisoner when Grant forced the surrender of Fort Donelson. He was sent to Camp Morton near Indianapolis. He, Patterson, and several others escaped when they overpowered their guards, who had taken them to a stream to bathe.

They fled to Newburgh, Indiana, where Clarke masterminded a brazen plan to capture the garrison there. It surrendered, and Clarke took many weapons and supplies. They returned to Kentucky, where the federals captured Patterson, who was wounded and lost his eyesight. Clarke was deeply affected by the incident and vowed never to take a federal prisoner.

Clarke joined John Hunt Morgan's raiders and fought during many of Morgan's campaigns, first as a scout and later as an artillerist. After Morgan's death in September 1864, Clarke returned to Kentucky where he joined Sam "One-Armed" Berry, Henry C. Magruder, and others in a guerrilla band that terrorized the state from mid-1864 until the war's end. The origin of the name Sue Mundy is uncertain, although Clarke's shoulder-length hair and almost feminine beauty gave rise to the tale that he was in fact a woman. His exploits were written about by GEORGE PRENTICE, editor of the *LOUISVILLE DAILY JOURNAL*. Prentice called him Sue Mundy, a name supposedly borrowed from Suzanna Monday, a free black woman in Nelson County known for her cruel nature.

Though the band was guilty of shootings and train robberies as well as the burning of bridges and at least one courthouse, the crimes attributed to the outlaws were exaggerated. Early in 1865 Clarke and his band joined Missouri's William "Bloody" Quantrill for a raid in central Kentucky. Shortly thereafter, Clarke and three others were ambushed in Hancock County. The survivors took refuge in a tobacco barn near Webster in Meade County. When the news reached Louisville, troops were sent, and on March 12, 1865, Clarke surrendered. He was taken by riverboat to Louisville where a military court found him guilty of guerrilla activities. On March 15, 1865, he was hanged at the old fairgrounds on BROADWAY near Eighteenth St. before a crowd of thousands, and his body was returned to Simpson County for burial.

The next morning the *Louisville Daily Jour-*

nal carried an interview with the prisoner and an extensive description of the execution. Mundy declared that he was not guilty of one-tenth of the outrages with which he was charged and stated that his death was a great injustice. Nevertheless, he was led to an elevated platform, and at the word *three* the prop was pulled from under the trap. The fall, not more than three feet, did not break his neck, and he choked to death. The crowd witnessed hard struggles and convulsions. It was feared for a time that he would break the lashings. His sufferings, however, were of short duration. He was left hanging for some twenty minutes before he was cut down. Immediately a crowd gathered around the body, some trying to cut off parts of his clothing as a memento.

See L.L. Valentine, "Sue Mundy of Kentucky," *Register of the Kentucky Historical Society* 62 (July 1964): 175–205, (Oct. 1964): 278–306; James A. Ramage, *Rebel Raider: The Life of General John Hunt Morgan* (Lexington 1986); *Louisville Daily Journal*, March 7 and March 16, 1865; *Louisville Times*, Oct. 27, 1938.

Richard Taylor
Rhonda Abner

CLARK MARITIME CENTRE. Located on the bank of the OHIO RIVER in JEFFERSONVILLE, INDIANA, the center is a river port/industrial complex that provides twelve-month ocean access to shippers via the Gulf of Mexico, as well as easy access to truck and rail transportation. The public port, situated on 830 acres, was established in 1985 and is administered by the Indiana Port Commission, a seven-member bipartisan panel appointed by the governor. With large storage, lift, and processing capabilities, the site handles a wide variety of commodities and cargo products ranging from fertilizer to steel. In 1997, Clark Maritime Centre landed three large companies when GEA Parts LLC, a General Electric subsidiary; Ohio-based Wayne Steel; and longtime Louisville manufacturer Vogt Valve Co. all moved into the complex.

CLARK'S GRANT. Officially the Illinois Grant, the Clark Grant was a tract of land in southern Indiana awarded to Gen. GEORGE ROGERS CLARK (1752–1818) and his regiment in recognition of a triumphant Illinois campaign during the Revolutionary War. Lying primarily in CLARK COUNTY, INDIANA, the 150,000-acre tract also extended into later FLOYD and SCOTT COUNTIES, Indiana.

When the campaign into the Illinois Territory was initiated, Clark was assured that awards in land would be given to him and his men upon their success. Clark's Illinois Regiment captured British forts at Kaskaskia, Cahokia, and Vincennes in 1778–79. In 1783 the Virginia Assembly granted Clark 150,000 acres to be awarded to him and his men for their wartime service. A board of commissioners made up of Clark and nine others was established to settle and determine claims to the land. Claimants were required to present their claim to the commissioners on or before April 1, 1784, and, if approved, were required to pay one dollar for every hundred acres of such claim for the cost of surveying and appropriating the lands.

The land selected was across the OHIO RIVER from Louisville, extending from below the FALLS OF THE OHIO, a little below SILVER CREEK, upriver to the farthest end of Eighteen-Mile Island. Appointed principal surveyor was William Clark, a cousin of George Rogers Clark, and he worked with a corps of assistants. The land was originally intended to be laid off in tracts of fifty-five acres each, but, due to errors, tracts often ran larger. Overall three hundred men were allotted land. One thousand acres of the grant was designated as the town of CLARKSVILLE. Officially founded in 1784, it was the first American settlement in the Northwest Territory. Clark was the first town council president and built a home on the "Point of Rocks" overlooking the Falls, where he lived from 1803 to 1809. When Clark County was formally organized on April 7, 1801, it took the general's name.

See William Hayden English, *Conquest of the Country Northwest of the River Ohio 1778–1783 and Life of Gen. George Rogers Clark* (Indianapolis 1896); James Alton James, ed., *George Rogers Clark Papers* (New York 1972).

CLARK STATE FOREST. Clark State Forest is located on U.S. Highway 31, ten miles south of SCOTTSBURG and one mile north of Henryville, just off of INTERSTATE 65. In May 1903 the state of Indiana acquired two thousand acres of land in the knob area of CLARK COUNTY near Henryville to establish Indiana's first state forest. Seedling trees were to be raised here and distributed throughout the state in an effort to restore Indiana's role as a major producer of hardwood. Unless this was done, many woodworking industries would have been forced to close or move to other areas. Other purposes of the facility were to teach forestry and to convert what was considered worthless land into something of value.

To add to the scenic beauty and to promote water conservation, artificial lakes were built by the WORKS PROGRESS ADMINISTRATION during the New Deal era of the Franklin D. Roosevelt administration (1933–45). At that time, young men in the Civilian Conservation Corps were working and learning forestry.

There are now twenty-four thousand acres of heavily forested timberland with winding roads and paths. Clark Forest is a multiple management facility concerned with timber, wildlife, water conservation, and recreation. Timber management is its primary purpose. This involves raising and harvesting trees. Plantings include both native and introduced species.

Foresters select trees between seventy and a hundred years old to mark for cutting in the fall. Only selectively marked trees are sold. The timber is sold to the highest bidder, with the state reserving a low bid. Group demonstrations of the proper techniques of marking and harvesting timber are available and encouraged.

Another function is wildlife management. Cutting certain trees gives deer the open space they need and encourages brush growth necessary for the survival of many small animals. Hunting is allowed in season, except in recreational areas. All state regulations apply.

Recreation is a sideline. The campsites and recreational areas are primitive. There are two hiking trails, but campers are encouraged to equip themselves with a topographic map and a compass and hike off trails into the forest. Camping is restricted to designated campsites and within a quarter of a mile off the Knobstone Trail. There are a hundred miles of bridle trails and camping sites for horsemen. Fishing, backpacking, boating, and picnicking facilities are also available.

See Louis C. Baird, *Baird's History of Clark County* (Indianapolis 1909).

Charline Judd Hall

CLARKSVILLE, INDIANA. Clarksville is situated on the north side of the OHIO RIVER at the FALLS. In CLARK COUNTY, it is bounded by JEFFERSONVILLE on the east and by NEW ALBANY on the west and north, and located across the river from Louisville.

In 1783 the Virginia Assembly set aside a 150,000-acre grant to be awarded to the veterans of GEORGE ROGERS CLARK's Revolutionary War Campaign in the Illinois country. One thousand acres of that grant was designated as the town of Clarksville, making it the first settlement under the United States in what became the Northwest Territory, officially created by Congress. General Clark was the first town council president and built a home on the "Point of Rocks" overlooking the Falls. He lived there from 1803 to 1809, when ill health forced him to remove to LOCUST GROVE, the home of his sister, outside Louisville. His original homesite is now a state park.

Despite high hopes for the new town (by 1784 twelve of the half-acre lots had been sold and occupied), it did not flourish. By 1788 Dr. Saugrain, a French visitor, found "only seven or eight houses," although he described the land as "splendid and even amazing in goodness." Another physician, Dr. George Hunter, touring the area in 1796, noted "a few scattered Cabbins, with one indifferent farm." In 1828 Increase Allen Lapham, an employee of the contractor of the LOUISVILLE AND PORTLAND CANAL, then under construction, wandered through the town and reported "about ten houses and a flouring mill which are very old and neglected situated without any attention to regularity." The mill had been built by George Rogers Clark in 1784, and the waterway that powered it became known as Mill Creek.

SILVER CREEK, which empties into the Ohio

at the western end of Clarksville, is the border between Clark and FLOYD Counties. The buffalo trace was a path used by buffalo since prehistoric times. It became an important pioneer road that crossed the Ohio into Clarksville and led across Silver Creek into Floyd County and from there west to Illinois.

The LEWIS AND CLARK "Corps of Discovery" left from Clark's Point in 1803 and returned in 1806.

By 1850 Clarksville had become little more than a name, with few, if any, new residents moving in. An attempt to form the first suburban residential area—known as Andalusia and located at what is today Greenacres—was not attracting the number of homesteaders needed to keep the town alive. In 1854 a more ambitious project was launched, as a city with docks and train lines running as far north as Lake Erie was surveyed and planned. But this town, to be located near the area of the modern FOURTEENTH ST. RAILROAD BRIDGE and known as Falls City, also failed to come to fruition.

In 1861, Camp Joe Holt at Little Eddy was established as a training site for Kentuckians wishing to join the Union army. It was created across the river so as not to violate Kentucky's neutrality and possibly anger Kentucky governor Beriah Magoffin into siding with the South.

By the 1870s, Clarksville had practically vanished as a community, with no governmental structure and devoid of all but a few residents. An attempt to found another town, Ohio Falls, met opposition from the landowners, who thought such a move would only increase their taxes. The opposition fought the annexation all the way to the Indiana Supreme Court, which ruled that as the town had been chartered by the Virginia legislature—under "An act for surveying and apportioning the lands granted to the Illinois Regiment"—the high court had no jurisdiction. Thus the town survived in its modern entity, and the threat of oblivion spurred increased development as the Town Council was reformed. The Town Council elects a president of the town who serves as a chief executive officer.

The COLGATE-PALMOLIVE Co. has operated a plant in Clarksville since 1923. All the Colgate Total toothpaste produced in the United States is made there. The world's second-largest clock, which measures forty feet in diameter, is atop the plant. Prior to the plant's opening, the location was occupied from 1845 to 1861 by the Indiana Reformatory for men, which was the only state prison in Indiana. The reformatory was converted to the Colgate-Palmolive plant, and some new construction has been added. Other points of interest are the Derby Dinner Playhouse (1974) and Clarksville Little Theatre (1947). The latter is one of the oldest continuously operated community theaters in the country.

Interstate 65 is the major highway through Clarksville, and CSX TRANSPORTATION tracks traverse the town. The former Pennsylvania Railroad bridge, or Fourteenth Street Bridge, carries rail traffic between Indianapolis and Louisville through Clarksville. This bridge, completed in 1919, was constructed on some of the original piers of the Louisville Bridge of 1870, which was the first to cross the Ohio River between Kentucky and Indiana.

Clarksville's growth was slow but steady during the next century, and it remained a small residential community until 1968 when the construction of Green Tree Mall began a period of vigorous growth as a commercial and shopping area. In 1990 the River Falls Mall opened with a variety of stores, shops, and the River Fair Family Fun Park.

Despite its growth, Clarksville has retained the town form of government and is one of the largest communities with this form of government in Indiana. The governing body is a Town Council, consisting of seven elected officials. In 1995 the town government moved into the first structure that was built in Clarksville for government purposes. The Municipal Center houses the Town Hall, where town meetings are held.

The FALLS OF THE OHIO STATE PARK, located on the river in Clarksville, is alongside the world's largest exposed FOSSIL bed of the Devonian Age. This limestone reef occupies 220 acres and offers a display of 350-million-year-old fossils. Located above the fossil beds is the interpretive center, with displays that tell the story of the Falls area. The fossil beds and adjacent portions of the Falls of the Ohio have been designated by Congress as a National Wildlife Conservation Area. The town maintains eleven parks as well as the Clarksville Aquatic Center, a multi-activity water park. Lapping Park, on Potter's Ln., includes a softball complex and Wooded View, an eighteen-hole golf course.

Clarksville had a population of 13,806 in 1970, 15,164 in 1980, 19,838 in 1990, and 19,749 in 1996.

See Lewis C. Baird, *Baird's History of Clark County, Indiana* (Indianapolis 1909); Margaret Sweeney, *Fact, Fiction and Folklore of Southern Indiana* (New York 1967); Andrew R.L. Cayton, *Frontier Indiana* (Bloomington, Ind., 1996); "Early Clarksville," *Indiana Magazine of History* 41 (Dec. 1945).

Jane M. Sarles

CLAY, HENRY INDEPENDENCE "HARRY" (b aboard the USS *Independence* off Lisbon, Portugal, November 17, 1849; d Louisville, September 22, 1884). Lawyer and politician. Harry Clay's father, James Brown Clay, served as a diplomat in Lisbon. A grandson of Henry Clay, Harry was related to Louisville's Jacob family through his mother, Susan Maria (Jacob) Clay. One of ten children, Harry was educated by private tutors at Ashland, the Clay home in Lexington.

Clay attended McGill College in Canada and Washington College (Washington and Lee University) from 1865 to 1869. He then studied law in Louisville with BASIL DUKE. He practiced in San Francisco, Denver, and St. Louis, then joined the firm of Baskin and Richards in Louisville in 1875. In 1878 he was elected city prosecuting attorney, and a political career seemed assured. In 1880, however, he resigned to join the Howgate Expedition to the Arctic.

Clay spent a year in Greenland with the expedition, then returned to Louisville. He often spoke about his adventures in the Northland, gaining a degree of fame. Clay entered Louisville politics a second time. Loosely associating himself with reform elements, Clay lobbied for campaign reform in Louisville and Frankfort, charging powerful men such as JOHN G. BAXTER, Henry Murrell, JOHN WHALLEN, and his uncle, CHARLES JACOB, with corruption. He angered the same leaders when he ran against Isaac Caldwell in 1883 for state representative from Louisville's Sixth and Seventh WARDS. Narrowly defeated in one of the city's more corrupt elections, Clay established himself as a serious opponent of Whallen's efforts to become city boss.

A year later, Eleventh Ward city councilman Andrew Wepler, a supporter of Whallen, shot and killed Clay. The issue seemed to be one of honor when Wepler cast aspersions on the Clay family. Given the earlier conflicts and the number of Whallen supporters who petitioned Gov. Procter Knott for Wepler's pardon, Clay was probably an early victim of Louisville bossism. Wepler was not pardoned but served only two years in prison. Clay is buried in Lexington Cemetery.

See William Elsey Connelley and Ellis Merton Coulter, *History of Kentucky*, 5 vols., Charles Kerr, ed. (Chicago and New York 1922); Lindsey Apple, "In Search of a Star: A Kentucky Clay Goes to the Arctic," *Filson Club History Quarterly* 71 (Jan. 1997): 3–26.

Lindsey Apple

CLAY, HENRY, JR. (b Lexington, Kentucky, April 10, 1811; d Buena Vista, Mexico, February 22, 1847). Lawyer and soldier. The third son of famed Kentucky statesman Henry Clay and his wife, Lucretia, Henry Clay Jr. graduated at the age of sixteen from Transylvania College, where he made the acquaintance of Jefferson Davis, who would become a lifelong friend. Clay graduated with high honors from West Point in 1831 and, a year later, resigned his military commission to pursue a LAW career.

Clay's connection to Louisville began when he married Maria Julia Prather, daughter of prominent Louisville merchant THOMAS PRATHER, on October 10, 1832. Afterward, the couple moved to New Orleans, where Clay briefly practiced law. In the spring of 1833 he returned to Kentucky, where he purchased a farm near his father's Ashland estate near Lexington. During the 1830s he and his family spent time traveling in Europe, and Clay served two terms in the Kentucky House as a representative from Fayette County.

In 1840 Clay's beloved wife died shortly af-

Clifton Market and Saloon, 2044 Frankfort Avenue (west side) in 1883.

ter giving birth to a son. Following her death, Clay moved to Louisville, where he practiced in the law firm of John J. Jacob Jr. With the outbreak of the MEXICAN WAR in 1846, Clay enlisted and was commissioned a lieutenant-colonel in the second regiment of the Kentucky Volunteer Infantry. He was killed a year later at the battle of Buena Vista. Four months after his death, Clay's body, along with other Kentuckians killed in the same battle, was transported by the steamer *Ringgold* from New Orleans to Louisville, where a funeral procession was conducted through the downtown streets of the city past buildings draped in mourning black. From Louisville, Clay's body was given a military escort to Lexington and Frankfort. He is buried in Frankfort Cemetery in the Kentucky Veterans War Memorial.

Clay and his wife Julia were the parents of five children: Henry Clay III, Anne, Thomas Julian, as well as Matilda and Martha, both of whom died in infancy.

See *Louisville Times*, July 26, 1956, Aug. 2, 1956; Robert Remini, *Henry Clay: Statesman for the Union* (New York 1991); Richard Collins, *History of Kentucky* (Reprint, Frankfort 1966).

CLAY V. THE UNITED STATES. The MUHAMMAD ALI (Cassius Clay) draft case is historically significant because it promoted public debate on the VIETNAM WAR nationally as well as locally. Ali's draft case first became controversial in 1964 when he was classified "1-Y" (exempted) because he did not pass intelligence standards at the age of twenty-two. That was the same year he became heavyweight BOXING champion of the world and it was first reported that he had joined the Nation of Islam. The federal government tried to suppress public debate on Vietnam, but Ali's fame and draft exemption created acrimonious discussion of the war and Ali's exemption from military service. The government lowered the mental-aptitude requirement for conscription, and Ali was re-classified "1-A" (eligible) in 1966. The champ filed for conscientious objector (CO) status, and his case quickly created a public debate. Ali based his CO claim on his MUSLIM religion and being a minister. He believed Vietnam to be an "unholy war" in Islamic teaching, and he concluded that the Vietnamese were another dark-skinned people struggling for their freedom. Despite the fact that the Justice Department's hearing examiner recommended conscientious objector status for Ali, the department itself nonetheless advised the draft board to reject his claim. The rejection was based on three conclusions: first, that Ali's beliefs did not bar military service of any form, but rather were limited to military service in the U.S. Army; second, the teaching of the Nation of Islam was defined as racial and political rather than religious; and last, that Ali's claims were not consistent since they appeared only when he faced military service. He was indicted and stripped of his heavyweight title and license, forced out of boxing in his prime. In 1971 upon appeal, the Supreme Court ruled in Ali's favor; he returned to boxing and regained his heavyweight title.

Benjamin T. Harrison

CLIFTON. The Clifton neighborhood, located east of Downtown Louisville, is composed of approximately 423 acres bounded by Brownsboro Rd. to the north, Interstate 64 to the south, Ewing Ave. to the east, and Mellwood Ave. to the west. The neighborhood derives its name from one of the area's most important early landholders, gentleman farmer Col. Joshua B. Bowles, who built an estate near what is now the corner of Vernon and Sycamore Avenues between 1817 and 1842. He called it Clifton in reference to the area's topography, and the name eventually spread to the surrounding community.

Two early-nineteenth-century transportation systems that had a major impact on how Clifton was later developed are the Louisville and Shelbyville Turnpike (a toll road dating from the 1830s that was built on a ridge line trail originally formed by buffalo and migrating Native Americans) and the LOUISVILLE AND FRANKFORT RAILROAD (by 1850 it intersected the toll road and facilitated the movement of goods and people). As the turnpike road and the rail line made areas east of the city more accessible, an increasing number of people moved out to the countryside.

By the mid-1800s emerging industries began to attract residents to the area. The constant water supply provided by the Middle Fork of BEARGRASS CREEK brought DISTILLING as well as the slaughtering and processing of meats to areas nearby, while an abundance of limestone attracted quarrymen who slowly carved away huge chunks of hillside. A variety of religious denominations were represented and are noted in the presence of St. Francis of Rome Catholic Church, Clifton Unitarian, James Lees Memorial Presbyterian, and Clifton and Beargrass Baptist Churches.

In 1853 the KENTUCKY SCHOOL FOR THE BLIND, a state-supported grade and high school, relocated to Clifton. Eventually, other businesses related to the blind would emerge, among them the AMERICAN PRINTING HOUSE FOR THE BLIND (manufacturer of large-print and Braille literature), Recordings for the Blind (talking books and taped recordings), and Industries for the Blind (brooms and handicrafts). All continue to have a strong presence in the neighborhood.

While some subdivision of land occurred as early as the 1850s, it was not until after the CIVIL WAR that it was in full swing. The western tip

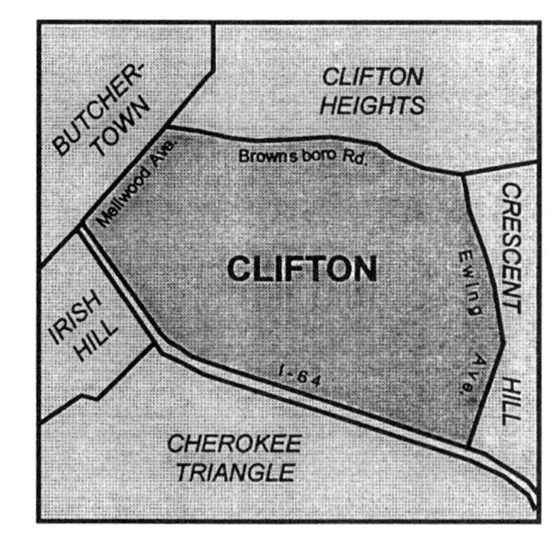

of Clifton was annexed by Louisville in 1856. In 1876, with a population of seventy-five, a group of civic-minded residents successfully petitioned the state legislature to grant a charter to the town of Clifton. It was engulfed by subsequent annexations that occurred in 1895 and 1897.

With time, a mature, mixed-use neighborhood emerged that was largely late Victorian in design. Modest one- and two-story frame and brick houses lined the side streets, with Frankfort Ave. serving as the primary commercial core. Residential building styles reflected the architectural fashions popular between 1880 and 1910, the area's major period of development, and included buildings in the Italianate, Queen Anne, Princess Anne, Tudor, Gothic Revival, and Craftsman Bungalow styles. With the popularization of the automobile and the extension of city streetcar lines, the Frankfort Ave. corridor began to take on a "layered" effect, with newer storefronts added onto older residential and commercial buildings.

Remnants of Clifton's historic past have served the neighborhood well. The neighborhood has felt a resurgence in recent years as people discover its unique historic character, and younger people have moved there to remodel the wide variety of houses. Neighborhood groups such as the Clifton Community Council and the Frankfort Avenue Business Association have bolstered community pride as well. A wide variety of new businesses has sprung up along Frankfort Ave., especially restaurants.

See Louisville Historic Landmarks and Preservation Districts Commission, Clifton National Register District nomination form, Louisville 1983 and 1994; *Louisville Survey East Report,* City of Louisville Community Development Cabinet, 1979; *St. Frances of Rome Parish: Story of Seventy-Five-Years (1887–1962)* (Louisville ca. 1962); Samuel W. Thomas, *Crescent Hill Revisited* (Louisville 1987); *Courier-Journal,* Feb. 17, 1901, Feb. 15, 1953.

Joanne Weeter

CLIFTON HEIGHTS. Triangular-shaped neighborhood in eastern Louisville bounded by Brownsboro Rd., Birchwood Ave., Interstate 71, and Mellwood Ave. Development started in the area in 1892 when the Kentucky Excelsior Manufacturing Co. planned the neighborhood of Summit Park. Three years later, Gottlieb Layer platted the subdivision of Clifton Heights, which derived its name from its higher elevation than the surrounding area. However, the area received marginal attention from prospective buyers due to its lack of a nearby STREETCAR line or any major institutions and an unfavorable terrain. Few moved into the neighborhood until the automobile permitted easier access after WORLD WAR I. The area's sporadic growth pattern, coupled with numerous developers' preferences, led to the neighborhood's discordant ARCHITECTURE ranging from simple ranch to classical revival. In 1950, the mixed residential and commercial neighborhood, traditionally known as an AFRICAN AMERICAN enclave, was replatted to accommodate the expanding city. Today African Americans constitute between 10 and 20 percent of population in the area. A local landmark is the FISCHER PACKING CO.'S meat-processing plant, established in 1909 on Mellwood Ave.

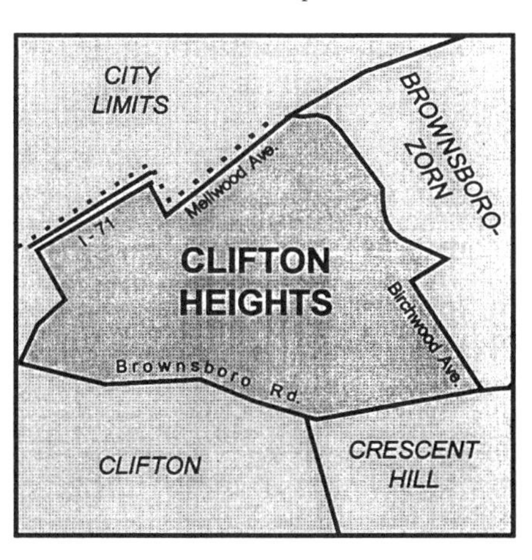

See "Louisville Survey: East Report" (Louisville 1980).

CLOISTER/URSULINE ACADEMY OF THE IMMACULATE CONCEPTION AND CONVENT. The Cloister was created by Ray Schuhmann of Photography Inc. when he bought the former URSULINE ACADEMY OF THE IMMACULATE CONCEPTION and its adjoining convent at Chestnut and Shelby Streets for sixty thousand dollars in 1977. The school had closed in 1972, but there was much public interest in saving the historic brick structures, and Louisville was then hailed nationally as a leader in HISTORIC PRESERVATION. The buildings were renovated into shops, offices, and RESTAURANTS and opened as an upscale collection of boutiques in the fall of 1977. Raposo's, a gourmet restaurant, opened in the former chapel in 1978. In July 1978, the buildings were added to the NATIONAL REGISTER OF HISTORIC PLACES.

The revitalization of the neighborhood, however, did not keep pace, and the Cloister foundered. It was difficult to keep the shops rented. Raposo's closed in December 1980.

The LOUISVILLE SCHOOL OF ART bought the property for $425,000 in 1981 and moved its campus from ANCHORAGE. The school's administration hoped that the downtown location would be an easier commute for low- and middle-income city residents, who comprised the bulk of the student body. The school renovated the buildings again to accommodate art classrooms, making large rooms with big windows and skylights. In 1983 the school added three shotgun houses, at 617–21 Shelby St., to the campus. These also were renovated into art classrooms. Later that same year, however, declining enrollment and escalating costs caused the Louisville School of Art to merge into the UNIVERSITY OF LOUISVILLE.

The buildings were left vacant until 1989 when Temple Beth Shalom, a congregation of Messianic Jews and Gentiles, began meeting in the chapel. When fire gutted the chapel that same year, seriously damaging the Johann Schmitt murals on its walls, the congregation moved to the basement, where it continues to meet.

The rest of the buildings were renovated into thirty-four apartments. This complex was dedicated in December of 1990 to provide low-income housing for single-parent households.

See Landmarks Commission report 29, Oct. 1976; *Courier-Journal,* July 27, 1978, May 22, 1981, Jan. 24, 1982, Jan. 12–13, 1983, July 13, 1983.

Otis Amanda Dick

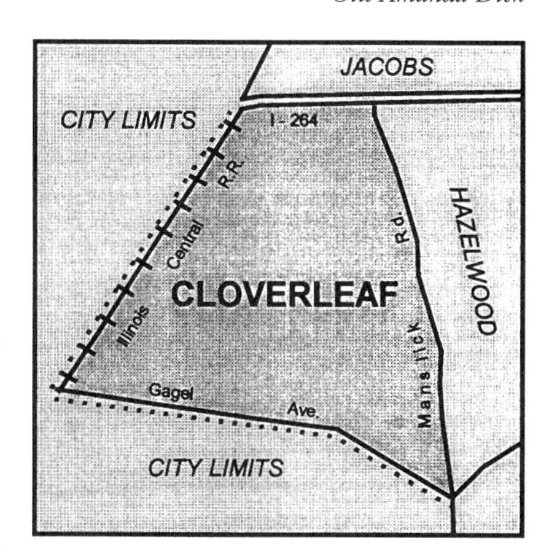

CLOVERLEAF. Neighborhood in southwestern Louisville bounded by the WATTERSON EXPRESSWAY to the north, Manslick Rd. to the east, Gagel Ave. to the south, and the ILLINOIS CENTRAL RAILROAD tracks to the west. In 1965 Thruston M. Crady purchased land south of Mill Creek and called it Cloverleaf Acres. From the beginning the Cloverleaf neighborhood has been a residential area. In 1958 it was annexed by the city.

CLOWES, MOLLY (b Birmingham, England, January 21, 1906; d Louisville, April 19, 1992). Journalist. Molly Clowes may have been the first woman to head the editorial page of a major United States newspaper, the *COURIER-JOURNAL.* She came to Louisville in 1923 when her father, a former police officer with Scotland Yard, was hired as a police sergeant. She attended school in England until the age of fifteen but was largely self-educated.

Clowes was first a reporter for Louisville's *Herald-Post* until 1936, when it closed and she joined the *Courier-Journal* as a reporter and feature writer. While still a reporter, she began writing editorials in the late 1930s. In 1941, Clowes became a full-time editorial writer, a position she held until 1966 when she was named editor of the editorial page. Specializing in writing about foreign affairs and PUBLIC HEALTH and welfare, she was editor until her retirement in 1971. Friends said she enjoyed

French cooking, disliked local politics, and enjoyed discussing developments in Europe. Clowes was married to French-born J. Willy Walsh, a WORLD WAR I pilot and later a teacher of French and history at the UNIVERSITY OF LOUISVILLE. Both were naturalized United States citizens. They had no children.

See *Courier-Journal*, Feb. 6, 1971, April 21, 1992.

Mary Lawrence Young

COAL HOLE COVERS. During the nineteenth and early twentieth centuries, coal was used extensively to heat Louisville factories and office buildings as well as homes. The coal was supplied by local purveyors and delivered by workmen using carts or wagons. Stopping in front of a business to remove the CAST-IRON coal hole cover from the sidewalk, they would shovel the coal into a chute to a basement storage bin, where it would form a pile next to the coal-fired furnace. The coal could be then easily shoveled by the building custodian into the furnace as needed. Although most coal furnaces have long ago been replaced by gas, oil, or electric heat, coal hole covers can still be seen embedded in some sidewalks in Louisville's older commercial districts.

Coal hole covers are part of a larger group—manhole covers that give access to underground utility installations and to water reservoirs for use by the fire department in fighting fires. Many of these are on the street and are as artistically designed as those of coal holes.

Louisville, a major supplier of cast iron during the mid- to late nineteenth century, had a dozen or more foundries operating during the industry's peak in the 1880s. The same foundries that cast the iron for Louisville's Victorian era storefronts also manufactured coal hole covers. These functional objects were round, came in a variety of sizes, and were held in place by a custom-made (and often ill-fitting) fixed ring. Sometimes the name of the casting foundry was integrated into the cover's design as a form of advertisement. These artifacts of the Industrial Age were often aesthetically pleasing as well as functional. Many were embellished with strikingly beautiful and highly ornamental geometric designs.

Perhaps the most widely recognized of Louisville's coal hole cover designs was cast by the Snead & Co. Iron Works, the area's most prolific cast iron manufacturer. A preservation advocacy group, PRESERVATION ALLIANCE of Louisville and Jefferson County Inc., used the Snead design as its organization's logo, embracing its distinct design of concentric circles. Later this same design served as the inspiration for the custom protective grates installed at the base of trees along historic W MAIN ST. Mimi Melnick also chose the Snead & Co. logo to grace the cover of her book *Manhole Covers*.

Awareness of the importance of coal hole covers as unique local examples of industrial art has increased. In the 1970s the UNIVERSITY OF LOUISVILLE and the Kentucky Arts Council joined forces to conduct an extensive study of these covers. Their photographic survey of extant coal hole covers in Louisville's downtown confirmed that over seventy were still in use at that time. Later, rubbings were taken of the decorative surfaces of selected covers using techniques popularized by British brass monument societies. These rubbings were later photographically reproduced to a uniform size and displayed as part of an exhibition on the subject.

In 1985 COURIER-JOURNAL columnist Byron Crawford declared, "In America's gallery of accidental art, Louisville is the Louvre of [coal hole] covers." Melnick used eleven Louisville examples to illustrate her book and declared, "I would rate Louisville's manhole covers Number 1, not only nationwide but worldwide [in terms of their aesthetic appeal and because of their high concentration]."

Although many of Louisville's coal hole covers have been removed from their original locations in recent years, a half-dozen have been saved and re-installed as part of a public art interpretation project in the sidewalk in front of the Hart Block Building at 726 W Main St. A commemorative plaque reveals their history.

Coal hole covers manufactured by Snead & Co. Iron Works and Merz Architectural Iron Works, c. 1960.

See Mimi Melnick, *Manhole Covers* (Cambridge, Mass., 1994); *Courier- Journal,* Jan. 8, 1995; Margot Gayle and Edmund V. Gillian Jr., *Cast-Iron Architecture in New York* (New York 1974).

Joanne Weeter

COCHRAN, ARCHIBALD PRENTICE (b Louisville, March 28, 1898; d Louisville, May 2, 1970). Industrialist and civic leader. Archibald P. "Archie" Cochran, the son of Margaret Lee and Heywood Cochran, was educated at MALE HIGH SCHOOL and graduated from the Massachusetts Institute of Technology in 1920. After completing his education and serving as a Marine Corps flight instructor during World War I, he returned to Louisville and rose from mill helper to plant manager at United States Foil Co., which was later bought by REYNOLDS METALS.

In 1936 Cochran married Mary "Polly" Zimmer of Richmond, Virginia, and in 1940 founded Cochran Foil Co. During WORLD WAR II, the plant's products included chaff foil, which was thrown out of aircraft to confuse enemy radar. Cochran Foil was later sold to Anaconda Aluminum.

While traveling in Europe, Cochran had become impressed by the way cities such as Paris had successfully integrated their waterfronts into the lives of their citizens. Convinced that Louisville could gain the same benefits, Cochran founded the Louisville River Area Foundation Inc. in 1959 (it was later renamed RIVER FIELDS Inc.). River Fields is the ninth-oldest river-conservation organization in America. Cochran, acting with River Fields, was the key citizen leader in the drive to revitalize Louisville's waterfront in the late 1960s. At first no one wanted to invest in the area; finally, developer Al J. Schneider built the GALT HOUSE, and that paved the way for construction of the Riverfront Plaza Belvedere, under Cochran's guidance.

During the final decades of his life, Archie Cochran used his business and financial acumen to bring other civic projects to fruition. He was president of the local YMCA chapter and the Louisville Area Chamber of Commerce as well as vice president of the State Fair Board, and he served on the Louisville and Jefferson County BOARD OF HEALTH. In 1965 he spearheaded the issuing of municipal bonds that led to improvements throughout the city. From 1966 until his sudden death in 1970, Cochran was chairman of the board of trustees at the University of Louisville and was instrumental in having the university made a state institution.

After Cochran's death, his wife quietly carried on his work to beautify the city waterfront and preserve riverfront property. She joined the board of River Fields, serving as vice president from 1974 to 1980 and secretary from 1991 to 1994. The group flourished, accumulating eighty acres of river corridor and increasing its roster of members. He and his wife are buried in CAVE HILL CEMETERY.

See Tom Owen, *Inside U of L* 5 (June 30, 1986): 3; *Courier-Journal,* March 27, 1997.

Meme Runyon

COCHRAN HILL. In 1868 Archibald P. Cochran (1823–89), a wealthy IRON FOUNDRY businessman, purchased the property of Judge Joshua Fry Bullitt east of downtown, and he and his wife, Harriet, built a large estate called Fern Cliff in what is now Cherokee Park.

In 1887 Col. ANDREW COWAN proposed the concept of a city park system. His goal was to form three large suburban PARKS called east, west, and south parks. It was proposed that the eastern park was to encompass the Morton and Griswold woods and the Alexander, Cochran, Bonnycastle, Barret, Wilson, and Belknap estates. Cowan proposed that the eastern park be named "Beargrass," but the name Cherokee was selected instead in 1891.

After Cochran's death in 1889, his wife sold the forty-three-acre estate to the Board of Park Commissioners. The house was converted into a museum, called the Jefferson Institute of Arts and Sciences, with R.C. BALLARD THRUSTON as its benefactor. The museum operated out of the home from 1911 to 1914, when the institute closed. The museum collection was given to LOUISVILLE FREE PUBLIC LIBRARY and is now a part of the LOUISVILLE SCIENCE CENTER'S collection. The house has been demolished.

Cochran Hill is still located in Cherokee Park, although Cochran Hill Rd. lies outside the park boundaries and runs through the Eastleigh subdivision. The hill became the focus of attention when in 1966 the federal government proposed to run Interstate 64 through Seneca and Cherokee Parks. To appease challenges from citizens groups such as Save Our Parks, the federal government agreed to pay 90 percent of the estimated $1.2 million to make a twin-bored tunnel through the hill near Lexington Rd. and Grinstead Dr. The tunnels, which average 424 feet in length and are approximately 65 feet below the crest of the hill, opened in August 1970.

See Samuel W. Thomas, *Crescent Hill Revisited* (Louisville 1987).

COCKE, WILLIAM A. (b 1796; d Louisville, May 9, 1844). Mayor. Little is known of Cocke's early life. He was elected to a one-year term on the City Council in 1834 to represent the First Ward, and again in 1838 and 1843 representing the Sixth Ward after the city was redistricted. He was Louisville's first marshal for the Chancery Court. Cocke was elected marshal by a wide majority in 1828 along with Louisville's first MAYOR, JOHN C. BUCKLIN.

Cocke was elected Louisville's third mayor on March 21, 1836, and served for one year, until March 15, 1837. He was the first mayor to be elected by the City Council after an act of the General Assembly took the authority to select the mayor away from the governor and state Senate. This new method of selection was problematic, since it often took several balloting attempts to place an individual in the office. In the 1836 council election it took three council meetings before the council was able to reach a majority. During this three-week period, a resolution was introduced to refer the election to the people of Louisville, but it was defeated. Cocke eventually was selected mayor over Levi Tyler by a vote of 7 to 3.

Cocke ran for mayor again in 1841 but was not elected even though he received the majority of the votes. His opponent in that election, James Harrison, gave various reasons why Cocke should not take office. Cocke then requested a new election, but in that election both Cocke and Harrison were defeated by DAVID L. BEATTY, who received a plurality of 135 votes over the other candidates.

Cocke also served as secretary of the Kentucky & Louisville Mutual Insurance Co., organized in 1839. He was married to Matilda Cocke, and the couple had five children: Thomas, William, Edward, James, and Eliza. The family lived on the corner of Sixth and Grayson Streets at the time of his death.

See Richard and Lewis Collins, *Historical Sketches of Kentucky* 2 vols. (Frankfort 1874); Attia Martha Bowmer, *The History of the Government of the City of Louisville 1780–1820,* M.A. thesis, University of Louisville, 1948; *Louisville Daily Journal,* May 7, 1841, May 10, 1844.

COLE, HIRAM (b Prospect, Kentucky, ca. 1806; d Harrods Creek, Kentucky, March 21, 1829). Ferry operator. The story of Cole, known for his outrageous tales of those he reportedly ushered across the OHIO RIVER from HARRODS CREEK to UTICA, INDIANA, remains shrouded in mystery, as no sources exist outside of local tradition. Cole reportedly grew up around the Sand Hill area (modern-day PROSPECT) and worked as a farmhand during his childhood. After realizing the demand for a ferry following the discontinuation of James Noble's service in 1825, Cole proceeded to the Harrods Creek basin east of Louisville, where he constructed a ferry he named *Fanny* after his boyhood love, Francis Dearing. Popularly known as the river's fastest ferrier, Cole had a taste for eccentric items and would barter with his customers for anything that caught his eye. He also grew quite gifted at storytelling and would embellish the tales of those whom he had escorted across the river, who reportedly included local giant JIM PORTER and Andrew Jackson during his 1829 visit. According to legend, Cole claimed that Porter once fell off of the ferry and appeared to be drowning until Cole told the 7' 8" Porter to stand up, at which time the water was only up to the man's chest. Cole's untimely demise occurred during the winter of 1829 when his ferry, overloaded with dry goods, tipped in the frigid Ohio River waters. Unable to right the sinking ferry, Cole drowned. His body was never recovered.

See "Harrods Creek," *Louisville Historical League Newsletter*, May 1982.

COLE, I. WILLIS (b Memphis, Tennessee, January 22, 1887; d Louisville, February 19, 1950). Publisher and civic leader. The son of James Henry and Roberta Cole, I. Willis Cole graduated from LeMoyne College in Memphis at the age of nineteen. From there he moved to Chicago and entered the Garrett Bible Institute. While on a trip to Louisville to sell bibles, Cole decided to quit school and settle here.

Shortly thereafter, in 1917, he founded the I. Willis Cole Publishing Co. and produced the inaugural issue of the *LOUISVILLE LEADER*, a weekly newspaper for AFRICAN AMERICANS. In his editorials, Cole adamantly condemned racial discrimination, stressed the importance of black pride, and often encouraged blacks to withhold their patronage from businesses owned or operated by whites. The *Leader* soon became Louisville's foremost black newspaper, and Cole continued as publisher until his death.

Cole was actively involved in a number of community and business activities. He was a board member of the MAMMOTH LIFE INSURANCE Co., president of the Mammoth Realty Co., and president of the Falls City Chamber of Commerce. He was also involved with the URBAN LEAGUE and served for a time as president of Louisville's NAACP branch. He was the first African American to sit on the advisory board of the Kentucky National Youth Administration, one of the agencies established by the federal government during the presidency of Franklin D. Roosevelt.

Cole and his first wife, Katherine Walker, had four children: I. Willis Junior, Ruthlyn, Katherine, and Anna. After Mrs. Cole's death in 1921, he married Rosa Long. Their children were Lattimore and Tella. Cole is buried in Louisville Cemetery.

See George C. Wright, *Life Behind a Veil: Blacks in Louisville, Kentucky, 1865–1930* (Baton Rouge 1985).

John A. Hardin

COLE, WHITEFOORD RUSSELL (b Nashville, Tennessee, January 14, 1874; d near Cave City en route to Louisville aboard train, November 17, 1934). Railroad executive. Whitefoord, who corrected anyone who omitted the additional "o" from his name, was born the only child of Col. Edmund "King" William and Anna Virginia (Russell) Cole. His was one of the most prominent families in Tennessee; his mother was a well-known socialite and the founder of the Southern Sociological Congress, while his father founded the American National Bank of Tennessee and ran the Nashville & Chattanooga Railroad (later the Nashville, Chattanooga, & St. Louis) and the East Tennessee, Virginia, & Georgia Railroad.

After finishing his education at Vanderbilt University (1890–94), Whitefoord joined the

Nashville, Chattanooga, & St. Louis Railroad as a director and worked his way up to the presidency of the Sheffield Coal, Iron, and Steel Co. in Sheffield, Alabama, and the Napier Iron Works in Bevier, Kentucky. Upon his father's death in 1899, Cole became the managing director of Sheffield Coal, Iron, and Steel and eventually the president in 1918.

Cole's reputation, after he served as the president of the Nashville and Decatur Railroad and the Nashville, Chattanooga, & St. Louis, earned him the presidency of the LOUISVILLE & NASHVILLE RAILROAD in 1926 after the untimely death of Wible Mapother. During his tenure, Cole fought excessive governmental regulation, battled new competition, urged the rebuilding of the aging rails, and guided the railroad through the GREAT DEPRESSION without losing revenue.

During his years in Louisville, Cole also was president of the Southeastern President's Conference, which represented railways before the federal government. He also held high positions on the LOUISVILLE BOARD OF TRADE, the Vanderbilt Board of Trustees, and in numerous RAILROADS, TELEPHONE companies, and banks, including the local branch of the FEDERAL RESERVE.

Cole married Mary Conner Bass on April 21, 1901; they had one son, Whitefoord Russell Jr. While riding back from Nashville in an office car on the L&N's premier train, the Pan American, to see his newly born grandson, Cole collapsed of heart failure near Cave City, Kentucky. After services in Louisville, the body was returned to Nashville for burial in the Mt. Olivet Cemetery.

See Jesse C. Bart Jr., "Whitefoord Russell Cole—A Study in Character," *Filson Club History Quarterly* 28 (Jan. 1954): 28–48; Maury Klein, *History of the Louisville & Nashville Railroad* (New York 1972).

COLE, WILLIAM (b Jefferson County, ca. 1820; d Louisville, April 6, 1881). Barber and musician. Cole, who was born a free African American, joined JAMES C. CUNNINGHAM'S popular band as a violinist in the late 1840s. In 1855 Cole, who lived near Seventh and Green (now LIBERTY) STREETS, organized his own string band. Cole's Cotillion Band became very popular and played for a wide variety of functions, including cotillions, balls, picnics, barbecues, parades, political rallies, and steamboat excursions. His band was in great demand by trade groups and social organizations such as firemen, butchers, carpenters, and Odd Fellows. He was best remembered for his dance music at picnics and barbecues. He and his wife, Anna Graves, had two children, Ida and Lizzie. He is buried on a small farm he owned in Jefferson County.

Cornelius Bogert

COLGAN, JOHN (b Louisville, December 18, 1840; d Louisville, February 1, 1916). Pharmacist. The son of William and Elizabeth (Christopher) Colgan. He was orphaned by the age of twelve, at which time he was taken in by his uncle, Henry Christopher. He was educated in Louisville's public schools and attended St. Joseph's College in Somerset, Ohio.

In 1858 Colgan began an apprenticeship in a local drugstore, and in 1860 he established his own drug business on the northwest corner of Tenth and Walnut (now Muhammad Ali Blvd.) Streets. Colgan's business flourished, but it was not until the 1870s that he became widely known as the reputed first manufacturer of flavored chewing gum.

Though the precise date of Colgan's creation is not known, it is believed that he was making his "Taffy Tolu" gum as early as 1873. The product was a substance made by adding balsam tolu extract, a cough syrup flavoring, to chicle. Certainly the use of chicle was known prior to Colgan's gum. It is the addition of a flavoring that may merit him the distinction of the first person to combine the two.

Around 1880 he entered into a partnership with James A. McAfee under the company name of Colgan & McAfee. In 1890, with the "Taffy Tolu" a success, they decided to focus solely on the production of chewing gum. A few years later, Colgan and McAfee's association ended, and Colgan established the Colgan Chewing Gum Co., originally located on Seventh St. between MARKET and Jefferson, and later on W Breckinridge between Seventh and Eighth Streets. His popular "Taffy Tolu" gum was marketed throughout the United States, Canada, and Australia. Colgan retired about 1911, and the Colgan Chewing Gum Co. was sold to the Autosales Gum and Chocolate Co. of New York.

John Colgan married Mattie McCrory in 1866, and they had five children: Bettie, William, Henry, Mabel, and Clifton. Colgan is buried in Cave Hill Cemetery.

See J. Stoddard Johnston, ed., *Memorial History of Louisville* vol. 2 (Chicago 1896).

COLGATE-PALMOLIVE PLANT AND CLOCK. Located in CLARKSVILLE, INDIANA, overlooking the OHIO RIVER, the Colgate-Palmolive Co. plant occupies surviving portions of the former Indiana Reformatory for Men. Constructed in stages during the late nineteenth and early twentieth centuries, the Romanesque structure functioned as a prison until 1922. The Colgate-Palmolive-Peet Co. bought it in 1923 and reopened it the following year as a soap factory. Since then it has produced a variety of soap, detergent, and personal-care products. Despite significant workforce reductions, the plant remains one of southern Indiana's leading private employers.

The Colgate Clock, a major local landmark, was built in 1908 and stood for sixteen years atop the Colgate plant in Jersey City, New Jersey. At that time it was the world's largest timepiece. It was replaced by a larger clock and moved to Clarksville in 1924. Measuring forty feet in diameter, with hands of sixteen and twenty and one-half feet in length, it is still the second-largest clock in the world, exceeding London's Big Ben.

See Carl E. Kramer, *Brief History of Jeffersonville, Clarksville, New Albany and Corydon,* (Jeffersonville, Ind., 1997); Lewis C. Baird, *Baird's History of Clark County* (Indianapolis 1909).

Carl E. Kramer

COLLINS, LEE (b Priceville, Kentucky, April 26, 1892; d Shelbyville, Kentucky, March 26, 1976). Inventor. When Lee Collins was four years old, his father closed down the general merchandise store he ran in Priceville in Hart County, Kentucky, and moved his young family to Louisville, where he operated a grocery store. The family moved in with Collins's paternal grandparents, who were given custody of the child. As a youth he showed early signs of interest in all things mechanical. He insisted that he be the one to wind all clocks in his house, ran a miniature train set, and constructed a string telephone for his friends.

In 1905 Collins began making more profitable devices. His gum dispenser was installed in several stores around the neighborhood. It was also this year that he began delivering papers for the *COURIER-JOURNAL*. His career there was extended when, in 1911, as Collins was preparing to leave home to attend college, his father and grandfather passed away, leaving him to care for his family. He studied engineering, physics, and chemistry under private tutors while working as nighttime advertisement manager for the newspaper.

In the following years Collins was to have countless promising ideas rendered useless by lawsuits. His ideas, however, did catch the attention of THOMAS EDISON, who was serving on the United States Naval Consulting Board during WORLD WAR I. It was through this connection that Collins was to achieve his first great success. He devised a system by which long-range artillery on United States ships could automatically aim and fire in the direction of approaching subs, which the military quickly put to use.

Another wartime invention of Collins came in answer to the difficulty the country was having in spreading propaganda on the German lines. A shortage of airplanes left military leaders seeking other methods, and Collins had the idea to suspend the propaganda from gas-filled balloons that would ride the prevailing easterly winds into Germany and release their cargo when a fuse burst the balloon. This invention was cited by both American and German leaders as important in the propaganda aspects of the war.

Other notable inventions included an early method of recording sound and film at the same time, a projector for the first talking pictures, and a method of guiding airplanes by radio control, used by U.S. forces in the KOREAN WAR.

While Collins never received a great deal of money for any of his inventions, he was considered one of the brightest inventors of his day.

In 1921 Collins married Virginia Ruth Montgomery, and they had one son. In 1957 Collins retired from the *Courier-Journal* and continued to work on his inventions. He is buried in Resthaven Memorial Park.

See Richard L. Collins, "Collins Laboratories," University of Louisville Local History Series, vol. 2, University Archives and Records Center.

COLLINS, MARTHA LAYNE (HALL) (b Bagdad, Kentucky, December 7, 1936). Governor. Martha Layne Collins is the daughter of Everett and Mary Taylor Hall. She spent a year at Lindenwood College in Missouri, then transferred to the University of Kentucky, where in 1959 she received a degree in home economics. Soon afterward she married William Collins; they had two children, Steve and Maria "Marla." While her husband completed his dentistry degree at the UNIVERSITY OF LOUISVILLE, she taught in area high schools, including Fairdale and Seneca. The couple moved to Versailles, Kentucky, in the mid-1960s, and Collins taught at Woodford County Junior High School.

She became interested in Democratic politics and showed a talent for organization. She served as Wendell Ford's campaign manager for governor, taking a leave of absence from teaching and never returning. When Ford was elected in 1971, he named Collins to represent Kentucky on the Democratic National Committee. She then worked to elect Walter "Dee" Huddleston to the U.S. Senate in 1972 and continued to work behind the scenes until 1975, when she made her first bid for public office.

Collins won the party's nomination for clerk of the Court of Appeals in 1975 and defeated Republican Joseph E. Lambert, 382,528 to 233,442, in the general election. In 1979 she was one of six major candidates who sought the party's endorsement for lieutenant governor. The vote was so divided that her 23 percent won the nomination. She then defeated Republican Harold Rogers 543,176 to 316,798, becoming the state's second female lieutenant governor. Several times as president of the state senate, she took controversial stands on legislation. In 1980 she voted against a professional negotiations bill for teachers, and in 1982 she voted against a bill that would allow multibank holding companies to buy banks across county lines. In the administration of John Y. Brown Jr. (1979–83), Collins kept her distance from the administration and maintained close ties with the party machinery. When she announced her candidacy for governor in 1983, she had the support of many party regulars and record campaign funds. The primary was a close race, in which Collins won the nomination with 223,692 votes to 219,160 for HARVEY SLOANE and 199,795 for Grady Stumbo. In the general election, she defeated state senator Jim Bunning, 561,674 to 454,650.

During her campaign for governor, Collins promised to avoid new taxes and to give priority to educational reforms. However, recovering from the recession of 1982–83, Kentucky faced a revenue shortage even as demands for quick action on education became more insistent. Collins asked the General Assembly for $324 million in additional funds in 1984, most of it committed to public schools. When it became apparent that the House would not vote that sum in an election year for its members, she withdrew her tax proposals and substituted a continuation budget. Critics of the governor stressed her failure to control the newly independent legislature and the resultant defeat of major parts of her program during the first session. The legislature in 1984 enacted a tougher drunk-driving law and the multibank bill that allowed state banking companies to purchase other banks in the state. Later that year Governor Collins chaired the Democratic national convention and was one of the vice presidential hopefuls interviewed by former vice president Walter F. Mondale.

One of her major accomplishments came when the Japanese company, Toyota Motor Sales, USA, decided to establish a large automobile plant near Georgetown. Some detractors, including Wallace Wilkinson, her successor, charged that the $125 million in incentives (with an ultimate cost of $300 million in bonds) was excessive, but criticism was blunted as dozens of Toyota suppliers set up plants across the state. A record number of new job opportunities were brought to Kentucky under Collins's national and international economic development program.

Upon leaving office in December 1987, Collins became an international trade consultant; she taught at the University of Louisville in 1988 and at the Institute of Politics at Harvard University in 1989. She served on the boards of the SOUTHERN BAPTIST THEOLOGICAL SEMINARY and Midway College. In June 1990 she became president of St. Catharine College in Washington County, a position she held until June 1996. She then became director of the International Business and Management Center at the University of Kentucky, and in 1998 she went to Georgetown College, where she works out of the president's office.

See *Courier-Journal*, Aug. 22, 1998, May 8, 1996; "Governor Martha Layne Collins," *Register of the Kentucky Historical Society* 82 (Summer 1984): 211–13; Lowell H. Harrison, *Kentucky's Governors 1792–1985* (Lexington 1985); Robert A. Powell, *Kentucky Governors* (Lexington 1989).

COLONNADE CAFETERIA. The Colonnade Cafeteria opened in 1913 above the Boston Shoe Co. on S FOURTH ST. and remained in that location until 1924. When the STARKS BUILDING annex was erected in 1925–26, the cafeteria moved to its now-familiar spot in the building's basement. It serves luncheon fare to office workers in the building above, other nearby businesses, and shoppers in the downtown area.

Whether in Cincinnati, Cleveland, Detroit, Houston, Philadelphia, or Pittsburgh, most Colonnade Cafeterias were located on the lower level of downtown office buildings. Since the word "colonnade," means "a support for a roof, ceiling, cornice, or the like," the name probably symbolized their subterranean location.

Throughout its first eighty-three years in Louisville, the Colonnade Cafeteria was never locally owned until the company, based in Ohio, was purchased in December 1996 by Louisville-based Krill Enterprises Inc., a three-person partnership, with plans for expansion. The Colonnade opened a second, short-lived location in Dupont Square, at 4040 Dutchmans Ln., in September 1997. It closed in December of the same year.

Joseph Krill

COLORED ORPHANS' HOME. An orphanage formed in 1877 by a coalition of African American churches in Louisville to offer education and a stable social environment for children, it was also the first welfare institution opened in the city for people of color.

Originally founded at Taylor Barracks at Third and Oak Streets, the home moved to a larger facility at Eighteenth and Dumesnil in 1878. The site was donated by the American Missionary Society. The home received financial and material support from black churches and civic groups throughout the city. The Ladies Sewing Circle made the home its special project, donating furniture, blankets, sheets, and clothing. Other women's groups held annual fund-raising events at the home, baking cakes and pies for residents and for sale.

Larger churches, notably the FIFTH STREET BAPTIST CHURCH, and FRATERNAL ORGANIZATIONS such as the United Brothers of Friendship gave annual contributions and helped with the home's upkeep. At its peak, the home supported around seventy children and operated on a budget of less than five thousand dollars annually.

For three decades the Colored Orphans' Home was supported only by contributions from the city's black community. In 1909, Rev. Elijah Harris was elected president with the goal of attracting white benefactors. One of his first supporters was JAMES B. SPEED, who gave five hundred dollars in 1910, an amount greater than the total from all other white contributors. It soon became fashionable for wealthy whites to support the home. Soon the Board of Directors was dominated by this group. Eventually a yearly grant from the Louisville Welfare League was established, providing 90 percent of the home's funds.

In 1921, the annual report of the Louisville Welfare League described the home as "unsanitary and totally unfit for any use. Yet this building continues to house children. . . . This is the only colored orphanage in the city, and the conditions are so wretched that it should either acquire a new building or cease to operate." Yet children were still living in the home two years later, with sixty-seven children housed in a facility with a capacity for twenty-five, often with three children to a bed. The home moved to larger facilities at 1224 Dixie Hwy. in 1928 and closed in 1935.

See George C. Wright, *Life Behind a Veil* (Baton Rouge 1985); idem, "Blacks in Louisville 1890–1930," Ph.D. thesis, Duke University, 1977.

COLUMBIA BUILDING. The Columbia Building, Louisville's second skyscraper (surpassing the six-story Kenyon Building), was a culmination of the efforts by the Commercial Club to attract attention to the city and modernize downtown. Construction of the ten-story building, which began in 1888, was completed late in 1890 at a cost of $1 million. This allowed for a grand opening on the first day of 1891.

The building, which was first called the Commercial Club Building and later the Columbia, was the tallest building in the city for a decade. It was finished only five years after the completion of the country's first skyscraper, the Home Insurance Co. Building in Chicago. Designed by architects Cornelius Curtin and Pike Campbell of the Louisville firm Curtin and Campbell, the round-arched Romanesque-style building at the northwest corner of Fourth and Main Streets was constructed of pressed red brick and sat upon a foundation of red sandstone, akin to the work of Henry Hobson Richardson.

In 1964 the City Urban Renewal Agency purchased the Columbia Building along with several other properties in the area as part of its riverfront revitalization plan. Demolition of the Columbia Building began on September 30, 1966, and was completed by the end of the year. On the site of the old structure, the Louisville Trust Co. erected a twenty-four-story high-rise; the site is currently occupied by the Commonwealth Bank and Trust Co. As a reminder of the previous structure, a block of the original foundation from the Columbia Building was placed in front of the new building.

Columbia Building, north west corner Fourth and Main Streets, 1910.

See George H. Yater, *Two Hundred Years at the Falls of the Ohio* (Louisville 1987); "Meanwhile, at Fourth and Main," *Louisville* (March 1966): 43.

COLVIN, GEORGE (b Washington County, Kentucky, September 7, 1875; d Louisville, July 22, 1928). Educator and lawyer. He was the second of eight children of William Arthur and Lucy Allen Harris Colvin. After attending public school in Willisburg, he entered Centre College in Danville in 1891 and graduated in 1895. He was captain and quarterback of Centre's noted football team of 1894. After a year spent studying law at Centre, Colvin went to Springfield, Kentucky, and taught school. In 1900 he joined the Louisville Title Co., where he did legal work. In 1903 he returned to Springfield, practiced law for a few months, then became the town's superintendent of public schools.

In July 1919 Colvin won the Republican Party's nomination for state superintendent of public instruction, and in November was elected to office, along with the entire Republican ticket headed by gubernatorial candidate Edwin P. Morrow (1919–23). As state superintendent, Colvin worked for higher teacher salaries, a compulsory attendance law, health education, and an elected board of education for each county that would appoint the county superintendent. He was instrumental in the passage of the state's County School Administration Law in 1920. He urged the adoption of a longer school year for rural children and higher educational and professional standards for teachers and administrators, and he supported the Kentucky Education Association.

In May 1923 Colvin announced his candidacy for governor, but he failed to secure the Republican nomination. Colvin resigned his state post and returned to Louisville in November to accept appointment as superintendent of the Louisville and Jefferson County Children's Home. Formerly called the Louisville Industrial School of Reform, it was a city-owned facility for orphans and delinquent children on S Third St. He instituted reforms and oversaw the institution's move to its new Ormsby Village site in February 1925.

After the death of University of Louisville president Arthur Y. Ford, the university's board of trustees appointed Colvin to that position on August 1, 1926. As the school's eighth president, Colvin resisted faculty efforts to strengthen graduate programs and concentrated on developing the undergraduate curriculum. When he limited faculty contracts to one year, he faced strong opposition.

Louis R. Gottschalk, who taught history at the university from 1923 to 1927, resigned when his colleague, a professor of ancient history named Rolf Johannesen, delayed signing his one-year contract and was dismissed. Gottschalk then called for an investigation by the American Association of University Professors and issued a public statement critical of Colvin. Although thirty-nine of the forty-seven liberal arts faculty members petitioned for Colvin's resignation, he was supported by most of the trustees and continued to serve as president until his death in 1928.

On January 20, 1904, Colvin married Mary McElroy of Springfield. They had a daughter, Lovey Mary, and two sons, George and Palmer. Colvin died after surgery for appendicitis. He is buried in Springfield.

See Kitty Conroy, "George Colvin: Kentucky Statesman and Educator," *Bulletin of the Bureau of School Service, College of Education, University of Kentucky* 16 (March 1944): 5–57.

William J. Morison

COMBS, BERT THOMAS (b Clay County, Kentucky, August 13, 1911; d Powell County, Kentucky, December 3, 1991). Governor. The son of Stephen Gibson and Martha Jones Combs. He studied two years at Oneida Institute, then graduated from Clay County High School in 1927. After three semesters at Cumberland College, Combs worked three years with the highway department. He took another semester of classes at the University of Kentucky before being admitted to its law school.

After graduating with honors in 1937, he began practicing law, first in Manchester and then in Prestonsburg. After enlisting in the army as a private, Combs became a captain and served on Gen. Douglas MacArthur's staff and assisted in prosecuting Japanese war criminals in the Philippines.

Combs returned to Prestonsburg in 1946 and became city attorney in 1950 and commonwealth's attorney in 1951. In April 1951 he was appointed to a vacancy on the Court of Appeals, then Kentucky's highest court. Later that year he won election to the unexpired term but resigned in 1955 to seek the Democratic nomination for governor. He lost to former governor A.B. Chandler, who derided Combs's assertion that the state needed $25 million in additional revenue. In 1959 Combs won the nomination by twenty-five thousand votes over Harry Lee Waterfield when Wilson Wyatt, also seeking the governor's office, agreed to run with Combs as the candidate for lieutenant governor. The Combs-Wyatt ticket defeated Louisville Republican John M. Robsion Jr. by a record 516,549 to 336,456 votes.

Combs got additional revenue by securing

a 3 percent sales tax to pay a veterans' bonus, although less than 1 percent was needed for the bonus itself. Larger sums were spent on roads, parks, education on all levels, human resources, and social services. A merit system was implemented for state employees, and Combs appointed the state's first civil rights commission. An executive order desegregated public accommodations in 1963. He moved quickly to halt incidents of misconduct. A truck lease deal resulted in a split with former governor Earle C. Clements, who was serving as highway commissioner. Combs's most galling defeat was the voters' refusal to revise the archaic state constitution.

In 1967 Combs was appointed to the U.S. Sixth Court of Appeals in Cincinnati. He resigned in 1970 and sought the party's nomination for governor in 1971. Although an early favorite to win, he lost to Wendell F. Ford. Combs then became a major partner in the Louisville firm of Bullitt, Dawson, and Tarrant (later Tarrant, Combs, and Bullitt). Although active in Democratic Party affairs, Combs did not seek office again. He moved to Lexington in 1981 to the law firm's office there. He was the lead attorney who filed suit for sixty-six poorer school districts and won a 1988 decision that the public school system was unconstitutional due to the inequitable funding that resulted in vastly different qualities of instruction. This decision led to the Kentucky Education Reform Act of 1990.

As Combs reduced his law practice, he divided time between Lexington and his Powell County farm. He was returning to the farm on the night of December 3, 1991, when his car was swept away by the flooded Red River. He is buried in the Beech Creek Cemetery in Clay County.

Combs married Helen Hall of Hindman in 1937. Their children were Ann (1945) and Thomas George (1947). After a 1969 divorce Combs married Louisvillian Helen Clark Rechtin. Following their divorce, Combs married Sara Walker in 1988, a fellow attorney who survived him.

See George W. Robinson, ed., *Bert Combs, The Politician: An Oral History* (Lexington 1991); idem, *The Public Papers of Bert T. Combs, 1959–1963* (Lexington 1979); John Ed Pearce, *Divide and Dissent: Kentucky Politics, 1930–1963* (Lexington 1987); Lowell H. Harrison, ed., *Kentucky's Governors, 1792–1985* (Lexington 1985).

Lowell H. Harrison

COMMISSIONERS OF SEWERAGE. Although the first commissioners of sewerage unit was formed in 1906, the board's existence was divided into two different time periods: 1906 to 1912 and 1919 to 1942. Dating back to the 1820s, the city had constructed a few drain lines running north and south in the business district, although they consisted mainly of street-side gutters that channeled the water toward the river following heavy rains. The first real sewer in the city was built in 1850 and consisted of a roughly three-thousand-foot line running along First St. from Walnut St. (Muhammad Ali Blvd.) to BEARGRASS CREEK.

By 1870 the high number of malaria cases, thought to be caused by waste in the streams and streets, prompted city engineer Gen. I.M. St. John to study future needs of the growing city. Upon his recommendation, the first major trunk line, known as the Western Outfall, was constructed between 1871 and 1873, running from Lexington St. (modern-day Breckinridge St.) between Fourteenth and Fifteenth Streets westerly to the river. Additional sewers made of concrete, which was found to be smoother, cheaper, and more durable than the brick used in the past, were built, including the East End line from Caldwell St. to Beargrass Creek, which was extended to Third and A (Gaulbert) Streets in 1884. By 1896 the city had approximately seventy-three miles of sewer lines laid throughout Louisville.

Although this had grown to 113 miles by 1906, the city desperately needed additional sewer lines but had no funding after sewerage bond issues were defeated by voters in 1902 and 1904. In 1906, with the support of Mayor PAUL C. BARTH and several prominent citizens, the state legislature passed an enabling act for the creation of the Commissioners of Sewerage, an appointed board of four members with the MAYOR acting as an ex-officio member. The funding for the commissioners' projects was to come from a $4 million bond issue that was finally approved by voters in November 1906. In January 1908 construction of several projects began, with J.B.F. Breed as the chief engineer and PETER L. ATHERTON as chairman of the board. The commissioners decided upon a plan that called for a majority of the money to go toward the construction of large trunk lines, relief sewers for flood-prone areas, and the renovation of deteriorated lines. The balance of the funds would be used for lateral sewers, of which there would be very few.

The most important projects undertaken by the early board were the construction of the Southern Outfall, which ran from Dry Run near Floyd St. to the OHIO RIVER; the South Louisville branch; a trunk line for the northwest district; a connector for the sewers on Twenty-first and Twenty-seventh Streets; the improvement of the Beargrass Creek passage with long stretches being placed in concrete channels; an intercepting line of the Beargrass Creek channel along its southern fork; and a separate system that divided sewage and storm water into two different channels for the northeastern areas such as CLIFTON and CRESCENT HILL.

With the remainder of the funds, the board commenced several other projects after 1910, including additional improvements of the Beargrass Creek channel, the improvement of the northwestern sewer along Larkwood Ave. and Cedar St., the reconstruction of the Thirty-fourth St. outlet in the PORTLAND neighborhood, and the connection of the northwestern, western, and southern sewers with the western interceptor. By the end of 1912, when the board's funding—and therefore its tenure—expired, the commissioners of sewerage had completed over 54 miles of sewers, placing the city's total above 177.

Upon the dissolution of the first board, the state legislature passed an additional enabling act in 1912 to prevent a stoppage in the work. However, because of an uncertain economic climate in the city, the $2 million bond issue was not approved by the voters, and the second board did not convene until 1919. From 1912 until 1915, sewer work, which consisted mainly of improvements to the existing system and the Beargrass Creek channel, continued under the Board of PUBLIC WORKS, with approximately $1.4 million derived from the sale of Louisville Gas Co. stock owned by the city.

When the second commissioners of sewerage began work in 1919, it had $2 million and a long list of work that needed to be completed. When a proposed plan was submitted to the city, it became evident that further funding was required. To meet these ends, two additional bond issues, $5 million in 1924 and $10 million in 1928, were accepted by the citizens of Louisville. During this term, 134 sewer lines were constructed by the commissioners, with the largest projects being the Brownsboro Rd. line, the Beals Branch line, a line along the middle fork of Beargrass Creek with additional work along the south fork, the Grinstead Dr. line, lines along Fourth and Eighth Streets, additional work in the Portland area, and the completion of another large trunk line south of the Southern Outfall named the Southwestern Outfall.

The system, based primarily on gravity, required only one pumping station (completed in 1939) near THE POINT neighborhood, although the commissioners recommended additional stations along with purification facilities to treat the sewage before returning it to the river. By the end of 1942 the commissioners had completed almost eighty-seven miles of sewers, which provided a majority of the trunk lines and outfalls for the four hundred miles of connections laid by the city engineer and Department of Public Works. In 1946 the Louisville and Jefferson County METROPOLITAN SEWER DISTRICT (MSD) took over the work of the commissioners of sewerage.

See *Report of Commissioners of Sewerage, January 1907–January 1910* (Louisville 1910); *Final Report of Commissioners of Sewerage of Louisville, 1919–1942* (Louisville 1942).

COMMITTEE FOR KENTUCKY. Civic-minded citizens in Louisville organized the nonpartisan Committee for Kentucky near the end of WORLD WAR II to help make Kentuckians aware of political issues. From 1945 to 1950 the committee published studies dealing with AGRICULTURE, education, health, housing, welfare, industry, LABOR, natural resources, taxation, and the Kentucky constitution. The committee's members were businessmen, lawyers, teachers, labor leaders, and other professionals, none of whom were ever candidates for public office. Though some efforts were made to promote a statewide operation, the group's strength originated in and remained primarily in Louisville. Harry Schacter, president and general manager of the KAUFMAN-STRAUS Department Store and president of the Kentucky Merchants Association, chaired the committee during its five-year existence.

Each committee report challenged Kentuckians to recognize what was wrong with the state and go to work to correct those problems. The reports had the approval of representatives from as many as eighty-eight state-interest groups who served as delegates to the committee's central organization. The committee also sponsored a radio program, "Wake Up Kentucky," later called "Kentucky on the March." Committee-sponsored speakers visited Kentucky communities and met with students on college campuses. The committee stirred up thought about state problems, awakened citizen interest, caused awareness of the need for cooperation, and prompted many to participate in improvement efforts.

See Harry W. Schacter, *Kentucky on the March* (New York 1949).

George Robinson

COMMONWEALTH INDUSTRIES INC. In 1965 the Harvey Aluminum Co. completed the construction of an aluminum rolling mill in Lewisport, Kentucky. Within a year, the plant produced 274 million pounds of rolled aluminum used by the transportation, marine, appliance, and beverage industries.

In 1969 the Martin-Marietta Corp., an aircraft/aerospace firm, purchased the Lewisport plant in an effort to control its own source of aluminum and invested $33 million in a recycling facility and mill expansion. Martin-Marietta sold the aluminum production side to Comalco Ltd. of Melbourne, Australia, in 1985. At this time the subsidiary of Comalco was renamed Commonwealth Aluminum Corp.

Citing the desire to be closer to its customers in the southeast and its production facility in Lewisport, Commonwealth's management moved its American headquarters from Bethesda, Maryland, to Louisville in 1988. In 1995 Comalco divested itself of its non-core businesses, including Commonwealth Aluminum, which had an annual production of almost 600 million pounds. After an initial stock offering that summer, Commonwealth became an independent company.

In 1996 Commonwealth Aluminum acquired the CasTech Aluminum Group of Long Beach, California, for approximately $275 million. CasTech, which owned several facilities in Ohio and California, consisted of Alflex, an innovator of lightweight aluminum wiring products, and Barmet, a leader in continuous cast technology, a process that casts aluminum directly into slabs from its molten form. The complementing technologies created the nation's largest independent aluminum rolling company.

To reflect its growing product line, customer reach, and strategic position, Commonwealth Aluminum Corp., with offices in the Citizens Plaza Tower at Fifth and Jefferson Streets, changed its name in 1997 to Commonwealth Industries Inc. By the end of the year, the company, with over $800 million in sales, produced more than 1 billion pounds of aluminum in its facilities at Lewisport, Kentucky; Uhrichsville and Bedford, Ohio; and Carson, Torrance, Long Beach, and Rancho Dominquez, California.

See *Courier-Journal*, May 13, 1988.

COMMUNITY FOUNDATION OF LOUISVILLE INC. Louisville was among the first cities in the United States to create a philanthropic trust and community foundation when Judge John Stites established the Louisville Foundation in 1916. After being inactive for many years, it was converted to a private foundation in 1977.

In 1984 the foundation was reorganized as a corporate form community foundation and received classification as a public charity. From 1984 to 1999 the Community Foundation of Louisville grew from six charitable funds and assets of $1.4 million to more than seven hundred funds totaling $162 million. Although commingled as a lasting community resource, each fund has its own name and charitable purpose as defined by its donors. In 1999 the foundation awarded $18.6 million in grants and distributions to nonprofit organizations.

The Community Foundation provides services to help individuals, businesses, and organizations carry out their charitable giving at minimum cost, with maximum tax benefits and convenience. The foundation administers charitable giving accounts for donors and corporations. Donors may make gifts of cash or marketable securities, receive a tax deduction for the full fair-market value of the gift, and later request the foundation to make distributions to the charities they select.

Endowment funds may be created with $10,000 or more to support a donor's charitable interests forever and to reduce income and estate taxes. An endowed fund may be established by a lump sum, periodic contributions to build a fund, a bequest, or a life-income gift that pays income to the donor or a loved one before it becomes a charitable fund.

Donors determine if the income earned on endowed funds supports the community's changing needs ("unrestricted fund"), a specific nonprofit organization ("designated fund"), a particular field such as the arts or HOMELESSNESS ("field of interest fund"), or they may recommend their own grantees ("donor advised fund"). Funds can also be endowed to provide scholarships.

By creating a fund in the Community Foundation, individuals, businesses and organizations can leave a lasting legacy for their charitable interests and enrich Louisville's quality of life for generations to come.

J. Mark Stewart

COMMUNITY HEALTH BUILDING. In 1893 Louisville Medical College completed its new building at First and Chestnut Streets, located between the central business district and the city's incipient medical center just to the east. Construction of the college came at a time when Louisville was one of the nation's foremost centers of medical education, reportedly graduating more physicians annually than any city other than New York.

The medical schools in the city were consolidated into one program in 1908–9. These programs included the medical department of the UNIVERSITY OF LOUISVILLE, which was then housed in a GIDEON SHRYOCK–designed building completed in 1838 at Eighth and Chestnut Streets and demolished in 1971.

The University's School of Medicine remained at First and Chestnut for more than sixty years. The design of the four-story medical college and adjacent two-story dispensary building was by the local architectural firm of Clarke and Loomis, one of the city's most successful practices from the 1870s well into the 1920s. CHARLES J. CLARKE (the senior partner) and ARTHUR LOOMIS designed the medical school in the new Romanesque Revival style championed by Henry Hobson Richardson and so popular in Louisville at the time. Clarke and Loomis specified a rusticated Indiana limestone for the college, giving the tall, round-arched, corner building a fortresslike appearance, a feeling reinforced by its battered corner towers and tall, hipped roof system. Delicate carvings around the entrances and elsewhere depict the "LMC" monogram, the sinuous salamander symbolic of Francis I (the sixteenth-century French monarch most closely identified with the original Romanesque), and the fleur-de-lis associated with Louisville's early FRENCH ties.

The building was constructed between 1891 and 1893 at a cost of $150,000. The university used the building as a teaching facility until 1968 when the new medical complex was completed. In 1970, the school moved to its present facility at 500 PRESTON ST. between Chestnut and Muhammad Ali Blvd., in the heart of the burgeoning Medical Center. Nearly eight thousand medical students and other health professionals had been trained in the old building, listed on the National Register of Historic Places and designated a Louisville Landmark.

A desire to save the building, especially among the members of the medical community, led to its restoration and conversion to a community health building in 1981, securing the building's future. As of 1998, the building houses the Visiting Nurse Association, the JEFFERSON COUNTY MEDICAL SOCIETY, a University of Louisville metals research organization, and the medical foundation that runs the building.

Douglas L Stern

COMMUNITY MINISTRIES. Community Ministries is a term that has become identified in metropolitan Louisville with nonprofit organizations that are developed and governed by a group of religious congregations of more than one denomination, within an identified geographic area. Some community ministries are ecumenical (intra-Christian); some are interfaith. These religious congregations via their community ministries have chosen to combine their resources of people, facilities, and finances to meet the needs of persons living in an identified geographic area while at the same time promoting fellowship and unity among the member congregations.

On the local level, community ministries were conceived in the 1960s in NEW ALBANY, INDIANA, and in the HIGHLANDS of Louisville. By the late 1970s several more groupings of congregations formed nonprofit community ministries organizations in neighborhoods across Louisville and Jefferson County. In 1983 six community ministries organizations in metropolitan Louisville sponsored a national consultation on community ministries entitled "Doing the Gospel in our Neighborhoods." This first consultation gave birth to a national event every two years hosted by community ministries in different regions of the United States. This supportive effort among the community ministries nationally has resulted in the Interfaith Community Ministries Network (ICMN). ICMN is a national network of community ministries—ecumenical or interfaith created to provide a link for mutual support, leadership development, and promotion of community-based cooperative ministry.

By 1998, a network of fifteen community ministries had been organized within Louisville and Jefferson County. Every resident within the county has a community ministry to which that household can relate, at least in an effort to prevent HOMELESSNESS. Some community ministries have developed a wide range of services based on needs of the people within the area. These community ministries work closely together through the Association of Community Ministries (ACM). The mission of ACM is twofold: (1) promote awareness of the services available through the community ministries and (2) facilitate the work of its faith-based community ministries and their member organizations and congregations through collaboration, education, support, and fundraising.

Stan Esterle

CONCORDIA LUTHERAN CHURCH. Concordia Lutheran Church at 1127 E BROADWAY was organized February 3, 1878, as the First German Evangelical Lutheran Church. Its first meeting place was in a Presbyterian chapel at Clay and Broadway. In 1880 the growing congregation purchased the German Methodist church building on Clay St. near Market. While there the congregation started a Christian day school. When the congregation and the school outgrew this facility, the decision was made to move to the suburbs. Property was purchased on E Broadway just east of Barret Ave. in the PHOENIX HILL neighborhood where the street begins its gradual ascent into an area that became the HIGHLANDS.

The congregation, not financially able to build both a school and a church building, opted in 1892 to build a dual-purpose building on the rear of the property and later build the church in front. This arrangement served adequately until the present church was built. In the 1920s "German" was dropped from the name, and discussion began about building the church that had been delayed. A building fund was begun at this time. Through diligent effort by then-pastor Carl A. Eberhard, America's foremost Gothic Revival church architect, Ralph Adams Cram (1863–1942) of New York City, was engaged to design the new church building. Cram was responsible for such works as the Cathedral of St. John the Divine in New York City. While Concordia's facility is relatively small, the sanctuary, its carvings, and its Connick stained-glass windows are considered by many to be among the finest in Louisville. Cram was able to combine nave, transepts, separate chancel, baptistry, and sacristy in a form both simple and dignified by means of an exquisitely adjusted sense of proportions and his respect for the nature and quality of materials. The dedication of the sanctuary was on December 7, 1930. Early in 1930, the name of the congregation had been changed to "Concordia Lutheran Church." The word *concordia* is Latin for peace, harmony, accord.

Concordia not only served its members spiritually but served the community as well. It played a part in the rescue operation during the 1937 FLOOD when two-thirds of Louisville was under water. The water came within two hundred feet of the church property. An aid station was established in Concordia's auditorium to assist people rescued from their homes. Immunization shots were given, along with food and clothing. Volunteers worked in shifts around the clock. Not many of the church members were personally affected by the high water, but many of the members were volunteers. In July 1976, Concordia, jointly with the Redeemer Lutheran Church congregation, sponsored a Laotian refugee family. Living quarters were provided for them in what had been the janitor's apartment in Concordia's parish building. The Laotian parents and their three children were baptized. After about a year in Louisville, the family decided to move to Houston, Texas, to live with relatives. In October 1984, Concordia became Workcenter #1702 of Lutheran Braille Workers, printing and mailing sermons in Braille worldwide to the blind. Also in the 1980s, partial renovation of the parish building was accomplished. In 1997 Concordia acquired all the property from the church building to Barret Ave. to accommodate growing membership and activities.

See Douglass Shand-Tucci, *Ralph Adams Cram: Life and Architecture* (Amherst, Mass., 1975). Walter E. Langsam, *Preservation* (Louisville 1973).

Arthur L. Kurk

Confederate Home, Pewee Valley in 1890s.

CONFEDERATE HOME. On March 17, 1902, the Kentucky General Assembly approved a Kentucky Confederate Home for the care of infirm veterans. The United Daughters of the Confederacy and Confederate veterans bought Villa Ridge, a Victorian-style summer resort in PEWEE VALLEY, OLDHAM COUNTY, to house the former soldiers. Gov. J.C.W. Beckham (1900–7) was host at its opening on October 23, 1902. By 1904 about three hundred veterans resided at the health-care facility. Perhaps the most famous gathering of veterans was that of twenty-five of Gen. John Hunt Morgan's former Raiders, many of whom lived there. On

March 25, 1920, most of the facility burned. The remaining one wing was large enough to house the few remaining veterans.

More than seven hundred soldiers resided at the home during its existence, but by 1934 only five veterans remained. Despite the high cost of operating the facility, the United Daughters of the Confederacy successfully stopped its proposed sale on several occasions. On March 17, 1934, the legislature approved the sale of the property and allocated an annual allowance of eight hundred dollars to the remaining veterans, who were transferred to the Pewee Valley Sanitorium. By the end of June 1934 the Confederate Home had closed.

Of the veterans who had lived on the grounds, 313 were buried in the Pewee Valley Confederate Veterans Cemetery. In 1952 the state restored the cemetery, which had fallen into disrepair; and in 1957 Gov. A.B. Chandler (1955–59) rededicated it. The Kentucky State Parks Department has maintained the site since 1968.

CONFEDERATE MONUMENT.

The Confederate Monument at Third St. and Brandeis Ave. was erected in 1895 by the Kentucky Women's Confederate Monument Association to honor the rank and file of Confederate soldiers who died in the Civil War. The idea originated in 1887 during a meeting in the basement of the Walnut Street Baptist Church to arrange for decorating the graves of Confederate dead at Cave Hill Cemetery. The monument cost twelve thousand dollars, a considerable sum for the time and one that took the ladies of the Monument Association several years to accumulate.

A competition was held to select a design. The winner, young Louisville sculptor Enid Yandell, already was developing a national reputation. Today she is probably best known to most Louisvillians for her statue of Daniel Boone in Cherokee Park. However, the selection of Yandell started a mostly genteel, but heated, local conflict. Much of the outrage seemed due to a woman's being awarded the contract for a large public monument, and a war memorial at that. The expressed charge was that Yandell's friends on the selection committee had influenced the vote in her favor, although no identification of the designer had been permitted on the designs themselves. The newspapers made the most of the controversy.

Despite vigorous denials of impropriety by Yandell and her supporters, the contract was eventually awarded to Michael Muldoon of the Muldoon Monument Co. of Louisville, who had erected an almost identical monument in Raleigh, North Carolina. In fact, the figures on the two monuments were identical; only the shafts varied slightly.

The Muldoons did the granite work themselves and imported from Germany the three bronze figures of Confederate soldiers featured on the monument: an artilleryman on one side, a cavalryman on the other, and an infantryman standing sentinel at the top. In the mid-1950s Dr. Justus Bier, professor of art history at the University of Louisville and art editor of the *Courier-Journal*, established that they had been sculpted by Ferdinand Von Miller the Younger (1842 or 1843–1929). Von Miller was a member of the family that owned the foundry where the sculptures were cast.

After World War I local officials began to press for the monument's removal. In 1921 engineers claimed that it needed expensive repairs, in addition to causing traffic problems. Plans were made to dismantle the monument and rebuild it in nearby Triangle Park. However, because of public opposition the project was dropped. It was renewed in 1947, but again the monument was saved. A third and perhaps more serious effort to relocate the monument in the early 1950s finally led to a compromise. Mayor Andrew Broaddus agreed to reduce the grassy area around the base of the monument. Ground was taken from the sides of the forty-eight–foot-diameter circle, leaving a smaller, elliptical plot that would interfere less with traffic.

See Justus Bier, "A Forgotten Work by Ferdinand Von Miller the Younger, A Contribution to the History of Confederate Monuments," *Register of the Kentucky Historical Society*, 4 (April 1956): 125–33.

Audrea McDowell

CONGREGATION ANSHEI SFARD.

Anshei Sfard is the smallest of Louisville's Jewish congregations, is its only Orthodox congregation, and is dedicated to perpetuate traditional Orthodoxy. It was organized in 1883 by a group of Russian Jewish immigrants unhappy with the congregations then in existence. Its first High Holy Day services were held in a meeting hall on Seventh St., with Nathan Baer as the first president.

When Temple Brith Sholom moved to Second and College Streets in 1903, Anshei Sfard bought the structure it vacated at 511 S First St. This building remained its home until 1958. Notified that it would be evicted by construction of Interstate 65, the congregation purchased 17.5 acres adjoining the Jewish Community Center on Dutchmans Ln. and erected a new building on that site.

In 1971 Anshei Sfard merged with a younger congregation, Agudath Achim, which had existed since 1922 at 1113 W Jefferson. Nearly all of Agudath Achim's members had moved eastward by that time.

Anshei Sfard's rabbi from 1930 to 1945 was Charles B. Chavel, who won international fame for his commentary on Nachmanides, a medieval Jewish sage. Chavel was succeeded by Solomon Roodman, whose fiftieth year in Louisville was celebrated in 1996, after his retirement. Rabbi Avrohom Litvin was installed in 1989.

Herman Landau

CONGRESSIONAL MEDAL OF HONOR RECIPIENTS.

The Congressional Medal of Honor is the United States' highest military decoration, awarded for personal heroism. The criterion of "uncommon valor" in selecting the recipients has kept the medal, awarded to 3,408 men and women since 1861, highly respected. The ten listed below won the award between 1861 and 1997 and were born or lived in Jefferson, Bullitt, Shelby, or Oldham County in Kentucky or Clark, Harrison, or Floyd County in Indiana. Merely enlisting in one of these counties did not merit inclusion on this list.

Medal of Honor Recipients

Recipient	Date/Place of Action
Kentucky	
Army	
Col. J. Franklin Bell Shelbyville	September 9, 1899 Porac, Philippine Islands
Pvt. John H. Callahan Shelby Co.	April 9, 1865, Ft. Blakeley, Ala.
Corp. Charles E. Kelly Louisville	November 13, 1943 Altaville, Italy
Lt. John J. McGinty III Louisville	July 18, 1966, Republic of Vietnam
Pvt. James J. Nash Louisville	July 1, 1898, Santiago, Cuba
Sgt. John C. Squires Louisville	April 23-24, 1944 Padiglione, Italy
Dr. Mary E. Walker Louisville	July 21, 1861, Battle of Bull Run; October 1861, U.S. Patent Office, hospital, Washington, D.C.; September 1863, Chattanooga, Tennessee following Battle of Chickamauga; April 10 August 12, 1864, prisoner of war, Richmond, Virginia; September 1864, Battle of Atlanta
Major John F. Weston Louisville	April 13, 1865, Westumpka, Ala.
Indiana	
Army	
Sgt. Charles H. Seston, New Albany	September 19, 1864 Winchester, Virginia
Navy	
Lt. Jonas H. Ingram Jeffersonville	April 22, 1914, Vera Cruz, Mexico

See *The Congressional Medal of Honor: The Names, The Deeds* (Forest Ranch, California 1984).

CONGRESSIONAL OFFICEHOLDERS.

Louisville and Jefferson County were first represented in the U.S. House of Representatives by Christopher Greenup of Frankfort, beginning on November 9, 1792. Greenup served until 1797 and later served one term as Kentucky's governor (1804–8). Kentucky had two seats in the 142-member body, and Louisville was a part of the district described as "all counties lying on the south side of the Kentucky River."

In 1966, after the U.S. Supreme Court ruled that congressional districts should be equal in population within states, Kentucky's districts were reapportioned, giving Jefferson County all of one district (the Third) and almost one-half of another (the Fourth). For eighty-four years before that time, Jefferson County was a district unto itself, while Kentucky's number of congressional seats fell from eleven to seven, and fell to six after the 1990 census. This means that Jefferson County was underrepresented by almost half by 1966. Following the 1990 census reapportionment, 92 percent of Jefferson County's residents are in the Third District, with the remaining 8 percent now being a part of the Second District.

Before 1883, when Jefferson County became one district, it had been combined with groups of counties including, at various times, Breckinridge, BULLITT, Carroll, Green, Hardin, Henry, Nelson, OLDHAM, Owen, SHELBY, Trimble, and Washington. In the election of 1932, nine members were elected on an "at large" basis, none of whom were from Jefferson County.See Joel D. Treese, *Biographical Directory of the American Congress, 1774–1996: The Continental Congress, September 5, 1774, to October 21, 1788, and the Congress of the United States, from the First through the 104th Congress, March 4, 1789, to January 3, 1997* (Alexandria, Va., 1997).

Mike Ward

Members of the U.S. House of Representatives elected from districts containing Jefferson County, 1797–1997

Representative	*Dates served*	*County*	*District*	*Affiliation*	*Reason for leaving*
Christopher Greenup	Nov. 9–Mar. 3, 1797	Franklin	First	Anti-administ./ Democrat-Rep.	Unknown
Thomas T. Davis	Mar. 4, 1797–Mar. 3, 1803	Mercer	First	Democrat-Rep.	Retired
Matthew Walton	Mar. 4, 1803–Mar. 3, 1807	Washington	Third	Democrat-Rep.	Unknown
John Rowan	Mar. 4, 1807–Mar. 3, 1809	Jefferson	Third	Democrat-Rep.	Unknown
Henry Crist	Mar. 4, 1809– Mar. 3, 1811	Bullitt	Third	Democrat-Rep.	Unknown
Stephen Ormsby	Mar. 4, 1811–Mar. 3, 1813	Jefferson	Third and Eighth	Democrat-Rep.	Defeated
	April 30, 1813–Mar. 3, 1817, elected to fill vacancy upon death of Representative-elect John Simpson				
Richard C. Anderson Jr.	Mar. 4, 1817– Mar. 3, 1821	Jefferson	Eighth	Democrat-Rep.	Retired
Wingfield Bullock	Mar. 4, 1821–Oct. 13, 1821	Shelby	Eighth	no party	Died
James D. Breckinridge	Nov. 21, 1821–Mar. 3, 1823	Jefferson	Eighth	Democrat-Rep.	Defeated
Charles A. Wickliffe	Mar. 4, 1823–Mar. 3, 1833	Nelson	Ninth	Democrat	Retired
	Mar. 4, 1861–Mar. 3, 1863		Fifth, not including Jefferson County	Union Whig	Retired
Patrick H. Pope	Mar. 4, 1833–Mar. 3, 1835	Jefferson	Eighth	Democrat	Defeated
William J. Graves	Mar. 4, 1835–Mar. 3, 1841	Henry	Eighth	Anti-Jackson and Whig	Retired
James C. Sprigg	Mar. 4, 1841–Mar. 3, 1843	Shelby	Eighth	no party	Defeated
William P. Thomasson	Mar. 4, 1843–Mar. 3, 1847	Jefferson	Seventh	Whig	Retired
W. Garnett Duncan	Mar. 4, 1847–Mar. 3, 1849	Jefferson	Seventh	Whig	Retired
Humphrey Marshall	Mar. 4, 1849–Aug. 4, 1852	Henry	Seventh	Whig	
	Mar. 4, 1855–Mar. 3, 1859		Seventh	American Party	Retired
William Preston	Dec. 6, 1852–Mar. 3, 1855	Jefferson	Seventh	Whig	Defeated
Robert Mallory	Mar. 4, 1859–Mar. 3, 1865	Oldham	Seventh and Fifth	Union Democrat	Defeated
Lovell Harrison Rousseau	Mar. 4, 1865–Mar. 3, 1867	Jefferson	Fifth	Unconditional Unionist	Retired
Asa P. Grover	Mar. 4, 1867–Mar. 3, 1869	Jefferson	Fifth	Democrat	Retired
Boyd Winchester	Mar. 4, 1869–Mar. 3, 1873	Jefferson	Fifth	Democrat	Retired
Elisha D. Standiford	Mar. 4, 1873–Mar. 3, 1875	Jefferson	Fifth	Democrat	Retired
Edward Y. Parsons	Mar. 4, 1875–July 8, 1876	Jefferson	Fifth	Democrat	Died
Henry Watterson	Aug. 12, 1876–Mar. 3, 1877	Jefferson	Fifth	Democrat	Retired
	Appointed to fill the vacancy caused by the death of Edward Parsons				
Albert S. Willis	Mar. 4, 1877–Mar. 3, 1887	Jefferson	Fifth	Democrat	Defeated
Asbel G. Caruth	Mar. 4, 1887–Mar. 3, 1895	Jefferson	Fifth	Democrat	Defeated
Walter Evans	Mar. 4, 1895–Mar. 3, 1899	Jefferson	Fifth	Republican	Defeated
Oscar Turner	Mar. 4, 1899–Mar. 3, 1901	Jefferson	Fifth	Democrat	Retired
Harvey S. Irwin	Mar. 4, 1901–Mar. 3, 1903	Jefferson	Fifth	Republican	Defeated
J. Swagar Sherley	Mar. 4, 1903–Mar. 3, 1919	Jefferson	Fifth	Democrat	Defeated
Charles F. Ogden	Mar. 4, 1919–Mar. 3, 1923	Jefferson	Fifth	Republican	Retired
Maurice H. Thatcher	Mar. 4, 1923–Mar. 3, 1933	Jefferson	Fifth	Republican	Retired
	"At Large" representatives, none from Jefferson County				
Emmet O'Neal	Jan. 3, 1935–Jan. 3, 1947	Jefferson	Third	Democrat	Defeated
Thruston Ballard Morton	Jan. 3, 1947–Jan. 3, 1953	Jefferson	Third	Republican	Elected to U.S. Senate
John M. Robsion Jr.	Jan. 3, 1953–Jan. 3, 1959	Jefferson	Third	Republican	Defeated
Frank W. Burke	Jan. 3, 1959–Jan. 3, 1963	Jefferson	Third	Democrat	Defeated
Marion Gene Snyder	Jan. 3, 1963–Jan. 3, 1965	Jefferson	Third	Republican	Defeated.
	Elected to the newly created Fourth District, which covered about one-third of Jefferson County along with the counties going up the Ohio River (Oldham, Trimble, Carroll, Gallatin, Boone, and parts of Kenton and Campbell) Jan. 3, 1967–Jan. 3, 1987; Retired				
Charles P. Farnsley	Jan. 3, 1965–Jan. 3, 1967	Jefferson	Third	Democrat	Retired
William O. Cowger	Jan. 3, 1967–Jan. 3, 1971	Jefferson	Third	Republican	Defeated
Romano L. Mazzoli	Jan. 3, 1971–Jan. 3, 1989	Jefferson	Third	Democrat	Retired
Michael D. Ward	Jan. 3, 1995–Jan. 3, 1997	Jefferson	Third	Democrat	Defeated
Anne M. Northup	Jan. 3, 1997–Present	Jefferson	Third	Republican	

CONNOLLY, JOHN (b York County, Pennsylvania, ca. 1745; d Montreal, January 30, 1813). Early landholder. John Connolly was the first person to recognize the potential for a town at the FALLS OF THE OHIO. He was the son of John and Susanna (Howard) Connolly. Young Connolly, whose father was a physician, studied medicine with Dr. Cadwallader Evans in Philadelphia and enlisted in the British forces in America as a surgeon's mate, serving during the French and Indian War that resulted in a British victory in 1763. In the years following, Connolly traveled extensively in the newly won Ohio Valley and Illinois country. The future site of Louisville particularly attracted his attention. He settled in Pittsburgh, where he practiced medicine and became a figure of some importance.

George Washington, also interested in Ohio Valley land, met Connolly at Pittsburgh in the fall of 1770 and found him "a very sensible Intelligent Man" (John C. Fitzpatrick, ed., *The Diaries of George Washington, 1748–1799,* New York, 1925, 447–48). Connolly informed Washington of his scheme to settle a hundred or more families in Kentucky as the nucleus of a new British colony. The chance to implement this hope came in 1773 during the turbulent dispute between Pennsylvania and Virginia over sovereignty of a wide area around Pittsburgh. Virginia royal governor Dunmore, also caught up in the western land fever, was pushing the Virginia claim and sought allies in Pittsburgh.

He found several, including the ambitious Connolly and JOHN CAMPBELL, the latter doing well as the agent of Philadelphia merchants in the Indian trade.

Since Connolly had achieved officer status in the British forces in the colonies, he was entitled to a land grant for his services. A deal was struck: Dunmore would see that Connolly acquired the two thousand acres (now downtown Louisville) that he wanted at the Falls of the Ohio, and Connolly would head the Virginia faction around Pittsburgh. Another two thousand acres (now Louisville's West End) was to be awarded to Charles DeWarrensdorf, another Pennsylvanian who had served in the French and Indian War. It was apparently agreed beforehand that Connolly would purchase this tract, and to do so he turned to Campbell for financial aid. He gave Campbell a half-interest in his original grant and a mortgage note for half the DeWarrensdorf tract. The land was surveyed in 1773 by THOMAS BULLITT, apparently including lots for a town, but this survey was held to be illegal and was repeated in 1774 by JOHN FLOYD's surveying party. In that same year Connolly and Campbell advertised the lots for sale in the Williamsburg *Virginia Gazette* and in Pittsburgh, but the outbreak of Dunmore's War with the Ohio Indians in late 1774, followed by the American Revolution, halted development.

Connolly, meanwhile, was making himself obnoxious to the Pennsylvania faction in and around Pittsburgh, where he occupied old Fort Pitt (renamed Fort Dunmore) as commandant of a ragtag Virginia garrison. A visitor in the spring of 1775 described him as "a haughty, imperious man" (The *Journal of Nicholas Cresswell*, 1774–1777, New York, 1924, 65). Connolly created so much turmoil by arresting Pennsylvania adherents, demolishing their cabins, and suppressing Pennsylvania courts that Pennsylvania governor John Penn ordered his arrest in June 1775. However, the Virginia faction protested so vigorously that he was released and shortly after fled Pittsburgh. With the American Revolution in its early stages and Connolly an ardent Tory, he was commissioned a lieutenant colonel in the British forces on November 5, 1775. He had visited British general Thomas Gage in Boston and proposed a plan to raise a Tory regiment to leave Detroit and, with Indian allies, attack frontier settlements and continue east to join Governor Dunmore at Norfolk. Thus, Connolly thought, the northern and southern colonies would be divided. Before he could carry out this ambitious plan, he was captured near Hagerstown, Maryland, in November 1775 and imprisoned in Philadelphia until 1780, then paroled as an exchange prisoner. He joined Gen. Charles Cornwallis's troops at Yorktown, Virginia (thus violating parole), and was captured on September 21, 1781. He was again imprisoned in Philadelphia until March 1782, when he was permitted to go to New York to sail to England.

Meanwhile his land, since 1778 occupied by the settlers of Louisville, was seized in 1780 by Virginia as the property of a Tory. Louisville was chartered that year primarily to protect settlers, who were given first rights of land purchase from Virginia. Connolly was compensated by the British government for the seized land and went to Canada as a British officer on half pay. In 1788 he appeared in Kentucky, ostensibly to assess the value of his lost land, but actually to promote his scheme to bring Kentucky under the British flag. He met with his former partner, John Campbell, and even rented a cabin in Louisville. Connolly's presence disturbed James Wilkinson, who was pursuing a devious course to establish Spanish dominion. Wilkinson claimed in reports to Spanish governor Miro in New Orleans that he attempted to frighten Connolly to cause him to leave Kentucky and even hired a hunter to assault him on the pretext that the hunter's son had been killed by Indians incited by the British. Whatever the reasons, Connolly departed in late 1788 or early 1789, having failed in his mission. He also failed to gain British government posts he sought in Canada and spent the last years of his life in Montreal.

See Clarence M. Burton, "John Connolly, A Tory of the Revolution," *Proceedings of the American Antiquarian Society* 20 (Oct. 1909): 70–105; Percy B. Caley, "The Life and Adventures of Lieutenant Colonel John Connolly: The Story of a Tory," *Western Pennsylvania Historical Magazine* 11 (Jan., April, July, Oct. 1928); Gayle Thornbrough, ed., *Outpost on the Wabash, 1787–1791* (Indianapolis 1957); *A Narrative of the transactions: Imprisonments, and sufferings of John Connolly, an American Loyalist, and lieutenant-colonel in His Majesty's Service*, (London 1783, reprinted in New York for C.L. Woodward 1889); Nicholas B. Wainwright, "In Turmoil at Pittsburgh: Diary of Augustine Prevost 1774," *Pennsylvania Magazine of History and Biography* 2 (April 1961): lll–62; George H. Yater, *Two Hundred Years at the Falls of the Ohio* (Louisville 1979 and 1987).

George H. Yater

CONRAD/CALDWELL HOUSE. Commonly known as "Conrad's Folly" at the time of its construction in the mid-1890s, this architectural gem is located at 1402 SAINT JAMES CT. Recognized for its unusual combination of Richardsonian and Romanesque revival–style architecture, the home was built for local leather manufacturer Theophilus Conrad and designed by ARTHUR LOOMIS of the Louisville architectural firm of Clarke and Loomis.

The exterior is characterized by ashlar masonry, foliated capitals, and a wealth of detailed carving, including gargoyles, arabesques, and carved window frames. The luxurious interior is marked by the use of stained glass, parquet floors, and elaborate woodwork in a variety of woods, including oak, cherry, and maple. Following the death of Conrad on February 13, 1905, William E. Caldwell purchased the house. Then, in 1947, the Presbyterian church obtained ownership of the home, using it as the Rose Anna Hughes Home for Retired Women until 1987. Its current owner, the St. James Court Foundation Inc., has opened the Conrad/Caldwell House to the public as a museum.

See Samuel W. Thomas and William Morgan, *Old Louisville: The Victorian Era* (Louisville 1975).

COOK, CHARLES LEE (b Louisville, November 7, 1871; d Louisville, April 25, 1928). Inventor. Infected with a form of polio after his first birthday and wheelchair-bound his entire life, Cook accomplished more than the average person. Removed from school at the age of seven, he spent most of his time in his father's stables working with anything that was mechanical. His father played a principal role in the reconstruction of the LOUISVILLE AND PORTLAND CANAL in the 1870s.

By the time the younger Cook was eight, he had already built a steam engine of a thousand pieces of discarded junk. While observing a locomotive, Cook noticed steam loss from the steam chest. Over the next few days he was able to develop a packing ring device that solved the problem. It worked so well that he bought a lathe and a four-horsepower engine to produce more packing rings at a faster rate.

In 1888 at the age of seventeen, Cook had made enough money to move his business out of his father's stable to a small factory at 916 S Eighth St. The Cook Manufacturing Co. was a leader in the metallic packing industry, producing metallic packing for Emergency Fleet Corp. ships. It also built lathes for the French during World War I that were used in the production of cannon shells.

Cook also built an efficient creosoting plant that brought him much fame. Although successful in his work, a lack of formal education was evident in his speech, and his poor use of grammar drew attention away from a topic. Cook began to study English and the humanities. Later he demonstrated a vocabulary of more than thirty-seven thousand words. Besides having a wide vocabulary, Cook was an authority in the fields of law, art, history, architecture, and politics. In April 1920 Cook came to the attention of the American public when B.C. Forbes wrote about him in the *American Magazine*. The story revealed his optimistic philosophy that hard work and learning would inevitably bring success, regardless of physical handicaps.

Cook died at his home at Sixth and Ormsby Streets and is buried in Cave Hill Cemetery. His house, which contains a swimming pool in the basement and an elevator, still stands. Cook Manufacturing Co. remains at 916 S Eighth St. A sign on the building is inscribed with the words, "C. Lee Cook, Division of Dover Corp."

See *Courier-Journal Sunday Magazine*, Jan. 9, 1921.

COOK, MARLOW WEBSTER (b Akron, New York, July 27, 1926). United States senator, Jefferson County judge. The son of Floyd T. and Mary Lee Webster Cook, he moved to Louisville in 1942 and, at seventeen, joined the U.S. Navy, serving on submarines in both the Atlantic and Pacific Oceans during World War II. In 1946 he enrolled at the University of Louisville, receiving a bachelor of arts degree in 1948 and a law degree in 1950.

Cook practiced law in Louisville until 1957, when he was elected to the Kentucky House of Representatives. He was reelected in 1959. While there, he was vice chairman of the Kentucky Special Committee Investigating Education and a member of the Kentucky Legislative Research Commission planning and zoning committee.

Cook, a Republican, was twice elected Jefferson County judge, serving from January 1, 1962, until December 17, 1968. In 1961 he teamed with William O. Cowger, Republican candidate for mayor, to unseat the Louisville Democratic organization, which had been in office twenty-eight years. He defeated Democrat Thomas L. Ray, majority leader of the Kentucky House of Representatives, by 20,097 votes (95,699 to 75,602). As county judge/executive, Cook helped to streamline Kentucky's largest and most complex local government. His administration also assisted in the purchase of the *Belle of Louisville* steamboat for the city.

In his 1965 reelection bid, Cook trounced Democrat William B. Stansbury by more than 50,000 votes (121,481 to 71,280), solidifying the Republican party's control over city and county government. In 1967 Cook was defeated by Louie B. Nunn in a bitterly fought Republican gubernatorial primary. But in 1968 Cook was elected to the U.S. Senate, defeating Democrat Katherine Peden and Independent Duane Olson. Cook received 484,260 votes to Peden's 448,960 and Olson's 9,645 and became the first Roman Catholic to win a major statewide office in Kentucky. He was elected on November 5, 1968, and began serving as a senator on December 17, 1968, filling the unexpired term of Thruston B. Morton, who retired early.

He was appointed in October 1969 by President Richard Nixon to represent the United States at the Fifteenth Commonwealth Parliamentary Conference in Trinidad. He was also one of the first Republicans to denounce Nixon after Watergate and to call for the president's resignation.

Cook lost his bid for reelection to Wendell Ford in 1974, 399,406 to 328,982 votes. He resigned his seat on December 27, 1974, and began practicing law in Washington, D.C. He moved to Sarasota, Florida, in 1989.

He was married to Nancy Remmers of Louisville in 1947, and the couple had five children: Christy, Caroline, Nancy, Mary Louise, and Marlow Junior.

See *Biographical Directory of the American Congress 1774–1971* (Washington, D.C., 1971); *Courier-Journal*, Nov. 6, 1968.

CORE. The Congress of Racial Equality (CORE) was founded in Chicago, Illinois, in 1942. It began as an intellectual and interracial civil rights organization. Members sought to abolish segregation through nonviolent direct action. CORE developed slowly. The organization remained a northern-based group with a predominantly white membership throughout its early years of existence. It did not attract a large following. By 1957 there were fewer than ten affiliates nationwide.

In 1956 CORE tried unsuccessfully to establish a chapter in Louisville. Exactly why this effort failed is unclear. It may have been because of the low national profile of the organization. However, as the civil rights movement spread throughout the South and the philosophy of nonviolent protest became acceptable and useful, CORE garnered more interest and support. The Louisville Chapter of CORE was founded April 30, 1960, with fourteen active and four associate members. Thirty-one names were listed on the chapter's initial mailing list. Louisville CORE was not the first chapter organized in Kentucky, nor was it ever the largest or most active. But there were several committed persons, black and white, who worked with the organization throughout its existence in Louisville.

In the few years the organization was active, Louisville CORE was engaged in several different civil rights demonstrations in the city. Members held stand-ins at Kaufman-Straus Department Store, picketed Stewart's Dry Goods Store, and participated in sit-ins at Taylor Drug Stores and Ben Snyder's Department Store. CORE worked with several civil rights groups in the city, such as the Louisville Unitarians for Social Action, the Kentucky Conference of the African Methodist Episcopal church, and the NAACP.

Aside from these activities, Louisville CORE tried to expand employment opportunities for African Americans. The organization launched boycotts against the Coca-Cola Co. and Sealtest dairy products. As a result of these non-buying campaigns, both companies began gradually to hire African Americans in jobs that had been traditionally reserved for whites.

While individual members of Louisville CORE remained active in the civil rights movement throughout the sixties, the organization itself declined significantly after 1962. The effort to recruit new members suffered drastically because of organizational problems and the inability to attract a large following from the local NAACP. Meanwhile, in 1966, the national office advocated a "New Direction" for the organization that espoused black nationalism instead of promoting nonviolent direct action. By the mid-1960s Louisville CORE ceased to exist. Despite its brief existence, Louisville CORE did make an important and lasting contribution to the struggle for civil rights in Kentucky.

See Aldon D. Morris, *Origins of the Civil Rights Movement* (New York 1984); August Meier and Elliot Rudwick, *CORE: A Study in the Civil Rights Movement 1942–1968* (Urbana, Ill., 1975); Papers of the Congress of Racial Equality, reels 20 & 40, series 5.

Gerald L. Smith

CORHART REFRACTORIES. Located at 1600 W Lee St. in Louisville's West End, Corhart is a leader in industrial ceramics technology. It was founded in 1927 by Corning Glass Works with an initial workforce of thirty employees. Corning, in conjunction with Hartford-Empire, a company closely tied to glass manufacturing and its machinery, began the manufacture of Corning's newly discovered "Electrocast" refractories, heat-resistant ceramics used to line glass industry furnaces.

The success of these products led the firm to add a research laboratory in Louisville in 1936. Corhart, in addition to glass industry refractories, also began production of refractories for the steel industry shortly after World War II. However it abandoned that market in the 1980s because of the decline of steelmaking in the United States. In 1961 Corhart opened a facility in Buckhannon, West Virginia, that produces sintered refractories. Today the Louisville plant continues to manufacture fused cast refractories as well as products that resist abrasion in mining.

In 1985 a group of company managers completed a leveraged buyout of Corhart from Corning, which was looking to create capital for new business ventures. Two years later, the company was acquired by the industrial ceramics division of Compagnie de Saint-Gobain of France, one of the top one hundred industrial firms in the world.

See Bob Hill and Dan Dry, *Louisville: A River Serenade* (Memphis 1995); Martin E. Biemer, *In Celebration of Louisville* (Northridge, Calif., 1988).

CORNERSTONE 2020. The Louisville and Jefferson County Planning Commission had not adopted a new set of guidelines governing the county's growth since 1979, although they were moderately revised in 1986. In 1992 County Judge/Executive David L. Armstrong initiated the Cornerstone 2020 project to rewrite the existing comprehensive land use plan to better balance economic and environmental concerns and prepare for the estimated influx of sixty-seven thousand new residents by 2020. The goal was to define the objectives for the next twenty-five years of development in Jefferson County, an area with farms, suburbs, ninety-three small cities, and the city of Louisville.

It was begun with a small number of participants, then advisory groups and committees were formed until hundreds of people served. With the help of more than five hundred selected citizens representing a variety of interests, a mission statement for the project was developed during 1993. Later in the year, an additional 150 citizens chose transportation, economic development, land use, and environmental resources as themes that would facilitate discussions and provide the foundation for the new plan.

By the end of 1993 another panel of 150 people began the process of using these themes to chisel the goals and objectives for the new plan out of more than 50 selected topics. This portion of the project, funded by public and private sources, cost $3.5 million and was supposed to have lasted two and a half years.

However, as the project continued into 1996 amidst resignations and grumbling by committee members that it would never be completed, the planning commission predicted that a final draft would require another year of work. In early 1997 the committees, composed of neighborhood activists, environmentalists, developers, transportation officials, and business and industrial representatives, began to release their resolutions, which they hoped would eliminate the old, incoherent zoning laws by defining twelve new "form districts." In April the JEFFERSON COUNTY FISCAL COURT accepted the proposal even though business leaders and environmentalists alike deemed certain aspects of the document unfair. By November all thirteen of the county's legislative bodies with zoning powers, including Louisville, had passed the goals and objectives, and opposition to the plan subsided.

The goals and objectives fall into four categories: livability, mobility, marketplace, and community form. The livability section covers environmental issues such as PARKS, open space, and sewer and water services. The mobility section focuses on various transportation strategies for people and goods, and the marketplace section focuses on economic growth. The community form section covers development and land use, ensuring compatibility of new development with the character of existing NEIGHBORHOODS by requiring that site and building design standards be met before building permits are issued, thus keeping the character of our neighborhoods intact. The next phase covered policies and regulations.

Major changes in how the Louisville-Jefferson County Planning Commission reviewed development proposals raised unresolved questions that kept Cornerstone 2020 from meeting its December 1998 deadline. Concerns about how the elements were organized and how the transition was to be made from the old plan to the new one were highlighted when an examination of plan elements uncovered several issues and organizational problems that needed further review and study.

See *Courier-Journal*, June 11, 1995, April 9, 1997, Dec. 6, 1998.

CORN ISLAND. Corn Island has become the touchstone of Louisville history, the area's equivalent of Plymouth Rock. It was on this island's some seventy acres of verdant growth that the first settlers of Louisville established themselves on May 27, 1778. Initially dubbed Dunmore's Island (for the royal governor of Virginia) by THOMAS BULLITT's surveying party in 1773, the now-vanished island was close to the Kentucky shore at the head of the FALLS OF THE OHIO near the foot of what would become Twelfth St. Perhaps sixty civilian settlers accompanied GEORGE ROGERS CLARK's Virginia militia on its expedition to wrest control of the Illinois country from the British. The settlers were left behind on Corn Island after Clark had trained his troops and departed on June 24.

Remains of Corn Island, at right, in 1912.

From the crop of corn planted that spring, the island took its name. The settlers moved to the mainland in the fall after Clark's successes in Illinois. They established what historians have come to call Fort on Shore near the foot of Twelfth St. The island was quite fertile; one of the 1778 settlers thought that he "could hear the corn go tick-tick—it grew so fast." After the move to the mainland, the island became the site of barbecues, religious camp meetings, and a place to fish. It also continued its agricultural role. One Louisvillian recalled that in the 1850s, "There was a considerable farm on it; possibly twenty acres under cultivation." He noted that other lures to visit the island were "snipe-shooting on the rocks and the abundance of black haws and persimmons that one could gather in their season."

But the doom of the historic spot was already sealed by then. The limestone rock around the island was used early for building purposes and perhaps for the first paving of several blocks of MAIN ST. in 1813. As early as 1806 a notice was published in the *FARMER'S LIBRARY*, Louisville's first newspaper, that "All persons are hereby warned against taking Stone off the Quarry adjoining Corn Island without applying to Francis Battle or Thomas Inch and obtaining *Liberty*."

In 1824 a powder mill was built on the island. It exploded in 1830, killing several workers. The quarrying operations killed the willows growing along the island's shore, and erosion followed. Louisville attorney and historian REUBEN T. DURRETT as early as the 1850s and 1860s attempted to persuade the city of Louisville to take over the island and preserve it, but to no avail. The final insult followed the discovery during the building of the LOUISVILLE & PORTLAND CANAL in the 1820s that the limestone of the Falls is of the proper chemical composition to make natural cement. Manufacture of cement on a small scale was begun before the CIVIL WAR and blossomed after the war's end.

The formation of the LOUISVILLE CEMENT CO. in 1866 and other companies later brought large-scale excavation of the rock, including Corn Island itself. When the boiler of a stationary engine on the island exploded in 1878, the *Louisville Commercial* explained that it was used "in pumping water out of the rocks" so that they could be quarried.

A Louisville visitor in the early 1890s noted: "Little is now left of Corn Island, and that little is, at low water, being blasted and ground into cement by a mill hard by on the main shore." What remnants may have been left were flooded by construction of a dam and hydroelectric plant in the 1920s. The site of Louisville's founding now lies deep under water.

See *Farmers Library*, April 16, 1806; A.J. Webster, "Louisville in the Eighteen Fifties," *Filson Club History Quarterly* 4 (July 1930): 135; Reuben G. Thwaites, *Afloat on the Ohio*, (New York 1900).

George H. Yater

CORN ISLAND STORYTELLING FESTIVAL. Started in 1976, this festival was named for CORN ISLAND, the settlement that was the birthplace of Louisville but now is submerged beneath the OHIO RIVER. It was sponsored by JEFFERSON COMMUNITY COLLEGE and held on the BROADWAY campus. One of the founders was Louisville writer and former Jefferson Community College professor Dr. Lee Pennington.

From its beginning, when twelve storytellers performed to a small audience, the festival has grown to become one of the largest storytelling festivals in the country, drawing thousands of people from almost every state and numerous foreign countries. Because of the size of the event, an organization was created to produce the festival. The group, known as the International Order of EARS (the acronym's meaning is a secret known only to initiates) was created in 1980 to support storytelling worldwide and publishes the *Tale Trader* newspaper.

The festival takes place over a weekend and features a storytelling cruise on the *BELLE OF LOUISVILLE*; a storytelling olio, or mixture of tales; a day-long storytelling festival at LOCUST GROVE HISTORIC HOME; and an evening of ghost stories at Long Run Cemetery. The festival has attracted dozens of Kentucky centenarians as well as established international, national, and local amateur and professional storytellers. The most celebrated visitor was a Huli tribesman from Papua New Guinea, one of two members of the million-plus tribe who had ever ventured off the island. He left the highlands of his South Pacific home and stepped into the twentieth-century world in Louisville, bringing with him stories passed down for generations amongst his Stone-Age tribe.

Gail Ritchie Henson

CORRECTIONAL FACILITIES. Before Kentucky's statehood in 1792, the punishment for all felonies was hanging, while lesser offenses involved whipping or confinement on a public pillory. The first prison built in the commonwealth was erected in Frankfort in 1799. While hanging continued to be utilized for persons convicted of capital crimes, it was usually carried out in the county seat where the crime was committed and prosecuted.

From Louisville's earliest history into the twentieth century, lawbreakers in the area have been imprisoned in a number of local facilities, while long-term felony offenders have been sentenced to the state prisons at Frankfort, LAGRANGE, or Eddyville. Louisville was settled in 1778; and in March 1789, as recorded in the Jefferson County Minute-Order Book 2, it was ordered that a jail be built. A two-story jail was erected about 1790 at an unknown location. Six years later Thomas Smith constructed another prison at the northwest corner of Jefferson and Sixth Streets. Complaints from the sheriff about inadequate facilities impelled the city to hire EVAN WILLIAMS to build a new five-room, two-story stone jail on the northeast corner of Jefferson and Sixth Streets in 1802–3. Historian HENRY MCMURTRIE in his *Sketches of Louisville* (1819) described it as "a most miserable edifice, in a most filthy and ruinous condition, first cousin to the blackhole of Calcutta." Although leaders discussed replacing this structure for several years, it was not until late 1819 that it was supplanted by a new L-shaped facility. Located at the northwest corner of Sixth St. and Court Pl., the jail was constructed by Dr. James Chew Johnston for nearly ten thousand dollars.

By 1844 the old "gaol" had been replaced by a new city/county jail on the north side of Jefferson St. between Sixth and Seventh Streets. It was designed in the Gothic style by city architect John Jeffrey and included forty-eight cells. Although this jail was enlarged during the 1860s, the community had outgrown the facility by the end of the century, and the CITY HALL Annex was built on its site in 1909.

In 1902 the JEFFERSON COUNTY FISCAL COURT approved plans by the architectural firm of D.X. MURPHY AND BROTHER for a new jail. Located on the former site of the FIRST PRESBYTERIAN CHURCH on Green St. (LIBERTY) between Sixth St. and Armory Pl., the structure of stone and red brick was completed in 1905. It was considered one of the most modern in the nation. Originally four groups of inmates were segregated by means of an elaborate system of corridors and it provided separate facilities for men and women, black and white prisoners. A tunnel to and from the courthouse to the jail was constructed at the same time. The edifice was a reflection of the Chicago school of architecture.* The jail's administration wing was in the castellated style, and its front office has an arch entranceway bordered by protruding turrets that go up through the corbelled parapet. The faintly Egyptian-style cell block, housing 240 units, has tall, slender windows that stretch from near sidewalk level to the cornice. The structure was vacated in 1976 upon completion of the new Hall of Justice. After being placed on the NATIONAL REGISTER OF HISTORIC PLACES in 1973, the old jail was remodeled in 1982–83 for use as government offices and the Jefferson County Law Library.

In 1976 the county celebrated the opening of the new Jefferson Hall of Justice at the corner of Sixth and Jefferson Streets. The six-story, concrete-and-glass structure cost $15 million and was designed to accommodate approximately 350 prisoners. The facility also housed the city Police Court, the county's Quarterly Court, Magistrate Court, and all divisions of the Circuit Court.

An additional facility used to incarcerate prisoners in the 1970s was the Community Treatment Center. It was first located at the corner of Clay and Walnut (Muhammad Ali Blvd.) Streets. In 1975 the center changed its name to the Community Correction Center when it moved into the former Youth Center building on Chestnut St. between Floyd and PRESTON STREETS. In 1989 a new 210-bed wing was opened to alleviate overcrowding; the older portion of the structure was renovated in 1991. The Jefferson County Youth Center moved to a new sixty-four-bed facility at the corner of Eighth and Jefferson Streets at that time. A thirty-two-bed addition was dedicated in 1998.

The city WORKHOUSE had its beginning in 1830 to deal with misdemeanor cases. From a downtown location it was moved to Payne St. near Lexington Rd. in 1879. Prisoners served their sentences by toiling under the hot sun in the Cave Hill quarry and nearby Breslin quarry, hewing the stone from which alleys and fences were made throughout the city. Although the quarry work was abolished in later years, the facility remained in use until 1954.

As a temporary CIVIL WAR measure, a large prison at Tenth St. and W BROADWAY was built by the federal government to house military prisoners. Some prisoners were hanged there in the courtyard. Female prisoners were housed in the Wiles Mansion on the southwest corner of Thirteenth and W Broadway.

In 1936 the Kentucky General Assembly appropriated $3 million to build the new KENTUCKY STATE REFORMATORY (KSR) at LaGrange in nearby OLDHAM COUNTY on a twenty-eight-hundred-acre farm. The new medium-security prison was built to relieve overcrowding at the Kentucky State Penitentiary at Eddyville. In 1937 the Kentucky National Guard supervised the moving of thirty prisoners to KSR. They lived in tents until prison construction was completed. The new facility was dedicated later in the year by Gov. A.B. Chandler before a crowd of four thousand spectators. Soon twenty-six hundred prisoners took up residence in the new prison.

By 1940 it was becoming increasingly difficult to attract men as prison guards because of low pay and stressful working conditions. To solve the problem, prisoners were assigned civilian jobs inside the prison, and the prisoners literally ran the LaGrange prison. In 1942 there were three thousand male prisoners at KSR even though six hundred had been paroled to military service in WORLD WAR II. Lax security during this time allowed prisoners and guards to leave the prison freely, many of whom were often found drunk in LaGrange. Despite attempts to tighten up prison security, 117 prisoners managed to escape in 1946. As rules became more strictly enforced, violators were usually punished by either having their heads shaved, being forced to work in the rock quarry under armed guard, or spending the night in a dark hole. Also during this time, compulsory religious services and mandated elementary education became part of the prison regimen. In the 1980s, KSR expanded to include a hospital and a geriatric center for the growing population of aging prisoners.

Responding to mounting public anger over the housing of male and female prisoners in the same facility, the General Assembly ordered the Women's Division at KSR to build a separate prison for women in the small rural community of Pewee Valley near LaGrange. Because women prisoners were the wives, mothers, daughters, and sisters of Kentucky citizens, correctional officials tried to soften the image of prison by euphemistically naming the new facility Pine Bluff. However, this was short-lived, and the prison was eventually renamed the Kentucky Correctional Institution for Women. By 1950 there were sixty-seven women prisoners at the facility, a majority of them murderers.

Racial disturbances at the reformatory during the 1950s and 1960s were aggravated by overcrowding and poorly trained and unmotivated prison guards. Because of this, the federal courts ordered the population at KSR to be reduced in 1963. Four years later a reception and diagnostic center for new prisoners, called the Roederer Correctional Complex, was opened nearby. By 1976 a farm center had been opened at the complex, and in 1987 a military-style boot camp for first offenders was added.

Despite initial complaints from LaGrange residents who questioned the need for another facility in their community, the new Luther Luckett Correctional Complex opened in 1981 with William Seabold as warden. Seabold, like Luther Luckett for whom the new prison was named, believed in rehabilitation with firm discipline. The prison, originally designed for six hundred prisoners, in time held more than double that number. In 1981 the former Central State Hospital for the criminally insane was replaced by the Kentucky Correctional Psychiatric Center (KCPC) on the grounds of the Luckett complex. Unlike Luckett, KCPC is staffed entirely by employees of the Cabinet for Human Resources.

From early statehood days persistent overcrowding and violence in the Louisville-area jails have been a problem. In 1983 a federal court in Louisville ruled that no more than thirty convicted felons could be confined at the Jefferson County Jail. The court further ordered that the prisoners could not be kept there longer than thirty days after they were convicted. In an effort to ease violence and overcrowding at the Hall of Justice and the Community Corrections Center, Judge Charles Allen of the federal court in Louisville issued a "consent decree" in 1985 limiting the number of prisoners who could be confined in these facilities to 823. The court order remained in effect into the late 1990s, mandating the release of many nonviolent and minor offenders to make room for serious and violent long-term offenders. While approximately fifty to one hundred offenders were released each week under the program, penology experts agree that the decree was effective in reducing overcrowding, easing violence, and forcing alternative sentencing.

The court order also encouraged corrections officials to utilize community release programs such as home incarceration (wearing electronic monitoring devices), work release, and "Bond Vacate" orders issued by a federal district judge. Desperate for solutions and attempting to comply with federal court orders, the city and county signed a contract with U.S. Corrections Corp., a private for-profit company, to operate the home incarceration programs using electronic monitoring to follow the movements of prisoners serving their sentences at home.

The concept of community corrections began to gain favor with state officials, who saw it as a convenient way to reduce prison populations. In 1986 Dismas House (a halfway house for released prisoners) could boast the cost of $18.75 per day as opposed to the $35 per day it cost to house a prisoner in Kentucky's growing prison system. This amount may be misleading, however, since it lists only the operating costs and ignores the sixty thousand dollars it costs to build a single new prison bed. New ways were sought to reduce prison populations including the use of early release for older prisoners who no longer posed a threat to society.

Facing severe restrictions on jail overcrowding from the courts, the Louisville area witnessed the construction of new facilities and renovations to old ones during the 1990s. In 1998 the fifth and sixth floors of the Hall of Justice were renovated to accommodate an additional 180 beds. Areas to educate and counsel prisoners in efforts to help them avoid crime and become taxpayers were also added during this time. In 1999 Jefferson County converted the former Metropolitan Sewer District building at Sixth and Liberty into a jail at a cost of $20 million. The new facility, with approximately nine hundred beds, relieved overcrowding as mandated by the federal courts and replaced the private work-release jails at the Dismas Center in Portland and the River City Corrections Center on Market St.

CORRECTIONAL FACILITIES, GREATER LOUISVILLE AREA

Adult facilities

Hall of Justice, 600 W Jefferson St., Louisville: Temporary holding facility

Jefferson County Community Correction Center, 316 E Chestnut St., Louisville: An adult detention facility that incarcerates both sentenced misdemeanants and pretrial detainees

Kentucky State Reformatory, 3001 W Highway 146, LaGrange: Medium- and minimum-security prison for adult males

Luther Luckett Correctional Complex, LaGrange: Medium-security prison for adult males

Roederer Correctional Complex, 4000 Morgan Rd., LaGrange: Medium- and minimum-security prison for adult males

Kentucky Correctional Institution for Women, 2401 Ash Ave., Pewee Valley: Maximum-, medium-, and minimum-security prison for women

U.S. Army Military Stockade, US 31W, Ft. Knox: Holding facility for U.S. Army prisoners

Community Correctional Facilities

River City Work Release Program
Cornerstone Halfway House
Diersen Halfway House
Dismas Halfway House #1 for state prisoners
Dismas Halfway House #2 for jail release
St. Ann's Halfway House
St. Patrick's Halfway House

Juvenile Correctional Facilities

Juvenile Justice Center
Central Kentucky Treatment Center
Cardinal Treatment Center
Johnson-Breckinridge Treatment Center
KCH-Rice Audubon Center
Phoenix House Temporary Shelter

CORRECTIONAL FACILITIES, SOUTHERN INDIANA

Clark County

Clark County Jail, 501 E Court Ave., Jeffersonville

Clark County Detention Center for Juveniles, 501 E Court Ave., Jeffersonville

Clark County Youth Shelter, 118 E Chestnut St., Jeffersonville

Henryville Correctional Facility, Clark County State Forest, Henryville

Floyd County

Floyd County Jail, 311 Hauss Square, New Albany
Floyd County Youth Shelter, 3005 Grantline Rd., New Albany

Harrison County

Harrison County Justice Center, 1445 Gardner Ln., Corydon

Scott County

Scott County Security Center, 111 S First St., Scottsburg

See Samuel W. Thomas, *An Inventory of Jefferson County Records* (Louisville 1970); Falls of the Ohio Metropolitan Council of Governments, *Metropolitan Preservation Plan* (Louisville 1973).

Lou Torok

CORYDON. Corydon, Indiana, the Harrison County seat, is located in Harrison Township at the junction of Big Indian and Little Indian Creeks, about ten miles north of the Ohio River. The town was founded in 1808 after Harvey Heth purchased the site from William Henry Harrison, the territorial governor of Indiana. The town's name was derived from one of Harrison's favorite songs, "The Pastoral Elegy," that mourns the death of a shepherd named Corydon.

In 1813 the Indiana territorial legislature voted to move the capital from Vincennes in southwestern Indiana to Corydon, which was closer to Indiana's population centers. For a time, territorial officers shared quarters with Harrison County officials in a half-finished log structure at the corner of High St. and Capitol in downtown Corydon. When delegates to the constitutional convention met in June 1816, they held many of their sessions under the shade of a nearby giant elm tree, which became known as the "Constitutional Elm."

From 1816 to 1825 Corydon was Indiana's capital. Completed in 1816 at a cost of three thousand dollars, the capitol was initially intended as a new county courthouse. Erected under the supervision of Dennis Pennington, a local stonemason and politician, it is constructed of rough blue limestone that was quarried locally. The House of Representatives occupied the lower room, while the Senate and Supreme Court met on the upper floor. When Indianapolis became the capital in 1825, the structure assumed its original purpose as the Harrison County Courthouse.

In early July 1863, Corydon was one of several southern Indiana towns visited by Gen. John Hunt Morgan and his Confederate raiders. On July 9 Morgan and approximately 2,000 of his cavalry confronted about 450 members of the Indiana Home Guard on the outskirts of town. Morgan drove the outnumbered guardsmen from the field and shelled the town. The battle lasted about a half-hour, during which eight rebels were killed and thirty-three wounded, while two guardsmen were killed and eight wounded.

From its founding into the mid-twentieth century, Corydon served primarily as a government and commercial center for farmers and other rural residents of Harrison and surrounding townships. Except for local roads linking it with other nearby towns, Corydon lacked significant transportation connections until construction in 1883 of the Louisville, New Albany, & Corydon Railroad. This standard-gauge line linked Corydon with the Louisville, Evansville, and St. Louis Railroad (now Norfolk Southern) at Corydon Junction, eight miles to the north.

Corydon's first major industrial firm was Keller Manufacturing Co., which began producing wagons in 1901. The company later replaced wagons with furniture and is still one of the town's largest employers. Completion of Interstate 64 in 1974 opened Corydon and its environs to new POPULATION and industrial growth. The town's population has remained stable, growing from 2,719 in 1970 to 2,742 in 1990, but declining to 2,652 in 1996. Harrison County's population grew from 20,423 to 29,890 in 1990, and 33,349 in 1996.

Many of the new residents moved from Louisville to new subdivisions outside Corydon in Harrison Township. Population and expansion of the workforce, combined with improved transportation, have attracted several new industrial employers, particularly in the areas of automotive parts, food processing, and wood products.

Corydon is a town governed by an elected clerk-treasurer and board of trustees. In 1996 Frank O'Bannon, an attorney and publisher of the *Corydon Democrat*, was elected governor of Indiana after several terms as a state senator and two terms as lieutenant governor.

Carl E. Kramer

COSBY, FORTUNATUS, JR. (b Harrods Creek, Jefferson County, May 2, 1801; d Louisville, June 15, 1871). Poet and educator. The son of Fortunatus Sr. and Mary Ann (Fontaine) Cosby, Fortunatus Jr. moved with his family to Louisville shortly after his birth. Educated at both Yale and Transylvania Universities, Cosby decided not to practice LAW, which he had studied, but instead to follow his literary and scholarly talents.

For a time, he was the director of a private girls' school; and in 1829, when Louisville's first free public school opened, Cosby was appointed to the board of trustees. He served as superintendent of the public schools from December 1839 to September 1841, from May 1843 to July 1846, and from January to June 1849.

While a leader in education, Cosby was also an accomplished poet and literary critic whose work regularly appeared in the newspapers and magazines of the 1840s and 1850s, such as *Graham's Magazine*. Though historian J. STODDARD JOHNSTON noted that many of Cosby's stanzas were of a "sober" tone, he did occasionally produce verses of a lighter nature. A friend of newspaper editor GEORGE D. PRENTICE, Cosby often contributed to the *Louisville Daily Journal*. In 1847 he became the assistant editor and, in 1848, the editor of the *Examiner,* a paper "devoted to the cause of gradual emancipation of the slaves." Cosby also wrote the ode that was sung at the dedication ceremony of CAVE HILL CEMETERY in 1848.

In 1850, Cosby moved to Washington, D.C., to serve in the Treasury Department, and in 1861 President Abraham Lincoln nominated him for appointment to be consul to Geneva, Switzerland. Though Congress finally confirmed his nomination and commissioned him in February 1863, Cosby's loyalty had been questioned because one of his sons and a son-in-law were Confederate soldiers. Cosby's term as consul was short-lived. Later that same year, he was relieved of his post after controversy arose from a visit he had received from former Kentucky governor Charles Morehead, who was falsely suspected of being an overseas Confederate agent. Cosby remained in Geneva until after the end of the CIVIL WAR. Then he returned to Louisville, where he lived until his death.

Cosby married Ellen Mary Jane Blake in 1826, and they had seven children: Robert Todd, Ellen Blake, George Blake, Alice Gray, Mary Fontaine, William Vernon, and Frank Carvill. His first wife died in 1848. In 1854, Cosby married Anna T. Mills, who died in 1864. He is buried in Cave Hill Cemetery.

See J. Stoddard Johnston, ed., *Memorial History of Louisville,* vol. 2 (Chicago 1896).

COSBY, FORTUNATUS, SR. (b Louisa County, Virginia, December 20, 1767; d Louisville, October 19, 1846). Attorney, legislator, judge. Fortunatus Cosby was the third of twelve children of Charles and Elizabeth (Sydnor) Cosby. He received a good education, graduated from William and Mary College at age nineteen, and then read LAW. Cosby must have been an excellent student and talented practitioner of the law, because he became a district attorney in 1790, serving to 1795. In 1798 he moved with his wife's family to Jefferson County, settling on HARRODS CREEK, and opened a successful law practice. After he and his wife fulfilled family obligations to her widowed father and her younger siblings, and due to a growing legal and political career, Cosby moved his family to Louisville in the early 1800s.

He served in the Kentucky legislature, 1802–3 and 1805–6, and as a circuit court judge, 1810–16. He was one of Louisville's largest real estate holders, including owning a large tract that once belonged to JOHN CAMPBELL encompassing an area from the proximity of Tenth St. to PORTLAND. He is said to have built one of the earliest brick houses in the city and in 1804 founded its first market house at the corner of FOURTH and MARKET STREETS. Joblin described him as "large-hearted, generous to a fault, and [someone who] entertained with true Kentucky liberality. . . . His society, was everywhere sought after by the cultivated."

Johnston described him as having an "exceedingly genial disposition and graceful wit, he was considered one of the most brilliant conversationalists of his day." Cosby married Mary Ann Fontaine (b ca. 1779), oldest daughter of AARON FONTAINE, on November 1, 1795, in Louisa County, Virginia. They had seven children: Eliza Sydnor, Fortunatus Junior, Fontaine, Barbara, James Smiley, William Vernon, and Thomas Prather.

See M. Joblin & Co., *Louisville Past and Present: Its Industrial History* (Louisville 1875); J. Stoddard Johnston, ed., *Memorial History of Louisville* vol. 2 (Chicago 1896); Malcolm H. Harris, *History of Louisa County, Virginia* (Richmond 1936).

James J. Holmberg

COSSAR, MAUDE (WOODSON) (b Memphis, Tennessee, ca. 1869; d Louisville, November 24, 1931). Columnist, politician. She was the daughter of Maj. William Orville and his wife Texie (McPherson) Woodson. The family moved to Louisville when she was still young.

In 1905 Cossar became society editor for the *COURIER-JOURNAL*. Later she wrote a popular daily advice column for the *Louisville Herald* under the name Cynthia Gray. Cossar's first marriage to Morton Cassedy, a writer on the editorial staff of the *Courier-Journal,* ended in divorce. Later she married Louisville newspaperman and advertising agent Aubrey Cossar. She had no children.

Developing an interest in politics, Cossar

entered the political arena soon after women received the right to vote. She defeated her Democrat rival, Adolph Schmitt, by 5,547 votes to win the November 8, 1921, race for city treasurer in the HUSTON QUIN administration. She was one of four female Republican candidates elected to office in Louisville that year. At the time of her term, Cossar, who resided at 312 W Oak St., was chairman of the Fifth District Republican Women's Organization and also a member of the Republican State Central Committee.

She was active in other organizations, including serving as first president of the local Business and Professional Women's Club and director of the Altrusa Club. In her spare time Cossar won acclaim for her unique decoration of pianos. She is buried in CAVE HILL CEMETERY.

See Bess A. Ray, ed., *A Dictionary of Prominent Women of Louisville* (Louisville 1940); *Courier-Journal*, Nov. 9, 1921, Nov. 25, 1931.

COTTER, JOSEPH SEAMON (b Nelson County, Kentucky, February 2, 1861; d Louisville, March 14, 1949). Educator and poet. The son of Martha Vaughn, a freed slave of the Rowan family of Federal Hill (*My Old Kentucky Home*), Cotter was born into poverty in a log cabin near Bardstown, Kentucky. Eight years later he and his mother moved to a farmhouse at Thirty-sixth St. and Virginia Ave. in Louisville. Cotter's early education was limited and was derived mainly from the songs sung and stories told by his mother, who had taught him to read by the age of four.

His early schooling ended when he was forced to quit the third grade to help support his family. He went to work as a manual laborer at a local brickyard and later became a teamster. At twenty-two, he entered night school and, upon graduation, began a fifty-year career as an educator in Louisville's PUBLIC SCHOOLS.

From 1889 to 1893 Cotter taught at Western Colored School, and from 1893 to 1911 he was principal of the Paul Lawrence Dunbar School. He was then appointed principal of Samuel Coleridge Taylor School, where he served until his retirement in 1942. As an educator, Cotter was credited with winning approval for the practice of naming schools in African American neighborhoods after famous AFRICAN AMERICANS.

Cotter discovered a talent for storytelling as a child, and as an adult he published several books of POETRY, folk tales, drama, and SONGS, achieving local and national recognition as one of Louisville's most accomplished and significant African American writers. Cotter's writing was generally solemn in tone with a deep spiritual basis. His stories of African American life were straightforward and bold, and many of his poems paid tribute to local civic leaders.

His first book, *A Rhyming*, was published in 1895. His other works include *Links of Friendship* (1898), *A White Song and a Black One* (1909), *Negro Tales* (1912), *Collected Poems* (1938), *Sequel to the "Pied Piper of Hamlin" and other Poems* (1939), and *Caleb the Degenerate: A Play in Four Acts - A Study of the Types, Customs and Needs of the American Negro* (1940). Cotter was a strong supporter of LIBRARIES for African Americans and was an organizer of storytelling contests in those libraries. He was also a member of the National Storyteller's League, the NATIONAL ASSOCIATION FOR THE ADVANCEMENT OF COLORED PEOPLE, and the Author's League of America.

Professor Joseph Seaman Cotter with winners of story telling contest, about 1919.

Cotter married Maria F. Cox in 1891, and they had three children. Their son, Joseph S. Cotter Jr., was also a promising poet until his untimely death at the age of twenty-four. Cotter Sr. was remembered for his dedication to education and his pride in his African American heritage. The Cotter Homes housing project and the Joseph S. Cotter Elementary School were named in his memory in 1956. Cotter is buried in Greenwood Cemetery.

See Joseph S. Cotter Sr., *Twenty-Fifth Anniversary of the Founding of Colored Parkland or "Little Africa"* (Louisville 1916); Ann Allen Shockley, "Joseph S. Cotter, Sr.: Biographical Sketch of a Black Louisville Bard," *CLA Journal* 18 (March 1975).

J. Blaine Hudson

COUNTRY LAKE CAMP INC. The Louisville area has had many summer camps for youth. While not as popular at the end of the twentieth century as earlier, both public and private residential and day camps were an important part of a child's summer group experience. There children could take part in such various activities as SWIMMING, hiking, archery, and horseback riding. One important private resident summer camp was opened in June 1966 at Underwood, Indiana, by Louisvillians Everett and Martha Ballard and family. Located approximately twenty-five miles north of Louisville, the camp was situated on 250 acres of pine forest, contained a 15-acre lake, and bordered the 22,000-acre CLARK STATE FOREST.

The noncompetitive co-ed camp featured a high ratio of staff to camper and small group activities of many kinds, with one counselor and six campers living together and carrying their daily activities with their cabin group. Some of the programs most popular with the campers were hikes and overnights on a thousand-foot knob and early morning escorted lake swims. Out-of-camp trips made use of the Clark State Forest riding trails and fire tower areas and of nearby lakes for water skiing and advanced sailing.

Until it closed in 1981, Country Lake Camp served families from over twenty-eight states and foreign countries and was continuously accredited by the American Camping Association.

Everett E. Ballard
Martha Stoll Ballard

COURIER-JOURNAL, THE. Kentucky's leading newspaper for more than a century was not founded so much as it evolved. In November 1830 GEORGE D. PRENTICE, a young Whig New Englander who had come to Kentucky to write a biography of Henry Clay and took a liking to the area, accepted the editorship of the new Whig organ, the *LOUISVILLE JOURNAL*. For forty years Prentice waged a war of words for the WHIG PARTY. He took little part in the slavery controversy, but as a strong advocate of the Union he denounced slavery when the CIVIL WAR threatened.

Prentice was strongly opposed by the *LOUISVILLE COURIER*, established in 1844 by WALTER N. HALDEMAN, which took sides against the North and in 1861 was suppressed by Union forces. For four years it was published on the run in Nashville, but when the war ended Haldeman brought it back to Louisville and resumed publication under its original name.

A third paper, the *Louisville Democrat*, was also organized in 1844, by prominent businessman and Democratic leader JAMES GUTHRIE. In 1868, the three papers were merged into the *Courier-Journal*, with HENRY WATTERSON as editor. The son of a Tennessee congressman, Watterson was born in Washington, D.C., worked on *Harper's Magazine*, the *New York Times*, and the *New York Tribune* but returned to his father's home state when war loomed and worked on the *Nashville Banner* before enlisting in the Confederate army. In 1865, sensing that the war was being lost, Watterson went to Cincinnati, where he became editor of the *Evening Times*. He returned to the *Banner* at war's end, where he came to the attention of Isham Henderson, who chose the young editor as his successor on the *Journal*, though they had

Courier-Journal editorial board, 1869.

been on opposing sides in the war.

Watterson soon became one of the nation's outstanding editors, and under his direction the *Courier-Journal* became recognized as the region's leading newspaper. His florid, often caustic, style and his editorials supporting the DEMOCRATIC PARTY and urging industrial development of Kentucky and the South won a wide audience. He also sparked controversy with his attempts to prove that Christopher Marlowe had actually written the works attributed to Shakespeare. Watterson won the PULITZER PRIZE in 1917 with editorials demanding United States entry into WORLD WAR I, declaring "To hell with the Hapsburgs and Hohenzollern." He then opposed the League of Nations, saying, "We have plenty to do on our own continent without seeking to right things on other continents."

In the meantime, the afternoon *LOUISVILLE TIMES,* founded by Walter N. Haldeman in 1884, flourished alongside the morning *Courier-Journal,* with Emmett Logan and E. Polk Johnson as its editors. When Haldeman died in 1902, his son Bruce became president and editor. A family dispute, however, put the papers in the hands of his brother, William, and Henry Watterson. It was from them and sister Isabel Haldeman that in 1918 and 1919 Judge ROBERT WORTH BINGHAM, who had come to Louisville from North Carolina and married the widow of railroad magnate Henry Flagler, bought a majority interest in the *Courier-Journal* and *Times.* He built the two into a formidable combination that triumphed in a bitter intra-city battle with the *Herald-Post* and established what amounted to a monopoly in the city's daily news field.

Bingham was as strong in his support of President Woodrow Wilson and the League of Nations as Watterson was opposed, and, though the two men maintained cordial relations, it soon became apparent that they were too far apart on such issues as the League, government supervision of saloons, and woman suffrage, all of which Bingham supported. In 1919 Watterson asked that his name be removed from the masthead, and he retired from the paper after fifty years as editor. He died on December 22, 1921.

Watterson was succeeded as editor by Harrison Robertson, who was more scholarly and mild-mannered than his predecessor and served until 1939. One of Watterson's protégés, TOM WALLACE, left the editorial board of the *Courier-Journal* to become editor of the *Louisville Times.* Tall, courtly, but fiery in his defense of the environment, Wallace for years fought off attempts by private utilities to develop Kentucky's Cumberland Falls for hydroelectric power and championed the establishment of state parks and nature preserves.

Under Judge Bingham's direction, the *Courier-Journal* became an ardent supporter of conservation; international cooperation; more spending for education, especially for improvement in schools for AFRICAN AMERICANS; and woman suffrage. He was among the first southern publishers to hire women in the newsroom for duties other than society and home economics. One woman who joined the *Courier-Journal* in 1936 and rose from the ranks of reporter and feature writer to full-time editorial writer was MOLLY CLOWES. In 1966 she was named editor of the editorial page, a position she held until her retirement in 1971.

In 1922 Bingham founded the STANDARD GRAVURE CORP., which grew to be an operation almost as large as the NEWSPAPERS. It printed not only the *Courier-Journal Magazine,* which replaced the rotogravure section, but color magazines for other newspapers and a variety of commercial catalogues.

The *Courier-Journal* and *Times* were aggressive in their support of the Democratic Party. Judge Bingham became an enthusiastic backer of Franklin D. Roosevelt for president in 1932 and was named to the committee that drafted legislation establishing the Agricultural Adjustment Act. In 1933 he was appointed ambassador to the Court of St. James's, leaving his son, George Barry, in charge of the newspapers. Bingham had two other children, Robert and Henrietta, neither of whom showed an interest in managing the newspapers.

George Barry, known always as Barry, had shown an interest from boyhood. After graduating from Harvard, where he met and later married Mary Caperton of Richmond, Virginia, he traveled for a year in Europe, tried fiction writing, and came home to begin an apprenticeship on his father's papers, assuming control at age thirty-one when his father died on December 18, 1937. Before that he had hired, upon the recommendation of President Roosevelt and with his father's approval, MARK ETHRIDGE, who came to Louisville in 1936. In 1937 BARRY BINGHAM became president and publisher of the Bingham holdings; Ethridge became vice president and general manager; and Lisle Baker, a native of Monticello, Kentucky, came from a bank in Frankfort, Kentucky, to be secretary and later treasurer of the company.

Ethridge brought to Louisville a cadre of seasoned southern newsmen, among them James S. Pope, who became one of the nation's outstanding managing editors. The news and editorial staffs were enlarged, new bureaus were established, and the magazine began publication. Under the Bingham-Ethridge-Baker leadership, the *Courier-Journal* and *Louisville Times* enjoyed what became known as the golden era.

Even before Ethridge came to Louisville, sports coverage was significant under Earl Ruby, the sports editor for thirty years whose daily column, "Ruby's Report," became a fixture on the sports page. Ruby started as an office boy at the *Courier-Journal* in 1921 and continued on the staff until 1989. He wrote more than ten thousand columns and was outdoor editor for more than twenty years after serving as sports editor. Ruby has had more stories published in *Best Sports Stories,* an annual anthology of sports reporting and photography, than any other sports reporter. He won a National Headliner Award in 1945, was a cofounder of the KENTUCKY DERBY FESTIVAL in 1956, and was founder of the Kentucky Athletic Hall of Fame in 1969. He is the author of three books.

During his career John Ed Pearce was one of the most widely read writers in Kentucky as an editorialist, columnist, and author. Called by Barry Bingham "the best writer ever to serve on the *Courier-Journal,* he won a Nieman Fellowship to Harvard, a Governor's Medallion for Public Service, a share in a Pulitzer Prize, and numerous other national and local awards. He has written several books about Kentucky and Kentucky politics.

In 1941 Barry Bingham joined the U.S. Navy, from which he retired in 1945 as a commander, USNR. During his absence, Herbert Agar was brought in to direct the editorial page, and MARY BINGHAM became active in the editorial and book departments. Ethridge assumed the title of publisher; and it was during the ensuing decade, when Bingham was often absent on Navy duty or diplomatic missions, that Ethridge left his indelible imprint on the papers.

In the years following the war, the *Courier-Journal* won seven Pulitzer Prizes for editorial excellence (giving it a total of nine, including one received by the *Louisville Times,* more than all but four other papers). It pioneered in the extensive use of photographs, headlines below the front-page fold, continuation of front-page stories to the back page of the front section, and it was among the first to develop an op-ed page for opinion other than that expressed in editorials.

The *Courier-Journal* has attracted outstanding political cartoonists. GROVER PAGE was followed by HUGH HAYNIE, who was political cartoonist from 1958 to 1995, followed by a stint as part-time contributor. Nick Anderson overlapped Haynie's last years before becoming the primary local cartoonist. Haynie used pen and brush in a distinctive, sardonic style in open, uncluttered compositions, drawing widely from popular culture, comics, and nursery rhymes for his images. He won a National Headliners Club Award in 1966 and received other national recognition. He was awarded an honorary degree from the UNIVERSITY OF LOUISVILLE and received the Alumni Medal from the College of William and Mary.

In 1922 Judge Bingham had also begun BROADCASTING over station WHAS, a radio station that won national fame during the historic OHIO RIVER FLOOD OF 1937 when it stayed on the air throughout the crisis, helping to organize and direct relief and rescue efforts. In 1950 WHAS-TV went on the air, the second TELEVISION station to telecast in Kentucky. The station was part of a revolutionary development that would change the nature of journalism and shake the role of newspapers in America. The *Courier-Journal* was not to escape.

Before the advent of television, the *Courier-Journal* dominated the daily paper field in Kentucky, enjoying circulation in every county; it was repeated by many knowledgeable Kentuckians that "only two things hold Kentucky together—the University of Kentucky and the *Courier-Journal.*" Television, dismissed at first as an interesting entertainment medium, soon began to challenge newspapers for followers and, as a consequence, for advertisers.

The Bingham papers, however, continued to be vigorous and influential. In 1962 Barry Bingham took his first step toward retirement, positioning his oldest son, Robert Worth Bingham, to run the newspapers, and a younger son, George Barry Jr., to operate WHAS and WHAS-TV. But in 1966 Worth was killed in an accident, and Barry Jr .was named editor and publisher in 1971, while Barry Sr. became chairman of the board.

George Barry Bingham Jr. was born September 23, 1933, in Louisville. He graduated from Harvard University in 1956 with a B.A. in history. After his father retired, he was made editor and publisher and held this position until 1986. Barry Junior raised eyebrows in March 1984 when he restructured the family's business, removing from the boards of directors his wife, his mother, and both sisters, setting in motion the events that led to sale of the family's interests. From April 1989 to December 1991, Bingham was publisher of *Fine Line,* a newsletter on media ethics.

With ADVERTISING rates based on a circulation area that was not expanding or growing in population, the papers began for the first time to feel deep financial pressures. In 1985 the *Courier-Journal Magazine* was discontinued. In the same year, the *Courier-Journal* and the *Louisville Times* news staffs were merged. Both papers continued, but it proved to be a temporary reprieve, and on February 14, 1987, the *Louisville Times* discontinued publication.

In the meantime, however, a fierce struggle erupted between Barry Jr. and his sister Sallie, who threatened to sell her considerable block of company stock to the highest bidder. Rather than see the paper torn apart, Barry Sr. and Mary Bingham decided to sell the papers, stations, and other family properties. In 1986 the *Courier-Journal* was bought by Gannett Inc. and became one of the Gannett chain of papers.

George N. Gill, who had been president of all the Bingham-owned companies before they were sold, was named publisher. Michael Gartner, a former editor of the *Des Moines Register and Tribune,* became editor for a year and then was succeeded by David V. Hawpe. Most of the management team of the newspaper remained in place under Gannett until their retirements. Gill was president and publisher from 1986 until retiring in 1993. He first joined the paper in 1960 as copy editor. His career developed swiftly as he moved to reporter, city editor, and then managing editor from 1966 to 1974. From there he transferred to the business side of the paper as general manager. Gill was also instrumental in bringing local government and business together to focus on expanding the local economy as chairman of the GREATER LOUISVILLE ECONOMIC DEVELOPMENT PARTNERSHIP. Gill is a 1957 graduate of Indiana University in journalism and GOVERNMENT.

In 1987 David Hawpe became editor of the paper, remaining in that position until 1996 when he was reassigned as vice president and editorial director in a management shuffle. A native of Pikeville, he grew up in Louisville, graduated from the University of Kentucky, joined the *Courier- Journal* as a summer intern in 1965 and later worked as a reporter, editorial writer, copy editor, assistant state editor, city editor, and managing editor.

Gill was succeeded as publisher by longtime Gannett executive Edward E. Manassah. The *Courier-Journal* won the Pulitzer Prize for general news reporting in 1989 for coverage of a school bus–pickup truck head-on collision near Carrollton that killed twenty-seven people. The newspaper continues to have the largest circulation of any in Kentucky, and space devoted to news has increased.

Throughout its history, the *Courier-Journal* has attracted the best in journalism—people whose names became household words throughout Kentucky and southern Indiana as a result of their work on the pages of the newspaper. There were the writers, the likes of JOE CREASON and ALLAN TROUT and John Fetterman; the photographers, men such as Billy Davis, whose remarkable aerial photos highlighted many a front page, and Harold Davis, the pioneer in newspaper color PHOTOGRAPHY; the indomitable CISSY GREGG and her mouth-watering recipes; and many others. Their places have been filled by current columnists Byron Crawford, Bob Hill, Rich Bozich, Pat Forde, Sarah Fritschner, and Rochelle Riley. Twenty-six individuals from the *Courier-Journal* have been inducted into the Kentucky Journalism Hall of Fame.

The *Courier-Journal* has been located in four buildings. The first was on Jefferson St. between Third and FOURTH STREETS. In 1876 it moved into a new building (designed for the company by Louisville architect JOHN ANDREWARTHA) on the southeast corner of Fourth and Green (LIBERTY) STREETS. In 1912 it moved one block away to the southwest corner of Liberty (Green) and Third Streets and occupied the former post office and custom house. In 1948 the company moved to its new quarters on the northeast corner of BROADWAY and Sixth St.

See Donald B. Towles, *The Press of Kentucky, 1787–1994* (Frankfort 1994); John Ed Pearce, *Memoirs: 50 Years at the Courier-Journal and Other Places* (Louisville 1997); Maurice Horn, ed., *Contemporary Graphic Artists,* vol. 3 (Detroit 1988); Charles Press, *The Political Cartoon* (East Brunswick, N.J., 1981).

John Ed Pearce

COURIER-JOURNAL/WILL SALES BUILDING. The Courier-Journal Building stood at the southeast corner of Fourth and Green (LIBERTY) STREETS from 1876 to 1979. Attributed to architect JOHN ANDREWARTHA, it was a splendid example of High Victorian Gothic ARCHITECTURE, with a mansard roof and Second Empire details. The dark red and black brick facade had incised stone trim, encaustic tiles, and cast-iron details. The statue of editor GEORGE PRENTICE (1802–70), later placed in front of the main branch of the LOUISVILLE FREE PUBLIC LIBRARY, once sat above the main entrance.

The structure, which was built for the COURIER-JOURNAL newspaper, suffered a fire in 1907. The newspaper's offices moved one block east to the southwest corner of Third and Green (Liberty) Streets in 1912. Over the years the building had its mansard roof removed until only one section remained. Many different businesses and services occupied the upper floors of the building, including dentists, doctors, a beauty salon, and a loan company. Will Sales Jewelers occupied a part of the building from 1927 until close to the demolition.

When the Louisville GALLERIA was planned,

there was a valiant but failed effort by preservationists to preserve the building and have it incorporated into the Galleria. The site is now occupied by the BROWN AND WILLIAMSON TOBACCO CORP. headquarters.

See Walter Langsam, *Metropolitan Preservation Plan* (Louisville 1973); R.C. Riebel, *Louisville Panorama* (Louisville 1954); Samuel W. Thomas, *Views of Louisville since 1766* (Louisville 1971).

Elizabeth Fitzpatrick "Penny" Jones

The Courier-Journal/Will Sales Building, southeast corner of Fourth and Green (Liberty) Streets, c. 1880. Demolished 1979.

COURTS. The court systems in Louisville are fully integrated into the larger federal and state judicial branches. Since federal courts deal only with crimes against the national laws and with civil conflicts that affect interstate issues, each system operates independently. There is occasional overlap, particularly in the criminal area, since some criminal activity can trigger prosecution in both courts.

Federal Courts

Kentucky was originally part of Virginia. The Judiciary Act of 1789 passed by the first congress elected under the new United States Constitution established one district court for all of Kentucky. President George Washington appointed Harry Innes (1752–1816) to be the first district judge of Kentucky. Congress dictated that court sessions be held at "Harrodsburgh," but five years later the location was changed to Frankfort. It was not until 1901 that Kentucky was divided into two federal districts. The Eastern District holds court in Frankfort, Covington, London, and Richmond. The Western District holds court in Louisville, Paducah, Bowling Green, and Owensboro. The United States Sixth Circuit Court of Appeals in Cincinnati, Ohio, supervises both districts.

There are currently five judges sitting in the Western District of Kentucky. Judges are appointed by the president of the United States, approved by the Senate, and serve for life. Judges hear both civil and criminal cases.

Because of the large volume and variety of cases, federal district courts have been authorized to establish and supervise lesser tribunals to handle certain routine or highly specialized matters. Most important of these tribunals is bankruptcy court, established in 1984. There are currently three bankruptcy judges in Louisville. Each is appointed for a fourteen-year term and may be reappointed.

Magistrates are also appointed by the district court judges to conduct many routine civil and criminal proceedings of district court, although they may not handle felony trials. Full-time magistrates serve eight-year terms, while part-time magistrates serve four-year terms. Currently two full-time magistrates serve the district court in Louisville. While most litigation occurs in state courts, federal courts do carry substantial caseloads. During 1996 there were 1,736 civil cases, 204 felony cases, and 508 misdemeanor cases filed in district court in Louisville. Many of the latter cases concerned drug trafficking.

Local Courts

Kentucky has a unified state court system that now incorporates all local courts. Before the judicial reforms of 1976, Louisville had a hodgepodge of police, municipal, and quarterly courts with overlapping jurisdictions, conflicting rules, and more than a hint of political favoritism. The reforms instituted in 1976 were the result of an amendment to the Kentucky constitution ratified by voters in 1975. Since that time, all local courts are integrated into a four-level structure organized along county lines. District and circuit courts are trial courts where all cases begin. The Court of Appeals is an intermediate court that hears appeals from both district and circuit courts. At the top is the Kentucky Supreme Court.

The circuit court, with jurisdiction over Louisville and the rest of Jefferson County, has sixteen judges. It hears all civil cases involving more than four thousand dollars and has jurisdiction over capital offenses, felonies that might result in a year or more incarceration, contested probate, divorces, adoptions, and termination of parental rights. Circuit courts also hear some appeals from district court and various administrative agencies. In the 1995–96 fiscal year, Jefferson County Circuit Court judges heard 3,673 criminal cases, 6,112 civil cases, 2,961 domestic and family cases, and several hundred miscellaneous cases.

District court in Jefferson County has twenty-three judges. It is a court with limited jurisdiction over lesser crimes, primarily misdemeanors (crimes that could result in penalties of less than twelve months in jail), civil cases involving less than four thousand dollars, domestic violence and abuse, traffic offenses, juvenile matters, uncontested probate of wills, guardianship for disabled persons, and mental commitments. It has a small claims division that handles disputes over amounts of less than fifteen hundred dollars, and a mediation program. The latter programs tend to function with less formality than regular court proceedings and do not require lawyers' assistance.

District courts handle the vast majority of cases. In fact, 90 percent of people who have contact with a court in Kentucky will deal only on the district court level. In the 1998–99 fiscal year the district court judges in Louisville/Jefferson County handled 74,779 criminal cases, 99,060 traffic cases, 31,775 civil cases, 12,979 juvenile cases, 3,256 small claims, 5,294 probate cases, 1,356 disability and health cases, and 4,335 cases involving claims of domestic violence.

Judges

While the president appoints federal court judges for life, all other judges in Kentucky are elected. The seven Supreme Court justices, fourteen Court of Appeals judges and ninety-seven circuit court judges are elected for eight-year terms. The 126 district court judges are elected for 4-year terms. Justices and judges must run on a nonpartisan basis. As a result, endorsements by NEWSPAPERS, labor unions, and unofficial judicial review committees play an important role in judicial selection. Some scholars claim that name recognition is the most important factor of all. For a sitting judge running for reelection, the evaluation of judges by attorneys published in newspapers each year can mean the difference between winning and losing. For the most part, judicial races are financed by donations from businesses and attorneys, many of whom may expect to appear before the judge should he or she be elected. To lessen any potential conflict of interest or even appearance of impropriety, the Kentucky Bar Association has considered a rule to prohibit attorneys from donating to judicial races. Such a provision, however, might well violate attorneys' right to participate freely in the political process.

If a vacancy occurs on the bench through death or retirement, a judicial nominating committee from the affected circuit will submit three names to the governor, who appoints one person from this list to fill the unexpired term. The person selected must then run for a full term whenever the unexpired term is completed. A judge or justice may also be removed or retired involuntarily for disability or cause by the Judicial Retirement and Removal Commission. Any such action, however, may be appealed to the Kentucky Supreme Court.

Juries

Juries in the American legal system serve only in trial courts, never at the appeals level. Their role is primarily fact-finding, although in criminal cases they may also recommend sentences. Juries on the circuit court level in Kentucky may have six to twelve members. District court juries have six members. All criminal trials require a unanimous verdict by a jury to find a defendant guilty. Civil trials in circuit court require a three-fourths majority to find for one or another party. In district court civil trials, a five-sixths majority is required.

Since 1976 Kentucky courts have been among the most innovative in the nation. They pioneered pretrial mediation, the end of bail bonding, release on recognizance, and a pilot project creating family courts in Louisville/Jefferson County.

Family matters that come before the courts are often complex, involving a variety of issues, overlapping jurisdictions, civil and criminal dimensions, and oftentimes several social service agencies. Under traditional conditions various family members may be working with different service agencies, social workers, and court personnel. It is not unusual for agencies and the courts to inadvertently work against each other or for some family members to fall between the cracks. Delays and scheduling conflicts are unavoidable. The goal of those creating a family court is to provide an integrated, focused process within which all affected parties can work together for the good of the family as a whole, as well as for each member. The guiding principle is "One judge, one staff, one family."

The Jefferson Family Court Pilot Project consists of four circuit court judges and five district court judges who have volunteered for what is called "Family Session." One unusual feature is that circuit judges are sworn in as special district court judges to have jurisdiction over district court matters, and district court judges are sworn in as special circuit court judges to have jurisdiction over circuit court matters. Each judge is given specialized training in family law and family dynamics.

Paul J. Weber

COWAN, ANDREW (b Ayreshire, Scotland, September 29, 1841; d Louisville, August 23, 1919). Businessman and civic leader. He was born to William Strong and Margaret Isabella (Campbell) Cowan. Young Andrew's family immigrated to the United States and settled in Auburn, New York, in 1848. Cowan attended Madison (Colgate) University until President Lincoln made his first call for troops in 1861, at which time Cowan enlisted as a private. At war's end, Cowan, who had achieved the rank of lieutenant colonel, relocated to Indianapolis. In 1866 he moved to Louisville and joined James E. Mooney and Charles H. Mantle in a partnership known as Mooney, Mantle, and Cowan. The firm on W Main St. supplied leather and railway and mill products and passed on to the Cowan family as the other two partners left the business. Cowan became more involved in the leather business as he was elected the president of the National Oak Leather Co. of Louisville and vice president of the Louisville Leather Co.

Cowan was best remembered, however, as one of the leading proponents of a comprehensive public park and parkway system for Louisville and for the recruitment of Frederick Law OLMSTED as its architect. In an 1887 speech to the SALMAGUNDI CLUB, a gentlemen's conversation group, Cowan first publicly argued the healthful and economic merits of a system of three large urban PARKS connected by tree-lined parkways. This vision was realized with the hiring of Olmsted's firm in June 1891. Cowan was elected as one of the first park commissioners and was primarily responsible for securing the lands for Cherokee and Shawnee Parks. He later served as the Board of Park Commissioner's president and remained active with the park board after his retirement. Philadelphia architect Wilson Eyre designed Cowan's 1907 home overlooking BEARGRASS CREEK and Cherokee Park near Big Rock. Cowan married Mary Adsit of Palmyra, New York, in February 1864; they had one son named Albert Andrew. After Mary's death in 1867, Cowan married Anna L. Gilbert of Utica, New York, in 1876; they had one son named Gilbert Sedgwick. Cowan is buried in CAVE HILL CEMETERY.

See J. Stoddard Johnston, ed., *Memorial History of Louisville*, vol. 2 (Chicago 1896).

Douglas L Stern

COWGER, WILLIAM OWEN (b Hastings, Nebraska, January 1, 1922; d Louisville, October 2, 1971). Louisville mayor and United States congressman. Cowger was the son of Dr. R.H. and Catherine (Combs) Cowger. He enrolled at Texas A&M University in 1940 but received his bachelor's degree in 1944 from Carleton College in Minnesota. After college he was commissioned a naval officer and served during World War II in the Atlantic and Pacific theaters. In 1946 he started a Louisville mortgage realty firm, Thompson and Cowger Inc., serving as its president.

Cowger, a Republican, ran unsuccessfully for the General Assembly in 1951. He served as party campaign chairman in 1953 and is generally credited with revitalizing the party in Jefferson County. In 1954 he directed the campaigns of United States senator John Sherman Cooper and Third District congressional candidate JOHN ROBSION.

In 1961 he became the first Republican to be elected Louisville MAYOR since WILLIAM B. HARRISON in 1929. He defeated William S. Milburn by a vote of 61,651 to 50,219. The central focus of the campaign was the thirty-year dominance by the DEMOCRATIC PARTY machine of city politics. Cowger is credited with helping to dismantle that machine built by MICHAEL "MICKEY" BRENNAN. Cowger served as mayor until 1965.

Cowger's administration was marked by many URBAN RENEWAL projects that altered the appearance of the downtown area. He had strong support from Louisville's African American community and received national recognition for supporting the first public accommodations act in a southern city. By law, Cowger was not able to succeed himself, but his personal choice for mayor, KENNETH A. SCHMIED, was easily elected.

In 1966 Cowger was elected United States representative from Kentucky's Third District, defeating Norbert Blume by 66,577 to 46,240. He was reelected in 1968. In Congress he pushed hard for federal legislation to relieve the plight of urban areas. He chaired the Republican Congressional Urban Affairs Committee and was also elected chairman of the freshman GOP representatives. In 1970 he lost a reelection bid to ROMANO MAZZOLI by 211 votes. Cowger was considering running again for mayor in 1973 or contesting Mazzoli in 1972 when he died of a heart attack.

Cowger married Cynthia Thompson on March 19, 1945. The couple had two children, David and Cynthia. He is buried in CAVE HILL CEMETERY.

COXE, GLOUCESTER CALIMAN (b Carlisle, Pennsylvania, May 7, 1907; d Louisville, July 24, 1999). Artist. For four decades G.C. Coxe was the dean of Louisville's African American artists, founder of significant art organizations, mentor to a constellation of young artists, and a daringly experimental abstract painter.

Coxe was born to Della (Caliman) and P.J.A. Coxe, a Presbyterian minister. The family moved to a mission post in Louisville in 1924, where Coxe attended CENTRAL COLORED HIGH SCHOOL and contributed to founding the Bourgard School of Music and Art at Twenty-seventh and Walnut (Muhammad Ali Blvd.) Streets.

At age forty-four Coxe enrolled at the UNIVERSITY OF LOUISVILLE, becoming the first African American to receive an ALLEN R. HITE Art Scholarship and the university's first black fine arts graduate. In 1959 he helped found Gallery Enterprises, and later the Louisville Art Workshop that provided exhibition and studio space for artists of all races from the mid-1960s to mid-1970s. In 1999 he was honored at the annual African American Invitational Art Exhibition for his impact on the Louisville art scene and for nurturing generations of artists, who called him "G.C."

While admired by artists, Coxe was often frustrated by the lack of local support and sales, and he periodically held bonfires of his inventory to make way for new work. In 1999 he wrote, "I have thought many times of quitting. [But] How can I, when at the finish of a piece there comes another image. I hope that with each finished piece, the viewer will look beyond the surface, the form and color and see and understand the indescribable—the other part of me—of all of us. God? Spirit?"

Coxe's enigmatic paintings suggest the pulsating rhythms and mystery of life. His radical use of nontraditional materials began with the

"Minimal Series," 1968–70, where Coxe used wire woven through monochromatic canvas. Continuing to discover the extraordinary in the ordinary, the spiritual in the mundane, Coxe later incorporated molded cardboard, carpet remnants, upholstery fabric—even pantyhose—into his dynamic abstractions.

At the time of his death Coxe had almost completed writing an autobiography. With his wife, the former Jodie Brown, he attended GRACE HOPE PRESBYTERIAN CHURCH and is buried in Highland Memory Gardens in MOUNT WASHINGTON, Kentucky. Following his death, a *COURIER-JOURNAL* editorial praised Coxe as one who "never stopped stretching and straining the boundaries of artistic convention."

See *Gloucester Caliman Coxe, A Retrospective: Rags and Wires, Sticks and Pantyhose Too,* Allen R. Hite Art Institute, University of Louisville, 1995; *Courier-Journal,* July 27, 1999.

John Franklin Martin

CRADDOCK AFFAIR. On the morning of August 26, 1856, the body of Paschal D. Craddock was found sprawled in a lane leading to Bardstown Rd., about six miles from Louisville. The sixty-five-year-old farmer's body, horribly mutilated by hogs, bore three bullet wounds in the thigh. The coroner subsequently determined that the cause of death was a broken neck caused by being thrown from his horse. This event was far from rare in nineteenth-century Louisville, but Craddock's reputation as one of Jefferson County's most notorious criminals made his death at the hands of some midnight assassin headline news.

A native of Virginia, the victim was the son of Archer Craddock, who migrated from Barren County to Jefferson County in the 1830s. Paschal Craddock was described as "bold and aggressive" by nature, a man whose "greatest fault" was the "inordinate desire to steal and drive off stock of all kinds."

His neighbors eventually regarded his home as a haunt for the criminal element throughout the region. After two horse thieves were reportedly arrested in his home in early 1856, his outraged neighbors finally took action. In a public meeting held on February 27 in the vicinity of Two-Mile Town, located on the Bardstown Rd. southeast of Louisville, the leading citizens of the community ordered Craddock and two alleged accomplices to "settle their business and leave the state of Kentucky within six months."

The two accomplices complied with the demand, but Craddock openly defied the order. On the night of August 25, two days before the committee's ultimatum fell due, Craddock was summoned from his home by the slave of Andrew Hikes, a neighbor, who said that his master wanted to see him. Despite the pleas of his wife, Craddock rode off into the night. A subsequent investigation of the murder scene revealed that he was ambushed by three men concealed along the roadside. Hikes's slave, Washington, was afterwards charged with being an accomplice in the killing but was released for lack of evidence. The killing was shrouded in mystery until one John Miller, a thirty-one-year-old MEXICAN WAR veteran who resided in BULLITT COUNTY, came forward in November 1857 and made an alleged confession to the commonwealth's attorney. According to Miller, he and two other men, Col. Jack Allen of SHELBY COUNTY and an unidentified Mexican War veteran, were hired by several prominent citizens to assassinate the notorious criminal.

On the basis of Miller's confession, Allen; his brother, Dr. Joseph Allen; and Stephen Beard, both of SPENCER COUNTY; Joseph Wright and Austin Hubbard of Bullitt County; and Andrew and Frederick Hikes of Jefferson County were indicted for murder. The news caused an immediate sensation, and the trial received nationwide press coverage. As the *Louisville Democrat* reported, "The community was appalled upon hearing of the mangled remains of Craddock, but no more astonished that his death should be charged to his neighbors and other respectable men of position and fortune." Indeed, the Hikes family were the virtual founders of the Two-Mile community, while Col. Jack Allen, who had been home on leave from Gen. William Walker's "filibuster" army in Nicaragua at the time of the murder, was one of Kentucky's leading military heroes.

All of the defendants provided solid alibis and were acquitted on December 4, 1857. The *LOUISVILLE COURIER* reported, "This announcement was received by the spectators with wild applause. Hundreds of persons crowded around Colonel Allen and the others offering their congratulations." Miller's own confession contained little that would support a conviction, and he was released shortly afterward. The "Craddock Affair," the *Courier* concluded, must remain a "mystery deep and seemingly impenetrable." However, evidence indicates that the residents of the Two-Mile community always believed that Craddock was the deserving victim of vigilante justice.

One of the most sensational trials in Louisville history, the Craddock affair was not as controversial as the famous MATTHEW S. WARD trial of 1854. Nevertheless, the incident contributed to Kentucky's growing reputation as one of the most violent states in nineteenth-century America.

See contemporary Louisville newspapers for details of the murder and subsequent trial, and *History of the Ohio Falls Cities and Their Counties* (Cleveland 1882).

James M. Prichard

CRAIK, CHARLES EWELL (b Jefferson County, Kentucky, May 7, 1851; d Louisville, December 22, 1929). Clergyman. The Reverend Dr. Charles Ewell Craik was the son of the Reverend Dr. JAMES and Juliet (Shrewsbury) CRAIK. After receiving his early education in Louisville, he attended Shattuck School in Faribault, Minnesota, and studied at Trinity College, Hartford, Connecticut, and at Berkeley Divinity School in Middletown, Connecticut, where he became a deacon in the Episcopal church. He received his D.D. degree from Trinity College in 1914.

After two years as assistant rector at Grace Church, Brooklyn, New York, Craik served as rector of the American Episcopal Church in Geneva, Switzerland. In 1881 he returned to Louisville as assistant to his father at CHRIST CHURCH CATHEDRAL and the following year succeeded the elder Craik as rector. Craik became one of the most conscientious, respected, and well-known Episcopal clergymen of the South. During his thirty-eight years at Christ Church, he served as a trustee of and took great interest in the EPISCOPAL CHURCH HOME and Infirmary. He was a longtime member of the standing committee of the diocese of Kentucky and six times was elected deputy to the general convention of the Episcopal church. Also during his tenure, the Christ Church Cathedral House was built.

Craik was a member of the Louisville Country Club, PENDENNIS CLUB, the SONS OF THE AMERICAN REVOLUTION, and the Masonic Order. Until injured in an automobile accident in later life, he was an avid sportsman, taking particular interest in golf and quail hunting. Craik married Nellie Hite Wilder on February 19, 1889, and the couple had four sons: James, Charles Ewell Jr., Oscar, and Whitney. Craik is buried in CAVE HILL CEMETERY.

See Alwin Seekamp and Roger Burlingame, *Who's Who in Louisville* (Louisville 1912); Harry James Boswell, *Representative Kentuckians* (Louisville 1913).

Kenneth Dennis

CRAIK, JAMES (b Alexandria, Virginia, August 31, 1806; d Louisville, June 9, 1882). Clergyman. The Reverend Dr. James Craik was the son of George Washington and Maria (Tucker) Craik. He was the grandson and namesake of Dr. James Craik, George Washington's personal friend and physician and the chief physician and surgeon of the Continental Army during the American Revolution.

Having completed his early education in Alexandria, Craik came to Transylvania University in Lexington in 1825 with the intention of studying medicine. However, his attention soon turned to the study of law; and after leaving the university in 1826, he established a successful law practice in Kanawha County, Virginia. During his ten years as a practicing lawyer, Craik undertook the study of theology and eventually determined that it was in the church that his life's work lay. Craik was ordained deacon in the Episcopal church in 1839 and became a priest in 1841. His initial rectorship was in Charleston, Virginia (now West Virginia), and he remained there until 1844, when he was called to be rector at CHRIST

CHURCH CATHEDRAL in Louisville. Here he would spend the rest of his life and earn his reputation as one of the most eminent and influential clergymen of his day.

Craik was a forceful speaker and a prolific writer. Prominent among his works were *The Search of Truth* and *The Divine Life and the New Birth* (1869). It was largely through his efforts that a split in the Episcopal church was avoided during the turbulent CIVIL WAR years. Craik served as president of the General Convention of the Episcopal church from 1862 to 1874. Louisville's Orphanage of the Good Shepherd and the EPISCOPAL CHURCH HOME and Infirmary owed him much for their existence. An able theologian and administrator, Craik saw Christ Church parish grow and prosper greatly during his tenure.

Craik married Juliet Shrewsbury in 1829, and they had seven children. Their son CHARLES EWELL CRAIK succeeded his father as rector of Christ Church in 1882. Craik is buried in CAVE HILL CEMETERY.

See J. Stoddard Johnston, ed., *Memorial History of Louisville* (Chicago 1896); Frances Keller Swinford and Rebecca Smith Lee, *The Great Elm Tree* (Lexington 1969).

Kenneth Dennis

CRANE HOUSE. Crane House (The Asia Institute Inc.) is a regional nonprofit organization established to foster mutual understanding between people of the United States and Asia through educational services and cultural programs. The organization began operations in 1987 in OLD LOUISVILLE as a CHINESE cultural center. The founder, Helen Lang, is Chinese-American. It was Lang's desire to learn more about her native land and to share this heritage with other Americans that led her to establish Crane House. In 1997 the Board of Directors broadened the mission to include other Asian cultures in addition to Chinese.

Crane House is a resource center specializing in programs about Asia. The organization collects and maintains Asian artifacts and a library of information about Asia. It conducts classes and sponsors educational workshops and programs for individuals, schools, and businesses. Crane House offers lecture series, business seminars, and discussion groups. A target audience is families with adopted Asian children. Crane House also sponsors a summer teaching program in Asia.

Crane House is funded by membership support, private and corporate contributions, program grants, fund-raising events, and participant fees. Although most programs serve the greater Louisville area, there is an educational outreach to schools throughout Kentucky and nearby states. In order to accommodate its growing audiences, in July 1997 Crane House moved to a larger facility at 1244 S Third St.

See *Courier-Journal,* April 13, 1988, April 10, 1997.

CRAWFORD, THOMAS HOWELL (b Rockbridge County, Virginia?, March 1, 1803; d Pewee Valley, Kentucky, June 17, 1871). Mayor. He was the son of Thomas and Jane (Todd) Crawford. Crawford's mother was the first woman to have an ovariotomy. The operation was performed by the noted surgeon Ephraim McDowell in Danville, Kentucky, on December 25, 1809. The tumor weighed seven pounds. Jane Todd Crawford died in 1842 at age seventy-eight. She had four children: James, Alice, Samuel, and Thomas Howell.

In 1857, Thomas Crawford was elected to the BOARD OF ALDERMEN on the KNOW-NOTHING PARTY ticket and served until 1858. He was president of the Board of Aldermen for about six months in 1858.

Crawford was elected MAYOR of Louisville on April 2, 1859, and served until April 6, 1861. A strong supporter of the North during the CIVIL WAR, he ran again for mayor in 1863 representing the Union Party but was defeated by WILLIAM KAYE, a marginal Union supporter who was backed by the secessionist element in the city.

Crawford worked as a real estate agent in the mid-1860s. In 1870 he was an agent for the Piedmont and Arlington Life Insurance Co. of Virginia. He also was president of the Central Savings Bank of Pewee Valley until his death in 1871.

Crawford was killed in a gas explosion at his home. He had been one of the first Kentuckians to install gas lights in the home. The accident occurred on May 27, 1871, when Crawford and his sister-in-law Matilda G. Martin went into the Crawford's basement to find out what was the trouble with lighting the gas works. The two, armed with burning candles, opened the door to the basement, setting off a large explosion almost immediately. Matilda died in the fire, but Crawford survived three more weeks before succumbing to his injuries. He is buried in CAVE HILL CEMETERY.

See "Death of Hon. Thomas H. Crawford," *Courier-Journal,* June 18, 1871.

CREASON, JOE CROSS (b Benton, Kentucky, June 10, 1918; d Louisville, August 14, 1974). Journalist. One of Kentucky's best-known newspaper writers of the twentieth century, Creason was the son of Herman and Reba Cross Creason. He graduated from the University of Kentucky in 1940 and became the editor of his hometown *Benton Tribune-Democrat.* After a short time, he moved to the Murray, Kentucky, *Ledger and Times* before finally joining the *COURIER-JOURNAL* early in 1941.

Although he started as a sportswriter, he was moved to the *Courier- Journal Magazine* staff later in the year, where he stayed except for navy service from 1944 to 1946, until 1963. At that time he was given his own column, "Joe Creason's Kentucky," which featured "people and places and things" from every corner of the state. It was said that he traveled half a million

Joe Creason, 1972.

miles during his tenure to explore Kentucky's history, its modern-day struggles, and its hope for the future. Excerpts from "Mr. Kentucky's" columns were collected in *Joe Creason's Kentucky* (1972), which was followed by *Crossroads and Coffee Trees* (1975). Creason was also published in *Reader's Digest,* the *Saturday Evening Post,* and *Coronet.*

Creason married Shella Robertson, and they had two sons, Joe Cross Junior and William Scott. Creason died of a heart attack while playing tennis with television and radio personality Milton Metz. He is buried in Longview Cemetery in Bethel, Kentucky. In 1975, the old Collings estate property on Trevilian Way across from the LOUISVILLE ZOOLOGICAL GARDENS was named Joe C. Creason Park in his honor.

See *Courier-Journal,* Aug. 15, 1974.

CRESCENT HILL. Aside from the shops on tree-lined Frankfort Ave., which bisects the community, Crescent Hill is primarily a residential neighborhood bordered by Brownsboro Rd. to the north; a combination of Coralberry Rd., the MASONIC HOME, and Fenley Ave. to the east; Lexington Rd. to the south; and a combination of Grinstead Dr. and Ewing Ave. to the west. Lying to the east of downtown Louisville, the Crescent Hill area slowly developed as transportation routes linked the city to Lexington and Frankfort. By the early 1800s the Shelbyville Pike (Frankfort Ave.) was reportedly a well-used stagecoach road. In 1817 the artery was upgraded and renamed the Lexington and Louisville Turnpike. As toll gates were set up, the first being the Three Mile House near the intersection of Frankfort and Keats Avenues, families began to establish country estates as early as 1828. The area, then known as Beargrass, began to attract more residents after the LOUISVILLE AND FRANKFORT RAILROAD CO.

Louisville Water Company Building on Reservoir Avenue in Crescent Hill, 1921.

laid tracks (now owned by CSX CORP.) through the community in the late 1840s.

Because of the area's easy accessibility, the Southwestern Agricultural and Mechanical Association purchased thirty-eight acres adjacent to the rails for use as the state fairgrounds (the modern-day site of the ST. JOSEPH CHILDREN'S HOME). In 1857 the enlarged site gained a national audience as it hosted the fifth annual National Agricultural Fair, the first time it had not been in an eastern metropolis. With its Floral Hall, Power (or Machinery) Hall, and ten-thousand-seat amphitheater for livestock exhibitions, it attracted an estimated twenty thousand people on its busiest day. After costly damages incurred as a result of Union troops' occupying the grounds during the CIVIL WAR, the land was sold in 1863 to the Louisville and Jefferson County Association, which went bankrupt and auctioned off the property in 1874. The portion of land not occupied by the children's home was subdivided into lots in 1875 as Fair View.

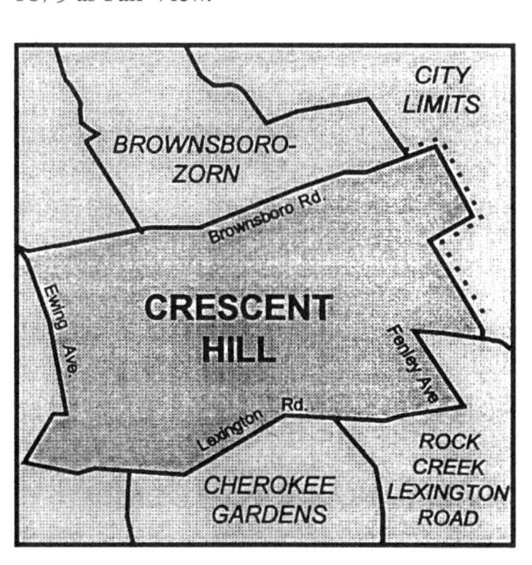

By the 1880s the once sizable lots began to be carved into smaller tracts, inciting additional residents to move to the area. In 1884 the community, which had grown beyond the fairgrounds land and contained a store and a post office, was incorporated as the sixth-class town of Crescent Hill. Three stories have been offered as to the origins of the name: the first claims that the city was named after New Orleans, known as the Crescent City; the second states that a resident, Catherine Anderson Kennedy, noted the crescent-shaped reservoir at Reservoir Park as she ascended its hill one day; and the third, and most likely explanation, referred to the uphill curve of Frankfort Avenue as it rose from Clifton Avenue to the site of the old fairgrounds. Although most of the neighborhood was platted by the end of the century, development, aided by the arrival of the electric STREETCARS in 1901, continued into the 1920s. In 1894 most of the town was annexed by Louisville, with the remaining portion brought into the city limits in 1922.

Through the years, the Crescent Hill community has been home to many well-known institutions. In 1876 ZACHARIAH SHERLEY sold a hundred-acre tract, with an additional ten acres from the Arterburn family, to the LOUISVILLE WATER CO. By 1879 the water company had finished its new reservoir, which was fed by large pipes running under Pipe Line Rd. (Zorn Ave.) to the pumping station on River Rd. The company also built a filtration plant across Frankfort Ave. in 1909.

The SOUTHERN BAPTIST THEOLOGICAL SEMINARY moved to its campus at "The Beeches" on Lexington Rd. in 1927. Also on Lexington Rd., the Ursuline Order of Roman Catholic nuns has operated the motherhouse and Sacred Heart Academy since 1877. The order also ran the URSULINE COLLEGE from 1938 until its merger with BELLARMINE COLLEGE in 1968. The area was once the site of three ORPHANAGES. Woodcock Hall, a home for boys started in 1870 by the Episcopal church on Crestwood Ave., was closed and sold to the Ursulines in 1955. The other two homes, both on Frankfort Ave., are the St. Joseph Children's Home, which was founded in 1849 by German Catholics and moved to its present site in 1886, and the Masonic Widows and Orphans Home, which was organized in 1867 and relocated to its present site in 1927. A CARNEGIE LIBRARY branch was built in 1908 and has since served the area. The Crescent Theater, located along Frankfort Ave., was a well-attended cinema house for many years before becoming a restaurant.

After the tornado of 1974 ripped through the area, the Crescent Hill Community Council took a leading role in rebuilding the neighborhood.

See Samuel W. Thomas, *Crescent Hill Revisited* (Louisville 1987); *Louisville Survey: East Report* (Louisville 1980); *A Place in Time: The Story of Louisville's Neighborhoods* (Louisville 1989).

CRESCENT HILL BAPTIST CHURCH. The church was organized January 12, 1908, under the leadership of its first pastor, John F. Griffin. Originally located at 2644 Frankfort Ave., it moved to 2810 Frankfort in 1911 with the erection of the first building on its site at Frankfort and Birchwood Avenues. In 1926 the church built its current sanctuary, designed by architect Otto Davis Mock, for a growing congregation. SOUTHERN BAPTIST THEOLOGICAL SEMINARY moved from downtown to its location on Lexington Rd. in the early twenties with classes opening in 1926, which placed Crescent Hill Baptist within two blocks of the campus. Over the years the seminary developed close ties of support and friendship with the church.

In the twenties and thirties Crescent Hill Baptist contributed significantly to the $75 Million Campaign, a massive effort to rebuild and expand Baptist work worldwide. Members also contributed to the Anti-Saloon League, the Billy Sunday revival, and relief for the victims of the 1937 GREAT FLOOD. The onset of the GREAT DEPRESSION brought the church a financial crisis that was bridged by members who willingly mortgaged their homes to prevent foreclosure on the church property. During the turbulent years of WORLD WAR II, the church continued to grow and expand under the leadership of Dr. William C. Boone, a descendant of Daniel Boone. In addition, 123 members of Crescent Hill served in the armed forces. During the fifties and sixties the church sustained strong growth. Racial crisis was a major focus of concern, and the church created staff positions, including social ministry and counseling. Dr. H. Stephen Shoemaker, who began his eleven-year ministry in May 1981, sought to oppose forces seeking a hostile takeover of the Southern Baptist Convention. By 1990 fundamentalist trustees controlled the seminary. Crescent Hill Baptist was the home church of many faculty members who left Southern Baptist Seminary because they disagreed with the conservative ideology. Among those were Molly Marshall, who was pressured by the seminary president in 1994 to resign from Southern's faculty; Glen Stassen, who was active in civil rights and peace initiatives; and Diana Garland, whom the president fired in 1995 as dean of the seminary's Carver School of Church Social Work. Women were regularly invited to preach from the pulpit of Crescent Hill Baptist. While the church retained its Southern Baptist affiliation, the congregation chose to align itself as well with the more liberal American Baptist Churches in the U.S.A., which allowed ordination of women as pastors. In 1999 the church was affiliated as well with the Southern Baptist Convention and the Cooperative Baptist Fellowship.

CRESTWOOD. Sixth-class city located in southern Oldham County, centered near the intersection of KY 22 and KY 146. In 1839 Joseph Beard moved from Fayette County onto land just outside of LaGrange and established an estate, which he called Woodland Cottage. After the tracks of the Louisville & Frankfort Railroad (later purchased by the Louisville & Nashville Railroad Co.) were laid nearby in 1851, Beard donated a warehouse and part of his land for the town's train station. To honor Beard's generosity, the town adopted the name of Beard's Station in 1857 when the area's first post office was opened. In the early 1880s, railroad conductors and workers playfully altered the shortened name of "Beard's" and redubbed the town "Whiskers," to the dismay of several residents. After an increase in commercial and tourist business following the arrival of the interurban line in 1905, the town was renamed Crestwood in 1909. The name reportedly was chosen because of the town's position upon a small crest and the area's abundant trees.

Many of the town's improvements, such as streetlights and stop signs, were carried out by the Crestwood Civic Club after it was established in 1914. However, these duties were transferred to the town's government after its incorporation in 1970. The 1970s marked a dramatic increase in residential developments after the extension of the Louisville Water Co.'s lines into the area. By the 1990s Crestwood, with its proximity to railroad lines and Interstate 71, had become one of Oldham County's fastest-growing commercial and residential centers. The population in 1980 was 531, 1,435 in 1990, and 1,841 in 1996.

See *A Place in Time: The Story of Louisville's Neighborhoods* (Louisville 1989); Robert M. Rennick, *Kentucky Place Names* (Lexington 1984).

CRIMMINS, JOHN WHALLEN (b Louisville, December 29, 1911; d Louisville, April 22, 1999). Political leader. John "Johnny" Whallen Crimmins was the son of Stephen B. and Bertha Crimmins. He was godson of the late-nineteenth-century Democratic political power broker John Whallen, who died in 1913, two years after Crimmins's birth. Growing up in a political family, Crimmins was active in the Democratic Party in the 1930s and was a member of the historically powerful Mose Green Democratic Club. Crimmins served as organizational director for the Jefferson County Democratic Executive Committee from 1947 to 1962. He helped recruit more than a thousand precinct captains, co-captains, and district leaders in Louisville. He and Lennie McLaughlin, or "Miss Lennie" or "Miz Lennie" as she was known, wielded enormous political influence in the selection of Jefferson County and city candidates, and were known as "political bosses."

When the election of Republican William O. Cowger as mayor broke the power of the machine, Crimmins resigned his position in 1962 and was appointed the U.S. collector of customs for Louisville by President John F. Kennedy. In 1969 Crimmins ran for Jefferson County clerk but was defeated by the incumbent, James P. Hallahan. In 1972 he was named to the state Alcohol Beverage Control Commission. In 1985 Jefferson County judge/executive Bremer Ehrler appointed him administrator of the county's Alcohol Beverage Control Commission. In 1988 as secretary of state, Ehrler appointed Crimmins as his division director of land and, eight months later, director of corporations.

He and his wife Virginia had two daughters and four sons. He is buried in Calvary Cemetery.

See *Courier-Journal*, April 23, 1999.

CRIST, HENRY (b Fredericksburg, Virginia, October 20, 1764; d Shepherdsville, Kentucky, August 11, 1844). U.S. congressman. Crist moved to Pennsylvania at a young age and, after some basic schooling, came to Kentucky with a land surveyor, Jacob Myers, and settled at the Falls of the Ohio in 1780. Crist's participation in land transactions made him aware of the potential for profit from the many salt licks in the area that is now Bullitt and Nelson Counties. Crist, along with business partner Solomon Spears, acquired the Long Lick claim, near the Salt River in Nelson County, in 1784.

On May 26, 1788, Indians attacked a flatboat owned by Crist and Solomon Spears. The boat, occupied by a small band of men, was heading down the Salt River toward Bullitt's Lick near present-day Shepherdsville. The ensuing engagement, referred to as the Battle of the Kettles because of the many salt-processing kettles on the flatboat, lasted almost two hours. Spears was killed and Crist severely wounded in the heel. Crawling the remaining distance to Bullitt's Lick, Crist survived.

Taking up permanent residence near Shepherdsville, Crist served in the Kentucky House of Representatives in 1795 and 1806 and in the Senate from 1800 to 1804. In 1808 Crist was elected to Congress and served from March 4, 1809, until March 3, 1811. On January 17, 1811, Gov. Charles Scott commissioned Crist a general in the Kentucky state militia. He became a Whig after the organization of that party. He is buried in the Frankfort Cemetery.

See *Biographical Directory of the American Congress 1776–1961* (Washington, D.C., 1961).

CROGHAN, JOHN (b Jefferson County, Kentucky, April 23, 1790; d Jefferson County, January 11, 1849). Physician and entrepreneur. John Croghan was born to William and Lucy (Clark) Croghan, the oldest of eight children. He was reared at Locust Grove, the family home in eastern Jefferson County. His uncle, George Rogers Clark, lived at Locust Grove from 1809 until his death in 1818.

In 1806 and 1807 John Croghan was a student at Dr. Priestley's Seminary in Danville. He left to attend the College of William and Mary from 1807 until his graduation in 1809. Croghan then traveled to Philadelphia to begin private instruction and an apprenticeship with Dr. Benjamin Rush. Rush, a friend of his uncle William Clark, had provided medicine and treatment advice for the Lewis and Clark Expedition. In the fall of 1810 Croghan enrolled as a student at the University of Pennsylvania's School of Medicine, graduating on April 1, 1813.

He set up practice in Louisville in the fall of 1813. He became involved in the Louisville Hospital Co. in 1817 and worked toward the founding of the Louisville Marine Hospital, constructed in 1823. He served as a director of that institution until 1832.

In 1827 John Croghan began a salt-producing operation on inherited land near the Cumberland River. This and other diversions soon led him to limit his medical practice to the care of family and friends. In 1832 John accompanied his brother Charles to Europe in search of a better climate for the ailing young man and to escape cholera in the United States. While in Paris, Charles died of tuberculosis. John remained in Europe until 1833.

The cholera epidemic struck Louisville in 1833 and resulted in the death of John's sister Eliza Croghan Hancock. Eliza and her husband, George Hancock, had purchased the family estate from brother William Croghan Jr. in 1828. With Eliza's death, Hancock sold Locust Grove to John Croghan, who established himself as a gentleman farmer and experimented with the cultivation of grapes.

In October 1839 Croghan purchased two thousand acres in the Green River area that included Mammoth Cave. He had two plans for the use and exploration of the cave. He considered the steady climate potentially beneficial in the treatment of tuberculosis. This effort proved unsuccessful, particularly because of the accumulation of smoke from oil-burning lamps and cooking and heating fires within the cavern, and the death and departure of his patients led to the termination of the hospital project. Croghan also saw great potential for the site as a tourist destination, and early on began designing improvements and activities to attract visitors. Extensive mapping of the cave's vast interior was led by African American slave STEPHEN BISHOP. Interest in the cave as a natural wonder grew.

Beginning in 1845, declining health forced Croghan to spend most of his time at Locust Grove. He remained closely involved in the development and operation of Mammoth Cave, even after renting the property out in 1846. Croghan never regained his health and died of tuberculosis. In his will he emancipated his slaves and left Locust Grove and Mammoth Cave in trusteeship for his brother George and his nieces and nephews.

See Eugene H. Conner and Samuel W. Thomas, "John Croghan, An Enterprising Kentucky Physician," *Filson Club History Quarterly* 40 (July 1966): 205–35; Gwynne Bryant, *The Croghans of Locust Grove* (Cincinnati 1988).

Julia C. Parke

CROGHAN, WILLIAM (b Ireland [Dublin?], 1752; d Jefferson County, September 21, 1822). Soldier, farmer, and businessman. The son of Nicholas Croghan, he received a good education and came to America in 1769 to pursue a mercantile career. Landing at Philadelphia, he soon went to work for the Shipboy merchants of New York, a job acquired through the influence of his uncle George Croghan, the Indian superintendent. In 1771 he received an ensign's commission in the British army, joining the 16th Regiment of Foot. Sometime during 1774 he apparently resigned from the army and moved to western Pennsylvania.

At the outbreak of the Revolutionary War he served as a captain in the West Augusta (Virginia) militia, 1775–76, and on April 9, 1776, received a captain's commission in the Eighth Virginia Regiment. Croghan served throughout the war and participated in numerous campaigns. On April 7, 1777, he was appointed brigade inspector of Charles Scott's brigade, and on May 16, 1778, he was promoted to major in the Eighth Virginia. On September 14, 1778, he was transferred to the Fourth Virginia. He was captured at Charleston on May 12, 1780, paroled in 1781, and was at Fort Pitt until the end of the war.

On February 9, 1784, he and GEORGE ROGERS CLARK received their surveying commissions from the College of William and Mary and were appointed the principal surveyors for Virginia military grants in Kentucky. That same year Croghan settled in Louisville. He was involved in business, land investments, and politics. He was one of three men ordered by the county court in April 1788 to lay out the site for the JEFFERSON COUNTY COURTHOUSE and contract for its construction. In the spring of 1789 he succeeded George Rogers Clark as the head surveyor of Virginia State Line military lands. He also served on the commission that surveyed the CLARK or Illinois GRANT (across the OHIO RIVER from Louisville), and laid out Clarksville, Indiana.

On April 10, 1790, Croghan purchased the tract of land on which he would build LOCUST GROVE. He was living in a cabin on the tract in 1790, and it is believed he started construction of the house that year. Croghan's home was a center of hospitality and enjoyed many a famous visitor, including James Monroe, Andrew Jackson, WILLIAM CLARK, and Meriwether Lewis. In 1790 Croghan served as a Jefferson County delegate to one of the Kentucky statehood conventions held in Danville, and he frequently served in temporary appointed positions regarding county government.

He was a charter member of the Society of the Cincinnati, 1783; a Mason; an original subscriber and trustee of the JEFFERSON SEMINARY, 1798; and a director of the Indiana Canal Co., 1805. He maintained a public ferry below SIX MILE ISLAND and established the town of Smithland at the mouth of the Cumberland River, 1805. He was buried at Locust Grove, although, on May 3, 1916, he and other family members were reinterred in CAVE HILL CEMETERY.

Croghan married Lucy Clark (1765–1838) on July 14, 1789. He had known her since at least 1781 when he visited the Clark family in Caroline County, Virginia, as a guest of fellow officer and comrade Jonathan Clark. His business association and friendship with George Rogers Clark furthered his ties to the Clark family, and the relationship was renewed when John and Ann Clark settled with their family, including Lucy, in Jefferson County in 1785. The Croghans had nine children: John, George, William, Charles (died as an infant), Ann, Elizabeth, Charles and Nicholas (twins), and Edmund.

See Samuel W. Thomas, "William Croghan, Sr., [1752–1822]: A Pioneer Kentucky Gentleman," *Filson Club History Quarterly* 43 (Jan. 1969): 30–61.

James J. Holmberg

CRONAN, CHARLES J., JR. "JUNE" (b Louisville, Kentucky, September 10, 1895; d Louisville, Kentucky, September 6, 1985). Businessman and horseman. Born to Charles Joseph and Anita Hamel Cronan, Charles Jr. graduated from the JEFFERSON SCHOOL OF LAW and was admitted to the Kentucky bar in 1917. His stint in LAW was short-lived, however, as he enlisted in the U.S. Army Field Artillery the day after his admission. Cronan remained in the 138th Field Artillery of the Kentucky National Guard after WORLD WAR I and saw active service in WORLD WAR II, attaining the rank of colonel before his discharge in 1946. Following World War I, Cronan returned to Louisville and established a fire and casualty INSURANCE company, while also becoming involved in the horse industry.

A lover of horses since he received his first at the age of eleven, Cronan founded the Kentucky American Saddlebred Futurity horse show in 1927, an event held annually at the KENTUCKY STATE FAIR. In 1932 Cronan became secretary of the American Saddlebred Horse Association and held that post until 1979, when he was made executive vice president. His love of horses and his involvement in the industry continued as he served as a director of the American Horse Shows Association, the United States Pony Club, the American Saddlebred Pleasure Horse Association, and the American Horse Council.

Involved in breeding and training as well, Cronan in 1936 produced American Model, that year's three-gaited world grand champion. Upon his retirement in 1983 (although he remained active on the board of directors), the association gave him a plaque officially designating him "Mr. Saddlebred." This award had been preceded seven years earlier with his selection as horseman of the year by the United Professional Horsemen's Association.

In 1918 he married Laura Virginia Ewing; they had two children: Charles III and Virginia Clarke. He is buried in St. Aloysius Cemetery in PEWEE VALLEY.

See Lynn P. Weatherman, *American Saddlebred Magazine* (Lexington 1985).

CRUSADE FOR CHILDREN INC. The Crusade began as a simple telethon in 1954. It was the creation of station manager Victor Sholis and WHAS-TV and radio owner BARRY BINGHAM SR. Its purpose was to raise money for local agencies providing direct services to children with special needs. Crusade One raised $156,725. Expenses were 10 percent. The 1997 Crusade raised $5 million. Expenses were 3.7 percent. The Crusade raised $5.5 million in 1998. The expenses were 3.95 percent. In 1999 Wayne Perkey, the charity's master of ceremonies for twenty years, retired, but not before setting an all-time record with donations totaling $5,962,355.

The Crusade's phenomenal growth is attributed to a number of factors. First, during the second Crusade, members of the Pleasure Ridge Park Volunteer Fire Department issued a challenge to other fire departments to join in helping raise money. The challenge was quickly accepted, and in 1997 over 230 fire departments in Kentucky and Indiana raised 55 percent of the dollars donated to the Crusade. Second, the Crusade does not rely on corporations for donations. Besides fire departments, other funds come from volunteer groups—churches, employee groups, clubs, and special events. Third, Crusade funds are granted to local agencies by a panel of seven area ministers. They alone make the decisions on where Crusade dollars go. Another factor in the success of the Crusade is public trust.

The public supports the Crusade because it has few expenses and shows, via TELEVISION, where the money goes and who is being helped. Three times *LOUISVILLE* MAGAZINE has asked readers to name their favorite charity. All three times the Crusade was a winner by a wide margin.

The Crusade has become the largest single-station telethon in the nation. It now collects money all year long but still ends its fiscal year with the annual two-day radio/telethon in June. Many local and national entertainers are featured in the entertainment. Donors appear live, and names of others are read in recognition of monetary gifts. In its long history, more than $77 million has been raised.

See *Courier-Journal,* June 7, 1999.

Louis "Bud" Harbsmeier

CSX CORP. This Virginia-based corporation specializing in international transportation was created in November 1980 with the merger of two holding companies that owned the Chessie System Railroads (Baltimore & Ohio and Chesapeake & Ohio) and Seaboard Coast Line Industries (parent of LOUISVILLE & NASHVILLE and Seaboard Coast Line railroads). In CSX's corporate name, the "C" stands for Chessie, "S" represents Seaboard, and "X" denotes multiplication or "coming together."

CSX Transportation was the unit formed by the corporation in 1986 to operate the merged RAILROADS as one system, which by 1996 totaled over eighteen thousand route miles of lines in twenty states, the District of Columbia, and Ontario, in Canada. CSX transportation's major holdings in Louisville and southern Indiana include buildings, tracks, and yards of the former B&O and L&N (some of their properties were sold to the city of Louisville for redevelopment). In March 1997, CSX and Conrail, a northeast rail system and successor to the bankrupt Penn Central, agreed to merge. The agreement called for Conrail to be divided evenly between CSX and Norfolk Southern.

CSX Corp.'s founding officers were Prime F. Osborn, president of the L&N after 1972, and Hays T. Watkins, who was born in FERN CREEK, Kentucky, and headed the Chessie System. Watkins later succeeded Osborn as chairman and CEO and served until his retirement in 1992.

The corporation's other major local holding was American Commercial Lines Inc. (ACLI), the JEFFERSONVILLE, Indiana–based barge line, and its barge-building and marine construction subsidiary, JEFFBOAT, also in Jeffersonville. With CSX Transportation, ACLI's Louisiana Dock Co. subsidiary also jointly operated a rail-to-water transfer facility for coal and other bulk commodities. As of December 1999, CSX had reduced its ownership (or "holdings") in ACLI to about one-third.

See George H. Drury, *Train-Watcher's Guide to North American Railroads* 2nd edition (Waukesha, Wis., 1992); CSX-2 "Fast Facts, Commonwealth of Kentucky," Backgrounder from CSX Transportation, Jacksonville, Fla., Oct. 1994; "CSX, A Corporation with Roots in Kentucky and Branches to the World," *Kentucky Business* (Spring 1988).

Charles B. Castner

CUBANS. Beginning with a series of treaties with Spain in the late 1790s, the economy of the Mississippi/OHIO RIVER basin became linked with the Spanish colony of Cuba. The key to this new trade was access to the important port of New Orleans, opened to American river traffic by the Spanish treaties of the 1790s, then sold to the United States by the French in the Louisiana Purchase (1803). In the 1830s, one could buy a steamship ticket from Louisville to Havana because Kentucky's TOBACCO and hemp economy linked it with New Orleans, which was second only to New York City in trade with Cuba. It might have been like bringing coals to Newcastle, but it is likely that many of the cigars puffed in Louisville's fine HOTELS came directly from Havana, as did much of the sugar consumed in the city. That was an increasing amount of sugar, because the United States developed a sweet tooth in the nineteenth century.

Kentucky was a hotbed of expansionist sentiment during that century, which called for the United States to annex Cuba from Spain by purchase or conquest. The *LOUISVILLE COURIER* editorialized in favor of a move on Cuba in 1850, saying, "Take her, Uncle Sam, she is ready!" That same year, a number of Kentuckians took part in a private invasion of Cuba, called a *filibuster,* led by Narcíso López.

No Kentucky or Indiana regiments were engaged in any of the battles of the Spanish-American War of 1898, but Kentuckians and Hoosiers served in the war. Pvt. James J. Nash of Louisville, Co. F., Tenth U.S. Infantry, was awarded the CONGRESSIONAL MEDAL OF HONOR during the advance against Santiago. After the war the 161st Regiment of the Indiana Volunteer Infantry, with company C from Shelbyville (116 men) and company E from JEFFERSONVILLE (114 men), was assigned to Cuba as part of an occupation force. They were stationed at Camp Columbia, near Havana, Cuba, from December 17, 1898, until March 29, 1899.

The leader of the Cuban Revolution of 1895, the war that prompted U.S. intervention in 1898, was José Martí. There is a monument to this "Apostle of Cuban Independence" in SHIVELY in the park behind city hall, across from the fire and police stations. Fulgencio Batista, the dictator who was ousted by Fidel Castro in 1959, presented the five-foot bust of Martí, who died in the revolution against Spain, to the people of the city after the Youth Ambassadors of Jefferson County visited the island in 1955. On the pedestal are the words "a tribute to the valiant Kentuckians who fought for the liberation of Cuba in 1850."

The U.S. Census Bureau estimated the total Hispanic population of Jefferson County in 1997 to be 5,163, up from 4,365 in 1990. The World Communities group of Hispanic organizations estimates the 1999 population of the Louisville metropolitan area to be at least twenty-five thousand. It is unclear how many of these people are Cuban; the 1990 census listed 320 Cuban residents in Jefferson County, although the figure had significantly increased by 1999. Cuban immigration to Louisville boomed after August 1994, when the most recent exodus by boat from the island occurred. Moreover, the Cuban population in Louisville is bound to increase with migration of Cubans from Florida and the likely reduction of tensions between the governments of both nations.

Eric Paul Roorda

CULBERTSON MANSION STATE HISTORIC SITE. This three-story mansion in NEW ALBANY, Indiana, at 914 E Main St. was constructed between 1867 and 1869 at a cost of about $120,000. The twenty-five-room Indiana landmark was commissioned by wealthy dry goods merchant William S. Culbertson as a gift for his second wife, Cornelia. It was constructed by master builders James and William Banes. Culbertson, once thought to be Indiana's wealthiest citizen, moved to New Albany from Pennsylvania and became a clerk in a dry goods store. This began an amazing business and philanthropic career. When he died in 1892 he left a fortune of $3.5 million.

Considered by architectural historians to be one of the country's best residential examples of French Second Empire design, the Culbertson mansion's magnificence is evident in its marble fireplaces, carved rosewood staircase, and hand-painted ceiling murals. It is these *trompe l'oeil* paintings, done by German immigrant Ernst Linn, that are probably the home's most distinctive feature. Many of the frescos on the first and second floors had been painted over by past owners, but in the 1990s an extensive restoration project tackled the painstaking task of restoring the paintings to their former glory.

Sold during an economic downturn in New Albany following the depression of 1897, the Culbertson mansion, along with its remaining furnishings, brought a mere $7,100 at auction in 1899. It was purchased by John S. McDonald. In 1946 the home became the club site for the American Legion. The Legion sold the house in 1964 to Historic New Albany. In 1976, the state of Indiana took possession of the mansion to maintain it as a historic site.

See *Courier-Journal,* Aug. 13, 1995.

CUNNINGHAM, JAMES C. (b St. George, Bermuda, May 3, 1787; d Louisville, June 18, 1877). Violinist, bandleader, and dancing teacher. Cunningham came to Louisville around 1835 and joined a band led by Henry Williams, an early free African American violinist. In 1847 Cunningham formed his own band, and it quickly became the most popular band in the city. His band, which included other free AFRICAN AMERICANS as well as German immigrants, played at fancy balls and cotillions, as well as for various trade groups such as carpenters, mechanics, and firemen. In 1849 the band was selected to perform at the ball honoring President-elect ZACHARY TAYLOR, and in 1850 it played at a famous masquerade ball hosted by SALLIE WARD. Cunningham's band was also in great demand during the summers at watering places such as PAROQUET SPRINGS and Drennon Springs.

Cunningham was active in the UNDERGROUND RAILROAD. He was implicated, but not arrested, in an attempt by Rev. Calvin Fairbanks to help a slave escape to Indiana in 1851. The next year Cunningham traveled to Pittsburgh to hear Frederick Douglass speak at a Free Soil Convention, and in 1855 he was accused of helping five slaves escape.

He married Lucinda B. Steele, and their children played important roles in Louisville's African American community. Their daughter, Mary V. Cunningham (1842–1919), was a well-known organist; and their son, JAMES R. CUNNINGHAM (1853–1943), led his own brass band. James C. Cunningham is buried in Eastern Cemetery.

Cornelius Bogert

CUNNINGHAM, JAMES R. (b Louisville, July 10, 1853; d Louisville, November 10, 1943). African American cornetist and bandleader. He was the son of JAMES C. and Lucinda B. (Steele) CUNNINGHAM. His father led one of the most popular bands in Louisville. The younger Cunningham was working as a full-time musician by the time he was seventeen.

About 1874 he founded the Falls City Cornet Band, which quickly became one of the city's most popular bands. The group, which later became the Falls City Brass Band, played regularly on STEAMBOATS. It also performed for St. John's Day parades, festivals organized by the LOUISVILLE COLORED MUSICAL ASSOCIATION, train excursions, the Louisville Colored Fair, and even gave concerts on the frozen OHIO RIVER. In 1895 Cunningham's "famous brass band" was selected to play for a huge barbecue in WILDER PARK during the GRAND ARMY OF THE REPUBLIC ENCAMPMENT.

Cunningham counted among his many admirers songwriter WILL S. HAYS and newspaperman HENRY WATTERSON. In the 1890s Cunningham toured England, where he performed for Queen Victoria. His band was one of the first African American brass bands to tour Japan. Around 1900, the Falls City Brass Band began to play what was then known as "syncopated music"—RAGTIME-influenced dance music. Cunningham remained active in MUSIC as a teacher through the 1920s. He is buried in Eastern Cemetery.

Cornelius Bogert

CUNNINGHAM'S RESTAURANT. Located at the corner of Breckinridge and Fifth Streets, it began in 1870 as a combination delicatessen and horse stable. A Mr. Melton was the first proprietor of the grocery, but he sold the business in 1871 to Dave Oswald, who was employed as a meat cutter in Melton's delicatessen. In 1890 Oswald installed the beer bar with large mirrors and carved wood supports that became a Cunningham's fixture.

Between the late 1890s and the 1920s, the building was used for a variety of purposes. During the 1920s the upstairs was used as a bordello or "rooming house" by a Mary Polly and her "sisters." Photographs of many of the working girls still adorn the walls in Cunningham's.

In 1922 James Cunningham, a captain in the LOUISVILLE POLICE DEPARTMENT, acquired the property and opened "Cunningham's Delicatessen." While he did away with the rooming house, he also had some questionable business enterprises. During PROHIBITION, "Cap" went into business with a bootlegger named Coleman and started "Cunningham's Soft Drink Stand." The enterprise was so successful that they opened another establishment at 1822 S Third St. Cunningham's "soft drink" business was closed down after a federal agent discovered that the men were selling liquor.

During the 1930s the stable and blacksmith area of Cunningham's was closed. In 1942, Cap utilized the large parking area to start Louisville's first drive-in restaurant with full waiter service.

In 1967 Cap sold the business to four restaurateurs. Between 1967 and 1981, Cunningham's passed among numerous owners before finally being sold to Don George and his family. The restaurant decor is greatly influenced by its origins as a horse stable. The walls are replete with pictures of KENTUCKY DERBY winners dating back to 1919's Sir Barton. In addition, the walls are covered with old photographs of Louisville, including several taken by the well-known photographer R.G. Potter.

See Maryann Davis, "Cunningham's Can Be Proud of Its Burger," *Louisville Skyline*, Dec. 5, 1983; George H. Yater, *Two Hundred Years at the Falls of the Ohio* (Louisville 1978).

CURTIN, CORNELIUS A. (b Louisville, March 20, 1853; d Louisville, January 17, 1928). Architect. The son of John Curtin from Philadelphia, Pennsylvania, Curtin designed some of the most notable buildings in the area. Among his works were the City Hall Annex (1909), one of the city's best examples of the Beaux Arts style.

As a young man, Curtin worked as an office boy for architect H.P. Bradshaw, who steered him into the field of architectural design. He started his own firm in 1878 and was a partner with L. Pike Campbell for a couple of years in the late 1880s. From 1890 until 1897 he was in partnership with Louisville native JOHN BACON HUTCHINGS, another well-known architect, who designed the Kentucky Building for the Tennessee Centennial in 1897. After 1898 Curtin worked alone.

In 1890 Curtin and Campbell designed the ten-story COLUMBIA BUILDING, then Louisville's tallest building and an excellent example of the Richardsonian Romanesque style. The Columbia Building, which was located on the northwest corner of FOURTH and MAIN STREETS, was demolished in 1966 by the Urban Renewal Agency.

Curtin also designed ST. BRIGID and St. Charles Borromeo Roman Catholic Churches and the Louisville Steam & Power Co., part of which became the Morris parking garage on Third St. In addition, he designed twenty-nine churches in Kentucky, Illinois, and Indiana, as well as many private homes in the area.

Curtin, who lived at 121 Galt Ave., died of peritonitis at the age of seventy-four at St. Joseph's Infirmary. He is buried in St. Louis Cemetery. Curtin had one daughter, Mrs. L. Lyne Smith. His son, John, died as the result of a swimming accident in 1913 at the age of eighteen.

See *Courier-Journal*, Jan. 18, 1928; C. Julian Oberwarth and William B. Scott Jr., *A History of the Profession of Architecture in Kentucky* (Louisville 1987).

CURTISS-WRIGHT AIRCRAFT FACTORY. Constructed on the west side of Standiford Field (now LOUISVILLE INTERNATIONAL AIRPORT) during WORLD WAR II, the government-owned Aircraft Defense Corp. climate-controlled plant was assigned to the Curtiss-Wright Corp. to build their twin-engine C-76 Caravan cargo aircraft. Fear of a wartime shortage of aluminum prompted the design of the all-wood C-76. Work on the 1,550- by 394-foot factory began in May 1942. The first aircraft completed flew on May 3, 1943. Seven days later it crashed south of the airport, killing the three crewmen. With design flaws in the aircraft and plentiful supplies of aluminum, the C-76 program was canceled in mid-1943, although twenty aircraft were produced.

In May 1944 production was underway to complete the first of 439 Curtiss C-46 Commando twin-engine, all-metal cargo aircraft. The last was assembled during June 1945. Between Caravan and Commando production runs, the factory modified Curtiss SB2C Helldivers and C-46s, both built at other locations. Again in 1945 modifications resumed on aircraft, notably the Consolidated B-24 and Boeing B-17 and B-29. Curtiss-Wright vacated the factory on August 1, 1945.

By October 1945 the Laister-Kauffmann Co. of St. Louis leased the factory for production of its predominantly wooden CG-10 Trojan Horse assault glider. In early 1946 contracts were canceled, although two aircraft were built in Louisville, with the first flying on February 2, 1946. The factory would reopen as INTERNATIONAL HARVESTER and be demolished in 1997.

In a similar operation, an Aircraft Modification Center was constructed on the east side of Standiford Field in 1942 and operated by the Consolidated Vultee Co. to modify B-24 bombers built in Fort Worth and Detroit. Many were delivered to the British Royal Air Force. The one-thousandth modification was completed in October 1944. After the war, the facility became the Bremner Biscuit Co. and was demolished during the mid-1990s.

See Peter M. Bowers, *Curtiss Aircraft 1907–1947* (London 1979); Walt Boyne, "C-76, The Basketcase Bummer," *Airpower* (May 1974): 60–65; David W. Ostrowski, "The Trojan Horse from St. Louis," *Journal of the American Aviation Historical Society* (Fall 1992): 190–201; *Louisville Times,* Feb. 2, 1946.

Charles W. Arrington

D

DAINTY. Street game. Revived in 1971 by George Hauck and Charlie Vettiner as the World Championship Dainty Contest, this game was perhaps introduced to Louisville in the mid-1800s by GERMAN immigrants. The contest is based on a European children's game known in England as "tip-cat." It involves placing one small, pointed stick (about five inches long) on the ground and flipping it off the ground by tapping an end with another stick (about three feet long), then attempting to strike the airborne "dainty" as far as possible.

While some claim the smaller stick was named for its size, the origin of the "dainty" name may be related to the ice cream confection peddled by pushcart vendors in the neighborhoods where the game was popular. The "dainty man's" treats, wrapped in wax paper and resembling a small stick, suggest a connection. The modern contest is open to adults age forty-five and older and is surrounded by a day of celebration in the SCHNITZELBURG area of GERMANTOWN on the last Monday in July. The unofficial dainty world's record is held by Gene Klein at 145 feet and 6 inches.

See Robert Cogswell, "Dainty: A Louisville Street Game," *In Kentucky* (July 1984): 35–37.

Gene Klein

DAIRIES. The production, processing, and distribution of milk and milk products have been essential activities in the Louisville area from an early date, although the beginnings are somewhat obscure. In examining what has happened to the milk industry, we need to look at the history of three facets of dairy products handling: SANITATION, refrigeration, and distribution. To arrive at where we are today, there have been dramatic developments in each of those areas.

The dairy industry started as a profoundly local business. Most households in pioneer Louisville owned a cow and produced their own milk by milking twice a day. As Louisville was settled, all lots were one-half acre or larger in size, since it was expected that each household would need space for pasturage and a kitchen garden. Therefore, there was plenty of pastureland within the city to graze cattle. Some cities even had common grazing lands for a relatively large number of cows. The Boston Common was a prime example. Simple cow ownership during most of the nineteenth century was the primary source of milk for families.

As the village that was Louisville became a town and urban center, specialized dairy farms were established on the city's outskirts to provide milk. "Dairymen" were not listed as a specialized occupational group until shortly after the CIVIL WAR. In 1869 there were seven such listings. Most of these dairymen had GERMAN names, and four of them were in the area that came to be known as GERMANTOWN. Ten years later the total had grown to twenty, mostly German, of which half were in Germantown. The West End, thinly settled at that time except for PORTLAND, counted only one dairy farm in both years. Others were scattered about on the urban fringe.

By the middle of the nineteenth century the dairy farmers began what would later become regular milk routes by putting the latest milking in a small tank of about twenty-gallon capacity on a wagon and delivering it about town. The wagons from Germantown usually reached Shelby St. over a short stretch of road that became known as Milk St. as early as 1858. It now is part of Oak St. east of Shelby.

These deliveries were usually made twice a day after each milking, because refrigeration was nonexistent and the milk would spoil if it were not immediately consumed. A typical farmer would milk his cows, possibly cool the milk in the SPRINGHOUSE, load it on his wagon, and make his rounds. Customers would leave a container outside, and the dairyman would dip from his tank into the customer's container. This method of distribution continued to some extent until about 1930 in the smaller Jefferson County towns around Louisville. At that time, too, farmers often could not dispose of all the milk they could produce, and hence the surplus milk was manufactured into products that would keep longer—butter and cheese, for example. The making of butter in wooden churns became a common practice and was generally left for women to do.

There were interesting developments that would have significant impact on the local dairy industry in the twentieth century. First, in 1856 Louis Pasteur began experimenting with what became pasteurization. Testing of cows for disease, primarily for tuberculosis, began. The milk bottle was invented in 1884, and it was in use in Louisville shortly after the turn of the twentieth century.

By 1907 eighty-three dairymen and seventy-one depots were listed in the Louisville phone directory. Farmers delivered milk to the depots, which were forerunners of the later milk processing plants, and it was put into bottles. The depots separated cream and made butter and distributed these with milk, which was still unpasteurized. Milk was also brought into Louisville in large metal cans from distant points in Kentucky and southern Indiana by passenger trains. The cans were picked up at special platforms and returned empty in the evening. Because these "milk trains" made frequent stops to pick up cans, they were avoided by passengers in a hurry. The electric interurban lines that began to stretch outward from Louisville in the early twentieth century also brought many milk cans into the city. Refrigeration was in the form of ice boxes, and not everyone could afford one, making daily milk purchases an imperative.

An entry from the family journal of C. Oscar Ewing sheds light on how the dairy industry was evolving at that time. "Mr. D.H. Ewing, my father, started the business in 1876 on a small farm located near the city of Louisville. The foundation of the herd was one small black cow costing the sum of $20.00, $10.00 of which was paid down. This herd finally grew to number about twenty-five head at which time it became necessary to move to another farm nearer the city. The product of the dairy was made into butter and sold as such. No whole milk was delivered while the dairy operated on

Oscar Ewing Dairy delivery wagons.

the farm. This herd grew to be of such an enormous size that it became necessary to either move to a larger farm farther removed from the city or give up entirely."

The family moved to the city, opened up a small plant, and formed a partnership called D.H. Ewing's Sons in 1888. They continued to operate in that way until 1919 when it was incorporated under the same name. The journal continues: "The company was engaged in the sale and distribution of high grade butter and bottled milk and cream. Of course during this period there was a great amount of development from the beginning until the time it was merged with National Dairy in 1930. The centrifugal separator (for separating milk and cream) came into the field, the Babcock tester (for testing for butterfat), pasteurizing equipment, and other modern conveniences, all making for a better and safer product for the public." A price list dated in 1928 shows a quart of pasteurized milk costing thirteen cents.

From this plant, and others like it, milk and milk products began to be distributed early in the morning by wagons specifically made for milk delivery and pulled by horses shod with rubber shoes so as not to disturb NEIGHBORHOODS during predawn delivery. The horses knew the routes better than the milkmen and would know exactly where to stop and when to head to the barn. With improved refrigeration (ice poured over milk bottles), the deliveries could be reduced to one per day. Horse-and-wagon delivery continued in some form until 1940 when the last route, which happened to be along FOURTH ST., was discontinued. That same year a city ordinance was passed requiring daylight delivery of dairy products, a measure instituted primarily for the safety of milkmen, who sometimes were confused with prowlers.

Some processors used milk bottles with a special bulge at the top to capture the cream, which would rise to fill the bulge, enabling the customer to pour it off if he or she desired. Freezing weather often left the customer with a two- to three-inch column of frozen milk sticking out of the top of the milk bottle.

During the 1930s, trucks began replacing wagons, improved refrigeration techniques were being developed, and improved processing and packaging equipment was being used. The Louisville Health Department became active in attempting to insure a clean, wholesome supply of milk from the farm, through the plant, and to the customer.

Records of the Health Department give an excellent picture of what was happening during that time. For example, in 1905 no milk was being pasteurized. By 1920, 50 percent of the milk sold was pasteurized; by 1940, the figure was 98 percent. Complete pasteurization came in 1941, and the records of the Health Department claim that Louisville was the first "Southern City" to offer 100 percent pasteurization without a law. Other figures help fill out the picture at that time: daily consumption of milk by 1940 was about 29,000 gallons; a majority of milk shipped to processors came from farms that had mechanical refrigeration; sanitation was greatly improved, indicated by reduction in bacteria counts in raw milk; and per-capita consumption was increasing. In 1935 there were twelve hundred dairy farms in seventeen counties surrounding Louisville supplying the dairy processors.

WORLD WAR II brought about many changes in distribution. In 1943 every-other-day delivery was instituted, which helped the war effort by saving on precious fuel, tires, and the general need for additional trucks. This also was of benefit in reducing the need for manpower, which became very critical. This method of delivery continued even after the war, and some dairies even went to a three-days-a-week delivery, with a Monday, Wednesday, and Friday pattern, or Tuesday, Thursday, and Saturday, allowing for an off day on Sunday.

At the end of the war, there were thirty-eight dairy processors listed in the phone book, and twenty ice cream manufacturers. Among them were Cherokee Sanitary Milk (Bardstown Rd.), Cream Top Creamery (Bardstown Rd.), Oscar Ewing (S Floyd St.), Ewing-Von Allmen Dairy Co. (W Oak St.), Kentucky Dairies (S Third St.), Mellwood Dairy (Mellwood Ave.), Model Farms Dairy (Baxter Ave.), Sure Pure Milk (E Kentucky St.), Von Allmen Brothers (Taylorsville Rd.), Walnut Grove (Frankfort Ave.), and Zehnder Brothers Creamery (Frankfort Ave.). Ninety percent of the milk consumed was sold on home delivery, with the rest of it sold through grocery stores, RESTAURANTS, and schools.

Changes in lifestyles, improved sanitation and refrigeration, the development of supermarkets, improved transportation equipment and highways, new packaging, and improved milk handling served to bring about massive changes in the industry. A major change was the development of bulk shipment of milk from farm to processing plant. Until the early 1960s, milk was shipped in ten-gallon milk cans picked up daily at the farm and delivered to the plant. The cans were heavy and time-consuming to clean. Even though there was mechanical refrigeration on the farm, proper cooling seldom was accomplished. With bulk shipment all of that changed. Milk went from the cow through pipelines to a refrigerated stainless-steel storage tank to be picked up by modern trucks carrying stainless-steel insulated tanks holding up to ten thousand gallons each. More than any other thing, this change improved the quality and shelf life of milk and milk products. The old milk cans are now sold in antique shops.

Supermarkets, with their mass purchasing power, developed into the primary method for the retail distribution of milk. They could sell at lower prices. Improved refrigeration and sanitation allowed for perhaps a once-a-week pickup at the store, and no one would have to stay home waiting for the milk delivery. Improved packaging also lent itself to supermarket distribution. Milk went from being packaged in a round quart returnable glass milk bottle; through glass half-gallons; into wax-coated, one-way paper containers; to plastic-coated paper containers; to glass gallon returnable jugs; up to one-way plastic gallon and half-gallon containers. The dominant package today is the recyclable plastic gallon container.

The necessity of large volumes of milk to justify ever-increasing costs of processing equipment and delivery equipment put a strain on small processors. Between 1945 and 1990, most of them merged, sold out, or went out of business. Even though today there are still several dairies supplying the Louisville market, there is now only one processor left with a plant in Louisville, Dean Foods Co. Some of the other milk comes from plants several hundred miles away. This really is a tribute to the quality of milk, which has improved to such an extent that it is not unusual to have milk keep under proper conditions for up to a month. Consumers can take for granted that they will have a plentiful supply of wholesome dairy products. In most cases ice cream is also made in distant plants and shipped to supermarkets for sale. While some ice cream continues to be locally made, most of it is sold by nationwide outlets such as Baskin-Robbins. An exception is locally owned White Mountain Creamery.

Niels O. Ewing

DARE TO CARE INC. Prompted by the 1969 Thanksgiving eve starvation death of nine-year-old Bobby Ellis of Louisville's RUSSELL neighborhood, Rev. John E. Jones, pastor of St. John Catholic Church, joined with others moved by the tragedy. Two years later they formed the St. John's Emergency Food Program. Incorporated as the Dare to Care Food Program in 1973 and shortened to Dare to Care six years later, the nonprofit agency spent its early years supplying food to a handful of emergency food shelters for inner-city families but soon thereafter focused countywide.

In the beginning the organization was run solely by volunteers and did not hire a paid staff member until 1977. As donations and the agency's reach increased, a larger staff was required (the first full-time director was hired in 1981), but the bulk of the workers continued to be made up of volunteers who sorted, picked up, and delivered food; worked in the offices; and helped at food drives. In need of a storage facility, Dare to Care moved into warehouse and office space at the Louisville Air Park in 1977.

In 1981 the board of directors decided to expand the scope of Dare to Care with a food bank program that would provide food to nonprofit agencies such as soup kitchens, missions, and nursing homes. Two years later this became part of Second Harvest, a national food-banking program headquartered in Chicago that supplies bulk food to its nearly two hundred certified members. After learning that Dare to Care's facilities were needed for the UPS expansion at LOUISVILLE INTERNATIONAL AIRPORT, city and county officials pledged $375,000 to relocate Dare to Care. A new thirty-five-thousand-square-foot warehouse on Fern Valley Rd. was dedicated in 1987, more than doubling storage space.

Dare to Care began a new program in 1993 called Kids Cafe. With food provided by Dare to Care as well as local restaurants and food suppliers, Kids Cafes are food kitchens where children can get hot meals three nights a week. Placed in neighborhoods with a high concentration of children below the poverty level, the volunteer-run operations also provide a safe environment for children under the age of seventeen. By mid-1998 there were six Kids Cafes in the Louisville area serving approximately sixty thousand meals per year.

Dare to Care is financed by a combination of fund-raisers such as the Hunger Walk and the Kroger Golf Tournament; donations from individuals and area businesses; and city, county, and federal funds. By 1998 Dare to Care had expanded its reach to seven Kentucky and five Indiana counties. Annually the organization supplied approximately 6 million pounds of food to over 340 area agencies through its food bank program and helped roughly 90,000 people at its 29 area distribution centers.

See *Courier-Journal*, Sept. 18, 1996.

DAVIS, BRINTON BEAUREGARD (b Natchez, Mississippi, January 23, 1862; d Louisville, June 27, 1952). Architect. Brinton was the oldest son of Jacob Brinton and Mary (Gamble) Davis. He trained with his architect father and with architects in New York City, Chicago, and St. Louis prior to establishing a practice in Paducah, Kentucky, in 1892. He moved his practice to Louisville in 1902. His best-known works include the Jefferson County Armory (1905, later THE GARDENS OF LOUISVILLE), the Inter-Southern Insurance Building (1911–13, later the Kentucky Home Life Building), the Kentucky and Watterson Hotels, the interior remodeling of the JEFFERSON COUNTY COURTHOUSE, and eleven structures at Western Kentucky University.

Davis married Clara Benbrook on February 23, 1889. The couple had two daughters, Gladys and Mildred. Davis is buried in CAVE HILL CEMETERY.

See Jonathan Jeffrey, "The Hill Builder: Brinton B. Davis and Western Kentucky University," *Filson Club History Quarterly* 69 (Jan. 1995): 3–24.

Jonathan Jeffrey

DAVIS, FINIS E. (b Lead Hill, Arkansas, August 29, 1911; d Louisville, May 15, 1998). Educator of the blind. Born to John Preston and Mary Elizabeth (Cagle) Davis, Finis Davis was educated in the Arkansas public schools before receiving his B.S. in education from the University of Arkansas. His interest in the blind was due to a sight-impaired classmate. He taught for five years at the Arkansas School for the Blind in Little Rock and was named its superintendent in 1939. In his eight years at the school, Davis helped establish a social adjustment program for the visually impaired and an internationally recognized vocational training center, known as the Lions World Service for the Blind, that teaches blind persons independent living and job training skills.

In 1947 Davis resigned from the Little Rock school to become the superintendent of the AMERICAN PRINTING HOUSE FOR THE BLIND in Louisville. During his tenure, Davis collaborated with Brazil, Mexico, and India in their attempts to set up small printing presses for the blind. The American Printing House assisted the developing countries by training stereograph operators and by helping to build stereograph machines that could produce braille in the native languages.

Davis also spearheaded a cooperative effort with IBM to develop computer translation software that could turn ink print into braille. He developed a process for producing braille plates using plastic instead of metal. This move cut costs by 90 percent, meaning that blind children in all schools around the country could have their own textbooks. After serving in later years as its vice president and general manager, Davis retired from the printing house in 1976 and became president of Label Specialties Inc.

Ever interested in assisting the visually impaired, Davis first joined the Lions Club, a civic organization whose primary focus is to aid and educate the blind, while in Little Rock in 1941. He continued his association with the club upon moving to Louisville and was elected president of the local chapter in 1951. After serving Lions International in several capacities, Davis was named president of the parent organization in 1960.

The Kentucky Lions Eye Center, located at the corner of Floyd St. and Muhammad Ali Blvd., was dedicated to Davis in 1997 after a $4.8 million addition was completed. Davis had chaired the fund-raising drive in 1968 that had led to its establishment. The building houses the UNIVERSITY OF LOUISVILLE Department of Ophthalmology and the Kentucky Lions Eye Research Institute.

Davis married Ethlyn Watkins in 1933. They had three children: Marybel, Juliann, and Linda Sue. Davis is buried in CAVE HILL CEMETERY.

See *Courier-Journal*, May 17, 1998; *Voice-Tribune*, May 20, 1998; *New York Times*, May 21, 1998.

DAVIS, THOMAS TERRY (b ?; d Jeffersonville, Indiana, November 15, 1807). U.S. congressman. Davis was admitted to the Kentucky bar on June 28, 1789, practicing in Mercer County. After a brief term as deputy attorney for the commonwealth, Davis served in the state House of Representatives from 1795 through 1797. He was elected to Congress and served from March 4, 1797, to March 3, 1803, when he was appointed United States judge of Indiana Territory on February 8, 1803. Davis held this position until 1806, when he became the head of equity court of Indiana Territory until his death.

Circa 1911 architect's rendering of the interior of the Watterson hotel, Louisville. Brinton B. Davis, architect.

See *Biographical Directory of the American Congress 1774–1961* (Washington, D.C., 1961).

DEARING, J. EARL (b Vinton, Virginia, March 29, 1921; d Louisville, August 22, 1969). Attorney and civil rights activist. Dearing, born in Virginia and raised on a farm, moved to Louisville in 1950. In the days of SEGREGATION, he walked three miles each way to attend the local grade school because school bus service was for whites only. He attended the closest African American high school, the Lucy Addison High School, in Roanoke, Virginia, an eight-mile bicycle ride. In 1942 he graduated from the Virginia Union University in Richmond, a black Baptist college, and entered the army. After four years of military service he enrolled in law school, under the G.I. Bill, at Western Reserve University in Cleveland.

A tall, soft-spoken man with a penchant for bow ties, Dearing was both an attorney for and president of the local and state chapters of the National Association for the Advancement of Colored People (NCAAP). In this capacity he advocated, for five years, a local ordinance outlawing discrimination in public accommodations, that passed in 1963. Dearing had been upset when he was prevented from taking his son to see *Bambi* in a downtown theater. That event resulted in his campaign for integrating all public facilities.

Locally, Dearing was the first African American to be appointed to the position of deputy clerk of the police court in Jefferson County. He was appointed to positions of assistant police court prosecutor and Municipal Court judge. Dearing was, in 1965, the first black to be elected Police Court prosecutor. In 1969 he was also the first black nominated by the voters in a primary election for a circuit court judgeship, (the 4th Division of Common Pleas Court), but died before the general election. A Republican, he served on the party's national advisory committee on crime and law enforcement and a national task force on crime and delinquency.

He married Mary Alice Hambleton of Louisville, and they had two children, David Earl and Frances Penn. He is buried in CAVE HILL CEMETERY.

See *Courier-Journal and Times*, Aug. 24, 1969; *Louisville Defender*, Aug. 28, 1969.

DECORATIVE ARTS. The interior-design profession in America did not achieve recognition as a separate and distinct entity until the years following WORLD WAR II. As the profession is so closely linked to social and cultural events, those factors shaped its early development in the Louisville area.

Significant residential ARCHITECTURE has been a part of the Louisville area scene from its inception, two notable examples being LOCUST GROVE and FARMINGTON. Louisville has been fortunate to have had settlers from a variety of ethnic and cultural backgrounds. Settlers from Virginia were often accustomed to a more gracious way of life, thus fostering a demand for the goods and services necessary for a genteel lifestyle. Immigrants from Europe brought special skills and talents. Strassel Painting and Roofing Co., established in 1854, and BITTNERS, established in 1854 by a German cabinetmaker, Gustave Bittner, would become two of Louisville's most prestigious interior-design firms in the twentieth century.

The designing of fine interiors had usually been the responsibility of architects, and, with some notable exceptions, architects had relied on the services of experts such as artists, artisans, upholsterers, and cabinetmakers. But by the middle of the nineteenth century the Industrial Revolution had created an increasingly prosperous middle class, a fact that would alter the manner in which these services would be rendered.

The Philadelphia Centennial Exposition of 1876 presented exhibitions that played a significant role in the enhanced appreciation of the public for the importance of art in daily life. New monthly and weekly publications on art and the home were initiated. Gradual improvement in comfort, speed, and safety aboard trains and ocean liners coincided with the growth of a new leisured class who now had the opportunity to travel to Europe, further enhancing a greater art consciousness. By the last quarter of the nineteenth century, American firms such as Poitier and Stymus, Leon Marcotti and Co., and Herter Brothers were providing this clientele with stylish interiors. These establishments laid the groundwork for the large number of interior-design firms that opened after the WORLD WAR I.

Louisville's position as a large manufacturing and commercial center in the second half of the nineteenth century spawned the rise of a new leisure class that led to the development of fine residential NEIGHBORHOODS stretching along the streets lying south of BROADWAY. This fact in turn attracted artists and artisans having the talents required for these upscale residences.

Mirroring events on the East Coast, Louisville was the site for the SOUTHERN EXPOSITION of 1883–87. This annual event would further public awareness of the importance of art in daily lives. The site for this exposition became ST. JAMES CT. and BELGRAVIA CT., the crown jewels of new upscale neighborhoods.

Since most American schools of art did not offer courses in the decorative arts, practitioners had to look to Europe for such knowledge. The École des Beaux Arts in Paris offered studies in both architecture and the decorative arts. Museums, art galleries, and extensive travel on the continent provided additional information and inspiration. However, to acquire such a body of knowledge would have required that the student come from an affluent background or have a wealthy patron. Therefore, if the interior-design profession were to meet growing demand, schools of interior design would be required. Realizing this fact, Frank Alvara Parsons established Parsons School of Design in New York City in 1908. The city was in a position to provide its designers with everything necessary for the successful completion of important commissions. This included craftsmen, artisans, and manufacturers of the first rank dealing with fine textiles, furnishings, and antiques. Another fine program was introduced at the University of Cincinnati. With few exceptions, these became some of the first major schools offering serious programs in interior design until the middle of the century.

In Louisville, firms offering services in interior design did not appear until after World War I. Both Bittners and Strassel introduced interior-design services to the public. G. Bittner and Sons hired Fred Krazeise, an upholsterer skilled in the art of fabric selection, including drapery design. Then in 1918 Thomas Kruse joined Fred Krazeise to develop Bittners' design division. In the early 1920s the Strassel Painting and Roofing Co. reorganized, spinning off the roofing division. The firm became known as Strassel and Sons; and Thomas Jefferson Kelly, a new addition to the firm, was responsible for developing its interior-design division. These were the leading firms in the Louisville area until after World War II.

The postwar years became a pivotal time for the interior-design profession and the nation. Three pieces of legislation enacted by Congress would transform American society. The G.I. Bill offered veterans an opportunity for a college education; the Federal Housing Administration offered veterans low-interest home loans, allowing many families to become homeowners for the first time; and the introduction of the interstate highway system would make the automobile the major mode of transportation, leading to the development of suburbia. A fourth factor was the emergence of the baby-boom generation, which would bring a large increase in POPULATION.

These dramatic changes in lifestyle spawned a demand for the services of interior designers. The retail industry quickly recognized this new customer base. At that time STEWART'S DRY GOODS, Louisville's largest department store, added an interior-design department. The firm was in an excellent position to establish such a service, for it already had a large, upscale furniture department; an excellent drapery department; and one of the best drapery workrooms in the city. Stewart's became one of Louisville's major interior-design firms until it closed in 1987.

Burdorf's, another fine furniture store, also opened an interior-design department. HUBBUCHS, initially specializing in draperies and wallpaper, established both a residential-design department and one of the largest contract-design departments in the nation. In the 1960s and 1970s, contract design became a major area of practice, dealing with the broad variety of commercial interiors. Other interior-design firms established in the last quarter of the twentieth century include Allen House Inc., E.S. Tichenor Co., and Ewald Associates. The practicing designer now has a broad choice of options in employment—for example, joining an established design firm or ARCHITECTURAL FIRM as an in-house designer in commercial or institutional establishments, or as a freelance designer.

In the 1930s during the depths of the Depression, prominent designers recognized their lack of professional standing in the eyes of the general public. They formed the first professional organization, the American Institute of Interior Designers (AID) in 1931. Membership depended on the recommendation of a member in good standing and an examination of the applicant's design portfolio.

As the number of designers proliferated in the postwar years, those not accepted for membership in AID formed their own organization, the National Society of Interior Designers (NSID). They were often younger, and their expertise was often in commercial design.

These differences in objectives brought the two organizations into conflict in the 1950s. Cooler heads in both organizations realized that if the profession was to be recognized, they would have to join forces. Members of AID were insistent that a qualifying exam be the major qualification for membership; members in NSID believed licensing was the way to go. After a prolonged period of debate, the two organizations merged, forming the American Society of Interior Designers (ASID) in 1975. This merger brought two major factors into focus: the qualifying exam and the accreditation of schools of design. This would require the establishment of two separate entities to fulfill these tasks.

The National Council for Interior Design Qualification (NCIDQ), was established to develop and grade the qualifying exam. A second body, Interior Design Education Council (IDEC), is responsible for accrediting schools of interior design. It sets the guidelines, gives support to programs under consideration, and arranges the visitation of the programs in both schools of design and departments of interior design at colleges and universities.

The profession in Louisville has seen the development of an active local chapter of ASID as well as the development of an interior-design program in the Fine Arts Department at the UNIVERSITY OF LOUISVILLE. This degree program is fully accredited.

Nancy Lee Pearcy

DEER PARK. Neighborhood in eastern Louisville bounded by Newburg Rd. to the west, Eastern Pkwy. to the north, Bardstown Rd. to the east, and a combination of Richmond Dr. and Douglass Blvd. to the south. In the 1890s developers began to subdivide the deer-filled wooded farmlands as the streetcar line was extended down Bardstown Rd. to Bonnycastle Ave. While most of the area was platted by 1917, the primarily residential neighborhood, with commercial establishments lining the major thoroughfares, saw its last development originate in 1935. A local landmark is the King's Daughters and Sons Home on Stevens Ave. It is an institution dedicated to caring for the ill and disabled, dating from 1909.

See "Louisville Survey: East Report" (Louisville 1980).

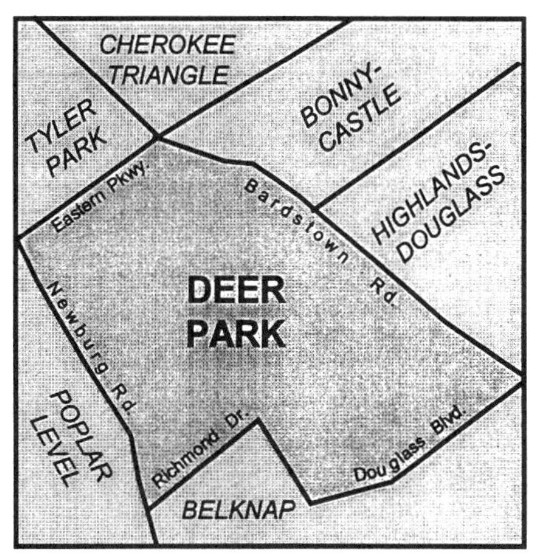

DELPH, JOHN MILLBANK (b Madison County, Virginia, August 18, 1805; d Louisville, December 16, 1891). Mayor. He was the youngest of four children of Daniel and Ann (Millbank) Delph. Delph's father died when he was three years old, and the family moved from Virginia to Scott County, Kentucky, with Delph's grandfather. Until he was sixteen years old, young Delph divided his time between the farm and school. He apprenticed to Matthew Kennedy in Lexington to learn the carpentry trade. He worked with Kennedy for four years and, near the end of the apprenticeship, married Eliza F. Spurr, of Fayette County. He moved back to Scott County for two years and then came to Louisville to become a carpenter and builder. His wife died in 1831, leaving one son.

Delph opened a bagging and bale-rope manufacturing firm in Lexington that operated for two years. He eventually came back to Louisville and entered real estate, where he made his fortune. He was appointed city tax collector by the City Council, and he also held the positions of constable, sheriff of Jefferson County, and deputy marshal of the chancery court during the next ten years. He was elected to the City Council in 1844, 1848, and 1849.

Delph took office as MAYOR on May 13, 1850, after emerging from a field of nine candidates with a plurality of the votes. His closest rival, WILLIAM S. PILCHER, a future mayor of Louisville, received 762 votes to Delph's 883.

Delph served as mayor for one year under the old CITY CHARTER. Then, on March 24, 1851, the Kentucky General Assembly enacted the new voter-approved city charter, and Delph became the first mayor to serve under the new charter. It changed the mayor's term of office to two years, created a bicameral City Council composed of a BOARD OF ALDERMEN and a Board of Councilmen, and it changed election day to the first Saturday in April.

But the new charter caused problems for the city because the wording created some confusion over whether the election was to be held in specific years or starting from the date the new charter was enacted. Delph, who was chosen to serve in 1851, resigned his office after several months but was elected by the common council to serve as mayor pro tem until April 26, 1852.

During his first administration, Louisville finally experienced the cholera EPIDEMIC that had plagued other parts of the state for several years. Delph distinguished himself by an all-out drive for sanitary conditions throughout the city. In 1853 he was elected to fill a vacancy for one year on the Board of Aldermen.

On April 6, 1861, less than a week before the start of the CIVIL WAR, Delph was again elected mayor. He was nominally an old-line Whig during his first term of office, but during the war he became a staunch Union supporter. After serving as mayor until April 1863, he was elected to the state legislature in that year, serving until 1865.

Delph also was one of the founders of the WALNUT STREET BAPTIST CHURCH. After his first wife died, he married Ellen L. Schwing in 1837. She was the granddaughter of Augustus Kaye, the father of Mayor FREDERICK A. KAYE. The couple had nine children. He is buried in CAVE HILL CEMETERY.

See *Louisville Past and Present: Its Industrial History* (Louisville 1875); J. Stoddard Johnston, ed., *Memorial History of Louisville* (Chicago and New York 1896); Attia Martha Bowmer, "The History of the Government of the City of Louisville," M.A. thesis, University of Louisville, 1948.

DEMBITZ, LEWIS NAPHTALI (b Zirke, Prussia, February 1833; d Louisville, March 11, 1907). Attorney and scholar. Lewis Naphtali Dembitz was the son of Sigmund Z. and Fanny (Wehle) Dembitz. He was educated in Poland, graduating in April 1848 from the gymnasium at Golgau in Silesia province. In the winter of 1849, Dembitz attended lectures on Roman law at Charles University in Prague. In May 1849 the family emigrated to the United States, where his parents settled in New Orleans while Dembitz moved to Cincinnati. There he studied LAW with the firm of Walker and Kilber for two years. In 1851 he moved to Madison, Indiana, where he studied with the firm of Dunn and Hendricks. In 1852 he was admitted to the bar and moved to Louisville, where he spent the rest of his life. For a year Dembitz edited and wrote for the German daily *Der Beobachter am Ohio*, and he wrote one of the earliest known German translations of Harriet Beecher Stowe's classic novel, *Uncle Tom's Cabin*.

In 1853 Dembitz left the newspaper to practice law, quickly gaining recognition as a leading attorney in Louisville. His partners were Martin Bijur during 1856–64 and Otto A. Wehle during 1870–74. Dembitz was involved in virtually every important case involving land disputes in Louisville and Indiana. His two-volume *Dembitz on Land Titles* was published in 1885. In 1884 he drew up a tax law for Louisville that enabled the city to collect taxes that had been evaded. He was city attorney for tax collection during 1884–88.

In 1888 Dembitz drafted the bill passed by the state legislature that required use of the Australian ballot (secret ballot) in Louisville elections. Known as the Wallach Law, it was the first of its kind in the United States. He wrote many scholarly works on American law, including *Kentucky Jurisprudence* in 1890. Dembitz was also a leading influence in the legal career of his nephew, Louis Dembitz Brandeis, who served on the U.S. Supreme Court from 1916 until 1939. Brandeis changed his middle name from David to Dembitz in honor of his uncle.

Dembitz served as a delegate to the Republican National Convention in 1860, where he was one of Abraham Lincoln's strongest supporters. He was just as well known in Kentucky for his writings on Jewish theology as for his legal works, his most famous work being *Services in Synagogue and Home*, published in 1892. Dembitz married his cousin Minna Wehle in 1852; they had eight children: Abraham L., Emily, Stella, Henry C., Annette, Milly, Ruth, and Martha. Dembitz is buried in Brith Sholom Jewish Cemetery in Louisville.

See John J. Weisert, "Lewis N. Dembitz and Onkel Tom's Hutte," *American- German Review* 10 (Feb. 1953): 7–8; Jewish Historical Society, *A History of the Jews of Louisville, Kentucky* (New Orleans 1901).

Nelson L. Dawson

Democratic campaign workers at Floyd and Oak Streets, 1921.

DEMOCRATIC PARTY. "Politics is Kentucky's major industry," so said Democratic sage Mike Barry, editor and publisher of the old *Kentucky Irish American*.

The Democratic Party traces its origins to the political organization that grew up around Thomas Jefferson and his alternative policy program to George Washington's agenda. Initially called the Republican Party, it was later modified to Democratic-Republicans and finally to Democratic Party after the 1828 presidential election in which the party split into two factions. Andrew Jackson, the successful candidate in that election, adopted the Democratic Party label. The other faction in that election, the National Republican Party, was absorbed by the Whig Party by 1834.

The Whigs were primarily made up of anti-Jackson forces and were led by Kentuckian Henry Clay. Because of Clay's affiliation with the Whigs, there was a time in Kentucky's mid-nineteenth-century history when many in Louisville and throughout the state joined the anti-Jackson party. Clay and Jackson were strong adversaries. Clay, who finished fourth in a large field of candidates in the 1824 presidential race, used his influence in the House of Representatives to help get John Quincy Adams elected over Jackson. In the 1828 election Clay actively supported Adams's reelection bid, but Jackson emerged victorious.

Jackson, following the lead of Jefferson, established the basic agenda of the party that would last into Franklin D. Roosevelt's New Deal programs in the next century. Democrats favored states' rights, supported the interests of the farmer, and defended a limited role for the national government.

It was mainly opposition to Jackson that caused the formation of the Whig Party as a successor to the Federalists. The Clay-Jackson feud was personal but also a matter of principle, in that Clay favored the establishment of a national bank that Jackson opposed. Clay died in 1852, and several circumstances combined so that the Whig Party disappeared.

The political fortunes of the Democratic Party in Kentucky mirrored the national party, although the party enjoyed greater success locally after the Civil War than in the country at large. When the country went Republican in the 1890s, 1920s, and late 1950s through the 1960s, the party also enjoyed its greatest success locally.

One of the great influences in the development of the Democratic Party in Louisville was the arrival of the Irish and Germans in large numbers in the 1840s and 1850s. Many of them, especially the Irish, became Democrats. The collapse of the Whig party, the rising tide of immigrants, and schism over the extension of slavery into "free-soil" lands led to the formation of the American Party to replace the Whig agenda.

The newly formed American, or Know-Nothing Party prevailed for a time both in Louisville and throughout Kentucky. This anti-Catholic, anti-foreigner political organization reached its zenith of popularity in the 1850s, but the riots of Bloody Monday were a turning point for the Know-Nothings. By the late 1850s Know-Nothing supporters began drifting to either the Democrats or the fledgling Republican Party.

Democrats in Louisville were weak except in areas where the German population was strongest. Louisville was mostly for the Union during the Civil War but favored avoiding war. However, the *Louisville Courier* (later the *Courier-Journal*), a newspaper that was to become perhaps one of the strongest political voices in Kentucky, stridently favored the South. Its editor, Walter N. Haldeman, a Democrat, spoke for the minority with considerable influence. Opposing forces had a leader in James Speed, Louisville attorney and strong Lincoln supporter. Speed was elected to the state General Assembly in 1861.

Lincoln's preliminary emancipation proclamation of September 22, 1862, did not affect Kentucky as a neutral state, but the Thirteenth Amendment to the U.S. Constitution in 1865 ended slavery in the commonwealth. The resulting turmoil put Kentucky in the Democratic ranks for decades to follow. Democrats dominated Louisville until 1895, when Republicans took control of the Louisville BOARD OF ALDERMEN, despite the fact that HENRY S. TYLER, a Democratic MAYOR, was midway through his term. Tyler died in 1896, leaving a vacancy to be filled by the Republicans. Disorganized Democrats soon fell under the control of JOHN WHALLEN, a political boss without precedent in Louisville.

John Whallen came to Louisville from Newport, Kentucky, in 1871 and opened a saloon on Green (LIBERTY) ST. His brother James later joined him in the opening of the Buckingham Theater. John became known as the "Duke of Buckingham," the theater having been made headquarters for the Whallens' political maneuvering. The Whallen machine, by mobilizing the Irish and Germans, was heavily Catholic. Periodically, the Whallens had the support of Walter N. Haldeman, publisher of the *Courier-Journal*. Popular Democratic mayor CHARLES D. JACOB fought the Whallen-supported Democrat William B. Holt in 1887. Jacob won despite considerable vote-buying and other Whallen skullduggery. Corruption in the election of 1887 prompted adoption of the secret ballot in 1888. However, Whallen ingenuity discovered ways to overcome the minor obstacle of a secret ballot. In 1897 Whallen supported Democrat CHARLES P. WEAVER, who defeated Republican GEORGE D. TODD. Weaver won in a narrow election characterized by some Republicans as the rankest fraud in Louisville history.

The twentieth century provided the shaping of the Democratic Party in Louisville and Jefferson County, making it the primary political force in the region. From the election of Weaver in 1897 to 1997, Louisvillians have chosen nineteen Democratic mayors and seven Republicans. In some cases, Republicans were able to carry the city and county in reaction to the misdeeds of Democrats. Democrat PAUL C. BARTH became mayor in 1905, having defeated a FUSIONIST group of Democrats and Republicans seeking reform. The Whallen machine pulled every trick in the book for Barth, and, after a long and tedious litigation by the Fusionists, the whole Barth ticket was thrown out by the Kentucky Court of Appeals in May 1907. Barth and other Democrats were removed from office, and Gov. J.C.W. Beckham appointed as mayor ROBERT WORTH BINGHAM, a reform Democrat who favored Prohibition. Saloons were thought to be the main power implements of Boss Whallen. Bingham took office Saturday, June 29, and the next day, Sunday, every saloon in town was closed under a law that hitherto had not been enforced. Bingham held office only four months, but in that time he made many reforms, including sending police to raid the red-light districts. His changes assured his successor, Republican JAMES E. GRINSTEAD, the first nearly fair election in many years. The Whallen organization never gave up and succeeded in electing two more Democrats in 1910 and 1913. Republicans and reform caught on shortly thereafter, and there were four successive Republicans out of five mayors from 1917 to 1933.

The Democrats also used the Kentucky court system to their advantage in the 1920s when the Republicans, led by party boss CHESLEY SEARCY, were at the pinnacle of their power. In the 1925 election, Democrats challenged the Republican sweep of city and county elections, led by Mayor-elect ARTHUR WILL and County Judge–elect HENRY FOX. Democrats leveled allegations of vote fraud, and the Kentucky Court of Appeals sided with the party and threw out the Republicans, thus allowing Gov. William J. Fields to fill the positions with fellow Democrats, including JOSEPH T. O'NEAL JR. as mayor and BEN EWING as JEFFERSON COUNTY judge. Both O'Neal and Ewing ran against the Republicans in the 1925 election but were defeated. O'Neal had been a last-minute replacement when it was discovered that the Democratic nominee for mayor, William T. Baker, had ties to the Ku Klux Klan.

When John Whallen died in 1913, the party mantle was briefly passed to his brother, James, before Democratic boss MICKEY BRENNAN, a strong Catholic organizer, eventually took the reins. Brennan, proud of his moniker "Portland Irish," built the party organization that would control local politics for almost thirty years, starting with the 1933 election of Democratic mayor JOSEPH SCHOLTZ. Brennan's organization included the political talents of such personages as LENNIE "MISS LENNIE" MCLAUGHLIN and JOHNNY CRIMMINS. Their political savvy is seen in the fact that from the 1933 election to 2000, the mayors were all Democrats with the exception of two Republicans, William Cowger in 1961 and Kenneth Schmeid in 1965. Those Democratic mayors helped to define the party locally, particularly mayors like NEVILLE MILLER, who carried the banner of the Roosevelt revolution in the 1930s; WILSON WYATT during WORLD WAR II; CHARLES FARNSLEY in the late 1940s and early 1950s; HARVEY SLOANE in 1973 and again in 1981; and JERRY ABRAMSON from 1985 to 1999. Republican victories in 1961 were due in part to dissatisfaction with Democratic "machine" control. No comparable party organization from either the Democrats or the Republicans has appeared since.

Other major factors in the recent development of the Democratic Party in Louisville include the influence of its largest newspaper, the *Courier-Journal*, which attained national prominence with the editorials of HENRY "Marse Henry" WATTERSON. Robert Worth Bingham bought the *Courier-Journal* in 1918, pledging to the previous owner, BRUCE HALDEMAN, continued support for the Democratic Party and liberal causes. Watterson later gave up his position as editor when a clash of wills occurred with Bingham over such issues as women's suffrage and the League of Nations; Bingham favored the liberal causes, and Watterson was against them. With some diversions, the paper under Robert Worth Bingham's son, BARRY BINGHAM SR., and grandson, Barry Bingham Jr., continued to support the liberal agenda of the national party organization until the sale of the papers to the Gannett chain in 1986.

Another prominent recent force within the Democratic Party in Louisville and Jefferson County has been the growing power of black voters. After the Civil War, most AFRICAN AMERICANS tended to identify with the party of Lincoln. When Franklin Roosevelt started instituting New Deal reforms in 1933, many of which benefited poor blacks, he increasingly gained support in the African American community. New Deal programs, President Harry S. Truman's desegregation of the military, and the Great Society programs of President Lyndon B. Johnson all contributed to make the African American community one of the most consistent interest groups to support the Democrats.

The Louisville Democratic Party attained some national recognition when the nation as a whole seemed to be leaning to Republicans in 1995. Democrats in Jefferson County gave the party's gubernatorial candidate, Paul Patton, his largest majority of any county in the entire state. Patton's Louisville victory was attributed chiefly to his strength with organized LABOR and black voters.

Louisville and Jefferson County voters were more sympathetic to the North during the Civil War. The rest of the state largely favored the Confederacy. Now it appears the situation is somewhat the reverse. Liberal Democratic strength seems mostly concentrated in Louisville. The western part of Kentucky, once a Democratic Party stronghold, has been represented by Republicans in Congress in the 1990s. There are some signs that an increasing number of black voters are supporting the GOP.

Bob Johnson, a longtime political observer for the *Courier-Journal*, suggests that many party changes in recent years are the result of TELEVISION. As a major means of communication, it bears upon everything from POLITICS to changing family relationships. The lessening cohesiveness of political parties generally, according to Johnson, can be laid to the changing of all social relationships by television.

See Lowell Harrison and James Klotter, *A New History of Kentucky* (Lexington 1997); and George Yater, *Two Hundred Years at the Falls of the Ohio* (Louisville 1979).

Philip Ardery

DENTISTRY. When Louisville received its first charter in 1780, pioneer physicians already practiced their trade in the city. Among the first physicians who provided the city with necessary dental care were RICHARD FERGUSON and George Hart. Ferguson and Hart, like most medical doctors of the time, performed routine oral care such as extracting teeth, treating gum disease, and dealing with toothaches. White's and Hahn's Toothache Drops were available locally and were probably sold as a general elixir as well.

Drs. Joshua Drummone, Thomas G. Dunlap, and Samuel Griffith were some of the first local physicians-dentists who plied their trade in the 1820s. They followed the tradition of tooth extraction and elixir prescriptions. The preceptor model was the accepted pedagogy for students: students read a course in MEDICINE with a practicing physician, paid fees for the course, and, upon completing it, entered medicine and/or DENTISTRY. Some unscrupulous preceptors existed who accepted fees from students and immediately issued a certificate of competency before training was completed.

Dental technology had not evolved much either. The "pelican" instrument was the most common tool used by local dentists from the early to middle nineteenth century. Forceps replaced the pelican, but stumps of teeth and roots proved resistant to removal with forceps. Out of necessity, the screw extractor was developed and was widely used in Louisville. About 1830 Louisville had more than a dozen dentists, including Thomas Armstrong, J. Braselman, J.W. Bright, Edwin B. Church, Nicholas Clute, Thomas G. Dunlap, Sam Griffith, Edward Griffith, John Harris, W.C. Hobbs, D. Illingham, Orien Jerome, Theodore Phillips, A. Van Camp, and Rufus Somerby. Practitioners began specializing in children's care partly because of so many cases of broken and fractured teeth from boys playing catch. When the break was deep into the tooth, it was extracted. When not deep, the tooth was plugged with gold foil. For a loose tooth a thread or wire was used until the errant tooth tightened.

Dentists practiced in making pivot crowns for patients. The root of the tooth was retained and prepared, a human tooth was selected or one was made of some substitute material such as ivory, walrus tusks, hippopotamus tusk, or sea horse or sea cow teeth. Porcelain teeth were not in general use.

In 1841 Abraham Lincoln visited JOSHUA SPEED at his friend's FARMINGTON estate near Louisville. During his visit Lincoln developed a toothache and decided to walk the five miles to downtown to have it examined. Back in Illinois Lincoln wrote Speed and mentioned that he did not have the tooth removed. What happened is not exactly known. Perhaps Lincoln's condition improved, perhaps he lost his nerve, or maybe the dentist was not able to pull the tooth. The many biographies of Lincoln do not refer to the dental problem, and even in his papers no mention is made.

The Louisville Dental Society was founded in 1850, when more than two dozen dentists came together for professional and social interaction. Papers were presented, educational standards discussed, ethics reviewed, and clinical techniques examined. Also in 1850 the Kentucky General Assembly authorized the Transylvania School of Dental Surgery. Early sources contend that there was an association between the Louisville Society and the Transylvania School, but no reliable evidence has been found.

In September 1851 the Mississippi Valley Association of Dental Surgeons held its annual meeting in Louisville. Participating dentists read papers on their clinical experiences and discussed the latest technologies such as vacuum chambers and atmospheric plates. Plaster was a common tool for taking impressions so that dentures could be crafted. Local dentists participated in this meeting, including Drs. William H. Goddard, W.H. David, and Ben Dudley.

On April 18, 1865, at the National Hotel at Fourth and Main Streets, the Central States Dental Association elected Louisvillians to office: Dr. W.G. Redman, second vice president; Dr. W.H. Shadoan, secretary; and Dr. J.A. McClellan, corresponding secretary. This professional organization sought "to cultivate the science and art of dentistry and all its collateral branches; to elevate and sustain the professional character of dentists; to promote among them a mutual improvement, social intercourse and good feeling and to collectively represent and have cognizance of the common interests of the dental profession in the Central States."

In January 1868 Kentucky's regulation of dentistry began, but with a slow start, when the first bill introduced before the General Assembly to regulate trade died in committee. As introduced, the legislation would have established standards and qualifications for the practice of dentistry. Improvements did occur when the Louisville College of Dentistry was established in 1886 as a branch of the Hospital College of Medicine. The first students were admitted in January 1887. Medical and dental students attended the same classes and used the same rooms for study. Dr. James Lewis Howe served as dean of both the medical and dental divisions. In order to graduate, students completed two years of study, and the first class graduated in the spring of 1888 with four members. The school was on the south side of Chestnut, near Preston. In 1900 the Dental School moved to a new building at Brook and BROADWAY, breaking away from the medical school.

When Central University of Richmond and Centre College of Danville consolidated as the Central University of Kentucky, headquartered in Danville, the Louisville College of Dentistry affiliated with this institution until 1918. In that year the School of Dentistry was reorganized as a school of the UNIVERSITY OF LOUISVILLE. The Dental School moved again in 1970 to the Health Sciences Center on Preston St. in the Medical Center.

The Blair Dental Manufacturing Co., a nationally recognized company in the production of dental equipment, provided a unique technological development arising out of Louisville's dental community. Dr. John C. Blair in 1908 developed a cuspidor that featured running water and a fountain for patient convenience.

Over the course of the twentieth century, dental professionals became interested in procedures for the oral health of the local community, including better brushing techniques, flossing, and rinsing. Community dental health was one of the primary causes for the forming of the Jefferson County Dental Society in 1910. During the nineteenth century the society had been known as the Falls City Dental Club.

The dental profession grew and prospered in Louisville just as professional dentistry grew throughout the United States in the twentieth century. In 1948, when prevention of dental problems became a concern, the University of Louisville established a training program for dental hygienists. Today dental hygienists and dental assistants are important members of the dental profession. The University of Louisville School of Dentistry continues to attract full classes of students who seek to be trained in all areas of oral health. Dental health research continues, attracting some of the top researchers and practitioners in the country at the end of the twentieth century.

See Robert L. Sprau and Edward B. Gernert, *History of Kentucky Dentistry 1636–1960* (Louisville 1960).

Hoyt D. Gardner Jr.

DEPARTMENT STORES. Founded in 1846 on New York City's Broadway, Alexander T. Stewart's dry goods store, known as the Marble Palace, had become successful enough by 1862 that it moved to a new eight-story building. Soon thereafter Rowland Macy of New York, John Wanamaker of Philadelphia, and Marshall Field of Chicago opened their stores. Their department stores became emporiums and trade palaces where all classes of society could see, touch, and, of course, buy the merchandise. Because of the sizes of the institutions, less-personal relationships between owners and workers resulted. In addition, haggling between clerks and customers over item costs was replaced with a uniform, fixed-price policy.

The name reflects the fact that fabrics, clothing, notions, and wares were separated into different sections of the immense interiors. Cast-iron columns made possible great expanses of open space, and larger glass windows admitted more light to the displayed merchandise. Occupying areas called departments, sales clerks no longer stood at the front doors of the buildings waiting for customers. They were assigned to specific locations and vested with specific product knowledge that addressed the concerns of the increasing number of female patrons. As a result of the overwhelming switch from male to female shoppers, the "saleslady" became the heart of the business.

Louisville's first dry goods store appeared in 1783. Located on the north side of MAIN ST. between Fifth and Sixth Streets, Daniel Brodhead's double-sized log cabin featured glass panes in the windows (known as window-lights) and goods from Pittsburgh and Philadelphia.

By 1852 the community boasted 275 dry goods dealers with 25 of these establishments dedicated exclusively to the wholesale trade.

It was along Market St. that the retail trade first congregated. Running parallel to the Ohio River, the stores were ideally positioned to receive from riverboats their shipments of goods. To present the wares, front-page newspaper advertising was a commonly accepted form of commercial news. By the 1870s many of Louisville's merchants were abandoning their initial locations for outlets along Fourth St. Shopping became a social event along this new north-south corridor of stores, restaurants, theaters, and hotels. The area's southern boundary was Broadway, established by the opening on that corner of the Brown Hotel in 1923.

As in eastern cities, department stores replaced smaller mercantile outlets. A 1907 pamphlet published by the Retail Merchants Association listed three department stores in Louisville: J. Bacon & Sons, Stewart's, and Kaufman-Straus. Though Bacon's appeared first in the community (1845), it was Louis Stewart's New York store that became the standard by which all others were measured. Founded on Market St. in 1846 as Durkee and Heath's New York Store, the name changed after Stewart's leadership in the late 1800s. The store moved to the corner of Fourth and Jefferson Streets in 1853 before settling in 1907 at the southeast corner of Fourth and Walnut (Muhammad Ali Blvd.). Combining its impressive seven-story building of sixty-two departments, tearooms, rest rooms, doormen, and elevators with its New York buying practices, this institution defined the downtown shopping experience. Kaufman-Straus (1879), though possessing all of the conveniences associated with upscale retailing, including a signature building on Jefferson St. between Seventh and Eighth Streets, was unable to capture the Stewart image. Bacon's, and eventually Ben Snyder's, were identified with blue-collar patrons. As the growing middle class slowly moved away from the city to the suburbs, their customer loyalties were maintained. People continued to make the trek downtown until these stores were forced to follow their clientele into the suburban areas by the 1960s.

Two other important early stores were Oak Hall and The Fair. Opened in 1878 on the southwest corner of Fourth and Jefferson Streets, Oak Hall was in what had been Mozart Hall, an entertainment venue. The southern agent of Philadelphia's Wanamaker store, the Louisville branch received daily arrivals of fashionable East Coast clothing. The Fair opened in 1885 on Jefferson St. between Second and Third Streets with political leaders John and James Whallen as the principal owners. After only three years, the unsuccessful venture closed and was turned into the Grand Opera House and later the Buckingham, a burlesque theater.

Ben Snyder Department store, south side Market Street between Fourth and Fifth Streets, 1929.

Situated among Louisville's department stores were a variety of men's and women's specialty stores. These family-owned and -operated businesses functioned apart from the large buying groups such as Mercantile, City Stores, and Associated Dry Goods, and were owned and managed by men and women who maintained a close identity to the community. Living in the very neighborhoods they served, local owners often extended their commercial integrity and reputations into civic causes and affairs. Their sense of caring and involvement extended far beyond the sales counters to the lives of the people who entered their buildings. Examples of these stores included H.P. Selman and Co., founded in 1915 and closed in 1970; Byck Brothers and Co., founded in 1902 and closed in 1991; Levy Brothers, founded in 1861 and closed in 1979; Loevenhart and Co., founded in 1898 and closed in 1995; Appel's, founded in 1883 and closed in 1963; Bon Ton, founded in 1916 and closed in 1961; and Rodes-Rapier (Crutcher & Starks), founded in 1890.

The store owners saw the value of some cooperation among themselves. Beginning with the Retail Merchants Association in 1904, a variety of organizations appeared to promote unified standards of advertising integrity, working hours, and special events. Shoppers clearly developed loyalties to specific businesses and to those employed in them. However, shopping normally involved a daylong commitment to the experience. A typical visit was described as going downtown. It was generally understood that Fourth St. was the destination. Arriving by streetcar and later by bus was the transport style of most, since these vehicles could drop off and pick up patrons near the stores. After paying a visit to an establishment where one might be called by name, a meal and a movie could divide the day. A special treat would be lunch inside the department store itself. Only Kaufman's and Stewart's provided this amenity. Undoubtedly it was Stewart's fifth-floor Orchid Room that gave added importance to the trip. Expensive plates, crystal glasses, and quality silverware, along with food prepared by an accomplished chef, could transform a purchase into a memory. As the afternoon wore on, other stores could be visited, but transportation schedules dictated when it was time to head home.

The impact of the stores on the metropolitan area was instrumental in shaping a sense of community. Initially they served as a part of the commercial foundation of the town. Dry goods houses, churches, banks, hotels, and homes were the necessary building blocks that transformed an outpost into a permanent settlement. The products found there from East Coast cities and beyond maintained a link between the materialistic desires of those west of the Appalachian Mountains and their efforts to identify themselves with the lifestyles associated with urban America. Citizens could assess their economic and social standing within the larger community by where they shopped. The stores themselves were identified with class structure. Fourth St. purchases implied quality and service. Beyond it in any direction indicated an acceptance of less. As the magnet that pulled people downtown long before a significant retail presence existed outside the city limits, they brought thousands of local area residents together in their elevators, their restaurants, along the sidewalks traveled to arrive there, and in the streetcars and buses on which they were transported.

In a variety of ways the stores assumed a subtly distinct southern flavor. Dress codes for women were enforced, and men were expected to wear suits and exhibit the behaviors thus implied. Additionally, for most of the existence of these establishments, African Americans were relegated to service roles. Blacks shopped at stores along Walnut St. (Muhammad Ali Blvd.), which had a thriving African American business district west of Sixth St. With the few exceptions of some of the Jewish-owned businesses, especially along Preston St., that possessed a greater sensitivity to the injustice of racism and the commercial value of serving this market, the majority of the retailers actively participated in maintaining the barriers. As the exterior signs of Jim Crow faded outside the buildings, so too did the restrictions disappear within the stores as managers began to welcome African American shoppers. This courting eventually had an adverse effect on Walnut St. shopping.

Stores consciously cultivated loyalties with color-coded sacks and boxes, recognizable logos, and uniform appearances of the delivery trucks and those who drove them. Pins replaced medals as employees were publicly decorated for years of faithful service. Military veterans were honored with newspaper advertising and bronze plaques in waiting areas. A couple of the menswear specialty stores supplied uniforms to Confederate Civil War veterans. For years following World War I, department store employees and patrons recognized a minute of silence on Armistice Day.

By the late 1960s and early 1970s the downtown shopping trade was disappearing as stores moved to the suburbs. Rather modest shopping centers that had first appeared in the early 1950s around the fringes of the city were soon challenged by expansive malls that began to appear in the early 1960s. Enormous complexes such as Mall St. Matthews (1962), Oxmoor (1971), Bashford Manor (1973), and Jefferson Mall (1978) attracted branches of local favorites such as Stewart's, Kaufman's, and Rodes. They also housed national and regional stores such as Sears, J.C. Penney, Shillito's (Lazarus), Lord and Taylor, and Dillard's. Huge discount stores such as Zayre's, Kmart, Ayr-Way (Target), Woolco, Kohl's, and Wal-Mart, and later mega-stores such as Bigg's and Meijer's eventually doomed five-and-dime variety stores such as Woolworth's and McCrory's, both of which closed their Louisville affiliates in 1997.

Some downtown stores attempted to maintain their customer base by following their patrons to suburban outlets as sales figures in their downtown locations dropped and Fourth St. stores began to close their doors. The process of shopping had subtly switched from a dress-up, day-long event to a casual, quick-trip experience to a nearby shopping center or mall where parking spaces were both plentiful and free. Though downtown continued to witness its morning influx of people, office occupations became the primary reason they commuted. Despite this trend, in 1982 the Galleria shopping center opened on South Fourth St. The building contained, as part of its eastern wall, the exterior facade of the 1903 Kaufman-Straus building.

Gone were the electric neon and brass marquees with the familiar names. Gone were the Christmas parades and window displays. Gone were the odors of food, candy, and popcorn mixed with the smells of warm pavement and exhaust fumes. Gone were the days of the retailing energy that had helped fuel the growth of Louisville. Only two major stores (Rodes and Bacon's) continued to survive in the downtown environment into the 1990s.

See Daniel J. Boorstin, *The Americans: The Democratic Experience* (New York 1973); Bill Bryson, *Made in America* (New York 1994); Ben Casseday, *The History of Louisville* (Louisville 1852); Reuben T. Durrett, *The Centenary of Louisville* (Louisville 1880); Ken Miller, *Stewart's: A Louisville Landmark* (Louisville 1991); George H. Yater, *Two Hundred Years at the Falls of the Ohio* (Louisville 1987).

Kenneth L. Miller

DE PAUW, WASHINGTON C. (b Salem, Indiana, January 4, 1822; d New Albany, Indiana, May 5, 1887). Philanthropist, entrepreneur, Victorian capitalist. De Pauw was a descendant of Huguenots who first came to America with the Marquis de Lafayette in 1776 and was the second son of John and Elizabeth (Battiste) De Pauw. Achieving success as a banker in Salem at an early age, he moved his bank to the thriving river city of New Albany in 1850. Before the Civil War his fortune was estimated at one-quarter of a million dollars; after the war he profited greatly from earlier investments in government bonds and securities.

By 1868 he was a pillar of New Albany society, one of the richest men in Indiana, and financially involved in enterprises totaling over $11 million in annual sales. As the largest holder of capital in New Albany, he helped other businesses to expand, and when the community was hit by the panic of 1873 he saved a number of these budding enterprises and gained control of numerous others. In 1882 it was estimated that his manufacturing enterprises in New Albany alone represented an investment of $2 million.

At the time of his death, his estate was valued at several million dollars, and he owned or held majority control in textile mills, glass works, rolling mills, iron works, three banks, and a utility. His major interest, however, was making a success of the glass works his cousin John B. Ford had started. Eventually he did, taking over the business and establishing efficiencies that reduced the price of American plate glass to 75 cents a foot, as compared to European glass at $2.50 a foot.

A deeply religious man, De Pauw's philanthropies were many; the most noteworthy was saving the financially distressed Indiana Asbury University in Greencastle, Indiana, which was renamed De Pauw University in his honor in 1884. He was married three times—to Sarah Malott, Katharine Newland, and Frances Marion Leyden. He is buried in Fairview Cemetery in New Albany.

See *Dictionary of American Biography* (New York 1974); *History of the Ohio Falls Cities and Their Counties* (Cleveland 1882); Betty Lou Amster, *New Albany on the Ohio* (New Albany, Ind., 1963).

Betty Lou Amster

DERBY-PIE® There are many tales about the name and origins of DERBY-PIE®, but these are the facts. DERBY-PIE®, a chocolate nut pie with a flaky crust and a rich, sweet filling, was created in the 1950s as the specialty pastry of the Melrose Inn in Prospect, Kentucky. The restaurant owners, Walter and Leaudra Kern, with the help of their son George, spent many hours finding a unique blend of ingredients that would produce a classic dessert. However when the perfect recipe was finally achieved, each family member had his or her own idea about the perfect name. So everyone wrote down his or her favorite, and the name DERBY-PIE® was literally pulled from a hat.

In the early 1960s the Kerns sold the restaurant but continued to produce pies for select customers. Then in 1969 they registered the name DERBY-PIE® with the U.S. Patent and Trademark Office and the Commonwealth of Kentucky. Since then the trademark has been continually renewed. DERBY-PIE® is a federally registered trademark on the principal register.

In 1973 the Kerns' grandson, Alan Rupp, took over the family business. When the name "Derby Pie" began showing up in unauthorized cookbooks as a name for pies that were obvious imitations of the original pie, Rupp took legal action to defend the family trademark. In April 1982 a federal judge issued a preliminary injunction against a local cookbook. Unsold copies were returned to the publisher "so that the offending page describing Derby Pie" could be deleted. But in May 1987, the DERBY-PIE® trademark was ruled generic in ongoing litigation with *Bon Appetit* magazine. Kern's Kitchen appealed, and the U.S. Court of Appeals for the Sixth Circuit completely reversed the previous ruling. *Bon Appetit* "failed to introduce scientific survey evidence to support their assertion that the public views 'DERBY-PIE' as generic." Since then Kern's Kitchen has fought several lawsuits against other infringers, and all have been ordered by federal district courts to cease infringing.

For over forty years DERBY-PIE® has been

baked exclusively by Kern's Kitchen. It is sold in Restaurants, Hotels, Kentucky state resort parks, through mail order, and in select retail outlets across the United States. And while most people recognize the real chocolate chips and walnut pieces, no one has ever been able to duplicate the special filling, which remains a family secret.

See *Courier Journal,* May 1, 1989; *Washington Post,* April 28, 1982; *Louisville Times,* May 6, 1972; *Charlotte Observer,* April 5, 1989.

Alan S. Rupp

DIEHL, CONRAD LEWIS (b Neustadt, Germany, August 3, 1840; d Louisville, March 25, 1917). Pharmacist. The son of Conrad and Therese Diehl and the eldest of three children, the family immigrated to America in 1849, having fled politically troubled Europe.

Diehl attended Oakland Academy near St. Louis and graduated in 1862 from the Philadelphia College of Pharmacy. He then enlisted in the Fifteenth Regiment of the Pennsylvania Volunteer Cavalry. Diehl was wounded at the Battle of Stone's River; upon recovery he became assistant chemist in the United States Army Laboratory in Philadelphia until 1865.

Diehl's Louisville connections began when he became manager of the Louisville Chemical Works in July 1865. In 1868 he married Catherine Zimmerman, and in June 1869 he purchased and operated a drugstore at First and Walnut Streets. In 1874 he opened a new store at Third and Broadway.

Diehl's business activities belie his more important contributions to pharmacy in the United States and Kentucky. Beginning in 1873 he served as recording secretary on the progress of pharmacy for the American Pharmaceutical Association (APhA) for nearly forty years. In 1874–75 he served as president of the APhA.

Following Charles Rice (1841–1901), who established the first *National Formulary* in 1888, Diehl chaired the NF Committee during its crucial early years. He founded the Louisville College of Pharmacy (now part of the University of Kentucky) in 1870, serving as president of the college (1870–81) and professor of Pharmacy until 1916. He was instrumental in organizing Kentucky's first statewide Board of Pharmacy in 1874 and remained an active member throughout most of his professional life.

Diehl was survived by his wife and three daughters: Eleanor, Jennie, and Emily. He is buried at Cave Hill Cemetery.

See Michael A. Flannery, "C. Lewis Diehl: Kentucky's Most Notable Pharmacist," *Pharmacy in History* 39 (1997): 101–12; Gordon L. Curry, *Proceedings of the Fourteenth Annual Meeting of the Kentucky Pharmaceutical Association* 14 (1917): 90–95; Joseph P. England, ed., *The First Century of the Philadelphia College of Pharmacy, 1821–1921* (Philadelphia 1922); "Conrad Lewis Diehl 1840–1917," *Journal of the American Pharmaceutical Association* 6 (1917): 423–27; Glenn Sonnedecker, *Kremers and Urdang's History of Pharmacy* (Philadelphia 1976).

Michael A. Flannery

DISTILLING. When Louisville was first settled in 1778, chances are that someone owned a still and made whiskey. This was the era of the farmer/distiller, and whiskey-making was a vital part of the economy. The stills used by these farmer/distillers were small and easily transported down the Ohio River or across the Appalachian Mountains. There were no government registrations of stills or whiskey-making, so there are no official records as to who owned a still. Evan Williams of Louisville is often credited as being Kentucky's first distiller in 1783, but there are several other people who are better candidates for the title of Kentucky's first distiller. It cannot be proved that Evan Williams was Louisville's first distiller.

A typical farmer/distiller owned one or two small copper stills with a capacity of 60 to 120 gallons. The farmer would build a still-house near a limestone water source such as a spring. The iron-free water was important for making good whiskey. The grain used to make the whiskey was produced by the farmer/distiller on his farm. This means that most of the whiskey being made was straight corn whiskey. The "heads" is the first whiskey that comes off the still, and this whiskey was separated from the run to be re-distilled. The "tails" is the last whiskey of the run and was also separated. A good distiller only took the "heart of the run" for beverage purposes. The whiskey was usually distilled a second time to make it a better product, but not everyone did this. Some distillers had other methods of rectifying their whiskey to make it a palatable product. These methods included filtering the new whiskey through charcoal to mellow it or by adding flavoring agents such as wild cherry bark and roots to make a "cherry bounce" liqueur out of the new whiskey. The whiskey was then placed in barrels and sometimes allowed to age before the whiskey was sold.

Farmer/distillers played an important role in the Economy of Louisville. In a specie-starved economy, the whiskey could be used to barter for supplies needed on the farm. The farmer/distiller would also allow his neighbors to make, or would make for them, whiskey with his stills. He would take part of the whiskey as payment for this service. When local merchants accumulated enough whiskey, they would ship it down the Ohio and Mississippi Rivers to New Orleans, where it was sold for hard currency. This currency could then be used to purchase merchandise to be traded for more whiskey from the farmer/distillers.

Under the prodding of Alexander Hamilton, the federal government enacted a tax in 1791 to help reduce the government debt stemming from the American Revolution. This tax led to the first trial of the government's authority—the Whiskey Rebellion. The government required registration of all stills, with a tax on the still's capacity and on the product from the still. The product tax was to be based upon the proof of the whiskey, as measured by a hydrometer. The tax hurt the farmer/distiller who had very little hard currency with which to pay it.

Legend has it that the Whiskey Rebellion drove Pennsylvania distillers into Kentucky, but Kentucky had plenty of distillers before the Whiskey Rebellion. Kentucky was also part of

Advertisement for Sunny Brook distillery.

Hauling distillery waste for animal feed and fertilizer. Stitzel Distillery.

the rebellion. The federal government played down Kentucky's role in the rebellion for two reasons: the government was not sure it could handle the logistics of moving troops over the Appalachian Mountains into Kentucky, and the government also was afraid that a show of force in Kentucky would drive the West into the arms of Spain. The legal maneuvering of Judge Harry Innes spared Kentucky's distillers from government pressure to collect the tax. The lack of strong government action allowed Kentucky to survive the Whiskey Rebellion with little violence. Congress repealed the whiskey tax in 1802, but it was brought back for a short period between 1814 and 1817 to pay government debts from the War of 1812.

The first attempt at large-scale whiskey production in Louisville came from the Hope Distillery which was built about Fifteenth St. and Portland Ave. in 1817 by New England investors. This large scale pot still distillery could make twelve hundred gallons per day. This first attempt at large-scale production failed within three years, and the distillery buildings were turned to other uses.

Louisville became an important center for Kentucky's distilling industry in the early part of the nineteenth century. America's oldest surviving spirits company, W.L. Weller and Sons (1849), dates from this period. Louisville became the home of spirits merchants or rectifiers. They would buy whiskey from the small farmer/distillers and rectify the whiskey by blending or adding other substances to it. The respectable rectifiers would simply blend the whiskeys produced by several distillers until they had a taste profile that they could sell. Less reputable rectifiers would add anything from caramelized sugar to sulfuric acid.

As Louisville's distilleries became more important, the farmer/distiller declined. The railroad and the steamboat allowed for grain to be shipped at low cost from the surrounding country, thus allowing cities to support larger distilleries. The finished product also could be shipped to distant markets. Most whiskey sold in the nineteenth century was sold by the barrel to saloons or drugstores. The consumers would bring in their own jugs or bottles to be filled. The term "brand name" comes from this period because of the name of the whiskey branded into the barrel head.

The invention of the column still in the 1830s also hurt the farmer/distiller. This device is a continuous still that allows the production of a large amount of alcohol at a reduced cost. It was also a very large and expensive piece of equipment—four stories tall and made of copper. The column still, combined with the railroad and Steamboats, allowed large-scale distilleries to succeed in Louisville in the late 1860s.

The final factor that spelled an end to the farmer/distiller was the Civil War and the renewed liquor tax. The tax was collected as soon as the spirit came off the still. Since whiskey must be aged before it can be sold, this created a financial burden that could only be met by distillers with the money to pay this tax before the whiskey was sold.

The period following the Civil War was a golden age for Louisville's distilling industry. Louisville was the bourbon capital of the world. Main St. near the wharf became known as "whiskey row" because of the number of distillers' and rectifiers' offices located there. Even if a distillery was located in another county, chances are it had an office in Louisville and shipped its whiskey to market from the city. Many new and larger distilleries were built after the war. Most were located either in the neighborhood of Twenty-sixth and Broadway or in the East End near Beargrass Creek. These distilleries drilled deep wells that supplied them with the limestone water needed to make good bourbon. Grain brought to the city by the Railroads supplied the huge demand of these distilleries.

The Louisville distilling industry of the late 1800s was responsible for two important innovations. The first change came from George Garvin Brown. George Garvin and his brother J.T.S. Brown founded a company called J.T.S. Brown and Bro. in 1870. This wholesale spirits company created the Old Forester brand of whiskey. Whiskey was one of the few medicines available to doctors and was prescribed for many ailments. Doctors were complaining because the quality of the whiskey was not always the same from one week to the next.

Brown decided to create a market by selling Old Forester only in bottles, so that doctors would know that the quality would always be the same. There had been bottled whiskeys sold for over fifty years, mostly by grocers who bottled their own brands from bulk whiskey purchased from distillers, but Old Forester was the first brand to be sold by a wholesale company only by the bottle and not in bulk lots by the barrel. This started a trend that eventually led to the Bottled-in-Bond Act of 1897.

The next innovation came from Fredrick Stitzel of Stitzel Bros. Distillery. He saw problems with the way barrels of whiskey were being stored in warehouses for aging. The barrels were stacked on top of each other, and the pressure caused the bottom barrels to leak or burst. He patented a system of racks that not only allowed barrels to be stored individually but also improved the air circulation in the warehouse, thus eliminating a lot of musty whiskey. This system of barrel-racking quickly became standard in all whiskey warehouses.

The end of the nineteenth century saw the growth of the Prohibition movement. This movement climaxed in 1920 when national Prohibition began. Louisville quickly became a center for the legal trade in "medicinal spirits." Four of the six companies allowed to sell medicinal spirits were based in Louisville: Brown-Forman, Frankfort Distilleries, Glenmore Distilling Co., and W.L. Weller and Sons. The other two companies, American Medicinal Spirits Co. (later National Distillers) and Schenley Distillers Corp., were based in New York City. There were only four legal markets for alcohol during Prohibition. One was wine sold to churches for sacramental purposes. Physicians and dentists could buy twelve pints of distilled spirits a year for office use. Bakers could buy twelve pints of brandy or rum a year for cooking. A PHARMACY could buy alcohol to fill prescriptions. This was the largest market. In 1928 the government allowed these medicinal spirits companies to replenish their dwindling stocks of whiskey through limited production. A Louisville distillery, A. Ph. Stitzel Co., which had close ties with W.L. Weller and Sons, made the whiskey for Weller, Brown-Forman, and Frankfort Distilleries.

When Prohibition ended in December 1933, there was an explosion of growth in the distilled spirits industry in Jefferson County, mostly in the southwest. In the area that was to become the incorporated community of SHIVELY, there were seven distilleries built before 1940: Glencoe, STITZEL-WELLER, Seagram, Hill and Hill, OLD KENTUCKY, Four Roses, and TAYLOR AND WILLIAMS. Distilleries in the city included Old Sunnybrook at Twenty-sixth and Broadway, Bonnie Bros. in Portland, BERNHEIM at Seventeenth and Breckinridge, A. Ph. Stitzel on Story Ave., and Old Grand Dad at Lexington Rd. and Payne St. At the urging of several local distilleries—which included Stitzel-Weller, Brown-Forman, Frankfort, National, Yellowstone, Schenley, and Joseph E. Seagram and Sons Inc.—who wished to avoid Louisville taxes, Shively decided to seek incorporation in 1938. The city annexed the eager distilleries and increased its tax base by approximately $20 million.

During WORLD WAR II, distilleries were forced to convert all their production facilities to the distillation of 190-proof alcohol for the war effort. In June 1942, conversion of the Louisville distilleries was complete, and, except for one three-month period in 1943, only industrial alcohol was commercially produced in Louisville until 1945. From 1942 to 1945, Kentucky distillers had provided nearly one-third of all high-proof alcohol made.

Industrial alcohol had many vital uses for military production. Although antifreeze, plastics, and smokeless ammunition needed 190-proof alcohol in their production, the most strategic use of industrial alcohol was in the manufacture of synthetic rubber. Since Louisville's West End and Shively had such a large concentration of distilleries and were located near the Ohio River, the military built a butadiene and synthetic rubber manufacturing center in the west end of the city. The plant's close proximity allowed Louisville distillers to feed their entire industrial alcohol production directly into a central plant. Louisville became known as a rubber manufacturing center, or RUBBERTOWN, when other distillers in the Midwest also shipped their alcohol to the West End facility.

Changes in AGRICULTURE in the period following World War II changed the local impact the distilleries had on the economy. Hybrid grains were imported from the Midwest, and less local grain was bought for distilling bourbon.

The economic Depression of the 1930s and World War II had taken a toll on distilleries. In the 1930s giant industries absorbed small distilleries that could not operate because of economic difficulties. The industry consolidated as stronger companies acquired the weaker distilleries and brands. By the 1950s, SEAGRAM'S acquired Frankfort Distilleries and the Four Roses brand. National Distillers had Old Grand Dad, Old Sunnybrook, Hill and Hill, and Glencoe properties. Schenley owned Bernheim and Bonnie Bros., and Glenmore acquired Taylor and Williams. Brown-Forman bought the Old Kentucky distillery and changed its name to EARLY TIMES. As bourbon sales started to decline in the 1960s, consolidation continued. In the 1970s more distilleries were simply closed and the production of their brands moved to new sites. By the end of the 1980s there were only three sites in Jefferson County where whiskey was aging. These were the Stitzel-Weller and Early Times distilleries in Shively and the Bernheim Distillery in Louisville. In 1999 the Bernheim Distillery was sold to Heaven Hill Distilleries Inc.

In the 1980s and 1990s, consumption of bourbon continued to decline, forcing distillers to diversify or find new markets. Products such as vodka and tequila took their share of the bourbon market. Some distillers began to diversify by acquiring and selling California, Italian, and French wines and champagnes. A market has developed for premium, aged small-batch, and single barrel brands of specialty bourbons. There is a steady growth of markets in foreign markets such as Japan and Eastern Europe. In addition new ADVERTISING strategies began to take place. The industry took a fresh look at advertising on TELEVISION, where it has to compete with beer and wine manufacturers for a bigger share of the domestic market. Distillers began to focus on younger customers. As consumption of bourbon declined, Brown-Forman diversified into the new area of consumer durables. Lenox China and Crystal, Dansk casual and contemporary tableware, and Hartmann Luggage and Business Cases became an essential part of the corporation's product line.

Fine American Whiskies (Shelburne, Vt., 1995); Henry Crowgey, *Kentucky Bourbon* (Lexington 1971); John Ed Pearce, *Nothing Better in the Market* (Louisville 1970); Aaron D. Purcell, "Bourbon to Bullets: Louisville's Distillery Industry during World War II, 1941-1945," *The Register of the Kentukcy Historical Society* 96 (Winter 1998): 61-87; *Courier-Journal*, Feb. 25, 1999.

Michael R. Veach

DIXIE HIGHWAY. Louisville's Dixie Hwy. is a stretch of U.S. 31W running 18.8 miles from BROADWAY on the north through southwestern Jefferson County to the SALT RIVER Bridge in West Point at the Hardin County line. It starts as an urban street, turning into a suburban artery traveling south-southwest through the heart of SHIVELY, PLEASURE RIDGE PARK, VALLEY STATION, and KOSMOSDALE, before becoming a rural highway in the very tip of Jefferson County and then continuing to FORT KNOX and Nashville.

The stretch of Dixie Hwy. in Jefferson County is part of a much larger and more elaborate highway system that extends from Sault Sainte Marie, Michigan, to Miami, Florida, covering 3,989 miles of paved roads. It was constructed between 1915 and 1927 under the supervision of the Dixie Highway Association (DHA), which was composed principally of the new motor clubs, entrepreneurs, and others interested in the growing potential of the automobile for industry and transportation in the South. The idea for the highway system came from Carl Graham Fisher of Indianapolis, a manufacturer of battery-powered automobile headlights and one of the organizers of the Indianapolis Speedway. Fisher, along with Indiana native William S. Gilbreath, helped to gather support among area governors, businessmen, and car enthusiasts.

At a May 1915 meeting of the DHA, after a heated debate among members of the route selection committee, it was decided to build both an eastern and western branch of the highway. The western route runs through Louisville and Nashville, and the eastern route through Cincinnati and Knoxville, reflecting the powerful lobbying interests of the four cities at the meeting. There are also east-west connections throughout the route, notably between Indianapolis and Dayton, Ohio; Augusta and Atlanta in Georgia; and between Jacksonville and Tallahassee in Florida. The DHA disbanded in 1927 after the highway was completed. The several connections, with another joining Chicago to Indianapolis, bring the total miles to 5,706.

In Louisville, parts of the old LOUISVILLE AND NASHVILLE TURNPIKE were used in the construction of the Dixie Hwy. in the early 1920s. In 1924 a Louisville chapter of the DHA was formed to put pressure on the state Highway Commission to fund construction and maintenance of the road from Louisville to the Tennessee border. The LOUISVILLE AUTOMOBILE CLUB, the local affiliate of the American Automobile Association (AAA), and a variety of area merchant associations were also instrumental in supporting early construction and maintenance efforts.

In the 1950s the WATTERSON EXPRESSWAY (I-264) was connected to Dixie Hwy. in Shively. Their place of merger is one of the highest traffic areas in the county. In 1987 the GENE SNYDER FREEWAY (I-265), which runs from U.S. 42 in east Jefferson County, ended at the Dixie Hwy. just south of Valley Station.

Since the 1930s Dixie Hwy. in Jefferson County has been one of the state's most dangerous roads, earning it the title "the Dixie Dieway." A May 1969 article in *Life* magazine named it one of the nation's "deadliest highways." Traffic fatalities in the 1950s led to a lowering of the speed limit from sixty to fifty along the southern part of the highway. The speed limit is even lower inside the city limits. Annual fatalities peaked in 1951 and 1952 with nineteen each. As late as 1997 Dixie Hwy. was named the second-most-dangerous highway in Kentucky behind U.S. 27 in Garrard, Jessamine, Fayette, and Bourbon Counties. Between 1990 and July 1996, Dixie Hwy. in Kentucky had sixty-five fatalities, sixteen of them pedestrians.

Over the years there have been numerous renovations, expansions, and drivers' education programs undertaken to ease the congestion and lower the number of traffic accidents. Some of these included expanding the southern stretch beyond Watterson Expressway to six lanes, adding traffic lights and turning lanes to make it easier to enter and exit, and creating a state-sponsored program to post "Drive Smart" signs along the highway.

Many of the accidents over the years were a result of drivers crossing over into oncoming traffic. There have also been a number of pedestrians killed over the years after dark, with driver and/or pedestrian frequently intoxicated. The Dixie Hwy. reflects an example of a commercial strip that has developed without planning and contains an almost endless stream of service stations, RESTAURANTS, BARS, motels, shopping areas, strip clubs, billboards, and neon signs.

See Howard L. Preston, *Dirt Roads to Dixie: Accessibility and Modernization in the South, 1885–1935* (Knoxville, Tenn., 1991); *Courier-Journal*, June 14, 1970.

DODD, WILLIAM JAMES (b Chicago, September 21, 1862; d Los Angeles, June 14, 1930). Architect. Little is known of Dodd's early life and education, but he is thought to have worked in Chicago as a draftsman for William Lebaron Jenney and later for Solon S. Beman, where he designed buildings for the new town of Pullman. He came to Louisville in 1884 and worked alone or in partnership with other architects until moving to Los Angeles in 1913. He was associated with C.C. Wehle from 1887 until joining MASON MAURY in 1889. Maury and Dodd's most notable work was the LOUISVILLE TRUST CO. (now the First Trust Centre) completed in 1891 at Fifth and MARKET STREETS.

About 1896 Dodd formed a partnership with Arthur Cobb, an engineer who came from Cleveland to Louisville in 1889. Dodd is generally considered the design person in this practice. Associates until 1904, Dodd and Cobb designed the FOURTH AVENUE METHODIST CHURCH (1900) at Fourth and St. Catherine Streets, Samuel Grabfelder house (1897) on Third between Magnolia and Burnett Ave., the Atherton Building (1901–2, razed 1980) at Fourth and Muhammad Ali Blvd., the Masonic Temple/Strand Theatre (1900–2, razed in 1955) on Chestnut between Third and FOURTH STREETS, LOUISVILLE PRESBYTERIAN SEMINARY (now JEFFERSON COMMUNITY COLLEGE, 1902) at Second Street and BROADWAY, and the Edwin H. Ferguson house (now the FILSON CLUB HISTORICAL SOCIETY, 1901–4) on Third St. Dodd is also credited with designing ST. PAUL'S EPISCOPAL CHURCH (1895–97) during this period, and he worked with Frank Andrews on the SEELBACH HOTEL (1905).

In 1906 Dodd and KENNETH MCDONALD became partners and practiced together until 1913. Described as the leading ARCHITECTURAL FIRM in Louisville during those years, McDonald and Dodd designed some of the city's outstanding commercial and institutional buildings and residences. These included the Lincoln Building (ca. 1906, razed 1973) on Market St., Atherton Building/Mary Anderson Theatre (1906) on Fourth between Chestnut St. and Broadway, Western Branch Library (1907–8) at Chestnut and Tenth Streets, FIRST CHRISTIAN CHURCH (1910–11) at Fourth and Breckinridge Streets, the YMCA building at Third St. and Broadway (1912–13), Citizens National Life Insurance Building in ANCHORAGE (1911), and the Louisville Country Club (1909–10). Notable residential commissions included the John Caperton house, "Rio Vista" (1911–12, razed); Alfred Brandeis house (1912); Louis Seelbach house (1910–12); and Lincliff, the William R. Belknap house (1911). In 1913 McDonald and Dodd dissolved their firm, and Dodd moved to Los Angeles. There he practiced with William Richards until his death in 1930.

See Marty Lyn Poynter Hedgepeth, "The Victorian to the Beaux Arts, A Study of Four Louisville Architectural Firms: McDonald Bros., McDonald and Sheblessy, Dodd and Cobb, and McDonald and Dodd," M.A. thesis, University of Louisville, 1981; Henry F. Withey and Elsie Rathburn Withey, *Biographical Dictionary of American Architects, Deceased* (Los Angeles 1956).

Mary Jean Kinsman

DOERR, J. HENRY (b Gaumbach, Germany, March 12, 1847; d Louisville, February 18, 1906). Photographer. At the age of five, Doerr immigrated to the United States with his parents. After briefly settling in New York City, the family moved to Louisville, where Doerr was educated.

At the age of fourteen he began to study photography with EDWARD KLAUBER, eventually opening his own business. During the CIVIL WAR, Doerr followed the federal army, taking photographs. At the war's end, he briefly settled in JEFFERSONVILLE, Indiana, but returned to Louisville, where he opened a photography business on Market St. He organized the Kentucky and Tennessee Photographer's Association and was a member of the LOUISVILLE BOARD OF TRADE.

In 1895 Doerr was authorized to make the first set of photographs of CAVE HILL CEMETERY. His images, showing driving alleys set off by raised curbs, reveal the transformation of Cave Hill's farm fields into a landscape that increasingly paralleled the city. Embedded in the curbs were lot and section numbers, markers like street addresses.

Self portrait of photographer J. Henry Doerr, whose studio was at Twelfth and Market Streets.

In 1904 Doerr invested in an abandoned gold mine outside Cripple Creek, Colorado. The following year he sank a shaft and worked it for four weeks. He struck a vein of gold and sold his claim for two hundred thousand dollars. Returning to Louisville, Doerr retired from photography. He died after contracting pneumonia on a winter visit to the mine and is buried at Cave Hill Cemetery.

When Doerr was quite young, he wed Jennie Pope, who died three months later. For many years he lived with his widowed mother, Katherine Doerr. On January 16, 1902, he married Mrs. Christina Cawein, the widow of Dr. William Cawein, and adopted her daughter, Lillian. He was a stepfather to her other children, William, John, Charles, and MADISON CAWEIN, a noted poet.

See Samuel W. Thomas, *Cave Hill Cemetery* (Louisville 1985).

DOLFINGER'S. German immigrant Jacob Dolfinger began his business career in Louisville around 1851 as a gold and silversmith. Seven years later he established his own business as a jewelry and silverware manufacturer on FOURTH ST. between Market and Jefferson Streets. However in 1862 under the name of J. Dolfinger and Co., the business moved farther down Fourth St., under Wood's Theater, and began specializing in the sale of china and fine giftware. As the business grew, the need for bigger accommodations did also.

Over the years Dolfinger's was located at 316 W Market, Fourth and Walnut (Muhammad Ali Blvd.), the HEYBURN BUILDING, and, in 1932, at 325 W Walnut St. That same year

Dolfinger retired as president, and in 1933 he died. In 1934 the business was sold to its president, Jerome Kopp, who ran the firm for thirteen years before selling it to John Laird in 1947. In the mid-1950s, Dolfinger's opened its first branch store at 3938 Frankfort Ave. and, in 1955, its second branch store in the Gardiner Lane Shopping Center on Bardstown Rd.

Dolfinger's continued to expand until the 1980s, when it encountered financial difficulties. Under its fourth owner, William Steiden, who had acquired the business in 1977, the firm declared bankruptcy in 1983, and the company's five Louisville stores were closed as well as those in CLARKSVILLE, INDIANA; Owensboro; and Lexington. That same year, William B. Bellis Sr. bought the troubled business and consolidated it into one store at 4201 Shelbyville Rd. Dolfinger's quickly rebounded and, in 1989, was sold again to the firm's president, William Hamman. Dolfinger's moved once again to Lexington Rd. in the early 1990s. It opened a sister store next door at 3738 Lexington Rd. known as Butler's Barrow, specializing in the sale of casual and contemporary housewares and giftware. In 1997 Butler's Barrow closed, and Dolfinger's moved to the Forum Center on Hurstbourne Pkwy.

See *Courier-Journal*, April 17, 1983; *Louisville*, June 20, 1957.

DORRIS, MICHAEL ANTHONY (b Louisville, January 30, 1945; d Concord, New Hampshire, April 10–11(?), 1997). Author, educator, advocate. Dorris was the only child of Jim Leonard and Mary Besy (Burkhardt) Dorris; on his father's side he was part American Indian (Modoc tribe). After local primary and secondary schooling, he majored in English and classics at Georgetown University, Washington, D.C., graduating in 1967. Inspired by his Native American heritage, he studied anthropology at Yale, from which he received a Master of Philosophy degree in 1970.

The following year, Dorris became one of the first single men in America to adopt a child, a three-year-old Sioux boy named Abel. He later discovered that his son, who had developmental disabilities, suffered from fetal alcohol syndrome (FAS), a result of his birth mother's excessive drinking during pregnancy. Dorris chronicled the story of his son (under the name Adam) in *The Broken Cord* (1989), which won the National Book Critics Circle Award, among other honors, and in 1992 was filmed for TELEVISION.

That work, complemented by Dorris's testimony before Congress, helped lead to labels on alcoholic beverages and signs in bars warning pregnant women not to drink. Abel was struck by a car and died at the age of twenty-three. While still single, Dorris adopted two more children of Indian descent, Sava and Madeline, both of whom had fetal alcohol effect, a subtler form of FAS.

In 1972 Dorris founded the Native American Studies Program at Dartmouth College, where he taught until 1989. In 1981, he married Louise Erdrich, a poet of German and Turtle Mountain Chippewa heritage, whom he had first known casually as a student at Dartmouth. Erdrich adopted his three children, and the couple also had three daughters—Persia, Pallas, and Aza.

Dorris's numerous publications include novels for adults (*Cloud Chamber* [1997] takes place largely in Louisville) and for children, a book of short stories, a collection of essays, and nonfiction volumes on Indians and on refugees in Zimbabwe. He collaborated with Erdrich, also an author, on magazine fiction under their pseudonym Milou North; on a travel memoir; and on a novel. He had other works in varying stages of completion, or under contract, when he died.

Dorris committed suicide in a motel in Concord, New Hampshire. He and Erdrich were separated and in the midst of divorce proceedings. Michael Dorris is buried in Cornish, New Hampshire.

See L. Elisabeth Beattie, ed., *Conversations with Kentucky Writers* (Lexington 1996); *Contemporary Authors*, new revision series, vol. 46 (1995); *Washington Post*, July 13, 1997; *New York Magazine*, June 16, 1997: 30–37; *Courier-Journal*, April 27, 1997; *New York Times*, April 15, 1997.

John Spalding Gatton

DOSKER, HENRY ELIAS (b Bunschoten, Netherlands, February 5, 1855; d Louisville, December 23, 1926). Minister and educator. In 1869 Nicholas Dosker and his family emigrated from the Netherlands to America. A friend and fellow minister in Grand Rapids, Michigan, had invited the family to take his place upon his retirement at Central Reformed Church.

Henry Dosker attended Hope College in Holland, Michigan, where he received an A.B. degree in 1876 and an A.M. in 1879 and was known as one of the college's most distinguished alumni. In 1879 he graduated from McCormick Presbyterian Seminary in Chicago. After graduating from the seminary, Dosker served as minister at churches in Ebenezer and Grand Haven, Michigan. His first wife passed away a few months after they married. Returning to Holland, Michigan, he taught church history at the Western Theological Seminary. In 1882 he married the cousin of his first wife, Wilhelmina Doornink, and they had two daughters and three sons. Raised in the Dutch Reformed church, he later joined the Presbyterian church. In 1894 he received a Doctor of Divinity degree from Rutgers University. He received an LL.D. from Central Kentucky University at Richmond in 1905.

Dosker came to Louisville in 1903 and served as professor of church history at the LOUISVILLE PRESBYTERIAN THEOLOGICAL SEMINARY. Throughout his career, Dosker was one of the most distinguished church historians of his era. He often contributed to such works as Louisville's *Christian Observer* and other religious journals. His writings included *Outline Studies in Church History* (1913), *De Zondagschool* (1882), and *Life of Doctor A.C. Van Raalte* (1893), as well as many articles and reviews.

Funeral services for Dosker were held at Louisville Presbyterian Theological Seminary and at Warren Memorial Presbyterian Church. His body was then returned home for burial services at Central Reformed Church in Grand Rapids, Michigan, where he is buried where his father had first preached.

Alwin Seekamp and Roger Burlingame, eds., *Who's Who in Louisville* (Louisville 1912).

DOUGLAS PARK RACE COURSE. Douglas Park Race Course opened in 1895, coinciding with the GRAND ARMY OF THE REPUBLIC convention in September that same year. Developed by James Douglas, the track, located south of Louisville in the BEECHMONT suburbs where Southside Dr. joins Second St., originally was built as a trotting track. In its heyday, Douglas Park had a grandstand and clubhouse and became a popular source of entertainment. The track closed from 1906 to 1912. In 1913 the property was renovated and the venue changed to Thoroughbred racing. In 1918 the owners merged their interests with CHURCHILL DOWNS, and Douglas Park ceased to function as a racetrack. The Kentucky Jockey Club became the owner of the property and used the track as a place to exercise horses and to stable Thoroughbreds that could not be accommodated at Churchill Downs. Although the track itself remained, the grandstand and clubhouse deteriorated until finally in 1939 they were torn down. Fires in 1945 and 1951 damaged several of the horse barns. A fire on October 26, 1952, completely destroyed the largest horse barn, killing sixty-eight horses. Churchill Downs, which had again acquired the property, began selling parcels of land beginning in 1954. Eventually it became tracts for light industry, a church, a school, and housing. Stately brick columns leading to the HOLY ROSARY ACADEMY are all that remain of the old racecourse.

See Lyons Local History Series, vol. 11, *Southern Parkway and Adjacent Communities*, University Archives and Records Center, University of Louisville; *Courier-Journal*, Oct. 27, 1952.

Margaret Merrick

DOUGLASS BOULEVARD CHRISTIAN CHURCH. Founded in 1846 and originally known as the Second Christian Church, the Douglass Boulevard congregation began as a mission of Louisville's FIRST CHRISTIAN CHURCH. The new congregation first occupied a facility on Hancock St. east of downtown. Within months, the church had out-

Douglas Park Race Track on Douglas Avenue, east of First Street in the Beechmont neighborhood.

grown that structure and moved to PRESTON ST. By 1850 a third move had returned the congregation to a new building on Hancock St.

In 1864, as a result of their continuing growth, the congregation moved again. This time, to reflect the church's new location, they changed the name to the Floyd and Chestnut Streets Church of Christ. (During the nineteenth century, it was not uncommon for churches within the Campbellite movement that sought a return to simple New Testament Christianity to use the names Disciples of Christ, Christian Church, and CHURCH OF CHRIST interchangeably.) In 1865 Disciples founder Alexander Campbell visited Louisville and preached at the Floyd and Chestnut Streets church. During this period, the church was also active in founding several other Disciples congregations in the city, such as the Campbell Street Christian Church, Portland Avenue Church of Christ, Third Christian Church, and the Highland Park Christian Church.

In 1891 the church again changed both its name and location and became the Broadway Christian Church (on BROADWAY between Floyd and Preston Streets). On the move again, in 1939 the church relocated to 2005 Douglass Blvd. and renamed itself the Douglass Boulevard Christian Church.

Local ecumenical activity has characterized much of the life of the church since the late 1970s. Douglass Boulevard, along with St. Paul United Methodist Church and St. Francis of Assisi Catholic Church, have for several years held joint worship services and engaged in official dialogue, both theological and practical, in order to promote greater understanding among Christians of various denominations.

See Vicky Fuqua, *Douglass Boulevard Christian Church: 150 Years of Building a Future* (Louisville 1997); *Courier-Journal,* Oct. 16, 1991.

DOUGLASS HILLS. Douglass Hills is a residential city adjoining MIDDLETOWN in eastern Jefferson County. It is located in an area roughly bounded by Shelbyville Rd. to the north, Watterson Trail to the east and south, and Moser Rd. to the west. The city is surrounded by Middletown on its east, JEFFERSONTOWN to the south, and Plainview to the west.

One of the region's earliest settlers was John Womack, who married Sarah Boone Bryan in 1813 and built an elegant brick house at what was then the west end of Middletown. He helped organize the Middletown Christian Church in 1836 and was its first elder. After his death in 1859, his family lived on the estate for several years. The house and several of the outbuildings were standing as late as the 1970s, although the house was partly burned during the CIVIL WAR. The Womack property was later owned by Nicholas Finzer, a Swiss immigrant and Louisville TOBACCO merchant who established it as a stock farm. His widow, Agnes E. Finzer, sold the three-hundred-acre estate to Col. James J. Douglas, who moved there in 1896 and lived in elegant style until his death in 1917. Douglas, an ardent racing patron, raised many fine horses on the estate known as Douglas Place. Douglas also built a stone waiting shelter named Douglas station on Shelbyville Rd. along the INTERURBAN LINE to Louisville. He was the founder of DOUGLAS PARK, a racecourse opened in 1895 in Louisville.

After Douglas's ownership, the property passed through several hands until the house was demolished and the farmland developed into a residential subdivision in the early 1970s. The subdivision, named Douglass Hills, was incorporated as a sixth-class city in 1973 and was upgraded to fourth-class in 1976. The population of the city was 4,384 in 1980, 5,431 in 1990, and 5,195 in 1996.

See Edith Wood, *Middletown's Days and Deeds: The Story of 150 Years of Living in an Old Kentucky Town* (Middletown, Ky., 1946).

James G. Strohmaier

DOWNTOWN DEVELOPMENT. Louisville's founding and its first one hundred years of growth were tied to the river. The OHIO RIVER was a willing path for westward expansion, and Louisville was to be an important milepost. The river was the primary source of transportation and commerce; correspondingly, physical growth followed the river.

The 1791 plan of Louisville, which ABRAHAM HITE copied from WILLIAM POPE'S "original plan" of the city done in 1783, showed a simple grid pattern on an east/west axis with the river. Three ninety-foot-wide streets—MAIN, MARKET, and Jefferson—ran east/west, parallel to the river, and were followed by sixty-foot-wide Green (now LIBERTY) ST. Numbered streets, also with a width of sixty feet, ran north/south perpendicular to the Ohio. Commercial activity was concentrated close to the water's edge on Main St.

By 1830 Louisville, with a population over ten thousand, was Kentucky's largest city. The onset of the steamboat era, the opening of the LOUISVILLE AND PORTLAND CANAL, and the founding of banks and manufacturing signaled a period of rapid physical and commercial expansion. Downtown and Louisville's boundaries stretched southward to Prather St. (now BROADWAY), eastward to BEARGRASS CREEK, and westward to Twelfth St. Yet even with this fast-paced growth, the city and downtown were a compact unit of two- to three-story buildings where people lived and worked in close proximity. Main and Market Streets remained the heart of the city, the center of activity.

With the founding of the LOUISVILLE & NASHVILLE RAILROAD and completion of the FOURTEENTH STREET BRIDGE across the Ohio River to Indiana in 1870, Louisville gained an important role in the national railroad network. Technological innovations in transportation and building methods were changing the look and sense of downtown. The city center was a bustling place to live and work, but the orientation of the city was changing. Increased mobility and immigration spurred expansion, pushing development outward to the west to the RUSSELL neighborhood, south to what was to become OLD LOUISVILLE, east to PHOENIX HILL and the HIGHLANDS, and southeast to GERMANTOWN. With the rise of RAILROADS, the river—and in turn Main and Market Streets—began to lose importance as commercial and transportation lifelines.

As the turn of the century approached, Louisville continued to be engulfed in change. The rate of technological change in the mid- to late 1800s had not slowed. Exciting building methods and early efforts at city planning were making a profound imprint on the cityscape. During the 1890s Louisville saw its first "skyscraper," the COLUMBIA BUILDING at the northwest corner of Fourth and Main, and witnessed the birth of one of the city's dearest possessions—a park and parkway system designed by the firm of Frederick Law OLMSTED. With development of the STREETCAR and park system, the city experienced the emergence of its first true suburbs. Development followed the streetcar lines east along Frankfort Ave. to CRESCENT HILL, up Broadway to the Highlands, and south along Second and Fourth Streets to Old Louisville and the South End. The city fathers and Olmsted combined good access and scenic beauty along a parkway system to create luxurious new neighborhoods.

The movement at the city's edges was mirrored by the shift in the downtown activity center from Main St. south along Fourth St., a movement that began shortly after the CIVIL WAR. For the first quarter of the twentieth century, Louisville continued the expansion that had typified the late 1800s. Like the rest of America, Louisville experienced a surge of growth following WORLD WAR I. The city was growing, industry was thriving, and advances in auto, air, and public transit services were nurturing an increasingly mobile population. During this period of growth and success, two changes in particular had the most significant effect on the look and feel of the center city—one immediate and the other a more gradual transformation. First the Municipal Bridge (now Clark Memorial) opened in 1929, forming the first vehicular link across the Ohio River in the downtown area. Second, by the 1920s the intersection of Fourth St. and Broadway, which the *Herald Post* called the "magic corner," had become the heart of the city. With movement of the city's activity center south from Fourth and Main Streets to Fourth and Broadway, downtown—literally and figuratively—was turning away from its historical and commercial links to the Ohio River.

The growth and prosperity of the early 1920s was halted with the GREAT DEPRESSION. Recovery from the economic downturn was slow, and for impoverished residential neighborhoods flanking the Fourth Ave. core, the 1940s and 1950s brought no sign of recovery. The city's overall economy was boosted by the pre– and post–WORLD WAR II production periods, yet these benefits were felt mainly outside the central business district.

Suburbanization was taking hold. Grandiose expressway and interstate highway plans of the 1940s, 1950s, and 1960s were envisioned to bring throngs of shoppers and businesses to downtown. They did just the opposite, drawing businesses, shoppers, and residents away. These roads imposed an additional liability on downtown: they served to divide—and at points sever—the central business district. The route of Interstate 65 through downtown was debated for almost nine years. But when finally completed in 1963, it separated the Medical Center from the downtown and cut in half many traditional NEIGHBORHOODS.

The decades of the 1950s through the 1970s saw numerous reactions to the physical and economic decline of the inner city and to the changing retail and financial role of downtown relative to suburban growth. In the 1960s Louisville—like most American cities—utilized URBAN RENEWAL as a tool to revitalize or "suburbanize" the inner city. Although many of downtown's historic resources were lost to urban renewal, a good deal was gained through the process as well. The HISTORIC PRESERVATION movement emerged in the early 1970s, both as a reaction to urban renewal and as a recognition of the built environment as an important resource. At the same time, public and private sectors joined forces to coordinate efforts to rejuvenate downtown. Civic and business leaders cooperated with the government to help revitalize downtown. The Hyatt Regency Hotel, the GALLERIA, the reopened SEELBACH and BROWN Hotels, and Theatre Square are a few examples of such cooperative efforts. The RIVERFRONT PLAZA/BELVEDERE; First National Tower; the KENTUCKY CENTER FOR THE ARTS; rehabilitation in the 600, 700, and 800 blocks of W Main St.; and the HUMANA Building provide a glimpse of the future and of the past, including Louisville returning to Main St. and the river. Activity and interest on the riverfront and Main St. are both exciting and historically familiar.

See Samuel W. Thomas, *Views of Louisville since 1766* (Louisville 1971); George H. Yater, *Two Hundred Years at the Falls of the Ohio* (Louisville 1979).

Patricia A. Clare

DRAKE, DANIEL (b near Bound Brook, New Jersey, October 20, 1785; d Cincinnati, Ohio, November 5, 1852). Physician. Daniel was the son of Isaac and Elizabeth (Shotwell) Drake. In 1788 his family moved to Mays Lick, Kentucky, and in 1800 his father apprenticed him to a physician in Cincinnati, Dr. William Goforth. In 1805–6 Drake studied medicine at the University of Pennsylvania in Philadelphia, where he became a student and friend of the noted American physician Benjamin Rush. He practiced medicine for a year in Mays Lick before assuming the Cincinnati practice of Dr. Goforth in 1807. He completed his medical degree at the University of Pennsylvania in 1815–16.

Returning to Cincinnati, Drake proved instrumental in the founding of the Medical College of Ohio (now the University of Cincinnati College of Medicine) in 1819, the Commercial Hospital and Lunatic Asylum (now The University Hospital) in 1820–21, and the *Western Medical and Physical Journal* in 1827. Drake's renown led to academic appointments elsewhere, but he always returned to his Cincinnati home. He was a professor in the medical department of Transylvania University in Lexington during 1817–18 and 1823–27. In Lexington, he was befriended by Henry Clay. In 1830 Drake served as a professor at the Jefferson Medical College in Philadelphia. In 1835, he spearheaded the establishment of a medical department at Cincinnati College, an institution that he had helped to found in 1819. The medical department closed in 1839, prompting his move to Louisville.

In 1839 Drake accepted a position as professor of clinical medicine and pathological anatomy at the LOUISVILLE MEDICAL INSTITUTE (now the School of Medicine of the UNIVERSITY OF LOUISVILLE). In 1841 he organized the Physiological Temperance Society of the Louisville Medical Institute, and in 1841–42 he delivered a series of lectures detailing methods to teach the blind and challenging his audience to establish a school for them. Drake's suggestions reached fruition in the 1842 establishment of the KENTUCKY SCHOOL FOR THE BLIND in Louisville.

At Louisville, Drake and other colleagues edited the *Western Journal of Medicine and Surgery* (1840–49). During academic breaks his extensive travels from the city to collect information on diseases carried him throughout the South, the Midwest, the North, and Canada. Accepting a professorship at the Medical College of Ohio, Drake returned to Cincinnati in 1849. In the following year, his major work on diseases in North America was published. In 1851–52, he taught in the medical department of the University of Louisville (formerly the Louisville Medical Institute) but returned to Cincinnati in 1852, where he died.

Drake's publications included *Notices Concerning Cincinnati* (1810–11); *Natural and Statistical View, or Picture of Cincinnati and the Miami Country* (1815); *A Practical Treatise on the History, Prevention, and Treatment of Epidemic Cholera, Designed for both the Profession and the People* (1832); and *A Systematic Treatise, Historical, Etiological, and Practical, on the Principal Diseases of the Interior Valley of North America, as They Appear in the Caucasian, African, Indian and Esquimaux Varieties of Its Population* (vol. 1, 1850; vol. 2, posthumously, in 1854). He served as an editor of the *Western Journal of Medical and Physical Sciences* (1828–38) and of the *Western Journal of Medicine and Surgery* (1840–49). Drake's *Pioneer Life in Kentucky 1785–1800* (posthumous, 1870) is the basis of much information about early Kentucky social history.

In 1807 Drake married Harriet Sisson. They had five children: Harriet, Charles Daniel, John Mansfield, Elizabeth Mansfield, and Harriet Echo. Drake is buried in Spring Grove Cemetery in Cincinnati.

See Dwayne Cox, "The Louisville Medical Institute: A Case History in American Medical Education," *Filson Club History Quarterly* 62 (April 1988): 197–219; Daniel Drake, *Pioneer Life in Kentucky, 1785–1800* (Cincinnati 1870; reprint, edited by Emmet F. Horine, New York

1948); Emmet F. Horine, *Daniel Drake (1785–1852) Pioneer Physician of the Midwest* (Philadelphia 1961); Henry D. Shapiro and Zane L. Miller, eds., *Physician to the West: Selected Writings of Daniel Drake on Science and Society* (Lexington 1970).

Paul A. Tenkotte

DRAKE, SAMUEL (b Devonshire, England, November 15, 1768; d Oldham County, Kentucky, October 16, 1854). Actor. Born Samuel Drake Bryant (a name he later dropped), his parents and family history are unknown. Drake, his wife, Alexina (Fisher), and their five children arrived in America in 1810. By 1814 they were performing at Green Street Theatre in Albany, New York. While there, Samuel received an invitation from Luke Usher of Lexington, Kentucky, to come and perform in his theater. Drake's wife had recently died, and Usher's description of the "new" country was appealing. Drake brought his children; Frances Denny, an eighteen-year-old daughter of the proprietor of Albany Inn; and a hired African American couple to Lexington. By 1816 this theatrical family began performing at Louisville's City Theatre, where they remained until it burned during the 1850s. Afterwards, Drake retired to his country home, Harmony Landing, on the Ohio River above Louisville in Oldham County. It is possible that he was buried at Harmony Landing. In 1893 his remains were re-interred in Cave Hill Cemetery.

See George D. Ford, *These Were Actors: A Story of the Chapmans and the Drakes* (New York 1955); West Hill Jr., *The Theatre in Early Kentucky, 1790–1820* (Lexington 1971).

Warder Harrison

DREAM FACTORY. "I slept and dreamed that life was beauty. I woke—and found that life was duty; Was my dream, then, a shadowy lie? Toil on, sad heart, courageously, and thou shalt find thy dream shall be a noonday light, and truth to thee." So noted the little-known poet Ellen Sturgis Hooper, who died prematurely at the age of twenty-five in 1841. The Dream Factory of Louisville aspires to be that "noonday light."

The Dream Factory is a national nonprofit organization dedicated to fulfilling the dreams of critically and chronically ill children. Founded in 1980 in Hopkinsville, Kentucky, by Charles Henault, it has grown into one of the nation's largest wish-granting organizations, with its national headquarters at 1218 S Third St. in Louisville. In addition to being the national headquarters, Louisville also has one of the earliest local chapters. Founded in 1985 by a group of local South Central Bell employees, it now has more than two hundred volunteers and has granted the dreams of more than six hundred local children. The organization numbers more than fifty local chapters throughout the United States. Each focuses its efforts on addressing the needs of its own community, and ninety cents of every dollar raised is directly used to benefit the children and their families of that community.

Working with volunteers, corporations, and other nonprofit organizations, the Dream Factory grants more than twenty-five hundred dreams each year to children between the ages of three and thirteen, and in some cases up to the age of seventeen. The most common wish made by younger children is a trip to Disney World or Disneyland. The most common wish of older local children is to own a computer.

DRUG ABUSE. The expenditure of money and suffering caused by those who choose to abuse drugs continues to seriously undermine the quality of life in greater Louisville, perhaps more nowadays than ever before.

When the first corn was grown offshore on Corn Island and later on shore, it is quite likely that part of it was used for bourbon whiskey. Corn Island has disappeared, but we still have a Corn Alley in the west end, where a huge field of corn was grown.

Evan Williams in 1783 started operating his distillery on Fifth near Market St. A swig from the bottle cost sixpence. It did not take long before innkeepers found an ounce glass was more profitable—the gulp was smaller.

Coffee houses were all over the city and advertised in the local newspapers. The following advertisement appeared in an 1828 *Louisville Public Advertiser*: "Western Coffee House - With all kinds of liquors - Hot Punch Lemonade - Hot Toddies - Fresh beer from Cincinnati - also on hand - pigs feet - pickled Tripe and soused Sturgeon." Most said nothing about coffee.

During the 1840s and for many years thereafter, newspaper advertisements similar to the following were published: "Ginseng For Sale at all 'fine' drugstores. Is warranted to contain no preparation of antimony, mercury or opium. The preparation is now attracting the attention of the medical world both in Europe and America. A treaty afforded the secret to be smuggled from China. It is the great remedy for coughs, colds, asthma, bronchitis, pain in the breast and all other affections of the lungs."

During the 1850s John Bull had one of the quality sarsaparilla businesses in Louisville, exporting fluid sarsaparilla to Mexico and Cuba. Sarsaparilla is made from various tropical plants and several American species of smilax, and it was used as a drug before it was used as a flavoring for soft drinks. It was used to treat psoriasis. In its day, it was advertised as being "good" for everything from good luck to a cure-all.

By 1837 there was one liquor store for every seventy people. On December 3, 1869, an ordinance to allow grocers to sell beer was adopted. Within a decade the *Louisville Commercial* in December 1878 observed: "Louisville has a population of 140,000 or 150,000 and its population supports thousands of drinking saloons. Go in whatever direction you will, and you will hardly be able to walk two squares without finding a place where liquor is retailed. There are 5,000 places in Louisville where liquor is retailed. Nearly every corner grocer has its customers who drop in for a morning toddy. Ice cream saloons also set out the drinks." So pervasive was the sale that in 1907 Marshall Bullitt, chairman of the Board of Public Safety during the brief administration of Mayor Robert W. Bingham, ordered the chief of police to put the "lid" on selling liquor on Sunday. He declared that "Police are ignoring booze laws."

Louisville had a prohibition movement, smaller than many cities, and on January 16, 1920, the eighteenth amendment to the U.S. Constitution prohibited the manufacture, sale, import, and export of liquor. Prohibition caused many a pocketbook in the community to become anemic. Much of Louisville's commerce centered around alcohol, where twenty-four distilleries had been responsible for thousands of jobs.

Of course, many residents went from legal work to an illegal occupation. Speakeasies were all over town. Some new words became prominent in the community—bathtub gin, alky, firewater, spirits, strong drink, homebrew. During June 1923 the federal agents went after a hundred alleged bootleggers in Louisville and its vicinity. In 1926 some three thousand spectators gathered in the 800 block of E Broadway to watch police pour forty-two barrels of whiskey mash down the sewer after a raid.

Prohibition was repealed December 5, 1933. On December 6, the city issued 325 beer licenses. As early as 1940 it was realized that alcoholism was a disease, yet the Board of Aldermen extended the drinking hours. The number of drinking-related incidents increased, including drunk driving. Many alcoholics are well known by the police. Some are arrested over a hundred times before death. It is quite evident that "street alcoholics" do not benefit from being arrested. In April 1983 MADD (Mothers against Drunk Driving) located its business office in the Louisville Fraternal Order of Police headquarters. It is a strong organization that is dedicated to keeping alcohol abusers from driving.

Tobacco continues to play a role in the economic life of Louisville, although most of the jobs of yesteryear pertaining to tobacco have moved from the community. During 1783 Col. John Campbell built the community's first tobacco warehouse in Shippingport, below the Falls of the Ohio. The first tobacco warehouse within the city limits was built in 1808 by Elisha Applegate. By 1819 there were many plants manufacturing chewing plugs, snuff, and smoking tobacco.

Before World War I, tobacco was most often used for chewing, dipping snuff, cigars, and pipes. Selling spittoons was a lucrative business. Most Louisville homes had at least one cuspidor, and businesses had brass ones. Chief of Police Thomas A. Taylor, at the request of the health department, insisted on stricter enforcement of the "expectorant ordinance." Six detectives were detailed to stop people from spitting in public places (buildings, STREETCARS, STREETS, etc.) as no one carried anything in which to spit tobacco juice. The health department felt that germs in saliva caused most of the tuberculosis in the community.

As early as October 29, 1908, Chief Haager, in an effort to break up the unhealthy habit of youngsters smoking, issued the following order: "Police will take the names and addresses of all boys under sixteen years of age smoking cigarettes or having cigarette tobacco and papers (for rolling cigarettes) in their possession. The names will be turned over to the Juvenile Court for the purpose of warrants against such offenders who will be prosecuted in Juvenile Court."

People completing an application for employment by the Police Department were required to state if they smoked. In time cigarettes became more popular. During World War I cigarette manufacturers, doing their part for the war effort, furnished free "puff sticks" for military personnel. Most of the young men accepted the gift and came home addicted. During WORLD WAR II military personnel were required to pay only fifty cents a carton for cigarettes in military sales outlets.

In 1993 the city legislated cigarette smoking to designated areas or outdoors. The Environmental Protection Agency advised that secondhand cigarette smoke was a health hazard and that there were thousands of toxins in tobacco smoke often inhaled by a nonsmoker.

For over two hundred years the marijuana plant has been a part of Louisville. Its first lawful use was for making rope. The city had a number of ropewalks in which marijuana was manufactured into hemp rope.

It is impossible to pinpoint when muggles, now called marijuana cigarettes, first became part of our history, or when phang, hemp-based drugs, became popular. Hashish, the rosin part of the marijuana plant, also became popular.

The *LOUISVILLE TIMES* on December 4, 1930, explained marijuana to a city that knew little about it: "Loco weed cigarettes, manufactured from a plant that has killed millions of animals are being sold to hunters who lack the price of morphine or opium shots. The cigarettes are chiefly known as 'muggles,' 'bujees' or 'mariwanas.' Chief buyers are newspaper boys. The fags sell at thirty-five cents a piece or three for a dollar. There are sellers at Eighteenth and Jefferson, Third and Jefferson and Second and LIBERTY STREETS." The boys bought, used, and sold marijuana.

A federal law took effect October 1, 1934, putting a fine on the sale of marijuana at not more than two thousand dollars and imprisonment for not more than five years. Federal narcotics agents described Louisville as "as bad as any of them." NEWSPAPERS reported that cooperation between the city police and federal agents was expected to effectively control the evil that led in many instances to murder, assaults, robberies, and suicides.

In time the marijuana laws became more lenient. Marijuana itself was recognized as not being as dangerous as once thought, but it did lead to the abuse of harder drugs such as morphine. Morphine is derived from the dried juices of the opium poppy. Morphine or morphine sulfate is the major active ingredient in opium and is most often taken by mouth or injected. It is often used by heroin addicts as a substitute when heroin is not obtainable. Heroin is the most potent narcotic and is produced synthetically by heating morphine in the presence of acetic acid. It is more addictive than morphine. For many years in the early nineteenth century, bottles with five hundred medical opium tablets were advertised in local newspapers and sold without prescription. It was said that no matter what ailment, the little pill would make one feel better. Laudanum was often taken for pain caused by cancer. It was one of the derivatives of opium, often mixed with alcohol.

Complaints against opium smoking were numerous. Mayor CHARLES D. JACOB, on January 14, 1884, advised the chief of police, Thomas Taylor, to close "vile opium dens." The chief had a difficult assignment, since there was no opium law in Kentucky. Keeping a disorderly house was the best charge available when something was going on that police did not think was proper. The charge was indictable and punishable with a heavy fine, but a heavy fine seldom was imposed.

Narcotics were sold over the counter in the United States until the Opium Exclusion Act of 1909. Even after the exclusion act, the illegal sale of morphine and cocaine continued. In those early years few wealthy people were involved with hard drugs. The arrest and prosecution of low-income drug addicts was frequent, while some doctors, druggists, and the chief agents in the billion-dollar drug abuse problem conducted business, most often without problems with the law.

The Harrison Narcotics Act of 1914 provided for control of narcotic drug traffic within the United States or any territory or place subject to its jurisdiction. This act restricted doctors to prescribing narcotics for medical reasons only, and not to furnishing drugs to addicts to satisfy addiction.

During the 1920s and 1930s, police were often assigned special duty assisting federal agents in arresting narcotic violators. On March 20, 1935, Louisville detectives George Moss and C.J. Burns assisted United States agents in dope case raids that resulted in the indictment of twenty-two men, the biggest drug bust to that date in Louisville.

During the 1960s the drug problem escalated nationwide. The foremost problem within metropolitan Louisville was the influx of illegal drugs. Heroin, cocaine, marijuana, LSD, barbiturates, and amphetamines were readily available. Drugstore narcotics and dangerous drugs were being sold by the use of prescription.

Codeine is less potent and addictive than other narcotics. It is found in prescriptions for cough suppressants and minor pain relievers. It can be changed into a form that can be injected. Codeine is often the last resort when an addict is in need of a "fix."

Depressants such as barbiturates and tranquilizers are often used as a mild sedative. They also have a great potential for serious abuse. Tolerance to depressants builds up rapidly in the body, causing psychological and physical dependency. Sudden withdrawal can cause fatal consequences.

Another group of abused drugs are stimulants. There are a large number of illegal stimulants, but the two most widely used are amphetamines and cocaine. Abuse of these drugs can result in psychological disorders such as anorexia nervosa, autism, catalepsy, depression, hysteria, nervous breakdowns, and neuroses. Participants are often called "speed freaks." Cocaine, known in South America for at least a thousand years, is a white, powdery substance made from the leaves of the coca plant. Soon after being brought into the United States in the nineteenth century, it became the main ingredient in many medicines and imparted vigor to many who used it. Cocaine earned a reputation as a drug for the rich in the late 1960s. Crack rock cocaine, possibly the most sought-after drug of the late 1990s, has become, in a very short time, the drug of choice amongst many of the most hardened drug users. A crystallized form of freebase cocaine first appeared in 1985, and in Louisville shortly thereafter.

Hallucinogens, the psychedelic drugs, are substances that can change the way people view the world around them for much longer than the length of time the drug is present in the body. They have an extreme effect on the senses and can distort the thinking processes, interfere with self-awareness, and confuse emotions. Hallucinogens include marijuana, mescaline, psilocybin, and PCP (Phencyclidine), also known as "angel dust." "Angel dust" was developed in 1967 as an anesthetic and tranquilizer for veterinary use and is now an illegal hallucinogen.

Another substance-abuse problem became more obvious to police during the late 1950s. The *Louisville Times* on July 20, 1961, reported that "Louisville police are going to ask medical advice on what danger there may be in a new teen-age fad, sniffing glue for supposed 'kicks.' The glue fumes can be potentially physically dangerous or fatal as one doctor has already said could be the case. The Crime Prevention Bureau said the police may ask for an ordinance to control the sale of the glue."

Several private and federally sponsored groups have attempted to solve the problem by educating and informing parents and users. There were several successful undercover drug busts during the sixties, but the city had its most successful undercover operation during 1970. Secret indictments of more than a hundred people on charges of selling drugs or narcotics were made, and most of those charged were arrested within twenty-four hours. All were found guilty except two.

Money needed for drugs is often stolen or earned by addicts who sell their bodies. Drug use brings about more crime and murder in the community. As a result, the Anti-Drug Abuse Act of 1986 provided for increased federal financing for law enforcement, treatment, educational programs, stiffer penalties in federal drug cases, and life prison terms for principals in drug enterprises. By the end of the twentieth century the problem was far from a solution. Without a more sustained effort by the community, more people will commit more crimes than ever before, and tax payers will continue to pay the bill for drug abuse. That cost is seen in the number of arrests. For example, in 1998 the total number of arrests by the LOUISVILLE POLICE DEPARTMENT totaled 34,806 (31,248 adults and 3,558 juveniles). Of that number 5,441 adults and 621 juveniles were arrested for drugs/narcotics crimes.

Morton O. Childress

DUDLEY, THOMAS UNDERWOOD (b Richmond, Virginia, September 26, 1837; d New York City, January 22, 1904). Episcopal Bishop of Kentucky. Born the son of Thomas and Maria (Friend) Dudley, he received his early education in private schools, then entered the University of Virginia, graduating in 1858. Dudley taught school for several years and was assistant professor of Latin and Greek at the University of Virginia until the outbreak of the CIVIL WAR. He joined the Confederate army, enlisting in the Hanover Artillery, but was soon assigned to the commissary department, where he served as assistant commissary with the rank of major until the war's end.

Dudley briefly studied law before entering Virginia Theological Seminary, where he graduated in 1866. Following his ordination, he took up his first rectorship at Harrisonburg, Virginia. In 1869 Dudley became rector of Christ Church in Baltimore, Maryland; and in 1875 he was named assistant bishop of Kentucky, moving shortly thereafter to Louisville. After the death of Bishop Benjamin Bosworth Smith in 1884, Dudley became bishop. In 1896 the diocese split, creating the Diocese of Lexington in the eastern half of the state and the Diocese of Kentucky in the western half. Dudley remained bishop of the Diocese of Kentucky, with CHRIST CHURCH in Louisville as his cathedral.

Possessing a keen sense of humor and a beautiful voice, Dudley was much in demand as a speaker and was reported to be at the time of his death one of the "foremost pulpit orators of the country." Under his direction, the Episcopal denomination enjoyed great prosperity in the state. He was a powerful exponent of the missionary cause and held a lifelong interest in the Christian education and evangelization of AFRICAN AMERICANS. He was the only Louisvillian to address the 1893 Congress of Religions at the Columbian Exposition in Chicago. In addition to his duties as bishop, Dudley served as chancellor of the University of the South in Sewanee, Tennessee (1894–1904), was chairman of the House of Bishops (1901–4), and was active in various Masonic functions.

Dudley married Fanny B. Cochran in July 1859, and the couple had four daughters before her death in 1865. In April 1869 he married Virginia F. Rowland, with whom he had two sons and a daughter. His second wife died in 1877, and he was married for the third time in June 1881 to Mary E. Aldrich, who survived him. There were two children, a son and a daughter, from this last marriage. While in New York City for his mother-in-law's funeral, Dudley died, only three days short of twenty-nine years as bishop. He is buried in CAVE HILL CEMETERY.

See Frances Keller Swinford and Rebecca Smith Lee, *The Great Elm Tree* (Lexington 1969); J. Stoddard Johnson, ed., *Memorial History of Louisville* (Chicago 1896).

Kenneth Dennis

DUELS. The duel constituted a formal way for sensitive gentlemen, often from the South, to avenge insults. According to the code of honor, a popular standard of manly social behavior between the Revolutionary War and the CIVIL WAR, gentlemen had a duty to demand satisfaction for unresolved slights to their reputation. Combatants fought duels according to the *code duello*, which provided elaborate rules for the appointment of seconds and the selection of weapons and the place of the duel. Seconds sometimes negotiated a settlement, thus avoiding bloodshed. If a settlement could not be reached, to avoid arrest the duelists usually fought their duel in an isolated place, sometimes across a state boundary.

Of forty-one recorded duels fought by Kentuckians between 1790 and 1867, three involved Louisvillians. The most celebrated, that involving HENRY C. POPE and JOHN T. GRAY in 1849, embodied many of the characteristics of the typical duel. As was often the case, alcohol fueled the duel between Pope and Gray, close friends until the drunken Pope insulted Gray during a card game at the GALT HOUSE on June 11, 1849. Gray responded by bashing Pope over the head with a cane and then punching him in the face. The next morning, Pope challenged Gray to a duel, and Gray accepted the challenge. Their seconds could not negotiate a settlement, so the two squared off in Indiana opposite SIX MILE ISLAND in the OHIO RIVER. Gray's choice of weapons, a pair of twelve-gauge shotguns each loaded with a single ball to be fired at a distance of sixty feet, guaranteed bloodshed. Both parties fired simultaneously, Pope's shot being wide of the mark and Gray's fatally wounding Pope. Gray moved to Maryland to avoid public outrage and prosecution.

Only briefly reported, the duel between Maj. Thomas Marshall of Louisville and Col. Charles S. Mitchell "of Kentucky" was fought on February 19, 1812, opposite Maysville in Ohio. Mitchell wounded Marshall in the leg, but apparently the victim survived.

The most sensible duel between Louisvillians involved John Thruston and Johnson Harrison, who met each other in the summer of 1792 in the woods along where BROADWAY currently runs. Manifesting uncommon sense, the two parties decided to settle their trivial disagreement by shooting at an inanimate target rather than at each other, the winner to receive a gallon of whiskey. Harrison won the match and the liquor.

Outrage over the Pope-Gray duel contributed to a decision of the framers of Kentucky's third constitution (1850)to require all would-be state officeholders to take an oath that they had neither fought nor aided and abetted the fighting of a duel. This oath, and statutes enacted earlier that outlawed the duel, did not end the practice. Only the gradual transformation of social custom and public opinion altered the duel from an accepted method of conflict resolution to a controversial relic of the past.

The de facto duel or street fight constituted a more deadly and popular form of conflict resolution for nineteenth-century Kentuckians, and Louisville had its share of these affairs. Men of honor often did not bother to challenge each other to a formal, regulated duel, but rather hauled out their weapons at the moment of insulting behavior and fought until one or more of the combatants lay dead or seriously wounded. One such affair involved a fight in the barroom of the Galt House in November 1838 between three aristocratic Mississippians and friends of a local tailor, whom they had insulted and assaulted because of an ill-fitting wedding suit he had made for one of them. The Mississippians prevailed in the combat, killing two of their adversaries. Tried for murder in April 1839 in Harrodsburg on a change of venue, the three were acquitted after their celebrated counsel persuaded the jury that the killings represented a vindication of honor rather than premeditated murder or criminal manslaughter.

See J. Winston Coleman, *Famous Kentucky Duels: The Story of the Code of Honor in the Bluegrass State* (Frankfort 1953); Robert M. Ireland, "Homicide in Nineteenth-Century Kentucky," *Register of the Kentucky Historical Society* 81 (Spring 1983): 134–53.

Robert M. Ireland

DUKE, BASIL W. (b Scott County, Kentucky, May 28, 1838; d New York City, September 16, 1916). Soldier, lawyer, historian. The child of Nathaniel W. and Mary Pickett (Currie) Duke, Basil Duke attended Georgetown and Centre Colleges and studied law at Transylvania University. In 1858 he moved to St. Louis and began practicing law. While there he became deeply involved in the Missouri secessionist movement. He moved to Lexington upon his marriage in 1861 to Henrietta Hunt Morgan, a sister of John Hunt Morgan. In October 1861 he enlisted in the Confederate army as Morgan's second-in-command and rose to the rank of colonel.

Duke was wounded both at Shiloh and near Elizabethtown on a raid in December 1862. Captured on the Great Raid in Ohio, he was a prisoner from July 19, 1863, to August 3, 1864. After Morgan was killed, Duke took command of Morgan's men on September 15, 1864 with the rank of brevet brigadier general. At the end of the war he led the force that escorted Jefferson Davis on his retreat from Richmond, Virginia.

In 1868 Duke began practicing LAW in Louisville and served as chief counsel and lobbyist for the LOUISVILLE & NASHVILLE RAILROAD, where he led the opposition to construction of the Cincinnati Southern Railroad and its efforts to build a line through Kentucky to Chattanooga. As a result, construction of the line was delayed for several years, a move that exacerbated the rivalry between Louisville and Lexington. A Democrat, he was elected in 1869 to the Kentucky House of Representatives and served until 1870, when he resigned. He was elected commonwealth's attorney for the Fifth Judicial District, 1875–80.

Duke was prominent in city affairs and veterans' groups and in demand as a speaker. He was a founder of the FILSON CLUB HISTORICAL SOCIETY in 1884 and delivered papers for the historical society. Filson Club president REUBEN T. DURRETT introduced Duke to Theodore Roosevelt, and in 1901 President Roosevelt appointed Duke a commissioner of Shiloh National Park. He edited *Southern Bivouac* magazine, 1885–87, and wrote *History of Morgan's Cavalry* (1867) and *History of the Bank of Kentucky 1792–1895* (1895). His children were Johnnie "Reb," Basil, Thomas, Currie, Calvin, Henry, Julia, and Frances Key. He died after surgery and is buried in Lexington.

See James W. Henning, "Basil Wilson Duke, 1838–1916: One of the Founders of the Filson Club," *Filson Club History Quarterly* 14 (April 1940): 59–64; Lowell H. Harrison, "General Basil W. Duke, C.S.A." *Filson Club History Quarterly* 54 (Jan. 1980): 5–36; Basil W. Duke, *Reminiscences* (New York, 1911).

James A. Ramage

DUNCAN, WILLIAM GARNETT (b Louisville, March 2, 1800; d Louisville, May 25, 1875). Congressman. Duncan studied LAW at Yale and graduated in 1821. He returned to Louisville in 1822 and practiced law until his election to Congress in 1846 as a member of the WHIG PARTY. He declined his opportunity to be a candidate for renomination to Congress after his first term, instead moving to Louisiana to practice law there. He retired in 1860 and returned to Louisville to live with his son. He is buried in CAVE HILL CEMETERY.

See *Biographical Directory of the American Congress 1774–1961* (Washington, D.C., 1961).

DUNCAN MEMORIAL CHAPEL. Duncan Memorial Chapel is in the Floydsburg Cemetery, one mile southeast of CRESTWOOD in OLDHAM COUNTY, Kentucky. Used primarily as a nondenominational wedding chapel and for special events, the chapel was constructed in 1936 and dedicated to the memory of Flora Ross Duncan by her husband, Alexander Edward Duncan. Duncan was born in 1878 in Floydsburg and briefly operated a general store in Crestwood. In 1903 he moved to Cincinnati, and in 1907 he removed to Baltimore and founded the Commercial Credit Corp., one of the largest credit firms in the country in the 1920s and 1930s.

The Floydsburg Cemetery was originally the William Boulware family cemetery, begun on three-quarters of an acre of land about 1799. In 1818 an acre of land containing the cemetery was deeded to the trustees of the Methodist Episcopal Church in Floydsburg by William and Charity Boulware for one dollar. A log church was constructed in 1818 and replaced by a stone church. In 1850 the stone church was razed and replaced by a brick church. In 1909 the Methodist congregation moved to Crestwood, and the church was demolished. In 1936 Duncan bought property adjacent to the cemetery and donated it to the Floydsburg Cemetery Co.

The chapel, designed by Louisville architect Fred H. Elswick, of Wischmeyer, Arrasmith, and Elswick, is in the English Gothic style with transept and nave. It was constructed of native stone taken from old fences in the countryside. The Abbott-McMillan Co. of Louisville built the chapel. The interior is trimmed with cut Indiana limestone, and the roof and floor are of slate. The medallion-style stained glass windows, which use medallion shapes for both figures and symbols, were designed and executed by Henry Lee Willet of Philadelphia. A portion of one of the windows above the altar was selected by the Rockefeller Foundation to be exhibited at the 1937 Paris Exposition as an outstanding example of American stained glass. On the altar is a woodcarving of Leonardo da Vinci's "The Last Supper" by F. Pescosta of Wisconsin. Both Duncans are buried in the chapel's chancel.

See Oldham County Historical Society, *History and Families of Oldham County, Kentucky* (Paducah, Ky., 1996)

Susan Buren Eubank

DUNNE, IRENE MARIE. (b Louisville, December 20, 1898; d Los Angeles, September 4, 1990). Star of stage and motion pictures. She was the daughter of Joseph John and Adelaide (Henry) Dunn. The final "e" was added to the name at the beginning of Dunne's Hollywood career, and she variously reported her birth year as 1901, 1904, and 1905, although the 1900 census shows her living at her father's home at 1803 Edward St. Her father was a U.S. government steamship inspector. Her mother, an accomplished pianist, was Dunne's first music teacher. Dunne spent the first eleven years of her life in Louisville, attending CEDAR GROVE ACADEMY in Louisville and studying voice and piano with private teachers.

Following her father's death in 1910, Dunne and her family relocated to Madison, Indiana. In 1919 she graduated from the Chicago College of Music and in 1920 made her professional acting debut in Chicago in the touring company of the musical *Irene.* Dunne soon found herself on the New York stage, beginning a ten-year period of theater work. While appearing as Magnolia in *Show Boat,* she attracted the attention of Hollywood producers. She made her film debut in *Leathernecking* in 1930.

Dunne's twenty-two-year film career earned her five Academy Award nominations. Although an actress of considerable range, she usually epitomized the lady of grace and charm. Among her most memorable films were *Cimarron* (1931), *Theodora Goes Wild* (1936), *The Awful Truth* (1937), The *White Cliffs of Dover* (1944), *Anna and the King of Siam* (1946), *Life with Father* (1947), and *I Remember Mama* (1948).

Dunne returned to Louisville for the premiere of *My Favorite Wife* in 1940 and again in 1965 to become the first woman recipient of the Bellarmine Medal. She served as an alternate delegate to the United Nations Twelfth General Assembly in 1957-58 and received Kennedy Center Honors in 1985.

Dunne married Dr. Francis D. Griffin, a dentist, on July 16, 1928. They had one child, an adopted daughter, Mary Frances. She is buried in Los Angeles.

See *Current Biography* (New York 1945).

Kenneth Dennis

DU PONT, ALFRED VICTOR (b Wilmington, Delaware, April 18, 1833; d Louisville, May 16, 1893). Entrepreneur. Alfred "Uncle Fred" Victor du Pont was the third son of Alfred Victor Philadelphe and Margaretta (Lammot) du Pont. After his uncle, Henry du Pont, made it clear that there would be no position at the family's company in Delaware, Fred and his younger brother, ANTOINE BIDERMANN DU PONT, moved to Louisville in 1854 to seek their own fortunes. The elder brother purchased a paper mill at Tenth and Rowan Streets and made Bidermann his partner. Three years later, du Pont founded the A.V. du Pont Co., and the business thrived. He soon branched into other ventures including the Central Passenger Railway Co. in Louisville and invested in other street railway companies in Cleveland, Brooklyn, and Chicago. Because of his popularity and wealth, Alfred became the vice president and director of the First National Bank in Louisville.

Du Pont involved himself in several iron, coal, and steel companies—most prominently, the Central City Coal and Iron Co. in Central City, Kentucky. Since his brother, Bidermann, actually ran the day-to-day affairs of the company, battled the unions, and broke the strikes, Fred was well liked by his workers. He later turned over control of the Central City Co. to his favorite nephew, THOMAS COLEMAN (known as Coly or T.C.) DU PONT.

Du Pont loved children and acted as guardian for the fifteen children of his deceased brothers, Irènèe and Lammot. He also remained close to the du Ponts in Delaware and returned there often for family meetings, weddings, and funerals. Known for his generosity, du Pont donated to philanthropic organizations (most often anonymously), and in 1892 he helped found a technical school for white males known as du Pont Manual Training High School (later changed to DU PONT MANUAL HIGH SCHOOL) at the corner of Oak and Brook Streets. The school later moved into Halleck Hall at Second and Lee Streets. Du Pont was unusually tight with money spent on himself and refused to place fans in his sweltering office until his nephew Coly found a cost-free way of installing them. Threadbare clothes accented his usual unkempt appearance. Although relatives commented on his lack of personal style, his thrift influenced several generations of du Ponts.

However, he was best known for his independent and, at times, eccentric behavior. Despite his staggering fortune, for the forty-four years du Pont lived in Louisville, he resided in one room of the GALT HOUSE hotel that he never permitted the staff to renovate. Although he once thought of moving out of room 422 after purchasing the home of Rev. STUART ROBINSON in the area that is today Central Park, du Pont decided not to leave and instead allowed his brother Bidermann to live at the estate with his family.

He never married but instead regularly visited bordellos, a penchant that eventually led to his mysterious death. The *COURIER-JOURNAL* reported that Fred had died of a heart attack in front of the Galt House. However, two days later, the *Cincinnati Enquirer* published the truth: Fred had been shot by Maggie Payne, the proprietor of a bordello at Eighth and York Streets, apparently over a paternity dispute. *Courier-Journal* editor HENRY WATTERSON, who owed large back payments to du Pont's company for pulp paper, and the du Pont family continued to maintain that Fred died of natural causes for years before finally admitting the circumstances surrounding his death. Coly smuggled the corpse out of Louisville under cover of darkness, and du Pont was buried at the family estate along the Brandywine River in Delaware.

See Joseph Frazier Wall, *Alfred I. du Pont, the Man and his Family* (New York 1990); Marc Duke, *The du Ponts, Portrait of a Dynasty* (New York 1976).

Charles H. MacKay

DU PONT, ANTOINE BIDERMANN (b Wilmington, Delaware, October 13, 1837; d Wilmington, Delaware, October 22, 1923). Industrialist. The youngest son of Alfred Victor Philadelphe and Margaretta (Lammot) du Pont. With little prospect of employment at the family's business in Delaware, Bidermann relocated with his older brother, Alfred "Fred," to Louisville in 1854. Fred and his cousin Charles I. du Pont Jr. bought a paper mill and renamed it the A. V. du Pont Co. The mill, located at Tenth and Monroe (Rowan) Streets, with offices and warehouses on Sixth between MAIN and MARKET STREETS, specialized in the manufacture of newsprint to be sold in the West. Bidermann first worked as a clerk in the paper mill but became Fred's partner in 1857 when their cousin sold his interest in the company. The paper mill prospered, and Bidermann's business interests grew to include the presidency of the Central Coal and Iron Co., with offices in both Central City, Kentucky, and Louisville, and the Central Passenger Railway Co., which operated mule-drawn STREETCARS in the city. Later Bidermann bought the Republican newspaper, the *Louisville Commercial*, which became the *Louisville Herald* in 1902.

In 1862 a number of concerned Louisville businessmen, including du Pont, organized the LOUISVILLE BOARD OF TRADE as a pro-Union organization. Members were required to take an oath declaring their determination not to aid the Confederacy. The Board's closed membership and the disunity caused by the CIVIL WAR led to reorganization in 1879. Du Pont was elected to the new board of directors. Soon thereafter he was voted one of its five vice presidents. It later became the Louisville Area Chamber of Commerce.

On April 18, 1861, du Pont married Ellen Coleman of Louisville. Having amassed a fortune, the du Ponts built a house on the corner of fashionable FOURTH ST. and Park Ave. They had seven children: Margaretta, Thomas Coleman, Antoine Bidermann Jr., Dora, Zara, Pauline, and Evan, who died at birth shortly after his mother, Ellen, on May 10, 1876. Du Pont remained close to the "Delaware du Ponts" and frequently visited the family estates with his children. He later returned to live in Delaware. He is buried in Louisville's CAVE HILL CEMETERY.

See J.M. Elstner, *The Industries of Louisville and of New Albany, Indiana* (Louisville 1886); William H.A. Carr, *The du Ponts of Delaware* (New York 1964).

Charles H. MacKay

DU PONT, ETHEL B. (b Louisville, 1896; d Louisville, October 17, 1980). Labor organizer and social activist. The second daughter of Antoine Bidermann Jr. and Mary Ethel (Clark) du Pont. In 1909, when the family lived in Cleveland, Ohio, Ethel's mother died, and her Aunt Zara du Pont moved in to raise the children. From her father and aunt, Ethel became interested in liberal politics. After graduating from college she moved to Louisville, supported the right of women to vote, joined the SOCIALIST PARTY and later the DEMOCRATIC PARTY, and in 1947 was selected to serve on the Executive Committee of Louisville's chapter of the NATIONAL ASSOCIATION FOR THE ADVANCEMENT OF COLORED PEOPLE. She helped form the Greater Louisville Committee to Defend Civil Liberties and the Citizens Committee for Welfare Legislation in Kentucky. She was active in the LEAGUE OF WOMEN VOTERS. However, she devoted most of her life to LABOR concerns. From 1938 until 1951 she wrote "With Labor's Ranks" twice a week in the *LOUISVILLE TIMES*. The column was popular with skilled labor unions but helped to isolate her from "high" society. In 1945 she attended a General Motors stockholders' meeting, and, as a stockholder herself, she demanded that the company open its books for the United Auto Workers.

Du Pont spent most of her life trying to improve working conditions for teachers. She taught economics at the UNIVERSITY OF LOUISVILLE. In 1954 she helped organize a teachers' strike in Edmonson County. She traveled ceaselessly throughout the state, especially in the mountains, organizing teachers into labor unions. She also served as president of the Kentucky Federation of Teachers.

Her activities came at great personal cost, though. Since she came from a prestigious and wealthy family, she was expected to act like a young socialite, and many of her peers abandoned her because of her efforts to support civil, labor, and women's rights. Although she wanted to marry, she never did, and she constantly had to face false assertions that she was a lesbian. Also, because of her family connections, labor leaders and rank-and-file members suspected her motives until she had proven her loyalty. Du Pont is buried in CAVE HILL CEMETERY.

See Joseph Frazier Wall, *Alfred I. duPont: The Man and His Family* (New York 1990).

Charles H. MacKay

DU PONT, THOMAS COLEMAN (b Louisville, December 11, 1863; d Wilmington, Delaware, November 11, 1930). Entrepreneur. Thomas Coleman was the oldest child of Thomas Bidermann and Ellen Susan (Coleman) du Pont. Coleman—"Coly" or "T.C.," as he was called—attended Urbana University in Ohio before finishing his degree in engineering at the Massachusetts Institute of Technology in 1884. Handsome, tall, a favorite with women, captain of the FOOTBALL and baseball teams, and a track and crew star, Coleman went to work for his uncle (Fred du Pont) and his father driving a mule in the mines of the Central City (Kentucky) Iron and Coal Co. in 1883. Initially popular with the miners, he joined a labor union, the Knights of Labor, and rose rapidly to the position of president of the local chapter. However in 1884 when the Knights of Labor struck, Coleman used prisoners under guard to break the strike. After guards shot and killed one prisoner, the miners abandoned their strike. Following the sudden death of his favorite uncle, ALFRED VICTOR "Uncle Fred" DU PONT, in 1893, Coleman helped cover up the mysterious circumstances of his death and took over Uncle Fred's vast holdings in and outside of Kentucky. His interests, however, turned to politics. After a failed attempt to become Central City's mayor, he left Kentucky to become general manager of the Johnson Steel Co. in Johnstown, Pennsylvania. He relocated to Wilmington, Delaware, in 1900 to operate a button factory and then began to speculate on real estate, including the purchase of a posh private country club where he entertained his friends and business associates. He also operated two Kentucky companies, the Jellico Mountain and McHenry Coal Companies. He and two other first cousins bought the family's gunpowder business in 1902, and he served as its president until 1915. During that time, the Du Pont Co. supplied a majority of the United States' gunpowder, saltpeter, dynamite, and sporting powder, and held an absolute monopoly on military smokeless powder. Gregarious and sometimes flamboyant, ruthless and cunning in business, Coleman made the du Ponts the richest family in the United States by the 1920s.

However, politics remained Coleman's passion. He led the National Security League, an organization designed to bring the United States into the first world war, and in 1916 he received thirteen votes as a presidential candidate on the second ballot of the 1916 Republican National Convention. He publicly opposed restrictions on immigration but strongly favored "Americanizing" foreign-born workers. Delaware governor William Denney appointed Coleman to fill the U.S. Senate vacancy caused by J.O. Wilcox's resignation. He served from July 7, 1921, to November 7, 1922, and was elected to his own senatorial seat in 1924. He gave generously to the REPUBLICAN PARTY, helped elect Warren G. Harding president in 1920, and became an influential part of Harding's inner circle of friends. After a senatorial committee uncovered his involvement in the famous "Teapot Dome" scandal, Coleman resigned his Senate seat on December 9, 1928, rather than face an investigation. In that same year he donated $230,000 to buy 2,300 acres of land for a state park in the Cumberland Falls area of Kentucky to save it from commercial development by a dam and water-powered electric generating station. A land development scandal in Florida, the stock market crash of 1929, and his declining health forced Coleman out of the public eye in 1929.

Coleman married Alice du Pont, a second cousin, in 1889. They had five children: Renee de Pelleport, Thomas Coleman II, Alice Hounsfield, Ellen Coleman, and Francis Victor. Coleman died of throat cancer and is buried in the family cemetery along the Brandywine River.

See Leonard Mosley, *Blood Relations: The Rise and Fall of the Du Ponts of Delaware* (New York 1980); Louisville *Board of Trade Journal* 13 (Aug. 1940): 22–24; *Courier-Journal*, Aug. 13, 1941.

Charles H. MacKay

DU PONT MANUAL HIGH SCHOOL. Du Pont Manual High School, named for ALFRED VICTOR DU PONT, opened in October 1892 with 121 students. Originally called du Pont Manual Training High School, it "set out to help the average boy," according to early yearbooks. Du Pont, whose family owned du Pont Powder Co., contributed $150,000 to the school board for the purchase of property at the corner of Brook and Oak Streets and construction of suitable buildings. Du Pont died only sixteen days after the school's dedication in May 1893.

The school was equipped with new furniture and the up-to-date tools and machinery necessary for a reputable manual training school. No special trade was taught, and no articles were manufactured for sale. Manual training continued to be the educational focus for the school as expansion contributed a foundry, drawing room, and power plant to the complex. In 1915, when it was consolidated with LOUISVILLE MALE HIGH SCHOOL to form Louisville Boys High, the manual training courses were still located at Brook and Oak Streets. The two schools were again separated at the end of the 1918 school year.

In 1921 Manual hired Neal Arntson, just graduated from the University of Minnesota, as FOOTBALL coach and athletic director for the specific purpose of defeating the Male football team in their annual meeting. By 1923 enrollment almost topped seventeen hundred boys, and the faculty numbered fifty-six. To accommodate the growing student body, an annex and gymnasium were built. Arntson, who had been calling for the building of a stadium to accommodate the school's football team since his arrival, finally got his wish. In the thirty-year history to this point, the school had no athletic field of its own, and teams were practicing and playing on any space, public or private, that could be afforded to them, including the Fair Grounds and Male High Park. Because of the efforts of Arntson and J.N. Dennis, the president of the Manual Parent-Teacher Association, who along with Edward G. Isaacs of the Alumni Association selected the lot at 1230 E Burnett Ave., the school board purchased the six and a half acres between Texas Ave. and Eastern Pkwy. for ten thousand dollars. The purchase was approved by the athletic committee of the BOARD OF EDUCATION, composed of Dr. A.B. Weaver, Edward Gottschalk, and E. LELAND TAYLOR. The field was immediately cleared and graded, and a fence and temporary seating were put in place for the fall football season.

In December of 1923, fresh from winning the "Rivalry" game against Male, Manual began its fund-raising drive for the stadium. The money was to be raised through a subscription drive, with dedication of box seats to subscribers of five hundred dollars and a section of the stadium dedicated to those who subscribed one thousand dollars. A feature of the drive was the sale of perpetual rights to the purchase of tickets in certain boxes. Contributions of a thousand dollars were made by THEODORE AHRENS, Mrs. Mary R. Beutel, John W. Klein, and Levelle McCampbell, a Manual graduate living in Pittsburgh and manager of the first Manual football team to defeat Male in 1899. A contribution of a thousand dollars also came from the students of Male High School. Several five-hundred-dollar donations were made by individuals such as Arthur G. Tafel and Mr. and Mrs. Van Buren Ropke, companies such as

Third year shop class at du Pont Manual High School, 1894.

HILLERICH & BRADSBY and the *COURIER-JOURNAL* and *LOUISVILLE TIMES*, and groups such as the students of the UNIVERSITY OF LOUISVILLE.

On November 15, 1924, du Pont Stadium, which seats up to eighty-five hundred football fans, was opened and dedicated. The highlight of the dedication game against the team from Washington High School of Cedar Rapids, Iowa, was the halftime show. At halftime a mock football game was held in which Joseph Burge, chairman of the Stadium Campaign and Building Committee, and the "Campaigners," representatives of the different groups that helped raise the money for the stadium, faced Edward Gottschalk and the "Educationers," members of the Jefferson County School Board, with Mayor HUSTON QUIN as the referee. A conference was called midfield by the mayor in which the stadium was presented to the school board.

On September 21, 1946, a lighting system was dedicated in the stadium along with a bronze plaque with the names of all Manual men who had gone off to battle in WORLD WAR I and II and never returned home. It was the opening game of the 1946 season, which Manual lost to Cleveland High School of St. Louis, Missouri, 41 to 7. The lights and plaque were dedicated at halftime, this time without the show of the stadium dedication.

One of the most popular events at the stadium was the annual Manual and Male football game, first played on November 18, 1893. Originally the game was played on Thanksgiving Day; however, it is presently played on the last Friday of October. Male won the most recent game on October 30, 1998, with a score of 55 to 10, and they lead the series 71–38–6.

For many years Manual High's counterpart was nearby LOUISVILLE GIRLS HIGH. Socializing between the boys at Manual Training and the girls from Girls High was encouraged by joint ventures such as senior plays and mixed membership in clubs. The two schools were segregated by sex until 1950, when du Pont Manual Training High School relocated and changed its name to du Pont Manual High School. It moved to Reuben Post Halleck Hall at 120 W Lee St., former home of the Louisville Girls High School, and in 1951 graduated its first coed class.

In 1984 it became known as the du Pont Manual Magnet High School. Besides offering academic classes for students in the nearby Youth Performing Arts School, four magnet programs were introduced. The High School/University Academic Center provides a strong college-preparatory curriculum for students, offering an opportunity to earn free-of-charge college credit from nearby University of Louisville while attending du Pont Manual. The Communications/Media Arts program is designed for students who want to complete the liberal arts graduation requirements while gaining experience in BROADCASTING, ADVERTISING, and journalism. The Visual Arts Magnet Program combines specialized art classes in design, ceramics, sculpture, photography, drafting, and graphic arts. The Math, Science, and Technology Magnet offers accelerated four-year programs in mathematics, science, and state-of-the-art technology, preparing students for admission to some of the nation's leading technological colleges and universities.

Du Pont Manual is recognized by the U.S. government as a National School of Excellence; its students have won the Governor's Cup for Academic Excellence three times in the last decade (1990s) and held the state's highest number of National Merit Semi-Finalists in 1996, 1997, and 1998. In 1998 the science class won over $13 million in college scholarships.

See *Courier-Journal*, Aug. 3, 1923, Dec. 11–12, 14–15, 19, 1923, Sept. 22, 1946, Aug. 29, 1950; Eustace Williams, *That Old Rivalry, Manual vs. High School, 1893–1900* (Louisville 1940); Elva Lyon, ed., *University of Louisville Local History Series: Schools*, vol. 26, University of Louisville Archives and Records Center; Dedication Program, Nov. 15, 1924, Dedication Program, Sept. 21, 1946.

DURRETT, REUBEN THOMAS (b Henry County, Kentucky, January 22, 1824; d Louisville, September 16, 1913). Attorney and historian. Durrett was the son of William and Elizabeth Rawlings Durrett. He attended Georgetown College and received a B.A. degree in 1849 from Brown University in Rhode Island. In 1850 he received an LL.B. degree from the UNIVERSITY OF LOUISVILLE. He was awarded the A.M. degree by Brown University in 1853. From 1850 until 1880 Durrett practiced LAW in Louisville. He served on the City Council in 1853. In 1857 he bought a half interest in the *LOUISVILLE COURIER* and served as its editor from 1857 to 1859. For his pro-southern leanings, he was confined briefly in Fort Lafayette in Indiana. In 1870 he helped found the Public Library of Kentucky in Louisville.

In the 1850s Durrett wrote POETRY. After 1880 his interest turned to Kentucky history, and articles he wrote on aspects of the state's history were published in magazines and newspapers. Some of his work is suspect, however, reflecting his own opinions and his penchant for making a good story better. Durrett was one of the founders of the FILSON CLUB in 1884 to collect, preserve, and publish historic matter relating to Kentucky, and he was president of the club from 1884 to 1913. The club published five of Durrett's books on history. Among his books were *Centenary of Louisville* (1893) and *John Filson the First Historian of Kentucky* (1884).

Durrett's celebrated library at his home at Brook and Chestnut Streets was the Filson Club's meeting place from 1884 until 1913. The library was used for research by many scholars, including Theodore Roosevelt while writing *Winning of the West* (1889–96). When Durrett died in 1913 his collection, considered the finest and most comprehensive gathering of materials on Kentucky, was sold to the University of Chicago. It consisted of 20,000 volumes, 250 pamphlet boxes, 200 volumes of atlases and maps, hundreds of newspaper titles, and thousands of original manuscripts. The university still holds the Durrett Collection.

On December 16, 1852, Durrett married Elizabeth Humphreys Bates of Cincinnati. He died in Louisville, survived by his son, William. Durrett is buried in CAVE HILL CEMETERY.

See Thomas D. Clark, "Reuben T. Durrett and His Kentuckiana Interest and Collection," *Filson Club History Quarterly* 56 (Oct. 1982): 353–78; Edward M. Walters, "Reuben T. Durrett, The Durrett Collection, and the University of Chicago," *Filson Club History Quarterly* 56 (Oct. 1982): 379–94.

James R. Bentley

DUVALLE, LUCIE N. (b Louisville, August 16, 1868; d Louisville, December 1, 1928). Educator. The child of Peter and Ann Du Valle, Lucie was the eldest of four daughters. She received her education in Louisville's public schools, and, though still only a girl herself, in 1878 she began her teaching career at the Eastern Colored School at the corner of Breckinridge and Jackson Streets. Five years later DuValle transferred to the Western Colored School. In 1890 she became the first female principal in the Louisville public school system when she was appointed to head the California Colored School, later renamed Phillis Wheatley School. During her thirty-eight-year tenure there, she was credited with instituting the first "parents meetings," which were precursors to the Parent-Teacher Association, and with establishing a number of programs at Wheatley such as health and vocational training.

In honor of DuValle's contributions to education, the Lucie N. DuValle Junior High School was opened at Ninth and Chestnut Streets in September 1952 in the old Central High School facility. In 1956 the DuValle junior high was moved to 3500 Bohne Ave. in a structure it shared with Joseph S. Cotter Elementary School. Thirty years later DuValle junior high was renamed the DuValle Education Center, which offered various opportunities to the surrounding community such as GED courses, vocational training, and a Head Start program.

Lucie DuValle died of a heart attack and is buried in Eastern Cemetery.

E

Eclipse Park, 7th and Kentucky Streets, 1913.

EARLY TIMES. The whiskey brand of the Brown-Forman Corp. was created about 1853 by John H. "Jack" Beam, grandson of pioneer distiller Jacob Beam and uncle of James B. Beam. Beam chose the name and his distinctive label illustrating the distilling process to reflect his interest in the early methods of making bourbon. His distillery was on Stuart's Creek near Beam's Station in Nelson County, four miles south of Jim Beam Distillery. The neighborhood subsequently became known as Early Times and had its own station on the Louisville & Nashville Railroad (now csx).

Paducah native B.H. Hunt became a partner in the enterprise in the 1880s, serving as president, with Beam serving as vice president and distiller. Hunt sold his interest back to Beam soon after the turn of the century, and general manager John Shaunty purchased one-third interest. Searles Lewis Guthrie entered the company about 1908, purchased one-third eight years later, and became sole owner about 1920. But Prohibition soon followed and Guthrie found himself unable to sell his bourbon, since, according to the terms of the Eighteenth Amendment, it could be dispensed only by prescription.

In 1923 Guthrie sold Early Times to Louisville's Brown-Forman Corp., which had a license to sell "medicinal" spirits and needed a new supply of bourbon to satisfy the increasing prescription demand. Brown-Forman moved the company's offices to Louisville the following year. After Prohibition was repealed, a new Early Times distillery was built there in 1933.

Anticipating a renewed public interest in straight bourbon after the war, Brown-Forman emphasized production of Early Times. Returning to the market in 1949, it soared in popularity and by 1953 was the number-one straight bourbon in the United States. It also became Brown-Forman's biggest seller and top income-producer.

To reduce internal competition with its Old Forester brand, Brown-Forman changed the Early Times available in the United States to an "old style Kentucky whisky" in 1983. It is now aged in a combination of new and previously used white oak barrels. Though not available domestically, Early Times bourbon is sold in several foreign markets and is especially popular in Japan.

See William L. Downard, *Dictionary of the History of the American Brewing and Distilling Industries* (Westport, Conn., 1980); Harry H. Kroll, *Bluegrass, Belles, and Bourbon* (New York 1967).

Thomas E. Stephens

ECKSTEIN NORTON INSTITUTE. In 1890, Dr. William J. Simmons resigned as president of State University in Louisville to establish the Eckstein Norton Institute, a school specializing in the industrial training of African Americans. With funding from prominent Louisville businessmen such as Louisville & Nashville Railroad (L&N) executives Eckstein Norton and Milton Smith, Simmons purchased seventy-five acres of land across the Bullitt County line near the L&N rail line in Cave Springs. In mid-September, the school, consisting of one central brick building surrounded by six additional frame structures, opened with twenty-four students and sixteen teachers, many of whom had followed Simmons from State University. Although the institute, with its motto of "Education of the hands, head, heart, and mind," offered business classes such as bookkeeping, the pride of the school was its industrial department that offered training in carpentry, blacksmithing, farming, painting, cooking, tailoring, and dressmaking. Simmons believed that, after firmly establishing Eckstein Norton, he would be able to open a branch closer to Louisville and train competent domestic servants. However, Simmons died at the end of October later that year. Undaunted, the Louisville businessmen continued to fund the school and convinced Simmon's assistant, Dr. Charles Parrish Sr., to assume the presidency, a post he held until the school's closing. After donations from the Louisville benefactors slowed, the Eckstein Norton Institute merged with the Lincoln Institute in Simpsonville in 1912. By that time, it reportedly had provided aid to 1,794 students while graduating 189.

See George C. Wright, *Life Behind a Veil: Blacks in Louisville, Kentucky, 1865–1930* (Baton Rouge 1985).

ECLIPSE HALL. Located at 1230 W Walnut St. (Muhammad Ali Blvd.) Eclipse Hall was opened in 1872 as a market and saloon under the ownership of Henry Koch. By 1876 part of the building was rented to African American groups for dances and balls, and the Grand United Order of Odd Fellows (GUOOF) began to hold meetings there. In 1885 the GUOOF bought the building and renamed it Odd Fellows Hall. The building was destroyed by the 1890 tornado but was rebuilt and enlarged. In 1908 the Bijou Theater, the first black-owned theater in Louisville, opened in the rear of the building under the management of Edward D. Lee. The theater offered vaudeville acts by both white and black artists and operated under several different names before it closed its doors in 1921. The building remained under the ownership of the GUOOF until it was razed in the 1960s.

See H.C. Weeden, *Weeden's History of the Colored People of Louisville* (Louisville 1897).

Cornelius Bogert

ECLIPSE PARK. During its existence as one of Louisville's foremost ballparks, Eclipse Park was home to amateur, semipro, and professional baseball. Constructed in 1871, its first location was in Louisville's West End at Twenty-eighth and Elliott Streets. Fire destroyed that ballpark in September 1892, and shortly thereafter a new Eclipse Park was erected nearby on the southwest corner of Twenty-eighth and Broadway.

The park lay within the city limits of Parkland, which prohibited baseball playing on Sundays. Baseball club administrators appealed to Louisville officials for aid. In response,

Louisville annexed Eclipse Park in 1893, and Sunday games were reinstated. Games continued to be played at that location until fire razed the wooden grandstands in 1899. This second Eclipse Park is of particular historic importance because it was the site of the last major-league game played in Louisville. It was on September 2, 1899, when Louisville defeated Washington 25 to 4.

The third Eclipse Park was established at the northwest corner of Seventh and Kentucky Streets in 1902, and its opening was marked by much fanfare and a parade. The new grandstands and bleachers seated about eighty-five hundred people. Though FOOTBALL games also were played there, the park was primarily the home for the LOUISVILLE COLONELS semiprofessional baseball club until 1922. Fans going to the games often got off the FOURTH ST. trolleys and took a shortcut to the park through an alleyway located on the north side of Memorial Auditorium that became known as BASE BALL ALLEY.

On November 20, 1922, the third Eclipse Park was ravaged by fire. It was replaced in 1923 by PARKWAY FIELD on Eastern Parkway. The grounds of the old Eclipse Park lay empty until 1938 when a government housing project, College Court, was erected.

See A.H. Tarvin, *Seventy-Five Years on Louisville Diamonds* (Louisville 1940).

ECLIPSE VS. A.L. SHOTWELL. American steamboat enthusiasts remember the greatest race between two post–CIVIL WAR steamboats, the *Robert E. Lee* and the *Natchez,* in 1870. The race started in New Orleans and ended at St. Louis. The *Robert E. Lee* won the championship of the Mississippi River by six hours and fifteen minutes. Both steamboat captains were natives of Kentucky. This highly publicized contest has obscured other steamboat races that were equally interesting and exciting.

The race between the *Eclipse* and *A.L. Shotwell* in the spring of 1853 is among these. The two boats were built in NEW ALBANY, Indiana, and demonstrated superior design and craftsmanship. The *Eclipse* was built by Dowerman and Humphrey shipyard in January 1852, and its machinery was installed by Phillips, Hise, and Co. Then it was moved to PORTLAND where its cabins and finery were laid on. The boat was designed to eclipse everything on the western waters because it was bigger, more luxurious, and faster. Its cost was $150,000, the highest of any western steamboat up to that time. Its captain and one of the principal owners, E.T. Sturgeon, closely followed the construction process.

The *A.L. Shotwell* came out of John Evans's boatyard in December 1852. Its machinery was produced and installed by Phoenix Foundry of New Albany. The boat was named after its principal owner, a well-known figure among navigators; and its captain was B.L. Elliot. The *Shotwell* was also of the finest and latest type of construction and emerged as the main rival to the *Eclipse*.

At the beginning of 1853 there were some informal discussions among representatives of the two boats to try them in a race. It was set for May 1853. The boats would run from New Orleans to Louisville, a distance of about fourteen hundred miles. Rather than race simultaneously, they left three days apart. The *Eclipse* departed New Orleans on May 14, and the *Shotwell* left on May 17. *Eclipse* arrived at Louisville in record time of four days, nine hours, and thirty minutes; but three days later *Shotwell* beat *Eclipse's* record by one minute, reaching the city in four days, nine hours, and twenty-nine minutes.

The slim margin resulted in quarrels among their supporters. *Shotwell* partisans questioned the validity of clocking procedures and suggested a new race. The tremendous amount of betting made the stakes high, and the issue was crucial. Both captains, each convinced he was the winner, were required to publish extensive documentation with many sworn affidavits. The information and growing controversy made an objective verdict almost impossible.

On June 6 Captain Elliot of the *Shotwell*, in an elaborate ceremony, was designated the winner, while Captain Sturgeon still insisted on his victory. There was no rematch, and most of the bettors held tightly to their money. The race and lengthy dispute reflected how essential were the STEAMBOATS in the culture of river towns in the 1850s.

See Victor M. Bogle, "The *Eclipse* vs. the *A.L. Shotwell*; Memorable Contest Almost Forgotten," *Filson Club History Quarterly* 35 (April 1961): 125–37.

ECONOMY. Cities typically spawn around critical military, religious, and economic points. Louisville grew initially due to its location at the then-treacherous FALLS OF THE OHIO, the only break in river traffic from Pittsburgh to New Orleans. Historian George Yater wrote, "That a city would rise here at the break in navigation was inevitable." In 1778 GEORGE ROGERS CLARK was en route down the OHIO RIVER to snatch the vast Illinois country from British control during the Revolutionary War. He strategically chose the Falls area as a base, both to protect the increasing flow of frontier settlers from Indian attack as they stopped and also as a base for his foray into the Illinois country.

Beyond that necessary for survival of the early settlers, the first economic activity in the Louisville area appears to be wood-processing (to make boats) and SALT-MAKING (to preserve food). The flatboats of the eighteenth century favored the export of simple Kentucky agricultural products downriver to New Orleans and the import of settlers and basic household provisions from the Pittsburgh area.

The STEAMBOATS of the early nineteenth century, with their relatively large cargo capacities and quick speed up or downstream, made Louisville an economic powerhouse on the frontier. Because the steamboats could pass the Falls only during high water, their stops helped warehousing, wholesaling, and distribution industries flourish in Louisville, as well as INSURANCE and BANKING enterprises. Manufacturing operations—in shipbuilding, cotton, paper, wagons, cooperage, soap, lumber, GLASS, CEMENT, steam engines, beef, pork, leather, flour, TOBACCO, and liquor—took root around this important shipping point. And the sheer flow of people—riverboat workers, speculators, and frontier families—created a thriving hospitality industry. All early accounts cite the numerous taverns and HOTELS as well as the muddy STREETS and rough clientele. Newspaper operations, federal courts, and law offices all grew rapidly in Louisville as the population in the Ohio River Valley grew at its fastest rate in history.

RAILROADS, the freight transportation innovation of the second half of the nineteenth century, brought the next wave of economic development to Louisville—then the tenth-largest American city. More dependable and flexible than river transportation, yet bound to link all the major river cities, rail created new demand for both Louisville's producer and consumer goods. Local IRON FOUNDRIES, steam engine plants, and timber mills sprang up to build the rail system west of the Appalachians. And Louisville-produced pork, wool, cotton, and FURNITURE could be sold in new markets such as Nashville and Atlanta that were not easily accessible by water.

Factories, offices, and shops were primarily family-owned and family-run propositions until the twentieth century. By modern standards the scale of production was small, but most proprietors were also residents of the city in which their enterprises were sited. The families enjoyed the wealth of their business successes, and they suffered the ruin of their failures. With the advent of the corporation, business owners could place at risk only their investment in an enterprise, not their total private wealth. This legal innovation unleashed an explosion of economic activity, fueled by newly attracted capital and the unit cost advantages of large-scale production and distribution. It also induced a new round of competition among regional economies. Early in the twentieth century, Louisville gained automobile and plumbing fixture factories but lost paper and leather operations.

The major technological and commercial developments of the twentieth century—automobiles and trucks, interstate highways, air travel, pervasive electricity and gasoline-powered activity, electronics, telecommunications, and computers—each played a role in shaping the current characteristics of the Louisville area economy. The federal interstate highway system connected all major cities and provided daunting competition to the rail freight industry in particular. Louisville is served by three interstate highways; and, combined with its enviable barge, rail, and air freight service, it remains an important transportation, warehousing, and logistics hub.

The westward movement of the center of the United States population has passed just north of Louisville, making the city a natural point of adding value before shipment of high-value products to consumers. Louisville's central location and strong transportation linkages ensure a prosperous distribution industry. Proximity to so many large consumer markets, combined with inexpensive energy, give Louisville a competitive advantage in manufacturing big-ticket consumer durable goods, including autos, appliances, and furniture. In the early 1980s, UNITED PARCEL SERVICE (UPS) chose Louisville as its international hub for overnight and next-day air freight service. In 2000, with sixteen thousand employees in Louisville, UPS was the largest private employer in the metro area as well as the state of Kentucky. The UPS presence, combined with major investments in infrastructure and aggressive state and local economic development programs, have encouraged a wide array of warehousing, inventory control, computer-repair, and logistics operations, primarily in the industrial parks near the two interstate highway belts in Jefferson County.

While technological changes in the transportation of goods— flatboats, steamboats, rail, truck, and air—have historically blessed Louisville's economy, other innovations have not benefited the city to the same degree. Buoyed by advances in computers, audio and visual communications, and the rising general education of the world population, the most lucrative sectors of the U.S. economy at the close of the twentieth century involve the discovery, enhancement, and transmission of information. This includes medical, financial, legal, engineering, design, marketing, ADVERTISING, PUBLIC RELATIONS, entertainment, consulting, and research and development enterprises. These industries have thrived primarily in and around clusters of highly educated workers, often attracted by natural and cultural amenities, and in locales where risk-taking is encouraged and rewarded. On average, Louisville's workforce lags in formal educational attainment. While nearly all of the technical, professional, and creative occupations are represented in the area to some degree, the growth in the service economy here has been disproportionately at the lower end of the skill and earnings profile.

Louisville's most prominent service-sector success stories have been in insurance and health care. HUMANA, the community's largest homegrown corporation, was founded by David Jones and WENDELL CHERRY in the 1960s. What started as a single Louisville nursing home became a management company for nursing homes around the country, then an owner and manager of HOSPITALS, and finally a health insurance/health maintenance organization. According to the 1999 *Fortune Magazine* rankings, it was the 165th-largest United States company in terms of revenues. Humana sold its hospitals in 1994 to Columbia HCA, at first headquartered in Louisville, then Nashville. In 1998 Humana employed around forty-five hundred persons at its Louisville headquarters.

Another major health-care employer in Louisville is VENCOR, the largest owner and operator of long-term-care hospitals in the United States. In 1997 the company was named to the Fortune 500 list and in 1999 was ranked 464th in terms of revenue. In 1999 the company encountered legal and financial problems, however, and delayed indefinitely its planned $50 million riverfront headquarters building designed by architect I.M. Pei and his firm.

The talent and financial resources attracted to these major insurance and health delivery organizations have spawned other emerging ventures, including ResCare, a provider of at-home health-care services, and Atria, a developer of assisted- and independent-living communities for the elderly.

To the east of the banking, legal, insurance, and management firms in Louisville's central business district, there is the Medical Center, an important cluster of hospitals providing acute care, teaching, and research. The cluster includes Jewish Hospital along with its Frazier Rehabilitation Center and Rudd Heart and Lung Center; NORTON HEALTHCARE with its Women's Pavilion and KOSAIR CHILDREN'S HOSPITAL; and the UNIVERSITY OF LOUISVILLE Hospital and its medical, dental, nursing, and other health science schools. The cluster has become a regional economic engine, attracting patients from a large radius and winning federal research grants.

The three largest Louisville banks from the regulated (pre-1980) era—First National, Citizens Fidelity, and Liberty—have each been purchased by larger out-of-state banks. Now owned and managed by, respectively, NATIONAL CITY, PNC, and BANK ONE, they remain the largest local banks in terms of customers and assets. Many of the former banks' high-level functions and employees, however, have been transferred to the home offices in Cleveland, Pittsburgh, and Columbus. Louisville has gained some operations centers under the consolidations, most notably National Processing Corp. and Liberty Payment Services—clearinghouses for checks and other financial instruments spun off by National City Corp. and Bank One, respectively. The high profitability of banking during the mid-1990s, combined with Louisville's general economic revitalization, has generated a recent wave of local bank start-ups and expansions.

The international wave of mergers and acquisitions cost Louisville two *Fortune 500* firms in the mid-1990s. Columbia/HCA, which grew out of Humana, moved to Nashville in 1995 as part of a merger with Health Trust. In 1997 Providian Corp., a large diversified financial services company headquartered in downtown Louisville, was acquired by AEGON Inc., a Dutch insurance giant. Many of Providian's operations were moved to Baltimore, home of Aegon's U.S. company. Providian grew out of Capital Holding and Commonwealth Insurance, a company built on selling life, homeowners, and other insurance products at the retail level throughout the rural South.

Louisville has generally been successful in attracting clerical, data processing, and consumer service centers in banking, insurance, catalog sales, and telemarketing. Most of the jobs supported by these operations, however, are part-time, require little formal education, pay relatively low wages, and generate wealth primarily for out-of-town owners.

Another strong sector of the Louisville economy has been the beverage and food-service industry. Louisville is home to BROWN-FORMAN, a major distiller and consumer products company, as well as several national or regional restaurant companies, including KFC (Kentucky Fried Chicken), PAPA JOHN'S Pizza, Chi Chi's Mexican Restaurants, and TUMBLEWEED MESQUITE MEXICAN GRILL. In 1997 TRICON GLOBAL RESTAURANTS, a company with $20 billion in annual sales, was spun off from PepsiCo and established its international headquarters at the KFC site off the WATTERSON EXPRESSWAY. Tricon oversees nearly thirty thousand KFC, Pizza Hut, and Taco Bell franchise and company-owned stores in ninety-five countries and is the world's largest restaurant company in terms of retail outlets. With annual revenues of $8.5 billion, it ranked 199th on the 1999 *Fortune 500* list of American companies.

Beyond selling rooms and food to the overnight commercial and recreational traveler, Louisville's hospitality industry is based primarily on its large trade show and convention business. The state-owned KENTUCKY FAIR AND EXPOSITION CENTER, adjacent to the main airport, has the sixth-largest indoor floor space for exhibitors in the United States. The facility has long attracted major space-intensive annual shows such as the National Street Rod Association Expo; the Mid-American Trucking Show; the International Lawn, Garden, and Power Equipment Expo; the NORTH AMERICAN INTERNATIONAL LIVESTOCK EXPO; the National Farm Machinery Show; the Recreation Vehicle Industry Association Trade Show; and Equitana. These shows each bring ten to twenty thousand exhibitors and attendees to Louisville for multiday stays. They perennially fill the thirteen thousand area hotel rooms. The low hotel rates, Louisville's central midwestern location, and easy interstate highway access also regularly attract some major national conventions such as that of the JEHOVAH'S WITNESSES, the National Quartet Society, the National Head Start Association, United Way of America, and FFA. A major renovation and doubling of floor space at the downtown Kentucky International Convention Center made it a popular convention gathering place.

A solid network of museums, artistic venues, and natural and manmade amenities lures other visitors to Louisville and enhances the quality of life for all residents. Most notable of these are the KENTUCKY CENTER FOR THE ARTS; ACTORS THEATRE; the LOUISVILLE ORCHESTRA, Ballet, and Opera Companies; the KENTUCKY DERBY FESTIVAL; the KENTUCKY STATE FAIR; ST. JAMES ART SHOW; the LOUISVILLE SLUGGER MUSEUM; the J.B. SPEED ART MUSEUM; the LOUISVILLE SCIENCE CENTER; the LOUISVILLE ZOO; Derby Dinner Playhouse; Stage One; Comedy Caravan; CHURCHILL DOWNS and its KENTUCKY DERBY MUSEUM; CAESAR'S Glory of Rome Casino; the FALLS OF THE OHIO STATE PARK in CLARKSVILLE, INDIANA; and the downtown Waterfront Park. Tourism-related sales and payrolls at area hotels and RESTAURANTS are comparable to those of similarly-sized cities in the central United States. The lack of more first-class hotel rooms and of better air connections to large cities in North America have been mentioned as constraints on the growth of Louisville's hospitality industry.

Louisville's locational and energy cost advantages have led to a natural concentration of producers of high value-to-weight commodities. While Louisville was known for its tobacco processing and alcoholic beverage industries in the first half of the twentieth century, the second half has been led by home appliance and automobile assembly. GENERAL ELECTRIC and FORD MOTOR CO. have major plants in Louisville. These two companies directly account for about sixteen thousand of Louisville's ninety thousand manufacturing jobs. Given that nearly all of their output is sold to consumers outside of the local economy, these sales and the payroll they generate are the major source of export earnings for Louisville. Other area manufacturers—plastics, CHEMICALS, PAINT, fabricated metals, PRINTING, paperboard—have prospered by serving these large producers of consumer durable goods. Their high wages and strong upstream and downstream linkages to other local companies mean that auto, truck, and appliance production continue to be the most important economic activities in Louisville.

General Electric's Appliance Park in Louisville, operating since 1953, became the largest site for the production of major home appliances in the world. At its peak in the early 1970s it employed over twenty thousand Louisville-area residents. With less than half its peak workforce in 1999, GE is still the largest manufacturing employer in the Louisville area and the state of Kentucky. Its shipments of dishwashers, refrigerators, and home laundry equipment have grown, but less and less labor is required for fabrication and assembly. The average worker at the plant earned over forty thousand dollars per year, compared to an overall average of around twenty-nine thousand for all jobs in the Louisville market.

Ford has two plants in Louisville, with a combined payroll of over eight thousand employees. The plant just south of the main airport has made many popular models including the LTD luxury car, the Ford Ranger pickup, and the Explorer sport utility vehicle. The plant in the far eastern part of Jefferson County produced mid-sized and large trucks, but in 1997 Ford sold its heavy truck line to Daimler Benz AG Freightliner Corp. and began switching production to light and medium trucks. Ford's workers also average around forty thousand dollars per year, and, like GE, its employees have excellent fringe benefits. Furthermore, since the late 1970s, the center of the U.S. automobile industry has moved southward from Michigan, Indiana, and Ohio into Kentucky, Tennessee, Alabama, and South Carolina. This includes not only auto and truck assembly but also the manufacture of steel, plastics, glass, and aluminum, as well as their fabrications and shapings. Louisville has benefited from the regional shift of this important industry.

Other major exporting industries include printing, cigarettes, distilled liquor, aluminum foil, chemicals, and paper and wood products. In addition, Louisville has a rich complement of manufacturers that serve primarily local consumers—bakeries, wood flooring, cabinetmakers, and printers. Manufacturing as a whole directly generates about $4 billion in payroll annually in the Louisville area, accounting for roughly one-fourth of the total payroll in the metropolitan area.

Though still perhaps the most important layer of the Louisville economy, manufacturing now accounts for a smaller share of employment and worker earnings than at any time since WORLD WAR II. At its peak employment level, 137,000 workers in 1973, manufacturing payrolls made up 27 percent of the workers and 36 percent of all worker earnings in the metro area. In 1997 manufacturing accounted for about 18 percent of area jobs and 25 percent of area earnings. The decline in the size of Louisville's factory workforce relative to the total is due to a worldwide increase in manufacturing productivity as well as the rapid growth in service enterprises where machines cannot so easily replace labor.

Looking back over the twentieth century, Louisville's share of national manufacturing activity has been remarkably steady. For example, the local share of national manufacturing production workers (as distinct from supervisors and management) has fluctuated in a fairly narrow band around one-half percentage point, even as Louisville's share of population has fallen to less than four-tenths of a percentage point. Perhaps most impressive is that Louisville's operations have on net held their ground during the rounds of energy crises, high interest rates, global competition, and technological change so challenging during the last three decades of the twentieth century. The post–WORLD WAR II buildup in value added by Louisville area manufacturers is evident, reflecting the massive investments by General Electric at Appliance Park, by Ford Motor Co., and by firms selling parts to the major plants. As of 1992 Louisville's share of United States manufacturing value added (the difference between the value of shipments and the cost of materials) was approaching its historic peak, and it was double Louisville's share of the nation's population.

In manufacturing, Louisville has historically been a high value-added, high-wage town. Louisville area manufacturers tend to produce more complicated and more expensive items than are manufactured in other areas of the United States. For example, Louisville has a high concentration in automobile assembly and a low concentration in apparel manufacturing. The strong growth in manufacturing employment throughout much of the century, combined with Louisville's specialization at the high end, led to solid payroll growth for the entire community. However, since at least the late 1970s manufacturing employment has declined throughout the United States. The lack of new manufacturing jobs in Louisville has exposed a weakness in the human capital of the local workforce and in the area's climate for new venture creation for the emerging lucrative service sectors. Indeed, since the early 1980s the annual earnings per job in the Louisville market has failed to keep pace with national gains, despite the strong growth in raw jobs in the local distribution, office, and retail sectors during the most recent decade.

Metropolitan Louisville's population has hovered just below the one-million mark since 1975. Slightly less than 1 in 250 Americans live in the Louisville metro area, roughly the same ratio as at the turn of the nineteenth century, although well below its mid-nineteenth century status (one in 190 U.S. residents). Longer lives and the resultant fall in mortality rates have been offset by a local decline in fertility rates, generating little natural growth in the POPULATION. The rising female labor force participation rate, in Louisville and around the country, as well as changing lifestyle preferences, has led to smaller family sizes. In addition, Louisville has not seen the influx of foreign immigrants (and their typically large families) common to cities near America's borders. Finally, Louisville's lack of natural amenities, a major research university, or enough booming professional industries has made it difficult to keep educated young people in their hometown.

For those firms that have incubated in Louisville or have moved here, there have been several common keys to their success in attracting and retaining an educated workforce. Louisville is consistently regarded as a "great place to raise a family." Century-old NEIGHBORHOODS and church groups provide a bedrock foundation for the community. Hundreds of small family-run retail businesses provide excellent value for everyday items like car repair, hair styling, produce, and home maintenance. The large pre-1970 layer of inexpensive well-built homes in coherent central neighborhoods makes it easy for a young family to own a solid home. The crime rate is low, as are local property tax rates. There is a wide mixture of good public and private, primarily Catholic, schools. And commuting to work and shopping—if one can find a way to avoid the infamous Spaghetti Junction downtown, where three interstate highways awkwardly merge, and a few other bottlenecks—is fairly brisk around the metro area.

In 1996 business and civic leaders undertook a study that identified a number of important impediments, and initiatives, to enhance economic prosperity in the Louisville area. One was that the bi-state region needs to start behaving as the economic entity it is. The report said that precious energy and dollars are often wasted in turf battles between Kentucky and southern Indiana jurisdictions, and among local jurisdictions in Kentucky. Two more bridges over the Ohio River were proposed to complete the interstate loop around the central business district, to divert some heavy truck and hazardous materials traffic, to provide access to new industrial land, and to symbolize the seamlessness of the community.

Second, to increase the number of high-paying professional and technical jobs, the study urged the community to improve its climate for entrepreneurship and enhance its higher education infrastructure. Venture capital is scarce in Louisville, at least in comparison to nearby markets such as Nashville and Indianapolis. Kentucky state tax rates on personal income, wealth, and consumption are among the highest in the United States. Louisville has been handicapped by the lack of a major research university. It has meant a less-educated and older workforce, a climate weak in discovery and commercial development, and a net cash outflow for the community. At the University of Louisville a number of newly endowed faculty positions are being funded in biotechnology, neurosciences, cardiology, and logistics. The new faculty will bring with them established research programs and federal funding. By concentrating fresh investments in research areas most aligned with Louisville's past economic success and competitive advantages, it is anticipated that some new companies, and perhaps new industries, will emerge.

Geographically, economies are most naturally defined as spatial concentrations of economic markets for workers, housing, retail purchases, industrial and commercial goods, and services. The closest statistical concept for measuring economies in the United States is the METROPOLITAN STATISTICAL AREA (MSA)—groups of counties typically clustered around a central business district with relatively dense and inward-looking commuting and shopping patterns, one that generates a distinct market for housing, jobs, entertainment, communication, and daily purchases. The Louisville MSA includes BULLITT, Jefferson, and OLDHAM Counties in Kentucky, and CLARK, FLOYD, HARRISON, and SCOTT Counties in Indiana. The wider Louisville economic area includes, in order of population size, Hardin, Nelson, Jefferson (Indiana), SHELBY, Meade, Washington (Indiana), Grayson, Breckinridge, Marion, Henry, Larue, Washington, Crawford (Indiana), Carroll, SPENCER, and Trimble Counties.

To many casual observers, the term "Louisville economy" refers to economic conditions in the city of Louisville—city with a capital C. While the City contains the central business district and many of the most important industries and neighborhoods, the Louisville economy has always encompassed a much wider GEOGRAPHY. In fact, there was a Louisville economy before there was a City of Louisville. When the present City was founded in 1778 with a dozen families and around thirty troops, Jefferson County already had perhaps a thousand inhabitants. Census records show that the majority of Jefferson County residents lived outside the City of Louisville until the 1830s. By the end of the nineteenth century, nearly 90 percent of county residents lived in the City. The share has fallen steadily since, and today the City of Louisville is home to less than 40 percent of Jefferson County residents and less than 30 percent of MSA residents.

Farming, trading, transportation, and low-volume manufacturing activities were prevalent in the Falls of the Ohio region for decades before the urbanization of Louisville, JEFFERSONVILLE, NEW ALBANY, and other important area cities. Farming and horticulture remain an important industry in the Louisville area, generating hundreds of millions of dollars annually from sales of crop, equine, livestock, nursery, and greenhouse products. Several major manufacturing operations are located in more sparsely populated parts of the Louisville area, including PUBLISHERS' PRINTING in Bullitt County, Budd's auto body stamping facility in Shelby County, and the Ford Truck plant in far eastern Jefferson County. FORT KNOX, in adjacent Hardin County, has economic links with Louisville area firms and workers. The largest entertainment establishment in the history of the Louisville area, the CAESARS RESORT, is in Harrison County, Indiana. All of these enterprises tap the large metropolitan workforce, rely upon area schools to prepare workers, use the area's transportation system, and purchase heavily from local vendors. All too have a stake in the health of the city's core.

See George Yater, *Two Hundred Years at the Falls of the Ohio* (Louisville 1979); U.S. Bureau of the Census, decennial censuses, 1780 to 1990; U.S. Bureau of the Census, *Census of Manufacturing,* 1900, 1905, 1910, 1914, 1919, 1935, 1939, 1947, 1954, 1958, 1963, 1967, 1972, 1977, 1982, 1987, 1992; U.S. Bureau of the Census, Historical Statistics of the United States, Colonial Times to 1970.

Paul A. Coomes

ECUMENISM. Ecumenical developments in Louisville grew from two major twentieth-century catalysts: the foundation in 1948 of the World Council of Churches (WWC) and the reform initiatives of the Roman Catholic church's Second Vatican Council (1962–65). These postwar events afforded new models for interdenominational collaboration and interconfessional dialogue to parallel the WCC's "Life and Work" and "Faith and Order" branches.

The city had seen some notable interfaith forerunners, including Monsignor Michael Bouchet (1827–1903), inventor (he patented an adding machine in 1882) and rector of the CATHEDRAL OF THE ASSUMPTION; Bouchet's close friend Rabbi ADOLPH MOSES (1840–1928); and Rev. EDWARD L. POWELL (1860–1928), civic leader and pastor of FIRST CHRISTIAN CHURCH for over forty years.

An event in Louisville history that anticipated later interfaith cooperation was the memorial service on April 21, 1912, for those lost in the sinking of the *Titanic.* Held at the city's new Armory (now GARDENS OF LOUISVILLE at Sixth and Muhammad Ali Blvd.), this religious service drew over ten thousand worshipers and featured speakers from all the city's major denominations.

The late 1950s and early 1960s saw the first formal cooperation between Protestant congregations, giving birth to the Louisville Area Council of Churches. This structure grew directly out of informal neighborhood ministerial associations. Following the joint efforts by church leaders in the CIVIL RIGHTS movement of the 1960s and their opposition to the war in Vietnam, in 1971 ROMAN CATHOLICS and Orthodox Christians were included in a new, broader ecumenical partnership, the Louisville Area Interchurch Organization for Service (LAIOS). In the late 1950s and until his death, the Cistercian monk THOMAS MERTON (1915–68) held informal ecumenical meetings at the Abbey of Gethsemani in Nelson County, attracting ecumenical leaders from around the country. Merton first welcomed the students of Dr. E. Glenn Hinson from the SOUTHERN BAPTIST THEOLOGICAL SEMINARY in the late 1950s; students and faculty from Lexington Theological Seminary also visited with Merton at the abbey.

By 1979 Louisville ecumenism had matured to form the Kentuckiana Interfaith Community (KIC) with the Reverend Dale Tucker as its first interim director and Father Stanley A. Schmidt as its first president. KIC allowed for both denominational (or judicatory) membership and individual local congregational membership, reflecting the diverse church order structures; more significantly, KIC was the first formal "covenant" in which a local metropolitan ecumenical structure broadened its mission to include the membership of Jewish congregations. The first full-time director of KIC was the Reverend Kenneth MacHarg (1980–90) of the UNITED CHURCH OF CHRIST. Greek Orthodox Reverend Dr. Gregory Wingenbach served as the second director of KIC (1990–98); he was followed by Baptist Reverend Reba S. Cobb (1998–).

Networks of neighborhood COMMUNITY MINISTRIES in Louisville provided models for KIC by providing services ranging from day care for children and the elderly to food pantries to formal covenants between local congregations and parishes. The first such agency, Highlands Community Ministries, was founded in 1971 under the direction of Stan Esterle. Its activities have been awarded recognition by the National Council of Churches. KIC also convenes a Forum of Christian Churches in which the churches can address doctrinal or confessional issues and developments through multilateral dialogue. Louisville also provided one of the leaders of the National Community Ministries Network in the person of the Reverend A. David Bos, former director of St. Matthews Area Ministries.

Louisville was the site of the Consultation on Church Union's (COCU) fifteenth plenary meeting in 1979. The Faith and Order Commission of the WCC convened for its international consultation on baptism at the Southern Baptist Theological Seminary in 1979. In 1974 a jointly funded Ecumenical Center was constructed on the campus of the UNIVERSITY OF LOUISVILLE. Throughout its history it has been served by Catholic priests and religious, Protestant and/or Episcopal ministers, and Jewish rabbis or staff members through collaborative programming. Following three-part dialogues in the 1980s and 1990s involving JEWS, Christians, and MUSLIMS, the campus center changed its name to reflect this broadening ministry, becoming the Interfaith Center. From 1980 to 1996 Louisville's Council on Religion and Peacemaking began its political advocacy ministry on issues of peace and justice and developing nonviolent skills.

In May 1983 the National Workshop on Christian Unity met in Louisville at the Hyatt Hotel and featured a plenary presentation by local ecumenists on the importance of the Louisville churches' consensus on baptism as a response to the WCC's Baptism, Eucharist, and Ministry study of 1982. In 1988 the international Disciples of Christ–Roman Catholic Dialogue met in Louisville and at the Abbey of Gethsemani near Bardstown.

The PRESBYTERIAN CHURCH (USA) moved its headquarters in 1988 from New York City to Louisville. Efforts by civic leader David A. Jones and Dr. John M. Mulder, president of the LOUISVILLE PRESBYTERIAN THEOLOGICAL SEMINARY, proved vital to this move. The Presbyterian headquarters serves as a frequent locus for national ecumenical activity and, consequently, a significant contributor to local ecumenical enterprises.

In September 1989 the North American Academy of Ecumenists held its annual meeting at the GALT HOUSE in Louisville. Local ecumenists presented a panel of Louisville interchurch couples to highlight the 1988 formation by the Reverend Dr. Gregory Wingenbach and Rev. George Kilcourse of the American Association of Inter-church Families in collaboration with KIC.

Louisville's broadcast industry contributed to the development of local ecumenism by launching in May 1952 WHAS Radio's *The Moral Side of the News*, a panel including a rabbi, a priest, and Protestant ministers. The program went on to be televised and continues weekly broadcasts. The panel also administers funds collected by WHAS's CRUSADE FOR CHILDREN, which assists physically and mentally handicapped children in Louisville and southern Indiana. In 1987 the Faith Channel was founded by KIC, the Archdiocese of Louisville's Communications Center, and the Southern Baptist Theological Seminary and its network of cooperating Baptist churches. The Faith Channel has continued as the only full-time ecumenically sponsored cable TV station in North America. It broadcasts a spectrum of denominational programs sponsored by all of KIC's membership churches.

A unique development in Louisville ecumenism began in 1983 with the CATHEDRAL HERITAGE FOUNDATION. The foundation was established to restore the historic 1852 Cathedral of the Assumption on Fifth St. and to create an Interfaith Spiritual Center for the entire community. Its committees include members from the wide spectrum of religious communities in the city. Plans include the construction of the nation's first Museum of Faiths, a dining hall for the homeless, and a meditation chapel and inner-city garden. Each November since 1996 the Cathedral Heritage Foundation has convened a four-day Festival of Faiths with exhibits, speakers, and events manifesting the developing interreligious cooperation in Louisville.

George A. Kilcourse Jr.

EDGEWOOD. Neighborhood in southern Louisville bounded by Fern Valley Rd. to the south, Interstate 65 to the west, Preston Hwy. to the north, and the city limits to the east. Originally laid out in the mid-1920s by two developers, the area grew slowly because of the

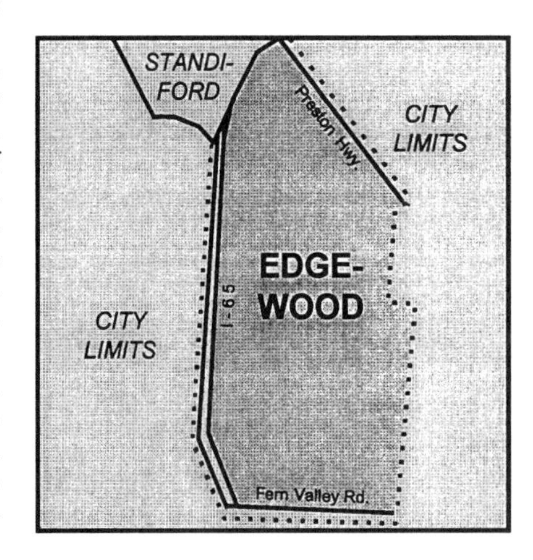

GREAT DEPRESSION, the location's poor drainage, and the distance from the city. The neighborhood flourished after WORLD WAR II with the increased use of Standiford Field (now LOUISVILLE INTERNATIONAL AIRPORT) and the improved sewage system that followed Louisville's annexation of the area in 1957. The airport expansion in the late 1980s and early 1990s required the city to purchase some of the homes in the neighborhood. Remaining families complained about the increased airport noise levels until the city agreed in 1996 to purchase the rest of the homes through a voluntary acquisition plan. Officials expect the buyout to be completed by 2005.

See *Louisville Survey: Central and South Report* (Louisville 1978).

EDISON, THOMAS ALVA (b Milan, Ohio, February 11, 1847; d West Orange, N.J., October 18, 1931). Inventor. Edison spent nearly two years in Louisville as a young telegrapher. The son of Samuel and Nancy (Elliott) Edison, he was perhaps the best-known inventor of the nineteenth century, especially noted for developing the incandescent electric light. He was in the city by late March 1866 (just past his nineteenth birthday), coming from Memphis, Tennessee, where he had been discharged as a TELEGRAPH operator for an inventive violation of rules.

Edison had devised a repeating mechanism that permitted messages from New York to New Orleans to be automatically relayed to the New Orleans wire. Ordinarily a Memphis operator transcribed this copy, then turned to his telegraph key to send it on to the Crescent City. Since this was Edison's task, the local manager considered that the young operator was not performing his assigned task when Edison used the repeating mechanism. In addition, according to Edison, the manager was attempting to develop a similar mechanism.

Edison found immediate employment in Louisville handling Western Union's night press wire (Associated Press copy). The office was then located in a shabby building on the south side of MAIN ST. between Second and Third. He lodged in a boarding house kept by Mrs. Agnes Smith on Third St. near Guthrie, not far from the telegraph office.

Intrigued by telegraphic opportunities in Brazil, Edison and two fellow operators left Louisville on August 1, 1866, for New Orleans to take ocean passage. Fortunately, Edison changed his mind and returned to Louisville and Western Union. His two companions reportedly died in Mexico of cholera.

Edison recalled that, upon his return, he found living quarters "in a room above a saloon." This may have been on Jefferson St. between First and Brook. During this second Louisville sojourn the Western Union office was moved to a newly constructed building on the southwest corner of Second and Main Streets. Constantly experimenting, Edison accidentally

Mr. and Mrs. Thomas Edison, Fort Myers, Florida, 1910.

spilled several gallons of sulfuric acid as he was attempting to fill a battery he had built. The acid leaked through the floor into the newly furnished office of manager T.R. Boyle. Edison was discharged the next day, sometime in the summer of 1867. By August he was handling press copy for Western Union in Cincinnati.

Only a dozen years later, when he first demonstrated his incandescent light, Edison's name became a household word. Interestingly, one of his financial backers was Dr. NORVIN GREEN of Louisville—who had been involved in forming Western Union in 1866. Green became Western Union's president in 1878 and also president of the Edison Electric Light Co. As early as January 4, 1880, Dr. Green's son, Pinckney, discussed progress on the incandescent bulb in a *COURIER-JOURNAL* interview.

It might have been this connection that prompted Louisville's SOUTHERN EXPOSITION, opened in August 1883, to opt for Edison's light. The forty-six-hundred-lamp system that was installed was the world's largest at the time. It set the norm for all future large expositions worldwide to be lighted electrically. The inventor left installation of the light system to trusted associates. He apparently never visited Louisville again after his days as a telegrapher, despite local legend that he was present at the Exposition's opening.

Nor is there hard evidence that Edison rented a room in the small double cottage at 729–31 E Washington St. in the BUTCHERTOWN neighborhood. However, *Edwards' Louisville City Directory* for 1866–67 lists Western Union operator Amos Eggleston as living at 337 E Washington between Clay and Shelby Streets. This became the 700 block in 1881, and 337 appears to have been the present 729 E Washington.

See Reese V. Jenkins and others, eds., *The Papers of Thomas A. Edison,* vol. 1 (Baltimore 1989); Frank L. Dyer and Thomas C. Martin, *Edison: His Life and Inventions,* 2 vols. (New York 1910, reprinted 1929); Harold C. Passer, *The Electrical Manufacturers* (Cambridge 1953).

George H. Yater

EGAN, EILEEN (b Boston, January 11, 1925; d Louisville, December 3, 1997). Educator. Eileen Egan was the daughter of Eugene O. and Mary (Condon) Egan. She joined the Roman Catholic Sisters of Charity of Nazareth in 1944. In 1956 she received her bachelor of arts degree from now SPALDING UNIVERSITY and went on to obtain her master's and doctorate from the Catholic University of America in Washington, D.C. Egan also earned a law degree from the UNIVERSITY OF LOUISVILLE. She served as chair of the English Department at Spalding from 1966 to 1967. In 1968 she became vice president of the university and a year later its president.

President of Spalding from 1969 to 1994, Egan was also a member of the American Association for Higher Education, the LOUISVILLE BAR ASSOCIATION, and the Kentucky Bar Association. Despite her impressive educational and professional accomplishments, she remained approachable and interested in people from all backgrounds.

Affiliated with several community organizations, she was known as a true humanitarian. She served on many boards, including the Louisville branch of the FEDERAL RESERVE BANK OF ST. LOUIS, the state Commission on Higher Education, the BETTER BUSINESS BUREAU of Greater Louisville, the Louisville Area Chamber of Commerce (GREATER LOUISVILLE INC.), Kentucky Country Day School, and Jewish Hospital. In 1987 Egan, along with others, including David Jones of HUMANA INC., successfully encouraged the PRESBYTERIAN CHURCH (USA) to locate its headquarters here rather than Kansas City, Missouri. In 1991, after creating the Jefferson County Office for Women, Judge-Executive DAVE ARMSTRONG chose her to head a thirty-two-member advisory committee on the issue of domestic violence.

During Egan's tenure at Spalding she led efforts that developed the small women's college into a successful coeducational university. She added seven undergraduate and eleven graduate degrees and a weekend college and helped with expansion of the campus. She was listed in *Who's Who in America* and eleven other biographical directories. She was showered with awards by groups as diverse as the LOUISVILLE URBAN LEAGUE and the Louisville chapter of the American Jewish Committee. She was awarded the Equality, Brotherhood, and Blanche B. Ottenheimer Awards for her community service. She died in a car accident. Egan is buried in the Nazareth Community Cemetery near Bardstown, Kentucky.

See *Who's Who of American Women* (New Providence, N.J., 1989); *Courier-Journal,* Dec. 4, 1997.

Michelle Thompson

EGREGIOUS STEAMBOAT JOURNAL. Steamboat Masters & Associates Inc. (SM&A) was incorporated in 1989 in the Commonwealth of Kentucky by Jack E. Custer and his wife, Sandra Miller Custer. SM&A specializes in river and steamboating history, and its principals have been actively engaged in river research since the 1970s. The company's primary focus is on the history of STEAMBOATS, the inland waterways, and the people who worked and traveled on them. The company's mission is to promote and make available accurate information on these subjects to writers, artists, television producers, educators, federal and state agencies, museums, boat or model designers, archaeologists, and individuals. SM&A accomplishes this through consulting, lectures, and publishing. It became clear that there was a need for a more scholarly journal for river and steamboat researchers to take advantage of modern research techniques and resources made available through computerized databases. SM&A began publishing the *Egregious Steamboat Journal* (ESJ) in 1991. The journal is dedicated to the history of the inland waterways, steamboats, diesel towboats, and the people who worked and traveled on them, past and present. Since the adjective "egregious" is usually known for its negative connotation, the name caught many by surprise.

"Egregious" is frequently used to mean "notably bad" or "flagrant." The word "egregious" had a positive connotation in English until the sixteenth century and then gradually became a pejorative. "Egregious" comes from the Latin *ex grege,* which literally means "out of the flock." The Latin adjective egregius, *-a, -um,* based on *ex grege,* means "exceptional, singular, uncommon, distinguished, illustrious" in a most positive sense, without any negative connotation whatsoever.

Part of the latent humor behind the title is that the editor of *ESJ* and the late Capt. Frederick Way Jr., the former editor of the *S&D Reflector*, another steamboat journal, had long maintained a facetious effort to find the other's "egregious" errors in their writings and research.

The *Egregious Steamboat Journal* is widely read and quoted. Each issue features many unusual topics about steamboats and rivers. While most steamboat periodicals have tended to become very provincial and feature only certain sections of the rivers, the *ESJ* has covered steamboats on the Mississippi and its tributaries as well as the Columbia, Sacramento, Hudson, and Potomac Rivers. It has also featured Canadian steamboats. In particular it includes Louisville's river history and its steamboats. It covers underwater ARCHAEOLOGY and features a variety of singular historical topics. Each issue has a photo essay covering some unusual aspect of steamboats and their architecture. It even features historic diesel towboats.

Jack E. Custer
Sandra Miller Custer

EHRLER, BREMER (b Louisville, July 10, 1914). Jefferson County judge/executive, Louisville postmaster. Ehrler's grandfather, Dominic E. Ehrler, started the well-known family dairy in Switzerland, immigrating to America in the latter part of the nineteenth century. Bremer worked in the family dairy farm on Poplar Level Rd. as a boy. He graduated from DU PONT MANUAL HIGH SCHOOL in 1931.

His public service career began in 1936 when he joined the United States Post Office Department. In 1962, he became the first career employee to serve as Louisville postmaster. He was president of the National Association of Postmasters and served on the Postmaster General's Advisory Committee. As Kentuckiana district manager/postmaster, he was responsible for thirteen hundred POST OFFICES and a $100 million annual budget statewide.

In 1973 he retired from the postal service and was elected to the first of three terms as Jefferson County clerk. During his eleven-year tenure he instituted the first computerized vehicle registration system in Kentucky. In 1984, as chairman of the Jefferson County Board of Elections, he established the first electronic voting system in the state.

On December 21, 1984, Ehrler, a Democrat, was appointed by Gov. MARTHA LAYNE COLLINS to serve out the remainder of United States senator MITCH MCCONNELL'S unexpired term as JEFFERSON COUNTY JUDGE/EXECUTIVE. He served until January 6, 1986.

In 1987 he was elected Kentucky secretary of state, serving until 1992. In 1993 he was appointed to complete an unexpired term as Jefferson County sheriff.

Ehrler volunteered for the army in 1942, serving in the adjutant general's branch during WORLD WAR II. After serving four years of active duty, he continued in the Army Reserve, retiring in 1968 with the rank of lieutenant colonel.

He married Elizabeth Greive in 1941. The couple had six children, four sons and two daughters. Bremer Way and Ehrler Drive, both located just east of Poplar Level Rd., are named for Ehrler and his family.

EHRMANN'S BAKERY. In 1848 William Ehrmann began operating a confectionery on MARKET ST. between Floyd and PRESTON STREETS. When William's brother, George G., became a partner in 1865, the name was changed to William Ehrmann and Bro. Co. In 1875 the two brothers began operating separate stores on Market St. George's sons, George H., Julius C., and Emil A., joined their father, and the company was named G.G. Ehrmann and Sons. By 1889 William's store had closed, and in 1891 Emil started his own store on Baxter Ave. However, Emil left the business in 1903 and began working for Bradas and Gheens, local candy manufacturers. George H. then took control of the store and operated it for the next forty years. After the street numbering change in 1909, the address became 1120 Bardstown Rd.

Ehrmann sold the store to Emil F. Miller in 1946, who ran it until 1956 when Arthur J. Steilberg bought it. In 1961 Steilberg facilitated the move to the bakery's current location in the Mid-City Mall on Bardstown Rd. The current owner, Gerald R. Driskell, has been involved in the bakery since the 1960s. When he became owner of the company in 1980, Driskell kept Ehrmann's true to its historic charm. It is one of the few bakeries or drugstores in the city that still operates a soda fountain serving ice cream, sodas, and sundaes. Small antique tables are provided for eating. Ice cream has always been the most popular item on the menu since William Ehrmann began serving it in 1848, with caramel and banana as popular flavors.

See *Courier-Journal*, July, 4, 1998; *Business First*, May 11, 1998.

E.I. DU PONT DE NEMOURS & CO. The history of the E.I. du Pont De Nemours & Co. manufacturing plant in Louisville dates to the 1940s. In 1941 construction of du Pont's Louisville Works began on 251 acres. The plant was designed for the manufacture of neoprene—a synthetic rubber invented in 1931 and used in products ranging from shoe soles to tires and adhesives to rocket fuels. At the outbreak of WORLD WAR II, the plant was purchased by the federal government as a war production facility, and du Pont operated the plant. The company repurchased the plant after the war and it operated as a du Pont plant for the first time on January 1, 1949.

In 1955 the company began making freon, and in 1962 the company added difluoroethane and vinyl fluoride. In 1996 du Pont Elastomers and Dow Chemical Co. formed du Pont-Dow Elastomers to make neoprene and hydrochloric acid. The six hundred workers are represented by two unions: The International Brotherhood of DuPont workers, Local 788, and Chemical Protection Employees Independent Union.

The plant has not been without its problems. In 1965 an explosion killed twelve workers. Du Pont rebuilt the plant, and it reached full production a year and a half later. The company has invested millions, including a $50 million investment announced in early 1993 to modernize equipment and to meet tougher environmental standards. In October 1993 a federal judge approved a $14 million settlement against the plant to satisfy a racial discrimination suit that had lasted three decades.

See Martin E. Biemer, *In Celebration of Louisville* (Northridge, Calif., 1988); *Courier-Journal*, Aug. 14, 1993, Sept. 2, 1994.

Eric Benmour

ELEMENTARY SCHOOLS—CENTENNIAL. The earliest history of primary education in Louisville and Jefferson County is characterized by private or denominational schools and academies scattered throughout the county. These were located in villages and field schools that served many small communities. In 1838 the Kentucky legislature established a system of common schools and by 1850 was supplying some aid throughout the state. Nearly all of the early schools disappeared from the scene as public elementary education became the norm; however, a number of public elementary schools are able to boast more than a century of educating thousands of Louisville's young boys and girls of all races. The centennial elementary schools include:

Benjamin Franklin Elementary School. Located in the CLIFTON neighborhood at 1800 Arlington Ave. in its original building. The two-story, red brick, Italianate/Victorian structure first opened in 1892 on the northwest corner of Smyser and Prospect Avenues as Smyser Avenue School. During 1910 it was renamed Benjamin Franklin Elementary School. In 1965 the building was renovated and an addition constructed. In 1999 the school was combined with Breckinridge Elementary School to form the Breckinridge-Franklin Elementary School at 1351 Payne St. In February 1998 Alderman Bob Butler submitted a proposal for the city to purchase the original school building and convert it to a community center for the Clifton, CLIFTON HEIGHTS, and CRESCENT HILL areas.

Cane Run Elementary School. Though the first official record is for 1876, it is widely believed that the school was founded in 1832 in a log cabin on the property of Madison Miller and located near what is now the northern edge of SHIVELY. Miller's father, Robert, hired Cane Run School's first teacher, Thomas Bohannan, a sixteen-year-old from Richmond, Virginia. In the years that followed, Miller family members continued to contribute to the school. Some donated land for new and larger structures, while others were teachers who became memorable figures and gave continuity throughout various moves. In 1972 the school moved into its current facility at 3951 Cane Run Rd.

Charles D. Jacob Elementary School. The school was named in honor of CHARLES DONALD JACOB, a four-term mayor of Louisville. When it began in 1892, Jacob Elementary was a county school whose first location is unrecorded. In 1898 a new two-room school building was completed at the southeast corner of Woodruff and Camden Avenues. Fourteen years later, a larger Jacob was opened on the corner of Camden and Wheeler Avenues. In 1922 the growing JACOBS neighborhood and school was annexed by the city. A new building at 3670 Wheeler was constructed next to the old one in 1932. By 1991 Jacob Elementary School moved to its present facility at 3701 E Wheatmore Dr. in the city's South End. The old building on Wheeler was renamed Jacob Annex and houses various school district programs.

Fairdale Elementary School. It is widely believed that this school originated in 1842 in a log structure on what is now Mt. Holly Rd. Two succeeding schools were built between 1842 and 1910, when the surrounding community was named FAIRDALE. Three years later a new school was built because its county school district was divided into five separate schools—Pine Grove, Berry, Mitchell, South Park, and Fairdale. In 1928 the five districts were consolidated to form Fairdale Grade and High School on the south side of Manslick Rd. In the 1950s the elementary school and high school were divided. A new Fairdale Elementary was built in 1973 at 10104 Mitchell Hill Rd.

Fern Creek Elementary School. The first official record of Fern Creek Elementary School is 1876. By 1911 a one-room school at the intersection of Bardstown and Fern Creek Roads was built for eighty-five children of the rural FERN CREEK community. Conditions in the original one-room frame structure were so crude that a Fern Creek Improvement League, later renamed the Mothers' League, was formed to remedy the situation. As a result of that organization's efforts, a larger, three-story brick building was constructed on the west side of Fern Creek Rd. in 1922. During the 1923–24 school term, two years of secondary school were added. By 1941 a separate Fern Creek High School was constructed. The development of GENERAL ELECTRIC APPLIANCE PARK in 1951 so strained the school's capacity that in 1967 a new Fern Creek Elementary was built on its present site at 8703 Ferndale Rd.

Gavin H. Cochran Elementary School. Cochran was first established in 1900 at 1507 S Second St. The school was named in honor of Gavin H. Cochran, a trustee and later president of the BOARD OF EDUCATION for several years. Located near the fine homes and distinguished families who lived in the OLD LOUISVILLE neighborhood, Cochran was regarded as an elite school. Before many county schools existed, Cochran often accepted, on a tuition basis, students living outside the city limits. In January 1991, after the state had declared the original building to be substandard for elementary students, Cochran School moved into a new facility at 500 W Gaulbert St. in the Old Louisville neighborhood. District outreach programs are now located in the old structure.

Greathouse Elementary School. This school has been serving the children of ST. MATTHEWS since at least 1877. It was first established as a one-room private school on Browns Ln. opposite the home of Philip Brown. The second one-room structure was located at the junction of Shelbyville Branch Turnpike (Frankfort Ave.) and the main Shelbyville Turnpike (Lexington Rd.). When the school moved to St. Matthews Ave., Miss Tommie Greathouse was appointed teacher, and, after thirty-four years as both teacher and principal, the school was named in her honor in 1915. The school shares its present site at 2700 Browns Ln. with Shryock Elementary School. The school's best-remembered location at 3796 Grandview Ave. became the new St. Matthews City Hall in February 1994.

Greenwood Elementary School. There is some reason to believe Greenwood Elementary School is the oldest school in Jefferson County. Unofficial school histories contend that it was first established in a building erected with handmade bricks by slaves belonging to Jack Waller. By the early 1880s the attendance had grown to twenty-one pupils, so a larger one-room frame structure was built on the north side of Greenwood Rd. By 1912 a third building was completed, but it was destroyed by a tornado in 1925. A new four-room school was constructed on the same site. The present Greenwood Elementary School was completed in 1957 in response to a growing population of families in the PLEASURE RIDGE PARK neighborhood who were employed at FORT KNOX and Louisville. It is located next to Pleasure Ridge Park High School.

I.N. Bloom Elementary School. Located at 1627 Lucia Ave. in Louisville's TYLER PARK neighborhood, Bloom Elementary has been housed in its original building for more than a hundred years. Constructed in 1896, the school was then known as Lucia Avenue School. It was renamed I.N. Bloom Elementary in 1923 in honor of a local physician who was a member of the Louisville BOARD OF EDUCATION from 1911 to 1922 and was its first president. Additions and renovations were made to the facility in 1968.

Isaac M. Shelby Elementary School. Named after Kentucky's first governor, Shelby Elementary was once known as the GERMANTOWN School, after the neighborhood where it is located. Germantown School began in a one-room building at 130 Mary St. near Swan St. in the mid-1860s. In 1870 the Louisville city directory listed Sue Smith as the first principal, earning a salary of eight hundred dollars. The school was moved to a new three-story structure at 930 Mary St. in 1891, and in 1915 the name was changed to Isaac M. Shelby Elementary School to honor the state's first governor. In 1968 the school was renovated and expanded.

Jeffersontown Elementary School. Though official records reveal that a school in the JEFFERSONTOWN area existed before 1900, available written histories begin in 1911. That year land for a new school was donated by the Jefferson Heights Land Co. and John B. McFerran, its president. Shortly thereafter, donations were collected from area citizens to help pay school construction costs. Jeffersontown School was opened at 3300 College Dr. in 1913. In 1963 Alexander-Ingram Elementary School was consolidated with Jeffersontown's school. A larger school building was constructed at its present site at 3610 Cedarwood Way in 1973.

Joseph B. Atkinson Elementary School. The school began in rented rooms at Twenty-sixth and Duncan Streets in 1893. Three years later, the BOARD OF EDUCATION purchased a building and lot at Twenty-eighth and Duncan Streets, and the existing building was converted into a school and named Park School. In 1902 a new school was constructed on the site. Designed in the Second Renaissance Revival style by the prominent architectural firm of D.X. MURPHY and Brother, it was later placed on the NATIONAL REGISTER OF HISTORIC PLACES. The name was changed to Joseph B. Atkinson Elementary School after a longtime member of the Louisville school board. In January 1991 a facility was completed at 2800 Alford St. behind the older building on Duncan St. The old building was demolished.

Kerrick Elementary School. Located in southwestern Jefferson County, Kerrick Elementary School is said to have begun in 1878 in the home of a Stallings family on DIXIE HWY. as a public school on private land. As it grew, the school was named for the Kerricks—George, Harry, and C.H.—who donated land for a new building in 1892 and served as trustees to the fledgling school. Early in the century, school district boundary lines were not adhered to, and many students rode the new Louisville/Orell interurban to attend the school because of its popular principal, Alice Waller. The Kerrick land on the Lower Hunter's Trace and DIXIE HWY. corner often flooded, so another building was erected in 1919 on a two-acre site on the east side of Eighteenth Street Rd. north of Blanton Ln. When larger facilities became necessary, the current structure at 2210 Upper Hunters Trace Rd. was built in 1959.

Medora Elementary School. The southwest Jefferson County school began in 1877. It originated in and took its name from the railroad station in a small rural area east of DIXIE HWY. and a little north of the BULLITT COUNTY line known as Medora, in honor of the daughter of a prominent family. The school soon became a gathering place for community events such as ice cream socials. In 1954 Medora Elementary School was moved from its site at Orell and Pendleton Roads in the Orell neighborhood to 11801 Deering Rd., two miles north in the Bethany neighborhood.

Middletown Elementary School. The first public school in the MIDDLETOWN area was opened by a Presbyterian minister in 1799. By 1905 the children of Middletown were served by a green frame two-room structure on Harrison Ave. with a student capacity of 120 and suitable outhouses. In 1918 the school boasted a new two-story red brick building of eight rooms at 218 N Madison Ave. Viola Caldwell served as principal of the new school, and there were four teachers. In 1941 James F. Crosby was appointed principal and held that post for thirty years. The school continued in its N Madison

Ave. location when the present structure replaced the original building in 1971.

Milburn T. Maupin Elementary School. Opened in 1891 on the southeast corner of Catalpa and Dumesnil Streets, the school was first known as the Parkland Public School, after the surrounding neighborhood. In its first year the principal was Atlanto H. Taylor, who was replaced by Frances H. Crothers in 1892, according to city directories. The original Victorian-style building has been placed on the NATIONAL REGISTER OF HISTORIC PLACES. The school building was expanded in 1910 and again in 1968 when a large addition was constructed. In 1985 the school was renamed for MILBURN T. MAUPIN, a prominent educator, and in 1997 its present building was constructed across the street from the old location at 1309 Catalpa St.

Mill Creek Elementary School. Mill Creek School has been a SHIVELY institution since 1896. It began in a one-room frame building on land donated by brothers Jacob and Christian Shively. In 1912 the schoolhouse was transformed into a two-room structure by a partition. By the mid-1920s, a five-room facility had been constructed, and in 1942 the school moved a little south of its original location, to 4205 Dixie Hwy. Rapid population growth and the resulting overcrowding in the school's district forced it to be divided, and a new Mill Creek Elementary was opened at 3816 Dixie Hwy. in 1970.

Newburg Elementary/Middle School. Located in the NEWBURG area southeast of Louisville, the school dates back at least to 1875. Originally designated as a "colored" school, it remained so until desegregation in the 1950s. After it had outgrown its first two buildings, a third Newburg School was constructed in 1929 on Newburg Rd. between the Southern (Norfolk Southern) Railroad tracks and Indian Trail. The school moved again in 1953 to 5008 Indian Trail and served elementary and junior high students. In 1968 Newburg again became an elementary school. Another transformation took place in 1975 when, after a $250,000 renovation, the school was converted into Newburg Middle School, housing grades six to eight. In the fall of 1997 the school moved to 4901 Exeter Ave.

Phillis Wheatley Elementary School. Located at 1107 S Seventeenth St., the school is a combination of the California Colored School, founded in 1870 on Harney St. (now 1638 W Kentucky St.) in the CALIFORNIA district of the city, and the old Phillis Wheatley School erected in 1884 at 1624 W St. Catherine St. After the consolidation of the two schools, the name Phillis Wheatley was retained. Wheatley, a slave from Senegal, was the protégé of a Boston family who educated her and encouraged her renowned talent as a poetess. In 1962 a new building was constructed.

Portland Elementary School. This school at 3410 North Western Pkwy. was founded as a four-room schoolhouse in the PORTLAND neighborhood. In 1870 the Louisville city directory locates Portland Elementary School on the corner of Portland's Commercial and Third Streets. The principal was George E. Roberts, and there were enough children to require ten teachers. In 1906 Portland was annexed by Louisville, and the school was added to the city school system. Although many additions to the original structure have been made, the most extensive renovation and expansion project was undertaken in 1968. That year the existing school building was remodeled and completely surrounded by a new addition designed by Louisville architect Jasper Ward. The new design of Portland Elementary garnered an Honor Award from the Kentucky Society of Architects in 1968.

Samuel Coleridge-Taylor Elementary School. Established in 1853, Coleridge-Taylor Elementary School was originally a white school known as the Tenth Ward School, located at Thirteenth and Green (Liberty) Streets. In 1911 the name was changed to the Tenth Ward Colored School when it became a facility for AFRICAN AMERICANS. Another name change came in 1913 when principal JOSEPH S. COTTER SR. renamed the school after the black British musical genius, Samuel Coleridge-Taylor. After 116 years in the same building, the school moved to its current site at 1115 W Chestnut St. in the RUSSELL neighborhood in 1970.

Victor H. Engelhard Elementary School. The school was opened in 1886 at 119 E Kentucky St. in what is now the OLD LOUISVILLE neighborhood. The original building, called the Kentucky Street School, was later placed on the National Register of Historic Places. In 1919 the school was renamed in honor of Victor H. Engelhard, a member of the Louisville school board (1911–15) who promoted innovative methods to improve the administration and finances of the Louisville schools. The school moved to a new building one block west at 1004 S First St. in 1965 to better serve its inner-city children.

ELEVEN JONES'S CAVE. The most famous cave in Louisville and the source of a reliable spring, Eleven Jones' Cave is sixteen hundred feet southwest of the intersection of Eastern Pkwy. and Poplar Level Rd., on the west bank of the south fork of BEARGRASS CREEK bordering the Louisville Cemetery.

Eleven Jones' Cave is a typical limestone crawlway conduit cave with a stoopway entrance passage two and one-half feet wide, four and one-half feet high, and forty feet long. The entrance passage intersects the first turn that leads to the right, while the entranceway terminates twenty-five feet farther in a small room. The ninety-foot passageway between the first and second turns is a tubular crawlway, intersected by a canyon passage about five feet high. A twenty-five-foot sewer-type tubular passage connects the second and third turns. A fifty-foot composite tube and canyon passage between the third and fourth turns contains a small room large enough to stand in. Between turns four and five is a hundred-foot stoopway. To the left from turn five is a sewer-type passage extending for fifty feet. Beyond the sixth turn are several sharp bends. The cave continues past the measured area at the eighth turn 450 feet from the entrance, but lack of air circulation makes exploration difficult beyond that point. The farthest portions of crawlway remain open but unsafe.

Its name is shrouded in mystery and varies according to the storyteller. Eleven Jones's Cave is the oldest name, but 'Leven Jones, Leben Jones, Leven Jones, and Eleven Jones Brothers Cave have all been used. The name probably derived from Levin Powell and John Jones, who were early nearby residents, although neither man owned the main spring or cave entrance.

The cave's fame comes from legends that began in the mid-nineteenth century. The best-known tale is about mythical Jones brothers who were said to have used the cave as a base for their illegal activities as bank robbers, counterfeiters, and killers. The story has it that the brothers carved out rooms for living quarters and hid their treasure of silver, gold, and jewels there. Finally the mysterious Joneses died or left the area, leaving their treasure behind. The treasure supposedly remained, hidden by collapsed roofs in distant passageways.

One old tale describes three-inch iron bars that form a gate to keep adventurers from finding the Jones's treasure. A more recent legend tells of finding a CIVIL WAR–era army saber in 1949. Two physical survey trips into the cave in 1967 found nothing to verify any legend, nor did the survey find any evidence of entrances other than the main spring entrance on Beargrass Creek.

See Angelo I. George, "The Legend of Eleven Jones' Cave, Jefferson County, Kentucky," *Filson Club History Quarterly* 48 (Oct. 1974): 342–59.

ELIOT, THERESA (GARRETT) (b Louisville, June 8, 1884; d Cambridge, Massachusetts, March 20, 1981). Artist. The daughter of George Hurst and Belle (Frazee) Garrett, she studied at the St. Louis School of Fine Arts, Art Institute of Chicago, École des Beaux Arts of Paris, and Art Students' League of New York. She married Henry Ware Eliot Jr. (only brother of poet T.S. Eliot) on February 15, 1926. Her etchings and paintings were exhibited in New York, Chicago, and Boston; and she designed liturgical pieces for Groton School. She became the curator of Harvard's Houghton Library. Eliot is buried beside her husband at CAVE HILL CEMETERY.

See *Courier-Journal,* Aug. 26, 1984.

Clyde F. Crews

ELM TREE GARDEN. Elm Tree Garden was Louisville's first AMUSEMENT PARK. It was opened as the Elm Tree Pavilion by Frenchman

Joseph L. Detiste on June 6, 1829, in SHIPPINGPORT at the foot of the Eighteenth Street Canal Bridge. The Garden centered around a giant elm tree with a large wooden platform, more than three hundred feet in circumference, that was constructed in the branches. The platform was home to a tavern featuring mirrors, bars, customer seating, and a variety of activities, including drinking and GAMBLING. Twenty-four branches of the tree came through the floor of the tavern and were said to represent the twenty-four states of the Union at the time. Below the treetop tavern were mazes, puzzle gardens, and a racetrack where the Kentucky Giant, JIM PORTER, supplemented his family's income as a jockeyprior to his tremendous growing spurt at age seventeen.

In early 1831 Detiste added a small locomotive and train track as an amusement ride, and by June 1832 there was a China pavilion, pagoda, tree arbor, a dance pavilion, and a gondola service to ferry people across the OHIO RIVER. The flood of 1832, which nearly destroyed Shippingport, marked the end of Elm Tree Garden's heyday. It reopened but never achieved its former level of popularity. The amusement property eventually closed by 1873.

See J. Stoddard Johnston, ed., *Memorial History of Louisville* (Chicago 1896); Rick Bell, "This Week in Portland History," *Portland Anchor*, May 19, 1983.

ELY NORMAL SCHOOL. In January 1866 Gen. Clinton B. Fisk ordered that the work of the Bureau of Refugees, Freedmen, and Abandoned Lands (the Freedmen's Bureau) be extended from Tennessee into the commonwealth, even though the bureau's authority was supposed to extend only to former Confederate states. Fisk, who was the bureau's assistant commissioner for Tennessee and Kentucky, extended the bureau's activities into Kentucky in response to widespread racial violence and the state's refusal to ratify the Thirteenth Amendment and rescind its antebellum slave code. By March 1866 Gen. John Ely, bureau superintendent for Kentucky, divided the state into three subdistricts, with Louisville as the state headquarters. In the field of education, the Freedmen's Bureau, although despised by many whites, had its most lasting impact as a catalyst in the creation of educational opportunities for AFRICAN AMERICANS. This impact was particularly significant in urban areas such as Louisville where United States Army units could protect school property, personnel, and students until public funds for and public acceptance of the education of African Americans could be secured.

An important example of the work of the bureau was the Ely Normal School, which opened in April 1868 on the northeast corner of Fourteenth and BROADWAY. The eight-room, two-story brick school was named in honor of General Ely, who was considered a strong advocate of black education and who had resigned from the army in November 1867. The Ely school was jointly financed by the bureau and the American Missionary Association at a total construction cost of twenty-five thousand dollars. Its purpose was the training of African American teachers, both to extend educational opportunities to larger numbers of African American children and to replace white northern teachers in increasingly segregated schools for blacks.

As the only public school for African Americans in Louisville, Ely could not restrict its role to teacher training and enrolled 396 students initially, only 40 of whom were enrolled in its "normal" department. John Hamilton and O.H. Robins, white graduates of Oberlin College, served as the first two principals; and the school employed up to seven teachers, only one of whom was African American. However, although Ely's enrollment was large, its capacity was far from sufficient to accommodate the numbers of African Americans seeking an education.

On September 22, 1870, the Louisville BOARD OF EDUCATION responded to repeated petitions from the local African American community and established PUBLIC SCHOOLS for African American children and appointed a "Colored Board of Visitors" in July 1871 to advise the board on matters related to the staffing and operations of these schools. Because the public schools available to African Americans were still inadequate and too few in number, HORACE MORRIS, secretary of the Board of Visitors, negotiated a lease of the Ely Normal School at an annual cost of nine hundred dollars, and the building was used as a public school in 1872 and 1873. However, after the Freedmen's Bureau was discontinued in 1872 and additional public school facilities were made available in Louisville, the Ely Normal School building was abandoned and allowed to deteriorate.

See George R. Bentley, *A History of the Freedmen's Bureau* (Philadelphia 1955); Alice A. Dunnigan, *The Fascinating Story of Black Kentuckians: Their Heritage and Traditions* (Washington, D.C., 1982); *Louisville City Directory*, 1872, 1873; Marion B. Lucas, A *History of Blacks in Kentucky: From Slavery to Segregation, 1760–1891* (Frankfort 1992); Donald G. Nieman, *The Freedmen's Bureau and Black Freedom* (New York 1994); George D. Wilson, A *Century of Negro Education in Louisville, Kentucky* (Louisville 1941).

J. Blaine Hudson

ENGLISH-SPEAKING UNION—KENTUCKY BRANCH, THE. Founded in Great Britain in 1918 and in the United States in 1920, the English-Speaking Union (E-SU) has branches throughout the United States, the British Commonwealth, and many non-English-speaking countries. According to the mission statement, "The English-Speaking Union of the United States is committed to promoting scholarship and the advancement of knowledge through the effective use of English in an expanding global community."

The Kentucky Branch carries out the E-SU's mission by sponsoring a variety of educational and cultural programs. Best known is the scholarship program, which provides summer study and travel in Great Britain for Kentucky college students. Students from seven Kentucky colleges and universities—BELLARMINE, Berea, Centre, Kentucky, Louisville, SPALDING, and Transylvania—attend Oxford, Cambridge, London, or the London School of Economics each summer. Since the program began in 1960, more than four hundred young Kentuckians have been E-SU Scholars.

Throughout the year, the branch offers a variety of activities for members. Regular dinner and brunch meetings feature timely speakers and entertainment. A book discussion group examines classics and contemporary works. Each February the branch holds a Shakespeare competition for high school students at ACTORS THEATRE. The local winner competes for a trip to England at the E-SU's national Shakespeare competition in New York.

English-in-Action provides volunteers to conduct weekly conversational English classes for refugees. Each holiday season the E-SU decorates a tree in the British style for Kosair Charities' Festival of Trees and Lights. From time to time, the branch hosts trips to England and to local places of interest. For example, a branch trip to Keeneland for the Queen Elizabeth Cup Race has proven popular.

The Kentucky Branch maintains ties with a "twin branch" in Winchester, England. Kentucky donates American books winning E-SU Ambassador Book Awards to historic Winchester College. Fund-raising is a vital part of the branch's year. The annual Queen's Birthday Garden Party, honoring Queen Elizabeth II on her official birthday, benefits the scholarship fund. In addition, there are the scholarship fund campaign and the silent auction. Providing hospitality for overseas visitors is also part of the E-SU's work.

S. Norman McKenna

EPIDEMICS. River and port towns have been known throughout history for having high illness and death rates, and nineteenth-century Louisville was no exception. Cursed with swampy areas along the banks of the OHIO RIVER and with ponds southward from the Falls to the SALT RIVER, the area was visited annually with various kinds of fevers, the causes of which were unknown in the nineteenth century. Moreover, the city's large number of visitors brought with them communicable diseases from other areas.

During the town's first century, smallpox (a highly contagious viral infection) reached epidemic proportions on at least two occasions; Asiatic cholera (a diarrheal disease caused by the ingestion of water contaminated by the vibrio cholerae bacteria) killed thousands of

Kentuckians during its four sweeps across the nation; yellow fever (a virus transmitted from person to person by the bite of the Aedes aegyptae mosquito) made at least two visits; and endemic fevers and enteric disorders, including malaria (a parasitic malady spread by the bite of a mosquito), typhoid, and dysentery (caused by ingesting food or water contaminated by bacteria and protozoa) annually claimed the lives of many Louisvillians. Early in its history the Falls City earned the nickname, "Graveyard of the West."

Little is known of Louisville's 1804 smallpox epidemic, but some information is available on the 1817 visitation. Probably introduced by a river traveler, smallpox ravaged the town, especially overcrowded areas inhabited by the poor. To quarantine the sick, John Gwathmey's large textile factory on the edge of town became a makeshift hospital. Local authorities also tried to convince area residents of the benefits of being vaccinated; unfortunately, many resisted. Earlier in the year the legislature had incorporated the Louisville Hospital Co., and the epidemic reinforced the need for the facility. Nevertheless, construction was slow; and the Louisville Marine Hospital on Chestnut St. at Preston, which served visitors and residents, did not open until 1823. Smallpox continued to menace area residents even into the twentieth century, but the city would not again experience an outbreak of epidemic proportions.

Another frequent complaint during the antebellum era was "bilious remitting fever." The health of any area depends on its climate and topography, wrote Louisville's first historian, Henry McMurtrie, in 1819. He believed that Louisville's ponds and marshy grounds, together with the intensity of summer heat and "decomposition of animal and vegetable matter" caused foul air to spread pestilence and death; next to smallpox, bilious remitting fever (sometimes called autumnal fever, malaria, or ague) was the area's most deadly visitor. McMurtrie urged that the area's "laboratory of disease" be drained and filled and that the town be cleaned of its excessive filth. He also encouraged the construction of a hospital or dispensary where "indigent victims of disease or accident might find relief." Louisville could not escape forever a visit from the "destroying angel," he warned.

In the summer of 1822 the destroyer struck. Called "bilious fever" but probably yellow fever, it swept away at least 140 of Louisville's 4,000 residents. In his monumental work of 1850 on the *Principal Diseases of the Interior Valley of North America*, midwest physician Daniel Drake recalled that the fever scourged the town "almost to desolation" by slowing the town's growth and economic development. The town trustees appointed a Board of Health—the community's first—to examine the malady's cause and make suggestions for a remedy. The board reiterated McMurtrie's earlier plea that ponds created a disease-producing miasma and should be drained and filled. An engineer was appointed to head the effort, the Louisville Theater held a benefit performance for the "pond fund," and for a half-decade draining and filling ponds and low spots was one of the town's chief enterprises.

Yellow fever continued to plague areas along the lower Mississippi River, but not until 1878 did the malady again threaten Louisville. The scourge appeared along the Gulf Coast earlier than usual that summer and by early August had reached Kentucky's borders. The town's medical community held differing opinions on how the disease spread. Theodore S. Bell, a medical professor at the University of Louisville who probably had never treated a case, insisted that even if arrivals from the South were ill or introduced fever-infected clothing, the necessary environmental conditions did not exist for the disease to spread; yellow fever never had and never would visit Louisville. To bar refugees from a haven in the Falls City would be inhumane, he advised.

Luke Blackburn, future governor of Kentucky and a veteran of many fever epidemics, insisted that the fever could affect any locale and that quarantine was the only means of preventing the "saffron scourge" from devastating Louisville as it had other towns along the Mississippi. City officials accepted Bell's advice and ordered that the city open its gates. The local Board of Health supervised the "cleaning and disinfecting" of streets and alleys, called for the creation of a yellow fever hospital on the grounds of St. John's Eruptive Hospital, which was located to the east of the House of Refuge, arranged to meet each boat and train and take sick arrivals to the hospital, and appointed Dr. E.O. Brown to oversee all efforts on behalf of afflicted visitors.

The eruptive hospital was used until two fifty-foot by thirty-four-foot pavilions, which constituted the fever hospital, were completed in early September. Brown hired a cook, nursing corps, and a resident and several visiting physicians to care for the fever patients. Between early August and October 22, when the hospital closed, at least eighty-nine refugees were treated; thirty died. In addition to itinerants receiving care at the hospital, more than fifty indigenous cases, twenty-eight of which were fatal, appeared among residents living near, and in some cases employed in, the Louisville & Nashville Railroad's (L&N) "baggage car shop" at Eleventh and Maple Streets. In his official report, Brown insisted that cleaning the town had assured Louisville of its relatively lucky escape from the scourge—Hickman reported more than two hundred deaths and Bowling Green lost more than thirty residents—and urged that in the future a national quarantine be instituted to prevent yellow fever's entry into the Mississippi Valley. He also insisted that the local Board of Health be strengthened and given full control of the sanitary condition of the whole city. Cholera "is now raging over the waters," he admonished. "Cleanliness is next to godliness and my belief is that Providence cares for and protects those that care for themselves."

The idea of cleanliness as a means of preventing disease grew out of the earlier cholera epidemics. Indigenous to India, usually fatal, and its cause unknown prior to the 1880s, Asiatic cholera is spread with water contaminated by the fecal matter of other cholera victims. The scourge made its first appearance in the United

Scene at Camp Taylor during flu epidemic, 1918.

States in 1832, and, as it spread westward from the East Coast, it created panic and fear and left an enormous death toll in its wake. In early October a cook employed on a Cincinnati-to-Louisville steamboat died of the disease in Louisville, and, within a seven-week period, Louisville experienced 122 deaths. The majority of the cases appeared in a low area along the Ohio River and BEARGRASS CREEK. The City Council convened a temporary Board of Health, and area residents hastily established a cholera hospital and urged the mayor to secure nursing aid from the Sisters of Charity of Nazareth. Area residents also initiated a short-lived campaign to rid the city of miasma-producing filth. With the appearance of cold weather, the threat of cholera vanished, to return the following summer when it afflicted the entire state. Reports differ concerning its Louisville appearance in the summer of 1833. A visitor from Virginia wrote that the disease ravaged the town and countryside. Perhaps wishing to alleviate its readers' fears, the newspaper reported only fifteen to twenty deaths among transients who contracted the disease elsewhere. Whatever the death toll, the disease apparently left a number of orphaned children, for the women of St. Louis Church held fairs and raised money for an orphanage to care for cholera waifs.

Physicians from Louisville wrote extensively on cholera. Although they differed on their favorite treatments and cures—today it is treated with antibiotics—they cited miasma (airborne gases produced by filth), decaying vegetation, stagnant ponds, marshy inlets, and temperature variations as the major culprits, with sinful ways, "ardent spirits," indigestible fruits and vegetables, strong emotions, and even the "abuses of Venus" as the "exciting" causes. No one seemed to connect the pestilence with water supplied by easily contaminated wells.

Following a thirteen-year absence, cholera returned to the United States and in the early summer of 1849 reached Louisville by the plague's principal carrier, the steamboat. Once again it appeared in wretched areas along the creek and riverfront. The mayor created a Board of Health and joined the NEWSPAPERS in their call for a general cleaning of the town. When only a few cholera deaths were reported, the MAYOR assumed that few fatalities occurred. The disease reappeared the following summer, however, and the papers' daily cholera reports indicated that the disease struck with greater fury than in the previous summer, especially in low, damp, and filthy portions of the town. The Board of Health announced that cholera was a "health inspector" and urged that the town be cleaned, that ponds along FOURTH ST. be drained, and that individuals observe personal cleanliness, shun vegetable and animal impurities, avoid cold drink and excessive fatigue, wear wool or flannel belts around their mid-sections, and air their bedding daily. As the number of cholera cases lessened each summer between 1851 and 1854, officials continued to credit their cleaning project. However, at least one physician doubted that the city was clean or that there was a correlation between clean streets and an absence of cholera. Louisville's roads, wrote medical professor LUNSFORD YANDELL, "afforded the condition of disease to a high degree—the offence is rank and smells to Heaven." Disease had been known to abate "in the midst of dirty streets and the worst sort of weather," he insisted. No one seemed to notice that the town's more prosperous areas, which were relatively free of the disease, were not only cleaner than some of the hard-hit NEIGHBORHOODS but were also areas where concrete-lined cisterns fed by filtered streams provided the water supply.

During the 1850s Louisville began to construct sewers, establish a waterworks, and build a station to pump water from the river to the city's reservoir. By the spring of 1866, when cholera returned to the United States, the water supply for many of the town's residents no longer came from easily contaminated wells but rather from cisterns and the new system. A few cholera cases were confirmed in May of that year among army recruits from New York who had just arrived at Taylor Barracks at Third and Oak Streets. The army surgeon ordered that the post be cleaned, that large quantities of disinfectants be scattered about, that bedding be aired daily, and that recruits be warned against intemperance. Apparently all cases were confined to the post, but, fearing that it might spread, the newspaper urged residents to be on the lookout for possible cholera-producing filth and pointed out areas needing attention. Concerning a particularly nasty area, a reporter invited health officials to "take a pleasure excursion to the delightful spot some pleasant night." On another occasion a newspaper suggested that someone "died of the intolerable stench in O'Neal's Alley." When the pestilence made its final visit to the commonwealth in 1873, it devastated many small towns. Louisville, however, remained free of the disease, and officials credited the city's safety to "cleanliness."

Louisville has enjoyed greater (but certainly not universal) cleanliness and a reduced death rate in the twentieth century than during the previous one hundred years. An improved water supply, better SANITATION, a greater understanding of the link between hygiene and health, and inoculations against infectious and communicable diseases have lowered the city's mortality statistics. Nevertheless, the epidemic that killed the most Kentuckians occurred in the fall and winter of 1918–19. Spanish influenza, a viral infection with serious secondary complications, including pneumonia (usually fatal prior to the availability of sulfa, penicillin, and the mycin drugs), probably entered the nation with soldiers returning from Europe. Kentucky's first cases were reported in late September at CAMP ZACHARY TAYLOR, a large training base located on the southern edge of Louisville. Within a brief period, the malady increased so rapidly that fifteen barracks were converted into hospital wards. Twenty physicians from Connecticut came to Louisville, and nurses were recruited throughout the Midwest. The YMCA, Knights of Columbus, and SOUTHERN BAPTIST THEOLOGICAL SEMINARY sent volunteers to help keep medical records. The Red Cross issued a plea for bed linens; local residents sent wagonloads of garden produce, soups, and jellies; students at LOUISVILLE GIRLS' HIGH SCHOOL prepared chicken broth; and a group of young folks fixed food trays for the hospitalized soldiers. The entire community rallied to aid the men at Camp Taylor.

The epidemic raged for more than a month, hospitalizing one-sixth of Taylor's sixty thousand men; fifteen hundred died. As the rate of new cases lessened in camp, flu began to ravage other communities, eventually striking every area of the state. Louisville reported sixty-four hundred cases, of whom more than five hundred died. Deaconess Hospital set aside an entire ward for flu sufferers, and Louisville's other HOSPITALS opened new contagion wards. The state Board of Health urged that local newspapers carry daily instructions on prevention and treatment, and on October 7 ordered that all schools, churches, and places of amusement be closed until further notice and that Kentuckians remain at home and refrain from travel.

These dictates—and fear of contracting the disease—forced the cancellation of numerous public gatherings, including the Columbus Day parade and election campaign activities; the flu bug even stifled the oratory of Kentucky politicians. In late October the epidemic began to abate, and the Board of Health withdrew its restrictions, although it admonished the public to beware of crowds. Reports of flu continued to remain high throughout the winter and early spring of 1919 but ceased to be epidemic. Throughout the visitation, the state Board of Health kept records of the cases and death rate. The statistics are appalling. The "Spanish lady" killed sixteen thousand Kentuckians, severely hampered the state's industrial production and agricultural ECONOMY, temporarily curtailed education, and caused untold hardships and financial losses. Although various strains of flu have threatened the nation from time to time since 1920, the availability of vaccines and "miracle drugs" has prevented illness and death rates like that of 1918–19.

The most persistent epidemic disease of the twentieth century was infantile paralysis. In earlier days, everyone was exposed to filth and thus to polio. Mothers passed to their babies a passive immunity, and, when older children and young adults contracted a mild and usually undetected case, they acquired a lifetime immunity, which women then transmitted to the next generation. The sanitation improvements in the years of the late nineteenth and early twentieth centuries interfered with this passive immunity and inadvertently exposed the nation to the polio virus. As early as 1904 the commonwealth's physicians began to write about polio, and, as the number of cases increased, so did the attention given to the disease. Four hundred Kentuckians suffered with polio in the 1920s; the number rose 132 percent in the 1930s and in the 1940s increased 160 percent over the previous decade; between 1938 and 1958 polio afflicted at least seventy-five hundred Kentuckians. Most of the malady's victims were children from all walks of life, although the incidents were slightly higher in inner-city areas. Physicians and health officials speculated on the cause and effective treatment of the crippling, often fatal, malady; and because it struck the younger more often than older segments of the population, mention of the disease created panic but also strengthened the determination to find a preventive. The solution, Americans believed, lay in research laboratories.

Answering the call for funds to help polio victims and for polio research, nearly every Kentucky community organized fund-raisers. As part of Franklin D. Roosevelt's nationwide "President's Birthday Ball," the Falls City held its first gala in 1934. At the armory, six thousand Louisvillians danced to the music of a band financed by the BROWN HOTEL, ate auctioned cake resold at ten cents a slice, and watched a blind pugilist demonstrate shadow boxing. Celebrations were held throughout subsequent years, raising thousands of dollars for the polio fund and March of Dimes, an impressive feat especially during the GREAT DEPRESSION and war years.

During Kentucky's worst polio years—1944, 1949, 1952, and 1954—Louisville's KOSAIR CHILDREN'S HOSPITAL made room for polio patients by dismissing others and called for volunteers to aid its exhausted staff. Sometimes the opening of school was delayed, and children under fourteen were barred from the state fair and other public gatherings. The L&N usually offered free transportation for patients to treatment centers; and Louisvillians, like Kentuckians elsewhere, held dances, fairs, and neighborhood get-togethers to raise money. To care for victims of the 1952 epidemic, the state's worst, Louisville women (and a few men who wore hat bands saying, "Tonight I am a mother") held a Mother's March and collected over ten thousand dollars for the polio fund.

Louisville was among the municipalities involved in early testing of the Salk vaccine. In the spring of 1954, nearly 200 volunteer nurses and physicians inoculated 6,175 second-graders in Jefferson County. The program continued the following years, and by the summer of 1957 the Louisville-Jefferson County Health Department reported that 92 percent of those under twenty years of age had been inoculated. By 1963, 70 percent of the state's residents had received the oral vaccine, and, for the first time since it began to keep polio records, the Kentucky Board of Health reported no incidents of infantile paralysis. During the next two decades the board recorded only five cases.

Continued improvements in sanitation and advancements in methods of diagnosis, therapeutics, and inoculation programs have controlled or eliminated many of the diseases that threatened the lives of previous generations. Unfortunately, other killers remain, and a few new ones have surfaced. AIDS and other terrible conditions annually claim thousands of Kentuckians. Louisville's medical community continues the fight against these and other "assassins" that strike down residents of the Falls City and the commonwealth.

See Nancy Disher Baird, "Asiatic Cholera's First Visit to Kentucky: A Study in Panic and Fear," *Filson Club History Quarterly* 48 (July 1974): 228–40; Nancy Disher Baird, "Asiatic Cholera: Kentucky's First Health Inspector," *Filson Club History Quarterly* 48 (Oct. 1974): 327–41; Nancy Disher Baird, "The Spanish Lady in Kentucky," *Filson Club History Quarterly* 50 (July 1976): 290–301; Nancy P. Bradshaw, "Polio in Kentucky," M.A. thesis, Western Kentucky University, 1987; E.0. Brown, *Official Report of Dr. E.0. Brown, Physician in Charge of the Yellow Fever Hospital, Louisville, Kentucky, 1878* (Louisville, 1878).

Nancy D. Baird

EPISCOPAL CHURCH HOME. The Episcopal Church Home, at 1201 Lyndon Ln., is a retirement center serving senior citizens desiring various levels of care. The home has been in operation for over 115 years and is affiliated with the Diocese of Kentucky of the Protestant Episcopal church. The institution was founded largely through the efforts and philanthropy of JOHN P. MORTON (1807–99), a prominent Louisville textbook publisher. Morton's generosity grew out of an illness and long convalescence he experienced shortly after moving to Louisville in the 1820s. His surroundings during that illness were so grim that Morton vowed that if he ever prospered he would one day build a facility to care for the sick.

True to that early resolution, Morton in 1872 obtained an Act of the Kentucky General Assembly authorizing the incorporation of a home and purchased land at 1508 Morton Ave. in Louisville's HIGHLANDS. When fund-raising efforts proved unsuccessful, Morton in 1881 decided to personally finance construction of the facility. The home was dedicated November 2, 1884, and operated at the Morton Ave. address for ninety-six years. Although officially named the Church Home for Females and Infirmary for the Sick, for many years the facility was commonly called the Morton Home. In addition to donating the land and building, Morton bequeathed to the home a sixty-thousand-dollar endowment.

Annual reports submitted to the diocese by the trustees reveal that the home has enjoyed efficient management and community support throughout its history. Some of the credit for the early achievements must go to Miss Julia T. Maury, who served as home matron from 1885 to 1920. Since 1974 the home has been administered by Thomas Horton.

By the 1960s the five-story building on Morton Ave. was showing signs of aging. Its heating, plumbing, and electrical systems were either outdated or beyond repair. A 1962 study recommended that the home expand its mission from solely residential to a more health-oriented role and build a new enlarged building in a suburban setting. In the early 1970s the Morton Ave. property was sold to Louisville's BOARD OF EDUCATION, a professional administrator was hired, and a fund-raising campaign was conducted. In 1975 construction began on the new site on Lyndon Ln., and on October 3, 1977, thirty residents moved into the new facility. In 1998 the home had 145 residents. The home's mission expanded once again in 1994 with the construction of Dudley Square, a thirty-six-unit townhouse project that provides housing for active retirees.

See Proceedings of the Annual Council of the Protestant Episcopal Church in the Diocese of Kentucky, 1888–1997, Office of the Diocese of Kentucky, Louisville; *Acts of the General Assembly of the Commonwealth of Kentucky, 1871–72,* vol. 2: 70, Frankfort, Kentucky; "Historical Sketch and Report of Trustees to November 21, 1905," unpublished, Episcopal Church Home Archives, Louisville; J. Stoddard Johnston, ed., *Memorial History of Louisville* (Chicago 1896).

Olivia M. Frederick

EPISCOPAL CHURCH OF THE ADVENT. Located since 1888 at 901 Baxter Ave., the Church of the Advent is one of Louisville's more important architectural landmarks. The church began as a Sunday school of CHRIST CHURCH CATHEDRAL. Founded by Mr. and Mrs. William Babb in 1870, the group met in a storefront on the southeast corner of E BROADWAY and Baxter Ave. The congregation soon numbered about two hundred persons, and, on the First Sunday of Advent in 1870, the Reverend Dr. JAMES CRAIK named it "the Sunday School of the Advent." In 1872 the congregation moved into its first facility, a wooden structure on E Broadway near Underhill (Rubel) St. In December 1873 a parish organization was effected, and the congregation was admitted into union with the Council of the Diocese in May 1874.

As population moved up Broadway and into the HIGHLANDS, the congregation was determined to have a new building. When New Broadway (Cherokee Rd.) was constructed, a triangle of land was separated from the main tract of CAVE HILL CEMETERY. Because the land was useless for burials, the cemetery officials were anxious to have a suitable tenant for the property. The church secured a ninety-nine-year lease, with a guaranteed ninety-nine-year renewal, and later purchased the land. The services of New York architect Frederick C. Withers (1828–1901) were secured. The cornerstone was laid in 1887 for the limestone church in a late Victorian Gothic style, making use of a slate roof, a series of gables, and a tower to complete the effect. It is reported that the pastor, the Reverend Mortimer Benton, watched the placement of every stone. The first service was held on April 15, 1888, the second Sunday after Easter.

The church, part of the CHEROKEE TRIANGLE Preservation District, has been listed on the NATIONAL REGISTER OF HISTORIC PLACES, which described the building as "the architectural and historical keystone of the district." The best-known feature is the stained glass windows. Angels depicted in some of the chancel windows memorialize deceased congregation members. In 1994 a British firm specializing in collectibles known as Lilliput Lane commissioned NEW ALBANY, Indiana, artist Ray Day to complete a miniature model of the church, which was marketed internationally as part of the company's "American Landmarks Collection."

See "Cherokee Triangle, Jefferson County, Kentucky," *National Register of Historic Places* (Teaneck, N.J., 1984); *Courier-Journal,* Nov. 30, 1988.

Otis Amanda Dick

EPISCOPALIANS. The Episcopal church in Kentucky dates from 1775 when an Anglican minister, Rev. John Lythe, preached the first public Christian service near Harrodstown (now Harrodsburg). So strong was the influence of the Church of England (Anglican) in the colonies that two-thirds of the signers of the Declaration of Independence were avowed members, and the constitution of the renamed Protestant Episcopal Church in America was modeled after the United States Constitution. However, the antipathy toward the British during and after the American Revolution was so severe that it was not until 1789 that the Protestant Episcopal church in America could complete its organization. It was several years after that before evangelistic efforts west of the Appalachians and Kentucky began.

The Diocese of Maryland was largely responsible for supplying the first Episcopal clergy to serve Kentucky. These ministers were mainly settled in Lexington, and the records of their activities are fairly well documented. The records for similar efforts by Episcopal clergy in Louisville are scant. However, an Episcopal church presence in Louisville probably dates from 1797, and certainly as early as 1803, when the Reverend Williams Kavanaugh, an Episcopal minister, conducted services "on lot 89 . . . 'next the fort' at Main and Twelfth Streets in a 20 X 30 foot house of rough-hewn logs . . . which was used by followers of various faiths, when opportunity, or inclination, prompted a service."

From those early beginnings, a small congregation of Episcopalians developed in Louisville. Reverend Joseph Jackson wrote to Bishop James Kemp of Maryland in 1820, "Certain it is that an Episcopal clergyman ought to have been settled here some years ago," and in later correspondence Jackson bemoaned the lack of Episcopal missionaries, established seminaries, and a bishop for the area. However, barely two years later, on May 31, 1822, fifteen communicants became the charter members of CHRIST CHURCH, and, despite the financial crisis of the times, registered 185 subscribers and soon raised over $6,000 for the erection of a church. The "temporary building" was "a frame structure on the present Court House lot near the corner of Jefferson and Fifth Streets." In Casseday's *History of Louisville*, the author noted that in the next two years there was nothing of much historical interest to note in the town, "save the building in the winter of 1824–25 of an Episcopalian Church on Second Street," between Green (Liberty) and Walnut (Muhammad Ali Blvd.). This building is Christ Church, the oldest church edifice in Louisville.

The first bishop of Kentucky was Benjamin Bosworth Smith (1794–1884), who also served as the presiding bishop of the Protestant Episcopal church from 1876 to 1884. He established the Episcopal Seminary in Lexington and was the superintendent of public instruction for Kentucky. Under his leadership the diocesan headquarters was moved from Lexington to Louisville in 1841 as the population of the river city continued to surge past the inner Bluegrass city.

During the nineteenth century Episcopalians made their marks in POLITICS, merchandising, LAW, and MEDICINE, and counted among their number some of the most prominent and influential of Louisville's citizenry. Thomas Hopkins Shreve (of the Hopkins family for whom Hopkinsville, Kentucky, and Johns Hopkins University were named) was an editor of the *LOUISVILLE JOURNAL*. Samuel Bullitt Churchill was active in politics in several states and Kentucky's secretary of state from 1868 to 1872. George Hancock established several farms in the region, most notably "Hayfield" on present-day Tyler Ln. James Stewart's dry goods business and its successor operated until 1985, and W.L. LYONS was a partner in a stock and bond brokerage company that continues to this day. Louisville's landscape also retains the names of some of her early Episcopalian citizens: Baxter, Ormsby, Tyler, Castleman, Gray, Jacob, Watterson, and Barbee, to name a few. In addition, the EPISCOPAL CHURCH HOME, Norton Infirmary, the HOME OF THE INNOCENTS, and other social institutions were founded through the philanthropy of the Diocese of Kentucky and its churchmen and women. SHELBY COLLEGE at SHELBYVILLE was organized in 1836 and transferred to the Episcopal church in 1841. During its thirty years of existence it prepared many men and women for service to the community.

During the CIVIL WAR, Episcopalians served both armies of the conflict, and Union soldiers encamped in Indiana were said to have ferried the OHIO RIVER to attend services at Christ Church. In 1884 THOMAS UNDERWOOD DUDLEY became the second bishop of the diocese. Dudley was well known for his establishment of churches in rural areas and among the African American population of Kentucky. He presided over a greatly expanding church, which included all those in Kentucky. By 1895 the number of parishes in the diocese had grown too large to be administered as one see. A special convention was held that year; and the Diocese of Lexington, comprising roughly the eastern part of the state, and the Diocese of Kentucky, which includes all of Kentucky from about Shelbyville west to the Missouri state line, were formed.

Charles Edward Woodcock became the third bishop of Kentucky in 1905. He was active in social and political concerns of the day. He fought political corruption in Louisville, advocated support for the League of Nations, and defended the teaching of evolution in PUBLIC SCHOOLS during the famous "Scopes Trial" in 1925. He was an early ecumenist and invited non-Episcopal clergy to give a series of lectures at Christ Church Cathedral aimed at understanding what each denomination could offer toward a united Christian Church. He was also a staunch supporter of women in leadership roles in the church. The Woodcock Society, the oldest honorary scholastic organization at the UNIVERSITY OF LOUISVILLE, is a living legacy of this bishop.

During the twentieth century, Louisville's Episcopalians have continued the support of the nineteenth-century institutions the church founded and have begun others, such as St. Francis School, St. Francis High School, and St. George's Community Center. Charles Clingman became the fourth bishop of the diocese in 1936. His episcopacy spanned the tumultuous years of the 1937 FLOOD, the GREAT DEPRESSION, and the second world war. Much of his energies were devoted to shoring up Episcopal institutions deeply affected during these times. Bishop Clingman also forbade "raffles, bingo parties and the like," declaring them "undignified and unworthy."

Charles Gresham Marmion succeeded Bishop Clingman in 1954. Bishop Marmion provided leadership during an intense period of CIVIL RIGHTS activity in the diocese. He asserted that the church must take a stand on issues of moral and human values. During the Companion Relationship with Haiti, he provided frequent services for five years following the expulsion of the Episcopal bishop there. Bishop Marmion supported the ECUMENISM promoted during the Second Vatican Council of the Roman Catholic church (1962–65). He also contributed to the national liturgical revision efforts of the Episcopal church in the 1970s. Under Bishop Marmion, All Saints' Conference Center near Leitchfield was founded as a camp, retreat center, and meeting facility for children and adults.

David Benson Reed became the sixth diocesan bishop in 1974. Bishop Reed brought to Kentucky a background of diverse cultural experiences within the church. He had ministered to the Lakota (Sioux) Indians in South Dakota and had spent a total of fifteen years in South America before becoming the first bishop of Colombia (which included Ecuador) in 1964. He led the diocese in the formation of area ministries and encouraged churches to find more ways to work together. In his official capacities, Bishop Reed was a strong supporter of diversity and inclusivity and was one of the first bishops to ordain women priests. During his episcopacy, Rev. Geralyn Wolf, the first woman dean of any cathedral in the worldwide Anglican Communion, was installed at Louisville's Christ Church Cathedral.

In 1994 Edwin Funsten Gulick was elected the seventh bishop of the Diocese of Kentucky. Bishop Gulick is known as an energetic and charismatic leader with strong liturgical and oratorical skills. As of the 1998 Annual Diocesan Convention, the Diocese comprised thirty-eight congregations, with seventy-two canonically resident clergy and seven deacons.

Episcopal Bishops of the Diocese of Kentucky

Rt. Rev. Benjamin Bosworth Smith: 1832–84
 Rt. Rev. George D. Cummins D.D.: 1866–74, Bishop Coadjutor
Rt. Rev. Thomas U. Dudley D.D.: 1875–84, Bishop Coadjutor; 1884–1904, Bishop
Rt. Rev. Charles Edward Woodcock: 1905–35
Rt. Rev. Charles Clingman: 1936–54
Rt. Rev. Charles Gresham Marmion: 1954–74
Rt. Rev. David Benson Reed: 1972–74, Bishop Coadjutor; 1974–94, Bishop
Rt. Rev. Edwin F. Gulick Jr.: 1994 to present

See J. Stoddard Johnston, ed., *Memorial History of Louisville* (Chicago 1896); Richard Lightburn McCready, *The History of Christ Church Cathedral* (Louisville 1937); Ben Casseday, *The History of Louisville from its Earliest Settlement Till the Year 1852* (Louisville 1852); Sharon Receveur, Catherine Luckett, Rt. Rev. David Reed, "A Brief History of Seven Bishops in the Diocese of Kentucky" (Louisville, April 17, 1994); *1998 Journal of the Diocese of Kentucky, The Proceedings of the 170th Annual Convention, February 27 and 28, 1998, together with the Canons of the Diocese.*

Sharon Receveur

E.P. "TOM" SAWYER STATE PARK. On September 10, 1971, Gov. Louie B. Nunn named the first state park in Jefferson County for the late Republican Jefferson County judge E.P. "Tom" Sawyer. Nunn announced that 377 acres of the parkland on Freys Hill Rd. south of Westport Rd. would be open that fall. However, the next year, when Democrat governor Wendell Ford took office, the park project slowed. It was not until June 1, 1975, that the park finally opened.

The park's $2.5 million recreation center offered a large gym, an Olympic-sized swimming pool, twelve tennis courts, a picnic area, and a parking lot for twelve hundred cars. In spite of the new facilities, the park's flat, open spaces and few trees did not attract many visitors. In the early 1980s Gov. John Y. Brown's administration began to cut the park's budget and staff and considered turning its management over to Jefferson County. The park's patrons and visitors began a series of protest rallies to save it. These events led to the formation of the Sawyer Park Foundation in 1982.

Dozens of the foundation's dedicated volunteers began to lobby on the park's behalf and to raise money for its development. In 1981 E.P. "Tom" Sawyer Park was chosen for the Kentucky State triathlon competition. In 1983 the park introduced trails for walkers and runners, and softball fields were built in 1985. Since 1984 Sawyer Park has hosted the BMX (bicycle racing) Grand National Championships, which brings together about ten thousand people each year. Over the years the Sawyer Park Foundation has continued to work on the park's landscape with the aim of creating more green and shady areas. Extensive tree planting took place in the 1990s with the help of a Mary Bingham Fund grant. In 1992 Sawyer Park began the tradition of a July Third celebration. The event gathers thousands of people every year. In addition, the park hosts "dive-in movies" at its pool on Friday nights in the summer. In 1998 the state gave the park forty-seven acres of surplus land from neighboring CENTRAL STATE HOSPITAL. Sawyer Park provides facilities for TENNIS, soccer, BASKETBALL, and SWIMMING.

See *Courier-Journal*, Sept. 7, 1998.

ETHRIDGE, MARK FOSTER (b Meridian, Mississippi, April 5, 1896; d Moncure, North Carolina, April 5, 1981). Journalist. Mark Ethridge was the son of William Nathaniel and Mary (Howell) Ethridge Sr. The life of a newsman came to him early. After several years as a carrier for the *Meridian Dispatch*, founded by his attorney father, he went to work in the newsroom at age fourteen. It was a bond that would continue for the rest of his life.

Ethridge spent a year after his high school graduation in 1913 working as a reporter for the *Meridian Star*, then went to the University of Mississippi. After college, Ethridge moved to Georgia, where he worked at newspapers in Columbus and Macon. He served in the navy in WORLD WAR I before returning to Macon, where he was promoted to city editor. In 1920 he married Willie Snow, also a journalist, and together they skipped across the eastern United States as Mark's career flourished. He worked at the *New York Sun*, the *Washington Post*, and the Associated Press. By 1934 he was named president and publisher of the *Richmond* (Virginia) *Times-Dispatch*, where he drew the attention of President Franklin D. Roosevelt for his support of New Deal policies.

When Ambassador ROBERT W. BINGHAM asked Roosevelt for advice about someone to help run the *COURIER-JOURNAL* and the *LOUISVILLE TIMES*, FDR proposed Mark Ethridge. In 1936 Ethridge moved to Louisville as general manager of the NEWSPAPERS. Within two years, Judge Bingham had died. In tandem with Judge Bingham's son, BARRY BINGHAM, Ethridge made sweeping changes to improve the quality of the two newspapers' content. Not only did Ethridge hire top-notch reporters and editors, he also studied new trends in design, PHOTOGRAPHY, and typography. During his tenure, the *Courier-Journal* became known as one of the best-looking newspapers in America, often serving as a model for others.

Ethridge gained much attention, and some criticism, as he emerged as a leading southern liberal, a fact that endeared him to the Binghams if not to many of their more conservative readers. Throughout the 1930s and 1940s, he was a vigorous advocate of anti-lynching legislation; he denounced the poll tax and racial violence. In 1941 Roosevelt appointed Ethridge chairman of the Fair Employment Practices Commission, which was designed to ensure that AFRICAN AMERICANS and other minorities had equal opportunities in federal defense industries.

It was a visible national forum for Ethridge's views on integration. His progressive New Deal views extended to other fields including health care (he was an advocate of more federal involvement in MEDICINE) and housing. And in the war years he occasionally lashed out at FDR for failing to live up to the promise of his earlier policies. While Barry Bingham Sr. served with the navy, Ethridge worked closely with his wife, MARY BINGHAM, who became more active in editorial decisions during her husband's absence. They were ideologically compatible.

In the postwar era Ethridge became an international troubleshooter for the U.S. State Department. In 1945 he was sent to Bulgaria and Romania to report on the effect of new Communist regimes in those countries. He was a key figure in Middle East diplomacy in the years before and after the nation of Israel was created in 1948. Like his colleague, Barry Bingham, he was a visible and ineluctable foe of the anti-Communist McCarthy movement. He was important in shaping the peaceful response in Louisville to the desegregation of public education in 1956.

In 1963 Ethridge retired from the Louisville newspapers, but this lifelong newspaperman did not end his career. He spent two years on Long Island at *Newsday*, an increasingly influential suburban New York daily. In 1965 he moved to Moncure, North Carolina, and he taught journalism at the University of North Carolina until 1968. Soon after his death in 1981 he, Barry Bingham, and HENRY WATTERSON were among the first inductees into the Kentucky Journalism Hall of Fame at the University of Kentucky. Ethridge was cremated and buried in Moncure.

Keith L. Runyon

Willie Snow Ethridge, 1952. Photograph by Whit Wootton.

ETHRIDGE, WILLIE (SNOW) (b Savannah, Georgia, December 10, 1900; d Key West, Florida, December 14, 1982). Author and humorist. Ethridge's parents, William Aaron and Georgia (Cubbedge) Snow, moved the family to Macon, Georgia, while Willie was a child. In high school, she met MARK ETHRIDGE, a talented young reporter with the *Macon Telegraph*. During World War I, while Ethridge served in the navy, Snow became a *Telegraph* staffer, and she studied journalism and English at Georgia Wesleyan College and Mercer University in Macon. In 1920 she and Mark Ethridge were married.

Her earliest publications were in magazines, among them *Good Housekeeping* and the *New Republic*. The first of her many books was *An Aristocracy of Achievement* (1929), a biography of Benjamin F. Hubert, a prominent black educator. Her first popular success was *As I Live and Breathe*, a spirited memoir of her life as the wife of a newspaperman, which was published in 1937, the year after her husband had accepted a position in Louisville as general manager of the *COURIER-JOURNAL*. During the family's twenty-eight years in Louisville, Willie Snow Ethridge published ten additional books. Several, like *I'll Sing One Song* (1941), were engaging descriptions of life with her husband, Mark, and the four Ethridge children, Georgia Cubbedge, Mark Foster Jr., Mary Snow, and William Davidson. "As American as cinnamon buns and as warm and spicy," the *New York Times* on March 7, 1937, said of Ethridge's domestic memoirs, which sometimes used gentle satire to dissect the male-controlled worlds of civic affairs and newspaper publishing. Critics praised her as a "vital new name in American humor" (*Christian Science Monitor*, Feb. 11, 1948), a reputation that grew through five books, beginning with *It's Greek to Me* (1941), and continuing with *Going to Jerusalem* (1950), *Let's Talk Turkey* (1955), *Russian Duet* (1959), and *There's Yeast in the Middle East* (1963), which recounted her impressions as she accompanied her husband on his assignments in Europe and the Middle East as a United Nations commissioner and U.S. State Department troubleshooter.

Ethridge wrote serious works as well, including *Mingled Yarn* (1938), a pro-labor novel about life in a southern mill town, and *Strange Fires* (1971), a study of Methodist cofounder John Wesley's love affair in colonial Georgia. It was her informal autobiographical volumes, however, that earned the respect of critics and the loyalty of a large readership. When her husband retired from the *Courier-Journal* in 1963, they moved first to Garden City, New York, then in 1965 to Moncure, North Carolina. Ethridge's other works include *This Little Pig Stayed Home* (1944), *Nila: Her Story As Told to Willie Snow Ethridge* (1956), *Summer Thunder* (1958), *You Can't Hardly Get There from Here* (1965), *I Just Happen to Have Some Pictures* (1964), and *Side by Each* (1973). Her body was cremated and the ashes scattered near Big Carpet and Cudjoe Keys north of Key West.

See William Ward, *A Literary History of Kentucky* (Knoxville, Tenn., 1988).

Anthony Newberry

EUDY, MARY CUMMINGS (b Louisville, February 17, 1874; d New York City, June 7, 1952). Fashion designer and poet. She was the daughter of Enoch Hale and Kate (Moore) Paine. Her father, who worked in transportation during the CIVIL WAR and RECONSTRUCTION era, founded the Rip Van Winkle Sleeping Car Co. and later became associated with the Pullman company.

Eudy was educated in Louisville's private schools. In 1896 she married William Harrison Eudy, and their son, Enoch Harrison Eudy, was born in 1899. In 1914 Eudy opened a clothing-designing firm, Mary Cummings Inc., which flourished at 222 W Magnolia Ave. for a quarter-century until WORLD WAR II. The firm was famous for hand-embroidered dresses and imported fine fabrics. Each spring and fall Mary Cummings Inc. issued a *Book of Designs* containing original watercolors of dresses and samples of embroidery and fabrics.

Eudy had clients in many cities. One of her most prominent customers was Sara Delano Roosevelt, mother of President Franklin Delano Roosevelt. Eudy at one time employed about four hundred women, many of whom had young children and did hand embroidery at home. With the beginning of World War II, Mary Cummings Inc. went out of business because it became impossible to get imported fabrics and embroidery materials.

Twenty-five years after beginning her business, Eudy began to write POETRY. Her poems were published in several magazines and poetry journals, including *Harpers*, *Scribners*, *Palms*, and *The Lyric*. Her poem, "Oxen," was set to music by Alma Steedman, also of Louisville, and performed by the Westminster Choir of Princeton, New Jersey. In 1935, G.P. Putnam's Sons published her first volume of poetry, *Quarried Crystals*. In his introduction to the work, Joseph Auslander judged it "an original achievement" that "translates and transcends individual experience." Harper and Brothers published a second volume of her work, *Quicken the Current*, in 1949. The book was described as a collection of witty and compassionate poems that express the author's feelings and thoughts on life, events, and people.

She left most of her estate, worth $657,000, to her son, E. Harrison Eudy, but also provided a life income for a friend, Anne F. Rutherford. She is buried in CAVE HILL CEMETERY.

See Bess A. Ray, *Louisville Library Collection*, vol. 2, (Louisville, 1941); *New York Times*, June 9, 1952; *Courier-Journal*, Jan. 23, 1986.

Candace K. Perry

EVANS, WALTER (b Glasgow, Kentucky, September 18, 1842; d Louisville, December 30, 1923). U.S. congressman. Evans attended public schools in Logan, Todd, and Christian Counties, Kentucky, and then moved to Hopkinsville in 1859, where he worked as deputy county clerk until 1861. He served as a captain in the Union army from 1861 until 1863. After his stint in the war he returned to Hopkinsville and studied LAW while working again as deputy and later as chief clerk. In 1864 he began practicing law. He served as state representative and then state senator from 1871 until 1874. In 1874 he moved to Louisville and resumed practicing law. He unsuccessfully ran for Congress in 1876 and received the Republican nomination for governor in 1879. He was defeated by Democrat LUKE PRYOR BLACKBURN by a vote of 125,790 to 81,882. Between 1883 and 1885 he was the commissioner of the Internal Revenue Service. In 1894 Evans was elected to Congress from Louisville as a Republican, serving two terms from March 4, 1895, to March 3, 1899, before failing to be reelected in 1898. He returned to Kentucky, and the day after he left office he was appointed by President William McKinley as district court judge for the District of Kentucky and served in that position until his death. He is buried in CAVE HILL CEMETERY.

See *Biographical Directory of the American Congress 1776–1961* (Washington, D.C., 1961).

EWING, BENJAMIN FRANKLIN (b St. Matthews, Kentucky, 1881; d Louisville, June 3, 1959). Jefferson County judge. He was educated in Louisville's public schools and was a graduate of KENTUCKY MILITARY INSTITUTE and Centre College at Danville. From 1905 to 1908 he was a teacher at the institute. In 1910 he received a LAW degree from the JEFFERSON SCHOOL OF LAW and began practicing in Louisville that same year.

In 1923 Ewing, a Democrat, ran for City Council but was defeated. However, the election was contested by the DEMOCRATIC PARTY, and a Kentucky Court of Appeals ruling in June 1925 declared that the election was invalid. The BOARD OF ALDERMEN, Board of Councilmen, and two parks commissioners, all of whom were Republican, were removed from office due to election fraud. Ewing subsequently was appointed to serve out the remainder of the term by Gov. William J. Fields. He also served as president of the Board of Councilmen during his four-month tenure on the City Council.

Ewing was also appointed county judge by Governor Fields in 1927 after another Kentucky Court of Appeals ruling declared the 1925 election invalid. Ewing, who was defeated in the 1925 race by Republican HENRY I. FOX, served as county judge from June 1927 until the special election in November 1927. In November he ran against Fox again but was defeated.

Ewing was elected JEFFERSON COUNTY JUDGE in November 1933 and served from January 1, 1934, until December 31, 1937. He was elected over Republican challenger Stanley Briel by more than 6,000 votes out of 148,000 counted. The 1933 election was marred by violence, particularly in Louisville's black NEIGHBORHOODS. One elderly black man was shot to death, and several blacks were beaten in predominantly black-on-black violence between Democratic and REPUBLICAN PARTY supporters. Ewing ran for another term as county judge in 1937 but was defeated.

In January 1938 Ewing was appointed by Gov. A.B. "Happy" Chandler to fill a vacancy as county commissioner. Ewing was later elected to fill the remaining term and was reelected county commissioner in 1939. He resigned in 1943 to accept a post as deputy circuit court commissioner. Ewing was twice elected Sixth Ward alderman. He served on the board from 1947 until 1951. On the Board of Aldermen, he served as chairman of the Finance Committee, and he also served as acting mayor and acting aldermanic president at various times during his tenure.

Ewing was a former law partner of county judges BERTRAM C. VAN ARSDALE and BOMAN L. SHAMBURGER during WORLD WAR II. He also served as first president of the United Service Organization (USO) in Louisville that provided relaxation and entertainment for soldiers. He was also director of the War Fund. He directed tin and scrap metal salvage operations in Jefferson County outside the city during the war. He had earlier served as an infantryman on the Mexican border in 1916 and as a first lieutenant in the field artillery in WORLD WAR I, stationed in England and France.

Ewing, who lived at 1364 S First St., was married to Ruth Graham on October 12, 1912. The marriage lasted briefly, and the couple had no children. He later married Willie Carnes Kendrick, of Louisville, on July 26, 1917. The couple had two sons, Ben F. Junior and William K. Ewing, and a daughter, Betsy K. Ewing. He died of cancer at St. Anthony Hospital. He is buried in ZACHARY TAYLOR NATIONAL CEMETERY.

See *Courier-Journal*, June 4, 1959; Mary Young Southard and Ernest C. Miller, eds., *Who's Who in Kentucky; A Biographical Assembly of Notable Kentuckians* (Louisville 1936); W.T. Owens, *Who's Who in Louisville* (Louisville 1926).

FAIRDALE. Suburb located eleven miles south of Louisville and bounded by Outer Loop on the north, the L&N Railroad tracks or the South Park Rd. on the east, the BULLITT COUNTY line on the south, and New Cut, Manslick, Keys Ferry, Jefferson Hill, and Top Hill Roads on the west. The suburb includes the communities of Coral Ridge and South Park and the sixth-class city of Hollyvilla.

The area just north of modern-day Fairdale developed as MANN'S LICK. A natural repository for salt, probably named for John Mann, a member of Capt. THOMAS BULLITT's surveying party, it drew hundreds of workers into the area to extract the salt. As the labor supply multiplied at Mann's Lick, the new residents began settling on 150 acres of nearby land owned by pioneer James F. Moore, who secured a charter for the town of Newtown in 1794.

About the turn of the nineteenth century, the owners of the region's two largest SALT LICKS, with nearby BULLITT'S LICK being the most prominent, decided to monopolize the local business. While their cooperative effort dominated the market for some years, the licks' limited supply, coupled with the arrival of STEAMBOATS importing cheaper salt, caused the town's population to dwindle to practically nothing by 1830. A change in the state constitution requiring cities to elect officials and have meetings to remain incorporated, eliminated the community in the 1890s.

Several small communities emerged in the area after Newtown's disappearance, including Coral Ridge, South Park, and Mount Holly, which developed in the 1840s with the founding of the Mount Holly School and the Mount Holly Methodist Church. These sites are miles away from the center of the modern community.

The territory drew an increasing number of residents during the 1850s when the LOUISVILLE & NASHVILLE RAILROAD established the Old Deposit Station—named for a salt warehouse once there. However, the present-day district had its origin in 1881 when John and Si Morgan opened a grocery store at the intersection of Mount Holly Rd. and Mitchell Hill Rd.

By the turn of the century, the area surrounding present Fairdale was referred to simply as the "Woods Precinct" because of its proximity to the marshy "WET WOODS" region to the north. This area not only provided an abundant supply of wood for charcoal, which the locals sold in Louisville, but was also reputed to harbor dangerous criminals. At a meeting in 1910, the residents attempted to distance their town from this negative image and decided upon the more flattering name of Fairdale.

Situated near the JEFFERSON COUNTY MEMORIAL FOREST and Forest View Park, the mainly working-class suburb supports a mix of commercial and residential properties. It also contains SOUTH PARK COUNTRY CLUB, which dates its establishment back to an 1854 fishing and boating club.

See *A Place in Time: The Story of Louisville's Neighborhoods* (Louisville 1989); Robert M. Rennick, *Kentucky Place Names* (Lexington 1984); Robert Emmett McDowell, "Bullitt's Lick: The Related Salt Works and Settlements," *Filson Club History Quarterly* 30 (July 1956): 240–69.

FALLS OF THE OHIO. The Falls of the Ohio is located immediately downstream from the MCALPINE DAM spillway below the FOURTEENTH STREET BRIDGE, at the west end of Riverside Dr. in CLARKSVILLE, CLARK COUNTY, INDIANA. Much of the lower bedrock exposed at low water is actually in Kentucky. Geologically and paleontologically, the rocks visible at the Falls of the Ohio are famous and unique, for they compose one of the largest horizontally exposed fossil coral reefs in the world. In addition to the FOSSILS, many types of birds, including shore BIRDS, and several species of fish are found at the Falls. The Falls is now part of the Falls of the Ohio National Wildlife Conservation Area created in 1982 and administered by the U.S. Army Corps of Engineers. In 1990 the FALLS OF THE OHIO STATE PARK was created by the Indiana legislature. An interpretive center was opened on the Indiana shore in 1994.

The Falls of the Ohio was originally a two-mile-long series of rapids (dropping about four feet at most at any one level, and some twenty-six feet overall). It formed on the Devonian Jeffersonville Limestone and the underlying Silurian Louisville Limestone (visible only at lowest water), which trend across the river at this place due to their gentle westward slope on the western flank of the Cincinnati Arch, a regional structure. The rock layers were raised locally by a small anticline in the downstream portion of the Falls. The bedrock exposure, the only obstruction in the entire Ohio River, served at low water as a passage for PREHISTORIC INHABITANTS and buffalo and other animals, and was the west end of the Wilderness Trail from Cumberland Gap. It is this rapids in the river that brought about the establishment of Louisville and the communities of NEW ALBANY, Clarksville, and JEFFERSONVILLE. This happened because most boats stopped here so that pilots could come aboard to steer them safely through, and cargo and passengers could portage around the Falls. The names of the early towns of PORTLAND and SHIPPINGPORT located west of Louis ville reflect this activity.

Some believe Europeans may have reached the Falls quite early, and the French explorer LaSalle is claimed to have visited in 1669. That claim is doubtful, but George Croghan, a British agent, did come in 1765. He referred to the Falls as no more than a rapids. Various maps of the Falls were made beginning with that of Brasier in 1766. GEORGE ROGERS CLARK founded the first settlement at CORN ISLAND at the head of the Falls in 1778. Soon settlers moved to the Kentucky shore and established a town named Louisville in 1779.

A canal around the Falls was proposed in the early 1800s, and in a few years excavation began on both sides of the river. The only canal

The Falls of the Ohio River as seen from Clarksville, Indiana, in 1922.

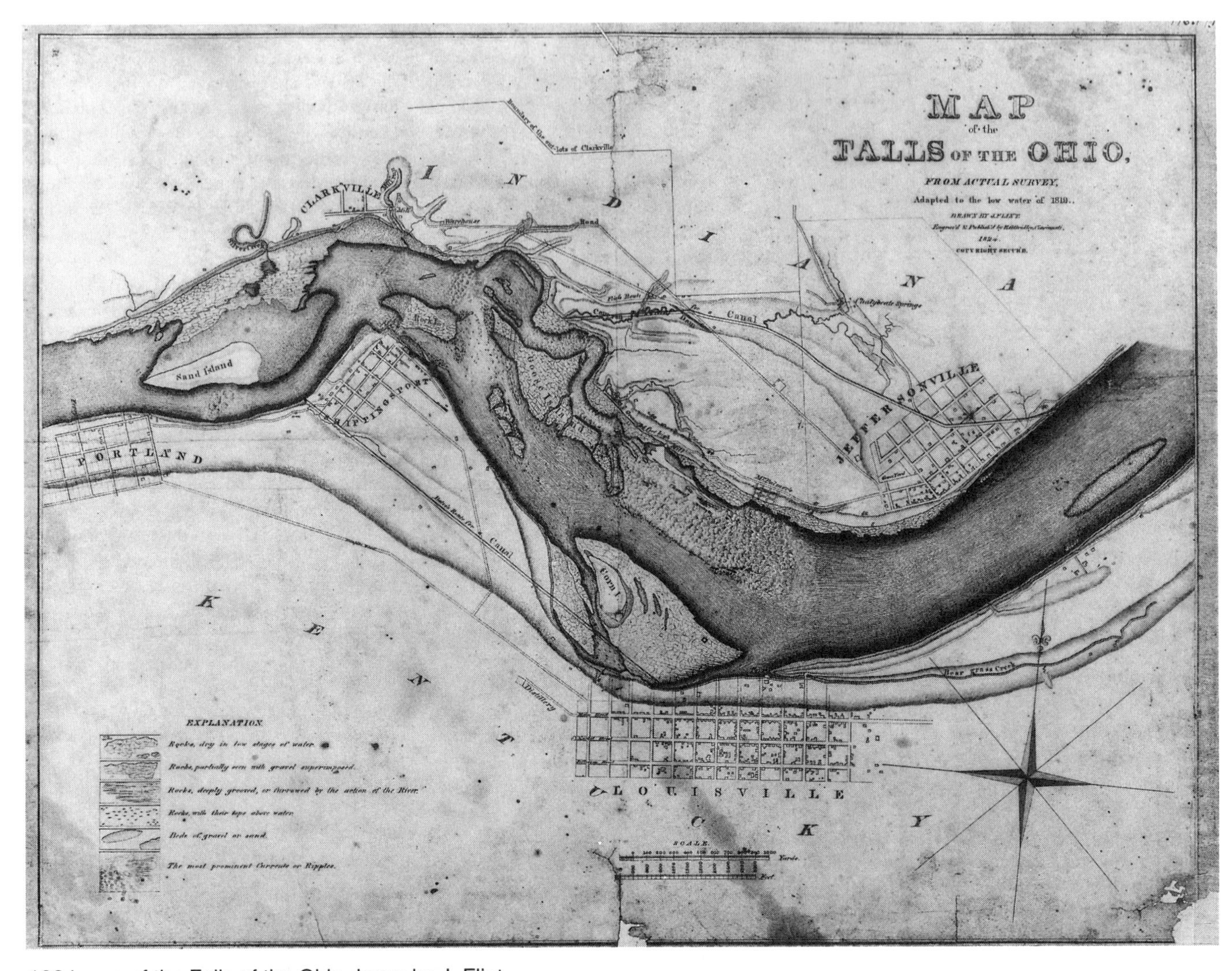

1824 map of the Falls of the Ohio drawn by J. Flint.

completed was the LOUISVILLE AND PORTLAND CANAL on the Kentucky side in 1830. River-related commerce and business sprouted, including ship-building, IRON FOUNDRIES, mills, fishing, and quarrying of building stone. The first bridge (for the LOUISVILLE & NASHVILLE RAILROAD) at Louisville was opened in 1870 and the first dam in 1881. Other larger dams were later constructed. The so-called wicket dam and the first hydroelectric station were both constructed in 1927. In 1929 the Municipal Bridge at Second St. opened for automobile traffic. Presently the McAlpine Dam and Locks, completed in the 1960s, control the flow of water and shipping. Until that time boats and barges often used the Falls at high water, crossing the old wicket dam.

See James E. Conkin and Barbara M. Conkin, *Handbook of Strata and Fossils at the Falls of the Ohio* (Louisville 1980); Stephen F. Greb, Richard Todd Hendricks, and Donald R. Chesnut, *Fossil Beds of the Falls of the Ohio* (Lexington 1993); George H. Yater, *Two Hundred Years at the Falls of the Ohio* (Louisville 1987).

Barbara Conkin

FALLS OF THE OHIO STATE PARK. The Falls of the Ohio State Park was established in 1990. Located in CLARKSVILLE, INDIANA, it is managed by the Indiana Department of Natural Resources, Division of Parks and Reservoirs. The park is sixty-eight acres and includes the fossil beds along the Indiana shoreline and the GEORGE ROGERS CLARK homesite near the mouth of SILVER CREEK.

The Falls of the Ohio National Wildlife Conservation Area (NWCA), established in 1982, was created to preserve the fossil beds that cover approximately 170 acres, as well as to protect fish, wildlife, and water quality. The NWCA encompasses 1,404 acres and is managed by the U.S. Army Corps of Engineers.

The park is within that larger area. Its interpretive center has exhibits and a short movie examining 400 million years of history at the Falls. Geologic, natural, and cultural history are highlighted. Two large marine aquariums with exhibits allow visitors to compare a living coral reef to a similar environment 387 million years ago. A two-thousand-gallon OHIO RIVER aquarium displays live paddlefish, sturgeon, and other more common river fish such as sauger. Visitors may picnic, fish, birdwatch, and explore the woods and fossil beds. FOSSILS can be viewed in boulders near the Center when the beds are flooded.

Nearby is the George Rogers Clark homesite where Clark's cabin was located. Clark was the founder of Louisville, and the town of Clarksville is named in his honor. The site has a commanding view of the west end of the FALLS OF THE OHIO, including MCALPINE DAM'S lower tainter gates and the hydroelectric power plant of Louisville Gas and Electric Co. (LG&E). The best time of the year to see the fossil beds is late summer and fall when the river is at the lowest levels. It is possible to explore the outer fossil beds when the upper tainter gates are closed (located by the FOURTEENTH STREET BRIDGE). A siren sounds before the gates open to warn explorers to quickly leave the fossil beds.

Alan Goldstein

FARMER'S LIBRARY. Louisville's first newspaper was established by Samuel Vail, a native of Pomfret, Vermont, born in 1778. Vail worked for the *Farmer's Library* in Fair Haven, Vermont, then came to Louisville in 1800 to establish an anti-Federalist newspaper. The first issue appeared on January 19, 1801, under the title *Farmer's Library, or Ohio Intelligencer*, a name later shortened. The *Farmer's Library*, a weekly newspaper, was a folio sheet, nineteen by eleven inches, printed with long primer type on coarse paper made at Georgetown, Kentucky. The type was brought from Vermont and had been used there in a newspaper called *Scourge of Aristocracy and Repositories of Political Truth*, published by Matthew Lyon. The *Farmer's Library* was anti- Federalist to the core and printed some of Thomas Paine's work.

Vail relied heavily on the financial support of his longtime friend, Matthew Lyon, who also moved to Kentucky and became the founder of Eddyville and a United States congressman. Money matters caused difficulty when Vail became unpopular, apparently for refusing to take part in the political fighting between parties in Kentucky. People turned to new competitors, such as the *Louisville Gazette* (1807). Although the date of the final issue is uncertain, the latest known copy is July 23, 1807. There are original and photocopies of some issues at the FILSON CLUB HISTORICAL SOCIETY. Vail considered the possibility of starting a new newspaper and, in fact, advertised in St. Louis the coming of the *Missouri Correspondent & Illinois Gazette*; instead he joined the army in 1808. He later took part in the battle of New Orleans. The place and time of his death are unknown.

See J. Stoddard Johnston, *Memorial History of Louisville* (Chicago 1896); *History of the Ohio Falls Cities and Their Counties* (Cleveland 1882); Mary Verhoeff, "Louisville's First Newspaper, The Farmer's Library," *Filson Club History Quarterly* 21 (Oct. 1947), 278–79.

FARMINGTON HISTORIC HOME.

The home, located at Bardstown Rd. and the WATTERSON EXPRESSWAY, was built for John and Lucy Gilmer (Fry) Speed and was the center of a sprawling, five-hundred-acre hemp plantation. The house may have been designed from a plan by THOMAS JEFFERSON.

John Speed was a thirty-six-year-old widower with two young daughters when he met and married twenty-year-old Lucy Gilmer Fry. Both had come across the WILDERNESS ROAD from Virginia at the age of ten, along with their respective families and slaves. Sometime after his 1808 marriage to Lucy, John, together with David Ward and William Pope Jr., purchased over two thousand acres of fertile land along BEARGRASS CREEK in Jefferson County. The land was divided among them; and John, his young bride, and two daughters settled into log cabins on his portion of the property in 1809.

The fourteen-room Federal-style house was begun in 1815 and completed in 1816. A contract (discovered in 1998) for construction of the house identified Robert Nicholson as the builder and Paul Skidmore as the individual who drew up the plan for the Speeds, quite possibly based on a plan for a house by Thomas Jefferson. Close similarities between the Farmington plan and the plan by Jefferson, which both include octagonal rooms and enclosed staircases in the same locations, have led scholars to suggest the Jefferson connection with Farmington. Family associations between Lucy Fry's family and Jefferson provide additional circumstantial evidence for this idea. Lucy's maternal grandfather, Thomas Walker, was a guardian of Thomas Jefferson, and her aunt's house in Charlottesville, also named Farmington, received an addition designed by Jefferson in 1802.

John Speed developed into a successful hemp planter, though he sought to diversify with other crops at Farmington. Livestock, apple orchards for cider production, a small dairy, corn, wheat, and TOBACCO rounded out the plantation's production.

Enslaved AFRICAN AMERICANS were involved with every aspect of the plantation's operation, from probably firing and laying bricks for the house and its dependencies to tending the dairy and livestock, maintaining the house, serving the family, weaving, spinning, gardening, and creating income from their hire-out status. At the death of John Speed in 1840, fifty-seven slaves were listed in the inventory of the property. Among them was forty-one-year-old Morocco, who sometimes functioned as a courier, and Rose, who, along with Morocco, frequently traveled to market with farm goods to sell.

John and Lucy Speed saw eleven children reach adulthood from his two marriages—five sons and six daughters. All the children played prominent roles in the growing young river city. The Speed daughters, with the exception of Mary and Eliza, married and became leading matrons of Louisville. Susan Speed Davis contributed to the establishment of the Home for Friendless Women. Mary became a noted pianist and lived with Eliza all her life. Sons Joshua and James would have a significant influence in both local and national politics.

In 1835 JOSHUA SPEED moved to Springfield, Illinois, to open a mercantile store. After two years in business, Speed met another young man—ABRAHAM LINCOLN—who was beginning his own career. Lincoln sought credit at the store. He received both credit and an offer to share quarters with Speed in his room above the store. Over the next three years, Speed and Lincoln became political allies and intimate friends, entertaining the rising young men who congregated in the store after hours to sort out the latest political developments in the region. They remained roommates until 1841 when Speed returned to Louisville after the death of his father.

In August 1841, Lincoln, suffering from depression after a break in his relationship with Lexington-born Mary Todd, traveled to Louisville at the request of Joshua to regain his spirits. Joshua was clearly disturbed by his friend's state of mind and felt that a few weeks at Farmington would be beneficial. Lincoln spent an undetermined amount of time, probably about three weeks, visiting with the Speeds and aiding young Speed's courtship of Fanny Henning. Both men spoke at length about their relationships with women. This bond would continue throughout Lincoln's life.

During this 1841 trip, Lincoln frequently traveled into Louisville to visit with fellow lawyer JAMES SPEED, who remembered Lincoln's often-ribald joking. In 1864, Lincoln asked James Speed to serve as attorney general in his Cabinet. Speed served beyond Lincoln's death but resigned in 1866.

By 1845 widow Lucy Speed moved into town to live with various of her children, while another daughter, Peachy, along with her husband, Austin L. Peay, operated the plantation. Much of it had been subdivided and sold both to family members and others. After the 1849 death of Austin Peay in a cholera epidemic, Peachy ran Farmington herself along with her slaves. These included David Spencer, reported to be a master bricklayer, and Martha, a young girl who later married David and served as a cook for Peachy Peay. By 1865 the CIVIL WAR was over, SLAVERY had been abolished, and Peachy sold Farmington to German farmers.

In 1959 Farmington Historic Home became the flagship house of Historic Homes Foundation Inc. and opened for tours. Farmington is listed on the NATIONAL REGISTER OF HISTORIC PLACES.

See Ann I. Ottesen, "A Reconstruction of the Activities and Outbuildings at Farmington, An Early Nineteenth Century Hemp Farm," *Filson Club History Quarterly* 59 (Oct. 1985): 395–425; Construction Contract, Bullitt Papers, Microfilm Reel #7, in Filson Club Historical Society.

Deborah Spearing

FARNSLEY, ALEXANDER THURMAN

(b Louisville, Feb. 9, 1869, d Louisville, Oct. 28, 1941). Distiller. The son of Alexander Pericles and Mary Elizabeth (Thurman) Farnsley, he was educated at LOUISVILLE MALE HIGH SCHOOL. He joined the firm of W.L. WELLER and Sons in 1905. In 1908 he and JULIAN VAN WINKLE gained controlling interest in this liquor company.

By the end of PROHIBITION Farnsley had become the president of W.L. Weller and Sons, vice president of the STITZEL-WELLER DISTILLERY Co., vice president of A.Ph. Stitzel Inc., president of the Bank of St. Helens, and vice president of the LOUISVILLE WATER CO. He also served two terms as president of the PENDENNIS CLUB.

Alexander Farnsley married Marie Antoinette Danforth of Louisville in 1905. They had two daughters, Florence Danforth and Elizabeth Thurman. He is remembered in the city of SHIVELY by a par-three golf course that is named for him.

Michael R. Veach

FARNSLEY, CHARLES ROWLAND PEASLEE (b Louisville, March 28, 1907; d Louisville, June 19, 1990). Louisville mayor, United States congressman. He was born in the Peaslee mansion at 1243 S Third St., the son of Burrel Hopson and Anna May (Peaslee) Farnsley. His father was an attorney and circuit court judge in Louisville. The Farnsley family's Jefferson County roots date back to 1782.

Farnsley attended LOUISVILLE MALE HIGH SCHOOL and continued his studies in political science at the UNIVERSITY OF LOUISVILLE. After two years he entered the university's law school, receiving his law degree and admittance to the bar in 1930. Farnsley joined his father's law firm.

Farnsley, a Democrat, ran unsuccessful election bids in 1932 and 1934 for the United States Congress before reaching the Kentucky House of Representatives in 1935. He was reelected in 1937. After his term in the General Assembly, he became one of the state's most powerful lobbyists, representing distillery and brewery interests in the state capital.

In 1940 Farnsley ran in the primary for United States senator against incumbent Albert B. "Happy" Chandler but was soundly defeated. Declared 4-F in WORLD WAR II, he returned to college to complete his undergraduate degree, studying public administration at the University of Chicago, Columbia University, and the University of Kentucky.

Farnsley served as Louisville's MAYOR from 1948 until 1953. He was considered by many to be one of Louisville's best. He was originally selected to serve out the unexpired term of E. LELAND TAYLOR, who died of a heart attack in February 1948. Farnsley was initially considered a dark horse to succeed Taylor. The BOARD OF ALDERMEN, of which Farnsley was a member, chose Farnsley as the mayor's successor as a compromise candidate when neither attorney Eli Brown III nor investment banker Tom Graham could garner enough votes. In November 1948 he was elected to serve out the one year remaining on Taylor's term. Then in 1949, he was elected to a four-year term.

Charles P. Farnsley with President Harry Truman at the Seelbach Hotel, Sept. 30, 1948.

Farnsley, who was seldom without his trademark black string tie, was one of the most innovative of Louisville's mayors. He was described as a "true eccentric" and iconoclast, known for his constant references to Eastern philosophy and Jeffersonian democracy. He also had a strong affection for the Confederacy, evidenced in his defense of the CONFEDERATE MONUMENT on S Third St. When the city proposed moving the monument from its location near the family home on Confederate Place, he stood guard with a musket to protect it.

As mayor, Farnsley was a pioneer of the use of the occupational tax to fund local projects. He created the Louisville Fund, later renamed the Greater Louisville FUND FOR THE ARTS, to expand the city's art community through financial assistance to such organizations as the LOUISVILLE ORCHESTRA. The fund, which served as an umbrella organization, was one of the first of its type in the country. He was a champion of quality-of-life issues, promoting the expansion of the LOUISVILLE FREE PUBLIC LIBRARY and park system, improving the city's STREETS, and developing creative new recreational facilities for children. Under his administration, Louisville also began to dismantle many forms of racial SEGREGATION.

Farnsley was known for his weekly "beef sessions" held every Monday night at CITY HALL. During this exercise in civic participation, Farnsley invited the public to air their thoughts and grievances directly to the mayor and his department heads. Farnsley and the city were frequently the focus of national media attention, through profiles in such publications as *Life*, *Reader's Digest*, and *Collier's*, and in editorials in the *New York Times* and *New York Herald-Tribune*.

After his tenure as mayor, Farnsley worked behind the scenes to promote various projects. A 1960s Indiana University study of Louisville URBAN RENEWAL ranked him as among the city's twelve most influential men. Farnsley was the only man on the list who did not presently hold political office, head a major corporation, or possess substantial wealth.

Farnsley reentered politics, defeating Republican incumbent M.G. "GENE" SNYDER for the United States congressional seat. He served in the United States House of Representatives from January 3, 1965, to January 3, 1967. He chose to leave the House after a single term of office to return to Louisville. Although never a wealthy man while in office, he was successful later in life through such ventures as the Lost Cause Press, which published rare historical and literary works on microfilm.

Farnsley was married to Nancy Hall Carter on February 27, 1937; the couple had three sons, Alexander, Burrel, and Douglass, and two daughters, Sally and Ann Peaslee. He died of Alzheimer's disease and is buried in CAVE HILL CEMETERY.

See William Manchester, "Louisville Cashes in on Culture," *Harper's Magazine* 211 (Aug. 1955): 77–83; James Nold Jr., "Rebel with a Cause," *Louisville*, Oct. 1990; idem, "An Affair to Remember," *Louisville*, Nov. 1990; George Dent, "Here's a Mayor Who Knows How to Get Things Done," *Reader's Digest*, Nov. 1949.

FATHER MALONEY'S BOYS' HAVEN. In the 1940s the Reverend James C. Maloney was the Catholic chaplain at ORMSBY VILLAGE, the home for children operated by Jefferson County in LYNDON, a suburb of Louisville. When he noticed that dependent, neglected, and abused adolescent boys were housed with delinquent adolescent boys, he felt that they should be cared for separately. Maloney went to the Catholic parishes in the Archdiocese of Louisville to raise funds for a separate home. Fund-raising began in 1948 and, with support from the Maloney family and the people of the archdiocese, Boys' Haven accepted the first residents in 1950 at what is now Goldsmith Ln. and WATTERSON EXPRESSWAY. Over the years, it grew to have a capacity for fifty adolescents.

During the 1980s the name was changed from Boys' Haven to Father Maloney's Boys' Haven. During the 1990s changing needs called for innovative programs to which the home responded. Intensive therapy is employed, a program for family restoration is in place, and an independent living program is provided.

Maloney, described as a simple and humble man who wanted to give boys a home and a future, retired as director in 1983 but stayed on as a member of the board of trustees. He died on August 28, 1998, and is buried in Calvary Cemetery.

See *Courier-Journal*, Aug. 23, 1998.

Herman J. Naber

FAUNA. Arising at the junction of the Allegheny and Monongahela Rivers at Pittsburgh, Pennsylvania, the OHIO RIVER is a modern tracing of the southern edge of Pleistocene Period glacial masses. It flows 975.5 miles to meet the Mississippi River at Cairo, Illinois. The cutting of its valley and its meandering across the glacial outwash have created the physical landscape around Louisville. In this "Falls Region" the river descends twenty-four feet within a distance of two and a half miles, cutting through ancient reefs of limestone. This area was the only natural barrier to navigation on the Ohio River.

The limestone rocks of the Falls contain FOSSILS of the Devonian Period, also called the "Age of Fishes," a time over 375 million years ago when Paleozoic Era life increased in complexity and diversity in the seas of our world. Bryozoan "moss animals" have left imprints of intricate branched structures in these rocks, mixed with the Crinoid "sea lily" stem segments that bear star-shaped cavities linking them in evolutionary history with modern-day starfish. Large balls of colonial corals, rugose horn corals, and the now extinct colonial hydrozoan "stroma-toporoids" dominate the rock ledges. Embedded in the rock can be found the casts of the many-chambered straight nautiloid, an ancient type of shelled cephalopod related to modern-day squids. Here also is *Turbonopsis shumardi*, the large fossil snail.

The great proliferation of sharks and bony fish is evidenced in the rocks of the Falls with tiny bone beds containing fish teeth. The ancient trilobites, a group of arthropods whose cousins evolved into such diverse creatures as lobsters, crabs, and insects, are present in these rocks.

Rock strata of the area describe other ancient life. In the older Silurian Period limestone one can find the unique chain coral (*Halysites* sp.), the fossil indicator of the Louisville Limestone. Atop the KNOBS, in younger Mississippian Period stone, there are fossil blastoids, the heads of which once waved in sea current on long columnal stalks. Brachiopod fossils, with their uneven mussel-like shells, are abundant.

A great display of fossils in this area can be seen today by traveling to the Indiana side of the river and visiting the FALLS OF THE OHIO STATE PARK. After studying the educational exhibits, one can climb down the rock beds themselves and look for brachiopods in the *Brevispirifer gregarious-Moellerina greenei* subzone or finger corals in the lower *Amphipora ramosa* zone.

Dug gently in river and stream sediment today are the mussels, freshwater mollusks akin to clams and oysters. These freshwater bivalves are members of the family Unionidae and are filter feeders. They are some of the first sensitive animal species to be affected by pollution and excessive sedimentation. They produce thousands of parasitic, larval glochidia that attach to fish. Mussel shells were formerly used for buttons but are now regulated as a source of starter pearls utilized by the Asian cultivated pearl industry.

Kentucky is at the center of evolutionary diversity for mussels. Yet many species in this region are threatened with extinction. Hence the fanshell (*Cyprogenia stegaria*), the orangefoot pimpleback (*Plethobasus cooperianus*), the pink mucket *(Lampsilis abrupta),* and the fat pocketbook *(Potamilus capax*) are listed as endangered and are protected by both state and federal law.

Betraying evidence of continental drift, the Ohio River harbors fish known as "living fossils." Early fish groups evolved when Kentucky was connected in a single land mass with Europe and Asia. Accordingly, fishermen still snag the paddlefish (*Polyodon spatula*) with the long spatulate head protrusion in the Ohio River. The only other species of paddlefish in the world is found in the Yangtze River in China. The bowfin (Amia calva) is the freshwater descendant of the dominant order of sea fishes in the Jurassic Period, the "Age of Dinosaurs." It is the last species of the ancient bowfin family, fossils of which can be found in European rocks.

The primitive alligator gar (*Atractosteus spatula*) once reported in Jefferson County waters, can grow to ten feet in length and weigh three hundred pounds. Likewise, the large, long-living lake sturgeon (*Acipenser fulvescens*), a source of roe caviar, was once found here. Large fish such as the flathead catfish (*Pylodictis olivaris*), commonly weighing fifty pounds, have been found in Kentucky waters.

In streams, bluegill (*Lepomis macrochirus*), smallmouth bass (*Micropterus dolomieu*), largemouth bass (*Micropterus salmoides*), freshwater drum (*Aplodinotus grunniens*), and white crappie (P*omoxis annularis*) are examples of some of the more than thirty sport fish in the state. One need not travel far to fish for walleyes (*Stizostedion vitreum*), sauger (*Stizostedion canadense*), common carp (*Cyprinus carpio*) and muskellunge *(Esox masquinongy).*

In Kentucky's streams and lakes, smaller fish are also of interest. Shiners (*Cyprinella spp. and Notropis spp.),* bluntnose minnows (*Pimephales notatus*), stonerollers (*Campostoma spp.*) and the logperch (*Perina caprodes)* swim amidst the rocks, pebbles, and bigger fish. The colorful darters, miniature fishes of the trueperch family, inhabit the tumbling environment of stream and river riffles. The rainbow darter *(Etheostoma caeruleum)* and the spotted darter (*Etheostoma maculatum*) are seldom seen scurrying among the highly oxygenated riffle rocks.

There are also unusual species of animals swimming in these waters. Lampreys (*Ichthyomyzon spp.*), some of which are sucking parasites, grow about one foot in length and, in their larval form (*Ammocoetes*), are called "mud eels" because they burrow into the sediment as filter feeders. The American eel (*Anguilla rostrata*) is also found here.

The fierce-looking hellbender (*Cryptobranchus alleganiensis*) is really a predatory aquatic amphibian that can grow to two feet in length. Likewise, the mudpuppy (*Necturus maculosus*), an aquatic salamander, can grow to a foot in length and often surprises fishermen who hook one and find the squirming body with four legs. The eel-like salamander, the lesser siren (*Siren intermedia*), which is smooth-skinned with small pairs of legs, may also be found.

Aquatic insects are the food for many aquatic animals. Notable species winter as larvae in lakes, rivers, and streams and show themselves during summer as adult swarms or unusual insects on porch screens. Hence the mayflies (*Order Ephemeroptera*) are important fish foods. Their larvae have three hair-like tails (*cerci*). In spring, adults swarm in a reproductive frenzy with females, falling back to the water to deposit eggs. Artificial lures used by fishermen are often made to look like adult mayflies, an excellent fish food.

Caddisflies (*Order Trichoptera*) are aquatic grub-like larvae that build cases of sand grains and plant remains under rocks as houses for their bodies. The adult dobsonfly (*Suborder Megaloptera*) has two-inch-long wings and threatening pincer-like mandibles three times the length of its head. Its aquatic larval form, the helgrammite, is often sought for fishing bait.

Climbing around the edges of water bodies will be found many amphibians and reptiles. Those sticky, slimy salamanders are present but often hidden under moist rocks and leaves. Look for the small-mouthed salamander *(Ambystoma texanum)*, the dusky salamander (*Desmo-gnathus fuscus*), or, around limestone cave openings, the black, red-speckled cave salamander (*Eurycea lucifuga*). The newt (*Notophthalmus viridescens*) may be found swimming in water.

Frogs are often hidden but announce their presence to potential mates. Spring peepers (*Hyla crucifer*), with high-pitched birdlike tweets, and chorus frogs (*Pseudacris triseriata*), with a sound often compared to a finger running over the teeth of a comb, are harbingers of spring, filling the evening air with sounds of life. Later in the season, the rumbling bullfrog (*Rana catesbeina*), and the trilling American toad (*Bufo americanus*) dominate the amphibian symphony.

Snapping turtles (*Chelydra serpentina*) are often seen "migrating" to different farm ponds. Weighing up to thirty-five pounds, these creatures have a jagged rear shell edge, a spike-like tail, and a determined eye. One can look for mud turtles (*Kinosternon subrubrun*), stinkpots (*Sternothaerus odoratus*), soft shell turtles (*Trionyx* spp.), and the pond slider (*Chrysemys scripta*) at water's edge or on logs protruding therefrom. In woods the mostly terrestrial box turtle (*Terrapene carolina*) can be found.

Snakes are well represented in this region, although poisonous snakes are relatively rare. The copperhead (*Agkistrodon contortrix*) and the timber rattlesnake (*Crotalus horridus*) may be found in the Knobs region but are unlikely to be found in the lowlands around Louisville. The interesting eastern hognose snake (*Hetero-don platyrhinos*) is sometimes confused with a Rattlesnake. This blunt-nosed, two-foot-long creature will coil up, flatten its head and neck, raise up, hiss, and make striking motions. It may even make a "rattling" noise by shaking its tail under dead leaves. If that does not scare away an intruder, the hognose snake will roll over and "play dead." If righted, the snake will roll back over again.

Another common local snake is sometimes confused with the poisonous cottonmouth found in the western part of Kentucky. This local water snake (*Natrix sipedon*) is a heavy, aggressive snake and when confronted can bite viciously with several rows of tiny teeth. Like many snakes, they secrete a foul musk when handled.

Other interesting snakes include the black racer (*Coluber constrictor*), a sleek, swift, up-to-five-foot-long snake that may be territorially defensive. The king snake (*Lampropeltis getulus*) is a constrictor and is reported to be immune to rattlesnake venom. The milk snake (*Lampropeltis triangulum*) is two feet long and got its name from its common presence around farm barns, giving rise to the false impression that it would suck milk from cows. Two snakes, the copperbelly water snake (*Nerodia erythrogaster*) and Kirtland's water snake (*Clonophis kirtlandii*), are considered rare.

Snakes and other animals prey on the small rodents and other mammals (*Class Mammalia*) in the environment. The abundant short-tailed shrew (*Blarina brevicauda*) travels through small runways in grass and under leaves. The white-footed mouse (*Peromyscus leucopus*), also abundant throughout the state, does not make runways, choosing instead to scamper around overland. The house mouse (*Mus musculus*) and the Norway rat (*Rattus norvegicus*) were introduced from Europe and are widespread, following human settlement.

The eastern mole (*Scalopus aquaticus*) feeds on earthworms, grubs, and other insects by digging a series of underground tunnels. It has tiny eyes and poor vision but has keen hearing and scent. It is rarely seen aboveground. Another tunnel-digging mammal is the groundhog or woodchuck (*Marmota monax*). This relative of the squirrel is often seen in the sun and can swim and climb trees. It eats many types of vegetation and burrows in tunnels leading to a nesting or hibernation chamber with a bed of grass five feet below the surface of the ground. Raccoons (*Procyon lotor*) and the state's only marsupial, the oppossum (*Didelphis virginiana*), are nocturnal, omnivorous, active all year, and often nest in trees.

Other interesting mammals inhabit the area. The striped skunk (*Mephitis mephitis*) often lives in an old groundhog or fox den but does not hibernate during winter. It is often the prey of the great horned owl (*Bubo virginianus*). There are two foxes in the area, both nocturnal, the red fox (*Vulpes vulpes*) and the gray fox (*Urocyon cinereoargenteus*). The gray fox is more common in forested regions, and the red fox is more common on farmlands. Cottontail rabbits make up almost half of their diet. The eastern cottontail (*Sylvilagus floridanus*) is primarily nocturnal, hiding in shrubbery during the day. Nests are made in depressions in the ground. There are three squirrels in the region. The gray squirrel (*Sciurus carolinensis*) is smaller and does not have the yellowish underside that marks the red squirrel (*Sciurus niger*). The nocturnal flying squirrel (*Glaucomys volans*), which spends the day in woodpecker cavities, does not really "fly," but rather glides on extended folds of skin.

There are many members of the class Mammalia in this area. The long-tailed weasel (*Mustela frenata*) hunts for chipmunks (*Tamias striatus*), often at night. The mink (*Mustela vision*), with a furry tail and a white spot on its chin; the muskrat (*Ondatra zibethicus*), in reality a large, aquatic rat; and the flat-tailed, tree-chewing beaver (*Castor canadensis*) are all found near water. The river otter (*Lontra canadensis*) was historically found here, as the name in Louisville's Otter Creek Park implies.

Bats are also mammals and well represented here. During twilight one may look carefully to the sky and see these creatures darting about gathering up insects. Some live in caves or trees, and many can be found in buildings. Our species include the little brown bat (*Myotis lucifugus*), the eastern pipistrelle (*Pipistrellus subflavus*), the big brown bat (*Eptesicus fuscus*) and the hoary bat (*Lasiurus cinereus*). Two bats, the gray bat (*Myotis grisecens*) and the Indiana bat (*Myotis sodalis*), are listed federally as endangered species. The gray bat lives in caves, and the Indiana bat hibernates in caves during the winter, raising young under loose bark on old trees in the summer.

The white-tailed deer (*Odocoileus virginianus*) is now abundant in the area. The deer mate (rut) in November and December, and their antlers fall off naturally soon thereafter. Their white tails, shown as they bound off into the woods, are often seen in the shadows of dawn and dusk. The coyote (*Canis latrans*) has recently extended its range into Kentucky from the West. Primarily nocturnal, the eerie yelping and whining betray its presence. Ninety percent of the coyotes' diet is composed of mammals. The buffalo, or bison (*Bison bison*), was once lured to Kentucky by the presence of SALT LICKS and Native Americans using fires to maintain the "barrens" for grazing. Excavations in archaeological sites indicate the use of turtle, elk (*Cervus elaphus)*, white-tail deer, beaver, rabbit, possum, squirrel, black bear (*Ursus americanus)*, Bobcat (*Lynx rufus)*, Wolf, Fox, raccoon, skunk, wild turkey (*Meleagris gallopavo*), and mussels by local inhabitants.

The avian fauna is rich in this area. The large great blue heron (*Ardea herodias*) and the smaller green heron (*Butorides virescens*) are often seen by canoeists, silently lifting from the water and ascending on powerful wings. The Canada goose (*Branta canadensis*) with its black neck is often heard "honking" as flocks settle in on farm ponds in the region. The male wood duck (*Aix sponsa*) surprises the observer with its colorful iridescence. This year-round resident breeds in Kentucky, and the white-eyed female is often seen proudly paddling before a line of young, downy chicks.

Driving along a road, one can frequently see large red tailed hawks (*Buteo jamaicensis*) with white chests sitting on a naked limb. This foot-and-one-half tall hawk is seemingly patient in review of its surroundings until its deep, muscular wings raise its body silently into the air. Its shriek is telling, and it is often seen being attacked by smaller BIRDS seeking to drive the hawk away. Hovering above the median of the interstate the American kestrel (*Falco sparverius*) is often seen. Also called the sparrow hawk, this Falcon preys on small mammals and large insects. The soaring, grey underwinged turkey vulture (*Cathartes aura*) is two feet in length with a potential wing span of over five feet.

The tall red-crested pileated woodpecker (*Dryocupus pileatus*) is infrequently seen in Louisville's PARKS along with the red-headed woodpecker (*Melanerpes erythrocephalus*), the widespread red-bellied woodpecker (*Melanerpes carolinus*), the black and white downey woodpecker (*Picoides pubescens*), and the ant-eating, yellow-undersided, northern flicker (*Colaptes auratus*).

The native quail species, northern bobwhite (*Colinus virginianus*), is often found in coveys and is identified by its call sounding like "poor bob-white." The shorebird killdeer (*Charadrius vociferus*) tweets noisily and scampers about often feigning a broken wing to lure an intruder away from its nest.

Around structures can be found the originally western house finch (*Carpodacus mexicanus*), the European house sparrow (*Passer domesticus*), and the mud-pack nests of the eastern phoebe (*Sayornis phoebe*). Common blackbirds include the red-shouldered, red-winged blackbird (*Agelaius phoeniceus*), the shiny-headed grackle (*Quiscalus quiscula*), the foreign, flock-forming European starling (*Sturnus vulgaris*), and the brown-headed cowbird (*Molothrus ater*), which lays its eggs in nests for other birds to raise.

Passing splashes of blue may be the small indigo bunting (*Passerina cyanea*), the favorite eastern bluebird (*Sialia sialis*), or the larger, aggressive bluejay (*Cyanocitta cristata*). Red patches among the green vegetation may be the familiar American robin (*Turdus migratorius*) or the equally familiar crested northern cardinal (*Cardinalis cardinalis*) feeding on the seeds of the tulip poplar tree and announcing itself with the sound of "cheer, cheer, cheer." Yellow swatches may betray the black-bibbed, yellow-breasted eastern meadowlark (*Sturnella magna*); the all-yellow yellow warbler, (*Dendroica petechia*) which builds its nests in shrubbery; or the summer yellow, American goldfinch (*Carduelis tristis*), which in its more modest winter coloration is frequently found at thistle feeders. Other winter feeder favorites are the white-bellied slate-sided junco (*Junco hyemalis*), also known as the "snow bird"; the upside-down-hopping white-breasted nuthatch (*Sitta carolinensis*); and the small, dark-crested tufted titmouse (*Parus bicolor*) with its announcement, "here, here, here."

Some interesting birds were noted early in Kentucky history but are no longer found here. In 1784 early Kentucky historian John Filson found "The Perraquet a bird in every way resembling a Parrot but much smaller; the ivory bill Woodcock of a whitish colour with a white plume, flies screaming exceeding sharp." One colony of the passenger pigeon (*Ectopistes migratorius*) in 1808 was estimated at more than a billion birds in a single roost forty miles long and three miles wide with up to ninety nests per tree. The Carolina parakeet (*Conuropsis carolinensis*) and the passenger pigeon are now extinct. The ivory-billed woodpecker (*Campephilus principalis*) is no longer found in the United States.

Kentucky is a storehouse of animal diversity, much of it within a short drive of Louisville. Known species in Kentucky include 347 bird species, 230 fish species, 105 amphibian and reptile species, 103 mussel species, and 69 species of mammals. The number of invertebrate species in Kentucky is indeterminately large, but there are approximately seventy-five thousand species of insects in North America.

See Diana J. Taylor, *Kentucky Alive: A Report of the Biodiversity Task Force* (Kentucky 1995); J.E. Conkin and B.M. Conkin, *Handbook of Strata and Fossils at the Falls of the Ohio* (Louisville 1980); B.L. Monroe Jr., *The Birds of Kentucky* (Bloomington, Ind., 1994).

Ronald R. Van Stockum, Jr.

FEDERAL RESERVE BANK OF ST. LOUIS, LOUISVILLE BRANCH. In 1913 the Federal Reserve Act established the Federal Reserve System to serve as a holding and lending facility to the BANKING community and the United States government. In December 1917 the Louisville office was opened on the second floor of the COLUMBIA BUILDING at Fourth and MAIN STREETS as the first branch of the eighth district (based in St. Louis). Strategically located at the crossroads of major railroad and river traffic, the Louisville branch was placed in charge of sixty-four counties in western Kentucky and twenty-four counties in southern Indiana.

By the end of the first day of operations, approximately $7 million in deposit accounts and $2 million in cash had been transferred to the branch from St. Louis. Within two years the branch had outgrown its facility and moved into the Louisville National Bank Building at the corner of Fifth and MARKET STREETS. These offices were expanded and a new vault was added in 1925 on property along Fifth St.

By the late 1940s the St. Louis office determined that the Louisville branch, which had increased its staff from 100 to 250 to handle war bonds during and after WORLD WAR II, needed a larger space. In 1954 a new site at the southwest corner of Fifth and LIBERTY STREETS was purchased, and construction began two years later. The $3.9 million, five-story building was opened in 1958.

By 1998 the Louisville office had approximately 150 employees. Its duties include regulating and acting as the repository for banks in its district, processing approximately 1.2 million checks per day, maintaining the policies and guidelines of the Federal Reserve System, and circulating coin and currency to its territory.

The branch is overseen by a seven-member board of directors that consists of bankers, business persons, educators, and others from the district who serve a three-year term. Four of the members are selected by the existing Louisville board members, with the remaining three elected by the Board of Governors at the St. Louis office.

See *Courier-Journal*, Dec. 1, 1917, May 26, 1958.

FERGUSON, RICHARD BABINGTON (b Londonderry, Ireland, 1769; d Louisville, April 9, 1853). Pioneer surgeon. Ferguson immigrated to Louisville in 1802. He originally intended to move downriver to New Orleans but was persuaded by a friend and a coin toss to remain in Louisville. His decision to stay was cemented when he married Elizabeth Aylett Booth of Virginia on February 3, 1803. The couple had seven children. The Fergusons built a new log house on MAIN ST. between Third and Fourth.

In 1809 Ferguson, who had a medical practice in Louisville at the time, earned notice after he successfully amputated the leg of Gen. GEORGE ROGERS CLARK above the knee. Ferguson undertook the operation after a consultation with Drs. WILLIAM GALT and John Collins. To divert the patient and allay the severe pain of the knife and saw, General Clark was serenaded by a fife and drum corps during the two-hour operation, which was performed without the benefit of anesthesia. Clark's injuries were the result of extensive burns he had received when he fell into his fireplace at his CLARKSVILLE, INDIANA, home. After the operation Clark retired to his sister's home, LOCUST GROVE, where he lived until his death in 1818.

Ferguson helped to pioneer Louisville's PUBLIC HEALTH system. He stressed the need for a hospital, and in 1817 he became the city's only practicing physician on the twelve-member board of the newly established Louisville Hospital on Chestnut St. between Floyd and PRESTON, serving in both an administrative capacity and as a member of the professional staff until his retirement. He promoted compulsory vaccination. In 1841 he became the first president of the Louisville District Medical Association and was named president of the boards of the JEFFERSON SEMINARY and the Hibernian Benevolent Society. He also helped start the CHRIST CHURCH CATHEDRAL, the oldest Episcopal church in Louisville.

Ferguson is buried in CAVE HILL CEMETERY a short distance away from the plot for General Clark.

See Evelyn Crady Adams, "Dr. Richard Ferguson (1769–1853), Pioneer Surgeon of Louisville, Attended General George Rogers Clark," *Filson Club History Quarterly* 36 (April 1962): 177–83.

FERN CREEK. The area of southeastern Jefferson County known as Fern Creek was named for the local stream along which wild ferns once grew in abundance. Fern Creek had its beginning in the 1780s at the convergence of the Guthrie, Sheppard, and Shafer LAND GRANTS. It extends from Watterson Trail on the north, south to the BULLITT COUNTY line, east to the JEFFERSONTOWN city limits, and west to the Highview Fire District line. It encompasses the communities of Fairmount, Ashville, and Hays Springs and contains fifty-five square miles. This area is approximately twelve miles from the JEFFERSON COUNTY COURTHOUSE in Louisville.

The log home at 7602 Bardstown Rd. was built in 1789 and is the oldest home still in existence in Fern Creek. It was originally a one-room log house situated on land granted to Col. William Fleming. By 1816 the home was owned by William G. Johnson.

The earliest thoroughfare in the area was the Stage Rd. that connected Bardstown and Louisville. In 1831 the Kentucky legislature chartered the Bardstown-Louisville Turnpike Co. to build a toll road that was completed July 1, 1838, at a cost of $203,598. One of the toll gates was placed at Fern Creek. This twenty-nine-mile turnpike later became part of U.S. Highway 31E, also known as the Jackson Highway. The community was initially known as Stringtown because of its strung-out appearance along the main road. Residents changed the name to Fern Creek in the 1870s after being inspired by a fern-lined stream located beside the original post office.

In June 1908 the interurban railway line to Fern Creek was opened, with the loop located at the junction of Bardstown and Fern Creek Roads. It was discontinued in December 1933 and replaced by the Blue Motor Coach bus line.

Pioneer families who settled in the Fern Creek area cleared the land, which became well known for its orchards, strawberries, and vegetables. This agricultural area's proximity to Louisville provided good markets for these products. Residents were victims of both armies who passed through during the CIVIL WAR. The JEFFERSON COUNTY FAIR Co. was organized and incorporated in 1900. The fairground was located one-fourth mile from the Bardstown Pike on Fairground Rd. It contained a track for horse and dog racing, exhibitions of livestock, agricultural products, home economics, arts and crafts displays, and other things typical of county fairs. The fairground closed in 1928.

Some of the well-known places in Fern Creek include Hays Springs, a watering station for travelers from points south to Louisville, and the Nicholson Hotel, originally known as Fruitland Farm. This residence was built by Civil War veteran Col. Noah Cartwright near the intersection of Bardstown and Ferndale Roads. Later, fine home-cooked meals were served and overnight accommodations provided there, and, until its closing in 1962, it was frequented by many celebrities who visited Louisville, especially at KENTUCKY DERBY time.

The first record of a school is a log cabin built in 1792. Another early school was located at a stagecoach stop on property now owned by Dr. Robert J. Seebold. It was in operation from 1858 to 1897. The Morrison Academy was a private school located at Bardstown and Seatonville Roads in the home of William Morrison. In 1923 land was donated by S.A. Stivers as a site for a new two-year Fern Creek School, and in 1925 it became a four-year high school. The community raised funds for the four-room building, which became the consolidated elementary and high school. A new high school building was completed in 1941.

Since the completion of the GENE SNYDER FREEWAY in 1987, Fern Creek has experienced rapid growth, with thriving businesses, new shopping centers, and many new homes in the area where the expressway crosses the Bardstown Rd. Even though several attempts have been made for incorporation, Fern Creek remains an unincorporated town.

See Fern Creek Woman's Club, *Fern Creek Lore and Legacy 200 Years* (Louisville 1976); *Courier-Journal*, June 3, 1998.

Rosetta Stasel Melton
Iris Biggs Peers
Doris Metcalf Thompson
Mary Rush McCaulley
Phyllis Glover Bunnell

FERRIES. The OHIO RIVER, one of the most convenient routes to the territory west of the Allegheny Mountains until the railroad era, was also an obstruction to north-south travel. At Louisville the river could be forded at the foot of the FALLS OF THE OHIO during periods of drought or solid ice, but otherwise ferries were needed. The earliest were simply skiffs or scows propelled by oars, poles, or horses powering treadmills or turntables to turn a paddle-wheel. They were not regularly scheduled but crossed on demand.

One of the earliest was operated by James Noble Wood between Transylvania (HARRODS CREEK) and UTICA, INDIANA, from about 1794 until about 1825. The Oatman family in Indiana operated a ferry beginning in 1807 from below present NEW ALBANY (established in 1813) to the foot of present Duncan St. in Louisville. By 1816 AARON FONTAINE owned or had an interest in this operation, which became known as Fontaine's Ferry and gave its name to the much later AMUSEMENT PARK nearby. HENRY M. SHREVE, an important figure in early river history, ran a ferry between Ferry St. (now Thirty-sixth St.) in PORTLAND to New Albany by 1815. It was soon acquired by John Conner of New Albany. A horse-powered ferry between SHIPPINGPORT and CLARKSVILLE, INDIANA, was operating by 1830. Proprietor William Wright advertised stock-holding pens and a "House of Entertainment" at his Shippingport landing. Other early ferries operated from Clay St. in Louisville to Spring St. in Jeffersonville from an early date until 1867.

The first steam-powered ferry in the Louisville area began operation to Jeffersonville in 1831, but it exploded soon after with seven fatalities. It was replaced in 1835 by another steamer operated by the Louisville and Jeffersonville Ferry Co. The New Albany and Portland Ferry Co. operated steam ferries between the two communities but fell on hard times after the opening of the KENTUCKY AND INDIANA BRIDGE between those points in 1886. The bridge company, apparently seeking a monopoly of cross-river traffic at that point, purchased the ferry company about 1890 but discontinued service about 1896.

The last ferry operation was between Louisville and JEFFERSONVILLE. The original company, facing difficult competition from electric interurban car service over the BIG FOUR BRIDGE beginning in 1905, was reorganized as the Falls City Ferry and Transportation Co. in December 1920, with David B.G. Rose as principal shareholder. Among the minority shareholders was HARLAND D. SANDERS, later of Kentucky Fried Chicken fame. Though the passenger load declined through the 1920s, vehicular traffic increased as automobiles proliferated. There was as yet no vehicular bridge between Louisville and Jeffersonville. Fares were low. During the 1920s pedestrians were carried for five cents. Once aboard they could ride all day for that modest fee.

Both the Portland–New Albany and the Louisville-Jeffersonville services often used more than one boat simultaneously. During busy daylight hours two were used, usually on a twenty- or thirty-minute headway, with a third on standby. During slow traffic times, especially on Sundays, one or more boats were used for excursion work. A popular destination for the New Albany boat was SUGAR GROVE, downriver on the Indiana side. The Jeffersonville boat went upriver to Fern Grove, later called ROSE ISLAND, also on the Indiana shore. Moonlight excursions and charter trips for picnic parties were also common.

Although vehicular traffic boosted revenues of the Louisville-Jeffersonville route, the sheer volume grew so rapidly that the ferries were unable to cope with it efficiently. Calls for a vehicular bridge between Louisville and Jeffersonville became more insistent. The LOUISVILLE BOARD OF TRADE and Louisville mayor WILLIAM HARRISON finally came up with a solution to financing such a venture: bond issues with tolls on the bridge dedicated exclusively to paying off the bonded debt. The George Rogers Clark Bridge (originally the Louisville Municipal Bridge) was opened on October 31, 1929, and was the death blow to the last ferry service in the Falls Cities. The last run of the diesel-powered *Froman M. Coots*, made to complete the charter provisions, was at 6:00 p.m., December 31, 1929, after two hours of free rides. Twenty-six or more muscle-powered and thirty-six steam ferry boats had served the Louisville area during 185 years of cross-river service.

Ferries Serving Louisville Area

Ferry Name	*Dates*	*Between Louisville and*
James Noble's Ferry	1794–1825	Harrods Creek and Utica
Croghan's Ferry	1799–1803	Locust Grove and Six Mile Island
Aaron Fontaine's Ferry	1816-23	Mouth of Falling Run
Oatman Family's Ferry	1807–16	Portland and New Albany
Trublood's Ferry	1811–13	Portland and New Albany
Sproud's Ferry	1813–20	Portland and New Albany
Scribner's Ferry	1820s-?	Portland and New Albany
William Wright Ferry	1824–ca. 1835	Shippingport and Clarksville
About sixteen other ferries whose names and routes are obscure	1807–35	Jeffersonville
Steam Ferry Boat	1831–31	Jeffersonville
Black Locust	1834–47	Jeffersonville
Second *Black Locust*	1847–67	Jeffersonville
New Albany	1849–51	Portland and New Albany
Otto	1849–54	Portland and New Albany
Walk in the Water	1850–55	Portland and New Albany
A. Wathen	1852–66	Jeffersonville
Adelaide	1853–65	Portland and New Albany
John M. Martin	1853–60	Portland and New Albany
Ben South	1860–64	Portland and New Albany
Isaac Bowman	1860–70	Jeffersonville
Union	1860–?	Jeffersonville
James Thompson	1862–73	Jeffersonville
John Shallcross	1863–77	Jeffersonville
Excelsior	1864–69	Portland and New Albany
Thomas Conner	1865–87	Portland and New Albany
Frank McHarry	1867–90	Portland and New Albany
James Wathen	1870–85	Jeffersonville
Music	1873–80	Portland and New Albany
Z.M. Sherley	1873–91	Jeffersonville
New Shallcross	1873–91	Jeffersonville
Music	1880–1901	Portland and New Albany
W.C. Hite	1882–1914	Jeffersonville
Sunshine	1888–1907	Jeffersonville
Rush	1889–96	Portland and New Albany
City of Jeffersonville	1891–1914	Jeffersonville
Columbia	1892–1913	Jeffersonville
Corona	1914–16	Jeffersonville
Pilgrim	1916–l924	Jeffersonville
George Rogers Clark	1916–29	Jeffersonville
Transit	1918–18	Jeffersonville
Perryville	1920–24?	Jeffersonville
W.S. McChesney Jr.	1920-1924	Jeffersonville
Andrew Christy	1920–23	Jeffersonville
Henry Watterson	1923–29	Jeffersonville
*Froman T. Coots**	1925–29	Jeffersonville

*diesel-powered

Ferry "City of Jeffersonville" at landing on Louisville Wharf, ca. 1905.

See Lewis C. Baird, *Baird's History of Clark County, Indiana* (Indianapolis 1909; reprinted Evansville, Ind., 1972); Charles P. Fishbaugh, *From Paddlewheels to Propellers* (Indianapolis 1970); Victor M. Bogle, "New Albany as a Commercial and Shipping Point," *Indiana Magazine of History* (Dec. 1952): 371–72; Frederick Way Jr., *Way's Packet Directory, 1848–1973* (Athens, Ohio, 1983); Indiana Magazine of History (Sept. 1999): 255-283.

Alan L. Bates
Martin C. Striegel

FETTER PRINTING CO. Founded by George G. Fetter Sr. in 1888 on Fifth St. between MAIN and MARKET STREETS, Fetter Printing Co. originally did commercial PRINTING and sold office furniture and stationery supplies. After taking over the business in the mid-1920s, Fetter's two sons, George Junior and John, split up the furniture and printing businesses in 1939, with George Junior taking control of the printing side. The furniture business, located for years at 425 S FOURTH ST., closed in the early 1970s. To meet the growing need for storage and printing space, the printing firm moved to its present site on Locust Ln. in the BRADLEY neighborhood in 1958. In 1967 the Fetter family sold the company to Harold Braun, who sold it to E.A. Ford III, who was responsible for upgrading the facilities in 1978. After being diagnosed with Lou Gehrig's disease in 1992, Ford offered ownership of the company to its employees through a stock ownership program. By 1997 Fetter Printing Co. had expanded its capabilities to include labels and direct mailings, in addition to commercial printing.

FIELD HOUSE. The house of Judge Emmet Field, located at 2909 Field Ave., was built about 1878 by Jonathan C. Wright, who dealt in mill supplies. Wright's widow sold the property in 1890 to the Field family, which had occupied the house since 1886 when Field was first elected to the common pleas branch of the Jefferson Circuit Court.

The house, a large Victorian structure, was built on the old fairgrounds on a forty-three-acre tract between Shelbyville and Brownsboro Roads. Its original address was listed as the Fairgrounds. For a number of years Field's address was listed simply as CRESCENT HILL, and then as Field Ave. in 1900. Seven years after Judge Field's death in 1909, his widow Susan turned the house into apartments and lived there until her death in 1938. The younger Field, William Hill, lived in the upper apartment with his wife for a short time. He was elected to succeed his father and served thirty-six years as judge of the common pleas branch. In 1998–99 the house was extensively renovated.

FIFTH STREET BAPTIST CHURCH. An AFRICAN AMERICAN church founded in 1829. Fifth Street Baptist Church was the second such church in the state, following behind the Separate BAPTISTS organized in Lexington.

Originally known as the African or First Colored Baptist Church, it was on MARKET ST. between Seventh and Eighth Streets. The church was founded in 1839 as a house of worship for the slaves of white parishioners of the First Baptist Church. The Reverend Henry Kiger was the first pastor and was assisted by the white members. A slave owner dedicated the ground at Fifth and York Streets in approximately 1835 for a place of worship for his slaves. A meeting house was erected beyond the city limits in a place described as swampy and difficult to reach. Under the leadership of pastor HENRY ADAMS, who came to preach in 1839, black members were taken out of the white Baptist church three years later. At the time of separation from First Baptist, the church had a charter membership of 475 members. The church also holds the distinction of being the first piece of real estate owned by blacks in the city. In 1848 it established itself on Fifth St. south of Walnut (now Muhammad Ali Blvd.).

Though not free from the influence of the white standing committee, the church largely controlled its own affairs. In 1866 it began a movement for a hospital for freed slaves. In the 1870s the church revolutionized the concept of social welfare by assigning a deacon to supervise visitation in each of the city's WARDS. It provided boxes of clothing for poor members and gave financial support to destitute members during the 1873 depression. By June 1876 the church was able to give three dollars a week to the poor, comparable to a laborer's weekly wage. The church gave annual financial support to and held fund-raising drives for the COLORED ORPHANS' HOME and St. James home for the elderly. In addition, it awarded a college scholarship. The church also sponsored missionary work in Africa. It established several branch missions, some of which became churches. The church is located at 1901 W Jefferson St., its fourth location.

See J.H. Spencer, *History of Kentucky Baptists,* vol. 2 (Cincinnati 1885); *General Association of Colored Baptists in Kentucky* yearbook (Louisville 1943); Marion Lucas, *A History of Blacks in Kentucky,* vol. 1 (Frankfort 1992); George C. Wright, *Life Behind a Veil* (Baton Rouge 1985).

FILM-MAKING. Since the days of silent movies, film-makers have been frequently fascinated by the heritage and magical sound of Kentucky. As early as 1904 *Kentucky Squire* was filmed by the American Mutoscope and Biograph Co. In 1905 *A Kentucky Feud* was filmed, and in 1908 *The Kentuckian.* In 1915 the following films were produced: *A Night in Kentucky, A Kentucky Episode,* and *A Kentucky Idyll.*

Until the mid-1950s almost all movies were studio-bound. On occasion footage would be shot on location. Beginning in 1919, Anita Stewart Productions made its way to Kentucky with an army of technicians, including Anita Stewart and the president of the company, Louis B. Mayer, to partly film *In Old Kentucky.* This was a screen version of Charles E. Dazey's record-breaking play that ran for twenty-five years throughout the country. It utilized many old mansions around Lexington and used Louisville's CHURCHILL DOWNS for the climactic race scenes.

Once again, the Kentucky spirit of love for the horse was portrayed on the screen in the 1938 film *Kentucky,* a drama directed by David Butler. Aside from the superb Technicolor photography and Butler's unerring ability as a director, Walter Brennan did such a fine job of characterizing Peter Goodwin that the role garnered Brennan his second "best supporting actor" Academy Award. As with all productions supervised by Darryl F. Zanuck, *Kentucky* was a first-class production. It starred Loretta Young and Richard Greene. Although portions were filmed in and around Louisville, the film's world preview was at the Cathay Circle Theatre in Los Angeles on December 15, 1938. Aside from the many Hollywood celebrities, the list of guests included Kentucky governor A.B. Chandler, his wife, and two daughters.

In 1931 the film *Sporting Blood* was filmed and cast Clark Gable in his first starring role opposite Madge Evans. The film included an audience-rousing KENTUCKY DERBY climax. In 1939 MGM sent director S. Sylvan Simon to Kentucky to film yet another movie entitled *Sporting Blood* (1940). Again filmed partly on location in Lexington and at Louisville's Churchill Downs, it starred Maureen O'Sullivan, Robert Young, and Kentuckian Lynn Carver.

The Bugle Sounds—a 1941 MGM production—was a pre–WORLD WAR II movie about the substitution of tanks for horses in the United States cavalry. This film was directed by S. Sylvan Simon, with all exterior shots filmed at FORT KNOX. The cast included Wallace Beery, Marjorie Main, Donna Reed, and William Lundigan. Five weeks after the bombing of Pearl Harbor, the world premiere, accompanied by a large parade, was held in Louisville's Loew's Theatre (later the Palace). In attendance were Wallace Beery, his brother Noah Beery, and Marjorie Main.

The 1951 Warner Brothers film, *The Tanks Are Coming,* was mostly filmed at Fort Knox. However, little of the military camp was recognizable, as technicians used props and such to change the scenery around Fort Knox to resemble the Reich and the Siegfried Line. This film shows the part the Third Armored Division played in the St. Lo breakthrough during the advance through Normandy in the summer of 1944. The film was directed by Lewis Seller and starred Steve Cochran and Phil Carey.

Glory was filmed by RKO Studios in 1955. The author of this story was Gene Markey, who was formerly married to Myrna Loy, Hedy Lamarr, and Joan Bennett before taking for his fourth wife Lucille Parker Wright, the owner of Calumet Farm in Lexington. The majority of the exterior shots for this film were shot at Calumet Farm in Lexington and at Churchill Downs. This was the first film Margaret O'Brien appeared in as an adult. It was directed by David Butler, and the cast included Walter Brennan and Charlotte Greenwood.

The third James Bond movie, *Goldfinger,* starring Sean Connery, cost more money than both of the previous Bond pictures combined. The main expense was due to the remarkable Ken Adam set designs—in particular the full-scale replica of Fort Knox built at Pinewood Studios in England. Many of the exterior shots for the film were shot at Fort Knox, Louisville's BOWMAN FIELD, and Lexington.

Asylum of Satan, released in 1972 by Studio I Productions (headquartered in Louisville), was written by J. Patrick Kelly III and Louisville native William B. Girdler. Filmed entirely in Louisville on the Schmutz estate in GLENVIEW, this satanical horror flick was directed by Girdler. Included in the cast were Louisvillians Charles Kissinger, Nick Jolley, Louis Bandy, Claude Fulkerson, Sherry Steiner, and James Pickett.

Girdler filmed three other low-budget independent films in Louisville during the 1970s. His relatively unknown *Three on a Meathook,* loosely based on the same story as *Psycho,* starred local actor Charlie Kissinger as a madman similar to Wisconsin killer Ed Gein.

Carol Speed played the title character in *Abby,* released in 1974. Filmed by Mid-America's Pictures Corp. (formerly Studio I Productions) entirely in Louisville, this unheralded movie reached thirteenth place in *Variety*'s weekly listings of the fifty top-grossing films in the United States for 1975. *Abby* was completed in six weeks at a cost of six hundred thousand dollars and grossed over $12 million, making it the fourth-largest-grossing black movie at that time.

Girdler's last film, *Sheba, Baby,* was released a year later in 1975. In 1978 Girdler and several others were killed when their helicopter crashed in the Philippines. He is buried in CAVE HILL CEMETERY.

MUHAMMAD ALI played himself in *The Greatest.* It also starred James Earl Jones, Ernest Borgnine, and Robert Duvall. The film follows Ali's life from a youngster growing up in Louisville to his winning the Olympic gold medal. Many exterior shots for this 1976 film were shot in and around Louisville.

The 1976 film *Thoroughbred*—later renamed *Run for the Roses*—was another story about Lexington horse breeders and the winning of the Kentucky Derby. The entire film was shot on location around Lexington and at Churchill Downs. In starring roles were Vera Miles and Stuart Whitman.

Stripes was filmed during a six-week schedule on location in Clermont, where a distillery was transformed into a Russian army barracks, and at the Louisville juvenile-detention center, Ormsby Village, which became an Italian military base. This movie starred Kentuckians Warren Oates and Sean Young, plus Bill Murray and John Candy.

Eight Men Out, filmed in 1988, used nearly eighty local residents during its shooting at Churchill Downs. The cast included Charlie Sheen and John Cusack.

A screenplay by Oldham County native Naomi Wallace, called *Lawn Dogs,* was partially filmed on the Prospect farm of her father, Henry Wallace, in 1996. The cast included Mischa Barton and Sam Rockwell.

Another 1996 film, *Fire Down Below,* starring Steven Seagal, was shot on a twelve-week location in Jackson, Hazard, and Louisville. The film was released in September 1997 and brought in $6.1 million during its first week's run.

In 1997 a low-budget movie, *Winner Takes All,* was filmed for more than a month in Louisville and southern Indiana. Approximately 150 Louisville extras and several rap stars, including Flesh-N-Bone, made up the acting ensemble of this film.

Another film shot locally in 1997 was the romantic comedy, *Nice Guys Sleep Alone.* Directed by native Louisvillian Stu Pollard, who adapted the screenplay from a book, the film was shot primarily at Hermitage Farm on U.S. 42 in Oldham County, with other scenes filmed at such Louisville sites as Genny's Diner, Churchill Downs, Jack Fry's restaurant, J. Harrod's restaurant on Upper River Rd., and Kentucky Country Day School in eastern Jefferson County. Sean O'Bryan, formerly of Louisville, was cast in the lead role.

In May 1997 an award-winning documentary by Louisville filmmaker Walter Brock premiered at the Baxter Avenue Theaters. *If I Can't Do It,* a biography of disability activist Arthur Campbell who was originally from eastern Kentucky but later moved to Louisville, won the Golden Sphere award for Human Rights at the San Francisco Film Festival.

In 1998 filming took place on Croydon Circle in Hurstbourne for a movie starring Al Pacino and directed by Michael Mann. The movie, called *The Insider* and based on a *Vanity Fair* story by Marie Brenner, is a drama about Jeffrey Wigand, a former Brown & Williamson Tobacco Corp. executive, and the inside information on company policies he gave to *60 Minutes* investigative reporter and producer Lowell Bergman, played by Pacino. Russell Crowe played Wigand. The house where the movie was filmed was located near where Wigand actually lived.

Louisville has been the birthplace of many film stars. Among the best known are Victor Mature, Irene Dunne, and Ned Beatty. Beatty was born on July 6, 1937, in St. Matthews to Charles William, a salesman, and Margaret (Fortney) Beatty. He won a hundred-dollar prize as Louisville's "best breast-fed baby" of 1938 in a contest sponsored by the city Department of Health. Beatty attended Eastern High School in Middletown. After a year at Transylvania University in Lexington, he began his professional career as a singer in the 1957–58 stage production of *Wilderness Road* in Berea. He was a member of repertory stage companies including Actors Theatre of Louisville. Beatty made his Broadway debut in *The Great White Hope* in the 1960s.

In 1972 Beatty began his movie career with a featured role as a rape victim in *Deliverance.* Beatty has worked with the Kentucky Film Office to attract location shooting to the commonwealth and has served as an adviser to Appalshop Productions in Whitesburg. Beatty is the celebrity sponsor of the annual Ned Beatty Hope for Children Classic Golf and Tennis Tournament beginning in 1997 and held the first two years at the Oxmoor Country Club. He is the father of eight children from three marriages.

Warder Harrison

FILSON CLUB HISTORICAL SOCIETY, THE. In 1884 a group of Louisville citizens, concerned that Kentucky's history was being lost, formed a private association to "collect, preserve, and publish historical material, especially that pertaining to Kentucky." That year marked the centennial of the publication of John Filson's *The Discovery, Settlement, and Present State of Kentucke* (1784), a promotional work that Filson, a frontier land speculator, mapmaker, and surveyor, hoped would draw settlers to Kentucky. To honor Kentucky's first historian, the founders named their organization The Filson Club. It is the state's oldest continuously operating historical society.

The Filson Club is among the 8 percent of historical societies established in the United States prior to 1900. Its early leaders created an association, or "club," whose members shared a common object—the study of Kentucky's history—and were willing to support this endeavor through financial contributions and donations of historical material. As one of the South's leading independent history research centers, The Filson Club receives no government funds in support of its operating budget.

For much of its early history, the membership met at the home of Reuben T. Durrett (1824–1913) at Brook and Chestnut Streets. Durrett led the society from its founding until his death in 1913. Rogers Clark Ballard Thruston (1858–1946) subsequently became the institution's major supporter, serving as president from 1923 until 1946. It was under Thruston's leadership that the organization purchased its first permanent home at 118 W Breckinridge St. Thruston made important contributions to the library and manuscript collections, as well as significant donations to the endowment fund. In 1984 The Filson Club, having outgrown its old headquarters, celebrated its centennial by launching a fund-raising drive to acquire a new home, the ca. 1905 Beaux Arts Ferguson mansion at 1310 S Third St. The society moved to its new home in 1986.

Researchers are drawn to The Filson Club because of the national reputation of its library and special collections. The noncirculating library collection specializes in the history and culture of Kentucky and the Upper South. It contains more than fifty thousand titles, more than fifteen hundred eighteenth to twentieth century maps, three thousand reels of microfilm, eight hundred newspaper titles, and almost three thousand pieces of sheet music. The special collections department includes approximately 1.5 million manuscript letters, diaries, and business records that are the most significant in the state for the frontier, antebellum, and Civil War eras. The photographs and prints collection houses more than forty thousand images and hundreds of lithographs and engravings. The museum department has one of the state's most extensive nineteenth-century portrait collections, as well as important holdings of Kentucky coin silver, quilts, and Civil War artifacts.

Immediately after its founding, the historical society took steps to provide greater access to historical documents and interpretations by establishing a publications program. In 1926 *The Filson Club History Quarterly* was founded to provide a forum for scholarly writings on Kentucky history. Today, in addition to supporting the state's oldest continuously operating historical society, the society offers the public an ambitious schedule of lectures, institutes, seminars, tours, and workshops that explore the history and sense of place that makes Kentucky unique.

See Lowell H. Harrison, "A Century of Progress: The Filson Club, 1884–1984," *Filson Club History Quarterly*, 58 (Oct. 1984): 381–407.

Mark V. Wetherington

FILSON CLUB HISTORY QUARTERLY, THE. The Filson Club began publishing historical monographs in 1884, the year of its founding. This first publication series (1884–1938) had become a significant contribution to Kentucky historiography when in 1926 the club augmented its publication program by launching the *History Quarterly* in cooperation with the history department of the University of Louisville. This joint sponsorship resulted in a journal with an unclear focus—one article in 1928 was entitled "A Roman Town in Africa." In 1928 the Filson Club assumed sole responsibility for the journal and renamed it *The Filson Club History Quarterly.* Over the years the *Quarterly* has become a highly regarded regional history journal that focuses on Kentucky but maintains a broad perspective on the South and Midwest in both the articles published and the books reviewed.

In 1982 the *Quarterly* became a refereed journal, with a twelve-member editorial advisory board. A refereed journal is a journal in which authors submit their work for peer review prior to publication. In 1983 the Otto A. Rothert Award for the best article published each year was established. The first editor was Robert S. Cotterill (1926–28), followed by Otto A. Rothert (1928–45), Lucien Beckner (1946), Richard H. Hill (1947–71), Robert E. McDowell (1971–75), and Nelson L. Dawson (1975–). Over the years there have been incremental design changes. The once-familiar gray cover was replaced in 1992 with a glossy, two-color cover showing a portion of John Filson's map of Kentucky. Special theme issues have devoted particular attention to various historic milestones, including the Filson Club centennial (1984), the Kentucky bicentennial (1992), and the fiftieth anniversary of World War II (1994).

See Lowell H. Harrison and Nelson L. Dawson, eds., *A Kentucky Sampler: Essays from The Filson Club History Quarterly* (Lexington 1977).

Nelson L. Dawson

FINK, ALBERT (b Lauterbach, Germany, October 27, 1827; d Louisville, April 3, 1897). Civil engineer and railroad executive. He graduated in 1848 from the Polytechnic School of Darmstadt, where he studied architecture and engineering. He immigrated to the United States in 1849 after the failure of the democratic uprising of 1848.

Beginning as a draftsman for the Baltimore & Ohio Railroad, he soon became principal assistant to the chief engineer. By 1852 his Fink truss design was being used by the B&O. In 1857 he was recruited by the Louisville & Nashville Railroad as assistant engineer for bridges and buildings. His five-span Fink truss bridge across Green River just south of Munfordville was the second-longest iron bridge in the United States. In 1859 he became the L&N chief engineer. That same year, at the behest of James Guthrie, vice president of the L&N, Fink completed the Jefferson County Courthouse that had stood unfinished for almost twenty years.

After the outbreak of the Civil War in 1861, Fink and his engineering corps were kept busy repairing damage to the L&N line by Confederate raiders. Repair gangs were sometimes so quickly on the scene that they themselves came under attack. At war's end, Fink was named general superintendent of the L&N. He simultaneously designed and superintended construction of the Fourteenth Street Bridge over the Ohio between Louisville and Indiana, connecting railroads of the North and South. It was completed in 1870 and has been called Fink's "crowning achievement as an engineer." (It was replaced by a new bridge in 1918–19.)

Following his appointment as an L&N vice president in 1871, he made what is regarded as the first sophisticated accounting analysis of railroad operating expenses. This brought him the commissionership of the newly organized Southern Railway and Steamship Association in Atlanta in 1875. Designed to stabilize rates, to bill through freight handled by several roads, and to solve similar problems, it was the model for the Trunk Line Association formed by northeastern railroads in 1887 with Fink as its head.

Tall and muscular, Fink was known as "the Teutonic giant." He married Sallie Moore Hunt of Louisville on April 24, 1865; they were the parents of a daughter, Eleanor. In 1889 failing health caused Fink to resign the Trunk Line post and return to Louisville from New York City. He is buried in Cave Hill Cemetery.

See Ellen Fink Milton, *A Biography of Albert Fink* (Rochester, N.Y., 1951); John E. Tilford Jr., "The Delicate Track—the L&N's Role in the Civil War," *Filson Club History Quarterly*, 36 (July 1962): 209–21; Carl W. Condit, *American Building Art* (New York 1960): 122–24.

George H. Yater

FINK, MIKE (b Fort Pitt [now Pittsburgh, Pennsylvania] ca. 1770; d Montana area, 1823). Keelboatman and frontiersman. Fink's parents were of the Scots-Irish emigration who followed the frontier westward. His education was in the western woods and along the Ohio and Mississippi Rivers. As a bargeman or keelboater, he in time became known as "King of the Mississippi Keelboatmen." At best the life of a boatman on the western waters was a challenging one. It was beset by dangers from nature and man in about equal proportions. Mike Fink in time was able to cope with both.

Not only was Mike Fink a master with the poling oars of a keelboat, he was an extraordinarily accurate marksman with a flintlock gun. He once shot the tails off of nine pigs on the shores of the Ohio River from his boat fifty yards away. He was also a fighter and a well-known prankster. In the neighborhood of Louisville he and his crew engaged in two capers that landed them in court. Once he doped sheep with snuff and convinced their owner that they had the deadly "black murrain." He offered to destroy the sheep and throw them into the river. However, Mike returned later to collect the carcasses and turn them into mutton for his own profit. In the second incident, Jefferson County justices had procured a reward for Mike's capture because of his many devious deeds. Mike was convinced by an old friend who was struggling financially to turn himself in. The friend would in turn receive the reward. Mike agreed to go to court peacefully if he and his crew could go in their keelboat. However, the keelboat was used as an easy escape. Mike, along with his boatmen, was allowed to jump out of the courtroom windows and quickly retreat down the Ohio River in the craft.

The coming of the steamboat drove Fink and the keelboatmen off the river and onto the trails of the Rocky Mountain trappers and fur traders. He became a trapper for the Missouri Fur Co. Fink and his companion of the river days, a man named Carpenter, followed the famous fur trader William H. Ashley into the fur rendezvous in the Rocky Mountains in early 1822. Fink and Carpenter had on occasion shot marked cans off each other's heads. In a drunken moment Mike Fink shot at a can on Carpenter's head but hit him between the eyes instead. Mike was accused of having willfully murdered Carpenter and was murdered in turn by a man named Talbott. Fink is buried at Fort Henry, Montana, near the confluence of the Yellowstone and Missouri Rivers.

It is difficult to distinguish fact from fiction about Mike Fink. Part of his legendary fame rests upon the boast accredited to him that "I can out-run, out-hop, out-jump, throw down, drag out and lick any man in the country. I am a Salt-River roarer, I love the wimmin and I'm full of fight."

See Walter Blair and Franklin J. Meine, *Mike Fink, King of the Mississippi Keelboatmen* (New York 1933); Blair and Meine, *Half Horse, Half Alligator: The Growth of the Mike Fink Legend* (Chicago 1956); Ben Casseday, *The History of Louisville, From the Earliest Settlement till the Year 1852* (Louisville 1852).

Thomas D. Clark

FIRST CHRISTIAN CHURCH. While reportedly organized in the early nineteenth century, this congregation splintered from its Baptist origins and changed its name from the Baptist Church of Jesus Christ to the Disciples of Christ in 1833. Continuing to worship in the same house as the Baptists until March 1835, it then severed all ties by moving services to a rented house on Second St. between Market and Jefferson Streets. The congregation grew, necessitating the construction of a new place of worship in 1836 on Fifth St. between Walnut (Muhammad Ali Blvd.) and Chestnut Streets. In only nine years this structure became too small. The congregation sold the church to the Reverend Henry Adams for his Colored Baptist Church. While awaiting construction of a new church on Walnut St. at Fourth, the group held services at a schoolhouse on Grayson St. The church's name was changed to Walnut Street Baptist Church upon completion of the new building. Continued growth again forced the congregation out of its structure, and it moved services to the Masonic Temple at Fourth and Jefferson Streets about 1859, as the fifteen-year-old church was demolished to make way for a larger one on the same site. Although the basement of the new church was completed by 1860 and the services were moved there, the Civil War interrupted the remaining construction, which was not finished until a decade later. In 1876 the name of the congregation was changed to First Christian Church.

By 1904, the church had established thirteen branches in the Louisville area, with four thousand members. Five years later, John Starks purchased the church site for $350,000 for the

First Christian Church building, northeast corner Walnut (now Muhammed Ali) and 4th Street. Razed(?) in 1911.

future site of the Starks Building. By 1911 the church's sixth structure was completed at the corner of Fourth and Breckinridge Streets. In 1977 this house of worship was sold to the African American Lampton Baptist Church, and services for First Christian Church were divided between Kammerer Middle School in the east and Fourth Avenue United Methodist Church in Old Louisville. Two years later, the congregation moved into its latest church on U.S. 42 at the intersection of Wolf Pen Branch Rd.

See Herbert L. Drane Jr., "Study of the History of the First Christian Church of Louisville, Kentucky," Master's thesis, The College of the Bible, Lexington 1959; *Courier-Journal*, Sept. 22, 1979.

FIRST PRESBYTERIAN CHURCH. In 1815 the Presbyterian Synod of Kentucky created three new Presbyteries, one of which was Louisville. The following year the city's oldest Presbyterian congregation, First Presbyterian Church, was founded by the Reverend Daniel C. Banks, a Congregationalist minister from New England. In 1817 the congregation constructed its first meetinghouse on the west side of Fourth St. between Market and Jefferson. In 1836 that building was destroyed by fire (along with, according to legend, a church bell cast by Paul Revere). Consequently, a lot was purchased on Green (Liberty) at Sixth St.; and a new church, designed by Louisville architect John Stirewalt, was built.

During the 1830s the Presbyterian church was shaken by a dispute known as the Old School/New School controversy. In 1834 the congregation at First Church passed a resolution that placed it solidly within the Old School party, meaning that the church generally: 1) favored presbytery control over church activities, 2) adhered to a strict Calvinism, 3) opposed the aggressive revivalism employed during the Second Great Awakening, and 4) favored "gradual emancipation" of slaves over outright abolitionism.

During the early 1860s, as the nation plunged deeper into the Civil War, the northern branch of Presbyterianism (the Presbyterian Church in the United States of America) became increasingly insistent that its member churches endorse from the pulpit such Union political positions as the abolition of slavery and loyalty to the federal government. Louisville's First Presbyterian Church openly opposed mandatory obedience to Washington. As a result, at the end of the war, in June 1865, the church facilities were commandeered by Union general John M. Palmer for temporary use as a hospital and military station. In 1868 the congregation finally split with the Northern Presbyterian body and united itself with the Southern General Assembly (the Presbyterian Church in the United States).

In 1874 the congregation at First Church suffered a division when its pastor, Rev. Samuel R. Wilson, attempted to withdraw himself and a faction of the church from the supervision of the Southern General Assembly over a dispute concerning the extent of the pastor's powers. However, the Wilson faction exited the denomination without relinquishing their claim to the use of the church's facilities. The recognized remainder of the congregation was forced to hold services at Library Hall on Fourth St. until the Kentucky Court of Appeals decided in *First Presbyterian Church of Louisville v. Wilson* (1878) that implicit in the Wilson faction's renouncing of the Presbyterian hierarchy's authority was the forfeiture of their interest in the church's property. Consequently, the holdings on Green St. were restored to the part of the congregation that remained in harmony with the Southern Presbyterian organization.

In 1889 the Green St. property was sold to the Louisville Gas Co., and the congregation again moved, to Fourth near York St. In 1910 the membership of Louisville's Westminster Presbyterian Church was annexed into the First Presbyterian Church's congregation. However, plans for another merger, this time with Warren Memorial Presbyterian Church, were crushed in 1919, largely because of opposition from within First Church. By 1922 First Church had again relocated, this time to a building at W Ormsby and First St.

By the 1990s, membership at First Church had dwindled to about a dozen individuals. In February 1998, the church closed its doors and the church facilities were sold to the Abundant Life Ministries Church, a nondenominational evangelical congregation.

See *Manual of the First Presbyterian Church Louisville, Kentucky, 1816–1916* (Louisville 1916); *Courier-Journal*, Feb. 7, 1998; Edward L. Warren, *The Presbyterian Church in Louisville: From Its Organization in 1816 to the Year 1896* (Chicago 1896).

Timothy L. Wood

FIRST STANDARD BANK. The evolution of African American businesses in Louisville unfolded in several stages, beginning with the establishment of small shops and service enterprises in the 1830s. By World War I, larger-scale businesses emerged with the opening of Mammoth Mutual Co. (later Mammoth Life and Accident Insurance Co.) in July 1915. Domestic Life and Accident Insurance Co. followed in June 1920, and its executives, while awaiting their charter, immediately began soliciting capital subscriptions for a bank to create both a depository for its funds and an engine to drive community economic development.

On January 17, 1921, the banking commissioner of Kentucky authorized the First Standard Bank to conduct regular banking operations. Touted as the "million dollar bank," First Standard became the first African American bank in Kentucky when it opened on February 5, 1921, with Wilson Lovett as president, W.W. Spradling as vice president and chairman of the board, and Dr. L.R. Johnson and Bishop G.C. Clement as vice presidents. Lovett resigned in July 1929 to assume the treasurership of Supreme Life Insurance Co. and was succeeded as president by longtime First Standard cashier, J.R. Ray.

Located first at Seventh and eventually at Sixth and Walnut (Muhammad Ali Blvd.) Streets, First Standard served both as a symbol of community pride and a source of working capital for African American businesses, which could not borrow at reasonable rates, if at all, from local white-owned financial institutions. By the mid-1920s, First Standard boasted $375,000 in total deposits, $500,000 in total assets, and more than $300,000 loaned to local African American entrepreneurs. Based on the success of Domestic Life and First Standard, Lovett and his partners also established other companies; e.g., the Standard Building and Loan Association and the Parkway Building and Loan Association.

Despite their many accomplishments, African American businesses, even in this "Golden Age" of the 1920s, were fragile institutions marginal to the larger national economy and dependent upon the limited earning (and purchasing) capacity of African Americans in a racially segregated society. This fragility was exposed most graphically with the onset of the Great Depression. When their depository institution, the Louisville Trust Co., closed after the failure of the National Bank of Kentucky, First Standard and the American Mutual Savings Bank, an extension of Mammoth Mutual, failed to open on November 17, 1930.

In an effort to salvage these key financial institutions, First Standard and American Mutual merged in January 1931 under the leadership of W.W. Spradling to form the Mutual Standard Bank. With strong community support, Mutual Standard opened briefly in April 1931. However, while factors external to the African American community caused the failure of First Standard, the economic weakness of that community in the throes of the Great Depression undermined Mutual Standard from its inception. Mutual Standard closed on May 7, 1931, and was liquidated subsequently by the Kentucky Banking Commission. More than forty years would pass before another African American bank would be established in Louisville.

See "The Crisis," *NAACP* 20 (July 1920): 148; "The Crisis," *NAACP* 20 (Feb. 1, 1921): 175; *Louisville Leader*, Jan. 12, 1921, July 6, 1929, Sept. 14, 1929, Sept. 21, 1929, Nov. 22, 1930, Dec. 6, 1930, Jan. 10, 1931, Feb. 7, 1931, Feb. 14, 1931, Feb. 28, 1931, April 4, 1931, May 9, 1931, May 16, May 16, 1931; May 14, 1932, Sept. 23, 1932, Oct. 15, 1932; George C. Wright, *Life Behind a Veil* (Baton Rouge 1985).

J. Blaine Hudson

FIRST UNITARIAN CHURCH. The First Unitarian Society of Louisville was established on July 3, 1830. In 1829 a group of Louisvillians interested in liberal religious philosophy began meeting in the schoolroom of Francis E. Goddard on Green (Liberty) St. They invited a Unitarian minister, the Reverend John Pierpont of Boston, to give a series of sermons, which inspired the formal organization of the society. Interest in Unitarian ideas had been kindled in Kentucky during Horace Holley's presidency of Transylvania University (1818–25). Holley, a Unitarian, resigned under pressure from those opposed to his liberal religious views.

The first building of the First Unitarian Church was on the southeast corner of Fifth and Walnut (Muhammad Ali Blvd.) Streets. The classical style building was dedicated on May 27, 1832. The first two ministers, George Chapman and James Freeman Clarke, served the church from its founding until 1840, when John Healey Heywood (1818–1902) became minister. Heywood's ministry continued for forty years. He was well known for his civic activities, which included fourteen years as president of the school board. During his presidency, the city's first high schools—separate ones for boys and girls—were established.

In 1869 the Universalist Church (founded 1840) joined with First Unitarian Church. With funds from the sale of the Universalist Church building on Market St. between Eighth and Ninth and other funds from the two congregations, a new church was built on the southeast corner of Fourth and York Streets. This Gothic building was designed by H.P. Bradshaw and constructed from local golden limestone. It was dedicated on January 16, 1871. At the end of that year, the church was severely damaged by fire. Funds were raised to repair the damage, and services resumed on December 15, 1872. When the Louisville Unitarian and Universalist congregations joined in 1869, the church was incorporated as The Church of the Messiah. It was, however, commonly known in the community as First Unitarian Church, and this name was officially restored in 1924.

The Dickens Club, a dramatic society organized in 1858 by members of the church, raised money through its productions for charitable causes in the city. Among them was the Old Ladies' Home. The home, founded in 1865, later became part of the Cook Benevolent Institution. During the Civil War the congregation supported the United States Sanitary Commission and the Refuge Commission, both of which were led by the minister, Mr. Heywood.

In his long ministry to the church (1946–60), Robert Terry Weston was known throughout the community as a panelist on the radio program *The Moral Side of the News*. Robert Reed, minister from 1968 to 1985, led the congregation in working to promote social justice on both local and national levels. Virginia Knowles followed as interim minister in 1985 and in 1986 Richard Beal became the minister. The congregation was active in founding a number of community organizations, including the Help Office, Neighborhood Development Corp., and Council on Peacemaking and Religion. First Unitarian serves as a site for meetings of many diverse community groups and performances by Louisville musicians and performing artists.

On December 14, 1985, the church building was severely damaged by a spectacular fire. Nothing remained of the 1871 building but the stone walls. The congregation decided to rebuild at the same downtown location. A new church building was designed by Louisville architect John Grossman. It incorporated the original stone walls of the church and the 1881 Heywood House, a next-door residence that had been purchased by the church in 1977. The new church was dedicated on March 26, 1989.

See J. Stoddard Johnston, ed., *Memorial History of Louisville* (Chicago 1896); Edith Fosdick Bodley and Gustave Breaux, *An Historical Sketch of the First Unitarian Church of Louisville* (Louisville 1930); *Courier Journal*, Oct. 7, 1979.

Carol Brenner Tobe

FIRST VIRGINIA AVENUE BAPTIST CHURCH. The predecessor church of First Virginia Avenue Baptist Church was organized in 1884 by Jake Oldham, C.C. Bates, J.M. Mitchell, Richard Hyman, and John Jackson. Initially, the church was named Nebulan Baptist Church, and services were held in a private home on Orleans (Dumesnil) Ave. Sunday school activities were conducted in a house at Thirty-sixth St. and Virginia Ave. The church was reorganized as First Virginia Avenue Baptist Church in 1891 by R.H.L. Mitchem.

A church was erected at the Thirty-sixth St. and Virginia Ave. location that same year. When the original church was completed, the name was changed from Nebulan to its present name. The identification "First" was added to distinguish the church from the Virginia Avenue Methodist Episcopalian church in the same neighborhood. The pastor at the time, Rev. W. Augustus Jones, implemented the name change. The church was the first black church in the original African American section of the Parkland neighborhood. The present church was built in 1919 and has undergone several renovations since that time.

See Ethel I. King, *From Parkland to the River's Edge* (Louisville 1990); "First Virginia Avenue Baptist Church, 87th Anniversary, 1891–1978," Western Branch Library, African American Collection.

Margaret Merrick

FISCHER PACKING CO. This family-owned firm, which advertised itself as "the bacon makin' people," operated for almost six decades until it was sold to a larger corporate buyer. Founder Henry Fischer emigrated from Zweibrucken, Germany, in 1893. After learning the grocery trade in Louisville, he and a partner started a small wholesale meat business that offered hand-ground sausage. Fischer took over the business in 1909, which he first ran from his backyard on Mellwood Ave. Soon after he added a shed and slaughterhouse.

During World War I Fischer, a member of the Socialist Labor Party, opposed American entry into the conflict. This prompted a federal investigation that was dropped after the intervention of top LABOR leaders, including American Federation of Labor president Samuel Gompers. Fischer's good labor relations had earned friends among the unions.

In 1923 the firm was incorporated as the Henry Fischer Packing Co., with Fischer as president and a son, Carl, as vice president. A new plant, also on Mellwood Ave., which covered a city block, was later erected near the site of Fischer's house; employment in 1939 was 285 persons. Principal products, which included pork, beef, veal, lamb, and sausage, were sold wholesale under the trade names Mellwood Brand and Summit Brand.

Carl T. Fischer Sr. took over as president in 1942, expanded the firm's market regionally, and upgraded operations with modern packaging and refrigeration equipment. He and his two sons, Carl T. Junior and Terry, both of whom had joined their father in management, sold the plant to Wilson Foods Corp. in 1969. The plant was sold again in 1988 to International Fish & Meat USA but continues to operate at its longtime location. In 1993 the company experienced a bitter, nineteen-week strike by the Food and Commercial Workers Union. The strike focused on improving wages and benefits that had been reduced in previous contracts in order to assure the company's long-term profitability. Founder Henry Fischer died in 1973 at age ninety-seven, and Carl Senior, who was born in 1899, died in 1992.

See *Henry Fischer, President, Fischer Packing Co.* (Indianapolis 1939); *Courier-Journal*, Dec. 29, 1992; Hilton E. Hanna and Joseph Belsky, *The "Pat" Gorman Story: Picket and Pen* (Yonkers, N.Y., 1960).

Charles B. Castner

FISHERVILLE. A small community in southeastern Jefferson County, roughly centered around old TAYLORSVILLE Rd. between Fisherville Rd. and English Station Rd. In the early nineteenth century, farmers from Virginia and Pennsylvania came to the region to settle in the fertile valley along FLOYDS FORK. By 1833 the community had attracted enough inhabitants for Edward Currey to open the area's first post office. Two entrepreneurs, John Fisher and his son Robert, moved to the area in 1835 and established a five-story grist mill along the creek's banks. Two years after Robert's death in 1845, the town of Curreys was renamed Fisherville in his honor. With the extension of the Louisville, Fisherville, and Taylorsville Turnpike in the 1850s, the small community prospered as people visited on their way through and others moved to the town permanently. Developing in a pattern similar to other "stringtowns," the town was divided into two districts, with the eastern half containing most of the businesses, while the suburbs—although the entire stretch was only approximately three-fourths of a mile—were in the western half.

In the late nineteenth and early twentieth centuries, Fisherville was not only a growing business community, boasting over a dozen enterprises, but also a popular resort spot for Louisville vacationers. With the arrival of the Southern Railroad tracks in 1888, people could easily make their way out to the Currey Hotel and, after 1903, to the nearby Blue Rock Hotel. The latter hotel was established by Stephen Beard as a health spa after some of his workers discovered a MINERAL WATER well. While some of the water, which reportedly contained sixteen minerals, was bottled and shipped for consumption, the runoff was channeled into a bathing lake for hotel guests. After the well dried up in 1914, the number of visitors steadily dwindled; and the hotel, along with the area's reputation as a playful retreat, came to an end in 1921. After several attempts to reopen it during summers, it was demolished in 1939. After the completion of the new Taylorsville Rd. in the early 1980s, Fisherville was bypassed by regular traffic and retained its small-town feel.

See *History of the Ohio Falls Cities and their Counties*, vol. 2 (Cleveland 1882); *A Place in Time: The Story of Louisville's Neighborhoods* (Louisville 1989); Carl E. Kramer, "Fisherville: Jefferson County's Stringtown on the Turnpike," *Filson Club History Quarterly* 69 (Jan. 1995): 67–84.

FISHPOOLS. Clay deposits in the southern and southwestern parts of Jefferson County formed a perched water table resulting in swampy ground and precluded much early large-scale settlement in those areas. Originally located in the Cross Roads precinct south of modern-day OKOLONA between Blue Lick Rd. and Preston Highway at Interstate 265, Fishpools was a well-known landmark in early Jefferson County. Fed by a tributary of Fishpool Creek, which branched southward from Oldham Pond in the swampy WET WOODS region in southern Jefferson County, the concentration of springs formed excellent fish breeding grounds. James Francis Moore, a colonel with the Jefferson County militia, moved to the area in the 1780s and established a salt work at the nearby MANN'S LICK furnaces. According to family tradition, his cabin was moved across the creek to Preston Hwy. following his death in 1810, where it still constitutes part of a house standing in the 1990s. Although the pools have dried up, possibly after the Wet Woods region was drained in the early 1900s, Fishpool Creek continues to flow from the Southern Ditch to McNeely Park.

PTRL Environmental Services bought and created a new wetland in the area in 1998–99. The 11.7-acre site, at the confluence of Fishpool Creek and Southern Ditch, is able to hold up to 80 acre-feet of water. After a heavy rain, water in those tributaries backs into the wetland. As the creeks' levels fall, water flows back into them from the wetland. The site has been planted with water-loving trees.

See Leslee F. Keys, ed., *Historic Jefferson County* (Louisville 1992); *Courier-Journal*, Sept. 14, 1998.

FITZBUTLER, HENRY (b Canada, December 1837; d Louisville, December 27, 1901). Physician, publisher, and CIVIL RIGHTS activist. Born to slave parents who had escaped north to Canada, Fitzbutler became the first black graduate of the University of Michigan's medical school in 1872. That summer, Fitzbutler moved his family from Ontario to Louisville and opened a small office. While Fitzbutler's practice struggled the first few years, it served a vital role in assisting the city's fifteen thousand AFRICAN AMERICANS who were turned away from physicians and HOSPITALS.

After the passage of the CIVIL RIGHTS Acts of 1875, which prohibited discrimination in HOTELS, RESTAURANTS, public transportation, and public amusement places, Fitzbutler became a vehement advocate for the equal use of these facilities. He was considered outspoken by more conservative AFRICAN AMERICANS who desired the use of these places only when white leaders felt it was possible. Fitzbutler took a more demanding position and claimed that each citizen had a right to public facilities, although he too disapproved of the use of force. To publicize his and other African American opinions on political issues, Fitzbutler established a weekly newspaper, the *Ohio Falls Express,* in 1879. It condemned SEGREGATION and discrimination and was published until 1904. Fitzbutler's continued interest in politics, coupled with his desire to improve African American education, prompted him to run without success for the school board several times during the 1880s. In so doing he was the first African American to campaign for an elective post in Louisville. He continued his participation in politics when he formed the R.B. Elliott Club in 1894. Named for a prominent African American politician from South Carolina, the club lobbied to get equal-rights Republicans into office.

In 1886 Fitzbutler joined several local African American physicians who had recently moved to the city, including Drs. W.A. Burney, Rufus Conrad, E.S. Porter, B.F. Porter, and one white physician, John A. Octerlony, to establish a medical college and free infirmary. In the fall of 1888, the state-chartered LOUISVILLE NATIONAL MEDICAL COLLEGE opened its doors to all races and became one of five MEDICAL SCHOOLS in the nation to offer degrees to African Americans. The school, which held classes for the first year in a fraternal lodge building, had three teachers (Fitzbutler, Burney, and Conrad); taught bacteriology, histology, and pathology; and graduated six students in its first class, who had been studying under Fitzbutler, in the spring of 1889. Later that year, the school purchased the Louisville College of PHARMACY building on Green (now LIBERTY) St., between First and Second Streets, and reopened with an expanded faculty. In 1891, it became affiliated with State University, which later became Simmons University, and initiated a nurse-training program a year later. The three-year program attracted approximately thirty students per year, mainly men and women from Kentucky, Indiana, and Tennessee, and had graduated 175 students by the time its doors closed in 1912.

Fitzbutler married Sarah McCurdy in 1866. They had five children: Prima, Mary, James, Myra, and William. Fitzbutler is buried in Greenwood Cemetery.

See Marion B. Lucas, *A History of Blacks in Kentucky*, vol. 1 (Frankfort 1992); George C. Wright, *Life behind a Veil* (Baton Rouge 1985).

FITZBUTLER, SARAH McCURDY (b Canada, ?; d Chicago, ? 1922). Physician. The first African American woman to earn a medical degree in Kentucky, Sarah McCurdy Fitzbutler was the daughter of William H. McCurdy, a prosperous cattle and horse farmer in southern Ontario. In 1866, she married Henry Fitzbutler. During the first years of their marriage, the young couple resided in New Canaan and Amherstburg, Ontario. In 1871 Henry decided to attend the Detroit Medical School. After one year he transferred to the University of Michigan, where in 1872 he became the first African American to earn a medical degree. Sarah and their two children remained in Amherstburg until the family moved to Louisville following Henry's graduation. For the next two decades, Sarah raised their family, which grew to six children, five of whom survived to maturity, and supported Henry in his efforts to advance the status of blacks in Louisville.

After her children were older, Sarah entered the Louisville National Medical College and, following her graduation in 1892, joined her husband's practice. Sarah also served as the primary nursing instructor at the medical college and as the superintendent of its teaching hospital. She was noted for her work in obstetrics and pediatrics. Following Henry's death in 1901, Sarah continued to practice medicine in Louisville. In the last years of her life, she moved to Chicago, where several of her children were pursuing their careers. A memorial to the Fitzbutlers and their work is located in Louisville at the Church of Our Merciful Saviour, 473 S Eleventh St.

See Leslie L. Hanawalt, "Henry Fitzbutler: Detroit's First Black Medical Student," *Detroit in Perspective: A Journal of Regional History* 1 (Winter 1973): 126–40.

FITZGERALD, FRANCIS SCOTT (b St. Paul, Minnesota, September 24, 1896; d Hollywood, California, December 21, 1940). Author. The popular twentieth-century author was named for his great-great-grandfather's brother, Francis Scott Key, who penned the words of the *Star-Spangled Banner*. F. Scott was the third child and first son of Edward and Mollie (McQuillen) Fitzgerald.

Fitzgerald was educated at Roman Catholic boarding schools and attended Princeton University. In his senior year, 1917, he left Princeton and enlisted in the army during World War I. In March 1918 he was shipped to the Forty-fifth Infantry Regiment at Camp Zachary Taylor, near Louisville, where he stayed for a month. In his third novel, *The Great Gatsby* (1925), Louisville was the meeting place of fictional characters Daisy Fay and Jay Gatsby. It was also where she married Tom Buchanan in the summer of 1919. Tom rented an entire floor of the Muhlbach (Seelbach) Hotel and brought a hundred friends down from Chicago in four private Pullman cars. Fitzgerald is said to have drunk so heavily at the Seelbach Hotel that he passed out on the ballroom floor. In April, Fitzgerald left Louisville for Montgomery, Alabama.

In July 1918, while stationed at Camp Sheridan, Alabama, he met Zelda Sayre, whom he married April 3, 1920. Their only child, Frances Scott, was born October 26, 1921.

Fitzgerald's first novel, *This Side of Paradise*, published in 1920, was an instant success. His second novel, *The Beautiful and the Damned* (1922), proved less popular. Fitzgerald supported his expensive lifestyle by writing short stories. Some 46 of his more than 150 stories appeared in 4 books published between 1920 and 1935. *The Great Gatsby*, generally considered his finest work, sold poorly. Fitzgerald's personal life crumbled as his alcoholism worsened and Zelda slipped into schizophrenia. *Tender is the Night* (1934), Fitzgerald's fourth novel, was not well received, and he suffered a breakdown. He recovered enough to move to Hollywood in 1937 to become a screenwriter but was unsuccessful. While in Hollywood, Fitzgerald began writing *The Last Tycoon* but died of a heart attack. The unfinished novel was published in 1941 and brought Fitzgerald considerable posthumous popularity. Buried in the Rockville, Maryland, Union Cemetery, Fitzgerald and Zelda, who died in 1948, were reinterred in St. Mary's Cemetery in Rockville in 1975.

See Jeffrey Meyers, *Scott Fitzgerald: A Biography* (New York 1994); Andrew Turnbull, *Scott Fitzgerald* (New York 1962).

Rhonda Abner

FLAGET, BENEDICT JOSEPH (b Auvergne region of France, November 7, 1763; d Louisville, November 11, 1850). Catholic missionary and bishop. "The First Bishop of the West" became a priest of the Society of St. Sulpice in 1788. Because of the anti-clerical tumult of France in revolutionary times, young Flaget came to America as a Catholic missionary, arriving at Baltimore in 1792.

That same year, on his way to Vincennes, Indiana, as a frontier priest, Flaget stopped in Louisville and offered the first documented Mass in that city. He returned east in 1795 and taught at Georgetown (Washington) and St. Mary's (Baltimore). In those years, he met President George Washington. Flaget was named by Pope Pius VII as first Bishop of Bardstown in 1808 but did not arrive at his post until 1811.

His new diocese, the first in the West, was vast; its jurisdiction touched over eight states. From Bardstown he oversaw a growing Catholic network of parishes, academies, colleges, sisterhoods, and institutions of benevolence. Because of Louisville's rapid growth, the seat of the diocese was transferred there from Bardstown in 1841, and thus Flaget became the first Bishop of Louisville. In his new city, as at Bardstown, he was noted for his holiness, kindness, and ecumenical spirit. Among the last acts of his life were the welcoming of the monks who arrived in 1848 to found the Abbey of Gethsemani and the blessing of construction of the new Cathedral of the Assumption, begun in 1849. He died at the Cathedral rectory and is buried in the undercroft of the Cathedral of the Assumption.

See Charles Lemarie, *Le Patriarche de l'Ouest* (Angers 1983); M.J. Spalding, *Sketches of the Life of the Rt. Rev. Benedict Joseph Flaget* (Louisville 1852).

Clyde F. Crews

FLAGET HIGH SCHOOL. In 1941 Louisville Archbishop John A. Floersh initiated a capital campaign for the construction of new Catholic schools, including a boys' high school in the West End. The next year, the James Whallen home at Forty-fourth and River Park Dr. was purchased to house Flaget Memorial High School, named for Benedict Joseph Flaget, the first Catholic bishop of Kentucky. Flaget was to be staffed by Xaverian Brothers, who also taught at St. Xavier High School.

Flaget High School was opened on October 21, 1942, to classes of seventy freshmen and fifty sophomores. The school's first faculty was composed of Brother Clarence Herlihy, CFX, its first principal from 1942 to 1946, and three other Brothers. Brother Clarence encouraged the formation of the first Flaget Parent-Teacher Association in March 1943.

Flaget organized its first varsity sports teams in the 1944–45 school year, and the Flageteers, a sports booster organization, were formed to help support athletics. The nickname "Braves" was chosen for the school. Flaget's colors, originally maroon and gold, were changed when the school received a gift of blue and white basketball uniforms. Flaget won its first-ever championship, a city championship in golf, in 1945. Flaget's first graduating class, composed of thirty boys, received diplomas on June 6, 1945.

In 1944 work began on a new school building that was first occupied during the 1946–47 school year. The Whallen home was razed in late 1947 to add an east wing to the new building, which included Brothers' quarters and a chapel. The new school building was formally dedicated by Archbishop Floersh on October 31, 1949. A gymnasium was included in the original plans of the school but was not built until 1964.

By the 1949–50 school year, Flaget's enrollment had reached 1,012, making it one of the largest Catholic boys' high schools in Kentucky. Of the thirty-six faculty members, thirteen were Brothers.

Flaget produced numerous state champions and All-State players in all sports. Perhaps the best known are former UNIVERSITY OF LOUISVILLE football coach Howard Schnellenberger and 1956 Heisman Trophy winner Paul Hornung.

In the 1970s Flaget experienced financial difficulties as enrollment declined to several hundred students. The school won its last state championship in any sport, a tie for the FOOTBALL title, in 1971. In its last year of existence, 1973–74, Flaget admitted female students from LORETTO HIGH SCHOOL, which had closed the previous year. The 1974 graduating class included sixty-five students, of whom eighteen were females. Flaget's last principal was Brother Kirby Boone, CFX. who served from 1968 to 1974. In all more than forty-two hundred students graduated from Flaget High School in its thirty-two-year existence.

The most significant contribution of Flaget to the West End of Louisville was that it afforded the opportunity of a structured college-preparatory high school education to boys who, for the most part, were sons of blue-collar families. Many graduates of Flaget were the first in their families to attend college. Some notable graduates of Flaget include Rohm and Haas president Daniel Ash, singer-songwriter Mickey Clark, businessman and former University of Louisville trustees chairman Charles Fischer, former WHAS radio executive Robert Sherer, and former Citizens Fidelity Bank (now PNC BANK) president Daniel Ulmer.

The old Flaget school building was converted to an apartment complex for the elderly in 1982. Flaget Field, the former athletic practice field at 45th and Greenwood Ave., is managed as a recreation center by the Metropolitan PARKS and Recreation Department.

See David N. Aspy and Paulie Miller, *Burning Desire: A History of Flaget High School, 1942–1974* (Louisville 1991).

C. Robert Ullrich

FLEXNER, ABRAHAM (b Louisville, November 13, 1866; d Falls Church, Virginia, September 21, 1959). Physician and educational reformer. Flexner, the son of Morris and Esther (Abraham) Flexner, earned a B.A. degree from Johns Hopkins University in 1886, developing an admiration for the rigors of the German university system, which Hopkins had adopted. Flexner returned to Louisville in mid-1886 to teach at LOUISVILLE MALE HIGH SCHOOL. Four years later he opened a college-preparatory school that he operated for fifteen years; it drew the attention of many educators, including Harvard University president Charles W. Eliot.

In 1905 Flexner studied psychology at Harvard University, where he earned an M.A. degree in 1906. He then studied comparative education at the University of Berlin, from which he earned an M.A. in 1907. His book, *The American College: A Criticism* (1909), reflected his belief that German universities were far superior to their United States counterparts. The book brought Flexner to the attention of Henry S. Pritchett, head of the Carnegie Foundation for the Advancement of Teaching, who asked Flexner to prepare a report on the state of medical education in the United States.

Flexner spent two years working on what has come to be called the Flexner Report, published in June 1910 by the Carnegie Foundation for the Advancement of Teaching as *Medical Education in the United States and Canada.* The report, which received much public attention, served as a catalyst for reform movements already under way. It also helped to speed the process by which the weaker, commercial proprietary schools of MEDICINE were phased out, a four-year standard curriculum was adopted, and the basic sciences achieved prominence in the nation's colleges of medicine.

After writing *Medical Education in Europe* (1912), Flexner joined the permanent staff of the general education board of the Rockefeller Foundation in 1913. He worked there in a variety of positions (including head of the division of studies and medical education) until 1928. He was instrumental in securing tens of millions of dollars for the advancement of scientific medical education and for the establishment of full-time research faculties in the basic sciences within U.S. colleges of medicine. In 1930 Flexner became the first director of the Institute for Advanced Study at Princeton University, a post he held until his retirement in 1939. The institute reflected his personal vision of educational excellence, and he brought a number of brilliant scholars—including Albert Einstein—to work in its ideal atmosphere for research. Flexner's autobiography, *I Remember* (1940), was revised and published posthumously as *Abraham Flexner: An Autobiography* (1960). For his contributions, *Life Magazine* numbered him among the hundred most important Americans of the twentieth century.

In 1898 Flexner married Anne Laziere Crawford; the couple had two daughters, Jean Atherton and Eleanor. When he died the *New York Times* ran his obituary on the front page. Nearly twenty years earlier, the *Times* had written that many recipients of medical care owed their lives to Abraham Flexner's pursuit of excellence. Flexner is buried in CAVE HILL CEMETERY.

See Steven C. Wheatley, *The Politics of Philanthropy: Abraham Flexner and Medical Education* (Madison, Wis., 1988); Charles Vevier, ed., *Flexner: 75 Years Later: A Current Commentary on Medical Education* (Lanham, Md., 1987).

Allen J. Share

FLEXNER, BERNARD (b Louisville, February 24, 1865; d New York City, May 3, 1945). Lawyer and Zionist. Flexner was one of nine children born to immigrants Morris and Esther (Abraham) Flexner. Among his siblings were SIMON FLEXNER, discoverer of the "Flexner bacillus" and the "Flexner serum" and director of the Rockefeller Institute for Medical Research, and ABRAHAM FLEXNER, author of an influential critique of MEDICAL SCHOOLS that changed the direction of the nation's medical education.

Bernard Flexner attended LOUISVILLE MALE HIGH SCHOOL, the UNIVERSITY OF LOUISVILLE, and University of Virginia law school. He was admitted to the Kentucky bar in 1898 and practiced LAW with the Louisville firm Bodley, Baskin, and Flexner during 1903–5, independently during 1906–7, then finally with Flexner, Campbell, and Gordon during 1908–11. He moved to Chicago in 1911, then to New York City in 1919.

A successful lawyer, Flexner wrote various monographs on juvenile courts, delinquents, and neglected children. He was a joint author with Roger N. Baldwin of *Juvenile Courts and Probation* (1914) and co-authored *The Legal Aspect of the Juvenile Court* with Reuben Oppenheimer in 1927. In 1923 he promoted and assumed responsibility for publication of and free distribution to libraries throughout the world a complete record of the controversial 1921 trial of Sacco and Vanzetti, Italian immigrants found guilty of murder.

Flexner was interested in public welfare. In 1912 he was a member of the Kentucky Tuberculosis Commission, and in 1917 he went to Rumania as a member of the American Red Cross to study wartime conditions. He was well known for his devotion to various Zionist and philanthropic organizations to aid displaced Jewish scholars and refugees around the world. He served as the counsel to the Zionist delegation at the Paris Peace Conference at Versailles in 1918–19. He organized and headed the Palestine Endowment Funds Inc., and he was active in the works of the American Jewish Joint Distribution Committee and the Jewish Agency for Palestine. These activities gave him an opportunity to work with such intellectuals as Supreme Court justice LOUIS BRANDEIS.

A benefactor of the University of Louisville School of Law, he donated five thousand dollars in 1940 for the "Bernard Flexner Scholarship" to pay annually the tuition of students. He also willed $150,000 to the school for the "Bernard Flexner Professor of Law Endowment," endowing a chair of law. Flexner never married. He is buried in the Temple Cemetery in Louisville.

See *Courier-Journal,* Feb. 24, 1920, May 4, 1945; *New York Times,* May 4, 1945.

FLEXNER, GUSTAV (b Shelbyville, Kentucky, September 8, 1895; d Louisville, December 30, 1960). Banker. Gustav Flexner's parents, Soloman and Frances, immigrated to the

United States from Alsace-Lorraine in the mid-1800s and settled in SHELBYVILLE. Flexner completed his education there and in 1908 moved to Louisville. His first employment was at the KAUFMAN-STRAUS Co. department store, where he stayed for six years. In 1914 Flexner helped to organize a savings and loan association, later known as the Greater Louisville First Federal Savings and Loan Association. In 1934 it became a federally chartered institution. Flexner held several positions, including secretary (1914–34), secretary-treasurer (1934–45), and executive vice president (1945–60). He was credited with having a major role in the growth of the association through his emphasis on ADVERTISING. Flexner was the radio and TELEVISION spokesman for the association.

Other various BANKING and financial affairs interested him. He was president of the Southeastern Conference of the United States Savings and Loan League in 1942, committeeman of the United States Savings and Loan League in 1946, and president of the Kentucky Building and Loan Association in 1950.

Flexner was also active in various philanthropic groups, a member of the Masonic order, and affiliated with Congregation Adath Israel. He married Ruth Berg in 1917 and had two daughters. After her death in 1939, he married Claudia Husak in 1944. He is buried in the Temple Cemetery.

See *Courier-Journal*, Dec. 31, 1960.

FLEXNER, SIMON (b Louisville, March 25, 1863; d New York City, May 2, 1946). Pathologist. Simon Flexner, discoverer of the "Flexner bacillus" and the "Flexner serum" and director of the Rockefeller Institute for Medical Research, was the fourth child of nine born to immigrants Morris (Bohemia) and Esther (Abraham) Flexner (Alsace). Among his siblings were lawyer and Zionist BERNARD FLEXNER and ABRAHAM FLEXNER, author of the influential critique of MEDICAL SCHOOLS that changed the direction of medical education in America.

Graduating in 1882 from the Louisville College of PHARMACY, Flexner received his M.D. from the UNIVERSITY OF LOUISVILLE in 1889, leaving the next year for Baltimore to study pathology at Johns Hopkins Hospital, where he joined the staff of the Johns Hopkins Medical School. From 1899 to 1903 he was professor of pathology at the University of Pennsylvania. In 1902, at age thirty-nine, he was named director of the Rockefeller Institute in New York City. In 1903 he married Helen Whitall Thomas, member of a prominent Baltimore Quaker family. They had two children, mathematician William Welch Flexner and author and historian James Thomas Flexner.

Flexner was an acknowledged leader of American medical science when elected president of the American Association for the Advancement of Science in 1920. His fame came from his 1905 development of a serum that reduced the mortality rate from cerebrospinal meningitis to 25 percent from 75 percent in untreated cases. On August 19, 1911, he received the Cameron Prize for this work. After retiring in 1935 from the Rockefeller Institute, he continued his investigations and publications until his death at the Presbyterian Hospital. He wrote more than 350 scientific papers and was the author of *William Henry Welch and the Heroic Age of American Medicine* (1941).

See James Thomas Flexner, *An American Saga: The Story of Helen Thomas and Simon Flexner* (Boston 1984); *Dictionary of American Biography* (New York 1974).

Betty Lou Amster

FLEXNER, STUART BERG (b Jacksonville, Illinois, March 3, 1928; d Greenwich, Connecticut, December 3, 1990). Lexicographer, author, editor. Flexner was born in 1928 to David and Gertrude (Berg) Flexner. His family moved from Illinois to Louisville when he was thirteen. He skipped his senior year at LOUISVILLE MALE HIGH SCHOOL and entered the UNIVERSITY OF LOUISVILLE as a sixteen-year-old sophomore. He changed his major from chemistry to English after developing a fascination with criminal argot while working with Dr. David Maurer. After graduating in 1947, the next year, at the age of twenty, Flexner became the youngest student to earn a master's degree at the university.

Flexner left Louisville to study at Cornell University and then joined the publishing business in New York City, compiling the *Dictionary of American Slang* (1960). He spent six years in Mexico and worked with the Mexican Board of Education to publish books for an adult literacy campaign. Returning to New York, Flexner joined Random House and became a senior vice president responsible for the publisher's dictionary series. Flexner and his wife, Doris, had one daughter, Jennifer, and one son, Geoffrey.

Among his other works were a two-volume history of the American language, *I Hear America Talking* (1976); *How to Increase Your Word Power* (1971); and *The Family Word Finder* (1975).

See *Courier-Journal*, Dec. 15, 1976, Dec. 20, 1987, Dec. 5, 1990.

Bob Edwards

FLOERSH, JOHN ALEXANDER (b Nashville, Tennessee, October 6, 1886; d Louisville, June 11, 1968). Archbishop. John A. Floersh, first prelate to hold the rank of archbishop of the Roman Catholic Archdiocese of Louisville, was the fourth of eight children of John A., a cigar manufacturer, and Minnie O. (Alexander) Floersh. Floersh, influenced by his devout family life, began his study for the priesthood at age sixteen. He earned doctor of philosophy and doctor of divinity degrees in 1907 and 1911, respectively, from the Propaganda Fide College in Rome. Archbishop (later Cardinal) Giovanni Bonzano, the college's rector, was his mentor. Floersh was ordained to the priesthood in Rome on June 10, 1911, and returned to Nashville to serve a year as a diocesan priest.

With Bonzano's appointment as papal apostolic delegate to the United States in 1912, Floersh was named secretary to the apostolic delegation, a post he held for a decade. In 1917 he was made a monsignor. Floersh was sent to Louisville in 1923, at the age of thirty-six, as coadjutor bishop to the elderly and ailing incumbent Bishop Denis O'Donaghue, with the right of succession. Floersh would ultimately serve longer than any other ordinary in the Louisville diocese. O'Donaghue retired officially in 1924, and Floersh became bishop of Louisville. In 1937 the diocese of Louisville was elevated to the status of archdiocese, raising Floersh to the rank of archbishop.

Floersh said that his main goal as bishop was "trying to save souls." His tenure was noted for the expansion of parishes, schools, and other Catholic institutions, and for his personal expertise in financial and real estate matters. Floersh established Catholic Charities, the annual Corpus Christi processions, and ST. THOMAS SEMINARY (1952–70). At Floersh's retirement in 1967, the archdiocese included 100 parochial elementary schools, 19 high schools, 5 colleges, and 2 seminaries, educating 50,000 students, nearly 130 parishes, and the highest number ever of diocesan priests (286).

Floersh was described as being aloof from most political and economic controversies of his time, but exceptions included his public criticism of the COURIER-JOURNAL for printing a full-page advertisement for a means of artificial birth control in 1941 and his 1963 statement urging Kentucky Catholics to be personally involved in racial harmony. He is buried in Calvary Cemetery.

See *The Record*, Archdiocese of Louisville, Louisville, June 13, 1968; *Courier-Journal*, June 12, 1968; Clyde F. Crews, *An American Holy Land* (Louisville 1987).

Mary Margaret Bell

FLOOD OF 1937. In early 1937 one of the largest FLOODS in American history inundated the OHIO RIVER Valley. Kentucky river cities from Ashland to Paducah were affected by the immense rainfall; however, the heaviest hit was Louisville.

Intense rainfall in Louisville began on January 9, and continued until January 15, raising the Ohio River to a crest of thirty feet, two feet above flood stage, on January 17. The rain resumed that day and fell without interruption until January 23. This second surge was accompanied by colder temperatures, which produced sleet and freezing rain. By January 23, the river reached a crest of 51.1 feet. Because of the rising waters, city officials restricted water use and ordered the rationing of food, fuel, and electricity.

On January 24, known as "Black Sunday,"

Fourth Street during 1937 flood, looking south toward the Brown Hotel from the middle of the 600 block.

the Waterside electric generating plant filled with water and ceased to operate. For the next four days, Louisville was without electricity. Power to the downtown area was not completely restored until February 12. The floodwaters turned downtown Louisville into an island, with thousands of people confined to an area bounded by MAIN ST. on the north, BROADWAY on the south, Shelby on the east, and Twenty-sixth and Eighteenth Streets on the west. Flooded STREETS became navigable channels; and boats, instead of horses, raced at the submerged CHURCHILL DOWNS. Still the rain continued to fall.

As the situation worsened, Louisville's media supplied information and relief. Radio station WHAS sent its programming by TELEPHONE to Nashville, Tennessee, where it was broadcast over WSM-Radio. During the disaster, WHAS broadcasted 187.5 hours of uninterrupted service and carried official flood news to stranded citizens and rescue teams. Louisville's two NEWSPAPERS, the *COURIER-JOURNAL* and *LOUISVILLE TIMES*, also helped spread the word. Starting on January 25, the papers printed combined flood editions at newspaper plants in SHELBYVILLE, and later in Lexington.

On January 25, Mayor NEVILLE MILLER asked Gov. Albert B. Chandler for assistance. The next day, with over twenty thousand people marooned in the downtown area, Chandler declared martial law for the city of Louisville. With the help of federal troops and other rescue agencies, by January 27, about 230,000 of Louisville's 350,000 residents had been evacuated to higher ground and towns throughout the state. A PONTOON BRIDGE built on empty whiskey barrels provided an exit from Jefferson St. to Baxter Ave. and the dry HIGHLANDS. On January 27 the river crested at 57.15 feet, which surpassed the 1884 record. The river slowly returned to its banks, and on Saturday, February 6, it dropped below flood level. The great cleanup began and, by May, Churchill Downs was ready for the KENTUCKY DERBY.

In total, during the 1937 flood more than 60 percent of Louisville (thirty to thirty-five square miles) was under water. During the flood, the river stayed above flood stage for twenty-three days, with a period when rain fell for fifty-three consecutive hours. Louisville's January 1937 rainfall totaled a record 19.17 inches, still by far the most ever in a month. Ninety deaths were attributed to the conditions created by the flood, and financial losses for Louisville totaled $54.3 million. The 1937 flood was one of Louisville's greatest natural disasters. Despite the extensive destruction, the city recovered quickly. By the 1940s construction of floodwalls, levees, and pumping stations to control future of flooding was well under way.

See Lowell Thomas, *Hungry Waters: The Story of the Great Flood* (Philadelphia 1937); *Courier-Journal Magazine,* Jan. 18, 1987; *Courier-Journal and Louisville Times*, (combined editions) Jan. 25–Feb. 5, 1937; U.S. Department of Agriculture, Weather Bureau, "Daily Local Record," Jan. 1937.

Aaron D. Purcell

FLOODS AND FLOOD CONTROL. Calamitous floods have wreaked havoc in the Louisville area on numerous occasions: 1832, 1883, 1884, 1913, 1945, 1964, and 1997. None, however, reached the ravenous level of the Great Flood of January 1937. It was described as an "inundation of almost biblical proportions." The OHIO RIVER at Louisville was flooded for twenty-three days, cresting at 57.15 feet above flood stage on the upper gauge, nearly ten feet above the previous record level in 1884.

More than 60 percent of the city was under water, along with an additional sixty-five square miles of Jefferson County. The flood damaged more than 30,000 residences, and more than 230,000 thousand residents had to evacuate; property damage was estimated at $50 million. Flood waters extended as far south as CHURCHILL DOWNS; the familiar cry, "Send a boat!" was heard throughout the city; fish were reportedly caught in the lobby of the BROWN HOTEL at FOURTH and BROADWAY; and public utilities were inoperable for days.

After the 1937 flood, the UNITED STATES ARMY CORPS OF ENGINEERS was assigned an expanded role in flood protection. Construction of the first phase of the city's protection system was begun by the Louisville District of the Corps in 1948 and completed in 1957. It consisted of 4.5 miles of concrete wall in the downtown area, 12.5 miles of earthen levee, 13 pumping stations, and 50 street closures. One of the pumping stations, located on BEARGRASS CREEK, was designed to pump 2.5 million gallons of water per minute, making it the largest pump of its kind in the world at that time. The second phase, the Southwest Jefferson County Protection Project, was completed in 1988, bringing the total length of the system to twenty-nine miles of concrete wall and earthen levee. The entire system was constructed by the Corps of Engineers and is operated and maintained by the Metropolitan Sewer District.

See Leland R. Johnson, *The Falls City Engineers: A History of the Louisville District, Corps of Engineers, United States Army*, 2 vol. (Louisville 1975 and 1984); Historical files, Louisville District, U.S. Army Corps of Engineers, Louisville.

Charles E. Parrish

FLORA. The flora of the Louisville area reflects the glacial origin of the OHIO RIVER and its subsequent meandering across the glacial outwash plain that now lies beneath Louisville. Accordingly, much of the original surface of this land was composed of hydric soils with many ponds, lakes, and wetlands. These marshy conditions hosted a variety of wetland species. The same conditions, however, created inhospitable living conditions for settlers, who promptly set about draining and filling and making the area more habitable. As a result, the diverse flora that once occupied these wetland areas of Louisville is greatly restricted. Remaining wetlands are protected by law, and native wetland species can still be found today bordering ditches and creeks and within marshy areas and bottomland hardwood forests. Such a wetland ecosystem today can be explored at Caperton Swamp along River

Rd. in Jefferson County.

The lowland of southern Jefferson County lies above New Albany Shale. This area, more poorly drained than the limestone bedrock uplands, contains a unique flora including breakrush (*Rhynchospora corniculata*), purple fringeless orchid (*Habenaria peramoena*), prairie dodder (*Cuscuta campestris*), buttonbush (*Cephalanthus occidentalis*), and willow (*Salix humilus*). Trees native to this area include shingle oak (*Quercus imbricaria*), bur oak (*Q. macrocarpa*), pin oak (*Q. palustris*), and black gum (*Nyssa sylvatica*).

Aquatic and semi-emergent plants live in a world easily examined by the interested observer. Duckweed (*Lemna* sp.*), one of the tiniest flowering plants, is often seen floating like a carpet of green dots on the surface of a pond. Sweet flag (*Acorus calamus*), rosemallow (*Hibiscus* sp.), and southern blue flag (*Iris virginica*) raise prominent flowers and spikes around marshy edges. One can expect to see, on certain ponds, the serene floating leaves of the white water-lily (*Nymphaea odorata*) and the yellow pond lily (*Nuphar lutea*) with their beautiful large flowers resting open on stems just above the water surface. The large truncate, conical seed box of the American lotus (*Nelumbo lutea*), when dried, can make a child's rattle or a prominent addition to a winter floral arrangement.

Peering into the water, one can see the jelly-coated water-shield (*Brasenia schreberi*) and feathery coontail *(Ceratophyllum demersum)* floating amongst the pondweed (*Potamogeton* sp.). Stoneworts (*Chara* sp.), with lime-crusted, whorled branchlets, may be found at the water's edge. On cool, moist rocks, under ledges or at springs, mosses like sphagnum (*Sphagnum* sp.) and the flat green liverwort (*Marchantia* sp.) grow.

Moving through the high foliage, the air may be bombarded by the elastic valves of the touch-me-not *(Impatiens capensis)* fruit capsules disturbed in passing. Pausing and inspecting the small stream crossings may result in the recognition of a sweet odor rising from the crushed vegetation under foot. Here a fragrant mint, such as the Derby favorite, spearmint (*Mentha spicata*), another European import, may be found. The South American water hyacinth (*Eichhornia crassipes*), with expanded blades and inflated petioles, a scourge in waterways in the southeastern United States, has also been reported here.

The abundant algae of the area are of note. In the clean, fast-flowing streams of the KNOBS, freshwater representatives of red algae (*Botrachospermum* sp. and *Lemanea* sp.) cling to the rocks. Blue-green algae such as the filamentous *(Oscillatoria* sp.) grow in dense mats in the water. The green algae (*Spirogyra* sp.) when examined under the microscope are found to grow as a clear, linear group of cells within which green chloroplasts conspicuously spiral. Microscopic diatoms such as *Navicula* sp., single-celled plants housed in finely sculptured silica walls, inhabit the water. They mix with other microscopic organisms such as the euglenoids, with one hairlike flagellum for motion, and the dinoflagellates with two.

A perennial plant to be found on stream banks and floodways in the area is the tall, native cane (*Arundinaria gigantea).* This is the only North American representative of the great bamboo family so prominent in China. It is this cane that reportedly hid Kentucky pioneers from attackers and served as torches for Native Americans exploring caves. It can be found growing under the whitish, bark-shedding sycamore (*Platanus Occidentalis*) and the three-leaflet member of the maple family, box elder (*Acer Negundo*), growing at the streamside.

If one looks closely and thinks in geologic time, one can find the small descendants of the great forests that reigned three hundred million years ago in the Pennsylvanian Period and were responsible for Kentucky's great beds of coal. Once represented by towering forest giants, these plant groups now can be found here only as siliceous, reed-like horsetails (*Equisetum* spp.), used by pioneers as "scouring rushes" to clean pans, and the feathery club mosses (*Lycopodium* spp.**), also called "ground cedars" and "ground pines."

Walking on the dry, thin, limestone soils of areas supporting glades of cedar trees (*Juniperus Virginiana*), one might discover the adder's tongue fern (*Ophioglossum* sp.) with lanceolate fronds bearing long, clublike sporangia. Cedar wood is famous for aromatic cabinetry and its heartwood, which is rot resistant and can be seen in many old fence posts in the area. The spreading rattlesnake fern (*Botrychium virginianum*) is common in woodlots throughout our area. Its spore-laden frond reaches up like a tiny grape cluster, heavy with oil, that flashes brightly when thrown in a fire. There also can be found the evergreen Christmas fern (*Polystichum acrostichoides*) rolling out from "fiddleheads" into two rows of waxy fronds reaching to the reduced, grainy, spore-bearing tips. The maidenhair fern (*Adiantum pedatum*) fans out above moist soils. The abundant ebony spleenwort (*Asplenium platyneuron*) is found in dry areas, its small fronds running ladder-like up a dark stem. The walking fern (*Camptosorus rhizophyllus*) has thin, evergreen fronds that arch out from clusters on calcareous rocks. These fronds "walk" by allowing their tips to sprout new plants that root where the fronds touch.

The flora of eastern North America, including the Louisville region, has much in common with Asian plant groups and their diversity. As part of an ancient landmass with Asia, this area shares both the place of origin of many plant groups as well as a temperate climate. Lacking east-west mountain barriers, eastern North American plant communities weathered the glacial ages by migrating south or surviving in isolated refuges.

Lucy Braun, an early-twentieth-century botanist in Kentucky, described the Louisville area as part of the Western Mesophytic Forest. It overlaps the geographic area known as the Interior Low Plateau. In this area certain species found in the more complex forests of the eastern mountains of Kentucky tend to become more dominant. In Jefferson County, Braun reported a forest composition at Cedar Creek as being composed of fifteen tree species dominated by tulip tree (*Liriodendron tulipifera*), white oak (*Quercus alba*), and black oak (*Quercus velutina*). The tulip tree, a majestic member of the magnolia family, is now the state tree of Kentucky.

Regions of the native sedimentary limestone of Kentucky extend into the Louisville area, including the areas of CRESCENT HILL, the HIGHLANDS, and the KNOBS to the south. These upland areas support a drier xeric flora that include oaks (*Quercus* spp.) and hickories (*Carya* spp.) in dominant association. In the Knobs area, typified by Muldraugh's Hill and outliers like IROQUOIS PARK, such communities intermingle with the smooth, silvery-barked beech (*Fagus grandifolia)* and the tulip tree. The Jefferson Memorial Forest in southern Jefferson County contains many of these associations.

Bernheim Forest is a large forest preserve in the Knobs section of Kentucky, south of Louisville. There chestnut oak (*Quercus prinus*), scarlet oak (*Quercus coccinea*), and black oak are found on the knob tops. Hickories and white oak rise in dominance on the slopes. The presence of beech increases until a beech–tulip tree–white oak forest develops in the lowest areas.

Beautiful flowering trees can also be found in the native forest community of this area. The white dogwood (*Cornus florida*) and the crimson-flowered redbud (*Cercis Canadensis*) are small trees that draw our vision into the light green tapestry of spring. Shiny muscular ironwood (*Carpinus caroliniana*) and its shaggy-barked cousin, hop hornbeam (*Ostrya virginiana*), are small trees with exceptionally hard wood useful for utensils and tool handles. The aromatic sassafras (*Sassafrass albidum*), prized by early American settlers for European trade, is abundant here and is evident along many fence rows by the numerous upright, parallel branches on its young trees.

The tall Kentucky coffeetree (*Gymnocladus dioica*), with long leaves broken into doubly pinnate leaflets, is locally rare. Wide, stout, black seedpods hang from high branches and give evidence of the coffeetree's presence. Another tree, the pawpaw (*Asimina triloba*), which grows wide, greenish-yellow seedpods bearing large seeds and a yellow custard-like flesh, is often called the custard apple or the Kentucky banana.

Louisville was, at one time, replete in its upland areas with the American chestnut (*Castanea dentata),* that most stately and important lumber tree. It has been extinguished from its range by the foreign parasitic fungus *Endothia parasitica,* first detected in New York in the early

1900s, and can no longer be found in the backyards or PARKS of Louisville. Coppice growth can be occasionally seen sprouting from the roots of these dead giants, but in time they succumb to the deadly fungus. Likewise, it is probable that the stately elms will suffer as they are attacked by another foreign fungus, Dutch elm disease (*Ceratocystis ulmi),* carried by the European elm bark beetle (*Scolytus multistriatus).* Regardless, the great parks of Louisville, designed by the company of landscape architect Frederick Law Olmsted at the end of the nineteenth century, continue to maintain and display the rich flora that inhabit this area.

The FALLS OF THE OHIO form one of the most unusual habitats in America. Short's goldenrod (*Solidago Shortii)* was originally discovered at the falls by noted Kentucky botanist Dr. CHARLES W. SHORT in the early 1800s. This Kentucky endemic plant is now extinct at the Falls, and its last remaining populations in the world can be found only near Kentucky's Blue Licks Battlefield State Park. Another plant, the stipuled scurf-pea (*Psoralea stipulata*), was known only from the Falls and is now feared to be extinct. The Kentucky State Nature Preserves Commission lists twenty-two plants as either threatened, endangered, or of only historic status in Jefferson County.

Andre Michaux, the noted French botanist, visited the Louisville area three times in the 1790s. During at least one such expedition in 1793, Michaux, acting on behalf of French Minister Genet, bore a letter and a French commission for GEORGE ROGERS CLARK encouraging General Clark to raise an army of Kentuckians to attack the Spanish legions in New Orleans. While in Louisville, Michaux took the time to note the presence of the pecan tree (*Carya illionensis*) and measured a tulip tree near Louisville to be "twenty-two feet in circumference, making it more than seven feet in diameter."

In 1819 Dr. HENRY MCMURTRIE published *Sketches of Louisville and Its Environs* that contained a "Florula Louisvillensis." It is probable that Constantine Samuel Rafinesque, the famed naturalist who worked in Kentucky for seven years in the early 1800s, provided this list of plants to Dr. McMurtrie. Rafinesque was a contemporary of JOHN JAMES AUDUBON. He collected and named thousands of plants, including many from Kentucky.

There were even grass prairies on the high terraces in this region, populations reminiscent of the great American prairies and the barrens of Kentucky's Green River country. These local prairie populations may have been encouraged by buffalo migrations and burning by Native Americans. In the 1940s, botanists found the Great Plains wild rye (*Elymus canadensis*) and the prairie rosinweed (*Silphium integrifolium*) in remaining examples of prairie communities. Unfortunately, these species have not been found here since then. The endangered running buffalo clover (*Trifolium stoloniferum*), however, can still be found in one local area perhaps once grazed by the buffalo. The famed Kentucky bluegrass (*Poa pratensis*) thrives here, but it is greatly disputed whether it is of native or European origin.

Colorful wildflowers are easy to encounter in spring. The harbinger-of-spring (*Erigenia bulbosa*), as its name implies, is one of the earliest of wildflowers. It is commonly known, however, by the name of "salt and pepper" due to the presence of black anthers in its small white flowers. Spring-beauty (*Claytonia virginica*) is another early spring favorite and, with five small white petals tinged with pink, can be found in woods and shady lawns. Jack-in-the-pulpit (*Arisaema atrorubens*) and the yellow trout-lily (*Erythronium americanum*) grow on moist slopes and along creeks. Orchids, such as puttyroot (*Amplectrum hyemale*) and rattlesnake-plantain (*Goodyera pubescens*), can be found in hilly areas. The multitude of wildflowers in the area awaits only interest and a good guidebook to be discovered, identified, and enjoyed.

The passing of summer brings the great growth of tall annual herbaceous plants. The Kentucky state flower, goldenrod *(Solidago* sp.), spreads a swath of sallow yellow across the landscape. The six-foot-tall purple-mottled plant, poison hemlock *(Conium maculatum),* crowds the roadways and the farm fields and, with lacy leaves, can be confused with Queen Anne's lace, also known as wild carrot (*Daucus carota*). Both are European imports, but the poison hemlock (not the native hemlock tree *Tsuga Canadensis*) is the infamous hemlock responsible for the tragic death of Socrates in ancient Greece.

The weeds in our environment include pesky European imports such as the garlic mustard *(Alliaria petiolata)* and Japanese honeysuckle (*Lonicera japonica*) crowding out our native flora. Curious hitchhikers, including both native and exotic weeds, line our roads and railways. These species include Johnson grass *(Sorghum halepense),* ragweed (*Ambrosia* sp.), peppergrass (*Lepidium virginicum*), mullein (*Verbascum Thapsus*), and chicory (*Cichorium intybus*). Plants we call weeds represent a mixture of reproductive strategies and family groups. We have all noted with annoyance socks decorated with "stick tights" and clothing infested with seeds known as "beggar ticks."

We know from archaeological evidence that ancient North Americans exploited the botanical resources of the area. Nut-bearing trees such as oak, chestnut, hickory and walnut (*Juglans nigra*) provided food thousands of years ago in the Archaic Period, along with wild fruits such as blackberries and raspberries (*Rubus* spp.), grape (*Vitis* spp.), mulberry (*Morus rubra*), persimmon (*Diospyros virginiana*), and pawpaw. In the later Woodland Period they collected sunflower kernels (*Helianthus Annuus*), sumac (*Rhus* spp.), purslane seeds (*Portulaca* sp.), butternut (*Juglans cinerea*), and honey locust (*Gleditsia triacanthos*).

It is not difficult to visualize Native American families collecting pigweed, a cousin of spinach also known as "lamb's-quarter" (*Chenopodium* sp.), to mix as a potherb with their stews of local meats. It is possible that these early people dug the potato-like root of the groundnut (*Apios americana*). Likewise, cattails *(Typha* sp.) from the marshy areas of Louisville may have been a source of pollen for flour, cattail roots for starchy soup stock, and cattail leaves could have been woven into baskets and mats for village use.

Although metropolitan Louisville is becoming increasingly urban, AGRICULTURE is still an important component of the ECONOMY. This area supports intensive cultivation of corn, soybeans, wheat, and alfalfa and other hays. Burley TOBACCO (*Nicotiana Tobacum*) is a traditional agricultural product. The fiber in the Asian import hemp (*Cannabis sativa*) was, in the past, a thriving industry producing rope and cordage.

The Ohio River Valley is a lush, wet area with abundant rainfall and vegetative growth. The average annual temperature of Louisville is 56.1 degrees Fahrenheit, and the average annual precipitation is 44.4 inches. The average first fall freeze is in October, and the average last freeze is in May. The soil freeze line is fourteen inches deep. The United States Department of Agriculture places the Louisville region in Hardiness Growing Zone Six, stretching from New Jersey and southern Pennsylvania through Kentucky to northern Texas.

* Single species

** Multiple species

See Charles R. Gunn, *The Flora of Jefferson and Seven Adjacent Counties, Kentucky* (Frankfort 1968); E. Lucy Braun, *Deciduous Forests of Eastern North America* (New York 1950); Ernest O. Beal and John W. Thieret, *Aquatic and Wetland Plants of Kentucky* (Frankfort 1986); Ray Cranfill, *Ferns and Fern Allies of Kentucky* (Frankfort 1980); Donald Culross Peattie, *A Natural History of Trees* (New York 1966).

Ronald R. Van Stockum Jr.

FLOYD, DAVIS (b Virginia, 1772; d Florida, before July 9, 1834). Politician and businessman. He was the son of Robert and Lillian Floyd. The Floyds lived in both Amherst and Hanover Counties, Virginia, prior to moving to Jefferson County, Kentucky, in 1779, so it is probable that Davis Floyd was born in one of those Virginia counties. He was reared on the Kentucky frontier and received at least a basic education. On May 22, 1798, Floyd was commissioned a second lieutenant of cavalry, First Regiment, in the Jefferson County militia. By 1799 the Floyd family had moved across the river to Indiana Territory, but Davis remained in Jefferson County. By 1801 the Floyds, including Davis, had settled in CLARKSVILLE, where Davis and his father operated a ferry at the base of the FALLS OF THE OHIO. In December 1803 Davis became one of the first licensed Falls pilots and guided boats through the Falls until 1808. In 1801 he was appointed deputy sheriff of newly formed CLARK COUNTY, INDIANA, and from 1803 to 1806 served as sheriff of Clark County. In 1807 he was secretary of an antislavery meeting at now-vanished Springville, at that time the Clark County seat. Floyd also served other county and territorial positions, including that of circuit court judge (1814?–23), militia sergeant and officer (including participation in the Battle of Tippecanoe in 1811), member of the territorial and state legislature from Clark and Harrison Counties (1805–6, 1816–17), and member of the 1816 Indiana Constitutional Convention in Corydon.

In 1807 he was tried and found guilty of involvement in the Aaron Burr conspiracy. His sentence was only three hours in jail and a fine of ten dollars. This episode apparently did not affect his career in the least. Just a few days after this sentencing, the Indiana Territorial legislature elected him clerk of the lower house, and he remained active and successful in political, military, civic, and business affairs. About 1815 he moved to CORYDON, HARRISON COUNTY, INDIANA Territory. He was an unsuccessful candidate for lieutenant governor in 1816 and for the U.S. House of Representatives in 1822. In 1823 he was appointed a United States commissioner to settle Florida land claims and moved to Florida Territory the following year.

In 1794 he married Susanna Johnston Lewis in Jefferson County, Kentucky, and, after her death, Elizabeth Robards in 1816. The brick house he built in 1817 is now an Indiana historic site. He had four children, two being born to each union. He was a Methodist and a freemason. Floyd was the older brother of Sgt. Charles Floyd of the LEWIS AND CLARK Expedition. FLOYD COUNTY, INDIANA, and Floyds Knobs are possibly named for Davis Floyd, who was instrumental in forming the county in 1819.

See *A Biographical Directory of the Indiana General Assembly* (Indianapolis 1980); Lewis C. Baird, *Baird's History of Clark County, Indiana* (Indianapolis 1909); Floyd family file, Filson Club Historical Society, Louisville; Andrew R.L. Cayton, *Frontier Indiana* (Bloomington, Ind., 1996); *Indiana: A New Historical Guide* (Indianapolis 1989); *Louisville Commercial,* Nov. 22, 1897.

James J. Holmberg

FLOYD, JOHN (b Amherst County, Virginia, 1750; d Jefferson County, Kentucky, April 10, 1783). Pioneer. John Floyd, an early surveyor and military figure in Kentucky, was the son of William and Abadiah (Davis) Floyd. His father, of Welsh descent, was an apparently successful small planter. His mother's genealogy included an Indian woman. Floyd and his brothers were of a somewhat dark hue, and all had jet-black straight hair. Floyd's educational background is unknown, but his penmanship and spelling were above average for the time.

At age eighteen he married Burnell Burford, who died a year later while giving birth to their first child, a girl named Mourning. Shortly after, he went to Botetourt County to seek employment as a deputy surveyor to Col. William Preston, official surveyor for the newly created Fincastle County, which included most of present Kentucky. He received the appointment in 1772 and in 1774 led a group into Kentucky to survey land tracts around the FALLS OF THE OHIO and in the Bluegrass. These were warrants by the British Crown to Virginia militia officers for service in the French and Indian War. Some STREETS in Louisville and roads in Jefferson County still follow the 1774 survey lines.

The following year Floyd brought a party of some thirty settlers to Kentucky and established a camp at St. Asaph's on Dick's (now Dix) River. This was only twenty miles from Boonesborough, headquarters of Richard Henderson's abortive Transylvania settlement. Henderson described Floyd as a man "with a great show of Modesty and open honest countenance and no small share of good sense" (Henderson's Journal, May 3, 1775). Floyd even accepted a post as surveyor for the Transylvania Co. He also participated in one of the great adventure stories of pioneer Kentucky, when in July 1776 three young girls were abducted near Boonesborough by Indians: Bessie and Frances Callaway and Jemima Boone. Floyd joined the rescue party (the one led by Daniel Boone). After two days of pursuit the girls were rescued near the Upper Blue Licks.

In 1776, Floyd was offered a partnership in a privateer that would prey upon British sea shipping. The privateer was soon captured by a British man-of-war, and Floyd spent time in a British prison. He did not return to Virginia until 1778.

That same year he married Jane "Jenny" Buchanan, the ward of Col. William Preston. In late 1779 the couple, with an infant son and other family members, set out for the Falls of the Ohio by way of Cumberland Gap. Floyd moved upon the land he had surveyed for himself in 1774, authorized by miliary warrants he had purchased. This land, which included what was to be future ST. MATTHEWS, became the site of FLOYD'S STATION, one of six fortified stations along the Middle Fork of BEARGRASS CREEK. He found that squatters had already built eleven cabins on his land. During the summer of 1780 he commanded a militia regiment during GEORGE ROGERS CLARK'S campaign against the SHAWNEE in Ohio, and in 1781 he was named commander of the Jefferson County militia, with the rank of colonel. That same year he was wounded in a battle with a force of Indians and British near Jefferson County. He was with Clark on a 1782 foray into Ohio and in 1783 was appointed one of the three judges of the new District Court of Kentucky, which held its first session on March 3 of that year in Harrodsburg.

Scarcely a month later he was fatally wounded in an Indian ambush on April 8 on the way to BULLITT'S LICK near present SHEPHERDSVILLE in BULLITT COUNTY. He died April 10, at the FISHPOOLS Plantation of Col. James Francis Moore. The plantation was along what became Preston Highway. He was buried at the site of his station along Beargrass Creek about one-half mile west of Breckenridge Ln. He and Jenny had three sons—William, George, and John—the last born shortly after Floyd's death. Son John became a governor of Virginia as did a grandson, also named John.

See Anna M. Cartlidge, "Colonel John Floyd, Reluctant Adventurer," *Register of the Kentucky State Historical Society* 66 (Oct. 1968): 317–68; Hambleton Tapp, "Colonel John Floyd, Kentucky Pioneer," *Filson Club History Quarterly* 15 (Jan. 1941): 1–24; Neal Hammon and James Russel Harris, "In a Dangerous Situation, Letters of Col. John Floyd, 1774-1783," *Register of the Kentucky Historical Society* 83 (Summer 1985): 202-36.

Neal O. Hammon

FLOYD COUNTY, INDIANA. Indiana's second-smallest county was created by the Indiana General Assembly in early 1819 from land carved from Clark and Harrison Counties. Bounded on the southeast by the OHIO RIVER, it is bordered on the east and north by CLARK COUNTY and on the west by HARRISON COUNTY. Its most prominent geographic feature is its forested limestone KNOBS that rise from nine hundred to a thousand feet above sea level. It is also ribboned by several creeks, including Silver, Falling Run, Big Indian, Little Indian, Richland, and Jacobs Creeks. The county's land area is 150 square miles.

Before the beginning of European settlement, Floyd County was a hunting ground for the SHAWNEE, Piankeshaw, Wyandotte, and Delaware tribes. The first permanent settlers arrived in 1804 when Robert LaFollette and his wife built a cabin in the southern part of the county in what became Franklin Township. Patrick Shields and his family arrived from Virginia the following year. In 1807 Pennsylvanian George Waltz laid out the town of Georgetown and began promoting land sales to farmers and the creation of shops and mills. Six years later, Joel, Abner, and Nathaniel Scribner established NEW ALBANY on an 826-acre tract overlooking the Ohio River.

By 1818 New Albany was large enough that leading citizens wanted to create a new county so that the town could be designated a county seat. They dispatched Nathaniel Scribner and John K. Graham, the town's original surveyor, to CORYDON, then the state capital, to lobby the General Assembly on the community's behalf. On January 2, 1819, the assembly approved boundaries for the new county, effective February l. The board of county commissioners created to oversee organization met on

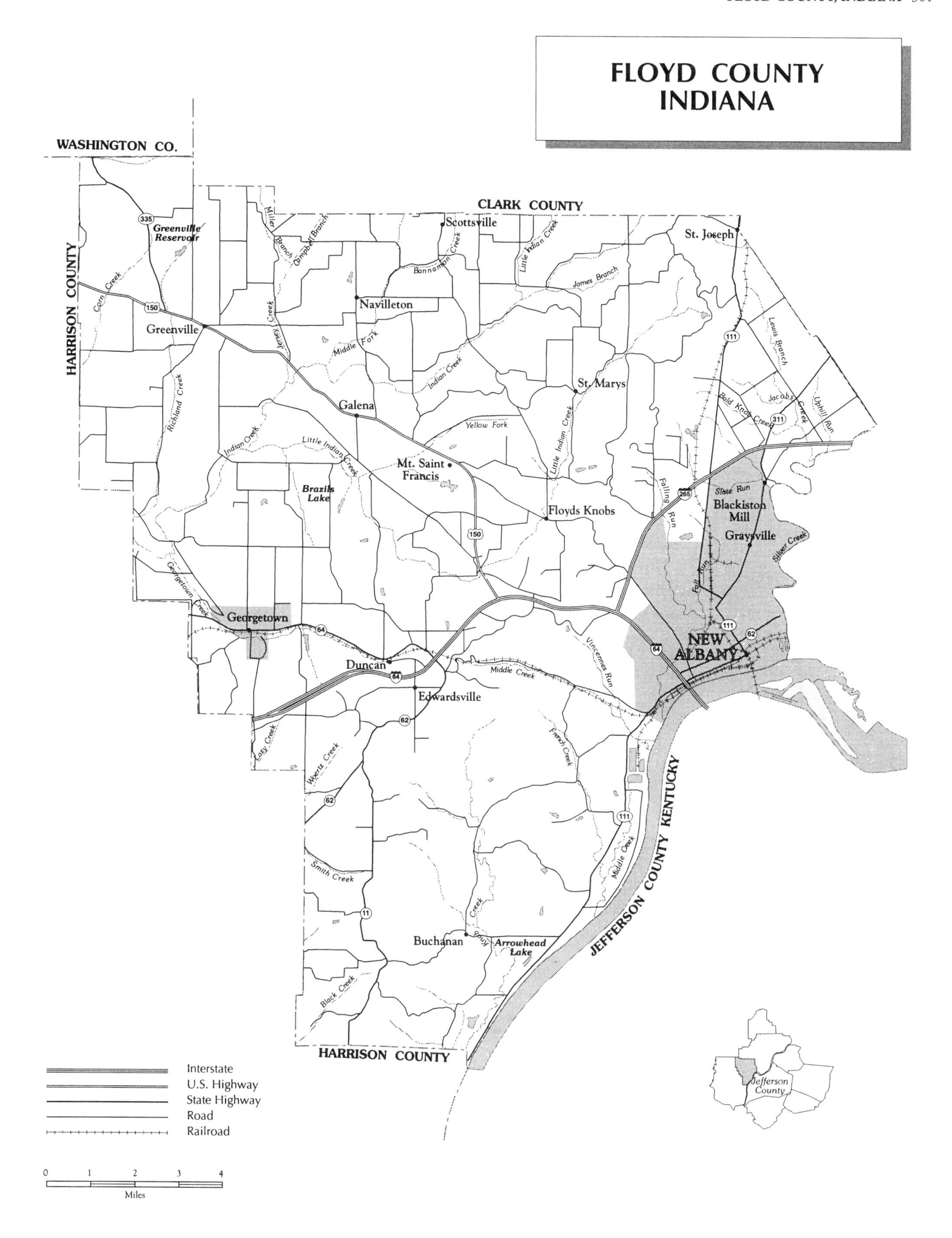
FLOYD COUNTY
INDIANA
WASHINGTON CO.
CLARK COUNTY
HARRISON COUNTY
HARRISON COUNTY
JEFFERSON COUNTY KENTUCKY
Greenville Reservoir
Scottsville
St. Joseph
Navilleton
Greenville
St. Marys
Galena
Mt. Saint Francis
Brazils Lake
Floyds Knobs
Blackiston Mill
Graysville
Georgetown
NEW ALBANY
Duncan
Edwardsville
Buchanan
Arrowhead Lake
Corn Creek
Jersey Creek
Middle Fork
Indian Creek
Richland Creek
Little Indian Creek
Yellow Fork
Bannamon Creek
James Branch
Lewis Branch
Jacobs Creek
Bold Knob Creek
Uphill Run
Slate Run
Falling Run
Silver Creek
Fall Run
Vincennes Run
Middle Creek
French Creek
Georgetown Creek
Lazy Creek
Woertz Creek
Smith Creek
Black Creek
Interstate
U.S. Highway
State Highway
Road
Railroad
Miles
Jefferson County

February 8, 1819, and divided the county into three townships—New Albany, Greenville, and Franklin.

On March 4 the commissioners selected New Albany as the county seat. As the county grew, Lafayette Township was organized in 1828 and Georgetown Township in 1837. There are two main theories regarding the origin of the county's name. One attributes it to DAVIS FLOYD, a prominent Clark County politician who participated in the county seat campaign and became the county's first circuit court judge. Another attributes the name to Davis Floyd's uncle JOHN FLOYD, a leading Jefferson County, Kentucky, pioneer who lost his life in 1783 when a party of men with whom he was traveling were attacked by Indians near BULLITT'S LICK near the present Jefferson-BULLITT COUNTY line.

An important factor in Floyd County's early development was the Buffalo Trace, an old trail created by herds of buffalo making their way from their grazing areas in Illinois to SALT LICKS in Kentucky. Traversing Floyd County in a northwesterly direction from the Ohio River near SILVER CREEK, the Buffalo Trace became the primary route of pioneer travel between the FALLS OF THE OHIO and Vincennes in western Indiana. Shortly after Indiana became a state in 1816, the legislature launched an ambitious internal improvements program. One of the first projects was a paved road that approximated the Buffalo Trace, linking New Albany and Vincennes. It was completed to Paoli when the state reached the brink of bankruptcy and was forced to lease the road to a private company, which operated the road as a turnpike. In 1820 Indiana's first stagecoach route was established on the New Albany–Paoli Turnpike.

In addition to providing transportation to hinterland towns, the Buffalo Trace and its subsequent improvements also served as a path for town development in Floyd County, notably the nineteenth-century towns of Greenville, Galena, and Floyds Knobs. Greenville, about twelve miles northwest of New Albany, was laid out in 1816 by Arthur Mundall, a former Kentucky schoolteacher, and Benjamin Haines, who owned adjoining tracts of land. The source of the town's name is unclear, but Greenville soon became a stop on the stagecoach route to Paoli. This traffic helped support several hotels, a post office, and numerous other businesses. By 1819 it was of sufficient size that some residents pressed to have it named the county seat.

Galena, situated about eight miles from New Albany, was platted in 1837 by George Sease, who hoped to profit from selling lots on the turnpike. Known at first as Germantown, it was renamed Galena to avoid getting confused with another Germantown in the area when the post office was opened in 1860. Early businesses included a store operated by Isaac Parks, a steam-powered flour mill erected in 1857, a blacksmith shop, and a couple of cooperages. Floyds Knobs, about two miles northwest of New Albany, was platted in the late 1830s as Mooresville in honor of James Moore, a prominent local landowner and native New Yorker. The name held until 1852 when a post office was established. Because another Mooresville in Morgan County already had a post office, the name was changed to Floyds Knobs. Many of the community's early settlers were FRENCH, IRISH, and GERMAN immigrants who united to organize St. Mary of the Knobs Catholic Church shortly after the War of 1812. In 1820 they built a log edifice near Little Indian Creek and replaced it with a permanent brick church in 1837.

An important road was the New Albany–Corydon Turnpike, which carried traffic to the state's first capital. Approximating the route of later State Road 62, it provided access to Edwardsville, about five miles west of New Albany. First owned by Charles Paxon, the original townsite was platted in 1853 by Henry Edwards, for whom it was named. The town functioned primarily as a rural market and postal and toll-gate stop on Corydon Pike until 1870, when the Louisville, New Albany, & St. Louis (Airline) Railroad reached the knobs. A short time later the company began constructing a tunnel through the hills. Construction of the 4,689-foot tunnel, the longest in Indiana, was completed in 1881, and it is used by the Norfolk Southern Railroad.

While most residents of Floyd County, especially those living outside New Albany, were small general farmers, shipbuilding was the foundation of the county's industrial ECONOMY during the first half of the nineteenth century. Because of its position as the northern terminus of traffic between New Orleans and the Falls of the Ohio, New Albany quickly attracted shipbuilders. In 1818 the partnership of Shreve & Blair, whose senior partner was the famed builder HENRY SHREVE, built the *Ohio*, which measured about 140 feet in length and weighed 443 tons. Only a few boats were launched between 1819 and 1825, but twelve vessels were constructed during the next five years. Business increased rapidly over the next three decades, with construction of 244 STEAMBOATS between 1825 and 1854. By the mid-1850s the firms of Jacob Dowerman & Thomas Humphreys, William Jones, Charles Wible, John Evans, Peter Tellon & Jacob Alford, and George Armstrong had established New Albany's position as the Ohio Valley's premier shipbuilding center. Among the more famous steamboats to slide down New Albany's ways before the CIVIL WAR were the *Eclipse* (1852), *A.L. Shotwell* (1853), and *Baltic* (1856).

But New Albany's shipbuilding fortunes declined rapidly after the Civil War began. The coming of the RAILROAD gradually diverted considerable traffic away from the steamboat. More important, because of the city's position below the Falls, local shipbuilders built for the southern market. When the war came, rebel ship owners not only ceased ordering vessels from Yankee builders, they also refused to complete payment for some boats already in service. However, some shipbuilding continued after the conflict, and in 1866 a New Albany yard launched the famed *Rob't E. Lee*, which four years later defeated the *Natchez* in one of the most famous matches in steamboat racing.

Floyd County's romance with the railroad began in 1847, when local merchants and other affluent residents raised ten thousand dollars in stock and New Albany City Council appropriated one hundred thousand dollars for bonds to launch the New Albany & Salem Railroad. By 1851 the line was completed to Salem, the Washington County seat. During the 1850s the line was extended in sections to Bedford, Bloomington, and finally to Michigan City on Lake Michigan. In addition to providing a much-needed intercity transportation link, the railroad provided a major stimulus to the local economy. The railroad company built repair shops near its new depot on Pearl St. Pork packers established slaughterhouses on the riverfront to take advantage of the connection between river and rail traffic. Hotel operators opened new hostelries to accommodate travelers. By the late 1850s, however, the New Albany & Salem had outgrown the ability of local sponsors to provide expansion capital. When eastern bankers decided to invest in 1858, the line became the Louisville, New Albany, & Chicago Railroad, better known as the Monon.

Floyd County attracted a substantial immigrant POPULATION during the nineteenth century, particularly French, Germans, Irish, and AFRICAN AMERICANS. Substantial numbers of French immigrants settled in Floyds Knobs and the Budd Rd. area southwest of New Albany, where they made their mark in farming, barrel-making, stone-quarrying, and truck-gardening. French priest Louis Neyron was instrumental in building St. Mary of the Knobs Church, which he served from 1836 to 1854. Irish immigrants began arriving in Floyd County in 1817. They came in large numbers during the 1830s and 1840s to work on construction of roads, canals, and railroads.

Many settled in the neighborhood north of the MONON RAILROAD yards, which became known as Limerick Hill. German immigrants congregated in western New Albany, where they built slaughterhouses, tanneries, and breweries, and practiced trades such as tailoring, stone-carving, and furniture-making. Many German farmers settled in Lafayette Township, near St. Mary of the Knobs Church and near St. Joseph's Church, just across the Clark County line. German Protestants established the forerunner of the present St. Mark's United CHURCH OF CHRIST in downtown New Albany in 1837.

By 1850 immigrants composed 17 percent of New Albany's population. Like many other American cities with large foreign-born populations, it experienced a period of nativist hysteria that reached a fever pitch during the 1854 election campaign between the Democrats, who courted the immigrant vote, and a Fusion party that included old Whigs, free soilers, TEMPERANCE advocates, and nativist Know-Nothings. The tension culminated on October 10, 1854, in a series of election day riots in which a number of Irishmen were badly beaten, predominantly Irish Holy Trinity Catholic Church was stoned, and immigrant-owned businesses were attacked. The FUSIONISTS won the election, but their electoral success was short-lived. During the next two years, Lt. Gov. ASHBEL P. WILLARD, a New Albany Democrat, frequently attacked nativist bigotry and PROHIBITION laws and swept to victory in his 1856 campaign for governor. In 1860 he also became the only Indiana governor to die in office.

Because of its immediate proximity to a slave state, New Albany was a haven for African Americans fleeing from slavery via the UNDERGROUND RAILROAD. By 1860 the city had the highest black population in Indiana, almost 8 percent of the total. Many lived in an area on the city's western edge known as West Union or, more commonly, "Contraband Quarters." Although some white residents participated in the Underground Railroad, economic and social conditions for African Americans were quite poor, and prejudice and discrimination were rampant.

New Albany and Floyd County escaped the physical ravages of the Civil War, but the conflict had an enormous impact locally. Shortly after hostilities began, the Floyd County Fairground near Silver St. and Charlestown Rd. was converted to Camp Noble, an assembly and training site for Union troops recruited from the surrounding area. Particularly notable was the Thirty-eighth Indiana Volunteer Infantry Regiment. Commanded by Col. Benjamin F. Scribner, grandson of Joel Scribner, it fought at Perryville, Stones River, Chickamauga, Chattanooga, Atlanta, and in Sherman's March to the Sea.

A number of African American residents joined the Twenty-eighth Regiment of U.S. Colored Volunteers. Among its members was Dr. William A. Burney, who became a member of the Floyd County Board of Health and served briefly as president protem of the Floyd County Medical Society after the war. Many city schools were converted to HOSPITALS to treat sick and wounded soldiers, and local school children lost two years of education.

During the decades that followed the Civil War, New Albany developed a thriving industrial economy based on the manufacture of plate glass, textiles, and iron products. By the mid-1890s, however, many of these firms were out of business, either because of the loss of resources, such as natural gas, or economic reverses in the depression that followed the Panic of 1893. During the early twentieth century, the city became a major center for production of plywood, veneer, and other wood products, largely on the strength of large nearby stands of native hardwood timber. Outside the city, Floyd County remained largely agrarian, dominated by small general farms that produced a few milk and beef cattle, hogs, chickens, wheat, corn, oats, and other grain and vegetable crops. This pattern prevailed until well after WORLD WAR II.

Several New Albany and Floyd County residents attained regional and national acclaim during the nineteenth and twentieth centuries. GEORGE W. MORRISON, born in Baltimore in 1820, moved to New Albany in 1840 and became a prominent portraitist and landscape painter. WASHINGTON C. DEPAUW, born in Salem, Indiana, in 1822, arrived in New Albany in 1854 and became the city's leading industrialist, with investments in several of the city's leading manufacturing firms. Because of his contributions to Indiana Asbury College in Greencastle, the institution changed its name to DePauw University before his death.

Pennsylvania native Michael Crawford Kerr established his law practice in New Albany in 1852 and was elected to the United States House of Representatives in 1864. He was elected speaker of the House in December 1875 and served until his death eight months later at age forty-nine. William Vaughn Moody, born in Spencer, Indiana, in 1869, was reared in New Albany and went on to become professor of literature at the University of Chicago and a distinguished poet and playwright. CHARLES ALLEN PROSSER, born in New Albany in 1872, served as New Albany superintendent of schools from 1900 to 1908 before moving into the field of vocational education. He served as director of the Dunwoody Industrial Institute in Minneapolis and is known as the father of vocational education in the United States. New Albany native BILLY HERMAN, a talented second baseman for the Chicago Cubs during the 1930s and 1940s, went on to coach for the Brooklyn Dodgers and Milwaukee Braves and to manage the Boston Red Sox. He was elected to the Baseball Hall of Fame in 1975. EDWIN HUBBLE, born in Marshfield, Missouri, in 1889, taught physics, mathematics, and Spanish, as well as coached the basketball team, at New Albany High School from 1913–14. Hubble left the teaching field and went back to the field he received his degree in, ASTRONOMY. He spent much of his life developing larger, more effective telescopes. The Hubble Space Telescope, named for him, was released into orbit in 1990. Floyd County's most famous citizen is the late SHERMAN MINTON. Born in Georgetown in 1890, he was appointed by President Harry Truman to the United States Supreme Court in 1949. He served until his retirement in September 1956.

Like other parts of the Louisville metropolitan region, Floyd County experienced significant population growth during the post–World War II decades, with much of the growth coming in the suburban fringe. Between 1940 and 1950 the county's population increased more than 25 percent. In 1960 the population stood at 51,397, with New Albany's 37,812 citizens accounting for 73.6 percent of the total. In 1970 Floyd County's population was 55,622 and New Albany's was 38,402. In 1980 Floyd County had 61,169 and New Albany 37,103. By 1990 the county's population had grown to 64,404, while New Albany's 36,322 residents comprised only 56.4 of the total. In 1996 Floyd County's population was 70,746, and New Albany's was 38,224. Most of the county's residential growth during these decades occurred in suburban townships, especially Lafayette, Georgetown, and Greenville, along U.S. Highway 150, which parallels the old Vincennes Rd. Floyd County is the third-largest county in the Louisville metropolitan region, with an increasingly diverse economy that includes not only AGRICULTURE but plastic moldings, label manufacturing, refrigerated dough products, fireproof file cabinets, automobile parts, air filters, and electronic components.

See Betty Lou Amster, *New Albany on the Ohio: Historical Review, 1813–1963* (New Albany 1963); *This Is Our Community* (New Albany 1994).

Carl E. Kramer

FLOYD'S DEFEAT. On September 12, 1781, because of hostile Indians, a number of families abandoned SQUIRE BOONE'S STATION in present SHELBY COUNTY and were attacked on the road to Louisville by a force of Indians led by Alexander McKee. There were about a dozen killed, including ten women and children.

When news of this massacre reached Col. JOHN FLOYD, commander of the Jefferson County militia, he immediately mobilized all the mounted men at the BEARGRASS STATIONS. They rode to Linn's Station, which Floyd surmised would be the next to be attacked. His force was smaller than he had hoped, for that very afternoon twenty-five horses had been stolen from the Low Dutch Station (or New Holland) by the Indians. Early the next morning, on September 14, Floyd gathered twenty-seven men and this "Horse Militia" headed for Long Run.

Prior to reaching this creek, Floyd's columns ran into a party of two hundred Indians. A battle began, with the militia on the defensive. In a few minutes, Floyd's troops were down to nine men, all fleeing for their lives. Capt. James A'sturgus was killed, and Floyd was wounded in the foot and his horse killed. As he was being closely pursued, Floyd was given another horse by Samuel Wells, upon which he made his escape.

The fact that the mounted militia company was so quickly surrounded and defeated led everyone to believe the Indians had prepared an ambush. This story was later reinforced by Bland Ballard's statement that "he could not persuade Floyd not to pursue. He was decoyed onto a ridge in pursuit of some indians that showed themselves and the indians just fired on them from both sides, their shot crossing up the hill. His men would have been, as many of them were, just shot down, but they charged through the ranks [of the enemy]. Floyd was wounded but 6 or 7 men brought him off."

A more careful study suggests that the Indians were more surprised to see Floyd than he was to meet them. Most of the Indians were off the road, collecting the goods discarded by the settlers the day before, and, upon seeing the militia riding along the ridge, the Indians were able to attack from both sides and the rear. Being greatly outnumbered, the only chance for Floyd's men to survive was to wheel about and retreat through the enemy.

Floyd's men had killed only three Hurons and a Miami, but one of the dead Hurons was their chief. This man was their principal warrior and had been a great supporter of the British efforts to keep the Indians organized against the Americans. The British Indian agent, Alexander McKee, tried to convince the Indians to follow up on their success, but the Huron would not listen and started for home. McKee followed with most of the Miami.

See Neal O. Hammon, "Early Louisville and the Beargrass Stations," *Filson Club History Quarterly* 52 (April 1978): 146–66.

Neal O. Hammon

FLOYDS FORK. Floyds Fork of Salt River has its origin near Floydsburg in OLDHAM COUNTY and enters Jefferson County approximately one mile north of Aiken Rd. The creek, which provides drainage for much of eastern Jefferson County, traverses over thirty miles in the county. It is subject to FLASH FLOODS, particularly in the FISHERVILLE area, but is reduced to a series of ponds during periods of severe drought. Floyds Fork enters BULLITT COUNTY approximately two and a half miles west of U.S. 150. It joins SALT RIVER near SHEPHERDSVILLE.

Confederate and Union forces skirmished at Floyds Fork and what is now U.S. 60 on October 1, 1862. The vastly outnumbered Confederates retreated after Union artillery joined the battle.

The creek is named for Col. JOHN FLOYD, an early surveyor and the first county lieutenant commander of the militia of Jefferson County. Much of the surrounding land is undeveloped. To maintain the natural setting, a "Floyds Fork Areawide Rezoning Plan" was approved by JEFFERSON COUNTY FISCAL COURT on March 9, 1993. This established rural residential zoning for much of Floyds Fork south of Interstate 64.

See J. Andrew White, *On the Fingertips of an Invasion* (Louisville 1993).

Blaine A. Guthrie Jr.

FLOYD'S STATION. Floyd's Station was begun on November 3, 1779, by Col. JOHN FLOYD. He built the station on the north side of BEARGRASS CREEK, nearly in the center of his property, which he had acquired with two thousand-acre military surveys. When Colonel Floyd arrived at this site, he discovered that eleven cabins had already been built on his property by squatters.

A small fort was built west of the present Breckenridge Ln., behind the present-day Jamestown Apartments. The family cemetery can still be visited. Floyd named the station Woodville, but it was generally called Floyd's Station. Initially this settlement contained only his family, a few friends, and a slave; but, by February 20, 1780, he wrote that he had ten families settled at the station and expected five more families to join him soon.

After Floyd's death in 1783, Jane Floyd married ALEXANDER BRECKINRIDGE. After his father's death, William Preston Floyd inherited the property, although his mother and the other children continued to live at the old station.

Several historians have reported inaccurately that John Floyd built another station closer to Louisville before moving to his land near ST. MATTHEWS. This is refuted by Robert Breckinridge, who stated that Floyd "removed to that place in the fall of 1779 . . . and that Mrs. Floyd continued her residence in that place while the widow of Col. Floyd and until her death which was in May of 1812" (Draper Mss., 17CC125).

See Neal O. Hammon, "Early Louisville and the Beargrass Stations," *Filson Club History Quarterly* 52 (April 1978): 147–66.

Neal O. Hammon

FONTAINE, AARON (b Charles City, Virginia, November 30, 1753; d Louisville, April 1823). Ferryman. Aaron Fontaine's name (mispronounced as "Fountain") was given to FONTAINE FERRY PARK, Louisville's beloved amusement park on the OHIO RIVER at the west end of MARKET ST. His parents were the Reverend Peter Fontaine, rector of Westover Parish Church, and Elizabeth (Wade) Fontaine. The Fontaines were a French Huguenot family who had fled to England in 1685 after the revocation of the Edict of Nantes. The Reverend Fontaine was born in England in 1691 and came to Virginia in 1716.

Aaron Fontaine was commonly known as Captain Fontaine because of his service in the Virginia militia from Louisa County as an ensign in the Revolutionary War. Though there was no record found of his promotion to this rank, he apparently achieved it. In 1798 Aaron, well-endowed with this world's goods, moved to the Louisville area with his large family—twelve children and his wife, Barbara (Terrell) Fontaine, who died on the overland trail. One daughter in the entourage, Mary Ann, was accompanied by her husband, FORTUNATUS COSBY Sr., and their infant daughter. They first settled along HARRODS CREEK but later moved into town. In 1806 Fontaine and Cosby jointly purchased a large tract of land, part of JOHN CAMPBELL's two thousand acres from JOHN FLOYD's 1774 survey. Then, in 1814, Fontaine purchased an adjacent tract of several hundred acres on the river, where he established a plantation and a spacious home. With the purchase he acquired the right to a ferry established in 1807 across the river to Indiana. The ferry reached the HOOSIER shore a short distance below NEW ALBANY. Named for its various operators, it was known first as Carter's, then Oatman's, and finally Fontaine's Ferry.

A letter in the *Vincennes* (Indiana) *Western Sun* in 1816 noted that a branch of the road from CORYDON, Indiana, turned south before reaching New Albany and went "to [Joseph] Oatman's ferry, opposite to which, on the Kentucky side, is the farm and present dwelling of Captain Fontaine, who, I believe, it is truly said, keeps the neatest and best boats &c on the Ohio. The distance from here up to Louisville is 4 miles over a handsome road well causey'd, which I am informed, the Captain opened, and for which he has my thanks." The road is now W Market St., but it was formerly the Fontaine Ferry Rd.

Fontaine married again in 1805. His bride was a widow, Elizabeth T. Thruston, who had ten children and bore Fontaine four more. He died at the age of 70. His grave site is unknown, but he was probably buried in the old Western Cemetery. Many bodies buried there were later moved to CAVE HILL, but his is not among them. With his numerous progeny, most of whom married into prominent Louisville families, his descendants in the urban area probably number in the hundreds.

See J. Stoddard Johnston, ed., *Memorial History of Louisville* (Chicago 1896); George R. Wilson and Gayle Thornbrough, *The Buffalo Trace* (Indianapolis 1946).

George H. Yater

FONTAINE FERRY PARK. Called "Fountain Ferry" by generations of patrons, Fontaine Ferry Park was Louisville's foremost AMUSEMENT PARK and family recreation center from 1905 to 1969. Located at 230 South Western Pkwy. at the western terminus of MARKET ST., Fontaine Ferry's sixty-four acres offered more than fifty rides and riverside attractions under a tall canopy of whitewashed, spreading trees.

Forerunner to contemporary theme park attractions, "Fountain Ferry" offered an entire day of family activities: picnicking, roller skating, rides, games, shows, and amusements for all ages, plus SWIMMING beneath a cascading waterfall in a pool second in size only to Louisville's CRESCENT HILL pool. Prominent musicians and entertainers graced Fontaine Ferry's theater building stage or Gypsy Village outdoor dance garden throughout the park's history. Those who appeared included the John Philip Sousa Band, the Dunbar Light Opera Co., Mary Pickford, Will Rogers, Fred Astaire, Louis Armstrong, the Tommy Dorsey Orchestra, Frank Sinatra, and Perry Como.

The park evolved from Capt. AARON FONTAINE's OHIO RIVER estate and flatboat ferry service landing, originally called Carter's Ferry, purchased in 1814 from William Lytle.

Fontaine, a Virginia militiaman, settled in Kentucky at HARRODS CREEK in Jefferson County in 1798 with his twelve children. His wife did not survive the perilous journey. The twenty-six children in the combined families of Fontaine and his second wife, Elizabeth Thruston, included daughters who married names prominent in Louisville's early history: Cosby, Floyd, Jacob, Pope, Prather, and Todd.

In 1887 entrepreneur Tony Landenwich purchased Fontaine's Ferry and established a riverside hotel, outdoor restaurant, bandstand, and a world-class, one-third-mile bicycle racetrack with grandstand. Hopkins Amusements of St. Louis entered in 1903. John Miller, architect of Palisades Park in New Jersey, was commissioned to design a grand-scale amusement park on the Landenwich property. Following two years of construction, Fontaine Ferry Park opened to the public in May 1905. Immensely popular from the start, the ornate, Victorian-style attraction soon passed into the managing hands of the Park Circuit and Realty Co., owner and operator of other stockholder amusement properties in the Midwest, including Forest Park Highlands in St. Louis. Carefully nurtured under the administrations of Judge CHARLES A. WILSON, Benjamin G. Brinkman, and, later, John F. Singhiser, the corporation of Fontaine Ferry Enterprises emerged following the appointment of the park's last general manager and president, John R. "Jack" Singhiser (son of John F. Singhiser), in 1947.

From the park's inception to the 1940s, throngs of visitors arrived by STEAMBOAT, debarking at a small Market St. beach and pontoon landing along the Ohio River. Others came via open-sided "summer car" trolleys; Fontaine Ferry was the turnaround point for the Market St. trolley line. These rail lines allowed the park to be powered free of cost for almost twenty years. When the park threatened to close around 1932, the Louisville Railway Co., alarmed about the possible loss of riders, provided their excess direct current to power Fontaine Ferry's rides. By oversight, the power source was not removed until the lines were taken up in 1952, at which time the railway company sent a bill (later compromised) for the electricity.

Following the post–WORLD WAR II automobile boom, thousands crowded the park grounds on summer weekends, their numbers augmented by special annual promotions such as County Days, Nickel Days, and well-attended company picnics. The Scooters, the Rocket, the Whip, a hand-carved 1910 Dentzel carousel, the Old Mill, Hilarity Hall, and the Penny Arcade enticed young and old alike. Fontaine Ferry's most popular ride was its wooden roller coaster. There were four in the park's history: the original Scenic Railway (1905–10); the Racing Derby (1910–36); the Velvet Racer (1936–48); and the breathtaking Comet (1951–69), which featured a world-class ninety-foot drop and thirty-eight-hundred-foot track.

Racially integrated in 1964, Fontaine Ferry Park was heavily vandalized during racial unrest on May 4, 1969. Soon thereafter, the property was sold. It was renovated in 1972 as Ghost Town on the River, then renamed River Glen Park for its unsuccessful last season in 1975. Following a series of spectacular fires, the city purchased and cleared the site and, since 1981, has maintained a park adjacent to Shawnee Park. In the mid-1990s an outdoor sports complex and other surface improvements were added to the original Fontaine property, which in turn has spurred new private residential development adjacent to the former Fontaine Ferry landing.

See Jerry L. Rice, "Fontaine Ferry Park, A Time of Innocence," video, Louisville 1992; Lou Block, "Fontaine Ferry Fun & Fantasy," *Louisville Magazine* 17 (May 20, 1966): 18–21.

Jerry L. Rice

Entrance to Fontaine Ferry Park, 230 South Western Parkway, about 1930.

FOODS. The history of food in Louisville is closely tied to the city's commercial role as a river port, stockyard, and agricultural market. Breweries and distilleries made their mark in local culinary inventiveness, as well. Because of GEOGRAPHY, Louisville fare has reflected the cooking customs of both the American South and the Midwest. Indeed, regional foods are more popular in Louisville than ethnic foods. Although large numbers of GERMANS and IRISH settled in the city, few RESTAURANTS represent their tastes.

In the early to mid-twentieth century, restaurant menus revolved around such traditional dishes as fried chicken, country ham, pork chops, steak, catfish, and trout. Side dishes included ham-flavored green beans, corn pudding, and potatoes cooked many ways. But the 1980s and 1990s were marked by the emergence of eateries influenced by international and ethnic cooking traditions. After flirtation with these foods, many Louisville chefs began experimenting with regional ingredients and used Continental techniques to create an emerging Kentucky fine dining movement.

Dishes commonly found in the city's finer restaurants have included Bibb lettuce salad with country ham and black-eyed pea vinaigrette, bourbon-soaked hickory-smoked trout, and free-range chicken stuffed with country ham and pesto. Bourbon has found its way into every course as an ingredient in salad dressings, sauces, and soufflés. The spent sour mash from the distillation process at Brown-Forman distillery is even used to bake a distinctive multigrain bread served at the Oakroom of the SEELBACH HILTON HOTEL. Chefs Kathy Cary (Lilly's), Joe Castro (The English Grill), and James Gerhardt (The Oakroom) were recognized with profiles in national food magazines such as *Gourmet* and *Food & Wine,* and honored by the James Beard Foundation.

Such inventiveness is not just a late-twentieth-century phenomenon. Several famous dishes have their origins in Louisville restaurants, clubs, and catering establishments dating from late in the nineteenth century. Oysters were all the rage across America by the 1880s. Swift transportation by STEAMBOAT up the Mississippi and OHIO RIVERS meant a ready supply of the mollusks for Louisville markets. In 1884 Italian immigrant Philip Mazzoni started a bar that specialized in serving oysters. Pan-fried, stewed, and raw oysters were menu staples. Mazzoni also invented the ROLLED OYSTER, a hand-sized snack of two or three oysters rolled in bread crumbs and deep-fried. Initially the rolled oyster was a giveaway with the purchase of a mug of beer. Later, MAZZONI'S charged a nickel.

A Polish actress inspired another 1880s invention, the candy known as MODJESKAS. Helena Modjeska performed the American premiere of Ibsen's *A Doll's House* at MACAULEY'S THEATRE in 1883. One of the theatergoers was a local confectioner, Anton Busath, who was inspired to create a melt-in-the-mouth caramel candy with a soft, marshmallow center. He asked Modjeska for permission to name the sweet after her and was granted it. They are often referred to by Louisvillians as "Majestics."

Louisville's PENDENNIS CLUB, a private men's club, opened its doors in 1881. Among its employees was a young AFRICAN AMERICAN elevator operator named Henry Bain. Bain eventually became the club's headwaiter. Known affectionately as Captain Henry, he created his eponymous gourmet sauce in the club's dining room at the request of several members who wanted something to put on their steaks. HENRY BAIN SAUCE has a sharp, savory flavor, derived from its blend of chili sauce, Worcestershire sauce, Tabasco, and chutney. It is as successful an accompaniment to pork as it is to beef. A frequent addition to Louisville hors d'oeuvre trays is a dollop of Henry Bain sauce added as a topping to cream cheese on crackers.

Caterer JENNIE BENEDICT also lent her name to a Louisville delicacy. Benedictine is a light green cream cheese–based spread flavored with cucumber and mild onions. (Green food coloring provides the distinctive hue.) The spread remains a popular filling for sandwiches and is a staple of hor d'oeuvre selections. It makes a fine chip dip, too. Benedict ran a tea room and soda fountain shop on S FOURTH ST. between 1893 and 1925. There is an account that a group of patrons from St. Louis tried to talk her into moving to that city to cater to St. Louis society. When her loyal Louisville following found out, they begged her publicly and vociferously to stay, and she remained in her home city.

Probably the most famous dish to be created in Louisville is the HOT BROWN sandwich. It was invented by Chef Fred K. Schmidt at the BROWN HOTEL in the 1930s. The dish consists of sliced turkey, ham or crisp bacon, toast, and two different kinds of savory sauce (béchamel and mornay) placed in a small baking dish. Cheddar and Parmesan cheeses combine to give the Hot Brown its distinctive sharpness. The sandwich is placed under the broiler until the cheese is bubbly. Later variations showing up at other restaurants contain tomatoes, but this was not an original ingredient, and Hot Brown purists shun tomatoes. Schmidt also introduced a Cold Brown, but it never gained a following.

A true American classic was also served in the 1930s at KAELIN'S RESTAURANT. The story goes that Carl Kaelin, owner and kitchen manager, was determined to make his hamburger, a menu staple, the best in the city. One day Kaelin was presiding over the kitchen and noticed the slices of American cheese kept on hand. He decided to add a slice to a ground beef patty in the last few moments of cooking so that it would melt over the meat and add extra flavor to the sandwich. Thus the cheeseburger was created. Other places have claimed the distinction of making the first cheeseburger, but Kaelin's may well have been the first to put it on a menu.

Given that Louisville is the home of the KENTUCKY DERBY, it is surprising that more dishes have not been created to commemorate the most famous two minutes in sports. DERBY-PIE® virtually stands alone. Leaudra and Walter Kern came to Louisville in the 1950s and assumed the management of the Melrose Inn, located several miles outside the city limits. For many years, members of the inn staff had been baking the pie. (They even peddled a tart-sized version through the fence to racing patrons at CHURCHILL DOWNS.) The Kerns copyrighted the recipe, and ever since Kern's Kitchens has had the exclusive rights to bake authentic Derby-Pie®, which is a registered trademark. The pie is made with walnuts, chocolate chips, and a touch of bourbon. It is best served warm, with a dollop of whipped cream or vanilla ice cream. Another hometown favorite dessert was created by food writer, cookbook author, and one-time caterer Camille Glenn. Camille's Golden Cointreau Cake (sometimes simply called Camille's Orange Cake) is a light-as-air sponge cake flavored with orange juice and finished with a luscious Cointreau-laced buttercream frosting.

See John Egerton, *Southern Food: At Home, On the Road, in History* (New York 1987); John Finley, ed., *Courier-Journal Kentucky Cookbook* (Louisville 1985); Camille Glenn, *The Heritage of Southern Cooking* (New York 1986).

Susan H. Reigler

FOOTBALL. Football has been a part of Louisville almost since 1876, when Walter Camp, the father of American football, transformed English rugby into the game we know today. While sandlot games, mimicking the new "American College" game played in the East, were probably being played in Louisville in the 1880s, no official football team was organized in the Louisville area until the fall of 1892, when the LOUISVILLE ATHLETIC CLUB team was formed.

One of the first organized games became Kentucky's oldest football rivalry and one of the oldest high school rivalries in the country. On November 18, 1893, LOUISVILLE MALE HIGH SCHOOL and du Pont Manual Training High School (now DU PONT MANUAL HIGH SCHOOL) played their first game of organized football against each other. For eighty-seven years the "Old Rivalry" was a Thanksgiving Day tradition. The 1948 matchup between the two schools has the distinction of being the first program broadcast on a local television station on WAVE-TV.

Louisville has had several forays into professional football. In the early 1900s, Louisville fielded a semiprofessional club team, the Louisville Brecks, who played at the lowest skill level. The Brecks took their name from the location of their home field on Breckinridge St. and were one of several teams in the East and Midwest to earn money for playing. Others were the Buffalo Niagaras, Rochester Jeffersons, and Racine Cardinals. The teams were made up primarily of local talent and loosely guided by player-managers who handled the scheduling—usually with whatever teams were willing and available to play—and finances, which basically amounted to paying players a cut of the gate.

One of the most successful and beloved of the city's professional teams was the Louisville Tanks, which was organized in 1935 after another semiprofessional team, the Louisville Bourbons, folded. The team was made up of every class of athletes, from former National Football League players to local high school talent, earning an average salary of two hundred dollars a season. The Tanks were organized by AMERICAN STANDARD Inc., a plumbing and fixtures manufacturer. The team got its name from a company product and chose green and gold for the team colors. The Tanks were organized and coached by plant manager H.M. "Harry" Reed. In 1936 the team started the Midwest Football League with teams from Cincinnati, Indianapolis, Dayton, Columbus, and Springfield, Ohio. The team made its debut on October 4, 1936, at PARKWAY FIELD in front of three thousand fans. Over the next two seasons the team played in both the Midwest Professional League and the American Professional Football League. The final game was played in Los Angeles on December 18, 1939. The team, after winning three league championships and compiling a record of 35–14–3, disbanded two weeks later.

Another professional team, the Louisville Raiders, was organized in March 1960, for the short-lived United Football League. The team lasted only through the 1962 season and played teams from Michigan, Ohio, and Indiana. The team, which was put together by the KENTUCKIANA Professional Football Club Inc., led by former University of Kentucky BASKETBALL star Lucian "Skippy" Whitaker, played at Fairgrounds Stadium.

In the late 1970s Louisville was host to the most recent attempt at professional football—the Kentucky Trackers, an American Football Association franchise known for its dubious, short-lived history. Between the team's opening game on June 2, 1979, at Fairgrounds Stadium and July 29, 1980, when the franchise was revoked, the Trackers were known primarily for "violating every rule in the book," according to AFA chairman Bob Williams. The team failed to pay league fines totaling ten thousand dollars for several rules violations, had players' checks bounce, and had phantom ownership when Louisville developer John Waits sold the franchise without filing the appropriate papers with the league. The team was also accused by its own players of playing college-eligible players under aliases. Although the Trackers, which finished with a 0–8 record for the abbreviated 1980 season, were the city's last professional franchise, a semiprofessional team, the Louisville Bulls, currently plays throughout the region.

The UNIVERSITY OF LOUISVILLE (U of L) played its first intercollegiate football game in 1912. Between 1912 and 1998 the team has posted a 351–379–17 record, for a .470 winning percentage. The team, whose mascot is the Cardinal, has a 3–2–1 record in bowl appearances, including the 1958 Sun Bowl when U of L beat Drake 34–20, and the 1991 Fiesta Bowl when the Cardinals, led by quarterback Browning Nagle, defeated Alabama 34–7. The Cards also won the 1993 Liberty Bowl game against Michigan State. The Cardinals' Missouri Valley Conference Championship team tied Long Beach State at the 1970 Pasadena Bowl 24–24. The team's only losses in bowl appearances occurred in the 1977 Independence Bowl when the Cards were defeated by Louisiana Tech 24–14, and in the 1998 Motor City Bowl when Marshall won 48–29 in the Pontiac (Michigan) Silverdome. The LOUISVILLE MUNICIPAL COLLEGE Bantams, from the former African American division of the University of Louisville, also made a bowl appearance on New Year's Day 1947, losing to the Tennessee A&I State Tigers in the Vulcan Bowl, 32–0.

In 1925 the University of Louisville, along with Western Kentucky State Normal School (Western Kentucky University), Kentucky Wesleyan, and Transylvania University, became a member of the Kentucky Intercollegiate Athletic Conference (KIAC). This organization soon encompassed nearly every college in the state except the University of Kentucky, which maintained its affiliation with the Southern Intercollegiate Athletic Association, the forerunner of the Southeastern Conference.

With the hope of creating a more equitable athletic structure, Roy Stewart, athletic director at Murray State University, in 1941 proposed a new division, the Ohio Valley Conference (OVC), but WORLD WAR II prevented forming the OVC until 1948. The OVC was made up of the University of Louisville, Eastern Kentucky University, Western Kentucky University, Morehead State University, Murray State University, and Evansville (Indiana) College. Except for Evansville, it was another All-Kentucky conference. Louisville left the conference in 1949.

Throughout much of its history, the Cardinal football team has played as an independent. From 1975 until 1995, the team was not affiliated with any collegiate football conference. Prior to the 1975 season, the school had been a member of the Missouri Valley Conference since 1963. In 1996 the University of Louisville joined Conference USA (C-USA), along with Southern Mississippi, Cincinnati, Houston, Memphis, and Tulane. East Carolina was added in 1997 and Army in 1998. The University of Alabama-Birmingham, a charter member of C-USA, started conference play in football in 1999.

The rivalry between the University of Louisville and the University of Kentucky extended to football in the 1990s. In 1993 the squads squared off for the first of the Governor's Cup contests. After 1998, Kentucky led the series 3–2. In 1998 the contest was played in U of L's new forty-five-thousand-seat football arena, Papa John's Cardinal Stadium, located on Crittenden Dr. just south of campus.

Under Coach Howard Leslie Schnellenberger in the 1980s, U of L began to rebuild its football program. He was born on March 16, 1934, in St. Meinrad, Indiana, to Leslie and Rosena (Hoffman) Schnellenberger. The family moved to Louisville in 1936, where he became an All-State basketball and football player at FLAGET HIGH SCHOOL. Schnellenberger enrolled at the University of Kentucky (UK) in 1952 on a football scholarship, playing end for both Paul Bryant and Blanton Collier, and became an All-American in 1955. After earning a B.S. degree at UK in 1956, he played briefly in the Canadian Football League, then returned to UK as an assistant coach in 1959. He became assistant coach at the University of Alabama (1961–65), the Los Angeles Rams (1966–69), and the Miami Dolphins (1970–72) and 1975–79), and head coach of the Baltimore Colts (1973–74). In 1979 he took over the coaching reins at the University of Miami and led Miami to the national championship in 1983. In December 1984 Schnellenberger moved to the University of Louisville, where he was determined to build a national football power. By 1990 he had compiled a 32–33–2 record, with his best year (1990) culminating in a Fiesta Bowl victory over the University of Alabama. In 1994 Schnellenberger abruptly left the University of Louisville to become head football coach at the University of Oklahoma, where he stayed one season. In 1998 Schnellenberger became director of football operations at Florida Atlantic University in Boca Raton, Florida, where he was hired to build a Division 1-A football program from scratch. Schnellenberger married Beverlee Donnelly of Montreal on May 3, 1959. They had three sons.

After Schnellenberger's departure, the Cardinals were coached by Ron Cooper, the school's first African American head football coach. After Cooper compiled a record of 13–20 over three years, his contract was bought out amidst controversy in 1997. In November 1997 John L. Smith, former head coach of Utah State, was signed to coach the Cardinals.

U of L football has had several successful coaches in its past. Frank Camp, head coach from 1946 to 1968 with a 118–95–2 record, was considered one of college football's early innovators. Lee Corso coached U of L for four seasons from 1969 to 1972, posting a 28–11–3 record, but they were some of the most successful seasons in the school's history.

The list of U of L legends is topped by Baltimore Colts quarterback John Constantine "Johnny" Unitas. He was born to Leonard and Helen (Superfiski) Unitas on May 7, 1933, in Pittsburgh. The University of Louisville offered him a scholarship, and Unitas played there for four years (1951–54). The Cardinals rarely won, but Unitas threw twenty-seven touchdown passes during his career and set a school record with four in one game in 1951. Unitas was selected by the Pittsburgh Steelers in the ninth round of the 1955 National Football League (NFL) draft, was subsequently released, and was playing sandlot football for $6 a game when a Baltimore Colts scout discovered him. He played most of his career with the Colts (1956–72) and finished with the San Diego Chargers (1973–74), retiring that season.

Unitas played on two Super Bowl teams, losing in Super Bowl III in 1969 to Joe Namath's New York Jets and winning the title in Super Bowl V against the Dallas Cowboys in 1971. He was league MVP three times, in 1957, 1964, and 1967; made Pro Bowl appearances in 1957–59, 1964–65, and 1967; was voted Player of the Decade in 1970; and was elected to the Pro Football Hall of Fame at Canton, Ohio, in 1979.

A life-sized statue of Unitas fronts the entrance to PAPA JOHN'S Cardinal Stadium, which also houses a small museum display in his honor. The Johnny Unitas Golden Arm Award, established in 1987 and presented annually to the nation's outstanding college senior quarterback by the Johnny Unitas Golden Arm Educational Foundation Inc. and the Kentucky Chapter of the National Football Foundation and Hall of Fame, is named in his honor.

After leaving football, Unitas was a broadcaster with CBS Sports and a restaurateur in Baltimore; he then became a marketing representative for Atlantic Electric Corp. and later vice president. His first wife was Dorothy Jean Hoelle; they had five children. He then married Sandra Lemon; they had three children.

Other U of L legends include running back Lenny Lyles (1954–57). Lyles, a Louisville businessman, owns several U of L records. Other greats include Bruce Armstrong (1983–86), an offensive tackle with the New England Patriots since 1987 and frequent Pro Bowl selection; Mark Clayton (1979–82), a wide receiver with the Miami Dolphins from 1983–92 and one of U of L's all-time leading receivers; Chicago Bears linebackers Otis Wilson (1977–79), a two-time Pro Bowl selection who played ten seasons with the Bears from 1980–90, and Doug Buffone (1962–65), who played fifteen seasons in the NFL from 1966–80; Houston Oilers wide receiver Ernest Givins (1984–85), who played from 1986–94, and in 1995 with the expansion Jacksonville Jaguars; Dwayne Woodruff (1976–78), a cornerback with the Pittsburgh Steelers from 1979–90; ESPN sports analyst Tom Jackson (1970–72), who played linebacker for the Denver Broncos from 1973–87; and

Washington Redskins offensive tackle Joe Jacoby (1978–80), playing in four Super Bowls and winning three (1983, 1988, 1992). Jacoby, who was a member of the Redskins' famous "Hogs" offensive front line from 1980–93, attended Western High School in Louisville. The list of U of L standouts also includes cornerback Frank Minnifield (1979–82), with the Cleveland Browns from 1984–92, and running back Ernie Green (1958–61), also with the Browns from 1962–68.

The Louisville area has also produced many talented players who went on to find success at other colleges and in the professional ranks. Paul Hornung (b Louisville, December 23, 1935), nicknamed "Golden Boy," was a multisport athlete at Louisville's Flaget High School before becoming an All-American quarterback at Notre Dame, where he won the Heisman Trophy in 1957. Elected to the Pro Football Hall of Fame in 1986, Hornung, a first-round selection of the Green Bay Packers in the 1957 National Football League draft, played nine seasons in the NFL, including three championship teams in 1961, 1962, and 1965 under Hall of Fame coach Vince Lombardi. Hornung, who lives in Louisville, was suspended for a year in 1963 from professional football for gambling on football games. He is featured on a televised one-hour interview sports show called "Paul Hornung's Sports Showcase," based on his personal relationship with some of sport's most recognized and controversial sports figures.

Other local football celebrities include former New York Giants quarterback Phil Simms; thirteen-year NFL veteran offensive lineman Will Wolford, a graduate of St. Xavier and Vanderbilt University who played for the Buffalo Bills in three Super Bowls in the 1990s; William "Bubba" Paris, a college All-American offensive tackle at the University of Michigan and a member of the San Francisco 49ers from 1982–90; Sherman Lewis, a Heisman Trophy hopeful at Michigan State University and a college and professional assistant coach for the San Francisco 49ers and offensive coordinator for the Green Bay Packers; Steve Raible, a wide receiver with the Seattle Seahawks from 1976–81 and a radio announcer for the Seahawks; and Maurice "Mo" Moorman, a guard from Texas A&M who played on the 1969 Super Bowl IV Champions Kansas City Chiefs and is currently a local beer distributor in Louisville.

Next to Hornung, Simms (b Louisville, November 3, 1956) is perhaps the area's best pro football product. Simms grew up in Louisville, graduating from Southern High School. He played at Morehead State University before being drafted into the pros as the Giants' first pick in 1979. Simms, an All-Pro quarterback and fifteen-year NFL veteran, led the New York Giants to victory in Super Bowl XXI in 1987, earning MVP honors. In an on-field interview directly after the game, Simms was asked how he planned on celebrating the victory. He replied that he was "going to Disneyland," a phrase that has become part of sports vernacular. Simms has covered the NFL for network television since 1995, serving as lead analyst for NBC and CBS. In 1998, Simms's son, Chris, signed a letter of intent to play quarterback for the University of Tennessee.

By 1914 football was being played in Louisville at the majority of larger high schools. Player eligibility was a problem, with numerous schools allowing non-students to participate. In 1914 representatives from schools in Mt. Sterling, Winchester, Paris, Georgetown, Frankfort, Somerset, and Lexington organized the Central Kentucky High School Athletic Association and established eligibility rules. In April 1916 the association ended when its members helped to create the Kentucky High School Athletic Association.

Kentucky State Champions from the Louisville Metropolitan Schools since 1959

Year	*Team*	*Class*
1959	Manual	AAA
1960	Male	AAA
1961	Flaget	AAA
1962	St. Xavier	AAA
1963	Male	AAA
1964	Male	AAA
1965	Seneca	AAA
1966	Manual	AAA
1967	Flaget	AAA
1968	Trinity (Louisville)	AAA
1969	St. Xavier	AAA
1970	Butler	AAA
1971	Thomas Jefferson and Flaget	AAA (tie)
1972	Trinity (Louisville)	AAA
1973	Trinity (Louisville)	AAA
1974	St. Xavier	AAA
1975	St. Xavier	AAAA
1976	Trinity (Louisville)	AAAA
1977	Trinity (Louisville)	AAAA
1978	St. Xavier	AAAA
1979	Butler	AAAA
1980	Trinity (Louisville)	AAAA
1983	Trinity (Louisville)	AAAA
1985	Trinity (Louisville)	AAAA
1986	St. Xavier	AAAA
1987	Shelby County	AAAA
1988	Trinity (Louisville)	AAAA
1989	Trinity (Louisville)	AAAA
1990	Trinity (Louisville)	AAAA
1992	St. Xavier	AAAA
1993	Male	AAAA
1994	Trinity (Louisville)	AAAA
1995	St. Xavier	AAAA
1997	St. Xavier	AAAA
1998	Male	AAAA*

*The first year of the three-tiered class system

Currently, high school football is organized into a system of four classes—A, AA, AAA, and AAAA. The system was established by the Kentucky High School Athletic Association in 1975. Jefferson County has eighteen high school teams in AAAA, five teams in class AAA, no teams in AA, and three in A. There are approximately three thousand high school football players in the county. The state championship for all four divisions is held annually at Cardinal Stadium in Louisville.

The playoff system, also established in 1975, has four regions statewide, with two regions making up Jefferson County. Each region is divided into two districts, with four teams from each district meeting to determine the regional champion. Louisville is composed of Region Two and Region Three. Region One, from the western half of the state, plays Region Two; and Region Three plays Region Four, from the eastern half of Kentucky, to determine who will play for the state AAAA championship. From 1959 to 1974, high school football was divided into three classes. The playoff system for the state AAA champion was determined by a Louisville-Jefferson County championship game. The winner would play the representative from the state.

Currently, the most intense gridiron rivalry in Louisville football is between the Catholic high schools Trinity and St. Xavier. Started in 1956, by the 1980s the annual match was drawing the largest attendance among all one-night high school sporting events in the state. In the 1992 game, a record crowd of 35,262 fans witnessed Trinity's defeat of St. Xavier. By 1996 St. Xavier led the rivalry in number of games won, 26–22–2.

See Eustace Williams, *That Old Rivalry, Manual vs. High School, 1893–1900* (Louisville 1940); Robert W. Peterson, *Pigskin: The Early Years of Pro Football* (New York and Oxford 1997); *Courier-Journal*, Sept. 19, 1976.

FORD, ARTHUR YOUNGER (b Parkville, Missouri, November 11, 1861; d Louisville, June 8, 1926). Journalist, banker, and educator. About four years following his birth, Ford's parents, Salem Holland and Sarah (Beauchamp) Ford, moved to Owensboro, Kentucky. Ford attended Centre College in Danville for a short time and then Brown University, from which he graduated in 1884. He then returned to his boyhood home and became part-owner and editor of the *Owensboro Inquirer*. In 1890 he moved to Louisville and joined the LOUISVILLE *TIMES*. After a few months, he transferred to the *COURIER-JOURNAL*, becoming state editor, then editorial writer, then managing editor. In 1907 he resigned to become treasurer of the Columbia Trust Co. After it became the Fidelity & Columbia Trust Co., Ford served as vice president. From 1913 until 1922, he was president of Goodwin Preserving Co.

In 1914 Ford succeeded Judge David W. Fairleigh as chairman of the UNIVERSITY OF LOUISVILLE Board of Trustees, and in 1921 he became the university's first full-time president. Ford centralized the university's administrative offices; improved the academic standing of its medical and law schools; acquired use of the Louisville City Hospital as a teaching facility for the medical school; and added a dental school, a school of PUBLIC HEALTH which was later absorbed into the medical school, and the

Speed Scientific School. To fund a new campus and to lay the groundwork for postsecondary educational opportunities for blacks, Ford campaigned successfully for a city bond issue in 1925. That year he moved the College of Arts and Sciences from its downtown site to what became the Belknap Campus on Third St.

Ford served as president of the Kentucky Commission for the St. Louis World's Fair of 1904, chairman of the local draft board during WORLD WAR I, and president of the Kentucky Tax League (later the Kentucky Tax Reform Association), from which came the state's 1917 tax law. He died in office in 1926.

Ford married Esther Annie Brown of Cloverport, Kentucky, in 1887. They had three children: Emmett B., Margaret, and Salem. Ford is buried in CAVE HILL CEMETERY.

William J. Morison

FORD, JOHN BAPTISTE (b Danville, Kentucky, November 17, 1811; d Creighton, Pennsylvania, May 1, 1903). Manufacturer. Born of pioneer parents Jonathan and Margaret Ford, he was a colorful inventor, river captain, and manufacturer. Apprenticed to a saddler in Danville, he ran away, making his first fortune in saddles, feed boxes, and a general store in Greenville, Indiana. He moved to NEW ALBANY, Indiana, in the 1850s to build STEAMBOATS, launching thirty-eight hulls, at least six of which were steamers for the Louisville–New Orleans and St. Louis–New Orleans trade. Also in New Albany he set up various successful enterprises, including the John B. Ford & Co. Glass Works in 1867, importing workers from England.

The *New Albany Ledger* of November 20, 1869, said of him: "If there is one man in our community to whom our city is indebted for its rapid material prosperity, that man is Capt. John B. Ford, senior proprietor of the Star Glass Works." He lost everything, however, at age seventy and moved to Creighton to start another glass factory. The founder of successful plate glass manufacturing in the United States, his name lives on in the Libby-Owens-Ford Glass Co. He was interred in the family mausoleum in Allegheny Cemetery, Pittsburgh, Pennsylvania.

See John Baptiste Ford entry, *Dictionary of American Biography* (New York 1974); William Earl Aiken, *The Roots Grow Deep* (Toledo, Ohio, 1957); Betty Lou Amster, *New Albany on the Ohio* (New Albany, Ind., 1963).

Betty Lou Amster

FORD MOTOR COMPANY ASSEMBLY PLANTS. The first Ford automobile was sold in Kentucky in 1910, and three years later an assembly operation was established in Louisville at 931 S Third St. Its seventeen employees (including sales force) produced twelve vehicles per day, and entry-level workers earned eight cents per hour. On September 12, 1915, a new assembly plant was completed on a two-and-one-third-acre site at 2500 S Third St., south of Eastern Pkwy., and the first automobile rolled off the lines on January 2, 1916.

Building Model A's at the Ford Motors assembly plant on South Western Parkway in 1925.

Initially the plant employed fifty-three people and produced between fifteen and seventy vehicles per day. By 1923 the success of Ford's Model T and its variants had resulted in an expansion to six hundred employees and a maximum production of two hundred vehicles per day, the limit at that site. Production was halted from June 1918 until March 1919, and the plant was taken over by the U.S. Army Mechanical and Medical Corps for use during WORLD WAR I. By 1924, 205,395 vehicles had been assembled there.

On February 2, 1925, a new $1.5 million plant was completed on a 22.5-acre site, located on part of the old Kentucky State Fairgrounds at 1400 South Western Pkwy. The plant was designed for a thousand employees and production of four hundred vehicles a day. With the changing nature of the automobile business, the plant completed its last Model T on June 3, 1927, but began assembling the new Model A on January 13, 1928, as well as V-8 engines six years later. Although it survived the FLOOD OF 1937, 9 feet of water in the factory required a 60-day shutdown and the disassembly of 325 water-damaged vehicles. Between February 1942 and July 1945 Ford converted the assembly lines to produce military trucks and jeeps during WORLD WAR II.

With a pressing need for additional storage and production space, the last of the 1,608,710 vehicles manufactured at the plant on the OHIO RIVER rolled off the lines on April 13, 1955. Five days later work began at the Fern Valley Rd.–Grade Ln. location, referred to as the Louisville Assembly Plant. This factory, with space of more than 2 million square feet, was located on a 180-acre tract; the initial employment of 2,850 workers constructed both cars and light trucks. By July 1957 employment had grown to forty-seven hundred, after the expansion of the light-truck operations and the addition of the mid-priced Edsel. The plant made five hundred Edsels a day until the model was discontinued late in 1959. The same plant began to make ten different models of heavy trucks in early 1958.

On August 4, 1969, production of heavy trucks was transferred to a new 68-acre factory on a 415-acre site at 11200 Westport Rd. The Kentucky Truck Plant represented an investment of $100 million and was designed to produce three hundred units a day on three assembly lines. By August 1, 1997, the plant had produced its two millionth truck and employed approximately five thousand.

Faced with the energy crisis, a recession, and the globalization of the auto industry, Ford switched production of automobiles to plants specially designed for the smaller cars of the 1980s. After assembling the last full-sized LTD on June 12, 1981, which was also the last of the 3,433,660 Louisville-produced passenger vehicles, $750 million was spent on the Louisville Assembly Plant by 1983 to convert its operations to make the Ranger (a compact pickup truck) and the Bronco II (a light sport-utility vehicle).

Between 1987 and 1989, $263 million was

invested, and 163,000 square feet were added to the factory in preparation for the Explorer line, which replaced the Bronco II in 1990. During the 1980s Ford invested approximately $1 billion in both the Louisville Assembly Plant and the Kentucky Truck Plant.

In February 1997 Ford announced that it was selling its heavy truck division at the Kentucky Truck Plant to Freightliner Corp. and that it would discontinue heavy truck production by the end of the year. In October Ford announced its plan to add 130,000 square feet to the truck facility and hire approximately 1,000 additional workers to boost the production of its F-series light trucks and add the manufacturing of a large sport utility vehicle to compete with GMC's Suburban.

By the end of August 1997 approximately 10.6 million Ford vehicles had been produced in Louisville, and the plants together employed roughly eighty-four hundred workers.

See *Ford 75th Anniversary in Louisville: 1913–1988* (Louisville 1988).

FORMAN, GEORGE (b Louisville, August 7, 1844; d Louisville, November 19, 1901). Distiller. Forman's father was Thomas Seabrooke Forman, a successful bagging and rope manufacturer who came to Louisville from Mason County, Kentucky, in the early 1800s. The younger Forman was one of five children.

Forman was an employee of the local Brown whiskey distillery when, in 1881, he was made a partner in the company along with James Thompson. The firm used the name Brown, Thompson, and Co. for several years, until Thompson eventually withdrew. In 1889 the name was changed to Brown, Forman, and Co. When Forman, who had worked as a bookkeeper before becoming a partner in the firm, died, George Garvin Brown purchased the entire business. Brown incorporated the firm under the name Brown-Forman shortly after Forman's death in compliance with a written agreement he had made with Forman to retain the name.

Forman was married to Hannah Bartley, and the couple had a daughter, Emily Forman. The family lived at 1403 Second St. Forman, who had been in bad health for several years, died after a long illness and is buried in Cave Hill Cemetery.

See *Courier-Journal*, Nov. 21, 1901.

FORT DUFFIELD. In order to protect the Ohio River and the southern approach to Louisville during the Civil War, Gen. William T. Sherman, headquartered in Louisville, ordered a fort built at the confluence of the Salt and Ohio Rivers. Construction of the fort began in November 1861 on Pearman Hill, a bluff overlooking the rivers and the city of West Point in Hardin County. The first garrison consisted of men of the Thirty-seventh Indiana Infantry, from Lawrenceburg, Indiana, and the Ninth Michigan Infantry, from Ft. Wayne, Michigan. Other units serving in the fort included the First Wisconsin Infantry, First Ohio Infantry, the Eighteenth Ohio Infantry, and Lambert's Coldwater Artillery from Michigan. Approximately 950 soldiers were garrisoned at the fort during the winter of 1861–62.

The fort was strategically located at a site overlooking the Ohio and Salt Rivers and the Louisville and Nashville Turnpike. The fort worked as a deterrent to marauding Confederate forces such as those led by Gen. John Hunt Morgan, who in 1863 crossed the Ohio into Indiana at Brandenburg, downriver from West Point.

The fort hugged the side of a high bluff. It was so secure when it was completed that when the request was made for locks for the gates the quartermaster sent two toy locks as a joke. The fortification was constructed of earthen mounds, seventeen feet from the top of the wall to the bottom of the ditch, and nine feet wide at the top of the wall. The fort had ten faces so as to allow line of fire in all directions. It was never challenged. The soldiers constructed their own shelters, a cross between a log cabin and a tent, and also dug their own well, although most water was carried up the steep hill from the river.

After the war the site of the fort remained in private hands until it became part of the Fort Knox Military Reservation. In 1978 the land was given to the city of West Point and named Fort Duffield in recognition of the commander of the Ninth Michigan. In 1992 the Fort Duffield Heritage Committee was appointed by the City Council to raise funds and preserve the site, recognized as one of the most significant Civil War sites in Kentucky because of the size of the earthworks. In 1995 the fort was placed on the National Register of Historic Places.

The earthworks are still visible, although eroded from their original size. The Fort Duffield Preservation Committee works to restore and preserve the fort. An annual "Civil War Days" event has been held at both the fort and West Point since the creation of the committee, with proceeds going toward the preservation of the fort.

W. Daniel Sturgeon

FORT HILL. The neighborhood known traditionally as Fort Hill (but dubbed Meriwether by the city of Louisville about 1975) takes its name from Civil War Fort Horton that occupied a large area of elevated land in the southwest angle of the junction of Meriwether Ave. and Shelby St. This was one of a series of fortifications surrounding Louisville to protect the city from possible Confederate attack. Much of the hill on which the fort stood has been graded away, although it was more or less intact as late as 1905.

The neighborhood is bounded by Shelby St. and the "Schnitzelburg" area of the Germantown neighborhood to the east, and by Preston St. to the west. It extends north to about Ormsby Ave. and south to about Eastern Pkwy. Meriwether Ave. cuts through the neighborhood on an east-west axis. Little is known of the development of the area in the years immediately after the Civil War. By the mid-1880s, however, farmland was being slowly converted to residential and commercial use. Industrial operations sprang up along the railroad opened through the area in 1871. Mule-drawn streetcars on Shelby St. had reached the northern edge of Fort Hill by the late 1870s, but much open land remained and small dairy farms persisted until early in the twentieth century.

The sparse early population was mixed black and white, but by the end of the nineteenth century there were few white residents west of Shelby St. That area west to Preston was practically all African American, most of whom lived on Meriwether and on north-south Bland St. Most are listed in the city directories as laborers. They found employment in the factories along the railroad, the sand and clay quarry that stretched north from Bergman (part of the street was dug away), the Gernert Lumber Yard, and two brick manufacturers. One brickyard was operated by J.H. Egelhoff, who also had a park on Preston St. at the railroad crossing. The park was used by black workingmen for the annual labor celebration held on May 1. (White workingmen observed the day at Phoenix Hill Park on Baxter Ave.)

In 1894 the Shelby Street Colored School, a small frame building, was opened at Shelby and Burnett Ave. During that decade black churches made their appearance. Both the Bland Street Baptist Church and Miles AME Chapel (Methodist), also on Bland St., were founded in the 1890s. In 1905 the Red Cross Sanitarium (no connection to the American Red Cross), the only private medical institution that treated African Americans, moved from downtown Sixth St. to the Fort Hill area at 1436 Shelby St. Red Cross was a two-story frame dwelling that stood almost alone. It operated the only nurse-training program in Kentucky for African Americans. The hospital was later expanded, and in 1951 a new brick building was erected. With the end of segregation in Louisville hospitals, this pioneering institution closed in 1975. The building later housed several programs of the Volunteers of America in Kentucky.

Another institution that closed with the end of segregation in schools in 1956 was the Lincoln Colored School on Bland St. at Morgan Ave. The two-story brick structure had been opened in 1912 to replace the inadequate Shelby St. Colored School. It was located within what is now Lincoln-Preston Park, which memorializes the school in its name.

See *Sanborn Insurance Atlas*, 1892 and 1905 editions; "Street Directory" section of *Caron's Louisville City Directory*, 1884–1915 editions; U.S. Geological Survey topographical map, Eastern Louisville, surveyed 1904–5; U.S. Engineer Corps "Map of Louisville and its Defenses" 1865 (reproduced in *Courier-Journal Magazine,* Sept. 30, 1956); G.T. Bergmann, "Map of Jefferson County," 1858; and *Louisville Post*, April 9, 1891.

George H. Yater

FORT KNOX. Fort Knox lies approximately thirty-five miles south of Louisville in Hardin, Bullitt, and Meade Counties, with its main entrance on U.S. Hwy. 31W. The post encompasses 170.4 square miles, or 109,000 acres, which includes ranges, training areas, and the cantonment area. In its scope of operations and population served, Fort Knox ranks as one of the largest communities in Kentucky. Known as the Home of Mounted Warfare, the post provides training for armor officer and enlisted personnel in both the active and reserve components. Fort Knox offers a unique mix of simulator facilities, gunnery ranges, and maneuver space that attracts units from across the country. The Armor Center also generates armored warfare doctrine and training strategies, and oversees the development of new materiel for armor and cavalry units. Fort Knox provides basic training for new soldiers and houses the U.S. Army Recruiting Command, responsible for worldwide recruiting operations. The Reserve Officer Training Corps Basic Camp, also on post, prepares college students for future army commissions.

Two rivers run through or near Fort Knox—the OHIO and the SALT. Prior to white settlement, these rivers supported an abundance of fish and game, including buffalo. The area became a favored hunting ground for Indian tribes. Between the 1790s and the 1820s, the three counties that Fort Knox now spans were formed—Hardin, BULLITT, and Meade. Further development included the completion of the LOUISVILLE AND NASHVILLE TURNPIKE that now follows the trace of Wilson Rd.

During the CIVIL WAR, troops of both sides operated in the area, and Union fortifications guarded the approaches to Louisville, including FORT DUFFIELD near West Point. In 1862 the Sixth Michigan Infantry built fortifications atop Muldraugh Hill, a ridge within the present-day military reservation. In December 1862 Confederate general John Hunt Morgan, leading the Second Kentucky Cavalry, raided the area and captured Union troops. At Brandenburg in Meade County, just west of Fort Knox, Morgan led his troops across the OHIO RIVER to raid Indiana and Ohio in July 1863.

In 1903 the War Department began seriously considering the Fort Knox area for a permanent military reservation when it established Camp Young as a maneuvers headquarters near West Point. After the United States entered World War I, Congress, on June 25, 1918, allocated $1.6 million to purchase forty thousand acres for Camp Knox. Named after Maj. Gen. Henry Knox, the Revolutionary War chief of artillery and first secretary of war, the post served as an artillery training center. The climate permitted continuous training throughout the year, railroad and roadways provided easy access to the site, and the army had already leased land there as an annex to CAMP ZACHARY TAYLOR in Louisville. The Camp Knox purchase included towns, homes, churches, and farms. The inhabitants dispersed, resulting in the disappearance of many small towns or—as in the case of Stithton—their relocation.

New construction included Godman Army Airfield, which opened in 1918 and became the first airfield in Kentucky. Plans for developing and expanding the post ended with the war. In 1925 it was renamed the Camp Knox National Forest. The National Guard and Reserves continued to use the site for summer training, but only after the assignment of two infantry companies to Camp Knox did it reopen in 1928.

In 1931, when the army was struggling with the concept of mechanization and motor transport of its weapons and troops, Camp Knox became identified with the form of warfare that has become its hallmark. The arrival of the Seventh Cavalry Brigade (Mechanized) transformed the post from an undeveloped training camp into a permanent installation. Its redesignation by Congress as Fort Knox in January 1932 denoted this change. Further expansion and an increase in the scope and pace of activities soon followed. The arrival of more troops on post acted as a boon to local economies still suffering from the GREAT DEPRESSION. A $2.8 million allotment in 1933 went for construction of much of the brick housing, along with the headquarters building, hospital, storage warehouses, barracks, and ordnance facilities. In addition to training and doctrine development for the mechanized cavalry, Fort Knox continued to support National Guard and Reservist training and directed Civilian Conservation Corps work camps. In 1937 the mechanized cavalry personnel provided relief to Louisville and nearby areas devastated by the highest known flood on the Ohio River.

During the 1930s federal authorities determined that gold storage sites, located along the nation's coasts, might be vulnerable to enemy attack. Removed from the threat of air or amphibious attack, accessible by road and rail, and defendable by the Seventh Cavalry Brigade (Mechanized), Fort Knox was chosen as the new location for a bullion depository. Constructed of granite and concrete, the building is 105 feet by 121 feet with a height of 42 feet. The U.S. Bullion Depository opened when the first shipments of gold arrived from New York and Philadelphia in 1937.

The vault has held more than gold. During the second world war many documents were sent from Europe and Washington for safekeeping, including the Lincoln Cathedral copy of the British Magna Carta, the St. Blasius–St. Paul copy of the Gutenberg Bible, the U.S. Declaration of Independence, the U.S. Articles of Confederation of 1778, the signed copy of the Constitution of the United States, ABRAHAM LINCOLN's Gettysburg address of 1863, and the autographed copy of Lincoln's inaugural address of 1865.

WORLD WAR II changed the status of the post. The war's onset quickly demonstrated the value of large armored formations. The army therefore established the armored force with its headquarters at Fort Knox. This new organization bore responsibility for creating armored divisions and corps. By 1945 the armored force had grown to sixteen divisions and more than a hundred separate tank battalions and mechanized cavalry squadrons. The need to train large numbers of officers and enlisted personnel in the operation of armored units resulted in a deluge of military personnel on post.

The establishment of the Armored Force School and Armored Force Replacement Training Center followed in 1940. An initial shortage of military maintenance instructors led to the hiring of civilian instructors from local vocational schools. The post expanded through new construction and land purchases from 864 buildings and 30,000 acres in 1940 to 3,820 buildings and 106,861 acres by 1943. The large-scale construction that occurred during the war years marked Fort Knox's transformation from a small military post to one of the largest communities in Kentucky. Much of the installation's current infrastructure was built during this time. Unfortunately, at the onset of this expansion, the volume of traffic to and from the post made the roads linking Fort Knox to nearby towns among the most dangerous in the country, and DIXIE HWY. was often referred to as "Dixie Dieway."

The end of World War II reduced the scale of Fort Knox's activities, but the rapid onset of the Cold War with the Soviet Union and its allies generated a continuous demand for armored soldiers. Training remained a primary function of the post. The assignment of the 194th Separate Armored Brigade to Fort Knox in 1968 underscored the post's importance and resulted in a steady influx of federal money that filtered into the local communities, fueling their development. Louisville benefited in many ways, including the visitation by soldiers on leave. The presence of Fort Knox was also apparent from the large numbers of soldiers flooding onto the post for training prior to overseas deployment, especially during the KOREAN and VIETNAM WARS. In addition, field testing of vehicles often occurred at nearby Otter Creek Park, owned by the city of Louisville. In 1989 the Eighth Attack Helicopter Battalion and the 229th Aviation Regiment were activated at Fort Knox, filling local skies with the sound of "choppers."

The 1990s opened with the Gulf War in the Middle East. Fort Knox commenced continuous operations to assist units deploying to the Persian Gulf. The post received its largest mobilization since the Vietnam War, resulting in large numbers of activated reservists arriving at the installation for training. The Armor Center in turn contracted additional support from the surrounding communities. Following the war's conclusion, however, Fort Knox felt the effects of army downsizing. Although the U.S. Army Recruiting Command relocated to the post in 1992, the 194th Separate Armored Brigade was deactivated in 1995, and the civilian workforce steadily shrank throughout the decade.

The Armor Center, however, remains an important contributor to the army's ongoing modernization. It continues to establish new precedents in the use of computer-based and simulation-based training. Army needs drive Armor Center work upon the next generation of combat vehicles and the application of information technology to the battlefield. The Armor Center also works to keep soldiers prepared to operate anywhere in the world, evidenced by the construction of an urban training site. This emphasis upon soldier preparedness has been a central feature of the post's continuing history, and it is embodied in the large numbers of retired military personnel who reside in the surrounding communities and represent Fort Knox's heritage.

See Katherine Grandine, Leo Hirrel, Deborah Cannan, and Hampton Tucker, "Inventory, Evaluation, and Nomination of Military Installations: Fort Knox, Kentucky," Feb. 17, 1994; Gary Kempf, "Fort Knox History: Battles, Maps, Extinct Towns, Churches, Schools, and Historic Vignettes,"unpublished survey, 1996; Addison F. McGhee, "Fort Knox, Home of Armored Command," Presentation to Filson Club, 1944; United States Army Armor Center, *1998 Fort Knox Post Guide*; United States Army Armor Center, *Fort Knox Pam 360–2: This is Armor; Forging the Thunderbolt*, June 1, 1998; Lucian K. Truscott Jr., *The Twilight of U.S. Cavalry: Life in the Old Army, 1917–1942* (Lawrence, Kans., 1989).

Robert S. Cameron

FORT NELSON. The establishment of a settlement at the FALLS OF THE OHIO during the Revolutionary War (1775–83) was a perilous advance into hostile territory. When the settlers, who came to the Falls with GEORGE ROGERS CLARK, left CORN ISLAND in 1779, they built a fort at what is now the foot of Twelfth St. This fort, referred to by several names including Fort-on-Shore, was soon superseded by a much larger fortification, Fort Nelson, named after Gov. Thomas Nelson of Virginia. The fort was built north of present-day MAIN ST. between Seventh and Eighth Streets. Construction was probably begun by Clark's troops under the command of George Slaughter late in 1780 and completed by March 1781. RICHARD CHENOWETH, an early settler, also played an important role in the construction of the fort. He contributed money and supplies to the project, for which his heirs later sought compensation.

Fort Nelson was an impressive structure that covered an acre. It was surrounded by a ditch with spikes in the bottom. The dirt from the ditch was used to help strengthen the outer walls of the fort, which supposedly were capable of resisting cannon fire.

Fort Nelson was called the strongest fort in the West besides Fort Pitt, and its strength undoubtedly discouraged attack. Ironically the fort was built late in the Revolutionary War when the need for it had almost disappeared. By the late 1780s there were reports that the fort had been abandoned and was in poor condition, particularly after the construction of Fort Finney (later FORT STEUBEN) at the future site of JEFFERSONVILLE, INDIANA, by the United States Army in 1786. A marker commemorates the site of Fort Nelson.

See Nelson L. Dawson, "A Note on Fort Nelson," *Journal of Kentucky Studies* 2 (1985): 225–27.

Nelson L. Dawson

FORT STEUBEN. Fort Steuben was established by the United States Army in 1786 at present JEFFERSONVILLE, INDIANA, as part of a defensive system of forts north of the OHIO RIVER to help defend settlers against hostile Indians. Originally christened Fort Finney in honor of Capt. Walter Finney, it was renamed Fort Steuben in honor of Revolutionary War hero Baron Friedrich Wilhelm von Steuben in 1789.

Located at the foot of present Fort St., it was described by Lt. Erskurius Beatty in 1787 as being on a "beautiful bank about half a mile above the beginning of the Rapids, on the Indiana shore . . . a very strong defensible fort, built of block houses and pickets about 90 yards from the margin of the river." A deep trench, covered with logs and dirt in order to make a tunnel, was dug from the fort to the river in order to assure a supply of water and an escape route.

Fort Steuben served as the center of military activity in the Falls area. The garrison comprised two companies from the First U.S. Infantry, but in 1791, as the threat to the area declined and the theater of operations against the Indians shifted elsewhere, it was reduced to sixty-one soldiers. Its commanders included Captain Finney, Maj. John Wyllys, Capt. John Armstrong (who is buried on the property he owned in Clark County), and Capt. Joseph Ashton. Fort Steuben apparently was abandoned as an official army post in 1791, although U.S. troops continued to use it until at least 1793. It was used until the late 1790s or early 1800s by militia troops. A diagram and sketch of the fort are in the John Armstrong papers at the Indiana Historical Society. All trace of the fort has vanished, and in 1843 the post cemetery was relocated to the Mulberry St. cemetery in Jeffersonville.

See diary of Erkuries [sic] Beatty, New York Historical Society, published in the *Magazine of American History*, vol. 1, no. 7 (1877); Lewis C. Baird, *Baird's History of Clark County, Indiana* (Indianapolis 1909).

James J. Holmberg

FOSSEY, DIAN JEANNE (b San Francisco, California, January 16, 1932; d Virunga Mountains, Rwanda, Africa, December 27, 1985). Zoologist. Daughter of George and Kitty Fossey, Dian received a degree as an occupational therapist from San Jose (California) State College in 1954 and, after two years of further study, moved to Louisville. Although the world-renowned zoologist was said to have taken an interest in horses, among other animals, during her undergraduate years, little is known of her reasons for relocating to the Ohio Valley. Upon her arrival in 1956, she rented a cottage at Glenmary Farm, south of FERN CREEK and off of Bardstown Rd. She became the director of the occupational therapy department for the KOSAIR CHILDREN'S HOSPITAL on Eastern Pkwy.

However, Fossey's desire to work with animals and travel to Africa, which she claimed to be her destiny, impaired her work in the hospital. After scraping together some funds and taking out an eight-thousand-dollar loan, Fossey set out on a seven-week African safari in September 1963. During a stop at the Olduvai Gorge in Tanzania, she told Louis and Mary Leakey of her desire to study the mountain gorilla in its natural habitat.

Fossey returned to Louisville, studied the piano, joined the Louisville Writers' Club, and moved into a house north of McNeely Lake Park on Pennsylvania Run Rd. When Louis Leakey, in Louisville for a speaking engagement, encouraged the burgeoning scientist to head to Africa with a National Geographic grant, Fossey did so. In late 1966 Fossey left for Zaire, Rwanda, and fame.

Gorillas in the Mist, her memoirs and tales of her findings, was published in 1983, two years before her brutal murder by unidentified assailants in the jungle at the Karisoke Research Institute in Rwanda. In the book, Fossey details her findings concerning the behavioral patterns, identifying sounds, and nurturing family life of the endangered gorilla and also discusses the poaching that had decimated the gorilla population. Her life story was made into a motion picture, *Gorillas in the Mist*.

See Charles Mortiz, ed., *Current Biography Yearbook, 1985* (New York 1985); Farley Mowat, *Woman in the Mists* (New York 1987).

FOSSILS. A fossil is evidence of prehistoric life, usually preserved in rock. Plants and animals are the most common fossils; bacteria and fungi are rare. A trace fossil is indirect evidence of an animal, such as tracks, trails, borings, and coprolites (excrement).

The most ancient fossils are the more-than-3-billion-year-old single-celled bacteria. The youngest fossils may be leaf impressions or bones in travertine (calcium carbonate) in caves and only a few years old (not prehistoric).

A view of the exposed Devonian period fossils at the Falls of the Ohio.

Fossils are found throughout the Louisville metropolitan area. Rocks with fossils were deposited mainly during the Paleozoic era and include Ordovician (445 to 440 million years ago), Silurian (440 to 425 m.y.a.), Devonian (390 to 365 m.y.a.), and Mississippian (365 to 345 m.y.a.) periods. Younger rocks are absent in the Louisville area except for deposits of the Pleistocene (Ice Age) and Holocene (Recent) Epochs. Pleistocene fossils are associated with river and cave deposits and are typically ten thousand to fifty thousand years old. Holocene fossils are associated with cave springs such as those in Cherokee Park or two-thousand–year-old lake deposits along the OHIO RIVER. Charles Butts published a comprehensive survey of Louisville area fossils in 1915.

The Louisville area contains over a thousand species of fossils ranging from microscopic single-celled foraminfera to large colonial corals and mammoth and mastodon skeletal remains. Ten animal phyla are present as well as algae, rushes, and woody plants. Only groups of fossils found in area rocks are described here.

Kingdom Protista is represented by one-celled radiolarians and foraminifers that lived in marine environments. Some foraminifers and radiolarians from the Louisville area are illustrated by Conkin and Conkin (1976).

Sponges (Phylum Porifera) are among the most simple multicellular organisms. Relatively rare in the fossil record, they are occasionally found in some Silurian, Devonian, and Mississippian formations in the metropolitan area.

Stromatoporoids have only recently been classified in the Phylum Porifera, and not all paleontologists are in agreement with that assignment. Locally, stromatoporoids are much more common than regular sponges. In the Upper Ordovician "coral reefs," *Aulocerас*, a tubular stromatoporoid, is one of the easiest to identify. The Middle Silurian Louisville Limestone has mound- or sheet-shaped varieties that are generally less than twelve inches (30 cm.) across. The Middle Devonian Jeffersonville Limestone varieties show the greatest variation in size. Some are as small as six inches (15 cm.) wide but commonly are much larger. The FALLS OF THE OHIO has a sheet-like stromatoporoid that is traceable for more than seventy-five feet (23 m.) on one rock ledge!

Corals (Phylum Cnidaria) are among the most common fossils in Jefferson County. There are several hundred species that have been described. Modern corals are exclusively marine and are commonly found at tropical latitudes. Paleozoic species likely inhabited a similar environment. Soft-bodied cnidarians, such as jellyfish, are unknown from area rocks.

Within local Devonian rocks, over two hundred corals have been described, more than anywhere else in the world (Stumm, 1964, discusses and illustrates most of them). However, many were described from poorly preserved specimens, and further studies may reduce the number of species. Local Silurian rocks contain over seventy coral species. Ordovician and Mississippian formations contain significantly fewer.

Three of the six orders of "true" corals can be found in the Louisville area. Those in Order Tabulata are commonly called "honeycomb" corals because of their superficial resemblance to honeycomb in a beehive. The largest may exceed fifteen feet (3 m.) in diameter, but most are less than two feet (0.6 m.).

Corals of Order Rugosa are called "horn corals" because of their resemblance to a cow's horn. There are great variations among them; some are solitary, others colonial. Some are button-like, while others are as straight as a building column. The largest known solitary rugose coral is *Siphonophrentis elongata.* One curved specimen at the Falls of the Ohio measures over four feet (1.2 m.) in length! The smallest "horn" coral (found in southern Indiana) is *Hadrophyllum orbignyi,* which may be the size of a dime and only slightly thicker.

Colonial rugose corals form mounds from a few inches to many feet across. Some varieties resemble tubes of a pipe organ. Others have individual corals in contact forming hexagonal shapes.

Order Heliolitida is found in Silurian rocks and is distinguished by a sponge-like texture between corallites (the individual coral cells within a colony).

Conularids are organisms that are sometimes placed with cnidarians, although most paleontologists have doubts about this assignment. In the Louisville area they are most common in Mississippian-age rocks. Conularids resemble a slender, four-sided pyramid with a four-part "trap door" at the wide end. The exoskeleton is closely grooved and may be composed of chitinous or phosphatic material.

Of the fourteen phyla of worms, only Phylum Annelida has a significant fossil record. Annelid jaw elements are found in area rocks; soft body parts are not preserved. Jaws are composed of glossy black calcium phosphate and are usually less than five millimeters in length.

Evidence of other worms (including annelids) occur as trace fossils within many rock strata, especially the Upper Ordovician Drakes Formation, Middle Silurian Osgood Formation, Middle and Upper Devonian New Albany Shale, and the Lower Mississippian Borden Formation.

Trilobites are in the phylum Arthropoda, the joint-legged animals. Some trilobites had the ability to roll up like a garden pill bug.

Many trilobites are known from the Louisville area. Most are molts shed by the growing animal. Heads, tails, or tail/mid-section combinations are typically observed. Whole trilobites are rare but include the Ordovician *Flexicalymene meeki,* Silurian *Calymene breviceps,* Devonian *Phacops rana,* and Mississippian *Phillibole conkini.*

The largest trilobites that lived in our ancient seas include the Ordovician *Isotelus*, perhaps twenty inches (50 cm.) long; Silurian *Arctinurus*, up to ten inches (25 cm.) long; and Devonian *Odontocephalus*, known to be as long as sixteen inches (40 cm.). The *Silurian Maurotarion christyi* is the smallest. Two would fit end to end on a dime.

Ostracods are a tiny bivalved arthropod that

can still be found in freshwater ponds and streams in the Louisville area. The carapace resembles a tiny bean. Reported from many of the Paleozoic rocks of the metropolitan area, they are abundant in the Hitz Limestone Bed of the Saluda Dolomite Member of the Drakes Formation (Ordovician).

Representatives of Phylum Mollusca in area rocks include the classes Pelecypoda or Bivalvia (clams), Gastropoda (snails), Cephalopoda (relatives of the squid and octopus), snail-like Monoplacophora (tergomya), and bivalve-like Rostroconchia.

Pelecypods (bivalves) are common in the Ordovician as internal casts. There are many varieties. *Caritodens* is one of the most recognizable, like a scallop without ribs crossing the shell. *Paracyclas* and *Modiomorphia* are among the most common Devonian pelecypods. Silurian and Mississippian clams are less common.

Gastropods are more abundant than clams in local rocks. *Cyclonema* is the most widespread Ordovician snail in the area. *Platystoma* dominates the Silurian snail FAUNA. In the Devonian rocks, the giant *Turbonopsis shumardi* is the largest, up to four inches (10 cm.) across. The most bizarre gastropod, *Platyceras dumosum,* was protected by long spines. The Mississippian Coral Ridge fauna is dominated by a single gastropod, *Glabrocingulum ellenae.* Faunal remains have been replaced by iron sulfide, or pyrite, rather than the more common calcium carbonate or silicon dioxide.

Cephalopods are related to the squid and octopus. The modern *Nautilis* is one of the few remaining living species. Nautiloid cephalopods (ancestors of the modern form) are commonly found in Ordovician rocks. Its shell may be coiled or cone-shaped, divided into many chambers. Cephalopods are usually found incomplete, often an inch wide (2.5 cm.) and from a few inches to a foot (30 cm.) in length.

Silurian and Devonian cephalopods are rarer. The orthocone (straight-coned) shapes are more common than the coiled species. The Silurian *Dawsonoceras* has a zigzag pattern on the suture.

The Mississippian Coral Ridge fauna has a number of species of goniatites, a variety of coiled nautiloid cephalopods. Most are smaller than a dime. The most common variety is *Polaricyclus*, some of which are as small as BBs. It, along with the somewhat less common disklike *Michiganites greeni* have sinuous sutures.

Monoplacophorans are snail-like mollusks that are only found in the deep ocean. *Cyrtolites Ornatus* is an Ordovician species, while *Sinuitina annae* is from the younger Coral Ridge fauna.

Rostroconchs are the only extinct order of mollusks. Their shells resemble a trilobite but are heart-shaped in cross-section. Most common is the Devonian genus *Hippocardia.*

Brachiopods (Phylum Brachiopoda) are the most abundant fossil shells in the Louisville area. Many rock formations contain a few to dozens of species. Whereas the top and bottom valve of a clam are generally symmetrical, that is not the case with brachiopods. Their left and right sides are symmetrical, but the top and bottom valves are not. In life, they were filter-feeders attached to a substrate for life (much like barnacles).

Inarticulate brachiopods are usually attached to a hard substrate or buried deep in the sediment. The two valves are held together by muscles. Articulate brachiopods have a tooth-and-socket system to keep the valves aligned. Five orders of articulate brachiopods can be found in area strata. They vary from the size of a large sand grain to five inches (13 cm.) in diameter.

Members of Phylum Bryozoa are colonial organisms composed of dozens to thousands of individual members called zooids. Colonies form a variety of shapes and sizes. Among the most interesting are the fenestrate bryozoa, which look like lace or netting. Others form antler-like branches, mounds, flattened/erect, interconnecting branches, or irregular shapes.

Well-known living members of Phylum Echinodermata include starfish, sea urchins, and sand dollars. Echinoderms are exclusively marine and are characterized by five-fold symmetry. During the Paleozoic Era, they were dominated by crinoids. Paleozoic crinoids were stalked animals with a small body supporting long comb-like arms that filter-fed on plankton. Crinoids are common in the fossil record, especially as disk-like columnals that are sometimes called "Indian beads." Some rock layers, like the Beechwood Limestone member of the North Vernon Limestone (Devonian) and parts of the New Providence Shale member of the Borden Formation (Mississippian), are composed of countless numbers of columnals. Complete crinoid "crowns" containing the arms and body (the calyx) are rarely preserved in area rocks.

"Horn" corals found at the Falls of the Ohio.

Blastoids were similar to crinoids, with a more robust nut-shaped body. The delicate tentacles and stalk are never preserved. Blastoids are rare but can occasionally be found in Devonian and Mississippian rocks.

Cystoids have been divided into two echinoderm classes, Rhombifera and Diplopora. While relatively rare, the rhombiferan *Caryocrinites* is the most common variety found in the area. Cystoids existed from the Ordovician into the Devonian Period.

Echinoids (sea urchins) are first known from the Ordovician Period. Locally, their spines and plates can be found in Mississippian rocks in the southwestern part of the county. Complete echinoids are very rare. Starfish (asteroids) and brittlestars (ophiuroids) are virtually unknown from area rocks, although they no doubt lived in the warm shallow Paleozoic seas.

Graptolites (Phylum Hemichordata) are colonial marine organisms that may be found as carbonized remains in some layers. Although not very common, some Ordovician layers may have hundreds per square foot. Planktonic graptolites are often black and linear with a serrated edge. Bottom-dwelling graptolites have a web of interconnecting branches.

Plant fossils are found in the Louisville area. The largest are logs of petrified "driftwood" in the Devonian New Albany shale. Specimens up to a thousand pounds are known. On the small end of the scale, eggs of freshwater charophyte algae *Moellerina greeni* are common in some layers of the Devonian Jeffersonville Limestone. Their association with marine fossils indicates that islands with freshwater pools were located nearby.

Holocene plants can be found in two-thousand-year-old lake beds along the Ohio River, especially near SILVER CREEK. Leaves are typical of trees of a cooler climate. Microscopic pollen is preserved in some sediments.

Vertebrate fossils are rare in the Louisville area. Fish remains (teeth, isolated bones, and scales) are occasionally found in Devonian and Mississippian rocks. Most remains are very small but may exceed six inches (15 cm.). Fossil fish material are from sharks, arthodires (extinct armored fish), and paleoniscids (ancestors of modern bony fish).

Pleistocene mammal remains are known from river and cave deposits. Bones, teeth, and tusks of mammoths, mastodons, and other animals have been found in sand and gravel deposits. Complete peccary (pig) and smaller mammal skeletal remains have been found in some cave sediments.

See James E. Conkin and Barbara M. Conkin, *Guide to the Rocks and Fossils of Jefferson County, Kentucky, Southern Indiana, and Adjacent Areas* (Louisville 1976); W.R. Jillson, *The Paleontology of Kentucky,* series 6, vol. 36, 1931; S.F. Greb, R.T. Hendricks, and D.R. Chesnut

Jr., *Fossil Beds of the Falls of the Ohio*, Kentucky Geological Survey, series 11, Special Publication, 1993; E.C. Stumm, *Silurian and Devonian Corals of the Falls of the Ohio,* Geological Society of America Memoirs, vol. 93, 1964; Charles Butts, *Geology and Mineral Resources of Jefferson County, Kentucky,* Kentucky Geological Survey, series 4, vol. 3, part 2, 1915.

Alan Goldstein

FOSSILS AT THE FALLS OF THE OHIO. The FALLS OF THE OHIO is world famous for its fossil beds, notably abundant corals and stromatoporoids (ancestral calcareous sponges), in the Devonian Jeffersonville Limestone (385 million years old). Coral FOSSILS include patch reefs and extraordinary specimens of solitary, horn-shaped corals. Other prominent invertebrate fossils include crinoids (sea lilies), brachiopods (lamp shells), bryozoans (moss animals), snails, clams, trilobites, ostracods (bean-shaped crustaceans), and blastoids (bud-shaped echinoderms). The total number of valid species may exceed four hundred.

Several fish-bone beds occur at the Falls. Layers of rock with concentrations of teeth and tiny bone fragments of fish, often too small for the human eye to detect, are associated with brief intervals between sediment deposition. Fish-bone beds and fossils are generally used by geologists and paleontologists as a tool to correlate rock beds in different areas.

Studies of fossils from the Falls began in the 1820s. The fossil beds in the Jeffersonville Limestone have been divided into five zones, named after prominent fossils and listed below along with their thickness and common fossils:

Middle Devonian
New Albany Shale
Sellersburg Limestone
  Beechwood Limestone Member
  Silver Creek Limestone Member
Jeffersonville Limestone
  Paraspirifer acuminatus (brachiopod) zone (6 feet thick)
    brachiopods fenestrate bryzoans, snails
  Bryozoan-brachiopod zone (6 feet thick)
    fenestrate bryozoans, brachiopods, crinoids, blastoids, snails, solitary and colonial corals
  Brevispirifer gregarius (brachiopod) zone (4.5 feet thick)
    brachiopods, solitary and colonial corals, snails, clams
  Amphipora ramosa (stromatoporoid) zone (8.5 feet thick)
    stromatoporoids, solitary and colonial corals
  Coral Zone (10 feet thick)
    Solitary and colonial corals, stromatoporoids, fenestrate bryozoans, crinoids, brachiopods

Middle Silurian
Louisville Limestone (oldest exposed rocks)

During Middle Devonian time, the Falls area was covered by a shallow, tropical sea. The earth's continents had not yet moved into their present positions, and the site of the Falls was located fifteen to twenty degrees south of the equator. The reef at the Falls presents fossil evidence of the shallow, clear, tropical waters associated with milder latitudes and of plate tectonic movement (continental drift). The intermixing of fresh- to brackish-water stonewort algae with marine organisms and bone-bed beach deposits overlying wave-cut surfaces of marine erosion indicate the presence of a nearby land mass as well as widespread shallow seas.

See David Dale Owen, *Second Report of the Geological Survey in Kentucky during the years 1856 and 1857* (Frankfort 1857); Erwin C. Stumm, *Silurian and Devonian Corals of the Falls of the Ohio* (New York 1964); Henry Nettleroth, *Kentucky Fossil Shells, A Monograph of the Fossil Shells of the Silurian and Devonian Rocks of Kentucky* (Frankfort 1889); E.M. Kindle, *The Devonian Fossils and Stratigraphy of Indiana* (Indianapolis 1901); James E. Conkin and Barbara M. Conkin, *Guide to the Rocks and Fossils of Jefferson County, Kentucky, Southern Indiana, and Adjacent Areas,* second edition (Louisville 1976); J.E. Conkin et al., *Devonian and Mississippian Foraminiferans of Southern Indiana and Northwestern Kentucky* (Falls Church, Va., 1979); J.E. Conkin and B.M. Conkin, "North American Primitive Charophytes and Descendants" in Robert C. Roman, ed., *Geobotany* (New York 1977); Stephen F. Greb, R. Todd Hendricks, and Donald R. Chestnut Jr., *Fossil Beds of the Falls of the Ohio* (Lexington 1993); R. Todd Hendricks, Frank R. Ettensohn, T. Joshua Stark, and Stephen F. Greb, *Geology of the Devonian Strata of the Falls of the Ohio Area, Kentucky-Indiana: Stratigraphy, Sedimentology, Paleontology, Wtructure, and Diagenesis* (Lexington 1994).

James E. Conkin

FOUNDERS SQUARE. In December 1966 Mayor Kenneth Schmied revealed plans for a new plaza to be built on the north side of Walnut St. (MUHAMMAD ALI Blvd.) between Armory Place and Fifth St. The plaza, opened in 1970 at a cost of $1 million, was financed by four hundred thousand dollars in federal funds and a bond issue passed in 1965. The centerpiece of the plaza was a visitors' center run by the Convention Bureau and the Chamber of Commerce. The ultramodern structure designed by Louisville architect Lawrence Melillo consisted of large glass panels supported by spider-like girding outside the glass. It had surrounding fountains within a moat. The center was originally in an ideal location, directly across from the Convention Center (later Louisville Gardens, now THE GARDENS OF LOUISVILLE), and attracted as many as three thousand visitors per month. But it began to decline when the new Commonwealth Convention Center opened several blocks away in the late 1970s. By the mid-1980s, the center had fallen upon hard times and into disrepair. The number of visitors had dwindled to a thousand per month, half of whom were local residents. The tourist information center closed in 1987, and the structure was razed in 1992. The square was converted into a landscaped plaza with walkways that ran from each corner toward the center. Wood benches were added to the polished granite benches left over from the original Founders Square. Although a 1991 Massachusetts landscape architectural firm's proposed $1 million plan to redevelop Founders Square with shade trees, a fountain, and glass pillars never materialized, in 1998 it got a facelift with new walkways and landscaping. It hosts music festivals during the spring and summer months.

See *Courier-Journal,* Oct. 2, 1998.

FOURTEENTH STREET (RAILROAD) BRIDGE. Although an attempt was made to bridge the OHIO RIVER at Louisville as early as the 1830s, not until 1870 was the river—a mile wide at this point—spanned to Indiana. The first attempt to build a bridge was spearheaded in 1829 by JAMES GUTHRIE through the Ohio Bridge Co.

The bridge was to be a wooden structure built by Ithiel Town, a New England architect/engineer, using his patented Town lattice truss. Although a cornerstone was laid at the foot of Twelfth St. in 1836 amid great ceremony, nothing more was done. The panic of 1837 brought the project to a halt. Attempts to finance a bridge in the 1850s also failed, as did a proposal for a tunnel under the river.

But with the construction of the LOUISVILLE & NASHVILLE RAILROAD and a railroad stretching north from JEFFERSONVILLE to Indianapolis, the project became not only feasible but essential. The Louisville Bridge Co., financed largely by the L&N Railroad, headed by Guthrie, began work on August 1, 1867. Stone from QUARRIES at UTICA, INDIANA, and Bardstown Junction, Kentucky, were used to construct the piers. The bridge was designed by German-born ALBERT FINK, using his Fink truss. At one mile in length, the twenty-seven-span bridge was the longest iron bridge in the United States at the time. Two of the spans were built with overhead trusses to give clearance to STEAMBOATS passing through the Kentucky and Indiana chutes of the FALLS OF THE OHIO. The LOUISVILLE AND PORTLAND CANAL was crossed on a revolving span that swung open to permit boats to pass. The first train crossed the completed bridge on February 18, 1870, and the expanding rail networks of the North and South were connected. Soon, commuter trains known as "Dinkeys" served Louisville, NEW ALBANY, and Jeffersonville.

In the mid-1870s the trackage between Jeffersonville and Indianapolis came under the control of the giant Pennsylvania Railroad, which also acquired L&N's 60 percent interest in the bridge. Traffic boomed, and by 1882 there

Fourteenth Street Bridge designed by L&N chief engineer Albert Fink and completed in 1870.

were 150 train movements each day. The pioneer use of semaphore signals on single track was instituted to handle the flow. But as traffic continued to increase (over three hundred movements per day early in the twentieth century) and train weights grew heavier, the 1870 bridge became inadequate.

In May 1916 work began on a new double-track, steel superstructure erected on the original reinforced piers. The new bridge was opened in January 1919. It included one span of 645 feet over the Indiana Chute, replacing two of the original spans. The pier in the chute was removed to improve navigation. The swing span over the canal was replaced by a lift span.

The bridge has had several owners and informal names through the years. Unlike public bridges, railroad bridges generally do not have a formal name. It was known as the Pennsylvania bridge during that railroad's ownership until 1968. Then the Pennsylvania and New York Central RAILROADS merged to form Penn-Central. The latter, in turn, was included in the Consolidated Rail Corp. (Conrail), formed in 1976. In March 1994 Conrail sold the bridge and the line to Indianapolis to the Louisville and Indiana Railroad. Regardless of ownerships the structure has not changed location. It has been at Fourteenth St. since 1870 in both its incarnations.

See *Louisville Daily Journal*, Aug. 2, 1867; *Louisville Commercial*, Feb. 19, 1870; Carl W. Condit, *American Building Art: The Nineteenth Century* (New York 1960).

George H. Yater

FOURTH AVENUE UNITED METHODIST CHURCH. Fourth Avenue United Methodist Church, 318 W St. Catherine St. at the corner of Fourth, is on the NATIONAL REGISTER OF HISTORIC PLACES (1979). Its 111 charter members, drawn largely from three other congregations of the then–Methodist Episcopal church, South, first worshiped together on December 16, 1888. Their original church is now a parlor, and the current sanctuary was opened in January 1902.

Fourth Avenue's exterior is English Perpendicular Gothic Revival, appropriate to Methodism's birth in the Church of England during the eighteenth century. The interior employs the semicircular seating configuration, gently sloping floor, raised pulpit dais, and elevated central choir loft; it is an auditorium model designed primarily for preachers, singers, and listeners. The mahogany of the pews, wainscoting, gallery rail, and hammerbeam arches of the vaulted ceiling, plus the elaborate stained glass windows, testify to the turn-of-the-century affluence that generated a hundred thousand dollars to realize the design of WILLIAM J. DODD, architect of many houses and churches in OLD LOUISVILLE. Altogether Fourth Avenue's building manifests the church's origins and early development during the height of the power of urban Protestantism.

Until 1957 Fourth Avenue was a so-called "transfer church." These large urban churches had pastors assigned from all across the denomination, not from the regional conferences in which they were located. One of Fourth Avenue's pastors, William B. Beauchamp (1906–10), and one of its associate pastors, Edward L. Tullis (1944–47), became bishops. The 1920s through the 1940s were boom decades for the church. Membership grew from 650 to 1,462 in the 1920s under Pastor J.W. Johnson (1920–31), requiring the addition of an education building in 1922. The WORLD WAR II decade under Pastor Ira M. Hargett (1939–51) was the church's golden era in terms of the traditional indices of institutional strength. The membership went from 1,631 to 2,318 to become the largest membership METHODIST church in Kentucky. Beginning in 1944, Easter Day services were held in Memorial Auditorium, one block away, to accommodate the crowds. Membership began to decline in 1951, and the Auditorium Easter services ended in 1955.

Pastors Fred R. Pfisterer, James O. Thurmond, and William W. Bowling (covering 1964–81) led the church into COMMUNITY MINISTRIES. Dr. Pfisterer was an organizing force and the first president (1969) of the Neighborhood Development Corp. that addresses housing, social services, economic development, and ethnic relations in Old Louisville. Fourth Avenue member Mae Salyers served ten years as executive director of NDC (1971–81).

Under its first AFRICAN AMERICAN pastor, Edgar S. Goins Sr. (1991–97), Fourth Avenue achieved full commitment to being a metropolitan, intercultural, diverse community of faith. Symbolic of this new direction for a historic congregation was Fourth Avenue's leadership role in the 1992 United Methodist General Conference, which met in Louisville. William O. Yates cochaired the annual conference committee to host this gathering of the United Methodist world parish, and the major Sunday service of the denomination's global governing body was held at Fourth Avenue. Fourth Avenue Church was selected in 1998 by the President's Initiative on Race as a promising practice toward one America. In 1999 the official full membership was 331 with a total pastoral constituency of 412.

See "A Brief History of Fourth Avenue Methodist Church, 1888–1968"; "Fourth Avenue United Methodist Church: 105th Anniversary Celebration 1888–1993": Marjorie Anderson Circle, "Fourth Avenue United Methodist Church: 1888–1973"; R. Kenneth Lile, *Thy Hand Hath Provided: A Historical Rhapsody in Five Movements* (Franklin, Tenn., 1996).

Charles W. Brockwell Jr.

FOURTH STREET. Once the residence address of prominent merchants, Fourth St. became downtown Louisville's primary retail, corporate, and entertainment corridor throughout much of the nineteenth and twentieth centuries. Stretching from BROADWAY north to the OHIO RIVER, the seven blocks comprising inner-city Fourth St. have seen a dramatic, two-hundred-year transition from pastoral to residential use, followed by rapid commercial growth, urban decay, and sweeping revitalization.

A natural radius from the Louisville wharf's bustling STEAMBOAT trade and post–CIVIL WAR building boom, Fourth St. of the nineteenth century evolved to become the bedroom counterpart of MAIN and MARKET STREETS' commerce: a resplendent neighborhood of fine brick homes, many of the city's founding churches, and leisurely entertainment. Typical were *COURIER-JOURNAL* editor HENRY WATTERSON's two-story home of the 1880s located opposite Fourth Street's St. Joseph Infirmary (1853–1926) between Broadway and Chestnut St., and Union general DON CARLOS BUELL's 1862 headquarters on the west side of Fourth near Walnut St. (Muhammad Ali Blvd.). Buell's three-story command post was a neighbor of the

Fourth Street looking north from south of Walnut (Muhammad Ali Blvd.), ca. 1908.

WALNUT STREET BAPTIST CHURCH, constructed in 1853–54. Beginning with the PRESBYTERIANS' 1816 house of worship between Market and Jefferson, Fourth St. soon became the axis along which many of Louisville's new churches were built: First Christian at Fourth and Walnut, Warren Memorial at Fourth and Broadway, the Church of the Messiah at Fourth and York Streets, and Calvary Episcopal on Fourth south of York.

Fourth St. was the place for generations of diners, shoppers, theatergoers and urbanites to see and be seen. The city's finest confectionery since the 1870s, SOLGER'S (later the site of the BROWN HOTEL in 1923), was a popular stroll across Fourth and Broadway from the HA-WI-AN GARDENS dance hall on the northwest corner (site of the Martin Brown Building in 1926; enlarged to the 1955–94 Commonwealth Building).

JENNIE BENEDICT'S Tea Room, at two Fourth St. locations in 1900 and 1911, was also a gracious and relaxing destination for downtown shoppers. The Canary Cottage, Thompson's restaurant, the Orange Bar, the BLUE BOAR, and COLONNADE CAFETERIA, among other landmark RESTAURANTS, satisfied Louisville appetites for decades. KUNZ'S, with eight former downtown locations, still remains as Fourth Street's oldest restaurant, continuously operating since 1892.

The SEELBACH HOTEL, opened in 1905, helped transform Fourth and Walnut into the crossroads of downtown, known for its "four-S" corners of Seelbach, Selman's, the STARKS BUILDING, and Stewart's. Constructed in 1907, the massive STEWART'S DRY GOODS CO. competed with KAUFMAN-STRAUS, J. BACONS, Jefferson Dry Goods, Livingston's, plus an entire promenade of other Fourth St. department, specialty, and dime stores. Until the advent of enclosed suburban malls and a convenient expressway system, walking along Fourth St. was a treasured way of life for Louisville families intent upon a day-long mix of shopping, dining, and perhaps the reward of a movie or stage performance. Often included on the itinerary was the opulent Rialto, Louisville's first grand motion picture and vaudeville palace, which, in 1921, immediately outshone the adjacent MARY ANDERSON Theatre and smaller one-reel movie houses. Almost directly across Fourth, Loew's State (later Loew's/United Artists/Penthouse) opened in 1928 as a Spanish Baroque adventure. It later became the Palace. In 1968 the thirty-five-hundred-seat Rialto joined the Majestic, Old Masonic, Rex, Star, Kentucky, and later the Ohio, on Fourth Street's obituary of THEATER memories.

By 1969 aging buildings and dwindling crowds along the once-bustling thoroughfare signaled the need for change, resulting in the 1970s' RIVER CITY MALL for pedestrians only. (The name was changed to Fourth Avenue in 1981 to reflect a longtime unofficial use dating back to the early century). However, the people and their automobiles that had once been the lifeblood of Fourth St. were to be found at outlying malls, cinemas, and restaurants. Cleared lots and vacant storefronts peppered along Fourth reflected fears of inner-city blight and crime. The GALT HOUSE, RIVERFRONT PLAZA/BELVEDERE, Commonwealth Convention Center, and Hyatt Hotel of the 1970s marked major commitments to downtown redevelopment, as did the major 1980s restorations of the Brown and the Seelbach Hotels. Soon, opening of the block-long GALLERIA in September 1982, followed by TOONERVILLE II trolley shuttle service in 1987, pumped new life into Fourth Street's heart. The 1990s Palace Theatre restoration, Providian Tower and Plaza, and reopening of parts of Fourth to two-way auto traffic continued the theme of downtown redevelopment with Fourth St. as a vital element. By the late 1990s the Galleria was being reviewed for possible removal to permit more of the street to be reopened to traffic.

To illustrate the importance of Fourth St. in the commercial life of Louisville, the following businesses are a sample of those found in the 600 block between Chestnut St. and Broadway in 1951:

Southern Optical Co.
Taylor Drug Stores
First National Bank
Gem—The Gift Shop
Leo L. Baach Co. (children's clothes)
Beck Jewelry and Optical Co.
Rhoads Jewelers
Thom McAn Shoes
DeBro Frocks (women's clothing)
Lula Glasscock (dressmaker)
King's Men's Clothing
Taylor Trunk Co.
Mary Anderson Theatre
Rudolph's Inc. (confectioners)
Betty Maid Dress Shop Number One
Rialto Theatre
California Orange Bar
Fowlers Bootery Co.
Bartenders Local No. 79
Fischer's Hobby Service
Kay Jewelry Co.
J Kunz and Co. (delicatessen and restaurant)
Shackleton Piano Co. (music)
Lovely Legs Hosiery
Grasso Shoes
Loew's Theatre
Brown's Booterie
Louisville Flower Shop
Baynham's Inc. Shoes
Bennets Womens Clothing
Katherine Wells Shop—The Childrens Clothiers
Steiden Stores (grocery)
Burdorf's Furniture
Zellner's (women's clothing)
Blue Boar Cafeteria
Variety Record Shop
Tropical Orange Bar
Readmore Card Shop
Kentucky Theatre
Chilton's Jewelry Shop
California Orange Bar (two within the block)
Ohio Theatre
Baron-Atlas Cocktail Lounge
Baron Atlas Liquors
Edwards Linens
Kleinman's Furriers
New York Furriers
Younger's Furriers
Walgreen Drug Stores
Foley's Re-Nu Shop Shoe Repairs
Berkeley Hotel
Muth Optical Co.
Federal Bake Shop
Wilderness Road Book Shop
John R. Thompson Restaurant
Hafner Brothers Jewelers
W.D. Gatchel and Sons Photographic Supplies
Brown Hotel Tea Shop
T.J. Howe Opticians
Eastern Airlines ticket shop
Rebecca's (women's clothing)
Martin Brown Building
Brown Hotel

See Jerry L. Rice, "Fourth Street, Louisville's Street of Yesterdays," video (Louisville 1995); George H. Yater, *Two Hundred Years at the Falls of the Ohio* (Louisville 1979); R.C. Riebel, *Louisville Panorama* (Louisville 1960); *Courier-Journal*, April 20, 1981.

Jerry L. Rice

FOX, FONTAINE TALBOT, JR. (b Louisville, June 4, 1884; d Greenwich, Connecticut, August 9, 1964). Creator of TOONERVILLE TROLLEY comic series. Born near the corner of Brook and Oak Streets and energized by lively activities of nearby DU PONT MANUAL HIGH SCHOOL, Fox spent his memorable boyhood days in that neighborhood. The son of Fontaine Senior, a lawyer, editorial writer, and book reviewer, and Mary Pitkin Fox, he attended LOUISVILLE MALE HIGH SCHOOL.

During those formative years his inventive imagination was forged for the ready depiction of ideas to use in hilarious cartoon classics.

Heated rivalries and battles between Manual and Male students were legend. Fox grew up in that rough and tumble existence. Other teenage turf battles were being waged throughout the city. Foremost enemies were GERMANTOWN, LIMERICK (IRISH), and hostile South and West Enders. Fox picked up on this with a tamer "Little Scorpions" in his cartoons. Tough guy Mickey McGuire was a composite of several bullies he remembered. Hotly contested sandlot BASEBALL games became favorite topics in cartoons. While still in his teens, he played semi-pro ball in the West End for the "Dusty Rhodes" team.

For refining his personal style, Fox studied illustrations of world-renowned caricaturist John Leech, a British artist, and discovered *Comic History of England* in his father's library. He practiced and perfected a knowledge of Leech's expertise in facial expressions and "body language" to depict fear, anger, sadness, joy, laughter—all the tricks of the trade he needed in cartooning. He learned how to delineate characters with rapid, defining strokes of his pen, a trait that identified the genius of the mature cartoonist.

The unreliable tiny Brook St. trolley sparked his creative genius. The whimsical trolley became the centerpiece of his success. The streetcar had only four wheels, providing a very delicate balance. Students discovered it was easy to rock it off its tracks as it "waddled" along. Pranksters also pulled the trolley pole from the overhead power wire. Former Manual High School students claimed the schoolboys nicknamed the motorman "The Skipper," although this was never verified by the cartoonist. In early manhood, Fox rode the trolley daily to his job as an editorial cartoonist at the *Louisville Herald*. He learned quickly why angry passengers "railed" at its always being far behind schedule. In disgust, he often lampooned the trolley in cartoons that delighted readers.

From 1908–10 he worked for the *LOUISVILLE TIMES*. At age twenty-six, he made it to the big leagues of journalism, moving to Chicago and cartooning for the *Evening Post*. He also married the former Edith Hinz of Chicago. By 1915 he had negotiated a contract for national representation with the Wheeler Syndicate. Fox moved to New York City and enlarged his stock of characters. His father was supposedly the prototype of the bad tempered Mr. Bang. His wife contended it was a combination of Fox himself and his father. Powerful Katrinka was a merger of his family's African American female cook and Ole Olson, a football character with super strength in a novel by George Fitch.

Toonerville adventures were syndicated in an estimated three hundred metropolitan dailies at the height of his popularity. Fox moved to Greenwich, Connecticut, and hobnobbed with F. SCOTT FITZGERALD, Grantland Rice, Ring Lardner, and cartoonist H.T. Webster. Golfing buddies, they also fed off each other's rich experiences and keen insights.

Cartoon by Fontaine Fox Jr.

The Toonerville Trolley cartoon made its last run in 1955 when Fox retired at seventy. He moved to Vero Beach, Florida, concentrating on golf and watching baseball's spring training camps. Fox had two daughters, Elizabeth (Shonnard) and Mary. Fox denied that either one provided the inspiration for Tomboy Taylor.

See *Fontaine Fox's Toonerville Trolley* (New York 1972); *Courier-Journal*, April 24, 1960; *Courier-Journal*, Nov. 22, 1987.

Lew Miller

FOX, FRANCES BARTON (b Gap-in-Knob, BULLITT COUNTY, Kentucky, January 19, 1887; d Louisville, February 4, 1967). Novelist. She was the daughter of Mary Barton and Fontaine Fox, an attorney. Fox attended public and private schools in Louisville before beginning her writing career with a novel for adolescents, *The Heart of Aresthusa* (1918). It relates the story of an eighteen-year-old girl who makes a trip to Europe with her father. Although she falls in love there, she ultimately returns to Kentucky and her first beau.

In 1934 her second novel, *Ridgeways*, was published under the pen name Frances Renard. Set in Kentucky's Bluegrass region, this novel takes a fictitious family through five generations. In *A Literary History of Kentucky*, William S. Ward wrote that the novel "is a moving story, told simply and straightforwardly and with a fine sense and sweep of history that leaves the reader with the tragic realization that what happened to Ridgeways also happened throughout the South."

In 1928 Fox moved to New York City, where she was a member of the New York Society of Kentucky Women and the Pen and Brush Club. She returned to Louisville in 1963.

Fox was the sister of FONTAINE FOX JR., the creator of the "TOONERVILLE TROLLEY" comic strip. She never married and left her estate of $125,000 to her brother, sister, and two nephews. She donated her unpublished manuscripts to the University of Kentucky library.

See William S. Ward, *A Literary History of Kentucky* (Knoxville, Tenn., 1988).

FOX, HENRY IRVIN (b Jefferson County, Kentucky, May 19, 1882; d Louisville, December 5, 1957). Jefferson County judge. The son of Henry and Matilda (Katzman) Fox, he was educated in Louisville's PUBLIC SCHOOLS and received his law degree from the UNIVERSITY OF LOUISVILLE in 1907. He was a court reporter for the *Louisville Herald* and a member of the legal firm of Fox & Lucas.

Fox, a REPUBLICAN, was Jefferson County judge from January 1, 1926, until he was forced out of office in June 1927 because of voting irregularities. He had run against and defeated Democrat BEN F. EWING, but the DEMOCRATIC PARTY alleged instances of voting fraud on the part of the Republicans, particularly in Louisville's AFRICAN AMERICAN neighborhoods. Instances included missing ballot boxes, irregular polling hours, and ineligible residents casting ballots. One charge was that as many as three thousand names ordered stricken from voting rolls were not removed. Democrats filed a lawsuit in Jefferson Circuit Court. In June 1927 a Kentucky Court of Appeals decision invalidated the election. Fox was ousted as county judge, and Ewing and other Democratic candidates were chosen by Gov. William J. Fields to serve out the remainder of the term.

In a 1927 special election, Fox ran against Ewing and defeated him a second time as the Republicans again took over most of the city and county offices. Fox was reelected in 1929 and served until December 31, 1933. Fox served as a member of the City-County Air Pollution Control Board from 1952 until 1957. For several years he led West End residents in a fight against area pollution, heading an organization called the Joint Committee on West End Air Pollution.

He married Genevieve Stroud, a Canadian, on October 21, 1911. The couple had two daughters, Mary Elizabeth and Sarah Katherine. He divorced his first wife in 1937 and later married Marie Maurer. Fox, who had been a practicing attorney for fifty years, retired from practice only three days before his death. He is buried in CAVE HILL CEMETERY.

See "Jefferson Ex-Judge Henry Fox Dies," *Courier-Journal*, Dec. 7, 1957; W.T. Owens, *Who's Who in Louisville* (Louisville 1926).

FRANKFORT DISTILLERY INC. Frankfort Distillery Inc. was founded in 1902 when several rectifying companies merged. Rectifying was a process practiced ca. the 1860s, by which whiskey wholesalers would blend several batches of bourbon to get a consistent taste. Later the term "rectifier" would fall into disrepute, implying someone who mixed straight bourbon whiskey with plain alcohol—neutral spirits—as opposed to "blenders," who mixed together several straight bourbons to constitute what they insisted was a better and more uniform product than that which could be produced by any single distiller.

Frankfort Distillery's portfolio of brands included Old Oscar Pepper, Mattingly and Moore, and Antique. Their distillery was near the forks of Elkhorn Creek near Frankfort, but sales offices were in Louisville. When Prohibition came in 1920, Frankfort Distillery was one of six companies to receive a license to sell medicinal spirits.

In 1922 the PAUL JONES Co. acquired Frankfort Distillery Inc. and changed its own name to Frankfort Distillery Inc. to retain the license to sell medicinal whiskey. This acquisition added the Paul Jones Whiskey and Four Roses brands to the portfolio. Lawrence Jones, Paul Jones's nephew, became president of the new company. When the government allowed limited DISTILLING in 1928 to replenish dwindling stocks of medicinal whiskey, Frankfort Distillery did not have a distillery, so they contracted with the A. Ph. Stitzel Distillery on Story Ave. to make their share of the new whiskey. When PROHIBITION ended in 1933, Frankfort Distillery purchased the Stitzel Distillery when Stitzel merged with W.L. Weller and Sons and built the STITZEL-WELLER DISTILLERY in Shively. Frankfort Distillery also invested in a new distillery in SHIVELY and built the Four Roses Distillery on DIXIE HWY.

When Lawrence Jones died in 1943, Frankfort Distillery was acquired by Joseph E. Seagram & Sons. SEAGRAM ran it as a subsidiary until the 1960s, when it dissolved the company. The Frankfort Distillery on Story Ave. was closed in the 1950s. The Four Roses Distillery in Shively was closed and production of the brand transferred to another Seagram distillery in the early 1960s.

See John Ed Pearce, *Nothing Better in the Market* (Louisville 1970).

Michael R. Veach

Arch built at Fourth and Broadway in 1895 for the Louisville conclave of the Knights Templar.

FRATERNAL ORGANIZATIONS. Fraternal organizations constituted a vital part of Louisville's social structure from an early date. Benevolent, ethnic, fraternal, patriotic, and religious organizations abound throughout a great deal of the city's history.

By 1832 there were four Freemason lodges. Within twenty years the number increased to fourteen chapters and continued to expand. On June 16, 1851, Masons laid the cornerstone of their first Masonic Temple Building, designed by Louisville architect ELIAS E. WILLIAMS. It stood on the west side of FOURTH ST., occupying the entire block from Jefferson to Green St. (LIBERTY). The *Louisville Democrat* described the building-to-be as "one of the most beautiful ornaments of the city. . . . The Temple will be when completed one of the largest, most elegant and costly structures of its kind in the Union." In 1857 the Temple formally opened.

The FREEMASONS were one of numerous organizations established in Louisville during the nineteenth century. Among other fraternal organizations were the Odd Fellows with over twenty lodges by the 1880s. During the late nineteenth century the number of social organizations increased. The United Order of Foresters, the Knights of American Brotherhood, the Benevolent Protective Order of Elks, the Loyal Order of Moose, Benevolent Order of Buffaloes, Knights of Columbus, Catholic Knights of America, Knights of Honor, Knights of Pythias, Knights of St. John, Improved Order of Red Men, Fraternal Order of Eagles, Temples of Honor, Ancient Order of Hibernians (IRISH, or Irish descent), and the Woodmen of the World were among the many active fraternal organizations in Louisville. These lodges, orders, temples, and tribes drew their members from all walks of life. Professionals and laborers alike joined these groups in large numbers. Women joined the female counterparts of the major organizations. The Order of the Eastern Star, Rebekah Lodges, and Pocahontas Councils were among the social outlets for women.

Minorities in Louisville were also active in fraternal organizations. AFRICAN AMERICANS had the Courts of Calarthe and their own chapters of a number of the popular societies. By 1935 there were eleven white lodges of Odd Fellows and fourteen black. The Knights of Pythias had two white lodges and seven black in 1935.

The CIVIL WAR produced two large and very active fraternal groups. The Grand Army of the Republic (GAR) was founded as a Union veterans association. The GAR had both female and black auxiliaries. The Sons of Confederate Veterans gave the descendants of Confederate soldiers an organization to remember those who had fought for the South. Later the veterans of the Spanish-American War established the United Spanish-American War Veterans.

The American Legion and the Veterans of Foreign Wars became popular with the Louisvillians who served in the armed forces. Jefferson Post No. 15 of the American Legion, the first in Louisville, was founded in July 1919. By 1929, when the American Legion national convention was held in Louisville, Jefferson Post was the largest unit of the American Legion in the world. The Peter Salem Post No. 45, founded in 1927, was the first and only post in Louisville for African American servicemen. The first Kentucky Veterans of Foreign Wars post, Louisville Post No. 440, was organized on May 5, 1920. Louisville's only African American VFW post, Sgt. Scott Razdell Post No. 2822, was organized as an African American post on April 4, 1936.

A number of Louisville fraternal associations combined benevolent, fraternal, and social aspects in their organizations. Among them were the Senior Order of United American Mechanics, The Royal Arcanum, The Hebrew Relief Society, The Knights of the Golden Rule, The Knights of the Ancient Essenic Order, The Knights of Honor, The American Legion of Honor, The United Order of the Golden Cross, The Knights of the Maccabees, and the Oriental League. In addition to these groups, The YOUNG MEN'S CHRISTIAN ASSOCIATION was formed in July 1853. A number of TEMPERANCE societies, including the Women's Christian Temperance Union and the Temple of Honor and Temperance, also came into existence at about this time.

The men and women of the Louisville fraternal organizations not only participated in social activities associated with their respective groups but also did a great deal of charitable work for the needy, providing scholarships for educational advancement and funding for cultural programs. Many of these organizations provided insurance policies and retirement homes for their members. Ethnic groups retained some of their Old World culture by becoming a part of an ethnic social organization. The intellectual, social, and cultural life of Louisville was greatly enhanced by its number of fraternal organizations.

In the late twentieth century, membership in many of these groups declined as other activities vied for attention. TELEVISION became an especially important detriment to club membership. Many lodges closed and others struggled with declining membership as the age of members increased.

See J. Stoddard Johnston, ed., *Memorial History of Louisville* (Chicago 1896).

Ron D. Bryant

FREEDMEN'S PLEASURE GARDEN. Although after 1865 AFRICAN AMERICANS in Louisville were no longer prohibited from gathering for public and private occasions such as parades, picnics, and steamboat excursions, they were denied access to the city's popular PARKS and gardens such as WOODLAND GARDEN and Lion Garden. Consequently, there was no single location where African Americans could gather on a regular basis to hear speakers, listen to summer band concerts, or enjoy other activities.

In 1870 John McCarthy, a sixty-year-old, IRISH-born lawyer, purchased about four acres in the CALIFORNIA neighborhood on Fifteenth St. between Gallagher and O'Hara Streets for the development of a "complete pleasure resort for the colored population of the city" (*Louisville Commercial*, April 12, 1870). The new "pleasure resort" was named Freedmen's Pleasure Garden, although it was sometimes called California Garden. It opened, under black management, on May 21, 1870, and featured speakers and Sunday night sacred concerts by WILLIAM COLE's Brass Band. The Freedmen's Pleasure Garden included a dancing hall, roller skating rink, speaker's stand, and a BASEBALL field. It closed after the 1871 season, and the property was sold to the Martin Senn & Bro. brewery.

Cornelius Bogert

FREEDOM HALL. Freedom Hall is a 19,500-seat arena located at the KENTUCKY FAIR AND EXPOSITION CENTER, I-264 at Phillips Ln. This brick, glass, and steel building is home to the national championship UNIVERSITY OF LOUISVILLE BASKETBALL team and the annual WORLD'S CHAMPIONSHIP HORSE SHOW. It is part of the vast meeting and event complex commonly referred to as the state fairgrounds, Kentucky's premier venue for trade shows, sporting events, and, of course, the annual state fair.

The idea for the facility, designed by the firm of Joseph & Joseph, dates to 1945, when the KENTUCKY STATE FAIR Board proposed a grand plan to replace the obsolete fairgrounds on the west side of Louisville. Local architect Fred Elswick submitted a rough sketch the next year for the new facility, along with an initial construction estimate of $6 million. It took until 1950 to begin construction on the complex. The KOREAN WAR slowed progress, but the doors finally opened in 1956 with that year's state fair. Gov. A.B. "Happy" Chandler presided over the opening to great fanfare, the *New York Herald* calling the new facility "a magnificent showplace."

A contest was sponsored by the American Legion and the State Fair Board to name the facility. State high school students were asked to send both a name and an essay. A seventeen-year-old DU PONT MANUAL HIGH SCHOOL student, Charlotte Owens, submitted the winning name and essay. More than sixty-five hundred students participated, and it was Owens's essay that distinguished her from the other five who suggested the same name, ideal in the Cold War era, and won her a thousand-dollar prize.

Freedom Hall has been greatly expanded and altered over the years, including the addition of air conditioning in 1966 and a $12 million overhaul in 1984. Its original style might only be loosely referred to as Modernist Functional, an appearance in keeping with the stripped-down ahistoricism of the postwar period. The facility is remarkable, however, in terms of its vision, scope, and planning. In 1956, it was unique, a comprehensive events facility all under one roof, convenient to the then-incipient Interstate highway system and the community's principal airport. Its uniqueness even inspired the Reverend Billy Graham who, after a 1956 crusade in Freedom Hall, said, "It's the most beautiful auditorium in the world. . . . Louisville's new fairgrounds and coliseum offer unlimited potential for our purposes."

See *Courier-Journal*, Dec. 20, 1956.

Douglas L Stern

FREEMASONS. Masons are members of what is generally regarded as the oldest and largest male-only fraternal organization in the world. The earliest document that refers to ancient Masonry is the Regius Poem, or Halliwell Manuscript. Paleographists have concluded from the type of parchment, language, and lettering that this document was written in approximately 1390 A.D.

Masonry, or more properly Freemasonry, characterized by an elaborate system of rituals and degrees, is believed by many scholars to have evolved from the medieval craft guilds on the British Isles and throughout Europe. Four of these early lodges joined together in 1717 to form the first grand lodge. The Grand Lodge of England was formed on St. John the Baptist's Day (June 24) 1717 at the Goose and Gridiron Ale House in London. The Grand Lodge of Ireland dates from 1730 and the Grand Lodge of Scotland from 1736. The fraternity was in existence in America by 1730. However, the first properly constituted lodge was St. John's Lodge of Boston, Massachusetts, which was founded on July 30, 1733. This lodge is still in existence.

Until recently, only a few American Masonic lodges included AFRICAN AMERICANS among their ranks. Traditionally, only white men are initiated as members. However, though many American Masons refused to recognize its existence, black freemasonry, known as Prince Hall Masonry, developed in the United States during the Revolutionary War. Prince Hall, an African American soldier, was initiated into British Military Lodge No. 441 in Boston in 1775. He went on to establish the first lodge in the U.S. for African Americans, which was chartered by the Grand Lodge of England in 1784. In regard to Kentucky, Marion Lucas has noted that blacks in Louisville were extremely active in FRATERNAL ORGANIZATIONS such as Masonry. By the mid-1870s, there were three African American lodges, operating under a dispensation from the Grand Lodge of England, with a total membership of four hundred. Just a few years later, in the early 1880s, the number of black lodges had increased to fifteen.

In 1778 six lodges organized the Grand Lodge of Virginia. By 1788 there were enough Freemasons in Kentucky to form a lodge. Lexington Lodge No. 1, under the Grand Lodge of Virginia, was chartered on November 17, 1788. By 1800 there were five lodges in Kentucky, including Solomon Lodge No. 5 in SHELBYVILLE. In October 1800 the Grand Lodge of Kentucky, Free and Accepted Masons, was organized in Lexington. The Grand Lodge continued to meet in Lexington until 1833. It met in Louisville from 1834 to 1838, Lexington in 1839, Louisville in 1840, Lexington from 1841 to 1858, and finally in Louisville from 1859 to the present.

From the beginning, Masons have taken care of their own. In 1867 the Kentucky legislature granted a charter for the incorporation of the Masonic Widows' and Orphans' Home in Louisville, the first Masonic Home in North America. The home, which admitted its first resident in 1871 and was completed in 1873, was originally located about Second and Lee Streets. It later moved to Frankfort Ave. in ST. MATTHEWS in the late 1920s.

The first lodge to meet in the Louisville area was Abraham Lodge No. 8, founded in MIDDLETOWN in 1801. In 1803 it moved to Louisville, consolidating in 1886 with three other Louisville lodges: Clarke No. 51, which first met September 16, 1817; Mount Moriah No. 106, which initially met August 29, 1839; and the Lodge of Antiquity No. 113, which was chartered in 1840. One of the more memorable Masonic events in Louisville took place in the spring of 1825, when General Lafayette visited Clarke Lodge No. 51 jointly with Abraham Lodge No. 8, then located on the third floor of a building at Fifth and Green (Liberty) Streets.

The next surviving lodge was Mount Zion No. 147, which was chartered in 1846. PHILIP TOMPPERT, who later became mayor of Louisville, was its first master (presiding officer). This lodge transacted its business and ritual work in the GERMAN language until after the turn of the twentieth century.

Lewis Lodge No. 191 operated under dispensation as St. John's Lodge prior to August 1849 until a charter was granted on August 28, 1850. The lodge, chartered in PORTLAND, was named in honor of Past Grand Master Asa K. Lewis. Philip Swigert Lodge No. 218 was chartered in 1851. Compass Lodge No. 223 was chartered August 27, 1851.

St. George Lodge No. 239 was chartered September 2, 1852. It met with other lodges in a building on the southeast corner of Third and MARKET STREETS. Its first master was the Reverend W.Y. Rooker, rector of ST. PAUL'S EPISCOPAL CHURCH. This lodge met on the north side of Jefferson St. between FOURTH and Fifth Streets. The senior warden was James C. Ford, a southern planter who built a fine residence on the southwest corner of Second and BROADWAY. This lodge is now composed of many Jewish Masons.

Louisville's first Masonic Temple opened in 1857 on the southwest corner of Fourth and Jefferson Streets. Designed by principal architect E.E. WILLIAMS, the temple not only hosted Masonic meetings but also housed the Temple Theater, where a number of famous theatrical performers and speakers appeared, including Oscar Wilde in 1882. Destroyed by fire in 1902, the structure was replaced with a new Masonic Temple in 1903, on Chestnut between Third and Fourth Streets. It too had a THEATER called the Schubert Masonic Theater. In 1916 the theater began to show motion pictures, and its name was changed to the Strand Theater (it was demolished in the mid-1950s). The present Grand Lodge Building is located on the grounds of MASONIC HOMES INC. on Frankfort Ave. in St. Matthews.

By 1893, a *Louisville Post* article noted that the city was home to about fourteen Masonic lodges (white) with a cumulative active membership of about three thousand. Since then over twenty other lodges have been chartered in Louisville and Jefferson County, many named for the area in which they were located.

In addition to symbolic lodges, Louisville has been the home for a number of appendant Masonic organizations. The York Rite has three chapters of Royal Arch Masons, three councils of Royal and Select Masters, and two commanderies of Knights Templar. The oldest chapter was chartered May 19, 1818, as Louisville Chapter 5, Royal Arch Masons; however, its name was changed in 1896 to King Solomon Chapter 5, Royal Arch Masons.

There were two early commanderies of Knights Templar that developed considerable national prominence in drill team competitions. They were Louisville Commandery No. 1 (chartered September 11, 1840) and DeMolay Commandery No. 12 (chartered June 27, 1867). They were consolidated in 1933 to form Louisville-DeMolay Commandery No. 12, Knights Templar. This commandery is believed to be the only one in the United States that owns its own building. The structure, on GARDINER LANE, was dedicated in 1990.

The Scottish Rite came to Louisville on August 20, 1852, being chartered as a Grand Consistory. The Scottish Rite Temple on the southeast corner of Brook and Gray Streets was completed and dedicated in 1931.

Kosair Temple, Ancient Arabic Order of the Nobles of the Mystic Shrine, was established in 1884. It built its own temple on Broadway in 1924 but had to sell the structure during the GREAT DEPRESSION. The current temple is located at 812 South Second St. A major contribution to the community was the Kosair Crippled Children's Hospital, which opened in 1926. Today, Kosair Charities has assumed this function.

AAHMED Grotto, Mystic Order of Veiled Prophets of the Enchanted Realm, a social organization for master masons, was chartered December 16, 1941. The Downtown High Twelve Club, a noon luncheon club for master masons, was chartered May 23, 1947. This club has produced four High Twelve International presidents during its short history.

In addition to the organizations for men, the Louisville area has been home to a number of Masonic-affiliated organizations for women and for youth. The Order of the Eastern Star, the Order of the Amaranth, and the Order of the White Shrine of Jerusalem, along with the Order of DeMolay, the International Order of the Rainbow for Girls, and the International Order of Job's Daughters, have all been active for many years.

See J. Stoddard Johnston, ed., *Memorial History of Louisville* (Chicago and New York 1896); Marion B. Lucas, *A History of Blacks in Kentucky,* vol.1 (Frankfort 1992); S. Brent Morris, *Masonic Philanthropies* (n.p., 1997).

Roland T. Stayton

FRENCH. The French came to America in three significant migrations, each time for a different reason, and each time inevitably they added something of themselves and their culture to the existing American mix. Huguenots fleeing France after the revocation of the Edict of Nantes, which had guaranteed them religious toleration, began to arrive in 1685. The total immigration, primarily affecting the coastal states, was probably close to fifteen thousand Frenchmen. Huntley Dupre, writing in the April 1941 *FILSON CLUB HISTORY QUARTERLY*, said, "These Huguenots, however, exerted an influence and contributed a leadership in colonial days that belied their numbers." By the time members of this group reached Louisville, they were second- and third-generation American-born French. THOMAS BULLITT, an early surveyor of Louisville, was a descendant of such Huguenot refugees.

The second influx occurred during the American Revolution, after France had allied itself with the Americans. Dupre remarked that "a great number of French military men and nobles came over to participate in the American cause. Along with them came dancing masters and hairdressers, French mirrors, French goods, French styles and French balls." Most Frenchmen who came for the war eventually returned to France, but their influence continued. Father Stephen Theodore Badin, himself French, remarked much later that "the Americans like the French very much and endeavor to acquire their politeness and their gaiety. They recall with gratitude the services which they have received from the martyred king." Louisville itself was named in honor of LOUIS XVI, America's ally in the Revolution.

The third major migration occurred after 1783, during the French Revolution, and included nobles, aristocrats, clergy, and others threatened by the revolutionary government. Some traveled to Kentucky, and many of these settled in or near Louisville. Those who stayed eventually comprised the largest segment of Louisville's French community.

Smaller groups of French immigrants came to Louisville from Kaskaskia and other French settlements in the Mississippi valley, and from the French islands in the Caribbean. Bloody slave uprisings on some islands forced plantation owners to abandon everything. Both JOHN JAMES AUDUBON and John D. Colmesnil were among these later immigrants. John D. Colmesnil was born in Haiti in 1787, the year of a major uprising. His father, Louis Gabriel de Colmesnil, and a native nurse managed to save the infant John. The rest of the family were killed. The older Colmesnil chartered a ship and brought the baby, some neighbors, and a few slaves to America. They went first to New Jersey and later moved to Georgia.

After his father's death, Colmesnil journeyed to Louisville to visit LOUIS AND JOHN TARASCON, kinsmen by marriage. He remained and became a river trader and one of the city's wealthiest merchants. He was said to have owned one of the largest warehouses near the docks. John Colmesnil established the popular PAROQUET SPRINGS spa near SHEPHERDSVILLE about 1838.

Even though the earliest French settlers in Louisville had little influence on the city's religious life, their ties to famous French Catholics of the day were strong. Frenchman Bishop BENEDICT JOSEPH FLAGET was a frequent visitor, and the French frontier priest Father Badin founded the first Catholic church in Louisville, St. Louis Church on Tenth St. between Main and the river, in 1811.

From the beginning, French influence showed itself in business and commerce. Barthelemi Tardiveau arrived at the Falls about 1781, supplied GEORGE ROGERS CLARK's Virginia regiments with flour, and was repaid in Kentucky land. With his partner, Jean A. Honoré, he established a firm that traded in furs, flour, and land. In 1782 theirs was the first business to exploit the New Orleans trade, which was responsible for Louisville's early importance. Tardiveau and Honoré eventually settled in Louisville.

Later, the Tarascons were the leaders of the French business community at the FALLS. In 1819 John built a large water-powered flour mill at SHIPPINGPORT, then the center of French settlement. Shippingport also had a rope walk twelve hundred feet long, called "one of the finest in the United States." AARON FONTAINE developed such a busy boat landing at the bend of the Ohio that the tract became known as Fontaine Ferry. After the devastating flood of 1832, most of the French community shifted to PORTLAND, though some families, like the Berthouds, moved to Louisville.

By the mid-nineteenth century the French in Louisville were engaged in a wide range of business activities. Robert A. Burnett explained (*Filson Club History Quarterly*, April 1976) that M. Hugonin erected a sawmill near the river. The French firm of Twis and Barbaroux owned a hydraulic foundry on Washington Street at Floyd Street, and C.I. and A.V. DU PONT operated a paper mill on Twelfth Street near the river. John Colmesnil was a member of the first planning committee for building a bridge across the OHIO RIVER. James Berthoud was instrumental in incorporating the second insurance firm in the state and the first in Louisville, and in chartering the first BANK OF KENTUCKY. His son Nicholas was a charter member of the LOUISVILLE AND PORTLAND CANAL CO. WILLIAM FONTAINE BULLOCK, a descendant of French Huguenot stock, was prominent in helping form the LOUISVILLE & NASHVILLE RAILROAD, and Messrs. Biedermann du Pont and S.M. Lamont were among the organizers of the LOUISVILLE BOARD OF TRADE."

The French had as much cultural as professional influence in Louisville. They lived well, had commodious homes, and were hospitable and determined to make their surroundings attractive and comfortable. The French seem to have had no problem combining business and culture. Hector St. John Crévecoeur, a native of Normandy, left New York for Kentucky in 1784, and built a sawmill here. By virtue of his *Letters from an American Farmer* which he had written in 1782 he also became Louisville's first prominent author in residence. MICHAEL LACASSAGNE, a leading merchant, built a French cottage with a veranda on three sides and a beautiful garden in the French tradition. This home apparently challenged the community to investigate new architectural styles and soon was followed by the first brick and stone houses. Lacassagne was the first postmaster of Louisville and a member of the Kentucky convention of 1787.

John James Audubon (originally Jean-Jacques Fougère Audubon), the naturalist, was born in Haiti and lived for thirteen years in Louisville and Henderson, Kentucky. He first came to Louisville in 1807. After failing in business, Audubon moved to Henderson but later returned to Louisville, where he lived with Nicholas Berthoud (his wife was the sister-in-law of James Berthoud) and for income painted landscape panels for STEAMBOATS and five-dollar portraits. Audubon's portraits of the Berthoud family are owned by the SPEED ART MUSEUM.

The French played a vital part in the first century of Louisville's history, and their descendants continue to do so. An abundance of French names and family traditions remind us that a small but vigorous outpost of La Belle France once existed at the FALLS OF THE OHIO.

See Robert A. Burnett, "Louisville's French Past," *Filson Club History Quarterly* 50 (April 1976): 5–27; Huntley Dupre, "The French in Early Kentucky," *Filson Club History Quarterly* 15 (April 1941): 78–104; *Louisville Past and Present* (Louisville 1875).

Audrea McDowell

FRIENDS MEETING OF LOUISVILLE. About 1937 a few Friends and a varying number of conventional church members began to hold Sunday afternoon worship meetings after the manner of classic Quakers—silent meditation occasionally interrupted with inspirational messages from participants. In 1954 Joan and Lee Thomas moved to Louisville and insisted on a full-time meeting for the proper development of their growing family, even if the only attendees were their own family. Regular First Day (Sunday) morning meetings for worship at the old NEIGHBORHOOD HOUSE on First St., Monthly Meetings for business, study groups, and a First-Day school were established at that time.

Up to that time the meeting was really only a group of people acting like Quakers but having no official membership in the Society of Friends. In 1959 the Louisville meeting, as a first step toward membership, became a Preparative Meeting under the East Cincinnati meeting of Miami Quarterly meeting, of Indiana yearly meeting of the Friends General Conference, one of the national organizations of Quakers.

The Monthly Meeting is the basic unit of Friends, and the Preparative Meeting is an apprentice monthly meeting. The Quarterly Meeting consists of two or more Monthly Meetings that meet together three times a year for fellowship and to conduct business on common concerns. The Yearly Meeting in turn consists of two or more Quarterly Meetings that meet annually. In 1962 the Louisville meeting became a full-fledged Monthly Meeting of the Quarterly Meeting.

In 1964 a house at 3050 Bon Air Ave., formerly part of the Roederer farm, was bought for a meetinghouse. Built before the CIVIL WAR, it was made of bricks from the FARMINGTON estate kiln, with American chestnut joists and hand-wrought, square-headed nails. The meeting repaired and expanded it under the supervision of MANSIR TYDINGS, an architect and community activist, and it is still the home of the meeting.

Almost from the beginning, meeting members were involved, and continue to be involved as individuals, in the Quaker social concerns for peace and justice. The meeting as a group took out an organizational membership in the newly formed Kentucky Council of Human Relations in 1956. Later a Social Concerns Committee was formed to work on race relations and urban affairs. At that time members of the meeting were particularly active in efforts to integrate public accommodations such as RESTAURANTS and stores.

In 1959 after the failed Hungarian revolution, the meeting sponsored a Hungarian refugee family even though it probably had only about fifteen adult attendees itself at the time. From time to time meeting members participated in projects organized by the American Friends Service Committee: Interns in Industry at Plymouth Community Renewal Center, student volunteer units at CENTRAL STATE HOSPITAL, Family Camps, and LearnMore—EarnMore, a pilot project in adult evening education for the un- and underemployed.

During the VIETNAM WAR, the meeting was actively involved in seeking an end to the conflict. A Peace and Conscientious Objectors Committee, later joined by other organizations to form the KENTUCKIANA Military and Draft Counseling Center, assisted young men who had problems of conscience with the draft and military service.

In 1977 the Friends Council for Social Concerns was set up to manage the social concern projects of the meeting. The first project was the Student-Parent Aid & Resource Center (SPARC), which worked with other organizations to assist parents and educators with children who had learning and school discipline problems. It later was spun off as an independent not-for-profit agency but closed because the school system improved its own methods and the agency was unable to obtain funding.

Later the Friends Pre-School was established to provide not just a preschool but an enriched experience for children from various economic levels and ethnic groups as well as handicapped children. It later expanded to include regular grades as "Friends School." In 1981 a Peace Education Program initiated a program of conflict-resolution training in the PUBLIC SCHOOLS, which branched out to the community at large, notably in the housing projects. Both Friends School and Peace Education are now independent not-for-profit agencies, although their bylaws require a Friend on the board.

Also in the early eighties, Ploughshares was started to develop decent cooperative housing for low-income residents. Later that project was turned over to New Directions, a private not-for profit agency that builds or rebuilds and manages quality low-income housing.

Joan E. Thomas

FULTON CONWAY CO. Founded in 1860 by Thomas L. Clarke and William Fulton under the name Clarke and Fulton, it manufactured wagon wheel hubs, spokes, and felloes at a factory on Ormsby Ave. between Eighth and Ninth Streets. By 1871 John T. Smith had replaced Clarke at the renamed firm of Fulton, Smith, and Co. The business added buggy bodies and shafts to its products in the early 1880s, as George W. Conway joined the firm. The firm's name then became Fulton, Conway, and Co. During this time, the company moved to its new site on MAIN ST. between Eighth and Ninth Streets. The factory was constructed as a four-story building, but the top two stories were ripped off as the TORNADO OF 1890 swept down Main St.

In 1898 the Fulton family sold the company to Andrew G. Whitley, although he retained the Fulton Conway name. Within ten years, the business had added automobile parts and supplies and moved solely into that wholesale field as the need for wagon and buggy parts dwindled. By 1998 the Fulton Conway Co. continued to sell automobile supplies.

FUND FOR THE ARTS. The Fund for the Arts, founded in 1949, is solidly rooted in the community. Its board of directors comprises civic and community leaders. It provides programming and administrative support for nineteen Louisville area arts agencies and programs. The fund also provides grants and resources to neighborhood groups that offer cultural opportunities to minorities and in underserved communities, and also supports the annual Arts Leadership Institute, which supplies a framework for the professional development of those whose skills and commitment are needed to shape our arts and to ensure their future.

The Fund for the Arts also administers the six-member Youth Arts Council, established in 1993 to serve as a facilitator and catalyst for youth arts programs and to provide exceptional performance opportunities for young people. Another project supported by the fund is the Arts Administration cluster of the YMCA's Black Archives Program that underwrites scholarships and summer internships in the arts. In addition, the fund provides bus subsidies for schoolchildren to attend arts performances and regular workshops on such subjects as fund-raising, marketing, and diversity for a broad range of arts organizations.

In 1998, in a separate campaign, the fund raised over $4 million to restore the historic Brown Theatre, which was deeded to the fund in 1997. The theater was renamed in honor of former chief executive of BROWN-FORMAN CORP., W.L. LYONS BROWN.

The fund has raised over $80 million for the arts in Louisville, a long way from its first campaign initiated by former Mayor CHARLES FARNSLEY. Farnsley, who served as Major of Louisville from 1948 to 1953, contacted several prominent Louisvillians about establishing a united arts fund that would raise funds for the city's major arts organizations. He based the fund's structure on the Community Chest (now METRO UNITED WAY). The idea was enthusiastically received, and the articles of incorporation were signed on March 4, 1949. The Louisville Fund became the first united arts fund in the nation and would become a national and international leader and example for other arts funds to follow.

The fund's first office was a room with five desks in the basement of the main public library at FOURTH and York Streets. The first campaign, chaired by fund board president (and later judge) Alexander G. Booth and overseen by a part-time executive secretary, William R. Dunton III, raised ninety-nine thousand dollars. The first member agencies included the Louisville Institute of Architectural Design, the Louisville Little Theatre Co., and the LOUISVILLE ORCHESTRA.

The second part-time head of the fund was Richard H. Wangerin, who took over as executive secretary from 1954 to April 1968. At the time Wangerin also managed the Louisville Orchestra, the Louisville Theatrical Association, and the Brown Theatre. Fund-raising in those early years was a struggle, despite hundreds of volunteers and broad community support. The annual campaigns sometimes failed to reach their goals, which generally increased only slightly from year to year. It was not until the 1960s that the campaign raised more than two hundred thousand dollars.

The first full-time executive secretary, C. Dennis Riggs, a Louisville native and former college athlete, was hired in September 1971. In 1972 offices were moved to a larger space at Fourth and Walnut St. (now MUHAMMAD ALI Blvd.), and the name was changed to the Greater Louisville Fund for the Arts. In 1974 the offices moved once again into the balcony of the Liberty National Bank branch at 511 W BROADWAY.

In 1976, Allan Cowen, who later became president and CEO, was hired. His first fund-raising campaign was in 1977. The name was simplified to the Fund for the Arts to reflect its involvement in southern Indiana and other regions in Kentucky. The offices moved two more times before relocating in 1989 to its own nine-hundred-thousand-dollar downtown home at 623 W MAIN ST.—the first quarters actually owned by the fund. Under Cowen's leadership the campaign totals rose from about six hundred thousand dollars in 1977 to over $6 million in 1999, making Louisville the largest per-capita arts-giving base in America, with over thirty-four thousand donors.

The fund's growth in recent years has been primarily fueled through its employee campaigns, conducted in workplaces throughout Louisville. The employee campaign has risen from five participating companies in 1980, with a few hundred donors, to over two hundred companies in 1999, with more than thirty thousand donors. The fund's popular ArtsCARD, providing donor discounts to member agencies' arts events, was introduced in 1983 as an incentive to donate and as a valuable audience development tool.

By 1999 the fund's member agencies and programs included ACTORS THEATRE OF LOUISVILLE, Community Partnerships Program, the KENTUCKY ART AND CRAFT FOUNDATION, the KENTUCKY OPERA Association, the KENTUCKY SHAKESPEARE FESTIVAL, the LOUISVILLE BACH SOCIETY, the LOUISVILLE BALLET, the Louisville Orchestra, the Louisville Theatrical Association, the LOUISVILLE VISUAL ART ASSOCIATION, the Louisville Youth Choir, the LOUISVILLE YOUTH ORCHESTRA, Music Theatre Louisville, Stage One, West Louisville Boys Choir, WALDEN THEATRE, and Youth Arts Council. That year the effort raised a record $6.128 million from more than thirty-four thousand donors.

Largest Area Performing Arts Organizations (1999 Budget)

Actors Theatre of Louisville (Louisville) ($8.4 million)
PNC Bank Broadway Series (Louisville) ($7.2 million)
The Louisville Orchestra Inc. (Louisville) ($5.55 million)
Derby Dinner Playhouse (Clarksville, Indiana) ($3.7 million)
Louisville Ballet (Louisville) ($2.5 million)
Kentucky Opera (Louisville) ($2.1 million)
Stage One (Louisville) ($1.43 million)
Comedy Caravan (Louisville) ($1 million)
Music Theatre Louisville (Louisville) ($529,340)
Kentucky Shakespeare Festival (Louisville) ($500,000)
APPLE Inc./The Blue Apple Players (Louisville) ($445,000)
Walden Theatre (Louisville) ($278,000)
New Performing Arts Inc. (Louisville) ($25,000)
Louisville Youth Orchestra (Louisville) ($205,000)
Louisville Bach Society (Louisville) ($164,000)

See *Business First Book of Lists* (Louisville 1999).

Trish Pugh Jones

FURNITURE FACTORIES. Prior to the CIVIL WAR, furniture manufacturing in Louisville was centered in small cabinetmakers' shops. In 1832 the city's first directory listed nineteen cabinetmakers and five chair makers, of which only one, Ward and Stokes cabinetmakers, was ambitious enough to list its enterprise in boldface type. Little is known about these early artisans, but city directories suggest that their individually hand-crafted wares were likely produced in small shops located either below, adjacent to, or in the rear yard of the manufacturer's residence. The apprentice system trained these furniture makers.

By the mid-nineteenth century, furniture-making centers appeared following improved transportation and the mechanization of the industry. Louisville's location on the OHIO RIVER and its mid-century POPULATION boom spurred the growth of local furniture production. CITY DIRECTORIES from 1848 to 1860 point to larger operations than those previously carried on by individual artisans in cabinet shops. Among the firms that existed were T.M. Duffy's Chair Manufactory on Second St. between MAIN and MARKET; William C. Dodge, on FOURTH ST., manufacturer of cabinetware, upholstery, chairs, and Venetian blinds; John Simms' Cabinet Furniture Ware-Rooms, at the corner of Main and Seventh Streets; and Louisville Cabinet Warehouse, on Fourth St., manufacturers and wholesale suppliers of mahogany sofas and dressing bureaus and a variety of chairs, tables, and beds. Some businesses boasted that they could furnish STEAMBOATS and HOTELS at a moment's notice. In 1860 the U.S. manufacturing census reported 14 furniture and cabinet-making firms in Jefferson County, employing a total of 194 men.

Not until the end of the Civil War and the decade following did the city's first large-scale furniture factories appear. Utilizing steam-powered equipment and employing more workers, the result was mass-produced furniture. During the 1860s and 1870s at least five large three- to five-story furniture complexes were constructed in Louisville.

One of the first was likely the Wrampelmeier and Schulte Furniture Co., established in the early 1860s. By 1865 the company, which produced sofas, bureaus, tables, and beds, was located at the corner of Fifteenth St. and Portland Ave. and billed itself as the Southern Steam Furniture Factory. About 1880 the factory moved into a larger, five-story complex at the corner of Fifteenth and Lytle Streets. Though by 1895 the Wrampelmeier furniture factory had ceased production, the 1880 building still exists and is listed on the NATIONAL REGISTER OF HISTORIC PLACES.

The Louisville Furniture Manufacturing Co. first appeared in the city directory for 1866–67. Located at the corner of Ninth and Jefferson Streets, its complex, now demolished, consisted of a three- and four-story factory and warehouse. The J.W. Davis Furniture Manufacturing Co. and the Dickinson Furniture Manufacturing Co. both, between 1875 and 1880, either built new factories or moved into existing structures. These were located on Preston St. between Lampton and Ross, and on Jacob St. between Hancock and Clay, respectively. Neither factory survives.

Yet another early furniture company that grew to become a large-scale enterprise was Greve, Buhrlage, and Co., which dated back to 1853. About 1868 the firm constructed two adjacent, but separate, four-story brick structures, one a steam factory and the other a showroom, at 1501 Lytle St. and 1500 Portland Ave. Though it ceased operation as a furniture factory in the early 1890s, the buildings are extant and are listed on the National Register.

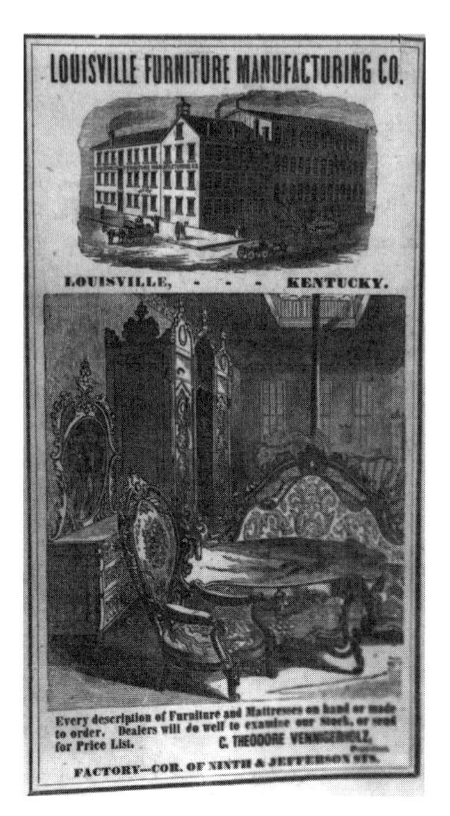

An advertisement for the Louisville Furniture Manufacturing Co. from an 1868 city directory.

Lastly, of the factories that reached prominence in the years following the Civil War, Harig, Koop, and Co./Columbia Mantel Co. was the city's longest-surviving furniture factory, with a history that spanned over a hundred years. The firm of Harig, Koop, and Co. was formed in 1868 by a merger of two separate companies owned by Frederick Harig and August Koop. Harig had been in the chair-manufacturing business since at least 1858, and Koop had been producing furniture since the mid-1860s. In 1871 the firm built a new factory at Ninth and Breckinridge Streets to replace its previous facility at the northwest corner of Third and Madison (now Guthrie) Streets, which had been destroyed by fire. The two buildings of the complex were separated by a drive in the middle, a feature that was intended to reduce the risk of fire damage, a particular hazard in the furniture business because of the highly flammable glues and solvents that were used in production.

About 1899 Harig sold his interest in the company to his partner, and the firm continued on as A. Koop and Sons until shortly after Koop's death in 1904. In August 1905 the property and factory, along with much of the machinery, were bought by the Columbia Mantel Co., a producer of wood mantels that was owned by Charles P. Brecher. By 1913 the company was also manufacturing furniture, an increasingly more important aspect of the business as consumer demand for mantels decreased sharply during the GREAT DEPRESSION and WORLD WAR II. Columbia ceased making mantels in 1958. Furniture production continued until 1986 when the Columbia Manufacturing Co., the successor of Columbia Mantel, was liquidated.

By 1880 furniture manufacturing had assumed a prominent position in Louisville's growing industrial base. The 813 workers designated in the 1880 census as employees in local furniture production plants comprised the fifth-largest group of workers involved in manufacturing. Though Louisville still fell behind its largest regional competitor, Cincinnati, in furniture production, it placed ahead of neighbors such as Indianapolis, St. Louis, and Nashville with sales exceeding $1 million.

NEW ALBANY, Indiana's few furniture factories existed primarily between the 1870s and 1930s. The factories owned by Henry Klerner on Oak St. at the corner of Fifth and by John Shrader on Main St. were more successful and managed to stay in business longer than others. JEFFERSONVILLE mainly had furniture retail stores. Both cities faced competition from Louisville in furniture production, and by the 1930s most of the furniture business in southern Indiana became retail or simply disappeared.

From 1880 to 1915 the furniture industry in Louisville continued to change as new firms appeared and others were dissolved and reorganized under new names, often moving from one established plant site to another. For instance, sometime between 1885 and 1890 a new factory was erected at 1800 Portland Ave. by the Kentucky Furniture Manufacturing Co. By 1930 the same plant site had been home to two other furniture companies as well, Palmer and Hardin, and G.E. Gans Manufacturing. Likewise, a large furniture factory at 620–24 S Thirty-first St. was constructed by the Gimnich Furniture Manufacturing Co. between 1901 and 1905. Not long afterward it housed Wilson Furniture Manufacturing and later housed what was likely the city's largest furniture manufacturer, Consider H. Willett. By 1935 Consider H. Willett had established a second operation at Thirtieth and Kentucky Streets, which had originally been constructed and used by the Inman-Pierson Co. in the early 1900s.

Between 1909 and 1939 census figures reflected the large increase in workers employed in and profits garnered by the furniture industry in Louisville. In regard to profits created, furniture-manufacturing ranked as the seventh-largest industry in Kentucky in 1929, with most of that production taking place in Louisville. The city's furniture industry made it through the Great Depression relatively well, and in 1939 Louisville was home to sixteen household furniture plants (not including those that produced office furniture), which employed over twenty-five hundred workers and had an annual product value of over $8 million, putting it among the city's most important industries and surpassing that of its regional rival, Cincinnati.

Throughout the 1950s and 1960s furniture production continued to be an important industry in Louisville. However, beginning about 1970 its prominence gradually declined. In this way the decline paralleled the loss of other manufacturing jobs by the city. Furniture manufacturing concentrated in fewer locations, most notably in other parts of the South. By 1997 only two companies were listed in the telephone directory as furniture manufacturers, Crown Division of the Allen Group Inc. on Electron Dr. and KFI on Bank St. The city directory, however, listed twenty-four, many of them manufacturers of cabinets or general woodworking. Eighteen businesses were listed as repairing or refinishing furniture.

Carolyn Brooks

FUSIONIST MOVEMENT. The Fusionists were a group of Louisville Republicans and disaffected Democrats who banded together to fight the Whallen brothers' political machine in the 1905 mayoral election. The wing of the group representing Democrats was made up of several of the city's best-known and most influential businessmen and religious and civic leaders, including Helm Bruce; Col. Thomas W. Bullitt; William Marshall Bullitt; William Belknap; Augustus E. Willson, who became governor of Kentucky in 1907; William Heyburn; ex-Confederate general Basil W. Duke; Richard Knott, editor of the *Louisville Evening Post*; and several clergymen such as the Reverend E.L. Powell of the First Christian Church, Episcopal Bishop Charles E. Woodcock, and the Reverend Edgar Y. Mullins, president of the Southern Baptist Theological Seminary. The group represented the city's reform element that was tired of seeing the local Democratic Party apparatus controlled by political bosses—in this case Charles F. Grainger, who had temporarily wrested party control from John Whallen and his brother, James. The Democratic machine drew its support from the area's lower-income groups, immigrants, saloonkeepers, prostitutes, gamblers, corrupt city officials, police and firemen, and, most important, the Louisville & Nashville Railroad.

The Fusionists, who were interested in curbing the corrupt practices of the machine in the wards and the strong-arm tactics of the police, formed the City Club, an organization committed to getting Louisville and Jefferson County politics back on an honest footing. One of the central issues leading up to the election was voter registration. Democrats and Fusionists had a showdown over "repeaters"—individuals, usually drifters, who were not legal residents of the wards and precincts where they registered. Fusionists had several confrontations with these registrants and police in the months leading up to the November election, including a well-publicized altercation between police and Fusionist Arthur D. Allen, an official of the Belknap Manufacturing Co.

These Democrats banded together with Republicans to field attorney Joseph T. O'Neal as the Fusionist mayoral candidate for the 1905 election, which was to be one of the most blatantly corrupt in the city's history. Fusionist anger over political corruption reached its apex on November 4, 1905, when a crowd, which was variously reported from fifteen hundred to ten thousand, of Fusionist supporters gathered in front of the Jefferson County Courthouse and City Hall to listen to speeches by many of the City Club members. Duke presided over the rally, which was repeatedly disrupted by the efforts of the Democratic bosses. At the instigation of local bosses, trolley cars converged on the crowd and rang bells demanding passage through. Horse-drawn fire engines also attempted to cut a path through the throng of people. Other disruptions to the meeting included policemen weaving through the crowd writing down the names of those in attendance and catcalls from Democratic Party supporters who were stationed in the courthouse to drown out Fusionist speakers.

On November 7, election day, the Democrats perpetrated several different forms of voting fraud at numerous polling stations, although Fusionists as well were responsible for contributing to the lawlessness. Ballot boxes were stuffed or stolen. Police manning the stations would discourage Fusionists from voting; many went so far as to physically assault Fusionist officials or arrest them for disorderly conduct, including William Heyburn, Alexander Scott Bullitt, and C.A. Wickliffe. In several precincts Democrats used a technique called "alphabetical voting" in which voters were required to go to the polls in alphabetical order, thus preventing many from ever casting their ballot before polls closed.

Needless to say, the Fusionists had little success at the polls, electing only three candidates—a state representative, a Jefferson County constable, and a city school trustee. The Fusionist mayoral candidate O'Neal was soundly defeated by Democrat Paul C. Barth by more than forty-eight hundred votes.

Immediately after the election the Fusionist Campaign Committee and the Executive Committee of the City Club, led by Col. Thomas W. Bullitt, drafted a resolution to Mayor Charles Grainger to investigate election fraud. On November 11 a group of enraged Fusionist sympathizers met at the Galt House to discuss what to do about the election abuses. A Citizens Committee of One Hundred was formed, and ten thousand dollars was contributed to take the case before the courts. Much of the funding for the legal proceedings was secured by the committee.

On December 2, 1905, the election fraud case went to trial before Shackelford Miller and Samuel B. Kirby, Jefferson County chancellors of the circuit court. The plaintiffs were led by Helm Bruce, William Marshall Bullitt, and Alex G. Barret, all prominent Louisville attorneys. The Democrats' cause was championed by John L. Dodd, J.C. Dodd, A.J. Carroll, W.W. Davies, and others. Numerous depositions were filed on the case from both sides; the paperwork was so extensive that the court proceedings, when printed, filled nine large bound volumes.

On March 23, 1907, Miller and Kirby handed down a 184-page decision that ruled against the plaintiffs and in favor of the Democrats. While the decision supported the findings of fraud, the chancellors said it was not pervasive enough to warrant the declaration of "no election." The chancellors ruled that almost all of the candidates would have won regardless of the vote-tampering and the police assaults.

Fusionists immediately appealed the decision to the Kentucky Court of Appeals. On May 23, 1907, the Court of Appeals rendered an opinion on the case prepared by Judge John B. Lassing, reversing the lower court's decision by a vote of 4 to 2. All the officials elected in 1905 in Louisville and Jefferson County were immediately removed from office, and Kentucky governor J.C.W. Beckham was called upon to choose replacements for those positions until another election could be held in November. Beckham, who had recently won election in part as a result of strong Democratic Party support from Jefferson County, found himself in the untenable position of having to pick suitable replacements for mayor, county judge, and other posts that were not part of the local machine. For mayor, Beckham chose county attorney Robert Worth Bingham, a Democrat but also something of an outsider.

By the November 1907 election the Fusionist movement had all but disappeared, as the Republican Party decided not to collaborate with independent Democrats. Although Bingham had some success with a progressive agenda of cleaning up politics and the city, Democrats increasingly fell out of favor with the electorate in 1907 and the Republicans were able to elect James F. Grinstead, the city's second Republican mayor, in November to serve out the two years left on Barth's term of office. Augustus E. Willson, a leader in Louisville's Fusionist movement in 1905, became Kentucky's second Republican governor.

See George Yater, *Two Hundred Years at the Falls of the Ohio* (Louisville 1987); Thomas D. Clark, *Helm Bruce, Public Defender: Breaking Louisville's Gothic Political Ring, 1905* (Louisville 1973); William E. Ellis, *Robert Worth Bingham and the Southern Mystique* (Kent, Ohio, 1997).

F. WOLKOW & SONS. This hair-care products company at 2001 Magazine St. was founded in 1894 by Fannie Wolkow. She was a

Russian immigrant who started the business as a wig manufacturer at 437 E Jefferson St. for Orthodox Jewish women in the new world. Later the company also made wigs for men and dolls as well as hairstyling products. The factory was moved several times until it was established in its current location in 1963.

It is one of the world's largest producers of hair straighteners, combs, curling irons, and heating devices marketed under the "Kentucky Maid" insignia. This status came in the early twentieth century after an endorsement by Madame Walker, a successful hair-care products dealer who was also the first female African American millionaire. Offering the "Kentucky Maid" products along with her own line of grooming items and using her wide-ranging distribution system, she helped to give the company national name recognition. Operations were managed by Fannie and her sons, Leo and Joseph, until her death in 1933. Leo took control from 1936 to his retirement in 1955 when the company was bought by Louisville dentist Sidney Meyer. Meyer moved the business to Magazine St. and headed the company until 1970 when it was bought by Abraham Rolnick.

Allejandro Magallanez

GAFFNEY, JAMES J. (b Louisville, June 18, 1863; d Louisville, November 30, 1946). Architect. Gaffney was born to Michael and Anna (McMullen) Gaffney, IRISH Catholic refugees from the potato famine of 1845–47, and grew up in what is now the PHOENIX HILL area. There is no evidence of Gaffney receiving any formal training as an architect, and he is known to have attended only one year of school, probably in order to receive the Sacrament of Confirmation. In 1881 Gaffney took a job as a draftsman with architect CHARLES JULIAN CLARKE, where he learned the skills that would later earn him his fame. His widely diverse commissions included ecclesiastical, institutional, residential, and commercial buildings. His individual style built upon a variety of influences, ranging from Victorian to Byzantine to Arts and Crafts. Some of his more notable structures included St. James Catholic Church (1912, Bardstown Rd. and Edenside Ave.), ADATH JESHURUN synagogue (1919, 757 S Brook St., now Unity Temple), Waverly Hills Tuberculosis Sanitorium, the Besten and Belvoir APARTMENTS, and the J.D. Taggart mansion. Gaffney contributed greatly to the ARCHITECTURE of Louisville, breaking the conventional barriers of his time period with his unusual stylistic combinations.

A quiet man, Gaffney was deeply committed to his family. In 1892 he married Ella Gross, and in 1895 she gave birth to two sons, THOMAS JAMES and James Louis; both died of dysentery in 1896. Gaffney is buried in the family plot at St. Louis Cemetery.

See Julian Oberwarth, *A History of the Profession of Architecture in Kentucky* (Louisville 1987).

Lisa Grace Carpenter

GAITHER, WILLIAM "BILL" (b Belmont, Kentucky, April 21, 1910; d Indianapolis, October 30, 1970). Guitarist and BLUES singer. The son of Samuel Gaither and Bertha Kennison, he moved to Louisville in 1920 and made his first recordings for Victor Records in December 1931. In 1932 he moved to Indianapolis and from 1935–41 enjoyed success recording for Decca and OKeh Records under the names of "Little Bill" and "Leroy's Buddy" (a reference to pianist Leroy Carr). He returned to Louisville in 1940, operating a radio repair shop on Seventh St. In 1942 he was drafted into the army, assigned to the all-black Twenty-fourth Infantry Regiment, and saw active duty in the Solomon Islands. He was discharged in 1945 and moved back to Indianapolis in 1948, where he died and is buried in the New Crown Cemetery.

Brenda K. Bogert

GALLERIA. The Louisville Galleria is a large office and retail complex that sits astride Fourth St. and is bounded by Third, Fifth, and LIBERTY Streets and Muhammad Ali Blvd. in downtown Louisville. The complex consists of two office towers and a glass-enclosed retail mall that contains over sixty-five DEPARTMENT STORES, service and specialty shops, and RESTAURANTS. The structure also includes the facade of the former KAUFMAN-STRAUS building.

The idea of such a project dates to the *Louisville Center City Development Program,* commissioned by the Center City Committee and published in 1968 by Gruen Associates Inc. An initial effort to implement the concept collapsed in 1971, but LOUISVILLE CENTRAL AREA Inc. (LCA) began promoting it again in 1975. Instrumental in making it work were Mayor Harvey I. Sloane, bankers Maurice D.S. Johnson and A. Stevens Miles, and Wilson W. Wyatt Jr., LCA director. Oxford Development Corp. of Edmonton, Alberta, was selected in 1976 as the developer; and Skidmore, Owings, and Merrill was chosen to design the complex. In 1978 Gov. Julian Carroll committed $8 million in state funds to the project, the United States Department of Housing and Urban Development followed in 1979 with a matching Urban Development Action Grant, and Teachers Insurance and Annuity Association provided $65 million in construction financing. The project was slowed for a time by a controversy over the architecturally and historically significant Will Sales and Atherton Buildings, which local preservationists wanted included in the project against Oxford's will. The dispute ended in October 1979 when the federal Advisory Council on HISTORIC PRESERVATION approved demolition. Ground was broken two months later, and the Galleria opened in September 1982. Construction cost was approximately $130 million.

Carl E. Kramer

GALT, WILLIAM CRAIG (b Williamsburg, Virginia, April 8, 1777; d Louisville, October 22, 1853). Physician. The son of John Minson Galt, M.D., and Judith (Craig) Galt, he was trained in MEDICINE by his father, who had attended medical lectures in Edinburgh, Scotland (1767). Galt married Matilda Beall in Virginia. Coming to Louisville in 1802, they made their home at Second and MAIN Streets. He became a widely known practitioner and soon was sought as a preceptor-teacher by medical students. As was customary in the early nineteenth century, Dr. Galt sold medicine from his shop, ADVERTISING in Louisville NEWSPAPERS as early as August 1806. He also was involved in civic and medical affairs. He was appointed a trustee of the town of Louisville in 1805 and 1808.

A much-respected and frequent medical consultant in communities on both sides of the OHIO RIVER, Galt assisted in the medical care of Gen. GEORGE ROGERS CLARK in 1809 when Dr. Richard B. Ferguson amputated the general's leg. An incorporator of the Louisville Library Co. (1816), Galt was also a founding member of the first Louisville medical society (1819) formed by sixteen physicians for advancing professional science and establishing a fee schedule. In 1823, with four other physicians, he was appointed to the first health board. When the Louisville Marine Hospital (later Louisville City Hospital) opened in 1823, he served as an attending physician and later (1839) as consulting physician. Involved in medical education since his arrival in town, Galt was one of the twelve physician incorporators (1833) of the LOUISVILLE MEDICAL INSTITUTE, which began classes in 1837. He received an honorary M.D. from the Institute (1838). He was also a capable botanist/horticulturist, but no publications by him have been located.

See *Louisville Weekly Courier*, Oct. 29, 1853.

Eugene H. Conner

GALT HOUSE. Four HOTELS on Louisville's riverfront, two of them contemporary, have carried the name Galt House. The first, so named because it was built on land purchased from Dr. William C. Galt, opened about 1835 at the northeast corner of Second and MAIN Streets. Its most quotable guest—and among its most notable—was Charles Dickens, who wrote in his *American Notes* of his 1842 visit, "We slept at the Galt House; a splendid hotel; and were as handsomely lodged as though we had been in Paris, rather than hundreds of miles beyond the Alleghenies."

Before the CIVIL WAR, southern planters brought their families to the Galt House to escape the summer heat of Louisiana and Mississippi, often staying from early spring through late fall. The hotel became a social and political center widely known for its lavish food and mint juleps. It was also the scene of occasional violence, including a barroom brawl in 1838 that resulted in two deaths.

With the coming of the Civil War, the leisurely visits of southern planters were gone forever. Instead the hotel was filled with northern guests, many of them military. Gen. William Tecumseh Sherman made his headquarters at the hotel in 1861, and Gen. U.S. Grant stayed there. On September 29, 1862, the hotel was the scene of the shooting death of Union major general William L. Nelson by Union brigadier general Jefferson C. Davis in response to an insult. In the turmoil of war, Davis was never tried and eventually returned to duty.

Louisville's original Galt House was destroyed by fire on January 11, 1865. The rooms were heated by coal fires, and metal chutes had been installed in the walls from top to bottom to facilitate the removal of ashes. A watchman

The second Galt House, completed in 1869 on the northeast corner of First and Main Streets.

spotted the fire in one of the chutes shortly after midnight and roused the 250 or so guests. Nevertheless, there were several deaths, variously reported as two to six, and a number of injuries.

The second Galt House, larger and more elegant than the first, was designed by architect HENRY WHITESTONE and completed in 1869 at the northeast corner of First and Main Streets. In this era of post–Civil War prosperity, guests still arrived by steamboat in large numbers, and Louisvillians held fancy dinners and debut parties at the hotel.

Over the years, presidents, from U.S. Grant to Theodore Roosevelt, and entertainers stayed there. An event described as the "most brilliant ball ever seen in Louisville" honored the Grand Duke Alexis of Russia during an overnight stay in 1872. In 1877, twenty thousand well-wishers rallied in front of the hotel to greet President Rutherford B. Hayes.

With the demise of steamboat traffic, Louisville's commercial center moved away from the river. The second Galt House closed in 1919 and was torn down in 1921 to make way for BELKNAP Hardware and Manufacturing Co.'s new headquarters and warehouse.

In 1972 developer/builder Al Schneider opened Louisville's third Galt House. Alton "Al" J. Schneider was one of the first modern developers to risk his own money for riverfront revitalization. Schneider dropped out of high school during his first year when his father's construction business fell victim to the GREAT DEPRESSION. His grandfather built houses, including many of the Victorian homes on South Third and FOURTH Streets. He struck out on his own in 1938. He began branching out from housing during WORLD WAR II, building military structures and afterwards schools, hospital additions, office buildings, shopping centers, and churches across Jefferson County. Beginning in the 1950s, Schneider moved to develop office buildings and HOTELS, including the Medical Arts building on Eastern Parkway, the Louisville Inn, the Executive Inn, and the Executive West. In the 1960s, as a member of the URBAN RENEWAL Commission, Schneider became involved in efforts to have a national hotel chain locate on riverfront urban renewal property in order to justify building a parking garage. When the commission could find no one interested, the chairman, ARCHIBALD COCHRAN, urged Schneider to undertake it. "From a monetary standpoint [it] was kind of a stupid thing to do," according to Schneider. He did it anyhow, succeeding in building the Galt House and anchoring the rebirth of Fourth and Main Streets.

Designed by architect Thomas Nolan, the 658-room hotel at Fourth St. overlooks the OHIO RIVER. The Galt House East, a 610-room sister hotel across Fourth St., opened in 1985. A third building with sixteen floors was constructed at the same time but remained unfinished until 1999, when it added extra-large hotel suites with prime river views for short- or long-term residence. With three RESTAURANTS and fifty-two banquet rooms, the Galt House hotels are the sites of meetings and conventions; and, like the earlier hotels, these have hosted entertainers and politicians. Presidents Jimmy Carter, Ronald Reagan, and George Bush have been guests, as well as President and Mrs. Bill Clinton when he was governor of Arkansas. Other famous guests have included MUHAMMAD ALI, Rosemary Clooney, Bob Hope, Bishop Desmond Tutu, and John Wayne.

See *The Story of the Galt House* (Louisville 1914); George Yater, *Two Hundred Years at the Falls of the Ohio* (Louisville 1979); *Louisville Herald,* Dec. 12, 1909; *Courier-Journal,* Feb. 9, 1999.

Kay Gill

GAMBLING. Controversy over GAMBLING in Louisville has proven immune to the passage of time. Since the city's birth, citizens, politicians, and religious leaders alike have debated the merits of gambling's ever-changing forms, many of which have blurred the lines between amusement, sport, fund-raising, and racketeering. Some have argued that gambling is a harmless social activity—indeed, promoting a democratic transcendence of class and culture—while others have viewed gambling as an unmistakable vice, leading individuals, families, and communities down a path of ruin. Despite the perennial controversy, one certainty remains: gambling has throughout its history changed the nature of Louisville's gathering places and fitfully occupied its participants with dreams of striking it rich.

Gambling has existed since before recorded history. Therefore, it is no surprise that the onset of stagecoach and steamboat transportation in the late 1700s and early 1800s brought men jaded from weeks of travel and those looking for adventure and fast profit to Louisville's TAVERNS and boardinghouses, especially along the wharf. These establishments thus became prime spots for spontaneous and organized gambling, including poker, billiards, and faro, a popular card game of European import. Games of cards and dice flourished, as they required little preparation and even less honesty. Professional gamblers, roving on the riverboats of the Ohio and arriving in Louisville by stagecoach, often posed as amateurs looking for an innocent game of poker. One of the country's most notorious stagecoach gamblers, Sam Austin, was shot to death in Louisville following an argument ostensibly ignited around a card table.

Early-nineteenth-century Louisville witnessed the emergence of lotteries, frequently drawn at local taverns. Utilized by schools, churches, relief funds, medical organizations, and, in its early days, the military, lotteries offered a means of raising money without the burden of taxation. This "civic fundraising" saw its most active years during times of recession and depression (1798, 1816, 1818, and 1822), as lawmakers realized a need to counterbalance the paucity of money. In 1818 a lottery raised fifty thousand dollars for a hospital in Louisville, and in 1822 forty thousand dollars was amassed to drain city ponds.

Despite the lotteries' great humanitarian potential, corruption and protest quickly ensued. The humanitarian crusade of the 1830s, whose other battles included slavery and TEM-

PERANCE, began an anti-lottery campaign. Lotteries, it was claimed, were just another form of gambling and a scourge on the common working man. Although Kentucky's General Assembly finally outlawed all existing lottery privileges in 1852, the edict lasted only three years. By 1862 Kentucky was one of only three states in the nation with a statewide lottery, an object of defiance to a then-national anti-lottery crusade.

Horse-racing was in its infancy in Louisville just as lotteries were emerging. As early as 1815, the Louisville Turf, a race track on Sixteenth St. and adjacent to the HOPE DISTILLERY, was conceived. Far out of town, Beargrass Track, situated near the present-day HURSTBOURNE Pkwy. area, was established in the mid-1820s. By 1832, Oakland Racecourse replaced Louisville Turf on what is now Seventh St., south of Magnolia Ave., creating a more elegant venue for horse-racing. Though the city's number of racetracks increased from early to mid-nineteenth century, the races themselves were largely private affairs. Bets were placed by horse owners, their close friends, and, on occasion, the servants and slaves who accompanied them. The mid-1850s witnessed a decline in horse-racing, the closing of the Oakland Racecourse, and the onset of a national economic recession.

The years of the CIVIL WAR initiated a widespread loosening of restraints on social activities. Gambling dens, which had dotted the city since the 1820s, proliferated at a dizzying pace. By 1862, the estimated eighty thousand Union soldiers stationed in and around Louisville had at their disposal "an almost continuous line of gambling establishments offering keno, faro, roulette and poker games" which "lined the north side of Jefferson from Fourth to Fifth, turned the corner on Fifth to Market, and continued on the south side of Market back to Fourth" (*COURIER-JOURNAL*, February 20, 1920).

In 1871 Louisville hosted the largest single lottery held in the United States at the time. The "Grandest Scheme Ever Presented to the Public" was a series of five "gift concerts" running from 1871 to 1875, apparently used to finance the building of the Public Library of Kentucky in downtown Louisville. The bill authorizing the event never mentioned a "lottery" but instead described "fine public, literary, musical, or dramatic entertainment, at which they may distribute by lot, to patrons a portion of the proceeds." The concerts culminated with a group of blind children drawing winning numbers from a glass wheel. In the end, more than $6 million was collected in ticket sales, 7 percent of which actually benefited the new library. The once-celebrated lottery ended in controversy, leaving many Louisvillians wondering whether their city had actually hosted a fund-raiser.

After the Civil War, horse racing re-emerged a different event than it once had been. With the abolition of slavery, running horses was no longer the sole province of the landed gentry. Along with democracy, gambling would become a more important facet of a day at the racetrack. CHURCHILL DOWNS, organized in 1874 under the auspices of the Louisville Jockey Club, opened on May 17, 1875, for the "first running of a new stakes race."

Early trackside betting at Churchill Downs evolved from auction pools, to bookmakers, to pari-mutuel machines. Bookmakers reluctantly yielded to pari-mutuels only after the city GOVERNMENT declared bookmaking illegal in 1908. The pari-mutuels, first imported from France by Col. MERIWETHER LEWIS CLARK, founder of Churchill Downs, were initially invented to eliminate dishonest bookmakers. Kentucky was the first state in the nation to legalize the new betting machines, and Louisville was home to the first American-made pari-mutuel device, produced at CHARLES GRAINGER's downtown iron foundry.

The 1920s introduced a widespread challenge to Louisville's racetrack and gambling industries. The tide of PROHIBITION was accompanied by a potent anti-gambling sentiment, both elements of the Progressive movement. Leading the way was the Churchmen's Federation, a group chartered in 1910 to combat immorality. After the Churchmen's Federation established the Kentucky Anti-Racetrack-Gambling Commission, the issue penetrated Louisville politics in 1923 and became a staple Democratic campaign issue. When the commission received a vote of support from the local Ku Klux Klan chapter, the cause lost momentum due to its extremist ties. The attempt to create both a moral and economic issue also backfired, effectively ending the Progressive anti-gambling movement after the 1927 gubernatorial election, in which Republican Flem D. Sampson secured the popular vote.

Although lotteries had been prohibited in Kentucky in 1891, lottery betting continued under new guises well into the twentieth century. The state legislature permitted "bank night lotteries" in MOVIE THEATERS in the 1930s. Bank nights were evenings in which merchants distributed "gifts by drawing" to select patrons for the price of a theater ticket. Some patrons would arrive before the drawing and depart before the movie started. Bank nights were eventually outlawed in 1941.

The 1930s also witnessed the popularity of the numbers racket, an illegal lottery game descended from the streets of Detroit and Harlem. The game was based on a random selection of numbers, sometimes established by the day's pari-mutuel payoffs or stock sales. The Green House, on the 700 block of Wall St. in JEFFERSONVILLE, INDIANA, was home to the oldest and most infamous numbers den in the area. Patrons of the Green House were admitted only by recognition after climbing the club's famed flight of rickety stairs. By 1939 the numbers racket was considered the largest and most profitable form of gambling in Louisville.

When bookmakers were outlawed from Churchill Downs and city streets in 1908, their operations shifted to Louisville's gambling underground. Handbooks, or clandestine racetrack betting parlors, multiplied during the 1930s. It was estimated that seven handbooks were tucked within a block and a half of the Courier-Journal Building at Third and LIBERTY Streets during the GREAT DEPRESSION and that an average of $6 million changed hands in the city's handbooks each year. Louisville lost its claim as the local gambling center for high-rollers when luxurious betting centers sprang up in southern Indiana. The Turf Club and the Greyhound Night Club, opened in the early 1930s near Jeffersonville, offered Louisvillians free rides across the Ohio River and a posh evening of chance.

In October 1938 the Louisville chief of detectives took hold of the Cumberland News Service in the Breslin Building at Third and BROADWAY in response to an ordinance prohibiting the transmission of race news to bookmakers. Since the wire service was an essential vehicle for a bookmaker's livelihood, the city's continued action crippled the underground operations. In 1939 the Greyhound Night Club near Jeffersonville closed following the actions of the Clark circuit judge, who had prohibited big gaming in the county.

Prevalent in the late 1800s to early 1900s, pinball machines reemerged in the 1930s and 1940s to find a new popularity in BARS, poolrooms, RESTAURANTS, and drugstores. These "counter games" or "plank and peg devices" were attractive for merchants because of their small size, affordability, and innocuous reputation. To camouflage pinball's resemblance to gaming devices such as slot machines or "five-cent one-arms" and roulette wheels, machine operators installed gumball dispensers and pasted "for amusement only" signs on the machines. Despite assertions that pinball was purely a game of skill, the city levied taxes on pinball owners and operators. In 1936 an estimated eleven hundred pinball machines were being operated without licenses in the Louisville area.

Gaming devices received greater scrutiny in the 1950s and 1960s. The Johnson Act deemed unlicensed gambling machines illegal, and by 1953 federal law required a fifty-dollar gambling tax stamp per machine prior to operation. By 1957 the cost of tax stamps increased to $250; and by that time dice games, poker, and roulette were outlawed in Louisville bars. A 1960 survey calculated that 1,179 gaming devices occupied 773 locations in Jefferson County.

Beginning in the 1950s BINGO became a popular means of entertainment. Exemptions to the state's anti-gambling laws were made for churches and other nonprofit groups to hold bingos as a means of fund-raising. In time bingo parlors sprang up independently of these groups, and their numbers increased. Bingo games could be found many nights and every weekend in converted buildings along Dixie Hwy.

Ninety-seven years after lotteries were outlawed in Kentucky, voters approved a constitutional amendment permitting the operation of a state-run lottery in the autumn of 1988. Section 226 of the 1891 Kentucky Constitution had been officially voided. On April 4, 1989, Louisvillians participated in the first legally sanctioned lottery sale their state had observed in nearly a century.

The Kentucky State Lottery and Churchill Downs, both vibrant local enterprises, headed into the 1990s with a formidable competitor on their horizons. Effected in 1993, the Indiana Riverboat Gambling Act gave the Indiana Gaming Commission the ability to grant state licenses to eligible casino operators on riverboats. On November 19, 1998, CAESAR'S World Casino was inaugurated on the banks of the Ohio River in HARRISON COUNTY, INDIANA. Reminiscent of the extravagant handbooks that thrived near Jeffersonville in the 1930s, Caesar's caught the attention of Louisville gamblers looking for good fortune. Profits soared during the first year of operation.

See J. Winston Coleman, *Stage-Coach Days in the Bluegrass* (Lexington 1935); Richard Sasuly, *Bookies and Bettors: Two Hundred Years of Gambling* (New York 1982); George H. Yater, *Flappers, Prohibition and All That Jazz* (Louisville 1984); George H. Yater, *Two Hundred Years at the Falls of the Ohio* (Louisville 1989).

Susan Crowell Berigan

GARDENCOURT. Fourteen-acre estate located along Alta Vista Rd., overlooking Cherokee Park in eastern Louisville. The twenty-room residence, a two-and-one-half-story Beaux Arts–style mansion, was completed in 1906 under the guidance of the Boston architectural firm of George F. Shepley, Charles H. Rutan, and Charles A. Coolidge. Later that year, a carriage house and a gardener's cottage/greenhouse, both in the Adamesque style and presumably designed by the same firm, were added to the property. The surrounding pastoral grounds, comprising a pergola garden, a rose and terrace garden, and an entry court garden, were developed by the Olmsted Brothers landscaping firm of Brookline, Massachusetts.

At the conclusion of the construction, Lucie Underwood Norton, Martha A. "Mattie" Norton, and Minnie Norton Caldwell (widowed in 1880), the daughters of Louisville financier George W. Norton, moved into the house. After the death of Mattie in 1946, her executors, knowing her unwritten wishes for the grounds, presented GARDENCOURT to the UNIVERSITY OF LOUISVILLE for its School of Music.

The school added the Emily Davidson Recital Hall in 1962. The hall, named for the internationally prominent singer from Louisville, had hosted distinguished musicians such as Igor Stravinsky and Aaron Copland before the School of Music moved to the Shelby Campus in 1969. For nearly two decades, Gardencourt served as the offices and practice hall of the KENTUCKY OPERA Association and as the Urban Studies Center for the University of Louisville. Then school officials decided to auction the property due to the rising cost of maintenance and repairs. In April 1987, Helen Combs purchased the property for $2.2 million. Within two months, she sold it to the LOUISVILLE PRESBYTERIAN THEOLOGICAL SEMINARY for $2.25 million. After a three-year, $6.7 million restoration project, the structures and gardens were renovated for classrooms, offices for the seminary, and meeting halls, and reception areas.

GARDENS OF LOUISVILLE, THE. Located in the block between Sixth St. and Armory Place along MUHAMMAD ALI Blvd., the GARDENS OF LOUISVILLE, initially known as the Jefferson County Armory, was completed late in 1905 as the home of the LOUISVILLE LEGION militia battalion. The Beaux Arts–style building, designed by Louisville's Brinton B. Davis, was erected in less than ten months at a cost of $440,000. It opened to much fanfare as the county fiscal court members, hoping that the structure would attract local and national gatherings, presented the largest building in the commonwealth to the legion and to the city's residents.

While the structure was used throughout the first half of the twentieth century as a military training hall and an induction center during major wars, the Kentucky National Guard eventually outgrew the facilities and moved its headquarters to the State Fairgrounds in 1946. By that time the Armory had become more than an arsenal and frequently drew large crowds to a variety of events. Benefits for international and local causes such as the Children's Welfare Association usually received the arena free of charge and substantial coverage by the local press. Numerous entertainment acts graced the Armory's stage, including Ray Charles, Louis Armstrong, Frank Sinatra, Mary Wells, Igor Stravinsky, Elvis Presley, Stevie Wonder, Bob Dylan, Aaron Copland, and a national broadcast of the Tommy Dorsey Orchestra in 1936. The structure also hosted several national conventions for corporations such as the Eastman Kodak Co.; rallies for prominent figures such as President Harry S. Truman and Martin Luther King Jr.; and athletic contests such as hockey, BASKETBALL, roller derby, and even miniature race car driving. Additionally, the Armory served as a beacon of hope to the ten thousand citizens who attended a memorial service following the Titanic disaster in 1912 and the six thousand refugees who sought dry accommodations during the FLOOD OF 1937.

After an extensive renovation in 1963, the renamed Convention Center assumed a different role in the community by hosting smaller meetings, musical acts, and sports, while complementing the larger State Fairgrounds and FREEDOM HALL. The name was changed again in 1975 to avoid confusion with the new Commonwealth Convention Center being constructed a few blocks away. Dubbed Louisville Gardens, the Convention Center Operation Co. chose the name to evoke images of the celebrated Boston Garden and Madison Square Garden. In 1980 the building was added to the NATIONAL REGISTER OF HISTORIC PLACES and, beginning in 1991, was managed by the Kentucky Center for the Arts. In December of 1998, the name was changed to The Gardens of Louisville, and the arena underwent a $350,000 renovation.

See *Courier-Journal*, June 20, 1905; *Louisville Times*, April 17, 1963.

Craig M. Heuser

The Gardens of Louisville, formerly the Jefferson County Armory, on Muhammad Ali between Sixth Street and Armory Place.

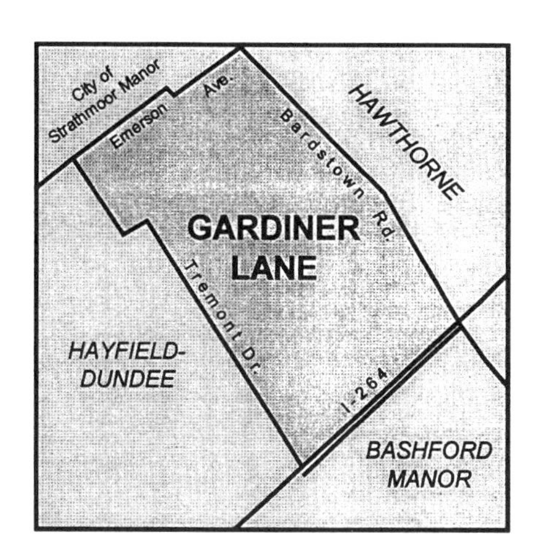

GARDINER LANE. Neighborhood in eastern Louisville bounded by Emerson Ave. to the north, Bardstown Rd. to the east, the WATTERSON EXPRESSWAY to the south, and Tremont Dr. and Lovers Ln. to the west. Mostly farmland until the early 1900s, this mixed residential and commercial community developed mainly between 1913 and 1950. A local landmark is Assumption High School for girls, established in 1954.

See *Louisville Survey: East Report* (Louisville 1980).

GARLAND, EDWARD (b Goochland County, Virginia, 1810; d Louisville, October 12, 1882). Jefferson County judge. Garland immigrated to Louisville in 1836. He practiced LAW for a number of years before being elected the first judge of Jefferson County under Kentucky's 1850 constitution. That constitution established county judgeships as elected, rather than appointed, positions. Garland served in the post from June 2, 1851, until September 5, 1858. Garland was one of the original members of the board of managers of the Industrial School of Reform, a public reformatory and house of correction for juvenile delinquents. The school, which was originally organized as the HOUSE OF REFUGE, was incorporated in 1854 by an act of the state legislature. He was married and had several children. He is buried in CAVE HILL CEMETERY.

See *Courier-Journal*, Oct. 13, 1882; J. Stoddard Johnston, ed., Memorial History of Louisville, (Chicago 1896).

GARVIN, WILLIAM (b Londonderry, Ireland, 1795; d OHIO RIVER near Warsaw, Kentucky, December 4, 1868). Businessman. The son of Hugh and Jane Garvin, he immigrated to the United States in 1816. In Philadelphia Garvin worked as a clerk in a wholesale grocery house. From there he moved to SHELBYVILLE, Kentucky, where he worked as a salesman, and then to Glasgow, Kentucky, where he went into business for himself. While there, he and his wife, Sarah Veech, had two sons and two daughters.

In 1827 Garvin and his family moved to Louisville, and he started a wholesale dry goods business with David S. Chambers under the name Chambers and Garvin. In 1835 Chambers retired, and the partnership was dissolved. Garvin continued independently for about two years and then went into business with his brother James, Thomas J. Carson, and Samuel Getty. Carson retired after a few years, and the firm became WILLIAM GARVIN and Co. In 1855 Garvin's son-in-law John Bell, Samuel Gwin, and Robert RUSSELL formed Garvin, Bell, and Co. In October 1861 the firm closed because of financial problems and remained closed throughout the CIVIL WAR. In 1866 it reopened with Garvin, his daughter, Jane G. Bell, Russell, and John T. Fisher as Garvin, Bell, and Co.

Garvin died in one of the era's most spectacular maritime accidents on the Ohio River. On December 4, 1868, near midnight, two Louisville and Cincinnati mail steamers, the *United States* and the *America*, collided almost head-on near Rail's Landing, twenty-two miles upriver from Madison, Indiana. The *America's* bow crashed through the side of the *United States,* and some petroleum on the *United States* caught fire and quickly burned. The *America* also caught fire but was able to make it to shore. Of the approximately three hundred passengers on both boats, between fifty and sixty—all but about two aboard the *United States*—lost their lives in the wreck. Garvin, who was a passenger on the *United States*, was found two weeks later still inside a cabin. Speculation was that he died of suffocation, because the body was not badly burned.

At the time of his death Garvin was the oldest member of the Board of Trade and one of the oldest merchants in the city. His untimely death prompted a substantial outcry of public sympathy. The Board of Trade published a tract honoring him, and his funeral was one of the largest in the city's history. According to newspaper accounts, the FIRST PRESBYTERIAN CHURCH was packed to overflowing, and several hundred people spilled into the streets. The funeral procession to CAVE HILL CEMETERY was more than a mile long.

A section of Fifth St. between Zane and Ormsby Streets was renamed Garvin Place in his honor.

See Louisville Board of Trade, *A Tribute to the Memory of William Garvin* (Louisville 1869); M. Joblin and Co., *Louisville Past and Present* (Louisville 1875).

GARVIN BROWN PRESERVE. The Garvin Brown Preserve, opened to the public in 1996, comprises forty-six acres of farmland and wetlands along fifteen hundred feet of the OHIO RIVER in eastern Jefferson County, adjacent to Hays Kennedy Park. Once part of Sutherland Farm, it was named in honor of the late Garvin Brown II, chairman of the board of Brown-Forman Corp, who owned and managed the farm from the time he purchased it in 1945 until his death in 1969. His widow, Trudy Polk Brown, assumed ownership and management until her death in 1983. The property was then sold to Joe Cross, who placed it for sale in 1994. Laura Lee Brown, who grew up on Sutherland Farm and wanted it preserved, was joined in its purchase by her sister, Dace Polk Brown, and her brother, GEORGE GARVIN BROWN III. Collectively they donated $1 million to help RIVER FIELDS INC., a nonprofit land conservation organization, purchase the property. Owsley Brown raised five hundred thousand dollars to maintain the preserve in perpetuity, and Joe Cross donated one hundred thousand dollars in challenge money. The Trust for Public Land donated funding, negotiated the purchase, and covered some legal costs. The land is mostly open fields and wetlands. There are no hiking trails and no admission fee to gain access to the property.

Hope L. Hollenbeck

GAST, ROBERT HENRY (b Louisville, March 2, 1896; d Hangchow Bay, China, April 10, 1934). Aviator. In 1917 he trained as a pilot with the Royal Flying Corps in Canada and served in England, Ireland, and France during WORLD WAR I. In 1919 he was instrumental in establishing BOWMAN FIELD and is said to have selected its site.

Gast was among those who founded the Aero Club of Kentucky in 1922 to promote local aviation. In the same year, he became an

Robert H. Gast, c. 1918.

officer in the Army Reserve's 465th Pursuit Squadron at BOWMAN FIELD. He also made exhibition flights and flew passengers during this period. Gast was appointed to the first group of federal aviation examiners in 1927 but soon became the personal pilot for Col. William McCormick of the *Chicago Tribune*.

In July 1929 Gast, with Parker Cramer as copilot, attempted a Chicago-to-Berlin polar flight in McCormick's Sikorsky S-38 amphibian airplane. After a water landing in northern Labrador for refueling, a wind shift drove floating ice into their airplane, and it sank. Several weeks were required for the airmen to return to civilization by ship, land tractor, and train.

Gast joined China National Aviation Corp. in 1934 and was a pilot on its passenger routes out of Shanghai. On April 10 of that year he became disoriented in dense fog over Hangchow Bay and crashed into its waters. His remains were found four months later, and he was buried in Shanghai.

In 1937 a bronze memorial to Gast was unveiled in the Administration Building lobby at Bowman Field. After WORLD WAR II the name Gast Blvd. was given to the principal north-south street of the airport.

See Lester Gardner, *Who's Who in American Aeronautics* (New York 1925); Frank Jerdone, *Pilot of Fortune* (New York 1986).

Edward Peck

GAY MEN. The history of GAY MEN in Louisville closely parallels that of other cities in the South and Midwest. In light of the environment, before the 1980s the gay community was quiescent and unobtrusive. Even later, the majority of Louisville's gay men preferred to keep their homosexuality private, opting not to become openly involved in gay cultural or political organizations.

Little is known of Louisville's gay life before the 1940s. Tantalizing clues surface here and there, but, because of the stigma attached by American culture to homosexuality, few records have survived.

If gay life was prevalent in the Victorian Era, city leaders apparently were not aware of it. The first sign of a gay subculture in Louisville came during a visit by Oscar Wilde to Louisville in 1882. Wilde's reputation as a dandy and fop preceded him. His favored flower at the time was the green carnation. When he spoke at the Masonic Temple in February, several single young men sported green carnations in their lapels. Presumably, many were gay. In the wake of Oscar Wilde's tragic fall from grace in 1895, discretion became simply a means of survival.

A 1915 vice committee report notes that "perverts," a rarity only a decade before, had become more noticeable in the intervening years. More than likely, the incidence of homosexuality has remained constant throughout Louisville history. Before the later decades of the twentieth century, the only relatively safe places for gay men to meet were public PARKS such as Cherokee; certain streets such as the YORK St. circle in front of the LOUISVILLE FREE PUBLIC LIBRARY, or Fourth near Central Park; BURLESQUE houses; or the balconies of second-run MOVIE THEATERS. The YMCA, with rooms for men only, proved convenient, as did public bathhouses. One such bath at the Windsor Hotel on Fifth near Breckinridge survived well into the 1970s.

In the absence of an established visible community, informal social networks became important. Louisville's gay life tended to center around OLD LOUISVILLE and the HIGHLANDS. Though gay men and LESBIANS might be seen entering homes together for private parties, once inside they would pair off with members of their own gender. Neighbors seldom suspected what was going on behind closed curtains.

Most certainly gay men had gathered discreetly in specific SALOONS and TAVERNS for years, but the first known "gay BARS" in Louisville date from the 1930s. Many were located in HOTELS. The Beau Brummel at the Seelbach was one such place. While not gay per se, gay men found it safe if they were discreet. Another, dating from the 1940s, was the Beaux Arts on street level in the Henry Clay Hotel. Because it catered to lesbians as well, a casual customer might not realize that the men and women sitting together in booths or at tables were gay men and lesbians out on dates with members of their own gender. A 1950 gay bar guide lists two others: the Plantation Room in the Kentucky Hotel and Gordon's at 1001 W BROADWAY. About three years later, Louisville's most successful gay entertainment operation, the Downtowner, opened on Chestnut near Fourth St. After a fire in 1974, the owners moved it to MAIN St. In 1989 it moved to Brook St. and changed its name to the Connection Complex, one of the largest gay bars in the country.

The gay bars of an earlier day little resembled the ones of today. Same-sex dancing and touching were prohibited. If customers showed overt affection, they were asked to leave. Fear of arrest was constant. Only with the surge of POPULATION known as the Baby Boom and the countercultural movement of the late 1960s did the gay subculture begin to change. When gay men and lesbians revolted against police harassment at New York's Stonewall Inn in the summer of 1969, little did they know that within five years gay men and lesbians would start to go public nationwide. In Louisville, initial efforts at organizing were tentative and brief. In 1970, a few men who had participated in the Stonewall riots came through Louisville on a "consciousness raising" mission. In response, a few young men and women formed Kentucky's first gay group, the Gay Liberation Front.

Almost immediately it ran into controversy. The UNIVERSITY OF LOUISVILLE had established a "Free University," a system of free classes on such subjects as astrology, tarot card reading, and psychic phenomena. The Gay Liberation Front proposed that Free University include classes on gay life in the curriculum. Some state legislators objected and threatened to cancel the entire Free University. But U of L's president argued successfully in favor of the class, and the first was held in September. Ironically, most attendees were reportedly non-gay.

The same group would go on to organize a community center in the HIGHLANDS, publish Kentucky's first gay newspaper (*Trash*), and establish the state's first gay counseling line. But in October 1971 Louisville police raided the community center on a tip that marijuana was being smoked there and teenagers were allowed inside. The Louisville gay community would show little interest in organizing again in the same magnitude for another ten years.

Nonpolitical organizing proved more enduring. On September 9, 1972, two lesbian women invited some friends over for a Bible study. Two years later they began meeting at the FIRST UNITARIAN CHURCH, where the group grew to mission status of the Metropolitan Community Church. After a difficult beginning, the group was recognized as a chartered church on November 17, 1985. When First Unitarian burned on December 14, 1985, space was found at the Comm-Ten Community Center. In October 1988 the congregation moved to a facility on Bank St. On July 6, 1997, with the Reverend Dee Dale leading the congregation, it moved into the former Trinity Lutheran Church building on Highland Ave. A chapter of Dignity, a support group for gay Catholics, was also founded in the early 1970s.

In April 1978 the *LOUISVILLE TIMES* published an article about Kelly King, the stage name for a local female impersonator. Reader response was overwhelmingly negative, prompting WLKY-TV News to run a series on gay men in Louisville the following month. In the final segment, a local realtor, Jack Kersey, proclaimed his homosexuality publicly: the first gay man in Kentucky to do so. Kersey would go on to help organize several groups, including the Gay and Lesbian Hotline and Community Health Trust, the leading local agency in the fight against AIDS.

But Louisville's gay community would not find its cause celèbre until 1981. That fall, Sam Dorr, branch manager of a local bank, was elected president of Dignity. Because he felt he might have to speak out on gay issues, he told his supervisors about his election. They objected and asked him to resign from the bank, which he did, but the following year he filed suit in federal court, charging that the bank had violated his religious rights, among others. He settled out of court four years later. His problems bothered many of his friends. In early 1982, several banded together to found Gays and Lesbians United for Equality (GLUE), a coalition group. Other groups soon formed, including a hotline, an ARCHIVES and library, and support groups targeted at various populations. Many remain active. A gay newspaper, the *Lavender Letter,* had begun publication the previous year. By 1983 *Lambda Louisville News* joined it. A cable access gay and lesbian TELEVISION show followed in June 1984.

Political organizing remained difficult within the gay community but not impossible. An early victory came in March 1986 when the Greater Louisville Human Rights Coalition convinced the Louisville and Jefferson County Human Relations Commission to vote in favor of extending CIVIL RIGHTS protections in the area of sexual orientation. The aldermen chose to ignore the vote.

The political establishment couldn't ignore the gay community completely, however. In July 1983, Kentucky's first death from AIDS occurred in Lexington. By the late 1980s, the epidemic was expanding in Louisville. Community Health Trust took an early lead, establishing Glade House, a residence for people with AIDS, and helping them financially in other ways. It would go on to become the state's premier community-based AIDS organization. In 1989 the aldermen passed an ordinance to prohibit discrimination against people with AIDS after heated debate punctuated by protests from local church members. The following year they also approved a hate crimes ordinance extending protections to gay men and lesbians. After the state attorney general found it unconstitutional, they approved a second ordinance in 1991 that passed muster.

The year 1991 proved to be a major turning point. In the primary elections that year, two gay-supportive aldermen were defeated. Gay leaders quickly realized that if the aldermen were ever to approve a gay civil rights ordinance, they would have to take the issue up before the end of the year. The board initially tabled it, prompting a vigorous campaign by a new group, the Fairness Campaign. The seeds of Fairness were found in the Lesbian Feminist Union of the 1970s. It was formally launched in June 1991 to work for a community in which all are treated equally.

Frank G. Simon headed up the fight against the Fairness Campaign. Simon, a conservative Republican, leads the political action committee Freedom's Heritage Forum—a local group formed in 1986 that opposes legal protection for homosexuals and abortionists. The organization uses mailings and a TELEPHONE network to mobilize its members. Simon also directs the Kentucky chapter of the American Family Association best known for its efforts to boycott television programs and other media that contain obscene or immoral materials. Simon is a ST. MATTHEWS allergist who had a Christian conversion experience in 1975.

The Fairness Campaign has prioritized both the strengthening of relations within the gay and lesbian community and the building of bridges with others working for a more just society. Its primary goal is comprehensive civil rights legislation prohibiting discrimination on the basis of sexual orientation. But on August 25, 1992, the Fairness Amendment was defeated by the aldermen 8 to 4. A second attempt three years later on March 28, 1995, also failed to get employment discrimination banned. Following that vote, twenty-three protesters were arrested in aldermanic chambers for refusing to leave. A third vote failed in 1997. On January 26, 1999, by a vote of 7 to 5, the BOARD OF ALDERMEN adopted an ordinance that banned workplace discrimination based on sexual orientation. It was signed into law a few days later by Mayor Dave Armstrong.

David Williams

GENERAL ELECTRIC APPLIANCE PARK. In 1950 the General Electric Corp., with Ralph J. Cordiner as president, decided to consolidate its various major appliance businesses into one location. Corporate predictions anticipated phenomenal growth in the Major Appliance division, which at that time accounted for about 10 percent of the corporate giant's $3-billion-a-year volume. However, GE's manufacturing facilities were scattered throughout the United States.

General Electric chose the Louisville area because of its easy access to water, rail, and air transportation systems. The city was also a central location for national distribution and possessed a very favorable business climate and a good LABOR supply.

In May 1951, seven hundred acres of land in BUECHEL were purchased, and three hundred more were rezoned "industrial" for future use. Groundbreaking ceremonies for the first building took place in July. Construction continued through 1952. Massive landscaping was completed, with more than four hundred acres of land grassed and planted with some seven hundred varieties of trees and shrubs.

Today's completed complex covers about 920 acres. There are twelve miles of paved road, twenty miles of railroad track, and a postal zipcode, 40225, just for Appliance Park. The 140 acres of buildings include 5 manufacturing plants, an enormous warehouse, and a research-and-development center. Building One was designed to produce home laundry equipment; Building Two, electric ranges; Building Three, dishwashers and disposers; Buildings Four and Five, refrigerators and, in the 1960s, air conditioners.

In 1953, as the park produced its first products, it leased a UNIVAC computer from Remington Rand. At that time there were only six in existence, and the U.S. GOVERNMENT owned five of them. GE at Appliance Park became the first company to make industrial application of computers. It was also one of the first companies to promote its products on the then-infant industry called TELEVISION. *GE Theater* made its debut on CBS Television in April 1953. In January 1953 the first dryers and dishwashers were assembled. By March ranges from Building Two, the first appliances to be completely manufactured at and shipped from the park, made their appearance. So, also, did clothes-washing machines. In April Disposall-brand food waste disposers began production. In October 1954 the refrigerator line began production; and in 1958, after completion of a $40 million expansion program, GE began production of air conditioners at the park.

The tenth anniversary of Appliance Park was 1961, and a statistical overview of the park's effect on the Louisville area at that time is amazing: an annual $63 million company payroll, 50,000 new residents, 10,000 new homes, 3,500 new retail stores, about 10 new schools, $1.7 million in philanthropic contributions to local HOSPITALS, direct employment for as many as 16,000 workers (1955), and approximately $250,000 paid annually in Union dues. Appliance Park itself used about a hundred thousand tons of steel a year. On a daily basis it used close to 10 railroad cars of Kentucky coal, enough electricity to power 120,000 average homes, and enough water to supply 60,000 homes. In short, Appliance Park had a phenomenal impact on every aspect of Louisville life.

The 1960s was a decade of great development for GE. A 1961 company advertisement said Appliance Park employed more than ten thousand people and could produce sixty thousand major appliances a week. In 1963 GE introduced the revolutionary self-cleaning oven, a major development in the industry, and GE engineers garnered over 100 patents as a result. The years 1964 through 1968 were great growth years for the U.S. ECONOMY, and especially for the home appliance industry. Appliance Park in 1964 had an annual payroll of $80 million and a workforce of about ten thousand people. By 1970, as reported by the Louisville Chamber of Commerce, the park had an annual payroll in excess of $150 million, with eighteen thousand employees. The present was booming, and the future looked rosy. The industry projected a growth rate of 80 percent by the end of the next decade. But the end of this decade, 1969, saw the company embroiled in the longest and most costly strike in its history. The issue was wages and the cost of living. The strike began on October 27, 1969, and ended on February 1, 1970, with the acceptance of a negotiated national contract. With Donald I. Rock as president of Local 761 of the IUE, 14,000 union workers participated in the 101-day national walkout.

Still, the 1970s promised huge growth in the country's major appliance needs. The decade would show wild fluctuations, however, beginning in champagne but ending in swamp water. The first four years saw very rapid growth in the industry and also at Appliance Park. In 1970 employment reached twenty thousand. In 1971 the Applied Research and Design Center at the park was completed, with a 5,000-volume technical library and 182,000 square feet of laboratories. In 1972 employment peaked at an all-time high of about twenty-three thousand workers, nearly fifteen thousand of these union members of Local 761 of the IUE, of which Ken Cassady was president. The appliance industry had its best year ever in 1973, but 1974 and 1975 marked the beginning of a U.S. recession that would be the most severe since the 1930s. Nationwide unemployment in 1975 reached 9 percent of the total labor force, with Kentucky unemployment reaching 8.4 percent. Appliance manufacturing in these years was characterized by low profitability, rising costs, and excess capacity. U.S. factory productivity fell behind many other industrialized nations. The weakness of the dollar, large international trade deficits, and high inflation also bedeviled the economy. High mortgage rates and depressed housing starts brought the decade to a close. Between 1979 and 1980 industry sales of major appliances fell 7 percent. These woeful economic patterns would continue until 1983.

In 1977 Appliance Park noted its twenty-fifth anniversary, and in 1978 General Electric its one hundredth anniversary.

The first three years of the 1980s were characterized by a continuing attempt to turn the economic corner. The first robotics were introduced at Appliance Park in 1980. In 1981 GE earmarked $38 million for the modernization of the dishwasher department, despite the fact that all major appliances except room air conditioners and microwave ovens showed declining sales. One 1981 financial bright spot, however, was the export market. GE boosted its exports dramatically from $1.9 billion in 1976 to $4 billion in 1981. Finally, in 1983, as housing starts more than doubled, the economy of the major appliance industry began its recovery. Industry-wide sales rose 21 percent. The last half of the decade saw employment at Appliance Park slip from 13,500 in 1984 to about 11,300 in 1990. The same trend would continue through the decade of the 1990s.

The 1990 Appliance Park employment figure of 11,300 would fall to 9,550 by 1997, according to the Louisville Chamber of Commerce and the Kentucky Cabinet for Economic Development. Automation, intense foreign and domestic competition, and attractive lower-wage foreign labor have all been cited as reasons for the loss of manufacturing jobs at Appliance Park. Nonetheless, despite local employment problems, GE Appliances in the late 1990s, with Appliance Park as its designated global headquarters, sold annually, under 5 different brand names, more than 12 million units in 150 world markets.

Throughout its Louisville history, Appliance Park, GE, and its employees have been unstintingly generous in their support of local hospitals, youth organizations, and educational programs through donations, in-kind services, and countless volunteer hours. This tradition of serving the community includes an on-site volunteer center and the Employees' Community Fund, which has donated over $25 million to area community service organizations.

February 1998 saw the park cut fifteen hundred jobs with an announcement to move the production of ranges and dryers to plants in Mexico and Georgia. August 1999 brought another formal notice, to close the plant's refrigerator line and move it to Mexico. In Louisville fifteen hundred jobs could be lost; in Bloomington, Indiana, another thirty-two hundred. At the time of the latter announcement there were about 5,000 hourly workers at the park—most of them members of IUE 761, of which Charles Smith was president—averaging $17.50 an hour. Mexico held out the prospect of lower labor costs.

In July 1999 the Research and Development Center at the park announced the development of the GE Advantium Oven. It is considered the first new invention in cooking technology since the microwave oven and cooks food using only halogen lights. Also in July, GE announced that Appliance Park's Building Three would be the site of a new line of dishwashers called the Triton. The new line represents a $34 million investment by GE.

See Franklin Friday, *A Walk through the Park* (Louisville 1987); *Courier-Journal*, April 29, 1951, May 20, 1951, Jan. 8, 1960, Nov. 19, 1961, Jan. 25, 1970, Feb. 15, 1970, July 30, 1999, Aug. 1, 1999.

Mark Reilly

GENE SNYDER FREEWAY. Along with the plans for an inner-belt highway (modern-day WATTERSON EXPRESSWAY), the Jefferson County PLANNING AND ZONING Commission announced its approval in 1946 of the construction of an outer-belt highway ringing the city. After land acquisition problems, numerous changes in the route, money concerns, and protests from outlying cities such as ANCHORAGE, the first stretch of the highway opened between SHELBYVILLE Rd. and Interstate 64 in 1961, almost two years before the final plans for a proposed thirty-four-mile route were completed. In 1964 the artery was renamed Jefferson Freeway to avoid confusion with the existing Outer Loop. By 1975 construction had stalled, with only $30 million of work finished out of an estimated $205 million, and state Highway Commission officials doubted if the freeway ever would be completed. However, state officials renewed their efforts late in 1980 and guaranteed the completion of the route between Dixie Hwy. and Interstate 65 by 1985. Two years after this promise, the end was in sight as the state began purchasing the land for the final link between Smyrna Rd. and TAYLORSVILLE Rd. U.S. Representative MARION GENE SNYDER included $52 million in a PUBLIC WORKS bill for the Jefferson Freeway's construction. To commemorate Snyder's efforts, United States Senator MITCH MCCONNELL convinced the state to rename the route GENE SNYDER FREEWAY in 1985. After a total cost of $250 million, the final stretch of the expressway opened in 1987, completing the thirty-seven-mile stretch from U.S. 42 to Dixie Hwy. Its completion has hastened the movement of POPULATION to settle along its route, while many of its interchanges show growth and development.

See *Courier-Journal*, Jan. 28, 1990.

GEOGRAPHY. "Geography" listings in gazetteers reveal Louisville's geographic location to be 38 degrees, 15 minutes north latitude and 85 degrees, 14 minutes west of the Greenwich Meridian (at a point near the intersection of First St. and BROADWAY). Other sources note that Louisville is located on the left bank of the OHIO RIVER about six hundred miles downstream from the confluence of the Monongahela and Allegheny Rivers at Pittsburgh. Both citations are correct and, more important, reveal the absolute and relative geographic location; that is, the site and the situation of Kentucky's largest metropolitan center.

In 1997 the city limits of Louisville included an area of sixty-six square miles within Jefferson County, Kentucky. A large portion of the city occupies a low, flat area along the Ohio River floodplain about 460 feet above sea level. Along the city's northern boundary the river flows southwest, turns to the northwest to cross the Falls, and then continues on a sweep directly to the south where it becomes the western city limits. The city is bounded on the east and south by Jefferson County and on the north and west by the river.

An eastern portion of the city's site is on a limestone upland called the HIGHLANDS located about fifty-five feet above the floodplain to the west. It was the Highlands and adjacent CRESCENT HILL that served as havens for residents displaced by the 1937 flood. The Paleozoic sedimentary rocks that are found here have been weathered over geologic time to form caves and sinkholes. Nineteenth-century Louisville breweries often used these caves to cool their wares. Perhaps the best-known cemetery in Louisville, CAVE HILL CEMETERY, is also located here, where the existence of caves offered early residents convenient kinds of natural mausoleums.

A second upland area is found in the southern region of Louisville consisting of KENWOOD HILL and IROQUOIS Hill. The latter is the highest elevation in the city (761 feet), and the "Overlook" at its peak is a popular spot for viewing a panorama extending into southern Indiana. The lowest elevation is generally considered to be the point where the Ohio River leaves southwestern Louisville at the western end of Gibson Lane, 384 feet above sea level.

Parts of the Highlands are drained by BEARGRASS CREEK, which entered the Ohio near the present-day intersection of Fourth St. and River Rd. before the channel was moved upstream to the "cutoff," a point near Towhead Island. Stream drainage to the south and west is through Pond Creek and Mill Creek, tributaries of the Salt River.

The physical site of Louisville included two additional natural characteristics associated with water. The first was the poor natural drainage on the floodplain often leading to stagnant pools of water that provided breeding grounds for mosquitoes throughout the central and western portions of the city. These swampy areas were generally thought by early residents to be unhealthy or insalubrious sources of a number of human ailments known collectively as "consumptive diseases." The second characteristic is the multiple layers of unconsolidated material lying on the floodplain between the surface and the limestone bedrock below. These layers of sand, gravel, silt, and clay make up what is known as the LOUISVILLE AQUIFER. Water running through and around these layers moved north and northwest toward the river and is still used as a natural source of seasonal cooling and heating for large buildings located in the Central Business District. The natural heating and cooling effect is possible because the groundwater in the aquifer maintains a relatively constant temperature, cooler than surface water in the summer and warmer than surface water in the winter.

Louisville's metropolitan region includes seven counties, three in Kentucky (Jefferson, Oldham, and Bullitt) and four across the Ohio River in Indiana (Clark, Floyd, Harrison, and Scott). While not officially so designated in 1997, SHELBY COUNTY, Kentucky, is very much a part of Louisville's geographic region culturally and economically, and it is included by most geographers as part of the metropolitan region.

In a larger geographic sense, Louisville lies at the western limits of the Outer Bluegrass physiographically, and, as a town, between the Midwest and South culturally. This latter situation was reinforced by a large electric sign that was located for many years at the southern end of the Clark Memorial Bridge on the Louisville Gas and Electric Power Plant proudly proclaiming Louisville as the "Gateway to the South."

Without question, the most important physical element of Louisville's GEOGRAPHY is the FALLS OF THE OHIO, the only natural barrier to water transportation on the river. One of the earliest accounts of travel on the Ohio River is contained in the journal of John Howard and John Peter Salley, who negotiated the Falls of the Ohio in May of 1742. While a falls in name, a more appropriate title might have been "rapids," for the twenty-six-foot descent of the river here occurred over a distance of some two and one-half miles. Before the advent of high-lift dams, the falls must have been spectacular to behold as water, drift, and on occasion even unsuspecting travelers were carried downstream over this outcropping of 300-million-year-old limestone. During times of low water the ledge was exposed in places, and the natural erosive power of water upon stone left a series of low mounds that came to be described as "petrified wasps' nests."

In times of low water, downstream travel over the Falls was impossible; however, in high water, "shooting the rapids" was possible. Three passages or "chutes" were available to river travelers. On the north side was the Indiana Chute, on the south the Kentucky or Town Chute, and in the middle the appropriately named Middle Chute. Thus one of the first opportunities for employment was the role of river pilot, whose job it was to direct watercraft safely across the barrier via one of the chutes. While it was possible then to cross the Falls going downstream during high water, uninterrupted travel upstream was quite difficult until the opening of the LOUISVILLE AND PORTLAND CANAL in 1830. Thus the river, both as transportation route and as a barrier to continuous movement of goods and people, was the primary natural influence in the growth and development of early Louisville.

Even before the growing volume of river traffic on the "Western Waters" followed the east-to-west flow of the Ohio, the geographic hinterland of Louisville had already expanded to the territories north of the river. In 1787 Hector St. John Crevecoeur, a FRENCH traveler and trader, noted Louisville's importance as a center for commerce. He wrote: "This little city, already the metropolis of the country, contains merchandise for the trade in skins from Venango and the Peninsula of Lake Erie by the river Miami, Muskingham, Scioto, etc., and also goods to descend the Ohio to supply the wants of farmers of Indiana, Kentucky, the Wabash, and even Illinois." Venango was a fortification on the Allegheny River route connecting Presque Isle (Erie, Pennsylvania) with Fort Duquense (Pittsburgh).

Louisville's geographic location as a transfer point led to an increasingly important role as an entrepôt between the settled East and the growing western frontier. Goods shipped on downstream via the Ohio and Mississippi to New Orleans could be sold or traded there for imported goods that could then be shipped back upstream. The volume of commerce on this route was of sufficient concern to Congress to make Louisville an official "Port of Entry" in 1799, complete with a collector to impose tariffs and prevent the smuggling of goods into the country. The office was closed in 1803 after the Louisiana Purchase.

The growth of Louisville as a trading center and transfer point for commercial traffic at the Falls was greatly enhanced in 1811 with the advent of steam navigation on the Ohio River. Launched at Pittsburgh in the summer of 1811, the *New Orleans* was the first STEAMBOAT on the Ohio. On its maiden voyage downstream the craft arrived at Louisville on October 28, 1811, when the low water level prevented crossing the Falls. To the astonishment of the citizenry and perhaps as a precursor of things to come, the *New Orleans* steamed upstream against the current toward Cincinnati and was then turned downstream once again to travel across the Falls on its voyage to its namesake city. Thus began Louisville's love affair with the steamboat.

The growth in numbers of steamboats built and traveling on the Ohio by the year 1830 (over two hundred) guaranteed Louisville's growth. While the Falls was an important break for steamboat navigation on the Ohio, the city, along with NEW ALBANY and JEFFERSONVILLE, INDIANA, served as a shipbuilding, outfitting, and repair center. The resultant growth of POPULATION saw Louisville triple in size between 1820 and 1830, surpassing Lexington as Kentucky's largest city. Here was the "ripple effect" at work, with increased employment in transportation and river commerce creating numerous opportunities in other sectors of the ECONOMY. And even as late as 1870, when the magic of the railroad marked the decline of the steamboat, Louisvillians, one hundred thousand strong, could boast of their ranking as the fourteenth-largest city in the United States.

As a river town, Louisville, especially the waterfront, developed a reputation as a rough place where transients and locals were often given to rowdy and bawdy behavior. To meet the growing need for efficient and effective law enforcement, Louisville was granted city status by the Kentucky General Assembly in 1828. This also allowed the city to develop plans for a city court as well as the improvement of local streets and roads and the creation of new thoroughfares.

In addition to internal road building, other roads or turnpikes were built to provide overland linkages with other regions of Kentucky, notably Frankfort, Bardstown, and Bowling Green. This latter road came to be known as the LOUISVILLE AND NASHVILLE TURNPIKE. Chartered in 1829, the road was to connect Louisville with Elizabethtown via West Point and then go on toward Bowling Green and finally the Tennessee line. Work began in 1837, and by mid-century over a hundred miles had been completed, with other portions at various stages of construction. The road system was superseded by the arrival of the railroad and later became a part of U.S. Highway 31W (Dixie Hwy.), a major north-south route.

As was the case with other regional cities in mid-nineteenth-century America, Louisville's age of transportation by turnpike, riverboat, and canal was followed by yet another epoch, the coming of the railroad. If the city was to survive as a transportation point, it would require the development of overland rail linkages to complement the river traffic that had been the major influence in Louisville's early growth.

The first rail connection from Louisville was to Frankfort and on to Lexington's Bluegrass Region in 1851. Because of competition between Louisville and Cincinnati for access to the South, local capital was used to form the LOUISVILLE & NASHVILLE RAILROAD. In 1859 the line from Louisville was completed to Nashville, where it connected with lines to other southern cities. In addition, other branch or trunk lines were built to connect smaller towns with the main lines and thus with Louisville.

During the CIVIL WAR the L&N was a major transportation system for Union forces operating west of the Appalachians. Following the war, growth and the acquisition of other rail lines extended the L&N to ports on the Gulf of Mexico as well as the coal fields of eastern Kentucky, eastern Tennessee, and western Virginia. Thus the geographic connections afforded by a growing rail system continued the transportation linkages provided by the Ohio River.

The advent of air transportation in Louisville was also influenced by geographic factors. The first commercial airport, BOWMAN FIELD, was opened in 1928. During WORLD WAR II this airport was chosen as a training location for glider pilots because of its accessibility and because the region's irregular field patterns and TOPOGRAPHY were similar to those in the European war zone and thus were ideal training sites.

A second airport, STANDIFORD FIELD (now LOUISVILLE INTERNATIONAL AIRPORT), was opened in 1947 to handle the growing volume of commercial air traffic. In part the result of its geographic location, it was chosen as the site of UNITED PARCEL SERVICE's main United States air hub, with operations beginning there on August 28, 1987.

See Ralph H. Brown, *Historical Geography of the United States* (New York 1948); Thomas D. Clark, *Beginning of the L&N.* (Lexington 1933); Ellen Churchill Semple, "Louisville: A Study in Economic Geography," *Journal of School Geography* (New York 1900); George H. Yater, *Two Hundred Years at the Falls of the Ohio* (Louisville 1987).

Dennis L. Spetz

GEOLOGY. All of the bedrock that one sees in Jefferson County—the rocky ledges in creek beds, roadcuts along highways, shaley slopes on hillsides—all of these outcropping rocks were deposited in environments quite different from those found in the county today. At the time of their deposition several hundred million years ago during the Paleozoic Era, the area of the North American continent that is now the site of Louisville and Jefferson County was moving through the southern latitudes, between five and twenty-five degrees south of the equator.

Geologic deposits presently exposed at the surface in Jefferson County consist of sedimentary rocks deposited in marine environments during the middle part of the Paleozoic Era, from about 445 to 345 million years ago, and unconsolidated sediments laid down in terrestrial environments during the latter part of the Cenozoic Era, from at least 20,000 years ago to the present time, but possibly from as much as 150,000 years ago to the present. The rocks consist of limestone, dolomite, shale, and siltstone; the sediments are composed of silt, clay, sand, and gravel.

A total of about 1,040 feet of Ordovician, Silurian, Devonian, and Mississippian sedimentary rocks are exposed in Jefferson County. An additional 5,350 feet of dolomite, limestone, shale, and sandstone of Cambrian and Ordovician age (570 to 445 million years old) are present beneath the surface. They were encountered in a deep well in western Jefferson County that was drilled through the Paleozoic sedimentary section into Precambrian igneous rock. The well bottomed out in a Precambrian gabbro, which has been dated as being at least 1.6 billion years old or older.

Jefferson County is on the western flank of the Cincinnati Arch, a north-south-trending anticline extending across central Kentucky. Rock formations in the county generally dip to the west, away from the arch. The regional dip causes older rocks to dip beneath progressively younger formations from east to west across the county.

The oldest surface rocks crop out in eastern Jefferson County and consist of limestone, dolomite, and shale in the Grant Lake Limestone and Drakes Formation of Late Ordovician age (445 to 440 million years old). The limestones, commonly interbedded with shales, were deposited in warm, shallow seas. They contain abundant FOSSILS, including zones of colonial corals. The dolomite, finely crystalline and partly mudcracked, accumulated in shallower lagoons and tidal flats. About 230 feet of Ordovician strata are exposed in the county.

In the adjacent metropolitan counties of Shelby and Spencer, as much as an additional 450 feet of older Ordovician limestone and shale crop out at the surface. These older Ordovician rocks dip westward beneath the Grant Lake and Drakes formations and are below the surface in Jefferson County.

Younger Paleozoic rocks deposited during the Silurian and Devonian Periods crop out in an irregular belt trending north to south across central Jefferson County. The Silurian and Devonian outcrop belt extends southward through BULLITT COUNTY and northeastward across OLDHAM COUNTY.

Limestone, dolomite, and shale of Silurian age (440 to 425 million years old) form five geologic rock units consisting of, in ascending stratigraphic order, the Brassfield Formation (limestone and dolomite), Osgood Formation (shale and minor dolomite), Laurel Dolomite (dolomite and minor shale), Waldron Shale (shale and minor dolomite), and Louisville Limestone (dolomitic limestone and dolomite). The five formations have a combined thickness of about 170 feet.

Silurian limestones, which are abundantly to sparsely fossiliferous, were deposited in environments ranging from wave-agitated sea floors to lagoons and tidal flats. Several limestones were later altered to dolomite by magnesium-enriched fluids moving through the rock. The original calcium carbonate (calcite) was replaced by calcium magnesium carbonate (mineral dolomite). Shales in the Osgood and Waldron formations, derived from an eastern source area, accumulated in a deeper open-marine setting.

An unconformity, which is a break in the geologic record, occurs between rocks of Silurian and Devonian age in the Louisville area. It was caused by a lengthy interruption in deposition, accompanied by erosion of the Silurian deposits. The gap in the rock record between the Louisville Limestone (Silurian) and the overlying Jeffersonville Limestone (Devonian) represents about 35 million years, based on the absence of fossil zones that occur in Silurian and Devonian rocks elsewhere. Unconformities between rock units commonly are characterized by a very irregular erosional surface, but only an obscure planar contact separates these two limestones in much of the area. This contact between the Louisville and Jeffersonville Limestones in Jefferson County is cited in geologic LITERATURE as a classic example of a "paraconformity," one of the four major types of geologic unconformities.

Unconformities of lesser magnitude occur at the contact between the Ordovician Drakes Formation and Silurian Brassfield Formation, between the Silurian Brassfield and Osgood Formations, and between formations in the Devonian sequence. The Silurian Brassfield locally contains rock fragments eroded from underlying Ordovician rocks. Each of these unconformities represents a change in sea level and interruption of deposition.

Three formations of Devonian age (390 to 365 million years old) are present in the Louisville area and consist of, in ascending order, the Jeffersonville Limestone (fossiliferous limestone), SELLERSBURG Limestone (fossiliferous limestone and argillaceous, dolomitic limestone), and NEW ALBANY Shale (black, silty, carbon-rich shale). The formations have a combined thickness of about 150 feet. The abundantly fossiliferous Devonian limestones, the principal rocks forming the FALLS OF THE OHIO, were deposited in shallow seas ranging from quiet depths, where larger corals flourished, to wave-agitated shoals. Vertical changes in the types of marine FAUNA that are preserved in the limestones generally reflect changes in sea level between shallower and deeper waters. In contrast to the abundance of life on the sea floor during deposition of Devonian limestones, the overlying carbon-rich black shale of the New Albany accumulated in the anaerobic bottom layer of a restricted inland sea. Scattered remains of tree trunks, washed into the sea from forested coastal areas, are preserved in the black shale.

The youngest Paleozoic rocks are in the knobs of southwestern Jefferson County and, in ascending stratigraphic order, consist of the Rockford Limestone (dolomite), Borden Formation (shale, siltstone, dolomite, and limestone), and Harrodsburg Limestone (limestone and minor dolomite), all of Mississippian age (365 to 345 million years old). The Rockford, up to three feet thick, occurs only locally in the county. Total thickness of the three Mississippian formations is about 490 feet. To the south, knobs in BULLITT COUNTY are capped by as much as an additional 230 feet of younger Mississippian limestone, dolomite, and shale.

A delta advancing westward toward Kentucky during Early Mississippian time started filling in the Devonian sea with sediments that became shale and siltstone of the Borden Formation. Clay and silt were transported onto the sea floor and slope out in front of the approaching subaerial delta. The accumulating sediments built up to form a shallow platform where dolomitic siltstone, silty dolomite, and limestone of the upper Borden were deposited. This mixture of carbonate and detrital sediments was succeeded by fossiliferous limestone of the Harrodsburg, indicating a rise in sea level. A distinct unit consisting of siltstones interbedded with shales occurs near the lower middle part of the Borden Formation and is named the Kenwood Siltstone Member of the Borden, for exposures on KENWOOD HILL in southern Louisville. Kenwood siltstones were deposited from sediments carried by turbidity currents, which are bottom-flowing density currents laden with suspended sediment that move swiftly down a subaqueous slope. The turbidity currents probably were set in motion by seismic shocks, or earthquakes, in a source area to the east.

Rocks and sediments representing the period of time from about 345 million to roughly about 150 thousand years ago are absent in the county. They were either never deposited, or, if deposited, they have been removed by erosion. This unconformity, which is a major break in the geologic record, encompasses the latter part of the Paleozoic Era, all of the Mesozoic Era, and most of the Cenozoic Era.

The site of Louisville and Jefferson County on the North American continent moved north of the equator early in the Mesozoic Era, probably about 250 to 240 million years ago. It has remained in the northern hemisphere since that time.

During the Pleistocene (Ice Age) and Holocene (Recent) Epochs of the Quaternary Period in the latter part of the Cenozoic Era (from at least 20,000 years ago to the present time, but possibly from as much as 150,000 years ago to the present), silt, clay, sand, and gravel were deposited in parts of Jefferson County, mainly in the VALLEYS of the OHIO RIVER and its tributaries. Transport and deposition of alluvial sediments continues in the valleys today. Of these unconsolidated sediments, the most extensive is the Pleistocene glacial outwash, as much as 135 feet thick, that forms a broad plain on which much of western and downtown Louisville has been built. The glacial outwash, mainly sand and gravel, was swept down the Ohio Valley by meltwater from Wisconsinan-stage ice sheets when they began retreating northward across Ohio and Indiana after the last glacial advances of the Pleistocene (about twenty thousand and fifteen thousand years ago). The Ohio Valley had been deeply eroded during the Yarmouthian interglacial stage (about 200,000 to 170,000 years ago), near the middle of the Pleistocene, and outwash deposits now are the principal sedimentary fill in this part of the valley. Outwash sand and gravel in the subsurface of western Jefferson County are a major groundwater aquifer.

The flood of Wisconsinan glacial outwash in the valley of the Ohio River blocked and ponded tributary streams. Lake bottom (lacustrine) sediments, mainly clay and silt (as much as sixty feet thick), accumulated in the ponded valleys of HARRODS CREEK, Little Goose and Goose Creeks, Muddy Fork, and BEARGRASS CREEK, and, in southern Jefferson County, across the broad drainage basin of Pond Creek.

Older Pleistocene sediments, consisting of silt, clay, sand, and gravel transported by water and wind, are preserved in terraces, occurring mainly in western and southern Jefferson County. Windblown silt and sand, also of Pleistocene age, cover sediments and bedrock in parts of the county.

Wisconsinan-age glaciers, the principal source of outwash deposits in the Ohio Valley, did not reach Kentucky, but deposits from earlier Pleistocene glaciers (possibly as old as eight hundred thousand years) have been found in northern Kentucky and adjacent to the Ohio Valley northeast of Jefferson County. Remnants of glacial drift, composed of gravelly, clayey silt, and scattered glacial pebbles, cobbles, and boulders, occur in northwestern OLDHAM COUNTY on uplands bordering the Ohio Valley and, locally, in the valley along the base of the uplands.

Folding of bedrock by tectonic forces has produced two subparallel linear structures, the downwarped Lyndon Syncline and the upwarped Springdale Anticline. These features extend from Oldham and Shelby Counties southwestward across Jefferson County. The thickness of the Silurian-age Brassfield Formation increases in the axial area of the Lyndon Syncline, indicating that movement occurred along this structure either during or immediately before deposition of the formation. At the FALLS OF THE OHIO, strata have been folded upward to form a low northeast-trending anticline. The origin of rapids, or "falls," in the Ohio River at this site may be related to the laterally migrating and downcutting river encountering this locally upwarped bedrock.

No surface faults have been found in Jefferson County, but faults offset surface rocks locally in Bullitt, Oldham, and Shelby Counties. Of particular interest is the complexly faulted JEPTHA KNOB in eastern SHELBY COUNTY, because it may be a meteoroid-impact structure. Highly disturbed Ordovician rocks are overlain by undeformed strata of Early Silurian age, indicating that the event occurred in Late Ordovician time.

Western Jefferson County and adjacent southern Indiana are underlain by a major positive magnetic anomaly that is associated with a deep-seated, intrusive igneous body composed of gabbro. The anomaly, named the Louisville Anomaly or the Louisville Accommodation Structure, extends southward into west-central Kentucky. Magnetic and gravity data indicate that the gabbro body is cut by several west-northwest-trending strike-slip faults. Earthquake epicenters in the Louisville area may be related to these deep faults.

See Charles Butts, *Geology and Mineral Resources of Jefferson County, Kentucky* (Kentucky Geological Survey, series 4, vol. 3, part 2, 1915); James E. Conkin and Barbara M. Conkin, *Guide to the Rocks and Fossils of Jefferson County, Kentucky, Southern Indiana, and Adjacent Areas,* 2nd revised edition (Louisville, University of Louisville Reproduction Services, 1976); R. Todd Hendricks, Frank R. Ettensohn, T. Joshua Stark, and Stephen F. Greb, *Geology of the Devonian Strata of the Falls of the Ohio Area, Kentucky-Indiana: Stratigraphy, Sedimentology, Paleontology, Structure, and Diagenesis* (Kentucky Geological Survey, series 11, 1994); Robert C. McDowell, ed., *The Geology of Kentucky: A Text to Accompany the Geologic Map of Kentucky* (U.S. Geological Survey Professional Paper 1151–H, 1986).

Garland R. Dever Jr.

GERMAN-AMERICAN CLUB. The German-American Club was founded in 1878 by Louis Vormbrock at Beck's Hall on Jefferson St. The fifteen men who met there called themselves the Sozialer Männerchor. They hired Otto Schuler as their first music director and gave their first concert in June 1879 at the gardens of Beck's Hall. In 1884 a constitution was drawn and a society flag was designed. Prof. Gustav Clausnitzer became music director, a position he held for more than two decades. Professor Clausnitzer led the chorus to many national singing festivals, where it distinguished itself. In 1914 Louisville hosted the national festival of the North American Singers Union, maybe the largest collection of singers ever to visit the city.

In 1937 the club amended its constitution to admit women as members. In 1942 the club moved into its first permanent home on Jackson St. and changed its name to the Social Male Chorus. In 1964 URBAN RENEWAL caused the club to relocate to 1840 Lincoln Ave.

In 1989 the National Saengerfest was held in Louisville, and the club distinguished itself by raising more money than any other Saengerfest to date. In 1993 the Club was renamed the German-American Club Gesangverein.

Michael Daniel
Kenneth Johnston

GERMAN INSURANCE BANK BUILDING. This Beaux Arts–style landmark at 207 W MARKET St. was designed by one of Louisville's most accomplished German-born architects and marked the city's second major wave of German immigration. The highly carved, two-story Indiana limestone building was begun in 1887 to the designs of architect Charles D. Meyer. Additions were made in 1900

German Insurance Bank building at 207 West Market Street, 1920.

and 1919. A lovely Rookwood Pottery drinking fountain (designed by Louisville sculptress Enid Yandell) was added to the lobby. The building's clock tower became a famous landmark.

The bank itself was established in 1854 when Louisville saw its first major wave of native Germans, who tended to be Protestant, entrepreneurial, and Republican. The city's late-nineteenth-century German immigrants, who prompted the new bank building, tended to be Roman Catholic, blue-collar, and Democrat. The building continued to serve as a bank, although the name was changed during World War I to Liberty Insurance Bank (later Liberty National Bank and Trust Co.). Threatened with demolition on more than one occasion, it was saved and served for a time as the home of Metro United Way and later for the firm of Godsey Associates Architects.

Douglas L Stern

GERMANS. German families such as the Bruners, the Blankenbakers, and the Funks, immigrated to colonial America and settled in Pennsylvania, Maryland, and Virginia. Many of their descendants moved to Kentucky after the Revolutionary War and settled in eastern Jefferson County. In 1797 they founded Brunerstown, later renamed Jeffersontown. The German Reformed Church, established there in 1809, was the first German church in Jefferson County. Many settlers of German ancestry also were found in Louisville in the late eighteenth century. Among these was a man named Kaye who built the first brick house in the city in 1789. The first German immigrant to settle in Louisville is believed to have been A.D. Ehrich, a master shoemaker who arrived in 1817. In the early nineteenth century, growth in Louisville was stimulated by the introduction of steam navigation on the Ohio River. Many German immigrants traveled to river cities such as Louisville, St. Louis, and Cincinnati via steamboat from New Orleans.

By the 1830s significant numbers of German-speaking immigrants were living in Louisville, and they began to establish churches in which German was spoken rather than English. St. Boniface, the first German Catholic church, was founded by Father Joseph Stahlschmidt in 1836; in 1849 the administration of St. Boniface was assumed by Franciscan priests from the province of St. Leopold in Tyrol, Austria. The Church of the Immaculate Conception (St. Mary's) was established in 1845, followed by St. Martin of Tours (1853) and St. Peter's (1855). Also, St. John's Cemetery (1849) and St. Michael's Cemetery (1851) were established for German Catholics. Land for St. Stephen's Cemetery was purchased by the St. Boniface Benevolent Society, but the cemetery was not sanctioned by the Diocese of Louisville.

The first German Evangelical church in Louisville was St. Paul's Evangelical Church, founded in 1836 under the leadership of the Reverend George Brandau. St. John's Evangelical Church was founded in 1843, followed by St. Peter's (1847) and St. Luke's (1850). Other German Protestant churches established before the Civil War were the Second German Methodist Church (1848) and the German Baptist Church (1856). Additionally, Temple Adath Israel, founded by German immigrants in 1838, was the first Jewish temple established in Louisville.

The St. Joseph's Orphan Society was founded in 1849 in the wake of a cholera epidemic. Father Karl Boeswald of St. Mary's Church and Father Otto Jair of St. Boniface Church collaborated in the establishment of the society, which later had branches at six German Catholic parishes. The German Protestant Orphans' Home was founded in 1851.

In the early 1850s the German population of Louisville had grown to eighteen thousand, about 35 percent of the total population. There were also many German-speaking Swiss and some Austrian immigrants who associated closely with the Germans.

Germans influenced Louisville schools in two ways: the introduction of kindergarten and bilingual education. The first of the German schools, the Freie Buergerschule, was founded in 1852. The Hailman School, attended by Justice Louis Brandeis, was begun in 1855. The school at the German Protestant Orphans' Home was regarded as one of the best of its kind. At the suggestion of Bishop Martin Spalding, Catholic churches organized parish schools; St. Boniface School and St. Martin's School were the largest of these. German language instruction was introduced in Louisville public schools in 1854; German was taught at both Male and Female High Schools by 1872.

The Liederkranz Singing Society was founded in 1848. The society suggested the formation of a North American Singing Federation and hosted its second singing festival in 1850. The Orpheus Choral Society was founded in 1849 and was prominent among Louisville singing groups. In 1865 the Singing Federation of Louisville was founded and included the Liederkranz, Orpheus, and Frohsinn singing groups, and the singing section of the Turnverein. The first Liederkranz Hall, located on Market St., was completed in 1873 and became the center of German social life in Louisville. Germans were prominent in the Louisville Philharmonic Society, which was formed in 1866 and was conducted by Bavarian native Louis Hast. Also, Germans were enthusiastic opera supporters and performers.

The Louisville Turnverein, among the first of the German gymnastics societies in the United States, was founded on September 2, 1850. The first Turnfest in Louisville was held in 1852 on the Stein and Zink farm on Salt River Rd. (Dixie Hwy.). In 1854 the Turnverein dedicated its own hall, the Turnhalle on Floyd St. Many of the early Turners had liberal political views and were regarded with suspicion by American-born citizens.

In all, there were approximately thirty German language newspapers in Louisville. The first of these, the *Volksbuehne*, appeared in 1841 but was short-lived. The *Beobacher am Ohio*, which had the support of liberal Germans, lasted from 1844 to 1856. By far, the most successful German language newspaper was the *Louisville Anzeiger*, first published on February 28, 1849. The *Anzeiger* became a daily publication several months after its founding.

The unsuccessful Revolution of 1848 in Germany resulted in the immigration of many educated Germans to the United States, where they became known as Forty-eighters. The Forty-eighters, who advocated liberal political views, were extremely outspoken. Most German immigrants, especially those with strong religious beliefs, did not agree with the Forty-eighters, whose actions colored the opinions of American-born citizens about Germans. The Forty-eighters, unable to align themselves with any of the established national political parties, formed the *Bund Freier Manner* in 1853. The party held a state convention in 1853 and adopted the liberal Louisville Platform, which included the abolishment of slavery and voting by women. Many of the tenets of the Louisville Platform conflicted with the philosophy of the anti-foreigner, anti-Catholic American Party ("Know-Nothing" Party), which found broad support in Louisville. George Prentice, the editor of the *Louisville Daily Journal*, supported the American Party in a series of inflammatory editorials preceding the gubernatorial and congressional elections of August 1855.

On election day, Monday, August 6, 1855, American Party committees, supported by the police, took control of the polls and attempted to allow only card-carrying American Party members to vote. Fights broke out and violence escalated as nativist mobs ransacked and burned German businesses and homes in the Shelby St. area and the IRISH neighborhood west of downtown.

German immigrants were among the strongest supporters of the Union during the CIVIL WAR. They voted overwhelmingly for pro-Union candidates in state elections in 1861, helping ensure that Kentucky stayed in the Union. Out of a total German population of only thirteen thousand, more than a thousand men joined the Union army. In addition, many Germans were members of Louisville's Home Guard units. One to four German companies were in each of the Fifth, Sixth, Twenty-second, Twenty-eighth, and Thirty-fourth Kentucky Volunteer Infantry Regiments. Three German companies fought in the Fourth Kentucky Volunteer Cavalry Regiment. Also, German-born residents of Louisville contributed money to the Union cause, volunteered for work in HOSPITALS, and prepared meals and made clothing for soldiers. The Louisville Turnhalle was converted into a hospital for sick and wounded soldiers. German contributions to the Union cause did much to change the attitudes of native-born Louisvillians toward them. Even *Louisville Daily Journal* editor George Prentice wrote articles praising the German immigrants. In 1865 Louisvillians elected their first German-born mayor, PHILLIP TOMPPERT.

German immigration to the United States waned during the Civil War but resumed in earnest afterward and reached a peak in 1882. Germans were active participants in the economic and professional expansion of Louisville in the post–Civil War period. By the end of the century, manufacturers such as Ahrens & Ott Manufacturing Co. (plumbing fixtures), HENRY VOGT MACHINE CO. (steam boilers), C.C. Mengel Jr. & Brother Co. (wood products), Peaslee-Gaulbert Co. (paint and glass products), and Ewald Iron Co. (iron works) were a large presence in Louisville. German businessmen were included on the boards of directors of many local banks. Financial institutions established by Germans included the German Security Bank, the German Insurance Bank, and the German Insurance Co. Germans were important in the DISTILLING and brewing businesses. Prominent among the distillers were the BERNHEIM BROTHERS and J.B. Wathen & Brother Co. German brewmasters practiced their skills in many breweries, both small and large, such as the Frank Fehr Brewing Co., Senn & Ackermann Brewing Co., and the Oertel Brewing Co. German BEER GARDENS abounded, the most popular of which was Woodland Garden, founded in 1848. Zehnder's Garden was a popular country garden located at the point of Baxter Ave. and Bardstown Rd.

Germans were well represented in the food industries, such as wholesale and retail GROCERIES that sold meat, produce, and dairy products. BUTCHERTOWN was an area of Louisville where many Germans established meatpacking businesses. The FISCHER PACKING CO. was founded in 1899 by Henry Fischer, a German immigrant. Many German-speaking Swiss were prominent in dairy farming. German bakeries and confectioneries were found throughout Louisville. Also, large numbers of Germans were engaged in the construction trades.

Embalmers and undertakers were prominent in Louisville's German community. Best known among these were Henry Bosse and John Rattermann. Also, Henry Nanz, who established a floral business in 1850, won an award for his arrangements at the SOUTHERN EXPOSITION held in Louisville in 1883–87.

In 1900 Louisville's population totaled 204,731, which included 13,263 Germans and about 35,000 persons who claimed at least one German-born parent. As the German immigrant population of the nineteenth century was assimilated, identifiable German customs and institutions began to fade. German NEIGHBORHOODS such as Uptown (PHOENIX HILL), Butchertown, and Germantown gradually changed as businesses encroached and the population moved to newer neighborhoods. Sermons at German Catholic churches and services at German Protestant churches began to be conducted in English rather than German. Catholic parish schools that had previously taught solely in German began instruction in English.

In 1914, as WORLD WAR I engulfed Europe, American sympathies identified with the Allied cause. *COURIER-JOURNAL* editor, HENRY WATTERSON, who had professed admiration of Germans, reversed himself to take a staunch anti-German position. As anti-German sentiments pervaded Louisville's culture, many German institutions in Louisville changed names to downplay their German identity; for example, the German Security Bank became simply the Security Bank, and the German Insurance Bank became the Liberty Insurance Bank. Also, German books were removed from the LOUISVILLE FREE PUBLIC LIBRARY, and the city renamed many streets that had German names.

As WORLD WAR II approached, many of the early German Catholic and Evangelical churches, located in inner city neighborhoods, were in decline. Many closed after the war. The *Louisville Anzeiger*, which had existed as a German language newspaper for eighty-nine years, ceased publication on March 4, 1938. Among the thousands of Louisvillians who fought to defeat Nazi Germany in World War II, many were descendants of German immigrants to Louisville.

Today, almost one in three persons in Jefferson County claims Germanic heritage. The Germanic heritage of Louisville is preserved in a number of social, cultural, and civic organizations. The German-American Club Gesangverein, founded by German immigrants in 1878, is a social organization for recent German immigrants and those of Germanic heritage. The Gruetli-Helvetia Society (originally the Gruetli Benevolent Society) was founded by Swiss immigrants in 1850; the society operated the popular Swiss Hall from 1923 to 1993. The KENTUCKIANA Germanic Heritage Society, founded in 1991, seeks to promote awareness and preserve Louisville's Germanic heritage. The city of Louisville began a civic and cultural association with Mainz, Germany, in 1977; the two cities officially became Sister Cities in 1994.

See Robert C. Jobson, "German-American Settlers of Early Jefferson County, Kentucky," *Filson Club History Quarterly* 53 (Oct. 1979): 344–57; *Louisville Anzeiger Jubilaums Ausgabe*, March 1, 1898; Raymond C. Riebel, Louisville Panorama: A Visual History of Louisville, (Louisville 1960); Elsie Rowell, "The Social and Cultural Contributions of the Germans in Louisville from 1848–1855," M.A. thesis, University of Kentucky, 1941; Ludwig Stierlin, Der Staat Kentucky und die Stadt Louisville mit besonderer Beruecksichtigung des Deutschen Elementes, (Louisville 1873); George H. Yater, *Two Hundred Years at the Falls of the Ohio* (Louisville 1987).

C. Robert Ullrich
Jane K. Keller
Joseph R. Reinhart

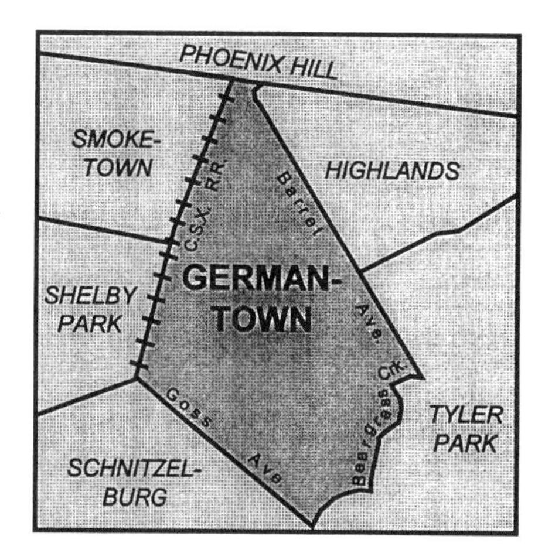

GERMANTOWN. The Germantown neighborhood, bordered roughly by Goss Ave., Barret Ave., BEARGRASS CREEK, BROADWAY, and the CSX Railroad tracks, was a popular settling spot in the 1850s for German Catholic immigrants. The land was once part of a thousand-acre grant to Col. Arthur Campbell of Virginia to reward his services during the Indian hostilities in the Northwest Territory. Campbell's daughter, Mary Beard, inherited part of the land in 1811 but found no purchasers for the swamp-laden property at the will-stipulated price of twenty dollars per acre. She challenged her father's will and was able to subdivide and sell the land at cheaper rates to the newly-arrived immigrants.

The marshy condition of the Germans' new neighborhood, which spawned the nickname "Frogtown," isolated the residents and forced many to maintain their own vegetable gardens and bread ovens in their backyards. Others became dairy farmers. The area experienced its largest growth in the late nineteenth century as the neighborhood became known for its candlemaking, butcher shops, ice houses, brickyards, and a paper mill. In the early twentieth century, the residents increasingly turned to blue-collar LABOR and constructed the highest concentration of SHOTGUN COTTAGES in the city. Many of the cottages are camelbacks, constructed with one story in front and two stories at the rear.

Paristown, to the northeast of Beargrass Creek and settled by FRENCH Huguenots, once existed as a separate community. However, in 1907 a bridge was built over the creek to allow Catholics on the north side to attend church in GERMANTOWN. This led to the consolidation of the two communities, which culminated in the establishment of the German-Paristown Neighborhood Association in 1973.

See *A Place in Time: The Story of Louisville's Neighborhoods* (Louisville 1989).

GHEENS, CHARLES EDWIN (b Louisville, 1878; d Louisville, November 11, 1961). Businessman and civic leader. The son of Charles W. and Mary B. Gheens, C. Edwin Gheens was educated at LOUISVILLE MALE HIGH SCHOOL and the Flexner's School for Boys. Though he went on to become a prominent figure in Louisville's business community, he never attended college, having been stricken with typhoid fever right before entering Yale University.

In 1899, after his recovery, Gheens became a partner of Louisville candymaker James Bradas. The newly christened firm of Bradas and Gheens was on W MAIN St. Upon the retirement of Bradas in 1920, Gheens became the sole owner and president of the company, where he remained for the next forty-one years. Gheens's other business endeavors included owning and managing Koch's Dairy Farm as well as the Golden Ranch Plantation in Gheens, Louisiana, where he raised sugar cane and, later, cattle. In 1957 Gheens and his wife, Mary Jo, established the Gheens Foundation Inc., a nonprofit organization dedicated to quietly improving the quality of life in the two regions where the Gheens family and fortune were centered: Louisville and Lafource Parish, Louisiana. The foundation is unique in its proactive selection of grant recipients, choosing areas of need with a potential for major, long-term impact on community life.

Grantees are encouraged to develop fresh approaches to their problems. With a strong focus on education, cultural programs, and social services, the Gheens Foundation underwrites such things as building projects, operating costs, program development, and scholarship funds. For example, the foundation contributed $250,000 to BELLARMINE COLLEGE for a new library in 1993, and in the mid-1980s it granted $4 million to fund the Gheens Professional Development Academy on Preston Hwy., a public-private partnership with the Jefferson County PUBLIC SCHOOLS.

The mission of the Gheens Academy is to ensure a qualified workforce for Louisville through leadership and support for teachers, and improved student learning. Since its inception the academy has become a nationally recognized center for training teachers and educational administrators through programs such as its Leadership Development Center and the Leadership Center Network. It is also well known as a center for innovation in education. Many proven strategies for educational reform have originated at the Gheens Academy. The Professional Development School, a means to promote a culture of inquiry and teacher research in schools while providing intensive induction for new teachers, has been adopted by the Holmes Partnership (a national coalition of universities, school districts, and professional associations).

Gheens was also a longtime Baptist leader. Not only was he a deacon and trustee of the BROADWAY BAPTIST CHURCH, where he had been a member most of his life, but he also served for forty years as a trustee of the SOUTHERN BAPTIST THEOLOGICAL SEMINARY in Louisville. In 1959 the school's main lecture hall was named in his honor. The Gheens Lectureship, which invited prominent scholars to speak at the seminary, was endowed by Gheens as well.

Gheens's civic activities were numerous. He was the director of the Cook Benevolent Institution and the Louisville River Area Foundation, belonged to the PENDENNIS CLUB, and was a life member of the Historic Homes Foundation. Gheens's wife, Mary Jo Lazarus Gheens, served for many years as the vice president of Bradas & Gheens and, after her husband's death, continued to support many of the family's civic and religious interests. Gheens is buried in CAVE HILL CEMETERY.

See *Courier-Journal*, Nov. 13, 1961.

GIBSON, WILLIAM H. (b Baltimore, Maryland, May 1829; d Louisville, June 3, 1906). Teacher, musician, and community leader. Gibson was born free to Phillip and Amelia Gibson. He moved to Louisville in 1847 and taught schools at the Fourth Avenue Colored Methodist Church and at QUINN CHAPEL AME Church. Gibson helped form the first African American Masonic lodge in Kentucky in 1850, and he was one of the founders of the United Brothers of Friendship. After the CIVIL WAR (1861–65) he served in a variety of important public and private positions: in 1870 he was appointed a U.S. mail agent, he was president of the Colored Musical Association, he was one of the founders of the COLORED ORPHANS' HOME, and he played an indispensable role in the development of post–Civil War AFRICAN AMERICAN educational institutions in Louisville. Gibson wrote the earliest history of African Americans in Louisville in 1897. He is buried in Eastern Cemetery.

See William H. Gibson, *History of the United Brothers of Friendship and Sisters of the Mysterious Ten* (Louisville 1897).

Cornelius Bogert

GILES, JANICE HOLT (b Altus, Arkansas, March 18, 1905; d Adair County, Kentucky, June 1, 1979). Author. She was the daughter of John and Lucy (McGraw) Holt. She graduated from Fort Smith (Arkansas) High School in 1922. In 1923 she married Otto Moore of Fort Smith, and on September 28, l924, their daughter, Elizabeth Ann "Libby," was born. The Moores divorced in 1933. Janice and Libby moved to Louisville in 1941, where they lived at 1437 Hepburn Ave. in the HIGHLANDS. She became secretary to Dr. Lewis J. Sherill, dean of the Presbyterian Theological Seminary. Janice Holt Moore and Henry Giles, a soldier from Knifley (Adair County), Kentucky, met on July 12, 1942, aboard a Greyhound bus going from Louisville to Texas. Their courtship through letters, marriage on October 11, 1945, and their life in Louisville is fictionalized in Giles's first novel, *The Enduring Hills* (1950), which she wrote in the kitchen of the Hepburn Ave. apartment at night. *Miss Willie* (1951), Giles's second novel, was completed before the couple moved to a forty-acre farm near Knifley. In 1952 the Gileses returned to Louisville and lived on Cherokee Rd. They moved back to Adair County in 1954. In time, Giles became one of Kentucky's best-known and most prolific novelists.

Giles wrote twenty novels, co-authored four books, and wrote a few short stories between 1949 and 1975. Giles's fiction and nonfiction place characters in their natural settings and traditional patterns of life. English professor Bonnie Jean Cox has written that Giles has been critically overlooked, perhaps because of her prolific output as well as her appeal to popular tastes. She is buried in the Caldwell Ridge Separate Baptist Church Cemetery, Knifley, Kentucky.

See Dianne Watkins Stuart, *Janice Holt Giles: A Writer's Life* (Lexington 1998); Dianne Watkins (Stuart), *Hello, Janice* (Lexington 1992); William Ward, *A Literary History of Kentucky* (Knoxville, Tenn., 1988); Clara L. Metzmeier, ed., *Janice Holt Giles: Papers from Giles Symposium* (Campbellsville, Ky., 1991).

Clara L. Metzmeier

GILLOOLY, JOHN F. (b Jackson, Mississippi, September 18, 1855; d Louisville, April 17, 1926). Coast guardsman. Often called "Captain Jack" and "Hero of the Falls," Gillooly is said to have been involved in the rescue of five thousand people from the OHIO RIVER. He was the son of James and Annie Gillooly. At age four he moved with his parents to Louisville and was educated at St. Patrick's Catholic school. Gillooly spent his boyhood days on the banks of the Ohio River, where he became a strong swimmer and excellent oarsman.

About 1870 he became a volunteer lifesaver, rescuing people from boats stuck on the FALLS

OF THE OHIO. Gillooly and co-workers Capt. Billy Devan and John Tully gained national attention for their rescues and were awarded gold medals of honor by a special act of Congress. By special act of the Kentucky General Assembly, they were presented gold medals by Gov. LUKE BLACKBURN (1879–83) on February 18, 1880. Also in 1880 Gillooly was involved with the rescue of seventy-five people when the steamer *Virgie Lee* sank at the Falls. So successful were their efforts and so hazardous was the Falls that in 1881 the United States GOVERNMENT established the first inland lifesaving station in the country at Louisville. The floating station was built at JEFFERSONVILLE, INDIANA, and placed in operation at the foot of Second St. on November 4, 1881. Known as Life Saving Station number 10 (now ANDREW BROADDUS WHARF BOAT/Louisville Life Saving Station), its crew performed rescue duties by rowing out in skiffs to save passengers and cargo stranded at the Falls. In 1915 the Life Saving Station Service was combined with the Revenue Cutter Service to become the U.S. Coast Guard. Gillooly was a member of both.

Gillooly also rescued people stranded in their homes during the 1883 and 1884 FLOODS. In May 1911 Gillooly became commander of the Louisville rescue team following the death of Devan. During the flood of 1913, he rescued thousands marooned by flooding at Dayton, Ohio. Lifesavers from various stations were on duty, but the work of the Louisville crew stood out prominently, since they were the first to cross the Miami River to unpenetrated flood sections, where they took provisions to four thousand people marooned in their homes and rescued five hundred families from housetops and trees. For that service Gillooly received commendation from William Gibbs McAdoo, the secretary of the treasury, under whose department the Life Saving Station Service was operated. One of the biggest rescues occurred on February 17, 1914, when the steamer *Queen City* sank at the Falls en route from Pittsburgh to New Orleans. Two hundred fifteen passengers and crewmen were rescued.

Gillooly retired in August 1917. Records of the station disclose that during his career the Life Saving Station was responsible for saving 6,312 lives and $5 million worth of property and for recovering the bodies of 400 drowning victims. Following his retirement he was made manager of the CRESCENT HILL SWIMMING pool. He married twice; his first wife was Annie L. Schweer, and his second wife was Mary. He had five sons, John F. Junior, James, Robert, Hite, and Barret, and three daughters, Anna, Frances, and Mary. Gillooly died of heart disease and is buried in St. Louis Cemetery.

See *Louisville Times,* April 17, 1926.

GIRDLER, TOM MERCER (b SILVER CREEK Township, Indiana, May 19, 1877; d Easton, Maryland, February 4, 1965). Executive and innovator. One of five children, Girdler was born on a farm near SELLERSBURG. Girdler crossed the OHIO RIVER to attend du Pont Manual Training High School in Louisville and stayed for an additional year, teaching students in exchange for an additional year of study. In 1897 he left Louisville to attend Lehigh University in Bethlehem, Pennsylvania, where he earned a degree in mechanical engineering. Girdler entered the steel industry as a factory foreman for Oliver Iron and Steel Co. in Pittsburgh before moving to Atlanta in 1907 to become the superintendent of the Atlantic Steel Co. In 1914, Girdler returned to Pittsburgh as the assistant superintendent of the Aliquippa plant at Jones and Laughlin Steel Corp. and left the company as its president in 1929. He was named chairman of the Republic Steel Corp. upon its formation in 1930 and was noted for his battles against LABOR unions. Girdler later became the chief executive officer at Republic and also served as a director of Goodyear Tire and Rubber Co. and the Cleveland and Pittsburgh Railroad. During WORLD WAR II, while serving as chairman of Consolidated Corp. and Vultee Aircraft, two companies which he later merged into Consolidated Vultee Aircraft, Girdler is credited with helping to introduce the assembly line process and mass production methods to the construction of aircraft.

Girdler married four times and had four children: Jane, Betty, Tom Junior, and Joseph, all by his first wife, Bessie Hayes of Louisville.

See Tom Girdler with Boyden Sparks, *Boot Straps* (New York 1943); *Courier-Journal*, Feb. 5, 1965.

GIRL SCOUT COUNCIL OF KENTUCKIANA. Girl Scouting began in the United States when it was founded by Juliette Gordon Low in Savannah, Georgia, in 1912. As membership grew rapidly, local councils were chartered by the national headquarters in New York.

The GIRL SCOUT COUNCIL of Louisville, formed by members of the Louisville City Women's Club, was chartered on April 4, 1923. In 1932 the name was changed to Louisville Council of Girl Scouts. Twenty years later, as nearby Kentucky counties were added to its jurisdiction, it became the Louisville Area Girl Scout Council and then, in 1958, the Kentucky Cardinal Girl Scout Council. With the addition of Indiana counties in 1965, the name changed again to KENTUCKIANA GIRL SCOUT COUNCIL.

Because of jurisdictional mergers spanning approximately thirty years, the Kentuckiana Girl Scout Council currently includes fifty Kentucky counties, six southern Indiana counties, and a portion of one county in Tennessee. What began in 1923 as a fledgling council of fewer than fifty girls and twenty-five adults had grown to a membership of nearly nineteen thousand girls and more than sixty-five hundred adults by the late 1990s. Since 1923, the council has had its offices in Louisville on Chestnut St., Third St., Jefferson St., Cherokee Rd., and MAIN St.; it is now located at 1325 S Fourth St. The council also has other offices in the Kentucky communities of Elizabethtown, Bowling Green, Owensboro, and Paducah.

Girl Scouting in KENTUCKIANA provides an opportunity for girls to explore their own interests, take leadership roles, learn skills that will serve them throughout their lifetime, and contribute to the betterment of their community.

Kadie Engstrom

GLASS INDUSTRY. Southern Indiana has long been known as an important center of glass manufacturing. It is generally believed that the first U.S.-produced plate glass was installed as a store window in a tailor shop at 318 Pearl St. in NEW ALBANY.

JOHN BAPTISTE FORD, who became the father of the American plate GLASS INDUSTRY, introduced glassmaking in NEW ALBANY. He had previously lived in Greenville Township in Floyd County, close to a huge bed of sand located near the Washington County line. The proximity of abundant raw material led him to study the art of glassmaking and to conclude that New Albany was an ideal place for a glassworks. He secured backing from several New Albany businessmen and established the John B. Ford and Co. Glass Works in 1865. Principal products were bottles, fruit jars, and window glass. Unfortunately, Ford's expertise lay more in glassmaking than moneymaking, and within a year the company was reportedly owned by Samuel Montgomery and Henry Hennegan. The works burned in 1866 but was soon rebuilt and resold to Ford. Records of 1866 and 1867 show a Montgomery, Ford, & Co. in the glass business, but that venture failed.

By February 1867, however, Ford had secured enough capital to go back into glassmaking. His New Albany Glass Works, located on riverbank property between Eleventh and Thirteenth Streets, was established on a much larger scale. Instead of one frame building, there were three brick and three frame structures. An 1868 New Albany directory reported that the firm had 120 employees. It further states that, in ten months, 165,000 bushels of coal, 500 tons of soda ash, 1,500 tons of sand, 9,000 bushels of lime, and 600 barrels of salt were used in production. The value of the goods manufactured was three hundred thousand dollars annually. The silvering and finishing of plate glass mirrors and the making of window glass and bottles were the primary endeavors. Always more of a scientist than a businessman, Ford devoted himself to learning the process of making and polishing plate glass that would compare with that made in Europe. He perfected the technique in 1870 and received awards for his excellent plate glass in 1871 and 1872. Even the FRENCH Academy of Science gave him honorable mention.

In 1869 another plate glass manufactory was established by Ford's step-cousin, WASHINGTON

C. DePauw. The new enterprise was called Star Glass Works and had a five-pointed star as its trademark. The main line of products consisted of plate glass, window glass, bottles, jars, and insulators for TELEGRAPH poles. In addition, such items as rolling pins, paperweights, and green glass doorstops were made of slag from the mill. There is also evidence that some stained glass church windows may have borne the Star trademark. A year later, DePauw bought controlling interest in Ford's company. When the New Albany Glass Works faced financial difficulties, it was acquired by Star in 1872. Thus Star Glass Works became the only glass manufacturing company in New Albany. That same year, DePauw forced his step-cousin out of the Star works. There is no evidence that this caused any family problems or raised any eyebrows. It was considered to be simply good business practice.

In 1874 and 1875, Ford was affiliated with the Louisville Plate Glass Co. In 1875 notices appeared to the effect that a plate glass company would be built in Jeffersonville if twenty thousand dollars of stock "can be subscribed." On November 1, 1876, construction of the Ford Plate Glass Co. began on a site donated by the city of Jeffersonville. A reorganization of the company occurred in 1880, and the name was changed to Jeffersonville Plate Glass Co. The outlook for this enterprise was very promising. The product was of high quality, and the demand was great. Finished plate glass was sold for about $1.60 per square foot in 1881, and the sales figures amounted to $250,000. The company was in production until the middle of the 1880s. Ford later moved to Creighton, Pennsylvania, where he established the Ford Plate Glass Co. He and his sons became major stockholders in Pittsburgh Plate Glass. Ford eventually became part of the Libby-Owens-Ford Co.

Meanwhile the Star Glass Works of New Albany was an extensive and elaborate industry. DePauw hired many glassmakers from England, and his polished plate glass compared favorably with the best of that made in Europe. The quality of the product and the fact that it could be made and sold cheaper than imported plate glass was extremely attractive to the buyers of the day. A news report on the opening of Louisville's City Hall in 1873 stated that the windows in the building were made from glass rolled in DePauw's works in New Albany.

The location of the works was ideal from several standpoints. Good glass sand abounded in nearby Borden, Indiana; coal arrived by barge; and the finished product was shipped out by river and rail. Ford had the same advantages and certainly an impressive knowledge of the art. But DePauw had a million dollars to invest, as well as other enterprises generating a good cash flow until he took his first profits in 1879.

In 1881 Star Glass Works became DePauw's American Plate Glass Works, and the Star trademark was no longer used. A Courier-Journal article of August 24, 1881, reported that DePauw's American Plate Glass Works covered twenty-five acres and was the greatest manufactory in Indiana. It was said to positively affect every working person in New Albany, including the merchants who sold to the workers and the farmers who sold to the merchants. At that time, the works employed 1,500 to 2,000 men producing 1.4 million feet of polished glass, 150,000 boxes of window glass, and 30,000 gross of fruit jars per annum. In addition, some beautiful glass ornaments were made. The works paid out more money than any other company in the Falls area, and its products were distributed to all parts of the world.

Although DePauw died suddenly in 1887, an 1889 issue of the *New Albany Ledger* noted that his American Glass Works was the largest and most complete plate glass works on the American continent.

The demise of the glass industry in this area began with the discovery of natural gas in central and eastern Indiana, which would make the use of coal in the manufacture of glass obsolete. Another contributing factor was the financial panic of 1893. The New Albany plant went into receivership in 1895. By 1900, the glass industry in New Albany no longer existed.

Other glassworks in the New Albany area were New Albany Ornamental Glass Co.; New Albany Silvering, Beveling, and Ornamental Glass Co.; and the New Albany Novelty Glass Works. The names are the only thing known about these companies, and the constant changing of names in the industry makes tracing them difficult.

See Lewis C. Baird, *Baird's History of Clark County* (Indianapolis 1909); Gerald 0. Haffner, *The Glass Works* (New Albany, Ind., 1982); L.A. Williams & Co., *History of the Ohio Falls Cities and their Counties,* vol. 2 (Cleveland 1882); *Who Was Who in America Historical Volume 1607–1896* (Chicago Revised 1967).

Charline Hall

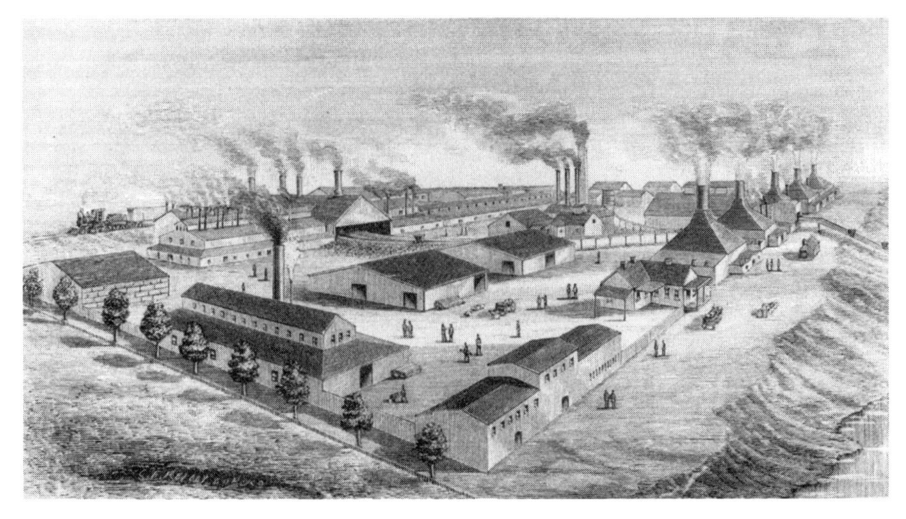

DePauw's American Glass Works advertisement, 1886.

GLENVIEW. Sixth-class city located in northern Jefferson County bordered roughly by Lime Kiln Ln. to the east, River Rd. to the north, Brittany Woods Circle to the south, and the Knights of Columbus property on River Rd. to the west. In the mid- to late 1800s, several wealthy families from Louisville moved eastward and erected large estate homes on the high cliffs overlooking the Ohio River.

In order to live outside the city while continuing to work downtown, several local businessmen cooperated with other families living farther east in Harrods Creek to open a commuter rail line. In 1877, the Louisville, Harrods Creek, and Westport Railroad was completed, running from First St. to Prospect. The new railroad permitted easy transportation for the residents of the area and drew visitors to the outlying community during the summer months. The line, later incorporated into an electric interurban commuter system, was abandoned in the 1950s, but two of the train stations continued to be used into the 1990s—one as the Glenview post office and part of another as a carpool pick-up at the base of the hill below the Chance School.

Three years before the railroad came, meat packer James C. McFerran unknowingly named the future city when he established Glen View—later changed to Glenview Farms—on land formerly owned by Virginia-born planter James Smalley Bate. In 1868, McFerran purchased the inheritance of Bate's youngest son, which was the largest of his father's seven allotments, and opened a trotting-horse farm. After McFerran's death in 1885, developer John E. Green acquired the land and renamed the property Glenview Stock Farm.

A social club was constructed in the area in the late 1880s for recreation and entertainment. It was dubbed the Fincastle Club, reputedly after Virginia's Fincastle County that once included Kentucky. The club furnished a gathering place for summer guests while also providing "cottages" for five families. As more families (including the Binghams, BELKNAPS, and Ballards), moved permanently into the neighborhood after the turn of the century, the club closed and an amphitheater was built on the site, by then part of the Bingham estate.

After a 1983 attempt by Louisville to annex the residential area, the residents moved to form their own city. This led to the 1985 creation of the sixth-class city of Glenview. In the mid-1980s, the county established the Glenview Historic District and added several of the residences to the NATIONAL REGISTER OF HISTORIC PLACES. Some of the homes were designed by local architects such as JOHN BACON HUTCHINGS and the firm of Nevin and Morgan. A number of the houses and gardens were included in a "country estates historic district" nominated to the National Register of Historic Places in 1999. The POPULATION of Glenview in 1980 was 511, in 1990 it was 653, and in 1996 it was 686.

See *A Place in Time: The Story of Louisville's Neighborhoods* (Louisville 1989); *Courier-Journal*, Feb. 1, 1999.

GLOVER, ANNIE CASEY (b County Galway, Ireland, March 31, 1861; d New York City, April 20, 1947). Fashion designer. The eldest daughter of IRISH immigrants William and Julia (Devley) Casey, Madame Glover, as she was known professionally, gained international recognition for her dress designs. She is first mentioned in the Louisville city directory of 1880, in which her occupation is listed as seamstress.

Little is known of her early life before the family arrived in the United States in 1876. She lived at home with her parents and siblings. Three years later her father died, and Glover went to work for a local wholesale and dry goods company, Close & Wasson, located on Fourth St. Shortly thereafter, she accepted a position in the dressmaking department of Sharpe and Middleton's New York Store (later Stewart Dry Goods), and it was there that her creations began to attract attention. Glover, who at the time specialized in bridal wardrobes, was praised by the *COURIER-JOURNAL* in 1886 for her talent and ingenuity. It was noted that she had "probably made more trousseaus in the last two or three years than any dressmaker in town."

In June 1886, Annie Casey married Walter E. Glover, and the couple combined their talents—he as business manager and she as designer—to open the first of Madame Glover's dress shops on S Fourth St. in 1891. Later, she operated her shop in the Tyler Building on Jefferson St. Glover, who often made excursions to Europe to study fashions, was renowned for her elegant creations that ranged from ladies' formal wear to dress suits. By the turn of the century, her clientele included women from across the United States and Europe. In 1912, following the death of her husband, she retired. Sometime later she removed to New York City, where she remained until her death. She was the mother of two daughters, Marie and Antoinette. Madame Glover is buried in CAVE HILL CEMETERY.

See *Louisville Times*, Oct. 25, 1956; *Courier-Journal*, June 4, 1886, April 22, 1947.

Candace K. Perry

GOLF. *The Kentucky Magazine* in 1917 published a preamble to the "Introduction" written by former governor of Kentucky Augustus E. Willson for an article by Julia A. Muldoon describing GOLF in the commonwealth: "The worldwide progress of the noble game of golf, so marked in recent years, seems not to have overlooked Kentucky. On the contrary, its sanctuaries and devotees in the Bluegrass State afford convincing evidence that it finds here a royal habitat. Nowhere else, it appears, can the game be played with greater zest the year 'round.'" As indicated by the growth of the sport over the past century, Louisville and the surrounding communities continue to offer that same "royal habitat" described in 1917.

Golf had its beginning in the Louisville area in 1886 when George C. Patton, an Englishman working in the TOBACCO business, established, with the help of other prominent businessmen, a golf course and clubhouse. The first course, consisting of six holes and clubhouse, was located on S Third St. For a few years, the clubhouse proved to be ample; however, the continuously growing membership soon necessitated the construction of a then "regulation" nine-hole course. Restricted by the rapid growth of the city, it was impossible to expand, and steps were taken to secure a larger site. A "picturesque" tract of land on Upper River Rd. along the OHIO RIVER, five miles from downtown, was selected and leased from the LOUISVILLE WATER CO. In 1895 the Louisville Golf Club opened at what is now Zorn Ave. and Upper River Rd. In 1899 the *National Golf Guide* noted that the club was "five miles from the city, but easily reached by the Narrow-Gauge Railway, which has a depot opposite the entrance to the club grounds."

The first golf professional at Louisville Golf Club was a Scotsman named Tom Cunningham. He was succeeded by another Scot, Robert White, who, in 1899, formed a partnership with another of his countrymen, Robert Andrews. The two opened a blacksmith's shop across the road from the course, where they produced "hand-forged" irons that were shipped throughout the nation. Gilbert Nichols, David Ogilvie, and Alex Smith were among the golf professionals who were known to play with "McAndrews' Irons."

In 1902 the standard caddy fee was ten cents for nine holes of golf. Caddies were required to provide their own tools and materials to clean the golfer's clubs, the fee for which was five cents. Although the course offers bent grass greens and rye grass fairways today, the original greens were bluegrass. The responsibility of greenskeeper was awarded to a local farmer who "had the knack for growing grass." At that time, two thousand sheep were used to help fertilize the grass on the fairways as well as keep it cut and maintained.

The property that houses Louisville's first "regulation" course is still owned by the Louisville Water Co. It continues to function as a golf and country club, although it has been the home of four different clubs over the course of the past century. Originally opening as the Louisville Golf Club, it later merged with the Country Club of Louisville to form the Louisville Country Club. In 1910 the Louisville County Club relocated to "higher ground," safely out of the floodplain along the Ohio River, to its current location between Mockingbird Valley Rd. and Indian Hills Trail. The original course and facility was then assumed by the Standard Country Club, which also eventually relocated, to Brownsboro Rd., leaving the property available. Two years later, the facility at Upper River Rd. was renovated and established as River Road Country Club. The club opened after several weeks of effort from members of three hundred families who worked until after midnight on the third of July to have the club ready to open on the Fourth of July, 1952.

Golf's introduction and growth in Louisville occurred nearly simultaneously with the rest of the nation. In 1888 John G. Reid, with the help of four friends, established a six-hole course in Yonkers, New York. That course was forerunner of the famous St. Andrews Golf Club. The first United States Open was played in 1894, and the first United States Amateur Open was played in 1895, the same year that both the Louisville Golf Club and Cherokee Golf Club and course (only the fifth municipal course to open in the United States) were established. Though constructed in 1895, Cherokee Golf Course in Cherokee Park saw little use until 1897. It was not until 1907 that the Cherokee Golf Club was incorporated.

Golf clubs and courses opened at a rapid pace throughout the area. By 1917, only thirty years after its introduction to the city, Louisville was the home of four courses: AUDUBON Country Club, Cherokee Golf Club, Louisville Country Club, and Standard Country Club. By the late 1920s the local communities provided the home for fourteen courses including CRESCENT HILL Course, Big Spring Country Club, NEW ALBANY Country Club, Standard Oil Golf Course, P.W.P. (Producer's Wood Pre Co.) Golf Course, Owl Creek Country Club, Jefferson Country Club, L&N Country Club, and Shawnee Golf Club. One hundred years after the introduction of the sport to the Louisville area, there were over fifty public, semiprivate, and private courses in Louisville and the surrounding communities.

Metropolitan Louisville has also been the home of several famous professional golfers. Robert "Bobby" Herman Nichols, golf's long-hitting "LOUISVILLE SLUGGER," was born April 14, 1936, in Louisville to Owen and Artie Nichols. He attended ST. XAVIER HIGH SCHOOL

Golf at the Louisville Country Club, 1912.

where he was a starting player in FOOTBALL, BASKETBALL, and golf. Nichols entered Texas A&M on a football scholarship but instead played golf. He graduated in 1958 and turned professional in 1959. Nichols won his only major championship, the Professional Golfers Association tournament title, in 1964. In the top sixty money earners every year from 1960 through 1975, Nichols made the top twenty a total of eight times (1962–74) and was fifth in 1964. He has played for many years on the senior pro golf circuit.

Frank Beard was born May 1, 1939, in Dallas, Texas. While a young man, Beard's family moved to Louisville. In 1961 he graduated from the University of Florida. Following his graduation, Beard returned to Kentucky in order to play amateur golf. He won the state championship in 1961 and 1962. After his 1962 win, he decided to go pro. By 1969 Beard had become the tour's top money winner. In 1989 Beard joined the senior golf tour. He was widely known as being cool and steady, with a masterful putting stroke.

Frank Urban "Fuzzy" Zoeller Jr. [the nickname was acquired from his initials] was born November 11, 1951, in New Albany, Indiana, to Alma and Frank Zoeller Sr. His childhood home was located on the fourth fairway of the old Valley View Golf Club. Zoeller attended Edison Junior College in Fort Myers, Florida, and the University of Houston. He turned professional in 1973. Zoeller is owner of two of the most coveted titles in golf, winning the 1979 Masters on his first attempt and the 1984 U.S. Open. By 1999 Zoeller had an additional eight PGA tournament victories for a total of ten. Zoeller, a favorite with fans and the media, is an unflappable competitor with a powerful playing style and a contagious sense of humor. Zoeller has taken an interest in golf course design and development, including the Covered Bridge Golf Club in SELLERSBURG, Indiana. In 1997 he inaugurated the Fuzzy Zoeller Wolf Challenge at the Covered Bridge course. Zoeller is married to Diane Thornton, and they had three daughters and one son.

The Metro PARKS Golf Courses have men's, women's and juniors' associations to help individuals attain their United States Golf Association Handicap. Association membership includes participation in weekly tournaments, outings, and other social events.

GOLF COURSES IN LOUISVILLE AND THE SURROUNDING COMMUNITIES

Metro Parks Golf Courses:

Cherokee Golf Course 9-Hole
The fifth-ever municipal course in the United States and Louisville's oldest public course, Cherokee's unusual design leads to many challenging shots and offers ample opportunities to test short games.

Crescent Hill Golf Course 9-Hole
Hilly, long, and narrow, the "quarry hole," a 476-yard par five, challenges even the most experienced golfers.

Iroquois Golf Course 18-Hole
The South End's finest course: hilly and long with water hazards on seven of its eighteen holes.

Long Run Golf Course 18-Hole
This course is very long and narrow.

Bobby Nichols Golf Course 9-Hole
This hill-laden short course is a fine test for golfing skills. Nichols Creek comes into play on eight of the nine holes.

Seneca Golf Course 18-Hole
This is Louisville's most popular Metro Parks course. It is utilized for professional and amateur golf events annually.

Shawnee Golf Course 18-Hole
Short and flat, Shawnee runs along the Ohio River in Louisville's West End.

Charlie Vettiner Golf Course 18-Hole
Hilly and long, this course offers variety with fifty white-sand bunkers, creeks, and three lakes.

Public Courses:

Different Strokes at English Station	9-Hole
Different Strokes at New Cut Rd.	9-Hole
Golf World International	9-Hole
Hidden Creek Golf Club	18-Hole
Maplehurst Golf Course	18-Hole
Penn Run Golf Course	18-Hole
Shively Municipal Golf Course	9-Hole
Sleepy Hollow Golf Course	9-Hole
Sultan's Run Golf Course	18-Hole
Sun Valley Golf Course	18-Hole
Tanglewood Golf Course	18-Hole

Semiprivate Courses:

Bellarmine College Course	9-Hole
Covered Bridge Golf Club	18-Hole
LaGrange Woods Golf Course	18-Hole
Indian Springs Golf Club	18-Hole
Nevel Meade Golf Course	18-Hole
Oldham County Country Club	18-Hole
Persimmon Ridge	18-Hole
Quail Chase	27-Hole

There are many exclusive golf courses and country clubs in the Louisville area, including Audubon, Louisville Country Club, Big Springs, and Hunting Creek. There are courses designed by the biggest names in golf, including Fuzzy Zoeller's Covered Bridge and Arnold Palmer's Lake Forest designs. Valhalla, however, is Louisville's premier golf challenge. The course, designed by Jack Nicklaus, has been recognized as the St. Andrews of the PGA. Valhalla Golf Club played host to the 1996 and 2000 PGA Championships. Valhalla will host the 2004 PGA Championships and the 2007 Ryder Cup.

Private Courses:

Audubon Country Club	18-Hole
Big Spring Country Club	18-Hole
Glenmary Golf Recreation Club	18-Hole
Glen Oaks Country Club	18-Hole
Harmony Landing Country Club	18-Hole
Hunting Creek Country Club	18-Hole
Hurstbourne Country Club	27-Hole
Jeffersonville Elks Golf Club	18-Hole
L&N Golf Course	18-Hole
Lake Forest Country Club	18-Hole
Louisville Country Club	18-Hole
Midland Trail Golf Club	18-Hole
New Albany Country Club	9-Hole
Oak Meadow Country Club	18-Hole
Owl Creek Country Club	9-Hole
Oxmoor Golf & Steeplechase Course	18-Hole
Polo Fields Golf Club	18-Hole
River Road Country Club	9-Hole
South Park Country Club	18-Hole
Standard Country Club	18-Hole
Valhalla Golf Club	18-Hole
Wildwood Country Club	18-Hole
Woodhaven Country Club	27-Hole

AMATEUR AND PROFESSIONAL TOURNAMENTS

The United States Amateur Public Links Championship had its inception in 1922, giving exposure to many public-course players who otherwise would not have an opportunity to compete in a national championship. The championship continues to attract amateur golfers from all walks of life including bus drivers, educators, bartenders, public servants, waiters, and tradespersons. The tournament has also worked as a springboard for such notable golfers as United States Open champions Ed Furgol, Tommy Bolt, and Ken Venturi; British Open champion Tony Lema; PGA champions Dave Marr and Bobby Nichols; and Masters winner George Archer. Louisville was the home of the Amateur Public Links tournaments in 1932 when the event was held at Seneca Golf Course and in 1950 at Shawnee Golf Course.

On April 20, 1958, Gary Player won his first American tournament, the Kentucky Derby Open at Seneca Golf Club. Player shot a pair of sixty-eights and a sixty-nine to win by three over Chick Harbert.

BUSINESS OF GOLF

In 1916 Louisville's Hillerich & Bradsby Co. (H&B) manufactured its first golf club. H&B has since become one of the oldest continuous golf club manufacturers in the United States. With the popularity of its "new" golf club in 1925, H&B purchased a warehouse from the American Tobacco Co. at Jackson and Finzer Streets to house its offices and a new golf-club-manufacturing plant. In 1933 the Hillerich & Bradsby Co. used the name "Power Bilt" on its golf clubs for the first time. H&B moved its golf production to Jeffersonville, Indiana, in 1973 because of inadequate production and warehousing facilities. In 1996 Hillerich & Bradsby opened a new corporate complex in Louisville on W Main St. at Eighth St. The new facility includes business offices, bat and golf factories, and the Louisville Slugger Museum.

Although titanium clubs are apparently the way of the future for many, Louisville Golf Co., founded in 1974, has focused on the manufacturing of persimmon woods and putters. In the early 1980s sales suffered, and the fledgling manufacturer was facing the prospect of bankruptcy. However, in the 1990s, Louisville Golf made a resurgence, and in 1997 the company experienced its strongest sales ever.

See *Courier-Journal,* Oct. 20, 1998; *Kentucky Golf Guide,* 1998.

Robert F. Magers

GOODWILL INDUSTRIES OF KENTUCKY. Dr. Edgar James Helms, Methodist minister, founded the national organization—GOODWILL INDUSTRIES—in the Boston slums in 1902. Following several name changes, it eventually became the Goodwill Industries International. Dr. John Lowe Fort, Methodist minister and first agency president, founded GOODWILL INDUSTRIES OF KENTUCKY in October 1923. After several years of working from the basements of various local churches, space requirements forced the organization to find a larger, more permanent home, this time at 814 W Market in May 1927. The foundation remained at that location until April 1990 when it moved to 909 E BROADWAY.

Goodwill's goal is to help those of limited employability to realize a more abundant life, regardless of physical impairments or emotional problems. There is particular concern for those with dependents and those who have been or may become a burden to the community. Their objective is to restore dignity and self-respect, with the philosophy "not charity but opportunity." This is done by teaching trades and literacy skills and providing work and social services to the physically disabled and the needy. The collection, repair, and sale of unwanted clothing and household items have been a major source of income, training, and employment for the nonprofit organization. Goodwill Industries has been active on state/federal levels concerning unemployment compensation, sheltered workshops, rehabilitation services, and transportation for elderly and handicapped persons.

In 1934 the local branch became part of the Goodwill Industries International. The 1937 flood found Goodwill providing disaster and emergency services, offering food and shelter, and sorting and packing clothes and other daily living necessities for victims. That same year, Goodwill first employed the services of Edmund D. Redmon, a man who, despite the disability of polio, rose from being the organization's bookkeeper to chief financial officer in a career spanning thirty-eight years. In 1992 Goodwill dedicated a conference center and community room to Redmon's legacy, recognizing his services to improving the lives of Kentucky's handicapped and disadvantaged.

Lillian C. Milanof

GORDON, JAMES FLEMING (b Madisonville, Kentucky, May 18, 1918; d Sarasota, Florida, February 9, 1990). Jurist. The son of John Fleming and Ruby JAMES GORDON, his father sat as a circuit judge and continued a family law practice established in 1807. Gordon earned a LAW degree from the University of Kentucky in 1941. After serving in the army during WORLD WAR II and in the military GOVERNMENT in postwar Japan, he returned to the family law practice and Democratic state politics.

Gordon's tenure on the federal bench (1965–84) is memorable for two cases. The first, occurring almost as soon as he assumed the job as United States district judge for Western Kentucky, involved a $2 million libel suit filed by retired army major general Edwin Walker against the *COURIER-JOURNAL* and WHAS-TV for their coverage of Walker's participation in a protest against the admission of James Meredith to the University of Mississippi. Gordon dismissed the suit on the grounds that Walker was a public figure who had thrown himself into the "vortex of the news."

Gordon's most controversial action came in 1975 when, under orders from a higher court, he drafted the BUSING plan to desegregate the Louisville and Jefferson County school systems. The original suit, brought against the public schools by a coalition of civil rights groups in 1973, had been dismissed by Gordon, who ruled that segregation in local schools was the result of housing patterns and other factors rather than the policies of school officials. In the summer of 1975, the U.S. Circuit Court of Appeals reversed the ruling and ordered Gordon to implement a desegregation plan by the start of the fall term.

Working with school officials and local leaders, Gordon merged the city and county school systems on April 1, 1975, and imposed a busing plan that integrated the community's public schools. When put into operation, the plan generated enormous resistance, including school boycotts and violent demonstrations. Yet Gordon enforced the busing plan evenhandedly and won praise from leaders of civil rights groups.

But to those opposing the busing plan, Gordon symbolized the busing order that touched every school in the county and became a target of vilification. After leaving the bench, Gordon remarked that he "was . . . shocked by the bigotry of the white community." The result was to have an adverse impact upon his health, and he moved to Florida. He died six years after retiring from the bench and is buried in Odd Fellows Cemetery in Madisonville, Kentucky. He and his wife, the former Iola Young, had one daughter, Marianna Dyson, and two sons, Maurice II and James Junior.

See *Courier-Journal,* Feb. 11, 1990.

Olivia M. Frederick

GOSPEL, SOUL, AND RHYTHM-AND-BLUES MUSIC. Louisville enjoys an especially rich musical tradition in the black Baptist community. In the 1960s this translated into churches having multiple choirs, such as West Chestnut Baptist Church, which had as many as ten at one time. By the 1980s the number of choirs per church was dropping as churches began the practice of traveling to other churches on Sunday morning and taking their music programs along; the more people involved, the harder it was to do this. Average black church choirs now number between forty and seventy people.

The modern gospel movement in Louisville can be traced to Cable Baptist Church at 314 S Wenzel St. in the late 1970s when at Sunday services musicians began using instruments other than piano and organ, including the Hammond B3 organ, drums, conga drums, bass guitar, rhythm guitar, and a children's percussion section including tambourines, blocks, and bells. The church's choirs began giving concerts in addition to providing music for Sunday worship services and drawing national names such as Albertina Walker and Milton Bronson to sing with them. St. Stephen and CANAAN MISSIONARY BAPTIST CHURCHES joined Cable Baptist as leaders in Louisville's Gospel scene. There has also been an active gospel choir (The Black Diamond Choir) at the UNIVERSITY OF LOUISVILLE since 1969, led for many years by Lamott Bush.

Gospel music since the 1980s has been dominated by artists such as Keith Hunter, Archie Dale and the Tones of Joy, and especially Tommy Jones and the Christian Workshop Choir, who in addition to their activity in Louisville do gospel music workshops throughout the United States and frequently work with the James Cleveland Workshops of America. Largely due to Jones's work, Louisville has also become a popular site for these workshops. The Louisville Choral Union, formed in 1941, serves to connect and coordinate the active gospel scene in the city.

Though the city has not been home to as much activity in rhythm-and-BLUES (R&B) or soul as it has in gospel, there have still been some notable groups. In the early 1970s, New Birth included members and writers from Louisville, although it was based in Detroit. Prince Philip Mitchell began in Louisville in the late 1970s as did Reggie Calloway's Midnight Star before moving to Los Angeles, and Playa and Southern Comfort have been mainstays in the 1990s.

Rap music has not been a major part of the creative scene in Louisville, although the Underground Mafia was popular in the late 1980s.

Soul/R&B groups traditionally have played in Louisville in large arena spaces such as Louisville Gardens and the W.L. Lyons Brown (formerly Macauley) Theatre, because there are no mid-size venues for them. Thus, promoters often book national acts, hoping to fill them with audiences from St. Louis, Cincinnati, and other neighboring cities, and book local groups to open for them. These large venues have not been a problem for gospel artists, since large halls are necessary to accommodate the choir. African American music has been served in the city since 1982 by Ben Jones's Better Days Records, a major black-owned independent label.

See various issues of *Louisville Music News*, University of Louisville music library.

Jack Ashworth
Ben Jones

GOTTHELF, BERNARD HENRY (b Bavaria, Germany, February 5, 1819; d Vicksburg, Mississippi, September 7, 1878). Jewish leader, chaplain. Gotthelf married Sophie Landauer in 1840 just before immigrating to the United States at age twenty-one. He served as spiritual leader of several Jewish congregations in the East, including KENESETH ISRAEL in Philadelphia, before coming to Louisville in 1849 to serve as cantor, teacher, and "lecturer" for Congregation Adath Israel. In 1855, he represented Adath Israel in Cleveland, Ohio, at the first conference of Reform-oriented congregations in America. Gotthelf apparently had not received rabbinic ordination and was asked to deliver sermons at Adath Israel only after 1862.

During the CIVIL WAR, following a protracted campaign by leaders of American Jewry to amend the requirement that military chaplains be "regularly ordained minister[s] of some Christian denomination," Gotthelf was selected as the second Jewish chaplain in the Union army. Appointed on May 6, 1863, he served primarily in the HOSPITALS of Kentucky and was mustered out on August 26, 1865. In 1866, Adath Israel hired Leopold Kleeberg as its first rabbi but retained Gotthelf as cantor. Within a year, however, Gotthelf moved to Vicksburg, Mississippi, with his wife, four sons, and four daughters. There he led Congregation Anshe Chesed until his death in the yellow fever epidemic of 1878.

See Bertram W. Korn, *American Jewry and the Civil War* (Philadelphia 1955); Charles Goldsmith, "History of Congregation Adath Israel" in *History of Congregation Adath Israel, Louisville, Kentucky, and the Addresses Delivered at the Dedication of its New Temple* (Louisville 1906); Gertrude Philippsborn, *The History of the Jewish Community of Vicksburg* (Vicksburg, Miss., 1969).

Lee Shai Weissbach

GOTTSCHALK, LOUIS REICHENTHAL (b Brooklyn, New York, February 21, 1899; d Chicago, Illinois, June 23, 1975). Author, historian, and educator. The sixth of eight children, born to Jewish Polish immigrants Morris and Anna Krystal Gottschalk, he entered Cornell University in 1915 and had received his Ph.D. by 1921. Later that year, Gottschalk accepted a teaching position at the University of Illinois. He joined the history department at the rapidly growing UNIVERSITY OF LOUISVILLE in 1923 during the school's move from downtown to the BELKNAP Campus. The abrupt death of university president ARTHUR FORD not only altered the philosophy of the university but Gottschalk's career as well, due to the trustees' appointment of GEORGE COLVIN as the school's new president in 1926.

Colvin immediately initiated changes and incurred the wrath of the faculty as he reportedly told history and economics professors to avoid controversies in the classrooms, abolished the college art department, admitted FOOTBALL players of questionable backgrounds, and indicated that research and graduate instruction would take a back seat to undergraduate work. As an added insult to the faculty, Colvin announced his intention to abolish tenured positions and to distribute only one-year contracts. The two sides clashed in 1927 when the administration mistakenly concluded that history professor Rolf Johannsen's extended consideration of his contract renewal signaled his refusal and fired him.

When Gottschalk heard of his friend's dismissal, he immediately resigned and issued a statement critical of what he deemed the anti-Semitic policies of Colvin and the board of trustees. The board accepted Gottschalk's resignation with the claim that he was "the sole or principal cause for the trouble at the university." Although the board promptly recanted this statement, Gottschalk asked for an investigation by the American Association of University Professors, which eventually condemned the president and the board for their actions. Gottschalk accepted a position in the fall of 1927 at the University of Chicago, where he became a renowned historian specializing in the American and FRENCH Revolutions. He retired in 1964 as the Gustavus and Ann Swift Distinguished Service Professor Emeritus. Later University of Louisville administrations attempted to repair the relationship several times when they honored Gottschalk at the sesquicentennial in 1948, hosted him as a Bingham Professor of Humanities in 1968, and gave him an honorary doctorate in 1970.

Notable works by Gottschalk include *Jean-Paul Marat* (1927), *The Era of the French Revolution* (1929), and *Lafayette Comes to America* (1935). He was active on the Social Science Research Council; worked on the *Journal of Modern History,* serving as associate editor from 1929–43 and acting editor from 1943–45; was the author-editor of the UNESCO universal history project titled *Foundations of the Modern World, 1300–1775* (1969); and was the president of the American Historical Association in 1953.

After a failed first marriage to poet/critic Laura Riding from 1920 to 1925, Gottschalk married Fruma Kasdan in 1930; they had two sons, Alexander and Paul. He was cremated at Oakridge Cemetery, Hillside, Illinois.

See Works Progress Administration, *Centennial History of the University of Louisville* (Louisville 1939); Dwayne Cox, "A History of the University of Louisville," Ph.D. dissertation, University of Kentucky, 1984.

GOVERNMENT. A county is a subdivision of state GOVERNMENT created to carry out state functions at a local level. In a rural nation, counties were often the only government and were charged with recording important actions or events including births, deaths, marriages, and property deed transfers. As an area became more urban, municipalities were created that could provide a greater level of services (i.e., urban services), including police and fire protection, and roads. The state, by legislative act, would create a municipal corporation or municipality (city) and grant it a charter that specified what authority that city had and how it would govern itself. In some states, the process of incorporating municipalities was routinized. Instead of granting a specific charter to a city, a process was created for cities to be incorporated if they met certain conditions, often POPULATION. State law would define what powers that city had based upon its classification.

The origins of local government in Louisville and Jefferson County date back to the early days of the new Republic. The town of Louisville and county of Jefferson were created by acts of the Virginia legislature in 1780. The first Jefferson County was one of three original counties carved from Kentucky County, which had been created on December 31, 1776, out of land owned by Virginia. Today, Jefferson is one of the twenty-eight counties eventually created out of the larger Jefferson County.

Kentucky's 1891 Constitution established a classification system of cities based upon population size. State law defined the powers and organization of cities within each of the six classes of cities that replaced prior CITY CHARTERS. Only one city, Louisville, met the population threshold of a hundred thousand people required for a first-class city. Other classes were second class, twenty thousand people; third class, eight thousand people; fourth class, three thousand people; fifth class, one thousand people; and sixth class, three hundred people. The constitution prohibited the legislature from passing special acts for particular cities and required that laws apply to classes of cities. Of course, the fact that only one city, Louisville, was a first-class city meant that the legislature could still pass special acts intended only to affect Louisville, which had been made a city in 1828.

There are 125 local governments in Jefferson County. This includes ninety-five general purpose governments—Jefferson County government and ninety-four city governments. There are another thirty special-purpose governments. Among the special-purpose governments are two school districts (Jefferson County and ANCHORAGE) and twenty-eight special taxing districts, including twenty-two volunteer fire districts, a sewer district (Metropolitan Sewer District), and a transportation district (TRANSIT AUTHORITY OF RIVER CITY). In addition to the 125 local governments in Jefferson County, there are another 22 subordinate local government organizations including joint city-county agencies and public authorities set up under interlocal agreements.

Louisville operates under a mayor-council form of government based upon a separation of powers with checks and balances between the executive branch (the mayor) and the legislative branch (the BOARD OF ALDERMEN). The mayor is elected for a four-year term. The mayor is responsible for preparing and submitting a budget to the Board of Aldermen, appoints department heads and members of boards and commissions, and is charged with overseeing implementation of the laws of the city. The mayor can veto acts of the Board of Aldermen.

There are twelve members on the Board of Aldermen, who serve two-year terms. Candidates for Board of Aldermen run in one of twelve districts (WARDS) in a party primary. Winners of the Republican and Democratic primaries then face off in "at-large" (citywide) general elections. Given the predominance of Democrats in the city, Republicans rarely compete for aldermanic seats. For all practical purposes, the winners are decided in the smaller ward Democratic primary elections. The Board of Aldermen is responsible for appropriating money, setting tax rates, determining zoning, and adopting city ordinances within the confines of the state constitution and laws. The Board of Aldermen may override executive vetoes. The city provides a number of urban services including fire and police protection, garbage collection, PUBLIC WORKS, PUBLIC HOUSING, PARKS, and URBAN RENEWAL.

Jefferson County operates under a variation of a commission form of government. The Fiscal Court is made up of four members—the county/judge executive and three commissioners who are nominated in district party primaries and elected in at-large general elections. The Fiscal Court combines legislative and executive powers. The Fiscal Court is responsible for tax rates, zoning in fifth- and sixth-class cities and unincorporated areas (unincorporated area refers to land in a county that is not in a city), passing a budget, and generally overseeing administration of county programs.

The judge/executive presides at Fiscal Court meetings and serves as the executive of county government. However, the judge/executive is more limited than a chief executive in a strong mayor system. For example, the power to appoint many top officials in county government is shared with the Fiscal Court. Other separately elected constitutional officers include the sheriff, county clerk, county attorney, and property valuation administrator. These officials operate their departments independently of county government and the judge/executive.

Reformers have long sought to reduce the fragmentation in local government or establish more unified government. The quest for metropolitan government was hastened by the rapid suburbanization of business and people and new incorporations of suburban cities after WORLD WAR II. In the 1940s and 1950s, a number of Louisville and Jefferson County officials called for the consolidation of the city and county governments. The most far-reaching proposal and the only one put to the voters during this period was the Mallon Plan in 1956. The Mallon Plan would have extended Louisville's boundaries to encompass all urban areas of the county and provide residents in outlying areas with urban services such as garbage collection and fire protection. The Mallon Plan was essentially a major annexation that would have added forty-six square miles and sixty-eight thousand residents to the city. The proposal was defeated by suburban voters.

It took more than twenty-five years before another governmental reorganization plan was put before the voters. In 1982, Judge/Executive MITCH MCCONNELL and Mayor Harvey Sloane asked the legislature to allow Jefferson County the option of consolidating with Louisville. Other counties were permitted this option in 1972, and Lexington and Fayette County had merged that year. The legislature passed a bill permitting Louisville and Jefferson County to consider merger after an amendment was added guaranteeing small cities their continued existence. The mayor and county judge appointed a charter commission to study and recommend a new consolidated government.

The 1982 merger proposal was defeated in a referendum, losing by 1,450 votes. The closeness of the election led to a second merger effort in 1983. This 1983 merger was defeated by a larger margin, 5,600 votes. A major factor in the defeat of the 1982 and 1983 merger proposals was suspicion by West End AFRICAN AMERICANS and South End blue-collar whites about the motives of the downtown business community and East End elites in pursuing merger. African Americans were concerned that consolidation would dilute their political strength and obstruct their aspirations to elect an African American mayor as they increased their proportion of the city POPULATION. A strong anti-merger coalition united police bargaining units, the National Association for the Advancement of Colored People (NAACP), eighteen state representatives, and five members of the Louisville Board of Aldermen, among others, to defeat the effort.

Between 1960 and 1980, Louisville had lost nearly a hundred thousand people and close to 25 percent of its population, thousands of manufacturing jobs, and millions of dollars in annual revenues. Since merger was not politically feasible, the Board of Aldermen proposed to annex all remaining unincorporated areas in Jefferson County in 1985. This seriously threatened county revenues because employees working inside the boundary of the city do not pay county occupational taxes. The annexation proposal also threatened the interests of residents of unincorporated areas hopeful of forming their own cities or being annexed to a smaller city. Smaller cities objected as well, since this would limit their ability to expand. The level of conflict among local governments competing for economic development and revenue and the apparent rifts between different segments of the community—racial, ethnic, and socioeconomic class (East, West, and South)—were tearing the community apart. The proposed annexation plan indicated the city would fight for its financial survival, including annexing many who wanted to be separate from the city.

In November 1985 Mayor Harvey Sloane was elected judge/executive of Jefferson County. At the same time, Jerry Abramson was elected mayor of Louisville. Between the elections and the time they took office in January 1986, they negotiated the Louisville and Jefferson County Compact, which provided for tax sharing, a moratorium on annexation and new city incorporations, and new arrangements for financing and managing joint city-county agencies. The state legislature passed an act authorizing the two governments to enter into this agreement. In June 1986 the compact was passed as an ordinance by the city Board of Aldermen and adopted as a resolution of JEFFERSON COUNTY FISCAL COURT. The compact was set to last for twelve years and would expire unless extended or renegotiated.

Essentially, the compact was a peace treaty between the city and county governments. It removed or reduced major sources of tension between the city of Louisville and Jefferson County. With respect to tax sharing, the two governments agreed to split the occupational tax. The city would receive about 58 percent and the county about 42 percent of the total occupational tax revenues collected by the two governments. This formula was based upon the distribution of revenues in 1985. Separate formulas provided for adjustments for inflation and for new economic growth. This tax sharing arrangement ensured that the city would have a stable revenue source. This meant the city no longer needed to pursue annexation to gain revenue. Further, since both governments shared the revenues, regardless of where growth went, there was no longer an incentive to compete for new businesses coming into the area.

The moratorium on annexation and new incorporations assured Louisville that its interests would be protected should the compact not be renewed. If or when the compact expires, the city of Louisville has the right to pursue all the annexations it had filed in 1985, prior to the adoption of the compact. Technically, the compact does not prohibit Louisville annexation efforts, but it requires a dual majority referendum—a majority vote in the city and the area to be annexed—for an annexation to succeed. Annexations requiring dual majority votes rarely are approved. Permitting new incorporations would prevent the city from annexing these areas, as would allowing small cities to annex. Small cities have objected to these provisions in the compact, arguing that they were not a party to the agreement and therefore the limitations should not apply to them. The courts have not yet ruled on this issue. However, since the compact is enacted by the state as well as Louisville and Jefferson County, it is unlikely that the COURTS will overturn this provision of the compact.

The third part of the compact deals with the financing and management of the dozen joint city-county agencies. The joint agencies were a mechanism to provide urban services throughout the county. The joint agencies were operated under independent boards appointed by the mayor and county judge/executive. The two governments shared equally the budgets of these agencies. The agencies were rather independent of the two governments that were obligated to fund them. Two problems were associated with the joint agencies. First, the agencies were not always responsive to the two governments, and they could play them against each other in the budget process. Second, by 1970 Louisville no longer held 50 percent of the population of the county, yet under the joint agency arrangement, the city still shouldered half the costs of providing these services.

Under the compact, the boards overseeing the agencies were made advisory. Eight of the agencies were directly assigned to one or the other government. The city ended up with Disaster and Emergency Services, the Human Relations Commission, the History and Science Museum, and the zoo. The county ended up with the Air Pollution Control Board, the BOARD OF HEALTH, the Crime Commission, and the Planning Office. Each government was free to run the agency as it saw fit, including appointing the directors, integrating the agencies into regular city or county administrative structures and policies, and setting the budgets. Four agencies remained joint: the library, Parks and Recreation, TRANSIT AUTHORITY OF RIVER CITY (TARC), and the Metropolitan Sewer District (MSD). The executive directors of these agencies were jointly appointed by the mayor and judge/executive instead of by an independent board. The financing remained equally shared. In addition, one new joint agency, the Office of Economic Development, was created. In the re-sorting of services associated with reorganizing the independent joint agencies, the county agreed to take on an additional $1 million in public service obligations as compensation to the city for giving up annexation and to reflect the reduced proportion of the population residing in the city.

The compact worked remarkably well in its first twelve years. It allowed the city and county to cooperate on economic development initiatives and provided the basis for a public-private partnership for economic development. The airport expansion could not have been successful without the compact in place. The city and county evolved a cooperative if occasionally antagonistic relationship. The county objected to the amount of money, more than $20 million, transferred to the city under the terms of the compact. However, both governments saw their revenues grow and profited from the end of battles over annexation and economic development.

The compact did not end calls for government reorganization. In 1998, the compact was set to expire, setting the stage for community debate over whether the compact should be renewed or some other government reorganization plan should be considered, including possibly city-county consolidation. A Chamber of Commerce Regional Economic Development (REDs) strategic planning process called for local government reorganization in 1993. The major concern was that the community lacked a unified leadership, resulting in conflicting state legislative agendas and community priorities such as whether and where to build a new bridge across the OHIO RIVER. In 1994, as the result of compromise among the city Board of Aldermen, mayor, Fiscal Court and judge/executive, a Local Governance Task Force was created. It was financed by the GREATER LOUISVILLE ECONOMIC DEVELOPMENT PARTNERSHIP and managed by the Chamber of Commerce. There were 128 people appointed to the task force. In December 1995, after a year of study and at a cost of approximately $350,000, the task force produced a set of recommendations for local government reorganization.

The task force rejected city-county consolidation. It proposed that a number of services be consolidated under county authority, including "police protection, emergency medical services, parks and recreation, public works, human relations, public housing, indigent care, the library system, air pollution, land use planning, economic development, TARC, MSD, and the airport authority." At the same time, revenues to support these activities were to be transferred to the county. Accompanying the shift in services to the county was to be modernization of county government, which was viewed as an anachronism more suitable to a rural age. The Fiscal Court was to be replaced by a county executive and a separate twelve-person county council elected on a nonpartisan basis. *A Report to the Jefferson County Fiscal Court on Final Recommendations of the Jefferson County Governance Project* concluded that, if enacted, these changes would leave the city a shadow of its former self and that the proposal was an incremental step toward eventual consolidation of the city and county governments. Questions were raised about the adequacy of the evidence to support the recommendations.

The task force sought to have the legislature place a referendum on the ballot on restructuring county government in the fall 1996 elections. If passed, the city and county were to negotiate the transfers of services and revenues. Although the Senate passed a bill setting the referendum, the House did not act after it was clear that there was no consensus among members of Fiscal Court, the Board of Aldermen, mayor, and county judge to support the proposals.

This left renegotiation and renewal of the compact in the hands of Mayor Jerry Abramson and Judge/Executive David Armstrong. After about one year of negotiations the compact was renewed, with minor revisions, for an additional ten-year period. The arrangement for sharing revenues and funding joint agencies remains unchanged. To promote a more unified economic development effort, an Economic Growth Fund was created to facilitate business attraction. Each government is to contribute $1 million annually for the first five years of the compact extension. Subsequent to the compact's extension, the Office of Economic Development (OED) was eliminated. Many of the economic development functions previously provided by OED were taken over by GREATER LOUISVILLE INC. (the former Chamber of Commerce). Thus, public and private economic development efforts are now integrated in a single public-private partnership.

Other changes included provision of a short time span in which small cities could annex a small amount of land (no more than 10 percent of existing land area). All residents in areas to be annexed had to favor the annexation, which also had to be approved by the Board of Aldermen and Fiscal Court. A handful of annexations were approved.

An outgrowth of the compact renegotiations was a proposal by Judge Armstrong for merging of city and county police departments and a General Assembly mandate to consider local government reorganization, including possibly merger of city and county government. Initially, Armstrong had proposed that police consolidation could be completed before Abramson left office at the end of his second term in December 1998. (There is a two-term limit on the OFFICE OF MAYOR of Louisville). The Louisville and Jefferson County Crime Commission Merger Study Advisory Committee examined the issue, but it was tabled when newly elected Judge REBECCA JACKSON indicated that a decision on police consolidation should be considered as part of the broader issue of city-county consolidation.

The General Assembly set up a special Task Force on local government in Counties containing a City of the First Class in June 1998 to consider reorganizing local government in Louisville and Jefferson County, including possible merger. The task force consists of fifty-four elected officials including the local state legislative delegation, the Board of Aldermen, Fiscal Court, mayor, judge/executive, and several small city mayors. In September 1999, Judge Rebecca Jackson and David Armstrong, who took over the position of Louisville mayor, formally proposed city-county consolidation. The merger proposal exempts the small cities. The task force is to make a recommendation to the General Assembly in January 2000 on whether to authorize a local merger proposal or otherwise restructure city and county government.

Momentum has been building behind a merger proposal stemming in part from concern that Lexington may surpass Louisville as the state's largest city sometime after the 2000 census. Lexington, a consolidated city-county, had 225,000 residents in 1990 compared to Louisville's 269,000. (Jefferson County had a population of about 670,000 persons in 1990.) Ironically, as public leaders debate merging the city and county governments, in July 1999, some African American leaders including Mattie Jones and the Rev. Louis Coleman have proposed creating a separate city of West Louisville. West Louisville is predominantly African American. This proposal stems from concern about police brutality and the failure of the city to create a civilian police review board.

At the time this entry was written, it is unclear if the Task Force will recommend local government reorganization. The structure of local government sets the framework within which urban politics occurs. Any governmental structure works to the advantage or disadvantage of different community interests. Restructuring or changing local governmental institutions likely would alter the distribution of winners and losers in the urban politics of the community. Therefore, efforts to reorganize local government highlight the cleavages in society that get reflected in political struggle. In Louisville's recent past, lower socioeconomic classes and African Americans have seen city-county consolidation as a threat to their communities and their ability to benefit from local government through public services, infrastructure investments, and local policies. More affluent residents and community leaders have been more likely to see unified government as increasing economic development opportunities and leading to greater efficiency and effectiveness in the delivery of urban services. These divergent views of city-county consolidation are reinforced by geographic separation in different sections of the community. African Americans predominate in western Louisville, working-class whites in the south end, and more affluent whites in the eastern cities and unincorporated areas. In this respect, efforts to restructure local government are at the core of urban politics and will never be wholly settled.

Basketball Team sponsored by Grace Hope Presbyterian Church in 1926.

See League of Women Voters of Louisville and Jefferson County, *Your Government at Your Fingertips: A Handbook of Local Government* (Louisville 1994); Legislative Research Commission, *The Multiplicity of Local Governments in Jefferson County* [report no. 130] (Frankfort 1977); H.V. Savitch and Ronald K. Vogel, "Louisville: Compacts and Antagonistic Cooperation" in H.V. Savitch and Ronald K. Vogel, eds., *Regional Politics: America in a Post-City Age* (Thousand Oaks, Calif., 1996); H.V. Savitch and Ronald K. Vogel, *Report to the Jefferson County Fiscal Court on Final Recommendations of the Jefferson County Governance Project* (Louisville 1996); Bob Schulman, "A Splitsville Called Louisville," *Urban Resources* 4; Ronald K. Vogel, *Local Government Reorganization* [Goldstein Report no. 1] (University of Louisville 1994).

Ronald K. Vogel

GRACE HOPE PRESBYTERIAN CHURCH. In 1898 six students from the Louisville Presbyterian Seminary—E.V. Dickey, H. McDowell, E.P. Piller, J. Little, E.H. Mosley, and D.D. Little—decided to establish a mission among AFRICAN AMERICANS. The downtown area south of BROADWAY, which was called SMOKETOWN, and north of Broadway, called Uptown, (east of the central business district) constituted the city's largest and poorest black settlements. These areas harbored saloons, GAMBLING houses, and prostitutes. Student missionaries wanted to address the problems caused by their presence and bring hope to these long-neglected areas.

In 1898 they opened a Sunday school in a small house on Preston St. near Pearl St. with twenty-three people in attendance. This was the founding of Hope Mission in Uptown. The following year, the second Sunday school was opened at the corner of Jackson and Lampton Streets with thirty people present. This school was the beginning of Grace Mission in

Smoketown. Under the leadership of the young students, with help from the seminary and local residents, the two missions grew rapidly to about one hundred attending during the first year.

In the fall of 1899 the Presbytery of Louisville decided that the missions should be permanently maintained. JOHN LITTLE, one of their founders and a graduate of the Presbyterian seminary, became the first director of the missions. Both missions expanded and moved to new sites. Grace Mission moved to the corner of Roselane and Hancock Streets in 1902. Hope Mission purchased the building at 314 S Hancock St. in 1911. The missions became important parts of the community. The attendance and interest in the services increased rapidly, and by 1907 both missions had more than five hundred members. In 1910 the Sunday school of Grace Mission organized as Grace Presbyterian Church, a part of the Presbyterian church in the USA, with Dr. W. Sheppard as its pastor. In 1935 the Hope Mission became the Hope Presbyterian Church with Dr. Charles Allen as pastor. URBAN RENEWAL and construction in the Uptown area forced many residents to move eastward in the 1950s and 1960s. This led to a drop of attendance in the Hope Church. In 1964 the GRACE AND HOPE CHURCHES merged as GRACE HOPE PRESBYTERIAN CHURCH at the corner of Hancock and Roselane Streets.

The executive directors and many staff members of Grace and Hope community centers had always been white. In the mid-1950s and 1960s there was a gradual increase in the number of black staff members. In 1966 Rev. Irvin S. Moxley became the first black executive director of the community center at Grace Hope Presbyterian Church. In 1977 Grace Hope Church moved to a brick building at 702 E Breckinridge St. Rev. Keith O. Paige began his service in 1991. In 1998 Grace Hope Presbyterian Church celebrated one hundred years of ministry.

See Elder Charles E. Richardson, *Grace Hope Presbyterian Church* (Louisville 1998).

GRAHAM, CHRISTOPHER COLUMBUS (b Fort WORTHINGTON, near Danville, Kentucky, October 10, 1784; d Louisville, February 3, 1885). Physician, antiquarian, and historian. Graham was the son of James Graham, a longhunter who was a pioneer settler of Kentucky in 1778. In 1819 Graham received his medical degree from Transylvania University in Lexington. Upon graduation he worked briefly as a railroad surgeon but never became a regular practitioner.

From the early 1820s his life was connected to Harrodsburg, where his father-in-law, Capt. David Sutton, owned Harrodsburg Springs, a nationally famous health resort. Graham built a large hotel at the spa that he operated until 1852. Harrodsburg's Christian Baptist Female College and Presbyterian Female College owed their existence in part to Graham, who was a supporter of those schools.

Throughout his life Graham collected and studied minerals, FOSSILS, coins, and other relics from the local area. Later he donated his extensive collection to the LOUISVILLE FREE PUBLIC LIBRARY and other institutions.

Beginning in 1872 he spent most of his time in Louisville while writing a history of Kentucky. Several of his articles about pioneer life in Kentucky were published in the *Louisville Monthly Magazine* in 1879. Among them were works on historic figures GEORGE ROGERS CLARK, Bland Ballard, Simon Kenton, William Whitley, Benjamin Logan, and Col. Ben R. Milam. Graham also published books on science and philosophy such as *Man from His Cradle to His Grave* (1859), *The True Science of Medicine* (1866), and *The Philosophy of Mind* (1869). In 1884 friends and colleagues celebrated Graham's one hundredth birthday at the LOUISVILLE HOTEL. Graham is buried in Danville.

See Brent Altsheler, "C.C. Graham, M.D., 1784–1885," *Filson Club History Quarterly* 7 (April 1933): 67–87; *Louisville Past and Present* (Louisville 1875); *The Biographical Encyclopaedia of Kentucky* (Cincinnati 1878).

GRAINGER, CHARLES F. (b Louisville, January 23, 1854; d Louisville, April 13, 1923). Mayor. He was the son of William H. and Emily P. Grainger. His father was the proprietor of the Phoenix Foundry, later known as Grainger & Co., a successful iron manufacturing plant. Charles eventually became president of the company, which furnished the steel for many buildings in the Louisville area, including the Seelbach Hotel and the Tyler Building.

Grainger spent more than twenty years in public service. He was first elected from the Seventh Ward to the BOARD OF ALDERMEN in 1890. In 1893 he became president of the board. He was appointed chairman of the Board of PUBLIC WORKS by Mayor Charles P. Weaver. In 1901 he succeeded Weaver as mayor and served until 1905. He was a lifelong Democrat.

During Grainger's tenure, he was instrumental in expanding the park system and in road and sewer construction. He also assisted in the creation of the Jefferson County Armory. The jail and the Free Public Library were built during his tenure. After his term as mayor he became president of the LOUISVILLE WATER CO. He promoted improvements in the city's water supply, including construction of the filtering building at the Frankfort Ave. plant.

Throughout his life, Grainger was active in Kentucky's horse-racing industry. He was a member of the first Kentucky State Racing Commission. In 1902 he became president of the Louisville Jockey Club and held the position until 1918. Grainger, acting as a trustee for a syndicate, purchased the land upon which the Jockey Club sat from the Churchill family in 1905. By then the place was called CHURCHILL DOWNS. In 1918 he became resident manager of Churchill Downs, a position he held until his death.

During his years at the Downs, Grainger helped to make the Kentucky Derby one of the greatest sporting events in America. While he headed the Jockey Club, the purse for the KENTUCKY DERBY rose from five thousand to fifty thousand dollars. He also introduced the pari-mutuel betting system in the United States. Grainger also financed a school for jockeys and exercise boys at Churchill Downs.

Grainger was president of the PENDENNIS CLUB from 1919 to 1921. Grainger married Jeannie Miller, daughter of Silas F. Miller, the proprietor of the second GALT HOUSE. They had no children. He died of heart disease and is buried in CAVE HILL CEMETERY.

See Samuel W. Thomas, *Churchill Downs: A Documentary History of America's Most Legendary Race Track* (Louisville 1995).

Candace K. Perry

GRAND ARMY OF THE REPUBLIC ENCAMPMENT. Louisville's opportunity to host the twenty-ninth annual encampment of the Grand Army of the Republic (GAR) in September 1895 was a coup for the growing city of approximately two hundred thousand citizens. In October 1893, the Commerce Club of Louisville, with the support of local Confederate veteran organizations that had initiated the idea, voted to solicit the yearly meeting of CIVIL WAR Union veterans. The convention had never previously ventured south of the OHIO RIVER, although two conventions had been held in Washington, D.C. Louisville's proposal was accepted at the convention at Pittsburgh in 1894, and the citizens of Louisville formed a citizens planning committee of a hundred men led by T.H. Sherley (president of the Citizens Committee), ANDREW COWAN, George W. Griffiths, R.M. Kelly, Charles L. Jewett, Isaac F. Whitesides, John H. Milkie (director general of the committee), and William Cornwall Jr., and chaired by ex-Confederate John H. Leathers. Confederate general John B. Castleman was head of the reception committee. To bring the GAR would be a matter of civic pride, economic infusion, and a symbol of unity.

During the planning stages an article appeared in several African American NEWSPAPERS in the North saying the black veterans would be unable to get rooms or food and would be shown only the river or the work camps. Committee members reassured black veterans that such would not be the case. Black chapters were promised free quarters as centrally located as white free quarters in a new school building and were told that, if chapters wanted black members boarding with white members, there would be no objection. Louisville delivered on its promise, and there was much pleasant surprise among African American delegates.

As the city prepared for the anticipated crowd of 150,000 soldiers, every business and organization, hoping to make money, was in

Parade during the 1895 Grand Army of the Republic Encampment.

some way involved with the celebration. Newspaper advertisers capitalized on the event by selling flags and other patriotic goods while publicizing their establishments as being directly on the parade route, as standing on historic ground, or as simply the best in the city. Scrapbooks and GAR plaques were for sale (or free with certain purchases), and one guidebook for the city featured local THEATERS, PARKS, and popular brothels in Louisville's red-light district, many of them located along Green (LIBERTY) St. Official badges and souvenirs were made from bronze taken from a Union and a Confederate cannon melted down together to reinforce the theme of unity.

To house the visitors, a three-hundred-tent city, known as "Camp Caldwell," was raised on the ground bounded by Preston, Floyd, Oak, and Camp Streets. Schools were closed for the week and emptied of their furniture to provide shelter, while HOTELS and rented homes were filled to capacity with Union veterans and their families.

Extra transportation was readied by the railroad carriers, and the Louisville Railway Co. reorganized its entire trolley system to concentrate on the convention's major activities. Most of the nation's RAILROADS, especially those east of the Mississippi River, agreed to the cut rate of one cent per mile from destination to Louisville. Other communities sent extra policemen, firemen, and public safety equipment, while temporary first-aid centers were established on street corners and in drugstores. The city also contracted for additional lighting, public decorations, and SANITATION facilities.

When the conventioneers began arriving on Monday, September 9, 1895, the *COURIER-JOURNAL* greeted them with a headline reading: "Louisville, the Gateway to War in 1861, is to the Veterans in 1895 the Gateway to a Prosperous South." After a ceremonious welcome of the GAR's commander-in-chief later in the day, the celebration was under way. While the convention's official agenda simply called for the election of officers, discussions of pensions and holidays, and a decision on the site of the next meeting, these events were overshadowed by the happenings throughout the city. Planned and spontaneous gatherings and reunions known as campfires (army) or dogwatches (navy) popped up throughout the city. Nightly concerts were held in the PARKS, and musicals were performed daily at the Grand Opera House and the Buckingham and the Macauley theaters. Louisville's two racetracks—Douglas Park and CHURCHILL DOWNS—carried full cards during the week and competed with vaudeville shows, city tours, receptions, and balls, all of which received attention in the NEWSPAPERS.

After the general meeting on Wednesday, thirty thousand veterans marched in a parade down BROADWAY from Shelby St. to Fourth St., then north to Jefferson, west to Eighth, north to Market, and turned east and ended at First St. Later that day at PHOENIX HILL PARK, veterans enjoyed a campfire for the remainder of the evening. On Thursday, the festivities continued as the celebrants lined the Ohio River at night for a fireworks show in which the city's two bridges were used. On Friday, the last day of the convention, a day-long picnic featuring a barbecue of a hundred cattle, three hundred sheep, two hundred pigs, and seventy-five gallons of burgoo was held in WILDER PARK (near present-day Third St. and Central Ave.) for approximately a hundred thousand visitors.

While most of the celebrations remained orderly and passed without incident, two episodes marred an otherwise perfect week. Before the Wednesday parade, a cannon loaded with sixty pounds of black gunpowder exploded, killing four members of the LOUISVILLE LEGION'S Battery A and a carriage driver. The Thursday fireworks show was delayed after an overcrowded grandstand collapsed and injured approximately thirty people. Despite these accidents, the city received high accolades from the departing visitors.

See William E. Cummings, "Pomp, Pandemonium, and Paramours: The GAR Convention of 1895," *Register of the Kentucky Historical Society* 81 (Summer 1983): 274–86; J. Stoddard Johnston, ed., *Memorial History of Louisville,* vol. 1 (Chicago 1896).

GRAVES, WILLIAM JORDAN (b New Castle, Kentucky, 1805; d Louisville, September 27, 1848). U.S. congressman. Graves was a practicing member of the Kentucky bar until he was elected to the state House of Representatives in 1833 and served in the 1834 session. In 1834 he was elected to Congress as a member of the WHIG PARTY and served three consecutive terms from March 4, 1835, to March 3, 1841. During that time he engaged in a duel with and killed Jonathan Cilley in Maryland. Following his return to Henry County, Graves was reelected to the state House of Representatives in 1843. He is buried at his former residence in Henry County.

See *Biographical Directory of the American Congress 1776–1961* (Washington, D.C., 1961).

GRAWEMEYER, HENRY CHARLES (b Louisville, September 3, 1912; d Louisville, December 8, 1993). Businessman and philanthropist. His father, Adolph, emigrated from Germany to Louisville and married Emily Elise Sheirich of Indianapolis. Adolph, a cabinetmaker by trade, started a picture-framing business, expanding to include wallpaper, art supplies, and greeting cards. When the business collapsed during the GREAT DEPRESSION, young Charles helped support his three brothers and one sister by raising chickens, selling eggs, and organizing a neighborhood garage rental service by finding available space that owners were willing to let.

He graduated from the UNIVERSITY OF LOUISVILLE Speed Scientific School in 1934 and began working for Reliance Paint and Varnish Co. as a laboratory chemist. He soon moved to management and from 1942 to 1962 was vice president in charge of the Tomlinson Products division in Chicago. In 1962 he returned to Louisville as CEO of Reliance Universal, a position he held until 1967. In 1968 he founded Plastic Parts Inc. in SHELBYVILLE, Kentucky, and served as president until his retirement in 1977. A sophisticated investor, Grawemeyer accumulated his fortune while maintaining a modest lifestyle.

In 1970 Grawemeyer established a small endowment for the modern language department at the University of Louisville to fund study in German language and culture. In 1981 he established a METROVERSITY award for innovative college teaching. Faculty of six colleges and universities in the Louisville metropolitan area are eligible for four annual awards of one thousand dollars plus an extra thousand dollars for the outstanding proposal. A panel of three experts from other universities chooses the winners.

In 1984 he endowed the University of Louisville GRAWEMEYER AWARDS, annual international competitions in music, political science, education, RELIGION, and psychology. The administration building at the University of Louisville is named in his honor. He made numerous smaller awards, often anonymously, to the William F. Ekstrom Library and other community nonprofit organizations.

In 1937 Grawemeyer married Lucy Martin of Louisville. They had three daughters: Nancy Robbins and twins, Martha Colton and Marian James. He is buried in CAVE HILL CEMETERY.

See Allan E. Dittmer, Paul J. Weber, and W. Eugene March, *The Power of Ideas: University of Louisville Grawemeyer Awards* (Ashland, Ky., 2000); *Courier-Journal*, Dec. 10, 1993.

Allan E. Dittmer
Paul J. Weber

GRAWEMEYER AWARDS. The UNIVERSITY OF LOUISVILLE GRAWEMEYER AWARDS were endowed over several years beginning in 1984 by HENRY CHARLES GRAWEMEYER, a 1934 graduate of the university's Speed Scientific School. Grawemeyer gave an initial gift of twenty thousand dollars and four thousand shares of stock to which he added periodically until his death in 1993. The 2000 value of the endowment was approximately $31 million.

The donor envisioned five international awards in the humanities and social science areas not adequately recognized by the Nobel or other awards. Currently each annual award is $200,000, making them among the largest in the world in their respective fields. Winners who meet certain criteria are selected by international and university juries and must come to the University of Louisville for a lecture and an awards banquet. Customarily the awards were announced in April and presented in October. However, beginning in 1999, the winners were announced in November and presented in April in conjunction with Founders' Day.

The award in music composition is given for outstanding achievement by a living composer in a large musical genre. It was established in 1985 and first won by Polish composer Witold Lutoslawski for his *Third Symphony*. The second award, for ideas improving world order, is given for outstanding proposals that can lead to more just and peaceful international relations. It was initiated in 1988 and won by Harvard professors Richard Neustadt and Ernest May for their 1986 book, *Thinking in Time: The Uses of History for Decision-Makers*. The education award is given for outstanding ideas that have potential to bring about significant improvement in educational practice and attainment. It was offered a year later in 1989 and won by FRENCH citizen Bertrand Schwartz, who developed a plan for a national network of agencies to locate, train, and find jobs for school dropouts and the chronically unemployed. The RELIGION award is given to honor and publicize insights into the relationship between human beings and the divine and the ways this relationship may empower human beings to attain wholeness, integrity, or meaning. The LOUISVILLE PRESBYTERIAN THEOLOGICAL SEMINARY and the university jointly offer this award, and it was first given in 1990 to E.P. Sanders for his 1985 book, *Jesus and Judaism*. The fifth award, in psychology, will begin in 2000.

Among later winners are former Soviet president Mikhail Gorbachev for his 1988 speech to the United Nations; Norwegian prime minister Gro Harlan Brundtland on behalf of the UN Commission on Environment and Development for *Our Common Future*; Carol Gilligan for her book, *In a Different Voice*; and Stephen L. Carter for his book, *The Culture of Disbelief*.

AWARD RECIPIENTS

Music Composition

1999 - Thomas Ades, "Asyla"
1998 - Tan Dun, opera "Marco Polo"
1997 - Simon Bainbridge, "Ad Ora Incerta: Four Orchestral Songs from Primo Levi"
1996 - Ivan Tcherepnin, "Double Concerto for Violin, Cello, and Orchestra"
1995 - John Adams, "Violin Concerto"
1994 - Toru Takemitsu, "Fantasma Cantos"
1993 - Karel Husa, "Concerto for Violoncello and Orchestra"
1992 - Krzystof Penderecki, "Adagio for Large Orchestra"
1991 - John Corigliano, "Symphony No. 1"
1990 - Joan Tower, "Silver Ladders"
1989 - Chinary Ung, "Inner Voices"
1988 - No Award given
1987 - Harrison Birtwistle, "The Mask of Orpheus"
1986 - Gyorgy Ligeti, "Etudes for Piano"
1985 - Witold Lutoslawski, "Symphony No. 3"

World Order

1999 - Margaret E. Keck and Katheryn Sikkkink, *Activists Beyond Borders*
1998 - No Award given
1997 - Herbert Kelman, "Interactive Problem-Solving"
1996 - Max Singer and Aaron Wildavsky, "The Real World Order: Zones of Peace—Zones of Turmoil"
1995 - Gareth Evans, "Cooperative Security and Intra-State Conflict"
1994 - Mikhail Gorbachev, "1988 speech to the United Nations"
1993 - Donald Harman Akenson, "God's Peoples: Covenant and Land in South Africa, Israel, and Ulster"
1992 - Samuel Huntington, "The Third Wave: Democratization in the Late Twentieth Century;" Herman Daly and John Cobb, "For the Common Good: Redirecting the Economy Toward Community, the Environment, and a Sustainable Future"
1991 - The United Nations World Commission on Environment and Development, "Our Common Future"
1990 - Robert Jervis, "The Meaning of the Nuclear Revolution: Statecraft and the Prospect of Armageddon"
1989 - Robert Keohane, "After Hegemony: Cooperation and Discord in the World Political Economy"
1988 - Richard Neustadt and Ernest May, "Thinking in Time: The Uses of History for Decision-Makers"

Education

1999 - Vanessa Siddle Walker, *Their Highest Potential: An African-American School Community in the Segregated South*
1998 - L. Scott Miller, "An American Imperative: Accelerating Minority Education Advancement"
1997 - Mike Rose, "Possible Lives: The Promise of Public Education in America"
1996 - Victoria Purcell-Gates, "Other Peoples Word: The Cycle of Low Literacy"
1995 - Shirley Brice Heath and Milbrey W. McLaughlin, "Identity and Inner City: Beyond Ethnicity and Gender"
1994 - John T. Bruer, "Schools for Thought"
1993 - Ron Gailmore and Roland Tharp, "Rousing Minds to Life: Teaching, Learning, and School in Social Context"
1992 - Carol Gilligan, "Gender Differences in Psychological Development"
1991 - Kieran Egan, "Teachers as Storytellers"
1990 - Howard Gardner, "Theory of Multiple Intelligences"
1989 - Bertrand Schwartz, "Innovations in Social and Vocational Preparations for Disadvantaged Youth"

Religion

1999 - Jürgen Moltman, *The Coming of God: Christian Eschatology*
1998 - Charles Marsh, *God's Long Summer: Stories of Faith and Civil Rights*
1997 - Prof. Larry L. Rasmussen, *Earth Community, Earth Ethics*
1996 - No Award given
1995 - Prof. Diana L. Eck, *Encountering God: A Spiritual Journey from Bozeman to Banaras*
1994 - Prof. Stephen L. Carter, *The Culture of Disbelief: How American Law and Politics Trivialize Religious Devotions*
1993 - Sister Elizabeth A. Johnson, *She Who Is: The Mystery of God in Feminist Theological Discourse*
1992 - Prof. Ralph Harper, *On Presence: Variations and Reflections*
1991 - Dr. John Hick, *An Interpretation of Religion:*

Human Responses to the Transcendent
1990 - Dr. E.P. Sanders, *Jesus and Judaism*
1989 - No Award given

See Allan E. Dittmer, Paul J. Weber, and W. Eugene March, *The Power of Ideas: University of Louisville Grawemeyer Awards* (Ashland, Ky., 2000); *Courier-Journal*, Feb. 28, 1984, April 28, 1991, Dec. 10, 1993, April 27, 1995, April 3, 1997, Sept. 21, 1997; Richard Griscom, *The Grawemeyer Collection of Contemporary Music, 1985–1991* (Louisville 1992).

Allan E. Dittmer
Paul J. Weber

GRAY, JOHN THOMPSON (b Louisville, September 9, 1815; d Louisville, July 17, 1902). Attorney and businessman. Although widely regarded in early Louisville as a scholarly "old school gentleman," JOHN THOMPSON GRAY was best remembered for his role in a tragic act of violence. The son of John Thompson Gray and Mary (Ormsby) Gray, he was educated in local schools and graduated from Harvard University law school. Young Gray practiced his profession in Louisville, where he became close friends with fellow attorney HENRY CLAY POPE. Following the death of his father in 1845, Gray abandoned the LAW to manage the large estate he inherited.

Gray's role in one of Kentucky's most famous DUELS marked a tragic turning point in his life. During the course of an 1849 card game at Louisville's original GALT HOUSE, Henry Clay Pope, whose hot temper and heavy drinking had tarnished his MEXICAN WAR record, became increasingly violent. Gray's effort to calm his drunken friend led to a physical altercation in which Pope received a sound thrashing. Mortified by his public chastisement, Pope challenged Gray to a duel. Both antagonists met on the Indiana shore on June 14, 1849, where Pope fell mortally wounded at the first fire. Pope forgave his friend before he died.

Despite the fact that he had strictly adhered to the code duello, Gray was condemned by many as a cold-blooded killer. Indicted for murder in Indiana and pilloried by Louisville public opinion, he fled to Maryland, where he remained in self-imposed exile for a number of years. This duel led to the implementation of the anti-dueling clause that was put into the 1850 Kentucky Constitution. Upon returning to Louisville, he dabbled in local politics but devoted most of his time to farming and literary pursuits. Reportedly a friend of Longfellow, Oliver Wendell Holmes Sr., and other distinguished men of letters, he wrote one novel, *A Kentucky Chronicle*, published four years after his death.

Gray was married three times. His first marriage to Anita Anderson produced one daughter, Anita. His second marriage to Miss Hook of Baltimore produced one son, Frank. His third wife was Caroline DeButts. They had two sons and three daughters, Ormsby, Charles, Mary, Sophie, and Annette. He is buried in CAVE HILL CEMETERY.

See J. Winston Coleman, *Famous Kentucky Duels* (Lexington 1969); *Courier- Journal*, July 18, 1902.

James M. Prichard

Bread line during the Louisville flood of 1937.

GRAYMOOR-DEVONDALE. Fourth-class city in eastern Jefferson County, centered around the intersection of WESTPORT Rd. and Herr Ln. and bordering the cities of LYNDON, ST. MATTHEWS, and Crossgate. Most of the community's land was originally granted to Col. WILLIAM CHRISTIAN, whose wife was the sister of Virginia governor Patrick Henry, for his service during the FRENCH and Indian War. Throughout the nineteenth and into the twentieth century, much of the land was purchased by families, including the Herrs and the Rudys, who established large estates and farms.

Midway through the twentieth century, developer John A. Walser purchased part of O.A. Winkler's farm and opened the Graymoor neighborhood, naming it after the monastery of the Friars of the Atonement in Garrison, New York. In 1959 the residents joined with the nearby Woodstock community to become the sixth-class city of Graymoor. The following year, the community of Devondale, located just to the east of Herr Ln., was similarly incorporated as a sixth-class city. Through annexations and mergers, the city grew until Devondale was reclassified as a fifth-class city in 1980.

Desiring fourth-class status in order to gain zoning control over the flourishing WESTPORT Rd.–Herr Ln. intersection, the two cities merged in 1986 to create the fifth-class city of GRAYMOOR-DEVONDALE. By 1992, the city's POPULATION had reached the minimum of three thousand residents for fourth-class status.

An important landmark in the area is the Albert G. HERR HOUSE, located on what was the Magnolia Stock Farm. The farm was known for its Jersey cattle, trotting horses, and Merino sheep. Originally owned by John Herr Jr., the land passed to his son Albert in 1863. Albert constructed a new Italianate-style home in 1877. The house was the site of a disastrous wedding in the spring of 1891. During the reception, approximately sixty people fell ill and roused the possibility of arsenic poisoning. Suspicions were heightened after six people, including the bridegroom, died within two weeks. However, a team of doctors from the UNIVERSITY OF LOUISVILLE School of MEDICINE discovered that in fact the cause was bacterial infection in a batch of spoiled chicken salad.

The POPULATION of the primarily middle-class city in 1980 was 3,191 and in 1990 was 2,911. In 1996 the population was 3,074.

GREAT DEPRESSION. October 29, 1929, "Black Tuesday," when the stock market crashed, is generally considered the starting point of the GREAT DEPRESSION. But it was not until the collapse of BancoKentucky in 1930 that the full weight of the crisis hit the Louisville area. Trouble for BancoKentucky, a holding company made up of the National BANK OF KENTUCKY and the Louisville Trust Co. and operated by Louisville eccentric James B. Brown, started when the National Bank of Kentucky and two smaller institutions controlled by BancoKentucky—the Louisville Trust Co. and Security Bank—were closed by their respective directors on November 17.

Major investors, such as Standard Oil of Kentucky and the LOUISVILLE & NASHVILLE RAILROAD, began withdrawing sizable funds from the bank after it merged with a Tennessee bank on June 1930—Nashville-based Caldwell & Co., headed by Rogers C. Caldwell. The Nashville institution was practically insolvent at the time of the merger. So great was the impact of the failure of Caldwell & Co. that, of the 143 American banks that failed in November 1930, 129 could be traced to the collapse of Caldwell.

Because of the extensive control of BancoKentucky over other regional financial institutions, a general panic in Louisville's financial community spread quickly. In rapid succession the Bank of St. Helens and two African American BANKING institutions—the American Mutual Savings Bank and the FIRST STANDARD BANK—all in Jefferson County, closed, primarily because they used BancoKentucky as a repository for their assets.

By 1930 the GREAT DEPRESSION was starting to affect several important economic indicators in the Louisville area. The value of new construction, a major source of employment in the late 1920s, was down almost 50 percent in 1930 from a year earlier—from $11.3 million in 1929 to $5.9 million, and down from the high of more than $28 million in 1925. Construction values further declined to less than $1 million by 1933. Manufacturing was also affected. In 1930 eleven local manufacturing firms with net liabilities of more than $1.3 million went bankrupt. Unemployment as a whole was around 9 percent in the city, and average wages at thirty-seven large manufacturing concerns had fallen by 4 percent in 1930 alone. Even though Louisville instituted an employment program in 1930, putting people to work at odd jobs for a few days each week at thirty cents an hour, only one thousand jobs were available for the more than eleven thousand who showed up to work.

The following year was worse as economic indicators continued a downward spiral. Bank deposits in 1932 were a mere $1.24 billion, only 49 percent of the 1929 high mark. Building permits, another indicator of the failing ECONOMY, dropped from 1,107 in 1930 to a paltry 293 in 1933, which was only 6.3 percent of the total number of permits in 1925. By 1932 Louisville's unemployment rate had reached 23.5 percent among whites and 37.2 percent for AFRICAN AMERICANS. More than thirty-five thousand were out of work in 1933. Many who continued to work found themselves on short hours earning lower wages. Retail sales were down about 60 percent from 1929 levels, and new construction had fallen off by 62.9 percent from pre-Depression totals.

Although most Louisville industries suffered, some, such as the TOBACCO industry, actually experienced growth. The reason may be that smoking brought pleasure and relaxation to a tense situation. Between 1931 and 1932 Louisville's three tobacco producers manufactured three times the pre-Depression volume of cigarettes. BROWN & WILLIAMSON TOBACCO CORP., which got its start in Louisville in 1929, was producing at or near capacity, averaging about three thousand workers throughout the Great Depression.

Louisville's political response to the crisis was similar to much of the country in November 1932, voting the Democrats, led by Franklin Delano Roosevelt, into the White House. Roosevelt got 51.3 percent of the local vote in 1932, but by the 1936 election his New Deal programs earned him 60.2 percent. Before Roosevelt took office in March 1933, Louisville continued to feel the effects of the Great Depression, particularly the collapse of the nation's financial system in the period between the election and the inauguration. Another run on the banks by depositors prompted some states to close all financial institutions. Kentucky ordered all banks closed on March 1, 1933. The day after Roosevelt took office, Congress and the president declared a "banking holiday" and closed all financial institutions to stave off the complete collapse of the system.

Roosevelt's early initiatives had a direct impact upon Louisville. He pushed through the Volstead Act to permit the sale and manufacture of 3.2 percent alcoholic-content beer, and Louisville immediately began issuing beer licenses, the first one to a city police captain, James B. Cunningham. Repeal of the Eighteenth Amendment was put on the ballot in Kentucky in November 1933, and Louisville voted overwhelmingly—62,040 to 7,151—to end PROHIBITION. By December, the two-thirds of the states needed to rescind the "noble experiment" had voted to repeal it. Several distilleries opened shortly thereafter, including Brown-Forman, Stitzel, and Bernheim (later Schenley Distillers). As many as twenty-five new DISTILLING plants were opened in 1933. In 1935 Louisville became the site of the new Joseph E. Seagram & Sons distillery. The $4.5 million facility, which was completed by 1937, was then the world's largest.

While Louisville was not immune to the Great Depression's ravaging effects, because of its diversified industrial economy the city was in better shape than some, such as Detroit, which were dependent on a single industry. In addition to tobacco and liquor manufacturing, several smaller firms were brought into the city during the 1930s, frequently led by the efforts of the LOUISVILLE INDUSTRIAL FOUNDATION, headed by a former Louisville mayor, WILLIAM HARRISON. To speed recovery, the city's first comprehensive plan was developed by the City PLANNING AND ZONING Commission, the city administration, and other local agencies. Enacted in the mid-1930s, it involved a major street improvement plan, recreation plan, riverfront development, aviation plan, and civic art projects.

Louisville also benefited by Roosevelt's "pump priming" initiatives, such as the National Industrial Recovery Act (NIRA) of 1933, which created the National Recovery Administration (NRA) to stimulate business activity through the use of self-governing codes for production, wages, and employment. Businesses would enact codes establishing minimum wages, prices, and production levels and in exchange would be certified by the federal GOVERNMENT to post the "Blue Eagle" banners indicating the company was doing its part to end the Great Depression. Some of the companies participating initially were the Enro Shirt Co., Louisville Textiles Co., BELKNAP Hardware, Wood-Mosaic, MENGEL CO., and International Harvester. The act was declared unconstitutional in 1935.

Although the city had its own relief programs, there was a gradual shift toward federal programs to aid the unemployed and destitute. Early work relief efforts were headed by UNIVERSITY OF LOUISVILLE professor Kenneth P. Vinsel, who was picked by Mayor NEVILLE MILLER (1933–37) to supervise the Municipal Relief Bureau (MRB). When the federal PUBLIC WORKS Administration (PWA) took over all work-related relief efforts, the city MRB began providing emergency relief and was renamed the Municipal Bureau of Social Services. By 1934 there were five thousand families receiving some form of direct aid.

The NIRA, which created the Public Works Administration in 1933, and the 1935 Works Progress (later Projects) Administration (WPA) helped ease the impact of the Great Depression on Louisvillians. The PWA, begun in 1933, and later the WPA, were federal programs designed to quickly put people back to work by funding public construction projects. These agencies were partly responsible for the building of the Fiscal Court Building, the IROQUOIS Branch Library in Beechmont, the IROQUOIS AMPHITHEATER IN IROQUOIS PARK, the University of Louisville School of Law building on the Belknap Campus, and many transportation and sewer projects. In 1938 alone about six thousand people were working in WPA jobs.

While Louisville was experiencing an economic upturn, the city was inundated by the worst flood in the area's history. Coming in January the water level surpassed by eleven feet the old record set in 1884. Not until mid-February was the river back to normal. More than thirteen hundred homes and businesses received assistance from the Federal Disaster Loan Corp., which provided $1.2 million in relief loans. WPA workers helped to clear away tons of mud and river debris from city streets, homes, and businesses. The RECONSTRUCTION put people to work and pumped money into the local ECONOMY for building supplies. Perhaps the most famous photograph of Louisville was taken by Margaret Bourke-White for *Life* magazine during the flood. It depicted a group of African Americans waiting in line for food while a billboard behind them showed a happy white family (dog and all) in an automobile. The sign read

"World's Highest Standard of Living" and "There's no way like the American Way."

The PWA was also involved in efforts to secure public housing for low-income families. The emergency housing program, started in June 1933, targeted an area east of the central business district for construction of a low-income housing project. Construction of what would eventually become the Clarksdale housing project was initially delayed by a lawsuit from property owners who claimed the city overstepped its powers of eminent domain in acquiring the thirty acres of land. With the court decision pending, Louisville built a public-housing complex, dubbed College Court because of its proximity to the LOUISVILLE MUNICIPAL COLLEGE, at Seventh and Kentucky Streets. Another complex, LaSalle Place, was built at Seventh and Algonquin Pkwy. The two, which were unofficially segregated, with whites occupying LaSalle and blacks housed in College Court, were opened in 1938. The go-ahead was finally given to build the Clarksdale project, and it and another project west of downtown, called Beecher Terrace, were complete by 1940. The four facilities, which totaled more than nineteen hundred units of PUBLIC HOUSING, were managed by the Municipal Housing Commission.

The WPA also helped to support local artists and writers in Louisville as part of several federally sponsored programs. A series of murals were produced at the LOUISVILLE FREE PUBLIC LIBRARY by Orville Carroll, a student at the Louisville Art Center, as part of the WPA's public works of art project. Other artists from the Louisville Art Center who received WPA commissions included Paul Childers, Charles Goodwin, Ollie Patton, and Mary Spencer Nay. The Louisville Free Public Library also assisted in other WPA projects, including a series of books on such subjects as Kentucky's artists, authors, prominent women, statesmen, and a guide to the city and its institutions.

By the end of the decade Louisville had seen the worst of the Depression. In 1940 the economy was on the rebound, with unemployment dropping to 11.5 percent. Still, it was not until the start of WORLD WAR II that the country and the city were able to return to and surpass pre–Great Depression levels of production and employment.

See George H. Yater, *Two Hundred Years at the Falls of the Ohio* (Louisville 1987); *Louisville Survey: Central and South Report* (Louisville 1978); Lowell H. Harrison and James C. Klotter, *A New History of Kentucky* (Lexington 1997).

GREATER LOUISVILLE ECONOMIC DEVELOPMENT PARTNERSHIP. During the early 1980s the Greater Louisville area was suffering from an economic and social depression. During this time the city lost thirty-four thousand manufacturing jobs, had an increase into double-digit unemployment, and saw the POPULATION decline. Louisville had turned into a rust-belt city and was fading into obscurity. In 1987, after a study was released showing how far Louisville was behind other cities in economic development and business attraction, the local GOVERNMENT and business launched a $10-million fund-raising campaign to make the city more competitive.

After a year of fund raising culminating in 1988, the Campaign for Greater Louisville, a joint business and government venture, resolved to spend the bulk of its $10 million budget on attracting industry and jobs to the area and supporting and coordinating local economic growth initiatives. Later that year, the Louisville Area Chamber of Commerce, dating from 1862, transferred its office of industry and job recruitment to the campaign, leading to the formation of the GREATER LOUISVILLE ECONOMIC DEVELOPMENT PARTNERSHIP. At that juncture the chamber returned its focus to assisting its members and lobbying for them in the state legislature.

From 1991 to 1994 the area's ECONOMY grew by 9 percent (the nation's growth rate was 5 percent), and, in 1994 alone, the regional economy gained 18,000 jobs and set an all-time employment record of nearly 526,000 jobs. In addition to recruiting business, the partnership had been involved in a number of important community development projects including a $530 million upgrading of the LOUISVILLE INTERNATIONAL AIRPORT, a $650 million expansion of the local Ford plant, and the Regional Economic Development Strategy that enhanced Louisville as a community and not just as a place of business.

In 1996 both organizations sponsored a study by an economic development consulting firm based in Vail, Colorado, to determine the city's national economic position and develop an outline for its future. The study found that, for Louisville to move from a solid second-tier city to an emerging center of economic activity, it would need to pursue technology and high-growth companies, improve local research and education, and streamline several of its decision-making bodies. The chamber and the partnership embraced the last suggestion and consolidated their operations the following year to create a single voice on business issues.

Under the merger agreement, which was finalized September 18, 1997, the partnership's activities, capital, and employees were absorbed into the chamber. A new governing board was created containing thirty chamber and twenty partnership representatives, although a nineteen-member board of directors oversaw operations. In its nine-year existence, the partnership claimed to have created or preserved approximately twenty-four thousand jobs.

See *Courier-Journal,* Oct. 26, 1988, April 17, 1997.

GREATER LOUISVILLE INC. Greater Louisville Inc., known as the Louisville Area Chamber of Commerce prior to 1998, traces its beginning to 1862 when two hundred dues-paying members established the Board of Trade, meeting in the old United States Customs House at Third and Green (LIBERTY) Streets. They paid one dollar to join and discuss dynamics of the local ECONOMY.

The present chamber grew out of the LOUISVILLE AREA DEVELOPMENT Association (LADA), founded by Louisville's mayor, Wilson Wyatt, in 1943. By 1950 the Chamber was officially launched as an umbrella group encompassing the old Board of Trade, LADA, the Retail Merchants Association, and the Convention Bureau. Former UNIVERSITY OF LOUISVILLE professor K.P. Vinsel moved from his position as executive director of LADA to head the new organization, one of the early local chambers to be accredited by the United States Chamber of Commerce. Vinsel directed the chamber during an expansion period that saw General Electric locate a major facility in Louisville and the first expressway built. Thomas A. Ballantine Jr., the Chamber's first president, founded LOUISVILLE CENTRAL AREA in 1959 to focus on DOWNTOWN DEVELOPMENT.

When Vinsel retired in 1966, Charles F. Herd came from the top Knoxville, Tennessee, chamber post to head the organization. Herd stressed consensus-building in community decision-making, public-private partnerships, and linkages with regional business support organizations, changing the name to the Louisville Area Chamber of Commerce. During his tenure the Louisville Development Committee was launched in 1971 to promote Louisville nationally. One of its direct mail tools was the Chamber-published magazine *Louisville,* which redirected its editorial focus toward citywide interests. Meanwhile, the LDC's corollary, the Louisville Development Foundation, funded a chamber-staffed study that paved the way for the creation of the Kentucky Center for the Arts.

The chamber also helped revitalize the KENTUCKY DERBY FESTIVAL, operated the local effort in carpooling, and began a business development program for minorities. In 1974 the chamber led the development of the Bicentennial Corp., which operated the highly popular Heritage Weekends on the RIVERFRONT PLAZA-Belvedere. Among other activities during Herd's tenure were the development of the Riverport Authority, designation of Riverport as a foreign trade zone, and the funding of a national consultant report on needed educational improvements. In 1978 the chamber initiated Leadership Louisville, a program aimed at broadening the horizons of local leaders.

Herd was followed in 1983 by economic development expert James O. Roberson. A Development Finance Center was established to help provide venture capital for emerging businesses. The ensuing years saw the beginning of a break between the chamber and another business development group. In 1987 the GREATER LOUISVILLE ECONOMIC DEVELOPMENT PARTNERSHIP was organized to become the major business attraction agency in the area. Roberson was succeeded in 1991 by South Carolina native Robert H. Gayle Jr., who, in his five-year tenure as president and CEO of the Louisville Area Chamber of Commerce, managed to garner national recognition for his work with the organization. Among the awards received were the National Association for Membership Development Award of Excellence as the nation's top chamber of commerce, Regional Entrepreneur of the Year Award as the Best Supporter of Entrepreneurism, an Equity Award from the LOUISVILLE URBAN LEAGUE, and a rating of excellent from the United States Chamber reaccreditation process. Gayle spearheaded an $8 million AFRICAN AMERICAN Venture Capital Fund and a workforce development initiative through the KENTUCKIANA Education Workforce Institute, and he created the Area Councils program to include members in outlying areas. As president, Gayle also supervised the chamber's relocation to the Commerce Center at 600 W Main, sold the *LOUISVILLE* MAGAZINE, and played an active role in the privatization of the Naval Ordnance Station, passage of Workers' Compensation Reform, and higher education reform.

When Gayle left Louisville in late 1996 to head the New Orleans Chamber of Commerce, he was serving as chairman of the board of the Louisville Area Chamber of Commerce. Local entrepreneur and chairman of the chamber board Douglas Cobb was chosen as the new CEO. Cobb was born October 6, 1957, to Ann (Ford) and Stewart Cobb. The younger Cobb is a Louisville native who came home in 1984 to begin a successful entrepreneurial business. Cobb; his wife, Gena; his brother, Steve Cobb; and his friend and colleague, Tom Cottingham, formed the Cobb Group, which became the world's largest publisher of computer-related newsletters. It was sold to Ziff-Davis Publishing Co. in 1991, which moved the company to Rochester, New York, in 1998. Cobb is a graduate of Williams College with a degree in political economics in 1979, and of New York University in 1981 with a degree in ACCOUNTING. Cobb began a consulting firm in Cambridge, Massachusetts, co-authoring the how-to book for Lotus 1–2–3 as the extremely popular Lotus spreadsheet program first hit the market. After retiring from the Cobb Group in 1994, Cobb became a partner in the venture capital firm Chrysalis Ventures Inc.

In 1997 the Louisville Area Chamber of Commerce and the Greater Louisville Economic Development Partnership merged. In January 1998 the chamber's board voted to change the organization's name to GREATER LOUISVILLE INC. The move was intended to reflect the association's expanded economic development role as it became the key organization in attracting and keeping businesses in the Louisville area. This role was solidified later that summer when the city-county Office for Economic Development was disbanded. Its duties, which included among other things retaining jobs and helping local companies expand, were placed solely under Greater Louisville Inc. for a more unified approach to attract and keep businesses.

See *Louisville,* Jan. 1975; *Courier-Journal,* March 28, 1997, Sept. 19, 1997.

Betty Lou Amster

GREEKS. The Greek community in Louisville has been established primarily by three groups: the early pioneers who came about 1910, their descendants, and the Greek professionals who arrived after the 1960s. In 1997 the Greek community consisted of about three hundred families. According to the 1990 census sample estimates, there were approximately 1,140 citizens living in the Louisville metropolitan area who identify their ancestry as Greek, as compared to 3,280 for the whole state of Kentucky (U.S. Census, 1990).

In a classic tale of European emigration, it was because of poor economic and political conditions that most of the early Greek immigrants came from the Arcadia, Carpenisi, and Peloponnesus areas. They were primarily in the restaurant and dry-cleaning businesses located in the area called "Greek Town," from Market to LIBERTY Streets and from Third to Fifth Streets. James Pappas was the first to come and was later joined by restaurateur John Marineris. Chris Thodis operated the Union Quick Restaurant for many years and became a friend of MARK ETHRIDGE, the publisher of the *COURIER-JOURNAL.* He initiated the "Greek Flag Day," which is celebrated on March 25th, Greek Independence Day. Louis Maniatis, a native lawyer and a founding member of the local American Hellenic Educational and Progressive Association (AHEPA) George Dilboy chapter, moved to Washington, D.C., and later was appointed by Vice President Spiro Agnew as an Immigration Appeals Board Member.

During 1911-90 the Gianacakes brothers operated the 4th Avenue Candy Shop. A roster of other successful early GREEKS would include the families of Tolakis, Geftos, Angelo, Damaskis, Georgacopoulos, Jackson, Johnson, Georgantas, Mallos, Calas, Stamos, Poulos, and Zervos. The Doumas family had a son, John, who has left his mark as an architect. One of the well-known restaurants from the 1930s is Masterson's, which was originally founded by Nicholas Mastoras, whose descendants also own the Captain's Quarters restaurant at HARRODS CREEK. Other RESTAURANTS have been operated since that time by the Geromes and later Karageorge families. The business community has also produced two multimillionaires, Pete Gianacakes and Savas Mallos, who live out of town. Most of the local Greeks are professionals: physicians, educators, lawyers, or in managerial positions. Lou Tsioropoulos, a retired Jefferson County public school principal, played BASKETBALL at the University of Kentucky and for the Boston Celtics in the early 1950s.

The center of the community is the ASSUMPTION GREEK ORTHODOX CHURCH, the first Orthodox church in Kentucky, located at 932 South Fifth St. The church was built in 1927 and enlarged in 1967. This is where the religious, social, and political functions take place. Teddy Georgacopoulos was a longtime Greek teacher and church chanter for about forty years,

Baptism in the Avgerinos family apartment at 208 East Madison Street, 1926.

starting in the 1930s. Priests have included Fathers Iatrides, Panagiotis, and Lambert Venoutsos. Beginning in the 1970s, American-born priests have held church leadership positions. Archbishop Athenagoras, who later became the Patriarch in Constantinople, Turkey, visited here on August 5, 1941. Groups that use the Greek Orthodox church as a center for various activities include the Greek School, which is usually taught by the priest to perpetuate the Greek language; the Sunday school; the GOYA (Greek Orthodox Youth Association); the Philoptochos, which is a church-affiliated women's philanthropic group; AHEPA chapter, which is a national fraternal educational and social organization; the Daughters of Penelope, which is a Greek American Women's cultural, educational, and philanthropic organization; and the Greek dancing groups.

The major social event that unifies the Greek community is the Summer Greek Festival, which was revitalized in the early 1990s. Previously the festival took place on the Plaza/Belvedere as part of the Heritage Weekends. In 1974, George Fexy, who was the president of the board of directors of the church, initiated both the Belvedere Greek Festivals and also the annual Greek Glendi, an annual dinner-dance preceding Lent. In 1934 the AHEPA sponsored a district convention at the Brown Hotel, and again in 1988 at the Hyatt Regency Hotel under the direction of Nicholas Johnson, a lawyer. AHEPA also sponsored the visit by Andreas Jacovides, ambassador of Cyprus to the U.S., in 1986.

See Marios Stephanides, "The Greek Community of Louisville," *Filson Club History Quarterly* 55 (Jan. 1981): 5–26; U.S. Census of Population, 1990, *General Social and Economic Characteristics, Ancestry, Kentucky/Indiana.*

Marios Stephanides

GREEN, JOHN WILLIAMS (b Henderson County, Kentucky, October 8, 1841; d Louisville, June 13, 1920). Banker, broker, and soldier. Green was born on his grandfather's plantation to Hector and Ellen (Ruggles) Green. The family soon moved to Louisville, where Green attended the public SCHOOLS and graduated from LOUISVILLE MALE HIGH SCHOOL. He went to work for Louisville bankers Hunt and Badger and then found employment with the firm of McAllister and Co. in Florence, Alabama, where he was living at the outbreak of the CIVIL WAR.

Green returned to Kentucky and enlisted in the Confederate army at Bowling Green on October 7, 1861, one day before his twentieth birthday. Serving in the Ninth Kentucky Infantry, which was part of the famous First Kentucky (or Orphan) Brigade, Green saw action throughout the war. Among the engagements in which he fought were Shiloh (where he was wounded twice), Vicksburg, Stones River, Chickamauga, Missionary Ridge, and the Atlanta campaign. The casualty rate of the Orphan Brigade was astoundingly high, its numbers dwindling from over 3,000 men to 513 by September 1864. Green finished the war with the rank of regimental sergeant major. About 1890 he compiled his wartime notes and diaries into a journal for the benefit of his children. This journal gives an interesting and informative account of Civil War life in the field.

After the war Green entered the Louisville BANKING firm of Quigley and Morton. Several years later he joined the firm of Morton, Galt, & Co. He then formed a brokerage business with Lucian Galt that operated until 1879. At that time Green formed a brokerage partnership with his brother, David Simmons Green. This partnership was to last the remainder of his life. He was a director of the Louisville Title Co. and of the Fidelity & Columbia Trust Co., two of Louisville's largest financial houses. Long active in the affairs of the Episcopal Diocese of Kentucky, Green was a member of ST. PAUL'S EPISCOPAL CHURCH and sat on the board of managers of the Morton (Episcopal Church) Home.

Green married Annie Amis on February 28, 1881. The couple had three children: Elizabeth, Marion (who became a well-known columnist for the *Courier-Journal)*, and a twin brother of Marion who lived only a few days. Following a prolonged and painful attack of neuritis, Green shot himself. He is buried in CAVE HILL CEMETERY.

See Albert D. Kirwan, ed., *Johnny Green of the Orphan Brigade* (Lexington 1956); William C. Davis, *The Orphan Brigade* (Baton Rouge 1980).

Kenneth Dennis

GREEN, NORVIN (b NEW ALBANY, Indiana, April 17, 1818; d Louisville, Feb. 12, 1893). Physician and entrepreneur. His parents were Joseph and Susan (Ball) Green, both Virginia natives. When he was still a youngster, the family moved to Breckinridge County, Kentucky, where his father engaged in various enterprises, including an 1833 flatboat trading trip down the Ohio and Mississippi Rivers with his son. Most of their goods, including livestock, were lost in a violent storm. The family then moved to Cincinnati, where young Norvin engaged in a successful flatboat trading venture down the Ohio. Green then settled in Carrollton, Kentucky, where he launched a business cutting cordwood for steamboat fuel. He earned enough to attend the UNIVERSITY OF LOUISVILLE School of MEDICINE, graduating in 1840.

Green practiced medicine in Carrollton and the surrounding area as well as in Louisville, and also entered politics. He was rewarded in 1852 with the post of disbursing agent for the Custom House and Post Office being constructed in Louisville on the southwest corner of Third and Green (LIBERTY) Streets.

In Louisville he became intrigued by the possibilities of the still-infant TELEGRAPH business and leased the Morse line between Louisville and New Orleans. In 1854 he arranged a merger with the competing O'Reilly line and became president of the successor Southwestern Telegraph Co.

In 1857 he went to New York and engineered a merger of the six largest telegraph companies as the North American Telegraph Co. In 1866 he was active in bringing all telegraph companies in the United States together as the Western Union. That same year Green became vice president of the new company. In 1878 he became the company's president, a position he held until his death. He made his home in New York after 1871.

Green intended to retire in 1882 and purchased the Louisville mansion of the late James Ford (designed and built by HENRY WHITESTONE) on the southwest corner of BROADWAY and Second St., but he was pressed to remain in office. On his usual Christmas visit to Louisville in 1892 he became ill and died at his home. He is buried in CAVE HILL CEMETERY.

See J. Stoddard Johnston, ed., *Memorial History of Louisville*, vol. 1 (Chicago 1896); and *Louisville Commercial*, Feb. 12, 13, 1893; Lester G. Lindley, "Norvin Green and the Telegraph Consolidation Movement," *Filson Club History Quarterly* 48 (July 1974), 253–64.

George H. Yater

GREEN RIVER WRITERS INC. Creative writers' organization, established in 1985 by Mary Beam of Hodgenville, Kentucky, and James O'Dell of Louisville, and open to any person who writes in any form or genre.

In the summers of 1985 and 1986 in Campbellsville, Kentucky, nineteen writers met for Green River Retreats. During the 1986 Retreat, Jim Wayne Miller, a professor at Western Kentucky University, and novelist Sharyn McCrumb offered workshops. In 1987 and 1988, retreats were held at Western Kentucky University with workshops by Miller, McCrumb, Leon Driskell (UNIVERSITY OF LOUISVILLE), Lee Pennington (University of Kentucky), and novelists Betty Receveur, John Birkett, and Roberta Dorr.

In June 1988, GREEN RIVER WRITERS was recognized as a nonprofit organization. Founding board members were Mary Beam O'Dell, James O'Dell, Deborah Adams, Charles Winstead, Ruth Clark, BRADLEY Law, and Barbara Greer.

In 1989, Green River activities moved to the University of Louisville's Shelby Campus. In January 1991, Green River Writers held its first Novels-in-Progress Workshop, featuring novelists Betty Receveur, John Birkett, Jim Wayne Miller, Ann Gabhart, and Michael Williams teaching thirty-five participants in small groups. Several publishing houses and agents were present.

Green River Retreat and the Novels-in-Progress Workshop have become annual events, and in 1997 the group held its first POETRY-in-Progress Workshop. Other activities include an annual writing contest, publication of a quarterly newsletter, local reading/critiquing sessions, and operation of Grex Press, which publishes volumes of poetry.

Mary E. O'Dell

GREENE, SAMUEL WEBB (b Montgomery County, Kentucky, April 15, 1876; d Miami, Florida, September 3, 1958). Jefferson County judge. He was the son of Lucien B. and Sarah F. (Johnson) Greene. Greene was a graduate of the KENTUCKY MILITARY INSTITUTE, where he later taught for eight years. He started practicing law in Louisville in 1903.

Greene, a Democrat, was Jefferson County judge from January 1, 1914, until December 31, 1917. Supported by the Whallen brothers' Democratic machine, he defeated the candidate from the Progressive Party, Matthew J. Holt, by 8,818 votes. Greene received 29,983 votes, Holt received 21,165, and Republican candidate Judge W.G. Dearing received only 1,722. In an ironic twist, Holt was arrested election day for accosting a voter on his way to an election booth. Greene was also elected to the City Council three consecutive terms, serving from 1910 until 1915. He also served two terms as president of the City Council's Board of Councilmen, from November 1909 to November 6, 1912.

Greene became a lecturer for the CHRISTIAN SCIENCE church, speaking throughout the United States and in several foreign countries. He was first reader for the mother church at Boston, Massachusetts, from 1926 to 1929. Greene was also a major in the First Kentucky Regiment of the National Guard, 1906–07.

Greene married Anna Woolfolk. The couple had three children: Gault, Blanche J., and Adelaide. He was later married to Viola Greene. The family lived at 1144 Garvin Place. He is buried in CAVE HILL CEMETERY.

See Alwin Seekamp and Roger Burlingame, eds., *Who's Who in Louisville* (Louisville 1912); *Courier-Journal*, Sept. 6, 1958.

GREEN STREET BAPTIST CHURCH. First known as Second African Church, this house of worship originated at First and MARKET Streets on September 29, 1844, and moved to Green (LIBERTY) St. and took its current name in 1860. The first deacons were elected in 1845 under church organizer George Wells, who served until his death, possibly from cholera, in 1850. At the time of his death, the congregation numbered 280. During the CIVIL WAR, the church organized a Soldiers' Aid Society to support black troops enlisting in the Union army. By April 1865, the end of hostilities was imminent, and the church organized a day school to educate soon-to-be-freed slaves.

From its founding, the church worked to instill moral values in the congregation. On May 10, 1846, the church voted to discipline members "for acts such as disorderly conduct; Sabbath breaking; nonattendance of church; attending a carnival or circus; failure to speak to one another; wife beating; cursing; drunkenness; dancing; playing cards, checkers or dominoes; adultery; fornication; lying; fighting; fussing; GAMBLING; malicious gossip; having to appear in court; and shooting marbles on Sunday." The church later required members to receive a marriage license from the state within ninety days of marriage, ending the old informal ceremony from slavery times that only required a bride and groom to jump over a broom to be considered united. Any members failing to comply would be excluded from the church.

In 1879 the first National Convention of Colored BAPTISTS was held at the church. In 1886 the church took a bold step forward in seeking equal recourse under the law in Kentucky, circulating a petition for the state legislature to pass a CIVIL RIGHTS bill. On September 29, 1930, the church moved to 519 E Gray St. On August 3, 1967, the Reverend Dr. Martin Luther King preached at Green Street in support of a black voter registration drive. This was his last visit to Louisville. The church's membership lists include the names of many who are descendants of the church's original charter members.

See J.H. Spencer, *History of Kentucky Baptists*, vol. 2 (Cincinnati 1885); General Association of Colored Baptists in Kentucky (Louisville 1943).

GREER-PETRIE, CORDIA (b Merry Oaks, Kentucky, February 12, 1872; d Louisville, July 15, 1964). Author. The daughter of Newton Mulkey and Sallie Elizabeth (Settle) Greer, Cordia moved to Louisville as a young girl with her parents. She was educated in the city's PUBLIC SCHOOLS, graduated from Eminence (Kentucky) College, and studied expression for a time with Letitia Kempster Barnum in Chicago. After marrying Dr. Hazel G. Petrie on July 18, 1894, Greer-Petrie spent a number of years in eastern Kentucky and Tennessee, where her husband was a physician for coal mining companies. It was during that period that she was exposed to the mountain dialect and surroundings that would figure so prominently in her literary works.

Greer-Petrie began her writing career when she co-authored a short story, "When the Bees Got Busy," for the August 1904 issue of *Overland Monthly*. The character of Angeline Keaton was first introduced in that piece. Greer-Petrie and her husband moved back to Louisville about 1920 and purchased the Park APARTMENTS at 1345 S Fourth St. While her husband settled into semi-retirement, Cordia pursued her literary endeavors in earnest. Her 1921 publication, *Angeline at the Seelbach*, was an instant success, with thirteen editions issued over the following two years. Greer-Petrie produced a series of books featuring the adventures of Angeline, a simple mountain girl from Bear Holler whose humorous interactions with metropolitan life and refined society were the source of the books' entertainment. These works included *Angeline Steppin' Out* (1922), *Angeline Doin' Society* (1923), *Angeline Gits an Eyeful* (1924), *Angeline Hittin' on High* (1925), *Angeline of the Hill Country* (1925), *Angeline Fixin' fur the Queen* (1926), *Angeline Tames Her Sheik* (1927), *Angeline Goes on Strike* (1928), and *Angeline on Them Big Republicans* (1929).

Greer-Petrie toured throughout the southern states promoting her books. She gave lectures and delivered readings from the "Angeline" series to clubs and organizations, often wearing a mountain woman's dress. One of her most notable appearances was in front of the Kentucky Society in Washington, D.C. She also appeared on WHAS radio. Greer-Petrie is buried in CAVE HILL CEMETERY.

See Mary Ann Southard and Ernest C. Miller, eds., *Who's Who in Kentucky* (Louisville 1936).

GREGG, MARY HANSON "CISSY" (b Cynthiana, Kentucky, April 26, 1903; d Cynthiana, May 10, 1966). Food columnist. The daughter of Hanson and Mary (Jouett) Peterson, Cissy, as she was nicknamed by her sister Minnie, graduated from Cynthiana High School in 1920. In 1924 she received her undergraduate degree in AGRICULTURE and home economics from the University of Kentucky.

Shortly thereafter, Gregg took a job with the home extension service of Mississippi A&M College (now Mississippi State University at Starkville) and later moved to Cincinnati, Ohio, where she was employed as an assistant buyer for the H&S Pogue Department Store. In 1930 she married Edd R. Gregg, a Louisville architect. In April 1942, her food column began in the *COURIER-JOURNAL*'s first Sunday magazine section printed in color. Over the next twenty years, Gregg contributed regular food columns to the daily *Courier-Journal* and a weekly food article for the magazine section. For a number of years, she also wrote a gardening feature for the Sunday newspaper.

She was often asked to judge food competitions, and she spoke extensively about the American diet, which she criticized for including too much meat, bread, and potatoes and too few green vegetables. She had a collection of over seven hundred cookbooks. In the 1950s, the *Courier-Journal* published two collections of Gregg's recipes and food columns: *Cissy Gregg's Cookbook and Guide to Gracious Living* (October 1953) and *CISSY GREGG'S Cookbook* (November 1959).

In her food columns and cookbooks, Gregg included select recipes that reflected the flavor of Kentucky, such as "chicken fried in lard, North MIDDLETOWN beaten biscuits, and Eastern Kentucky stack cake." Readers often wrote to Gregg to request recipes. Among the most popular were Kentucky Pecan Bourbon Cake and Margarella, a tuna dish.

Gregg's husband died in 1961. She retired from the *Courier-Journal* in 1963 and returned

Cissy Gregg, 1957. The Courier-Journal (Louisville).

to her native Cynthiana. She is buried in the Battle Grove Cemetery in Cynthiana.

See Lillian Marshall, *Courier-Journal and Times Cookbook* (Louisville 1971); *Courier-Journal*, May 11, 1966.

GREGORY, JAMES PARKER (b Boyle County, Kentucky, December 12, 1862; d Louisville, May 9, 1940). Jefferson County judge. He was the son of Allen Kendrick and Maria (Eastland) Gregory. The family moved to Louisville when he was young, and he graduated from LOUISVILLE MALE HIGH SCHOOL in 1884. In 1896 he received his law degree from the UNIVERSITY OF LOUISVILLE and began practicing law that same year in Maj. Allen Kinney's law firm. In 1894 he was made a partner in the firm of Kinney, Gregory, & Kinney. In 1911 Gregory became an instructor at the JEFFERSON SCHOOL OF LAW. He taught moot court and real property law for more than twenty-five years. He also authored the legal text *Gregory's Kentucky Criminal Law*.

Gregory, a Democrat, was elected Jefferson County judge for two consecutive terms, serving from January 1, 1898, until December 31, 1905. In the 1897 race he defeated the Republican incumbent Charles G. Richie by a mere 426 votes out of the more than 44,000 cast. He was reelected in 1901, defeating former state representative WILLIAM KRIEGER by 7,236 votes. In 1907 he served as a member of the Board of Public Safety; and he was judge of the Jefferson Circuit Court, Criminal Division, from 1910 until 1916. In 1932 he was appointed by local attorneys to serve on Louisville's civil service board.

Gregory ran for circuit court judge in 1933 but was defeated by William H. Field in the Democratic primary. Field was backed by the wing of the DEMOCRATIC PARTY led by future mayor E. Leland Taylor, while Gregory was backed by MICKEY BRENNAN's wing of the party. Gregory was the Brennan organization's only judiciary candidate to lose in that primary.

Gregory served under Col. John B. Castleman in the Spanish-American War. He became a lieutenant colonel of the old First Kentucky Regiment of the National Guard; he also served as a first lieutenant of infantry during WORLD WAR I.

He married Ruth Miller, daughter of Dr. William F. and Alice G. Miller, and the couple had four children: William Kendrick, Alice Miller, Ruth Elizabeth, and Mattie Ellis. Gregory was elected judge of the chancery branch of circuit court in November 1939. The strain of the primary and election campaign was said to have contributed to his death six months later. He is buried in CAVE HILL CEMETERY.

See Alwin Seekamp and Roger Burlingame, eds., *Who's Who in Louisville* (Louisville 1912); W.T. Owens, *Who's Who in Louisville* (Louisville 1926); *Courier-Journal*, May 10, 1940.

GRIFFITH, DAVID WARK (b OLDHAM County, Kentucky, January 22, 1875; d Hollywood, California, July 23, 1948). Film pioneer and the industry's first major producer-director. He was born on his family's 264-acre farm about 20 miles from Louisville. His parents were Col. Jacob Wark Griffith, a Confederate veteran of the CIVIL WAR, and Mary (Oglesby) Griffith. Colonel Griffith died when his son was ten years old. In 1889 the debt-ridden family moved to Louisville, where Mary Griffith took in boarders. The following year young Griffith quit school. For the next six years he held a succession of jobs, including errand clerk in a dry goods store and cub reporter for the COURIER-JOURNAL. His favorite employment during this period, however, was in Flexner's Bookstore, where he was allowed to spend hours among the stacks absorbing the great works of LITERATURE.

After seeing Julia Marlowe perform at MACAULEY'S THEATRE, Griffith was stagestruck and sought work as an actor with an amateur touring stock company. To spare his family the embarrassment of his taking up a career on the stage, he performed under the name of Lawrence Griffith. From 1896 until he left Louisville for New York City in 1899, Griffith met with very limited success as an actor.

It was while on tour that he met Linda Arvidson, a young actress, in San Francisco. The two were married on May 14, 1906, in Boston. They settled in New York City, where Griffith decided to try his hand as a playwright. His play, *A Fool and a Girl*, opened and played one week in Washington, D.C., ran one more week in Baltimore, and then closed. Discouraged and his funds exhausted, Griffith returned to New York City to try his luck acting in the new medium of motion pictures.

Griffith's first film appearance was in the Edison Co.'s *Rescued from the Eagle's Nest* (1908). He then shifted to the Biograph Co. where he appeared in *When Knighthood Was in Flower* and a number of one-reelers. His acting at Biograph led to writing scenarios and then to directing. His first job as director was the ten-minute *The Adventures of Dollie*, which was released in July 1908.

Over the next five years at Biograph, Griffith was responsible for innovations in filmmaking that would have a dramatic and lasting effect on the art of motion pictures. Often assisted by his cameraman, Billy Bitzer, Griffith pioneered such film techniques as the close-up, long shot, fade-in, fade-out, iris or eye-opening effect, flashback, soft focus, cross-cutting of action, backlighting, and high- and low-angle shots. He was the first director to depart from the standard one-thousand-foot film and frequently drew on historical themes, literary adaptations, and social problems for his film subjects.

Griffith also displayed a remarkable eye for spotting talent. Among the actors and actresses who owed their film careers to him were Mary Pickford, Lillian and Dorothy Gish, Douglas Fairbanks, Blanche Sweet, Richard Barthelmess, Donald Crisp, Lionel Barrymore, Harry Carey, Mack Sennett, Mabel Normand, Joseph Schildkraut, and the Talmadge sisters. Griffith's last film for Biograph was the four-reel *Judith of Bethulia*, which he made in 1913 before leaving to become head of production for the Mutual Film Corp.

Griffith's position with Mutual allowed him greater creative freedom, but his 1915 film, *The Birth of a Nation*, was largely his own independent project. With its controversial subject matter and planned twelve-reel length, studio executives were apprehensive, and Griffith secured financial backing himself. The film, which was based on Thomas Dixon's novel, *The Clansman*, dealt with the Civil War and RECONSTRUCTION.

Tending to glorify the Ku Klux Klan and to depict the worst racial stereotypes, the film aroused protests from a number of sectors, especially the National Association for the Advancement of Colored People. Nevertheless, the film took in an estimated $60 million at the box office, showing a tremendous profit for a picture that cost one hundred thousand dollars to produce.

Griffith's next screen effort was *Intolerance* (1916). Shot on a grand scale with four parallel stories set in four different historical periods, it ran an unheard-of eight hours after the first editing. Eventually cut to two and one-half hours, it was a critical success but a huge financial failure, leaving Griffith with a million-dollar debt he was years in paying off.

Following this debacle, Griffith made several films for various production companies before joining Charlie Chaplin, Mary Pickford, and Douglas Fairbanks in 1919 to create the United Artists Co. Within the next five years, Griffith made a quartet of silent film classics: the poetic and tragic *Broken Blossoms* (1919), the melodramatic *Way Down East* (1920), the spectacular *Orphans of the Storm* (1921), and the mammoth *America* (1924).

His years of prominence in the motion picture industry ended then. The sentimental Victorian viewpoint of his films put him out of vogue in the materialistic 1920s and out of business by the 1930s. His only talking pictures were *ABRAHAM LINCOLN* (1930) and *The Struggle* (1931), the latter a study of alcoholism. His personal finances ruined by poor investments, Griffith sold his United Artists partnership in 1933.

Although he continued planning various projects, Griffith was never again active in filmmaking. In the mid-1930s he returned to Kentucky with the stated intention of living in LAGRANGE in OLDHAM COUNTY. He spent much of his time, however, in Louisville, where he set up quarters in the Brown Hotel. He became a familiar figure in the local BARS, visited CHURCHILL DOWNS, and was a guest at meetings of the Arts Club.

Having divorced his first wife, Griffith married Evelyn Marjorie Baldwin, some thirty-five years his junior, on March 2, 1936. Three days later the couple left for Hollywood, where Griffith received a special Academy Award. Returning to Kentucky, Griffith and his wife divided their time between a home in LaGrange and the Brown Hotel. They also found much time for traveling. Griffith left Kentucky for the last time in 1939, moving back to Hollywood in hopes of finding regular film work. These hopes were not to be realized.

In 1945 the University of Louisville awarded Griffith an honorary doctorate of literature, but he did not return to receive it. He and his second wife were divorced in November 1947, and Griffith moved into the Hollywood Knickerbocker Hotel, where he lived in virtual seclusion. He died of a cerebral hemorrhage and was buried in the family plot at Mt. Tabor Cemetery in Oldham County. Two years later his remains were moved to a new grave also in Mt. Tabor Cemetery, surrounded by rails from the old Griffith farm and marked with a stone donated by the Screen Directors Guild.

See Lillian Gish, *The Movies, Mr. Griffith, and Me* (Englewood Cliffs, N.J., 1969); Richard Schickel, *D.W. Griffith: An American Life* (New York 1984); Robert M. Henderson, *D.W. Griffith: His Life and Work* (New York 1972).

Kenneth Dennis

GRIFFYTOWN. GRIFFYTOWN is an African American neighborhood between the cities of ANCHORAGE and MIDDLETOWN. The community has its origins in the post–CIVIL WAR RECONSTRUCTION era, a time of changing settlement patterns in rural Jefferson County.

The community appears to have been settled by Dan Griffy, who purchased a single isolated lot from Silas O. Witherbee of MIDDLETOWN in 1879. According to property records, Griffy, who was black, had been living on the land prior to his purchase. Local tradition holds that Griffy purchased a log cabin that had once belonged to early Middletown settler Minor White and moved it to his lot. Witherbee filed a plat to create Calloway's Addition in 1892, including the lot where Dan Griffy lived. It appears that by the 1890s the community was being referred to as Griffithtown and later GRIFFYTOWN. Lots were sold to AFRICAN AMERICANS by Witherbee into the early 1900s. The original lots were further subdivided and sold throughout the twentieth century. The community underwent an URBAN RENEWAL project in the 1960s.

See Leone W. Hallenberg, *Anchorage* (Anchorage, Ky., 1959); Louisville and Jefferson County Planning Commission, "Griffytown Redevelopment Plan" (Louisville 1976).

Donna M. Neary

GRINSTEAD, JAMES FONTLEROY (b Glasgow, Kentucky, November 15, 1845; d Louisville, November 13, 1921). Mayor. Grinstead's grandfathers were brothers who fought in the Revolutionary War and came to Kentucky from Virginia about 1818 to settle in Glasgow in Barren County. Grinstead was the son of William and Levina Grinstead. William Grinstead was a wagon maker.

Grinstead had a common school education. He moved to Louisville in 1866 at the age of twenty-one and went to work in a wholesale grocery house. By 1871 he was a full partner in Glazebrook, Grinstead, and Co. and worked for the firm for twenty years. In 1892 Grinstead formed the wholesale company of Grinstead and Tinsley, a successful firm with business ties throughout Kentucky and several neighboring states.

In 1901 the REPUBLICAN PARTY sought out Grinstead, then a well-known MAIN St. merchant, to run in the party primary for mayor. The Republican Party was headed by Charles Sapp, the city's collector of internal revenue. Elements of the party that opposed Sapp put PAUL BOOKER REED, a former mayor of Louisville, in as a primary candidate. Sapp's forces were accused of stealing the nomination from Reed. When Grinstead learned of Sapp's tactics, he declined the nomination, earning the nickname "Honest Jim" John A. Stratton accepted the Republican nomination but was defeated handily by Democrat CHARLES F. GRAINGER.

Grinstead was elected mayor of Louisville in 1907 and served through November 16, 1909. He was elected to fill the unexpired term of PAUL C. BARTH, who was thrown out of office when the mayoral election of 1905 was ruled invalid by the Kentucky Court of Appeals. Grinstead ran for reelection in 1909 but was defeated by the Democratic machine's candidate, William 0. Head. In that election there was some debate over whether Grinstead would be eligible to succeed himself as mayor since he had not served a full term. The city charter had a provision that no mayor could succeed himself. This was a contributing factor to Grinstead's 1909 defeat.

After a County Commission was established to replace the Fiscal Court in Jefferson County, Grinstead was elected a county commissioner in 1917. In 1919 he was reelected for a four-year term but died in the middle of his term. Grinstead Drive in Louisville's East End is named in his honor. In 1874 Grinstead married Margaret Perkins and had two children, Martha and Bailey. She died in 1882. He married Katie Hume in 1882 and had one child, Carrie. Katie died in 1888, and Grinstead then married Annie W. Harwood, a native of SHELBY COUNTY, Kentucky, on July 21, 1892. They had a son, Durward. Grinstead died of a stroke at his home. He is buried in CAVE HILL CEMETERY.

See Charles Kerr, ed.. *History of Kentucky*, 5 vols. (Chicago and New York 1922); E. Polk Johnson, *History of Kentucky and Kentuckians*, 3 vols. (Chicago and New York 1912); George H. Yater, *Two Hundred Years at the Falls of the Ohio* (Louisville 1987).

GRISWOLD, HOWARD CLIFTON (b Louisville, February 28, 1866, d Louisville, January 29, 1941). Businessman and philanthropist. He was the son of Howard and Anna Griswold. HOWARD GRISWOLD entered the Stevens Institute of Technology at Hoboken, New Jersey, after graduating from Louisville's public school system, and received a degree in civil engineering. From 1889 to 1895 he worked with the LOUISVILLE & NASHVILLE RAILROAD in Louisville and Lebanon, Kentucky. In 1895 he went to work for the Illinois Steel Co. in Chicago until news of his father's death in 1915 brought him back to Louisville to take over as president of his father's business, John

P. Morton & Co, printers and publishers. The company had been founded in 1823 by Howard C. Griswold's grandfather and his brother-in-law, John P. Morton.

Griswold was a member of the Transportation Club of Louisville, the American Society of Civil Engineers, the American Iron and Steel Institute, the AUDUBON Country Club, and onetime director of the Ben Franklin Club. He also gave freely and often of his time and money to the Community Chest (METRO UNITED WAY), CHRIST CHURCH CATHEDRAL, and various city charities. Griswold was also an avid amateur photographer. His collection is kept in the UNIVERSITY OF LOUISVILLE Photographic ARCHIVES.

Griswold's first wife, Mec MacIntyre Young of Thomasville, Georgia, died in 1914, and Griswold married Mary Ruth Lewis in Nashville, Tennessee, on January 10, 1925. They had three daughters: Charlotte Lewis, Anna Grant, and Mary Clifton Griswold. He is buried in CAVE HILL CEMETERY.

GROCERIES. In the spring of 1783, Daniel Broadhead opened the first grocery store of any kind in Louisville. Broadhead's "general store" was contained in a large log cabin situated on the north side of MAIN St. between Fifth and Sixth. This general store contained every item that was bought by the pioneers, from dry goods to GROCERIES to hardware and furniture. The majority of these products originated in Philadelphia. They were transported by wagon to Pittsburgh and loaded onto flatboats for delivery to Louisville. As the barter system was well at work in the early community (mostly due to the currency shortage), Broadhead often accepted corn, TOBACCO, whiskey, and other agricultural products as payment for goods purchased by the pioneers. He could then ship these bartered products to New Orleans for sale and use the proceeds to buy more goods from his suppliers in eastern cities.

As Louisville's POPULATION grew, so did its need for an increasing number of places from which settlers could buy staple products. In order to meet this need, in 1802 the Louisville Board of Trustees repealed the law requiring a market house to be built on the public square and got authority from the Kentucky General Assembly to erect it on MARKET St. Until the new market house could be constructed, Peter Bass was allowed to erect a temporary market house on Sixth St. between Main and the river. That house was even less sophisticated than that of Broadhead, but it served people until better was erected. In 1804 FORTUNATUS COSBY and George Wilson were commissioned to draw a plan for the market house later erected in the center of Market between Fourth and Fifth Streets. Eventually, Market St. grew to contain five "market houses," together known as the Market Houses of Louisville. The Market Houses were said to be "profusely supplied with every production of this latitude." (Casseday, *A History of Louisville,* 227) These markets, held daily, offered goods at prices much lower than could be found in eastern cities.

The structure of the retail trade industry changed dramatically as Louisville grew. There was a significant change in shopping trends—no longer were there the large markets that everyone frequented, but instead, small, family-owned grocery stores began to appear. It was much more convenient for someone to shop somewhere nearer to their home than to travel a distance into town to shop at the crowded market, especially since there was not a significant variation in the price of goods. By 1832 there were nearly twenty grocery stores.

The localization trend in grocery stores continued through the nineteenth and into the twentieth centuries. There have, however, been some changes in the grocery trade. In the early twentieth century, grocers began delivering groceries as a convenience to their customers. The customers appreciated the service, and the grocers saw it as a small price to pay to maintain customer approval. In 1973, however, a prophetic technological development occurred in the grocery business. Named Call-a-Mart, this new kind of grocery store would take customers' orders via phone and enter them into a computer. This computer would total the order and even plot the customer's house on a map of the city so that the delivery person would know where to deliver the groceries. Unfortunately for its owners and investors, Call-a-Mart did not catch on in the way that they had hoped, and so it went bankrupt. It was around this time that Louisville saw a decline in grocery delivery; instead, people were going back to the stores to do their shopping.

With the decline in transportation costs due to a multitude of factors, shoppers were again becoming willing to drive a distance in order to find a bargain. This trend led to the larger, chain-owned supermarkets. The chains were able to buy in larger quantities and take advantage of large-scale distribution and thus provide lower prices than the smaller corner grocery stores were able to match. It was not long before many small "mom-and-pop" grocery stores were forced to close. The Louisville city directory of 1925 listed more than 1,080 retail grocery stores. Since 1990 there have been three major grocery store chains in Louisville: Kroger (41.2 percent market share), Winn-Dixie (16.6 percent), and SuperValu (15 percent). These three players have composed nearly three-fourths of the Louisville grocery market. While these stores carry the same types of items as their predecessors, they are physically much larger and are geographically dispersed.

Recently, however, a new player has come to town with a new concept for the grocery store, the "hypermarket." Grand Rapids, Michigan–based Meijer is a chain of combination supermarket/DEPARTMENT STORES that announced it would open five stores in the Louisville area by early 1999. Jeffrey Thomison, an analyst with the Louisville-based investment firm J.J.B. HILLIARD, W.L. LYONS INC., predicted serious price cuts and a very competitive grocery market to befall Louisville. Cheap milk is one way Meijer makes its presence known when entering a local market.

The Meijer chain of stores further sets itself apart from others in that it is more than a grocery store. Many shoppers think of their local Meijer store as a Kroger and a Wal-Mart combined. Meijer carries everything from produce to clothing to tires. Meijer also sells gasoline. Much like in the dairy market, Meijer buys in such large quantities that it can buy gasoline for less per gallon than individual gas station operators. People like the low prices Meijer offers, and they love the convenience of having everything they need for their home in one location. In an attempt to compete with Meijer, Kroger renovated stores and installed gas pumps at some stores.

In a return to neighborhood grocery shopping, many convenience stores appeared throughout the metropolitan area beginning in the 1980s. They offered a limited selection of products but provided the convenience of shopping close to home. Traditional gasoline stations quickly disappeared to be converted into a one-stop place for groceries and gasoline.

See Ben Casseday, *The History of Louisville* (Louisville 1852); Reuben T. Durrett, *The Centenary of Louisville* (Louisville 1880); Carl E. Kramer, *The City-Building Process: Urbanization in Central and Southern Louisville* (1981); *Courier-Journal,* June 15, 1973; J. Stoddard Johnston, ed., *Memorial History of Louisville* (Chicago and New York 1896); George H. Yater, *Two Hundred Years at the Falls of the Ohio* (Louisville 1987).

Adam Kirby

GROSS, SAMUEL DAVID (b Northampton County, Pennsylvania, July 8, 1805; d Philadelphia, May 6, 1884). Physician, surgeon, educator, and author). He was the son of Philip and Juliana (Brown) Gross. Educated in local schools, Gross, who had wanted to study MEDICINE since boyhood, was apprenticed to a country doctor at the age of seventeen. However, he soon realized his need for further education and entered the Wilkesbarre Academy for a year of study and then attended Lawrenceville High School in New Jersey. In 1828 he earned a medical degree from Jefferson Medical College in Philadelphia.

From 1828 to 1830, Gross operated a private practice in Philadelphia. Business was slow and allowed him the time to translate certain FRENCH and German medical works, including Alphonse Tavernier's *Elements of Operative Surgery* (1829). In 1830 Gross returned to Easton, Pennsylvania, in an effort to build a more successful practice. That same year he published a *Treatise on the Anatomy, Physiology, and Diseases and Injuries of the Bones and Joints.* In 1833 he accepted the position of demonstrator of anatomy at the Medical College of Ohio in Cincinnati. Two years later he transferred to Cincinnati Medical College, where he was named chair of pathological anatomy. While there, Gross published the seminal work that brought him international recognition, *Elements of Pathological Anatomy* (1839), the first thorough examination of the subject in English.

In October 1840 Gross took over as the chair of surgery at the UNIVERSITY OF LOUISVILLE. He spent the next sixteen years here, except for the winter of 1850–51 when he taught at the University of the City of New York. Tireless in his devotion to his profession, Gross continued practicing surgery and publishing, in addition to his teaching duties. While at Louisville he wrote three major treatises: one on intestinal wounds, another on diseases of the urinary system, and the third on *Foreign Bodies in the Air Passages* (1854). In late 1856 Gross and Dr. T.G. Richardson founded the *Louisville Medical Review*, the first issue of which was released in May 1857. Only six issues of the journal were published. While in Louisville, Gross also helped to establish the Kentucky State Medical Society, of which he was also named president.

In September 1856 he left Louisville to accept a professor of surgery position at his alma mater, Jefferson Medical College. Gross always looked back fondly on his days spent in Kentucky, calling them "among the happiest of my life" (Gross, vol. 1, 103). The night before he and his family departed for Philadelphia, a ball was held in his honor at the GALT HOUSE. Gross left half of his personal library consisting of many volumes at the University of Louisville for "safe keeping." However, just two months after his departure, those books and other materials were destroyed by fire.

Gross served on the faculty of Jefferson Medical College from 1856 to 1862. During this time he published his most acclaimed work, *System of Surgery, Pathological, Diagnostic, Therapeutic and Operative* (1859), a two-volume textbook that became a standard reference for the field and was translated into many different languages. Between 1859 and 1882 it went through six editions. In 1861 *The Lives of Eminent American Physicians and Surgeons of the Nineteenth Century* was published, a work that Gross had edited. That same year, Gross's *The Manual of Military Surgery* was also published.

Gross was the inventor of the modern technique of intestinal resection and the suturing of intestinal wounds. He was a founder of the American Medical Association, of which he became president in 1867, and was also an originator of the American Surgical Association (1880). During his career he belonged to a long list of other surgical and medical associations.

In 1875 Gross was at the height of his career when American artist Thomas Cowperthwait Eakins approached him with a request to paint him at work. Eakins observed anatomy lessons and surgical operations at Jefferson Medical College taught by Gross. In his PAINTING *The Gross Clinic* (1875), Eakins depicts the college's surgical amphitheater where Gross explains the procedures of surgery to students while his assisting physicians huddle over the patient. Gross's dominating figure is lit by a strong light that embodies the triumph of knowledge. Dramatic red strokes of blood on the patient's thigh and the surgeon's hand and the figure of the patient's horrified mother at the corner of the painting add intensity to the represented scene and elicits a strong emotional response from the viewer. After completion the painting was shown publicly at the annual exhibition of the Pennsylvania Academy of the Fine Arts in 1876. *The Gross Clinic* received extensive coverage in the press and became one of the important works in American art. In 1878 the painting was purchased from Eakins by the alumni association of Jefferson Medical College. It is still housed in a wing at the medical college in Philadephia.

Gross married Louisa Weisell in 1828. They had four children. After his funeral, Gross's body was taken to Washington, Pennsylvania, where it was cremated and buried in the Woodlands Cemetery.

See Samuel D. Gross, *Autobiography of Samuel D. Gross, M.D.* (New York 1972); John Duffy, *The Healers, A History of American Medicine* (Urbana and Chicago 1979); Martin Kaufman, Stuart Galishoff, Todd L. Savitt, eds., *Dictionary of American Medical Biography*, vol. 1, (Westport, Conn., 1984); Darrel Sewell, *Thomas Eakins—Artist of Philadelphia* (Philadelphia Museum of Art 1982).

GROVER, ASA PORTER (b Phelps, New York, February 18, 1819; d Georgetown, Kentucky, July 20, 1887). U.S. congressman. Grover moved to Danville, Kentucky, in 1837 to attend Centre College. He taught school while studying LAW until he was admitted to the bar in 1843, and he then moved to Owenton, Kentucky, to practice there. He served in the Kentucky Senate from 1857 until 1865. In 1866 Grover was elected to the fortieth Congress as a Democrat, serving one term from March 4, 1867, to March 3, 1869, before returning to his law practice. In 1881 he moved to Georgetown, Kentucky, and practiced law until his death. He is buried in Georgetown Cemetery.

See *Biographical Directory of the American Congress 1776–1961* (Washington, D.C., 1961).

GUTHRIE, JAMES (b Nelson County, Kentucky, December 5, 1792; d Louisville, March 13, 1869). Attorney, politician, and city promoter. He was the son of Adam and Hannah (Polk) Guthrie. His early education in a log schoolhouse was completed at McAlister's Academy in Bardstown and was followed by several trips in the flatboat trade to New Orleans, carrying local agricultural produce. Finding this business laborious and not very remunerative, he took up the study of LAW with the prominent Judge JOHN ROWAN. He was admitted to the bar in 1817 and quickly gained a reputation as an able practitioner.

James Guthrie, 1850.

Appointed commonwealth's attorney in 1820 by Gov. John Adair, he moved to Louisville, which was henceforth his home. His legal abilities won him an outstanding reputation and a lucrative practice. His memorable achievements, however, were in Louisville civic affairs. He made his debut in this role in 1824 as a member of a committee to draft a legislative act to confer city status on Louisville, giving it more HOME RULE than it possessed under its archaic 1780 town GOVERNMENT. That same year he was elected to the board of town trustees and soon became chairman. He would remain a principal actor in Louisville's progress for nearly fifty years.

The 1824 city status effort failed, but in 1828 Guthrie (who had been elected to the state House of Representatives in 1827) mustered the support to pass the act making Louisville a city. It was the first Kentucky town to achieve this status. He was elected a member of the new City Council and soon was chairman of the finance committee, the most powerful post in the new regime. In 1831 he was elected to the state Senate, a position he held until 1840. He also served in the state House and presided over the 1850 state Constitutional Convention. From these positions, aided by a dominating personality, he initiated a host of projects to advance the development of his adopted city. One was the construction of a building "of hewn stone" to house city and county offices. There is little doubt that Guthrie's hidden agenda was to make Louisville the state capital, with the new structure—the JEFFERSON COUNTY COURTHOUSE—the capitol. He also pushed for construction of a bridge across the OHIO RIVER to

Indiana, with the city purchasing stock in the enterprise. A waterworks was also on his agenda, and the city purchased land at Campbell and Main Streets for a reservoir.

All of these projects were put on hold by the panic of 1837, and the uncompleted courthouse earned the title of "Guthrie's Folly." All were eventually completed some years later, but Louisville never became the state capital, although the unfinished courthouse was offered as a lure in 1842.

One effort did come to fruition, however. Guthrie headed a City Council committee investigating the possibility of establishing a medical school. An 1836 internal dispute among the medical faculty at Transylvania University offered the opportunity. Guthrie encouraged the faculty to move to Louisville and pushed through the City Council an ordinance to establish the Louisville Medical Institute, which became the seed for the University of Louisville. Guthrie served as president of the university from 1846 until his death in 1869.

Improved transportation facilities for the city were among Guthrie's long-term goals. He was a director of the Louisville and Portland Canal Co. from its inception in 1825. At his behest, the City Council in the 1830s authorized purchase of stock in the Lexington and Ohio Railroad, Kentucky's first, that was to connect Lexington and Louisville. The 1837 financial panic stopped construction at Frankfort; not until 1851 was the gap filled. Guthrie was also a promoter of the railroad completed in 1852 between Jeffersonville and Indianapolis, Indiana.

President Franklin Pierce recognized his financial ability and in 1853 appointed him as secretary of the treasury. He soon became the most influential member of the cabinet and was regarded by many as the ablest secretary since Alexander Hamiliton. In 1857 he left Washington and returned to Louisville to become vice president of the Louisville & Nashville Railroad, which had encountered fiscal difficulties. Noted as a financier, Guthrie solved the financial difficulties, and the road was completed in 1859. He became the road's president in 1860 and saw it through the difficult Civil War years.

A committed Unionist, Guthrie led the National Peace Conference in Washington, D.C., in February 1861 in an effort to compromise the differences between North and South, but Congress failed to act on the proposals. President Abraham Lincoln approached him about accepting the position of secretary of war, but Guthrie declined due to his age and health. However, he did return to Washington. Elected to the United States Senate in 1865, he resigned on February 7, 1868, because of ill health, and he stepped down from the L&N presidency on June 11.

Although a Jacksonian Democrat, his strong personality gave him political power in Louisville, which was a Whig stronghold. The Whig *Louisville Daily Journal*, his implacable foe, spoke of his "despotic sway" in the City Council but admitted that "The city [of Louisville] is but another name for Mr. Guthrie."

Guthrie married Eliza Churchill Prather in 1821. They had three daughters: Mary, Augusta, and Sarah "Sallie." He is buried in Cave Hill Cemetery.

See Ann Ruth Spiegel, "Public Career of James Guthrie, (1792–1869)," M.A. thesis, University of Louisville, 1940; J. Stoddard Johnston, ed., *Memorial History of Louisville* (Chicago and New York 1896); *Louisville Past and Present* (Louisville 1875).

George H. Yater

HADASSAH, LOUISVILLE CHAPTER. Hadassah, the women's Zionist organization, is now the largest women's Zionist group, with chapters around the world. Henrietta Szold of New York City had visited Palestine in 1909 and was distressed by the plight of the Jews and Arabs living there, especially the poor health and sanitation conditions. On her return, Szold gave an account of her trip to the study group, the Daughters of Zion. They determined to do something to alleviate the suffering. In 1912 the study group changed its name to Hadassah, the Hebrew name for Queen Esther. They chose that name because it was the time of the Jewish holiday of Purim, which commemorated the heroism of Queen Esther and her devotion to her people. Two American-trained nurses were sent to set up a maternity center in Jerusalem and to fight the spread of trachoma, an eye disease.

From that beginning the Hadassah Medical Organization developed into the Hadassah-Hebrew University Medical Center, one campus established in Ein Karem in 1961 and another in 1972 at Mount Scopus, both in Jerusalem. The HOSPITALS include a medical school; nursing, dental, and pharmacy schools; and clinics. All of Hadassah Medical Organization's work is nonsectarian. Through Youth Aliyah, of which Eleanor Roosevelt was the first patron, Hadassah has helped settle and rehabilitate in Israel thousands of Jewish youth from around the world. In the early 1940s Hadassah started two vocational education colleges.

The Louisville chapter of Hadassah was founded in 1919 after three Louisville Jewish women attended a national convention of Hadassah and came home enthusiastic about its projects. The Louisville chapter had fifteen charter members and has since grown to about a thousand members. Men are invited to become associate members. The chapter participates in fund-raising for Hadassah projects in Israel and for Young Judea youth groups in this country. Another facet of the organization is education. Meetings always include Zionist and American affairs discussions, as well as study groups on diverse topics.

Shirley Schramm

HADDAD, FRANK ELIA, JR. (b Louisville, June 28, 1928; d Louisville, April 7, 1995). Trial lawyer. Haddad was born to Clara (Gallo) and Frank Elia Haddad Sr., a Lebanese immigrant, and grew up in the HAYMARKET district over the family meat store. He worked his way through high school, college, and law school, graduating from the University of Louisville with an L.L.B. in 1952.

Haddad was an important and respected courtroom attorney when he died. He was known for undertaking the largest cases and clients, including corrupt politicians, fellow lawyers, rock stars, and accused killers as they sought his counsel and his connections. Haddad equally represented the hapless, applying his work ethic and experience regardless of fortune. A *Louisville Today* article asserted, "If you are guilty, get Frank Haddad," an opinion held by many.

Haddad practiced law for over four decades and was not only famous for his courtroom success but also his skills as a storyteller and his keen sense of humor. He died suddenly from a heart ailment at age sixty-six before he was able to write a long-planned book drawn from his experiences. Haddad was a devoted family man who had a love of fishing.

He served as president of the Kentucky Bar Association, the Louisville Bar Association, the Kentucky Association of Trial Attorneys, and the National and the Kentucky Associations of Criminal Defense Lawyers. He was a member of dozens of boards and legal committees.

Haddad married JoAnn Seymour on June 20, 1954; they had two children, Frank E. Haddad III and Debbie Haddad Reed. He is buried in CAVE HILL CEMETERY.

See Dan Bischoff, "Big Fish in the Legal Pond: Frank Haddad," *Louisville Today* 28 (Oct. 1977): 37–41; *Courier-Journal,* April 8, 1995, April 6, 1996.

HADLEY, MARY ALICE HALE (b Terre Haute, Indiana, May 11, 1911; d Louisville, December 26, 1965). Pottery artist. She was the daughter of Frank R. and Hattie Alice Hale. Hadley, whose father was the founder of Vigo-American Potteries, a building tile producer, exhibited artistic talent at an early age, often making clay figures for her childhood friends. Educated in Indiana public schools, she later attended Indiana State University at Terre Haute, and in 1933 graduated from Depauw University at Greencastle, Indiana.

Mary Alice and her husband, George E. Hadley, whom she had married in 1930, then briefly settled in Louisville before moving to New York City. There she took art classes at Columbia University. The Hadleys returned to Louisville. In 1939, after an unsuccessful search for suitable dinnerware for their houseboat, Mary Alice decided to make her own. Friends in New York and Chicago, impressed by her work, showed it to others, and orders began to arrive at her home for mugs, plates, and platters. Many of her earthenware pieces, before being glazed, were adorned with hand-painted figures of pigs, chickens, horses, sheep, and farmers. Hadley also created a children's pottery line and did custom designs.

Mary Alice Hadley, 1957.

Hadley's first commercial outlet was a gift shop, for which she personally filled special orders. In 1945 she and her husband opened HADLEY POTTERY at 1570 Story Ave. She gained national recognition for her pottery designs. In 1947 the American Craftsmen's Education Council hosted an exhibit of her work at New York City's America House. In 1952 Hadley was honored with a good design award from the Museum of Modern Art for her brown pottery with cream "coin" polka dots. Her pottery then was exhibited as part of the Good Design Institute's show at Chicago's Merchandise Mart. She was also involved in painting and interior decorating; and she started, along with C.C. Vatter Jr., Deco Paper Products, a company that made paper plates, napkins, and gift wrap that Hadley designed.

See *Courier-Journal Magazine,* Oct. 8, 1950; *Courier-Journal,* Sept. 28, 1952, Dec. 27, 1965.

HADLEY POTTERY. In 1939 MARY ALICE HADLEY, an established Louisville artist, wanted some dinnerware for her boat. She painted nautical designs freehand directly on unglazed greenware purchased from Louisville Pottery Co., then located at 228 E Bloom St. The unfired pottery, shaped by molds made by Perry Day, was dipped in a porcelain-like glaze known as "underglaze decoration" and fired in gas kilns at 2300 degrees F. This unique "single-fire process" bonded the painted design, body, and glaze, creating durable stoneware.

Mary Alice began to design clay pottery for friends at her home on St. James Court, and founded Hadley Pottery. The pottery was fired by Day at Louisville Pottery. Hadley sold her unique pottery in specialty shops until a backlog of a thousand orders created the need for more space. In 1945 Mary Alice's husband, George E. Hadley, joined Mary Alice in business by purchasing the Semple Cordage Mill and moving Hadley Pottery there. The new location was 1570 Story Ave. in BUTCHERTOWN. Hadley, a mechanical engineer, designed kilns, drying racks, and moulding and glazing tables, which Perry Day built and installed.

By 1949 Hadley Pottery produced two hundred unique pieces daily. The signature "M.A. Hadley" appeared on each piece. Mary Alice continued to create new designs from her original Country pattern. It featured motifs of whimsical farmers and animals, which became the most popular design over the years. Flora Watkins, who became head decorator in 1947, trained twelve freehand decorators. In time the company produced a complete line of dinnerware featuring Mary Alice Hadley's designs: the Blue Horse, Ship and Whale, and Pear and Grape, along with customized door plaques and personalized children's and Christmas items.

Mary Alice Hadley continued to paint and design pottery, and some of her works were exhibited at the American House in New York. She also won first prize for painting from the ARTS CLUB OF LOUISVILLE in 1949. Her Hot-Brown Fleck pottery won a good design award from the Museum of Modern Art in 1952. Mary Alice Hadley died in 1965, and Lavida Lynch became head decorator at the pottery.

The Mary Alice Hadley Foundation and Little Gallery, founded in 1967 to promote ceramic arts, was continued by George Hadley until his death in 1991. In 1989 George donated five hundred ceramic pieces to the J.B. SPEED ART MUSEUM.

George Hadley was president of Hadley Pottery Co. Inc. until majority control was bought in 1979 by Kenneth W. Moore. In 1988 Moore hired Gene Hewitt to succeed Virgil Kendall as vice president and general manager of Hadley Pottery Co. Inc.

See Mary Alan Woodward, "House of Stone(Ware)," *Louisville* 42 (May 1991): 20–2.

Lynn Olympia

HALDEMAN, BRUCE (b Chattanooga, Tennessee, November 5, 1862; d Naples, Florida, November 29, 1948). Newspaperman. Haldeman was the son of Walter N. and Elizabeth Metcalfe Haldeman. His father was the publisher of Louisville's pro-Confederate newspaper, the *COURIER*. The Haldeman family had been forced to flee Union martial law in Kentucky. At war's end the family returned to Louisville. The *Courier* was merged with the *LOUISVILLE JOURNAL* to form the *COURIER-JOURNAL* in 1868. The afternoon *LOUISVILLE TIMES* was started in 1884 to compete with the *Evening Post*.

After a period at the University of Virginia and a tour abroad, Haldeman went to work at the newspaper in the financial end of the business. The newspaper, emphasizing news rather than opinion, flourished, growing in prosperity and influence. When Walter N. Haldeman died in 1902, his will specified that his elder

Walter N. Haldeman family, c. 1871.

son, William B. Haldeman, was to be editor of the *Louisville Times* and that Bruce Haldeman would be president of the company. In 1911 his mother died. With only 40 percent of the corporation's stock, Bruce Haldeman asked his siblings to agree to his continued management of the paper. The agreement was not signed by HENRY WATTERSON, editor of the *Courier-Journal*, an omission that later led to Bruce Haldeman's loss of a landmark lawsuit, *Haldeman v. Haldeman*, which defined the rights of the minority stockholder.

In 1917, longstanding resentments between the brothers surfaced, and the directors of the company ousted Bruce Haldeman. He sued his fellow stockholders but ultimately lost in the Court of Appeals. Henry Watterson was the minority stockholder who had not been consulted in the earlier agreement. The lawyer for Bruce Haldeman's opponents was ROBERT WORTH BINGHAM, who a year later bought a controlling interest from Watterson and the Haldeman relatives. Bruce Haldeman then retired to GOLF, hunting, and wintering in Naples, Florida. He is buried in CAVE HILL CEMETERY.

See Dennis Cusick, "Gentleman of the Press: The Life and Times of Walter Newman Haldeman." M.A. thesis, Univ. of Louisville, 1987; J. Stoddard Johnston, ed. *Memorial History of Louisville* (Chicago and New York 1896); George Yater. *Two Hundred Years at the Falls of the Ohio* (Louisville 1987).

Charles Price Jr.

HALDEMAN, WALTER NEWMAN (b Maysville, Kentucky, April 27, 1821; d Louisville, May 13, 1902). Newspaper entrepreneur. The son of John and Elizabeth (Newman) Haldeman, he started his career in 1840 as a clerk in the business office of the *Louisville Daily Journal*, one of the leading Whig NEWSPAPERS in what was then the West. He left after three years to go into business for himself, opening a bookstore with a three-hundred-dollar loan from an aunt. Within months Haldeman took over a fledgling newspaper, the *Daily Dime*, after its owners defaulted on credit for printing supplies and for the out-of-town newspapers and magazines that were their chief sources of news.

With Haldeman as publisher, the newspaper prospered to the point that after only four months he invested in new type, increased the paper's physical size, and, at advertisers' request, changed its name to the *Louisville Morning Courier*. At first the newspaper was moderately Whig in political orientation, although it attempted to attract readers of all political viewpoints by emphasizing news. The editorial philosophy of the *Courier* shifted wildly as Haldeman's own views lurched from Whig to nativist to abolitionist, and eventually to Southern Democrat and radical pro-slavery spokesman.

When the CIVIL WAR started, the *Courier* expressed strong sympathy for the Confederacy. This prompted the Union troops to seize the newspaper's office and seek Haldeman's arrest as soon as Kentucky abandoned its neutrality in September 1861. Fleeing to Nashville, he established a *Courier* in exile that was distributed to Confederate troops and to Confederate-held parts of Kentucky. Publication ceased when Confederate forces withdrew from Nashville in February 1862. Haldeman eventually settled in Madison, Georgia, where he and his family sat out the war as refugees.

At war's end, he returned with a hero's welcome to a Louisville that had developed Confederate sympathies during four years of Union military presence. With the help of friends, he reestablished the *Courier*, which quickly eclipsed the other surviving Louisville dailies in circulation. In 1868 Haldeman bought out the competing *LOUISVILLE JOURNAL* and *Louisville Democrat* and merged the staffs of the *Courier* and *Journal* under the *Journal's* editor, HENRY WATTERSON.

Watterson, who remained editor of the *COURIER-JOURNAL* for fifty years, became a nationally recognized spokesman for the South in his editorial columns. Haldeman concentrated on the business side of the newspaper and on community interests. When baseball's National League was being organized in late 1875, the businessmen behind Louisville's entry into the league gave the Louisville club presidency to Haldeman to lend credibility to the enterprise. The club disbanded after just two seasons, however, when Haldeman's son John discovered that several players had accepted bribes from gamblers.

Haldeman founded the *LOUISVILLE TIMES* in 1884 as an afternoon counterpart to the *Courier-Journal* and competitor to the new *Evening Post*. In the late 1880s, Haldeman and several associates developed the town of Naples, Florida, as their vacation resort.

He was twice a key player in presidential campaigns: in 1876 when he and other publishers facilitated a compromise on the disputed Tilden-Hayes tally and in 1896 when the *Courier-Journal* first bolted the Democratic Party and supported a third-party ticket rather than the party's nominee, William Jennings Bryan. Haldeman kept control of his newspaper company until his death. He was struck by a streetcar while on his way to the office and died three days later. He left an estate valued at more than $1 million, most of it in the stock of his newspapers.

Haldeman married Elizabeth Metcalfe in October 1844, and they had five children: William, Bruce, John, Isabel, and Lizzie. He is buried in CAVE HILL CEMETERY.

See Dennis Cusick, "Gentleman of the Press: The Life and Times of Walter Newman Haldeman," M.A. thesis, University of Louisville, 1987; J. Stoddard Johnston, *Ed., Memorial History of Louisville* (Chicago and New York 1896); George Yater, *Two Hundred Years at the Falls of the Ohio* (Louisville 1987).

Dennis Cusick

HALLECK, ANNIE AINSLIE (b Louisville, December 15, 1867; d Louisville, October 31, 1946). Women's advocate and LABOR reformer. Halleck was the daughter of James Wellstood and Annie (Clark) Ainslie. She was the granddaughter of the Scottish poet Hew Ainslie, who immigrated to the United States in 1822 and settled in Louisville in 1828 after taking part in Robert Owen's utopian experiment in New Harmony, Indiana. Her father was a partner in the Ainslie-Cochran Co., said to be the best-equipped foundry south of the OHIO RIVER, and was involved in various other business interests. On October 29, 1896, she married author and educator Reuben P. Halleck, who served as principal of Male High School in Louisville from 1896 to 1912.

Early in life Halleck developed an interest in social welfare reform, professional social work, and the labor movement. In 1901 she organized the Consumer's League of Kentucky and served as its president from that time until 1930. The organization in Kentucky was affiliated with the National Consumer's League, which was dedicated to improving wages and working conditions for women and children in industry. The league identified employers, especially those in the garment industry, who treated their employees well, and it encouraged women to purchase products displaying a white label of approval it provided manufacturers.

Under Halleck's leadership, the league supported child labor laws, juvenile court laws and minimum wage laws. It also assumed responsibility for verifying state enforcement of labor laws and wrote its own industrial SANITATION code.

In 1909 Halleck became a member of the board of the Family Service Organization in Louisville and continued to serve on it until her death. In 1917 and again in 1924 she was elected president of the Louisville Women's City Club. She attended virtually every session of the Kentucky General Assembly, where she lobbied for legislation on behalf of women and children. In 1933 she was one of four Louisville women honored at the annual National Conference of Social Work.

After her retirement as president of the Consumer's League of Kentucky, Halleck continued to be involved in the league's activities as well as in other social welfare projects. These included chairing a committee to raise money to send women to the Southern Summer School for Workers, an adult education program established under the WORKS PROGRESS ADMINISTRATION, and supporting the National Labor Relations Act and other New Deal legislation. In the 1940s she led the campaign to establish a professional school of social work at the UNIVERSITY OF LOUISVILLE and contributed twenty-five thousand dollars of her own funds to the project. These efforts resulted in the establishment of Kent School of Social Work, named after Dr. Raymond A. Kent, who was president of the University of Louisville.

Halleck died at her residence on Third St. and is buried beside her husband in CAVE HILL CEMETERY. The larger portion of her estate, valued at $571,879, she left to her sister, Maud Ainslie, a painter and patron of the arts.

See Ainslie family papers, Filson Club Historical Society, Manuscripts Division, Louisville, Kentucky.

Melba Porter Hay

HALLECK, REUBEN POST (b Long Island, New York, February 8, 1859; d Louisville, December 24, 1936). Educator. Reuben Post Halleck's father, Rev. Luther Calvin Halleck, was a Congregationalist minister, and his mother, Fannie (Tuthill) Halleck, was a schoolteacher.

In 1874 Halleck enrolled in Gen. William A. Russell's college preparatory school, the Commercial and Collegiate Institute at New Haven, Connecticut. Upon his graduation in 1877 Halleck was accepted at Yale University. He began his studies there in 1878 and was graduated with a B.A. degree in English in 1881. He was immediately appointed principal of the Cherry Valley Academy (formerly the Lancaster School) in Cherry Valley, New York. Halleck held this position until August 13, 1883, when he accepted the position of psychology and English professor at LOUISVILLE MALE HIGH SCHOOL on Chestnut St. between Eighth and Ninth Streets.

Halleck made an immediate impression on the high school and quickly earned the respect of his peers for his research abilities and the close bonds he forged with his students. Every Saturday he took students on nature hikes. Such dedication led to his appointment as vice principal of the high school on July 5, 1896. Later that year he received his M.A. degree in English from Yale. On October 29, 1896, Halleck married Annie Ainslie, daughter of wealthy industrialist and president of the Louisville Bridge & Iron Works, James W. Ainslie.

On January 18, 1897, following the death of principal Maurice Kirby, Halleck was promoted to the position of principal of Louisville Male High School. As principal, Halleck made improvements to the already acclaimed school. Students continued to receive a B.A. upon graduation, a policy that had been in effect since before Halleck's arrival in Louisville and that lasted until 1913, but several changes were made to the curriculum. The school focused more on the liberal arts. He took great pride in the school and ensured its faculty's quality by personally selecting and hiring every teacher. It was during this period, at the turn of the century, that Halleck began writing textbooks in psychology, literature, and history. In addition, Halleck organized several societies and clubs for the students including the printing of the school newspaper, the *Spectator,* in 1901. Halleck placed great emphasis on the value of physical fitness. He equipped his school with exercise equipment and facilities, which allowed him to indulge in one of his passions, athletics. He made it possible for Male to field championship squads in almost every sport from track and field to football and baseball. Students excelled academically as well as athletically during his tenure as principal. From 1907 to 1912 over half the graduates furthered their education in science, classics, law, and medicine. In 1906, following a confrontation with the school board over allocation of funds, Halleck tendered his resignation as principal. The public outcry was so great that the Board of Education refused to accept the resignation, choosing rather to give in to his terms.

Halleck was acclaimed across the nation. In 1904 he was elected president of the National Educational Association's Department of Secondary Teachers. In 1907 Halleck was elected chairman of the National Educational Association Committee of Seventeen, which met to discuss educational reform. For his service to education, the University of Kentucky presented Halleck with an honorary LL.D. in 1912.

In 1898 the high school was moved from the Chestnut St. site where it had originally been established in 1830 to First and Chestnut Streets, formerly the location of the Girls' High School, which moved to a new building at Fifth and Hill Streets. Because of the dilapidated condition of the old building, Halleck headed an effort to raise funds for the construction of a new facility. He succeeded, and the new building was erected and opened in 1910 at Brook and Breckinridge Streets.

In that same year Halleck retired but did not stop working. He continued to write textbooks; edited the national secondary school publication, *School Review*; and toured the country as an inspirational lecturer. A final honor was bestowed upon him in 1934 when Louisville constructed and opened a new building to house both the Louisville Girl's High School and the Louisville Junior High School. On November 23, 1934, the new building between First and Second Streets and Lee and Avery Streets (now Cardinal Blvd.) was officially dedicated as Reuben Post Halleck Hall. Although now home of DU PONT MANUAL HIGH SCHOOL, the building continues to bear his name.

Halleck bequeathed a portion of his estate to educational institutions. He is buried at CAVE HILL CEMETERY.

See Patricia Kurtz Bowling, "Reuben Post Halleck: A Biography," M.A. thesis, University of Louisville, August 1968.

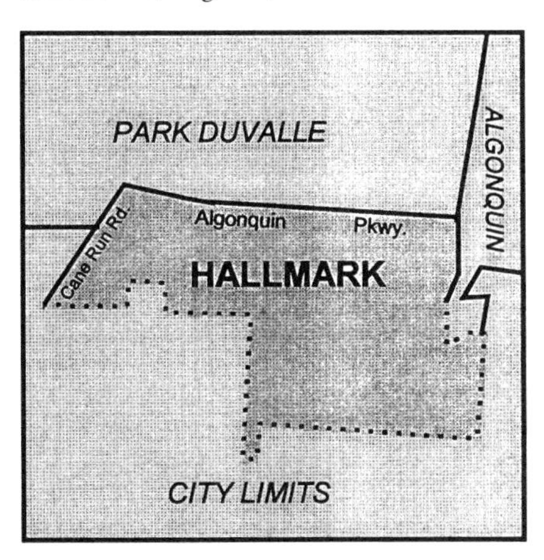

HALLMARK. A primarily residential neighborhood in western Louisville bounded by Cane Run Rd. to the west, Algonquin Pkwy. to the north, Cypress St. to the east, and the Louisville city limits to the south. The origin of the neighborhood name is unknown.

HAMILTON, LEE HERBERT (b Daytona Beach, Florida, April 20, 1931). U.S. congressman. Hamilton moved to Evansville, Indiana, in 1944 with his family, where he attended public school. He graduated from DePauw University in Greencastle, Indiana, in 1952 and then spent a year studying at Goethe University in Frankfurt, Germany. In 1956 Hamilton received his law degree from Indiana University, and after a brief stint with a law firm in Chicago he began to practice law in Columbus, Indiana, in 1958.

Hamilton, a Democrat, was first elected to the United States House of Representatives from the Ninth Indiana District in 1964. He has served in Congress since January 3, 1965. During his career he chaired the Select Committee on Intelligence and was cochair of the Select Committee to Investigate Covert Arms Transactions with Iran. He was the former chairman and ranking member of the House International Relations Committee, also known as the Joint Economic Committee. Hamilton resides in Nashville, Indiana, with his wife, Nancy. They had three children: Tracy Souza, Deborah Hamilton, and Douglas Hamilton. In 1997 Hamilton announced he would not seek reelection to Congress. His last term ended in January 1999.

See *Biographical Directory of the United States Congress, 1774–1989* (Washington, D.C., 1989).

HAMMON, STRATTON OWEN (b Louisville, March 6, 1904; d Louisville, October 22, 1997). Architect. The son of John and Emma (Miller) Hammon, his paternal great-great-grandfather was the revolutionary war hero John Hammon, descended from Ambrose Hammon, who landed at Old Rappahannock County, Virginia, in 1666. Hammon's ancestors were in Louisville as early as 1790.

A graduate of DU PONT MANUAL HIGH SCHOOL, where he studied art and mechanical drawing (and seven decades later was inducted into Manual's Hall of Fame), he attended the School of Architecture at the UNIVERSITY OF LOUISVILLE, affiliated with the Beaux Arts Institute of Design in New York City, and designed his first house when he was sixteen.

In 1930 Hammon became the thirty-fifth architect registered in Kentucky. For the next ten years, he published house designs and accompanying articles in *Ladies Home Journal*, *Better Homes & Gardens*, *McCall's*, and *Good Housekeeping*. Appointed to the State Board of Examiners and Registration of Architects in 1945 and elected secretary-treasurer in 1947, he was also vice president of the Kentucky Chapter of the American Institute of Architects.

In 1942 Hammon was called to active duty as captain in the U.S. Army Corps of Engineers. In this capacity he helped build two air fields, one in Columbus, Indiana, and another in Sturgis, Kentucky. He also began construction on Standiford Field (LOUISVILLE INTERNATIONAL AIRPORT) and extended the runways at Bowman Field. Unearthing a latent love of law, he studied international law at the University of Virginia and attended military government school in Schriveham, England.

He participated in the Normandy invasion of France on June 6, 1944, and was ordered to Versailles in 1945 to serve as the fine arts and monuments officer at Supreme Headquarters Allied Expeditionary Forces. France presented him with the Legion of Honor and the Croix de Guerre for his work in that country during WORLD WAR II. He was discharged with the rank of lieutenant colonel. After the war, he formed the firm of Hammon and Hammon, architects and engineers and vibration damage specialists, with his son, Neal.

During his lifetime Hammon was architect (known for his design of Georgian Revival houses), engineer, explosives expert, writer, photographer, canoeist, soldier, genealogist, historian, and was active in architectural and engineering law. Crusty and opinionated, he was an inveterate writer of letters to the editor and to all and sundry. As an avid reader, concentrating in history and archaeology, he was a member of the FILSON CLUB HISTORICAL SOCIETY and the KENTUCKY HISTORICAL SOCIETY and wrote numerous articles for their publications. Three-time president of the Kentucky Chapter of the Sons of the American Revolution, he was also a member of the State Historical Marker Committee.

Hammon was married in 1924 to Bertha Lee Fieldhouse. Two sons, Neal Owen and Keath Edwin, were born to that marriage. In 1933 he married Helen Louise Jones. One daughter, Helen Stratton, was born to that marriage of fifty-seven years. After his second wife's death, he married Carol Fears Trautwein in 1991. Hammon is buried in CAVE HILL CEMETERY.

Helen Hammon Jones

HAND SURGERY. Kleinert, Kutz, and Associates Hand Care Center in Louisville is one of the largest hand care practices in the world, pioneering achievements in hand and microsurgery, research, therapy, and orthotics. The physicians offer expertise in comprehensive upper extremity care from major trauma and replantations to minor injuries and diseases or conditions affecting the upper extremities. A number of world "firsts" have been achieved by the physicians including first reported repair of a digital artery, technique for successful primary flexor tendon repair, first bilateral forearm replantation on a man injured by sheet metal, first bilateral upper arm replantation, pioneering work in primary reconstruction using free tissue transfer, and the first transplant of a human hand in the United States.

The hand transplant was a joint project of Kleinert, Kutz, and Associates; Jewish Hospital; and the UNIVERSITY OF LOUISVILLE. Dr. Warren Breidenbach, the head of the hand transplant team, performed the surgery on January 24–25, 1999, on patient Matthew Scott from New Jersey. The Louisville hand transplant took place just four months after such surgery was performed by doctors in France. The first known hand transplant was in Ecuador in 1964, but it failed after two weeks.

The practice began in 1953 when Harold Earl Kleinert came to Louisville from Detroit to teach surgery at the University of Louisville School of Medicine. Kleinert received a B.A. from the University of Michigan in 1943 and an M.D. at Temple University in 1946. He was born October 7, 1921, in Montana to Amil and Christine Kleinert, growing up on a ranch outside Sunburst. He had six children.

Joseph E. Kutz became a Christine M. Kleinert hand surgery fellow in 1963 and subsequently became Kleinert's first partner. He graduated from the University of Michigan Medical School in 1958. Kutz was born June 11, 1928, and is a native of Standish, Michigan. He and his wife, Mary Jane, had two sons and one daughter.

Kleinert, Kutz, and Associates provided leadership for the development of the University of Louisville's Microsurgical Training Laboratory. The lab is a model training facility for surgeons and the site for the development of new microsurgical techniques. In 1997 a Division of Hand Surgery was established at the University of Louisville Department of Surgery.

By 2000, in conjunction with the Christine M. Kleinert Institute for Hand and Micro Surgery, the research and educational component of the practice, more than one thousand Hand Fellows from fifty countries had been trained by the practice since 1960. The institute continues a long-term training relationship with Duke University to provide hand surgery rotations for their plastic and surgery residents

Kleinert, Kutz, and Associates was also instrumental in the development of the International Hand Library located on the Jewish Hospital Medical Campus. The not-for-profit library serves as a repository and comprehensive resource for all scientific, medical, and general information related to the hand.

See Harold E. Kleinert, M.D., *CIBA-Geigy Clinical Symposia Replantation* 43 (1991); American Society for Surgery of the Hand, *The Hand: Primary Care of Common Problems* (New York 1990); Christine M. Kleinert Institute for Hand and Micro Surgery Inc., *First Hand News* (Louisville 1989–97); *Courier-Journal,* Jan. 26, 1999.

Barbara Kuprion Mackovic

HAPPY BIRTHDAY SONG. In 1893 Clayton F. Summy Co. of Chicago published a songbook by two Louisville sisters: *Song Stories for the Kindergarten.* The book consisted of seventy-two songs written for children from three to six years of age. The music was composed or arranged by MILDRED JANE HILL, and the words were written or adapted by PATTY SMITH HILL. Both women were involved in early childhood education.

Local history recounts that during a birthday party in the LITTLE LOOMHOUSE on KENWOOD HILL for Lisette Hast, daughter of organist LOUIS HAST, Patty Hill suggested that the words of the first song in *Song Stories,* "Good Morning to All (sometimes listed as "Good Morning to You.")," be changed to "Happy Birthday to You."

Without authorization, the words and music of "Happy Birthday to You" were included in *Harvest Hymns,* compiled and published by Robert H. Coleman in Dallas in 1924. The first authorized publication of "Happy Birthday," with credit to the sisters, was as a march for piano, published by Clayton F. Summy Co. On December 6, 1935, two arrangements, with words, retitled "Happy Birthday to You," were copyrighted. After that date, payment was required for commercial use of the song.

The song has appeared numerous times in films, documentaries, commercials, and cartoons. Igor Stravinsky used it as the basis for his forty-five-second work, "Greeting Prelude." Aaron Copland employed it in his "Happy Anniversary." The most bizarre rendition of the song was by actress Marilyn Monroe, who crooned it seductively at a public party for President John F. Kennedy's forty-fifth birthday in Madison Square Garden in New York City.

See James J. Fuld, *The Book of World-Famous Music* (New York 1995); *Courier-Journal,* Feb. 15, 1948, June 29, 1981.

Robert Bruce French

HARLAN, JOHN MARSHALL (b Boyle County, Kentucky, June 1, 1833; d Washington, D.C., October 14, 1911). United States supreme court justice. John Marshall Harlan moved to Louisville in 1861 and, except for a few years, lived there until he left for Washington to take up his seat on the Supreme Court in 1877. Harlan was the son of James Harlan, a lawyer and politician, and Eliza Shannon (Davenport) Harlan. Harlan was educated at Centre College in Danville and at the Transylvania University Law School in Lexington. Following graduation in 1852, he joined his father's Frankfort law practice and plunged into politics. He began his career as a Whig follower of Henry Clay, then made brief alliances with many other parties before settling down as a Republican in 1868.

Elected county judge of Franklin County in 1858, Harlan resigned in 1861 and moved to Louisville. He set up a law practice, but at the outbreak of the CIVIL WAR he entered military service. A firm supporter of the Union, he raised a regiment in Louisville and served with distinction as a colonel in the Union cavalry. He left the army in early 1863 after the death of his father and returned to Frankfort. Later that year he was elected Kentucky attorney general. In 1867, his term over, he moved back to Louisville, residing at Brook and Jacob Streets and then on Broadway between First and Second Streets. He practiced law out of offices on Jefferson St. between Fifth and Sixth Streets and spent a lot of time campaigning. Harlan was the Republican candidate for governor in 1871 and 1875. He lost both times but is credited with putting the party on the map in Kentucky. In 1876, he delivered the Kentucky delegation to Rutherford B. Hayes at the national nominating convention. Shortly after Hayes became president in 1877, he appointed Harlan to the Supreme Court.

Harlan's reputation rests on his Supreme Court opinions, especially those defending the CIVIL RIGHTS of AFRICAN AMERICANS. Harlan grew up in a slaveholding family and had owned slaves himself. Like many Kentuckians, he defended slavery while fighting for the Union during the Civil War. But when he joined the REPUBLICAN PARTY, which stood for black rights, Harlan said he had changed his mind; and his nearly thirty-four years on the Supreme Court (1877–1911) proved that he had. He wrote 1,161 opinions. The most famous are his dissents in civil rights cases. His masterpiece was an eloquent protest against the court's approval of separate but equal status for blacks in *Plessy v. Ferguson* (1896). "Our constitution is colorblind," he wrote. "All citizens are equal before the law." He was vindicated almost sixty years later when the court struck down the separate but equal doctrine in *Brown v. Board of Education* (1954). A quiet southern gentleman in private life, Harlan was a passionate jurist, and many of his views were ahead of their time. He has been included on some modern lists of the court's greatest justices.

Harlan married Malvina French Shanklin of Evansville, Indiana, on December 23, 1856. The marriage produced six children. One of their grandchildren, also named John Marshall Harlan, was appointed to the Supreme Court in 1955. Harlan died at his home in Washington. He is buried in that city's Rock Creek Cemetery.

See Tinsley E. Yarbrough, *Judicial Enigma: The First Justice Harlan* (New York 1995); Loren P. Beth, *John Marshall Harlan: The Last Whig Justice* (Lexington 1992); Leon Friedman and Fred L. Israel, *The Justices of the United States Supreme Court 1789–1969,* vol. 2 (New York 1969); Alan F. Westin, "John Marshall Harlan and the Constitutional Rights of Negroes, The Transformation of a Southerner," *Yale Law Journal* 66 (1957): 637–710; John Marshall Harlan Papers, University of Louisville, Louis D. Brandeis School of Law and Library of Congress, Washington, D.C.

Charles Thompson

HARNEY, BENJAMIN ROBERTSON "BEN" (b Louisville, March 6, 1871; d Philadelphia, March 1, 1938). Musician and composer. Benjamin Robertson "Ben" Harney was the son of Benjamin and Margaret (Draffen) Harney and the grandson of John Hopkins

Harney, editor of the *Louisville Democrat*.

Though he promoted himself as the "inventor of RAGTIME" music, Harney almost certainly was not. However, he was in the forefront of that turn-of-the-century musical style, and music historians credit him with two important distinctions. His "You've Been A Good Old Wagon, but You've Done Broke Down" (1895, Greenup Music Co., Louisville) was the first published ragtime song, and his popularity as a performer in New York City took the nation's music publishing capital by storm the following year, contributing significantly to the ragtime craze that soon swept the country.

According to Jessie Boyce Harney, his wife and stage partner, Harney composed "Good Old Wagon" and another staple of the Harney act, "Mister Johnson, Turn Me Loose," while living in Middlesboro, Kentucky, in the early 1890s. (Jessie Harney, also a Kentuckian, performed under the stage name of Jessie Haynes.)

After returning to Louisville, Harney performed his songs in minstrels before persuading Greenup to publish "Good Old Wagon" in 1895. John Biller, conductor of the MACAULEY'S THEATRE orchestra, helped Harney transcribe the song for piano, and Biller received equal billing as composer on the original sheet music. Isidore Witmark, the New York publisher who reissued both Harney songs in 1896, was dubious that Harney actually had composed the pieces, so Witmark took a train to Louisville to verify that Harney was the composer.

Starting in 1896 Harney performed at several New York vaudeville houses, but appearances at Tony Pastor's Fourteenth Street Theatre sealed his fame. Isidore Witmark recalled later: "Harney . . . quickly became a New York fad. . . . Those who remember the sensation caused by the earliest jazz pianists will imagine the furor created by Ben Harney's ragging the scale. . . . Ben Harney had the huskiest voice most people had ever heard in a human being, and this quality made his voice just right for ragtime singing." Harney's dexterity as a pianist and stick dancer was a source of amazement. Stick dancing was used by Harney to accompany his song "You've Been a Good Old Wagon, but You've Done Broke Down." Harney performed this dance while he was sitting at the piano with a cane in one hand and tap danced with one or both feet and the cane during the rests of the stop-time section.

Because of his dark complexion, his ability to emulate the African American style of music, and his use of black players in his act, Harney's racial roots have been debated by some ragtime commentators. However, the historical evidence strongly suggests that he was white and not of mixed race.

Harney's vaudeville performances took him all over the country and to Europe and the Pacific, including visits to Australia and the Fiji Islands. He composed more than two dozen songs, including "The Cake-Walk in the Sky" (1899) and "Ben Harney's Rag Time Instructor" (1897), a ten-page manual explaining how to "rag" other music.

JAZZ and other musical forms supplanted ragtime after WORLD WAR I, and Harney's career was cut short by a heart attack in 1923. He died fifteen years later in impoverished circumstances. He is buried in Philadelphia's Fernwood Cemetery. Funds were raised for a grave marker, which Harney's widow had inscribed: "In Memory of My Beloved Husband / Ben R. Harney / Creator of Ragtime."

See Edward Berlin, *Ragtime: A Musical and Cultural History* (Berkeley, Calif., 1980); Rudi Blesh and Janis Harriet, *They All Played Ragtime* (New York 1971); William H. Tallmadge, "Ben Harney: The Middlesborough Years, 1890–93," *American Music* 13 (Summer 1995): 167–94; Isidore Witmark and Isaac Goldberg, *The Story of the House of Witmark: From Ragtime to Swingtime* (New York 1939).

William L. Ellison Jr.

HARPER, NATHANIEL R. (b Indianapolis, Indiana, February 17, 1846; d Louisville, January 27, 1921). Attorney. Nathaniel R. Harper was the eldest son of Hezekiah and Elizabeth Harper. As a child he moved to Detroit, where he was educated, and migrated to Louisville in 1869 with his wife, Drusilla. He was the first African American admitted to the Kentucky bar (November 23, 1871) and quickly became Kentucky's best-known black lawyer.

During the era of SEGREGATION, Harper, like most African American attorneys, was dependent on predominantly poor black clients and was often treated disrespectfully in open court by white lawyers. Although he often found it difficult to make a living as a practicing attorney, Harper's basic conservatism made him an attractive candidate for numerous political patronage positions. In 1878 he became the first black notary public in the state and in 1888 Kentucky's first black judge. In the 1890s, he was instrumental in founding the Central Law School, which became affiliated with black-controlled State (later Simmons) University in Louisville.

In 1895 Harper was nominated for the Kentucky General Assembly but withdrew, to the consternation of his black supporters, under pressure from Republican officials. In recognition of his loyalty to the "Party of Lincoln," he was appointed commissioner of the Bureau of Agriculture, Labor, and Statistics of the Colored People of Kentucky by Gov. WILLIAM O. BRADLEY (1895–99). Harper was a choirmaster, a playwright, and was active in civic and church affairs. He was the father of six children and a longtime resident of 1302 W Madison St. He is buried in Louisville Cemetery.

See Alice A. Dunnigan, *The Fascinating Story of Black Kentuckians: Their Heritage and Traditions* (Washington, D.C., 1982); *Louisville Leader*, Feb. 5, 1921; Marion B. Lucas, *A History of Blacks in Kentucky* (Frankfort 1992); George C. Wright, *Life behind a Veil: Blacks in Louisville, Kentucky, 1865–1930* (Baton Rouge 1985).

J. Blaine Hudson

HARRIS, EVERETT G. (b Amelia Court House, Virginia, February 1867; d Louisville, December 11, 1936). Minister and settlement house founder. After graduating from Howard University's School of Religion, Harris was sent to Louisville in 1893 by the American Missionary Association to shepherd the small assembly that would become the PLYMOUTH CONGREGATIONAL UNITED CHURCH OF CHRIST. At the time of Harris's arrival, the church was meeting at Ninth and BROADWAY, but by 1902 a new meeting place had been built at 1630 W Chestnut St., a location that was on the edge of the African American community's westward expansion. The church's present structure was erected at the same location in 1929.

Though Harris concentrated his early efforts on increasing the membership numbers of his congregation, he also became especially concerned with the needs of the area's children and domestic workers. By 1911 he had conceived of the need for an arm of the church directed specifically at social ministry, in particular a settlement house. It took six years for the plan to come to fruition, but in the fall of 1917 the Plymouth Settlement House opened at 1624–26 W Chestnut, next door to the church. The settlement, which featured a large auditorium, classrooms, and dormitory rooms for black female servants, stressed both religious and domestic training and provided a number of youth programs for the community's children. One of the more notable services Harris offered at the settlement was an employment bureau that found placement for black female domestics. In 1919 Plymouth Settlement House became a member of the Louisville Welfare League. Harris continued as the settlement's superintendent and pastor of Plymouth Congregational until his death in 1936. The house is now called the Plymouth Community Renewal Center.

In addition to his ministerial duties, Harris was active in the civic affairs of the city. He was a board member of the Commission on Interracial Cooperation, a moderate organization that sought to "improve race relations and elevate the status of blacks." Harris also served with the Interdenominational Ministerial Alliance and was, for a time, on the board of directors of the Louisville COLORED ORPHANS' HOME.

Not long after coming to Louisville, Harris married Rachel Davis, known for her work at the western branch of the public library. Both his wife and a son, J. Everett Harris, survived Harris, who is buried in Louisville Cemetery.

See Benjamin Donaldson Berry Jr., "Plymouth Settlement House and the Development of Black Louisville, 1900–1930," Ph.D. dissertation, Case Western Reserve University, 1977; George C. Wright, *Life behind a Veil* (Baton Rouge 1985).

HARRIS, RACHEL DAVIS (b Louisville, May 10, 1869; d ? 1969). Teacher and librarian. After graduating from Central High School in 1885, Harris began her career as a teacher in the public schools at a time when teaching was one of the best salaried professions open to black women. She soon became a children's librarian in an effort to help AFRICAN AMERICAN children develop an interest in reading. As a librarian at the Western Colored Branch of the LOUISVILLE FREE PUBLIC LIBRARY, she succeeded in a profession virtually nonexistent for black women. In the 1920s Harris worked at the Eastern Colored Branch and became a senior assistant there.

Although Harris never had formal training and education as a librarian, she gained experience while working with THOMAS BLUE, the head of the first Colored Department of the Louisville Free Public Library. They became close friends and professional partners. Together Blue and Harris developed a standard training course that educated black librarians from across the South.

Recognizing the significance of a public library in the lives of black children, Harris and Blue also collaborated to make libraries both community centers and important gathering places for young blacks. They enlisted elementary school principals, teachers, and ministers to become actively involved in the library's programs for children. Wide-ranging discussions, lectures, and exhibitions were organized at library branches to entice children to become involved in reading. In 1923 Harris created fifty-eight classroom library collections in the thirty African American schools of Louisville and JEFFERSON COUNTY. In 1935 she succeeded Blue as head of the Colored Department of the library.

She was married to Rev. Everett G. Harris, pastor of PLYMOUTH CONGREGATIONAL CHURCH. She participated in many church activities and sometimes preached there. In 1954 the Harris Recreational Center located at 1723 S Thirty-fourth St. in the Cotter Homes housing project was dedicated and named for Reverend Harris, while the library it housed was named for Rachel Harris.

Harris was a member of the American Library Association and the Woman's Missionary Union.

See *Louisville Times,* March 22, 1954; United States Works Projects Administration, *Libraries and Lotteries: A History of the Louisville Free Public Library* (Cynthiana, Ky., 1944); Cheryl Knott Malone, "Louisville Free Public Library's Racially Segregated Branches, 1905–35," *Register of the Kentucky Historical Society 93* (Spring 1995): 159–79.

HARRISON, JAMES (b Louisville, May 1, 1799; d Louisville, December 23, 1890). Businessman and politician. The youngest son of Mary Ann (Johnston) and Maj. John Harrison and a distinguished officer in the Revolutionary Army, he was educated at JEFFERSON SEMINARY in Louisville. From 1818 until 1820 he worked as an assistant to Worden Pope, clerk of the Jefferson County and Circuit Court, where Harrison devoted himself to the study of law. In 1823, after being admitted to the bar, he married Mary P. Overstreet and entered into a partnership with her father, the Reverend James Overstreet, in the manufacture of TOBACCO products and cotton cloth at the same time running a sawmill and a real estate business. The partnership ended in 1834 when Harrison sold his interest in the sawmill. By 1840 his business interests had failed, and in 1843 he started practicing law.

In 1827 he was elected Justice of the Peace of Jefferson County. In 1846, by virtue of his tenure in office, he became high sheriff of Jefferson County and served in that position two years.

After Louisville was incorporated in 1828, Harrison was elected on March 1829 to serve on the Board of Councilmen. He was elected eight times to serve as a councilmen, the last in 1847. His influence permitted him to introduce and secure passage of many ordinances, including an ordinance establishing local PUBLIC SCHOOLS. In 1840 he was employed by the City Council to codify the city charter and laws relating to the city and Jefferson County.

In 1864 he was elected to fill the unexpired term of state senator Gibson Mallory, who died in office. Among the most important measures he introduced while in the Senate was one to repeal laws against those who sympathized with the Confederacy, and another to regulate the status of black citizens in the state. Harrison was urged to run for reelection but declined. His first wife died in 1832, and he married Susan Howard. After Howard's death in 1854, Harrison married Virginia Corlett in 1858. He fathered eleven children. He is buried in CAVE HILL CEMETERY.

See *History of the Ohio Falls Cities and Their Counties* (Cleveland 1882).

HARRISON, WILLIAM BENJAMIN (b Louisville, July 28, 1889; d Wequetonsing, Michigan, July 13, 1948). Mayor. The son of William and Virginia L. (Trelevant) Harrison, he graduated from LOUISVILLE MALE HIGH SCHOOL in 1907 and from the University of Virginia with a law degree in 1910. He served two years as a captain in the army during WORLD WAR I. He was secretary of the Foundry Products Co. until 1925, and from 1922 until 1929 he was president of the Kentucky Refrigerating Co.

Harrison, a Republican, was mayor of Louisville from 1927 until 1933. He was elected to a two-year term as mayor after the Kentucky Court of Appeals threw out the election of Republican ARTHUR A. WILL, who had been mayor from 1925 to 1927. Following the court's decision in June 1927, Joseph T. O'Neal was appointed to serve as mayor until November 1927. Harrison, who was head of the Board of PUBLIC WORKS, then ran against and defeated O'Neal in the 1927 election by a vote of 65,168 to 61,760. The court also approved Harrison's bid to run again in 1929 for a full term as mayor, succeeding himself. He defeated Edward F. Reidling, a Democrat, in 1929 by a majority of 37,000 votes.

During his administration, Harrison was responsible for arranging the financial plan for the building of the Municipal Bridge (now Clark Memorial) across the Ohio to Jeffersonville. The original bond issue for the bridge had been defeated, but Harrison was able to secure the $5 million funding for the bridge from an Ohio investment company. Harrison's administration was also responsible for the formation of the city PLANNING AND ZONING COMMISSION, the Model Registration law, civil service for the city's police and fire departments, and the purchase of the Von Zedtwitz estate from the federal government for use as Seneca Park and BOWMAN FIELD.

During his administration the state legislature enacted the City Government Bill of 1929, which strengthened the position of mayor. It revamped local government by consolidating the BOARD OF ALDERMEN and Councilmen and the Boards of Public Safety and Public Works into a single legislative body, the Board of Aldermen. The mayor was then given the responsibility for governing and appointing city department directors. Harrison, an articulate and moving speaker, was chosen as the Republican candidate for governor in 1931, but he was defeated by Democrat Ruby Laffoon by a vote of 446,301 to 374,239.

When his term as mayor ended, Harrison became president of the LOUISVILLE INDUSTRIAL FOUNDATION, which helped to attract industry to the area. He worked for the foundation for fourteen years, retiring as president two months before his death.

Harrison married Margaret W. Allis of Louisville in 1912. The couple had five children. He died of lung cancer and is buried in CAVE HILL CEMETERY.

See George H. Yater, *Two Hundred Years at the Falls of the Ohio* (Louisville 1979).

HARRISON COUNTY, INDIANA. Harrison County, Indiana, was organized October 11, 1808, by the Indiana Territorial Legislature, effective December 1 the same year. The fourth oldest Indiana county, it was created from land carved from Knox and Clark Counties and was named for territorial governor William Henry Harrison, who resided at Vincennes, the territorial capital. The same legislation designated CORYDON as the county seat. At the time of its creation, Harrison County encompassed approximately sixteen hundred square miles, including all or parts of present Washington, Orange, Crawford, Floyd, Perry, Lawrence, Jackson, Scott, and Clark Counties.

By the time it reached its present configuration in 1852, the county's land area had been reduced to 479 square miles. Today Harrison County is bordered by the OHIO RIVER on the south, Floyd County on the east, Washington County on the north, and Crawford County on the west. Blue River serves as the Harrison-Crawford boundary line and is one of the county's dominant geographic features. Much of the county is hilly and heavily forested, with a number of caves.

European settlement in Harrison County began about 1792, with one of the first recorded settlers being SQUIRE BOONE, younger brother of Daniel Boone. Most pioneers were of English, Scots-Irish, French, or German stock and had migrated overland from the coastal states through Tennessee and Kentucky. Smaller numbers came down the Ohio River from Pennsylvania, New York, and New England. With completion of federal land surveys in 1807, many began purchasing land at auctions conducted under supervision of the government land office at Jeffersonville. The first two entries were made by John Harbison, but the largest land purchasers included government surveyor Hervey Heth, who purchased six tracts, and Governor Harrison, who bought five.

Harrison's tracts included a quarter-section at the junction of Big and Little Indian Creek that became the site of the town of Corydon. He assigned his certificate to Heth, who laid out the town in 1808. Harrison named the town Corydon for a popular song, "The Pastoral Elegy," in which a young woman lamented the death of her lover, a shepherd named Corydon. It has been said that the name reflects Harrison's bad taste in music.

Since the statute creating Harrison County made no provision for appointing county officials, the responsibility fell to Governor Harrison. On December 8, 1808, he appointed Spier Spencer, sheriff; Richard M. Heth, recorder; Samuel Black, coroner; and Patrick Shields, John George Pfrimmer, and Boone, justices of the court of common pleas. The court conducted administrative and judicial duties, including appointment of several minor officials such as road supervisors and fence viewers. One of the court's first duties was to divide the county into townships.

The first townships were Exeter, in the south; Harrison, in the center; and Washington, in the north. Townships were restructured numerous times over the next four decades as territory was carved away to form new counties. Today the county has twelve townships—Blue River, Morgan, Spencer, Jackson, Harrison, Franklin, Washington, Webster, Posey, Heth, Boone, and Taylor.

From 1808 until 1811 Harrison County had no permanent courthouse. Most county officials conducted business from their residences. The court of common pleas met in members' homes or in rented property. In 1811 the county purchased the unfinished home of County Clerk George F. Pope at the northwest corner of Capitol and High Streets and converted it into a courthouse. But in 1813 the territorial capital moved from Vincennes to Corydon, and territorial officials began sharing space with county officers.

This arrangement proved so inconvenient that in 1814 the county contracted with Dennis Pennington, a prominent stonemason and politician, and carpenter John Smith to build a stone or brick courthouse for three thousand dollars. Built under Pennington's supervision, it was constructed of rough blue limestone. The walls are two and one-half feet thick on the first floor and two feet thick on the second floor.

Although intended as the county courthouse, the structure was completed in 1816 just in time to become the first capitol for the newly organized state of Indiana. The House of Representatives occupied the lower floor, and the Senate and Supreme Court occupied the upper floor. The county and district courts used the building when the legislature was not in session. Corydon served as the state capital until 1825, when the seat of government moved to Indianapolis. At that time the structure assumed its original purpose as the county courthouse.

During the nine years it served as the state capital, Corydon was a bustling center of economic and cultural life as well as political activity. In addition to hosting sessions of the legislature, Corydon became the residence of Governors JONATHAN JENNINGS and William Hendricks and other state officeholders. Both men had served in Washington, and they and their wives were experienced in the social graces of the nation's capital. When President James Monroe and Gen. Andrew Jackson visited Corydon in June 1819 to discuss Indian affairs with Governor Jennings, they were treated to a quiet but elaborate banquet. Statehood also brought an improvement to the town's housing situation. When the territorial assembly began meeting in 1813, most legislators crowded into a handful of taverns and boarding houses. Within three years the shortage had been eliminated.

As the state capital, Corydon had an immediate need for newspapers, resulting in the establishment in 1816 of both the *Indiana Gazette*, which lasted until 1824, and the *Indiana Herald*, which folded in 1818. Similarly, by the early 1820s the town had no fewer than nine attorneys, including John Boone, DAVIS FLOYD, Daniel C. Lane, Patrick Shields, Robert A. New, W.P. Thomason, H.H. Moore, John N. Dunbar, and John W. Payne. Lane was the first state treasurer and New the first secretary of state.

In 1819 New and editor R.W. Nelson established the Corydon Seminary to educate students in the rudiments of Greek, Latin, mathematics, English, and other traditional subjects. Three years later, Mrs. Mitchell and Mrs. Baker opened a school for young ladies. Dr. W.C. Chace opened Corydon's first medical practice in 1819; the following year Dr. David G. Mitchell opened his own practice. Also in 1819 the Reverend John Finley Crowe, who founded Hanover College, helped organize a Presbyterian church in Corydon. The first church building was erected on S Capitol Ave. in 1826. Meanwhile, in 1820 Harvard graduate Henry P. Coburn, clerk of the Indiana Supreme Court, established a Sunday school for local children in the senate chamber; by 1824 three churches had been organized in Corydon. The town also had a bank and a lending library at Jamison Tavern.

The capital also attracted numerous craftsmen and businesses. A tailor from New York City, a hatmaker, a milliner, and a boot and shoemaker opened shops in Corydon. Pennsylvanians Jacob and Peter Kintner established leather, harness making, and saddle shops; and general stores advertised all of life's necessities, including goods and fashions from the East Coast, as well as imports from abroad.

Although Corydon is located several miles to the north, the Ohio River served as an economic lifeline for both the capital and the rest of Harrison County. Several pioneer entrepreneurs recognized the opportunity to profit on cross-river transportation and established FERRYING operations at various points along the river. In 1807 William Smith opened a ferry between Eight Mile Creek on the Indiana side and Salt Landing in Kentucky. Because he failed to post the required bond, he was forced to sell to John Brinley. Downstream were Colvin and Trueman's ferries. Samuel McAdams had a ferry at New Amsterdam; and the operator at Lick's Run, Frederick Mauck, gave his name to the town of Mauckport. Within a few years crude roads began reaching out from these ferrying sites, creating a network of roads that would eventually provide connections with towns and villages, including Laconia, Elizabeth, White Cloud, Ramsey, DePauw, Milltown, Frenchtown, Bridgeport, Lanesville, Crandall, Bradford, and Palmyra.

One of the most important roads into Harrison County was the old Buffalo Trace, which crossed the northern part of the county and brought travelers from the FALLS OF THE OHIO. Governor's Trace extended from Corydon to Governor Harrison's grist and saw mill at Big Fish Spring on Blue River and then angled northwest toward French Lick, crossing the Buffalo Trace in the meantime. Another route to the Falls of the Ohio was the Ridge Rd. or Big Rd., which followed a ridge from Corydon about twelve miles to the KNOBS at the river. From there it followed the river to Clarksville, approximating present State Rd. 111. While most pioneer roads were of very poor quality, they formed the foundation for much of Harrison County's present road system.

One of the most divisive political issues in early Harrison County was slavery. Although the Northwest Ordinance had forbidden slavery in Indiana, numerous settlers from southern states had nevertheless brought their slaves with them and hoped to establish a pro-slavery

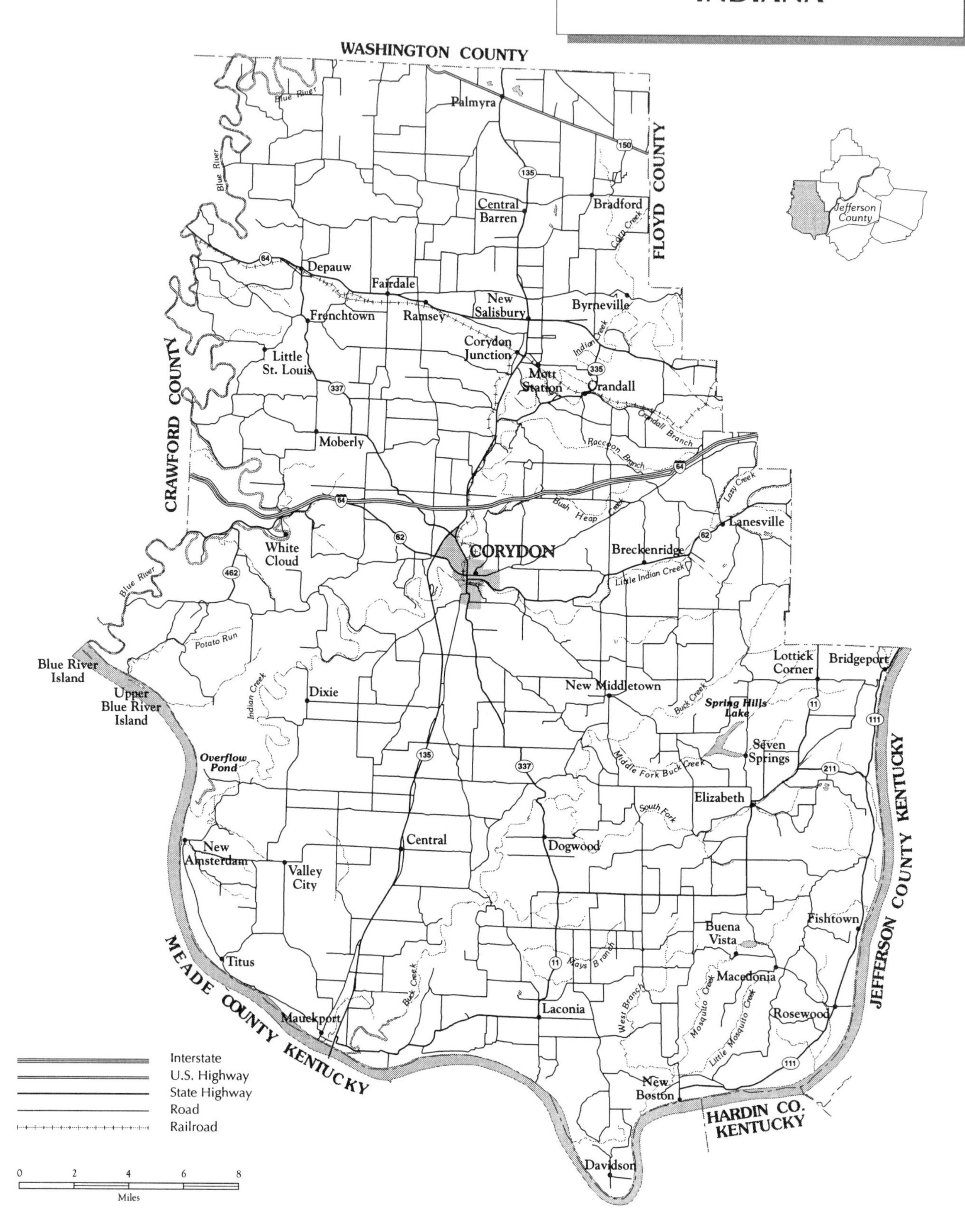
HARRISON COUNTY
INDIANA
WASHINGTON COUNTY
FLOYD COUNTY
CRAWFORD COUNTY
MEADE COUNTY KENTUCKY
JEFFERSON COUNTY KENTUCKY
HARDIN CO. KENTUCKY
Jefferson County
Palmyra
Central Barren
Bradford
Depauw
Fairdale
Frenchtown
Ramsey
New Salisbury
Byrneville
Corydon Junction
Little St. Louis
Mott Station
Crandall
Moberly
CORYDON
White Cloud
Breckenridge
Lanesville
Blue River Island
Upper Blue River Island
Dixie
New Middletown
Lottick Corner
Bridgeport
Spring Hills Lake
Seven Springs
Overflow Pond
Elizabeth
Central
Dogwood
New Amsterdam
Valley City
Fishtown
Buena Vista
Macedonia
Titus
Laconia
Rosewood
Mauckport
New Boston
Davidson
Blue River
Potato Run
Indian Creek
Corn Creek
Crandall Branch
Raccoon Branch
Bush Heap Creek
Lazy Creek
Little Indian Creek
Buck Creek
Middle Fork Buck Creek
South Fork
Mays Branch
West Branch
Mosquito Creek
Little Mosquito Creek
Interstate
U.S. Highway
State Highway
Road
Railroad
0 2 4 6 8
Miles

constitution when Indiana became a state. They had every reason to believe they could achieve their goal, since the 1810 census showed 237 slaves in the Indiana Territory, including 15 in Harrison County. Furthermore, William Henry Harrison, a Virginian who served as territorial governor until 1812, advocated slavery. On the other hand, most northerners, and numerous southerners who had left the South because they opposed slavery, firmly endorsed the constitutional prohibition of slavery.

When the issue came to debate during the Constitutional Convention in Corydon in 1816, the antislavery faction, led by Jonathan Jennings of Charlestown, triumphed, inserting provisions that not only prohibited the introduction of slavery, but that refused to recognize the indentured servitude of any African American or mulatto, whether the contract was made inside or outside Indiana, if the contract was a clear subterfuge to avoid the antislavery provision. While these provisions officially made Indiana a free state, slavery continued in Harrison County until well into the mid-nineteenth century.

During the CIVIL WAR, Harrison County was the site of Indiana's only pitched battle of the bloody conflict. On July 7, 1863, Confederate cavalry under the command of Brig. Gen. John Hunt Morgan captured two STEAMBOATS, the *John B. McCombs* and the *Alice Dean*, at Brandenburg, Kentucky; lashed the vessels together; and used them to ferry Morgan's brigade across the Ohio River to Morvin's Landing near Mauckport. From there Morgan's 2,000 troops made their way toward Corydon, where they confronted about 450 members of the Indiana Home Guard on July 9. Morgan drove the outnumbered guardsmen from the field and shelled the town. In an encounter that lasted about a half-hour, eight rebels were killed and thirty-three wounded, while two guards died and eight were wounded. The battle occurred five days after the end of the battle of Gettysburg, the only other Civil War battle fought above the Mason-Dixon Line, the boundary between the North and the South that covered the line of the Ohio River from the Pennsylvania boundary to its mouth, where it flows into the Mississippi River. Morgan learned of the South's defeat at Gettysburg while still in Corydon. A monument erected on the battle site in 1977 bears the names of the Union dead on its north side and the names of the Confederate dead on the south side.

The Civil War's most notable participant from Harrison County was Gen. Walter Quinton Gresham. Born in Lanesville in 1832, he clerked in a local store, read law, and was admitted to the bar in 1854. He was practicing in Corydon in 1860 when he was elected to the Indiana General Assembly as a Republican. Despite a falling out with Gov. Oliver P. Morton, when the war came he raised a company of soldiers and in 1862 was promoted to colonel of the Fifty-third Indiana regiment. The regiment performed well at the battle of Vicksburg, and Gresham was elevated to brigadier general. A wounded knee during the Atlanta campaign ended his military career, and he returned to Indiana, setting up a law practice in NEW ALBANY. After Gresham was defeated in two runs for public office, President Chester A. Arthur appointed him postmaster general in 1883. He served briefly as secretary of the treasury in 1884 before accepting appointment as United States circuit judge. Although a Republican, he supported Democrat Grover Cleveland for president in 1892 and was appointed secretary of state as a reward. He died in office in 1895.

Throughout the nineteenth century and well into the twentieth century, Harrison County's economy was heavily agricultural. Because poor roads limited access to urban centers, most citizens lived off the land, operating highly self-sufficient general farms and harvesting wood products from abundant stands of hardwoods. The oldest manufacturing firm in the county is Keller Manufacturing Co., which today employs about 475 persons. The firm was founded near the turn of the century by William Keller, the son of a German immigrant who arrived in Corydon in 1847. Keller began manufacturing farm wagons, and between 1901 and 1935 his firm turned out more than 250,000. As trucks and other mechanized implements began replacing wagons during the 1930s, Keller began replacing wagon production with solid wood furniture. The firm is now one of Southern Indiana's leading producers of fine home and office furniture.

In November 1883 Corydon was linked to the nation's expanding railroad network with completion of the Louisville, New Albany, and Corydon Railroad. It connected with the Louisville, Evansville, and St. Louis Railroad (later Norfolk Southern) at Corydon Junction, some eight miles to the north. The railroad in the 1970s began developing an industrial park near Corydon Junction that has attracted a number of new industrial operations to Harrison County. The railroad also operates a summer tourist train under the name Corydon Scenic Railroad.

Completion of Interstate 64 through Harrison County in 1974 increased transportation options and brought a new wave of population growth and economic development. In 1960 the county's population stood at 19,207; a decade later it had increased by just 6.3 percent to 20,423. But it grew to 27,276 in 1980 and 29,890 in 1990, for an increase of 46.4 percent between 1970 and 1990. Much of the growth consisted of migrants from Louisville, and Clark and Floyd Counties in southern Indiana, most of whom settled in new subdivisions that sprang up along county roads near Corydon, Lanesville, Milltown, Palmyra, New Salisbury, and other small communities. However, these new residents added only minimally to the population of existing towns. Indeed, in 1990 Harrison County's ten incorporated towns had a combined population of only 5,656, with Corydon having nearly half the total. By 1996 the population of Harrison County was 33,349, and Corydon's was 2,652.

The combination of increased population and improved transportation also stimulated economic expansion. During the 1980s several communities improved their water and sewer capacities, making the county even more attractive to new industry. In the mid-1980s Corydon attracted two major automotive parts manufacturers—A.O. Smith Automotive Products Co., now Tower Automotive, and Lobdell-Emery Manufacturing Co., now Oxford Automotive—with a combined workforce of nearly six hundred employees. A related firm is Exide Corp., which produces battery separators. Other relatively new firms include Hudson Foods Inc., a poultry processor in Corydon; Norstam Veneers Inc. in Mauckport; and Schmidt Cabinet Co. in New Salisbury. A unique manufacturing firm is Zimmerman Art Glass, a Corydon firm founded in 1963 that manufactures handcrafted items such as paperweights, ashtrays, and vases. Its artistry is displayed in the Smithsonian Institution.

TOURISM is also a vital part of Harrison County's economic base. The twenty-four-thousand-acre Harrison-Crawford State Forest, adjoining two-thousand-acre Wyandotte Woods State Recreational Area and Wyandotte Caves, and Squire Boone Caverns are very popular outdoor attractions. Harrison County also has one of Indiana's outstanding county park systems, with seven PARKS located throughout the county. The Corydon Capitol State Historic Site, which includes the old state Capitol, Constitutional Elm Monument, the home of Gov. William Hendricks, the first state office building, and numerous historic retail, financial, and professional offices in downtown Corydon, are on the NATIONAL REGISTER OF HISTORIC PLACES. Many of these structures have been restored, including the law and publishing offices of Harrison County's most notable twentieth-century citizen, Gov. Frank O'Bannon, who was elected to Indiana's highest office in 1996 after two terms as lieutenant governor and several terms as a state senator.

In 1998, CAESARS Riverboat Casino, then touted as the world's largest riverboat casino, opened on the Ohio River in the Harrison County town of Bridgeport. Although its construction was hindered by numerous delays, the most recent being the discovery of human bone fragments on the site that date over five thousand years old, Caesars has spurred tremendous growth in the county, generating more than two thousand jobs and $25 million in tax revenues.

See Frederick P. Griffin, *Harrison County's Earliest Years* (Corydon, Ind., 1984); Gerald O. Haffner, *Everyday Life in Indiana's Old Capital, 1813–1825* (New Albany, Ind., 1976); *Courier-Journal*, Feb. 3, 1999.

Carl E. Kramer

HARRODS CREEK. The area is bordered roughly by the OHIO RIVER on the west, U.S. 42 on the east, Lime Kiln Ln. to the south, and the area near Hays Kennedy Park to the north. Formerly known as the Seminary Land, the area was first laid out by the Transylvania Co., a frontier firm that also established Transylvania Seminary (now Transylvania University) in Lexington. The company sold lots, but the planned town never developed. The HARRODS CREEK area developed as an important depot for goods making their way to inland Kentucky or south to Louisville via the Louisville-Westport Pike, which later became River Rd.

The area was named for either James Harrod, the founder of Fort Harrod (modern-day Harrodsburg), or Capt. William Harrod, the commander of the first fort in Louisville. Flat-bottomed cargo boats frequently stopped at the mouth of Harrods Creek in the late eighteenth century to avoid going as far as the dangerous FALLS OF THE OHIO and to visit the famous Harrod's Tavern, the site of the modern-day Captains Quarters Restaurant.

Although many cargo boats began bypassing Harrods Creek by the beginning of the nineteenth century, the overland ferry to UTICA, INDIANA, was still popular. Farmers began to populate the fertile soils surrounding the Harrods Creek area and nearby Goose Creek and Little Goose Creek. The farmers shipped their well-known ground flour and cornmeal to Louisville.

Transportation into town became easier after 1877 with the completion of the narrow-gauge Louisville, Harrods Creek, and Westport Railroad. In 1904 the interurban line was adapted to electric service, which opened the area to suburbanization. Wealthy families such as the Browns and the Hilliards constructed summer homes and weekend retreats that eventually became permanent residences.

AFRICAN AMERICANS have also played an important role in the area. After emancipation, many of Harrods Creek's slaves moved into the region known as "The Neck" near present-day Hoskins Beach Rd. The racial mixture of the district was solidified in the 1920s when farmer and developer James Taylor purchased a large tract of land north of the creek and sold the subdivided lots solely to other African Americans.

In the 1990s, citizens of the Harrods Creek area fought a proposal that would have bisected their community by building a bridge to the Indiana side of the river.

See *A Place in Time: The Story of Louisville's Neighborhoods* (Louisville 1989); *History of the Ohio Falls Cities and Their Counties*, vol. 2 (Cleveland 1882).

HARRODS CREEK BAPTIST CHURCH. Founded in 1797 and originally known as the Regular Baptist Church on Harrods Creek, this congregation is one of the oldest AFRICAN-AMERICAN Baptist churches in the Louisville metropolitan area. The church's first minister was the Reverend William Keller, a Virginia carpenter who was known for his skill as both a hunter and a brewer. During its early life, the church was affiliated with several local Baptist organizations, such as the Salem Association, which it joined in 1797. The church then switched to the Long Run Association in 1803, and finally the Sulphur Fork Association in 1855. In 1822 the church constructed a modest stone sanctuary at BROWNSBORO that still exists as one of Oldham County's oldest church buildings.

After the death of Keller in 1817 (according to legend, killed by a bear), the Reverend Benjamin Allen built the church to well over 200 members. However, while serving as the church's minister, Allen came under the influence of the reformer Alexander Campbell, who advocated a departure from the elaborate doctrines of existing denominatioins and a return to simple Biblicism. Allen converted to the teachings of Campbell and in 1831 took all but seventeen members of the Harrods Creek congregation with him in founding what would become the Brownsboro Christian Church.

In 1966 a modern brick worship facility was built on the property next to the original stone edifice at 7610 Upper River Rd. In 1976 the old sanctuary was added to the NATIONAL REGISTER OF HISTORIC PLACES. Nevertheless, due to the expense of maintenance, considerable controversy existed during the early 1980s concerning the fate of the previous building. However, in 1981 the church voted to undertake a restoration project, an effort which has occupied them well into the 1990s.

See *The Courier-Journal*, November 1, 1989, August 8, 1997; Frank M. Masters. *A History of Baptists in Kentucky* (Louisville 1953); Kenneth Ray Norris. "The Impact of Interpersonal Conflict on Kiononia within the Harrods Creek Baptist Church, Brownsboro, Kentucky." D.Min. dissertation, Southern Baptist Theological Seminary, 1983.

Timothy Wood

HART, MARVIN (b FERN CREEK, Kentucky, September 16, 1876; d Fern Creek, September 17, 1931). Heavyweight champion boxer and referee. Born to Samuel and Carthage (Swope) Hart, Marvin grew up attending the public school at Fern Creek, where he first discovered his talents as a boxer in the local schoolyards. After completing the elementary grades, Hart began to learn the trade of plumbing and continued to fight in his free time. On December 12, 1899, Hart fought "Big Bill" Schiller, one of the best-known pugilists in Louisville. Hart defeated Schiller with a knockout in the sixth round and instantly became a local hero.

From 1899 to 1902 Hart scored seventeen successive knockouts in Louisville prizefights. Although BOXING had been a felony in Kentucky since 1896, enforcement had been lax. However, the Kentucky Court of Appeals on June 20, 1903, in the case of *Commonwealth v. McGovern* clarified the illegality of boxing. The case defined prizefighting and specifically stated that it was the duty of the courts to "suppress and prevent" boxing as a public nuisance. Hart never again fought professionally in Louisville and rose to national prominence with matches in Philadelphia, Boston, and Chicago. On March 28, 1905, in San Francisco, Hart battled the great African American boxer Jack Johnson.

Scene on Harrods Creek, c. 1890.

Sportswriters of the day labeled Johnson the better fighter but gave Hart a chance based on his aggressiveness and tenacious determination. Referee and fight promoter Alex Greggains awarded the decision in the twenty-round fight to Hart, although Johnson, who claimed he was "robbed," dominated much of the contest.

On July 3, 1905, in Reno, Nevada, Hart defeated Jack Root, a former light heavyweight champion, for the heavyweight championship, which was vacant after the retirement of James Jefferies. Although Root was an 8–1 favorite, Hart landed a powerful right-arm jolt that ended the match in the twelfth round. Noted sportswriter and former lawman Bat Masterson described the 190-pound, 5-foot, 10-inch Hart as "an awkward appearing fighter when in action in the ring, but his awkwardness is more apparent than real."

Hart had the misfortune to be champion during a time of declining national interest in boxing. Purses declined, racism and violence (both in and out of the ring) were rampant, and the sport was under attack from Progressives such as Theodore Roosevelt, who at one time had boxed himself. Nevertheless Hart spent seven months touring the country promoting his title. On February 23, 1906, in Los Angeles, Hart lost the title to Canadian Tommy Burns by a decision. The fight was a dull affair that attracted little interest. Hart fought eleven more times and was managed by Louisville businessman John F. Seitz during 1909. With a final record of 28–7–4, Hart retired to his home at Fern Creek in 1910. In 1920, after the General Assembly passed the Perry-Bryson Bill legalizing professional boxing, Hart became the first official referee in Kentucky. After ten years of refereeing, he was forced to retire due to ill health. Hart married Florence Ziegler of Fern Creek. They had no children. Hart is buried in Resthaven Memorial Park.

See Randy Roberts, *Papa Jack: Jack Johnson and the Era of White Hopes* (New York and London 1983); *Courier-Journal*, July 4, 1905, July 9, 1905, Sept. 18, 1931.

HASENOUR'S RESTAURANT. Located at the corner of Barret Ave. and Oak St., Hasenour's Restaurant & Bar was a Louisville fixture for nearly forty-four years. Ed Hasenour started in the RESTAURANT business in 1934, opening a cafeteria at the corner of Floyd and Breckinridge Streets with a partner. The cafeteria closed in the 1970s.

The restaurant, opened in 1952 as an upscale steak-and-potatoes dining establishment, had its share of notoriety. In 1964, AFRICAN AMERICANS protested when the restaurant refused to serve them, and eleven were arrested. A week later, the Rev. E. Deedom Alston, a black minister, was served in the restaurant. In 1965, Hasenour's liquor license was suspended for ten days due to gambling. State officials found that pinball machines on the premises were paying off to customers.

But times changed in 1974 when Ed Hasenour was named "Restaurateur of the Year" by the Kentucky Restaurant Association, an association he had founded. In 1979 Lee Hasenour, Ed's son, opened the Atrium, an adjoining section of the restaurant. When Ed died on January 27, 1988, Lee and his wife, Barbara, became the proprietors. In 1989, animal rights activists protested Hasenour's plan to serve zebra meat to promote the new zebra-striped carpet. The restaurant canceled its plans.

The restaurant was seized and closed on June 13, 1995, by agents of the Kentucky Revenue Cabinet for failure to pay forty-two thousand dollars in delinquent sales and payroll taxes. The restaurant had been experiencing declining revenues since the early 1990s. This was attributed to the growing number of restaurants in the area, fewer affluent would-be diners living and eating in the city, reliance on an elderly clientele, and the decision to open the Atrium rather than make it a separate eatery in the HURSTBOURNE area.

Lee Hasenour filed for reorganization on June 15, 1995, and the family was given ten months to reorganize the restaurant. But the restaurant liquidated when it was unable to meet its financial obligations or find a buyer for the restaurant. The business closed in April 1996. On June 29, 1996, the entire inventory was sold at auction to pay off the more than $460,000 owed to creditors. The restaurant building was sold and became the Barrett-Nusz Funeral Home.

See *Courier-Journal*, June 14, 1995, June 16, 1995, May 25, 1996.

HAST, LOUIS HENRY (b Gochlinger, Bavaria, January 13, 1822; d Louisville, February 12, 1890). Musician. Louis Henry Hast was the son of Cornelius and Lizette (Reither) Hast. After graduating from the Munich Conservatory of Music, he and his brother, an artist, came to Kentucky in 1849 and settled in Bardstown. On the death of his brother in 1854, Hast moved to Louisville, where his musical talent and teaching ability were quickly recognized. He was the first organist at the old St. Louis Cathedral on Fifth St., now the site of the CATHEDRAL OF THE ASSUMPTION. In 1878 he was appointed organist of the Episcopal CHRIST CHURCH CATHEDRAL.

His home became a center of musical activity after his elopement and marriage to Emma Sorgenfrey Wilder on June 18, 1860. In addition to his church work, he was director of La Reunion Musicale, the Philharmonic Society, the Beethoven Quartette Club, and the Mozart Society. As a teacher, his most accomplished pupil was Hattie Bishop Speed.

On a trip to Germany in the late 1880s, he suffered attacks of vertigo that sent him into bouts of depression. Hast took his own life by cutting his throat with a straight razor. He is buried in CAVE HILL CEMETERY.

See J. Stoddard Johnston, Ed., *Memorial History of Louisville* (Chicago and New York 1896; *Courier-Journal*, Feb. 13, 1890; Lisette Hast, *Classical Music in Early Kentucky, 1850–1889, Taught Conducted, Arranged by Louis H. Hast* (Louisville 1947); James D. Bennett, "A Tribute to Louis H. Hast, Louisville Musician," *Filson Club History Quarterly* 52 (Oct. 1978): 323–29.

Robert Bruce French

HAUPT, CHRISTIAN (b Darmstadt, Germany, 1829; d Louisville, February 1, 1876). Cornetist, brass band leader, and tavernkeeper. Haupt and his father, Henry, immigrated to the United States and settled in Louisville about 1848. In the early 1850s young Haupt played in Sigismund Arbogast's Saxhorn Band. About 1858 Haupt formed the Kentucky Cornet Band, and it quickly became one of the most popular bands in Louisville. In 1860 he organized the Louisville Silver Cornet Band and was much in demand for balls, exhibitions, and other events organized by the Marion Rifle Battalion, Falls City Guards, and other groups. His most popular band, the Great Western Star Band, was formed in 1869 and was hailed as "one of the finest brass bands in the country" (*Louisville Commercial*, 1870). His saloon was located on Green (now LIBERTY) St. between Third and FOURTH STREETS. Haupt is buried in Eastern Cemetery.

Cornelius Bogert

HA-WI-AN GARDENS. A dancehall built by hotelman J. Graham Brown, it opened on October 17, 1917, at the northwest corner of Fourth and BROADWAY. Created specifically as a place of entertainment for soldiers from CAMP ZACHARY TAYLOR, the Gardens was operated under the supervision of the War Recreation Board. This ballroom, once known as the Arcadia, was a popular dance spot in Louisville that featured live big band, jazz, and orchestral music. It even drew a visit from silent film star Rudolph Valentino, who tangoed there in 1923. At times, the dance floor would serve as a basketball court, with the UNIVERSITY OF LOUISVILLE playing a few games. On the morning of October 2, 1923, fire damaged the building in which Ha-Wi-An Gardens occupied the second floor. The Gardens was destroyed, and first-floor businesses suffered damage to their inventories. Ha-Wi-An Gardens was demolished, and Brown replaced it with the Martin Brown Building.

See *Courier Journal*, Oct. 17, 1917, Oct. 21, 1917, Oct. 30, 1917, Oct. 3, 1923; Samuel W. Thomas, *Louisville since the Twenties* (Louisville 1978); George H. Yater, *Flappers, Prohibition and All That Jazz* (Louisville 1984).

HAWLEY-COOKE BOOKSELLERS. Hawley-Cooke Booksellers opened the largest independent bookstore in the greater Louisville area in June 1978 at the site of a former Walgreen Drug Store at 27 Shelbyville Road Plaza.

HA-WI-AN Gardens, northwest corner Broadway at Fourth Street, 1925.

At the time, the Louisville market was dominated by small, chain-owned bookstores.

The store was founded by William Schuetze and Graham Cooke, who had met in law school. Both practiced at the Legal Aid Society, and their wives, Martha Neal Cooke and Audrey Schuetze, were both English teachers. The bookstore's name combines the Cookes' last name with Hawley, the name of the family who raised William Schuetze's orphaned grandfather.

Before settling on the idea of running a bookstore, the group researched opening a restaurant, an Earth Shoe store, and a dinner theater. The Cookes and Schuetzes enlisted the help of former Louisvillians Tom and Louis Borders, owners of the Borders chain of bookstores and Book Inventory System, a book wholesale operation, for advice.

A second store was opened at 3024 Bardstown Rd. in the GARDINER LANE Shopping Center in June 1981. Hawley-Cooke operated a store at 609 W MAIN ST. in downtown Louisville from 1982–84. A third store opened at 2400 Lime Kiln Ln. at Glenview Pointe in November 1996. The stores offer comfortable seating, alcoves rather than aisles, oak shelving, and a diverse selection of books, periodicals, newspapers, posters, records, greeting cards, and reading accessories. The Shelbyville Rd.store has a cafe and all feature a variety of programs for adults and children.

See *Louisville Times,* April 3, 1980; *Courier-Journal,* July 4, 1982; *Publishers Weekly,* Jan. 18, 1985.

Ellen Birkett Morris

HAWTHORNE. Neighborhood in eastern Louisville bounded by Taylorsville Rd., Hawthorne Ave., Bardstown Rd., and the WATTERSON EXPRESSWAY. At one time, most of the land was part of John Speed's Farmington estate. It is the site of his Federal-style residence, listed on the NATIONAL REGISTER OF HISTORIC PLACES and thought to have been built in 1815–16. Hawthorne is primarily a residential neighborhood, although businesses exist along the major roads. The area was first subdivided in 1909 but attracted few residents until the mid-1920s. The area got its name from Hawthorne Ave. Many of the streets in the area are named after famous poets and writers. The sixth-class city of Wellington is surrounded by the neighborhood. SULLIVAN COLLEGE is located in the neighborhood as well.

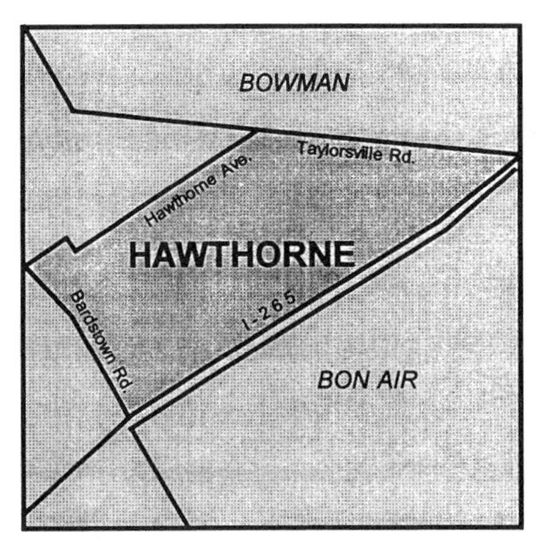

See *Louisville Survey: East Report* (Louisville 1980).

HAYES, CLIFFORD (b near Glasgow, Kentucky, March 4, 1895; d Ohio, May 1957). Fiddler. Born into a family of talented African American musicians, Hayes learned to play the fiddle at an early age and performed with his brothers in a string band. About 1914 the family moved to Louisville, where Hayes became an integral part of EARL MCDONALD's Louisville Jug Band, playing blues and popular tunes. From 1915 to 1927 he traveled with McDonald, visiting New York, Chicago, and Atlanta for recording sessions and performances. By 1927 he was fronting his own band, playing more JAZZ and BLUES and fewer of the jug band standards. He continued playing music until his death.

Brenda K. Bogert

HAYES, ROLAND WILTSIE (b near Curryville, Georgia, June 3, 1887; d Boston, Massachusetts, January 1, 1977). African American tenor. Hayes was one of seven children of William and Fannie (Mann) Hayes, a former slave. He studied voice in Chattanooga with Arthur Calhoun and later attended Fisk University in Nashville. Moving to Louisville in 1910, he became a waiter at the PENDENNIS CLUB. There he attracted the attention of the city's business and musical elite, who arranged for him to study in Boston. His debut was made there on November 11, 1915, at Jordan Hall.

During his career of almost sixty years, Hayes sang hundreds of recitals in America and Europe. Between 1918 and 1961 he presented sixteen programs in Louisville halls that included QUINN CHAPEL AME Church; Macauley's, Brown and National THEATERS; LOUISVILLE MEMORIAL AUDITORIUM; and Central High School. To acknowledge his status as an artist and role model for succeeding generations of AFRICAN AMERICAN singers, the UNIVERSITY OF LOUISVILLE awarded him an honorary Doctor of Humanities degree in 1972.

In 1932, Hayes married Helen Alzada Mann, his first cousin, in California where he was appearing at the Hollywood Bowl. One daughter, Afrika Fanzada Hayes, was born in 1935. Hayes died of pneumonia and is buried in Mt. Hope Cemetery in Mattapan, Massachusetts.

See MacKinley Helm, *Angel Mo' and her Son, Roland Hayes* (Boston 1942; *Courier-Journal,* Feb. 19, 1990; F.W. Woolsey, "Conversation with Roland Hayes," *Black Perspective in Music* 2 (Fall 1974): 179–85; Marva Griffin Carter, "In Retrospect: Roland Hayes—Expressor of the Soul in Song," *Black Perspective in Music* 5 (Fall 1977): 189–220; Warren Marr II, "Conversation with Roland Hayes," *Black Perspective in Music* 2 (Fall 1974): 186–90.

Robert Bruce French

HAYFIELD-DUNDEE. Neighborhood in eastern Louisville bounded by Dundee Rd. and Emerson Ave. to the north, NEWBURG Rd. to the west, the WATTERSON EXPRESSWAY to the south, and Lovers Ln. and Tremont Dr. to the east. Louis A. Arru's Gerald Realty Co. began developing the area around Gardiner Ln. in

The Haymarket, between Jefferson and Liberty, Brook and Floyd, 1920s.

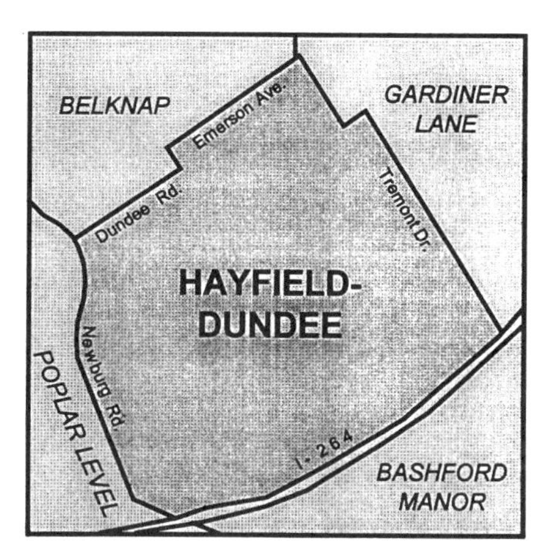

1944. However, most of the growth occurred in the 1950s and 1960s as developers platted the Dundee Estates community and subdivided Hayfield Farm. The farm was owned by Dr. Charles Wilkins Short, a founding professor of the UNIVERSITY OF LOUISVILLE Medical School. Local landmarks include Atherton High School and the Alpine Ice Arena, formerly known as the GARDINER LANE Ice Skating Club, established in 1960.

See *Louisville Survey: East Report* (Louisville 1980).

HAYLOFT HOEDOWN. One of the most popular locally produced programs of TELEVISION'S early days, *Hayloft Hoedown* played for nineteen years between 1951 and 1971. The idea for the half-hour country music show originated with WHAS general manager Harold Feher. The early show starred Randy Atcher, Tom "Cactus" Brooks, Janie Workman, the Red River Ramblers, the House Sisters, Joe Masterson, "Tiny" Thomale, Bernie Smith, Shorty Chesser, Sleepy Marlin, and George Workman. The moderator was Atcher, who was born in Tip Top, Hardin County, Kentucky, on December 7, 1918, one of eight children of George C. and Mary (Ray) Atcher.

Educated at West Point, Kentucky, public schools, he attended what later became Western Kentucky University for one year. Atcher came from a musical family and as early as 1933 he and his brother Bob were entertaining across Kentucky and southern Indiana. Atcher played guitar and mandolin and sang. In 1933 he and Bob first performed on WHAS. After the year at college, he returned to WHAS in 1937. While working at KMOX in St. Louis he accepted Bob's offer to join him in Chicago in 1939 to work for WJJD and WBBM. Atcher served in the South Pacific during WORLD WAR II. Following the war he spent a brief time in Savannah and then returned to Louisville, working first at WHAS, then at WGRC and WKLO. In 1950 he returned to WHAS and remained there until his retirement in 1971. Atcher married Daphne Fuller and, following her death, Elizabeth Blankenbaker.

Hayloft Hoedown appeared on Friday evenings and featured country music, a comedy routine by Brooks, solo and group instrumental pieces, a square dance (by the Hayloft Hoedowners), and ended with a gospel song. Members were like a family. Guest stars were often featured, including Eddie Arnold, Homer and Jethro, Marty Robbins, Roy Rogers, and Frankie Carle. For many years, it had the highest rating of any Louisville-originated television program. For nineteen years it was an important part of the CRUSADE FOR CHILDREN. The show ended in 1971 when WHAS concluded that a single station could not afford to produce the big-budget, slickly produced, expensive kind of country show the public demanded. Atcher's other popular television program, *T-Bar-V Ranch,* began on March 27, 1950, and ended in June 1971.

HAYMARKET. The Haymarket refers to Louisville's colorful outdoor downtown market, where farmers sold fruits and vegetables but very little (if any) hay. The market occupied the square block between Jefferson and LIBERTY Streets on the north and south and Brook and Floyd Streets on the west and east. A small section also extended along Floyd St. south of Liberty. The Haymarket was established in 1891 by the Gardeners and Farmers Market Co. It was on the site of the city's first railroad station, built in the early 1850s by the Louisville and Frankfort Railroad, which entered the city on Jefferson St.

When the station was relocated to First St. and River Rd. in 1881, the site was cleared. Its use during the next ten years is unclear. Louisville tradition holds that local truck farmers began using the open space as an informal market, selling directly to consumers. What may have been informal became formal in 1891 when some of the farmers formed a stock company and purchased the space as a permanent market. This development may have been spurred by the closing of the nearby municipal market house in the center of MARKET ST. between Clay and Shelby Streets in 1888. That market was the only one remaining of at least seven market houses that had been located on Market St. between Clay on the east to Seventeenth on the west. Another nearby market house at Preston and Market had been closed and demolished in 1871.

With the Haymarket in operation, other food-related marketing activities sprang up along the sidewalks in the area. In 1894 the city formalized and set limits on these small operators. They were permitted to use certain sidewalks on Jefferson, Second, and Floyd Streets. This became a thriving market area for agricultural produce, so much so that in 1898 the city declared a larger area from Third east to Jackson St. and from Market south to Liberty (then Green St.), to be a "Public Market Place." Hucksters of fruits, vegetables, and "other products" could use three feet of the sidewalks along the curbs for their sales stands (*Third Biennial Compilation of Ordinances of the City of Louisville,* 1900). The centerpiece of this Public Market Place was the Haymarket.

Commission merchants who handled sales of agricultural produce in large lots and wholesalers who brought in produce from distant points also flocked to the designated area. Louisville grocers picked up fresh fruit and vegetables at the crack of dawn to offer to their customers that day. Nearby truck farmers arrived before dawn and napped in their wagons until the sun rose.

"Housewives of means come face-to-face with the producers," the *Courier-Journal* noted on August 2, 1914, and added that these were called the "curb buyers" because they bargained with the sellers along the street curb. The same newspaper on June 1, 1919, described a typical transaction in which a "pretty bride from out on Cherokee Dr. [Lexington Rd.] braves the strenuous bargaining with the Italian woman at a vegetable stand and pays four cents a bunch instead of six cents" and is whisked home in her limousine. Many of the sidewalk stands were conducted by ITALIANS and LEBANESE, recent immigrants to the United States.

In the mid-1920s a series of long, open-sided sheds were erected in the Haymarket to provide protection from the weather and bring a modicum of order to the busy scene. But twenty years later it was obvious that the colorful but congested Haymarket was outdated and inadequate. The rise of chain GROCERIES with their own warehouses and rail sidings cut the market's volume. Many wholesalers traded in more efficient markets elsewhere, and the quality of Haymarket produce declined. By 1953 some wholesalers were contemplating a new and larger produce terminal outside the city. By 1955 they had firmed plans for the Louisville Produce Terminal on a thirty-two-acre site with railroad connections on Jennings Ln. When it opened in 1962 it included twenty booths for individual vendors.

The Haymarket, seemingly determined to hold on, was doomed by the construction of Interstate 65 through downtown. An expressway exit cut through the seventy-one-year-old institution, and the Haymarket closed on September 1, 1962. The closing was not good news to dozens of smaller vendors who wanted to remain in the vicinity. The downtown URBAN RENEWAL program was in full swing, and the result was the formation of Louisville Produce Plazas Inc. in 1962. The Urban Renewal Agency cleared a square-block site between Jefferson and Market Streets and Floyd and PRESTON Streets. The new Produce Plaza, informally called the Haymarket, was designed by Louisville architect Jasper Ward and opened in 1966. Like its predecessor, the new market is filled by late fall with Christmas trees. Hundreds of Louisvillians continue the tradition of choosing their trees at the Haymarket.

George H. Yater

HAYNIE, HUGH SMITH (b Reedville, Virginia, February 6, 1927; d Louisville, November 26, 1999). Political cartoonist. Haynie, remembered as a soft-spoken yet intensely self-critical man, was born and raised in the Chesapeake Bay area of Virginia, the son of Raymond and Margaret (Smith) Haynie. The family operated a large menhaden fishing business founded by his grandfather. After high school graduation, Haynie, at age 17, enlisted in the Coast Guard. He served from 1944 to 1946. In 1950 he graduated from the College of William and Mary with a degree in fine arts, and then served another year in the Coast Guard during the KOREAN WAR. From his first political cartoon in college, he went on to draw for the *Richmond Times-Dispatch,* the *Greensboro Daily News,* and the *Atlanta Journal,* before coming to the *LOUISVILLE COURIER-JOURNAL* in 1958.

Haynie's career with the Courier-Journal, beginning at the age of 31 and ending at the age of 70 with the appearance of his last original cartoon on July 25, 1997, encompassed, at a conservative estimate, more than eight thousand original drawings. As an editorial cartoonist his critical eye, hard-hitting, virulent style of drawing, and political liberalism aroused anger and admiration, rage and rapture. He once commented, "Cartoons are not to pat people on the back." Nonetheless, his popularity in Kentucky was instant and considerable.

A committed critic, Haynie was most critical of himself. He once confessed to a reporter, "I've never been satisfied with one of my cartoons." Later, he added, "Not being a very good artist and a perfectionist, my work is never up to what it should be." This minority opinion of one, however, never gained public credence.

During his career in Louisville his work was syndicated in more than eighty newspapers around the nation, and was frequently reprinted in national news magazines. Haynie cartoons are included in the collections of the Eisenhower, Kennedy, Johnson, Nixon, Ford, and Carter presidential libraries. His most popular cartoon may well have been the "Christmas Shopper," first printed in the *Courier-Journal* on Christmas Eve, 1961. It pictures a middle-aged man, with the image of Christ behind him, ruminating over his Christmas shopping list and asking, "Now, let's see, have I forgotten anyone?" In 1962, th U.S. Chamber of Commerce named Haynie one of th ten outstanding young men of that year.

During the course of his career Haynie received many honors: the National Headliners Club Award (1966), the Freedoms Foundation Medal (twice), an honorary doctorate of humane letters from the UNIVERSITY OF LOUISVILLE (1968), alumnus member of Phi Beta Kappa, and Alumni Medal from the College of William and Mary (1977), and the Distinguished Service Award and Bronze Medallion from Sigma Delti Chi (now the Society of Professional Journalists). In 1978 the Kentucky Civil Liberties Union named him Civil Libertarian of the Year. In 1987 he was inducted into the Kentucky Journalism Hall of Fame.

Haynie was twice-married. His first wife was Lois Cooper, of Norfolk, Virginia. (The word "Lois" was often hidden within the details of his earlier cartoons, and eagerly sought for by readers.) His second wife was Oleta Joanna Stevens. He had one son by his first marriage, Hugh Smith Haynie Jr. He is buried in CAVE HILL CEMETERY.

See Maurice Horn, ed., Contemporary Graphics Artists, vol. 3 (Detroit 1988); *The Courier-Journal,* November 27, 1999.

Donald B. Towles

HAYS, WILLIAM SHAKESPEARE (b Louisville, July 19, 1837; d Louisville, July 23, 1907). Songwriter, journalist. William Shakespeare Hays was the most successful native Kentucky songwriter of the nineteenth century. He began writing poems and songs about the age of twenty. By the time of his death, he had published some 350 SONGS. His tunes sold over 6 million copies in sheet music form—a phenomenal performance for that era.

Hays was a colorful and controversial individual. A reporter for the *Louisville Democrat* during the CIVIL WAR, he later became a river captain on the Ohio and Mississippi Rivers. He returned to journalism and was for many years the popular and influential river editor for the *COURIER-JOURNAL.* Apparently composing in his spare time, Hays claimed he never made money from his music. Contemporaries considered him a composer of "charming melodies" while noting his "rough ways and his profane language," mannerisms he demonstrated while a steamboat captain but had given up after his marriage. He also published three volumes of POETRY.

Hays's music gained popularity during the Civil War, when he wrote "Evangeline" (his first published tune), "The Drummer Boy of Shiloh" (which came out in northern and southern versions), and "My Southern Sunny Home" (which got him in trouble with Union army authorities in New Orleans). Hays also wrote "The Union Forever," the first nationally popular Civil War song—at least in the North. "Mollie Darling" appeared in 1866. It was Hays's most famous song; it alone sold perhaps 2 million copies. Other popular pieces included "Nora O'Neil," "Write Me A Letter from Home," "Shamus O'Brien," "Save One Bright Crown for Me," "Roll Out!" "Heave Dat Cotton," "Sweet Bess o' Bonnie Doon," and "We Parted by the River Side."

Many of his songs entered the folk music repertoire and enjoyed renewed success in the early days of radio and recorded music. One of the first country music recordings was Fiddlin John Carson's 1923 performance of "The Little Log Cabin in the Lane." That tune had inspired parodies like "The Little Red Caboose behind the Train." Hays said he wrote one of the most famous songs in American history—"Dixie." However, this claim remains unsubstantiated, and credit for composing this southern anthem must remain with Ohioan Daniel Decatur Emmett.

Opinions of Hays's body of work vary. Nineteenth-century writers praised his "easy and effective accompaniments" and "genuine feeling"—"written for the masses and by the masses appreciated." However, a modern critic declared that "his writing generally lacked depth of feeling and was too topical to achieve universal quality."

The son of Pennsylvanian Hugh Hays, Will S. Hays married Belle McCullough in 1865. The couple had two children. Hays is buried in

Cave Hill Cemetery.

See Edwin Anderson Alderman, ed., *Library of Southern Literature* (New Orleans 1909); F.O. Jones, ed., *A Handbook of American Music and Musicians* (New York 1971); *Courier-Journal,* July 19, 1987; William S. Ward, *A Literary History of Kentucky* (Knoxville 1988); Charles K. Wolfe, *Kentucky Country: Folk and Country Music of Kentucky* (Lexington 1982).

Nickey Hughes

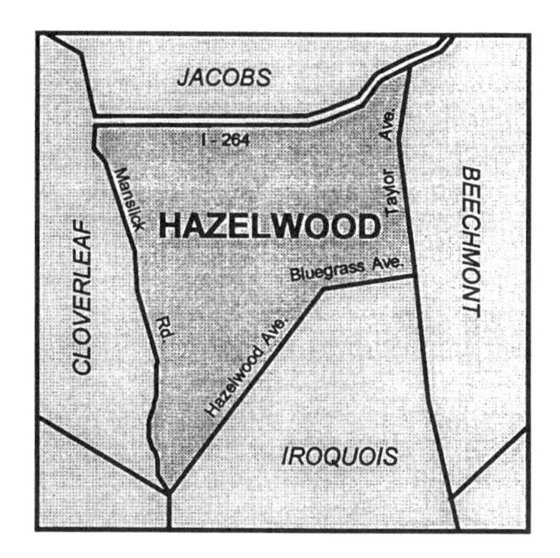

HAZELWOOD. Neighborhood in southern Louisville bounded by Manslick Rd. to the west, the Watterson Expressway to the north, Taylor Blvd. to the east, and Hazelwood Ave. and Bluegrass Ave. to the south. Sparked by the establishment of Iroquois Park to its south and a streetcar line into the area, the first land division occurred in 1899 by E.E. Meacham. In 1902, Alma Bergmann and the Columbia Finance and Trust Co. financed the Hazelwood subdivision of Bergmann's Addition. Three years later they added the Hazelwood Annex, providing the area with its name. Local landmarks include the Hazelwood Center, an open-air tuberculosis treatment clinic dating from 1907 that became a hospital for the mentally handicapped in 1971, and the Caritas Medical Center, formerly the Saints Mary and Elizabeth Hospital, which moved there in 1958.

See "Louisville Survey: Central and South Report" (Louisville 1978); Carl E. Kramer, "The City-Building Process: Urbanization in Central and Southern Louisville, 1772–1932," Ph.D dissertation, University of Toledo, 1980.

HEAD, WILLIAM O. (b Providence, Kentucky, July 29, 1859; d Clearwater, Florida, April 19, 1931). Mayor. He was the son of John W. and Mary A. Head. John Head was a captain in the Confederate army during the Civil War. William was educated in the public schools in Providence and grew up on a farm near there. When he was twenty-one years old, he came to Louisville and took a job with a tobacco warehouse and later became a manager for the People's Tobacco Warehouse Co. Head's entire business career was in the tobacco business.

In 1894, Head, a Democrat, was elected to the state legislature as a representative of the Eighth and Ninth Wards. The hand-picked successor for the mantle of the Whallen brothers' Democratic machine, Head served as mayor of Louisville from November 16, 1909, through November 18, 1913. He defeated incumbent mayor James F. Grinstead by fanning racist fears of the expanding African American community. Local newspapers, particularly those run by publisher Walter N. Haldeman, published several stories meant to scare white voters.

During Head's administration the Tenement House Commission, a group formed in 1909 to study Louisville's tenement housing problem, issued a report calling for greater city regulation of urban housing. As many as one-third of Louisville's inner-city families lived in tenements by 1900. In 1910 the Kentucky General Assembly passed the model housing law to curb the worst excesses of tenement housing. It was incorporated into the city's charter shortly thereafter. Also during Head's administration, annual appropriations from the city's budget were started for funding the University of Louisville. The appropriations were prompted, in part, by a scathing report on the state of medical education by Abraham Flexner.

Head served as a member of the Democratic State Central Committee from the Fifth District for four years. He was a delegate to the Democratic national convention in Baltimore in 1912. He also served as president of the Louisville Water Co. for four years.

Head married Lelia Bean, daughter of John W. and Eliza Redmond Bean, in 1896. He and his family lived at 1414 S Second St. Head moved to Florida in 1926 because of his wife's failing health. She died there in August 1927. Head married a second time to Mrs. W.Q. Williams of New Orleans in August 1928. He is buried in Cave Hill Cemetery.

See Alwin Seekamp and Roger Burlingame, eds., *Who's Who in Louisville* (Louisville 1912); *Louisville Times*, April 20, 1931; George Yater, *Two Hundred Years at the Falls of the Ohio* (Louisville 1987).

HEADY, JAMES MORRISON (b Spencer County, Kentucky, July 19, 1829; d Louisville, December 20, 1915). Poet and novelist. The "Blind Bard of Kentucky," Heady was the son of Dr. James Jackson and Lois (Eastburn) Heady. At age six he lost the sight in one eye and was totally blind at age sixteen. He became deaf when he was forty. A poet, novelist, musician, teacher, architectural designer, and inventor, Heady moved to Louisville in 1900.

He attended the Kentucky School for the Blind (1846) and the Ohio Blind Institute (1848). An early advocate of books for blind people, Heady was an agent for the American Printing House for the Blind.

Heady's first book, *The Farmer Boy* (1864), the story of George Washington's youth, was printed in raised letters by the American Printing House for the Blind (1873). Later, he published several novels and books of poetry. His poems appeared in the *Louisville Journal*.

His "talking glove," which had on it the letters of the alphabet, enabled his friends to communicate with him. Louisville's most prominent citizens were his friends. At his death he was eulogized by Rabbi Joseph Rauch, who said, "Mr. Heady was a man with the vision of a seer, the spirit of a philosopher and the soul of a poet." Heady is buried in Elk Creek Cemetery, Spencer County, Kentucky.

See *Louisville Herald,* Dec. 20, 1915; *Courier-Journal,* Dec. 21, 1915.

Carol Brenner Tobe

HEIGOLD HOUSE. Christian Heigold, a German immigrant and stonecutter, came to Louisville sometime prior to 1850. He built his home at 264 Marion St. in an area known as the Point between 1857 and 1866, a period of unrest and attacks on Irish and German immigrants. The infamous Bloody Monday incident had occurred in 1855. In order to prove his patriotism and loyalty to America, he carved inscriptions and busts of American notables into the front of the house. Among the incised mottoes is one reading, "Hail to the City of Louisville." He died shortly after the facade was completed in 1865, and his son Charles lived there until his death in 1925.

The house survived until 1953 when the city purchased the property in order to expand the city dump. Mayor Charles Farnsley saved the facade of the house from demolition by moving it to Thruston Park on River Rd. between Adams and Ohio Streets.

See *Courier-Journal*, March 17, 1954, Dec. 27, 1954, July 19, 1992; George H. Yater, *Two Hundred Years at the Falls of the Ohio* (Louisville 1979).

Dorothy C. Rush

HEIMERDINGER CUTLERY COMPANY. August Heimerdinger, the immigrant son of a German tailor, opened a cutlery and sewing machine repair and manufacturing business in 1861 at First and Jefferson Streets, later moving to W Market between First and Second Streets. In the 1870s Heimerdinger began to manufacture scissors and shears, which became the core of the business. In 1922 his grandson, W.G. Heimerdinger, patented a scissor-action grass shear that he manufactured and sold by the boxcar-load to such retailers as Sears, Roebuck, and Co. Manufacturing ceased in 1955, but the company continued to sell and service cutlery. In 1983, still owned and operated by the Heimerdinger family, it moved to 4207 Shelbyville Rd.

Charles Thompson

HEINEMANN, ALWINIA (b Kickenbach, Germany, April 21, 1908; d Mishawaka, Indiana, January 19, 1995). Nurse. Often called the unofficial mother of fifty-seven thousand babies born while she worked at St. Anthony

Hospital in Louisville (opened 1902), she revolutionized the way mothers and their families were cared for during labor and delivery. She was the daughter of Peter and Alwinia (Kramer) Heinemann.

She joined the order of the Sisters of St. Francis of Perpetual Adoration three years before she moved to the United States in 1934. She received a bachelor's degree in NURSING from St. Francis College in Fort Wayne, Indiana, and worked at St. Anthony Hospital for twenty-nine years, retiring in 1985. She became nursing supervisor in the obstetrics unit, a position she held for seventeen years.

Sister Alwinia opened the labor rooms to expectant fathers in 1956 and the delivery rooms in 1962. She later promoted unlimited visits by fathers, allowed newborns to stay with their mothers at all times, and eventually supported visits to newborns by their brothers and sisters. Other city HOSPITALS followed those practices, which were at first dramatic. Following retirement she lived at Our Lady of Angels Retirement Home in Mishawaka, Indiana. She died of kidney failure, pneumonia, and other complications and is buried at St. Francis Cemetery in Mishawaka.

See *Courier-Journal*, Jan. 20, 1995.

HEINRICH, ANTHONY PHILIP (b Schönbüchel, Bohemia, March 11, 1781; d New York City, 1861.) Merchant, self-taught musician, and composer. The publication in Philadelphia in 1820 of a series of musical compositions under the collective title of *The Dawning of Music in Kentucky* brought Heinrich his first extended notice as a composer. Most, perhaps all, of the works in the publication had been written in 1819 at Farmington, the Speed family plantation on Bardstown Rd. near Louisville.

Heinrich had come to the United States about 1809 in hopes of recouping his once-large fortune derived from a thriving manufacturing and wholesale business in linen, thread, and other commodities. He had inherited the business from his uncle, but the financial disarray created in the Austrian empire by the Napoleonic wars caused the business to falter. In Philadelphia, where he set up an importing business specializing in Bohemian glass, his love of music also found expression as the unpaid director of music at the Southwark THEATER. In 1811 the total collapse of the Austrian economy wiped out his remaining assets.

He turned to MUSIC as his profession and in 1815 became the salaried director of the orchestra of the theater in Pittsburgh. When the theater suffered financial reverses, Heinrich sought new fields in Kentucky, arriving in Lexington in late 1817. He almost immediately organized a concert that included works by Mozart, Haydn, and Beethoven's first symphony (*Sinfonia con Minuetto*), the first performance of a Beethoven symphony in the United States. This was quickly followed by a program in Frankfort of two musical farces. Then Heinrich retired to a log cabin near Bardstown, where he honed his violin skills. But soon, in January 1819, he moved as a guest of the Speed family to Farmington. Here he remained until at least the summer of 1820, devoting full time to composition.

Many of his works were dedicated to various members of the Speed family; others honored the estate: "Farmington March," "Visit to Farmington," and "Farewell to Farmington." Other compositions were "Hail to Kentucky" and "The Birthday of Washington," the latter written at the request of Farmington's owner, Judge John Speed. "The Minstrel's March, or Road to Kentucky" is a program piece describing Heinrich's travels from Philadelphia to Kentucky and Louisville. The program notes, printed at appropriate places on the score, include these for arrival at Louisville by boat: The Rapids, Standing in for Port, Casting Anchors, Landing and Cheers, and Sign of the Harp (apparently an inn). It was at the Speed estate, Heinrich noted, "where I first drew in my musical inspiration" (William T. Upton, *Anthony Philip Heinrich,* New York 1939, 44).

While a guest at Farmington, Heinrich presented what was undoubtedly Louisville's first concert. It was given on June 8, 1819, at SAMUEL DRAKE's Louisville Theatre on Jefferson St. between Third and FOURTH STREETS. More than twenty compositions and SONGS (many by Heinrich) were presented in what must have been a long evening. None of the presentations were of the quality of his Lexington concert, though some then well-known European composers were represented. One presentation was Heinrich's own variations on "Yankee Doodle," played on the violin by Heinrich. The *LOUISVILLE PUBLIC ADVERTISER* (June 12, 1819) found this a "specimen of his wonderful performance on the violin . . . in a style of excellence peculiarly his own."

Late in 1820 Heinrich left Louisville for Philadelphia, where he had been invited by Dr. HENRY MCMURTRIE to prepare a musical score for McMurtie's melodrama, *Child of the Mountain; Or, The Deserted Mother.* It was first presented on February 10, 1821. McMurtrie had in 1819 published the first history of Louisville, *Sketches of Louisville and Its Environs,* but returned to Philadelphia shortly after publication. He owed debts to his landlord and his printer. It is likely that Heinrich and McMurtrie had become acquainted in Louisville.

Heinrich apparently returned to Louisville but left permanently in 1823 to achieve fame on the East Coast as a composer and conductor. Music festivals on a grand scale were devoted to his music in New York, Boston, and Philadelphia, and even in London, Dresden, Prague, and Graz. In fact, the musical press of the time often called him "The Beethoven of America." Some of his compositions from *The Dawning of Music in Kentucky* were recorded in 1975 on a long-playing record by the Vanguard Recording Society.

See West T. Hill Jr., *The Theatre in Early Kentucky 1790–1820* (Lexington 1971); *Courier-Journal,* Oct. 21, 1951; William T. Upton, *Anthony Philip Heinrich: A Nineteenth Century Composer in America* (New York 1939); John J. Weisert, "The First Decade at Sam Drake's Louisville Theatre," *Filson Club History Quarterly,* 40 (Oct. 1965): 290–91.

George H. Yater

HENDERSON, JENNIE KATHERINE EDMONIA (b Jefferson County, Kentucky, ca. 1900; d Louisville, February 17, 1947). BLUES singer and evangelist. Between 1924 and 1926 she traveled to Chicago to make blues records for Paramount, OKeh, and Vocalion. Her accompanists included top JAZZ musicians such as Jelly Roll Morton, Tommy Ladnier, and Johnny Dodds. By 1928 she was teaching music and giving gospel concerts at the Griffith Conservatory of Music at 1412 W Chestnut St. in Louisville. By 1932 she had married and had become the Reverend Edmonia Buckner, pastor of the Church of the Living God at 1821 W Walnut St. (Muhammad Ali Blvd.). She is buried in Louisville Cemetery.

Brenda K. Bogert

HENNING, JAMES WILLIAMSON (b Anne Arundel County, Maryland, June 9, 1813; d Louisville, November 20, 1886). Real estate developer and investment banker. He was the son of Samuel and Elizabeth (Williamson) Henning. The family moved to the home of Elizabeth's brother, James Williamson, at ANCHORAGE in Jefferson County following the death of Samuel.

In 1836 James Henning went into business with EDWARD HOBBS, surveyor for the city of Louisville who had recently married Henning's sister Susan. As a surveyor and civil engineer, Henning is credited with making one of the early maps of Louisville. In 1851, in a partnership with JOSHUA FRY SPEED, husband of Henning's sister Fanny, he laid out a subdivision called Henning and Speed's Highland Addition (popularly known as the HIGHLANDS) in an area southeast of Louisville's core.

Speed, who had met ABRAHAM LINCOLN in Springfield, Illinois, is considered by many historians to have been Lincoln's closest friend. After he became president, Lincoln reportedly asked both Speed and Henning to serve in his cabinet, an honor that they both declined.

Henning had three children by his first wife, Mildred Maupin: Maria, Betty, and Fanny. By his second wife, Sarah Katherine Cowan, daughter of Samuel and Anne Woolfolk Cowan of SHELBY COUNTY, he had three children: James Williamson Junior, Samuel Cowan, and Lulie. Henning is buried in CAVE HILL CEMETERY.

See Temple Bodley and Samuel M. Wilson, *History of Kentucky* (Chicago and Louisville 1928); Charles P. Stanton, *Bluegrass Pioneers: A Chronicle of the Hunt and Morgan Families of*

Lexington, Kentucky (1996); George H. Yater, *Two Hundred Years at the Falls of the Ohio* (Louisville 1979).

R.R. Van Stockum Sr.

HENNING, SUE THORNTON (b Shelby County, Kentucky, August 14, 1866; d Washington, D.C., June 29, 1933). Sue Thornton Henning was a descendant of John and Ann (Polk) Allen of Frederick County, Virginia. On September 6, 1887, at the home of her mother, Bettie Allen Meriwether, in Shelbyville, she married James Williamson Henning Jr., a successful young Louisville financier and son of Joshua Fry Speed's business partner, James W. Henning Sr. During the period 1907–28 following the failure of her husband's brokerage firm in New York, Mrs. Henning returned to Allen Dale, her ancestral farm that had been in her family since 1795. Here, as owner and breeder, she established a prize-winning herd of registered Jersey cattle. In 1914 the farm produced the national grand champion Jersey bull. Under her direction, Allen Dale Farm became nationally and internationally renowned, and Henning became the first woman to serve on the board of the American Jersey Cattle Club. In 1909 Mrs. Henning's daughter Susanne, despite the adamant opposition of her mother, married Marquis Antoine de Charette, scion of a distinguished French military family. Before her death, Henning was dispossessed of her farm because of financial insolvency. She is buried in Grove Hill Cemetery in Shelbyville.

See R.R. Van Stockum Sr., *Kentucky and the Bourbons: The Story of Allen Dale Farm* (Louisville 1991).

R.R. Van Stockum Sr.

Sue Thornton Henning (right) with her mother, Bettie Meriwether, and daughter Susanne, c. 1908.

Henry Vogt Manufacturing Company, 222 South 12th Street, 1920s.

HENRY BAIN SAUCE. Created and served at the Pendennis Club, 218 W Muhammad Ali Boulevard. The recipe for the sauce, heralded as a "delightful concoction which seems to make even the finest cut of beef taste just a little better," is a closely guarded secret. It was named after its originator, an African American who was a forty-year employee of the club. He began work as an elevator operator in the 1880s and later became the head waiter of the club's dining room. Bain, who died on May 1, 1928, was also the uncle of the famed singer Roland Hays.

See "Centennial of the Pendennis Club" (Louisville 1981).

HENRY VOGT MACHINE CO. Henry Vogt was born in Louisville in 1856 to poor German immigrants. Shortly after becoming a journeyman machinist, he entered into business with Henry H. Sulzer in 1880 to form Sulzer-Vogt, a partnership with an office, machine shop, and foundry on E Main St.

Recognizing that an engineered proprietary product would have numerous advantages over a general machine shop, Sulzer and Vogt found early success in constructing hydraulic elevators. Sulzer died in 1892, and Vogt sold the elevator business to the Otis Elevator Co. seven years later. In 1902, Vogt constructed a new twenty-seven-acre plant just south of downtown at Tenth St. and Ormsby Ave. and opened the Henry Vogt Machine Co.

The modern facility allowed Vogt to explore the new process of manufacturing "artificial" ice. After learning of Edmond Carre's invention of the ammonia absorption refrigeration machine in France, which used steam to create refrigeration, Vogt applied Carre's principles, and later modifications by Carl von Linde of Germany, toward creating a new ice-producing device. This unique process replaced the expensive, noisy, and high-maintenance refrigeration compressor systems with cheaper and virtually trouble-free steam absorption machines. The large ice and cold-storage plants were the great "high-tech" products at the turn of the century and stimulated the growth and prosperity of the Henry Vogt Machine Co.

Requiring a heat source to power his absorption refrigeration machines, Vogt entered the boiler business by manufacturing gas, oil, and coal-fired boilers for his own company's use. As the business grew, it became one of the leading builders of industrial-size boilers. During World War II, the company dedicated a significant part of its daily business toward the production of boilers for ships. At its peak in 1942, Vogt was shipping one complete boiler a day to the Maritime Commission for use in its vessels.

Vogt was unable to find quality cast valves that did not leak ammonia for his early ice machines. This caused him to fabricate his own valves and propelled him into the forged-steel valve and fitting business. In 1917 he built a new forge shop with fifteen steam-driven forging hammers and a seven-floor machine shop to shape the forgings into finished valves, fittings, flanges, and unions.

As the company continued to grow, the production of ice dramatically changed from the days of Vogt's early experiments. The old absorption process evolved into the production of Tube-Ice®, which froze water inside of vertical tubes, then momentarily thawed the ice loose from the tubes and cut it into the familiar cylindrical shape with the hole in the center. Tube-Ice machines, along with plate ice machines, ranged in capacity from one thousand pounds to eighty tons per day. The machines supplied ice to national accounts such as the Walt Disney Co. and the Hyatt and Marriott Hotels.

As a result of restructuring and divestitures, Henry Vogt Machine Co. sold off various components of the company in 1996, including the valve and fitting division (to Edward Valve of Raleigh, North Carolina), the heat transfer division (to NEM), and the forge and die division (to Kentucky Forge) and formed the Vogt Industrial Commons on the Vogt plant site. This new enterprise, which leased nearly one million square feet of industrial and office space to a variety of tenants, managed the rental and support services. The company maintained control of the refrigeration and tube-ice divisions until 1998 when they were sold to Louisville-based Icelease Partners Ltd., one of the nation's largest lessors and distributors of commercial ice makers. Icelease incorporated the tube-ice division as Vogt Ice Inc.

Henry V. Heuser Sr.

HERMAN, WILLIAM JENNINGS BRYAN (b New Albany, Indiana, July 7, 1909; d West Palm Beach, Florida, September 5, 1992). Hall of Fame baseball player. Herman was one of the most consistent infielders of the 1930s and 1940s. During his Hall of Fame career with the Chicago Cubs and the Brooklyn Dodgers, Herman participated in ten All-Star games and was a member of four pennant-winning teams.

Herman was the next-to-youngest of ten children. His father was a machinist. His earliest experience with baseball did not portend his future as a Hall of Famer. He was not a member of the regular lineup for his New Albany High School baseball team, serving instead as a utility infielder. He was able to hone his skills as a player in Louisville by playing for a factory team at the veneer factory where he worked as well as in a church league where he pitched his club to a championship.

In 1928 Herman signed with the Louisville Colonels of the American Association for $250 per month. During the next few years, Herman played primarily for the Colonels, although he was farmed out to several other teams in different leagues. In 1931 he started his fourth minor-league season with Louisville but was called up by the Chicago Cubs near the end of the season, replacing player-manager Roger Hornsby at second base.

Herman played for the Cubs from 1931 until 1941. During that span he led National League second basemen a record seven times in putouts, also topping the league three times in assists. In 1932 as a starter, Herman tied for the league lead in games played. That year the Cubs reached the World Series against the Yankees, best remembered for Babe Ruth's "called shot" home run. Herman was on the 1935 Cubs World Series team, which lost to the Detroit Tigers. The Cubs also made it to the 1938 World Series, losing again to the Yankees in four games.

On May 6, 1941, Herman was traded to the Brooklyn Dodgers, joining the infield with Louisville-area Hall of Famer Pee Wee Reese and skipper Leo Durocher. With Herman at second the Dodgers won the pennant, taking on the Yankees in the World Series. Once again, Herman's club was on the losing end of the contest. In 1943 Herman batted .330, second in the league behind St. Louis's Stan Musial. During the 1944 and 1945 seasons, Herman served in the United States Navy in Honolulu, Hawaii. He returned to baseball in 1946, and, after a couple of trades, he was named the player-manager for the Pittsburgh Pirates. The day before the close of the 1947 regular season, Herman was fired from the team. He finished with a career batting average of .304.

During the next twenty years, Herman played with and coached numerous minor-league and professional teams. From 1952 until 1957 he coached for the Brooklyn Dodgers, which made four World Series appearances, including the 1955 championship. Herman also coached for the Boston Red Sox, managing the club for two seasons in the mid-1960s. He was elected to baseball's Hall of Fame in 1975 by the Veteran's Committee.

In 1927 Herman married Hazel Steproe. The couple had one child, Billy III, and divorced in 1960. He remarried in 1961. Although Herman kept ties in New Albany, where he owned partial interest in a paint factory, he moved to Palm Beach in 1956, where he remained until his death in 1992.

See Martin Appel and Burt Goldblatt, *Baseball's Best: The Hall of Fame Gallery* (New York 1977); *The Baseball Encyclopedia* (New York 1993).

HERMANY, CHARLES (b Lehigh County, Pennsylvania, October 9, 1830; d Louisville, January 18, 1908). Civil engineer. Charles Hermany, who served as the chief engineer of the Louisville Water Co. for nearly fifty years (1861 to 1908), was the son of Samuel and Salome Wannemacher Hermany. Young Hermany worked on the family farm but showed an early aptitude for mathematics. His aspirations turned to civil engineering. He was prepared for college in the Minerva Seminary in Easton, Pennsylvania, but family financial difficulties cut short his formal education. He returned to the family farm and also taught school but continued mathematics and engineering studies on his own. In 1853 he went to Cleveland, Ohio, and secured a post in the city's engineering department headed by Theodore Scowden, who recognized the unusual potential in his twenty-three-year-old assistant.

When Scowden came to Louisville in 1857 to design and supervise construction of the waterworks, he brought Hermany along as his principal assistant. Following completion of the work, Scowden resigned and Hermany succeeded him as chief engineer on January 1, 1861. He was to make a deep impression on the fledgling enterprise. Possessed of a keen mind and a fierce dedication to civil engineering, Hermany had to solve the early problems of the water system, and they were many. He was undoubtedly the one among the top officers who did most to shape the Louisville Water Co. into a viable, efficient concern.

As early as the 1870s Hermany was occupied with the problem of the sediment in the water pumped directly from the river. He initiated the long series of experiments that led to solving the problem and that has been adopted by all cities taking their water supply from muddy inland rivers. He designed and supervised construction of the Crescent Hill Reservoir, completed in 1879, and built the company's second pumping station also in 1879. He used his own labor force when private contractors turned down the job as too risky. He also had a hand in designing the huge steam-pumping engine installed in the new station. An operating model of the Leavitt-Hermany engine is on display at the Smithsonian Institution.

Hermany also found time to design and construct waterworks in Frankfort and Bowling Green, Kentucky, and Evansville, Indiana. He was a founder and first president in 1881 of the Louisville Engineers and Architects Club and served five successive terms. Experiments on filtering river water continued and were promising enough that work was begun on the Crescent Hill Filtration Plant in 1897 across Frankfort Ave. from the reservoir.

In 1900 Hermany turned seventy, an age when most men would have retired. He stayed on however, wanting to correct the unexpected problems that cropped up in the filtration process. In January 1908 he was scheduled to attain the crowning recognition of his professional career. He was to become president of the American Society of Civil Engineers, a rare honor for a self-taught individual. But early in the month he contracted pneumonia and died. He is buried in Cave Hill Cemetery. The nagging filtration problems were soon solved by others, but the sparkling clean water flowing to Louisville homes and businesses remains Hermany's triumph.

See George Yater, *Water Works: A History of the Louisville Water Company* (Louisville 1996); J. Stoddard Johnston, *Ed., Memorial History of Louisville* (Chicago 1896); *Louisville Times*, Jan. 18, 1908; *Courier-Journal*, Jan. 19, 1908.

George H. Yater

HERR HOUSES. An extraordinary group of houses exists within a three-mile radius in eastern Jefferson County, east of St. Matthews. The houses were built by the Rudy and Herr families and are listed in the National Register of Historic Places. The eight houses date from ca. 1790 to 1876 and are predominantly Federal I-style, with Greek Revival additions. All but one are brick, and many original outbuildings still exist. Many of the original families retained the houses into the twentieth century.

The house at 520 Old Stone Ln. is a stone and frame structure, built about 1790 with additions from 1810. It was built for Daniel Rudy when he married Mary Shively. He was the son of Revolutionary War hero Jacob Rudy, who came to the area in 1783.

The John Herr house, 726 Waterford Rd., was built ca. 1795 for Herr, an orphan who accompanied Jacob Rudy to Louisville and married his daughter, Elizabeth Susan.

The Edwards-Herr house, 4417 Westport Rd., was built ca. 1790 by Frederick Edwards, who married Mary Rudy, daughter of Jacob Rudy.

The Vulcan Rudy house, 4319 Westport Rd., was probably constructed about 1820 for Herr's daughter, Elizabeth, who married Rudy.

George Herr (1805–75), son of John Herr, built the house at 612 Rudy Ln. ca. 1825 when he married Sarah Simcoe, the daughter of his stepmother.

The Taylor-Herr-Oldham house, 1823 Ballard Mill Rd., was built in the early nineteenth century. John Herr acquired the house from ZACHARY TAYLOR's father.

The John Herr Jr. (1806–63)/Albert G. Herr (1840–99) house, 1705 Lynn Way, was built in 1830 on the foundations of an earlier house and enlarged in the Italianate style in 1876. It became known as Magnolia Stock Farm. John Herr Jr. married Susan Oldham. Albert married Mattie E. Guthrie in 1860. In April 1891 a tragedy occurred at the wedding of Albert Herr's daughter when twenty-six persons, including the bridegroom, died of food poisoning.

Richard S. Herr, son of George Herr, built the house at 260 Leland Court ca. 1857.

See Henry A. and Kate Ford, *History of the Ohio Falls Cities and Their Counties* (Cleveland 1882); Elizabeth F. Jones and Mary Jean Kinsman, *Jefferson County: Survey of Historic Sites in Kentucky* (Louisville 1981); Mary Cronan Oppel, *Herr-Rudy Houses, National Register of Historic Places Nomination Form* (Frankfort 1976).

Elizabeth Fitzpatrick "Penny" Jones

HERT, ALVIN TOBIAS (b Owensburg, Indiana, April 18, 1865; d Washington, D.C., June 7, 1921). Entrepreneur and political leader. The son of William and Isabel (Owen) Hert, he was educated in Owensburg's public school and ended his studies after graduating from the Bloomfield Academy. He began his business career as a traveling salesman in Indiana, working first for a Louisville shoe company and then selling cigars. Later, he opened a store in Brazil, Indiana. There Hert entered the political arena for the first time when he was elected mayor in 1895.

In August 1895 Hert was named warden of the Indiana Reformatory in Jeffersonville. He stayed until November 1902, when he resigned and moved to Louisville. Two years later, using money he had made in Indiana real estate deals, Hert founded the American Creosoting Co., with its first plant in Shirley, Indiana. The company grew to control fifteen other creosoting companies across the nation and had a governing interest in a Canadian firm. Hert was also active in other business venues. He was president of the Southern Motors Co., director of the NATIONAL BANK OF KENTUCKY, chairman of the American Tar Products Co. board of directors, and a trustee of the American Surety Co. of New York.

Hert also played a significant role in Republican politics. In 1916, he helped to manage the presidential campaign of Charles Evans Hughes, was a delegate to the national convention, and became the state's national committeeman. He headed the Kentucky delegation at the Republican Convention in Chicago and served as chair of the committee on arrangements.

In 1920 Hert was influential in securing the presidential nomination for Warren G. Harding and became a head adviser to Will H. Hays, Harding's presidential campaign manager. After Harding's election, Hert declined an ambassadorship and a position as the president's representative on the Government Reorganization Committee.

Hert married Sally Aley on November 20, 1893. The couple later purchased the historic SOLDIERS' RETREAT property. The Herts renamed the estate Hurstbourne Farms, and years later part of the property and the house became the site of the HURSTBOURNE Country Club. Mrs. Hert later became head of the GOP women's organization and gave the seconding speech for the nomination of Herbert Hoover in 1932.

Hert died suddenly of apoplexy, or a ruptured artery in the brain. He is buried in CAVE HILL CEMETERY.

HEYBURN BUILDING. Located at Fourth and BROADWAY in downtown Louisville, this local landmark, listed on the NATIONAL REGISTER OF HISTORIC PLACES, was one of a number of buildings constructed from 1900 to 1930 that furthered Broadway's transition from a posh residential area to a commercial and retail district. Its location at Broadway and Fourth St. helped to designate that location the "magic corner." Completed in 1928, the seventeen-story, Classical Revival–style skyscraper, owned by William R. Heyburn, president of BELKNAP Hardware and Manufacturing Co., was constructed on the site of the Avery mansion, which had become the home of the YMCA. The buff-colored brick and stone edifice was designed by the Chicago firm of Graham, Anderson, Probst, and White, and exhibited their penchant for using classical elements to adorn office buildings. The firm was also responsible for the design of the Belknap Hardware Building (1923) and the STARKS BUILDING addition (1926). Throughout its history, the Heyburn Building has had several different owners and undergone a number of renovations, one of the largest being a two-year project begun in 1983 that was financed through a $6 million city industrial-revenue bond issue. The building has served as a premier location for physicians, lawyers, and myriad businesses.

HICKMAN, JOHN JAMES (b Lexington, May 26, 1839; d Columbia, Missouri, April 29, 1902). Reformer. John James Hickman was to live in Louisville for about a decade beginning in 1867. He was born in Lexington, the son of James L. Hickman. In 1858 he married Lizzie Hollingsworth. Sometime before 1880 he moved to Missouri, where their two sons attended the state university.

Early in his life Hickman joined the Independent Order of Good Templars, a fraternal TEMPERANCE society. During the three years (1868–71) that Hickman led the Grand Lodge of Kentucky, its membership grew from fewer than three thousand to almost twenty-five thousand. Hickman headed the international Good Templar organization from 1874 to 1877 and again in 1879–81. He was renowned as a charismatic orator.

In the late 1860s and early 1870s, Louisville had been a Good Templar stronghold with as many as nine lodges. A succession of Louisville NEWSPAPERS such as the *Temperance Advocate* and the *Riverside News* served as official organs of the Grand Lodge. Louisville was the home of many Good Templar leaders such as Tim Needham, who practiced law from 1869 to 1878, and Green Clay Smith, pastor of the Twenty-second and Walnut Streets Baptist Church in the city during the 1880s.

At an international meeting held in Louisville in May 1876, a schism occurred out that lasted until 1887. Failing to get concessions intended to encourage African American membership, the British representatives fomented a secession. At the time of the 1876 meeting there was only a single Good Templar lodge in Louisville. That lodge closed in 1892.

The Good Templars were only one part of a growing movement that not only favored temperance, but PROHIBITION. Beginning at the local and state levels, it attracted men and women who became increasingly vocal in their denunciation of alcohol. In time localities and states did enact prohibition laws, but it was the federal government that saw to it that the Good Templars' goal of a sober society was reached with the passage of the Eighteenth Amendment. The thirteen-year period of Prohibition from 1920 to 1933 made the production and sale of alcoholic beverages illegal.

See John A. Garraty, ed., *American National Biography* (New York 1999); David M. Fahey, *Temperance and Racism: John Bull, Johnny Reb, and the Good Templars* (Lexington 1996); Tim Needham, *Good Templar Gem* (New York 1880), reprinted in Thomas F. Parker, *History of the Independent Order of Good Templars* (1882; revised edition, New York 1887).

David M. Fahey

HIGHLAND BAPTIST CHURCH. Located at Grinstead Dr. and Cherokee Rd. in the Highlands, the church held its first service May 7, 1893. The church's origins owe a great deal to GEORGE W. NORTON, banker and capitalist;

his brother WILLIAM F., an impresario and builder of the AMPHITHEATRE AUDITORIUM at FOURTH and Hill Streets as well as private banker and real estate entrepreneur; and George's three daughters, particularly Mrs. J.B. Marvin (formerly Juliette Norton). The two brothers, major benefactors of the SOUTHERN BAPTIST THEOLOGICAL SEMINARY, designated that some of their support was to be used for mission work. The building of the HIGHLAND BAPTIST CHURCH was based on a collaboration between the seminary professor in charge of mission work, Dr. Basil Manly, and Mrs. Marvin, who with her sisters, the Misses Lucie and Mattie Norton, provided the money to build the first church building.

While the stone church was being completed, prayer meetings were held at a private residence once a week, and a Sunday school was organized and conducted by theological students and members of the Ladies' Aid Society of the Highland Baptist Church, which had formed to support the new church. The Sunday school was held Sunday afternoon at the German Baptist Orphans' Home. Twenty-seven persons from five Louisville churches and one in Hopkinsville, Kentucky, became charter members of the church. In 1908 a Sunday school building was built behind the sanctuary. The church grew rapidly, and the sanctuary was replaced in 1915 with another larger stone sanctuary, this one in English Gothic style. Both this and the earlier building were constructed of stone from the Tucker quarry in JEFFERSONTOWN. A new education building was added on Cherokee Rd. in 1954.

Highland Baptist continued its missionary work by establishing four mission churches. The first was at Thirty-eighth and MARKET Streets in 1923 (now the Shawnee Baptist Church). The second was begun in 1937 and is now the Baxter Avenue Baptist Church. The third church, begun in 1940, is now the Vine Street Baptist Church, and the fourth mission was begun in 1960 and is now the BASHFORD MANOR Baptist Church. Highland Baptist has also contributed to foreign and domestic missions, has provided weekly devotion services to Parr's Rest Home and the Eastern Star Home in the HIGHLANDS, and tends toward moderate Baptist church policies.

Highland Park School, 205 East Adair Street, 1922.

HIGHLAND PARK. Neighborhood in southern Louisville roughly bounded by the CSX railroad tracks to the west, Farmington Ave. and the KENTUCKY FAIR AND EXPOSITION CENTER'S southern boundary to the north, the boundaries of the Exposition Center and LOUISVILLE INTERNATIONAL AIRPORT to the east, and Wabasso Ave. to the south. In 1889 the LOUISVILLE & NASHVILLE RAILROAD began expanding the switching yards in south Louisville. This prompted the Vance Land Corp., a subsidiary of the Highland Park Corp., to announce a "manufacturing suburb" in the area for the rail employees. Headed by T.C.H. Vance and Angus Allmond, the corporation procured a charter a year later for the town of Highland Park, named for its position on somewhat high ground, which included the neighborhoods of Beechmont and WILDER PARK.

In 1902, the area received another boost when the L&N announced plans to build car shops adjacent to the SOUTH LOUISVILLE yards. IRISH and AFRICAN AMERICAN rail workers from the LIMERICK neighborhood poured into the community with the promise of $125 lots, a park-like appearance, paved roads, transportation to the job site, and utilities such as sewers and gas lines. However, many of the promises were not kept. The neighborhood was labeled "an ugly duckling" as the parks were not developed, the dirt roads were impassable at times, and the sewers were not connected until 1917. This happened when the United States Army, worried about the soldiers' health at nearby CAMP ZACHARY TAYLOR, insisted on sewer installation.

These problems improved in 1922 when the city annexed the area after a five-year court battle that ended in the United States Supreme Court. Although Highland Park was predominantly populated by white railroad workers, a small African American community, known by locals as Buck Town as early as 1906, coexisted peacefully to the south of Saginaw Ave. in a three-square-block area.

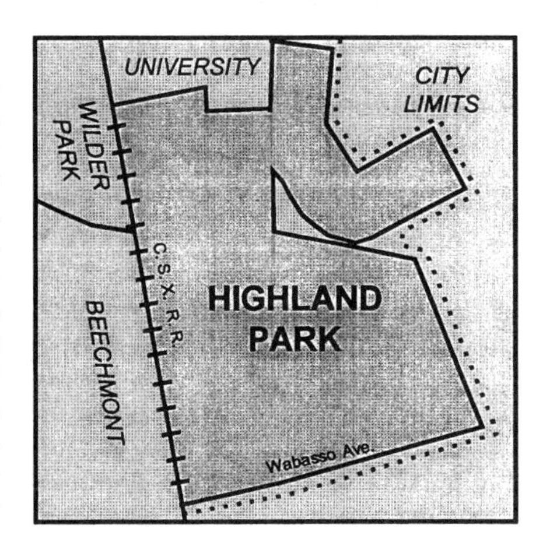

The entire community enjoyed prosperous times until the years following WORLD WAR II. Then the construction of the WATTERSON EXPRESSWAY, the transfer of commercial traffic from BOWMAN FIELD to Standiford Field (Louisville International Airport) in 1947, and the construction of the Fairgrounds in the early 1950s all caused the area to decline. With the expansion of Louisville International Airport in the late 1980s and early 1990s, much of the neighborhood was purchased by the city. Its residents were moved to other areas, and Highland Park ceased to be officially recognized as a Louisville neighborhood.

See *A Place in Time: The Story of Louisville's Neighborhoods* (Louisville 1989); *Louisville Survey: Central and South Report* (Louisville 1978).

HIGHLAND PRESBYTERIAN CHURCH. On May 15, 1882, twenty-five people gathered at the corner of Highland Ave. and E Broadway (now Cherokee Rd.) to meet with a committee appointed by the presbytery. It was unanimously resolved that the church organized there should be called the Highland Presbyterian Church of Louisville, Kentucky. This makes Highland Presbyterian the oldest church in the Highlands east of CAVE HILL CEMETERY. At the time it was organized, the setting was quite rural with few houses, each surrounded by plenty of land.

The history of Highland Presbyterian Church actually began in 1872 with the establishment of a Sunday school that met in the parlor of Mrs. Annie Cood's home at 904 Barret Ave. Weekly prayer meetings began in the fall of 1873 in the home of Mrs. John A. (Hattie N.) Larrabee, who lived on Baxter Ave. The Craycroft house was rented in 1874 for the purpose of housing the Highland Presbyterian Sabbath School, which opened with sixty-five students and nine teachers. The Sabbath School grew rapidly, but the Craycraft house was sold in 1876, making it necessary to find another facility. Joseph Gheens, one of the Sabbath School teachers and the first superintendent, purchased the site on which a frame chapel was erected during the summer of 1876. This chapel was built where the church now stands.

The early membership of Highland consisted of people coming from the two branches of the Presbyterian church, popularly known as Southern and Northern, which had split during the separation of 1861. The original church had been founded as a mission of College Street Church. In 1887, after steady growth, the frame chapel was moved to the rear of the lot, and construction of a new sanctuary was begun in front. In 1907, after several additions to increase seating and enlarge the Sunday school, adjoining land was purchased, and additional construction doubled the size of the facility. The Sunday school was remodeled and enlarged in 1916. Major renovation or construction projects were undertaken in subsequent years to expand or renovate facilities. The Walker-Nevin building was completed in 1960 to house the growing Sunday school and also to provide space for expanding the preschool weekday school.

Highland Presbyterian Church practiced involving itself strongly with the world around it. Beginning in 1983 it established a relationship with West Chestnut Baptist Church designed to proclaim the need for racial unity in the city. This led to yearly worship services shared between the two congregations and the yearly joint Court Education Project in the district courts in downtown Louisville, the Atkinson Elementary School Reading Project, and many other shared activities.

Beginning in 1990 the Kentucky Refugee Ministries established residence in the church and, at the peak of its work, brought over five hundred international refugees per year to the Louisville area, acclimating them to a new culture and lifestyle. Beginning in 1985 the church joined with the American Jewish Community in sponsoring a monthly dialogue between Jews and Presbyterians. Members of the church are highly dedicated to activities for the benefit of the community and include many business, political, and arts leaders.

Prominent pastors include Peter Pleune, William A. Benfield, Henry P. Mobley, and James O. Chatham. Traditionally the church has a strong music program, which has been led by the late Leon Rapier, among others.

HIGHLANDS. Neighborhood in eastern Louisville bounded by E BROADWAY to the north, Baxter Ave. to the east, Winter Ave. to the south, and Barret Ave. to the west. Originally owned by Col. WILLIAM PRESTON, the chief surveyor of Fincastle County, Virginia, the original Highlands land was inherited by his son, Maj. William Preston, upon the colonel's death in 1781.

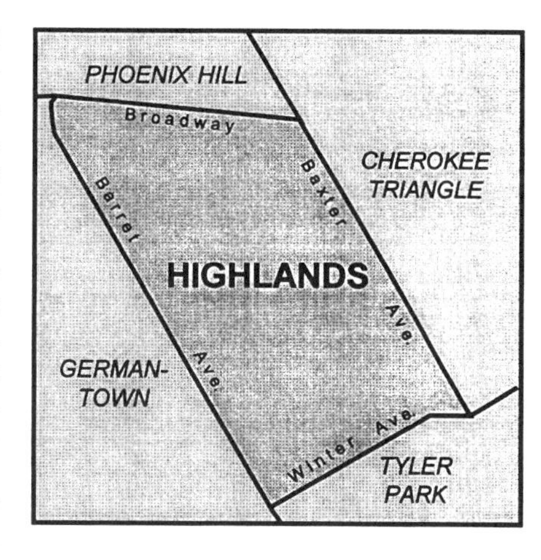

Major Preston and his wife, Caroline Hancock, moved onto the land in 1814 and established a plantation known as "The Briar Patch." After the Louisville and Bardstown Turnpike was constructed in 1819 in the area, the improved access persuaded citizens to move east of the south fork of BEARGRASS CREEK. This, combined with the 1848 opening of CAVE HILL CEMETERY, which also doubled as a park, induced further movement into the neighborhood.

The subdivision and development of residential communities began in earnest after the land passed into the hands of Major Preston's daughter, Susan Preston Christy. The area was also known as New Hamburg in the second half of the nineteenth century because of its heavily German population. The original Highlands continued to gain popularity with the extension of the streetcar line on Baxter Ave. to Highland Ave. in 1871 and the establishment of nearby Cherokee Park in 1891. By 1895 most of the building in the area was completed, containing a mixture of large Victorian ornamental houses alongside working-class SHOTGUN COTTAGES. Local landmarks include the VENCOR Hospital—formerly St. Anthony's Hospital, which was established in 1901 by a group of Franciscan sisters—and ACADEMY OF OUR LADY OF MERCY, an all-girl school established in 1885 by the Sisters of Mercy and located at its present site on E Broadway since 1901. Breckinridge Elementary School is located in the historic building at 1128 E Broadway that was once the site of Louisville Normal School.

HIGHLAND-DOUGLASS. Irregular-shaped neighborhood in eastern Louisville bounded by Speed Ave., Bardstown Rd., Park Boundary Rd., TAYLORSVILLE Rd., and the sixth-class city of Strathmoor Village. The core of this mixed residential and commercial neighborhood was originally assembled during the 1830s as the two-hundred-acre "Woodbourne" estate of Mississippi cotton planter Starks Fielding. The land was purchased by Western Union executive George Douglass in 1870 and then passed to his daughter, Mrs. S.R. Carter, upon his death. The home still stands, located be-

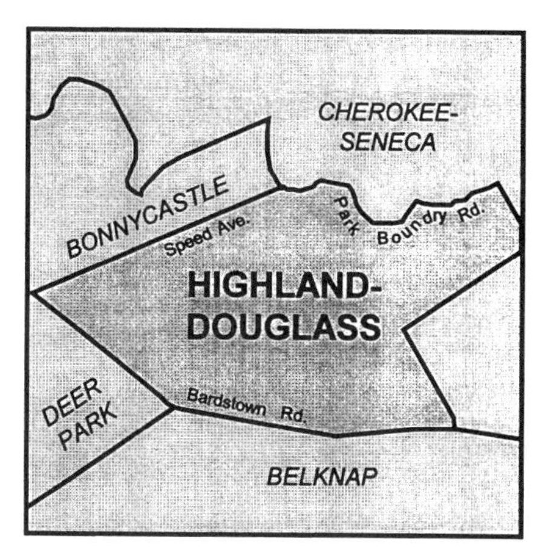

hind DOUGLASS BOULEVARD CHRISTIAN CHURCH. Development in the area exploded as the population continued to move toward the suburbs in the 1920s. The move was aided by the extension of the streetcar line, in 1912, out Bardstown Rd. to the present-day Douglass Loop. Dominated by the bordering Cherokee Park, the neighborhood also includes Douglass Park, a five-acre park located at Douglass Blvd. and Ellerbe Ave., a community center, and the First District police substation, in its interior.

HIKES FAMILY HOUSES. In southeastern Louisville a group of four homes, built between 1790 and 1830, is a legacy of the Hikes family, one of the earliest families in Jefferson County. The houses are now separated by residential developments, schools, and churches, but at one time only open farmland was between them. They are listed on the NATIONAL REGISTER OF HISTORIC PLACES.

Around 1790, former Revolutionary War officer George Hikes Sr. (1762–1832), a native of Lancaster, Pennsylvania, who migrated to Jefferson County from Ohio, purchased a four-hundred-acre tract of land on BEARGRASS CREEK in the triangular area that is today bounded by Bardstown Rd., Taylorsville Rd., and Hikes Ln. It was on this land that Hikes constructed one of the area's first saw and grist mills and a carding and fulling mill (used to thicken and cleanse cloth). He also built a stone home, known as the George Hikes Sr. House, at 3026 Hikes Ln., to which several additions were made. The original stone section was demolished in 1901 due to a faulty foundation. However, a three-bay, two-story stone portion, an early addition to the home, still remains. Hikes's son Andrew (1803–70) inherited the house, and it passed down in the family until 1960, when it was sold to the Saint Michael Eastern Orthodox Church to be used as a rectory.

As the sons of George Hikes Sr. reached adulthood, he gave each a parcel of his original tract of land. His oldest son, Jacob (1781–1857), received the portion of the land containing the fulling mill in 1820. He built a five-bay, two-story brick, center-hall, I-style house with Federal details at 2806 Meadow Dr. The house was inherited by Jacob's son John, and was the site of a horse farm and riding stable at the turn of the twentieth century. It remained in the family until 1972.

The George Hikes Jr. (b. 1788) House is at 2834 Hikes Ln. The two-story brick, Federal-style house built in 1824 has had several additions. A brick smokehouse is extant. The house remains in the family.

The third son of George Hikes Sr., John, built his home around 1830 at 4118 Taylorsville Rd. A Federal-style farmhouse, it is almost identical to the Jacob Hikes House, with the same elliptical fanlight at the entrance. John, who died in the 1870s, was married to Kitty Herr, daughter of John Herr.

See Carl E. Kramer, *Louisville Survey East* (Louisville 1980); Elizabeth F. Jones, "Hikes-Hunsinger House, National Register of Historic Places Nomination Form" (Frankfort 1975); Mary Cronan Oppel, "The Hikes Family Houses, National Register of Historic Places Nomination Form" (Frankfort 1978).

Elizabeth Fitzpatrick "Penny" Jones

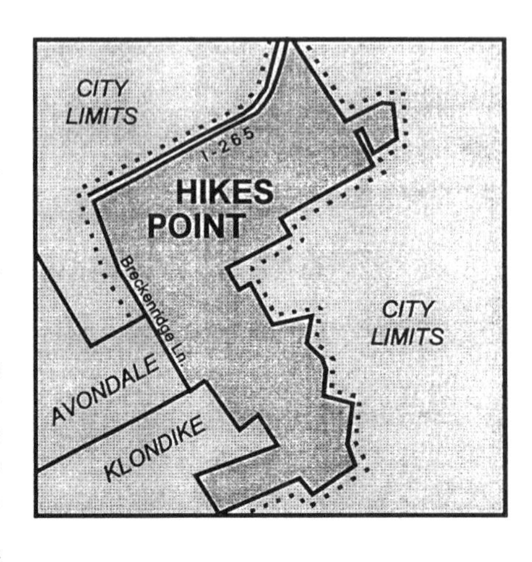

HIKES POINT. Neighborhood in eastern Louisville bounded by the WATTERSON EXPRESSWAY to the north, Breckenridge Ln. to the west, and an irregular boundary on the south and east following the city limits. The name comes from Revolutionary War veteran George Hikes, who settled in the area in 1791 on land sold to him by William Meriwether. Hikes built his own home with stone from a nearby quarry and dubbed the subsequent neighborhood Two Mile Town. As more people settled in the area, Hikes supported the community operation of a cloth industry and opened grist and saw mills that were used by people all over the region. In the early 1800s Hikes encouraged the building of schools and churches to increase development. Through the rest of the century, the Hikes family was responsible for growth and development in the area.

In the 1900s, several developers began to take interest in the potential for growth in the area, now officially named Hikes Point. These developers bought much of the land surrounding the old Hikes home, including present-day Melbourne Heights and land bordering Taylorsville Rd., Breckenridge Ln., Hikes Ln., and Stanton Dr. Despite investors' interests in the area, little development occurred until after World War II.

In 1946, Roy F. McMahan, the president of Louisville Tool and Die Co., purchased the Eberle farm at the corner of Taylorsville Rd. and Breckenridge Ln. After several residential buildings were in place, McMahan had the Louisville and Jefferson County Planning Commission rezone much of the area for commercial use. By 1954 McMahan had developed the subdivisions of Lincolnshire, Yorkshire, McMahan Village, and Sunset Terrace. The next year, residential development began to taper off. By 1960, McMahan had also developed two major shopping centers in the area, McMahan Plaza on Richland Ave. and Breckenridge Ln., and Hikes Point Plaza on Taylorsville Rd. and Breckenridge Ln. These streets became a major intersection in eastern Louisville and even earned the dubious distinction of the worst intersection in the state of Kentucky, according to one Louisville-Jefferson County Traffic Engineer.

The favorable site of residential neighborhoods combined with the worsening traffic conditions due to the heavy commercial areas induced the city and county governments to cooperate for the first time on a neighborhood improvement project for Hikes Point. They pledged two hundred thousand dollars in 1993 for a three-year project to beautify the area, including installing sidewalks, planting trees, and doing additional landscaping along Taylorsville Rd., Breckenridge Ln., and Hikes Ln.

See *Louisville Survey: East Report* (Louisville 1980).

HILL, MILDRED JANE (b Louisville, June 27, 1859; d Chicago, June 5, 1916). Composer, educator, pianist, and music historian. Mildred was the oldest of six children of the Reverend William Wallace and Martha (Smith) Hill. She received her general education at the Bellewood Female Seminary in ANCHORAGE, Kentucky, of which her father was named director at the beginning of the Civil War. Her musical studies in piano, theory, and composition were taken in Louisville and Chicago.

In 1893 she collaborated with her sister, PATTY SMITH HILL, on the publication of a volume of seventy-two children's SONGS, *Song Stories for the Kindergarten.* This songbook ran through more than twenty editions and was published in seven languages. The words to one song, "Good Morning to All (sometimes listed as "Good Morning to You")," were later changed by Patty Hill at a birthday party to "HAPPY BIRTHDAY TO YOU," which became one of the world's most popular songs. In addition, Hill published *Songs of Nature and Childhood*, with words by Annie E. Moore; a collection, *Seven Songs*; and about thirty-five separate songs. In 1896 she contributed to the *Memorial History of Louisville* a comprehensive chapter, "History of Music in Louisville," which was the only complete record of musical life in the city to that date.

In later life she developed heart disease and died of an attack at her brother's home in Chicago. She is buried in CAVE HILL CEMETERY.

See *Courier-Journal*, June 6, 1916, Feb. 15, 1948, May 1, 1962, Oct. 22, 1988; *Louisville Post*, June 16, 1916; Louis S. Schafer, "Birthday Tradition Result of 1924 Musical Theft," *Back Home in Kentucky* 17 (July/Aug. 1994): 23–25; Marion Adams, "Four Misses That Made a Hit," *Bluegrass Music News* 34, No. 3: 16–17.

Robert Bruce French

HILL, PATTY SMITH (b ANCHORAGE, Kentucky, March 27, 1868; d New York City, May 25, 1946). Educator. She was the daughter of the Reverend William Wallace Hill, a Presbyterian minister who began the Bellewood Female Seminary at Anchorage in 1861, and Martha Jane Smith Hill. Hill's early years were spent amid the security and serenity of Bellewood. When she was six, the family moved to Fulton, Missouri. After her father died in 1878, the Hills moved to Louisville. She attended public schools before entering the Louisville Collegiate Institute (not to be confused with the present Louisville Collegiate School) in 1882. While at Collegiate, Hill was exposed to new theories on education. She became particularly interested in primary age schoolchildren, which resulted in her becoming an edu-

Patty Smith Hill, 1905.

cator. Patty was one of six to graduate from the first kindergarten training school in Louisville.

In 1887 a group of prominent Louisville women established the Free Kindergarten Association, and by the middle of the 1890s the association's ten kindergartens were directed by Hill. She believed in individual creative play within a stimulating environment and used music, poetry, stories, and plays as an integral part of her curriculum. In 1893, she and her sister Mildred published *Song Stories for Sunday School*, which included "Good Morning to You (sometimes listed as "Good Morning to All")." The tune was later amended to the universal "HAPPY BIRTHDAY TO YOU."

In 1900 Hill spoke before the Louisville Education Association on her theories of education through play. By then, though criticized, Hill's ideas were of interest to educators all over the world. In 1905 Dr. James Russell, the dean of Teacher's College at Columbia University, invited her to present a series of lectures. Three days after her final address she was asked to return for a semester. Hill, convincing Dean Russell of the need for a demonstration kindergarten, left Louisville to begin the Speyer School Experimental Playroom (forerunner of the Horace Mann Kindergarten). By the time the term was over, she agreed to be a permanent faculty member. In 1929, she received an honorary doctor of letters degree from Columbia University for her work in early education. She retired in 1936. Her portrait hangs in the halls of Columbia's Teachers College. She is buried in CAVE HILL CEMETERY.

See Frances Farley Gwinn, "Patty Smith Hill: Louisville's Contribution to Education," *Filson Club History Quarterly* 31 (July 1957): 203–27.

Laurie A. Birnsteel

HILLERICH, JOHN ANDREW "BUD" (b Louisville, October 15, 1866; d Chicago, November 28, 1946). BASEBALL bat innovator. Born to J. Frederick and Ella (Ward) Hillerich, he produced the first LOUISVILLE SLUGGER baseball bat in 1884. As an amateur baseball player, the young Hillerich made bats for himself and his teammates.

There are several stories of the origins of the first Louisville Slugger bat, but the younger Hillerich was most certainly involved in getting his father to make the company's signature item. According to company legend, the first bat was turned by Bud for PETE BROWNING in 1884. On a spring afternoon Hillerich, then seventeen, witnessed Browning break his favorite bat. Bud offered to make a bat for his hero, and Browning accepted. After the young woodshop apprentice lathed a quality specimen, according to the story, Browning got three hits with it in the next game.

The company's version of the story has been subject to challenges from baseball scholars for many years. Some claim that Hillerich did not make the first bat; his father did. That bat launched the new line of business for the company after Bud showed it to some professional players who requested that Bud's father, J. Fred Hillerich, make more bats for the team. As word of mouth spread about the quality bats, other teams began sending in requests. Another story, which has been given credence by no less than Bud Hillerich himself, suggests that the first Louisville Slugger was made for a player from a visiting team—Arlie Latham of the St. Louis Browns, who found himself in Louisville without a good piece of lumber and just happened to drop into a wood shop near his hotel. The origins of the bat continue to generate controversy, although most students of the game are convinced of the important role Bud played in orienting the company toward bat-making.

Bud Hillerich continued to improve the manufacturing processes of the new bat business, inventing a centering device for a lathe, and an automatic sander. In 1897 he became a partner with his father, and the firm became J.F. Hillerich & Son. In 1911 Frank W. Bradsby of Simmons Hardware in St. Louis joined the firm and took over the sales end of the business. Bradsby became a full partner in 1916, and the name of the company was changed to HILLERICH & BRADSBY CO.

Hillerich continued to be a strong influence on the company and the sporting goods industry until his death in 1946. He married Rose Ratterman, and the couple had two sons, Ward and John Andrew Junior, and one daughter, Cletus. Hillerich died in Chicago on the way to professional baseball meetings in Los Angeles. He is buried in CAVE HILL CEMETERY.

Bill Williams

HILLERICH & BRADSBY COMPANY. The BASEBALL bat called the LOUISVILLE SLUGGER is well known throughout much of the world, and Hillerich & Bradsby Co., maker of the bat, has a long and eventful history in Louisville.

In the late 1830s, J. Frederick Hillerich emigrated with his family from Baden-Baden, Germany, to Baltimore, Maryland. After a short while they moved to Louisville, where he started a woodworking shop in 1856. Two of his sons, Adam and John Andrew "Bud," were born in the United States and would later join their father in his business. By 1864 "J.F. Hillerich, Job Turning" was in operation at Clay St. It filled orders for businesses by custom-turning everything from balusters to bedposts.

The firm continued to thrive, and by 1875 the little woodworking shop had moved to First St. near MARKET ST. It had from fifteen to twenty employees. In 1880 BUD HILLERICH, who was an amateur baseball player, became an apprentice in his father's shop. Young Bud made his own baseball bats and bats for several of his teammates, but, according to company legend, the most important bat was turned in 1884. The story goes that in early spring Bud took the day off from work to watch Louisville's professional baseball team of the American Association play a home game. During that game, Pete "The Old Gladiator" Browning broke his favorite bat, and the young Hillerich brought Browning down to the woodworking shop after the game and turned a special custom-made bat for him out of a piece of white ash. Browning got three hits the next day.

The story's credibility has been questioned. Other versions claim that the first bat was turned in 1883 or 1884 for Arlie Latham, a third baseman with the American Association St. Louis Browns, when Latham was caught without a stick during a stand in Louisville. This version was supported by a 1942 letter by the turner of that first bat, Bud Hillerich. Another story, which predates all others, claims that the Louisville Slugger was born after Bud showed the bat his father made him to some Louisville players, including future star Gus Weyhing. The players were so enamored with the bat they asked Bud's father, J. Fred Hillerich, to make some for the team. Word of the quality of the bats spread and soon other teams were requesting their own. The debate over the origins of the first bat continues to generate controversy among baseball enthusiasts.

While the company had enjoyed success selling a patented swinging butter churn licensed from W.H. Curtice of Eminence, Kentucky, the baseball bat business started to grow. By 1890 Simmons Hardware of St. Louis was one of the prime customers for baseball bats. The bat was first known as the Falls City Slugger, but the brand name was changed to Louisville Slugger, which was registered as a trademark with the U.S. in 1894.

Bud Hillerich became a partner with his father in 1897, when the name of the firm was changed to J.F. Hillerich & Son. By 1899 the plant needed to expand even more, and property was purchased at the corner of Preston and Jacob Streets. This began a process of revitalization of the new factory, and a new plant sprang up in 1901. This new facility eventually encompassed the entire block bounded by Preston, Jacob (Finzer St.), and Jackson Streets.

The success of the growing bat company was enhanced beyond any expectations in 1905 when Honus "The Flying Dutchman" Wagner, a player for the Pittsburgh Pirates who had formerly played in Louisville, signed a contract as the first player ever to endorse a bat. His autograph was also the first ever to be used on a bat.

In 1911 Frank Bradsby, a successful salesman for Simmons Hardware, joined J.F. Hillerich and Son. He brought expertise and drive to the company, along with the game of GOLF. In 1916 he was made a full partner, and the company name was changed, for the last time, to Hillerich & Bradsby Co. The firm also began producing golf clubs that year.

The firm produced one million bats in a year for the first time in 1923. The success was marred the next year by the death of J. Frederick Hillerich.

Packing Louisville Slugger bats at the Hillerich & Bradsby Company.

A new golf club factory was built in 1925, and the corporate offices were moved to the Finzer and Jackson Streets location. This new golf club factory gave birth to the PowerBilt golf club brand in 1933. The Flood of 1937 did significant damage to the factory and offices on Finzer St. Working almost nonstop for weeks to repair the factory, Frank Bradsby became a physically broken man. His efforts during that terrible flood are believed to have led to his death that year.

Hillerich & Bradsby Co. served its country during World War II by producing carbine stocks, tank pins, and billy clubs for the armed forces. It also continued to make baseball and softball bats for the troops. Bud Hillerich, the maker of the first Louisville Slugger baseball bat, died in 1946. His son Ward took over. But after only three years as president, Ward died in 1949. His brother, John Andrew Hillerich Jr., succeeded him.

In 1954 the company purchased Larimer & Norton Inc., a lumber company in Moscow, Pennsylvania, and created its own timber division. In 1966 it purchased Wally Enterprises in Wallaceburg, Ontario, Canada, a manufacturer of ice hockey sticks. The new hockey sticks were called Louisville Slugger, but the name was changed to Louisville Hockey in the 1980s. The firm moved its corporate headquarters to the Portland Federal Building at 200 W Broadway in 1968. The following year John Hillerich Jr. died. He was succeeded by his son, John Andrew Hillerich III.

The company produced its first aluminum bat in 1970, and in 1978 it purchased the Alcoa Aluminum plant in Santa Fe Springs, California. Making almost 7 million wood bats and 750,000 golf clubs per year, the company, for the first time since 1903, began to look around for new facilities. Between 1972 and 1974, the firm moved to its Slugger Park manufacturing facility in Jeffersonville, Indiana. In 1984 the firm celebrated its one-hundredth anniversary. Declining sales in both wood bats and golf clubs led to its move back to Louisville in 1995. A new complex housing corporate offices, a bat factory, a golf club factory, and a new museum was built on W Main St. and occupied in 1996. In July of that year, the Louisville Slugger Museum officially opened on Eighth and Main Streets. A huge baseball bat stands adjacent to the building. The bat is 120 feet tall, made entirely of steel, and weighs 68,000 pounds. It resembles an R43 model baseball bat, the same model that Babe Ruth used. In July 1998 a seventeen-ton limestone statue of a baseball glove and ball was added to the museum's atrium. In the museum's first year it attracted more than 230,000 visitors.

See Philip Von Borries, *Louisville Diamonds: The Louisville Major-League Reader, 1876–1899* (Paducah, Ky., 1996); Philip Von Borries, *Legends of Louisville: Major-League Baseball in Louisville 1876–1899* (West Bloomfield, Mich., 1993).

Bill Williams

HILLVIEW. Fourth-class city in northern Bullitt County just across the southern Jefferson County line along U.S. 61 (Preston Hwy.). Although the area was originally used as farmland, it began attracting new residents in 1954 after the completion of the Kentucky Turnpike, which connected Bullitt County with Louisville. Between 1960 and 1970, Bullitt County's population, which grew at a state-high rate of 66 percent, was propelled by the 103 percent growth rate in the northern part of the county due to the platting of the Overdale, Lone Acres, and Maryville subdivisions.

Maryville, named for the wife and daughter of developer John A. Walser, was begun in 1960. It provided the core for the city with approximately twenty-four hundred new homes. In 1972 residents grew frustrated with the low funding being supplied by the county government for public services and began to push for incorporation.

Two years later, the sixth-class town of Hillview, which maintained the name of an existing subdivision, was incorporated. After an effort to disband the area failed in 1976, the town continued to grow and reached the level of a fifth-class city. This was followed in 1978 by another reclassification as a fourth-class city. By the 1980s, Hillview was the county's largest town. It continued its expansion in 1986 with further annexations and the opening of the Brooks Hill Rd. exit off nearby Interstate 65, which allowed the town to begin attracting commercial businesses.

The population of Hillview was 7,124 in 1980, 6,119 in 1990, and 5,815 in 1996.

See *A Place in Time: The Story of Louisville's Neighborhoods* (Louisville 1989).

HISTORIC PRESERVATION. The historic preservation movement in Louisville and Jefferson County mirrored the national movement to preserve the tangible remnants of our national and local past. During the nineteenth century, private efforts had been organized to preserve the homes of the founding fathers of the United States. Other communities had worked to preserve the monuments of their local pioneer past.

The National Trust for Historic Preservation was chartered by Congress in 1949 to foster historic preservation as a national value. That same year Congress authorized the Urban Renewal program of categorical grants to local communities to eliminate slums and blight. As most of the slum conditions and blight were in older urban areas, conflict between these programs was assured.

The local and national preservation movement initially concentrated on preservation of individual sites with patriotic appeal or, for aesthetic reasons, buildings of architectural merit. In Louisville Barry Bingham Sr. and Judge Macauley Smith joined forces to purchase the Speed family home, Farmington, in 1959. They formed the Historic Homes Foundation Inc. to manage the property. The Commonwealth of Kentucky and Jefferson County Fiscal Court partnered in 1961 to purchase Locust Grove, the final home of Louisville founder Gen. George Rogers Clark. The home was opened to the public in 1964, with full ownership having been transferred to Jefferson County Fiscal Court. The county entered into a long-term agreement with Historic Homes Foundation Inc. to manage the property.

Through several decades of economic decline, significant clusters of Louisville's Main St. cast-iron and limestone storefronts were just left alone. Several blocks of similar structures were torn down with little public concern in the mid-sixties to make way for the Riverfront Plaza/Belvedere and new skyscraper banks, but recognition of the value of Main St. real estate began to emerge in response to the successful projects of pioneering investors.

Jasper Ward moved his architectural office, and Cornelius Hubbuch and Fred Burdorf moved their interior design firms to buildings they renovated on Main St.; Actors Theatre prospered in the former Illinois Central Railroad Station at Seventh St. and the Ohio River; Paul O'Brien opened the Normandy Inn Restaurant across Seventh St.; Preservation Alliance moved its headquarters to 712 W Main St.; and others followed. The West Main Street Historic District was listed on the National Register of Historic Places in 1974 and within a year became the city's second local preservation district.

A boost in development activity was generated by the July 1977 opening of the Natural History Museum (Louisville Science Center) in the old Carter Dry Goods Building at 727 W Main St. The project's financial feasibility was secured by the city's lease of the upper floors for its development offices. The pro-preservation message thus delivered by the city was important, but the dramatic increase in pedestrian activity on the street had an equally beneficial effect.

The first seeds of interest in neighborhood historic preservation were planted in 1955 by *Louisville Times* reporter John Rogers's series on Louisville neighborhoods. The series was so well received that the articles were reprinted as a booklet.

By the early 1960s, the St. James Court Association was already mature, but the architecture of the surrounding area—later to become the hotbed of historic preservation activity—was largely overlooked. The older neighborhoods closer to the Ohio River had much-used names: Butchertown and Smoketown on the east and Portland and Limerick on the west.

The Urban Renewal and Community Development Agency was established in 1962. In quick succession, east and west downtown projects were begun, followed by the Riverfront Project in 1964 and Old Louisville south of Hill St. in 1965, with a second phase in 1967. These massive clearance and redevelopment projects were undertaken between 1954 and 1963, while construction of Interstate 65 cut a swath through the east side of the Central Business District. When urban renewal became a concentrated, visible reality, citizen reaction was largely negative. Excepting the Riverfront Plaza/Belvedere and office towers, new development in the resulting voids did little to improve opinion. Subsequent historic preservation achievements and vigorous architectural criticism owe much to the collective dismay experienced by local citizenry. Significantly, there were no new urban renewal projects for twelve years, and some of the most ardent historic preservation activists came from the ranks of former urban renewal staff, namely Herbert Fink and Katie Miller Kamin.

University of Louisville academics saw the carnage coming and documented what was about to be lost. Walter Creese and Robert Doherty did a late 1950s photographic survey of downtown when it still had single-family residences, and of north Old Louisville when it was still largely intact. The survey was limited in scope but well devised and served as a solid basis for later work. In 1960 Theodore Brown and Margaret Bridwell researched and photographed Old Louisville, publishing a handsome booklet of their joint work.

A handful of Old Louisville homeowners kept their property up and stuck it out through the hard times, but the earliest investor rehabilitation recorded was that of Eli Brown III, who started in 1961 on the west end of Belgravia Ct. Interior designer Bob Smith and rehabilitation contractor Ernie VonKannel were also involved in many early restorations there and nearby on Third and Fourth Streets.

In 1966 Congress passed the National Historic Preservation Act (NHPA). This first major federal historic preservation mandate established the National Register of Historic Places to recognize property with local as well as national significance. The survey and nomination process was designed to be conducted at the local level by State Historic Preservation Officers (SHPO) appointed by governors to administer a review process and make qualifying nominations to the Keeper of the National Register, a position in the National Park Service. The legislation also created the President's Advisory Council on Historic Preservation to provide guidance to federal agencies concerning the impact of their actions on property listed on the National Register. The program was paid for through annual appropriations to the states from the National Historic Preservation Fund. In the same session of Congress, the Department of Transportation implemented Section 4F, a policy to preserve natural and man-made sites; and the Demonstration Cities Act allowed HUD to use funds to rehabilitate existing homes, rather than demolish and build new construction.

Ida Lee Willis, widow of former governor Simeon Willis (1943–47) and executive director of the Kentucky Heritage Commission (now Council), was Kentucky's first SHPO. Assisting her with critical early survey and nomination work were architectural historian Walter Langsam and historian Charles Parrish, both Louisvillians. The NHPA was passed with the idea that a national survey would be completed in ten years. Understanding the enormous task of identifying all eligible Kentucky property, Mrs. Willis recruited a network of volunteer county representatives.

Recognizing the increasing deterioration and loss of population surrounding them, a coalition of downtown, mostly Old Louisville, religious and educational institutions formed the Neighborhood Development Corp. (NDC) in 1967. Its goal was to reverse the neighborhood's post–World War II decline. Longtime resident Mae Salyers became the organization's first executive director. She developed a partnership with Hal Richards, executive director of New Directions, which, in effect, became the hammer-and-nails arm of NDC. In keeping with their charitable purposes, the partnership renovated approximately fifteen buildings within a few years' time, mostly for first-time homebuyers and low- to moderate-income residents.

NDC recognized early that the neighborhood needed to be organized for effective advocacy. Salyers recruited a network of block captains to act as watchdogs for zoning and land-use violations and to serve as conduits for complaints about vacant property and unsatisfactory city services. When the network began to have a life of its own, it was spun off as the Old Louisville Neighborhood Council. In turn, the council spun off the Old Louisville Information Center, incorporated to receive charitable contributions.

In the early years of neighborhood turnaround, few real estate brokers and fewer lending institutions showed interest in Old Louisville. Buddy Cohen, realtor, was among the first to be convinced of the value of the neighborhood, and he became a force for positive change.

While renovation fever was taking hold in Old Louisville, James Segrest was working for the Louisville and Jefferson County Planning Commission on a neighborhood plan and downzoning proposal for Butchertown. Soon he took a personal interest in the neighborhood by buying and rehabilitating several houses himself and then founding Butchertown Inc. to do more. Butchertown Inc. later spun off Butchertown Neighborhood Government so that the former could concentrate exclusively on housing rehabilitation.

The Cherokee Triangle Association was formed to preserve the integrity of the well-mannered historic property on Cherokee Rd. Interior designer Donald Allen and real estate broker Edward Lang were resident property owners and early and effective advocates for neighborhood planning and downzoning to encourage single-family rehabilitation and occupancy. They were also strong supporters of local legislation to protect historic property through regulation of exterior changes. The Cherokee Triangle was to become the city's third preservation district.

Working toward preservation of the Cherokee Triangle included the 1970 formation of the Citizens Task Force on Zoning. The task force comprised a number of prominent residents, among them Helen Abell and Barry Bingham Sr., and included a determined and vocal coalition of other civic leaders, politicians, preservation-minded architects, real estate professionals, and neighborhood activists. The group was chaired by Kathleen Sloane, wife of Harvey Sloane, who was to become mayor in November 1973 (following a campaign whose chief themes were urban revitalization, housing rehabilitation, and neighborhood empowerment). Research and technical assistance were provided to the task force by member Donald Ridings, executive director of the Planning Commission, and his staff.

Increasingly, the federal government has mandated regional planning before federal money is spent. The first such local agency was the Falls of the Ohio Metropolitan Council of Governments. That agency funded a survey of historic property by Walter Langsam, published in 1971 as the *Metropolitan Preservation Plan.* Indiana counties across the Ohio River were added to the local Standard METROPOLITAN STATISTICAL AREA, and the agency was renamed the Kentuckiana Regional Planning and Development Agency (KIPDA).

In 1972 the Citizens Metropolitan Planning Council (CMPC) chairman was architect John Cullinane, later to become the first executive director of Preservation Alliance of Louisville and Jefferson County. Preservation Alliance was incorporated in October 1972 to coordinate private-sector forces and to teach, advocate, and demonstrate the value of historic preservation. Ann Hassett, CMPC's newsletter editor, became assistant director of Preservation Alliance and later the first executive director of the Historic Landmarks and Preservation Districts Commission.

In April 1973 the Louisville Landmarks Commission was established under HOME RULE authority, finally raising historic preservation to the level of public policy. The commission's job was to identify historically and architecturally significant property and to protect it through designation of qualifying districts and landmarks, with subsequent regulation of exterior changes. Frank Rankin was the agency's charter chairman.

Almost before the ink was dry on the June 1974 report designating Old Louisville as the Landmarks Commission's first preservation district, the WOMAN'S CLUB OF LOUISVILLE at 1320 S Fourth St. applied to demolish three neighboring buildings it owned at the corner of Fourth and Park for a "model parking garden." A controversy followed. The houses were purchased by the City of Louisville through a condemnation action and transferred to new owners for rehabilitation.

The Housing and Community Development Act of 1974 ended the federal categorical grants for urban renewal and instituted the Community Development Block Grant Program. Entitled communities were allowed to decide for themselves how the federal money should be spent, but planning and public comment were required more than ever. City government responded to the decision-making challenge by forming mostly volunteer committees. They included economic development, PARKS and recreation, housing rehabilitation, conservation and preservation, social services, and environmental programs. At first, the committees worked separately to assess and set priorities in their respective areas, but then they were asked to come together to slug out details of the 1975 application for CDBG funds. The process worked; consensus was reached.

The benefit to Louisville's older neighborhoods was substantial. Housing rehabilitation proposals were approved, along with improvements to nearby parks. A citywide survey of historic property was funded through the Landmarks Commission. The Louisville Community Design Center, under the direction of architect Ronald Gascoyne, was funded to help affected neighborhoods plan and implement housing rehabilitation and other projects. Established neighborhood organizations received money to hire staff.

The city's Neighborhood Development Office launched an eventually successful effort to identify every square inch of the city as being within some neighborhood's boundaries. Notable was the pioneering work of Stan Esterle, director of the HIGHLANDS COMMUNITY MINISTRIES, who orchestrated a self-identification process for the eastern neighborhoods.

In 1976 Congress passed a Tax Reform Act that made historic building rehabilitation financially attractive and viable. This incentive brought renewed interest to the buildings of downtown Louisville.

The first survey of historic property in Jefferson County was compiled in 1977, funded by the state historic preservation office. This survey was the first comprehensive documentation of historically significant properties outside the city of Louisville. County Judge/Executive MITCH MCCONNELL and his wife, Sherrill Redmon McConnell, initiated preservation activity in Jefferson County that led to the establishment in 1979 by Jefferson County Fiscal Court of the Jefferson County Historic Landmarks and Preservation Districts Commission. Bruce Yenawine was appointed its first chairman. Elizabeth F. "Penny" Jones, former research director at the Louisville Landmarks Commission, was appointed director; and Mary Jean Kinsman, research assistant at the city Landmarks Commission, moved to the county staff. Its mission was to identify historically and architecturally significant property in the unincorporated areas of Jefferson County and in the incorporated small cities. It offered protection to those properties through designation of historic districts and landmarks and regulation of exterior changes.

Louisville and Jefferson County were leaders in the national preservation movement in the 1970s and 1980s, hosting the annual conference of the National Trust for Historic Preservation in 1982. Local players in the preservation movement have expanded toward the end of this century. They include RIVER FIELDS INC., a riverwatch group; the Louisville and Jefferson County African American Heritage Committee; Historic Homes Foundation Inc.; and the Louisville Historical League.

See William Murtaugh, *Keeping Time: The History and Theory of Preservation in America* (Pittstown, N.J., 1988); "Special Report: Preservation/Redevelopment," *Louisville* 31 (Feb. 1980): 30–59; Leslee F. Keys, ed., *Historic Jefferson County* (Louisville 1992).

Ann S. Hassett
Donna M. Neary

HISTORIC PRESERVATION IN SOUTHERN INDIANA. The roots of historic preservation in southern Indiana vary from community to community and until the mid-1970s reflected efforts to preserve specific structures as memorials or museums. CORYDON and Harrison County have the longest preservation tradition, dating to 1917 when the Indiana General Assembly voted to purchase the old State Capitol as a state memorial. The structure was restored in 1929 and opened to the public in 1930. In 1938 the federal WORKS PROGRESS ADMINISTRATION encased the trunk of the Constitution Elm in a sandstone monument to commemorate the drafting of Indiana's first Constitution in 1816. Meanwhile, the Hoosier Elm Chapter of the Daughters of the American Revolution (DAR) bought the home of Col. Thomas L. Posey and opened it as a museum in 1925.

NEW ALBANY and Floyd County's preservation movement began in 1922 when the Piankeshaw Chapter of the Daughters of the American Revolution purchased the home of New Albany founder Joel Scribner, built in 1814, and restored it for use as its headquarters. In 1946 New Albany attorney John A. Cody and his wife, Bebe Cody, revived the Floyd County Historical Society. In 1964 veneer manufacturer Richard Stem led the organization of Historic New Albany Inc., which purchased the CULBERTSON MANSION for twenty-five thousand dollars to prevent its demolition for a service station. The Indiana Department of Natural Resources acquired the structure in 1976 and made it a state memorial. In 1969 the New Albany–Floyd County Public Library occupied new quarters; the original structure, a 1903 gift from Andrew Carnegie, reopened as the Floyd County Museum in 1971.

In Clark County the movement dates to 1958 when Loretta Howard established the HOWARD STEAMBOAT MUSEUM in the Romanesque Revival mansion built in the 1890s by her father-in-law, Edmonds J. Howard, son of James Howard, founder of Jeffersonville's Howard Shipyard.

The preservation initiatives of the 1960s and early 1970s in New Albany and Jeffersonville paralleled an even stronger movement in Louisville, which prompted preparation of *Preservation: Metropolitan Preservation Plan* by the Falls of the Ohio Metropolitan Council of Governments in May 1973. This document identified fifty-six nationally, regionally, or locally significant structures and districts in New Albany and Floyd County and thirty-six in Jeffersonville and Clark County. Written by UNIVERSITY OF LOUISVILLE architectural historian Walter E. Langsam, it provided a political justification and a sound professional rationale for long-term preservation planning and an impetus to move beyond preservation for museums and other not-for-profit uses to continuing and adaptive use for residential and commercial purposes.

With publication of the *Metropolitan Preservation Plan*, preservation gained momentum in both Floyd and Clark Counties. In 1974 local preservation advocates founded Main Street Preservation Association Inc. to preserve the historic homes of "Mansion Row" along E Main and E MARKET STREETS in New Albany and to educate the community about the values of historic preservation. The same year, the Culbertson mansion was listed on the NATIONAL REGISTER OF HISTORIC PLACES. Two years later, the Indiana Department of Natural Resources, through its Division of Historic Preservation and Archaeology (DHPA) and Historic Landmarks Foundation of Indiana (HLFI) published the *Indiana Historic Sites and Structures Inventory: Floyd County Interim Report*, which identified nearly five hundred historically significant buildings, either scattered structures or in districts in New Albany and Georgetown. By the end of 1982 three more structures, including the Scribner house, had been listed on the National Register. Mansion Row was added in 1983, and three more structures had followed by 1996.

The city of New Albany officially recognized the importance of preserving its historic resources in 1986 when the City Council adopted a Local Historic District Ordinance and established a historic review board. Five years later, Mayor Robert L. Real and Phyllis Garmon, then chief executive officer of Key Communications Inc., organized Develop New Albany Inc. to implement the city's participation in the Main Street Program. During the mid-1990s, with organizational and financial assistance from Main Street Preservation Inc., DHPA, and other local donors, Develop New Albany became a prime mover in renovating the 1837 Indiana State Bank building. In 1995 Develop New Albany began a $450,000 rehabilitation of the former White House department store on Pearl St. for reuse as a small business incubator.

Meanwhile, in 1994 DHPA and HLFI updated the 1976 Floyd County historic sites inventory with preparation of the *City of New Albany Interim Report* that encompassed the entire city and its unincorporated two-mile fringe. It identified 19 historic districts containing 3,758 individual properties plus 287 properties outside historic districts. In 1998 the city wrote a new historic district ordinance and design guidelines. The same year the Floyd County Museum underwent a $1 million renovation, supervised by RCS Associates Architects and K. NORMAN BERRY Architects. It reopened in 1999 as the Carnegie Center for Art and History.

Preservation did not move so fast in Clark County as it did in Floyd County after publication of the *Metropolitan Preservation Plan*, but significant progress occurred nevertheless. In 1973 the Howard Steamboat Museum was placed on the National Register, followed in 1974 by the original site of Clarksville. The major impetus for preservation in Clark County came in 1981 when fire gutted the Federal-style Grisamore house, built in 1837 and located on Chestnut St. in downtown Jeffersonville. Soon thereafter, Clarksville civic activist Rosemary Prentice and Jeffersonville businessman Harvey Russ purchased the structure. In 1982 they organized Jeff-Clark Preservation Inc. and donated the building to the new organization for restoration. In May 1983 the Grisamore house was listed on the National Register, and in September it was rededicated and became the offices of the Southern Regional Office of HLFI. Jeff-Clark remains a force in historic preservation, having renovated or restored several endangered structures through effective use of revolving loan funds and volunteer labor.

Several major initiatives occurred during the remainder of the 1980s. In 1984 HLFI commissioned preparation of a National Register nomination for downtown Jeffersonville and its adjoining residential NEIGHBORHOODS. The Old Jeffersonville National Register of Historic Places District was officially listed in 1987. Meanwhile, in July 1984, the Jeffersonville City Council created a seven-member Historic District Board of Review, and in December it enacted a historic district ordinance that designated a downtown preservation district encompassing Spring St. and Riverside Dr.

In 1983 several historically minded citizens in Charlestown founded the Charlestown Architectural Preservation Society. By the end of 1984 CAPS had successfully nominated the Benjamin Ferguson, Ward Watson (1898), and Thomas Downs houses to the National Register. In 1988 DHPA and HLFI published the *Indiana Historic Sites and Structures Inventory: Clark County Interim Report* that identified 1,506 historically significant structures in 9 districts in Jeffersonville, Clarksville, and Charlestown or as scattered sites in all 12 townships. The following year, several Jeffersonville business and civic leaders founded Jeffersonville Main Street Inc. to revitalize the city's downtown business district. During the 1990s it became a major force in promoting the rehabilitation and reuse of several endangered commercial structures along Spring St.

Harrison County was not included in the *1973 Metropolitan Preservation Plan*, but the movement there paralleled developments in Floyd and Clark Counties. In 1973 the Corydon Historic District, which embraces a large section of downtown adjacent to the Corydon Capitol State Historic Site, was listed on the National Register. Six years later the Gov. William Hendricks Headquarters was added to the Corydon Capitol Site, followed by the First State Office Building (Old Treasury Building) in 1988. Meanwhile, DHPA and HLFI conducted a countywide inventory, which was published as the *Indiana Historic Sites and Structures Inventory: Harrison County Interim Report* in February 1987.

The 1980s and 1990s witnessed several important private initiatives. The Corydon Capital Preservation Alliance, formed in 1983, promotes preservation of the Corydon Historic District and other historic sites throughout Harrison County. In 1985 Corydon was one of five target communities in Indiana selected to participate in Indiana's Main Street Program. Main Street Corydon was established to revitalize the town's commercial district while maintaining its historical character.

The Friends of Corydon Capitol State Historic Site acquired the former Corydon Presbyterian Church in 1997 with the intention of restoring it as an interpretive center for the historic site. In addition, private individuals have undertaken efforts to preserve such notable sites and structures as the Kintner House Inn, the Heth House, Cedar Glade home, and the Corydon Colored School, all in Corydon, and Cedar Farm, which overlooks the Ohio River south of Corydon. Playing pivotal roles in many preservation initiatives in Corydon and Harrison County were Frederick P. Griffin, a local businessman and amateur historian whose decades of research helped document the significance of many historic sites and structures, and banker Blaine Wiseman, whose financial and leadership acumen helped bring projects to fruition.

Carl E. Kramer

HISTORIES OF LOUISVILLE. The first book that might be called a history of Louisville was published in 1819. *Sketches of Louisville and its[sic] Environs* was the work of Dr. Henry McMurtrie, a Philadelphia native and medical graduate of the University of Pennsylvania who came to Louisville in 1816. It is in this volume that the myth of the "White Indians" at the FALLS OF THE OHIO first appeared in print. Since the book was published only some forty years after the founding of Louisville, there was an opportunity to gather first-hand recollections of the town's early days, but McMurtrie did not avail himself of the opportunity. The work remains, however, an invaluable description of Louisville in 1819 and its commercial and manufacturing status. It also contains geological and botanical information. The work includes descriptions of SHIPPINGPORT, PORTLAND, NEW ALBANY, Clarksville, and SHELBYVILLE. McMurtrie's work (including the fold-out map) was reprinted with an added index in 1969 by the G.R. Clark Press, formed by a group of Louisville scholars.

The first coherent historical account of Louisville appeared in 1832 as a lengthy essay by educator Mann Butler that appeared in the city's first directory. "An Outline of the Origin and Settlement of Louisville, in Kentucky" relied on primary sources and recollections of the few living persons who were present at the events they described. Butler in 1834 published the first generally reliable history of Kentucky. *The Louisville Directory for the Year 1832* was reprinted by the G.R. Clark Press in 1970, including the fine fold-out map of the city.

In 1852 the *History of Louisville* by journalist Ben Casseday was published. In format it anticipated the later nineteenth-century habit of year-by-year chronology of events without analysis or interpretation. However, it contains some interesting observations by Casseday: among them, he deplores the preference for the ballroom to the cultivation of knowledge, and he described the German immigrants flocking to the city as "careful pains-taking and industrious people, of quiet, unobtrusive manners: and . . . in a majority of cases, men of some ability and education." This was only three years before BLOODY MONDAY. Casseday's volume was also reprinted by the G.R. Clark Press in 1970, including the fold-out map of the city.

In 1875 a "Historic Sketch" of the city appeared in *Louisville Past and Present*, a volume of 358 pages, most of which were devoted to biographies of prominent citizens. The short history, based on the works described above, especially Casseday's (in some cases verbatim) contributed little to original research but did include brief addenda on the rise of banks and RAILROADS. The sketch is uncredited but was probably written by P.A. Towne, first librarian of the Louisville-based Public Library of Kentucky, who edited the entire volume (See *Louisville Monthly Magazine,* Sept.–Oct. 1879, 512–14).

The first history of the area that can be called comprehensive was the two-volume *History of the Ohio Falls Cities and Their Counties* published in 1882 by the L.A. Williams Co. of Cleveland, Ohio, a firm that undertook similar ventures in other cities. It includes New Albany, Jeffersonville, and Clark and Floyd Counties in Indiana as well as Louisville and Jefferson County. Like most nineteenth-century popular histories it is chronological, decade by decade, and it contains a generous number of biographies of individuals on both sides of the river. Unfortunately, though comprehensive, it is ill-digested. Even so, it remains a valuable adjunct for research. A number of topics are covered separately, including railroads, roads, STEAMBOATS, schools, charities, and the press. This was the most ambitious effort so far but was followed by one even more ambitious.

The *Memorial History of Louisville* appeared in 1896 in two hefty volumes edited by J. Stoddard Johnston and published by the American Biographical Publishing Co. of Chicago and New York. Contributions by numerous Louisvillians in their special areas of expertise give the volumes an authority that none of the earlier works could muster. In addition to a narrative history of the city and the usual biographies, there are chapters devoted to the TOBACCO trade, DISTILLING, other industries, banks, railroads, navigation, THEATERS, PARKS and PARKWAYS, authors, and many more subjects, even CEMETERIES. This work is more extensive and expertly done than the 1882 predecessor.

In 1954, to mark its one-hundredth anniversary, Liberty National Bank (later BankOne) sponsored a book on local history, *Louisville Panorama.* Subtitled *A Visual History,* it lacks a connected narrative but is instead a scrapbook of Louisville history. *Views of Louisville since 1766* was published by the COURIER-JOURNAL and LOUISVILLE TIMES Co. in 1971. In the nineteenth-century style, the work provides a chronology interrupted by short pieces on various topics. The illustrations are the work's strongest suit.

This pictorial story of Louisville's development flowered in a series of volumes by Dr. Samuel W. Thomas. After *Views of Louisville*, a sequel titled *Louisville since the Twenties* followed in 1978. Thomas also was the author of other books on aspects of Louisville's history: *Old Louisville: The Victorian Era*, which was coauthored with William Morgan (Courier-Journal and Louisville Times 1975); *Cave Hill Cemetery* (Cave Hill Cemetery Co. 1985); *Crescent Hill Revisited* (George Rogers Clark Press 1987); and *Churchill Downs: A Documentary History* (Kentucky Derby Museum 1995). All are well illustrated. The first *Views of Louisville* volume has been reprinted. In 1999 Thomas's *St. Matthews: The Crossroads of Beargrass* was published by the Beargrass-St. Matthews Historical Society. It is a comprehensive account of this eastern suburb of Louisville.

In connection with the bicentennial of the founding of Louisville in 1778, George H. Yater produced *Two Hundred Years at the Falls of the Ohio: A History of Louisville and Jefferson County* (1979). A revised, updated edition appeared in 1987. After undergraduate studies in history at the UNIVERSITY OF LOUISVILLE and graduate studies at Columbia University, Yater pursued a career in writing and journalism. His book, an amply illustrated volume, is meticulous in its scholarship and easy to read. The work is of special significance for two reasons: 1) the writing and research were reviewed and overseen by an editorial advisory board of some twenty-five individuals, most of whom were historical scholars and published writers; and 2) the text consciously set about to cover many individuals and groups that had long been under-reported or neglected in previous Louisville histories. Yater dedicated his book to the men and women who had built a community at the Falls of the Ohio. None of Louisville's early histories were so generous in recognizing the contributions of the "common people."

George H. Yater
Clyde F. Crews

HITE, ABRAHAM. (b Germantown, Pennsylvania, May 10, 1720; d Louisville, January 17, 1790). Pioneer settler. Hite was the seventh child of Jost Heydt (Hite) (1685–1758), founder of the German settlements in the Shenandoah Valley in Virginia, which is now Winchester, Virginia. Familiar with land acquisition, the family sought to enhance its fortune in the new frontier in Kentucky. In 1773 Abraham's oldest son, Isaac (1753–94), accompanied THOMAS BULLITT's party on a surveying trip down the OHIO RIVER to the Falls. In the spring of 1774 he re-surveyed with JOHN FLOYD. In 1781 Isaac was appointed by the governor of Virginia as one of the justices of the Lincoln County court, the first convened in Kentucky.

Although settlers were killed nearby by Indians in the 1780s, Isaac established a self-sufficient frontier outpost on Goose Creek in Jefferson County. He called it Cave Spring Plantation and resided there after 1781–82. "Hite's Mill" is identified on Filson's 1784 map of Kentucky, as are the fortified stations along BEARGRASS CREEK. This land was sold by the Hite heirs to the state of Kentucky in 1869 and is presently the site of CENTRAL STATE HOSPITAL and E.P. "Tom" Sawyer Park.

About 1784 Abraham Senior and sons Abraham Junior (1755–1832) and Joseph (1757–1831) moved their households from Virginia to occupy a portion of the thousands of acres of land they had claimed in Jefferson County. The houses they built are maintained as residences to the present day on Starlight Ln. near Bardstown Rd. In 1968 the Revolutionary War service of Abraham Senior was recognized by the Fincastle chapter of the Daughters of the American Revolution with the erection of a marker at his gravesite in the family cemetery near Starlight Ln.

Abraham Junior, who later dropped the Junior, was a Jefferson County delegate to the Danville conventions for Kentucky statehood. He also became a trustee of the town of Louisville. He assumed the role of head of this venturesome and prolific family. He deeded land on Goose Creek to an orphan nephew William (1756–1828), who had accompanied the family from Virginia. William's grandson, William Chambers Hite (1820–82) was owner of a steam ferry, the *W.C. Hite*, that operated between Louisville and Jeffersonville. His son, Allen R. Hite (1865–1941), left a sizable estate from which a million-dollar bequest established the fine arts department of the UNIVERSITY OF LOUISVILLE in 1946 as the Allen R. Hite Art Institute.

See Robert C. Jobson, "German-American Settlers of Early Jefferson County, Kentucky," *Filson Club History Quarterly* 53 (Oct. 1979): 344–58. Sallee, Helen Hite, *Col. Abraham Hite and His Three Sons,* Fincastle Chapter, Daughters of the American Revolution.

Mildred Ewen

HOBBS, EDWARD DORSEY (b Jefferson County, Kentucky, November 16, 1810; d AN-

CHORAGE, Kentucky, September 6, 1888). Politician and business leader. The son of Basil N. and Polly (Dorsey) Hobbs, Edward began his long and varied career at the age of nineteen when he established Louisville's first real estate office. In 1831 he was the youngest man ever elected city surveyor, and for five years he surveyed the city's streets and riverfront. At that time, Hobbs published maps of Louisville and its environs. In 1835 he founded the Louisville Savings Institution.

In 1843 Hobbs was elected to the Kentucky General Assembly and was twice reelected. In 1847, he was elected to the state Senate but shortly resigned to focus his energies on the development of a rail line between Louisville and Frankfort.

As president of the LOUISVILLE & FRANKFORT RAILROAD, Hobbs oversaw its construction, which began in 1848 and was completed in 1851. In 1869, the railroad merged with the Lexington and Frankfort to become the Louisville, Cincinnati, and Lexington Railroad, now part of CSX Transportation.

Hobbs returned to politics during the CIVIL WAR (1861–65), when President ABRAHAM LINCOLN appointed him a special agent of the Treasury Department for northern Kentucky. His chief duties were to oversee the supply of arms and equipment to volunteer troops. Aside from his business and political interests, Hobbs was an ardent horticulturist who founded one of the country's largest nurseries before the Civil War. He was responsible for the planting of hundreds of trees and shrubs in his community of modern-day Anchorage, then named Hobbs Station.

Hobbs married Susan Henning on December 4, 1833, but she died two years later. In 1839 he married Mary A. Craig. The couple had six children.

See Marion Castner Browder, "Edward Dorsey Hobbs, 1810–1888, A Kentucky Gentleman," *Filson Club History Quarterly* 6 (Jan. 1932): 88–99; *A Place in Time: The Story of Louisville's Neighborhoods* (Louisville 1989); *Courier Journal*, Sept. 7, 1888.

Edward Dorsey Hobbs, c. 1884.

HOBLITZELL, BRUCE, SR. (b Louisville, June 25, 1887; d. Louisville, August 11, 1970). Mayor. The son of Bruce and Jane A. (Bradley) Hoblitzell, he attended grade school in Louisville and graduated from du Pont Manual Training High School. After graduating in 1907 from the KENTUCKY MILITARY INSTITUTE in LYNDON, he returned to the family real estate business, succeeding his father. He quit real estate in 1906 and went to work as an assistant superintendent for the Kentucky Heating Co., where he stayed until 1912. He resigned from Kentucky Heating to organize the McClellan-Hoblitzell Realty Co. with J.A. McClellan in 1912. The firm was dissolved in 1919 and became Bruce Hoblitzell Realtors and Insurance Agency.

Hoblitzell, who was known throughout the city as "Mr. Hobby," was elected mayor of Louisville on November 5, 1957, succeeding ANDREW BROADDUS. He defeated Republican Robert B. Diehl 57,027 to 47,874. He served from December 1, 1957, until December 1, 1961, when Republican William O. Cowger took office. Hoblitzell, a Democrat, was a fiscal conservative who had a reputation for not spending money. During his administration the city transferred programs costing about $2 million a year to the state and county. Hoblitzell did have the city contribute more than $6 million to the UNIVERSITY OF LOUISVILLE for improvements.

Most of the impact of his administration centered on PUBLIC WORKS projects such as the installation of street lights, paving city streets, and renovating substandard housing. He also acquired approximately two hundred acres of PARKS and playgrounds for the city's park system.

Before serving as mayor, Hoblitzell was elected sheriff of Jefferson County in 1953, an office he used to institute reforms in prison conditions. He served as president of the LOUISVILLE BOARD OF TRADE, the Louisville Chamber of Commerce, and the Better Business Bureau. He was also president of both the Louisville and Kentucky real estate boards before serving as mayor. He was on the boards of the Metropolitan Sewer District and the Louisville Gas & Electric Co.

Hoblitzell devoted much of his energy to improving conditions for handicapped children in the city. He was president of the Kosair Crippled Children's Hospital's Board of Governors for thirty years, as well as chairman of the annual fund-raising picnic held by the hospital. A plaque at Kosair honors Hoblitzell's years of service to the institution. He visited the hospital every Sunday to spend time with the children.

Hoblitzell married Irene Oatey Forbes of Louisville on January 31, 1910. The couple had one son, Bruce Junior, and two daughters, Jane and Margaret. Hoblitzell suffered a stroke in December 1962 and was bedridden for much of the rest of his life. He died at his home at 1415 St. James T. Court and is buried in CAVE HILL CEMETERY.

See W.T. Owens, *Who's Who in Louisville* (Louisville 1926); *Louisville Times*, Aug. 11, 1970.

HOGAN'S FOUNTAIN. In 1903 Mr. and Mrs. W.J. Hogan of Anchorage announced that they wished to erect a drinking fountain for dogs and horses in the eastern part of Louisville. In a letter submitted to the Board of Park Commissioners, they offered to donate seven thousand dollars. On their behalf, the board announced a competition for the fountain's design and asked the park system's architect, OLMSTED and Associates, to select the site. The top of a small hill in Cherokee Park was chosen. The work of sculptor ENID YANDELL was selected for the fountain's design. Louisville-born Yandell was a well-known artist who worked in various studios in Chicago and New York City and had lived in France and sculpted with Auguste Rodin.

Mrs. Hogan actively participated in the choice of subject matter, and the figure of the Greek god Pan, known as "Faun" in Roman mythology, was selected. The god of the forest and herds had found refuge in fountains when the woods were cut down by man. The sculpture consists of three parts. The first is a circular fourteen-foot-wide granite basin with four bronze dog heads on its outer walls. These heads spew water from their mouths into troughs from which dogs can drink. A granite pedestal springs from the basin on which the third part, a bronze figure of Pan, is placed. Pan, who has a hairy human-like body, short horns, and goat's feet, is depicted dancing while holding a pipe in one hand. He is surrounded by four large turtles that spout water from their mouths into the basin. The fountain was officially unveiled on August 31, 1905. It immediately became a popular gathering spot for Louisvillians.

See Donna Wiseman, "The Story of Hogan's Foundation," unpublished paper, 1981, University of Louisville Records and Archives.

HOKE, WILLIAM BAIRD (b Fisherville, Jefferson County, Kentucky, August 1, 1838; d Louisville, August 5, 1904). Jefferson County judge. Hoke was the son of Cornelius and Jane (Dunbar) Hoke. Hoke's great-grandfather George Hoke came to the United States from Germany sometime before the American Revolution, first settling in New York, then in Pennsylvania. Hoke's grandfather George Hoke Jr. left Pennsylvania about 1793 and traveled down the Ohio River by flatboat before settling in Louisville. The Hoke family settled in Jefferson County near Jeffersontown. Although Hoke had several children, only Cornelius stayed in the Louisville area.

William Hoke was born at the Hoke plantation in Fisherville near Floyd's Fork Creek. He attended a country school and went to Hanover College at Hanover, Indiana, before completing his studies at Centre College in Danville, Kentucky. He attended the University of Louisville Law School and graduated as valedictorian of his class at the age of twenty-one.

He became a law partner with his father-in-law, Col. Samuel S. English. He had a successful practice until the outbreak of the Civil War, when he joined Confederate general John Hunt Morgan's regiment. He was captured by Union soldiers on an expedition to Louisville to find recruits and was held until he took the oath of allegiance.

Hoke, a Democrat, was Jefferson County judge from September 3, 1866, until December 31, 1894. He was elected to the office seven times during his career until he was defeated by Republican Charles G. Richie. Hoke ran for mayor of Louisville in 1887 but was defeated by Charles D. Jacob, who ran as an independent. It was a bitterly contested three-way race that also included Republican Samuel Avery.

In 1859, Hoke married Sarah Wharton English, daughter of his law partner and Nancy (Demint) English, of Louisville. Hoke and his wife had four children: McClure, English, Nannie, and Mrs. Allen E. Smith.

Hoke died of a stomach ailment at the age of sixty-six. He is buried in Cave Hill Cemetery.

See J. Stoddard Johnston, ed., *Memorial History of Louisville* (Chicago and New York 1896); *Courier-Journal*, Aug. 6, 1904.

HOLDOVERS FOR PRISONERS. Lawmen have always needed a holdover for prisoners waiting for their "day in court." The very first arrested persons were held in makeshift places of confinement such as barns, rooms in homes, cellars, or sheds.

The Louisville Board of Trustees in December 1810 resolved that a watch house be built at the east end of Market St. The night watchmen made this building their headquarters and it functioned as a holdover for prisoners.

It is necessary to know that police holdovers were often thought of and called jails. Indeed the County Jail is often called the City Jail. Jail confinement, most often, is for no more than a year for a misdemeanor.

In 1866, with the growth of the city, Police Chief Robert Gilchrist announced the building of four new station houses, each with a holdover. They were No. 1 on Shelby St. between Jefferson and Green (Liberty) Streets, No. 2 on First St. between Jefferson and Green Streets, No. 3 on Fifth St. between Walnut (Muhammed Ali Blvd.) and Chestnut Streets, and No. 4 in the lower portion of the city, the exact location not yet decided in 1866. The second stories of the buildings were set apart for female prisoners.

The job of stationhouse keeper was a position most officers desired. They had the responsibility of the paperwork and for seeing that prisoners were cared for and were in court on their court days, and they had officers who helped with the upkeep of the stationhouse. Many officers resigned rather than wash windows, mop floors, or keep the fires going. On June 2, 1920, officer R.W. Galway was accused of insubordination by his superior, who noted, "When I told him to mop the cell room and keep the station house clean, he said, damn if he would mop the cell room."

Over the years the city's stationhouses furnished stragglers, many from other cities, a place to sleep for one or more nights. As early as 1871 stragglers (now called street people) were people whom the police wanted to be rid of. Their numbers were always greater in winter months (spring months 306, summer months 115, fall months 465, winter months 938 in 1871). Running the holdovers remained a police function for many years before the responsibility shifted to trained civilian guards.

For years women were arrested and put in stationhouse holdovers. Between August 1893 and August 1894, fifteen hundred women were arrested and taken into holdovers. By law, women, like men, had to be searched to ascertain if they had stolen property, valuables, poison, or deadly weapons upon their person. At times an officer would get a nearby woman from the neighborhood to do the search, but "ladies of the night" frequently hid contraband. During 1913 a designated stationhouse for females and child prisoners was put into operation and a matron was provided for it.

For a short time after 1921 a small section of the northwest corner of City Hall's basement was used as a holdover for persons arrested by city police. It was called "Dover Hotel" in honor of Officer Tom Dover, known for his ability to convince "visitors" not to cause problems while staying at his domain. The holdover was indeed a hellhole. There were six rather small cells and a woman's bullpen. On a busy weekend—and most were busy—there would be as many as ten to twelve men packed in each cell waiting to be booked. Murderers, thieves, drunks, and "good guys" were all packed together. Prostitutes and women arrested for minor offenses were all put in the same cage. The single toilets in the cells were fully exposed. The air conditioning was two exhaust fans. Prisoners were constantly yelling for water. There were times the turnkey was overpowered while alone among the cells and had to be rescued. A prisoner or two might be taken to the hospital when an officer was disrespected.

Customers were pleased with the city's new jail/holdover located at police headquarters, which began operating in June 1956. Police officers were in charge, and prisoners did the chores such as cleaning, clothes washing, floor polishing, and cooking. Prisoners who helped with the cleaning and other chores were called "trusties." The jail area, which was located on the third floor, was not air-conditioned, unlike the rest of the building. Most prisoners were kept fewer than thirty days. The jail in the Hall of Justice, after being built in 1976 took over holdover duties.

Morton O. Childress

HOLLENBACH, LOUIS JACOB III "TODD" (b Louisville, February 23, 1940). Jefferson County judge. The son of Louis Jacob Junior and Marie (O'Meara) Hollenbach, he received his early education at Sacred Heart Model School and Holy Spirit Elementary School. Hollenbach was a member of Trinity High School's first graduating class in 1957. He earned his B.A. degree from the University of Notre Dame in 1962 and his law degree from the University of Louisville in 1965.

He was elected county judge in 1970, defeating incumbent county judge W. Armin Willig by more than four thousand votes. Hollenbach's victory was part of the local Democratic Party's return to power after eight years of Republican domination. Hollenbach immediately initiated measures that would make his first term in office one of the most innovative and progressive in the county's history.

Legislation made it possible to begin planning for the construction of the Hall of Justice, a new Jefferson County jail, and a regional government center. Land was also purchased for the construction of two additional government centers. Funds were obtained for a major expansion of the flood wall in southwest Jefferson County, and a wide range of drainage improvements were made. More effective law enforcement was high on the agenda of Hollenbach's administration. As a result, the total number of crimes in Jefferson County was reduced by 23 percent during Hollenbach's first term. Under Hollenbach's direction there was strict enforcement of air pollution laws and the creation of an ecology court, which was copied both nationally and elsewhere around the world. To provide better direct personal contact between the local government and the citizenry, he started the community relations department, and a federal programs office was set up to provide county government with expertise in acquiring available federal funds.

In court administration, four full-time prosecutors were hired, a public defender program was established, and a full-time juvenile court judge was appointed. Also, plans were put in motion to build a modern juvenile detention facility.

During Hollenbach's administration, all Fiscal Court meetings, including executive sessions, were open to the news media. For the first time, on-site public zoning hearings were held in the neighborhoods most likely to be affected by the rezoning being sought. In August 1973, with Hollenbach's strong support, the Fiscal Court formally took action to reduce the county's property tax rate by 5 percent.

Defeating Republican Edwin A. Schroering Jr., the commonwealth's attorney, by an overwhelming margin of nearly fifty-four thousand votes, Hollenbach began his second term as county judge in 1974. This term brought to fruition projects started during his first term. Hollenbach arranged for the initial funding and planning for the restoration of the JEFFERSON COUNTY COURTHOUSE. The second term, however, soon found the administration dealing with a gigantic emergency when a tornado cut a swath of destruction across the county on April 3, 1974. The following year the county was torn by dissension and strife resulting from the federally mandated BUSING of school children for DESEGREGATION. In an effort to calm the highly volatile situation, the administration arranged for a series of community forums to be held and hosted a national forum dealing with equality of educational opportunity.

In 1975 Hollenbach ran for the Democratic nomination for governor. It was thought by many that Hollenbach had a better chance at winning the lieutenant governor's office instead of running against the popular incumbent Julian Carroll. Carroll, as lieutenant governor, had succeeded Governor Wendell Ford when the latter resigned to run for the U.S. Senate. Hollenbach was defeated by Carroll by over a hundred thousand votes.

In 1977 Hollenbach was unsuccessful in his bid for a third term as county judge, being defeated by MITCH MCCONNELL by just over eleven thousand votes. A major factor in this loss was the emotionally charged busing issue. Also, Hollenbach had called for a grand jury investigation of some questionable fund-raising by friends for his primary campaign for governor. The grand jury found no laws had been broken but criticized Hollenbach for not keeping closer watch on how money was solicited. Nor was he helped by the fact that earlier on he had irked some influential civic leaders by opposing parts of a city-county merger proposal.

Hollenbach made unsuccessful runs for lieutenant governor in 1979 and 1983 before winning election to the office of commonwealth's attorney in 1984, defeating George Kunzman by sixty thousand votes. As commonwealth's attorney, Hollenbach set up the first domestic violence strike force of prosecutors in Kentucky and one of the first in the nation. He helped get legislation passed for a truth-in-sentencing law that allows previous criminal convictions to be made known in the sentencing phase of a trial. After leaving office in 1988, Hollenbach made a losing bid for the post of Kentucky attorney general and then returned to the private practice of law.

Hollenbach married Carroll DeHart on December 17, 1959, and the couple had three children: Louis Jacob IV, John Philip, and Caroline. They were divorced in 1977.

Kenneth Dennis

HOLT, JOSEPH (b Breckinridge County, Kentucky, January 6, 1807; d Washington, D.C., August 1, 1894). Attorney and statesman. The son of John and Eleanor (Stephens) Holt, Joseph Holt was educated at both St. Joseph's College at Bardstown and Centre College at Danville, Kentucky. He began his law career in 1828 when he established an office in Elizabethtown and was a partner of the renowned jurist Benjamin Hardin Jr. At that time, Holt became active in DEMOCRATIC PARTY politics and within a few years established a reputation as a skilled orator. In 1832 he moved to Louisville and spent a year as the assistant editor of the *LOUISVILLE PUBLIC ADVERTISER*. Holt was appointed the commonwealth's attorney for the Jefferson circuit in 1833, a position he held for the next two years.

Holt moved to Mississippi in 1835 and continued his law practice there until 1842, when he retired and moved back to Louisville to recover from tuberculosis, the same disease that had killed his first wife, Mary Harrison. Over the next few years, he made occasional campaign speeches, married Margaret Wickliffe, and spent time traveling in Europe. Then, in 1857, President James Buchanan appointed Holt commissioner of patents to reward his contribution to the 1856 Democratic victory. In 1859 he became postmaster general, and in 1861 he succeeded John B. Floyd as secretary of war. Though he was formerly a Douglas Democrat, the weight of his duties and South Carolina's secession had convinced Holt that the South had to be dealt with firmly. After President ABRAHAM LINCOLN'S inauguration, Holt, now considered a War Democrat, gave his full support to the new administration and the Union cause. He openly condemned Kentucky's neutrality policy and made every effort to change it by keeping in close contact with the state's Unionist leaders and by making pro-Union speeches throughout Kentucky and the border states. His efforts were rewarded in September 1861 when the Kentucky legislature acted to keep Kentucky in the Union camp. A recruiting camp named Camp Joe Holt was opened just west of JEFFERSONVILLE, INDIANA, in July 1861 by Col. Lovell H. Rousseau. By September 1861, the camp had recruited over two thousand local citizens for the Union army.

On September 3, 1862, Holt was given the rank of colonel and appointed by President Lincoln to the newly created post of judge advocate general of the army, which gave him "certain powers of arrest and of holding persons in arrest without writ of habeas corpus." Holt was named head of the Bureau of Military Justice upon its establishment in 1864 and promoted to the rank of brigadier general. During his term as judge advocate general, Holt participated in a number of military commissions and courts-martial, including the Clement L. Vallandigham and Lambdin P. Milligan cases, as well as the military trial of President Lincoln's assassination conspirators. In 1865, he was breveted a major general.

Many of Holt's decisions as judge advocate general won him popularity among radical Republicans, but, as political tides changed after the war and a more conservative element gained control, some of Holt's actions drew criticism. He was most notably accused of suppressing evidence in the Lincoln assassination trial and of keeping the military commission's recommendation of clemency for Mrs. Mary Surratt from President Andrew Johnson. Holt, who retired from his post in 1875, spent many of his remaining days trying to vindicate his name.

See H. Levin, *Lawyers and Lawmakers in Kentucky* (Chicago 1897).

HOLY ROSARY ACADEMY. The Holy Rosary Academy was founded in 1867 by the Sisters of the Dominican Provincial in the Louisville Roman Catholic Diocese. Dedicated in the name of the Virgin Mother Mary, Holy Rosary Academy began as a convent where Dominican Sisters engaged upon their missions. Sisters Angela Lynch and Sybillina Sheridan came from the Dominican motherhouse to Louisville to found the school at the behest of the Bishop of Louisville, Joseph Lavialle, due to the influx of Catholic immigrants.

The academy opened in March 1867 across from ST. LOUIS BERTRAND CATHOLIC CHURCH, with which the academy was associated. Financial difficulties brought closure to the first location of the academy at Garvin Place. The sisters continued the academy in a family house on Sixth St. until they obtained a house on Kentucky and Eighth Streets. This former home of Captain Pennington had been purchased at a reduced price. Sister Louise Hayden became the first principal and superior of the Holy Rosary Academy.

In 1894 Holy Rosary moved again because of the expansion of railroads and industry in the area. Only elementary classes continued in unused rooms of St. Louis Bertrand School until 1897 when Holy Rosary Academy reopened at 418 Ormsby Ave. Its first graduate, Katherine Morthorst, completed studies in 1902.

In 1914 the Academy moved to Fourth St. and Park Ave. Enrollment continued to increase, and, by the late 1940s, the sisters recognized that they needed larger accommodations. The motherhouse purchased a tract of land on Southside Dr. The cornerstone was laid in May of 1955. Holy Rosary Academy for Girls still remains at this location.

See Dominican Sisters of Louisville, "Centennial Anniversary: Holy Rosary Academy," Anniversary annual/brochure, 1967; Clyde F. Crews, *American and Catholic* (Cincinnati 1994).

Paul Wolf Holleman

HOME FOR THE AGED AND INFIRM (ALMSHOUSE). Louisville built its first almshouse in the 1830s at Eighth and Chestut Streets, where it served as a shelter for the poor, aged, and infirm. It was soon moved to the city's recently purchased tract of land east of downtown known as Cave Hill. There the almshouse was combined with the Louisville workhouse, an institution for misdemeanor offenders. When people could not take care of themselves or their children because of old age, lack of financial resources, or mental incapacity, the children were sent to this institution to work the city farm along with those incarcerated in the workhouse. There they were fed, given a bed, and, most important, provided with companionship. The two institutions, the almshouse and the workhouse, were separated again in 1851. The almshouse then moved to Duncan St. between Twenty-eighth and Twenty-ninth Streets. A second almshouse was opened by Jefferson County in 1858. The Jefferson County Home for the Aged (Jefferson County Poorhouse) was built in JEFFERSONTOWN on a seventy-acre tract adjacent to the present-day library building on Watterson Trail. Later converted to a branch of the LOUISVILLE FREE PUBLIC LIBRARY, the old almshouse now serves as home to a senior citizens' activity center.

In 1872 the city of Louisville purchased a 225-acre tract of land approximately 6 miles southwest of downtown Louisville in present-day SHIVELY for the purpose of building a new almshouse for the poor. The site is today bounded by Seventh Street Rd., Manslick Rd., Berry Blvd., and Gagel Ave. Construction began soon after, and in 1874 the Home for the Aged and Infirm was opened. The building itself had 142 rooms (room enough to house almost 300 wards of the city) and was surrounded by a large farm that was worked by prisoners at the city workhouse. The property also contained a cemetery west of Manslick Rd. (now east of Manslick Rd.) where inmates of the institution and other indigents could be buried. In October 1874 the first inmates arrived at the home. Residents earned their keep by performing tasks such as sewing, cooking, or helping with the gardening. Tradegy struck on January 31, 1879, when the home caught fire and was badly damaged. The inmates were forced to survive in makeshift shelters until December 1879, when reconstruction of the building was completed.

The Home for the Aged and Infirm came under a different kind of fire from a grand jury in June 1922. The home was said to be overcrowded and the grounds in a state of disarray. This resulted in a transfer of some inmates to the City Hospital. The facility then received a quick cosmetic makeover to satisfy the courts. Not satisfied for long, in 1930 another grand jury investigation described the institution's condition as "deplorable" and "filthy," citing several grotesque health code violations.

Things improved in 1933 when Garner G. Denton became superintendent. He immediately instituted several improvements, including cleaning and refurbishing. Denton also was responsible for bringing electric lighting to all the rooms. New floors were laid, and the halls and rooms were plastered and repainted. In addition Denton purchased the home's first refrigerator. Lastly, six more hospital rooms were added to the building. Most important, whereas inmates had had nothing to do but "sit and stare" and "wait to die," they now had several activities to engage in. Services for a wide variety of religious persuasions were held in addition to dances, shows, musical performances, and the like.

The Home for the Aged and Infirm was closed in 1953, after which the property was sold and the building razed. In 1961 ground was broken for construction of the Southland Shopping Center where the home once stood. Since the Manslick Rd. cemetery was filled, the city opened a new cemetery for the poor and infirm on Cane Run Rd. next to the Louisville Gas & Electric Co. plant in 1988.

See Virginia Conn, "Faith, Hope and Charity," *University of Louisville Local Historical Series*, vol. 16 (January 1940).

HOMELESSNESS. Homelessness captured the attention of Louisville and Jefferson County in 1984 when several homeless people were found dead in abandoned buildings within the city. Mayor Harvey Sloane called a community meeting that evolved into a task force to explore why this had occurred and how such tragedies could be prevented.

The task force issued a report in 1985 identifying a day shelter as the community's top need. The following year the task force was incorporated as the Coalition for the Homeless, and planning began on what became St. John Day Center. Over the next few years the coalition was primarily a governing body for St. John's. It was not until it separated from it, in 1988, that the coalition became closely involved in the overall service and shelter care system.

In its new role, the coalition developed a programs council, a subcommittee structure of its board of directors that serves as a mechanism for networking with others. This has proven to be an effective model for identifying issues, sharing concerns, problem-solving, coordinating the allocation of funds, and implementing change.

One of the coalition's key efforts is the quality assurance standards program, created and implemented in 1991 to monitor the quality of care and range of programs offered by shelters. Participating shelters choose to be monitored by the coalition's volunteers. The shelters agree to meet certain standards.

Another program of the coalition is its computerized data collection project begun in 1992 to establish the first informational baseline on the number and needs of homeless single men. In 1994 the coalition began receiving the same data from shelters serving single women. In addition, the survey form was amended for both men and women to collect information on abuse. In 1995 it took over METRO UNITED WAY's responsibility to collect similar data on homeless families.

The coalition has played a major role in the development of a comprehensive shelter and service system that has brought the Louisville community national attention. These services have helped those using them and have had a positive impact on the overall community by creating an environment that is welcoming to visitors and is rarely a problem to local businesses.

Between 1986 and 1997, more than $36 million in federal Stewart B. McKinney Act funds have been allocated to the community to serve the needs of the homeless. These funds have supported shelter and food services, building renovations for emergency shelters and transitional facilities, case management services, health-care services, education/job training programs, and research. In addition, both city and county governments and Metro United Way have provided funding.

In 1998 twenty-two local agencies provided shelter to homeless people, and several had services at more than one location. That year in the city and county, the homeless shelter system served 12,403 persons There were 7,641 single men (62 percent), 1,209 single women (10 percent), 799 youth on their own (6 percent), and 2,754 family individuals (21 percent).

As high as these numbers are, they are only a part of the true picture of homelessness in the community. Countless others did not ask for help from the homeless shelter system, and chances are there would not have been room for them if they had. For every family that was served—1043 of them—another 3 to 4 more families were turned away for lack of space.

Poverty is a primary cause of homelessness. According to the 1990 United States Census, 13.7 percent of all people in Jefferson County and 22.6 percent within Louisville live in poverty. If a family has a child under the age of five, the figures increase to 21.8 percent in the county and 37.2 percent in the city. If that household is headed by a single mother the rates are 63.7 percent in Jefferson County and 74.1 percent in the city.

Other contributing factors to homelessness include drug and alcohol abuse and mental illness. The local picture is much like the national, where about one-third of people who are homeless abuse alcohol and another one-third abuse other drugs. Between one-fourth and one-third of people who are homeless have a mental illness. One-tenth to one-fifth are diagnosed with both a substance abuse disorder and a mental illness. Many who work in the area of homelessness believe all of these figures are likely even higher.

Family violence is also a factor. In 1996 local shelter residents were asked whether they were homeless because of abuse. A total of 24.3 percent of the single women, 3.8 percent of the single men, and 61.1 percent of the family members answered yes. As people flee their homes to escape violence, they are confronted with the lack of safe, affordable housing. According to city and county studies for 1993, there were twenty-eight thousand households where shelter costs exceeded half of the household's income. As of June 1999, there were 8,781 eligible households on waiting lists for rent subsidies.

Soni Castleberry

HOME OF THE INNOCENTS. First opened at 108 W BROADWAY by Dr. James Taylor Helm in conjunction with CHRIST CHURCH CATHEDRAL, the home was incorporated by a special act of the Kentucky General Assembly on April 23, 1880. The goal of the institution as stated in its acts of incorporation was to "provide for the comfort and care of children of poor families, children of working and destitute mothers, and protection of the latter." The home cared for infants, preschool children, and young mothers with their babies regardless of religious affiliation.

In 1930 the home merged with the Protestant Episcopal Orphan Asylum. The former REUBEN DURRETT house at 202 E Chestnut St. was purchased in 1942 and modified to provide temporary care for eighteen children. By 1969 the home agreed to sell that property to Norton Children's Hospital for proposed expansion of the hospital's facilities. In 1972 the home moved into a new facility at 505 E Chestnut. The fifteen-year period between 1972 and 1987 saw increased capacity from thirty to ninety children. In 1977 the expansion of University Hospital required the home again to relocate to 485 E Gray St. Another home at 522 E Gray served as a dormitory for twenty children.

Among the programs and services offered by the Home of the Innocents to benefit children is the Pediatric Convalescent Center. As the only fully dedicated pediatric nursing facility in Kentucky, it is a skilled NURSING facility with forty-six beds to care for children who are medically fragile. The convalescent center is the only nursing home in Kentucky exclusively for the care of children, from birth to age twenty-one, with a variety of medical problems and birth defects. When residents reach twenty-one, the home helps their families find residences for them. In addition the home furnishes assistance to children through its Childcare Center. Among the services offered are the Emergency Shelter, which provides a safe environment for children who have been removed from their homes because of neglect or abuse; the Pregnant and Teen Parenting Services, which furnishes support services to pregnant teenage girls; the Transitional Housing Program, which provides a supervised life experience for young homeless mothers and their children; Home to Home Services, which helps maintain severely emotionally disturbed children in their families and communities; and the Therapeutic Loving Foster Care Services, which offers a family-based alternative to long-lasting institutional confinement for seriously ill children.

Each year the home serves about twelve hundred abused, neglected, and fragile children and pediatric nursing home patients from Kentucky and southern Indiana. The full- and part-time staff includes a pediatrician, child development specialist, nurses, counselors, social workers, medical social workers, child-care workers, and recreational specialists. Occupational, speech-and-hearing, and physical therapists are also available. Volunteers help in various capacities.

On March 5, 1999, the Home of the Innocents purchased the 20.5 acre BOURBON STOCK YARDS from Lincoln International Corp. for $3.4 million. Located at the east end of MARKET ST., the new facilities, designed by Michael Koch and Associates and Luckett and Farley Architects, are slated to be opened in 2001. Funding for the project combined proceeds from the sale of the Grey St. properties, a capital campaign fund, and specific donations. On November 17, 1998, Kosair Charities, which benefits children, donated the largest gift in its history, $6.2 million to the organization to finance a new pediatric convalescent center.

See *Courier-Journal,* Nov. 12, 1998, March 25, 1999.

HOME RULE. Louisville and Jefferson County were governed until 1972 by special legislation that made them agents of state GOVERNMENT exercising only those specific powers delegated by the Kentucky General Assembly. Their status was governed by Dillon's Rule, which states that cities and counties have no inherent power but owe their existence to and exercise only those powers expressly granted by the state legislature. In 1972 the General Assembly allowed Louisville and Jefferson County to escape the limitations of Dillon's rule by enacting home rule statutes.

The county home rule statute, Senate Bill 165, provided all Kentucky counties with a broad grant of powers stating that "the fiscal court of any county is hereby authorized and empowered to exercise all rights, powers, franchises, and privileges including the power to levy all taxes not in conflict with the constitution and statutes of this state." The Kentucky Supreme Court, wedded to Dillon's Rule, struck down the statute. In *Fiscal Court of Jefferson County* v. *City of Louisville* (1977), the court held that the legislature could grant counties governmental powers, but "it must do so with the precision of a rifle shot and not with the casualness of a shotgun blast." In response, the 1978 General Assembly salvaged county home rule by enacting House Bill 152, the current statute, which provides fiscal COURTS with legislative authority to enact ordinances, issue regulations, levy taxes, issue bonds, appropriate funds, and employ personnel to perform twenty-five specified public functions.

The home rule statute for cities of the first class (House Bill 355) provided Louisville, as the only city of the first class, with a broad grant of home rule powers virtually identical to those initially given to counties. House Bill 355 empowered the BOARD OF ALDERMEN to exercise "all of the rights, privileges, powers, franchises, including the power to levy all taxes, not in conflict with the Constitution."

Louisville's home rule statute also confronted a legal challenge. The dispute began when the Board of Aldermen enacted an ordinance to give them subpoena power to investigate the mayor. In *Stansbury* v. *Maupin* (1979), the Jefferson Circuit Court granted the mayor an injunction holding that the home rule statute did not expressly confer the subpoena power upon the board. The Court of Appeals, relying upon the shotgun language of the *Fiscal Court* case, agreed that the home rule statute did not confer specific authorization to issue subpoenas. But then it reversed the circuit court by holding that the subpoena power was necessarily implied by the statute's express grant of power to enact legislation. The Kentucky Supreme Court agreed with the circuit and appellate courts that the statute did not specifically include the subpoena power, but then decided the case in favor of the mayor by holding that, in the absence of utter necessity, the subpoena power was "too powerful and too susceptible of abuse, to be implied from the express power to enact legislation."

So far, the Kentucky Supreme Court decisions have not allowed the General Assembly to completely escape the strictures of Dillon's Rule. The court's decision in the *Stansbury* case avoided the issue and permitted Louisville to exercise broad home rule powers, while its decision in the *Fiscal Court* case required the legislature to specify the powers it grants to counties. As a consequence, the General Assembly has continued to amend the county home rule statute because that statute with its detailed list of powers could not anticipate every possible power a county government might need.

See Charlie Bush, ed., *Citizen's Guide to the Kentucky Constitution,* Kentucky Legislative Research Commission Research Report No. 137 (Frankfort 1991); Mark E. Mitchell and Cheryl J. Walters, *County Government in Kentucky,* Kentucky Legislative Research Commission Informational Brochure No. 115 (Frankfort 1996); J. David Morris, *The New Municipal Law: Kentucky's Cities under Home Rule,* Kentucky Legislative Research Commission Informational Bulletin No. 138 (Frankfort 1981).

William Crawford Green

HONORABLE ORDER OF KENTUCKY COLONELS. The Honorable Order of Kentucky Colonels has maintained its headquarters in the Louisville/Jefferson County area since its formation in the early 1930s. Located at 6100 Dutchmans Ln., this nationally known group comprises individuals who have been commissioned honorary Kentucky Colonels by a Kentucky governor—beginning with Gov. Isaac Shelby in 1812. The first recipients of the award were soldiers who had served with Shelby in battle and often functioned as members of his personal guard.

Under the leadership of Gov. Flem Sampson, a group known as "The Kentucky Colonels" was formed in 1931. A year later, Gov. Ruby Laffoon helped reorganize the group into the "Honorable Order of Kentucky Colonels," reflecting its members' honorary status. Col. Anna Bell Ward, a prominent Kentuckian and Hollywood movie producer, was appointed the first secretary for the Honorable Order, and Col. Charles Pettijohn as first national commanding general.

After the appointment of Col. Anna Friedman as secretary in 1938, the order began evolving from primarily a social organization to one of the premier grant-making charities in Kentucky. Recognized as a nonprofit organization by the IRS in 1944, the order began its charitable work by providing decorations and furnishing recreation halls for soldiers stationed at FORT KNOX during WORLD WAR II and involving itself in various other projects in subsequent years. In 1951, the order awarded its first grants totaling sixty-one hundred dollars to four Kentucky institutions. By the end of the century it had awarded over $20 million to Kentucky philanthropic organizations.

The social aspects of being a Kentucky Colonel are fulfilled through the sponsorship of two Derby weekend events, the annual banquet held Derby Eve at the GALT HOUSE in Louisville and the Annual Kentucky Colonels Barbecue held at the Wickland Estate in Bardstown, Kentucky, the day after the KENTUCKY DERBY.

The affairs of the order are managed by a Board of Trustees who serve without compensation.

James H. Molloy

HOOSIER. Hoosier is the nickname for Indiana residents. The origins of the term are obscure, and many derivations have been suggested. Several authorities have theorized that it derived from "Hoozer," a word in English dialect meaning anything unusually large. It supposedly evolved to describe an unpolished person—an apt description of many Indiana pioneers. Another popular theory attributed "Hoosier" to a slurring of the inquiry "Who's here?" in response to a knock on a settler's door. Nearly as popular is the notion that the name derived from "husher," an Indiana settler capable of finishing off an opponent with a few well-placed blows. Popular but unfounded is the attribution to Sam Hoosier, a mythical contractor on the LOUISVILLE AND PORTLAND CANAL. He supposedly favored Indiana workers, who became known as "Hoosier men." Although it does not explain the term's origin, John Finley's 1833 poem "The Hoosier's Nest" promoted its popular acceptance in Indiana.

Carl E. Kramer

HOPE DISTILLERY. Founded in 1815 by a group of primary eastern investors headed by James D'Wolf Jr., the Hope Distillery was intended to mass produce whiskey for the East Coast market. The origins of the name are uncertain though it may have derived from the single-word motto of the investors' home state. Armed with the knowledge that the Internal Revenue tax, used to pay federal debts from the War of 1812, would be abolished in 1818, the company raised approximately one hundred thousand dollars in capital for its revolutionary venture. Construction of the distillery began in 1816, with the first production in mid-1817. Located on one hundred acres at MAIN ST. and Portland Ave. purchased in 1814 by D'Wolf, the Hope Distillery was a technological experiment in its day. A 45-horsepower steam engine served two English stills of 1,500-gallon capacity and a 750 gallon doubler. The distillery produced twelve hundred gallons per day in 1819 and reached a maximum capacity of fifteen hundred gallons a day in 1821. The spent beer, or slop, would feed nearly five thousand cattle or hogs, according to the owners' somewhat optimistic estimates.

The New England–based company was ahead of its time in both vision and method. It was the first venture to attempt mass production of Kentucky bourbon, and the process it used to separate the alcohol from the mash became popular only after PROHIBITION. However, management miscalculated in several critical areas. They failed to realize that mass production created a different taste than that of whiskey made in small pot stills. The public preferred the latter. They also remained outsiders in an industry characterized by a closely knit group of producers who acted like an extended family. They also underestimated the power of TEMPERANCE forces that used the huge operation as a symbol of the dangers of the liquor industry. Finally, there was dissension among the owners and mismanagement of the plant. Litigation went on from the 1820s to the 1870s, with at least one case going to the U.S. Supreme Court and involving such famous Kentuckians as Henry Clay, Richard M. Johnson, Robert Wickliffe, James Prentice, and Charles Thruston. The distillery closed in 1850. The building fell into disrepair and burned after standing idle for many years. The land was developed into a subdivision called DeWolf's Western Addition. The distillery remains part of Louisville folklore because of its connection to the legendary Jim Porter. Porter was so tall, it was said, he could remove a bird's nest from the steeple of Old Hope.

See Gary Regan and Mardee Haidin Regan, *The Book of Bourbon and Other Fine American Whiskeys* (Shelburne, Vt., 1995); H.W. Coyte, unpublished papers, University of Louisville Archives, Sanborn Insurance Maps, 1894, University of Kentucky Map Room; Henry G. Crowgey, *Kentucky Bourbon* (Lexington 1971); William L. Downard, *Dictionary of the History of the American Brewing and Distilling Industries* (Westport, Conn., 1890), 19; J. William Stone, "The Hope Distillery Co.," *Filson Club History Quarterly* 27 (Jan. 1953): 29–35. James F. Hopkins, ed., *The Papers of Henry Clay* (Lexington 1963) vol. 3, 1–3, 109–10, 453–54.

Lindsey Apple
Albert Young

HORINE, EMMET FIELD (b Brooks, BULLITT COUNTY, Kentucky, August 3, 1885; d Brooks, February 1, 1964). Physician. Emmet Field Horine, the son of Dr. George H. and Elizabeth (Barrell) Horine, graduated from Emory College in Atlanta in 1903 and received his M.D. degree from the Kentucky School of MEDICINE in Louisville in 1907. Later he studied cardiology, pathology, and anesthesiology in Europe and Louisville. During WORLD WAR I Horine was a captain in the Medical Corps, U.S. Army, and chief of the cardiovascular service at Camp Hancock, Georgia.

In private practice, Horine was the first cardiologist in Jefferson County. For nearly fifty years, Horine taught medicine at the UNIVERSITY OF LOUISVILLE School of Medicine and was chief of the section on medical history. He also served as president of the Medico-Chirurgical Society of Louisville and of the Ohio Valley Medical Association. In 1955 he became professor emeritus of medicine. Between 1935 and 1963 he was the historian of the Kentucky State

Medical Association.

During his long career, Horine accumulated a medical history collection of manuscripts, classic treatises, and other documents that he bequeathed to the rare books departments of libraries at the University of Louisville, University of Kentucky, and Transylvania University. His most enduring contribution to medical history is *Daniel Drake, M.D. (1785–1852): Pioneer Physician of the Midwest* (1961).

On June 30, 1914, Horine married Helen B. Ruthenburg; they had four children. He was cremated and his ashes are buried in the Horine family cemetery, which is now within the Jefferson County Memorial Forest.

See E.H. Conner, "Emmet Field Horine, 1885–1964," *Journal of Kentucky State Medical Association* 62 (1964): 216.

Eric Howard Christianson

HORSE RACING. Since the early 1800s racing horses has been a popular, although somewhat sporadically supported, seasonal sport in Louisville. Unlike Lexington, where horse racing has always been a deeply ingrained tradition, Louisville has embraced racing primarily for its commercial value, distinguished by virtue of the KENTUCKY DERBY being the prime spring destination on the North American racing circuit.

The blooded horse (an animal of known ancestry) that Virginians, North Carolinians, and Marylanders brought through the Cumberland Gap into Kentucky's Bluegrass Region traced its aristocratic heritage to England, where, following the Battle of Bosworth Field (1485), Henry Tudor reigned as Henry VII. A century of civil war had decimated the island kingdom's equine population. Henry forbade the exportation of all bloodstock and established a royal stud. There, small, fleet-footed Irish Hobby and Scottish Galloway mares were mated with imported Arab stallions to produce faster, lighter-boned cavalry horses suitable for modern warfare. Speed and maneuverability, not full body armor, as the Crusades and Bosworth Field proved, determined victory. Elizabeth I, finding the royal stud no more than a muddled mix of breeds at the beginning of her reign, systematically reinstituted proper breeding and record-keeping techniques.

In 1607 a company of adventurous English gentlemen with little practical knowledge of survival established a colony in Virginia, naming the settlement Jamestown to honor their patron king, James I. They brought no horses with them. Six mares and a stallion sent to the colony in 1610 became food for the starving colonists. Just before the remnant of this ill-prepared band determined to abandon their colony, additional men, supplies and horses arrived. A decade later, the Virginia Co., operating under James's royal charter, underwrote the expense of shipping twenty mares to the colony, where these animals sold for premium prices.

Charles I (r. 1625–49) loved sporting life. His reign was marked by a bloody civil war beginning in 1642. Seven years later, the Puritan-controlled Long Parliament ordered Charles beheaded, the royal stables disbanded, and public amusements suppressed. For the next decade, racing was confined to the estates of out-of-favor Royalists, some of whom emigrated to the colonies.

In 1649 there were two hundred horses in Virginia. Twenty years later, Virginia's equine population was so large that breeders began exporting surplus animals to other coastal settlements. By then, Charles II (r. 1660–85), "Father of the British Turf," was England's monarch, and the sport of kings was in full flower. Charles not only oversaw the importation of North African Arab stallions for the royal stud; he jockeyed his own horses at public meets and was an arbiter and authority in racing matters. Subsequent monarchs, especially Queen Anne (r. 1702–14) encouraged the sport and sponsored the construction of new tracks.

English racing developed around meandering grassy courses where horses lumbered along for several miles, out of sight of spectators, then accelerated nearing the finish line. In contrast, colonial dash-racing—two animals running full speed on a flat straightway—was informal, exciting, and a ready-made betting opportunity for the working classes, who, by law, were forbidden the gentleman's privilege of wagering.

Eventually the flat grassless stretches of worn-out TOBACCO fields provided novel footing—a compacted dirt surface—for testing horses' speed. As the coastal population grew, men of all social classes migrated inland. By the 1770s they had ventured through the Cumberland Gap into Kentucky. Climate, soil, and grazing conditions in the Bluegrass were well suited to the development of racing stock. With the colonies on the brink of revolution, Daniel Boone, a delegate to the four-day May 1775 Transylvania convention at Boonesborough, introduced a bill to improve the breed of horses in the Kentucky territory. That bill was one of nine that became law. The first recorded races in the state had taken place at Harrodstown in 1773.

True to their intent, Bluegrass horsemen bought pedigreed stallions from Virginia breeders and reported births to nationally circulated gentlemen's sporting journals. The first volume of the *American Turf Register,* published in 1830, listed seven thoroughbreds standing in Kentucky. That number tripled by 1837. All were Bluegrass-based; there were no farms of note in or around Louisville. Louisville's culturally diverse population never had the mindset or the slave-based plantation economy crucial to the development of Thoroughbred racing. Early accounts of the sport in Louisville are sketchy at best.

In the 1820s, members of the Louisville Jockey Club raced horses below town in the "Bottoms" at the HOPE DISTILLERY turf course adjacent to PORTLAND, after safety-minded citizens objected to impromptu races on MARKET ST. There was a track on SHIPPINGPORT where young Jim Porter, before he grew to "Kentucky Giant" stature, made his living as a jockey. On the other side of Jefferson County, Peter Funk built the Beargrass track at what is today the intersection of Taylorsville Rd. and Hurstbourne Pkwy. Both tracks were well patronized. A visitor from SHELBY COUNTY wrote his brother in 1829 complaining about the "dirty mechanics who crowded in the stagecoach at Middletown—all anxious to get to the Louisville races."

OAKLAND RACE COURSE, on the Oakland Turnpike at roughly Seventh and Magnolia Streets, opened in 1832. It was an outgrowth of racing sponsored by the Louisville Agricultural Society, which, in 1831, had reorganized as the Louisville Association for the Improvement of the Breed of Horses. Samuel Churchill was the group's president when Oakland was built on land the association purchased from him. The 57 1/2-acre facility, located a mile from the southern boundary of the city, boasted a 3-story clubhouse and stabling facilities for 120 horses.

The nationally advertised fourteen-thousand-dollar, three-heat match race between Louisiana's Wagner and Grey Eagle—the pride of Kentucky—took place at Oakland in 1839, attracting "the Bench, the Bar, the Senate and the Press." Louisville grew, but Oakland waned, a victim of financial difficulties. Oakland ran its last official race around the mid-1850s. Informal trotting races were held there until the stables fell in ruins and grass reclaimed the track.

The aged stallions Wagner and Grey Eagle appeared in the arena at the inaugural Southwestern Agricultural Association exposition in 1853. That facility, located in CRESCENT HILL, included a track for "trotters" bred and raced by affluent gentlemen farmers in Jefferson and surrounding counties. During the CIVIL WAR, the association site became a campground for Union soldiers. The tract was subdivided and auctioned the week M. Lewis Clark Jr.'s Louisville Jockey Club opened.

In the late 1850s Louisville and Bluegrass horse interests joined forces to establish what they envisioned as the National Race Course of America. They purchased 150 acres adjacent to the LOUISVILLE & NASHVILLE RAILROAD tracks along Westport Rd., east of the fledgling community of ST. MATTHEWS. Supporters raised fifty thousand dollars, issuing stock in the name of the Louisville Association for the Improvement of the Breed of Horses. Investors included some of the wealthiest men in Lexington. WOODLAWN RACE COURSE featured both a racing and a trotting track. The Civil War made scheduling regular meets there impossible. The site was subdivided and auctioned in 1872, although harness races were held there as late as 1876.

In 1869 *The Turf, Field and Farm*'s editorialist noted that the Greenland Course, later part of SOUTH LOUISVILLE'S WILDER PARK, had sprung up like a mushroom following

Woodlawn's demise. The track was poorly managed and short-lived, "a blot on the escutcheon of racing which true lovers of the sport would not patronize," the writer correctly concluded.

Louisville businessmen and Bluegrass horsemen, calling themselves the Louisville Jockey Club and Driving Park Association, built another South End track in 1875. By 1883 turfwriters referred to it as CHURCHILL DOWNS, acknowledging the role three generations of that family played in Louisville racing.

Churchills trace their roots to the south of England, where they were landholders of record by the reign of Edward III (1327–77) and Royalists during the Protectorate. William Churchill (ca. 1650–1711) immigrated to Virginia in 1674, purchased land on the Rappahannock River, married a wealthy widow, and became a man of position and prominence. Armistead Churchill, his grandson, was born at the family plantation, Bushy Park, in 1733. Armistead was fifty-four old when he brought his family to Louisville. Samuel, his youngest son, was then eight years old. Armistead Churchill's three-hundred-acre tract included today's AUDUBON PARK, the Eastern Pkwy.–Preston Hwy. intersection, parts of the UNIVERSITY OF LOUISVILLE Belknap Campus, and Churchill Downs.

Samuel's signature can be found on early nineteenth-century Jefferson County estate inventory filings. His specialty was appraising livestock, especially horses. Samuel married Abigail Oldham. Their daughter Abigail married MERIWETHER LEWIS CLARK, son of William Clark of the LEWIS AND CLARK expedition. After Abigail's death, six-year-old Meriwether Lewis Clark Junior was passed along to his bachelor brothers, John and Henry, to raise. The Churchills were astute businessmen who lived off the income from their well-invested fortunes. They raced thoroughbreds only as a hobby, but they understood the importance of an accessible racetrack to landlocked Lexington horsemen and to Louisville's burgeoning convention trade.

Since 1875 Louisville racing, principally at the Downs, has survived because of its affiliations with local transportation and hotel and TOURISM interests. Clark and his eventual successor, Matt Winn were the industry leaders because they blended Bluegrass sport with river city commerce and updated tradition with technology.

Clark created the KENTUCKY DERBY and the Oaks, patterning these races on classic British events. He imported French pari-mutuel wagering machines but had no success teaching the public how to use them. In an attempt to unify racing and codify racing rules, he convened the first American Turf Congress at Louisville's GALT HOUSE, but the various jockey clubs could not reach a consensus. In 1884 he created the Great American Stallion Stake, the prototype for the modern Breeders' Cup, but the race was short-lived. He was forced to turn his debt-ridden Downs over to bookmakers in 1894. Within seven years, the track became little more than an attractive nuisance that civic-minded citizens were anxious to avoid.

After 1902 Winn developed Churchill Downs as a multipurpose entertainment site. He brought in baseball's caterer, Harry M. Stevens, and hired big-name bands to play there in the summer. He reintroduced pari-mutuel wagering at the 1908 Derby, using newspaper advertising to teach bettors how to use the new-fangled machines. Embracing twentieth-century technology, he promoted racing through movie house newsreels. WHAS radio provided nationwide coverage of the Derby from a lookout in the Twin Spires in 1925. A public address system allowed fans to hear a race call in 1930. WAVE, the forty-first television station in the country, did a live on-site telecast of the Diamond Jubilee Derby in 1949. Stevens's commercialization of the mint julep souvenir glass became part and parcel of the Derby's success.

In 1956 Derby day guest John Steinbeck wrote, "This Kentucky Derby, whatever it is—a race, an emotion, a turbulence, an explosion—is one of the most beautiful and violent and satisfying things I have ever experienced." Those wishing to experience Derby magic the rest of the year visited the one story concrete block KENTUCKY DERBY MUSEUM, completed in 1962. Mary Ann Cooper, the third woman licensed to train thoroughbreds in Kentucky, was curator.

For the next twenty years, American racing rested on its laurels, vying only with baseball to attract record crowds. Smaller tracks around Louisville came and went; Churchill Downs and the Derby reigned supreme. Late in 1981 Downs president Lynn Stone announced that a new $5 million Kentucky Derby Museum, funded by the J. Graham Brown Foundation, was in the works.

The Chamber of Commerce Derby Festival, a weeklong civic celebration, has supported "the greatest two minutes in sports" since the 1950s. At the festival's April 23, 1982, "They're Off!" awards luncheon, prominent horseman John R. Gaines announced plans for the Breeders' Cup, an annual multimillion-dollar fall day of racing beginning in 1984. Downs management was forced to take a new look at its operation. The track had no turf course and could not qualify as a Breeders' Cup host site.

By the end of the year Churchill's board not only approved plans to build a turf course but also extended the 1983 spring meet into the summer. It was too much racing for Louisvillians. Losses were so high Lynn Stone resigned in August 1984 after a second summer of racing proved equally disastrous.

Warner L. Jones, a Churchill descendant whose sole business was breeding and racing Thoroughbreds, was elected chairman of the board, and Thomas H. Meeker, the track's general counsel, was appointed president. Meeker toured Churchill Downs and reported that he saw a rundown track in a blighted neighborhood. Through his Three-C initiative—capital improvement, community relations, and customer service—he began turning the track and the nearby community around. In July 1987 Churchill Downs was named host track for the 1988 Breeders' Cup. The 71,237 attendance figure eclipsed the 69,155 record set at Santa Anita in 1986. In 1991 Breeders' Cup Day attendance at the Downs dipped to 66,204, then set a new record, 71,671, in 1994, assuring the track a fourth Breeders' Cup on November 7, 1998. Racing's richest day—$13.2 million in purses—unfolded before an all-time record crowd of 80,452. When California's Santa Anita Park backed out early in 1999, Churchill Downs won back the event an unprecedented fifth time.

Louisville racing has long given the city an international identity and supported tourism and business development large and small. Since 1979 Louisvillian Becky Biesel's mail order business has shipped Derby party supplies worldwide. Ben Isaacs's Festival Gallery has been a downtown fixture since 1981. William Friedberg has published three reference books on racing's most sought-after collectible, the souvenir mint julep glass.

Before his death in 1997, turf writer Jim Bolus produced seven volumes of Derby stories. For the 1995 Twin Spires centennial, Lynn Renau wrote and published histories of Thoroughbred racing, documenting the history of parimutuel wagering and long-forgotten African American contributions to the sport. That same year, the Kentucky Derby Museum published Samuel W. Thomas's *Churchill Downs: A Documentary History of America's Most Legendary Race Track.*

See Roger Longrigg, *The History of Horse Racing* (New York 1972); Lynn S. Renau, *Racing around Kentucky* (Louisville 1995); idem, *Jockeys, Belles and Bluegrass Kings* (Louisville 1996); Samuel W. Thomas, *Churchill Downs: A Documentary History of America's Most Legendary Race Track* (Louisville 1995); George H. Yater, *Two Hundred Years at the Falls of the Ohio* (Louisville 1987). *Courier-Journal,* May 6, 1956.

Lynn Renau

HORSE SHOWS AND COMPETITIONS. By the 1790s Kentuckians were paying top dollar for imported pedigreed livestock. Lewis Sanders advertised an agricultural fair in the May 27, 1816, *Kentucky Gazette*: "On Thursday, the 25th day of July next there will be exhibited at Sanders Gardens, Sandersville, two and a half miles northwest of Lexington, fine cattle, sheep, hogs and horses. Premiums will be given to the owners of the best stock. etc. P.S. Silver cups will be given as prizes, valued at $15.00 each."

The following year, a State Agricultural Organization, predecessor of the later Louisville-based KENTUCKY STATE FAIR, was formed. By 1830, Bourbon, Franklin, Mercer, and Jefferson Counties had broken away from the state organization, and all held HORSE SHOWS. In the decade before the Civil War, the Louisville Agricultural Society sponsored both harness racing and agricultural competitions at the Southwest Agricultural Society's fairgrounds in Louisville's now CRESCENT HILL neighborhood.

Horses competing there were primarily Kentucky Saddlers, the forerunner of the American Saddlebred, a flashy high-stepper that performs three natural gaits—walk, trot, and canter—and two manmade gaits—slow-gait and rack. The state fair, where annual competitions date to 1902, has crowned the world's grand champion five-gaited American Saddlebred since 1917. The world's grand championship three-gaited and fine harness classes have been held there since 1936.

America's horse population declined following World War I, only to rebound after the Korean War as the interstate highway network and specialized horse-hauling equipment made long-distance horse transport practical. During the 1970s the Rock Creek Horse Show and the Long Run Horse Show were strong regional competitions. ANCHORAGE youngsters competed in the St. Luke's Horse Show held on the church grounds in eastern Jefferson County. By the early 1980s, Long Run and St. Luke's, highlighting the talents of Thoroughbred-type horses capable of jumping elaborately designed fences, had fallen victim to their own success, as entries required more space and manpower than the volunteer organizations sponsoring them could provide.

In contrast, the Kentucky State Fair WORLD'S CHAMPIONSHIP HORSE SHOW, under the direction of Bill Munford, grew from a 5-day show awarding $155,000 in prize money and trophies in 1974 to a 6-day show awarding $1,125,000 in premiums, the largest amount of any American Horse Show Association–sanctioned show in America. The World's Championship Horse Show is the only breed show controlled by a state rather than a breed association, guaranteeing that it will always be held in Louisville. In 1998 the show drew 2,020 entrants, exhibitors from 40 states, and, with a profit of over half a million dollars, was the state fair's most successful event.

Because of the heavy shoe that enhances a Saddlebred's gait, a farrier must be stationed ringside, ready to replace a shoe in the five-minute timeout allotted each exhibitor for emergency tack repairs. For over seventy-five years, three generations of Louisville's Ernst family have served as farriers at the Kentucky State Fair Horse Show. In recognition of their service to the horse industry, Phil, Forrest, and Jack Ernst became charter members of the International Horseshoers Hall of Fame in 1993.

See Anna Virginia Parker, *The Sanders Family of Grass Hill* (Madison, Ind., 1966); The American Saddle Horse Museum, Kentucky Horse Park, Lexington, Ky.

Lynn Renau

HOSPICE & PALLIATIVE CARE OF LOUISVILLE. This first hospice in Kentucky began providing compassionate care for incurable patients and their families in 1978. Hospice & Palliative Care of Louisville cares for the physical, emotional, and spiritual needs of all patients and their families, regardless of their ability to pay. Hospice care also includes bereavement support, education, and counseling.

The idea that there should be a hospice in Louisville was first explored in 1974. After groundbreaking efforts by Sherrill Thirlwell, Dr. Harper Ritchie, and Gerald Swim, Hospice of Louisville was incorporated June 29, 1976. The Reverend Richard Humke was the first board chair. In June 1978 the first patients were accepted.

The word *hospice* comes from the Latin root *hospes,* from which our words *hospital, hospitality, hostel,* and both *host* and *guest* are derived. In medieval times, a hospice was a place of shelter and refuge for a person on a difficult journey—the outward journey undertaken as pilgrims sought to visit holy places or the inward journey faced by widows, orphans, lepers, and dying individuals. We can trace the existence of hospices from that time until now. However, the modern hospice movement is considered to have begun in England in the 1960s with the founding of St. Christopher's Hospice by Dame Cicely Saunders.

Hospice & Palliative Care of Louisville does not duplicate any existing service. It is nondenominational and nonprofit; available in Bullitt, Henry, Jefferson, Oldham, Shelby, Spencer, and Trimble Counties; and serves adults and children. It is one of the few hospices in the country to have a pediatric program.

Each year Hospice & Palliative Care of Louisville, Hospice & Palliative Care of Central Kentucky, and Hospice of Southern Indiana offer special weekend camps for children ages six through eleven at Camp Evergreen, and sponsor Tsunami, a weekend gathering for youth ages twelve through seventeen. Both programs help children develop skills to cope with the death of a loved one. The Bridges Center meets both the bereavement needs of the families of hospice patients and those of the general community.

Hospice & Palliative Care of Louisville is funded through Medicare, Medicaid, insurance, and donations from individuals, memorials, businesses, and foundations.

Robert J. Mueller

HOSPITALS. The first Louisvillians found themselves living near disease-breeding ponds that were the source of fevers, smallpox, and waterborne illnesses. Even on the frontier it was considered the responsibility of a town to provide not a hospital for the sick but a pest house to quarantine the poor who contracted a known contagious disease. Often towns were forced to designate specific buildings as pest houses in order to avoid an epidemic or the panic that some diseases created. Such was the case for Louisville in June 1817 when a virulent smallpox epidemic broke out. The need to quarantine the contagious was so acute that John Gwathmey's cotton textile mill at the edge of town was commandeered as makeshift quarters for victims, and all town physicians volunteered their services. The improvised facility housed the infected poor, who were relegated to the pest house not for care but specifically for quarantine. The wealthy and middle class were fortunate enough to be quarantined in their homes, where they often flew yellow flags to warn others of illness.

Although Louisville's first charter in 1828 authorized establishment of an adequate pest house, another smallpox epidemic ravaged an unprepared Louisville again in 1840. The need for emergency relief was met this time by temporarily taking over a warehouse at Ninth and MAIN Streets. A more permanent pest house was not built until 1848 because residents refused to have it located nearby. The situation was resolved by the purchase of WILLIAM JOHNSON's old brick residence, which had formerly been used as a poorhouse. There victims of yellow fever, smallpox, and other contagious diseases languished but did not infect others. By 1878 Saint John's Eruption Hospital officially became the permanent home to quarantine the city's contagious poor. The staff was supplied by the Catholic order of Sisters of Charity of Nazareth. Its site, Seventh Street Pike five miles from the courthouse, was chosen for its remoteness from the city and its proximity to the Illinois Central Railroad tracks to make transportation for the sick by rail easier. Early in 1817, the same year as the first smallpox epidemic, plans were set in motion by the Commonwealth of Kentucky for a Louisville Marine Hospital. The facility was planned to provide care for local citizens and the many boatmen who become sick on the OHIO RIVER and disembarked at Louisville to recuperate or die. The hospital was incorporated in 1817 but was still unfinished in 1822 when a yellow fever epidemic swept the town. Even the head of the hospital project was among its 140 victims. By 1823 the still-unfinished building opened at Chestnut St. between Floyd and Preston on land donated by two wealthy resdients. Although the site was remote at the time, it was largely responsible for the location of Louisville's current medical complex.

An 1832 charter of the Kentucky General Assembly authorized the trustees of the Louisville Marine Hospital to transfer their medical department to the planned Medical Institute, which would be located on Chestnut St. between Eighth and Ninth. The institute functioned informally as the University (of Louisville) School of Medicine but did not change its name to reflect that until 1846 when it was renamed UNIVERSITY OF LOUISVILLE Medical Department.

For the next 150 years, area hospitals developed largely in response to POPULATION growth

City Hospital, north side of Chestnut Street between Floyd and Preston, 1941.

and specific needs. The Marine Hospital itself, with only eighty beds, became woefully inadequate as the city grew. In 1836 a remodeling project added two new wings, and the name was changed to Louisville City Hospital to reflect the patients it served. In 1910 the need for more beds was so critical that the city authorized a bond issue. A new structure was begun on Chestnut St. between Brook and Preston Streets in 1911 and completed in 1914. In 1943 it was renamed Louisville General Hospital. In 1979 General Hospital was deeded to the University of Louisville and renamed the University of Louisville Hospital. There followed mergers with various hospital corporations, first HUMANA INC., then Galen Health Care, Columbia, and Columbia/HCA. In 1996 the University of Louisville Medical Center assumed management. The University of Louisville Hospital is located at 530 S Jackson St.

As medical knowledge improved and the town grew into a city, specific needs of ill citizens were identified and responded to with varying degrees of success. Several hospitals for women were founded but did not last long. The first two, the Kentucky Infirmary for Women and Children, founded in 1877 on the northeast corner of Green and Eleventh Streets, and Forest Hill Lying-In Hospital, which was established in 1878 on Workhouse Rd., did not survive. In 1892 the Jennie Casseday Free Infirmary for Women on Sixth St. between Magnolia and Hill Streets opened its doors.

The hospital was founded by the Order of King's Daughters as a memorial to the philanthropist Cassady who had founded the Louisville chapter. It had twenty-two beds and, for over five years, maintained both free and private wards to serve poor and middle-class women of Louisville.

At the end of the nineteenth century an interest in good health for children began to gain national prominence, but Louisville did not respond until a TORNADO forced many children to live in damp, unsanitary conditions. A yearlong fundraising drive collected enough money to finance Children's Free Hospital, which was built at 220 E Chesnut in 1892. It was joined in 1929 by the Kosair Crippled Children's Hospital, founded by Louisville's Kosair Shriners and located on Eastern Pkwy. between Preston St. and Poplar Level Rd. Kosair Crippled Children's Hospital became known for offering the "Kenny Treatment," named for Sister Elizabeth Kenny of Australia, to the youngest victims of the polio epidemics of the 1940s and 1950s. It is now known as KOSAIR CHILDREN'S HOSPITAL.

As was the national norm, AFRICAN AMERICANS were treated in separate wards in local hospitals or in separate infirmaries. From 1905-1912, Citizen's Hospital, listed as a colored facility in city directories, served blacks at 112 W Green St. Fraternal Hospital, founded in 1922 at 2125 W Chestnut, was also exclusively for blacks. The Red Cross Tuberculosis Sanitarium was established around 1905 at 1436 S Shelby for black patients only. It was staffed with both black and white physicians. Louisville City Hospital and Waverly Hills Tuberculosis Sanatorium accepted both black and white patients but in segregated wings.

In 1837 the federal government, acting as interstate commerce agent, determined that Louisville's location on the busy Ohio River required a hospital to serve the needs of mariners who worked the waterway. In 1843 a site in PORTLAND at Portland Turnpike and High St. (Portland Ave. and Northwestern Pkwy.) was purchased for six thousand dollars from George W. Gwathmey. The United States Marine Hospital, with a unique viewing tower so that boats could identify its location near the Portland Canal, was completed in 1847.

Although the U.S. Marine Hospital was a government facility, it only served war-wounded and veterans when the need for beds was acute. Two other hospitals in Louisville trace their origins directly to the need to serve veterans. During the CIVIL WAR, all available buildings, including warehouses, factories, schools, and some private homes, were turned into hospitals for the Union and Confederate wounded. Army hospitals were located at Ninth and BROADWAY, at Eighth and Green (LIBERTY), on Main between Seventh and Eighth, at Seventh and Main, Seventh and Green, and Fifteenth and Main. By February 1863 nineteen temporary hospitals had been established in Louisville. When the hospitals were disbanded at the end of the war, Confederate veterans were cared for at the Confederate Veterans' Home located in PEWEE VALLEY.

With a thousand beds, Nichols U.S. Army General Hospital was Louisville's largest hospital during WORLD WAR II. It was built at Berry Blvd. and Manslick Rd., south of the city, as a temporary facility to treat sick and wounded soldiers. In 1946, when the U.S. Army turned the facility over to the Veterans Administratioin, it was remained Nichols Veterans Administration Hospital. In 1952 a new hospital, Louisville Veterans Affairs Medical Center, was built on a hilltop near Zorn Ave. and later renamed the Department of Veterans Affairs Medical Center. The original site was used by the federal government until 1957, when it was razed for private development.

Tuberculosis, a highly contagious disease, required very lengthy treatment. In the beginning patients were treated at the Tuberculosis Dispensary, a part of the Louisville City Hospital, but were moved to separate quarters on July 26, 1910. The facility was renamed Waverly Hills Sanatorium. It was located outside the city in a rural setting to take advantage of the beneficial effects of fresh air and sunshine. Hazelwood Sanatorium, organized and run by the Louisville Tuberculosis Association, opened in 1907. When the drug streptomycin became widely available, both hospitals closed, Waverly Hills in 1961 and Hazelwood in 1971.

Locally known as Lakeland Hospital, Central Kentucky Asylum for the Insane was founded in 1873. Now known as CENTRAL STATE HOSPITAL, it continues in newer quarters at the same location at 10510 LaGrange Rd. Although overcrowding had always been a problem at the state facility, there were few private alternatives for long-term care until 1952. In that year, responding to the need for a private facility, the Sisters of Charity of Nazareth opened Our Lady of Peace Hospital (Caritas Peace Center) in a quiet, park-like setting overlooking Newburg Rd. Other private psychiatric hospitals currently serving the Louisville area are Charter Behavioral Health System at 1405 Browns Ln. and Ten Broeck Hospital at 8521 Old LaGrange Rd.

There have been a number of important Catholic hospitals in Louisville. Most were established by CATHERINE SPALDING, the founder of the Sisters of Charity of Nazareth, whose mission is to minister to the sick. The earliest, St. Vincent Infirmary, opened in 1836 in two rooms of the St. Vincent Orphanage, housed in a brick building on Jefferson St. once owned by James Marshall. Staffed by the Sisters of Charity of Nazareth, Kentucky, its superintendent was Mother Catherine Spalding. In 1853 a move to FOURTH St. between Chestnut and BROADWAY allowed room for more beds. It was renamed St. Joseph Infirmary. In 1926 it moved from downtown to a large campus on Eastern Pkwy. between Preston St. and Bradley Ave. With room for expansion, St. Joseph's developed into the largest private hospital in Louisville. In 1970 the hospital was purchased by Humana Inc., and the building was razed. A new facility located on Poplar Level Rd., Humana Hospital-Audubon, was named for the nearby AUDUBON PARK neighborhood. It later merged with Galen Health Care and Columbia/HCA Healthcare Corp. In the fall of 1998 Alliant purchased Audubon from Columbia/HCA and in 1999 changed the hospital's name to Norton Audubon Hospital.

The second Catholic hospital in Louisville was Sts. Mary and Elizabeth Hospital, opened in 1874 at Thirteenth and Magnolia by the same order, Sisters of Charity of Nazareth. At that time neither Sts. Mary and Elizabeth nor St. Joseph Infirmary used professional nurses; all NURSING care was provided by the sisters themselves. In 1995 the Sisters of Charity of Nazareth formed the health-care corporation CARITAS HEALTH SERVICES. Its one remaining hospital in Louisville is the Caritas Medical Center. In 1900 the Franciscan Sisters founded St. Anthony, the third Catholic hospital. It has been known since 1995 as Vencor Hospital Louisville, located at 1313 St. Anthony Place.

The first Protestant hospital in Louisville was the John N. Norton Memorial Infirmary. Named for a local Episcopal priest known for his philanthropy, the infirmary was opened in 1886 at the corner of Third and Oak Streets and included the Norton School of Nursing, Kentucky's first nursing school. In 1969 the Norton Infirmary merged with the Children's Hospitals Inc. In 1973 a new building was built that separated the adult-care facilities, known as Norton Hospital, and the child-care facilities, the Children's Hospital. In 1981 Kosair Crippled Children's Hospital merged with the Children's Hospital and was renamed Kosair Children's Hospital. The two later formed a parent corporation, NKC Inc.

The Methodists have had two hospitals in Louisville, starting with Deaconess Hospital, established on S Eighth St. in 1895. Like Norton, it had its own nursing school. Although Deaconess closed in 1951, it was followed by Methodist Evangelical Hospital, which opened on E Broadway in 1960. In 1989 Methodist Evangelical Hospital was renamed Alliant Medical Pavilion after a merger with NKC Inc. to form the Alliant Health System (now NORTON HEALTHCARE).

The Baptists opened a hospital in the HIGHLANDS east of downtown Louisville in 1924. Kentucky Baptist Hospital, at Barret Ave. and DeBarr St., closed in 1989 and consolidated with Baptist Hospital East at 4000 Kresge Way in the St. Matthews area and is managed by the Baptist Health System Inc.

Jewish Hospital was incorporated in Louisville in 1903 to offer medical care for East European Jewish immigrants and at the same time provide a place that welcomed Jewish physicians. A thirty-two-bed facility was built at Floyd and Kentucky Streets, convenient to the Preston St. neighborhood where many Jewish immigrants lived. in 1955 a new 145-bed Jewish Hospital was built at 217 E Chestnut. It was expanded again in 1960 to two hundred beds. In that decade Dr. Harold Kleinert established the Christian M. Kleinert Institute of Hand and Micro Surgery. Kentucky's first kidney transplant and first open-heart surgery, in 1964 and 1965 respectively, were both performed by Dr. Allen M. Lansing in Jewish Hospital. In 1973, with the opening of Wheeler Tower, the hospital's capacity grew to 403 beds. In 1977 the world's first bilateral forearm reimplantation was performed.

The later decades of the twentieth century continued to bring numerous firsts to Jewish Hospital. In 1981 Dr. Ronald Masden performed the state's first angioplasty. In 1984 the hospital received national attention for the first Kentucky heart transplant performed by Dr. Laman Gray Jr. In 1985 Dr. Gray implanted a ventricular assist device on a sixteen-year-old boy, only the third time in the world that such a device was used for a bridge to a transplant. In 1987 Kentucky's first pancreatic transplant took place. In 1999, Jewish Hospital was the site of the first hand transplant operation in the United States, performed by a team led by Dr. Warren Breidenbach on patient Matthew Scott.

In the late 1980s Jewish Hospital underwent structural reorganizations to become Jewish Hospital HealthCare Services. In 1995 these services included the Amelia Brown Frazier Rehabilitation Center, the Rudd Heart and Lung Center (with the state's largest cardiac program), and an expanded regional network including thirty-six locations, twelve hospitals, and twenty-four hundred beds. Jewish Hospital HealthCare Services also established the Jewish Hospital Foundation, which supports medical research and has established health and information centers in four local shopping malls.

The Louisville metropolitan area is also served by five Indiana hospitals: Clark Memorial Hospital at 1220 Missouri Ave. in JEFFERSONVILLE, Harrison County Hospital at 245 Atwood St. in Corydon, Scott Memorial Hospital at 1451 N Garner St. in Scottsburg, the Medical Center of Southern Indiana at 2200 Market St. in Charleston, and Floyd Memorial Hospital and Health Services in NEW ALBANY.

Hospitals in Greater Louisville

Alliant Medical Pavilion
315 W Broadway, Louisville
Baptist Hospital East
4000 Kresge Way, Louisville
Caritas Medical Center
1850 Bluegrass Ave., Louisville
Caritas Peace Center
2020 Newburg Rd., Louisville
Central State Hospital
10510 LaGrange Rd., Louisville
Charter Behavioral Health System
1405 Browns Ln., Louisville
Clark Memorial Hospital
1220 Missouri Ave., Jeffersonville, Indiana
Department of Veterans Affairs Medical Ctr.
800 Zorn Ave., Louisville
Floyd Memorial Hospital and Health Services
1850 State St., New Albany, Indiana
Frazier Rehab Center
220 Abraham Flexner Way, Louisville
Harrison County Hospital
245 Atwood St., Corydon, Indiana
Jewish Hospital
217 E Chestnut St., Louisville
Jewish Hospital
727 Hospital Dr., Shelbyville, Kentucky
Kosair Children's Hospital
231 E Chestnut St., Louisville
Norton Audubon Hospital
One Audubon Plaza, Louisville
Norton Hospital
200 W Chestnut St., Louisville
Norton Southwest Hospital
9820 Third Street Rd., Louisville
Norton Suburban Hospital
4001 Dutchmans Ln., Louisville
Scott Memorial Hospital
1451 N Gardner St., Scottsburg, Indiana
Southern Indiana Rehab Hospital
3104 Blackston Blvd., New Albany, Ind.
The Medical Center of Southern Indiana
2200 Market St., Charlestown, Indiana
Ten Broeck Hospital
8521 LaGrange Rd., Louisville
Ten Broeck Hospital
518 Washington St., Shelbyville, Kentucky
Tri-County Baptist Hospital
1025 New Moody Ln., LaGrange, Kentucky
University of Louisville Hospital
545 S Jackson St., Louisville
Vencor Hospital Louisville
1313 Saint Anthony Pl., Louisville

See Haven Emerson and Anna C. Phillips, *Hospitals and Health Agencies of Louisville 1924: A Survey* (Louisville 1925); Gail McGowan Mellor, *Kosair Children's Hospital: A History, 1892–1992* (S.1., 1992); Betty Lou Amster and Barbara G. Zingman, *The Mission: The History of Methodist Evangelical Hospital, 1960-1993* (Louisville 1994); Samuel W. Thomas, *Changing Medicine, Constant Care: Kentucky Baptist Hospitals* (Louisville 1990); Barbara Zingman and Betty Lou Amster, *A Legendary Vision: The History of Jewish Hospital* (Louisville 1997); State

Department of Health in Kentucky and the Kentucky State Medical Association, *Medicine and Its Development in Kentucky* (Louisville 1940); Elva Anne Lyon, ed., *University of Louisville Local History Series*, vol. 18, Hospitals (np).

Penelope Papangelis

HOT BROWN. Not long after the Brown Hotel, at W Broadway and Fourth St., opened in 1923, head chef Fred K. Schmidt created the now-famous Hot Brown. Developed as an alternative to the hotel's usual late-night fare of ham and eggs, the open-faced sandwich was an immediate success, quickly becoming the most requested item on the Brown's regular luncheon menu. In the ensuing years it has become closely associated with Louisville as its quintessential indigenous dish.

Known for its "light and fluffy" cheese sauce, the original Hot Brown consisted of white toast topped with slices of turkey, which at the time was a meat usually reserved for the holidays. The dish was then topped with Mornay sauce and a dash of Parmesan cheese, set under the oven broiler until bubbly, and garnished with pimiento and two crossed strips of bacon.

In later years, a number of variations on the original recipe were developed by professional and amateur chefs. These included the use of American and cheddar cheeses in the sauce, and garnishing with tomato or slices of mushroom. At times even canned peaches have been used as trimming, a practice generally frowned upon by purists.

See Kay Gill, *The Brown Hotel and Louisville's Magic Corner* (Louisville 1984).

Kosair Hotel and Temple (after Fort Nelson Hotel) and now a medical office building, south side of Broadway between Brook and Floyd Streets, 1924.

HOTELS AND MOTELS. As J. Stoddard Johnston noted in his *Memorial History of Louisville,* "hotels, called in those days taverns, were established in Louisville as soon as the people ventured outside the forts" (1: 52). In 1793, with a tavern license allowing a charge for meals and lodging in private homes, Maj. John Harrison opened one of the first Louisville hotels or taverns, at Sixth and Main Streets. Textile mill owner John Gwathmey established an inn called the Indian Queen around 1803 at the northeast corner of Fifth and Main Streets. The first hostelry to offer patrons more than just the bare necessities, it was later renamed Union Hall. Included among its famous guests were John James Audubon and his wife, Lucy, who lived there when they first arrived in Louisville in 1808. The Marquis de Lafayette stayed at Union Hall during his 1825 visit. Gwathmey sold the inn in 1819 to Archibald Allen, who himself had operated a hotel for a number of years near Second and Main Streets known as Washington Hall. Washington Hall was a small inn with meals at one sitting and no specialized services.

In Middletown, the Middletown Inn opened about 1800. Nearby was the Davis Tavern, opened in the early 1840s as a hotel, stagecoach stop, and slave-trading post. It was famous for its homemade cheese and attracted guests such as Henry Clay and John C. Breckinridge.

In 1832 the Louisville Hotel, Louisville's first large hotel, was built at 610 W Main. It was built on the plan of Boston's Tremont House and had sixty rooms, including parlor-bedroom suites and a dining room, bar, baggage room, and shops. It closed in 1938 and was razed in 1949 for a parking lot. Also nearby, the original Galt House, with sixty rooms, was built in 1835 on the site of Dr. William Galt's home at Second and Main. This hotel hosted Charles Dickens and several U.S. generals. It was destroyed by fire in 1865. A new Galt House was opened at First and Main in 1869. It closed in 1919 and was torn down in 1921 to make way for the new headquarters and warehouse of Belknap Hardware and Manufacturing Co. In 1972 developer Al Schneider opened the third (714-room) Galt House at Fourth and Main.

A number of hotels catered to a particular clientele. For instance the Falls View Hotel, at Fourth and the river, was opened in 1865 by a Captain Dougherty and catered primarily to steamboat pilots. Dougherty lost the hotel due to a gambling habit. It came into the possession of Eliza Birch, whose husband had loaned Dougherty money, and she ran the thirty-eight-room hotel until her death in 1900. The Falls View was demolished in 1937 after its closure a few years before.

The Commercial Hotel at the southwest corner of Bullitt and Water Streets operated in the 1840s and billed itself as a "homelike place for all river men"; likewise, the Opera Hotel at Fourth near the river catered to steamboatmen. The Bourbon House on E Main St. in Butchertown was a favorite of stockmen who had driven their cattle and hogs to Louisville for sale. Establishments such as the Hotel Preston at Third and Main Streets and the Nick Bosler Hotel (named the Antler Hotel during World War I) on the southeast corner of Second and Jefferson were popular haunts for theater performers in the early 1900s. Proximity to a railroad station was a selling point for some hotels. The Victoria on Broadway near Ninth St. was close to Union Station. The Fountain Hotel, on the northeast corner of Floyd and Jefferson, advertised in 1865 that it was opposite the city's first railroad depot (Louisville and Frankfort Railroad, 1851) at Brook and Jefferson. The Normandy Hotel, opened in the 1890s, was located on N Seventh St., across from Central Station. The St. Charles Hotel on the corner of Seventh and Main Streets was opened in 1869. Although it ceased operation as a hotel, it remained one of the oldest building on West Main St. and was purchased by Brown-Forman Corp. in 1998 and renovated for office space.

By 1870 Louisville counted thirty-five hotels. They included the National Hotel (1856) at Fourth and Main Streets, which provided its guests with ticket offices for the city's railroads; the Willard Hotel, known in the 1850s and '60s as the Croghan House, on Jefferson at Armory Place; and the United States Hotel at Fourth and Jefferson Streets. In 1856 C.C. Rufer opened Rufer's Hotel on Fifth St. between

Market and Main, with improvements such as electric call bells, annunciators, and steam heating. It catered to businessmen and was close to the Louisville business area, the steamboat landing, depots, and amusements. In 1866 Mrs. Smyser's Hotel was built near today's BOWMAN FIELD, east of the city. In the late 1800s several HOTELS/APARTMENTS were built along Broadway—Seneca Hotel, which was originally built in 1864 as a residence and later became Chesterfield Bachelors Apartments; Welsworth Hotel (1870), initially the home of banker Woodford H. Dulaney; and Rossmore Apartments (1894) on Fourth near Broadway, Louisville's first apartment house, which later became the Berkeley Hotel. In 1880 Seelbach's original "European Hotel" opened at Sixth and Main, but in 1902 brothers Louis and Otto Seelbach began building the downtown hotel at Fourth and Walnut (Muhammad Ali Blvd.) with elegant materials and goods imported from around the world. Opening in 1905, the Seelbach, which was alluded to in F. Scott Fitzgerald's *The Great Gatsby* as the Muhlbach, had gourmet dining and has hosted seven U.S. presidents. Closed in 1975 due to financial difficulties, the hotel was sold in 1978 to a pair of local businessmen, Gil Whittenberg and Roger Davis, who initiated an elaborate renovation project and reopened the hotel in 1982. In 1997 the hotel's name was changed to Seelbach Hilton after it was purchased by the CapStar Hotel Co. of Washington, D.C., in association with Hilton Hotels.

In the early 1900s hotels continued to be built, such as the Colonial Hotel at 422 W Chestnut. In 1910 the Girls' Friendly Society of the Episcopal Church opened the Girl's Friendly Inn at 219 E Chestnut to provide a chaperoned residence for girls; the inn later was the site for Jewish Hospital. In 1910 the Tyler Hotel at Third and Jefferson Streets was opened and was later named the MILNER HOTEL after its owner, Earle Milner. The Milner suffered fires and low occupancy in a block with adult entertainment and eventually was razed for the expansion of the KENTUCKY INTERNATIONAL CONVENTION CENTER. In 1912 J.B. Pound of Chattanooga contacted HENRY WATTERSON, the editor of the *COURIER-JOURNAL,* who was on a Mediterranean cruise, to request use of his name for a hotel. Pound built the Watterson Hotel at 415 W Walnut St. (Muhammad Ali Blvd.). In 1916 the Hermitage Hotel at 543 S Fifth opened, and in 1917 the Puritan Apartments-Hotel at Fourth and Ormsby Streets.

Tyler Hotel on the northeast corner of Third and Jefferson Streets, 1938.

To accommodate persons traveling in automobiles and by inter-city motorbus, hotel space increased. In 1923 JAMES GRAHAM BROWN opened the fifteen-story Brown Hotel at Fourth and Broadway, with six hundred rooms, a street-level restaurant, and shops. In the mid-1920s the Brown Hotel's head chef, Fred K. Schmidt, created the HOT BROWN specialty. Like the Seelbach, the Brown also closed for a time, but was reopened as part of the effort to revitalize the Fourth and Broadway area. The Camberley Hotel Co. began to manage the Brown in 1988.

In 1924 the 155-room Kosair Hotel on E Broadway was constructed at a cost of $1.5 million. It was sold in 1928 by the Kosair Temple Association to become the Fort Nelson Hotel. Beset by the GREAT DEPRESSION and an unsuitable location, it became the U.S. Farm Credit Association building in 1934. In 1925, at Fifth and Walnut, the eighteen-story Kentucky Hotel opened. It became Kentucky Towers Apartments about 1970. Then in 1926 the Mayflower at 425 W Ormsby Ave. opened as an apartment hotel and restaurant. In 1928 the eight-story Elks Club (1924) at Third and Chestnut Streets became the Henry Clay Hotel, the only Louisville hotel with a swimming pool.

In the decades before DESEGREGATION, AFRICAN AMERICANS were usually denied accommodations in the city's hotels. For instance, the Brown and Kentucky Hotels prohibited overnight lodging for blacks, while the Seelbach, the Watterson, and the Henry Clay would only allow lodging for black guests on a limited basis. All of these hotels refused to serve blacks in the public dining areas and only allowed them to dine in the private dining rooms if they were there as part of a primarily white organization. Thus, separate establishments were opened for African Americans. For instance, the Allen Hotel, opened in the 2500 block of West Madison about 1926, was owned by black insurance agent B.W.P. Allen. It hosted former world heavyweight boxing champion Joe Louis. Sadie's Restaurant and Rooming House on W Green St. was advertised in a 1909 program for a meeting of the National Negro Business League. The Hotel Imperial was at 726 W Walnut by 1915. The formerly white Coker's Hotel at 720 W Chestnut became Hook's Hotel for an African American clientele about 1952 but was demolished a few years later as part of the URBAN RENEWAL activity.

During WORLD WAR II, the war effort of plant construction, visiting relatives of FORT KNOX troops, and business travelers increased the hotel business. Additionally, in the late 1940s Standiford Field (LOUISVILLE INTERNATIONAL AIRPORT) opened as a commercial airport; and in 1956, the WATTERSON EXPRESSWAY opened. New expressways resulted in businesses moving to the suburbs rather than the suburbanites coming downtown. During the 1950s and 1960s, Louisville's motel business boomed. In 1956 J. Graham Brown opened BROWN SUBURBAN HOTEL with an initial 133 rooms near the Watterson Expressway, on Bardstown Rd. at Goldsmith Ln. Built to resemble a Florida hotel, it had a white stucco exterior and an eighty-five-foot, guitar-shaped outdoor swimming pool. It later became part of the Motel 6 chain and then Junction Inn. Other Bardstown Rd. motels included Hidden Valley Motel (1940s), Collier's Motel (1950s), Holiday Inn Southeast (1960s), and Admiral Benbow (1960s), which later became Quality Inn.

Motels opened on Dixie Hwy. included Maples Motel (1930s), named for the property's maple trees; Alamo Plaza Court (1940s); Parks Motel (1940s), which was later renamed Clarke's Motel; Capri Motel (1945); Trimer's Valley Motel (1950s), named for owner Norman Trimer; Knott's Motel (1950s), renamed Little Biff's Motel; Churchill Inn (1960s), later renamed Scottish Inn, then the Royal Inn; Holiday Inn Southwest (1962); and Louisville Manor Motor Court.

Motels opened in the vicinity of the airport included Executive Inn (1963); Holiday Inn Airport South (1970); Thrifty Dutchman (1970's); Colonel Sanders' Inn (1971), which later became Holiday Inn Airport East; Royce Hotel (1973), which later became the Ramada Plaza–Airport East; Executive West Hotel (1975); Red Roof Inn–Louisville Airport (1980s); Red Roof Inn–Louisville Southeast (1985); Louisville Airport Super 8 (1988); Wilson Inn Airport (1990); and Hampton Inn–Louisville Airport (1995).

Motels opened in the East End included Holiday Inn Northeast (1960s), which later became Ramada Inn–Brownsboro; Howard Johnson's (1960s), which later became Days Inn–Louisville East; Holiday Inn–Rivermont (1970s); and Breckenridge Inn (1972). In 1965 the opening of Bluegrass Industrial Park and the later shift in the economy to the information/knowledge/service sector saw a boom in hotel development in the HURSTBOURNE area. These included Holiday Inn Hurstbourne (1963); Ramada Inn (1970), which later became Hurstbourne Hotel and Conference Center and then Doubletree Club Hotel; Scottish Inn (1974), which later became Red Carpet Inn; Red Roof Inn (about 1980); Starlight Inn (early

1980s), which later became Travelodge-Louisville at Hurstbourne; Knights Inn (1983), which later became Days Inn Southeast; Residence Inn (1984), which became Marriott Residence Inn; Hilton Hotel (1986), which became the Radisson Hotel–Louisville East and then Louisville Marriott East; Hampton Inn (1987); Studio Plus and Studio Plus Hurstbourne (late 1980s); Signature Inn (1988); Courtyard by Marriott (1989); Wilson Inn East (1990), and Fairfield Inn Marriott (1991). As population moved eastward, later hotels opened even farther east in the Blankenbaker area—Comfort Suite, Best Western, and Choice Hotels' Sleep Inn.

Bucking the trend toward motels built on the fringe of the city, several downtown hotels were built in the 1960s and 1970s in addition to the 1972 GALT HOUSE. These include Howard Johnson's (mid-1960s), which later became Master Hosts Inn and then Inn at Jewish Hospital; Travelodge–Convention Center (1962); Stouffer's Louisville Inn (1964), which became Holiday Inn Downtown/Select; Rodeway Hotel (1972), which became Day's Inn Downtown and then Club Hotel by Doubletree; Hyatt Regency Hotel (1978); Galt House East (1985); and the Courtyard by Marriott (1999).

In the late 1990s bed-and-breakfast businesses such as Ashton's Victorian Secret, Towne House, and Old Louisville Inn opened. As of May 1997 there were approximately thirteen thousand hotel rooms in the Louisville metropolitan area, with about eighteen hundred added in the previous year.

Largest Area Hotels and Motels (1998)

Hotel	*Location*	*No. of Rooms*
The Galt House	Louisville	714
Executive West	Louisville	600
Galt House East	Louisville	600
Executive Inn	Louisville	465
Holiday Inn Airport South	Louisville	405
Club Hotel by Doubletree	Louisville	399
Hyatt Regency Louisville	Louisville	388
Holiday Inn Lakeview	Clarksville, Ind.	356
The Seelbach Hilton	Louisville	321
Camberley Brown Hotel	Louisville	292

See J. Stoddard Johnston, ed., *Memorial History of Louisville* (Chicago 1896); *Courier-Journal,* July 24, 1937, Nov. 11, 1956; George H. Yater, *Two Hundred Years at the Falls of the Ohio* (Louisville 1987).

Gay Helen Perkins

HOUSE OF REFUGE. Because of an escalation in juvenile delinquency, in March 1854 the Kentucky legislature appointed a Board of Managers, including such notable men as William F. Bullock, James Pirtle, and James S. Speed, to establish a new correction facility in Louisville. After investigating a similar establishment in Cincinnati, the directors decided that the local institution was to be not only a refuge but also a place of reformation where children received moral and religious instruction, occupational training, and a general education.

In July 1859 the city appropriated sixty thousand dollars for construction purposes, and, after five years without a site, the first House of Refuge building was started a year later on eighty-two acres formerly reserved for the defunct Oakland Cemetery on South Fourth St. Just before the completion of the first buildings, the CIVIL WAR erupted, and Union army soldiers seized the structures for use as HOSPITALS. The grounds were turned back over to the city at the end of the conflict, and the first child was admitted to the House of Refuge in July 1865.

Louisville House of Refuge in an illustration from the 1875 annual report.

While the original charter opened the House of Refuge to both sexes, only 1 girl was admitted out of the first 136 inmates. Originally boys between the age of seven and eighteen and girls between seven and sixteen could be admitted, although the age limits were often ignored. Other stipulations stated that children must be residents of the city (although children were also accepted from other counties in the state) and had to be committed by either a judge, magistrate, parent, or guardian. Orphans were initially not considered by the committee due to the belief that those children had family members or charitable institutions to care for them. However, many of the early residents were orphans who did not qualify for the religious ORPHANAGES and had nowhere else to go.

Led by superintendent Peter Caldwell from 1866 until 1909, the institution grew from one building for white boys of all ages to a campus that included not only separate accommodations for older and younger boys and girls, but buildings for colored boys (added in 1877) and girls (added in 1894) as well. A library, workshops, laundries, additional classrooms, and a chapel were also constructed. Caldwell eliminated the use of corporal punishment and solitary confinement as means of discipline. In 1886 the institution's name was changed to the Industrial School of Reform. By 1896 the institution averaged 301 inmates per day (the number grew to 439 twenty years later) who were schooled in subjects such as arithmetic, geography, and writing and learned trades such as cabinetmaking, gardening, and needlepoint.

Soon after Caldwell's retirement, plans were made to move the school to a more rural setting. After merging with the Parental Home and School Commission in 1920 to create the Louisville and Jefferson County Children's Home, the school was moved to the new four-hundred-acre site in LYNDON. The UNIVERSITY OF LOUISVILLE purchased the Fourth St. property in 1923 and continues to use some of the old structures such as Ford, Gardiner, Jouett, and Gottschalk Halls. Popularly known as ORMSBY VILLAGE, the home on LaGrange Rd. closed in 1968.

See J. Stoddard Johnston, ed., *Memorial History of Louisville* (Chicago 1896); George H. Yater, *Two Hundred Years at the Falls of the Ohio* (Louisville 1987).

Lorna Sprague Zeck

HOWARD SHIPYARD AND DOCK CO. The Louisville vicinity has long been a center for boat-building. One of the great steamboat building firms was established in JEFFERSONVILLE, INDIANA, in May 1834, by James Howard.

Although he was a lad of only nineteen years, James Howard had fully learned his craft from William Hartshorn, a master builder in Cincinnati. By the end of the year Howard established a boatyard and built the 125-ton Steamer *Hyperion* for Capt. James Leonard. He did not build the entire boat, only the hull. The cabin and machinery were finished by others in Louisville or NEW ALBANY. The next year he built the Louisville-Jeffersonville steam catamaran ferry *Black Locust*, the boat that established his reputation for building lasting hulls. She was built of black locust wood and was so durable she lasted a dozen years, at a time when most STEAMBOATS wore out in five years. The hulls even may have been reused under the second *Black Locust*, which continued until the winter of 1866–67.

In 1837, after he had built six hulls, James Howard was obliged to leave boat-building owing to the economic panic. Starting in 1841 he again worked as a steamboat carpenter and engineer until 1846, then resumed boat-building in SHIPPINGPORT at the lower end of the LOUISVILLE AND PORTLAND CANAL. Disaster struck when the spring flood of 1847 floated two nearly finished hulls to their destruction. After the 1847 flood he was joined by John Enos, a tavern keeper in Shippingport. John Enos died in a few months; and, in order to settle his estate, the yard, near Towhead Island, was sold. James Howard's brother, Daniel, finished the seven hulls then under construction. James moved his residence to Jeffersonville, where the boatyard was located until 1942.

James Howard ran the yard until his death in 1876, by which time he had built at least 231 hulls. His son, Edmonds J. Howard, took over the firm and ran it until he suffered a stroke in 1916. The largest and most elaborate steamboats in American history were built at the Howard Yard under his leadership. These were the fabulous floating palaces of romantic song and story. At least 771 hulls were built during this time, ranging from the gigantic *J.M. White* to a lowly horse-powered ferry only seventy feet long. In addition, the yard did repairs to many steamboats, constructed lock gates, built at least one storefront, and even made benches for Jeffersonville's park.

In 1916, when Edmonds's sons, Clyde and James E., took over the business, conditions on the river had changed drastically. The days of the gorgeous packet boat–boats carrying mail, goods, and passengers along regular routes on rivers and coastlines—had almost ended owing to competition with RAILROADS, INTERURBANS, and private automobiles and trucks. The rivers had not been improved to the docile system that exists today. The last packet boat, the *Cape Girardeau,* was built in 1923, after which the yard built barges, towboats, and other workboats, such as dredges. The sons' partnership ended in 1923, and James E. Howard took over until 1942, when the firm was bought by the Defense Plant Corp. for the United States Navy.

The Howards built a grand total of 1,123 hulls, of which 692 were steam-, gasoline-, or diesel-powered boats, and 431 were non-powered barges. The last Howard-built boat was the diesel towboat *Frank Costanzo* of 1940.

The name of the firm changed a number of times over the years because of partnerships, adapting to corporate law, and refinancing. At first it was simply James Howard. He soon was joined by David Barmore, whose sister, Rebecca, became James's wife in the fall of 1836. After the panic of 1837, James Howard joined P. Emerson at Madison, Indiana. The firm was known as Howard and Emerson and lasted until 1841. James again went on the river as a carpenter. He returned to boat-building in 1846 with a yard in Shippingport as James Howard. In partnership with Daniel Howard, his brother, he formed the D. & J. Howard Co. in 1848. The name lasted until 1865. The next name was James Howard and Co., a partnership with his brother John and his son, Edmonds J. In 1876, with the passing of James, the firm became the E.J. Howard Co. In 1902 a conglomerate was formed called the American Rivers Shipbuilding Co., consisting of E.J. Howard Co., the Queen City Marine Railway and Dock Co. in Cincinnati, and Mound City Marine Railway and Dock Co. in Mound City, Illinois. The firm soon acquired the Mississippi Valley Marine Railway and Dock Co. and the Paducah Marine Railway. It was an unwise expansion. This woefully undercapitalized firm was reorganized as the Howard Shipyard and Dock Co. in 1903. In 1923 Clyde T. Howard was bought out by James E. Howard, but the company name remained the same until it was sold to Jeffersonville Boat and Machine Co. through the Defense Plant Corp. in 1942.

In 1938 the J.M. Sweeney yard, just below the Howard Shipyard and Dock Co., was acquired by American Barge Line, which changed its name to Jeffersonville Boat and Machine Co. In 1942 this firm took over the management of the Howard yard and soon changed the name of the combined enterprises to JEFFBOAT. After a number of corporate mergers, Jeffboat became a part of the CSX conglomerate of railroads, gas and petroleum pipelines, and a barge line.

The steamer *Alton* sliding down the ways at the Howard Shipyards in 1906.

Some Famous Howard-Built Boats

Fanny Bullitt	*J.F. Pargoud*
Glendy Burke	*Ben Franklin*
General Lytle	*Ruth*
Morning Star (two of them)	*Belle Memphis*
City of Providence	*Robert E. Lee* (2nd)
John W. Cannon	*J.M. White*
Ed Richardson	*Kate Adams* (1st, 2nd, and 3rd)
City of Louisville	
Cape Girardeau	*Belle of the Bends*

See Charles P. Fishbaugh, *From Paddlewheels to Propellers* (Indianapolis 1970); Louis C. Hunter, *Steamboats on the Western Rivers* (Boston 1949).

Alan L. Bates
Martin C. Striegel

HOWARD STEAMBOAT MUSEUM. The 1894 Howard mansion was built by the second generation of the Howards of JEFFERSONVILLE, INDIANA, premier STEAMBOAT builders. The massive brick-and-limestone structure now houses the Howard Steamboat Museum, 1101 E Market St. in Jeffersonville. Displays include a large collection of rare half-breadth hull models, steamboat models, tools, paintings, photographs, documents, and artifacts from Howard-built as well as other boats. Material dealing with WORLD WAR II vessels (LSTs—or Landing Ship Tank) is also included. Original furnishings comprise approximately half of the collection, including brass chandeliers, fine china, art glass, and bathroom fixtures. Among the distinctive architectural features are the terra-cotta decorations, seven soaring chimneys, a grand staircase, and intricately carved spandrels.

A nonprofit organization, the Howard Steamboat Museum was incorporated in 1958 and is governed by a volunteer twenty-five-member board of directors. Guided tours are offered to the public, and it is open year-round. Operating funds are generated by tour and gift shop revenues, special events, promotions, memberships, and donations. Interest from the Frances Howard Kohlhepp Endowment is restricted to capital improvements. The mission of the museum includes preserving the history of western river steamboats, the Howard story, their collection, and the family home.

See Steven G. Savage, "James Howard of Jeffersonville, Master Builder of Steamboats," M.A. thesis, Indiana University, 1952; Robert H. Smith, *The Naval Institute Guide to Maritime Museums of North America* (Annapolis, Md., 1990); Charles Preston Fishbaugh, *From Paddle Wheels to Propellers* (Indianapolis 1970); Kevin Haydon, "On the Ohio, the Howard Shipyard—Largest and Oldest of Them All," *Sea History* 74 (Summer 1995): 19.

Yvonne B. Knight

H.P. SELMAN AND COMPANY. This exclusive women's wear concern was located on the northwest corner of Fourth and Walnut (Muhammad Ali Blvd.) Streets at 466 S Fourth. It was the principal occupant of the five-floor Atherton Building. In 1915 a local women's outfitter known as Gutman's changed ownership. It was renamed H.P. Selman's for its new proprietor, Louisville resident Homer P. Selman. With the stock market crash of 1929, the store relinquished its local control to out-of-town investors, who in 1953 passed on the business to the Thal family of Dayton, Ohio. In 1961 the business changed hands for a final time to a New York firm. The store closed in 1970. Gus Mayer, another women's wear business, moved to the location. Throughout its fifty-five-year existence and a variety of owners, the business maintained the name Selman's. From 1933 to 1946 the business was managed by Norman Fallot. Fallot was a president of the Retail Merchants Association and active in civic affairs. Selman's never opened a suburban location. A bronze plaque on the Walnut St. side of the building read "SELMAN'S Louisville, London, New York, Paris." The Atherton Building was leveled in 1979, and in 1981 the Meidinger Tower was erected at that location.

Kenneth L. Miller

HUBBLE, EDWIN POWELL. (b Marshfield, Missouri, November 20, 1899; d San Marino, California, September 28, 1953). Astronomer. Hubble was the son of John Powell and Virginia Lee (James) Hubble. After receiving a degree from the University of Chicago he spent the summer of 1910 with his family at 928 Bland Ave. in Shelbyville, Kentucky. His father, a manager for National of Hartford Insurance, had moved them there from Chicago in 1909 so that they could live in a small town. Edwin had been awarded a Rhodes Scholarship, and he departed Shelbyville by train in September to begin his journey to Oxford, England. There he received a B.A. in law, following a path sEt by his father, who strongly objected to Edwin's interest in a career in astronomy. The family moved to 1318 Brook St. in Louisville in 1911. His father died at home in the winter of 1913 while Edwin was still in England, and he is buried in CAVE HILL CEMETERY. Edwin returned to Louisville that summer to look after his mother, two sisters (Helen and Lucy Lee), and brother (Henry). Of others in the family, a sister (Virginia) had died as a child, and a brother (William), a student at the University of Wisconsin, spent the summer of 1913 with the family in Louisville. To provide enough room for everyone when Edwin arrived, the family moved to 1287 Everett Ave., where Edwin lived with them for the following year. During the summer Edwin translated Spanish documents for an import company, and that fall he was hired to teach Spanish, physics, and mathematics at NEW ALBANY High School, and to coach basketball. An accomplished athlete himself, he led the team to a third place finish in the state championship tournament, and his popularity as a teacher is recorded in the school yearbook. When the term ended in May 1914, Hubble applied to return to the University of Chicago as a graduate student in astronomy. He left Louisville for good in August 1914 when he moved to Williams Bay, Wisconsin, to begin his career as an astronomer at the University of Chicago's Yerkes Observatory. The family moved to Madison, Wisconsin, two years later.

In 1931 Hubble announced his discovery of a law now named for him, that the spectra of galaxies were shifted to the red in proportion to their distance from us. When this shift is interpreted as a speed of recession, the Hubble Constant which characterizes it measures the age of the universe. The discovery was instrumental in the development of the "Big Bang" theory of cosmology.

Hubble dedicated much of his career to the use of the largest telescopes to measure distant and faint galaxies. The Hubble Space Telescope, released into orbit April 25, 1990, was designed to observe the heavens without interference from the Earth's atmosphere. One of its primary objectives is to determine a precise value for the Hubble Constant.

See Joel Gwinn. "Edwin Hubble in Louisville, 1913-1914." *Filson Club History Quarterly* 56 (October 1982): 415-19; Gale E. Christianson. *Edwin Hubble, Mariner of the Nebulae* (New York 1995).

HUBBUCH AND COMPANY. In 1933, with $1,750 borrowed from an aunt, Cornelius Hubbuch Sr. founded a floor- and wall-covering business that grew to become one of Kentucky's largest architectural and interior-design firms. Originally located on E Broadway and known as Hubbuch Wall and Floor Covering, the company supplied architects and interior designers with materials, often installing the products as well. In 1937 the firm, renamed Hubbuch on Broadway, combined its existing services with a new focus as a residential and commerical interior design company.

By the early 1950s the company had changed its name to Hubbuch in Kentucky, relocated to E Gray St., and then moved to 324–26 W Main St. It also branched out, adding gallery locations in Lexington and Owensboro, Kentucky. In 1974 Hubbuch expanded with the establishment of an architectural division. Twenty-three years later the firm became Hubbuch & Co., an umbrella title for its interior design, ARCHITECTURE, and residential and commercial furnishings operations.

The Louisville headquarters of the firm include an extensive resource center, administrative and design offices, and showrooms with conference centers. A 150,000-square-foot warehouse at 2418 W Main St. houses the company's accounting, furniture, and floor and wall covering divisions. As a nationally prominent design firm, Hubbuch has served clients in thirty-three states. The firm has been responsible for such projects as the renovation and expansion of the historic MAKER'S MARK DISTILLERY in Loretto, Kentucky; remodeling of CHURCHILL DOWNS Turf Club; and the design of Valhalla Golf Club, Commonwealth Bank and Trust Co., and St. Xavier High School's Arts, Athletic, and Fitness Center.

See *Courier-Journal*, Sept. 19, 1993.

HUGHES, EDWARD (b Louisville, February 1, 1828; d Beechwood, Kentucky, July 19, 1903). Fire chief. Hughes was the son of Irish immigrant Edward Hughes. He began his career at Union Volunteer Fire Co. #2 and was mustered into the paid department when it began on June 1, 1858. He was chief of the LOUISVILLE FIRE DEPARTMENT from 1880 to 1902. His twenty-two-year tenure was the longest of any Louisville fire chief. During his term, he persuaded the City Council to pass an ordinance requiring fire escapes on all public buildings, warehouses, and city schools. His other successes included improving the cistern system and installing an electrical communications system for dispatching fire companies.

He also pushed for an underground cable system that would operate an electric alarm system and invented the hose-drying racks used in Louisville fire stations. Hughes, who never married, was known for his acts of charity. Every Christmas the city's ORPHANAGES received turkeys from the chief. Hughes retired on December 31, 1902, and died several months later when he was struck by an electric suburban railway car. He is buried in CAVE HILL CEMETERY.

See *Historical Sketch and Souvenir of the Louisville Fire Department* (Louisville 1894); *Courier-Journal*, July 20, 1903; Fillmore Tyson, chief, *Report of the Louisville Fire Department* (Louisville 1903).

Rhonda Abner

HULL, HENRY WATTERSON (b Louisville, October 3, 1890; d Cornwall, England, March 8, 1977). Leading actor of the THEATER and motion picture character actor. The son of William Madison and Elinor (Vaughn) Hull, his early education was acquired in the public schools of Louisville. When his father secured a position as publicist for theatrical producer David Belasco, the family moved to New York City. He later enrolled in Cooper Union and Columbia University, where he studied engineering. He left school for work in a Canadian cobalt mine but was back in New York by 1911, when Belasco offered him his first stage role.

Hull's rich bass voice and distinctive presence firmly established him among the first rank of Broadway performers. His crowning theatrical achievement came in 1933 with his creation of the role of Jeeter Lester in the Broadway production of Erskine Caldwell's *Tobacco Road,* which ran for 3,182 performances.

Hull's film career, which began in silent pictures, consisted of some forty-five roles. He was a highly sought after character actor, especially in later years. He is remembered for parts in such films as *Boys' Town* (1938), *Jesse James* (1939), *High Sierra* (1940), *Lifeboat* (1943), *Mourning Becomes Electra* (1947), and *The Proud Rebel* (1958).

Hull married Juliet van Wyck Frémont, granddaughter of John C. Frémont, on November 30, 1913. The couple had three children: Henry, Shelley, and Joan.

See Alfred E. Twomey and Arthur F. McClure, *The Versatiles* (Cranbury, N.J., 1969).

Kenneth Dennis

HUMANA INC. In 1961 two young Louisville lawyers built Heritage House, a new kind of NURSING home, one that would offer personal attention to its residents while making a profit. David A. Jones and WENDELL CHERRY recruited four friends and each of the six invested one thousand dollars in what is now Humana Inc.—in 1999 the third-largest health insurer in the United States with 6 million customers and one of only five Kentucky-based *Fortune 500* companies. Humana offers products in all areas of the health insurance market, serving employers, the military, and Medicare and Medicaid beneficiaries. The company's specialty lines include dental, worker's compensation, and life insurance. Humana's operations were concentrated in fifteen states and Puerto Rico at the end of 1999.

David A. Jones is chairman of the board of Humana Inc., serving as chief executive officer from 1961 until his retirement in December 1997. He was born August 7, 1931, to Evan Logan and Elsie T. Jones in Louisville. In 1949 he graduated from LOUISVILLE MALE HIGH SCHOOL. Jones worked a year for R.J. Reynolds Tobacco Co. before enrolling at the UNIVERSITY OF LOUISVILLE on a Navy ROTC scholarship. Jones graduated with a bachelor's degree in 1954 from U of L, where he earned the outstanding senior award. He then served three years in the U.S. Navy.

Jones married the former Betty Ashbury in 1954 and that year became a certified public accountant. After his navy service, he enrolled in Yale University's law school, earning his law degree in 1960. While at Yale, he taught management accounting at Yale and at another local college. On graduation Jones was recruited by a Louisville law firm and returned to his home city, where he met Wendell Cherry. For the next thirty-one years, until Cherry's death in 1991, the two men were partners in business and in numerous civic activities.

Jones has long been active in support of the arts, economic development, and education in Louisville. The Humana Foundation has sponsored the annual Humana Festival of New American Plays, the world's premier forum for emerging playwrights, at Actor's Theater since 1981. In 1986 Jones donated a building that attracted the headquarters of the Presbyterian Church (USA) to Louisville. He also played a leadership role with the Partnership for Kentucky Schools, helped found the African American Venture Capital Fund, and raised critically needed disaster-relief funds for victims of TORNADOES in 1996 and the flood of 1997.

Jones serves as a member of the board of directors of Abbott Laboratories. He serves on the executive committee of the Healthcare Leadership Council, an organization he has also chaired. Jones serves on the board of the American Association of Health Plans and is a former member of the Business Roundtable, where he served on the health and retirement task force. Since 1990 he has spearheaded efforts to provide urgently needed medical information and training to eastern Europe through the Romanian Assistance Project and neonatology program in Poland. Jones and his wife, Betty, are the parents of five children: David Junior, Susan, Daniel, Matthew, and Carol.

Humana's history has been marked by innovation. Several times the company has reinvented itself in response to market conditions and the needs of its customers. What began as a nursing home company in the 1960s became a hospital corporation in the 1970s and a leader in the health INSURANCE INDUSTRY in the 1980s and 1990s.

The company, at first called Extendicare, went public on January 31, 1968, selling 250,000 shares of stock at $8 per share. That year it also began its first transformation, buying its first hospital—Medical Center Hospital in Huntsville, Alabama. Four years later, in August 1972, Extendicare sold its nursing homes to focus on its hospital business. To reflect this change in direction, Extendicare became Humana Inc. on January 21, 1974.

Within a few years, the company was operating more than ninety HOSPITALS at home and abroad, becoming the largest hospital company in the country in 1978. Among Humana's innovations in hospital management was its sixty-second emergency room response standard. Treatment came before paperwork, a change that required emergency rooms to be rebuilt so that a "triage" nurse, capable of initiating treatment, was the first point of contact.

In 1982 Humana solved a major health-care crisis caused by the University of Louisville's refusal to continue operating the city's unaccredited and money-losing public hospital or to open the new replacement hospital. In an innovative partnership with local and state government, Humana agreed to lease, open, and operate the new hospital named Humana Hospital–University. Humana also agreed to provide necessary hospital care to all patients without regard to their ability to pay, thereby solving Louisville's indigent care problem. The contract also limited government's annual cost increase to the lesser of the percentage increase in their tax revenues or the consumer price index, saving government tens of millions of dollars during Humana's ten-year stewardship.

Also during the 1980s, Humana launched its centers of excellence program. Hospitals designated as centers of excellence supplemented innovative care with one or more teaching and research efforts. The best-known outcome of this program was the pioneering artificial-heart research conducted at the Humana Hospital–Audubon in Louisville. It was there on November 25, 1984, that Dr. William C. DeVries implanted the JARVIK-7 artificial heart in William Schroeder.

The same year that DeVries performed that operation, Humana began its third transformation, although the results would not become apparent for several years. Humana sold its first health-plan products, setting the stage for its transformation into a leading managed-care insurer.

In 1993 the company spun off its hospitals to shareholders, creating Galen Healthcare, a $4 billion company. (Galen merged in 1994 with Columbia/HCA Healthcare Corp.) That move left Humana as a $2.8 billion health-insurance company. Carl F. Pollard served as chief executive officer of Galen Healthcare, while David A. Jones remained CEO of Humana. (Co-founder Wendell Cherry died of cancer in 1991.) On February 3, 2000, Humana named Michael B. McCallister as its president and chief executive officer.

Humana had grown to 6.2 million health-plan members and $8 billion in annual revenues by December 1997. At the time, one eight-dollar share from the 1968 Extendicare initial public offering was worth forty-eight hundred dollars with dividends reinvested, for a compound annual growth rate of 24 percent. After Jones's retirement as CEO in December 1997, his duties were taken over by Gregory H. Wolf, who had been president and chief operating officer.

Humana's history has been marked by challenges as well. In October 1998, a Louisville jury awarded more than $13 million to plaintiff Karen Johnson for her claim that Humana acted in bad faith by refusing to pay for a hysterectomy. The surgery was recommended by her doctor in order to remove cancerous tissue.

Johnson paid for the surgery by herself and sued Humana for treatment costs and damages for breach of contract.

In the early 1980s when Humana was looking for new office space, it saw an opportunity not just to meet its practical and functional requirements but also to create a headquarters building of national significance that would integrate well with downtown Louisville and spur the development of quality architectural design in the city.

In January 1982 the company invited five internationally known architects to compete for the design of such a building. Michael Graves of Princeton, New Jersey, won the award that May. Groundbreaking took place on October 20, 1982, and the postmodern building was completed in May 1985. It has won numerous architectural awards; *Time* magazine hailed the structure as the Building of the Decade.

Despite its impressiveness, the Humana Building is not the biggest way that Humana has given back to the Louisville community. Through 1997 the company and its Humana Foundation had donated more than $111 million to initiatives in the fields of education, the arts, community development, parks, and health and human services, with much of that money going to Louisville and Kentucky organizations.

Mark A. Ray

HUMANA TOWER. The construction of the twenty-seven-story Humana Tower, an example of late-twentieth-century postmodern ARCHITECTURE, brought Louisville international publicity. The design competition included notable architects Cesar Pelli, Norman Foster, Ulrich Franzen, and Helmut Jahn, but it was Michael Graves who won in May 1982. Ground was broken on October 20, 1982, and the building was completed in May 1985. Located at 500 W Main St., it is the corporate headquarters for Humana Inc., a healthcare company founded in 1961 as Extendicare.

Graves, professor of architecture at Princeton University, designed a building that presents a slightly different design on each side and is crowned by a pyramid-shaped top. The north, main facade is visually more complex, with its twenty-fifth floor radiating terrace supported by a truss-like structure, and the rich columned entrance loggia. Such details give a nod to local traditions, reflecting the downtown bridges and keeping the building in scale with smaller Victorian storefronts. Graves gave the building a large amount of natural light by placing evenly spaced windows and centrally located window shafts on each side. The light shaft on the south side is gently curved, allowing a gathering commons for each floor.

The entire structure is covered in a variety of lush stone. Outside, the loggia's piers and pilasters are covered in dark pink and green granite. The majority of the exterior is flat pink granite. Inside, the lobby features a variety of colored, imported marble surfaces.

Response to the Humana Tower has varied from, "It looks like Graves put together remnants of Greek and Mayan temples, a rocket assembly hangar, and architectural doodads culled from the back lot of a Hollywood studio" (Paul Gapp, "Bizarre Design Takes the Prize in Louisville," *Chicago Tribune,* Jan. 30, 1983), to "a building of international significance that testifies to the continuing vitality of American architecture" ("AIA Honor Awards 1987," *Architecture,* May 1987).

See Charles K. Grandee, "Humana," *Architectural Record* 173 (Aug. 1985): 102–3; *Chicago Tribune,* Jan. 30, 1983, Aug. 4, 1985; *New York Times,* Jan. 20, 1985; *Courier-Journal Magazine,* Aug. 22, 1982; John Pastier, "Strong, Quirky, Abstract, Monumental," *Architecture* 74 (Nov. 1985): 57–63; Peter Arnell and Ted Bickford, *A Tower for Louisville: The Humana Competition* (New York 1982); George H. Yater, "Who is This Man Michael Graves and What is He Up to at Fifth and Main," *Louisville* (Sept. 1982): 61–64.

Rod A. Miller

HUMES, HELEN (b Louisville, June 23, 1909; d Santa Monica, California, September 13, 1981). JAZZ singer. Humes was the daughter of John and Emma (Johnson) Humes. As a child she performed with Bessie Allen's Booker T. Washington Community Center Band. She graduated from Central High School in 1926 and in 1927 traveled with guitarist SYLVESTER WEAVER to St. Louis and New York City for her first recording sessions. From 1938 to 1942 she sang with the Count Basie band. Her hit records include *Be-Baba-Leba* (1945) and *Million Dollar Secret* (1950). In 1967 she retired from music and moved back to Louisville to care for her parents. In 1973 she came out of retirement to perform at the Newport Jazz Festival, which led to a successful comeback. In 1975 she was presented the key to the city of Louisville.

See Linda Dahl, *Stormy Weather: The Music and Lives of a Century of Jazzwomen* (New York 1989); Sheldon Harris, *Blues Who's Who* (New York 1979); Jim O'Neal, "Helen Humes," *Living Blues* 52 (Spring 1982): 24.

Brenda K. Bogert

HUNT, THOMAS H. (b Lexington, January 2, 1815; d New Orleans, May 6, 1884). Confederate soldier. The son of John Wesley and Catherine (Grosh) Hunt, he attended Transylvania University and in 1834 entered the wholesale business with his father. In 1838 he opened a hemp factory; and in 1848 he moved to Louisville, where he operated a commission business that shipped hemp and imported wool from New Mexico.

In 1860, as a colonel in the State Guard, the pro-Southern state militia, he organized a training camp at SHEPHERDSVILLE and later at Muldraugh's Hill. When the state legislature went Unionist in September 1861, he resigned and, on October 3, 1861, as a Confederate colonel, organized the Ninth Kentucky Infantry Regiment in the First Kentucky Infantry Brigade, the famous Orphan Brigade. The regiment included the Citizen Guards company from Louisville.

His men admired "Uncle Tom," and his commanders commended him for reliability, courage, and gallantry. He resigned on April 22, 1863, and resided in Augusta, Georgia, until after the war, when he moved to New Orleans. Hunt married Mary Tilford of Lexington, and they had six children: Mary Tilford, Thomas, Catherine, Tilford, Anne Francis, and Walter Eugene. He is buried in Lexington.

See Clement A. Evans, ed., *Confederate Military History*, vol. 9 (Atlanta 1899), 403–4; William C. Davis, *The Orphan Brigade* (Garden City, N.Y., 1980).

James A. Ramage

HUNTOON, BENJAMIN BUSSEY (b Milton, Massachusetts, January 30, 1836; d Louisville, August 9, 1919). Educator. Benjamin Bussey Huntoon, a national leader in the education of blind children, became superintendent of the KENTUCKY SCHOOL FOR THE BLIND and the AMERICAN PRINTING HOUSE FOR THE BLIND in 1871. He served the school for forty-one years, resigning in 1912, and led the printing house until his death.

Huntoon was the son of Susan Pettingill and Benjamin Huntoon, a Unitarian minister. He earned an A.B. (1856) and an A.M. (1859) degree from Harvard and established a school in Louisville in 1857. He married Sarah Josephine Huntoon in 1860, and daughter Mary was born in 1861.

At the Kentucky School for the Blind, he was a dedicated teacher and administrator who read aloud to the students each evening. He established the Colored Department in 1884. As superintendent of the printing house, he developed methods and apparatus to improve tactile printing and mapmaking. In 1879 he secured an annual federal appropriation for producing tactile books.

Huntoon was an officer in the American Association of Instructors of the Blind. He was active in Louisville civic affairs, a member of FIRST UNITARIAN CHURCH, and literary editor for the *COURIER-JOURNAL* from 1868 to 1873.

See George S. Wilson, "Benjamin Bussey Huntoon," *Outlook for the Blind* 21 (Dec. 1927): 5; Col. Andrew Cowan, "In Memorium, B.B. Huntoon," *Outlook for the Blind* 13 (Autumn 1919): 79–81; *Louisville Times,* Aug. 9, 1919.

Carol Brenner Tobe

HURSTBOURNE. A fourth-class residential city located in eastern Jefferson County, Hurstbourne is bounded by Shelbyville Rd. (U.S. 60) on the north, Interstate 64 on the south, Hurstbourne Pkwy. on the east, and the OXMOOR estate on the west.

One of the first settlers to the region was Maj. William Linn, a veteran of George Rogers Clark's Illinois campaign against the British. Linn was one of the thirty-nine signers of the 1779 petition to the Virginia legislature to establish the town of Louisville. He moved his family to a site along Beargrass Creek in 1779 and established what would become known as Linn's Station. The pioneer station, located on the road from the Falls of the Ohio to Fort Harrod, was one of the first of several settlements on Beargrass Creek. In the fall of 1781 the survivors of the Long Run Massacre sought shelter there. By the 1790s the Indian attacks had begun to taper off.

During this time the heirs to Linn's estate discovered that the station was built on land belonging to someone else, and they left. The area, which was included in the 1774 surveys directed by John Floyd, was originally part of a land grant to Virginia officer Henry Harrison for service in the French and Indian War. After the Linn family departure, the stockade deteriorated quickly. It was probably located on the east side of what is now Hurstbourne Pkwy. in the Plainview community.

One of the earliest entries recorded in the Jefferson County Deed books recorded Harrison's sale of one thousand acres to Peyton Short of Lincoln County, Kentucky, in 1786. In 1789 Short sold five hundred acres to Col. Richard Clough Anderson Sr. The Anderson estate, known as Soldiers' Retreat, made up much of what is now Hurstbourne. Anderson built a substantial two-story stone house and raised a large family. The stone mansion was struck and damaged by lightning in 1840 and was razed several years later. Four of the original stone outbuildings on the estate still exist, as does the family burial ground.

By 1842 the farm was owned by John Jeremiah Jacob, a wealthy Louisvillian whose son, John J. Jacob Jr., built a Gothic Revival house on the land and named the estate Lynnford. In 1915 the property, which was already known as Hurstbourne Farm, was acquired by the Hert family. Mrs. Alvin T. Hert remodeled and enlarged the house, which is now the center section of the clubhouse of the Hurstbourne Country Club. Funk's Ln., which bordered the property, was widened in 1935 and renamed Hurstbourne Ln., now Hurstbourne Pkwy.

After the death of Mrs. Hert, L. Leroy Highbaugh Sr. and his son, L. Leroy Junior, acquired the property and renamed it Highbaugh Farms. In 1965 the younger Highbaugh began developing the residential and commercial community of Hurstbourne. In the late 1970s an archaeological excavation uncovered the foundations of the old Anderson house. L. Leroy Highbaugh Jr. reconstructed the house to original specifications and moved there with his family in 1983. The rebuilt Soldiers' Retreat home is considered by many to be the centerpiece of the community.

With the building of I-64 along the area's southern boundary, development in Hurstbourne expanded quickly. The quick access to Louisville encouraged commercial, as well as residential, growth. In August 1982 the city of Hurstbourne was incorporated to prevent annexation by Louisville. By 1990 residential building in the subdivision was nearly complete and the city contained several churches, office complexes, and a shopping area. Hurstbourne had a population of 3,530 in 1980, 4,420 in 1990, and 4,698 in 1996.

James Strohmaier

HUTCHINGS, JOHN BACON (b Louisville, 1857; d Louisville, January 17, 1916). Architect. He was the son of Eusebius Hutchings, a prominent Louisville financier, and his wife, the former Elizabeth Bacon. The particulars of Hutchings's education and architectural training are unknown. From 1890 to 1897 he was in partnership with Cornelius Curtin in the firm of Curtin and Hutchings. Except for a brief association with Henry Hawes, he then practiced independently until he took his two sons into his business about 1909. In 1914 the firm was advertised for the first time as John Bacon Hutchings and Sons. John Bacon Hutchings Jr. was a civil engineer; Eusebius Theodore "E.T." Hutchings, born in 1886, was an architect trained at Cornell University. When Hutchings died in 1916, survived by his wife, Lena (Schwartz) Hutchings, his two sons, and his two daughters, the family firm closed. Following service in World War I, E.T. Hutchings returned to Louisville and practiced as an architect until the year before his death in 1958. He and his wife Heloise (Bullitt) Hutchings, had two daughters.

J.B. Hutchings's obituary refers to the many manufacturing plants and warehouses he designed. In 1897 he was selected as the architect for the Kentucky Building at the Tennessee Centennial. He drew the plans for the remodeling of the old Courier-Journal Building at Third and Green (Liberty) Streets. At the time of his death he was engaged in the remodeling of the YWCA building at Second and Broadway (the former James C. Ford mansion) and was serving as president of the Louisville chapter of the American Institute of Architects. Today, J.B. and E.T. Hutchings are best known for their residential work for wealthy clients. Individually and in partnership they designed a number of the grandest early twentieth-century houses along River Rd. at Glenview. J.B. Hutchings is credited with a residence for Maj. Charles J.F. Allen and another for Charles T. Ballard, later owned by Robert Worth Bingham. E.T., either alone or in collaboration with his father, designed houses for two of Major Allen's sons. Later in his career, E.T. was the architect of the Fourth Avenue (Central) Presbyterian Church, the Woman's Club of Louisville clubhouse, and, among many other residences, the Attilla Cox house on Upper River Rd. Both J.B. and E.T. Hutchings are buried in Cave Hill Cemetery.

See *Courier-Journal*, Jan. 18, 1916, Dec. 1, 1958; Eusebius Theodore Hutchings, Application for Registration as a Registered Architect, Sept. 17, 1930; C. Julian Oberwarth, *A History of the Profession of Architecture in Kentucky* (Frankfort 1987); City directories and Cave Hill Cemetery records.

Carolyn Brooks

I

ICE COMPANIES. The storage and sale of ice and later the manufacture of "artificial" ice have been closely connected to the cold-storage warehouses used to store fresh meat, fruits, eggs, and vegetables. Sometimes a company (B&B and Polar) would sell both ice and coal in order to take advantage of seasonal demands. While ice suppliers certainly existed before CITY DIRECTORIES, the first companies appeared in the 1855-56 directory. A majority of these were operated by one man who carted ice from door to door to houses or businesses. In 1864 John T. Monsch, a wholesale and retail dealer in Northern Lake Ice with offices in Louisville and New Albany, promised to deliver ice–or oysters and game, which he also sold–to any part of the city.

Locke & Jacquemin also established themselves as wholesale and retail ice dealers in 1879. They harvested their ice from three hundred acres of lake surface and had a storage capacity of more than twenty-five thousand tons in a depot at Main and Thirteenth Streets. Because of a dearth of large lakes nearby, many dealers continued to purchase natural, or lake, ice from regions farther north, transporting it down the Ohio River to be stored for summer use. Another major ice supplier during this time was the Talmage Lake Ice Co. With its main office on Third St. between Walnut (Muhammad Ali Blvd.) and Green (Liberty) Streets, the firm also had branch offices in Nashville, Tennessee, and Lafayette, Indiana.

The industry began to change after the Pictet Artificial Ice Co., located on Kentucky between Brook and Floyd Streets, introduced manufactured ice to Louisville in 1881. In 1834 Jacob Piterkins had patented an ice-making machine in England. Pictet stated that his product was "made with pure spring water from a well seventy feet deep, with a daily capacity of thirty-five tons." The company's trade was essentially local, and it had more than two thousand subscribers from householders in addition to public establishments such as HOTELS and TAVERNS. After the introduction of this innovation, mass commercial production decreased the price while increasing ice's availability. The spring water used in the manufacture of ice was gradually replaced by distilled water, and there was no lake ice advertised for sale by 1900.

Louisville Cold Storage Co., on W Jefferson St., opened in 1891. S.M. Lemont, president, offered ample cold-storage facilities and the latest refrigerating machinery, with the capacity of producing forty-five tons of ice a day from distilled water.

Henry Vogt began to experiment with the manufacturing process after moving his plant to Tenth St. and Ormsby Ave. in 1902. His new machines, which utilized ammonia absorption, replaced the noisy and high-maintenance refrigeration compressor systems with cheaper and virtually trouble-free machines. The absorption process eventually evolved into the production of Tube-Ice®, which froze water inside vertical tubes, momentarily thawed the ice loose from the tubes, and cut it into the familiar cylindrical shape with the hole in the center (generally in three-hundred-pound blocks).

John Rohrman, with offices at 518 Third Ave. and factory and cold storage at Fourteenth and Magazine, opened for business in 1894. The plant was operated by a twenty-five-horsepower engine and a twenty-horsepower electric motor. By 1903 his company was producing 150 tons of ice daily, which he sold wholesale.

The Louisville Ice Co. was established in 1894 by Mathias Poschinger, a native of Germany and a Louisville resident for fifteen years. Located on E Main St., it provided cold storage and produced one hundred tons of ice daily. Poschinger was also the president of the New Albany Ice Co., which he had founded four years earlier.

The Inman Ice Co., located on E Caldwell St., was established in 1897 and incorporated in 1902. J.T. Duffy was president. The company's two ice machines used distilled water to produce a large amount of ice daily, which was sold wholesale and retail throughout the entire city and state.

The American Ice and Storage Co. was incorporated in 1906 with C.J. O'Connor as president. It manufactured ice for family use, distilled water for the family table, and offered cold storage of all kinds. The plant was located at Floyd and Pearl Streets and had an ice-making capacity of 180 tons daily.

The Arctic Ice Co. (modern-day Merchants Ice and Cold Storage Co.) was established in 1909 with Henry M. Brennan as president. Located first on S Seventh St., it had ice houses that acted as relay stations around the city and county. Since that time there have been many presidents of the company: John T. Malone, L.W. Breed, Gilbert J. Stecker, Mary Sweeney, and W. Clyde Glass.

There were many other ice dealers and manufacturers about which little or nothing is known beyond their names in the city directories. Most of them offered home delivery. The iceman, making the route with horse-drawn wagon or truck, would know the amount to deliver by means of an "ice card" placed in a window. Depending on the way it was turned, he would use tongs to place the product in the ice box. The presence of the iceman was a delight to youngsters who sought ice "slivers" on hot summer days.

The number of retail ice dealers continued to increase until refrigerators became available for households beginning in the 1920s. Artificial ice-makers cut into the business to taverns and RESTAURANTS. The result was the closing of the companies, and the iceman seldom came. Grocers Ice and Cold Storage company began in 1906 and, along with Merchants Ice and Cold Storage, Pure Ice Co., AAA Ice Delivery, and Polar Ice Co., was one of the few still in operation in the late 1990s. They mostly service grocery and convenience stores with bagged ice, while block sale is now a rarity.

Grocers Ice and Cold Storage Company, 603 East Main Street in 1937.

Illinois Central Railroad roundhouse at Fourteenth and Oak Streets.

See *Louisville, Kentucky, the Falls City, the Industrial Center of the Southwest* (Louisville 1903); *Illustrated Louisville: Kentucky's Metropolis* (Chicago 1891); *Greater Louisville-Illustrated* (Louisville 1908); *Louisville of Today* (Louisville 1895); *Industries of Louisville* (Louisville 1881).

Dorothy C. Rush

ILLINOIS CENTRAL RAILROAD. The historic railroads of western Kentucky, Illinois Central (IC) and its predecessor, Elizabethtown & Paducah (E&P), provided access from Louisville and north-central Kentucky to the Pennyroyal and Purchase Regions of the state and their valuable coal deposits. Chartered in 1867, E&P was supported not only by local interests, including that of stagecoach operator Samuel Thomas of Elizabethtown, but also by the city of Louisville and the L&N, both hopeful of securing business from the western counties.

Construction proceeded westward from Elizabethtown. Caneyville was reached in 1870, and tracks were opened to Greenville by June 1871. The du Pont family of Louisville were also heavily involved in the Western Kentucky coalfields in the late 1870s, founding the trackside town of Central City in connection with their Central Coal and Iron Co.

The entire line was in operation by September 1872. The L&N conveyed passengers and freight from the E&P north to Louisville, but in September 1874 the road finished its own route from Cecelia (west of Elizabethtown) to Louisville via Vine Grove, West Point, and Valley Station. In 1881 the E&P was bought by Collis P. Huntington and consolidated into his Chesapeake & Ohio Southwestern as part of a proposed transcontinental rail system.

After collapse of the Huntington empire in the 1890s, IC purchased the line, which became its Kentucky Division. Before 1900, IC helped develop the Western Kentucky Coalfields, and well into the twentieth century it supplied Louisville industries and power producers with coal. The IC also transported thousands of troops and military supplies to and from Fort Knox after that base was organized by the United States Army. In 1972, the IC merged with the parallel Gulf, Mobile & Ohio Railroad to form Illinois Central Gulf. The acquisition included GM&O's mainline through Western Kentucky.

Downsizing its system in 1985-6 and returning to its original name, IC sold the Kentucky Division to CG&T Industries Inc. of western Kentucky, which formed the Paducah & Louisville Railway. Ownership was transferred in 1995 to Four Rivers Transportation, a holding company jointly owned by P&L management and CSX Transportation.

See Carleton Corliss, *Mainline of Mid-America, Story of the Illinois Central* (New York 1950).

Charles B. Castner

INDEPENDENT SCHOOLS. Independent, or private schools, afford local children an alternative to the public and parochial school systems of the Louisville metropolitan area. The schools are nonprofit; supported by tuition, donations, and endowments; guided by a board of trustees; and provide a secular education, although some do maintain religious affiliations. Curricula vary from kindergarten through twelfth-grade programs, to specialized teachings to help children with specific needs. Independent schools have a long tradition in Kentucky education.

By 1998, only eight schools, enrolling nearly twenty-eight hundred students, with approximately 20 percent receiving financial aid, comprised the Louisville Independent School Council (LISC) and were also members of the Kentucky Association of Independent Schools (KAIS). These independent schools are characterized by high academic standards, large libraries, and a low student-teacher ratio, with many of the faculty holding advanced degrees. For the upper-level schools, many of the programs include competitive varsity and junior varsity athletics, community service, college placement courses, student publications including yearbooks and newspapers, study abroad, and fine arts.

Independent schools in the area include Chance School (founded in 1950), the de Paul School (1970), Kentucky Country Day School (formed in 1972 with the merger of Kentucky Home School for Girls (1863) and Louisville Country Day School (1948)), Louisville Collegiate School (1915), Meredith-Dunn School (1971), St. Francis School (1965), St. Francis High School (1976), and Walden School (1975).

INDIANA ARMY AMMUNITION PLANT. The Indiana Army Ammunition Plant near Charlestown encompassed 10,650 acres in 1997, bounded by the Ohio River on the east and Indiana State Rd. 62 on the west. The plant was a U.S. government response to the outbreak of World War II in Europe. Originally three separate facilities, it was constructed between 1940 and 1945. The first was the smokeless powder plant, the Indiana Ordnance Works Plant 1, built and operated by E.I. du Pont de Nemours & Co. The second was the bag manufacturing and load, assembly, and pack facility, the Hoosier Ordnance Plant, operated by Goodyear Engineering Co., a subsidiary of the tire and rubber company. The last facility, never completed because of the end of the war, was to be a rocket propellant plant. The smokeless powder plant came on line in May 1941, before U.S. entry into World War II, and soon was producing nearly 1 million pounds of smokeless powder each day. In that month twenty-seven thousand workers were active at the plant (many were doing construction jobs, soon gone), and about five thousand at the ordnance plant. The plants were major employers in the area throughout the war.

After the war the plants were consolidated as the Indiana Arsenal and kept on standby. Goodyear and du Pont signed new contracts for the Korean conflict. Goodyear became the maintenance contractor for the entire facility in 1959, then handed control to the Olin Mathieson Chemical Corp. in 1961, when the facility was renamed the Indiana Ordnance Plant. In 1963 it was renamed again as the Indiana Army Ammunition Plant. ICI Americas Inc. became the operating contractor in May 1972. As the cold war drew to a close, the facility was deemed unnecessary and was shut down in 1993. ICI Americas, acting for the plant owner, the U.S. Army, converted 8,000 of the

Seamstresses sewing powder bags at the Indiana Army Ammunition Plant, Charlestown, Indiana, 1948.

9,790 acres remaining into a business and industrial park, known as Facility One. Other acreage was given to the state of Indiana and became Charlestown State Park.

See Steve Gaither and Kimberly L. Kane, *The World War II Ordnance Department's Government-Owned Contractor-Operated (GOCO) Industrial Facilities: Indiana Army Ammunition Plant Historic Investigation* (Plano, Tex., 1995); Cary Stemle, "Battle Escalates as Officials Attack ICI Management at Facility One," *Business First*, Sept. 15, 1997; *Courier-Journal*, Sept. 28, 1997.

William W. Struck

INDIANA UNIVERSITY SOUTHEAST. One of eight campuses comprising the Indiana University system based at Bloomington, Indiana, University Southeast's establishment dates back to the 1940s. The fully accredited four-year college, located on 180 acres of land at the base of Floyds Knobs in NEW ALBANY, offers both undergraduate and graduate programs.

In 1941, the Falls Area Center in Jeffersonville opened as an extension campus of Indiana University, with classes held at Jeffersonville and New Albany High Schools. Four years later, the school purchased the National Youth Administration Building in Jeffersonville's Warder Park and renamed the center the Southeast Center of Indiana University. Between 1957 and 1967, the campus sprouted as the school added five buildings, did major renovations to the old center, renamed East Hall, and expanded its mission to include additional degrees. With its increased enrollment during the 1960s, the school witnessed several changes. In 1963 it was renamed Southeastern Campus of Indiana University and dubbed Indiana University Southeast five years later. As the school's grounds rapidly approached capacity in the late 1960s, New Albany civic leaders began raising five hundred thousand dollars to aid in the construction of a new campus. Ground was broken at the new site in 1971, with the move from Jeffersonville occurring two years later.

By 1999 the school offered more than seventy majors, minors, options, and certificates as part of its ten different undergraduate and graduate degrees. There were over fifty-eight hundred commuter students.

See George H. Yater, "Indiana University Southeast: Moving Up by Degrees," *Louisville* (Sept. 1973): 36-38.

INDIANS. The history of natives of India who settled in Louisville prior to 1961 is nearly unknown. It is doubtful if any Indian was settled here prior to the year 1900. It is known that some students received higher education degrees in the 1950s.

A well-known Indian immigrant was P.J. Ouseph, a physicist who joined the UNIVERSITY OF LOUISVILLE faculty in 1961. Another notable local Indian educator, Bellarmine professor of history Thomas Davasia, also arrived early in the 1960s and would later help to found Gandhi University in India. But these were atypical until 1965 when immigration policies changed to permit waves of Indian professionals to enter the country. These included primarily physicians and engineers, most of whom stayed as citizens. Many of them came for education, but many left the city to settle elsewhere after training. Noteworthy is the fact that rural medical support in Kentucky is to this day heavily provided by Indian physicians, many of whom trained in Louisville. In 1999 there were about four hundred families living in Louisville. Only about fifty of those families had lived here for more than twenty-five years and produced second and third generations.

The Indian community in Louisville reflects the overall pattern of Indian population in the United States. Most of them are physicians in nearly all specialties, engineers, university professors, top-level scientists, software specialists, and businessmen. Major religious groups comprise Hindus, Jains, Sikhs, MUSLIMS, and Christians. The Hindu Temple of Kentucky (4213 Accomack Dr. at Interstate 265 and Westport Rd.) occupies a twenty-two-acre site and is the first Hindu architectural landmark for the Louisville area. The temple hall was completed in 1989, a year after the Hindu Temple of Kentucky was founded. Before that devotees met in homes. The temple (expanded and dedicated on June 20, 1999) offers a place for worship, lectures on the philosophy of Hinduism, yoga classes, meetings of young adults, festival events, weddings, and priestly services.

Other small groups (Sikh Gurudwara, Sai Baba, Devi Jagran, Gujrati, and Karnatic music) meet at residences representing diverse religious and cultural heritage. The Sai Baba group participates in hospice, nursing homes, Meals on Wheels, and prayer sessions. A Masjid (Islamic Cultural Association of Louisville, 1911 Buechel Bank Rd.) is the place of worship for Muslims. Ethnic and social backgrounds bind Indians from the eighteen states of India, primarily from Gujarat, Punjab, Bengal, Southern States, and from the central Indian regions. Intermarriages commonly occur. Among the important dignitaries who have gone through Louisville are Rabindranath Tagore, a Nobel laureate in literature, and Ravi Shankar and Hari Prasad Chaurasiya both musicians.

The cultural heritage of India is advanced by such groups as the Indian Academy of Dance, which educates youngsters in classical dancing. A women's group, the LILA (Louisville Indian Ladies Association) organizes charitable events such as feeding the poor and helping the Red Cross, and provides volunteers for many other things. Since 1968 the India Community Foundation and the India Student Association have engaged in the dissemination of knowledge about India.

Kunwar Bhatnagar
Indu Bhatnagar

INGRAM, FRANCES McGREGOR (b Loup City, Nebraska 1875(?); d Louisville, March 29, 1954). Social worker. A Nebraska native, Frances Ingram moved to Louisville with her family at the age of seven. In 1894 she graduated from Louisville Girls High School and two years later graduated from Louisville Normal School. Having enjoyed her education and time spent in school, she returned as a teacher, first in kindergarten and then at the Normal School.

Ingram attended a lecture on the importance of monitoring the activities of children outside of the home and school and decided to go into social work. She began working at the NEIGHBORHOOD HOUSE on First St. in 1905 and quickly became involved in social causes throughout the city. In 1909 she served on the Louisville Tenement House commission, followed by several years of service with the City-County Children's Home board. From 1920 to 1922 she was the president of the Kentucky Child Welfare Commission and then served as chairman of the public welfare committee of the KENTUCKY FEDERATION OF WOMEN'S CLUBS. In 1928 she earned her bachelor's degree at the UNIVERSITY OF LOUISVILLE, all of this while serving at Neighborhood House, becoming president there in the late 1920s.

Ingram became noted throughout the state and the country for her articles on the work taking place in Neighborhood House. She also became popular with immigrants, helping them to earn their citizenship. In 1933 Ingram appeared before Congress to report on child labor conditions. This trip, as a culmination of her efforts in social work, led the University of Louisville to bestow upon her an honorary master of arts in 1938, citing "outstanding service in bettering social conditions." When she retired from Neighborhood House in 1939, she was named president emeritus. She is buried in CAVE HILL CEMETERY.

See *Courier-Journal,* March 30, 1954.

INGRAM, JAMES MAURICE (b Paducah, Kentucky, 1905; d Louisville, December 20, 1976). Architect. Ingram was the only child of Morris and Maggie Ingram. Upon graduation from Notre Dame in 1928, he apprenticed with Paducah architect Tandy Smith. In 1929 he established his own practice in Bowling Green and remained there until he moved his office to Louisville in 1943. In Louisville he designed many residences and a number of buildings or additions for Baptist and Catholic churches such as CEDAR CREEK BAPTIST CHURCH, Ninth and O Baptist Church, Mother of Good Counsel, St. Thomas More Church, and Third Avenue Baptist Church. He married Ruby Stephens, and they had one son, James. Ingram was a member of the National Society of Engineers and the American Institute of Architects. He is buried in Paducah's Oak Grove Cemetery.

See James M. Ingram papers, Manuscripts and Archives, Western Kentucky University, Bowling Green, Kentucky.

Jonathan Jeffrey

INGRAM, JULIA ADELINE (b Charlestown, Indiana, February 6, 1852; d Louisville, September 23, 1933). Physician. Born to William and Nancy (Fouts) Ingram, she received her early education in the JEFFERSONVILLE, INDIANA, public schools and later attended DePauw University in Greencastle, Indiana. She returned to Jeffersonville after earning her degree and taught in the public school system until 1871, when she enrolled at the Woman's Medical College in Philadelphia. After interning at the New England Hospital in Boston, Ingram moved to Louisville in 1882 and practiced MEDICINE, reportedly as the city's first female doctor, for thirty years. In 1887, along with Jennie Casseday and Dr. A. Morgan Vance, Ingram established the city's first training school for nurses at the old City Hospital.

Upon her retirement, Ingram devoted herself to the development of Louisville's social services, especially for women and children. She served as the director of the Kentucky Children's Home and of the Louisville and Jefferson County Children's Home (ORMSBY VILLAGE), was a devoted supporter of the juvenile court system, and was one of the charter members of the Woman's Club.

Ingram never married. She is buried in Walnut Hill Cemetery in Jeffersonville.

See Bess A. Ray, ed., *Dictionary of Prominent Women of Louisville and Kentucky* (Louisville 1940); *Courier-Journal,* Sept. 24, 1933.

INSURANCE INDUSTRY. The end of the eighteenth century was marked by increasing activities on the Louisville riverfront. More valuable goods were being transported, stored, and sold there. These activities created a need for marine insurance to protect cargo against loss or damage. Marine insurance long preceded fire and life insurance. The first marine insurance contracts were written by private individuals, usually merchants. For example, in 1784 merchant Daniel Broadhead wrote a cargo contract on a shipment from Pittsburgh to Louisville for James Wilkinson. The cargo was valued at seven hundred pounds with a premium of forty-two pounds.

The earliest information on the city's insurance companies dates to 1818 when the Louisville Insurance Co. was incorporated with one hundred thousand dollars. THOMAS BULLITT, William S. Vernon, and Anderson Miller were among its first incorporators. It was a joint fire and marine insurance company authorized to insure vessels, boats, or crafts against fire. In 1832 Louisville Marine and Fire Insurance Co. was founded by James Marshall. The city directory of 1836 mentions two other companies– Firemen's Insurance Co. and Merchant's Louisville Insurance Co.

As Louisville grew in population, so did the number of insurance companies. Some out-of-town insurance companies opened offices in the city. In the 1830s and 1840s Farmer's Fire Insurance Co. and Loan Insurance Co. were based in New York City. Aetna Insurance Co. and Protection Marine and Fire Insurance Co. were from Hartford, Connecticut. As the names suggest, the insurance of the first half of the nineteenth century primarily provided fire and marine damage coverage. Many early fire insurance groups started as a combination of volunteer fire companies and insurers.

In 1854 the Board of Underwriters was founded, the first insurance agents' organization. It was first composed of local fire insurance companies and agents from out-of-state insurance companies. The board took a major step toward better protection of the city against fire through its insistence that Louisville in 1857 began to employ a steam fire engine. The board took an active part in the creation of the city fire department in 1858, installation in 1865 of an electrical fire alarm telegraph to report fires, and the use of automatic sprinklers in 1882. In the 1980s this organization, then known as the Louisville Board of Insurance Agents, merged into the Independent Insurance Agents of Kentucky.

Along with marine and fire insurance companies, there was some insurance available on slaves. Union Mutual Insurance Co. and Knickerbockers Insurance Co. advertised insurance on slaves in the *Daily Courier* of 1855. They offered recompense to owners whose slaves became ill, were injured, or died prematurely. No compensation was offered for slaves who ran away.

The second half of the nineteenth century witnessed the growth of life insurance companies. These companies had a variety of contracts to pay set sums upon the death of policyholders. Premiums were based on mortality tables calculated on the expectation of longevity. Among the first life insurance companies in Louisville were Kentucky Title Co. (1874), Sun Life Insurance Co. of America (1891), and Citizen's Mutual Life Insurance Association of New York (1887). Later accident insurance was added, for example, by the Kentucky Life and Accident Co. of Louisville (1890).

In 1870 the Insurance Bureau of Kentucky was established by act of the legislature to regulate the growing insurance industry. It set standards of conduct and specified types of insurance permissible under Kentucky law. The bureau laid the groundwork for the Kentucky Department of Insurance. Over the years the department became a full-service organization that offers the public advice on all types of insurance. It protects the interests of policyholders and examines and approves insurance policy forms offered by companies.

In 1890 a disastrous tornado struck the city. More than six hundred buildings were destroyed and nearly a hundred people died. This event showed the need for windstorm insurance. Some insurance companies began to offer protection for storm, explosion, tornado, and sundry other disasters.

In 1903 the Commonwealth Life Insurance Co. opened at 308 W Chestnut St., offering not only life insurance but a full line of health coverage for Louisvillians. Health insurance began in the early 1900s. It included protection against income loss due to sickness or accident and provided for hospital and surgical expenses. Commonwealth signaled a major growth in the industry for Louisville and Kentucky and remained a successful business entity throughout the twentieth century.

The first decade of the twentieth century witnessed further development and growth in the insurance business for automobile coverage. By the 1910s every major insurance company in Louisville had added auto insurance policies. Over the years it became one of the major types of insurance coverage.

In 1915 MAMMOTH LIFE AND ACCIDENT INSURANCE CO. was established, the first insurance company in the city owned and operated by AFRICAN AMERICANS. Many blacks were either denied coverage by white-owned insurance companies or were charged inflated premiums. Mammoth helped poor people obtain insurance through small weekly installments instead of monthly or annual payments. Mammoth successfully operated through the mid-1990s when it was merged into Atlanta Life Insurance Co.

Between 1920 and 1950 there was a growing trend toward formation of mutual insurance companies. Mutual companies required little capital and offered policyholders a share in profits. Many mutual companies were able to survive the uncertainties of the Depression era. One of the oldest was the Kentucky and Louisville Mutual Insurance Co.

Beginning in 1940 the primary market for health insurance shifted from individuals to employer-sponsored group policies. Pressure from labor unions coupled with the emerging economic realities of WORLD WAR II brought about this change. As unions demanded health coverage for their members, the federal government, by making the cost of premiums tax deductible and the value of benefits tax exempt, encouraged the purchase of group policies by employers.

Equine insurance began in the city in the mid-1950s, first offered by the English company Lloyd's of London through individual underwriters. Later, local equine insurance companies were established in response to the growing demand from the area's Thoroughbred industry.

One of the most important and successful insurance companies in Louisville is HUMANA INC. It started in 1961 as a nursing home business, grew into a chain of HOSPITALS in the 1970s, and in the 1980s and 1990s blossomed into a successful health insurance company. The architects of the company's success were WENDELL CHERRY and David Jones.

There are many reasons for the success of the insurance business in Louisville. The city is centrally located in relation to the rest of the nation and has also benefited from its proximity to Indianapolis–only 110 miles away and an important insurance center. Many of the companies that expanded into growth markets in Louisville are based in Indianapolis. Louisville provides a direct outlet for the growth of those insurance companies as a link to the South.

State regulations have also had a powerful impact on the local insurance business. Kentucky has consistently been a hotbed of activity with regard to insurance laws and regulations. While a few of these have had negative effects, many have stimulated growth and provided greater profit margins. One such regulation is the no-fault insurance code, which negates responsibility for many types of auto accidents. Most insurance codes and laws in Kentucky are consumer-oriented, and thus residents are more willing to purchase insurance.

State and federal regulations concerning medical insurance have also had a profound effect on insurance. Since the laws of Kentucky are consumer-oriented, Kentuckians, including small businesses, have been willing to invest in insurance coverage programs offered by companies such as Humana. This is part of the success of Humana, which has utilized both the consumer and the professional ends of the medical market to bring both groups together in a collection of insurance programs.

The health-care debate of the 1990s had positive and negative effects on insurance. The debate in the General Assembly revolved around reform of community coverage. A push for universal coverage had both its proponents and its detractors. The insurance industry's resistance was stimulated by the potential for lost revenue, while proponents saw universal coverage as a way to gain equity and a reduction in state costs for noninsured patients.

The national debate over health-care reform has had a more positive connotation for insurance companies in Louisville and across the nation. The concerns about the kinds of reform in regard to a national insurance law have provided the insurance companies with an influx of customers and clients switching to privately based insurance. This provided the insurance companies with an incentive to create a more diversified set of options for existing and potential clients.

One of the most significant reasons for the success of the insurance business in Louisville is the growth of medical services. This has generated positive returns for insurance companies. The success and growth of Jewish Hospital, Humana, Caritas, and VENCOR, among others, have also promoted the increase of specialized areas and centers of MEDICINE such as artificial heart surgery and hand transplants. A strong symbiotic relationship between the insurance industry and the medical services industry promotes the financial success and stability of both. This environment of interdependency has created both medical and insurance giants.

Largest Kentucky Insurers (1998)

Property and Casualty:

KENTUCKY FARM BUREAU Mutual Insurance Co. (Louisville)
State Farm Mutual Automobile Insurance Co. (Bloomington, Ind.)
Allstate Insurance Co. (Northbrook, Ill.)
Anthem Insurance Cos. Inc. (Indianapolis, Ind.)
State Farm Fire & Casualty Co. (Bloomington, Ind.)
West American Insurance Co. (Indianapolis, Ind.)
Grange Mutual Casualty Co. (Columbus, Ohio)
Allstate Indemnity Co. (Northbrook, Ill.)
Cincinnati Insurance Co. (Fairfield, Ohio)
Nationwide Mutual Insurance Co. (Columbus, Ohio)

Life and Health:

Monumental Life Insurance Co. (Baltimore, Md.)
Metropolitan Life Insurance Co. (New York, N.Y.)
Northwestern Mutual Life Insurance Co. (Milwaukee, Wisc.)
Prudential Insurance Co. of America (Newark, N.J.)
United Healthcare Insurance Co., (Hartford, Conn.)
Teachers Insurance & Annuity Association (New York, N.Y.)
Connecticut General Life Insurance Co. (Bloomfield, Conn.)
Aetna Life Insurance Co. (Hartford, Conn.)
American General Life and Accident Insurance Co. (Nashville, Tenn.)
New York Life Insurance Co. (New York, N.Y.)

See J. Stoddard Johnston, *Memorial History of Louisville,* (Chicago and New York 1896); Victor Gerhard, *Commonwealth Life Insurance Co.* (Louisville 1985); George H. Yater, *Two Hundred Years at the Falls of the Ohio* (Louisville 1987); *Caron's Louisville City Directory,* from 1832 to 1981; *Courier-Journal,* Feb. 23, March 23, July 17, and Sept. 30, 1997; *Business First Book of Lists* (Louisville 1998).

Paul Wolf Holleman

INTERNATIONAL HARVESTER COMPANY LOUISVILLE WORKS. The original building was located on Crittenden Dr., just south of LOUISVILLE INTERNATIONAL AIRPORT. The one-million-square-foot former Curtiss-Wright Corp. airplane plant was purchased by Chicago-based International Harvester, now known as Navistar International Transportation Corp., from the U.S. government in 1946. Tractors were produced on an assembly line there beginning in March 1947. A $15 million gray iron foundry was completed in 1948, making the Louisville works, at $58 million, the company's largest single investment to that time.

By 1950 Louisville Works was the biggest factory in Kentucky and the largest wheel tractor plant in the world, with 1.7 million square feet of floor space in 23 buildings on 132 acres. It employed sixty-two hundred people and manufactured its Farmall brand small farm tractors. The foundry produced tractor parts, castings for washing machines used at General Electric's Appliance Park, and refrigeration and automotive parts. While it grew in size, LABOR disputes that included more than 250 walkouts and strikes, some of the wildcat variety, plagued Louisville Works.

By the early 1960s emphasis at the Louisville plant had changed to manufacturing the

Construction of northbound exit ramp from I-65 to Brook Street at Chestnut Street in 1963.

smaller Cub Cadet lawn and garden tractor and portions of products assembled elsewhere. Employment had settled to about thirty-five hundred. A $22 million expansion and modernization program was initiated in the early 1970s, and employment had risen to about sixty-five hundred by 1974.

However, the recession of the 1970s and early 1980s and a 1979-80 strike left the company fighting bankruptcy. It lost $393 million in 1980 and $397 million in 1981. A 1982 restructuring effort closed numerous plants in the United States, Canada, and Great Britain. The assembly portion of the Louisville plant was closed on January 28, 1983, and the foundry closed the following August. The forge remained in operation until it was sold to Louisville Forge and Gear Works Inc. on April 12, 1985. The remaining hourly employees were laid off, though some supervisors and office workers were hired by the new owner. The site was purchased under the airport expansion plan in June 1996, and Louisville Forge and Gear Works moved to Georgetown, Kentucky.

See "International Harvester . . . Helping Farmers Feed the World," *Kentucky Business*, Nov. 1953; *Courier-Journal*, July 30, 1982; *Louisville Times*, Jan. 28, 1983.

Thomas E. Stephens

INTERSTATES AND EXPRESSWAYS.

The Federal-Aid Highway Act of 1956 authorized construction of the forty-one-thousand-mile National System of Interstates and Defense Highways. Under the act, the federal government provided 90 percent of the cost, and the states would cover the other 10 percent for the interstates within their boundaries. Jefferson County and Kentucky embarked on a major program of highway building that for the most part was not finished until 1976. Jefferson County and Louisville's highway system is marked by three interstates (64, 65, and 71) and two expressways (the WATTERSON EXPRESSWAY and Snyder Freeway).

One of the earliest ideas for the establishment of a system of major thoroughfares throughout the city was ANDREW COWAN'S proposed parkway system, conceived during the nineteenth century. Those PARKWAYS were to be the links that tied together Louisville's growing PARKS system. However, the idea of a highway ringing the far outskirts of Louisville was not seriously considered until the late 1940s. In early 1949 construction of the first leg of the highway, known as the Inner-Belt, was begun with a plan to eventually extend the route nearly thirteen miles from Shelbyville Rd. west to Dixie Hwy. Federal funds paid for the early road work, and a two-and-a-half-mile stretch opened between Bardstown Rd. and Breckenridge Ln. later in 1949. Initially intended as a limited-access road, planners projected that by 1970 it would carry twenty thousand vehicles per day. However, as more connections opened in the 1950s, some stretches were conveying 23,500 vehicles per day. It became obvious that the two-lane highway, complete with grade interchanges and accompanying sidewalks, was inadequate.

In 1952 the route was officially renamed the Henry Watterson Expressway in honor of the former editor of the *Courier-Journal*. With the passage of the Federal Highway Act of 1956, the Watterson received a much-needed infusion of money. In 1958 the Watterson Expressway was designated Interstate 264 in order to qualify for federal funds for an expansion to create a superhighway. The federal funds were used to construct a four-lane highway with underpasses and overpasses, and to complete the Watterson as originally intended from Shelbyville Rd. to Dixie Hwy. In 1968 the expressway was extended north to Brownsboro Rd. to connect with Interstate 71. An additional $400 million widening project was completed in 1995 after eleven years of work. In 1995 the expressway carried approximately 117,000 vehicles per day. This was expected to rise to 135,000 vehicles by 2005.

Along with the plans for an inner-belt highway, the Jefferson County PLANNING AND ZONING Commission announced its intention in 1946 to build an outer-belt highway ringing the city. After land acquisition problems, numerous changes in the route, money concerns, and protests from outlying cities such as ANCHORAGE, the first one-and-a-half-mile stretch of the highway opened between Shelbyville Rd. and Interstate 64 in 1961, almost two years before the final plans for the finished route were completed. In 1964 the artery was renamed Jefferson Freeway to avoid confusion with the existing Outer Loop. By 1975 construction had stalled, with only $30 million of work finished out of an estimated $205 million, and the state highway commission doubted if the freeway ever would be completed.

However, state officials renewed their efforts late in 1980 and guaranteed the completion of the route between Dixie Hwy. and Interstate 65 by 1985. Two years after this promise, the end was in sight as the state began purchasing the land for the final link between Smyrna Rd. and Taylorsville Rd., and U.S. representative Gene Snyder included $52 million in a public-works bill for Jefferson Freeway's construction. To commemorate Snyder's efforts, United States senator MITCH MCCONNELL convinced the state to rename the route GENE SNYDER FREEWAY in 1985. After a total cost of $250 million, the final stretch of the expressway opened in 1987, completing the thirty-seven-mile stretch from U.S. 42 to Dixie Hwy. Interstate 265 was also developed in southern Indiana. In the late 1970s, work was completed on the highway linking Interstate 64 and Interstate 65. This was extended eastward to route 62 at the CLARK MARITIME CENTRE in 1994. In 1996, Interstate 265 in Indiana was named for U.S. representative LEE HAMILTON, who was instrumental in securing funds for the highway.

Louisville's interstate system has three highways that converge in the downtown. The first is Interstate 65, a north-south route through the center of the city that heads south to Nashville, Tennessee, and on to the Deep South, and north to Indianapolis, Indiana, and on up to the Great Lakes. Next is Interstate 64, an east-west route that runs to Lexington, Kentucky, and out to the Atlantic coast in the east, and to St. Louis and past the Mississippi River basin in the west. Finally Interstate 71, which originates in downtown Louisville, runs northeast through the county to Cincinnati and, eventually, Cleveland, Ohio. All those interstates meet at Spaghetti Junction, a tangled interchange at the foot of the John F. Kennedy Memorial Bridge.

Interstate 65 was designed to integrate within it both the already-existing KENTUCKY TURNPIKE, a four-lane highway running from the Watterson Expressway south to Elizabethtown, Kentucky, and the North-South Expressway. The North-South Expressway was a four-lane northward extension of the Kentucky Turnpike into the center of the city. Work began on this expressway in 1954, and it was originally supposed to follow a path slightly west of what it actually did, ending at Third and MAIN STREETS. The expressway got only as far as St. Catherine St. when plans to absorb it into Interstate 65 directed its path to the east, where it would continue over the OHIO RIVER by means of a new bridge. Interstate 65 was completed through Jefferson County when the bridge and its southward extension were opened for traffic on December 3, 1963. On November 26, 1963, just four days after the assassination of President Kennedy, the Kentucky state Senate named the new bridge the John F. Kennedy Memorial Bridge, the first such memorial in the nation. The effect of this interstate route was to essentially divide Louisville's downtown in two by cutting a path directly through its inner core. It was necessary to build the road on an elevated level through this area.

In December 1966 the first section of Interstate 71 in Jefferson County opened between Spaghetti Junction and Zorn Ave. It was extended to the Watterson Expressway in July 1968 and to the Jefferson Freeway the following month. This provided easy access to downtown for citizens of northeast Jefferson County and Oldham County. In July 1969 Interstate 71 was opened all the way to Cincinnati, shortening the distance between the two cities from 109 miles by use of U.S. Route 42 to 98 miles.

The construction of Interstate 64 through Jefferson County was the longest and most difficult project. This was because routing the highway directly east would cut through prime real estate, including a path through Seneca and Cherokee Parks. Various sections opened up in the West End, downtown, and just east of downtown throughout the 1960s. Land acquisition, routing debates, and the rough terrain of the path chosen delayed the opening of Interstate 64 between Grinstead Dr. and the Watterson Expressway. A citizens committee founded in 1958 called Save Our Parks objected to any proposed highway through the parks. The group was headed by Dr. Richard M. Kain, an English professor at the University of Louisville. The committee's protests took the form of petitions and letters to residents of the area, to the *COURIER-JOURNAL* and *LOUISVILLE TIMES*, and to various public officials. During its most active years it boasted three hundred thousand supporters, although no official record exists of its membership. An earlier attempt to route an expressway through the parks in 1947, based on accommodating Louisville's future traffic needs, failed mostly due to the efforts of the residents of Alta Vista Rd., the street that runs north-south between Cherokee and Seneca Parks.

On June 21, 1961, the Kentucky State Highway Commission held a public hearing to determine an exact location of the expressway within the corridor already chosen through the parks. This hearing became the focal point of the committee's activities. It was there that Save Our Parks made its case to reroute the expressway somewhere else, possibly along the Frankfort Ave. railroad tracks. Their argument was that the New Jersey engineering firm contracted to find the best route had considered no other less-damaging options in the routing of the expressway. Despite the efforts of the committee, Interstate 64 was routed through the parks and opened in August 1970.

Interstate 64 crossed the Ohio River at the far west end of the city by a bridge built and financed by Indiana, with the Kentucky extension up to the bridge built by Kentucky. Completed in 1962, the bridge was named after United States supreme court justice Sherman Minton (1890-1965) of NEW ALBANY, Indiana. With the completion of the Ninth St. overpass in December of 1976, Interstate 64 was complete from Charleston, West Virginia, to St. Louis, Missouri. The construction along the river effectively separated Louisville from its source of origin, the Ohio River.

The inner loop was not completed until Interstate 264 was extended from Dixie Hwy. to the Interstate 64 interchange near the Sherman Minton Bridge. Rather than extend the Watterson Expressway, this stretch of Interstate 264 was named the Shawnee Expressway. It was completed on January 25, 1971, when the last section from Ralph Ave. to the Dixie Hwy. exchange opened. For the first time, a driver could enter Interstate 71 from Spaghetti Junction, transfer to Interstate 264 and travel the Watterson and Shawnee Expressways, and transfer to Interstate 64, leading back to Spaghetti Junction, making a complete circle.

By the early 1990s, it was becoming very difficult for Spaghetti Junction to handle the increasingly heavy rush-hour traffic. With an exceptionally high accident rate and with several key ramps slightly above full capacity, relatively minor accidents often tied the junction in knots for several hours. After years of wrangling, in 1997 a bi-state Transportation Policy Committee, responsible to the governors of both Kentucky and Indiana, decided to build two bridges, one downtown and one linking Interstate 265, to relieve the traffic at the junction. In December 1997 the governors of Kentucky and Indiana met and formally launched the two-bridge construction project. In the late 1990s the Transportation Policy Committee had also considered the metropolitan area for a light rail system that would help alleviate some of the congestion on the interstates and expressways.

See George H. Yater, *Two Hundred Years at the Falls of the Ohio* (Louisville 1987); *Louisville,* Feb. 20, 1954; *Courier-Journal,* Dec. 14, 1996.

INTERURBANS. Electric interurban cars came to the Louisville area in 1893 when the Kentucky & Indiana Bridge Co. (K&IB) electrified its steam-powered commuter line from downtown Louisville to NEW ALBANY, Indiana. This was the first change from steam to electric interurban operation in the country, and by 1901 interurban lines were under construction on both sides of the OHIO RIVER. The Louisville, ANCHORAGE & PEWEE VALLEY (LA&PV), later to be reorganized as the Louisville & East-

Interstate Public Service car with parlor-dining car.

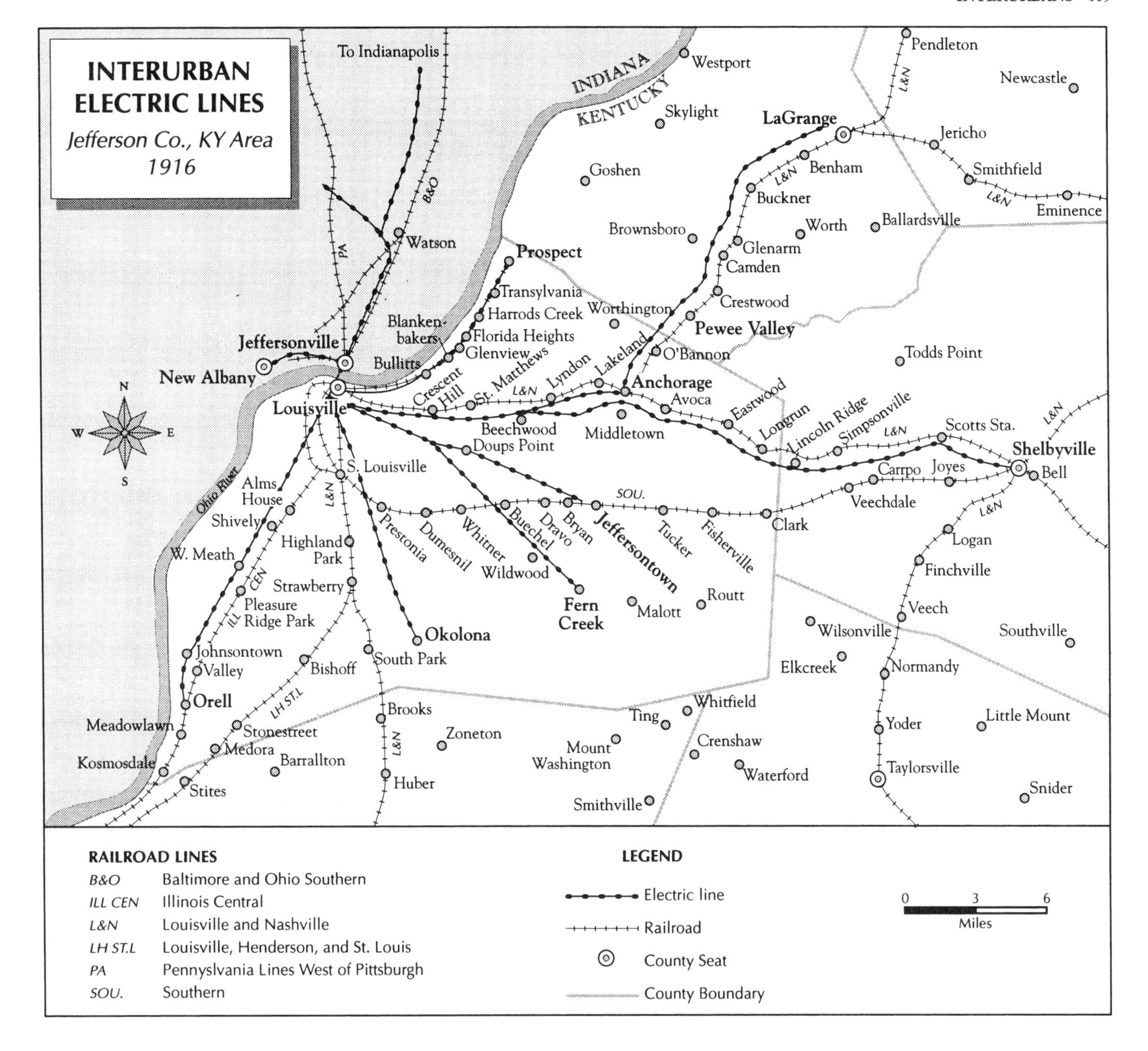

ern (L&E), had started construction of a line to the towns mentioned in its corporate title. The Southern Indiana Interurban Railway (SIIRy), later to become Louisville and Southern Indiana Traction Co. (L&SIT), began constructing a line between Jeffersonville and New Albany, and in 1902 began negotiating with the Louisville and Jeffersonville Bridge Co. (Big Four) for trackage rights into Louisville.

The Louisville and Interurban Railroad Co. (L&I) was incorporated in January 1903 and began constructing lines radiating from downtown Louisville to five towns in the metropolitan area. Service on these divisions began to JEFFERSONTOWN on May 2, 1904, PROSPECT on December 17, 1904, OKOLONA on May 1, 1905, Orell on April 13, 1907, and FERN CREEK on June 6, 1908.

The L&E reached LAGRANGE on April 1, 1907. Construction was started by the L&E on a line to SHELBYVILLE in 1908, and service began on August 19, 1910. Construction of the Shelbyville line through hilly countryside was very costly, and the L&E was forced into bankruptcy. It was acquired by its principal stockholder, the Louisville Traction Co., a holding company for the Louisville Railway. The company was then consolidated with the L&I in January 1911.

The Louisville and Northern Railway and Lighting Co. was organized in 1905 and began operating a shuttle service over the BIG FOUR BRIDGE between Louisville and Jeffersonville. In 1906 it extended its services to Charlestown and extended them to SELLERSBURG, Indiana, in 1907. In 1908 the Indianapolis and Louisville Traction company closed the gap between Sellersburg and Seymour, Indiana. It was now possible to ride an interurban car from Louisville to Indianapolis. In 1912 the Interstate Public Service Co. was formed and soon controlled all the interurban properties operating in southern Indiana, including the former KENTUCKY AND INDIANA BRIDGE Co. line between Louisville and New Albany. The completion of the Louisville and Eastern line to Shelbyville in 1910 ended the construction period for metropolitan area interurban lines.

Interurban travel was safe, reliable, convenient, and fast. The cars on the long runs generally operated on an hourly schedule with extra runs added during the morning and evening rush periods. Local service between Louisville and southern Indiana operated on a fifteen- to thirty-minute headway. Passenger terminals were conveniently located in downtown Louisville. The Louisville and Interurban terminal was on Jefferson St. between Third and FOURTH Streets. The Interstate terminal was on Third St. between LIBERTY and Walnut (Muhammad Ali Blvd.).

The Louisville and Interurban was a subsidiary of the Louisville Railway Co.; and all L&I cars, except on the Prospect line, entered the city on Louisville Railway tracks. The Prospect line and the Interstate line from Indianapolis were built to the standard railroad gauge of 4' 81/2." The Louisville Railway city tracks were 5'0". The terminals of both the L&I and the Interstate could accommodate cars from either line by a system of dual-gauge tracks. However, the different track gauges prevented the two RAILROADS from interchanging cars.

The interurban offered a complete freight service, although interurban freight equipment was not interchanged with the steam railroads. Freight originating on the L&I with a destination in Indiana, Ohio, or Michigan would be transferred to an Interstate box trailer at the dual gauge L&I freight terminal on Liberty St. between Brook and Floyd Streets. The Interstate freight terminal was on First St. between Liberty and Walnut (Muhammad Ali Blvd.). Freight hauled on the interurban lines included cement, cattle, lumber, milk, farm implements, and farm produce.

Passenger equipment on the L&I consisted of twenty-one cars delivered by the St. Louis Car Co. in 1903-04. These cars could be operated from either end and had a deck roof. They closely resembled city cars operated by the parent Louisville Railway. The Louisville and Eastern operated a variety of passenger cars. The L&E cars were longer, heavier, and faster than the suburban-type cars operated by the L&I. After acquiring the L&E in 1911, the L&I immediately placed an order with the Cincinnati Car Co. for five motor cars and five matching trailers, which were delivered in 1912. The L&I then owned forty-one passenger cars and five trailers. Freight business was handled with ten freight motor cars and four box trailers.

The Interstate was one of the premier interurban lines in the nation. Its aging fleet of passenger equipment was upgraded in 1921 when seven heavy steel cars were delivered by Cincinnati Car Co. These cars were assigned to the celebrated Dixie Flyer and Hoosier Flyer runs. In 1923-24 five parlor-dining cars and three sleeping cars were delivered. These cars were built at the Jeffersonville plant of AMERICAN CAR AND FOUNDRY CO. (AC&F). In 1927 Interstate upgraded local and suburban service when it received six new cars from the G.C. Kuhlman Car Co. These were assigned to Louisville-Jeffersonville-New Albany service using the Big Four Bridge. Freight business on the Interstate provided a major source of revenue. Equipment was upgraded in 1923 when Interstate ordered three freight motors and three express trailers from the AC&F plant in Jeffersonville.

The interurban lines thrived until the 1920s, when vastly improved highways and increasing use of automobiles began to seriously erode passenger revenues. More serious was the onset of the GREAT DEPRESSION that began in late 1929 and was severely felt by both Interstate and L&I in 1930. The Interstate was reorganized and its name changed to Public Service Co. of Indiana (PSCI) in 1931.

Interurban lines were being abandoned everywhere when the Indiana Railroad System (IRR) was formed in 1930. This new company was a consolidation of the largest interurban operations in Indiana. The IRR leased the PSCI, former Interstate line, from Indianapolis to Louisville and the suburban line between Louisville-Jeffersonville-New Albany via the Big Four Bridge. Thirty-five lightweight, high-speed cars were ordered by IRR in an attempt to reduce costs and stem the tide of declining ridership. The new cars were probably the finest interurban cars ever built. Thirteen cars were coach-lounge design. These cars were placed in service in July 1931 between Louisville and Indianapolis and continued the train names of Dixie Flyer for southbound runs and Hoosier Flyer for trips going north. The new cars were designed to be operated by the motorman only, eliminating the need for a conductor. The extensive use of aluminum resulted in a car that weighed half as much as the heavy steel cars they replaced. Newly designed motors also saved electricity and gave the cars a top speed of eighty to eighty-five miles per hour. Normal operating speeds on the Louisville line were seventy miles per hour.

The new cars were popular with the riding public, but proliferation of automobiles and trucks continued. The Indiana Railroad discontinued local service between Louisville and Jeffersonville in 1932. The parlor-dining and sleeping cars were also withdrawn from service that year and the branch from Watson Junction to Charlestown was abandoned. Service between Jeffersonville and New Albany was discontinued in 1934, and the original K&IB Daisy Line that ran over Louisville's city streets and the K&I Bridge was sold to the New Albany and Louisville Electric Railroad Corp. This service operated until late 1945 when the Louisville Railway, whose tracks it used, converted the Portland Ave. line to buses.

The L&I was suffering the same fate as the Indiana lines, and the Okolona line was abandoned May 5, 1931. Each year saw more abandoned lines. The Jeffersontown line ended service on December 1, 1932. The line to Fern Creek ended service on December 26, 1933, to Shelbyville on May 15, 1934, to Orell August 17, 1935, to LaGrange August 24, 1935, and to Prospect on October 31, 1935. Rails were removed shortly after a division was abandoned and cars were scrapped. The L&I, as a company, was dissolved in 1936.

The Indiana Railroad discontinued interurban passenger service between Louisville and Seymour, Indiana, on October 31, 1939. Freight service to and from Louisville to points on the Indiana Railroad was continued using trucks.

See Louisville Transit Collection, Filson Club Historical Society, Louisville, Ky.; *Sentinel-News*, Shelbyville, Ky., Bicentennial Edition 1974; Jeffy Marlotte, *Interstate: A History of Interstate Public Service Rail Operations* (Polo, Ill., 1990); George K. Bradley, *Indiana Railroad: The Magic Interurban* (Chicago 1991); George W. Hilton and John F. Due, *The Electric Interurban Railways in America* (Stanford, Calif., 1960): 279-80, 291-93.

James Burnley Calvert

IRANIANS. Prior to the late 1970s the few Iranians in Louisville were primarily those sent by their families or the Iranian government to gain higher education. The fields of engineering and medicine were particularly valued. The UNIVERSITY OF LOUISVILLE drew many students, even actively recruiting students from Iran.

Between 1978 and 1981, at the beginnings of the Islamic revolution, many families left Iran because of increased political and religious oppression. Although the majority planned to return to Iran eventually, it was evident to some that return to their homeland would be unlikely. This was especially true of members of the Bahá'í Faith, whose persecution had greatly increased under the new regime. Other religious faiths represented by Louisville's Iranians are Islam (the majority) and Christianity.

Like cities all over the country, Louisville became attractive to these immigrants because friends and family members were in the city. The new arrivals found Louisville to be welcoming and helpful in assisting newcomers to adapt. Many of the Iranians in Louisville became United States citizens.

As the twentieth century ended, the number of Iranians in Louisville was difficult to pinpoint, since the census does not separate Iranians from other Caucasians. Estimates range from a few hundred to a thousand.

Nancy D. Harris

IRISH. The Irish were the largest non-English immigrant group to enter this country during the colonial period. They came to Louisville in two distinct patterns. The first to arrive were primarily the "Scotch-Irish" or "Ulster Scots" who dominated the colonial period. The latter group were largely refugees of "An Gorta Mor" (The Great Hunger), commonly known as the Irish Potato Famine. Both sought new opportunities but as often as not traveled out of necessity: the former fleeing religious persecution by the established Church of England and the latter to survive a virtually malign governmental indifference.

The earliest settlement in Louisville on CORN ISLAND included several Irish, including John McManus and family, Neal Doherty, William Coomes, and Dr. George Hart. The city could have become known as "Campbelltown" or "Connollyville," as the original survey of a two-thousand-acre tract of what is now the central area of the city was undertaken by two Ulster Scots from Pittsburgh, JOHN CAMPBELL and JOHN CONNOLLY. Connolly was a nephew of George Croghan, a native of Ireland who was Great Britain's agent in securing Indian support during the French and Indian War (1755-63). Connolly fled to Canada with fellow Tories after England lost thirteen of its American colonies. Campbell reemerged and, having purchased Connolly's interests, was an active partisan among those seeking Kentucky's severance from Virginia. GEORGE ROGERS CLARK, who ferociously fought the British and the Indians and is generally credited as Louisville's founder, was the brother-in-law of County Longford native WILLIAM CROGHAN. Croghan built Locust Grove, one of Louisville's most revered historic places, where Clark spent his last days. The stone walls on the estate and several features of the house have designs that are said to be uniquely Irish.

Louisville's outer reaches were also settled by the Irish. In 1780 James Sullivan erected a stockade on a site now occupied by real estate and insurance offices at 3411 Bardstown Rd. In 1805 there was a small settlement of some native Irish families living on Fifth St. near the river, which by 1850, was dissipated by intermarriage and relocation to other parts of the city. Apart from Ulster, most of the Irish immigration did not come until after the War of 1812. In that year James Anderson immigrated from Ireland with his son James Junior. He was successful in the wholesale dry goods business and became a director of the Louisville branch of the Bank of the United States and a member of the Louisville Common Council. One of the first Irishmen to be mentioned in histories of early Louisville is David Ferguson, who came by way of Pittsburgh to set up a bakery shop at Fifth and MARKET Streets in 1814.

After 1825 an increasing number of Irish settled in Louisville undertaking a wide variety of pursuits: Patric Maxcy, Bernard "Barney" McGee, and John Lyons, candle-markers; Thomas K. Byrne, clerk; John O'Beirne, secretary of the Firemen's Insurance Co.; EDWARD HUGHES, boardinghouse proprietor; Edward Kirwan, sawmill owner; Frank McKay and Martin Crowe, grocers; and John Kearney, attorney. The Collins directory of 1838-39 shows a considerable number of Irish engaged as teamsters, grocers, boardinghouse proprietors, merchants, carpenters, tanners, stonecutters, bricklayers, and riverboat porters. Several of these early immigrants achieved commercial success. Patrick Bannon from County Down eventually owned the Kentucky Vitrified Paving Brick Co. Dennis Long of Derry became the owner of the Louisville Pipe Foundry and built the pumping engines for the city waterworks in the 1860s. Arriving from County Cork in 1835, Thomas C. Coleman achieved great wealth in the rolling mill business and built an elegant house at what is today Fourth Ave. and Muhammad Ali Blvd. William and Ellen Banon moved to Louisville in the 1830s and owned a hundred acres in PORTLAND. A successful grocer, William was one of the original trustees of Notre Dame du Port Church (now called "Our Ladys"), which opened in 1840. Irish immigrants sometimes took jobs that had been done by slaves. This undercut the value of chattel slaves and partly explains why their number decreased in Louisville in the decade between 1850 and 1860. An Irish Catholic priest, the Reverend Patrick Joyes, attracted a following from among the Irish settlers and in 1811, the first Catholic church, St. Louis Church, was established for them at Eleventh St. near the river. It was replaced in 1830 by the church on Fifth St. that is today the CATHEDRAL OF THE ASSUMPTION. The first church built exclusively for the Irish was St. Patrick's Church, established in 1853.

Some of the more successful immigrants were brothers John and Francis Quinn, who arrived in 1830. Ordained in 1839, John served at St. Louis Church and administered investments for immigrants, amassing a small personal fortune in the process. Francis inherited the money when John died in the 1852 cholera epidemic. With this money Francis built row houses between Tenth and Eleventh on Main St. that he rented to Irish. Known as "QUINN'S ROW," it was the scene of the most horrific incidents of the anti-Catholic riots in 1855 known as "BLOODY MONDAY" when "Know-Nothing" mobs had been inspired by newspaper editorials containing comments about "Rome Rule."[3] Irish men and women were shot by the arsonists as they fled their burning homes. Irish immigration to Louisville slowed as a result but did not stop.

The most concentrated Irish presence in Louisville was the neighborhood still known as "LIMERICK" (from Kentucky St. on the north to Ormsby on the south between Fifth and Tenth Streets). One of Louisville's first "SUBURBS," two factors led to its development in the 1860s: the LOUISVILLE & NASHVILLE RAILROAD needed laborers and the Dominican Order was in search of a parish. Father William Dominic O'Carroll established a convent and "studium" (house of studies). By 1873, Bishop McCloskey presided over the ceremonies officially dedicating St. Louis Bertrand Church, which included the Galway orator Fr. Thomas N. Burke and the "Sarsfield Rifles." Notable Limerick families included Collins, O'Doherty, Keeley, Murphy, Fahey, and Barry. The beginning of the end of an era began in 1902 when the Louisville & Nashville Railroad moved its shops to HIGHLAND PARK in south Louisville and many of the Irish laborers moved also. Although thousands were in the line of march through Limerick, the last St. Patrick's Day Parade in Louisville until the late 1970s was held in 1918. By the 1920s Limerick had virtually lost its Irish identity.

The *KENTUCKY IRISH AMERICAN* newspaper was published in Louisville from 1896 to 1968. The paper included articles relating to Irish history and its current affairs and, not surprisingly, had an anti-British tone. It was also defensive of Catholic causes, editorializing against the AMERICAN PROTECTIVE ASSOCIATION, the Ku Klux Klan, and the anti-Catholic opposition to the presidential candidacy of Al Smith. The Barry family sustained the paper in its last half century until the logistics and cost of publication became overwhelming.

Local Irish raised money for famine relief, sent twenty-seven volunteers on the quixotic campaign to wrest Canada from Britain in 1866, and turned out in great numbers to greet President Eamon De Valera, the first president of the Republic of Ireland, when he visited during his campaign to raise funds for the newly independent nation. The Whallen brothers, John and James, were sons of Irish immigrants who came to Louisville in the 1870s. Entering the theater business, they soon drifted into Democratic politics. John was widely known for his charities, and he amalgamated into a political base the working-class Catholic and Irish immigrants. The local Irish joined together in less serious endeavors as well. Moonlight river excursions and grand picnics at PHOENIX HILL PARK were diversions for a community that was increasingly able to enjoy its leisure. The Phoenix Hill Park picnics had Irish from all over Louisville in attendance. Counties Sligo, Galway, Limerick, Cork, and Kerry were especially well represented. Irish neutrality in the second world war and successful integration into mainstream American life combined to obscure a strong Irish identity. Emblematic of this was the steady decline of the local Ancient Order of Hibernians (AOH), which had seven chapters in its heyday but had dissolved entirely by 1944.

Although Irish immigration to Louisville has declined to an imperceptible number, those arriving today may be surprised to find a continuing Irish presence. The folk revival and the CIVIL RIGHTS movement renewed American interest in Ireland. The AOH was revived in Louisville in 1966 and, for the second time, hosted the National Convention at the Galt House Hotel in 1994. The first was in 1888 when the bulk of the representatives were lodged at the original GALT HOUSE Hotel at Second and Main Streets. Mayor Harvey Sloane reestablished a St. Patrick's Day Parade as a civic event in Louisville. The Sons and Daughters of Erin was formed in 1975, declaring as its mission to promote "Irish heritage, culture and friendship." The Greater Louisville Irish Cultural Society was founded in 1996 to support an officially sanctioned "feis" (pronounced *fesh*), or competition (principally) of Irish step dancing. The Louisville Irish Family Fest began in 1989 to feature Irish music, dance, and DECORATIVE ARTS, with emphasis on exposing Louisvillians of all ages to Irish culture. The number of Irish music groups in Louisville exceeds that of any city in the region outside of Chicago. The "Irish

Rover" and "Molly Malone's" are two local "authentic" Irish pubs that serve an increasing appetite for an Irish experience. Although the Irish have thoroughly "melted in Louisville's pot," their love of the ancestral island is yet resilient and joyful.

See Michael I. O'Brien, "Irish Pioneers in Kentucky," *The Gaelic American* (New York); Stanley Ousley Jr., "The Irish in Louisville," M.A. thesis, University of Louisville, 1974; Stephan Thernstrom, ed., *Harvard Encyclopedia of American Ethnic Groups* (Cambridge, Mass., 1980); George H. Yater, *Two Hundred Years at the Falls of the Ohio* (Louisville 1987).

Paul B. Whitty

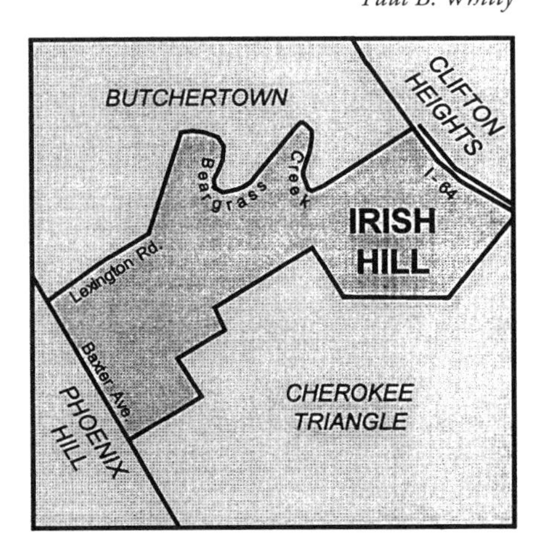

IRISH HILL. A small, primarily residential neighborhood on high ground roughly bounded by Baxter Ave. to the west, Lexington Rd. and the middle fork of BEARGRASS CREEK to the north, Interstate 64 to the east, and Eastern and Cave Hill Cemeteries to the south. Originally known as BILLY GOAT HILL due to the numerous goats that grazed on the hillside of an area farm, the neighborhood was later named for nineteenth-century Irish-Catholic immigrants, although a large number of Germans also settled there. Irish Hill's first subdivision was laid out in 1859 by John C. Hull and Benjamin J. Adams, with the rest of the community being developed five years later by Ward Payne.

Soon after, in 1873, ST. BRIGID CATHOLIC CHURCH was established on the east side of Baxter Ave. between Payne and Rogers Streets, where it remained until 1890 when the parish moved to its present-day location at the corner of Baxter at Hepburn Ave. In 1891 St. Aloysius Church was established in the former quarters of St. Brigid, and then it moved to the 1100 block of Payne St. A school was built next to the church in the early 1920s, but both were closed in 1996.

From the 1850s until its demolition in 1968, the city WORKHOUSE, which until 1954 housed prisoners convicted of lesser crimes, stood at Payne St. and Lexington Rd. across from Distillery Commons, which was the OLD KENTUCKY DISTILLERY and warehouse. Breslin Park was established on the site of the workhouse in 1974. The neighborhood area was also the site for a firehouse constructed for Steam Engine 11 in 1893 (closed 1977) on Rogers St. In 1884 Stottman's Grocery and Bar, a typical corner saloon, opened at Payne and Cooper Streets and later became Baxter Station Bar and Grill. Although a majority of the homes in Irish Hill are SHOTGUN COTTAGES, an important historic structure is the two-story Renaissance-revival home of Swiss-born tobacco merchant Nicholas Finzer, constructed in 1866 on Hull St.

See *Louisville Survey: East Report* (Louisville 1980); *A Place in Time: The Story of Louisville's Neighborhoods* (Louisville 1989).

Dona Schicker

IRON FOUNDRIES. Iron-casting foundries were one of Louisville's leading industrial operations in the latter part of the nineteenth century. The proprietors, the city's "Iron Men," were among its prominent citizens. The first foundry was established in 1812 by Paul Skidmore, about whom little is known. It produced such small items as pots and pans, fireplace andirons, grates, stove lids, and smoothing irons. Previously such items had been brought downriver from Pittsburgh.

Skidmore sold out to Joshua Headington about 1814. When Headington died about 1816, the foundry was purchased by David Prentice, who began the first large-scale operations in Louisville. Prentice, a Scots millwright who arrived in the United States before 1811, was by 1813 the proprietor of the Eagle Works, an iron foundry near Philadelphia. When the British blockade of Chesapeake Bay during the War of 1812 cut off coal supplies from Virginia, he agreed to go to Henderson, Kentucky, to install a steam engine in the saw and grist mill erected by JOHN J. AUDUBON and Audubon's brother-in-law, English-born Thomas Bakewell. The mill was a financial failure, and Prentice came to Louisville and purchased Headington's foundry. Soon he was joined by Bakewell. Louisvillian GEORGE KEATS, brother of English poet John Keats, was an investor in the venture.

The foundry scored early successes and in 1819 produced the first steam engine made in Louisville. It was built to power a cotton mill. The advent of STEAMBOATS and their need for steam engines was the principal factor in stimulating the growth of iron-working in the city in the early 1820s. As the demand for steamboat engines increased, the foundry expanded. It had at one time sixty employees and in one year constructed eight engines for steamboats and two for stationary use, as well as small castings for local sale. But a sudden drop in orders brought an end to the partnership in 1821, although Prentice continued operation until his death in 1827. Bakewell ascribed the firm's failure to Prentice, whose engines, he said, lacked sufficient power and were subject to breakage, resulting in frequent lawsuits.

One of the foundrymen employed by Prentice and Bakewell was DAVID L. BEATTY, who had become the first apprentice iron molder in Louisville in 1815 when Headington operated the foundry. (Other workers presumably had been recruited in Pittsburgh.) Beatty soon became the foundry foreman. Following Prentice's death, Beatty, in partnership with John Curry, in 1829 launched a new venture, the Jefferson Iron Foundry, at Ninth St. and the river.

In 1838 this foundry was to make a particularly intricate casting for a steamboat engine, a casting that seemed beyond the skills of local molders despite the fact that since 1819 Louisville foundries had turned out 246 engines for use in steamboats, mills, and factories. A call was sent to Pittsburgh for aid. Dennis I. Long, a young Irish-born molder, came promptly. After the first attempt at casting proved a failure, Long declared that it could be done if he were allowed to handle it his way. It was successful, and Long was induced to remain in Louisville.

Within a few years, in partnership with Bryan Roach, Long established the Union Foundry, taking over the Jefferson Foundry from Beatty and Curry. Here, in the shop where Long made the successful casting, were turned out many steamboat and stationary engines, including the two engines for the new LOUISVILLE WATER CO. in 1860. Roach died just as the pumping engines were being completed, and Long turned to the specialty of producing cast-iron pipe for water and gas mains. The pipes were used in Louisville and many other cities, including Chicago and St. Louis.

Much of the pig iron, the raw material of the foundries, came from nearby Nelson and Bullitt Counties, where iron ore was found. The Belmont Furnace in BULLITT COUNTY and the Nelson Furnace in Nelson County sent pig iron down Salt River and up the Ohio to Louisville. When author Washington Irving stopped off at Louisville on a western trip in 1832, he noted that the wharf was piled with goods, including "heaps of iron." The *Louisville Daily Courier* of March 23, 1855, reported that the Belmont Furnace had unloaded two hundred tons of "the celebrated Salt River Iron" at the wharf and was sending more to Wheeling at thirty-three dollars a ton. Fifteen years later, the *Louisville Commercial* reported on January 4, 1870, that 121 tons of pig iron had arrived in Louisville in a single 36-hour period. (By 1887 the year's total was 48,813 tons, but this came from Alabama.) With iron close at hand and the alluvial sand underlying much of Louisville ideal for forming molds, the city by 1850 had twelve foundries. By 1860 employment reached 1,380, making foundries the single largest employer. Often the maker of machinery would oversee its installation as well. The Hydraulic Foundry of Emile Barbaroux and Richard Snowden at Floyd and Washington Streets produced the usual line of steam engines and varied machinery. The *Louisville Daily Journal* of October 13, 1858, reported Snowden's death of yellow fever in Mississippi, where he had gone "to put up machinery made by his firm."

Another early shop, founded about 1830, was the Fulton Foundry at Ninth and MAIN STREETS, operated originally by Shreve, Anderson, and Co. Later owners changed the name to the Washington Foundry, and it became the seedbed of what was to emerge as the city's premier establishment–the Louisville Foundry and Machine Shop, operated by Ainslie, Cochran, and Co. George Ainslie, born in Edinburgh, Scotland, in 1814, came to the United States with his family in 1823. They joined Robert Owen's utopian community in New Harmony, Indiana, but came to Louisville in 1837. Ainslie became an apprentice in the Washington Foundry and later a foreman and eventually a partner.

In 1857 he and the younger ARCHIBALD COCHRAN, also connected with the Washington Foundry, established the large Louisville Foundry and Machine Shop at Tenth and Main Streets, adjacent to the Boone Foundry. The latter establishment closed at the outbreak of the Civil War and was converted to the Boone Tobacco Warehouse. Ainslie and Cochran's shop by the mid-1870s was described as "the largest foundry in the West" (*Louisville Past and Present,* Louisville 1875, 348). Like most Louisville foundries it turned out a variety of products, but in larger volume. Cochran later erected an imposing country residence on a hillside (COCHRAN HILL) along what became Lexington Rd. By the mid-1870s Louisville, with thirty-two foundries and machine shops, was an important iron center that the Iron Molders Union in 1878 chose as the site of its annual convention.

An important iron-working establishment was the Phoenix Foundry and Machine Shop begun in 1833 by William H. Grainger. He was born in 1808 near Sheffield, England, and came to the United States about 1825. After serving a foundry apprenticeship in Belleville, New Jersey, he came to Louisville in 1832. He opened the Phoenix Foundry and Machine Shop on the riverfront between Sixth and Seventh Streets. By the 1850s his foundry had expanded into a larger plant on Tenth St. near the river, where he produced steam engines, coal-mine machinery, saw and grist mills, and other machinery. In 1888 his son, Charles, became a partner in the renamed Grainger and Co. Charles, who served as Louisville's mayor from 1901 to 1905, moved the company into the production of structural iron.

Foundries had appeared in NEW ALBANY, Indiana, home of several boatyards, by the 1850s. Both the Union Foundry (later Webster and Pitt) and the American Foundry were in operation by then, producing steamboat machinery and iron castings to order. Both were along the riverfront. The American Foundry later became part of the New Albany Rail Mill. The most important and longest-lived in New Albany, however, was Charles Hegewald and Co., founded in 1873 as a partnership between Hegewald and Washington C. De Pauw. This establishment, on Water St. between Pearl and Bank Streets, specialized in steamboat machinery and equipped nearly two hundred boats. It also produced the pumping engines for the New Albany Water Works, the De Pauw Glass Works, and other New Albany manufactories.

In Jeffersonville, an important boat-building center, the Jefferson Foundry on Watt St., was in operation by the 1870s. Later Michael A. Sweeney founded M.A. Sweeney and Co. on Market St. between Mechanic and Fulton Streets. Both foundries made steam engines as well as castings to order. Most Jeffersonville boats, however, were probably equipped with machinery made by Hegewald or in Louisville.

Ohio Falls Iron Works advertisement from an 1889 city directory.

Architectural Foundries

By the 1850s some specialized foundries had appeared in Louisville, producing only one type of product, such as architectural castings. Cast-iron fronts for commercial buildings were not only fireproof but cheaper than stonework and permitted larger windows. Cast-iron columns for interior support also became common. Many of these cast-iron-front buildings survive along Main St.

The first foundry specializing in such work was opened by Charles S. Snead about 1852 in a failed stove foundry on MARKET ST. near Ninth. Here he produced iron fronts, railings, porches, stairs, skylights, bank vaults, and ornamental items. He also became a partner in the Metropolitan Foundry on Fourteenth St., also specializing in architectural work. By the mid-1870s Louisville architectural ironwork was being shipped "as far north as Chicago and as far south as New Orleans" (*Centennial Report of the Business of Louisville . . . and . . . New Albany and Jeffersonville,* Louisville 1876). Snead's foundry later expanded its metalworking capacity to include wrought iron and sheet steel. In the late 1890s it manufactured all the steel bookcases for the new building of the Library of Congress. Both of Snead's works, along with the smaller architectural foundry of F.W. Merz on Green (Liberty) St. near Third and some of the machinery-oriented foundries, also produced ornamental manhole covers. When the Snead foundry on Market St. was destroyed by fire in 1898, it was replaced by the Snead Building (817-27 West Market St.), designed to house various small manufacturing enterprises. It was one of the earliest pre-stressed concrete buildings in Louisville. After the fire, the business was moved to Jersey City, New Jersey, but a small foundry operation continued at Tenth and Hill Streets until about 1960.

Agricultural Foundries

Production of agricultural implements, specifically cast-iron and cast-steel plows, began as early as 1845 when Daniel H. Avery arrived in Louisville with wooden plow patterns provided by his uncle, Benjamin F. Avery. The latter had grown up on a farm near Aurora, New York, and had devised an improved plowshare. He had earlier formed a partnership with a practical molder for the production of his plowshare. When the partnership ended in the early 1840s (Avery had been named executor of his father's large estate), he sent his nephew with the patterns to find a suitable southern site for further production.

The younger Avery picked Louisville, and the first plowshares were cast in the Jabez Baldwin Foundry on Main St. between Floyd and PRESTON STREETS. Soon Benjamin Avery came to Louisville and by 1852 had purchased Baldwin's foundry. Within a few years he built a much larger plant at Fifteenth and Main Streets. (It was used as a Union army hospital during the Civil War.) In 1868 he took his son and son-in-law into the business as B.F. Avery and Sons. Other farm equipment, such as cultivators and reapers, was added to the firm's output, and Avery products were sold all through the South and Southwest. In 1910, pressed for greater manufacturing capacity, the company built a complex of modern shops on a fifty-seven-acre tract on the outskirts of Louisville at 1721 Seventh Street Rd. near Algonquin Pkwy.

When Daniel Avery arrived in Louisville in 1845, a young man in SIMPSONVILLE (twenty miles east of Louisville in SHELBY COUNTY) had been making plowshares of his own design for a number of years. Thomas E.C. Brinly, grandson of noted English botanist John Bradbury, had learned the blacksmith trade from his father, who also made plowshares. Production was limited at first because of lack of capital and limited manufacturing facilities. Nevertheless, his plowshares proved popular in his neighborhood and attracted the attention of Louisville iron merchant William B. Belknap. Soon almost all of Brinly's output was sold to Belknap, who developed a market for the plows throughout the South.

As demand outstripped production facilities, Brinly moved operations to Louisville in 1859, with a Mr. Dodge as his partner in Brinly, Dodge, and Co. The new foundry was on Main St. between Brook and Floyd Streets. A year later it was moved a block east between Floyd and Preston to the foundry in which B.F. Avery had begun business. Because of its strong southern market, the Brinly firm had established production centers in several southern cities to supplement its Simpsonville operations. Many of the branch shops were destroyed during Civil War actions and were not rebuilt.

In 1863 James E. Hardy had joined the firm, followed soon after by Brinly's brother-in-law, A.D. Miles, and the name became Brinly, Miles, and Hardy. Plows and other agricultural implements were produced until about 1948. Since then it has concentrated on attachments for lawn-and-garden equipment. In 1900 Miles had sold his interest and the name became BRINLY-HARDY CO., which it has retained since. It has been owned by the Hardy family since that year (the last Brinly died in 1900), and fifth-generation Jane W. Hardy became president in 1994. In 1964 the company purchased a large brick structure on the northeast corner of Preston and Main Streets to use as a distribution warehouse. It was built in 1902 as a railroad freight station.

When the city of Louisville opted to build a new baseball stadium for the Louisville Redbirds along the riverfront near Preston St., it purchased the Brinly-Hardy distribution warehouse to use as a primary entrance to the planned Slugger Field, which opened in 2000. In its search for a new home, Brinly-Hardy decided to move to the CLARK MARITIME CENTRE in Indiana, upriver from Jeffersonville.

Stove Foundries

Another specialty among foundries was the production of wood- and coal-burning heating and cooking stoves. These were made in Louisville until World War II and found a ready market in the South and Southwest. The major names in the field were James Bridgeford's Louisville Stove and Grate Foundry; James S. Lithgow's Eagle Foundry; Baxter and Fisher; Fischer, Leaf, and Co.; and Terstegge, Gohmann, and Co., New Albany. Most, perhaps all, of these foundries also turned out cast-iron mantels (often painted to resemble marble) for the many fireplaces in Victorian homes.

Louisville's pioneer stove manufacturer was James Bridgeford, a Jefferson County native who had served an apprenticeship in the copper, brass, and sheet-iron trade. In 1829 he became a partner in a firm devoted to this business. Bridgeford's partners (and the name of the firm) changed from time to time, but in 1842 the manufacture of stoves was begun. The firm in later years claimed to be the first stove foundry south of the Ohio River. In 1860 Bridgeford purchased the interest of his then-partners and adopted the name of Louisville Stove and Grate Foundry. In 1880 it was incorporated as Bridgeford and Co. At the turn of the century the enterprise moved from its longtime location on Sixth St. between Main and Market to a large new plant at 2007-23 Portland Ave.

In 1923 a group of Louisvillians formed the Southern Signal Co. to produce railroad grade-crossing signals and purchased the Bridgeford foundry, where the odd combination of railroad signals and stoves were produced. This enterprise was a victim of the GREAT DEPRESSION. The foundry was purchased in 1934 by the Stiglitz Furnace and Foundry Co. (dating from 1883), which made stoves as well as coal furnaces. After World War II the burgeoning use of gas furnaces brought a steep decline in the demand for coal furnaces. This, coupled with the falling demand for stoves, caused the foundry to be closed in 1948. Reorganized as the STIGLITZ CORP., it made sheet-metal stampings for manufacturers of home appliances and air conditioners and in 1967 moved to 1747 Mellwood Ave. in Butchertown. It is a job shop that stamps parts, paints, and provides light assembly. Douglas Stiglitz is the fifth-generation president.

What became the largest stove foundry in Louisville, J.S. Lithgow and Co., was begun only two years after James Bridgeford founded his enterprise. James S. Lithgow, born in Pittsburgh in 1812, was apprenticed in that city in 1826 to master the copper, tin, and sheet-iron trade, just as Bridgeford had been. In 1832 he came to Louisville and found employment in his trade. In 1836 he and partner Allen S. Wallace launched a sheet-metal shop as Wallace and Lithgow on Market St. Eight years later they began manufacturing heating and cooking stoves in the Eagle Foundry they erected at Second St. and the river.

When fire destroyed the foundry in 1857, they built a new and larger one at Main and Clay Streets. After Wallace's death in 1861, Lithgow took his two sons-in-law into the business as J.S. Lithgow and Co. It was a success and by the 1870s processed more iron than any other stove foundry south of the Ohio River. Lithgow served as mayor of Louisville from late 1866 until late 1867. The partnership was incorporated as Lithgow Manufacturing Co. about 1890. Following Lithgow's death in 1902, the company faltered and was closed. The Kentucky Lithographing Co. occupied the premises for many years thereafter but moved in the early 1980s to a suburban location in Bluegrass Industrial Park. The large building was then converted to apartments.

John G. Baxter, another graduate of an apprenticeship in copper, tin, and sheet-iron work, founded a third Louisville stove foundry. Baxter, born in Lexington, Kentucky, in 1826, came to Louisville in 1847 to join his brother Archibald in the sheet-metal business on Main St. between Seventh and Eighth Streets. Just a block away the same type of business was conducted by R.G. Kyle and Co.

About 1860 Baxter and Kyle, along with William H. Fisher (foreman of Kyle's establishment), joined forces to manufacture stoves as Baxter, Kyle, Fisher, and Co. Kyle later withdrew, and the firm became Baxter and Fisher. The foundry was at Thirteenth and Main Streets. Although the enterprise never achieved the volume of business of Bridgeford or Lithgow, it was a profitable operation, and Baxter became a prominent citizen. In 1870 he was elected mayor of Louisville and was elected again in 1879. He received much of his support from workingmen, probably because of his humble origins. Baxter died in 1885, and in 1887 his heirs moved the business to the rising iron-producing city of Birmingham, Alabama, to save the cost of shipping pig iron from Birmingham to Louisville. (Dennis Long also considered moving his pipe foundry to Birmingham, even buying land there, but decided to stay in Louisville.)

The fourth large stove foundry was established in 1866 by eight stove molders, some of whom worked for Lithgow and others for Bridgeford. At first called Hare-Leaf and Co. for two of its founders, it became the Fischer-Leaf Co. in 1870 following the death of Sidney Hare and the admission of John Fischer as a partner. In 1884 the enterprise was incorporated with Fischer as president. From a small beginning at Sixteenth and High Streets the venture grew into a large operation. Its line of heating and cooking stoves, retailed under the name Arizona, was sold throughout the South and Midwest. About 1925 the company was purchased by the Hart Manufacturing Co., which had begun business in 1922 at 2006-36 High St., across the street from Bridgeford. It was operated as the Fischer-Leaf Division of

Hart, and all operations were moved to the Hart plant. As the demand for wood and coal stoves and ranges plunged after World War II, the production of stoves ceased. The Hart Heating and Cooling Co., 754 Logan St., became the successor operation.

There were a number of other small manufacturers of stoves, including LOUISVILLE TIN AND STOVE CO., O.K. Stove and Range Co., and the Kentucky Stove Co.

Plumbing Equipment

What became American-Standard Inc., one of the largest plumbing equipment foundries in the United States, had its origin in 1859 in a small brass foundry and machine shop established on Louisville's Market St. by German-born Theodore Ahrens Sr. He had completed his machinist's training in his native Hamburg and came to the United States in 1853 and to Louisville in 1858. Here he worked as a toolmaker at the Barbaroux and Snowden Hydraulic Foundry, but he soon established his own business. He specialized in brass plumbing fixtures such as faucets, drains, and valves. In 1866 Henry Ott became a partner in Ahrens and Ott, which expanded into commercial plumbing and heating.

The expanding market for brass plumbing fixtures as more Louisville homes and businesses were supplied with running water led to incorporation in 1880 as Ahrens and Ott Manufacturing Co., with Ahrens as president. In 1888 the two founders created the Southwestern Iron Works to manufacture enameled iron bathtubs, kitchen sinks, and bathroom basins and toilets for a national market. Located first at Sixteenth and Maple Streets, the works soon outgrew this plant and by 1890 was in a newly built foundry on the southwest corner of Sixth and Shipp Streets. By the middle of the decade, employment at the plant was near seven hundred.

Ahrens and Ott was by then a major player in the plumbing supply business nationwide. THEODORE AHRENS JR., who had by the late 1890s succeeded his father as head of the enterprise, initiated a move to combine the company with ten of the other large manufacturers of sanitary ware across the nation. The result was the Standard Sanitary Manufacturing Co., formed in 1900 with the younger Ahrens as president. In 1901 the corporation built a massive new foundry at Seventh and Shipp Streets on a fifty-three-acre site. It was not only the largest foundry in Louisville but was also the largest industrial plant in Kentucky at that time. Through the years the facilities were expanded, and at one time employment numbered five thousand.

Another merger in 1929 with the American Radiator Co. resulted in a name change to American Radiator and Standard Sanitary Manufacturing Co., shortened later to American Standard Inc. Modernization of the plant was considered in the 1950s but never carried out, although a research facility was established at Broadway and Campbell St. in 1950. During this period, when the post–World War II housing boom was in full swing, the plant turned out an average of five thousand enameled cast-iron bathtubs each week, in addition to sinks, basins, and other plumbing items.

An aging plant, strikes, and changes in technology were to spell the foundry's doom, however. An American Standard plant in Salem, Ohio, was producing steel tubs by a less expensive process. Bathtub production in Louisville was slowly phased out, along with other cast-iron items. Other plumbing items, such as brass faucets, continued to be made at the plant, but the workforce was steadily cut. Finally, at the end of May 1992, operations ceased.

The closing of International Harvester and American Standard were the end points of a long, slow decline in Louisville foundry operations that had reached their apex about 1890. The eleventh decennial census taken that year reported thirty-two independent foundries with machine shops and seven architectural and ornamental foundries. Total employment was almost two thousand. Most of these foundries were relatively small operations. A number of factors were responsible for the decline in the early twentieth century.

The dwindling of the steamboat trade with the coming of railroads cut the demand for boat engines, while the coming of electrical power in the late 1890s obviated the need for steam engines to power manufacturing plants. In addition many large industries maintained their own foundries, such as the LOUISVILLE & NASHVILLE RAILROAD'S sprawling SOUTH LOUISVILLE repair shops, HENRY VOGT MACHINE CO., Peerless Manufacturing Co., American Standard, and International Harvester.

The first major closing was Ainslie and Cochran's Louisville Foundry and Machine Shop, the city's largest independent foundry, about 1892. It may have been a victim of the troubled economic times of that decade. Dennis Long's Union Foundry and its cast-iron pipe business was purchased about 1890 by the United States Cast Iron Pipe and Foundry Co., headquartered in Chicago. It continued in operation until World War II. It was closed probably because of wartime restrictions and an outmoded plant.

The once-thriving Grainger and Co. switched to producing and distributing structural iron before the 1920s but was closed about 1932 during the GREAT DEPRESSION. B.F. Avery and Sons, whose most important products by the 1940s were farm tractors, merged in 1951 with farm-machinery producer Minneapolis-Moline Co. It continued in operation as the B.F. Avery Division until 1956, when the plant was closed. The large site and its buildings were turned into what was called an "industrial park," housing numerous smaller-scale machine and manufacturing enterprises. It was the first of its kind in Louisville, a predecessor of such built-from-scratch entities as Bluegrass Industrial Park and Riverport Industrial Park.

See Carroll W. Pursell Jr., *Early Stationary Steam Engines in America* (Washington, D.C., 1969) 66-68; *House Executive Document 21* (the Woodbury Report), Twenty-fifth Congress, Third Session (Washington, D.C., 1838); Bruce Sinclair, ed., "Thomas Woodhouse Bakewell's Autobiographical Sketch and Its Relation to Early Steamboat Engineering on the Ohio," *Filson Club History Quarterly* 40 (July 1966): 235-48; John F. McDermott, ed., *The Western Journals of Washington Irving* (Norman, Okla., 1954). 70; *Industrial and Commercial Louisville* (n.p., n.d., ca. 1887), 38; D.P. Robbins, *Advantages and Surroundings of New Albany, Indiana* (New Albany 1892), 52-53; *Fifty Years Ago* (Louisville 1923), 92; various editions of Louisville, New Albany, and Jeffersonville city directories; various decennial census returns, especially manufacturing censuses; *Courier-Journal Magazine,* May 8, 1949.

George H. Yater

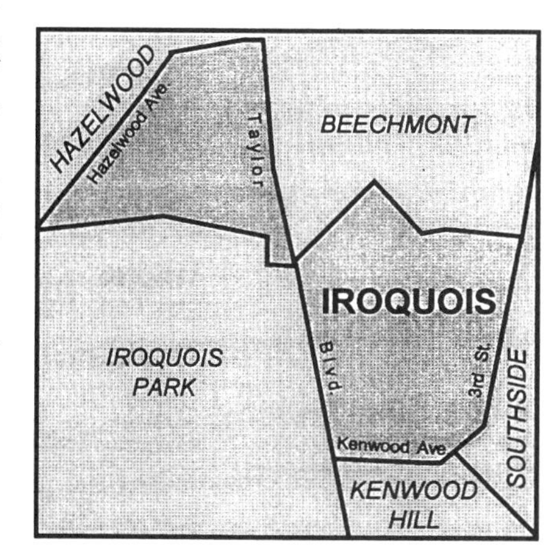

IROQUOIS. Neighborhood in southern Louisville split into two parts by the southern tip of the Beechmont neighborhood. The north section of the neighborhood is bounded by HAZELWOOD Ave. to the west, Bluegrass Ave. to the north, Taylor Blvd. to the east, and the Iroquois golf course to the south. The southern section is bounded by Taylor Blvd. to the west; Southern Pkwy., Auburndale Ave., and Southland Blvd. to the north; Third St. to the east; and Kenwood Dr. to the south. As citizens moved farther from the city's core after World War II, this primarily residential area became a popular site for development, especially during the 1950s. The area is located west of LOUISVILLE INTERNATIONAL AIRPORT. The Iroquois Neighborhood Association joined others in the area to challenge the proposed expansion of the airport in the late 1980s and early 1990s because of concerns over noise pollution.

IROQUOIS AMPHITHEATER. The thirty-five-hundred-seat Iroquois Amphitheater, located on the eastern side of IROQUOIS PARK, is a product of the WORKS PROGRESS ADMINISTRA-

TION of the GREAT DEPRESSION years. The open-air amphitheater has offered entertainment in the Olmsted-designed park since 1938. The desire for such a facility had been raised at least fifteen years earlier, spurred by a group of music lovers and a local interest in light opera. However, it was not until March 1938 that the city's Board of Park Commissioners approved the building project. The amphitheater was built in seventy-five days and cost fifty thousand dollars. The facility included an outdoor stage, an orchestra pit, a building with dressing rooms, storage areas, a box office, and terraced seating.

The amphitheater's grand opening was July 4, 1938, and featured the musical *Naughty Marietta.* Early patrons remember that an evening at the musicals was a special occasion calling for dress clothes. A water curtain, used to hide the stage crew during scene changes, was one of the features fondly remembered by the THEATER patrons of the 1940s and 1950s. By the late 1950s, however, attendance began to decline; by 1959 the decision was made to stop production of the summer musicals.

The city of Louisville took over the management in 1961. Between 1961 and 1974 very few events were staged, and the facility fell into disrepair. In 1975 the Iroquois Amphitheater Association was organized to renovate the amphitheater. It cleaned, painted, and helped to return the theater to its original condition. Along with Metro Parks, the administrative body that eventually replaced the Board of Park Commissioners, the organization assisted in managing the theater. In 1981 the Iroquois Park Players began staging musicals. This policy continued after another production company, Music Theater of Louisville, began producing shows in 1987. In addition, Metro Parks and the Iroquois Amphitheater Association also continue to provide a wide range of entertainment at the amphitheater.

Throughout its history, the Iroquois Amphitheater has offered theater patrons quality entertainment. In the early years, Robert Whitney, conductor of the LOUISVILLE ORCHESTRA, often directed the orchestra supporting the singers. Moritz Bomhard, founder of the KENTUCKY OPERA Association, also conducted productions. Actors such as Elaine Stritch, Janet Blair, Jeanette MacDonald, Don Ameche, Larry Parks, Gordon MacRae, Audrey Meadows, Gene Barry, and Liberace appeared in productions at the amphitheater and have become part of the enduring memories of the outdoor theater. The amphitheater also hosts the annual Kentucky Music Weekend, a folk-music festival with workshops.

In 1999 plans were approved for a massive renovation of the facility. Designed by the Bravura Corp., the $7 million plan was intended to increase the available seating by about 640 as well as provide a roof for the stage and most of the audience. Additional parking and better road accessibility to the amphiteater were also considerations.

See *Courier-Journal,* Nov. 20, 1996, May 21, 1999.

Margaret Merrick

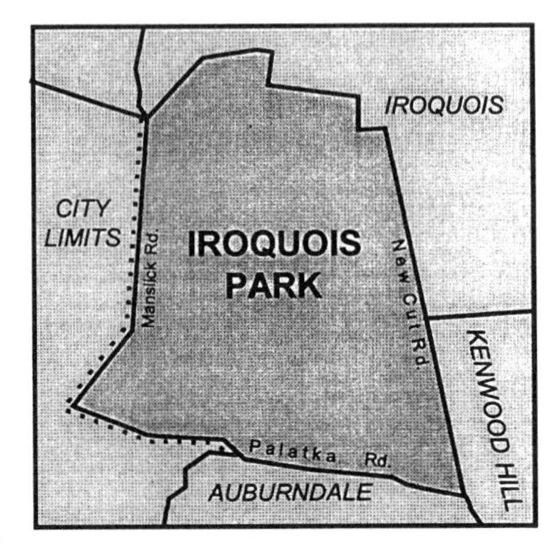

IROQUOIS PARK. Neighborhood in southern Louisville comprising the homes surrounding the park within the boundaries of Manslick Rd. to the west, Palatka Rd. to the south, New Cut Rd. to the east, and the Iroquois golf course to the north. Carved into the hilly terrain, the two-part community, separated by the 739-acre wooded park reserve, developed on the eastern and southwestern fringes of the park's borders.

IRWIN, HARVEY SAMUEL (b Highland County, Ohio, December 10, 1844; d Vienna, Virginia, September 3, 1916). Congressman. After graduating from high school in Greenfield, Ohio, Irwin began studying law but left his studies to serve in the Union army during the CIVIL WAR and helped raise a volunteer regiment of artillery. He also served in a special corps of the regular army. Following the war he resumed his law studies in Louisville, where he served as assistant internal revenue assessor, deputy clerk of the United States District Court, and chief deputy collector for an internal revenue district in Kentucky. In 1895 he was elected a Kentucky railroad commissioner, which post he filled until his election to Congress in 1900 as a Republican. After failing to be reelected in 1902, Irwin practiced law in Washington, D.C., where he was later licensed as an evangelist. He is buried in CAVE HILL CEMETERY.

See *Biographical Directory of the American Congress 1776- 1961,* 1107.

ISAACS, NORMAN E. (b Manchester, England, March 28, 1908; d Santa Barbara, California, March 7, 1998). Newspaper editor. Isaacs moved with his family first to Canada and then to Indianapolis. He dropped out of high school and went to work for the *Indianapolis Star.* He was editor of two other Indianapolis NEWSPAPERS and served as managing editor of the old *Star-Times* in St. Louis before his tenure as executive editor of the *COURIER-JOURNAL* and the *LOUISVILLE TIMES.* He also served as the vice president of the Courier-Journal and Louisville Times Co. for several years.

In 1967, after reading an article in the *New York Times Magazine* by editorial page editor A.H. Raskin, Isaacs appointed the first newspaper ombudsman in the United States to serve both Louisville newspapers. The ombudsman acts as a liaison between the public and the newspaper, handling reader complaints and promoting improved community services. The idea caught on, and many metropolitan and community newspapers now have an ombudsman.

Isaac became managing editor of the *Louisville Times* in 1952. In 1953 he served as president of the Associated Press Managing Editors Association. In 1969 and 1970 he was president of the American Society of Newspaper Editors. In 1970 he retired from the Louisville newspapers and joined the faculty of Columbia University.

He served as editor-in-residence at Columbia's Graduate School of Journalism from 1971 to 1980. In 1975 and 1976 he was also president and publisher of the News Journal Co. in Wilmington, Delaware, and, from 1977 to 1982, he served as chairman of the old National News Council, which assessed complaints about major news organizations. He was also a member of the Nieman Fellows selection committee and the Pulitzer Prize advisory board.

He married Dorothy Ritz in 1932, and she died in 1977. They had a son, Stephen, and a daughter, Roberta Mathews of Washington. He married the former Mildred L. Wade of Santa Barbara in 1979. Isaacs died of heart failure.

See *Courier-Journal,* March 8, 1998; *New York Times,* March 10, 1998.

ITALIANS. It is unknown when the first Italians arrived in Louisville, but their number increased in the great southern European exodus in the late eighteenth century, when an Italian community began to form. A majority came after the turn of the twentieth century. Italians never came to the south-central states in large numbers, and the Louisville area was no exception. In 1870 the city had only 234 native Italians, about 0.2 percent of the city's total population. By 1900 there were only 679 Italian-born immigrants in Kentucky, with almost half residing in Louisville. The total population of Italians in the city in 1900, both foreign-born and those born in this country, was almost twelve hundred.

The first decade of the twentieth century was the peak for Italian immigration to Louisville. There were 654 native Italians in 1910, making up 0.3 percent of the city's total population—the high point up until that time. During the next twenty years Louisville's Italian immigrant population actually declined in both real numbers and percentage of the population. Although the Italian immigrant population never reached 1 percent of the total population of the city, it did expand as a percentage of the total number of immigrants during this peak period. In 1880 Italians made up just over 1 percent of the city's foreign-born. That number had grown to 5.8 percent by 1930. Although always a small percentage in comparison to Louisville's German and IRISH communities (GERMANS constituted as much as half the city's immigrant population in 1900), the Italians did continue to move up in the rankings of Louisville's largest immigrant communities. In 1900 Italians were the ninth-largest immigrant community, and they had risen to fourth by the 1930s behind Germans, RUSSIANS, and the Irish. However, if the extended ethnic communities of both foreign-born and second- and third-generation Italians are added together, then Italians ranked as only the seventh-largest ethnic group in the city in 1930, falling behind the English, Swiss, and FRENCH communities, as well as others. Immigration of these groups had fallen off, but they still made up a much larger percentage of the ethnic communities.

Although there were never any distinctly Italian communities such as the Irish in PORTLAND or the Germans in GERMANTOWN, there were concentrations of Italians in the central WARDS of the city. Still, Italians resided in every ward in the early decades of the twentieth century. After 1930, according to oral histories and other informal sources, many Italians moved to East End neighborhoods. Many Italians who worked in the produce business lived near Louisville's market district. In the late 1800s there were large concentrations of Italian households in an area bounded by Main, Floyd, Green (now LIBERTY), and Seventh Streets, with clusters on Jefferson, Market, and Green Streets in the heart of downtown.

During the nineteenth century, Italians, with their skills of artistry, masonry, SCULPTURE, PAINTING, mosaics, woodcarving, moldings, and their knowledge of farming and horticulture, came to Louisville to find a better life. Masonry was one of the first art forms to be in demand in the growing city. Since most Italian homes and buildings were made of stone, it was only natural that Italian stonecutters, stonemasons, and stone carvers were invited to ply their trades in Louisville. The masons took care of the outside of houses. Next the interior of the houses had to be completed. The Rosa family came to Louisville from the Udine region of Italy and started the Rosa Mosaic and Tile Co. The building that housed this company was located at the northeast corner of BROADWAY and Floyd St. The other part of the Rosa family started the Keno Rosa Tile Co., and it was located on Brook St. between Chestnut St. and Walnut St. (now Muhammad Ali Blvd.). These two Italian companies did marble facades on buildings and houses. They were also responsible for terrazzo floors as seen today in HOSPITALS, churches, schools, and other public buildings, as well as the marble sills and battiscopo installed where the wall meets the floor.

Wall and ceiling decorations were in demand. Zeffiro Grisanti came to Louisville to start the Grisanti Statuary Co. at 304 South Campbell St. (between Jefferson St. and Green St. (now Liberty). Zeffiro Grisanti was responsible for bringing the following plaster workers to Louisville: Florindo Grisanti; Constantino Mattei; Monte Togneri; Ernesto Lucchesi; Vincenzo Mattei, son of Romulo and Domencia Mattei; Antonio Pellegrini; "Guiseppe" Albanese; Zeffiro's brother Paciffico Grisanti; Alfredo Lena; Amadeo Casani; and Ricardo Casani. Also coming to Louisville to work for the Grisanti Statuary was architect Anziani. Sculptors such as Alfred Bertoli and Ricardo Casani were employed for making original cartouches, finials, rosettes, mantels, niches, statuary, crown moldings, and other plaster works. Examples of the work of the Grisanti Statuary Co. can be seen in Louisville at St. Theresa and St. James Catholic Churches and at the Brown and Seelbach HOTELS.

In 1892 the C.G.I. Mattei Co. was started by Giovacchino Mattei, Casmiro Mattei, and Innocente Mattei to supply plaster decor for homes. The printer mistakenly printed "J" instead of "I" so the name became C.G.J. Mattei Co. This company began supplying the F.W. Woolworth Co. with home decorations. This company also sold wares to S.H. Kress, Kresge Co., McCrory Stores, W.T. Grant, and all of the major "5 and 10 cent" stores.

Italians are responsible for much of the city's produce business. In the early 1900s Italians routinely comprised about two-thirds of the city's fruit peddlers. Such names as Datillo, Denunzio, Lombardo, Campisano, Passafiume, Cieresi, Polio, Michael, and Conti came and went in the vegetable business. Most of these people came from the southern part of Italy and Sicily. It is this region of Italy that produces the best fruits and vegetables, and, like other artisans, their knowledge of the business added greatly to the Louisville ECONOMY. Indeed, Gus Dattilo informed his customers and suppliers that he wanted his invoices mailed on Saturday so that he could have them by Monday morning. He satisfied his creditors and debtors by Wednesday. Today, because of Gus Datillo, nationally, all wholesale food sales are on a seven-day schedule.

Joseph Denunzio was one of the city's largest wholesale suppliers of fruit and produce in the late 1800s and early 1900s. He opened a fruit and produce business in the 1870s. By the end of the century the Joseph Denunzio Fruit Co., located on W Jefferson St., was one of the largest in Louisville. Denunzio was known for starting the auction of fruits and vegetables early in the morning so that other wholesalers could bid for his produce. In fact, his grave monument in Calvary Cemetery shows him in the pose of an auctioneer with produce at his feet. JOSEPH DENUNZIO SCHOLTZ, mayor of Louisville in the late 1930s and early 1940s, was the son of Charles Scholtz, who served as president of the Denunzio Fruit Co. for many years. Other successful fruit companies of the day include Passalacqua's, DeSopo's, and J.B. Corso and Sons.

Antonio Ciresi operated his retail fruit business in the mid-thirties on Jefferson St. between Second and Third Streets. Julio Polio had his retail business on South Brook St. between Jefferson and MARKET STREETS, almost oppo-

The Philip Passafiume Fruit Co. in the Haymarket was in the 500 block of East Jefferson Street, 1926.

site St. Michael's Roman Catholic Church, which was considered the Italian church after 1924 when Father Delphin Autheman, a native Italian, was appointed pastor. This area was actually "Little Italy," and any Italian immigrant automatically moved in to this area upon arrival in Louisville. So much was this Little Italy that the Italians bought an old Jewish synagogue on the south side of Jefferson St. between Jackson and PRESTON STREETS and started the Italian-American Society Club, which would sponsor the annual Columbus Day celebrations in the city. This club functioned until the start of the GREAT DEPRESSION.

The Italian restaurant business began when three Italian brothers arrived in Louisville. Phillip, Charles, and Angelo came from Genoa and opened a tavern that served, among other things, a ROLLED OYSTER. Mazzoni Oysters was located on the west side of Third St. between Jefferson and Market Streets for more than ninety years until URBAN RENEWAL forced its removal. Although they had at first given them away, Mazzonis amassed a fortune selling rolled oysters at five cents apiece. Another Italian restaurant was Luvisi's on the west side of Fifth St. between Walnut (now Muhammad Ali Blvd.) and Liberty Streets. Luvisi was in operation until the mid-1950s.

During the Depression era and World War II, an Italian doctor cared for the Italian community. Vincent Stabile had his offices at the junction of Garden (now Chestnut) St. and Baxter Ave. He was a great asset to the Italian community, since he was able to minister to his patients and understand their descriptions of ailments in the Italian language. Dr. Stabile was also a diplomat in his work, bringing together the Societa di Fratelanza, which was mostly northern Italians, and the Italian-American Society, which was predominantly southern Italians. This was accomplished in the late 1940s and early 1950s.

In the post-World War II era when the Italians were returning from the war, they made themselves known with the establishment of Codispoti's Restaurant and Lentini's Restaurant. The G.M.G. Art and Novelty Co. was founded by Albert Grisanti, his brother Ferdinand, and his cousin Dorina Mattei. After about ten years in this business of manufacturing plaster novelties, the three principals started Casa Grisanti. For many years it was a premier Italian restaurant located on Liberty St.

Although they tended to specialize in the trades of their native country, Italians soon were absorbed into the mainstream of Louisville life. Their presence strengthened the Catholic RELIGION. Although Germans and Irish were more noted for their political acumen, Romano Mazzoli was a United States representative from 1971 until his retirement in 1995.

See F.S. Aprile, "Louisville's Italian Community: 1870 to 1930 and Points Between," student papers, University of Louisville Archives, 1978. Gregory Kent Stanley, "Making a Home: Italians and Jews in Louisville." *The Filson Club History Quarterly* 68 (January 1994):35-57

Dominic Mattei

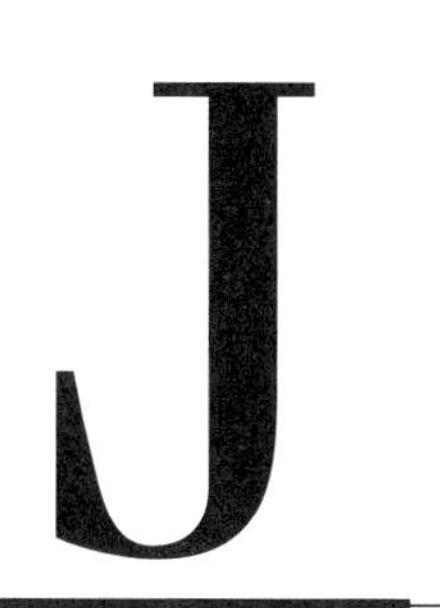

JACKSON, REBECCA DAY (b Short Creek, Grayson County, Kentucky, April 12, 1949). County judge/executive. Rebecca Day Jackson was born to Jesse Thomas and Louise Dennis Day. In 1998 she became Jefferson County's highest-ranking elected official and the first woman to hold the post with her election as Jefferson County judge/executive. Jackson was the first Republican to win the office since 1981.

Jackson served two terms as Jefferson County clerk (1990-98). Building on her 1990 victory over an incumbent, Rebecca Jackson captured an overwhelming 74 percent of total votes cast in her 1993 reelection.

Jackson's background includes extensive experience in business, administration, and education. She has served as a teacher, administrator, and coordinator for the Jefferson County Public Schools and the University of Louisville. As an entrepreneur, she started Consultants for Educational Programs Inc., which designed and implemented programs for educational institutions. She also founded JobCenter Inc., an employment agency for persons with handicaps. Her awards have been numerous, with none more important than being named "Public Official of the Year" in 1998 by the National Association of County Recorders, Election Officials, and Clerks.

Jackson served on two teams representing the United States for the International Republican Institute. The first bipartisan team observed Russia's parliamentary elections in December 1993, and the second in February 1996 devised a candidate selection process in Bulgaria for the presidential elections. In 1997 the National Association of Counties selected Jackson to serve as one of seven American elected officials in a delegation to foster relations with local governments in China in the areas of business, trade, technology, environmental protection, and city planning.

Rebecca Jackson received a bachelor of science from the University of Louisville in 1973 and a master of education in 1977. She graduated from Southern High School in Jefferson County in 1969. She married Ralph Wallace Jackson Jr. on June 14, 1969. They had three sons: Wesley Alastaire, Garett Reid, and Derrick Brice.

JACOB, CHARLES DONALD (b Louisville, June 1, 1838; d Louisville, December 25, 1898). Mayor. Jacob was one of the more popular mayors in the city's history, having been elected to office four times during his career. He was the son of John J. and Lucy Donald Robertson Jacob of Louisville. His father was the first president of the Bank of Kentucky, one of the city's largest real estate owners, and one of the wealthiest men in the city in the early and mid-1800s. He owned several properties in Louisville's early business district and also owned land, known as Jacob's Woods, comprising the area bounded by Fifth, Preston, Broadway, and Breckinridge Streets.

Charles Jacob was the next-to-youngest of ten children. He grew up on the Jacob homestead, which made up an entire city block, bordered by Third, Fourth, Walnut (Muhammad Ali Blvd.) and Chestnut Streets. His brother Richard T. served as lieutenant governor of Kentucky. He was educated by private tutors in Louisville and attended Harvard College. He contracted diphtheria about 1857 and had to return to Louisville. After a period of recuperation in Europe in 1857 and 1858, he intended to finish his studies but never did. Between 1860 and 1868, Jacob's poor health prevented him from engaging in civic affairs. Bad health would be a constant problem.

In 1870 he received the Democratic nomination for Seventh Ward councilman, winning the office by a large margin. He was reelected to a second term as councilman without opposition. In 1872 he ran for mayor in one of the city's most famous political battles. Jacob had been selected to challenge incumbent mayor John G. Baxter. Jacob defeated Baxter by approximately nine hundred votes, becoming at age thirty-two the youngest mayor in the city's history. He easily won reelection in 1875. He left office in January 1879 because the city charter was changed so that he could not be reelected to another consecutive term, and he was succeeded by Baxter.

Jacob went to Europe in August 1879 following the death of his wife, returning in September 1880. In 1881 he again ran for mayor and won by an outstanding margin (14,260 out of the 15,000 votes cast). He served until 1884. Shortly after the completion of this third term, he served for two years as ambassador to Colombia during the first administration of President Grover Cleveland (1885-89).

In 1887 he ran as an independent candidate and defeated the two party representatives to win his fourth term as mayor. He took on the Democratic nominee, County Judge William B. Hoke, and Republican Samuel Avery, son of Benjamin F. Avery and the first Republican candidate for mayor. Jacob's 11,339 votes easily bested Avery's 5,987 and Hoke's paltry 3,326. In 1890, while serving as mayor, his health forced him to take a leave of absence for several months, during which time he took a round-the-world trip with a traveling companion, William Ward, the janitor at City Hall.

He sought the Democratic Party nomination in 1893 but was defeated by Henry S. Tyler, who went on to win the mayor's post. In 1896 he ran again for mayor to fill the unexpired term of Tyler, who had died in office. Jacob refused the Democratic Party nomination because of his lack of support for the free silver plank of the party's platform. The political machine of the Whallen brothers chose Louisville postmaster Charles P. Weaver to carry the mantle of the Democrats. The Republicans went with incumbent George D. Todd, who had been chosen by the Republican City Council to serve until the election. Jacob lost, coming in second to Weaver.

During his last term, Jacob acquired the land that was later used to create Iroquois Park (often referred to by its original name, Jacob's Park) south of Louisville. In 1889 Jacob had preempted the passage of the necessary park legislation and personally purchased 313 acres of land, then known as Burnt Knob, to be used as part of the city's new park system. He sold the land to the city for the same ninety-eight hundred dollars he initially paid for it, although a substantial amount of controversy surrounding the acquisition and sale of the property was generated by the local press. Many of the city's leaders, especially those connected with the Salmagundi Club, which provided the original impetus for the park system, were angered by Jacob's bold initiatives to purchase the land without prior approval. He also acquired land to create Southern Pkwy., known originally as Grand Blvd., which stretched from the end of Third St. to the park. The boulevard was to resemble the Champs-Élysées in Paris.

The elegant Jacob, who was never without his signature yellow rose, a Marechal Niel, in his lapel, also influenced the construction of the Home for the Aged and Infirm. He ushered Louisville into the age of electricity when, in the 1880s, the city granted the first franchise to light the streets. It was also during his tenure

Charles D. Jacob.

as mayor that granite and asphalt were first used to pave streets. From 1871 until 1873 he served as president of the Central Savings Bank of Louisville, and from 1886 until his death he served as president of the Mutual Life Insurance Co. of Kentucky.

He married Addie Martin of Louisville on January 12, 1859. The couple had three children: Jennie, who married ISAAC CALDWELL; Lucy Donald; and Charles Junior, a soldier in the LOUISVILLE LEGION. He was killed on July 1, 1898, during the Spanish-American War at the battle of San Juan Hill while trying to save a wounded man. The loss of his son was believed to have contributed to Jacob's death on Christmas Day in 1898. His first wife had died in 1878, and he was remarried in 1897 to Edith Bullitt, a member of one the city's most prominent families. He is buried in CAVE HILL CEMETERY.

See Temple Bodley, *History of Kentucky*, vol. 1 (Chicago and Louisville 1928); *Courier-Journal*, Dec. 26, 1898; George H. Yater, *Two Hundred Years at the Falls of the Ohio* (Louisville 1979).

JACOB, RICHARD TAYLOR (b Oldham County, Kentucky, March 13, 1825; d Louisville, September 13, 1903). Political leader. His father, John Jeremiah Jacob, at one time was considered the largest real estate owner in Louisville, contributing largely to the founding of the City Hospital (predecessor of the University of Louisville Hospital) and donating the original site for the Blind Asylum, a large lot on BROADWAY between First and Second Streets and extending south to Jacob St. His mother, Lucy Donald Robertson Jacob, was the granddaughter of Commodore RICHARD TAYLOR of the Virginia navy in the Revolutionary War.

As a young man, poor health forced Jacob first to Brazil and then to California, where he served as captain of a forty-six-man company under John C. Fremont during the MEXICAN WAR (1846-48). After the fighting in California ended, Jacob returned to Kentucky. He was married on January 17, 1848, to Sarah Benton, the daughter of Col. Thomas H. Benton of Missouri. Jacob resided in Missouri as a farmer until 1853, when he returned to Kentucky and purchased a home overlooking the OHIO RIVER near WESTPORT in OLDHAM COUNTY.

In 1859 Jacob was elected to the Kentucky House of Representatives. In the 1860 presidential election, Jacob served as an elector for southern Democrat John C. Breckinridge but rejected the idea of secession. When the Kentucky General Assembly convened in January 1861, he played an active role in the defeat of a call for the secession of the state. Jacob was reelected by an overwhelming majority in the 1861 regular election, and he continued his efforts to keep Kentucky in the Union in the ensuing session.

In July 1862 Jacob, frustrated with efforts to stop Confederate general John Hunt Morgan's raids into the state, issued a call for fifteen hundred to two thousand young men. However, the project collapsed when Morgan retired from the state. Union general Jeremiah T. Boyle, commander of the Military District of Kentucky, then called on Jacob to raise a regiment of cavalry for one year's service, and in 10 days he had 1,244 men in camp at Eminence. Designated the Ninth Kentucky Cavalry, Jacob's command rode in support of Union general DON CARLOS BUELL'S army. Jacob was shot twice, in the left arm and above the heart, in a hand-to-hand encounter with Confederate cavalry near Lawrenceburg.

In March 1863 Jacob accepted his party's nomination for lieutenant governor on the condition that he would be permitted to remain in the field with his command. Jacob was then ordered to the Cumberland River with the Twentieth Michigan Infantry Regiment, two units of the Twenty-fourth Indiana Light Artillery, and three cavalry regiments–his own Ninth, along with the Eleventh and Twelfth Kentucky. Returning from an expedition south of the Cumberland River to Monticello, in Wayne County, part of his command fought off an attack by Morgan's cavalry on May 10, 1863, at Horseshoe Bend in RUSSELL County, then successfully recrossed the rain-swollen Cumberland River. Jacob participated in the pursuit of John Hunt Morgan during his raid through Kentucky, Indiana, and Ohio. A portion of his command was present at Morgan's capture in Ohio. Soon thereafter, the Ninth Kentucky was mustered out.

Elected lieutenant governor in November 1863, Jacob supported George B. McClellan in the 1864 presidential election and was denounced by Lincoln administration supporters. After Lincoln's reelection, Jacob was seized and placed outside Union lines at Catlettsburg, Kentucky, by order of Union general Stephen G. Burbridge. After making his way to Richmond, Virginia, Jacob wrote Lincoln, demanding that he be allowed to return to Kentucky. Lincoln issued an order permitting Jacob to travel to Washington, D.C., where Lincoln gave him a letter of unconditional release. Returning to his native state, Jacob served out his term as lieutenant governor.

Following the CIVIL WAR, Jacob ran for Congress and then for the Court of Appeals clerkship but was defeated both times. In 1876 Jacob was elected as judge of OLDHAM COUNTY to fill a vacancy but refused to run for a regular term of office. Jacob's first wife, Sarah Benton, died in January 1863 after bearing two children–Richard T. and Sally Benton. He was married a second time, on June 15, 1865, to Laura Wilson of Lexington, who bore five children–John, William, Donald, Brent, and Laura. Jacob is buried in CAVE HILL CEMETERY.

See Jacob-Johnson family papers (1798-1928), Filson Club Historical Society, Manuscripts Division, Louisville; W.H. Perrin, J.H. Battle, & G.G. Kniffin, *Kentucky: A History of the State* (Louisville 1887); E. Merton Coulter, *The Civil War and Readjustment in Kentucky* (Chapel Hill, N.C., 1926); Edwin Bryant, *What I Saw in California* (New York 1848).

Ed Cahill

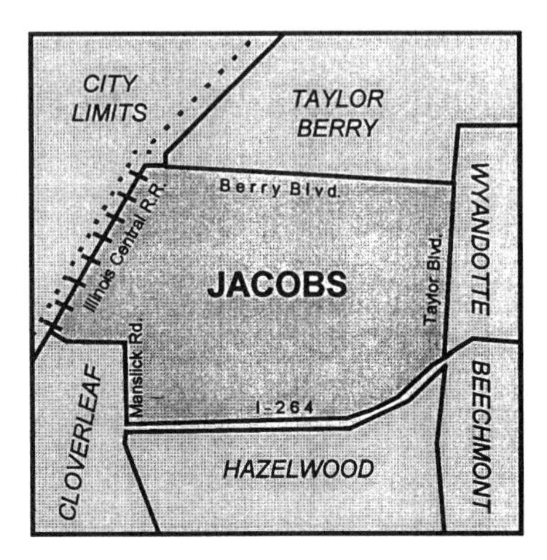

JACOBS. Neighborhood in southern Louisville bounded by Berry Blvd. to the north, Taylor Blvd. to the east, the WATTERSON EXPRESSWAY to the south, and SEVENTH St. and the ILLINOIS CENTRAL RAILROAD tracks to the west. The Starks Realty Co. began to develop the area as Jacob's Addition in 1892 after the opening of nearby Jacob's Park (modern-day IROQUOIS PARK,) and the Grand Blvd. (modern-day SOUTHERN PKWY.). From WORLD WAR II until a new facility opened on Zorn Ave. in 1952, the area housed the Nichols General Hospital, a temporary facility for the treatment of soldiers and veterans. Local landmarks include Manslick Cemetery, a burial site for indigents dating from the 1870s, the adjacent Watterson Lake Park, and the city Animal Control and Protection Center.

See Carl E. Kramer, "The City-Building Process: Urbanization in Central and Southern Louisville, 1772-1932," Ph.D. dissertation, University of Toledo, 1980.

JAMES, GRACE (b Charleston, West Virginia, ca. 1924; d Louisville, January 25, 1989). Physician, professor, health-care advocate. Grace Marilynn James was the fourth of seven children born to Edward L. James Sr., owner of a produce company, and Stella Grace (Shaw) James, postmistress of Institute, West Virginia. James graduated from West Virginia State College in 1944 and did postgraduate work at the University of Chicago and West Virginia State College before entering Meharry Medical College in Nashville, Tennessee. She graduated from Meharry in 1950. James worked during her internship and residency at Babies Hospital and Vanderbilt Clinic and in New York City at Columbia Presbyterian Hospital and Harlem Hospital, where she completed her studies. She was also a fellow in the care of handicapped children at the Children's Evaluation and Rehabilitation Clinic of the Albert Einstein College of Medicine at Yeshiva University's Jacobi Hospital.

James was one of the first two AFRICAN AMERICANS appointed to the faculty of the University of Louisville School of Medicine. She was assistant clinical professor of pediatrics and among the first African American women to gain membership in the JEFFERSON COUNTY MEDICAL SOCIETY and be appointed a staff member of the old General Hospital.

In 1973 James founded at 2209 W BROADWAY a health-care facility serving the poor in the West End. Located at 2209 W. Broadway, it was known as the West Louisville Medical Center and served people in the RUSSELL, CALIFORNIA, SHAWNEE, and PORTLAND NEIGHBORHOODS. By 1980 the project had failed financially. She also founded the Teen Awareness Project, designed to help reduce the teenage birth rate among blacks. James served with many medical and minority advancement groups, including the Falls City Medical Society and the Council on Urban Education, a citizens' group concerned with education problems facing black children. As president of the Louisville chapter of the National Association for the Advancement of Colored People, James was a vocal opponent of inadequacies in the education of African Americans in PUBLIC SCHOOLS.

James was married to Charles Carlisle O'Bannion of Madison, Indiana, from 1952 to 1957. Following their divorce, James adopted a son, David. After her death of a heart attack at home, a scholarship fund in her name was created at Meharry Medical College in Nashville, Tennessee.

See *Courier-Journal,* Jan. 25, 1989, Dec. 3, 1980.

JAMES, THOMAS (?). Minister. A freeman from New York, the Reverend THOMAS JAMES came to Louisville during the CIVIL WAR to work among the city's African American refugees and soldiers. He was acting as an agent for the American Missionary Association, which had been founded in 1846 to promote the peaceful abolition of slavery and to further the belief that blacks deserved the full and equal rights of citizens. In 1864 James took over as supervisor of a large refugee camp located on BROADWAY near the city limits. Plagued by rampant disease and substandard shelter, the refugee camp improved under James, who constructed a refugee home on the site and established the first school for the city's refugee children.

In 1865, in response to James's allegations that many blacks were being imprisoned in slave pens across Louisville, the military commander of Kentucky, Union major general John M. Palmer, gave James the authority to investigate the situation by attaching him to the office of the provost marshal. As a result, James was responsible for the freeing of hundreds of former slaves from the city's slave jails and from slave traders. During the time he spent in Louisville, James was a controversial figure who drew criticism from certain city leaders and ministers who believed his tactics to be too radical. Pro-slavery forces were particularly hostile toward him, and James often received death threats. James eventually left Louisville, and little is known of him afterward.

See Marion B. Lucas, *A History of Blacks in Kentucky, From Slavery to Segregation, 1760-1891* (Frankfort 1992).

JAMES THOMPSON AND BRO. Liquor wholesaler. JAMES THOMPSON came from Ireland to Louisville in 1871. By 1876 he had found employment as a wholesale liquor salesman with Chambers and Brown. He was a cousin of the firm's GEORGE GARVIN BROWN. In 1881 Chambers retired, and Thompson became a partner with Brown in a new company called Brown-Thompson. In 1889 he sold his share of the company to GEORGE FORMAN and created his own spirits company with his brother, Francis P. Thompson. JAMES THOMPSON AND BRO. was a wholesale liquor company.

Francis died in 1891, but the company kept its name. James purchased the building vacated by the N.M. Uri Co. in 1900 at First and MAIN Streets, making it one of the most complete blending houses on Louisville's "Whiskey Row."

In 1901 James Thompson and Bro. acquired the Glenmore Distillery in Owensboro. Thompson put his brother-in-law, Harry S. Barton, in charge of the distillery. Barton remodeled the distillery, making it the largest distillery in the nation at that time.

James Thompson and Bro. was one of the six companies that were allowed to sell "medicinal" whiskey during PROHIBITION. When James died in 1924, the company was reorganized and renamed the Glenmore Distillery Co. in 1927. When Prohibition ended, Glenmore was in excellent condition to compete in the bourbon market.

Glenmore grew to be one of the largest DISTILLING companies in the United States. In 1944 Glenmore acquired SHIVELY's Taylor and Williams Distillery, with its Yellowstone brand. In 1960 Glenmore acquired the Columbia Distilling Co., and in 1969 it acquired Foreign Vintages Import Co. of New York. The Old Mr. Boston Co. was the next acquisition by Glenmore, purchased in 1970. The Medley Distillery became part of Glenmore in 1988 and the Fleischmann's Distilling Co. in 1989.

In 1991 Glenmore was acquired from the Thompson family by United Distillers, a subsidiary of Guinness PLC of London. Guinness created United Distillers Glenmore in 1992 as a subsidiary company. In 1996 United Distillers Glenmore was reorganized and renamed United Distillers USA.

Michael R. Veach

JAY'S CAFETERIA. Jay's Cafeteria was opened in April 1974 by owner-proprietor Frank Foster and his wife, Barbara Jean. Originally at 504 S Eighteenth St., the cafeteria moved in 1994 half a block west to a larger facility at 1812 MUHAMMAD ALI Blvd. The 100 percent black-owned and -operated restaurant has grown from a 150-seat local eatery to a spacious, 400-seat mauve and dark green dining and catering establishment worth an estimated $1.7 million. The name *Jay's* was derived from Foster, who is a junior, and his wife's name, Barbara Jean.

The cafeteria is part restaurant and part community center to the inhabitants of the west Louisville neighborhood. There are bulletin boards announcing activities and meetings as well as several private rooms at the site often used for these meetings. Jay's has been a lunch mecca to employees of the United States Postal Service, Brown-Forman, Philip Morris, and Courtaulds Coatings. The clientele is a unique mixture of the city's POPULATION.

Jay's thriving business is based on big portions of homemade food served at reasonable prices. The menu fare is traditional American, with features such as liver and onions, pot roast, barbecued ribs, pork chops, a variety of vegetables, and its signature dessert, sweet potato pie. A large part of the business is in catering, and the restaurant has catered events for many of the city's largest corporations and civic celebrations.

Jay's has been a regular stop for many famous people, including Vice President Al Gore, Muhammad Ali, Don King, Wesley Snipes, Patti LaBelle, and the Temptations. The restaurant is also a popular stop for GOVERNMENT employees, including Louisville mayors, county judge/executives, and Kentucky's governors.

See *Courier-Journal,* March 11, 1995.

JAZZ. While no single definition can be attached to JAZZ, this uniquely American art form traces its origins to the intermingling of African, European, and Creole musical cultures in New Orleans during the late 1800s. With the passing of each decade, jazz musicians developed a complex and expressive tonal language that emphasized rhythmic variation and syncopation, a sophisticated harmonic vocabulary and a fluid melodic line whose bent notes and chromaticism echoed its roots in the BLUES and gospel tradition. Distinct musical styles emerged (RAGTIME, New Orleans and Chicago jazz, swing, bebop, progressive, avant-garde, fusion, and mainstream) that continue to evolve.

It is unclear how Louisvillians first became acquainted with these new, intoxicating sounds. Unquestionably the OHIO RIVER and the RAILROADS were two vital transportation avenues along which many jazz pioneers migrated. As early as 1909 Boston novelist Elliot Paul, writing in *My Old Kentucky Home,* was enthralled by a black musician in a "sporting house" at Seventh and MARKET Streets, when he wrote, "Whatever else I remember about Louisville, my most poignant recollections have to do with hearing...jazz."

The Island Queen and other excursion boats on the Ohio River booked New Orleans styled jazz bands, such as Sidney Desvigne's Southern Syncopators. From the 1900s until WORLD WAR I, jazz was performed primarily in shady brothels and SALOONS. However, after the Army shut down the red-light district and PROHIBITION forced the closure of the BARS, the music moved to mainstream nightclubs and dance halls that featured local jazz ensembles. During the 1920s, Magnolia (later Rainbow) Gardens at Third and Avery Streets, Edgewater Garden on Upper River Rd., and the MADRID BALLROOM at Third and Guthrie Streets were some of the favorite spots which hosted ORCHESTRAS such as Bernie Cummings' band. Prior to WORLD WAR II, Louisville played host to the greatest practitioners of this fledgling art form. Louis Armstrong, George Gershwin, Duke Ellington, and Benny Goodman all demonstrated to Louisville audiences the virtuosity and elegance inherent in this musical genre.

The 1950s and early 1960s are generally considered to be the halcyon days of Louisville jazz, attested to by the popularity of area venues that showcased local talent. Encompassing all points of the city's GEOGRAPHY–from the East End's Topaz (969 Baxter Avenue) and the Kentucky Tavern (Lexington Rd. and Grinstead Dr.), the Idle Hour (545 Fifteenth St.) and the Top Hat (1210 Walnut St. (Muhammad Ali Blvd.); from the South End's Iroquois Gardens (5306 New Cut Rd.) to downtown's Riney's (414 Walnut St.) and the Arts in Louisville (519 Zane St.)–small jazz combos entertained nightly. This was a period when many of the "white clubs" were strictly segregated. Not until 1967 did the white Musicians' Union (Local 11)and the black Musicians' Union (Local 637) merge to become the local 11-637.

After a decline of the jazz scene in the 1970s, a jazz renaissance of improvisational music occurred througout the 1980s when such clubs as the Fig Tree and Othello's, (both at Third and Broadway), Just Jazz (2901 Bardstown Rd.) and various downtown hotel lounges catered primarily to a jazz clientele. Formed originally in 1967 as the Louisville Jazz Council, the Louisville Jazz Society promotes the music through educational programs and monthly concerts featuring both local and national performers. The city and its active arts community continued to attract outstanding jazz musicians to its major concert settings (the Brown Theatre and the Kentucky Center for the Arts) and outdoor music festivals, such as Jazz in Central Park, a series of Kentucky Center for the Arts-sponsored concerts started in 1992 funded by the Lila Wallace-Reader's Digest National Jazz Network.

The future of jazz improvisation appears promising locally, due in large part to the efforts of jazz educators dedicated to guiding students' tonal imagination. James Aebersold, a NEW ALBANY, Indiana, saxophonist of international renown in the field of jazz education, has conducted a summer jazz workshop in Louisville annually since 1975. BELLARMINE COLLEGE and INDIANA UNIVERSITY SOUTHEAST include jazz coursed in their curriculum. The University of Louisville School of Music has offered a bachelor of arts degree in music with emphasis in jazz since 1996. WFPL/WFPK-FM has presented jazz as a staple of its broadcast format since 1980.

A listing of nationally known jazz performers born in Louisville chronicles the entire history of this improvisational medium: vocalist Sarah Martin (1884-1955), vocalist and dancer John Bubbles (1901-84), vibraphonist Lionel Hampton (1909-), trumpeter Jonah Jones (1909), vocalist HELEN HUMES (1913-81), guitarist Jimmy Raney (1927-95), pianist Rahn Burton (1934-), and saxophonist Don Braden (1963-), who moved to Louisville at age four.

Lionel Hampton, jazz musician and vibraphonist, was born on April 20, 1908, in Louisville. Hampton's parents, Charles Edward and Gertrude (Morgan) Hampton, moved there when his father went to work for the railroad. Since railroad work kept the elder Hampton away, the new mother returned to Birmingham, Alabama, her hometown. Hampton first recorded with Louis Armstrong in 1930, and by 1936 he was playing in the Benny Goodman Quartet. Hampton became one of the best known jazz musicians, recording extensively and touring worldwide. "Flying Home" and "Hamp's Boogie Woogie" were his two indispensable trademarks. In 1936 Hampton married Gladys (Riddle) Neal.

Robert Elliot "Jonah" Jones, jazz trumpeter, was born in Louisville December 31, 1909. A student of Bertha Ella Allen's Sunday school music class of the Booker T. Washington Community Center at Ninth and Magazine Streets, Jones began his music career at age ten. Many of Bertha Ella Allen's child musicians later became active band members because they could read music. By age fourteen Jones had started his professional career in the pit orchestra at the Palace Theatre at Eleventh and Walnut (now Muhammad Ali Boulevard) Streets. At seventeen he began playing on a riverboat. He joined Jimmie Lunceford's band in 1931, moving through some of the best bands of the 1930s and '40s including McKinney's Cotton Pickers, Fletcher Henderson, Benny Carter, and Cab Calloway. In 1954 Jones toured Europe with a solo act returning to form a quartet that maintained its popularity in New York City clubs throughout the 60s. Making his home in New York City, Jones continued to perform and record mainstream jazz albums through the early 1990s.

See *The Courier-Journal,* August 24, 1980, January 27, 1984, August 25, 1985, February 9, 1992, March 30, 1996; Rick Mattingly, "Jazz Educators Speak," *Louisville Music News,* February 1995; George H. Yater, *Flappers, Prohibition and All that Jazz* (Louisville 1984).

Steve Crews

J.B. SPEED ART MUSEUM. The J.B. SPEED ART MUSEUM on South Third St., Kentucky's oldest and largest art museum, was founded in 1925 by Mrs. JAMES BRECKINRIDGE SPEED as a memorial to her husband, a prominent Louisville businessman and philanthropist. Designed by Louisville architect ARTHUR LOOMIS, the museum opened January 15, 1927, with an exhibition sponsored by the Louisville Art Association. Over a hundred American and European painters were represented and nearly two thousand visitors attended the opening. In 1933 the museum was incorporated as a privately endowed institution, and its board of governors was established. Although the museum is adjacent to the UNIVERSITY OF LOUISVILLE on land conveyed by deed from the university, the museum is not a part of it.

In 1934 the museum received its first major donation, a valuable collection of North American Indian artifacts given by Dr. Frederick Weygold. In 1941 Dr. PRESTON POPE SATTERWHITE made a significant gift to the museum–his collection of fifteenth- and sixteenth-century FRENCH and Italian DECORATIVE ARTS. In 1944 he donated the English renaissance room, which was moved in its entirety from Devonshire, England. Dr. Satterwhite's gift necessitated an enlargement of the building, and in his will he provided for the addition that bears his name. Completed in 1954, it was the first of three additions to the original building.

The north addition, designed by Brenner, Danforth, and Rockwell of Chicago, opened in 1973, and the south addition, designed by Robert Geddes of Princeton, New Jersey, opened in 1983. In 1995 architect Peter Rose unveiled a master plan for the renovation of the museum. In 1996 construction began on the first phase of the project, which included a twenty-eight-hundred-square-foot interactive art learning center, a collections storage facility, and a complete renovation of the Satterwhite gallery to display the museum's collection of renaissance and baroque decorative arts and tapestries. The museum closed for the one-year renovation and reopened in November 1997. In 1998 a parking garage was built behind the building in a cooperative venture with the University of Louisville on land that had been occupied by the Rauch Memorial Planetarium. Plans for the disposition of the 1996 bequest of $50 million made by Alice Speed Stoll, granddaughter of James Breckinridge Speed, were also formulated at the time of the museum's renovation.

Mrs. James B. Speed was the first president and director of the museum. After her death her niece, Jenny Loring Robbins, held the position. Catherine Grey, a friend of Mrs. Speed, was acting director until 1946, when Paul S. Harris became the first professional director. During his tenure, acquisitions were mainly in decorative arts and furniture. In 1962 he left to become deputy director of the Henry Francis du Pont Museum in Delaware and was succeeded by Addison Franklin Page, curator of contemporary art at the Detroit Institute of Arts, who served until 1984. During his tenure, the museum collection was enriched and expanded, and the north and south additions were built. He was followed as director by Peter Morrin, formerly curator of twentieth-century art at the High Museum in Atlanta, who arrived in 1986. He continued the enrichment of the collection and initiated an outreach program to involve the communities the museums serve.

The Museum Alliance, an organization of volunteer members, was established in 1972 to interest the public and museum members in museum activities and to raise funds for special projects. The charter collectors and the new collectors are composed of museum members interested in contributing to the growth of the collection through the purchase of pre-twentieth century and contemporary art. The museum has changing exhibitions, programs, films, a shop, a library, a cafe, and a 350-seat auditorium. The museum is supported entirely by special gifts, endowments, grants, and memberships.

The focus of the collection is Western art, from antiquity to the present. Holdings of PAINTINGS from the Netherlands, French and Italian works, and contemporary art are particularly strong, with SCULPTURE prominent throughout. Representative artists include Rembrandt Van Rijn, Peter Paul Rubens, Giovanni Tiepolo, Henry Moore, Thomas Gainsborough, Claude Monet, Pablo Picasso, and contemporary artists Frank Stella, Helen Frankenthaler, Sam Francis, Petah Coyne, Sam Gilliam, Vito Acconci, and Deborah Butterfield.

See William F. Bradbury, *A Brief Chronicle: The Museum in Four Decades 1925-1961* (Louisville 1961).

Mary Jane Benedict

JEFFBOAT INC. America's largest inland shipyard was founded in 1938 as Jeffersonville Boat and Machine Co., a wholly-owned subsidiary of American Barge Line Co. The firm was located on the former Sweeney Shipyard property adjacent to the Howard Shipyard in Indiana. In 1939 the firm began building barges, and in 1940 it launched the towboat *National*. In 1942, following American entry into WORLD WAR II, the navy acquired the moribund Howard Shipyard and turned it over to JEFFBOAT to construct vessels for the war effort. After making extensive improvements, the company began producing LSTs (Landing Ship Tank), oilers, and submarine chasers. By the war's end, the firm's yards encompassed sixty-four acres of riverfront land, and it employed approximately thirteen thousand persons.

After the war, Jeffboat returned to its roots, producing barges, towboats, and other commercial vessels. In 1947 it bought the old Howard Yards from the navy, including sixty acres of land and buildings, ways, gantry cranes, outfitting dock, rail spur, machines, and tools installed during the war. The company also installed a large floating dry dock, which gave it one of the best-equipped marine repair yards on the OHIO RIVER.

In 1957 Jeffboat's parent firm, American Barge Line Co., merged with Commercial Transport Corp. to create American Commercial Barge Line Co. In 1964 the new parent firm became known as American Commercial Lines Inc., and Jeffersonville Boat and Machine Co.'s name was formally changed to Jeffboat Inc. Four years later American Commercial Lines Inc. was acquired by Texas Gas Transmission Corp., which subsequently became the Texas Gas Resources Corp. In 1983 CSX CORP. acquired the former firm, including American Commercial Lines.

In addition to towboats and barges, by 1997 Jeffboat had built over fifty specialty vessels, including the *Mississippi Queen*, a luxury steamboat; the *General Jackson*, an Opryland showboat; the *City of Evansville*, which houses the Casino Aztar in Evansville, Indiana, and several Clipper Cruise ships. Other special projects included numerous car and passenger ferry vessels, ocean tankers and deck barges, an ocean seismographic vessel, and drill platform components. Along with its construction work, Jeffboat operates an around-the-clock marine repair division. In 1997 the company took on the responsibility of repairing the *BELLE OF LOUISVILLE* after it partially sank at the Louisville wharf.

During the 1990s Jeffboat made many production innovations, including installation of plasma-burning equipment, an advanced hopper barge bottom panel line, and other technological improvements. In 1997 it entered an exclusive distributorship arrangement with Proform Co. LLC to deliver a new generation of fiberglass barge covers. Such innovations enabled the company to significantly expand its production capacity. In 1995 Jeffboat signed its largest-ever civilian contract, committing to build sixty-eight barges for ASHLAND INC. The contract resulted in a major increase in the workforce, and by mid-1997 the firm employed more than a thousand workers, making it the largest private employer on the Indiana side of the Louisville metropolitan area. The same year, Jeffboat completed its eight-thousandth hopper barge.

In April 1998, American Commercial Lines was combined with National Marine Inc. of New Orleans. The new company, called American Commercial Lines Holdings LLC, is based in Jeffersonville. In the transaction, CSX Corp. sold a majority of ACL to a company controlled by Citicorp, a worldwide bank-holding company. Vectura Group of New Orleans, a company controlled by Citicorp Venture Capital, owns the majority of the new company. With 4,500 barges and 195 towboats, the new company had almost 25 percent of the total United States inland fleet. The company assets totaled $1 billion.

Carl E. Kramer

JEFFERSON, THOMAS (b Albemarle County, Virginia, April 13, 1743; d Charlottesville, Virginia, July 4, 1826). Statesman and president. Born to Peter and Jane (Randolph) Jefferson, young Jefferson attended the College of William and Mary and later studied LAW. His wealthy family's standing allowed him to enter politics, and he entered the Virginia House of Burgesses in 1769, where he served for six years. A patriot, Jefferson attended the Second Continental Congress and eventually drafted the Declaration of Independence.

During the American Revolution, Jefferson stayed active in politics, becoming the governor of Virginia in 1779. In 1780 the Virginia General Assembly divided the Kentucky lands into Lincoln, Fayette, and Jefferson Counties. With Louisville as its seat, Jefferson County was named after the governor. At the conclusion of his term, Jefferson became a member of the Continental Congress in 1783 and served as the American ambassador to France from 1785 until 1789, when he returned home to become the nation's first secretary of state (1789-97) under President George Washington. In 1791 he worked with others to guarantee individual rights by adding the first ten amendments to the Constitution. Six years later Jefferson received three less votes than John Adams and became his vice president.

Jefferson became the leader of the REPUBLICAN PARTY (forerunner of the modern DEMOCRATIC PARTY) and favored a GOVERNMENT that protected the rights of individuals. His party was popular in Kentucky, especially after the Federalists imposed a whiskey tax in 1793. In 1801 he was elected president by the House of Representatives after tying with Aaron Burr in the initial election. First-term highlights include the purchase of the Louisiana Territory from France in 1803 and his sponsorship of the LEWIS AND CLARK Expedition. He was reelected in 1804, and foreign policy dominated most of his second term as Jefferson attempted to remain neutral in the Napoleonic Wars. His unsuccessful policy incited both the British and FRENCH navies to attack American merchants on the high seas. At the conclusion of his second term in 1809, Jefferson retired from politics and returned to his estate at Monticello. He subsequently designed the University of Virginia campus and created its curriculum. A life-size statue of Jefferson stands in front of the JEFFERSON COUNTY COURTHOUSE.

In 1772 Jefferson married Martha Wayles Skelton, and they had two daughters. He died at Monticello on the fiftieth anniversary of the signing of the Declaration of Independence.

Jefferson's long career in public service permitted him to do several things that had an impact upon Louisville. As governor, he signed the act of the Virginia Legislature incorporating the town in May 1780. As secretary of state he had negotiated Pinckney's Treaty, which gave local merchants assurances that the Mississippi River and the city of New Orleans would not be closed to American commerce by the Spanish GOVERNMENT. As president Jefferson purchased Louisiana, which proved an additional boon to trade and traffic on the OHIO RIVER. It was from the Louisville area that Jefferson's Corps of Discovery, headed by MERIWETHER Lewis and WILLIAM CLARK, departed in 1803.

See Dumas Malone, *Jefferson and His Time* (Boston 1948).

Charles H. MacKay

JEFFERSON, THOMAS LEWIS (b Baltimore, Maryland, February 15, 1826; d Louisville, March 23, 1884). Businessman and civic leader. The son of Thomas and Elizabeth (Smallsread) Jefferson, Thomas L. moved to Louisville with his family in 1831. He attended school until the age of sixteen, having studied under such local scholars as Noble Butler and J.H. Harney. Then in 1842 he went to work as a clerk in the profitable little grocery store started by his mother. Ten years later, Jefferson formed a partnership with Charles Gallagher in the wholesale grocery business. This association was short-lived, and by January 1853 he had opened his own wholesale/retail grocery trade on MARKET St.

Shortly thereafter, as his business flourished, Jefferson moved his enterprise into a new building at the southeast corner of First and Market Streets, where it remained for the next twelve years. Due to the growth of the wholesale element of his business, Jefferson was compelled to open a branch facility, in association with his two brothers and A. Jennison, as T.L. Jefferson & Brothers at the northwest corner of First and Main, where their dominant commodities were salt and flour. In 1875 Jefferson retired from his position with the firm to focus on his duties as executor of sarsaparilla millionaire JOHN BULL'S will. However, he resigned in 1879 because of the legal disputes that had arisen.

Though the wholesale trade had been Jefferson's primary enterprise, he was extremely active in the business and civic affairs of Louisville. At various times, he served on the board of directors of the HOUSE OF REFUGE and as a trustee of both the Louisville Female College and the AMERICAN PRINTING HOUSE FOR THE BLIND. Jefferson was a director and vice president of the LOUISVILLE BOARD OF TRADE and in 1859 was appointed a director of the first BANK OF LOUISVILLE. From 1872 to 1874, he served as director of the Louisville & Frankfort and Lexington & Frankfort Railroad Companies. In 1878 he was named a director of the Kentucky and Louisville Mutual Insurance Co. and the following year became its president. Jefferson was also a trustee of the Kentucky Institute for the Blind. He was a founder of the Masonic Widows' and Orphans' Home and served first as its director and then as president from 1869 until his death.

As an extension of his civic activism, Jefferson also entered the realm of politics. In 1851, at the age of twenty-five, he was elected to fill a vacancy on the city's Common Council, to which he was reelected three more times. In 1860 he was elected to a two-year term on the BOARD OF ALDERMEN, and in 1867 he was elected to the Kentucky state legislature, where he served for two sessions as a representative. He was elected to the state senate in 1873 and served for one term. A Democrat, Jefferson served for a number of years on both Louisville's Democratic City Executive Committee and the state Central Committee. In 1868 he was a delegate to the National Democratic Convention in New York City.

Jefferson married Elizabeth Ann Creagh in May 1848. They had nine children–Ann Eliza, Catherine Louise, Mary Holman, Thomas Lewis Junior, John Wesley, Lillie Emma, Henry Theodore, Charles William, and another son who died at birth. Jefferson is buried in CAVE HILL CEMETERY.

See *Courier-Journal*, March 23, 1884.

JEFFERSON COMMUNITY COLLEGE. Jefferson Community College is an open-door institution of higher learning. It offers associate degrees for those who wish to earn the first two years toward a baccalaureate degree or who wish to earn applied science degrees that lead to immediate employment in such areas as allied health, engineering, business, commercial art, and computer technology. The college operates three primary campuses: one in downtown Louisville located between BROADWAY, Chestnut, First, and Second Streets; the second, the Southwest Campus near VALLEY STATION; and the third at 324 MAIN St. in downtown Carrollton, Kentucky.

The college opened in 1968 in the refurbished Presbyterian Seminary Building at First and Broadway. Eight hundred students attended the college that first semester, and enrollment grew quickly from that point. The Southwest Campus opened in 1972 in what was then Jesse Stuart High School. The campus moved to its permanent location in 1980. The Carrollton Campus opened in 1990 on Hwy. 227 near the main entrance of Butler State Park and moved to its downtown location overlooking the OHIO RIVER in 1992. In 1998, the enrollment overall was approximately nine thousand students.

Jefferson Community College was part of the University of Kentucky community college system from 1968 to 1997, when it became a part of the Kentucky Community and Technical College System. All public community colleges in Kentucky with the exception of Lexington Community College, which remains part of the University of Kentucky, are part of this system of colleges. Funding for Jefferson Community College comes from four primary sources: student tuition, state allocations, private donations, and a variety of grants.

The college serves as a springboard for students seeking to improve their occupational skills as well as preparing for new careers. Many students who attend Jefferson Community College intend to transfer to four-year colleges in Louisville or elsewhere in the state of Kentucky. Numerous matriculation and transfer agreements between Jefferson Community College and other institutions of higher learning guarantee that class credits can be transferred.

Many students also come to Jefferson Community College who need remedial work in reading, mathematics, or English composition before they can successfully complete college-level classes. Jefferson Community College offers such students remedial classes to help prepare them for success at the college level. Financial aid and scholarship opportunities are also available. Jefferson Community College is accredited by the Southern Association of Schools and Colleges (SACS).

See David Patrick Ecker, "The Emergence of Jefferson Community College: Politics and the Search for Identity," Ph.D. dissertation, University of Kentucky, 1991.

David Patrick Ecker

JEFFERSON COUNTY COURTHOUSES. Because of the constant threat of Indian attacks, the early settlers of the Louisville area used different forts around the area, such as Sullivan's old station on BEARGRASS CREEK, Cox's station on the Salt River, or FORT NELSON at the foot of modern-day Seventh St., as sites for the county court sessions. In 1784 it was decided to establish a permanent courthouse in Louisville. Tradition holds that it was a sixteen- by twenty-foot, one-story log cabin with a board roof. Erected by George Wilson, the structure was completed in 1785 for what was considered to be an expensive $309.79. After it burned in 1787, a sixteen- by eighteen-foot temporary log cabin, with an adjoining twelve- by twelve-foot jury room, was constructed in August under the supervision of RICHARD TAYLOR (the father of President ZACHARY TAYLOR) and Richard Eastin.

In May of the following year, the county court decided upon a design for the third courthouse, which was to be a two-story, forty-eight- by thirty-six-foot stone building with a spire and belfry on top. Located on the south side of Jefferson St. between Fifth and Sixth Streets, the courthouse, designed and built by Capt. John Cape, was also used as a town hall and for religious purposes.

By 1810 larger facilities were required, and within two years construction had begun on the fourth JEFFERSON COUNTY COURTHOUSE, located at the corner of Jefferson and Sixth Streets. Designed by amateur architect John Gwathmey, the building was a two-story brick structure with two side wings. The main body was topped with a cupola and spire and fronted by an Ionic portico. The portico was supported by four enormous wooden columns cut from local poplar trees that were said to have provided ample whittling material for lawyers and bystanders alike. A description of this courthouse can be found in HENRY MCMURTRIE'S *Sketches of Louisville* (1819). Because of its poor condition and the need for additional space, the courthouse was vacated in 1835 and sold two years later to Stephen Sanders for four hundred dollars.

The fifth and present Jefferson County Courthouse, ridiculed in its early years and at one time called an "elephantine monstrosity of ARCHITECTURE," (*Louisville Daily Journal*, Sept. 1, 1858) is a monumental Greek Revival structure that originated as a joint venture of Jefferson County and the city of Louisville. Construction began in 1836, but, because of the financial panic of 1837, the building was not completed until 1860, forcing the county court to hold sessions in the Union Engine House and local churches. An often-repeated legend, not confirmed by any official records, says that leading citizens of Louisville, including JAMES GUTHRIE, hoped to have the state capital moved from Frankfort and believed that construction of a grand building to house the legislature would advance their cause.

GIDEON SHRYOCK, the first professionally trained Kentucky architect, designed the courthouse, although additions and modifications have covered much of his original designs. With completion expected at an earlier date, the eager city and county GOVERNMENTS moved into the partially completed structure in 1842. By then Shryock had, for unknown reasons, resigned or been fired from the project. The courthouse stood unfinished until 1858 when ALBERT FINK, a bridge designer and chief engineer for the LOUISVILLE & NASHVILLE RAILROAD, was appointed architect along with Charles Stancliff.

They completed the courthouse in 1860 by simplifying Shryock's original plans (which had included a cupola and side porticos), while keeping the basic temple form. Most of the architectural details are their work, including the dramatic rotunda (in which the full-sized marble statue of Henry Clay stands) and its cast-iron floor and staircase. After a damaging fire in 1905, Louisville architect Brinton B. Davis fireproofed the courthouse and added major interior architectural details.

The city government moved from the building to the Louisville CITY HALL after its construction in 1871-73 but kept partial ownership of the courthouse until 1980. Although it was threatened with replacement several times, renovation projects completed in 1981 stabilized and refurbished the courthouse, removing many inappropriate alterations while retaining significant architectural elements. The courthouse is listed on the NATIONAL REGISTER OF HISTORIC PLACES.

See Samuel W. Thomas, "An Enduring Folly: The Jefferson County Courthouse," *Filson Club History Quarterly* 55 (Oct. 1981): 311-43; Samuel W. Thomas, "An Inventory of Jefferson County Records," *Filson Club History Quarterly* 44 (Oct. 1970): 321-51; John W. Carpenter, *Kentucky Courthouses* (London, Ky., 1988).

JEFFERSON COUNTY FAIR. The Jefferson County Fair had its origins in the annual agricultural exhibitions begun in 1878 by the Fern Creek Farmers and Fruit Growers Association. FERN CREEK, located along the Bardstown Rd. south of Louisville, then among the leading fruit-growing sections of the state, enjoyed immediate success with its exhibitions, which were first held in the Beulah Church area on Bardstown Rd. In 1880 the exhibitions were formally organized as the Fern Creek Fair, with Dr. R.D. Porter elected president; Edward J. Heikes, vice president; J. Decker, secretary; and M.F. Johnson, treasurer. A permanent location having a grandstand and a racetrack was established on Fairgrounds Rd. Additional impetus was received in 1883 when a selection of the best fruit shown at the Fern Creek Fair won first place at the SOUTHERN EXPOSITION in Louisville.

In 1900 incorporation of the Fern Creek Fair was allowed to lapse, and the Jefferson County Fair Co. was formed. At that time Fern Creek's annual fair became the Jefferson County Fair, with Frank M. Williams, president; W.P. Hays, vice president; H.P. Stivers, secretary; and E.B. Berry, treasurer. With its grandstand, racetrack, agricultural exhibits, dining hall, and nightly dances, the county fair was popular with all ages from both town and country. However, the last fair was held in 1928. Its failure was due in part to the emergence of JEFFERSONTOWN'S Community Fair and the popularity of the state fair, which eventually supplanted both.

See *The Jeffersonian*, March 18, 1909, and July 4, 1907, Filson Club Historical Society; *The Jeffersonian Historical and Christmas Supplement*, Dec. 1909, private collection; Fern Creek Woman's Club, *Fern Creek Lore & Legacy* (Fern Creek, Ky., 1976); Joellen Tyler Johnston, *Jeffersontown, Kentucky: The First 200 Years* (Jeffersontown, Ky., 1997).

Joellen Tyler Johnston

JEFFERSON COUNTY FIRE SERVICE. Fire protection and other rescue services are provided outside the corporate limits of Louisville and SHIVELY by twenty-one fire districts (1997) organized pursuant to Kentucky LAW. Most of the fire departments operated by these districts are staffed by VOLUNTEER FIREFIGHTERS, though many are combination departments that employ paid firefighters during the daylight hours and rely chiefly on volunteers at night and on weekends. In most districts, the chief of the department is a full-time paid professional, but in a few the chief is also a volunteer. Collectively, the twenty-one fire districts are referred to as the Jefferson County Fire Service.

While each district is a legally independent entity, separate from county GOVERNMENT and from any city governments within their respective districts, they function in practice in a highly cooperative way. All departments share a common radio dispatch alarm channel with additional emergency operation channels allocated to departments in adjacent geographic areas. Individual volunteer firefighters are alerted by alarm pagers worn on their belts that sound an alarm tone and identify the type and location of an emergency. These pagers are much louder than those commonly used by business people and are designed to wake firefighters if necessary and to overcome background noise. Firefighters are authorized by state law to equip their private vehicles with red lights and sirens and have the legal right of way in emergency situations, just as do police cars and ambulances.

It is the usual practice for one or more chief officers (including deputies or assistants) to go directly to the fire scene or other emergency and determine whether the occupants or motorists are safe. All other volunteers report to their stations and travel to the scene on firefighting apparatus. Many of the fire districts have mutual aid agreements under which alarms in certain areas are answered by firefighters from more than one district. Even residential alarms may be answered pursuant to a "closest station response" policy, in which the closest engine company will respond to the alarm even if the scene actually lies in another district. It is common for more than one district to be dispatched on the first alarm to high-risk locations, such as HOSPITALS, NURSING homes, churches, and schools. Persons familiar with the fire service on a national level often refer to Jefferson County as an example of effective cooperation.

Most areas of Jefferson County are served by effective fire hydrant systems. However, some of the more rural areas still rely on water tanker operations to provide water beyond that carried on the fire engine. The fire districts work closely with county planning officers and developers to ensure that new residential subdivisions, industrial PARKS, and other new construction projects comply with fire safety requirements such as fire hydrant placement, road widths with proper turning space for fire trucks, and enforcement of sprinkler requirements where applicable.

The fire service is subject to a national rating system operated by the Insurance Services Office (ISO). The classifications established by ISO are used by fire insurance companies in determining fire insurance premiums for property, and a change in classification can have a substantial effect on the insurance premiums paid by the property owner. Most fire departments in Jefferson County range from class two to class five, while others throughout the state are mostly rated from seven to nine, indicating a lower level of fire protection.

Each fire district is operated pursuant to law

by a seven-member board of trustees composed of three members appointed by the county judge/executive, two members elected by property owners of the district, and two members who are active firefighters in the district. It has the power to employ a chief officer, appoint other officers, and discipline any member of the department. The board also has the power to levy taxes upon real property (up to .10 percent on each hundred-dollar valuation on real estate, motor vehicles, and boats). These property taxes principally fund the purchase of fire apparatus and the operation of the individual districts. State law requires that each district be audited annually by independent auditors and that each district publish an annual budget, which is a public record.

The various districts are equipped with sophisticated firefighting apparatus and tailor their training to the fire threats that exist in the respective districts. Some areas of Jefferson County are heavily industrial, with many chemical plants, while many others are largely residential. Even the latter are laced with heavily traveled highways and railroad lines where accidents commonly call for emergency service. Certain specialized equipment owned by one district will be shared immediately with other districts on radio request. For example, trucks with large fans to move smoke, lights to illuminate dark accident scenes, and compressors to refill firefighters' air bottles are frequently sent from one district to another. More than one aerial apparatus may be needed for certain fires, or more than one rescue vehicle for multiple vehicle accidents. These are dispatched by the radio center operated by the Jefferson County Police. Some districts provide supplemental emergency medical service, using their equipment and personnel to provide first responder medical care and to stabilize the patient in areas where they can reach the patient more quickly than the Jefferson County Emergency Medical Service ambulance.

Some districts sponsor Boy Scout Explorer posts in which young people not yet old enough to become active firefighters can participate in certain aspects of firefighter training and assist the districts in other ways. This opportunity introduces them to disciplined volunteer firefighters and officers who have committed to serve their community and who put the interests of the community ahead of their own each time an alarm sounds.

Robert I. Cusick

JEFFERSON COUNTY FISCAL COURT. Jefferson County was created in 1780, but its Fiscal Court, the county's legislature, was not established until 1892. When the county was first created, it had no legislative body, nor was one established by the Kentucky constitutions of 1792 and 1799. They did provide for the appointment of justices of the peace but did not specify their duties. Subsequently, the General Assembly created a county court made up of justices of the peace who exercised legislative, executive, and judicial powers.

Jefferson County's current governmental structure had its origins in the constitution of 1851. It provided for one county judge to conduct judicial and administrative affairs of the county court but required that decisions on fiscal matters involve the justices of the peace. In 1854, the General Assembly, acting with respect to Jefferson County alone, placed fiscal affairs under the authority of a Levy Court composed of the county judge and one justice of the peace from each of the districts. The 1891 constitution converted Jefferson County's Levy Court into a fiscal court and permitted the county to choose either a justice of the peace form or commission form of fiscal court. In 1892 Jefferson County voters elected a county judge as the county's executive officer and presiding officer of the Fiscal Court, which was composed of eight justices of the peace, one from each precinct.

As Jefferson County's Fiscal Court "became unequal to the increasing governmental burden of paving roads, building and administering schools, [and] preventing crime," a move toward the commission form gained support. In 1913, a local referendum favoring the change was approved by the voters, but the county refused to hold an election. The General Assembly broke the deadlock in 1916 by enacting a statute that required the county to abide by the referendum. Three commissioners were elected the following year, and, on January 1, 1918, Jefferson County became the first Kentucky county to adopt the commission form of government. Still Jefferson County did not have the authority to address public problems and meet the needs for GOVERNMENT services.

In the 1970s, constitutional and statutory changes in the offices of fiscal court and the county judge made substantial improvements in Jefferson County government. The Judicial Article, ratified by the voters in 1975, streamlined the court system and relieved county judges of their judicial duties. Subsequently, the General Assembly changed the name of the office to county judge/executive and strengthened its executive, administrative, and fiscal powers.

The Kentucky Supreme Court had struck down the first county home-rule statute in *Fiscal Court of Jefferson County* v. *City of Louisville* (1977) as an overly broad delegation of legislative power. In response, the General Assembly enacted the current home-rule statute, which provides fiscal COURTS with legislative authority to enact ordinances, issue regulations, levy taxes, issue bonds, appropriate funds, and employ personnel to perform twenty-five specified public functions. Now the Jefferson County Fiscal Court and Jefferson County judge/executive have the legal autonomy to meet the changing needs of a metropolitan county.

See Charlie Bush, ed., *Citizen's Guide to the Kentucky Constitution* (Frankfort 1991); Samuel W. Thomas, "An Inventory of Jefferson County Records," *Filson Club History Quarterly* 44 (Oct. 1970): 321–47; William Wiley and William Van Arsdall, *Duties of Elected County Officials;* Kentucky Legislative Research Commission Informational Bulletin No. 114 (Frankfort 1993).

William Crawford Green

JEFFERSON COUNTY HISTORIC LANDMARKS AND PRESERVATION DISTRICTS COMMISSION. Jefferson County GOVERNMENT, through Fiscal Court, established the county landmark process by ordinance on June 12, 1979. A Jefferson County landmark is defined as a cultural resource that is a visible reminder of the history and heritage of Jefferson County, with architectural, archaeological, and/or historical qualities.

There are many reasons why Jefferson County codified its commitment to HISTORIC PRESERVATION in 1979, but the overriding cause was a force called the "Preservation Movement." Across the United States, as a reaction to URBAN RENEWAL programs that fueled the destruction of historic buildings and sites, many municipalities started to adopt HISTORIC PRESERVATION ordinances on the local level, including historic districts with design review commissions, historic landmark designation, and more sensitive policies that helped to protect our cultural inheritance. On the federal level, the Historic Preservation Act of 1966 was the enabling legislation for the NATIONAL REGISTER OF HISTORIC PLACES, under the jurisdiction of the National Park Service, Department of the Interior. On the state level, the system of state historic preservation offices was also established at that time.

While many city landmarks ordinances were enacted in the 1960s, Jefferson County is one of the first county governments to enact a historic preservation ordinance. This act did not happen without precedent. The city of Louisville Landmarks Commission and the nonprofit PRESERVATION ALLIANCE helped to define the first steps at establishing historic districts and promoting the preservation movement on the local level. Probably the most influential group to effect the revitalization in Louisville and Jefferson County NEIGHBORHOODS and sites were the private citizens who risked their resources and dedicated their time to historic neighborhoods and structures. This grassroots action was indirectly responsible for creating an environment where local government officials responded to the historic preservation efforts in their community.

The Jefferson County Historic Landmarks and Preservation Districts Commission is responsible for designating Jefferson County landmarks outside the Louisville city limits. This commission is appointed by the JEFFERSON COUNTY FISCAL COURT and is composed of Jefferson County citizens who have an interest and expertise in history, architectural history, historic preservation, or ARCHAEOLOGY.

Consent of the property owner is required

by state law before a resource may be designated a county landmark. Final approval of the landmark designation rests with Jefferson County Fiscal Court. A Jefferson County landmark is protected from neglect, destructive alterations, or demolition. Any changes to the landmark that require a building permit must be reviewed and approved by the commission. The commission will determine whether or not the proposed changes affect the historic or architectural integrity of the landmark and may impose a waiting period before granting approval for a building permit. This waiting period gives the property owner and the commission an opportunity to work out a compromise on the proposed alterations.

The Jefferson County Historic Landmarks and Preservation Districts Commission requires any potential landmark site to meet at least one of the following criteria:

1. Its character, interest, or value as part of the development or heritage of Jefferson County, the commonwealth of Kentucky, or the United States.
2. Its exemplification of the historic, aesthetic, architectural, archaeological, educational, economic, or cultural heritage of Jefferson County, the commonwealth, or the nation.
3. Its location as a site of a significant historic event.
4. Its identification with a person or persons who significantly contributed to the culture and development of the county, the commonwealth, or nation.
5. Its embodiment of distinguishing architectural characteristics.
6. Its identification as a work of a locally or nationally recognized architect or master builder.
7. Its embodiment of elements of architectural design, detail, materials, or craftsmanship that represent a significant architectural innovation.
8. Its unique location, significance, physical characteristics, significant architectural, or historic characteristics, representing a neighborhood or district within the county or representing an established or familiar visual feature within a neighborhood or district in the county.

The Jefferson County Department of Public History serves as staff for the Jefferson County Historic Landmarks and Preservation Districts Commission. It provides research service, publications on restoration techniques, and information on legislation affecting preservation.

The landmark sites are diverse. The current sixteen landmarks represent a variety of architectural styles, rural contexts, and guideposts for Jefferson County history that can be interpreted through the lives of those who are associated with these significant places. Sixteen landmarks are listed below, each with its JF number, which is a state-designated survey number of historic structures along with the historical name of the site and its address. Landmarks without historical information below have separate entries.

JF13
Riverside, the Farnsley-Moremen Landing
7410 Moorman Rd.
Louisville, Ky. 40272

JF30
Clover Hill/Youngland
2618 Dixie Hwy.
Louisville, Ky. 40216

In 1826 Robert Nicholas Miller built the main block of the two-story, five bay, Kentucky center-hall house as the centerpiece of his plantation, Clover Hill. He lived there until his death in 1877. In 1804 Miller had come with his parents from Charlottesville, Virginia, to Jefferson County and shortly thereafter erected a substantial log dwelling. It later served as the kitchen, located behind the newer dwelling. The Flemish- and American-bond brick house included end chimneys, a gable roof, and nine-over-six double-hung sash windows.

A son, Howard Miller, lived on the farm, overseeing its operation for his father and keeping detailed diaries of the activities. Miller's diaries describe construction of the house's additions. The rear and east wings can be dated to 1857 and 1859. Clover Hill's octagon room–a rare architectural feature in Jefferson County–is detailed from its beginning in August 1863 to its completion in November 1863.

In 1908 Col. Bennett H. Young bought a small portion of the farm, using the house for a summer home and renaming the site Youngland. Young had been a Confederate officer with Gen. John Hunt Morgan's brigade. His political sympathies remain in evidence at Youngland through the consciously planted "stars and bars" pattern of trees. Young was a lawyer and an amateur archaeologist who published *Prehistoric Men of Kentucky* in 1910. He was a founder of Bellewood Seminary and was instrumental in establishing the LOUISVILLE FREE PUBLIC LIBRARY system.

JF116
Pennsylvania Run Church and Cemetery
Vaughn Mill Rd.
Louisville, Ky. 40228

Pennsylvania Run Church is a typically austere, frame rural church in a rectangular form. The open square tower is placed off-center on the gable end facade and serves as a vestibule with a single door. A pair of four-paneled doors also provide access to the interior space. The church was built in 1840, and the belfry is a later addition.

The Pennsylvania Run congregation may have been organized informally as early as 1789. The minutes of Transylvania Presbytery note that a "supply" minister was sent for one Sunday in October 1789 to preach at Pennsylvania Run. According to local tradition, the first church building was a log structure perhaps located near the present site. The cemetery that surrounds the present church contains gravestones dating from as early as 1795. The church was formally organized and a minister "called" in 1799.

JF196
Omer-Pound House
6609 Billtown Rd.
Louisville, Ky. 40299

The Omer-Pound house is an interesting ensemble of two houses of different forms and construction dates joined by a one-story frame wing. The oldest portion of the house is a one-room-and-loft stone house with an exterior end chimney, enclosed corner staircase, and built-in cupboards on each side of the fireplace. The stone house may have been built as early as 1796-1800 by Daniel and Ann Sellinger Omer.

An 1812 lawsuit indicated that Omer bought the land and was given possession in 1795, but because of title disputes he did not receive legal title until 1820. Ten years later, Peter Omer, a son, acquired the farm and in the 1870s built the two-story, frame vernacular farmhouse that forms the main block of the dwelling.

In 1906 Dr. Thomas Pope Dudley Pound, a well-known SEATONVILLE physician, bought the property, and it remained in his family until 1979. The site also includes a log-and-stone springhouse. The stone house bears evidence of a one-room log structure being attached to it at an early point in its history.

JF217
Westwood Farm
3503 Westwood Farms Dr.
Louisville, Ky. 40220

Valentine and William Conrad came from North Carolina to JEFFERSONTOWN about 1800. There they served terms as town trustees and operated a pottery until 1837, when they sold the business and moved to farms in the Six Mile Ln. area. This site was part of a farm that was deeded to Valentine Conrad's son Samuel.

In 1857 George Seebolt of Springbank Farm bought this property and conveyed it to his son-in-law, Benjamin L. Alderson. In the 1840s Alderson had come to Louisville to manage the Hotel de Raine after successes in the stocks and commodities trade in New Orleans. He named the farm "Westwood" and, according to an 1882 description, turned it into a showplace.

The house is a Kentucky center-hall form with a facade of Flemish-bond brickwork and a corbeled brick cornice, interior end chimneys, and brick jack arches above six-over-six sash windows. Alderson and his wife, Nancy, added a long, two-story brick ell with second-story balconied window treatment for the center bay. Original woodwork and chair rails remain in the main block of the house. The parlor mantel has a carved shell motif.

The house, a collapsed springhouse, and archeological evidence of a substantial slave dwelling remain on the six-acre tract. The remainder of the farm has been subdivided for residential use.

JF224
Harriet Funk Hise House/Nunnlea
1940 South HURSTBOURNE Pky.
Louisville, Ky. 40220

Harriet Funk married Alfred Hise in 1854, and in 1862 she received title to one hundred acres from her parents, Peter and Harriet Hite Funk. Most likely, this house was built during that time period. The house, with its one-story, hipped roof, double-pile construction, is similar to several others in the vicinity. The front door has sidelights and an elliptical fanlight. A kitchen wing projects from the rear of the building.

The Doric-columned front porch and side wing were designed by architect E.T. Hutchings following the 1937 Flood. A brick slavehouse and smokehouse remain on the site.

JF249
Fisher House
15103 Old TAYLORSVILLE Rd.
FISHERVILLE, Ky. 40299

In 1834 John Fisher and his son Robert bought 271 acres on FLOYDS FORK and a ca. 1823 grist mill. The Fishers are credited with building a hall-parlor plan house on a small rise overlooking the mill about one-quarter mile to the west. This section forms the rear wing of the current dwelling. In 1854 Dr. Stephen H. Reid purchased the Fisher house and 118 acres. Fisher and Reid CEMETERIES are located near Taylorsville Rd.

After 1879 John H. Gilliland of the pioneer family purchased the farm and built what is now the main block of the house. It is a two-story frame ell-shaped building with a gabled roof and interior chimneys. The first story has a bay window and an Eastlake-inspired porch. Windows have flat-topped molding hoods with small brackets. The cornice features brackets and modillions.

The sixteen-acre farm remnant includes, in addition to the main house and cemetery, a root cellar, frame smokehouse, TOBACCO barn, and the original farmland and fence lines.

JF317
SOLDIERS' RETREAT Site
9300 Seaton Springs Pky.
Louisville, Ky. 40222

JF333
Eight-Mile House
8111 SHELBYVILLE Rd.
Louisville, Ky. 40222

This small stone house is one of the best-known historic buildings in Jefferson County. It was probably built in the late 1790s or early 1800s, although the builder and first owner is unknown. Local tradition has long held that the building was a stage stop and tavern. The earliest record of a tavern on the site is found in 1879 when the owner was granted a tavern license. The building was shown on an 1879 map as the "8 Mile Ho.," reflecting its probable use as a tavern.

While the origins of this structure are not known, it was most likely a dwelling in the early years of the nineteenth century. It is an excellent example of early stone construction and features a dirt-floored basement kitchen. The carefully shaped and fitted stones in the arches above the openings are refined details. The three dormers and the east wing are twentieth-century additions.

JF436
Bellevoir
1 Bellevoir Circle
Louisville, Ky. 40252

Bellevoir, or "beautiful to see," is an outstanding example of an Italianate country house. It is a two-and-one-half-story brick dwelling with a low, hipped roof and paired interior chimneys. The forward-projecting center bay contains a recessed entrance and paired, round-arched windows on the second story. There are elaborate hood molds above the windows and a brick stringcourse beneath the small attic windows. Quoins at the corners and wide eaves with paired brackets and small dentils are embellishments typical of the Italianate style. A graceful, curved iron porch spans the center of the facade.

Hamilton and Edmonia Taylor Ormsby built this house between 1864 and 1867 to replace an earlier house that had burned. Ormsby was a grandson of Judge STEPHEN ORMSBY. The site of Bellevoir was originally part of his farm, *Maghera Glass*. Mrs. Ormsby was a niece of President ZACHARY TAYLOR of nearby SPRINGFIELDS.

In 1912 Ormsby heirs sold Bellevoir, which became incorporated as ORMSBY VILLAGE, a facility for dependent and orphaned children. The house and surrounding acreage remain in the ownership of JEFFERSON COUNTY FISCAL COURT.

JF454
Wilhoyte House
8610 Westover Dr.
PROSPECT, Ky. 40059

This two-story brick Italianate farmhouse was built by Jacob Evans Wilhoyte in the late 1850s or early 1860s. Wilhoyte's family had come to Jefferson County from Culpeper County, Virginia, about 1808 and later moved to OLDHAM COUNTY. The Wilhoyte (Wilhoite) family were part of the original Wilhoyte emigrants from Alsace in Europe, and formed the Germanna Colonies in Virginia.

The house is designed in the Italianate style with a symmetrical, five-bay main facade. Although common for urban buildings of this period, the Italianate style was seldom chosen for farmhouses in Jefferson County. The main entrance to the house is detailed with sidelights and a three-light transom. A portico over the main entrance replaces an earlier porch. Wide eaves are accented by brackets on all four elevations. The low, hipped roof is pierced by paired interior chimneys.

JF469
Long Run Church Site
Long Run Rd.
Louisville, Ky.

JF524
Locust Grove
561 Blankenbaker Lane
Louisville, Ky. 40207

JF527
SPRINGFIELDS
5608 Apache Rd.
Louisville, Ky. 40207

JF629
Hanna House/ANCHORAGE CITY HALL
1306 Evergreen Rd.
ANCHORAGE, Ky. 40223

An example of the Gothic Revival style, this three-bay, two-story building probably dates from the 1840s. Its details are characteristic of the period, with ornate trim embellishing the central gable and the one-story porch supported by clustered posts. There is also an unusual iron grille in the side gable.

Built upon land that originally formed part of the Brengman farm, the house evidently existed before the railroad tracks were laid almost across its front entrance in 1849. In 1870 Valerie Hanna, who taught at the Bellewood Seminary, bought the house from John H. Brengman, selling it back to him in 1873. It is now used as the Anchorage City Hall.

JF637
Hobbs Memorial Chapel and Cemetery Site
Evergreen Rd.
Anchorage, Ky. 40223

Although only the gate and entrance doorway remain standing, the chapel once located on the site was a Gothic Revival structure built of brick trimmed with stone. For many years oral tradition attributed the design of the building to EDWARD DORSEY HOBBS, who donated the land for the church; however, a newspaper article of the period credits Louisville architect William H. Redin with the design.

Completed in 1877, the Hobbs Chapel was used for both Methodist and Episcopal church services. During the twentieth century it stood empty and unused for many years. In 1954 the structure was heavily damaged by fire, and after several years of deterioration it was razed in 1957.

Its original iron gates and vestibule gable were later deeded to the city of Anchorage by Hobbs's heirs. Decorated with Gothic motifs, these now serve as an entrance to a small park. The Henning-Hobbs family cemetery adjoins the site.

See Leslee F. Keys, ed., *Historic Jefferson County* (Louisville 1992).

Donna M. Neary
Chris A. Wilson

JEFFERSON COUNTY JUDGE/EXECUTIVE, OFFICE OF. The county judge/executive of Jefferson County, like his or her counterparts in all other counties in Kentucky, is one of the elected officials of the county as established by the state constitution. The office combines both executive and legislative aspects. The judge/executive serves as a member and pre-

Jefferson County Judges

Judge	*Years in Office*	*Political Party*
Edward Garland	1851-58	N/A
Andrew Monroe	1858-66	N/A
William B. Hoke	1866-94	Democrat
Charles G. Richie	1895-97	Republican
James P. Gregory	1898-1905	Democrat
Charles A. Wilson	1906-June 29, 1907 (removed from office by the Kentucky Court of Appeals)	Democrat
Walter P. Lincoln	June 30-November 14, 1907	Democrat
Arthur Peter	1907-10	Republican
Muir Weissinger	1910-13	Democrat
Samuel W. Greene	1914-17	Democrat
William Krieger	1918-21	Republican
Harry E. Tincher	1922-25	Republican
Henry I. Fox	1926-June 1927 (removed from office by the Kentucky Court of Appeals)(re-elected November 8, 1927, sworn in November 23, 1927) (re-elected November 5, 1929, sworn in January 6, 1930)	Republican
Benjamin F. Ewing	June 27,-November 22, 1927 lost to Fox in 1927, won in 1933, sworn in January 1, 1934) 1934-37	Democrat
James Mark Beauchamp	1938-45	Democrat
Horace M. Barker	1946-49	Republican
Boman L. Shamburger	1950-53	Democrat
George S. Wetherby	1954-March 25, 1954 (died in office)	Democrat
Robert T. Burke Jr.	March 25-June 7, 1954	Democrat
Bertram C. Van Arsdale	June 15, 1954-1961	Democrat
Marlow W. Cook	1962-December 17, 1968	Republican
Erbon P. "Tom" Sawyer	1968-September 23, 1969 (died in office)	Republican
W. Armin Willig	September 29, 1969-January 4, 1970	Republican
Louis J. "Todd" Hollenbach III	1970-78	Democrat
Mitch McConnell	1978-84	Republican
Bremer Ehrler	December 21, 1984-1985	Democrat
George Harvey I. Sloane	1986-89	Democrat
David L. Armstrong	1990-98	Democrat
Rebecca Jackson	1999	Republican

siding officer of JEFFERSON COUNTY FISCAL COURT and acts as the county's chief executive and administrative official (Constitution, Section 124; KRS 67.040 and 67.710). KRS 67.710 designates the county judge/executive the chief executive of the county. The judge/executive is specifically charged with the execution of all ordinances and resolutions of Fiscal Court, all contracts entered into by the Fiscal Court, and enforcement of all state laws subject to enforcement by him/her or by officers under his/her supervision. The judge/executive has the authority to create, abolish, or combine any county department or agency and to transfer functions from one agency or department to another. The fiscal responsibilities include preparation of the county budget, oversight of county funds, financial reports to Fiscal Court, and fiscal record-keeping. The judge/executive has the authority to appoint, supervise, suspend, and remove county personnel, with Fiscal Court approval, unless state law provides otherwise.

The Jefferson county judge/executive and the three Jefferson County commissioners together compose Jefferson County Fiscal Court. The judge/executive has the same legislative powers as any other Fiscal Court member, including the right to vote on all matters coming before the court.

Although county court is the oldest form of local GOVERNMENT in Kentucky, deriving from Virginia and English antecedents, the office of county judge/executive (county judge before January 1, 1978) is newer. The Kentucky constitutions of 1792 and 1799 did not provide for county judges. Under these constitutions, the justices of the peace were responsible for administrative matters of county government. The Kentucky Constitution of 1850 did provide for a county judge who presided over the county court, the court of claims, and quarterly court. It was the court of claims, or levy court, that became the predecessor of fiscal court. Still, most executive and administrative functions were, at that time, the collective responsibility of the court rather than of the county judge.

The present constitution, enacted in 1891, gave county government much of its present-day form. It reformed county governmental structure by combining judicial, legislative, and administrative duties under the office of the judge of the county court. The county judge was the chief judicial officer of the county court and quarterly court, a member and the presiding officer of the fiscal court (the county legislative body), and chief executive of the county, performing executive and administrative duties assigned by the General Assembly. However, even under the fourth constitution, counties (and by extension the person serving as the chief executive and administrative officer, the county judge) were agents of the state whose role was to govern rural territory. This was still true of Jefferson County for the first half of the twentieth century, when over eight of ten residents of Jefferson County were also residents of the city of Louisville. The citizens of Jefferson County did reform the county government early in the twentieth century when, by referendum in 1913, they opted for the commissioner form for fiscal court, which took effect in 1918.

In the 1970s, the office was changed by two reforms, beginning with the authorization of limited HOME RULE for counties in 1972 and 1978 by the General Assembly, and by the judicial amendment to the constitution in 1975, which, while reorganizing the structure of the court system in Kentucky, also removed all judicial functions of the office of county judge and strengthened its role as the chief executive and administrative officer of county government. The office was renamed county judge/executive in 1978 to reflect this new shift in responsibility.

Probably the most profound changes to the office of judge/executive of Jefferson County resulted from the post-1950 suburbanization of Jefferson County and the expansion of the responsibilities of Fiscal Court. Throughout the latter half of the nineteenth century and the early decades of the twentieth, the overwhelming majority of the residents of Jefferson County lived in the city of Louisville. The RAILROADS allowed only a limited form of suburbanization in the county. Even so, in 1940 only 7 percent of the residents of Jefferson County lived in the county outside of Louisville. Moreover, there were only seven other incorporated cities.

By 1990, after fifty years of suburbanization based on the automobile, approximately 40 percent of the county population lived in the county outside of Louisville or any of the other incorporated cities, 20 percent lived in incorporated cities other than Louisville, and 40 percent lived in Louisville. For the residents in unincorporated areas of the county, Jefferson County Fiscal Court, led by the county judge/executive, is the principal provider of local government services. For the 20 percent living in the ninety-three incorporated areas other than Louisville, county government shares responsibility for local government services with those municipal governments in varying degrees, depending on their size. County government and Louisville have joint authority over city/county agencies and the special service districts.

Many of the responsibilities of the Jefferson County judge/executive are unique to that office because they apply only to counties with cities of the first class (i.e., Jefferson County). The complex relationship between county government, the city of Louisville, the other incorporated areas, joint city-county agencies, countywide special service districts, and special districts created by fiscal court, all combined with the demands of Kentucky's most urban and populous county, make for a unique political office.

See Prentice A. Harvey, *Research Report No. 130: The Multiplicity of Local Governments in Jefferson County* (Frankfort 1977); William Wiley and William Van Arsdall, eds., *Informational Bulletin No. 114: Duties of Elected County Officials* (Frankfort 1993) and *Informational Bulletin No. 115: County Government in Kentucky* (Frankfort 1994); League of Women Voters of Louisville and Jefferson County, *Your Government at Your Fingertips: A Handbook on Local Government* (Louisville 1988).

David B. Morgan

JEFFERSON COUNTY MEDICAL SOCIETY. Since 1819 physicians of Jefferson County, Kentucky, have assembled as societies under various names for the purpose of improving medical care by discussing methods of treatment, prevention of disease, and the results of research. On March 4, 1892, the present JEFFERSON COUNTY MEDICAL SOCIETY (JCMS) was established. After one year, there followed nearly a decade of dormancy, but the society has been active since 1902.

The JCMS and its members effected many measures improving the health and welfare of citizens by providing impetus and leadership for different projects. A Milk Commission was established by the society in 1905, which made available milk with low bacteria count, known as "certified milk." A Medical Foundation was established in 1957 by JCMS as its nonprofit educational and public service arm. The foundation was supported by annual voluntary subscriptions from JCMS members, from which scholarships were funded at the UNIVERSITY OF LOUISVILLE School of MEDICINE.

With the advent of a successful single-dose vaccine (Sabin) against poliomyelitis, JCMS and the Junior Chamber of Commerce cosponsored a campaign to vaccinate, in two successive years, every citizen of Jefferson County over the age of six weeks. One Sunday each in October, November, and December 1962 were selected as vaccination days. Over 98 percent of the targeted POPULATION was vaccinated against three strains of polio.

Occupying its new facilities in the HEALTH SCIENCES CENTER in 1971, the University of Louisville virtually abandoned its building at First and Chestnut Streets. Robert S. Howell, M.D., president of JCMS, approached the U of L Board of Trustees in July 1976 concerning purchasing the building. Receiving pledges from former students and local practitioners, with additional support from local business and two grants from the J. Graham Brown Foundation, the medical foundation obtained the deed to the property in May 1977. The steering committee embarked on a carefully planned restoration of the building. Finances, as well as construction details, were overseen by Richard S. Wolf, M.D. JCMS moved into its new quarters on March 17, 1981, when the first floor was completed. By June 1987, all floors had been renovated and leased. Later, the dispensary building and the medical school annex were renovated to meet the requirements for the Ronald McDonald House, and a long-term lease was obtained. This facility provides inexpensive quarters for out-of-town families whose children are hospitalized in Louisville.

A JCMS committee, Supplies for Overseas (SOS) collects and sorts unused medical and surgical supplies salvaged from local and regional HOSPITALS, which are then distributed to war-torn or third-world countries. UNITED PARCEL SERVICE and Rotary International have joined SOS, simplifying overseas shipments.

The foundation of JCMS has sponsored public forums, seminars on the history of medicine, and specific grants in support of short-term projects.

In 1970, Will W. Ward Jr., M.D., and Harold W. Blevins, M.D., began staffing a medical clinic one evening a week at Father John Morgan's Mission House, a shelter for homeless men. A psychiatric clinic was soon added. In 1988 plans were made for JCMS to acquire Mission House. A new Foundation was formed, and by 1991 Mission House became the Healing Place, a full-service recovery and rehabilitation facility for substance-abusing and homeless men. Four years later a similar shelter/recovery program for women became operational. Later, shelter and treatment were provided for battered women and their children.

See E.H. Conner, "History of the Jefferson County Medical Society," *Louisville Medicine* 40 (Oct. 1992): 20, 22, 24, 26, 28; idem, *A History of the Medical Society Foundation of the Jefferson County Medical Society* (Louisville 1996); E. Lee Heflin, "History of the Jefferson County Medical Society," *KMJ* 39 (May 1941): 188-92.

Eugene H. Conner

JEFFERSON COUNTY MEMORIAL FOREST. The Jefferson County Memorial Forest is the largest forest owned by any local GOVERNMENT in the United States. Jefferson County government maintains this urban forest of approximately fifty-two hundred acres and continues to add acreage. The forest annually attracts thirty-five thousand visitors.

The forest was begun in August 1945 by the creation of the Jefferson County Forest Commission, charged by Fiscal Court to establish a community forest. The court noted that recreation outlets were few in southwestern Jefferson County.

Forester Paul Yost was appointed in April 1946. L.H. Weir, field secretary of the National Recreation Association, was hired as a recreation consultant. Fiscal Court budgeted ten thousand dollars for the Forest Commission for fiscal year 1946. A purchase area was identified by the commission and Yost.

The first annual report by Yost indicated three obstacles in creating the forest. He reported that there was "excessive abuse and malpractice" of the existing forest and concern about the possibility of increased forest fires and increased real estate prices in reaction to government purchases for a forest. Nevertheless, 932.2 acres had been purchased by 1947, and another 111 acres optioned by Yost. He recommended that an appraisal be done for each individual tract of land at the time of the purchase.

A hundred-foot tower was ordered from the Aeromotor Co. of Chicago in 1947 and placed on top of Holsclaw Hill as a lookout to help detect forest fires. The tower was equipped with a TELEPHONE and two-way radio and provided a normal visibility of thirty-five thousand acres of forest land. A volunteer fire crew, including students from FAIRDALE High School called the "Minute Man" crew, was formed to respond to fires. In addition, managed timbering was done to clean out dead trees and underbrush.

Wildlife was scarce in the forest because of the small water supply, uncontrolled fires, and unregulated hunting. Through the construction of a dam to create TOM WALLACE Lake; fire prevention techniques; the release of squirrels, raccoons, quails, and rabbits into a 150-acre nature preserve; and a PROHIBITION against guns in the reserve, wildlife began its return.

A management plan included selling wood products to create revenue to operate other programs in the forest. Wood was milled into lumber and cut as fenceposts and fuel. The 7,688 board feet of lumber processed in 1948 and 1949 were stored for construction projects in the forest.

The Jefferson County Memorial Forest was dedicated October 10, 1948, as a memorial to the veterans of WORLD WAR II. It was later rededicated to all veterans of foreign wars.

Land acquisitions increased the size to thirteen hundred acres by the end of 1947. The county accumulated another four hundred acres by 1954. Purchases for the forest between 1979-84 brought the acreage to four thousand. Two hundred fifty acres were named the Paul Yost Section in honor of the forester. The donation by the heirs of EMMET HORINE of a thousand acres in 1989 brought the total acreage to five thousand. In 1990, a new master plan was established and new hiking paths designed. An additional 120 acres was added to the forest in 1997 and Louisville water was brought to the forest.

An alpine tower, designed for developing climbing skills and endurance, became very popular with schoolchildren and adults. The Emmet Horine house was rehabilitated as a conference center and retreat and renamed the Horine Manor House in 1993. The site boasts an outstanding view of the county from atop Holsclaw Hill. The Mitchell Hill School, built in 1915, was rehabilitated as the welcome center for the forest in 1994. It features a recreated schoolroom and a modern classroom for programs. A Jefferson County Employee Trail was completed in 1997 to memorialize employees who died while in service to Jefferson County. In July 1998 an overused piece of land in the Horine Reservation, a section of the Memorial Forest, was turned into a native-plant garden. The garden taught visitors the identity of native plants and demonstrated how to create an inexpensive native-plant habitat in a backyard. By the end of 1998 another 337 acres were under option and awaiting purchase.

See Paul Yost, First Annual Report, April 30, 1946, to June 30, 1947, to the Jefferson County Forest Commission Inc.; second Annual Report, July 1, 1947, to June 30, 1948; Third Annual Report, July 1, 1948, to June 30, 1949.

David L. Armstrong

JEFFERSON COUNTY POORHOUSE. In about 1858 the county established a poorhouse in a log structure on seventy acres purchased near JEFFERSONTOWN. About twenty years later the log building was replaced with several one-story residences, a small hospital, a two-story dining hall, and housing for the superintendent–all built of frame and painted white. The facilities were used by men and women, young and old, black and white in the hope of creating a caring family atmosphere in which the homeless poor could find relief.

In 1914 a new, beautifully designed two-story brick-and-stone facility replaced the worn frame buildings. The new poorhouse included a basement, electric lights, hot and cold running water, and steam heat. A separate one-story, fifty-room facility housed African American residents, and a 1.5-million-gallon spring-fed reservoir supplied ample water. Later the poorhouse ceased to operate as such and became the Jefferson County Home for the Aged. More recently the building housed the Jeffersontown Branch of the LOUISVILLE FREE PUBLIC LIBRARY and then was used commercially.

See *Louisville Times*, Feb. 8, 1908; Joellen Tyler Johnston, *Jeffersontown, Kentucky-The First 200 Years* (Jeffersontown 1997).

Joellen Tyler Johnston

JEFFERSON SCHOOL OF LAW. Founded October 2, 1905, to provide night and Saturday classes for working students aspiring to a legal education, the Jefferson School of Law opened in the Louisville Medical College at First and Chestnut Streets. Judge Shackelford Miller was dean of the faculty. Sixty-three seniors comprised the first class. Another founding faculty member was Benjamin F. Washer, who became dean in 1930, a post he held until 1950 when the school merged with the UNIVERSITY OF LOUISVILLE School of LAW, now the Louis D. Brandeis School of Law. Judge Miller's family held a special niche: one of his sons, NEVILLE MILLER, who was a popular mayor of Louisville (1933-37), became a dean at the university law school after teaching at the Jefferson School; another, Shackelford Miller Jr., taught at the night school for many years.

The quality of education was high, as seen by the success of graduates in passing the bar and later functioning as first-rate practitioners, judges, and law teachers. At first the course duration was one year. Later it was extended to two years, and finally three years. Evening classes met from 7:30 to 9:00 p.m.

The school averaged sixty students; the part-time faculty was drawn from members of the Louisville bar who were the leaders in their profession. In this way the students had contact not only with the theory of law but with the lawyers who were daily applying legal principles in the courtrooms.

A healthy rivalry existed between the campus school and the downtown school, although a number of the founders of the Jefferson School had received their degrees from the university law school. Dean Washer, for instance, graduated from the University of Louisville in 1892.

When merger of the two schools was discussed in the 1940s, the subject was clouded with controversy. A Jefferson School faculty member summed up the anti-merger feelings in a commencement address, objecting to any plan that would "place a wall of exclusion around the legal profession, the gates to which could be unlocked only with a key of gold." The merger, however, was a foregone conclusion, since the American Bar Association was pressing to raise standards for legal education. The university law school's lack of accreditation was holding up accreditation for the entire University of Louisville, and limited resources prevented either school from achieving ABA goals.

After merger, the Jefferson School of Law classes of 1951 and 1952 became students of the University of Louisville, and all former graduates became eligible to receive degrees from the university. Jefferson School of Law had graduated 1,513 students.

See *University School of Law 1846-1896* (Louisville 1996); also unsigned typescripts in the University of Louisville Law Library: "The Jefferson School of Law" and "The Merger of the University of Louisville and the Jefferson School of Law."

Betty Lou Amster

JEFFERSON SEMINARY. In February 1798 the Kentucky General Assembly chartered the Jefferson Seminary in Louisville, along with six thousand acres in the southern part of the state that was to be sold in order to pay for the construction of the school. In April eight prominent citizens–Richard Clough Anderson, WILLIAM CROGHAN, John Thruston, JAMES MERIWETHER, ALEXANDER SCOTT BULLITT, Henry Churchill, John Thompson, and William Taylor–began seeking donations for the fledgling high school and were constituted as its board of trustees.

Due to slow land sales in southern Kentucky, ineffective fund-raising, and criticism of the trustees, the board was reformed in 1800, 1804, and again in 1808. There is some speculation as to when the seminary began operation. *The Kentucky Encyclopedia* listed classes as beginning in 1816 when the schoolhouse was built; however, a site was purchased and building began in 1813. Students were enrolled that year, and the school opened in temporary quarters with EDWARD MANN BUTLER as the principal. The institution relocated to a building on Eighth St. between Green St. (now LIBERTY) and Walnut (now Muhammad Ali Blvd.).

By the time the new schoolhouse was completed in 1816, Jefferson Seminary, with high school and college classes in English, GEOGRAPHY, FRENCH, Latin, geometry, and trigonometry, had approximately forty-five to fifty students paying twenty dollars for a six-month term. Although the school's initial progress was encouraging, this growth slowed because of perpetual faculty turnover, internal dissent, and financial difficulties.

By the mid-1820s, Jefferson Seminary came under attack from Shadrach Penn Jr., the editor of the *LOUISVILLE PUBLIC ADVERTISER*, who claimed that the school was an elitist institution that did not teach practical education to Louisville's children. Although the curriculum was revised shortly thereafter, the school received too much competition from the city's new PUBLIC SCHOOLS and was closed in 1829.

See Works Progress Administration, *Centennial History of the University of Louisville* (Louisville 1939); David Post, "From the Jefferson Seminary to the Louisville Free School: Change and Continuity in Western Education, 1813-1840," *Register of the Kentucky Historical Society* 86 (Spring 1988): 103-18.

JEFFERSON SQUARE. Located just west of the Citizens Plaza Building and bounded by Jefferson, LIBERTY, and Sixth Streets, Jefferson Square was created in the late 1970s after the old Center Building was torn down. Because of its location in the middle of the GOVERNMENT center (the former jail, the county courthouse, the hall of justice, and CITY HALL), the park-like plaza has hosted numerous rallies as well as festivities such as "Light Up Louisville," an annual celebration following Thanksgiving that kicks off the holidays with the illumination of the downtown area. Within the common is a large fountain surrounded by benches, the flags of Louisville's sister cities, the Law Enforcement Officers Memorial (dedicated in 1992), and the Louisville-Jefferson County-SHIVELY Firefighters Memorial (dedicated in 1996).

JEFFERSONTOWN. Peter Shepherd, a native of Berkeley County, Virginia, and a veteran of GEORGE ROGERS CLARK'S 1778 campaign in the Northwest Territory, obtained warrants for several thousand acres of land, some of which lay on Chenoweth Run, a major tributary of FLOYDS FORK of the Salt River in what is now eastern Jefferson County. In 1794 Adam and Michael Shepherd, heirs of Peter, deeded 500 of those acres to Frederick Geiger, who sold 122 acres to Abraham Bruner. On May 3, 1797, the Jefferson County Court approved Bruner's petition to establish a town on his forty acres of land. Named the Town of Jefferson, in honor of THOMAS JEFFERSON, the name changed with time, becoming Jefferson Town and finally Jeffersontown, although for many years inhabitants referred to it as Brunerstown. The first trustees were Robert McCowan, Samuel Blankenbaker, John Stuart, August Frederick, Michael Leatherman, John Stucky, and Philip Bence.

Located on the old pike between Louisville and TAYLORSVILLE at the junction of today's Ky. 1065 and Ky. 155, Jeffersontown served the needs of the surrounding agricultural community. Early STREETS were packed dirt, while buildings were of log and/or locally quarried stone. Several HOTELS catered to travelers, and a variety of cottage industries made some manufactured products available locally. A movement to improve roads resulted in a plank turnpike from Louisville through Jeffersontown in 1851, which was later covered with broken rock. Although the area's earliest explorers and settlers were heavily SCOTS-IRISH, after 1790 many people of German descent migrated to Jeffersontown and by the mid-nineteenth century a growing number of AFRICAN AMERICANS had become part of the community. The surrounding farmland produced potatoes, onions, and vegetables, while Jeffersontown served as a supply center.

Except for the occasional passing of Union troops, Jeffersontown saw little of the CIVIL WAR. However, in 1864, four Confederate prisoners were brought there for execution in retaliation for the murder of a Union soldier. Two of them are buried in the town cemetery, where a marker was placed for them in 1904 by the United Daughters of the Confederacy. The other two were reinterred by their families.

About 1858 Jefferson County established a poorhouse in a simple log structure on seventy acres purchased near Jeffersontown. Twenty years later the original structure was replaced by several one-story residences that included a small hospital, a two-story dining hall, and housing for a superintendent–all built of frame and painted white. The facilities were used by men and women, young and old, black and white in hope of creating a caring family atmosphere in which the homeless poor could find relief. In 1914 a two-story brick-and-stone facility was built as a poorhouse and was later the Jefferson County Home for the Aged. In the 1960s it became the Jeffersontown Branch of the LOUISVILLE FREE PUBLIC LIBRARY. Today the historic building stands completely renovated by the city of Jeffersontown, which owns and operates it as a senior citizens' activities center.

In 1896 HENRY WATTERSON, noted editor of the *COURIER-JOURNAL*, built an estate just south of town; in 1905-6 MARVIN HART, a descendant of one of the town's early families, became the BOXING world's heavyweight champion; and in 1913 locally born Roscoe Goose rode Donerail to victory in the KENTUCKY DERBY. By 1890 the Southern Railway had a depot near town; and on May 2, 1903, the Beargrass Railway began operating its Jeffersontown line of the interurban, providing speedy transportation to and from Louisville. Fire was a constant hazard, and in November 1921 the entire northwest corner of the town square was consumed. After this event all new structures in the town center were built of fireproof materials such as brick, concrete block, or tile.

On June 13, 1907, the first edition of the *Jeffersonian*, a weekly all-county newspaper, was printed in Jeffersontown by W.C. Barrickman and J.C. Alcock. Although centered in and on Jeffersontown, coverage extended to areas as distant as Spencer and Bullitt Counties. Within a few years of the paper's inception as many as forty correspondents were writing news from their local communities. Workers employed from the Jeffersontown area included T.R. "Tommy" Jones, who began work in 1913 as a printer's devil and eventually became sole owner. By mid-century the paper, no longer the only county publication, was suffering financially from a lack of local advertisers. When Kentucky statutes were changed requiring that legal advertisements be printed in the area newspaper having the largest circulation, a major source of revenue was lost. In 1959 the *Jeffersonian* was sold to Al Schansberg, who merged it with the *Voice of ST. MATTHEWS* in about 1965. At this time the Jeffersontown issue was a remake front and back page sharing other pages with the *Voice*. Attempts of successive owners to revive the *Jeffersonian* failed, and eventually publication ceased entirely.

Jeffersontown grew slowly. By 1920 the official POPULATION numbered only 320, but after 1950 changes came swiftly. General Electric's Appliance Park opened to the southwest, bringing many newcomers to the area; roads were improved; expressways put downtown Louisville within easy reach; and adjacent subdivisions were annexed. In the 1960s Bluegrass Research and Industrial Park was developed, becoming by 1997 the workplace of more than thirty-three thousand people and making Jeffersontown Kentucky's third-largest employer. Today a white-columned CITY HALL, a large community center, a renovated public square, and nearby PARKS and recreational facilities reflect this fourth-class city's prosperity. It is one of the county's fastest-growing cities, as new subdivisions open south of town toward the GENE SNYDER FREEWAY. The community celebrates its heritage with an annual Gaslight Festival, and each summer a popular farmers' market promotes business while reflecting the town's agricultural roots. The population was 9,701 in 1970, 15,795 in 1980, 23,223 in 1990, and 25,596 in 1996.

See Robert C. Jobson, *A History of Early Jeffersontown and Southeastern Jefferson County, Kentucky* (Baltimore 1977); William E. Cummings, *Jeffersontown's Past 175 Years* (Jeffersontown, Ky., 1972); Robert C. Jobson, "German-American Settlers of Early Jefferson County, Kentucky," *Filson Club History Quarterly* 53 (Oct. 1979): 344-57; Joellen T. Johnston, *Jeffersontown, Kentucky-The First 200 Years* (Jeffersontown, Ky., 1997); *The Jeffersonian Historical and Christmas Supplement*, Dec. 1909; *Voice of St. Matthews*, Jan. 5, 1983.

Joellen Tyler Johnston

JEFFERSONVILLE, INDIANA. Jeffersonville, the seat of GOVERNMENT in CLARK COUNTY, INDIANA, lies above the FALLS OF THE OHIO, just across the river from Louisville. The area was opened for settlement in 1783 when the Virginia General Assembly awarded a 150,000-acre tract at the Falls of the Ohio to Gen. GEORGE ROGERS CLARK and his Illinois regiment in honor of their capture of the British forts at Kaskaskia, Cahokia, and Vincennes during 1777-78. Settlement in the Jeffersonville vicinity began about 1786 with construction of Fort Finney on a site near the present John F. Kennedy Bridge. The fort was named for its

Ferry *City of Jeffersonville* with Jeffersonville, Indiana in the background.

Jeffersonville Mayors

Name	*Term*	*Party*	*Profession*
Isaac Heiskell	1839-43		
Christopher Peasley	1843-45		
William Cross	1845-48		
William F. Collum	1848-54		Surgeon
John D. Shryer	1854-55		
U.G. Damron	1855-56		
Thomas J. Downs	1856-57		
William Lackey	1857-58		
John D. Shryer	1858-61		
O.C. Woolley	1861-65		
John Ware	1865-67		
Gabriel Poindexter	1867-69		
Levi Sparks	1869-73	Democrat	Merchant
Burdet Clifton Pile	1873-75	Democrat	Hardware Dealer
Luther Fairfax Warder	1875-83	Democrat	Attorney
John M. Glass	1883-85	Republican	Real Estate
Herman Preefer	1885-87	Democrat	Insurance, Real Estate, Dry Goods
Luther Fairfax Warder	1887-91	Democrat	Attorney
Benjamin H. Robinson	1891-94	Republican	Merchant
Isaac F. Whiteside	1894-98	Republican	Industrial Baker
Thomas B. Rader	1898-1902	Democrat	Real Estate, Insurance
Abraham Schwaninger	1902-4	Republican	Shoemaker
Henry A. Burtt	1904-6	Democrat	Attorney
Edward N. Flynn, M.D.	1906-9	Republican	Physician
James E. Burke	1910-12	Democrat	Coal Merchant
Jonas G. Howard Jr.	1913	Democrat	Attorney
Ernest W. Rauth	1914-17	Democrat	Real Estate
Newton H. Myers	1918-21	Republican	Manufacturer
Joseph H. Warder	1922-25	Democrat	Attorney
Harry C. Poindexter	1926-29	Republican	Bookseller
Allen W. Jacobs	1930-38	Republican	Grocer
Homer G. Vawter	1939-42	Republican	Real Estate
Samuel G. Shannon	1942-51	Republican	Dairy Owner
Charles W. Hoodenpyl	1952-63	Democrat	Druggist
Richard L. Vissing	1964-83	Democrat	Auto Dealer
Dale L. Orem	1984-91	Republican	Sporting Goods
Raymond J. Parker Jr.	1992-95	Democrat	Law Enforcement
Thomas R. Galligan	1996-present	Democrat	Building Contractor

first commander, Maj. Walter Finney. In 1787 it was renamed FORT STEUBEN in honor of Baron von Steuben, the German officer who had helped Gen. George Washington train the Continental army. Fort Steuben served as a base for campaigns against the Indians in southwestern Indiana and Illinois until about 1791, when it was relegated to militia status.

The settlement became known as Jeffersonville in June 1802 when Lt. Isaac BOWMAN, recipient of Section No. 1 of Clark's Grant, placed a portion of his land in the hands of a board of trustees for division into streets and lots. The town was platted initially according to concepts provided by President THOMAS JEFFERSON at the invitation of territorial governor William Henry Harrison. Jefferson recommended a checkerboard plan, with an alternating pattern of open and subdivided squares. The open squares were to be left for "turf and trees," providing a means to clear the air of diseases such as yellow fever. Jefferson's plan was altered by the addition of diagonal streets, which crossed in the open squares. This modification proved impractical and in 1817 town officials received state approval to replat the town into a regular gridiron.

Jeffersonville became the Clark County seat in 1802, a status it held until 1811 when it gave way to Charlestown. From 1813 to 1816 Jeffersonville was Indiana's unofficial capital because territorial governor Thomas Posey disliked CORYDON and chose to do state business from his home in Jeffersonville, where he could be close to his physician in Louisville. Jeffersonville remained a town governed by a self-perpetuating board of trustees until 1839 when trustee and state legislator Dr. Nathaniel Field secured legislation to make it a city with a mayor and council. In April the voters elected Isaac Heiskell the city's first mayor.

Since the OHIO RIVER served as Jeffersonville's economic lifeline, transportation was an important force in shaping the city's growth. As the Indiana terminus for traffic between Pittsburgh and the Falls of the Ohio, the town quickly became a primary center of ferrying operations with Louisville and a hub for interior surface transportation. In the SUBURBS several small towns sprang up including Port Fulton on the east, Ohio Falls City on the west, and Claysburg on the north. Within a generation of the town's founding, primitive roads ribboned out to communities such as Charlestown, NEW ALBANY, Utica, and Salem.

Between 1800 and 1830 Jeffersonville was involved in efforts to build a canal around the Falls of the Ohio. In 1805 the territorial legislature created the Indiana Canal Co. Its incorporators included such figures as George Rogers Clark and former vice president Aaron Burr, but the enterprise failed to raise enough capital to begin construction. In 1818 the Indiana General Assembly incorporated the Jeffersonville Ohio Canal Co. It excavated a ditch that began at the foot of Meigs Ave. and meandered through downtown Jeffersonville before emptying into the river near Clarksville. This project also ran out of money before it could be completed, and opening of the LOUISVILLE AND PORTLAND CANAL in 1830 ended Jeffersonville's canal dreams.

Jeffersonville entered the steamboat era in 1819 when several investors built the *United States,* a seven-hundred-ton vessel capable of carrying three thousand bales of cotton. Its success inspired several other entrepreneurs to enter the steamboat-building business. The most notable of these pioneers was James Howard, who launched the *Hyperion* in September 1834. In 1848, after similar ventures in Madison Indiana, and Louisville, Howard returned to Jeffersonville and joined with his brother Daniel to open a new yard. The Howard family developed a reputation as master craftsmen whose vessels reflected both artistic excellence and technical proficiency. By the CIVIL WAR the Howard Ship Yard was one of the leading steamboat builders on the inland waterways, a status it retained until the 1930s when it succumbed to the GREAT DEPRESSION and the 1937 flood.

The coming of the railroad increased Jeffersonville's transportation role. In 1846 the Indiana legislature incorporated the Jeffersonville Railroad Co., empowering it to build a line north to Columbus and then to use the Madison & Indianapolis tracks to complete the road to Indianapolis. The two companies merged sixteen years later to create the Jeffersonville, Madison, & Indianapolis Railroad. The JM&I came under control of the Pennsylvania Railroad in 1873.

Jeffersonville was a military support center during the Civil War. The city's riverfront was a primary gateway for Union troops, supplies, and equipment headed to the western THEATER of operations. Located a few blocks to the north in what is now Warder Park was a bakery that produced hardtack, a staple in the military diet. The United States Quartermaster Corps had operations spread throughout the central part of the city, including stables, ordnance warehouses, commissary stores, transportation facilities, and administrative offices. In February 1864 Jefferson General Hospital opened a few blocks north of the river on property seized from former United States senator Jesse D. Bright, who had been expelled from the Senate in 1862 because of his apparent Southern sympathies.

The city's earliest settlers were largely English and Scots-Irish pioneers who emigrated from western Virginia, Pennsylvania, and North Carolina. They established businesses and religious institutions such as Howard Ship Yard, Citizen's National Bank, Wall Street Methodist Church, St. Paul's Episcopal Church, and First Presbyterian Church. But Jeffersonville also attracted numerous German and Irish immigrants as well as many African Americans who escaped slavery or moved north after the Civil War. By the end of the nineteenth century, all three groups had made their impact on the city's demographic, economic, and institutional structure.

The post-Civil War years saw substantial industrial development in Jeffersonville. Near the end of the war, several local businessmen organized the Ohio Falls Car & Foundry Co. on a riverfront tract bisected by the Jeffersonville-Clarksville boundary. It evolved into the Ohio Falls Car Manufacturing Co. during the 1870s and became a major producer of railroad rolling stock before being absorbed into the American Car & Foundry Co. in 1899. Sweeney's foundry, opened in 1869 at Court Ave. and Pearl St., moved to the riverfront in 1881 and became an important producer of ship engines and machinery. The Jeffersonville Quartermaster Depot moved into permanent facilities in 1874 and occupied more than ten blocks by World War II. The Ford Plate Glass Co., opened in 1878, was reorganized two years later as the Jeffersonville Plate Glass Co. and employed some two hundred workers. Such economic expansion and consequent population growth fueled a movement to return the county seat to Jeffersonville. In 1878 county records were returned to the city, where they were housed in a new courthouse financed through a fund-raising campaign led by Mayor Luther F. Warder.

Jeffersonville's population was 10,774 in 1900, and it grew very little during the next 40 years. Nevertheless, the city witnessed several important developments during the decades that preceded World War II. The Jeffersonville Free Public Library, financed by a grant from Andrew Carnegie, opened in 1904; Clark Memorial Hospital was organized in 1922; and the Louisville Municipal Bridge (now Clark Memorial Bridge) opened in 1929.

Arctic Springs was a favorite Jeffersonville resort community on the Ohio River upstream a mile from the town's center on Utica Pike. Summer cottages were built around a spring that provided frigid water year-round. In the 1920s hundreds came to the springs for weekend dancing under the stars on an outdoor dance floor managed by the Jeffersonville Elks Club. Later Arctic Springs provided water for the city through wells dug into the aquifer.

Beginning in the 1930s and continuing for twenty years, Jeffersonville was known for open, illegal gambling that drew many players from Louisville and elsewhere to establishments such as the 110 Club, 322 Club, 125 Club, Antz's Cafe, and the Municipal Bar in downtown Jeffersonville and to posh casinos like the Log Cabin, the Club Greyhound, and the Silver Creek Country Club on the city's outskirts.

The World War II years brought a resurgence in shipbuilding as the newly organized Jeffersonville Boat & Machine Co. took over the old Howard yards and several adjoining properties and began building landing craft and warships for the United States Navy. Growth triggered by wartime labor demands, postwar residential development, and annexation of adjoining neighborhoods such as Ingramville, Port Fulton, and Claysburg during the 1940s caused the city's population to jump to 14,685 by 1950. Jeffersonville experienced moderate growth over the next thirty years. Closure of the Quartermaster Depot in 1957 was an economic blow, but its impact was largely offset by opening of the Census Bureau's processing center and the sale of many buildings to private industrial firms. The establishment of Jeffersonville Research and Industrial Park in the early 1970s and opening of the Clark Maritime Centre in 1985 substantially enhanced the city's economic base. The city's population was 20,008 in 1970, 21,220 in 1980, 21,830 in 1990, and 25,787 in 1996.

See Lewis C. Baird, *Baird's History of Clark County* (Indianapolis 1909); Gerald O. Haffner, *A Brief, Informal History of Clark County, Indiana* (New Albany, Ind., 1985).

Carl E. Kramer

JEHOVAH'S WITNESSES. Jehovah's Witnesses are well known in the Greater Louisville area, having been a part of "Kentucky soil" since the late 1800s. The Witnesses are a dynamic part of the community, having grown from only a small band of Bible students. They meet together regularly for Christian Bible study and in 1997 worshiped in twenty-four congregations throughout the Louisville area.

The activity of Jehovah's Witnesses in Louisville dates back to at least 1881 when a small group began meeting together to study the Bible. By 1901 another group of Jehovah's Witnesses (who were then known simply as Bible students) had started meeting in New Albany, Indiana, while yet another twenty formed a small group for Bible study in Magnet, Indiana, about sixty miles by road west of Louisville. A congregation was formed, and by 1906 a group of twenty-six Witnesses was meeting every other week in Louisville.

The first formal meetings of Jehovah's Witnesses in Louisville were held in the home of Dr. Walter D. Pelle. Louisville resident Mrs. Charles Hickey, a Witness whose son was receiving medical treatment from Dr. Pelle at the time, introduced the doctor to the Witnesses. Meanwhile, another group of Bible students in Jeffersontown, Kentucky, began meeting at the home of Fannie House.

Because the number of Witnesses in the Louisville area was growing steadily, it became necessary for them to rent buildings for weekly meetings. Among the premises used by Witnesses were a Christian Science church, a former Jewish synagogue near downtown, and buildings at 223 W Breckinridge St. and 409 W Oak St. The Oak St. building, which contained an auditorium and four small rooms, served for several years as the Witnesses' general headquarters for the Greater Louisville area. The Witnesses occasionally rented larger facilities–such as Lewis Hall, Macauley's Theatre, and the Strand Theater–to house special assemblies and larger public meetings.

Eventually, in 1940, the Witnesses decided to build their own meeting hall–called a Kingdom Hall–when Yoder Same, owner of the Same's Sand and Gravel Pit in Jeffersonville, Indiana, donated property. A few years later another congregation was formed in Louisville's West End, with a Kingdom Hall at Eighteenth and Anderson Streets. Continued growth has called for the building of more Kingdom Halls. From 1947 to 1970 ten more Kingdom Halls were constructed in Louisville, all by volunteer labor.

Jehovah's Witnesses are active in the community–working in local businesses, sharing in school events, and participating in a number of other civic activities. Regardless of occupation, all Witnesses take part in a voluntary educational work that reaches out to people of all religious faiths in the community. Recent literature campaigns by the Witnesses have focused on issues such as the environment, crime, sexual harassment, literacy, domestic violence, and child abuse. The Witnesses perform their educational work and distribute Bible literature in cooperation with the Watch Tower Bible and Tract Society, a philanthropic organization supported entirely by voluntary donations and volunteer workers.

Louisville has played host to a number of special events involving Jehovah's Witnesses, including repeated personal visits by Charles T. Russell, whose writings in the 1870s were integral to the spread of Witness beliefs and who founded the *Watchtower*, the chief periodical printed and distributed by the Witnesses. Another noteworthy event held in Louisville was the presentation of the *Photo-Drama of Creation*, an eight-hour motion picture and slide presentation with synchronized sound, produced by the Watch Tower Bible and Tract Society of Pennsylvania. The *Photo-Drama* was a dazzling technological accomplishment at the time. Its extensive use of synchronized sound predated the commercial production of sound movies by more than a decade. It was shown to capacity crowds in Louisville's Strand Theater in April 1914, and portions of it continued to be shown free of charge in Louisville through 1916.

Freedom Hall at the Kentucky Fair and Exposition Center was the site of one of 194 district conventions held by Jehovah's Witnesses in the continental United States during 1997. In the past, Jehovah's Witnesses have held both large-scale conventions and smaller assemblies in Louisville at locations such as PARKWAY FIELD and Broadbent Arena. From 1980-97, 28 conventions have been held in Louisville, with an economic impact of over $700 million.

To assist doctors and HOSPITALS in their use of alternatives to blood, the Witnesses organized a Hospital Liaison Committee in the Greater Louisville area in December 1987. In cooperation with the committee, the Jewish Hospital of Louisville introduced a Bloodless Surgery Program in 1991 and has successfully treated hundreds of patients who wish to avoid treatment that involves using blood products, since Witnesses refuse to accept the transfusion of blood and blood products.

See *Jehovah's Witnesses: Proclaimers of God's Kingdom* (Brooklyn, N.Y., 1993).

James F. Gates

JENNINGS, JONATHAN (b Hunterdon County, New Jersey, 1784; d near Charlestown, Indiana, July 26, 1834). Governor of Indiana. The son of a Presbyterian minister, this future governor of Indiana moved to Fayette County, Pennsylvania, with his parents, Jacob and Mary (Kennedy) Jennings, when he was a young boy. Jennings received his early education at a private Presbyterian academy in Canonsburg, Pennsylvania, and later studied LAW. At the age of twenty-two Jennings came down the OHIO RIVER from Pittsburgh and settled for a brief time in JEFFERSONVILLE, INDIANA Territory. From there he moved in quick succession to Charlestown and then Vincennes, Indiana, where he was admitted to the bar in 1807. In addition to a small law practice, Jennings supplemented his income by working in the Vincennes land office and later as an associate editor of the *Western Sun* newspaper.

He returned to Charlestown, and in 1809 he was elected a delegate to Congress from the Indiana Territory on a platform that supported preserving the anti-slavery clause in the Northwest Ordinance. As a delegate, Jennings guided the enabling act for Indiana statehood through Congress. He continued as a territorial representative until 1816 when Indiana was admitted to the Union. As president of the state's constitutional convention, held in CORYDON in June 1816, Jennings oversaw the framing of Indiana's GOVERNMENT and called for the state's first elections, during which he ran a successful bid for the governorship, assuming office in November 1816.

In 1818, while governor, Jennings was appointed an Indian treaty commissioner by President James Monroe. Jennings, along with Lewis Cass and Benjamin Parke, negotiated the New Purchase Treaty that ceded to the government most of the central part of Indiana. Jennings was reelected to the governor's post in 1819 but resigned after being elected as a representative to Congress in 1822, serving from December 2, 1822, until March 3, 1831. He then retired to his farm near Charlestown, Indiana, where he lived until his death. Jennings County, Indiana, is named for him.

Jennings was twice married, first to Ann Hay in 1811 and later to Clarissa Barber in 1827. He had no children. Jennings is buried in Charlestown Cemetery.

See R. Carlyle Buley, *The Old Northwest* (Bloomington 1983); Joseph E. Kallenbach and Jessamine S. Kallenbach, *American State Governors, 1776-1976* (Dobbs Ferry 1981); Andrew R.L. Cayton, *Frontier Indiana* (Bloomington 1996).

JEPTHA KNOB. Located in SHELBY COUNTY seven miles east of SHELBYVILLE, Kentucky, Jeptha Knob is actually a series of hills in the form of a horseshoe, open at the western end. The highest, which is easily visible from both Interstate 64 and U.S. 60, is approximately 2 miles in diameter, rises 1,188 feet above sea level, and represents the highest point in the Bluegrass Region. Though formed during the Ordovician and Silurian geological periods and consisting of alternating layers of shale and limestone, geologists disagree about the source of the formation. One theory posits that the knob is the result of a volcanic upthrust coupled with erosion of the surrounding countryside, a second argues that it is a meteoroid-impact structure, and a third suggests that it is the result of the processes of differential erosion. Jeptha Knob is unique in that it lies more than thirty miles from the Knobs Region of the state.

Mysteries concerning its origin notwithstanding, Jeptha Knob seems to have figured prominently in the history of the state before and after white settlement. Local legend claims that American Indians regularly used the hills as the site of intertribal "festivals" where archery, tomahawk throwing, and other such contests were held. In the late 1700s Daniel Boone reportedly hunted the area while a member of his party, Daniel Goodman, claimed land near the knob. Goodman died at Boonesborough in 1777. Many years later, Boone, in August 1795, returned to Shelby County to issue a sworn statement that Goodman indeed had claimed the land and that it belonged to his family. Apparently the family experienced trouble from other settlers who tried to claim the tract.

Throughout the remainder of the frontier period, the knob was probably best known as a landmark on a route from Harrodsburg to the FALLS OF THE OHIO. In the late twentieth century the geologic formation still serves that function for travelers along I-64 and U.S. 60. Aviators also use the knob as a navigational mark. Local media companies also have made use of the knob. In 1998 nine communications towers resided on top of Jeptha Knob.

In 1996 one last mystery concerning the knob, the source of the name, was solved–at least to the satisfaction of some Shelby County residents. An 1809 deposition from James F. Moore, a cousin of James Harrod, credits SQUIRE BOONE, Daniel's brother, with naming the knob after Jepthah, the biblical warrior who sought God's deliverance from battle. Prior to this discovery, it was thought to be named for Jeptha Layson, who owned the land in the 1880s.

See Arthur McFarlan, *Geology of Kentucky* (Lexington 1943).

Thomas J. Kiffmeyer

JERUSALEM. There is an area known to some as Jerusalem, located off Spring St. east of the CSX Transportation railroad tracks in the BUTCHERTOWN neighborhood. In *Butchertown of Yesterday* Father Diomede Pohlkamp in 1946 wrote that the area was most likely named "for the farm of Jacob Schiebe, a native of France who for many years was a confidential valet to the Governor of Syria, who lived in JERUSALEM. The former valet, after becoming a resident of Louisville, never tired of speaking of the glories of ancient Jerusalem and in consequence the quaint house with its small vineyard and kitchen became known as 'Jerusalem.'" A newspaper once said it got that name because several Jewish families had lived there, but old-timers at the time questioned that statement. There is no record of any Jewish families ever having lived in the area.

Herman Landau

JEWISH COMMUNITY CENTER. Founded in 1890 as the Young Men's Hebrew Association (YMHA), it is the nation's third-oldest Jewish community center in continuous operation. It was organized at a meeting called by philanthropist Isaac W. Bernheim, who became its first president. Its original home was on First St. north of Chestnut. It started out as only a gymnasium, but in 1895 a three-story addition was erected.

A 1913 building fund drive raised nearly eighty thousand dollars, and two years later the YMHA moved into a new building at Second and Jacob. This building remained the center of Jewish life in Louisville until 1955. By then it had been renamed the Jewish Community Center and had outgrown its downtown space. The center acquired a site at 3600 Dutchmans Ln. and raised $550,000 in a building fund drive. A new building was constructed. There was an outdoor SWIMMING pool and space remaining for outdoor activities. A program of day camping was inaugurated on the grounds. The new building also provided classrooms for the LOUISVILLE HEBREW SCHOOL.

The YMHA pioneered in many ways. It started women's gym classes in 1891, a year ahead of New York. It helped organize the National Jewish Welfare Board (now the Jewish Community Centers Association) in 1913. Ten years later it became one of the organizers of the Community Chest (now METRO UNITED WAY). There were activities for women as well as men, and in 1979 Frankye Gordon was elected the center's first woman president.

When the country entered WORLD WAR I, an influx of Jewish soldiers at CAMP TAYLOR led to a wide-ranging hospitality program. This proved so successful that it was copied by the National Jewish Welfare Board and during World War II by the USO. In WORLD WAR II, this program was reactivated on a larger scale. The gymnasium became a weekend dormitory for service personnel.

The YMHA Orchestra was founded in 1916 and metamorphosed into the LOUISVILLE ORCHESTRA, but a second orchestra, the Jewish Community Center Orchestra, was developed and has continued under the direction of Rubin Sher. A drama group survives as the Heritage Theatre. A summer camp was operated on Upper River Rd. from 1913 until the OHIO RIVER FLOOD OF 1937 demolished it. The YMHA also started holding English classes for new Americans. It conducts cultural, social, and athletic programs for all age groups and houses the Naamani Library, named for Dr. Israel Naamani, a UNIVERSITY OF LOUISVILLE faculty member and the former director of the bureau of Jewish education.

Since 1960, as a result of a twenty-five-thousand-dollar bequest from Blanche B. Ottenheimer, the JCC has presented the Ottenheimer Award annually to persons who have performed outstanding civic service to the city at large. Its first recipient was Mayor CHARLES FARNSLEY.

The facility was refurbished in 1988 with the addition of twenty-five thousand square feet to house a second gymnasium and fitness track and two new youth lounges. A cybernetics laboratory for computer training was opened in 1996. A 1997 flood caused more than $1 million in damage. A salutary effect was that it speeded up a project for refurbishing and expanding some facilities. A three-story health-lifestyle center was opened in 1997. Jewish Hospital contributed $1.5 million to the project. This allowed for a health-evaluation area and a preventive heart maintenance program.

Herman Landau

Groundbreaking for Jewish Hospital at the southwest corner of Kentucky Street at Floyd, c. 1903.

JEWISH COMMUNITY FEDERATION. The Jewish Community Federation of Louisville developed from two wartime emergencies and is now looked upon as the voice of Louisville's Jewish community. It is an umbrella organization that raises funds for local, national, and overseas Jewish needs. It also engages in community relations, civic observances, services to the elderly, and absorption of immigrants.

Cooperative activities began when the American Jewish Joint Distribution Committee sought to raise a sizable Jewish war relief fund in 1922-23. With Col. Fred Levy as state chairman, $150,000 was raised here to meet the pressing need of JEWS who survived WORLD WAR I.

When Hitler came to power, further needs developed, and in 1934 attorney Charles W. Morris, who had worked on the first drive, called together a broadly representative group to raise funds for international Jewish relief and for several local institutions. This group styled itself the Conference of Jewish Organizations and was incorporated in 1951. The Conference launched an annual United Jewish Campaign to support social services in Israel. At one time there was a separate women's committee, but now women have assumed a major role in the overall organization.

In 1971 the name was changed to the Jewish Community Federation of Louisville to keep in line with other communities in the nation. It has a voice in matters of national concern through its membership in the Council of Jewish Federations and the Jewish Policy Association.

Responsibilities of the federation grew as it coordinated fund-raising and intensified its work in the field of human relations. In 1978 it built Shalom Tower, providing 150 low-cost APARTMENTS for the elderly. A vital subdivision of the Federation is its Community Relations Council.

It works with the schools to avoid calendar conflicts and holds workshops for teachers. It also holds an annual observance of Yom Hashoah in memory of the Jews killed by Hitler. The federation sponsors the Louisville Board of Rabbis and Cantors, which brings together all of the city's pulpit rabbis to discuss matters of mutual concern.

The federation is managed by a board of directors that represents all segments of the Jewish community–Orthodox, Conservative, and Reform–but each congregation remains fiercely independent. The board employs an executive director to supervise the fund-raising, long-range planning, and other activities.

See Clarence F. Judah, *Unity in Community* (Louisville, 1974).

Herman Landau

JEWS. The first Jewish settlers in the Louisville area—men such as John Jacob, who was apparently resident near the city as early as 1802 and later became a Louisville councilman, and the Heymann or Hyman brothers, who came about 1814—had no real possibility of perpetuating Jewish life on the frontier. They tended to abandon most Jewish practices, marry non-Jews, and raise families that identified with Christianity. It was in the decade of the 1830s that the first Jewish communal institutions arose in the city. An Israelite Benevolent Society with at least ten members was listed in the first Louisville city directory of 1832, and, although this original Jewish organization seems to have ceased functioning as its earliest members moved on, new Jewish arrivals established regular religious services about 1838. Louisville's first Jewish congregation, which was also Kentucky's, dates from 1842 when the Jews who had been meeting for worship gave their prayer group the name Adath Israel (Congregation of Israel) and acquired a charter from the state.

During the decades of the 1840s and 1850s Louisville's Jewish POPULATION grew substantially, as hundreds of immigrants from the German states of Europe or from adjacent areas, such as Alsace or Prussian Poland (Posen), arrived in the city. A second Jewish congregation, known first as the Polish House of Israel and soon after as Beth Israel, was established in the city in 1851; and a third congregation, Brith Sholom, was organized in 1880. In that year

Louisville was home to some twenty-five hundred of Kentucky's thirty-six hundred Jews, and its Jewish community was the thirteenth-largest in the United States.

Like most Jews arriving in the United States in the middle decades of the nineteenth century, those who settled in Louisville came both to escape the discrimination they faced in Europe and to seek economic advancement. In several ways these so-called "German Jews" maintained their distinctive identities; they not only organized congregations but also schools, welfare associations, burial societies, and social organizations. As early as 1852 a lodge of the fraternal order B'NAI B'RITH was chartered in Louisville, and the Standard Club (later the Standard Country Club) was established as a downtown gathering place for Jews in 1883. Like other German immigrant groups, Louisville's early Jews also maintained elements of their specifically German culture; some synagogue minutes were still being written in German as late as the 1880s.

Nonetheless, Louisville's German Jews became integrated into local society quite rapidly. Their acculturation is reflected in the fact that many were early supporters of the Reform movement in Judaism. Reform was championed by Rabbi Isaac Mayer Wise of Cincinnati and promoted the idea that, in adapting to a modern environment, Jewish practice should abandon strict adherence to Jewish law and borrow some of the religious customs of the majority culture. Among Louisville's three earliest congregations, only the relatively small Beth Israel remained strictly Orthodox. Symbolizing both the integration and the self-confidence of the local Jewish community was the impressive temple erected by congregation Adath Israel in 1868. Designed by H.P. Bradshaw, one of Louisville's foremost church architects, it was prominently located on BROADWAY at Sixth St.

The entry of Louisville's German-Jewish citizens into local civic and political affairs and their central roles in local commercial development were also indicators of their rapid acculturation. Although many of Louisville's German Jews began their lives in America as peddlers, store clerks, or small shopkeepers, a few rose to prominence as leading entrepreneurs in the city. By the end of the nineteenth century, Jews were liberally represented in the professions as well. Around 1900 the city's most prominent Jews included the distiller and philanthropist Isaac W. Bernheim; clothiers Henry and Moses Levy; dry goods magnate Henry Kaufman; attorney Aaron Kohn, Jefferson County prosecutor and a three-term Louisville alderman in the 1880s; and lawyer and scholar LEWIS DEMBITZ, city tax attorney from 1884 to 1888 and the uncle of Brandeis. Louis Brandeis, born and raised in Louisville, served on the Supreme Court from 1916 to 1939, making him the first Jew to hold the position. A liberal, Brandeis supported reforms of the Progressive Era and upheld the constitutionality of most New Deal legislation.

By the beginning of the twentieth century, the character of Louisville's Jewish population had begun to change dramatically, for in the half century after 1880 a new wave of Jewish immigrants arrived in the city, this time coming from Eastern Europe rather than the German states. Like their predecessors, the East Europeans came to America in search of more tolerant conditions (one cause of their migration was the series of pogroms that followed the assassination of Czar Alexander II in 1881). They were also seeking economic opportunity. Some of the new immigrants entered into commercial activity in the same way that Louisville's German Jews had, but the East Europeans were far more likely than their predecessors to become wage earners in trades such as tailoring or cigar-making. By 1927 Louisville's Jewish population had expanded to 12,500, and it was one of the nation's 39 cities with Jewish communities of more than 10,000.

Despite the similarities between the German Jews and their East Europe successors, there was also some distance between these two groups. Jewish society in Eastern Europe had been rather isolated and inward-looking. As East Europeans sought ways to adapt to their new surroundings, they found it difficult to identify with the Americanized Jewish lifestyle that had developed in Louisville during the nineteenth century. For their part, many of the more established Jews of Louisville found the East Europeans quite alien. While most of the German Jewish families of the city had achieved at least middle-class status and a great many of them had abandoned traditional Jewish practice, the East Europeans arriving in the city tended to be of a lower social and economic order, and they were much more comfortable with traditional Judaism. Even if not all were rigorously observant, they knew Judaism only in its Orthodox form, and they retained a strong ethnic and cultural identity tied intimately to their Yiddish vernacular.

Louisville's East European Jews tended to cluster in a highly cohesive downtown neighborhood centered on Preston St., which some referred to as a shtetl, using the Yiddish term applied to the self-contained Jewish communities of East European villages. Because the city's existing organizations often did not fulfill their needs, they created a whole new set of Jewish institutions. As the accompanying table indicates, five new Jewish congregations were established in Louisville between 1882 and 1905, and at least four of these were Orthodox in outlook, by-products of the influx of East European Jews. Moreover, the Orthodox congregations of Louisville, together with the traditionalist congregation Adath JESHURUN, tried to replicate the kind of integrated, organic Jewish community that had characterized Jewish life in Eastern Europe by centralizing many communal functions and creating a single rabbinic authority for the city. In 1902 they established the United Hebrew Orthodox Congregations, and they brought Rabbi Asher L. Zarchy to Louisville as its head. Zarchy was succeeded in 1933 by Ben Zion Notelevitz.

The attempt to maintain a unified ecclesiastical structure for Louisville's Jewish community was doomed to failure in an environment where recognition of a central religious authority could not be enforced and where individual congregations soon developed their own identities. However, the United Hebrew Orthodox Congregations did undertake several initiatives that were essential for the maintenance of traditionalist Jewish life in Louisville. This umbrella organization supervised the provision of kosher food, maintained the community's ritual bath, and organized the Louisville Talmud Torah Society to provide the kind of Jewish education that was considered vital by the city's East European Jews.

Because East Europeans thought of their Jewishness in ethnic and cultural terms as well as in religious terms, the new institutions they created were not limited to those that would serve religious needs only. There was a Yiddish Literary Society established in Louisville sometime around World War I, and there were also a number of Zionist associations organized in the city to promote the creation of a Jewish national home in Palestine. As early as 1907 there were already three Zionist circles in Louisville, and a chapter of the women's Zionist organization HADASSAH was established in 1919.

Despite the differences between Louisville's more established Jews and their newly arrived East European co-religionists, the two groups were not completely divorced. Some organizations supported primarily by German Jews, such as the local branch of the National Council of Jewish Women that was established in 1893, initiated projects to aid Jewish immigrants. The city's indigenous Jews also founded several new philanthropic institutions to help immigrants adjust. Among these was a restructured Young Men's Hebrew Association (YMHA), incorporated in 1890, the forerunner of the JEWISH COMMUNITY CENTER. In the early 1900s, the YMHA sponsored activities such as gym classes, outings to PARKS and playgrounds, English language courses, and a cooperative program with NEIGHBORHOOD HOUSE, itself organized in 1896 as a social service agency on First St., within Louisville's so-called shtetl district.

Another institution created by the established community was Jewish Hospital, founded in 1903 to provide facilities for Jewish doctors who were routinely denied staff privileges elsewhere and also to cater to the needs of the growing number of East Europeans in the city who required medical care. These Yiddish-speaking patients were frequently indigent, and they were likely to be uncomfortable in medical centers that were unfamiliar with Jewish dietary laws and religious customs.

By 1909 the number of welfare organizations to aid Louisville's expanding Jewish population had proliferated to such an extent that a

Federation of Jewish Charities was created to bring some order to Jewish welfare work. This body became the Jewish Welfare Federation by 1918 and the Jewish Social Service Agency in 1951. In 1934 a second coordinating body was established: the Louisville Conference of Jewish Organizations. Intended primarily as a fund-raising agency, over time the conference developed into the local Jewish community's main coordinating, planning, and community relations body as well, adopting the name JEWISH COMMUNITY FEDERATION of Louisville in 1971.

By the late 1920s, the dramatic growth of Louisville's Jewish population slowed as restrictionist American legislation reduced Jewish immigration from Europe to a trickle. In the interwar period, some Jews, including musicologist Gerhard Herz and art historian Justus Bier, did arrive in Louisville as they fled Nazi Germany, but in general the size of the city's Jewish community began to decline by the 1940s. Louisville's Jewish population was estimated to be 13,800 in 1937, 9,000 in 1947, 8,500 in 1960, and 9,200 in 1980. In the latter decades of the twentieth century, the only significant Jewish immigrants arriving in Louisville from overseas were perhaps eight hundred new Americans from the former Soviet Union. However, domestic migration remained an important factor in the composition of the city's Jewish community. In 1991, Louisville's Jewish population was reported to be eighty-seven hundred, with only about 38 percent of Jewish Louisvillians having lived in the city all their lives.

In the decades after World War II, many of the national trends in American Jewish life were reflected in Louisville's Jewish community. For example, the increasing acculturation of all American Jews resulted in faded distinctions between German Jews and East European Jews. The latter became as visible in public life as the former. For example, in 1983 CHARLES LEIBSON became a justice of the Kentucky Supreme Court, and in 1985 Jerry Abramson was elected mayor of Louisville.

Another postwar development was the movement of Jews out of the city's downtown area, reflecting the increasing affluence of the community. This migration, which had begun in the interwar period, accelerated after World War II. Initially, Louisville's Jews moved primarily into the HIGHLANDS neighborhood, and their institutions followed. Brith Sholom was the first synagogue to relocate, in 1949, and the Jewish Community Center opened its new facility on Dutchmans Lane in 1955. By 1965 four of Louisville's five synagogues were in the Highlands; and in 1979, next door to the Jewish Center, the Shalom Tower was erected. This building provided 150 units of subsidized housing for senior citizens. It also housed the offices of the Louisville Jewish Federation and of the Jewish Family and Vocational Service, created in 1978 by the merger of the Jewish Social Service Agency and the Jewish Vocational Service.

Toward the end of the twentieth century, Louisville's Jews began to move even farther away from the central city. Although the Highlands remained home to three of Louisville's older congregations and to the informally organized Beth Israel congregation (an Orthodox group not associated with the original Louisville congregation of that name), only about 20 percent of Louisville Jews lived in the 40205 postal zone, which includes the Highlands. The city's Reform congregations also were located away from this first area of suburban settlement as well. In 1976 Adath Israel and Brith Sholom had merged to form The TEMPLE, and that congregation had dedicated a new sanctuary on Brownsboro Rd. in 1980. A group that opposed the merger of the two congregations established TEMPLE SHALOM, and that congregation dedicated a synagogue on Lowe Rd. near Jeffersontown in 1989.

Other national patterns reflected in local Jewish life include an increasing departure from endogamous marriage practices and a tendency to disregard ritual observance. A 1991 study revealed that, whereas more than 95 percent of married Louisville Jews over age sixty-five were wed to others who were born Jewish, only about 80 percent of married Louisville Jews between the ages of twenty-five and forty-five had spouses who were born Jewish. Only 25 percent of Louisville Jews reported regularly lighting Sabbath candles on Friday night or attending religious services often, and fewer than 20 percent said they observed the Jewish dietary laws, even at home. On the other hand, at 77 percent, congregational affiliation among Louisville Jews was very high by national standards, and in the mid-1990s the Jewish Federation's United Jewish Campaign was raising about $2.5 million annually to meet Jewish needs locally, nationally, and overseas, mainly in the state of Israel. In Louisville, as in many other American cities, some aspects of local Jewish life suggest great vitality, while others indicate a decline in Jewish identity.

See Herman Landau, *Adath Louisville: The Story of a Jewish Community* (Louisville 1981); Lee Shai Weissbach, *The Synagogues of Kentucky: Architecture and History* (Lexington 1995); Jewish Historical Society, *A History of the Jews of*

Louisville Synagogues

Congregation	*Location*	*Dates*
Adath Israel		1842–1977
	Fourth St. between Green (Liberty) and Walnut (Muhammad Ali Blvd.)	(1849–66)
	Sixth and Broadway	(1868–1906)
	832 Third St.	(1906–77)
Beth Israel		1851–94
	127 W Green St.	(1857–94)
Brith Sholom		1880–1977
	613 First St.	(1881–1903)
	753 S Second St.	(1903–50)
	1649 Cowling Ave.	(1950–77)
B'nai Jacob		1882–1926
	454 E Jefferson St.	(1891–1926)
Beth Hamedrash Hagodol		1887–1926
	339 S Preston St.	(1905–26)
Anshei Sfard		1893–present
	613 First St.	(1903–58)
	3600 Dutchmans Ln.	(1958–)
Adath Jeshurun		1894–present
	228 E Chestnut St.	(1894–1919)
	757 S Brook St.	(1919–57)
	2401 Woodbourne Ave.	(1957–)
Agudath Achim		1905–71
	1115 W Jefferson St.	(1917–64)
Keneseth Israel		1926–present
	339 S Preston St.	(1926–29)
	232 E Jacob Ave.	(1929–64)
	2531 Taylorsville Rd.	(1964–)
Temple Shalom		1976–present
	4220 Taylorsville Rd.	(1981–89)
	4615 Lowe Rd.	(1989–)
The Temple		1976–present
	1649 Cowling Ave.	(1977–80)
	5101 Brownsboro Rd.	(1980–)
Beth Israel		1985–present
	1663 Almara Circle	(1985–)

Louisville, Ky. (New Orleans 1901); Gary A. Tobin and Gabriel Berger, "The Jewish Community Federation of Louisville Demographic and Attitudinal Study" (Waltham, Mass., 1991); Ira Rosenwaike, "The First Jewish Settlers in Louisville," *Filson Club History Quarterly* 53 (Jan. 1979): 37-45; Betty Lou Amster and Barbara Zingman, *A Legendary Vision: The History of Jewish Hospital* (Louisville 1997).

Lee Shai Weissbach

JIM BEAM DISTILLERY. The Jim Beam Distillery, located on 430 acres of land in Clermont, BULLITT COUNTY, is Kentucky's oldest continuing business. The turn of the millennium will mark its third century of bourbon distillation.

Six generations have guided the Beam family enterprise. Jacob Beam, family patriarch, farmer, and miller, emigrated from Germany and came through the Cumberland Gap and settled in Kentucky shortly before statehood. Within twenty miles of the present distillery, Jacob operated a water millstone that ground grain, principally sweet corn. He distilled surplus corn, rye, and barley into whiskey. By 1795 he had devoted his entire operation to the commercial production and sale of bourbon. The operation prospered. By 1820, when his son David had taken over the business, Beam family bourbon was being shipped by river to New Orleans and then overseas.

David's son, David M. Beam, was born in 1833. At the age of seventeen he became head of the family concern. With the death of his father in 1854, he relocated the distillery, now called the Clear Spring Distillery, to Nelson County to be nearer to the railroad.

In 1864 James "Jim" Beauregard Beam, son of David M., was born. At the age of sixteen he began work in the distillery and by 1894, at the age of thirty, had become head of the family business. Under his leadership the business prospered for twenty-five years. PROHIBITION, in 1920, closed the distillery. Beam sold all of his liquor holdings, and for the next fourteen years he pursued other business interests unrelated to bourbon. Prohibition was repealed in 1933. On August 14, 1934, septuagenarian Beam founded and incorporated the James B. Beam Distilling Co. in Clermont. In 1947, at the age of eighty-three, he died, having devoted fifty-two years to the Kentucky bourbon industry. In 1946 his son, T. Jeremiah Beam, became president and treasurer of the company. He, in turn, trained his nephew, F. Booker Noe Jr., who in 1999 was master distiller emeritus for the company.

The distillery has a tourist facility on its grounds, the Jim Beam American Outpost. In 1999, on a daily basis, the distillery produced thirty thousand cases of bourbon. A total of 750 barrels, each barrel containing 53 gallons of aged whiskey, is dumped daily for bottling. There are fifty-one warehouses, each with a capacity to store twenty thousand barrels, on the distillery grounds. Outside the United States, Jim Beam bourbon is bottled in seventeen foreign countries and is the world's best-selling Kentucky bourbon.

Mickey List Jr.

JIM CROW. Some authors claim Cincinnati or Pittsburgh as the origin of the usage of the term "Jim Crow," which came to mean SEGREGATION of AFRICAN AMERICANS. However, two eyewitness accounts place the event in Louisville during a performance at SAMUEL DRAKE's City Theatre (the former Louisville Theatre) on May 21, 1830. Located on the north side of Jefferson St. between Third and FOURTH Streets, the THEATER housed a traveling company of players from New York. THOMAS D. RICE, a bit player in the company, appeared in "The Kentucky Rifle, or a Prairie Narrative," as Sambo. He incorporated a song and dance described in the program as "the comic Negro song of 'Jim Crow.'"

Near the City Theatre was a livery stable kept by a man named Crowe, who owned an arthritic slave named Jim Crowe. As Jim Crowe worked, he sang, shuffled his feet, and hopped about on his stiff limbs in a peculiar dance while tending to the horses. Rice studied Jim Crowe at work and created a new stage character modeled on the old man: a blackface character who danced and sang a song called "Jump Jim Crow."

The first night Rice performed as Jim Crow, the act was such a success that he received twenty curtain calls. This stage act quickly became nationally famous, and the phrase "Jim Crow" entered the vernacular. The song was published in Pittsburgh in 1830 by William C. Peters. "Jim Crow," which paved the way for the blackface minstrel show, was an almost instant success, catapulting Rice to national fame and earning him the title of "father of American MINSTRELSY."

See Dale Cockrell, "Jim Crow, demon of disorder," *American Music* 14 (Summer 1996): 161–84; Laurence Hutton, *Curiosities of the American Stage* (New York 1891); *Louisville Public Advertiser,* May 1830; Molly N. Ramshaw, "Jump, Jim Crow! A Biographical Sketch of Thomas D. Rice (1808–1860)," *The Theatre Annual* 17 (1960): 36–47; George H. Yater, *Two Hundred Years at the Falls of the Ohio* (Louisville 1987); West T. Hill Jr., *Theatre in Early Kentucky* (Lexington 1971).

Jane D. Julian

J.J.B. HILLIARD, W.L. LYONS INC. Hilliard Lyons is among the largest investment BANKING and securities brokerage firms in the Ohio Valley as well as one of the oldest. The firm and its predecessors have been serving investors since 1850, although in recent years, 1854 has become recognized as the founding date.

The banking house of Quigley, Lyons & Co. was begun in 1857 in the booming OHIO RIVER trade center of Louisville. However, during the CIVIL WAR, Thomas Quigley died and Henry J. Lyons went to Montreal and then New York, where he established the private banking firm bearing his name. He died in 1867 at the age of 39. His son, WILLIAM LEE LYONS, and James Heffernan formed a brokerage firm, W.L. Lyons & Co., dealing in provisions and grain in 1881. When Heffernan departed, W.L. Lyons took in his brother, Harry J. Lyons, and in 1905 purchased a seat on the New York Stock Exchange for his son, Samuel Clay Lyons. When the latter retired in 1933, his brother, W.L. Lyons, Jr., assumed direction of the firm.

In the meantime, North Carolina native John James Byron Hilliard was in the cotton trade in New Orleans when he met Maria Henning Hobbs of Louisville. They were married in 1871 and in 1872, the 1852 graduate of the Harvard Law School and GEORGE KEATS Speed joined A.D. Hunt in his firm, A.D. Hunt & Co., which Hunt had established in Louisville in 1850. After Hunt died in 1885, Hilliard struck out on his own. In 1897, his son, J.J.B. Hilliard, Jr., joined the firm. Subsequently, his sons, Isaac and EDWARD HOBBS HILLIARD, were taken in, while the firm retained the name, J.J.B. Hilliard & Son. In 1924, the firm purchased a seat on the New York Stock Exchange.

When J.J.B. Hilliard & Son and W.L. Lyons & Co. merged in 1965, J. Henning Hilliard continued his role of managing partner. He served 1968-71 as the only governor of the New York Stock Exchange from Kentucky. When the firm incorporated in 1972, Hilliard became chairman of the board.

By 1988 the company, located since merger in The Madrid Building at Third and Guthrie streets, had outgrown its headquarters. The former Stewart Dry Goods building at Fourth and MUHAMMAD ALI Boulevard was purchased and renovated as the Hilliard Lyons Center. Currently the firm operates more than a hundred branches in 16 states, serving a quarter of a million investors.

In 1998 PNC Bank Corp reached an agreement to acquire Hilliard Lyons for $275 million in cash and stock. While Hilliard Lyons remains autonomous, its affiliation with PNC BANK provides access to new markets in eastern states.

Stephen Brown

JOE HUBER FAMILY FARM AND RESTAURANT, HUBER ORCHARD AND WINERY. Home to seven generations of Hubers since 1843, the Joe Huber Family Farm and Restaurant in Starlight, Indiana, has become a favorite country-style restaurant and working farm open to visitors year-round. Simon Huber migrated from Baden-Baden, Germany, in 1843, bringing apple trees to plant at his new home in Starlight.

A member of the fourth generation, Joseph Huber Sr., and his wife, Mary, bought the land now known as the Joe Huber Family Farm in

1926. They and their family of eleven children grew fruits and vegetables and raised cattle and chickens. Joe Huber Jr. continued to help on the farm as an adult but also worked for the Indiana Gas Co. Following Joseph Senior's death in 1967, Joe Junior and his wife, Bonnie, purchased the farm and moved there with their five children. Joe Junior left the gas company to farm full-time, supplementing his income by driving a school bus. The same year they acquired the farm, the younger Hubers invited the public to pick their own green beans and began opening the farm to visitors. They soon constructed a farm market to sell the pickers the vegetables they gathered. In 1983 they added the country-style restaurant. The farm offers guided tractor and wagon rides and is well known for its seasonal offerings of pumpkins and Christmas trees.

The nearby Huber Winery is Indiana's largest estate-bottle winery, with its own farm market, cheese factory, petting zoo, wine tastings, and vineyard tours. The winery was established in the early 1970s by Gerald and Carl Huber, who were also descendants of Simon Huber. Gerald's son, Ted, succeeded him as the winemaker and operator of the winery.

See promotional material, Joe Huber Family Farm and Restaurant brochure, *The World Looks Different from Here, Starlight, Indiana*; Robin Garr, "Growing the Grape," *Louisville 49* (Sept. 1, 1998): 44-48.

Mary Margaret Bell

JOE LEY ANTIQUES. Joe Ley, an orphan, started this unique business in the early 1960s repairing cast-off furniture. It has developed into one of Louisville's most unusual establishments, as much a museum as it is an antique store. In 1982 Ley moved the antique business to 615 E Market St. in the former Hiram Roberts Normal School, built in 1890. This three-story building with two acres of floor space is filled with acquisitions from various estates. They include architectural and builders' antique supplies such as doors, mantels, balconies, hardware, fences, gates, posts, newels, and ornaments. One finds clowns, carousel animals, chandeliers, brass of all kinds, antique toys and furniture, china, silver, and collectibles of all types.

Joe Ley has provided special pieces for hundreds of restaurants. Constantly changing inventory attracts people from all points of the United States and abroad who might have read of the establishment in *House Beautiful, Travel & Leisure,* or *Apartment Life*. Joe Ley Antiques imports, exports, provides rental props for the movie industry, and is a popular place for filming of country music videos, movies, and commercials. Some customers of note include Mark Harmon, Jonathan Winters, Penny Marshall, Johnny Cash, Andy Williams, and Robert Goulet.

Jerome W. "Jerry" Ostertag

JOHN CONTI COFFEE COMPANY. The john conti Coffee Co. is Louisville's largest coffee company and the only coffee roaster that imports, roasts, grinds, and packages high-quality whole-bean and ground gourmet coffees. In 1997 the company had four divisions that served over fifty-four hundred office, restaurant, and institutional customers.

John Conti began his company in 1962 with an eighteen-hundred-dollar loan and a 1949 Chevrolet from which he delivered and filled cigarette machines. It was at this time that the john conti Vending Co. was founded. Conti had a burning desire to develop the best vending service in town. Growth was imminent, and in 1971 the john conti Co. installed its first coffee unit in an office location.

The first john conti Gourmet Coffee Shoppe opened in OXMOOR Center on December 13, 1976. One year later the second shop was inaugurated in the BASHFORD MANOR Mall. As the gourmet coffees' popularity increased, the need for better-quality coffee in fine RESTAURANTS and HOTELS became apparent. In 1977, the company began to supply restaurants, hotels and HOSPITALS with "The Best Coffee in Town®" through its institutional division.

In order to concentrate on growth and development of the coffee company, the vending operation was sold in 1982. In that same year John Conti installed his first coffee roaster to assure that each roast upholds his high standards of quality. In 1988, the wholesale division was established to sell gourmet coffees to supermarkets and specialty stores.

Noted for buying the very best 100 percent Arabican coffee beans available in the world, JOHN CONTI COFFEE CO. was first selected in 1977 by *LOUISVILLE TODAY MAGAZINE* as "The Best Coffee in Town®" and has won that distinction in every contest since. In 1990, the company was awarded a federal copyright on "The Best Coffee in Town®."

Debbie Redmond

JOHNSON, LYMAN TEFFT (b Columbia, Tennessee, June 12, 1906; d Louisville, October 3, 1997). CIVIL RIGHTS leader and educator. Lyman Tefft Johnson, grandson of slaves, pursued the twin beacons of education and equality to become a legendary educator, reformer, and social activist in Louisville. He was the eighth of nine children of Mary Dew and Robert Graves Johnson. He was named after Lyman Beecher Tefft, who had been one of his father's instructors at Roger Williams University in Nashville, Tennessee. College Hill School, where his father was principal, took him through eleven grades, which was as far as the only school for black students in Columbia could go. Two additional years at Knoxville Academy, a division of Knoxville College, enabled him to gain his high school diploma in 1927. In 1930 Virginia Union University in Richmond awarded him a bachelor's degree following his studies of ancient languages, history,

Lyman Johnson.

and English. After a year at the University of Michigan, he received his masters degree in history in 1931.

Beginning work in 1933 as a teacher of history, economics, and mathematics at Louisville's Central (Colored) High School, he took on the additional duties of athletic business manager for twenty-five of his thirty-three "perfect attendance" teaching years at Central. Seven years as an assistant principal at PARKLAND Junior High, Manley Junior High, and FLAGET HIGH SCHOOL for Boys capped a remarkable forty-year span in Jefferson County schools. Four additional years as a member of the Jefferson County BOARD OF EDUCATION, from 1978 to 1982, closed out his formal career as an educator.

The more noteworthy of his numerous accomplishments are: successful plaintiff in federal court to desegregate the University of Kentucky (1949), successful equalization of white and Negro teachers' salaries in Louisville (1941), and a principal plaintiff in federal court for the "merger and desegregation" of Louisville and Jefferson County PUBLIC SCHOOLS (1972-75). His leadership in sit-ins and protests led to eventual opening of public accommodations, RESTAURANTS, THEATERS, LIBRARIES, PARKS, and PUBLIC HOUSING.

Johnson filled leadership positions in numerous organizations such as Louisville Association of Teachers in Colored Schools, American Federation of Teachers, Louisville Education Association, KENTUCKY EDUCATION ASSOCIATION, Kentucky Negro Education Association, National Association for the Advancement of Colored People, Alpha Phi Alpha Fraternity Inc., and PLYMOUTH CONGREGATIONAL UNITED CHURCH OF CHRIST, where he was a deacon for forty years, including twelve years as chairman. Throughout his distinguished career, awards, accolades, honors, and distinctions kept pace with his multiple endeavors. He was recognized by presidents; governors; mayors; elected officials; religious, political, and educational leaders; peers; colleagues; associates; and former students. In the documentation of over three hundred personal citations are included four honorary doctorate degrees, a national commendation from Common Cause (1996), the Governor's Distinguished Service Medallion (1995), and the All-American Award from the University of Kentucky Alumni Association (1993). A local school has been renamed in his honor.

Johnson married Juanita Morrell in 1936. They had two children, Florence Yvonne and Lyman Morrell. Johnson was a navy veteran of WORLD WAR II. His body was donated to the UNIVERSITY OF LOUISVILLE School of MEDICINE.

See the collected papers of Lyman T. Johnson, University Archives, University of Louisville; Wade Hall, *The Rest of the Dream: The Black Odyssey of Lyman Johnson* (Lexington 1988).

Walter W. Hutchins

JOHNSON, TOM LOFTIN (b Blue Spring, Kentucky, July 18, 1854; d Cleveland, Ohio, April 10, 1911). Street railway entrepreneur, inventor, and politician. Johnson was the son of Col. Albert and Helen (Loftin) Johnson. The family's support of the Confederate cause led to the loss of the family fortune, necessitating a move to Stauton, Virginia, where the colonel's family had its roots. There the eleven-year-old Johnson acquired a monopoly selling newspapers on a train, enabling him to pay for his family's return to Kentucky, where they settled this time in Louisville. In 1869 he took a job with the Central Passenger Railway Co., a street railway owned by brothers Bidermann and Victor du Pont. He became superintendent in 1873 and worked there through 1875, building his fortune with such inventions as the see-through glass fare box for streetcars that prevented drivers from stealing fares. With that money and a thirty-thousand-dollar loan from Bidermann du Pont, he began his street railway ventures.

The first business acquired by Johnson was the Indianapolis Street Railway, purchased about 1876 on a trip to sell his fare boxes in that city. Johnson helped reorganize the company with financial assistance from the du Pont brothers, John Churchill, and other Louisvillians before selling to a Chicago company for a profit. Over time his interests in the street railways spread to St. Louis, Cleveland, Detroit, and Brooklyn, including the first traction line over the Brooklyn Bridge. In 1879 Johnson moved to Cleveland with his wife, Margaret, to take advantage of what he perceived to be a great business opportunity. After establishing a street railway strongly competitive with the existing system controlled by Mark Hanna, Johnson expanded his interest to steel, establishing companies in Johnstown, Pennsylvania, and Lorain, Ohio. These plants produced steel rails, including a new type of streetcar rail invented by Johnson while he was in Louisville. His plants were later absorbed by United States Steel Co.

In 1890 Johnson entered the political arena, his interest sparked by the writings of Henry George and the topics of free trade and the single tax. He was elected that year to Congress as a Democrat and served two terms from March 4, 1891, to March 3, 1895. After returning to Cleveland and retiring from his business interests, in 1901 Johnson was elected mayor. During his admininstration Cleveland became known as the best-governed city in the United States. As mayor he encouraged open discussions of city issues, arguing against monopolistic practices and for municipal control of utilities. He also organized a municipally owned streetcar system with a three-cent fare. Bidermann du Pont Jr. served as president. In 1909 Johnson failed to win reelection largely because of his attempts at reform, which were not looked upon favorably by local businessmen; however, his attention to the will of "common people" earned him the respect and high regard of many. He is buried in Greenwood Cemetery in Brooklyn near Henry George.

Annie Fellows Johnston (right) with Hattie Cochran, c. 1907.

See *Biographical Directory of the American Congress, 1776-1961* (Washington, D.C., 1961); David D. Van Tassel, *The Encyclopedia of Cleveland History* (Bloomington, Ind., 1987); Eugene C. Murdock, *Tom Johnson of Cleveland* (Dayton, Ohio, 1994); Michael Massouth, "Technological and Managerial Innovation: The Johnson Company, 1883-1898," *Business History Review* (Spring 1976): 46-68; idem, "Innovations in Street Railways before Electric Traction: Tom L Johnson's Contributions," *Technology and Culture 18* (April 1977): 202-17; Tom Johnson, *My Story* (New York 1915).

JOHNSTON, ANNIE FELLOWS (b Evansville, Indiana, May 15, 1863; d PEWEE VALLEY, Kentucky, October 5, 1931). Children's author. Her parents were Rev. Albion and Mary (Erskine) Fellows. After attending the McCutchansville, Indiana, district school and Evansville PUBLIC SCHOOLS and then studying one year at the State University of Iowa, Johnston taught school, worked in an office, and traveled in New England and Europe. She married her cousin, William L. Johnston, on October 11, 1888, in Evansville, Indiana. When he died four years later, she supported herself and her three stepchildren (Mary, Rena, and John) through publication of more than thirty books. Her first is entitled *Big Brother* (1893) and is based on an Iowa summer with her sister, Albion. It is representative of her work, blending personal experience with imagination.

Best known for the "Little Colonel" series–twelve novels published between l895 and 1912–Johnston immortalized Pewee Valley, a commuter village in OLDHAM COUNTY, as "Lloydsboro Valley." There, Johnston met young Hattie Cochran, the prototype for her main character. At the time, Cochran, later Mrs. Albert Dick of Louisville, was visiting her grandfather, Confederate colonel George Weissinger, at his home, the Locust. The "Little Colonel" series chronicles Lloyd Sherman's experiences from age five until her engagement and includes allegories and legends later published as the "Johnston Jewel" series. Most "Little Colonel" volumes were written in less than a year and marketed by L.C. Page and Co. at Christmas. Johnston inspired her readers to dream, yet tackle simple tasks cheerfully. Encouraging children to "only mark the hours that shine," she introduced *The Little Colonel Good Times Book* as a record for joys to sustain its diarist during bad experiences.

As her popularity grew, Johnston allowed her readers' letters to influence her work. Emulating the characters they loved, American children formed Little Colonel clubs, wore Tusitala rings as symbols of the road of the loving heart, strung strands of pearls for days well spent, and presented charity performances of the play *The Rescue of the Princess Winsome*. Two other popular titles were *Georgina of the Rainbows* (1916) and *Georgina's Service Stars* (1918).

In 1898 Johnston moved to Pewee Valley, where she resided most of the rest of her life. Her only significant period away from Kentucky occurred between 1901 and 1910, when her stepson's health caused the family to travel to New York and to reside in Arizona, California, and Texas. In April 1911 Johnston purchased the Beeches in Pewee Valley, the destination of many fans' pilgrimages.

An active member in the Author's Club, a Louisville group of women writers, Johnston was elected vice president of the League of American Pen Women in 1922. In 1935 Shirley Temple's film version of *The Little Colonel* premiered in Louisville and sustained Johnston's popularity. As early examples of marketing to child moviegoers, *Little Colonel* investors created merchandise as diverse as girls' clothing, shoes, toothbrushes, pocketbooks, puzzles, games, and notebook paper. Johnston is buried in Evansville, Indiana.

See Annie Fellows Johnston, *The Land of the Little Colonel: Reminiscence and Autobiography* (Boston 1929); Sue Lynn McGuire, "The Little Colonel: A Phenomenon in Popular Literary Culture," *Register of the Kentucky Historical Society* 89 (Spring 1991): 121-46; Ray B. Browne et al., *Challenges in American Culture* (Bowling Green, Ohio, 1970).

Sue Lynn Stone

JOHNSTON, JOSIAH STODDARD (b near New Orleans, February 10, 1833; d Clayton, Missouri, October 4, 1913). Historian and journalist. Johnston was born on a plantation to John Harris and Eliza Ellen (Davidson) Johnston. After studying LAW at Yale, he married Eliza Johnson in 1854, and they had five children: Mary, Eliza, George, Harris, and Stoddard Junior. During the CIVIL WAR Johnston served in the Confederate army and reached the rank of lieutenant colonel. Following the war he relocated to Frankfort to pursue a career in journalism. There he served as editor of the *Kentucky Yeoman*, helped establish the Kentucky Press Association, and from 1875 to 1879 served as secretary of state. By the 1870s Johnston was well established as a popular political writer and an orator, and was one of the leading forces in Kentucky's Democratic Party.

In 1889 Johnston moved to Louisville to continue his writing career. During the late 1890s he published three scholarly accounts of Kentucky history, *A Memorial History of Louisville* (an edited work) (1896), *First Explorations of Kentucky* (1898), and *A Confederate History of Kentucky* (1898). Johnston also served as vice president of the Filson Club from 1893 to 1913 and was associate editor of the *COURIER-JOURNAL* from 1903 to 1908. He is buried in CAVE HILL CEMETERY. An elementary school, now closed, was named after him on Bradley Ave. in the St. Joseph's neighborhood.

See George Baber, "Colonel J. Stoddard Johnston," *Register of the Kentucky State Historical Society* 14 (Jan. 1916): 9-13.

Aaron D. Purcell

JOHNSTON, WILLIAM PRESTON (b Louisville, January 5, 1831; d Lexington, Virginia, July 16, 1899). Lawyer, educator, and writer. Johnston was the eldest son of Henrietta (Preston) and Confederate general Albert Sydney Johnston. His mother died when he was four years old, and his father left for Texas soon after, leaving Johnston to be raised by his mother's family. He attended PUBLIC SCHOOLS in Louisville and later the academy of S.V. Womack in SHELBYVILLE, Kentucky. Johnston attended Centre College at Danville and the Western Military Institute at Georgetown, Kentucky. He graduated from Yale in 1852 and studied LAW at the UNIVERSITY OF LOUISVILLE. In the spring of 1853 he opened a practice in Louisville.

At the outbreak of the CIVIL WAR, Johnston joined the Confederate army and was made a major in the Second Kentucky Regiment. He rapidly advanced to lieutenant colonel. After being stricken with pneumonia, Johnston served as aide-de-camp to President Jefferson Davis, with the rank of colonel, starting in May 1862. At the end of the war, Johnston was held captive and kept in solitary confinement along with Davis for several months at Fortress Monroe in Virginia.

After being released, he spent nearly a year in exile in Canada before returning to his Louisville law practice. In 1867 he became chairman of the department of history and English LITERATURE at Washington University in Lexington, Virginia, a position offered by the university's president, Gen. Robert E. Lee. He held this position until 1877. Johnston was made president of Louisiana State University at Baton Rouge in 1880. Two years later he began to organize the University of Louisiana in New Orleans. It was renamed Tulane University in 1884, and Johnston was its president until his death.

Johnston's biography of his father, *The Life of General Albert Sidney Johnston* (1878), describes his father in the grandest and noblest terms and is one of the best accounts of the Battle of Shiloh. His other works include *The Prototype of Hamlet and Other Shakespearean Problems* (1890), a series of lectures delivered at Tulane University, as well as three books of POETRY: *My Garden Walk* (1894), *Picture of the Patriarchs* (1895), and *Seekers after God: Sonnets* (1898). He also wrote his family record, *The Johnstons of Salisbury*, published in 1897.

Johnston married Rosa Elizabeth Duncan of New Orleans on July 7, 1853. They had six children–Albert Sydney, Henrietta, Rosa, Margaret, Mary, and Caroline. His first wife died on October 19, 1885, and he married Margaret Henshaw Avery of Louisiana on April 25, 1888. Johnston is buried in CAVE HILL CEMETERY.

See William Preston Johnston, *The Johnstons of Salisbury* (New Orleans 1897); *Courier Journal*, July 18, 1899.

JOINER, HARVEY (b Charlestown, Indiana, April 8, 1852; d Lincoln Heights, Indiana, May 30, 1932). Artist. Born to Charles and Elizabeth (Tophouse) Joiner, Joiner worked as a house painter and journeyman sign painter during his teens. With no formal artistic training, he began his career at the age of sixteen by sketching AFRICAN AMERICANS on Mississippi River boats. In the spring of 1874, he became an assistant to a German-born portrait painter named Hoffman in St. Louis. The following year he worked in Illinois and UTICA, INDIANA, where he received a substantial commission from the Christian church to paint "Ruth Gleaning in the Fields of Boaz." In 1880 he moved to Jeffersonville and opened a portrait studio in Louisville's COURIER-JOURNAL Building. After a fire in 1907 destroyed his office, he moved his studio to the Equitable Building at the northeast corner of Fourth and Jefferson Streets.

Following a short time in Pittsburgh, Joiner returned to Indiana and completed a series of portraits of the first five governors of Indiana, which were hung in the former capitol at CORYDON. Early in the 1920s Joiner toured the West, where he painted landscapes of Colorado's Rocky Mountains. Among his best-liked works are scenes of Kentucky beechwood trees, many of them found in Cherokee Park.

Joiner married Helen Annette Cain of Jeffersonville in 1878; they had one son. Joiner is buried in Walnut Ridge Cemetery in Jeffersonville.

See *Courier-Journal*, May 31, 1932.

JOLAS, MARIA MCDONALD (b Louisville, January 1893; d Paris, France, March 4, 1987). Magazine founder and translator. Maria Jolas was the daughter of Donald and Betsy (Carr) McDonald. After an early education in Louisville, in 1925, while studying voice in Paris, she met journalist and critic Eugene Jolas (1894-1952). They married in 1926 and had two daughters, Betsy and Tina. Her brother-in-law Jacques Jolas became the first dean of the UNIVERSITY OF LOUISVILLE School of Music (1932-35).

In Paris the couple, with Elliot Paul, founded the influential literary review *transition* (1927-30, 1932-39), whose contributors included Gertrude Stein, Ernest Hemingway, Samuel Beckett, and James Joyce. Jolas corrected proofs of Joyce's novel, *Finnegans Wake* and, after WORLD WAR II, rescued his papers and possessions from a Paris attic. She also translated into English the novels of Nathalie Sarraute.

Maria Jolas is buried beside her husband in Chérence, France.

See *Courier-Journal*, Feb. 25, 1964; Shari Benstock, *Women of the Left Bank: Paris, 1900-1940* (Austin, Tex., 1986); *A Paris Anthology*

(New York 1990); Richard Ellmann, *James Joyce* (New York 1982); Hugh Ford, *Published in Paris* (New York 1975).

John Spalding Gatton

JONES, EPAPHRAS (b Hartford County, Connecticut, February 10, 1764; d New Albany, Indiana, February 14, 1847). Eccentric. In an age of rapid expansion in the Ohio River Valley, this veteran of the American Revolution attempted to found a town called Providence upriver from NEW ALBANY, Indiana, but his efforts failed. Providence was later absorbed by New Albany. He then purchased several hundred acres from WILLIAM CROGHAN of Louisville on July 21, 1818, and had the tract surveyed and laid out in streets. The town extended westward to Eleventh Street. To attract lot purchasers, Jones established a ferry at the point where the Kentucky & Indiana Railroad bridge was later built. From this point he planned a road to Vincennes that would bypass New Albany to the east and north, connecting with the road to Vincennes and diverting travel away from New Albany. The road was never finished, probably because of the expense of cutting its dense forest. The finished portion is today's Vincennes Street.

Because he served in the Revolution and owned property that was part of the Clark Grant, it was assumed by later New Albany historians that Jones served with George Rogers Clark on the 1778 expedition to the Illinois country. In fact, he served with the Connecticut militia as a musician (he was only 14 at the time) and spent the winter of 1778-79 in barracks at Newton, Massachusetts, and was discharged in 1780.

Jones continued to wear eighteenth-century attire throughout his life: knee breeches with knee buckles, powdered wig, ruffed shirt front, cockade hat, and a cane. He was deeply religious and considered the American Indians to be descendants of the lost tribes of Israel. He published at his own expense two books on the subject, both printed in New Albany. *On the Ten Tribes of Israel and the Aborigines of America* appeared in 1831. Ten years later he published *On the Aborigines of America.* He was opposed to the Mexican War of the 1840s, since he considered it a strike against the lost tribes. At the time of his death he was attempting to produce silk from silkworms.

After the death of his first wife (name unknown) he married Ann Silliman of New Albany on January 25, 1822. He was buried on his own property in what was known as Jones Graveyard, apparently along East Market Street near Vincennes Street. There is no trace of it today.

See *History of the Ohio Falls Cities and their Counties,* vol. 2 (Cleveland, 1882); *Hoosier Genealogist 30* (June 1990): 30; Jones's Revolutionary pension application, National Archives, file S-16889; *Roster of Soldiers an Patriots of the American Revolution Buried in Indiana,* Daughters of the American Revolution (Washington, D.C. 1938); Clark County Deed Book 1:410.

George H. Yater

JONES, PAUL (b Lynchburg, Virginia, September 6, 1840; d Louisville, February 24, 1895). Distiller. Paul and his brother, Warner, joined the Confederate army at the outbreak of the CIVIL WAR. Paul saw very little action during the war, but Warner was killed during the siege of Atlanta. After the war, Paul and his father, Paul Jones Sr., moved to Atlanta and entered the whiskey and TOBACCO business. Paul Jones Sr. died in 1877, and the younger Jones continued the business. In 1884 the Georgia legislature passed PROHIBITION in that state, and Paul Jones moved his business to Louisville.

The Paul Jones Co. was located at 138 MAIN St. in the heart of Louisville's "whiskey row." His investment in the city quickly grew as Jones became the president of the J.G. Mattingly Distillery at Thirty-ninth and High Streets. He also was a director and vice president of the American National Bank and president of the Louisville Fair and Driving Association, which founded Douglas Park racetrack.

Paul Jones registered the Four Roses trademark for whiskey in 1892. His name and his brand names soon became known across the country. He believed in ADVERTISING, and in New York he rented space on a building at Madison Square for a sign of incandescent electric lights at a cost of twelve hundred dollars per month.

Paul Jones was unmarried and lived at the GALT HOUSE while in Louisville. He developed Bright's disease (kidney disease) in the 1890s and died of complications. He is buried at CAVE HILL CEMETERY.

Michael R. Veach

JONES, WARNER LAVALLE, JR. (b Louisville, January 24, 1916; d OLDHAM COUNTY, Kentucky, February 6, 1994). Horse breeder. Born to Warner and Mina (Ballard) Jones, young Warner discovered his love for horses at the age of two when he was given his first pony. After attending prep school in New Jersey, Jones returned to Louisville and entered the breeding business. In 1935 he purchased Hermitage Farm near Goshen with fifty thousand dollars borrowed from his mother and developed it into one of America's premier breeding farms over the next several decades. Hermitage garnered international attention in 1985 when Jones sold Seattle Dancer, a colt by Nijinsky II, for $13.1 million, still a record price into 1997. Jones also became the first breeder, and the only one as of 1998, to breed the winners of the KENTUCKY DERBY, Oaks, and a Breeders' Cup Race. He bred 1953 Kentucky Derby winner Dark Star, 1967 Oaks winner Nancy Jr., and 1988 Breeders' Cup Juvenile winner Is It True.

Jones joined the CHURCHILL DOWNS Board of Directors in 1941 and was named chairman in 1984, a post he held until 1992. During his tenure, he oversaw a $25 million renovation of the racetrack and witnessed revenue, purses, and attendance figures rise substantially. Included in the improvements was the construction of a turf course allowing the Breeders' Cup, which Jones played a key role in establishing, to be held at Churchill Downs. Jones was also instrumental in organizing the American Horse Council in 1969, a national organization dedicated to representing the horse industry in Congress.

Jones's interest in horse-racing had links to his own Kentucky bloodlines. His great-great-grandmother was a Churchill, the family on whose land the track was built. Another distant relative, MERIWETHER LEWIS CLARK Jr., Capt. WILLIAM CLARK'S grandson, was the track's president when it opened in 1875.

Jones married Harriet Seelbach, and they had two daughters, Mina and Harriet. He died of lung cancer and is buried in CAVE HILL CEMETERY.

See *Courier-Journal,* Feb. 8, 1994.

JOUETT, MATTHEW HARRIS (b Mercer County, Kentucky, April 22, 1788; d Lexington, Kentucky, August 10, 1827). Portraitist. Born near Harrodsburg on land dubbed "Old Indian Fields," Jouett was the third of twelve children born to Capt. John "Jack" Jr. and Sallie (Robards) Jouett. Jouett's father, sometimes called the "Paul Revere of the South," is credited with delivering the warning that saved Gov. THOMAS JEFFERSON and the Virginia legislature from capture by British troops in 1781.

The young Jouett reportedly displayed talent for drawing at an early age after the family moved to Woodford County in 1793. When his brothers selected Matthew to be the only child to attend college, Jouett enrolled at Transylvania College in 1804 and graduated with honors in 1808. At the urging of his father, Jouett studied LAW in Frankfort under Judge George M. Bibb following his graduation, but he appeared more interested in PAINTING than in his studies.

Jouett had a year-long apprenticeship prior to his move to Lexington, where he opened his own practice in 1812. When the war with England was declared, he enlisted in September in the Third Mounted Regiment of the Kentucky Volunteers and served as a first lieutenant, paymaster, and captain. After he resigned from his post on January 20, 1815, the GOVERNMENT initially blacklisted Jouett, claiming over nineteen thousand dollars in missing funds. While Jouett could not prove his innocence due to the loss of his receipts in a boating accident, this total was later reduced to $1,339.84 and was finally repaid two months before his death.

Upon leaving the service, Jouett returned to Lexington and opened a painting studio, where he reportedly painted three portraits per week at twenty-five dollars each. He headed for New England in the summer of 1816 in search of further training and studied in Boston under the tutelage of well-known portraitist Gilbert Stuart. After several months in Boston, Jouett returned to Kentucky and doubled the price of his portraits. Unable to make a living in Lexington, Jouett spent winters in New Orleans and other Mississippi towns from 1817 until his death. He had a studio in New Orleans at 49 Canal St. in 1824 and opened a studio in Louisville in 1826. Although he gained prominence in the South, Jouett did not gain national recognition until samples of his work were exhibited at the Chicago Exposition in 1893. His first one-man exhibition was held between February 19 and March 11, 1928, at the J.B. Speed Art Museum, which owns many of his paintings. Several of his paintings are also on display at the Filson Club Historical Society.

Three hundred and thirty-four portraits and miniatures are attributed to Jouett between 1816 and 1827. One of his most celebrated is that of Marquis de Lafayette. Other subjects included Henry Clay, Gen. George Rogers Clark, Kentucky governor Isaac Shelby, Sen. Isham Talbot, Dr. W.C. Galt, Virginia governor James McDowell, Asa Blanchard, Henry Crittenden, and Dr. Horace Holley.

Jouett married Margaret "Peggy" Henderson Allen of Fayette County on May 25, 1812; they had nine children. After returning from an extended stay in Louisville where he had become ill with a fever, Jouett died eleven days later. He was buried in the family burial ground of his father-in-law, William Allen. Near the turn of the century the bodies of Jouett and his wife were moved to Cave Hill Cemetery.

See Samuel M. Wilson "Matthew Harris Jouett, Kentucky Portrait Painter," *Filson Club History Quarterly* 13 (1939): 75–97; William Barrow Floyd, *Jouett-Bush-Frazer: Early Kentucky Artists* (Lexington 1968).

JOYES, JOHN (b Louisville, January 8, 1799, d Louisville, May 31, 1877). Mayor. Joyes was the second son of the Irish pioneer Patrick Joyes, who came to Louisville in 1783 and settled on a lot on the northeast corner of Main and Sixth Streets. He was a representative of a mercantile house in Philadelphia.

After John completed his academic education, he studied law and was admitted to the Louisville bar. In 1827 he was elected to the state legislature from Jefferson County. The second mayor of Louisville after it was incorporated in 1828, he was elected on March 4, 1834, and served two terms until March 21, 1836. After serving as mayor, he was made judge of the city court in 1837 by the governor's appointment. The position, which was created by an act of the legislature, gave the judicial duties of the mayor to a separate city official. He remained in that position until 1851. He is buried at Cave Hill Cemetery.

Patrick Joyes's oldest son, Thomas, was born on December 9, 1787, at their Louisville home. Thomas served in the Wabash campaign of 1812 and was a captain in the Thirteenth Regiment of the Kentucky Militia at the battle of New Orleans in 1813. He was a member of the Kentucky legislature, representing Jefferson and Oldham Counties. He was also a member of the City Council and the Board of Trustees in the early 1800s. He represented Louisville in the state legislature several times, the last being in 1834-35. On May 4, 1866, Capt. Thomas Joyes died, one of the first white males born in Louisville to also die there. He is also buried in Cave Hill.

See L.A. Williams, *History of the Ohio Falls Cities and Their Counties,* 2 vols. (Cleveland 1882); *City Journal,* vol. 6, Unpublished Proceedings of the City Council (Louisville, March 21, 1836, 288).

JUG BANDS. Louisville has long been known to jazz record collectors as the home of jug bands, so called because their bass lines are provided by a musician skillfully blowing into a jug. The earliest jug-band musicians came out of Louisville's African American string bands. They played jazz, blues, ragtime, dance tunes, and popular music, performing on the streets, at train stations, and at downtown hotels. The most successful jug bands entertained white audiences at private parties, especially during Kentucky Derby week, where patrons would sing along on requests such as "Under the Chicken Tree" and "Titanic, Fare Thee Well." The best-known jug bands were led by jug-player Earl McDonald and fiddler Henry Miles. The Louisville jug band tradition lives on in the Juggernaut Jug Band and its entertaining presentation of jazz and popular tunes, as well as jug-band standards.

See *Courier Journal Magazine,* June 8, 1980.

Brenda K. Bogert

JULIUS SCHNURR & SONS. Founded in 1894 by Julius Schnurr, an immigrant from Obersasbach, Germany, Julius Schnurr & Sons was one of the important plaster businesses in Louisville. Along with his brother Gustav, Julius opened his first shop at 528 Center St. (Armory Pl.) between Green (Liberty) and Walnut (Muhammad Ali Blvd.) Streets. In 1898 another brother, Stephen, joined the business, and they formed Julius Schnurr & Brothers on Fifth St. between Green and Walnut Streets. There they remained until the turn of the century when the business moved to 1525 Shelby St. between Bancroft and Breckinridge Streets. In 1910 they moved to 825 S Shelby St.

In 1923 Gustav and Stephen left their brother Julius to form their own plastering business, Schnurr Brothers, at 753 S Shelby St. and remained in business until 1976. With their departure in 1923, Julius asked his two sons, Stephen V. and Urban, to join him, and together they formed Julius Schnurr & Sons. The business remained at 825 S Shelby St. for seventy-three years until 1983 when it moved to 820 Logan St. When Julius died in 1947 his two sons took over. Steven died in 1961. In 1972, Urban retired. The following year, on June 24, Julius Schnurr & Sons was incorporated. Stephen J. Schnurr, grandson of Julius, retired in 1993, and several of his children, nephews, and a niece joined the company. Together they own and operate the business their grandfather

Ballard Chefs jug band at the Kentucky State Fair, 1935.

and great-grandfather founded. They specialize in the patching, repairing, maintaining, and renovating of older buildings.

JUNIOR LEAGUE OF LOUISVILLE. The Junior League was founded by Mary Harriman in New York City in 1901. This scion of a wealthy family wished to help the less fortunate. First called the Junior League for the Promotion of the Settlement Movement, it worked in settlement houses of New York's Lower East Side to improve child health, nutrition, and literacy. The Junior League of Louisville, begun in 1921, is one of 293 international chapters with more than 193,000 members. They constitute an organization of women committed to promoting voluntarism, to developing the potential of women, and to improving the community through the effective action and leadership of trained volunteers. Its purpose is exclusively educational and charitable. The Junior League of Louisville reaches out to women of all races, religions, and nationalities.

Prior to the mid-1970s the league rented office space in different locations of the city. In 1974, while searching for permanent quarters, the league bought the 1892 warehouse at 627 W Main St., once the Harry Hibbs Hat Co. In so doing, the league manifested its commitment to the preservation of the historic district of MAIN St. With the help of local businesses, foundation funds, government grants, and individuals, the league made a $350,000 renovation of the five-story structure.

In the 1990s the league focused on the problems of families at risk and women's health. These are broad areas of concern under which were developed specific projects for the betterment of those involved. The league is the local organizer of the Race for the Cure, a three-mile run/walk for breast cancer. Proceeds funded national breast cancer research and local educational programs. Other funded projects during the 1990s addressed the needs of children and families at risk, such as the Rites of Passage Program in collaboration with Cabbage Patch Settlement House, where league volunteers mentor pre-teen girls. In addition, the league in the late 1990s completed three projects to meet the physical, mental, and spiritual needs of Louisville's children, particularly those living downtown: Playscape, the playground on the Waterfront, Kidscape at Louisville Science Center, and Artsparks at the J.B. SPEED ART MUSEUM. The league also offers a range of services for the membership. Members are trained through workshop formats as well as through hands-on experiences in such areas as fundraising and communications.

Anita P. Barbee

J.V. REED & CO. In 1875 Joseph V. Reed of JEFFERSONVILLE, INDIANA, started a printing business in Louisville. At first called Perkins & Reed, by 1878 it bore the name of J.V. Reed & Co. and was located downtown on the corner of Bullitt and MAIN Streets. From this location the first TELEPHONE directory for the city was printed, as well as pamphlets, broadsheets, books, signs, and ADVERTISING of every description. The company also owned one of the first imported metal lithographing presses in the United States, which it used in the production of metal tags used on TOBACCO sold in twists for chewing.

In 1905 J.V. Reed & Co. relocated to 1102 W MAIN St., the company's home for the next ninety-three years and corporate headquarters for all seven company presidents, from founder Reed to Andrew M. Blieden in 1999. On this site the plant eventually grew to thirty-five thousand square feet. By 1927, while George C. Weldon was president (1915-37), it was the world's largest manufacturer of metal tags for the chewing tobacco industry.

While Roy I. Lindley was president (1938-47), the firm purchased, sometime before WORLD WAR II, an out-of-state company making dustpans and wastebaskets. This was a natural extension of its work manufacturing light-gauge metal signs and advertising. Dustpans had to wait, however, while the company geared up to war-related manufacturing. The war years saw the company hire many more women, a policy that the company actively pursued after the war. In 1999 the workforce was still more than 60 percent female.

By 1977, under the helm of Pres. Ralph W. Ray (1969-86), it became the largest manufacturer of metal dustpans for residential use in the world. In 1977, for example, the company employed about a hundred men and women and could produce a dustpan in less than three seconds. It made more than 6 million every year and marketed 20 percent of the dustpans throughout the non-Communist world.

The company stopped printing on paper products in 1947 to concentrate solely on metal. Under Lewis A. Southwick (1947-69) the firm, in addition to a booming dustpan business, also produced millions of multi-colored, two-foot-high metal posters for cigarette advertising. The posters were printed in English and also in Spanish for the South American trade, and featured beautiful models.

Philip J. Campbell Jr. was president from 1986 until 1997. The company remained vigorous during these years despite the fact that plastics had cut heavily into the firm's traditional product lines. In December 1998, under Blieden, the company relocated to an eighty-five-thousand-square-foot facility at 1201 Story Ave. In 1999, 40 percent of its product line–about 2.5 million items a year–was dustpans, 20 percent was burner covers for stoves, 10 percent wastebaskets, 10 percent reproductions of nostalgic advertising, and the remaining 20 percent miscellaneous products.

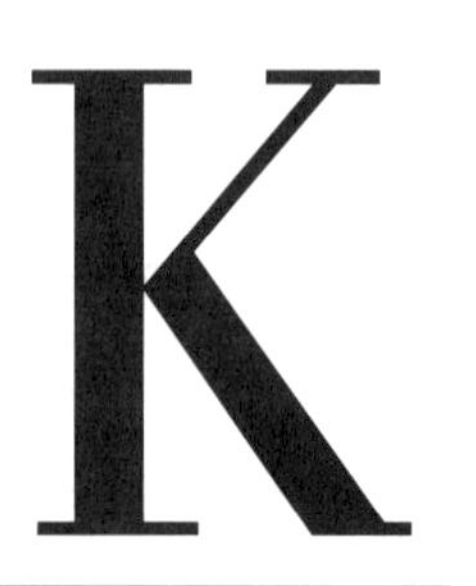

KADEN TOWER. Located at 6100 Dutchmans Lane in St. Matthews, this local landmark was built in 1965 for $2.7 million as the new home of the Lincoln Income Life Insurance Co. Opening in Louisville in 1937, Lincoln Income specialized in group life, health, and accident insurance. By 1966 the company sold insurance throughout the South and Southwest. Initially known as Lincoln Tower, the fifteen-story structure was designed by William Wesley Peters of the Scottsdale, Arizona, firm Taliesin Associated Architects. Peters, a pupil of architect Frank Lloyd Wright, was also known for his marriage to Svetlana Alliluyeva, the daughter of Soviet leader Joseph Stalin.

The unique appearance of the tower can be attributed to its cantilever, or hanging, style of construction. The upper floors are actually suspended from the large girders that form the central shaft of the building. The exterior is composed of lacework panels made of a special lightweight concrete material. These panels were specially designed by Taliesin to keep the offices cool by cutting down on direct sunlight and to permit viewing from inside.

In 1986 Lincoln Life was absorbed by Conceco, an Indianapolis-based insurance-holding company. Later the same year Conceco sold the building for approximately $3 million to the Kaden group, a consortium of local investors. The group spent an additional $2 million on renovations, which included repainting the exterior panels a distinctive salmon color and also changing the name of the building to Kaden Tower. The tower has been shared by several different businesses including insurance companies, computer repair shops, mortgage companies, and restaurants. In 1998 the New Orleans–based steakhouse chain, Ruth's Chris, moved into the top floor of the Kaden Tower. A walkway around the top offers panoramic views of Louisville's East End.

See *Courier-Journal*, March 13, 1966.

Cassie R. Roberts

KAELIN'S RESTAURANT. Kaelin's Restaurant, located at the corner of Speed Ave. and Newburg Rd., was opened on January 22, 1934, by Carl and Margaret Kaelin. It claims to be the birthplace of the cheeseburger. One afternoon in October 1934, Margaret Kaelin was preparing a hamburger for her husband. When he saw her putting away some American cheese, he asked her to melt a slice on top of the hamburger. Carl liked the combination so much he added it to the menu on October 12, 1934. These first cheeseburgers cost fifteen cents.

In 1990 a disagreement over the origins of the cheeseburger arose when a Louisville newscaster, Barry Bernson, discovered that Denver, Colorado, claimed to be the home of the cheeseburger. A memorial plaque commemorating the invention of the cheeseburger is located at the former site of Humpty-Dumpty's Barrel Drive-In in Denver. The plaque indicates that the cheeseburger was invented by Louis Ballast in 1935, a year after Kaelin's started serving it. While there has been no authoritative ruling on the legitimacy of Kaelin's claim, a spokesman at the Smithsonian Institution said it was possible that the Louisville restaurant was the first to market a menu item labeled a cheeseburger. The first meals served at the restaurant were for the students at St. Agnes Elementary School, located across the street from Kaelin's. Serving lunch to the students became a tradition that lasted for eleven years. In 1955 Kaelin's became one of the first restaurants to put Kentucky Fried Chicken on the menu. Kaelin's was also one of the first area restaurants to have curb service. Between 1962 and 1973, Kaelin's operated a carry-out restaurant on Dixie Hwy. in Pleasure Ridge Park. Kaelin's is also known for a sign in front of the restaurant saying, "If you can't stop, please wave!" In 1989, Irma Raque, the Kaelins' daughter, became the sole proprietor of the restaurant.

KAUFMAN-STRAUS. Kaufman-Straus Dry Goods first appeared in Louisville in 1879 in a storefront outlet on Jefferson St. between Seventh and Eighth Streets. Henry Kaufman, a local retail clerk, was its founder. In 1883 Benjamin Straus joined him as a partner. In 1887 the two men moved their business to S Fourth St., leasing space from the Polytechnic Society of Kentucky (predecessor of the Louisville Free Public Library). In 1903 a new Kaufman-Straus building designed by Louisville architect Mason Maury was completed at 533–49 S Fourth St. The Louisville Free Public Library continued to occupy space in the store until 1908. In 1925, after extensive interior renovation, the concern was touted in its grand reopening as Louisville's newest department store. As a member of the City Stores buying group of New York City, it had an extensive merchandise assortment.

Kaufman-Straus Building, 427-437 South Fourth Street, 1950s.

Today the exterior facade of the 1903 building may be viewed as part of the eastern wall of the Galleria shopping complex. At its height in the late 1950s, Kaufman's was one of Louisville's finest department stores. It possessed all of the conveniences associated with big-city facilities. It boasted suburban locations at the St. Matthews Mall and at Dixie Manor. By 1971, as a result of a corporate takeover of the buying group, Kaufman's became L.S. Ayres. In that same year the business announced it was terminating its downtown presence of ninety-two years because of dwindling sales. Later its two branches also closed their doors.

Kenneth L. Miller

KAYE, FREDERICK AUGUSTUS JR., (b Louisville, April 21, 1796; d Breckinridge County, Kentucky, April 29, 1866). Mayor. The son of Frederick Augustus and Mary Dorothy Kaye, both of Pennsylvania, who had nine children. The Kayes came to Louisville in the late 1700s, purchasing a half-acre of land from Jacob Bucher on March 3, 1789. It is believed that the Kaye family built the first brick house in the city of Louisville that year. It was on Market St. between Fifth and Sixth.

Kaye served as a councilman from the Fourth Ward in 1830, 1831, and 1832 before taking office as mayor on March 15, 1837. In the 1837 election, Kaye, a member of the Whig Party, was chosen by the City Council after a vote was taken thirteen separate times to decide who would serve as mayor.

Kaye was the first to be selected mayor solely by the qualified voters of the city. In 1838, in response to the difficulties caused by the selection of the mayor by the City Council, the state legislature amended the city charter to allow for direct popular election. The city charter was also amended to extend the mayor's term of office to three years and to prohibit the incumbent from running for reelection. Kaye served until May 17, 1841. After sitting out a term, he was again elected mayor, serving from May 10, 1844, until May 10, 1847. He defeated George B. Didlake, of the pro-slavery Democratic Locofoco Party, by a vote of 963 to 338. Turnout was less than two-thirds of eligible voters.

After his tenure as mayor, Kaye was a member of the Board of Aldermen from 1854 until 1856 and was its president in 1855–1856. He married Rachel C. McLaughlin (1802–64) in Louisville. They had six children. Kaye died at his son William's home. Both Kaye and his wife are buried in Cave Hill Cemetery.

See Josiah Stoddard Johnston, ed., *Memorial History of Louisville,* 2 vols. (Chicago and New York 1896); George Yater, *Two Hundred Years at the Falls of the Ohio* (Louisville 1987).

KAYE, WILLIAM (b Yorkshire, England, February 13, 1813; d Louisville, November 19, 1890). Mayor. William Kaye was the son of Joshua Kaye, a cloth manufacturer. In 1819 the Kaye family moved to Pittsburgh. Kaye trained as a machinist in 1827. In 1836 he came to Louisville and formed a partnership in business with a son of his former employer, under the firm name of Patterson & Kaye.

In 1841 he started Kaye & Co. Brass Founders and Machinists. The company was famous for its bell and brass works and sold its products in many parts of the world. The company also made artistic and heavy brass castings. One of its most famous castings was the bell in the Cathedral of the Assumption. His son succeeded him as the sole proprietor after his death.

In 1862 Kaye, a Democrat, was elected a member of the City Council of Louisville, holding the position for one year. On April 4, 1863, he was elected mayor, defeating Union Party candidate and former mayor Thomas H. Crawford by 820 votes out of the more than 4,300 cast. Although Kaye, who was backed by the *Louisville Democrat,* was not an open supporter of the Confederacy, he was able to put together a coalition of secessionists and some Union supporters to propel him to the mayor's office. He held the position almost until the close of the war in 1865. Kaye issued a proclamation calling for an official day of observance of the end of the war on April 14, 1865—five days after Lee's surrender.

Leaving office, he was elected by the City Council to fill a vacancy as the representative from his ward. While on the City Council, Mayor James S. Lithgow appointed him chief of police for one year. In 1870 Kaye was again elected a member of the City Council. He served again in 1871 and then was elected to the council from 1873 through 1876. In 1875 he was president of the Board of Councilmen.

He married Mary Patterson of Chillicothe, Ohio, in 1836. They had four children. He died of heart failure and is buried in Cave Hill Cemetery next to his wife, who died on February 17, 1864, and an infant child.

See *The Biographical Encyclopedia of Kentucky of the Dead and Living Men of the Nineteenth Century* (Cincinnati 1878); George Yater, *Two Hundred Years at the Falls of the Ohio* (Louisville 1987).

KAYE FOUNDRY. The Kaye Foundry was located at Second and Water Streets. William Kaye, Louisville mayor from 1863 to 1865, started the foundry in 1841. After Kaye died in 1890, his son Samuel J. Kaye ran the business, which closed in 1895. The Kaye Foundry specialized in manufacturing bells of all sorts for steamboats, plantations, churches, schools, factories, and courthouses. According to William Kaye's obituary, "his success speaks for itself, for there are few cities in the United States where the Kaye bell is not known. Every engine house and nearly every church in his city has bells of his make, and he had a very large trade in the South. Even in the North and West, his trade reached." A bell cast by the foundry tolled V-E day in St. Louis in 1945. A Kaye bell still hangs in Louisville's Cathedral of the Assumption, and another is on the well-known steamboat *Delta Queen.* The foundry also manufactured brass castings, burning brands, chimes, and peals. The Kaye Foundry was also known as Kaye & Co., and Kaye Bell and Brass Foundry.

See *The Biographical Encyclopedia of Kentucky of the Dead and Living Men of the Nineteenth Century* (Cincinnati 1878); *Illustrated Louisville: Kentucky's Metropolis* (Chicago 1891); *Courier-Journal,* Nov. 20, 1890, May 9, 1945.

Vivian Keinonen

KEAN, WILLIAM LEE "BILL" (b Louisville, October 12, 1899; d Louisville, April 29, 1958). High school coach and athletic director. Kean was athletic director for Central High School for thirty-three years, from 1923 until 1956. He also coached the then all-black school's football and basketball teams as well as baseball, track, and tennis. Kean was a graduate of Central High School and was captain of the football, basketball, and baseball teams.

Although slightly built at just over 5 feet, 1 inch and 140 pounds, Kean made the football team at Howard University in Washington, D.C. In 1922, the year he graduated, he was named to the Negro All-American Team as a quarterback. Kean earned letters in three other sports, making him one of Howard's first four-letter athletes. He also earned a master's degree from Indiana University.

Kean, who was also a health and physical education teacher at Central, was one of the most successful high school football and basketball coaches in the state. During his tenure as head football coach, the Yellow Jackets won 225 games and lost 45. He also coached Hall of Famer and University of Louisville football standout Leonard Lyles, who played with the Baltimore Colts. Kean, a soft-spoken man, had perhaps his greatest success with the school's basketball team, winning 857 out of the 940 games he coached. His teams won five state championships in the Kentucky High School League, the league for black schools prior to integration. After the league was dissolved and Central was made a member of the Kentucky High School Athletic Association, the Yellow Jackets won the Louisville Invitational Tournament two consecutive years. The school's basketball teams also won the national Negro high school championship four times. In 1952 he was named "Coach of the Year" by the Kentucky High School League. He also served as state commissioner of Negro high school athletics.

In 1956, with his health failing, Kean turned over some of his coaching responsibilities to J. Dan White, an assistant football coach and former student, although he continued to work until his death. Kean was inducted into several halls of fame, including the Kentucky High School Athletic Association's Hall of Fame in 1988, National High School Sports Hall of Fame in 1993, and the Afro-American Hall of Fame in 1995.

Kean lectured at the former Municipal College in Louisville and also taught at Kentucky State and Tennessee State Colleges. He was a deacon at Calvary Baptist Church. He married Helen Anthony in 1939. The couple had a son, William Anthony, and a daughter, Alice Carolyn, who married former University of Louisville assistant basketball coach Wade Houston. Their son, Allan Houston, is a professional basketball player. Kean is buried in Eastern Cemetery.

See *Courier-Journal,* April 30, 1958.

KEATS, GEORGE (b London, England, February 27, 1797; d Louisville, December 24, 1841). Businessman. Born into a lower-middle-class English family, Keats amassed a fortune in the lumber business in Louisville. He was a younger brother of John Keats, considered one of the greatest of English poets. Orphaned at an early age, George and his brothers, John and Tom, were reared by Richard Abbey as guardian. George received some commercial experience in Abbey's tea-importing firms but resigned as he approached his majority when he received a trust fund from his grandfather's estate. Realizing that his brothers were unfit for business, he determined to invest this in a profitable enterprise as the breadwinner of the trio.

In 1818 he and his sixteen-year-old bride, Georgiana Wylie, set out for the United States, where he hoped to make his fortune. They perhaps intended to go to one of the English colonies in Indiana or Illinois but settled in Henderson, Kentucky, living with the John James Audubon family. George invested heavily in a flatboat load of merchandise with Audubon, but, when the boat sank and the cargo was lost, relations between the men became strained.

The following year George and Georgiana moved to Louisville. When brother Tom died, George returned to London in 1820 to settle the estate and to claim his share of the inheritance, which he invested in a Louisville lumber mill. This proved profitable, and he invested in real estate and in a flour mill. By 1835 he built a columned mansion on the south side of Walnut St. (Muhammad Ali Blvd.) between Third and Fourth Streets. One of the most impressive residences in the city, it became known as "the Englishman's palace."

Samuel Osgood, assistant minister of the

Unitarian church where Keats was a member, recalled him thus: "One of the most delightful and hearty men in the social walk was an English gentleman who had come out to seek his fortune. . . . The brother of one of our most ideal and gifted poets, he did not lose sight of the ideal world in the prosaic business of a lumber merchant. He was always ready for a literary conversation, and took delight, at any time, in turning from his ledger to his library, and from numbers arithmetical to numbers poetical."

Like his brother John, George wrote poetry; many critics believe that at least three poems attributed to John were written by George. When John died in 1821, George paid all of the poet's outstanding debts. He also attempted to have his biography written, but none appeared until 1887. However, some of John's poems, copies of which had obviously been sent by the poet to George, made their first American appearance in a Louisville literary publication, the *Western Messenger*, founded about 1835 by Unitarian minister James Freeman Clarke.

On a timber inspection trip in 1841, Keats contracted a cold that led to tuberculosis, the "family disease," and died on Christmas Eve that year, leaving a family of eight children. Within a year Georgiana remarried; her second husband was Scotsman John Jeffrey, a civil engineer who had come to the United States about 1830 as an expert in installing gas-lighting systems. Jeffrey installed the Louisville system, first operated in 1837.

George Keats was buried in the Western Cemetery, but in April 1879 was reinterred in CAVE HILL CEMETERY, along with Georgiana and two of their daughters. John Jeffrey died in February 1881 and is buried in the Keats plot.

See Naomi Kirk, "George Keats," *Filson Club History Quarterly* 8 (April 1934): 88–96; Frank R. Shivers Jr., "A Western Chapter in the History of American Transcendentalism," *Bulletin of the Historical and Philosophical Society of Ohio* 15 (April 1957): 117–30.

George H. Yater

KELLY, ELEANOR (MERCEIN) (b Milwaukee, Wisconsin, August 30, 1880; d Louisville, October 11, 1968). Novelist and traveler. Kelly was born to Thomas Royce and Lucy (Schley) Mercein. She received her high school education at Georgetown Convent of the Visitation in Washington, D.C., where she was valedictorian of her class in 1898. Mercein moved to Louisville in 1901, and there she married Robert Morrow Kelly Jr. on June 4 of that year.

Kelly did much of her writing in her tri-level house, a renovated barn located on Edgehill Rd. She contributed regularly to the *Saturday Evening Post,* which ran fifty-four of her stories. She wrote twenty-two novels and numerous short stories. Kelly's first novel, *Toya the Unlike* (1913), was about a Japanese girl in America. Her next novel was the first of three novels set in Kentucky. All have strong female characters. The first of this trilogy, *The Kildares of Storm* (1916), is about a woman in the foothills of the uplands who bears her hard-drinking, hard-riding husband; rears her two daughters; and falls in love with another man. *Why Joan?* (1919) describes the three courtships of a young society woman in Louisville. This novel was written particularly for female readers and draws a good picture of society among the "good families." *The Mansion House* (1925), the final book in the trilogy, tells the story of an orphan and her rearing in the ancestral "Treaty Oak," the MANSION HOUSE.

Kelly traveled to the Basque country in Spain, where she studied the region, the people, the customs, and the way of life. This experience resulted in her trilogy about the Basque country, which would prove to be some of her best writing. *Basquerie* (1927) chronicles the life and romantic adventures of a wealthy family there. Kelly drew a great deal of attention from this novel, which was made into a movie in 1931. The other Basque novels are *The Book of Bette* (1929) and *Nacio: His Affairs* (1931). Her last book, *Proud Castle* (1951), is about the Magyars of Hungary, reflecting Kelly's many travels to Southern and Eastern Europe. Kelly was the director of the Louisville Arts Club and held memberships in the Woman's Club of Louisville, Colonial Dames of America, and the National Arts Club of New York. She died in Louisville. Her body was cremated and buried in a family lot in Milwaukee, Wisconsin.

See William S. Ward, *A Literary History of Kentucky* (Knoxville 1988); *Courier-Journal Magazine*, Jan. 3, 1960.

KENDALL, WILLIAM H. (b Somerville, Massachusetts, March 24, 1910; d Jacksonville, Florida, March 31, 1989). Railroad president. The son of Warren C. and Helen (Hodgkins) Kendall, he was a second-generation railroad officer. Kendall graduated from Dartmouth College and its Thayer School of Civil Engineering in l933. He began his career in the engineering department of the Pennsylvania Railroad, later joining Atlantic Coast Line Railroad's operating department. Before coming to the LOUISVILLE & NASHVILLE RAILROAD as assistant to the president in l954, he served as general manager of the Clinchfield Railroad, jointly owned by ACL and L&N. Kendall became vice president and general manager of the L&N in l957 and was elected president in l959. During his presidency, he oversaw merger with three railroads, two of them (Chicago & Eastern Illinois and Monon) taking L&N to Chicago. Following Seaboard Coast Line Industries' acquisition of the L&N in l972, he was named vice chairman of SCLI's Board of Directors. He retired in l975 but remained in Louisville until just before his death. In 1957, during Kendall's presidency of the L&N, the railroad donated steam locomotive No. 152 to the fledgling KENTUCKY RAILWAY MUSEUM. This locomotive (of the Pacific 4–6–2 type) was built in 1905 and has been restored to active service with the museum, now headquartered in New Haven, Kentucky, but originally in Louisville. Married to the former Lucille Hayworth, he had two children, William Thomas Kendall and Roberta Ann Kendall. William Kendall died at St. Luke Hospital, Jacksonville, Florida. He is buried in Bristol, Tennessee.

See *L&N Magazine*, April 1959.

Charles B. Castner

KENESETH ISRAEL. In 1927 two Orthodox congregations—B'nai Jacob and Beth Hamedrash Hagodol—merged to form Keneseth Israel. The two were the result of the large-scale emigration from Eastern Europe toward the end of the nineteenth century. B'nai Jacob was founded in 1887 and fourteen years later moved to 432 E Jefferson. Beth Hamedrash Hagodol was founded in 1887 and occupied a building at the northeast corner of Preston and Green (LIBERTY) Streets.

Keneseth Israel joined the United Synagogue of Conservative Judaism in 1994. It built its first home at Floyd and Jacob Streets, a building designed by architects Joseph & Joseph. The outward movement of its members to the HIGHLANDS led the congregation to seek a new site, and in November 1971 the congregation dedicated a sanctuary at 2531 Taylorsville Rd. An outstanding feature of the building is its twelve stained glass windows designed by local artist William Fischer, each depicting some phase of Jewish religious life. Joseph & Joseph designed this building also.

In its early years the congregation was rocked by some turbulence, which led its first leader, Rabbi Albert N. Mandelbaum, to leave before his contract expired. Some years later there was an altercation over mixed gender seating, which disrupted services. A number of families left the congregation over this issue. In 1952 mixed seating was adopted. Mixed seating is forbidden in Orthodox ritual, so Keneseth Israel styled itself Traditional until it joined the Conservative movement in 1994. Under the leadership of Rabbi Shmuel Mann, who came in 1992, women participated in occasional egalitarian services, which were held at the same time as traditional services and which are open to men and women. The congregation elected Elaine Lerner in 1981 as its first woman president.

See *Adath Louisville: The Story of a Jewish Community* (Louisville 1981).

Herman Landau

KENT, RAYMOND ASA (b Plymouth, Iowa, July 21, 1883; d en route to Louisville, February 26, 1943).Educator. Born on a farm, he was the son of Thomas Oliver and Ellen (Stevens) Kent. His father, a native of St. Blazey, Cornwall, England, came to the United States in 1862 and served with the 31st Wisconsin Infantry in the CIVIL WAR before settling in Iowa. The younger Kent was educated in PUBLIC SCHOOLS and received his A.B. degree from

Cornell College in Mount Vernon, Iowa, in 1903. Following graduation, he attended Drew Theological Seminary in Madison, New Jersey, but returned to the Midwest in 1904 and began his career in education as the principal of graded schools in Fountain, Minnesota.

In Minnesota, he was the superintendent of schools in Mabel (1905–07), Lanesboro (1908–09), and finally in Winona (1911–13). During this period, he also studied at Columbia University (1907–08), where he received an A.M. degree in 1910 and a Ph.D. in 1917.

Kent served as president of the UNIVERSITY OF LOUISVILLE from 1929 until his death. Under Kent's administration, the university raised its academic standards and improved its physical plant. The LAW school was a particular concern of Kent's. In the first five years of his tenure, the law school was accredited by several local and national boards. In addition, a new law library was built with the financial support of Supreme Court Justice Louis D. Brandeis and with a grant totaling one hundred thousand dollars, half of the library's cost, from the Works Progress Administration. Kent also reorganized the College of Liberal Arts. More than two dozen departments of the college were consolidated into three main divisions: natural sciences, social sciences, and languages and LITERATURE. The school's curriculum was revised to shift from narrow departmental concentrations to broader divisional ones. Kent applauded the increased availability of independent study in the college, believing that it encouraged student initiative.

The university also added two new schools during Kent's first half decade. The Louisville Municipal College for Negroes opened as a junior college accredited by the University of Kentucky on March 27, 1931, and became a four-year college of liberal arts accredited by the Southern Association of Colleges and Secondary Schools in December 1932. The university opened the college with one hundred thousand dollars allotted for AFRICAN AMERICAN higher education in Louisville's million-dollar bond issue of May 1, 1926, and a gift of twenty-five thousand dollars from the Rockefeller Foundation. The second addition to the university was the school of music, added in 1932 following the closing of the Louisville Conservatory of Music.

Kent believed that the university, funded by the city, should serve its community. To this end, he introduced night extension courses and opened a division of adult education in 1935. The following year the university opened a graduate division of social administration. As a permanent memorial to Kent, the university expanded the division of social administration into the Kent School of Social Work in 1944.

Among his publications were *Higher Education in America* (1930), *Foreign Language Equipment of 2,325 Doctors of Philosophy* (1929), and numerous articles in the *Journal of Higher Education*, *School and Society* and *The Educational Record*.

He was married to Frances Stanton Morey on December 23, 1911. They had three children: Charles Stanton, Constance Frances, and Roger Betts Kent. Kent died in a Pullman berth on a Chesapeake and Ohio train traveling from Washington, D.C., to Louisville. He was found dead after the train arrived in Louisville. He is buried in Winona, Minnesota.

See *National Cyclopædia of American Biography,* vol. 32 (New York 1945); J.J. Oppenheimer, "Raymond Asa Kent, 1883–1943," *Educational Record* 24 (April 1943): 148–56.

Annette Chapman-Adisho

KENTUCKIANA. The word "Kentuckiana" was coined at some unknown date (perhaps in the 1940s) by the *COURIER-JOURNAL* and *LOUISVILLE TIMES* to describe in brief the area of Kentucky and Indiana encompassed in the single economic and population unit that includes Jefferson County, Kentucky, and Clark and Floyd Counties in Indiana. Divided by the Kentucky-Indiana state line and the OHIO RIVER, the three counties have nevertheless always shared the same types of industries and job bases. Many residents in the Indiana counties commute to jobs in Louisville, and the reverse is true for Jefferson County residents, although on a smaller scale. Basic economic and POPULATION changes affect both sides of the river in an identical way.

The urban centers (Louisville, NEW ALBANY, and JEFFERSONVILLE) all were established as Ohio River–oriented communities. Clarksville began along the river directly on the shore at the Falls of the Ohio, an ill-chosen site that prevented development of a shipping trade. It faded away, and not until the late nineteenth century did it revive farther from the river as a suburban community.

Since at least the 1980s the term "Kentuckiana" has come to include a larger area on both sides of the river, although the boundaries are indefinite. Occasionally the Kentucky media uses the term "North Side" (which dates back to at least 1913) to describe the Indiana communities alone. The word "Kentuckiana" is sometimes disparaged by Hoosiers as demeaning by giving too much weight to Kentucky and as an example of urban imperialism by the Louisville media. Of 108 commercial and service organizations listed in the 1999–2000 Louisville metro area telephone directory, only three were on the Indiana side of the Ohio River.

George H. Yater

KENTUCKIANA ANTIQUE BOTTLE AND OUTHOUSE SOCIETY. The Society was formed in 1974 at Louisville by a group of bottle collectors and diggers. It is a group infected by the bottle bug and whose members dig, buy, sell, and collect rare bottles—whiskey, ink, bitters, wine, cola, perfume—plus marbles, pottery, clay pipes, old coins, and other items. All of these items have been found in old outhouses.

Member Charles Pentecost recalled that one of the first digs was at the old Frank Fehr Brewery site at LIBERTY and Pearl Streets. It was discovered in 1967 after a bulldozer had removed the side of a woodwall privy in a sandy hillside. CIVIL WAR–era soft drink, ale, and porter bottles fell out in quantity or could be pulled out by the necks. It also gave up a perfect LOUISVILLE GLASS WORKS ribbed eagle flask.

A unique anatomical "Whimsy" bottle was found in a nearby privy. The Founders Square area, at Fifth St. and Muhammad Ali Blvd., also produced a number of first-class bottles, mocha pottery, and other artifacts. Many early digs were carried out just ahead of the bulldozers and concrete trucks. One digger was looking for missing parts of a Canton China vase when a dozer blade swept up his nearby earlier finds, including a brass hanging lamp. Other diggers report being ordered off digs by ill-natured foremen or workmen, forcing the diggers to come back at night.

The club sponsors a nationally recognized spring bottle show. Several club members have written books on various phases of bottle collecting. Club members include attorneys, journalists, artists, pharmacists, physicians, teachers, and printers.

Shirley Shields Settle

KENTUCKY AIR NATIONAL GUARD. The Louisville-based Kentucky Air National Guard (ANG), Kentucky's only ANG unit, began with federal recognition on February 16, 1947, although groundwork started in 1945. As a reserve component of the United States Air Force, the Kentucky ANG serves a dual role commanded by the governor through the adjutant general in a nonmobilized status and by the president and/or Congress upon being mobilized into federal service.

Locating in the former World War II Vultee B-24 Bomber Modification Center (later Bremner Biscuit Co.) at Standiford Field (now LOUISVILLE INTERNATIONAL AIRPORT), the Kentucky ANG's first aircraft, including twenty-five North American F-51D Mustangs, arrived during May 1947. Under the command of Lt. Col. Philip Ardery, a decorated World War II bomber pilot, the unit was designated the 123rd Fighter Group (FG)/165th Fighter Squadron (FS). Molded around a group of experienced World War II veterans, its first years were devoted to organization, recruitment, and training.

On October 10, 1950, the 123rd FG was called to federal service by President Truman in response to the KOREAN WAR. At this time the 123rd FG headquartered in Louisville included, in addition to the 165th FS, the 167th FS (West Virginia ANG) and the 154th FS (North Carolina ANG). All were ordered to report to Godman Field at FORT KNOX under the command of Colonel Ardery. While at Godman Field, the 123rd was redesignated the 123rd

Fighter Bomber Wing (FBW) and assigned to train replacement pilots for the Korean War. At this time several Kentucky ANG pilots were assigned to combat squadrons in Korea on a temporary basis, with five men lost either in action or during captivity.

On September 18, 1951, the 123rd FBW was moved to Manston Royal Air Force Station near Margate, England. Its mission was to support NATO units in Europe and provide air defense for the United Kingdom. Pilots were assigned to fly the Republic F-84E Thunderjet. On July 9, 1952, the 123rd FBW was returned to the Kentucky ANG. This was a paper move only, as personnel and equipment remained in Europe. It was another year before most of the officers and enlisted ranks returned to Standiford Field and resumed flying the F-51D Mustang.

On September 13, 1956, the first of twenty-five North American F-86A Sabre Jets arrived in Louisville. Preceding this, the Kentucky ANG was redesignated the 123rd Fighter Interceptor Wing/165th Fighter Interceptor Squadron. Sabres were used to supplement the air defense of a three-hundred–mile sector around Louisville. Four pilots were put on alert during daylight hours to be airborne within three minutes of a scramble.

Flight operations with the F-86A were short-lived, and by 1958 conversion was under way to the Martin RB-57B Canberra. The Canberra brought an entirely new mission to the Kentucky ANG, aerial photographic reconnaissance. A realignment and redesignation of the wing followed, resulting in the creation of the 123rd Tactical Reconnaissance Wing (TRW)/165th Tactical Reconnaissance Squadron (TRS). In time the wing included, in addition to the 165th TRS, the 117th TRS (Kansas ANG), 154th TRS (Arkansas ANG), and the 192nd TRS (Nevada ANG). Capable of taking detailed photographs at high and low altitudes, Canberras participated in numerous military exercises far and wide. During 1960 the base was moved to a new fifty-one–acre site on the south side of Standiford Field. At this time, Philip Ardery, now a brigadier general, accepted an assignment to the Pentagon. He was replaced on a temporary basis by Brig. Gen. William D. Ott and then by Col. William H. Webster as permanent wing commander in 1961.

During 1965, with the nation engaged in the Vietnam War, Air National Guard Canberras were recalled by the Air Force for combat duty in Asia. On February 16 it was announced that the 123rd TRW would replace its RB-57s with McDonnell RF-101 Voodoos. When delivered, Voodoos were a mix of F-101A and F-101C fighters and would undergo a period of conversion to reconnaissance, then being designated RF-101G and RF-101H. The RF-101 provided the Kentucky ANG with its first supersonic aircraft and an airplane that was capable of air-to-air refueling. With military forces heavily engaged in Vietnam during 1968, President Lyndon B. Johnson mobilized the 123rd TRW on January 26 in response to North Korea's capture of an intelligence ship, the USS *Pueblo*. The wing was ordered to Richards-Gebaur Air Force Base, Missouri, near Kansas City, for a period of active duty. To bolster forces in Korea, the entire 123rd TRW (now without the 117th TRS) deployed to Itazuke Air Base, Japan, on a rotational basis. The Kentucky ANG went last, preceded by the 154th TRS and 192nd TRS. Kentuckians served in Japan from January into April 1969. By June 9, the entire 123rd TRW was deactivated and returned to state control. Among the many awards and commendations earned during the recall, Wing Commander Brig. Gen. Jack Owen accepted for the entire wing a Presidential Proclamation from President Richard M. Nixon in December.

Leadership changes through the remainder of the Voodoo years (into 1976) saw the following serving as wing commander: Col. Verne M. Yahne, Col. William J. Semonin, Brig. Gen. L.A. Quebbeman, and Brig. Gen. Fred F. Bradley. During 1972 the fleet of Voodoos, now consisting of only RF-101Hs, was exchanged for standard production-line RF-101C aircraft. After a deadly series of tornadoes devastated parts of Kentucky, including Louisville, on April 3, 1974, Kentucky ANG Voodoos crisscrossed the areas, producing aerial photos to help assess the damage.

A major upgrade in reconnaissance came on March 11, 1976, when it was announced that the Kentucky ANG would reequip with the McDonnell Douglas RF-4C Phantom II. During the 1970s, the Pentagon initiated the "total force" concept, where the Reserves and National Guard would take more responsibility in the nation's defense. In this regard, the Phantom-equipped Kentucky ANG made several major deployments to Europe.

Airlift became the primary mission of the Kentucky Air National Guard in 1989, when C-130B Hercules transports were assigned to replace the RF-4C. With the Hercules, a large, four-engine turbo-prop aircraft, a complete retraining of ground and flight crews was needed. Although not federally mobilized during Operation Desert Shield and in Desert Storm, the Kentucky ANG, using volunteers, airlifted more cargo in support of the effort than any other ANG unit. On February 6, 1992, a C-130B on a training flight practicing takeoffs and landings at the Evansville, Indiana, airport crashed into a nearby hotel. Fatalities included the five crew members aboard the aircraft and eleven on the ground.

Deliveries of twelve new C-130H Hercules commenced during May 1992. Included in the dozen was the two-thousandth C-130 built by the manufacturer, Lockheed Aircraft Co. Into the 1990s, the Kentucky ANG has participated in numerous humanitarian airlift missions worldwide. Among these were relief flights in 1993 into Somalia for Operation Restore Hope and Provide Relief. The same year it was deliveries of food and supplies to Bosnia to support Operation Provide Promise. During Operation Support Hope, relief missions were flown into Rawanda and Zaire in 1994. Personnel assisted in security and cleanup efforts after the 1996 BULLITT COUNTY tornado and 1997 Ohio River FLOODS.

As a result of Air Force restructuring in 1992, the Kentucky ANG received its current designation, the 123rd Airlift Wing/165th Airlift Squadron. No longer are any out-of-state units attached to the 123rd. Wing commanders from the 1970s into the late 1990s have been Maj. Gen. Carl Black, Brig. Gen. John L. Smith, Col. Joseph L. Kottak, Col. John V. Greene, Maj. Gen. Stewart R. Byrne, and Col. Michael L. Harden. During 1995, as a result of the expansion of Louisville International Airport, the base was moved to a new 81.5-acre facility on the northeast side of the airport.

In 1997 the Kentucky ANG celebrated its fiftieth anniversary. Over this period of time, it has been recognized with many awards including three Spaatz Trophies, the Metcalf Trophy, ANG Distinguished Unit Plaque, Air Force Safety Plaque, and nine Air Force Outstanding Unit Awards.

See Donald L. Armstrong and James S. Long, eds., *KYANG: Mustangs to Phantoms 1947–1977* (Kentucky Air National Guard 1977); Rene J. Francillon, *The United States Air National Guard* (Aerospace Publishing Ltd. 1993); Lt. Gen. John B. Conaway with Jeff Nelligan, *Call Out the Guard* (Paducah, Ky., 1997); Col. Larry L. Arnett, *Call to Arms: A Collection of Fascinating Stories, Events, Personalities, and Facts about Kentucky's Military History* (Kentucke *[sic]* Publishing Co. 1995); Charles W. Arrington, "Kentucky Air National Guard: Forty Years over the Bluegrass State, Part Two," *Air Classics* (April 1987): 48–63; Tom Ivie and Charlie Arrington, "Kentucky's Air National Guard: A New Look and a New Mission for an Historic Unit," *Air Combat* (Dec. 1993): 44–47.

Charles W. Arrington

KENTUCKY AND INDIANA BRIDGE. The Kentucky and Indiana Bridge (popularly, the K&I Bridge), completed in 1886, was the second to span the Ohio River between Louisville and Indiana and the first through-cantilever-truss bridge erected in the United States. It was built by the Kentucky and Indiana Bridge Co., incorporated in Kentucky on April 1, 1880, and crossed from Louisville's Portland neighborhood to New Albany, Indiana. Primarily a railroad bridge, it also included vehicular lanes extended from each side of the main trusses. This provided the first road crossing of the river in the Louisville area.

Its chief promoter was Bennett H. Young, at the time the president of the Louisville, New Albany, and Chicago Railroad (Monon), which sought an independent entrance to Louisville. Young, who also became president of the bridge

Kentucky and Indiana Terminal (K&I) Bridge, 1886.

company, foresaw an expansion of the Monon into the Kentucky coalfields through subsidiary companies. The bridge would provide a direct connection between the coalfields and the Chicago market. The capital was raised in New Albany and Louisville and from some outside investors such as William T. Grant, who had made a fortune in the dime-store business.

A cornerstone-laying ceremony was held in New Albany in the fall of 1881, but financial difficulties delayed the start of construction until 1883. The designer was John MacLeod, who had a number of Kentucky railroad bridges to his credit. He opted for the relatively new cantilever designs in which each of the wrought-iron, self-supporting trusses was extended outward from its pier toward a similar truss, obviating much of the need for supporting falsework. A swing span, seldom used, was put over the downriver end of the Indiana Chute to permit passage of boats in high water. The approaches were of wood, replaced with steel in 1893.

The vehicular lanes, on which tolls were charged, were opened on June 22, 1886, with a procession of "carriages, buggies, dog carts and phaetons." The single-track rail line was opened on October 16 of that year with a special train for dignitaries. A commuter service in competition with the "Dinkey" on the FOURTEENTH STREET BRIDGE was started immediately. These trains, which ran to Louisville's downtown riverfront and to Parkland in the West End, were known as "Daisies," apparently from the yellow coaches. In 1893 the Daisy trains were changed to electric operation, the first switch of steam to electric operation in the United States. In 1907 the commuter service was taken over by the Louisville & Northern Railway and Light Co., controlled by utility magnate Samuel Insull, and the electric cars were removed from the riverfront route and operated to a downtown station on Jefferson St., and later to one on Third St.

Within twenty years of its construction the bridge was inadequate to handle the volume of traffic and the increased weight of trains using it. A new double-track, steel bridge was put under construction beside the 1886 structure on the upstream side and completed in 1912. It included vehicular lanes on each side, as had the original. The old bridge was dismantled.

The completion in 1961 of the Sherman Minton Bridge between the Portland area and New Albany sharply reduced automotive traffic on the K&I Bridge's vehicular lanes. When an overloaded truck caused severe damage in February 1979, the lanes were closed permanently. Since 1899 the bridge had been owned jointly by three railroads: the Baltimore & Ohio, the Southern, and the Monon. Mergers in the railroad business ended this tripartite arrangement, and, on January 1, 1982, the bridge became the property of the Norfolk Southern Railroad as an essential element of its route between Louisville and St. Louis.

See David Plowden, *Bridges: The Spans of North America* (New York 1974). *Courier-Journal,* Oct. 29, 20, 1881; April 19, 1979; *Louisville Commercial,* June 23, Oct. 17, 19, 1886, Jan. 7, 1893; *Louisville Post* Nov. 27, 1912.

George H. Yater

KENTUCKY AND INDIANA HISTORICAL HIGHWAY MARKER PROGRAM. Historical markers recognize important historic sites and provide information for travelers on Kentucky's highways. In August 1949 the commonwealth of Kentucky began erecting them, with the Kentucky Historical Highway Markers Committee responsible for the selection process. In March 1962 the committee became a part of the Kentucky Historical Society. It works in conjunction with the Kentucky Department of Transportation. Up until 1992 the funding for markers had been provided either by the state or by private interests. Since then markers are funded only by individuals or organizations.

Developing a marker can take much time and effort. Any individual or organization may submit, following guidelines made available by the Kentucky Historical Society, a recommendation to a county chairman. After the chairman's approval, it is submitted to an advisory committee, which is made up of eighteen members appointed by the director of the society. Following committee approval the entry is placed on a list where more research and review is initiated.

The highway markers have been in two different styles, white letters on a black background and gold leaf letters on a dark green background.

The metropolitan area historical markers as of the spring of 1999 are listed below:

Jefferson County

ABRAHAM LINCOLN
(U.S. 60, 1 mi. E of Eastwood)

ALICE VIRGINIA COFFIN (1848–88)
(Jefferson St. between Preston and Floyd Streets, Louisville)

ARTIST OF CONFEDERACY
(Cave Hill Cemetery, Baxter Ave. and E Broadway, Louisville)

AUGUSTUS E. WILLSON (1846–1931)
(Cave Hill Cemetery, Baxter Ave. and E Broadway, Louisville)

BANK OF LOUISVILLE
(316 W Main St., Louisville)

BEARGRASS BAPTIST CHURCH
(Shelbyville Rd. at Bowling Blvd., St. Matthews)

BEECHLAND
(#2 Rebel Rd. just off Brownsboro Rd., Louisville)

BELKNAP CAMPUS
(University of Louisville Campus, Third St., Louisville)

BERRYTOWN
(Haefer Ln. and LaGrange Rd.)
(Reverse)
BERRYTOWN

BIRTH OF TRUTH IN ADVERTISING
(First and Main Streets, Louisville)

BOWMAN FIELD
(Bowman Field, Taylorsville Rd., Louisville)
(Reverse)
BOWMAN FIELD

BOWMAN FIELD—East
(Dutchmans Ln. and Gast Blvd., Louisville)
(Reverse)
BOWMAN FIELD—East

CALVARY BAPTIST CHURCH
(Twenty-eighth and Woodlawn Ave., Louisville)

CALVARY EPISCOPAL CHURCH
(821 S Fourth St., Louisville)
(Reverse)
CALVARY EPISCOPAL CHURCH

CATHEDRAL OF THE ASSUMPTION
(Fifth St., Louisville)
(Reverse)
CATHEDRAL OF THE ASSUMPTION

CEDAR CREEK BAPTIST CHURCH
(7709 Bardstown Rd., Fern Creek)

CENTER ST. CME CHURCH (CHESTNUT ST. CME CHURCH)
(809 W Chestnut St., Louisville)
(Reverse)
BROWN MEMORIAL CME CHURCH

CHARLES W. ANDERSON JR.
(Sixth and Jefferson Streets, Louisville)
(Reverse)
CHARLES W. ANDERSON JR.
CHARLES H. PARRISH JR.
(Parrish Ct., U of L Belknap Campus, Louisville)
(Reverse)
CHARLES H. PARRISH JR.
CHENOWETH MASSACRE
(Junction of Shelbyville and English Station Roads, Middletown)
CHURCHILL DOWNS
(Kentucky Derby Museum, 704 Central Ave., (Louisville)
Reverse)
KENTUCKY DERBY
CITY OF AUDUBON PARK
(3100 Preston Hwy., Audubon Park)
(Reverse)
NATURAL GARDEN SPOT
DISCOVERY OF THE OHIO RIVER
(Clark Memorial Bridge, Second and Main Streets, Louisville)
DR. JAMES BOND (1863–1929)
(930 W Chestnut St., Louisville)
(Reverse)
EARLY LEADER AND EDUCATOR
EARLY BLACKSMITH SHOP
(3612 Brownsboro Rd., Louisville)
EARLY FOURTH ST.
(Just S of the Galleria, Fourth St., Louisville)
(Reverse)
LATER FOURTH ST.
EARLY JEWISH CONGREGATIONS
(5101 Brownsboro Rd. at Lime Kiln Ln.)
(Reverse)
EARLY JEWISH CONGREGATIONS
FARMINGTON
(Junction of Bardstown Rd. and Wendell St. at the Watterson Expressway, Louisville)
FILSON CLUB HISTORICAL SOCIETY
(1310 S Third St., Louisville)
(Reverse)
FERGUSON RESIDENCE
FLOYD'S STATION
(Breckenridge Ln. at Hillsboro Ave., Louisville)
FORREST HOME CEMETERY
(Petersburg Rd. near Indian Trail)
FORT SOUTHWORTH
(4522 Algonquin Pkwy., Louisville)
FORT WILLIAM
(Junction of Shelbyville Rd. and Whipps Mill Rd., St. Matthews)
(Reverse)
COL. WILLIAM CHRISTIAN
FOUNDING OF JEFFERSON SEMINARY
(U of L, near Grawemeyer Hall, Belknap Campus, Louisville)
(Reverse)
FOUNDING OF JEFFERSON SEMINARY
FOURTH ST.
(Near N entry to Galleria, Fourth St., Louisville)
(Reverse)
A CIVIL WAR COMPASS
GALT HOUSE
(Second and Main Streets, Louisville)
GEORGE ROGERS CLARK
(Cave Hill Cemetery, Baxter Ave. and Grinstead Dr., Louisville)
(Reverse)
GEORGE ROGERS CLARK
GRAVE OF STEAMBOAT CAPTAIN MARY MILLICENT MILLER
Entrance to Portland Cemetery,Bank St., (Louisville)
GRIFFYTOWN
(401 Old Harrods Creek Rd., Griffytown)
(Reverse)
GRIFFYTOWN
HARRODS CREEK HISTORIC COMMUNITY
(River Rd. and Shirley Ave.)
HAYFIELD
(3000 Bunker Hill Dr., Louisville)
HENRY WATTERSON (1840–1921)
(525 W Broadway, Louisville)
(Reverse)
JOURNALIST-POLITICIAN
HOME OF FOUNDER
(202 E Chestnut at Brook St., Louisville)
(Reverse)
THE FILSON CLUB
I. WILLIS COLE
(2217 W Muhammad Ali Blvd., Louisville)
IRENE DUNNE (1898–1990)
(Kentucky Center for the Arts, 501 W Main St., Louisville)
ISAAC HITE'S HOME
(12215 Lucas Ln., Anchorage)
(Reverse)
ISAAC HITE
JAMES GUTHRIE (1792–1869)
(Fourth St. and Guthrie Green, Louisville)
(Reverse)
JAMES GUTHRIE (1792–1869)
JEFFERSON COUNTY
(Courthouse lawn, Sixth and Jefferson Streets, Louisville)
JEFFERSON COUNTY COURTHOUSE
(Sixth and Jefferson Streets, Louisville)
(Reverse)
CITY AND COUNTY NAMED
JEROME CLARKE ("SUE MUNDY")
(Eighteenth St. and W Broadway, Louisville)
(Reverse)
"SUE MUNDY" EXECUTED
JOHN B. CASTLEMAN—SOLDIER
(Cherokee Rd. and Cherokee Pkwy., Louisville)
(Reverse)
JOHN B. CASTLEMAN—CITIZEN
JOHN FLOYD'S GRAVE
(Breckenridge Ln. at Hillsboro Rd., Louisville)
KNIGHTS OF PYTHIAS TEMPLE
(930 W Chestnut St., Louisville)
(Reverse)
HUB OF CULTURE AND HISTORY
LEWIS & CLARK EXPEDITION
(At the Wharf, Fourth St., Louisville)
(Reverse)
WILLIAM CLARK (1770–1838)
LOCUST GROVE
(Junction of U.S. 42 and Blankenbaker Ln.)
LONG RUN MASSACRE
(U.S. 60, Eastwood)
LOUIS DEMBITZ BRANDEIS
(Entrance to University of Louisville Law School, Louisville)
(Reverse)
U.S. SUPREME COURT JUSTICE
LOUISVILLE & NASHVILLE RAILROAD
(Tenth St. and W Broadway, Louisville)
(Reverse)
L&N EXPANSION
LOUISVILLE CEMETERY
(1339 Poplar Level Rd., Louisville)
(Reverse)
WILLIAM WALKER MEMORIAL MARKER
LOUISVILLE CITY HALL
(Sixth and Jefferson Streets, Louisville)
(Reverse)
SIXTH AND JEFFERSON
LOUISVILLE CONVENTION, 1845
(Fourth St. between Market and Jefferson Streets, Louisville)
(Reverse)
UNITED METHODIST CHURCH
LOUISVILLE FREE PUBLIC LIBRARY
(Fourth and York Streets, Louisville)
(Reverse)
REPRESENTATIVE LOUISVILLE AUTHORS FROM KY. COLLECTION
LOUISVILLE GIRLS HIGH SCHOOL
(Second and Lee Streets, Louisville
LOUISVILLE LEGION
(Cherokee Rd. and Cherokee Pkwy., Louisville)
(Reverse)
LOUISVILLE LEGION
LOUISVILLE MEDICAL COLLEGE
(101 W Chestnut St., Louisville)
LOUISVILLE WESTERN BRANCH LIBRARY
(604 S Tenth St., Louisville)
(Reverse)
LOUISVILLE WESTERN BRANCH LIBRARY
LOUISVILLE'S STEAMBOAT ERA
(At the waterfront, end of Fourth St., Louisville)
(Reverse)
VISITORS AT LOUISVILLE WHARF
LOW DUTCH STATION
(Junction of Brown's Ln., Bowling Blvd., and Kresge Way, St. Matthews)
LYMAN T. JOHNSON
(exact location to be determined)
LYNDON
(LaGrange Rd., Lyndon)
MEMORIAL AUDITORIUM
(Fourth and Kentucky Streets, Louisville)
(Reverse)
PERFORMERS AT MEMORIAL
MERIWETHER HISTORIC HOME
(6421 Upper River Rd.)
"NEIGHBORHOOD HOUSE"
(428 S First St., Louisville)
(Reverse)
SETTLEMENT HOUSE
NOTED SCHOOL SITE
(550 W Kentucky St., Louisville)
OLD CATHOLIC HIGH SCHOOL
(428 S Eighth St., Louisville
OUR LADY CHURCH
(Northwestern Pkwy. at Cedar Grove Terrace, Louisville)
(Reverse)
PORTLAND
OXMOOR—1790
(Shelbyville Rd. east of Watterson Expressway, St. Matthews)
PARKLAND HISTORIC COMMUNITY
(Twenty-eighth St. and Virginia Ave., Louisville)
PERRYVILLE PRELUDE
(Shelbyville Rd. west of Middletown)
PETERSBURG
(Indian Trail and Newburg Rd.)
(Reverse)
NEWBURG
PRENTICE SCHOOL
(525 S Sixth St., Louisville)
PRESENTATION ACADEMY
(861 S Fourth St., Louisville)
(Reverse)

PRESENTATION ACADEMY
(525 S Sixth St., Louisville)
PRESTON PARK SEMINARY
(At Bellarmine College, 2001 Newburg Rd., Louisville)
(Reverse)
BELLARMINE COLLEGE
RESTORATION PROJECT
(Taylorsville Rd., Jeffersontown)
RUFF MEMORIAL WHEELMEN'S BENCH
(Third St. and Southern Pkwy., Louisville)
(Reverse)
CYCLE CARNIVAL, 1897
RUSSELL HISTORIC COMMUNITY
(Twenty-first and Chestnut Streets, Louisville)
ST. JOHN'S EVANGELICAL CHURCH
(637 E Market St., Louisville)
(Reverse)
ST. JOHN'S EVANGELICAL CHURCH
SCOTTISH RITE TEMPLE
(200 E Gray St., Louisville)
(Reverse)
GRAND CONSISTORY OF KENTUCKY
SECOND AFRICAN BAPTIST CHURCH
(First St. between Market and Main Streets, Louisville)
(Reverse)
SECOND AFRICAN BAPTIST CHURCH
SIMMONS UNIVERSITY
(1811 Dumesnil, Louisville)
(Reverse)
SIMMONS UNIVERSITY
SINCE 1842 (The Kentucky School for the Blind)
(Frankfort Ave., Louisville)
(Reverse)
SINCE 1858 (American Printing House for the Blind)
SLAVE TRADING IN LOUISVILLE
(Second and Main Streets, Louisville)
(Reverse)
GARRISON SLAVE PEN SITE
SLAVERY LAWS IN OLD KENTUCKY
(First St. between Market and Jefferson Streets, Louisville)
(Reverse)
SITE OF ARTERBURN BROTHERS SLAVE PENS
SMOKETOWN
(Hancock St. and E Broadway, Louisville)
(Reverse)
HISTORIC AREA
SOLDIER'S RETREAT
(Shelbyville Rd. east of St. Matthews)
SOLDIER'S RETREAT
(Nottingham Pkwy. and Seaton Springs off Hurstbourne Pkwy.)
(Reverse)
SOLDIER'S RETREAT
SPRING FORT
(McCready Ave. and Trinity Rd., Louisville)
STURGUS STATION
(Shelbyville Rd. east of Watterson Expressway, St. Matthews)
THOMAS EDISON BUTCHERTOWN HOUSE
(729 E Washington St., Louisville)
(Reverse)
THOMAS EDISON BUTCHERTOWN HOUSE
THOMAS MERTON (1915–1968)
(Fourth St. just south of the Galleria, Louisville)
(Reverse)
A REVELATION
TRAINER AND JOCKEY
(Watterson Trail and Taylorsville Rd., Jeffersontown)
TYLER SETTLEMENT
(Sweeney Ln. and Taylorsville Rd., Jeffersontown)
(Reverse)
TYLER SETTLEMENT
WALNUT ST. RETROSPECTIVE
(Sixth St. and Muhammad Ali Blvd., Louisville)
WATER WORKS PUMPING STATION
(Near water tower, off River Rd. and Zorn Ave., Louisville)
(Reverse)
WATER TOWER
WILDERNESS RD.
(Junction of Preston Hwy. and Outer Loop, Okolona)
WOODLAWN RACE COURSE
(Perryman and Westport Rds., Louisville)
YOUNGLAND
(Dixie Hwy., Shively)
ZACHARY TAYLOR HOME
(5608 Apache Rd. off Blankenbaker Ln., Louisville)
ZACHARY TAYLOR HOME
Blankenbaker Ln. N of Brownsboro Rd.)
ZACHARY TAYLOR NATIONAL CEMETERY
(4701 Brownsboro Rd.)
ZION BAPTIST CHURCH
(Twenty-second and Muhammad Ali Blvd., Louisville)

BULLITT COUNTY
BELMONT FURNACE
(On KY 61, near Belmont)
(Reverse)
IRON MADE IN KENTUCKY
BRASHEAR'S STATION
(KY 44, Shepherdsville)
(Reverse)
BRASHEAR'S STATION
BULLITT'S LICK
(Three mi. NE of Shepherdsville on KY 44)
COUNTY NAMED, 1796
(Courthouse lawn, Shepherdsville)
L&N BRIDGE IN CIVIL WAR
(KY 61 at Salt River bridge, Shepherdsville)
MILESTONES, ca. 1835
(Near Mt. Washington Baptist Church, U.S. 31–E, Mt. Washington
(Reverse)
AN EARLY TURNPIKE
MORGAN—ON TO OHIO
(KY 61 near Salt River bridge, Shepherdsville)
MYSTERY CEMETERY
(KY 245 near junction with KY 1604, Lotus)
SALT RIVER FURNACE
(Beech Grove Rd. and KY 61, Bardstown Junction)
(Reverse)
IRON MADE IN KENTUCKY
SHERMAN HERE
(KY 434 at railroad crossing, Lebanon Junction)

OLDHAM COUNTY
CSA CEMETERY
(Maple Ave., Pewee Valley)
DAVID WARK GRIFFITH
(KY 22, Crestwood)
FUNK SEMINARY SITE
(Junction of KY 53 and 146, LaGrange)
MASONIC LEADER
(KY 53, LaGrange)
OLDHAM COUNTY, 1824
(Courthouse lawn, KY 53, LaGrange)
PEWEE VALLEY
(Old L&N Depot, Pewee Valley)
WESTPORT
(KY 524, Westport)

Shelby County
ARMSTRONG HOTEL
(Sixth and Main Streets, Shelbyville)
BENJAMIN LOGAN—PIONEER
(U.S. 60, 4 mi. W of Shelbyville)
(Reverse)
JAMES KNOX—PIONEER
CAPTAIN JOHN SIMPSON
(U.S. 60, Simpsonville)
GENERAL JOSEPH WINLOCK (1758–1831)
(on KY 55, 2 mi. S of I-64)
(Reverse)
DR. JOHN KNIGHT (1748–1838)
JEPTHA'S KNOB
(U.S. 60 at Jeptha Knob Rd., Clay Village)
LINCOLN INSTITUTE CAMPUS
(U.S. 60, Simpsonville)
(Reverse)
LINCOLN INSTITUTE CAMPUS
MAJOR BLAND W. BALLARD
(U.S. 60 at Cross Keys Rd.)
(Reverse)
TICK CREEK MASSACRE
OLD STONE INN
(U.S. 60, Simpsonville)
PIONEER STATION
(KY 55, 2 mi. north of Shelbyville)
(Reverse)
SQUIRE BOONE
SCIENCE HILL SCHOOL
(U.S. 60, Shelbyville)
SHELBY COUNTY, 1792
(Courthouse lawn, U.S. 60, Shelbyville)
SHELBY COUNTY HEMP
(Junction of U.S. 60 and KY 714, E of Shelbyville)
(Reverse)
HEMP IN KENTUCKY
SHELBYVILLE FOUNTAIN
(Public Square, U.S. 60, Shelbyville)
SQUIRE BOONE'S STATION, 1779
(Across from courthouse, U.S. 60, Shelbyville)
WHITNEY M. YOUNG JR. (1921–1971)
(U.S. 60, Simpsonville)
(Reverse)
WHITNEY M. YOUNG JR. (1921–1971)

Spencer County
COUNTY NAMED, 1824
(KY 44, Taylorsville)
COURTHOUSE BURNED
(Courthouse lawn, KY 44, Taylorsville)
GUERRILLA QUANTRILL
(KY 55, 5 mi. S of Taylorsville)
SPENCER HOUSE
(Main St., Taylorsville)
TAYLORSVILLE
(KY 55, Taylorsville)
"VAUCLUSE"
(Two and one half mi. N of Taylorsville)

Indiana

Application for Indiana state historical markers is directed to the Indiana Historical Bureau, which is headquartered in Indianapolis and is the organization responsible for the dispensation of markers. Funding for markers can be either state or private. Markers are distinguished by gold lettering affixed to a dark blue background. There are two types of markers: state format markers have an outline of Indiana at the raised top, while Civil War Centennial Commission markers have a straight top with no state outline. Southern Indiana historical markers as of the summer of 1998 are as follows:

Clark County
CLARKSVILLE
(Clark Blvd. and Harrison Ave., Clarksville)
CIVIL WAR HOSPITAL
(Holt Masonic Orphans' Home, Jeffersonville)
GENERAL JEFFERSON C. DAVIS, 1828–1879
(U.S. 31, Memphis)
GRAVE OF JONATHAN JENNINGS, 1784–1834
(SR 3, Charlestown)
BIRTHPLACE AND CHILDHOOD HOME OF COLONEL HARLAND SANDERS
(SR 160 and I-65, Henryville)
LEWIS AND CLARK EXPEDITION, 1803–1806
(Falls of the Ohio State Park, Clarksville)
CLARK STATE FOREST
(U.S. 31, Clark State Forest, Henryville)
BORDEN INSTITUTE SITE
(301 W Borden St., Borden)

Floyd County
SITE OF CAMP WHITCOMB
(Beharrell Ave. and Spring St., New Albany)
NEW ALBANY
(W Spring St. at I-64, New Albany)
NEW ALBANY
(Spring St. and Woodrow Ave., New Albany)
MICHAEL C. KERR HOME
(1109 E Main St., New Albany)
CLARK'S GRANT
(Indiana University Southeast, 4201 Grant Line Rd., New Albany)
STATE BANK OF INDIANA
(203 E Main St., New Albany)
CULBERTSON MANSION
(914 E Main St., New Albany)
SCRIBNER HIGH SCHOOL
(First and Spring Streets at City-County Building, New Albany)

Harrison County
INDIANA CAPITOL
(Capitol Grounds, Corydon)
BATTLE OF CORYDON, JULY 9, 1863
(Capitol Grounds, Corydon)
FIRST STATE OFFICE BUILDING
(Walnut St., Corydon)
FIRST STATE CAPITAL
(SR 62, west side of Corydon)
FIRST STATE CAPITAL
(NE corner of Capitol grounds, Corydon)
SITE OF THE BATTLE OF CORYDON, JULY 9, 1863
(Old SR 135, 1 mi. S of Corydon)
MORGAN'S RAID, JULY 8–13, 1863
(SR 135, Mauckport-Brandenburg Bridge)
POSEY HOUSE
(Oak St., Corydon)
HARRISON COUNTY JAIL
(N Capitol Ave., Corydon)
GOVERNOR'S HEADQUARTERS
(Walnut St., Corydon)
PRESBYTERIAN CHURCH
(Walnut and Elm Streets, Corydon)
LAST HOME OF SQUIRE BOONE
(SR 135, Mauckport-Brandenburg Bridge)
WALTER Q. GRESHAM
(Post Office, Lanesville)
MT. SOLOMON LUTHERAN CHURCH
(SR 62, 5 mi. W of Corydon)
CEDAR HILL CEMETERY
(E Summit St., Corydon)

Harrison County
(Capitol Grounds, Corydon)
CORYDON UNITED METHODIST CHURCH
(214 N Elm St., Corydon)
CEDAR GLADE 1808
(772 N Capitol Ave., Corydon)
LEORA BROWN SCHOOL
(400 E Summit St., Corydon)

Scott County
PIGEON ROOST
(U.S. 31, entrance to Pigeon Roost Historic Site, S of Scottsburg)
PIGEON ROOST
(U.S. 31, Pigeon Roost Historic Site, S of Scottsburg)
MORGAN'S RAID, JULY 8–13, 1863
(SR 203, Lexington)
BOUNDARY OF CLARK'S GRANT
(SR 3 at Clark's Grant Park, W of Lexington)
JOHN KIMBERLIN
(Nabb-Lexington County Rd., 1/4 mi. NW of Nabb)
SITE OF WILLIAM HAYDEN ENGLISH HOME
(SR 203, Englishton Park, Lexington)
SITE OF WESTERN EAGLE
(Main and Mulberry Streets, Lexington)

KENTUCKY & INDIANA TERMINAL RAILROAD. A terminal railroad that owned switching yards and an OHIO RIVER bridge, the K&IT also operated 130 miles of tracks in Louisville and Jefferson County. The original corporation, Kentucky & Indiana Bridge Co., was formed in 1880 to give the Baltimore & Ohio (B&O), Monon, and Southern their own access to Louisville. By 1886, the company had constructed an Ohio River bridge between PORTLAND and NEW ALBANY. On the bridge, the single-track rail line was straddled by two roadway lanes, providing the first vehicular crossing of the river at the Falls Cities.

K&I also operated a steam commuter train service called the "Daisy Line" (named for its yellow cars) that ran from downtown Louisville along the Portland Canal and then across the bridge to New Albany. The service, one of the first in the country to be electrified (in 1893), was taken over sometime after 1900 by the Louisville & Northern Railway and Light Co., which in 1908 shifted the cars to run on city streets from Portland to reach downtown Louisville.

In receivership by 1893, the bridge company was reorganized and acquired in 1899 by its three user railroads, which also changed its corporate name to "Kentucky & Indiana Terminal Railroad Co."

K&I's first tracks looped around the west and south ends of the city to connect with the IC and L&N, and were later extended to reach several new industrial districts on property K&I owned and helped develop. A large, fifty-track switching yard, locomotive terminal (with twenty-four-stall roundhouse) and shop, built between 1918 and 1926, supplanted smaller yards laid out earlier for the owner RAILROADS. In 1951, K&IT had 1,177 employees and directly served 200 local industries, more than any other railroad in the city. It handled more than 1.3 million freight cars annually. Corporate headquarters were in the old Irvin mansion (built about 1860) at 2910 Northwestern Pkwy. K&IT and its bridge and terminal facilities were sold to the Southern Railway in December 1981. Norfolk Southern became the new owner on January 1, 1982, after the Southern and the Norfolk & Western merged. Bennett H. Young was K&I Bridge Co.'s first president, serving from 1880 until the late 1890s. Top K&ITRR officers were William Mitchell, William S. Campbell, Carroll W. Ashby, and Joseph H. Gaynor.

See unpublished manuscript by John E. Hartline, retired general freight agent, K&ITRR, 1991; "K&IT Develops Industrial Areas," *Louisville*, May 20, 1952; George W. Hilton, *Monon Route* (Berkeley, Calif., 1979)

Charles B. Castner

KENTUCKY ART AND CRAFT FOUNDATION. In 1980 Phyllis George Brown, then married to Gov. John Y. Brown, began to promote Kentucky crafts, giving them as gifts from the state and helping to organize craft shows. A year later Mrs. Brown, together with Mary Shands, a Louisville patron of the arts, set up a private, nonprofit Kentucky Art and Craft Foundation to provide educational and promotional opportunities for Kentucky craftspeople. One of the earliest educational workshops taught business skills to craftspeople, helping them to market their works.

Brown was instrumental in setting up retail shops in New York City at Bloomingdale's Department Store and later in Neiman-Marcus in Dallas and Marshall Field in Chicago, where wood sculptures, woven baskets, clay pots, wooden bowls, rugs, garden bonnets, quilts, and many other works from Kentucky were sold. Brown's actions brought national attention to Kentucky crafts.

In 1984 the foundation opened the Kentucky Art and Craft Gallery and a gift shop in its 609 W Main St. headquarters. The gallery contains two exhibition areas with several different shows annually. The Kentucky Art and Craft Foundation launched notable exhibitions in its gallery including "Head, Heart and Hands: Native American Craft Traditions in Contemporary World" and "A Marriage of Fire and Earth: Kentucky Glass."

Rita Steinberg was the executive director from 1984 to her resignation in 1998. During her fourteen-year tenure the foundation firmly established itself as the center of arts and crafts in Kentucky, hosting numerous exhibitions and expanding educational programs, focusing on children. Under her leadership gallery sales rose from $80,000 to $475,000 annually. In 1996 the Kentucky Art and Craft Foundation, together with the SPEED ART MUSEUM and the LOUISVILLE VISUAL ART ASSOCIATION, opened TriArt Gallery and gift shop at 400 W MARKET St. The partners' aim was to sell visual arts and use the proceeds for educational purposes. The foundation is noted for its annual fund-raising extravaganza—the Bourbon Ball.

In 1996 the main exhibition space at the Kentucky Art and Craft Gallery was named for longtime patrons and collectors the Reverend Alfred R. and Mary Shands. Mary (Norton) Shands, daughter of George and Jane (Morton) Norton, was born in Louisville June 12, 1930. Mary Shands attended Sarah Lawrence College near New York City. The Reverend Alfred R. Shands was born to Elizabeth and Alfred R. Shands in Washington, D.C., December 19, 1928. Shands graduated from Princeton with a B.A. and went on to receive his M.Div. at the Virginia Theological Seminary in 1954.

In 1997 Mary Shands became a partner in Triad Development, which supplied the land for the creation of a village-style community, the first of its kind in Kentucky, on the WAVE Farm. The farm, which had been in Shands's family since 1938, provided six hundred acres along the Jefferson-Oldham County line for the development of a wide range of housing and was named Norton Commons. The architect, Andres Duany, designed Seaside in the Florida panhandle and Kentlands in Gaithersburg, Maryland, near Washington, D.C.

See *Courier-Journal,* Dec. 26, 1996, April 21, 1996, April 27, 1997, Oct. 18, 1998, Feb. 7, 1999, May 16, 1999.

KENTUCKY ASSOCIATION OF ELECTRIC COOPERATIVES. Established in 1948, the Kentucky Association of Electric Cooperatives (KAEC) provides various services for all of Kentucky's twenty-eight electric cooperatives. Those co-ops serve approximately one-third of Kentucky's population. With headquarters on Bishop Ln. in Louisville, KAEC provides coordinated services in the areas of safety, communications, public relations, meeting coordination, GOVERNMENT and regulatory representation, and sponsorship of youth activities. Primary among youth activities is support of a statewide 4–H club and young farmer activities.

KAEC was established to help in extending electrical services to rural areas in Kentucky. Today Kentucky has one of the five largest rural electrification programs in the country, with electric rates among the lowest. The association is a voluntary membership organization, with its board of directors composed of one manager and one director from each of its member co-ops. KAEC's *KENTUCKY LIVING* is the state's most widely circulated monthly magazine. The magazine covers cultural, social, agricultural, educational, and technological topics about rural Kentucky.

KENTUCKY BANKER'S ASSOCIATION. The Kentucky Banker's Association (KBA) was organized in 1891 in response to the turmoil that rocked Kentucky's BANKING system in the late nineteenth century. The most immediate event that prompted the organization of the association was the monetary stringency of 1890. The stringency resulted in the failure of the Falls City Bank, the Masonic Savings Bank, and the private banking house of Theodore Schwartz & Co., all in Louisville. The failures of the Masonic Bank and Schwartz & Co. were the most disastrous failures and were more widespread in their effects than any failures that had occurred in the city until then. Hundreds of small depositors, mostly among the German population in Louisville, lost their lifetime savings. The failures of those banks shattered the confidence some people had in banks and aroused suspicion against all banking institutions. Thus the KBA was formed to reinstill confidence in the banking system by guaranteeing healthy banks.

The first meeting of the organization was held in Louisville at the Board of Trade building at Third and MAIN Streets on October 21–22, 1891. One hundred sixty members attended this inaugural meeting. The first officers were Thomas L. Barrett, of the BANK OF KENTUCKY, as president; Clinton C. McClarty, of Louisville's Second National Bank, as secretary; and E. Palmer of Paducah as treasurer. The constitution of the KBA declared that the association was formed to promote fiscally healthy and service-oriented banks and banking institutions.

In addition, the KBA promoted unity and cooperation between banks and other commercial, industrial, and agricultural interests of the commonwealth. The KBA promoted the organization as a proponent of legitimate and conservative banking. Through the years the KBA advanced banking interests through the educating of its members, developing products and services for the industry, lobbying the state and federal governments on legislation, and initiating legal actions to protect the industry.

See Kentucky Bankers Association, *KBA—A Command Performance* (1991).

Margaret Merrick

KENTUCKY CENTER FOR THE ARTS. The Kentucky Center for the Arts, established by the legislature as "the Commonwealth's official performing arts center," opened on the north side of MAIN St. between Fifth and Sixth Streets on November 19, 1983, following ten years of planning and development. Kentucky Center was funded and built through a unique partnership between the state, city, county, and private sectors.

The center was designed as a major cultural hub to promote the development of the arts in Louisville and Kentucky by providing a home for the classical performing arts. It would also provide support for downtown tourism and the city's convention and hotel industry. The urban renewal focus included improvement of the downtown area and increased foot traffic from popular, well-attended attractions. Broadway road shows sometimes displace the classical groups.

In the decade after its opening, the governor-appointed Kentucky Center Board of Directors followed the national trend of shifting focus away from classical offerings that attracted small audiences to more lucrative Broadway shows. Popular interest in diversified scheduling for broader audience appeal focused on showcasing a wide variety of regional, national, and international talent. The LOUISVILLE BALLET and the Broadway Series call the center home. The LOUISVILLE ORCHESTRA and the Kentucky Opera Association, while not based at the center, conduct productions at the center's theaters. As a result, in the late 1990s, one-half million visitors each year enjoyed performances in the facility's 2,406–seat Whitney Hall, the 626–seat Bomhard theater, the intimate Martin Experimental or "black box" theater, rehearsal halls, meeting rooms, and the vaulted lobby. The center is also used for civic events, business meetings, dinners, and conventions. Performances are broadcast by Kentucky Educational Television statewide on its "Kentucky Center Presents" programs, some of which are distributed nationally. One of only four arts centers in the United States with a fully staffed comprehensive education program, the center serves the students and teachers of Jefferson and surrounding counties with a variety of educational programs and acts as an educational resource for the entire state. Since its opening, Kentucky Center has given Kentucky's school districts learning opportunities either by bringing students and teachers to Louisville or through outreach programs that take ideas directly into the schools. The center manages the Governor's School for the Arts, an intensive three-week program held each summer.

Kentucky Center for the Arts is visually striking as well as technically state-of-the-art. A sweeping glass facade reflects the surrounding Victorian ARCHITECTURE, back terraces complement the Belvedere Plaza on the riverfront, and seven works of twentieth-century sculpture, which include the works of Alexander Calder, Jean Debuffet, Miro, Tony Smith, Malcolm Morley, Louise Nevelson, and John Chamberlain, grace the interior and exterior spaces. Caudill, Rowlett & Scott, a Houston architectural firm, designed the building with assistance from the Design and Construction Department of HUMANA INC.

See George H. Yater, "Kentucky Center for the Arts: A 17–Year Production," *Louisville* 34 (Nov. 1983): 34–43, 47–55; *Courier-Journal,* Dec. 6, 1998.

Marlow G. Burt

KENTUCKY COLONELS BASKETBALL. One Kentucky foray into professional BASKETBALL ranks was the Colonels of the American Basketball Association (ABA), a marginally successful competitor to the National Basketball Association. The league was inaugurated on March 31, 1967. Nicknamed "The Lively League," the ABA was known for its colorful team promotions such as bikini-clad ballgirls, women's half-time basketball scrimmages, and wrestling bears, to lure fans. The league was also an innovator in several aspects of the game, including the three-point shot.

The Colonels were one of the league's eleven charter members. On March 6, 1967, the franchise was awarded to Don Regan for thirty thousand dollars, but the Colonels were quickly bought by Mamie Gregory, the daughter of a U.S. senator from North Carolina and heiress to a $50 million family fortune; her dog-breeder husband, Joseph; and William C. Boone. The Gregorys, who put up the $64,900 franchise fee for the team, also gave the team its first mascot, a champion Brussels Griffon dog named Ziggy. The first team logo was Ziggy chasing a goateed Kentucky Colonel in a basketball uniform.

The red, white, and blue basketball was the signature emblem of the ABA. And, although the Colonels used chartreuse and white for team colors the first three years, the team eventually settled on its trademark red, white, and blue. The team played home games the first three seasons at the fifty-four-hundred–seat Louisville Convention Center (The GARDENS OF LOUISVILLE), but from 1970 until the league folded in 1976, games were held at FREEDOM HALL.

On June 7, 1967, the Colonels made their first acquisition, Louie Dampier, an All-American guard from the University of Kentucky. Dampier became the most prolific scorer in ABA history, with 13,726 career points. He also set several other records in the ABA, including career assists (4,044), career three-pointers (794), total games played (728), and total minutes played (27,770). Other team greats included Hall of Famers Dan Issel and Artis Gilmore. All three were perennial ABA All-Stars. Issel, a two-time college All-American and the University of Kentucky's career scoring leader, joined the Colonels in 1970 and quickly became one of the most accomplished players in the league. Issel, who was known as "the Horse," was second only to Dampier in career scoring (12,823), and that was in 228 fewer games. Issel was also second in career-scoring average (25.6 points per game) and was in the top ten in career rebounds.

Gilmore, at seven feet, two inches, was the most dominating center in the ABA. Known as "the A-train," he led the league in career field goal percentage (.557) and finished second in career rebounding (7,169) and fourth in career scoring average (22.3 ppg).

There were a number of talented professionals who played with the Colonels, including UK–standout Cotton Nash; Walt Simon, a vice president with Louisville's KFC CORP. until his death in 1997; and Darel Carrier, a standout guard at Western Kentucky University. One of the potential acquisitions who got away was Wesley Unseld, an All-American at the University of Louisville and a future Hall of Famer with the NBA's Washington Bullets. The Colonels offered Unseld a contract for five hundred thousand dollars over two years in 1967, but he eventually signed with the NBA.

The team also had several colorful players of less-than-spectacular abilities, including Orb Bowling, a native of Sandy Hook, Kentucky, who averaged 1.9 PPG; Howard Bayne, a team enforcer skilled primarily at fouling the opposition; and Jim "Goose" Ligon, an Indiana high school star who never played college ball. Ligon, who made it to the Colonels via the Indiana prison system, would respond with "Penn State" when asked what college he attended. There was also crowd favorite Wendell Ladner, who once sustained fifty-four stitches after diving through a glass water cooler trying to retrieve a loose ball.

The Colonels had a variety of coaches in the team's nine-year history. John Givens was the first head coach but lasted only seventeen games before being replaced by Gene Rhodes in the 1967–68 season. Rhodes, a Louisville native who had played at Male High and led St. Xavier High School to a state basketball championship, coached more than two more years before being replaced by Frank Ramsey early in the 1970–71 season. Ramsey quit after the season and was replaced by Joe Mullaney, who coached from 1971 until the end of the 1973 season. In 1973 Babe McCarthy took over for a season, but then in 1974 star-coach Hubie Brown became the last and most successful of the Colonels' coaches.

While few of the ABA teams stayed in one city during the league's history, the Colonels (like the Pacers in Indiana and the Nuggets/Rockets of Denver) never left Louisville. The team earned numerous league accolades, including winning the most regular-season games in ABA history. The Colonels were also the first professional basketball team to play a woman in a game, however briefly.

The Colonels were also known for having regular-season success but struggling in the playoffs. In the 1971–72 season the Colonels set the league's regular-season record of 68–16 but were surprised by the New York Nets, led by Ricky Barry, in six games in the first round of the playoffs. The Colonels made it to the championship in 1971, 1973, and 1975 but were only able to capture the league crown in 1975. In 1971 and 1973 the team took the opposition to a seventh and deciding championship game only to come up short. But on May 22, 1975, before a Freedom Hall crowd of 16,622, the Colonels finally finished off the Indiana Pacers four games to one to become ABA champions. Many sports analysts thought the 1975 Colonels team could have competed against the best in the NBA.

On October 30, 1969, the franchise was purchased from the Gregorys by a consortium headed by HUMANA founder WENDELL CHERRY that included David Grissom, Stuart Jay, David Jones, and John Y. Brown Jr. The group then hired Mike Storen as president and general manager. Storen came from the Indiana Pacers.

Although the Colonels had relative success on the court under the new owners, the consortium continued to lose money. Cherry worked out a deal to sell the team to Cincinnati investors, but on July 31, 1973, John Y. Brown Jr. stepped in and purchased 51 percent of the team and made his wife, Ellie, the majority stockholder.

Finally, on June 17, 1976, Brown folded the team after reaching a $3 million financial agreement with the rest of the teams in the league as part of the merger agreement between the ABA and the NBA. The New York (later New Jersey) Nets, Indiana Pacers, Denver Nuggets, and San Antonio Spurs were the only four teams to make it into the NBA under the terms of the merger. Brown, who estimated the team's losses at about $1 million annually, was unwilling to put up the $3.2 million sign-up fee to join the NBA. The lack of local interest in salvaging the team, coupled with the deal Brown got in the league merger, brought an end to professional basketball in Kentucky.

Many of the Colonels, such as Issel, Dampier, and Gilmore, enjoyed success in the NBA after the league merger. In October 1975, in a move that shocked Colonels fans, Issel was traded to the Baltimore Claws for five hundred thousand dollars, but within weeks he was retraded to the Denver Nuggets. Issel played nine years for Denver, earning a spot in the Basketball Hall of Fame in 1993. As of 1998 he was the Nuggets' vice president and general manager.

Gilmore also enjoyed success in the NBA. In 1976, Gilmore, who was chosen by the Chicago Bulls in the ABA dispersal draft, was the first player chosen by the NBA. He played twelve seasons in the NBA, first with the Bulls (1976–82, 1987), then five seasons with the San Antonio Spurs (1982–87), a season with the Boston Celtics (1988), and one in Italy. He finished with an NBA career scoring average of 17.1 PPG, and he still holds the NBA record for career shooting percentage (.599). In 1998 he was a nominee to the Basketball Hall of Fame.

Dampier also played three seasons with the San Antonio Spurs in the NBA (1976–79). In 1998, after an extended absence from professional basketball, he was named an assistant coach for the Denver Nuggets by his old teammate, Dan Issel.

See David Kindred, *Basketball: The Dream Game in Kentucky* (Louisville 1976); *Lexington Herald-Leader*, June 16, 1995.

James Strohmaier

KENTUCKY CORRECTIONAL INSTITUTION FOR WOMEN. The Kentucky Correctional Institution for Women (KCIW) began in 1938 as an extension of the Kentucky State Reformatory at LaGrange. The Kentucky Federation of Women's Clubs had tried to establish a home for girls on Shelby County property after World War I but were forced to abandon the project due to lack of funds. The federation donated the 270 acres to the commonwealth, and the Pine Bluff Prison Farm was dedicated there on November 4, 1938. The single building was designed by Associated Architects of Newport, which had charge of all welfare construction programs in Kentucky. Ninety inmates were housed in the two-story brick structure that had cost $250,000. The women were transferred from a former school building in Frankfort where they had been lodged after the old prison in Frankfort flooded in 1937.

Gov. A.B. Chandler had gone to Washington, D.C., seeking federal funds from President Franklin D. Roosevelt for prisons, asylums, and hospitals in Kentucky. He spoke at the dedication, as did Mrs. T.C. Carroll, president of the State Federation of Women's Clubs.

Fanniebelle Sutherland, a judge in Paris, Kentucky, and an officer of the state Federation of Women's Clubs, was named superintendent of the farm. She was reported to want to eliminate the use of the words *prison* and *reformatory*. She encouraged inmates to read and sew in their spare time until she was able to begin a vocational education program. The surroundings were supposed to be as pleasant as possible under the circumstances. Windows had no bars, but rather were constructed of small panes of glass set into steel frames. The dining room had small tables with white tablecloths; beds had white counterpanes.

In 1962 the General Assembly separated the farm from the Kentucky State Reformatory. The Kentucky Correctional Institution for Women became an autonomous unit with its own warden. Betty Greenwell Kassulke was appointed to that post in 1968 at the age of twenty-five, the youngest person in the country to be appointed warden of a major institution. She became the first American woman ever to head a major men's prison when she served as interim warden of the Kentucky State Reformatory in 1986, and again in 1998 was interim warden at the Luther Luckett Correctional Complex.

KCIW is the only women's correctional facility operated by the commonwealth and therefore houses prisoners serving sentences from one year up to life imprisonment. Any women sentenced to the death penalty would also be held at KCIW. Women may be placed in minimum to maximum security. Residents have opportunities for basic education through high school classes, vocational training, college classes through Jefferson Community College, and self-help programs including parenting, anger management, and substance abuse.

See *Courier-Journal,* Nov. 5, 1938.

Otis Amanda Dick

KENTUCKY COUNCIL OF CHURCHES. The Kentucky Council of Churches was established in Louisville on December 11, 1947, by representatives of six Protestant denominations. As the successor to the Kentucky Sunday School Union, established in October 1865, it represents more than a century of interchurch cooperation in Kentucky. Formal membership in the council was held in 1990 by twenty-seven jurisdictional groups (conferences, dioceses, presbyteries) representing eleven Christian denominations—African Methodist Episcopal, African Methodist Episcopal Zion, Christian (Disciples of Christ), Christian Methodist Episcopal, Cumberland Presbyterian, Episcopal, Lutheran, Presbyterian Church USA, Roman Catholic, United Church of Christ, and United Methodist. The Roman Catholic dioceses in Kentucky joined the council in 1984. Two divisions of the Salvation Army hold observer membership, and liaisons represent three local ecumenical groups and several Southern Baptist congregations. By January 1951 the organization relocated to Lexington, Kentucky.

The council serves as a channel for cooperative ministry to identify and meet the social, economic, and spiritual needs of the people of Kentucky. The council's Task Force on Hunger has gained national recognition for its assistance to the hungry. The Commission on Religion and Public Policy keeps churches informed on legislative issues and directs the churches' response. The council has sponsored seminars and publications on baptism, eucharist, and ministry, as a sequel to the World Council of Churches study of the three topics.

Donald F. Hellmann

KENTUCKY DERBY. The Kentucky Derby is a one-and-one-quarter-mile stake race for three-year-old Thoroughbred colts, geldings, and fillies. The Derby and the Kentucky Oaks are the oldest continuously contested American sporting events and the only Thoroughbred stake races run annually at the same site since their inception in 1875. At that time, these events were innovative approaches to spring racing that showcased young stock competing over distances that old-time trainers considered too grueling for all but their fittest animals.

The Derby and the Oaks are the creation of Meriwether Lewis Clark Jr. (1846–99), whom Louisville businessmen and Bluegrass horse breeders sent abroad in 1873 to study successful racing ventures in England and France. Clark was nephew and heir-apparent to John and Henry Churchill, wealthy Louisville urbanites who owned and raced Thoroughbreds as a hobby. Clark's wife was John Churchill's teenage ward, Mary Martin Anderson (1854–1934). Her considerable fortune came not only from investments in Louisville enterprises but from a plantation near Greenville, Mississippi, where Clark's younger brother, George Rogers Clark, practiced law and raced horses. Her grandfather was founding secretary of the Lexington Jockey Club. Anderson had been raised by her aunts, one of whom, Pattie Anderson Ten Broeck (d. 1873), was married to Richard Ten Broeck (1811–92), a horseman and track owner of international reputation. In the late 1850s he became the first American to successfully race American Thoroughbreds in England.

The Civil War took a heavy toll on Bluegrass farms, particularly those belonging to Southern sympathizers. Louisville businesses, on

The parade to the post for the 1942 Kentucky Derby.

the other hand, profited both from the conflict and the southern expansion of the LOUISVILLE & NASHVILLE RAILROAD, whose postwar manipulation of rates, routes, and schedules all but shut Bluegrass AGRICULTURE out of Louisville's lucrative river trade.

After Woodlawn, eastern Jefferson County's ill-fated track, closed in 1870, Thoroughbred owners desperately needed an accessible urban racetrack complemented by HOTELS, restaurants, and theaters—amenities that attracted wealthy eastern buyers to meets. Lacking the means to showcase promising young stock, the Bluegrass racing industry's future appeared bleak. Long-term stability lay in the plan to link central Kentucky with northern markets via the Cincinnati Southern Railway. Ground was broken in 1873 but completion of that system was years in the future. When the panic of 1873 depressed already rock-bottom yearling prices, Clark's mission, backed by Churchill money and Ten Broeck's name, became vital to Bluegrass breeders' economic survival. It also signaled L&N management's interest in wooing Lexington commerce back to Louisville.

As the guest of Adm. Henry John Rous (1795–1877), longtime president of the English Jockey Club, Clark studied all aspects of the sport, including the Oaks and the Epsom Derby, classic races then almost a hundred years old. Edward Stanley, twelfth Earl of Derby, had suggested a one-and-one-half-mile race for fillies to senior members of the English Jockey Club in 1778. Named the Oaks for Derby's country retreat near Epsom, the race was run in June 1779. The success of the Oaks led to plans for a mile-long race—lengthened to one and one-half miles in 1784—at Epsom, open to three-year-old colts and fillies, to be run in the spring of 1780. Tradition has it that Lord Derby and fellow Jockey Club member Sir Charles Bunbury set the terms of the race, agreeing the event should be named for one of them, the decision to be made on the toss of a coin. The coin fell to Derby. Bunbury's Diomed won the race and then faded into oblivion. Twenty years later the aged stallion was sold to Colonel Seldon, a Virginia horse breeder. Diomed was champion sire of 1803, the first year his offspring competed at Virginia tracks. Horsemen termed his death in 1808 "a great natural disaster." Diomed's offspring reflected their sire's worth for the next half century before the Civil War brought regularly scheduled meets to a halt. A decade later, when Kentucky racing was near ebb stage, a Diomed descendent made history again.

Clark returned from Europe late in 1873 to superintend the building of the racetrack on his uncle's property just south of the city limits. As president of the Louisville Jockey Club and Driving Park Association, he scheduled the Kentucky Derby as the track's inaugural event on Monday, May 17, 1875. The Oaks was run on Wednesday. Clark and his associates assumed the track's big draw would be the Louisville Cup, a well-publicized handicap race for older, bet-

Kentucky Derby Winners

Horse	*Jockey*	*Date*	*Time*
Aristides	O. Lewis	May 17, 1875	2:37 3/4
Vagrant	B. Swim	May 15, 1876	2:38 1/4
Baden-Baden	W. Walker	May 22, 1877	2:38
Day Star	J. Carter	May 21, 1878	2:37 1/4
Lord Murphy	C. Shauer	May 20, 1879	2:37
Fonso	G. Lewis	May 18, 1880	2:37 1/2
Hindoo	J. McLaughlin	May 17, 1881	2:40
Apollo	B. Hurd	May 16, 1882	2:40 1/4
Leonatus	W. Donohue	May 23, 1883	2:43
Buchanan	I. Murphy	May 16, 1884	2:40 1/4
Joe Cotton	E. Henderson	May 14, 1885	2:37 1/4
Ben Ali	P. Duffy	May 14, 1886	2:36 1/2
Montrose	I. Lewis	May 11, 1887	2:39 1/4
Macbeth II	G. Covington	May 14, 1888	2:38 1/4
Spokane	T. Kiley	May 9, 1889	2:34 1/2
Riley	I. Murphy	May 14, 1890	2:45
Kingman	I. Murphy	May 13, 1891	2:52 1/4
Azra	A. Clayton	May 11, 1892	2:41 1/2
Lookout	E. Kunze	May 10, 1893	2:39 1/4
Chant	F. Goodale	May 15, 1894	2:41
Halma	J. Perkins	May 6, 1895	2:37 1/2
Ben Brush	W. Simms	May 6, 1896	2:07 3/4
Typhoon II	F. Garner	May 12, 1897	2:12 1/2
Plaudit	W. Simms	May 4, 1898	2:09
Manuel	F. Taral	May 4, 1899	2:12
Lieut. Gibson	J. Boland	May 3, 1900	2:06 1/4
His Eminence	J. Winkfield	April 29, 1901	2:07 3/4
Alan-a-Dale	J. Winkfield	May 3, 1902	2:08 3/4
Judge Himes	H. Booker	May 2, 1903	2:09
Elwood	F. Prior	May 2, 1904	2:08 1/2
Agile	J. Martin	May 10, 1905	2:10 3/4
Sir Huon	R. Troxler	May 2, 1906	2:08 4/5
Pink Star	A. Minder	May 6, 1907	2:12 3/5
Stone St.	A. Pickens	May 5, 1908	2:15 1/5
Wintergreen	V. Powers	May 3, 1909	2:08 1/5
Donau	F. Herbert	May 10, 1910	2:06 2/5
Meridian	G. Archibald	May 13, 1911	2:05
Worth	C.H. Shilling	May 11, 1912	2:09 2/5
Donerail	R. Goose	May 10, 1913	2:04 4/5
Old Rosebud	J. McCabe	May 9, 1914	2:03 2/5
Regret	J. Notter	May 8, 1915	2:05 2/5
George Smith	J. Loftus	May 13, 1916	2:04
Omar Khayyam	C. Borel	May 12, 1917	2:04 3/5
Exterminator	W. Knapp	May 11, 1918	2:10 4/5
Sir Barton*	J. Loftus	May 10, 1919	2:09 4/5
Paul Jones	T. Rice	May 8, 1920	2:09
Behave Yourself	C. Thompson	May 7, 1921	2:04 1/5
Morvich	A. Johnson	May 13, 1922	2:04 3/5
Zev	E. Sande	May 19, 1923	2:05 2/5
Black Gold	J.D. Mooney	May 17, 1924	2:05 1/5
Flying Ebony	E. Sande	May 16, 1925	2:07 3/5
Bubbling Over	A. Johnson	May 15, 1926	2:03 4/5
Whiskery	L. McAtee	May 14, 1927	2:06
Reigh Count	C. Lang	May 19, 1928	2:10 2/5
Clyde Van Dusen	L. McAtee	May 18, 1929	2:10 4/5
Gallant Fox*	E. Sande	May 17, 1930	2:07 3/5
Twenty Grand	C. Kurtsinger	May 16, 1931	2:01 4/5
Burgoo King	E. James	May 7, 1932	2:05 1/5
Brokers Tip	D. Meade	May 6, 1933	2:06 4/5
Cavalcade	M. Garner	May 5, 1934	2:04
Omaha*	W. Saunders	May 4, 1935	2:05
Bold Venture	I. Hanford	May 2, 1936	2:03 3/5
War Admiral*	C. Kurtsinger	May 8, 1937	2:03 1/5

Horse	*Jockey*	*Date*	*Time*
Lawrin	E. Arcaro	May 7, 1938	2:04 4/5
Johnstown	J. Stout	May 6, 1939	2:03 2/5
Gallahadion	C. Bierman	May 4, 1940	2:05
Whirlaway*	E. Arcaro	May 3, 1941	2:01 2/5
Shut Out	W. Wright	May 2, 1942	2:04 2/5
Count Fleet*	J. Longden	May 1, 1943	2:04
Pensive	C. McCreary	May 6, 1944	2:04 1/5
Hoop Jr.	E. Arcaro	June 9, 1945	2:07
Assault*	W. Mehrtens	May 4, 1946	2:06 3/5
Jet Pilot	E. Guerin	May 3, 1947	2:06 4/5
Citation*	E. Arcaro	May 1, 1948	2:05 2/5
Ponder	S. Brooks	May 7, 1949	2:04 1/5
Middleground	W. Boland	May 6, 1950	2:01 3/5
Count Turf	C. McCreary	May 5, 1951	2:02 3/5
Hill Gail	E. Arcaro	May 3, 1952	2:01 3/5
Dark Star	H. Moreno	May 2, 1953	2:02
Determine	R. York	May 1, 1954	2:03
Swaps	W. Shoemaker	May 7, 1955	2:01 4/5
Needles	D. Erb	May 5, 1956	2:03 2/5
Iron Liege	B. Hartack	May 4, 1957	2:02 1/5
Tim Tam	I. Valenzuela	May 3, 1958	2:05
Tomy Lee	W. Shoemaker	May 2, 1959	2:02 1/5
Venetian Way	B. Hartack	May 7, 1960	2:02 2/5
Carry Back	J. Sellers	May 6, 1961	2:04
Decidedly	B. Hartack	May 5, 1962	2:00 2/5
Chateaugay	B. Baeza	May 4, 1963	2:01 4/5
Northern Dancer	B. Hartack	May 2, 1964	2:00
Lucky Debonair	W. Shoemaker	May 1, 1965	2:01 1/5
Kauai King	D. Brumfield	May 7, 1966	2:02
Proud Clarion	B. Ussery	May 6, 1967	2:00 3/5
Forward Pass	I. Valenzuela	May 4, 1968	2:02 1/5
Majestic Prince	B. Hartack	May 3, 1969	2:01 4/5
Dust Commander	M. Mangenello	May 2, 1970	2:03 2/5
Canonero II	G. Avila	May 1, 1971	2:03 1/5
Riva Ridge	R. Turcotte	May 6, 1972	2:01 4/5
Secretariat*	R. Turcotte	May 5, 1973	1:59 2/5
Cannonade	A. Cordero Jr.	May 4, 1974	2:04
Foolish Pleasure	J. Vasquez	May 3, 1975	2:02
Bold Forbes	A. Cordero Jr.	May 1, 1976	2:01 3/5
Seattle Slew*	J. Cruget	May 7, 1977	2:02 1/5
Affirmed*	S. Cauthen	May 6, 1978	2:01 1/5
Spectacular Bid	R. Franklin	May 5, 1979	2:02 2/5
Genuine Risk	J. Vasquez	May 3, 1980	2:02
Pleasant Colony	J. Velasquez	May 2, 1981	2:02
Gato Del Sol	E. Delahoussaye	May 1, 1982	2:02 2/5
Sunny's Halo	E. Delahoussaye	May 7, 1983	2:02 1/5
Swale	L. Pincay Jr.	May 5, 1984	2:02 2/5
Spend A Buck	A. Cordero Jr.	May 4, 1985	2:00 1/5
Ferdinand	W. Shoemaker	May 3, 1986	2:02 4/5
Alysheba	C. McCarron	May 2, 1987	2:03 2/5
Winning Colors	G. Stevens	May 7, 1988	2:02 1/5
Sunday Silence	P. Valenzuela	May 6, 1989	2:05
Unbridled	C. Perret	May 5, 1990	2:02
Strike the Gold	C. Antley	May 4, 1991	2:03
Lil E. Tee	P. Day	May 2, 1992	2:03
Sea Hero	J. Bailey	May 1, 1993	2:02 2/5
Go for Gin	C. McCarron	May 7, 1994	2:03 3/5
Thunder Gulch	G. Stevens	May 6, 1995	2:01 1/5
Grindstone	J.D. Bailey	May 4, 1996	2:01
Silver Charm	G. Stevens	May 3, 1997	2:02
Real Quiet	K. Desormeaux	May 2, 1998	2:02
Charismatic	C. Antley	May 1, 1999	2:03 1/5
Fusaichi Pegasus	K. Desormeaus	May 6, 2000	2:021.12

* Triple Crown Winners

ter-known horses, set for Thursday of Spring Meet week.

To boost first-day attendance, Clark opened the infield to the public free of charge. Thus a crowd estimated at ten to twelve thousand saw Diomed's descendant, Kentucky-bred ARISTIDES, outrun fourteen other entrants and set a new American record for the one-and-one-half-mile distance. The Kentucky Derby took on a prestige the Louisville Cup never achieved even though there was no trophy to accompany the $2,850 purse Clark handed to Aristides's owner, H. Price McGrath.

Flush with success, Clark boasted that within the decade a Derby winner would be worth more than the farm on which he was foaled. Clark did not envision fillies winning against colts. The Oaks, he emphasized, showcased the abilities of distaff runners.

For the next fifteen years Derby winners subsequently proved themselves champions, and Derby publicity grew apace. Then Clark's track, popularly known as CHURCHILL DOWNS, became mired in feuds with bookmakers. In 1894 Clark turned his debt-ridden operation over to the New Louisville Jockey Club, an association of local bookmakers that leased the grounds from John Churchill as had the original Louisville Jockey Club. By then Clark was estranged from his wife, and relations with John Churchill, his surviving uncle who controlled the family fortune, were cool at best. When John's will was probated in 1897, Clark had been virtually disinherited. After living in greatly reduced circumstances for five years, acting as steward at tracks rife with corruption, Clark committed suicide in Memphis thirteen days before the 1899 Derby.

Under New Louisville Jockey Club ownership, Churchill Downs became an attraction fit only for the dregs of society. Following the 1902 spring meet, which featured a four-horse Derby field, even the bookmakers wanted out. Rallying to save the Downs, Louisville clothier Matt Winn convinced local businessmen to invest in a facelift for the failing track. Building on that success, Winn took over the track's management and systematically realigned national racing interests in Churchill's favor. Although fields remained small for the next decade, four Derbys put the Louisville race back in the spotlight.

Outflanking a religious coalition of anti-GAMBLING advocates intent on closing the Downs, Winn reintroduced pari-mutuel wagering at the 1908 Derby, where a $5 win ticket on Stone Street paid $123.50. Five years later, Donerail not only set a new track record (2:04 4/5) but returned $184.90 on a $2 pari-mutuel ticket. In 1914, the heavy favorite, Old Rosebud, clipped more than a second off Donerail's record-setting time with a time of 2:03 2/5. Then, in 1915, H.P. Whitney's Regret became the first filly to win the race.

Winn courted New York racing writers and publicists, who milked Derby stories for all they were worth. When Sir Barton won the Kentucky Derby, the Preakness, and the Belmont in 1919, turf writer Charlie Hatton, mimicking English ways, dubbed the sweep "the Triple Crown," coupling the Derby with racing's moneyed strongholds in Maryland and New York. Winn's only significant public relations defeat came in 1920 when he failed to secure Man o' War as a Derby entrant. Samuel Riddle, Man o' War's owner, was one of those horsemen who believed a colt should not be sent the punishing one-and-one-quarter-mile distance so early in the spring.

The year 1921 marks the first time researchers have found newspaper accounts of Derby attendees singing Stephen Collins Foster's "My Old Kentucky Home" before the race. It became the state's song in 1928.

When Churchill Downs celebrated its fiftieth anniversary in 1924, Winn commissioned Lemon and Son Jewelers to create unique trophies for the Kentucky Derby and the Oaks. The Derby trophy was a fourteen-karat-gold-lidded cup topped by the statue of a horse and jockey. One of identical design has been presented to the winning owner every year since. Winn's valet, Andy Phillips, always had the dubious honor of draping a hand-stitched, satin-backed swag of roses across the sometimes-still-fractious winner's withers. The presentation of a "blanket of roses" had been standard practice since 1908.

Winn teamed with Bluegrass horsemen, especially professional gambler and philanthropist E.R. Bradley, to fill Derby fields during the GREAT DEPRESSION. Bradley named 1932 winner Burgoo King for famed Lexington caterer James T. Looney. The 1933 Derby was spiced with a stretch scuffle between the jockeys riding Head Play and Bradley's Brokers Tip. Few spectators realized what had happened until the *COURIER-JOURNAL* printed a head-on shot of the race on its front page the next day. The "fighting finish" exemplified the depths of Depression desperation; newsreel reruns of the race appeared in MOVIE THEATERS around the country. Man o' War's son, War Admiral, won the Derby and the Triple Crown in 1937, signaling better times to come. Ethel Mars's Milky Way Farm's Gallahadion paid a whopping $72.40 to win in 1940.

During World War II, Winn turned Churchill Downs into a patriotic mecca for war-weary civilians and armed forces personnel. Faced with a government-ordered ban on racing in 1945, Winn took Derby nominations as usual and ran the race on June 9, a month after V-E Day. By 1949, the first year WAVE televised the Derby, the race was America's best-known sporting event, celebrating its Diamond Jubilee. For the next thirty years, Derby winners such as Swaps, Carry Back, and Northern Dancer were national stars. In 1968 stewards disqualified Dancer's Image after routine post-race testing identified a then-prohibited medication in the winning colt's urine. Owner Peter Fuller's appeals dragged on for several years until the Kentucky Racing Commission finally declared that, except for pari-mutuel wagering, Calumet's Forward Pass was the 1968 Derby winner.

In 1970 Diane Crump became the Derby's first female jockey, finishing fifteenth on W.L. Lyons Brown's colt Fathom. Crump and a handful of women riders have faced brickbats, boycotts, and court tests to gain the right to ride. Only three other women have ridden in the Derby since them: Patricia Cooksey (1984, So Vague, eleventh), Julie A. Crone (1992, Ecstatic Ride, fourteenth, and 1995, Suave Prospect, eleventh), and Andrea Seefeldt (1991, Forty Something, sixteenth).

During the 1970s three Derby victors—Secretariat, Seattle Slew, and Affirmed—were added to the twentieth-century roster of triple-crown winners. Fillies Genuine Risk and Winning Colors won the 1980 and 1988 Derbies respectively in a race that worldwide viewing audiences had come to know as "the greatest two minutes in sports."

Those two minutes, however, no longer supported the track year-round. Beginning in 1984 Churchill Downs' Board of Directors made significant leadership shifts. Derby tradition bowed to the realities of survival. In short order, the best Derby boxes were sold to corporate sponsors, leaving many Louisvillians who wanted to participate in the hoopla no choice but to party at home or attend the Oaks. In 1987 track management, ignoring public outcry, terminated its long-standing contract with local Derby rose supplier Kingsley Walker Florist and awarded the floral contact to Kroger, a Cincinnati-based grocery chain.

The Derby has attracted a crowd in excess of 100,000 every year since 1969, hitting a record 163,628 for the hundredth running in 1974, before construction of the Matt Winn Turf Course considerably diminished the space available for infield partying. On May 1, 1999, what was probably a record per-square-foot 151,051 fans filled 48,447 seats, the infield, and the back side for the 125th Derby.

Reflecting in part a communications trend, interest in the televised Derby declined steadily throughout the 1990s. Early in 1998 Churchill Downs announced and the State Racing Commission subsequently approved an innovative approach to the centuries-old pre-race ritual, the pill pull, which determines horses' post positions. For the 1998 and 1999 Derbies, the pill pull determined the order in which trainers, after a maximum of one minute's consultation with their Derby horse owners, picked their spot in the starting gate. The goal of this unprecedented change was to enhance the strategic factor of the race and lure viewing audiences back to "the most famous two minutes in sports."

Images of the Twin Spires and slogans long associated with the Kentucky Derby, such as track president Bill Corum's "Run for the Roses," are now copyrighted and trademarked by Churchill Downs Inc. and cannot be used for promotional purposes without permission. Following professional FOOTBALL's lead, the corporation licenses all Derby souvenirs, from the "official" julep glass to the "official" country ham and bourbon balls. Long gone are the days of free infields and easy entrepreneurship upon which the Derby's fame was built.

In his heyday, Paducah-born country humorist and bon vivant Irvin S. Cobb was asked to explain the emotion the Derby evoked in Americans. "If I could do that," he said, "I'd have a larynx of spun silver and the tongue of an anointed angel. Until you go to Kentucky and with your own eyes behold the Derby, you ain't been nowheres and you ain't never seen nothin'!"

See Joe Hirsch and Jim Bolus, *Kentucky Derby: The Chance of a Lifetime* (New York 1988); Lynn S. Renau, *Racing around Kentucky* (Louisville 1995); Lynn S. Renau *Jockeys, Belles and Bluegrass Kings* (Louisville 1996); Jackie C. Burke, *Equal to the Challenge: Pioneering Women of Horse Sport* (New York 1997); Jim Bolus Collection, Kentucky Derby Museum Archives, Louisville;

Lynn S. Renau

KENTUCKY DERBY FESTIVAL. The Kentucky Derby Festival began in 1956 with the Pegasus Parade, produced for a mere $640. CHURCHILL DOWNS donated one hundred dollars toward that parade. Earl Ruby, Addison F. McGhee, Ray Wimberg, and Basil Caummisar are credited with getting the festival under way and sustaining it through the early years. Robinson R. Brown served as the first chairman of the board in 1957. The premise of the early festival was to create a celebration allowing the entire community to take part in the excitement surrounding the Kentucky Derby. An early version of the festival had been attempted in 1936. It had a parade, a wrestling match, concert, and fireworks. However, it was unable to sustain itself due to the 1937 Flood, World War II and a lack of interest.

In the early 1960s the schedule expanded to include more activities. When Jefferson County purchased the steamboat *Avalon* and renamed her the *BELLE OF LOUISVILLE* in 1963, the Great Steamboat Race was born. In the 1970s the festival board made an effort to stabilize the organization. The festival began positioning itself as an integral part of the community in both business and social contexts. It became part of the Chamber of Commerce, and the festival board expanded to include decision-makers.

A strong executive director, Jack Guthrie, was hired in 1972. The "They're Off!" luncheon featured famous speakers and became more popular. New events such as the Chow Wagon, balloon and bike races, the miniMarathon, and the Run for the Rosé were added. Its opening event, Thunder Over Louisville, has become the largest annual fireworks show in North America.

Through the 1980s and 1990s, the festival became more businesslike in its operations. Daniel A. Mangeot became president and CEO in 1979 and led the organization to international recognition as a special events industry leader. During his tenure, the budget increased from $700,000 to $4 million, contributions grew to an estimated $5 million, the number of corporate sponsors tripled from 110 to 325, Pegasus Pin distribution increased by more than 600 percent, and the festival's economic impact multiplied from $17.5 million in 1984 to more than $53 million by the time of Mangeot's death in 1997.

The private, not-for-profit festival is Kentucky's largest annual event. Attendance exceeds 1.5 million people, and two-thirds of the activities are free. Its mission is to provide creative and unique entertainment and community service for the people of greater Louisville. It aims to directly contribute to the aesthetic, cultural, educational, charitable, and economic development of the area. The festival operates under a seventy-five-member volunteer board of directors. Each year charitable organizations raise more than $250,000 by holding festival events. In addition, the Derby Festival BASKETBALL Classic has raised more than $595,000 for charity.

Clay W. Campbell

KENTUCKY DERBY MUSEUM. The Kentucky Derby Museum, newly-renovated in spring 2000, is a three-level, fifty-six-thousand-square-foot facility dedicated to expanding public awareness, appreciation, and understanding of the KENTUCKY DERBY and Thoroughbred racing. Located adjacent to historic Churchill Downs on Central Ave. in Louisville, the museum building, crowned with replicas of the grandstand's familiar twin spires, was dedicated April 28, 1985, a week before the 111th running of the Kentucky Derby. The museum is a nonprofit organization and is not legally or financially connected to the racetrack. It was funded in part by the J. Graham Brown Foundation, the philanthropic organization established by and named for the Louisville businessman and CHURCHILL DOWNS director.

A premier Louisville attraction, the museum features changing exhibitions of Derby and Thoroughbred racing artifacts, memorabilia, and fine art, as well as an award-winning, 360-degree, multimedia Derby presentation titled "The Greatest Race" that is updated yearly. Permanent exhibits include "AFRICAN AMERICANS in Thoroughbred Racing" and one of the most complete collections of Derby glasses. The museum also provides high-tech interactive devices, including a "Place Your Bets" exhibit that explains the mysteries of handicapping and the "Warner L. Jones Jr. Time Machine" that permits visitors to select footage of Derbies as far back as 1918. Popular special events at the museum include racing-related art exhibits, an annual fashion show, the Museum Gala, KENTUCKY OAKS and Derby Day parties, and educational programs for all ages.

Guides offer walking tours of Churchill Downs and the museum's paddock area (weather permitting), where the resident Thoroughbred lives with his companion, a miniature horse. Also located outside in the museum's garden is the actual finish line pole used at Churchill Downs for many years, as well as the grave sites of three famous Kentucky Derby winners: Carry Back (1961), Swaps (1955), and Brokers Tip (1933).

See *The Kentucky Derby Museum at Historic Churchill Downs, Louisville, Kentucky: An Official Souvenir Publication* (Louisville 1986); Samuel W. Thomas, *Churchill Downs: A Documentary History of America's Most Legendary Racetrack* (Louisville 1995).

Michelle Mandro

KENTUCKY EDUCATION ASSOCIATION. The first school established in Kentucky was opened by Mrs. William Coomes in Harrodsburg in 1775. During this early period, educational institutions were private. The formation of free common schools, or public schools as they are called today, was initiated by an 1836 federal grant given to Kentucky in the amount of $1,433,757. In 1837 the Kentucky General Assembly allocated $1 million of the grant to set up a system of common schools; in 1838 that figure was reduced to $850,000. The legislation also allowed for a superintendent of public instruction, who was to be chosen by the governor, and a three-member BOARD OF EDUCATION composed of the secretary of state, the attorney general, and the superintendent, who acted as chairman. However, due to gross misappropriations of funds supposedly designated for educational usage, the system did not flourish as expected.

The sixth man named superintendent, Louisvillian Dr. Robert J. Breckinridge (1847–53), sought to remedy this problem through his introduction of Article Eleven of the new state constitution. The article, approved in 1850, protected the educational system from misappropriations of state school funds and instituted a tax whose proceeds were to be used for educational purposes. Breckinridge retired in 1853 and is regarded as the man who "finally laid the foundation for Kentucky's system of free public schools."

His successor, Dr. John Daniel Matthews, continued to strengthen and advance the state public education system by inviting its leading supporters and educators to a conference in Louisville to discuss strategies for the furthering of the institution. The conference, held December 28 through 30, 1857, was quite innovative. The thirty-eight delegates attending made it the first teachers' meeting in Kentucky history with statewide representation. The meeting was successful in accomplishing many of its goals, including the formation of the Kentucky Association of Teachers and the adoption of its charter constitution. Dr. E.A. Grant of Frankfort was elected the first president. Dr. E.A. Holyoke of Louisville was named secretary, and ten others were named vice presidents to serve on the Board of Directors.

In the spring of 1858 the Kentucky General Assembly passed an act incorporating the Kentucky Association of Teachers. The charter, valid for twenty-five years, provided for the organization's legal establishment. The association met twice that year, first in Lexington in July and then in Louisville in December. This was the only time that the teachers met more than once in the same year. Due to political turmoil and the CIVIL WAR, there were no meetings from 1859 to 1864. The delegates met again in 1865 and drafted a second constitution, changing the group's name to the State Teachers Association of Kentucky. The conference returned to Louisville in 1871. It was here that Pres. Zachary F. Smith proposed an increased school tax and provisions for the appointment of a commissioner for Louisville schools. This began superintendency on a municipal level in Kentucky.

In 1873 the annual meeting took place in Winchester, where a third constitution was written. Under their president and superintendent of public institutions, Dr. Howard A.M. Henderson, the organization changed its name to the Teachers Association of Kentucky. Several innovations in teaching techniques were instituted under Henderson, including the establishment of a school system for Negroes, the enlargement of the State Board of Education, the creation of a board of examiners, and the proposal of uniform textbooks for all schools. In 1877 the Kentucky Teachers Association (State Association of Teachers in Colored Schools) was formed in Frankfort.

A fourth constitution was adopted at the 1892 conference in Paducah, and this time the organization changed its name to the Kentucky Educational Association. The association had been meeting annually since its inception, with the exception of the Civil War years and 1869, but it did not meet in 1893 because of the excitement generated by Chicago's Columbian Exposition and Louisville's hosting of the Southern Educational Association conference.

The association wrote its fifth constitution in 1907 in Winchester but kept its name. It was here that official high school and elementary school curricula were adopted. Music was added in 1914. In 1916 industrial education was added to the curriculum, and athletics became part of the regular school program. The association also formed the Kentucky High School Athletic Association in 1917.

Because of its large population, accessibility, and the fact that it had hosted one-quarter of the meetings already, Louisville was chosen to be the permanent location for the association's annual conferences beginning in 1912. In 1916, under J.H. Bently, the conference platform promoted higher teacher salaries, added vocational education to the curriculum, and advocated the improvement of teacher retirement and tenure systems. In addition the conference made a push for the equalization of educational opportunities for all Kentuckians.

Teacher training was also a growing concern during this period. Before 1906 Kentucky had only two normal schools for the training of teachers. One was at State University in Lexington (currently the University of Kentucky), established in 1880, and the second was the normal school for AFRICAN AMERICANS in Frankfort, established in 1887. In 1906 two more normal schools were opened, in Bowling Green and Richmond, followed by additional ones in 1923 at Morehead and Murray. It was in Louisville that the association adopted its sixth constitution, in 1926.

Prior to 1923 the association had no headquarters. Its offices were located wherever the secretary resided. This changed in 1923 when Louisvillian R.E. Williams, who had served as part-time secretary for the previous seven years, was named permanent executive secretary and treasurer. After his appointment he promptly opened a headquarters office in the Starks Building at Fourth and Walnut St. (now Muhammad Ali Blvd.). Membership in the association doubled over the next five years to almost twelve thousand, and the association was forced to relocate to a more spacious facility. The offices moved to the HEYBURN BUILDING at Fourth St. and BROADWAY in 1928. The association reorganized completely in 1932, dividing itself into eleven districts under their seventh constitution. It was at this meeting that the association changed its name to the Kentucky Education Association. In 1934 free textbooks for the students were purchased by the state for the first time. Meetings were once again canceled in 1944 and 1945 because of travel restrictions stemming from World War II.

In 1956 the Kentucky Education Association merged with the Kentucky Teachers Association, thereby integrating their memberships. For the association's centennial meeting in 1957, a newly constructed headquarters opened at 2303 S Third St. on the University of Louisville's Belknap Campus. The association remained at this location until moving to 101 W Walnut St. (Muhammad Ali Blvd.) in 1967.

In 1982 the Kentucky Education Association announced plans to relocate to Frankfort and sell its building. This was done because most of the important decisions concerning education are made in Frankfort and, as such, it was vital to the organization to be as close as possible to the legislature. The move was made in 1985.

See Porter H. Hopkins, *KEA: The First 100 Years* (Louisville 1957); *Courier-Journal,* Oct. 17, 1982.

KENTUCKY FAIR AND EXPOSITION CENTER. The Kentucky Fair and Exposition Center is a multipurpose complex that houses sporting events, trade shows, an AMUSEMENT PARK, flea markets, numerous special events, and the KENTUCKY STATE FAIR. Commonly known as "the Fairgrounds," the Kentucky Fair and Exposition Center is situated on over four hundred acres at 937 Phillips Ln. It consists of more than a million square feet of indoor exhibit space in FREEDOM HALL Coliseum; the East, West, and South Wings; East and West Halls; the Pavilion; Broadbent Arena; Newmarket Hall; and Cardinal Stadium. This puts KFEC in the top ten exhibit halls in the nation.

The "new" fairgrounds was just an idea in 1946 when the original design for KFEC was submitted to State Fair Board officials. By 1954, construction was underway for what the *New York Herald-Tribune* would call "a magnificent showplace." Fairgrounds Coliseum, soon named Freedom Hall, the East and West Wings, the Pavilion, and the Stadium were completed in 1956 at a cost of $16 million. Newmarket Hall was added in 1968. On April 3, 1974, a tornado caused considerable damage to Freedom Hall, the East Wing, and several horse barns.

Reconstruction costs reached $2 million. The East and West Halls were completed in 1976, and Broadbent Arena was added in 1977. By 1984 construction was underway once again at KFEC. Freedom Hall underwent a $12.5 million renovation including new lighting, new dressing rooms, new meeting rooms, and new VIP suites. Ground was broken for the South Wing in August 1989. Construction of Phase I was completed in 1989. Phase II, including a twenty-five-thousand-square-foot conference center, was opened in 1993.

Over four million people visited the KFEC in 1999, generating more than $401 million. KFEC hosts five of the largest annual trade shows, including the Mid-America Trucking Show; the International Lawn, Garden and Power Equipment Expo; and the Recreation Vehicle Industry Association Trade Show. KFEC is or was also home to minor-league baseball's LOUISVILLE COLONELS and later Redbirds, the American Hockey League's LOUISVILLE PANTHERS, University of Louisville BASKETBALL and FOOTBALL (the football team moved to the new Papa John's Cardinal Stadium in 1998), and the Kentucky Colonels ABA basketball team. Six Flags Kentucky Kingdom—The Thrill Park is also located at KFEC. Approximately eight hundred thousand people visited the Kingdom in 1999, a full-blown amusement park complete with roller coasters, the Thrill Park Theater, and Hurricane Bay Water Park. KFEC is operated by the Kentucky State Fair Board, an agency of the Kentucky Tourism Development Cabinet.

Donald R. Smith

KENTUCKY FARM BUREAU. During the difficult times of World War I, farmers faced very limited marketing opportunities and had no agricultural support. The Kentucky Farm Bureau (KFB) grew directly out of the efforts of business leaders who began to see that an organized and progressive AGRICULTURE would be a boost to the state's overall ECONOMY and their own bottom lines. In the late spring and early summer of 1919, the LOUISVILLE BOARD OF TRADE and the KENTUCKY BANKERS ASSOCIATION formulated the "Kentucky Plan for State Development." Central to the plan was a series of 42 three-day meetings in all regions of the state, bringing key leaders and teachers in the fields of agriculture, schools, roads, and health to rural areas. The meetings gave elemental instruction on such subjects as boosting garden yields, increasing the influence of the rural church, and building silos. These meetings served as a prime mover in the formation of the KFB.

On November 8, 1919, a meeting of several hundred farmers representing farm bureaus from thirty-five counties in Kentucky met at the Hotel Henry Watterson in Louisville and formally organized the bureau. The organization was to work with the University of Kentucky College of Agriculture, the United States Department of Agriculture, and the Kentucky State Board of Agriculture; and it was to become a member of the national organization. The KFB aimed to improve rural schools, stabilize farm prices, and study means for reducing the costs of production.

The KFB's first meeting was in February 1920, and it acquired office space in the Starks Building at Fourth and Walnut (Muhammad Ali Blvd.) Streets. However, financial difficulties followed, since the bureau relied solely on voluntary contributions. The situation grew so bad that in October 1925 the executive committee considered dissolving the organization. The financial problems continued well into the 1930s as the Depression brought unprecedented hardships for Kentucky farmers as prices bottomed out. In April 1933 Ben Kilgore became the executive secretary and began to lay the groundwork for a self-sustaining professional advocacy group. Under Kilgore, the KFB became a strong advocate of President Franklin Roosevelt's Agricultural Adjustment Act (AAA) to control production. KFB weighed into the debate over AAA, asking that a strong production control mechanism be adopted and extended to Kentucky's chief crop, tobacco.

In 1937 the future of the Kentucky Farm Bureau began to look brighter. In April the first issue of *Kentucky Farm Bureau News* rolled off the press. Later that year, Kilgore was one of five who went to Philadelphia to present the KFB's views on a program to control farm production and to make commodity loans available, saying that such a plan was the only way to preserve farmers' purchasing power. The program was approved by Congress, and its popularity brought tangible results to the KFB. Its membership went from five thousand at the beginning of the year to thirteen thousand at year's end. In February 1938 Congress gave final approval to new farm program legislation, including a provision allowing for production limits and price support on tobacco. This achievement was one of KFB's longest-standing and most cherished goals.

The bureau experienced enormous growth and prosperity during the 1940s. In 1941 the KFB ended its association with State Farm Insurance and created the Kentucky Farmers Bank Insurance Co. This company would grow into one of Kentucky's largest in the next fifty years. By the end of the forties, the bureau's membership had reached sixty thousand.

The changing times of the 1950s brought new challenges to the KFB. These challenges included maintaining growth despite the exodus from farm areas and reacting to new challenges facing tobacco from critics who had begun talking about health risks. One of the bureau's biggest issues was taxes. In 1965, at the bureau's urging, the state tax rate on farm real estate was reduced from 5 cents to 1.5 cents per $100 of valuation. Also the tax rate on livestock was lowered from fifty cents per hundred dollars' valuation to one mill. This in effect, eliminated that tax. During the 1968 session KFB pushed for the Farmland Assessment Amendment to the state constitution. This required tax assessors to value farmland for its agricultural value rather than its assumed market value for other purposes. Approved in 1970, the change in assessment procedures would prove to be the most beneficial piece of tax policy for farmers.

In the early 1970s things were looking up for Kentucky farmers. The free market philosophy of the federal government and the boosting of foreign trade brought farm prices to record levels. But after Watergate and President Richard Nixon's resignation, the tide turned. Trade initiatives were replaced with trade embargoes, and the free market farm policies were replaced with high price supports and production limits. Inflation swept through the economy, raising prices on consumer goods and farm inputs. Farmers were blamed for the price increases. KFB found itself defending these increases while at the same time searching for new ways to reduce costs. Another major event that occurred during the 1970s was the switch Kentucky burley farmers made from hand-tying bundles to baling. In 1975 the University of Kentucky began an experimental burley-baling project, but it was received negatively by some buyers who thought the procedure would cheapen the quality of the burley. The university discontinued the project because of the negative feedback. However, in 1976 KFB took up the project and tried once again to convince Kentucky farmers to switch over to baling rather than continue the slow and labor-intensive hand-tying of bundles. Although 175 farmers took part in the project and reaped the benefits in major reductions of LABOR, the project was cancelled again in 1978 after the government did not put price supports on baled burley. Nevertheless, some farmers kept using the new method, and each year the government relented a little more. By 1981 most farmers had embraced the concept.

The 1980s and 1990s saw Kentucky farmers beset on all fronts, especially from anti-tobacco legislation and by environmentalists' complaints of pesticide runoff into ground water. When studies done by KFB confirmed the validity of their complaints, KFB joined the environmentalists in dealing with the problem.

The state office and insurance company is located at 9201 Bunsen Ave. in the Bluegrass Industrial Park in eastern Jefferson County.

See Gary Huddleston, *Seventy-Five Years of Kentucky Farm Bureau, 1919–1994* (Louisville 1994).

KENTUCKY FEDERATION OF WOMEN'S CLUBS. On the hot days of July 9 and 10, 1894, representatives from sixteen women's clubs from across the state gathered at the historic Ashland estate in Lexington, Kentucky. Their purpose was to form the Kentucky Federation of Women's Clubs (KFWC), headquartered in Louisville since 1954. Their desire was to bring together and increase communication between club women involved in artistic, educational, philanthropic, and civic work. The KFWC was the first in a southern state to join its parent organization, the General Federation of Women's Clubs, founded in 1890, one of the world's largest nondenominational international service groups.

In 1921, just 17 years after the KFWC's inception, 150 clubs had joined its ranks; by the mid-1990s, the KFWC served 16,000 clubwomen in 9 state districts. Clubs that limit membership to women between the ages of eighteen and forty are eligible to join the KFWC as junior clubs. Juniorette status is given to those clubs with membership between the ages of fourteen and eighteen.

The KFWC has advocated education reform, child LABOR laws, woman suffrage, conservation, health awareness, and community betterment. In 1968 a treatment center in Jefferson County for delinquent girls, Jewel Manor, named in honor of former KFWC president Jewel Hamilton (1964–66), was dedicated. Though the house was operated by the Kentucky Child Welfare Department, the campaign to raise funds for the building had been spearheaded by the KFWC. Today, the KFWC divides its work into six main departments: education, art, conservation, home life, international affairs, and public affairs.

The KFWC did not have a permanent home until the 1950s, when the decision was made to center operations in Louisville. In 1954 a temporary office was rented on W LIBERTY St. Until then, the club's work and records were located with the KFWC president, a position that comes up for election every two years. In 1956 KFWC headquarters was permanently established at 1228 Cherokee Rd. in Louisville.

KFWC publications include the quarterly journal, *Kentucky Clubwomen*; a cookbook, *Kentucky Hospitality: A 200-Year Tradition* (1976); and *Tradition of Service: A History of the Kentucky Federation of Women's Clubs, 1894–1994* (1994). Louisville-area clubs affiliated with the KFWC include Beechmont Woman's Club, Buechel Woman's Club, FERN CREEK Woman's Club, Highland Woman's Club, HIKES POINT Woman's Club, Woman's Club of LYNDON, Meadow Heights Woman's Club, MIDDLETOWN Woman's Club, Okolona Woman's Club, Pleasure Ridge Park Woman's Club, Shively Woman's Club, Woman's Club of St. Matthews, and Valley Woman's Club.

See Janice Theriot, *Tradition of Service: A History of the Kentucky Federation of Women's Clubs, 1894–1994* (Louisville 1994).

KENTUCKY GOVERNOR'S SCHOOL FOR THE ARTS. The program, founded in 1987, provides training for outstanding high school students in the fine and performing arts throughout the commonwealth. The program includes a residential summer session, career and college days, and master classes in the arts statewide.

Each year more than 1,200 students entering their junior and senior years audition for 164 openings. Selected students attend classes with master instructors in dance, drama, instrumental and vocal music, creative writing, and visual art. The three-week summer program held at BELLARMINE COLLEGE culminates in a daylong festival of performances and exhibits.

Governor's School for the Arts (GSA) graduates are invited to participate and audition at a special college and career fair held for them in conjunction with the Youth Performing Arts School in Louisville each November. Students meet college and arts school representatives from many states. One of the outreach initiatives of GSA is a series of master classes held throughout the state. These provide an opportunity for students to learn more about their art and also prepare for GSA auditions and reviews.

This program is administered by the Kentucky Center for the Arts. GSA receives support from private and public donations and from the Kentucky Center's endowment fund, the Kentucky Education Arts and Humanities Cabinet, and more than a hundred corporations, parents, educators, and friends of the arts.

Gail Ritchie Henson

KENTUCKY HARVEST. In 1987 Louisville stockbroker Stan Curtis was going through a cafeteria line when a half-full tub of green beans was removed and replaced with a fresh batch. After learning that the old beans would be thrown out because of restaurant policy, Curtis began to develop the idea for a nonprofit agency known as Kentucky Harvest. Concentrating on perishable foods that restaurants, caterers, grocery stores, and other businesses would normally throw away, Kentucky Harvest distributes the surplus food to needy people in soup kitchens, missions, and other charitable agencies in Louisville and southern Indiana.

Dubbed "food-raisers" as opposed to fund-raisers, Kentucky Harvest receives no federal money and rarely accepts donations. Instead, the organization prefers that people offer their time to assist the other one thousand volunteers do such things as pick up food on a moment's notice and deliver it to shelters or to help with administrative work. After other cities formed similar organizations, Curtis formed USA Harvest as an umbrella agency with approximately 125 members by late 1997.

By 1998 Kentucky Harvest had distributed roughly 18 million pounds of food to over 130 organizations in the Louisville area with the assistance of more than 120 local restaurants and businesses.

See *Courier-Journal*, Jan. 16, 1997, Nov. 7, 1997.

KENTUCKY HISTORICAL SOCIETY. The Kentucky Historical Society was founded April 22, 1836, in Frankfort, Kentucky. A group of men dedicated to preserving Kentucky history met in the secretary of state's office and voted to form a state historical society. State senator John Brown was elected the first president of the organization. On February 16, 1838, the society received its charter and was incorporated. On March 29, 1839, the society met in Louisville and elected Judge John Rowan of Bardstown as president. The society's headquarters was located in the Telegraph Building, a brick structure on the corner of Third and MARKET Streets.

The constitution of the Kentucky Historical Society stated that the goal was to collect and preserve items of historical interest pertaining to Kentucky. The librarian of the society, Dr. Edward Jarvis, a leading Louisville physician, effectively carried out this mission. During his tenure as librarian, the collection of the society grew to several thousand volumes. Jarvis received gifts of books from such notable figures as John Quincy Adams, Ralph Waldo Emerson, and Henry David Thoreau. In 1841, the state legislature agreed to place copies of its acts and journals in the library of the society.

With the death of Judge Rowan in July 1843, the society experienced a decline. Another great loss in leadership came when Jarvis left Kentucky because of the slavery issue and returned to his native Massachusetts. By 1852 the society ceased to be active. The collection of the society was turned over to the Louisville Library, a short-lived group whose holdings eventually were passed on to the LOUISVILLE FREE PUBLIC LIBRARY when it was established in 1908.

In October 1878 historian George W. Ranck of Lexington and members of the Frankfort Lyceum revived the Kentucky Historical Society. Rooms were provided in the Old Capitol annex building in Frankfort for artifacts and books. However, interest in the society lapsed, and in 1889 the organization again closed its doors. On October 6, 1896, Mrs. Jennie Chinn Morton (1838–1920) and the Frankfort Colonial Daughters held a public meeting to reorganize the society. In June 1897 the Kentucky Historical Society was legally reestablished. Since 1906 the state has annually appropriated moneys for its operation.

In April 1999 the historical society moved into a state-of-the-art headquarters in the Kentucky History Center in Frankfort, where the society maintains an extensive museum and library collection.

See Williard Rouse Jillson, "A Sketch of the Bibliography of the Kentucky State Historical Society 1836–1943," *Register of the Kentucky Historical Society* 41 (July 1943): 179–230.

Ron D. Bryant

KENTUCKY HOME SCHOOL FOR GIRLS. In 1863 Belle Peers, daughter of an Episcopal clergyman, formed a school with twelve children in the vestry of CHRIST CHURCH CATHEDRAL. Five years later she and Henrietta Barbaroux created a school with both a junior and a senior department. Although the school was commonly known as the Home School for Girls, an act of the Kentucky legislature chartered the facility as the Kentucky Home Seminary in 1882. In 1904 the name was changed to the Davison-Dodge School. In 1908 Lelia Calhoun became the owner and first principal of the renamed Kentucky Home School. In 1910 Annie Stuart Anderson and Annie S. Waters bought the school, which was located on Fourth St. In 1927 the school moved to Cowling Ave., and in 1944 it was chartered as a nonprofit organization. The Kentucky Home School moved to its last home on Douglass Blvd. in 1948. The school was merged with Louisville Country Day in 1972 to become Kentucky Country Day.

See Florence Willey Dickerson, "A History of Kentucky Home School for Girls from 1863–1913," M.A. thesis, University of Louisville, 1963.

Sharon Receveur

KENTUCKY INTERNATIONAL CONVENTION CENTER. The Kentucky International Convention Center, located at 221 Fourth St. in downtown Louisville, is home to a variety of regional and national events such as conventions, expositions, trade shows, banquets, and worship services.

The center occupies two full city blocks. Designed by the Louisville architectural firm of Luckett & Farley, it was constructed between November 1974 and December 1976 and opened in 1977. Originally it consisted of 144,000 square feet of exhibit space. Inside, it contained a column-free 100,000-square-foot exhibit hall, a 15,000-square-foot lobby, 36 meeting rooms, and a 9,600-square-foot ballroom.

Almost eight hundred thousand people visited the center in 1996, attending such events as Fred Wiche's Lawn and Garden Expo, Jim Strader's Hunting and Fishing Expo, the Veterans of Foreign Wars annual convention, the Great American Train Show, and the Summer Bridal Expo. It was also host in 1996 to the African Methodist Episcopal (AME) church convention, which drew a daily average of twelve thousand delegates over nine days. In 1997 the center was also home to five of the top twenty area conventions and trade shows as determined by attendance figures, including the National Baptist Sunday Church School and Baptist Training Union Congress, the 1997 Convention of Presbyterian Women, and the International Science and Engineering Fair.

In the late 1990s a $71.8 million expansion doubled the size of the center. The early facility stands on the block between Third and FOURTH Streets, bounded by MARKET St. on the north and Jefferson St. to the south. Completed in December 1999, the expansion extends over Third St. and fills the block east between Third and Second Streets. The Convention Center was increased in size to 285,000 square feet, with 147,000 square feet of column-free exhibit space. A thirty-thousand-square-foot ballroom was added in the old half. The exterior of the old half was made "friendlier," and its fortress-like appearance was toned down by the insertion of glass and brick elements into the concrete facade. A canopied entrance to the new ballroom was added on Market St. The designers were Godsey Associates Architects of Louisville in collaboration with Ellerbe Becket of Minneapolis. The lobby floor design was primarily the work of Massachusetts artist Lejos Heder. The enlarged center added millions of dollars to the local ECONOMY because the expansion allowed the center to attract more and bigger conventions to Louisville.

The Kentucky International Convention Center is a member of the Kentucky Tourism Development Cabinet and is operated under the direction of the Kentucky State Fair Board.

See *Courier-Journal*, May 18, 1998.

Donald R. Smith

KENTUCKY IRISH AMERICAN. The ethnic weekly *Kentucky Irish American* (KIA) began publication on July 4, 1898, at 319 Green (LIBERTY) St. The founding editor was William M. Higgins (1852–1925), who employed John J. Barry (1877–1950) as his associate. The latter became editor in 1925, holding that position until his son John Michael "Mike" assumed the post in 1950 and kept it until the paper ceased publication.

After the death of Higgins, the KIA was a Barry family paper. Many of Mike Barry's brothers (and his wife Bennie) were involved in producing the journal. His brother Joseph served as business manager, and his own children aided in distribution. In 1966 the offices moved to 325 E Breckinridge St., and from

issue appeared on November 30, 1968.

The early KIA was distinctly IRISH, American, and Catholic. While it was never a religious paper as such, it reported initially to a predominantly Irish Catholic audience and was quick to defend that ethnic community against challengers. Its early enemies included Great Britain, the Ku Klux Klan, and the Republican Party. In the era of the first world war, the KIA opposed the League of Nations, Prohibition, and women's suffrage. The paper supported the candidacy of Catholic presidential candidate Al Smith in 1928 and, after his defeat, headlined its issue, "Bigotry Won the Day."

The 1930s saw a strong defense of President Franklin D. Roosevelt's New Deal, while a special feature of the World War II years was a column titled "Brothers in Arms," featuring letters home from the five Barry boys who were in military service around the globe. The annual St. Patrick's Day edition in March routinely featured green ink and a full-page map of Ireland.

Under the editorship of Mike Barry, the KIA identified itself strongly with the civil rights movement and became a strong supporter of President John F. Kennedy's New Frontier. Barry's acerbic comments against the *Courier-Journal* and against Kentucky governor A.B. "Happy" Chandler became legendary. The KIA counted President Harry S Truman and Franklin D. Roosevelt Jr. among its subscribers. Paying tribute both to the sports and general coverage of the journal, national sportswriter Red Smith once allowed that the KIA "was all the excuse any man needs for learning to read."

See Clyde F. Crews, *Mike Barry and the Kentucky Irish American* (Lexington 1995).

Clyde F. Crews

***KENTUCKY LIVING* MAGAZINE.** The Kentucky Association of Electric Cooperatives began publishing the *Kentucky Electric Co-op News* in April 1948 from its Louisville headquarters, to inform co-op members about the utilities they owned. In January 1951 the name was changed to the *Rural Kentuckian* and in April 1989 to *Kentucky Living*, recognizing the diversity of electric co-op consumer-owners. In 1999 *Kentucky Living* was the largest-circulation publication in the state, being sent to 475,000 homes and businesses. *Kentucky Living* is distributed through twenty-three of the state's twenty-five local, not-for-profit electric cooperatives that subscribe on behalf of their consumer-owners. Those cooperatives also produce local sections of between four and twenty-four pages. The magazine provides general Kentucky interest coverage, focusing on tourism, gardening, history, culture, business, and lifestyle trends as well as the electric utility industry.

Paul Wesslund

KENTUCKY LOTTERY CORPORATION. The creation of a state lottery, headquartered in Louisville, was a major plank in Wallace Wilkinson's successful gubernatorial campaign in 1987. The issue of a state lottery was put on the ballot in November 1988, and Kentuckians passed the referendum, as it was supported by 60 percent of the voters. In December 1988 the General Assembly created the Kentucky Lottery Corp. (KLC), making Kentucky the twenty-ninth state to operate a lottery. The lottery initially received strong public support because it was designed as a revenue source to help fund improvements in education without tax increases.

On April 4, 1989, the first lottery ticket was sold; sales the first day surpassed $5 million. The state contracted with Rhode Island–based GTECH to supply the computers and equipment for on-line services that run Lotto-type games for the lottery. In April 1995 GTECH lost the lottery contract after Atlanta-based Automated Wagering International Inc. (AWI) underbid the firm by $20 million. AWI eventually withdrew its bid after problems with the company's software surfaced in other states and after learning that their parent company was considering selling the firm.

In April 1997 Kentucky Lottery Corp. signed a five-year, $47.9 million contract with GTECH for them to be KLC's computer services vendor. During contract negotiations, the lottery considered running the games independently, but officials decided against operating a "run-your-own" system after a report by a Columbus, Ohio–based consultant indicated that the savings would not be substantial.

While generally considered a success, the lottery has been frequently marred by controversy over operations. In 1993 State Auditor Ben Chandler's office issued a scathing report on lottery operations. The report's findings indicated that Kentucky Lottery Corp. was poorly managed and criticized the extravagant spending practices of top officials and employees. Several lottery officials resigned after the audit was released.

In September 1997 Kentucky Lottery moved its headquarters from just off Dutchmans Ln. near the Watterson Expressway to a $7 million, newly renovated two-story brick building on W Main St. near Ninth St. The facility also houses the information-technology center, previously located in Bluegrass Industrial Park, and the regional sales office and warehouse, formerly located on Produce Rd.

As of 1998 there were several lottery games available to Kentuckians, including Powerball, Pick 3 and Pick 4, Cash Five, Lotto Kentucky, and Cash Quest. The most popular were Powerball, in which winners match numbers—including a red "powerball" automatic winner—for cash prizes, and Lotto Kentucky, a similar game where players can choose the "cash option" of a smaller one-time payoff rather than receive the prize in yearly installments. There are also dozens of instant-win games such as pull-tabs and scratch games.

See *Courier-Journal*, Dec. 16, 1988, Aug. 24, 1998, March 31, 1997, March 13, 1996.

KENTUCKY MILITARY INSTITUTE. The Kentucky Military Institute, popularly known as KMI, enjoyed a long history in the field of education. KMI was opened in 1845 by R.T.P. Allen, a graduate of the United States Military Academy at West Point, New York. On January 20, 1847, the school was given a charter by the state upon a written endorsement by Henry Clay. It drew students from all over the country, especially from the Ohio Valley and the South. When the school opened with thirty students, it was located at Farmdale, six miles southeast of Frankfort, then later at Lyndon, a Louisville suburb, with a winter campus in Venice, Florida. The school was operated as a quasi-military corps. In 1851 the first graduating class of four received degrees. One graduate was John G. Carlisle, who became secretary of the treasury under President Grover Cleveland (1893–97).

The school flourished until 1861, when most of the cadets and many of the faculty members left to join the Union and Confederate armies. Ten KMI alumni became generals. Associated with the names of KMI graduates and former cadets are such historic moments as Bull Run, Chickamauga, Missionary Ridge, Stone's River, the Wilderness, and Gettysburg. Chickamauga was the battle in which the most KMI students participated, serving on both Union and Confederate sides. Three of the more notable officers to come from KMI were Brig. Gen. Benjamin Hardin Helm (1847), Maj. Thomas Bell Monroe Jr. (1847), and Brig. Gen. Meriwether Lewis Clark (faculty). Helm, who led Confederate troops at Shiloh and at Chickamauga, was married to Emily Todd, sister-in-law of President Abraham Lincoln. Before joining the Confederate army, Monroe was mayor of Lexington and the publisher of the *Kentucky Statesman*. Clark was the son of William Clark of the Lewis and Clark Expedition. He commanded a brigade of the Missouri State Guard (CSA) and was chief of artillery. Clark served with Gen. Robert E. Lee and was with Lee at the surrender at Appomattox Courthouse.

In 1893 Charles Wesley Fowler bought KMI and decided that the school would benefit from being located in an urban environment. In early 1896 he acquired a historic plantation, formerly the home of Stephen Ormsby, located on LaGrange Rd. near Bashaw's Station, where operations continued until 1971. KMI prospered under Fowler, and extensive physical improvements were made. However, financial problems arose, and in 1925 Col. Charles B. Richmond and Col. Charles E. Hodgin purchased the school.

Their first order of business for the institution was to end the college program and become a college preparatory school. In 1933 two

come a college preparatory school. In 1933 two hotels were purchased in Venice, Florida, and the students began to spend January, February, and March there. Throughout the 1940s and 1950s KMI prospered, enrolling as many as 330 students. With the retirement of Richmond in 1965, Dr. William T. Simpson and Col. Charles A. Hodgin assumed command. They ran the school until 1971, when anti-military sentiment accompanying the Vietnam War caused many military schools to make drastic changes. KMI was no different. It closed in 1971, and in 1973 the facilities were merged with Kentucky Country Day School. KMI's alumni include former Kentucky governor and businessman John Young Brown Jr. and actors Jim Backus, Victor Mature, and Fred Willard.

See James Darwin Stephens, *Reflections: A Portrait-Biography of the Kentucky Institute, 1845–1971* (Georgetown, Ky., 1991).

William Simpson

KENTUCKY OAKS. In the 1870s Louisville gentlemen were trying to start a new track and racing association known as the Louisville Jockey Club (later Churchill Downs). While traveling in Europe in 1872, Col. Meriwether Lewis Clark Jr., a local businessman, viewed several prestigious races that he hoped would serve as models for stakes races at the new club. Of the four, which included the Derby, the Oaks, the Clark Handicap, and the Falls City, the Kentucky Oaks was modeled on the English Oaks. Founded by Lord Derby and Lord Bunbury in 1779, the one-and-one-half-mile race for fillies was named after Lord Derby's large house at Epsom where he entertained during the race meets.

The Kentucky Oaks was first run on Wednesday, May 19, 1875, as one of the four original stakes races at the club. It was won by Vinaigrette, owned by A.B. Lewis & Co., who received a purse of $1,175.

Between 1906 and 1930 the Derby was something of an Oaks trial. The Oaks did not yet have a traditional day and was usually run two weeks, or more, following the Derby. Fillies who had placed in the money in the Derby would often go on to win the Kentucky Oaks. They typically ended their racing careers as broodmares of still more champions.

By 1944 the Oaks had moved to the Friday before Saturday's Derby. At that point, city residents began to consider Oaks Day as "Louisville's day at the track," since locals, who had no luck obtaining Derby tickets, could more easily get tickets to it. Moreover, Churchill Downs would already be decked out in all its Derby finery and flowers. Many people preferred the comparative quiet of Oaks Day.

In 1985 attendance began to increase at both the mile-and-an-eighth Oaks and the mile-and-a-quarter Derby. So significant was the increase at the Oaks that in 1989 the infield was opened for the racing crowd.

In 1991 Kroger florists created an Oaks gar-

Kentucky Oaks Results

Winner	*Jockey*	*Date*	*Time*
Vinaigrette	J. Houston	May 19, 1875	2:39 3/4
Necy Hale	W. James	May 17, 1876	2:42 1/2
Felicia	W. James	May 24, 1877	2:39
Belle of Nelson	Booth	May 23, 1878	2:39
Liahtunah	Hightower	May 22, 1879	2:40 1/4
Longitude	J. McLaughlin	May 20, 1880	2:41 3/4
Lucy May	Wolfe	May 19, 1881	2:41
Katie Creel	J. Stoval	May 18, 1882	2:39
Vera	J. Stoval	May 23, 1883	2:39 3/4
Modesty	I. Murphy	May 10, 1884	2:48 1/4
Lizzie Dwyer	Fuller	May 16, 1885	2:40 3/4
Pure Rye	E. Garrison	May 17, 1886	2:41
Florimore	Johnston	May 14, 1887	2:40 3/4
Ten Penny	A. McCarthy Jr.	May 22, 1888	2:42
Jewel Ban	J. Sloval	May 16, 1889	2:41
English Lady	Hollis	May 21, 1890	2:42 1/2
Miss Hawkins	T. Britton	May 20, 1891	2:18 1/4
Miss Dixie	H. Ray	May 16, 1892	2:14 1/4
Monrovia	J. Reagan	May 15, 1893	2:16
Selika	A. Clayton	May 19, 1894	2:15
Voladora	A. Clayton	May 28, 1895	2:16 3/4
Souffle	C. Thorpe	May 11, 1896	1:54 1/2
White Frost	T. Burns	May 22, 1897	1:49
Crocket	J. Hill	May 19, 1898	1:51 1/2
Rush	J. Hill	May 20, 1899	1:52 1/2
Etta	M. Overton	May 19, 1900	1:48
Lady Schorr	J. Woods	May 11, 1901	1:53
Wain-a-Moinen	M. Coburn	May 24, 1902	1:51 1/4
Lemco	J. Reiff	May 19, 1903	1:49 3/4
Audience	G. Helgeson	May 18, 1904	1:51
Janeta	D. Austin	May 27, 1905	1:49 3/4
King's Daughter	E. Robinson	May 29, 1906	1:47 4/5
Wing Ting	J. Lee	June 6, 1907	1:50 1/5
Ellen-a-Dale	V. Powers	May 30, 1908	1:46 3/5
Floreal	Heidel	May 22, 1909	1:49 1/5
Samaria	R. Scoville	June 4, 1910	1:50 1/5
Bettie Sue	T. Rice	June 8, 1911	1:48
Flamma	J. Butwell	May 28, 1912	1:51 1/5
Cream	C. Ganz	May 24, 1913	1:47 3/5
Bronzewing	W. Obert	May 22, 1914	1:45 3/5
Waterblossom	E. Martin	May 21, 1915	1:46 3/5
Kathleen	R. Goose	May 27, 1916	1:47 2/5
Sunbonnett	J. Loftus	May 25, 1917	1:46 4/5
Viva America	W. Warrington	May 25, 1918	1:46 4/5
Lillian Shaw	T. Murray	May 31, 1919	1:45
Lorraine	D. Connelly	May 19, 1920	1:58 2/5
Nancy Lee	L. McAtee	May 14, 1921	1:50 2/5
Startle	D. Connelly	June 3, 1922	1:52 3/5
Untidy	J. Corcoran	May 26, 1923	1:53
Princess Doreen	H. Stutts	May 31, 1924	1:51 4/5
Deeming	J. McCoy	May 30, 1925	1:54
Black Maria	A. Mortensen	May 31, 1926	1:55 2/5
Mary Jane	D. Connelly	May 30, 1927	1:53 2/5
Easter Stockings	W. Crump	June 2, 1928	1:51 3/5
Rose of Sharon	W. Crump	June 1, 1929	1:51
Alcibiades	R. Finnerty	May 31, 1930	1:52 3/5
Cousin Jo	E. James	May 9, 1931	1:53
Suntica	A. Pascuma	May 21, 1932	1:52 1/5
Barn Swallow	D. Meade	May 20, 1933	1:51 1/5
Fiji	G. Elston	May 19, 1934	1:51 3/5
Paradisical	G. Fowler	May 18, 1935	1:51 1/5
Two Bob	R. Workman	May 16, 1936	1:52 3/5
Mars Shield	A. Robertson	May 15, 1937	1:53 2/5
Flying Lee	L. Haas	May 28, 1938	1:52 4/5

Winner	Jockey	Date	Time
Flying Lill	C. Bierman	May 13, 1939	1:51
Inscolassie	R.L. Vedder	May 11, 1940	1:54 2/5
Valdina Myth	G. King	May 17, 1941	1:52 3/5
Miss Dogwood	J. Adams	May 9, 1942	1:47
Nellie L.	W. Eads	May 8, 1943	1:48 3/5
Canina	J. Adams	May 5, 1944	1:48 3/5
Come and Go	C.L. Martin	June 8, 1945	1:49 4/5
First Page	J.R. Layton	May 3, 1946	1:51 2/5
Blue Grass	J. Longden	May 2, 1947	1:51 3/5
Challe Anne	W. Garner	April 30, 1948	1:48 3/5
Wistful	G. Glisson	May 6, 1949	1:47 2/5
Ari's Mona	W. Boland	May 5, 1950	1:43 3/5
How	E. Arcaro	May 4, 1951	1:45 3/5
Real Delight	E. Arcaro	May 2, 1952	1:45 2/5
Bubbley	E. Arcaro	May 1, 1953	1:45 3/5
Fascinator	A. DeSpirito	April 30, 1954	1:45
Lalun	H. Moreno	May 6, 1955	1:46
Princess Turia	W. Hartack	May 4, 1956	1:44 4/5
Lori-El	L.C. Cook	May 3, 1957	1:44 4/5
Bug Brush	E. Arcaro	May 2, 1958	1:44 4/5
(1) Wedlock*	J.L. Rotz	May 1, 1959	1:45
(2) Hidden Talent*	M. Ycaza		1:44 2/5
Make Sail	M. Ycaza	May 6, 1960	1:44 1/5
My Portrait	B. Baeza	May 5, 1961	1:47
Cicada	W. Shoemaker	May 4, 1962	1:44 3/5
Sally Ship	M. Ycaza	May 3, 1963	1:44 4/5
Blue Norther	W. Shoemaker	May 1, 1964	1:44 1/5
Amerivan	R. Turcotte	April 30, 1965	1:44 2/5
Native St.	D. Brumfield	May 6, 1966	1:44 4/5
Nancy Jr.	J. Sellers	May 5, 1967	1:44
Dark Mirage	M. Ycaza	May 3, 1968	1:44 3/5
Hail to Patsy	D. Kassen	May 2, 1969	1:44 2/5
Lady Vi-E	D. Whited	May 1, 1970	1:44 4/5
Silent Beauty	K. Knapp	April 30, 1971	1:44 1/5
Susan's Girl	V. Tejada	May 5, 1972	1:44 1/5
Bag of Tunes	D. Gargan	May 4, 1973	1:44 1/5
Quaze Quilt	W. Gavidia	May 3, 1974	1:46 3/5
Sun and Snow	G. Patterson	May 2, 1975	1:44 3/5
Optimistic Gal	B. Baeza	April 30, 1976	1:44 3/5
Sweet Alliance	C. McCarron	May 6, 1977	1:43 3/5
White Star Line	E. Maple	May 5, 1978	1:45 1/5
Davona Dale	J. Velasquez	May 4, 1979	1:47 1/5
Bold 'n Determined	E. Delahoussaye	May 2, 1980	1:44 4/5
Heavenly Cause	L. Pincay Jr.	May 1, 1981	1:43 4/5
Blush With Pride	W. Shoemaker	April 30, 1982	1:50 1/5
Princess Rooney	J. Vasquez	May 6, 1983	1:50 4/5
Lucky Lucky Lucky	A. Cordero Jr.	May 4, 1984	1:51 4/5
Fran's Valentine	P. Valenzuela	May 3, 1985	1:50
Tiffany Lass	G. Stevens	May 2, 1986	1:50 3/5
Buryyourbelief	J. Santos	May 1, 1987	1:50 2/5
Goodbye Halo	P. Day	May 6, 1988	1:50 2/5
Open Mind	A. Cordero Jr.	May 5, 1989	1:50 3/5
Seaside Attraction	C. McCarron	May 4, 1990	1:52 4/5
Lite Light	C. Nakatani	May 3, 1991	1:48 4/5
Luv Me Luv Me Not	F. Arguello Jr.	May 1, 1992	1:51 2/5
Dispute	J. Bailey	April 30, 1993	1:52 2/5
Sardula	E. Delahoussaye	May 6, 1994	1:51
Gal In A Ruckus	H. McCauley	May 5, 1995	1:50
Pike Place Dancer	C. Nakatani	May 3, 1996	1:49 4/5
Blushing K.D.	L. Meche	May 2, 1997	1:50 1/5
Keeper Hill	D. FLores	May 1, 1998	1:52
Silverbulletday	G. Stevens	April 30, 1999	1:49 4/5
Secret Status	P. Day	May 5, 2000	1:50.30

* The Oaks was run in two divisions in 1959.
Distance: 1875–90 (inclusive), 1 1/2 miles; 1891–95 (inclusive), 1 1/4 miles; 1896–1919 (inclusive), 1 1/16 miles; 1920–41 (inclusive), 1 1/8 miles; 1942–81 (inclusive), 1 1/16 miles; 1982–present, 1 1/8 miles.

land called the Lilies for the Fillies to be awarded to the winning filly. For the garland, 188 white star gazer lilies were edged with oak ivy leaves. The Star Gazer Lily was chosen for its burst of vibrant magenta radiating from the center of the blossom. It is a dramatic flower, but the overall effect of the garland is feminine in honor of the fillies. The winner's owner also receives a set of twelve sterling silver julep cups, and the filly's name is engraved on the Kentucky Oaks Trophy, which resides at the KENTUCKY DERBY MUSEUM.

By 1999 the Kentucky Oaks was one of a dozen Grade I events for three-year-old fillies. The purse is five hundred thousand dollars. The Friday before Derby is the second-largest-attended day of racing in America, with 94,415 people attending the 1998 Kentucky Oaks.

Otis Amanda Dick

KENTUCKY OPERA. Kentucky Opera, the state opera of Kentucky and the twelfth-oldest in the nation, was founded in Louisville in 1952 by Heinrich Hans Claus Moritz von Bomhard, a native of Germany who came to Louisville in 1949 to aid the University of Louisville in mounting a production of Mozart's *The Marriage of Figaro*. He was not only conductor of the opera in the early years but also the stage director, set designer, chorus master for a talented group of volunteer singers, and music director. The performances took place at the Columbia Auditorium, and the productions were presented in English.

In the 1950s the Louisville Philharmonic Society (later the LOUISVILLE ORCHESTRA) commissioned five operas to be presented jointly with the Kentucky Opera: Richard Mohaupt's *Double Trouble*, Rolf Liebermann's *School for Wives*, Peggy Glanville-Hicks's *Transposed Heads*, George Antheil's *The Wish*, and Nicolaus Nabakov's *Holy Devil*. WAVE-TV commissioned Lee Hoiby's *Beatrice*, to be presented on television for the dedication of the station's new facilities. In 1956 *School for Wives* was performed by the New York City Opera with Bomhard conducting.

In 1963, the productions were moved to the Brown Theater, where such operas as Janácek's *Jenufa* and Britten's *Peter Grimes* were added to the repertoire. Puccini's *Tosca*, produced in 1967, was the first produced-in-Kentucky opera sung in the original language.

Several outreach programs were started. Full-scale matinees of dress rehearsals for school children were begun in 1963. By 1967 the company was touring the state performing at schools and colleges. In 1973, Kentucky Opera performed Verdi's *Otello* at the opening of the Regional Arts Center at Centre College in Danville, Kentucky. In 1979 the dress rehearsal of Humperdinck's *Hansel and Gretel* was interpreted in sign language for the hearing impaired.

In 1981 Bomhard retired, and Thomson Smillie, a native of Scotland and former director of the Opera Co. of Boston, became general director. Mary Ann Krebs joined Smillie as executive director in 1983. She left the company in 1994. Smillie brought the opera to the Kentucky Center for the Arts, with such productions as Rimsky-Korsakoff's *The Golden Cockerel* and Verdi's *Aida*. He also began the use of "supertitles," short translations of the libretto projected onto a screen above the stage. The company moved its offices to the McKesson Building at Eighth and MAIN Streets in 1993. At that time, the Plumb-Boyer Library was established to act as an archive and a resource for the company. Thomson Smillie resigned in 1996, and William P. Winkler, retired army major general and physician, served as the company's executive director while a replacement was sought. In 1997 Deborah Sandler of the Opera Festival of New Jersey took the position of general director.

During its history the company has been known for two major fund-raising events: the annual book sale begun in 1973 and the Hard Scuffle Steeplechase begun in 1974. The first race attracted fifteen hundred guests and raised eight thousand dollars. By the time it was discontinued in 1996, a total of $2 million had been raised. It was called "one of the most romantic races in America."

The opera, a member of OPERA America, is overseen by a forty-three-person board of directors. The Opera Guild acts as a support group with outreach and development programs. Funding is provided by ticket sales, the FUND FOR THE ARTS, the National Endowment for the Arts, and the Kentucky Arts Council.

Doris J. Batliner

KENTUCKY QUILT PROJECT INC. Based in Louisville and established in 1981 by founding directors Shelly Zegart, Eleanor Bingham Miller, and Eunice Ray, the Kentucky Quilt Project was the first attempt to document the state's quilt legacy. It assembled over a thousand quilts for study by organizing quilt days throughout the state. In 1982 a catalog of the project's findings, *Kentucky Quilts, 1800–1900*, was published. In 1983 forty-four of the quilts studied were put on display at the Louisville Museum of History and Science (later the LOUISVILLE SCIENCE CENTER) in an exhibition entitled "Kentucky Quilts, 1800–1900." The exhibit traveled to twelve other museums in the United States and Ireland through the Smithsonian Institution Traveling Exhibition Service. In November 1991 the project hosted a seven-month-long event, "Louisville Celebrates the American Quilt," to which quilt scholars as well as those from related fields were invited. In the winter of 1992 the premiere issue of *The Quilt Journal: An International Review*, a semiannual journal, was published by the Kentucky Quilt Project in an effort to encourage and review quilt scholarship. In 1993 the Kentucky Quilt Project began working with the Library of Congress Folk Life Center and others to create both the Center for the Quilt, and the International Quilt Index, a database for quilt-related materials.

See Georgene Muller Lockwood, "History's Mirrors: The Kentucky Quilt Project Revisited after 15 Years, Still Going Strong and Growing," *Patchwork Quilts* (Aug./Sept. 1995): 5–9 and 58; Shelly Zegart, "The Quilt Projects 15 Years Later," *Folk Art* (Spring 1996): 28–37.

KENTUCKY RAILWAY MUSEUM. The Kentucky Railway Museum (KRM), one of the oldest of its kind in the United States, was formed over forty years ago by efforts of Louisville-area rail enthusiasts to preserve old steam locomotives and other rail equipment being displaced by newer technology. Chartered in 1954, the museum occupied a site provided by the city on River Rd. east of downtown. First displays were 1905–vintage Pacific-type locomotive No. 152 and a wooden coach and caboose, donated by the LOUISVILLE & NASHVILLE and MONON RAILROADS. The two railroads also provided track materials. The Parks Department lighted and fenced the six-acre site. KRM was dedicated on September 30, 1957, and opened to the public on May 30, 1958.

During the 1960s, volunteer members built more tracks to park their growing collection of historic rail cars and locomotives, but some were damaged beyond repair by a March 1964 Ohio River flood. By the 1970s, KRM began looking for a larger site away from the river. In December 1975, Jefferson County agreed to lease forty acres at Ormsby Village near LYNDON. KRM opened there in May 1978 but retained the River Rd. site to rebuild L&N 152 to operating condition to pull excursions, which the museum also began running with its own cars in the 1970s. After 1985 the trips were pulled by No. 152, on which members had spent thousands of hours during thirteen years of restoration. On March 6, 2000, No. 152 was designated the official steam locomotive of the commonwealth.

In 1985 the county announced plans for commercial development of all Ormsby Village properties, and KRM once again sought a new home, eventually purchasing seventeen miles of L&N's former Lebanon Branch in Nelson and LaRue Counties from CSX Transportation. In 1990 all equipment and train operations were moved to New Haven, where KRM has since built a station to house offices and displays, and a shop building to repair its rolling stock.

Charles B. Castner

KENTUCKY SCHOOL FOR THE BLIND. The Kentucky School for the Blind (KSB) is a state-supported PUBLIC SCHOOL for blind and visually impaired students from kindergarten through secondary school. Some of the students live on campus; others commute daily. Many attend local schools and come to KSB to learn special skills related to their visual impairment. Basic academic studies are taught using specialized teaching methods, technology, and adapted materials and equipment. Students also learn specialized skills in orientation and mobility programs and participate in classes in independent living and career development.

Originally named the Kentucky Institution for the Education of the Blind, KSB was the third state-supported school for the blind established in the United States. The school's founder was Bryce McLellan Patten, then President of the Louisville Collegiate Institute, who began teaching a class of six blind students in the summer of 1839. Patten became interested in the education of blind children because his brother Otis was visually impaired and a student of Dr. Samuel Gridley Howe, noted pioneer in the education of the visually impaired.

Bryce Patten invited his brother Otis to teach at the Louisville Collegiate Institute. Otis taught the sighted children in the morning and the blind children in the afternoon. In early 1841, in an effort to obtain funding for a school for the blind, Otis Patten presented an exhibition of his blind students' skills before the General Assembly. Unfortunately, funding was not granted.

Dr. Samuel Gridley Howe of the Massachusetts Institute for the Blind often traveled with his students to promote the education of blind children. The Patten brothers invited Dr. Howe and his students to Kentucky to make a presentation to the Kentucky legislature. Howe came in the winter of 1842, and, on February 5 of that year, the Kentucky Institution for the Blind was chartered with an appropriation of ten thousand dollars. The funding was granted on the condition that Louisvillians would raise the additional funds needed to get the school started. Louisville citizens raised twelve hundred dollars for equipment, and a "committee of ladies" furnished a house on Sixth St. The school opened in May 1842. Bryce Patten was the unpaid director and maintained his private school; Otis Patten was the teacher.

In less than a year, the school outgrew its building. The Collegiate Institute building was rented—Bryce Patten, the superintendent, had closed the Institute to devote his full attention to the blind students. The Prather House, on the same property (the block bounded by Third, FOURTH, Green [LIBERTY], and Walnut [Muhammad Ali Blvd.]) was also rented.

The school's first permanent home was designed by John Stirewalt and completed in 1845. It was located on the south side of BROADWAY between First and Second Streets on a lot purchased from Mr. John I. Jacob for fifteen hundred dollars. This building burned in 1851, and the Board of Visitors decided to move the school out of the city. They purchased the tract on the Frankfort Turnpike Rd. (now Frankfort Ave.) where the school is located today. The domed building was designed by architect Elias E. Williams. It was completed in 1855 and was a Louisville landmark until it was razed in 1967.

In 1884 the legislature appropriated twenty thousand dollars for a school for African Ameri-

Main building of the Kentucky School for the Blind (razed in 1967), Frankfort Avenue near Haldeman in the Clifton neighborhood, 1922.

can blind. Charles J. Clarke drew the plans, and the school formally opened in October 1886. It was located on Haldeman Ave., near the school for white students. Although a separate institution, the AMERICAN PRINTING HOUSE FOR THE BLIND occupied space in the KSB building until 1883, when a building was constructed adjacent to the school.

Bryce Patten, superintendent from 1842 to 1871; Benjamin B. Huntoon, superintendent from 1871 to 1912; and SUSAN BUCKINGHAM MERWIN, who served from 1912 until 1923, were nationally recognized leaders in education for blind people. These three early superintendents also served as the first executive directors of the American Printing House for the Blind. Merwin was the second woman to head a United States school for the blind.

See Otis Patten, "Reminiscences of the Origin of the Kentucky Institution for the Blind," *The Mentor* 1 (July 1891): 209–14; *Annual Reports 1842–1996*, Kentucky Institution for the Education of the Blind/Kentucky School for the Blind; *Louisville Journal*, Jan. 31, 1842, Feb. 5, 1842, Feb. 8, 9, 28, 1842, March 8, 1842, April 16, 1842; J. Stoddard Johnston, ed., *Memorial History of Louisville* (Chicago and New York 1896).

Carol Brenner Tobe

KENTUCKY SHAKESPEARE FESTIVAL. The Kentucky Shakespeare Festival—Louisville's oldest continuously operating professional theater and the longest-running free professional Shakespeare festival in North America—formally began in 1962 with a summer season of four plays produced in Central Park (Fourth and Magnolia) on an outdoor stage improvised from a BOXING ring and a circus wagon. Its founder, C. Douglas Ramey, was responding to community enthusiasm for such a festival. The Carriage House Players, an established local repertory theater also started by Ramey, constituted the acting company.

An hour-long version of *Much Ado about Nothing* at the St. James Court Art Fair in 1960 had marked the Players' first Shakespearean presentation in Central Park. In 1961–62, the troupe offered several of the Bard's plays at its usual theater, a remodeled carriage house on S Fifth near Kentucky St.

The success of the 1962 summer productions led to the construction of a permanent stage in Central Park in 1963. In 1976 the open-air amphitheater was named in honor of Ramey, who variously served the festival as director, actor, and producer until his death in 1979. He was succeeded as producing director by Bekki Jo Schneider (1980–84), Hal Park (1985–88), and Curt L. Tofteland (1989–). In 1984, the Kentucky legislature designated Shakespeare in Central Park as the Kentucky Shakespeare Festival. Most actors are hired from national auditions. The festival has also conducted such educational outreach programs as Shakespeare in the Schools (1963–73) and Will on Wheels (1990–), presented not only in Kentucky but also in Illinois, Indiana, and West Virginia. Corporate, foundation, and individual support helps ensure C. Douglas Ramey's vision of free summer theater for all in Central Park.

See Jane Elizabeth Davis, "A History of Shakespeare in Central Park, Louisville, Ky," M.A. thesis, University of Kentucky, 1981; *Courier-Journal & Times Magazine*, Aug. 1, 1971; *Louisville Times*, July 6, 1968; Glen Loney and Patricia MacKay, *The Shakespeare Complex* (New York 1975).

John Spalding Gatton

KENTUCKY SOCIETY OF NATURAL HISTORY. This organization of nature enthusiasts began on the University of Louisville campus in the late 1930s and was incorporated in 1943. Its first president was Dr. William Clay. Various chapters have developed across the state, but the largest and most active is the FALLS OF THE OHIO Chapter in Louisville. The statewide organization meets for spring and fall conferences, usually at Kentucky state resort parks. The goal of the organization is to foster greater understanding of the plants and animals of the commonwealth as well as its geology, hydrology, and ecology.

Allen L. Lake

KENTUCKY SOUTHERN COLLEGE. A Baptist liberal arts college founded in 1961 by the Long Run Association of BAPTISTS and the Kentucky Baptist Association, it initially offered classes at the Southern Baptist Seminary. In the fall of 1963, the college moved to its 238-acre campus on Shelbyville Rd. At its height in fall 1966, the college had nearly nine hundred students and one hundred faculty and staff. Kentucky Southern offered bachelor of arts, bachelor of science, and religious studies degrees on a trimester basis, allowing students to earn four-year degrees in three years.

The college encountered financial difficulties soon after opening because of construction and maintenance costs. Despite an "SOS" or "Save Our School" campaign in fall 1967, which raised over $1 million and allowed the college to continue another year, the debt-plagued school faced mortgage foreclosure after an attempt by Western Kentucky University to underwrite bonds for the college was ruled illegal by the state attorney general in 1968. In 1969 the campus, student body, assets, and an over-$4 million debt were absorbed into the University of Louisville college system at the urging of Gov. Louie Nunn. The former college became the University of Louisville's Shelby campus.

KENTUCKY STATE FAIR. Judging from its history and offerings, one might judge the Kentucky State Fair to be quintessentially American, an annual celebration of economic progress and cultural activity based on the agricultural fair tradition. The General Assembly initiated the Kentucky State Fair in 1902 and provided for financing it. The Livestock Breeders' Association was the driving force behind the fair. Some seventy-five thousand people attended the fair in September 1902, held at CHURCHILL DOWNS in Louisville. By 1998 attendance had grown to 655,000.

Owensboro served as the site in 1903 and

Lexington in 1905. There was no fair in 1904 because of a suit filed to test the legality of funds granted by the state to the Livestock Breeders' Association. The state auditor refused to authorize the money for the fair. The 1906 fair was again held at Churchill Downs, and the next year the Board of Agriculture decided on Louisville as the permanent site. One hundred fifty acres in the southwestern corner of the city at the end of Cecil Ave. lying west of Thirty-eighth St. and north of Gibson Ln. were purchased on December 6, 1907. The 1908 fair opened in the shadow of a newly constructed livestock pavilion, at that time the largest in the state. More impressive, however, was the Merchants and Manufacturers Building, which opened in 1921 accompanied by the proud announcement that it was larger than Madison Square Garden in New York City.

In time the facilities became antiquated so that the 1946 legislature authorized the sale of bonds to construct the KENTUCKY FAIR AND EXPOSITION CENTER on 357 acres (now over 400) south of Louisville, adjacent to Standiford Field (later LOUISVILLE INTERNATIONAL AIRPORT). The new facility, opened in 1956, was designed to be used throughout the year for exhibitions and sporting events.

The Kentucky State Fair retains its popular appeal as a late-summer, multidimensional festival. Held annually in the hot days of mid-August, it hosts livestock exhibitions and features among other activities a world championship horse show, cooking contests, rides and amusements, educational programs, nationally known entertainers, and judging of all kinds. One building wing is devoted exclusively to exhibitors. Food and drink concessions feature locally produced food products. An official part of state GOVERNMENT, this sprawling piece of popular American culture has not only endured but has grown in content and in appeal. In 1997 the fair offered 139 rides, 88 of which were a part of Six Flags Kentucky Kingdom AMUSEMENT PARK and the others located along a midway.

On the occasion of its 50th anniversary in 1953, the Kentucky State Fair counted 305,000 visitors. By 1990 that number had increased to 637,500. In 1996 the fair attendance was 673,874, the fourth-largest crowd ever; and the 1998 attendance was 655,000. The record stands at 684,356 in 1994. The event attracts large numbers of people to the city and is important to the Louisville ECONOMY.

See Kentucky Writer's Project, *Fairs and Fair Makers of Kentucky* (Frankfort 1942); H. Clyde Reeves and Lawrence A. Cassidy, "Fairs in Kentucky," *Filson Club History Quarterly* 34 (Oct. 1960): 335–57.

KENTUCKY STATE REFORMATORY.

Establishment of the Kentucky State Reformatory, a medium-security facility near LAGRANGE in Oldham County, was authorized by Gov. A.B. Chandler during his first term (1935–39). By late 1937 the old Kentucky State Reformatory at Frankfort had been razed, and construction of the new reformatory was well under way, with inmates living temporarily in corrugated iron buildings at the site. Once construction was complete, most inmates were housed in open-wing dormitories rather than in small cells.

In eleven separate housing units, inmates were classified, treated according to their needs, and prepared for release. A large farm provided both employment and food. Although academic, vocational, recreational, and religious programs were planned, personnel to carry out these rehabilitation programs were not hired until 1961. The number of security personnel was often inadequate to manage an institution that was frequently overpopulated.

In the beginning, inmates ate in silence, and mail was censored. Misbehavior was punished by work in the stone quarry, head-shaving, or solitary confinement on bread and water. Inmates marched to work in uniform and produced goods for state use, such as printed forms, metal furniture, road signs, license plates, and soap. However, providing adequate employment was a continuing problem. Investigations in 1963 and 1973 deplored the brutal and abusive conditions and prompted funding for additional treatment, custodial personnel, and programs to prepare inmates for release.

In 1977 the facility's dormitories were racially integrated, and in 1980 the settlement of a class-action lawsuit filed by inmates limited the prison population to fifteen hundred. In an effort to help reintegrate special needs inmates into the reformatory's general population, Boy Scout Troop 825 was founded in December 1990, the first of its kind to be established within the walls of an adult correctional institute in the United States. The program has helped its members, many of whom are mentally handicapped or suffer from psychiatric disabilities, function better in their environment by developing better personal hygiene and interpersonal skills.

T. Kyle Ellison

KENTUCKY TURNPIKE.

One of the notable achievements of Gov. Lawrence W. Wetherby's administration (1950–55), the Kentucky Turnpike was the state's first superhighway. Initially it was proposed as a section of an expressway from the Great Lakes to the Gulf of Mexico. It was built to connect Louisville and Elizabethtown. Ground was broken in BULLITT COUNTY on July 25, 1954. The turnpike was officially opened to traffic on August 1, 1956. Built at a cost of $39 million, it ran a distance of thirty-nine miles. Eight roads in Louisville gave access to the turnpike, and a later extension was built from the Watterson Expressway north to Eastern Pkwy. The terrain over which the turnpike was built was considered difficult; it included portions of the Kentucky KNOBS, several rivers, and steep hills. Advanced engineering design produced concrete-paved lanes twenty-four feet wide, blacktop outside shoulders ten feet wide, and no grade steeper than 3 percent. It followed the example of the Pennsylvania Turnpike.

During the Democratic gubernatorial primary campaign of 1955, candidate A.B. Chandler questioned the need for the road. An op-

Old Kentucky State Fair Grounds during the fair of 1923.

ponent of toll roads, he said it started nowhere and went nowhere. The issue helped him to defeat Bert T. Combs.

The road was financed with bonds, and tolls were established to pay off the bonds within forty years. Tolls were collected at two locations, Shepherdsville and Elizabethtown. Two service areas were established, one at Shepherdsville, where a Glass House Restaurant was located, and the other just south of the Rolling Fork of the Salt River, which provided a snack bar. The turnpike was heavily used, and an estimated 90 million vehicles, excluding local traffic in Louisville, traveled the road before the toll was lifted on June 30, 1975. That year the turnpike was officially made a part of Interstate 65, which connected with it on both the south and north ends. The road has since been widened to ten lanes south of the Watterson Expressway, and it is at least six lanes wide to Elizabethtown.

See "Future Superhighway," *Courier-Journal Magazine*, July 25, 1954; "Kentucky Turnpike Is in Business," *Louisville* 7 (Aug. 20, 1956): 18–19.

KENTUCKY WAGON MANUFACTURING COMPANY. Organized in 1879 with capital of sixty thousand dollars, the Kentucky Wagon Manufacturing Co. was incorporated on January 16, 1882. The firm's first president was Stephen E. Jones, and William C. Nones was its first secretary-treasurer-general manager. At the time of incorporation, the company's capital was in excess of three hundred thousand dollars. An office and salesroom were located on E Walnut St. (Muhammad Ali Blvd.). The factory, which could manufacture forty wagons a day, was on E Madison St. A local advertisement of the time noted that the firm was the proud manufacturer of Old Hickory brand farm and freight wagons and the American brand dumping and garbage wagons.

In less than twelve short years the company advertised itself as having "capital of $1 million." Under Jones, who was also a director of the Fidelity Trust and Safety Vault Co., and a board of directors steeped in the financial and BANKING establishments of Kentucky, the enterprise prospered. By 1889 it had relocated its manufacturing facilities to an area just south of the present-day Belknap Campus of the University of Louisville. Occupying thirty acres between Third, Brook, K (Montana), and N (Iowa) Streets, Kentucky Wagon had designed a manufacturing plant that was, as the 1891 edition of *Louisville Illustrated* noted, "the most complete and largest in the world." The main building alone measured two and one-half acres. With twenty-two acres of lumberyards; a full complement of shop buildings, kilns, machinery, and welding apparatus; and a complete electrical plant, the company could produce thirty-five thousand wagons a year. Five to six hundred workers produced wood vehicles of every description under the trade names of Tennessee, American, and Old Hickory.

By 1894 William C. Nones, who was also a director of the Kentucky National Bank, had succeeded Jones as president. Under his leadership, business continued to boom. The 1908 *Greater Louisville Illustrated* boasted that the farm wagons made by Kentucky Wagon were the "standard all over the world." But the halcyon days of horse and wagon were numbered. Automobiles and trucks were the future.

In 1914 Robert V. Board became president of Kentucky Wagon, and William C. Nones was chairman of the board. A new department within the company was formed, with Henry B. Hewett as manager, to manufacture electric vehicles. A battery-powered truck, called the Urban Electric, was produced. By 1916 the firm, in addition to wagons, was making gasoline and electric trucks. Urban Electric brand truck production ceased around 1917, but Old Hickory brand motor trucks continued to be made.

In addition to trucks, the firm also began to make automobiles. It purchased the Dixie Motor Co. and from about 1916 to 1924 manufactured the Dixie Flyer, a four-cylinder passenger car. The ADVERTISING of the day trumpeted, "An amply powered motor and approved engineering principles throughout give you that unusual sense of security that comes from owning and driving 'The Car That Takes You There and Brings You Back.'"

Despite these innovations, the Kentucky Wagon Manufacturing Co. saw the demand for its products dwindle and its markets shrink. So in 1922 the firm joined a grandiose $80 million automobile merger. The Kentucky Wagon Manufacturing Co. was to be a principal unit in a vast enterprise called Associated Motor Industries Co. Inc., with plants in several cities. The *COURIER-JOURNAL*, on January 22, 1922, said that the new company estimated that it would be producing ten thousand cars by the end of the year and would, it hoped, provide employment for five thousand Louisville workers within the next twelve months.

Associated Motor Industries Co. never materialized. What did materialize, beginning in March 1922, was an endless string of financial difficulties, petitions for receivership, allegations of mismanagement, plans for financial relief and restructuring, and legal maneuvering of every kind. On November 17, 1930, the National Bank of Kentucky failed. It and BancoKentucky claimed a $2.9 million mortgage against Kentucky Wagon property. Although the COURTS later disallowed this claim, saying that the bank really owned the property and could not give itself a mortgage, it nonetheless spelled the end of the Kentucky Wagon Manufacturing Co. In December 1930, it slipped into bankruptcy. In 1936 the company's thirty-two acres of land and eight acres of buildings were sold for fifty thousand dollars. On February 21, 1940, a federal judge adjudicated the company bankrupt.

See *Courier-Journal*, Aug. 10 1922; *Louisville Post*, March 28, 1922; *Louisville Times*, Feb. 11, 1936, Feb. 21, 1940; George Yater, *Two Hundred Years at the Falls of the Ohio* (Louisville 1987); *Louisville Illustrated*, 1891.

Kevin Collins

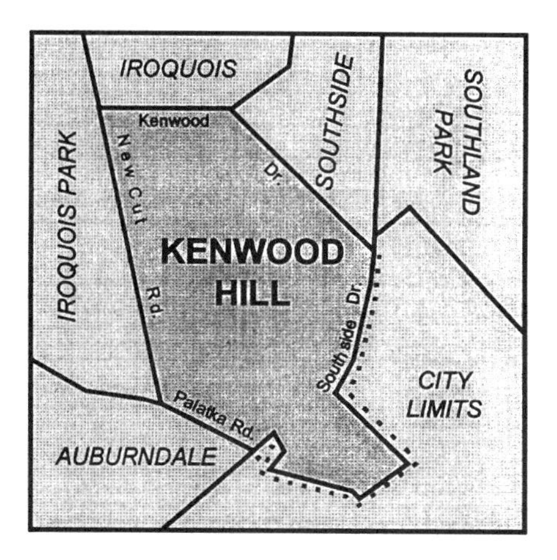

KENWOOD HILL. Neighborhood in southern Louisville bounded by New Cut Rd., Kenwood Dr., Southside Dr., and Palatka Rd. The summit, known in earlier times as "Sunshine Hill," was used by Native Americans as an outlook to spot buffalo on their way to the river and to cure the game they had killed. By 1868, Benoni Figg had purchased the area, known then as Cox's Knob, in order to clear the land for his charcoal business. He later built a small sawmill, opened a rock quarry, and constructed the LOUISVILLE & NASHVILLE RAILROAD Co.'s Strawberry Station at the intersection of New Cut and Third Street Roads. In 1876, Figg's daughter, Mary, and her new husband, Charles W. Gheens, acquired half of the heavily wooded property and fourteen years later sold it to the Kenwood Park Residential Co., who dubbed the area Kenwood Hill.

Although the opening of the Grand Blvd., modern-day Southern Pkwy., in 1893 allowed easier transportation to the area, the first suburban residents were wealthy families who built retreats in the area to escape the summer heat. While settlement remained sparse until the first subdivision was started in 1942, the hill was extensively carved up for residential use in the 1960s and required retaining walls in the 1980s to halt erosion and drainage problems.

The LITTLE LOOMHOUSE, located since 1939 in two of the old summer retreats and a building that once was Figg's office, is an institution that drew students from around the world to learn the art of handweaving. The establishment, with its extensive collection of genuine weaving drafts, some of which date from the 1700s, hosted crowds that included names such as Mrs. Lou Hoover, Mrs. Eleanor Roosevelt, and Frank Lloyd Wright to watch Louisa Tate Bousman, better known as Lou Tate, produce cloth samples on her weaving machine.

See *A Place in Time: The Story of Louisville's Neighborhoods* (Louisville 1989).

KFC CORPORATION. KFC Corp. (Kentucky Fried Chicken) has been a part of the Louisville landscape since 1968 when the company, then headquartered in Nashville, broke ground for its eighty-eight-thousand–square-foot corporate office building on Gardiner Ln. In April 1969 the company's headquarters formally moved to Louisville, settling in temporary office space in the Atkinson Square office complex just east of the building site.

In July 1970 the company moved into the $3.7 million building at 1441 Gardiner Ln., nicknamed "The White House" for its resemblance to the famous one in Washington, D.C. On September 16, the building was dedicated as part of KFC founder Col. Harland Sanders's eightieth birthday celebration. State and local GOVERNMENT officials, civic leaders, franchisees and their families, and KFC employees attended the celebration.

As the company grew, office space tightened. In the mid-1970s, about two hundred KFC associates moved to offices occupying several floors of the Watterson Towers office building, a mile east of the White House. In 1978, KFC Corp. opened another satellite office—its new KFC Training Center, which occupied a part of the main building housing Sullivan Junior College at the Watterson Expressway and Bardstown Rd. This facility boasted three kitchens, two restaurant-like service areas, and several classrooms, plus audiovisual production facilities and offices for the training and program development staff. Within several years, this facility, too, was bulging at the seams.

In October 1984 the Colonel's widow, Claudia Sanders, and then–KFC Chairman and CEO Dick Mayer broke ground for a new $23 million Colonel Sanders Technical Center adjacent to the headquarters building. It housed departments such as information technology, training, ACCOUNTING, engineering, real estate, and research and development. In it were a half-dozen high-tech test and training kitchens, equipment development and testing labs, a sophisticated consumer research "taste panel" room, offices and classrooms, and computer systems. It was connected to the headquarters building by an underground walkway.

On June 3, 1986, KFC dedicated its six-story, two-hundred-thousand-square-foot Colonel Sanders Technical Center. In the cornerstone of the new building are test tubes containing the Colonel's secret blend of eleven herbs and spices encased in acrylic. The cornerstone plaque reads, "Just as the Colonel's secret blend of eleven herbs and spices is the foundation of his world-famous fried chicken, the legacy of the man is the foundation of Kentucky Fried Chicken Corp. We dedicate this building in memory of Colonel Harland D. Sanders."

KFC Corp. has gone through several owners since its move to Louisville. In 1964 the Colonel sold his company, then headquartered in Shelbyville, Kentucky, to John Y. Brown Jr. (who later would become Kentucky's governor) and Jack Massey, a Nashville financier, for $2 million. In 1971 they sold to Heublein Inc. for $285 million. In 1982 Heublein became a part of R.J. Reynolds Industries Inc. (now RJR/Nabisco). Four years later, in 1986, RJR/Nabisco sold its restaurant business (which also included Zantigo Mexican Restaurants and H. Salt Fish & Chips) to PepsiCo Inc. for $840 million.

In March 1996, KFC restructured its operations to better focus on its frontline employees, who are viewed as the most important members of the restaurant team. The shift in focus was part of a multi-million-dollar reinvestment in training and field support for marketing, facilities development, and restaurant staffing. To demonstrate this new "restaurant-up" philosophy, KFC renamed its Louisville corporate offices the "KFC Restaurant Support Center."

In January 1997, PepsiCo Inc. announced that it would spin off its domestic and international restaurant divisions—KFC (support center in Louisville), Taco Bell (Irvine, California), and Pizza Hut and PepsiCo Restaurants International (both in Dallas)—in order to form a separate company. This company would become the world's largest restaurant company in number of units. Together, the company boasts nearly thirty thousand KFC, Taco Bell, and Pizza Hut restaurants worldwide, with combined revenue in 1996 of $20.8 billion.

Within a few months, word was out that Louisville and Kentucky officials were creating a package of incentives to convince the new company—now known as Tricon Global Restaurants Inc.—to select Louisville as its headquarters city.

On July 31, 1997, Tricon Global Restaurants Inc. announced that it would locate in Louisville. Tricon brought 250 jobs—many of them accountants, finance experts, and lawyers to the KFC complex on GARDINER LANE.

Jeannie Litterst Vezeau

KIDD, MINNIE MAE (JONES) STREET (b Millersburg, Kentucky, February 8, 1904; d Louisville, October 20, 1999). CIVIL RIGHTS activist. Minnie Mae Jones was born in 1904, the same year that the infamous Day Law, state legislation that effectively segregated Kentucky's public and private schools, took effect. She was the daughter of Charles Robert Jones, a white man, and Anna Belle Leer (Jones) Taylor, a black woman. By the racial calculus of the day she was legally a Negro, but, in fact, because she was at least 80 percent racially white, with fair skin and blond hair, she lived, culturally, in a no-man's-land where she was discriminated against by members of both races.

Once while shopping in downtown Louisville, she saw two black women that she knew well and she said hello to them. When they declined to acknowledge her presence, she was stunned and asked why. When told, in a whisper, that the two women thought that Kidd wanted to pass in public for white, she said, "Ladies, nooooo. I'm not trying to pass for white. If anything, I've been passing for black all my life because I'm almost 90 percent white."

Kidd attended the LINCOLN INSTITUTE in Simpsonville. Then, at the age of twenty-one, she moved to Louisville where she pursued a successful career with the black-owned and -operated Mammoth Life Insurance Co. In 1930 she married Horace Leon Street, who died in 1942. During World War II she served overseas with the American Red Cross, where she met her second husband-to-be, army officer James Meredith Kidd. They were married on August 27, 1947.

In 1968, despite her oft-repeated protestation that "I do not like politics," she was reluctantly persuaded to run, as a Democrat, for the General Assembly from Louisville's Forty-first Legislative District. She won this first election by a two-to-one majority and went on to win seven more elections. For seventeen years, from 1968 to 1985, she was known as the "Lady of the House." She was a diligent worker, an outspoken and indefatigable champion of civil rights and equal opportunity, and an advocate for disadvantaged children and the poor.

During her tenure in the legislature, Kidd became the first woman to serve on the Rules Committee, the first woman elected secretary of the Democratic caucus, and the first woman elected as chair of the Enrollment Committee. In 1968 she sponsored and helped pass a statewide open-housing bill with the power of enforcement vested in a Human Rights Commission. In 1970 she drafted the MAE STREET KIDD Act, which was passed by the legislature and signed into law by Gov. Wendell Ford in 1972. The act created the Kentucky Housing Corporation, an agency designed to lend money at low interest rates to home buyers of modest income. In these years she also championed having Dr. Martin Luther King's birthday declared a state holiday.

Her proudest achievement, she said, was the ratification by the commonwealth of Kentucky of the Thirteenth (abolition of slavery), Fourteenth (full citizenship), and Fifteenth (right to vote) Amendments to the U.S. Constitution. Although these amendments were the law, nonetheless, 112 years of Kentucky passivity had failed to ratify them. In 1976 Kidd saw that this embarrassing burden, for blacks and whites both, was rectified, and the ratification was unanimous.

In the 1984 general election, Kidd was defeated by Republican Tom Riner. In addition to her political life, she had been active for twenty years with the LINCOLN FOUNDATION, an educational organization for disadvantaged children. She had also worked with the YMCA, the Black Girl Scouts, and the LEAGUE OF WOMEN VOTERS; had organized an Urban League Guild; and was the recipient of *Esquire Magazine*'s annual achievement award for 1976.

Kidd was married and widowed twice. There were no children. She is buried in Zachary Tay-

See Wade Hall, *Passing for Black: The Life and Careers of Mae Street Kidd* (Lexington 1997); *Courier-Journal*, Oct. 24, 1999.

Kevin Collins

KINDERGARTEN MOVEMENT. Louisville played an important role in the kindergarten movement in the United States, based on the teachings of German educator Fredrick Froebel (1782–1852). The earliest kindergartens in this country were founded in German communities. Louisville had one of the first ten, established by William Hailman in 1865 at the German-English Academy at Second and Gray Streets. It did not last when he left Louisville to become a school administrator, translator of Froebel's work into English, and later the first chairman of the kindergarten section of the National Education Association.

Sustained kindergarten work began in Louisville in 1887 under the auspices of prominent Louisville women who were working with poor and immigrant children at the Holcombe Mission on W Jefferson St. These women were Mrs. Louise E. Yandell, Mrs. Albana C. Carter, Mrs. J.R. Clarke, Mrs. W.N. Little, Mrs. A.C. Bowser, Mrs. Albert S. Willis, and Ms. Mary L. Graham. The mission was run by converted gambler Steve Holcombe to Christianize and Americanize the immigrant population. At the mission's industrial school, which trained children in trades, the women began a kindergarten class in February 1887 for children too young to sew. Mrs. J.R. Clarke gave up the money for her new fur coat to pay the first teacher's salary. The Louisville matrons, after studying the kindergartens in other cities, decided to start a training school for kindergarten teachers in the fall of 1887, enrolling five students and using the mission kindergarten as their laboratory school. A Louisville native, Anna Bryan, trained at the Armour Institute in Chicago and was hired as the superintendent. She was invited to live at the home of Mr. and Mrs. John Carter of CARTER DRY GOODS. In October 1887 the Louisville Free Kindergarten Association was incorporated at a meeting at the Warren Memorial Presbyterian Church at Fourth St. and BROADWAY.

Kindergartens established by the association flourished. A second was started in February 1888 at the HOME OF THE INNOCENTS. When the first class graduated from the training school in February 1889, two more kindergartens were begun. They were directed by graduates PATTY SMITH HILL and Finnie Burton: Burton at the Sunbeam Kindergarten, Twenty-second and Walnut Streets, and Hill at the German Free Kindergarten at Clay and Market. By September 1889, four more were established, including one for black children. Training classes for black teachers were organized as well. By 1890 three more kindergartens were begun. The Louisville kindergartens began to get national attention, attracting over three thousand visitors in one year to see the experimental work. Included among the visitors were prominent educators John Dewey, Col. Francis Parker, and William Hailman, along with others who had heard Anna Bryan and Patty Smith Hill speak at national meetings about their kindergarten work.

The experimental work of Americanizing and modernizing the kindergarten was led by Bryan and Hill. Hill would become one of America's foremost leaders in early childhood education. Hill and Bryan went every summer to study with famous educators such as John Dewey; Dr. G. Stanley Hall, the father of child psychology; and Dr. Luther Gulick, the father of the playground movement. Bryan and Hill spoke about their work at National Education Association meetings. Patty Hill and her sister, Mary D. Hill, who was also a kindergarten teacher, wrote lessons for the national *Kindergarten Magazine*. Bryan turned over the principalship of the demonstration kindergarten to Patty Hill as the leadership of the association expanded to include Sunday school and nurses' training departments, taking more of Bryan's time. The school even added a boarding department in order to train students not living in Louisville. Some of the teachers trained here went as missionaries to start kindergartens in Brazil, China, and Japan. One of the most famous was Fannie Caldwell McCauley, who wrote *Our Lady of the Decoration,* a bestseller in 1907 about her experiences as a kindergarten teacher in Hiroshima.

When Bryan returned to Chicago in 1893, Patty Smith Hill became the association superintendent and exhibited the Louisville kindergarten work at the Columbian Exposition. At the same time, Patty and her musician-composer sister, MILDRED HILL, wrote a book of *Song Stories for the Kindergarten* that included the famous "Happy Birthday to You" for which the Hill sisters maintained the copyright for many years.

In 1894 the Louisville Free Kindergarten Association moved into its own building on the southwest corner of Floyd and Walnut (Muhammad Ali Blvd.) Streets. Mary D. Hill exhibited Louisville kindergarten's innovative methods at the Cotton States Exposition in Atlanta. By 1895 the influence of child psychology and concerns for the health and welfare of children led to the use of disposable handkerchiefs, water fountains, low hooks for children to hang up their own coats, and psychological and medical examinations of children. Hill introduced the child study movement to Louisville, which spawned the Parent-Teacher Association.

By 1903 the kindergartens became part of the public school system, with the Kindergarten Association still training and supervising the teachers. The presence in public schools led to closer collaboration with first-grade teachers and curriculum. Louisville kindergarten work was exhibited at the St. Louis World's Fair in 1904. The fame of the Louisville kindergartens became focused in Patty Smith Hill's lectures and debates with the conservative leaders of the movement at Columbia Teacher's College in New York City in 1905. This resulted in an invitation for Hill to teach at Columbia the following year.

The Louisville Kindergarten Association employed Mary D. Hill, who carried on the work until the association merged with the Louisville Normal School in 1909. At that time there were twenty-two white and seven African American kindergartens. Both Mildred and Mary Hill died in 1916, and Central School was later renamed for Mary D. Hill. Patty Smith Hill continued as leader of the kindergarten movement, publishing the first early childhood education series, including the conduct curriculum for kindergarten widely used throughout the United States. Much of the pioneering work was done in the Louisville kindergartens.

In 1922 the International Kindergarten Union met in Louisville. At that time the nursery school movement was beginning in the United States under the leadership of Patty Smith Hill and others. The conference evoked a task force to lobby for statewide kindergartens in Kentucky, which did not become a reality until 1985. However, nursery schools began with the founding of Mrs. Agnes P. Sawyer's nursery school (Country Nursery School) in the 1930s. During the Depression, Work Progress Administration nursery schools began, and teachers were trained at the University of Louisville. In 1939 Dr. Spafford Ackerly, director of the Bingham Child Guidance Clinic, began the Mental Hygiene Nursery School.

In 1956 public school kindergartens were closed due to a lack of sufficient funds, and church and private schools emerged to do much of the local preschool education. With the 1960s and the War on Poverty came the National Head Start program for children whose parents could not afford private preschools. The Louisville Head Start program began in 1964 with the University of Louisville training teachers and doing research and evaluation of the program. In 1966 public school kindergartens were reopened. The Patty Smith Hill Lectures at the University of Louisville and the Louisville Kindergarten Club kept the kindergarten dreams alive. By 1984 the Jefferson County Public Schools began a pilot preschool program to serve handicapped preschoolers and those who would benefit most from pre-kindergarten programs. Louisville had led the way in kindergarten education in both the state and the nation for almost a century.

See Martha K. Alexander, *Seventy-five Years of Kindergarten in Kentucky* (Nashville 1938); Mrs. J.R. Clark, "First Annual Report of the Louisville Free Kindergarten Association," 1888; Frances Farley Gwinn, "Patty Smith Hill in Louisville," M.A. thesis, University of Louisville, 1954; Patty Smith Hill Papers, Filson Club Historical Society, Louisville; J. Stoddard Johnston, ed., *Memorial History of Louisville*

Johnston, ed., *Memorial History of Louisville* (Chicago 1896); Louisville Free Kindergarten Association Reports 1894–1895, 1900–1901, 1904–1905, 1905–1907; Agnes Snyder, *Dauntless Women in Childhood Education, 1856–1931* (Washington 1972); Pearl Allen Williams, "History of the Kindergarten Movement in Louisville, Kentucky, 1887–1930," Jefferson County Public School Archives, Louisville, Kentucky.

Mary Anne Fowlkes

KING, ALFRED DANIEL WILLIAMS "A.D." (b Atlanta, Georgia, July 30, 1930; d Atlanta, July 21, 1969). Preacher and CIVIL RIGHTS activist. King was the son of the Reverend Martin Luther King Sr. and Alberta (Williams) King. Born in 1930, he was the youngest of three children. After completing his education at Morehouse College's Interdenominational Theological Center in Atlanta and preaching at First Baptist Church in Birmingham, Alabama, King accepted the pastor's post at Louisville's Zion Baptist Church on Twenty-second and Walnut (now Muhammad Ali Blvd.) in late 1964.

Reverend A.D. Williams King with civil rights marchers.

Soon after assuming his post in early 1965, King founded a state chapter of his older brother Martin's Southern Christian Leadership Council (SCLC), known as the Kentucky Christian Leadership Council. After playing a minor role in Louisville's civil rights battle for nearly a year and a half, King took a vocal stance in 1967 on the community's discriminatory housing policies. In early summer he and other leaders of the Committee for Open Housing organized nightly marches through the South End, at which time he was jailed for thirty hours and forced to pay a thirty-dollar fine after leading a protest during prohibited hours.

Although Martin Luther King Jr. attended a couple of the marches, the number of demonstrators dried up midway through the summer. However, the efforts were rewarded late in 1967 when the recently elected Democratic BOARD OF ALDERMEN passed a new open-housing ordinance. After his brother was assassinated in Memphis, A.D. stepped up his presence nationally in the civil rights movement. In June 1968 he announced his resignation from Zion Baptist Church, which had become the largest African American Baptist church in Kentucky, in order to succeed his brother at Ebenezer Baptist Church in Atlanta and play a larger role in the SCLC.

A.D. and his wife, Naomi Barber King, had five children. King was found dead in his backyard swimming pool, the victim of an apparent drowning.

See Wade Hall, *The Rest of the Dream: The Black Odyssey of Lyman Johnson* (Lexington 1988).

KING, HORTENSE (FLEXNER) (b Louisville, April 12, 1885; d Louisville, September 28, 1973). Poet and writer. Hortense Flexner was born to Jacob and Rosa Maas Flexner. She attended the Flexner School (founded by an uncle), Bryn Mawr, and the University of Michigan. She was a supporter of women's suffrage and worked as a reporter and women's section editor at the *Louisville Herald* from 1912 to 1919. She married cartoonist Wyncie King and became a writer for the Curtis Publishing Co. when he joined the *Saturday Evening Post.* She also taught at Bryn Mawr and Sarah Lawrence College.

Flexner wrote plays—*The Broken God* (1915), *The Faun* (1915), *Voices* (1916), and *The New Queen* (1920)—and children's books—*Clipper* (1941), *Wishing Window* (1942), and *Puzzle Pond* (1948), which her husband illustrated. She published nearly two hundred poems between 1911 and 1956 in publications such as *Harper's*, *North American Review*, *The New Yorker*, and *Poetry*. In 1920, *Clouds and Cobblestones*, her first collection of poems, appeared. She published *This Stubborn Root and Other Poems* in 1931 and *North Window and Other Poems* in 1943.

Flexner returned to Louisville after King's death in 1961. Her poetry gained renewed attention when British poet Laurie Lee edited a volume of her works in 1963 and Marguerite Yourcenar published *Presentation critique d'Hortense Flexner* in 1969. The University of Louisville granted her an honorary degree in 1971 and published *The Selected Poems of Hortense Flexner* in 1975. Consistently praised for her purity of style and gripping imagery, Flexner's later poems expressed concerns about postwar mechanization and materialism. Her body was cremated.

See Marguerite Yourcenar, *Presentation critique d'Hortense Flexner suivie d'un choix de poems* (Paris 1969); Hortense Flexner King papers, University of Louisville Rare Books and Special Collections; William S. Ward, *A Literary History of Kentucky* (Knoxville, Tenn., 1988); Harvey Curtis Webster and Joy Bale, *The Selected Poems of Hortense Flexner* (Louisville 1975).

Lindsey Apple

KING, PEE WEE (b Abrams, Wisconsin, February 18, 1914; d Louisville, March 7, 2000). Songwriter and musician. Born Julius Frank Anthony Kuczynski to John and Helen (Mielczark) Kuczynski, King began his musical career as a child by playing accordion and concertina in his father's polka band. Early in the 1930s King joined the *Badger State Barn Dance* on Milwaukee's WJRN radio. After one year he was discovered by manager/promoter J.L. Frank, who convinced him to move to Louisville with a group called the Log Cabin Boys. It was then that he changed his name to Pee Wee King. Early in his career, King could often be heard performing on WHAS and WAVE radio. King married Lydia Frank, daughter of J.L. Frank, in 1936. In 1937 King formed the band the Golden West Cowboys and was a major draw at the Grand Ole Opry, in Nashville, until 1947. King then hosted his own television show on WAVE-TV. In the years that followed, King hosted shows originating from Cincinnati, Cleveland, and Chicago. He even hosted the nationally syndicated *Pee Wee King* show on ABC from 1955 to 1961. In addition to his television career, King also had a nationally syndicated radio show on NBC and appeared in several feature films, all of them westerns.

Throughout his career, King continued to write music as well as record. He wrote or co-wrote more than 400 songs, including the "Tennessee Waltz." Written in 1946 and recorded for RCA Victor in 1948, the waltz, which King wrote in collaboration with Redd Stewart, is country music's most-recorded (500 times), most-sold (70 million records) song of all time. Patti Page's version was one of the biggest hits in modern popular music history. In 1965 "Tennessee Waltz" was designated an official song of the state of Tennessee. King personally re-one on the charts. "Slow Poke," written by King, Stewart, and Chilton Price, sold over a million copies and reached number one on both the country and pop music charts.

Known and respected for his talent and innovations to the country music genre, such as the addition of new sounds produced by drums, trumpets, and electric guitars, King was named director of the Country Music Foundation in 1969. In 1974 he was honored with induction into the Country Music Hall of Fame.

King was survived by his wife, Lydia; their three sons: Frank Jr., Gene C., and Larry and a daughter, Marietta Wuchterl. He is buried in Louisville Memorial Gardens East.

See Wade Hall, *Hell-Bent for Music: The Life of Pee Wee King.* (Lexington, 1996).

KING, ROBERT EMMET (b Louisville, 1848; d Louisville, November 11, 1921). Mayor. The son of John C. King, a well-known Louisville undertaker, King was elected to the BOARD OF ALDERMEN in 1894 when the Republicans were swept into power throughout the country. In Louisville, Republicans elected members of the City Council, a number of county officials, and elected Judge WALTER EVANS to Congress. King served as president of the Board of Aldermen from November 1895 through November 1897, with the exception of his brief tenure as mayor.

King served as mayor pro tem for two weeks from January 14 through 31, 1896, following the death in office of Henry S. Tyler. King was the first Republican to serve as mayor of Louisville, although George Todd is credited with being the first elected Republican mayor. Todd was later elected by the City Council to serve out the remainder of Tyler's term. King was leader of the "Big Seven" aldermen who banded together and controlled legislation during Todd's administration. After his public life, King retired to an Indiana farm and worked for the Adams Express Co. He is buried in CAVE HILL CEMETERY.

See "First Republican Mayor is Buried," *Louisville Times,* Nov. 12, 1921.

KINGSLEY, SUSAN DEE HURT (CARDWELL) (b Middlesborough, Kentucky, March 1, 1946; d Athens, Georgia, February 6, 1984). Actress. Born to Ballard Newton and Treecy (Cadle) Cardwell, she attended the University of Kentucky and won a place at the London Academy of Music and Dramatic Arts in 1970. She married David Garland Hurt in 1974, and had two children, Roxanne and Garland. Beginning in 1969 Kingsley appeared in many productions at ACTORS THEATRE OF LOUISVILLE (ATL), including *Crimes of the Heart* with Kathy Bates. Playwright, Marsha Norman wrote *Getting Out* with Susan in mind for the leading role of Arlene. The play premiered at ATL and it was repeated off Broadway to critical acclaim, then went on to Ireland, Yugoslavia, and Israel on ATL's first tour abroad. Given a choice between roles in two Broadway productions, *Night Mother*, a Pulitzer Prize–winning play by Norman, and Beth Henley's *The Wake of Jamie Foster,* she chose the latter because the contract allowed her more time with her two small children. Despite critical praise for her acting, the Henley play was not a success. Kingsley appeared in the films *Coal Miner's Daughter* (1980), *Popeye* (1980), and *Reckless* (1984), and the network television production of *The Dollmaker* (1984) with Jane Fonda. Ms. Kingsley's last ATL stage performance before her untimely death in an automobile accident was *The Three Sisters* by Anton Chekov.

Sylvia Cardwell Bruton

KLAUBER, EDWARD K. (b Louisville, February 24, 1887; d New York City, September 23, 1954). Broadcast executive. Edward K. Klauber was born to Morris and Ray (Forst) Klauber. He was a member of a family prominent in artistic and business circles in the late nineteenth and early twentieth centuries. Klauber's father and grandfather, also named Edward Klauber, were Louisville photographers during the early years of photography. An uncle, Henry Klauber, was a noted local art authority and owner of Klauber's Artistic Shop. Another uncle, Adolph Klauber, received recognition as a New York actor, an early producer of Eugene O'Neill's work, and drama critic for the *New York Times* from 1906 to 1918.

Klauber moved to New York City, where he was a reporter, editor, and ultimately executive vice president of Columbia Broadcasting System (CBS). He was considered by many to be the father of CBS News, which was the model for all subsequent news programs. He became interested in the development of BROADCASTING ethics and standards for news and was instrumental in the 1948 adoption of the "Standards of Practice for American Broadcasting" by the National Association of Broadcasters, providing the medium a code. Klauber hired commentator Edward R. Murrow in 1935, and he also offered Murrow the position as CBS European director in 1937.

Klauber graduated from Male High School in 1903 and went on to attend the University of Louisville and the University of Pennsylvania. He originally planned to study MEDICINE but along the way became interested in journalism. He worked as a reporter for the *New York World* from 1912 to 1916. Klauber worked for the *New York Times* from 1916 to 1928, starting as a reporter and becoming city editor in 1927. From 1928 to 1929 he was director of public relations at a New York advertising agency. In 1930 he began work for CBS, becoming executive vice president in 1931. He became director at CBS in May 1937 and chairman of the executive committee in March 1942, retiring in 1943. Klauber was appointed director of the Office of War Information from 1943 to 1945, succeeding Milton Eisenhower.

Klauber married Gladys Gustafson February 23, 1925. She died in 1943. He married Doris E. Larson in April 1945.

See M. Sperber, *Murrow: His Life and Times* (New York 1986); Alexander Kendrick, *Prime Time: The Life of Edward R. Murrow* (Boston 1969); *New York Times*, Sept. 24, 1954.

Ruth Spangler

KLEIN, SAMUEL H. (b Louisville, February 6, 1906; d Louisville, May 17, 1995). Banker. Klein was the son of a local grocer. He graduated from Male High School and started his business career in the 1930s as a used-car salesman, eventually acquiring his own company, National Auto Sales.

In 1950, Klein and his brother Isadore bought an interest in the Royal Bank and later got controlling interest. The bank eventually became Louisville's fourth-largest. In 1957 he was elected the bank's president. When in 1963 it merged with the BANK OF LOUISVILLE, he remained president. In 1970 he was named chairman and chief executive of the bank, also serving in the same capacity for Mid-America Bancorp, the holding company for the bank and its trust affiliates. He remained in that position until he retired in November 1985, when he turned control of the bank over to his nephew Bertram Klein.

Klein was active in promoting economic development. He provided some of the early financing for HUMANA INC. (originally Extendicare), started in 1961 when David Jones, WENDELL CHERRY, and four others began operating a nursing home.

Klein also promoted community service and was a member of the University of Louisville's Board of Trustees during the 1960s and 1970s. He served in a similar capacity for BELLARMINE COLLEGE. Klein was active in the Louisville Area Chamber of Commerce, Leadership Louisville, Temple Adath Israel, KOSAIR CHILDREN'S HOSPITAL, LOUISVILLE CENTRAL AREA, Salvation Army, FUND FOR THE ARTS, GOODWILL INDUSTRIES, and the KENTUCKY DERBY FESTIVAL.

In 1925 Klein married Hattie Brohm. He was survived by two daughters, Mrs. Stanley Yarmuth and Mrs. Stanley Atlas. He is buried in the Temple Adath Israel cemetery.

KLING, ARTHUR SOMMERFIELD (b Louisville, December 10, 1896; d Louisville, October 7, 1981). Humanitarian and businessman. The son of Benjamin and Anna (Sommerfield) Kling, he attended the University of Cincinnati and, for awhile, Hebrew Union College in Cincinnati before leaving rabbinical training for the Chicago Technical College. During World War I, he served as the morale officer for the National Jewish Welfare Board in Fort Oglethorpe, Georgia, before holding the same post at CAMP TAYLOR in Louisville during the 1918 flu epidemic.

Following the war, Kling joined his brother Morris and their father at the family's business, the Kling Stationery Co. on Sixth and Main

the Kling Stationery Co. on Sixth and Main Streets. After taking charge of the company and changing the name to the Kling Co., the brothers built the firm into a large wholesale distributor and a chain of variety stores known as Dimeco.

Kling's philanthropic nature drove him to aid a wide array of the city's population, although much of his energy went toward helping the Jewish community. He founded the Jewish Vocational Service (Jewish Family and Vocational Service), was a founder and lifetime board member of the JEWISH COMMUNITY FEDERATION, and was president of the Jewish Community Center. In 1959 he was chosen as man of the year by the Louisville chapter of the B'nai B'rith, while he and his brother were jointly honored with the B'NAI B'RITH National Humanitarian Award in 1978. He also was selected in 1969 as the recipient of the Blanche B. Ottenheimer Award for outstanding civic service. In broader community efforts, Kling was instrumental in the organization of both the Kentucky chapter of the American Civil Liberties Union and the Americans for Democratic Action, was the first white board member of the Urban League of Louisville, and was active on the board of the National Association for the Advancement of Colored People. In 1937 Kling, a social progressive, ran unsuccessfully for mayor of Louisville on the Socialist ticket.

Kling's later years were devoted to the cause of older Americans. He founded both the Kentucky Association of Older Persons and the Kentucky Combined Committee on Aging, and served on Gov. Wendell Ford's Task Force on Aging. During his lifetime, the Kling Center for senior citizens on W Ormsby Ave. was named in his honor.

Arthur Kling married Selma Marcus in 1920, and they had one child, David.

Suzanne Post

KLING, SIMCHA (b Dayton, Kentucky, January 27, 1922; d Louisville, February 26, 1991). Rabbi and scholar. The son of Eli and Ann (Niman) Kling. After graduating from Gymnasia Herzlia in Tel Aviv, he received a B.A. at the University of Cincinnati, and an M.A. at Columbia University, and in 1948 was ordained at Jewish Theological Seminary in New York City, where he also received a doctorate. He served as an assistant rabbi in St. Louis during 1948–5l; rabbi of Beth David in Greensboro, North Carolina, during 1951–65; then came to ADATH JESHURUN in Louisville. He was president of the North Carolina Association of Rabbis and of Louisville's Board of Rabbis. For twenty-five years he was president of Louisville's Hebrew Speaking Circle. He taught sociology of religion for five years at the University of Louisville and lectured at BELLARMINE COLLEGE in Louisville and elsewhere. Kling wrote *Embracing Judaism* (1970) and five other books, among them biographies of Zionist leaders and a historical account of Israel. He also wrote seventeen articles for *Hadoar*, an American Jewish weekly; translated essays; and wrote study guides, besides serving as editor of *Mercaz Newsletter*. He was a strong advocate for women's participation in Jewish life. He married Edith Leeman June 15, 1947. They had three daughters, Elana, Adina, and Reena. Kling is buried in Louisville's Adath Jeshurun Cemetery.

Herman Landau

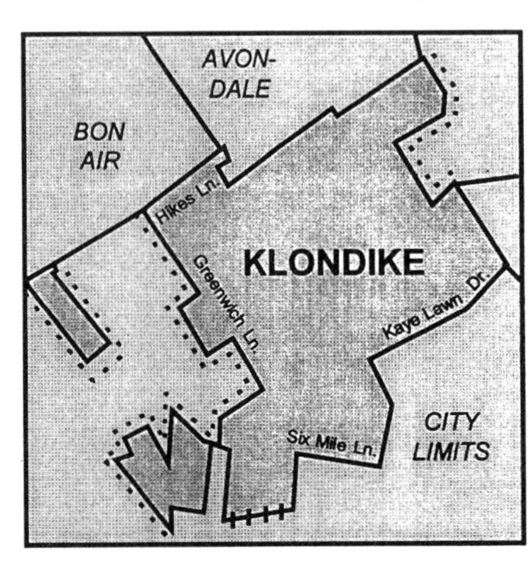

KLONDIKE. Irregular-shaped neighborhood in eastern Louisville, west of Breckenridge Ln. and to the south of Hikes Ln., bounded by the Louisville city limits. Like its surrounding neighborhoods, Klondike got its start after World War II as suburban sprawl, abetted by the automobile, began changing Jefferson County. In 1955 developers Edward Butler and Chester Cooper purchased forty-five acres of the Graff family farm and part of the Hikes family's Midlane Farm, and subdivided the area. A local landmark in the primarily residential neighborhood is Klondike Park, which, according to a longtime resident, was opened around the turn of the century by Frank Bumann, a prospector in the Yukon. The Klondike neighborhood derived its name from the park.

KNOBS. Knobs are isolated conical hills usually over two hundred feet in height. Together they form one of the six geographic regions of Kentucky, stretching in a 230–mile-long arch that runs roughly along the southern border of the Bluegrass Region. It reaches as far east as Lewis County, while Jefferson and Bullitt Counties constitute its western boundary. A typical knob is made up of a layer of loose sandstone, sometimes called knob freestone, atop a more dense layer of Devonian and Silurian shale mixed with Mississippian limestones. The slopes of the knobs are generally not favorable for plant growth. However, the summits have far richer soil. Poplars; white, red, and black oaks; gum; and elm trees are found atop most knobs. Along the Ohio River, knobs have long been desirable locations for homes and, in more recent years, have been used as sites for television- and radio-transmitting towers.

In the Louisville area, BULLITT COUNTY has the most distinctive grouping of knobs. Knobs extend from the Muldraugh Hill cuesta in the west, southeastward across Bullitt into Nelson County. The highest point in Bullitt County is 998 feet, the top of a knob located three and one-half miles northeast of Lebanon Junction.

The knobs were a source for economic opportunity in the early 1800s. Iron ores known as "Kidney" and "Blue Sheet" ores were found below the sandstone surface. These low-grade ores were taken from the ground and sent to local furnaces. These furnaces, such as the Belmont Furnace that operated in Bullitt County in the 1850s, used the timber from the top of the knobs for the manufacture of pig-iron. The pig-iron was then sent down the Salt River or on the LOUISVILLE & NASHVILLE RAILROAD to Louisville. At times the L&N had to station "pusher" engines throughout the knobs, particularly at the base of Muldraugh Hill, to help heavy freight trains up the steep inclines.

Knobs in Jefferson County are found in the southwest around Valley Station and do not extend any farther north than Mill Creek. Burnt Knob, later renamed Iroquois Hill, forms the northern border of IROQUOIS PARK. JEPTHA KNOB, in Shelby County, with an elevation of 1,188 feet, is one of the highest knobs in the area.

In southern Indiana, knobs refer to the hilly area lying immediately north of the Ohio River. The community of Floyds Knobs in Floyd County takes its name from surrounding peaks. Clark County has several knobs, among them Pine Knob (890 feet) and Round Knob (886 feet). Likewise, Harrison County has several well-known knobs such as Greenbriar Knob (802 feet), Pilot Knob (877 feet), and Wildcat Knob (886 feet).

See Preston McGrain and Jaces C. Currens, *Topography of Kentucky* (Lexington 1978).

Joe Wayne Roberts

K. NORMAN BERRY ASSOCIATES. K. Norman Berry Associates, a Louisville architectural firm, traces its roots back to architect Leo L. Oberwarth (1872–1939). Oberwarth, a native of New York State, came to Kentucky in 1894 and settled in Frankfort, where he became the city's major architect. The Capital Hotel of Frankfort was designed by Oberwarth in association with Frank L. Packard. In 1926, with the addition of his son Julian, his firm was renamed Leo Oberwarth and Son. In 1930 Julian, in recognition of his efforts to establish an architects' registration law in Kentucky, was assigned the first certificate as a registered architect. He designed, among other works, a number of school buildings in Frankfort, the Frankfort Municipal Building, and the State Police Barracks and Training Center. He also coauthored, with William B. Scott Jr., *A History of the Profession of Architecture in Kentucky.*

In 1964 K. NORMAN BERRY, James Burris, and Milton Thompson acquired the Oberwarth firm. They remained in Frankfort until their reorganization as K. Norman Berry Associates in 1971, when they relocated to Louisville. In 1994 the firm was again reorganized as a partnership between Norman Berry and Steven A. Eggers.

K. Norman Berry Associates has from its inception specialized in historical architectural renovation. Among its renovations are the old Jefferson County Jail; the Doe-Anderson Building; the building that formerly housed the Highland Branch of the LOUISVILLE FREE PUBLIC LIBRARY; Riverside, the Farnsley-Moremen historic home, which is located in southwest Jefferson County; Federal Hill (My Old Kentucky Home) in Bardstown; and the Governor's mansion. In 1985 the firm received the Ida Lee Willis Service to Preservation Award from the Kentucky Heritage Council.

In addition to historical renovation work, the firm has designed many projects of new construction such as the University Club at the University of Louisville; a convent and nursing home facility for the Little Sisters of the Poor; the Fenley Office Park, located at Hurstbourne Green in Louisville; and several classroom buildings at Kentucky State University in Frankfort. The latter won for the firm a national American Institute of Architects Design Award in 1968. The firm is located at 611 W MAIN St. in a renovated Victorian building.

KNOW-NOTHING PARTY. In the early 1850s a third political party emerged as a powerful influence, upsetting the two-party system of Whigs and Democrats firmly entrenched in American politics. The tremendous influx of predominantly Catholic IRISH and German immigrants beginning in 1846 gave rise to strong anti-foreign, anti-Catholic sentiment. Some native-born Americans perceived the rush of foreigners as a threat to undermine Americanism and open the door for a papal takeover of the country. The hysteria associated with this xenophobia gave birth to the American Party, whose members were commonly called Know-Nothings.

The so-called nativist movement that eventually jelled into the Know-Nothing/American Party began around 1850. Originally known as the Order of the Star-Spangled Banner (later the Order of United Americans) in New York and the Order of the Sons of America in Pennsylvania, these societies formed secret lodges throughout the Union. Only native-born, Protestant male citizens with Protestant parents and not joined by marriage to a Roman Catholic could join a lodge. Members used cryptic hand signals and passwords and swore an oath never to divulge the activities of the party meetings. If outsiders questioned them, members replied, "I know nothing."

When Whig Party leaders Henry Clay and Daniel Webster died a few months apart in 1852, that party began to disintegrate, badly split over the slavery issue. Generally, northern Whigs were antislavery and joined the fledgling Know-Nothing Party due in large part to its stance against Catholic immigrants who were at the time inundating the northeast United States. The southern faction of Whigs supported the nativist movement in part because the massive numbers of immigrants in the North increased the population and gave the North more representation in Congress, where they could outvote the South.

Each faction had definite views on the free/slave status of new states but let that issue remain unresolved, choosing to ride the unifying wave of strong anti-foreign fervor that was a welcome diversion from the slavery issue. Though the party never officially advocated violence, its vehement xenophobic rhetoric gave rise to the use of thugs to control elections. The best known of these were the Plug Uglies, who organized in several cities to prevent foreigners from going to the polls. By 1854–55, the stunning Know-Nothing success resulted in one hundred congressional seats, eight governorships, and thousands of local offices.

By 1854 Louisville was fruitful ground for the growing hatred of "non-Americans." German and Irish immigrants flooded into the city. Many Irish were poor and illiterate, and according to the Know-Nothings owed blind obedience to the Pope. A greater concern was that the Irish were almost unanimously flocking to the DEMOCRATIC PARTY. This fueled the former Whigs' fear of a shift in the balance of power. Equally frightening were the German Forty-Eighters, who escaped political oppression in Germany following the failed revolutions of 1848. Members of this foreign element were generally educated, intellectual, politically active, and inclined to express their radical ideas in print.

A few of these radicals formed the League of Free Men in Louisville and espoused their views in the LOUISVILLE PLATFORM of 1854. This document called for women's rights and emancipation of slaves, among other issues. The platform incensed Louisville Whig/American Party members and fueled the violent fires of Know-Nothingism.

Enter former Whig Walter Haldeman, editor of the *Louisville Daily Courier*, who had advocated nativist thinking for many years. His daily written railings against foreigners inflamed native-born Americans to a white-hot anger as city elections approached.

Haldeman's rival, George Prentice of the *Louisville Daily Journal*, also took up the banner of Louisville's Know-Nothings. In part, it was an act of survival. Prentice's beloved Whig Party had breathed its last, and his newspaper's circulation was in decline. Prentice took up his pen against foreigners and Catholics with a venom that exceeded even Haldeman's rhetoric, at one point railing against the pope as an "Italian despot" who sent forth hordes of Catholic immigrants to take over the country and do his bidding.

In question that spring of 1855 was the debate over the election of mayor. James Speed, elected in 1852, contended his term lasted until 1856. The Know-Nothing–dominated City Council disagreed, called for an election, and declared JOHN BARBEE the American Party candidate. Though Speed was an able mayor, he had one deplorable fault, unspoken by council members but most likely the cause for their actions. Speed was a convert to Catholicism.

John Barbee won the election held on April 7, and Speed filed suit. The judge ruled in Speed's favor, but the Know-Nothings took the matter to the Kentucky Court of Appeals, which declared Barbee the winner. Know-Nothings also dominated the magistrate elections held that May, as ruffians beat GERMANS and Irish who attempted to vote.

The violence dismayed even WALTER HALDEMAN, who backed off his fervent nativist stance. He completely abandoned Know-Nothingism after the American Party convention in June 1855 wavered on the slavery issue. The debate over the free and slave balance that brought the downfall of the Whigs now threatened the American Party. As tempers grew hotter with the sultry summer days of 1855, a showdown was inevitable. On state election day, August 6, 1855, the minor skirmishes that had taken place all summer culminated in the BLOODY MONDAY riots that claimed the lives of at least twenty-two people. There may have been more victims, but an official inquiry was never conducted amidst the frenzy of finger-pointing that followed. The American Party swept the election statewide.

Bloody Monday was the climactic and defining moment for Know-Nothingism in Louisville. The nativist movement temporarily diverted attention from the seething slavery issue, but it was a matter that could not be ignored and its presence was obvious within the party.

The American Party remained a dominant political force in the city and state. By the summer of 1857, things began to change. The Kentucky American Party, although "one of the strongest and best organized in the South," experienced a net loss of four offices in statewide elections that year. Louisville, "where mobs of Plug Uglies had controlled the polls for several years, remained in American Party hands."

Nationally, the American Party decline was underway. Its downward spiral nearly equaled its rapid rise. The slavery issue again took center stage, and the Know-Nothing effort to make immigration the issue of the day failed. Working for a constitutional amendment to forbid Catholics and foreigners to hold public office, fighting to require a twenty-one-year wait before an immigrant could vote, and forming a Joint Special Committee on the Inspections of Nunneries and Convents proved ghastly mistakes. The northern faction began embracing the new Republican Party, while the pro-slavery southern wing reluctantly leaned toward the Democratic Party, its reputation as the party of choice among immigrants apparently forgotten. On state levels, Know-Nothings were responsible for surprisingly enlightened legislation that gave women more rights and created the first desegregation law, in the state of Massachusetts.

Louisville, the border city, was a study in contrast. It was a gateway town, pro-slavery and pro-Union, with strong trade ties to both North and South. There were also a great many slaves and free blacks, though their numbers in Louisville and Jefferson County were in decline as the slavery debate heightened. In the 1860 election, Louisvillians resoundingly rejected Kentuckian ABRAHAM LINCOLN, the Republican candidate, and John C. Breckinridge of the Southern Democrats. They gave a dignified second-place nod to regular Democrat Stephen A. Douglas. But it was John Bell of Tennessee under the banner of Constitutional Unionists, made up of old-line Southern Whigs and former Know-Nothings, who solidly carried Louisville and Jefferson County.

Nationwide, the death knell sounded for the Know-Nothings. The party passed away in the maelstrom that saw foreign and native blood flow together on the fields of civil conflict. By 1861, the American Party had no representation in Congress and soon completely vanished from the political scene.

The final say against Know-Nothingism in Louisville came two weeks before the end of the CIVIL WAR. On April 1, 1865, less than ten years after Bloody Monday, German Philip Tomppert was elected mayor of Louisville.

See Kenneth M. Stampp, *America in 1857: A Nation on the Brink* (New York 1990); George H. Yater, *Two Hundred Years at the Falls of the Ohio* (Louisville 1987); Thomas P. Baldwin, "George Prentice, *The Louisville Anzeiger* and the 1855 Bloody Monday Riots," *Filson Club History Quarterly* 67 (Oct. 1993): 482–95; William G. O'Toole and Charles E. Aebersold, "Louisville's Bloody Monday Riots from a German Perspective," *Filson Club History Quarterly* 40 (Oct. 1996): 419–25.

Rhonda Abner

KOHLHEPP, NORMAN (b Louisville, December 22, 1892; d Louisville, June 8, 1986). Artist. The son of William and Emma (Miller) Kohlhepp, he did not begin painting until he was in his mid-thirties. His studies at Manual Training High School led him to enroll in the University of Cincinnati in 1915, where he received a degree in metallurgical engineering. After graduation, he worked for General Fireproofing, a manufacturer of steel office furniture, in Boston. In 1917 he left his career and enlisted in the French army. After World War I he returned to his former company but made frequent visits to France.

In 1928 at the American Students and Artists Club, which he founded in Paris, he met his future wife, Dorothy, an art student at the Academy Julian. After their marriage in 1930, she encouraged him to study painting, and he began his study at the Academie Calarossi. In 1933 he and Dorothy became pupils of the cubist painter, Andre Lhote, an association that lasted twenty years.

He returned to engineering and Louisville but continued to paint. In 1938 he and Dorothy had a joint exhibition at the J.B. SPEED ART MUSEUM, sponsored by the Junior League. In 1948 the museum exhibited their recent works, many inspired by their travels to the Far East, India, Spain, and Mexico. In 1979 the museum held a retrospective show of his work titled "50 Years in the Arts." From 1936 through 1979 he constantly exhibited at the Kentucky State Fair. In 1979 he and four other Louisville painters were honored by the KENTUCKY FAIR AND EXPOSITION CENTER and the Kentucky Department of the Arts.

Throughout his life he supported the art community of Louisville and was active in the Art Center and the LOUISVILLE SCHOOL OF ART. His work is in the collections of the J.B. Speed Art Museum, the University of Louisville, and the National Museum of American Art. The Smithsonian Institution acquired his "Purple Tree and Ohio River Steamboat" in 1980. He is buried in Cave Hill Cemetery.

See *Courier-Journal*, June 9, 1986.

Mary Jane Benedict

KOREANS. The first Koreans living in the Louisville area were visiting professors and college students, especially at the University of Louisville. In the late 1950s most of the early Korean functions were limited to seasonal outings among students and professors.

Within twenty years, more than six hundred Koreans had settled throughout the Louisville metropolitan area. Based here since 1975, the Korean-American Association of KENTUCKIANA supported the new immigrants and promoted the socioeconomic status of the entire Korean population in the state of Kentucky and the southern Indiana Region.

The Korean population in the Louisville area grew immensely in the late twentieth century. More than two thousand strong, they excelled in medical, engineering, and technical fields as well as entrepreneurial ventures. About 10 percent of the population consisted of full-time students in local universities, colleges, and graduate seminary schools.

The Korean Association coordinates activities with other ethnic communities and participates in functions such as the Derby Parade. Korean churches of different denominations in the Louisville area play a major role in preserving and nurturing the native culture and heritage. Mayor Jerry Abramson once declared Labor Day as the Day of Koreans, in appreciation of Korean-Americans' participation in enrichment of the city's culture.

The Korean School of Louisville at 8101 Brownsboro Rd. teaches the native heritage and language. Also, the Tae-Kwon-Do academies in the Louisville area teach American students the martial art discipline as well as basic Korean customs. Korean-American Community Services Inc. provides numerous social services to those in need and prepares immigrants for citizenship examination and offers court translation.

Sung John Suh

KOREAN WAR. After communist North Korea invaded South Korea on June 25, 1950, President Harry Truman hastily committed American forces to blunt the North Korean Army's push to the south. In the first American battle on July 5, 1950, north of Oson, Pvt. Norman G. Cawthorne, a member of "Task Force Smith," a reinforced infantry battalion up against an enemy division, became Louisville's first serviceman killed in action. As America's piecemeal commitment continued, other units of the army's Twenty-fourth Infantry Division were gathered up in Japan and thrown into action. Louisville's Col. Robert Martin—Kentucky's highest-ranking casualty in the war—lost his life in a one-man standoff against a tank.

During that first month of heavy casualties, Louisville lost two more of its heroes, Chaplain Herman G. Felhoelter and PFC Charles Allen Taber. As the enemy overran their positions, Father Felhoelter chose to stay and administer to the wounded who were unable to withdraw. The enemy shot the priest and killed about thirty wounded men on stretchers. Taber continued to fire his mortar until he was killed. Private First Class Taber, Chaplain Felhoelter, and Colonel Martin were awarded the Distinguished Service Cross posthumously—the nation's second-highest award for valor. Lt. Leonard L. Preston, a former University of Kentucky FOOTBALL star, was wounded in that early action.

With the immediate need for replacements, reservists in all branches, many of them WORLD WAR II veterans, were called to active duty. Enlistments in the Louisville recruiting stations increased dramatically. The city draft board geared up to induct its first draftees in September. In October, doctors, dentists, and veterinarians registered for the draft in Louisville—altogether about a hundred.

Soon, city reserve and national guard units received orders to report for active duty. Co. D, Sixteenth Marine Infantry Battalion, was the first reserve unit called. Woman's Air Force reservists in the 436th Carrier Wing received their orders. Louisville National Guard units called included the 413th Ordnance Heavy Maintenance Co., the 198th and 452nd Field Artillery Battalions, and the 123rd Air National Guard Group. None of these guard units went overseas, but individuals in the units went to Korea as replacements. Maj. Meade Brown and First Lieutenants Lawrence B. Kelly and Eugene L. Ruiz, pilots' replacements out of the 123rd, were killed in action.

In September 1950 the North Korean offensive was halted at the Pusan Perimeter about the same time Gen. Douglas MacArthur launched an amphibious landing behind enemy lines. Soon American, South Korean, and other United Nations (UN) forces drove the disintegrating North Korean army back across the Thirty-eighth parallel. As the UN forces approached the Yalu River on the Chinese border, hidden Chinese armies struck hard. In the bitterly cold retreat in November and December, Louisville lost ten young men, among them Lt. William A. Dean, a marine who had survived Iwo Jima in World War II, and Pvt. Earnest A. Taylor. Taylor received the Distinguished Service Cross. After the Chinese intervention, the high initial public approval rating of the war dipped dramatically.

By July 1951 the lines stabilized near the Thirty-eighth parallel. For the next two years, while bitter negotiations continued first at Kaesong and later at Panmunjom, the front lines were bunkered in with connecting and fighting trenches. Casualties dropped drastically, and the war moved off the front pages. This was the beginning of what would become known as the "forgotten war."

SFC Henry C. Gamble was the city's first AFRICAN AMERICAN killed in the war. Lt. Comdr. John J. Magda, a World War II ace, was the city's only Navy officer killed in the war. Others not mentioned above who are known to have received the Distinguished Service Cross were Lieutenants Herbert B. Condor and George M. Gividen Jr. and M.Sgt. James R. Mills. In the last battle, Marine PFC Jack B. Reesor was killed in action two days before the armistice ended the shooting on July 27, 1953. Thus, Louisville lost a son in two small battles—the first and last.

About 1.5 million Americans served in Korea—fifty-four thousand died. On the city's Korean War Memorial, located in McNeely Park off Cooper Chapel Rd., there are 170 names of men who sacrificed their young lives for their country in the conflict. It was a war that ended in stalemate, enshrined Truman's containment policy, introduced the limited war concept, and in some ways charted how the cold war would be played out.

Arthur L. Kelly

KOSAIR CHILDREN'S HOSPITAL. Kosair Children's Hospital ranks among the nation's top ten pediatric HOSPITALS. Opened as Children's Free Hospital in 1892, it was, moreover, the tenth pediatric hospital in the United States, the first in the South, to serve a mountain region, and the first nondenominational pediatric hospital in Louisville. A part of the Norton Health Care corporation and the downtown LOUISVILLE MEDICAL CENTER, designated by the American College of Surgeons as the region's Level I trauma center, it is Kentucky's only freestanding pediatric facility.

Founded by MARY LAFON, Hallie Quigley, Dr. Ap Morgan Vance (surgeon), and Dr. John Albert Larrabee (early pediatric specialist), it opened in the Cornwall House on the south side of E. Chestnut St. near Floyd St. Lafon headed its volunteer administration from 1892 until 1918 and Vance its volunteer medical staff until 1917. Children's Free Hospital pioneered regionally in pediatric care, orthopedic surgery, professional nursing, the fight to end child LABOR, mountain outreach, provision of free pasteurized milk, and outpatient pediatrics clinic service; and was the seventh in the nation to provide education for disabled children (1913), and the third to offer child psychology (1923).

A full-service acute and chronic care facility serving Kentucky, Tennessee, Virginia, and Indiana, it became a teaching hospital of the University of Louisville in 1930. In its second quarter century, it provided Louisville's first burn unit, and was the first in Kentucky to correct esophageal blockages and congenital heart defects and to offer child psychiatry, a heart-lung machine, open heart surgery, and penicillin. CFH expanded from 1918 on to fill the south side of the block between Floyd and Brook streets.

Dropping "Free" from its name in 1946 but continuing free care, Children's Hospital with the University of Louisville and General Hospital founded the Louisville Medical Center in 1950, and was a co-founder in 1967 of the National Association for Children's Hospitals and Related Institutions. In 1969 Children's Hospital consolidated with Norton Memorial Infirmary, creating Norton-Children's, Inc.

Meanwhile, the Kosair Charities Committee, Inc., of Kosair Shrine Temple, had in 1925 created a second Louisville pediatric facility, for orthopedics only. Kosair Crippled Children's Hospital, located at 982 Eastern Pkwy., expanded its plant steadily through 1952. The major regional facility for the treatment of polio, it was by 1944 treating three times more disabled children than any other state facility.

Offering Sister Elizabeth Kenny's rehabilitative approach, the Kosair institution spearheaded the creation of mountain orthopedic clinics and state-funded pediatric care for indigent children, regionally pioneering in scoliosis surgery and treatment, and preventive and rehabilitative pediatrics programs. In 1981, Children's Hospital and Kosair Crippled Children's Hospital merged, forming the Kosair Crippled Children's Hospital. In 1986, it moved to a new building on the northeast corner of Floyd and Chestnut Streets. The hospital network has steadily expanded becoming (1981) NKC Inc., then (1989) Alliant Health System, then (1999) Norton Health Care.

See Gail McGowan Mellor, *Kosair Children's Hospital: A History 1892–1992* (Louisville 1992).

Gail McGowan Mellor

KOSAIR SHRINE CIRCUS. Kosair Shrine Circus is a project of Kosair Temple, Ancient Arabic Order Nobles of the Mystic Shrine. Kosair Temple began operating on December 5, 1884, under dispensation from its parent organization, the Imperial Council, A.A.O.N.M.S., an appendant organization of what is commonly called the "Masonic Order."

Shriners Hospitals for Children were founded by the Imperial Council in 1922. Kosair Crippled Children's Hospital of Louisville was founded by Kosair Charities Committee Inc., the charitable arm of Kosair Temple, in 1925.

Local shrine temples throughout the country found that circuses were ideal ways to help their temples run and, in turn, support their HOSPITALS for indigent children. So in 1924, Kosair Temple signed a contract for "Kosair's Big Indoor Circus" under the personal direction of the world-famous circus man, John G. Robinson, for a week of performances beginning March 23, 1925. The contract between Robinson and Kosair Temple was for eight thousand dollars plus 15 percent of all circus revenue.

Kosair Temple contracted in 1940 with Polack Bros. Indoor Circus for performances at the Jefferson County Armory (now Louisville Gardens). General admission tickets were forty-eight cents. In 1958 the circus moved to FREEDOM HALL at the Fairgrounds, then returned to The GARDENS OF LOUISVILLE in 1964, and then moved to Broadbent Arena at the Fairgrounds in 1988. George Carden Circus International became the producer in 1992. Ticket prices in 1997 were eight dollars. Kosair Shrine Temple provides free circus admission annually to twenty thousand underprivileged children who otherwise would not have the opportunity to attend a live circus performance.

John T. Wilson Jr.

KOSMOSDALE. This small community in southwestern Jefferson County is on Dixie Hwy. approximately three miles north of the Salt River. While the area was known as Grassy Pond in 1854 and then dubbed Riverview in 1860, the most substantial growth, and an additional name change, occurred a year after the establishment of the Kosmos Cement Co. in 1904. The company reportedly was named after someone claimed that the product would be sent around the cosmos and later substituted the "k" to indicate the connection with Kentucky.

Soon after its founding, the company constructed twelve duplexes, half for white workers and half for African American workers, and opened a local school, a medical office, and a company store, creating its own community surrounding the factory. In the early 1900s, the owner and founder of the company, Samuel J. Horner, persuaded the ILLINOIS CENTRAL RAILROAD to run a spur line, with commercial and freight service, to his growing business. In exchange, Horner agreed to construct the depot, along with railroad spurs to connect with the Illinois Central Railroad tracks. The local depot still stood (in deplorable condition) in 1997 near Dixie Hwy. and was listed as one of the county's historic sites.

Although the company continued to grow throughout the century, the town's population dwindled in the 1950s and 1960s as many of the workers and their families moved to surrounding areas such as Valley Village and Valley Station. The factory was sold by the Horner family in 1957 to the Flintkote Co. of New York, who modernized the facility in 1979 to increase its capacity to 720,000 tons per year. The facility changed hands several times until 1988, when it was purchased by Houston-based South Down Inc. In the 1990s the plant's efforts to incinerate waste and tires for cement production were successfully opposed by the few remaining nearby residents.

See *A Place in Time: The Story of Louisville's Neighborhoods* (Louisville 1989); Robert M. Rennick, *Kentucky Place Names* (Lexington 1984).

KREMENTZ, JOSEPH (b Kriftel, Germany, March 15, 1840; d New Albany, Indiana, April 12, 1928). Artist. Krementz was the son of Martin and Catherine Krementz and had three brothers and four sisters. His family moved to Weisbaden in 1847 and immigrated to the United States in 1851, settling in New Albany, where he remained the rest of his life.

From boyhood, he displayed unusual talent as an artist. When he was nine he won first prize for a drawing in competition with the other school children of Weisbaden, where he studied under the internationally known artist Ludwig Knaus. His formal training was directed by Louisville artist CARL FETSCH. Krementz was associated for many years with Kentucky artist Carl Brenner and New Albany artist and operator of the Art Shop, James L. Russell.

Krementz maintained studios at the corner of Fourth and LIBERTY Streets in Louisville and one at his residence on E MARKET St. in New Albany. A lover of nature, he often went to the fields and forests to sketch. Beech trees were among his favorite subjects. His portraits and landscapes hang in numerous public and private collections. A portrait of Krementz and his wife, along with several landscapes, hang in the New Albany Public Library gallery, and he is represented in the permanent collection at the New Albany High School. He was a frequent exhibitor in New York, Chicago, Nashville, Indianapolis, Louisville, and New Albany. He also dabbled in photography and is credited with being the first in New Albany to use the dry plate process, which was the latest advancement at the time. Krementz loved music and played the violin and flute. He married Maria Louisa Keller in 1870. They had four children, twins George and Ann, Adam Edward, and Mary Catherine. He is buried in St. Mary's Cemetery in New Albany.

See *New Albany Tribune*, April 13, 1928.

KRIEGER, WILLIAM (b Louisville, April 2, 1868; d Louisville, November 14, 1941). Jefferson County judge. The son of Jacob and Mary Louise (Conrad) Krieger, he was educated at public schools and received his undergraduate degree at Transylvania College in Lexington. He received a LAW degree from the University of Louisville in 1887.

As a young man, Krieger was elected to the Kentucky House of Representatives from Louisville's Third District in 1891 and served until 1893. Krieger was elected as a Democrat, but he later became a member of the Republican Party. In 1906 Krieger was appointed judge of the Police Court by Mayor JAMES GRINSTEAD. He was elected judge of the Jefferson County Court, including Juvenile Court, in 1917 by defeating Democrat Loraine Mix in a Republican sweep of city and county political offices. In that election, the Whallen's Democratic machine, headed by James P. Whallen after his brother John had died in 1913, suffered its final defeat.

Krieger served as Jefferson County judge from January 1, 1918, until December 31, 1921. In November 1921, he was elected judge of the Jefferson Circuit Court, Common Pleas Branch. He was reelected in 1927 and served until 1933. He also served as director of the Avery Building Association, and he was a captain in the LOUISVILLE LEGION, serving in Frankfort after the state militia was called out following the assassination of Gov. William Goebel in 1900.

He had two children, W. David and Ethel. He retired from his law practice on January 1, 1941. Krieger died at his home on Sixth St. and is buried in CAVE HILL CEMETERY.

See Mary Young Southard and Ernest C. Miller, eds., *Who's Who in Kentucky: A Biographical Assembly of Notable Kentuckians* (Louisville 1936); *Courier-Journal*, Nov. 15, 1941.

KROCK, ARTHUR (b Glasgow, Kentucky, November 16, 1886; d Washington, D.C., April 12, 1974). Journalist. The son of Joseph and Caroline (Morris) Krock and winner of four Pulitzer Prizes, he got his first newspaper job on the *Louisville Herald* in 1906. He covered the 1908 presidential conventions for it. He became editor-in-chief of the *LOUISVILLE TIMES* in 1919 and in 1923 left Louisville to become Washington correspondent for the *COURIER-JOURNAL* and the *Louisville Times*. He acted as intermediary in the purchase of the two Louisville newspapers by ROBERT W. BINGHAM but later left because of a policy disagreement. He attended the Versailles Peace Conference and was one of three American reporters on a committee that urged open sessions for the World War I settlement talks. France honored him with the Legion d'Honneur, and Norway gave him the Order of St. Olaf.

He left journalism to be assistant to the chairman of the Democratic National Committee during the 1920 presidential campaign and worked briefly for Will Hays, who headed the Motion Picture Producers and Distributors of America. He joined the *New York Times* in 1927 and became head of its Washington bureau in 1932. His coverage of the New Deal won him a Pulitzer Prize in 1935, and three years later he won another for an interview with President Franklin D. Roosevelt. A third Pulitzer came to him for an interview with President Harry Truman in 1950, and five years later he was honored for distinguished Washington coverage. He was considered the outstanding conservative political commentator for his column, "In the Nation," which ran in the *New York Times* for thirty-three years.

Krock attended Lewis Institute in Chicago and Princeton University. He received honorary degrees from the University of Louisville in 1939, Centre College in 1940, and the University of Kentucky in 1956. He wrote two autobiographical works, *Memoirs: 60 Years on the Firing Line* (1968) and *Myself When Young: Growing up in the 1890s* (1973). He compiled the *Editorials of Henry Watterson* (1923).

Krock married Marguerite Pelleys on April 22, 1911. They had a son, Thomas Pelleys. Mrs. Krock died in 1938, and the next year Krock married Martha Granger Blair, bringing into the family two stepsons, William Granger and Robert H. Blair.

Herman Landau

KRUPP, HEINRICH (b Bavaria, Germany, January 30, 1831; d Louisville, December 18, 1890). Entrepreneur. Krupp left Germany at eighteen and moved to New Orleans for two years before relocating to Louisville, where he took employment as a butcher. After working in a brickyard in the early 1860s, Krupp started his own brickyard on Shelby St. between Breckinridge and Kentucky Streets. In 1873 his company, Krupp and Brothers, moved to a larger location on Rammers Ave. near its intersection with Dandridge Ave. (now Oak St.). As the company expanded into construction, it undertook projects such as the sewer line along Brook St. and assisted in building the state penitentiary in Eddyville in 1888. By the time of his death, Krupp's company had become one of the largest brickyards in the city.

Krupp also expanded into other ventures; he was a part owner of a textile mill, a partner in and president of the Shaefer-Meyer Brewery, and owner of a substantial portion of the Central Iron and Coal Co. in Muhlenberg County. He also owned large amounts of land, including a 420–acre farm in the West End, a 328–acre farm near FAIRDALE, a 102–acre farm near Okolona, and approximately 20 other pieces of property around the county.

Krupp and his wife, Frances, had eleven children, three of whom died in infancy. At the height of his fortune, Krupp was bitten on the arm by either a snake or spider one morning while visiting one of his properties. After he refused to allow the arm's amputation, Krupp died within a week. He is buried in St. Michael's Cemetery.

See *Courier-Journal*, Dec. 19, 1890.

KUNZ'S RESTAURANT. In 1892 Jacob Kunz Jr., of Swiss heritage, opened a wholesale liquor and wine establishment on MARKET St. in Louisville. When a group of local businessmen calling themselves the Peachtree Club began socializing there, Kunz added cheese and crackers. In 1905 the business was moved to 239 S Second St., and in 1912 a delicatessen and catering establishment were added. In 1933 the Kunz family opened a delicatessen at 608 S Fourth St., and in 1937 another location was opened at 322–24 W Jefferson St. After moving in 1941 to 619 S Fourth St. as a restaurant, grill, delicatessen, and fancy grocery, Kunz's changed the name to "The Dutchman" to promote its Dutch style of interior decoration and hearty meals. At this location Kunz's began to offer a charbroiled steak, baked potato, and salad dinner that became an industry standard. In 1962 the restaurant relocated to 526 S Fourth St., and in August 1987 an additional restaurant was opened four blocks north at the northeast corner of Fourth and Market Streets. In January 1988 a fire forced the banquet facility at 526 S Fourth St. to close. In the late 1990s Kunz's remained downtown Louisville's oldest continuously family-owned and -operated restaurant.

Gay Helen Perkins

LABOR. An exact date is not known for the beginnings of organized labor in Louisville, but it may be reasonably conjectured that there were union activities when the city was incorporated in 1828. A rather brief but mysterious entry in one of the city's earliest histories refers to an 1815 meeting between manufacturers and mechanics at a "union hall." In the early half of the nineteenth century, *mechanics* was a widely used generic term for skilled workers of one or more trades. The name *union hall* is suggestive, since at that time the use of the word *union* was not employed in describing North-South differences. In 1831 the city enacted a mechanics lien ordinance that protected workers from imprisonment for debt. This was the first such enactment in Kentucky.

The earliest available Louisville City Directory is that of 1832. It contains references to societies for coppersmiths/tinplate workers and painters. By 1835–36, there were seven such organizations and a reference to a strike by the city's tailors. There was also a central labor body known as the "trades union," and it sponsored a parade and a celebration in a local Methodist church, complete with a sermon. This group also sent a letter of protest to the federal printer Duff Cooper, in Washington, about what appears to have been an unfair labor practice.

The panic of 1837, the first significant national depression, seriously crippled the local labor movement. However, there is little documentation on the detailed impact of this event in Louisville. Documentation is also scarce on the movement's revival, possibly occurring in the early 1840s. The first known mention states that a delegation of union printers attended an "Industrial Congress" at New York in 1847.

The growing tensions between North and South led a number of unions in Kentucky to hold a meeting at Lexington in 1849 to emphasize the urgency of protecting the Federal Union of States. Several Louisville trade unions took part. In 1850 the incorporation of the Louisville & Nashville Railroad led to increased union activity in the years to come. The city's increasing industrialization signaled the emergence of Louisville as a vital manufacturing center. In October, German-American workers from several local unions took part in the first German-American Union Convention in Philadelphia. In December the local printers union sent George E. Greene, James L. Gibbons, and Raymond Lynch to New York City for the formative convention of the International Typographers Union. Greene initiated and piloted to passage a decisive motion concerning its organization, and this resulted in his being elected the organization's first vice president. The following year Louisvillian Gibbons was elected president in Baltimore.

The degree of involvement of workers in "BLOODY MONDAY" (August 6, 1855) is uncertain, but the group included IRISH and German trade unionists. Not long after this tragedy, the molders were among the city's leading trade unionists, and their national leader, William Sylvis, made the first of several visits here. As the CIVIL WAR approached, that union and Louisville working men from fourteen unions called and took part in a vigorous meeting at CITY HALL on December 28, 1860, that strongly declared a vital need to preserve the Federal Union. They clearly saw the necessity of preventing open hostilities. Molder Will Horan was elected to national office for the first of several times; two other local molders were also among the International's leaders during this decade. Labor played a key role as well in the election of John M. Delph as mayor, which explains his selection of molder Robert Gilchrist as police chief.

The outbreak of war did not put an end to union activity. A Kentucky Court of Appeals decision in 1863 upheld the right of workers to form combinations to raise wages. At least twice the molders struck, and once Union army soldiers with bayonets were used to control the strikers. This action led Commanding General Burbridge to earn the sobriquet of "butcher." Gilchrist then called and presided over a convention held in Louisville on September 21, 1864, seeking to form the "Industrial Trade Union Assembly of North America." Eight unions from several cities took part. Though this assembly did not continue, it was to be a factor in the National Labor Union, which first met in 1867 and lasted for several years afterward.

Just before the postwar years began, there was the first organization of a local lodge by the Brotherhood of Locomotive Engineers. Louisville carpenters and joiners solicited funds from merchants for a bell in the courthouse to signify the start and end of the workday. Various other organizations of workingmen such as musicians, butchers, bricklayers, cigar makers, and blacksmiths were getting under way in the city as the United States entered into the throes of industrialization. The depression of 1873 affected labor adversely, but no details have been found. Louisvillians took part in the National Labor Union, and Maurice Coll took part in an 1874 meeting at Rochester, New York, from which emerged the Industrial Brotherhood. Strikes at the L&N and the *COURIER-JOURNAL* also occurred that year, while Louisvillian Mike McDonough wrote the platform for the Workingmen's Association.

The 1870s also saw considerable unionization elsewhere in Kentucky, including both the eastern and western coalfields. The year 1877 should be remembered in Louisville for several landmarks in the history of labor. First of all, a railroad employee, Frank Alley, became grand master of the lodge for the Brotherhood of Locomotive Firemen. Also, the L&N was experiencing considerable labor unrest but not as extensively as other cities such as Baltimore. A large number of Louisville workers allied themselves with the Workingmen's Party, which appears to have had a strongly socialist orientation and affiliation. On August 9, more than 60 percent of those voting for state legislators elected five out of seven candidates from that party. In addition, the Knights of Labor, then with an oath of secrecy, was becoming well established in Louisville and Kentucky. By 1880, they had thirty-six local assemblies whose membership included workers in all kinds of jobs. There were also twenty-three craft unions.

The 1880s saw continuing labor activities in the city. In 1882 the first labor paper was published in Louisville, and a central body, the Trades and Labor Union Assembly, got under way. The newly formed central labor body began to exchange visits for recreation and reinforcement with its Cincinnati counterpart. Both activities involved a printer, Edward F. Cronk, and soon the city would have its own celebration of Labor Day on May 1 with a parade, visiting celebrities, and speeches. In 1885 another Louisville printer, SAMUEL GREEN, became first vice president of the American Federation of Labor. The following year he lost the election for presidency of its legislative committee to a New York City cigar maker named Samuel Gompers.

This decade also witnessed other significant activities for and by unionists here and on the national scene. A federal law established the U.S. Bureau of Labor Statistics in 1883. The following year, Kentucky enacted its first law about mine safety inspection. The year 1884 saw Louisville experience both a major flood and its share of economic panic. The Knights of Labor nationally reached the peak of its numbers and influence just prior to the ill-fated Haymarket Riots in Chicago in mid-l886. Meanwhile, the craft unions grew ever stronger. During this time Louisville featured many visiting speakers including Peter McGuire, a New York City carpenter who is partially credited with founding Labor Day; the anarchist Albert Parsons, later linked to and executed for his involvement in the Chicago riots; Henry George, the proponent of the single tax; J. Keir Hardie, the Scottish coal miner who would soon found the British Labour Party; and Eleanor Marx Aveling, the daughter of Karl Marx.

During these years, some labor leaders in Kentucky sought a political alliance with the farmers and Populists. One result was a third political party with a complete slate, including a Louisville printer as a candidate for lieutenant governor. The results were this party's first and last appearance, but labor continued vigorous political activities. Both the Knights of Labor and the Trades and Labor Assembly sought to influence and evaluate the work of the Constitutional Convention of 1890–91, which produced the document that is still in force.

The 1880s also witnessed women's familiarity with organization and willingness to unionize and strike. Women made up a significant part of the city's growing workforce. Although the majority of Louisville's working women could still be found as seamstresses, dressmakers, servants, and laundresses—traditional nineteenth-century female occupations—a trend toward industrial employment was clear. The woolen mills employed more women than any other industry. In 1880, 145 women worked in the mills. Ten years later, their number had increased to nearly six hundred. Of Louisville's other major industries, only TOBACCO employed large numbers of women. The number of female steamers, packers, and wrappers employed in Louisville cigarette, chewing, and snuff factories was comparable to that in woolens.

As early as 1883, operatives in woolen mills struck for higher wages and successfully resisted mill owners' attempts to import strikebreakers. In 1885, women workers formed their own union, the Spinners and Weavers Association. Like many Louisville workers in the 1880s, they affiliated with the Knights of Labor. The Knights of Labor pushed for women's rights and civil rights in the workplace and in politics. The organization emphasized "equal pay for equal work." Even more women workers were unskilled than men. The order had hired a women's organizer and established a women's department by 1886. By 1888, about twelve thousand women throughout the nation had become Lady Knights. Black women as well as white women joined the Knights.

An example of Louisville's women workers on strike occurred in late July 1887. Two hundred fifty-six workers in the city's Eclipse Woolen Mill staged a walkout. They were joined by workers in two other Louisville plants, the Louisville Kentucky Woolen Mill and the Old Kentucky Mill. About three-fourths of the strikers were young women. Although the operatives eventually lost, about two hundred workers remained on strike until mid-December 1887, when the private funds of the Knights of Labor ran out.

Labor Day 1890 brought widespread attention to Louisville largely through the visit and keynote address of Gompers, who drove home his point, "Man is not a mule!" That year also witnessed Louisville machinists hosting their International's second convention, and a destructive tornado that preceded the other two events. But overall the 1890s were not successful in and for Louisville. The year 1893 marked the beginning of the worst depression the city had known. One historian estimates there were some ten thousand laborers out of work. That year also witnessed the largest strike (fourteen hundred men) at the L&N shops, which was a disastrous failure. The year 1897 was also the year that the Knights of Labor held their first and last convention in Louisville. Labor had something of a paradoxical champion in Kenton County senator William Goebel (1856–1900), the legislature-declared governor-elect in the heated and controversial election of 1899. He defended striking members of the ill-fated America Railway Union, and he was an avowed enemy of the L&N. What he would have done as governor remains unknown. Nevertheless, he was the first candidate for the state's highest office who had piloted bills to passage that had benefited working people.

The 1890s also saw a certain amount of internal dissension within labor and the founding of several labor papers. Mayor Henry Tyler declared Labor Day a legal holiday; he also worked to mediate labor's difficulties with the L&N. But after relatively short-lived attempts, plumber George Roser successfully launched a local building trades council. The "laundry girls" got a profit-sharing clause in their contract after a strike. And eleven of the city's eighteen industrial disputes during this decade were settled without strikes. Unionist Humphrey Knecht became the first labor union member to be elected to the BOARD OF ALDERMEN. Eugene Debs worked here on behalf of his ill-fated American Railway Union. Advocacy for use of the union label was vigorously pushed by the Louisville Allied Printers Council. Louisville union leader James McGill spearheaded the movement, which led to the formation of the Kentucky Federation of Labor (AFL). A member of one of the city's two musician unions, Andrew Ludwig, brought them together, and, in 1897, he was the local central body's delegate to the annual convention of the American Federation of Labor. An increasing number of floats took part in the city's Labor Day parade. In 1899 the Amalgamated Association of Street Car Employees of America held their annual convention in Louisville; they took advantage of this event to revive their local union.

Louisville labor then snagged a big prize by becoming the host city for the annual convention of the American Federation of Labor. The hospitality drew both surprise and praise from many quarters, including Sam Gompers, who allowed himself to wonder out loud whether the convention would get its work done.

Another characterization of the 1890s involved the incidents in which blacks were assimilated into certain facets of the labor movement. Though the AFL attempted to assure that union ranks were open to black as well as white workers, the autonomy of each craft union made this goal difficult to achieve, especially in the South. Louisville's black unionists held a separate May day celebration in 1890, for instance, although later that year black and white hod carriers held a joint parade and picnic. The Tobacco Workers International Union, headquartered in Louisville, imposed no racial qualifications for membership in its early years (perhaps because most tobacco workers were black), and in 1895 a Louisville local elected a black officer who eventually became second vice president of the international union.

The beginning of the current century, in spite of the Goebel assassination, presaged a significant and favorable era for organized labor in Louisville. The AFL Convention witnessed a substantive amount of goodwill on the part of local business. Louisville unionists provided significant leadership for the newly formed State Federation. Kentucky enacted its first child labor law and a factory inspection statute. The first inspector was Andrew Ludwig, who proved himself to be a tireless worker as well as an articulate and courageous spokesman for all laborers. In the next few years, the child labor law was improved, and the inspection statute was amended to include a woman inspector, Mrs. Charles Musgrave.

But there were also other developments of a different kind whose results were not favorable to workers in general and organized labor in particular. Internal dissension within the latter led to suspension of the state federation's charter in 1904. There were difficulties between the central labor body and the building trades council as well as more than one labor paper. There were jurisdictional strikes in which one union clashed with another. Some of these conflicts were aided and abetted by hostile activities encouraged by manufacturers who were strongly anti-union then and remained so for the next two decades. The factory inspector's reports became less useful; the budgets for this work were extremely modest. The panic of 1907 adversely affected many workers.

Nevertheless, the state federation was rechartered in 1908, and, by 1914, it was strong enough to secure passage of the state's first worker's compensation law and a substantially improved mine safety statute. Though the former was soon declared unconstitutional, the law enacted during the next session withstood all challenges. The newly elected governor, A.0. Stanley, was a declared foe of using injunctions in labor disputes and was favorable to unions. When the United States entered WORLD WAR I in 1917, labor was expected not to strike but to pull together for victory. A vigorous young Louisvillian named Patrick Gorman was a strong influence on his own Butcher Workmen and Meat Cutters Union as well as the larger union organizations, both city and state. Louisville plumber Peter Campbell began a long-time tenure as full-time head of the state federation and, along with John Schneider, gave vigorous service to labor in its many-sided relations with state government, including full-time lobbying.

Labor activity that involved women workers escalated at this time. In 1910 Lula Spading promoted female and black involvement in labor relations by leading thirty-five hundred to

Union Labor Temple, 127-131 West Market Street, 1926.

four thousand tobacco workers in Louisville in a three-week strike for higher wages. In 1911 an outspoken leader of the Kentucky Consumers' League, Mrs. Reuben Post Halleck of Louisville, agitated for labor legislation relating to women and children. She served as secretary to the 1911 Governor's Special Committee on women's working conditions in Kentucky.

Also in 1911 the first complete report and investigation of Kentucky women's working conditions was produced. The survey covered 11,048 women in 186 establishments in various cities in Kentucky, including Louisville. The committee in charge of the report found women working in unfavorable conditions. Women worked six days a week and lived in fear of losing their jobs; two-thirds of the women received $6.50 a week or less, and one-fourth were paid $4 or less. The committee concluded the report by recommending the installation of seats for use when not working; separate and cleaner restrooms; two more inspectors, both of whom would be women; greater care for ventilation and sanitation; and a minimum wage.

The report was acted upon by the 1912 legislature, which passed a law limiting the hours of work for females under twenty-one with the exception of domestic workers and nurses. The law also responded to most of the recommendations made in the 1911 report. Moreover, the State Labor Inspector law was amended in 1912 to provide for a women's factory inspector. Madge Nave of Louisville became the first to occupy the post.

Other surveys were conducted, including one in 1921 that proved that women workers' salaries were low. White women received $7.50 to $14.50 per week, while black women received $8.15 to $10.15 per week. In 1921 the clothing and tobacco industries employed approximately 40 percent of all Kentucky women workers.

The aftermath of World War I witnessed a period of anxiety for labor and opposition to it. This lasted until the New Deal in 1933. The overthrow of Csarist rule in Russia, followed by its communist replacement, resulted in a widespread reaction to anything considered radical. A particularly difficult strike of Telephone workers in Louisville was followed by a similar situation involving employees at the L&N roundhouse. Gov. Edward Morrow (1919–23) sent troops to deal with three strikes in as many parts of the state. The Factory Inspector was changed to the Department of Labor by the General Assembly in 1924. Edward Seiller, a youthful unionist, was appointed to head the department. But its budget was not significantly increased, and in this situation the unions and the department were to face the many-sided upheaval of the 1929 stock market crash and the Great Depression. The same year the department began, the Butcher Workmen and Meat Cutters concluded a twelve-year strike with an employer that then went out of business.

By January 1931 it was estimated that 55 percent of organized labor was out of work. Many of the L&N shop employees had only part-time employment, and the Axton Fisher Tobacco Co. was the only local employer not to reduce wages. In the depth of the Great Depression, the year 1932, two Republican congressmen, Fiorello La Guardia of New York and George Norris of Nebraska, secured passage in a Democratic Congress of a bill that outlawed "yellow dog contracts." These documents allowed employers to dismiss workers for belonging to a union.

The presidential election of 1932 brought Franklin D. Roosevelt and the New Deal to the fore. Roosevelt signed the National Recovery Act, which contained a clause (7a) legally recognizing the right to join a union. Though the Supreme Court declared the clause unconstitutional in 1935, Sen. Robert Wagner of New York piloted the National Labor Relations Act to passage, and it withstood Supreme Court scrutiny. During these years, some of the most active unions in Louisville were the building trades, whose leaders were A.C. Kaiser, Pat Reardon, and Fred Kirk. They aided in the passage of the new governor A.B. Chandler's (1935–39) comprehensive reorganization act that enlarged the Department of Labor into the Department of Industrial Relations. The department's first commissioner was union printer William Burrows, whose work put the new department on solid ground.

Economic difficulties revealed that at the local, state, and national levels unskilled workers, including those on the assembly line, were particularly vulnerable and needed union organization. This realization came about in the aftermath of a verbal and physical confrontation at the 1935 AF of L convention, with Miners International Union president John L. Lewis spearheading the organization of the Committee for Industrial Organizations within the AFL. Later this group became the Congress of Industrial Organizations (CIO). This movement cut deeply into the state federation, whose leader, Peter Campbell, left to head the new organization in Kentucky. Its membership at first drew heavily from the garment workers and the steelworkers. Along with a disastrous OHIO RIVER flood in January 1937, that year saw the state federation elect carpenter Ed Weyler to replace Campbell.

Diplomacy and recognition of a common concern for the well-being of workers enabled the two statewide organizations to work well. The CIO was more widely known as the Kentucky Industrial Workers Union. It aggressively pursued organization of the unskilled workers. One of the CIO's most significant achievements was the organization of assembly workers at Louisville's Ford plant. Weyler proved to be a courageous and thoughtful leader who gained wide respect. The AFL also made substantial gains in Louisville; its apprenticeship program with carpenter Fred Kirk and the Building Trades Council was a chief reason. Both organizations worked on a statewide basis. Legislation on wages and hours was an enviable achievement for which persons from both organizations could take just pride.

In the midst of all this activity, the Japanese attack on Pearl Harbor on December 7, 1941, brought the United States officially into WORLD WAR II. The unions pledged and kept their word to avoid, as much as humanly possible, strikes in defense-related industries; total time lost was less than 1 percent of the total work time. They also vigorously supported rebuilding Europe through the Marshall Plan and the United Nations. But the postwar period also had some major difficulties. The abandonment of labor-supported wage-and-price controls was a factor in any number of strikes. A Republican Congress amended the National Labor Relations Act, better known as the Taft-Hartley Act, to such an extent that it was referred to among unionists and their supporters as a "slave labor law." Senator Taft's widely respected integrity and reputation for plain and courageous speech could lead students of this controversial legislation to have second thoughts about its real intent and purpose. There can be little doubt that anti-union forces did use it as a club for their cause, but Taft was not known to have commented pro or con about such uses.

At the beginning of the postwar period, International Harvester converted Louisville's Curtiss-Wright facility into a factory for building farm equipment. A struggle for the employees' union allegiance followed between the Farm Equipment Workers and the United Auto Workers, as well as some other traditional labor organizations. This jurisdictional strife was not without some violence. There was also fallout from difficulties resulting from activities between Harvester and unions at the national level. By 1949 Louisville labor was experiencing severe and widespread unemployment. The rash of strikes in 1946–47 led to the formation of the Louisville Labor-Management Committee, which has a highly commendable record. This effort was enhanced significantly by the Federal Mediation and Conciliation Service, with special recognition to Joseph Kirkham. The Kentucky Federation of Labor, still headquartered in Louisville, launched a widespread education program under Frances Kaufman that soon received national acclaim. Its activities included formation of the League for Political Education. The CIO was also active in this field. Other names of significance in these endeavors were Annie Post Halleck, Robert Woerner, James Wolfe, "Spike" Duvalle, and Sam Ezelle. Ed Weyler also was adept at securing impartial arbitrators among the local clergy for vexing labor disputes.

Among the many notable local leaders during the 1940s was "Pat" Ansbury, who helped revive and strengthen the Teamsters so that, in time, they would become Louisville's largest union. Another commendable person was George Burton, a hard worker and talented leader, who was designated the title of Commissioner of Industrial Relations.

North Korea's invasion of South Korea in June 1950 revived the draft and gave the economy a boost. William Taylor was doing for the CIO much of what Ed Weyler was doing for the State Federation, Owen Hammons for the Auto Workers, Emma Saurer for the Garment Workers, and Tobacco Union officer Thelma Stovall for her local. Ansbury's sudden death led to Paul Priddy becoming Teamster 89 leader. Together with Marion Winstead and Howard Haynes and a number of able aides, they comprised a formidable local. All these persons were active civic leaders.

During the 1950s, Sam Ezelle emerged as Weyler's successor after an aggressive campaign. In 1958 the state CIO merged with the KFL. The Teamsters withdrew from the State Federation in a move not entirely unrelated to the union's national activities and other reactions by organized labor. ETHEL DU PONT, a member of the teachers union, wrote a weekly column, "In Labor's Ranks," in the *LOUISVILLE TIMES* for almost a generation. General Electric, (GE) opened a huge plant in Louisville in the early 1950s, and peak employment reached twenty-three thousand. The plant experienced considerable labor unrest for a variety of reasons, including strong demands for a state "right to work" law by the plant's manager of industrial relations and the Associated Industries of Kentucky. Although unsuccessful, this struggle led to tensions for many years. Matters became calmer when GE executive John Clarke and union president Ken Cassady developed mutual respect. A rather serious strike occurred at the L&N in 1954–55, and eventually the railroad merged with other lines (CSX Transportation), moving its headquarters to Jacksonville, Florida.

Since the 1960s, perhaps the most significant developments involving and affecting organized labor in Louisville would include the following: increasing use of automation in and by local industry; publication and many-sided responses to the 1982 series of articles in the *Courier-Journal* characterizing Louisville as "strike city"; the multiple activities of the Louisville Labor-Management Committee with special emphasis on the twenty-one years of leadership by its Executive Director Henri Mangeot; the changes in the local economy from manufacturing to service highlighted by the location of a principal branch of UNITED PARCEL SERVICE (UPS); increasing community activities involving the Central Labor Council, the Greater Louisville Building and Construction Trades Council, Teamster locals 89 and 783 and others; legalization of collective bargaining for more than fifteen hundred Jefferson County employees; and the Labor Management Center at the UNIVERSITY OF LOUISVILLE.

Labor has been less successful in winning NLRB elections. Surveys taken by the University of Kentucky for the years 1985, 1986, and 1987 gave individuals a range of choices to describe their opinions on organized labor in Kentucky. Fifty-three and a half percent of the respondents from Louisville were positive about organized labor in the state, and only 11.5 percent had no opinion. The local building trades council included twenty-three different trades. In the 1990s significant strikes took place involving the LOUISVILLE ORCHESTRA, General Electric, and United Parcel Service. Teamsters #89 is the city's largest local, and the 1998 city directory numbers 120 locals in Louisville and Jefferson County.

Largest Area Labor Unions (1999)

Teamsters Local 89, AFL-CIO (16,620 members)
United Food and Commercial Workers International Local 227, AFL-CIO (16,335 members)
United Auto Workers Local 862, AFL-CIO (8,362 members)
Electronics Workers IUE Local 761, AFL-CIO (5,800 members)
Teamsters Local 783, AFL-CIO (4,608 members)
Electrical Workers, IBEW Local 369, AFL-CIO (2,405 members)
Machinists Local 681, AFL-CIO (1,596 members)
Electrical Workers, IBEW Local 2100, AFL-CIO (1,456 members)
Plumbers and Pipefitters Local 522 AFL-CIO (1,303 members)
Firemen and Oilers Local 320, AFL-CIO (1,250 members)
Communication Workers of America, Local 3310, AFL-CIO (1,239 members)
Bakery and Tobacco Workers Local 16, AFL-CIO (1,238 members)
Service Employees International Local 541, AFL-CIO (1,226 members)
Laborers Local 576, AFL-CIO (1,223 members)
Sheet Metal Workers Local 110, AFL-CIO (1,132 members)
National Association of Letter Carriers, Branch 14, AFL-CIO (1,120 members)
Service Employees Local 557, AFL-CIO (1,020 members)
Teamsters Local 2727, AFL-CIO (963 members)
Ironworkers Local 70, AFL-CIO (606 members)
American Federation of Grain Millers Local 33, AFL-CIO (560 members)

Plumbers and Pipefitters Local 107, AFL-CIO (523 members)
United Steelworkers of America Local 155, AFL-CIO (409 members)
Graphic Communications Local 619 (362 members)
Hotel Employees, Restaurant Employees, Local 181, AFL-CIO (323 members)
United steelworkers of America Local 1693, AFL-CIO (321 members)

See Herbert Finch, "Organized Labor in Louisville 1880–1914," Ph.D. dissertation, University of Kentucky; George N. Stevens, "The Development of Labor Law in Kentucky," *Kentucky Law Journal,* vol. 28, no. 2; *Business First Book of Lists* (Louisville, Oct. 22, 1999).

Henry C. Mayer

LACASSAGNE, MICHAEL (b France ca. 1750; d Vincennes, Indiana, October 1797). Entrepreneur. Lacassagne is one of a number of almost-forgotten FRENCH entrepreneurs, and nothing is known of his background before his appearance on the local scene in 1783. Presumably he first arrived in Philadelphia during the American Revolution and spent some time there before his arrival at the FALLS OF THE OHIO. He was closely associated with Jean Holker, who was sent to Philadelphia in 1777 by the French court as agent to the revolutionary colonies. Lacassagne also acquired land in Maryland. Shortly after his arrival in Louisville, he began to play an important role in providing goods and provisions for sale to the settlers as well as to GEORGE ROGERS CLARK's Virginia militia. He was engaged as well with other (French?) traders in a venture to New Orleans with Kentucky produce, perhaps TOBACCO. Their vessel, however, was captured by the notorious James Colbert and his river pirates. The venturers lost all but were released unharmed. They made their way to New Orleans and Philadelphia, and Lacassagne was back in Louisville by 1785.

During the next several years his trading activities were quite successful, and he reputedly became the wealthiest merchant at the Falls. Another French trader, Barthélemi Tardiveau, explained the market in a letter to Holker in 1783: "The inhabitants of Kentucky are in need of absolutely everything, and the few commodities they receive from travelers who come to explore the country are always sold to them at 3 or 4 hundred percent profit." (Original letter at the Cincinnati Historical Society.)

Lacassagne's residence on the north side of Main at Fifth was built in the manner of a French cottage, with a veranda around three sides, and was painted in attractive colors. It was a startling contrast to the rude cabins that stood nearby. The grounds surrounding Lacassagne's home were landscaped. All notable visitors to Louisville were entertained there. French botanist Andre Michaux was invited to dine with Lacassagne (Michaux spelled it La Cassagne) on August 2, 1795, and noted that his host had been "a resident of Louisville for more than fifteen years" (*Early Western Travels* 3: 66). Either Lacassagne exaggerated or he actually came first in 1780, although there is no record until 1783. Lacassagne also had as a guest French-born BENEDICT FLAGET (later bishop of the See of Bardstown and the Diocese of Louisville) in 1792. Flaget was on his way to an assignment in Vincennes, Indiana. Lacassagne supposedly pressed Flaget to remain in Louisville, promising to leave his home to the young priest. Flaget declined.

Although never married, Lacassagne was reported in 1787 as "sighing to Miss Sally Christian," daughter of early Jefferson County settler WILLIAM CHRISTIAN (*The Intimate Letters of John Cleves Symmes and His Family* [Cincinnati 1956]: 108). Lacassagne's mercantile pursuits were widespread and took him through Kentucky and to Vincennes and New Orleans. Some of his dealings were with the infamous James Wilkinson, later involved in the Burr Conspiracy. Jean Holker in 1788 named Lacassagne his agent to collect debts from persons "on the waters of Ohio and Mississippi Rivers" (*Filson Club History Quarterly* 7 [Jan. 1933]: 56). Civic affairs also attracted him. He served as a Jefferson County delegate to the 1787 Danville convention, one of the series seeking separation of Kentucky from Virginia. He was named a trustee of Louisville by the Virginia legislature in 1789 and was Louisville's first postmaster. He took the post January 1, 1795, and served until his death. The office was probably in his house.

He also purchased more than 2,000 acres of land from grantees in the 150,000 acre Clark's Grant across the OHIO RIVER from Louisville. On some of this land he attempted to found a town on or near the site of what became Jeffersonville. His town, named Cassania, was a failure. By 1796 it could boast only two houses and one store. The only reminder of his hopes for profits from Indiana land is the small stream flowing into the Ohio River above Jeffersonville. It is shown on modern maps as Lankasang Creek and no doubt preserves the American pronunciation of his name.

There is little doubt that he had imbibed the goal of égalité from the French philosophes. In 1790 he wrote to President Washington to complain about the arbitrary power of the commanding officer at FORT STEUBEN (in present Jeffersonville), who sentenced a civilian to forty lashes at the public whipping post. In his will he made various bequests of Clark's Grant lands. In one case he stipulated that if the recipient should die, the GOVERNMENT was to use sales proceeds to educate children of poor parents. He also devised one hundred acres in the grant to Charles Clark, an African American.

Lacassagne's will mentions a sister, Jenny, "of the Republic of France," to receive five hundred acres in the grant. As late as March 11, 1802, a public notice appeared in the *FARMER'S LIBRARY* (Louisville's first newspaper) ordering her to appear at the Court of Quarter Sessions in regard to her brother's will. The *Farmer's Library* did not circulate in France, and it is doubtful that Jenny received her five hundred acres. He also provided that his "two mulatto children" be taught to read and write and that they receive their freedom at age twenty-five. Although Lacassagne died in Vincennes, his body apparently was transported to his estate, Richmond, upstream from present Jeffersonville. His will provided that a "well-built brick house" be erected over his grave. Perhaps this accounts for the tradition that Richmond was haunted.

See Richard L. Pangburn, "Michael Lacassagne," *Filson Club History Quarterly* 59 (July 1985): 368–70; Howard C. Rice, *Barthélemi Tardiveau: A French Trader in the West* (Baltimore 1938); Thomas P. Abernethy, *The Burr Conspiracy* (New York 1954); Louis Cohen, *Postal History of Louisville, Kentucky* (Louisville 1987); viii; Jefferson County, Kentucky Will Books, 1:76.

George H. Yater

LAFAYETTE'S VISIT. A decorated soldier and FRENCH spokesman, the Marquis de Lafayette (b Auvergne, France, September 6, 1757; d Paris, France, May 20, 1834) is best known in American history for his distinguished service in the Revolutionary War. His military career began in 1771 when he entered the French Royal Army. In 1777 Lafayette sailed to America to serve the colonies in their struggle for independence from Great Britain. He served as a major-general under the command of Gen. George Washington.

In 1824 President James Monroe invited Lafayette to visit the United States. He arrived at Staten Island, New York, on August 15, 1824, for a yearlong tour. Accompanied by his son George Washington Lafayette; his personal secretary, Auguste Levasseur; and his servant Sebastien, Lafayette began with visits along the eastern coast.

Lafayette's arrival in Louisville in 1825 was highly anticipated. The trustees of the city authorized the expenditure of two hundred dollars for a reception, and broadsides were printed and distributed that directed citizens to where they should gather to greet the honored guest. Businesses were asked to close during Lafayette's procession through the streets, and people were asked to wear "Lafayette badges." Gov. Joseph Desha of Kentucky assigned a reception committee to represent the state upon Lafayette's arrival. The members included Gen. Robert Breckinridge, Gen. Thomas Bodley, James W. Denny, William Taylor Barry, J. Bledsoe, and Charles S. Todd.

On May 8, 1825, Lafayette departed Shawneetown, Illinois, aboard the steamer *Mechanic,* headed for Louisville. That night the boat struck an obstacle in the water and began to sink. Lafayette and the other passengers were able to make it safely ashore, where they spent the night. The next morning the cargo steamer *Paragon,* heading downriver to New Orleans, came into view. One of the stranded passengers, a Mr. Neilson, was the owner of the *Paragon,* and he ordered it to turn around and take Lafayette and his party to Louisville. On the morning of May 11, 1825, Lafayette arrived at PORTLAND, below Louisville. Although it was raining, he was met with an enthusiastic welcome.

Upon his arrival, welcoming speeches were given by the attorney general of Kentucky, Solomon P. Sharp, and Senator JOHN ROWAN, with Lafayette responding. Then he entered an open carriage and was escorted by the Lafayette Cavalry, the Louisville Light Infantry, and a crowd of citizens into the city. There the procession was greeted by an estimated ten thousand people. Lafayette's procession made its way up MAIN St. to Third St., then south to Jefferson St. and west to Fifth St., and finally to Union Hall at Fifth and Main Streets, where he was to stay during his visit.

On the evening of May 11, 1825, Lafayette, a Mason himself, met with members of Louisville's two Masonic lodges, Clark Lodge and Abraham Lodge, at the Clark Lodge. There he listened to an address given by the Reverend H.M. Shaw, after which Lafayette made a short response. He then greeted the members, and refreshments were served. Later that night a grand ball was held at Washington Hall and was attended by approximately 350 people.

On Thursday, May 12, Lafayette and his retinue crossed the OHIO RIVER on the *General Pike* to JEFFERSONVILLE, in response to the governor of Indiana's invitation. Salutory speeches were given, and in the early afternoon a dinner was held. At six in the evening Lafayette and his party returned to Louisville, where a barbecue had been planned. It was canceled because of inclement WEATHER. That night Lafayette attended the circus and the THEATER. At the theater he was met by a standing ovation from his fellow audience members. On the morning of Friday, May 13, Lafayette presented a banner to the Lafayette Guards. He then left Louisville for Frankfort. A reminder of his visit was Lafayette St., which ran for one city block and was located half a block south of Green St. (now Liberty) between Floyd and Preston. The city of LaGrange was named for his French country estate.

See Edgar E. Hume, *Lafayette in Kentucky* (Frankfort 1937).

Tanya S. Evans

LAFON, MARY (b near Lexington, Kentucky, 1840; d Louisville, December 5, 1925). Children's health and women's rights advocate. The daughter of John and Mary Ann (Barkley) Lafon, she was the descendant of Huguenots and eighteenth-century IRISH independence fighters. The family settled in Kentucky in 1793. She was educated at Maplewood Academy in Pittsfield, Massachusetts, an early female boarding school. In the 1850s she went to Europe to pursue advanced linguistic study. Later Lafon, who did not marry, moved to Louisville.

In the early 1870s she formed the Presbyterian Mission Society of Kentucky. She then linked the Kentucky society to those of other states, helping to create a united national mission. In the late 1870s she became administrator of the Louisville Presbyterian Orphans' Home and turned it into a model institution in excellent financial condition.

In the 1880s she was one of the leaders in the local Free KINDERGARTEN MOVEMENT, a supporter of the Kentucky Infirmary for Women and Children, and an officer in the Louisville Equal Rights Association. In the 1890s she became a charter member and first vice president of the WOMAN'S CLUB OF LOUISVILLE. During this time she was actively involved in the founding of the Louisville Children's Free Hospital (later KOSAIR CHILDREN'S HOSPITAL). It became the tenth pediatric hospital in the United States, the first in the South, and the first nondenominational hospital in Louisville. Lafon was the hospital's president from 1890 to 1918.

Always an advocate for women's rights, she was a founder in 1900 of the Louisville Suffrage Association. As late as the 1920s, as an elderly woman, she was active with the League of Women Voters, movements to equalize marriage laws, child labor legislation, women voter registration, and GOVERNMENT support for child health and public education. A 1926 plaque in Kosair Children's Hospital reads, "If You Would See Her Monument/Look About You." She is buried in CAVE HILL CEMETERY.

See Gail McGowan Mellor, *Kosair Children's Hospital: A History, 1892–1992* (Louisville 1992).

Gail McGowan Mellor

LAGRANGE. This fourth-class city, the seat of Oldham County, lies at the junction of KY 53 and 146 just north of Interstate 71, twenty-four road miles northeast of downtown Louisville. It was founded by Maj. William Berry Taylor on a fifty-acre tract he offered in 1827 for the first relocation of the county's seat from WESTPORT. The site was first called simply the Cross Roads, for it was the junction of early routes connecting Louisville with the Bluegrass Region and Westport with SHELBYVILLE.

It was renamed by Taylor in 1827 for the country estate in France of the Marquis de Lafayette, who had been Taylor's guest on the general's brief visit to that area on his 1824–25 American tour. The town was laid off by William T. Barbour in the summer of 1827, and the LaGrange post office was also established that year, with Thomas Berry as the first postmaster. Due to political pressure, the county seat was returned to Westport in April 1828, but it was permanently relocated at LaGrange ten years later. The town was incorporated on January 23, 1840.

LaGrange's early years were relatively undistinguished. Its growth and economic development, especially in competition with earlier and larger towns in the county—Westport, Floydsburg, and Brownsboro—began only with the arrival in 1851 of the Louisville & Frankfort Railroad (which later became the Louisville, Cincinnati, & Lexington, then the Louisville & Nashville, and ultimately CSX Transportation). The completion in 1869 of an extension to Covington, the so-called "Short Line," provided direct rail service to both Louisville and Cincinnati.

Like most of the county's other extant communities, LaGrange is essentially suburban to Louisville and Jefferson County. These ties began, in effect, with the completion in 1907 of the Louisville and Eastern electric railroad, an early commuter line providing hourly runs to and from Louisville until the late 1930s, when improved highway ties with the larger city brought an end to the service. Yet the railroad continues to influence the town, with freight trains passing directly down the main street through its center, holding up vehicular traffic and interfering with regular urban routines.

LaGrange's development as a Louisville suburb came in earnest only with the completion of the interstate, which facilitated commuter traffic, for now most of the town's residents must commute to jobs in Jefferson County. Though the city had only about 1,700 residents in 1970, this number grew to 2,971 in 1980 and to 3,853 by 1990. The U.S. Census's 1994 estimate placed LaGrange's POPULATION at 4,527, an increase of over 250 percent in only the past twenty-five years, making it one of the fastest-growing towns in the region. The population had increased to 5,040 by 1996.

In recent years LaGrange's ECONOMY has been diversifying to some extent. While still the county seat and its major trade and service center as well as a bedroom community for Louisville and Jefferson County, the town has enjoyed modest industrial development. Six manufacturers, with at least fifty employees each, produce magnetic wire and copper products, veneer and plywood, plastic injection molding, engraved stationery, electronic security systems, and steel conveyors. Most of the town's industrial labor force comes from within the county.

Oldham's only extant newspaper, the weekly *Oldham Era,* began publication at LaGrange in 1876. LaGrange has also experienced some of the other trappings of modern urbanization: urban fringe development with retail and service outlets at the Interstate 71 interchange with KY 53 and the recent establishment of two upper-middle-class subdivisions, Cherrywood and Glen Eagles, also at the south end of town.

See *Courier-Journal,* Oct. 14, 1991; *History and Families of Oldham County, Kentucky (The First Century, 1824–1924)* (Paducah, Ky., 1996).

Robert M. Rennick

LAINE, JOSEPH F. (b Winchester, Kentucky, April 9, 1881; d Louisville, August 18, 1967). Physician. Educated at Berea College,

Laine completed his medical training in 1906 at Meharry Medical College, an institution in Nashville, Tennessee, which was established in 1876 for the education of AFRICAN AMERICANS. He did postgraduate work at Meharry as well as the Tuskegee Institute and Talladega College, both in Alabama. As a practicing physician for over sixty years, Laine spent the majority of his career in Kentucky.

At the request of Dr. John E. Hunter, Laine established an office in Lexington, where he practiced for approximately eighteen years. He then moved to Louisville and in the late 1920s founded the Laine Medical Clinic at 1120 W Walnut (now Muhammad Ali Blvd.). Laine, who was influential in bringing other African American doctors to practice in Kentucky, was a member and former president of both the Falls City Medical Society of Louisville and the Bluegrass State Medical Association. He was also active in civic affairs as a member of the NAACP and the Urban League.

Laine, who was survived by his wife, Bruce (Simpson) Laine, son, Joseph F. Jr., and daughter, Pauline, is buried in the Louisville Cemetery.

Beach at Lake Louisvilla in Oldham County, 1926.

LAKE DREAMLAND. Lake Dreamland, once a popular vacation site for wealthy Louisvillians, is located in southwestern Jefferson County with the OHIO RIVER on the west, Camp Ground Rd. on the east, Senn Rd. to the north, and Bramers Ln. to the south. Developer Ed Hartlage began the resort area in the early 1930s. He dammed Bramer's Run to form the lake and leased waterfront property to citizens willing to erect their own cottages. To entice additional builders, Hartlage converted an old dairy barn into a tavern and dance hall in 1937 and dubbed the structure Hartlage's Barn. The hall later became known as Club El Rancho and was a popular rock and roll club until it burned in 1967.

However, the need for costly repairs after the 1937 flood and a lack of modern conveniences such as public water, sewers, electricity, and paved roads caused many owners to abandon their cottages. Left with deteriorating houses and a flood wall dividing the neighborhood, Hartlage was forced to rent the properties at reduced rates to low-income families. During and after WORLD WAR II many workers from neighboring RUBBERTOWN lived in the area. Hartlage continued to maintain ownership of the land, which prevented the area from receiving any GOVERNMENT aid to update the utilities or improve the structures.

Organized in 1983, the neighborhood association defeated a 1988 arrangement in which the flood-prone area would have received government aid but would have eventually reverted back to the county to become a vacant "land trust" upon the departure of the original homeowners. However, a new plan was instituted in the early 1990s that promoted individual property ownership and provided government funds for the restoration of the homes and the environment.

See *A Place in Time: The Story of Louisville's Neighborhoods* (Louisville 1989).

LAKE LOUISVILLA. Lake Louisvilla was a summer resort south of KY 22 in OLDHAM COUNTY, about two miles from the Jefferson County line. It was developed in the early 1920s by New York developer and speculator Warren Smadbeck as a resort featuring SWIMMING, boating, a hotel, clubhouse, bathhouse, and two-story diving platform.

Lake Louisvilla provided a summer retreat for many of Louisville's city dwellers. Two Louisville NEWSPAPERS of the times, the *Post* and the *Herald* promoted the sale of 20- by 100-foot lots along the lake for $58.50, along with a 6-month subscription to either of the newspapers. The hotel burned in the late 1920s after only three years of operation.

Lake Louisvilla continued in popularity until the GREAT DEPRESSION, when unpaid taxes and fees caused the properties to fall into disrepair. Some of the property reverted to Oldham County. The mid-1950s marked the area's end as a retreat and its emergence as a year-round residential area. In 1989 state officials decided to drain the lake because money could not be raised to pay for dam repair and possible septic pollution.

See *A Place in Time: The Story of Louisville's Neighborhoods* (Louisville 1989).

Susan Buren Eubank

LANDAU, SARA (b Philadelphia, November 4, 1890; d Louisville, September 17, 1986). Economist, educator, activist. Sara Landau, the oldest of three sisters, attended school in Louisiana before moving to Kentucky. In 1916, she graduated from Bowling Green (Kentucky) Business University. The following year, she enrolled at the UNIVERSITY OF LOUISVILLE, earning a bachelor's degree in 1920 and a master's degree in economics in 1921.

Landau began teaching at the University of Louisville while an undergraduate. She continued until 1928, when she resigned her associate professorship in protest over the university's perceived anti-semitic attitude, which caused the firing of historian LOUIS GOTTSCHALK. She went to the University of Chicago where she taught and worked toward a doctorate, teaching also at Wheaton College. She returned to Louisville for most of the 1930s, holding GOVERNMENT jobs and managing family-owned property.

During the 1940s, Landau taught at McNeese Junior College (Louisiana), Alabama College, Women's College of the University of North Carolina, and Simmons College (Boston). She did research for the federal Treasury Department during the war years. Hired to teach at the new Roosevelt University in Chicago in 1946, she argued successfully for the same salary as male faculty. Upon retirement in 1954, she was recruited to teach at Berea College, where she spent the next ten years, finally retiring at the age of seventy-two.

Landau was active in many organizations, including the American Association of University Women, the League of Women Voters, the National Council of Jewish Women, and the Women's Overseas Service League. In 1980 Louisville's JEWISH COMMUNITY CENTER gave Landau the Blanche B. Ottenheimer Award for outstanding civic service.

Landau wrote academic works, short stories, plays, and book reviews. She traveled extensively, embarking on a year-long world tour at age seventy. She is buried in ADATH JESHURUN Cemetery.

Katherine Burger Johnson

LAND GRANTS IN JEFFERSON COUNTY. In 1763 the French lost control of the Ohio Valley as the outcome of the French and Indian War, but it was not until 1766 that the British government managed to officially inspect its new acquisition. The first English party to explore the Ohio and Illinois country included Capt. Harry Gordon and Ens. Thomas Hutchins. As a result of this expedition the river was mapped, and a good drawing was made of the Falls, the future site of Louisville.

Seven years later Capt. THOMAS BULLITT led a party of surveyors to the Falls with the intention of locating land for officers who had served in the late war with France. This party camped on the site of Louisville in July and August of 1773, during which time surveys were made and town lots were laid out along the shore. Each man in Bullitt's company was given one lot as a reward for his services, so James Harrod, who was present, owned a lot in Louisville before he established Harrodsburg.

When Captain Bullitt returned from Kentucky, he attempted to have all his surveys entered, but Col. WILLIAM PRESTON, the surveyor of Fincastle County, Virginia, refused to honor them. Bullitt then appealed to Lord Dunmore, the governor of Virginia, who subsequently ordered Preston to issue the patents for two of the surveys made at the Falls. These grants, each for two thousand acres, were awarded to Dr. JOHN CONNOLLY, a surgeon's mate who served with the British in the war, and Charles DeWarrensdorff, an ensign in the Pennsylvania regiment, and included practically all the land in Louisville north of BROADWAY. Connolly's claim to the land was bolstered by his friendship with the governor. The land patents were issued in December 1773. Thus the two tracts at the Falls became the first land grants west of the Appalachian Mountains. Early in 1774 Connolly and Col. JOHN CAMPBELL contracted to purchase DeWarrensdorff's two thousand acres. In exchange for helping to finance the DeWarrensdorff purchase, Campbell (for whom Campbell County was named) acquired a half-interest in Connolly's original two thousand acres.

While Connolly and Campbell owned the large tracts of land near the Falls, there were still unclaimed lands south and east of the fledgling settlement. On April 22, 1774, another party of surveyors started west to survey land on "Western Waters" for persons with certificates "agreeable to his Majesty's Proclamation of October, 1763"—that is, veterans who had served in the French and Indian War. The group of thirty-six men included four deputy surveyors from Fincastle County: JOHN FLOYD, Hancock Taylor, James Douglas, and Isaac Hite.

The party arrived at the Falls on the afternoon of May 29, 1774, and camped on Dunmore Island, later called CORN ISLAND. The following day the men split into two groups, one headed by Floyd and the other by Taylor, and began to run large surveys ranging from one thousand to six thousand acres. Thirty such surveys were made, including those for Col. William Byrd, William Preston, Alexander Spotswood Dandridge, WILLIAM CHRISTIAN, and Henry Harrison. The largest survey, six thousand acres for Southall and Charlton, ran from the OHIO RIVER southward and included much of present eastern Louisville. John Floyd and Hancock Taylor also surveyed land for themselves on warrants purchased from veterans.

These military surveys almost completely covered the Louisville area, extending as far east as present ANCHORAGE and PROSPECT; and, with three exceptions, Virginia issued land grants to the owners of the surveys. In 1780 the two tracts north of Broadway awarded to Connolly and DeWarrensdorff and another three-thousand-acre survey for Robert McKenzie reverted to the state, with the land from the Connolly survey being used to establish the town of Louisville. Connolly and McKenzie were found by a Lexington jury to be British subjects, allowing for the land to be confiscated.

In 1779 the Virginia Land Act allowed the original settlers and others to acquire land in Kentucky. Commissioners were sent west to hold court and determine the best claims. Members of the Hite family were active in claiming land near the Falls. Isaac Hite had explored Goose and HARRODS CREEKS in 1773, so he made claims in this area for members of his family. ABRAHAM HITE also purchased the settlement and preemption claims of William Linn and Vangelist Harden, just south of the old Southall and Charlton survey, thereby acquiring twenty-eight hundred acres on the headwaters of Beargrass and FERN CREEKS. Those who had an early "settlement" claim could acquire 1400 acres, although they had to pay for it. James Nourse acquired grants on Goose Creek with military warrants that he sold to the Hites.

One of the commissioners, William Fleming, was granted a thousand-acre preemption claim adjacent to his brother-in-law, William Christian. Capt. James Knox, who originally came to Kentucky in early 1774, acting as a guide to surveyor, John Floyd, and was awarded fourteen hundred acres on a settlement and preemption on the South Fork of BEARGRASS CREEK, but he sold it before it was surveyed.

In the present MIDDLETOWN area, a number of large surveys were made on treasury warrants, purchased from the state, to John Williams, Anthony Bartlett, John Minor, Joseph Combs, and others. John Handly had a preemption in the same area.

Down the Ohio, below the old military surveys, Cuthbert Bullitt received two grants by rights of settlement and preemption, one as assignee of Thomas Bullitt, then deceased. Ben Roberts received a grant that overlapped Bullitt's land, and the heirs of William Madison were granted a preemption that also overlapped part of Bullitt's grant.

Farther down the river Richard Grayham was granted fourteen hundred acres on a settlement and preemption, but it overlapped land granted to Mary Byrd. George Slaughter, WILLIAM POPE, Jacob Myers, and Robert Breckinridge also had conflicting land grants in the area.

One interesting grant that resulted in a lengthy lawsuit was that of James Terry, alias Luth, deceased. This tract overlapped the old military survey of William Byrd. A number of pioneers, including Daniel Boone, appeared before the commissioners to verify that Terry had a settlement claim on the Ohio near the mouth of Harrods Creek. The land was awarded to his estate, the executors being James Douglas and William Fleming. One sold the Terry land to RICHARD TAYLOR, and the other sold the same land to James Bate.

The only grant in central Kentucky relating to military service during the Revolutionary War was 560 acres to WILLIAM OLDHAM, as assignee of GEORGE ROGERS CLARK, about 4 miles south of the Falls. The state presented this land warrant to Clark in lieu of $750 for recruiting his battalion.

See Neal O. Hammon, *Early Kentucky Land Records, 1773–1780* (Louisville 1992); "The Fincastle Surveyors at the Falls of the Ohio, 1774," *Filson Club History Quarterly* 47 (Jan. 1973): 14–28.

Neal O. Hammon

LANDMARK BUILDING. When it opened for business in October 1858, the new Post Office and Custom House at Third and Green (Liberty) Streets caused the Louisville press to exhaust its stock of adjectives. The structure, with massive limestone walls, became the Morrissey Building in 1979 and the Landmark Building in 1996. It was described in 1858 by the *LOUISVILLE COURIER* as the "most convenient, the most substantial and the best built Custom House in the West." (Though the frontier era was long past, the city still thought of itself as western in 1858.) The *LOUISVILLE JOURNAL* found it "one of the most massive buildings we have ever seen."

It is undoubtedly the first large building to have been constructed of the famed Indiana limestone from the QUARRIES around Bedford, Indiana. This was possible only because of the completion of the NEW ALBANY and Salem Railroad (Monon) to Bedford in the spring of 1853, which made it feasible to transport large blocks of the heavy stone to Louisville. This first federal GOVERNMENT building project in Louisville replaced an insubstantial custom house on the wharf and the post office at Third and Jefferson, both in rented quarters.

The architect was ELIAS E. WILLIAMS, one of Louisville's leading practitioners of the building art. Little is known of his background except that he was born near Shepherdstown, Virginia, (now West Virginia) on November 22, 1791; probably learned the carpenter's trade in Hagerstown, Maryland; and came to Louisville in early 1838. He advertised that he had twenty years of experience as "architect and house builder."

Whether he was self-taught or served an apprenticeship with an established architect is unknown, but he was an accomplished designer and builder. He had just completed the impressive Masonic Temple at Fourth and Jefferson in 1857 and had built numerous other commercial buildings and residences. The Landmark Building is the only example of his work that survives.

He proposed a totally fireproof building in the then-popular Italianate mode and probably incorporated suggestions of Capt. Alexander H. Bowman of the Army Engineer Corps, who headed the Treasury Department's Office of Construction. It was the most technically advanced building in Louisville at the time. It was provided with running water, including water closets, supplied by a lead reservoir on the third floor. A pump forced water from a well into the reservoir. (Not until 1860 did the LOUISVILLE WATER CO. begin operation.) Hot-air furnaces supplied heat. Iron stairs, floor beams, and window frames, plus concrete floors and interior brick walls, were all fireproof. Postal facilities were on the first floor, the federal courtroom with a twenty-five-foot ceiling was on the second floor, and various offices were on the third. The basement housed bourbon-in-bond.

Spacious for the needs of 1858, the building by 1880 was inadequate for the volume of mail being handled. Ironically, Elias E. Williams died that year. A new post office and custom house at Fourth and Chestnut, long planned, was finally completed in 1892. The vacant building was sold at auction in June 1896 to Walter N. Haldeman, publisher of the *Courier-Journal* and *Louisville Times,* for fifty thousand dollars. He had planned to move his newspapers there but for some reason did not. Instead, he converted it to Haldeman's Warehouse, advertised as "absolutely fireproof."

It continued in this role until 1907 when Haldeman's son Bruce announced plans to demolish it, no doubt with the thought of erecting a new newspaper plant on the site. Apparently the cost of demolition (the building's outer walls are three feet thick) saved it from destruction. Instead in 1911–12 it was totally remodeled on the interior as the newspapers' new home. Architect John B. Hutchings's plan also altered the exterior. Only the third-floor windows retain their original form. It was in this building that WHAS, Louisville's first radio station, went on the air in 1922.

The newspapers occupied the building until September 1948 when they moved to a newly constructed building at Sixth and BROADWAY. In 1950 the former post office was remodeled into rental office space, with the Louisville Chamber of Commerce as the anchor tenant. The building was sold to the Old South Life Insurance Co. in 1963, which sold it in 1979 to James and Kay Morrissey, proprietors of the local Weight Watchers program and real estate developers. They named it the Morrissey Building and expended $2 million on renovation. It had been placed on the NATIONAL REGISTER OF HISTORIC PLACES in 1977. In January 1996 the Morrisseys sold the property to Legacy Properties Inc., formed by a group of Louisville investors. They changed the name to the Landmark Building.

In 1999 the Landmark Building was purchased by Whittington Realty Partners LLC. Citing the excellent location near the Commonwealth Convention Center, plans were initiated to renovate the lobby and rent the building for office space. It offered high-quality office space in an older, smaller building, a rarity in Louisville.

See George H. Yater, *The Morrissey Building: 130 Year Saga, 1858–1988* (Louisville 1988); *Courier-Journal,* July 20, 1999.

George H. Yater

LA SALLE, RENÉ ROBERT CAVELIER, SIEUR DE (b Rouen, France, November 22, 1643; d near the Brazos River in present Texas, March 19, 1687). FRENCH explorer. Although he was originally educated by Jesuits for the priesthood, La Salle's sense of adventure inspired him to leave France for New France (Canada) in 1666. There he received a land grant near Montreal and established a fur-trading post. La Salle's passion for exploration was fueled by Indian reports of the regions beyond New France and was further encouraged by the Count de Frontenac, the governor of New France (1672–82). He began his explorations in 1669. In 1677 he was granted vast exploration powers by King Louis XIV.

One of the highlights of La Salle's career came when, accompanied by his lieutenant, Henri de Tonti, he led an expedition into the interior of North America to the Mississippi River, which he descended to the Gulf of Mexico. There in 1682 La Salle laid claim to the entire Mississippi Valley in the name of Louis XIV. He dubbed the area Louisiana.

Controversy has surrounded the idea that La Salle also explored the OHIO RIVER and followed it as far as the Falls at present-day Louisville during his explorations of 1669–70. Histories such as Francis Parkman's *La Salle and the Discovery of the Great West* (1875) and *The History of the Ohio Falls Cities and Their Counties* and F.E. Wood's *The Louisville Story* (1951), while acknowledging the doubt that surrounds it, all support this belief.

Some histories point to La Salle's own claims and to the maps of his rival, Louis Joliet, which designate La Salle as the explorer of the Ohio. Even as late as 1976, Robert Burnett, in a *FILSON CLUB HISTORY QUARTERLY* article, maintained that La Salle was likely the first European explorer to reach the Falls. However, most modern historians refute this claim. George Yater's *Two Hundred Years at the Falls of the Ohio: A History of Louisville and Jefferson County* (1987) makes no mention of La Salle. Canadian historian J.M. Bumsted makes the best statement of the case in his book *The Peoples of Canada* in which he says "La Salle left Montreal in July 1669, with nine canoes and spent two years wandering in the western Indian territory, undoubtedly learning about the native people and their ways, although probably not making any of the major discoveries later claimed by him and attributed to him." Another Canadian historian, Lawrence Burpee, wrote in 1944, "whether or not he discovered the Ohio at this time has for years been a matter of dispute. All that we can be sure of is that he intended to go to the Ohio, and had the energy and the will to do so."

See Robert Burnett, "Louisville's French Past," *Filson Club History Quarterly* 50 (April 1976): 5–27; Francis Parkman, *La Salle and the Discovery of the Great West* (Boston 1897); *The History of the Ohio Falls Cities and Their Counties* (Cleveland 1882); F.E. Wood, *The Louisville Story* (Louisville 1951); Lawrence Burpee, *The Discovery of Canada* (Toronto 1944); J.M. Bumsted, *The Peoples of Canada* (Toronto 1992).

LATIN AMERICANS. It is not clear when the first Spanish-speaking person came to Louisville. For all practical purposes the history of Latin Americans in Louisville may have started early in the twentieth century. Soldiers of Latin American heritage were stationed at FORT KNOX during WORLD WAR II. Some young women living in the Louisville area began dating those soldiers. The first of those known cases is that of José Peña, who met his wife, Willa Jo Corrigan, while doing his military service in 1950. He later moved from Laredo, Texas, his native town, to make VALLEY STATION his home. His brother, Jesús, followed him and eventually married Elfrieda Gravatte. Some military personnel, stationed elsewhere, also married Latin Americans and brought them back to Louisville. Among them were Nora Colson from Laredo, Texas, and Marta Wood from Costa Rica. Some Louisville-based companies had international business. When their employees worked in Latin America, a small number of them found spouses and brought them to Louisville.

In the 1950s the UNIVERSITY OF LOUISVILLE and other educational institutions attracted students from Latin America, some of whom made their home in Louisville after their studies. Some married local residents, among them Miguel Lagunas from Mexico, Gloria Marshal from Nicaragua, and Carmen Newman from Puerto Rico. Until that time there was no established pattern for any organized immigration from any Latin American country to Louisville. Each person decided whether or not to stay and where to live. As a result the very small Latin American community was not concentrated in a specific neighborhood, and therefore Louisville does not have the typical "Latin Quarter."

In a broader sense, students from Spain and other Latin American countries attended exchange programs in local high schools and colleges. Long-lasting romantic relationships were formed, and some ended in marriage. In some cases, residents of Louisville brought their spouses from those countries. This perpetuated the demographic distribution of Hispanics. The term *Hispanic* refers to people whose culture has been influenced, in one way or another, by the Spanish culture but who are not necessarily natives of Spain.

Following the revolution in the early 1960s, the first wave of CUBANS came to the community. This was a group of highly motivated people with good education, a strong work ethic, and a desire to succeed. Many of them eventually left for Florida in search of warmer WEATHER, but a sizable group settled in Louisville and has made a positive contribution to the ECONOMY and culture of the area.

The University of Louisville and the medical community were also responsible for bringing Hispanic doctors to Louisville. By the 1970s the Hispanic community was the minority group with the highest percentage of contributors to the local economy and the largest percentage of professionals who practice their profession. While Hispanics remain distinct in Louisville, they have been able to integrate to an amazing degree.

In the early 1970s Professor Fortuna Gordon, who taught Spanish at the University of Louisville, invited some of her Latin American friends to her house. Among them were America Dunhan and Miguel Lagunas, both from Mexico, and Delma Durig from Colombia. They discussed the founding of a club where Latin Americans in the area could get together to socialize and preserve their culture. The Community Club of the Americas was formed first, but shortly afterward the name was changed to the Latin American Club of Louisville. Club members Julio Ramirez and his wife, Mariela, were responsible for making Louisville a sister city of La Plata in Argentina. The club cooperates with other local organizations dedicated to improving relations between the United States and other countries that facilitate exchanges in the areas of education, culture, business, and government.

The club actively participates in the Hispano /Latino Coalition sponsored by Seven Counties, an organization that helps people in the community deal with crisis situations. This coalition promotes mutual understanding between Louisville residents and the growing Latino POPULATION of this area. It also helps the newcomers function within Louisville's social structure.

The 1980s and 1990s can be described by the phrase "Mexico Discovers Kentucky." A large number of Mexican and Central American workers came to Kentucky, attracted by the tobacco farms that were losing their traditional workforce as labor costs increased. In an attempt to survive, TOBACCO farms hired migrant workers. Many of these workers found work in Louisville during the times of slow farm work and have stayed in Louisville.

Miguel Lagunas

LAW. The city of Louisville was incorporated in 1780 by the Virginia legislature as a town in Jefferson County, in part as an answer to a petition from settlers who feared their new property would not have clear title due to conflicting claims from pre-Revolutionary surveys. Virginia agreed, incorporated the frontier town, and forfeited the lands of convicted Tory Dr. JOHN CONNOLLY, the main stumbling block in the settlers' claims.

As property rights set the litigation stage from the earliest period, so did the complexity of pursuing justice. At the time of Louisville's settlement, all legal matters, excepting misdemeanors, had to be heard in a superior court of Virginia, involving travel to Williamsburg and later to Richmond over dangerous trails. Lesser matters were heard by justices of the peace, appointed by the governor. The "bench" was literally a bench in those pioneer days of justice rendered in crude log cabins by justices of the peace. These cabin COURTS handled misdemeanors and litigation involving not more than $4.16. As the court system developed through attempts to move justice closer to the pioneer settlements, matters were settled in Harrodsburg and Danville and later in Lexington and Bardstown.

When Kentucky became a state in 1792, the Virginia legal model was adopted with few exceptions. The major change occurred, however, in 1802, when Louisville for the first time became the home of one of the circuits established by a reformed judicial system.

By this time the Louisville bench and bar were gathered in the second courthouse built since 1785 and were anticipating the construction of a larger building to accommodate the needs of a POPULATION that was to double in the decade. (That structure opened in 1818; the present courthouse opened in 1842.)

The first circuit court convened in Louisville in 1803 with an able lawyer as judge: STEPHEN ORMSBY, appointed by the governor. Prominent lawyers later appointed were FORTUNATUS COSBY, A. Metcalf, HENRY PIRTLE, J.P. Oldham, Henry Price, T.Q. Wilson, J.M. Hewitt, T.T. Crittenden, J.J. Marshall, and W.F. Bullock. The circuit court had jurisdiction over all criminal, civil, chancery, and equity proceedings until 1835, when the accumulated load was too heavy for one judge to carry and the Louisville chancery court was established.

After 1850 the third constitution called for judicial election; William F. Bullock, the last to be appointed, was the first elected circuit judge. A city court was established in 1837, a county court in 1854, and a court of common pleas in 1865. In September 1891 a new constitution sought uniformity in the court system, which proved impractical in view of the different nature of the circuits. For example, the Louisville area needed a special division for juvenile offenders as early as 1906 and magistrate courts in 1934.

The Louisville bar has seen outstanding lawyers since the earliest days, when judges did not have to know law and attorneys held sway by virtue of superior knowledge. Historians have noted that, while the bench might have been crude, the bar embraced many distinguished members, a number of whom attained prominence in state and national politics. The first recorded lawyer in Louisville history was James Brown, brother of John Brown, Kentucky's first U.S. senator. Brown was admitted to the Jefferson County circuit court on August 13, 1795. These early lawyers tended to be farmers as well. Their private and professional characters were often modeled after those members of the bar in Virginia, under whom many had studied. Thomas Nelson Page expressed the character of these early lawyers in this way: "The profession of the law was to him the highest of all professions. It was brotherhood; it was sacred; it maintained the rights of man, preserved the government, and controlled the administration of the law" (Levin, 18). Among the pioneers was Revolutionary hero and famed Indian fighter Col. WILLIAM CHRISTIAN, who had studied law with Patrick Henry before settling in Louisville in 1785 as county lieutenant in charge of the Jefferson County militia. His daughter married ALEXANDER SCOTT BULLITT, starting a dynasty of lawyers, including William Marshall Bullitt, who became solicitor general of the United States. A.S. Bullitt led Kentucky's second constitutional convention in 1799; fifty years later WILLIAM CHRISTIAN BULLITT, together with Col. WILLIAM PRESTON, represented Louisville in the third convention. President of the 1849 convention was attorney JAMES GUTHRIE, considered the community's first civic leader. He was admitted to the Kentucky bar in 1817 and, after a distinguished career in the Kentucky legislature, was appointed secretary of the treasury by President Pierce in 1853.

In 1832 the city's population was 10,341, of whom 40 were attorneys. Among the prominent lawyers who settled in Louisville after the CIVIL WAR was Louisville & Nashville Railroad attorney BASIL DUKE. As a Confederate soldier, Duke rode as a raider with his brother-in-law, John Hunt Morgan, and frequently destroyed the Louisville & Nashville's track. A fellow Confederate soldier, Bennett Young, moved to Louisville in 1868 to become one of the city's foremost courtroom attorneys, entrepreneurs, and civic leaders. Young helped develop the MONON RAILROAD, the KENTUCKY AND INDIANA

Bridge, and the Louisville Southern Railway; he also was noted for liberal politics and social philanthropy. Another famous attorney during this early period was John Marshall Harlan, who eventually rose to the position of associate justice of the U.S. Supreme Court. In 1885 noted attorney John Chaplin, in the landmark case of John Loree versus 116 residents in northern Kentucky, put an end to land disputes dating back almost a hundred years. By 1902 almost four hundred lawyers had set up practices in Louisville. In 1914, six years before the Nineteenth Amendment allowing for women's suffrage, three women, Marguerite Dravo, Elizabeth Marshall, and Laura Wehner, graduated from the law school at the University of Louisville. The most famous attorney of this period was Louis Brandeis, who was named to the Supreme Court by President Wilson in 1916.

The citizen-lawyer was perhaps best exemplified by Wilson W. Wyatt, who founded one of Kentucky's largest law firms. Wyatt was inaugurated mayor of Louisville in 1941. In 1959 he was inaugurated lieutenant governor.

In November 1975 Kentucky voters, prodded by a group led by citizen lawyers, including Wilson Wyatt, approved an amendment to the Kentucky constitution that replaced a judicial system not changed since 1891. The Judicial Article, as the amendment was called, was long overdue. Population growth, property damage suits stemming from the arrival of the automobile, domestic relations, regulatory expansion, growth in environment and consumer legislation, plus a burgeoning crime rate had created a docket backlog of monumental proportions. Respected former jurist Lawrence Grauman issued a call for reform in 1964, calling the system "cluttered and antiquated," but voters turned down an amendment at the polls in 1966. The successful 1975 amendment, however, contained many of the earlier reformers' suggestions, including a four-tier court system, the elimination of police and magistrate courts, and the addition of a requirement that all county judges be lawyers. "County judge/executives" were to be administrators, not judicial officers.

A special session of the Kentucky legislature was called in 1976 to implement the article. Under the reform, a supreme court, consisting of seven judges, was established at the top level; the court of appeals, now the second tier, included fourteen judges; the eighty-six-judge circuit court moved to the third tier; and a new district court, with a minimum of fifty-six judges, replaced the former lower courts—county, quarterly, police, and magistrate.

The modern era has seen the rise of African Americans in the profession, notably Charles W. Anderson, the first to be elected to the Kentucky legislature (1936), where he fought to extend educational opportunities to African American students. Later he was appointed an alternate delegate to the United Nations General Assembly.

Women, too, began to achieve prominence in the legal community in modern times, including Lillian Fleischer, Kitty Meuter, Olga Peers, Ellen Ewing, Ann Oldfather, and Rebecca Westerfield. Some of these women lawyers are included in oft-mentioned names of lawyers who inspired young students to study for the bar. The list also includes the lawyers' lawyer defense attorney Frank Haddad; federal judge Charles Allen; Stanley Chauvin, former president of the American Bar Association (ABA); Herbert Segal, chair of the ABA's labor section; Gordon Davidson, one of Wyatt's protégés who followed the citizen lawyer path; labor lawyer Ralph Logan; Neville Miller, former U of L law school dean and former Louisville mayor; Ben Shobe; Ben Washer, former dean of the Jefferson School of Law; First Amendment specialist Edward Zingman, another Wyatt protégé; Charles Dawson; Kennedy Helm Sr.; and Kentucky Supreme Court Justice Charles Leibson.

Men and women in modern practice cover the gamut of specialization. However, practice in earlier days focused on title law, then later on transportation and maritime law as steamboats and railroads entered the scene, and still later on commercial and corporate law. Also, perhaps because Kentucky's founding corresponded with Revolutionary fervor for individual rights, an underlying theme of constitutional protection has been a hallmark of the local and state practice.

As early as 1917 in *Buchanan v. Warley*, the high court ruled against a city ordinance preventing blacks from buying property in predominantly white neighborhoods. The appearance of Louisville lawyers arguing cases before the Supreme Court was not unusual in the twentieth century. Outstanding among the local cases credited with making law through high court decisions is *Thompson v. City of Louisville*. In 1960 the court ruled that the loitering law under which a black man had been convicted was unconstitutional—a decision that blocked police interference with the coming civil rights struggle.

In 1985 the ruling in *Batson v. Kentucky* set the standard against exclusion of members of the defendant's race from the jury selected to try him. Also in the 1980s, the U.S. Supreme Court ruled against the validity of "voluntary confessions" obtained while the defendant was in custody; another case lowered the eligibility for capital punishment to age sixteen; still another rule prohibited the Kentucky Bar Association from interfering with a lawyer's right to advertise.

The development of legal education in Louisville was a rocky road. From pioneer days well into the 1920s, prospective attorneys read the law with someone who had passed the bar. An act of the General Assembly of 1796 set the standards: a practicing attorney must have a license issued by two or more judges of the Court of Appeals or district court who would attest to his character and training. In 1902 delegates to the first annual meeting of the Kentucky Bar Association raised concerns about the lack of educational requirements for admission. In 1918 a board of bar examiners was established to administer the examinations, but no educational requirements were set. Recommendations of the KBA requiring at least a high school education were finally adopted by the Court of Appeals. After 1928 admission requirements were raised to include at least one year in a law school. It was not until 1934 that Kentucky had a mandatory bar that required practicing attorneys to belong to the appropriate bar association.

The School of Law, conceived in 1837 and established in 1846, was ready to receive students who wanted formal education long before pressures from the state and national bar associations were being felt. Beginning as a department in the newly formed University of Louisville, today the Louis D. Brandeis School of Law, as the university law school is now named, ranks as fifth-oldest in continuous operation in the United States.

Among the subjects of the school when new were constitutional law, commercial law and equity, the practice of law and criminal law, the science of law, and law of nations. Out of the first class of thirty-seven students, twelve graduated the following year with the degree of bachelor of law after passing an oral examination conducted by the professors and two outside practitioners.

The law department started out in the basement of the Jefferson County courthouse (students brought their own candles for evening classes) and moved to five other downtown locations before settling at the Belknap Campus in 1938. One of the few law schools in the mid-nineteenth century to confer an academic degree, the school boasted an excellent faculty, including three lawyers who resigned from the U of L Board of Trustees to teach in the department. Henry Pirtle, a prominent member of the Louisville legal community, was dean de facto. Other distinguished professors included James Speed, appointed attorney general by President Abraham Lincoln in 1864, and Garnett Duncan, who served in Congress.

During the 1920s the school of law began to benefit from the attention of Supreme Court justice Louis Dembitz Brandeis. A Louisville native, Brandeis was a nephew of Lewis Dembitz, who had published the landmark *Kentucky Jurisprudence* in 1890 after a distinguished career as a practicing attorney and legal scholar in Louisville.

Justice Brandeis's vision that the school's "aim should be high and the vision broad" was difficult to realize in the days when the school was not accredited, the library was inadequate, and resources were extremely limited. However, under the leadership of U of L president Raymond A. Kent and law school dean Neville

Largest Area Law Firms
(Ranked by number of area lawyers as of Dec. 14, 1998)

Name	*Lawyers**	*Office**	*Notable Clients*	*Services*	*Locally founded*
Brown, Todd and Heyburn	131/183	2/5	Bank One, Brown-Williamson, General Electric, Jewish Hospital, L.G.& E., Louisville Water Co., Rescare, Unidial, UPS, Vencor	U.S. and International Business, Litigation and Dispute Resolution	1972
Wyatt, Tarrant and Combs	108/232	2/9	Alliant Health System, Churchill Downs, City of Louisville, DuPont, Ford, General Electric, Jefferson County Public Schools, PNC Bank, United Catalysts, Henry Vogt Machine Co.	Business Law and Litigation	1812
Greenebaum, Doll, and McDonald	87/151	1/5	Ashland Oil, Atria Communities, Columbia/HCA, Commonwealth Industries, Gallatin Steel, Hillerich & Bradsby, Humana, LG&E, Toyota, Vencor, Papa John's	Corporate and Business Law, Litigation, Labor Unemployment, Trusts-Estate Planning, Environmental	1952
Stites and Harbison	79/136	2/6	Modis Professional, Alcan Aluminum, Brown-Forman, Tricon/KFC, Kentucky Medical Ins., National City Bank, Regional Airport, Anthem Health, Steel Technologies, Stock Yards Bank	Business Law, Litigation, Real Estate, Regulatory Law, Personal Services	1832
Boehl, Stopher, and Graves	47/67	2/4	Allied Signa, Jeffboat Inc., Baptist Hospitals, Bristol-Meyers Squibb, City of Louisville, CSX Railroad, Ford, Bank of Louisville, Southern Baptist Theological Seminary, Transit Authority of River City	General Trial and Appellate Practice, Administrative, Probate-Estate Planning, Corporate	1895
Middleton and Reutlinger	39/39	2/2	Arm Financial, Borden Chemical, Bridgeman Foods, Brown and Williamson, Hillerich & Bradsby, Kroger, Logan Aluminum, MCI Telecommunications, Norfolk/Southern, Vermont-American	Corporate, Environmental, Intellectual Property, Litigation, Estate Planning, Probate and Tax	1854
Ogden, Newell, and Welch	39/39	1/1	Bank of Louisville, Bell South, Brown-Forman, J.J.B. Hilliard-W.L. Lyons, Kentucky Medical Ins., LG&E, Publishers Printing, Sodrel Truck Lines, United Medical Corp., Vencor Inc.	Corporate and Tax, Employee Benefits and Labor, Estate Planning and Administration, Litigation, Utility	1898
Woodward, Hobson, and Fulton	38/44	1/2	Bank One, Brown-Forman, Caritas Health, Catholic Health Initiatives, CSX Transportation, Different Strokes Golf, General Motors, Louisville Water Co., Res-Care, Wal-Mart	Product Liability Defense, Hospital, Administrative Law, Corporate and Tax, Employment, Labor, General Trial	1917
Segal Sales Stewart Cutler and Tillman	24/26	5/6	Kentucky State AFL-CIO, United Auto Workers, JCTS, Bank of Louisville, IBEW, Amalgamated Transit Union, American Federation of State, County, and Municipal Employees, Machinists Union, Kentucky Laborers District Council	Labor and Employment Law, Litigation, Personal Injury/ Workers Compensation, Bankruptcy, General Law	1955
Goldberg and Simpson	22/22	1/1	Bank of Louisville, Jefferson County Board of Health, Kentucky Center for the Arts, Liberty Mutual Insurance, Bank One, Breed Technologies, Commonwealth of Kentucky, U.S. Corrections, Jewish Hospital, Spector Entertainment	Corporate, Litigation, Family Law, Real Estate, Labor, Insurance Defense, Construction, Health Care	1981
Seiller and Handmaker	21/22	2/3	Arby's, Bank of Louisville, Carlson-Wagonlit Travel, Cumberland Surety Ins., Fire King Inc., John-Kenyon Eye Center, Kentucky Racing Commission, Neil Huffman Auto, Jillian's Entertainment, Tony Roma's Restaurant	Civil/Criminal Litigation, Bankruptcy, Corporate, Intellectual Property, Domestic Relations, Trusts, Estates, Employment Law	1990
Ackerson Mosley and Yann	20/20	1/1	Home Supply Co., Brown Noltemeyer, Bank One, Commonwealth Bank, Swope Auto, AAA of Kentucky, Vanderlande Industries, Mercer Transport, Kingfish Restaurants, Gateway Press, Galt House	Corporate Law, Litigation, Real Estate, Estate Planning and Administration, Family Law, Tax, Employee Benefits, Zoning	1998
Conliffe Sandman and Sullivan	19/19	3/3	Waste Management, Fruit of the Loom, United Companies Lending Corp., Fidelity Finances, United General Title Ins., A.I. Management and Profit Liability Claims, J.C. Bradford, Advest Securities, AT&T, United Defense.	Civil Trial and Appeal; Corporate Law, Environmental Law, Estate Planning, Securities Law	1964

Name	*Lawyers*	*Office*	*Notable Clients*	*Services*	*Locally founded*
Lynch Cox Gilman and Mahan	19/19	2/2	Akzo Nobel, Corradino Group, First Star, Gates Rubber Industrial Equipment, Yellow Cab, Kentucky-Indiana Lumber, Nabisco, Sud Chemie, Underwriters Safety & Claims, United Catalysts, Zoeller Co.	Corporate, General Trial, Insurance Defense, Patent, Probate-Estate Planning	N/A
Weber and Rose	19/19	2/3	Healthcare Indemnity, Jewish Hospital, Alliant Health, V.G. Reed, Winn-Dixie, P&I Railway, Vencor, WDRB-TV, WLKY-TV, Volunteers of America, Metro United Way	Medical Malpractice, Insurance Defense, Trials, Appeals, Labor-Employment, Probate-Estate Planning	1981
Pedley Zielke Gordinier Olt and Pence	18/18	1/1	Metro Sewer, Convention and Visitors Bureau, Coltec Industries, Intermedia, Desa International, Atlas Concrete, Service Welding & Machine, Papa John's, Advanced Lifeline Services, Healthcare Recoveries	Commercial Litigation, Business and Insurance Regulation, Governmental, Criminal, Media Communications	1981
Dinsmore and Shohl	17/216	1/7	Allstate Insurance, Jewish Hospital, Humana, Winn-Dixie, Chi-Chi's, Courier-Journal, Landmark Community Newspapers, Bluegrass Cellular, Key Communications Services, Kentucky Press Assoc., Brandenburg Telephone Co.	Labor and Employment, Healthcare, Business, Commercial Litigation, Media/First Amendment, Telecommunications, Appellate	1997
Morgan and Pottinger	17/22	2/3	Bank One, Fifth Third, National City Bank, PNC Bank, Republic Bank, Star Bank, Stock Yards Bank, GMAC, Oxmoor Toyota, Town and Country Ford	Bank and Lending, Retail and Commercial Collections, Civil Litigation, Real Estate, Estate Planning	1974
Borowitz and Goldsmith	16/16	1/1	Bank of Louisville, Bank One, Collins Auto, Blacketer Builders and Developers, Colston Group, Chemical and Industrial Engineering, Rhodes, Safetran, Kentucky Transportation Cabinet, Fred Grimm and Associates	Corporate and Banking Law, Litigation, Personal Injury, Taxation/Employee Benefits, Estate Planning and Administration	1972
Tilford Dobbins Alexander Buckaway and Black	16/16	1/1	Alumintec, Abel Construction, City of Louisville, Coast Midwest Transport, Kosair Charities, Sachs Co., Sprint PCS, Commonwealth of Kentucky, WKB Development, Tritel Communications	Corporate Law, Workers Comp., Domestic Relations, Personal Injury, Civil Litigation	1903
Morris Garlove Waterman and Johnson	15/15	1/1	Armco Inc., Dixie Associates Shopping Centers, McMahan Group Shopping Centers, Medical Center Anesthesiologists, Miller Transportation, U.S. Fidelity and Guaranty, General Shoelace, Bluegrass Cardiology, Metropolitan Urology, Industrial Services of America	Probate, Estate Planning, Tax Insurance, Business Litigation, Real Estate, Business, Corporate Law	1928
O'Bryan Brown and Toner	15/15	1/1	GCU Insurance, Kentucky Employers Safety Association, Kentucky Hospital Insurance Co., Medical Protective Co., Owens Corning, Providian, Royal InsuranceCo., St. Paul Insurance, Co., TIG Insurance Co.	Medical Malpractice Defense, Product Liability Defense, Association Trust, Kentucky Medical, Professional Liability Insurance, Workers Comp. and Premises Liability	1991
MacKenzie and Peden	14/14	2/2	Rapid Industries, United Electric Inc., Central Farm Supply, Raymond Equipment, Manning Equipment, EPI Corp, Topworx, State Automobile Insurance Co., Nationwide Mutual Insurance Co., Shelter Insurance Co.	Business Law, Commercial Litigation, Tax Law, Estate Planning/Wills and Trusts, General Corporate Law, Insurance Defense Litigation	1941

*Local/total

Miller, the school was reorganized in 1933. With four full-time professors plus part-time lecturers and a library of seventeen thousand volumes, it was accredited by the American Bar Association. In 1938 a handsome new building was begun. The school's resources, however, could not cover an evening division. In 1950, urged by the Court of Appeals, the university law school merged with the Jefferson School of Law, the night school committed to provide legal education for young people who might not otherwise have the opportunity to study law.

The merger of the two schools brought additional accreditation pressures. The American Bar Association, closely monitoring promised progress in faculty, library facilities, and moves toward a four-year program—improvements that were to accompany the merger—threatened to withdraw accreditation in 1969 and again in 1976. Under the leadership of Dean James R. Merritt, with support from university and state administrators and the legal community, an extensive program was undertaken to add space, enhance the library, and improve the faculty-student ratio. By 1982 the major challenges had been met.

See *University of Louisville School of Law 1846–1996* (Louisville 1996); J. Stoddard Johnston, ed., *Memorial History of Louisville*, vol. 2 (New York 1896); H. Levin, *Lawyers and Lawmakers of Kentucky* (Chicago 1897); *Littell's Laws of Kentucky* (Frankfort 1809); Samuel W. Thomas, "An Inventory of Jefferson County Records," *Filson Club History Quarterly* 44 (Oct. 1970): 321–49; Vince Staten, *Law at the Falls: A History of the Louisville Legal Profession* (Dallas 1997). *Business First Book of Lists* (1999).

Betty Lou Amster

LEADERSHIP LOUISVILLE FOUNDATION. In 1979 Leadership Louisville was founded "to foster interest in and promote educational, civic and social service activities." Community leaders Wilson Wyatt Sr., BARRY BINGHAM Sr., and Maurice D.S. Johnson started the program to ensure that Louisville's future leaders would be knowledgeable about community issues, well networked, and passionate about the success of the community. Initially Leadership Louisville was organized under the auspices of the old Louisville Area Chamber of Commerce. As it expanded and matured, the Leadership Louisville Foundation became an independent umbrella, with a mission of developing a diverse group of leaders to serve as catalysts for a stronger community.

The Leadership Louisville program and its companion programs, Focus Louisville and the Bingham Fellows, are regarded as national models because of their continued popularity and scope. Focus Louisville, established in 1985, is a two-and-a-half-day community orientation. Through this experience, participants have the opportunity to have hands-on interaction with schools, GOVERNMENT, the arts, leisure activities, and distinctive NEIGHBORHOODS. The Bingham Fellows, a program for graduates of Leadership Louisville, began in 1988 through an endowment from the MARY AND BARRY BINGHAM Sr. Fund. Initially the program was structured as a yearlong problem-solving experience. In 1997 the program was redesigned to offer educational "fellowships" in topics related to Louisville's community agenda.

Selection for the Leadership Louisville program results in approximately fifty community leaders from all walks of life being chosen to participate. The program is one year in length, and participants continue their experience afterward through member activities. Monthly topics focus on community issues such as education, business, government, human needs, quality of life, and the criminal justice system. The Leadership Louisville Foundation is a member of the National Association for Community Leadership.

Christine Johnson

LEAGUE OF WOMEN VOTERS OF LOUISVILLE AND JEFFERSON COUNTY. The League of Women Voters of Louisville and Jefferson County is a nonpartisan political organization dedicated to increasing informed citizen participation in GOVERNMENT. The structure of the League of Women Voters parallels that of the government, with local, state, and national levels. Each level is a separate corporation, linked through its bylaws and dues structure with the other levels. At the national, state, and some local levels, each league comprises two legally distinct corporate entities that are linked through their bylaws and other agreement documents. These consist of a 501(c)(3) corporation that conducts voter service and education activities, and a non-501(c)(3) that lobbies on issues on which the league has developed consensus positions.

The league was created in 1920 to "finish the fight" after passage of the Nineteenth Amendment to the Constitution, which gave women the right to vote. At each structural level, the league was an outgrowth of the suffragette organizations. With the passage of the Nineteenth Amendment, the National American Woman Suffrage Association dissolved and immediately reestablished as the National League of Women Voters, later renamed the League of Women Voters of the United States. Also in 1920, the Kentucky Equal Rights Association became the League of Women Voters of Kentucky. The Louisville League of Women Voters was formed on November 26, 1920, by the joining of the School Election League and the Louisville Women Suffrage Association and the election of its first president, Julia Duke Henning, and vice president, Mrs. Herbert Mengel. The Louisville League, one of the oldest local leagues in the country, was later renamed the League of Women Voters of Louisville and Jefferson County to reflect the larger metropolitan area actually served by the organization.

At all levels, the purpose of the league was to "develop a citizenship worthy of the long struggle for the ballot." Although originally created to educate newly enfranchised female voters about the political process, over time the mission was expanded to encompass all voters, but the basic mission has remained virtually the same for more than three-quarters of a century. Membership in the league, originally limited to female citizens of the United States, was opened to men in 1972. All of its programs are open to the general public.

The league sponsors candidate debates, speak-outs, and forums, as well as forums on specific public policy issues. In 1984 the League of Women Voters of Louisville and Jefferson County hosted the debate between presidential candidates Ronald Reagan and Walter Mondale. League volunteers worked full-time for weeks in preparation for the debate. The local league typically hosts four or more public forums each year on policy issues, consistently producing events that bring people together for dialogue and discussion.

The league develops materials that are published and distributed to other organizations, schools, libraries, and the public. *Your Government at Your Fingertips* is a handbook defining the local government of Louisville and Jefferson County, its departments, and their responsibilities. No such publication was available in the community until the handbook was created by the league in 1962. The publication is researched, written, and published by the league, and updated as needed. The handbook was used extensively in 1994–96 by a task force sponsored by the local administrations and the Chamber of Commerce to study and develop a proposed plan for local government reorganization. Other publications included a handout on "Voting and the College Student" and a packet of information on the restoration of civil voting rights following the completion of the terms of a felony conviction. The league also prepares and distributes non-partisan voter guides that list candidates running for office, the offices sought, and candidates' comments on issues of interest to voters.

League members assist in voter registration; provide voting information; participate in a speakers' bureau; serve as representatives or observers on community boards; and provide information about nongovernmental organizations and the democratic process to international visitors.

See files in League of Women Voters of Louisville and Jefferson County office, and at the University of Louisville Archives and Records Service.

Katherine K.M. Kamin

LEBANESE-SYRIANS. There is general agreement that the first Lebanese-Syrian to arrive in Louisville was Lahoud "Louis" Karem, from the small village of Bsharri in the mountains of Lebanon. It was also the birthplace and home of the famous poet Kahlil Gibran. Karem arrived in 1884, having first gone to New Orleans but having left there because of his strong dislike of the climate and his understanding that Louisville was a major mercantile center. In his lifetime, Lahoud became a very powerful force in Democratic politics. The early Lebanese-Syrians were generally sent for or came because of Lahoud Karem. Later immigrants came because of the positive word that filtered back to their villages. To this day, most Lebanese families in Louisville can be traced to just three or four villages. Most of the early Lebanese were merchants, butchers, or fruit and vegetable vendors, and much of their activity centered around the Downtown HAYMARKET. Many learned English and prepared for citizenship at the NEIGHBORHOOD HOUSE, then located at 428 S First St. While these early families were called Syrians here, because Lebanon was a Syrian Protectorate, they always thought of themselves as Lebanese and had strong nationalistic feeling toward Lebanon, which finally became independent after WORLD WAR II.

The first immigrants were Marianite Catholics (in union with Roman Catholicism). Because of the strong Roman Catholic community in Louisville, they had no trouble joining local parishes. St. Boniface and St. Mary Magdalene were particular centers of the early immigrants. Other Lebanese were primarily Antiochian Orthodox and, interestingly, some joined the Episcopal church, also strong here in Louisville. Records of CHRIST CHURCH CATHEDRAL reflect such membership in the early part of the twentieth century. Probably the real

Five generations of the family of State Senator David Karem (fourth from left, second row) 1950.

mainstay of the Lebanese, and in fact the whole Middle Eastern community, was St. Michael's Antiochian Orthodox Church, founded in 1934.[3] This church has been, and remains, not only a spiritual center for its members but also a cultural center and connection point for the entire Lebanese and Middle Eastern population. St. Michael's annual ethnic fair has become an entree for all of Louisville to sample the Middle Eastern food and experience the culture. Food has remained a major tie to the old country. While the Arabic language has been lost to subsequent generations, a strong cooking tradition has remained. Some dishes have now even become accepted westernized food, such as pita bread, tabbouleh, hummus, and falafel.

There appears no evidence of a significant influx of the Muslim faith until after WORLD WAR II. Specifically, in the 1950s and 1960s there began to be a Muslim presence of immigrants, primarily from Lebanon, Syria, and Jordan, and those who consider themselves Palestinians. Religious differences and hostilities that exist in the Middle East fortunately have made virtually no transition to this country. Lebanese who came and set up their merchant businesses in the Haymarket area did so literally side by side with early Jewish immigrants. The unique relationship of the Christian and Jewish communities in Louisville has frequently been cited as a positive model. The churches and synagogues have held mutual functions and peace services over the years.

The loss of the Arabic language, while unfortunate, was caused by the early immigrants pushing their children strongly toward social and economic assimilation. The Lebanese community finds itself in a very comfortable relationship with Louisville and is now a mix of professionals, merchants, and craftsmen.

David K. Karem

LEIBSON, CHARLES MORRIS (b Louisville, June 30, 1929; d Louisville, December 10, 1995). Jurist. Charles Morris Leibson was born into a family of lawyers. His parents, Oscar and Pearl (Isler) Leibson, were first-generation Americans who had one son and one daughter.

He was a graduate of Male High School and attended the UNIVERSITY OF LOUISVILLE as an undergraduate for only two years before being allowed to enroll in its law school. After graduating at the top of his class in 1952, he completed a two-year tour of duty in the army Judge Advocate General corps before entering private practice in Louisville with his father and brother-in-law.

Over the next twenty-one years, Leibson made an indelible mark on the practice of law and gained a national reputation as a trial lawyer. He worked on behalf of his clients while always maintaining the highest professional standards. Along the way, he pioneered legal remedies for individuals who were injured or otherwise wronged and blazed new trails in the presentation of testimonial and documentary evidence. He won many important trial victories including *Nazareth Literary and Benevolent Institution v. Stephenson* (1973), the first multimillion-dollar verdict in Kentucky. He was elected to the International Academy of Trial Lawyers in 1972 and the prestigious Inner Circle of Advocates in 1975.

In 1976 he was elected judge of the Jefferson Circuit Court. He presided over many trials and hearings involving issues ranging from whether a horse should run in the KENTUCKY DERBY to murder cases carrying the death penalty. He was a trial judge for six years before being elected to the Kentucky Supreme Court in 1982. He served on the court for thirteen years, during which time he became known as the court's leading intellectual.

He was a prolific writer whose opinions brought a new level of scholarship and intellectual rigor to the court. His influence derived from an outstanding legal mind, a passion for fairness, and an intellectual honesty that refused to bend the law or the state constitution to fit the prevailing public mood. He led the court to revise its thinking to further permit individuals to sue government or corporations for injuries and WRONGDOING, thus narrowing the doctrine of sovereign immunity, which shields government from lawsuits. He authored the opinions in which the court adopted the doctrine of comparative negligence, recognized an individual's "right to die," and reaffirmed the right of privacy under the Kentucky constitution.

Even after his ascension to the Supreme Court, he continued to study law. He obtained a master's degree in "The Judicial Process" in 1986 from the University of Virginia, where he had received his Judge Advocate General (JAG) training. He also held several teaching positions—at U of L (adjunct professor from 1969 until shortly before his death), Harvard Law School, University of Kentucky, and the National Judicial College in Nevada.

He was named Judge of the Year in 1979 by the Louisville Bar Association. The Association of Trial Lawyers of America named him Outstanding State Trial Judge in America for 1980 and the Outstanding State Appellate Judge in America for 1985. He was also inducted into the International Academy of Trial Judges in 1980. In 1995 he received the Lawrence Grauman Award, the highest alumni tribute from U of L. He was survived by his wife, Margaret "Meg" (Burnett) Leibson, and three sons, Steven, Marc, and James, from his first marriage. He is buried in the Adath Jeshurun Cemetery.

Margaret "Meg" Leibson

LELAND, LOUISE (b Springfield, Illinois, March 20, 1902; d Louisville, September 9, 1956). Architect. The daughter of Jerome and Gertrude (Akin) Leland, her family was prominent in the hotel business throughout the Northeast and Midwest. Leland graduated from the Cambridge School of Architecture and Landscape Architecture in 1931. In 1934 she applied to the Kentucky State Board of Architecture for admission, although she did not pass the examination until January 4, 1938. She became the state's first female registered architect and the only one until 1975.

Leland came to Louisville in 1934 and teamed with classmate and landscape architect

Anne Bruce Haldeman to form the firm Haldeman and Leland, with offices located in the Francis Building at 606 S Fourth St. The two lived together in GLENVIEW. During WORLD WAR II, Leland served as a tool designer in the engineering department at the Curtiss-Wright aircraft plant in Louisville, where she also earned a professional rating as an aeronautical engineer. The firm continued operation until Leland's death.

See Julian Oberwarth, *History of the Profession of Architecture in Kentucky* (Louisville 1987).

LEMON & SON. Louisville's oldest continuous retail business first appeared in the community in 1828 at 535 Main St. This many-generation jewelry business was founded by James Innes Lemon, who had begun his career in the Lexington area as a diamond and silver tradesman. Mr. Lemon's grandfather was a captain in the Revolutionary War. In 1862, a son, James K. Lemon, joined the business. From its initial location on Main St., the business moved to S Fourth St., where it stayed until 1992. It then moved to the AEGON CENTER. For a time the business operated a suburban branch at the Holiday Manor Shopping Center on Brownsboro Rd.

In 1924 the business became the exclusive supplier of the official KENTUCKY DERBY trophy. Prior to the cup's classic design, what was awarded as the winner's trophy varied from year to year. Artist George Graff was commissioned by Col. Matt Winn in 1924 to design the trophy, which has been changed only twice: once for the 100th Derby in 1974, and again in 1999, for the 125th Run for the Roses.

See Louisville Board of Trade, *Louisville Fifty Years Ago* (Louisville 1923).

Kenneth L. Miller

LEONARD BRUSH AND CHEMICAL SUPPLY COMPANY. In 1879 local brush manufacturer Frank B. Leonard opened a brush supply business on Market St. between Eighth and Ninth Streets. Working in partnership with his brothers Christopher and Richard, Leonard was one of several brush suppliers in the Louisville area. Leonard's success outpaced the other manufacturers so rapidly that the company moved in 1881 to a larger facility on MARKET ST. between Fourth and Fifth Streets.

Following Frank Leonard's death in 1905, his widow sold her interest in the business, and it became Leonard Brush and Woodenware Co. at 651 W Market St. About that time W.T. Adams, who had begun working for Leonard in 1896, became the manager of the facility and continued to operate the company until 1946. His son, Walter T. Adams, then took over the operation at 901 W MAIN ST., and it became the Leonard Brush and Chemical Supply Co.

In the 1950s the business expanded its operations to include the manufacturing and sale of janitorial and cleaning supplies as well as offering repair services for the equipment they manufactured. In 1988 W. Terry Adams became the third generation of Adamses to run the company. In 1995 he moved the facilities to 1450 Mellwood Ave. The company sells janitorial products and supplies to HOSPITALS, schools, and offices throughout much of Kentucky and some locations in Indiana.

LESBIANS. Louisville has a significant history of lesbian activists, culture, and community. Lesbian culture surely existed before the tumultuous 1960s, but there is little documentation on such activity. However, beginning in the early 1970s, groups of women began to openly focus on creating a lesbian community in the city.

Lesbianism in the 1960s and 1970s was often coupled with activism and politics, and the lesbian community consisted of a range of different individuals. Some lesbians in Louisville chose to promote the lesbian cause through activism or feminism, while others limited their involvement to little or no activism or community connection at all. Some lesbians who spent the early years of their political involvement in Louisville working for equal rights under the labels of "feminist" or "CIVIL RIGHTS worker" eventually chose a path of total independence. Degrees of lesbian activism existed, including radical lesbianism, which strove to maintain a separate identity from other activist movements and to create a lesbian culture called "Lesbian Nation," a world that was self-sufficient and detached from patriarchal oppression. Probably a small minority of lesbians were "radical," but their influence was profound.

Lesbian cultural achievements include the first lesbian bar in Louisville, Mother's Brew. In addition to featuring live music by a local female band, River City Womyn, Mother's Brew hosted nationally known musicians, sponsored lectures by early lesbian leaders such as Rita Mae Brown and Kathie Sarachild, and housed a lesbian resource center that provided women with information about the development of lesbian activism. The Brew also influenced another significant element of lesbian culture in Louisville—softball. Softball teams were often sponsored by local BARS or women-owned businesses. Mother's Brew sponsored the city's only all-lesbian team, the Matriarchies.

Although Mother's Brew closed in 1978, lesbian culture was still strong throughout the following years. Forms of personal expression such as writing, works of art, clothing, and spirituality were encouraged by the lesbian community. Louisville photographer JEB became one of the most widely recognized artists in the community. She produced two photographic anthologies, *Eye to Eye: Portraits of Lesbians* and *Making a Way: Lesbians Out Front.* In 1988 a second all-woman band was started in Louisville. Carol Kraemer, Laura Shine, and Dana Shelter named the band CLD, representing the first letters of their first names. In the fall of 1988, Shine and Kraemer joined three other musicians to form Yer Girlfriend. The Lesbian Feminist Union (LFU) published *Free Our Sisters,* a collection of POETRY dedicated to "sisters who are imprisoned in the jails and asylums of the patriarchy." Lesbian groups also created their own childcare centers, food co-ops, health-care clinics, skills centers, and bookstores. Believing in financial as well as cultural independence, the community opened the Bluegrass Feminist Federal Credit Union in 1976. There was a small membership fee, and the services of the credit union ranged from savings accounts to supplying small loans to lesbians.

As a result of this expression of spirituality and community-mindedness, the Metropolitan Community church was founded nationally for homosexuals by Rev. Troy Perry. In Louisville the branch at 1432 Highland Ave. was started by two lesbians on September 9, 1972. The church is still in existence with current pastor Rev. Dee Dale, who has served since 1983.

The lesbian movement in Louisville was not completely disconnected from local and national political influence. In 1971 the Gay Alliance was formed to fight oppression and ignorance in Louisville; however, the majority of its members and officers were men, and the organization tended to exclude women's issues from its list of concerns. Feminist Cell was established to host consciousness-raising groups to discuss women's sexist treatment in the civil rights movement. The group lasted three years and published a newsletter called *Woman Kind.* However, straight members of Feminist Cell would not support the newly forming homosexual groups in the community. As a result, most lesbians left the organization. Feminist Lesbians of America was formed soon afterwards. This group sought an alternative to the local bar scene. The group did not initially have a political agenda but eventually embraced the concept of a Lesbian Nation.

The Lesbian Feminist Union (LFU), founded in 1974 by five women, initiated a movement in the mid-1970s toward greater rights for lesbians who also considered themselves feminists. The LFU was a direct result of lesbians' dissatisfaction with both gay liberation and the women's liberation movement. The group increased to fifty members within six months. The LFU encouraged members to seek a world free from racism, sexism, and economic inequality. Along with many projects such as attempting to establish a publishing company and jointly supporting the opening of lesbian-run businesses, LFU developed a library and ARCHIVES for the community, published a monthly newsletter, and eventually bought a house. However, because of a decline in membership and decrease of funds, LFU was forced to disband in 1979.

Called "the footsoldiers of every previous civil rights movement" by today's lesbian and gay leaders, these women were the initiators of Pride Week, AIDS support, and civil rights rallies. This early effort sparked the creation of the Greater Louisville Human Rights Coalition (GLHRC), which, in 1984, launched its effort to pass what came to be called the Fairness Amendment, to protect the rights of lesbian and gay citizens.

In 1978 the LFU held a conference with the theme of "Reunifying Our Nation." Unfortunately it did not prove sufficient to keep the group together. The organization eventually faded away as diversity within the group increased, radical and activist feminism lessened, and attacks on both gay and lesbian communities brought the two into alliance.

Since that time, lesbians and gays have primarily worked together to improve Louisville's homosexual community's situation. In 1981 Gays and Lesbians United for Equality (GLUE) served as an umbrella organization for all Louisville-area nonprofit groups that were supportive of gay rights. In 1986, following discussions with GLHRC members and the Kentucky American Civil Liberties Union, the Louisville and Jefferson County Human Relations Commission voted to recommend passage of this legislation to the BOARD OF ALDERMEN.

While the board chose not to follow the recommendation of the commission, the GLHRC was nonetheless an influential group. According to the curator of the Kentucky Gay and Lesbian Library and Archives, it was a fertile group for the development of future community leaders, and it helped bring about the first March for Justice in Louisville in 1987.

The early 1990s saw continuing efforts to gain equality in Louisville. Following the perceived threat from some members of the state legislature as well as local groups, the Kentucky Fairness Alliance (KFA) was formed in 1992. KFA seeks to "promote equality for all people regardless of their sexual orientation, educate the public about the lesbian and gay community, facilitate the passage of information between local and statewide efforts, and support local efforts to achieve equality." Fairness Alliance members in 1998 numbered over nine hundred in the Louisville area. Through the Alliance's educational and lobbying efforts, many pieces of legislation hostile to the lesbian and gay community were stopped, and KFA has established a positive relationship with most governmental officials.

In November 1994, some users of the LOUISVILLE FREE PUBLIC LIBRARY filed four complaints against the book, *Heather Has Two Mommies*, written by Leslea Newman. The book features a little girl whose parents are lesbians and explores examples of different family models. Library director Harriet Henderson said that the people who complained didn't want their children exposed to the lesbian relationship in the book. In late December 1994 it was decided by a committee of seven reviewers—who included library employees and outside reviewers—that the book would be retained.

Often working with KFA is the Louisville Fairness Campaign. This organization and its political action committee CFAIR (Committee for Fairness and Individual Rights) were created in 1991 to support the initiation and passage of the Fairness Amendment, which would prohibit discrimination in employment, housing, and public accommodations in Louisville on the basis of sexual orientation.

In 1995 the Fairness Campaign of Louisville promoted two narrower ordinances that would have banned only employment discrimination; thus it would have been illegal to fire, or not to hire, someone on the basis of sexual orientation. But these, too, were rejected by the board in a 7 to 4 vote. But the Fairness Amendment, in its broadest form (to prohibit discrimination in employment, housing, and public accommodations), received another hearing when it was reintroduced before the Board of Aldermen's Affirmative Action Committee on August 12, 1997. It was once again defeated. In addition to banning employment discrimination, it would have prohibited landlords from refusing to rent an apartment to someone just because she or he is gay. Also, a taxi driver could not refuse to transport, or a restaurant refuse to serve, someone on the basis of his or her sexual orientation. During past hearings on the measure, members of the Fairness Campaign have testified to numerous instances of discrimination, concluding that this amendment is needed to create equal treatment. However, the bill's opponents define the issue much differently—not as ending unfair treatment but as creating special rights for lesbian and gay residents. On January 26, 1999, the Board of Aldermen passed a bill banning employment discrimination based on sexual orientation. The two other proposals to the city's civil rights laws were not called up for a vote.

While Fairness Campaign members have usually faced an uphill battle, they have used a number of strategies to help secure passage of the amendment. Literature explaining the need for the amendment and countering anti-gay misinformation and stereotypes has been produced and disseminated to aldermen and the public. Project Fair Vote sponsors radio and TELEVISION ads and voter registration drives. Members and volunteers have canvassed door to door and offered public testimony about the unfair acts of discrimination they have encountered. Fairness Campaign leaders have engaged in coalition building with women's rights groups, African American groups, and area churches.

Like members of the Fairness Campaign and KFA, students at the UNIVERSITY OF LOUISVILLE are also actively promoting fairness and tolerance. Members of Common Ground, the campus organization for lesbians as well as gay, bisexual, and transsexual individuals and groups, frequently speak to classes, other student groups, and administrators about university policies, "coming out" issues, tolerance, AIDS awareness, and legal and workplace issues facing lesbian and gay people. In 1997, along with KFA, Common Ground cosponsored the annual Come Together Kentucky meetings that included more than thirty workshops aimed at education, leadership development, and HIV prevention.

See Jonathan Ned Katz, *Gay American History* (New York 1976); Joan Nastle, *A Restricted Country* (Ithaca, N.Y., 1988); Kathie Denise Williams, *Louisville's Lesbian Feminist Union* (Department of History, University of Louisville, 1995).

Marilyn Mote-Yale

LESCH, ALMA (WALLACE) (b Kevil, McCracken County, Kentucky, March 12, 1917; d Louisville, May 15, 1999). Fiber artist and teacher. Lesch was the daughter of Ruth (Burnley) and Rollie "Tot" Wallace. She received her B.S. degree from Murray State University in 1941 and a master's degree in education in 1962 from the UNIVERSITY OF LOUISVILLE. After retiring as a teacher of the third grade in the Louisville public school system, she taught textile arts at the LOUISVILLE SCHOOL OF ART (1961–78) and was adjunct professor at the University of Louisville (1975–82).

She became internationally known for her fabric collages, having exhibited in the United States, Canada, and Europe. In 1970 her classic text, *Vegetable Dyeing*, was published. In 1974 she was named a master craftsman by the American Crafts Council. In the same year she was chosen as one of five fiber artists to have their work chosen for the first World Crafts Exhibition in Toronto.

She received numerous awards including the Fellow Award from the Kentucky Guild of Artists and Craftsmen in 1986 and the Governor's Award for Lifetime Achievement in the Arts in 1987. Lesch's work is in many private collections and is represented in the collections of the SPEED ART MUSEUM, Evansville Museum of Art, Mint Museum (Charlotte), American Crafts Museum (New York City), and the Flint Institute of Art (Michigan). Her husband, Ted Lesch, a pharmacist and weaver, died in 1994. Alma Lesch is buried at Maple Lawn Cemetery in Paducah.

Mary Jane Benedict

LEVY BROTHERS. This menswear store, owned and operated for three generations by the Levy family, traced its history back to Henry and Moses Levy, who immigrated to America in 1853 from Nierstein, Germany. Beginning their retailing careers in rural Kentucky as peddlers, the brothers established a retail presence on Louisville's Market St. in 1861. In 1893 the Levy Brothers Building was completed at Third and MARKET Streets, where it currently stands. It is listed on the NATIONAL REGISTER OF HISTORIC PLACES. In 1908 the building was outlined by electric lights and, as a result, the phrase "Lit up like Levy's" became a part of Louisvillians' vocabularies. In 1955 the concern

Levy Brothers, northeast corner Third and Market Streets, 1940s.

established its first of four suburban locations at the Shelbyville Road Plaza. Others were to open at Bashford Manor Mall, Jefferson Mall, and Dixie Manor. In 1979 the family's 118-year retail presence at 235 W Market came to a close. Soon thereafter, as a result of a decreased involvement by the family, Levy's ceased all of its business operations in the community.

See Henry Levy scrapbooks, Filson Club Historical Society, Louisville.

Kenneth L. Miller

LEWIS, LOCKWOOD (b Kentucky, ca. 1891; d Louisville, October 24, 1953). Singer and bandleader. Little is known about the early life of Lewis, an African American, but by 1912 he was living in Louisville and working as a musician. Around 1918 he joined the John Embry Band on alto sax. During the early 1920s he led the Booker T. Washington Community Center Band and performed regularly with Louisville's JUG BANDS. In 1926 he left town to tour with the Fess Williams Orchestra. From 1927 to 1930 he led the Missourians, a JAZZ band from St. Louis that reputedly "could outswing anybody within earshot." In 1930 the Missourians became Cab Calloway's band, and Lewis returned to Louisville, where he performed with local bands and operated a music studio until his death.

See Gunther Schuller, *The Swing Era: The Development of Jazz, 1930–1945* (New York 1989).

Brenda K. Bogert

LEWIS AND CLARK EXPEDITION. The Lewis and Clark Expedition of 1803–6 generally is considered the most famous exploring venture in United States history and one of the most perfect examples of exploration in world history. Conceived by THOMAS JEFFERSON, it had been his hope for some twenty years to send a United States party into the unknown West of the North American continent, going as far as the Pacific Ocean if possible. The catalyst for the expedition was his fear that Great Britain would exploit and claim the Pacific Northwest. Jefferson wanted to learn more about what lay up the Missouri River and beyond its headwaters to the Pacific, try to confirm the presence of the fabled Northwest Passage, and promote United States trade with the Indians and possibly the Orient.

The leader of the expedition was Capt. Meriwether Lewis, on leave from the army while serving as Jefferson's private secretary. It was decided that a second officer was needed in case of Lewis's illness or death and to help maintain discipline. Jefferson recently had received a letter from his friend GEORGE ROGERS CLARK, who recommended his brother William for anything the president needed doing in the West. Lewis, because of this letter or on his own, remembered his former commanding officer and friend WILLIAM CLARK, who had resigned from the army in 1796 and returned to his home, MULBERRY HILL, near Louisville. Lewis asked Clark to be co-commander of the expedition in June 1803, and Clark accepted. Thus was formed one of the most famous duos in American history. On July 5, 1803, Lewis departed the capital for Pittsburgh via Harpers Ferry. By the end of August the keelboat for the trip finally had been completed, and Lewis left Pittsburgh for Louisville on August 31 with a temporary party. By the time Lewis arrived at Louisville on October 14, 1803, Clark had recruited some men. These, together with two Lewis had recruited, became known as the "nine young men from Kentucky" and were the nucleus of the Corps of Discovery, as the party was known.

These nine men, who were not all necessarily Kentuckians, were Charles Floyd (ca. 1782–1804), Nathaniel Hale Pryor (1772–1831), Reubin Field (ca. 1781–1822 or 1823, probably the latter), his brother Joseph Field (ca. 1780–1807), John Shields (1769–1809), George Gibson (d 1809), William Bratton (1778–1841), John Colter (ca. 1775–1813), and George Shannon (ca. 1785–1836).

They made important contributions to the success of the expedition, and several of them were among those receiving the highest praise of the captains. Floyd was fated to be the party's only fatality, Colter would gain fame as the "father of the Mountain Man," and Shannon would become a politician and judge. Clark's slave, York, became an unofficial member of the expedition and made important contributions to its success. In addition, five soldiers recruited from frontier posts are believed to have been Kentuckians. They were Hugh McNeal, William Werner, Joseph Whitehouse (b ca. 1775), Alexander Hamilton Willard (1778–1865), and Richard Windsor. Not only did half the members of this famous expedition have Kentucky connections, but almost one-third of them were from KENTUCKIANA.

The group stayed in Louisville and Clarksville for twelve days before setting off down the Ohio from the latter town on October 26, 1803. The starting point of the Lewis and Clark Expedition still is debated today, with St. Louis generally perceived as the point of origin; but only the captains and a couple of men actually were in St. Louis during the winter of 1803–4. Camp Dubois, where they wintered in 1803–4, also is considered a starting point, as is Pittsburgh, but the FALLS OF THE OHIO has a strong claim to this honor. It was here that Lewis and Clark actually joined forces, and it was here that the nucleus of the party was recruited. Clark himself considered Louisville the starting point.

After a winter of preparation and training, the Corps of Discovery set off up the Missouri on May 14, 1804. The group at this time consisted of thirty-two members of the permanent party, as those going all the way to the Pacific are known, and about twenty temporary members, traveling with the corps for assistance and support in ascending the river. The temporaries returned with the keelboat once the Mandan villages were reached. The fifty-five-foot keelboat was accompanied by two pirogues. By late October the party had reached the Mandan villages some sixteen hundred miles up the Missouri. The winter of 1804–5 among the Mandan brought brutal cold but a happy time. The Mandan were friendly. There was much visiting back and forth between their villages and Fort Mandan, the stockade where the corps wintered across the river; and the two groups hunted and traded with each other.

It was here that the captains met and hired the FRENCH-Canadian interpreter and trader Toussaint Charbonneau. The captains did not think much of Charbonneau's abilities but did appreciate those of his wife, the teenage Shoshone woman Sacagawea. Although the popular belief that she guided the explorers to the Rocky Mountains and beyond is incorrect, she provided valuable assistance as an interpreter and peace symbol and in recognizing a few landmarks of her homeland in the Three Forks re-

William Clark. Portrait by Joseph H. Bush.

gion of the Missouri.

On April 7, 1805, the permanent members set off up the river into what for white men truly was unknown territory. In June they arrived at the Great Falls, and for the next month made an eighteen-mile portage around the ten-mile stretch of waterfalls. By August the party was well into the foothills of the Rocky Mountains. They searched for the Shoshoni Indians, from whom they had to get horses if they were to cross the mountains. Contact finally was made on August 13, and, in a great stroke of luck, Sacagawea's brother Cameâhwait was the band's chief. This connection undoubtedly helped in the negotiations for the horses, as did the trade goods and the promises of more.

The trip across the Rockies proved to be some of the hardest and most miserable going of the entire expedition—not the easy mountain portage generally anticipated. At the end of the Lolo Trail, the corps encountered the Nez Percé Indians on September 20. A brief stay with the Nez Percé allowed some recuperation from the rigors of the ordeal and time to build dugout canoes for the trip down the Clearwater, Snake, and Columbia Rivers to the Pacific. On November 15, the corps reached its goal of the Pacific. The estuary of the Columbia is so wide that they had mistakenly believed they had sighted the ocean on November 7. Shortly after reaching the Pacific, they took a vote (including York and Sacagawea) that decided they would build their winter quarters on the south side of the Columbia.

The winter of 1805–6 was spent at Fort Clatsop. It was a miserable four months of rainy, gloomy WEATHER; poor food; poor relations with the local Indians; and homesickness mixed with anticipation of returning home. Fort Clatsop was abandoned on March 23, 1806, and the trek home prematurely begun. Snow in the Bitterroots forced the corps to be the guests of the Nez Percé for some six weeks.

On July 3, at Traveler's Rest on the eastern front of the Rocky Mountains, the captains divided the force in two, determined to follow different routes to the confluence of the Missouri and Yellowstone Rivers in order to maximize their exploring efforts. Lewis traveled due east with part of the corps to the Great Falls. He then went on a northern reconnaissance with George Drouillard and Reubin and Joseph Field up the Marias River toward Canada. Lewis and his men made a forced march back to the Missouri after a violent confrontation with a party of Blackfeet Indians in which two braves were killed, and reunited with the party that had stayed on the river. Clark and his detachment retraced part of the previous year's route and then cut overland to the upper reaches of the Yellowstone. Part of the group under Clark traveled down the river and encountered no problems. The party under Sergeant Pryor followed the Yellowstone with the horses that had not already been stolen by Crow Indians and had them soon stolen, but they safely reunited with Clark's party. The entire corps reunited on August 12, downstream from the mouth of the Yellowstone. Making excellent time traveling downstream on the Missouri, Lewis and Clark and men arrived in St. Louis on September 23, 1806. The captains settled accounts over the next few weeks and discharged the men on or about October 10.

In late October they set out with some of their men and an Indian delegation for Washington. They arrived in Louisville on November 5 and regaled family and friends with tales and souvenirs of their adventure. On November 8, Lewis and Clark visited with the Croghans at Locust Grove. At Louisville the captains parted company, continuing on to Washington at different times. The lives of the members of the Corps of Discovery after the expedition ranged from the successful to the tragic. A few enjoyed long lives and successful careers. Most returned to the obscurity they had emerged from when they joined the expedition. And a number of them, both the forgotten and the well-remembered, met premature, often violent, ends.

See Gary E. Moulton, ed., *The Journals of the Lewis and Clark Expedition,* 13 vols. (Lincoln, Neb., 1983–2000); Bernard DeVoto, ed., *The Journals of Lewis and Clark* (Boston 1953); George H. Yater and Carolyn S. Denton, *Nine Young Men from Kentucky*, supplement to *We Proceeded On,* WPO Publication No. 11 (May 1992); Stephen E. Ambrose, *Undaunted Courage: Meriwether Lewis, Thomas Jefferson, and the Opening of the American West* (New York 1996).

James J. Holmberg

LG&E ENERGY CORPORATION. In 1990, responding to the rapidly growing independent electric power business, the management of Louisville Gas and Electric Co. formed LG&E Energy Corp. to provide electric power and/or gas under negotiated private contracts to large industrial and business users. Such private contracts do not fall under utility regulatory constraints. Louisville Gas and Electric Co., a regulated public utility, became a subsidiary of the new corporation.

LG&E Energy's first move was to purchase Hudson Power Systems of California, a pioneer in the construction and operation of such private power plants selling energy under contract. The federal Energy Policy Act of 1992, designed to increase competition among utility companies, expanded the field for LG&E Energy and other similar entities created by traditional electric and gas companies. The corporation could now broker wholesale sales of power from any regulated utility to any part of the nation, a process known in the trade as merchant trading and sales. Roger Hale, CEO of LG&E Energy, noted, "The days of the traditional utility are over."

In 1994, for example, a brokered arrangement was made by LG&E Energy with the East Kentucky Power Cooperative to supply it with forty megawatts of power per hour for ten years. The power cooperative resells it to the Gallatin Steel plant in Warsaw, Kentucky. LG&E Energy can tailor its price to the market, since the contract is private and not regulated. East Kentucky Power Cooperative, which does not have enough capacity to provide all the power the steel plant needs, gained a good customer. The needed power comes from Louisville Gas and Electric Co., but, if demand in the Louisville area is too high to permit that, LG&E Energy can buy power anywhere in North America to meet the contract. However, in 1998, the company withdrew from merchant trading and sales because of the unpredictable volatility of that market. It expects to return to that market at some time in the future. Meanwhile it concentrates on marketing power from its own generating facilities.

In 1998 LG&E Energy merged with KU Energy Corp. of Lexington, formed by Kentucky Utilities Co. LG&E Energy is the surviving corporation. Kentucky Utilities Co. thus joined Louisville Gas and Electric as a regulated utility subsidiary of LG&E Energy.

The energy corporation in the late 1990s had operations in fourteen states, Canada, Spain, and Argentina. Through its two Kentucky regulated power companies it served some 630,000 gas and electric customers in 77 Kentucky counties and 5 counties in Virginia. In 1998 LG&E Energy executed a twenty-five-year lease of the electric-generating facilities of the Big Rivers Electric Corp. in Henderson, Kentucky, serving that company's member cooperatives totaling ninety thousand customers. It also gave LG&E Energy access to the seventeen hundred megawatts of generating capacity, increasing the amount of energy it has to sell in the wholesale market. On Feb. 28, 2000, the British-based energy company PowerGen announced plans to purchase LG & E for $3.2 billion and assume the company's $2.2 billion debt.

See LG&E *Energy Corporation 1997 Annual Report. Courier-Journal,* Nov. 17, 1993.

George H. Yater

LIBERTY STREET. Downtown street, approximately two and three-quarters of a mile long, lying south of Jefferson St. and north of Muhammad Ali Blvd., stretching from Baxter Ave. in the east to Roy Wilkins Ave. in the west. Originally called Green St., it once extended westward as far as Eighteenth St. Both names were significant. It was called Green St. because it was originally a long strip of grass used as common land where horses could graze. In 1911 the *Louisville Herald* ran a contest to rename the street. Because of the patriotic fever during WORLD WAR I, and the fact that the word *liberty* was a catch phrase at the time, the name Liberty St. was chosen. The official name change came on April 5, 1918.

The southeast corner of Fourth and Liberty Streets was the location of a THEATER that burned and then later the COURIER-JOURNAL Building (later the Will Sales Building) from 1876 to 1979. The *Courier-Journal* moved from this location one block east when the building was damaged by fire in 1907. The site is now occupied by the Brown & Williamson headquarters. The first Presbyterian Church (1836-1889) was located on Green St. on the same site on which the old Jefferson County Jail was built in 1905. It was listed on the NATIONAL REGISTER OF HISTORIC PLACES in 1973. The jail was replaced by a new facility on Jefferson St. in 1976, and the old jail was renovated in 1982 to house county offices and the Jefferson County Law Library. St. BONIFACE CHURCH, a German Catholic church established in 1838 is at 531 E. Liberty St. In 1848 the parish established the first parochial German school in the city on an adjoining lot. This was later converted into Liberty House, a shelter for homeless teens. In 1899 a new church was built.

Green St. was known as "Newspaper Row" in the mid-nineteenth century. On the north side of the street between Third and Fourth St. was the *LOUISVILLE JOURNAL*, a pro-Union paper. On the south side between the same two streets was the *LOUISVILLE COURIER*, a pro-Confederate paper. Before the name change, the street was known for a large number of SALOONS, GAMBLING establishments, and houses of PROSTITUTION. The United States Army required that the street be cleaned up as a prerequisite before building CAMP ZACHARY TAYLOR. Mayor GEORGE WEISSINGER SMITH (1917–21) cleaned it up for this as well as economic reasons.

The Jewish Hospital Medical Campus Office Building is at the corner of Floyd St., just north of the LOUISVILLE MEDICAL CENTER. Although the street is heavily characterized by commercial establishments, it does have some residential areas. During the late 1930s a federal housing project (Clarksdale) was built along the street east of Preston St. In this area is East Liberty Park. One of Louisville's former premier RESTAURANTS, Casa Grisanti, was on the street near Baxter.

LIBRARIES. In 1816 the General Assembly of Kentucky incorporated the Louisville Library Co., a joint stock company, under the administration of Mann Butler, Dr. William C. Galt, Brooke Hill, Hezekiah Hawley, and William Tompkins. In 1819 the library was located on the second floor of the east side of the courthouse on Jefferson St. and possessed five hundred books, most notably valuable histories acquired by Butler himself and an impressive collection of books on scientific subjects. The efforts of Butler and others to establish a useful and successful library in the city fell short, however, because of poor funding.

The most valuable books of the collection were lost, and those remaining were acquired by the city's next library at the KENTUCKY HISTORICAL SOCIETY, established in 1838. This library was also short-lived but did serve to connect the first library to the succession of libraries, passing the dwindling collection of the Louisville Library Co. to each new facility. The library also served to preserve some important documents from early Louisville and Kentucky history.

In 1840 a number of Louisville businessmen founded the Louisville Franklin Lyceum. This library attempted to create a circulating collection of books but was unable to become a permanent establishment. Not until 1842 was there a temporarily successful library in Louisville, instituted by a large number of investors headed by Simon S. Bucklin. During its first year it was known as the Mercantile Library and had acquired three thousand volumes, primarily on American history but also containing science, reference, and literature collections rivaling any public library in the country. As the library grew, it came to offer lecture courses along with this impressive collection of circulated texts. Still, and despite efforts to place the company in the hands of city officials, it was not long before the library weakened and was dispersed due to lack of financial support.

In 1847, as the Mercantile Library Association was dissolving, legislative permission was granted to form the "President, Directors, and company of the Louisville Library." This group struggled for the next three years to be granted a suitable location from the city, until in 1850 it was allowed to house the collection in the courthouse on the corner of Sixth and Jefferson Streets. The library then came under the control of the city, which appointed several directors to deal with the running expenses. However, the citizenry's interest in a public library seemed to wane.

In 1871 Louisville's most successful private library was founded by 217 members of the Louisville Library Association, each of whom donated either thirty dollars or twenty books deemed acceptable by the directors. Attorney Alexander G. Booth, the first president of the library, was especially instrumental in the early success of this library, located on the northwest corner of Third and Walnut (Muhammad Ali Blvd.) Streets.

Also in 1871 the Public Library of Kentucky was founded in Louisville as a free public institution for the state, funded initially by the selling of stock. Books were obtained in large part from the YOUNG MEN'S CHRISTIAN ASSOCIATION'S library that had become the benefactor of many of the city's earlier attempts at libraries.

In 1902 construction of the LOUISVILLE FREE PUBLIC LIBRARY was begun with the help of Andrew Carnegie's offer to build a library for any city willing to handle the operating costs of the facilities. On July 24, 1908, the main library building at Fourth and YORK Streets was opened to the public. Carnegie and the city also worked together to build eight branches in the city.

The Louisville Free Public Library system was an ambitious one from the beginning, training librarians to develop a completely professional staff and opening branches specifically for the use of AFRICAN AMERICANS. The system grew rapidly until the FLOOD OF 1937 that damaged twenty-five thousand books and the museum collection in the Main Library's basement.

In the 1940s and 1950s, the task of bringing the library back up to standards and continuing to expand its services was trusted to the leadership of C.R. Graham. During this time the library received national recognition for its circulation of audiovisual materials and was an early pioneer in the use of microforms.

In 1965 the library's services were extended to include more of Jefferson County, expanding to thirty-one branches and two bookmobiles by the early 1970s. This growth, however, was more than the library's finances could handle, and several attempts were made to fund the library through increased taxes. In 1993 a committee made up of city, county, and library commission representatives developed a five-year plan that would get the library's budget back in order while increasing hours and staff, relocating and improving branches, and increasing services for children.

Louisville's Free Public Library has been able to maintain its successful operations due in part to the volunteer work and funds provided by the Friends of the Library and the Library Foundation. Funding from these institutions has allowed the library to increase the availability of research technology and books.

The Louisville Free Public Library is one of many libraries in the metropolitan area. Taken together they provide every resident with books and other learning materials for research and leisure reading. Technology has transformed the use of libraries as computers expand resources and facilitate retrieval capabilities.

Bullitt County Library. The Bullitt County Library was founded January 24, 1924, by the Bullitt County Women's Club. A room in Saint Aloysius Church housed the facility until it went under in 1945. SHEPHERDSVILLE was then without library facilities until 1954 when the citizens saw fit to establish library services, even if they were unsure where to house the facility. In 1955 Dorothea Stottman was hired as the first librarian and would follow the library during its many relocations over the next twenty-nine years. On July 21, 1963, the former home of Dr. Ridgway of Shepherdsville was made available and became the Ridgway Memorial Library. Four years later a library tax was enacted, providing funding for a modern facility that opened in January 1973. Stottman continued to serve as librarian until 1984. By the late 1970s the library had branches in Mount Washington, Lebanon Junction, and HILLVIEW.

Oldham County Public Library. In 1944 Mary F. Duerson donated her house and property in LaGrange for a public library to be established in memory of her daughter, who had served as a teacher in OLDHAM COUNTY. In 1968 the Kentucky Department of Libraries and Archives aided the expansion of the facilities into the Oldham County Public Library. Following a petition for a library tax in 1969, a new library was completed in 1974. Because of the greatly increased POPULATION of Oldham County in the following years, the South Oldham Library was opened in CRESTWOOD in 1981. In 1990 the Mahan branch of the library was opened in Goshen.

Shelby County Public Library. In 1898 the Woman's Club in SHELBYVILLE donated two hundred books to a library facility above a former fire station. In 1902 Shelbyville took advantage of Andrew Carnegie's offer and had the Woman's Club collection and other donated books moved to a permanent facility. In 1962 a taxing system was developed within the county to support the library. The original building of the library has been expanded three times, the most recent improvement was completed in 1997.

Spencer County Public Library. The first library in SPENCER COUNTY was built in 1909 on land donated to the city of TAYLORSVILLE, where it was still located in 2000. The building was funded by the Ambassador Circle of the King's Daughters and later provided for financially by the Fidelis Circle of King's Daughters. In the 1920s the library was closed because of lack of interest and financial difficulties. In 1966 the public library facilities of the county were reestablished there as the city of Taylorsville and the county agreed to fund the continuing operations.

Clark County, Indiana, Public Library. For the first sixty years of its existence, beginning in 1907, the library service of Charlestown, Indiana, and the surrounding area was located in the Charlestown township trustee's office. In 1966 a board was organized to construct a permanent building that was dedicated February 9, 1973. In 1977 the library received a grant that allowed branches to be established in Borden, Henryville, New Washington, and SELLERSBURG, and to begin bookmobile services. A new library district had to be formed in 1979 to continue service. In 1994 a branch was opened in Utica.

In Jeffersonville local women's literary clubs and other supporters joined to form a library association with a small collection of books from the township trustee's office library. In 1902 the association contacted Andrew Carnegie to secure funding for library facilities. Arthur Loomis designed this new structure, completed in 1904 and opened the following year. This building, too, would be outpaced by the growing demands of the community, and in 1970 the new Jeffersonville Township Public Library was opened at 211 E Court Ave. In 1986 circulation at the library was automated, and in 1997 the library offered Internet access. A branch library in Clarksville was opened in 1993.

Floyd County, Indiana, Public Library. Library facilities have been available in the Floyd County area since 1854 when the NEW ALBANY township trustees opened a private library. In 1884 the oldest continuous public library in the metropolitan area was opened in New Albany. Since that time the library has moved to five different locations. One of these buildings, opened with the help of Andrew Carnegie, in 1999 housed the Floyd County Museum, a department of the library. The new main library was opened in 1969 and has continued to expand as demand for library facilities has increased.

Harrison County, Indiana, Public Library. The history of libraries in Harrison County begins with the law library for the state of Indiana in CORYDON, at that time the state capital, established in 1820 as the first such library in the state. Public libraries, however, were not developed in the area until at least 1839, at which time there is evidence of a Harrison County Library. This library operated until about 1878. In February 1909 the Corydon Library Association announced the renting of the second floor of the Luckett building for a reading room and library. The facilities were moved to a number of such rooms around the town until it became clear that a separate building would be necessary for the library, and the Carnegie Corp. was contacted. In 1914 the town's collection was moved to the new building, which was still its home in 1999. In 1988 the building was renovated, and the Heather Eckart Children's Center was opened in the basement.

Scott County, Indiana, Public Library. While records do not allow further inquiry, Scott County has had public library services since at least 1851, one year before a law provided for county and township libraries in the area. But libraries established at that time in Scottsburg and the surrounding area were not provided with adequate funding for new books, and the old ones deteriorated, so, in the years following the CIVIL WAR, no public libraries could be found in Scott County. In 1917 Dr. Theophilus E. Biery founded a collection of books to be circulated from his office for the public of Scottsburg, using seventy-five hundred dollars collected for that purpose by a law enacted in 1818. Also in 1917 Mrs. Rachel Wells, president of the Civic League of Scottsburg, presented a petition to the county commissioners for a grant of five hundred thousand dollars for the maintenance of a free public library. Andrew Carnegie was instrumental in the funding of the library facilities built in 1919 at its current site in Scottsburg. Since that time, the Scott County Public Library has continued to grow in its physical size and in the number of services it has provided to the community.

In 1999 the following libraries existed in the Louisville metropolitan area:

KENTUCKY

Bellarmine College W.L. Lyons Brown Library, 2001 Newburg Rd
Church of Jesus Christ of Latter Day Saints Genealogy Library, 1000 Hurstbourne Pkwy
Dorothea Stottman Library, 1251 Hillview Blvd
Filson Club Historical Society Research Library, 1310 S Third St
International Hand Library, 100 E Liberty St
J.B. Speed Art Museum Library, 2035 S Third St
Jefferson Community College Library, 109 E Broadway
Jefferson Community College Library Southwest, 1000 Community College Dr
Jefferson County Law Library, 514 W Liberty St
Jewish Community Center Naamani Library, 3600 Dutchmans Ln
Louisville Free Public Library Bon Air, 2816 Del Rio Pl
Louisville Free Public Library Crescent Hill, 2762 Frankfort Ave
Louisville Free Public Library Fern Creek, 5725 Bardstown Rd
Louisville Free Public Library Highlands–Shelby Park, 1250 Bardstown Rd
Louisville Free Public Library Iroquois, 601 W Woodlawn Ave
Louisville Free Public Library Jeffersontown, 10635 Watterson Trail
Louisville Free Public Library Main Branch, 301 York St
Louisville Free Public Library Middletown, 200 Juneau Dr
Louisville Free Public Library Okolona, 7709 Preston Hwy
Louisville Free Public Library Portland, 3305 Northwestern Pkwy
Louisville Free Public Library Saint Matthews, 3940 Grandview Ave
Louisville Free Public Library Shawnee, 3912 W Broadway
Louisville Free Public Library Shively Newman, 3920 Dixie Hwy
Louisville Free Public Library Southwest Region, 10375 Dixie Hwy
Louisville Free Public Library Valley Station, 375 Dixie Hwy
Louisville Free Public Library Western Branch, 604 Tenth St
Louisville Free Public Library Westport, 8100 Westport Rd
Louisville Presbyterian Seminary Library, 1044 Alta Vista Rd
Our Lady of the Rosary Library, 4016 Preston Hwy
Southern Baptist Theological Seminary Library, 2825 Lexington Rd
Spalding University Library, 853 Library Ln (Main Campus, S Fourth St)
University of Louisville Dwight Anderson Music Library, Belknap Campus
University of Louisville Margaret M. Bridwell Art Library, Belknap Campus
University of Louisville Ekstrom Library, Belknap Campus
University of Louisville Kersey Library, Belknap Campus
University of Louisville Kornhauser Medical School Library, Health Sciences Center
University of Louisville Law Library, Belknap Campus
University of Louisville Speed School Library, Belknap Campus
Bullitt County Public Library, 113 Snapp St, Mt Washington
Bullitt County Ridgway Memorial Library, 127 N Walnut St, Shepherdsville
Bullitt County Lebanon Junction Library, 276 Main St, Lebanon Junction

Oldham County Public Library, Main Library, Mahan Library, 12501 Harmony Landing Rd
Oldham County Public Library South Oldham County, 6720 W Highway 146
Shelby County Library, 309 Eighth St, Shelbyville
Spencer County Library, 168 Taylorsville Rd, Taylorsville

METROPOLITAN INDIANA
Clark County Borden Public Library, 117 W Main St, Borden
Clark County Charlestown Library, 51 Clark Rd, Charlestown
Clark County Henryville Public Library, 214 W Main St, Henryville
Clark County Jeffersonville Township Public Library, 211 E Court Ave, Jeffersonville
Clark County New Washington Library, 210 Poplar St, New Washington
Clark County Sellersburg Library, 430 N Indiana Ave, Sellersburg
Harrison County Corydon Public Library, 117 E Beaver St, Corydon
Indiana University Southeast, 4201 Grant Line Rd, New Albany
New Albany–Floyd County Public Library, 180 W Spring St, New Albany
Scott County Public Library, 108 Main St, Scottsburg

See United States Works Progress Administration, Kentucky; *Libraries and Lotteries* (Cynthiana, Ky. 1944).

LIEDERKRANZ SOCIETY. The Louisville Liederkranz, one of the earliest singing societies in the United States, was founded in 1848 by German immigrants who brought with them their love of music and fellowship. These "Forty-Eighters" were closely connected with the political refugees from the 1848 revolutions in Europe. In 1849 the Louisville Liederkranz collaborated with choral clubs of Cincinnati and Madison, Indiana, in establishing the North American Saengerbund. Among the diverse singing societies flourishing in Louisville in the nineteenth century, the Liederkranz held a position of leadership. Its members were performers and sponsors of choral concerts, ORCHESTRAS, bands, coffee concerts, opera, German THEATER, galas, and folk festivals. They succeeded in making music an essential part of the cultural life of Louisville. The Liederkranz sponsored National Saengerfests in Louisville in 1866, 1877, and 1914.

In 1873 the society moved into the first hall of its own, having previously rented various places for its meetings. Liederkranz Hall was located on MARKET St. between First and Second Streets. Twenty-three years later, a new Liederkranz Hall opened on the northwest corner of Sixth and Walnut (now Muhammad Ali Blvd.). That structure burned down on January 6, 1900, but was rebuilt at the same location.

Due to the hostility toward those of German descent that arose after WORLD WAR I, the Liederkranz Society voted to suspend their activities. Meetings were resumed at the end of 1921, taking place in private homes until 1923, when meetings were moved to Liberty Hall at Second and Walnut. The singing group continued through the 1930s and 1940s. By the 1950s they still sang together but no longer presented concerts. The Louisville Liederkranz dissolved in 1959 after the death of its last president, Fred Nuetzel. Among the society's prominent members were Jacob Dolfinger, Georg Zoeller, J.J. Fischer, LOUIS HAST, G.S. Schuhmann, August Hollenbach, and Karl Schmidt.

See Erna O. Gwinn, "The Liederkranz in Louisville, 1848–1877," M.A. thesis, University of Louisville, 1973; "The Liederkranz in Louisville, 1848–1877," *Filson Club History Quarterly* 49 (July 1975): 276–90; "The Liederkranz in Louisville, 1877–1959," *Filson Club History Quarterly* 55 (Jan. 1981):40–59.

Erna O. Gwinn

The Liederkranz Society of Louisville, 1865.

LIGHT AND POWER. Louisville was among the earliest cities to have gaslights on its streets and in homes and businesses. The gas was provided by the Louisville Gas and Water Co., chartered on February 15, 1838. The company had the right to construct a waterworks if Louisville residents gave their approval at a public meeting, but this privilege was later withdrawn.

BANKING privileges were also given in the charter. The country was deep in the financial panic of 1837, and President Andrew Jackson had vetoed the renewal of the charter of the Bank of the United States. Banks were set up and notes issued independently that other banks would not honor. Businessmen were reluctant to accept any kind of bank notes. By granting the new company banking powers, the commonwealth assured that the Louisville Gas and Water Co. would be able to collect fees for its services.

The state charter also stated that the company should provide gas lights and fixtures used in lighting the streets for a sum not to exceed twenty dollars a year for each gaslight. To aid the infant enterprise, the city of Louisville subscribed for more than nine thousand shares of stock and held them for seventy-five years, earning handsome dividends.

On Christmas Day 1839 a crowd gathered at the home of L.L. Shreve, president of the Louisville Gas and Water Co., on Jefferson St. between Fourth and Fifth Streets, to watch the lighting of the first residential gaslight in Louisville. That same year gas lighting made the waterfront a much safer place. Louisville was the first city west of the Allegheny Mountains to have gaslight and only the fifth city to have gaslight in the United States. John Jeffrey, the first engineer of the Louisville Gas and Water Co., was an Englishman who had learned engineering in London, where the world's first gas street lamps were installed on Pall Mall in 1806. Jeffrey was in charge of building the works for the new company.

The gas, made by roasting coal at high temperatures in airtight ovens, was to be "of such purity as not to be offensive or injurious to health" (1838 *Acts,* Chapter 824). To this end the gas was "scrubbed" to remove ammonia, a by-product. Tar and coke were also by-products and found a ready market. The gas was pumped into large storage tanks called gas holders. The gas works was on Jackson St. at its crossing of BEARGRASS CREEK before that stream was diverted by the upriver Beargrass Cutoff in the 1850s. Coal barges from Pittsburgh were taken up the creek to the plant. Although natural gas was known to exist, no technology had been developed to transport it long distances.

When it was obvious that no waterworks was to be built at that time, the state legislature revoked this privilege in January 1842. The same act amended the charter by eliminating banking privileges and changing the name to Louisville Gas Co. The first streetlights were put into operation in 1840, confined to the area between First to Ninth Streets and Water to Walnut (Muhammad Ali Blvd.) Streets. In 1842 Louisvillian James Russell exulted that the lights made "the streets lighter than the full moon....Gas is employed in all the churches and in numerous stores and houses . . . the gas works are a great curiosity" (John T. Flanagan, "Six Letters by James Russell," *Journal of the Illinois Historical Society* [Spring 1951]: 36). Still, some Louisvillians mistrusted gas and would not allow it above the first floor of their residences.

Louisville's POPULATION was 10,341 in the 1830 federal census; by 1840 it was 21,240. In 1850 the population had doubled again to 43,194. These gains can be attributed in part to Louisville's expansion of gaslight. The streets were safe, and the presence of gaslight in homes made the community look prosperous and inviting. The general use of streetlights had the additional effect of reducing crime and increasing business. The *Louisville Public Advertiser* noted on October 14, 1838, that stores would be able to stay open twelve hours instead of eight. By 1848 the business district had 461 gas streetlights, and by 1859 it had added another 464, all fed by 35 miles of underground piping.

In the decades after the CIVIL WAR, the Louisville Gas Co. entered an era of expansion as the city grew in population and territory, passing the hundred-thousand mark in 1870. With a burgeoning market, competition soon appeared. James S. Lithgow visited the Brush Co. in Cleveland, Ohio; and on November 15, 1881, he and Thomas W. Tobin formed the Brush Electric Light Co. at the Lithgow Foundry at Clay and Main Streets. Their foundry had its blast each day from 2:00 to 4:00 P.M. Lithgow and Tobin planned to use the steam left over from the blast to generate electricity from dusk until 1:00 A.M. Nevertheless, Brush went bankrupt.

The Citizens Gas Light Co. entered the market in 1885, but Louisville Gas obtained a restraining order that prevented the newcomer from manufacturing or vending gas in Louisville. The so-called "Gas War" was not settled until the U.S. Supreme Court ruled in favor of the Citizens Co. on December 7, 1885.

More serious competition also appeared. Natural gas had been discovered in nearby Meade County in 1865, and in 1887 the first attempts were made to exploit this resource. The Union Gas Co. drilled a well in July of that year, but, before it could be capped, the gas caught fire, sending flames forty feet into the air. STEAMBOATS took hundreds of excursionists to Meade County to see the spectacle. The Kentucky Rock Gas Co. was the first to complete a pipeline to Louisville in the fall of 1888. The gas boom soon crashed, however, as the Meade County reserves proved inadequate. Reorganized as the Kentucky Heating and Lighting Co., the former Rock Gas Co. constructed its own gas production facility in Louisville.

Another competitive development—electric lighting—was also looming at this time. In 1876 the LOUISVILLE INDUSTRIAL EXPOSITION (predecessor of the grander SOUTHERN EXPOSITION), at Fourth and Chestnut Streets, was illuminated by gas in its first years but by electric arc lights in its last three years. The Exposition featured an arc dynamo, loaned by the Wallace Farmer Electric Manufacturing Co. Dr. C.L. Mees, who came to Louisville as professor of chemistry and physics at Male High School, convinced the company to leave the equipment so that he could experiment with this primitive form of electric lighting. He managed to put the entire contraption onto a steamboat, making night excursions more exciting and night handling of cargo possible. The lights also scared many on the shore who first saw the brilliant illumination moving along the OHIO RIVER. Hence, boat owners were not inclined to embrace the new technology. Arc lighting was also used for theatrical effects in Louisville and to make dances brighter. Dr. Mees had to return the equipment in June 1877, and his experiments ended. Arc lighting would continue to be the electric lighting in Louisville for several more years.

The first commercial electric arc lamp in Louisville was switched on on Christmas Eve 1881 in Denunzio's Fruit Market on Jefferson St. In December 1882, James Clark and Associates founded the United States Electric Light Co. in Louisville to install electrical generating equipment at the Louisville Gas Co. This was the first company to use the incandescent lamp, invented by THOMAS EDISON in 1879. Arc lights were too brilliant for use except in large spaces. Incandescent lamps were to become the standard streetlight in the 1890s.

It was Edison's incandescent bulb that was to make interior lighting common. Louisvillians were introduced to it—and dazzled by it—at the Southern Exposition of 1883–87, with its forty-five thousand incandescent bulbs, plus some arc lights. Thomas Edison returned to the city to throw the switch to light the thousands of incandescent bulbs at the huge industrial exhibition. Reporters noted that the electric lights did not give off excessive heat, had no dangerous open flame, and did not consume oxygen. In addition to the general lighting, individual booth sponsors wanted electric lights in their exhibits. The generators for the Exposition could accommodate them. The entire installation had been supervised by Col. H.M. Byllesby.

The first large installation by the Louisville Electric Light Co. was inaugurated on Christmas Eve 1883. The next day the *COURIER-JOURNAL* reported, "The electric light was in use on Fourth Avenue and on Market and Jefferson Streets. You could tell the old-timer by the way he dodged it." Several stores were "ablaze with daylight," the newspaper added, noting that the most elaborate display was on Jefferson St. at John and James Whallen's Buckingham Theater, a noted BURLESQUE house. The new electric lights often went off before one o'clock, yet they were enthusiastically installed on the waterfront and in the GALT HOUSE and downtown stores. Some people claimed that merchants locked workmen in their stores overnight as an incentive to finish the wiring as soon as possible.

The first Louisville business use of the incandescent bulbs was on May 10, 1883, at a woolen mill in BUTCHERTOWN. Seemingly, Louisville would be in the forefront of electrified cities. The post of electrical inspector was created in 1888, and the first electric streetcar ran on Louisville streets on September 21, 1889. In the 1890s the incandescent light slowly began to replace gas in residential, business, and industrial settings. To meet this challenge, the Louisville Gas Co. in 1890 acquired the electric light company as a subsidiary and in 1891 erected the first large-scale electric generating station in the city at Fourteenth and Magazine Streets.

Gas companies and electric companies proliferated throughout the 1890s, generating power for their own use and selling the excess mostly to nearby businesses. After the turn of the century H.M. Byllesby and Co. of Chicago took over management of the Louisville Gas and Electric Co. Byllesby had built a team of skilled technicians, and he ran a number of utilities across the country.

Other electric power companies appeared, including the Citizens Light and Power Co. in 1890. This company was merged on April 1, 1903, with the Louisville Electric Light Co. to form the Louisville Lighting Co., continuing as the electrical arm of the Louisville Gas Co. A newcomer, the Kentucky Electric Co., was formed in 1906 and competed so successfully that it was able to erect a large generating station on the riverfront between Second and Third Streets. In 1913, the two gas companies and two electric companies were merged as the Louisville Gas and Electric Co. The riverfront station of the Kentucky Electric Co. became the Riverside station of LG&E and in the late 1990s remained as a standby source of power.

Within a short time the LG&E system was providing thirty-seven thousand customers with gas and nineteen thousand customers with electricity. Rising demand for both gas and electricity necessitated infrastructure investments. H.M. Byllesby was specifically charged with constructing a pipeline to the West Virginia gas fields. A gas pipeline 12 inches in diameter and 178 miles long (the longest gas line built at that time) was completed in 1914 to bring natural gas from eastern Kentucky and West Virginia.

Continuing concern over developing reliable sources of supply led to the steady acquisition of coal mines and gas wells, and a new manufactured gas plant was built on River Rd. in the mid-1920s. Demand for gas increased 100 percent every four years from 1914 to 1926. A hydroelectric generating plant, powered by the FALLS OF THE OHIO, was completed in 1927 as part of construction of a new dam at the falls by the U.S. Army Corps of Engineers.

During January 1937 and the Great Flood, Louisville Gas & Electric maintained 50 percent of its gas service and in less than six weeks had its electric generators back on line. Both of the company's plants were either partially or entirely flooded, but employees worked nonstop, many of them camping in the crippled facilities.

By 1938 most of the 140 individual steam power plants in the city in 1914 had disappeared. In 1939 the board of directors ordered two twenty-five-thousand-kilowatt steam-powered electrical generators. Two weeks later, in anticipation of the war that was to come, the federal government banned all utility expansion projects. LG&E's contract was one of the few that would be filled, enabling the company to build and open the Paddy's Run generating station. Located southwest of Louisville at the site of the confluence of Paddy's Run Stream and the Ohio River, Paddy's Run Station began operation in 1942. The additional capacity enabled LG&E to be designated a national defense utility and helped Louisville to meet its normal growth requirements.

The GREAT DEPRESSION brought profound change, reducing demand while increasing regulatory standards, but LG&E used this time to prepare for future demands. By the time of WORLD WAR II, the company was well positioned to respond to increased wartime demands and, later, to the postwar building and manufacturing boom. RUBBERTOWN developed to manufacture neoprene, butadiene, and other synthetics for the war effort. Airplanes, trucks, uniforms, medical supplies, and hundreds of other goods were churned out. Factories and power to run them were in place to turn out the consumer goods everyone wanted as soon as the war was won. The city had never known such growth and prosperity, even in frontier days.

Cane Run Station was constructed in the early 1950s in response to Louisville's booming electricity needs during the "dynamic decade" of progress and growth. LG&E purchased more than six hundred acres of land in 1951 located on the Ohio River about three miles down from Paddy's Run and seven miles southwest of Louisville. Construction of the Cane Run coal-fired generating plant was started in 1952 to help meet the demand for electricity by industries that had located in the city during World War II.

Appliance Park, constructed in 1952 by the General Electric Co. (GE), was served by LG&E and located on about a thousand acres near BUECHEL. The park was committed to planning for community growth and anticipating future needs of government, industry, and private customers. GE became LG&E's largest customer, using more than 440 million kilowatt hours of electricity and 570 million cubic feet of gas each year. Also in the 1950s LG&E added Reddy Communication's personification of the value of electric energy, Reddy Kilowatt, and a blue natural gas flame symbol to its simple "Pioneers in Public Service" shield to create a new version of the company's logo. The Reddy Kilowatt trademark, established in 1957, was adapted to many different aspects of LG&E's operations through the years.

The 1960s were equally as successful as the previous decade. In 1964 LG&E became the first company in the electric utility industry to use new jet engines to drive existing generators. The company installed four jet engines at Waterside, the oldest existing station in Louisville, to replace obsolete coal-fired steam boilers and turbines to run units seven and eight, two standby generators.

In addition, in 1969 the city began construction of Mill Creek Station. In 1967 LG&E purchased a 415-acre site, located on the Ohio River near KOSMOSDALE, Kentucky, about 10 miles downstream from Cane Run Station, for a new electric generating plant. Four generators were eventually built at Mill Creek Station, ranging in capacity from 330,000 to 495,000 kilowatts.

On March 19, 1972, disaster struck the LG&E's Ohio Falls Station. Several barges broke loose from their tow and floated straight towards LG&E's Ohio Falls Station. One barge settled against the plant's headworks; the other lodged in the tainter gates of the dam. The second barge carried four tanks of liquid chlorine that were eventually pumped out on April 16 into a waiting tank barge under the careful scrutiny of military personnel. PORTLAND was evacuated for the day while the unloading operation was successfully completed. Two years later, on April 3, 1974, several TORNADOES touched down in the Louisville area, causing massive damage. The tornadoes severed all the lines that interconnected LG&E with other electric utilities. Twenty-nine of the company's substations were rendered inoperative, and about eighty-four thousand electric customers were without power. Fortunately, LG&E's electric generating stations were undamaged; the company's problems were confined to transmission and distribution facilities. The company's entire cost of damages caused by the tornadoes totaled $2 million.

A few months later, LG&E added a closed-condenser circulating water system with a mechanical draft-cooling tower to unit two at Mill Creek Station. The cooling system, which reuses the condensation in steam heat produced by the plant, limited the amount of heat discharged into the OHIO RIVER, thus avoiding any harm to aquatic life. The cooling systems, which are an integral part of LG&E's new generating plants, were not the only significant environmental action taken by the company. In the early 1970s, the company decided to begin an extensive research and development program on sulfur removal equipment. Coal, the primary source of energy for LG&E's generating plants, produces a large amount of sulfur when burned, causing harm to the environment and contributing to air pollution. In compliance with the Clean Air Act of 1970, LG&E helped to develop a system known as a scrubber, which removes sulfur oxides from stack emissions produced by coal in the electric generation process. The success of the scrubbers led to LG&E's introduction of technology for the disposal of sludge and fly ash, which are by-products of the removal of stack-gas pollution. In 1976, LG&E received a research grant of about $2 million from the Environmental Protection Agency for a program to develop practical and environmentally acceptable methods for the disposal of waste materials. The establishment of the company's first waste-processing plant followed in 1980.

In 1982 LG&E launched Project WARM to weatherize homes of elderly and handicapped persons. Winter help was begun in 1983. LG&E worked with various civic groups to ensure that heating bills were paid and no one was cut off from heat in the winter. In 1986, in conjunction with the Kentucky Cabinet for Human Resources, WARM II expanded weatherization service to low-income families. In 1984 LG&E's messages began appearing on commercial TELEVISION stations, as Louie the Lightning Bug promoted electric safety to children.

In 1990, responding to the rapidly growing independent electric power business, the management of Louisville Gas and Electric Co. formed LG&E Energy Corp. to provide electric power and/or gas under negotiated private contracts to large industrial and business users. Such private contracts do not fall under utility regulatory constraints. Louisville Gas and Electric Co., a regulated public utility, became a subsidiary of the new corporation.

LG&E Energy's first move was to purchase Hudson Power Systems of California, a pioneer in the construction and operation of such private power plants selling energy under contract. The federal Energy Policy Act of 1992, designed to increase competition among utility companies, expanded the field for LG&E Energy and other similar entities created by traditional electric and gas companies. The corporation could now broker wholesale sales of power from any regulated utility to any part of the nation, a process known in the trade as merchant trading and sales. Roger Hale, CEO of LG&E Energy, noted, "The days of the traditional utility are over" (*COURIER-JOURNAL*, Nov. 17, 1993).

In 1994, for example, a brokered arrangement was made by LG&E Energy with the East Kentucky Power Cooperative to supply it with forty megawatts of power per hour for ten years. The power cooperative resells it to the Gallatin Steel plant in Warsaw, Kentucky. LG&E Energy can tailor its price to the market, since the contract is private and not regulated. East Kentucky Power Cooperative, which does not have enough capacity to provide all the power the steel plant needs, gained a good customer. The needed power comes from Louisville Gas and Electric Co., but if demand in the Louisville area is too high to permit that, LG&E Energy can buy power anywhere in North America to meet the contract. However, in 1998, the company withdrew from merchant trading and sales because of the unpredictable volatility of that market. It expects to return to that market at some time in the future. Meanwhile in concentrates on marketing power from its own generating facilities.

In 1998 LG&E Energy merged with KU Energy Corp. of Lexington, formed by Kentucky Utilities Co. LG&E Energy is the surviving corporation. Kentucky Utilities Co. thus joined Louisville Gas and Electric as a regulated utility subsidiary of LG&E Energy.

The energy corporation in the late 1990s had operations in fourteen states, Canada, Spain, and Argentina. Through its two Kentucky regulated power companies it served some 630,000 gas and electric customers in 77 Kentucky counties and 5 counties in Virginia. In 1997 LG&E served 356,082 electric customers and 283,690 gas customers in 17 Kentucky counties, with the greatest concentration in Jefferson County.

In 1998 LG&E Energy executed a twenty-five-year lease of the electric generating facilities of the Big Rivers Electric Corp. in Henderson, Kentucky, serving that company's member cooperatives totaling ninety thousand customers. It also gave LG&E Energy access to the seventeen hundred megawatts of generating capacity, increasing the amount of energy it has to sell in the wholesale market. On Feb. 8, 2000, the British-based energy company PowerGen announced plans to purchase LG&E for $3.2 billion and assume the company's $2.2 billion debt.

See LG&E *Energy Corporation 1997 Annual Report; Courier-Journal,* Feb. 13, 1938; *Light Years: A History of Louisville Gas and Electric Company, 1838–1988* (Louisville 1988); George W. Morris, "Gas and Electric Light Companies," *Memorial History of Louisville* (Chicago and New York 1896); George H. Yater, *Two Hundred Years at the Falls of the Ohio* (Louisville 1979); *LG&E: The First 148 Years,* University of Louisville Archives and Records Center.

Otis Amanda Dick
John S. Gillig

LIMERICK. This neighborhood, originally an enclave of IRISH immigrants, extends roughly from Breckinridge St. on the north to Oak St. on the south, and from the CSX (formerly Louisville & Nashville) railroad tracks and Ninth St. on the west to Fifth St. on the east. The community began to take shape about 1860 on a largely undeveloped tract owned by William A. and Samuel A. Churchill. The tract was in close proximity to the growing L&N repair shops, freight yard, and depot. This provided

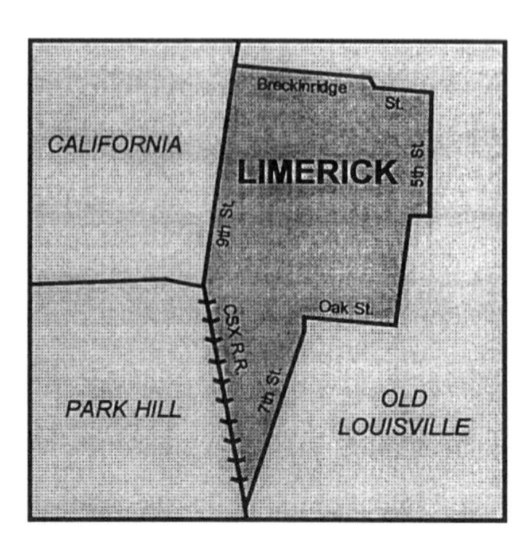

employment for the newcomers, many of whom were from the PORTLAND neighborhood.

ST. LOUIS BERTRAND CATHOLIC CHURCH, established in 1866 and staffed by priests of the Dominican order, became the focal point for the developing area. The original wood-framed church on Seventh St. was replaced by an impressive stone structure on Sixth St. in 1872. Much of the hard labor on the church was contributed by parishioners.

The name "Limerick" was adopted in 1869 at a meeting called for that purpose by the Reverend D.J. Meagher, pastor of the church. Since most were from County Limerick in Ireland, that name easily carried the day. The Irish built SHOTGUN COTTAGES along the streets, while numerous AFRICAN AMERICANS (who may have been there before the Irish) populated the ALLEYS. Some of the "lace-curtain" Irish, who had done well, built substantial homes, especially on St. Catherine St.

An annual event was the St. Patrick's Day parade from St. Louis Bertrand Church north on Sixth St. to BROADWAY. The paraders (all men and boys) wore green sashes over their shoulders and marched eight abreast to the cadence of the Limerick Band's Irish tunes.

The black presence, however, was substantial enough that the CENTRAL COLORED School was opened in 1873 at Sixth and Kentucky Streets. It was probably the first tax-supported public school for African Americans in Kentucky. In 1879 the General Association of Colored Baptists in Kentucky opened an institution of higher education that became SIMMONS UNIVERSITY. Located between Seventh and Eighth Streets south of Kentucky St., it became the Municipal College for Negroes in 1930 as a part of the UNIVERSITY OF LOUISVILLE. It was closed in 1951 when segregated education ended in the state.

With the removal of the L&N shops to South Louisville in 1905 the character of Limerick began to change. Many of the railroad workers moved to SOUTH LOUISVILLE; younger, upwardly mobile Irish moved to more fashionable areas. The last St. Patrick's Day parade was held in 1918. African Americans moved from the alleys to the vacated cottages. Since the 1970s the neighborhood has been positively affected to some extent by the "gentrification" of the nearby OLD LOUISVILLE area. Limerick is a designated Louisville Historic Preservation District.

See Stanley Ousley, *Limerick: An Irish Neighborhood* (Louisville 1974); Carl Kramer, *Old Louisville: A Changing View* (Louisville 1982); and Richard J. Meany, "Louisville Scenes: The Autobiography of Fr. Richard Meany," *Filson Club History Quarterly,* 56 (April 1982): 170–80 and 58 (Jan. 1984): 5–39.

George H. Yater

LINCOLN, ABRAHAM (b Berks County, Pennsylvania, May 13, 1744; d Jefferson County, Kentucky, May 1786). Pioneer and grandfather of President Abraham Lincoln. Lincoln moved from Pennsylvania to Rockingham County, Virginia, where his father gave him title to his first tract of land. In 1770 he married Bathsheba Herring (d 1836). The two had three sons, Mordecai, Josiah, and Thomas, and two daughters, Mary and Nancy. While in Virginia, Abraham served as a captain in the militia from 1770 through the Revolutionary War.

Lincoln first visited Kentucky in 1780 after being captivated by the tales of the land as told by his friend and distant relative, Daniel Boone. In the spring of 1782 he purchased three tracts of land, one in Lincoln County six miles below Green River Lick and two in Jefferson County (one at Floyd's Fork and the other in downtown Louisville). In 1782 he moved his family from Rockingham to the wilderness territory of Lincoln County, then still a part of Virginia. He removed from there on May 7, 1785 to his Jefferson County farm, fifteen miles east of Louisville on a branch of Floyd's Fork called Long Run. In May 1786, while clearing the forest in order to build a farm with his three sons, Abraham was shot and killed by Indians. Immediately his two eldest sons ran for help, leaving behind their youngest brother Thomas. Josiah fled to the nearby fort at Hughes's Station, while Mordecai rushed to the family cabin for his father's gun. After retrieving the gun, he peered out of the cabin just in time to see an Indian preparing to make off with Thomas. Mordecai shot and killed the Indian, thereby rescuing his brother. When Josiah returned with men from the fort, Abraham lay dead and there was no sign of the Indian attackers. Lincoln is buried on his property in the area where the Long Run Baptist Church was erected. He was survived by Bathsheba and their five children, including Thomas, the father of the future president.

For Thomas Lincoln the problem was not Indians but the beautiful but none-too-fertile hillsides of Hardin (now Larue) County. Life was never easy for the orphaned Thomas as he struggled to provide himself with the barest necessities on his little farm on Nolin Creek. In 1806 he married Nancy Hanks, and they briefly resided in Elizabethtown before he bought the

Sinking Creek farm, where his father's namesake would be born in a log cabin in 1809.

See Joseph H. Barrett, *Life of Abraham Lincoln* (New York 1865); William E. Barton, *The Lineage of Lincoln* (Brooklyn 1929); Henry Lea, *Ancestry of Abraham Lincoln* (Boston 1909).

Aaron J. Bohnert

LINCOLN, WALTER PIERCE (b Louisville, December 17, 1857; d Louisville, February 1, 1939). Jefferson County judge. The son of Dennis and Catherine (Murray) Lincoln, he was educated in parochial schools and attended St. Xavier High School before graduating from Male High School. He studied law under James F. Clay at Henderson, Kentucky, where he was admitted to the bar in 1877 at the age of nineteen. He worked in the Louisville law firm of Lieber & Lincoln with Mace Lieber from 1882 until 1910.

Lincoln, a Democrat, was Jefferson County judge from June 30, 1907, until November 14, 1907. The Court of Appeals declared all city and county officials of Louisville and Jefferson County disqualified following irregularities in the 1905 election, and Gov. J.C.W. Beckham appointed Lincoln county judge until a special election could be held to choose new officers. Lincoln was also elected judge of the Jefferson Circuit Court, Common Pleas Branch, Third Division, serving from January 1, 1910, until January 1, 1922. In 1917 he was elected president of the Circuit Judges Association, after speaking out against the use of "third degree" interrogation methods employed by Louisville police.

On November 30, 1892, he married Ida May Adams of Mount Vernon, Kentucky. The couple had one daughter, May Adams. The family lived at 1137 Garvin Place. When he died at his home, Lincoln was considered to be the oldest practicing attorney in the state. He is buried in Mount Vernon, Kentucky.

See W.T. Owens, *Who's Who in Louisville* (Louisville 1926); "Judge Lincoln, Dean of City Bar, Lawyer 62 Years, Dies at 82," *Courier-Journal*, Feb. 2, 1939.

LINCOLN FOUNDATION. In 1910 the Lincoln Foundation was established to oversee and manage the assets of the Lincoln Institute, a school for African Americans in Simpsonville, Kentucky.

Following the 1954 Supreme Court ruling ordering the desegregation of schools, enrollment at the Lincoln Institute began to decline. In 1966 it closed; however, the Lincoln Foundation continued its work. It moved to Louisville and occupied different locations in the downtown area before the mid-1980s when it moved to 233 W Broadway. The foundation began to assist students and teachers to address the challenges of integrated education. Its "The Youth Speaks" program, developed under its executive director, Mansir Tydings, was crucial in understanding desegregation and other community issues. Students and representatives from all school systems held annual forums and regular discussions on WAVE-TV.

Beginning in the 1970s the foundation explored other ways to serve the educational needs of students. Under the leadership of Samuel Robinson, who succeeded Tydings as executive director, the foundation offered various educational, cultural, and support programs to economically disadvantaged youth. It helped to place gifted students in academic institutions by providing scholarships. The foundation developed several career-oriented training programs for high school students. It created workshops where, through the knowledge of arts and humanities, students could learn about African and African American culture and history. Because of its leadership in innovative educational programs, the foundation attracts financial support from corporate and governmental organizations.

LINCOLN INDEPENDENT PARTY. In August 1921, the Lincoln Independent Party (LIP) was formed when Louisville leaders of the National Association for the Advancement of Colored People (NAACP) could no longer tolerate the feelings of political slavery that pervaded the local African American community at that time. One leader, Arthur D. Porter, noted that blacks were "in the very unenviable position of being owned by the Republican party and hated by the Democrats." The LIP was formed to consolidate the black community's political voice within Louisville.

In 1924 the city Board of Park Commissioners adopted a resolution specifying certain parks within the city as exclusively for whites and other parks as exclusively for blacks. Prior to this, however, there were understood restrictions on where blacks could go. Officially, city government was generally unwilling to segregate parks until 1921, when signs were erected in the parks designating areas for blacks. The signs were removed when I. Willis Cole and William Warley, prominent black journalists, protested vehemently. Then, at the state fair, blacks were confronted with signs designating hot dog stands and toilets "For Colored People." Although this treatment was not unusual, for black community leader and local businessman Wilson Lovett it was an impetus for action. Outraged by these segregation attempts, Lovett announced his candidacy for the state legislature. After receiving the endorsement of several black groups, Lovett was disqualified from the election by a legal suit filed by the Republican Party.

Following this maneuver by the Republicans, Cole, Warley, Lovett, Porter, and other young community leaders met to form the LIP. Citing the link between the Republican political machine and political corruption and crime in the black communities, along with terrible race relations and insufficient black political power within the Republican Party, the founders announced that, on the LIP ticket, Porter would run for mayor, Lovett for the state legislature, Cole for the state senate, and Warley for magistrate. Their platform called for absolute equality of opportunity, racial representation "at the forum where laws are made to tax our property," and a "proportional share of the emoluments of official preferment"; and it insisted that they owed no allegiance to either party and could not be "bought or bluffed."

The formation of the party was denounced by conservative black leaders and, of course, the Republican Party. Conservative blacks hinted that the LIP had been created by the Democratic Party to disperse black political power and foster racial animosity. The party was also not strongly supported by local African American religious leaders, a fact that Cole also attributed to the political machine.

Besides this verbal opposition, physical abuse was also visited upon the party leaders. At one LIP meeting a black opponent of the party fired a shot into the crowd. The police appeared immediately, as if on cue, and ordered the members to leave the area, claiming that they had incited the disturbance. As they left, rocks and eggs were thrown at the party members by a group of black men and women involved with the Protective Aid Society, which had ties to Louisville underworld leader Harvey Burns. The candidates themselves were especially prone to violent attacks, with each having his home or office ransacked by opposing blacks, and culminating in the physical assault of Lovett while he was waiting to vote. While his assailant was allowed to go free, police arrested Lovett for disturbing the peace.

The LIP was predictably defeated. Porter received only 274 votes for the mayor's office versus 63,332 Republican votes and 56,199 Democratic votes. The other candidates faced similar defeats. Although they suspected that there had been some tampering with ballot boxes, the LIP members were not discouraged. Indeed, they had never really expected victory. Their party experiment was still a success. Amelioration between dissenting black community members following the split allowed each group to better understand, if not agree with, the stance taken by the other.

Warley and his cohorts insisted on changes within the Republican Party before they would return. The Republican Party began hiring blacks for clerical and lower echelon city government jobs, and blacks were finally hired as policemen and firemen in the city. While it would be years before the black community could unite more completely to oppose the standard political practices that continued to oppress them, the Lincoln Independent Party had proved that blacks were to be taken seriously in Louisville politics and that they would not continue to settle for less power than they knew they deserved.

See George C. Wright, *Life Behind a Veil* (Baton Rouge 1985) 246–52.

LINCOLN INSTITUTE. Founded in 1912 some twenty miles east of Louisville in SIMPSONVILLE, this African American educational institution came about as a result of Kentucky's Day Law. In 1903 state representative Carl Day, from Breathitt County, visited the campus of Berea College, which at the time was Kentucky's only integrated college. Day was disturbed by the intermingling of blacks and whites.

In response, he sponsored the bill that later bore his name, which passed the Kentucky legislature in 1904. It mandated the SEGREGATION of public and private schools. Although Berea officials fought the law all the way to the United States Supreme Court, they lost their case in 1908. Still, their sense of commitment to black education remained.

In 1906 the president and board of trustees of Berea, along with Dr. JAMES BOND and Kirke Smith, who were African American alumni, began to raise funds for a new private school for blacks. By 1909, thanks in large part to a two-hundred-thousand-dollar donation by Andrew Carnegie, a Berea board member at the time, all the moneys had been raised.

In 1910 the Lincoln Foundation was created to oversee the assets of the new institution, and the following year construction began on the first building. On October 1, 1912, under the direction of its first president, A. Eugene Thomas, the Lincoln Institute opened with a racially mixed faculty and an initial enrollment of eighty-five students.

While the Lincoln Institute did offer a small number of college-level classes, it was primarily a high school. It had a strong emphasis on vocational training, having been modeled after Booker T. Washington's Tuskegee Institute in Alabama. Much of the school's 444 acres served as farm ground on which most of the school's food was raised and where students were instructed in modern agricultural methods. Home economics and maintenance engineering were also among the skills taught, alongside traditional subjects such as mathematics and English. Lincoln Institute served as a normal school as well, being the site where Kentucky State College education students received their practical teacher training. White students from the Southern Baptist Seminary in Louisville prepared for the mission field training program at Lincoln.

In 1935, hard-hit by the Depression, the Lincoln Institute would likely have shut its doors had it not been for the efforts of the school's newly elected president, Whitney M. Young Sr. With his guidance and a faculty who was willing to make salary sacrifices, the school was able to WEATHER the storm. After only two years as president, Young, who remained at Lincoln for thirty years, was credited with increasing enrollment and soliciting larger donor contributions. In 1941 the Lincoln Institute profited greatly when the Kentucky General Assembly passed a law requiring local school boards to provide all students within their districts access to a high school education. If no such facilities existed, they were obligated to bus students to another district or pay for tuition at a boarding school. Since about half of the state's school districts did not offer such education for black students, many of them contracted with Lincoln to provide it.

In 1947 the Lincoln Institute became an accredited, state-supported high school and was put under the auspices of Kentucky State College (now a university). The institute closed its doors in 1966 after desegregation made it no longer feasible to operate a separate black high school. However, the next year the campus became the site of Lincoln School, a facility for academically gifted, yet financially disadvantaged, students from throughout Kentucky. The program operated until 1970, when the state legislature cut its funding, forcing it to close. In 1972, the Whitney M. Young Jr. Job Corps Center opened on the property.

See *Kentucky's Black Heritage* (Frankfort 1971); Edwina Ann Doyle, Ruby Layson, and Anne Armstrong Thompson, *From the Fort to the Future: Educating the Children of Kentucky* (Lexington 1987).

LINCOLN MASSACRE. Abraham Lincoln (frequently spelled Linkhorn in early records), the grandfather of the president, was born May 13, 1744, in Berks County, Pennsylvania, the eldest son of John and Rebecca Flowers Morris Lincoln. The family moved to Virginia's Shenandoah Valley in 1768.

In 1773, Abraham purchased two hundred acres on Linville Creek. He became a captain in the Augusta County militia in 1776. Lincoln sold his holdings in 1780 and purchased Virginia land warrants for five thousand acres. He visited Kentucky that year and later established a claim for four hundred acres on Long Run Creek in Jefferson County, which was recorded in 1785. Lincoln was a slaveholder.

In May 1786 he was planting corn with his three sons, Mordecai, Josiah, and Thomas (the president's father), when Lincoln was killed by a marauding Indian band. Mordecai shot and killed one of the Indians.

President Abraham Lincoln wrote, "The story of his death by the Indians, and of Uncle Mordecai, then fourteen years old, killing one of the Indians, is the legend more strongly than all others imprinted upon my mind and memory."

See Louis A. Warren, "Abraham Lincoln, Senior, Grandfather of the President," *Filson Club History Quarterly* 5 (July 1931): 137–52; Lucien Beckner, "John D. Shane's Interview with Mrs. Sarah Graham of Bath County," *Filson Club History Quarterly* 9 (Oct. 1935): 228–29; R.C. Ballard Thruston, "The Lincolns in Jefferson County," *Filson Club History Quarterly* 11 (July 1937): 197–206.

Blaine A. Guthrie Jr.

LIND, JENNY (b Stockholm, Sweden, October 6, 1820; d Malvern, England, November 2, 1887). Soprano. On Sunday, April 6, 1851, the celebrated thirty-one-year-old Swedish soprano Jenny (Johanna Maria) Lind arrived in Louisville. She had been met by Mayor JOHN DELPH and other prominent citizens ten miles south on the Elizabethtown Pike, where four matched white horses were hitched to her coach for a triumphal entry into the city.

Plans had been made for her to stay at the LOUISVILLE HOTEL, but, since the building was undergoing repairs she was taken to the home of Louisville & Nashville Railroad president Levin Lawrence Shreve on Walnut St. (Muhammad Ali Blvd.), now the site of the GARDENS OF LOUISVILLE. Lind's manager, Phineas Taylor Barnum, and his daughter, Caroline, registered at the GALT HOUSE hotel. Sixteen members of the accompanying orchestra, conductor Julius Benedict, and baritone Giovanni Belletti were housed in the LOUISVILLE HOTEL.

Jenny Lind's journey to America began when Barnum offered her a contract with a guaranteed fee of $1,000 for each of the 150 concerts, plus half of all receipts in excess of $5,500 for each of the programs. Lind arrived in New York harbor on September 1, 1850, where she was greeted by over thirty thousand cheering fans. After the initial concert in New York City's Castle Garden, she embarked on a tour of all the major cities down the eastern coast to Havana, Cuba. Barnum then chartered a boat that took her through New Orleans to Memphis and Nashville. From there she traveled by carriage to Mammoth Cave, Elizabethtown, and Louisville. Her fame preceded her in Louisville with the publication of *Jenny Lind's Favorite Polka* (1848) by Anton Wallerstein and *Swedish Nightingale Polka* (1850) by James Bellak, both for piano.

Lind's concerts were scheduled as the inaugural programs in the newly completed Mozart Hall on the corner of Fourth and Jefferson Streets. As in other cities, tickets were auctioned at ten o'clock on the morning of the performance. An admission fee of ten cents was charged to the auction room, it being agreed that the money would be given to the poor.

For the concert on Monday, April 7, Louis Tripp, a music teacher, bid $175 for the first seat. Many others passed the hundred-dollar mark, and the cheapest tickets went for twenty to fifty dollars. After all the seats were sold, sixty "standee" tickets were disposed of for three dollars each.

That evening the program consisted of two overtures by the orchestra, a violin solo, three SONGS by Giovanni Belletti, and a trio for voice (Lind) and two flutes. Lind's solo songs included operatic arias by Rossini and Donizetti, *The Bird Song* by Taubert, *Home, Sweet Home* by Bishop, and *The Herdsman's Song*, commonly called the *Echo Song*—a Swedish melody. In this song she simulated an echo with her voice, an effect that never failed to impress the audience. The second program on Wednesday included the famous aria from Handel's *Messiah*, "I Know That My Redeemer Liveth," and the IRISH ballad *The Last Rose of Summer*.

As a result of the overwhelming demand for tickets, a third concert was added on Thursday evening. On that program she was joined by Signor Salvi, a tenor who had just arrived from New York. Lind presented a *Tyrolean Duet* (with Belletti), *Within a Mile of Edinburgh Town*, and, again, *Home, Sweet Home*. The next morning the company left for Cincinnati on the steamer *Ben Franklin*. As the boat pulled away from the wharf, it hoisted the Swedish flag and fired two guns.

Lind completed her tour and returned to Europe in the summer of 1852. On November 2, 1887, she died of cancer at the age of sixty-seven near London. She was survived by her husband, pianist Otto Goldschmidt, and three children. In 1894 a bust and a plaque were placed in the Poet's Corner of Westminster Abbey in recognition of her exceptional contribution to music.

See Gladys Denny Shultz, *Jenny Lind, the Swedish Nightingale* (Philadelphia 1962); Melville O. Briney, *Fond Recollections: Sketches of Old Louisville* (Louisville 1955).

Robert Bruce French

LINN, WILLIAM (b New Jersey, 1734; d Jefferson County, Kentucky, March 5, 1781). Soldier and pioneer settler. Linn, sometimes spelled Lynn and whose name is perpetuated in the Linn Station Rd. in eastern Jefferson County, was the son of Andrew Linn. His mother's name is unknown. The family moved ca. 1750 to western Maryland and later to southwestern Pennsylvania near Red Stone, now Brownsville. Linn served as a scout for Gen. Edward Braddock's forces in the unsuccessful British attempt in 1755 to capture Fort Duquesne (now Pittsburgh) during the FRENCH and Indian War. In 1758 he was with Gen. John Forbes's army in the campaign that finally ousted the French.

Linn's first venture into Kentucky, which was attracting interest as an area of settlement, was in 1775 along the Licking River. He built a rude cabin and claimed land at the Big Blue Lick, now part of Blue Licks Battlefield State Park. At the outbreak of the Revolution, he enlisted in the company of Virginia militia riflemen commanded by Capt. George Gibson. They were dubbed "Gibson's lambs" because they were quite the opposite. In 1776, when powder was desperately needed on the frontier, Gibson and some of his "lambs," including Linn, were dispatched to New Orleans to obtain powder from the Spanish and bring it back upriver with Linn in command.

At the FALLS OF THE OHIO, all three thousand pounds of the powder in kegs had to be carried by hand around the obstruction and here the party rested. It was probably at this time that Linn explored the virgin countryside and found the site that later became Linn's Station. In 1778 Linn, a widower, and at least some of his children were among the civilians who accompanied GEORGE ROGERS CLARK's expedition to the Illinois country. The civilians had been left behind on CORN ISLAND at the Falls. In late June a message came downriver to Clark from JOHN CAMPBELL in Pittsburgh, reporting the news of the French alliance with the colonists. Clark, however, had departed on June 24. Linn, realizing how important this information would be, took the message and set out alone by canoe to deliver it. He found Clark and the militia, then stayed on with the expedition, eventually becoming a major in the Illinois Regiment.

When the short-term enlistment of Clark's militia expired in the fall of 1778, some seventy men decided not to reenlist and marched overland from Vincennes on the well-known Buffalo Trace to the Falls under Linn's command. In May 1779 he moved out to a point on the Middle Fork of BEARGRASS CREEK east of present Hurstbourne Pkwy., the site that he had likely scouted in 1776. Linn's Station was the earliest of the stockaded points along the creek. Five more were established in 1780, but Linn's was the easternmost and the most likely to suffer Indian attack. Many early settlers avoided Linn's because they thought it too dangerous.

Jefferson County, established by the Virginia legislature in 1780, held the first meeting of its county court on March 5, 1781, in Louisville. A group from Linn's Station planned to attend, and Linn rode out ahead of the group. A short time later rifle shots were heard, and a party was sent from the station to investigate. Linn's body was found, probably along the creek in the area that became the golf course of the Hurstbourne Country Club. His burial site is unknown but was likely in or near his station. The land east of Hurstbourne Ln. and south of the Middle Fork of Beargrass Creek Pkwy. was described in deeds for many years after as the "Linn Station tract." It was farmland until about 1965, when it was turned to commercial uses.

See George W. and Helen P. Beattie, "Pioneer Linns of Kentucky," *Filson Club History Quarterly* 20 (July 1946): 220–50.

George H. Yater

LITERATURE. The literature created by Louisville writers encompasses a broad range of topics, styles, and genre. A fascination with Kentucky settings, local humor, and optimism generally characterizes the literature, but considerable diversity also is reflected. The poetry, fiction, and drama by Louisville writers provide a glimpse into the literary landscape.

Poetry

One of Louisville's first writers was Hew Ainslie, from Ayrshire, Scotland, who moved to Louisville in 1828 after leaving Robert Owen's utopian community of New Harmony, Indiana. Ainslie had published poems and conversations with Robert Burns's friends in 1822 under the title *A Pilgrimage to the Land of Burns* and added to that *Scottish Songs, Ballads, and Poems* in 1855. His topics reflected his Scottish roots rather than the excitement of the emerging West.

Soon a writer emerged who reflected the excitement of the new West: Amelia B. Welby (1819–52). Welby became Kentucky's most widely regarded female poet of the mid-nineteenth century. Her topics were chosen from the stuff of life itself: faith, children, love, nature; "The Rainbow" was considered her best poem. Even Edgar Allan Poe and Rufus Griswold identified her as a significant poet of the time. In 1837 her work was published in the *LOUISVILLE JOURNAL* by its editor, George Prentice. He called her "the finest branch of his poetical tree." Her works were so popular, despite their sentimentalism, that when she compiled her poetry in 1845 in *Poems by Amelia*, subsequent editions were published until the seventeenth in 1860.

Poet FORTUNATUS COSBY JR. (1801–71) became the editor of the *Louisville Examiner*, a newspaper advocating the emancipation of all slaves. His poetry was lyrical enough to win him acclaim as a songwriter. His works include "Fireside Fancies" and "Ode to the Mocking Bird." His poetry was never published as a whole, but it was well represented in collections of United States poetry.

As the nineteenth century came to an end, two other names in poetry stood out: Madison Cawein, considered Louisville's most famous early poet, and the African American poet Joseph S. Cotter. Cotter's son Joseph S. Cotter Jr. also went on to write poetry.

MADISON CAWEIN (1865–1914), also known as "Louisville's Lark" and "Kentucky's Keats," received national recognition in *Harper's* magazine. He chose nature as his subject, immortalizing the dogwood, the redbud, and other aspects of nature he could find in his OLD LOUISVILLE neighborhood and surroundings. His works include vivid descriptions of Kentucky flowers and BIRDS. Mythological references and superstitions permeated his works, such as "The Vale of Tempe," "The Dream Oread," and "The Haunted House." His works include *Myth and Romance* (1899), *Kentucky Poems* (1902), *Vale of Tempe* (1905), and the prose *Nature Notes and Impressions* (1906).

JOSEPH COTTER (1861–1949) was hailed as Kentucky's first significant AFRICAN AMERICAN writer. He published five volumes of poetry as well as other volumes of drama, fiction, and assorted other pieces. His *Links of Friendship* (1898) was a collection of poetry that attracted the attention of William Dean Howells and Paul Laurence Dunbar. Cotter dealt with black-white relations in his poetic drama *Caleb the Degenerate* (1903). Other works include *Sequel to "The Pied Piper of Hamelin" and Other Poems* (1939) as well as *Negro Tales* (1912) and *A White Song and a Black One* (1909), dealing with relationships between blacks and whites.

Cotter's son Joseph Cotter Jr. (1895–1919) attended Louisville's Central High School and Fisk University until tuberculosis forced him to withdraw. His poetry also dealt with the identity and treatment of African Americans, as seen in his poem "The Mulatto and the Critics." Despite his untimely death, he wrote sufficiently to attain critical acclaim in his volume of poems, *The Band of Gideon and Other Lyrics* (1918).

Another Louisvillian, WILLIAM SHAKESPEARE HAYS (1837–1907), found fame as a poet and a songwriter. Literary historian William Ward estimated that 6 million copies of Hays's SONGS were sold during his lifetime, most notably "Dixie." His poem, "Mollie Darling" (1866), was his most successful, selling 2 million copies in its own right. His poems were published in *The Modern Meetin' House and Other Poems* (1874), *Will S. Hays Songs and Poems* (1866), and *Poems and Songs* (1895).

CALE YOUNG RICE (1872–1943), husband of Alice Hegan Rice, published a prodigious twenty-one volumes of poetry and ten volumes of poetic drama between the publication of *Dusk to Dusk* in 1898 and *High Perils* in 1933. He enjoyed mixed popularity in the United States and in England for his poems about nature, love, and places he had traveled.

Sonneteer DAVID MORTON (1886–1957) published from 1914 until 1955. Known primarily as a lyric poet and sonnet writer, he published poems in *Harper's, Poetry,* and *North American Review.* He won first prize from the Lyric Society of New York and Poetry Society of America for his poem, "Ships in Harbor" (1921). Other volumes of poetry include *Harvest: A Book of Sonnets* (1924), *Nocturnes and Autumnals* (1928), *Earth's Processional* (1932), *Spell against Time* (1936), *Angle of Earth and Sky* (1941), and *Poems* (1945). In 1945 the *Saturday Review of Literature* called him "probably the foremost American nature lyricist in the years 1920–1945." He wrote about the literary history of the sonnet in *The Sonnet Today and Yesterday* (1928). He received the Borestone Prize for Poetry for his volume *Like a Man in Love* (1955).

Hortense Flexner (1885–1973) published several volumes of poetry that earned acclaim from *Bookman* and the *New York Times: Clouds and Cobblestones* (1920), *The Stubborn Root, and Other Poems* (1930), and *North Window, and Other Poems* (1943). Her poetry ranged from light verse to probing questions of life. Flexner wrote several children's books: *Chipper* (1941), *The Wishing Window* (1942), and *Puzzle Pond* (1948).

Contemporary Louisville poets include Wade Hall, Jeffrey Skinner, Lee Pennington, Frederick Smock, and Sarah Gorham. Wade Hall (1934–) is professor emeritus of English at BELLARMINE COLLEGE. He has provided a forum for Kentucky poets since 1964, when he founded *Approaches* with author Joy Bale Boone; this was the poetry journal that became the *Kentucky Poetry Review.* Hall's poems were published in *The High Limb* (1973).

Lee Pennington (1939–) enjoys popularity as a poet as well as a storyteller. He has published poetry collections, including *Wildflower, Spring of Violets, Songs of Bloody Harlan,* and *I Knew a Woman.*

Jeffrey Skinner (1949–) is professor of English and director of creative writing at the UNIVERSITY OF LOUISVILLE. He has published three volumes of poetry: *Late Stars* (1985), *A Guide to Forgetting* (1988), and *The Company of Heaven* (1992). *A Guide to Forgetting* was chosen for the 1987 National Poetry Series by Graywolf Press. He has published a scrapbook of poems with his wife, Sarah Gorham, and other poets entitled *The Night Lifted Us* (1994). He has also compiled a book with Stephen P. Policoff called *Real Toads in Imaginary Gardens: Approaches to Creative Writing for Young Writers* (1991).

Frederick Smock (1954–) has published two books of poems, *12 poems* and *Gardencourt.* He is the founding editor of the *American Voice,* an international literary journal based in Louisville. His poetry, including "Through the Gap," "The Night Lifted Us," "Kentucky Voices," and "Savory Memories," has appeared in numerous anthologies.

Sarah Gorham (1956–) has published a number of volumes of her poetry, including *Don't Go Back to Sleep* (1989), *The Night Lifted Us* (1991, with Jeffrey Skinner), *The Tension Zone* (1996), and *Last Call: Poems on Alcoholism, Addiction, and Deliverance* (1997, with Jeffrey Skinner). Her prizes include the Poetry Society of America 1983 Gertrude Claytor Memorial Prize, 1990 Carolyn Kizer Prize for her work in the anthology *Poetry Northwest,* and the 1994 Four Way Books Award in Poetry.

Fiction

Louisville writers have produced a wealth of short stories and novels since the nineteenth century. Early fiction writers embodied the local color movement characteristic of nineteenth-century Kentucky writers. Included in this category would be Alice Hegan Rice and Cordia Greer Petrie, both of whom employed folksy dialect in the new urban environment of Louisville.

Alice Hegan Rice (1870–1942) brought recognition to the CABBAGE PATCH area of Louisville, the former OAKLAND RACE COURSE, in her novel, *Mrs. Wiggs of the Cabbage Patch* (1901). As William Ward writes, "The conventions of the form were well established: a family in reduced circumstances or actual poverty because of a father dead, absent, sick, or feckless, is held together by an indomitable mother who manages her brood of bright, active children with good humor, and whose ingenuity, hard work, simple virtue, and faith . . . are finally rewarded, but only after many vicissitudes, some comic, some pathetic." *Mrs. Wiggs* was number two on the *New York Times* bestseller list in 1902 and by 1912 had had its forty-seventh printing. It was adapted for films four times, twice as a silent movie (1910 and 1925) and twice with sound (1934 and 1942). It was also serialized for radio. Other works by Rice include *Lovey Mary* (1903), *Sandy* (1905), *Captain June* (1907), *A Romance of Billy-Goat Hill* (1912), and her serious novel *Mr. Opp* (1909) about a newspaper editor who cares for his sister. This received favorable reviews in such publications as *The Bookman, Nation,* and *The Spectator.* Other novels that dealt with Louisville scenes and social problems included *Calvary Alley* (1917) and *Mr. Pete & Co.* (1933). While some criticized her work as "the dreariest herbage of sentimental commonplace" (*Saturday Review* on *Sandy*), her work was bright, cheery, and appealing to those who needed sunshine in their lives, and it was well suited to the culture in which it was written.

Evelyn Barnett (1861–1921) was the founder of the AUTHORS CLUB, worked as a literary editor for the *Courier-Journal,* and was the author of a collection of short stories, *Mrs. Delire's Euchre Party and Other Stories* (1895), *Jerry's Reward* (1903), and *The Dragnet* (1909)—the first murder mystery worth noting by a Kentuckian. She also introduced a new form of lecture into the Redpath Chautauqua program—the oral book review.

Mary Finley Leonard (1862–1948) was born in Philadelphia and moved to Louisville at an early age. She was the author of at least thirteen children's stories such as *The Story of the Big Front Door* (1898), *The Christmas Tree House* (1913), *The Little Red Chimney* (1914), and *The Way of Jane* (1917). Her best-known story, which received national attention, was *Everyday Susan* (1912).

Cordia Greer Petrie (1872–1964), the folksy writer who delighted readers, moved to Louisville from Barren County, Kentucky, and drew on that experience in her writing. She created a character named Angeline who was from Barren County and lived at Louisville's Seelbach Hotel. Angeline bumbled into society and expressed her amazement at the "brazen hussies" on the hotel walls, JAZZ ORCHESTRAS, and the chance to meet the First Lady, Mrs. Calvin Coolidge. Of the nine volumes in the *Angeline* series, (1922–28), the most popular was *Angeline at the Seelbach* (1922), which went through thirteen printings. Petrie put her native Barren County dialect into Angeline's voice, to the delight of her readers.

ANNIE FELLOWS JOHNSTON (1863–1931), author of popular children's books, was born in Evansville, Indiana. After the death of her husband in 1892, she made trips to PEWEE VALLEY, OLDHAM COUNTY, where her three stepchildren were staying with their aunt. Pewee Valley became the inspiration for her 12 volume *Little Colonel* series (begun in 1895), which documents the life of five-year-old Lloyd Sherman, a little girl who lives with her widowed grandfather. She created charming characters of high integrity who encounter situations where simple virtues and good intentions always triumph. When she moved to Pewee Valley in 1898, she had already published three novels, *Big Brother* (1894) *Joel, a Boy of Galilee* (1895), and *The Little Colonel* (1895).

Another writer at this time was Harrison Robertson (1856–1939). Robertson wrote numerous novels, including *How the Derby Was Won* (1889), *If I Were a Man* (1899), *Red Blood and Blue* (1900), and *The Pink Typhoon* (1906). In addition, Robertson was on the staff at the *Courier-Journal* for more than sixty years. He became editor-in-chief in 1929 and held that position until his death in 1939.

Abby Meguire Roach (1876–1966) published poetry and short stories in *Harper's* monthly, *Century Magazine, Cosmopolitan,* and *Criterion.* Born in Philadelphia, her family moved to Louisville in 1881. Roach was a graduate of LOUISVILLE GIRLS' HIGH SCHOOL and Wellesley College. Roach's novel, *Some Successful Marriages* (1906), was among the best- sellers of that time and dealt with marital problems.

A little-known short story and novel writer who lived in St. James Ct. in Louisville was Charles Neville Buck (1879–1930). A lawyer by training and a cartoonist and editorial writer for the *Louisville Evening Post,* Buck wrote *The Key to Yesterday* (1910) and *The Lighted Match* (1911). The first dealt with mental illness and the second with an international love affair. Buck incorporated mountain people and a feud in his work, *The Portal of Dreams* (1912). He spent some time at the Pine Mountain Settlement as well as in the mountains, recording details of mountain life with a popular appeal. Like Rice and Greer, his characters were presented in stereotypes. Feuds and the actions resultant from warring loyalties were recorded in the novels *The Call of the Cumberlands* (1913), *Battle Cry* (1914), and *The Code of the Mountains* (1915). His last and perhaps best mystery novel, *Mountain Justice* (1932), involves a Louisville surgeon accused of murder who flees to the mountains until he is vindicated. It treats themes characteristic of Depression-era writing: hunger, unemployment, the growing number of Communist organizers, and violence.

Another Louisville author who began writing during the GREAT DEPRESSION was WILLIE SNOW ETHRIDGE (1900–82), author of fifteen books, most notably *As I Live and Breathe* (1936), *I'll Sing One Song* (1941), and *This Little Pig Stayed Home* (1944). These reflected her experiences as the wife of a journalist (husband Mark was publisher of the *Courier Journal* and the *LOUISVILLE TIMES*) and as a mother. Her novels include *Mingled Yard* (1938), a social commentary about textile mills in Georgia; *Strange Fires: The True Story of John Wesley's Love Affair in Georgia* (1971); and *Summer Thunder* (1972), about James Oglethorpe.

Gwen Davenport (1910–) recorded life during WORLD WAR II in her 1947 novel, *Belvedere,* a humorous story about an aspiring writer who takes a position as nanny to a young couple's three children. The novel was made into a movie in 1948, starring Clifton Webb as Belvedere and Robert Young and Maureen O'Hara as the young couple, Harry and Tracey King. The movie's popularity brought new acclaim to the novel. Davenport's next novel, *Family Fortunes* (1949), features the misadventures of a family keeping their Revolutionary-era Bluegrass mansion afloat by turning it into a tourist attraction. Other novels include *Candy for Breakfast* (1950), *The Bachelor's Baby* (1958), and *The Wax Foundation* (1961), all of which feature satire as well as warm humor. Her latest novel in *Time and Chance* (1993).

JANE MORTON NORTON (1908–88) published *Blackbirds on the Lawn* in 1944, receiving kudos from the *New York Herald Tribune* and the *New York Times.* This story traces a feud that started between two Bluegrass landowners and continued to the 1940s in a small Kentucky town. The town is a microcosm of the struggle between good and evil, hate, envy, and prejudice. Her fame came from this one novel as well as from her career as a painter. Her family's business in radio and TELEVISION in Louisville absorbed much of her time in later years.

Another media-related writer is Sallie Bingham (1937–), a member of the Bingham family that owned the *Courier-Journal* newspaper as well as radio and television enterprises. Her first novel, *After Such Knowledge* (1959), was published while she lived in Boston. She published *The Touching Hand* (1967) and *The Way It Is Now* (1972), two collections of short stories. She has also written plays, including *Milk of Paradise* (1980) and *Paducah,* which opened in 1984. Other works include the autobiographical work, *Passion & Prejudice: A Family Memoir* (1989), and other novels such as *Upstate* (1993), *Small Victories* (1993), *Matron of Honor* (1994), and *Straight Man* (1996).

Cousin to Human brought attention to Louisville-born Jane Mayhall (1921–), with its *Catcher in the Rye* style. Its setting is Louisville during the mid-1930s, and it deals with everyday situations in the life of Lacy Cole, a teenager, and her family.

Betty Layman Receveur (1930–) traces her Louisville heritage to 1795 when the Layman ancestors floated down the OHIO RIVER from Pennsylvania. She grew up in Louisville near the St. Louis Bertrand Church and school on S Sixth St., which she attended. She went to HOLY ROSARY ACADEMY near Central Park for one semester, then eloped at the age of fourteen. She never finished high school and received her training from the Louisville Writers Club. Her first two books, *Sable Flanagan* and *Molly Gallagher,* were historical romances. *Molly* achieved national popularity and was published in Germany as well. Her best-known historical romance novel is *Oh, Kentucky!* (1990), which reflects her heritage from her female ancestors. It was conceived while jogging around the track at BELLARMINE COLLEGE. Her other work is *Kentucky Home* (1995).

Michael Dorris (1945–97) was born in Louisville. His adult fiction includes *The Crown of Columbus* (1991), co-authored with his wife, Louise Erdrich, and the story collection *Working Men* (1993). Among his nonfiction works are *The Broken Cord: A Father's Story* (1989), winner of the National Book Critics Circle Award, and a collection of essays, *Paper Trails: Collected Essays, 1967–1992* (1994). *Cloud Chamber* (1997) is a critically acclaimed novel set principally in Louisville.

Leon Driskell (1932–95) was a writer of fiction and poetry. He was professor of American literature at the UNIVERSITY OF LOUISVILLE, where he cultivated various writing and performing groups, known as the Friday Group, the Tuesday Group, and Minerva. These groups provided an important venue for writers to listen to and critique each others' works. At the university he published a literary magazine called *Adena.* His collection of short stories, *Passing Through,* was published in 1983. These stories, presented in chronological order, revolve around six people who live in fictional Owen County, Kentucky, during the 1970s. The emotional connections between people, the passage of time, commitment, and even the significance of the death of Elvis Presley unite these stories.

Sue Grafton (1940–), born and educated in Louisville, is a prolific writer of novels, television screenplays, and mysteries. Her novels include *The Monkey Room, Sparrow's Field, Keziah Dane* (1967), and *The Lolly-Madonna War* (1973). Some of her television plays include *Killer in the Family,* starring Robert Mitchum, and two Agatha Christie adaptations, *Caribbean Mystery* and *Sparkling Cyanide.* She is best known for her mysteries presented in alphabetical order, starting with *A Is for Alibi.* The mysteries feature Kinsey Millhone, a baby-boomer who reflects life toward the end of the twentieth century.

Another Louisville mystery writer is Taylor McCafferty (1946–), whose career began with *Pet Peeves* (1990), written for a contest sponsored by the Private Eye Association of America. The main character is Haskell Blevins, a detective who appears to be a country bumpkin but who has an eagle eye. Other books include *Ruffled Feathers* (1992), *Bed Bugs* (1993), *Thin Skins* (1994), *Hanky Panky* (1995), *A Killing in Real Estate* (1995), and *Double Murder* (1996).

Kristina McGrath (1950-) is a Louisville writer of fiction and poetry. She is the author of the novel *House Work* (1994), and her writing is published in the anthologies *Catholic Girls* (1992) and *Women on Women* (1990). She was the winner of the Pushcart Prize for fiction in 1989. She has also published poetry in a number of magazines such as *Prairie Schooner, Ironwood, Yale Review, Harper's,* and *Woman Poet-the East.*

Sena Jeter Naslund (1942–) is a short story

and fiction writer. She is a professor of English and former director of creative writing at the University of Louisville. Her first novel, *Ice Skating at the North Pole* (1989), treats the theme of women becoming friends. Her novel *The Animal Way to Love* (1993) deals with the theme of isolation and loneliness. A lighter novel, *Sherlock in Love* (1993), features Sherlock Holmes's smarter sister.

Susan Dodd also is a writer of short stories. Born in Chicago in 1946, Dodd received her M.S. from the University of Louisville in 1972. Her works include a collection of short stories that received the 1984 Iowa School of Letters Award for short fiction and several novels, including *No Earthly Notion* (1986) and *Old Wives' Tales* (1984).

Gerald Toner (1950–), Louisville attorney and writer whose chosen topic is holiday fiction, has published three titles: *Lipstick Like Lindsay's and Other Christmas Stories* (1990), *Whittlesworth Comes to Christmas* (1991), and *Holly Day's Cafe* (1996). Toner's themes are often regional and familiar, contributing to their local holiday appeal.

Louisville was the birthplace of one of the most distinctive practitioners of the "New Journalism" and the epitome of the expression "Gonzo Journalism." Hunter Stockton Thompson (1939–) grew up in the HIGHLANDS. Controversy characterized the topics he chose to write about for such magazines as *Scanlon's, National Observer,* and *Rolling Stone.* Thompson's *Rolling Stone* article "Fear and Loathing in Las Vegas" became a book in 1972. In 1998 it was made into a movie starring Kentuckian Johnny Depp. Thompson depicts the moral wasteland of the late twentieth century, revolving around drugs, sex, and money. Also in 1972, Thompson covered the presidential race for *Rolling Stone;* these articles were collected into the book *Fear and Loathing on the Campaign Trail* (1973). Thompson left *Rolling Stone* in 1976 after numerous disputes and has spent most of his time since in Colorado. Other works include *The Great Shark Hunt* (1979), *The Curse of Lono* (1988), *Songs of the Doomed: More Notes from the Death of the American Dream* (1991), and *The Proud Highway: The Saga of a Desperate Southern Gentleman, 1955–1967* (1997). In 1980 his life was depicted in the motion picture, *Where the Buffalo Roam.* Garry Trudeau also modeled a character after Thompson in his nationally syndicated comic strip, "Doonesbury."

Drama

Theatergoers in Louisville prior to 1873 attended the Louisville Theater, located at the southeast corner of Fourth and Green (Liberty) Streets, where they could see famous actors of the time, including John Wilkes Booth, Julia Dean, John Drew, and Charlotte Cushman. Louisville drama began to flower after the CIVIL WAR, particularly once MACAULEY'S THEATRE, 115 Walnut St. near Fourth St., opened in 1873. However, not much in the way of significant drama was written by Louisville writers until some began to write about contemporary problems. Some of these attempts included Bronson Howard's *Saratoga* (1870); Clyde Fitch's play about social issues, *The Climbers* (1901); and his play about jealousy, *The Girl with the Green Eyes* (1902).

Ann Crawford Flexner (1874–1955) lived in Louisville until 1905, then spent the remainder of her life in New York City. She dramatized Alice Hegan Rice's *Mrs. Wiggs of the Cabbage Patch* (1904), and it premiered at Macauley's Theatre in Louisville. Louisville journalist Thompson Buchanan (1877–1937) wrote the successful *A Woman's Day* (1909), which had considerable success in New York, Chicago, and Los Angeles.

Cleves Kinkead (1882–1955) achieved fame for his play *Common Clay.* It was written in the George Pierce Baker 47 Workshop at Harvard, a groundbreaking playwriting class at a time when most drama courses focused on the history of plays. Kinkead's sociological study depicted the problems of a young woman who works as a domestic. It ran for a year in New York and played also in London. It was made into a movie twice.

Two names of Louisville artists deserve inclusion with regard to theater: William Thompson Price and JOHN MASON BROWN.

William Thompson Price taught in the American School of Playwriting, contributed criticism as critic for the *New York Star,* and wrote *The Technique of the Drama* (1892), *Analysis of Play Construction and Dramatic Principle* (1905), and *The Philosophy of Dramatic Principle and Method,* an unpublished textbook.

John Mason Brown (1900–69) became one of America's most distinguished drama critics. The performance of *King Lear* at Louisville's Macauley's Theatre in 1909 made an impression on him that carried through his years at Harvard to his first position of dramatic critic with *Theatre Arts Monthly Magazine* (1926–28). He also served as drama critic for the *New York Evening Post,* the *New York World-Telegram,* and *Saturday Review of Literature.* He published *Dramatis Personae: A Retrospective Show* (1963), a collection of his essays, reviews, and criticism, and his 1930 work, *Modern Theatre in Revolt,* a history of the preceding hundred years of theater. His reviews incorporated insights on human life as well as a comprehensive understanding of theater history.

John Patrick (1906–) wrote *The Hasty Heart* and the Pulitzer Prize–winning play, *Teahouse of the August Moon* (1953). *The Hasty Heart, which* enjoyed a run of 205 performances in the Hudson Theatre in New York, was based on patients he knew while in a Burma hospital. His screen adaptations became famous, as seen in *Three Coins in a Fountain* (1954), *Love is a Many Splendored Thing* (1955), *High Society* (1956), *Les Girls* (1957), and *The World of Susie Wong* (1960). He had written thirty plays by 1930, co-authored nineteen film scripts, and adapted many plays for film. *Teahouse* brought him international fame and the New York Drama Critics Prize. *Teahouse* treats the theme of an American occupation force sent to Okinawa to teach American ways to the people there.

Marsha Norman (1947–) has been a prolific writer of drama for stage and screen. Her first play, *Getting Out* (1977), received the John Gassner Playwriting Medallion, the Newsday Oppenheimer Award, and a citation from the American Theatre Critics Association. She wrote two one-act plays with distinctive Louisville themes, *Third and Oak: The Laundromat* (1978) and *The Pool Hall* (1985). She won a Pulitzer Prize in 1983 for her play *'night Mother.* It was made into a movie, starring Anne Bancroft and Sissy Spacek. It has been translated into twenty-three languages and performed around the world. Another receiving acclaim was her libretto for the Broadway musical, *The Secret Garden.* She received a Tony Award and a Drama Desk Award for that work. In addition to other works such as *Loving Daniel Boone, Trudy Blue,* and *The Red Shoes,* she has published a novel, *The Fortune Teller* (1987). Norman has also worked in film and television, including *Face of a Stranger,* starring Tyne Daly, which won an Emmy Award.

Jane Martin is a pseudonym for the anonymous author or combination of authors responsible for *Talking With,* a collection of monologues. It was first produced at ACTORS THEATRE OF LOUISVILLE and won Best Foreign Play of the Year in Germany from *Theatre Heute* magazine. Other plays include *Cementville, Keely and Du* (winner of the 1994 American Theatre Critics Association New Play Award and nominated for a Pulitzer Prize), *Criminal Hearts, Middle Aged White Guys,* and *Jack and Jill,* winner of the 1996 American Theatre Critics Association New Play Award.

Naomi Wallace (1960–), playwright and poet, grew up a Kentucky farm girl near Prospect. Grandaughter of TOM WALLACE, longtime editor of the *Louisville Times,* and daughter of Henry Wallace, former *Time* and *Life* correspondent, she uses Kentucky themes in most of her works. Two of Wallace's works have been presented by the HUMANA Festival of New Plays: *One Flea Spare* in 1996 and *The Trestle at Pope Lick Creek* in 1998. Wallace also wrote the screenplay for the motion picture *Lawn Dogs* (1997), which was filmed in the PROSPECT area. Wallace was a 1999 recipient of a John D. and Catherine T. MacArthur "genius grant."

See L. Elisabeth Beattie, *Conversations with Kentucky Writers* (Lexington 1996); Sister Mary Carmel Browning, *Kentucky Authors: A History of Kentucky Literature* (Evansville, Ind., 1968); William S. Ward, *A Literary History of Kentucky* (Knoxville, Tenn., 1988); Gale Research Co., *Contemporary Authors: A Bio-bibliographical Guide to Current Authors and Their Works* (Detroit, Mich., 1962–).

Gail Ritchie Henson

LITHGOW, JAMES SMITH (b Pittsburgh, Pennsylvania, November 29, 1812; d Louisville, February 21, 1902). Mayor. James was the only son of Walter and Frances (Stevenson) Lithgow. Lithgow went to school until he was thirteen and then was apprenticed to a tin and coppersmith in Pittsburgh.

In 1832 he moved to Louisville and became an employee of Bland and Coleman, a copper, tin, and sheet iron manufacturing company. From 1833 until 1836 he worked for a Louisville merchant, Allen Barnett. After returning to Pittsburgh for a short time, he came back to Louisville in August 1836. In October 1836, he started Wallace & Lithgow, a copper, tin, and sheet-ironware business on MARKET St., with Allen S. Wallace. The business was successful, and Lithgow made a fortune.

In 1861 Wallace died and Lithgow continued the business alone until 1862, when he went into partnership with two of his sons-in-law, Clark O. Smith and J.L. Smyser, and another partner. He and his sons-in-law, along with Vincent Cox, started J.S. Lithgow & Co. at Third and MAIN Streets. Lithgow erected what became the Board of Trade Building in Louisville shortly before the financial panic of 1873. It was designed by HENRY WHITESTONE and was one of the largest, most expensive buildings in Louisville's financial district.

After the panic, Lithgow was wiped out and lost control of the building and lost other assets to creditors. He started over and built a stove manufacturing company, Lithgow Manufacturing Co., into another successful business. Lithgow also served as chief director and president of the Mechanics Fire Co. for several years. He was president of the Northern Bank of Kentucky at Louisville. He was also on the directorates of the Louisville, Frankfort, & Lexington, and the Elizabethtown & Paducah railroad companies. He was elected one the first directors of the LOUISVILLE WATER CO., serving for several years. He was active in the Methodist Episcopal Church, South.

Lithgow was elected to the City Council for the first time in 1849. Under the new city charter he was elected to the Board of Aldermen in 1852 and again in 1853. In 1866 he was a member of the city charter convention that helped to draft a new charter. Lithgow, a Democrat, was unanimously chosen by the councilmen and aldermen, not by voters, to fill the vacated mayor's post after the council and BOARD OF ALDERMEN impeached Philip Tomppert. Lithgow took over on January 2, 1866, and served until February 14, 1867. He resigned the post when Tomppert was reinstated by the Kentucky Court of Appeals.

He was married in November 1837 to Hannah Cragg, of English parentage, who had come to Louisville in her youth. The couple had eight children. His wife died on March 28, 1891. He is buried in CAVE HILL CEMETERY.

See *Louisville Past and Present: Its Industrial History* (Louisville 1875); Josiah Stoddard Johnston, ed., *Memorial History of Louisville*, 2 vols. (Chicago and New York 1896).

LITTLE, JOHN (b Tuscaloosa, Alabama, 1874; d Louisville, October 26, 1948). Presbyterian minister. After graduating from the University of Alabama, Little came to Louisville, where he enrolled in the LOUISVILLE PRESBYTERIAN THEOLOGICAL SEMINARY. While a student at the seminary, he founded the city's first settlement houses for AFRICAN AMERICANS. In February 1898, Little, along with five other members of the seminary's Student's Missionary Society, embarked on what was supposed to be a temporary project in home missions when they opened the Hope Mission Station in an old lottery office at 642 Preston St. as a Sunday school for the surrounding black community. With the success of Hope, the decision was made to open a second mission in the spring of 1899, at Jackson and Lampton Streets, serving the Smoketown community as Grace Mission. After graduating from the seminary in 1899, Little, who had originally intended to serve in the mission fields of Africa, was persuaded by the Louisville Presbytery to stay on as the director of the Grace and Hope Missions, a position he held until his death nearly fifty years later. Gradually, services at the missions expanded. Although Little's primary purpose was to teach Christianity, great importance was also placed on vocational and educational training, as well as basic health and hygiene. In fact, Hope Mission was responsible for Louisville's first public bathhouse for blacks. Thus, what started as two experimental Sunday schools evolved into nationally recognized, top-rated African American settlement houses under Little's guidance. In the mid-1950s, the name of the missions was changed to the John Little Presbyterian Centers in honor of their founder, who had died in 1948. In 1965, the name was changed again when the two centers were merged into one PRESBYTERIAN COMMUNITY CENTER in the old Grace building at 760 S Hancock.

Little, who was also one of the founders of Grace Presbyterian Church (1910), remarried after the death of his first wife and was survived by his second wife, Bertha (Tarrent) Little, and a daughter and son. He is buried in CAVE HILL CEMETERY.

See Anne F. Vouga, "Presbyterian Missions and Louisville Blacks: The Early Years, 1898–1910," *Filson Club History Quarterly* 58 (July 1984): 310–35; *Courier-Journal*, Oct. 27, 1948.

LITTLE AFRICA. With little recorded about the community known as Little Africa, its reputed boundaries have ranged as far north as Virginia Ave., east to Wilson Ave., south to Algonquin Pkwy., and west to the South Western Pkwy. Following the CIVIL WAR, the area became known as Needmore after thousands of poor freedmen settled on the swampy lands during their northern migration. It was known also as "black PARKLAND," and its flimsy shacks (although some sturdier houses existed) and muddy streets stood in stark contrast to the elegant homes and tree-lined boulevards in "white Parkland" farther east along Virginia Ave. and Dumesnil St. By the turn of the century AFRICAN AMERICANS living in downtown Louisville began calling the community Little Africa, and the name Needmore was forgotten.

Local leaders such as educator Joseph S. Cotter and Dr. A.J. Duncan, the "mayor" of Little Africa, worked through the Parkland Improvement Club to better the community by adding sidewalks and mailboxes, and by cleaning and leveling the streets. In 1916 Little Africa proudly celebrated its twenty-fifth anniversary after tracing its origin back to the erection of several houses on Virginia and Dumesnil and the opening of Virginia Avenue Baptist Church in 1891. During the festivities, Cotter boasted in a report of seven hundred homes, six churches, six GROCERIES, and a public school serving the area.

However, by the mid-1940s conditions in the community, known by then as Southwick, had improved very little. The destitute conditions caught the eye of Louisville officials, who earmarked the area for a PUBLIC HOUSING project. Despite the clearance of slums and the completion of the $7 million, 650-unit Cotter Homes in 1953, a *COURIER-JOURNAL* reporter visiting the area 2 years later related the continuing squalor. Claiming that he heard frogs croaking in the muddy streets, the reporter called Southwick "a generally shabby, rundown area with a high percentage of unmade streets, vacant, rubbish-filled lots, open dumps, many poor people and many poor dwellings." The addition of the $8 million, five-hundred-unit Lang Homes five years later alleviated further housing problems but did not bring about the neighborhood's turnaround. In 1956 the LUCIE DUVALLE Junior High School was moved into the area from Ninth and Chestnut Streets. After that time, the community began to be known as PARK DUVALLE.

As the area's crime, drug, infant-mortality, and poverty rates escalated throughout the 1960s, 1970s, and 1980s, city officials and federal agencies such as the Urban Renewal Agency continued to pump money into failing rehabilitation and renovation efforts. In the early 1990s the city, along with local residents, discussed the best way to solve the area's numerous problems. It was decided that, in order to revive the community, it was necessary to raze 118 public housing buildings and start over. In mid-1996 the city started a $165 million redevelopment plan. Funded by local and federal dollars, the project involved replacing the public housing with a mix of APARTMENT BUILDINGS, duplexes, townhouses, and single-family homes. The project is expected to be completed by 2007.

See *Courier-Journal,* July 4, 1972, Feb. 1, 1989, Jan. 14, 1996; Joseph S. Cotter Sr.,

Twenty-fifth Anniversary of the Founding of Little Africa, 1916.

LITTLE LOOMHOUSE, THE. The Little Loomhouse, a complex of three rustic cabins, is located on the north ridge of KENWOOD HILL in Louisville's South End. The area has gone through four distinct periods of development. First, it was an Indian hunting ground; then, a business and caretaker's quarters for a quarry located on the hillside; next, a turn-of-the-century artists' colony; and finally, during LOU TATE BOUSMAN's residence, a weaving center.

Each cabin has its own design and tradition, and each has acquired a personality of its own. The lower cabin, called Esta from an old Norse saying meaning, "May God's presence be in this dwelling," was Lou Tate's home for forty years. Built in 1870, it has undergone a number of changes through the years. The middle cabin, Wisteria, was built in 1895 by developer Sam Stone Bush from native oak trees cut from the hillside. It is of board-and-batten construction, with a corridor down the center and French doors on each end for ventilation. Tate used it mainly for her children's programs. The upper cabin, Tophouse, was also built of board-and-batten siding, with a second-story gable. An open porch on two sides of the cabin was later glass-enclosed.

Tate used the upper cabin for loom weaving. Experimental weaving groups, visiting weavers, and well-known textile artists were all headquartered there. In-house and visiting exhibits there emphasized new patterns and innovative ideas throughout Tate's working years. When Tate died in 1979, she left the Little Loomhouse and all its contents to a foundation devoted to HISTORIC PRESERVATION, education, and arts participation. The nonprofit Lou Tate Foundation Inc. carries on the unique work she started and promoted during a lifetime of artistic endeavor.

See Alice S. Davidson, *The Little Loomhouse, A Brief History* (Lou Tate Foundation 1997).

Alice S. Davidson

LITTLE SISTERS OF THE POOR. The Little Sisters of the Poor, a Roman Catholic charitable and religious order, opened a home in Louisville September 26, 1869, at 622 S Tenth St. The order, founded by Jeanne Jugan in France in 1839, performs a worldwide mission of charity to the elderly in need, regardless of race or creed. The order's Louisville home was named in honor of St. Joseph. A paralyzed woman became the first of more than four thousand patients cared for by the sisters during their first century. In 1977, however, the sisters announced they would close the home. Much of the building no longer met state codes for healthcare facilities. The 135 residents were moved to other homes operated by the Little Sisters in nearby cities or to alternate NURSING facilities in Louisville. As they left Louisville, the Little Sisters promised to return. In 1989 they launched a fund drive to raise money for new facilities at 15 Audubon Plaza Dr., off Poplar Level Rd., on a sixteen-acre property donated by the Archdiocese of Louisville. The Little Sisters dedicated their new 125,000-square-foot nursing home on May 15, 1991. Additional facilities included a day center for the elderly and APARTMENTS for assisted living. A brick from the old building was placed in the cornerstone of the new home. As the new residence was also named for St. Joseph, the old home's statue of the saint holding an infant Jesus was brought out of storage and installed on the front lawn.

See *Courier-Journal*, March 1, 1977, March 29, 1989, May 2, 1989, May 5, 1989, July 6, 1989, Dec. 1, 1989, Feb. 6, 1990, May 15–16, 1991, July 1, 1992; *The Record*, Archdiocese of Louisville, May 16, 1991; *Harper-Collins Encyclopedia of Catholicism* (San Francisco 1995).

Mary Margaret Bell

LOCK MANUFACTURERS. Rim locks were being manufactured in Louisville before 1843. One of the first was the large, wrought-iron "Patterson" lock, seen in many historic homes. John Patterson began manufacturing locks in Birmingham near Pittsburgh but at an early date set up another plant in Louisville. It was located on Third St. near Market. By 1855 this plant was being operated as Augustus C. Harig, Lock Manufacturer. After 1859 the company was called the Kentucky Lock Manufactory.

In 1859 locks were also being made on Jefferson St. by a partnership consisting of John Eberhard and Henry Speckman. A short time later George Bahr and Jacob Ernwin were also manufacturing locks. Their company, located on Sixth St., was called the Louisville Lock Factory.

After the CIVIL WAR several more companies began to manufacture locks. The Gibson & Hemler Co. was located on Green St. (Liberty), and Deally, James, & Co. was operating on W Jefferson St.

By 1872 one of Louisville's first lock manufacturers, Augustus Harig, had died. The Bahr & Ernwin partnership had split up, with each man running his own company. In 1875 two other lock companies were started, one by Frederick Illig on W MARKET St. and another by Joseph Siebert at First and Ferry St. in PORTLAND.

Before the turn of the century, Henry P. Speckman acquired the manufacturing rights of George Bahr, and his company began to make locks that had been designed and previously sold by Bahr. By then Speckman was operating from a Market St. store and beginning to deal in all types of hardware, not just locks. By 1915 the company stopped making locks and began selling hardware made by others.

Neal O. Hammon

LOCUST GROVE HISTORIC HOME. Built in 1790 by WILLIAM CROGHAN and his wife Lucy Clark Croghan, sister of GEORGE ROGERS CLARK, the 12-room brick house stands on 55 of the original 693.5-acre tract 6 miles east of downtown Louisville. The ARCHITECTURE is Georgian, reflecting a popular style in the colonies during the eighteenth century. William Croghan served as his own architect, and the five-bay house is simple and symmetrical. Most construction materials came from the property, with brass hardware and glass windowpanes imported from Pennsylvania. Another imported element was the FRENCH arabesque wallpaper designed by the Reveillon Studio in Paris, France. It dates back to 1786 and is reflective of the neoclassical revival. Enslaved Africans and other laborers, possibly indentured servants, provided labor for the construction. Some detail work likely was completed by traveling craftsmen, as elements of very similar design are found in other Jefferson County houses built at this time.

An IRISH immigrant, William Croghan briefly served with the British army during the Revolutionary War before joining the Eighth Virginia Regiment. He was captured and held in Charleston, South Carolina, where he met Jonathan Clark, oldest son of John and Ann Clark. Croghan later became acquainted with Jonathan's brother, Revolutionary War hero George Rogers Clark. In 1784 William Croghan traveled to Kentucky with a commission to survey military lands. Clark's parents, Ann and John, and his siblings still residing at home moved from Virginia to Kentucky in 1785, and Croghan married Lucy Clark in 1789. They began construction on Locust Grove in the following year.

Locust Grove served as a social center at the end of the eighteenth and in the early nineteenth century. In 1805 former vice president Aaron Burr (1801–05) visited Locust Grove during his travels through the region. In 1806 Meriwether Lewis and WILLIAM CLARK, younger brother of Lucy and George Rogers, stopped at Locust Grove following their famed discovery expedition to the Pacific Ocean. In 1809 George Rogers Clark, aging and in poor health, moved to Locust Grove and lived there until his death in 1818. Other famous visitors included President James Monroe (1817–25) and Gen. Andrew Jackson, who visited in 1819 during a tour of western military installations. Jackson later returned with his wife, Rachel. Neighbor and future president ZACHARY TAYLOR (1849–50) grew up at his father's farm, Springfield, about one mile east of Locust Grove and likely was a frequent visitor. Naturalist and artist JOHN JAMES AUDUBON was a family friend and did some of his Louisville area work at Locust Grove. In 1841 noted abolitionist Cassius Marcellus Clay fought a duel there with Robert Wickliffe Jr. Neither participant was wounded.

William and Lucy Croghan reared eight children at Locust Grove. Their eldest, Dr. JOHN

CROGHAN, was an important early developer of Mammoth Cave during the 1840s. Third son William Croghan Jr. inherited Locust Grove from his father in 1822. He married Pittsburgh heiress Mary Carson O'Hara in 1823 and resided at Locust Grove until her death in 1828. At that time William moved to Pittsburgh to manage the O'Hara estate, and Locust Grove was sold to his brother-in-law, George Hancock. Hancock had married Eliza Croghan in 1819. Eliza died in 1833 in a cholera epidemic, and Hancock sold Locust Grove to Dr. John Croghan. John Croghan maintained the property until his death in 1849, when Locust Grove fell to the supervision of nephew St. George Croghan. St. George rented out the property until his death in 1861. Then Locust Grove was placed in trust for his infant son. In 1878 the property was purchased by riverboat captain James Paul. The Paul family held the property only five years before it was sold to Richard Waters, whose family operated Locust Grove as a general farm.

In 1961, after almost eighty years in the ownership of the Waters family, Locust Grove was to be sold at auction. There was much local interest in saving the property from demolition, and the commonwealth of Kentucky and Jefferson County purchased the site to ensure its preservation. Research on the history of Locust Grove, restoration of the main house, and archaeological studies of the outbuildings began soon after. The house museum opened for public tours in 1964.

Locust Grove Historic Home is a National Historic Landmark, is listed on the NATIONAL REGISTER OF HISTORIC PLACES, and is only the second site, after Mount Vernon, listed on the National Register of the Surveyors Historical Society.

See Samuel W. Thomas, *The Restoration of Locust Grove* (Louisville 1984); Gwynne Bryant, ed., *The Croghans of Locust Grove*, Locust Grove division of Historic Homes Foundation Inc. (Louisville 1988); Clay Lancaster, *Antebellum Architecture of Kentucky* (Lexington 1991).

Julia C. Parke

LOEVENHART AND COMPANY. Loevenhart's menswear store began at the southeast corner of Louisville's Third and MARKET Streets in 1898. The business was brought to the community by Henry and Lee Loevenhart, who had immigrated from Wolfhenhasen, Germany. The brothers began their retail careers as watchmakers and jewelers in a variety of outlets in rural Kentucky and Tennessee. At their initial West Market location in downtown Louisville, they employed such shopping innovations as neon lighting, air-conditioning, street-level display windows, and Louisville's first air-freight delivery of dry goods.

By 1971 the family-run business had left downtown and centered its retailing efforts at its sole suburban outlet. Four generations of Loevenhart retailing expertise came to a close in December 1995 when the company's OXMOOR Mall location closed.

Kenneth Miller

LOGAN, WILLIAM HUME (b Marion County, Kentucky, November 28, 1862; d Louisville, October 21, 1948). Businessman. William Logan, known as "W.H." to friends and family, was the son of William Tinsley and Eva (Duncan) Logan. His first exposure to business was at the age of seven selling apples on the streets of Lebanon, Kentucky. Later he sold produce from a truck garden on his parents' farm.

After attending Columbia Christian College and Transylvania University in Lexington, Logan traveled to Louisville seeking employment. He was hired to do menial work by A.G. Dow in Dow's Wire Works Co. and was soon made bookkeeper and eventually president of the company.

W.H. Logan married Susan Viola Smith in 1888. They had four sons and a daughter. The daughter, Eva Viola Logan Littell (1894–1958), was the only child not to join W.H. in running the Logan Co. Logan Co. evolved out of Dow's Wire Works. The oldest son Robert Smith "R.S." Logan (1889–1987) was the first to succeed W.H. Logan as president of Logan Co. Edward Carter "E.C." Logan (1892–1973) ran the engineering portion of the company. William Hume Logan Jr. (1898–1992) managed ADVERTISING at Logan, while Zack Smith Logan (1900–81) ran the manufacturing end of the business. Each son served as president of the company when his older brother reached age sixty-five.

W.H. Logan is buried with his wife in CAVE HILL CEMETERY.

Zack H.Logan

LOGAN COMPANY. The Logan Co. was founded in 1876 by A.G. Dow under the name Dow's Wire Works Co. Mr. Dow hired William Hume Logan of Marion County, Kentucky, as bookkeeper in 1884. The earliest location of the business was in Mr. Dow's residence at 726 W MARKET St. Early records indicate twelve to fifteen employees. W.H. Logan purchased controlling interest in 1889 and was named president by 1891. By 1910 offices were moved to Franklin and Buchanan Streets in the BUTCHERTOWN area of Louisville.

In 1925, when the name was changed to Logan Co., W.H. Logan was president and his four sons, Robert S., Edward Carter, W. Hume Junior, and Zack S., were working in the business. Logan's earliest products were builders' wire and iron, ornamental iron, innerspring mattresses, bedding, summer furniture, and fireplace equipment.

Logan Co. was one of the first to develop the roller conveyor bearing. Using a fixed steel shaft and iron tubing from its bedding business, the simplest gravity roller conveyor was built. The Logan Co. grew in its Butchertown location to encompass over three hundred thousand square feet of manufacturing space and had over six hundred employees. Plant and office expansion in the same neighborhood moved the principal address to 200 Cable St.

The ornamental iron was sold under the trade name Colonel Logan and enjoyed nationwide sales prominence in the 1950s. The in-house development of automated weaving machines positioned Logan Co. as the nation's largest manufacturer of woven wire partitions in the 1960s. At that time, it was the largest conveyor manufacturer in Kentucky.

A majority of the Logan family interest in the company was sold in 1966 to George Meyer Manufacturing Co. of Milwaukee, Wisconsin. Automatic Sprinkler Corp. of America (also known as A-T-0 and subsequently Figgie International) bought both the Meyer Co. and the remaining Logan family interest in 1968. Under the new management, Logan Conveyor increased sales to become, at one time, the fifth-largest package-handling conveyor company in the world.

Changing technology and financial losses by the parent company, Figgie International, caused the company to be shut down in 1994. At the end of its 118-year history, Logan Co. had only 6 employees.

Zack H.Logan

LONG RUN BAPTIST CHURCH. Located in eastern Jefferson County on Flat Rock Rd., the Long Run Baptist Church is one of the oldest existing Baptist congregations in the Louisville area. Named after a nearby tributary of Floyd's Fork, the church was constituted in 1794. Upon leaving the Salem Baptist Association of churches, which had grown too large, Long Run Baptist Church joined with Beargrass, Chenoweth's Run, and Cane and Back Run Churches to form the Long Run Baptist Association in 1803. The church established itself as a leader among these churches and hosted the first annual meeting of the Long Run Association the same year. The church ran into difficulty as soon as it rose to prominence. In 1804, at a neighborhood log-rolling, several members of the church engaged in a heated argument concerning whether it would be permissible to lie under certain circumstances. A hypothetical situation was proposed regarding whether it would be justifiable for a father to lie about hiding his only remaining child to a group of Indians who had already killed four of his children. Two groups emerged over the issue, and the church split. Those who affirmed the permissibility of lying became known as "the lying party" and left Long Run Baptist Church to form Flat Rock Baptist Church, later Pleasant Grove Baptist Church. In all, six new churches have sprung from Long Run Baptist throughout its history, some as a result of internal splits and others from missionary endeavors.

Two pastors in the nineteenth century helped Long Run prosper. John Dale, who

Long Run Baptist Church, 1922.

served the church from 1823 to 1849, baptized 305 persons at Long Run Baptist Church during his ministry. W.E. Powers, pastor from 1862 to 1892, further established the church's reputation and served as the moderator of the Long Run Baptist Association for thirty-four years.

During the twentieth century, Long Run Baptist Church has been recognized for its historic character, partly because the original church was built on the site of Abraham Lincoln's grandfather's log cabin (some say on his grave site). Long Run was recognized as a national landmark in the 1960s. The 1840s single-story brick church building, which had been built to replace an earlier structure, was destroyed by a fire ignited by the sanctuary's potbellied stove on Christmas Eve in 1960. A new building was completed in 1961, the same year that the site, with the ruins and the cemetery, was deeded to the JEFFERSON COUNTY FISCAL COURT, which maintains it as a public shrine. The current congregation, composed of a largely rural constituency, struggles to define itself in the increasingly affluent eastern end of Jefferson County.

See Ira V. Birdwhistell, *Gathered at the River: A Narrative History of the Long Run Baptist Association* (Louisville 1978); Thomas C. Fisher, "Morgan Hughes Station and Long Run Baptist Church," *Filson Club History Quarterly* 20 (Oct. 1946): 279–90; George Barry Harkness, "Adapting to a Changing Community at Long Run Baptist Church," D.Min. dissertation, Southern Baptist Theological Seminary, 1991; Frank M. Masters, *A History of Baptists in Kentucky* (Louisville 1953); J.H. Spencer, *A History of Kentucky Baptists,* vol. 1 (Cincinnati 1886).

Gregory A. Thornbury

LONG RUN MASSACRE. The Long Run Massacre occurred September 13, 1781, east of present-day Eastwood on the Falls Trace. At the massacre site, the trace intersects the Long Run of Floyd's Fork; hence the name. It was one of the frontier battles that pitted American settlers against the British and their North American Indian allies during the Revolutionary War.

The previous day, settlers at SQUIRE BOONE'S Painted Stone Station (north of present-day SHELBYVILLE) had learned that a large war party (estimated at some four to five hundred) would raid their area. The majority decided to abandon their exposed position and seek refuge in the BEARGRASS STATIONS. The party was escorted by a light horse troop commanded by Capt. James Welch from the FORT NELSON garrison.

The Indians ambushed the party at the thirteen-mile tree, approximately eight miles from Linn's Station. A running battle resulted for almost a mile, with the settlers continuing to rush toward the Beargrass stations located to the west. Some fought with bravery, while others abandoned their neighbors. Thomas McCarty, one of the men who stood fast, later recalled "seeing a cowardly fellow in the act of driving a woman off her horse" and told the unidentified person to cease and desist or he would shoot him.

At least seven pioneers were killed, but some estimate the casualties to exceed ten. The Indian losses, if any, are unknown. Most of the survivors reached the safety of Linn's Station that night. This defeat was followed the next day by FLOYD'S DEFEAT, an even costlier battle with the Indian-British force.

See Draper MSS, 19C, 90, 91, and 95; Lou Catherine Clore, "Long Run Massacre," *Register of the Kentucky Historical Society* 10 (Jan. 1912): 75–76.

Blaine A. Guthrie Jr.

LOOMIS, ARTHUR (b Westfield, Massachusetts, January 28, 1859; d Louisville, January 8, 1935). Architect. Loomis was the son of Dr. John and Clarissa (Robinson) Loomis. He came to JEFFERSONVILLE, INDIANA, with his family just prior to the CIVIL WAR. There he was educated and spent most of his adult life, moving to Louisville about 1910.

Loomis designed some of the city's well-known buildings and churches. Beginning in 1876, he began working with noted Louisville architect Charles J. Clarke, taking over as head draftsman in 1885. In 1891 he became a partner in the firm of Clarke and Loomis, one of the most prestigious Louisville firms, for the next twenty years. In 1902 the firm completed Louisville's second ten-story skyscraper, the TODD BUILDING, commissioned by Louisville businessman James Ross Todd and located on the northeast corner of Fourth and MARKET Streets. The building, principally designed by Loomis, was the first steel-framed, fireproof structure in Kentucky.

The firm, which was quite prolific, designed numerous residences in the Richardsonian Romanesque style popular during the late Victorian period, including the residences of Theophilus Conrad on St. James Ct. and George A. Robinson on Fourth St. They also designed the Levy Brothers Store at Third and Market Streets in 1893, the Louisville Medical College in 1891, and the Manual Training School in 1893.

After Clarke's death in 1908, Loomis worked independently, then took on Julius Hartman as a partner after 1910. It was around this time that Loomis began to design structures in the newly popular Italian Renaissance style advocated by the Ecole des Beaux-Arts in Paris. Some of his most important works in this style include the Shelby Park Library (1911) and the CARNEGIE LIBRARY in Jeffersonville, Indiana (1904).

After 1920 Loomis worked alone, producing some of his most noted architectural works. Perhaps his best-known work was the J.B. SPEED ART MUSEUM, which opened in 1927 on South Third St. It was inspired by the Cleveland Museum of Art, an example of the neoclassical style known more for function and security than aesthetics. He also helped design several structures at the SOUTHERN BAPTIST THEOLOGICAL SEMINARY, working with noted New York architect James Gamble Rogers. He also designed homes for former governor Augustus E. Willson and Louisville businessman Alvin T. Hert.

Loomis is generally considered the first president of the Kentucky chapter of the American Institute of Architects. Although Clarke was elected the first president, he died before taking office, and Loomis was picked to succeed him. Loomis was married to Carrie Dorsey in 1902 but was a widower at the time of his death. He died of a heart attack while recovering from a hip injury he received when struck by a folding bed in his home on Belgravia Ct. He is buried in CAVE HILL CEMETERY.

See Harry James Boswell, *Representative Ken-*

tuckians (Louisville 1913); Kentucky Resources and Industries (Louisville ca. 1902), 157; Lewis C. Baird, *Baird's History of Clark County, Indiana* (Indianapolis 1909), 653.

LORETTO HIGH SCHOOL. Formerly known as CEDAR GROVE ACADEMY and founded by the Sisters of Loretto in 1842, the institution was forced to move out of the PORTLAND neighborhood in 1925 for financial reasons. The school reopened in 1926 with its new name and a new location in the Basil Doerhoefer mansion at the corner of BROADWAY and 45th St. In 1951, a new two-story brick building was added to the existing structure. By the early seventies, the school, which had become predominantly African American following the exit of many white families from the Shawnee neighborhood after WORLD WAR II, was having financial troubles.

Declining enrollment, coupled with rising operating costs and increased salaries for lay teachers, forced the school to close in 1973 amidst cries of racism. The remaining students were transferred to nearby FLAGET HIGH SCHOOL, creating the area's first Catholic coeducational high school. Flaget closed a year later. In 1974 Loretto High School's former building was dedicated as the Christ Temple Apostolic Church.

See Clyde F. Crews, *An American Holy Land: A History of the Archdiocese of Louisville* (Louisville 1987).

LOUIS XVI (b Saint-Germain-en Laye, France, August 23, 1754; d Paris, January 21, 1793). King of France. Born Louis-Auguste to Louis the dauphin of France and Marie-Josèphe of Saxony, he became heir when his father and two elder brothers died, and he inherited the throne in 1774. Louis's two younger brothers would rule over postrevolutionary France between 1814 and 1830 as Louis XVIII and Charles X, respectively. His youngest sister, Elizabeth, shared his imprisonment in THE TEMPLE. At sixteen, Louis married Marie-Antoinette of Austria in order to seal a Franco-Austrian alliance. They had four children. The second son, Louis-Charles de France, duc de Normandie, became dauphin in 1789 and Louis XVII at his father's death, but in most historical accounts he did not survive the Revolution.

Louis initially supported revolutionary reforms of the National Assembly in 1789 but withdrew support as transformations became more radical. After attempting to flee the country in 1791, the royal family remained under house arrest. The provisional revolutionary GOVERNMENT tried and convicted Louis of conspiracy against France and of threatening national security. He was executed by the guillotine.

Although Louis XVI has historically been portrayed as an incompetent buffoon incapable of perceiving revolutionary ideals and personal consequences, his actions before the French Revolution demonstrated a willingness to advance reforms. Nevertheless, he lacked the necessary political acumen and strength of character. His chief advisors receive credit for attempts to reconcile financial and political imbalances. As foreign secretary, Charles Gravier, comte de Vergennes, initiated French involvement in the American Revolution. A 1778 defensive treaty signed by Louis and American representative Benjamin Franklin secured troops, supplies, and naval support for the colonies, ensuring both American independence and French financial ruin.

In 1774 French and Indian War veterans from Virginia acquired government land grants on the site of what would become the city of Louisville and parts of Jefferson County. By sometime in 1779 the town founded at the FALLS OF THE OHIO the year before was being called Louisville in honor of France and Louis XVI's aid to the young United States. In 1780 the Virginia legislature chartered the town, which then officially received the name *Louisville.* Despite his faults and early death, Louisvillians remember the monarch for his role in aiding the American War for Independence. Michael Barone's *Almanac of American Politics* points out that only one other American city, St. Paul, Minnesota, is named for a man who was executed.

A Carrara marble statue of King Louis XVI now stands on the lawn of the JEFFERSON COUNTY COURTHOUSE. The statue, commissioned by Louis's daughter Marie-Therese and sculpted by Achille-Joseph Valois, stands three and one half meters tall and weighs nine tons. Soon after the original unveiling of the statue in Montpellier, France, in 1829, the second French Revolution began.

The statue was moved to a military installation for safekeeping, then to a hall in Montpellier University, and finally to the storage basement of the municipal ARCHIVES. There the statue was found in 1899, severely damaged, with one of the arms missing. The statue remained there until the mid-twentieth century. In 1956 Louisville and Montpellier, France, proclaimed themselves to be sister cities. In 1966 the mayor of Montpellier announced that he planned to present the statue to the city of Louisville as a display of friendship. After seven months of transit, the statue finally arrived in Louisville. On July 17, 1967, Mayor Francois Delmas presented the statue, in person, to Louisville mayor Kenneth Schmied at the unveiling ceremony. The ceremony was attended by over three hundred people, including several American and French notables.

See John Hardman, *Louis XVI* (New Haven 1993); Samuel F. Scott and Barry Rothaus, eds., *Historical Dictionary of the French Revolution, 1789–1799* (Westport, Conn., 1985); François Furet and Mona Ozouf, eds., *A Critical Dictionary of the French Revolution* (Cambridge, Mass., 1989); Vincent Cronin, *Louis and Antoinette* (London 1974); Leslie C. Tihany, "Louis XVI in Louisville: Background and History of a Statue," *Filson Club History Quarterly* 73 (Jan. 1999): 62–76.

Alana Cain Scott

LOUISVILLE, USS. Four Navy ships have been named for Kentucky's largest city. The first was an ironclad paddlewheel steamer built during the CIVIL WAR for service on the Ohio and Mississippi Rivers and their many tributaries. Commissioned on January 16, 1862, the *Louisville* participated in numerous engagements, often in conjunction with army operations where the ironclads patrolling the rivers could offer close support. *Louisville* thus assisted in the capture of Fort Donelson; the occupation of Columbus, Kentucky; the capture of Memphis, Tennessee; and the siege of Vicksburg, Mississippi. The ironclad *Louisville* served with distinction to the end of the war.

The second *Louisville* appeared briefly during WORLD WAR I, when the name was given to a requisitioned passenger liner converted into a troopship. After several round trips to Europe, the liner was returned to her owner and her original name.

The third *Louisville* (CA-28), the most famous of them all, was a Northampton-class heavy cruiser commissioned January 15, 1931, and known affectionately as the Lady Lou. With a main battery of three turrets (each with three eight-inch guns) complemented by four five-inch gun mounts, the *Louisville* was a powerful warship that was to prove its worth in many hostile engagements during WORLD WAR II. The *Louisville* helped carry the war in the Pacific, island by island, closer to the Japanese mainland, participating in campaigns off the Solomons, Guadalcanal, the Marshalls, Eniwetok, the Philippines, and nearly every other corner of the Pacific. *Louisville* was in the battle line at Surigao Strait, the Philippines, on October 25, 1944, helping to defeat a large Japanese force in the biggest naval engagement of the war. The ship was struck by two kamikazes off the Philippines in January 1945. Thirty-two men were killed, and the ship was forced to return to CALIFORNIA for repairs. *Louisville* was back in action for the Battle of Okinawa, where, on June 5, 1945, it was once again struck by a kamikaze; however, the ship was able to continue the campaign.

On June 17, 1946, the *Louisville* was decommissioned and placed in reserve. Despite efforts in Louisville to raise enough funds to purchase the ship, in 1959 the Lady Lou was sold for scrap.

The fourth and current *Louisville* (SSN-724) is a Los Angeles–class attack submarine commissioned on November 8, 1986. As of 1998 it was still serving in the navy.

See *Man of War: Log of the United States Heavy Cruiser Louisville* (Philadelphia 1946); Navy Department. *Dictionary of American Naval Fighting Ships*, vol. 4 (Washington, D.C., 1969); Larry A. Pearson, "Remembering the

Lady Lou," *Kentucky Monthly* 3 (Jan./Feb. 1982).

John S. Gillig

LOUISVILLE ACADEMY OF MUSIC. The founding of the academy on February 15, 1954, at 1577 Bardstown Rd. was the result of a partnership between Robert Bruce French and Donald Christie Murray. French assumed the administrative duties and provided income by copying symphonic scores and parts, and Murray taught piano and JAZZ workshops. A staff of eight gave vocal and instrumental lessons; and the Academy Chorale, a twenty-member choral group, was formed by faculty member Richard Dales.

In 1956 the school moved to 1020 S Fifth St. A board of directors was organized, and, on March 25, 1957, the school was incorporated as a nonprofit, tax-exempt educational institution. In July 1957 the academy leased the Victorian home of JAMES BRECKINRIDGE SPEED at 505 W Ormsby Ave. With larger quarters the school was able to organize a piano technology department, headed by Russell Sturgeon. In addition, the LOUISVILLE YOUTH ORCHESTRA was founded there in 1958.

In 1960 the academy bought the St. Matthews School of Music for use as a branch, and in 1971 a building at 2740 Frankfort Ave. was purchased. The branch was closed in 1978.

The present building on Frankfort Ave. consists of studios, a recital hall, a library and archive that contains thousands of books, records, and files on Kentucky musicians and organizations. The academy has presented more than a thousand programs and has trained over seven thousand students, many of whom have become composers, teachers, chamber music performers, and members of major ORCHESTRAS.

See Agnes Crume, "Music Still Has a Home in the Old Speed Mansion," *Courier-Journal*, July 20, 1969.

Robert Bruce French

LOUISVILLE AND JEFFERSON COUNTY RIVERPORT AUTHORITY. Responsible for promoting industry and commerce along the navigable waterways of the county, the riverport authority was created by the city and county a year after the Kentucky General Assembly passed an act in 1964 enabling local officials throughout the state to establish port authorities. The county judge/executive chooses its director and six-member board; the latter serve three-year terms.

The Riverport Authority began with high hopes in the mid-1960s, as the Louisville Chamber of Commerce and local officials planned a large riverside industrial complex in southwestern Jefferson County. Fearful of diminishing industrial property and increasing residential development, leaders chose the flat land primarily because of its availability and its location near major transportation routes. By the middle of the 1970s, a $6.3 million county bond issue had paid for the 1,623-acre site, and consultants optimistically claimed that it could provide 26,000 jobs by 1980. Although the flood wall was extended from the Mill Creek cutoff to KOSMOSDALE and protected the site, by 1982 the acreage remained mostly farmland. After $65 million of local and state money had been spent to supply the area with roads, sewers, water mains, and railroad lines, development included only a small warehouse and a Foreign Trade Zone (FTZ) building. The Foreign Trade Zone, granted by a national FTZ Board comprising the secretaries of Treasury, Commerce, and Army, allows companies to either defer import duties until the goods actually enter the U.S. market or avoid paying duties altogether if the components are shipped separately and assembled in the FTZ. The authority, which was $11 million in debt, blamed the undeveloped complex's woes on the recession and the lack of a port.

In 1983 the federal GOVERNMENT gave $2 million and the local government gave another $2 million for construction of a port. By the end of the year, two companies had agreed to move their operations to the site, located between the OHIO RIVER and Mill Creek and bisected by the Greenbelt Hwy. and Lower River Rd. Louisville's ECONOMY began to grow rapidly by the late 1980s, and the Riverport Industrial Park began attracting regional distribution facilities. UPS's nearby air freight hub improved interstate highway access, and aggressive state and local tax incentives also contributed to the rapid development of the park in the 1990s. By 2000 Jefferson Riverport International contained ninety manufacturing, service, and distribution companies that employed more than seven thousand workers.

In addition to managing Jefferson Riverport International, the riverport authority provides services to other local industrial PARKS such as Hurstbourne Green and Eastpoint Business Center.

See *Courier-Journal*, Nov. 21, 1982; George H. Yater, "Riverport: New Kingdom for the Southwest," *Louisville* 25 (July 1975): 39–43; John T. Adams III and Terry A. Below, "Louisville around the World," *Louisville* 27 (June 1976): 42–47.

First locomotive repaired in new L&N shops, June 1905.

LOUISVILLE & NASHVILLE RAILROAD COMPANY (L&N). L&N, Louisville's leading railroad, was, of all area rail carriers, the most closely linked with the city's growth and development. A corporate entity from 1850 to 1983, the L&N was born in Jefferson County and after the CIVIL WAR was expanded to become the first major rail system in the South. General offices, extensive terminal facilities, repair shops, and a large workforce all contributed to L&N's long and significant presence in Louisville. From the city's business community came the railroad's early leadership, and for years afterwards city businessmen filled chairs of its directorships.

It was Louisville's need for improved transportation that led to the chartering of the L&N in March 1850. That need was further spurred by rivalry with Cincinnati and Nashville for southern markets. The city subscribed more than $3 million in stock over the next decade to capitalize construction of L&N's main line to Nashville, and businessmen Leven L. Shreve and JAMES GUTHRIE became its first and third presidents, respectively. Construction forces pushed south from the city during 1855. Muldraugh Hill was assaulted and Elizabethtown reached in June 1858. The Green River at Munfordville was bridged a year later.

Through service was inaugurated to Nashville in October 1859. By then, there was reliable year-round travel, and shipping schedules could be measured in hours instead of days or weeks—ten hours by passenger train to Nashville versus two or three days by stage or horseback; twelve to sixteen hours for freight moving by rail between the two cities, compared with five days or longer by wagons or STEAMBOATS, the latter dependent on seasonal vagaries of rivers. At Nashville a through rail route continued on to Atlanta, Macon, and Savannah, while, after 1861 and completion of L&N's Memphis Line, connections to that city, New Orleans, and the Gulf Coast became available to local shippers and travelers alike.

With main line and branches periodically sniped at by Gen. John Hunt Morgan and other Confederate raiders, the L&N struggled to maintain operations throughout the Civil War. However, at war's end, the road emerged in strong-enough fiscal and operational condition to undertake expansion, by 1880 growing from a regional carrier to become the South's first major rail system. That growth was accomplished by purchase and rehabilitation of war-damaged lines in Tennessee and Alabama to reach Birmingham, Montgomery, and the Gulf Coast, and by construction of new routes through northern Alabama and southeastern Kentucky.

In 1867–70, L&N supported construction of the first OHIO RIVER bridge at Louisville, the railroad believing that access to the Midwest and Northeast should be sought. ALBERT FINK, the road's chief engineer, designed the bridge, which utilized his truss design in its twenty-seven spans.

Participation with other RAILROADS in so-called express car and fast freight routes enabled the L&N to offer Louisville shippers expedited service to many southern cities from the late 1860s on and, in turn, tap the recovering resources of the region. Until the late 1870s and completion of competing railroads into the South, the L&N was the only line that ran between the Ohio Valley and the central south and Gulf Coast. That fact enabled it to prosper and gain a lead over its competitors. Such geographic circumstances also benefited Louisville businesses that depended on L&N freight cars to roll their products southward.

In 1881, L&N purchased the former Louisville, Cincinnati, & Lexington (which had built the LaGrange-Cincinnati Short Line in 1867–69 and the earlier Louisville-Frankfort-Lexington links) and properties of the St. Louis & Southeastern. Ownership of Southeastern gave L&N access to St. Louis and Evansville as well as trackage through western Kentucky. Completion in 1885 of its Ohio River bridge at Henderson provided L&N a direct Midwest-to-central-South route, eliminating a time-consuming river ferry.

Additional line construction and purchase of smaller regional railroads by the L&N continued into the twentieth century. That growth took L&N rails deep into the eastern and western Kentucky coalfields, helping to develop those districts and providing faster transport for that fuel to the city's industries and domestic markets. Purchase of the Louisville, Henderson, & St. Louis in 1929 offered a line to Owensboro and Evansville. Merger in 1957 with the Nashville, Chattanooga, & St. Louis (which L&N had controlled since the 1880s) produced more direct routes to Atlanta and Memphis.

Access to Chicago was achieved in 1969–71 with purchase of the Chicago & Eastern Illinois Railroad's Evansville line and the Monon main line through Bloomington and Lafayette, Indiana. At its full geographic growth in 1971, the L&N operated sixty-five hundred route miles of main and secondary lines in thirteen midwestern and southern states and ranked as the sixteenth-largest railroad in the nation. Six main lines—from Chicago, Cincinnati, Lexington–eastern Kentucky, Corbin–southeastern Kentucky, Nashville–Gulf Coast, and Evansville–St. Louis—converged on Louisville, making the city a key L&N hub and placing L&N first among its eight line-haul rail carriers. L&N tracks reached more than sixty Kentucky counties, also ranking the road largest in the state in mileage and employment.

Early in the twentieth century, the Atlantic Coast Line acquired a minority stock interest in the L&N. Ultimately the long association with ACL and its successor Seaboard Coast Line led to purchase by Seaboard's holding company, SCL Industries, of all L&N stock in 1971–72 and, later (1983), to full merger and loss of L&N identity. Finally, in 1986, CSX Corp. of Richmond, Virginia, brought under one ownership the Seaboard and the Chessie System (Baltimore & Ohio and Chesapeake & Ohio) families of railroads to form its rail unit, CSX Transportation.

From the outset, Louisville became L&N's headquarters city. First offices were housed in the combination freight and passenger station at Ninth & BROADWAY. In 1851 a corporate office was established in a building at Main and Bullitt Streets. In 1877 all offices moved into a new building L&N had constructed at Second and Main, its rooms said to be ample enough to hold all company stockholders. After completion in 1907 of the eleven-story brick building at Ninth and Broadway, offices of most departments were centered at that location. An addition, finished in early 1930, filled up the remainder of the block to Tenth St., making the expanded general office building one of the nation's largest devoted exclusively to one railroad's use. Over two thousand men and women worked there, about a fifth of L&N's total Louisville workforce (in 1930). A neon L&N sign on the top east end of the building made it a downtown landmark. After the Seaboard merger, the building was sold in 1984 to the commonwealth of Kentucky.

Needing a repair shop, the young L&N in 1858 purchased the old Kentucky Locomotive Works at Tenth & Kentucky Streets. Over the next four decades, that shop (with smaller shops elsewhere) kept the line's growing fleet of cars and engines in repair and built new rolling stock when needed. The engine *Southern Belle,* assembled in 1871, inspired verse and song from the city's bard, Will S. Hays. Many shop workers lived in the Limerick neighborhood just to the east.

L&N's great expansion by 1900 dictated need for a much larger repair facility, and between 1902 and 1905 the railroad erected a vast complex of twenty buildings on sixty-eight acres

Louisville & Nashville Railroad Company's Union Station and headquarters building, Broadway between Ninth and Eleventh, 1933.

in SOUTH LOUISVILLE. The big plant became L&N's system repair base, functioning until 1990 when closed by CSX Transportation. Its buildings later were razed for a new UNIVERSITY OF LOUISVILLE stadium. During the South Louisville shops' eight decades of activity, employees repaired thousands of cars and engines as well as producing 400 new locomotives (282 to L&N's own designs) and more than 14,000 freight and passenger cars. Peak employment totaled about four thousand men and women, who represented a dozen crafts and trade unions.

For eighty-five years, or from September 1891 to October 1976, UNION STATION at Tenth and BROADWAY served as L&N's principal passenger terminal for the city. In its heyday, Union received and dispatched nearly sixty trains a day. A much smaller station built in1881 at First St. and the riverfront by the Louisville, Cincinnati, & Lexington accommodated L&N trains to and from Lexington and HARRODS CREEK until after 1910. For many years, some L&N through and local passenger trains stopped at Baxter Ave., CRESCENT HILL, Gaulbert St., Fourth St., HIGHLAND PARK, and ST. MATTHEWS.

L&N also maintained extensive facilities for its freight traffic. The original combination freight and passenger depot at Ninth and BROADWAY was later expanded to transfer freight between local drayers and railroad box cars. Trains were made up on tracks just south of the freight terminal. After 1905 L&N shifted its freight train makeup to the larger South Louisville and Strawberry Yards; its smaller switching yards and numerous sidings about the city served local industries. Over the decades, the railroad also helped attract new industries to the city and county and built tracks to reach their sites. In 1977 L&N opened its new Osborn Yard in southern Jefferson County and concentrated all local switching and train makeup at the huge four-mile-long automated facility. Smaller yards in town were closed and redundant properties turned over to the city for redevelopment.

During its 132-year history, L&N was led by 21 presidents, some serving lengthy tenures and others in office for only a few months. Most resided in Louisville during their presidencies. L&N's first chief executive was Leven L. Shreve, a prominent Louisville businessman who helped organize the road; he was followed in 1854 by former Kentucky governor John L. Helm, long active on behalf of the road. It was during Helm's tenure that construction of the main line and Lebanon branch was accomplished.

Louisvillian James Guthrie, who succeeded Helm in 1860, had pushed for railroads since the 1830s. Active in state and national politics, he had led meetings in 1849–50 to promote construction of and financing for the L&N. Guthrie oversaw L&N's operation during the Civil War and kept the road solvent so that, upon the return of peace, it was able to embark on its great expansion southward.

Guthrie's strong right hand was L&N's chief engineer, Albert Fink, who had emigrated from Germany in 1849, helped build the Baltimore & Ohio's main line through the Alleghenies, and joined the L&N in 1857. Fink's designs were utilized to erect the first Louisville station as well as the Green and Ohio River bridges, and he kept the line in repair during the Civil War. Although never president, he eventually served L&N in high leadership roles.

Louisvillians Horatio and Victor Newcomb, father and son, led L&N from 1868 to 1874 and for eight months in 1880, directing the road (with Fink) during its southward expansion and securing eastern and overseas financing to pay for that work. Dr. E.D. Standiford, who grew up near Louisville, left MEDICINE to enter business; he served between the two Newcombs, continuing the road's push to the Gulf and its support of industrial development in and around Birmingham. Thomas J. Martin, Edward H. Green, C.C. Baldwin, and J.S. Rogers served only briefly during the 1870s and early 1880s; and New York banker Eckstein Norton, a native Kentuckian who had helped finance several other railroads in the state, led L&N between 1886 and 1891. During the 1880s, control of L&N's financial policy and makeup of its directorship also shifted from Louisville to New York and Wall St.

More than any other chief executive, it was MILTON HANNIBAL SMITH who profoundly influenced the course of L&N's history. Joining the L&N after the Civil War, Smith rose to become president between 1884 and 1886, then served from 1891 until his death in office in 1921. Persuasive and visionary, yet controversial, Smith accomplished much: reorganization of administrative departments, retention of operational control in Louisville (separating it from finances in New York), building extensive lines to serve the Alabama steel industry and the Kentucky coalfields, and system-wide upgrading for anticipated twentieth-century traffic. Upon Smith's death, Louisvillian Wible Mapother served from 1921 to 1926, succeeded by WHITEFOORD COLE (1926–34) and James B. Hill (1934–50). Coming from the presidency of subsidiary Nashville, Chattanooga, & St.Louis, Cole and Hill each helped the road weather the Depression years. They also continued equipment and line modernization and programs started by Smith and Mapother. John E. Tilford (1950–59) oversaw system dieselization and merger of the NC&StL in 1957. Tilford also led the company during the prolonged spring l955 strike. WILLIAM H. KENDALL (1959–72) presided over the L&N during its last full decade as a corporate entity, and he introduced intermodal and unit-train services, along with fleets of specialized cars tailored to shipper needs.

With Seaboard Coast Line's acquisition of L&N in 1972, former L&N attorney Prime F. Osborn of Jacksonville, Florida, followed Kendall as president. He effected closer coordination of Seaboard and L&N staff operations that led to merger of the two systems in 1983. Richard D. Spence, from Conrail and Southern Pacific, was L&N's last resident president, serving between 1978 and 1982.

For many years one of Louisville's largest employers, the L&N also helped start the University of Louisville's engineering school. Individually and corporately, company employees and officers gave generously to charities and numerous civic endeavors. "Kiddie Special" excursions were run many winters for schoolchildren of Jefferson and neighboring counties. During the 1937 flood, special L&N trains shuttled refugees from downtown Louisville to Crescent Hill, Highland Park, and other dry NEIGHBORHOODS to escape rising waters. Long known as "The Old Reliable," the railroad was generally well managed, was never in receivership, and paid conservative dividends to its stockholders during many years of its corporate existence.

See Thomas D. Clark, *The Beginning of the Louisville & Nashville Railroad* (Louisville 1933); Kincaid A. Herr, *Louisville & Nashville Railroad, 1850–1959* (Louisville l959); Maury Klein, *History of the Louisville & Nashville Railroad* (New York l972); Charles B. Castner (with Patrick A. Dorin and Ronald C. Flanary), *Louisville & Nashville Railroad, "The Old Reliable"* (Lynchburg, Va., 1996); *Courier-Journal*, April 19, 1950.

Charles B. Castner

LOUISVILLE AND NASHVILLE TURNPIKE. The Louisville and Nashville Turnpike was the common name for the toll road that extended from Louisville through Elizabethtown, Munfordville, Glasgow Junction (now Park City), Bowling Green, and Franklin to the Tennessee state line. In a message to the General Assembly in 1825, Gov. Joseph Desha (1824–28) promoted the construction of two turnpike roads, one being a Louisville-to-Nashville route by way of the Green River. In 1829 the legislature chartered the Louisville, West Point, and Elizabethtown Turnpike Road Co. to build a road from Louisville by way of West Point to Elizabethtown. The road had not been built after the stipulated three-year limit, and in 1833 a new charter was issued to build a road from Louisville to Bowling Green. In a series of amendments (1837, 1838, and 1847), the legislature approved the division of the road into five sections, each managed by a separate company. The road was projected to extend a total of 143 miles and was to be constructed of macadamized materials, with toll gates placed every 5 miles. Work began in 1837 and within 12 years the Board of Internal Improvements reported nearly 106 miles completed, with much of the remaining route graded.

While the legislature used various names for the company it chartered to build the turnpike—among them the Louisville Turnpike Road Co., the Louisville and Nashville Turnpike Road Co., and, most commonly, the Louisville and Elizabethtown Turnpike Co.—the turnpike itself was never given an official name. The road from Louisville to Nashville through Bardstown, New Haven, Buffalo, Uno, Bear Wallow, Glasgow, Scottsville, and Gallatin, Tennessee, was sometimes referred to as the Louisville and Nashville Turnpike, but the name was more commonly applied to the route through Elizabethtown.

Travel accounts of the day report heavy traffic in both directions throughout the 1850s. After the Louisville & Nashville Railroad was completed in 1859 to serve much of the same area, the turnpike declined in popularity. Much of the road fell into disrepair, and maintenance of various sections was taken over by local county authorities. In 1901 Jefferson County purchased part of the turnpike, by then called the Valley Turnpike, that lay within the county.

By 1924 portions of the turnpike had become part of U.S. 31W, which ran from Sault Ste. Marie, Michigan, south through Louisville, where it was dubbed DIXIE HIGHWAY, to Fort Myers, Florida.

See S.G. Boyd, "The Louisville and Nashville Turnpike," *Register of the Kentucky State Historical Society* 24 (May 1926): 163–74; Frank Dunn, "The Official Opening of the Eastern Dixie Highway," *Kentucky Outlook* 1 (Oct. 17, 1925): 38–41.

LOUISVILLE AND PORTLAND CANAL. When the trustees of the new town of Louisville met for the first time on February 7, 1781, they adopted a petition to the Virginia General Assembly for the right to construct a canal around the FALLS OF THE OHIO, the only serious impediment to OHIO RIVER traffic between Pittsburgh and its juncture with the Mississippi River. During the next half-century, both Kentucky and Indiana made numerous failed attempts to build a canal. It was not until 1830 that the falls were bypassed with a man-made channel, the Louisville and PORTLAND CANAL.

Upriver cities, especially arch rival Cincinnati, blamed Louisville for hampering construction of a canal, since the forced break in the river journey was the basis of the warehousing, commission, and forwarding businesses; drayage, HOTELS and inns; and steamboat provisioning on which Louisville prospered. There was opposition to the canal among some Louisvillians, but others favored it. The *Louisville Public Advertiser* (Feb. 24, 1824), declared that with a canal "the storage and forwarding business would be diminished—and there might be less use for hacks and drays," but that a canal would provide "the necessary power for manufacturing,"

The overriding obstacle to a canal was the cost; the Ohio Valley itself did not have the resources. When outside aid, both public and private, became available; the Louisville and Portland Canal Co. was chartered in 1825. The private investment came almost exclusively from Philadelphia, which had close commercial ties with the Ohio Valley. Convinced by statistics of boats lost on the falls, the United States Congress authorized GOVERNMENT purchase of canal company stock. Construction began in 1826, and in December 1830 the *Uncas* became the first steamboat to pass through.

Some segments of Louisville business did lose trade, and attempts were made to sabotage the lock gates. Within a few years, however, Louisville's "carrying trade" reached probably a greater volume than ever before, as the spread of cotton plantations to Alabama and Mississippi in the 1830s immensely increased the demand for farm produce and manufactured goods from the Ohio Valley. The increase in the size of STEAMBOATS rendered the fifty-foot-wide "ditch" around the falls inadequate; by the 1850s nearly 40 percent of vessels were too large to pass through the canal, and their cargoes were carried by land around the falls.

Enlarging the Portland Canal, c. 1868.

Agitation for widening the canal began in the 1840s, but the company did not begin the project until 1860, adopting the plan proposed by hydraulic engineer Theodore Scowden, who had just completed the Louisville Water Works. The CIVIL WAR and inflation brought the project to a halt in 1866, before the new eighty-foot-wide lock was completed. Upriver cities were disturbed by this development. A Cincinnati group posed the dilemma thus: "And now the question recurs with awful significance; how are we going to get past Louisville? There are no balloons that we know of. There is no money in Kentucky that we ever heard of. If we don't finish that canal in some way, we may as well return to wheelbarrows."

Finally the federal government, which after 1855 owned a majority of the stock, agreed to fund completion of the widening, carried out under the supervision of the UNITED STATES ARMY CORPS OF ENGINEERS. The work was completed in 1872, and in 1874 the canal came under outright federal ownership. Tolls that had ranged upward to sixty cents per ton of cargo were reduced to ten cents, and in 1880 were eliminated. In 1910 Congress authorized a plan for "canalization" of the Ohio River by a series of locks and dams that would provide a minimum nine-foot depth of water for navigation. Since all locks were to be one hundred feet wide, a new lock was completed in 1921 beside the 1872 work.

By the 1950s the immense increase in barge tonnage required a radical reconstruction of the canal. The work, completed in 1962, widened the canal to five hundred feet so that barge tows upbound could pass tows downbound. A new five-hundred-foot-wide lock was also built, along with a surge basin that wiped out what was left of SHIPPINGPORT. The lock and a new dam replacing one constructed in 1927 were named McAlpine Lock and Dam, honoring William H. McAlpine, principal engineer of the Louisville District of the Army Engineer Corps from 1917 to 1929. The dam, in conjunction with others along the Ohio, provides a minimum twelve-foot depth of channel year-round.

See Leland R. Johnson, *The Falls City Engineers: A History of the Louisville District, Corps of Engineers United States Army* (Louisville 1975); Louis C. Hanter, *Steamboats on the Western Rivers: An Economic and Technological History* (Cambridge, Mass., 1949).

George H. Yater

***LOUISVILLE* ANZEIGER.** A German language newspaper, the *Louisville Anzeiger* was founded by George Philip Doern and Otto Scheesser in 1849. The first edition, February 28, 1849, was printed at a location on Jefferson St. near Third St. The paper's goal was to provide news of the city's growing German community and news of their homeland. Many young Germans versed in trades, plus bankers, artists, and merchants, had arrived in Louisville after the failure of the democratic revolution of 1848 and were key in the *Anzeiger's* founding.

The *Louisville Anzeiger* became the only German-language paper to publish continually into the twentieth century, surviving its competitor, *Beobacher am Ohio*. In 1877 Doern, sole proprietor for almost twenty-eight years, incorporated the Louisville Anzeiger Co. with himself as president. Upon Doern's death in 1878, Martin Borntraeger took office, followed by George S. Schuhmann in 1892 and Richard J. Schuhmann in 1910. Among other well-known newspapermen with the *Anzeiger* were Ludwig Stierlin, Carl Neumeyer, E. Von Schleinitz, Clem Engelsing, A.F. Stiefvater, John Krauss, Sigmund Gottschalk, John H. Nold, Paul Wolff, M. Von Nostiz, William Rammacker, Herman Cohn, Leo C. Schuhmann, and Rudolph Heckel.

A fiftieth-anniversary jubilee issue in March 1898 confirmed the *Anzeiger's* role and status in the city's life. In the hysteria of anti-German feeling during the war years of 1917–18, the *Anzeiger's* masthead included the statement, "A Loyal Patriotic Newspaper, Published Solely in the Interest of American Ideals and Principles." Its editor, John F. Horina, was required to submit an English translation of editorials to an official of Jefferson County before their publication.

Experiencing a gradual decline in circulation and ADVERTISING, the *Anzeiger*, at 321 W Liberty St., declared bankruptcy and reorganized in 1933. The last daily issue appeared that year. A weekly feature-type rotogravure magazine, *Deutsch Amerika,* continued until March 4, 1938. At that time Schuhmann family members owned most, if not all, of the assets of the Louisville Anzeiger Co. On October 11, 1940, its name was changed to the Schuhmann Printing Co., organized as a job printing business.

See *Louisville Anzeiger*, microfilm copy on reserve at the Filson Club, Louisville; *Louisville Anzeiger Jubilaums Ausgabe,* March 1, 1898; *Louisville Times*, July 31, 1967; Ludwig Stierlin, *Der Staat Kentucky und die Stadt Louisville mit besonderer Beruecksichtigung des Deutschen Elementes* (Louisville 1873).

Marie A. Heckel

LOUISVILLE AQUIFER. The Louisville aquifer is Louisville's primary source of groundwater. Water flowing from melting glaciers during the Pleistocene epoch (ca. 1,000,000 to ca. 8000 B.C.) eroded the Ohio Valley into its present shape. The sand and gravel in the glaciers was deposited to form an alluvial aquifer extending throughout the valley and, ordinarily, about half a mile from each bank. It is much wider at Louisville, though. It begins to broaden opposite JEFFERSONVILLE, INDIANA. The boundary then runs south-southwest from the west side of CAVE HILL CEMETERY to the intersection of Preston Hwy. with the Southern Rairoad track just east of the KENTUCKY FAIR AND EXPOSITION CENTER, where it makes a right-angle turn to run west-southwest to the intersection of Lower Hunters Trace Rd. and Dixie Hwy., where it again begins to run parallel to the river.

Almost all of the aquifer's water originates in the OHIO RIVER, seeping into the aquifer above Louisville and back into the river southwest of the city; very little is rainwater. The aquifer's water temperature is nearly constant at 57 degrees Fahrenheit (14 degrees Celsius), enabling Louisville distilleries to use groundwater as a cooling agent. Groundwater was in demand for downtown air-conditioning until the early 1960s, when the Metropolitan Sewer District started charging fees for dumping groundwater into sewers. Groundwater is also cleaner than surface water. Its purity and coolness keep Louisville aquifer water in use despite the availability of city water from the Ohio. In 1997 approximately 22 million gallons of groundwater were pumped daily in Jefferson County, down from the peak of 61.5 million gallons used industrially in 1943, but still representing about one-sixth of the county's water usage.

The high water table produced by the 1937 flood gave way to a groundwater shortage in 1944. This was caused by heavy pumping by distilleries and by rubber plants doing war work. Three distilleries suspended pumping during spring 1944 and recharged the aquifer with river water from the LOUISVILLE WATER CO. In 1945 the United States Geological Survey (USGS) began to monitor groundwater levels, which rose steadily as groundwater use declined in the 1960s and 1970s. High water levels in 1980 led to fears that the foundations of downtown buildings might be undermined. USGS's monitoring ended in 1997 because of lack of funds. In 1994 the Louisville Water Co. dug a test well on Zorn Ave. near the riverbank to determine the possibility of extracting all city water from the aquifer. The company noted that groundwater was cleaner than river water and free from zebra mussels, an ever-increasing threat to river intakes.

See Karen Durham Lippert, "A Study of Rising Groundwater Levels in Louisville, Kentucky," M.A. thesis, University of Louisville, 1980; Edwin A. Bell, Robert W. Kellogg, and Willis K. Kulp, *Progress Report on the Ground-Water Resources of the Louisville Area Kentucky*, 1949–55 (Washington, D.C., 1963); United States Geological Survey, *Ground Water* (pamphlet) (Washington, D.C., 1994); United States Geological Survey, *Water Resources Data for Kentucky, Water Year 1980* (Louisville 1981); *Courier-Journal*, Feb. 22, 1994.

William Duane Kenney

LOUISVILLE AREA DEVELOPMENT ASSOCIATION. The Louisville Area Development Association (LADA) was organized in 1943 by Mayor Wilson W. Wyatt as a public-private agency for planning Louisville and Jefferson County's postwar development. By mid-1943, 40 percent of local workers were employed in war production, and Louisville had become a major center for the manufacture of synthetic rubber, aircraft, and war-related goods. Looking ahead to the war's end, Mayor Wyatt and other political and business leaders wanted to preserve wartime economic advances, avoid postwar unemployment, and rebuild deteriorating public facilities. As president of the American Society of Planning Officials and president-designate of the American Municipal Association, Wyatt was eager to attack postwar problems in a manner that could be emulated in other cities.

Formally launched in October 1943 with Wyatt as its first president, LADA had an initial budget of one hundred thousand dollars, contributed primarily by local corporations, with smaller donations by labor unions and about fifteen thousand from city and county GOVERNMENT channeled through the Louisville and Jefferson County PLANNING AND ZONING Commission. The first governing board consisted of the mayor, the Jefferson County judge, and nine prominent business and labor leaders. Hired as executive director was Dr. Kenneth P. Vinsel, a former UNIVERSITY OF LOUISVILLE political scientist who had administered local social services programs during the GREAT DEPRESSION and then moved to a post with the War Production Board in Washington, D.C.

LADA operated primarily through a series of task forces of interested citizens who set out to study and prepare action plans for virtually every facet of community life, including POPULATION trends, economic development, education, fine arts, PUBLIC HEALTH, housing, PARKS and recreation, public buildings, smoke abatement, state fair, streets and highways, public transportation, and welfare.

During its eight-year life span, LADA produced reports and plans that laid the groundwork for completion of the flood wall, construction of the expressway system, development of Louisville's medical center, initiation of downtown revitalization, creation of the Metropolitan Sewer District, passage of the occupational license tax, relocation of the KENTUCKY STATE FAIRGROUNDS, and acquisition of new parks and playgrounds. While some recommendations went unrealized, by 1950 most of LADA's plans had been completed, and many community leaders believed a different organizational structure was necessary to translate the blueprints into action. In that year, the Louisville Board of Trade, the Retail Merchants Association, and the Louisville Convention and Publicity League merged with LADA to form the Louisville Chamber of Commerce. To assure continuity between planning and action, Dr. Vinsel was appointed the chamber's executive vice president.

See Carl E. Kramer, "Two Centuries of Urban Development in Central and Southern Louisville," in *Louisville Survey: Central and*

South Report (Louisville 1978); Wilson W. Wyatt, *Whistle Stops: Adventures in Public Life* (Lexington 1985).

Carl E. Kramer

LOUISVILLE ARTESIAN WELL. The presence of spas and the resorts that grew up around them are an integral part of Kentucky's history. During the nineteenth century thousands of people flocked to these sites both to "take the cure" and to vacation. The chemical makeup of each flow was meticulously analyzed, promoted, and hawked as containing medicinal powers.

In April 1857 Charles I. and ALFRED VICTOR DU PONT, to procure a source of pure and soft water for papermaking, sank a well at Tenth and Rowan Streets. After 16 months, the well reached the remarkable depth of 2,086 feet, producing a flow of 330,000 gallons per day. The water, gushing from sandstones that were cavernous and water-bearing, came out at a temperature of 76.5 degrees Fahrenheit.

A chemical analysis showed it heavily laden with chlorides and sulfates. Although the mineral contents made it useless in the paper-manufacturing process, it was considered to be good in the treatment of "dyspepsia, cortiveness, derangements of the liver, nervous diseases, kidney and glandular problems," as well as for external use on "scrofulous affections, lymphatic tumors, gout, and rheumatism." A brick bathhouse of three stories was erected, and a lawn area with a large fountain was built. The price of a bath was thirty-five cents.

In 1859 there was speculation that completion of the Louisville & Nashville Railroad would make Du Pont's Artesian Well a place for visitors. The CIVIL WAR disrupted those plans, and the well never proved to be a large tourist attraction. In 1923 the Tobacco Realty Co. sealed the top of the well with concrete and diverted the water to the sewer system. In 1930 the Walker Bag Co. once again opened it to public view and ran it through pipes that made it look like a miniature Cumberland Falls. In July 1948 the well was plugged because the caustic action of its salt- and sulfur-rich waters interfered with the construction of the flood wall along the riverfront.

See J. Lawrence Smith, *Du Pont's Artesian Well: Report, Analysis, and Medical Properties of its Water* (Louisville 1859).

John E. Kleber

LOUISVILLE ATHLETIC CLUB. The Louisville Athletic Club, first known as the Athletic Club of Louisville, was founded in 1888. The club was organized for the promotion of health, physical culture, and sports for area young men. However, the club soon became a social center of Louisville and was used for dances and parties as well as for sporting events like BOXING, SWIMMING, and wrestling.

During its heyday, 1888–96, it was located at the corner of Zane and Garvin Place. The building was built by local sports enthusiasts who later organized the athletic club. Organizers included George Norton, HELM BRUCE, CHARLES GRAINGER, Lee Robinson, James P. Hill, and architect Kenneth McDonald.

Louisville Athletic Club, 1890s.

Once described as "Louisville's most fashionable club," its membership was over four hundred and included many prominent families. In 1896 membership began to decline as older members joined newer clubs, and toward the end of the year it was dissolved. However, in 1901 the club was revived as the New Athletic Club and again flourished in its original location until it was dissolved in 1906.

The original four-story Victorian building, which was reduced to two stories in 1922, was multifaceted, with a turret and gables. It housed numerous businesses after 1906, including the Columbia Riding School, Hampton School for Young Women, the short-lived New Louisville Athletic Club, Ewing-Von Allmen Dairy Co., Union News Co., Midwest Foil Co., and the Arts in Louisville House. Before the structure was destroyed by fire in May 1969, it was transformed into a psychedelic hangout for teens, first named Changes Unlimited and later called Kaleidoscope.

See *Courier-Journal*, May 17, 1969.

LOUISVILLE AUTOMOBILE CLUB. In February 1903, five years after John E. Roche drove the first self-powered vehicle through the streets of Louisville and six months after the organizatin of the American Automobile Association, several Louisvillians met at the GALT HOUSE hotel in order to establish a social organization of car owners known as the Louisville Automobile Club. While there were only approximately six hundred cars in the entire state of Kentucky, the twenty-nine original members, working together with the Louisville Automobile Dealers' Association, sought to secure national legislation governing the use of automobiles, protecting the rights of the owners, encouraging the improvement of highways, and promoting careful and proper use of cars while discouraging reckless behavior.

In time they would achieve all these goals and much more. In 1904 the city enacted its first motor vehicles ordinances providing for, among other things, license plates, illumination, a horn or noisemaker of some sort, and a speed limit of twelve miles per hour. One of the pioneer automobile associations in the country, it became affiliated with the American Automobile Association in 1908 and released its first annual tour book for members two years later. To increase automobile awareness and promote its benefits, the club sponsored "No Accident Weeks," advocated pedestrian crosswalks, assisted in the creation of the state Department of Public Roads, pushed for the establishment of Mammoth Cave as a national park, promoted better roads statewide, posted directional signs along the highways, paid rewards for the arrest and conviction of violators of the state Motor Vehicle Act, and sponsored a law that made it illegal for revenuers to fire weapons indiscriminately at automobiles.

By the end of the 1920s, the club began a campaign to establish other branches in the state and sponsored a Kentucky Hospitality Tour in order to promote state TOURISM. During the same decade the seven thousand members began receiving exclusive benefits such as roadside service and towing twenty-four hours a day, legal advice and service, and nationwide touring information. The association moved into its present headquarters at Jackson St. and BROADWAY in 1965. To reflect its broader service, the Louisville Automobile Club changed its name to AAA Kentucky in 1988.

See Dave Stucker, "85 Years of Service," *Home and Away: Louisville Edition* (Jan./Feb. 1988): 6a–7a.

LOUISVILLE BACH SOCIETY. The Louisville Bach Society was founded in 1964 by Melvin and Margaret Dickinson following their return from two years' study in Germany with world-renowned organist Helmut Walcha. Specializing in choral masterpieces by Bach, Handel, Haydn, Mozart, Brahms, and many others, the society also performs music by leading contemporary composers.

The Dickinsons' search for works seldom performed in Louisville has led to presentations of Bach's *B Minor Mass* and *St. Matthew Passion,* Mozart's *C Minor Mass,* Beethoven's *Missa Solemnis,* Bruckner's *F Minor Mass,* and over one hundred of Bach's sacred cantatas, among other works.

Local performance locations include the Kentucky Center for the Arts, CALVARY EPISCOPAL CHURCH, St. Agnes and Holy Spirit Roman Catholic Churches, SECOND PRESBYTERIAN CHURCH, Macauley Theatre (Brown Theatre), and the UNIVERSITY OF LOUISVILLE's Comstock North Recital Hall. The society has also performed throughout Kentucky and neighboring states. Concerts regularly feature regionally and nationally acclaimed soloists. Many of the group's family and children's concerts have been taped and broadcast on national TELEVISION.

In 1988 MARY and BARRY BINGHAM Sr. funded a five-year project for performance of a complete *Messiah* as their Christmas gift to the community, a grant that was later extended for five more years. The first performance, held December 11, 1988, at the Macauley Theatre, was dedicated to the memory of Barry Bingham Sr. Later performances were presented at the Kentucky Center for the Arts. The Binghams' first grant to the society, made in 1970, had funded a performance of Beethoven's *Missa Solemnis.* The February 22, 1998, concert at Holy Spirit Catholic Church memorialized the Binghams for their generosity.

Chorus members include individuals from all walks of life. The group is accompanied by members of the LOUISVILLE ORCHESTRA and other local musicians. The society ranked fifteenth on *BUSINESS FIRST*'s 1998 list of the Louisville area's largest performing arts organizations because of its annual budget of $161,438.

Mary Kagin Kramer

LOUISVILLE BALLET. The Louisville Ballet, the state ballet of Kentucky, was founded by Thomas Jordan and Nancy Dysart in March 1952 as the performing arm of the Louisville Dance Council, a volunteer organization promoting dance locally. The first performance featured selections from four local dance studios. Subsequent productions were directed by guest artists, including Alexandra Danilova, Mia Slavenska, and Leon Danielian. In 1965 Larry Gradus was engaged as the first full-time resident artistic director. At that time the ballet season consisted of three performances, including the *Nutcracker,* plus lecture demonstrations in schools and statewide tours.

In 1971–72 Richard and Cristina Munro became artistic directors of the Louisville Ballet, and in 1974–75 the company attained professional status with eight local dancers, plus a nonprofessional corps de ballet. The Academy of the Louisville Ballet (now Louisville School of Ballet) was founded to train future company members, with Alun Jones as associate director. In 1976 the Louisville Ballet received permission to perform its first Balanchine ballet, *La Sonambula,* or *Night Shadow,* a milestone in local ballet's history. Alun Jones became the ballet's artistic director in 1978. In the following twenty years the company grew to thirty professional dancers from many states and foreign countries and a civic company chosen from the ballet school. In addition to its regular subscription series of five productions annually, the Louisville Ballet presents the *Nutcracker* at Christmas and a series of educational outreach programs. These included student matinees at the THEATER, lecture demonstrations in schools, and programs at the award-winning new ballet headquarters on E MAIN St., adjacent to the WATERFRONT PARK.

The Louisville Ballet is the only regional company with which Mikhail Baryshnikov has performed in its repertory productions. He performed with the company in the 1978–79 and 1979–80 seasons, after which the Louisville Ballet supported him in performances in Dallas and Houston. Other guest artists and choreographers have included Patricia McBride, Galina Samsova, Valery and Galina Panov, Jean-Pierre Bonnefous, Merrill Ashley, and Sean Lavery. The Ballet's repertory includes works by Erik Bruhn, George Balanchine, John Cranko, Antony Tudor, Kurt Joos, Choo-San Goh, and Eugene Loring, as well as Petipa, Fokine, and Bournonville. Among its full-length ballets are *Swan Lake, Romeo and Juliet, The Sleeping Beauty, Coppelia, Giselle,* and *Cinderella.* The Louisville Ballet had the largest per-capita subscription audience of all regional professional ballet companies in the United States in 1998. In 1995 the company moved to a new $2.2 million facility on E Main St.

Nancy S. Dysart

LOUISVILLE BAR ASSOCIATION. The oldest continuously operating bar association in Kentucky, the Louisville Bar Association (LBA) was founded in 1900, twenty-three years after the American Bar Association and one year before the failed Kentucky Bar Association (KBA) was revived. The early bar associations were started to address concerns about the status of the profession, to consider ethical questions, to improve the justice system, and to provide fellowship for attorneys.

A voluntary association located at 600 W MAIN St., LBA had three thousand members in 1998, representing some 70 percent of Jefferson County lawyers. Membership is open to attorneys in good standing with the KBA or the bar of any other state or the District of Columbia.

A growing number of member and public services are provided by the LBA. Best-known of these is the annual evaluation of judges in Jefferson County. Another widely used program is the Kentucky Lawyer Referral Service, which handles TELEPHONE calls from people seeking assistance with legal matters. More than twelve thousand individuals a year use the service, which provides thirty minutes of free consultation with an attorney. In addition, LBA is a partner with the Legal Aid Society in the Louisville Pro Bono Consortium, a legal protective arm for indigent and low-income persons.

In 1981 the Louisville Bar Foundation was established to direct grant funds to organizations providing legal services to the poor, to promote a better judicial system, and to educate the public about the law. By 1998 the endowment fund had grown to $2 million, and more than $750,000 in grants had been distributed.

One of the most important member services is Continuing Legal Education (CLE), now mandatory for Kentucky attorneys. LBA is a leading provider of this service, offering about a hundred seminars annually. Knowledgeable lawyers volunteer to conduct a wide variety of CLE seminars. LBA also works with the UNIVERSITY OF LOUISVILLE Brandeis School of Law to operate the Louisville Institute for Continuing Legal Education.

See *Law at the Falls* (Dallas 1997).

Betty Lou Amster

LOUISVILLE BEDDING COMPANY. In 1889 Samuel D. Cruse opened a pillow-manufacturing plant on the south side of MARKET St. between Jackson and Hancock. Cruse aptly titled his business the Louisville Pillow Co. In 1900 the first of three fires that plagued the company occurred. After the plant was rebuilt on the same site, a mattress division was started, and the company changed its name to the Louisville Pillow and Mattress Co.

In 1903 Cruse's business was incorporated, with himself as president, and "mattress" was dropped from the title. However, two years later, for unknown reasons, Cruse sold the company to a group of investors headed by Milburn P. Kelley, the company's secretary and treasurer. Kelley, who had begun working as a driver in 1894, became the president of Louisville Pillow Co. until its name was changed in 1917 to the Louisville Bedding Co. Kelley subsequently served as president of Louisville Bedding until his death in 1930. It was thought that the new name would reflect all the products that the company manufactured, including Spring Air mattresses, down and goose feather pillows, comforters, Old Kentucky quilts, mattress pads, furniture pads, and cotton batting for upholstery.

With the slogan "Invest in Rest" and a growing national market, business took off. When more space was needed in 1937, a three-story eighty-eight-thousand-square-foot building was erected at 418 E Main St. In April 1945 the pillow line was shut down for a few months following the OPA order to lower pillow prices. This made the cost of manufacturing higher than the price set by the Office of Price Administration. In June 1957 the company sold off its mattress line to expand its quilted goods line largely because the quilted goods sales had quadrupled from 1948 to 1956. In 1963 the company was doing so well that a second plant was needed. Munfordville, Kentucky, was chosen as the site. The Munfordville plant took over the manufacturing of mattress pads, and the Louisville plant started manufacturing a new line of comforters.

Two acquisitions in 1966 and 1968, National Sure-fit Quilting Co. and Holland Cotton Products Co., a maker of mattress pads, put sales over the $10 million mark. A major acquisition of Reed Handcrafts in 1971 greatly expanded the company as a maker of napkins, placemats, table runners, and chair pads. In addition to its plants in Louisville and Munfordville, the company has two distribution centers, one in Louisville and one in Los Angeles. In 1995 the company vacated the Main St. building and moved its plant to 2109 Carton Dr. and its headquarters to 10400 Bunsen Way, both in Bluegrass Industrial Park in eastern Jefferson County. D&W Silks bought the facility on Main St. in 1996. In 1980 John Minihan became the president of Louisville Bedding Co., a position he presently holds. Sales for 1996 were $117.5 million, with a profit of $4.8 million.

See *Business First*, March 24, 1997; *Courier-Journal*, Feb. 14, 1939.

LOUISVILLE BIBLE COLLEGE. In 1923 McGarvey Bible College was founded in downtown Louisville. In 1924 it merged with the Cincinnati Bible Seminary. In 1948 a group from that school returned to begin the Louisville Bible College. The Louisville Bible College was originally located at 1707 S Third St. and moved to Damascus Rd., near the GENE SNYDER FREEWAY and Beulah Church Rd., in 1990.

The Louisville Bible College, affiliated with the Christian Churches/Churches of Christ, is a Gospel training school used to prepare ministers, missionaries, and lay persons for church leadership. The school is "uncompromisingly committed to the Bible as infallible and final." It is licensed by the Kentucky Council on Higher Education and offers associate, bachelor's, and master's degrees.

The college has had five presidents: Ira M. Boswell (1949–50), Ralph R. Records (1950–65), Frank W. Buck (1965–71), Thomas R. Omer (1971–90), and Tommy W. Mobley (1990–).

LOUISVILLE BOARD OF FIRE UNDERWRITERS. The property insurance marketplace in Louisville prior to 1854 was a bewildering maze of rates and wordings to the average buyer. The idea of having licensed agents representing more than one insurance company was barely developing; most fire coverage insurance policies were sold directly by insurers who devised their own pricing and policy forms.

To add to the difficulties in procuring property insurance, Louisville's burning rate had reached an alarming high by 1854. Due principally to ineffective firefighting by Louisville's volunteer firemen using hand-pumped fire engines with unreliable water supplies, fire insurance costs were becoming prohibitive. Something had to be done, and quickly. On February 15, 1854, twelve Louisville tradesmen met at the Merchants Exchange and formed the Board of Underwriters. These founders were merchants, insurance agents, and officers of local insurance companies. Their purpose was to "secure uniformity in the rates of insurance, harmony in the conditions of insurance, and concurrence in policies issued." Present were William Riddle, J.W. Simrall, JOHN MUIR, N. Burge, W.S. Vernon, G.W. Meriwether, P.B. Atwood, T.S. Kennedy, J.E. Tyler, William Prather, and B.H. Gwathmey.

This board met at regular intervals, primarily to establish and/or review fire insurance rates on property located within the city limits of Louisville, and marine rates for cargoes and boats on inland waterways. Insurers doing business in Louisville agreed to accept these rates.

During its 128-year existence the board was known as Board of Underwriters, 1854–64; Louisville Board of Underwriters, 1864–74; Louisville Board of Fire Underwriters, 1874–1951; Louisville Board of Insurance Agents, 1951–69; Louisville Board of Independent Insurance Agents, 1969–76; and Louisville Board of Independent Insurance Agents Inc., 1976–82. The most familiar and affectionate name was the one in longest use, the Louisville Board of Fire Underwriters.

At an August 24, 1854, meeting, the board granted a general reduction in fire rates in anticipation of Louisville receiving a steam-powered fire engine, six sections of riveted leather fire hose (one thousand feet), and various-sized nozzles. The city also promised additional fire cisterns to reinforce the water supply. The steamer was built by Lawson & Pearce, a local company, under a contract with the city. Upon completion, the fire engine performed as required by its specifications, but, due to a change in administration, the city refused to honor the contract with the builder. With this turn of events, the board withdrew its fire rate reductions.

Acutely aware of the high cost of fire insurance, the board resolved at its April 16, 1857, meeting to assist in the procurement of another steam-powered fire engine. This pumper would be operated by a municipally owned LOUISVILLE FIRE DEPARTMENT, which would replace the volunteer fire laddies but would remain the property of the board, merchants, and other citizens who funded it. A general reduction in fire rates was granted by the board in April 1859.

The CIVIL WAR almost put the board out of business when it was reduced to one member in 1863. The board continued its rate-making activities for fire and marine insurance, taking due note of the increased hazards brought on by the war. The cessation of hostilities returned the insurance markets to normal underwriting.

With the new steam-powered fire pumpers in use in the city, the protection of property from water damage during a fire presented a new problem. In 1878 assistant fire chief Benjamin Franklin Bache proposed to the board that a salvage corps be organized. Since 1867 Hook & Ladder Co. No. 1 had been doing salvage work of sorts. Early in 1887 the board submitted to its member insurance companies a plan to establish a specialized group to protect property exposed to damage from firefighting. Such protection would reduce insured losses, and it was the board's plan that such a group could be funded by insurers. The member companies agreed, and the salvage organization was chartered by the Kentucky legislature in 1888, with the name of the Louisville Fire and Life Protective Association. In later years, the name became the Salvage Corps. The purpose of the Salvage Corps was to protect property and life during and after a fire, regardless of insurance, and to try to ascertain the cause of the fire. (The corps was disbanded in 1941, and its work was transferred to the Louisville Fire Department.)

Louisville was visited by a highly destructive tornado on March 27, 1890. Property losses were severe, and, while fire losses resulting from the tornado were insured under the then-current fire policies, there was no recovery from losses resulting from the tornado where there was no fire. Windstorm insurance had not yet been invented. The board recognized the serious gap and produced the necessary policy wording to provide windstorm coverage at an additional cost. The board established tornado (windstorm) rates based upon building and roof constructions at its April 5, 1890, meeting.

During 1890 the board instituted a special committee to pass on "patents and devices" for fire safety, on which manufacturers sought board approval. This service was a forerunner to that provided by the Underwriters Laboratories Inc., which was founded in 1894. As far back as 1882 the use of automatic sprinkler fire protection had been strongly endorsed by the board; in 1894 it created its sprinkler department to spread knowledge of this important firefighting tool. A pamphlet of standards titled "Rules Governing the Installation of Automatic Sprinkler Equipments[6]" was published by the board in 1896. Properties with automatic sprinklers installed in accordance with these standards received a considerable fire insurance rate credit.

Since 1854 the board had made its own fire and marine rates, and the member insurance carriers had accepted them without question. Fire rates for cities other than Louisville, Covington, and Newport were now being produced by the Western Actuarial Bureau in Chicago; this organization began to urge Louisville to use its new and more scientific fire-rating system known as the Dean Analytical Rating Schedule. Resistant at first, the board adopted this method of rating on February 8, 1911. The Kentucky General Assembly on March 6, 1912, passed a bill creating a state agency to approve all insurance rates. The board fought a losing battle over this legislation. To make rates on behalf of all of the insurance companies, the board created the Kentucky Actuarial Bureau, to be located in Louisville. The board turned over to the bureau all of its files relating to rates.

Two years after creating an insurance rate regulatory agency, the Kentucky General Assembly passed a bill further regulating insurance business; this was done over the strong objections of both the insurers and the board. This bill was so onerous that more than a hundred insurance companies withdrew from writing business in Kentucky. Modifications were made to the bill, with the result that all interests were satisfied and Kentucky ended up with an excellent insurance code in 1916. Between 1885 and 1917, the board drafted fire policy forms for its member agents and insurers. In 1917, however, this service was taken over by the uniform forms committee of the Western Actuarial Bureau. The general manager of uniform forms was J. Barbour Gray, a former member of the Louisville board. These standard forms became available to all insurance agents at no cost.

During the 1920s the board fought another losing battle to prevent insurance companies from appointing as agents banks, real estate companies, and others who did not have the "solicitation and placing of insurance" as their only business. More and more, the board was spending its time and resources handling disputes between members and nonmembers. The venerable organization was slowly seeing its control of insurers and agents being diluted.

Two other Louisville board rules caused much friction in Kentucky. Its mutual rule read: "No member may place business with a mutual property or casualty company or receive commission from a policy in a mutual property or casualty company." Its direct writer rule stated: "No member of this board shall operate or be affiliated with a direct writing company branch office." (A direct-writing company sells directly to the public through its sales personnel.)

By 1951 the United States Department of Justice became interested in all boards having the three foregoing restrictions. The justice department charged that these and other such rules comprised restraint of trade. By January 1962, in view of court decisions, the board withdrew its three controversial rules. The era of the Board's real power over insurers had now ended.

The character of the board continued to evolve until it became merely an association of independent insurance agents. On July 1, 1982, it ceased to exist when its members voted to merge into the Independent Insurance Agents of Kentucky.

See Louisville Board of Independent Insurance Agents Inc., minutes books, Feb. 15, 1854–July 1,1982, Manuscript Department, Filson Club Historical Society; *Louisville Board of Independent Insurance Agents Inc., 125 Years of Service* (Louisville 1980); David Winges, *Volunteer Firefighters of Louisville* (Louisville 1992).

David Winges

LOUISVILLE BOARD OF REALTORS.

The buying and selling of land was a high-profit revenue-generating activity on the frontier. Louisville's location on that frontier at the FALLS OF THE OHIO ensured a steady supply of customers for those intent on a quick profit from land. JOHN CONNOLLY's two-thousand-acre land grant of 1774 was followed by others, many of them of one-thousand- and two-thousand-acre tracts. As the POPULATION and the number of buildings grew, land in the city gradually became scarce and valuable. By the mid-nineteenth century Louisville was a growing and prosperous river town, and profit could be made in the purchase and sale of real estate.

The city directory for 1848 assured its readers that the growth in real estate was not due to the "visionary schemes of speculators" but the consequence of its enterprising and industrious citizens. The 1848 edition of *Collins' Louisville and New Albany City Directory* boasts the first local enterprising individual to use the term *real estate agent.* He was John N. Wright, doing business on Third between Market and Jefferson Streets. In his advertisement he described himself as a real estate agent "For the Purchase, Sale and Renting of Real Estate."

By the late nineteenth century, Louisville offered so many opportunities for land development that the city was considered a bonanza for the real estate market. In 1890 fourteen real estate firms were located in the first four blocks of Fifth St. alone, between the river and MAIN St., and by 1910 the number of agents had almost tripled. By 1892 ten of those real estate agents saw the need for standardization and regulation of their profession. Together they organized the Louisville Real Estate Exchange to formulate and standardize rules, regulations, and commission schedules. Alfred V. Oldham was secretary of the organization, located on Fifth St. Not long after its auspicious beginning the group dissolved.

However the continued expansion of Louisville's residential and commercial developments increasingly demanded some form of organization and regulation. To fill that need the Louisville Real Estate Association was incorporated in 1907 with Clarence R. Gardiner as president. Gardiner was to bequeath a large sum of money to the UNIVERSITY OF LOUISVILLE at his death, and Gardiner Hall was named for him. First located in small quarters on Fifth St., within two years the organization moved to a larger location on Fifth St. when it had grown to fifty-two members. After a dispute over providing a central property listing service, several prominent developers, banks, and real estate agents such as the Hieatt Brothers and Mueller and Martin, formed the Real Estate Exchange of Louisville in May 1909. It functioned much as the name implies, as a central exchange of information through a list of properties for sale that was available to all members for a fee of one dollar plus 5 percent of the commission on the sale. The Exchange was one of the first members of the National Association of Real Estate Boards to operate such a listing system.

The relationship between the two real estate associations was generally cooperative, and they often formed mutual committees on matters of interest to the industry, but they did not merge until January 9, 1914. Caldwell Norton was elected the first president of the newly merged group, and the name Louisville Real Estate Board was selected. Meetings were held at the Tyler, Seelbach, and Watterson Hotels. From its inception civic matters occupied its attention, including an extension of the city limits in 1916, an annexation of eleven square miles in 1922, and Louisville's first real estate training course in 1920. Louisville shared the wave of prosperity and frenzied growth that swept the country in the 1920s. Rapid and unregulated expansion of both residential and commercial development caught city officials unprepared; but the Board of Realtors, realizing the need for zoning, joined with the Engineers and Architects Club and the Women's City Club to back the more orderly and uniform development spearheaded by architect James C. Murphy.

Louisville's rapid development between 1919 and 1929 completely changed real estate. An expanded and refined multiple listing system was initiated in 1922. In response to the "Own Your Own Home Movement," the Board of Realtors organized the first home show—the Better Homes and Building Exposition—in October of the same year. Overwhelming growth of the industry spurred unsuccessful attempts in 1924 to standardize the discipline. They included the Real Estate License Bill, ruled unconstitutional the following year, and the Kentucky Real Estate Commission, which was soon disbanded. However the introduction of uniform sales and purchasing contracts was successful.

As the real estate business expanded, so did membership—from 177 in 1921 to 445 in 1924—which spurred the board to purchase a house and lot at 508 W Jefferson St. across from the JEFFERSON COUNTY COURTHOUSE. By 1926 the board again needed larger facilities to accommodate new services and its growing membership. A vacant lot at 610 W Jefferson was acquired, and plans were drawn. In the spring of 1927 the old property was sold, and the board moved into its new home. It remained at that location for forty-one years.

The phenomenal progress of the 1920s was soon replaced by the GREAT DEPRESSION of the

1930s. Survival of the real estate business was in question, but the Multiple Listing System and the Model Home Show survived, continuing to offer an opportunity to display homes to the public. Rapid deflation of real estate required a total reevaluation of city properties to bring taxes in line with lowered values. The Louisville Real Estate Board, in conjunction with the United States Postal Service, carried out a comprehensive survey of the city's houses and APARTMENTS to better determine municipal housing needs while reassessing property values.

By the mid-1930s the New Deal programs were beginning to have an impact, and, despite a setback caused by the 1937 flood, signs of interest in real estate began to reappear. Membership in the Board of Realtors was barely seventy, but it was still dedicated to standardization and regulation of the business. After a decade of work, the board was successful in getting the Kentucky General Assembly to enact the Valid Act, which required all real estate brokers and salespeople to register with the Kentucky Real Estate Commission and post a bond of one thousand dollars. Amendments specified written examinations and licensing that the Louisville Board of Realtors had insisted on since the 1920s.

By 1945 membership had grown to 148. For the next fifteen years civic activities and responsibilities on an organizational and individual level were the focus of the membership as the board worked to make Louisville an inviting place for industry to locate. Some of the concerns gaining interest among real estate agents were eliminating postwar rent control and reducing real estate tax increases. To recognize members' civic involvement the board initiated the Louisville Realtor of the Year Award in 1957.

Throughout its history the Louisville Board of Realtors has encouraged its membership to adapt to changes in the workplace as well as the marketplace. Women have played an active role in the organization since Margaret Fox and Hattie Henn were elected to active membership in 1942. By 1946 there were enough women real estate agents to organize the Women's Council of Realtors. A trend toward improved professionalism during the 1970s led to the implementation and sponsorship of a two-year associate degree program in real estate at local colleges and universities, largely through the efforts of then-board president Nat Sanders. After many years in its familiar urban location in the center of downtown Louisville, the Louisville Board of Realtors purchased 1.2 suburban acres on Dutchmans Ln. as the site for a $1.2 million two-story building.

Throughout the 1990s the board provided information on national and local trends in real estate for local home buyers. It has also continued its long-standing interest in community development projects by funding the Kentucky Housing Foundation, providing both time and money to Habitat for Humanity, a nonprofit organization that uses volunteer hours and donations to build houses for people who cannot afford them; contributing trees for Louisville's PARKS and its zoo; and sponsoring Jefferson County's community garden projects.

See Pamela L. Hess, *A History 1892–1979: Louisville Board of Realtors* (Louisville 1979); *Business First Book of Lists* (Louisville 1999).

Largest Area Commercial Real Estate Firms (1999)

Firm	*Sq. Ft. Brokeree*	*#of Agents/ Offices*
Harry K. Moore Co.	6,021,224	10/1
CB Richard Ellis/Nicklies	5,192,607	14/1
Commercial Kentucky, Inc.	4,593, 801	11/1
Walter Wagner Jr. Co.	4,181,000	21/1
Hogan Development Co.	3,540,000	5/1
NTS Development Co.	2,776,068	4/1
Re/MAX Commer. Brokers	2,998,330	18/1
Trammell Crow Co.	2,216,411	4/2
Hoagland Commercial Realtors	1,368,124	5/1
Williamson-Mulloy Commercial Group	1,352,170	9/1
Century 21 Joe Hagan	1,004,953	12/8
Fenley Real Estate Group	925,000	2/2
Stephen C. Gault Co.	837,000	3/1
The Prudential Parks and Weisberg Realtors	712,523	6/1
Vantage 7 Realtors	654,758	6/1

Largest Area Residential Real Estate Firms (1999)

Firm	*Closing*	*$Sales*	*Agents/ Offices*
Paul Semonin Realtors	5,995	$868.7 Mil.	555/9
Century 21 Joe Guy	3,884	$467.2 Mil.	343/9
Re/MAX Properties East	2,106	$308.6 Mil.	104/1
Coldwell Banker McMahan	1,850	$200 Mil.	130/4
Schuler Realty	1,237	$123.9 Mil.	98/3
ERA Kepple Keene Realtors	1,169	$139.8 Mil.	74/1
Re/MAX Associates of Louisville	1,032	$155.8 Mil.	41/1
Prudential Parks & Weisberg Realtors	947	$129.2 Mil.	85/4
Bauer Blake Biery Inc. Realtors/Better Homes and Gardens	745	$80.8 Mil.	70/3
Re/MAX Professionals	730	$102.5 Mil.	36/1
Century 21 Reisert, Baker, Walker & Associates	570	$50.8 Mil.	63/3
Coldwell Banker Action Realtors	570	$58 Mil.	35/1
Re/MAX 2000	557	$59.2 Mil.	26/3
Re/MAX Connectiona	504	$53.2 Mil.	20/1
Inno-Max Realty	416	$42.4 Mil.	22/1

LOUISVILLE BOARD OF TRADE. Founded in 1862 by businessmen, merchants, and manufacturers who favored the Union cause in the CIVIL WAR, the Board of Trade was created for their "mutual protection" and to encourage the "transportation of commodities." The association met for the first time on March 25 to accept its state-granted charter and admit a number of firms. Within one week, sixty-eight additional members, who each paid one dollar, had joined the board and elected George W. Morris president. Pro-Union sentiments continued to rise within the organization, and, a year after its founding, all members were required to swear allegiance to the North.

Aside from the establishment of the Merchant's Exchange in 1864, the disunity caused by the Civil War and the board's closed membership hindered its growth and usefulness. It recovered slowly until it was reorganized in 1879 with Gen. John B. Castleman as chairman and expanded to include Jeffersonville and NEW ALBANY. That same year, the organization purchased the Lithgow Building at Third and Main Streets for one hundred thousand dollars. Eleven years later, the board made seventy thousand dollars' worth of renovations and added an enormous exchange hall on the second floor. Although preservationists pushed for the building's restoration, it was demolished in 1975 for the widening of Third St. between River Rd. and MAIN ST.

Throughout the years, the board tried to entice domestic and foreign businesses and was instrumental in promoting and advancing the commercial and industrial interests of the city. This was seen in the prominent role it played during the SOUTHERN EXPOSITION, Louisville's bid during the 1880s to showcase her commodities to an ever-growing national market. The board also provided aid during the TORNADO OF 1890 and the New Albany tornado of 1917 by spearheading fund-raising drives that gathered $150,000 and $52,000 respectively. The group published a monthly magazine, the *Louisville Board of Trade Journal*, the forerunner to *LOUISVILLE* MAGAZINE, once published by the Chamber of Commerce. The board also spawned the Junior Board of Trade in 1932—the modern-day Louisville Jaycees.

In an effort to streamline several agencies, the Board of Trade, the Louisville Area Development Association, the Louisville Retail Merchants Association, and the Louisville Convention Bureau combined their organizations in 1950 and created the Louisville Chamber of Commerce. While a majority of the Board of Trade's duties were placed in the hands of the chamber, the organization continued to perform grain inspections until the late 1980s, when the Federal Grain Inspection Services branch of the United States Department of Agriculture took it over. The board was officially dissolved in 1995. It became a part of the agribusiness department of the Chamber of Commerce after transferring part of its funds to the chamber,

Board of Trade Building, northwest corner of Main at Third Street.

with the remainder going toward agricultural scholarships.

See Louisville Board of Trade, *Louisville, Fifty Years Ago* (Louisville 1923); J. Stoddard Johnston, ed., *Memorial History of Louisville,* vol. 1 (Chicago 1896).

LOUISVILLE CEMENT COMPANY.

The roots of the former Louisville Cement Co. date to 1830, when the builders of the Louisville & Portland Canal discovered huge deposits of natural cement in the bedrock of the OHIO RIVER. At that time John Hulme and Francis McHarry began grinding cement at the Tarascon brothers' grist mill at SHIPPINGPORT, near Louisville, and selling it to the canal company. In 1845 J. Hulme & Co. bought the mill and began selling cement beyond the Louisville region. Six Louisville businessmen purchased the company in 1866 and incorporated it as the Louisville Cement & Waterpower Co. It became the Louisville Cement Co. in 1869, and traveling agent JAMES BRECKINRIDGE SPEED was appointed general manager. In 1871 the firm opened a new plant at Petersburg in CLARK COUNTY, INDIANA. Located adjacent to the Jeffersonville, Madison, & Indianapolis Railroad, the plant grew quickly, attracting new residents in the process. By 1900 it was the largest producer of natural cement in the world, and Petersburg had been renamed Speed in honor of J.B. Speed, then the firm's president and chief stockholder.

With the development of PORTLAND cement, which was superior to natural cement for large construction projects due to its strength and consistent high quality, demand for natural cement began to decline. But the discovery of nearby shale deposits, which provided essential minerals for the new product, led to construction of a new Portland mill in 1905. Soon the Louisville Cement Co. was a leading producer of Portland cement. However, the transition to Portland cement did not end the production of natural cement. In 1916 Harry D. Baylor, a chemical engineer at the Speed plant, perfected a process for making masonry cement from natural cement rock. The product was patented as "Brixment," and it remains one of the leading masonry products on the market.

After WORLD WAR I, the Louisville Cement Co. adopted a policy of welfare capitalism that transformed Speed into a company town. In 1919 it built the Speed Community House as a recreational, cultural, and social center. In 1922 a large park was built behind the community house for picnicking, sports, and other forms of outdoor recreation; a gymnasium was added in 1925. The company also built scores of homes that were rented to employees and was instrumental in founding Speed Memorial Church in 1924 and Silver Creek High School in 1925. Other elements of the program included a company store, BASEBALL field, SWIMMING pool, and GOLF course. Speed remained a company town until the mid-1950s, when the firm began selling the homes to employees and gradually closing the store and recreational facilities or transferring them to outside operators.

Louisville Cement Co. grew rapidly after WORLD WAR II, and by 1965 it was the thirteenth-largest cement producer in the United States. Three years later it purchased Bessemer Cement Co., then based in Cleveland, Ohio. However, the company's growth eventually made it an acquisition target, and in October 1984 Coplay Cement Co., a Pennsylvania firm, purchased it for about $112.5 million. The company's Louisville connections ended in 1985 when local administrative functions were consolidated at the Speed plant. Now known as ESSROC Cement Inc., the firm is owned by Italcementi Group of Bergamo, Italy.

See Carl E. Kramer, *Sellersburg: A Century of Change* (Sellersburg, Ind., 1990).

Carl E. Kramer

LOUISVILLE CENTRAL AREA INC.

After a December 1958 meeting of the Louisville Chamber of Commerce (now GREATER LOUISVILLE INC.), Michael O'Dea, chairman of the chamber's URBAN RENEWAL committee, proposed the creation of a private planning organization for the central business district. The Louisville Central Area Inc. (LCA), a spinoff of the chamber's Downtown Louisville Committee, grew out of concerns that the central area needed special attention that it did not get from previous plans proposed by other local GOVERNMENT agencies and businesses. Thomas Ballantine, the chamber's first president and head of the downtown committee, organized the first meeting of the LCA. Hundreds of downtown businessmen attended the meeting held on March 9, 1959. It was decided that LCA's aim was to help plan, develop, improve, and maintain the central downtown area for trade, commerce, business, industry, culture, and entertainment.

LCA was created as a temporary organization to hire outside development agencies to evaluate special downtown needs. After raising three hundred thousand dollars from downtown businessmen, LCA, headed by Philip Geissal, a former chief planner for Kansas City, Missouri, defined a number of objectives for the central business district. Many objectives focused on improving traffic flow, the upkeep of area buildings, the cleanup of blighted areas, the promotion of special events to draw attention to downtown, and promotion of redevelopment. LCA quickly became the central focus of public-private downtown redevelopment efforts after Mayor BRUCE HOBLITZELL shepherded through a recommendation in October 1959 for the city to contract with LCA to plan the medical center on the east side of downtown and a civic center on the west side.

In 1960 LCA sponsored the first experimental pedestrian mall in downtown. The LCA demonstration project, named Guthrie Green because of its location on Guthrie St. between Fourth and Second Streets, was the predecessor of the RIVER CITY MALL, developed in the late 1960s and early 1970s.

In 1962 LCA released one of the first comprehensive plans for downtown redevelopment, the *Design for Downtown.* It included the creation of FOUNDERS SQUARE, converting the Armory (now the GARDENS OF LOUISVILLE) into a downtown convention center, a Fourth St. Mall, Guthrie Green, and a Ninth St. Thoroughfare to reroute through traffic around the downtown area.[7] Although the report was never officially adopted by the city, and many of the report's suggestions, such as a freestanding symphony hall for the LOUISVILLE ORCHESTRA (the Kentucky Center for the Arts was completed in 1983) and other major capital projects, went unfulfilled, *Design for Downtown* still became the blueprint for DOWNTOWN DEVELOPMENT for the next decade.

LCA also worked closely with the city's Urban Renewal Agency, the Retail Merchants Association, and city and county GOVERNMENTS on many of these projects. LCA, which by 1962 was headed by a former urban affairs editor at the *COURIER-JOURNAL*, J. Douglas Nunn, successfully encouraged Jefferson County government to purchase the *BELLE OF LOUISVILLE* to be used as a tourist attraction. During Nunn's tenure many important developments were completed in the downtown area, including the 800 Apartments, Trinity Towers, and the BANK OF LOUISVILLE's headquarters building.

In 1966 after Nunn resigned, Leslie J. Barr became executive director of LCA. Early in Barr's tenure, LCA endorsed the creation of a galleria on Fourth St. and a downtown beautification program, dubbed Prime Coat, to paint the facades of buildings. But in 1967 downtown development encountered several problems. Reynolds Aluminum Service Corp., a major supporter of riverfront development, announced it was pulling out of the project to build a hotel and waterfront plaza fronting the OHIO RIVER. This coincided with an LCA report that claimed downtown property values and rental rates had continued to decline since the mid-1950s, when redevelopment efforts had begun.

This prompted Barr to initiate a study that resulted in the most comprehensive, long-range action plan ever conceived for downtown. In 1968 the Louisville and Jefferson County Planning Commission formalized the program for the development of the central city, and in 1969 the city published the *Louisville Center City Development Program*, which became known as the Gruen Report because the primary consulting firm was Gruen Associates. It was a ninety-four-page blueprint for downtown redevelopment for the next two decades, and, unlike previous efforts, this was a cooperative venture to coordinate public and private activities and to bring business leaders and city officials under one planning organization, the Center City Committee. The plan envisioned creating a linear central area of development around Fourth St., which was to become a traffic-free commercial area for pedestrians.

In 1971 Wilson Wyatt Jr. took the reins from Barr and supervised an important period of development, culminating in the creation of the Fourth Street Mall, later renamed the River City Mall. It was a pedestrian shopping area running along Fourth St., stretching from Liberty St. to BROADWAY. LCA acted as developer for the mall, hiring the architect and obtaining the necessary state legislation. Wyatt, along with his father, who was then head of the Chamber of Commerce, and LCA were also instrumental in the development of the Commonwealth Convention Center and Hyatt Regency-Louisville Hotel, completed in 1977 and 1978 respectively.

In the mid-1970s LCA became involved in promoting the GALLERIA and the Kentucky Center for the Arts projects. In 1978 Wyatt stepped down and was replaced by Robert Bivens, who had served in a similar downtown development position in Atlanta. Bivens, who was executive director until 1984, helped LCA play a brokerage role in coordinating the Galleria and Kentucky Center for the Arts projects. In 1976 LCA also created Third Century, a special committee composed of LCA members and created to educate the public on downtown issues and projects. Third Century also sponsored such downtown events as Strassenfest. The name of the group reflected the fact that Louisville entered its third century in 1998.

Since 1986 LCA has played a role in almost every major development project in the central business district. In 1986 it provided private sector leadership for development of the Toonerville II Trolley, in 1988 it served as project manager for the LOUISVILLE FALLS FOUNTAIN, and in 1990 LCA put together another Louisville downtown development plan for the 1990s. LCA also obtained state legislation establishing a Louisville Downtown Management District (LDMD), which in 1992 began providing such services as cleaning, marketing, and crime prevention for central area businesses. In 1992 LCA also sponsored the first Work Downtown Week celebration, a weeklong event that showcases the opportunities and attractions that are available to the downtown employee.

In recent years LCA has played more of a promotional role, emphasizing business and residential opportunities in the center city. Since the mid-1980s LCA has given out its annual Cornerstone awards to companies that have invested $1 million or more in development projects in the downtown area during the past year. In 1997 LCA started bestowing annual Bricks & Mortar awards to those under the million-dollar mark who still make a significant contribution to downtown development. The organization also provided information during the planning stage for LOUISVILLE SLUGGER FIELD, as well as a host of other projects.

See George H. Yater, "It's Louisville to the Core," *Louisville* 24 (Aug. 1973): 39–46; *Louisville Survey: Central and South Report* (Louisville 1978); Carl Kramer, *Rebuilding Downtown: A Brief History of Louisville Central Area, Inc. 1959–1985* (Louisville 1985).

LOUISVILLE CENTRAL LAW SCHOOL. Louisville Central Law School was a major professional school for AFRICAN AMERICANS. Prof. John H. Lawson, who taught Greek and Latin at Kentucky Normal and Theological Institute (later State University and SIMMONS UNIVERSITY), established Central Law School at the institute in 1890 and became its first dean. Lawson received his bachelor of arts degree from Howard University and his law degree from Harvard University. It became the fourth law school for blacks in the nation after Howard University, Walden University School of Law, and Shaw University Law School.

Central Law School was a proprietary school owned by a private corporation and operated by instructors in affiliation with State University and was the only black-supported law school in the country. On May 10, 1892, the first five Central Law School graduates held their commencement at the Masonic Temple Theater. The graduates were Isaac W. Thomas of Hemphill, Texas; Charles W. Mason of Evansville, Indiana; Robert A. Goodall of Church Hill in Christian County; and John P. Jetton and William H. Perry, both of Louisville. The school was located on the campus at Seventh and Kentucky Streets.

Lawson died in 1896, and Albert S. White became the new dean, a position he held until 1911. In that year W.C. Brown, a graduate of the school in 1903, became the next and last dean. In 1930 UNIVERSITY OF LOUISVILLE purchased the property of Simmons University, which later became LOUISVILLE MUNICIPAL COLLEGE. SIMMONS UNIVERSITY was renamed Simmons Bible College and moved to its present location at Eighteenth and Dumesnil Streets. After 1930 the law classes continued to be conducted in the law offices of its dean. Between 1911 and 1941 there were approximately a hundred graduates of the school, including Sallie J. White, the first black female law graduate to be admitted to the Kentucky bar. After 1941 the records of Simmons University Central Law School ended.

See Lawrence H. Williams, *Black Higher Education in Kentucky: The History of Simmons University* (Lewiston, N.Y., 1987); George C. Wright, *Life Behind a Veil* (Baton Rouge 1985); George D. Wilson, *A Century of Negro Education in Louisville, Kentucky* (Louisville 1986); Kentucky Commission on Human Rights, *Kentucky's Black Heritage: The Role of the Black People in the History of Kentucky from Pioneer Days to the Present* (Frankfort 1971).

Bruce M. Tyler

LOUISVILLE CHAMBER MUSIC SOCIETY. In 1938 DWIGHT ANDERSON, dean of the UNIVERSITY OF LOUISVILLE School of Music, and Morris Belknap, a prominent local philanthropist and music lover, raised five hundred dollars to organize the LOUISVILLE CHAMBER MUSIC SOCIETY. The purpose was to present chamber music and to create an interest in forming chamber groups among Louisville musicians. Since then it has provided a regular series of concerts every year. The concerts were first held in the Playhouse on the University of Louisville's Belknap Campus.

From the beginning, the society set high standards in both its repertory and performances. Dr. Gerhard Herz, who taught music history at the School of Music, was an invaluable colleague who helped Anderson book outstanding chamber-music organizations for the society's concerts. He also worked closely with internationally famous groups to organize concerts that covered the broadest chamber music spectrum—from sixteenth-century vocal music to string quartets by such twentieth-century giants as Bartok and Hindemith. It was Herz who helped the society organize its 1976–77 season around a survey of Beethoven's sixteen string quartets, performed in series of five concerts by the Juilliard String Quartet.

In 1946 Anderson, because of increasing duties as dean, gave up the management of the society. His place was taken by Mrs. Macauley Smith and Fanny Brandeis, who together ran the organization for twenty years. It was a time of growth and prosperity. In 1952 the Chamber Music Society was incorporated as a nonprofit, educational, and cultural organization with a board of trustees.

In the late 1970s, the Playhouse on BELKNAP Campus was moved to make way for the construction of Ekstrom Library. This forced the Chamber Music Society to seek alternate halls for its concerts, which were given at such places as the Woman's Club Auditorium and Columbia Auditorium until the society took up permanent residence in the University of Louisville School of Music North Recital Hall in 1980.

See Agnes Crume, *The Chamber Music Society of Louisville Golden Anniversary Salute, 1938–1988* (The Chamber Music Society of Louisville, University of Louisville, 1988); Mari Sweeney Hammer, "History of Louisville's Chamber Music Society," M.A. thesis, University of Louisville, 1981.

LOUISVILLE CHESS CLUB. The Louisville Chess Club was founded in 1865 by O.B. Theiss, Bland Ballard, George Nicholas, H.M. Woodruff, Hiram Roberts, B. Frank Roberts, and J.T. Gaines, among others. One of the oldest chess clubs in the United States, it has met at various locations, including the YMHA Building, the Inter-Southern Building, Hermitage Hotel, the Fifth St. USO, the YMCA (at Third and BROADWAY), Mall ST. MATTHEWS, Bauer's Restaurant, St. Matthews Episcopal Church, SECOND PRESBYTERIAN CHURCH, GARDENCOURT, UNIVERSITY OF LOUISVILLE'S Shelby Campus, and the Douglass Blvd. Community Center. Famous chess players who have visited the club at these locations include Harry Pillsbury, Jackson Showalter, Johannes Zukertort, Frank Marshall, I.A. Horowitz, Sammy Reshevsky, George Koltanowski, Weaver Adams, Newell Banks, and Robert Byrne. Since 1946 the club has played twelve matches against out-of-town teams, winning four of eight versus Lexington, one of two versus Cincinnati, one versus Hanover, Indiana, and losing to FORT KNOX. Among the club's most successful players have been John Bloomer, Harold Branch, Edwin Cohen, Alex Conen, Pat Forsee, Dennis Gogel, Robert Jacobs, Robert Kannapell, Gary Klinglesmith, Jackie Mayer, Jack Moyse, Sergey Shchukin, and Richard Shields.

See Eric Yussman, *History of the Louisville Chess Club* (Louisville 1996).

Eric J. Yussman

LOUISVILLE CHORUS. In 1939 Father Joseph Emrich founded the Holy Name Band and Choral Club, which later became the Holy Name Choral Club (1968), the Choral Club of Louisville (1972), and finally, the Louisville Chorus (1987). Richard Spalding, conductor emeritus, devoted twenty years to the ensemble and made its 1985 European Sister Cities Concert Tour possible. In 1991, the chorus appointed Daniel Spurlock as its conductor. Therese Davis, executive director and pianist, has collaborated with the music directors since 1969 to ensure the growth and development of the chorus.

A member of Chorus America, this semiprofessional chorus, with offices on Fern Valley Pass, maintains approximately fifty singers who perform choral masterworks, pops, folk SONGS, musicals, and JAZZ. Through traditional, holiday, family, and fun series; joint ventures with other arts agencies; dinner concerts; commercial compact discs; and commissioned performances, listeners experience music filled with sparkle and personality. Additionally, the Opus 4 educational/outreach program offers vocal arts revues that encompass interactive audience participation. The Louisville Chorus gained an international reputation when it performed "My Old Kentucky Home" in Russian during the 1992 simulcast of the KENTUCKY DERBY viewed by citizens of the former U.S.S.R.

Darlene Welch

LOUISVILLE CIVIL WAR ROUND TABLE. A round table is a group of persons who meet to discuss a particular topic. The Louisville CIVIL WAR Round Table has a heritage of devoted study of the American Civil War from an objective historical perspective through lectures, discussions, and on-site visits to the battlefields.

It was founded at Big Spring Country Club in Louisville on January 19, 1961, upon the anniversary of Robert E. Lee's birth. Frank G. Rankin, a local historian, founded the group and was elected first president. Each year a president and board of directors are elected to one-year terms. Women and men from a variety of backgrounds and professions compose the membership roster.

The group meets from September through May at various locations for dinner and to hear a speaker. A roster of who's who in Civil War scholarship has spoken to the group, including James I. Robertson, Robert E. Krick, Shelby Foote, Kenneth Hafendorfer (also a member and past president of the round table), Ed Bearss, Gary Gallagher, Wiley Sword, and William C. Davis.

Charles Michael Mills

LOUISVILLE CLOCK. Initiated with the hope that it could be a landmark for the city comparable to the St. Louis Arch or the Space Needle in Seattle, a large, eye-catching clock was planned as part of the new RIVER CITY MALL along Fourth St. in the 1970s. With little time or money, however, the clock's intended platform sat empty at the mall's dedication ceremonies in August 1973. Hopes reemerged when former mayor Wilson W. Wyatt mentioned the lingering clock idea to a group of local leaders at a luncheon the following year and piqued the funding interest of Henry V. Heuser Sr., the president and director of the HENRY VOGT MACHINE CO.

A committee interviewed prospective sculptors from around the world for a year and finally chose Louisvillian BARNEY BRIGHT to design the showpiece. After scaling back the original concept and price, construction was started in 1974, and the Louisville Clock was dedicated December 3, 1976, in front of nearly 3,000 people.

Designed to look and act like a big windup toy, the clock played upon the area's love of horses and the KENTUCKY DERBY. A large, tilted racetrack sitting on eight ornamented columns was the focus of the forty-foot-high clock, and at noon each day a recorded bugle would call five hand carved contestants of local significance to the starting position. After a brief introduction, GEORGE ROGERS CLARK, Daniel Boone, the *BELLE OF LOUISVILLE,* King Louis XVI, and THOMAS JEFFERSON would circle the track to the delight of crowds. The daily contest led to the clock being popularly dubbed the "Derby Clock." Sitting atop the clock was a Victorian-style gazebo housing mechanical spectators, again with local ties. Motion picture director D.W. Griffith, actress MARY ANDERSON, U.S. president ZACHARY TAYLOR, trumpeter Oliver Cooke, and *COURIER-JOURNAL* editor HENRY WATTERSON all looked on as the figures raced below.

While the clock attracted lunchtime crowds, who often bet the cost of their meals on the outcome, mechanical problems plagued the intricate clock. The city, responsible for the maintenance costs that annually climbed to twenty thousand dollars, frequently posted a "No Race Today" sign out front, and the clock sat dormant for long spells. Coupled with these problems, the clock also had trouble finding a permanent home. When the GALLERIA was built over Fourth St. in 1981, developers paid one hundred thousand dollars to move the clock one block south near Guthrie Green. Five years later, in order to allow passage of the TOONERVILLE TROLLEY shuttle bus line, the clock was relocated near the west wing of the KENTUCKY FAIR

1928 Louisville Colonels team at Parkway Field.

AND EXPOSITION CENTER. In 1993, the city finally dismantled the clock after years of inactivity. Despite several attempts to resurrect the Louisville Clock, by 1999 it continued to sit in several pieces at various locations, with the racing figures on display at the Kentucky Derby Museum.

See *Courier-Journal,* March 3, 1993, Oct. 4, 1995, Oct. 27, 1996.

Craig M. Heuser

LOUISVILLE COMMITTEE ON FOREIGN RELATIONS. The Louisville Committee on Foreign Relations (LCFR) was formed in 1938 as an alliance between Louisville's Southern Regional Council and New York's Council on Foreign Relations and was one of its first affiliates. The LCFR was meant to serve as a nonprofit, nonpartisan discussion group. The meetings on U.S. foreign policy would be "off the record" to facilitate a productive exchange of ideas.

Membership of the committee generally ranges between sixty and eighty, and members are leading figures in the business, legal, and academic communities. Membership is by invitation only, and meetings are open only to members and their guests. There is approximately one meeting per month from September through May of each year.

Scores of prominent international figures have spoken to the committee, including ambassadors of various countries; representatives of defense, diplomatic, and intelligence communities of the United States and other nations; scholars and other foreign policy specialists; and journalists. In 1995 the Council on Foreign Relations terminated its ties with the LCFR and the other thirty-six regional committees; in response, the committees created a new parent organization, the American Committees on Foreign Relations (ACFR), based in Washington, D.C. The ACFR has assumed the Council on Foreign Relations' task of providing the regional committees with outstanding speakers on a regular basis.

Charles E. Ziegler

LOUISVILLE COLONELS. Louisville has a long and distinguished BASEBALL tradition. Its professional and semiprofessional teams from the 1870s through the 1890s used a variety of nicknames, but the early professional clubs officially were called the Louisvilles. The only exceptions were the 1882 and 1883 seasons when the team was called Eclipse, after the famous racehorse. Louisville's teams during that time were often referred to by a variety of nicknames such as the Falls City team, the Cyclones, the Grays, Night Riders, and Wanderers. But the most prevalent and longstanding team name was the Colonels.

In 1901 Louisville formed the city's first minor-league team in the Western Association and named the team the Colonels. The league did not last the year. In 1902 the Colonels became a charter member of the new American Association, staying in the league until 1962. From 1902 through 1938, the team was privately owned, but thereafter the club was either partially or wholly owned as a farm club by a big-league team, chiefly the Boston Red Sox.

In 1902 the first owner of the club, George "White Wings" Tabeau, built a new baseball stadium, ECLIPSE PARK, at Seventh and Kentucky Streets. It was the third park to bear that name. The park hosted the Colonels for twenty-one seasons until it was badly burned in November 1922. After the fire, team president William Knebelkamp announced construction of PARKWAY FIELD, the city's first steel-and-concrete stadium. It would serve as the Colonels' home until 1956, when the team started playing home games at Fairgrounds Stadium.

The first team captain was player-manager "Derby Bill" Clymer, an outfielder. The Colonels finished in second place in their first season, behind Indianapolis. Overall, the Colonels had an enviable record in American Association competition. They won their first pennant or league championship in 1909. They also won championships in 1916, 1921, 1925, 1926, 1930, and 1946. After the league adopted a playoff system to determine its representative in the Junior World Series—called the Little World Series through 1931—the Colonels won the championship in 1921, 1939, 1945, 1954, and 1960, and also played in eight additional championships.

Two of their most surprising playoff victories came in 1939 and 1954. During the 1939 regular season the team had a losing record but squeaked into the playoffs with a fourth-place finish. The team then beat both Minneapolis and Indianapolis leading up to the Junior World Series with Rochester. The series came down to an extra-inning seventh game that the Colonels won 7–3 with a four-run eleventh inning. The 1954 players finished ten games behind the pennant-winning HOOSIERS but won the last two games of the playoffs. Pitcher Hershel Freeman belted out a home run to win the last game and the championship. The Colonels then went on to defeat Syracuse for the Junior World Series title.

After the 1955 season the Colonels' affiliation with the Red Sox ended, and for several years the team played without a major-league affiliation. In 1956 both the team and the grandstand seating were racially integrated. After the 1962 season the American Association disbanded, and Louisville was without a professional baseball team for the first time in the twentieth century.

In 1964 Charles O. Finley, the owner of the Kansas City Athletics (later the Oakland Athletics), signed a contract to play American League games at Fairgrounds Stadium, but he was blocked by fellow league owners who instructed him to renegotiate a contract with Kansas City.

From 1968 through 1972 the Colonels were members of the International League. Evansville real estate developer Walter Dilbeck bought a Toronto farm team and moved the club to Louisville. The following year the team was purchased by Louisville attorney and shopping center mogul William Gardner. The team's record in the International League was less impressive. Though it won the pennant in 1972 and finished second in 1969, it lost out in the playoffs. After the 1972 season the KENTUCKY STATE FAIR Board decided to redesign the stadium mainly for FOOTBALL, and the team was evicted. Minor-league baseball would not return to the city until 1982, when the Redbirds, the St. Louis farm team, was brought to Louisville by banker Dan Ulmer and A. Ray Smith of Tulsa, Oklahoma.

Over the years the Colonels have had many noteworthy ballplayers and managers. A significant number of Colonels leaped to big-league fame, but manager Joe McCarthy (1919–25) undoubtedly leads the pack. McCarthy went on to manage some of the outstanding New York Yankees teams from 1931 to 1946. Seven of McCarthy's Yankee teams won World Series. He also managed the Chicago Cubs for five years and the Boston Red Sox for three. McCarthy's .615 winning percentage is among the game's best.

Big leaguers who played for the Colonels included pitchers Babe Adams, Grover Cleveland Lowdermilk, Fred Toney, Fred Schupp, Johnny Marcum, Tex Hughson, and Jim Wilson; catcher Hank Sevareid; infielders Bert Niehoff, Hall of Famer Billy Herman, a second baseman with the Chicago Cubs; Harold (Pee Wee) Reese, a shortstop with the Brooklyn

Dodgers; Tony Lupien; Johnny Pesky; Billy Goodman; Frank Malzone; and outfielder Earle Combs, a Kentuckian and future Hall-of-Famer who played for the Yankees. Stan Spence, Jim Piersall, southpaw Juan Pizarro, and Charley Maxwell also made the majors. Bob Uecker, better known for his work off the field in movies and on TELEVISION, played for the Colonels in the early 1960s.

Several Colonels who did not make it in the big leagues belong to a list of the club's greatest players and unique fan favorites. Among them are batting champs Jay Kirke, John Ganzel, Tom Wright, and Billy Hallman; the Colonels' only homerun champ, Elmer Smith; pitchers Nick Cullop, Joe DeBerry, Wes Flowers, Don Nottebart, and Roy Wilkinson; infielders Roxie Roach and Jose Olivares; and outfielders Mel Simons, Chet Morgan, Chick "One Hop" Genovese. Successful Colonels managers include Bill Burwell, Nemo Liebold, and Pinky Higgins, and 1960 American Association Manager-of-the-Year Bill Adair.

The Louisville team was also home to Jake Northup, a pitcher who won and lost more American Association games than any other. Another standout was Ben Tincup, a full-blooded Cherokee Indian and standout pitcher and hitter who played with the Colonels from 1919 until 1931. American Association Hall-of-Famers include, in addition to McCarthy, Herman, Reese and Combs, manager Burleigh Grimes from the 1936 team. From the International League days, major-league players who played with the Colonels include Cecil Cooper, Carleton Fisk, and Dwight Evans.

Three former Colonels executives also served as president of the American Association: Tom Chivington (1910–16), Bruce Dudley (1948–52), and Ed Doherty (1953–59).

See Philip Von Borries, *Louisville Diamonds: The Louisville Major-League Reader 1876–1899* (Paducah, Ky., 1996); Bill O'Neal, *The American Association: A Baseball History 1902–1991* (Austin, Tex., 1991), Henry C. Mayer, "The 1939 Louisville Colonels: The Team that Never Quit," *Filson Club History Quarterly* 70 (Jan. 1996): 39–61.

Henry C. Mayer

LOUISVILLE COLORED MUSICAL ASSOCIATION. The establishment of the Louisville Colored Musical Association in 1867 was made possible by the development of a talented cadre of musicians and a tradition of participation by black churches in musical events. Since the 1830s several of the most popular STRING AND BRASS BANDS in Louisville had been led by African American musicians such as JAMES C. CUNNINGHAM and WILLIAM COLE. Stringed instruments and organs were first introduced into black churches by music teacher WILLIAM H. GIBSON. Some of the churches held fund-raising fairs, with musical entertainment, as they struggled to establish themselves in antebellum Louisville.

On June 3, 1867, the Louisville Colored Musical Association held its first concert at the Center Street CME Church. The program featured the talented Lexington pianist Julia A. Britton. The first president of the association was Peter Lewis. Other leaders of the group included N.R. Harper, who was musical director from 1871 to 1881; William H. Lawson, a painter and photographer who served as president in 1877; and William H. Gibson, who was president in the 1880s. By 1877 the association had grown to over a hundred members, and its own Excelsior Brass Band provided accompaniment for its choral group, which was drawn from many of the city's black churches. In 1881 and 1882 it hosted two large musical festivals that featured outstanding performers from all over the country. The Louisville Colored Musical Association played an important role in the training of musicians, in providing concerts and music festivals for public enjoyment, and in the raising of funds for benevolent purposes.

See William H. Gibson, *History of the United Brothers of Friendship and Sisters of the Mysterious Ten* (Louisville 1897); H.C. Weeden, *Weeden's History of the Colored People of Louisville* (Louisville 1897).

Cornelius Bogert

LOUISVILLE COMMUNITY DESIGN CENTER. The Louisville Community Design Center (LCDC) was incorporated by Louisville architects John M. Shulhafer, Thomas E. Smith, and Ralph Hilton Kurtz in November 1972 "to improve the quality of the physical environment in the FALLS OF THE OHIO Region" by providing design service "in situations where professional assistance . . . would not otherwise be provided or would be inadequate."

At the end of the 1960s and into the early 1970s, Louisville was not unaffected by the social and political ferment precipitated by the VIETNAM WAR and by the CIVIL RIGHTS movement. Architects, whose professional focus is to shape the physical environment, felt increasingly challenged during this era to become involved as agents of social and economic justice—to build a just and more harmonious society by influencing the form and composition of the built environment. During the late 1960s, a cadre of young architects began pursuing these shared aspirations through their employment at a small number of Louisville firms and through occasional volunteer collaborations. Buoyed by the idealism of the age, they developed powerful personal relationships while contributing their talents to small community projects such as the design and construction of vest-pocket PARKS in poor Louisville NEIGHBORHOODS. Meanwhile, architects would occasionally come to the defense of neighborhoods against the URBAN RENEWAL Agency, such as when the agency announced plans to build a major street interchange that was considered by residents of OLD LOUISVILLE to be perilously close to Belgravia and St. James Courts.

The social awareness and volunteer activity among architects would ultimately converge with the American Institute of Architects' efforts through the founding of the Louisville Community Design Center in November 1972. An outgrowth of the AIA Central Kentucky Chapter, the community design center would originally be governed by a board composed of architects and neighborhood activists. At the time of its incorporation, the LCDC retained three graduates of the University of Kentucky College of Architecture, employed as VISTA volunteers, to serve as staff.

The founding of the Louisville Community Design Center creation preceded by just a few months the 1973 election of Harvey I. Sloane as mayor of Louisville. Among the hallmarks of the first Sloane administration (1974–78) was the creation and promotion of neighborhood associations to represent the interests and concerns of the city's diverse urban neighborhoods. With the passage of the federal Housing and Community Development Act of 1974, several of these associations would also serve as vehicles for the deployment of federal funds for housing rehabilitation and for the development of community facilities. In these new and expanded civic associations, the LCDC would discover a new ally and best client through which to channel its service to the poor. Meanwhile, the LCDC would briefly act as an agent for the city of Louisville as architect for a number of community facilities built or rehabilitated by the city with federal funds appropriated in the years following the 1974 housing act. While city funding enabled the design center to hire its first executive director, architect Ronald D. Gascoyne, in 1975, real and perceived threats thereafter to the organization's political independence led to a quick souring of the design center's relationship with the city and termination of the funding agreement in 1978. Nonetheless, in collaboration with urban writers Grady Clay and Jonathan Barnett, the design center produced an important study of Louisville's urban alley system. At the same time, LCDC conducted a comprehensive study of the Baxter-Bardstown Roads neighborhood commercial corridor from BROADWAY to Douglass Blvd. that promoted a renaissance for the corridor that would begin shortly thereafter. The design center served as the first consulting architect to the Art Center Association in the adaptive use of the city's historic River Rd. pumping station and standpipe as a museum of contemporary art.

Through the active and continuous involvement of a number of local architects on LCDC's governing board, the design center would continue to maintain a strong relationship with the local architectural community. However, the appointment of a planner rather than an architect as LCDC executive director in 1980 marked a change in direction for the design center. Rather than acting as a clearinghouse for volunteer architects serving the poor, or as a not-for-profit architectural practice, the design center would assume more the role of a community development agency. While LCDC's fundamental goals remained similar—to assist in improving the community where such assistance would otherwise be unavailable—the method of assistance rendered by LCDC had evolved considerably. Increasingly the design center emphasized the importance of the client as the source of vision on a project. It began to regard itself as the subordinate in its neighborhood collaborations, providing the technical planning and development assistance while relying on the tenacity of the neighborhood to lead the way.

In 1997 the Louisville Community Design Center had coalesced its method of service into three interrelated components: through education, the LCDC would enable neighborhoods to organize and to govern themselves more effectively in order to achieve the visions and goals to which they themselves aspired; through planning, the LCDC would assist neighborhoods to articulate their own inherent visions and goals and to formulate reasonable and manageable strategies for accomplishing those goals; and, through development assistance, the LCDC would provide neighborhoods with the technical tools and capacities required to accomplish certain neighborhood strategies such as housing rehabilitation and crime prevention.

John Trawick

LOUISVILLE CONSERVATORY OF MUSIC. The Louisville Conservatory of Music was founded with two thousand dollars on July 27, 1915, by Frederic A. Cowles, James Wesley McClain, and T.M. Gilmore Jr. as a for-profit corporation. Cowles was appointed director.

With 16 teachers and 250 students, classes began on September 7, 1915, in the former Dillingham mansion at 214 W BROADWAY. Artists' and teachers' diplomas were offered on graduation. As the school's reputation grew, enrollment increased, and more space was needed. In 1926 land on the northwest corner of Brook and Jacob Streets was bought for $60,000, and a 4-story building was erected at a cost of $170,000. By opening day in September 1927, there were sixty teachers and more than two thousand collegiate and preparatory students.

After the collapse of the stock market in October 1929, enrollment at the conservatory began to drop because parents could no longer afford tuition. On November 18, 1931, a petition of bankruptcy was filed; and on February 1, 1932, the conservatory closed its doors permanently. Today the building is gone, and Interstate 65 covers the site.

See Mary Grace Money, "A History of the Louisville Conservatory of Music and Music at the University of Louisville, 1907–1935," M.M.Ed. thesis, University of Louisville, 1976; *Courier-Journal*, April 1, 1915, Aug. 20, 1926, Nov. 19, 1931; *Louisville Herald Post*, June 20, 1926, Feb. 14, 1926, *Louisville Times*, Oct. 24, 1928.

Robert Bruce French

LOUISVILLE COURIER. The newspaper that merged with the *Louisville Journal* to form the *Courier-Journal* was started by WALTER NEWMAN HALDEMAN in 1844. Haldeman began his career as a clerk in the business office of the Whig newspaper, the *LOUISVILLE JOURNAL*, in 1840. After three years he went into business for himself, opening a bookstore. Within months, he took over a fledging newspaper, the *Louisville Daily Dime*, a small sheet issued without much success by an association of printers. He did this to protect his investments in the business. Under Haldeman the paper flourished, so after four months he invested in new type and increased its size. At the request of the advertisers, he changed the name to the *Louisville Morning Courier*.

The paper's editorial policy changed dramatically over time to match Haldeman's changing political views. He started as a moderate Whig and then shifted to a nativist, to an abolitionist, to a Southern Democrat, and then to a radical pro-slavery stance. At the start of the CIVIL WAR, the *Courier* supported the Confederacy, prompting Union troops to seize the newspaper's office and seek Haldeman's arrest when Kentucky compromised its neutrality in 1861. Fleeing the city, Haldeman published the *Courier* in Bowling Green, Kentucky, and Nashville until February 1862, when Confederate forces withdrew from there. Haldeman sat out the rest of the war in Madison, Georgia. He returned to Louisville after the war and reestablished the *Courier*, which soon became the dominant daily newspaper in the city. When HENRY WATTERSON became editor of the *Louisville Journal* in 1868, the *Courier* began to feel the heat of competition. Under Watterson's suggestion, Haldeman bought out the competing *Louisville Journal* and the *Louisville Democrat* and merged the staffs of the *Courier* and the *Journal* in 1868. Henry Watterson retained his position with the *COURIER-JOURNAL* while Haldeman concentrated on the business side.

LOUISVILLE DEAF ORAL SCHOOL. Upon hearing Spencer Tracy's wife describe the John Tracy Clinic in Los Angeles that aided hearing-impaired children, several members of the WOMAN'S CLUB OF LOUISVILLE began to consider establishing a similar school. In 1948 the Woman's Club joined with the Louisville branch of Kiwanis International, which had adopted aid to the deaf as a project, and welcomed three students to a makeshift facility in the Woman's Club basement on S Fourth St. A primary goal of the school, Kentucky's first preschool for the hearing-impaired, was to prepare children for easier transition into PUBLIC SCHOOLS.

As enrollment increased to fourteen, the institution moved into the first floor of the club's carriage house in 1951. Within three years, classes were held five days a week, with funding for the teachers coming from the Kiwanis Club and the Louisville Committee on Health. By the 1960s the school, which was incorporated in 1954, served roughly forty children and required the entire carriage house as classroom space.

Late in the 1970s it became evident that, with both its reputation and student body growing, the school needed a new structure. In 1981 the school moved again to a renovated three-story home donated by developer Al Schneider on W Ormsby Ave. In 1998 the school, with ninety students and thirty faculty members, kicked off a fund-raising campaign to pay for a new structure. A lot on Fourth St. in OLD LOUISVILLE between Oak and St. Catherine Streets was purchased by the Friends of the Deaf Oral School, using proceeds from its Fabulous Finds retail shop on Main St. In 1999 the school instituted plans to move to a newly reconstructed facility at First and Kentucky Streets. The school serves as a preschool for hearing-impaired children in the Jefferson County public schools as well as public school children in neighboring counties.

See Mary Adelberg, ed., *The Woman's Club of Louisville, 1890–1990* (Louisville 1990); *Courier-Journal*, Sept. 4, 1996.

Schuyler N. Heuser

LOUISVILLE DEFENDER. A leading weekly newspaper, it is the oldest still published by AFRICAN AMERICANS in Kentucky. It produced its first edition on March 20, 1933—an eight-page broadsheet that sold for a nickel. The founders were Alvin H. Bowman, a Louisville mortician, and John H. Sengstacke, owner of a black newspaper chain then expanding into the southern states and whose flagship publication was the *Chicago Defender*, now a daily tabloid.

Louisville then had two established black-owned papers: the *LOUISVILLE LEADER*, founded by I. WILLIS COLE in 1917 and dissolved after his death in 1950, and the *Louisville News*, founded in 1913 by WILLIAM WARLEY and discontinued in the mid-1930s.

Initially the *Defender* operated with part-time office staff, freelance writers, and commission-only ADVERTISING salespeople. But by 1936 it had six full-time employees producing twenty-five hundred copies weekly from offices at 623 W Walnut St. (now Muhammad Ali Blvd.). In April that year, Sengstacke bought controlling interest from Bowman and hired as general manager Frank Stanley Sr., who would become the paper's publisher and driving force for the next thirty-seven years, until his death in 1974.

The *Defender* grew steadily in influence and circulation in the intervening years, becoming Kentucky's leading advocate for racial justice. For example, in 1942 it published an exposé of segregated Army units at FORT KNOX, where black soldiers without barracks slept in tents.

News stories and editorials pushed aggressively in the 1950s for integrated public accommodations, and in the 1960s and 1970s for open housing, equal job opportunities, and desegregated PUBLIC SCHOOLS.

By 1943 it was circulating fifteen thousand copies weekly from offices at 418 S. Fifth St. It employed thirty-five news and business staff and operated bureaus in Lexington and Hopkinsville. Since 1968 it has occupied offices at 1720 Dixie Hwy.

Circulation peaked at seventeen thousand copies in 1948, dropped to about fifteen thousand when the paper became a tabloid in 1953, and fell to about ten thousand through the 1960s, when major daily papers such as the *COURIER-JOURNAL* and *Lexington Herald-Leader* began hiring black newsmen to cover CIVIL RIGHTS issues and compete successfully for African American readers. But the *Defender's* clout always exceeded its press run, thanks largely to its crusading publisher, Frank Stanley, who had become majority stockholder in 1950.

Stanley's sudden death prompted interfamily legal strife, with his oldest son, Frank Junior, unsuccessfully challenging the stock ownership of his brother and co-publisher, Kenneth, and stepmother, Vivian Stanley, then board chairman. Circulation plummeted to twenty-six hundred weekly by 1985, when Vivian Stanley sold her controlling interest to Consumer Communications Industries Corp., a holding company headed by Clarence Leslie, *Defender* general manager and executive vice president.

See *Louisville Defender*, March 24, 1983; *Courier-Journal*, March 22, 1983; *Kentucky's Black Heritage: The Role of Black People in the History of Kentucky from Pioneer Days to the Present* (Frankfort 1971).

Lawrence Muhammad

LOUISVILLE DOWNS. Situated on an eighty-seven-acre tract on Poplar Level Rd. just south of I-264, LOUISVILLE DOWNS, the city's half-mile harness track, opened on July 14, 1966, and closed on September 2, 1991. The track, notable for its crushed-limestone racing oval, large infield lake, and peppermint-striped, glass-enclosed grandstand, was the home of the Kentucky Pacing Derby, a major event on the harness-racing circuit.

The first president of the track and its guiding force for twenty-four years was William H. King, a Louisville promoter. In its heyday, from 1976–82, the track had a daily average of more than 3,000 fans and a handle of over $220,000. During its final season, the Louisville Downs' handle had shrunk to about fifty thousand dollars.

King introduced computerized wagering at the track, live CABLE TELEVISION coverage, such betting specialties as the Big L (a double perfecta wager), and Call-A-Bet, the first wagering-by-phone system in Kentucky and one of the first in the nation. In December 1988 the track was the first in Kentucky to accept wagering on a full simulcast card while conducting live racing.

In November 1986, King, who initially had invested five hundred thousand dollars in the track, purchased, along with his daughter and others, 100 percent of the track's stock for $5.1 million from Detroit businessman Raymond Kolowich and his family. Four years later, in September 1990, J. Chester Porter, Maria Bouvette, and Ched Jennings bought the track for a reported $7 million, and King's reign ended. Only a year later, in September 1991, CHURCHILL DOWNS bought the facility from Porter and Bouvette for a package deal of $6 million. The site became a Churchill Downs training facility and an intertrack wagering site called Sports Spectrum.

Joseph Woodson Oglesby

***LOUISVILLE ECCENTRIC OBSERVER* (LEO).** *Louisville Eccentric Observer* is an alternative, free circulation newsweekly founded in 1990 by John Yarmuth, who has been its only editor. Initially the paper was a journal of opinion and commentary, featuring regular columns by UNIVERSITY OF LOUISVILLE BASKETBALL coach Denny Crum as well as former *COURIER-JOURNAL* and *LOUISVILLE TIMES* writers Mary Caldwell, Robert Schulman, Dudley Saunders, and Yarmuth. The paper's first issue was published in July 1990, and it began a regular biweekly publishing schedule on November 1, 1990. In April 1993 the paper began weekly publication. Widely known as "LEO," the paper has been totally supported by ADVERTISING revenue. It is published on newsprint in tabloid format and is made available at no charge at approximately five hundred businesses and other locations throughout Jefferson County and Southern Indiana.

LEO was the first print medium in its market to popularize "personal" advertising, through which people seek social contacts. In its early years, the paper was largely known for satirical covers and colorful, opinionated commentary. After converting to a weekly publication schedule in 1993, *LEO* published a wider variety of news, arts and cultural information, and entertainment listings. It publishes a mix of local and nationally syndicated features including columns by Molly Ivins and Dave Barry; "News of the Weird," a collection of unusual but true events; and "Real Astrology." The newsweekly also publishes regular columns of media criticism, sports, and general commentary by local writers. In addition, *LEO* publishes reviews of movies, the performing and visual arts, books, and both live and recorded music.

Some of *LEO's* more significant feature stories have been an investigation of charges of racial discrimination by Dillard's department store, a critical examination of the *Courier-Journal's* reporting for an article critical of Louisville doctors, and an investigation of charges of abuse by a local Thoroughbred horse trainer. *LEO* occasionally publishes stories from other alternative publications.

In 1992 *LEO* began to devote a special issue to locally produced literature. Literary *LEO* is published once each year and comprises POETRY and short fiction submitted by writers and judged by the paper's staff.

In 1995, *LEO* was admitted to the Association of Alternative Newsweeklies (AAN), a trade association of more than one hundred members including papers such as the *Village Voice*, the *Chicago Reader*, and the *San Francisco Bay Guardian*. *LEO* had won more than twenty Louisville Metro Journalism Awards through 1996.

In January 1993 Blanche Kitchen became *LEO's* first publisher. Kitchen and her late husband had founded and operated *Bargain Mart*, a classified advertising publication, until its sale to the Landmark Publishing Co. in 1990.

As of January 1997 *LOUISVILLE ECCENTRIC OBSERVER* circulated thirty-three thousand copies weekly. Media Audit, a national audience research company, estimated *LEO's* readership at 113,000.

John Yarmuth

LOUISVILLE ECLIPSE. The Louisville Eclipse was a name used by both professional and semipro BASEBALL teams in the late 1800s. Originally a semiprofessional club, it became a charter member of the American Association, a professional league that started in 1881 and operated until 1891 as a counterpoint to the National League, although the team officially used the Eclipse name in only two big-league seasons (1882–1883). The name came from a successful semiprofessional club in Louisville, although its origin was a famous eighteenth-century racehorse that sired numerous legendary Thoroughbreds.

In the late 1860s and 1870s there were several semipro clubs playing baseball in the city. These teams were similar to gentlemen's clubs, usually charging annual membership fees and drawing players from the wealthier members of Louisville society. The games were free at first in the late 1850s, but later the teams would charge admission, sometimes giving players a percentage of the gate proceeds.

Louisville's first professional baseball team, the Grays, an original member of the first National League, was created in 1875 in response to the immense popularity of local semipro clubs. After an 1877 GAMBLING scandal cost the city its professional team, the semipro teams made a resurgence. Leading the group of new clubs was the Eclipse, with a then-seventeen-year-old slugger named PETE BROWNING helping the team to the state championship. Browning became known for his years as a professional player in the 1880s in the American Association.

By 1879 the Eclipse was the most popular semipro team in the area. It played home games at ECLIPSE PARK, which was built in 1871 at

Twenty-eighth and Elliott Streets in West Louisville. In 1881 the team became an openly professional squad, organized as a stock company and headed by distillery executive J.H. Pank. The stockholders pumped money into the team, getting the Central Passenger Railway Co., owned by brothers Alfred and Bidermann du Pont, to renovate Eclipse Park and build a new grandstand.

By the end of 1881 the Eclipse team was invited to join a new professional baseball league, the American Association (AA), with teams from Cincinnati (Reds), Philadelphia (Athletics), Pittsburgh (Alleghenies), St. Louis (Browns), and Baltimore (Orioles). On November 8, 1881, at the Gibson House in Cincinnati, Ohio, it was decided that the association would be operated under the "guarantee system," with each club operating its own affairs and allowed to charge such admission prices as each elected.

Formed to combat the National League, the new circuit went into action with vim and vigor and, for the first two years at least, outstripped its rival in attendance and popularity. This may be attributed to several causes. First, the quality of players in the league was equal, if not superior, to the National League. Second, each club charged a top admission price of twenty-five cents, thus cutting the National League rate in half. And third, in some cities such as Louisville, Sunday games were permitted. The American Association also allowed the sale of alcohol at the games, earning the nicknames "the beer and whiskey league" or the "Beer Ball League." The Louisville team frequently played to crowds of between eight hundred and twenty-five hundred on Sundays.

While the team was often referred to as the Eclipse, it was also listed as the Colonels and even the Louisville Baseball Club in the popular press. By 1885 the team had dropped the Eclipse name and was known primarily as the Colonels, although a scholar of Louisville baseball claims the team was officially listed as the "Louisvilles" throughout the rest of its big-league tenure.

Louisville had a professional baseball team until 1899 even though the American Association collapsed in 1891. The Louisvilles were one of only three teams to survive for the entire ten-year existence of the AA. The team had the worst overall winning percentage of any nineteenth-century club lasting a minimum of ten consecutive years (.429), and the second-worst in major-league history. The team, however, won the pennant in 1890, its lone standout year. The pennant was in part a result of the Players' League war that saw many of the AA's best players defecting to the new league. The high point for a Louisville team under the Eclipse name was the 1882 season when the team placed third in the new league. From 1892 until 1899, the LOUISVILLE COLONELS were a member of the National League.

In addition to Browning, who was also a two-time American Association batting champion, pitcher Guy Hecker and William Van Winkle "Chicken" Wolf were outstanding players. Browning was the dominant hitter in the American Association, taking the league batting titles in 1882 and 1885. A line-drive hitter with a lifetime batting average of .341, Browning is the best hitter in history not to be in the Baseball Hall of Fame, perhaps reflecting the bias against players who spent the majority of their careers in the American Association.

See Dean Alan Sullivan, *The Growth of Sport in a Southern City: A Study of the Organizational Evolution of Baseball in Louisville, Kentucky, as an Urban Phenomenon, 1860–1900,* M.A. thesis, George Mason University, 1989; Philip Von Borries, *Louisville Diamonds: The Louisville Major-League Reader 1876–1899* (Paducah, Ky., 1996).

Joseph Rettner Wells

LOUISVILLE FALLS FOUNTAIN. Anchored near the BELLE OF LOUISVILLE in the OHIO RIVER just west of the Clark Memorial Bridge, the Louisville Falls Fountain was dedicated August 19, 1988, just five days after the death of one of its donors, GEORGE BARRY BINGHAM Sr. Bingham, along with his wife, Mary, provided $2.1 million for the construction of the tallest computerized fountain in the world and granted an additional five hundred thousand dollars for its upkeep. The couple had hoped that their gift, which spews 15,800 gallons of water per minute in the shape of a fleur-de-lis, would become a representative landmark for the city, similar to the Gateway Arch in St. Louis. The Binghams had seen such a fountain in a lake in Geneva, Switzerland, and brought the idea back to Louisville.

After higher-than-expected costs and several early modifications due to malfunctioning sprays and a highly criticized appearance depleted the maintenance fund, an agreement was reached whereby the LOUISVILLE WATER CO. paid for the fountain's maintenance and operation while the city and the Waterfront Development Corp. split the cost of insurance and any additional expenses. Running from morning until midnight every day from Memorial Day until after Thanksgiving (unless high waters delayed its return from winter storage in UTICA, INDIANA), the illuminated fountain initially shot to heights of 420 feet, until energy costs forced the water company to reduce its zenith to 375 feet. Colored lights and a variety of spray patterns added diversity and an aesthetic quality. The fountain was clearly visible from the RIVERFRONT PLAZA and provided an interesting diversion for those sailing on the *Belle of Louisville* and dining at riverside RESTAURANTS.

In 1998 the fountain experienced serious mechanical problems and was shut down. There seemed to be little community support for the large expenditures that would be necessary to repair it. The fountain became an interesting part of Louisville's history and for a time offered a unique perspective to its skyline.

LOUISVILLE FIRE BRICK WORKS. Louisville Fire Brick Works was founded in 1889 at the corner of Louisville and Hiawatha Avenues by Karl Bernhard Grahn, a native of Hanover, Germany. Grahn, who became familiar with mining in Germany, immigrated to eastern Kentucky in 1886, where he became interested in finding iron-ore deposits. With friends Joseph Eifort and Henry Stoughten, Grahn bought extensive tracts of land in the Olive Hill district of Carter County, Kentucky. When flint and plastic fire clay were discovered there, Grahn opened a mining operation. Three years later, this discovery led Grahn, who had moved to Louisville, to establish a factory to produce the high-temperature-resistant bricks, known as firebricks, used to line industrial furnaces and ovens.

Most brick plants produced bricks on an automated production line system; fewer plants manufactured specialized hand-molded bricks. Louisville Fire Brick Works routinely produced individualized bricks and, as a result, developed a profitable enterprise catering to industries' needs for specially shaped firebricks. The company initially produced approximately five thousand hand-molded bricks a day using Kentucky flint and semi-flint clay. In 1905 Louisville Fire Brick Works was incorporated, and in 1913 a subsidiary plant in Grahn, Carter County, Kentucky, was opened. K.B. Grahn remained as president of the company until his death in 1922.

The Louisville plant continued to operate until 1959, when all brick production was shifted to the plant in Carter County where the raw materials were mined. However, the firm retained offices in Louisville. In 1965 the offices were moved from Louisville Ave. to a site on National Turnpike. In the mid-1980s, the Louisville offices returned to 4500 Louisville Ave.

Refractory bricks manufactured in Kentucky revolutionized steelmaking in America and abroad because of the superb quality of eastern Kentucky clays, which were well suited to withstand the intense heat required in steel production. Unfortunately, the economic stability of companies producing standardized refractory bricks was directly dependent on the economic stability of large steel manufacturing companies. Consequently, when the need for high-temperature fossil fuel furnaces declined, the need for furnace liner refractory brick also declined, causing many brick companies to go out of business. However, Louisville Fire Brick Works has remained an economically healthy enterprise at the beginning of the twenty-first century.

See *Courier-Journal*, March 23, 1952; Hubert V. Crawford and Paul L. Crawford.

Hubert V. Crawford
Paul L. Crawford

LOUISVILLE FIRE DEPARTMENT/FIRES. Fires have been endemic to the city of Louisville since its origin. The propensity to build with wood and the close proximity of buildings made fires a constant danger. As the city grew, so did the size of its fires. In time, to meet this growing threat, a volunteer firefighting force was replaced by professionals.

In 1780 firefighting consisted of a small, hand-pumped fire engine that was entirely supplied by a firefighting bucket brigade. The first record of money spent by Louisville for firefighting equipment was in 1807. At that time, a touring elephant was brought to town. The town trustees decided to levy a ten-dollar tax each time the animal was exhibited, and the profit was used to buy fire ladders for the community.

By 1821 Louisville firefighting efforts had been divided into three WARDS, each with a fire engine supported by a company consisting of forty men. The engine, which was hand-drawn, had four wheels and a nozzle protruding from the top. It was supplied by the bucket brigade and had to be lifted around street corners because it did not have a movable axle. It was fairly ineffective, having a water stream one inch wide that reached about a hundred feet.

In 1828 Louisville received its first city charter, and with it certain powers pertaining to fire protection passed from the General Assembly to the mayor and councilmen. The ordinance permitted the city to organize a fire department, members of which would receive no pay but would be exempt from serving on juries or performing militia duty during peacetime. The fire department, overseen by a committee, was responsible for the care, supervision, and inspection of all things connected with the department. The committee sent a monthly report to the mayor and the councilmen of Louisville. It also handled accounts of the firefighting companies and recommendations for equipment, oversaw any formation of a new firefighting company, and appointed able-bodied men who volunteered as firefighters.

By 1844 all six of Louisville's fire engines were able to suction water from various sources throughout the city, effectively ending the bucket brigades. Eight volunteer companies provided fire protection for the city at this time, but their hand-pump engines were inadequate and the bitter rivalries between the companies had intensified. The volunteers' feuds led to more fistfighting than firefighting at several fires.

During the early 1850s, Louisville experienced a number of fires, some of which were quite severe. The city's volunteer fire protection became less efficient because of the demands placed upon it, and in 1858 the Louisville City Council disbanded the volunteers. Concerned about the rising costs of insurance because of inadequate fire protection, the Louisville Board of Fire Underwriters purchased a steam engine, *Eclipse*, from the A.B. Latta Co. of Cincinnati in 1857. The board operated the engine independently for a year and presented it to the city along with two others when the new department formed. When the Steam Engine Fire Department of Louisville organized on June 1, 1858, it became the third fully paid department in the nation.

Louisville Fire Department Engine Company No. 11, 1122 Rogers Street in the present day Irish Hill neighborhood.

The seventy thousand inhabitants of Louisville were protected by three fire companies consisting of sixty-five men, twenty-three horses, and one chief engineer. The City Council appointed veteran volunteer Absalom Y. Johnson as the first chief. Old volunteer fire company Kentucky #5 became P.B. Atwood Engine Co. #1, equipped with the *Eclipse*. The Union #2 became the Gillis Engine Co. #2, and Lafayette #8 mustered in as E.D. Weatherford Engine Co. #3.

The first run for the new department occurred on July 2, 1858, to the home of a Mr. Waters on Campbell St. By the end of the year, sixty-two calls had sounded. There were forty-seven fires and fifteen false alarms. Fire losses dropped dramatically from the volunteer era, resulting in lower insurance rates for businesses in 1859.

Chief Johnson's success resulted in City Council approval for three additional companies: Baxter Hook-and-Ladder Co. #1, John Sargent Engine #4, and Sim Watkins Engine #5. Fire companies bore the names of prominent Louisville citizens, usually a member of the Board of Fire Underwriters, an elected official, or a high-ranking member of the department. Over the years, number designations remained the same, but names often changed. The practice continued until the turn of the century, when the department assigned new companies numbers only. In 1861 A.Y. Johnson resigned his position to enlist in the Union army. Veteran George Levi replaced him for a short time, then Michael J. Paul became chief in 1862. During his term the city's first general-alarm fire occurred. On July 1, 1864, a fierce blaze claimed eight hundred thousand dollars' worth of federal property. Louisville was under the military control of the Union army, which promptly arrested Chief Paul and thirty-nine others as Southern sympathizers. Paul spent the rest of the war in a federal prison, and A.Y. Johnson returned for a second term as chief.

In 1865 the department installed a Gamewell TELEGRAPH system consisting of 51 alarm boxes connected by 125 feet of cable strung across rooftops. A fire-alarm box in the nearest fire station received the telegraph code from the activated pull box. The fire-alarm box system was partially motivated by a fire at the GALT HOUSE on January 11, 1865, that cost several lives and caused an estimated damage of four hundred thousand dollars. The first alarm on this system sounded from Box 14 at Shelby and BROADWAY on May 21, 1865.

The General Assembly amended Louisville's city charter in 1868 to allow for the election of the fire chief. It later rescinded the amendment, but, ironically, the only Louisville fire chief ever elected by popular vote was former federal prisoner M.J. Paul.

Under the ordinance that formed the department, engine companies were to consist of one engineer, one captain, one pipeman, one fireman (who stoked the fire to build steam), two ostlers (who took care of the horses), and two horsemen, or drivers. The hook-and-ladder companies were to have one captain, one ostler, one steersman, and seven privates, or runners. Often manpower was much less, and, when George Levi began his second term as chief in 1870, he waged an annual battle with the City Council for more men and equipment. Within two years, Bunce Hook-and-Ladder #2 and three steamers, George Levi #7, James Leech #8, and J.A. Krack #9, had joined the ranks.

During the department's first twelve years, the city saw 939 fires, 1 general alarm fire and 96 false alarms. Net loss amounted to $1,721,260 for the period, one of the lowest fire loss totals in the country.

By 1874 the department added J.M. Letterle Engine #10, the Hose & Harness Repair Shop, and Chemical Engine #1. The chemical engine was a new firefighting concept. The two-horse wagon carried a reel of rubber hose and a chamber of bicarbonate of soda. A driver and a captain manned the company, which the department placed in areas that lacked cisterns and fireplugs. These companies initiated a fast attack with CHEMICALS to hold a fire in check until steamers (steam fire engines that operated the pump) arrived. The city placed four such units in operation as the city expanded. Steam engines replaced chemical units when sufficient water supply extended into annexed areas. Also in 1874, Jack Hunt became the first firefighter to die in the line of duty.

The City Council slashed the fire department budget by $8,538 during the economic depression in 1877. The cut reduced salaries, canceled plans for new steamers, and eliminated two assistant chief positions. George Levi lambasted the council and retired in 1878. George Frantz succeeded Levi and became the only civilian to be fire chief.

In 1880 EDWARD HUGHES began a twenty-two-year term (the longest of any Louisville fire chief) that saw massive changes in the department. Under pressure from the Board of Underwriters, the City Council approved a moderate pay increase for firefighters, who received only $1.50 for a 24-hour shift. Hughes also reinstated the assistant chief positions, remodeled stations, and replaced apparatus. His crowning achievement was the installation of an electrical communications system in 1882. When an alarm box was pulled, or activated, a signal was sent to the Fire Alarm Office (FAO). A series of holes, punched into a ticker tape, indicated a street or intersection where the activated box was located. The FAO sent the signal to all station houses. Each station was assigned certain box numbers, and the appropriate company responded to the call. Members of each company stood watch to receive the signal and alert the company. One drawback was the great number of false alarms received. The men dubbed the system the "joker," and the desk where the signal was received in the station house became known as the joker stand. By the time Hughes retired in 1903, the department consisted of the chief, 4 assistant chiefs, 190 firefighters, 31 substitute firefighters, 17 steamers, 5 hook- and-ladder trucks, 4 chemical units, a 55 foot Hale WATER TOWER, the hose and harness repair shop, and 102 horses.

Motorization of the department began in 1908 when the city purchased a twenty-horsepower automobile for Chief Fillmore Tyson. One year later his successor, Ben Dillon, became the only Louisville fire chief killed in the line of duty, when he crashed his car while responding to an alarm. In 1919 Chief Timothy Lehan established a fire-training school at Engine #17 on Garland Ave. In 1920 the Fire Prevention Bureau was established, and in 1921 Louisville observed its first Fire Prevention Day. This was later extended to become Fire Prevention Week, usually observed in October to commemorate the Great Chicago Fire of 1871.

The first all-black fire company formed at Engine #8 in 1923. When this company bade farewell to the last horse-drawn engine on St. Patrick's Day 1925, it left a fully motorized department of twenty-three engine and eight truck companies "roaring" through the 1920s under the command of Chief Alex Bache. In 1934 a fireboat was built. The boat could be towed to any location along the waterfront.

The pivotal year 1941 saw many changes. Firefighters won an eight-year battle for unionization when they joined Local 345 of the International Association of Firefighters. The Salvage Corps, which had done salvage work at fires since 1871, disbanded and the department assumed its duties. Many firefighters entered military service when President Roosevelt abolished the draft exemption for firefighters. Citizens manned the Civil Defense Auxiliary Fire Department to assist the regular department for the duration of the war.

In 1946 the department established the Arson Bureau, and during the 1950s companies received mobile radios. Prior to this, a company's only contact with the Communications Bureau was by telegraph key inside a fire-alarm box, or by TELEPHONE. The decade also saw 156 multiple alarm fires in the city. In 1955 it hired its first teenage firefighter. Eighteen-year-old firefighter Larry Bonnafon would later become the department's first African American chief in 1978. The work schedule for Louisville firefighters changed in 1964 by act of the General Assembly. The hours on duty were reduced from seventy-two hours per week to fifty-six hours per week. Instead of working twenty-four hours on/twenty-four off, firefighters worked twenty-four on/forty-eight off. A new pension plan went into effect in 1968. After an intense, three-month evaluation by the Insurance Services Office in 1973, the department was awarded a Class I rating, a distinction held at that time by only five other departments nationwide. The rating is still maintained by the department. On July 14, 1978, tempers flared when contract negotiations reached an impasse, and firefighters walked off the job for four days. Staff officers and National Guard members manned the fire stations.

Another milestone for the department occurred on March 18, 1984, when the first three women recruits entered drill school. They successfully completed the rigorous course. By 1997 nine women served on first-line fire companies.

In 1986 Chief Larry Bonnafon retired and Chief Russell E. Sanders assumed command of the department. During his tenure, the department established the state-of-the-art Louisville Fire Training Academy, which replaced the old drill school. During the late 1980s and early 1990s, the department also established several special-response teams. There are two fully equipped hazardous materials teams, a high-angle team, water rescue, and heavy-urban/trench rescue teams.

The BOARD OF ALDERMEN passed an ordinance in 1993 requiring all buildings 7 stories (or 751 feet in height) or higher to be completely sprinklered by the year 2005. In 1994 all companies began making first responder/basic life support runs to assist in medical emergencies. At least one member of each company is a certified firefighter/emergency medical technician. To better reflect its role, the department adopted the logo "Louisville Fire and Rescue" in 1994. The logo appears on apparatus, medical units, and department-approved shirts.

In December 1995, the department dedicated the Firefighters Flame Memorial outside fire headquarters to honor sixty-five heroes who have died in the line of duty since 1858. The date of the dedication commemorated the thirty-fifth anniversary of the Parkmoor fire that claimed the lives of three firefighters. When Russell Sanders retired in 1995, John Corso became chief. In 1999 Gregory W. Frederick was appointed chief.

Fires in Louisville

South side of Main St. between Third and Fourth Streets, 1827.

This was the first truly significant fire in the history of Louisville. It caused two hundred thousand dollars in losses. Only a torrential rainstorm prevented a major disaster.

John Hawkins Chair Factory, Eighth St. between Green (Liberty) and Walnut (Muhammad Ali Blvd.) Streets, March 27, 1840.

Known as the Great Fire of 1840, it spread rapidly in all directions, destroying nine stores, several homes, and a boarding house. Damage was estimated at three hundred thousand dollars. Since the inception of a fully paid department in 1858, Louisville firefighters have faced several major fires.

Federal warehouses, north side of Main St. between Eighth and Ninth Streets, July 1, 1864.

During the CIVIL WAR, the Union army controlled Louisville. On a hot summer night, ten buildings caught on fire, claiming eight hundred thousand dollars' worth of federal property. The army arrested thirty-nine citizens, including Fire Chief Michael J. Paul, as "Southern sympathizers."

Galt House, Second and Main Streets, January 11, 1865.

Just after midnight on a bitterly cold night, a fire started in the rear of Louisville's most prestigious hotel and raced through the open stairways and long hallways. The only warning for guests was sharp whistle blasts from a steamboat tied up at the wharf. Within minutes the fire, fanned by a strong north wind, burst through the front windows facing Main St. Hoses froze as firefighters struggled for six hours to extinguish the fire, which claimed several lives. Only two bodies were discovered; but four others, including a mother and two children, were never found, and they were believed to have perished in the flames. The estimated damage was four hundred thousand dollars from the blaze, which also destroyed a four-story building next to the hotel and severely damaged four other structures.

Bamberger, Bloom, & Co., Seventh and Main Streets, September 15, 1889.

On a late summer evening a night watchman activated Box 48 at Sixth and Main, signaling the department's deadliest night. The fire that began in the basement of the dry goods company spread rapidly. Firefighters scaled a three-story building at Seventh and MARKET Streets across the alley from the rear of Bamberger's shipping and receiving house. They battled bravely but lost ground. As firefighters were about to abandon their position, thirty thousand spectators gasped in horror as a brick wall of the shipping house, which towered two stories above the men, heaved and swayed. It collapsed onto the men, sending them crashing to the ground floor, killing five and severely injuring two others. Of the injured, one died fifteen months later, and the other lived out his days in an insane asylum. The fire destroyed seven buildings and caused $1.5 million in damage.

This was the first of the "Fatal 48" fires. Because so many fire-related fatalities occurred within a one-block radius of Box 48, firefighters gave the box its sinister name. In some cases, other boxes were activated, but all the fatalities occurred within that radius. From 1886 to 1897, thirteen firefighters and eight civilians died within the box's deadly domain.

Kentucky Distillery Co., Beargrass Creek, August 14, 1890.

Over a million gallons of whiskey and the Great Western Pork Packing Co. were destroyed, totaling $950,000 in damages. BEARGRASS CREEK is said to have become a river of fire that night as the flaming whiskey flowed into the water there.

Boone Paper Co., 637 W Main St., December 8, 1891.

When several firefighters of Hook-and-Ladder Co. #1 went to Cincinnati to attend a ball to raise money for the families of two fallen Cincinnati firefighters, three substitutes took their places. Within hours these and a regular perished beneath a collapsed wall. The first alarm sounded at six-twenty in the evening, and firefighters battled for hours. About two-thirty in the morning, as the men poured water on the smoldering remains, two thunderous explosions ripped the area. The fire had spread beneath the debris to the basement of several adjoining edifices. Quietly building its fury for hours, it burst forth, devastating the four-story Bamberger, Streng, and Co. (This business was located on the north side of Main, across the street from the ill-fated Bamberger and Bloom.) Once the second fire was under control about 4:30 A.M., the men searched frantically for their fallen comrades buried under eighteen feet of smoking debris. Less than four hours later, tragedy struck again.

Frank A. Menne & Co., 519 W Main St., December 9, 1891.

The next morning dawned sunny, as a tiny flame on the second floor of the four-story candy and fireworks manufactory intensified and spread rapidly through the old, poorly constructed building. Smoke and flames rushed up the narrow stairwells and elevator shaft. The third and fourth floors were half the length of the first two floors. Stairways were in the rear from the first to the second floors and in the front to the third and fourth floors. To escape, employees on the upper floors had to traverse the entire length of the building to reach the ground floor. The deadly nightmare took only minutes to claim its victims. People on the third floor jumped to the second-story roof, but those on the fourth floor were trapped. The fourth floor collapsed, hurtling six women and two men to their deaths. Several other employees were injured, some severely.

Old Vaudeville Theater/Southern Steam Motor, Third St. from Green (Liberty) to Walnut St. (Muhammad Ali Blvd.), May 2, 1893.

The fire originated in the THEATER and spread quickly, consuming Third St. from Green (Liberty) to Walnut (Muhammad Ali Blvd.). The conflagration killed one civilian and forty horses and destroyed fifty-three buggies.

Badgley Photo Supplies, The Graham Co., W.D. Gatchel and Sons, and Stewart Dry Goods, Third and Jefferson Streets, July 27, 1901.

The fire fueled two explosions that killed two civilians and injured five firefighters as Saturday night shoppers rushed to safety.

American Laundry, 1100 Story Ave., April 26, 1902.

Fierce high winds fanned the flames that injured two firefighters and destroyed thirty buildings, including a stable where fifteen mules burned to death.

Bourbon Stock Yard Co., 507 Johnston St., August 5, 1903.

Lightning struck the stock yards, igniting fourteen acres of wooden pens ranging from one to five stories in height. It was the largest fire (in area) up to that time. The stench from the 200 sheep, 175 hogs, and 35 cattle that burned to death inundated the surrounding NEIGHBORHOODS. Rainfall aided the arrest of the fire that injured 2 firefighters and caused $225,000 in damage.

Union Warehouse, Seventh and Magnolia Streets, July 21, 1903.

A pan of hot ashes carelessly discarded near a wooden fence started this fire. Chiefs from across the country, in town for the funeral of former fire chief Edward Hughes, rushed to the scene. Chief Myers of the Covington Fire Department was severely injured when a wall fell on his leg, necessitating the amputation of his foot.

David Baird & Son Millinery, 511–13 W Main St., September 23, 1911.

The curse of "Fatal 48" became more sporadic, claiming three salvage corps men beneath a collapsed wall at this fire.

Ox Breeches Manufactory, 827 W Main St., January 6, 1916.

Firefighters contended with a northeast gale to battle the blaze. The heavy snow and bitter temperatures hampered their efforts as the fire spread to adjoining buildings, causing more than $250,000 in damage.

Kentucky Drug Sundries Co., 503 W Main St., December 29, 1926.

Two more firefighters perished in falls from an icy roof in a blaze that engulfed this building. However, it was during the late 1800s that box 48 claimed most of its victims. Two of the worst incidents occurred in 1891.

Market and Floyd Streets, February 5, 1937.

A three-story brick building with two floors of APARTMENTS and a ground floor housing four businesses was the scene of a natural gas explosion that ripped through the building about two-forty-five on a Friday afternoon. When firefighters arrived, people were jumping from the second- and third-floor windows. The disaster killed ten people and injured scores.

Parkmoor Recreation Center, 2545 S Third St., December 17, 1960.

In a twenty-four-hour period, an elderly woman died in a house fire, a three-alarm blaze broke out at the Green Co. storage building, and fire destroyed three suites at the 310 Building on W Liberty St. But the worst was yet to come. At 7:25 P.M., steaks on a gas grill in the restaurant of the Parkmoor, which also housed a forty-lane bowling alley, coffee shop, bar, and nightclub, caught fire. Within thirteen minutes, three alarms, followed by three special alarms, sounded. In all, 110 firefighters, 14 engines, 2 hook-and-ladder, and 2 Quad companies responded. Suddenly, the super-heated interior sparked a backdraft that ravaged the building. One firefighter died of smoke inhalation en route to the hospital, and the bodies of two other firefighters were found in the rubble the following day.

Residence, 4300 block of River Park Dr., April 23, 1963.

House fires represent four of the city's most tragic blazes. This fire spread quickly, engulfing the home in minutes. Seven children, ages five to thirteen years, asleep on the second floor, died. The mother and five other children on the ground floor escaped, although two of those children died a few days later. An exact cause of the fire was never ascertained, although the Fire Prevention Bureau listed the cause as "children playing with fire."

Residence, 3834 River Park Dr., July 4, 1989.

Six children perished in this blaze. Louisville Gas & Electric Co. had shut off power to the house the month before, and it is believed candles caused the fire, although the cause was never established definitively. Firefighters found the children alone in the house, behind locked doors. Double-keyed deadbolt locks on all the doors prevented the children's escape. Investigators found one non-working smoke detector in the charred debris.

Standard Gravure, 643 S Sixth St., November 10, 1989.

Firefighters responded to a small fire in a press of the STANDARD GRAVURE Co. They extinguished the fire in the first-floor pressroom and discovered a second fire in the basement. Ink had seeped through the floor into the basement, where sparks of static electricity ignited it. A loud hissing noise filled the room as firefighters battled the second fire. Then two flash fires and an explosion ripped through the building, engulfing eighteen firefighters and three civilians in a deadly storm of heat and debris. The explosion hurled several firefighters into the parking lot, and the others were rescued from the basement. Many were seriously injured, but there were no fatalities.

Residence, 300 S Forty-second St., January 7, 1991.

Three more children perished in a house with a smoke detector without batteries. The fire department intensified its Operation Firesafe program, stressing the need for working smoke detectors and home fire safety drills.

Residence, 1929 Magazine St., April 3, 1999.

Four children and their mother perished in this house fire. Although the house had smoke detectors, the mother and children were killed in their sleep. The fire was considered the most tragic fire since 1989. The cause of the fire is unknown.

Other Major Fires:

American Tobacco Co., February 25, 1898.
Snead Building/Phoenix Hotel, June 23, 1898.
Matthews Tobacco Co., April 25, 1900.
Bonnie Brothers Whiskey House, December 29, 1902.
Masonic Temple, November 20, 1903.
Kentucky Public Elevator, February 25, 1917.
Hillerich & Bradsby, June 6, 1931. Injured forty-three and caused five hundred thousand dollars in damage.
Boston Building, November 29, 1947. Injured twelve firefighters and caused five hundred thousand dollars in damage.
Aetna Oil Co., June 26, 1948. Thirty-three tanks of fuel oil destroyed.
Ninth St. rooming house, March 6, 1953. Killed four tenants and injured five tenants and three firemen.
Aubrey Feed Mill, July 31, 1954. Five alarms, several firefighters injured.
Dixie Warehouse and Cartage, January 12, 1956. More than $2 million in damage.
Miles Park race course, May 19, 1964. Twenty-seven horses killed, $178,000 in damage.
Bronoco Chemical, May 5, 1969. Several explosions, hundreds evacuated.
J. Guthrie Coke Apartments, March 23, 1977. Two civilians killed, fourteen firefighters injured.
First Unitarian Church, December 13, 1985. Four alarms, three firefighters injured.
East Market St. businesses, April 23, 1989. Four alarms, three firefighters injured.
North American Fertilizer, April 1, 1990. Four alarms.
Vacant warehouse, Twenty-second and Rowan Streets, April 23, 1997. Three alarms, juvenile arson.

Fire Chiefs of Louisville

A.Y. Johnson, 1858–61, 1864–68
M.J. Paul, 1862–64, 1868–70
G.W. Levi, 1861–62, 1870–78
G.W. Frantz, 1878–80
Edward Hughes, 1880–1902
Fillmore Tyson, 1903–09
Ben Dillon, 1909–09
Timothy Lehan, 1909–17
A. Neunschwander, 1917–24
Alex Bache, 1924–27
J.H. Adams, 1927–34
Edward McHugh, 1924–27, 1934–43
J. Krusenklaus, 1943–63
Eugene Dodson, 1963–70
William J. Cummins, 1970–76
T.T. Kuster, 1976–79
Larry M. Bonnafon, 1979–86
Russell E. Sanders, 1986–95
John B. Corso, 1995–98
Gregory W. Frederick, 1999–

See *Louisville Fire Department History Volume II 1858–1997* (Paducah, Ky., 1997); David Winges, *Volunteer Firefighters of Louisville, Kentucky* (Louisville 1992); *Historical Sketch and Souvenir of the Louisville Fire Department* (Louisville 1894); *Louisville Fire Department History 1858–1989* (Paducah, Ky., 1989).

LOUISVILLE & FRANKFORT RAILROAD. This company, chartered in 1847 and operating between its namesake points in 1851, was the first line-haul common carrier railroad to serve Louisville and Jefferson County. While its organization came a decade or more after the building (in 1831–34) of Kentucky's first railroad, the Lexington & Ohio, to Frankfort, the histories of both lines were intertwined. The Lexington & Ohio fully intended to reach the OHIO RIVER in the vicinity of Jefferson County, and in fact, some grading and culvert construction went forward, west of Frankfort. However, attempts to push the work on to Louisville were unfulfilled during the 1830s, due in part to the panic of 1837 and the inability of the L&O to maintain track and sustain patronage. Only a short segment was completed in 1838 between downtown Louisville and PORTLAND.

In 1840, the L&O was sold to the commonwealth to satisfy debts and soon after was leased and upgraded for operation by William R. McKee and Philip Swigert. Several organizational meetings to revive the Louisville-Frankfort link took place in the city during the mid-1840s, followed by incorporation in March 1847. The L&F's charter granted it powers to finish the link as well as build east of Lexington to connect with other lines. Directors included John J. Jacob, William H. Field, John Hulme, Virgil McKnight, Thomas Smith, and Jacob Swigert. Smith, a prominent merchant of Newcastle in Henry County, Kentucky, was elected president. Upon his death in 1850, he was succeeded by Louisville's JAMES GUTHRIE.

Meanwhile, L&F's management bought out the commonwealth's interest the Lexington road held in the Frankfort-west segment and then proceeded to sell stock and raise funds to capitalize its new railroad. The city of Louisville contributed eight hundred thousand dollars to the project. Line surveys were conducted by Col. Stephen H. Long of the U.S. Topographical Engineers, who selected a favorable route between Louisville and Frankfort. Some of the Lexington's partially graded right-of-way west of Frankfort was utilized.

Beginning in March 1849, first rails, bought in London and shipped upriver from New Orleans, were laid eastward from the city. On February 6, 1850, a special train conveyed L&F directors and guests out to LaGrange and back. Work proceeded during 1850, with line construction completed in spring l1851. After a bridge across the Kentucky River at Frankfort opened, through service was inaugurated by late August between Louisville and Frankfort. Physical connection between the L&F and the Lexington line in Frankfort in 1852 made possible twice-daily train service from Louisville to Lexington, where connection with another railroad, the Covington and Lexington, later offered travelers service on to the greater Cincinnati area. On January 1, 1857, the L&F and Lexington lines agreed upon joint management and operations. They later merged corporately in 1867 to become the Louisville, Cincinnati, & Lexington and then built (from LaGrange) a more direct route to Cincinnati. In Louisville, the LC&L and Louisville & Nashville Railroad were connected after 1871 via the Railway Transfer, which skirted the southeast side of the city.

Principal L&F facilities included a one-story brick passenger station, its train shed spanning three tracks, and a frame freight shed and small roundhouse, all at Brook and Jefferson Streets. The LC&L later moved the stations to Brook & Water, also building a much larger roundhouse, repair shop, and train yard on East Jefferson at BEARGRASS CREEK. Corporate offices were on Main St. The LC&L's Cincinnati and Lexington lines were integrated in the larger L&N system after merger in 1881.

See Thomas D. Clark, *Beginning of the L&N RR* (Louisville 1933); Edward A. Hines, *Corporate History of the Louisville & Nashville & Roads in Its System* (Louisville 1905); "Louisville & Frankfort," unpublished manuscript by Dr. Wendell McChord, Dayton, Ohio, 1996; "Pioneer Kentucky Railroads" in Mechanical & Electrical Engineering Record, University of Kentucky, October 1908.

Charles B. Castner

LOUISVILLE FREE PUBLIC LIBRARY. The Louisville Free Public Library, founded in 1902, was the thirteenth in a succession of libraries established in Louisville. The first was the Louisville Library Co., which opened in 1816 and was modeled on the subscription library Benjamin Franklin established in Philadelphia. The library operated for six years but ceased operation during the yellow fever epidemic of 1822. The catastrophe nearly depopulated Louisville, and culture had to yield to more pressing problems after the epidemic passed.

Each of the successive libraries was witness to citizen recognition that Louisville needed a library to provide books and information for the self-improvement of its citizens. Lack of funding always caused their demise. In 1871 the Public Library of Kentucky was founded and took another approach to funding. It was to be free, with funds to be raised by means of five nationwide lotteries. These were held and grossed $6,250,000; the library's share was $424,396.

However, the library's income, after expenses, was not enough to continue its operation past 1878. The assets and debts were taken over by a new library venture, the Polytechnic Society, located on Fourth between Walnut (now Muhammad Ali Blvd.) and Green (Liberty). The assets included not only books but PAINTINGS, SCULPTURES, and natural history specimens. Its means of support were a small endowment and annual membership fees, but these were insufficient to maintain a vigorous enterprise. The society had its last meeting on January 9, 1913. The materials it held were given to the Louisville Free Public Library.

In 1902 Mayor CHARLES F. GRAINGER and a group of citizens met to plan a new library that would take advantage of philanthropist Andrew Carnegie's offer to cities to pay for library buildings if the city would maintain them, their collections, and staff. The proposal was accepted by Carnegie, and the Louisville Free Public Library began. On July 24, 1908, the present Main Library building at Fourth and York Streets was opened to the public. Carnegie not only underwrote the cost of this building but of seven branches throughout the city.

The Louisville Free Public Library instituted an ambitious plan of services to both children and adults. Western (opened in 1905) and Eastern (opened in 1914) Branch libraries were for the specific use of African American citizens, under the direction of Thomas F. Blue, Western Branch head. These branches for AFRICAN AMERICANS were the first in the country. Training classes for librarians at Western Branch and the Main Library were established in order to develop professional staff.

The library system maintained a steady growth throughout the first three decades of its existence. The 1937 flood was a disruption, damaging twenty-five thousand books and the museum collections in the basement of the Main Library.

During the 1940s and 1950s, under the leadership of C.R. "Skip" Graham, the library again expanded services. National recognition was received for its circulation of audiovisual materials. The Neighborhood College Program provided undergraduate courses in selected branches. Two radio stations (WFPL-FM [1950] and WFPK-FM [1954]) were also begun as an outgrowth of the concept that the availability of information should not be limited to the traditional printed media of books and periodicals. Both stations became part of the Public Radio Partnership. Their studios were in the downtown library building until 2000, when they moved to new facilities on downtown Fourth St.

Main building Louisville Free Public Library, York Street between Third and Fourth. 1920s.

The passage of the county occupational tax in 1965 led to the expansion of library branches into Jefferson County. By the early 1970s the library consisted of thirty-one branch libraries, two bookmobiles (begun in 1955), and the Main Library—the last having tripled its size by an addition that opened in 1969.

By the mid-1970s the growth in costs for services and branches had outstripped the available funds. Between 1985 and 1991 three attempts, by petition and referendum, to establish a library tax were defeated. Mayor Jerry Abramson and County Judge/Executive David Armstrong appointed a committee to develop a five-year plan for the library. The committee comprised city, county, and Library Commission representatives. Its report, accepted by the city and county in 1993, provided for additional funding, geographic equalization of branches, and a tiered system of sixteen branch libraries. Hours and staff were increased. Branches were relocated or renovated and expanded. Services to children were increased, and a special TELEPHONE information service was instituted.

The library system has benefited from the support of two groups: the Friends of the Library and the Louisville Library Foundation. Begun in 1977, the Friends of the Library has provided volunteers and funds generated through book sales and its annual Kentucky Author Dinner. The Louisville Library Foundation, established in 1980, has raised millions of dollars for a new book endowment. By early 1999 the foundation had raised five hundred thousand dollars for additional children's books and children's outreach programs. In 1994 the foundation began a campaign to fund up-to-date library technology; by 1996 $4.5 million had been raised.

Library authorities then set up an advisory group of experts to design a system-wide computer network. Four hundred new computers were purchased for use throughout the library system, most of them accessible to patrons. All the main system processing computers and hardware were replaced. Seventeen library buildings were rewired with new lines for information transmission and new lines to power the new equipment. All the buildings and equipment were hooked together and to the Internet with high-bandwidth phone lines capable of fast data transfer. Costly databases were added, allowing patrons access to vast storehouses of information. Additional money has been set aside for updating and replacing equipment as it wears out or becomes obsolete.

The technology upgrade has also made the library's resources available, via computer, to homes, offices, and schools. Patrons can find, reserve, or renew library books and can submit questions to reference librarians online. Searchable databases permit access to a wide range of current online indexes for newspaper and periodical articles, books, and associations.

The branch libraries are BON AIR Regional, CRESCENT HILL, FAIRDALE, FERN CREEK, HIGHLANDS-SHELBY PARK, IROQUOIS, JEFFERSONTOWN, Middletown, OKOLONA, PORTLAND, ST. MATTHEWS/Eline, SHAWNEE, SHIVELY/Newman, Southwest Regional, Western, and WESTPORT.

See *Libraries and Lotteries* (Cynthiana, Ky., 1944).

William Garnar

LOUISVILLE GIRLS' HIGH SCHOOL. Female High School, one of Louisville's first two public high schools, opened on April 7, 1856, at Center (Armory Place) and Walnut (Muhammad Ali Blvd.) Streets, with sixty-nine pupils and three teachers. It was the female counterpart to LOUISVILLE MALE HIGH SCHOOL, also established in 1856. Its first prin-

by an addition that opened in 1969.

By the mid-1970s the growth in costs for services and branches had outstripped the available funds. Between 1985 and 1991 three attempts, by petition and referendum, to establish a library tax were defeated. Mayor Jerry Abramson and County Judge/Executive David Armstrong appointed a committee to develop a five-year plan for the library. The committee comprised city, county, and Library Commission representatives. Its report, accepted by the city and county in 1993, provided for additional funding, geographic equalization of branches, and a tiered system of sixteen branch libraries. Hours and staff were increased. Branches were relocated or renovated and expanded. Services to children were increased, and a special TELEPHONE information service was instituted.

The library system has benefited from the support of two groups: the Friends of the Library and the Louisville Library Foundation. Begun in 1977, the Friends of the Library has provided volunteers and funds generated through book sales and its annual Kentucky Author Dinner. The Louisville Library Foundation, established in 1980, has raised millions of dollars for a new book endowment. By early 1999 the foundation had raised five hundred thousand dollars for additional children's books and children's outreach programs. In 1994 the foundation began a campaign to fund up-to-date library technology; by 1996 $4.5 million had been raised.

Library authorities then set up an advisory group of experts to design a system-wide computer network. Four hundred new computers were purchased for use throughout the library system, most of them accessible to patrons. All the main system processing computers and hardware were replaced. Seventeen library buildings were rewired with new lines for information transmission and new lines to power the new equipment. All the buildings and equipment were hooked together and to the Internet with high-bandwidth phone lines capable of fast data transfer. Costly databases were added, allowing patrons access to vast storehouses of information. Additional money has been set aside for updating and replacing equipment as it wears out or becomes obsolete.

The technology upgrade has also made the library's resources available, via computer, to homes, offices, and schools. Patrons can find, reserve, or renew library books and can submit questions to reference librarians online. Searchable databases permit access to a wide range of current online indexes for newspaper and periodical articles, books, and associations.

The branch libraries are BON AIR Regional, CRESCENT HILL, FAIRDALE, FERN CREEK, HIGHLANDS-SHELBY PARK, IROQUOIS, JEFFERSONTOWN, Middletown, OKOLONA, PORTLAND, ST. MATTHEWS/Eline, SHAWNEE, SHIVELY/Newman, Southwest Regional, Western, and WESTPORT.

See *Libraries and Lotteries* (Cynthiana, Ky., 1944).

William Garnar

LOUISVILLE GIRLS' HIGH SCHOOL. Female High School, one of Louisville's first two public high schools, opened on April 7, 1856, at Center (Armory Place) and Walnut (Muhammad Ali Blvd.) Streets, with sixty-nine pupils and three teachers. It was the female counterpart to LOUISVILLE MALE HIGH SCHOOL, also established in 1856. Its first principal, J.C. Spencer, remained only a short time. He was followed by Prof. Edward A. Holyoke, who presided over the first commencement held on June 18, 1858, in Mozart Hall at the corner of Fourth and Jefferson Streets. The diplomas were carried to the stage in a market basket.

In 1864 it moved to the former Hayden Curd house on First St., north of Chestnut, which was remodeled and enlarged. The property was purchased for sixteen thousand dollars, and improvements added another six thousand dollars. A new building, designed by Louisville architect Frank Vogdes, was completed in 1873 on the same site. The building had a graceful portico with eight stone Corinthian columns and a front of oolitic limestone. It was four stories in height with a basement. The school remained there until 1899. That year Female High School relocated to Fifth and Hill Streets. In 1912 the name was officially changed to LOUISVILLE GIRLS' HIGH SCHOOL. W.H. Bartholomew, principal from 1881 to 1911, suggested that additional high schools were needed to take care of growing enrollments. O.L. Reed became principal in 1911 and worked toward an additional high school. This came about in 1924 when Atherton High School was opened in the HIGHLANDS neighborhood. In 1929 SHAWNEE High School opened in the West End. Both of these schools became coed in 1950, yet, to the majority of Louisville girls who went to high school before 1924, Girls' High School was alma mater.

In 1934 Louisville Girls High School made its final move to Reuben Post Halleck Hall, at the corner of Second and Lee Streets. It remained there until its last class graduated in June 1950. That year Louisville Girls' High School became coeducational and merged with DU PONT MANUAL HIGH SCHOOL. The name du Pont Manual was given to Halleck Hall.

During its ninety-four years, Louisville Girls' High School was regarded as a thoroughly modern school, preparing its students for career opportunities or further education. Teacher-training courses were offered until the establishment of Louisville's Normal School in 1871, which took over the preparation of teachers. The curriculum was expanded in 1934 to include, among other courses, English, drama, mathematics, languages, history, science, office training, fine arts, physical education, and home economics. Louisville Girls' High School had nearly twelve thousand graduates.

Maxine Crouch McEwen
Virginia Leighton Orndorff

LOUISVILLE, HARRODS CREEK, & WESTPORT RAILWAY. Organized by city businessmen in 1870, this narrow-gauge railroad ran from the city to Harrods Creek and the Oldham County line. James Callahan was the road's first president. Construction commenced from First and River Rd. along Fulton St. in 1872; reached Goose Creek, about eight miles out, in 1874; and terminated a mile or so above Harrods Creek in 1877. The LHC&W intended to build beyond Oldham County, and amendments to its charter allowed it to consolidate with other lines, including a "Westport, Carrollton & Covington Railroad." That expansion never materialized, and the road was acquired in 1881 by the Louisville & Nashville, which widened its track gauge and continued service with four daily round trips. Residents living along upper River Rd. regularly commuted to and from downtown Louisville on the line. A modest freight service (by L&N at night) tapped a lime kiln, distillery, two quarries, and several farms. In 1904, L&N sold eight miles (from Zorn Ave. to Prospect) to the Louisville Railway Co., which electrified the route and ran trolleys hourly. All service ended in October 1935, and tracks were abandoned to Prospect. However, L&N and CSX (after 1986) retained former LHC&W tracks nearest Louisville to serve local industries.

See Edward W. Hines, *Corporate History of Louisville & Nashville R.R.* (Louisville 1905); Elmer G. Sulzer, *Ghost Railroads of Kentucky* (Indianapolis 1967).

Charles B. Castner

LOUISVILLE HEBREW SCHOOL. Louisville Hebrew School was founded in 1908 to provide youngsters with the background necessary for full participation in Jewish life. Its founders were stalwart Orthodox citizens; but the school, from its very beginning, taught girls as well as boys and enlisted students from Orthodox, Conservative, and Reform families. The founders included Rabbi A.L. Zarchy, Benjamin Mayer Kaplan, J.D. Wolkow, A.I. Shaffet, Julius Bass, and Sam Shenson.

Two years after it was established, the school moved into a two-story, yellow-brick building at 208 E Walnut (now Muhammad Ali Blvd.) that cost fifty thousand dollars. Although at that time a state of Israel was but a dream, the school treated Hebrew as a living language and allowed no English in its classrooms. After WORLD WAR I, outward POPULATION movement began to affect enrollment because its classes were held after public-school hours. The school countered this movement by opening a class for girls at the Young Men's Hebrew Association (now the JEWISH COMMUNITY CENTER) at Second and Jacob, and still later a full branch at Bardstown Rd. and Douglass Blvd. The school went through a series of financial ups and downs, and when Interstate 65 construction engulfed the Walnut St. property a new site had to be found. This problem was solved by adding classroom space to the Jewish Community Center, then under construction at 3600 Dutchmans Ln. The growth of congregational religious schools and the launching of the Louisville Jewish Day School (Eliahu Academy) in 1953 affected enrollment, but the school still serves the Jewish community.

Herman Landau

LOUISVILLE HISTORICAL LEAGUE. Founded in 1972 by Rev. Clyde F. Crews and Allan Steinberg, the league is a nonprofit, all-volunteer corporation whose purpose is to promote an interest in and appreciation for HISTORIC PRESERVATION and to develop an enhanced community awareness of the history and heritage of the Greater Louisville community. These goals are accomplished by conducting monthly Sunday afternoon events, which, with rare exception, are free and open to the public. A monthly newsletter is LHL's primary means of communication. During the annual meeting, preservation awards are given to individuals, organizations, and projects for their efforts to preserve, promote, and maintain the principles of historic preservation and education. A Founder's Award is presented to an individual who epitomizes lifetime achievement and dedication to the cause of preservation awareness, education, and community involvement. Its mailing address is the PETERSON-DUMESNIL HOUSE.

Laurie A. Birnsteel

LOUISVILLE HISTORIC LANDMARKS. When viewed collectively, Louisville's landmark buildings convey the citizens' firm commitment to HISTORIC PRESERVATION rather than providing a hierarchy of the best of Louisville's architectural history or heritage. The designation process begins with either a property owner's written request for designation or the submission of two hundred or more signatures provided to the Landmarks Commission by local citizens requesting consideration. After extensive historic and architectural documentation is gathered, the information is evaluated against established criteria; and a public hearing is held to consider the structure, site, or district in question.

Louisville's local landmarks represent a broad spectrum of architectural types, styles, and periods and provide a fascinating glimpse into the city's historic past. As of the summer of 1998 the list included seven educational buildings, six churches, five civic and five residential buildings, three commercial buildings, and two landmarks noted for their importance related to engineering. Some of the structures have been placed on the NATIONAL REGISTER OF HISTORIC PLACES.

Belknap Playhouse (1874)—Corner of Third St. and Cardinal Blvd. This board-and-batten, Carpenter Gothic–style building was built as a chapel for the HOUSE OF REFUGE for delinquent children and was later enlarged when the institution became the School of Industrial Reform. It was converted to a THEATER by the UNIVERSITY OF LOUISVILLE in the 1920s, and in 1980 it was dismantled and reassembled on its present site.

Brennan House (1868)—631 S Fifth St. This three-story brick Italianate residence was built in 1868 by TOBACCO merchant Francis S.J. Ronald. It was purchased almost a decade later by Thomas Brennan, whose descendants lived in the house for nearly a century. It is a rare surviving example of a mid-nineteenth-century townhouse and remarkably is furnished entirely with Brennan family furnishings. It was added to the National Register in 1975.

Cathedral of the Assumption Complex (1849–52)—433–43 S Fifth St. These three buildings (church, parish school, and rectory) are vital links to Catholicism in Louisville. Citizens have gathered at the cathedral, designed by William Keeley, since its dedication in 1852. It was added to the National Register in 1977.

Christ Church Cathedral Complex (1824–1912)—411 S Second St. The Cathedral, Louisville's oldest church building in continuous use, became the Cathedral Church of the Kentucky Diocese in 1894. The complex comprises a cathedral, cloister garden, and cathedral house. It was added to the National Register in 1977.

Church of Our Merciful Saviour (1912)—473 S Eleventh St. The African American Episcopal congregation held its first service in this church in 1912. Four years later the congregation sponsored the nation's first Negro Boy Scout troop. It was added to the National Register in 1983.

The Cloister Complex (1860–1946)—800 E Chestnut St. The Ursuline Sisters traveled from Bavaria in 1858 and within two years had built a convent and academy at this site. By 1868 the Romanesque Revival–style chapel was completed. It was added to the National Register in 1978.

Field House (1878)—2909 Field Ave. Built by Louisville businessman Jonathan C. Wright in 1878 and purchased by Judge Emmet Field a decade later, this CRESCENT HILL residence is one of the city's finest examples of Italianate-style ARCHITECTURE. It is part of the Crescent Hill National Register District.

Fifth Ward School/Monsarrat School (1855–57)—743 S Fifth St. This brick school was built in 1855 based on designs drawn by local architects Isaiah Rogers and HENRY WHITESTONE. It was one of the first schools built south of BROADWAY and was temporarily converted to a hospital during the CIVIL WAR. It later became the museum of the LOUISVILLE FREE PUBLIC LIBRARY and is now an apartment building. It was added to the National Register in 1978.

German Insurance Bank Building (1887–1900)—207 W Market St. This elaborate bank building was designed by architect Charles D. Meyer in 1887 and is a tangible reminder of the influence Louisville's large German POPULATION had on city commerce. It was added to the National Register in 1985.

Jefferson County Jail (1902–5)—514 W Liberty St. This city jail comprises a cell wing and an administrative wing, and was the most modern correctional facility in the country when it was completed in 1905. Based on designs by D.X. Murphy and Brothers, it reflected the latest trends in SANITATION, security, and mechanics. Two hundred forty cells had a remarkably innovative locking system that allowed guards the choice of opening only one cell or all cells on each tier. It was added to the National Register in 1973. The old jail now houses GOVERNMENT offices and the Jefferson County Law Library.

Little Loomhouse Complex (1870–96)—328 Kenwood Hill Rd. The Craftsman-style complex, composed of the Little Loomhouse, Wisteria Cottage, and Tophouse, has been used since the 1930s as a place for people to learn about the timeless American craft of weaving. Founded by Lou Tate, the Little Loomhouse holds one of the nation's finest collections of original weaving drafts. It was added to the National Register in 1975.

Louisville Male High School (1914)—911 S Brook St. Designed in the Jacobean Revival style by City Architect on Schools J. Earle Henry, Male High School is one of the city's outstanding examples of that style. Since its founding in 1856 it has been one of Louisville's prestigious secondary schools and counts among its graduates a number of local leaders. It was added to the National Register in 1979.

Louisville War Memorial Auditorium (1927–29)—970 S Fourth St. Built to commemorate the men from Jefferson County who died during World War I, it has been the site of musical concerts and theatrical performances for years. It was designed in the Beaux Arts style by the New York architectural firm of Carrere and Hastings in association with local architect E.T. Hutchings. It was added to the National Register in 1977.

Mary D. Hill School (1873)—524 W Kentucky St. This handsome building was designed by local architect J.B. McElfatrick as the first public school for AFRICAN AMERICANS and named the CENTRAL COLORED School. Later high school classes were added. In 1894 when the student body was relocated to a larger facility, it was renamed in honor of Mary D. Hill, kindergarten pioneer, and was then changed to an all-white student body. It was added to the National Register in 1976.

Municipal College (1879–1951)—1018 S Seventh St. For many years this college, which went by a variety of names over the course of the years (Kentucky Normal and Theological Institute, SIMMONS UNIVERSITY, and State University), was the only degree-offering institution in the state open to African Americans. One of its buildings, William H. Steward Hall, was designed by local African American architect Samuel Plato, who went on to build over forty United States post offices across the nation. It

Louisville Hotel, Main Street, south side between Sixth and Seventh Streets, c. 1860.

was added to the National Register in 1976.

Old Louisville Trust (1891)—208 S Fifth St. At the time of construction this building was declared "the finest office building yet erected south of the Ohio River." It was designed by local architects Mason Maury and William J. Dodd, who combined skyscraper and traditional masonry construction technology in the Richardsonian Romanesque style. It was added to the National Register in 1977.

Peterson Avenue Hill (ca. 1869)—Peterson Ave. Named for adjacent landowner Joseph Peterson, this stretch of Crescent Hill roadway is one of a dwindling number of brick streets still in use in the city. Surfaced with vitrified brick, the street and hill have been a proving ground for local automobiles for years. It was added to the National Register in 1980.

Peterson-Dumesnil House and Outbuilding (1869–70)—301 Peterson Ave. Named for a locally prominent family, this post–Civil War era mansion is one of the city's finest examples of the Italianate style and is one of the Crescent Hill area's oldest homes. Its design is attributed to Henry Whitestone. It was added to the National Register in 1975.

Saint Louis Bertrand Complex (1966–71)—1104 S Sixth St. The Dominicans established the St. Louis Bertrand parish near the Irish enclave of Limerick. The architect of the 1871 Gothic Revival–style church remains unclear. It is likely that either Patrick Keeley or H.P. Bradshaw was responsible. It is in the Limerick National Register District.

Saint Paul's Evangelical United Church of Christ and Parish House (1906)—217–19 E Broadway. St. Paul's, organized in 1836, is one of the oldest Evangelical congregations in Louisville. It built this Gothic Revival–style church and the adjacent parish house in 1906. It was added to the National Register in 1982.

Seelbach-Parrish House (1888)—926 S Sixth St. Built for Louis Seelbach and his bride, it was later sold to Charles Henry Parrish Sr., president of nearby Simmons University, who used it as rental property. The Richardsonian Romanesque–style house was designed by Oscar C. Wehle and William J. Dodd. It is in the Limerick National Register District.

Theodore Roosevelt Elementary School (1865)—222 N Seventeenth St. This was the oldest continuously operating public school in Louisville for many years. It was originally named the Eleventh Ward School, but its name was changed in 1922 to honor the president. It has been converted to apartments. It was added to the National Register in 1982.

Tyler Park Bridge (1904)—1400 Baxter Ave. Constructed by the City of Louisville Department of Public Works using turn-of-the-century bridge-building techniques, this structure not only serves suburban transportation needs but is an attractive aesthetic amenity as well.

Union Station Complex (1889–91)—1000 W Broadway. Designed by the Louisville & Nashville Railroad's chief architect, F.W. Mowbray (who worked on the Philadelphia Centennial Exposition), this structure exemplifies the importance of rail access to the city. The L&N played a major role in connecting Louisville to southeastern markets during the second half of the nineteenth century, which enabled the city to become an economic powerhouse. It was added to the National Register in 1975.

United States Marine Hospital Complex (1847–52)—2213 Portland Ave. Congress, in 1837, authorized the creation of a hospital for seamen along the western rivers and lakes. Construction of the Marine Hospital followed a decade later and is one of Louisville's few remaining pre–Civil War structures. The complex is composed of two hospital buildings that date from 1852 and 1933, an 1893 stable, and a 1911 laundry building. It was added to the National Register in 1997.

University of Louisville School of Medicine Complex (1891–1937)—550–54 S First St. Louisville's medical community used the Richardsonian Romanesque–style school as a medical research and teaching facility from 1891 until the 1970s. The school and infirmary were designed by local architects Charles J. Clarke and Arthur Loomis. D.X. Murphy and Brothers designed additions that date from 1937 and 1950. It was added to the National Register in 1975.

Application for exhibition space, Louisville Grand Industrial Exposition, 1873.

Western Branch Library (1908)—604 S Tenth St. In 1908 this Carnegie-endowed Beaux Arts–style building was constructed to serve Louisville's African American community based on designs by architects Kenneth McDonald and William J. Dodd. Since its construction the library has been a focal point of the black community. The Douglass Debating Club met here monthly to discuss such issues as woman suffrage. It was added to the National Register in 1975.

YMCA Chestnut St. Branch/Knights of Pythias Building (1914–15)—928–32 W Chestnut St. This building, designed by Henry Wolters, originally served as the state headquarters for the black Knights of Pythias. Many African American businessmen leased space in the building. In 1953 the YMCA purchased it to house an African American branch it had created ninety years previously. It continues to serve as an important professional and social center for the community. It was added to the National Register in 1978.

See Louisville Historic Landmarks and Preservation Districts Collection, Louisville Free Public Library, Main Branch.

Joanne Weeter

LOUISVILLE HOTEL. When the Louisville Hotel, the city's first elegant hostelry, opened in 1833, it was proudly described as larger than the ultra-fashionable new Tremont House in Boston, the prototype of the American hotel. Located on the south side of MAIN St. a bit west of Sixth St., the Louisville Hotel was a visible sign that Louisville had come of age as an urban center. The four-story structure was designed by Hugh Roland, the city's first professional architect. The facade boasted an impressive colonnade of ten Ionic columns. Louisville's first city directory, published in 1832 when the hotel was under construction, assured its readers that when completed the hotel "will surpass in elegance and arrangement, any in our western country."

Louisville's earlier hostelries could best be described as cozy inns, with rooms that often had to be shared with other guests. The Louisville Hotel was the first to provide such amenities as a baggage room, barber and tailor shops, and a private dining room. The new hotel had sixty rooms, some of them parlor-bedroom suites. Charles Fenno Hoffman, a New York City visitor, described the building as "much superior in external appearance and interior arrangement to any establishment of the kind we have in New-York" (*A Winter in the West,* New York 1835, I:123).

In 1853 the hotel was expanded eastward to Sixth St. by what was called "the Sixth Street ell." At the same time alterations to the facade removed the handsome colonnade. Interestingly the architects were HENRY WHITESTONE and Isaiah Rogers. The latter had designed Boston's Tremont House.

By the early twentieth century the hotel had lost its early prestige, although its dining room and bar were popular with Main St. businessmen through the 1920s. The Sixth Street ell had become the original Seelbach Hotel in the late nineteenth century and then the Old Inn when the Seelbach brothers built their new hotel at Fourth and Walnut (now Muhammad Ali Blvd.) Streets in 1905. But the venerable Louisville Hotel survived until October 1938, outliving its equally venerable rival, the original GALT HOUSE. The empty hotel stood as a stately ghost until it was razed in 1949 to make way for a parking lot. The Sixth Street ell has been renovated as office space.

See *The Louisville Directory for the year 1832* (reprinted Louisville 1970); *Louisville Daily Courier*, June 2, 1853; Elizabeth Jones, "Henry Whitestone: Nineteenth Century Louisville Architect," M.A. thesis, University of Louisville, 1974; George H. Yater, *Two Hundred Years at the Falls of the Ohio* (Louisville 1979 and 1987).

George H. Yater

LOUISVILLE INDUSTRIAL EXPOSITION. A showcase for the city's manufacturers to display their wares to potential buyers, the Louisville Industrial Exposition was opened on September 1, 1872, in a specially constructed building on the northeast corner of Fourth and Chestnut Streets. A precursor to the later, larger, and better-publicized SOUTHERN EXPOSITION, the Industrial Exposition continued annually through 1882. It did skip 1876 in deference to the Centennial Exposition in Philadelphia, marking the hundredth anniversary of the Declaration of Independence.

The Industrial Exposition was a testimonial to the shift in Louisville's economy to an industrial base following the CIVIL WAR. The city's value of industrial output rose from $14.2 million in 1860 to $18.5 million in 1870 and to $35.4 million in 1880. It is significant that the near doubling of output in the latter decade was during the time of the exposition. Directors of the private effort were largely the city's industrialists. They included furniture maker J.H. Wrampelmeier; foundrymen Charles S. Snead and George Ainslie; papermaker and railroad promoter Bidermann du Pont, who also developed coal mines in western Kentucky; and railroad financier H. Victor Newcomb, son of the Louisville & Nashville Railroad's new president, Horatio D. Newcomb. The exposition's president was John T. Moore, a partner in Bremaker, Moore, and Co., papermaker.

The brick building, 330 by 230 feet, was designed by Louisville architects Henry Struby and C.S. Mergell in a variation of the then-popular French Second Empire style. It opened with gas lighting but before the end of its life was equipped with the new electric arc lights. The principal exhibits were working machinery made in Louisville and displays of local products, but states other than Kentucky were also represented. "The knowledge of useful inventions cannot be conveyed by words, but by specimens of working machinery," the *Louisville Commercial,* which had proposed the exposition, declared on September 1, 1872. The aim was not only to display the city's productions to local residents and visitors but also to encourage local wholesalers and retailers to add these new items of a newly blooming industrial economy to their product lines.

The exhibits changed from year to year. The steps in processing Kentucky TOBACCO from field to consumer products was an attraction one year. The Louisville & Nashville Railroad displayed a newly built steam locomotive another year, although transporting it to Fourth and Chestnut Streets must have been a major undertaking. In 1877 Alexander Graham Bell's newly invented telephone was in operation, and visitors could speak by wire to someone in a remote part of the building. The TELEPHONE had first been shown publicly at the Centennial Exposition the year before.

An art gallery displayed work by popular artists of the day, including some aspiring Louisville artists such as CARL BRENNER and NICOLA MARSCHALL. Band concerts attracted visitors at night. The last season of the Industrial Exposition in 1882 was succeeded by the Southern Exposition. In 1883 the older building was converted to a hotel to help house the throngs of out-of-town visitors to the new exposition. It was demolished in the spring of 1884 to make way for the new United States Post Office and Custom House erected on the cleared site.

See *Louisville Commercial* and *Courier-Journal* for September of each year from 1872 to 1882, except 1876, and *Louisville Commercial,* May 29, 1884.

George H. Yater

LOUISVILLE INDUSTRIAL FOUNDATION. The Louisville Industrial Foundation (LIF), one of the nation's first urban industrial development agencies, was organized in 1916 during the depths of an economic recession that preceded American entry into WORLD WAR I. Its purposes were to establish new industries, improve existing firms, and create new payrolls. The LIF was composed of individual and corporate subscribers who purchased common stock in an industrial development revolving fund. Within one month after its formation, 3,118 subscribers purchased shares worth more than $1 million. As a result, LIF became known as "the million dollar factory fund."

LIF's charter empowered it to make loans to promising manufacturing enterprises that could not obtain adequate capital through banks or other conventional channels. From 1917 to 1922 the organization extended loans totaling approximately $803,000 to 18 firms. The foundation lent an additional $824,000 to 19 firms during the balance of the decade. In addition to its revolving fund loans, LIF also offered various forms of financial, managerial, and technical assistance.

Eastern Airlines plane at Louisville's Standiford Field, 1952.

LIF continued to make new loans and to attract new business during the Great Depression of the 1930s, but the impact of its efforts paled in comparison to the spiraling levels of bankruptcy, business closures, and unemployment that gripped the community between 1929 and World War II.

LIF's industrial development efforts continued after World War II. It was joined by new organizations that also sought businesses and industries for the Louisville area but did not provide financial assistance as LIF did. These included the Louisville Area Development Association, the Louisville Area Chamber of Commerce, and Louisville Central Area Inc. However, in 1986, shareholders decided to dissolve the agency. Gene Gardner, foundation chairman, claimed that LIF had not done enough to justify its existence in the past decade and was no longer needed.

See Leo F. Schnore and Henry Fagin, eds., *Urban Research and Policy Planning* (Beverly Hills, Calif., 1967); Carl E. Kramer, "The City-Building Process: Urbanization in Central and Southern Louisville, 1772–1932," Ph.D. dissertation, University of Toledo, 1980.

Carl E. Kramer

LOUISVILLE INTERNATIONAL AIRPORT. Since 1947 Louisville International Airport (originally Standiford Field) has served as the commercial airport for Greater Louisville and much of Kentucky and southern Indiana. Like air travel itself, the airport has undergone massive growth and change throughout its history, but its greatest period of growth occurred in the late twentieth century.

In the late 1990s Louisville International Airport was serving almost 4 million passengers each year. Seventeen airlines operated about a hundred daily flights to fifty-three nonstop or direct destinations. About 98 percent of the passengers flew on jet service. In addition to passenger flights, Louisville International Airport is home to one of the world's largest air cargo operations—the international hub of United Parcel Service. The airport also serves corporate, private, charter, military, and general aviation.

The airport is at the intersection of I-65 and I-264, some five miles south of Louisville's central business district, making it easily accessible from all parts of the community. Its close proximity to the downtown business district is unusual for a city of Louisville's size and is considered a major economic development advantage.

While Louisville's airport always handled mail and cargo delivery, its evolution into a major cargo facility began in 1981. In that year, United Parcel Service (UPS) selected Louisville as the main hub for its new overnight air delivery service. The phenomenal growth of that service made UPS Kentucky's largest private-sector employer and transformed Louisville International Airport into one of the world's largest cargo airports. More than 3 billion tons of air cargo moved through Louisville International each year in the 1990s.

Originally called Standiford Field, the airport's name was changed to Louisville International Airport in 1995 to reflect changes in the airport's operations and an expanded vision for its future. A trace of the airport's early history remains in its three-letter FAA designation—SDF. It was named for Dr. Elisha David Standiford, a businessman and Kentucky legislator, who owned much of the land on which the airport is built. It is ironic that Standiford was president of the Louisville & Nashville Railroad from 1875–80.

The airport's origin dates to 1941, when the U.S. Army Corps of Engineers constructed the first runway on the property, a four-thousand-foot strip used for World War II aircraft. Six years later the federal government turned the property over to the Regional Airport Authority, and all commercial flights began operating from that location. Bowman Field, the community's original airport, remained open to private planes and continued to operate as a general aviation facility. Standiford Field opened for business on November 15, 1947, serving some thirteen hundred passengers each week. An old cafeteria was pressed into service as a terminal, and the airport's three carriers—American, Eastern, and TWA—operated out of a converted World War II barracks.

Lee Terminal, constructed at a cost of $1 million, opened May 25, 1950. The 42,000-square-foot facility boasted 6 gates, a 300-space parking lot, and an annual capacity of 150,000 passengers. The terminal was named for Addison Lee Jr., who had served as chairman of the Regional Airport Authority's board for twenty years.

By the end of the 1950s, the airport had already seen tremendous growth. The terminal had almost tripled in size and included two indoor concourses. A motel had been built on the property, and the number of passengers had increased to nearly eight hundred thousand per year. The early 1970s brought still more growth. U.S. Air and Delta had joined the list of major airlines serving Louisville. The terminal was further enlarged, a new control tower was constructed, and the parking area was enlarged to accommodate two thousand cars. In 1983 construction began on a new landside terminal. The facility opened in 1985, followed by an adjoining nineteen-gate airside terminal completed in 1989.

During the early 1980s several issues pointed to a growing need for a major expansion of Louisville International Airport. Business and political leaders knew that inadequate air service was a major stumbling block to attracting new business development to the community. At the same time, UPS's air cargo business was growing at an overwhelming pace and showed no signs of slowing down. To increase the airport's capacity for both passenger and cargo operations, the airport embarked upon a comprehensive $750 million Louisville Airport Improvement Program. The massive program was designed to stimulate economic growth by expanding and improving Louisville International Airport. Begun in 1988, the centerpiece of the program was the construction of two new parallel runways with adjoining taxiways. They doubled the airport's capacity by allowing simultaneous takeoffs and landings in all weather conditions.

In addition to the runways, the program's major components included an air traffic control tower; relocation of Kentucky Air National Guard facilities; a U.S. Postal Service facility for airmail handling, including a customer service center; a forty-three-hundred-space parking garage, enabling passengers to travel between car and plane without going outdoors; and relocation of several NEIGHBORHOODS near the airport for noise mitigation purposes.

The expansion of Louisville International Airport has been essential for the economic growth of the city, which continues to attract new businesses and create more jobs. Air transportation in Louisville continues the tradition of the river and RAILROADS, which, in their day, were of equal economic importance to the city. Its expansion was generally supported by the public but also provoked some controversial reaction, especially from three neighborhoods—STANDIFORD, PRESTONIA, and HIGHLAND PARK. These neighborhoods were located next to the airport and were to be acquired under an URBAN RENEWAL plan in 1988. The neighbors, who were joined by residents to be affected by greater noise levels due to the realignment of the parallel runways for the airport, took the case to court. After three years of controversy a federal judge ruled against the use of urban renewal powers in the expansion project but allowed acquisition and relocation to proceed. Since 1988 more than 4,000 people in 1,100 homes and 115 businesses in Standiford, Prestonia, Highland Park, and neighboring areas have moved to make way for the expansion; other properties are yet to be acquired. In 1998 the General Assembly approved $20 million for relocating residents affected by airport noise. The program has been one of the largest residential acquisition and relocation programs ever carried out in the United States and is expected to be completed by the year 2010.

During the first stages of the controversial airport expansion, Joe Corradino gained public notice as a partner in Schimpeler-Corradino Associates (1970–92), which was responsible for airport planning and construction. In 1992 he became owner of the Corradino Group, a nationally recognized engineering firm. Besides building the two parallel runways at Louisville International Airport, Corradino is connected to the downtown trolley project operated by TRANSIT AUTHORITY OF RIVER CITY. In January 1999 Corradino took office as B District county commissioner, serving until he was defeated in the November 1999 election.

After a four-year stint with a Philadelphia engineering firm, Joe Corradino arrived in Louisville in 1970 with plans to start a business with his Purdue University classmate, Louisvillian Charles Schimpeler. Corradino, a native Philadelphian, was a graduate of Villanova University with a bachelor's degree in civil engineering and Purdue University where he earned a master's degree in urban planning. Born August 1, 1943, to Millie and Anthony Corradino, a construction worker, he planned to be an engineer from an early age. He and his wife, Vivian, have two sons and two daughters.

Louisville International Airport is owned and operated by the Regional Airport Authority of Louisville and Jefferson County (RAA). An independent, quasi-public agency, the RAA is responsible for the day-to-day operation of the airport as well as long-term planning. The RAA also operates Bowman Field. The RAA is governed by an eleven-member board of directors who set policy, approve the budget, and hire the airport's general manager. The board is composed of the mayor of Louisville and three mayoral appointees, the Jefferson County judge/executive and three judge appointees, and three members appointed by the governor of Kentucky. Daily management of airport business is handled by a general manager who reports to the RAA directors.

Louisville International Airport receives no tax support. The airport's annual operating budget is derived entirely from an array of airport user fees. The airport receives fees for the use of the airfield as well as revenues from a variety of concessions, lease agreements, business and operating permits, and passenger facility charges.

See Stratton Hammon, "The Phoenix of Standiford Airfield: A Military Incident of World War II," *Filson Club History Quarterly* 47 (April 1973): 161–70.

Robert S. Michael

LOUISVILLE INTERNATIONAL CULTURAL CENTER. Founded in 1984, the Louisville International Cultural Center (LICC) is a nonprofit, nonpartisan organization dedicated to developing and nurturing cross-cultural relationships among people and institutions in KENTUCKIANA and their counterparts elsewhere in the world.

Through its diverse activities, LICC programs and services reach individuals of all ages. LICC receives support from federal GOVERNMENT agencies, private foundations, corporations, and individuals. LICC is one of more than a hundred host agencies for the International Visitor Program of the United States Information Agency. In the late 1990s more than 250 official international visitors representing over seventy countries came each year to Kentuckiana to meet and exchange ideas with their American counterparts. Tomorrow's world leaders in business, government, and the arts visit the United States through this program. LICC's Business for Russia and Community Connections programs have served public administrators and entrepreneurs from Russia, Ukraine, Moldova, and other Eastern European countries.

Thomas Diener

LOUISVILLE JOURNAL. The *Louisville Journal* was first issued as a daily newspaper on November 24, 1830, and soon began publishing both a triweekly and a weekly edition that circulated throughout Kentucky, the South, and the Midwest. The newspaper, founded to promote Henry Clay's candidacy for the presidency, was financed and published by A.J. Buxton, with Clay's biographer, George D. Prentice, as the editor. The paper was initially coedited by EDWIN BRYANT, who had met Prentice in Providence, Rhode Island, and was asked to come to Louisville to be coeditor. When the fledgling newspaper failed to make enough money to support two editors, Bryant went to Lexington where he edited the *Lexington Observer* for two years and the *Lexington Intelligencer* (1834–44). On January 31, 1832, the *Journal* merged with the *Focus*, another Louisville daily, established in 1826. In December of 1833, Buxton sold his interest in the paper to John N. Johnson. Despite the success of the paper, Johnson sold his interest to George W. Weissinger, who continued to manage the *Journal's* business affairs until his death in 1850.

The *Journal* prospered and soon became one of the most widely circulated NEWSPAPERS west of the Appalachian Mountains, primarily because of Prentice's sparkling writing. In April 1831 Prentice boasted that the newspaper had fifteen hundred subscribers: two hundred daily, two hundred triweekly, and eleven hundred weekly. The *Journal* was enjoyed by western farmers, loggers, trappers, and rivermen. Prentice made the *Journal* a great supporter of the WHIG PARTY. As he watched his beloved Whig Party disintegrate in the mid-1850s, Prentice lent his pen to all-out support of the Know-Nothing Party. Prentice is credited with promoting anti-foreigner sentiment, which led to the BLOODY MONDAY riots against German and Irish immigrants in 1855. On January 15, 1855, he wrote in the paper: "It is evident that this foreign question is to override all others, even the slavery question, as we see men of the most opposite views on slavery, forgetting their differences and acting together." To his credit, Prentice later publicly regretted his role in the riots. The *Journal* also encouraged public education, municipal reform, and the commercial and economic development of Louisville. Prentice soon directed his attention to stimulating interest in Western literature. In December 1836 the *Journal* began publishing the *Literary News-Letter*, edited by Edmund Flagg. It was an eight-page weekly publication, designed to use contributions written by individuals living in the West and to publish articles about the Western country. Recognizing the need for education for the people in Kentucky and the entire West, the *Journal* began publishing in 1837 the *Western Journal of Education*, edited by B.O. Peers. Both publications were short-lived.

The *Journal* was involved in various editorial battles with other newspapers. Until 1830 the dominant editor of the state was Shadrack Penn, who edited the *Louisville Public Advertiser*, started in 1818. Prentice attacked Penn, a Democrat, at every point; Penn returned the fire in one of the greatest newspapers battles in the nation. Ultimately, Prentice won the battle and replaced Penn as the dominant publisher in Louisville. Following the Whig Party's demise, the *Journal* endorsed the Native American (or Know-Nothing) Party. In the presidential election of 1860, Prentice favored John Bell as the only candidate who could save the Union. Once Abraham Lincoln was elected, Prentice appealed to the Southern states to remain loyal to the Union; after Lincoln called for troops, Prentice urged Kentucky to remain neutral.

In 1868 twenty-eight-year-old HENRY WATTERSON was invited by the owners of the *Journal* to take over as editor. Watterson waged a six-month spirited campaign against Walter N. Haldeman of the *Louisville Morning Courier* and convinced him to merge the two newspapers. On November 8, 1868, the *COURIER-JOURNAL* made it first appearance.

See Betty Carolyn Congleton, "*The Louisville Journal*: Its Origin and Early Years," *Register of the Kentucky State Historical Society* 62 (April 1964): 87–103; Donald B. Towles, *The Press of Kentucky 1787–1994* (Frankfort 1994).

LOUISVILLE LEADER. The *Louisville Leader* was a weekly newspaper that covered issues important to the African American community during the first half of the twentieth century. It was founded by I. WILLIS COLE, a native of Memphis who came to Louisville in 1915 selling Bibles. With fifty dollars that he borrowed, Cole published the *Leader*'s first issue in November 1917. By the 1930s it had a circulation of twenty-two thousand and employed twenty AFRICAN AMERICANS, more that any other publishing house in Kentucky. In 1938 the I. Willis Cole Publishing Co. purchased the Berry Building located at 930 W Walnut St. (now Muhammad Ali Blvd.).

The *Leader* announced births and deaths, named those suffering from illness, listed Louisville churches and their schedules of services, and printed news items from black correspondents elsewhere in the state. It advertised black businesses and professionals and sponsored contests. The *Leader* had a children's page, a sports page, and a section titled "Hometown Correspondence" containing news from small towns around the state. A voice for CIVIL RIGHTS, the *Leader* styled itself "your newspaper—militant but stable." It implored African Americans to vote, opposed JIM CROW laws and black allegiance to the REPUBLICAN PARTY, and deplored lynching.

Cole, who strongly protested SEGREGATION and constantly informed his readers of the insults blacks received when patronizing white business establishments, urged them to boycott white businesses whenever possible. At the opening of Chickasaw Park in the West End in 1922, the newspaper labeled it an attempt by segregationists to mollify Louisville's black community. The *Leader* urged black leaders to stop bickering among themselves or else blacks would never progress. When Cole died in February 1950, his family, led by his widow, Rosa, published the newspaper until September, when it ceased operation.

See Alice Allison Dunnigan, ed., *The Fascinating Story of Black Kentuckians: Their Heritage and Traditions* (Washington, D.C., 1982); *Louisville Leader,* March 11, 1950; George C. Wright, *Life Behind a Veil* (Baton Rouge 1985).

LOUISVILLE LEGION. Since 1836, the Louisville Legion has been a proud part of Louisville's military heritage. In that year, a prominent citizen, Thomas Anderson, organized a company of infantry known as the Louisville Guards. Three years later, this company was incorporated into an organization chartered by the Kentucky General Assembly as the Louisville Legion. By 1845, six companies of infantry regularly drilled at the Oaklands racecourse on Seventh St. and marched in parades in the city.

When the news of hostilities with Mexico arrived in Louisville in the spring of 1846, the Louisville Legion was the first regiment offered for service. Designated as the First Regiment of Foot, Kentucky Volunteers, the regiment mustered into United States Service on May 17, 1846. STEPHEN ORMSBY was commissioned colonel of the Louisville Legion, as Thomas Anderson was considered too old for active duty. The regiment served in Brig. Gen. ZACHARY TAYLOR's army in Northern Mexico.

Although garrison duty comprised most of the Louisville Legion's service, the regiment was involved in the campaign for Monterrey in September 1846. The regiment was mustered out on May 7, 1847, in New Orleans. During its time in Mexico, the regiment lost fifty-three members to disease or to death at the hands of the enemy. Between the MEXICAN WAR and the CIVIL WAR, the Louisville Legion consisted of several companies commanded by prominent citizens of Louisville.

The outbreak of the Civil War caused division among the former members of the Louisville Legion. Many soldiers who had filled the ranks of the regiment during the Mexican War joined the Confederate army. Despite the division in sentiment among Mexican War veterans, the Louisville Legion of the Civil War was strongly committed to the Union cause. In the summer of 1861, President Abraham Lincoln authorized LOVELL HARRISON ROUSSEAU, a Louisville lawyer, state senator, and "brigadier general" of the Louisville Guards, to raise troops for the defense of the Union. However, to avoid violating the Kentucky legislature's proclaimed neutrality, the recruitment camp was located on the Indiana side of the OHIO RIVER. Camp Joe Holt was named in honor of JOSEPH HOLT, a prominent Louisvillian and subsequent judge advocate general of the army. On July 1, 1861, Rousseau led six campaigns of the Louisville Guards across the river to establish the camp. This force of 334 men formed the nucleus of the regiment. Within a short time, ten companies were raised from Louisville and surrounding counties. The Louisville Legion was originally designated the Third Kentucky Volunteer Infantry, but in November 1861 Gov. Beriah Magoffin ordered the unit renumbered the Fifth.

On September 9, 1861, the Louisville Legion was mustered into the service of the United States with Lovell H. Rousseau as colonel. In response to a rumor of Confederate invasion, the command was transported to Muldraugh Hill nine days later. On October 1, 1861, Colonel Rousseau was commissioned brigadier general, and Lt. Col. Harvey M. Buckley was promoted to fill the vacancy left by Rousseau's departure. Also promoted was William W. Berry to lieutenant colonel and John L. Treanor to major.

The Louisville Legion was assigned to Rousseau's Fourth Brigade of Brig. Gen. Alexander McDowell McCook's Second Division of the Army of the Ohio. The regiment participated in the occupation of Nashville, Tennessee, and was actively engaged in the fighting on the second day of the battle of Shiloh. The regiment was next engaged in the siege of Corinth, Mississippi, under Maj. Gen. Henry Halleck that resulted in the capture of that city on May 30, 1862.

In the summer of 1862, the Louisville Legion joined Maj. Gen. DON CARLOS BUELL's Army of the Ohio in the campaign against Chattanooga. The Confederate invasion of Kentucky caused the evacuation of Union forces from northern Alabama and middle Tennessee below Nashville. The Louisville Legion was part of the detachment under Brig. Gen. Joshua Sill sent to confront the Confederates at Frankfort during the Kentucky Campaign. The regiment was not involved in the Battle of Perryville on October 8, 1862, but skirmished with the Confederates a few miles southwest of Lawrenceburg, Kentucky, on that day.

The Louisville Legion next was engaged in the battle of Stone's River near Murfreesboro, Tennessee, on December 31, 1862, and January 2, 1863. In the fight, the Fifth Kentucky Infantry suffered 19 killed and 80 wounded of the 320 men engaged. After this battle, the regiment remained in Murfreesboro for the winter and spring of 1863. The legion, as part of the Army of the Cumberland, participated in the Tullahoma Campaign under Maj. Gen. William Starke Rosecrans. In late January 1863, Colonel Buckley resigned; the following month, William W. Berry was promoted to colonel.

At Chickamauga, the Fifth Kentucky Infantry was again heavily engaged in the fierce fighting and suffered its heaviest losses. On September 20, 1863, the regiment formed a part of the Union line that held their position against repeated Confederate attacks under the leadership of Maj. Gen. George Henry Thomas. During the Chattanooga Campaign, the Louisville Legion was prominently involved in the opening of the "Cracker line" at Browns Ferry, in the capture of Orchard Knob, and in driving the Confederates from their strong positions on Missionary Ridge.

In May 1864, Gen. William Tecumseh Sherman began his drive on Atlanta, Georgia, and the Louisville Legion bore a conspicuous part in the bloody journey. The Fifth Kentucky was engaged at Dalton, Resaca, Pickett's Mill, and Kenesaw Mountain, and in the siege of Atlanta.

On September 14, 1864, the regiment mustered out of service at Louisville, Kentucky. Of the 1,020 officers and enlisted men who had passed through the ranks of the regiment during the war, 302 lost their lives to disease or in battle. In a letter written after the Civil War, Gen. William T. Sherman wrote, "No single body of men can claim more honor for the grand result than the officers and men of the Louisville Legion of 1861" (Speed, *Union Regiments of Kentucky*, 324).

After the Civil War, the Louisville Legion was dissolved for more than a decade. In 1878 the legion was again reorganized as the First Regiment of Infantry, Kentucky State Guard. The organization consisted of eight companies, one of which was also trained for artillery service, under the command of a former Confederate officer, John Breckinridge Castleman. Over the next twenty years, the Louisville Legion was actively engaged in maintaining the peace and security of the commonwealth of Kentucky. Several times, the regiment was sent to eastern Kentucky during the disturbances known as the Rowan County War and the French-Eversole Feud.

The Louisville Legion was the first Kentucky unit to reach Puerto Rico during the Spanish American War (1898) and, under the command of Colonel Castleman, performed important duties. During the days following the assassination of Gov. William Goebel (1899–1900), the legion was called to Frankfort by Gov. William Taylor to preserve the peace. The regiment was next called to service along the Mexican border.

Before the first world war, the Louisville Legion became the 138th Field Artillery. In World War I and subsequent conflicts, the 138th Field Artillery has continued the military service and sustains the tradition of the Louisville Legion.

See Thomas Speed, *The Union Regiments of Kentucky* (Louisville 1897); Ernest MacPherson, *History of the First Regiment of Infantry: The Louisville Legion* (Louisville 1907); Robert Emmett McDowell, *City of Conflict* (Louisville 1962).

David R. Deatrick Jr.

***LOUISVILLE* MAGAZINE.** Founded in March 1950 as a quarterly publication of the newly formed Louisville Chamber of Commerce, *Louisville* magazine succeeded the *Board of Trade Journal.* The first editor was Glenn Ramsey; the first issue consisted of sixty-six pages and featured an aerial view of the city.

With an editorial focus on business and economic development news, subscribers were mainly chamber members who received copies as a part of association dues. Beginning in 1952 the publication became monthly; the editor was George H. Miller.

Helen G. Henry joined the staff in 1951, becoming editor in 1953. Her seventeen-year tenure was highlighted by forty-five awards from the American Association of Commerce Publications, including the top national award in 1968. She gradually broadened the magazine's focus to include community issues and upgraded the graphic content. Her obituary, published in the magazine in 1970, noted that her influence in leading chamber-published magazines to adopt technical modernization and wider journalistic focus was felt nationwide.

At the time of her death, the Louisville Development Committee (LDC) was preparing to launch a major economic development campaign with national newspaper ads and the use of the magazine as a city promotional tool. The LDC consequently underwrote the publication to provide for full four-color printing and wider distribution costs. The first issue of *Louisville* magazine to be used in this promotion was January 1971.

Succeeding Henry was Betty Lou Amster, who headed the magazine through the December 1989 issue. During her tenure the magazine received many additional local and national awards, including best chamber-published magazine and an art direction award from the National Association of Magazine Publishers. When she retired as executive editor, James Oppel became editor.

Louisville magazine joined the Audit Bureau of Circulations to enhance its ADVERTISING potential. Also, to obtain increased circulation, in 1984 the magazine included a monthly eight-page program guide for WKPC (Channel 15), the local public TELEVISION station. In April 1988 *Louisville* magazine published its largest issue to date—two hundred pages.

In 1993 the Chamber of Commerce sold its magazine to Dan Crutcher, who became publisher and editor. The new *Louisville* dropped the television program guide but continued to supply copies to GREATER LOUISVILLE Inc., successor to the Chamber of Commerce. Although circulation is not audited by ABC, Crutcher reported that in 1999 *Louisville* had a readership audit claiming seventy-six thousand readers, based on paid and unpaid circulation of thirty-seven thousand.

See *Louisville*, March 1950, Oct. 1970, Jan. 1971, Jan. 1975.

Betty Lou Amster

LOUISVILLE MALE HIGH SCHOOL. On April 7, 1856, Louisville Male High School, located at the corner of Ninth and Chestnut Streets, was established as a place to prepare Louisville's young men for leadership. It was one of the city's first two public high schools and was commissioned by the Louisville School Board along with its counterpart, Female High School. Admission was by examination, and students were held to the highest standards of conduct and curriculum. The school required a four-year course for graduation, and, until 1912, all graduates were awarded bachelor of arts degrees. The first class graduated in 1859 with only two members.

In 1899, under the leadership of Principal REUBEN POST HALLECK (1897–1912), Louisville Male High School moved to the west side of First St., between Walnut (Muhammad Ali Blvd.) and Chestnut Streets, in the former Female High School building. It remained there until 1915, when it moved to the corner of Brook and Breckinridge Streets. Here it grew and prospered for seventy-five years. It established a high reputation as a public institution, ranking with the best private schools in the United States for educational quality.

In 1915 it was consolidated with du Pont Manual Training High School and for four years was known as Louisville Boys High School. At the end of the 1918 school year the two schools were separated and their original names restored. Louisville Male High School kept its historic name until 1952, when it became coeducational and was given the name Louisville Male and Girls High School by the Board of Education. But the action encountered serious protest from students, faculty, and alumni regarding both the name change and its new coeducational status.

For ninety-six years, Male had been exclusively for young men. Many of its traditions and customs revolved around that status. The coeducational movement invaded Louisville's PUBLIC SCHOOLS in 1950, but Male had successfully resisted for two years. Finally in 1952, after several school board hearings, Male conceded. The only thing worse—in the eyes of the students (most boys and girls supported the old name), faculty, and alumni—than its new coeducational status was its new name. Even the new female students protested the name. Male stood for tradition, excellence, and reputation. On December 12, 1955, the Board of Education relented and agreed to have the name revert to Louisville Male High School. Its traditional name restored, Male thrived under the leadership of Principal W.S. Milburn (1931–61).

In 1977 Male was named the first traditional program high school in Jefferson County. This program holds that a structured, orderly learning environment is essential for student achievement. The primary goal of education is the acquisition of knowledge, but students are encouraged to think, analyze, and express their thoughts in a clear, concise, and logical manner. An emphasis is placed on patriotism, proper conduct, and self-discipline. These high standards are attained through the efforts of students, faculty, administration, and mandatory parental involvement.

In 1991 Male moved to the former home of Durrett High School, a forty-acre campus on Preston Hwy. The move doubled its space and allowed it to update its laboratories, library, and classroom facilities. The old facility on Brook and Breckinridge was sparsely used for years until the school board initiated controversial proceedings in 1997 for its demolition in order to make way for a new childcare center and stadium for Central High School. Many alumni and community supporters of HISTORIC PRESERVATION rallied to the cause of opposing the building's destruction. Supporters prepared detailed studies that argued it was economically feasible to recycle the building. However, the school board maintained their position, and the structure was scheduled to be razed during the summer of 1999. In April 1999 Superintendent Stephen Daeschner recommended that the school board approve the sale of old Male to a group headed by auto dealer Bill Collins for five hundred thousand dollars. The group plans to turn the old school into a community center, public auditorium, day-care center, and up to fifty apartments and offices. It was also announced that Central High will get a new stadium in the Russell neighborhood.

Male continued its high scholastic standards and has had many academic achievements. Male is the only high school in Kentucky to be recognized for consistently high achievement, with a flag of excellence given by the Kentucky Board of Education for seven consecutive years, 1984–90. Male has many notable graduates, including Wilson W. Wyatt, Hunter S. Thompson, William Belknap, Fontaine Fox Jr., Robert Bruce French, James S. Pirtle, Rev. Alexander Gross, Charles C. Stoll, Abraham Flexner, Madison Cawein, and Darrell Griffith.

See Sam Adkins and M.R. Holtzman, *The First Hundred Thirty-Five Years: The Story of Louisville Male High School* (Louisville 1991); *Courier-Journal Magazine*, March 11, 1956, April 26, 1999.

LOUISVILLE MEDICAL CENTER. The Louisville Medical Center occupies about twenty square blocks downtown, bounded roughly by Brook St., Muhammad Ali Blvd., Hancock St., and E BROADWAY. It is the location of three major health-care systems—Jewish Hospital HealthCare Services, NORTON HEALTHCARE, and the UNIVERSITY OF LOUISVILLE School of Medicine. The Medical Center is the largest concentration of health-care resources in the Louisville metropolitan region, each year serving more than sixty thousand inpatients, graduating more than one hundred medical students, and performing millions of dollars in contract research. In 1998 one in six jobs downtown was related to health care, including HOSPITALS, research labs, allied health services, and physicians' offices. In 1996 the Louisville Medical Center generated $1 billion in medical services, with approximately $46 million generated in tax revenues for state and local governments.

The center developed around the first city hospital and the University of Louisville School of Medicine. In 1823 the Louisville Hospital Co. was chartered by the Kentucky General Assembly. Known for a time as the Louisville Marine Hospital, ownership was transferred to the city in 1836, and it became Louisville City Hospital. A new building was erected in 1913 on Chestnut between Brook and PRESTON Streets and was renamed Louisville General Hospital in 1942. The hospital was charged with the care of indigent patients of Louisville and Jefferson County. The University of Louisville School of Medicine was founded in 1837 as the LOUISVILLE MEDICAL INSTITUTE, at Chestnut and Eighth Streets. In 1908 it was moved to First and Chestnut Streets, in closer proximity to the hospital. Louisville General Hospital was the primary teaching facility for students from the School of Medicine and the School of Dentistry (organized in 1918).

Children's Hospital was the second hospital built in the area. After a devastating tornado hit downtown Louisville in 1890, leaving in its wake hundreds of injured and homeless people, Mary Lafon began work to organize a hospital for children. In January 1892 the Children's Free Hospital admitted patients to its new twenty-five-bed hospital at Floyd and Chestnut Streets. In 1909 Children's Hospital started a NURSING school, and a larger hospital was constructed. In 1930 the hospital became affiliated with the University of Louisville School of Medicine, thus beginning its status as a teaching hospital.

By the 1920s a medical center had begun to evolve with the two hospitals and medical school as its core. The post–WORLD WAR II boom increased not only the population but accessibility to health care. Realizing the need to curtail overlapping efforts in health care, the Louisville Area Development Association and the Louisville Hospital Commission hired the Minnesota consulting firm, James A. Hamilton and Associates, to conduct a study. The 1948 report included ninety-five recommendations. The report emphasized the need for a central and organized medical center. The University of Louisville School of Medicine took the initiative in 1950 when it incorporated the Louisville Medical Center Inc. with General Hospital and Children's Hospital. The university worked hard in the early 1950s to attract other hospitals to the area, especially Jewish Hospital, which had been at Floyd and Kentucky Streets since its opening in 1905. The Hamilton Report noted that the fate of Jewish Hospital lay with the university medical school. Desperately needing a more modern facility, Jewish relocated to Brook and Chestnut Streets in January 1955. A revised plan, prepared in 1956 by Harland Bartholomew and Associates, brought the Medical Center proposals up to date and into harmony with the master plan for Louisville's and Jefferson County's URBAN RENEWAL project.

Other hospitals also relocated to the center, including Methodist Evangelical Hospital at Floyd and E Broadway in 1960. Methodist Evangelical was the successor of Methodist Deaconess Hospital on S Eighth St. (1895–1951). Deaconess closed in 1951, but plans were already under way to open a new hospital. In order to gain needed funding, board members of Methodist joined with the Evangelical Hospital Association, which was working toward the same goal, to form Methodist Evangelical Hospital (MEH).

MEH's first choice of sites was in the HIGHLANDS, but, unable to receive the federal funds that it needed unless it built at the Medical Center, MEH was compelled to build on E Broadway. The hospital was well known for its excellent medical staff and patient care and prided itself on providing the "personal touch." There was no affiliation with the university, since that would have required the hospital to have accepted university-appointed personnel to head the departments. By 1988 the occupancy rate was 44 percent and revenue was slipping. Unable to survive, Methodist Evangelical merged with Norton Hospital and Children's Hospital on June 27, 1989, to form Alliant Health System.

In 1969 Norton Memorial Infirmary made the move from Third and Oak Streets to the Medical Center. Norton was founded in 1886 by the Episcopal church. It pumped all its profits back into the hospital and patient care and thus suffered repeatedly during emergencies and depressions due to lack of savings. Thus, Norton board members welcomed the idea of working closely with other hospitals to ride out tough times. The opportunity to join the Medical Center came in the late 1960s as Children's Hospital faced financial disaster. In 1969 the two hospitals merged. Under the agreement they continue as separate facilities (under the same roof), with a single board made up of members from both hospitals.

Part of the university's plans was a modern health-sciences center for medical and dental students. Phase one was a four-building complex opened in 1970 on Preston St. between Abraham Flexner Way and Muhammad Ali Blvd. Located around a center courtyard stands a fourteen-floor tower housing the School of Medicine, the Health Sciences Building, and the Kornhauser Library and Commons Building. Phase two, completed in 1982, was a new University of Louisville Hospital to replace Louisville General Hospital. The Concentrated Care Building was designed as a 380-bed hospital. The Ambulatory Care Building handles 350,000 patients a year through a primary care center and dozens of clinics. Also included was the parking garage and Institutional Services Building.

Throughout the country many specialized pediatric hospitals went under in the 1970s and 1980s. The occupancy rate at Kosair Crippled Children's Hospital on Eastern Pkwy. was only 35 percent during the 1970s. The lack of patients threatened the life of the hospital, so in

May 1981 Kosair merged with Children's Hospital. The Eastern Pkwy. facility became Kosair Charities Centre, housing child services and advocacy groups. The corporation made up of Norton Hospital and KOSAIR CHILDREN'S HOSPITAL became Norton-Kosair Children's Hospitals Inc. (NKC Inc.). In 1986 Kosair moved from its home on the third floor of Norton Hospital, its location since 1973, to a new building directly across the street. On June 27, 1989, NKC merged with Methodist Evangelical Hospital, and Alliant Health System was formed. In 1993 the Methodist Hospital became the Alliant Medical Pavilion, the site of a broad range of outpatient services. Alliant Health System changed its name in 1999 to Norton Healthcare.

By 1997, along with specialized services and programs such as the Women's Pavilion, Kenton D. Leatherman Spine Center, Brain Institute, Cancer Treatment Center, Norton Psychiatric Center, Home Health, and Occupational Health Services, the Alliant Health System had entered into affiliation and management services agreements with over twenty hospitals in Kentucky, Indiana, and Illinois. In the fall of 1998 Alliant purchased from Columbia/HCA HealthCare Corp. its three remaining Louisville area hospitals—AUDUBON, Suburban, and Southwest—giving Alliant a total of six hospitals in Jefferson County.

Since its move to the Medical Center, Jewish Hospital has experienced enormous growth. In the mid-1960s the hospital ventured into HAND SURGERY, organ transplant, and open-heart surgery. This strengthened the hospital's ties with the university, which, up to that point, had been pro forma rather than vigorous. In 1968 the intensive care unit opened; and in 1974 the Wheeler Tower was completed, increasing the total number of hospital beds to 406 and adding more operating rooms. In 1982 Skycare, Kentucky's first hospital-based air ambulance service, was launched. Other expansions took place, including the outpatient center, completed in 1986, and the Rudd Heart and Lung Center, opened in early 1995. The Rudd Center houses the largest cardiac program in the area and was the largest financial commitment to the Medical Center in the 1990s. As of 1997 Jewish Hospital was the eighth-largest heart hospital in the country.

The Frazier Rehabilitation Center, a network of inpatient and outpatient rehabilitation facilities that includes a ninety-five-bed hospital in the Medical Center, was founded in 1954. Located at General Hospital for a number of years, it moved to 220 Abraham Flexner Way, near Jewish Hospital, in 1965. It had affiliated with Jewish in 1955. In 1984 Jewish Hospital HealthCare Services took over management of Frazier, and in 1994 the two merged. In 1998 the regional network of Jewish Hospital HealthCare Services was serving patients in thirty-six locations.

The UNIVERSITY OF LOUISVILLE HEALTH SCIENCES CENTER has been one of the largest contributors to the Medical Center. However, the University Hospital has had little financial stability since its construction. Due to a number of financial problems, the future of the hospital was threatened before it even opened. Skyrocketing inflation increased construction costs from the original estimate of $63 million to over $70 million. The rising cost of health care caused operational expenses to rise by 61 percent between 1979 and 1982, while GOVERNMENT appropriations rose by only 41 percent. Facing potential deficits of $5 million per year, the hospital was threatened with financial disaster. By the end of 1981 the hospital had begun to turn away some indigent patients. In July 1982, after exploring all options, the university issued a request for proposals to operate the hospital.

After seven months of intensive negotiations, the university, state, county, and city governments accepted a proposal by the Humana Corp. In the agreement, signed January 27, 1983, HUMANA leased the hospital for $6.5 million per year for four years, with options to renew. Humana assumed complete financial risk, continued to care for the area's indigent patients, and turned over 20 percent of the pretax profits to the university. The name of the hospital was changed to Humana Hospital University and changed again in the late 1980s to Humana Hospital University of Louisville. Despite predictions that the hospital would lose $10 million in the first year, it prospered.

In 1993 Humana discontinued hospital management and formed a spinoff company called Galen HealthCare Inc. to manage its contract hospitals. Five months later Galen merged with Columbia Hospital Corp. of America, based in Fort Worth, Texas, to become Columbia HealthCare Corp. Another merger with Hospital Corp. of America, based in Nashville, Tennessee, came just one month later and formed Columbia/HCA. In January 1995 Columbia/HCA moved its headquarters to Nashville, breaking a contract clause requiring that it keep its corporate headquarters in Jefferson County.

The university began searching for new management for the hospital, and in October 1995 University Medical Center Inc. was organized as a partnership between the University of Louisville, Jewish Hospital HealthCare Services Inc., and Alliant Health System Inc. Alliant and Jewish pledged a total of $45 million worth of support for training and for part of a planned medical research building at the university. Under the leadership of Chief Executive Officer Pat Davis, the transition took place smoothly in February 1996. By July of that year construction had begun on an expansion of the emergency department and trauma center, a $13 million project, enlarging it from twenty-one thousand square feet to fifty-six thousand square feet.

Other Health Sciences Center facilities include the James Graham Brown Cancer Center built in 1981 next to the hospital. Since 1973 the University Cancer Center had officially functioned as a special institute at the university. In 1977 civic leaders in Louisville organized a cancer center corporation to construct a facility to expand the program. Funding came strictly from private sources, half of it from the James Graham Brown Foundation. The center is run by the Regional Cancer Center Corp., a combined university-community board. The center pursues all three major areas of cancer activity: patient care, cancer research, and cancer education. The Henry Vogt Cancer Research Institute occupies the top two floors of the building.

The University of Louisville School of Allied Health Sciences, located in the K Building, was established in 1977. It also is the home of the university's nursing school, which gained full school status in 1979.

Other facilities in the University Medical Center include the Kentucky Lions Eye Center at Floyd St. and Muhammad Ali Blvd., housing the Department of Ophthalmology and Visual Sciences, the Kentucky Lions Eye Research Institute, the Rounsavall Eye Clinic, the Primary Care Eye Clinic, the University of Louisville Lions Eye Bank, and the Kentucky Lions Eye Foundation.

Directly across Muhammad Ali Blvd. is the Medical-Dental Research Building, used for medical research, and the Research Resources Center, a state-of-the-art animal care facility for research employing animal models to study the causes, mechanisms, and cures of human diseases. The Kidney Disease Center, located at Chestnut and PRESTON Streets, houses the division of nephrology, providing treatment for patients with renal disease and hypertension, recipients of kidney transplants, and patients on chronic dialysis.

The Keller Child Psychiatry Center located on Jackson St. studies and treats emotional disorders in families and children. The Comprehensive Health Care Center for High-Risk Infants and Children, is at Floyd St. and Abraham Flexner Way. is a model for comprehensive health care for children born to high-risk mothers and those residing in low socioeconomic areas. The Child Evaluation Center, operated as a nonprofit organization by the School of Medicine, was established in 1965 to serve children with developmental disabilities such as mental retardation, learning disorders, birth defects, or genetic disorders. Funds are provided by various local, state, and federal sources. Previously at 334 E Broadway, the center moved to Chestnut and Floyd Streets in 1996. The Irvin and Helen Abell Administration Center, located adjacent to the Child Evaluation Center, houses the administrative offices of the Health Sciences Center. At Preston and Gray Streets is the Medical-Dental Apartments, providing housing for medical and dental students and their families.

In the spring of 1998 the University of Louisville's Information Technology department began a research and development project to link the university's communication network with the hospitals of the medical center. The goal of the project is to spread physician access to patient information via a shared technological backbone, improving cooperation and patient care among members of the medical center. The network would allow the university and hospitals to take advantage of shared databases, patient data, research resources, Internet access, and more. In addition, doctors would be able to have access to information and conduct research online. Due to renegotiations of software vendor contracts, no completion date was predicted.

At the end of the twentieth century the Medical Center planned to expand beyond its traditional boundaries. In 1998 plans were under way by the Louisville Medical Center Development Corp. to devise a plan for financing the purchase of the HAYMARKET, on the west side of Interstate 65 between Market, Jefferson, Floyd, and Preston Streets. Plans are to turn the site into a health-related business park. To ensure that the community continued to benefit from leading-edge technology, Jewish, Alliant, and the university took a leadership role to support the construction of a $28 million medical research building. The facility was part of a plan to attract the growing pool of new talent in the medical field, to guarantee that the community would have access to the best health care available anywhere, and to help place Louisville's medical center in the ranks of other top centers such as the Mayo Clinic, Johns Hopkins Medical Center, and the Cleveland Medical Center.

See Barbara Zingman and Betty Lou Amster, *A Legendary Vision: The History of Jewish Hospital* (Louisville 1997); idem, *The Mission: The History of Methodist Evangelical Hospital 1960–1993* (Louisville 1994); Gail McGowan Mellor, *Kosair Children's Hospital, A History 1892–1992* (Louisville 1992); idem, *Norton Hospital: The First Hundred Years, 1886–1986* (Louisville 1986).

LOUISVILLE MEDICAL INSTITUTE. The institute grew out of an urban rivalry with Lexington, the home of Transylvania University and its Medical Department. When the school opened in 1837, its original faculty included three Transylvania defectors, led by CHARLES CALDWELL. Eventually, the faculty also included Charles Wilkins Short, DANIEL DRAKE, and SAMUEL DAVID GROSS, all of whom made significant contributions to American science and medicine. In 1838 classes moved into handsome new quarters, built and furnished at city expense, at Eighth and Chestnut Streets. Eventually, the Medical Institute drew students not only from Kentucky but from other states connected to Louisville by river. Matriculates attended two courses of lectures, submitted a thesis, and passed an oral examination before being awarded the M.D. degree. Outstanding graduates included David W. Yandell, who later taught in the Medical Department of the UNIVERSITY OF LOUISVILLE. In 1846 the Louisville Medical Institute became the Medical Department of the University of Louisville. This followed a series of attacks upon the school by local physicians jealous of the faculty and by advocates of a financial and administrative combination of the medical school with the less successful Louisville Collegiate Institute. The two were combined under a single board of trustees, but the medical school retained its financial independence.

See Dwayne Cox, "The Louisville Medical Institute: A Case History in American Medical Education," *Filson Club History Quarterly* 62 (April 1988): 197–219.

Dwayne Cox

LOUISVILLE MEMORIAL AUDITORIUM. "Erected by the citizens of the city of Louisville and the county of Jefferson in memory of their soldiers, sailors, and marines who served the nation in World War," states the official plaque on the massive Louisville Memorial Auditorium, with its imposing Greek Doric stone columns, which stands on the northwest corner of Fourth and Kentucky Streets. The auditorium was designed by Thomas Hastings of New York, and E.T. Hutchings of Louisville served as chief architect.

The idea for a new civic meeting hall seating two thousand people originated in 1912; however, following WORLD WAR I planning included the concept of a memorial auditorium honoring those who had fought and died in the war. A Louisville Auditorium Association was formed to raise monies for the project, and in November 1922 a $750,000 bond issue was also passed. These combined funds were administered by a memorial commission selected by the mayor of Louisville. This seven-member, mayor-appointed Louisville Memorial Commission continues to direct the operation of the facility today. After a series of setbacks, construction on the auditorium began in August 1927. The building opened on Armistice Day, November 11, 1929, and was known as the Louisville War Memorial Auditorium.

William H. Steward Hall, Louisville Municipal College, 1940s.

Louisville Memorial Auditorium's eighty-five-foot-wide stage has seen an impressive array of entertainers, including George Gershwin, Helen Hayes, George M. Cohan, Ethel Barrymore, Marian Anderson, Artur Rubinstein, Mikhail Baryshnikov, and the Peking Opera. Currently seating 1,765, the auditorium contains the world's largest—and only remaining—Pilcher Organ, manufactured in Louisville and equipped with 5,288 pipes. Used for a wide variety of programs, the multifunction building also houses various nonprofit groups (American Legion of Kentucky, Louisville Labor Management, City Employee Relations), the Skylight Ballroom, and the Louisville Department of Archives. A regal collection of flags of many nations lines the auditorium's inner corridors. The flags include some flown in World Wars I and II, plus personal banners and flags of famous American generals.

Jerry L. Rice

LOUISVILLE MOTOR SPEEDWAY. The Louisville Motor Speedway (LMS), at 1900 Outer Loop near Grade Ln. in southwest Jefferson County, was opened in 1988, cashing in on the booming popularity of National Association for Stock Car Auto Racing (NASCAR) throughout the country.

The track was opened by Andy Vertrees, its general manager, and Kenny Stilger, a drywall manufacturer and majority partner. Originally the track was a three-eighths-mile bowl-shaped asphalt oval costing about $1.8 million and designed primarily for stock-car racing. The track also featured lighting for Friday and Saturday night races and a grandstand seating nearly eight thousand. The first season scheduled fifty-six racing dates from April through October. Most of the drivers were local amateurs, with as many as a hundred cars in competition during a weekend of racing.

In order to accommodate more races, the track was expanded in 1994 to seven-sixteenths-mile. In 1997, to appease NASCAR officials, LMS refurbished the track, altering the D-shape to more resemble a tri-oval. Prior to the changes, drivers had labeled the track the "No. 1 weirdest" because of the banked turns, hills, dips, and other strange aspects of its layout.

One of the most popular races at the LMS was the figure-eight, a survival-of-the-luckiest contest where drivers traverse a figure-eight course, attempting to avoid oncoming cars as they pass through the eight's crossroads. The race, which virtually guarantees several crashes, was a big draw for the track, as it broadened its fan base. LMS also targeted family entertainment, featuring a playground for children and a clown named Dipstick. Vertrees was selected the 1995 Promoter of the Year by a national panel of auto-racing promoters.

In addition to sportsman stock-car racing, the track has also capitalized on a variety of promotional events such as truck rallies, bomber cars, midgets, late models, open-cockpit, and open-wheel sprint cars. LMS has also hosted several NASCAR-sponsored races, including the 1998 Kroger 225, part of the NASCAR Craftsman Truck Series with a purse of more than $335,000, and the Slim Jim All-Pro circuit.

LMS has also featured some of the best-known names in auto racing, including Darrell Waltrip, Bill Elliot, Terry Labonte, Ernie Irvan, Cale Yarborough, and Richard Childress. Local stars at LMS include the Kimmel brothers—Frank and Bill Junior—Tony Stewart, Scot Walters, Keith Gardner, and Chuck Winders. In 1994 LMS hosted the first victory of a championship-points feature race by a woman, Debbie Bartley. In 1996 Bartley became the first woman to win a NASCAR-sanctioned Winston Racing Series event, also at LMS.

In 1998 Stilger and Vertrees sold controlling interest in LMS for $5 million to Carroll Properties Inc., an investment group headed by Jerry Carroll, a northern Kentucky real-estate developer, who was planning a $132 million, one-and-one-half-mile super-speedway project in Kentucky's Gallatin County designed to attract NASCAR's prestigious Winston Cup Series.

The first Louisville Speedway was built by a group of Louisville investors in 1925 and opened for the 1926 racing season. Located on Dixie Hwy. just south of St. Helens (SHIVELY), the track was to be host to four major race meets annually on "Decoration Day," the Fourth of July, Labor Day, and the season-opening meet in April. According to the *COURIER-JOURNAL*, the track, which featured a sixty-five-hundred-seat grandstand, was designed for track records, safety, and convenience to Louisville, and was to host competitions between some of the most famous drivers in the country.

From 1931 until 1980 auto racing took place at the Fairgrounds Motor Speedway, a three-eighths-mile paved track operating during the summer months.

See *Courier-Journal*, Nov. 1, 1925, April 6, 1988, Aug. 27, 1998.

LOUISVILLE MUNICIPAL COLLEGE. The Louisville Municipal College, a liberal arts college for AFRICAN AMERICANS, enrolled its first students on February 9, 1931. Raymond A. Kent, then president of the UNIVERSITY OF LOUISVILLE, selected Rufus Early Clement as dean of the new institution, which was a division of the university. The school was located at Seventh and Kentucky Streets on property previously occupied by SIMMONS UNIVERSITY, which had closed in 1930.

Louisville Municipal was the result of a demand by a coalition of leading black taxpayers and white supporters that the city make provision for higher education for blacks. After defeating a bond issue in 1920, a second bond issue was passed in 1925 that set aside one hundred thousand dollars for African American higher education. The school was one of three such liberal arts colleges for blacks established in the United States at that time, and it assumed the role that Simmons University had once played as the principal institution for blacks in the city. The University of Louisville desegregated on the graduate level in June 1950 and on the undergraduate level in 1951. In April 1950, the University Board of Trustees voted to close Municipal and terminate its faculty and staff when desegregation occurred. After a bitter controversy, Municipal staff and nontenured faculty received severance pay. Three of the four tenured faculty—Dr. William Bright, Dr. George D. Wilson, and Dr. Henry Wilson—received assistance in securing jobs at other universities. The remaining Municipal faculty member, Dr. C.H. Parrish Jr., became the first African American faculty member on the main campus of the university when he joined the Department of Sociology in 1951.

See George D. Wilson, *A Century of Negro Education in Louisville* (Louisville 1986); Lawrence H. Williams, *Black Higher Education in Kentucky 1879–1930* (New York 1987).

Nettie Oliver

LOUISVILLE NATIONAL MEDICAL COLLEGE. Louisville National Medical College was a medical school that trained 150 African American doctors from 1888 to 1912. It was established by Dr. HENRY FITZBUTLER, a black graduate of the University of Michigan medical school who moved to Louisville in 1872 to establish his practice. On April 24, 1888, Fitzbutler and three other black doctors, Rufus Conrad, W.A. Burney, and W.O. Vance, received a state charter to operate the college. It was incorporated that year by the Kentucky General Assembly.

The college began in the United Brothers of Friendship Hall at Ninth and Magazine but moved to larger facilities on Green (Liberty) between First and Second Streets. In 1891 it awarded the first Doctor of Medicine degree to a Kentucky woman. In 1896 the college had been accredited as a four-year medical college and operated a twelve-room training hospital.

By 1897 the college enrolled fifty-four students from ten states and Jamaica. However, the tuition payments from these students were not enough to keep the college operating. In 1907 the college merged with State University (later called SIMMONS UNIVERSITY) in Louisville. On April 29, 1912, the university closed LNMC, and its hospital became the NURSING department of Simmons University.

See Alvin Fayette Lewis, *History of Higher Education in Kentucky* (Washington, D.C., 1899); Leslie Hanawalt, "Henry Fitzbutler: Detroit's First Black Medical Student," *Detroit in Perspective* 1 (Winter 1973): 126–40.

John A. Hardin

LOUISVILLE NATURE CENTER. The Louisville Nature Center is a place for environmental learning and community involvement located on the forty-one-acre BEARGRASS CREEK State Nature Preserve adjacent to JOE CREASON Park. The center provides classes to students and opportunities for the public to observe the more than 160 species of BIRDS; 180 species of trees, shrubs, and wildflowers; and the Louisville crayfish, an endangered species that lives in the urban forest. The Nature Center maintains the preserve through an agreement with the Kentucky State Nature Preserves Commission. A wetlands located on the preserve is part of an ongoing wetlands/watershed study. The center also serves as headquarters for a BEARGRASS CREEK study that works with the Metropolitan Sewer District, the city of Louisville, and other civic organizations to find solutions to the degradation of the creek's aquatic and riparian habitat. Also located on the site are remains of two-thousand-year-old Adena Indian homesteads and other pioneer homestead sites.

Gail Ritchie Henson

LOUISVILLE ORCHESTRA. Symphonic music in Louisville can be traced back to 1822 when the Society of St. Cecilia formed the first symphony orchestra, composed of musicians from several German Catholic churches. Other amateur and semiprofessional efforts followed, including the Louisville Philharmonic Society, founded by LOUIS HAST in 1866; the Louisville Symphony; the Philharmonic Society; the first Louisville Civic Orchestra; and the YMHA (Young Men's Hebrew Association) Orchestra, which has survived to the present day as the Jewish Community Center Orchestra.

Following the 1937 Ohio River flood, which halted all artistic endeavors in mid-season, the Civic Arts Association was in disarray and faced a substantial deficit. In the midst of that turmoil, however, the group's new president, Dann C. Byck Sr., engaged Robert S. Whitney, a young composer/conductor from Chicago, to establish the city's first professional orchestra.

The fifty-four paid musicians of the newly formed Louisville Civic Orchestra performed their first concert in the Memorial Auditorium on November 2, 1937. The orchestra rapidly grew to over seventy musicians, but the advent of WORLD WAR II brought unanticipated changes in personnel. Some of the musicians in the ensemble, by then known as the Louisville Philharmonic Orchestra, went off to war, to be replaced by musician-soldiers from nearby FORT KNOX.

The period following the war brought programming that has continued to define the orchestra's mission. Whitney expanded the "Making Music" children's concerts, which he had started in 1941, and in 1947 the orchestra inaugurated its statewide touring schedule. In 1948 Whitney and board president Mayor Charles P. Farnsley began formulating the orchestra's emphasis on commissioning and performing new compositions by twentieth-century composers. Those world premieres, many performed in Columbia Auditorium on Fourth St. during the late 1940s and early 1950s, eventually established the ensemble as "the world's busiest performer of new music," according to *Time* magazine (January 1955).

That mission sustained the orchestra during the 1950s and 1960s. In 1950 the newly renamed Louisville Orchestra was near bankruptcy when it premiered William Schuman's *Judith, A Choreographic Poem*, choreographed and danced by Martha Graham. The piece was a critical sensation and propelled the orchestra into national prominence, resulting in a Carnegie Hall performance with Graham on December 29, 1950.

In 1953 the Rockefeller Foundation acknowledged the orchestra's position in contemporary music by awarding it an unprecedented five-hundred-thousand-dollar grant to commission forty-six new compositions per year and issue a recording featuring these new works each month during a four-year period. The resulting flood of performances of works from composers all around the world, including Aaron Copland, Virgil Thomson, Paul Hindemith, Darius Milhaud, Lukas Foss, and Joaquin Rodrigo, prompted the orchestra to create its own recording label, First Edition Records. In many instances, the composers came to Louisville for the premiere of their compositions.

The Louisville Orchestra's reputation brought many prestigious performance opportunities. Prominent guest conductors, including Igor Stravinsky and Arthur Fiedler, enthusiastically accepted invitations to conduct the orchestra. In 1959 the U.S. State Department selected Louisville as a host city for a politically sensitive tour of Russian composers and music historians headed by Dmitri Shostakovich and Dmitri Kabalevsky. Then, in 1965, the Louisville Orchestra was the only orchestra chosen to perform in the White House Festival of the Arts in Washington, D.C., because of its "devotion to the music of American composers."

After thirty years at the orchestra's helm, Whitney retired in 1967. Under his successor, Jorge Mester, the orchestra performed 4 times at the Inter-American Music Festival in Washington's Kennedy Center, and he recorded more than 133 premiere performances on First Edition Records. Akiro Endo, who was appointed conductor in 1979, led the group on its first international tour with two weeks of concerts in Mexico City.

In 1981 the musicians went on strike. Picketing in formal attire, they won, for the first time, full-time status and full-time pay. Lawrence Leighton Smith was appointed music director in 1983. His tenure began with the move from the Macauley Theatre, the orchestra's home since 1962, into Robert S. Whitney Hall in the new Kentucky Center for the Arts. During its fiftieth anniversary year, the orchestra commemorated its commitment to contemporary music with Sound Celebration, a contemporary music festival featuring composers, critics, and musicians from around the world. Under Smith's direction this Grammy-nominated orchestra performed again at Carnegie Hall, and in 1990 at the Kennedy Center in Washington, D.C., for the national conference of the American Symphony Orchestra League. Smith continued to expand the orchestra's recording catalog with music by such twentieth-century notables as Gunther Schuller, John Corigliano, Joan Tower, Karel Husa, Ellen Taafee Zwilich, and Witold Lutoslawski.

Before Smith's resignation in 1995, the orchestra received its fifteenth American Society of Composers, Authors and Publishers (ASCAP) Award for adventuresome programming of contemporary music, giving it the distinction of winning more ASCAP awards than any other orchestra in the United States.

In 1995 Spaniard Max Bragado-Darman was appointed the orchestra's fifth music director, followed by Uriel Segal in 1999. Segal had been named the orchestra's first principal guest conductor in 1995. A native of Israel, Segal is conductor laureate of the Osaka (Japan) Central Orchestra, which he founded in 1991. As of 1999, under Segal's leadership, a resurgence in the "Making Music" program developed to great success in the Jefferson County Public School System, returning to Robert Whitney's original goal of making education a central part of the orchestra's mission.

See Robert Whitney papers and Louisville Orchestra records, University Archives and Records Center, University of Louisville; *Courier-Journal*, Jan. 26, 1999.

Clarita Whitney

LOUISVILLE PALACE THEATRE. At 10 A.M. on the morning of September 1, 1928, the Loew's State Theater at 625 S Fourth St. opened with a thirty-five minute program by Jan Garber and his stage band, followed by organist Haden Read, who accompanied an audience sing-along on the one thousand-pipe Wurlitzer THEATER organ. After a Fox Movietone Newsreel of current events, the silver screen was filled with the Metro-Goldwyn-Mayer comedy *Excess Baggage*, starring William Haines.

John Eberson, famed architect of many picture palaces, designed the L-shaped theater on the former site of St. Joseph's Infirmary at a cost of $1.2 million. The theater was designed in a lavish Spanish Baroque Revival style with fountains, statues, and tapestries calculated to transport the moviegoer to an imaginary place. Adding to the illusion, floating clouds and twinkling electric stars were set in a make-believe sky. In the foyer the "Ceiling of Celebrities" contained 141 medallion faces of famous men (including Eberson).

In 1954 the name was changed to United Artists Theatre, but it was popularly known as the Loew's. In 1963 the balcony was sealed off to accommodate the addition of the Penthouse Theater. With the decline of the downtown area and the POPULATION move to the SUBURBS in the 1970s, the movie theater closed in 1978. In August of that year, John J. Siegel Jr. and his Detroit partner, Maurice Kane, bought the building to be remodeled as a nightclub theater called the Louisville Palace. During the renovation, Siegel had a duplicate face of Shakespeare removed from the ceiling in the foyer and replaced with a likeness of himself.

After a successful opening on November 19, 1981, the theater drew large audiences for several years, but labor disputes and perpetual financial troubles caused the Palace to close in 1985. Siegel filed for bankruptcy in 1991, and controlling interest passed to principals of Sunshine Theatre, Inc. of Indianapolis. Siegel remained a minority partner. The Palace Theatre, along with its neighboring bar, Stage Door Johnnies, reopened June 29, 1994. However, burdened by a $4.8 million debt and sued by the state of Kentucky for back taxes, the Palace was ordered sold by a bankruptcy judge. At an auction on December 18, 1996, Fine Host Corp. of Connecticut bought the theater for $1.8 million.

On June 3, 1997, a four-alarm fire in the Electric Building just north of the Palace threatened to spread to the theater, but quick work by the LOUISVILLE FIRE DEPARTMENT limited the major damage to the Electric Building.

In January 1998 a group headed by theater-management professionals Brad Broecker of Louisville and David Anderson of Houston signed a lease to manage the Palace for the owners, Fine Host Corp. The group changed the name "Palace Theatre" to "Louisville Palace." On June 26, hoping to recapture some of FOURTH Street's golden years, the Palace began showing the first of fourteen vintage films. Beginning with the *Gold Diggers of 1935*, starring Dick Powell and Gloria Stuart (of the famed 1997 movie, *Titanic*), the series ran until September 7, when *Singing in the Rain* closed the festival.

The managers, under the name Palace Theatre Operating Group, bought the theater in December 1998 for $1.3 million. Included in the sale was the adjacent Stage Door Johnnies bar and restaurant, which was renamed the Palace Restaurant. The new owners also planned a wider variety of shows that included Broadway and cabaret-style entertainment.

See the *Courier-Journal* September 2, 1928; August 14, 1978; August 20, 1978; December 19, 1996; April 11, 1998; December 16, 1998; the *Louisville Times Scene* January 16, 1982; James Nold Jr., "The People's Palace," *Louisville* 42 (January 1991): 34-39; Rachel Kamuf, "A Royal Purchase," *Business First* 13 (November 18, 1996): 1.

Robert Bruce French

LOUISVILLE PANTHERS. On October 13, 1995, the Louisville RiverFrogs took the ice for the first time after the ownership of the Louisville Redbirds BASEBALL club had decided in 1994 to bring another sport to Louisville—a hockey team.

Louisville had hockey from 1990–94, with the Louisville IceHawks of the East Coast Hockey League(ECHL). The owner of the IceHawks then relocated the team to Jacksonville, Florida. After a one-year void the owners of the Redbirds brought the ECHL back to Louisville.

Prior to the IceHawks' brief stint, Louisville hosted several professional hockey teams during the 1940s and 1950s. The Louisville Blades of the International League was the city's first professional team, playing in the 1948–49 season and winning the pennant. The success of the Blades led the team to the higher-classified United States League in 1949. The team, which was known as both the Blades and the Stars during its brief tenure in the U.S. League, finished in the bottom half of the standings in 1949–50 and quickly folded. The Stars were revived during the 1953–54 season as part of the International Hockey League, but that club folded in mid-season. In 1957 the Louisville Rebels of the International Hockey League played, but, while the team was a success on the ice, it never enjoyed financial success. The team was taken over by the IHL in 1960 after the Louisville owners declared bankruptcy. In the mid-1970s the Louisville Blades returned as an amateur team, playing in CLARKSVILLE, INDIANA. There were also two attempts to bring professional hockey back to the city in 1977 and 1983, but problems with financing thwarted those efforts.

The city was awarded an expansion franchise for the 1995–96 season to join the then-twenty-three-team ECHL. Louisville joined the north division, along with Columbus, Erie, Toledo, Huntington, Wheeling, Dayton, and Johnstown. The name RiverFrogs was developed by vice president of sales Greg Galiette. The thought was that it could be marketed creatively and enjoyed by children of all ages.

Former National Hockey League (NHL) player Warren Young returned to Louisville to coach the RiverFrogs. Young also coached the Louisville IceHawks during every year of their existence.

The RiverFrogs opened their inaugural season against the Erie Panthers. The Frogs won in a 2–0 shutout by goaltender Alain Morissette. It was just the start of what would be an amazing first season for the Frogs and Morissette. Young and his RiverFrogs went on to a 39–24–7 record and a third-place finish in the North Division. Morissette won twenty-four games and was named the ECHL Goaltender of the Year. The RiverFrogs also enjoyed success at the box office. The Frogs sold out nine games in the final three months of the season.

Entertainment went with hockey. Broadbent Arena was called "The Swamp." Airship Froggie, a twenty-foot-long indoor blimp shaped like a frog, flew around the arena during intermission. The team skated onto the ice with a music and laser-light show. There were crazy chants, contests on the ice, and, of course, hockey. In the second season, the Frogs management added an improved laser-light show and a frog-shaped tunnel from which RiverFrogs players emerged during introductions.

Coach Young returned to the helm, but many players from the first season did not. With only six players returning, the team struggled to a 29–31–10 record. The team started 0–10–3—the worst start in ECHL history—but then a savior arrived. Young made a trade with the Richmond Renegades for goaltender Sandy Allan. Allan posted a 19–13–4 record with Louisville and almost led the team to the postseason. The Frogs missed making the playoffs by just six points (or three wins).

The RiverFrogs were affiliated in the second season, signing NHL agreements with the San Jose Sharks and New York Islanders and an American Hockey League affiliation with the Kentucky Thoroughblades of Lexington.

In March 1998 the owners of the RiverFrogs sold the team to a Miami partnership that relocated the team, renamed the Matadors, to southern Florida. This purchase cleared the way for the anticipated relocation of an International Hockey League or an American Hockey League team to FREEDOM HALL for the 1998–99 season. However, lease negotiations with the KENTUCKY STATE FAIR and Exposition Center postponed the transfer. In December 1998 an American Hockey League franchise signed a ten-year contract to play in Louisville at Freedom Hall starting in October 1999. The team, called the Louisville Panthers, is a feeder club for the parent organization, the National Hockey League's Florida Panthers.

Shawn H. Howe

LOUISVILLE PLATFORM. Economic and political turmoil in Europe caused immigration to increase sharply in Louisville during the 1840s, with the largest ethnic groups being the IRISH and the GERMANS, the latter being the larger. The German Forty-Eighters were often well-educated, liberal, radical leaders of the unsuccessful German revolution of 1848. They were politically oriented social reformers who brought with them sophisticated political ideas. Louisville became the national headquarters of a group called the Bund Freier Manner (League of Free Men), who were anticlerical, contemptuous of Puritan American culture, and very politically active. They offended both native-born Americans and pious German Catholics. In March of 1854 Karl Heinzen, along with other radical Germans, forged the Louisville Platform, which they hoped to be the foundation of a new political party.

The Louisville Platform bluntly stated what was wrong with the United States and contained twelve points addressed to "All true Republicans of the Union." It proposed an alliance between the liberal German element and progressive Americans "for the purpose of carrying into full effect these grand principles of the Declaration of Independence." Considered radical at the time, it advocated progressive ideas such as the abolition of slavery, direct elections, and equality between men and women. Germans who advocated such radical measures constituted a very small minority of the total POPULATION of the German immigration.

First published in German in the *Louisville Anzeiger,* it was also printed in English and was published in roughly thirty NEWSPAPERS around the country. The platform was formally endorsed by organizations of "free Germans" in Boston, Cincinnati, Indianapolis, and San Antonio. It was criticized by papers throughout the country such as the *Texas State Gazette,* which denounced it as "propaganda to undermine and uproot our institutions and laws, RELIGION and its ministers."

Historically considered a significant document in American political history in general and in German-American history in particular, the platform's main significance in Louisville was the backlash it created against foreigners. The influx of immigrants who came into the city in the late 1840s tended to join the DEMOCRATIC PARTY, threatening the dominance of the WHIG PARTY. At the same time, the Whig Party was torn over the slavery-extension issue, and many Whigs joined the American or Know-Nothing Party, which was both anti-foreigner and anti-Catholic. The Louisville Platform fanned the fear that immigrants threatened both Protestantism and democracy. To the nativists, the document was a flagrant example of the dangerous doctrines that immigrants imported to America. It incensed Louisville nativists and fueled the violent fires of Know-Nothingism that contributed to the BLOODY MONDAY riot on August 6, 1855, when at least twenty-two persons were killed, mostly German and Irish immigrants.

Principal Platform points

1. Slavery should be abolished.

2. Every religious coercion is illegal. That includes Sunday laws, thanksgiving days, the prayers in Congress and the legislatures, the oath on the Bible, the introduction of the Bible into free public schools, and the exclusion of atheists from judicial acts. These are a violation of human rights and the Constitution, and the platform demands their abrogation. The recognition of the Roman hierarchy standing under a foreign potentate is declared anti-republic and very dangerous to its existence. Every Roman priest and every Catholic obeying them is a subject of the pope and that the pope, "this murderer of a republic," must be a natural enemy of the American. Every Catholic is obligated, on the salvation of his soul, to overthrow the Constitution of the United States, if the

pope orders.

3. There should be measures for the welfare of the people. Included are release of public lands to cultivators and support of poor colonists for the first settling, promotion of immigration, and creation of a special department of colonization and immigration, to facilitate the getting of citizenship. Also proposed was liberation of "the working poor from the money interests, gaining from it, whereby the state must eventually function as arbitrator of all colliding interests. The work time should never last longer than ten hours. Since the work is the creator of property, the law of inheritance must be modified in such a way that a not-working money or land aristocracy becomes impossible."

4. Make changes and additions to the federal Constitution and those of the states:

a. All elections without exception proceed directly from the people.

b. Each eligible citizen of each state can be elected by the citizens of each other state as member of Congress and also each eligible citizen of each county by the citizens of each other county as member of the state legislature.

c. Any elected official or civil servant can be terminated at any time, and can be replaced by someone else.

5. Free trade should be established.

6. Public projects, such as RAILROADS, can be financed with federal money.

7. Foreign policy demands the giving up of the neutrality that has been in place until now, and demands a strong defense for the rights of the North American citizen and of those immigrants who declare their intention to become citizens, especially since every North American represents a person of the revolution who is against the despotism of aristocratic regimes.

8. Women's rights demand equal standing of women and men because the Declaration of Independence states that all men are born with certain inalienable rights.

9. Equal standing of the free Colored with all people.

10. All criminals laws are for the betterment, not punishment of criminals, and therefore the death penalty is against a logical mind, and therefore barbaric.

11. Military laws demand the dispensation of military justice during peacetime since the soldier as an armed citizen of the republic only takes up arms for the defense of the land.

12. Laws (such as TEMPERANCE laws) should not interfere with the individual's right to privacy.

See Joseph Wandel, *The German Dimension of American History* (Chicago 1979); Carl Wittke, *Refugees of Revolution: The German Forty-Eighters in America* (Philadelphia 1952); George Yater, *Two Hundred Years at the Falls of the Ohio* (Louisville 1987); A.E. Zucker, *The Forty-Eighters, Political Refugees of the Revolution of 1848* (New York 1950).

LOUISVILLE POLICE DEPARTMENT. Louisville's first police officer was engaged on October 6, 1785, when the trustees hired a town crier, who, along with shouting the time and the weather, reported any unusual happenings during the night in the city's streets. An additional move toward law enforcement occurred in 1797. Problems in and around the harbor of Beargrass Creek at the foot of Fourth St. compelled the trustees to appoint a harbor master with police power over the harbor itself and three hundred feet of the creek that reached into the town.

Members of the Louisville Police Department pose in front of City Hall in 1889.

The first true police force was recognized in 1806 when the town's trustees officially designated five men as "police officers," although they were commonly known as watchmen. They were of equal rank and reported directly to the trustees. Six years later the city constructed a fourteen- by fifteen-foot building where the officers worked.

In 1821 the trustees, needing someone directly responsible for the prevention of crime and the capture of violators, appointed a captain of the watch. Aside from overseeing the other watchmen, the captain was responsible for other tasks such as administering punishments, measuring the depth from the seat to the "filth" in outhouses with a "honey stick," and helping with baby deliveries. That same year the trustees designated the town's first sergeant. His duty, while mostly administrative, was to see that the trustees' wishes were carried forth.

Two years after the switch to the mayor-city council form of GOVERNMENT, an 1830 ordinance eliminated the office of the captain of the watch and established the new elected position of marshal as the chief of the watchmen. When the city charter was revised again in 1851, the mayor was put in charge of the police force, the members of which were selected by the city council. Five years later an ordinance created the two-thousand-dollars-a-year office of the chief of police, whose explicit responsibility was the police department. The term of office was one year, but, because the chief was selected by the mayor, the City Council and BOARD OF ALDERMEN customarily retained the selection for the mayor's entire term. In 1857 the mayor and City Council began reorganizing the department, modeling it after a number of progressive police departments in the East, and the watchmen became known as "policemen."

During the CIVIL WAR, policing became very difficult for the local authorities, as the federal army virtually took over the community, especially when the Confederate army of Gen. Braxton Bragg threatened. In 1862 Gen. Jeremiah T. Boyle, military commandant of Kentucky, declared that for a forty-eight-hour period anyone who would not fight to protect the city from nearby Confederate forces must stay in his house or be shot.

In 1868, after years of refinements in the police force, the Kentucky General Assembly passed an act for the reorganization of the department. Additionally the jurisdiction of the force was expanded countywide, and early efforts were made to patrol the entire region. In an attempt to separate the government and the growing force, one part of the act stated that "the government of said City may not hereafter interfere with the Board of Police of the city of Louisville and Jefferson County." However, corruption continued to reign in the force. Because the officers were selected by the council, politics dictated the enforcement of the laws, and a political party change meant much of the force would have to start looking for another job.

A year later, the city was divided along Sixth St. into the eastern and western divisions, with a first lieutenant in charge of each. Moreover the city was divided into several districts, four during the day and seven at night. A second lieutenant was placed in charge of each district with a sergeant as his aide. Through the years there have been as many as eleven districts and as few as four.

Corruption continued to be a problem for the department, and, in his 1875 annual report to the mayor, the chief of police stated that "we are working under probably the worst system of any large city." Aside from the frequent turnover due to the process of electing the policemen, officers were frequently accused of manipulating elections, operating PROSTITUTION rings, and taking advantage of citizens. However, the report was ignored. Unfortunately, politics remained an integral part of the police force until the 1929 state Civil Service law prohibited political or religious discrimination. State law requires that the Civil Service Board consist of three members of each political party, with the mayor breaking any tie vote. While patrolmen are protected, only two chiefs have remained in office after a change in political administrations.

As improved and affordable bicycles began causing accidents and other traffic problems on downtown streets during 1891, the police department purchased its first bikes. Later bicycle squads along with mounted police patrolled all city streets. While this practice tapered off through the twentieth century, the use of bikes in the downtown area was reinstituted in 1993 as an efficient alternative to automobiles. The mounted police, phased out in 1937, were not reestablished.

Soon after the introduction of the bicycle, automobiles began to cause an even greater number of problems on the Louisville streets. In order to apprehend fast-moving lawbreakers in their horseless carriages, the police department acquired three Cadillacs in November 1908 at a cost of forty-two hundred dollars. The automobiles had four-cylinder, thirty-horsepower engines and could attain speeds of fifty-five miles an hour, although this speed was prohibited by a city ordinance. In October 1932 the Louisville Police Department became the fifth department in the nation with radio-dispatched police cars. A few years after the first cars were purchased, motorcycles were acquired. They were utilized until expensive repair costs forced the department to discontinue their use in 1984.

In 1919 George Ragsdale, a faculty member at Male High School, instituted the first professional training school for the police department, known as the Police School. He presided over and taught at the school until 1937. Many aspiring officers with little more than three to six years of education received a broad training at the institute. Later a high school education was required for admission to the force. Additional educational opportunities became available in 1950 when the University of Louisville created the Southern Police Institute. Directed by David A. McCandless, the institute taught courses in police organization and administration and pioneered special techniques in handling disorders and tense situations.

The 1920s witnessed many changes in the police department as women and AFRICAN AMERICANS began joining the ranks. On May 20, 1921, Mrs. Alice Dunlop became the first white female officer, and on March 22, 1922, Bertha Whedbee became the first African American female officer appointed. Although the females had the same authority as male officers, the women were restricted to patrolling dance halls, apprehending thieves in downtown department stores, working with children, and performing female body searches. They were allowed to work only with members of their own race.

Heads of the Louisville Police

Name	*Title*	*Years*
Michael Woolston	Captain of the Watch	1821
John Laveneder	Captain of the Watch	1822
Nathaniel Melvin	Captain of the Watch	May 12, 1822
Michael Woolston	Captain of the Watch	Mar. 4, 1823
George B. Morrison	Captain of the Watch	1823
Daniel Robinson	Captain of the Watch	Sept. 9, 1823
E. Lord	Captain of the Watch	1826
W.A. Lock	Marshal	1830
Fredrick Turner	Marshal	1831
James S. Speed	Marshal	1848
William A. Arnold	Marshal	1851
William C. Kidd	Marshal	1854
James Kirkpatrick	Chief of Police	Mar. 7, 1856
Jacob B. Enrich	Chief of Police	1858
William R. Ray	Chief of Police	1859–61
Henry Dent	Chief of Police	Mar. 1862–May 9, 1862
Charles L. Stancliff	Chief of Police	Jun. 26, 1862–?
Richard Priest	Chief of Police	Jun. 24, 1863–Nov. 30, 1865
Alexander Gilmore	Chief of Police	Dec. 1, 1865–Jun. 30, 1866
William Kaye	Chief of Police	Jul. 1, 1866–Nov. 30, 1866
Robert Gilchrist	Chief of Police	Dec. 1, 1866–1869
George Shadburne	Chief of Police	Jan. 1, 1870–?
Walsworth Jenkins	Chief of Police	Apr. 1870–Dec. 30, 1872
Albert W. Johnson	Chief of Police	Jan. 18, 1873–Dec. 31, 1875
I.W. Edwards	Chief of Police	Jan. 8, 1876–Jan. 17, 1879
John A. Weatherford	Chief of Police	Feb. 25, 1879–Dec. 20, 1882
Thomas A. Taylor	Chief of Police	Jan. 1, 1883–Jan. 3, 1885
John A. Whallen	Chief of Police	Jan. 8, 1885–Aug. 8, 1888
T.J. Woods	Chief of Police	Sept. 1888–Jan. 1, 1890
Thomas A. Taylor	Chief of Police	Jan. 6, 1890–Dec. 12, 1897
Jacob H. Haager	Chief of Police	Dec. 18, 1897–Dec. 18, 1901
Sebastian Gunter	Chief of Police	Dec. 18, 1901–Jul. 21, 1907
Jacob H. Haager	Chief of Police	Sept. 7, 1907–Nov. 16, 1909
H. Watson Lindsey	Chief of Police	Nov. 17, 1909–Nov. 14, 1917
Ludlow F. Petty	Chief of Police	Nov. 20, 1917–Jan. 16, 1922
Forest Braden	Chief of Police	Jan. 16, 1922–Nov. 10, 1925
Roy W. Easley	Chief of Police	Apr. 8, 1926–Jul. 15, 1927
Jacob H. Haager	Chief of Police	Jul. 17, 1927–Nov. 22, 1927
Roy W. Easley	Chief of Police	Nov. 22, 1927–Dec. 31, 1929
George M. Ratcliff	Chief of Police	Jan. 1, 1930–Dec. 1, 1933
Edward P. Callahan	Chief of Police	Jan. 22, 1934–Nov. 11, 1937
John Malley	Chief of Police	Nov. 17, 1937–Jul. 10, 1939
Edward P. Callahan	Chief of Police	Jan. 1, 1940–Dec. 31, 1941
	(Remained chief while on disability through Dec.)	
Arthur Kimberling	Chief of Police	Dec. 2, 1941–Jul. 18, 1946
Carl Heustis	Chief of Police	? 1946–Jun. 14, 1960
William Binder	Chief of Police	Jun. 1, 1960–Mar. 1, 1968
Bert Hawkins	Chief of Police	Feb. 26, 1967–Feb. 27, 1967
Columbus J. Hyde	Chief of Police	Apr. 1, 1968–Oct. 8, 1971
Edgar Paul	Chief of Police	Oct. 10, 1971–Jul. 7, 1974
John H. Nevin	Chief of Police	Jul. 7, 1974–Jul. 18, 1977
Jon Higgins	Chief of Police	Nov. 30, 1977–? 1981
Richard Dotson	Chief of Police	Jan. 5, 1981–Aug. 31, 1990
John E. Aubrey	Acting Chief of Police	Jul. 31, 1990–Nov. 30, 1990
Douglas Hamilton	Chief of Police	Nov. 30, 1990–Mar. 31, 1999
Eugene T. Sherrard	Chief of Police	Apr. 12, 1999–Mar. 2, 2000

In February 1938 Louisville's four policewomen were dismissed because, in the opinion of the chief of police and the safety director, there were no duties requiring a policewoman. However, one policewoman was appointed in 1943 and nine more during the next nine years. When four of the sixteen policewomen on the force sought permission to take the Sergeant Promotional Test in March 1965, they were advised by the chief that the "Civil Service rules state only patrolmen can take the test." In 1969 Urania "Kitty" Laun became the first female appointed sergeant. Two years later she was appointed lieutenant and became the first female commanding officer assigned to a district. Women have held every position in the force except for chief of police.

In 1923 Page C. Hemphill and William Woods became the first male African American officers on the force. They were hired as non-uniformed detectives but were allowed to patrol only African American NEIGHBORHOODS. Additional advances came more slowly, as African American and white officers would not ride in the same cruiser as partners until 1965. Similarly it was not until 1973 that official policy yielded the same opportunities and responsibilities to every officer regardless of race or gender. In 1989 a federal court ruled that the police department had met the requirements of a 1979 consent decree to increase minority hiring by having African Americans as 15 percent of the force. On November 25, 1933, Officer William Woods became the first African American killed in the line of duty. He was one of the eighty-eight officers who have died of an injury received while on duty as of 1999.

During the 1970s and 1980s, the police department witnessed several changes. After thirty years of centralization, the police department began decentralizing in 1974. The traffic and the detective bureaus remained in the Headquarters Building at Seventh and Jefferson Streets, while outlying branches were established as district houses. There were six district houses by 1998. Also during this time the city and county government began merging such responsibilities as the photo and fingerprint labs, the narcotics bureaus, and the crimes against children departments in order to make both departments more efficient and cost-effective.

In 1982 the Board of Aldermen passed an ordinance at the mayor's request that allowed the chief of police to be removed for specific causes. This law was later amended to allow the mayor to both appoint and remove the chief after Mayor Jerry Abramson demoted Chief Richard Dotson in 1990.

With violence on the rise during the mid-1990s, the Board of Aldermen increased the number of police officers and approved extended overtime hours during the summers to set up checkpoints in high-crime areas. In 1998 the city budgeted for 716 officers.

Number of Homicides in Louisville (1950–99)

Year	Homicides	Year	Homicides
1950	54	1963	50
1951	45	1964	49
1952	44	1965	55
1953	41	1966	41
1954	41	1967	60
1955	40	1968	71
1956	34	1969	90
1957	31	1970	89
1958	36	1971	97
1959	43	1972	88
1960	42	1973	91
1961	43	1974	92
1962	42	1975	82
1976	82	1988	26
1977	66	1989	32
1978	61	1990	42
1979	70	1991	46
1980	69	1992	44
1981	57	1993	41
1982	44	1994	51
1983	54	1995	46
1984	42	1996	68
1985	32	1997	68
1986	41	1998	42
1987	45	1999	41

Police Departments in the Louisville Metropolitan Area

Kentucky

City of Anchorage Police Department
City of Audubon Park Police Department
City of Graymoor-Devondale Police Department
Douglass Hills Police Department
City of Hillview Police Department
Hollow Creek Police Department
Indian Hills Cherokee Police Department
Indian Hills/Rolling Fields Police Department
Jefferson County Police Department
City of Jeffersontown Police Department
Kentucky State Police
LaGrange Police Department
City of Louisville Police Department
Meadowvale Police Department
City of Minor Lane Heights Police Department
Oldham County Police Department
Plantation Police Department
City of Prospect Police Department
Rolling Hills Police Department
City of St. Matthews Police Department
City of Shelbyville Police Department
City of Shively Police Department
City of West Buechel Police Department
City of West Point Police Department
Westwood Police Department

Southern Indiana

Austin Police Department
Charlestown Police Department
Town of Clarksville Police Department
City of Jeffersonville Police Department
City of New Albany Police Department
City of Scottsburg Police Department
Town of Sellersburg Police Department
Pekin Police Department

Morton O. Childress

Fifth District Police Station at Clay and St. Catherine Streets, 1907.

LOUISVILLE PRESBYTERIAN THEOLOGICAL SEMINARY. The seminary (LPTS) originated in Danville, Kentucky, in 1853, when the synods of the old West and Southwest sought to establish a seminary in their region. (This was the more conservative, predominantly southern, Old School Presbyterian church.) The seminary thrived in its early years only to suffer a severe setback with the onset of the CIVIL WAR. After the Civil War the denomination—and the seminary—united with the New School church to form the predominantly northern Presbyterian Church in the U.S.A. The seminary never recovered from the exigencies of the war years, in part because of its location in Kentucky. The year 1870 found only six students enrolled, and for a period in the 1880s there was only one professor, after which faculty from Centre College in Danville taught at the seminary. The seminary struggled along until 1901.

As Danville maintained its tenuous existence, the majority of PRESBYTERIANS in Kentucky, who eventually joined the Presbyterian Church in the U.S. (a denomination within the bounds of the former Confederacy), sought a seminary of their own. With strong support from Louisville Presbyterians, the LPTS opened in 1893 in Sunday school rooms provided by SECOND PRESBYTERIAN CHURCH at Second and BROADWAY. Students were housed in rented rooms near the church. There were thirty-one students and six professors when the school opened. James H. Taylor, class of 1897, was Woodrow Wilson's pastor during his presidency and preached his funeral service. As was common at the time, most of the faculty were denominational leaders who had been ministers of large, wealthy churches and sometimes had taught in college. Francis R. Beattie, professor of theology, was the lone teacher with a Ph.D.

Despite the financial panic of 1893, the seminary opened with just over $104,000 in endowments. Louisville Presbyterians were key supporters of the project. Attorney Bennett Young, virtually bankrupted by the depression, sacrificially mortgaged some property to pledge twenty-five hundred dollars. W.N. Haldeman, owner of the *COURIER-JOURNAL*, gave ten thousand dollars and soon purchased the Barrett mansion at First and Broadway and donated it to the seminary. The large antebellum home provided classrooms and some dormitory space in 1895.

W.T. Grant served as the treasurer of the seminary from its opening until 1901; he and his wife left their entire estate of three hundred thousand dollars to the school and helped make possible the erection of the Gothic-style campus where the Barrett home had stood. The most important event in the seminary's early years came in 1901 when the Louisville Seminary merged with the seminary in Danville. The new entity was named the Presbyterian Theological Seminary of Kentucky (the name reverted to LPTS in 1928). The new seminary was the lone institutional connection between the two major Presbyterian denominations—the Presbyterian Church in the U.S.A. and the Presbyterian Church in the U.S.—that had divided during the Civil War. Although unable to effect a reunion, the seminary in Louisville played a key role in the twentieth century as a bridge between the two churches. Faculty, students, and board members were drawn from each denomination.

The Louisville community—particularly Presbyterians—supported the seminary, and LPTS sought to return that commitment. Professors regularly taught Sunday school, preached in area churches, and offered leadership in other ways. At least two Louisville Presbyterian churches, Meadowview and Bardstown Road, grew out of the work of seminary students. The social concern of the seminary manifested itself in 1898 when, responding to a plea for evangelical work among Louisville's African American community, a group of students organized a mission site on Preston St.

John Little took the lead in this work and in a second mission begun in the SMOKETOWN area south of Broadway. He remained with what came to be known as the Little Mission for almost fifty years (it later became the PRESBYTERIAN COMMUNITY CENTER). Prominent Louisville women, including Louise Speed and Lucy Belknap, volunteered in the mission. Another LPTS graduate, Richard Anderson, founded the Wayside Christian Mission. During WORLD WAR I, with the student body reduced, soldiers were housed in seminary rooms. The seminary also believed it was important to keep abreast of new needs in church work, and in 1915 added courses in Christian sociology, Christian ethics, religious education, and Christian missions.

In the seminary's early years there was no president; the chairman of the faculty assumed the necessary administrative responsibilities. In 1910 faculty member Charles Hemphill was named the first president of the seminary and served until 1920. John Vander Meulen succeeded him until 1928, followed by John R. Cunningham until 1936. That same year Frank Caldwell was called to be president; he would serve the seminary and the church until 1964.

In 1936 when the nation was still struggling out of the Depression, expenditures were outdistancing income by a wide margin despite heroic efforts at ECONOMY. Still, Caldwell managed to keep the seminary open; finances improved with the coming of WORLD WAR II. The FLOOD OF 1937 submerged the seminary's basement, and flood refugees were housed in the seminary, many sleeping in the chapel. In 1941, attempting to meet the needs of rural churches, the Todd-Dickey Rural Training Parish was organized under the leadership of Louisville graduate C. Morton Hanna. Hanna supervised students working in the twelve congregations that constituted the parish. The seminary soon realized this was not just an opportunity for students to earn money to help meet expenses but a chance for real field education, a laboratory experience for applying classroom knowledge.

Plans in the late 1950s to construct Interstate 65 within ten feet of the seminary building prompted a move from downtown. In 1928 land had been deeded to the seminary on Cannons Ln., and plans were made to move the seminary there, literally moving the Gothic structure. When it was learned that Interstate 64 construction would bisect the Cannons Ln. location, land was purchased on Alta Vista Rd. and new buildings erected. (The old downtown building now houses JEFFERSON COMMUNITY COLLEGE.) The seminary moved to its new location in 1963.

Upon Caldwell's retirement, Albert Curry Winn became president in 1965. He was succeeded as president by C. Ellis Nelson, who served from 1974 to 1981. The years following 1981, with John M. Mulder as president have been intensively active. The long-awaited reunion of the two largest Presbyterian denominations took place in 1983, and plans were made to relocate the national offices of the new church out of Atlanta and New York.

In an effort that involved both the seminary community and key people in the city, Louisville was chosen as the site—thanks in part to a gift of the old Belknap Building from Presbyterian David A. Jones, as the downtown location for the Presbyterian offices. On the same day that news came of Louisville's selection, LPTS negotiated the purchase of the GARDENCOURT estate adjacent to the seminary grounds. The integrity of the home was maintained in renovations; and the gardens, designed by the sons of Frederick Law Olmsted, were restored to their original plan.

During the 1990s, the seminary launched two new ventures aimed at church renewal. The Louisville Institute was created in 1990. It is a Lilly Endowment program for the study of American religion, based at the Louisville Seminary. With funds supplied by Lilly, the Louisville Institute provides support for a wide range of research and leadership education programs throughout the U.S. Through 1998, it has made $6.6 million in grants to more than 450 individuals and institutions. The Center for Congregations and Family Ministries was established in 1996. Through conferences, seminars, and other programs, the center strives to strengthen congregations in their ministries with families. The center also publishes a journal, *Family Ministry: Empowering through Faith*.

See I.S. McElroy, *The Louisville Presbyterian Theological Seminary* (Charlotte, N.C., 1929); Robert Stuart Saunders, *History of Louisville Presbyterian Theological Seminary, 1853–1953* (Louisville 1953).

Rick L. Nutt

LOUISVILLE PRONUNCIATION. Unlike many city names, that of Louisville has been open to various pronunciations depending on the era and, to some extent, place. Indeed, an old vaudeville joke went, "How do you pronounce the capital of Kentucky? Frankfort." There are two current pronunciations of the name Louisville: Louie-ville and Lou-a-vul. Both are heard in about equal measure and frequently one follows in close succession to the other on radio and TELEVISION BROADCASTING when announcers change. A certain tension exists between the proponents of each pronunciation. Louie-ville seems to be the earlier (and tends to be the pronunciation of older natives), but Lou-a-vul began rapidly gaining ground in the 1970s, heralded by bumper stickers proclaiming "I love Low-ah-vil" or "I Love Lou-a-vul." Indeed, newcomers (particularly radio and television personalities) are usually instructed that the latter is the "correct" pronunciation.

The origin of the Lou-a-vul pronunciation

is difficult, probably impossible, to pinpoint; but after the CIVIL WAR when manufacturing began to dominate the local ECONOMY, rural Kentuckians swarmed into the city to take industrial jobs, to drive the newly introduced mule cars, or to join the police force or fire department. They may have brought the Lou-a-vul pronunciation with them. For example, Eddyville in western Kentucky is pronounced Ed-a-vul, and Perryville in the Bluegrass Region is often called Perry-vul. In any event, this variant pronunciation has been in use for many years by some Louisvillians. In 1934 a street directory of the city felt obliged to note that the city "was named in honor of Louis XVI of France, and is, therefore, properly pronounced Loo-y-ville."

The earliest pronunciation, however, was neither of the above, but Lewisville, with the usual English pronunciation of Louis, as in St. Louis. GEORGE ROGERS CLARK, the city's traditional founder, spelled it Lewisville; and the spelling is found sporadically in deeds and deed books until about 1850, indicating that the pronunciation persisted. Some dictionaries cite Lou-a-vul as southern, but the towns of Louisville in Georgia and Alabama are pronounced Louie-ville; and in Mississippi it is Lewisville. Obviously, it is not southern but seems to be a Kentucky way of speaking.

George H. Yater

LOUISVILLE PUBLIC ADVERTISER. Louisville's first daily newspaper began publishing on June 23, 1818, as a weekly newspaper. It became a biweekly on January 27, 1819, and a daily on April 4, 1826. The paper, housed at the northwest corner of Third and MAIN Streets, was founded by SHADRACK PENN JR., who moved from Maryland to Kentucky as a boy. Penn became the dominant editorial voice in the state for a number of years. The paper soon rivaled Ben Casseday's *Western Courier*. Casseday later admitted that Penn was "an experienced politician, a forcible writer, and a man of extraordinary tact." During Kentucky's relief crisis of 1819–23, Penn, an anti-relief partisan, denounced the New Court and the idea of a Commonwealth Bank.

In 1828 Penn was offered a cabinet post by President-elect Andrew Jackson (1829–37), which he declined, preferring to make his voice heard through the vehicle of the press rather than through public office. The *Advertiser's* editorials were short, with very few local items, but its selections and letters to the paper were frequently long, the latter being chiefly political and generally marked with acrimony. With the coming of the steamboat, Louisville was in an ideal location to become the top commercial city in the state. Penn attracted attention to the city's advantages as a business port. The *Advertiser* saw its dominance challenged in 1830 by a new newspaper, the *Louisville Daily Journal*, edited by George D. Prentice, a staunch Whig. Provoked by Penn's open denunciation of Prentice, the two men engaged in editorial warfare for over a decade. Prentice's wit and humor won out, and Penn bowed out of the battle. He moved to St. Louis in 1841, where he began the *Reporter*, ending the twenty-three-year life of the *Louisville Public Advertiser*.

See Herndon J. Evans, *The Newspaper Press in Kentucky* (Lexington 1976); J. Stoddard Johnston, ed., *A Memorial History of Louisville* (Chicago 1896); Donald B. Towles, *The Press of Kentucky, 1787–1994* (Frankfort 1994).

LOUISVILLE PUBLIC WAREHOUSE COMPANY. A storage company founded in Louisville in 1884 to serve the needs of the railroad and steamship commercial shipping business. Originally created for storage of ironwork, wagons, furniture, cement products, leather goods, and TOBACCO, the company moved into bonded warehousing for whiskey as Louisville's spirits industry expanded. Its slogan, "Storage of every description—special warehouse for household effects—U.S. Bonded custom warehouse for importations," reflected the prosperity of the shipping ECONOMY of nineteenth-century Louisville.

Located first on MAIN St., in 1889 LPW moved to a large brick warehouse at Brook and Main built for general merchandise, while four warehouses at Brook and Washington were constructed specifically for customs, revenue, and shipments from Bremen, Germany. In 1891 the company boasted $150,000 in capital and was served by rail lines directly into their facilities.

The company's operations are now based at 4500 Progress Blvd., with warehouses in Louisville and southern Indiana and facilities in Houston, Dallas, Las Vegas, Phoenix, Atlanta, and Lakeland, Florida. The Louisville facilities offer more than 2 million square feet of storage space.

In 1952 the company was acquired by the Karp family. After James Karp became CEO in 1967, the business ceased storing whiskey and tobacco and began specializing in medical products storage and transportation. A wholly owned subsidiary, Medical Distribution Inc., was founded in 1986. It deals in medical disposables and equipment and also distributes blood for the American Red Cross. The company is also the owner and developer of America Place, an industrial park located in JEFFERSONVILLE, INDIANA.

LOUISVILLE RADIO BROADCASTERS ASSOCIATION. The association began in July 1976 as the Louisville Area Radio Stations, a trade association representing all of the radio stations in the Louisville market. The original purposes of the organization were to provide for the exchange of ideas and information beneficial to the operation of member stations, serve as a medium through which cooperative public service efforts could be undertaken, promote the use of radio as an ADVERTISING medium, encourage the maintenance of the highest standards of radio BROADCASTING, and encourage, promote, and foster better relations and understanding between the member stations and the general public.

Membership is open to any radio station licensed within the Louisville metropolitan area, including noncommercial stations, which have taken an active role in the association from its earliest days. The organization has had close to 100 percent participation from eligible stations since its inception. All stations have an equal vote in decisions. Each station designates one management-level employee as its official representative. Officers are elected annually. The first two presidents were Ernie Gudridge of WKLO and Jim Caldwell of WAVE.

One of the first undertakings of the group was establishment of a monthly revenue reporting system whereby each station reports its monthly revenue figures to an independent source. A monthly report is issued to each station, showing total amount of radio advertising in the market.

In the mid-1980s the name of the organization was changed to the Louisville Radio Broadcasters Association. It has been referred to since as the LRBA. Another significant development occurred in January 1993 when the group hired its first paid executive director, Louisa Henson. Initially the major source of funding for the association's activities was annual dues paid by members. However, since the mid-1980s the group's main revenue comes from noncommercial sustaining announcement programs.

Ed Henson

LOUISVILLE RIVERBATS. The Louisville RiverBats BASEBALL club is the latest chapter in the tradition of professional baseball teams in the city. Louisville lost the Colonels in 1972 when the team moved to Pawtucket, Rhode Island. The city went nine years without a baseball team. But in 1981 Louisville banker Dan Ulmer headed a group dedicated to obtaining an American Association club. A. Ray Smith, a native Texan who made his fortune in construction, bought the Tulsa, Oklahoma, club in 1961 and operated there until 1977. The team, which was the Triple-A affiliate of the St. Louis Cardinals, then moved to New Orleans and operated there for just one year before moving to Springfield, Illinois. On October 5, 1981, Ulmer's group introduced Smith as the man who was bringing a baseball team to Louisville. Smith was a hands-on owner who often walked through the stands and visited with fans. Under his leadership the Redbirds thrived, reaching unprecedented attendence records. He left the Redbirds in May 1987 to accept a job in St. Petersburg, Florida. Smith died in June 1999.

Ulmer's group raised $4.5 million for construction and renovation at Fairgrounds Stadium. There was a hurry-up project to get all of this done before April 17, 1982, when the Louisville Redbirds, as the RiverBats were known from 1982–98, began play. A crowd of 19,632 showed up that night to witness the Redbirds' first home game, a 7–4 loss to Iowa in the newly renamed Cardinal Stadium.

Soon after that first season began, it became apparent that Louisville was on track to break the minor-league single-season attendance mark of 670,563 set by the San Francisco Seals of the Pacific Coast League in 1946. On August 8 of the first season, the record fell. By August 29 and the end of the season, the new record was 868,418—passing the old mark by nearly 200,000.

The Redbirds then drew 1,052,438 fans in 1983, becoming the first minor-league team to ever surpass the million-fan mark. Louisville's per-game attendance that season of 16,191 exceeded that of five major-league clubs, including the Cincinnati Reds.

In 1982, Joe Frazier, former manager of the New York Mets, became the first manager of the Redbirds. Jim Fregosi took over in 1983 and was named AAA Manager of the Year. In 1984 Fregosi managed the team to the American Association championship. Vince Coleman stole 101 bases that season, a minor-league record. Fans of the Redbirds saw such great players as Lance Johnson, Todd Zeile, Joe Magrane, Jose Uribe, Ray Lankford, Brian Jordan, Todd Worrell, Tom Pagnozzi, Vince Coleman, Terry Pendleton, and Willie McGee. All went on to help the St. Louis Cardinals, parent organization of the Redbirds, or played on other big-league teams.

In 1986 Fregosi left to manage the Chicago White Sox of the American League, and the Redbirds sank to last in the American Association's Eastern Division. But the Redbirds continued to pull in the fans (660,200), leading all minor-league teams in attendance for the fifth consecutive year. Fregosi was succeeded by Dave Bialas in 1986, Mike Jorgensen from 1987–89, Gaylen Pitts in 1990, Mark Dejohn in 1991, Jack Krol in 1992–93, Joe Pettini from 1994 to 1996, Pitts again in 1997, Gary Allenson, 1998–1999, and Dave Miley, 2000. After the 1986 season, Ulmer persuaded Smith to sell the team to a group of Louisville investors for upwards of $4 million. Ulmer became chairman of the board.

Ulmer and his partners would have to wait almost ten years for the Redbirds to win a championship under their ownership. In 1995 Joe Pettini led a group of overachievers to the association crown. Ulmer and his partners announced in 1997 that a new baseball park (Louisville Slugger Field) would be built in downtown Louisville in an attempt to rekindle interest. In another change the Redbirds broke their longstanding relationship with the St. Louis Cardinals in September 1997 and announced a new affiliation with the Milwaukee Brewers. The team changed its name the following year to the RiverBats.

In 1998, the Redbirds' attendance dipped to 409,853, sixteenth among Triple-A teams and twenty-sixth among minor-league clubs.

Following the 1999 season, the Riverbats again announced an affiliation change when they became the Triple-A affiliate for the Cincinnati Reds. On April 12, 2000, Louisville Slugger Field opened to begin a new chapter of Louisville baseball in the twenty-first century.

Shawn H. Howe

LOUISVILLE RIVERWALK. On October 31, 1996, the dedication ceremony was held at Shawnee Park for the official opening of RiverWalk, a 6.9-mile walking path that runs along the OHIO RIVER from Fourth St. to Chickasaw Park. The walkway is paved and ranges from eight to ten feet wide. It is open to walkers, runners, in-line skaters, and bicyclists, and provides a beautiful view of the Ohio River, which is seldom more than 150 feet away. The RiverWalk provides great views of the Portland Canal, the Falls Fountain, and the McAlpine Locks and Dam. One stretch that is particularly attractive is between Thirty-first St. and Shawnee Park, a heavily wooded area that offers glimpses of the river and ends at the picturesque lily pond in the park. Three overlooks offer views of the river. Embedded in the asphalt walk at several points are groups of pavers reflecting different historical themes, names of local Native American tribes, and types of boats the plied the river. Developers of the walk added benches, distance markers every one-tenth of a mile, and markers showing water levels of the 1937 flood.

The RiverWalk was a project of the Louisville Waterfront Development Corp.'s plan to "reclaim Louisville's Waterfront." Funded completely by the city, the walk cost $3.5 million. The lead consultant was the firm of Wallace, Roberts, and Todd; and the contractor was Mac Construction and Excavating. Some discussion took place over naming the walk. Aldermen suggested naming it after Dr. Martin Luther King Jr. or for Shippingport Island near PORTLAND. Eventually, it was simply named the Louisville RiverWalk.

See *Courier-Journal*, July 10, 1996, Oct. 4, 1996, Oct. 11, 1996.

LOUISVILLE SCHOOL OF ART. The Louisville School of Art was a four-year professional college of art offering a bachelor of fine arts degree. Although the name was not adopted until 1968, its history went back to 1929 when Fayette Barnum, Morris Belknap Jr., Arthur Allen, Maud Ainslie, and members of the Louisville Handicraft Guild founded the Art Center. The name "Art Center" was chosen in the hope that all the arts would soon be assembled under one entity and would all work together.

The Art Center, first located in a three-story building at 125 E Jacob St., sought to promote local art and to provide art education for qualified young people. The school offered classes in drawing, PAINTING, SCULPTURE, CERAMICS, textile design, woodcarving, printmaking, PHOTOGRAPHY, and jewelry; it later added free art sessions for children. All classes were taught in a workshop method, which insured maximum contact of students and teachers combined with freedom of experimentation. In addition to art classes, courses in the humanities and art history were offered. Several years later the little gallery in the Art Center building opened for exhibitions and sale of works by members and students. The Art Center School was sustained by membership dues, tuition, fees, grants, and gifts from patrons.

In 1935 the Art Center School and the UNIVERSITY OF LOUISVILLE began to exchange students. Two years later the University of Louisville established a fine arts department offering classes in art history and art appreciation, but studio work of the department was held at the Art Center School, making it possible for students to major in art. Art history classes were taught by distinguished professors such as Dr. Richard Krantheimer and Dr. Justus Bier. Nationally renowned Romuald Kraus of the Cincinnati Art Academy taught sculpture. In 1939 the Art Center and its school moved closer to the university at 2111 S First St. The affiliation between the two schools ended in 1959 when the university developed its own creative department—the Allen R. Hite Art Institute.

In 1968 the Art Center changed its name to the Louisville School of Art; and the following year, because of the small office, studio, and storage spaces, it moved from the First St. building to 100 Park Rd. in suburban ANCHORAGE. While the school attempted to raise more money, get more publicity, and develop a greater involvement in community life, growing financial demands and its move to the SUBURBS began slowly to create a losing situation. In 1974 the school was separately incorporated because of the growing schism between those who wanted only professional school programs and others who were more interested in activities directed to the community. After incorporation, the Louisville School of Art was able to survive for another nine years.

In 1981, in an effort to gain accessibility and visibility, the Louisville School of Art sold the building in Anchorage and moved to the Cloister, former site of the Ursuline Academy, at 800 E Chestnut St. The downtown location did not help to solve the school's growing problems—escalating maintenance dues, increasing fees, and decreasing enrollments. In 1983 the Louisville School of Art closed and merged with the Department of Fine Arts at the University of Louisville.

LOUISVILLE SCIENCE CENTER. The Louisville Science Center, a nonprofit educational institution, strives to improve people's understanding of mathematics, science, and technology with interactive exhibits and programs. When founded in 1871 as part of the Public Library System of Kentucky, located on Fourth St. between Walnut (Muhammad Ali Blvd.) and

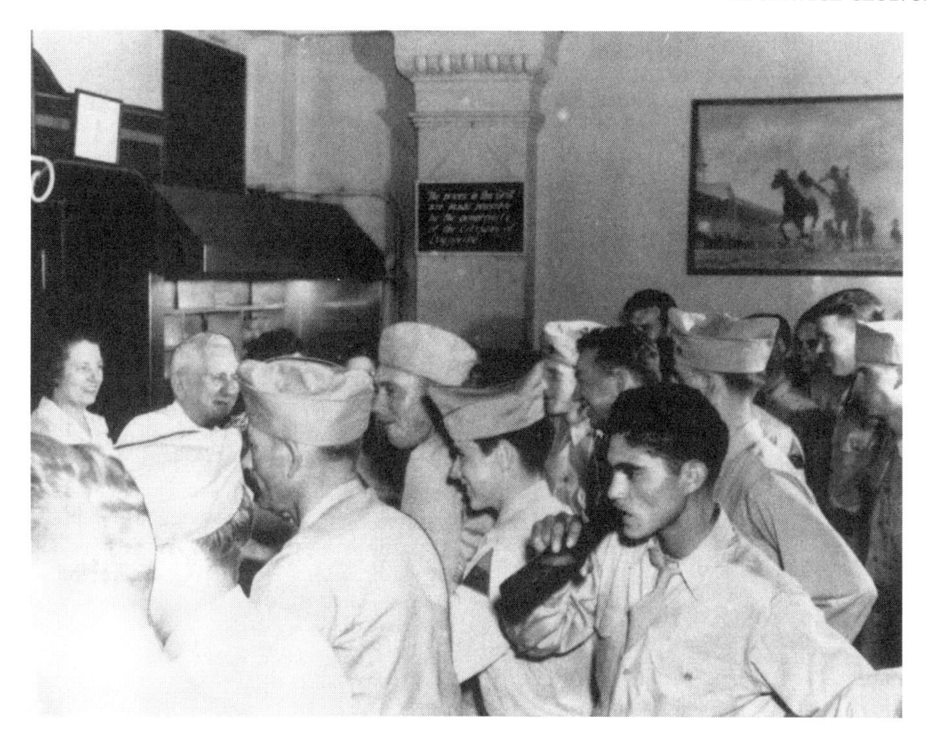

Snack Bar at Louisville Service Club, 1940s.

Green (Liberty) Streets, it was named the Natural History Museum. It began as a traditional "cabinet of curiosities" (*The Louisville Science Center Handbook*, 5–6). The museum's first acquisition was a fifteen-thousand-piece mineral collection.

The Polytechnic Institute, founded in 1876, was located in the same building. A predecessor of the LOUISVILLE FREE PUBLIC LIBRARY, the institute took over the museum when the Public Library of Kentucky closed in 1878 because of low funds. In the years leading up to 1908, the Polytechnic Institute moved several times to different buildings, and the museum accompanied the organization to its various locations.

When the Louisville Free Public Library was established at Fourth and YORK Streets in 1908, the museum was moved to the basement of the new building. In 1957, with an expanded collection, the museum moved its headquarters to Fifth and York Streets in the former Monsarrat School. In 1965 a six-hundred-thousand-dollar city of Louisville bond issue was passed to construct a permanent home for the museum. In 1975 the city purchased a nineteenth-century limestone and cast-iron warehouse building at 727 W MAIN St. It was originally built for Carter Brothers, a wholesale dry goods firm, in 1878 and enlarged in 1901 and 1907. When the museum moved into the building in July 1977, it was renamed the Museum of Natural History and Science. Because it was then operated by the city of Louisville, the third and fourth floors functioned as city offices. The renovated building, designed by the architectural firm of Louis and Henry, won several national design awards for the preservation and adaptive reuse of an old building.

In 1985 the museum became a nonprofit organization. A board of directors was named to oversee the museum, and the name was shortened to the Museum of History and Science. The board established a long-range strategic plan calling for a 40,000-square-foot renovation for additional exhibit galleries and a collections storage area, as well as a 230–seat IMAX Theater with a 4-story screen and 100,000-watt digital surround-sound system. These improvements and the addition were completed in 1988.

In 1992 an emphasis was placed on establishing permanent exhibits, and from this new mission grew three new exhibits, collectively called "Worlds of Wonder." "The World We Create," designed by the exhibit display firm of Ralph Appelbaum Associates and opened in 1997, illustrates the influence of mathematics and science on daily living. "The World Within Us" and "The World Around Us" will be opened by 2001.

Among the many additional permanent exhibits are a Space Science Gallery that houses items from the Apollo and Gemini missions, a thirty-four-hundred-year-old mummy in a simulated tomb, a multidiscipline exhibit on the unique and complex characteristics of the human hand, and exhibits involving earth science, physics, mathematics, and biology. There is interaction for children with presentations and hands-on experiments with staff members and volunteers. An interactive video conference room connects the science center to hundreds of sites throughout Kentucky with the Kentucky TeleLinking Network.

In 1994 the name was changed to the Louisville Science Center to emphasize its new mission of becoming a superior, hands-on science center.

Hope L. Hollenbeck

LOUISVILLE SERVICE CLUB/ UNITED SERVICE ORGANIZATION (USO). Early in WORLD WAR II, after France fell to the German army in 1940, President Franklin Roosevelt called for a massive mobilization of military personnel to bolster the nation's defenses and to prepare itself for war. In Louisville, the Curtiss-Wright Aircraft Co. built a production facility for its military transport aircraft at BOWMAN FIELD. In Charlestown, Indiana, the Indiana Ordnance Plant began to turn out huge quantities of smokeless gunpowder. Nearby FORT KNOX became the home of a newly formed division of mechanized infantry.

In August 1940 Louisville city leaders and civic officials voiced concern over the number of servicemen who would be flooding into the area. With support from future mayor ANDREW BROADDUS, chairman of the Louisville Defense Council, the Louisville Welfare and Recreation Center Committee was formed to address the problem of what to do with the soldiers. The Columbia Auditorium at 824 S Fourth St. was under the control of the Liberty National Bank and Trust Co. Originally built by the Knights of Columbus as their meeting hall, the auditorium had been vacant for some time. The city of Louisville purchased the building for $207,000 in October 1940 to use as a soldier's recreation center. Under a special agreement, the city leased the auditorium to the recreation committee at a low-enough rate that the committee could pay the mortgage and maintain a low operating cost.

On March 7, 1941, nine full months before the Japanese attack on Pearl Harbor, the Louisville Service Club opened its doors. At the time the club was the only one of its kind in the nation. The national United Service Organization (USO) would use the Louisville Service Club as a model when it began opening clubs around the nation in April 1941. The goal of the Service Club was not only to give the GIs a place to stay while on weekend leave but to provide entertainment as well. Nationally known bands such as Tommy Dorsey's and performer Jimmy Durante were among the acts.

Staff volunteers came from all walks of life. In the early days of World War II, local young women volunteered to be hostesses of the regular Friday night dances. Under the direction of Elizabeth A. Wilson, the women underwent a careful screening process. Only those between the ages of eighteen and twenty-five, unmarried, and not divorced could be a hostess. Girls under the age of eighteen could serve punch and food at the dances as junior hostesses.

Drawing on the community, the Service Club boomed. Between 1941 and 1946, the club saw thousands of young soldiers pass through its doors. In one thirty-hour period during the war, over forty thousand men in uniform came through the club's front doors. The numbers were so large that the club had problems housing the men overnight. With funds from a $160,000 federal grant, the Service Club remodeled the Monsarrat School at Fifth and York Streets to provide additional sleeping facilities. When they were complete, the new quarters could house eighteen hundred servicemen. During the war the club operated twenty-four hours a day and on weekends.

After the war, although the numbers of soldiers dropped significantly, the Service Club continued to expand. In 1950 a first club for African American servicemen was opened in the Brock Building at Ninth and Magazine Streets. In the late 1950s weekend activities took place at the JEWISH COMMUNITY CENTER on Dutchmans Ln. In 1963, just as the United States began military buildup for Vietnam, the Service Club moved its headquarters from Fourth St. to the YWCA building in the former Henry Clay Hotel at Third and Chestnut Streets.

In 1966 the Louisville Service Club announced that it would merge with the national USO and become a formal member of its national group of clubs. The facility at Ninth and Magazine was closed; and the new club, renamed the Louisville Service Club/USO, saw over five thousand visitors a month. By 1974, as the U.S. military faced considerable downsizing, the club had stopped its Friday night dances and set up a much smaller facility that included a reading room and a "rap" room where servicemen and servicewomen could discuss the topics of the day.

In the late 1990s the Louisville Service Club/USO modified its mission to fit the needs of the modern soldier. Since the days of rail and bus transports were long gone, the club moved to the flight deck of the LOUISVILLE INTERNATIONAL AIRPORT. Its goal was not to entertain but, rather, to aid in the soldier's travel from post to post. Although the mission of the Louisville Service Club has been modified over the years, the basic idea has not. The Service Club has been a shining example of the community's support for the armed forces personnel who have served the country.

See George Yater, *Two Hundred Years at the Falls of the Ohio* (Louisville 1987); *Courier-Journal,* May 30, 1946, Sept. 1, 1963, April 22, 1966, Sept. 22, 1974.

Joe Wayne Roberts

Ted Williams inspecting Louisville Slugger "rough-outs" in 1942. This photograph by Stern Bramson has been recreated as a diorama at the Louisville Slugger Museum. University of Louisville Photographic Archives: Royal Studio/Stern Bramson Collection R7222.

LOUISVILLE SLUGGER. John Andrew "Bud" Hillerich, an apprentice in his father's woodworking shop in Louisville, made the first Louisville Slugger BASEBALL bat in 1884 out of northern white ash, a sturdy but lightweight timber. It is the most famous product of its kind in the world.

According to company legend, the first Louisville Slugger bat was turned by Hillerich for Pete "The Old Gladiator" Browning in 1884. While playing hooky from work to see the city's professional team, the seventeen-year-old Hillerich saw Browning break his favorite bat. Supposedly, Bud jumped out of the stands and ran over to Browning, tugging on his sleeve to invite him down to his father's woodworking shop on First St. in downtown Louisville where Bud served as an apprentice. Perhaps humoring the young man, Browning accompanied him to the shop and watched Hillerich turn out a custom-made bat from a piece of white ash. The next day, Browning got three hits with his new bat, and an American sports icon was born.

Several baseball enthusiasts have questioned the veracity of the story. One of the earliest references to the company's origins was a 1914 *Louisville Herald* magazine story by Bruce Dudley, a sports editor and later president of the LOUISVILLE COLONELS and the American Association. Dudley interviewed BUD HILLERICH, who indicated that he had only carved a ring in a Browning bat to ensure hitting success for the superstitious slugger. The article, which made no mention of Browning receiving the first bat, claimed that the company gained fame for making bats after Bud showed a bat made by his father to minor-leaguer Gus Weyhing, who was working out with the Louisville professional team in 1884. Weyhing, who would later join the professional ranks, showed the bat to some of the members of the Louisville team, including Joe Gerhardt, Tom McLaughlin, and Monk Cline. They liked it so much they put in a request to Bud's father, J. Fred Hillerich, to make bats for the team. The elder Hillerich agreed only after extracting a promise from the players that they would request no more bats. Word about the quality of the bats spread, and soon players from other teams were requesting the Hillerich bats, as they were first called before receiving the moniker *Louisville Slugger* in the 1890s.

There is one other story about the origins of the first Louisville Slugger. In a 1937 interview for *Baseball Magazine*, seventy-seven-year-old Arlie Latham claimed that the first bat was made for him. Latham, a third baseman for the St. Louis Browns of the American Association, argued that he had broken a bat in Louisville in 1883 or 1884 and was unable to find another one. He stopped into the Hillerich wood-turning shop located near his hotel and asked J. Fred to have Bud turn a bat for him. The story is similar in many respects to the Browning story, which has been the official company line since 1939 when the head of HILLERICH & BRADSBY marketing first told the story to a trade publication. Latham's tale, considered as questionable as the Browning version, was buttressed by a 1942 letter in which Bud Hillerich verified the authenticity of Latham's story. Experts continue to debate the relative merits of each version.

In those early days, the bats were also called the "Falls City Slugger." In 1893 the brand name "Louisville Slugger" was first used. It was registered with the U.S. Trademark Office in 1894. The bat soon became popular with amateur ballplayers and members of the American Association. Eventually ballplayers from all over the country began to place orders with "J.F. Hillerich & Son" woodworking company.

In 1905 Honus Wagner, "The Flying Dutchman," of the Pittsburgh Pirates, became the first baseball player in history to sign a contract endorsing a bat. His autograph was branded on a bat, starting a trend that still exists. Ty Cobb signed with the company in 1908.

The success of the Louisville Slugger was due in part to the fact that amateur baseball players across the country could purchase the bat model of their favorite big-league player. In 1915 the Louisville Slugger first appeared in a youth-size model. In 1919 the company launched its first national advertising campaign. By 1923 more than one million Louisville Slugger bats were being sold each year. In 1927 Babe Ruth hit sixty home runs with his Model R43 Louisville Slugger bat, a record that stood until Roger Maris broke it in 1961 with a Louisville Slugger.

As of 1978, the Louisville Slugger name has also graced aluminum bats. In the late 1990s Louisville Slugger wood baseball bats still accounted for nearly 70 percent of all professional baseball use. The Louisville Slugger aluminum bat, as well as its wood counterpart, is available in adult baseball, youth baseball, and softball models. Professional baseball players still have their bats custom made at the Louisville Slugger wood bat manufacturing facility at 800 W Main St.

See *Louisville Herald*, Sept. 27, 1914.

Bill Williams

LOUISVILLE SLUGGER MUSEUM. The Louisville Slugger Museum, at 800 W MAIN St. in downtown Louisville, opened to the public on July 17, 1996. In its first year the new facility hosted over 230,000 visitors. The private museum, owned by HILLERICH AND BRADSBY CO., offers exhibits, displays, films, and factory tours. The museum celebrates the history of the LOUISVILLE SLUGGER BASEBALL bat and its relationship to professional baseball since 1884.

A fifteen-minute movie, *The Heart of the Game,* prepares the museum visitor for the museum itself. The museum offers a history of baseball as well as the Louisville Slugger bat and baseball in Louisville. Visitor-friendly exhibits and displays allow people to choose movies showing some of the greatest hitters in baseball history. A factory tour of the bat and golf facilities allows visitors to watch their favorite baseball players' Louisville Slugger baseball bats being made right before their eyes.

Bill Williams

LOUISVILLE SOUTHERN RAILROAD. Predecessors of this railroad envisioned a rail route from the Ohio Valley to southwest Virginia, and the earliest of its antecedents was chartered in March 1868 as the Louisville, Harrodsburg, & Virginia. No activity occurred until 1884, when, reorganized as the Louisville Southern (LS), the line commenced construction to Harrodsburg via SHELBYVILLE and Lawrenceburg. Impetus for the work also came from the Louisville, NEW ALBANY, & Chicago (LNA&C, later Monon), which hoped to reach the eastern Kentucky coalfields and compete with the Louisville & Nashville. Louisvillian Bennett H. Young, also president of the LNA&C between 1883 and 1884, became LS's top officer. Harrodsburg was reached in March l888, and a connection was made at nearby Burgin with the Cincinnati Southern's main line from Cincinnati to Danville, Somerset, and Chattanooga.

Later that year, the LS, intending to compete with L&N's parallel line to the Bluegrass, launched an extension from Lawrenceburg to Versailles and Lexington. It also acquired the Versailles & Midway Railroad, pushing tracks on to Georgetown. In 1889 the Chicago road (LNA&C) leased the LS, including the extension to Lexington, which was finished in August 1889. Service between Louisville and Lexington began in October 1889, with trains crossing the Kentucky River at Tyrone on a 1,625-foot-long steel trestle named "Young's High Bridge" after the LS's Young. In March 1890 the LNA&C's lease was dropped but was later picked up by the East Tennessee, Virginia, & Georgia, a Southern Railway System predecessor, which by then also leased the Cincinnati Southern. All came under formal control of Southern after 1894. In Louisville, the LS (and, later, Southern) used Kentucky & Indiana Bridge & Railroad Co. tracks and facilities, with its passenger trains terminating at Central Station at Seventh St. and the river. Its freight trains were handled at K&I's yard in the West End.

See David Morse, "History of the Louisville Southern," Bluegrass Railroad Museum newsletters, March–May 1994, Versailles, Ky.; Fairfax Harrison, *History of Legal Development of the Railroad System of the Southern Railway Company* (Washington, D.C., 1901); George W. Hilton, *Monon Route* (Berkeley, Calif., 1978)

Charles B. Castner

LOUISVILLE STONEWARE COMPANY. The Louisville Stoneware Co., founded in 1970 by John M. Robertson, formerly a ceramic engineer for American-Standard, a manufacturerer of bathroom fixtures, continues Louisville's rich stoneware tradition. Building on predecessors John Bauer Pottery and later the Louisville Pottery Co., its roots go back to 1879.

In 1905 S.O. Snyder bought John Bauer's pottery plant on Preston St. between Woodbine and Hill, which had been in the business of making pickle crocks and butter churns, and named it Louisville Pottery. Snyder moved the firm to 228 E Bloom St. in 1908. Red clay pots, collars for furnace pipes, pickling jars, and crocks bearing the "Cherokee Indian" insignia were manufactured. In 1936 John B. Taylor joined Louisville Pottery and served as its president from 1939 to 1970. In the 1930s and 1940s, the utilitarian line of products expanded to include colorful dinner pieces. Decorated dinnerware bore the trademark "Taylor Ceramics." At its peak, Louisville Pottery was the largest stoneware firm in the South, employing 125 people and manufacturing a line of about 300 items. In 1970 the URBAN RENEWAL Agency purchased the company's property, and Taylor sold the company's trademarks, molds, names, patterns, and equipment to John M. Robertson.

Robertson renamed his purchase the Louisville Stoneware Co., moved to 731 Brent St., and designed and built smaller, more efficient kilns. There the items are painted, glazed, and made durable by high firing. Norma Sydnor had a big impact on design patterns for more than twenty-five years. Artists continue to create some three thousand stylized items, handmade of clay that comes from the Clay City and Evansville, Indiana, area. Colorful dinnerware features fruit, flowers, birds, cats, gaggles of geese, precious pigs, Noah's Ark, and proverbs. Louisville Stoneware still produces one of its earliest patterns, the classic blue Cornflower, now named Bachelor Button.

Foreign competition for a wide variety of commodity items required innovation. New whimsical pieces including durable pet beds, character lamps, and birdhouses were created. Individualized Christmas ornaments and the ever-expanding official KENTUCKY DERBY items, started in 1973, are ordered nationally by retail customers from presidents of companies to presidents of the United States. In 1990 Robertson won the Small Business Administration's Kentucky Small Business Person of the Year award.

In March 1997 the company was bought by Christina Lee Brown, local preservationist and cofounder of the CATHEDRAL HERITAGE FOUNDATION, who recognized its value as a historic attraction for tourists as well as a commercial pottery. Robertson agreed to stay on as president. After Brown's arrival, a new feature, the paint-your-own-pottery section, was added. Customers were now able to go to the plant, choose an unfinished piece, decorate it with a personal design, and have their creation glazed in the firm's pottery kilns. Stressing to-order replicas, personal creations, and custom tableware has made custom designs the fastest-growing segment of the business.

In response to its flagging wholesale sales to upscale retailers and catalog companies, Louisville Stoneware expanded its Brent St. store and opened a second retail outlet in the Mall ST. MATTHEWS in 1998. The new location served upscale shoppers who had not visited the Brent St. store, and it served to showcase the Kentucky Heritage Collection that emphasized Louisville- and Kentucky-themed gifts such as replicas of nineteenth-century antiques.

See *Courier-Journal*, May 21, 1990, Sept. 19, 1996, March 13, 1997, Nov. 28, 1998.

Lynn Olympia

LOUISVILLE TIMES. The *Louisville Times* came into being on May 1, 1884, a four-page, eight-column afternoon newspaper created by *COURIER-JOURNAL* publisher WALTER HALDEMAN to compete with the *Evening Post*, which had long been an irritant. It was a "sister" newspaper to the *Courier-Journal*, giving Haldeman access to morning and evening readers.

From the outset, the *Times* had an advantage over the morning paper, covering breaking news with an immediacy and freshness not available the next day. The *Courier* was more heavily staffed and funded and won many prestigious awards, including PULITZER PRIZES, but the afternoon paper fulfilled an urban mission with verve and sauciness. The first editor, Emmet G. Logan, set the tone for the lifetime of the paper, which was bought from William, Isabel, and Bruce Haldeman and HENRY WATTERSON, along with the *Courier-Journal*, by Judge ROBERT WORTH BINGHAM in 1918–19.

The paper grew with the city and became more competitive with the *Courier*. Over the years it won plaudits on its own, including a Pulitzer for Robert York, the paper's political cartoonist from 1937 to 1974. It also had the nation's first media critic's column by Robert Schulman. Many of the paper's reporters won national recognition in larger markets, both in print and other media. Publisher BARRY BINGHAM Jr.'s famous remark, "The best thing *The Courier-Journal* has going for it is *The Louisville Times*" (*Louisville Times*, Feb. 14, 1987), adorned coffee mugs around the country.

As TELEVISION news encroached on the afternoon paper's turf, circulation dropped from 174,368 in 1965, its peak year, to 118,226 in 1987. The rivalry between the morning and afternoon papers continued to the end, although the staffs were merged in December 1985.

In the 1980s the Gannett company chain targeted the Louisville papers for takeover. The company, beset with the deep-seated resentments within the Bingham family, was vulnerable; and, to the dismay of many in the community, it was sold to Gannett in July 1986. The last issue of the *Louisville Times* was published February 14, 1987.

See *Louisville Times*, Feb. 14, 1987; David Leon Chandler and Mary Voelz Chandler, *The Binghams of Louisville* (New York 1987); James D. Squires, *Read All about It* (New York 1993); Isaac F. Marcosson, *"Marse Henry" A Biography of Henry Watterson* (New York 1951).

Mary Caldwell

LOUISVILLE TIN AND STOVE. Louisville Tin and Stove was incorporated in 1888 by J.B. Girdler, C.V. Edmonds, and C.L. Holmes as a tinware shop manufacturing stovepipes and tin utensils such as cream and lard cans. It was at 621 W MAIN St. By the turn of the century the company had evolved into a full-scale manufacturer and wholesaler of oil, wood, coal, and gasoline stoves, and in 1906 it added top-loaded iceboxes to the manufacturing line. It also sold hardware and household equipment that complemented the heaters and iceboxes. In support of the war effort, iceboxes were converted to powder boxes during WORLD WAR II.

The first foundry, located at Magazine St. between Sixteenth and Seventeenth Streets, was in operation by 1906 and was promoted as "the largest stove foundry in the South." Louisville Tin and Stove moved into its present three-hundred-thousand-square-foot facility at 737 S Thirteenth St. during the 1930s. In 1981 the wholesale operation was sold to allow the company to concentrate on manufacturing. In the 1990s the company manufactured Cozy gas heaters and, as a small sideline, Progress soft drink coolers for the bottling industry.

Craig R. Wilkie

LOUISVILLE TODAY. *Louisville Today* was a monthly magazine published in the Louisville area from 1976 until 1982. The magazine was founded by John Yarmuth, who later founded the *LOUISVILLE ECCENTRIC OBSERVER (LEO)* alternative newsweekly. Yarmuth was *Louisville Today's* first editor and only publisher.

Louisville Today was a glossy magazine sold on newsstands and by subscription. At its peak, the magazine had a paid circulation of approximately fifteen thousand.

The first two issues, October and November 1976, included the first in-depth interview with BARRY BINGHAM Jr., publisher of the *COURIER-JOURNAL*. In 1979 the magazine published the first public account of the dissension in the Bingham family that later led to the breakup of the Bingham media empire. The *Columbia Journalism Review* awarded *Louisville Today* a "Laurel" for a comprehensive article on erosion on the OHIO RIVER. Other notable articles included an examination of the prosecution in Cincinnati of *Hustler* magazine publisher Larry Flynt, a revealing profile of developer/actor Roger Davis, and several articles on local media.

Louisville Today's most popular annual feature was its "Best and Worst of Louisville Awards," which the magazine used to distinguish itself from *Louisville*, then a Chamber of Commerce publication, with which *Louisville Today* competed.

Louisville Today counted many successful writers and artists among its contributors, including Pulitzer Prize–winning playwright Marsha Norman, Alanna Nash, ABC radio correspondent John Winn Miller, and award-winning photographer John Ranard.

In 1978 *Louisville Today's* parent company purchased the *Manly Messenger*, a neighborhood newspaper serving the OLD LOUISVILLE neighborhood, and converted it into an alternative monthly publication, *City Paper*. It was discontinued in 1980, after having won several creative awards.

In 1981 Yarmuth agreed to sell *Louisville Today* to a group of investors. In fall 1981 the investors decided not to purchase the magazine, and Yarmuth closed the publication following the January 1982 issue.

John Yarmuth

LOUISVILLE TRUST COMPANY BUILDING. This Romanesque Revival building is at the southwest corner of Fifth and MARKET Streets in downtown Louisville. Completed in 1891, it is the city's finest commercial example still standing of the style most closely associated with the work of Boston architect Henry Hobson Richardson.

The architects, the Louisville firm of Maury and Dodd, created a seven-story pile of robust and lithic arches, punctuated by a corner tower. Original newspaper accounts noted the building's excellent workmanship and materials, inside and out, including polished granite columns, rusticated Ohio sandstone, and richly carved woodwork.

The Louisville Trust (United Kentucky Bank

after 1980) moved out in 1972 when the county purchased the building and moved in the police headquarters, driver's license bureau and other agencies. In 1985 the First Trust Restoration Partnership (a group of local investors) purchased the building from the county, spending $6 million on renovations. The building reopened in late 1986 as offices and a bank.

Douglas L. Stern

LOUISVILLE URBAN LEAGUE. As African Americans began migrating from rural areas to urban communities after the Civil War, they encountered an industrial world for which they were unprepared. In Louisville a group of progressive African American women became involved in the Big Brothers/Big Sisters program as a way of providing guidance and role models for African American children. They were joined by a group of African American and influential white men seeking to alleviate other problems within the black community.

In 1920 the Louisville Urban League emerged and became a member agency of the Community Chest. Incorporated in August 1921, it was initially known as the Urban League of Louisville for Social Service among Negroes, and as the Louisville Branch of the National Urban League, before becoming the Louisville Urban League. It was started with one thousand dollars raised at a public dinner. Elwood Street, serving as temporary chairman, appointed a five-person committee to create the framework for a local Urban League. Ehner S. Carter (1921–24) became the first executive secretary.

J.M. Ragland (1924–29) was the second executive secretary and J.A. Thomas, the third (1929–43). During these early years the league opened new opportunities in local businesses for African Americans, helped create two junior high schools for blacks, and coordinated an award-winning effort through Negro Health Week campaigns to improve the health of black families. Louisville Municipal College grew out of a bond issue led by the league during this period.

By the end of the term of Robert E. Black, fourth executive secretary (1943–46), African Americans held positions on the Municipal Housing Commission, the Louisville Free Public Library Board of Trustees, the defense council and subcommittee of the Louisville Postwar Planning Committee, and the mayor's interracial committee.

When Charles T. Steele assumed leadership of the league (1946–70), his title changed from executive secretary to executive director. During his tenure, former state representative Mae Street Kidd organized the Louisville Urban League Guild in 1948. It was the second guild formed in any of the affiliates nationwide. Guilds were organized as local information departments for the Urban League. Members identified particular areas of concern and aided the Central Organization in fund-raising and educational programs (always open to both sexes). In 1964 the league was the first agency in the Louisville area to develop and win a $210,000 Department of Labor grant for on-the-job training of disadvantaged workers. The grant, which preceded the National Urban League's involvement in on-the-job training, was a significant factor in integrating Louisville's nonunion workforce.

Under the leadership of Arthur M. Walters (1970–87), the Louisville Urban League became the first affiliate to select a female chairperson of the board, Thelma Clemmons. It created a personnel policy manual and an organization chart, with a job description for each function, which became a model for the National Urban League.

In the late 1970s the league established an affirmative action monitoring program directed to the downtown Galleria project, designed as part of the downtown revitalization effort. The project won one of five national awards based on the involvement of racial minorities and women in the workforce, the subcontractors, and the owned or operated businesses within the completed Galleria, as well as on the amount of money awarded to the project. Named an agent for affirmative action by the city of Louisville, the league held official status and negotiated with management and organized labor to include minorities in the Galleria project workforce. It instituted a pre-apprenticeship program permitting those involved to spend two nights a week learning a trade and the other three nights learning educational basics. This allowed unskilled workers to move to the skilled labor force while earning income during their training.

In 1985 the league relocated its headquarters to the entire third floor of Lyles Mall. Approval also was given to plan and implement a capital campaign to raise $1.2 million to purchase that space. Benjamin K. Richmond assumed leadership in June 1987 under the new title of president/CEO. His first responsibility was to revive the capital campaign. Having its own permanent location would be a first for an Urban League affiliate. Corporate Louisville contributed about 90 percent of the moneys needed.

Following construction of the new building (different from Lyles Mall) at 1535 W Broadway (at the corner of Sixteenth St.), the league purchased new state-of-the-art personal computer equipment and expanded its computer and office skills training program to include classes relating to telemarketing. From late 1989 to 1991, the league offered a Telemarketing Training Institute. Most graduates were hired to work in the telemarketing operation at Humana Inc. In 1992 the training curriculum was again expanded to include entry-level customer service skills for the retail and fast-food markets.

Attempting to avoid a local outbreak similar to the 1992 riots among young African Americans in Los Angeles, Louisville mayor Jerry Abramson assembled a group of African American civic leaders to discuss preventive measures. It was determined that employment assistance for young adults was needed. With support from the mayor and the city and in partnership with the local Private Industry Council, the league developed the Mayor's Urban Employment Program (MUEP), which primarily targeted at-risk African American males between ages sixteen and twenty-five. To guide them toward productive citizenship, these young men were given life skills training as well as other support services and were then found suitable employment.

In 1993 REBOUND Inc. (Rebuilding Our Urban Neighborhood Dwellings) was created to increase community development and neighborhood revitalization. REBOUND is a nonprofit, cooperative effort among the Louisville Urban League, the city of Louisville, and Main Street Realty, the private real estate firm of David A. Jones. Its goal was to build and sell ninety quality homes in the historic Russell neighborhood. REBOUND became one of the first single-family housing projects to act as a cornerstone in a neighborhood revitalization project involving diverse housing.

See George C. Wright, *Life Behind a Veil* (Baton Rouge 1985).

Hope L. Hollenbeck

LOUISVILLE VISUAL ART ASSOCIATION. On February 13, 1909, the Louisville Art Association was founded "to enhance the cultural life of the city" (Objectives of the Louisville Art Association, Minutes 1909–14). It was to go through many transformations and name changes before becoming the Louisville Visual Art Association. In 1910 the Louisville Artists League was formed to encourage and exhibit local artists, because the Louisville Art Association then emphasized New York talent. These two groups merged in 1920 and retained the Louisville Art Association name. In 1942 it merged with the Art Center, which had grown from the Handicraft Guild and became the Art Center Association.

In 1972 the Art Center Association held the first all-watercolor competition in the state of Kentucky. In 1978, in conjunction with the Hyatt Regency Corp. and the Speed Art Museum, it held the largest multimedia competition ever in Louisville.

In the 1980s when the organization moved its headquarters into the Water Tower, Louisville's original pumping station and a National Historic Landmark, it changed its name to the Water Tower Art Association. The riverfront Water Tower is located at the intersection of River Rd. and Zorn Ave., just off Interstate 71. TriArt sales and rental gallery was maintained in the Aegon Building until 2000. A Media Arts Center is located at Artopia on Shelbyville Rd. in St. Matthews.

In 1989 the Water Tower Art Association

The Louisville Water Company's pumping station on River Road, built in 1860. Circa 1875 photograph by Joseph Krementz.

merged with the Louisville Art Gallery to become the Louisville Visual Art Association, an organization dedicated to providing artist-oriented exhibition space and to being the foremost producer of professional art workshops and nonprofessional studio classes for Louisville.

In its mission "to foster an appreciation of today's visual art" and to remain a visual art advocate, the Louisville Visual Art Association, a non collecting organization, holds solo, group, competitive, or theme exhibitions on a six-week schedule. One of the exhibitions, the WATER TOWER Annual, was begun in 1910 by the Louisville Artists League "to encourage local artists and assure them an opportunity to exhibit" (compiled by Marian Lee Long, *Chronology of the Art Center Association*, 10). It also holds quarterly art classes, children's free art classes (begun in 1925) for talented and recommended youth, and open-door classes for special-needs constituents. Its Connections program places local artists in schools to work with teachers to establish a complete art experience.

Among the special events is the Art Auction, providing scholarships for student artists, which is held annually in cooperation with the Allen R. Hite Art Institute at the UNIVERSITY OF LOUISVILLE. The annual Boat Race Party is an official Derby Festival event.

The Media Arts Center in Artopia is a regional center for film and video, providing equipment use and multimedia training for a wide audience.

The Louisville Visual Art Association uses its own *Visual Art Review*, as well as area NEWSPAPERS and magazines, in an advocacy role for the visual arts, local artists, and the organization itself.

See Madeline Covi, Dorothy Kohnhorst Hodapp, Charlotte Price, *Tapestry of an Art Association, 1909–1984* (Louisville 1984).

Hope L. Hollenbeck

LOUISVILLE WATER COMPANY. Despite the abundant volume of OHIO RIVER water flowing past the city, Louisvillians did not have the benefit of piped-in water to homes, businesses, and manufacturing plants until 1860. Earlier attempts, beginning in the 1830s, to have the city construct a municipal waterworks were frustrated by citizen opposition. Water was easily obtainable from wells that tapped the aquifer that flows through the sandy soil under central Louisville, and residents were not inclined to pay for a commodity that was free of charge simply by sinking a well.

Not until the 1850s, after several devastating fires had caused enormous property losses, were Louisvillians finally convinced to expend public funds to create a waterworks. Even so, it took a spirited campaign to achieve that end. Under the prodding of Mayor JAMES SPEED, the Kentucky legislature in 1854 chartered a private corporation, the LOUISVILLE WATER CO., with the authority to raise capital through the sale of stock at one hundred dollars per share. But only fifty-one shares of stock found buyers, and it seemed that the project would fail again. An attempt to secure voter approval of purchase of stock by the city also failed.

A massive public-relations effort, stressing fire protection and promising to leave the corner pumps and their free water in place, finally won the day in 1856. The city purchased fifty-five hundred shares of stock to permit construction to begin. Again in 1859, when the work was nearly completed, another popular vote authorized city purchase of another twenty-two hundred shares. The city thus became almost the sole owner of a private corporation, with dividends paid to the municipality. Regular delivery of water began October 22, 1860.

The classic-style pumping station and its 169-foot-tall WATER TOWER, designed by chief engineer Theodore Scowden, were built along the river nearly two miles above the city. (In 1970 the American Water Works Association designated the station and tower a hydraulic engineering landmark, and in 1971 they were placed on the NATIONAL REGISTER OF HISTORIC PLACES.) The first reservoir was placed atop a nearby bluff. The twin steam pumping engines were constructed by the Roach and Long Foundry of Louisville. Although running water was now available through 26 miles of main, the vast majority of the original 512 customers were businesses of various kinds. Most homes continued to rely on wells or the corner pumps.

Water usage, however, rose in volume as manufacturing became a mainstay of Louisville's ECONOMY after the CIVIL WAR. By the early 1870s it was obvious that the original 7-million-gallon reservoir would soon be inadequate. Chief engineer CHARLES HERMANY, who had succeeded Theodore Scowden in 1861, chose CRESCENT HILL as the site of a new reservoir of 100 million gallons capacity, some fourteen times larger than the original reservoir. The Crescent Hill Reservoir was completed in 1879. To pump water to this new facility, it was necessary to make a deep, narrow cut through the river bluff for the pipelines. A road through the breach became Pipe Line Ave. and, later, Zorn Ave.

Hermany next turned his attention to removing the silt from the water, a problem shared by all communities that obtained water from inland rivers. In 1884 he began filtration experiments with the "slow" sand filters used in Europe. They were so slow and clogged so quickly on OHIO RIVER silt that they could not meet Louisville's increasing water demand. A "rapid" filter was needed. Hermany enlisted the aid of George Warren Fuller, father of sanitary engineering in the United States, who began his work in Louisville in 1895.

Armed with the results of his research, the company began the erection of the Crescent Hill Filtration Plant in 1897. But the high hopes for a quick solution to the silt problem were dashed. After many delays the first test on January 18, 1908 (the very day of Hermany's death), demonstrated that the goal had not been reached. Charles Warren Fuller was called into consultation again, and the changes he suggested finally produced the desired results. All the sand and mud that had discolored the city's water since 1860 had vanished, and eventually so did more than 99 percent of the bacteria. The authoritative volume, *Landmarks in Civil Engineering*, notes that "Everything that was learned in Louisville about sand filtration of turbid inland waters was eventually practiced in many other American cities and is now standard operation in municipal water purification." Many technical advances have been made since 1909, and Louisville water exceeds the strict standards of the Environmental Protection Agency in all categories.

The water distribution system had expanded as piped-in water became the residential norm and industrial use mounted. By 1920 there were 420 miles of distributing mains. New pumping capacity was added to the system from time to time to keep pace with demand. In 1928 the first electric pump was installed, a precursor to the demise of the giant steam-pumping engines by 1951. The Cardinal Hill Reservoir was completed in 1932, providing a capacity storage of 30 million gallons. Located on a hill south of IROQUOIS PARK, this additional reservoir helped provide water pressure to the growing southern and western parts of the city. It also provided a backup water source in case of pump outages.

The post–WORLD WAR II boom and the development of the new suburbia beyond the city limits posed problems for the water company. Owned by the city (the fifty-one private shares had been purchased in 1906), the company had seen the city as its area of primary responsibility and had extended its lines beyond the limits in only rare instances and special circumstances. Water users outside the city were charged 50 percent higher rates to help pay for the greater volume of water requiring treatment and the cost of booster stations to maintain pressure on longer lines.

In February 1959 the company called a halt to further extensions outside the city. But in July 1960 the Kentucky Public Service Commission ruled that municipally owned water companies must provide service within five miles of the city and that the benefited property owners must pay the full cost of the extension.

Then in 1963, when New Englander Horace Estey became the first non-Louisvillian to head the company, he took the position that Louisville was now part of a much larger metropolitan area, and the company must serve all of Jefferson County and perhaps beyond. Over the following years the company took over the various independent water districts in the county that had purchased water wholesale from the company. The once-parochial LOUISVILLE WATER CO. assumed a regional stance. To meet this expanded demand, a new riverside pumping plant and water-treatment facility was opened in 1977 in eastern Jefferson County near Harrods Creek.

By the mid-1990s the water distribution system had grown to nearly three thousand miles and the daily usage of water to 115 million gallons, plus reserve capacity to meet greater usage. The company is managed by a Board of Water Works with four members appointed by the mayor of Louisville and, because of expanded territory, two by the Jefferson County judge/executive.

In July 1998 the company headquarters moved from 435 S Third St., a location it had occupied since 1910, to the northwest corner of Third and Chestnut Streets. The new seventy-five-thousand-square-foot building, with a concrete and glass exterior, was designed by the Louis & Henry Group of Louisville, and the general contractor was Whittenberg Engineering and Construction Inc., also a local firm. Adjacent to the building is a 4-story, 240-space parking garage.

See George H. Yater, *Water Works: A History of the Louisville Water Company* (Louisville 1996); Charles Hermany, "The Louisville Water Works," *Memorial History of Louisville* (Chicago 1896), vol. 1: 344–52; Daniel L. Schodek, "The Louisville Waterworks," *Landmarks in American Civil Engineering* (Cambridge, Mass., 1987), 235–36; *Courier-Journal*, July 19, 1998.

George H. Yater

LOUISVILLE YOUTH ORCHESTRA. The Louisville Youth Orchestra, originally the Academy Youth Orchestra, began in September 1958 as the outgrowth of a summer program sponsored by the Louisville Academy of Music at 505 W Ormsby Ave. Rubin Sher, orchestra director at DU PONT MANUAL HIGH SCHOOL, was the conductor. William H. Sloane, faculty member, was assistant, and Robert B. French, the academy's president, was manager.

In 1960 the orchestra became independent and changed its name to the Louisville-Jefferson County Youth Orchestra, the name it holds again today, although over the years various names have been used. By 1962 the orchestra had grown too large to function as a single unit. It was divided into two groups, the advanced orchestra under Rubin Sher and the preparatory orchestra led by Renato Mastropaolo. A third group, the youth string orchestra, was created in 1972 and conducted by Eleanor Ritchie.

All three groups, now named the Symphony, Repertory, and Concert Orchestras, perform regularly in Louisville; the Symphony Orchestra has also performed in Chicago, Pittsburgh, Nashville, Buffalo, and Lausanne, Switzerland, where it had the honor of opening the Third International Festival of Youth Orchestras in 1971. They have premiered works by local and national composers and had guest conductors (Robert Whitney, Jorge Mester, and Karl Haas, among others) as well as soloists such as Lee Luvisi, Leon Rapier, and Miriam Fried.

Throughout its history the Louisville Youth Orchestra has had three permanent music directors: Rubin Sher (1958–75), Daniel Spurlock (1975–94), and Jim Bates (1996–).

See *Courier-Journal,* July 6, 1958, Nov. 16, 1975, May 19, 1968, March 3, 1974, May 21, 1973, *Courier-Journal Magazine,* Feb. 7, 1965, Sept. 19, 1971.

Robert Bruce French

LOUISVILLE ZOO. Lush botanical settings, creative exhibits, and over twelve hundred specimens make the Louisville Zoo (Louisville Zoological Garden) a multifaceted experience for discovering the world's most threatened animals. The zoo provides a home for endangered species by cooperating with conservation efforts such as the species survival plans of the American Zoo and Aquarium Association. Visitors not only see zebras, but endangered Hartmann's mountain zebras. They also see shy maned wolves from South America and Sumatran tigers, smallest of the remaining five tiger subspecies. Because of the zoo's involvement with international breeding programs, visitors can see the flightless Guam rail, the black-footed ferret of the North American Great Plains, and the Bali mynah—all species so threatened they had fewer than twenty individual specimens thirty years ago.

Opened in 1969 this 134-acre, city-operated zoo is located on Trevilian Way between Newburg and Poplar Level Roads. In the late 1990s it annually attracted over six hundred thousand visitors, including eighty thousand students. Educational programs coordinated through Kentucky and southern Indiana school systems offer interdisciplinary approaches to students and teachers alike. The zoo promotes conservation awareness through year-round animal demonstrations and outreaches, artistic performances and events such as "The World's Largest Halloween Party!" and popular festivals such as the annual Earth Day at the Zoo.

The zoo scientific study continues to attract international recognition for pioneering achievements in animal husbandry and exhibit design. The 1988 Edward H. Bean Award was given for the Woolly Monkey Propagation Program. The most prestigious of all first births was Equuleus (E.Q.), the name of the offspring, the first successful birth through transfer of an embryo from an exotic equine (Grant's zebra) to a domestic quarterhorse. This was done by veterinarians Scott D. Bennett and William R. Foster.

The original 1960s zoogeographic plan has grown with several exhibits that are contributing to zoo design around the world. The MetaZoo was the first combination education center and public exhibit in the nation. Reptiles, amphibians, and fish were the first in the nation to be combined in a bio-climatic setting of desert, forest, and water in the HerpAquarium. The Kentucky Wetlands Trail is an outdoor living classroom that champions natural resources. Now biodiversity is used to explain the complexities of the ecosystems we need to preserve. This is done with the new indoor and outdoor exhibits. The exhibits add the crucial cultural element and introduce the world's first multi-species rotational design that combines with operant conditioning (positive reinforcement for task) to enrich the daily life of the animals, encourage natural behavior, and give visitors the experience of entering the animals' world as the people travel along an island stream.

See *Courier-Journal,* Sept. 27, 1987, May 25, 1989, Sept. 22, 1990, June 18, 1991, Oct. 18, 1991, Sept. 17, 1992, July 6, 1997; Robert J. Wiese and Michael Hutchins, *Species Survival Plans: Strategies for Wildlife Conservation* (Bethesda, Md., 1994); Agnes S. Crume, "Zoo Genes," *Louisville* 36 (July 1985): 32–35; Mary Ellen Hill, "Perspective: The Louisville Zoo," *Business First* 12 (July 1, 1996): 25–31.

Diana DeVaughn

LOVELL, ETHEL MARTHA (b Astoria, Long Island, New York, January 20, 1878; d Louisville, November 19, 1946). Educator. Lovell's parents were English immigrants James and Eliza Lovell. After attending Louisville Girls High School, Lovell graduated from the Louisville Normal School in 1898. That same year she began teaching at the Seventh Ward School (later the MONSARRAT School). During that time she also attended summer programs at the University of Wisconsin at Madison in 1901 and 1902. Throughout her career Lovell continued her education. For example, she attended a summer program at Teachers College of Columbia University in 1920 and earned her Bachelor of Science degree from the UNIVERSITY OF LOUISVILLE in 1932.

Lovell's philosophy of education was based on her observations that traditional high school instruction had little value in the workplace. Instead schooling needed to stress and develop particular skills that could be used in life and "turned into cash." This turn-of-the-century philosophy was known as Progressivism. When she began her career as the first woman teacher of manual training in the city, she organized woodworking classes for grade schools. From that time on she devoted her adult life to vocational education.

In 1913 Lovell approached the Consumers' League of Kentucky with a plan to begin a separate vocational school for the Louisville BOARD OF EDUCATION to be housed in the Board's headquarters. Because of her interest in vocational education, her contacts with other educational experiments in the field, and her experience in teaching woodworking to elementary students, Lovell was selected, along with Lewis Bacon of the Indianapolis school system, to start the Prevocational School. The Consumers' League then sent Lovell to the University of Chicago for firsthand experience in the type of instruction the league envisioned for the project.

Upon completion of the work at the University of Chicago, Lovell continued with the project until 1915 when she accepted an offer with the Cincinnati PUBLIC SCHOOLS to be principal of their Sewing Trades School. Within a year the Louisville Board of Education lured her back with a substantial pay increase. Because the new vocational approach to learning was so popular, the school quickly outgrew its facilities on First St. near Chestnut St.

Prompted by the interest of THEODORE AHRENS, a local businessman and philanthropist, Lovell began to make plans for expansion of the program. Ahrens and Lovell spent many hours planning classrooms and curricula to serve the needs of students and of manufacturers who might hire graduates of the program. Pleased with the plans, Ahrens presented the results of their discussions to the Board of Education with a promise of three hundred thousand dollars in funding if the board would purchase the land and pay for some equipment. The board approved the proposal and erected a new building in 1926, which it named Theodore Ahrens Trade High School. Lovell was appointed principal, a position she held until her death in 1946.

As principal, Lovell became a widely acclaimed vocational administrator and leader. She held offices in various national organizations such as the Trade School Principals Association of the American Vocational Association. Her innovative approach to teaching students work skills to meet industry's ever-changing demands was responsible for her national reputation. She is buried in CAVE HILL CEMETERY.

See Edwin K. Linford, *Ethel M. Lovell, Pioneer in Vocational Education in Kentucky* (N.p.); *Courier-Journal*, May 17, 1930.

LUCAS, ROBERT HENRY (b Jefferson County, August 8, 1888; d Washington, D.C., October 13, 1947). Politician. Lucas was the son of Robert and Hattie (Galey) Lucas. He attended PUBLIC SCHOOLS in Louisville and graduated from Male High School. He received both his B.A. (1908) and his LL.B. (1909) degrees from the UNIVERSITY OF LOUISVILLE. In 1909–12 he served as captain of Company B, First Kentucky Infantry, National Guard. When the REPUBLICAN PARTY split in 1912 between the supporters of William Howard Taft and Theodore Roosevelt, Lucas supported Roosevelt and joined the Bull Moose Party. He was secretary-treasurer of the Progressive campaign committee for Louisville and Jefferson County.

Lucas began his legal practice in Louisville in 1909, and in 1917 he became the Police Court attorney, a position he held until 1921. He first gained recognition as a dominant political figure in the Republican Party in 1917 as a member of the team of "Chess, Matt, and Bob" (Chesley H. Searcy, Matt Chilton, and Lucas), where he helped defeat the Louisville Democratic machine of James and John Whallen. In 1921 he was appointed United States collector of internal revenue for Kentucky by President Warren G. Harding, a position he held until 1929. In 1927 Lucas lost the Republican primary for governor of Kentucky to Flem Sampson. In 1929 President Herbert Hoover appointed him United States commissioner of the Internal Revenue Service over the opposition of Secretary of the Treasury Andrew Mellon. He held this position for one year. From 1930 to 1932 Lucas was the executive director of the Republican National Committee.

After Lucas's stint in Washington, he reopened his legal practice, working in both Washington and Louisville. In 1936 he was unsuccessful in an attempt to unseat Marvel Mills Logan as United States senator, losing the election by a vote of 539,968 to 365,850. In 1939 he served as campaign manager for King Swope, Republican nominee for governor.

Lucas married Gertrude Losch on October 19, 1910; they had one daughter, Martha. Lucas is buried in CAVE HILL CEMETERY.

See *Courier-Journal*, Oct. 14, 1947.

LUCKY'S BEST BETS. A copyrighted Louisville horse racing tip sheet, it was started in December 1988 by Mike "Lucky" English at Turfway Park's winter meet. The tip sheet at one time was distributed in the Lexington and Elizabethtown areas as well as in metropolitan Louisville. English was one of the few turf writers in the country advising bettors on angles and strategies for better returns on investment in "exotic" wagering, which includes daily doubles, quinellas, pick threes, pick sixes, trifectas, and exactas. On May 23 and 24, 1991, he established a world handicapping record and was included in *Guinness Book of World Records* by picking twelve consecutive winners at CHURCHILL DOWNS.

Joseph Woodson Oglesby

LUSTRON HOUSES. Lustron is the trade name for a one-story, prefabricated, maintenance-free, metal ranch house developed in the mid-1940s by Chicago industrial engineer Carl Standlund (designer and builder of Standard Oil gas stations). Former mayor of Louisville Wilson Wyatt played a major role in its development when he, as National Housing Expediter under the Harry Truman administration (1945–53), agreed to allocate steel for its manufacture if the material was used exclusively to produce much-needed postwar housing (rather than five hundred Standard Oil gas stations as had originally been suggested).

By one account nearly twenty-five hundred Lustrons were erected in thirty-five states east of the Rocky Mountains (with a few in Alaska and Venezuela) between 1946 and 1950. Buyers could choose from three basic models and from eight standard pastel exterior colors. Sixteen Lustron houses (sold by local dealer E.D. Cross and Co. to first-time homebuyers as starter homes) were constructed in the Louisville area, and fourteen had survived into the 1990s. All but one are the two-bedroom Westchester model (the other models offered were the Newport and Meadowbrook). Company records have been located that indicate that sixteen Lustrons were erected in the Louisville area. The addresses and locations of two of the sixteen remain a mystery.

The complete house was shipped in one "package" on a specially designed trailer from the main plant, a former CURTISS-WRIGHT AIRCRAFT FACTORY near Columbus, Ohio, to the local builder-dealer for speedy erection on the site. It took approximately ten days and cost from $6,500 to $10,500 for skilled assembly crews to erect each house.

The Lustron Corp. boasted that these prefabricated building marvels, which had a steel roof and framing system and radiant heat panels situated in the ceilings, were "fireproof, ratproof . . . [and would never] fade, crack or peel, [and] never need PAINTING, refinishing or reroofing" because the interior and exterior were made with interlocking porcelain enamel-finished steel panels (similar to porcelain panels found on kitchen stoves and refrigerators). All surfaces could be wiped clean with a damp cloth, and pictures could be hung with magnets. Built-in cabinetry and a novel combination dishwasher-clothes washer that converted from one use to another "in a jiffy" were standard. The only parts of a Lustron home that were not steel were the aluminum window frames, asphalt floor tiles, and concrete foundations.

The local Lustron dealership's first open house attracted an estimated ninety-six thousand visitors who watched salesmen shoot small metal cannonballs at a sample Lustron panel in an attempt to put to rest any questions about the material's durability.

Sadly, the Lustron Corp. failed in 1950 because of financial and production difficulties, including difficulties with local building codes, trade unions, and conventional builders.

The Lustron houses still standing in 2000 were located at:
2408 Burwell Ave.
121 Cambridge Dr.
2523 Clarendon Ave.
547 Dover Rd.
2827 Eleanor Ave.
1911 Gladstone
4615 Greenwood Ave.**
325 N Hubbards Ln.
7238 Southside Dr.
319 Westport Dr.
1920 Winston Ave.
1922 Winston Ave.
125 Fifth Ave., LaGrange, Kentucky*
122 Old Forest Rd., Pewee Valley, Kentucky*
* Lacks original architectural integrity
** May no longer be standing or may be enveloped by new building

See Hays Birkhead Hendricks, "Louisville's Lustrons: Houses with Magnetic Appeal," M.S. thesis, Ball State University, 1994; *Courier-Journal,* March 22, 1953, Nov. 17, 1993; Robert A. Mitchell, "What Ever Happened to Lustron Homes?" *Association for Preservation Technology Bulletin* (Jan. 1992); Lustron Corp. Records Collection, MSS 861 (available on microfilm), Ohio Historical Society, Columbus, Ohio; H. Ward Jandl, "Yesterday's Houses of Tomorrow," *Preservation Press* (Washington, D.C., 1991).

Joanne Weeter

LUTHERANS. In the more than two hundred years since Lutheran pioneers first established churches in the Louisville area, the congregations, no matter what their synod, have proven themselves an integral part of Louisville's Christian community, as well as encouraging participation in local interfaith programs and dialogues. While retaining much of their German and Scandinavian heritage, they have reached out to the wider cultural community with vigor and passion, spreading the gospel in the historic tradition of Martin Luther. Though their numbers are small compared to the Baptist and Roman Catholic congregations in the area, they are a vital force in both Louisville and the larger community.

According to the *World Christian Encyclopedia* (1994 Update) some 33.6 percent of the world POPULATION, or 1.9 billion people, are classified as "in some sense Christians." Some 58.5 million of these, or 3 percent of the Christian population, are classified as Lutheran. In the late 1990s the world's Lutherans belong to 250 different autonomous Lutheran bodies. The 8.7 million Lutherans in North America belong to twenty-one of those bodies. The largest of these, at 5.2 million, is the Evangelical Lutheran Church in America (ELCA), founded in 1988 as the result of a merger between the Lutheran Church in America, the American Lutheran Church, and the Association of Evangelical Lutheran Churches. Next in size is the Lutheran Church–Missouri Synod (LCMS), now with better than 2.6 million baptized members. The Wisconsin Evangelical Lutheran Synod (WELS) has slightly under five hundred thousand members and is the third-largest Lutheran church in the U.S.A. All three synods are active in the Louisville area.

The ELCA counts slightly over 5 million members, over ten thousand congregations, and sixty-five synods in nine geographic regions. The Indiana-Kentucky Synod, with headquarters in Indianapolis, governs the Louisville area.

The LCMS was founded in 1847 and traces its origins to immigrants from Saxony who came to Missouri in 1839. The LCMS, (largely German in its makeup and language until the end of WORLD WAR I) reported a membership of 2.6 million in 1993 (the latest date for which accurate figures are available). They belong to more than 6,218 congregations. The Synod operates the world's oldest religious radio station, KFUO in St. Louis, and its program, *The Lutheran Hour*, has been continuoualy aired since 1930.

The Wisconsin Evangelical Lutheran Synod also dates from the mid-nineteenth century. It was founded in 1850 just outside Milwaukee, Wisconsin. At present the Synod counts twelve hundred congregations. Though their membership is small compared to the other two bodies, they operate in all fifty states as well as in twenty foreign countries and have more than sixty missionary families in twenty-four nations.

In Louisville the growth of the Lutheran churches reflected the growth of German immigration. The first German immigrants from North Carolina, Virginia, and Pennsylvania settled around JEFFERSONTOWN (then called Brunerstown), and in 1796 they built a log church in which Lutheran services were held on a monthly basis, sharing it with other denominations. This church was the forerunner of Christ Evangelical Lutheran Church, which was organized in 1817 as a congregation without synodical ties. In 1833 the congregation laid the cornerstone of its first building on N Watterson Trail in Jeffersontown, where it remained for the next 124 years. The current structure, at Taylorsville Rd. and Six Mile Ln., was begun in 1957.

The ELCA Louisville churches include: First Lutheran Church at 417 E BROADWAY, which was originally known as First English Lutheran Church. After several false starts, the church was finally organized in 1872 under sponsorship of the Home Mission Board of the General Synod. First English Lutheran began with only fourteen members, but in 1874 they built their very first house of worship on Broadway, and there the congregation has remained. Congregations established by First include Second English Lutheran Church (later named Fenner Memorial Church) in 1876, Third Lutheran Church in 1886, and, in 1892, the first Lutheran church in the HIGHLANDS area, Trinity Lutheran Church (now closed). In 1890 thirty-four of First Church's members were transferred to the new St. Paul's English Evangelical Lutheran Church at Second and Oak Streets. (In 1920, this congregation merged back with First Lutheran Church).

Third Lutheran Church was established in 1886 in the BUTCHERTOWN neighborhood, as many of the residents of that area were German immigrants with Protestant backgrounds. The first Sunday school classes, a precursor to the establishment of the church, met in a structure originally used as a curing house for meat. By 1887 the church had located on Frankfort Ave., near Story Ave., and the congregation remained there for forty-four years. In 1931 the congregation dedicated a new building at 1864 Frankfort Ave.

Ascension Lutheran Church, at 13725 Shelbyville Rd., was founded in 1988, when the national ELCA sent Rev. William Funk to establish a mission church. Funk personally knocked on eight thousand doors, inviting people to worship at Ascension. The church's first services were held at Eastern High School in Middletown. In 1992 the congregation moved into its new sanctuary near the Lake Forest subdivision. A new sanctuary was dedicated in February 1999.

Bethany Lutheran Church in the South End was the first Lutheran church in Louisville that was not established in a primarily German neighborhood. Founded in 1904, it was also, according to a history of the Indiana-Kentucky Synod, the first Lutheran church here to have an altar and was also the first Lutheran church in the area to build its own parsonage. While a leader in many movements, Bethany has never been a really large church. It is still located at 3938 Southern Pkwy., where its original founders purchased the lot in 1904.

Calvary Evangelical Lutheran Church was established officially in 1917 in the Highlands. One of its first meeting sites was a carpenter's shop. The Lutheran Men's League of Louisville presented Calvary with a lot at Bardstown Rd. and Roanoke Ave., and in 1919 the laymen and pastors of the city erected a frame chapel there in just one day. In 1928 it was replaced by a structure with Gothic elements. The church featured some of the most beautiful stained-glass windows in Louisville as well as a hand-carved altarpiece representing the Last Supper. Tragically, these were destroyed in 1979.

Good Shepherd Lutheran Church serves the VALLEY STATION area. It was established in 1958 when the ULCA sent a pastor there to survey the field and develop a congregation. Initial services were held at Valley High School, and later that year Good Shepherd was organized with seventy-eight names on the charter roll. The parish obtained its first full-time pastor in 1963 and dedicated its own church building at 9718 Dixie Hwy. in December 1966. During the pastorate of the Reverend Richard C. Duerr, a national Vietnam memorial was constructed on Good Shepherd's property. Consecrated on November 11, 1970, the project pays tribute to all Americans who gave their lives in Vietnam.

Grace Lutheran Church was established through the efforts of the Reverend Harlan K. Fenner and members of Second Lutheran Church. Following the traditional pattern, a Sunday school was first begun. In 1891 construction of a new building was begun in Louisville's West End, on Twenty-sixth St. just south of Bank St. By 1924 the church had grown so much that a large educational building was added. Then in 1926, the thirty-five-year-old frame church was condemned, and the congregation met for twelve years in the education building until 1939 when a new house of worship was built at 452 N Twenty-sixth. It was designated an official "urban church" in 1966 by the Board of American Missions.

The church first known as Messiah Lutheran Church was organized to serve the large number of Lutherans transferred here from Pennsylvania when General Electric moved to this area. Since the majority of the members had belonged to Messiah Lutheran Church in Wesleyville, Pennsylvania, they decided to keep that name. By 1961 the congregation had purchased property at 8701 Old Shepherdsville Rd. Beginning in January 1997, the church became a blended one, Messiah-Trinity Church, an amalgam of the Lutheran and Episcopal churches. It is the only truly blended congregation of its kind in the area.

New Creation African Lutheran Church serves Louisville's West End at 2111 W BROADWAY. One of the newest Lutheran churches in the ELCA, it was established in 1984.

St. John's Lutheran Church on Breckenridge Ln. was founded in 1948 when the congregation met at the old Greathouse School at Grandview and Fairfax Avenues, now the site of the ST. MATTHEWS/Eline Library and St. Matthews City Hall. The congregation has moved three times, finally in 1956 to 901 Breckenridge Ln.

St. Mark's Lutheran Church at 7153 Southside Dr. in the AUBURNDALE neighborhood was organized as a nondenominational Sunday school in 1907. It was known first as the Christian Union Church, or the Gheens Mission, since it was built on land donated by Charles E. Gheens. When the group decided to affiliate with an established Protestant church body in 1919, the Louisville Lutheran Men's League sponsored it. St. Mark's was officially organized in 1920 with thirty-three charter members, only two of whom had been Lutherans to begin with.

The second St. Paul's Lutheran Church (the original one was at Second and Oak Streets) serves the SHIVELY area. Originally the congregation met at the old Mill Creek School at the junction of the WATTERSON EXPRESSWAY and Dixie Hwy. A new site on Crums Ln. was purchased in 1955, and a new building was dedicated in 1960. In 1963 St. Paul's congregation was enlarged by the addition of the membership of (Fenner) Memorial Lutheran Church, which had been established in 1876 as Second English Lutheran Church.

St. Stephen's Lutheran Church in FERN CREEK was developed in 1956 as a mission of Trinity Lutheran Church (now closed). By 1959 the mission had grown to the point where it was organized on its own with seventy-two charter members, and a seven-acre site was purchased on Bardstown Rd. Groundbreaking ceremonies for a new modern church building were held in December 1962.

There are six Missouri Synod Lutheran congregations in the Louisville area. The oldest of these is CONCORDIA LUTHERAN CHURCH, which is actually the oldest Lutheran Church in Louisville proper. Concordia was established in 1878. The original name of the congregation was "The First German Evangelical Lutheran Church in Louisville." Meetings were held in the Presbyterian Chapel at Clay and Broadway until 1880, when the German Methodist Church building at Breckinridge and Clay was purchased. By 1892 the decision was made to buy the property on E Broadway. "German" was dropped from the name in 1920, and the name was changed to Concordia in 1930. The church played a large role in assisting the 1937 flood victims, when the water reached within two hundred feet of the church property.

Faith Lutheran Church was begun in 1954 by the Louisville Lutheran Federation to provide a congregation for the South End. Members of Concordia, Pilgrim, and Redeemer congregations were among the first members. The congregation was formally founded in 1955. Members worshiped at the Beechmont Women's Club until 1957. Land was then purchased at 7635 Old Third Street Rd., and the parish hall was built and dedicated in 1957.

Peace Lutheran Church, at 8913 Pennsylvania Run Rd. in southern Jefferson County, was begun in 1973 as a mission of Pilgrim Lutheran Church. Peace began as a mission congregation for the Fern Creek–OKOLONA area with only forty worshipers; twenty-six communicant members of Pilgrim then joined Peace Church. Soon after this, land near McNeeley Lake was purchased. In 1975 the church, along with classrooms and a fellowship area, was built.

Pilgrim Lutheran Church traces its beginning to 1927 when the Federation of Lutheran Churches—Missouri Synod was established in Louisville. By 1930 the federation had brought a missionary to Louisville for the express purpose of establishing a new congregation. The church's first location was at Shelby St. and Minoma Ave. As it outgrew that location, it moved to services in the old John J. AUDUBON Elementary School. In 1952 the rapidly growing congregation purchased property on Gardiner Ln., and the new church, designed by the Louisville firm of Hartstern, Louis, and Henry, was dedicated in 1955. Pilgrim established a Christian day school in 1931. In 1951 Pilgrim and Concordia agreed to establish a consolidated school (Concordia had its own school for approximately seventy years). By 1957 the school had grown so much that a new building was constructed next to the church. This school remained in operation, with help from Peace Lutheran and Redeemer Lutheran congregations as well, until 1989.

Our Savior Lutheran Church occupies an edifice on Nottingham Pkwy. off Shelbyville Rd. Like St. John's Lutheran, it too first met at the old Greathouse School in St. Matthews. It began as a mission in 1941, but the church's first building at Shelbyville Rd. and MacArthur Dr. was not constructed until 1947. The church remained there until 1968 when the congregation purchased the present site.

The history of Redeemer Lutheran Church is actually the history of two churches—St. James, a predominantly African American congregation, and Redeemer, predominantly white. The two congregations merged in 1974. Redeemer dates its history to 1888, and that history centers around the Christian day school that provided education for nearly one thousand children until it was closed in 1972. St. James began its work in 1947 and grew to a vital congregation at 3901 Greenwood Ave. but was never large enough to support a full-time pastor. Redeemer's building at 3650 River Park Dr., influenced by Gothic style, serves as a landmark for the area.

Hope Lutheran Church, 4200 Shenandoah Dr. in eastern Louisville, is the only congregation in the area belonging to the Wisconsin Evangelical Lutheran Synod. It was founded in 1973 and held its first services at the Jefferson County Farm Bureau Building, which was then on Hubbards Ln. in St. Matthews. In 1981 the congregation moved to its own facility on Chamberlain Ln., and in 1993 moved to its present facility.

See Henry G. Waltmann, *History of the Indiana-Kentucky Synod* (Indianapolis 1971).

Ann Hart Stewart

LYND, ROBERT STAUGHTON (b New Albany, Indiana, September 26, 1892; d Warren, Connecticut, November 1, 1970). Sociologist. Lynd was the son of Staughton Browning and Cornelia Lynd. He was educated in NEW ALBANY and received his B.A. from Princeton University in 1914. He then became managing editor of *Publishers Weekly* until 1918 when he served as a private in the United States Army during WORLD WAR I. In 1919, Lynd worked for a brief period as manager of ADVERTISING and publicity for the book department of Charles Scribner's Sons. The following year, he was assistant on the staff of B.W. Huebsch and the *Freeman*. He earned a divinity degree from the Union Theological Seminary in 1923 and his doctorate in sociology from Columbia University in 1931. From 1931 to 1960, he was a professor of sociology at Columbia University.

Lynd is best known for his book *Middletown: A Study in Contemporary American Culture* (1929), a product of a study he did as the director of the Institute for Social And Religious Research. Co-authored by his wife, Helen Merrell Lynd, it was a study of the town of Muncie, Indiana, and the first major profile of an American city. Its aim was to describe the behavior of the POPULATION and to cite its changes over a thirty-five-year period. The result was a close-up look at the governmental, social, educational, and economic realities of Muncie, down to the level of the methods of housekeeping the women used. The Lynds returned to Muncie in 1935 for their second survey. The result, *Middletown in Transition: a Study in Cultural Conflicts* (1937), was a reevaluation of the town in the light of the change brought about by the GREAT DEPRESSION. The study revealed a number of paradoxes, one being that people subscribed to the axiom that a worker could become an employer by hard work and by saving, even though the wage gap between the worker and the employer had widened. These two books became American classics and were used as required reading for junior and senior high school students. They were not only pioneer works but also gave rise to a whole new school of sociological research. Lynd also wrote *Knowledge for What? The Place of Social Science in American Culture* (1939) about the responsibility of social scientists to the public. He was a frequent contributor to sociological and general periodicals and, at the time of his death, was working on a book on social power. He was married to Helen Merrell in 1921. They had one son, Staughton, a historian, and one daughter, Andrea.

See Stanley J. Kunitz and Howard Haycraft, eds., *Twentieth Century Authors* (New York 1942); *New Albany Tribune*, Nov. 6, 1970; *New York Times*, Nov. 3, 1970.

LYNDON. This eastern Jefferson County fourth-class city is bounded by Westport Rd. to the north, Shelbyville Rd. to the south, Whipps Mill Rd. on the east, and the WATTERSON EXPRESSWAY on the west. It began in 1871 as a stop on the Louisville, Cincinnati, and Lexington Railroad that ran through the property of Alvin Wood. Wood built a depot so that area residents would not have to go into ST. MATTHEWS to catch the train. He named the station Lyndon, probably to honor Linn's Station, a pioneer fort built on nearby BEARGRASS CREEK by William Linn in 1779.

The area was first developed by STEPHEN ORMSBY, who came to Louisville in 1787 and was appointed Jefferson District Court judge. The judge, who served as a member of the U.S. Congress and later became president of the BANK OF LOUISVILLE, purchased about a thousand acres along Goose Creek in 1803. In the mid-1800s, Ormsby's only son, Col. Stephen Ormsby, built a late Greek Revival–style house on land that was part of his father's farm. The younger Ormsby was known for his exploits in the LOUISVILLE LEGION, an infantry regiment of Kentucky's state guard that fought in the MEXICAN WAR. The Ormsby estate was called Maghera Glass, a Gaelic phrase meaning "green meadows," and the family lived in the house located near what is now LaGrange Rd.

In 1896 the house and part of the estate were sold to the KENTUCKY MILITARY INSTITUTE (KMI), one of the oldest military schools in the country. KMI constructed several buildings on the campus. The school had both preparatory and college divisions until it closed in 1971. Ten Broeck Hospital, an institution specializing in drug and alcohol treatment, eventually acquired the school grounds and mansion.

In 1901 the Louisville and Eastern, an electric interurban railway, began serving Lyndon on the route linking Louisville and LaGrange. The area quickly grew into a commuter suburb. In 1912 the Hamilton Ormsby (Judge Stephen Ormsby's grandson) estate, Bellevoir, was sold and became ORMSBY VILLAGE, operated by Jefferson County as a home for needy and troubled youth. The complex was closed by county GOVERNMENT in 1979. In 1987 the mansion at Bellevoir was renovated. It is listed on the NATIONAL REGISTER OF HISTORIC PLACES and is owned by JEFFERSON COUNTY FISCAL COURT. The former Ormsby Village property has been developed as a commercial office park called Hurstbourne Green.

There were several unsuccessful attempts to start communities in the Lyndon area before the interurban railway encouraged the growth of residential housing and commercial businesses. In the 1890s George Washburn developed fifty acres into Warwick Villa, an early suburb near the railroad tracks. But the depression of 1893 forced Washburn to sell the lots to Henry Holzheimer Sr., who had some success with Warwick Villa. When the interurban railway discontinued service in 1934, the construction boom was temporarily stalled.

In the twentieth century, new single-family housing proliferated as expressways were built through the area. The community was incorporated as a fourth-class city in 1965 to avoid annexation by nearby St. Matthews. The POPULATION was 460 in 1970, 1,553 in 1980, 8,037 in 1990, and 7,675 in 1996.

See *A Place in Time: The Story of Louisville's Neighborhoods* (Louisville 1989).

James Strohmaier

LYNN'S PARADISE CAFÉ. Lynn's Paradise Café, located at 984 Barret Ave., was opened on Frankfort Ave. in the CRESCENT HILL–CLIFTON area in August 1991 by owner-proprietor Lynn Winter. In May 1994 it moved to the HIGHLANDS. Winter, a Louisville native, moved around the country with her family before settling in Lexington, Kentucky, where she graduated from Tates Creek High School. She learned about the restaurant business in CALIFORNIA, where she worked in such upscale dining establishments as Café Beaujolais, a Mendocino restaurant. She returned to Kentucky and opened the cafe shortly thereafter.

The restaurant, which is primarily a breakfast eatery, is known for its quirky decor and unusual menu items. The interior is an eclectic mix of furniture from flea markets and antique malls; Formica tables are adorned with plastic toys and the walls with colorful PAINTINGS and antique photographs. In the center of the restaurant is a large tree decorated with eggs hand-painted by employees and customers. Even the parking lot is distinctive and offbeat. There are brightly colored cement statues of animals in the front lot and a giant coffee pot that perpetually pours "coffee" into a mug. The food is described as American "with a twist," although the menu's anchor is the egg. Food items range from meat loaf to omelets, and the restaurant is consistently rated one of the best in Louisville by local food critics.

Both the restaurant and Winter have repeatedly been featured in the local and national media. In January 1997, a lengthy segment of the *CBS Evening News'* "Travels with Harry" with Harry K. Smith focused on the restaurant. Winter and the café have also appeared in articles in *Southern Living* magazine, *House Beautiful* magazine, and the *New York Times*. Winter has also won acclaim for her entrepreneurial skills, appearing on the cover of the book *Women's Ventures, Women's Visions*, a compilation of twenty-nine stories of successful women entrepreneurs, of which Winter's is one.

See *Courier-Journal*, Jan. 18, 1995; Steve Millburg, "Mom Would Love Lynn's," *Southern Living*, Aug. 1995.

LYONS, WILLIAM LEE (b Louisville, June 3, 1857; d Kenosha, Wisconsin, June 2, 1911). Stockbroker, mayor. He was the son of Henry J. Lyons, who was born in Washington, D.C., and Laura Simmons. Lyons's father was elected clerk of Jefferson County Court when he was twenty-one. He worked there until he joined the BANKING firm of Quigley, Lyons, & Co. He stayed with the firm until 1862, when he moved to New York to start Henry J. Lyons & Co. He died on April 4, 1867, and the family returned to Louisville.

Laura Lyons was the daughter of William and Ann (Lee) Simmons, both of whom were descendants of the first immigrants to Kentucky from Maryland—the Lee and Hill families of Bardstown and the Simmons family of BULLITT COUNTY. Laura Lyons died in Louisville on October 25, 1878.

William's early education began in New York City and continued in Louisville. He completed his studies at Highland Military Academy, Worcester, Massachusetts. Later he was a clerk for the Louisville & Nashville Railroad. In 1878 he became a broker in stocks and bonds, and by 1881 Lyons was the senior member of the firm of W.L. Lyons & Co, a precursor to the J.J.B. HILLIARD, W.L. LYONS INC. investment firm.

He was also active in several other Louisville companies. He was vice president of the

Louisville Silvering and Beveling Co., president of the Home Investment Co., and a member of the Board of Trade and the Commercial Club. Lyons was president of the Louisville Stock Exchange for three years prior to 1907. He then went to New York and was a member of the New York Stock Exchange for three years before returning to Louisville.

Lyons served as a city councilman for several terms. During much of his tenure, he was chairman of the finance committee of the Board of Councilmen. He also served as board president for three terms from 1891 to 1894. Lyons, a Democrat, was mayor pro tem for four months in 1890 during the Charles D. Jacob administration. When Jacob took a leave of absence to go overseas for his health, Lyons was elected mayor pro-tem unanimously by the council. He took over for Jacob on May 12 and served until the end of August.

Lyons, a surprise pick to serve as mayor, was to quell political rivalries on the council between Henry S. Tyler, president of the Board of Councilmen, and Albert A. Stoll, president of the BOARD OF ALDERMEN. Lyons also served as chairman of the Board of Public Safety under the administration of Mayor Charles P. Weaver and for several years was a member of the Democratic State Central Committee.

He was married to Mary Belle Clay, daughter of Samuel and Mary (Rogers) Clay of Lexington, in 1881. They had two sons and two daughters—Samuel Clay, Laura, Mary Rogers, and William Lee Lyons Jr. died of a stroke while convalescing at a Wisconsin sanitarium. He is buried in CAVE HILL CEMETERY.

See J. Stoddard Johnston, ed., *Memorial History of Louisville,* 2 vols. (Chicago and New York 1896).

M

MACAULEY'S THEATRE. Louisville's premier THEATER of the late nineteenth and early twentieth centuries was built by Bernard "Barney" Macauley, who had been an actor at the Louisville Theater at Fourth and Green (now Liberty) STREETS since the 1850s. His new theater on the north side of Walnut (now Muhammad Ali Blvd) between Third and FOURTH Streets made its debut on October 18, 1873, with a performance of the comedy *Extremes*. The building was designed by the architectural firm of McElfatrick and Sons and cost two hundred thousand dollars. But in 1879 debts compelled him to sell the playhouse, and it became the property of his brother John. Barney felt that John had profited deliberately from this financial stress, and he changed the spelling of his name to McAuley. The estrangement was permanent.

Under John Macauley's management the theater was a smashing success and was host to the stage's famed actors and actresses of the time. They included Sarah Bernhardt, Lily Langtry, Edwin Booth, George M. Cohan, and "Buffalo Bill" Cody. Likewise, Louisville's own MARY ANDERSON began her stage career at Macauley's on November 27, 1875, when, at age sixteen, she appeared as the lead in Shakespeare's *Romeo and Juliet*. Eight years later the renowned Madame Helena Modjeska starred in the American premiere of Henrik Ibsen's *A Doll's House*.

The early 1900s saw the appearance and growing popularity of movie houses. Even Macauley's showed an occasional motion picture such as DAVID WARK GRIFFITH'S *Birth of a Nation* in 1916. The theater continued to be the city's foremost outlet for legitimate theater until 1925. In that year it was razed to make way for the eastward expansion of the STARKS BUILDING at Fourth and Walnut Streets. It closed on August 29, 1925, with a performance of *The Naughty Wife*. The theatrical photos that had hung in its lobby were not lost but were removed to the UNIVERSITY OF LOUISVILLE'S BELKNAP PLAYHOUSE, where they are displayed.

With a performance of *Puzzles of 1925*, Macauley's Theatre was succeeded as the city's premier playhouse on October 5, 1925, by the Brown Theater on W BROADWAY next to the Brown Hotel. Both the hotel and the theater were built by JAMES GRAHAM BROWN. The fifteen-hundred-seat Brown was designed by Preston J. Bradshaw. Although it started out as a playhouse for legitimate theater, in the early 1930s it was converted to a movie house and hosted the October 2, 1957, premiere of *Raintree County*. It was not until 1962, after a remodeling project and grand reopening, that the Brown once again hosted stage productions. The Brown continued to operate until 1972, when, after a six-hundred-thousand-dollar renovation project, it was rededicated as the Macauley Theatre. Under the operation of the Louisville Theatrical Association, the theater opened under its new name on October 5, 1972, with a production of *Godspell*. In 1982 the Broadway-Brown Partnership bought the Macauley Theatre and the Brown Hotel, and, in 1995, the partnership donated the theater to the FUND FOR THE ARTS Properties Foundation. The theater was remodeled in 1997 at a cost of $2.9 million. A generous gift that year from the W.L. Lyons Brown Foundation resulted in the name the W.L. Lyons Brown Theatre in honor of the late board chairman of BROWN-FORMAN CORP. The Brown Theatre is operated by the Kentucky Center for the Arts.

See George H. Yater, *Two Hundred Years at the Falls of the Ohio* (Louisville 1979); Kay Gill, *The Brown Hotel and Louisville's Magic Corner* (Louisville 1984); West T. Hill Jr., "A Study of the Macauley's Theatre in Louisville, Kentucky, 1873–1880," Ph.D thesis, State University of Iowa, 1954.

Macauley's Theatre, north side of Walnut (Muhammad Ali) between Third and Fourth Streets, 1920s.

MACK, ESSIE (DORTCH) (b Louisville, April 4, 1883; d Louisville, August 2, 1940). Educator. Mack was the daughter of John and Emma (Talbert) Dortch. She graduated from Central High School in 1902 and attended LOUISVILLE MUNICIPAL COLLEGE. A lifelong promoter of African American education, Mack played a major role in the organization of the first kindergarten at the Phillis Wheatley Colored School (later Wheatley Elementary). Her belief that parents' involvement in their children's education was essential prompted her to serve as an officer of the Congress of Kindergarten Mothers, president of the parent-teacher organization at Phillis Wheatley, president of the Kentucky Colored Parent-Teacher Association for nine years, and president of the National Congress of Colored Parent-Teacher Associations for two terms.

Mack was married to Oliver P. Mack. She is buried in the Louisville Cemetery.

See *Second Report of the Board of Education of Louisville, Ky.* (July 1, 1912, to June 30, 1913); *Third Report of the Board of Education of Louisville, Ky.* (July 1, 1913, to June 30, 1914).

MADRID BALLROOM. As one of sixteen dance halls operated in Louisville at various times, the Madrid Ballroom, located on the southeast corner of Third and Guthrie STREETS and known as "The Place to Dance," opened on September 23, 1929, with five thousand people as guests. Couples danced to the music of Jan Garber and His Columbia Recording Orchestra on the one hundred- by fifty-foot floor.

Decorated in the style of a Castilian casa grande, the Madrid had golden walls that were hung with large, richly colored tapestries. Six wrought-iron balconies overlooked the stage. Adding to the romantic Spanish atmosphere, revolving dome lights and crystal chandeliers spread their magic over the couples. The first

Louisville Recreational Building, home of the Madrid Ballroom, southeast corner Third and Guthrie Streets, 1930.

season, a huge success, ended on May 18, 1930, with a "grand finale ball" and music by Paul Graham and His Crackers.

In the mid-1930s the ballroom became a nightclub with floor shows. Attendance records were broken in June 1944 when Louisville native Lionel Hampton and his band played an engagement. In January 1952 the lease on the hall was canceled, and the lights went out in the ballroom that was considered one of the most beautiful in America.

See *Courier-Journal,* Oct. 23, 1938, June 10, 1944, Feb. 8, 1945, May 9, 1971; *Louisville Herald-Post,* Sept. 24, 1929; *Louisville Times Scene,* March 18, 1978.

Robert Bruce French

MAIN STREET. An early major thoroughfare in the city of Louisville, Main St. stretches from Beargrass Creek/Mellwood Ave. in the east due west, with some gaps, to end at Forty-sixth St. Main St. was the site of Louisville's main land-based settlement, Fort Nelson, which was established in 1781. The gates of Fort Nelson opened near what is now Seventh and Main. Main St. was a hub of activity for settlers and travelers due to its close proximity to Louisville's waterfront and its position at the end of the Wilderness Road, an overland route from Virginia to Kentucky. By 1784 Nicholas Meriwether had opened one of the first houses of public entertainment on one of his lots on the north side of the street between Sixth and Seventh. The development of Louisville and Main St. was aided by their proximity to the Falls of the Ohio. Steamboat traffic stopped to unload passengers and cargo in Louisville. As river traffic grew, many warehouses for storing goods shipped along the Ohio River sprang up along Main St., as well as hotels and facilities serving the needs of riverboat travelers. The famous Galt House hotel was founded there. Starting in the 1850s, many tall buildings with decorative cast-iron facades were built, making Main St. the site of the second-largest number of cast-iron facades in the world (exceeded only by the SoHo area of New York City).

With the growth of railroads and the concomitant decline in river traffic, activity shifted away from Main St., leaving the area in a state of neglect. Commercial activity shifted south along Fourth St. and came to center around the "magic corner" of Fourth and Broadway. But in the early 1970s there was a move back toward the river, beginning with the hotel developments of Al Schneider. He built a new Galt House, while many historic buildings were renovated and put to new uses. Examples include the building that housed the original Seelbach Hotel at 600 W Main that became home to the Chamber of Commerce, the Carter Brothers wholesale drygoods establishment at 727 W Main that became home to the Louisville Science Center, and the 1837 Bank of Louisville building at 316 W Main that became home to Actors Theatre. Significant new construction continued to take place on Main St., including the Riverfront Plaza/Belvedere (1972), Humana Building (1982), Kentucky Center for the Arts (1983), and the Hillerich & Bradsby Co. headquarters and bat factory (1995) and baseball museum (1996).

See Ellen Birkett Morris, "Remaking Main Street," 12 *Business First* (Aug. 7, 1995): 1; Main Street Association, *Louisville's Time Machine: Your Guide to Main Street Association's West Main Walking Tour* (Louisville 1995); *Cincinnati Post,* Sept. 21, 1974; F.W. Woolsey, "Louisville's Rebound Main," *Courier-Journal & Times Magazine,* Sept. 11, 1977; George H. Yater, "Daring Rescue on Old Main Street," *Louisville* (Sept. 1982): 38–46.

Ellen Birkett Morris

MAKER'S MARK DISTILLERY. Although the Samuels family traces its bourbon-making days back to the late eighteenth century, the well-known bourbon did not get its modern-day start until 1953. In that year, T. William "Bill" Samuels Sr., a graduate of the

Main Street between Bullitt and Fifth Streets. From an ambrotype, c. 1858.

Speed Scientific School of the UNIVERSITY OF LOUISVILLE, destroyed his family's traditional bourbon recipe and sought a change that could distinguish his elixir. Armed with the new formula, which included locally grown corn, malted barley, and winter wheat as opposed to the traditionally used rye, Samuels purchased and rebuilt an aging distillery on two hundred acres in Loretto, Kentucky, that had originally housed Burks Spring Distillery.

After six years of development, the bourbon had been perfected to Samuels's wishes. Marker's Mark was launched in 1959, and only four hundred barrels were produced in that first year. Samuels's wife, Marjorie, a collector of fine pewter, explained that a maker's mark was only put on an artist's finest pieces, and the name was born. Marjorie Samuels also came up with the idea of the famous red wax seal after looking at an old cognac bottle.

Smaller than many other distilleries, Maker's Mark produces batches of less than one thousand gallons in its cypress vats and has won an international following with distinctive ADVERTISING and an award-winning taste. In 1975 T. William "Bill" Samuels Jr. took over the presidency of the company. Six years later, the family, concerned about estate taxes, sold the distillery to liquor conglomerate Hiram Walker and Sons of Canada. In 1987 Maker's Mark opened an office off of Dutchman's Ln. as their headquarters and administrative offices. Samuels Senior died on October 3, 1992.

Male-Manual football game, Thanksgiving, 1929.

MALE-MANUAL HIGH SCHOOLS FOOTBALL RIVALRY. Kentucky's oldest FOOTBALL rivalry, the annual game between Male and DU PONT MANUAL HIGH SCHOOLS, is also one of the oldest and most storied in all of high school sports. The inaugural game took place on November 18, 1893, pitting Louisville (Male) High School, founded in 1856, against one-year-old du Pont Manual Training High School (now du Pont Manual) in a game more similar to rugby than to modern football. The game was played over the objections of Male principal Maurice "Ole Hoss" Kirby, who forbade the boys from playing but also threatened to expel every member of the squad if Manual won the contest. Male won 14–12. Although both schools had been playing football as early as 1892, this was the first of many meetings between them. As of 1999 the teams had met 116 times, with Male leading the contest 72–38–6.

From 1894 until 1976 the "Old Rivalry" was played on Thanksgiving Day every year except 1915–18 when the two schools were consolidated. Following their four-year consolidation, the schools went their separate ways again in 1919. In the split-up, Male got most of the good athletes and more than twice as many students as Manual.

The contest became a city favorite almost immediately, routinely drawing crowds of close to twenty thousand by the 1930s. Since it was one of the most popular spectator sporting events in the area, the 1948 game was chosen as the first program broadcast on local TELEVISION station WAVE-TV. In 1966, at the height of its popularity, a record crowd of twenty-four thousand came out to witness the Thanksgiving Day contest; but, by 1984, when the teams played their one hundredth game, fan attendance had dwindled to fewer than twelve thousand. As other high school rivalries have taken center stage, most notably the matchup between Catholic powerhouses Trinity and St. Xavier, the Male-Manual game has garnered less attention. Although Male's football program excelled in the 1990s—winning state championships in 1993 and 1998—Manual has not been as successful on the gridiron.

Over the years the contest has generated much passion both on and off the field. For many years the two schools were located within a few blocks of each other: Male at Brook and Breckinridge Streets starting in 1915 and Manual at Brook and Oak Streets from 1892 until 1950. On the Wednesday before the game, students would meet after school along Brook St. to exchange taunts and engage in fistfights and rock-throwing. Some reported that more blood was spilled off than on the field. Students also participated in other forms of hazing such as painting each others' school buildings in the opposing school's colors. Sometimes students would attempt to kidnap the victory barrel before the game. The trophy was painted purple with a gold 'H' for Male, and red with a white 'M' for Manual and was in the possession of whichever team had won the last contest.

The last "Turkey Day" game was played on November 25, 1976. Today games are played on the last Friday night in October. The rivalry was nearly canceled in 1976 after Male's program experienced declining support following school BUSING. Manual was not included in the public school system's busing plan. After Male became Jefferson County's first traditional school in 1977, its sports programs experienced a resurgence.

See Eustace Williams, *That Old Rivalry* (Louisville 1940); *Courier-Journal*, Oct. 30, 1998, and Oct. 29, 1993; Jim Bolus, "Taps for the Old Rivalry," *Courier-Journal Magazine*, Nov. 21, 1976; Sam Adkins and M.R. Holtzman, *The First Hundred Years: The Story of Louisville Male High School* (Louisville 1957).

MALLORY, ROBERT (b Madison Court House, Virginia, November 15, 1815; d LaGrange, Kentucky, August 11, 1885). U.S. congressman. Mallory received his education in private schools and graduated from the University of Virginia at Charlottesville in 1827. He moved to LaGrange, Kentucky, to engage in agricultural pursuits and took up the study of law. He practiced law in New Castle, Kentucky, from 1837 until his election to Congress in 1858 and became a Union Democrat. He served in three successive sessions of Congress (March 4, 1859–March 3, 1865) until he lost the election of 1864. After leaving Congress he returned to pursue AGRICULTURE on his OLDHAM COUNTY farm. In 1876 he served as a vice president of the Centennial Exhibition in Philadelphia. He is buried in his family cemetery at Spring Hill, Kentucky.

See *Biographical Directory of the American Congress 1776–1961* (Washington, D.C., 1961).

MAMMOTH LIFE AND ACCIDENT INSURANCE COMPANY. Opened on July 12, 1915, at Sixth and Green (Liberty) Streets., Mammoth was founded by B.O. Wilkerson, Rochelle I. Smith, William H. Wright, and Henry E. Hall, who served as president of the company from its inception until his death in 1944. Mammoth was established as an alternative company for AFRICAN AMERI-

CANS who were often forced to pay inflated premiums by white-managed insurance companies, and many times were denied coverage.

Originally most of Mammoth's policies were of the home-service type, also called weekly debit, whereby an agent would make weekly door-to-door premium collections. This practice was intended to make it easier for low-wage earners to purchase insurance, because they were better able to pay the small weekly installments than the larger monthly or annual premiums. The sale of weekly debit policies was discontinued by the company in the 1980s in the face of consumer advocates' claims that the policies were more expensive in the long term.

The company received instant support from the black community and quickly became Louisville's largest black-owned and -operated company. Within two years of its founding, Mammoth had outgrown its facilities and moved into a three-story building at 422 S Sixth St. It also established branch offices in cities throughout Kentucky, including Lexington, Hopkinsville, Bowling Green, and Paducah. Though initially started as a mutual company, Mammoth became a legal reserve stock institution in 1924 following a statewide sale of capital stock. The next year Mammoth's success was shown in construction of a six-story home office building at 604–12 W Walnut St. (Muhammad Ali Blvd.). The previous building was maintained as the Louisville district office.

In 1928 Mammoth extended into other states, eventually establishing offices in eight states: Michigan, Illinois, Indiana, Ohio, Missouri, Tennessee, and Wisconsin, as well as Kentucky. Though many companies foundered during the years of the GREAT DEPRESSION, Mammoth weathered the storm, due in part to the loyalty of its employees, many of whom voluntarily donated a portion of their wages back to the company to help it meet its client obligations. During the FLOOD OF 1937, hundreds of people found temporary housing in the company's two downtown offices.

In the 1960s Mammoth, along with many other minority insurers, began to face increasing competition from white-owned firms that not only had discovered the profitability of doing business with the African American community but also had begun to entice accomplished black salesmen by offering higher salaries. Though this trend slowed Mammoth's growth, business remained strong, and in 1967 a $680,000 remodeling project of the company's headquarters was completed. In response to white competition, the company initiated a management training program in 1981 in an effort to "replenish the cells" of upper management.

In the mid-1980s, two other African American insurance companies, North Carolina Mutual and Atlanta Life Insurance, made unsuccessful attempts to take over Mammoth Life. However, two years later, Atlanta Life Insurance Co. succeeded in taking over Mammoth, and in 1992 Mammoth was merged into Atlanta Life. By 1994 Atlanta Life had closed the Mammoth office in Louisville.

See *Courier-Journal*, Aug. 9, 1981, June 3, 1985; Alice Allison Dunnigan, *The Fascinating Story of Black Kentuckians: Their Heritage and Traditions* (Washington, D.C., 1982); George C. Wright, *Life Behind a Veil* (Baton Rouge 1985).

Parade float advertising the Mammoth Life and Accident Insurance Co., 1920s

MANDOLIN ORCHESTRAS. Following the CIVIL WAR, America's fascination with fretted instruments grew. Although the banjo gained popularity first (among white East Coast urbanites during the 1880s), the mandolin was soon its rival. Players of both instruments were typically organized into social clubs, offering young people an opportunity to meet. A city of respectable size often had a dozen or more mandolin clubs.

An article in the *Louisville Post* in 1893 credits Mr. Emil Hess with founding Louisville's first mandolin group in the 1880s. This quartet of players, using instruments purchased from New York City, soon expanded to include others interested in the mandolin. The club was located at the corner of Walnut (Muhammad Ali Blvd.) and Fourth St. According to the *Memorial History of Louisville from its First Settlement to the Year 1896*, June 1891 was the year Richard W. Langan founded the Louisville Mandolin and Guitar Club (LMGC), the city's most accomplished mandolin ensemble of that era. A social group, LMGC began with eleven members, grew to fifteen, and occupied a club room on Fourth St. Between 1891 and 1897 or 1898, when it disbanded, the LMGC donated its concert revenues to local charities while earning a considerable regional reputation.

The *Louisville Post* on June 16, 1893, recognized the work of Emil Hess in promoting mandolin music when it wrote, "Mr. Emil Hess of the firm of Hess, Henle & Co. has done much toward creating a love for music in this city. He is the founder of that splendid organization, the Louisville Mandolin Club. Some years ago, when the Mexican Band had filled its engagement at the SOUTHERN EXPOSITION in New Orleans, and was giving a concert tour throughout the larger cities of the United States, it gave a concert at PHOENIX HILL. The playing of the mandolin was one of the distinctive features of the band. Mr. Hess had never heard of this instrument before, and at once fell in love with it. In the 1880's he wrote to New York and ordered several of the new instruments. Messrs. George and Henry Asper and himself soon became proficient. Other boys with a musical taste also desired to learn. Having no instruments and not being able to procure any at an early day, Mr. Henry Asper proved himself such a genius that he made several and distributed them to his companions who agreed to meet regular *[sic]* on certain evenings in order to practice. All the boys being congenial and devoted to music produced on string instruments, at last formed the Mandolin Club, which now has a large club room at the corner of Fourth and Walnut." This may well have been the first mandolin club in the city.

Louisville's mandolin orchestra activity peaked between 1891 and 1901. Volumes of *Caron's Directory of the City of Louisville* list the following mandolin clubs:

The Orpheus Mandolin Orchestra (1893 directory), a photo of the group from the

Orpheus Mandolin Orchestra, 1890s.

Durlauf Photo Collection lists its founding date as January 15, 1892, and identifies all twenty-two members, including Prof. Harry L.B. Sheetz as director.

The Calumet Mandolin and Guitar Club (1896 and 1897 directories), rehearsed on Tuesday nights on Eighteenth St., between Grayson St. and Walnut (Muhammad Ali Blvd.), directed by H.T. Brown, with secretary Eldridge Locke.

The Zahn Mandolin Orchestra and Guitar Club (1898 and 1899 directories), rehearsed on Tuesday nights on Eighteenth St., between Madison and Chestnut Streets, directed by club president Fred J. Zahn, with treasurer Carl O. Zahn and secretary Archie Hadfield.

The Cromwell Mandolin Quintette (1898 directory), located on Fourth St., between Walnut and Chestnut Streets, was directed by Herman Gallrein.

The Orient Mandolin and Guitar Club (1899 directory), rehearsed on Tuesday nights on MARKET St., between Clay and Shelby Streets.

The Saxton Mandolin and Guitar Club (1900 and 1901 directories), directed by J. Henry Brady, rehearsed on Monday evenings on Fourth St., between Green (Liberty) and Walnut Streets, the address that the LMGC had once occupied.

The Louisville Mandolin Orchestra (LMO) continues this tradition. Founded in June 1988 by Michael Schroeder to provide a classical outlet for local musicians, the group has earned an international reputation and has recorded compact discs under conductor Jim Bates. Between 1988 and 1998 the LMO performed by invitation in Germany (1994), France (1995), and Spain (1996). LMO appeared as part of the Lonesome Pine Specials Series at the Kentucky Center for the Arts (1988, 1989, 1997), and hosted the national convention of the Classical Mandolin Society of America (1990 and 1997) as well as international guest performers from Germany, England, Russia, and Italy.

See J. Stoddard Johnston, ed., *Memorial History of Louisville* (Chicago 1896); *Louisville Post*, June 16, 1893; *Caron's Directory of the City of Louisville* (Louisville 1871–1901); *Courier-Journal,* Dec. 27, 1940; Konrad Wolki, *History of the Mandolin: The Instrument, Its Exponents, and Its Literature, from the Seventeenth until the Early Twentieth Century* (Arlington, Va., 1984); Paul Sparks, *The Classical Mandolin* (New York, 1995).

James Bates
Robin R. Harris

MANN'S LICK. Mann's Lick, near present FAIRDALE in Jefferson County, was one of the major sites of salt manufacturing in Kentucky. On each succeeding frontier, the early explorers and settlers looked for salt springs, since salt was an essential element of diet and was used for preservation of meat. Wild animals such as buffalo and deer helped people to discover the salt springs at licks. These animals, which had a strong predilection for salt, licked up the places of earth rich with saline particles.

The lick was probably named for John Mann, a member of Capt. THOMAS BULLITT's 1773 surveying party. Bullitt himself claimed what became BULLITT'S LICK. In 1780 the land in the area was granted to Col. John Todd, who died in the Battle of Blue Licks in 1782. The land was patented by his daughter, Mary O. Todd, when in 1787 Joseph Brooks leased the property and began the saltworks at Mann's Lick.

While never as large nor as well known as the nearby Bullitt's Lick, Mann's Lick did become an important settlement and employed hundreds of white workers and black slaves. Its salt was considered of excellent quality and was advertised in Lexington's *Kentucky Gazette*. While its product was sold under several brand names, after 1810 the Little Sandy Salt was especially fine and highly promoted by merchants. Salt was not only sold, but it also served as an exchange product for tobacco, hemp, and linen. As late as 1808 it sold for $2.00 to $2.25 per bushel.

In the 1830s the supply of salt diminished and the works were closed. The settlement around Mann's Lick, however, continued to develop, and in 1910 it was renamed Fairdale. Today's Manslick Rd. running through Fairdale is the contracted version of the historic name.

See Marguerite Threlkel, "Mann's Lick," *Filson Club History Quarterly* 1 (July 1927): 169–76; Robert Emmett McDowell, "Bullitt's Lick: The Related Saltworks and Settlements," *Filson Club History Quarterly* 30 (July 1956): 240–69; Neal Hammon, "Pioneers in Kentucky, 1773–1775," *Filson Club History Quarterly* 55 (July 1981): 269.

MANSION HOUSE, THE. In 1838 Mrs. Margaret Wright Paget purchased a house on Fulton St. from Lloyd White. The house was built upon land that had been owned by Jacob Geiger and his father, Frederick Geiger. She then engaged a contractor to construct a new front wing onto the existing brick dwelling, with the front to face the OHIO RIVER. This dwelling was thereafter known as the Mansion House.

The original brick part of the house may have been built ca. 1800 and is perhaps one of the oldest buildings standing in Louisville. It was already so old that in 1838 it was necessary to replaster the ceilings. The contract specification was discovered by Stratton O. Hammon and later published in *National Architect* (March 1949). The house had a very fine wrought-iron balcony on the front, and the rim locks were imported from England. Tradition maintains that the plans were prepared by a New Orleans architect and were brought upriver by the captain of one of the STEAMBOATS owned by Mrs. Paget.

The city of Louisville purchased the Mansion House in 1937. Left vacant for many years without maintenance, it burned after being occupied by vandals and was boarded up. The house still stands, and plans have been made to restore the structure.

Neal O. Hammon

MAPS AND PRINTS, EARLY. Largely because of its location at the FALLS OF THE OHIO, the area around Louisville received early attention from mapmakers. A manuscript map was made when George Croghan's expedition was at the falls in June 1765. In 1773 and 1774, town plats were made for Capt. THOMAS BULLITT's plan and for JOHN CAMPBELL's and

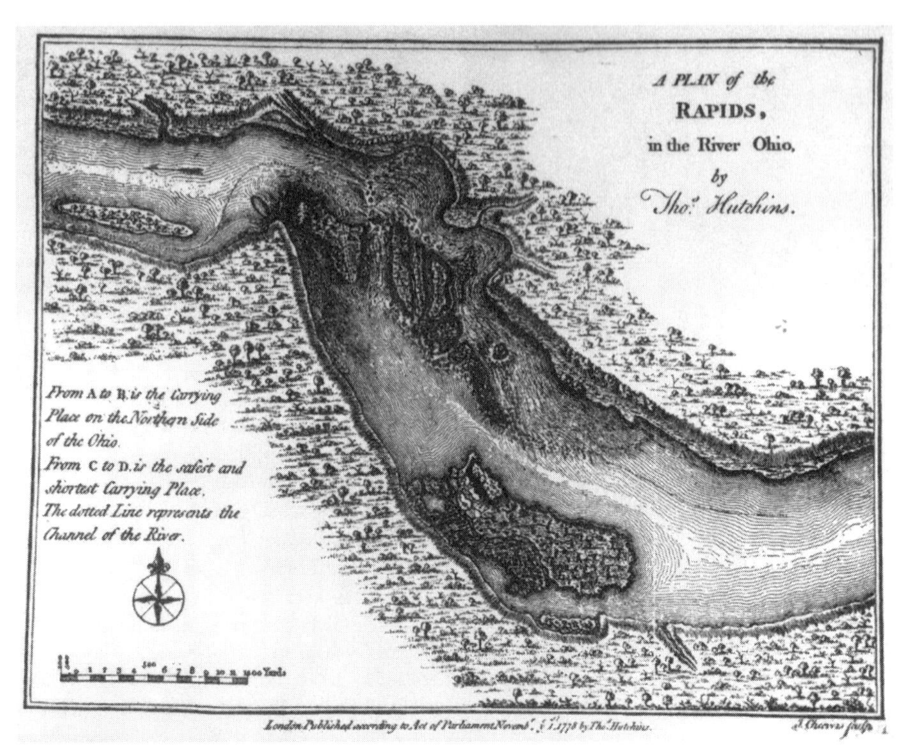

1766 map drawn by Thomas Hutchins.

John Connolly's offering of lots for sale.

In 1778, the year of Louisville's founding, a plan of the rapids was published in Thomas Hutchins's *Topographical Description of Virginia;* it had been drawn in 1766 by Hutchins, a British explorer at the falls.

John Corbly recorded a plat of a proposed town layout in 1779, and William Pope is believed to have made a detailed plan of the town in 1783, copied and recorded by Abraham Hite in 1791. About 1805 Jared Brooks published in Frankfort a more extensive map of the falls and surrounding area. The map included street plats of Louisville, Shippingport, Clarksville, and Jeffersonville, and proposed a location for a canal around the falls. A small section of this map, entitled "View of Louisville from near Clarksville," is the earliest known drawing of the town.

In 1796 Victor Collot drew a plan of the falls, as well as a view from their lower end. These were out of date when finally published in 1826 in Collot's *Journey in North America.* Dr. Henry McMurtrie published in 1819 his informative *Sketches of Louisville*, with a good map of the falls and the surrounding areas. However, the map platted far too many city blocks in Louisville and its extensions to be occupied by the then populace of less than four thousand.

Ohio River navigation guides, published first in 1801, supplied useful information for pilots and many others on charts of contiguous stretches on the river; the falls' reach took up one of these charts. The J. Flint/Gridley Louisville map of 1824 provided much-improved accuracy in details, and Louisville's first city directory, published in 1832, was associated with a good plan made by Edward D. Hobbs.

During the early 1800s some atlases of state maps included separate plans of important cities such as Louisville. An engraved view of the first state capitol at Frankfort appeared as early as 1795, and a small number of Louisville scenes can be found in a few early books and in travelers' accounts. However, the use of Kentucky and Louisville views was quite infrequent until the introduction of illustrated periodicals at mid-century.

Martin F. Schmidt

MARCOSSON, ISAAC FREDERICK (b Louisville, September 13, 1876; d New York City, March 14, 1961). Journalist. The youngest son of Louis and Helen M. Marcosson, at eighteen he became a reporter on the *Louisville Times* and later its assistant city editor. In 1903 he joined the staff of *World's Work*, a New York City magazine. From 1907 to 1910 he was financial editor of the *Saturday Evening Post*, and he was its foreign correspondent during World War I. Next, he became the *Post's* roving reporter, interviewing world leaders for more than two decades. Marcosson published numerous articles and twenty-three books, including seven biographies. Among his books were *Marse Henry: The Biography of Henry Watterson* (1951). Childless, Marcosson was survived by his third wife, Ellen Petts Marcosson.

See Isaac F. Marcosson, *Adventures in Interviewing* (New York 1919); *Turbulent Years* (New York 1938); *Before I Forget* (New York 1959).

Mary Boewe

MARKET STREET. A vital east-west artery of commerce through the heart of Louisville, Market St. stretches from Johnson St. outside the former Bourbon Stock Yards west to a half-block past South Western Pkwy. beside Shawnee Park and the Ohio River. Market St. is rivaled only by Broadway as the city's longest east-west thoroughfare, covering a total of 5.6 miles.

The history of Louisville and Market St. are inexorably entwined. The first map of Louisville shows the original four streets running parallel to the river: Water, Main, Market, and Jefferson Streets. Although street names were not officially designated until 1812, already the supplies and livestock that made Louisville thrive as an early western outpost were rolling down Market. Louisville was quickly becoming the center of commerce for the region and the emerging West, and Market St. fueled the westward expansion.

The first brick house built in Louisville was on the south side of Market St. between Fifth and Sixth Streets. Completed in 1789 by German immigrant Frederick Augustus Kaye (whose grandson William Kaye served as mayor in 1863–64), it was close to the first schools in Louisville, Langdon's at Sixth and Market and Dickenson's at Seventh and Market, both in existence by 1798. In 1804 the first markethouse was established at Fourth and Market by future circuit court judge, legislator, and real estate mogul Fortunatus Cosby and his partner George Wilson. Market became one of the first paved city streets shortly after Main St. was completed. The upper end of Market St. became the site of impromptu horse racing in the 1820s, a practice later abandoned when a more suitable track near the river around Fourteenth St. became available.

Market St. soon became the usual address of retail businesses and dry goods stores serving the drovers, rivermen, and settlers. By 1812 the first Methodist church in the city—a thirty-four- by thirty-foot wooden structure—sat on Market between Seventh and Eighth Streets. In later times, the street would have several large churches, including St. John's Evangelical United Church of Christ.

As Louisville began to swell in the early nineteenth century, so did Market St. The early 1800s continued to bring an increase in traffic from the river, and Market St. increasingly became a drover's lane, with livestock herds constantly en route between the Bourbon House on Story Ave. and adjacent livestock pens—better known as the Bourbon Stock Yards—and the river. The increase in traveling merchants and products necessitated a widening of Market St. to accommodate wagon traffic and the establishment of several market houses. These enlargements are still evident today, beginning at Floyd and Preston Streets between Campbell and Shelby Streets and again between Sixteenth and Seventeenth Streets. In the block between Shelby and Campbell there was a park in the center of the street enclosed by a fence, and the streetcars ran on each side close to the sidewalk. During this time the federal government also began renting a structure for a post office on Market St. between Third and Fourth Streets before moving into permanent quarters at Third and Green (now Liberty) Streets in 1858.

By the mid-1850s Market St. was the center for river goods. Soon the burgeoning prosperity required increased banking facilities, and institutions such as Farmer's and Drover's Bank at 115 Market were established. Five main market houses were eventually established along Market, although many businesses were damaged in 1840 by a fire that swept from Market north to Main and leveled the wooden structures lining the thoroughfare. But by 1852 the city directory noted "the entire extent of this street is given up to retail grocers, provisions dealers, and clothiers." Nearly everything for sale in Louisville originated from or ended up on Market St.

The onset of the Civil War saw Market St. become a part of both northern and southern supply lines, as Kentucky and Louisville profited from the state's short period of official neutrality. As the war dragged on, several times panicking residents who, fearing reported invasions of the city by Confederate forces, flooded the wharf and overflowed onto Main and Market Streets in hopes of escaping across the river to Indiana.

The end of hostilities and the economic hardship that affected the South was reflected along Market St., but soon the city and the street were busy again. By 1866 a streetcar line ran nearly the length of Market, stretching from Johnson to Twentieth St. Eventually Market St. and the streetcar line extended out to Fontaine Ferry Park, which became the destination for many city dwellers venturing out to escape the city heat or to enjoy the amusement park.

The March 27, 1890, tornado turned blocks of Market St. into piles of debris. The area of Tenth, Eleventh, and Twelfth Streets and Market had businesses and residences without roofs and fronts, and in some cases there were completely flattened structures.

The twentieth century saw Market continue to expand, becoming the home of Louisville's tallest building, the fifteen-story Lincoln Savings Bank on the northwest corner of Fourth and Market Streets; by the early 1990s that distinction had again been awarded to a Market St. building, the Aegon Center. Levy Brothers clothing, begun in 1861, was lighting up the Market and Third St. corner; Bacon's at Fourth and Market Streets began business in 1846; and Loevenhart's men's store at Third and Market opened in 1898. The German Insurance Bank (renamed Liberty Bank when the United States entered World War I) at Second and Market thrived after moving into its extravagant building in 1887. In 1916 Market St. was still full of horse collar makers, livery stables, and saddle shops, but more and more the names of the businesses were Italian, Jewish, and German, reflecting the soaring immigrant population. As in many other growing cities, immigrant shopkeepers would take up residence above the store, and, as a result, more and more people began calling Market St. their home address. Farther west on Market, a concentration of Catholics began around Thirteenth St. Churches such as St. Patrick's, especially during the antebellum period, and St. Anthony's arose to meet the settlers' religious needs.

Market Street west from Fourth Street, 1922.

The neighborhoods of W Market have changed little, with corner saloons and small shops still a part of its commercial life. The street twice passes under the railroad tracks, once at Fourteenth St. and again between Thirtieth and Thirty-first Streets adjacent to the "home of Beechnut Tobacco," the plant of the National Tobacco Co. at Thirtieth St. Although the tobacco plant was an industrial operation, much of W Market St. was still rural shortly after the turn of the twentieth century. A description of a streetcar ride out W Market noted, "For several miles toward the western end of the line the cars go whizzing past pleasant little farms, with the corn now waving in the breeze, with the cows standing knee deep in clover and with the fresh cool air from the river blowing in the face of excursionists."

By the early 1960s Market St. was a busy thoroughfare lined with something for everyone, including eighty-four furniture stores, twenty-six hardware and clothing stores, fourteen banking institutions, and fifty-three bars, taverns, or saloons. However, within a decade, the flavor of the street had changed as many of these shops had either closed or moved to the suburbs and were replaced with a number of second-hand junk or antique shops.

A change in the traffic patterns through downtown in the 1960s made Market St. between Ninth and Floyd part of U.S. 60 as well as U.S. 31W, while construction of Interstates 65 and 264 took the old street under the new highways. The construction of the Kentucky International Convention Center between Second and Fourth and Market and Jefferson Streets served as an attempt to bring people back downtown and return vitality to an area that has long been at the center of the city. At the close of the twentieth century, a rebirth of E Market St. brought a menagerie of art galleries, studios, and antiques stores to the grand old structures lining the way, keeping the heart of the city uniquely alive with commerce. Still the diversity of its life is seen in the presence of two homeless shelters.

See *Courier-Journal Magazine*, June 24, 1962, Sept. 20, 1970; Joseph Jacob Eisenbeis, "Recollections of Louisville, Kentucky, 1890–1920," *Filson Club History Quarterly* 65 (Jan. 1991): 5–37.

James Dale Kendall

MARRS, ELIJAH P. (b Simpsonville, Kentucky, January 1840; d Louisville, August 30, 1910). Preacher, writer, and educator. Marrs was born into slavery, the son of Andrew Marrs, a freedman, and Frances Marrs, a slave. Both were from Culpeper County, Virginia. Marrs learned to read and write by age eleven, a remarkable feat for a slave boy. He credited his early education to his daily trips to Simpsonville to pick up the farm's mail and also to a year he spent in a night school.

In September 1864, while en route to church in Simpsonville, Marrs decided to run away and join the Union army. He quickly convinced other slaves to join him, and, by the time he reached the Union recruiting office in Louisville on September 26, he had twenty-seven men with him. Marrs served out the war as a quartermaster and commanded troops that took part in the occupation of Bowling Green, Glasgow, Munfordville, and Elizabethtown.

After leaving the army, Marrs returned to his hometown, this time as a freedman and a schoolteacher. He later moved to LaGrange, where he taught for several years. Henry C. Weeden, a man who would record Louisville's African American achievements, was among Marrs's early pupils. In 1874 Marrs entered the Baptist College at Nashville, Tennessee, to become a minister but left the next year due to financial difficulties.

Marrs returned to SHELBYVILLE and then later began teaching in New Castle, where he taught more than one hundred students a year. He left there in late 1875 after he was elected to serve as messenger to the General Association of Colored Baptists of Kentucky convention in Paris. He was offered a position in the Paris schools but returned to SHELBYVILLE, where he was offered more money and authority.

In 1878 Marrs's brother Henry C. Marrs convinced him to assist in opening an institution of higher learning in Louisville. On November 25, 1879, Baptist Normal and Theological Institute opened at Seventh and Kentucky Streets. In 1883 the school changed its name to State University, and later to SIMMONS UNIVERSITY, then to Simmons Bible College. In 1880 Marrs took up the pastorate of Beargrass Baptist Church in CRESCENT HILL, and in 1881 he became pastor of the St. John Baptist Church in Louisville. In 1883 Marrs was invited by the Jefferson County School District to teach at a district colored school, a position he held for two terms.

Marrs was active in REPUBLICAN PARTY politics, influencing black voters and parishioners to support candidates sympathetic to the black plight. He was a delegate to every major political convention, constantly promoting African American political and CIVIL RIGHTS. He was active in voter registration campaigns in 1870, the first year blacks could vote. He is buried in Greenwood Cemetery in Louisville.

See Lawrence Williams, *Black Higher Education in Kentucky 1879–1930: The History of Simmons University:* (Lewiston, N.Y., 1983); Elijah P. Marrs, *Life and History of the Reverend Elijah P. Marrs* (Louisville 1885).

MARSCHALL, NICOLA (b Rhenish, Prussia, March 16, 1829; d Louisville, February 24, 1917). Confederate artist. Although the average Confederate soldier in the last years of the war for southern independence might have considered himself fortunate to possess a uniform of any standard design or color, the design of his official uniform and of the flag for which he fought were both attributable to a young German immigrant to Alabama who was to spend most of his life in Louisville. This was Nicola Marschall, the son of Emanuel Marschall, a wealthy TOBACCO manufacturer and wine merchant from St. Wendel, Germany, and his wife, Margaret Mohr.

Young Marschall began the study of both PAINTING and music at a very early age in his hometown and then went on as a young man to study in Italy and France as well as in several German cities. Perhaps due to a spirit of adventure, or in order to seek his fortune, he immigrated to the United States through New Orleans in 1849 and proceeded from there to Mobile, where he had a relative. He was employed almost immediately by the Marion Female Seminary, young as he was, to teach both painting and music. The seminary's brochure of 1851 not only boasts of his artistic and musical abilities but notes, "He speaks English fluently . . . and is highly competent to teach the German and FRENCH languages."

When the GOVERNMENT of the Confederate states was being formed in Montgomery, Alabama, in 1861, Gov. Andrew Moore of Alabama was visiting in Marion, where he mentioned to his relatives that the new country needed a design for its flag. Marschall's competence as an artist was immediately remembered, and he was asked for a design. Apparently he submitted three, and Governor Moore took these back to Montgomery, where the committee selected one. A recent bride contributed the material in her wedding dress so that the flag could be made at once.

The *Montgomery Advertiser* of March 5, 1861, noted, "The First Confederate Flag was raised on its staff at the Capitol . . . on March 4, 1861 by Miss Letitia Tyler, granddaughter of former President Tyler." This was the Stars and Bars. Marschall was also asked for designs for a Confederate uniform. The design he submitted, based on the uniform of a regiment of sharpshooters in the Austrian army that he had seen on a visit to Verona in 1857, was selected.

Marschall also served two periods in the Confederate army, where he was well known to Generals Nathan Bedford Forrest and RICHARD TAYLOR (son of President ZACHARY TAYLOR). After his discharge in 1865 he married an Alabama girl, Mattie Eliza Marshall. In 1873 they moved to Louisville, where he continued his career as a portrait painter, his studio being on the second floor of the McDowell Building at the southwest corner of Fourth and Green (Liberty) Streets. Dozens of his portraits hang in private homes and museums all over the country. He is buried in CAVE HILL CEMETERY.

See Marielou Armstrong Cory, "The True story of the first Confederate Flag," in *Stars and Bars*, (Montgomery, Ala., 1931)

Jo M. Ferguson

MARSHALL, HUMPHREY (b Frankfort, January 13, 1812; d Louisville, March 27, 1872). Soldier and politician. He was the son of John Jay and Anna Reed (Birney) Marshall, the nephew of antislavery leader James Birney and the grandson of Humphrey Marshall, author of the first history of Kentucky, published in 1812. Graduated from the U.S. Military Academy at West Point in 1832, Marshall soon resigned his commission for a career in the law and Whig politics. He moved to Louisville in 1834 and joined the state militia, serving as a colonel of the First Kentucky Cavalry during the MEXICAN WAR. In 1848 he was elected to Congress on the Whig ticket, serving from March 1849 until his resignation on August 4, 1852. He was then minister to China (1852–54) and was elected on the American Party ticket to two terms in the United States House of Representatives (March 4, 1855, through March 3, 1859). Marshall supported John C. Breckinridge in the 1860 presidential campaign but then lobbied for Kentucky's neutrality during the southern secession crisis. With the onset of the CIVIL WAR he accepted a commission as brigadier general in the Confederate army effective October 30, 1861, and was assigned to duty in eastern Kentucky.

Standing five feet eleven inches and weighing over three hundred pounds, Marshall was physically unfit for active duty in the rugged mountains, but he was obsessed with an independent command for his army of two thousand men. At Middle Creek in Floyd County on January 10, 1862, lesser numbers of Union troops under Col. James Garfield forced Marshall to withdraw. After playing a minor role in Confederate general Braxton Bragg's invasion into Kentucky in 1862, Marshall resigned his commission on June 17, 1863. Moving to Richmond, Virginia, he then served in the Second Confederate Congress until the end of the war, when he moved to Texas and then New Orleans. Marshall returned to Louisville in 1867, where he practiced law until his death. He is buried in the Frankfort Cemetery.

See Lowell H. Harrison, *The Civil War in Kentucky* (Lexington 1975); C. David Dalton, "Confederate Operations in Eastern Kentucky, 1861–1862," M.A. thesis, Western Kentucky University, 1962.

C. David Dalton

MARSHALL, JOHN (b Louisville, May 24, 1856; d Anchorage, Kentucky, August 19, 1922). Lieutenant governor and lawyer. Marshall was the son of David Marshall of Philadelphia and Mary Naomi (Ferguson) Marshall of Louisville. He attended PUBLIC SCHOOLS in Louisville and graduated from Centre College in Danville, Kentucky. Marshall attended Harvard Law School for one year but returned to Louisville due to his father's illness and received his law degree from the UNIVERSITY OF LOUISVILLE.

Soon after being admitted to the bar on June 27, 1879, he worked in the law offices of JOHN MASON BROWN. In 1884 he opened his own law practice with George R. Lochre, later joined by Charles H. Gibson. When Lochre left the practice, they were joined by Gibson's son, Barret.

Marshall is best known for the brief period he served as lieutenant governor, from December 12, 1899, to January 31, 1900, during the administration of Republican William Taylor. Taylor beat Democrat William Goebel by 2,383 votes, while Marshall defeated Democrat J.C.W. Beckham. Democrats filed a protest, citing the use of the militia in Louisville and accusing the Louisville & Nashville Railroad and the American Book Co. of corrupt use of funds to get Taylor elected. This resulted in a bitter battle and sharp division in the state, with hundreds of enraged voters flocking to the capital. In that charged atmosphere, Democratic contestant William Goebel was shot on January 30, 1900; he died four days later, having been named governor by the Democratic majority in the General Assembly. Until May, both parties claimed to be the legitimate holders of the office, but the United States Supreme Court eventually ruled in favor of the Democrats. Lieutenant Governor Marshall and Governor Taylor stepped down. Two months after his death, John Marshall was honored by a resolution of the Louisville Bar Association and the Jefferson Circuit Court for "refusing to countenance any measures that might invoke his native state in turmoil and civil strife."

Marshall retired in 1914 due to poor health. He was married twice, first to Ida Guthrie and then to Mary Barrett. He had one son, James Marshall Jr. He died in his home and is buried in CAVE HILL CEMETERY.

See *Courier-Journal*, August 20, 1922, October 15, 1922; Robert A. Powell, *Kentucky Governors* (Lexington 1989).

MARTIN, EDGAR BOYD (b Louisville, May 2, 1886; d Louisville, April 16, 1963). Drama critic, teacher, and director. The son of Silas D. and Pattie (Lovell) Martin, Boyd Martin graduated from DU PONT MANUAL HIGH SCHOOL and later attended the University of Kentucky and the UNIVERSITY OF LOUISVILLE. Without a hint of his future career as a drama critic or the impact he would have on the local THEATER scene, Martin went to work for the Grainger and Co. foundry in Louisville in 1904, where he rose to the position of chief engineer. Although he did not resign his position at the foundry until 1925, Martin years earlier had embarked on the career that would make him well known.

Martin's first assignment as a newspaper critic occurred by accident. In 1907, while visiting a friend at the offices of the *COURIER-JOURNAL*, Martin was mistaken for a reporter and told to review a newly opened BURLESQUE show, *The Burglar and the Lady*, at the Buckingham Theatre. He did, and thus began his fifty-five-year association with the newspaper. In 1909, the same year he became drama editor, Martin wrote his first movie review. His opinion of THOMAS EDISON's full-length feature, *The Great Train Robbery*, was that the film was "unrealistic." His lengthy tenure with the *Courier-Journal* was interrupted in May 1926 when he retired to become the publicity director and manager of the Strand Theater. This association was short-lived, however, and Martin returned to the paper as drama editor in September 1926. He continued writing theater and movie reviews until 1962, just months before his death. He was well known to those in the entertainment business from Hollywood to New York, and, in 1957, at the premiere of the movie *Raintree County*, actor George Murphy presented Martin with a gold watch from Metro-Goldwyn-Mayer in recognition of his distinguished career as a critic.

Martin's interest in the world of theater went beyond that of onlooker and extended to directing and teaching. In 1909 he began an affiliation with the University of Louisville that lasted until 1955. Martin directed the Dramatic Club's productions until the club dissolved in 1912. Two years later, Martin, acting as head director, reorganized the school's theater group, dubbing it the University of Louisville Players (1914–41). This was one of three acting companies Martin founded; the others were the Alumni Players (1927–32) and the Little Theater Co. (1932–60).

Martin directed over four hundred plays for the Little Theater Co. and its predecessors and also wrote some of the plays that were produced. He took on teaching duties at the university as well, becoming an assistant professor in public speaking and theater. Martin wrote *Modern American Drama and Stage* in 1943. Upon his retirement from the University of Louisville, Martin was presented with the school's highest honor, the Minerva award, in recognition of his civic, academic, and professional contributions.

In 1954 he began organizing the Boyd Martin Theater Train to New York City, a popular twice-a-year excursion to view Broadway plays. In 1960 Martin's wife of forty-eight years, Julia Johnson, died. He was remarried in 1962, to Jesse Strother Smith. Martin had no children. He is buried in CAVE HILL CEMETERY.

See *Courier-Journal*, April 17, 1963, Aug. 30, 1987; Barbara A. Elliott, "The Play's the Thing," M.A. thesis, University of Louisville, 1974.

MARTIN, GEORGE (MADDEN) (b Louisville, May 3, 1866; d Louisville, November 30, 1946). Author. The daughter of Frank and Ann Louise (McKenzie) Madden, in 1892 she married Attwood R. Martin, an officer of the Louisville Trust Co. (To avoid gender confusion, she often put Mrs. Attwood R. Martin in parentheses after her name.) The couple moved to Louisville when fire destroyed their ANCHORAGE, Kentucky, home. Author of eleven books, Martin is best known for *Emmy Lou, Her Book and Heart* (1902), stories about "the most charming child in Kentucky literature, a genuine creation" (Townsend, *Kentucky in American Letters*, vol. 2, 198). Other books included *Selina* (1914), *Children in the Mist* (1920), and *March On* (1921). During WORLD WAR I, Martin was on the staff of the *Red Cross Magazine*. In 1924–25, her articles about women in politics appeared in the *Atlantic Monthly*. During the twenties and thirties she served on various boards for racial and social reform.

See Jeannette L. Gilder, "Some Women Writers," *Outlook* 78 (Oct. 1, 1904): 281–89; John Wilson Townsend, *Kentucky in American Letters*, vol. 2 (Cedar Rapids, Iowa, 1913); William S. Ward, *A Literary History of Kentucky* (Knoxville 1988);

Mary Boewe

MARTIN, JOE ELSBY (b Louisville, February 1, 1916; d Louisville, September 14, 1996). BOXING coach and police officer. The son of Joe and Margaret (Shaw) Martin, he was orphaned before the age of one. He was reared by an aunt in Phoenix, Arizona, where he received his basic education. Martin returned to Louisville in 1937 and soon joined the city's police force, serving until his retirement in 1974. In 1938 he became a boxing coach at the Columbia Gym, which was located in the old Knights of Columbus building on Fourth, south of YORK ST. It later became a unit of SPALDING UNIVERSITY. The gym, which was operated by the Louisville Parks Department, provided a place of recreation for children off the streets. One of Martin's first acts was to integrate the gym racially.

It was at Columbia Gym in 1954 that Martin began his association with future heavyweight boxing champion MUHAMMAD ALI, then known as Cassius Clay. The twelve-year-old youngster went to police officer Martin to report the theft of his new bicycle and expressed his desire to "whip" the thief. Martin offered to teach him how to fight and became the guiding influence in the young boxer's career for the next six years. Beginning in the 1950s, Martin helped produce the weekly WAVE TELEVISION show *Tomorrow's Champions*, which was broadcast for twelve years and featured matches of amateur boxers. This was Ali's first television exposure. In 1960 Martin was chosen as U.S. boxing coach for the Olympic Games in Rome, where Ali won a gold medal. Upon returning from Rome, Ali began his professional career but kept in touch with Martin through the years.

Martin was known as a tough disciplinarian who stressed the fundamentals of boxing. While continuing his work as a full-time police officer, he was the sustaining force in amateur boxing in Louisville through four decades. In 1977 he was inducted into the Amateur Boxing Hall of Fame. He was the owner of the Joe Martin Auction Co. and twice ran unsuccessfully for sheriff of Jefferson County.

Martin married Christine Fentress on March 4, 1941. They had one son, Joe Jr. Martin is buried in Leitchfield Memorial Gardens in Leitchfield, Kentucky.

See *Courier-Journal*, Sept. 15, 1996.

Kenneth Dennis

MARTIN, SARAH (b Louisville, June 18, 1884; d Louisville, May 24, 1955). BLUES singer, actress, and church worker. The daughter of William Dunn and Kate Pope, she began singing in her church choir and in 1908 made one of her earliest appearances as a popular singer at the WHITE CITY AMUSEMENT PARK. In 1922 her recording of "Sugar Blues" was a hit, and she became one of the reigning blues queens, touring the country. Occasionally, her travels would bring her back to Louisville, where she performed at the Lincoln Theater, located at 814 W Walnut (now Muhammad Ali Blvd.). She made over one hundred records, recording on the Okey label, and appeared in several movies. In 1930 she retired from popular music and returned to Louisville, where she devoted the rest of her life to serving her church. In 1939 she opened a nursing home at 1728 W Walnut, which she managed until 1949. She was survived by three adopted children. She is buried in Louisville Cemetery.

See Sheldon Harris, *Blues Who's Who* (New Rochelle, New York 1979).

Cornelius Bogert

MARTIN'S MENS STORE. Martin's Mens Store was established in Louisville in 1930. Originally known as the Brown Hotel Men's Shop, it moved across the street to the Commonwealth Building in 1936. From their address at 684 S Fourth St., Charles and Ruth Martin maintained a competitive, locally owned business. Prior to opening his own concern, Charles had been a manager at Roche & Roche, another men's furnishings business along Fourth St.

Martin's operated in downtown Louisville at the "magic corner" until 1977. It opened a suburban outlet at OXMOOR Mall in 1971, where it continued to operate until 1992. The last location of Martin's was on HURSTBOURNE Pkwy. in suburban Louisville. The business ceased to function in 1997.

Kenneth L. Miller

Masonic Home showing destruction caused by 1875 tornado.

MARY ANDERSON CENTER FOR THE ARTS. The Mary Anderson Center for the Arts is a nonprofit artist residency facility on the grounds of Mount St. Francis, Indiana, a Franciscan friary and retreat center situated in the KNOBS of southern Indiana northwest of NEW ALBANY. The center was founded in 1989 by a group of Franciscan friars from the order of Our Lady of Consolation Province and by area artists. They sought to create a place for professional artists from across the nation to concentrate and work on creative projects of their own design within an environment where they can explore and develop unique visions. Through a juried application process, the center invites artists who are writers in all genres, including scholarship; visual artists and artisans; musicians and composers; and filmmakers and videomakers.

The center was named for Louisville actress Mary Anderson (1859–1940), who owned the property currently known as Mount St. Francis and deeded it to the friars of Our Lady of Consolation Province in 1885.

Sarah Yates

MASONIC HOMES OF KENTUCKY INC. On November 23, 1866, a group of Free and Accepted Masons (F&AM) met at the Masonic Temple in Louisville to discuss the idea of providing a widows' and orphans' home and an infirmary. The Ladies Masonic Widows' and Orphans' Home Society, with Susan P. Hepburn as president, helped raise ten thousand dollars in funds for the project. The charter for the incorporation of the Masonic Widows' and Orphans' Home was granted by the Kentucky legislature in January 1867. The cornerstone for the home was laid in 1869, and the first resident was admitted in April 1871. The original home was erected on Second St. at the corner of "A" St. (Gaulbert Ave.) and "B" St. (Bloom Ave.). The home primarily provided care for orphans of Kentucky FREEMASONS but also was home to many elderly Masonic widows.

On June 2, 1875, the building was hit by a tornado that tore off the roof and caved in the center walls. Miraculously, there were no injuries. In the early 1920s, the home began to outgrow its buildings; and, as the city continued to grow around it, a decision was made to erect a new home in the country, where the children could be provided with open space. A site was purchased east of Louisville along Frankfort Ave. in the small community of ST. MATTHEWS. Work began on the site in 1925, and, in mid-1927, the residents were moved. A campus of 176 acres became the home for several thousand widows and orphans over the years, providing them with care and nurturing.

The Masonic Widows' and Orphans' Home was called "the little city beautiful." All the resident needs were provided for by the home. This included formal and vocational education (the Masonic Home School operated from 1927 until 1955). The Masonic Home print shop, shoe shop, sewing room, cannery, and farm operation taught many children a trade that they continued after leaving the home. The St. John's Day League Infirmary cared for orphans and widows who needed the services of trained medical staff.

Strict state and health department regulations for facilities such as the Masonic Home no longer allow a farm operation to provide food products for use by the residents. The ninety-five acres of farmland were sold in September 1988. In the late 1990s, a community of single-family homes was built on the former farm acreage by a private developer.

The Grand Lodge of Kentucky, F&AM, occupies a building on the campus of the home, as does the St. John's Day League of Kentucky, the Masonic Homes of Kentucky development program, and the Grand Lodge Center for Education and Leadership.

On September 1, 1993, the Masonic Widows' and Orphans' Home Corp. and the Old Masons Home Corp. merged to become the Masonic Homes of Kentucky Inc. The organization is governed by a board of directors that includes elected members who serve three-year terms and the six elected Grand Lodge officers.

In June 1997, phase one of the Masonic Home Village Apartments was completed, and, in August, phase two was completed. The 103 studio, 1-bedroom, and 2-bedroom units provide affordable housing for persons age 62 and older. Over time, profits generated from apartment rentals will benefit the home.

See *History of the Ohio Falls Cities and Their Counties* (Cleveland 1882); *Courier-Journal*, Dec. 6, 1925, Sept. 24, 1997.

Roland Stayton

MASONIC UNIVERSITY. A preparatory and collegiate institution of higher learning was founded by the Masons of Kentucky at LaGrange, originally as an institution for educating the orphan sons of Masons. Funk Seminary was opened in 1841, funded by a ten-thousand-dollar bequest from William Funk of OLDHAM COUNTY. The school stood on four lots directly behind the public square, where the Oldham County Fiscal Court Building now stands, at the intersection of Hwy. 53 and Hwy. 146. This institution was incorporated into the Masonic school system in 1844. Each Mason in Kentucky was requested to donate one dollar for the school, and tuition fees of six dollars per student were assessed, with ten charity scholarships awarded. J.R. Finley was appointed president at an annual salary of $750. Finley began traveling and visiting Masonic lodges throughout the country in 1844–46, acquiring books, maps, and mineralogical specimens, in addition to raising $10,885. He also returned with 58 students, raising the total enrollment to 203, including 4 from France and 1 from Spain. Students were instructed in orthography (writing), reading, GEOGRAPHY, arithmetic, bookkeeping, Latin, and Greek, with collegiate studies on four grade levels added later. Students on charity scholarships were required to work in either horticulture, carpentry, coopering, smithing, or horseshoeing.

Students followed a strict set of bylaws, and no student expelled from another institution was admitted. Morality and RELIGION were woven into the curriculum, but, in keeping with Masonic tenets, sectarianism was prohibited. Under a vaguely worded resolution denying any financial responsibility, the Masonic Order agreed to incorporate an existing female school in 1847. They consented to educate local girls and offered eight students scholarships. The first commencement of Masonic College was July 23, 1847, when one earned and three honorary degrees were conferred. The valedictory was by the first graduate, George M. Bibb.

In 1848 the institution faced a deficit of nearly five thousand dollars. Subscriptions by Masonic lodges were going unfulfilled, causing the cancellation of scholarships. In 1850 the Kentucky School of Medicine was incorporated into the Masonic University with the intention of generating income; but, by 1851, disagreements between the two institutions led to the medical school disassociating itself and obtaining a separate charter from the state legislature. In 1860 the Kentucky School of Medicine offered to educate the sons of indigent Masons free.

The CIVIL WAR brought more problems with adjunct professor and principal of the grammar school Thomas Hines resigning to serve with John Hunt Morgan. Dr. Rob Morris, who headed the school from 1861 to 1865, is called the "poet laureate of Freemasonry." He also founded the Order of the Eastern Star for women. His home is preserved in LaGrange.

The school struggled on throughout the 1860s, and by 1870 the Masonic Lodge was attempting to end its financial obligations. The buildings were badly in need of repair. Lots were auctioned off in an attempt to keep the school afloat; but by 1881 the mounting costs and legal fees proved too much, and the Masonic University closed. The school had fallen short of its goal as a school for Masonic orphans, and, in attempting to become a university, resources were stretched too thin. Energies within the Masonic community were redirected to the Masonic Temple in Louisville and the Masonic Widows' and Orphans' Home.

See Charles Snow Guthrie, *Kentucky Freemasonry, 1788–1978: The Grand Lodge and the Men Who Made It* (Louisville 1981); Rob Morris, *The History of Freemasonry in Kentucky* (Louisville 1859).

MATTHEWS, KATE SESTON (b NEW ALBANY, Indiana, August 13, 1870; d PEWEE VALLEY, Kentucky, July 5, 1956). Photographer. Kate Seston Matthews was the daughter of Lucien and Charlotte Ann (Clark) Matthews and one of eight children. When she was very young, the family moved to Pewee Valley, Kentucky, where they lived in a fourteen-room residence known as Clovercroft. Because of a childhood illness, Matthews was educated at home.

At the age of sixteen she spent time in Vermont visiting her sister and brother-in-law, Lillian and Charles Barrows Fletcher, who introduced Matthews to PHOTOGRAPHY. Upon her return home, her father bought her a view camera and tripod with which she taught herself the art of photography.

Kate Matthews. Self portrait.

In an era when few women ventured into photography, Matthews made a name for herself when her photos were published in *Youth's Companion, Illustrated American, Cosmopolitan,* and *Good Housekeeping.* In 1895 *Southern Magazine* featured her, along with sculptor ENID YANDELL, in an article celebrating the young women as "bachelor maids" working in the arts. Her photographs were used in advertisements of the Old Flour Mill Co. and the J.B. Williams Co. Matthews chose as her subjects the people, ARCHITECTURE, and landscape of Pewee Valley. She is perhaps best known for her photographs used as postcards and promotional materials for ANNIE FELLOWS JOHNSTON's books in the *Little Colonel* series and as illustrations in Johnston's autobiographical *The Land of the Little Colonel* (1929). Matthews herself was portrayed as the character Miss Katherine Marks in *The Little Colonel's Knight Comes Riding* (1907).

Matthews won several prizes for her photographs at the KENTUCKY STATE FAIR and in Chicago and Pittsburgh. Her technique remained the same even after innovations in the art of photography. She disdained color photography, although she occasionally hand-colored photographs, and continued to make all her own prints.

Late in her career, Matthews began PAINT-

ING in oils. At the age of eighty-three, she won a prize for a painting in an exhibition sponsored by the KENTUCKY FEDERATION OF WOMEN'S CLUBS. In May 1956 an exhibition of Matthews's photographs was held at the UNIVERSITY OF LOUISVILLE. Her photographs are in the permanent collections of such places as the High Museum, the Whitney Museum of American Art, and the San Francisco Museum of Art. The Photographic ARCHIVES of the University of Louisville's Ekstrom Library has the largest collection of her prints.

Matthews is buried in the Pewee Valley Cemetery. Her family home, Clovercroft, was destroyed by fire shortly after her death.

See Norma Prendergast, "Kate Matthews, Photographer," *Kentucky Review* 1 (Spring 1980): 11–28.

Delinda Stephens Buie

MATURE, VICTOR (b Louisville, January 29, 1915; d Rancho Santa Fe, CALIFORNIA, August 4, 1999). Actor. Mature was born to George and Clara (Ackley) Mature and grew up in the GERMANTOWN neighborhood attending Roman CATHOLIC SCHOOLS, including ST. XAVIER HIGH SCHOOL, before completing his education at the KENTUCKY MILITARY INSTITUTE in LYNDON (1928–31). Mature, who planned to open a business locally, attended the Spencerian Commercial College during 1933. He sold candy and operated a restaurant until 1935, when he headed for Hollywood, where he became a successful actor.

Mature was spotted by Hollywood talent scouts at the Pasadena Community Playhouse. Soon afterward, he made his debut in the film *One Million B.C.* (1940). He starred in over fifty films, including *No, No, Nanette* (1940), *The Robe* (1953), *My Darling Clementine* (1946), *Samson and Delilah* (1949), and *Chief Crazy Horse* (1955). He often played the role of the tough leading man. Some of Mature's films had world premieres in what is now the LOUISVILLE PALACE THEATRE, and he often returned to Louisville to visit old friends and relatives. During his acting career Mature invested in real estate and retail stores, which allowed him to retire by the age of forty-five. He made few films during the last thirty-five years of his life, but these include the Italian farce *After the Fox* (1966) and *Every Little Crook and Nanny* (1972). He also appeared as Samson's father in a new TELEVISION version of *Samson and Delilah* (1984). Mature had appeared at a variety of charity events in Louisville, especially the Foster Brooks Pro-Am Golf Tournament for KOSAIR CHILDREN'S HOSPITAL.

Divorce ended Mature's first four marriages, to Frances Charles (1938–41), Martha Stephenson Kemp (1941–43), Dorothy Stanford (1948–55), and Adrienne Joy Urwick (1959–69). Mature married Lorey Sabina in 1972; they had a daughter, Victoria. He is buried in St. Michael's Cemetery in Louisville.

See *Courier-Journal,* Aug. 10, 1999.

MAUPIN, MILBURN TAYLOR (b Louisville, March 23, 1926; d Louisville, March 11, 1990). Educator. The son of Miller R. and Mary T. Maupin, Milburn was the eldest of seven children. He was educated in the PUBLIC SCHOOLS of Louisville and at the Oakwood Academy in Huntsville, Alabama. He received his bachelor of arts degree from the UNIVERSITY OF LOUISVILLE in 1949. In 1951, he was awarded a master's in education from Indiana University.

Maupin began his career in education in 1949 as a junior high social studies teacher in the Louisville public school system. In 1958, he became the assistant principal of the Jackson Junior High (later Meyzeek Middle School) –Booker T. Washington Elementary complex. The next year, he was promoted to principal, a position he held until 1965, when he was appointed the director of the BOARD OF EDUCATION's community school program.

As such, Maupin became the school system's first African American central office administrator. He also gained recognition as the first black president of the Louisville Education Association (1968–70). Maupin held a number of administrative posts, including assistant superintendent for federally related programs (1968–70), chairman of employee personnel services (1970–73), deputy superintendent of operations (1973–74), and interim superintendent (January–June 1975). He retired from the school system in July 1978 as the deputy superintendent of Jefferson County Public Schools.

Maupin also showed an interest in civic affairs, and in 1977 he was elected Louisville's First Ward alderman. He resigned in 1979 after he moved outside the city's limits. Maupin was also a veteran of WORLD WAR II, having served in the United States Army Medical Corps. He and his wife, Madeline Taylor Maupin, were the parents of two daughters, Madeline and Jacqueline. Maupin is buried in Evergreen Cemetery. In 1985 PARKLAND Elementary School was renamed Milburn T. Maupin Elementary in his honor.

MAURY, JOHNSTON MASON (b Louisville, May 1, 1846; d Louisville, January 1, 1919). Architect. The son of Matthew and Sally (Mason) Maury, MASON MAURY was educated in the Louisville public school system and reportedly graduated from Male High School. It is also believed that he studied civil engineering. Maury studied ARCHITECTURE with a firm in Boston and then returned to his home city, where, in 1877, he became a draftsman with the well-known ecclesiastical architect, William H. Redin. In the early 1880s, Maury opened his own office in Louisville; and over the course of his career, which lasted until shortly before his death, he became one of the city's prominent residential and commercial architects, partially known for his use of the "Chicago School" style of architecture. Among his more notable designs were the Kenyon Building (1886) and the Louisville Trust Building (1893), both on Fifth St.; the Liederkranz Hall at Walnut (now Muhammad Ali Blvd.) and Sixth Streets; and the Kentucky Building at the World's Columbian Exposition in 1893. He also designed the 1903 KAUFMAN-STRAUS Department Store on Fourth St. Its facade remains as part of the GALLERIA. Maury worked with Oscar Haupt for the year 1887, with William J. Dodd from 1889 to 1896, and with E. Walter Hillerich, his last partner, from 1907 to 1909. He had more than seven hundred buildings to his credit.

Maury married Gertrude Vaughan in November 1885. She died in 1889, and Maury was remarried on August 22, 1895, to Sarah Webb. He is buried in CAVE HILL CEMETERY.

See Tooba K. Latham, "Mason Maury and the Influence of the Chicago School in Louisville," M.A. thesis, University of Louisville, 1975.

MAYOR, OFFICE OF. The city of Louisville currently operates under what is commonly known as a "strong mayor" form of GOVERNMENT. Under this system, the mayor is the chief administrator, and all functional departments of the city operate under his aegis. The mayor annually develops and recommends the following fiscal year's departmental operating and capital budgets; and the BOARD OF ALDERMEN, the city's legislature, exercises its power to approve or deny these funding requests.

The office of the mayor had its origins in Louisville with the passage by the Kentucky General Assembly of the first city charter in 1828. Under that instrument a local government, to be administered by a mayor and a ten-member city council, was created to replace the trustee form of governance that had existed in the town of Louisville since 1780. The mayor and the City Council were to be elected annually on the first Monday of March by all free white male inhabitants who had been living in the city for at least six months prior to the election and were qualified under the state constitution to vote for members of the United States House of Representatives. Two councilmen were to be elected from each of the city's five WARDS established by the charter. In mayoral elections the names of the two persons with the highest number of votes were sent to the governor by the clerk of the City Council. The governor would choose one and submit his name for the advice and consent of the state senate.

The mayor was to have the powers of a justice of the peace of Jefferson County to arraign criminal offenders and send them on for trial, to deal out penalties for violation of the state laws and city ordinances, and to preside as justice of the peace over slaves and free blacks. In civil matters the mayor was to have no judicial authority. It was the duty of the mayor to be vigilant and active in the enforcement of the laws and ordinances. He was to inspect the conduct of all subordinate officers. The charter also states that if the mayor failed in his duty, he was to be prosecuted and punished. The mayor communicated to the Board of Councilmen all information and recommendations in all measures for the improvement of the finances, the police, health, security, cleanliness, comfort, and ornament of the city. Amendments to the 1828 charter in succeeding years altered and clarified the duties and responsibilities of city officials.

In 1851 a new city charter enabled the electorate to vote for all officers of the government, which was to comprise a mayor, a "lower house" Board of Common Council, and an "upper house" Board of Aldermen. The term of the mayor was fixed at two years from 1851 until the passage of the 1870 charter, when the term was increased to three years. The mayoral term was fixed at its current four years by an 1894 Act of the Kentucky legislature.

By the turn of the twentieth century, political patronage and graft at the highest levels of elected local offices were rampant, and political machines were the power brokers of the governments of both the city and Jefferson County. The 1905 election was so blatantly fraudulent that, after a year of lower court testimony, the Kentucky Court of Appeals declared the election of all the Democratic officeholders invalid. In 1925 the election of a Republican mayor was declared void for similar reasons. Overall, Democrats have occupied the office of mayor in all but twenty-five years of the twentieth century.

In 1929 the Kentucky legislature dictated another major change to the governmental structure of the city when it determined that

Mayor William O. Head delivers the first pitch in the 1912 opening day baseball game at Eclipse Park.

CITY OF LOUISVILLE MAYORS

Mayor	*Years in Office*	*Political Party*
John C. Bucklin	1828–34	N/A
John Joyes	1834–36	N/A
William A. Cocke	1836–37	N/A
Frederick A. Kaye	1837–41	
	1844–46	Democrat
David L. Beatty	1841–44	N/A
William R. Vance	1846–49	Democrat
John M. Delph	1850–53	Neutral first series of terms, then Unionist during the Civil War
	1861–62	
James S. Speed	1853–54	Whig
James Barbee	1855–56	Whig/American (Know-Nothing) Party/Democrat
William S. Pilcher	1857–August 1858	Democrat (died in office)
Thomas W. Riley	August 1858–April 1859	Whig
Thomas H. Crawford	April 1859–60	Unionist
William Kaye	1863–65	Democrat
Philip Tomppert	1865	Democrat
	1867–68	
James S. Lithgow	1866–Resigned February 14, 1867	Democrat
Joseph H. Bunce	1869	Democrat
John G. Baxter	1870–72	Democrat
	1879-1881	
Charles D. Jacob	1873–78	Democrat
Paul Booker Reed	1885–87	Democrat
William L. Lyons	1890 (pro tem)	Democrat
Henry S. Tyler	1891–January 14, 1896	Democrat (died in office)
Robert E. King	January 14–January 31, 1896	Republican
George Davidson Todd	January 31, 1896–November 1897	Republican
Charles P. Weaver	1897–1901	Democrat
Charles F. Grainger	1901–05	Democrat
Paul C. Barth	1905–June 1907	Democrat (removed from office by the Kentucky Court of Appeals)
Robert W. Bingham	June–November 1907	Democrat
James F. Grinstead	1907–09	Republican
William O. Head	1909–13	Democrat
John H. Buschemeyer	1913–17	Democrat
George Weissinger Smith	1917–21	Republican
Huston Quin	1921–25	Republican
Arthur A. Will	1925–June 1927	Republican (removed from office by the Kentucky Court of Appeals)
Joseph T. O'Neal Jr.	June–November 1927	Democrat
William B. Harrison	1927–33	Republican
Neville Miller	1933–37	Democrat
Joseph D. Scholtz	1937–41	Democrat
Wilson W. Wyatt	1941–45	Democrat
Edward Leland Taylor	1945–February 16, 1948 (died in office)	Democrat
Charles P. Farnsley	March 1948–1953	Democrat
Andrew Broaddus	1953–57	Democrat
Bruce Hoblitzell	1957–61	Democrat
William O. Cowger	1961–65	Republican
Kenneth A. Schmied	1965–69	Republican
Frank W. Burke	1969–73	Democrat
Harvey I. Sloane	1973–77	Democrat
	1982–85	
William B. Stansbury	1977–82	Democrat
Jerry Abramson	1985–99	Democrat
David Armstrong	1999–	Democrat

the Board of Aldermen would be the sole legislative body of Louisville's city government by abolishing the City Council. The evolution of the structure of city government since 1780 has continued throughout the twentieth century with the creation of a unified state court system and the abolishment of local COURTS in 1978. Each revision of the structure of government for Louisville since 1851 clarified the mayor's authority and responsibility for the administration of the public's business.

Today it is the role of the mayor to create the operating entities required to fulfill the mandates dictated by the voting public through the state constitution and the Kentucky legislature, and by the publicly elected members of the Board of Aldermen. The 1998–99 executive budget of the city of Louisville states, "The Mayor is the Chief Executive Officer of the City and holds broad powers of appointment of administrative officials and responsibility for preparing the annual city budget. Mayoral staff members perform a variety of duties, including research, planning, coordination, writing, responding to citizen complaints and information requests." The mayor's office staff has liaison functions with other city offices, the public, the private sector, various boards and commissions, and the media. In 1998–99, the mayor's office administrative budget, approved by the Board of Aldermen, was $1,432,150.

In 1986 through an amendment to the state constitution, mayors of cities of the first or second class were granted the right to succeed themselves twice, and to thereby serve a total of twelve consecutive years. Louisville is Kentucky's only city of the first class, and Jerry Abramson was the first to have served as mayor for three consecutive terms. However, owing to a change on the state level to streamline election year dates, Mr. Abramson served thirteen years.

Sharon Receveur

MAZZOLI, ROMANO LOUIS (b Louisville, November 2, 1932). U.S. congressman. He is the son of Romano and Mary (Ioppolo) Mazzoli. His early education was received at St. James Elementary School, and he graduated from St. Xavier High School in 1950. He earned his B.A. degree from the University of Notre Dame in 1954 and then spent two years on active duty with the U.S. Army, during which time he was stationed at Fort Knox, Kentucky; Fort Benjamin Harrison, Indiana; Fort Lewis, Washington; and Fort Richardson, Alaska.

Following military service, Mazzoli worked for a year in his father's business, the Mazzoli Tile Co., and then entered law school at the University of Louisville. As a law student, he clerked with the firm of Stites, Wood, Helm, and Peabody. Receiving his law degree in 1960, Mazzoli was engaged in legal work for the Louisville & Nashville Railroad. Beginning in 1962, he practiced law for six years with the firm of Jerry A. Lloyd. During this time, he also taught business law at Bellarmine College. Mazzoli entered his first political race when he ran as a Democrat for the Kentucky senate in 1967. He won and held this seat until 1970, when he was elected to the U.S. House of Representatives. Mazzoli's 1970 victory over Republican incumbent and former Louisville mayor William O. Cowger (by a margin of 211 votes) marked the beginning of his career representing Kentucky's Third Congressional District. Mazzoli would serve twelve terms, longer than anyone else who ever represented the Louisville district (January 3, 1971–January 3, 1995). During his early years in Washington he opposed President Richard Nixon's Vietnam policy and worked to bring about major changes in Congress's deeply rooted seniority system. He also successfully sponsored legislation to reform presidential campaign financing and to institute mandatory financial disclosure by candidates.

He was soon recognized for his individualism and independence. When Louisville was torn by dissension over the court-ordered busing of schoolchildren for desegregation in 1975, Mazzoli voted against anti-busing measures. A lifelong Roman Catholic who was strongly and consistently opposed to abortion, he nevertheless voted against prayer-in-schools legislation. He found inexcusable the efforts of the tobacco industry and some Kentucky lawmakers to avoid the health issue.

Rarely voting along strict party lines and defying ideological labeling, Mazzoli preferred to analyze the issues and act according to his analyses. While Mazzoli's inclination toward independence was generally respected by his colleagues, it was widely believed to have cost him his chairmanship of the House Judiciary Subcommittee on Immigration in the 1989–90 term. He regained the position, however, in 1991.

A centrist on immigration issues, Mazzoli was the House sponsor of the Simpson-Mazzoli Immigration Reform Act (1986), which controlled abuses but set no drastic limits on aliens with legitimate entry claims. He was long an advocate of campaign finance reform and made the decision in 1989 to stop accepting political action committee (PAC) contributions to his own campaigns. He accepted no honoraria from special interests for speeches, and in 1991 he set a hundred-dollar limit on individual campaign contributions.

Mazzoli proved invincible at the polls. His reputation for integrity, dedication, and hard work stood him in good stead in election after election, and his emphasis on constituent service kept his popularity high among district voters. A telephone call or letter to his office usually elicited a quick response and assistance in meeting the individual constituent's wants or needs. Mazzoli routinely held neighborhood forums where he would deal with voters' concerns and questions.

Although criticized by his opponents for not attracting more federal money to the district, Mazzoli was roundly applauded for his efforts to help save Louisville's Naval Ordnance plant in 1994. The federal government had slated the installation for closure, which would have resulted in the loss of two thousand jobs. Mazzoli was successful in leading the charge to convince federal authorities that the plant's work could not be done as effectively anywhere else in the military system or in the private sector, and the closure was forestalled.

He was also credited with obtaining $3.7 million in federal funding for construction of the Belvedere Connector, the stairways and overlooks that link the Riverfront Plaza and Belvedere to the downtown Louisville wharf. In recognition of his contributions, in 1995 Louisville's federal building was named the Romano L. Mazzoli Federal Building.

Mazzoli married Helen Dillon on August 1, 1959, and the couple had two children, Michael and Andrea. After leaving Congress, he was of counsel to the law firm of Stites & Harbison and was senior distinguished fellow in law and public policy at the University of Louisville.

See *Biographical Directory of the United States Congress, 1774–1989* (Washington, D.C., 1989).

Kenneth Dennis

MAZZONI'S CAFÉ. Mazzoni's Café, home of the rolled oyster, began in 1884 as a saloon at 212 S Third St. in downtown Louisville. It was opened by Phillip Mazzoni, an Italian immigrant who ran the business until the early 1900s, when a nephew, John, took over. In 1942 John sold it to his cousins Edward and Elsie Mazzoni, who sold it in 1966 to Edward's son-in-law, Kenneth Haner. In 1995, Haner sold the business to his son, Gregory.

Although the menu is varied, Mazzoni's Café is famous in the Louisville area for its rolled oysters. When it was a saloon, Mazzoni's served rolled oysters as free snacks for drinkers. When Prohibition took effect in 1920, Mazzoni's turned into a restaurant with the rolled oyster as its signature dish. It is still the centerpiece of the menu. Going to Mazzoni's for a rolled oyster is a popular exercise in Louisville nostalgia, and the restaurant sells thousands of them every week.

According to fourth-generation proprietor Gregory Haner, a rolled oyster is "three to four oysters, dipped in batter, and formed in more cracker meal. As you deep fry them the outside gets golden brown and the oysters on the inside steam and burst. Their liquor goes all through the dough on the inside, making it all taste like oyster. It's something different, it's indigenous to Louisville as far as we know, and we've been doing it the longest."

In 1974, construction of the Kentucky International Convention Center displaced Mazzoni's from its original location. The restaurant moved to 222 S Seventh and in 1975 opened a second location at 2804 Taylorsville Rd. In 1989 the downtown location was closed.

Charles Thompson

McALPINE LOCKS AND DAM. McAlpine Locks and Dam is located on the Ohio River 606 miles downstream from Pittsburgh, Pennsylvania. The navigation locks are

Steamer Tarascon navigates the Portland Canal and locks, c. 1905.

located on the Kentucky side of the river in the PORTLAND neighborhood, with access off Twenty-seventh St. at North Western Pkwy. The dam pools water about seventy-five miles upstream to Markland Locks and Dam. The Louisville and Portland Canal, with its three-flight lock system, was completed in 1830 and provided the first improvements to navigation at the FALLS OF THE OHIO. This project was built by a state-chartered stock company in which the federal GOVERNMENT became the largest stockholder. Army engineers assisted with improvements in the canal and new locks in the 1860s and 1870s, actually completing the project for the company. The federal government assumed jurisdiction in 1874, and the Army Corps of Engineers was charged with operation and maintenance. Since then the corps has undertaken several projects to provide improvements to navigation at the Falls. In the 1920s the Canal was widened and a 600-foot by 110-foot lock chamber was constructed as part of the canalization project for the OHIO RIVER; the hydroelectric generating station was built by the Louisville Gas and Electric Co. in that same era. As part of the navigation improvement for the Ohio, the project at Louisville was designated Lock and Dam No. 41 and consisted of a movable wicket dam. The wickets could be raised or lowered as needed. In the 1950s the corps began a navigation modernization program for the entire Ohio River to replace the old wicket dams.

At the Falls, construction of a lock chamber measuring 110 feet by 1,200 feet was begun in 1958 and completed in 1961. Work on a new dam started in 1961 and was completed in 1964. As part of the overall project, the canal was widened to five hundred feet. The dam is non-navigable, meaning all river traffic must pass through the locks. In 1960 the name was changed to McAlpine Locks and Dam in honor of William H. McAlpine, the only civilian to serve as district engineer at Louisville, and who later held key positions in the office of the Chief of Engineers.

The McAlpine project has the highest lift (thirty-seven feet) of any of the Ohio River locks. At McAlpine there are three locks; the oldest is what remains of the project completed in the 1870s and is no longer operable. There is also the 110- by 600-foot chamber built in the 1920s, which is used only as a backup to the main 1200- by 110-foot chamber. The corps has plans to replace both of the smaller chambers and construct another 1,200-foot lock in order to meet projected increases in barge traffic.

See Leland R. Johnson, *The Falls City Engineers: A History of the Louisville District Corps of Engineers, United States Army* (Louisville 1995 and 1984).

Charles E. Parrish

McCALL, JOHN "JACK" (b suspected in Jefferson County, approximately 1851; d Yankton, South Dakota, March 1, 1877). Villain. Known at the time also as Bill Sutherland, McCall is famous for having killed James Butler "Wild Bill" Hickok in Deadwood, South Dakota. After losing all of his money to Hickok playing cards the previous night, McCall entered Nuttall and Mann's Number 10 Saloon in midafternoon on August 2, 1876. Busy playing poker, Hickok never saw the gunman who entered the back door and shot him in the back of the head and then fled to a nearby butcher's shop. Following his capture, McCall's case was heard before an unofficial miner's trial on August 3 at McDaniels's Theater. Such a trial characterized the early stages of a mining camp before the establishment of traditional legal systems. The haste of the affair made the trial unofficial. McCall asserted that the shooting was to avenge the murder of his brother in Kansas. He was found not guilty and released. After this verdict was nullified because it was reached in Sioux country, an official trial began in a federal court on December 1, 1876, in Yankton, South Dakota, and ran until December 6. McCall, claiming this time that he had been a paid triggerman for a gambler named John Barnes, was found guilty and hanged on March 1, 1877.

While practically nothing is known of McCall's early years, shortly before the execution U.S. marshal J.H. Burdick received a letter from Mary A. McCall, a housekeeper at the Merchants' Hotel in Louisville who claimed to be the accused's sister. After acknowledging the relationship, Jack McCall apparently wrote back to his parents and three sisters in Louisville, whom he had left around 1870 to head west. Some believe that his family was from the PORTLAND area and that his father worked on riverboats.

See Joseph G. Rosa, *Wild Bill Hickok: The Man and His* Myth (Lawrence, Kans., 1996); Joseph G. Rosa, *Alias Jack McCall* (Kansas City, Mo., 1967).

McCLOSKEY, JOHN (b Louisville, April 4, 1862; d Louisville, November 17, 1940). BASEBALL advocate and promoter. Few persons have been as diversely active in promoting professional baseball in so many locations as Louisville's JOHN McCLOSKEY. He was widely known as "Honest John." Historian Philip Von Borries described him as "a trailblazing pioneer who spent his entire life spreading the gospel of baseball throughout the country."

Called the "Father of the Texas League," McCloskey also helped start the Pacific Northwest League (precursor of the Pacific Coast League), the Southern League, and a number of other minor leagues. Though never a big-league player, McCloskey managed several big-league teams, including serving a couple of years as skipper of Louisville's National League team in the mid-1890s and of the St. Louis Cardinals from 1906 to 1908. His career began in 1876 as a fourteen-year-old batboy for the Louisville Grays of the National League, the oldest continuous professional baseball league still in existence.

Possessing a keen eye for superior baseball talent, McCloskey found such all-time greats as Fred Clarke, Jimmy Collins, Joe Tinker, and Joe "Iron Man" McGinnity. It is believed that he managed a team every year from 1888 through 1932. He married Catherine O'Neill, and they had two children, Joseph and Mary. McCloskey is buried in Calvary Cemetery near another great Louisville diamond performer, Gus Weyhing.

See Philip Von Borries, *Louisville Diamonds, 1876–1899* (Paducah, Ky., 1996).

Henry C. Mayer

McCONNELL, ADDISON MITCHELL "MITCH", JR. (b Sheffield, Alabama, February 20, 1942). Senator. The only Republican in Kentucky history to be elected to three full terms in the United States Senate, McConnell is the son of A.M. and Dean McConnell. McConnell's renowned tenacity and focus were perhaps sown when overcoming a childhood bout with polio that required years of therapy and trips to nearby Warm Springs, Georgia, for treatments.

Moving with his family to Louisville as a young boy, McConnell's leadership abilities emerged quickly. He was president of the student body at DU PONT MANUAL HIGH SCHOOL, College of Arts and Sciences student body president at the UNIVERSITY OF LOUISVILLE (B.A. with honors, 1964), and president of the Student Bar Association at the University of Kentucky College of Law (J.D. 1967). McConnell's experience in Washington, D.C., began in 1964 as a summer intern for Sen. John Sherman Cooper. His post–law school career included tenure as chief legislative assistant (1968–71) to Sen. MARLOW COOK, private practice, and a stint in the Justice Department (1974–76).

Gradually building a public profile in Kentucky, McConnell was named one of Jefferson County's Outstanding Young Men of the Year in 1974 and one of Kentucky's Outstanding Young Men of the Year in 1977. McConnell succeeded in his first attempt at public office, ousting incumbent TODD HOLLENBACH to be elected Jefferson County judge/executive in 1977. McConnell was reelected in 1981, defeating James "Pop" Malone. McConnell first gained national recognition for his pioneering efforts on behalf of missing and exploited children, founding a state task force in 1982 that developed Kentucky's model legislation. The new legislation helped to ensure that perpetrators of abuse against children would be prosecuted for their crimes. In 1984 McConnell challenged, and defeated by a razor-thin margin (49.9 percent–49.5 percent), the seemingly unbeatable incumbent U.S. senator Walter "Dee" Huddleston.

Senator McConnell quickly used his vantage point on the Intelligence Committee to support sanctions against South Africa's apartheid regime. He became a lead proponent of lawsuit reform; championed Kentucky interests on the AGRICULTURE Committee, where he also passed legislation expanding child nutrition programs; and began leading a defining battle against campaign finance reform that found him aligned with the American Civil Liberties Union. Meanwhile, back in Kentucky, McConnell's successor as judge/executive, former two-term Louisville mayor Harvey I. Sloane, prepared to challenge him in the 1990 election. Sloane waged an aggressive campaign but ultimately came up short, as McConnell won the seat for a second time by a comfortable margin (52.2 percent–47.8 percent).

In McConnell's second term, he served on the Senate Ethics Committee, initially as vice chairman and later as chairman, and presided over the three-year investigation of sexual harassment charges against Oregon Republican senator Bob Packwood. McConnell led the fight on the Senate floor to enforce a committee subpoena demanding surrender of the Packwood diaries. In September 1995 McConnell moved to expel Packwood, prompting the senator from Oregon to announce his resignation. Though regarded as a fierce partisan, McConnell's second term was punctuated by conspicuous deviation from the party line not only on the Packwood matter but also on such highly charged issues as term limits for members of Congress and a Constitutional amendment to prohibit flag-burning, both of which he opposed.

Having secured a seat on the Appropriations Committee and the chairmanship of the Foreign Operations Subcommittee, McConnell became a major player in foreign affairs by working to reshape the multi-billion-dollar foreign aid programs into strategically targeted foreign policy tools. He preceded the Clinton Administration in utilizing foreign aid to secure the independence of the former Soviet Union states of Ukraine, Armenia, and Georgia. McConnell's position as an appropriator also enabled him to target significant allocations for Kentucky priorities such as the Land Between the Lakes and the Appalachian Regional Commission. He secured for Kentucky its only federal wildlife refuge.

McConnell is credited by political observers with transforming Kentucky into a two-party state, shepherding Republican candidates such as Congressman Ron Lewis and Ed Whitfield to victory in the 1994 special election, and Jim Bunning to his Senate victory in 1998. McConnell engineered a Republican rout of the Kentucky congressional delegation, turning it from a five-to-three Democratic advantage prior to 1994 to a seven-to-one Republican advantage after the 1998 elections.

McConnell established a privately funded program, based at the UNIVERSITY OF LOUISVILLE, to award scholarships to Kentucky high school students demonstrating leadership skills. The McConnell Center for Political Leadership's stated mission is to "train Kentucky's future generations of leaders."

McConnell began his 1996 reelection campaign in a state with lopsided voter registration strongly favoring Democrats. He faced a formidable opponent in former state attorney general and lieutenant governor Steve Beshear. However, McConnell's strength as a campaigner and his Senate record prevented the Beshear campaign from gaining any traction, and McConnell cruised to a landslide victory (55 percent–43 percent).

In the weeks following, McConnell was twice elected chairman of the National Republican Senatorial Committee, making him the party's chief Senate tactician for the 1998 and 2000 election cycles. He has grabbed press attention for unflinching opposition to campaign finance reform proposals that he called unconstitutional. Many credit McConnell with single-handedly blocking all of the federal campaign finance reform efforts of the 1990s.

In 1999, upon the retirement of Sen. Wendell H. Ford, McConnell assumed the role of senior senator from Kentucky and chairman of the Rules Committee and in that role changed the Senate's rules to permanently assign Henry Clay's desk to Kentucky's senior senator.

McConnell, a Baptist, married Elaine L. Chao in 1993. She is a Heritage Foundation distinguished fellow, former president of the United Way of America, and director of the Peace Corps. He is the father of three daughters from his first marriage, to Sherrill Redmon: Elly, Claire, and Porter.

See Michael Barone, *Almanac of American Politics* (New York 1986–present); *Congressional Quarterly-Weekly Report* (1984–present); Rich Lowry, "Louisville Slugger," *National Review* (Sept. 29, 1997): 22–25; David Mudd, "Mitch and the Machine," *Louisville* (April 1995): 26–31; Peter H. Stone, "Right on the Money," *National Journal* (Feb. 15, 1997): 314–17; Marc Fisher, "The Senator On the Eve of Obstruction" *Washington Post,* Oct. 12 1999: A1; Paul A.. Gigot, "Campaign Finance 'Reform' Meets its Mitch," *Wall Street Journal*, Sept. 17, 1999.

Tamara Somerville

McCONNELL, FRANCIS DEMAY (b Louisville, May 20, 1942; d Santa Barbara, CALIFORNIA, January 17, 1999). Writer. A graduate of Louisville's ST. XAVIER HIGH SCHOOL and Notre Dame University, McConnell received the Ph.D. from Yale in 1968 and taught English literature at Cornell, Northwestern, and the University of California, Santa Barbara.

A recipient of Woodrow Wilson and Guggenheim grants, he also taught briefly in Germany through the United States Information Agency. He served frequently on the Pulitzer Prize Fiction selection jury and published over two hundred essays and reviews on literature, film, music, politics, and popular culture. At the time of his death he was media critic for *Commonweal* magazine.

Among his publications were *The Confessional Imagination: A Reading of Wordsworth's Prelude* (1974), *The Spoken Seen: Film and the Romantic Imagination* (1975), *Four Post-War American Novelists* (1977); *The Science Fiction of H.G. Wells* (1981), *Storytelling and Mythmaking: Images from Film and Literature* (1979), and *The Bible and the Narrative Tradition* (1986). In addition he published four mystery novels and edited several texts, including Byron's poetry. He is buried in Santa Barbara.

See *Courier-Journal*, Dec. 31, 1981, Jan. 20, 1999; *Santa Barbara News-Press*, Jan. 18, 1999.

Clyde F. Crews

McDERMOTT, EDWARD JOHN (b Louisville, October 29, 1852; d Louisville, May 1, 1926). Lieutenant governor and attorney. The son of William and Catherine L. (Byrne) McDermott, Edward was educated in Louisville PUBLIC SCHOOLS, graduating from Male High School in 1871. Thereafter, he studied overseas for two years, first at Queen's College in Belfast, Ireland, and then at the University of Göttingen in Germany. McDermott returned to the states and graduated with an LL.B. degree from Harvard Law School in 1876. That same year he returned to Louisville and began private law practice.

In 1880 McDermott made his first foray into politics when he was elected to the Kentucky House of Representatives as a Democrat. While in the legislature McDermott's talent for oration became clear when he was chosen to give the welcoming address to the renowned IRISH leader, Charles Stuart Parnell, upon Parnell's visit to Frankfort in 1880. McDermott also served his party as a presidential elector from Kentucky in 1880. In 1888 he served as U.S. supervisor of elections for Kentucky, and in 1890–91 he was a member of the state constitutional convention. In 1892 McDermott chaired the committee of three that drafted a new city charter for Louisville. Earlier he had unsuccessfully sought to move the state capital from Frankfort to Louisville. Two years later, seeking to make his mark on the larger political stage, McDermott made an unsuccessful bid for a seat in the U.S. Congress. Though he won the Democratic primary, he was defeated in the general election by his Republican opponent, Judge WALTER EVANS. McDermott then settled back into his law practice.

As a prominent local attorney, McDermott was active in organizations related to his profession. From 1901 to 1907 he served as vice president of the Kentucky Bar Association. He was also president of the Louisville Bar Association from 1905 to 1906, and later, from 1913 to 1915, served on the executive board of the American Institute of Criminal Law and Criminology of Chicago, Illinois. McDermott was also an accomplished speaker whose services were in great demand at various universities, political functions, conferences, and civic events. For example, he spoke on behalf of Kentucky at the St. Louis World's Fair in 1904 and also delivered an address at the unveiling of the Lincoln monument in Hodgenville, Kentucky, in 1909. McDermott was the author of several essays and papers on criminal and civil law, which he contributed to various law journals. In addition McDermott was also founding president of the Louisville Literary Club in 1908.

McDermott reentered the political arena in 1911 when he was elected lieutenant governor of Kentucky, the highest elected post ever attained by a Catholic in the commonwealth. He served under Gov. James B. McCreary from December 1911 to December 1915. At the end of his term, McDermott became a candidate for the Democratic nomination for governor but was defeated by Augustus Owsley Stanley. In 1916 he was a delegate to the Democratic National Convention in St. Louis and from 1916 to 1920 was the president of the LOUISVILLE WATER CO. He received an honorary LL.D. degree from the University of Kentucky in 1913 and another honorary degree from the University of Notre Dame in 1917. From 1919 until 1926 McDermott taught law classes at the UNIVERSITY OF LOUISVILLE. He also continued in his private law practice up until his death from a heart attack.

In matters of RELIGION, McDermott was a devout Roman Catholic, but he was ahead of his time, showing wide sympathies for other doctrines. He was an early interfaith leader in the city. McDermott married Susan Rogers Barr on October 15, 1895. They had three children: Susan Barr, Edward J. Junior, and Catherine Watson Barr. McDermott is buried in St. Louis Cemetery.

See G. Glenn Clift, *Governors of Kentucky, 1792–1942* (Cynthiana, Ky., 1942); Clyde F. Crews, *An American Holy Land* (Wilmington, Del., 1987); *Courier-Journal*, May 2, 1926.

McDONALD, EARL (b Louisville ca. 1884; d Louisville, April 28, 1949). Musician. As a young man, McDonald learned to blow into an empty jug to create bass notes. By 1902 he had formed the Louisville Jug Band, which gained popularity playing at house parties and on the street. His band became a favorite with Louisville's elite, entertaining at country clubs and private parties, especially during KENTUCKY DERBY week. From 1924 to 1927 McDonald and his band traveled to New York, Chicago, and Atlanta to make records for OKeh, Vocalion, Victor, and Columbia. In 1931 they participated in a Victor field recording session held in Louisville. From 1929 to 1932 his band, dubbed the Ballard Chefs, broadcast its music over WHAS radio in a popular program sponsored by Louisville's Ballard and Ballard Co. flour mills. The Chefs often entertained both local people and city visitors. He is buried in Louisville Cemetery.

Brenda Bogert

McDONALD, HARRY PEAKE AND KENNETH (Harry, b Romney, Virginia, April 14, 1848; d Louisville, February 18, 1904; Kenneth, b Romney, Virginia, July 18, 1852; d San Francisco, November 17, 1940). Architects. The McDonalds were sons of Angus and Cornelia McDonald. Harry McDonald came to Louisville in 1869 after graduating from Washington University (now Washington & Lee) with a degree in civil engineering. He worked for a year with architect JOHN ANDREWARTHA on Louisville's CITY HALL and the Courier-Journal building, both designed by Andrewartha. In 1873 he established an architectural practice as H.P. McDonald.

Kenneth McDonald graduated from Virginia Military Institute in 1873 with a civil engineering degree and moved to Louisville, where he taught mathematics at the Rugby School and worked with his brother. In 1878 the architectural firm became H.P. McDonald & Brother. Two other brothers, Donald and Roy, joined the firm in the 1880s, and it was renamed McDonald Brothers. Harry and Kenneth McDonald were the principal design partners. Donald McDonald was the contract negotiator, and Roy McDonald worked as construction superintendent until they left the firm in the 1890s.

The McDonalds had a wide-ranging practice with commissions in Louisville, throughout Kentucky, and in other states. Most of their commissions were for public buildings, especially county courthouses and jails. The McDonalds designed Kentucky courthouses in the 1870s and 1880s in Adair, Carroll, Henry, Laurel, Simpson, Trimble, and Whitley Counties. They established the McDonald Bros. Jail Building Co. and designed approximately one hundred jails in seven states. Their best-known jail commission was the Chatham County Jail in Savannah, Georgia. In Louisville they designed the superintendent's house at the city WORKHOUSE (1878, razed 1968); the main building for the SOUTHERN EXPOSITION (with C.A. Curtin, 1883, razed 1889); completion of CALVARY EPISCOPAL CHURCH on Fourth St., begun by William H. Redin in 1872 (1886); St. Andrews Episcopal Church, Second and Kentucky Streets (1890, razed); Fire Department Headquarters (now the Sinking Fund Building), Jefferson St. (1891); and the M.S. Barker House on Cherokee Pkwy. (1892).

In 1895 Kenneth McDonald left the firm and practiced alone until forming a partnership with John Francis Sheblessy in 1901. He then joined WILLIAM JAMES DODD (ca. 1861–1930) in 1906. McDonald and Dodd worked together until 1913 when McDonald moved to San Francisco, where he died in 1940. Harry McDonald married Alice Keats Speed of Louisville. Kenneth McDonald married America Rouse Moore, and they had three sons.

See Marty Lyn Poynter Hedgepeth, "The Victorian to the Beaux Arts. A Study of Four Louisville Architectural Firms: McDonald Bros., McDonald and Sheblessy, Dodd and Cobb, and McDonald and Dodd," M.A. thesis, University of Louisville, 1981.

Mary Jean Kinsman

McDONOUGH, THOMAS J. (b Philadelphia, December 5, 1911; d Darby, Pennsylvania, August 4, 1998). Archbishop. McDonough entered St. Charles Seminary in Overbrook, Pennsylvania, in 1928 at the age of sixteen to prepare for the Roman Catholic priesthood. He was ordained a priest on May 26, 1938, in Philadelphia. He received a doctorate in canon law from the Catholic University of America in 1941. He began his ministry in Florida as a parish pastor and then administrator of the cathedral in St. Augustine. McDonough was named bishop of St. Augustine in 1947. At thirty-five he was then the youngest member of the American hierarchy. After a decade in that post, McDonough was transferred to the diocese of Savannah, Georgia, as the auxiliary bishop. He succeeded to the bishopric in 1960.

McDonough was named archbishop of Louisville as John A. Floersh's successor in 1967. McDonough showed the ability to adapt to the significant changes in the Catholic church following the Second Vatican Council (1962–65). McDonough had attended all sessions of Vatican II. His episcopal tenure in Louisville saw liturgical renewal, advances in ECUMENISM, and increased lay involvement in the church. The local church became more vocal in support of social justice, including efforts to seek the end of the war in Vietnam and participation in campaigns to combat hunger. One of McDonough's most notable policy statements declared that Louisville CATHOLIC SCHOOLS would not be havens for those seeking to escape school integration in the mid-1970s, and the archbishop urged parochial schools to integrate their teaching staffs and student bodies. McDonough retired in 1982 and was succeeded by Archbishop Thomas C. Kelly. McDonough retired to Palm Beach Gardens, Florida, where he lived until 1994. He returned to his native Pennsylvania to a retirement home for priests, St. Joseph Villa, in Darby, where he died. McDonough is buried in Calvary Cemetery in Louisville.

See *The Record*, Archdiocese of Louisville, Louisville, Aug. 6, 1998.

Mary Margaret Bell

The McHarry Hotel, Shippingport.

McDOWELL, ROBERT EMMETT (b Sentinel, Oklahoma, April 5, 1914; d Louisville, March 29, 1975). Author and historian. Robert Emmett McDowell, son of Robert Chester and Alice Lucile (Furnas) McDowell, was educated at the UNIVERSITY OF LOUISVILLE and began his writing career while serving in the merchant marine in WORLD WAR II. After first writing science fiction, he became a successful author of detective novels, mostly set in Kentucky. The best-known of these works include *Portrait of a Victim* (1964), *The Hounds Tooth* (1966), *Switcheroo* (1954), *Bloodline to Murder* (1960), and *Stamped for Death.* (1956).

McDowell was of pioneer Jefferson and Bullitt Counties ancestry and had a keen interest in history. His feel for history is evident in *Tidewater Sprig* (1964), a novel set at the BULLITT COUNTY salt works; *City of Conflict* (1962), a nonfiction account of Louisville in the CIVIL WAR; and his outdoor drama *Home Is the Hunter*, performed in Harrodsburg 1963–65.

In preparation for his novel *Tidewater Sprig*, McDowell and his wife spent years combing the circuit court records of Bullitt, Jefferson, and Nelson Counties, transcribing references to the salt and river trade, health conditions, slavery, crime, Indians, weather conditions, and other subjects between 1774 and 1869. These valuable records are preserved in seventeen volumes in the manuscript department of the FILSON CLUB HISTORICAL SOCIETY. McDowell wrote many articles on historical topics for the *Courier-Journal Magazine*, *Louisville*, and *THE FILSON CLUB HISTORY QUARTERLY*, especially his article "BULLITT'S LICK, the Related Saltworks and Settlements" (vol. 30, July 1956). McDowell wrote *Rediscovering Kentucky*, a tour guide, for the Kentucky Department of PARKS in 1971. He was editor of publications for the Filson Club from 1971 until his death.

McDowell married Audrea Adams in Louisville on August 31, 1940. They had one son, Robert Emmett McDowell III. McDowell is buried in CAVE HILL CEMETERY.

James R. Bentley

McHARRY, FRANCIS A. "FRANK" (b Indiana, April 25, 1805; d SHIPPINGPORT, Kentucky, February 15, 1857). Ferryboat captain and cement manufacturer. He was the son of Alexander McHarry from County Down, Ireland. Frank married Emily Beeler, and they had three children: Amelia Jane, 1830–70; Alexander, born 1837; and Florence, 1847–1900.

According to legend McHarry was buried upright in a stone tomb on the Indiana shore below Louisville and high above the OHIO RIVER. The various McHarry legends maintain that the bridges ruined his ferry business (even though the first bridge over the river at Louisville was not completed until 1870), and the eccentric man vowed revenge by building his tomb so that he could be buried standing up to curse passing rivermen and/or STEAMBOATS posthumously. Archaeologists who have surveyed McHarry's tomb have confirmed that all the crypts there were horizontal. Since McHarry was not buried upright, that part of the legend, along with the bridge stories, cannot be true.

"The real McHarry" was a construction worker on the Louisville and PORTLAND Canal in the 1820s and a canal toll collector in the 1840s. During the same time he was a partner of John Hulme in J. Hulme and Co. of SHIPPINGPORT. Hulme had been a canal toll collector and later treasurer and a director of the canal company. Their company produced flour, cement, and lime, and continued the operation of the Tarascon mill. In 1850 McHarry and Hulme operated a ferry between Shippingport and CLARKSVILLE, INDIANA. In June 1855 McHarry bought the Portland–NEW ALBANY ferry from Rebecca and Walker R. Carter. Instead of meeting a violent end on a steamboat, as some legends relate, McHarry died quietly at his home on Shippingport Island. At the time of his death, his estate was worth $190,000, and he owned about 2,050 acres of land in Indiana. His wife's family was also buried in the tomb. His daughter Amelia married James Irvin, who operated the ferry after McHarry's death. After Amelia's death in 1870, her sister, Florence, married Irvin.

One plausible part of the legend maintains that McHarry became irritated when passing steamboats' heavy wakes either delayed his ferry's landing or rocked the ferry and frightened horses aboard. That irritation could be the basis of his legendary anger. There is, however, no documented malevolent act done to McHarry to which his burial/cursing legend can be attributed. McHarry's wrath became legendary because of the overnight passenger steamboat tourist trade in the 1920s and 1930s. Cruise directors found that passengers especially enjoyed hearing tales of the river embellished into "better" stories. Many anecdotes were deliberately enhanced to provide more appealing stories for gullible passengers. In 1939 the trees and brush around McHarry's Tomb, from which his body had been long removed, were cut back to give steamboat passengers a better view.

Mrs. McHarry died in 1888. In 1905, seventeen years after her death, her husband's body was moved from the hillside tomb in Harrison County, Indiana, to join her at Cave Hill Cemetery in the Irvin tomb.

See *Louisville Courier*, Feb. 16, 1857; *Courier-Journal*, Oct. 12, 1888; *Corydon Democrat*, Oct. 8, 1919; *New Albany Tribune*, Sept. 26, 1939.

Jack E. Custer
Sandra Miller Custer

McKENDREE COLLEGE. McKendree College is an accredited nonprofit four-year college with a main campus in Lebanon, Illinois, and two off-campus branches in the Louisville area. The McKendree College Kentucky centers are located in east Jefferson County on Blankenbaker Rd. near Jeffersontown and on Lincoln Trail Blvd. in Radcliff.

McKendree College was founded in Illinois in 1828 by pioneer Methodist preachers who rode the Midwest circuit. The main campus is the oldest college in Illinois and the oldest in the country with continuous ties to the Methodist church.

The Illinois college was originally called Lebanon Seminary, but in 1830 Bishop William McKendree, the first American-born Methodist bishop, allowed the school's board of trustees to change the name to McKendree College. The head of the trustees, Rev. Peter Cartwright, a protégé of Bishop McKendree, was instrumental in getting the name changed.

The Kentucky program was started in 1973 after Air Force captain Michael Shirley, a graduate of McKendree's program at Scott Air Force Base in Illinois, suggested the school's unique format might appeal to adult learners in Louisville. That format included one-month evening classes designed to cater to nontraditional students unable to attend day classes.

Shirley persuaded McKendree's president to launch the program on a trial basis. The president gave Shirley, along with Hershel Finney, the Kentucky Center's first director of admissions, the authority to recruit students and faculty for the fledgling program. The Louisville program operated in rented office space downtown until 1990, when the east Jefferson County facility was opened. That center also offers classes at the Ford Motor Co., Louisville Assembly Plant, on Fern Valley Rd.

In 1975 a second college extension program was opened in the Fort Knox area and was operated in rented office space in a strip mall in Radcliff. In 1986 a separate facility was built to house the extension. The administration for both Kentucky Centers is on the east Jefferson County campus.

At the Kentucky Centers, the college offers bachelor's degree programs in business administration (specializing in accounting, management, or marketing), computer information systems, nursing, and organizational communication.

See "Take the Fast Path to Success," McKendree College pamphlet (Louisville 1998).

McLAUGHLIN, LENNIE LEE (WALLS) (b Breckinridge County, Kentucky, June 1, 1900; d Louisville, May 21, 1988). Political leader. "Miss Lennie" or "Miz Lennie" McLaughlin, as she was known by the public and by city workers, respectively, was the daughter of Lee and Mary Walls. She married William Lester McLaughlin in 1921. They were divorced in 1930. She never remarried and had no children.

She became nationally recognized as a Democratic Party leader and organizer for forty years, beginning her work as party secretary to local Democratic chairman Michael "Mickey" Brennan in the early 1920s.

McLaughlin was known for her careful record-keeping and precinct-organizing beyond that of any of her predecessors. She maintained close personal acquaintance with the entire Democratic party structure. After Brennan died in 1938, John W. "Johnnie" Crimmins, godson of an earlier Democratic boss, John Whallen, came in. Crimmins was selected somewhat as a compromise by Mayor Leland Taylor, who had won an election as an anti-organization candidate in 1945. Crimmins became chairman and McLaughlin became secretary of the party organization.

McLaughlin had on and off years and was forced out by Democratic mayor Joseph D. Scholtz in 1939. She then took her first work as a public jobholder and became clerk of the Fiscal Court in 1940. She returned as party secretary, working with Crimmins, in 1947.

Democratic mayor Leland Taylor died, leaving a vacancy in 1947. The Board of Aldermen, on a tie-breaking vote by Pres. Dann Byck, chose Charles Farnsley over McLaughlin's choice, Thomas Graham. Farnsley went on to win the remaining part of Taylor's term and a full term in the election of 1949. He made peace within the party, and McLaughlin reached the peak of her power in the following years.

A woman who wielded political power was unusual in the annals of Louisville history, but McLaughlin survived as a political leader by relying on the support of precinct workers, political patronage, legislative influence, primary and general election victories, organizational experience, and political savvy.

In 1960 McLaughlin warned the then-Democratic Fiscal Court members that if a proposed county occupational tax was passed, it would surely bring on defeat by the Republicans. The tax was passed, and McLaughlin's prophecy came true. The election of Republicans in both the city and county in 1961 brought in Mayor William Cowger and County Judge Marlow Cook. At issue, as well, was the strength and influence of the organization. Republican candidates promised an end to "machine" rule.

Lennie McLaughlin retired in 1965, bringing an era to a close. Democrats remember her as a brilliant, hard-working, effective political leader. She is buried in Ivy Hills Cemetery in Hardinsburg, Kentucky.

See Carolyn L. Denning, "The Louisville (Ky.) Democratic Party: "Miss Lennie McLaughlin," M.A. thesis, University of Louisville, 1981; George H. Yater, *Two Hundred Years at the Falls of the Ohio* (Louisville 1979).

Philip Ardery

McMEEKIN, CLARK. Clark McMeekin was the pen name of Louisville writers Dorothy (Park) Clark (b Osceola, Iowa, September 14, 1899; d Louisville June 23, 1983) and Isabel (McLennan) McMeekin (b Louisville, November 19, 1895; d Louisville, September 4, 1973). Between 1940 and 1961, they collaborated on a series of twelve successful historical novels, several local histories, and two plays. Dorothy (Park) Clark was the daughter of William and Eugenia (Dowden) Park. She moved to Kentucky at the age of five and received her higher education at Randolph-Macon Woman's College in Lynchburg, Virginia; College Conservatory of Music in Cincinnati; and Columbia University. She married Edward Clark in 1923, and they had two daughters, Christy and Martha. Isabel (McLennan) McMeekin was born to Alexander and Rosa (Harbison) McLennan. Educated at Westover School in Middlebury, Connecticut, and the University of Chicago, she married Samuel H. McMeekin in 1921. They were parents of three children: Isabel, Rosalind, and Paxton.

Both Clark and McMeekin individually produced a variety of literary work, including mysteries, short stories, poetry, and children's literature. It is for their collaborative historical novels, however, that they are best known. Beginning with *Show Me a Land* (1940), these books are set in nineteenth-century Kentucky and offer fairly accurate views of attitudes, morals, and manners of the time. The plots, which abound with action and romance, present realistic fictional characters whose paths often cross those of such historical figures as Henry Clay, Zachary Taylor, Mary Todd, Abraham Lincoln, and Aaron Burr. *City of the Flags* (1950) and *Tyrone of Kentucky* (1954) provide particularly vivid representations of life in Kentucky during the turbulent Civil War and Reconstruction periods. The Bluegrass, Louisville, and the Ohio River area are the usual settings for the stories. Their other collaborative novels include *Reckon with the River* (1941), *Welcome Soldier* (1942), *Red Raskall* (1943), *Black Moon* (1945), *Gaudy's Ladies* (1948), *Room at the Inn* (1953), *October Fox* (1956), and *The Fairbrothers* (1961). Both are buried in CAVE HILL CEMETERY.

See Dorothy Edwards Townsend, *Kentucky in American Letters*, vol. 3 (Georgetown, Ky., 1976); John E. Kleber, ed. *The Kentucky Encyclopedia* (Lexington 1992).

Kenneth Dennis

McMURTRIE, HENRY (b Philadelphia, 1793; d Philadelphia, 1865). Physician and historian. Educated at the College of William and Mary and the University of Pennsylvania, where he received his doctorate in MEDICINE in 1814, McMurtrie became a ship's surgeon during the War of 1812. He was held prisoner by the British after the capture of his ship, the *Penrose*.

Following his release, McMurtrie returned home, married, and decided to seek his fame and fortune along the OHIO RIVER. With his new bride, McMurtrie moved to Louisville and rented a house on MAIN St. While the city received many hopeful physicians at that time, McMurtrie found his niche by collecting historical, biological, and commercial information throughout the city. After more than a year of research, *Sketches of Louisville and Its Environs*, the first history of the city, was published in the fall of 1819 from the printing house of Shadrack Penn, the editor of the *Louisville Public Advertiser*. In his work, McMurtrie described the geological attributes of the area; wrote of the region's early history; detailed the backgrounds of local businesses, structures, and POPULATIONS; and cataloged over four hundred botanical specimens of the vicinity. As a frontispiece, his account also contained an updated 1806 map of the area drawn by Jared Brooks, whose daily observations of the earthquake of 1811–12 were included in the appendix.

McMurtrie did not stay to see the release of his book, as debt to his landlord and printer forced him to flee town in late summer 1819. He returned to Philadelphia, where he became a distinguished professor of anatomy, physiology, and natural history at the city's Central High School and helped edit one-time Louisville resident JOHN JAMES AUDUBON'S *Ornithological Biography* (1838).

See J. Stoddard Johnston, ed., *Memorial History of Louisville* (Chicago 1896); Henry McMurtrie, *Sketches of Louisville and Its Environs* (Louisville 1819).

MEATPACKING. Meatpacking has been a mainstay of Louisville's industrial ECONOMY since the early nineteenth century. As Kentucky's leading river port, Louisville captured control of a major segment of the state's agricultural trade between 1800 and 1830. During the first decade of the century, much cargo came into Louisville on flatboats, keelboats, or barges from Pittsburgh, Cincinnati, and other points along the river. But a major portion of the freight that passed through the Falls City consisted of Kentucky's own exports: TOBACCO, pork, beef, lard, flour, lumber, hemp, corn, and bourbon whiskey. With the advent of the steamboat on the OHIO RIVER in 1811, followed by the opening of the Louisville and PORTLAND Canal in 1830, trade became even more brisk.

Magnolia Ham advertisement, 1881.

During the late 1820s and 1830s Louisville entrepreneurs began to develop a network of turnpikes that reached out to interior towns like Brownsboro, Frankfort, SHELBYVILLE, TAYLORSVILLE, Bardstown, Shepherdsville, and Elizabethtown. With the linkage of road, steamboat, and canal, Louisville had the transportation system to support a terminal livestock market and MEATPACKING industry.

The center of Louisville's livestock industry was BUTCHERTOWN, a river neighborhood immediately east of downtown where several major roads converged. During the 1820s and 1830s a large number of butchers, many of them German immigrants, built homes facing Story Ave. Behind their homes they erected small slaughterhouses along BEARGRASS CREEK. Farmers drove their livestock from the Bluegrass and other regions of Kentucky into the city along Frankfort Ave. or other parallel streets to Story Ave. and transferred them to a slaughterhouse operator. Once animals had been killed and processed, they would be hauled to the wharf and loaded for shipment to Pittsburgh, New Orleans, or some other port.

As business expanded, so did the scale of slaughtering operations. During the late 1820s, two large pork houses were established, one by Patrick Maxey and the other by John D. Colmesnil and John O'Beirne. During the first six months of 1835 the combined export business of all Louisville porkpacking operations totaled 2.8 million pounds of bacon, 14,419 barrels of pork, 60,713 kegs of lard, and 149 barrels of tallow. Growth of the meatpacking business also resulted in creation of numerous related businesses such as manufacture of lantern oil, soap, and candles.

Between 1834 and the Civil War, Louisville was one of the nation's leading meatpacking centers, competing with Cincinnati for the title of "Porkopolis." The expansion of Louisville's meatpacking industry is easily traceable through statistics. In 1827, for example, pork houses operated by Patrick Maxey and Colmesnil & O'Beirne slaughtered a combined total of fifteen thousand hogs. As business grew, the latter firm opened a second pork house in 1837. By 1845, Louisville had four pork houses that together slaughtered and packed about seventy thousand hogs annually. The production of these operations was in addition to the smaller, family-owned and -operated slaughterhouses. Louisville's hog business mushroomed during the late 1840s and early 1850s. By the 1849–50 packing season, six houses were in operation, slaughtering 179,105 hogs annually. In addition, NEW ALBANY, Indiana, had its own stockyards and a porkpacking establishment by 1850. During the years 1857 to 1860, Louisville packers processed an average of 248,254 head annually.

An immediate spinoff of Louisville's expanding porkpacking industry was the development of specialty producers. For example, about 1850 Charles Duffield moved his famous ham-curing business from Cincinnati to Louisville. In 1852 the Charles Duffield Co. claimed to be the world's largest firm devoted exclusively to the curing of hams. The product was sold under the trade name "Duffield's American Westphalia Hams," exploiting the popularity of the famous hams imported from Westphalia in Germany.

Several factors contributed to the growth of Louisville's meatpacking industry during the antebellum years. One was the willingness of local agents to reach out to farmers for their business. Equally important was the fact that farmers found satisfaction with the Louisville market in terms of price and slaughtering conditions. Another important growth force was the westward movement of the geographic center of American hog production, which gravitated from Louisa, Kentucky, on the Big Sandy River in 1840 to Caneyville in Grayson County in 1860. Beginning in the 1850s, Louisville packers also benefited from the advent of the railroad, which enabled them to serve a much larger area. Because of its strategic position at the FALLS OF THE OHIO and as the northern terminus of the Louisville & Nashville Railroad, Louisville became the primary transportation and supply center for the Union's western THEATER during the CIVIL WAR. The city's packers obtained large contracts to supply meat for the western armies. Farmers began shipping all available livestock to slaughterhouses in Louisville, and packers worked day and night to fill military orders.

The RAILROADS became an even greater force in meatpacking after the Civil War, but not necessarily to Louisville's benefit. The gradual expansion of livestock production in the South, the development of the transcontinental railroad network, and the concentration of livestock trade at new western rail centers such as Chicago, Omaha, St. Louis, and Kansas City cut into Louisville's shipping business and severely eroded its standing as a national livestock market and packing center. The Falls City remained, however, a regional packing leader. In 1871 Louisville's 17 pork houses and 6 packing houses employed 1,470 people in processing $11 million worth of livestock. Approximately 127 million pounds of pork were sold, mostly to southern markets. By 1880 Louisville had dropped to sixth place among western porkpacking cities, but the industry remained an important component of the city's economy, ranking well ahead of both tobacco and distilled spirits in annual sales volume.

Meatpacking remained a heavily German, family-dominated industry during the post–Civil War decades, concentrated primarily in the BUTCHERTOWN neighborhood near the BOURBON STOCK YARDS. In 1875, for example, Herman F. Vissman, a former owner of the Bourbon House hotel, established his own packing firm, which became known as C.F. Vissman Co. when his son took control in 1890. Other firms in the neighborhood included the John M. Letterle Pork House; the Louis Bornwasser Co., producer of Corn Blossom hams; and smaller companies operated by residents with names like Koch, Pfaffinger, and Henzel. Not all firms were located in Butchertown. In 1876 Theodore Klarer opened a plant on Thirty-eighth St. near Amy Ave. in the West End that prepared pork products and sausage.

As the twentieth century dawned, Louisville's family-dominated meatpacking industry began to face competition from the large-scale national packers who applied mass production techniques to slaughtering and packing. By 1902, two of the so-called Big Five packers—Armour and Swift—had operations in the Falls City. But local firms such as Bornwasser, Pfaffinger, Rausch & Ruger, Vissman, and Klarer remained strong competitors. In 1909 Henry Fischer, a German immigrant, began grinding sausage in his backyard on Mellwood Ave., an operation that grew into the FISCHER PACKING CO. Six years later, Joseph M. Emmart and Theodore Klarer joined forces to organize Louisville Provision Co., and in 1921 Emmart established Emmart Packing Co. By mid-century, the Fischer, Klarer, Vissman, and Emmart firms, plus Louisville Provision Co., were major regional packers.

During the 1950s and 1960s the American meatpacking business experienced economic and technological changes that made it more difficult for smaller firms to make a profit and drove hundreds of them out of business. Many of those that survived did so by merging with stronger regional or national competitors. Louisville was not immune to this trend. In 1955 the city boasted at least thirteen packing companies, including C.F. Vissman & Co., which already had been acquired by Klarer; fifteen years later the number had dropped to eight. During that period, Emmart Packing Co. merged with Klarer, and the latter closed its Amy Ave. plant. In 1969 Armour acquired Klarer, which had undergone a major modernization program five years earlier, and Klarer became a subsidiary of Armour. The same year Fischer Packing Co. was purchased by Wilson & Co., a national giant, which itself had been acquired by the conglomerate Ling-Temco-Vought. Meanwhile, firms such as Fleischaker Co. and Morton Packing Co. folded.

The economic situation stabilized somewhat during the 1970s, although Swift & Co. closed its plant at 301 E MAIN St. In 1980 Louisville still had six active packers—Armour, Dawson Baker, Dryden Provision Co., Fischer, Hoerter & Son, and Koch Beef Co. But in 1988 International Fish and Meat USA, a subsidiary of a FRENCH food company, bought Wilson & Co., Fischer Packing Co.'s parent firm, from Doskocil, a Kansas firm that had acquired Wilson a short time earlier. A few years later, Montfort Inc. purchased the Armour Food Co. plant at 1200 Story Ave. It subsequently passed to Swift & Co., which is owned by ConAgra, one of the nation's largest food-processing companies.

In 1993 Fischer Packing Co. experienced a bitter, nineteen-week strike by the Food and Commercial Workers Union that focused on improving wages and benefits that had been reduced in previous contracts in order to assure the company's long-term profitability. In mid-1996 Swift & Co. announced long-term plans to close its Story Ave. plant and relocate in a more rural setting, closer to its supply of hogs. It subsequently expressed interest in a site in eastern CLARK COUNTY, INDIANA, but strong resistance from local residents caused the company to abandon that effort. Although labor-management relations at Fischer have improved and the Swift plant may remain open longer than anticipated, both the strike and the relocation controversy dramatized many of the economic issues that face the industry, as packers attempt to reduce costs and become more profitable by moving from the cities to the countryside, installing new technologies, and reducing labor costs.

See Carl E. Kramer, *Drovers, Dealers and Dreamers: 150 Years at Bourbon Stock Yards* (Louisville 1984).

Carl E. Kramer

MEDER, FLORENCE (b Louisville, March 6, 1877; d Louisville, September 16, 1932). Physician. Florence Meder was one of five children of Joseph and Margaret Meder. In addition to her two sisters, Lillian and Magdeline, she had two brothers, Frank and A.A., who were dentists. Meder graduated from LOUISVILLE GIRLS' HIGH SCHOOL in 1895. That fall she entered the Southwestern Homeopathic College of MEDICINE on S Sixth St., where she received gold medals in anatomy and physiology. She graduated in 1898 with the highest honors in her class.

Once established in medical practice in Louisville, she became interested in the study of mental illnesses. That interest led to her appointment in 1900 by Gov. J.C.W. Beckham as the third assistant physician at Western Kentucky Asylum for the Insane (Western State Hospital) at Hopkinsville. In 1906 Meder was transferred to a similar position at Eastern Kentucky Asylum for the Insane (Eastern State Hospital) in Lexington. There she became involved in civic affairs through the Woman's Club of Lexington and Lexington Associated Charities.

In 1908 Meder was transferred to Central Kentucky Asylum for the Insane (CENTRAL STATE HOSPITAL) at Lakeland in eastern Jefferson County. Two years later she was promoted to assistant physician to the superintendent, a post she held for ten years. During her years at the Lakeland facility she became known as one of Kentucky's pioneers in the field of mental illness. Among other things, she organized a training school for psychiatric nurses.

In addition to her work with the mentally ill, she remained active in civic affairs through the Civic League of the WOMAN'S CLUB OF LOUISVILLE. Meder never married. She is buried in St. Louis Cemetery, Louisville.

See Alwin Seekamp and Roger Burlingame, ed., *Who's Who in Louisville* (Louisville 1912); *Courier-Journal*, Sept. 18, 1932.

MEDICAL SCHOOLS. Louisville has had eleven medical schools, most of which, owing to closings and mergers, no longer exist. The only medical school in Louisville at this time is the University of Louisville School of Medicine. It is part of the UNIVERSITY OF LOUISVILLE'S HEALTH SCIENCES CENTER, which also includes the School of Dentistry, the School of Nursing, and the College of Health and Social Services. At this time the University of Louisville School of Medicine occupies a number of buildings in proximity to its administrative offices in the Irvin and HELEN ABELL Administration Center at 323 E Chestnut between Floyd and PRESTON Streets. There pre-clinical MEDICINE is taught, the Kornhauser Health Sciences Library housed, the Kentucky Lions Eye Research Institute's research laboratories and clinical facilities found, and medical and dental clinical studies and research conducted. The JAMES GRAHAM BROWN Cancer Center houses the Henry Vogt Cancer Research Institute; the Keller Child Psychiatry Research Center studies and treats emotional disorders in families and children; the Comprehensive Health Care Center for High Risk Infants and Children provides comprehensive health care for children born to high medical risk mothers and those residing in low socioeconomic areas; the Child Evaluation Center gives tertiary care to children up to the age of sixteen who may be at risk for or who have developmental disabilities; the Kidney Disease Center serves patients with renal disease and hypertension, patients on chronic dialysis, and recipients of kidney transplants; and the Research Resources Center is an animal-care facility supporting faculty research using animal models to study human disease.

The affiliated institutions of the School of Medicine are the University of Louisville Hospital, the major teaching hospital for University of Louisville medical students and house officers (junior full-time members of the staff, usually residents); the Veterans Administration Medical Center; Kosair-Children's Hospital; Jewish Hospital; Norton Hospital; Audubon Regional Medical Center; Trover Clinic; the Amelia Brown Frazier Rehabilitation Center; the Ackerly Child Psychiatric Service; and the Bingham Child Guidance Clinic.

The present University of Louisville School of Medicine was founded in 1837 under the name "LOUISVILLE MEDICAL INSTITUTE" at Eighth and Chestnut Streets. It was created by the transfer to Louisville of faculty of the Transylvania University medical department in Lexington. This transfer was brought about largely through the efforts of Dr. Theodore Stout Bell, who felt that Louisville could do a better job than Lexington of furnishing adequate clinical cadavers for the teaching of medical science.

At Transylvania, after six faculty members discussed and apparently agreed upon the advisability of the transfer, an allegation of conspiracy to remove the medical school to Louisville resulted in the Board of Trustees' immediately dissolving the whole faculty. Among the professors who subsequently made the move to Louisville were Drs. Lunsford P. Yandell Sr. and CHARLES CALDWELL. In 1839, only two years after the transfer, the Louisville Medical Institute opened the first clinical amphitheater in the West. It was attached to the Louisville Marine Hospital (predecessor of the University of Louisville Hospital), where the clinical teaching not offered by Transylvania was conducted. The Louisville Medical Institute was renamed the medical department of the University of Louisville in 1846. A final name change was made in 1922 to the University of Louisville School of Medicine.

The Kentucky School of Medicine, at Green (Liberty) and Fifth Streets, was started in the fall of 1850, taking almost its entire faculty from Transylvania, which had changed that year to a spring session, for which the Kentucky School of Medicine professors returned to teach in Lexington and then returned to Louisville in the fall. In 1866 a trustee of the Kentucky School of Medicine arranged for consolidation of the school with the medical department of the University of Louisville on condition of a professorship for a relative of his. This merger was brief, ending the next year when most of the former Kentucky School of Medicine faculty were dismissed and the trustee's act, which had been illegal, was revealed.

A second merger for the Kentucky School of Medicine took place in 1875 when it joined the Louisville Medical College, beginning an arrangement that would last another decade. The Louisville Medical College had been organized in 1869 by some physicians who had been military surgeons. The new Louisville Medical College immediately attacked what it called the "cheap fee schools" (the medical department of the University of Louisville and the Kentucky School of Medicine), while establishing what it called "beneficiary" scholarships that virtually every student received.

When the Central University of Kentucky opened another medical school in Louisville—the Hospital College of Medicine (on Chestnut between Preston and Floyd) in 1873—its fees, too, were competitive. Yet all three of these Louisville medical schools—the Kentucky School of Medicine, Louisville Medical College, and the Hospital College of Medicine—were absorbed by the medical department of the University of Louisville in 1908. (The year before, Louisville Medical College and the Hospital College of Medicine had merged to form the Louisville and Hospital Medical College.)

In 1886 medical education for AFRICAN AMERICANS in Louisville began with the LOUISVILLE NATIONAL MEDICAL COLLEGE, started by Dr. HENRY FITZBUTLER and associates and located on Green between First and Second St. Its 1889 graduate, Dr. William T. Peyton, was the first black man to receive an M.D. degree in Kentucky. In 1899 another black medical school, the State University Medical College, was organized in Louisville. It merged with the Louisville National Medical College in 1903.

An alternative medical school for Louisville, a school of homeopathy, was chartered in 1892 as the Southwestern Homeopathic Medical College. Homeopathy is a system of medical treatment in which small doses of medicines are administered that produce symptoms similar to those of the disease being treated, thus inducing the body to heal itself. The first woman to teach in a Kentucky medical school, Dr. Sarah J. Millsap, was one of the professors. The location was 635 S Sixth. In 1895 the allopathic medical schools of Louisville attempted to deny an equal footing to the homeopaths of this college. The school ceased to exist about 1910, quitting activity in Louisville at that time.

In 1882 another medical school for Louisville, the Jefferson School of Medicine, was organized. It was suspended after graduating one class. In 1898 there opened at BROADWAY and Brook St. another medical school, the Kentucky University medical department, born after a schism in the Kentucky School of Medicine. It merged with the medical department of the University of Louisville in 1907.

Finally, the Eclectic or American Reform movement in American medicine was reflected in Louisville by the Eclectic Medical College (chartered 1848). This movement spawned four other MEDICAL SCHOOLS in Louisville, which seem only to have existed on paper. They were the American Reform Medical Institute of Louisville (1850); the Louisville Homeopathic College of Medicine (1851); the People's Hydropathic, Literary, and American Reform College of Kentucky (1852); and the Clay School of Medicine (1854).

See Frederick Eberson, *Portraits: Kentucky Pioneers in Community Health and Medicine* (Lexington 1968); John H. Ellis, *Medicine in Kentucky* (Lexington 1977); Joseph McCormack, *Some of the Medical Pioneers of Kentucky* (Bowling Green, Ky., 1917); Medical Historical Research Project, *Medicine and Its Development in Kentucky* (Louisville 1940).

Penelope Papangelis

MEDICINE. When the first settlers came to the FALLS OF THE OHIO with Col. GEORGE ROGERS CLARK in 1778, no physician or surgeon accompanied them. This was not unusual, for these hardy pioneers seldom sought professional medical advice. Soon thereafter Dr. George Hart came to the tiny settlement here (1779) from Fort Harrod. Dr. Alexander Skinner came in 1783, following military service as a surgeon during the Revolution. The extent of his practice is unknown for the few years he was here. Drs. Absalom Bainbridge (1790), James O'Fallon (1791), and Benjamin Johnston (1791) followed, but nothing is known of their practices.

Seeking their fortunes in the West, physicians began to join the trek to this first frontier beyond the Appalachian Mountains, but they usually required other sources of income to supplement that obtained from practice. Some became merchants selling MEDICINE, dyes, surgical instruments, and books; while others became farmers, teachers, public servants, printers, newspaper publishers, or authors. By the turn of the century, some, such as Drs. William C. Galt and RICHARD B. FERGUSON, settled here permanently. Richard Ferguson and his assistant, John Collins, in 1809, became famous for the care they provided Gen. George Rogers Clark when a serious infection complicated a burn on his right leg, requiring amputation to save his life. Most people recognized what heroic steps were required to save a life if an open fracture, gangrene, or advancing infection involved an extremity.

Geographic location played an important role in developing the medical community of the city and surrounding counties, for river commerce brought money and people as well as diseases. The fledgling community was surrounded by marshy ground and numerous ponds, plus stagnant pools that developed when the river was low and provided breeding places for malaria-carrying mosquitoes. Mosquito and water-borne illnesses sickened much of the POPULATION. Fevers (malaria) were prevalent from summer until frost, and Louisville soon became known as a "sickly place."

By 1810 the growing medical community had become an important resource for medical student-apprentices. Richard Ferguson, soon after his arrival, advertised that he would be able to accept four apprentices. Medical education in the young United States was predominantly attained through apprenticeship, since by 1800 only three complete medical faculties had been assembled, and those were in cities along the eastern seaboard (Boston, New York, and Philadelphia). Since there was no state law regulating the practice of medicine until 1874, qualifications to practice were self-assessed, and some individuals were more courageous than knowledgeable of medical principles. Upon their arrival in Louisville between 1813 and 1823, thirty physicians announced in the NEWSPAPERS their intentions to practice medicine by offering their services to the residents of Louisville and the nearby communities. Although not all stayed, the profession was growing, and the physicians mentioned by HENRY MCMURTRIE in his *Sketches of Louisville* (1819) had increased from twenty-two to thirty-eight by the time the first directory of the city of Louisville appeared in 1832.

During 1819, two events occurred that, over the course of the next few decades, helped establish Louisville as a center of medical education: the chartering of a public hospital and the creation of a medical society. Both events benefited the practitioners, their students, and their patients, while nurturing the growing interest of the medical and lay communities in establishing a medical school.

During the first quarter of the nineteenth century, increased river traffic brought numerous riverboat crewmen and travelers. Those stranded by illness or injuries were initially cared for by private citizens in their homes. However, by 1819 the burden of such benevolence was addressed by chartering the first public general hospital in Kentucky—the Louisville Marine Hospital (later called City Hospital and General Hospital), which opened on Chestnut St. to receive patients in 1823. In April 1829 Benjamin H. Hall was appointed the first resident physician and provided with quarters in the hospital for his family. Hall soon advertised in the public press for medical students, offering them lectures, the use of books from his library, and access to the hospital's patients. This practice documents the earliest use of hospitalized patients for clinical teaching.

In June 1836 Hall established an "Infirmary" for the care of private patients and the teaching of medical students. His enterprise addressed a need and established an important trend. Physicians served the patients in their NEIGHBORHOODS. Infirmaries and eventually HOSPITALS developed as neighborhood institutions. Private infirmaries (later called SANATORIUMS), located in residential areas, continued to address the need for private care of the sick and injured into the first quarter of the twentieth century. Patients addicted to narcotics or alcohol, as well as those with psychological or psychiatric disorders, received specialized care in similar private facilities later in the nineteenth century.

Expanded accommodations in the public hospital (1830) heightened the interest of medical practitioners whose vision was focused on institutionalized medical education. Nearly forty physicians were already practicing here when one Alban Gilpin Smith (surname changed to Goldsmith in 1839), skilled surgeon and lithotomist of Danville, Kentucky, moved to Louisville primarily to offer his services as surgeon to the hospital trustees and patients. His interest in surgery and medical education had been developed in Danville, but that community was too small, provincial, and isolated to support a medical school. In 1833 it was this Dr. Smith who obtained the first charter for the Medical Institute of the City of Louisville, familiarly known as the LOUISVILLE MEDICAL INSTITUTE (LMI). The charter listed nine incorporators, all active practitioners in Louisville—R.H. Brodnax, J.Y. Dashiell, John P. Declary, William C. Galt, Robert P. Gist, John P. Harrison, Llewellyn Powell, Coleman Rogers, and Alban Gilpin Smith. This first charter, however, was unworkable, and a faculty could not be assembled. A revised and improved charter was written in February 1835 and was further revised in January 1836. Only one local practitioner, Henry Miller, became a member of the first faculty when the school opened in 1837.

In the mid-1830s a medical school was proposed in Louisville. This led to the eventual demise of Kentucky's only medical school, at Lexington's Transylvania University. During the school session of 1836–37 at the Transylvania University Medical Department, dissension became acrimonious. CHARLES CALDWELL and Lunsford Yandell, two professors of the medical department, were charged by the Board of Trustees with "treacherous and faithless conduct towards Transylvania University . . . having secretly conspired for the removal of the medical department from Lexington." As a result of the charges, their employment was promptly terminated. Eventually altercations between supporters of the proposed facility and non-supporters became so intense that the trustees of Transylvania University had no choice but to dissolve the entire faculty. Mindful of the tempest in Lexington, the mayor and City Council of Louisville saw an opportunity and met together to make a commitment to build a medical school in Louisville. Under the leadership of JAMES GUTHRIE, the chairman of the finance committee of the Louisville City Council, the council passed a resolution on March 6, 1837, designating a city square and approximately thirty thousand dollars to finance the construction of a medical school building. In order to gain public support for this project, Judge JOHN ROWAN and Guthrie invited Caldwell to Louisville to address a town meeting on March 30, 1837. Following Caldwell's address, the audience strongly favored a medical school in Louisville, despite a nationwide economic depression. This projected teaching institution would become the third important factor, in addition to the chartering of a public hospital and the creation of a medical society, in establishing Louisville as a medical center during the nineteenth and twentieth centuries.

The establishment of the only general hospital in the state attracted more physicians and surgeons to the city. As provided in its charter, the faculty of the new medical school (LMI) was to become the exclusive professional staff of the public hospital, assuring uninterrupted supervision and care for the patients. This dichotomy between practitioners in the community and the school faculty, however, created the first "town and gown" rift, which was rectified to some satisfaction in 1841 by appointing to the staff physicians practicing in the city and permitting them to instruct their private students there.

The increasing size of the medical community, in response to the growth of commerce and manufacturing as new waves of immigrants swelled the population, was a factor contributing to the increasing number of proprietary MEDICAL SCHOOLS. These schools were established under the charters of various institutions of higher learning, some virtually nonexistent except for valid charters that could be revived and revised. Schools such as these were important to the medical community because some physicians occupied chairs on the faculties from which they received fees from students who purchased their lecture tickets. Other faculty served gratis, but the prestige of being a medical school teacher attracted patients as well as medical students for preceptorships, thus increasing income.

Toward the end of the nineteenth century, medical schools throughout the United States were graduating too many poorly educated physicians. In Louisville there were 269 graduates in 1894 from the Kentucky School of Medicine alone. Graduates were not only living advertisements for their schools and faculty, but medical students were also of economic importance to the city, for they paid room and board for nearly five months of the year.

After the Louisville Medical Institute became the University of Louisville Medical Department (1846), other proprietary schools appeared in Louisville: Kentucky School of Medicine (1850), Louisville Medical College (1869), Hospital College of Medicine (1873), and Medical Department of Kentucky University (1898). At one time, in the 1890s, there were as many as eight medical colleges of varying sizes and quality in operation in the city. The majority of the schools were for education of regular physicians. There were also sectarian schools, perhaps chartered only or functioning but briefly, in the last half of the nineteenth century; e.g., Eclectic Medical College (1848), Louisville Homeopathic College of Medicine (1851), Clay School of Medicine (1854), and Southwestern Homeopathic Medical College (1893–1910). Before 1900 some schools admitted and graduated women (Southwestern Homeopathic and LOUISVILLE NATIONAL MEDICAL COLLEGE) but there was no medical college specifically for women.

During the 1880s and 1890s, neighborhood hospitals continued to address the more serious medical needs of nearby families. As technology helped improve the quality of medical care through more accurate diagnoses, the more specialized, unwieldy, and costly apparatus necessary to do so became a part of the hospital. Physicians developing expertise in x-ray techniques and interpretation were joined by those who conducted the clinical and pathological laboratories in affiliation with the hospitals. After WORLD WAR I, physicians providing anesthesia for hospitalized surgical and obstetric patients became identified closely with the hospitals. These practitioners, like their fellow medical practitioners, maintained their private practice autonomy.

In the latter decades of the nineteenth century, the numerous proprietary medical schools established dispensaries and infirmaries for the care of patients and the teaching of medical students and nurses. At the JENNIE CASSEDAY Free Infirmary for Women on Sixth St. in OLD LOUISVILLE, Dr. Lewis S. McMurtry, physician-in-charge, may have instituted the first specialized training for nurses in operating room antiseptic and aseptic techniques (1892). As the use of hospitals expanded during the late nineteenth and early twentieth centuries, a trend began that eventually removed the patient from the home to the hospital and the physician from house calls to hospital rounds, forever altering medical practice.

There were two medical colleges for African American students. The Louisville National Medical College, chartered in 1888, was co-founded by W.A. Burney and HENRY FITZBUTLER. Fitzbutler was the first African American medical graduate of the University of Michigan (1872). He came to Louisville and began practice in the fifteen-thousand-member African American community—the first African American physician to do so. Like others, he immediately began to train student-apprentices. He held the office of dean and the chairs of surgery and materia medica in his new school. In association with this new medical college, he established the Auxiliary Hospital and Dispensary (1895).

When his school became operational and after their children were old enough to allow his wife, Sarah, to do so, she attended the medical school and, in 1893, became the first female graduate in medicine in Kentucky. She then taught medical and NURSING students at the medical college and hospital. Fitzbutler edited two African American newspapers—the *Weekly Planet* and the *Ohio Falls Express.* He died in December 1901, but the medical school continued under Rufus Conrad until 1912. Over one hundred students had been educated in this pioneer school for African American medical students.

A second school, State University Medical College (1899), briefly served the African American community in Louisville before merging with the Louisville National Medical College in 1903. Since 1951 African American students and faculty have been a part of the University of Louisville School of Medicine.

Since first coming to the Falls of the Ohio, practitioners of this community have manifested an independence of spirit that, in some, occasionally became unyielding and even combative. As the medical community grew in numbers, physicians, united by a common interest in medicine and service, formed societies for mutual improvement for themselves and their apprentices. At first, medical societies consisted of "town" practitioners (an unnamed society of 1819 and Louisville Medical Society, 1833). As transportation and communication improved, a number of regional medical societies, which included Jefferson County practitioners, were established. Some functioned briefly, but others continue to the present (Louisville Surgical Society, 1888; JEFFERSON COUNTY MEDICAL SOCIETY, 1892; and Innominate Society, 1925). Although not identified by name or purpose, several of these early medical societies were dominated by "town" practitioners or by faculty members of several rival proprietary medical schools. Their discussions during the 1820s and 1830s were of equitable fee schedules. In time meetings lost their appeal and purpose in divisive discussions, and they disappeared (Louisville Medical Club, 1855, and the College of Physicians and Surgeons of Louisville, 1838–88).

The Jefferson County Medical Society, dormant for nearly a decade, was resurrected in 1902 and came to represent the profession as it gained an identity of its own after all the schools had been consolidated into one University of Louisville Medical Department (1908), later becoming the University of Louisville School of Medicine (1922). The medical community gained new focuses; i.e., medical society concerns such as PUBLIC HEALTH measures, control of quacks and patent medicines, and discussion of medical and surgical subjects for the edification of all members. Medical education improved, and practitioners were able to come together at their county medical society without disruptions related to the politics of proprietary medical schools. On November 17, 1953, Maurice F. Rabb became the first African American physician to become a member of the Jefferson County Medical Society.

All physicians practiced general medicine, while some claimed special knowledge of midwifery or special skill in caring for patients surgically whose disorders were deemed amenable to such treatment. But operations were infrequent before the advent of anesthesia, first used in Boston, Massachusetts, on October 16, 1846. The local medical community adopted the use of anesthetics much sooner than the concept of antisepsis, which emerged from the practical proof of the germ theory of disease by Scottish surgeon Joseph Lister's demonstrations of antiseptic surgery in 1865–67. The first published notice of the use of inhalation anesthesia in Louisville appeared in the *LOUISVILLE COURIER,* January 30, 1847, reporting an operation (not identified) performed by Samuel B. Richardson while the patient was anesthetized. Although locally there were not many such reports in the newspapers, extant medical student notebooks abound with accounts of the administration of ether, nitrous oxide, and chloroform to patients for surgical operations, delivery of babies, or for the student's own indulgence. There are a number of references to Samuel D. Gross operating on anesthetized patients; however, Dr. Gross is not recorded as including notice of anesthesia in his contemporary lectures.

Henry Miller, professor of obstetrics and diseases of women and children at the medical department of the University of Louisville, administered the first anesthetic (chloroform) to one of his obstetric patients in Louisville for delivery of her child on February 20, 1848. This was just over a year after the first use of anesthesia in obstetrics by James Y. Simpson in Edinburgh, Scotland. The storm of criticism generated by the clergy in their opposition to the use of anesthesia for delivery may account for the delay of over a year in Miller's making use of the discovery.

Prior to 1910 there were four physicians in general practice who administered anesthesia. W. Hamilton Long (1909) and W.A. Onderdonk (1910) were the first specialists to limit their practice to anesthesiology, and by 1916 these men had organized the Louisville Society of Anesthetists. Physicians administered all of the anesthetics for obstetrics and surgery (with one exception); and this professional attitude prevailed, except at federal hospitals, until nurse anesthetists were recruited to assist the anesthesiologists in several private hospitals (ca. 1970). Nurse anesthetists now work in most of the anesthesia groups in our community.

Anesthesiologists worked in several hospitals immediately following WORLD WAR II, but by 1957 there were private practice groups in each of the private hospitals. Professional relations were such that members from one group would assist others, and several private groups routinely assisted members of the University of Louisville Department of Anesthesiology at the General Hospital with their sometimes crushing load of emergency surgeries.

In addition to being an obstetrician, Miller was also a skilled surgeon, but he, too, was quite slow to recognize and acknowledge that puerperal (childbed) fever was transmitted by the "dirty" hands of the mother's attendant as had been described in 1843. Although Miller included a discussion of this deadly but preventable disease in his revised textbook (1858), he omits reference to its true cause and prevention; there was no adequate treatment at that time. Isolation and quarantine as general methods for controlling and preventing the spread of infectious disease and the more specific vaccination against smallpox had all been developed with scant knowledge of the cause or transmission of the disease.

Although the mode of transmission of childbed fever and surgical infections had been demonstrated during the middle decades of the nineteenth century, no causative organism could have been identified at that time. Ultimately, the work of Robert Koch proved the relationship between an infection and specific bacteria, and the germ theory of disease was born. Throughout the western world, physicians studying bacteria, the infections produced, and mechanisms of immunity had achieved the specific means for identifying and controlling many contagious diseases. These discoveries spawned the public health movement.

In order to be effective, health departments required a reliable Kentucky statewide Bureau of Vital Statistics (funded and established in 1911) and laws compelling registration of births, marriages, deaths, causes of death, and cases of epidemic disease. Such statistics provided methods of discovery, prevention, and treatment of many diseases, e.g. pulmonary tuberculosis. Facilities were established for sanatorium treatment of tuberculosis for Louisville (HAZELWOOD 1906) and Jefferson County (Waverly Hills 1910).

A health officer, William C. Galt, had been appointed temporarily in Louisville in 1822 in response to the "fever" EPIDEMICS (malaria) of 1821 and 1822, and a BOARD OF HEALTH soon followed in 1828. The first public health project became the draining of ponds in Louisville and Jefferson County, financed by a state lottery in 1822. However, endemic enteric diseases perpetuated by a contaminated water supply received no attention until the LOUISVILLE WATER CO. first began supplying untreated water in October 1860. Filtered and chlorinated water was not on line until 1909. A sewer system to replace privies developed slowly. Not until 1906 did voters support a bond issue to build extensive sewers, but mixed storm and sanitary sewerage was discharged untreated into the OHIO RIVER until after World War II.

Efforts of both state and Jefferson County (established 1866) health departments in "partnership" with local practitioners implemented programs against tuberculosis, venereal diseases, and the childhood diseases in the last decades of the nineteenth century. Although tuberculosis can now be effectively treated with medicines, the appearance of the "new" viral sexually transmitted diseases (STD) such as AIDS (HIV infection) characterized by depression of the host's immune system has resulted in a resurgence of tuberculosis in patients with that disease.

The devastating epidemics of poliomyelitis have been arrested by the immunization of all citizens in Jefferson County with oral polio vaccine by a combined effort of the Jefferson County Medical Society, Jefferson County Medical Foundation, and the Jefferson County Health Department in 1962 and 1963.

The first woman physician to practice in Louisville was Maria Guttermann (also listed as Mary Graf), from the University of Heidelberg, Germany, 1862, who came in the 1870s and practiced in an office in her home at 1016 E Walnut St. (Muhammad Ali Blvd.). Others arriving in the 1880s were JULIA INGRAM (1882), Alma F. Lawrence (1883), and Florence Brandeis (1887). Ingram became the first woman to be elected to office in the Jefferson County Medical Society—secretary-treasurer in 1895. Other women physicians beginning practice here were Mary Hopkins, a homeopath, 1904; Alice N. Pickett, 1913; and ANNIE S. VEECH, 1916.

Women physicians have made valuable contributions in Louisville and the state of Kentucky to maternal, infant, child welfare, and psychiatric care by establishing clinics; supervising children's affairs through juvenile court, federal bureaus, and the Kentucky Commission for Handicapped Children; and the teaching of medical and dental students at the University of Louisville Schools of Medicine and Dentistry.

The first practitioners in Louisville who declared their intentions to limit their practices to a specialty were surgeons. Joseph McDowell Matthews became a specialist in proctology and diseases of the rectum and colon (1878). Ap Morgan Vance limited his practice to surgery in 1880. He was quite interested in and adept at orthopedic surgery, to which he made many contributions. William Barnett Owen became the first to declare himself an orthopedic specialist (1906).

Preceding the rapid expansion in training programs for physicians, there had already been a system devised to assess the quality of hospital residencies by an on-site inspection team. First begun by the American College of Surgeons (1928), it evolved into the Joint Commission on Accreditation of Healthcare Organizations (JCAHO, 1951), which inspects hospital and training facilities every three years.

Physicians returning from World War II service were confronted by poorly maintained or inadequate hospital facilities. In 1946 Congress enacted the Hospital Survey and Construction Act (Hill-Burton Act) in response to the recommendations of a study begun in 1942 by the Commission on Hospital Care. The act was to provide funds to states for the orderly planning and construction of hospitals based upon surveys indicating the need and distribution of such institutions. Regulations also required matching funds (originally 66/33, soon revised to 50/50) and that the facilities funded and constructed be fully integrated in patient population and for the teaching of students of medicine and allied professions. Federal funds were sent to the Kentucky State Hospital Advisory Commission, which was the administrative pathway for Hill-Burton funds in the state.

The LOUISVILLE MEDICAL CENTER's future on E Chestnut St. was secured when the Jewish Hospital trustees decided to join the University of Louisville in the Medical Center Campus, and, on May 29, 1950, University Medical Center was incorporated. The University of Louisville had condemnation rights to clear the land for construction and, as owner of the property, leased it for ninety-nine years at a rent of a dollar per year.

Hill-Burton funds were made available and matching funds secured for the construction of the Jewish Hospital, which is a fully integrated teaching hospital of the University of Louisville School of Medicine. The Methodist-Evangelical Hospital joined the Medical Center and obtained Hill-Burton funds but did not become a full-fledged teaching hospital.

Hill-Burton funds and matching funds made Louisville's Medical Center a landmark for education, patient care, and treatment. Acquired clinical skills in the diagnosis and treatment of heart disease, coupled with the interpretation of the electrocardiogram in the early 1920s, evolved into the specialty of cardiology. Emmet F. Horine was the first to limit his practice to this new specialty in 1922.

The profession had become much more effective in preventing, treating, and curing disease during the years between World War I and World War II. Practices such as those of homeopaths and eclectics had largely disappeared by 1940. Psychiatry and neurology had secured their separate identities by the latter third of the nineteenth century. Early in the twentieth century, medicine had divided into other specialties such as dermatology, syphilology, and pulmonary medicine. Oscar O. Miller became one of the earliest specialists in pulmonary medicine, which was, in its beginning, primarily related to the diagnosis, care, and treatment of patients with pulmonary tuberculosis.

Returning veterans from the armed services sought opportunities to begin or further their medical education. The GI Bill, signed June 22, 1944, financed education based upon duration of military service. Medical school candidates increased, and positions for residency training quickly filled. Under the first full-time professor of surgery and chairman at the U of L School of Medicine, Rudolph J. Noer (1952), there was a revitalization of the department. New surgeons joined the established medical community as clinical teachers of students and residents in the Louisville General Hospital and other institutions affiliated with the teaching programs of the School of Medicine. Close affiliation between the U of L Department of Surgery and the Jewish Hospital was secured by the efforts of Alvin B. Ortner and Harold F. Berg.

One of these new members in 1953 was Harold E. Kleinert. A skillful, gentle surgeon and talented teacher, he became interested in treating injuries of the hand and started the first HAND SURGERY clinic at the Louisville General Hospital (LGH), which he continued to supervise for nearly a decade. By 1959 he performed most of his surgery at Jewish Hospital. His surgical expertise soon became widely recognized, eventually including reattaching traumatically amputated parts of fingers, entire fingers, and ultimately entire hands, forearms, and arms. An increasing volume of operative surgical cases required several operating rooms staffed twenty-four hours a day, associates to assist in providing surgical care, and the teaching of students, residents, and fellows. He established a fellowship in hand surgery (1960). In 1964, after taking Joseph E. Kutz as his first partner, he founded the Christine M. Kleinert Institute for Hand and Microsurgery at the Jewish Hospital, supporting his researches and fellowships in hand and microsurgery. The institute is named for his mother.

Kleinert's group continued to grow in numbers, becoming Kleinert, Kutz, and Associates, as its international reputation was established by innovative surgical techniques and training of over nine hundred Fellows from forty-nine countries. The addition in 1973 of Tsu Min Tsai, a talented vascular microsurgeon, added another dimension to the surgical skills available.

Innovators must possess and maintain an open mind, and Kleinert has utilized his open-mindedness to forge new techniques and perfect older ones. The most remarkable surgical accomplishment from the Kleinert, Kutz, and Associates Hand Care Center, as a joint effort with the University of Louisville Division of Plastic and Reconstructive Surgery and the Jewish Hospital Foundation, was the transplantation of a hand from a donor to Matthew Scott on January 24–25, 1999. The principal surgeons of the team were Warren C. Breidenbach III, Jon W. Jones, and Gordon R. Tobin.

Scott, who had lost his left hand in a fireworks accident in 1985, had been evaluated sometime prior to the surgery; and the medical, surgical, and ethical questions had been reviewed with the medical and lay community as well as with the recipient over a period of three months. This hand transplant was the first in the Americas and the second in the world. The patient had gained sufficient function to throw out the first ball as the major-league BASEBALL season began in 1999. By the end of three months, he was able to return to his home in New Jersey.

Hugh B. Lynn became the first professor of pediatric surgery and chief of surgery at the Children's Hospital, another private teaching hospital in the Medical Center. William W. Johnson, an adept surgeon, became a skilled associate of Lynn and received further training in Great Britain under the pioneering vascular surgeon Sir Russel C. Brock. Pediatric surgery was general surgery for children, and in Louisville in the 1950s and early 1960s it initially included repairs of major vascular anomalies (patent ductus arteriosis and coarctation of the aorta and "Blue Baby" operations), repairs of tracheo-esophageal fistula, and correction of pyloric stenosis.

The specialty of thoracic surgery was first brought to Louisville in 1935 when John S. Harter, a surgeon trained in the specialty, arrived, serving as chairman of the division of thoracic surgery at the Louisville General Hospital. Several other thoracic surgery specialists arrived in Louisville before World War II.

Following World War II, thoracic surgery began to change as better, more precise diagnostic techniques (cardiac catheterization and angiography) and better anesthesia care and intensive care nursing opened new possibilities for surgical interventions. These developments, among others, fostered the growth of the relatively new specialty of cardiovascular or cardiothoracic surgery.

Daniel E. Mahaffey, a University of Louisville School of Medicine graduate (1946), trained in general and cardiothoracic surgery at Baylor University Hospitals in Houston, Texas (1950–52, 1954–56). When he returned to Louisville from teaching at Tulane University in New Orleans in 1957, he had already accumulated some experience in operating on patients on cardiopulmonary bypass (with the heart-lung machine). He purchased a disc oxygenator and pump (heart-lung machine) and, with dedicated associates at the Kentucky Baptist Hospital (Sam D. Weakley, Lolita S. Weakley, Harold W. Bradshaw, and volunteer graduate and student nurses) and hours of practice, the first patient successfully underwent an operation (resection of an aneurysm of the heart) in August 1960. This was the first open-heart surgery with the patient on bypass performed in Louisville. Operations during cardiopulmonary bypass continued for nearly four years at the Baptist Hospital, but too infrequently to maintain perfection, and Mahaffey finally abandoned the project. In December 1960 at the Baptist Hospital he had implanted the first cardiac pacemaker in the city. Another group of surgeons, W. Fielding Rubel, William W. Johnson, and Charles K. Sargent, with technicians Betty Ann Potter, Dorothy Anderson, and Herbert T. Ransdell, M.D. (regulating the pump), began performing open-heart procedures at Children's Hospital as early as 1958. They used the disc oxygenator also.

A third addition to the University of Louisville's Department of Surgery was Allan M. Lansing, who came here from Canada in 1963 to become head of the U of L Cardio-Thoracic Surgery Program. He had been teaching at the University of Western Ontario in London,Ontario. Lansing was born in St. Catherines, Ontario, September 12, 1929, the son of a Canadian railroad worker and a teacher. Lansing received an M.D. degree from the University of Western Ontario in 1953. Lansing had trained in general and thoracic surgery and research in circulatory physiology, including experience with Drs. Michael De Bakey and Denton Cooley in Houston and Robert Gross in Boston. He and his wife, Donna, had two daughters and one son.

The heart-lung machine at Children's Hospital was needed for both pediatric and adult patients. Postoperative care for adult patients differs from that required for children, and the heart team needed another "home." Lansing, who had already moved the University of Louisville kidney transplant program from the General Hospital to Jewish Hospital and performed the first kidney transplant in Kentucky there in September 1964, discussed the needs of the cardiothoracic surgeons with Otis Wheeler, administrator of Jewish Hospital. In November 1964 the cardiothoracic program was inaugurated at Jewish Hospital. Before this could begin, however, the nursing staff required additional training to provide skilled nursing care for the cardiac surgical patients. The first Intensive Care Unit (ICU) in Louisville staffed by these nurses was opened in July 1964 at the Jewish Hospital.

The University of Louisville Department of Cardiothoracic Surgery, under Lansing's direction, continued its close association with Jewish Hospital, where the U of L cardiovascular training program was begun in 1965. Lansing continued to operate on his private patients at Jewish Hospital until 1983. He continued to direct the University of Louisville training program until the new professor and chairman of the University of Louisville Department of Surgery, Hiram C. Polk Jr. (1971), had an opportunity to appoint a replacement to this post in 1983.

HUMANA INC. invited Lansing to come to AUDUBON Hospital to become head of the new Humana Heart Institute in 1983. He accepted and soon (1984) had persuaded William C. DeVries, who with Robert K. Jarvik had pioneered the development of the totally artificial heart and performed its first implantation in man (University of Utah, 1982), to join him in Louisville.

While Lansing and DeVries worked to launch the mechanical heart project at the Humana Heart Institute, other events of consequence were to take place in Louisville. On August 24, 1984, Laman A. Gray Jr., professor and chief of the Division of Thoracic and Cardiovascular Surgery in the University of Louisville Department of Surgery, performed the first heart transplant in Kentucky. Ten days later

(September 3, 1984) Roland E. Girardet, at the Humana Heart Institute, performed Kentucky's second heart transplant.

On November 25, 1984, William C. DeVries and Allan M. Lansing at the Humana Heart Institute, for the first time in Kentucky, implanted the Jarvik-7 mechanical heart in a fifty-two-year-old patient whose heart had worn out. This was a successful implantation, and the mechanical heart itself functioned well until myriad difficulties arose and the heroic patient, William J. Schroeder, died after 119 days on the mechanical heart. DeVries and his team at the Humana Heart Institute implanted four other mechanical hearts and discontinued the project until some modifications could be made and approved by the Food and Drug Administration (FDA).

William DeVries arrived in 1984 from the University of Utah Medical School. He accepted a position at Humana Inc.'s Human Heart Institute after being offered donated care for one hundred artificial heart implants. DeVries, who is best known for implanting an artificial heart in retired dentist Barney Clark in 1982, brought with him the intense national media focus on artificial heart implants. DeVries graduated from the University of Utah in 1966 with a degree in molecular and genetic biology. Graduating from the University of Utah Medical School in 1970, he went on to complete a nine-year residency in general and thoracic surgery at Duke University Medical Center. In 1996 DeVries accepted an arrangement with Hardin Memorial Hospital in Elizabethtown, Kentucky, to start a heart-surgery program. He retired from practice in 1999.

DeVries was born December 19, 1943, to Henry and Cathryn Lucille (Castle) DeVries in Brooklyn, New York, but was brought up in Utah. DeVries and his first wife, Anne Karen (Olsen), had seven children. Linda Croan DeVries is his second wife.

Through the efforts of Allan Lansing, the disposable bubble oxygenator was introduced in Louisville. This allowed quick turnaround in the operating rooms and reduced the need for six or eight units of blood to prime the disc oxygenator before patients could be placed on cardiopulmonary bypass. Patients recovered quicker from anesthesia and surgery as these innovations were incorporated into intraoperative management. With the bubble oxygenator and careful technique, it has been possible to perform open-heart surgery without the need for blood transfusion. Since 1965, performing cardiopulmonary bypass surgery without the use of donor blood allowed Lansing to treat JEHOVAH'S WITNESSES, whose religious beliefs interdict the use of blood for transfusions.

A technique for improving myocardial oxygenation and function in patients with such severe vascular disease that coronary bypass surgery cannot be performed is called transmyocardial revascularization and uses a laser to make holes in the heart muscle. This technique was evaluated by Lansing at the Humana Heart Institute beginning in 1994. The results over the succeeding five years based upon 350 cases have been encouraging.

Since the first open-heart surgery was performed at Jewish Hospital in January 1965, many heart operations have been performed there: heart valve repair and replacement, coronary bypass operations, resection of aneurysms of the heart, and heart transplants. Benefits to patients have been enormous, but these operations, requiring high-tech support facilities, can only be performed where there is understanding and commitment by the administrative officers of the hospital that matches the foresight and requirements of the physicians, surgeons, and other health professionals caring for patients. Jewish Hospital continues to demonstrate the importance of this relationship. Jewish Hospital has absorbed all hospital costs for kidney transplants, heart transplants, extremity transplants, and reattachments.

The Humana Heart Institute, without academic ties but with strong commitments to medical progress, has made many contributions to the care of patients with heart problems throughout the world (Central and South America, Russia, and Korea). One program is known as "The Gift of Life." In conjunction with Rotary Clubs worldwide, it brings children from Third-World countries to Louisville's Humana Heart Institute for correction of congenital heart defects. Next, surgeons are brought here and taught cardiovascular surgical techniques. Soon after, ICU and OR equipment is sent to these countries. After that, the whole heart surgery team, five or six in all, is flown to the city where the equipment has been sent. Lastly, the local Rotarians in the community where this new surgical capability has been established guarantee a paid education for those children who are helped by the program.

The technique of cardiac catheterization, putting a thin tube into the heart, was developed during World War II and was of great help in providing correct diagnosis of congenital heart defects. The first cardiac catheterization laboratory (if it could be called that) was a reconstructed space in a stairwell in the old Louisville General Hospital in which Leonard Leight began performing cardiac catheterization studies. In his makeshift laboratory, x-rays were made following injection of a contrast medium into the heart. He and the radiologists obtained funds to purchase a rapid X-ray cassette changer—the Elema Machine—which enables serial X-rays as the dye flows through the heart. Catheterizations were eventually done by other cardiologists. Kareem Minhas established the first pediatric cardiac catheterization laboratory (WHAS-TV Crusade Heart Lab) in Children's Hospital (1966). The Thomas Cardiac Catheterization Laboratory at Jewish Hospital was opened in May 1971 by U of L cardiologist Leonard Leight, with others performing the catheterizations.

Transfusion of blood from person to person became possible at the beginning of the twentieth century when immunologic techniques identified the four major types of blood. Since then, blood transfusion has become the most common form of tissue transplantation. During the interval between World War I and World War II, blood became a commodity. Eventually there were four independent blood banks in the United States that controlled most of the country's blood supply, although a few communities did maintain banks. The American Red Cross, after prolonged difficulties related to who should administer community blood banks and the collection and distribution of blood, established a blood center in Louisville that began operating on May 23, 1949. Eventually, it moved to the Medical Center. It remains a distribution center for the KENTUCKIANA region.

Before and after the struggle about collecting and distributing blood, hospitals had their own blood banks, ultimately administered by clinical pathologists. Hematologist Marion Beard became involved in blood banking before World War II. Following the war he was a consultant to the Red Cross Blood Bank and was joined by his partner, Ellis Fuller. Together, they oversaw the distribution of blood in the 1950s and 1960s.

Since the late 1980s, typing of cells of all tissues, which, similar to blood cells, have their own identity, has developed. The first laboratory for tissue typing in Kentuckiana became a service of Robert S. Howell and the clinical laboratory at Jewish Hospital in the mid-1960s. This provided essential information to transplant surgeons.

Chemotherapy of various cancers and blood dyscrasias developed in the decade of the 1950s with drugs such as Methotrexate, 5–fluorouricil, and Cytoxan®. Two specialty groups pioneered in the use of these toxic cellular CHEMICALS and newer ones that followed. Hematologists Marion F. Beard and Ellis Fuller were among the earliest practitioners to alter their practice to include the use of chemical agents in the treatment of leukemia and cancer. Their specialty soon became known as oncology. Surgeons Malcolm D. Thompson and Blaine Lewis pioneered the direct infusion of these chemotherapeutic agents into the arterial blood supply of tumors (1966–89).

Emergency cases during the post–World War II era were usually taken by the police to the Louisville General Hospital, since a physician was always present day and night in the Emergency Room (ER). The ER at General Hospital was transformed in 1970–71 under the direction of Donald M. Thomas, an assistant professor of anesthesiology at the University of Louisville, who extended his teaching of cardiopulmonary resuscitation to the diagnosis and treatment of emergency problems in medicine. In 1972, Thomas began the residency training program in emergency medicine at

General Hospital. This was the second such program in the United States (the first was at Cincinnati General Hospital). In 1975, he was appointed professor of emergency medicine, and the department became the first to achieve academic status in a United States medical school. Thomas remained as chairman until 1988 when he resigned, but he remained in the department to practice and teach for several more years.

The police continued to bring the acutely ill or injured to the General Hospital until 1972, when, under the aegis of the Jefferson County Medical Society, a Louisville Emergency Medical Service (EMS) was begun. EMS functioned very well until the city transferred its control to the Fire Department in 1996–97. Since then, EMS has had difficulty maintaining full function.

Air evacuation of patients requiring emergency care was pioneered by the Jewish Hospital Skycare service, beginning July 1, 1982. Later, when the new University of Louisville Hospital was completed, a helicopter became a part of the University Hospital's Department of Emergency Medicine.

See J.N. McCormack, *Some of the Medical Pioneers of Kentucky* (Bowling Green, Ky., 1917); Irvin Abell, *A Retrospective of Surgery in Kentucky and the Heritage of Kentucky Medicine* (Louisville 1926); Works Projects Administration, *Medicine and its Development in Kentucky* (Louisville 1940); John H. Ellis, *Medicine in Kentucky* (Lexington 1977); Nancy Disher Baird, *David Wendel Yandell: Physician of Old Louisville* (Lexington 1978).

Eugene H. Conner

C.C. Mengel Company advertisement.

MENGEL COMPANY. First known as C.C. Mengel Jr. and Bro. Co. and later as the Mengel Box Co., the Mengel Co. was established in 1877 in Louisville by brothers Clarence R. (1858–1939) and Col. Charles C. Mengel Sr. (1856–1939). In 1890 they were joined by brother Herbert W. Mengel (1871–1930). These natives of Gloucester, Massachusetts, were able to take advantage of Louisville's proximity to hardwood forests, a need for tobacco boxes and whiskey barrels, and the city's strategic railroad network. C.C. Mengel was president of the company until his death and was active in civic affairs. Most noteworthy was his leadership of the Louisville Legion during the Gov. William Goebel assassination crisis of 1900.

By 1899 the Mengels' ten-acre plant on Kentucky St. between Tenth and Twelfth Streets employed upwards of six hundred workers and was one of the largest concerns of its kind south of the Ohio River. Fifty million feet of lumber was processed there, and nearly all of the plug tobacco boxes used by American tobacco companies were manufactured by Mengel. The firm exported lumber to Europe and eventually came to own a fleet of ships. Logging operations extended into Africa, British Honduras (Belize), and Mexico. Prosperity came with a price. When the U.S. fleet shelled Vera Cruz in 1914, the Mexican government seized $1.5 million worth of company assets. During World War I two of the company ships were sunk by German submarines.

The Mengel Co. was a giant in the field of wood products by the 1920s. It owned box factories in St. Louis; Jersey City, New Jersey; and Winston-Salem, North Carolina, in addition to the one in Louisville. In 1923 the Mengel Body Co. was built in Louisville at Fourth and G (Colorado Ave.) Streets. It was capable of producing 350 wooden automobile bodies a day with consumption of 100,000 feet of lumber every 24 hours.

During World War II the Mengel Co. produced wooden airplane crates and pioneered the development of plywood for airplanes. In 1942 the company contracted to supply plywood for the Curtiss-Wright airplane factory that was to be constructed at Standiford Field (Louisville International Airport). The war caused a shortage of male workers, and many African American women were employed with the Mengel Co.

After the war a combination of declining available wood resources and competition from other products caused company fortunes to wane. On November 8, 1960, Mengel Co. shareholders approved assimilation into the Container Corp. of America (later a subsidiary of Mobil Oil), effectively ending operations in Louisville.

See *Louisville Times*, Nov. 9, 1939; *Courier-Journal*, May 1, 1942.

MENTAL HEALTH. Organized mental health treatment and service trace their origins to the Central State Hospital, which was established at Lakeland near Louisville in 1873. The psychological laboratory was started by the Louisville school system in 1913 when there were only three other child guidance clinics in the country. This unit matured and grew to become the Bingham Child Guidance Clinic.

In 1932 Dr. Spafford Ackerly, the first full-time professor of psychiatry at the University of Louisville Medical School, was named to head the clinic. He introduced important changes in the teaching of psychiatry and the care of the mentally ill in Louisville and Kentucky. Dr. Ackerly was followed as professor and chairman of the department of psychiatry by Drs. William K. Keller, John J. Schwab, and Alan Tasman.

The Louisville General Hospital, opened in 1914, contained the first psychiatric unit in a general hospital in the state. After Dr. Ackerly arrived, he supervised the unit. He later recruited Dr. William K. Keller to administer the unit and to employ it as another teaching base in the University of Louisville Department of Psychiatry for medical students and postgraduate residents. This unit continued in the successor University Hospital.

In 1949 the Norton Psychiatric Clinic (inpatient and outpatient care) was dedicated under the leadership of Dr. Edward E. Landis. The Norton unit was also associated with Dr. Ackerly and the University of Louisville Department of Psychiatry. Norton included an inpatient service for disturbed small children and adolescents, and partial hospitalization service for children. The Veterans Hospital also developed a psychiatric section associated with the University of Louisville.

As the number of private psychiatrists increased, other hospitals were planned and built. Kentucky Baptist Hospital established a psychiatric unit, and in 1951 Our Lady of Peace Hospital (now Caritas Peace), sponsored by the Sisters of Charity of Nazareth, was opened. Later Charter Hospital and Ten Broeck Hospital were established.

During the early 1960s, Congress passed a series of laws to create, construct, and staff community mental health centers to be operated by local nonprofit boards. Kentucky was the first state to establish a statewide system of community mental health centers. In 1969, the Region Eight Mental Health Center board opened Waverly Mental Health Center (the first of four such area centers) on Dixie Hwy. under the direction of Theodore Ising Jr. The board then hired Theodore Frank as its regional director, and Dale Combs was named regional administrator.

In 1974 Region Eight became River Region under the same management structure. Early during this period, River Region managed CENTRAL STATE HOSPITAL. However, because of River Region's financial problems, this facility was forced into bankruptcy in 1978. In its final days, Hospital Management Associates (HMA) took over management of the organization and reopened the center with Dr. Howard Bracco as its assistant executive director. In January 1979, Bracco was named Seven Counties president and chief executive officer. Seven Counties is a private, nonprofit corporation that provides services in Bullitt, Henry, Jefferson, Oldham, Shelby, Spencer, and Trimble Counties. It is Kentucky's largest comprehensive mental health center and one of the nation's largest.

The Louisville Area Mental Health Association was established in 1951 under the presidency of BARRY BINGHAM Sr. The purpose of the association is to educate the public about mental illness, to promote care and treatment, and to serve as an advocate for the mentally ill. The Louisville Alliance for the Mentally Ill, a support group for families and friends of the mentally ill, is associated with a state and a national organization. The Coalition for Mental Health, with headquarters in Louisville, represents professional groups who work together for the mentally ill in areas such as health insurance, mental health laws, and housing.

Other mental health professionals were increasing in number and activity. Psychologists from the University of Louisville and other programs, social workers from the University's Kent School of Social Work, and pastoral counselors from the Southern Baptist Seminary were filling gaps in a much-needed service. Dr. WAYNE E. OATES at the Baptist Seminary first trained ministers to serve as hospital chaplains in state mental hospitals and other hospitals. As time went by, this became a wider program to train pastoral counselors to serve in their churches.

As hospital treatment improves, severely mentally ill persons stay in a hospital for shorter periods. However, these people need continuing care before they can return to families or live alone. This has led to the development of a number of followup systems such as Wellspring House to provide supervised care in a large house, with food and lodging. Patients start a rehabilitation service to regain lost skills of living and eventually move on to an independent apartment where they are helped on a lesser basis. Other agencies provide day care and help persons find work if they are sufficiently recovered.

Jefferson Alcohol and Drug Abuse Center (JADAC) operates under the supervision of Seven Counties Services. It provides hospital and outpatient service to abusers of alcohol and drugs. Other hospitals may provide similar services, but JADAC limits itself solely to drug and alcohol abusers.

Frank M. Gaines

MERCY, ACADEMY OF OUR LADY OF. In 1872, the Sisters of Mercy in Louisville began holding day classes at their Second St. location under the name of St. Catherine's Academy. In 1885, the first high school diploma was awarded under the name of the Academy of Our Lady of Mercy. In 1901 the academy moved to its current location at 1176 E BROADWAY. One year later, Mount Saint Agnes Academy closed its facility on NEWBURG Rd. and merged with Mercy Academy.

Mercy Academy educates young women in the tradition of the Sisters of Mercy, providing them a strong spiritual foundation. More than a century ago, Catherine McAuley began the Sisters of Mercy in Ireland to meet the needs of the uneducated, the poor, and the sick, especially women and children. The Sisters of Mercy continue McAuley's mission in HOSPITALS, churches, and schools around the world nationwide. Mercy Academy is one of over forty high schools in the Americas sponsored by the order.

Mercy Academy's goal is for each student to develop as a self-confident, self-reliant Christian individual with a strong educational and religious background. The academic program has produced students who were National Merit Semi-Finalists and Finalists and participants in the Governor's Scholars Program and the Governor's School for the Arts.

The athletic program has developed athletes who have captured eight state and twenty-one regional crowns in recent times. During the 1998–99 school year, Mercy Academy had 304 students, 5400 alumnae, and 30 full-time faculty members.

See Clyde Crews, *American Holy Land* (Louisville 1990); Mary Prisca Pfeffer, *In Love and Mercy: A History of the Sisters of Mercy in Louisville, Kentucky, 1869–1989* (Louisville 1992).

Jeanine P. Triplett

MERIWETHER. Triangular neighborhood south of downtown Louisville, bounded by Preston St., Shelby St., and the CSX railroad tracks. One of the three NEIGHBORHOODS, including BRADLEY and ST. JOSEPHS, known as

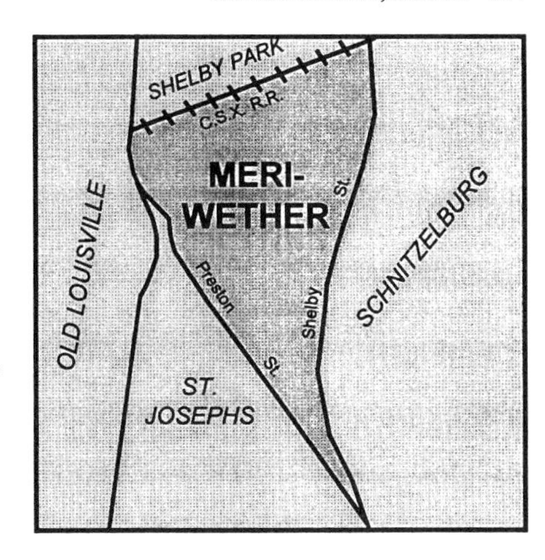

"Greater Schnitzelburg," the area derives its name from the nineteenth-century speculator who subdivided the area, David H. Meriwether. Although Meriwether platted the first community in 1871, residents did not begin moving into the neighborhood for another twenty years. The primarily residential area, which contains numerous SHOTGUN COTTAGES, was centered around Lincoln-Preston Park.

Meriwether was once a part of the old FORT HILL neighborhood, which took its name from CIVIL WAR Fort Horton built to protect the city against possible Confederate attack. Much of the hill on which the fort stood has been graded away. By the turn of the century most of the residents along Burnett Ave. were AFRICAN AMERICANS who found employment in the area's factories along the railroad, the sand and clay quarry, and brick manufacturers.

In 1905 RED CROSS HOSPITAL (no connection to American Red Cross) began to provide services to the black community at 1436 S Shelby St. It operated the only nurse-training program in Kentucky for African Americans. Racial integration of Louisville's hospitals and increasing operational costs resulted in the closing of the hospital in 1975.

See *Louisville Survey: Central and South Report* (Louisville 1978).

MERIWETHER, DAVID (b Louisa County, Virginia, October 30, 1800; d Jefferson County, Kentucky, April 4, 1893). Fur trader, political figure, and governor of the New Mexico Territory. He was the son of Elizabeth Winslow and William Meriwether (1760–1842), who had served with Col. GEORGE ROGERS CLARK's Illinois regiment in the 1778–79 campaigns that resulted in the capture of Kaskaskia, Cahokia, and Vincennes. In 1805 the family moved to southwestern Jefferson County, Kentucky, where William Meriwether had purchased a large tract of land on the OHIO RIVER.

In 1819 David Meriwether was employed by Col. John O'Fallon, sutler of the Yellowstone expedition of 1819–20, which was designed as a followup of the Lewis and Clark expedition. O'Fallon, a nephew of George Rogers Clark and his brother William and a friend of Meriwether's father, employed the young man as a combination trader and sutler to the troops. With this party Meriwether ascended the Missouri, visiting along the way Daniel Boone, who was living at La Charette, about twenty-five miles above St. Louis.

This expedition proceeded no farther than Council Bluffs (not present Council Bluffs, Iowa), about twenty-five miles above present Omaha, Nebraska. In 1820, having received exaggerated reports of gold and silver to be found in Spanish possessions in the Southwest, Meriwether suggested that an exploring party be sent to Santa Fe to determine the practicability of a route for wagons and the amount of gold and silver available in that area. This was approved; and Meriwether, accompanying a party of Indians, departed for Santa Fe in 1820, generally following the route later known as the Santa Fe Trail. He was captured by the Spaniards a few day's march from his objective and imprisoned in the Palace of the Governors in Santa Fe for a month. He was released after being warned by the Spanish governor never to return.

Upon returning to Kentucky, he married Sarah Hoar Leonard in February 1823. He was elected to the Kentucky House of Representatives from Jefferson County in 1832, serving for thirteen consecutive terms. In 1851 he was appointed by Kentucky governor Lazarus W. Powell to be secretary of state; and on July 6, 1852, he entered the U.S. Senate as a Democrat to fill the vacancy caused by the death of Henry Clay, holding this position until August 31, 1852. He was appointed by President Franklin Pierce to be governor of New Mexico Territory, a position he held from May 6, 1853, until his departure from Santa Fe in May 1857, prior to the official expiration of his term on October 31, 1857. It is ironic that he took the oath of office as governor in the same palace in which he had been imprisoned more than thirty years earlier. During his tenure he was responsible for resolving many disputes, including an Indian uprising and border disputes with Mexico.

In 1858 he was again elected to the Kentucky House of Representatives, becoming speaker when it convened in 1859. Intermittently for the next twenty-seven years he served as a legislator, the last time at the age of eighty-five. He died at his plantation eight miles below Louisville on the Ohio River and is buried in Cave Hill Cemetery. David Meriwether and Sarah Hoar Leonard had twelve children.

See David Meriwether, *My Life in the Mountains and on the Plains* (Norman, Okla., 1965); Nelson Heath Meriwether, *The Meriwethers and Their Connections* (Columbia, Mo., 1964).

Ronald Van Stockum Sr.

MERIWETHER, GEORGE (b Louisa County, Virginia, March 25, 1745; d Forks of the Monongahela and Cheat Rivers, February 4, 1782). Pioneer. The son of Nicholas (1719–58), a veteran of the French and Indian War, and Frances (Morton) Meriwether, he and his brother Nicholas (1749–1828) married sisters who were their first cousins, daughters of Capt. William Meriwether (1730–90) and Martha Cox Wood. George was elected in 1776 to the first Virginia legislature, which met in Williamsburg after Governor Dunmore sought safety in the king's ships in the harbor. He developed a great interest in Kentucky, where his brother Nicholas was locating land, visiting there as early as 1779.

On January 24, 1780, he addressed a prescient letter to George Rogers Clark, then in Kentucky:

> "I could wish that you would patronize a petition to have the town on Conelleys Land [Falls of the Ohio] established & have it sent with a plan of the Town to the Assembly in May, for was it established (& I think it would be of advantage to the whole Country by drawing trade) I would build some good houses on lotts as would likewise my friends that I purchased lotts for, & would settle there if the place should not be to sickley. Prosperity attend the Country & health & happiness attend you" (Draper Collection 50J2).

On May 1, 1780, the legislature passed an act officially establishing the town of Louisville at the Falls and appointing Meriwether as one of the original town trustees.

At the forks of the Monongahela and Cheat Rivers on February 4, 1782, about halfway between Louisa and Louisville, while waiting for water transportation for his family down the Ohio to Louisville, Meriwether died of what his distraught wife Martha described in a letter to her father, Capt. William Meriwether, as "a Violent Fever." "In all and every loss I ever sustain'd . . . none can be compared with This. . . . My situation is horrid almost without a Friend and Quite without money in a Strange Cuntry at a great distance from a most kind and tender Father." With the help of family and friends, Martha brought her family back to her father's home in Louisa County, where she died in August 1786.

See R.R. Van Stockum, "Nicholas Meriwether in Early Kentucky: Land Locator, Entrepreneur, Settler," *Filson Club History Quarterly* 59 (April 1985): 223–50; idem., "George Meriwether (1745–82)," *Filson Club History Quarterly* 72 (Jan. 1998): 76–86; Nelson Heath Meriwether, *The Meriwethers and Their Connections* (Columbia, Mo., 1964).

Ronald R. Van Stockum Sr.

MERIWETHER, JAMES (b Louisa County, Virginia, June 1, 1756; d Jefferson County, Kentucky, October 24, 1801). Revolutionary officer, landowner, and public figure. Son of James (1729–1801) and Judith Hardenia (Burnley) Meriwether, he served, as did his brother William, with George Rogers Clark's Illinois regiment in the 1778–79 campaigns that resulted in the capture of Kaskaskia, Cahokia, and Vincennes. He later served in the campaigns of Dabney's Virginia State Legion.

He married his first cousin, Sarah Meriwether, aunt of George Wood Meriwether of Louisville, the family chronicler. He acted as attorney for his father in the sale of the family's extensive land holdings in Kentucky. Meriwether was a representative of Jefferson County in the Convention of 1787 held in Danville to consider statehood for Kentucky, and in 1788 he became a commissioner of Jefferson County. He served in the Kentucky General Assembly as a member of the House of Representatives (1795, 1796, 1799, 1801). By act of the General Assembly dated February 10, 1798, he was appointed one of the original trustees for Jefferson Seminary, forerunner of the University of Louisville.

See Nelson Heath Meriwether, *The Meriwethers and Their Connections* (Columbia, Mo., 1964); *Collins' Historical Sketches of Kentucky, History of Kentucky, by Lewis Collins* (reprinted Frankfort 1966); Abstracts of Jefferson County Records, Filson Club Historical Society.

Ronald R. Van Stockum Sr.
Joan H. Meriwether

MERIWETHER, JESSE (b near Louisville, ca. 1812; d Louisville, May 16, 1892). Carpenter and educator. Meriwether was born a slave on the Samuel Churchill farm. He was emancipated in 1847 on the condition that he agree to be sent to Liberia. He did so but returned to Louisville in 1849. He prospered as a carpenter and took an active role in the affairs of the African American community. In 1850 the first black Masonic lodge in Louisville was organized in secret at his house on Walnut St. (Muhammad Ali Blvd). He traveled to a Free Soil Convention in Pittsburgh in 1852, where he heard Frederick Douglass and others give impassioned speeches against slavery. After the Civil War, Meriwether was appointed to the black Board of Visitors by the School Board, and he also served on the boards of the Freedmen's Savings Bank and the Louisville Cemetery Association. He is buried in Eastern Cemetery.

See William H. Gibson, *History of the United Brothers of Friendship and Sisters of the Mysterious Ten* (Louisville 1897).

Cornelius Bogert

MERIWETHER, NICHOLAS (b Louisa County, Virginia, June 4, 1749; d Shelby County, Kentucky, April 28, 1828). Land locator, entrepreneur, and pioneer settler. Nicholas Meriwether was the son of Nicholas Meriwether (1719–58) and Frances Morton. He and his brother George married sisters who were their first cousins, daughters of Capt. William Meriwether (1730–90). Meriwether first arrived at the FALLS OF THE OHIO in 1779 or possibly a year earlier. While not an officially appointed surveyor, he became one of the early Kentucky land locators, running private surveys through the virgin land of Kentucky for himself and his family, and for others from whom he extracted a fee.

Meriwether, who frequently used the OHIO RIVER for his travels to Kentucky, left many letters describing the threats of Indian attack along this route and how best to avoid them. "By no means take aney Stock on Board the Boat your familey comes in. Sail all night unless exceedingly dark & be upon the way earley in the mornings when you do stop, & stay but little time at a place."

Between October 4 and November 27, 1784, he lived on one of his lots on the north side of MAIN St. between Sixth and Seventh where he kept one of the first houses of public entertainment in Louisville. While there, Nicholas lost, through natural causes, his wife and four of his sons. On October 12, 1786, he married Elizabeth Daniel, sister of Walker Daniel, first attorney general for the court for the District of Kentucky who had been killed in an Indian ambush in 1784. A year later he purchased SQUIRE BOONE's old "Painted Stone" tract in Shelby County, which he called "Castle Hill" after the Meriwether estate in Albemarle County, Virginia. In 1804, the year after his cousin Meriwether Lewis departed the Falls with William Clark on the "Voyage of Discovery," Meriwether took his family down the Ohio and Mississippi to settle in West Bank, Mississippi, returning later to Shelby County where he died. Meriwether was an active and imaginative man who involved himself in many land deals and commercial ventures, creating enemies in the process, some real and some imagined; but through his drive and ambition he contributed significantly to the development of the Kentucky frontier.

See R.R. Van Stockum, "Nicholas Meriwether in Early Kentucky: Land Locator, Entrepreneur, Settler," *Filson Club History Quarterly* 59 (April 1985): 223–50; Nelson Heath Meriwether, *The Meriwethers and Their Connections* (Columbia, Mo., 1964); R.R. Van Stockum, *Kentucky and the Bourbons: The Story of Allen Dale Farm* (Louisville 1991).

Ronald R. Van Stockum Sr.

MERKLEY KENDRICK JEWELERS. Merkley Kendrick Jewelers has been a leader in fine jewelry sales and design in Louisville for more than a century. In 1832 William Kendrick founded a jewelry firm. By the 1880s his sons, William C. Kendrick and George P. Kendrick, had joined the firm, and the name was changed to William Kendrick and Sons. It grew to a business handling diamonds, fine jewelry, watches, silver, giftware, and art. In 1930 the store experienced the effects of the GREAT DEPRESSION and closed. However, it reopened in 1932 under the ownership of William P. Kendrick, grandson of the founder. It later moved to the 600 block of S Fourth St.

During the 1920s Joseph C. Merkley of Jasper, Indiana, became involved in the jewelry trade, studied in St. Louis, and then moved to Louisville. In the 1930s he began working in the store of Elmer L. Gray, soon forming a partnership. In the 1940s the E.L. Gray store became Gray and Merkley Jewelers, eventually moving from Eighteenth and Oak Streets to the Southland Terrace Shopping Center. In 1959 Merkley's sons, William and Donald, opened Gray and Merkley Jewelers in ST. MATTHEWS. In 1966 Gray and Merkley Jewelers merged with the Kendrick store and took the name Merkley Kendrick Jewelers.

In 1971 the downtown and Southland Terrace stores combined and moved to Chenoweth Ln. in St. Matthews. In July 1992 the partnership between Bill and Don Merkley was dissolved, and Bill and his wife, Carolyn, became the sole owners of Merkley Kendrick Jewelers. In December 1992 the Louisville and Lexington stores (opened in 1982) were combined in the Chenoweth Ln. store. In 1988 Nanette Merkley Vale, the first of the third generation, joined the business. Brian S. Merkley, also a member of the third generation, joined in 1996.

Nanette M. Vale

MERTON, THOMAS (b Prades, France, January 31, 1915; d Bangkok, Thailand, December 10, 1968). Monk and theologian. Thomas Merton was a Cistercian monk of the Abbey of our Lady of Gethsemani in Trappist, Kentucky, near Bardstown. His parents were artists; his father, Owen, a New Zealand native, was an accomplished watercolor painter, and his mother, Ruth Jenkins, born in the United States, was an artist-designer. Merton's mother died when he was six; his father died when he was fifteen. He was educated at Clare College, Cambridge University (1933–34) and at Columbia University, where he received a B.A. in 1937 and an M.A. in English literature in 1938.

In 1938 Merton converted to Roman Catholicism and taught English literature for a year and a half at St. Bonaventure University in Olean, New York (1940-41). On December 10, 1941, Merton entered the Abbey of Our Lady of Gethsemani. The Trappists live an austere, silent, agricultural lifestyle of prayer and work. However, Merton was encouraged by religious superiors to write. His first publication was *Thirty Poems* (1944). In 1948 his autobiography describing his conversion and early life at Gethsemani, *The Seven Storey Mountain*, became a publishing sensation and established Merton as an international postwar religious writer. In 1951, in a Louisville ceremony, Merton became a United States citizen.

In the later 1950s and throughout the 1960s, Merton developed his literary interests and emerged as a social critic, ecumenist, catalyst for monastic renewal, and mystic. His prolific writings include classics such as *Thoughts in Solitude* (1958), *New Seeds of Contemplation* (1961), *Conjectures of a Guilty Bystander* (1966), *Faith and Violence* (1968), and *The Geography of Lograire* (1968). A selection of his voluminous letters and his extensive journals have been published posthumously.

In 1965 he began living full-time in his hermitage on a wooded knoll at the abbey; this structure had been built in the early 1960s to facilitate his meeting with ecumenical guests, including students of E. Glenn Hinson from Louisville's SOUTHERN BAPTIST THEOLOGICAL SEMINARY. Merton's interest in dialogue with contemplatives from Eastern RELIGIONS led to his trip to Asia, including a visit with the Dalai Lama in India; trips to Sri Lanka and Singapore; and a conference on Buddhist-Christian monasticism in Bangkok, Thailand. It was there that he was accidentally electrocuted when he touched a fan with faulty wiring as he emerged from the shower. His body was returned in a military transport carrying bodies of American soldiers who had died in Vietnam, a war he opposed. He is buried at the Abbey of Gethsemani.

Among Merton's poems are "The OHIO RIVER—Louisville" and *Eighteen Poems* (1985), which include numerous references to Louisville locations. On March 18, 1958, he experienced a transforming "vision" at the corner of Louisville's Fourth and Walnut (now Muhammad Ali Blvd.) Streets, declaring that his monastic existence was not a separation from others and celebrating that he was a member of "the race in which God himself became incarnate." On several occasions, Merton wrote that he had visited and prayed in the nearby CATHEDRAL OF THE ASSUMPTION. His rare excursions into Louisville during the 1960s included visits to JAZZ clubs on Washington St. and to CUNNINGHAM'S RESTAURANT on Fifth St. His literary archives are housed at the THOMAS MERTON Center in the W.L. Lyons Brown Library of BELLARMINE COLLEGE in Louisville.

See Michael Mott, *The Seven Mountains of Thomas Merton* (Boston 1984); George Kilcourse, *Ace of Freedoms: Thomas Merton's Christ* (Notre Dame, Ind., 1993); Lawrence S. Cunningham, ed., *Thomas Merton: Spiritual Master* (New York 1992).

George A. Kilcourse Jr.

MERWIN, SUSAN BUCKINGHAM (b Louisville, November 24, 1874; d Louisville, May 6, 1923). An educator of the blind, Susan Merwin was the daughter of Samuel Miles and Mary (Irvine) Merwin. She was educated in Louisville and began her career as teacher and secretary at the KENTUCKY SCHOOL FOR THE BLIND in 1895. Merwin was elected vice president of the American Association of Instructors of the Blind in 1915 and served as associate editor of the national magazine, *Outlook for the Blind*. Locally she was president of the Louisville Conference of Social Workers and active in a number of Louisville organizations.

Merwin's concern for her students' education went beyond the academic. She obtained tickets so that they could attend concerts and lectures and started Boy Scout and Girl Scout troops at the school. Merwin's interests also extended to blind adults, and she was instrumental in establishing a workshop that provided not only employment but an opportunity for learning to read and type Braille.

She was the second woman in the country to be named superintendent of a school for the blind, the Kentucky School for the Blind. As superintendent of the American Printing House for the Blind, Merwin influenced the U.S. Congress to increase the annual federal appropriation to the institution from ten thousand to fifty thousand dollars. She also secured an appropriation from the Kentucky General Assembly for an addition to the building. She served in the superintendencies until her death. She is buried in Cave Hill Cemetery.

See "Susan B. Merwin," *Outlook for the Blind* 17 (Sept. 1923): 26–27; "Changes among the Superintendents," *Outlook for the Blind* 17 (Winter 1913): 104; Col. Ben. LaBree, ed., *Press Reference Book of Prominent Kentuckians* (Louisville 1916); T.L. Jefferson, "President's Report," *Report of the Kentucky School for the Blind* (1923).

Carol Brenner Tobe

METHODISTS. Methodism first entered Kentucky in 1786, six years before statehood and only two years following the Baltimore Christmas Conference that organized the Methodist Episcopal church in the United States. Between 1784 and 1796 American Methodism consisted of only one nationwide conference, overseen by the legendary Methodist Bishop Francis Asbury; but in 1796 the church established six conferences, and Kentucky was part of the Western Conference. At the time of the first Methodist conference in Kentucky (near Lexington in 1790), Methodism slowly became established around several Kentucky settlements, including Louisville.

At first Methodist preaching was in the open areas rather than in the towns and villages. The Salt River circuit, which included fifty-eight preaching places, was established in 1791. This circuit embraced Jefferson, Green, Washington, Nelson, Taylor, Spencer, Bullitt, Larue, Oldham, and Trimble Counties. According to church historians, Middletown United Methodist Church traces its beginnings (1800) to Salt River circuit activities. Even earlier, Methodists convened at the Mill Creek meetinghouse (also used by the Baptists) in the present Shively area. The original date and the composition of the Mill Creek Methodist congregation are unknown, but the congregation dates to at least 1793 and probably earlier. In 1816 Christian Shively (the namesake of Shively, at whose home Francis Asbury once stopped for breakfast) deeded land to the Methodists and asked that the church be named the Mill Creek Church. (That stone church burned, but the original stones may still be seen in the 1849 Mill Creek Church, just off Dixie Hwy. in Shively). Andrew Monroe, who was appointed to the Jefferson circuit in 1816, also organized the State Street Church in Bowling Green. Parkview United Methodist Church in Shively is descended from the very early Mill Creek Methodist congregation.

A Methodist society was organized in Louisville in 1806, the first inside the city limits. The first Methodist place of worship in Louisville was probably a private home; the second was a log schoolhouse at the present location of the county courthouse. A brick building used for worship was erected on the north side of Market St. between Seventh and Eighth Streets in 1809. Francis Asbury preached at that building three years later. In 1812 the Western Conference was divided into the Ohio and Tennessee Conferences, and Louisville was included in the Ohio Conference.

In 1816 the Market St. building was sold, and the proceeds were used to construct the Fourth St. church (a few other congregations dating from 1816 no longer exist). The church stood on the east side of Fourth St. on the southeast corner of the alley between Jefferson and Market Streets. The Fourth St. church is considered the first official Methodist church built in Louisville, although Methodists worshiped in the city for ten years prior to that time in other buildings. Bishop William McKendree dedicated that church when the Ohio Annual Conference met there in 1816. In 1835 the Fourth Street Church divided into three congregations: the Fourth Street Church, the Eighth Street Church, and the Brook Street Church. In 1853 the Fourth Street Church was sold, and the Walnut Street Church was constructed at Fifth and Walnut (Muhammad Ali Blvd.) Streets. That congregation remained until 1907 when it merged with the Chestnut Street Church to form the Union Church (the Methodist Temple), which in turn merged with the Trinity Church (founded in 1865) in 1940. The

Trinity Temple Methodist Church, northeast corner of Third and Guthrie streets, 1950.

Eighth Street Church at Eighth and Market Streets also merged into the Union Church in 1907. The Brook Street Church had its building on Brook St. between Market and Jefferson Streets until 1865, when the congregation moved to Broadway between Brook and Floyd Streets and changed its name to the BROADWAY Church. Broadway Church needed to move from that location in 1955 because of a planned medical center, so Bishop William T. Watkins helped the congregation plan a new site on Brownsboro Rd. Broadway merged with a "pilot church" in Indian Hills, and became Christ Church in the mid-1950s. Thus both Christ Church and Trinity trace their histories to 1816, through congregations descending from the original Fourth Street Church.

During the 1820s only one church, Cooper Memorial, was organized. It was called "the class at Coopers" when the congregation began in 1829. The congregation was called Bethesda Chapel when it finally erected a church in 1839. The second building, constructed in 1860, was called Cooper Chapel, and in 1896 the church took the name Cooper Memorial.

R.E. Jones United Methodist Church dates its history from the 1830s; blacks worshiped in a small building called Old Frog Pond Church near Shelby and Chestnut Streets before the Jackson Street M.E. Church was established at Jackson St. near Jefferson St. in 1832. The church moved to Sixth and Walnut Streets in 1923 (and eventually to Algonquin Pkwy.) and was named for the first black bishop, Robert Elijah Jones.

The Methodist Protestant church began from a schism in the Methodist Episcopal church in 1830. Actually the movement began in Louisville a year before that, when fifty members of the Fourth Street Church withdrew and formed the First Methodist Reformed Church at Fourth and Green (Liberty) Streets. The first pastor, Nicholas Snethen, was a close friend of Francis Asbury. Methodist Protestant work in Kentucky was not strong in Louisville.

In 1835 William Nast was appointed by the Ohio Conference as missionary to the Germans. Louisville, along with Covington and Newport, had large GERMAN POPULATIONS. Peter Schmucker organized the Market Street congregation in Louisville in 1840. The First German Methodist Episcopal church was constructed on Clay St. between Market and Jefferson Streets in 1842, a year after the congregation was founded. A second German Methodist Episcopal church began in Louisville in 1848 and constructed a building at Twelfth and Madison Streets in 1850. The church moved in 1912 to Eighteenth and Ormsby Streets. The congregation later merged with the St. Peter Church (formerly Davison Memorial) to form Crum's Lane Church (now Shively United Methodist). For a short time in the 1850s the Methodist Episcopal church South attempted a German mission in Louisville.

At the General Conference of the Methodist Episcopal church in New York City in May 1844, the slavery issue came to the fore. Bishop Andrew of Georgia had acquired slaves through marriage, and many delegates protested. Southern delegates objected to the criticism of Bishop Andrew. The denomination voted to separate into two jurisdictions. The organizing convention of the Methodist Episcopal church South assembled in Louisville on May 1, 1845, at the old Fourth Street Church. The Wesley Chapel Church (now Marcus Lindsey) was dedicated during the time of that organizing convention. In 1846 the Methodist Episcopal church South was organized in Kentucky as the Louisville Conference and the Kentucky Conference. The boundary between the two conferences was a diagonal line beginning at the mouth of HARRODS CREEK on the Ohio, down to the Tennessee border. Meanwhile, the northern Methodist church remained established in Kentucky via its Kentucky Conference.

Several Methodist Episcopal South congregations in Kentucky were racially integrated, although seating was usually separate. Eighth Street Church in Louisville had 546 black members and 180 white members, for instance. The Methodist Episcopal church South established three black congregations in the 1850s: Center Street, Green Street, and Jackson Street.

Several churches were organized in the 1840s. As stated above, the Market Street German Church, first known as the First German Church, and Second German Methodist Episcopal Church date from the early 1840s. In 1879 Market Street German Church was renamed the Market Street Church. Also dating from the 1840s are the Mt. Holly Church (1842), Marcus Lindsey Church (1843), Bethany Church (1843), ASBURY CHAPEL (1845), Sehon's Chapel (1848), and Jefferson Street Church (1848). Other Methodist churches established during the nineteenth century include PORTLAND (1860), JEFFERSONTOWN (1862), West Broadway (1867), Wesley (1870), Coke Chapel (1872, later New Coke and then Coke Memorial), CRESCENT HILL (1887), the Third German Methodist Episcopal Church (1887), the Fourth Avenue Church (1888), the Virginia Avenue Church (1889), the Fourth German Methodist Episcopal Church (later called St. John Church), the SHELBY PARK Church (1893), BEECHMONT (1893), Highland (1895), Epworth (1896), and Calvary (1900). In the early twentieth century, these churches were established: Davison Memorial (1904), Oakdale (1904), Jones Memorial (1909), HAZELWOOD (1912), FERN CREEK (1913), St. Paul (1915), St. Luke (1923), Grace (1933), St. Matthews (1938), Wetstein (1942, originally a chapel of the Market Street Church), Parkwood (1944), Emmanuel (1946), CLIFTON HEIGHTS (1947), and AUDUBON PARK (1947).

After the CIVIL WAR, many black members of the Methodist Episcopal church South left the denomination to join congregations of the Methodist Episcopal church, as well as new congregations of the African Methodist Episcopal church and the African Methodist Episcopal church, Zion. The latter two denominations became more active in Kentucky following the war. The Colored (now Christian) Methodist Episcopal church, organized as a new denomination in 1870, also began congregations in Kentucky. Two examples of historic black congregations are Young's Chapel and QUINN CHAPEL. Quinn Chapel African Methodist Episcopal Church was founded in 1838 as Bethel, House of God. It began when the Reverend David Smith organized a congregation in a room over a public stable, near a "Negro Pen" and slave auction block. William Paul Quinn had been the preacher who took African Methodism westward and spoke at Louisville. The Quinn Chapel church was considered an abolition church by some slaveholders. The congregation was closely associated with the antislavery movement and also with the 1960s CIVIL RIGHTS movement. Young's Chapel African Methodist Episcopal Church began in 1869 when the Reverend Octave Double gathered twenty-seven youth and adults together beneath a peach tree on Fifteenth St. and organized a Sunday school mission. It became the California Mission Church in the 1870s. The name was changed to Young's Chapel about 1887 to honor the Reverend Henry Young of Quinn Chapel African Methodist Episcopal Church. Stoner Chapel was established in late 1895 in the CABBAGE PATCH area at the home of the Reverend Thomas O. Stoner, and shortly after built a new church on S Twelfth St.

There are two other denominations of the Methodist tradition, the United Brethren, and the Evangelical Association. The United Brethren founded a congregation east of Louisville in 1811, but it did not survive. The Evangelical Association organized Zion Church in 1865. Zion eventually became an Evangelical United Brethren church and then a United Methodist congregation. It closed in the summer of 1998.

The Methodist Episcopal church, the Methodist Episcopal church South, and the Methodist Protestant churches united in 1939 at the Uniting Conference at Kansas City. The new denomination was called the Methodist church. In 1968 the Methodist church joined with the Evangelical United Brethren church, itself the result of a 1946 merger of the United Brethren and the Evangelical Association. The resulting denomination is named the United Methodist church.

Other church-related organizations include the Wesley Community House. Located in 1903 at 834 E Jefferson St., it later moved to 803 E Washington St. Wesley House serves as a settlement house for the needy. The Louisville Female Academy (1853–80) was a school of the southern church's Louisville Conference. The Methodist Widows' and Orphans' Home, owned by both the Louisville and Kentucky Conferences, was incorporated in 1871 and opened in 1883. The home was first located on

Fifth St. near Broadway and remained there until 1931, when it was moved to Versailles, Kentucky.

The Deaconess Hospital on Eighth St. began in 1896 and dedicated its hospital building in 1898. The Central German Conference owned the hospital until 1917, when the Kentucky Conference of the Methodist Episcopal church entered into joint ownership. When the neighborhood around Deaconess began to deteriorate and the hospital faced financial problems, a new Methodist hospital was authorized by the Louisville Conference in 1946. Called Methodist Evangelical Hospital (now NORTON HEALTHCARE Pavilion), the facility is on Broadway between Floyd and Preston Streets.

Wesley Manor, a facility for the elderly, was established from a 1914 fund from Mrs. Elizabeth Cluff Nettleton of the Broadway church. By 1958 the Louisville Conference fulfilled her dream and established Wesley Manor on Manslick Rd. in southern Jefferson County.

The General Board of Missions of the Methodist Episcopal church South was in Louisville from 1845–56, when it was moved to Nashville. The Board of Church Extension of the Methodist Episcopal church South was in Louisville from 1882–1939.

The Wesley Foundation began in the United States about 1920, first in the northern and then the southern church. The foundation provides a resource for planning and implementing ministries in higher education and offers a Methodist community for students, faculty, and staff of colleges nationwide. Student centers were developed at several Kentucky campuses, including Western Kentucky University and the University of Louisville.

Present-day United Methodist churches in the Louisville district are Advent(now Resurrection in LaGrange), Aldersgate, Audubon Park, Beechmont(now Gateway Community), Bethany, BUECHEL, Calvary, Christ Church, City Road Chapel, Coke, Cooper Memorial, Crescent Hill, Eastwood, Epiphany, Epworth, Fern Creek, Fourth Avenue, Genesis, Grace, Hazelwood, Highland, Hobbs Chapel, Jeffersontown, Louisville Korean(formerly Immanuel), Marcus Lindsey, Middletown, Mt. Holly, Mt. Tabor, Parkview, Parkway, Parkwood, PLEASURE RIDGE PARK, Preston Highway, R.E. Jones, St. John, St. Luke, St. Mark, St. Matthews, St. Paul, Shiloh, Shively, Spradling Memorial, Summit Heights, Sycamore Chapel, Trinity Towers Corporporation, Virginia Avenue, Watkins Memorial, West Broadway, and the Portland United Methodist Center. African Methodist Episcopal churches in the city and county include Acacia, Asbury Chapel, Quinn Chapel, St. Paul, and Young's Chapel. African Methodist Episcopal churches, Zion, include Broadway Temple, Brown Temple, Hughlett Temple, Spradling Memorial, Stoner Memorial, Taylortown, and Walter Clements. Christian Methodist Episcopal churches include Lampkins Chapel, Brown Memorial, Miles Memorial, Muir Chapel and Phillips Memorial, the First Congregational Methodist Church and St. John's.

See Walter I. Munday, "Louisville Methodism: Yesterday, Today, and Tomorrow" (n.p. 1949); Roy H. Short, *Methodism in Kentucky* (Rutland, Vt., 1979); A.H. Redford, *The History of Methodism in Kentucky* (Nashville 1863); J.H. Spencer, *A History of Kentucky Baptists from 1769 to 1885* (n.p. 1886); Othal Hawthorne Lakey, *The History of the C.M.E. Church* (Memphis 1985); William J. Walls, *The African Methodist Episcopal Zion Church: The Reality of the Black Church* (Charlotte, N.C., 1974); Frederick Norwood, *The History of American Methodism* (Nashville 1974); R. Kenneth Lile, *Thy Hand Hath Provided* (Franklin, Tenn., 1996).

Paul E. Stroble

METROPOLITAN SEWER DISTRICT OF LOUISVILLE AND JEFFERSON COUNTY. The Louisville and Jefferson County Metropolitan Sewer District (MSD) provides wastewater and drainage services for most of Jefferson County. It also operates and maintains the OHIO RIVER floodwall system, administers the floodplain management and hazardous materials programs, and manages the cooperative computerized mapping and data system for local GOVERNMENT agencies and utilities. It also is involved in many environmental and educational programs, most of them concerned with water quality.

The agency's responsibilities and services have expanded tremendously over the years. It was formed in 1946 for one basic reason: the city of Louisville, operating through its old COMMISSIONERS OF SEWERAGE, needed $60 million in sewer improvements, and it had only $6 million in bonding authority available. The district took over a sewer system, parts of which dated to the 1820s, that had never caught up with needs. By the end of WORLD WAR II, nearly one-fourth of the homes in the city were still without sewer service, and drainage problems were widespread. All of the wastewater was dumped into the Ohio River and local streams without any treatment. In addition to sewer improvements, the early tasks included designing and building the city's first sewage treatment plant, required under the Ohio River Valley interstate compact of 1948. Financial problems delayed the start of construction until 1956. The plant, later named for former MSD executive Morris Forman, was finished in 1959 off South Western Pkwy.

For income, MSD adopted a system of fees based on the quantity of water used—a system that would survive, with refinements, for the rest of the century.

MSD's challenges were so great in its early years that it could not begin to keep up with suburban expansion. Countywide sewer programs were discussed and planned from the late 1950s, but the costs seemed staggering. MSD's resources were concentrated on catching up with the problems in the city—and then upgrading its treatment plant to meet the increasing water pollution standards of the 1970s. This changed in the 1980s when MSD found the support it needed to expand. New laws enabled it to begin extending its network into the SUBURBS, eliminating dozens of small treatment plants and thousands of septic tank systems. In 1987 MSD took over the new drainage district, consolidating the fragmented drainage efforts of more than one hundred local government agencies.

Two disasters stand out in MSD's history, both involving hazardous materials. In 1977 a disposal company dumped highly toxic CHEMICALS into the sewer system, shutting down the treatment plant for three months. The chemicals required more than two years and nearly $2 million to clean up. The man responsible was the first person convicted of criminal charges by a federal jury for polluting a waterway. In February 1981 explosions ripped through more than two miles of sewers in OLD LOUISVILLE, leaving a series of craters and collapsed streets and four persons injured. The blasts were blamed on highly flammable hexane spilled into the sewer in an industrial accident at Ralston-Purina's soybean processing plant on Floyd St. (hexane is used to remove oil from soybeans). The company had reported a spill to MSD, but an inspector found no leaking chemicals. It was later confirmed that eighteen thousand gallons of hexane had escaped and run into the sewers. It took nearly two years and more than $18 million to repair the damage.

In the late 1990s, MSD worked with Oldham and Bullitt Counties on cooperative agreements that could extend sewer service to developments outside Jefferson County.

Martin E. Biemer

METROPOLITAN STATISTICAL AREA. Metropolitan Statistical Area, or MSA, refers to a concept created in 1949 by the United States Bureau of the Budget (later the Office of Management and Budget) so that a wide variety of statistical data on metropolitan areas might be collected and presented for a uniform set of geographic areas. The general concept is that of a geographic area consisting of a large urban POPULATION core together with adjacent communities having a high degree of economic and social integration with the core. MSAs are defined in terms of counties because these are the smallest geographical units for which a wide range of statistical data are regularly collected.

In order for a location to be considered an MSA it must have one or more central counties that contain its main population and have at least fifty thousand inhabitants. An MSA may also include outlying counties that have close economic and social ties with the central counties. The outlying counties must have a specified level of commuting to the central counties and must meet certain standards regarding metropolitan character such as population density, urban population, and population growth. The standards for the MSA are set by the Federal Committee on Standard METROPOLITAN STATISTICAL AREAS.

In general, the lower a county's percentage of workers commuting to the central core, the higher the population density and urbanization thresholds it must exceed in order for it to be included in the MSA. The definitions of individual MSAs are revised according to the results of each decennial census and are updated periodically between each census.

The original Louisville, Kentucky–Indiana MSA consisted of Jefferson County, Kentucky, and Clark and Floyd Counties in Indiana. The 1950 and 1960 censuses brought no change to this definition. Bullitt and Oldham Counties were added to the MSA after the 1970 census. After the 1980 census SHELBY COUNTY, Kentucky, and HARRISON COUNTY, INDIANA, were added to the Louisville MSA. And after the 1990 census Scott County, Indiana, was added to the Louisville MSA and Shelby County, Kentucky was dropped—primarily due to a decline in workers commuting to Jefferson County from Shelby County. The chart summarizes changes to the official MSA designation for the Louisville area during the last half of the twentieth century.

Louisville Metropolitan Statistical Area by Years

1949	Jefferson County, Kentucky
	Clark County, Indiana
	Floyd County, Indiana
April 1973	Jefferson County, Kentucky
	Clark County, Indiana
	Floyd County, Indiana
	Bullitt County, Kentucky
	Oldham County, Kentucky
June 1983	Jefferson County, Kentucky
	Clark County, Indiana
	Floyd County, Indiana
	Bullitt County, Kentucky
	Oldham County, Kentucky
	Harrison County, Indiana
	Shelby County, Kentucky
December 1992	Jefferson County, Kentucky
	Clark County, Indiana
	Floyd County, Indiana
	Bullitt County, Kentucky
	Oldham County, Kentucky
	Harrison County, Indiana
	Scott County, Indiana

Barry Kornstein

METRO UNITED WAY. United Way of America is a national system of volunteers, contributors, and local charities built on the proven effectiveness of local organizations helping people in their own communities. Metro United Way is one of those local, independent nonprofit organizations that resulted from a major community effort to efficiently plan and coordinate human services and to raise funds to support them. It is one of more than fourteen hundred local United Ways in the United States and is affiliated with the national organization.

Metro United Way began in 1917 as the Louisville Federation of Social Agencies. Brothers Arthur and Charles W. Allen and E.S. Tachau formed the volunteer-driven federation as a way to coordinate solicitations for support of human-service agencies. The first meeting of the federation's Board of Presidents was on October 25, 1917. Arthur Allen was elected the chairman, and W.G. Mun was elected secretary. Charles W. Allen served as the first campaign chair.

During that first campaign, which was a door-to-door canvass for donations, volunteers raised $108,000 from 5,450 contributors. These funds were distributed to twenty-five agencies that met certain accountability and coordination standards. The charter agencies were Associated Charities, Babies Milk Fund Association, Children's Free Hospital, Consumer's League of Kentucky, District Nurse Association, East End Day Nursery, Federation of Jewish Charities, Fresh Air Home, Home for Friendless Women, Henrie Barret Montfort Home, HOME OF THE INNOCENTS, Kentucky Child Labor Association, Kentucky Humane Society, King's Daughters Home for Incurables, Louisville Anti-Tuberculosis Association, Louisville Flower Mission, Louisville Santa Claus Association, Louisville Wesley House, Loyalty Charity Club, NEIGHBORHOOD HOUSE, Presbyterian Colored Mission, St. Thomas Orphan's Home, St. Vincent's Orphans' Home, THE SALVATION ARMY, and the Union Gospel Mission. Several of these agencies, although renamed, are still Metro United Way participating agencies.

In 1919 the federation changed its name to the Welfare League, and contributors were asked to "Invest in Louisville's welfare." In 1923 it became incorporated and changed its name to the Louisville Community Chest. The campaign that year raised $634,999.

Through the years the Community Chest played a vital and expanding role. In 1937 there was a heavy demand for volunteers to help the thousands of people left homeless by the Ohio River flood. This led to the development of the Central Volunteer Placement Bureau in 1938. Mary "Rip" McClure served as its first president. The current incarnation of the bureau is Metro United Way's Volunteer Connection, which places thousands of volunteers at more than two hundred nonprofit agencies throughout the community each year.

During WORLD WAR II the Community Chest incorporated the Louisville War Fund. The result was a campaign that went over the million-dollar mark for the first time, raising $1,535,748.

In 1943 payroll deduction allowed employees to donate a portion of each paycheck to the campaign, thus increasing a contributor's capacity to make a larger donation. The development of employee group solicitation and payroll deduction were two important aspects of effective cooperation between management and organized labor on behalf of United Way.

In 1947 the red feather—the badge of courage for American Indians and the legendary Robin Hood—became the familiar symbol of giving to the Community Chest. Ten years later the total surpassed the $2 million mark when in 1957 the campaign collected $2,043,388.

The 1960s brought "the war on poverty" and increased partnership among GOVERNMENT, the Chest, and nonprofit agencies. The Chest surpassed the $3 million mark and changed its name to the United Appeal to mark its new fund-raising partnership with the Louisville Chapter of the American Red Cross. To encourage involvement of organized labor, a union counselor training program was initiated in 1965 to introduce union members to the organization and programs it funded.

As fund-raising, health and human services programs, and the community grew and changed, so did the United Appeal, which changed its name to United Way of Louisville and Jefferson County in 1971. In 1972 the organization changed its name to Metro United Way to reflect the expansion to serve other counties in Kentucky and Indiana. It merged with United Way of NEW ALBANY and Floyd County that same year. The Jefferson County Southwest Resource Center was opened in VALLEY STATION in 1973, which brought agency services to the neighborhood level. SHELBYVILLE and SHELBY COUNTY joined in 1974. Campaign growth escalated to $6 million by 1978.

In the 1980s, Metro United Way moved from 207 W MARKET St. to 334 E BROADWAY. The organization grew to include Oldham and Hardin Counties in 1986 and HARRISON COUNTY, Indiana, in 1987. The campaign grew to $17.2 million in 1989.

To acknowledge the importance and contribution of volunteers to Metro United Way throughout its history, the organization established the Allen Society Community Service Awards and the Allen Society Leadership Awards, named for its founders. According to the 1991 Metro United Way annual report, "The award program recognizes local volunteers who have contributed to the quality of life in our community, supported its human services and furthered the cause of voluntarism through leadership or services to the Metro United Way and/or participating agencies."

With the dramatic increase of nonprofit organizations competing for donations in the 1990s, Metro United Way worked to position itself for continued growth and support of the community and people in need. In 1990 it merged with United Way of Clark County. In 1995 Combined Health Appeal, an umbrella organization for fourteen health-related agencies, joined the campaign as a fund-raising partner. Metro United Way's 1998 campaign raised $27 million.

Lillian C. Milanof

METROVERSITY. The KENTUCKIANA Metroversity Inc. was chartered May 7, 1969, as a nonprofit six-member higher education consortium. Charter members were Bellarmine College, Indiana University Southeast, Louisville Presbyterian Theological Seminary, Southern Baptist Theological Seminary, Spalding College (University since 1984), and the University of Louisville. Jefferson Community College was accepted as the seventh member on July 1, 1983.

Metroversity has been served by four executive directors: Dr. John Ford (1969–85); Dr. William F. Ekstrom (acting director for seven months in 1985); Dr. Thomas Diener (1985–95); and John F. Will III (1996–). A board of directors, composed of the chief executive officers of the member institutions, serves as the governing body of Metroversity.

Metroversity coordinates committees, councils, and task forces with representatives from each of the institutions. These groups aid in the development of cooperative programs among the institutions and oversee their implementation.

Students at all of the campuses may enroll in class offerings at another campus through the cross-registration program. With permission of the home school dean and registrar, a student can visit another campus to take a course and have the credit recorded on the home school transcript, the same as if the course had been taken there. Cross-registration allows students to take language courses, ROTC, music, drama, religion, and other courses that may not be offered on their home campus. Faculty and staff of all member institutions have the opportunity to take classes on other campuses.

Students have opportunities to participate in academic competitions, leadership conferences, and recreational activities with others from all member campuses.

Through the cooperation of the library council, students, faculty, and staff have access to the holdings of all libraries as well as to the public libraries of Louisville, Jeffersonville, and New Albany. A person at one of the institutions may request a book from one of the other libraries through the home school's interlibrary loan system. The book is picked up by courier, taken to the home campus library, and returned by courier to the original library.

When cable television came to Louisville and Jefferson County in 1980, a stipulation in the original contract provided for a higher education channel. Metroversity was chosen to program the channel, providing telecourses for college credit, religious roundtables, lectures, preparation for the GED, and various other types of educational material.

Since 1981 Metroversity has sponsored an annual faculty competition funded by the late H. Charles Grawemeyer. Professors enter new curriculum proposals for judging. Four entries are declared winners and receive monetary awards of one thousand dollars. Many new classes have been developed in member institutions from the entries in the Metroversity Instructional Development Award competition.

In 1977 Metroversity was awarded an Educational Opportunity Center (EOC) grant from the U.S. Department of Education. This community outreach project serves low-income, disadvantaged clients, providing them with college attendance information and workshops, one-on-one counseling services, aptitude testing, financial aid information, and help with forms completion, tutoring, and support as they enter postsecondary education.

An Education Talent Search (ETS) grant was made in 1988 by the U.S. Department of Education. The project provides counselors to work with at-risk, low-income middle and high school youth in certain designated schools. The ETS objective is to help the students stay in school, graduate, and eventually enter college or other higher education venues. Workshops on such subjects as math anxiety, study skills, and taking the ACT/SAT are provided for the program participants.

In 1996 Metroversity received a four-year grant from The Education Resources Institute in Boston, Massachusetts. The grant is funded by the DeWitt Wallace–Reader's Digest Fund as seed money to expand the outreach programs beyond the goals of the EOC and ETS grants. In 1998 the name of Kentuckiana College Access Center was adopted as the umbrella organization for all outreach projects.

Metroversity offices originally were on the Shelby Campus of the University of Louisville, later at Gardencourt, and since 1982 on the Ursuline Campus at 3113 Lexington Rd.

Dottie Weed

MEXICAN WAR. The war began when the United States, coveting California and lands of the Southwest, provoked fighting on the Texas border. The announcement of war with Mexico received mixed reactions from the citizens of Louisville. The *Louisville Morning Courier*, as advocate for the Democrat Party, and the Whig- oriented *Louisville Daily Journal* each portrayed the developing events to their readers through the partisan opinions of their editors. The *Courier* supported war, and the *Daily Journal* opposed it. The war with Mexico became official on May 13, 1846, when Congress passed the declaration of war submitted by President James K. Polk.

Many policies of the Polk administration had been unpopular with the large Whig contingent in Louisville. In the 1844 presidential election, Kentucky had supported the Whig candidate, Henry Clay, over Polk. As the voice of the Whig Party in Louisville, the *Daily Journal* was often critical of Polk and his administration. During the war, the *Daily Journal* continued to criticize the Polk administration and many of the president's decisions relating to the conduct of the war.

On May 22, 1846, Gov. William Owsley issued a call for two regiments of infantry and one cavalry regiment. Within four days, the governor announced that the requisite troops had been raised. Even before the governor's call, the First Regiment of Foot, Kentucky Volunteers, consisting of the companies comprising the Louisville Legion and companies from Louisville's surrounding counties, had been mustered into the service of the United States on May 17, 1846. On May 25, the First Regiment departed Louisville to join an army under the command of Gen. Zachary Taylor.

On June 9, Col. Humphrey Marshall's First Regiment of Cavalry, Kentucky Volunteers, and the Second Regiment of Foot, Kentucky Volunteers, arrived in Louisville. Both units camped at the Oakland Race Course on the Ashland Turnpike (Seventh St.), renamed Camp Owsley. Marshall's cavalry regiment included two companies containing Jefferson County troops. Co. E was commanded by Capt. William J. Hardy and Co. G by Capt. Aaron Pennington. The Second Regiment and Marshall's cavalry left Louisville in late June 1846 and were also assigned to Zachary Taylor's forces.

Taylor, the commander of American forces in northern Mexico, was born in Virginia but reared at Springfields, his father's home east of Louisville. Under General Taylor's command, the First Regiment was engaged in the siege of Monterrey. Colonel Marshall's cavalry was engaged in the Battle of Buena Vista on February 22 and 23, 1847. The First Regiment was mustered out of United States service at New Orleans on May 7, 1847, and arrived in Louisville on May 27. Colonel Marshall's cavalry returned to Louisville in mid-July and was mustered out of service.

On August 26, 1847, Governor Owsley announced that two additional regiments of infantry were to be raised in Kentucky. By September 20, 1847, the requisite number of volunteers to fill the regiment had been raised. The Third Regiment of Foot, Kentucky Volunteers, contained no companies from Jefferson County. Co. A of the Fourth Regiment of Foot, Kentucky Volunteers, was raised in Jefferson County by Capt. Timothy Keating. This regiment, commanded by Col. John S. Williams, was assigned to Gen. Winfield Scott's army in central Mexico. Colonel Williams's regiment was sent to Vera Cruz and on to Mexico City but arrived too late to be involved in the fighting around those cities. This regiment was mustered out in July 1848. The war ended with Mexico's surrender and the signing of the peace Treaty of Guadalupe Hidalgo in 1848.

The citizens of Louisville promoted the war effort in many nonmilitary ways. In May 1846, several local businesses acted as surety for a loan obtained from the Bank of Kentucky. The sum of fifty thousand dollars was raised and used for arming, equipping, and transporting the troops to Mexico. The citizens of Louisville followed the progress of the war through the accounts carried by the newspapers of the city. Besides the many editorials, the local newspapers also published official battle reports, casualty lists, and the letters of soldiers. In spite of continued Whig opposition, public support for the soldiers sent to Mexico remained high throughout the conflict.

See Ernest MacPherson, *History of the First Regiment of Infantry: The Louisville Legion* (Louisville 1907); John S.D. Eisenhower, *So Far from God: The U.S. War with Mexico 1846 to 1848* (New York 1989); Robert H. Ferrell, *Monterrey Is Ours: The Mexican War Letters of Lieutenant Dana 1845 to 1847* (Lexington 1990).

David R. Deatrick Jr.

MEYZEEK, ALBERT ERNEST (b Toledo, Ohio, November 5, 1862; d Louisville, December 19, 1963). Educator and CIVIL RIGHTS activist. Albert E. Meyzeek was the product of mixed parentage. His father, John E., was a white Canadian, and his mother, Mary Lott, was an African American. Meyzeek's maternal grandfather, John Lott, was one of the organizers of the OHIO RIVER UNDERGROUND RAILROAD in Madison, Indiana. Shortly after his birth, Meyzeek and his mother returned to the family's home in Toronto, where he received his early years of schooling. In 1875 the family moved to Terre Haute, Indiana, and he enrolled in Terre Haute Classical High School. The only black student in his class, Meyzeek graduated as valedictorian.

He initially enrolled at the Indiana State Normal School for teacher education. He continued his studies and later received a bachelor's degree in 1884 from Indiana University and a master's degree from Wilberforce in 1917.

Beginning in 1884 he taught school in Terre Haute. Meyzeek moved to Louisville in 1890, where he began an extraordinary tenure of more than fifty years of service in public education in Kentucky. His first appointment in Louisville was with the Maiden Lane School in BUTCHERTOWN, which later became Benjamin Banneker School. He was soon transferred to Western Colored School and then to the Eastern Colored School, where he served as principal from 1891 through 1893. For the next three years he was the principal at Central High School, where he expanded the curriculum from three to four years and established a reference library in the school.

In 1896 Meyzeek married Pearl E. Hill, who had been an elementary teacher in the public school system. That same year, he was appointed principal of the Eastern School District, which included the Jackson Junior High School and the Colored Normal School. While serving as principal of the Normal School over a fourteen-year period, he trained three-fourths of Louisville's black teaching staff. As a school principal, he reorganized the internal structure, offered new courses, sought college-educated teachers, established a school library, organized clubs for parents, and implemented discipline in his schools.

When the enrollment in Jackson Junior High increased, Meyzeek decided to concentrate all his talents at that institution. He remained principal of Jackson Junior High School until he retired in 1943. In April 1967 the Louisville BOARD OF EDUCATION renamed the school after Meyzeek as a tribute to his civic and educational accomplishments. Throughout his teaching career he sought opportunities to improve the schools in which he served. One of his accomplishments was having Louisville's black schools named for notable persons of African descent.

A champion of civil rights causes, Meyzeek spearheaded drives that desegregated the General Hospital, opened libraries to blacks, protested against ordinances for SEGREGATION in public facilities, worked to open the UNIVERSITY OF LOUISVILLE to blacks, and helped open a colored branch of the YMCA as early as 1892. He was also one of the founders of the LOUISVILLE URBAN LEAGUE, which he chaired for twenty-nine years. Meyzeek served as president of the Kentucky Negro Education Association in 1927 and was appointed to the Kentucky Board of Education from 1948 to 1956.

Among his many accomplishments, Meyzeek was one of the founders of a national black fraternity, Kappa Alpha Psi. He was the first man initiated into this organization. Meyzeek was also a successful businessman, serving as one of the founders of the Domestic Life and Accident Insurance Co. in Louisville, which became one of the leading black businesses in Kentucky. Meyzeek and others helped establish the Citizens Amusement Co. and the Palace Theater Co. of Louisville to provide entertainment opportunities for blacks. After Meyzeek retired from teaching he also worked as an assistant in the Office of Price Administration for Kentucky during WORLD WAR II. Meyzeek is buried in Eastern Cemetery.

See Jessie C. Smith, ed., *Notable Black American Men* (Detroit 1997); Alice A. Dunnigan, *The Fascinating Story of Black Kentuckians: Their Heritage and Tradition* (Washington, D.C., 1982); John Benjamin Horton, *Old War Horse of Kentucky* (Louisville 1986); *Who's Who in Colored America* (Yonkers, N.Y., 1938–40).

Karen C. McDaniel

MIDDLETOWN. Situated eleven miles east of downtown Louisville, Middletown is ringed roughly by the GENE SNYDER FREEWAY to the east, Interstate 64 to the south, the community of ANCHORAGE and Avoca Rd. to the north, and DOUGLASS HILLS to the west. Middletown was incorporated in 1797 when landowner Philip Buckner petitioned Jefferson County Court for permission to establish a town on five hundred acres of land "where the Sinking Fork of BEARGRASS CREEK crosses the road to SHELBYVILLE." The court named it Middletown for its location as midpoint between Shelbyville and Louisville. Others say it was because of its location between WESTPORT and SHIPPINGPORT.

Middletown quickly became a popular stagecoach stop along the Shelbyville Pike (upgraded to the Lexington and Louisville Turnpike in 1817) and served as a distribution center for the rich surrounding farmlands. By 1810 the town's POPULATION had grown to 241, and business was thriving—there were four inns, a post office, blacksmith, tannery, woolen mill, tailor, cabinet shop, cigar factory, bonnet factory, several TAVERNS, and a few general stores among other amenities. Middletown was important to neighboring communities where towns like Anchorage depended on its shops and services.

In 1862 Middletown witnessed CIVIL WAR action. Gen. Braxton Bragg, commander of the Confederate army invading Kentucky, sent a detachment of cavalry to take Middletown as a prelude to taking Louisville, which was an important strategic and supply route on the OHIO RIVER. On September 27, the Confederate Louisiana Cavalry under Col. John Scott captured the town, but their stay was brief. The fall of Middletown caused alarm in Louisville, and three days later Union troops pushed the rebels back toward southern Kentucky.

After the Civil War Middletown's importance as a regional trade center began to decline as Louisville continued to grow as the primary commercial center in the area. Middletown's main market street had some business, but the area largely remained agricultural. In 1871 the General Assembly amended the original incorporation to increase its limits. Because taxes were not being collected and regular elections were not held, Middletown was referred to as a ghost city in suspended animation municipally.

At the beginning of the twentieth century Middletown stepped to the fore again when in 1910 the Louisville and Eastern Railway Co. ran an electric interurban between Louisville and Shelbyville just to the north (along present-day U.S. 60) of Middletown's MAIN St. It ran until 1934, enabling citizens to expand their economic opportunities with employment in Louisville and to establish new businesses in the town. In the 1930s U.S. Hwy. 60 came through Middletown, and it was looped north away from historic Main St., which allowed many fine homes to be preserved.

There are seven pre–Civil War homes on Main St. The oldest existing structure, the Beynroth House, was originally built in 1784 of logs and was covered with wood siding during the 1800s. The original Middletown United Methodist Church, built in 1899 at the corner of Main and Madison Ave., has served as the town's most visible landmark. The Davis Tavern/Wetherby House was begun in 1797 and enlarged in the mid-nineteenth century. Another significant early structure near Middletown is the Chenoweth springhouse, which witnessed an Indian attack in summer 1789.

In 1960 Judge Macauley Smith of the Jefferson Circuit Court ruled that after years of governmental inactivity the town's charter was declared null and void. However on August 7, 1976, the town was reincorporated as a sixth-class city to prevent annexation by expanding JEFFERSONTOWN; later in 1982, Middletown's status was upgraded to a fourth-class city.

New transportation arteries contributed to the residential and commercial growth of the area when Interstate 64 and the GENE SNYDER FREEWAY were built in the 1970s and 1980s. Several new subdivisions and condominium and townhouse communities have been developed since. Commercial expansion is seen along Shelbyville Rd., where there are various small and large restaurants, offices, and businesses.

Middletown was the birthplace of Lawrence W. Wetherby, the only native-born Jefferson Countian to serve as Kentucky's governor (1950–55). Middletown's population was 4,262 in 1980, 5,016 in 1990, and 5,298 in 1996.

See Edith L. Wood, *Middletown's Days and Deeds* (Louisville 1946); *History of the Ohio Falls Cities and Their Counties* (Cleveland, Ohio, 1882); *A Place in Time: The Story of Louisville's Neighborhoods* (Louisville 1989); *Courier-Journal*, Nov. 8, 1989, April 30, 1997.

Blaine A. Guthrie Jr.

MIKE LINNIG'S. A popular seafood restaurant on Cane Run Rd. in southwest Jefferson County, it was founded in 1925 by Linnig as a roadside sandwich stand.

Linnig, whose family operated a hundred-acre farm along the OHIO RIVER, began selling produce at his stand sometime after his marriage to Carrie Wessel in 1915. All of Mike and Carrie's children—Bill, Leonard, Dorothy, Mel, Margie, Carolyn, and Mary Ann—helped operate the business, especially in their teen years. Gradually expanding his business to include ham sandwiches, SOFT DRINKS, and apple cider from the family's nearby orchard, Linnig added fish at the suggestion of a customer, who also donated a batter recipe that is still in use. After briefly catching fish for customers in the nearby river, Linnig began purchasing it from Louisville markets.

Cane Run Rd. was little traveled in the 1920s, and Linnig built a BASEBALL field and an outdoor dance floor to attract customers in summer months. String bands played country music at Saturday night dances. The Cane Run baseball team, founded by Linnig, competed in an independent league with other nearby teams and played on the field on Sunday afternoons. An African American team also played nearby for two years. Linnig also built cottages along the river for city dwellers wishing to escape summer heat.

At the end of PROHIBITION, Linnig added beer to his menu and opened a "garden," patterned after German BEER GARDENS, in what remained of his apple orchard. Maple and oak trees, which today tower over the site, gradually replaced the apple trees in the garden. The original produce stand was replaced by a larger frame structure as the business expanded.

The 1937 flood destroyed the ball field, dance floor, and cottages and flooded the restaurant. Linnig decided against replacing what had been lost, putting his resources into improving the restaurant portion of his business. More oaks were planted in the garden area by son Bill, and two small buildings with screened windows were built there. Oaks were also planted across Cane Run Rd., near where the baseball field and dance floor had been.

Bill and Leonard took over the business for good after the latter returned from service in the KOREAN WAR. They remodeled the building and installed gas heat and a tile floor. Large swing sets were also added about this time. Things ran smoothly until the restaurant burned on September 19, 1966, four weeks after Mike Linnig's death on August 21.

Bill and Leonard purchased the restaurant site from their father's estate; built a new, concrete block restaurant just south of the "garden"; and reopened for business on June 30, 1967. They also built a banquet room just north of the garden, about where the original restaurant had been.

Bill and his wife, Dorothy, and Leonard and his wife, Juanita, formed a corporation in 1971, with Bill as president, Leonard as vice president, Dorothy as secretary, and Juanita as treasurer. Leonard became president in 1979 upon Bill's death.

Thomas E. Stephens

MILES, HENRY (b Samuels, Kentucky, November 12, 1905; d Louisville, February 7, 1984). Fiddler and jug band leader. The son of Henry and Mattie Miles, he came to Louisville at the age of seventeen and learned to play the fiddle, guitar, and mandolin. From 1929 to 1932 he was a member of the immensely popular Ballard Chefs, whose music was heard Monday nights over WHAS radio in a program sponsored by the Ballard & Ballard Co. flour mills. In 1965 the HENRY MILES Jug Band performed at the World's Fair in New York. In January 1974 his band, without a jug player, appeared at the Smithsonian Folklife Festival in Washington, D.C. He is buried in Brownsboro Cemetery.

Brenda Bogert

MILES PARK. Miles Park was situated on the grounds of the old state fairgrounds at the southern terminus of Cecil Ave. and opened for Thoroughbred racing in 1956. The oval, later enlarged at a cost of $1 million, had previously been used for harness racing and was called the Fairgrounds Speedway Trotting Track. Owned by J. Fred Miles (1883–1963), an Ashland Oil company founder, the track featured the Junior Derby and Oh Susannah Stakes on its summer card.

On March 27, 1962, Miles sold the track for $2 million to Leonard Fruchtman, Joseph L. Arnold, and Bernard M. Kahn. Emprise, a Buffalo, New York, concessions conglomerate, acquired controlling interest in the track in 1969. The company completed a $2.5 million renovation in 1974 and renamed the track Commonwealth Race Course.

Commonwealth held its last racing meet in January 1975. In June of that year, the Kentucky Racing Commission had turned down Commonwealth's request for a 1975 summer meet, citing Emprise's 1972 conviction for "conspiring to aid racketeering in its role in acquiring an undisclosed interest in a Las Vegas casino-hotel," according to a published report in the *COURIER-JOURNAL*. In December 1975, the commission denied Commonwealth any 1976 racing dates, saying the track did not attract enough bettors to justify racing.

Whayne Supply Co., a heavy-equipment vendor, bought the 110-acre site in 1978 and is using it commercially.

Joseph Woodson Oglesby

MILLER, HENRY MANIA, JR. (b Glasgow, Kentucky, November 1, 1800; d Louisville, February 8, 1874). Physician and teacher. The son of Henry Miller, a Maryland native and one of Barren County's first settlers, Henry Jr. received his early education in the pioneer schools of Glasgow. At age seventeen, Miller began his professional studies with two Glasgow physicians, Drs. Robert P. Gist and Absolom Bainbridge. He went on to study at Transylvania University's medical school, from which he received his medical degree in 1822. Shortly thereafter, he was offered a position as an instructor of anatomy at Transylvania, and to prepare for this duty he attended a lecture series in Philadelphia in 1823, likely at a private school of anatomy. However, due to some degree of faculty opposition, Miller resigned his post without ever teaching. From 1824 to 1827, he practiced MEDICINE in his hometown of Glasgow. Then, in 1827, Miller moved to Harrodsburg, Kentucky, where he spent the next nine years in private practice with Dr. CHRISTOPHER COLUMBUS GRAHAM, owner of the Harrodsburg Springs resort.

In 1837 Miller became professor of obstetrics and diseases of women and children at the LOUISVILLE MEDICAL INSTITUTE, which became the medical department of the UNIVERSITY OF LOUISVILLE in 1846. From 1846 to 1858, he continued as a professor of obstetrics at the University of Louisville, and in 1859 Miller served as president of the American Medical Association. From 1858 to 1867, Miller went back into private practice in Louisville but returned to the classroom in 1869 when he was made professor of obstetrics at the Louisville Medical College, a position he held until 1874. In Miller's private practice, he pioneered in the use of anesthesia, particularly ether, during labor and childbirth. He is also credited with being one of the first in the state and the country to use the vaginal speculum in the field of gynecological diagnosis and treatment. Miller was an associate editor of the *Louisville Journal of Medi-*

cine and Surgery in 1838, and his extensive writings include *Principles and Practice of Obstetrics* (1858), one of the foremost texts on the subject. Miller married Clarissa Robertson on June 24, 1824. They had six children. Miller is buried in CAVE HILL CEMETERY.

See Franklin Gorrin, *The Times of Long Ago* (Louisville 1929); Martin Kaufman, Stuart Galishoff, and Todd L. Savitt, eds., *Dictionary of American Medical Biography*, vol. 2 (Westport, Conn., 1984); Dumas Malone, ed., *Dictionary of American Biography*, vol. 12 (New York 1933).

MILLER, MARY MILLICENT (b Louisville, 1846; d Louisville, October 30, 1894). Steamboat captain. Mary M. Miller was the first American woman to receive a steamboat master's license. She was born Mary Millicent Garretson, the daughter of Andrew Garretson, a steamboat engineer.

On August 3, 1865, she married George Miller, a widower of the PORTLAND area. They had four children: Lula Ann, George, Emma, and Norman. Steamboat men referred to George as "Old Natural Miller" because of his natural ability to build and navigate STEAMBOATS. With only a hatchet and a hammer, it was said, Old Natural could build his own boats. Miller became a river pioneer by being the first to take coal down the Mississippi. In 1829 he took two coal flats from Bon Harbor below Owensboro, Kentucky, to the La Branche Plantation just above Red Church, about thirty miles north of New Orleans.

One of several steamboats that George built was the *Saline*, a 178-ton packet. He built her at the boatyard at THE POINT on SHIPPINGPORT Island in 1882. The Millers' *Saline,* also known as the *Red Warrior,* carried passengers and freight on the Mississippi, Red, Ouachita, and other smaller rivers such as the Macon, Tensas, and Boeuf Bayous. George and Mary had a busy life running a steamboat and raising their children on board. She usually served as the clerk and kept the books. George's son by his first wife served as their engineer.

In the early 1880s, the bustling steamboat business out of New Orleans became highly competitive. Certain people wanted no further competition from George Miller and reported to the Steamboat Inspection Service (SIS) that he had been serving as both the *Saline's* master and pilot, a situation against the laws governing steamboats. When the SIS confronted Miller, he acknowledged that he was running as pilot and his wife, Mary, was acting as master. He noted that she would soon apply for her license and be fully tested. This infuriated their competitors, who felt that George Miller had outsmarted them and that no woman should be a steamboat master. The SIS inspectors in New Orleans quickly acknowledged their inability to act on the gender issue. They referred the question of the propriety of a woman steamboat master to the SIS headquarters in Washington, D.C., in November 1883. Finally, this matter reached the secretary of the treasury, whose question was, "Has Mrs. Miller a husband living?"

George L. Norton, the supervising inspector of the SIS tenth district in New Orleans, objected to issuing Mary Miller a master's license. He felt it was socially improper for a woman to take a position usually given to a man and that this situation would be degrading for a woman.

In January 1884, Charles J. Folger, secretary of the treasury, rendered an opinion. He advised the local SIS inspectors at New Orleans that "Mrs. Miller should be granted her license if she were fit for performing the duties required, without regard to her sex." She passed her examinations and took the required oath on February 16, 1884, at the age of thirty-eight. She gained national fame when her picture appeared in the *Harpers Weekly* of March 8, 1884.

As the *Saline's* master, she oversaw the boat's daily operations and managed the boat's fiscal matters. Although the Millers lived on board the *Saline* when working out of New Orleans, they always maintained a home in Portland. Various comments in New Orleans newspapers' river columns in the 1880s and 1890s indicate that prominent steamboat masters highly respected Mary Miller. Captain Miller was noted for her businesslike, fair, kind, and yet shrewd nature.

In 1891 George was ready to retire from the steamboat trade. Railroad competition had caused business to decline. That year George and Mary made their last trip together to New Orleans. They took the *Swan*, their sailboat, and went to the jetties at the mouth of the Mississippi River to spend the winter. During that trip, Mary Miller became ill. The towboat *W.W. O'Neil* towed the *Swan* back to Portland. Mary returned to the home on Bank St. in Portland that George had built for her as a wedding gift. She died there in 1894 and is buried in Portland Cemetery.

Capt. Mary M. Miller's sole reason for acquiring her license in 1884 was to keep the family's steamboat business solvent. She opened the door for a number of other notable women to become steamboat masters and pilots. She was inducted into the American Merchant Marine Hall of Fame at Kings Point, New York, in 1993 and recognized by the National Rivers Hall of Fame in Dubuque, Iowa, in 1995.

See E.W. Gould, *Gould's History of River Navigation* (St. Louis 1880); *New Orleans Daily Picayune*, Sept. 8, 1891; *Courier-Journal*, Oct. 31, 1894.

Jack E. Custer
Sandra Miller Custer

MILLER, NEVILLE (b Louisville, February 17, 1894; d Washington, D.C., March 27, 1977). Mayor. Neville, the son of Shackelford and Mary Floyd (Welman) Miller, was educated at LOUISVILLE MALE HIGH SCHOOL, where he was valedictorian of his 1912 class. He received a B.A. degree from Princeton University in 1916 and a law degree from Harvard Law School in 1920.

Miller began his legal practice in Louisville in 1920 with his father and brother, Shackelford Miller Jr., in the firm of Miller and Miller. His father had been chancellor of Jefferson Circuit Court and chief justice of the Kentucky Court of Appeals. After his father's death in 1924, he continued to practice law with his brother until 1930. He was an instructor at the JEFFERSON SCHOOL OF LAW from 1920 to 1925.

Miller was also a part-time instructor at the UNIVERSITY OF LOUISVILLE Law School from 1920 to 1930. In 1930 he became the first full-time dean of the law school, serving until 1933. Miller was instrumental in acquiring a number of books and papers for the law school's library, including contributions from Supreme Court Justice LOUIS BRANDEIS, a Louisville native.

Miller, a Democrat, was active in the party, chairing the speakers bureau and managing the unsuccessful 1929 Democratic race for mayor of Louisville. In February 1932 a "NEVILLE MILLER for Mayor" club was formed by Louisville-area businessmen, including Wilson W. Wyatt. Miller was elected on November 7, 1933, and served as mayor of Louisville until November 16, 1937. Miller's election as mayor ended more than fifteen years of Republican control of the office and began a period of domination by the Democrats that lasted more than twenty years. Miller won by a narrow margin of only 3,171 votes out of the 128,475 cast. Black voter turnout contributed significantly to Miller's and the Democrats' reasserting control over city hall.

Miller served during some of the worst years of the GREAT DEPRESSION, but his administration is forever tied to the 1937 flood, and he is known as Louisville's "flood mayor." From a city hall barricaded with sandbags, he directed the evacuations and relief efforts. He made appeals over nationwide radio for volunteers and supplies.

After leaving office he served as assistant to the president of Princeton University in 1938. From 1938 until 1944 he served as president of the National Association of Broadcasters and helped mobilize the radio industry for the war effort. He was senior deputy chief of the Balkan Mission of the United Nations Relief and Rehabilitation Association from 1944 to 1945. In 1945 he opened a private law practice in Washington, D.C., specializing in communications law. He was with the firm until he retired in 1974.

Miller also served as director of the LOUISVILLE WATER CO. He was a member of the Louisville Bridge Commission, commissioner of the Sinking Fund, and trustee of the Firemen's Pension Fund and Policemen's Pension Fund. He was a member of the LOUISVILLE FREE PUBLIC LIBRARY Board, the Park Board, and the Civil Service Board. He was president of the Kentucky Municipal League from 1935 to 1936 and a trustee for the United Conference of Mayors. He was also a member of the Louisville and Kentucky Bar Associations, serving as president of the Louisville bar in 1924–25.

Miller married Katherine Castleman Wilson of Summit, New Jersey, on September 20, 1924. They had four daughters: Barbara Neville, Gale, Katherine Wilson, and Mary Welman. The family lived at 1222 Bates Court in Louisville. He is buried in CAVE HILL CEMETERY.

See Mary Young Southard and Ernest C. Miller, eds., *Who's Who in Kentucky; A Biographical Assembly of Notable Kentuckians* (Louisville 1936); Janet Hodgson, "Neville Miller/Lawyer, Educator, Public Executive," *U of L Yesterday* 8 (Spring 1990); *Courier-Journal*, March 28, 1977.

MILLER, WILLIAM BURKE "SKEETS" (b Louisville, June 20, 1904; d Sebastian, Florida, December 29, 1983). Journalist. WILLIAM BURKE MILLER was a young reporter who yearned to be a concert singer. Instead he became a national celebrity by reporting an event that took place in February 1925. Born in the PARKLAND neighborhood, Miller was the only son of Charles J. and Julia (Burke) Miller. He attended LOUISVILLE MALE HIGH SCHOOL and in 1922 became a police reporter for the *Louisville Post*. In 1924 he moved to the *COURIER-JOURNAL*.

On Saturday, January 31, 1925, the newspaper received information from Cave City, Kentucky, that Floyd Collins, the discoverer of Crystal Cave, was trapped in a cave sixty-five feet underground. His left foot was caught under a huge rock, and he could not free himself. On Sunday the newspaper decided that the story warranted sending a staff reporter. Miller asked to go. Taking an express train to Park City, he arrived at the newly named Sand Cave on Monday morning.

At 5 feet, 5 inches in height, and weighing 120 pounds, "Skeets," as he was called because he was "no bigger than a mosquito," was small enough to squeeze into the cave's passageway. Crawling on his stomach, he carried food and drink to Collins, interviewed him, and tried to free him. Miller returned six more times in three days and filed daily reports to expectant readers across the country. Some of Miller's dispatches were routed to the rival *Herald-Post* in error, giving that newspaper several "scoops" on the *Courier-Journal*.

On Wednesday, February 4, a cave-in blocked the passageway. Hoping to reach the weakening explorer another way, rescuers worked with picks and shovels for twelve days and nights to open a new entrance. When they reached Collins on February 16, he was dead. Miller returned to the cave one last time through the new shaft and came out to report that it was too risky to remove Collins at that time. His body was finally brought up on April 23.

On the seventeenth anniversary of the Floyd Collins rescue effort, Miller wrote in the *Courier-Journal*: "It will be my everlasting regret that I did not effect his release but never will I be weighted down with a feeling of personal responsibility for the death of Floyd Collins."

Miller returned to his routine work on the *Courier-Journal* but soon moved to Florida to work in his father's ice cream business. In 1926 Miller was awarded the Pulitzer Prize for reporting. He intended to use the thousand dollars that went with the award for voice training, but ARTHUR KROCK, former editor-in-chief of the *Louisville Times*, invited him to join his staff on the *World* in New York City.

After one year, in June 1927, Miller left the newspaper to work for the National BROADCASTING Co. During his time there, he conducted experiments, testing how well a microphone could convey word pictures to radio listeners. He directed broadcasts from dirigibles, submarines, battleships, and lion cages at the Bronx Zoo. He also arranged a broadcast by a parachutist who leaped from a plane wearing a twenty-four-pound transmitter and described his sensations while falling. Another coup, the story of a disastrous earthquake in Italy, was aired from Guglielmo Marconi's yacht.

Miller retired to Vermont in 1961 with his wife, Madge Tucker Miller, but soon became an editor on the *Rutland Herald*. He is interred in the Melbourne Crematorium in Melbourne, Florida.

See Robert K. Murray and Roger W. Brucker, *Trapped!* (Lexington 1979); Billy Reed, *Famous Kentuckians* (Louisville 1977); Michael Lesy, "Dark Carnival: The Death and Transfiguration of Floyd Collins," *American Heritage* 27 (Oct. 1976): 34–45; *Courier-Journal*, May 4, 1926, March 25, 1930, Feb. 1, 1942, Jan. 1, 1984.

Robert Bruce French

MILLER'S CAFETERIA. Rudolph W. Miller Sr. and his wife, Margaret, purchased the property, located at 429 S Second St. between Walnut St. (Muhammad Ali Blvd.) and Green St. (Liberty), in 1898. The main section and rear porches of the building were built around 1826 and were originally owned by STEPHEN ORMSBY. The Millers ran a rooming house, renting sleeping rooms to many of the medical students attending the UNIVERSITY OF LOUISVILLE School of Medicine. The medical school was located one block away at First and Chestnut. Margaret Miller also served meals to the boarders, which was the beginning of the cafeteria.

The success of the food business led the proprietors to open their doors to the public soon after. In 1903 the Millers added a dining hall at the front of the main building to accommodate patrons. Bowls of fresh vegetables, meats, and bread were passed around to patrons sitting at long tables "home style."

During the 1937 flood the cafeteria remained dry. The National Guard used the building to serve meals to guardsmen and other workers. Rudolph W. Miller Jr., who had acquired the business from his father in the mid-1920s, persuaded the Guard to allow him and his wife to operate the kitchen and feed workers.

In the late 1990s the cafeteria was owned and operated by the third generation of the Miller family. Fourth and fifth generations of the Millers were also involved with the family business. The cafeteria closed on March 20, 1998, when the family decided it was time to end the business.

MILNE, COLIN ROSS (b Forres, Moray County, Scotland, March 26, 1813; d Owensboro, Kentucky, September 28, 1897). Lithographer. Born to Alexander and Jane (Smith) Milne, Colin studied lithography in Scotland in 1832 before coming to New York a year later. He apprenticed at the shop of Anthony Imbert on Wall St. before leaving for Baltimore in 1834. Shortly after arriving, Milne entered into a partnership for a lithographic press with artist THOMAS CAMPBELL. When Campbell decided to move to Louisville in 1835, Milne stayed behind to mind the shop but had sold it by June 1836 and joined his partner.

Campbell and Milne opened the first lithographic press west of the Allegheny Mountains, known as C.R. Milne and Co., on Jefferson St. across from the county courthouse. After Campbell's death in 1847, Milne went into business with German lithographer Charles Bruder until 1852. He left Louisville for Ghent in Carroll County and later moved to Daviess County in 1861, where he took up farming and eventually entered the funeral business. Among his works are lithographic drawings, including those for the *Kentucky Stock Book*, portraits, genre subjects, maps, and flowers. He married Mary Louise Fulton in 1845; they had seven children.

See Martin F. Schmidt, "The Artist and the Artisan: Two Men of Early Louisville," *Filson Club History Quarterly* 62 (Jan. 1988): 32–51.

Martin F. Schmidt

MILNER HOTEL. Formerly located on the northeast corner of Third and Jefferson Streets., this Louisville entry on the NATIONAL REGISTER OF HISTORIC PLACES was named the Tyler Hotel when it opened on December 14, 1911. The hotel was designed in the Beaux Arts style by the local architectural firm of McDonald and Dodd. Boasting that it was "so thoroughly fireproof that it carries the lowest insurance rate in the city," the Tyler took a utilitarian approach to hostelry, concentrating on providing modern accommodations at moderate prices, rather than aspiring to be the most elegant.

In the 1940s the MILNER HOTEL chain purchased the Tyler and renamed it the Earle Hotel. It operated as such until 1962, when the hotel was renamed the Milner shortly after a hotel of the same name, at First and Chestnut, was demolished to make way for the extension of Interstate 65. The Milner continued to accommodate lodgers until 1985, when it closed. Ten years later, on November 5, 1995, the old hotel, which was by then owned by the state, was imploded to make room for the expansion of the KENTUCKY INTERNATIONAL CONVENTION CENTER.

See "The Tyler of Louisville," *Hotel Monthly* 20 (July 1912): 36–45.

MINERAL RESOURCES. Extraction of mineral resources in Louisville and Jefferson County historically has concentrated on obtaining construction raw materials. Limestone, dolomite (limestone altered by magnesium-enriched fluids), sand, gravel, clay, and shale are the principal resources. Natural gas and siltstone have also been produced in the county.

In past years the Louisville Limestone of Silurian age was an important source of dimension stone for foundations, walls, curbs, fences, and dwellings. It was used to build several churches in the city. Many of the QUARRIES producing Louisville Limestone were located along the forks of BEARGRASS CREEK. Lesser amounts of dimension stone were obtained from the Laurel Dolomite (Silurian). In the upper Laurel, an interval of even-bedded dolomite, with shale partings commonly separating the beds, was easily quarried for building stone.

Building stone was also produced from other rock units. In eastern Jefferson County, thin-bedded limestones in the Drakes Formation and Grant Lake Limestone (both Ordovician) furnished fieldstone for fences, walls, and chimneys. Abutments for a railroad bridge near Eastwood were constructed using a thick-bedded dolomite from the upper part of the Drakes. Siltstone for foundations, walls, and dwelling facings was quarried from the Kenwood Siltstone Member of the Borden Formation (Mississippian) on KNOBS in southwestern Jefferson County.

Crushed stone for construction aggregate, road metal, and agricultural stone has been produced from the Laurel Dolomite and Louisville Limestone. In past years the Jeffersonville and SELLERSBURG limestones (Devonian) and the Drakes Formation also furnished crushed stone. During early road-building, small temporary quarries commonly were opened in bedrock near the construction sites to supply road metal. Today, stone is trucked to construction sites from permanent quarries and mines.

The Laurel is the principal source of stone in Jefferson and adjacent counties at the present time, being produced from both open-pit quarries and shallow underground mines. In 1998 work started on opening a mine in eastern Jefferson County to produce crushed stone from a deep deposit of limestone. A long haulageway slopes downward from the surface entry to a two-level room-and-pillar mine in limestone of the High Bridge Group (Ordovician). Depth of the lower level is 1,050 feet below the surface.

Sand and gravel are important raw materials for construction. They are obtained from the bed of the OHIO RIVER by dredging and from pits dug in the glacial outwash deposits (Quaternary) of western Jefferson County. To meet the area's demand for construction materials, sand and gravel are also transported to Louisville from deposits in the Ohio Valley upstream from the metropolitan area. Sand from several pits was used by foundries to make molds for metal castings.

Brick is manufactured near Coral Ridge in southern Jefferson County using shale from the New Providence Shale Member of the Borden Formation (Mississippian). In the past, local brick and tile plants also used residual clay, which accumulated from the weathering of Jeffersonville Limestone, and sedimentary clay from glacial outwash deposits, as well as shale from the New Providence. Lightweight aggregate formerly was manufactured from New Providence Shale in northern BULLITT COUNTY. Borrow pits in the NEW ALBANY shale (Devonian) furnish fill material.

In the nineteenth century, cement mills in Louisville and southern Indiana manufactured natural cement from argillaceous limestone in the SILVER CREEK Limestone Member of the Sellersburg Limestone (Devonian). The limestone, which contains sufficient quantities of calcium, silicon, and aluminum to make cement, was quarried along Louisville's riverfront and on CORN ISLAND. Since that time, natural cement generally has been replaced by PORTLAND cement for use in construction. Portland and masonry cements are produced in southwestern Jefferson County at a KOSMOSDALE plant, the only cement plant in Kentucky, and also at Speed, Indiana, just north of Louisville. Clay obtained from a nearby glacial outwash deposit furnishes silica and alumina for cement manufacture at Kosmosdale. Limestone, the source of calcium, is barged upstream to Kosmosdale from a company quarry in Meade County.

Shallow wells of the Meadow Gas Field in the vicinity of Kosmosdale, Meadow Lawn, and Orell in southwestern Jefferson County furnished landowners with natural gas for domestic use (heating, lighting, and cooking). Possibly as many as thirty wells were drilled in the gas field between 1890 and 1924, but commercial quantities of gas were never encountered. The gas was produced from the carbon-rich New Albany Shale (Devonian) at depths from 200 to 375 feet below the surface. Domestic gas has also been supplied by two wells near IROQUOIS PARK. Elsewhere in Jefferson County, several exploratory wells have been drilled for oil and gas, but only a few shows of gas and oil have been found in the Paleozoic rocks beneath the New Albany Shale.

Man-made lime and gypsum are by-products of industrial processes in Jefferson County. Manufacturing acetylene from calcium carbide at the Carbide and Graphite Group plant produces hydrated lime as a by-product. Louisville Gas and Electric Co. (LG&E) has used the lime as a reagent in flue-gas-desulfurization systems to remove sulfur dioxide from flue gas at their coal-burning power plants. Synthetic gypsum is a by-product of the flue-gas-desulfurization system at the LG&E Mill Creek power plant, where high-calcium limestone is now used as the reagent to capture sulfur dioxide emissions. The by-product gypsum is sold to the U.S. Gypsum Co. for manufacturing wallboard.

Residential, commercial, industrial, and public-works construction across the Louisville metropolitan area and the rebuilding and maintenance of the region's infrastructure require large quantities of mineral resources. In past years, mineral producers have been able to use low-cost local resources to meet much of the demand for construction raw materials. Meeting the region's resource requirements in the future, however, will be a challenge as urban expansion gradually covers and precludes use of the very mineral resources needed to support the growth.

See Wilber G. Burroughs, *Directory of Kentucky Mineral Operators* (Kentucky Geological Survey, series 6, vol. 32, 1930); Charles Butts, *Geology and Mineral Resources of Jefferson County, Kentucky* (Kentucky Geological Survey, series 4, vol. 3, part 2, 1915); Willard R. Jillson, *Natural Gas in Western Kentucky* (Kentucky Geological Survey, series 6, vol. 38, 1931); Roy C. Kepferle, *Geologic Map of Parts of the Louisville West and Lanesville Quadrangles, Jefferson County, Kentucky* (U.S. Geological Survey Geologic Quadrangle Map GQ-1202); Charles H. Richardson, *The Building Stones of Kentucky* (Kentucky Geological Survey, series 6, vol. 11, 1923).

Garland R. Dever Jr.

MINSTRELSY. AFRICAN AMERICANS were generally excluded from the American stage before the CIVIL WAR. However, northern white performers, with blackened faces, had been imitating what they thought to be black music, dialogue, jokes, and dance since the late eighteenth century. These caricatures of black culture became a dominant form of entertainment after 1830. In that year, THOMAS D. RICE achieved overnight success performing as "JIM CROW" in *The Kentucky Rifle* at Louisville's City Theatre. By 1837 Louisville book and music stores were ADVERTISING "New Negro Song Books" containing songs such as "Jim Crow," and "Coal Black Rose."

The first minstrel group was the Virginia Minstrels, which was formed in New York by Dan Emmett and others in 1843. It became very popular and set the standard for the groups that followed. Very quickly, numerous minstrel groups sprang up all over the North. Most of these groups performed in Louisville, including the Virginia Minstrels (Washington Hall, 1843), the Christy Minstrels (Washington Hall, 1844), and the Ethiopian Serenaders (Apollo Hall, 1845). The latter group consisted of blackface artists playing accordion, castanets, banjo, and tambourine.

There was even a steamboat named *The Minstrel* sailing on the OHIO RIVER in 1844. The first variety THEATERS in Louisville that featured minstrel acts were both established in 1859. The Concert Hall on MARKET ST. advertised Thomas Rice's old play *Oh Hush*! as well as "jig dancing contests," and Dodge's "Southern Varieties" on Jefferson St. offered "Negro performances."

After the Civil War talented African Americans interested in careers on the stage found that their only route to success lay in the incredibly popular minstrel shows. The first all-black minstrel troupe was organized in Georgia by Charles B. Hicks in 1865. It toured all over the United States and Europe. Its popularity was followed by other groups, including Sam Hague's Georgia Slave Troupe, Haverly's Minstrels, and Callender's Georgia Minstrels. All of these troupes were much larger ensembles (usually numbering more than twenty performers) than the antebellum minstrel groups, and their popularity created a demand for black musicians, actors, and actresses. The groups appeared regularly during the 1870s at local theaters, including the Masonic Theater, Library Hall, and the Metropolitan Theater.

Minstrel shows remained popular into the early 1900s. Early stars of black musical theater such as Bert Williams, Billy McClain, Ernest Hogan, Tom McIntosh, and Billy Kersands all started their careers in minstrel shows. The cruel irony of minstrelsy is that, while it provided employment and opportunity to many African American actors and actresses, it perpetuated caricatures and racial stereotypes that persist to this day.

See Robert C. Toll, *Blacking Up* (New York 1974); Henry T. Sampson, *The Ghost Walks* (Metuchen, N.J., 1988).

Cornelius Bogert

MINTON, SHERMAN (b near Georgetown, Indiana, October 20, 1890; d NEW ALBANY, Indiana, April 9, 1965). United States Supreme Court justice. Born on a farm near Georgetown, Indiana, to John Evan and Emma (Livers) Minton, Sherman "Shay" Minton rose through athletic scholarships, good looks, and grim determination to the pinnacle of his chosen profession—a seat on the U.S. Supreme Court.

After attending New Albany High School, he became an honor student at Indiana University and a varsity athlete in both FOOTBALL and BASEBALL. He ranked first in his class when he graduated with a law degree in 1915. After receiving a scholarship to Yale, he helped organize the Yale University Legal Aid Society and graduated with a master's degree in law in 1916.

Returning to NEW ALBANY to open a law practice, he married Gertrude Gurtz in 1917. They had three children: Sherman Jr., John, and Maryanne. Upon his return in 1919 from two years' service in WORLD WAR I as an army captain in France, he made a reputation in Indiana politics by espousing liberal positions against the policies of the Ku Klux Klan, which had a notorious hold on Indiana politics during the 1920s. Although he lost two congressional campaigns despite his oratorical skills and charisma, Minton was rewarded by Gov. Paul McNutt in 1933 with an appointment to the Public Service Commission. Elected to the U.S. Senate and serving from January 3, 1935, to January 3, 1941, he became a staunch supporter of the New Deal, even backing Roosevelt's court-packing bill, which would have enlarged the court.

Minton's allegiance to the New Deal program cost him reelection in 1940 after having served as the Democratic whip during the previous two years. His loyalty, however, resulted in an appointment to the U.S. Seventh Circuit Court of Appeals in May 1941. His good fortune continued in these years as his seatmate in the Senate, president-to-be Harry S Truman, elevated Minton to the Supreme Court on September 15, 1949.

Judicial scholars do not agree on Minton's ultimate contribution to the court. Many of his decisions did not fall on the liberal side; his political activism contrasted sharply with his judicial restraint. His alliance with Chief Justice Frederick M. Vinson and associate justices Tom C. Clark, Stanley F. Reed, Felix Frankfurter, and Harold H. Burton resulted in the court's swing away from its strong pro–Bill of Rights record of the 1940s, which distressed civil libertarians. Minton's explanation was that he believed justices should not undo the actions of the political branches of GOVERNMENT.

Minton retired from the court on October 15, 1956, in poor health, suffering from pernicious anemia and a failing memory. He returned to New Albany and was honored by the governors of Kentucky and Indiana when they agreed in 1963 to name the new Interstate 64 bridge connecting Louisville and New Albany the Sherman Minton Bridge. He is interred in Holy Trinity Catholic Cemetery in New Albany.

See William Franklin Radcliff, *Sherman Minton, Indiana's Supreme Court Justice* (Indianapolis 1966); Linda C. Gugin and James E. St. Clair, *Sherman Minton: New Deal Senator, Cold War Justice* (Bloomington, Ind., 1997).

Betty Lou Amster

MODJESKAS. This candy treat, distributed across the nation, was originated in Louisville by candy maker Anton Busath, probably in the 1870s. What became the Modjeska was originally the Caramel Biscuit, a specially made marshmallow dipped in liquid caramel. On December 7, 1883, Busath went to the old MACAULEY'S THEATRE on the north side of Walnut St. near Fourth St. to attend the premiere American presentation of Henrik Ibsen's controversial play, *A Doll's House*, retitled *Thora* for its American run. The title role of Thora was played by famed Polish actress Helena Modjeska, whose powerful performances held Victorian audiences spellbound.

Busath was so impressed that the next day he secured an audience with Mme. Modjeska and presented her some of his Caramel Biscuits. After she had sampled the treat, he asked

Display window at Busath's Candy Shop, 445 S. Fourth Street, featuring Modjeska caramels.

whether he could call the confection "Modjeska" in her honor and she agreed. It was an early example of product endorsement, although Mme. Modjeska received no pecuniary reward. Her signed portrait graced Busath's store.

Meanwhile, Joseph Rudolph and Frederick Bauer, both employees of wholesale confectioner C.G. Ehrmann, joined forces in 1889 to form the candy-making firm of Rudolph and Bauer. One of their products was the Caramel Biscuit—the exact counterpart of Busath's Modjeska. Then in 1923 Muth's Candy Store opened with one of its products, the Caramel Biscuit.

When Busath's downtown Fourth St. store was ravaged by fire in 1947, the firm ceased business, and the name Modjeska was transferred to the Caramel Biscuits made by Rudolph and Bauer, and Muth's. The latter remains in Louisville, while Rudolph and Bauer (now simply Bauer's Candies) moved operations to Mount Eden, Kentucky, about 1976 and to Lawrenceburg, Kentucky, in 1999. Between them they provide the entire national output of Modjeskas.

George H. Yater

MONON (LOUISVILLE, NEW ALBANY & CHICAGO RAILWAY). The Monon's oldest antecedent was the New Albany & Salem, chartered in 1847 and led by New Albany businessman James Brooks. Construction began in 1849, and track was opened to Salem in 1851 and to Bloomington in 1853. By 1854 the road had spanned the entire Hoosier state to reach Michigan City and connections to Chicago. The first New Albany station was a large, brick building, its facade fronting on Culbertson St. It was demolished about 1990. Anticipating the importance of Louisville and a link to the Louisville and Nashville, the road changed its name in 1859 to Louisville, New Albany & Chicago, and in 1897 to Chicago, Indianapolis & Louisville after an Indianapolis-Chicago line was acquired.

Long known as the Monon Route, from the north Indiana town where its main lines crossed, the road formally adopted Monon as its corporate name in 1956. Louisvillian Bennett Young was president in 1883–84, helping the road gain access to Louisville via the Kentucky and Indiana Bridge; and, for a brief time (1889–90), the road owned Young's Louisville Southern in an attempt to reach the Kentucky coalfields. In 1899 Monon joined Baltimore & Ohio and the Southern Railway in purchasing the bridge company and forming the Kentucky & Indiana Terminal Railroad.

Only moderately profitable, the Monon depended on local traffic and that delivered to it from connecting railroads. During the presidency of John W. Barringer (1946–52), the road was greatly modernized and became (by 1948) one of the first major United States railroads to fully dieselize all operations. In August 1971 it merged with the Louisville & Nashville (L&N). The twenty-five miles of former Monon mainline between Bedford and Bloomington were abandoned in the late 1980s.

See George W. Hilton, *Monon Route* (Berkeley, Calif., 1978); Gary W. and Stephen F. Dolzall, *Monon, The Hoosier Line* (Glendale, Calif., 1987).

Charles B. Castner

MONROE, ANDREW (b ?; d Louisville, January ?, 1868). Jefferson County judge. Monroe served as Jefferson County judge from September 6, 1858, until September 2, 1866. He was Jefferson County's second judge. He was also an attorney in private practice before being elected county judge. Monroe served on the Louisville City Council from the Fifth Ward from 1856 until 1857. He was the president of the Board of Councilmen in 1857.

On January 22, 1868, Monroe disappeared from his residence on Walnut (Muhammad Ali Blvd.) between Fifteenth and Sixteenth Streets and was not seen again until four months later when his body was found floating in the Louisville and Portland Canal. He was believed to have accidentally drowned. Monroe is buried in Frankfort, Kentucky, where he had family.

See *History of the Ohio Falls Cities and Their Counties* (Cleveland 1882).

MONROE, ROSE (LEIGH) WILL (b Science Hill, Kentucky, March 12, 1920; d Clarksville, Indiana, May 31, 1997). Riveter. Reared in Pulaski County, Kentucky, the daughter of Walter and Minnie (Calder) Leigh, she moved north after the death of her first husband in 1942 and took work riveting B-24 and B-29 aircraft at an assembly plant in Ypsilanti, Michigan, to support her two children; later she remarried and had a third child. It was there that a film crew selected her to play the part of Rosie the Riveter in a World War II war bonds film. The notion of Rosie the Riveter already existed in a patriotic song, and it was serendipitous that she had both the name and occupation of the preexisting character. She later worked at the Curtiss-Wright Corp. aircraft assembly plant in Louisville and settled in Clarksville, Indiana.

Unlike many other Rosies who returned to domestic life or low-paying jobs at the end of the war, the widowed mother continued to support her family through driving buses and cabs and by operating her own beauty shop and later her own construction firm, Rose Builders of Southern Indiana. She later realized a lifelong ambition and earned her aircraft pilot's license in the late 1960s, but a 1978 plane crash took her left eye and a kidney and ended her flying career.

She closed the construction firm in 1978, but her place in American popular cultural history as the personification of the American woman aiding the war effort was well-cemented by her role. Injuries sustained in the airplane crash eventually led to her death from kidney failure. She is buried at the Abundant Life Memorial Gardens in New Albany, Indiana.

See *New York Times*, June 2, 1997.

MONSARRAT, LAURA (LUCAS) (b Salem, Indiana, December 8, 1829; d Louisville, May 7, 1900). Educator. Monsarrat was educated in public and private schools of Louisville and in 1850 received a grammar certificate, the highest certificate granted by the Louisville Board of Education at that time. She was appointed a teacher in the Female Grammar School, and, when the Female High School opened in 1856 on First St. between Walnut (Muhammad Ali Blvd.) and Chestnut, she was given the job of instructor of mathematics. Monsarrat taught for one year in 1881 at the Holyoke Academy, a private school for girls on Broadway at Third St., before being promoted to the position of principal of the Seventh Ward School (formerly the Fifth Ward School) at Fifth and York Streets in 1882.

Laura married David T. Monsarrat on December 23, 1860, and the couple had one son, George L. Her husband died in 1871 and is buried in Memphis, Tennessee. Laura Monsarrat is buried in Cave Hill Cemetery.

On May 7, 1900, the Louisville Board of Education approved renaming the Seventh Ward School the Monsarrat School in honor of her fifty years of dedicated service to the education of Louisville children. At the beginning of World War II, the school closed because of declining enrollment and was used as a dormitory for soldiers, then by the Louisville Free Public Library Natural History Museum until 1975. In 1982 Monsarrat Preservation Limited Partnership carefully preserved much of the interior while converting the building into eighteen apartments. The first tenants moved into The Monsarrat Apartments in 1983.

Shirley J. Botkins

MONSARRAT/FIFTH WARD SCHOOL. The Fifth Ward School, at Fifth and York Streets, was built in 1857 on the site of a school destroyed by fire in 1854. Architects Isaiah Rogers and Henry Whitestone designed the Italian Renaissance Revival building with nine-foot-tall, round-arched windows that provided maximum light for the large classrooms. The curriculum was standard studies, with shop courses for the boys.

During the Civil War, the school was appropriated by the Union army for use as a hospital. After the war, Louisville political boundaries were changed, and the building became the Seventh Ward School.

In 1900 the school was renamed for its recently deceased principal, Laura (Lucas) Monsarrat. At the beginning of World War II, the school closed because of declining enrollment and was used as a dormitory for soldiers on leave from Fort Knox. Later it was occupied by the Louisville Free Public Library

Natural History Museum until 1975, then used for storage until 1980.

The following year the building was bought by the PRESERVATION ALLIANCE of Louisville and Jefferson County, which sold it to the Monsarrat Preservation Limited Partnership in 1982 for $215,000. Developers David Holobaugh and David Larue handled the conversion of the building into eighteen apartments at a cost of $750,000. Architect R. Jeffrey Points, who designed the remodeling, preserved much of the interior but added an elevator. The first tenants moved in before Christmas 1983. The building is now called The Monsarrat.

See *Courier-Journal*, Dec. 18, 1983, Jan. 4, 1984, May 30, 1984; "Monsarrat/Fifth Ward School," *Metropolitan Preservation Plan* (Louisville 1973); Elizabeth F. Jones, "Henry Whitestone: Nineteenth-Century Louisville Architect," M.A. thesis, University of Louisville, 1974.

Robert Bruce French

MOONLIGHT SCHOOLS. Convinced that illiteracy was a barrier to progress, Cora Wilson Stewart, superintendent of schools in Rowan County, Kentucky, opened the classrooms in her district to adult pupils in September 1911, thus beginning the Moonlight School movement, a Progressive Era crusade designed to eliminate illiteracy in one generation. Volunteers from PUBLIC SCHOOLS, churches, and civic organizations taught the basics of reading, writing, and arithmetic, but also included practical farming, homemaking, and health tips. Their motto, "each one teach one," characterized education as the responsibility of every literate citizen. The idea caught on quickly, and by 1914, when the state legislature created the Kentucky Illiteracy Commission, MOONLIGHT SCHOOLS were operating throughout the commonwealth and in several other states. Their focus on rural or small-town, native-born Americans differentiated them from adult education programs in urban areas.

Moonlight Schools were backed by the General Federation of Women's Clubs, the Women's Christian Temperance Union, the National Education Association, and many state education groups. Ultimately more than twenty states created illiteracy commissions. In the twenty-three years the schools operated, over seven hundred thousand Americans learned to read and write, of whom more than one hundred thousand were Kentuckians. The commonwealth's illiteracy rate dropped from 12.1 percent in 1910 to 8.4 percent in 1920 and to 6.6 percent in 1930, a decline at least partially attributable to the Moonlight Schools.

Louisvillians were active participants in the Moonlight School movement during the 1914 and 1919 statewide campaigns despite the fact that the city and Jefferson County enjoyed an illiteracy rate half that of the state of Kentucky (4 percent to 8.4 percent). Under the leadership of Mrs. Gilmer Speed Adams, the clubwomen of Louisville and Lexington raised more than eight thousand dollars for the cause as they publicized "Illiteracy Week" in November 1914. Many of the city's clubwomen also traveled to rural areas to teach in the Moonlight Schools. The 1919 campaign was boosted by energetic editorials in both the *COURIER-JOURNAL* and the *LOUISVILLE TIMES*.

See Yvonne Honeycutt Baldwin, *Cora Wilson Stewart and the Illiteracy Crusade: "Moonlight Schools" and Progressive Reform* (Forthcoming, University Press of Kentucky); Willie Everette Nelms Jr., "Cora Wilson Stewart: Crusader against Illiteracy," M.A. thesis, University of Kentucky, 1973; Wilson Somerville, ed. *Appalachia/America: Proceedings of the 1980 Appalachian Studies Conference* (Knoxville, Tenn., 1981).

Yvonne Honeycutt Baldwin

MORAL SIDE OF THE NEWS. The format for this WHAS radio and TELEVISION program is seven panelists (five of whom are regularly scheduled) representing the Catholic church, the Jewish faith, and members of conservative and liberal Protestant denominations. For a half hour, they discuss a variety of topics of local and international interest and their moral implications from their religious perspectives. The program was started in 1952 and produced by Dorcas Ruthenberg, who worked at WHAS. At that time there were only four ministers on *MORAL SIDE OF THE NEWS*. They included Dr. Duke McCall, president of the SOUTHERN BAPTIST THEOLOGICAL SEMINARY; Monsignor Felix Pitt, secretary, Catholic School Board; Dr. JOSEPH RAUCH, rabbi, Temple Adath Israel; and Dr. Robert Weston, pastor of the FIRST UNITARIAN CHURCH. Harry Schacter, a department store executive, was the moderator. On that first program the topic of discussion was the seizure of moonshine stills. Originally a radio show only, it was later broadcast on WHAS television as well. During the time before Vatican II (1962–65), when there were no formal relations between Catholics and Protestants, the show was an important step in promoting interfaith relations. In fact, Ruthenberg had entered the radio business because she saw it as the chief means of reaching a great number of people to increase an understanding among faiths. The program was one of the first of its kind in the country.

The first African American panel member was Presbyterian Irvin Moxley, who served from 1969 until 1972. The first female permanent member was Rabbi Gaylia Rooks, who became a panel member in 1994.

On one of the early programs in 1952, the ministers talked about corruption in government, concluding it was symptomatic of deeper cultural ills. A sample of other topics indicates the timeliness of the program: McCarthy hearings (1953), drugs in the military (1953), whether the city is obliged to provide bus service to all areas (1954), whether Red China should be admitted to the United Nations (1954), whether African American families have a right to move into a white neighborhood (1954), whether there is too much sex and violence in the movies and on television (1955), John Birch Society (1964), open-housing laws (1967), and necessity of marriage (1978). Later topics included the Supreme Court ruling on prayer in PUBLIC SCHOOLS and the ruling in the Paula Jones sexual misconduct charge against President Bill Clinton. The participants never shied away from hard topics. Panel members also serve to parcel out money raised by the WHAS CRUSADE FOR CHILDREN. Besides airing on WHAS radio and television, *The Moral Side of the News* has been picked up by WAMZ-FM and CABLE TELEVISION's *The Faith Channel*.

MORGAN, FREDERIC LINDLEY (b Loda, Illinois, January 6, 1889; d Louisville, May 29, 1970). Architect. Morgan was trained at the University of Illinois. He became a draftsman with Louisville BOARD OF EDUCATION architect J. Earle Henry and later joined Henry, Hugh Nevin, and Herman Wischmeyer as that partnership's chief designer. Working primarily in the Georgian Revival style, Morgan's earliest independent commission was the FIRST PRESBYTERIAN CHURCH at First and Ormsby St. (1921).

He designed many churches throughout his career, including Highland Methodist (ca. 1922), Second Presbyterian (1954), Broadway Baptist (1959), and St. Francis-in-the-Fields (1947–57). Morgan designed such Georgian landmarks as the PENDENNIS CLUB (ca. 1927–30), the Schuster Block at Bardstown Rd. and Eastern Parkway (1927), Louisville Collegiate School (1926), and Norton Chapel at the SOUTHERN BAPTIST THEOLOGICAL SEMINARY (1948–50). He also led the syndicate known as the Allied Architects that designed the Administration Building at the UNIVERSITY OF LOUISVILLE (ca. 1935), and he was one of the architects for Lee Terminal at Standiford Field (1950), now LOUISVILLE INTERNATIONAL AIRPORT.

He is best known for his domestic work—evocations of Tidewater Virginia and Georgian England found in eastern Louisville. Morgan also left an enduring legacy by bequeathing his estate to the University of Louisville; the FREDERIC LINDLEY MORGAN Chair of Architectural Design brings distinguished architects and historians from around the world to teach on the campus that he did so much to shape.

William Morgan

MORRIS, HORACE (b Louisville, 1832; d Louisville, April 3, 1897). African American leader. Horace Morris was born a free person. His father, Shelton Morris, moved to Louisville in 1828 after being emancipated in Virginia and became a barber, bathhouse owner, and real estate speculator. After the death of Morris's mother, Evalina Spradling Morris, in 1841 and a controversy over whether his father violated the law by voting in the 1840 presidential election, the family moved to Ohio. There Morris completed his education and became an active worker on the UNDERGROUND RAILROAD. He returned to Louisville in the late 1850s with his wife, Willeann, worked both as a riverboat steward and a storeroom clerk, and became involved in civic affairs.

After the CIVIL WAR, Morris became prominent in local and state REPUBLICAN PARTY politics. An eloquent speaker, he was politically moderate but committed to the struggle for CIVIL RIGHTS. He was considered a responsible leader by black and white Louisvillians. In December 1868 Morris was appointed cashier of the Louisville branch of the Freedmen's Savings and Trust Bank. He helped to make his branch one of the most successful in the nation and was the only AFRICAN AMERICAN cashier called to Washington in 1881 to assist in resolving accounts after the nationwide collapse of the bank.

He also led campaigns for suffrage and efforts that resulted in the creation of public elementary schools for African Americans in 1870 and a high school in 1873. As a secretary of the Colored Board of Visitors, he monitored these schools, and he helped found a Colored Orphan's Home in 1878. Morris later became the first African American to serve as steward at Louisville's Marine Hospital. He was also a pioneer, although unsuccessful, black newspaper publisher, launching the short-lived *Kentuckian* in the early 1870s and the *Champion* in the early 1890s.

Morris, a longtime resident of 1930 Magazine St., had five children. He was active in QUINN CHAPEL AME Church and was a prominent Mason. He is buried in Eastern Cemetery.

See William H. Gibson Sr., *Sketches of the Progress of the Colored Race in Louisville, Ky.* (Louisville 1897); Ruth Morris Graham, *The Saga of the Morris Family* (Columbus, Ga., 1984); Louisville City Directories, 1870–1900; *Louisville Commercial*, Oct. 8, 1873; *Louisville Courier*, Jan. 2, 1866, March 2, 1866; *Courier-Journal*, Dec. 2, 1873; Marion B. Lucas, *A History of Blacks in Kentucky: From Slavery to Segregation, 1760–1891* (Frankfort 1992); Henry C. Weeden, ed., *Weeden's History of the Colored People of Louisville* (Louisville 1897); George D. Wright, *A Century of Negro Education in Louisville, Kentucky* (Louisville 1941); George C. Wright, *Life Behind a Veil: Blacks in Louisville, Kentucky, 1865–1930* (Baton Rouge 1985).

J. Blaine Hudson

MORRIS, LOIS (WALKER) (b OKOLONA, Mississippi, June 15, 1919; d Louisville, January 27, 1989). Alderman and CIVIL RIGHTS leader. Morris was one of eight children of Tom and Clara (Lomax) Walker. She attended Clark College in Atlanta and received a master's degree in international law and political science from Catholic University in Washington, D.C. Upon graduation she returned to Mississippi and taught history at Alcorn College (later Alcorn State University). She also taught history at high schools in Maryland, Mississippi, and Virginia. In 1955 Morris moved to Louisville.

In Louisville she became actively involved in the struggle for the rights of AFRICAN AMERICANS, women, and the disadvantaged. In addition to being a member of the LOUISVILLE URBAN LEAGUE, Morris was the founder and president of the Louisville chapter of the National Council of Negro Women and the founder and executive director of the National Black Women for Political Action. She also served as a board member of the state chapter of the National Association for the Advancement of Colored People (NAACP). From 1979 to 1987 she served on the NAACP's task force on desegregating institutions of higher learning.

Morris served on various committees and commissions, including Louisville's first Human Relations Commission, the Kentucky Commission on Human Rights, and the Second Charter Commission on the merger of Louisville and Jefferson County.

In 1969 Morris ran in the Democratic primary for Twelfth Ward alderman. She won the primary and the next three general elections. She was defeated by E. Porter Hatcher in 1975. In 1977 she unsuccessfully ran for mayor in the Democratic primary.

In addition to her political contributions, Morris wrote, without compensation, a column for the *LOUISVILLE DEFENDER* called "Scribbling Socially." Morris, who was known for her fashionable dress and for wearing hats, was named to *Ebony* magazine's twenty-one best-dressed women list in 1963. She also helped organize the Miss Exposition beauty and talent contest and Miss Defender best-dressed list. Morris had several businesses at property she owned at 2000 W BROADWAY, including a consignment shop called "Lois' Old House of Bargains."

Morris was married to Dr. Ralph Morris, and they had one daughter, Roslyn. At KENTUCKY DERBY time the Morrises held a party at their West End home that attracted many celebrities and also received local and national newspaper coverage. Morris died in January 1989 from stomach cancer. She is entombed at the Evergreen Mausoleum. In 1996 the BOARD OF ALDERMEN commissioned a bust of Morris to be placed in the Shawnee Branch of the LOUISVILLE FREE PUBLIC LIBRARY.

See *Courier-Journal*, Jan. 28, 1989; "Women's Manuscript Collection," University Archives, University of Louisville.

MORRIS, SHELTON (b Louisa, County, Virginia, 1806; d Xenia, Ohio, 1889). Businessman and landowner. On April 2, 1820, his father and owner, Col. Richard Morris, completed a will that, upon the elder Morris's death, emancipated his "mulatto woman Fanny and her six children, Shelton, Richard, Hannah, Elizabeth, John and Alexander." This will provided for the education of Shelton and his siblings and directed that each receive six hundred acres of land in the "western country" and one slave.

On February 11, 1828, Shelton and his half-brother, James Maury Morris, had this will entered in the records of Jefferson County. This entry also indicates that Shelton took "Morris" as his surname and converted his claim to land and slave property into cash. As a free man, Morris then used his inheritance to purchase land and establish a business in Louisville.

Morris was a barber by trade, and he operated a shop on MAIN St. between Fifth and Sixth Streets. In 1832 he opened a bathhouse adjoining (or under) the LOUISVILLE HOTEL and became the first black businessman in the history of the city. Morris was joined in Louisville by his younger brothers, John and Alexander (his brother Richard having died before 1835), both of whom worked as barbers and lived in Louisville until well after the CIVIL WAR. Morris also became a small-scale real estate speculator and one of Louisville's first significant black landowners, buying lots in early downtown Louisville, in the Preston's Enlargement area east of downtown, and in the area that would later become the eastern section of the RUSSELL neighborhood west of downtown. As Louisville grew in the 1830s, much of this land appreciated in value. However, although Morris prospered, he moved to Cincinnati in 1841 after the death of his first wife and, according to the recollections of his contemporaries, after becoming embroiled in a potentially dangerous controversy; i.e., Morris, who was very fair-skinned, was accused of violating Kentucky law by voting in the presidential election of 1840.

Free people of color in the antebellum "West" were not numerous and comprised a close-knit regional community, often linked by intermarriage, that was instrumental in founding and leading local free black communities, in establishing African American institutions, and in the struggle against slavery.

Shelton Morris and his family belonged to and linked Louisville to this regional community. To illustrate, Morris's first wife was Evelina Spradling (married January 24, 1828), the sister of WASHINGTON SPRADLING, a key leader of African Americans in Louisville. Morris and Spradling were both barbers, purchased adjacent lots, and seemed to have followed a "family" business strategy. Evelina Morris bore three children: M.F., who did not live to adulthood; Horace (1832–97), and Benjamin (1838–71).

Morris moved to Cincinnati where his sister Elizabeth (or Eliza) lived with her first husband, Michael Clark, who may have been the black son of Louisville's WILLIAM CLARK of the 1804–06 Lewis and Clark Expedition. Michael Clark and Morris worked as barbers near the Cincinnati riverfront. Morris also worked as a barber and steward on STEAMBOATS plying the Ohio and Mississippi Rivers and, in this capacity, met his second wife, Mary (b 1831), in

Natchez, Mississippi. Mary Morris bore two daughters: Catherine F. (b 1850, died young) and Mary Leona (1856–1936).

By 1860 Morris had become a widower for the second time and had subsequently remarried. His third wife, Bridgett (b 1833), was an IRISH woman who bore him three children, all of whom lived to adulthood: William (b 1862), John (b 1866) and Ellena (b 1867). Morris had also moved to Wilberforce, near Xenia, Ohio, where he farmed and operated a barbershop and grocery. Not coincidentally, this "courtly gentleman" once again followed his sister Eliza, who, after being widowed in 1849, married Rev. Daniel A. Payne and moved with him when he founded Wilberforce College, the first black-controlled higher educational institution in the United States.

Morris's older sons, Horace and Benjamin, returned to Louisville in the 1850s, probably after Morris's third marriage. Horace became one of Louisville's most influential black leaders after the CIVIL WAR, and his descendants played prominent roles in the city for generations. Although Benjamin died in 1871, one of his children, Charles Satchell Morris, later became pastor of the Abyssinian Baptist Church in New York and a participant in Dr. W.E.B. DuBois's Niagara Movement, precursor of the NAACP.

See William H. Gibson Sr., *Sketches of the Progress of the Colored Race in Louisville, Ky.* (Louisville 1897); Ruth Morris Graham, *The Saga of the Morris Family* (Columbus, Ga., 1984); Ernestine G. Lucas, *Wider Windows to the Past: African American History from a Family Perspective* (Decorah, Iowa, 1995).

J. Blaine Hudson

MORRISON, GEORGE W. (b Baltimore, Maryland, 1820; d New Albany, Indiana, December 24, 1893). Artist. Best known for his portraits and landscape scenes, Morrison was regarded as one of Indiana's leading artists from the time he moved to NEW ALBANY in 1840 until his death. Shortly after his arrival in New Albany, Morrison advertised in the local newspaper the establishment of his studio on Main near Bank St. Though nothing is known of his early education, Morrison's technical skill is considered indicative of classical training, and it is thought that he studied with Rembrandt and Raphael Peale of Baltimore. During his lengthy career in New Albany, he painted portraits of many of the city's prominent citizens, including William A. Scribner and Mary Stewart Shields. He also drew commissions from elsewhere in southern Indiana. Morrison often exhibited his works at the Floyd County Fair and the Indiana State Fair, where they regularly merited high honors. His portrait of ASHBEL P. WILLARD, Indiana governor from 1857 to 1861, was his best-known work. It hangs in the statehouse in Indianapolis. The New Albany Public Library has also displayed Morrison PAINTINGS, including an early 1850s landscape of the city.

Morrison married Lydia Maynard of New Albany. He was buried on the grounds of their home in the Silver Hills area, but his remains were later moved to the Fairview Cemetery.

See Wilbur D. Peat, *Pioneer Painters of Indiana* (Indianapolis 1954).

MORTON, DAVID (b Elkton, Kentucky, February 21, 1886; d Morristown, New Jersey, June 13, 1957). Journalist and poet. Morton was son of Thomas B. and Mattie (Petrie) Morton. His boyhood was divided between Louisville and Elkton, and his initial education came from PUBLIC SCHOOLS in Louisville. He graduated from Vanderbilt University in Nashville in 1909. He worked as a reporter for the *Louisville Evening Post*, was subsequently employed by the Associated Press, and later became an editorial writer for the *COURIER-JOURNAL*. From 1915 to 1918, Morton taught English at LOUISVILLE MALE HIGH SCHOOL.

In 1918 he moved to Morristown, New Jersey, where he taught high school English from 1918 to 1924. While there he contributed articles to the *New York Sun* and the *New York Evening Post*. In 1924 he became a member of the English department at Amherst College in Massachusetts, a position he held until 1945, at which time he became poet-in-residence at the Deerfield Academy in Massachusetts. In the 1950s he became a professor of English at the American International College in the Azores, where he remained until his retirement in 1957 because of ill health.

Morton began his publishing career in 1914 when his verse began to first appear in such magazines as *Harper's Poetry*, *Smart Set*, and *The North American Review*. He published eleven volumes of POETRY and two volumes of prose. His first book, *Ships in Harbor*, was released in 1921 and was received favorably by critics. His other books include *Earth's Processional* (1931), *Angle of Earth and Sky* (1941), and *A Letter to Youth*, (1942). Morton was best known for his work as a critic. His first major work as a critic was *The Sonnet Today and Yesterday* (1928), where he said the fundamental principle of the sonnet "is the statement of a single idea, followed by another derivative or related statement." In preparation for his second volume about poetry, Morton went to Ireland to immerse himself in IRISH atmosphere and history and to gain the acquaintance of writers involved in the Irish Literary Renaissance.

The result, *The Renaissance of Irish Poetry, 1880–1930* (1930), was a systematic discussion of the subject matter and methods of the movement. His other critical writings have not been collected. Some of his most perspicacious remarks on poetry are to be found in his column "Poetry for Our Time," which appeared in several NEWSPAPERS, including the *COURIER-JOURNAL*. He selected a poem and commented on it in his weekly column.

Morton first attracted attention in 1919 when the Poetry Society of America gave him an award for his poem "Wooden Ships." In 1949 he was elected vice president of the Poetry Society of America; in 1952 and 1953 respectively, he was granted honorary degrees by the University of Kentucky and the University of Massachusetts; and in 1955 he received the Boreston Prize for Poetry for his *Like a Man in Love* (1955). He is buried in Morristown, New Jersey. Western Kentucky University is the repository for a collection of Morton's works.

See Marion Williams, *The Story of Todd County, Kentucky, 1820–1970* (Nashville 1972); William S. Ward, *A Literary History of Kentucky* (Knoxville 1988).

MORTON, JOHN PRICE (b Lexington, Kentucky, March 4, 1807; d Louisville, July 19, 1889). Businessman and publisher. Morton attended the school of Joseph Lancaster in Lexington and went on to study for two years at Transylvania University. After his father's business went bankrupt during Morton's sophomore year, he left school and began a clerkship at a Lexington bookstore.

In 1825 William W. Worsley established the Louisville Book Store on MAIN St. between Fourth and Fifth Streets and hired Morton to manage the shop. After reading unkind words in the *Public Advertiser* about his friend Henry Clay, Worsley started a newspaper known as the *Focus of Politics, Commerce, and Literature* (later shortened to *The Focus*) and put Morton in charge of the printing. Under the name of Morton and Co. (renamed Morton and Smith in 1829), Morton continued to print the newspaper until 1832, when it merged with the *LOUISVILLE JOURNAL* and became the *Journal and Focus* under editor George Prentice.

In 1838 Morton and his brother-in-law, Henry A. Griswold, opened a book, stationery, printing, and binding business known as Morton and Griswold on Main St. between Fourth and Fifth Streets. By 1858 the enterprise had changed its name to John P. Morton and Co. and moved into the publication of schoolbooks. The firm eventually became a large supplier to schools and colleges throughout the South and West, with well-known titles such as Noble Butler's *A Practical and Critical Grammar of the English Language* (1874) and George Frederick Barker's *Text-book of Elementary Chemistry* (1875), both part of the American Standard School Series. The company also published *The Western Farmer's Almanac* from 1822 until 1943. On April 1 of the latter year, the family business closed its doors, citing the lack of a male heir to assume the presidency. The building was sold to Lincoln Bank and Trust Co., which razed it for use as a parking lot.

One of the wealthiest residents of Louisville, Morton donated one hundred thousand dollars to establish the Church Home for Females and Infirmary for the Sick (popularly known as the Morton Home) on Morton Ave. in the HIGHLANDS. Placed under the auspices of the Episcopal church, the home cared for aged and invalid persons until the late 1970s at the Morton Ave. site. In 1977 a new facility was built on LYNDON Ln. in suburban Louisville.

Morton married Harriet Griswold in 1836; they had no children. He is buried in CAVE HILL CEMETERY.

See J. Stoddard Johnston, ed., *Memorial History of Louisville* (Chicago 1896); *Courier-Journal*, July 20, 1889, April 18, 1943.

MORTON, ROGERS CLARK BALLARD (b Glenview, Jefferson County, Kentucky, September 19, 1914; d near Easton, Maryland, April 19, 1979). Politician. A seventh-generation Kentuckian and a collateral descendant of Revolutionary War hero GEORGE ROGERS CLARK, he was the son of Dr. David Cummings and Mary Harris (Ballard) Morton and the brother of U.S. senator Thruston Morton (1907–82). He was educated in Jefferson County PUBLIC SCHOOLS as well as a college prep school, Woodberry Forest School in Orange, Virginia. In 1937 Morton graduated from Yale University. Prior to WORLD WAR II, he served in the naval reserve and later entered the United States Army as a private. During the war, he served in Europe and attained the rank of captain.

Following military service, Morton returned to Louisville and became the financial chair of the local REPUBLICAN PARTY. In 1947 he became president of his family's flour-milling business, Ballard & Ballard Co. In 1951 the business merged with Pillsbury Co., and Ballard moved to Maryland, where he established a farm and cattle operation.

In Maryland his political involvement deepened, and in 1962 he was elected as a Republican to the U.S. House of Representatives. He served in the House for four terms, from January 3, 1963, to January 29, 1971, when he resigned to become the secretary of the interior under President Nixon, a position he held until April 30, 1975. On May 1, 1975, Morton was appointed secretary of commerce, serving until February 2, 1976. From March 30 to November 2, 1976, Morton headed President Ford's election campaign committee, after which he retired from the political arena to his farm near Easton, Maryland, where he operated a custom boat-building business.

Morton married Anne Prather Jones in 1938. They had two children, Anne McCance and DAVID MORTON. He is buried in Old Wye Cemetery, Wye Mills, Maryland.

See *Louisville Times*, April 20, 1979; *Biographical Directory of the United States Congress, 1774–1989* (Washington, D.C., 1989).

MORTON, THRUSTON BALLARD (b Louisville, August 19, 1907; d Louisville, August 14, 1982). Politician. THRUSTON BALLARD MORTON was the son of Dr. David Cummings and Mary Harris (Ballard) Morton. Morton was the seventh Kentucky generation of the Ballard family, which had grain and milling interests in Louisville. Morton's grandfather, Samuel Thruston Ballard (1855–1926), served as lieutenant governor of Kentucky from 1919 to 1923. Morton attended PUBLIC SCHOOLS and the Woodberry Forest School in Orange, Virginia, and graduated from Yale University in 1929. He served as a lieutenant commander in the U.S. Naval Reserve from 1941 to 1946.

In 1946 Morton, a Republican, was elected to represent Kentucky's Third Congressional District, defeating incumbent EMMET O'NEAL by a vote of 61,899 to 44,599. He served three terms in the U.S. House of Representatives, from January 3, 1947, to January 3, 1953. Morton was appointed assistant secretary of state for congressional relations (1953–56) by President Dwight D. Eisenhower. He defeated Democratic incumbent Earle C. Clements in the 1956 election for the U.S. Senate by 506,903 to 499,922 in a bitterly fought campaign. In his 1962 reelection campaign he defeated Wilson W. Wyatt in another bitter race. Morton served in the Senate for two terms, from January 3, 1957, to January 3, 1969. He was chairman of the Republican National Committee from 1959 to 1961. He later became one of the first conservatives to withdraw his support for President Lyndon Johnson's VIETNAM WAR policies. Morton declined to run for reelection in 1968.

Morton married Belle Clay Lyons of Louisville in 1962. They had two children, Thruston Jr. and Clay Lyons. Morton served at various periods of his life as president of Ballard and Ballard, the grain and flour-milling business; vice chairman of the board and director of the Liberty National Bank; director of the Louisville Board of Trade; and chairman of the board and director of CHURCHILL DOWNS. Morton lived in Louisville until his death on August 14, 1982. He is buried in CAVE HILL CEMETERY.

MOSES, ADOLPH (b Kletchevo, Poland, May 3, 1840; d Louisville, January 7, 1902). Rabbi. Born into a scholarly and pious family, he was the son of Rabbi Israel Baruch and Eve Graditz Moses. His education was a mix of rabbinical and secular studies. Initially his father taught him the Torah and Talmud, but, since he showed particular promise, he was sent at the age of thirteen to study at a *yeshibot*, an orthodox Jewish college or seminary. He then pursued two years of secular studies. At the age of nineteen, he moved to Breslau, where he studied both at the university and the rabbinical seminary.

Twice Moses interrupted his studies to serve in nationalist struggles. In 1859 he joined Garibaldi's forces in Italy for eight months, and in 1863 he fought in the Polish uprising until he was captured by the RUSSIANS and briefly imprisoned in Warsaw. Returning to his studies, he followed Abraham Geiger, a prominent scholar in reformed Judaism, to Frankfurt am Main before moving to the University of Vienna, where he concluded his student life in 1867. From 1868 to 1870 he taught at Seegnitz in Bavaria.

In 1870 he immigrated to the United States and took charge of a synagogue in Montgomery, Alabama. A year later he moved to a congregation in Mobile, Alabama. When he arrived in the United States, many Jewish synagogues held their services in German. Convinced of the need to shift to English, Moses worked to master the new language. In 1881 he made his final move to Louisville's Temple Adath Israel.

Moses was an advocate of reformed Judaism, interpreting the faith as a universal RELIGION not limited to the Jewish race. He named his doctrine Yahvism after the Biblical name for the religion of Israel, "Torath Yahve," the moral law of Yahve. Under his leadership, Adath Israel introduced Sunday services in 1891 and an English prayer book. His liberal understanding of Judaism made him popular among Christian clergy, and he was remembered for his involvement in charitable projects and his friendship with Dr. John A. Broadus, the president of SOUTHERN BAPTIST THEOLOGICAL SEMINARY. In 1896 Gov. William Bradley (1895–99) appointed him to the Kentucky Institute for the Blind's Board of Visitors.

Moses never lost his enthusiasm for scholarship, and, in 1887, he enrolled in the UNIVERSITY OF LOUISVILLE's medical school, receiving his diploma in 1893. He also continued to contribute articles to magazines such as the *American Israelite* and published a book of sermons, *The Religion of Moses* (1894). Before coming to the United States, he wrote two novels, *Luser, the Watchmaker* and *The Cholera Bride*. Following his death, the Louisville section of the Council of Jewish Women published a selection of his writings under the title *Yahvism and Other Discourses* (1903).

Moses married Emma Isaacs in 1874. They had ten children: Alfred, Frederick, Garfield, Melville, Nathan, Mrs. Newmeyer, Beatrice, Octavia, Fannie, and Elsie. His funeral at the Temple Adath Israel was an interfaith gathering. He is buried in Adath Israel Cemetery.

See J. Stoddard Johnston, ed., *Memorial History of Louisville* (Chicago 1896); Herman Landau, *Adath Louisville* (Louisville 1981).

MOVIE THEATERS. The marquee lights have gone out on the majestic movie palaces of Louisville. Residents frequently recall the charm and grandeur of the larger theaters along downtown Fourth St., but the history of the motion picture THEATER in Louisville starts much earlier.

A storefront nickelodeon at 434 W MARKET St. called the Dreamland was Louisville's first moving-picture show. One of the earliest businesses of its kind in the country, Dreamland opened on April 6, 1904, and was operated by William "Billy" Baron. A sideshow barker would stand in front of the entrance to the hundred-seat theater and entice pedestrians to stop in for a look at the one-reel program that lasted about fifteen minutes.

The success of the Dreamland resulted in the building of the Bijou, 211 S Fourth St., the first real movie house on Fourth St. By 1908 seven electric theaters were operating in the city. They were the Bijou, Crystal Amusement Co., Dreamland, Empire, Marvel, Wonderland, and a second Bijou for "colored" patrons.

The Majestic Theater, 544 S Fourth St., opened on December 25, 1908. Admission was ten cents. In 1912 the original theater was torn down and replaced on the same site by the city's first large-scale picture playhouse, built specifically for motion pictures, with more than a thousand seats. Hundreds of electric lights illuminated the barrel-vaulted facade, enticing patrons into the exciting world of the moving-picture show. Still in its infancy, the movie industry had yet to garner full acceptance. When the Majestic's manager, Louis J. Dittmar, attempted to place an advertisement for the Sarah Bernhardt silent film *Camille* on the same page as legitimate theater, the NEWSPAPERS hooted at the idea. They said it would never happen. The Majestic was one of the most successful motion picture theaters and operated continuously until it was sold in 1928 to be replaced by an office building.

Grand Theater, 611 West Walnut Street, 1920s.

The Alamo Theater, 444 S Fourth St., opened on November 26, 1914, with Charlie Chaplin in *Dough and Dynamite*. The eleven-hundred-seat theater was designed by Joseph D. Baldez, who had also designed CHURCHILL DOWNS' famous twin spires in 1895. The Alamo was the second downtown Louisville theater to be equipped with sound, on September 1, 1928. Talkies premiered at the Alamo with Myrna Loy in *State Street Sadie*. In 1933 the Alamo's name was changed to the Ohio. (The marquee still standing at 657 S Fourth is from a second Ohio Theater built in 1941.) The Alamo was razed in 1940 to make way for a Woolworth's store.

The Mary Anderson Theater, 612 S Fourth St., opened on April 1, 1907, with the stage play *Happyland*. On May 30, 1909, Louisville experienced its first professional "talkie" at the Mary Anderson. It was billed as an Actologue. Actors stationed behind a screen attempted to speak their parts in sync with the performers in the picture. The effort was less than successful. In 1910 the MARY ANDERSON became part of the B.F. Keith Vaudeville circuit. By 1913 a screen was erected, and the theater was dedicated to motion pictures. The theater would continue to alternate vaudeville and pictures for nearly two more decades. The 1,250-seat auditorium operated as a first-run theater throughout the 1950s and 1960s before closing in 1972.

Like the Mary Anderson, the New Masonic Theater, 326 W Chestnut St., was built in 1902 as a legitimate stage theater. The theater was at various times also known as the Shubert and lastly as the Strand. It was significant in Louisville movie theater history as the first theater with true talking motion pictures. On January 15, 1927, just five months after its public debut in New York City, the Vitaphone came to Louisville. The Vitaphone system produced talking pictures by synchronizing a recorded disk with the film projector. Louisville's first talkie featured the New York Philharmonic, a vaudeville quartet, violinist Mischa Elman, and Metropolitan Opera star Giovanni Martinelli. The Strand closed in September 1952, and the building was demolished in 1956 for a parking lot.

The Walnut Theater, 418 W Walnut St. (Muhammad Ali Blvd.), opened in August 1910 and presented plays at moderate prices. By 1914 it went into motion pictures. On October 2, 1933, the 988-seat playhouse was renamed Drury Lane. The theater was rechristened again on April 17, 1942, as the Scoop, a newsreel house. The Scoop was the first theater in the South dedicated to the showing of newsreels, documentaries, and foreign films. It was particularly popular during the war, when Louisvillians were anxious to learn the latest about the war and perhaps catch a glimpse of their native sons and daughters. Admission was thirty cents, and programs ran continuously throughout the day. The Scoop was also the first theater in Louisville to have push-back seats, which allowed the occupant to slide back out of the way of people walking in front. A special paging system was also offered. An usher would carry an illuminated sign through the aisles to notify a patron that he or she was wanted on the phone. The Scoop closed in August 1952 following a series of labor disputes.

The National Theater, designed by Albert Kahn, opened at 500 W Walnut St. on November 24, 1913, to challenge the powerful B.F. Keith Vaudeville circuit. When the opening night headliner did not show up, it was rumored that the Keith syndicate had threatened to blacklist the performer. The National's management soon found it too difficult to compete with Keith and turned to showing pictures. Within a year, Keith interests had taken over the National and totally refurbished the twenty-eight-hundred-seat theater. When vaudeville declined years later, the National was one of the first to be dropped from the Keith circuit. In 1952 the theater was razed to make room for a parking lot for the nearby Kentucky Hotel.

As early as the 1870s, most theaters allowed AFRICAN AMERICANS to sit in designated areas, while the dress and parquet circles were reserved for whites. A few theaters did not allow blacks at all. In the early 1920s, black leaders protested these "peanut galleries" on the grounds that African Americans paid the same ticket price. A boycott was organized that resulted not only in the closing of the peanut galleries but also the closing of the theaters to blacks altogether. It was not until the public accommodations drive in the early 1960s that all theaters were opened to blacks. On May 14, 1963, the Louisville BOARD OF ALDERMEN passed the public accommodations law that made discrimination in all public facilities illegal.

During SEGREGATION, theaters on Walnut west of Sixth were for "colored" patrons, according to the CITY DIRECTORIES, earning the street the nickname "Black Broadway." The Bijou at 1230 W Walnut did business in 1908 and later as did the Pekin, the Taft, the Olio,

Rialto Theater, 616 South Fourth Street, Joseph and Joseph, architects, 1920.

and the Pearl. Louisville native John Bubbles (born John William Sublett), half of vaudeville's leading song-and-dance team "Buck and Bubbles," began singing as a boy in an all-black show at the Olio. In his teens, he and Buck (Louisvillian Ford Lee Washington) entertained at parties and worked as ushers at the Mary Anderson Theater (southwest corner of Fourth and Chestnut). The theater's manager once asked them to fill in for a weak act. As no black performer had ever appeared at the Mary Anderson Theater, they had to wear burnt cork and white gloves so that the audience would think they were whites in blackface; they were a hit, held over for two weeks.

The theater that was most recently known as the Savoy, 211 W Jefferson St., had the longest-running history of entertainment offerings in Louisville before its destruction by fire in 1989. In 1885 the site was home to Tivoli Gardens and later the Wonderland Museum, an exhibition of oddities and curiosities. The Grand Opera House, owned by John and James Whallen, opened in 1894 with a variety of touring productions. During the 1897 season the theater was rechristened the "new" Buckingham, which operated as a Burlesque and vaudeville house until 1916. In 1919 the theater changed its name to the Jefferson. Finally, in 1922, it became the Savoy. The theater presented an array of vaudeville and motion pictures for admission of ten cents. Wrestling came to the Savoy in 1954, and there were several seasons in which burlesque was revived. By the 1970s, the Savoy Art Theater had turned to triple-X-rated movies.

The Rialto, Louisville's million-dollar motion picture house modeled after the Capitol Theater in New York City, opened at 616 S Fourth St. on May 12, 1921. The initial program included entertainment by the thirty-piece Rialto Symphony Orchestra, along with the silent film, *The Witching Hour*, about the 1900 assassination of Kentucky governor William Goebel.

The Rialto's classical facade was created with white-glazed terra-cotta tiles from the Rookwood kilns of Cincinnati. Upon entering the grand lobby, patrons were bedazzled by ornate crystal chandeliers and brass torchères. From the lobby a spectacular twenty-six-step, white-marble staircase led moviegoers to the grand promenade, lined with eighteen-light candelabra. The house, with seating for thirty-five hundred, could be painted with colored lights from the gigantic ceiling fixtures equipped with X-Ray Culrlenz reflectors. The vast auditorium was spanned by an immense balcony unsupported by a single column. The walls were originally covered with blue silk damask, arabesqued in gold, and the seats were covered with blue velvet. The luxurious drapes of the grand triple stage were also blue velvet with gold satin. In 1965 the Rialto played host to more than three hundred thousand patrons during the longest-running film in local history—*The Sound of Music*, which played for sixty-four weeks. The Rialto closed on July 30, 1968, with *Doctor Dolittle*. After brief consideration as the site for a performing arts center, the Rialto was demolished in January 1969 for a parking lot.

The Kentucky Theater, 649 S Fourth St., designed by Joseph and Joseph Architects of Louisville, opened October 6, 1921, with Hope Hamilton in *Stardust*. The facade was created with carved stone and orange-glazed brick in a classical revival style. The lobby contained a large chandelier and two perfumed fountains. The 780-seat auditorium was topped by a huge stained-glass skylight that was lit from above by an array of colored lights. In accordance with the latest of styles, the Kentucky had an organ that "plays of its own accord." In 1940 the theater was remodeled and enlarged to include a balcony. The new interior design called for removal of many of the original lavish ornamental details. The Kentucky was redecorated again in 1951 and reopened as a first-run house. By the late 1970s, the Kentucky had established a reputation for attracting a rough crowd for its repertoire of horror movies and "kick flicks." The theater closed in 1981. Several attempts were made to revive the theater with a repertory cinema format in the early 1980s, but these attempts were short-lived. In 1982 the Broadway-Brown project threatened the destruction of the entire Kentucky Theater, but preservationists were able to save the facade, lobby, and a small seating area for about two hundred. From 1984 through 1988, the multimedia *Kentucky Show!* operated on the premises.

The Brown Theater, 317 W Broadway, was built in 1925 by James Graham Brown to replace the old Macauley, which was razed that year. Initially a legitimate theater, the Brown was wired for talkies in February 1930. The Brown operated as a first-run movie theater through the 1950s. In 1962 the Brown converted back to live theater. Following a refurbishing in 1972, the theater was renamed the Macauley. With a major renovation in 1998, for W.L. Lyons Brown, late chairman of the Brown-Forman Corp.

Considered one of Louisville's grandest movie palaces, Loew's State Theater (later the Palace) opened on September 1, 1928. The thirty-three-hundred-seat house at 625 S Fourth St. was designed by John Eberson, the originator of the popular atmospheric school of theater Architecture. Created in a Spanish baroque style, the theater is heavily textured and rich with jewel-toned colors. The interior walls depict a garden scene complete with statues, trees, and soaring birds. The ceiling, with its tiny twinkling lights, creates the illusion of a starlit evening sky. Eberson even developed a machine to project moving clouds onto the ceiling. The ornate lobby's ceiling of celebrities contains the busts of 130 historic figures such as Shakespeare, Socrates, Beethoven, and even Eberson himself. Loew's was originally designed as a silent-film house and therefore boasted an elaborate Wurlitzer organ with an extensive repertoire of sound effects ranging from the honk of a Model T to a brass band. During each performance, the spotlit organ would rise about fifteen feet above the stage on a mechanical lift for a featured presentation.

In 1958 Loew's was renamed United Artists. In 1963 the balconies of the theater were walled off from the main floor to create a second cinema called the Penthouse to show widescreen motion pictures. The Penthouse opened with *Lawrence of Arabia* on April 12, 1963. During the restoration of the theater in 1980, the Penthouse wall was removed, and the theater was restored to its original design. The partially renovated theater was renamed the Louisville Palace and reopened to the public for a brief period in the early 1980s as a live entertainment venue. Financial troubles closed the theater in 1985. Following further restoration, the Palace marquee was lit once again on June 29, 1994, primarily as a site for concerts and other performing arts.

As the popularity of the motion picture grew, dozens of theaters sprang up in NEIGHBORHOODS across the city. Neighborhood theaters generally ran movies after their first-run engagements in the larger downtown theaters. To the west were the Norman, the Ideal, the Park, and the SHAWNEE; to the south were the Cozy, the Crown, the Oak, and the Downs; to the east were the Baxter, the Bard, the Broadway, the Uptown, the Crescent, the Hill Top, and the Vogue, to name just a few.

On September 17, 1998, the Vogue, the last surviving neighborhood movie house, closed. Typical of the neighborhood theater, the Vogue had opened on December 22, 1939, at 3727 Lexington Rd. in ST. MATTHEWS. There were eight hundred seats, and tickets were sixteen cents. From its inception, the Vogue was equipped with the latest in cinematic technology. Renovations over the years allowed the Vogue to remain technologically current while keeping its 1930s Art Deco styling. Its clientele could choose from a wide variety: extended-run movies, art films, and independent films. Viewers came to prefer the newer multiplex theaters, however, and the Vogue did not survive.

In response to the American love affair with the automobile, movie theaters developed a unique American accommodation for their viewers in the 1950s. Most popular in the warm months, drive-ins offered a low-cost, form of entertainment. Admission cost would be based on the number of passengers, not counting the ones hiding in the trunk. A car would then pull up to a post holding a speaker that would be placed on the side window. Some offered heaters to warm the interior in colder months, although most closed during the winter. Drive-ins were a particular favorite of convertible owners. Play areas were sometimes provided for children, and chairs were available for those few who preferred to sit outside the confines of their car. Kenwood Drive In, the city's first drive-in theater, was built about 1948. Others quickly followed, enticing people to view second-run feature movies. Some of the drive-in theaters were the East, Skyway, Twilight, Parkway, Preston, Dixie, South Park, and Valley Auto Theater. By the 1970s, the popularity of this uniquely American movie forum had waned, and all but the Kenwood were gone by century's end.

Entering the twenty-first century, nearly all the majestic movie houses of the early twentieth century are gone. A few still stand, but their marquee lights have gone out.

Majestic Theater, 544 South Fourth Street. Joseph and Joseph, architects, 1920s.

Alamo: 444 S Fourth St. Opened Nov. 1914 thru ca. 1930. Also known as the Ohio.
Aristo: 1603 S Second St. Later known as the Ritz and New Ritz.
Bard: 2470 Bardstown Rd. Neighborhood theater. Building razed in 1998.
Baxter: 1055 Bardstown Rd. Later became the Airway.
Baxter Ave.: 1250 Bardstown Rd.
Bijou: 211 S Fourth St. Also known as the Columbia.
Bijou: 104 E Liberty St. Also known as the Liberty.
Bijou: 1230 W Walnut St. Also known as the Olio and Victory.
Broadway Theatre: 816 E Broadway. Opened in 1915 for vaudeville, later had movies and live theater. Closed as a theater in 1960. Building still stands (1998).
Brown: 317 W Broadway. Built by J. Graham Brown as part of the Brown Hotel. Stopped showing films in 1962. Later known as the Macauley.
Buckingham: 223–27 W Jefferson St. Burlesque. Closed in 1897.
Capitol: 2129 S Preston St. Neighborhood theater. Building still stands (1998).
Carriage House: 1101 S Fifth St.
Casino: 317 S Fourth St.
Cherokee: 1589 Bardstown Rd.
Cherokee: 326 W Market St.
Clifton: 2003–5 Frankfort Ave.
Colonial: 1801 W Market St.
Cozy: 3105 S Third St. Closed in 1965.
Crescent: 2862 Frankfort Ave. Also called the Masonic.
Crescent Air Dome: 2322 Frankfort Ave. Open-air theater.
Crown: 1215 S Seventh St.
Crystal: 456 S Fourth St.
Crystal: 314 W Market St.
Dixie: 941 S Preston St. Also known as the New Dixie.
Dixie Drive-in: 5131 Dixie Hwy., Pleasure Ridge Park.
Dixie Dozen: 6801 Dixie Hwy.
Downs: 3423 Taylor Blvd. First known as the Aljo.

Dreamland: 444 W Market St. Opened 1904.
East Drive-in: North side Shelbyville Rd.
Empire: 110 W Market St.
Empire: 736 E Market St. Also known as the Shelmar.
Evelann: Lexington Rd. and Frankfort Ave. (east of Wallace).
Gayety: 323 W Jefferson St. Burlesque with "style" 1910–36.
Germania: 1237 S Shelby St. Also known as the Palace.
Globe: 2010 Portland Ave.
Grand: 607–11 W Walnut St.
Grand: 138 E Market St., New Albany. Still operates in 1998.
Grand Opera House: 209 W Jefferson St. Later became the Savoy.
Green Tree 4: 701 E Hwy. 131. In Greentree Mall, Jeffersonville.
Greentree Cinemas 10: 701 E Hwy. 131. In Greentree Mall, Jeffersonville.
Highland: 1014–16 Bardstown Rd. Also known as Shibboleth Hall.
Highland Amusement Co.: 919 Baxter Ave. Later became the Gem.
Highland Park: 4506 Park Blvd. First known as the Hi-Land/New Superba (1924).
Hill Top: 1757 Frankfort Ave. Building still stands in 1998.
Hippodrome: 144–46 W Market St. ca. 1920. Red Skelton played here.
Hopkins: 133 W Market St. (1905).
Ideal: 2313–15 W Market St.
IMAX: 727 W Main St. In the Louisville Science Center.
J-Town 4: 9601 Taylorsville Rd. Closed 1998.
Kentucky: 649–41 S Fourth St. Closed in 1981.
Kenwood Drive In: 7001 Southside Dr.
Knickerbocker: 1801 W Market St. Also known as the Colonial.
Knox: 331 W Oak St. Also known as the Towers.
Loew's: 625 S Fourth St. Built between 1926 and 1928. Finished just before the stock market crash. Also known as Loew's State/United Artists/Palace/Louisville Palace.
LeRose: 331 Spring St., Jeffersonville.
Liberty: 104 E Liberty St.
Lyric: 604 W Walnut St.
Majestic: 544 S Fourth St. (at Guthrie). Designed by Joseph and Joseph Architects. Opened Christmas day 1908 for vaudeville and movies in lavish style. Closed New Years Day 1929.
Marvel: 348 W Jefferson St.
Mary Anderson: 610–12 S Fourth St. Became part of the B.F. Keith Vaudeville circuit.
National: 500 W Walnut St. Designed by Joseph and Joseph Architects. Opened in 1913 for vaudeville. Known for excellent acoustics but suffered many setbacks. Seated twenty-eight hundred persons on three levels. It was razed in 1952 by then-owner J. Graham Brown to make way for a parking lot for his Kentucky Hotel.
New Grand: 617 W Twenty-seventh St.

Victor Mature arrives at the Loew's (Palace) Theater, 625 South Fourth Street for the premiere of his movie One Million BC, 1940.

New Masonic: 326 W Chestnut. Also known as Shubert/Strand.
New Ritz: 1603 S Second St. The name was later changed to the Ritz.
Norman: 2051–53 Portland Ave. (through 1947).
Novelty: 408 S Fourth St. Also known as the Rex.
Oak: 1169 Dixie Hwy.
Ohio: 653 S Fourth St.
Oldham 8: 410 S First Ave., LaGrange.
Olympic: 326 E Market St.
Orpheum: 318–20 W Jefferson St. Also known as the Rodeo.
Palace: 1103 W Walnut St. Later 1224 W Walnut St.
Palace Airdome: Open-air theater.
Park: 4030 W Walnut St.
Parkland: 2817 Dumesnil St.
Parkway Drive-in: 2707 Millers Ln.
Portland: 2204 Portland Ave.
Penthouse: 624 S Fourth St. Opened in April 1963 and closed 1980.
Preston: 1249 S Preston St.
Preston Drive-in: 6705 Preston Hwy.
Preston Air-Dome: 1251 S Preston St. Open-air theater.
Princess: 328 W Jefferson St.
Pythian Air Dome: 613 S Tenth St.
Rex: 408 S Fourth St.
Rialto: 616 S Fourth St. Closed on July 30, 1968.
Ritz: 1603 S Second St. Originally the Aristo.
Rodeo: 320 W Jefferson St. Showed Westerns.
Royal: 1809 W Broadway.
Ruby: 914 W Walnut St. Also known as the Lincoln.
Savoy: 209 W Jefferson St. Originally opened in 1894 as the Grand Opera House, in 1897 becoming the New Buckingham, in 1916–18 the Jefferson (showing Westerns), and finally in the 1920s it became the Savoy. Destroyed by fire in 1989.
Savoy Airdome: 1014 Bardstown Rd.
Scoop: 418 W Walnut St. Showed newsreels and short features. Same location as the Drury Lane and Walnut.
Shawnee: 3725 W Broadway.
Shelby: 1224 S Shelby St.
Shubert: 316 W Chestnut St. Also known as Masonic Temple and Strand.
Shelmar: 736 E Market St. Also known as the Empire.
Showcase Cinemas Louisville: 3408 Bardstown Rd.
Skyway Drive-in: 3609 Bardstown Rd., Buechel.
South Park Drive-in: 9205 National Turnpike.
Star: 226 S Fourth St.
Star: 728 W Market St.
Stonybrook: 2745 S Hurstbourne Pkwy.
Sun: 1116 S Eighteenth St. Was called the "sauerkraut temple."
Superba: 406 W Market St.
Tinseltown: 4400 Towne Center Dr.
Towers: 331 W Oak St. Later known as the Knox.
Trolley: Operated out of Louisville's last trolley car.
Twin Drive-in: 4011–15 Crittenden Dr.

Twilite Drive-in: 4015 Crittenden Dr.
Uptown: 1504 Bardstown Rd. Facade still stands in 1998.
Valley Auto Theater: 14700 Dixie Hwy., Valley Station.
Victoria: 309 W Market St.
Village 8: 4014 Dutchmans Ln.
Vogue: 3727 Lexington Rd. Opening in 1938 with eight hundred seats; closed on September 17, 1998.
WEK: 208–12 S Twenty-eighth St.
Walnut: 418 W Walnut St. Later called the Ritz, the Drury Lane, and Scoop. The Scoop closed August 6, 1952.
West Broadway: 1738 W Broadway.
West End: 3312 W Broadway.
Westonian: Twenty-sixth and St. Cecelia Streets. Airdome theater.
Wonderland: 718 W Market St.
Zem: 2831 S Fourth St.

See *Courier-Journal*, Oct. 7, 1921, Jan. 2, 1922, Jan. 16, 1927, Feb. 11, 1940, Louisville *Herald-Post*, Sept. 1, 1928, Sept. 21, 1928, Dec. 25, 1928, Sept. 26, 1935; *Caron's 1908 Louisville City Directory; Louisville News & Enquirer,* Dec. 1, 1935; *Louisville Post*, May 10, 1921; *Louisville Herald*, May 1, 1921; *Louisville* (Sept. 1977): 65.

Jeff Rodgers

MT. WASHINGTON. Mt. Washington, in northeastern BULLITT COUNTY, is twenty miles from Louisville and ten miles from SHEPHERDSVILLE. It grew up at the junction of stagecoach roads connecting Louisville with Bardstown and TAYLORSVILLE with Shepherdsville. The town was laid out on fifty acres, part of a tract owned by Joseph Hough. On December 7, 1822, enough people had settled at the crossroads for the General Assembly to charter a town that was named Mount Vernon, after George Washington's Virginia home. The first trustees were Lewis Snapp, Craven Peyton, Joel Maynard, Willian Barnes, and Moses C. Hough.

A post office was established in 1830. When postmaster Jacob Fox applied under the city's name, it was discoverd another Mount Vernon existed, and the name was changed to MT. WASHINGTON. It was incorporated in 1833. By the 1850s the local economy was thriving, and the city was the county's largest, with a population of seven hundred. Businesses included a rifle factory, a coffin shop, two taverns, a tannery, and manufacturers of pianos, furniture, and hats. The Buck Mill was available for grinding flour and meal as well as turning wood on a lathe. A Masonic lodge was chartered in 1849. Part of the prosperity was explained by the construction in 1837 of the Louisville and Bardstown Turnpike. A bridge was built across Salt River a few miles south of town. After that, Mt. Washington became an important stagecoach stop.

In the fall of 1862, with the Confederate army occupying Bardstown, the area around Mt. Washington was held by elements of John Wharthon's Confederate cavalry. This posed a serious threat to Louisville, and Gen. Don C. Buell's Union army of 65,000 men was sent south to push the invaders back. The second Corps followed Bardstown Rd., and on October 2, 1862, Union soldiers under Gen. T.L. Crittenden skirmished with Wharthon's men north of Mt. Washington along Floyd's Fork. The Confederates were driven from their camp and fell back through the town while Union guns shelled it. Twenty-five Union soldiers were killed along the Bardstown Pike. By October 5, fighting had moved south of the city to the Salt River as the Confederates retreated toward Bardstown. The Confederates left Bardstown with Buell in pursuit, and on October 7 and 8 the two forces fought the battle of Perryville.

The POPULATION of the town declined in the post–Civil War years. Still, several new businesses were established to serve the agrarian area of northeast BULLITT COUNTY, including a funeral home, bank, carriage factory, and piano factory. The town had been hurt by the building of the main line of the Louisville & Nashville Railroad to the west at the county seat of Shepherdsville.

By the 1930s the town had relinquished its primary role in the county and had retained only a few of its original industries. Still its residents opened their homes to refugees from the 1937 OHIO RIVER flood. A disastrous fire swept through the business district on November 18, 1940, and destroyed the three-story Macabee Hall and several adjacent buildings. The town was reincorporated in 1955 and experienced rapid growth in the 1960s, especially because of the opening of General Electric's Appliance Park in Jefferson County. New residential areas reflect that it is one of the fastest-growing communities in the metropolitan area. In 1995 a bypass was begun around the business district. A four-lane highway was built from the FERN CREEK to Salt River, cutting the driving time between the town and Louisville. Along the bypass many new businesses opened.

The population of the fourth-class city was 2,020 in 1970, 3,997 in 1980, 5,256 in 1990, and 7,051 in 1996.

Tom Pack

MUIR, JOHN (b Dunbar, Scotland, April 21, 1838; d Los Angeles, CALIFORNIA, December 24, 1914). Naturalist and conservationist. John Muir immigrated to the United States with his family in 1849. They settled near Portage, Wisconsin, and Muir attended the university at Madison, although he ended his studies in 1863 without graduating. As a young inventor and machinist, he worked for a time in a Canadian factory and then in a carriage works in Indianapolis, where in 1867 he incurred an injury to his right eye that resulted in temporary blindness.

This experience had a profound effect on Muir, and, after regaining his sight, he quit his job and committed himself to his first love, the study of nature. Muir set out on a thousand-mile walk to the Gulf of Mexico, after which he traveled to Cuba and then on to California, where in 1868 he went to the Yosemite Valley.

Though Muir had taken a number of smaller botanical tours in parts of the upper Midwest, the Great Lakes region, and Ontario, the thousand-mile trek was by far his most ambitious venture up to that point. He began his journey in the Louisville area. On September 1, 1867, Muir left Indianapolis and went by train to JEFFERSONVILLE, INDIANA. He stayed overnight there and the next day he crossed the OHIO RIVER to Louisville. Muir wrote in his journal that he "steered through the big city by compass without speaking a word to anyone."

Once outside of the city limits, along the Louisville and Shepherdsville Plank Rd., Muir stopped to chart his trip. In a letter to a friend, he noted that he "spread out my map under a tree and made up my mind to go through Kentucky, Tennessee, and Georgia to Florida." Continuing south Muir entered BULLITT COUNTY and reached Salt River, which was nearly dry that fall. He came to the rolling hills called the KNOBS and encountered his first obstacle on Rolling Fork. A ferry house conveyed him across the stream, and he walked on to Elizabethtown. While in Kentucky, Muir marveled at the incomparable grandeur of the state's oak trees and took time to explore in Mammoth Cave. He reached the Gulf at Cedar Keys, Florida, on October 23, 1867. During his trip, he kept a journal of his experiences and observations, which was published in 1916 after Muir's death.

See John Muir, *A Thousand-Mile Walk to the Gulf* (San Francisco 1991).

MULBERRY HILL. Mulberry Hill was the Clark family home in Jefferson County and a significant historic structure in Kentucky and the early West due to its association with the Clarks. The site is within the city limits of Louisville along Poplar Level Rd., but in earlier times it was about three miles southeast of town on the South Fork of BEARGRASS CREEK. John Clark, father of GEORGE ROGERS CLARK, purchased the 256-acre tract from the heirs of GEORGE MERIWETHER on August 29, 1785. The Clarks already were living on the property, so apparently an agreement had been made prior to the actual sale. Additional land was added to the tract so that it totaled 318 acres by 1799. By 1803 it apparently totaled 343 acres.

John (1725–99) and Ann (Rogers) Clark (1728–98) and their four youngest children, Lucy (1765–1838), Elizabeth (1768–95), William (1770–1838), and Frances (1773–1825), arrived in Jefferson County in March 1785. They had begun their move to Kentucky from their home in Caroline County, Virginia, in 1784 and wintered at Redstone Landing on the Monongahela River. Son George Rogers Clark already had settled in Louisville and may have been living in the house. Tradition states, and there is some evidence to support it, that George, brother Jonathan (1750–1811), and some Clark family slaves built the house in 1784 in preparation for their family's move there.

The estate initially was christened Ampthill, possibly in honor of the Chesterfield County, Virginia, home of the same name owned at that time by the Temple family, Clark friends and relatives. At some point, probably within several years, John Clark changed the name of his estate to MULBERRY HILL. Information indicates it was christened Mulberry Hill because of the mulberry trees on the Poplar Level, as the area was called. One story states that mulberry logs were used to build the cabin. It originally might have been one story, but by 1799 it was a two-story log house, measuring forty feet by twenty feet and facing northwestward toward Louisville. The kitchen was a detached one-story log structure. There were also other structures such as slave cabins and a grist mill. Corn, wheat, and possibly TOBACCO were grown on the estate, and an orchard was maintained.

Mulberry Hill quickly became one of the most prominent estates in the area because of George Rogers Clark's residency there, the position of the Clark family in society, and the eligibility of the Clark girls. Elizabeth married Richard Clough Anderson Sr. in 1787; Lucy married WILLIAM CROGHAN in 1789; and Frances "Fanny" married Dr. James O'Fallon in 1791. Following O'Fallon's death she married Charles Mynn Thruston Jr. in 1796 and, after his death, Dennis Fitzhugh in 1805.

John Clark willed the property to his son William in 1799, and William deeded part of the property (including the house but not the mill) to his brother Jonathan on May 2, 1803. Jonathan and his family and their bachelor brother Edmund (1762–1815) had moved to the Louisville area the year before from Virginia. Both had been officers in Virginia regiments during the Revolutionary War, and Jonathan was a major general in the Virginia militia. Jonathan operated his plantation, Trough Spring, which bordered on Mulberry Hill. Edmund, in addition to being a merchant and a town trustee and clerk, purchased the mill from William and soon constructed a sawmill in addition to the gristmill.

Jonathan Clark's son Isaac (1787–1868) owned the house after his father's death. He lived there until 1863, when the loss of his slaves caused him to move in with his brother Dr. William Clark. The house eventually passed out of the family. The house stood until approximately 1900, when neglect caused it to partially collapse. The only surviving section had been incorporated into part of a wagon shed by 1907. This last remnant of the original house and its dependencies were completely razed in November 1917 after the property became part of WORLD WAR I facility CAMP ZACHARY TAYLOR.

In 1921 Clark family descendants Rogers CLARK BALLARD THRUSTON, his brother Samuel Thruston Ballard, and the family of their deceased brother, Charles T. Ballard, purchased the site of Mulberry Hill in order to establish a park. Today the homesite is included within George Rogers Clark Park. The family cemetery is there and includes the graves of John and Ann Clark, but some family members have been reinterred in Cave Hill Cemetery.

See Ernest M. Ellison, *Mulberry Hill Plantation: The Clark Family Home in Louisville, Kentucky* (Louisville 1991); John Frederick Dorman, "Descendants of General Jonathan Clark, Jefferson County, Kentucky, 1750–1811," *Filson Club History Quarterly* 23 (Jan. 1949): 25–32.

James J. Holmberg

MULDOON, MICHAEL McDONALD

(b County Cavan, Ireland, August 16, 1837; d Louisville, April 26, 1911). Monument maker. He was the son of Michael and Margaret (McDaniel) Muldoon. Dismal conditions prompted him to emigrate in 1849. He was proprietor of a marble yard in Steubenville, Ohio, before moving to Louisville in 1860. His partner, sculptor Charles Bullett (1824–73), established a studio in Carrara, Italy, where marble was fashioned and sent to Louisville to be inscribed and distributed to CEMETERIES throughout the South and Midwest. Muldoon and other partners erected Louisville CITY HALL, SECOND PRESBYTERIAN CHURCH, Lithgow (Board of Trade) Building, and other buildings. He married Alice Lithgow in 1865 when her father was mayor of Louisville. They had four daughters: Anita, an accomplished singer, who married Thomas S. Brown; Hannah, Margaret MacDonald, who married George W. Norton; and Aleen Lithgow, who married Byron Hilliard and then ROBERT WORTH BINGHAM. Muldoon is buried in CAVE HILL CEMETERY.

See J. Stoddard Johnston, ed., *A Memorial History of Louisville* (Chicago 1896).

Samuel W. Thomas

MULLINS, EDGAR YOUNG

(b Franklin County, Mississippi, January 5, 1860; d Louisville, November 23, 1928). Preacher and educator. The fourth of eleven children of Baptist minister Seth Granberry and Sarah Cornelia Barnes (Tillman) Mullins, Edgar grew up in Corsicana, Texas, and attended Texas A&M University and the SOUTHERN BAPTIST THEOLOGICAL SEMINARY. He served pastorates at Harrodsburg, Kentucky; Baltimore, Maryland; and Newton Centre, Massachusetts, before being appointed president of Louisville's Southern Baptist Seminary in 1899. Becoming president in the wake of the controversial William H. Whitsitt's tenure, Mullins espoused moderation.

During his presidency Mullins oversaw the construction of a new seminary plant at the Lexington Rd. campus. He combined the talents of a pulpit preacher with those of a scholar and administrator, writing ten major books and more than a hundred articles and book reviews. Mullins also excelled as a systematic theologian. While opposing the growing fundamentalism within his denomination, he also fought against the modernist tide among America's more liberal churchmen.

As the denomination grew, he increasingly took on the duties of leadership, including conciliating the moderate and fundamentalist factions among Southern Baptists. In the early 1920s he opposed the anti-evolution forces in the South, speaking in opposition to anti-evolution legislation in Kentucky. Mullins believed the legislation violated the old Baptist principle of separation of church and state. Mullins proposed a substitute bill that was less stringent and would protect Christianity only in general terms. Under his leadership Southern Baptists adopted a version of the New Hampshire Confession of Faith in 1925.

Mullins married Isla May Hawley on June 2, 1886. Their two children, Roy Granberry

Mulberry Hill, home of John Clark, 1898. Now the site of George Rogers Clark Park.

and Edgar Wheeler, did not survive to adulthood. Mullins is buried in CAVE HILL CEMETERY.

See William E. Ellis, "*A Man of Books and a Man of the People*": *E.Y. Mullins and the Crisis of Moderate Southern Baptist Leadership* (Macon, Ga., 1985); idem, "Edgar Young Mullins and the Crisis of Moderate Southern Baptist Leadership," *Foundations* 19 (April-June 1976): 171–85; idem., "The Early Ministry of Edgar Young Mullins," *Quarterly Review* 39 (Jan.-March 1979): 51–61.

William E. Ellis

MULLOY V. UNITED STATES. *Mulloy v. United States*, a suit brought by a Louisville resident against the actions of Louisville Selective Service Draft Board 47 (the same draft board involved in *CLAY V. UNITED STATES*), was a landmark decision in 1970 that provoked changes in the operation of draft boards in the United States. Joe Mulloy worked with the Council of Southern Mountains and the Appalachian Volunteers in eastern Kentucky and received an occupational deferment in 1966. His Selective Service Draft Board was located in Louisville.

When he attempted to renew his II-A status the following year he was classified as I-A and ordered to report for induction, despite the fact that his claim to conscientious objector status had not been properly reviewed. Over the next two years a series of procedural errors and time delays on the part of Draft Board 47 resulted in Mulloy's being taken into custody March 9, 1968, and charged with violations of the Selective Service Act. On June 15, 1970, in a unanimous and landmark decision on conscientious objection, the Supreme Court declared that Draft Board 47 wrongly denied Mulloy a hearing on his plea for conscientious objector status.

MULLOY V. UNITED STATES became the leading case in declaring that, when a prima facie claim for conscientious objector status is established, the local draft board must reconsider the classification and decide whether the registrant is entitled to the requested claim so long as the claim is made before the claimant has received his induction notice.

See Ruthe P. Holmberg, "Mulloy v. United States: A History," M.A. thesis, University of Louisville, 1985.

Ruthe Pfisterer Holmberg

MURPHY, DENNIS XAVIER (b Louisville, November 3, 1853; d Louisville, August 27, 1933). Architect. The son of Cornelius and Honora (McNamara) Murphy, both of Ireland, Murphy was hired as a draftsman by architect HENRY WHITESTONE in 1874. After Whitestone's retirement about 1881, Murphy changed the firm name to D.X. Murphy and Brothers, Architects. His brother James C. Murphy (1865–1935) joined the firm in 1890 and served as first chairman of the City Planning Commission in 1927; another brother, Peter J. Murphy (1869–1955), was also a member of the firm. Murphy and his brothers were ROMAN CATHOLICS and were architects for many Catholic churches and schools.

Little is known of Murphy's early work. Plans signed by him in 1878 for a house for Charles Merriwether on Third St. exist at the FILSON CLUB HISTORICAL SOCIETY. Several references to work by Murphy are in the *Inland Architect and News Record* in 1886 and 1887 for an opera building, a public school, and residences. A card file at Luckett and Farley Inc. lists structures from 1886 by Murphy, including the Engelhard School on Kentucky near Brook St., the Louisville Railway Co. car barn at Twenty-seventh and Chestnut Streets, and Turkish Bath rooms for the old GALT HOUSE.

The major work that occupied Murphy in the late 1880s was the U.S. Custom House and Post Office (demolished in the 1940s) at Fourth and Chestnut Streets. Murphy was the supervising architect for this project. This job probably came to him because of Whitestone's former position, from about 1865 to 1881, as supervisor of repairs for the old U.S. Custom House and Post Office at Third and Green (Liberty) Streets.

Some of the best-known works by D.X. Murphy and Brothers include PRESENTATION ACADEMY, S Fourth St. (1893); the grandstand with its twin spires at CHURCHILL DOWNS (1895); and the former Jefferson County Jail at Sixth and Liberty Streets (1905). Murphy also built the "Million Dollar Hospital" on Chestnut St. in 1914, so termed because of the added expense of duplicating all facilities for African American patients. Part of that building still stands as administrative offices for the University of Louisville School of Medicine. The firm also designed many residences. The firm later became Luckett and Farley Inc. Murphy is buried in Louisville's St. Louis Cemetery.

See *Inland Architect and News Record,* 7 (Feb. 1886): 13; 9 (June 1887): 85; 9 (May 1887): 50; Henry Whitestone Papers, Filson Club Historical Society, Louisville.

Elizabeth Fitzpatrick "Penny" Jones

MURPHY, ISAAC BURNS (b near Lexington, Kentucky, 1861-63?; d Lexington, February 12, 1896). Jockey. Isaac Murphy was born the son of free black man James Burns. He began riding as Isaac Burns in 1875 at the inaugural meeting of the Louisville Jockey Club (now CHURCHILL DOWNS). He placed fourth in the 1877 KENTUCKY DERBY, by which time he was also using his mother's maiden name, Murphy. He rode in nine Derbies, winning three (on Buchanan in 1884, Riley in 1890, and Kingman in 1891)—a record not equaled until 1930, nor beaten until 1948. He also won the Clark Stakes in Louisville four times, along with many other major races around the United States. He won 44 percent of his races (628 of 1,412, by his own count) or 33 percent (from other contemporary records), either figure surpassing the 20 percent achieved by Eddie Arcaro, the next three-time Derby winner.

Murphy's brilliance dispelled the lingering notion that a jockey's skill counted for little compared with the horse's talent. His control of pace was unmatched; his obituary in the *COURIER-JOURNAL* noted that, while he lost races by saving his horse's strength, he "stole ten times as many on inferior horses" that way. He exhibited this control most notably in the 1891 Derby, when his opponents all slowed their pace. Although the *Courier-Journal* stigmatized the race as a "funeral procession" in which Murphy "outwalked" his competitors in 2:52–1/4, it had only praise for Murphy's careful handling and precise pacing of the winning horse, Kingman.

Murphy died of pneumonia. He was inducted into the National Thoroughbred Racing Hall of Fame at Saratoga Springs, New York. In 1977 his body was reinterred at the Kentucky Horse Park in Fayette County.

See Jim Bolus, *Derby Magic* (Gretna, La., 1997); *Courier- Journal,* May 15, 1890, May 14, 1891, Feb. 13, 1896; Betty E. Borries, *Isaac Murphy: Kentucky's Record Jockey* (Berea, Ky., 1988).

William Duane Kenney

MURPHY, JAMES CORNELIUS (b Louisville, February 8, 1864; d Louisville, April 14, 1935). Architect and civic leader. Murphy was the second son of Cornelius and Honora (McNamara) Murphy. He attended LOUISVILLE MALE HIGH SCHOOL and the University of Louisville School of Law. His older brother, D.X. Murphy, was an accomplished architect with his own firm. Murphy became a partner in his brother's firm in 1890, and for the next forty years they operated one of the premier ARCHITECTURAL FIRMS of Louisville, designing such edifices as ST. BONIFACE CHURCH, the Jefferson County Jail, City Hospital, Norton Hospital, Waverly Hills Sanitorium, and numerous projects at CHURCHILL DOWNS.

While he was a member of various professional and civic groups, Murphy left his greatest mark on the city with his promotion of an urban planning commission. The urban planning movement began in Louisville in 1901 with Murphy's speech before the Louisville Engineers and Architects Club in which he called for more stringent land development controls. Despite Murphy's prodding and the obvious need for urban planning, nothing was done by local GOVERNMENT. Although Murphy would try for nearly thirty years to establish a city planning commission, it was not until 1930 that the General Assembly passed enabling legislation. Before 1930 the planning commissions and committees were merely nominal. After the legislation was passed, the Planning Commission, with Murphy as the chairman, was given broad PLANNING AND ZONING powers, and a comprehensive planning blueprint was developed. Murphy's hard work had finally paid off. Until his death, Murphy took an active role in seeing the comprehensive plan adopted. Murphy may well be considered the father of the city's urban planning movement.

Murphy was married to Mary Sue Strain and had three daughters: Mrs. John Guthrie, Honor, and Mary. He is buried in Calvary Cemetery.

See Carl E. Kramer, "James C. Murphy and the Urban Planning Movement in Louisville, 1901–1934," *Filson Club History Quarterly* 64 (July 1990): 317–59; George Yater, *Two Hundred Years at the Falls of the Ohio* (Louisville 1987).

MUSIC. Musical activity in Louisville is both strong and diverse, with classical music living side by side with various strands of traditional, popular, and commercial music, both European and African American derived, in a way that defies easy organization. The city has been known especially for its contributions to twentieth-century art music (the Louisville Orchestra's New Music Project; the Grawemeyer Award in Music Composition), rock music (*Playboy* magazine identified the city as a Rock Music "mecca" in 1998), gospel music, and, for a short period, Bluegrass Music. This article arbitrarily separates "art" music from traditional, commercial, and popular music, which are treated in separate articles—a ploy that makes organization somewhat easier yet does not produce a complete picture of the city's musical life at any given time.

Carl Ellis band performing at the Rathskeller at the Seelbach Hotel in 1941.

Before 1900

From its beginning as a lively river city, Louisville was the home of a flourishing musical scene at once amateur and professional. This activity rarely parceled itself into unambiguous groupings, a fact reflected in the proliferation of "bands," "Orchestras," "societies," and "clubs" with varying combinations of singers and with or without wind, brass, and string instruments. The first of these appears to have been the St. Cecilia Society (1822); others included the Mozart Society (from before 1845 until 1865; included singers), the Louisville Polka and Mazurka Club (1847), the orchestral Musical Fund Society (1857), the Philharmonic (1866; vocal and instrumental forces), and the Moebius Orchestra (1872).

An especially strong force in the city's early musical life was the male singing societies formed among the large German Population. The most important of these was the Louisville Liederkranz (wreath of Songs), whose organization in 1848 was largely due to the heavy influx of immigrants because of the failed democratic revolution in the German states. This group was part of, and indeed helped found, an active community of such organizations in the United States (Chicago, Cincinnati, Cleveland, Indianapolis, St. Louis, and many others) that met annually for conventions (Saengerfests), often held in Louisville. An 1870 Saengerfest attracted nearly sixteen hundred singers and instrumentalists, while the convention in 1914 drew about three thousand and was planned by a board including well-known Louisville names such as Ahrens, Bernheim, Oertel, and Seelbach.

The Liederkranz, which later merged with the Philharmonic Orchestra under the leadership of the indefatigable Karl Schmidt, was but one of about a dozen such groups documented in the nineteenth century. Others included the Orpheus Society (1849), Concordia Singing Society (1855), Mendelssohn Club (1867), Swiss Singing Society (Alpenroesli; 1877), Oratorio Society (1881), Harmonia Maennerchor and Musical Club (both 1882), and the Social Male Chorus (1878), still active as a social institution in the 1990s as the German American Club. A special, one-time event was the May Festival of 1891, to which organizers invited the Boston Symphony Orchestra under Nikisch, as well as several soloists, to participate with a special chorus prepared by Charles Shackleton of the Musical Club. The great success of the local singers in this performance led to Shackleton's invitation to bring a group to a festival associated with the Chicago World's Fair in 1893, where his Musical Club again made a strong and favorable impression.

The Louisville Mandolin and Guitar Club (1891) was the most well known of several such groups formed in Louisville during that period; the tradition was revived a hundred years later by the Louisville Mandolin Orchestra.

Some eight firms were in business printing sentimental ballads, polkas, waltzes, and the like between the 1830s and the 1870s. Various enterprises run by the Peters family were the most prolific of these, with W.C. Peters (no known relation to the European publisher C.F. Peters) active as a publisher as early as 1838. Pianos, organs, and other musical instruments were being manufactured in the city by the mid-nineteenth century, with the well-known organ manufacturer Henry Pilcher & Sons, from England by way of New York, St. Louis, and Chicago, in operation from the 1870s until 1944.

Anthony Philip Heinrich (1781–1861; worked in Louisville off and on between 1819 and 1823) was a Bohemian pianist called by some "The Beethoven of America" and is generally considered to be America's first professional composer. Among other things, he was a cofounder of the New York Philharmonic after leaving Kentucky. From Germany came Louis Hast (1823–90), who became organist of Christ Church Cathedral and was also a revered teacher and conductor (the choral/orchestral Philharmonic, 1866; La Reunion Musicale, an ensemble of vocalists and pianists, 1874) as well as William Frese, who followed Hast at Christ Church and was also an active choral leader and pianist.

John Mason Strauss (1870–1914) was an organist, string instrument player, and later an auto dealer who wrote waltzes, songs, and pieces for the musical stage; his popular *The Louisville Times Newspaper March* was published in 1894. Also active at this time was Zudi Harris Reinecke, an organist and composer in a time when women were not frequently either. And although Will S. (William Shakespeare) Hays (1837–1907), who rose to popularity with ballads such as *The Little Old Log Cabin in the Lane,* was probably the most well-known Louisville songwriter of the nineteenth century, certainly the city's most famous song is *Happy Birthday to You* (1893), published originally by sisters Patty and Mildred Hill in a children's songbook with the words *Good Morning to You,* as a student greeting "to" or "for" teachers, and still under copyright in the 1990s.

The many nineteenth-century concert facilities in Louisville included halls specifically built for the musical societies, including Mozart Hall on the northeast corner of Fourth and Jefferson (1851; Ole Bull, Louis Moreau Gottschalk, and Jenny Lind all performed here) as well as two different halls for the Liederkranz Society, the first on Market between First and Second (1872) and the second at the northwest corner of Sixth and Walnut (Muhammad Ali Blvd.)(1896). A special hall was built for the First National Saengerbund, held in Louisville in 1866. Situated on the southwest corner of Fifth and BROADWAY, it reportedly seated five thousand, with performance space for a thousand singers and an orchestra of sixty-nine.

There was also an auditorium at the SOUTHERN EXPOSITION (1883–87) that seated three thousand people and included a large organ, sold later to Warren Memorial Presbyterian Church. When the exhibition buildings were razed in 1889, millionaire concert hobbyist William F. Norton Jr., of the wealthy Norton family, bought the three thousand seats and built a new hall (called simply The Auditorium; 1889) a few blocks away at the southwest corner of Fourth and Hill, where for several years he presented everything from traveling orchestras and opera productions to John Philip Sousa's band, to prizefights. Norton's mother did not approve of such goings on, however, so in business matters this entrepreneur went by the name of Daniel Quilp, a repulsive character in Dickens's *Old Curiosity Shop.*

Bridging the nineteenth and twentieth centuries were the musical activities of Karl Schmidt and Hattie Bishop Speed. Schmidt, a cellist, was a tireless performer, composer, and entrepreneur who moved to Louisville in 1891 and continued to be active into the 1940s. In addition to composing and serving as organist/choirmaster at Temple Adath Israel, he was, with William Frese, a founder of the Louisville Quintet Club and also the Philharmonic Orchestra, which merged with the Liederkranz and was active for several years before what is now the Louisville Orchestra was organized under the aegis of a different musical faction. HATTIE SPEED (1858–1942), who began studying piano locally with Louis Hast, furthered her training in Boston and Europe. Upon her return to Louisville she was involved with several musical enterprises, including the Wednesday Morning Musical Club.

After 1900

Seibert's Greater Louisville Band and variously named groups led by the Italian immigrant Natiello brothers (Ernesto and Oreste) were popular from about the turn of the twentieth century and toured extensively in the East and Midwest until their untimely demise because of a freak accident in January 1922 in Washington, D.C., when the roof of the Knickerbocker Theatre collapsed under snow, killing 106 people, including Ernesto. By the mid-twenties Louisville musicians were following the lead of other cities and playing in company bands such as the Standard Sanitary Band, the Yellow Cab Band, the Post Office Band, the Ford Motor Co. Louisvillians, and the Louisville & Nashville Band that toured through the area covered by L&N trains from 1935 until the mid-fifties. The Ballard Chefs (of Ballard Mills) was a popular jug band, a type of music that is thought to have started in Louisville in the 1920s.

Orchestras were also formed at radio stations WHAS and WAVE, and players freelanced in the city's many dance halls and clubs, such as the MADRID BALLROOM, the HA-WI-AN GARDENS, the Trianon, and the Gypsy Village at Fontaine FERRY PARK, as well as playing on the roof gardens of the Brown and Seelbach Hotels and on the steamboat *Idlewild* (now *BELLE OF LOUISVILLE*).

Organized in 1919 by community activist Bessie Allen, the Booker T. Washington Community Center Band of Louisville comprised a marching band and dance orchestra for African American children, including later JAZZ and BLUES artists Dicky Wells, Jonah Jones, and HELEN HUMES. Other community bands have included the Holy Name Band and Choral Club, started in 1939 by Father Joseph Emrich, and the Commonwealth Brass Band, founded in 1989, which has perpetuated the tradition of nineteenth-century brass bands found in Louisville and other cities.

Three independent orchestras were active in the late twentieth century: the JEWISH COMMUNITY CENTER Orchestra, which traces its roots to the Louisville Civic Symphony orchestra, later the Young Men's Hebrew Association Orchestra, founded by Morris Simon in 1916; the LOUISVILLE YOUTH ORCHESTRA, founded at the Louisville Academy of Music in 1958 but later an independent entity; and the Louisville Orchestra, which hired Robert Whitney as its first conductor in 1937. The orchestra built a strong reputation for its association with twentieth-century music, thanks chiefly to the New Music Project in place between 1948 and 1957. The brainchild of energetic and visionary mayor CHARLES FARNSLEY and after 1953 funded largely by the Rockefeller Foundation, this project saw commissions of over a hundred works by composers such as Alan Hovhaness, Lukas Foss, Roger Sessions, and William Schuman. With the Rockefeller Foundation involvement also came First Edition Recordings, the world's only recording enterprise owned and operated by a symphony orchestra. The orchestra's commitment to contemporary music has led to its receiving more ASCAP awards than any other orchestra.

The city's strong tradition of amateur/professional choral singing continued in the twentieth century in the Louisville Male Chorus, founded by Frederic Cowles (1914), and the Louisville Women's Chorus, founded by Mildred Hill (1921), which eventually merged into the LOUISVILLE CHORUS under Cowles in 1926. Cowles, another organist, piano teacher, and choral conductor, was also a cofounder of the LOUISVILLE CONSERVATORY OF MUSIC in 1915 and joined the University of Louisville School of Music at its opening in 1932. The 1940s through 1970s saw a proliferation of choral groups of every size and repertory, including the Holy Name Choral Club (1940), formed one year after the companion Holy Name Band; the Louisville Gospel Choral Union, formed as part of the growing black gospel movement in the city (1941); the Philharmonic Chorus, formed and led by Edward Barret to provide a chorus for the Louisville Orchestra (1946); the Bell Singers, formed by employees of the Bell Telephone Co. (1957); the Louisville Boys Choir (1972); and Silver Notes, a senior citizen group (1974). By 1958 the Holy Name Choral Club was led by Joseph Herde and had become simply the Choral Club. The baton was then passed to Richard Spalding, during whose lengthy tenure the name was changed to The Louisville Chorus, the earlier "Louisville Chorus" having ceased operation some years before. The Louisville Bach Society formed a few years later (1964).

Strong academic choral programs have been built at the SOUTHERN BAPTIST THEOLOGICAL SEMINARY and University of Louisville School of Music, and by the 1980s and 1990s several

The Standard Sanitary Band (Standard Sanitary Company), 1920s.

independent groups existed in the city, including Voces Novae, the Louisville Youth Choir, Coro Favoriti, and Voices of KENTUCKIANA, a predominantly gay and lesbian chorus. Opera does not seem to have been produced locally until 1948 when MORITZ VON BOMHARD came to the city to mount a production of Mozart's *Marriage of Figaro* at the University of Louisville; he returned in 1952 to found the Kentucky Opera Association, later renamed KENTUCKY OPERA. In the early years, KOA productions were broadcast live on WAVE TELEVISION.

Chamber music has been an important feature of the city's musical life, beginning in the nineteenth century with groups such as the Mozart and Arion Quartets (both 1870) and the Louisville Quintet Club (1891). The Wednesday Morning Musical Club began its meetings in 1912 and continued for several years, expanding to include a Junior Wednesday Morning Musical Club in 1922. A major driving force through much of the twentieth century was Fanny Brandeis, a niece of Justice LOUIS BRANDEIS. A violinist, she performed in the ensemble Con Brio; wrote program notes for various groups, including the Louisville Orchestra; and helped found the LOUISVILLE CHAMBER MUSIC SOCIETY (1938), a group that sponsors touring chamber groups. The Louisville String Quartet, consisting of players from the Louisville Orchestra, was active in the 1960s and 1970s, and by the late 1980s chamber music was being performed by the period-instrument group Ars Femina, the Kentucky Center Chamber Players, and the Ceruti Chamber Players, among others. Touring chamber music groups as well as soloists have also been brought to the city under the aegis of the J.B. SPEED ART MUSEUM since 1945.

The city has produced nationally well-known figures such as recording catalogue guru William Schwann (1913–98) and composer and scholar of American music Karl Kroeger (b 1932), who received their B.M. degrees from the U of L School of Music in 1935 and 1954, respectively, and pianist Lee Luvisi (b 1937). Luvisi, a renowned pianist who has been Artist in Residence at the U of L School of Music since 1963, studied at the Curtis Institute of Music in Philadelphia with Rudolf Serkin and Meiczyslaw Horszowski, where, upon graduation in 1957, he joined its faculty as the youngest member in its history. Luvisi has appeared with nearly every important North American orchestra under conductors such as Bernstein, Marriner, Ormandy, Shaw, and Steinberg, and has collaborated with the Cleveland, Emerson, Guarneri, and Julliard quartets. He has been a member of the Chamber Music Society of Lincoln Center since the early 1980s.

The city has also been home to composer and theorist George Perle, who served on the U of L faculty between 1949 and 1957, as well as Maurice Hinson and Gerhard Herz, who each spent lengthy careers here. Hinson (b 1930), who joined the Southern Baptist Theological Seminary School of Church Music faculty in 1957, has an international reputation as a concert pianist, teacher, and writer; his comprehensive *Guide to the Pianist's Repertoire* is used by virtually every serious teacher of the piano. He has also been a major force in the American Liszt Society, receiving the Liszt Commemorative Medal from the Hungarian GOVERNMENT for his work on behalf of the composer. Hinson also received the Lifetime Achievement Award from the Music Teachers National Association in 1994.

Gerhard Herz (b 1911), an internationally famous Bach scholar, was born in Düsseldorf, Germany, received his Ph.D. in 1934 from the University of Zürich, and emigrated to the United States in 1936 with assistance from Albert Schweitzer. BERNARD FLEXNER helped find him an appointment at U of L, where he was professor and chair of the Music History department for over forty years. Herz quickly became a major contributor to the city's musical life. He was instrumental in development of the Louisville Chamber Music Society, served on the jury of the Louisville Orchestra's New Music Project, and was a member of the Louisville Orchestra's board for twenty years. Herz has published widely in English and German, including both articles and scholarly editions (Bach Cantatas 140 and 4), and is noted particularly for his work on dating the Bach cantatas as well as a catalogue of Bach Sources in America (1984). In 1943, Herz married Mary Jo Fink, who taught FRENCH at the University of Louisville and became the first female tenured professor in U of L's College of Arts and Sciences.

The LOUISVILLE CONSERVATORY OF MUSIC started in the Dillingham residence on Broadway, a large house that already had an organ installed in it. It moved to a building designed specifically for the institution in 1926. The stock market crash of 1929 had a serious impact, however, and declining enrollments forced its closure in 1931. A local group approached the Julliard Foundation of New York for assistance, and in 1932 music instruction resumed in the same building under the auspices of the University of Louisville School of Music with Jacques Jolas, a pianist on loan from Julliard, serving as dean until 1935. After a short time the school moved, first to ground floor quarters in the Speed mansion on Ormsby Ave., then to two different buildings on the University's BELKNAP Campus, and then for many years to GARDENCOURT, a spacious nineteenth-century mansion located in Cherokee Park. When this proved inadequate for the growing school, it moved (1969) to U of L's new Isaac Shelby campus in the eastern outskirts of the city and finally to a new building on the Belknap Campus in 1980. After Jolas's departure in 1935, the school was served by DWIGHT ANDERSON (dean 1937–56), a pianist who had been a student of Isador Philipp and had served on the faculty of the Louisville Conservatory, coming into the U of L School of Music at its opening. Anderson was assisted by Claude Almand, a composer who also served as head of music at the Southern Baptist Theological Seminary. Following Anderson were Robert Whitney (1956–71), who served simultaneously as conductor of the Louisville Orchestra, and Jerry Ball (1971–90), during whose tenure the school was given its own building. Since 1990 Paul Brink and then Herbert Koerselman served as dean. The School of Music administers the annual Grawemeyer Award for Music Composition, which at its founding by philanthropist Charles Grawemeyer in 1985 was, at $150,000, the largest cash prize given for musical composition in the world. Winners have included Gyorgy Ligeti, Witold Lutoslawski, Krystof Penderecki, and Joan Tower. The U of L School of Music has been central to the musical life of the city, with conductors, musicians, and board members of the orchestra, opera, Chamber Music Society, Louisville Bach Society, and other groups serving on its faculty. The presence of the school's alumnae in the city helped create a dedicated audience for the arts, given voice for many years in the consistently insightful work of the *Courier-Journal*'s chief music critic William Mootz, who graduated from the school in 1946. And since 1980, local groups and presenters alike have sought out the supreme acoustics of the school's Comstock Recital Hall.

Of the various other institutions offering music instruction in the city, two especially important ones include the Southern Baptist Theological Seminary, with a graduate program in church music, and the Louisville Academy of Music, cofounded in 1954 by Robert B. French and Donald C. Murray. Music has also been a strong feature of the curriculum at the KENTUCKY SCHOOL FOR THE BLIND.

Although pianos were not made in the city after the turn of the twentieth century, organs of the Steiner-Reck organ firm (which moved from Cincinnati in 1962) may be found in churches all over the United States. The publishing industry changed as well, with sheet music publishing giving way to recording studios and production companies.

The Louisville community has been a nurturing environment for art music in ways perhaps unexpected in a large midwestern/southern city. For example, it was the first city in the United States to incorporate music as part of its public school curriculum (1853); also, it has led the way in community coordination of arts patronage with the Greater Louisville FUND FOR THE ARTS, the oldest municipal arts support organization in the United States (1949). Further, the Louisville Orchestra has not been alone in the promotion of contemporary music: in 1947 John Schneider, a student at the University of Louisville School of Music, conceived the idea of having a Contemporary Music Festival in which local performers programmed works by living composers. This festival was held annually into the 1960s. The Kentucky Federation of Music Clubs has been a strong force in the promotion of music in the city, as have been women's clubs in various NEIGHBORHOODS. During the 1950s and 1960s Louisville produced two arts periodicals, *The Arts in Louisville Magazine* and *The Louisville Gazette,* and it was during this time that the Greater Louisville Music Teachers Association was formed (1960); in addition, for three decades listeners in the metropolitan area of under one million could enjoy two classical music stations, NPR affiliates WFPK-FM (began operation out of the Louisville Free Public Library in 1954) and WUOL-FM (at the University of Louisville from 1976). The two later joined with a third NPR station, WFPL-FM, to form the Public Radio Partnership, in which one station (WUOL) was devoted entirely to classical music programming. The city has been served by the monthly *Louisville Music News* since 1989.

Twentieth-century musical activity and support also included the Louisville Community Concert Association, a group that brought concerts to the city from the 1930s through the 1970s; the Sister Cities Scholarship project (in affiliation with the Louisville Sister Cities program), a music scholarship for a foreign student to attend the University of Louisville; Classics in Context, a citywide festival administered out of ACTORS THEATRE OF LOUISVILLE starting in 1986 in which arts groups (such as theater, orchestra, and art museum) coordinated productions along a single theme; and the presence at the University of Louisville of an endowed chair in the humanities that has brought noted musicians and scholars such as Alfred Deller, Karl Geiringer, and Bruno Nettl to the city for part or all of a year. The Youth Performing Arts School and Center was opened as part of the Jefferson County Public School System in 1979.

Instrument societies, or in some cases local chapters of national groups, have been found here since at least the 1960s for communities including cello, dulcimer, flute, guitar, harp, organ, and recorder players, among others.

Favored twentieth-century performance venues have included Memorial Auditorium (1929; contains the world's largest Pilcher organ), Columbia Auditorium (built originally as a Knights of Columbus Hall; 1925), the W.L. Lyons Brown Theatre (built as a movie house in 1925 and remodeled into a concert hall in 1972; also known for part of its life as the Macauley Theatre, not to be confused with the earlier MACAULEY'S THEATRE), the University of Louisville School of Music's Bird and Comstock Recital Halls (1980), and the Kentucky Center for the Arts' Bomhard Theatre and Whitney Hall (1983). Dozens of songs have been written for and about the city, of which the most famous may be *Eight More Miles to Louisville,* written by non-Louisvillian Louis Marshall "Grandpa" Jones.

Starting in the 1950s and continuing through the 1990s a diverse variety of popular/commercial/traditional music has appeared on the city's musical scene. In addition to barbershop singing, bluegrass, blues, gospel, rhythm and blues, soul, jazz, jug bands, rock and roll, and string and brass bands, all treated in separate entries, this has included dance bands (The Trademarks, Epics, Sultans, Monarchs, Mystics), German music (Rheingold Band, Hot Brats), Celtic music (Drowsie Maggie, Tight Squeeze, Ten Penny Bit, Galloglas), and others (Carribé, a steel drum band; Akordeonan, an accordion group; many more). National artists connected to the city in a small way include the NRBQ, which traces its beginnings at least in part to a SHIVELY basement in the summer of 1966, and Mary Allin Travers (of Peter Paul and Mary), born here in 1936 to parents who worked for Louisville newspapers (*Herald Post* and *Courier-Journal*). She left a year later for New York City and grew up in Greenwich Village, where she met folksinger Pete Seeger at age ten and later became associated with the contemporary urban folk music tradition.

See Jeanne Marie Belfy, "The Commissioning Project of the Louisville Orchestra, 1948–1958: A Study of the History and the Music," Ph.D. dissertation, University of Kentucky, 1986; Robert French, "Music," in *The Kentucky Encyclopedia* (Lexington 1992); Erna Ottl Gwinn, "The Liederkranz in Louisville, 1848–1877," M.A. thesis, University of Louisville, 1973; Mildred J. Hill, "History of Music in Louisville" in J. Stoddard Johnston, ed., *Memorial History of Louisville* (Chicago and New York 1896); Marion Korda, "Louisville" in H. Wiley Hitchcock and Stanley Sadie, *The New Grove Dictionary of American Music* (London 1986); Marion Korda, *Louisville Music Publications of the 19th Century,* Dwight Anderson Music Library, University of Louisville, 1981; Julie Salamon, "Happy Birthday. Sing it Out, Prepare to Pay," from *Wall Street Journal* in *Courier-Journal,* June 29, 1981; Brenda and Bill Wood, *Louisville's Own (An Illustrated Encyclopedia of Louisville Area Recorded Pop Music from 1953 to 1983*), privately published, 1983.

Jack Ashworth
Robert Bruce French
Gary Falk

MUSIC HALL CONVENTION. One of the most tumultuous of Kentucky's Democratic nominating conventions took place in Louisville's Music Hall on MARKET St. (between First and Second) in June 1899 and is thus known as the Music Hall convention. The candidates for governor were P. "Wat" Hardin, William J. Stone, and William Goebel. Hardin, a former state attorney general from Mercer County and 1895 gubernatorial candidate, had the support of business interests; the *Louisville Dispatch,* which had been recently acquired by Democratic political boss John Whallen; and, perhaps most important, the Louisville & Nashville (L&N) Railroad. Stone, a former speaker of the Kentucky House of Representatives and an ex-Confederate soldier from Lyon County, had the backing of rural areas in western Kentucky. Goebel, a lawyer and state senator from Kenton County, was strongest in urban areas and a foe of the L&N.

Goebel was trailing the field coming into the state party convention, partly because of the unpopularity of the recently enacted 1898 Goebel Election Law, giving the full legislature (which was overwhelmingly Democratic) and the state election commission the power to select county boards and board commissioners, who in turn selected polling booth workers. The law was seen as a potent weapon in the fight to reclaim political offices lost throughout the state to Republicans in the last election. However, members of both parties viewed the bill as a self-serving attempt by Goebel to strengthen his political power in the state. The day before the convention, Goebel and Stone combined forces against Hardin, the leading candidate, brokering a deal to select the composition of the convention's organization and chairman. They signed a pact in which Goebel agreed to give Stone half of his Louisville delegate support and to support Stone in the event that Goebel withdrew or was defeated. Stone agreed to do the same for Goebel.

The convention started on June 21, 1899, with Goebel and Stone forces electing Judge David B. Redwine of Breathitt County the temporary chairman of the convention over Hardin's man, William H. "Roaring Bill" Sweeney. The crucial task of deciding on contested delegates—those who would be selected to vote on the candidates for nomination—was left to the thirteen-man committee on credentials, which had been selected by Redwine and was made up of a majority of Goebel-Stone backers.

The more than three hundred contested delegates were a substantial number of unclaimed votes for the candidates and represented the momentum swing that could propel any one of the three candidates to the nomination. The committee's decision was delayed while the members sorted through the voting of the districts and counties, increasing the excitement and tension in the hall. Hundreds of people, mainly non-delegates and Hardin supporters, entered the hall in hope of disrupting the convention.

The *Dispatch* and the *COURIER-JOURNAL* differed in identifying these troublemakers. Redwine had requested the presence of city police to keep order, which further angered Hardin supporters, who accused Redwine of intimidation tactics. When the credentials committee report was released on June 23, it gave twenty-six of the twenty-eight contested cases to Goebel or Stone supporters. Hardin and his backers had lost nearly 160 votes through a procedural manipulation by Stone and Goebel backers.

The nominating process for governor began on June 24. Upset with the voting to accept the credentials committee's report, Hardin dropped out of the race briefly. John S. Rhea, a Stone handler, nominated him for governor. Stone's managers thought he and Goebel had an understanding that, with Hardin's withdrawal, Goebel would drop out of the race, while retaining dominance of the DEMOCRATIC PARTY. However, when Goebel was nominated, any understanding, perceived or real, vanished. When balloting reached the Louisville delegates, all roll-call votes were recorded for Goebel rather than being divided between the two candidates. Many Stone supporters then began to back Hardin as revenge on Goebel. At midnight on June 24, the convention adjourned deadlocked.

Redwine filled the hall with police on Monday, June 26. When Rhea requested that the police be removed to prevent intimidation, the chairman ruled the motion out of order. Stone and Hardin forces then joined in disrupting the business of the convention, standing on chairs, yelling, blowing tin horns, and singing. The *Courier-Journal*, which backed Goebel, blamed agents of the L&N Railroad as instigators of the disorder. Voting took place amidst the confusion, but many abstained because of the difficulty in hearing over the uproar. The day's proceedings for the most part halted, and the convention again adjourned without successfully nominating a gubernatorial candidate. The crowded hall was calm the following day, June 27, when voting proceeded. Stone and Hardin were unsuccessful in joining forces against Goebel, but both were ahead of him on the twentieth and twenty-first ballots.

Sheet music published in Louisville by D.P. Faulds & Co., 1858. The illustration is from a daguerreotype by Webster & Bro. Louisville.

By the twenty-fourth ballot, Goebel led by three votes. On the next ballot, a resolution to drop the third-place candidate from the race put Stone out of the running. On the last ballot, Goebel won Union County's sixteen votes, putting him ahead of Hardin (561 1/2 to 529 1/2) and securing the nomination. Opposition leaders gave a lukewarm approval of Goebel's nomination, and the rest of the party's slate of candidates was chosen quickly with little fanfare.

Goebel's political maneuverings throughout the convention had brought him new enemies as well as the nomination for governor. Some of these opponents left the party to organize another political party, the Honest Election League, also known as the Brown Democrats after their nominee, former Democratic governor John Young Brown. The party received 12,140 votes in the election—votes that could have ensured a Democratic victory and might have avoided the struggle between the Republicans and Democrats for control of the governor's office, a struggle that ended with Goebel's assassination in January 1900.

See James C. Klotter, *William Goebel* (Lexington 1977); Lowell H. Harrison and James C. Klotter, *A New History of Kentucky* (Lexington 1997); Hambleton Tapp and James C. Klotter, *Kentucky: Decades of Discord 1865–1900* (Frankfort 1977); Richard Conn, "The Music Hall Convention," *Courier-Journal Magazine*, June 21, 1959.

MUSIC PUBLISHING. In the fifty years between 1832 and 1882 Louisville held an important place in the early history of American music publication. A wide variety of instrumental and vocal music published in Louisville found its way into homes across America. Some publishers, such as Frank M. Burkett and R.S. Millar, were piano manufacturers as well, while others, like William C. Peters, were listed as "prof. of music" in the 1832 Louisville city directory.

The most prominent of Louisville's music publishers in the nineteenth century were William C. Peters, David P. Faulds, George Washington Brainard, and the Tripp family firms. Peters, who appeared in the city's first directory in 1832 as a music teacher and manager of a circulating music library on MAIN St. near Second St., was also a piano manufacturer. His later firm, Peters, Webb, and Co., included Benedict J. Webb, a book publisher; Frank M. Burkeet and R.S. Millar, piano manufacturers; and his brother, Henry J. Peters. The company stopped publishing music in Louisville in 1865 but continued to produce pianos. William Peters's sons were also active music publishers in Cincinnati, St. Louis, and New York. Peters, who returned to Pittsburgh in the 1830s, published Thomas Rice's song "JIM CROW" in Pittsburgh (premiered in Louisville) and Stephen Foster's early minstrel songs.

One of Louisville's most noted music store owners, David P. Faulds, also published music until 1882. As a member of the Board of Music Trade of the United States of America from 1855 to 1871, he served as vice president in 1860 and later as president. Faulds, who died in 1903, published about twenty-five hundred pieces during his lifetime and was affiliated with other top publishing firms in various cities. He also served as mentor to James Cragg, James Perry, Harry L.B. Sheetz, and William S. Hays, former employees who went on to start their own music publishing companies.

George Washington Brainard came to Louisville in 1851 and started a publishing house in Mozart Hall on the northeast corner of Fourth and Jefferson Streets. This enterprise was short-lived, and the store closed in 1854, with Brainard returning to Cleveland. However, until about 1856, he jointly published pieces with Faulds, and his link to Louisville was maintained through the companies of Brainard Brothers and G.W. Brainard Co.

Finally, from 1851 to 1880, the Tripp family was an active force in Louisville music publishing. Louis Tripp was first a partner with Thomas P. Cragg. From 1859 to 1871, Tripp and Cragg were members of the Board of Music Trade of the United States of America. After this partnership ended, Tripp spent a period publishing on his own. In 1871–72, an organization called the Harmony Club held bimonthly meetings at Louis Tripp's Harmony Hall. Tripp later went into business with G.W. Linton, with whom he also briefly published the magazine *Musical Monthly* in 1872. Louis Tripp later left his business to his wife, Emily.

Other local music publishers of the period included Francis W. Ratcliffe, William McCarrell, Julius C. Meininger, and Henry Knoefel. Louisville's music publishers had approximately half of their pieces printed in the city, and many of those were done by the noted engraver Jacob Slinglandt and his son Benjamin F. Slinglandt.

Louisville Music Publishers in the nineteenth century

Firm Name	*Location*	*Date*
Brainard, G.W. & Co.	Fourth St.	1851–54
Brainard Bros.		1856
Cragg, James H.	Fourth St.	1872–76
Faulds, David P. (listed separately below)		
Greenup Music Co.	W Market St. Fourth St.	1889–95
Knoefel, Henry (Knofel)	W Market St.	1871–86
McCarrell, William (Golden Harp Music House)	W Jefferson St.	1862–67
McCarrell & Meininger	W Jefferson St.	1865
Meininger & Co.	W Jefferson St.	1865
Morse, Nathan C. (see also Faulds)	Fourth St.	1858
Perry, James	W Market St.	1870–72
Peters, William C. (listed separately below)		
Ratcliffe, Francis W.	Third St.	1851–53; 61
Sheetz, Harry L.B.	Fourth Ave.	1879–87
Tripp & Cragg (Thomas P.)	Fourth St.	1851–64

Tripp, Louis	Fourth St.	1855–58
	Fourth St.	1865–66
	W Jefferson (Harmony Hall)	1865–71
	Main St.	1869–71 [74?]
Tripp & Linton, G.W.	Main St.	1870–72
Tripp, Emily (Mrs. Louis)	Fourth St.	1866–81
Washburn, L.	Fourth St.	1858

David P. Faulds

David P. Faulds	W Main St.	1851-61
Faulds, Stone & Morse (Nathan C. Morse)	W Main St.	1854-60
D.P. Faulds & Co.	W Main St.	1854–60
Faulds & Huber (James H.)	Main St. & Masonic Temple, W Jefferson	1858
D.P. Faulds	Main St.	1864–77
	Fourth St.	1877-87
Musical Inst.& Merchant	Fourth St.	1888–94
J.P. Simmons & Co.	Fourth St.	1894-95

Peters Family - Louisville, 1838–55 (56?)

W.C. Peters (store & "music saloon")	Fifth St.	1838–39
Peters, Browning & Co. (William C. & Samuel Browning)	Third St. Apollo Row (Apollo Hall)	1838–39
W.C. Peters	W Main St.	1842–49
	Apollo Saloon, Pearl St. (Third St.)	1844–46
Peters & Co. (Wm. C. & Henry J.?)	W Main St.	1842

Louisville Music Publications

Peters & Webster (W.C. Frederick)	Pearl (Third St.)	1846–47
W.C. Peters & Co. (W. C.W Peters with Alfred C.)	Main St.	1847–52
Peters & Webb (Henry J. & Benjamin J.)	W Main St.	1843–45; 1848
Peters, Webb & Co.	W Main St.	1848–55
Webb, Peters & Co.	Fourth St.	1851–55
	Fourth (Mozart Hall)	1853
Henry J. Peters	W Main St.	1845–50
Henry J. Peters & Co.		[1848]
Peters, Cragg & Co.	Fourth St.	1856
	W Main St., factory (music store and piano manufacturing only?)	

Louisville Music Publishers in the Twentieth Century

David P. Faulds	W Walnut
Finzer and Hamill	Fourth St.
A. Hauber and Son	W Market St.
McCullough Publishing Co.	Fourth St.
Tyler, Thompson, and Cook	W Broadway
House of Harmony	Bullitt Ln.
Ridgeway Music Publishers, Inc.	W Main St.
Lawrence J. Kaelin	Bobolink Rd.
FSM Music Management	Eastern Pkwy.
Meadow Creek Music	Meadowcreek Dr.
Music Management Co.	Ellwood Ave.
Music Warehouse	Bardstown Rd.
Mister Wonderful Productions, Inc.	Algonquin Pkwy.
River City Music News	Dixie Manor Office Building
Grawemeyer Industries	Grand Ave.
Media Beat Music	Bardstown Rd.

See Marion Korda, *Louisville Music Publications of the 19th Century* (Louisville 1991); Gilbert Chase, *America's Music* (New York 1954).

MUSIC SCHOOLS. Louisville's first music school was opened by pianist William Frese, a native of Osnabrück, Germany. In 1888 he, together with his brother Gustav, began teaching in a home on the southwest corner of Fourth and Chestnut Streets. The following year they moved to 424 W Walnut (Muhammad Ali Blvd.) and, with violinist Henry Burck, the leader of the orchestra at MACAULEY'S THEATRE, opened the Frese-Burck Music School. In 1891 they invited soprano Flora Marguerite Bertelle and cellist Karl Schmidt, who also taught theory and composition, to join the staff. The school continued in operation until 1894, when Frese died at sea on July 2 en route to Europe. After that Gustav operated the Frese Music School at Fourth and Walnut. On the third floor of the same building another brother, Rudolf, conducted the Rudolph Frese Piano School.

In addition, the C. Kollros Music School, the Vincent School of Music, and the Bell Margaret Ward School operated past the turn of the century. Notable among the many private teachers in the city was Patrick O'Sullivan, a former pupil of William Frese.

In 1915 the first full-curriculum music school was organized. In that year the LOUISVILLE CONSERVATORY OF MUSIC was incorporated by Frederic A. Cowles, James W. McClain, and T.M. Gilmore Jr. as a stock corporation. The school opened with 16 teachers and 250 students at 214 W BROADWAY in the former home of wealthy businessman W.H. Dillingham. The Victorian Gothic residence had been built about 1877 and was especially suitable because of its central hallway system and large rooms. Installed in the house was a pipe organ that had been used for recitals by Mrs. Dillingham, an accomplished organist.

The conservatory used the first floor for classrooms, business offices, reception rooms, and a recital hall that seated about two hundred people. The upper floors were used for studios, classrooms, and practice rooms. A carriage house in back was used for orchestra practice and public school classes.

By September 1926 the enrollment had grown to almost two thousand students, including the preparatory department. Having outgrown its location, the conservatory moved to a new four-story building at Brook and Jacob Streets. After the collapse of the stock market in 1929, the enrollment dropped and the school was forced to file for bankruptcy. The conservatory closed on February 1, 1932.

In 1922 pianist Alma Steedman, a former teacher at the conservatory, formed the Alma Steedman School of Music at 612 S Fifth St. In 1927 she moved the school to 1449 S Third St. and changed its name to the Alma Steedman Academy of Music and Fine Arts. Three years later she moved to 1445 S Second St. Classical and popular music was taught, and a glee club and orchestra were formed. In 1935 Steedman left Louisville to teach at the Westminster Choir College in Princeton, New Jersey. Her interest had shifted to composition, and Westminster's president gave her work high praise.

In March 1927 the Bourgard College of Music and Art, a school for African American children, opened with Caroline Bourgard as the first teacher. Unable to find African American teachers, she made arrangements with Frederic Cowles, director of the Louisville Conservatory of Music, to secure graduates for part-time teaching. In April 1927 Bourgard bought a building at 2503 W Walnut St. Within six weeks the enrollment had grown from eight to thirty-six pupils, and the faculty had increased to five. After Bourgard died in 1928, she was succeeded by G.P. Bruner, Iola Jordan, Elizabeth Buford, McDaniel Bluitt, and JoEtta Perkins.

Following the closing of the Louisville Conservatory of Music, the UNIVERSITY OF LOUISVILLE School of Music was established and opened on September 15, 1932, with twenty teachers, most of whom had been employed by the conservatory. At the request of the university, the Juilliard Foundation in New York City sent Jacques Jolas, a noted pianist, to serve as dean for three years.

The school was first housed in the former Conservatory building at 720 S Brook St. In 1946 the school was moved to GARDENCOURT, the private residence of the three daughters of George W. Norton at 1044 Alta Vista Rd. The home was given to the university by Mattie Norton and was occupied by the music school until 1969. It was sold to the LOUISVILLE PRESBYTERIAN THEOLOGICAL SEMINARY in 1987. In 1969 the school of music moved again. This time its new home was the former campus of KENTUCKY SOUTHERN COLLEGE on Shelbyville Rd., which had been absorbed by U of L in 1969. The school remained there until 1980.

The current building on BELKNAP Campus, eight years in the planning and two years in the building, was designed by Bickel-Gibson Associates of Louisville and completed in 1980. At a cost of $9.75 million, the school covered 131,000 square feet and had 76 practice rooms; 44 teaching studios; 12 teaching laboratories; a 506-seat concert hall that contained a 48-stop, 64-rank organ by Louisville builder Phares Steiner; 3 dance studios; and a 3-floor library covering 12,000 square feet.

The library contains a number of nationally known collections: the Grawemeyer Music Collection of orchestral scores and recordings submitted for the annual competition with a prize of $150,000, the Ricasoli Collection of eighteenth and early-nineteenth-century Italian music discovered in Italy by Dr. Robert Weaver, the Isidore Philipp Archive and Memorial Library of music and letters relating to the famous

French piano teacher, and a collection of fifteen hundred vocal and piano works published in Louisville in the nineteenth century. A list was compiled, annotated, and published by former music librarian Marion Korda. Deans that have served the school have been Jacques Jolas (1932–35); Dwight Anderson (1937–55); Robert Whitney (1956–71); Jerry Ball (1971–90); and Dr. Herbert Koerselman (1992–).

The School of Church Music and Worship of the Southern Baptist Seminary began in the fall of 1944, offering a bachelor of sacred music degree. Dr. Ellis Fuller, who became president of the seminary in 1942, envisioned as early as 1925 a school for the training of dedicated Baptists for a ministry of music. In 1943 V.V. Cooke Sr. bought the Callahan home on Lexington Rd. across from the seminary and donated it for use as a music school. In 1944 seventeen students enrolled. Early faculty members included composer Dr. Claude Almand, choral directors Donald and Frances Winters, and organist W. Lawrence Cook.

In 1970 a new building, Cooke Hall, was built behind the alumni chapel to house the expanding school. The first recital was given there on February 12, 1971, and the building was dedicated on April 19. Deans have been Frances Winters (1944–45), Donald Winters (1945–51), Dr. Forrest Heeren (1952–81), Dr. Shelby Melburn Price Jr. (1981–93), and Dr. Lloyd Mims (1993–).

In 1954 the Louisville Academy of Music, a preparatory school, was founded by Robert Bruce French and Donald Christie Murray. The Louisville Youth Orchestra was organized there in 1958 under the direction of violinist and conductor Rubin Sher. In 1971 the school moved from the historic J.B. Speed home on Ormsby Ave. at Garvin Place to 2740 Frankfort Ave. It continues to train young people and adults, some for careers in music.

Bellarmine College's Fine and Performing Arts Department has evolved from a small glee club and dance band to a department that offers a Bachelor of Arts in Music. Jazz has been at the heart of the studies since the early 1970s, when department head Gus Coin introduced it into the curriculum. To that end he hired pianist/composer Don Murray and guitarist Jeff Sherman to teach jazz to a new generation of students. In January 1985 the George W. Norton Fine Arts Complex, made possible by a $1 million gift from his widow, Jane, was dedicated. The complex consisted of two buildings, one for music and one for art. A third building, the Wilson W. Wyatt Lecture-Recital Hall, was built with gifts from friends of Wyatt. Department heads have been Gus Coin (1961–88), Dr. Lee Bash (1988–95), and Dr. Alexander T. Simpson Jr. (1995–).

In 1967 Dr. Wil Grechel was hired as the first full-time music teacher at Indiana University Southeast. He organized jazz ensembles and choral groups and taught music appreciation and music theory. In 1985 the Bachelor of Arts in Music program was established. A major facility was added in 1996 with the opening of the Paul W. Ogle Cultural and Community Center, which contained a five-hundred-seat concert hall, a one-hundred-seat recital hall, classrooms, and faculty offices. Dr. Grechel retired in December 1997.

The Ursuline School of Music was started in 1968 by Serena Summers with five part-time teachers and thirty students. In 1977 drama was added, and the name was changed to the Ursuline School of Music and Drama in 1987. Summers resigned in 1994, and Anna Jo Paul became director. The school is known for its annual productions of musicals such as *Hello, Dolly!* and *Meet Me in St. Louis.*

In January 1968 the Jefferson Community College opened with a music department that consisted of Larry J. Schenck, David S. Doran, and Sherree Zalampas. Classical guitarist Doug Jones joined the staff in 1979. A full two-year course was offered to students majoring in voice, piano, and instrumental music. Individual lessons later were dropped.

In addition to the preceding schools, a number of music stores and commercial schools have offered music instruction. Some of these are Bader Music Village, Bizianes Music Mart, Central Conservatory of Music, Cherokee School of Music, Durlauf Music Shop, Flying Hands School of Music, Folsom Academy of the Arts, Gittli Music Studios, Jerry Diggins School of Music, Louisville Music and Art Center, Mel Owen Music, Middletown Music Studios, Music Education Institute, Okolona School of Music, St. Matthews School of Music, Shackleton Piano Co., and Tiemann Academy of Music.

See Mary Grace Money, "A History of the Louisville Conservatory of Music and Music at the University of Louisville: 1907–1935," M.M.Ed. thesis, University of Louisville, 1976; David Norman Carle, "A History of the School of Church Music of the Southern Baptist Theological Seminary, 1944–1959," D.M.A. dissertation, Southern Baptist Theological Seminary, 1986; *Courier-Journal,* July 20, 1969, Jan. 9, 1985, March 25, 1987, Jan. 15, 1992, Sept. 22, 1996.

Robert Bruce French

MUSLIMS. Muslim is an Arabic word that means "one who submits to God." Muslims practice the religion of Islam, which was first preached in Mecca by Muhammad fourteen hundred years ago. Basic tenets of the faith are belief in one-ness of God (Allah, in Arabic), the prophethood of Muhammad, and the Qur'an, the Muslim scripture as the revealed words of God.

Muslims arrived in America at an early date. Although most slaves came from the west coast of Africa and practiced native religions, doubtless some African Muslims were brought to the country in bondage to work on plantations, including those in Kentucky. All were converted to Christianity. Arab Muslims began to immigrate to the United States in the nineteenth century, and the early twentieth century saw an influx of eastern European Muslims.

At the end of the twentieth century the Muslim religion is one of the fastest-growing in the United States, and the same is true in Louisville. In the late 1990s there were about 7 million Muslims in the United States, and more than 1.2 billion worldwide, mostly in the Middle East and Southeast Asia. In 1999 there were between five thousand and ten thousand in the Louisville metropolitan area who were recent immigrants from Afghanistan, Bosnia, Jordan, the Palestinian territories, India, Iran, Pakistan, Turkey, Bangladesh, Iraq, Lebanon, Kuwait, Libya, Kosovo, Albania, Egypt, Somalia and Senegal. Many of them have become naturalized citizens.

Several organizations serve the rapidly growing Muslim community: the Islamic Cultural Association of Louisville, founded in 1974 and located on Buechel Bank Rd.; the Islamic Center of Louisville (Fourth Street Mosque); Masjid Muhammad on Magazine St.; Faisal Mosque Inc. (River Road Mosque); Al-Zaharah Islamic Education Center on New Cut Rd.; and the Islamic Research Foundation Inc. on Shefford Ln. The United Muslim Foundation Inc. represents all the Muslims of greater Louisville.

About five hundred local Muslim citizens were Christian-born African American converts attracted to Islam's emphasis on equal justice and social acceptance. A significant segment of this group was introduced to the faith through the Nation of Islam or they were descendants of members of the Chicago-based organization, which was founded in the 1930s by Elijah Muhammad. The movement dates to the 1950s in Louisville and stresses racial pride and civic activism along with the basic Islamic religious beliefs. Today, it has about seventy members who are followers of Louis Farrakhan. They have their own mosque on W. Market St. Minister Jerald Muhammad is the leader.

Also, a smaller number of American-born whites converted to Islam or married immigrant Muslims. Black and white, American-born converts customarily shed their English names and adopt Arabic names legally. This was true of Louisville's most famous son, sports legend Muhammad Ali. Born Cassius Clay, he adopted the new name with his conversion. Muhammad Ali Blvd., a major east-west thoroughfare, is named after him.

Among African Americans, Muslims and Christian groups cooperate on a broad social agenda, and black churches have hosted Louisville appearances of Louis Farrakhan. Generally, African American Muslims are socially active and have influence beyond their numbers. Masjid Muhammad and Islamic Research Foundation coordinates a prison ministry at the Kentucky State Reformatory and Luther Luckett

Correctional Complex and other correctional institutions in Kentucky. The Nation of Islam has intervened in conflict between rival street gangs and has mobilized young black men to combat crime. It took busloads of Louisville men to the Million Man March held in Washington, D.C., in 1995. The Nation of Islam is sometimes associated with color prejudice because it once espoused black supremacy. It repudiated this principle after Elijah Muhammad died in 1975.

Some prejudice against Muslims exists, based primarily on media coverage of political turmoil in the Middle East. During the Gulf War in 1991, members of the Arab community, which is mostly Muslim, told Jefferson County Police and the Federal Bureau of Investigation they were harassed and threatened with violence. Also, the FBI instructed its field offices, including the one in Louisville, to question citizens of Middle Eastern descent about their war sympathies—a program widely criticized inside the Muslim community and out. However, the FBI contacts Muslim leaders to protect them from potential threats to their lives.

See Maulana Muhammad Ali, *The Religion of Islam* (Cairo, Egypt, 1961); E.U. Essien-Udom, *Black Nationalism in Chicago* (Chicago 1964); *Courier-Journal,* Feb. 13, 1991, Nov. 11, 1997.

Lawrence Muhammad
Ibrahim B. Syed

MUSSELMAN, WILLIAM M. (b near Carlisle, Cumberland County, Pennsylvania, ca. 1802; d Louisville, September 24, 1889). Pioneer tobacco manufacturer. He was the son of David and Margaretha Musselman. The family migrated to Covington, Kentucky, by 1826. In 1843, Birch, William's brother, established a tobacco factory at Tenth and Market Streets in Louisville. William and another brother, David, came to Louisville in 1845. An advertisement in the 1846 Louisville city directory indicates that the Musselmans were manufacturing tobacco in pound and half-pound lumps. By 1850 Musselman & Co. was producing three thousand boxes of tobacco with a value of sixty thousand dollars and employed seventy-five persons.

William had married Margaret Everson, who was born about 1804 in Baltimore, Maryland. They had eight children: Mary Elizabeth, wife of William M. Price; Stephen D., husband of Elizabeth Dundecker; Martha, wife of Frances Moore; Andrew J., husband of Ellen Lyons; Margaret, wife of William Hall; Sarah, wife of William S. Lampton; Frances S., wife of Sampson P. Dick; and David R., husband of Catherine "Kate" Perry.

Margaret died on January 12, 1876. Wife and husband are buried at Cave Hill Cemetery. Their three sons and their son-in-law S.P. Dick continued in tobacco manufacture after William's death.

Betty Rolwing Darnell

MUTH'S CANDY STORE. Muth's Candy Store was opened in 1921 by Rudolph Henry Muth and his wife, Isabelle Stengel Muth, at 533 E Market St. Using only the finest ingredients and their own recipes, the Muths became known for their handmade candy. Their motto was "Muth's sweets are fine treats."

When Rudolph died in 1953, Isabelle and her sister, Hildegard Bennett, operated the business until Isabelle's death in 1981. Hildegard then became the owner and, with her son, Stanley; his wife, Anna Rose; and their seven children, continued to operate the business, then at 630 E Market St. In 1991 Hildegard died. The tradition of doing everything by hand has made their bourbon balls and the caramel-covered marshmallows called Modjeskas two of the most popular delicacies.

See *Courier-Journal*, Dec. 17, 1984; James Nold Jr. and Julie D. Segal, *The Insiders' Guide to Greater Louisville* (Lexington 1995).

Robert Bruce French

NAACP, LOUISVILLE CHAPTER. The Louisville Chapter of the National Association for the Advancement of Colored People (NAACP) was organized in 1914 to fight against Louisville's residential SEGREGATION ordinance requiring separate black and white residential blocks for housing. At that time Dr. John A. Lattimore, a vocal Louisville CIVIL RIGHTS proponent, became a strong supporter of the organization. Dr. CHARLES HENRY PARRISH Sr. was the organizer of the local chapter. Parrish, as the chapter's first president, along with William H. Steward, William T. Amiger, and C.B. Allen, came together as a steering committee to form the Louisville chapter of the NAACP. The National NAACP granted formal recognition to the chapter that same year.

The chapter's efforts in the fight for civil rights resulted in early victories. Because of the chapter's legal work, the U.S. Supreme Court overturned Louisville's segregation ordinance, and in 1918 the chapter was instrumental in stopping, after two days, a showing of the controversial film *Birth of a Nation* at MACAULEY'S THEATRE. The Louisville NAACP also curtailed harassment of African Americans by soldiers stationed at CAMP ZACHARY TAYLOR after WORLD WAR I. It successfully campaigned in the state General Assembly for an antilynch and antimob bill in 1920 and fought against the Ku Klux Klan statewide. The chapter also worked to ban the local Klan's public activities. Among its other actions, the chapter helped with discrimination complaints and worked with local businesses in efforts to hire African Americans.

The Louisville NAACP also took up legal battles throughout the state, wherever and whenever it could. This widespread endeavor resulted in money problems, and because of this and other internal problems, the National NAACP was brought in to reorganize the local chapter. During the 1930s the Louisville chapter was less active, although it effectively used the vote to bring about change for African Americans. The 1940s saw a resurgence of activism under the leadership of Lyman T. Johnson. In 1947 the chapter filed suit to abolish segregation in public accommodations and in 1952 won the battle for African Americans to play GOLF on public courses. In 1956 the group began protesting segregation in stores and lunch counters. Its efforts were successful, and after the public accommodations ordinance was passed in 1963, the local NAACP turned its attention to advocating open-housing legislation; the Louisville open-housing ordinance was passed by the BOARD OF ALDERMEN in 1967.

In 1979 the Louisville chapter hosted the national convention of the NAACP. But by 1982 the local chapter had no permanent office, and its president had resigned. The members, however, still supported crime prevention programs, a scholarship program, and voter registration activities. In the course of the 1980s, a successful membership drive and efforts to make the officers more visible revived the organization. During the 1990s the chapter returned to the initiative of voter registration and encouraged the participation of Louisville's black population in the political process. The local NAACP remains active; its office is at 2600 W BROADWAY.

See the *Crisis,* Jan. 1921, Western Branch Library Archives; George C. Wright, "A Brief History of the Louisville Branch of the National Association for the Advancement of Colored People," University of Louisville Archives and Records Center; *Life Behind a Veil* (Baton Rouge 1985); *70th Annual NAACP Convention Souvenir Journal,* 1979, University of Louisville Archives and Records Center.

Margaret L. Merrick

NANZ & KRAFT FLORISTS. Currently headquartered at 141 Breckenridge Ln. in ST. MATTHEWS, Nanz & Kraft Florists was founded in 1850 by the German-born and German-trained horticulturist Henry Nanz Sr. He started his business by raising plants in a single greenhouse on Third St. south of Breckinridge, where he sold shrubs, ornamental and fruit trees, cut flowers, and hothouse plants. He was joined in the business by his son-in-law, H. Charles Neuner, in 1872, and the business was dubbed Nanz & Neuner. Their first store was on Fourth St. between Walnut (Muhammad Ali Blvd.) and Green (Liberty) Streets.

By 1880, as a result of greatly increased business and the need for more space, the company had moved its greenhouses to land purchased in 1866 in St. Matthews (then known as Gilman's Point). There the owners established thirty acres of flower gardens and thirty greenhouses. Henry Nanz Sr. died in 1895, and his only son, Henry Jr., assumed sole charge of the firm and incorporated it in 1896. About 1918 the Fourth St. store and office were moved to St. Matthews.

Henry Nanz Jr. was joined in the florist business by a brother-in-law Henry A. Kraft Jr., whose grandson Edward A. Kraft Jr. ultimately assumed the ownership and in 1958 changed the name to Nanz & Kraft Florists. When he died in 1967, ownership passed to his son, Edward Ramsey Kraft.

The company's store building in St. Matthews was completely destroyed by fire on November 22, 1976. The business moved to Rasmussen & Son's Greenhouse on Hubbards Ln. until the new 20,000-square-foot store was built on Breckenridge Ln. It opened in November 1977. Three of Edward Ramsey Kraft's sons, Edward R., Michael A., and David L. Kraft, have joined him in the business. The company has locations on Breckenridge Ln., HURSTBOURNE Pkwy., Brownsboro Rd., and Dixie Hwy.

Hope L. Hollenbeck

NATIONAL CENTER FOR FAMILY LITERACY. The center is a Louisville-based nonprofit organization supporting family literacy services across the United States. It is a leader in the field of family literacy in areas such as advocacy, research, training, and policy and program development. The organization promotes a four-component program model to bring parents and children together in a learning environment: families go to school together; children learn separately while their parents are taught in nearby classrooms; later, the parents and the children work and play together so that the parents can improve their skills as teachers within the family. Parent groups provide peer support and teach new parenting strategies.

In the mid-1980s a formal plan for developing programs for children and their caregivers to learn together was created at the Kentucky Department of Education. From that plan the Parent and Child Education (PACE) program was implemented in 1986 with state funding. By 1988 PACE had gained national attention from the Ford Foundation, and Harvard University's Kennedy School of Government named it one of the ten outstanding innovations in state and local GOVERNMENT.

Educator Sharon K. Darling founded the National Center for Family Literacy in 1989 to help focus the nation's attention on the link between a family's educational success and its economic and social well-being. Darling modified the successful PACE model, creating out of it the Kenan Family Literacy Project. She included more time for parent-and-child interaction and for parents to volunteer in the schools. She also increased the training provided for teachers and added a career education feature. The Kenan Trust supplied the initial funding to establish the center in 1989. Darling has been recognized with honorary degrees for her achievement. A graduate of the UNIVERSITY OF LOUISVILLE, she was an elementary teacher in Louisville before she began teaching and supervising adult basic education programs in the Jefferson County PUBLIC SCHOOLS. She directed the Division of Adult Community Education for the Kentucky Department of Education and was there when the PACE program was developed.

In the late 1990s approximately sixty thousand families each year were enrolled in literacy programs to help entire families at more than three thousand sites throughout the nation.

NATIONAL CITY BANK, KENTUCKY. The company that has become today's NATIONAL CITY BANK, KENTUCKY, has deep roots in Louisville dating back to 1874. In January of that year, the Louisville Abstract Co. was formed by a group of prominent Louisville attorneys. An abstract company was a forerunner of today's title companies. Over the ensuing twenty-six years, Louisville Abstract evolved, as its business grew and changed, becoming Kentucky Title Savings Bank and Trust on July 10, 1900. In 1910 Kentucky Title Savings Bank and Trust acquired the First National Bank of Louisville, which had been chartered in 1863, the first national bank south of the Mason-Dixon Line.

In 1925 a trust was established to hold all of the stock of both the First National Bank of Louisville and the Kentucky Title Bank & Trust Co. The trust issued trustee certificates, which were traded on the over-the-counter market. Then in 1974 common stock was issued in exchange for all outstanding trustee certificates. This was occasioned by a reorganization, transforming the trust to a bank holding company that was named First Kentucky National Corporation.

The history of this Kentucky bank illustrates how the BANKING industry has evolved over the years. Much of this was the result of bank failures in the early '30s. In 1930 the largest bank in Kentucky, the National Bank of Kentucky, failed. In 1931 capital was added to the First National Bank of Louisville, allowing it to purchase most of the deposits of the failed National Bank of Kentucky. First National also acquired the installment loans of the temporarily closed Louisville Trust Co. The purchase of these assets and deposits created much goodwill in the community and put First National in a prominent position among local banks.

After the Depression of the 1930s and the war years of the 1940s, banks exercised great caution, under close scrutiny by regulatory authorities. The 1950s saw an easing by the regulators, allowing banks to become more competitive. During this period, First National and its affiliate the Kentucky Title Bank & Trust Co.(renamed Kentucky Trust Co.) added branch banks and new services. Consumer installment lending became popular, and First National became a leader in that area. Trust and investment management was also emphasized with a special emphasis on investment performance.

In 1960 the Lincoln Bank & Trust was acquired, and its shareholders accepted First National trustee certificates for their stock. This merger vaulted the bank to a level of about two-thirds the size of Citizens Fidelity Bank & Trust Co., the largest at that time. The 1960s was a period of reorganization and assessment of future goals. The headquarters at Fifth and Court Streets had become too small, and the decision to become the anchor tenant and part owner of a thirty-seven-story tower signaled a strategic move to assume a much higher profile. This accompanied the larger strategy of expanding banking and trust services over a broader market region. In 1972 the new tower was occupied at Fifth and MAIN Streets and the era of regional expansion began.

The 1970s saw a new, younger management team elected. In 1974 the formation of First Kentucky National Corp., succeeding the trust, resulted in an increased trading volume in the shares of the company.

In the 1970s in keeping with the plan for regional growth, strategies were developed to extend the customer base over a wider geographic region and to develop new products to meet the needs of these customers. Leasing and international banking services were among the new products. More sophisticated employee benefit programs such as retirement fund management were added to the traditional investment management products. Item processing for national retailers grew so much that a separate subsidiary, National Processing Co., was formed. It became the second largest processor of credit card sales slips in the nation. In 1984 Kentucky law was changed to permit statewide banking, and First Kentucky National took advantage of this new opportunity by acquiring banks in Ashland, Bowling Green, Owensboro, and Lexington (two in Lexington). More followed, and when the law permitted, several banks were acquired in southern Indiana.

First Kentucky grew during the 1980s from $2.8 billion in assets in 1981 to $5.1 billion in 1986. Its net income during the period increased from $22.1 million to $50.1 million. By 1986 most states, including Kentucky, had passed laws permitting reciprocal interstate banking regionally or nationally. First Kentucky National considered a strategy for growth by making acquisitions of banks in other states, but the premiums required would have diluted per share earnings to an unacceptable level. In 1987 First Kentucky merged with National City Corp. of Cleveland to become National City Bank, Kentucky.

A. Stevens Miles Jr.

NATIONAL COUNCIL OF JEWISH WOMEN, LOUISVILLE SECTION. The Louisville Section of the National Council of Jewish Women, organized by Rebecca Rosenthal Judah in 1895, has pioneered many community social services. As early as 1897, it supported the city's first summer kindergarten. Education and public affairs have always been an important segment of section activities. Study groups, begun in 1910, informed members about such issues as slum clearance, decent housing, and child labor. In 1921 the section initiated a student loan fund. During the early years, section volunteers worked at Jewish Hospital and the Jewish Children's Home and originated pilot MENTAL HEALTH projects at General Hospital, Veterans' Hospital, and Our Lady of Peace Hospital (later Caritas). Their investigations into the need for a mental health halfway house led to the establishment of Bridgehaven. In 1956 the section opened the Nearly New Shop, a consignment operation to fund social projects and provide free clothing, household items, and furniture to new Americans.

The section provides programmed tutoring at Newburg Elementary School, financing for Community Coordinated Child Care, and volunteers for the Kentucky Youth Advocates. The section offers trained volunteers to monitor domestic violence cases in the courtroom, helps run senior adult day centers, and joins with other organizations in many youth and senior citizen projects. Funding is also provided for New Americans, a program for Jewish immigrants that is operated in conjunction with Louisville's Jewish Hospital and provides free health care.

Barbara G. Zingman

NATIONAL DISTILLERS. The Kentucky Distillers & Warehouse Co. (KDWC) was formed in 1899. It was an attempt to consolidate Kentucky distilleries, similar to the large combinations of steel and oil companies but on a more modest scale. The company fell short of its goals but did gain control of many distilleries in the central part of the state. By 1911 the KDWC owned nineteen distilleries. In Louisville and Jefferson County, the KDWC owned the J.B. Wathen & Brothers Co. at Twenty-eighth St. and BROADWAY; the J.G. Mattingly Co. at N 39th and High Ave.; the American Distilling, Anderson County; Elk Run, and Nelson County Distilling Companies at Gregory and Hamilton; and the Mellwood Distillery on Mellwood Ave.

Although PROHIBITION closed all the distilleries in the United States in 1920, one of the six companies allowed to sell spirits for "medicinal purposes" was the American Medicinal Spirits Co. (AMS). The National Distillers Products Co. owned 38 percent of the stock of AMS. In 1924 National Distillers acquired the KDWC and its brands and properties. In 1929 National Distillers acquired 100 percent of AMS, including its license to sell medicinal spirits. Under the leadership of president Seton Porter, who saw that the end of Prohibition was near, National Distillers acquired as much of the aged whiskey as it could in Kentucky, Pennsylvania, Maryland, and Illinois.

When Prohibition was repealed in 1933, National Distillers controlled about half of the spirits in the United States. It also owned many old and prestigious brands, such as Old Taylor, Old Grand Dad, Old Crow, Sunnybrook, and Hill and Hill. The Jefferson County area saw a huge investment by National Distillers in the period after Prohibition as it opened the Sunnybrook Distillery at Twenty-eighth and Broadway, the Hill and Hill Distillery in SHIVELY, and the Old Grand Dad Distillery at Lexington Rd. and Payne St. In 1940 the Old Grand Dad Distillery built a huge brick storage warehouse capable of holding 140,000 barrels of whiskey—almost seven times the capacity of a typical whiskey warehouse. These sites contained DISTILLING, aging, and bottling operations that employed several hundred people.

During the 1940s National, along with Schenley, Seagram, and Hiram Walker, was one of the Big Four distillers, which controlled 70 percent of the bourbon and rye whiskeys in the United States. In 1943 National acquired the Glencoe Distillery in Shively. This period of growth lasted until the late 1960s; then bourbon sales began to decline, causing an industry-wide consolidation. The smaller, older distilleries were closed and their operations moved to the larger, more modern plants. By the late 1970s, National closed all of its distilleries in Jefferson County, consolidating their operations at its distilleries in Frankfort. In the early 1980s, a group of investors bought the Hill and Hill distillery in Shively and during the brief period of their ownership, it was converted to a fuel alcohol plant. In 1987 National Distillers was sold to American Brands, which also owned the Jim Beam distilleries and brands. National Distillers was dissolved, and its brands and properties became part of Jim Beam Brands.

Michael R. Veach

NATIONAL REGISTER OF HISTORIC PLACES.

The National Register of Historic Places is the federal government's official list of the nation's cultural resources worthy of preservation. When a historic property is listed on the National Register, the property is considered in the planning for federally assisted projects, the owners may qualify for certain federal tax benefits, and the property may qualify for federal assistance when funds are available. Qualifying properties must be at least fifty years old and must exhibit integrity. Potentially eligible properties include districts, sites, buildings, structures, and objects that are significant in American history, ARCHITECTURE, ARCHAEOLOGY, engineering, and culture.

The city of Louisville and Jefferson County both have Historic Landmarks and Preservation Districts Commissions that administer the National Register program at the local level. Their work has resulted in the listing of more than thirteen thousand properties all over metropolitan Louisville, earning one of the highest rankings in the nation in total number of National Register listings. They include a broad spectrum of property types and settings—for example, rural farmsteads, urban residential enclaves, industrial and church-related complexes, and civic structures. Though the vast majority of the structures have been listed as elements of National Register Districts, there is also a wealth of buildings in Louisville and Jefferson County that have been individually recognized as significant.

National Register Districts in Louisville and Jefferson County, as of 1998

Anchorage
Audubon Park
B.F. Avery Industrial
Bowman Field
Brook and Breckinridge Streets
Butchertown
Cherokee Triangle
Clifton
Crescent Hill
Fifth and Market Streets
Gardencourt
Glenview
Green Tree Manor
Harrods Creek
Highlands
Limerick
Lower W Market St.
Marlow Place Bungalow District
Middletown
Nitta Yuma
North Old Louisville First St.
Oakdale
Old Louisville
Olmsted Park System of Louisville
Parkland
Phoenix Hill
Portland
Preston–St. Catherine St.
Russell
Savoy (demolished)
Second and Breckinridge Streets
Second and Market Streets (demolished)
Smoketown
Southern Heights–Beechmont
Third and Jefferson Streets
Third and Market Streets (demolished)
Tyler Settlement Rural Historic District
University of Louisville Belknap Campus
W Main St.
100 W Main St.

See Leslee F. Keys and Donna M. Neary, *Historic Jefferson County* (Louisville 1992); Louisville Historic Landmarks and Preservation Districts Commission Collection, Louisville Free Public Library, Main Branch.

Joanne Weeter

NATIONAL SOCIETY OF THE SONS OF THE AMERICAN REVOLUTION.

The National Society of the Sons of the American Revolution (SAR), headquartered in Louisville, is a hereditary, patriotic, educational, and historical organization of more than twenty-five thousand male descendants of those patriots who, during the American Revolution, rendered loyal service to the cause of winning our independence from Great Britain. The SAR consists of fifty state societies with more than 450 local or regional chapters. The Louisville-Thruston Chapter is located in Louisville. There are also societies in France, the United Kingdom, Germany, and Switzerland.

The National Society was formed in Fraunces Tavern in New York City on April 30, 1889, on the one-hundredth anniversary of the inauguration of George Washington as president of the United States. At this time similar organizations existed at the state level in fourteen states. The National Society of the SAR was incorporated on January 17, 1890, in Connecticut and chartered by the U.S. Congress on June 9, 1906. The first national congress was held at the GALT HOUSE in Louisville on April 30, 1890.

The SAR national headquarters, which has been located in Louisville since 1979, is at Fourth and Kentucky Streets. From 1927 to 1979 the national headquarters was in Washington, D.C. Before that the business of the society was conducted in the homes and businesses of the national officers and the SAR national headquarters was the president-general's home.

Any male is eligible for membership in SAR who is at least eighteen years of age, a citizen of good repute in his community, and a lineal descendant of a person who was at all times unfailing in loyalty to and who rendered active service to the cause of American independence.

Each state society is represented by a trustee to the national society. The national trustees meet at the headquarters in the fall and in the spring and at the annual national congress. The national congresses are held in major cities during June and July. Every several years the national congress is in Louisville. During the trustees' meeting, SAR committees responsible for various programs and operations convene.

The programs of the National Society of the SAR cover a wide range of activities that are patriotic, historical, and educational. Some programs are for youth (orations, essays, Eagle Scouts). Others recognize citizens' outstanding achievements and patriotism or bravery and self-sacrifice; still others recognize outstanding students and teachers of American history. There are programs to mark the graves of Revolutionary War soldiers, to maintain a grave registry, to highlight historical celebrations and places, and to monitor the quality and accuracy of textbook coverage of the history of the American Revolutionary War period and evaluate how this history is taught in schools. Other programs assist veterans in Veterans Administration HOSPITALS. The *SAR Magazine* is published quarterly.

Bruce Baird Butler

NATIONAL TOBACCO WORKS.

In the fall of 1879, a group of individuals combined their divergent talents to form the National Tobacco Works (or Pfingst, Doerhoefer & Co., as it was also known), which became a dynamic TOBACCO manufacturer. The senior partner of this plug manufacturer was Ferdinand J. Pfingst (1835–1901), who was a pharmacist by profession. He was the first manufacturer to use chemistry to make the flavor for tobacco. Joining with him were his brothers John (1849–1903) and Basil (1850–1923) Doerhoefer, who had been intimately familiar with tobacco manufacturing from their youth.

Almost from its inception, National's growth was "the most phenomenal in the history of the tobacco trade." (*Louisville Commercial,* Feb. 27, 1891)Its tremendous growth was due in part to the partners' good fortune in starting a business at the very beginning of the era of trademarked, mass-produced, and nationally distributed products and in part to their foresight in taking advantage of this new business environment. Pfingst "showed the rarest business ability. His methods were bold and daring. . . . Competition was not dodged . . . [but] prices were slashed down in reckless style. State after State was conquered by the enterprising firm... no business enterprise started in this city ever grew with more rapidity and apparent solidity than the National Tobacco Works." (*Louisville Commercial,* Feb. 27, 1891) It became one of the most profitable tobacco manufacturers ever established, in the nineteenth century.

The firm's growth can also be traced to its unique use of chemistry to flavor its tobacco. For instance, Piper Heidsieck—the brand by which the firm was "known in every city in the country and even abroad"(the City of Louisville, 51)—made use of the very best burley tobacco wrapped with spirit-cured wrappers from which all poisonous nicotine was removed. Other brands included Newsboy, People's Choice, Punch, and Battle Ax. National effectively marketed these brands by using attractive packaging and alluring advertisements, which were hallmarks of the new consumer age.

By 1891, when the partnership incorporated, National's factory, at 1806 W MAIN St., had expanded until its immense size made it one of the largest tobacco plants in the country and the largest in Louisville. By being in Louisville, this factory was well situated in the world's largest tobacco market, where it saved freight rates on raw material by being located at the base of supplies. The factory produced 6 million pounds of tobacco annually and employed five hundred workers. At the time, plug tobacco constituted over half of all tobacco manufactured.

In 1890 James B. Duke (1857–1925) organized the American Tobacco Co., which consolidated the fledgling cigarette industry. Because its brands showed larger profits than any others in the market, Duke decided to acquire National as American's first step into the important plug industry. National's four owners were paid at least $2.2 million (and perhaps as much as four times that amount).

After the sale, the owners remained as managers of the National Tobacco Works branch of American Tobacco. Under their continued guidance, National's growth was exponential. At the decade's end, several additional factories had been constructed, and National had increased its annual production to 27 million pounds of tobacco, which made it the country's largest plug manufacturer, with control of one-seventh of the U.S. plug market.

In 1911 American's tobacco monopoly was broken up by the federal government, and National became an undivided part of a much reduced American Tobacco.

See Robert K. Heimann, *Tobacco and Americans* (New York 1960); Jefferson County, Kentucky, Corporation Book, vol. 6, 568–70; J. Stoddard Johnston, ed., *Memorial History of Louisville* (New York, 1896); Richard Kluger, *Ashes to Ashes* (New York 1996); *The City of Louisville and Its Resources* (Louisville 1892); *Courier-Journal,* Feb. 27, 1891; Aug. 4, 1903; *Louisville Commercial,* Feb. 27, 1891; June 18, 1901; *Louisville Times,* June 18, 1901.

William Pfingst Carrell II

NAVAL ORDNANCE. Naval Ordnance Station Louisville, located between Southside Dr. and Strawberry Ln. in southern Louisville, provided equipment and maintenance to the U.S. Navy for more than fifty years before it was turned over to private industry. Ground was broken on January 29, 1941. The Louisville site for the ordnance-producing plant was chosen, among other reasons, because the inland location was less vulnerable to enemy air attacks.

Naval Ordnance was commissioned on October 1, 1941, and began production of gun mounts and torpedo tubes as well as other naval ordnance for the war effort. A private company, Westinghouse Electric Corp., held the contract for the work for the duration of the war. During peak production times, Naval Ordnance employed forty-two hundred people. The Westinghouse contract ended after the war in 1946, and the navy assumed command of Naval Ordnance. After WORLD WAR II, production and the number of employees decreased. During the KOREAN WAR, employment again rose and production increased.

The 1950s and 1960s saw changes in employee numbers and production output. Repair of navy equipment, both in the station and through sending personnel overseas to repair equipment on-site, kept the plant operating. The station manufactured ordnance, researched and developed gun weapon systems, and provided fleet technical and logistics support. Naval Ordnance continued to serve as a unique production facility for the navy until the 1990s.

After the end of the Cold War, Naval Ordnance, like many other defense companies, shifted production. On August 15, 1996, Naval Ordnance was officially turned over to United Defense and Hughes Missile Systems, private companies that assumed the role of contractor to the navy. The name of the site was changed from the Louisville Naval Ordnance Station to the Greater Louisville Technology Center.

Naval Ordnance was the first such facility to shift to a private operation that continued to supply services to the military under contract, but that survival has been at the expense of a much diminished level of operation. In the early 1990s, the ordnance station employed 1,850 people. In June 1999, the primary tenants, defense contractors United Defense and Raytheon Systems Co., accounted for only about 670 employees; there were also about 200 non-defense-related employees. One-third of the facility's manufacturing space—about 500,000 square feet—was vacant. In addition, the park developed environmental hazards because the buildings, some dating to the 1940s and 1950s, became subject to state and local building codes.

The park leases the property from the navy under an agreement that expires in 2004. To increase development and solve current problems, the authority(which manages the facility as the Technology Park of Greater Public Louisville) wants to either own the property or gain long-term control, which would allow it to obtain financing for development. Actions are also being taken to replicate the kind of skilled industrial jobs the facility offered under naval command, increase the number of positions by inviting new tenants to the park, and remedy environmental dangers.

See *Courier-Journal,* Oct. 10, Aug. 20, 1996; "Business & Industry: Naval Ordnance," Record Group 113, University of Louisville Archives and Records Center; Mike Ward Papers, Papers Relating to Naval Ordnance, University of Louisville Archives and Records Center.

Margaret L. Merrick

NEIGHBORHOOD HOUSE. In 1895 two Louisville theology students, Archibald Hill and W.E. Wilkins, invited future Nobel Peace Prize–winner Jane Addams, the founder of Chicago's Hull House, and Dr. Graham Taylor of Chicago Commons to visit the Louisville area and share their ideas and vision on the subject of social settlements. Lucy Belknap was in attendance and offered financial assistance to aid in the first local experiment in settlement house work. With Hill at the helm, by 1896 Kentucky's first settlement house was in operation at Jefferson and PRESTON Streets, east of the central business district. The sharing became mutual, "one neighbor shar[ing] his knowledge of life with another." NEIGHBORHOOD HOUSE's early neighborhood was settled by newly arriving immigrants, so English and citizenship classes, kindergarten, and legal aid were offered to help the neighbors assimilate into a new country. A new site, donated by BELKNAP, was located on S First at Walnut St. (Muhammad Ali Blvd.) and was in use by 1903. In 1996 the area, now cleared, was renamed Settlement House Park.

FRANCES INGRAM guided Neighborhood House from 1905 to 1939 and broadened the sphere of its influence. Under her leadership, the agency lobbied for labor laws for women (1911) and children (1912); developed social settlement training, which was later incorporated into the UNIVERSITY OF LOUISVILLE's social work curriculum; and cooperated with local agencies to form the Welfare League (1917), now METRO UNITED WAY.

In 1963 Neighborhood House relocated to 225 N Twenty-fifth St. in PORTLAND, offering programs for residents of all ages, from the first preschool to senior citizens' activities. With educational enhancement and cultural enrichment as cornerstones, Neighborhood House continues adapting its programming to meet Portland's changing needs, including planned year-round preschool. It also works to improve

Neighborhood House, 428 South First Street, 1921.

communication skills and provide conflict resolution training for teens, affordable summer day camp for children of single working parents, hot evening meals for children and teens, daily lunch and activities for seniors, and piano lessons.

Neighborhood House has collaborated with Portland's other youth-service agencies to prevent duplication and to better utilize resources and promote services targeting the underserved youth populations (1996). Drawing on the community's sense of tradition and pride, Neighborhood House developed the Portland Hall of Fame, into which inspirational Portlanders are inducted annually as role models and motivators for future generations of young people (1997).

See *Courier-Journal,* May 2, 1897; Jan. 20, 1955; March 10, Sept. 29, 1993; Sept. 28, 1994; May 15, 22, 29; July 31; August 14; Nov. 20, 1996; May 21, 1997; George H. Yater, *Two Hundred Years at the Falls of the Ohio* (Louisville 1979, 1987); Wade Hall and Nancy Jones, *Louisville 200: Reflections of a City* (Louisville 1978).

Jean McVickar

NEIGHBORHOODS. Louisvillians have historically demonstrated a strong sense of neighborhood identity. It is a tendency that has roots in the early days of settlement and reflects the dynamic interaction of demographic, technological, economic, social, and political patterns. When Louisville's first settlers moved from CORN ISLAND to Fort-on-Shore during the winter of 1778–79, they hung together out of a common need for defense against the dangers of frontier life. But as urban life became more complex, geographically definable neighborhoods that demonstrated a mixture of characteristics proliferated.

Louisville's earliest neighborhoods were incorporated river towns, including the present central business district, PORTLAND, and Shippingport. With economies based largely on river commerce, all three had riverfronts devoted to warehousing, draying, and other businesses that served shipping interests. They also had gridiron street plans, which made the sale of lots easy and economically efficient. Both commercial and residential lots tended to be deep and narrow. This compact development kept the urban area accessible and reflected the fact that most residents walked to and from work.

Setbacks were shallow, fostering an active street life. Despite their narrow lots, these neighborhoods demonstrated a mixture of housing styles, with people of greater economic means building their homes on two or more lots. Both Portland and Shippingport, which served as commercial centers below the FALLS OF THE OHIO, were strongly influenced by FRENCH immigrants such as LOUIS AND JOHN TARASCON during the early nineteenth century.

Between 1830 and 1860 Louisville experienced an influx of German and IRISH immigrants. Both groups had an indelible influence on the city's culture, but the GERMANS were particularly successful in stamping their ethnic character on their neighborhoods, notably BUTCHERTOWN, GERMANTOWN, and Uptown, known today as the PHOENIX HILL neighborhood. All three neighborhoods resembled Portland and Shippingport in basic physical character: they had gridiron or modified gridiron street plans; deep, narrow lots; shallow setbacks; and a mixture of housing styles. Unlike the river towns, none of these neighborhoods were ever incorporated before their annexation by Louisville. What made them distinctive were German businesses and cultural organizations such as Evangelical, Reformed, Lutheran, and Roman Catholic churches; German-dominated industries, such as MEATPACKING in Butchertown and brewing in Germantown and Uptown; and institutions like German-language NEWSPAPERS, physical culture clubs, and singing societies.

The city's social and economic elite had their special neighborhoods, notably downtown and the Southern Extension, now known as OLD LOUISVILLE. As early as 1830, affluent business and professional leaders erected large, stylish homes along Green (LIBERTY), Walnut (Muhammad Ali Blvd.), Chestnut, and BROADWAY between First and Seventh Streets. Homes accommodated carriages and included servants' quarters. Moderate to deep setbacks provided isolation from street noise, and land use was homogeneous since the residents had transportation such as carriages that enabled them to work and shop outside their immediate neighborhood. As commercial and institutional development encroached upon the downtown residential district near the time of the CIVIL WAR, the city's elite moved south of Broadway. Between 1860 and 1910 the area bounded roughly by Broadway, Floyd, and Sixth Streets and the present UNIVERSITY OF LOUISVILLE campus became the city's most prestigious neighborhood. Most residents occupied large two- and three-story homes, often designed by the leading local architects in the most fashionable styles and with modern utilities. In addition to the wealthy whites in the area, a number of AFRICAN AMERICANS and poor whites also lived in the area's small enclaves and along the alleyways.

The post–CIVIL WAR era also saw the development of what some scholars have called "zones of emergence"—neighborhoods such as SHELBY PARK, SCHNITZELBURG, and Limerick—that were settled by the children and grandchildren of immigrants. Laid out in a gridiron or modified gridiron street pattern with deep, narrow lots, these neighborhoods physically resembled the older immigrant neighborhoods. They also had their characteristic ethnic churches, businesses, and social institutions. However, the setbacks tended to be somewhat deeper, the land use became more homogeneous, and a broader range of housing styles and scales became available. These differences reflected growing social and economic diversity within the ethnic community.

Along with the zones of emergence came industrial neighborhoods such as MERIWETHER (FORT HILL), St. Joseph, Parkhill, and CALIFORNIA. Dominated physically and economically by heavy industry, these neighborhoods attracted industrial workers who occupied small, often identical cottages and bungalows erected by speculative builders. The setbacks are shallow to moderate; though the lots are still narrow, they are not so deep as those in older parts of the city.

Unique among postbellum neighborhoods

was Smoketown. Situated between Broadway and Shelby Park east of the Southern Extension, it was settled from the beginning by African Americans. Like most other nineteenth-century neighborhoods, Smoketown was platted in a gridiron, but the lots were narrower and shallower than other nearby neighborhoods. Another critical difference was that the developers retained ownership of the land and leased it to the residents, who erected small, wooden shotgun cottages at their own expense. Unfortunately, with much of their capital tied up in their houses, the residents frequently were unable to make their lease payments when the economy turned sour. As a result, they lost both their lot and their house, creating a substantial degree of residential and social instability in the neighborhood.

The decades between 1890 and 1930 marked the era of the streetcar suburb. Neighborhoods such as Cherokee Triangle and Crescent Hill in the East End, Beechmont and Southern Heights in the South End, and Parkland and Shawnee in the West End developed on the edges of Cherokee, Iroquois, and Shawnee Parks; an electrified streetcar system provided access. These neighborhoods were developed largely by professional real estate developers who used a variety of legal and marketing tools to ensure the high degree of uniformity favored by their middle-class market. Street patterns depended on topography, but most neighborhoods had large lots with deep setbacks, and the homes frequently were designed by architects or contractors using popular pattern books.

The advent of the automobile during the early twentieth century and its mass ownership after World War I, combined with new curvilinear residential development concepts advanced by planning pioneers such as Frederick Law Olmsted, gave rise to Arcadian neighborhoods such as Audubon Park, itself an incorporated city surrounded by Louisville, and Highlands neighborhoods such as Douglass, Belknap, Cherokee Gardens, and Braeview. The developers of such neighborhoods attempted to combine rural ambiance with urban amenities. Lots tended to be wide and shallow but with relatively deep setbacks. Homes often included attached garages and usually only a small porch, if any, reflecting people's increasing dependence on the automobile and the disappearance of street-oriented social activity. The latter tendency increased after World War II, with the growing popularity of television and the availability of air-conditioning in warm weather. Although it appealed initially to an upper-middle-class market, this pattern of neighborhood development prevailed across class lines during the postwar era, as the gridiron street pattern virtually disappeared, regardless of the topography.

Another postwar phenomenon was the proliferation of incorporated suburban neighborhoods and the suburbanization of historic unincorporated communities that had once served as rural market centers. By 1990 Jefferson County contained nearly one hundred fourth-, fifth-, and sixth-class cities. These "republics in miniature," as noted urban scholar Robert C. Wood dubbed them, provide a narrow range of municipal services such as police protection and garbage collection, while relying on volunteer fire departments for fire protection and on metropolitan agencies for water, sewerage and drainage, parks and recreation, and other urban services. In addition, fourth-class cities such as St. Matthews, Shively, Jeffersontown, and Douglass Hills have legislative authority for zoning. Regardless of class, however, these suburban neighborhoods use their corporate status to prevent annexation by Louisville. But except for the residential markets for which they were developed, these neighborhoods differ very little in their overall physical character from comparable neighborhoods in the city of Louisville or in unincorporated suburbs like Okolona, Fern Creek, Valley Station, and Pleasure Ridge Park, and Fairdale.

In the late twentieth century, many of Louisville's oldest neighborhoods went through a revitalization movement, often coupled with historic preservation, housing rehabilitation, and economic restructuring movements. In the early 1960s, through the leadership of groups such as Old Louisville Association and Restoration, Inc. residents of the former Southern Extension began rehabilitating the stylish old homes south of Broadway and renamed the neighborhood Old Louisville. The Neighborhood Development Corp., organized by area churches later in the decade, fostered a broader program of historic preservation, the enforcement of building codes, and the development of church-based social ministries.

During the War on Poverty of the late 1960s, the Louisville and Jefferson County Community Action Commission initiated neighborhood revitalization and housing improvement efforts in the Portland, Smoketown, and Russell neighborhoods in western Louisville. In 1966, in response to growing industrial encroachment, several residents and community institutions in Butchertown formed Butchertown Inc. and persuaded the Louisville and Jefferson County Planning Commission to downzone a large portion of the neighborhood. This encouraged the preservation and rehabilitation of much of the neighborhood's historic housing stock.

After the 1974 tornado, neighborhood action in Crescent Hill and Bonnycastle helped prevent the rezoning of damaged single-family dwellings for apartments and laid the foundation for other neighborhood improvements. In the old Uptown neighborhood, representatives of twenty-three businesses came together in 1976 to form the Phoenix Hill Association, which spearheaded a long-term effort to reverse the neighborhood's economic and residential deterioration. By the late 1970s, residents across the city were engaged in programs ranging from festivals and social action to rehabilitation and preservation designed to improve the physical structure and social quality of neighborhood life. Two decades later, neighborhood development and revitalization were fundamental components in the agendas of both city and county governments.

Many neighborhoods have conflicting names and boundaries, one traditional and historical and one determined by an act of local government. When the federal government switched from categorical grants to community development block grants in 1974, aldermen and city officials decided upon neighborhood names and defined boundaries. Although many reflected traditional names such as Butchertown and Portland, some designations were changed, such as from Oakdale to Wyandotte. This work has attempted to recover and list all names, past and present, and uses the 1974 boundaries to designate the neighborhoods' areas.

See Carl E. Kramer, "A History of Eastern Louisville," in *Louisville Survey—East Report* (Louisville 1979); Carl E. Kramer, "The City-Building Process: Urbanization in Central and Southern Louisville, 1772–1932" (Ph.D. diss., University of Toledo, 1980); George H. Yater, "Neighborhoods," *Louisville* 25 (Sept. 1975): 38–44; George H. Yater, "The Growth and Regrowth of Little Worlds in City Universe," *Louisville* 31 (May 1980): 22–26. Robert C. Wood, *Suburbia: Its People and Their Politics* (Boston 1958).

Carl E. Kramer

NELSON, WILLIAM (b Mason County, Kentucky, September 27, 1824; d Louisville, September 29, 1862). Military officer. William Nelson was the son of an eminent Maysville physician, Dr. Thomas W. Nelson, and Francis (Doniphan) Nelson. He was educated at the Maysville Academy and the U.S. Naval Academy. In 1840 Nelson was commissioned midshipman in the U.S. Navy. In the Mexican War, he participated in the landing of Winfield Scott's forces at Vera Cruz. During the shelling of that city, the captain of the USS *Scourge* commended Nelson for his command of a gun crew. Commissioned lieutenant on April 18, 1855, Nelson continued his naval career until the eve of the Civil War.

In the months following the firing on Fort Sumter, the Kentucky legislature officially adopted a position of neutrality. During this period, Nelson was authorized by Pres. Abraham Lincoln on July 1, 1861, to encourage the enlistment of volunteers without violating Kentucky's declared neutrality. To facilitate the enlistment, Nelson organized Camp Dick Robinson in Garrard County, Kentucky. On September 16, 1861, Nelson was appointed brigadier general of volunteers and began active campaigning in eastern Kentucky. In skirmishes at Ivy Mountain and Piketon (Pikeville), Nelson's men successfully drove the Confederate troops from the region.

Nelson was assigned command of the Fourth Division of the Army of the Ohio under Gen. DON CARLOS BUELL. A large man, standing over six feet tall and weighing nearly three hundred pounds, Nelson was a strict disciplinarian and earned the nickname Bull. He proved to be a reliable commander in the Army of the Ohio. General Nelson led the first reinforcements from Buell's army to arrive near Pittsburg Landing, Tennessee, on April 6, 1862. On the second day of the Battle of Shiloh, Nelson's troops were actively engaged in defeating the Confederates. His division participated in the siege of Corinth, Mississippi, and on July 19, 1862, he was promoted to major general of volunteers.

During the Confederate invasion of Kentucky in the fall of 1862, General Buell ordered Nelson to Louisville to take command of the defenses of the state. On August 30, 1862, a subordinate of General Nelson provoked a skirmish near Richmond, Kentucky. General Nelson arrived on the battlefield late in the day to find his troops defeated and retreating in disorder. Nelson was wounded while trying to rally his routed forces. He returned to Louisville after the battle and established his headquarters at the GALT HOUSE. There he set about organizing the numerous recruits from Ohio, Indiana, and other midwestern states who were pouring into the city.

On the morning of September 29, 1862, Nelson quarreled with a subordinate, Brig. Gen. Jefferson C. Davis of Indiana. Soon thereafter, a second confrontation occurred on the first floor of the Galt House, during which Davis shot and mortally wounded Nelson. Their disagreement was professional, based upon their dissimilar backgrounds and the fact that Davis was regular army under the command of a former naval officer. Nelson believed Davis to be incompetent. Nelson died about eight o'clock that morning.

He was buried at CAVE HILL CEMETERY, but his remains were moved to Camp Dick Robinson on August 21, 1863. At the request of his family, his remains were subsequently moved to the Maysville Cemetery.

See James B. Fry, *Killed by a Brother Soldier* (New York 1885); E. Hannaford, *The Story of a Regiment* (Cincinnati 1868); Ezra J. Warner, *Generals in Blue* (Baton Rouge 1964); Robert Emmett McDowell, *City of Conflict: Louisville in the Civil War* (Louisville 1962).

David R. Deatrick Jr.

NEW ALBANY. Situated below the FALLS OF THE OHIO and across the river from western Louisville, NEW ALBANY was founded in 1813 by Connecticut natives Joel, Abner, and Nathaniel Scribner, who had arrived from New York City a short time earlier. The three men settled north of the OHIO RIVER and bought 826 acres of land for $10 per acre.

The Scribners named the town for Albany, New York. The original town site in Clark's Grant was purchased from John Paul of Madison, Indiana. When the town was laid out, the Scribners gave sixty lots for school purposes and sixty for church purposes. The site was plotted by surveyor John K. Graham, who employed a regular gridiron orientation toward the river. High St., later renamed Main, was the major business and residential artery. It was paralleled by Market, Spring, Elm, and Oak Streets, and all five were bisected by State St.

The proprietors took pains to assure their own economic fortunes by declaring their perpetual right to offer ferry service to Louisville and conducting an extensive ADVERTISING campaign to sell lots. Likewise, Abner, a millwright, devoted considerable effort to a steam sawmill. But they also took care to provide for major public needs by reserving space for markets, schools, and churches.

In 1817 New Albany was incorporated as a town in Clark County. Two years later, the village and some surrounding territory were carved away from Clark and Harrison Counties and reorganized as Floyd County, with New Albany as its county seat. The county probably was named for DAVIS FLOYD, a prominent politician who was the first circuit judge. Joel Scribner was the first county clerk. In the 1820 census, New Albany had a POPULATION of about 1,000, and Floyd County had 2,776 residents.

New Albany quickly became an important boat construction and shipping center. Blessed with an excellent source of timber from the nearby KNOBS, shipbuilders attracted the skilled workers necessary to construct high-quality river craft. Four boats had been built and launched in New Albany by 1820. Between 1817 and 1867, New Albany yards such as the Jacob Dowerman and Thomas Humphreys yard and the Peter Tellon and Jacob Alford yard built more than 350 STEAMBOATS, including such fabled vessels as the *Eclipse*, the *A.L. Shotwell*, and the *Robert E. Lee*.

Unfortunately, because of New Albany's position below the Falls of the Ohio, local shipbuilders specialized in craft designed for Southern rivers. When the CIVIL WAR came, Southern steamboat owners not only ceased ordering vessels from Yankee builders but also refused to complete payment for boats already in service, sending the industry into a long-term decline.

Meanwhile, New Albany became a southern Indiana rail terminus. The creation of the New Albany & Salem Railroad in 1847 and its extension to Michigan City, Indiana, in 1854 opened new opportunities for interstate rail transportation. In 1859 the New Albany & Salem became the Louisville, New Albany & Chicago, popularly known as the Monon. During the late 1860s the Jeffersonville, Madison & Indianapolis laid track to New Albany. This line, along with a seven-mile stretch of track between New Albany and the Ohio & Mississippi Railroad at Watson in Clark County, gave New Albany an east-west connection via the Baltimore & Ohio. The completion of the Edwardsville Tunnel in 1881 by the Louisville, Evansville & St. Louis Airline Railroad gave the city access to national markets by four major RAILROADS. The opening of the KENTUCKY AND INDIANA BRIDGE in 1887 provided cross-river freight and interurban passenger connections with Louisville.

By the mid–nineteenth century, New Albany was Indiana's largest city, with a population of 8,181, which included substantial numbers of AFRICAN AMERICANS and German and Irish immigrants. The city also had acquired many of the cultural and social trappings of a thriving metropolis, including schools, churches, and mercantile houses. Indiana

Market Street, New Albany, Indiana, from Pearl Street, 1922.

Asbury Female College, established in 1852 and later renamed DePauw College for Young Women, was a forerunner of DePauw University in Greencastle. New Albany High School, opened in 1853, was Indiana's second public high school. One of the city's most popular politicians of the era was ASHBEL P. WILLARD, a young lawyer and state legislator who was elected lieutenant governor of Indiana in 1852 and governor in 1856.

The wealth generated by New Albany's rise to prominence created an elite class who erected many handsome residences along Main and MARKET Streets near downtown. Between 1830 and 1880 the city's commercial, professional, and industrial leaders, such as merchant William S. Culbertson, Dr. Asahel Clapp, congressman Michael C. Kerr, and industrialist WASHINGTON C. DEPAUW, built stately homes in the Federal, Italianate, Greek Revival, Gothic Revival, French Second Empire, and other Victorian styles.

After the war a host of new industrial enterprises sprang up. Many ancillary industries that had served the shipbuilders, such as foundries, machine shops, architectural ironworks, and cabinet and furniture makers, had found other customers for their products, especially during the war when the federal GOVERNMENT was a strong consumer. Although the Civil War crippled New Albany's steamboat industry, the city's industrial ECONOMY remained strong. This was the first of many economic setbacks the city was to receive. In each case, however, there has been some new development to absorb the shock.

In 1865 John B. Ford established the Star Glass Works (later known as the American Plate Glass Works) with financial assistance from his wealthy cousin, Washington C. DePauw. It was the largest glassworks west of Pittsburgh. Ford moved to Pennsylvania after the crash of 1873 and built a plant that eventually became part of Libbey-Owens-Ford in Toledo, Ohio. Meanwhile, American Plate Glass flourished under DePauw's management until fuel shortages forced the firm's relocation in 1893. The discovery of natural gas in northern Indiana and the incentives offered glass manufacturers by cities in that area helped kill off the New Albany GLASS INDUSTRY, which was the economic backbone of the town until about 1892.

Other prominent manufacturers established during the postwar period included New Albany Woolen Mills, Ohio Falls Iron Works, New Albany Forge Works, New Albany Rail Mill, and New Albany Hosiery Mills. The depression that followed the panic of 1893 severely damaged New Albany's industrial economy. But the city bounced back during the early twentieth century, becoming a national center for the plywood and veneer industry, with seven plants by 1923. The 1920 census listed New Albany as southern Indiana's second-largest city (behind Evansville) and the state's fifteenth-largest, with a population of 22,992. The GREAT DEPRESSION and the 1937 flood caused many to leave the city, and the 1940 census actually recorded a loss of more than 400 residents from the 1930 count. The economy rebounded during World War II, fueled by the military demand for wood products. That economic expansion also generated considerable population growth during and after the war. However, most of the new population growth occurred outside the city, resulting in a 1956 annexation move that more than doubled the city's area, increased its population by more than 8,000, and raised it from third-class to second-class status. In 1963 the city's population was about 40,000.

The postwar years saw many physical, economic, and transportation improvements. Floyd Memorial Hospital opened in 1953 and was followed in 1954 by the completion of a 3<1/2>-mile section of flood wall. In 1959 the Pillsbury Co. built a new plant on the city's northern edge; the City-County Building at W First and Spring was dedicated in October 1961; and the Sherman Minton Bridge, connecting Louisville and New Albany via Interstate 64, opened to traffic in 1962.

Since 1970 New Albany has focused on downtown revitalization, HISTORIC PRESERVATION, and economic development. The successful development of the New Albany–Floyd County Industrial Park has expanded the community's economic diversity and tax base. The relocation of INDIANA UNIVERSITY SOUTHEAST to a new campus on the northern edge of New Albany was an economic and educational boon to the city. In 1971 the former CARNEGIE LIBRARY became the Floyd County Museum, and in 1983 several blocks of the city's once-palatial residential district along Main and Market Streets were designated the Mansion Row NATIONAL REGISTER OF HISTORIC PLACES District. Among the historic homes (all located on Main St.) are the Joel Scribner house, the Indiana State Bank, the Culbertson Old Ladies Home, the Washington C. DePauw House, the Samuel Culbertson House, the Phineas M. Kent House, and the Michael C. Kerr House.

Despite such progress, New Albany has experienced a recent loss in population. Declining household size and movement to the suburban fringe appear to have been the primary forces behind this trend. In 1960 the population of Floyd County stood at 51,397, with New Albany's 37,812 citizens accounting for 73.6 percent of the total. In 1970 the Floyd County population was 55,622 and New Albany's was 38,402. In 1980 Floyd County had 61,169 residents and New Albany 37,103. By 1990 the county's population had grown to 64,404, while New Albany's 36,322 residents comprised only 56.4 percent of the total. In 1996 the population of Floyd County was 70,746 and New Albany's was 38,224.

NEW ALBANY MAYORS

Name	*Term*	*Party*
P.M. Dorsey	1839–40	Whig
Dr. Shephard Whitman	1840–43	Whig
Silas Overturf	1843–44	Whig
James Collins	1844	Whig
William Clark	1844–47	Whig
William M. Weir	1847–49 1850–52	Whig
John R. Franklin	1849–50	Democrat
Alexander S. Burnett Sr.	1852–53 1859–63	Democrat
Joseph A. Moffatt	1853–55	Know-Nothing
Jonathan D. Kelso	1855–56	Republican
Franklin Warren	1856–59	ran on Citizen ticket
Dumar M. Hooper	1863–65	Republican, but he ran on Reform ticket
William L. Sanderson (Died in office)	1865–68	Union Democrat
William Hart (Finished Sanderson's term and was elected to a two-year term)	1868–71	Democrat
Thomas Kunkle (Died in office)	1871–74	Democrat
William B. Richardson (Finished Kunkle's term of office)	1874–75 1875–77	Democrat
Solomon Malbon	1877–79	Democrat
Bela C. Kent	1879–83	Republican?
John J. Richards	1883–89	Republican
Morris McDonald	1889–92	Republican
William A. Broecker	1892–94	Democrat
Thomas W. Armstrong	1894–98	Republican
Edward Crumbo	1898–1902	Democrat
Frank L. Shrader	1902–4	Republican
William V. Grose (Impeached and removed from office)	1904–6	Democrat
Jacob Best	1907–11	Republican
Newton Green	1912–15 1928–31	Democrat
Robert Morris	1916–27	Republican
Charles B. McLinn	1932–35	Republican
Jacob G. Hauswald	1936–39	Democrat
Noble Mitchell (Died in office)	1940–42	Republican
C. Robert Brooks	1942–43	
Raymond Jaegers	1943–46	Republican
Irvin Streepy	1947–48	Republican
Pralle Erni	1948–63	Democrat
Garnett Inman	1964–71	Republican
Warren V. Nash	1972–75	Democrat
Robert L. Real	1975–83	Republican
Charles Hunter	1984–87	Democrat
Robert L. Real	1987–91	Republican
Douglas B. England	1992–99	Democrat
Regina Overton	2000-	Republican

See Betty Lou Amster, *New Albany on the Ohio: Historical Review, 1813–1963* (New Albany, Ind., 1963).

Carl E. Kramer

NEWBURG. An unincorporated residential community of 21,650 residents (1990 census), Newburg occupies the area roughly between Poplar Level Rd., Shepherdsville Rd., Newburg Rd., and Indian Tr., just west of the GENERAL ELECTRIC APPLIANCE PARK. It was settled in the late 1820s by four German families and within a decade had become a small village with several businesses and its own post office. As a "new town" it was appropriately named Newburgh.

The Newburgh post office was established on August 24, 1839, at the junction of the present Shepherdsville and Poplar Level Roads. It operated intermittently at several locations in that vicinity until it closed in early 1902. Several years before it closed, as part of the post office's name simplification process, the *h* was dropped from the name, and it became Newburg.

Since the late nineteenth century, Newburg has included the old African American community of Petersburg, centering just north and west of the junction of Shepherdsville and Newburg Roads and a mile north of Newburg's former post office sites. This was in a section of poorly drained land called the WET WOODS, 40 acres of which had been purchased in 1851 by Eliza and Henry Tevis, a free black couple who farmed and raised cattle in the area with slaves of their own. After the CIVIL WAR other AFRICAN AMERICANS acquired land in the area. Petersburg was named, probably after 1880, for one of these blacks, Peter Laws, who had built a cabin at a site just north and east of the Newburg Rd.

During most of the 1900s, the two communities were surrounded by farms. Slowly, Newburg became the name for the entire area, most likely because the post office bore that name. The biggest change came to Newburg during the urban renewal programs in the 1960s. The area gained more than a hundred new homes, along with paved roads, sidewalks, a community center, and sewer lines. Newburg is now largely an African American community. In the 1970s, following URBAN RENEWAL, hundreds of black families moved into the area from the West Louisville, SMOKETOWN, and Limerick NEIGHBORHOODS, as many whites moved farther out into the county.

Newburg was incorporated as a city for five years, from 1982 to 1987. A weak tax base and legal battles between residents about the need for a city finally resulted in its dissolution.

See M. David Goodwin, "Newburg," in *A Place in Time: The Story of Louisville's Neighborhoods* (Louisville 1989); Robert M. Rennick, "The Post Offices of Louisville and Jefferson County," in *Kentucky's Salt River Valley: A Survey of the Post Offices of the Greater Louisville Area* (Lake Grove, Ore., 1997).

Robert M. Rennick

The home of H.D. Newcomb, south side of Broadway between First and Second Streets.

NEWCOMB, HORATIO DALTON (b Springfield, Massachusetts, August 10, 1809; d Louisville, August 18, 1874). Businessman. Horatio Dalton Newcomb's father was Dalton Newcomb, a well-to-do farmer; his mother's name is not known. Because farming was not to his taste, he became a schoolteacher and then a traveling agent for a schoolbook publisher. This occupation brought him to Louisville in 1832, where he became a clerk in a small business dealing in pelts and furs. Called a born merchant, he was in a few years a partner in the firm of E. Webb & Co., commission merchants.

In 1837 Newcomb established a wholesale liquor business and about 1838, with his brother, Warren, entered the wholesale grocery business as H.D. Newcomb & Co., specializing in molasses, sugar, and coffee. The firm later became Newcomb, Buchanan & Co., whiskey rectifier and distributor. By 1859 Newcomb was one of Louisville's wealthiest men. He built a mansion, designed by HENRY WHITESTONE, on BROADWAY near Second St. From 1891 to 1961 it housed ST. XAVIER HIGH SCHOOL. Newcomb was also active in numerous other enterprises: the Cannelton (Indiana) Cotton Mill; coal mines at Cannelton; and the second GALT HOUSE, which replaced the original, destroyed by fire in 1865. He was president of Louisville's powerful Western Financial Corp. and, in 1862, during the CIVIL WAR, one of the organizers of the pro-Union Louisville Board of Trade. Despite these responsibilities, he accepted the presidency of the Louisville & Nashville Railroad in October 1868, succeeding JAMES GUTHRIE, and was reelected the following year. But in 1871 the railroad's directors reelected him only after he agreed to step down from executive office in any other corporation. It was during Newcomb's presidency that the growing L&N ceased to be dominated by Louisville mercantile interests and began a program of defensive expansion. Newcomb also had to deal with the first effects of the Panic of 1873.

He married Cornelia Read of Louisville on June 23, 1838. She later showed signs of mental instability and in 1852 threw the couple's four young children from an upper floor of their home on MAIN St. between Brook and First. Only two survived. She asserted that "God called for the children" and she "was sending them to Him," according to comments published in the *Louisville Daily Democrat* of December 22, 1852. Newcomb had her placed in the Massachusetts General Hospital for the Insane near Boston. In early 1871 he filed suit for divorce, taking advantage of a recent act of the Kentucky legislature that permitted insanity as grounds. He was granted the divorce by the Louisville Chancery Court on June 28, 1871, and, in a May–December match, shortly after married Mary C. Smith, daughter of John B. Smith, an officer of the Western Financial Corp. Two sons were born to this union.

Newcomb died of a stroke, though many in the business community, in a touch of black humor, declared that he "died of the Louisville and Nashville Railroad" (*Louisville Past and Present,* 83). The locomotives and depots of the L&N were draped in black for thirty days. Newcomb is buried in CAVE HILL CEMETERY.

His death set off a series of suits among his heirs. In 1875 a suit was filed in Louisville Chancery Court in the name of his first wife to break his will, on the ground that the second marriage was illegal. On April 6 of that year, nearly a year after Newcomb's death, the court agreed, declaring the divorce void and the second marriage illegal. Other suits followed, continuing to at least 1905.

See J. Stoddard Johnson, *Memorial History of Louisville* (Chicago 1896); *Louisville Past and Present* (Louisville 1875), 83; *Courier-Journal,* Aug. 19, 1874; March 2, April 7, 1875; Oct. 6, 1905; *Louisville Daily Democrat,* Dec. 22, 1853.

George H. Yater

NEW DEPARTURE DEMOCRATS. Favoring industrialization, natural resource development, improved transportation networks, and public education, the New Departure

Democrats broke with the traditions of the Kentucky DEMOCRATIC PARTY during the era of Readjustment (1866-77). Led by HENRY WATTERSON, editor of the *COURIER-JOURNAL*, the New Departure Democrats believed the state would serve its own best interests by aligning itself with the national Democratic Party; accepting the Thirteenth, Fourteenth, and Fifteenth Amendments providing protection for freedmen; and following the example of the industrialized North.

From their stronghold in Louisville, the New Departures challenged the Bourbon Democrats, who advocated the traditional southern plantation lifestyle. The Bourbon Democrats, representing the aristocratic Bluegrass Region, continued to dominate politics in Kentucky throughout the late nineteenth century. Nevertheless, the political influence of Watterson and his faction grew stronger over the years as more elements of the party accepted his tenets.

Despite their differing views, the two factions of the Democratic Party formed a coalition that proved strong enough to withstand all Republican challenges until the gubernatorial election of 1895. Badly divided over the free silver policy, which called for the minting of silver coins and an end to the gold standard, the Democrats failed to close ranks in 1895; and the state's first Republican governor, WILLIAM O'CONNELL BRADLEY (1895-99), was elected. By the late 1890s, however, the era of Bourbon domination of the organization had passed as Populism gained control of the state's Democratic Party.

See Hambleton Tapp and James Klotter, *Kentucky: Decades of Discord, 1865-1900* (Frankfort 1977).

NEW MADRID EARTHQUAKES. On December 16, 1811, the first of three great earthquake sequences began in what today is northeastern Arkansas and southeastern Missouri and were felt as far away as Louisville. These earthquakes, referred to as the NEW MADRID EARTHQUAKES or New Madrid Shakes of 1811–12, are some of the strongest ever recorded in North America. Major earthquakes occurred on December 16, 1811, at 2:15 and 8:15 A.M.; January 23, 1812, at 9:00 A.M.; and February 7, 1812, at 3:45 A.M.

With the aid of a pendulum, Jared Brooks, a Louisville surveyor, recorded 1,874 earthquakes between December 16 and March 15. Of these events, he classified eight as being violent, ten as being severe, thirty-five as being moderate but alarming, and the rest as being between generally and barely perceptible. According to accounts, the general effects of the earthquakes in Louisville were to crack brick walls, break off chimneys, stop pendulum clocks, throw small objects off tables and shelves, and greatly alarm the inhabitants. There were also reports of ground fissures near the Market House on MARKET St., indicating ground failure of the soils and loose sediments along the OHIO RIVER. At SHIPPINGPORT the steamboat *New Orleans,* the first on the Ohio River, was violently rocked by waves, causing some of the passengers to become ill. At Soldier's Retreat, Col. Richard Anderson's home in eastern Jefferson County, cracks appeared in the stone walls.

In the winter of 1811–12, Louisville was a small community where buildings would have typically been wood-frame or brick structures of one and two stories. Such structures are known to be particularly resilient to earthquakes. If earthquakes of a magnitude of the great earthquakes of 1811–12 were to occur in modern times, damage to multistoried structures, bridges, water and sewer lines, and other man-made structures could be appreciable.

See James Penick Jr., *The New Madrid Earthquakes of 1811–1812* (Columbia, Mo., 1976); M.L. Fuller, "The New Madrid Earthquakes," *U.S. Geological Survey Bulletin* 494 (1912): 119; Ronald Street and Otto Nuttli, *The Central Mississippi Valley Earthquakes of 1811–1812* (Lexington 1990); Henry McMurtrie, *Sketches of Louisville and Its Environs* (Louisville 1819).

Ronald L. Street

NEWSBOYS' HOME. Founded in 1895 as the Society for the Protection of Newsboys and Waifs, the home was started at a time when newsboys, or "newsies," were sleeping in doorways and cardboard boxes and were frequently hauled into criminal court and sent to jail or to a reform school. The home was a way to get the services of newsboys while providing them with care and shelter. Newsboys' Home was founded in an effort to improve their moral, social, intellectual, and religious life. A group of men, organized by Judge Reginald Thompson, A.B. du Pont, Louis Barkhouse, and Judge Charles A. Wilson, opened the home in a former mansion at 436 S Third St. between Green St. (Liberty) and Walnut (Muhammad Ali Blvd.). After selling editions of local NEWSPAPERS from early morning to late afternoon, the boys returned to the home for a variety of activities. There they were taught hygiene and good manners, as well as how to become studious, ambitious, honest, and gentlemanly in the best Horatio Alger fashion.

In 1915 the boys formed their own organization, the Newsboys' Protective Association of Louisville. Administered by the boys with help from an advisory committee, the organization stressed hygiene and warned against the evils of vulgarity, TOBACCO, GAMBLING, and other vices. Boys would be fined and even suspended through a demerit system for violating the rules. The boys also took part in several activities outside of selling newspapers. In 1914 the Newsboys' Band was organized with twenty-nine members; by 1916 it had increased to over fifty. The Newsboys' Home also housed a five-room night school, run by Principal Mattie B. Tucker, for all interested boys. More than a thousand boys graduated from the school.

In 1916, after a pronouncement by the fire marshal that the building was unsafe, the Newsboys' Home was renovated with several innovations and improvements. The library was expanded, and new electric lights and appliances were installed. In addition, the entire rear portion of the home was rebuilt to allow more room for the night school, as well as to add four new sleeping rooms equipped with showers. Several rooms of the home were designed for the boys' recreation: a reading room, a poolroom, and a music room. Serving as superintendent of the home were C.L. Martin, from the home's founding until 1901; G.M. Ridenour, 1902-14; R.E. McDowell, 1914-15; and H.M. Buckley, from 1915 until the home closed in 1918. Buckley's affection for the boys was undeniable. When the home was out of funds, he would make needed improvements at his own expense. He purchased several hundred books for the library. He also took it upon himself to give care and shelter to boys at his own expense when the home was filled to capacity. The Newsboys' Home closed in 1918 because the governing board felt its purpose had been accomplished. In addition, WORLD WAR I was a growing concern, and the charitable support of the community was required for other causes. The Newsboys' Home and all its properties were sold, and after all its debts were paid, the surplus funds were donated to the NEIGHBORHOOD HOUSE and the Children's Free Hospital.

See *Courier-Journal,* Nov. 6, 1915; June 5, 1918; *Louisville Herald,* Aug. 15, 1918; *Louisville Times,* Jan. 22, 1915.

NEWSPAPERS. Since its founding, Louisville has had more than two hundred newspapers, according to a list provided by the University of Kentucky library. Some were weeklies, others dailies. Some lasted but a short time; others remain today. The names ranged from the *Bee* to the *Critic,* from the *Bon-Ton* to the *Owl,* and included *Justice* and *Truth.* Some of the names were as peculiar as those who edited the early journals, and a goodly number of newspaper names resulted from mergers with other publications.

The first paper in Louisville was the *FARMER'S LIBRARY or Ohio Intelligencer,* started on January 1, 1801, by Samuel Vail and his partner, Matthew Lyon. Vail brought his press and type from Vermont and started with an 11 x 19 inch sheet that contained mostly foreign news and some ADVERTISING. In the early days newspapers would often pick up dispatches from other papers, thus increasing the amount of national and foreign news. The *Farmer's Library or Ohio Intelligencer* ceased publication in 1808, probably because of competition from the *Louisville Gazette,* started by Joseph Charless in 1807. It, too, had a relatively short life.

After the *Louisville Correspondent* began publication in 1810 and the *Western Courier* the following year, Louisville was never without a newspaper. Over the years the city saw papers of every imaginable political persuasion. Some paid little attention to politics but, like several German-language papers, concentrated on serving a particular segment of the POPULATION. The most notable was the *Louisville Anzeiger,* which started in 1849 and published until just before WORLD WAR II. There were several African American papers, including the *Louisville News,* which began publishing in 1912; the *LOUISVILLE LEADER,* 1917–50; the *Weekly Planet,* begun in 1874; the *Ohio Falls Express;* and the *LOUISVILLE DEFENDER,* founded by Frank Stanley Sr. in 1933, which continues today as a significant community voice. One weekly paper that gained a national reputation for its pithy editorial comments was the *KENTUCKY IRISH AMERICAN,* with Mike Barry as editor. That spicy paper stopped publication in 1968.

The first of Louisville's truly powerful newspapers was the *Louisville Public Advertiser,* started in 1818 by Shadrack Penn as a weekly publication; it soon become a semiweekly. When the paper went to daily publication on April 4, 1826, it became the first daily newspaper west of the Alleghenies. Penn held the dominant newspaper position in the state for several years until the arrival of George D. Prentice and his *LOUISVILLE JOURNAL.*

The *Focus of Politics, Commerce, and Literature* was started in 1826 by William Worsley and Dr. Joseph Buchanan to compete with Shadrack Penn's paper, but it lasted only six years. George D. Prentice had come to Kentucky to write a biography of his friend Henry Clay, who was running for president. Prentice joined the *Louisville Daily Journal,* established in 1830, and became its editor, making it the most influential paper in the state. His paper became the Whig Bible, for "every Whig to swear by and every Democrat to swear at," (Towles, 10) as one wag commented. Prentice was a powerful writer, perhaps as much so as HENRY WATTERSON, and not adverse to backing up his editorial opinions at the point of a gun.

No sooner had Prentice arrived in town than Penn leveled an editorial barrage at him for his Whig leanings, and a bitter newspaper war started. The rivalry knew no bounds and practically no ethics. At one point Prentice played a joke on Penn that almost brought the editors to blows. Prentice found a New Orleans paper, over a year old, with a story about a notorious murder in the city. He had the paper delivered to Penn as though it had come from an officer on a steamer just arrived in Louisville from New Orleans. Penn, not realizing the age of the paper, had his presses stopped and reprinted the entire story as though it were current news. He was shamed and embarrassed when he discovered he had been duped, and Prentice continued to rub it in at every opportunity. Eventually Prentice won the war and became the dominant editor in the area, holding that position for many years.

Meanwhile, in 1824 the owners of the *Louisville Morning Post,* Albert G. Hodges and William Tanner, wound up on opposite sides of the issue of how the state's highest court would be constituted, with each man writing his own separate opinion on the editorial page. Finally, they decided to toss a coin to see who would become the sole owner of the paper. Tanner won.

In 1844 Maysville native Walter N. Haldeman, who had worked for a short time for Prentice, established the *Louisville Morning Courier* after buying a failing newspaper, the *Daily Dime,* in which he had invested. Prentice had new competition.

With the WHIG PARTY in tatters, Prentice threw his editorial support to the Know-Nothing or American Party, a group violently opposed to foreigners and Catholics. As Prentice railed against the immigrant element in Louisville, tensions grew with the approach of the municipal election of August 1855. Prentice's shrill editorial attacks against immigrants continued, and violence flared on Monday, August 6; mobs of Know-Nothings burned the homes and businesses of GERMAN and IRISH residents. The "BLOODY MONDAY" riots cost the lives of more than twenty people.

Haldeman's *Courier,* which at first had supported the Know-Nothings, became a strong opponent of the group, charging Prentice with responsibility for the riots. Two other newspapers, the *Democrat* and the *Times* (no connection with the *LOUISVILLE TIMES* established in 1884) were in opposition to the Know-Nothings. Cassius Marcellus Clay, who had established the *True American* in Lexington to fight slavery, came to Louisville in 1847 and started the *Louisville Examiner,* another emancipatory paper that was highly regarded in the state. It lasted until 1849.

The outbreak of the CIVIL WAR found Prentice a strong Unionist and Haldeman supporting the Confederacy. Prentice was given credit for helping persuade Kentucky to remain in the Union, by means of his editorials. The occupation of Louisville by Union troops forced Haldeman from the city. He published the *Courier* from Bowling Green and Nashville until the end of the war, when he brought the paper back to Louisville and gradually began to overtake Prentice. The aging Prentice, who had lost his political party and many of his subscribers, looked for a way to breathe new life into his newspaper. Henry Watterson of the *Nashville Banner* was chosen as his successor. The twenty-eight-year-old Watterson, who had considerable political, military, and newspaper experience, brought to the city a fairly broad national and international view of events. Watterson quickly determined that a continuing fight between the *Journal* and the *Courier* would lead nowhere, so he approached Haldeman, saying, "You need an editor. I need a publisher." Haldeman, after Watterson announced that the *Journal* intended to put him out of business, agreed to a merger. On November 8, 1868, the two papers merged as the *Courier-Journal,* and Watterson wrote on the front page, "A double-headed monster with an unfamiliar hyphenated headline had taken possession of every man's doorstep . . . looking very much like it had brought its knitting and was come to stay." The bankrupt *Louisville Daily Democrat* became part of the merger and vanished. With Watterson directing the editorial and news operations and Haldeman watching over the business side, the *Courier-Journal* grew in daily circulation, advertising revenue, and influence throughout the South. The *Weekly Courier-Journal* was started and sent by mail throughout the South, becoming the region's largest-circulation paper, largely as a result of Watterson's writings.

In 1869 the *Louisville Commercial* was established as a Republican voice in the community; it was succeeded in 1903 by the *Louisville Herald.*

In 1884 Haldeman started the *Louisville Times* as an afternoon sister to the morning *Courier-Journal* and to meet the competition of the *Evening Post,* over the objections of Watterson. It was the *Times* that saved the *Courier-Journal* a few years later. William Jennings Bryan had been chosen as the Democratic nominee for president in 1896, but both Watterson and Haldeman opposed his views on free silver and refused to endorse Bryan. Taking the *Courier-Journal* out of the DEMOCRATIC PARTY was regarded as base treachery in the paper's circulation area.

Subscribers quit in droves, and advertising revenue dried up when Kentucky went Republican in a presidential election for the first time. The *Weekly Courier-Journal* was ruined, and the daily paper was faced with the prospect of bankruptcy. The *Louisville Times* made enough money to save the morning paper, because it had no strong editorial policy for anyone to be mad about. Earlier, the *Times* had attracted attention by hiring the first woman reporter in the area.

WALTER HALDEMAN died in 1902 after being struck by a streetcar on Fourth St., leaving control of the papers to his younger son, Bruce, who did not get along with his older brother, William, and his sister, Isabel. Family infighting raged, with Watterson in support of Isabel and William. In the meantime, quiet negotiations to buy the papers were begun by Judge ROBERT WORTH BINGHAM, a former mayor of Louisville and an influential attorney. On August 6, 1918, Bingham bought the controlling interest in the papers and gained the remaining shares the following year.

Watterson's editorials against the policies of Germany during WORLD WAR I won the papers the first of nine PULITZER PRIZES, journalism's highest award. Later Watterson was against the League of Nations, but Judge Bingham favored it. The aging and frail Watterson resigned in 1919 and died two years later.

The *Louisville Herald* and the *Louisville Post,*

combined in 1925 as the *Herald-Post,* were owned by financier James Brown, who fought the positions of Judge Bingham and his newspapers until Brown's papers went bankrupt in 1936.

Bingham's creed for newspapering appears today prominently displayed on the lobby wall of the papers' building: "I have always regarded the newspapers owned by me as a public trust and have endeavored so to conduct them as to render the greatest public service." He fought for the poor and minorities and for public education, while placing the papers on sound financial footing. Appointed by Pres. Franklin D. Roosevelt as ambassador to the Court of St. James's, he later died in 1937. Upon Judge Bingham's death, his twenty-seven-year-old son, BARRY BINGHAM Sr., became the publisher and set about upgrading the two papers. He chose Mississippian MARK ETHRIDGE and Kentuckian Lisle Baker Jr. to help run the organization, with Bingham directing editorial policy, Ethridge heading the news operations, and Baker attending to the business side. This leadership led to the *Courier-Journal*'s being consistently named as one of America's top ten newspapers in the 1960s and 1970s. Over the years, in addition to their nine Pulitzer Prizes, the papers won scores of other top national awards for journalistic excellence. Bingham was succeeded as publisher by his son, Barry Bingham Jr., in 1971.

As had been the case with the Haldeman family years earlier, dissension within the Bingham family resulted in Barry Bingham Sr. selling all his communications properties in 1986. The newspapers were bought by the Gannett Co. for more than $300 million. The *Louisville Times,* faced with falling circulation and advertising revenue, was discontinued in 1987. After the sale of the newspapers, George N. Gill became publisher and continued until his retirement in 1993.

The quality of the *Courier-Journal* was enhanced by capable journalists. Among the best-known was John Ed Pearce, who became one of the most widely read writers in Kentucky. Pearce was born September 25, 1919, in Norton, Virginia, to John Edward and Susan (Leslie) Pearce. He spent part of his boyhood in Kentucky and graduated from the University of Kentucky. Pearce served as a navy officer in World War II and in the reserve until 1977, retiring as a commander. He worked as editor of the *Somerset Journal* before joining the *Courier-Journal* in 1946. An editorial writer for twenty-five years, he is known to his fans as John Ed.

Pearce, admired as a newspaper columnist and an author and appreciated as a raconteur and historian, has attracted respect as a political pundit who wields a witty but caustic pen. He was a fixture at the *Courier-Journal,* where even after his retirement in 1986 he continued to write his Sunday column through December 1996. He also wrote a column regularly for the *Lexington Herald-Leader.* Pearce won a Nieman Fellowship to Harvard; a Governor's Medallion for Public Service; a share in a Pulitzer Prize; and Headliner, Meeman, and American Bar Association awards. He was named outstanding Kentucky Journalist by Sigma Delta Chi and is a member of the University of Kentucky Journalism Hall of Fame.

Pearce is a keen observer of the Kentucky political scene and was a close friend of Gov. Bert T. Combs. Among his many books dealing with that topic is *Divide and Dissent: Kentucky Politics, 1930–1963* (1987). He has recounted his life in his *Memoirs: 50 Years at the Courier-Journal and Other Places* (1997). Pearce has been married twice, to Jean McIntire and to Virginia Rutledge, and has five daughters: Susan, Martha, Virginia, Elizabeth, and Alida.

Writing in the 125th anniversary edition of the *Courier-Journal* in September 19, 1993, Kentucky historian Thomas D. Clark said, "Throughout the history of its publication both editors and reporters have been public watchdogs haunting the doors of governors, legislators, judges, and local officials. At times they have been public scolds, and often their probings have brought to light official misdeeds, much of which brought about political and social reforms. . . . Maybe, after all, the effectiveness of the *Courier-Journal,* on its reading constituency . . . is to be gauged by the fact that the paper has been a public organ 'to be sworn by and to be sworn at.'"

During the last half of the twentieth century, various alternative newspapers, usually published on a weekly or less-frequent basis, sprang up in the community. These were in addition to the weekly neighborhood papers and had a more narrow focus, offering the Louisville reader a different perspective on world and local happenings. Most did not last long. One exception was the *Louisville Eccentric Observer,* better known as *LEO,* which came into existence in November 1990 and offered a variety of observations and features that often appealed to younger readers.

Louisville Newspapers

Agriculturist
Amateur World
American Democrat & Weekly Courier
American Red Man
Argus and Louisville Literary Gazette
Baptist Banner and Western Pioneer
Bee
Black Rag
Bon-Ton
Bulletin
Business First
Catholic Advocate
Central Catholic Advocate
City Paper
Civic Opinion
Colored Democratic Voice
Columbian
Commercial Review and Louis Prices Current
Courier-Journal
Critic
Daily Dime
Daily Evening News
Daily Evening Sun
Daily Globe
Daily Journal and Focus
Daily Louisville Democrat
Daily Louisville Herald
Daily Louisville Herald & Commercial Gazette
Daily Louisville Public Advertiser
Daily Louisville Times
Daily Times
Democrat
Democratic Banner
Dollar Democrat
East End Voice
Emporium & Commercial Advertiser
Evening Bulletin
Evening Democrat
Evening Express
Evening Herald
Evening News
Evening Post
Evening Times
Examiner
Exposition Gazetteer
Falls City Amateur
Farmer's Library
Farmer's Library or Ohio Intelligencer
Focus
Focus of Politics, Commerce, and Literature
Fonda's & Klereff's Daily Review
Freedom's Banner
Free Press of Louisville
Free Republic
Gateway
Guardian
Haldeman's Monthly Gleaner
Herald
Herald-Post
Highland Citizen
Highlander
Highland Herald
Hill & Highlander
Indiana Times
Jefferson County Post
Jefferson County Republican
Jefferson Democrat
Jefferson Reporter
Journal and Focus
Justice
Katholischer Glaubensbote
Kent's Family Friend
Kentuckian
Kentucky Herald & Mercantile Advertiser
Kentucky Irish American
Kentucky New Era
Kentucky Red Man
Kentucky Reporter
Kentucky Tribune
Labor Union
Liberty News
Lincoln Republican
Lincoln Republican News
Louisville American
Louisville Anzeiger
Louisville Argus
Louisville Catholic Advocate
Louisville Chronicle
Louisville City Gazette
Louisville Commercial
Louisville Correspondent
Louisville Courier
Louisville Courier-Journal
Louisville Daily Courier

Louisville Daily Democrat
Louisville Daily Dime
Louisville Daily Express
Louisville Daily Focus
Louisville Daily Gazette
Louisville Daily Journal
Louisville Daily Ledger
Louisville Daily News
Louisville Daily Rover
The Louisville Daily Sun
Louisville Daily Union Press
Louisville Defender
Louisville Democrat
Louisville Democrat Extra
Louisville Dispatch
Louisville Eccentric Observer
Louisville Evening Bulletin
Louisville Examiner
Louisville Gazette
Louisville Gazette & Indiana Correspondent
Louisville Gazette, and Western Advertiser
Louisville Herald
Louisville Herald and Commercial Gazette
Louisville Herald Commercial
Louisville Idea
Louisville Industrial and Commercial Gazette
Louisville Journal
Louisville Journal Extra
Louisville Leader
Louisville Morning Courier
Louisville Morning Courier and American Democrat
Louisville Morning Post
Louisville National Union Press
Louisville News
Louisville News and Enquirer
Louisville Post
Louisville Public Advertiser
Louisville Republican
Louisville Skyline
Louisville Sun
Louisville Times
Louisville Tribune
Louisville Weekly Bulletin
Louisville Weekly Courier
Louisville Weekly Democrat
Louisville Weekly Dispatch
Louisville Weekly Gazette
Louisville Weekly Herald
Louisville Weekly Journal
Louisville Weekly Ledger
Louisville Weekly Public Advertiser
Louisville Weekly Union Press
Main St.
Messenger
Microscope
Midland Review
Morning Post and Commercial
Motor Weekly
National Granger
Nautilus
New Highlander
New Voice
Ohio Falls Express
Omnibus
O'Sullivan's Weekly
Our Weekly Youth
Owl
Portland Anchor
Portland Civic News
Post Sentinel
Prestonia Messenger
Public Advertiser
Public Ledger and Commercial Bulletin
Reporter
Republican Star
Riverside Weekly
Rough and Ready
Serviceman's Louisville Dispatch
Shawnee-Chickasaw Gleaner
Skyline
Sonntags Post
Southern Weekly
Star
Star Bulletin
Sunday Argus
Sunday Star
Tagliches Louisville Volksblatt
Times
True Democrat
Truth
Twice a Week Courier-Journal
Voice of the Nation
Voice-Tribune
Weekly Courier-Journal
Weekly Dollar Democrat
Weekly Louisville Commercial
Weekly Louisville Democrat
Weekly Louisville Times
Weekly Planet
West and Weekly News
Western American
Western Courier
Western Recorder
Western Ruralist
Western World and Weekly Messenger
Wochentlicher Louisville Anzeiger
Wochentliches Louisville Volksblatt
Young Spirit of the South and Central American

See Donald B. Towles, *The Press of Kentucky 1787–1994* (Frankfort 1994); Lowell H. Harrison and James C. Klotter, *A New History of Kentucky* (Lexington 1997); Herndon J. Evans, *The Newspaper Press in Kentucky* (Lexington 1976); George H. Yater, *Two Hundred Years at the Falls of the Ohio* (Louisville 1979); Thomas D. Clark, "A New Era, a New Kind of Paper . . .," *Courier-Journal,* 125th Anniversary Issue, Sept. 19, 1993, J10–J12.

Donald B. Towles

NICHOLAS, SAMUEL (b Lexington, 1796; d Louisville, November 27, 1869). Attorney and educator. Samuel Nicholas was the son of George and Mary (Smith) Nicholas. His father, a lawyer, was influential in framing Kentucky's first constitution. Nicholas's parents died while he was a child, and by the age of twelve he was working for an uncle in Baltimore. After a brief time operating a mercantile business in New Orleans, Nicholas moved to Frankfort, Kentucky, and studied law under George Mortimer Bibb. He was admitted to the bar in 1823 and two years later opened a law office in Louisville.

During his career as an attorney, Nicholas was a member of the Court of Appeals (1831–36), chancellor of the Louisville Chancery Court (1844–50), and a member of the Kentucky constitutional convention in 1849. In 1850 Gov. John J. Crittenden (1848–50) appointed Nicholas, Charles Wickliffe, and Squire Turner to revise the Code of Practice. Nicholas, a slaveowner who argued for gradual emancipation, remained a Union supporter during the CIVIL WAR and published several tracts on constitutional topics at the time.

Nicholas served as the first president of the newly chartered UNIVERSITY OF LOUISVILLE in 1846–47. At that time the university consisted of the recently merged Louisville College and LOUISVILLE MEDICAL INSTITUTE. A law department was established, and Nicholas granted degrees to the first graduating class. He also worked for the formation of the public school system in Louisville.

Nicholas married Matilda Prather in 1829; they had seven children. She died in 1844, and in 1848 Nicholas married his cousin Mary Smith, with whom he had three children. She survived Nicholas, who is buried in CAVE HILL CEMETERY.

Margaret L. Merrick

NIGHT WATCH. In 1810 Louisville's Board of Trustees formed a patrol, often referred to as the night watch, to protect people and their property. Louisville was one of the first towns south of the OHIO RIVER to establish a night watch. The town had a large slave POPULATION, and watching slaves constituted the patrol's first responsibility. Night watchmen did not allow any unlawful meetings of slaves, did not allow slaves to be out at night without a pass from their owners, and made certain that after ten o'clock all slaves had returned to their quarters.

The night watch had authority to jail slaves for the night if they did not follow the regulations. They could punish them with fifteen lashes for violations, but only if the fine of $2 was not paid. The watch patrol also imposed a penalty of $5 on any person who dealt or traded with slaves during the curfew, mainly to prevent the sale of alcohol.

Similarly, any person could be detained by watchmen because of his or her behavior, which included drunkenness or purposeless night wandering. Such persons were put in jail or in the watchhouse, a simple structure 12 x 14 feet with a shingled roof, which was built in 1811 at the east end of the market house.

The patrol was required to watch people's houses and businesses and to notify the owner of any unusual signs such as open doors or windows, lights, or strange noises. Night watchmen had the right to arrest any person found in a house or building who did not belong there. The patrol could also order the owner to remove wood or other obstructions on the streets or sidewalks.

At first the night patrol consisted of only two men, but by the late 1820s there were four. At that time two men started generally at six o'clock in the evening and the other two joined them at ten o'clock; all four stayed on duty throughout the rest of the night. One man was designated a captain. They patrolled on several streets, including Main, Market, and Jefferson.

At ten o'clock they would ring a bell announcing the slave curfew. It was also rung at any time in case of fire. Watchmen would cry out the hour throughout the night.

Watchmen were initially paid $1 per night, and the captain received an additional twenty-five cents. Later, when they started to ring a bell at ten o'clock, the whole patrol's pay went up seventy-five cents per night. Part of the money for watchmen's salaries was raised by the Board of Trustees through private subscriptions, and part came from existing revenues. Each watchman had a badge and carried with him a pike, a lantern, a rattle, and a trumpet. Since an additional task was the lighting of the town's oil street lamps, watchmen also carried a flaming torch, a small ladder, a pair of scissors, and two pot spouts.

In 1828, when the city was incorporated, the Board of Trustees was replaced by the City Council, which continued the tradition of the night watch and expanded it to include a day watch. The night watch was a forerunner of the city's night police patrol.

See Alice Mullins, "Establishing a Night Watch—Louisville 1810-1828," University of Louisville Archives and Records Center, 1987; Tom L. Owen, "Legislative Records of Louisville Kentucky," *Bound Volume 1791–1929,*[5] University of Louisville Archives and Records Center, 1975.

NILES, JOHN JACOB (b Louisville, April 28, 1892; d Lexington, March 1, 1980). Ballad singer, composer, and collector of folk music. Niles was born in the Portland neighborhood into a musical family; his grandfather was a composer, organist, and cello manufacturer.

His father, John Thomas, was a locally popular folksinger and square-dance caller, and his mother, Louise "Sarah" Niles, taught John music theory and piano skills. A quick study, Niles began singing publicly at the age of seven, composed his first song at the age of fifteen, and continued pursuing a musical career at the encouragement of Henry Watterson, editor of the *Courier-Journal.* Niles graduated from du Pont Manual High School in 1909 and began working as a mechanic at Burroughs Adding Machine Co. on Market St. In 1917 he enlisted in the aviation section of the Army Signal Corps and flew in France. He was discharged a year later following a plane crash that left him partially paralyzed. After his recuperation, he returned to music by using his disabled veteran benefits to attend the Cincinnati Conservatory of Music.

Although he preferred performing and toured with contralto Marion Kerby extensively throughout America and Europe, Niles is best remembered for his compilation of Appalachian folk music, which he collected from the mountains of eastern Kentucky from 1909 to 1917 and from 1928 to 1934. Niles arranged or composed more than a thousand ballads, folk songs, and carols. Among his best-known works are "I Wonder as I Wander" and "Black Is the Color of My True Love's Hair." His last major work was titled *The Niles-Merton Cycle.*

Niles married Rena Lipetz in 1934. He died at the age of eighty-seven and is buried at St. Hubert's Cemetery in Clark County, Kentucky.

Nancy Sexton

NITTA YUMA. The Nitta Yuma Historic District is located on bluffs above the Ohio River in the northeastern section of Jefferson County, eight miles from Louisville. *Nitta Yuma* is an Indian phrase meaning "high ground." A core of the original historic area remains. Other houses have been destroyed by fire and have been replaced with mid-twentieth-century dwellings.

The Nitta Yuma area was acquired in 1890 by three prominent Louisville businessmen who, desiring to form a summer enclave for their families, purchased land from the estate of James Todd, a Louisville attorney. The three were George Garvin Brown, founder of Brown-Forman Distillers Corp., and Charles Peaslee and William Frederick Booker, who were both associated with the Peaslee-Gaulbert Co., which produced paint, lamps, and oil. They hired the assistant engineer of the city of Louisville, Maj. Joseph D. Claybrook (1843–1921), to build the roads at Nitta Yuma. Claybrook, who lived in the Todd house until his death, was a military man, an engineer, and a physician, although he did not practice medicine. He was superintendent of the building of the Louisville Southern Railroad, the Mexican Central Railroad, and the Portland Canal. He was married to Mary Louise Booker, a member of the Booker family who, with the Browns and the Peaslees, founded Nitta Yuma.

The oldest of the structures is the Todd house, a two-story frame, vernacular farmhouse built about 1870. The Alex Galt Robinson house, built in 1905 and designed by E.T. Hutchings, a well-known Louisville architect, is a two-story frame house in the Neo-Colonial Revival style. The Gill house is a large, two-story frame house of the same style. On its north side there is a colossal Tuscan-Doric portico.

The Robinson Brown house is a one-and-one-half-story brick residence. The house was designed in 1929 by local architect William Arrasmith (1898–1965) and was one of his early residential commissions. Arrasmith also designed the Fifth and Broadway Greyhound Bus Station in Louisville (demolished) and Greyhound Bus Stations in Evansville, Indiana, and Washington, D.C.

See Elizabeth F. Jones, *Nitta Yuma Historic District, National Register of Historic Places Inventory—Nomination Form* (Louisville 1982).

Donna M. Neary

NORMAL SCHOOLS. Normal schools, derived from the Latin *norma,* meaning "standard" or "rule," were traditionally two-year institutions for the education and training of elementary teachers. Though normal schools were later established by the state of Kentucky, they began on the local level. The Louisville Normal School was founded in 1871 to train female teachers. It was the first teacher-training school established in Kentucky and among the first established in the United States. Elementary school classrooms housed within the school provided a model or demonstration school where normal school students could observe and practice teaching.

From 1871 to 1911, the normal school offered only one curriculum: preparation of teachers for grades one through eight. In 1911 the Louisville Free Kindergarten Training School became a department of the normal school. Two curricula were then offered. One prepared teachers for kindergarten and the primary grades, and the other prepared teachers for the intermediate and junior high school grades. The curricula included both academic and professional courses. In addition to offering preservice education, the normal school, after 1918, maintained an extension department to encourage graduates to continue their educational development.

The Main Street School at 537 E Main St. housed the normal school from 1871 to 1891 for all but one year. For that year, 1881–82, it moved into the Female High School on First between Walnut (Muhammad Ali Blvd.) and Chestnut. In 1891 it moved to the Hiram Roberts School at 615 E Market St., where it remained until 1916. In 1916 the school was relocated to 1128 E Broadway and stayed there until the normal schools closed in 1935.

The Louisville Colored Normal School was opened in 1897 by the Board of Trustees of the Louisville public schools. The primary purpose was to train teachers for the public elementary schools for African Americans. The two-diploma course prepared the teachers to teach either kindergarten and the primary grades or elementary school (first to sixth grades). Upon completion of the sixty-four semester hours required, graduates could apply to the state Department of Instruction, Division of Certification, for a standard elementary certificate. This normal school was located at Central Colored High School, Ninth and Magazine Streets, until 1907. In that year it moved to Booker T. Washington Colored School at Jackson and Breckinridge and remained there until 1925. In 1925 it was relocated to Paul Dunbar School at Ninth and Magazine and operated there until it closed in 1935.

The Louisville normal schools graduated a total of 2,348 students. When the Louisville Normal School began in 1871, the course of study was for one year. In 1895 it was lengthened to a year and a half. Then in 1898 the course of study became a two-year program. The closure in 1935 followed a growing tendency to require a four-year education of school teachers and an oversupply of normal-school-trained teachers.

See Bianca Esch, "History of the Louisville Normal School," in *Anniversary Number Louisville Normal School: 1871–1931* (Louisville 1931); Louisville Public Schools, *Louisville Colored Normal School Record Book* (Louisville n.d.); John A. Miller, "Statement of the Board of Education," in *Twenty-fourth Report of the Board of Education of Louisville: From September 1, 1934, to September 1, 1935* (Louisville 1935); "Training School," in *Report of the Board of Trustees of the Public Schools of Louisville for the Year Ending June 30, 1873* (Louisville 1873).

Jeanie Fridell

NORTH AMERICAN INTERNATIONAL LIVESTOCK EXPOSITION. North American International Livestock Exposition (NAILE), the world's largest purebred livestock show, was founded in 1974 by the Kentucky Department of AGRICULTURE with support from several national breed associations. Conducted each November at the KENTUCKY FAIR AND EXPOSITION CENTER in Louisville, the show was known originally as the North American Livestock Exposition and was confined to beef cattle. Sheep were added in 1975, with dairy cattle, swine, and quarter horses following in 1976. Dairy goats, llamas, and draft horses were added in later years. In 1978, after the closing of Chicago's Union Stock Yards and the suspension of the associated International Livestock Exposition, the North American inherited the International's Saddle and Sirloin Club and its portrait collection, which included 330 PAINTINGS of leading livestock men. At that time the Louisville show became known as the North American International Livestock Exposition. In 1996 NAILE attracted more than 19,500 entries. The exposition also hosts the North American Championship Rodeo and several national livestock-judging competitions, including the National 4-H Livestock Judging and the Junior College and Collegiate livestock judging contests.

Carl E. Kramer

NORTHUP, ANNE (MEAGHER) (b Louisville, January 22, 1948). U.S. congresswoman. Anne (Meagher) Northup is the daughter of James L. and Floy (Terstegge) Meagher and the sister of Mary T. Meagher, a swimmer who won an Olympic gold medal in 1984. Northup graduated from Louisville's Sacred Heart Academy and received a bachelor's degree in economics and business in 1970 from St. Mary's College in South Bend, Indiana. She had worked as a teacher at Atherton High School and in management at Ford Motor Co. in Louisville but was a stay-at-home mother when she entered politics.

In 1996 Northup became the first Republican in twenty-six years to serve as Third Congressional District representative when she narrowly defeated Democrat Mike Ward, a one-term incumbent, in the November election by 1,299 votes (126,625 to 125,326). She was sworn into office on January 7, 1997.

Attracting the support of Newt Gingrich, House Speaker at the time, Northup became one of only two House first-termers after the 1996 election to be appointed to the powerful House Appropriations Committee, which allocates all federal discretionary spending. Among the early issues that garnered her support were governmental deregulation, a balanced-budget amendment, capital-gains tax cuts, and antiabortion policies.

In 1998 she defeated former Kentucky attorney general Chris Gorman, receiving 51.5 percent of the popular vote to Gorman's 47.5 (100,690 to 92,865). The race was the most expensive U.S. House campaign in Kentucky history, with the two candidates spending a combined total of nearly $2.4 million. Northup also set an individual fund-raising record for a House campaign in the state, raising more than $1.8 million and beating her own record of $1.2 million set in the 1996 race against Ward.

Before her election to the U.S. Congress, Northup served five consecutive terms from 1987 to 1996 in the Kentucky General Assembly as a representative of the Thirty-second Legislative District. During her tenure in the Kentucky House, Northup supported efforts to regulate the sale of TOBACCO products to minors. She was also one of only five Republicans in the state House to side with Democrats and vote in favor of the Kentucky Education Reform Act in 1990.

Northup is married to Robert "Woody" Northup, owner of an electronics firm in Louisville. They have six children: David, Katie, Josh, Kevin, Erin, and Mark.

See *Courier-Journal,* Oct. 24; Nov. 6, 24, 1996; Nov. 4, 1998.

NORTON, GEORGE WASHINGTON (b Russellville, Kentucky, September 6, 1814; d Louisville, July 18, 1889). Banker and capitalist. Norton was one of eight children born to William and Mary (Hise) Norton. His father was a manufacturer of nails. Norton ran a dry-goods store before becoming the first president of the Southern Bank of Kentucky in 1850. He moved to Louisville in 1867 and established G.W. Norton & Co., a private BANKING and real estate concern that his brother WILLIAM FREDERICK NORTON joined in 1868. They purchased adjoining twin houses with mansard roofs on Fourth St. near BROADWAY. The two Nortons prospered from various investments and land holdings; W.F. retired in 1885 and died a year later. Their brother, Eckstein Norton, became a director and vice president of the Louisville & Nashville Railroad in 1884 and served as its president from 1887 to 1891, when he resumed private banking in New York.

When George Norton died, Louisville's leading NEWSPAPERS considered him perhaps the wealthiest man in the city and probably the state. A lifelong Baptist, he had helped subsidize the SOUTHERN BAPTIST THEOLOGICAL SEMINARY's move from Greenville, South Carolina, to Louisville in 1877, as well as its subsequent growth. The seminary's magnificent edifice, Norton Hall, was erected along BROADWAY between Fourth and Fifth streets several years before he died, and he served as the institution's treasurer. He married Martha Stuart Henry (1824–1911), a descendant of Patrick Henry, in Louisville in 1847, and they had seven children. Daughter Juliette married prominent physician J.B. Marvin, and Minnie married William Beverly Caldwell Jr., a grandson of JAMES GUTHRIE. Spinster daughters Lucie and Mattie and their widowed sister, Minnie Norton Caldwell, built GARDENCOURT on Alta Vista Rd., designed by the Boston architectural firm of Shepley, Rutan & Coolidge, the successor firm of the renowned H.H. Richardson. The magnificent Beaux Arts residence was bequeathed by Mattie Norton in 1947 to the UNIVERSITY OF LOUISVILLE, which used it for the School of Music. It was subsequently purchased in 1987 by the Presbyterian Theological Seminary and restored.

George Norton's son, George W. Norton Jr., also engaged Shepley, Rutan & Coolidge to design Norton Hall, his estate next door (ironically razed in 1961 to make way for the LOUISVILLE PRESBYTERIAN THEOLOGICAL SEMINARY). He was born in Russellville on September 12, 1865, attended Rugby School in Louisville, and graduated in 1885 from Yale University before becoming executor of his father's vast estate. He sat on various boards and succeeded his father as treasurer of the Southern Baptist Convention.

George W. Norton Jr. was instrumental in the Southern Baptist Theological Seminary's move to its present Lexington Rd. site, near his home. The centerpiece of the new campus, laid out by the Olmsted brothers of Brookline, Massachusetts, was Norton Hall, designed by James Gamble Rogers of New York and completed in 1926. He lived to see the Kentucky Baptist Hospital on Barret Ave. open in 1924 but not the seminary. He died on December 11, 1924, and is buried in CAVE HILL CEMETERY. He had served on the board of managers of the cemetery for twenty-two years and on the board of directors of its investment company for fourteen years.

In 1897 George W. Norton Jr. married Margaret MacDonald Muldoon, and they had three children. The family traveled extensively. Daughter Dorothy Lithgow Norton, a 1928 Vassar College graduate, married John Harris Clay, a gentleman farmer of Paris, Kentucky, and was instrumental in the preservation of the Shaker village at Pleasant Hill, Kentucky. Daughter Margaret MacDonald Norton studied in Rome and later married Leonard T. Davidson, M.D., who became head of the pediatrics department of the University of Louisville School of Medicine. She was on the Board of Governors of the J.B. SPEED ART MUSEUM.

Their brother, George W. Norton III, graduated from Yale University and the Harvard University School of Law (1926) and practiced law in the firm of Humphrey, Crawford & Middleton until serving in WORLD WAR II. After that, he devoted full time to the BROADCASTING business he had begun in 1933 with the purchase of a radio station he named WAVE. In 1948 WAVE-TV was the first TELEVISION station to broadcast in Kentucky, and in 1962 it pioneered locally the transmission of color. He was active in cultural, civic, and political (Republican) affairs, and he enjoyed farming. The Nortons had two working farms in eastern Jefferson County from which WAVE broadcast a live agricultural program thought to be the only one of its kind. They lived nearby on Wolf Pen Branch Road. He died in Jamaica following an automobile accident on February 13, 1964, and is buried in CAVE HILL CEMETERY. Like his father, he had served (1948–64) on the board of managers of the cemetery company as well as on the board of directors of the cemetery investment company.

George W. Norton III married Jane Lewis Morton, sister of Rogers Clark Ballard Morton and THRUSTON BALLARD MORTON, in 1928. They had two children, George W. Norton IV and Mary Norton. George W. Norton IV, a Yale University graduate and veteran of the KOREAN WAR, had just succeeded his late father as president of WAVE when he was killed at age thirty in an automobile accident on May 22, 1964. Jane (Morton) Norton, an author and accomplished painter, patron of the arts, civic leader, and philanthropist, became president and then chairman of the BROADCASTING company. She died on August 29, 1988. Daughter Mary Norton married Edwin Dulaney and, following a divorce, married the Reverend Alfred R. Shands, an Episcopal priest. The Shandses' collection of American folk art is recognized internationally, and they established the KENTUCKY ART AND CRAFT FOUNDATION. Mary Norton Shands, who has an abiding interest in medical wellness, created Foxhollow, a center for healing, in Crestwood.

See David Morton, *The Nortons of Russellville, Ky.: Reminiscences* (Philadelphia 1891); J. Stoddard Johnston, ed., *Memorial History of Louisville* (Chicago 1896).

Samuel W. Thomas

NORTON, JANE (MORTON) (b Louisville, 1908; d Great Barrington, Massachusetts, August 29, 1988). Philanthropist. The daughter of Dr. David C. and Mary (Ballard) Morton, Jane Norton attended Ballard School, Kentucky Home School, and Oldfield's Boarding School in Glencoe, Maryland. Following her graduation from Oldfield's, Norton attended the Art Student's League in New York City, and she spent one year studying art in Paris.

She was a member of a family prominent in Republican politics. Norton's brothers were Kentucky senator Thruston B. Morton and Maryland representative Rogers C.B. Morton. In 1928 she married George W. Norton III, an attorney and broadcaster, who founded WAVE radio station in 1933. In 1948 it became WAVE-TV—the first TELEVISION station in Kentucky. The Nortons had two children, George W. IV and Mary.

Jane Norton was vice president of WAVE from 1943 to 1945 while her husband served in the Army Air Force. She was a member of the Jefferson County Board of Education from 1945 to 1949. In 1964 personal tragedy forced her back into the BROADCASTING business. She became the president of WAVE-TV succeeding her son, George W. Norton IV, who was killed in an automobile accident; he had just succeeded his father, who had died three months earlier, also in an automobile accident. For two years, she was president of the station and its two affiliates, WFIE-TV, Evansville, Indiana, and WFRE-TV, Green Bay, Wisconsin. In 1966 Norton retired as president but remained chairman of the board and principal stockholder of Orion Broadcasting, which owned WAVE-TV and its affiliates and later expanded to include stations in Michigan and Iowa. In 1981 Norton sold Orion Broadcasting to Cosmos Corp., a BROADCASTING firm from South Carolina.

Norton was an accomplished artist who exhibited her works in New York City, Evansville, Louisville, Lexington, and other cities. She tried her hand at writing and in 1944 published a novel, *Blackbirds on the Lawn.* The story was set in a small Kentucky town during WORLD WAR II. At the time of its publication Norton noted that she would write another book only if it did not interfere with her civic work. She was known as a prominent patron of the arts and served on the boards of directors of the LOUISVILLE ORCHESTRA, the Kentucky Opera Association, the Kentucky Center for the Arts Endowment Fund, and the LOUISVILLE FREE PUBLIC LIBRARY Foundation. Norton supported art collections of the J.B. SPEED ART MUSEUM, the Kentucky Center for the Arts, the UNIVERSITY OF LOUISVILLE, and CHRIST CHURCH CATHEDRAL. She was a trustee of Shakertown in Mercer County and of Centre College in Danville, Kentucky.

A committed civic leader, Norton founded the Morton Center in Louisville to help people with chemical dependencies. She was president of the George W. Norton Foundation, where she gave priority to grants related to the community's social and welfare needs. In 1974 Norton was named "Man of the Year" by the Advertising Club of Louisville; that is the oldest award of its kind bestowed on community leaders in Kentucky. In 1977 SPALDING UNIVERSITY awarded her an honorary degree of Doctor of Humane Letters, and a year later she received the Brotherhood Award from the National Conference of Christians and JEWS.

Norton died after suffering a stroke at her summer home in Massachusetts. Her will demonstrated a continuing civic commitment, leaving $10 million to charity. She is buried in CAVE HILL CEMETERY.

See *Courier-Journal,* Aug. 31, 1988; Francis M. Nash, *Towers over Kentucky* (Lexington 1995).

NORTON, WILLIAM FREDERICK, JR. (b Paducah, Kentucky, December 6, 1849; d Coronado Beach, California, May 15, 1903). Impresario. The only child of William and Anne Eliza (Morton) Norton, Norton attended local schools, where he developed a love of literature, including Greek and Latin classics, and the works of William Shakespeare and Charles Dickens. After graduating from the men's Bethel College in Russellville, Kentucky, Norton moved to Louisville and worked for his father and his uncle, George W. Norton, at the G.W. Norton Co., a private BANKING and real estate establishment located on Jefferson St. near Fourth St. When the company closed in 1885, Norton assisted his father in managing the family's estate, an occupation that afforded him the time and money to pursue his interest in the arts.

After returning from a European tour in the 1880s, Norton began sponsoring several productions and concerts in du Pont Square (Central Park). For his first large-scale show, Norton decided that the city needed a spectacular fireworks show, one that would coincide with the SOUTHERN EXPOSITION. He had a special fireworks amphitheater built with a large stage and seating for ten thousand people on 4 acres adjacent to the exposition grounds. "The Last Days of Pompeii," with fireworks by specialist James Paine and a cast of over 250 characters, opened on August 23, 1886, and ran until October 23, with performances every Thursday and Saturday. The show's success caused Norton to look to new ventures.

Though not a religious man, Norton was raised by two devout BAPTISTS who disapproved of their son's association with show business. Not wishing to upset his parents, Norton insisted that all of his business transactions be conducted under the name Daniel Quilp, choosing the name of the abominable character from Charles Dickens's *Old Curiosity Shop* because he thought that no one else would ever want to use it.

In the spring of 1888, Norton learned that two of the era's greatest actors, Edwin Booth and Lawrence Barrett, were appearing in Nashville. Hoping to secure them for performances in Louisville, Norton sent his trusted business manager, James B. Camp, who hired Booth and Barrett for three nights at $10,000. With no venue for the shows, Norton leased the former Southern Exposition grounds and purchased three thousand seats, together with a carload of scenery. The May Festival began May 10 with *Julius Caesar, Hamlet, King Lear,* and *The Merchant of Venice* and brought in a profit of approximately $5,000.

The success of these shows, coupled with the three thousand chairs he now owned, convinced Norton of the need for a new auditorium. In the fall of 1888, he hired a contractor to build a stage and a three-thousand-seat amphitheater on a lot he owned on the southwest corner of Fourth and Hill Streets. Completed in late summer the following year at a cost of $200,000, the Amphitheatre Auditorium, which gained the motto "only for great attractions," presented operas and other theatrical attractions that had usually bypassed Louisville when it lacked a large stage. Opening week festivities kicked off September 23 with *The Merchant of Venice* performed by Booth and Barrett, who stayed the entire week for a selection of nine Shakespearean plays.

The auditorium quickly became a center of social activities and remained so for the next fifteen years as it attracted other great performers such as Adelina Patti, Sarah Bernhardt, Lillian Russell, and Henry Irving. Other performers included the New York Symphony Orchestra, Edward Strauss and the Viennese Orchestra and the Metropolitan Opera. New York governor and vice presidential candidate Theodore Roosevelt, delivered a political speech there in 1900. Any manager who filled the hall received either a gold-headed cane or an umbrella from Norton.

The eccentric Norton was forever an avid city patron as well as a critic of Louisville and its residents. He chided the citizens when a great performance did not sell out and deplored the collapse of the SATELLITES OF MERCURY, a group of area boosters who sponsored an annual festival and parade that attracted thousands from as far away as Richmond, New Orleans, and Baltimore. These and other failed ventures led Norton to label the city as "Dead Town," "Cemeteryville," and "Calamity Gulch"; he dubbed himself "The Duke of Dead Town." However, Norton was also a staunch supporter of his beloved city and gave generously to its residents. Friday mornings were known as "hard luck days" at the auditorium. Norton would dress as a policeman to hear a number of complaints, usually relating to money problems, and help those less fortunate. On his deathbed, Norton authorized that each employee of the auditorium be sent three months' salary.

Norton fell ill three months after his mother's death in 1901 and suffered a paralytic stroke two years later. He moved to Coronado Beach, California, where he had purchased property while on a visit in 1888, and oversaw from a wheelchair the construction of a fourteen-room home. From the Pacific coast, Norton attempted to convince Louisville to build a much-needed coliseum and even offered the property on which his auditorium sat. As it turned out, however, after the auditorium closed in April 1904, the property was sold at auction to real estate developer BRUCE HOBLITZELL for $900 and the structure was torn down and replaced by an apartment building and private homes.

Norton was cremated in Los Angeles, and his ashes were placed at the Maple Grove Cemetery in Russellville. He left the majority of his $900,000 estate to the Louisville Baptist Orphans' Home and divided the remaining $70,000 among family and friends.

See John Spalding Gatton, *"Only for Great Attractions"—The Amphitheatre Auditorium, Louisville, Kentucky: A Brief History and a Checklist of Performances, 1889-1904* (Louisville 1977); Raymond J. Randles, "A Biography of the Norton Family" (M.A. thesis, University of Louisville, 1961); *Courier-Journal,* May 16, 1903.

NORTON HEALTHCARE. The Alliant Health System was created on June 27, 1989, through the merger of NKC, owner of Norton and KOSAIR CHILDREN'S HOSPITALS, and Methodist Evangelical Hospital (MEH). Spearheaded by NKC president G. Rodney Wolford and MEH president E. Dean Grout after extensive consultation with the constituents of both organizations, the merger reflected changing realities in the American health care system as well as the peculiar needs and strengths of each corporation. NKC was growing rapidly during the late 1980s, especially in tertiary services, and had a serious capacity shortage. MEH had a strong base of primary care physicians but a surplus of rooms because of shorter hospital stays and a growing trend toward outpatient care. Studies by consultant Montague Brown indicated that a merger would address the needs and maximize the strengths of both organizations.

The merger created a new governance structure consisting of the Alliant Health System Board of Directors to set policy for the entire system; the Children's Services Operating Board to oversee Kosair Children's Hospital and related children's services; and the Adult Service Operating Board to oversee Norton and Methodist Evangelical Hospitals and other services for adult patients. Grout retired at the time of the merger, and Wolford became president of the new corporation. He was succeeded in 1993 by Stephen A. Williams.

The years following the merger witnessed many changes in internal organization, along with the expansion and realignment of services. Several top administrators from NKC and MEH took positions in the new corporation, while others left for positions elsewhere. The Norton and MEH medical staffs merged into a single adult medical staff. On June 1, 1993, Methodist Evangelical Hospital became the Alliant Medical Pavilion, offering a broad range of outpatient services. The Norton Hospital Foundation and the Methodist Evangelical Hospital Foundation consolidated to create the Norton-Methodist Evangelical Foundation in 1994.

By 1997, along with specialized services and programs such as the Women's Pavilion, the Kenton D. Leatherman Spine Center, the Brain Institute, the Cancer Treatment Center, the Norton Psychiatric Center, Home Health, and Occupational Health Services, the Alliant Health System had entered into affiliation and management service agreements with more than twenty HOSPITALS in Kentucky, Indiana, and Illinois. Nearby affiliated hospitals included Floyd Memorial Hospital and Health Services in NEW ALBANY, Indiana; the Medical Center of Southern Indiana in Charlestown, Indiana; and Harrison County Hospital in CORYDON, Indiana. Total operating revenues for 1996 were $348 million. In the same year the three Louisville hospitals admitted 28,824 inpatients and outpatients; the Southend Medical Center, community intermediate care centers and clinics, and the Norton and Kosair Children's emergency rooms had a total of 440,476 visits; the system employed approximately forty-eight hundred people; and the combined adult and children's medical staffs had nearly two thousand members.

In the fall of 1998, Alliant purchased from Columbia/HCA Healthcare Corp. its three remaining Louisville area hospitals—AUDUBON, Suburban, and Southwest, which gave Alliant a total of six hospitals in Jefferson County. Alliant also managed seventeen other hospitals in Kentucky, Indiana, and Illinois. The sale ended almost three decades of competition between for-profit and not-for-profit hospitals in Jefferson County. On October 20, 1998, Jefferson Fiscal Court voted to authorize the issuance of $225 million in tax-free bonds by Alliant Health System to help the company finance its purchase of the three Jefferson County hospitals. Alliant's remaining competitors were Jewish Hospital HealthCare services, the Baptist Healthcare System, and CARITAS HEALTH SERVICES, all of which are not-for-profit.

Alliant Healthcare System changed its name to Norton Healthcare on January 9, 1999. The new name, associated with an earlier hospital in Louisville, was chosen to reflect the company's commitment to remain headquartered in Louisville. The following health care servers are associated with the Norton name: Norton Medical Pavilion, Norton Hospital, Kosair Children's Hospital, Norton Audubon Hospital, Norton Southwest Hospital, Norton Spring View Hospital, Norton Suburban Hospital, and Norton Immediate Care Centers.

See Betty Lou Amster and Barbara G. Zingman, *The Mission: The History of Methodist Evangelical Hospital, 1960–1993* (Louisville 1994); Gail McGowan Mellor, *Kosair Children's Hospital: A History, 1892–1992* (Louisville 1992); *Courier-Journal,* May 20, 1998.

Carl E. Kramer

NUGENT SAND COMPANY. Most of central Louisville and the west end is underlain by a thick deposit of sand and gravel, glacial outwash sediments that were swept down the Ohio Valley by melted water from ice sheets when they began retreating across Ohio and Indiana after the last glacial advances of the

Pleistocene Epoch or Ice Age.

In earlier days the city was pockmarked with sandpits. Pits in the Fort Hill and Cabbage Patch areas and along Seventh Street Rd., now filled in, supplied molding sand for the iron industry as well as sand for the fertilizer industry. But most sand and gravel is used in construction, and in the Louisville area it has been supplied in abundance by the banks and bed of the Ohio River from either the shores of Louisville or sources upstream. River shipments of sand and gravel traditionally constituted one of the largest cargoes of water transportation from the Louisville port.

Many companies have participated in this important Louisville industry, but the Nugent Sand Co. is now the largest sand and gravel company in the state. Since the 1980s, the company estimates, its products have been used in about 70 percent of residential construction in Jefferson County. Both the ready-mix concrete industry and the asphalt industry used Nugent Sand products in the construction of Louisville International Airport, local highways, streets, and sidewalks.

In 1898 the Sand Island Sand Co. had an office at S Fifth St. It was owned and operated by three Nugent brothers as an adjunct to their principal business as contractors to the railroad. This company first provided ballast to be used under railroad track. By 1901 the three brothers—William F. (1870-1948), John R. (1873-1931), and Thomas C.L. (1880-1941)—had formed the W.F. Nugent & Bros. construction company. In January 1908 the Sand Island Sand Co. was incorporated as the Nugent Sand Co., with William, a former leveler with the city engineer's office, as its first president. In the earliest days neither sand nor gravel was in much demand. One yard of sand would serve to lay two thousand bricks or five perches of stone, one perch of stone measuring approximately 24 cubic feet; and today's concrete industry, using gravel aggregate, was still in its infancy.

As Louisville grew, however, the demand for gravel-aggregate concrete also grew. By 1930, with offices and yards near the junction of Beargrass Creek and the Ohio River, the Nugent Sand Co. had become the second-largest enterprise of its kind in the South. Its dredge boat could screen, wash and grade sand and gravel, and load four great barges simultaneously. A huge conveyor belt at the Clay St. yards would unload the barges and reload the cargo onto trucks for deliveries. Sometime in the 1930s, Thomas C.L. Nugent replaced William F. as president of the company.

From 1929 until about 1962 the firm's offices were located at 627 River Rd. When this land was purchased by the state highway department for construction of Interstates 71 and 64, the company relocated. During the presidency of T.C. Nugent Jr. (1941-81), a new flood-protected facility was built at 1833 River Rd. By 1963 the firm had completed its relocation to this, its present, address.

Thomas C. Nugent III became president of the company in 1981. In 1984 the Nugent Sand Co. merged with the E.T. Slider Co. and doubled its volume of business. In 1987 the firm redoubled its business. It acquired the assets of Martin Marietta's local sand-and-gravel operation. By 1999 it had mining sites and terminals in Columbus, Indiana; Milton, Kentucky; Bethlehem, Indiana; and Pittsburgh, Pennsylvania. New facilities in Utica, Indiana, and in Riverport in southwest Jefferson County opened at the end of the century.

See *Courier-Journal,* Feb. 28, 1930; April 1, 1962; Oct. 7, 1964; March 23, 1987; *Kentucky Progress Magazine,* Oct. 1930.

NURSING. The first "nurses" in the Louisville area, as in most areas around the country, were Roman Catholic sisters assisting in times of epidemic and war. The Sisters of Charity of Nazareth nursed those suffering during the cholera epidemic of 1833 and in 1836 opened an infirmary to care for the ill. They also offered their services as nurses to both Union and Confederate soldiers in their hospital, as well as in military hospitals (Hospital No. 1, in warehouse rooms at the corner of Broadway and Ninth St.; Hospital No. 2, Mr. Munn's Plow Factory at Eighth and Green (Liberty) Streets; Hospital No. 3, the Avery Plow Factory on Main St. between Thirteenth and Sixteenth Streets) and on hospital boats on the Ohio River from 1861 to 1865 in the Louisville area and other locations in Kentucky.

In 1869 the Sisters of Mercy of St. Louis, Missouri, sent a small group of their order to run the Louisville Marine Hospital (built in 1847) on Chestnut between Floyd and Preston Streets. The building and grounds were leased to the sisters for an initial period of two years. The order pledged to keep the building in good repair and to nurse, feed, and provide for seamen, for a fee of seventy-five cents per day per patient, with the U.S. government providing medical care and medications.

Although there were women (and men) nursing the sick and injured from the beginnings of settlement in the Louisville–Jefferson County area, nursing was not recognized as a profession until 1863, nor was there sanctioned education and training for nurses until late in the nineteenth century. The first nursing school in Louisville (and in Kentucky) was organized at Norton Memorial Infirmary (NMI) in 1886. When the NMI School of Nursing opened, it claimed to be the second established south of the Mason-Dixon Line, the eighth west of the Allegheny Mountains, and the thirty-sixth in the entire United States. The first graduate was Fannie Westbay, who graduated in 1887. The nursing classes remained fairly small, the numbers staying in the single digits until 1904. The school's two-year program was expanded to three years in 1903. Other training schools for professional nurses soon followed.

Local philanthropist Jenny Casseday lobbied for, supported, and pushed through the idea of a school connected with the Louisville City Hospital (LCH),also known as the Louisville Training School for Nurses, which also opened in 1886, graduating its first class in 1889. Methodist Deaconess Hospital added a nursing school in 1900. In the first quarter of the twentieth century, seven more nursing schools were established, all connected with local hospitals: Jewish Hospital, 1909; Waverly Hills Sanitorium, 1910; Saints Mary and Elizabeth, 1915 (the first Roman Catholic school of nursing in Kentucky); Saint Joseph Infirmary, 1919; Saint Anthony Hospital, 1923; Kentucky Baptist Hospital, 1924 and Red Cross Hospital, date unknown; Children's Hospital served as the training site for pediatrics for many of the schools. In 1914 the state of Kentucky established a board of examiners for trained nurses, thus beginning state governmental regulation and recognition of the profession. Licenses for practical nurses were first issued in 1950.

Nurses' training was rigid and difficult. The student nurses were required to sew their own uniforms, do cleaning as well as patient care, and work anywhere from 12-hour to 22-hour days. They kept the coal fires burning in the patients' rooms and used candles on their night rounds. They lived together in special housing, usually with several women sharing a room, and received room, board, training, and a small stipend each month while in school. The rules were strict and included criteria for grooming and personal behavior. Student nurses were suspended for getting their hair bobbed in the 1920s, and married women were still not allowed into some of the nursing schools as late as the 1940s.

Beginning in 1938, nursing education began a transition to an academic setting. Spalding College (now Spalding University) opened a nursing school that year. In 1952 the University of Louisville, with full support from the local Board of Health, tried to establish a nursing school independent of the Louisville General Hospital. The school never really got off the ground, attracting only twelve students. It was discontinued in July 1953. Other academic programs were begun at Jefferson Community College in 1968, the University of Louisville in 1974, and Bellarmine College in 1977. The move from the hospital setting to the university setting eventually forced all of the local hospital nursing schools out of business. Responding to the need for more highly educated nurses, from 1979 to 1984 the academic institutions added graduate programs in nursing.

Of course, African American women who wished to become trained nurses had few if any options in Louisville. Most of the nursing schools were restricted to whites; training for blacks was available only at the hospitals that were open to the black community. There may have been formal nurses' training at the Citizen's Auxiliary Hospital, connected with the Louisville National Medical College, but if so, it

Class at the nursing school of Sts. Mary and Elizabeth Hospital, Twelfth and Magnolia Streets, 1921.

lasted only for a few years, as the college closed in 1912. The Red Cross (Community) Hospital offered training for nurses from about 1909 through 1938 and was the only place for such training. The Louisville Council of Churches announced in 1940 that Louisville General Hospital School of Nursing would accept black students that year, but in reality, that did not happen until 1954. Saints Mary and Elizabeth and Saint Joseph accepted black women a year earlier, even though they did not admit black patients. Neither were male students accepted at some of the schools; LCH School of Nursing did not accept men until 1964, just three years before the program closed.

As during the CIVIL WAR, nurses from Louisville served during the Spanish-American War and in WORLD WAR I. A hospital unit with almost twenty nurses from Louisville General Hospital went to France, while others cared for those stationed locally at CAMP ZACHARY TAYLOR. In the fall of 1918, an influenza epidemic spread around the world, and Louisville was hit just as hard as anyplace else. The first diagnosed case in Kentucky of this flu, known as "The Spanish Lady," was at CAMP TAYLOR. Over the next few months, 1,500 died at the camp and another 879 in Louisville. There was already a shortage of medical personnel because of the war, and nurses were brought to Louisville from Ohio and Indiana, but there were still not enough to adequately care for the sick. In late October, the State Council of Defense asked Kentucky families to release any trained nurses in their employ for work where they were needed in other communities.

Louisville suffered through the GREAT DEPRESSION along with the rest of the United States, and the effect was felt in health care as in other aspects of life. One nurse, Elsie Delin, is credited with keeping Children's Free Hospital running throughout the 1930s with no nursing staff other than student nurses. January 1937 brought the great flood, and nurses were put to the test. Rising floodwaters forced Jewish Hospital to evacuate some of its patients, and at Louisville General Hospital, the almost one hundred student nurses worked around the clock alongside the regular graduate nurses and some additional volunteer nurses. Illnesses were compounded by the lack of SANITATION and the intense cold.

WORLD WAR II brought about another shortage of medical personnel as nurses and doctors joined the military. Hospital nursing schools around the country trained nurses for the newly formed Cadet Nurse Corps (1943–48), with Deaconess, Jewish, Baptist, Norton, Saint Anthony, and Saint Joseph serving as training sites. At one point it appeared that nurses might be drafted, and for the most part, this idea had the support of Louisville area nurses. The Red Cross stated that Louisville nurses were already applying for military service at four times the national rate. To meet the needs of the local hospitals, a series of lectures was offered through the Louisville General Hospital to help those women who were no longer working in the field prepare to assist in emergencies. The shortage continued even after the war ended, as married nurses left to join their husbands, single nurses left to get married, and few of the returning military nurses joined the staffs at local hospitals.

In 1942 the Army Air Force established the School of Air Evacuation at BOWMAN FIELD to train medical personnel, including flight nurses, for evacuation of patients from combat zones. The first class of nurses graduated in February 1943. The nurses accepted for this training had to meet age, height, and weight restrictions, and while in training studied aspects of the new specialized field of air medicine as well as tropical diseases and Arctic medicine. This, the first school of its kind in the world, was moved to Texas in 1944, but first it trained over a thousand nurses who assisted in the evacuation of wounded and sick soldiers from the frontlines in the European, Pacific, and Southeast Asian theaters of war.

In 1944 and again in 1952, Louisville was hit by an epidemic of infantile paralysis, commonly known as polio. During the first epidemic, as had happened during the influenza outbreak of 1918–19, there was a shortage of medical personnel because of the war. Hospitals were desperate, and nurses were recruited by the American Red Cross from out of state for temporary service in Louisville. Nurses worked shifts of up to sixteen hours, often with no days off, doing the exhaustive manual labor of caring for polio patients. One of the most famous nurses of the century, Sr. Elizabeth Kenney, visited Kosair Crippled Children's Hospital (the only hospital in Kentucky she visited), teaching her method of treatment for polio: application of heat and retraining of muscles.

The first organization of nurses in Louisville was the Louisville Graduate Nurses Club, founded in 1896, which later changed its name to the Jefferson County Graduate Nurses Club. In 1905 the alumnae of the Norton Memorial Infirmary founded their own organization, and in 1906 it merged with other groups around the state to create the Kentucky State Association of Graduate Nurses. This group, later known as the Kentucky Nurses Association (KNA), had units that negotiated contracts at various hospitals and political action committees that lobbied the Kentucky legislature on health-care-related issues.

After the KNA negotiated contracts at two Louisville hospitals in 1980, activists began an effort to unionize the seven thousand local nurses in 1989. The Nurses Professional Organization (NPO) was organized to address issues of working conditions and short staffing at local hospitals. Throughout the 1990s there were labor disputes between the NPO and some of the hospitals in Louisville, often resulting in charges being filed with the National Labor Relations Board. The NPO argued that patient care was compromised by the staffing levels. The organization also took its concerns to the state legislature, lobbying for restrictions on work that could be done by unlicensed aides and asking hospitals to disclose the levels of training of their nursing staff.

What began as a purely voluntary line of

work done almost exclusively by religious orders has evolved into a profession open to men and women, requiring a college education and state licensure. This evolution has also raised the status of the nurse from servant of the doctor to colleague of the doctor, in a highly technical and rapidly changing health care setting.

Nursing Schools in Louisville

Norton Memorial Infirmary/ Norton Hospital	1886–1976
Louisville City Hospital/ General Hospital	1886–1967
Methodist Deaconess Hospital	1900–1951
Waverly Hills Hospital	1910–1917
Jewish Hospital	1909–1947
Red Cross Community Hospital	1909-1938
Saints Mary & Elizabeth Hospital	1915–1970
Saint Joseph Infirmary	1919–1971
Saint Anthony Hospital	1923–1969
Kentucky Baptist Hospital	1924–1983
Spalding University	1938–present
Jefferson Community College	1968–present
University of Louisville	1974–present
Bellarmine College	1977–present

See Nancy Baird, "The 'Spanish Lady' in Kentucky 1918–1919," *Filson Club History Quarterly* 50 (July 1976): 290–301; Haven Emerson, M.D., and Anna C. Phillips, *Hospitals and Health Agencies of Louisville 1924* (Louisville 1925); Darlene Clark Hine, *Black Women in White: Racial Conflict and Cooperation in the Nursing Profession, 1890–1950* (Bloomington, Ind. 1989); Arnita Jones, *The Louisville General Hospital School of Nursing, 1887–1967* (Louisville 1988); *Kentucky Nurse* 32 (Jan.–Feb. 1984); *Courier-Journal,* Oct. 5, 11, 24, 1918; Jan. 30, 1919; June 21, 1940; April 26, 30; May 10; Dec. 6, 1942; Feb. 19; Sept. 15, 19, 1943; Oct. 4, 1944; Jan. 1, 22; May 19; Nov. 30, 1945; Nov. 14, 1948; May 27, 1950; Oct. 5, 1952; Feb. 6, 1954; Nov. 21, 1976; July 7, 1982; Feb. 22, July 19, Dec. 15, 1989; Feb. 8, April 1, 1995; *Louisville Times,* Jan. 23, Feb. 4, 1937; Dec. 12, 1956; May 12, 1976; Gail McGowan Mellor, *Kosair Children's Hospital: A History, 1892–1992* (Louisville 1992); Mary Prisca Pfeffer, *In Love and Mercy: A History of the Sisters of Mercy, Louisville, Kentucky, 1869–1989* (Louisville ca 1992); Justine J. Speer and Arnita A. Jones, "A History of Louisville General Hospital School of Nursing," *Filson Club History Quarterly* 67 (Oct. 1993): 462–81; World War II Flight Nurses Association, *The Story of Air Evacuation, 1942–1989* (Dallas 1989); Samuel W. Thomas, *Constant Medicine, Constant Care: Kentucky Baptist Hospitals* (Louisville 1990); Barbara Zingman and Betty Lou Amster, *A Legendary Vision: The History of Jewish Hospital* (Louisville 1997).

Katherine Burger Johnson

NUTT, GRADY LEE (b Amarillo, Texas, September 2, 1934; d near Vinemont, Alabama, November 23, 1982). Baptist minister and humorist. The son of a Baptist preacher, Grady Nutt was best-known for his warm, down-home sense of humor that often poked gentle fun at religious institutions. From the age of three, Nutt was involved in church activities, usually singing hymns at various church functions. When he was thirteen, Nutt decided to enter the ministry and was licensed as a Baptist pastor by his church. He went on to attend Wayland Baptist College in Plainview, Texas, and later Baylor University, where he majored in music and graduated in 1957. About that time Nutt met and married Eleanor Wilson.

In 1960 the couple, along with their two infant sons, Perry and Toby, moved to Louisville, where Nutt enrolled in the SOUTHERN BAPTIST THEOLOGICAL SEMINARY. Upon graduation, Nutt accepted a position at the seminary as an assistant to the president. From 1962 to 1964, he served as pastor of Graefenburg Baptist Church, in a small town near Frankfort, Kentucky. Then in 1966, a friend suggested that Nutt, a talented storyteller, try his hand in the entertainment business. Though at first reluctant, Nutt pursued the idea; after landing appearances on various TELEVISION talk shows, including *The Mike Douglas Show,* he decided in 1969 to become a full-time entertainer.

Nutt appeared on *The Mike Douglas Show* eleven times and over the course of his career made numerous appearances on television and radio programs, in addition to up to two hundred personal speaking engagements a year. About 1979 Nutt became a regular performer on the television show *Hee Haw.* For a brief time, Nutt also had his own program, *The Grady Nutt Show,* on NBC. Nutt had eight albums to his credit, including *The Gift of Laughter* and *All Day Singin' and Dinner on the Ground.* He also wrote five books, among them *Being Me* (1971) and his autobiography, *So Good, So Far* (1979). Nutt's life was tragically cut short in 1982 when the plane he was on crashed outside of Vinemont, Alabama. After a memorial service at CRESCENT HILL BAPTIST CHURCH in Louisville, where Nutt was a member, he was buried on his in-laws' farm in Somerville, Tennessee.

See *Courier-Journal,* Nov. 25, 1982.

OAKLAND RACE COURSE. Louisville's legendary CHURCHILL DOWNS owes at least part of its renown to Oakland House and Race Course. Oakland was the first Louisville track to gain national prominence and is thought by *Harper's* to have ensured for the city of Louisville and the state of Kentucky the title "racehorse region of America."

The racecourse, with no long stretches, was built in 1832 by the seventy-six-member Louisville Association for the Improvement of the Breed of Horses. The 55-acre site, located on the west side of Oakland Plank Rd. (Seventh St.) south of Magnolia Ave., offered picturesque views framed by the tall, graceful oaks that gave the track its name. On the beautiful grounds was the Oakland House, an imposing three-story Greek Revival building, which served as a clubhouse and visitors' hotel. Women were made welcome in the clubhouse by a handsomely furnished ladies' room and a private pavilion.

By the late 1830s the racecourse had become popular with Kentuckians. Samuel Osgood, a New England cleric who visited Louisville in 1837, though he disapproved of racing found himself intrigued by "the furor that prevailed . . . the whole city in commotion," while "the August head of Henry Clay towered up among the sporting magnates on the stand erected for the judges." The *Spirit of the Times* declared in 1838, "The Oakland Course is now probably one of the most complete in the country in its fixtures and appointments."

Oakland was then operated by Louisiana racing entrepreneur Yelverton N. Oliver, who had become a part owner. He used large purses, especially for match races, to promote the racetrack. The most famous match race pitted a Kentucky horse, Grey Eagle, against a Louisiana horse, Wagner, on September 30, 1839. The race was a grueling best-two-of-three contest in four-mile heats. The winner would receive the then unheard-of purse of $20,000.

The match was the talk of the South. It brought hundreds of famous racing enthusiasts to Louisville. "The Bench, the Bar, the Senate and the Press, the Army and Navy, and all the et cetera that pleasure and curiosity attracted were here," a racing magazine of the day reported. The less noteworthy who could not afford to be in the stands looked on from vantage points in treetops and carriages.

The first heat was won by Wagner. Just when it looked as if Grey Eagle had a chance to win the second heat, Wagner, the favorite of the Deep South, pulled ahead and won by a neck in 7:44—"best time ever south of the Potomac," the *Louisville Daily Journal* asserted. Wagner was declared the winner of the match, but disgruntled Kentuckians, who backed Grey Eagle, successfully pushed for a rematch. A week later, on October 5, 1839, the rematch was run with a third horse, Em Ward, as a pacesetter. Grey Eagle won the first heat by a length, and Wagner won the second. Excitement built as the two horses vied for the third and deciding heat. In the stretch Wagner bumped Grey Eagle, who was left to stumble and limp to the finish line behind the victorious Wagner. Sabotage was rumored by disappointed Kentuckians loyal to Grey Eagle, but nothing came of it. Some say the national publicity created by the match made Kentucky famous as the preeminent horse-racing state.

Despite good attendance at such widely publicized races, Oakland suffered financial reverses in the late 1840s and closed by the mid-1850s. It served as the rendezvous point for Kentucky troops during the MEXICAN WAR and as a cavalry remount station during the CIVIL WAR. The deteriorating property became the refuge of society's outcasts by the 1870s and a scene of frequent crime, which the press reported as occurring "on the Oakland." When Alice Hegan (who later married poet CALE YOUNG RICE) wrote *Mrs. Wiggs of the Cabbage Patch* (1901), she gave "the Oakland" a fictional name that has persisted. A short street at the north end of the old grounds bears the name Oakland, the only reminder of the once-famous track.

See Samuel Osgood, "Eighteen Years: A Reminiscence of Kentucky," in *Knickerbocker Gallery: A Testimonial to the Editor of the Knickerbocker Magazine* (New York 1855), 22–30; Tom Stephens, "Oakland House," *Kentucky Monthly* 2 (April 1999): 21–22.

George H. Yater

OATES, WARREN (b Depoy, Kentucky, July 5, 1928; d Hollywood Hills, California, April 3, 1982). Actor. Warren Oates was the son of Bayless E. and Sarah (Mercer) Oates and a fourth-generation Kentuckian. His life story could very well have been a novel penned by Hemingway. Oates grew up in the small coal-mining town of Depoy during hard times. However, by the time he was thirteen, his father's new job as an aide at the Kentucky Baptist Hospital in Louisville had improved the family's circumstances. After graduating from the LOUISVILLE MALE HIGH SCHOOL, Oates joined the Marines and served as an airplane mechanic for two years. After discharge he returned home to drift through several majors at the UNIVERSITY OF LOUISVILLE and to act in a student play that convinced him he wanted to be an actor. This led to his involvement with Louisville's Shakespeare in Central Park and his being tutored by C. DOUGLAS RAMEY, the founder. At twenty-five, upon the urging of Ramey, Oates went to New York with a head full of dreams and $200 in his pocket. He landed a job at CBS that had been vacated by James Dean. Oates's real break finally came in 1954 when he was cast in a Theatre Guild TELEVISION play. Fortunately, the show won a Christopher Award.

In 1958 Oates headed west, and the following year he made his film debut with a brief appearance in *Up Periscope. Yellowstone Kelly, The Rise and Fall of Legs Diamond,* and *High Country* quickly followed. Mixed in were television credits on *Have Gun, Will Travel, Gunsmoke,* and *The Rifleman.* In 1962, through the producer of *High Country,* Oates was chosen to play Jack Lord's buddy on a new television series, *Stoney Burke.* By 1966 his star shone brightly in the Yul Brynner western *The Return of the Seven,* and afterward in the Henry Fonda film *Welcome to Hard Times.*

In 1970s *Time* magazine praised Oates as being among the finest American actors for his title role in *Dillinger.* His increased popularity launched an extremely busy decade for Oates, averaging two or three films per year. In 1977 he married his third wife, Judith Jones, in Muhlenberg County, Kentucky. Oates died of a heart attack at age fifty-three and is buried in Hollywood's Forest Lawn Cemetery.

Warder Harrison

OATES, WAYNE E. (b Greenville, South Carolina, June 24, 1917; d Louisville, October 21, 1999). Theologian and author. Oates, the youngest of six children, was the son of Joseph A. and Lulu Oates, both textile mill workers in Greenville. As recounted in the autobiographical *Struggle to Be Free* (1983), Oates's earliest childhood memories are of poverty and an unremitting struggle with need. The family, abandoned by the father within weeks of Oates's birth, lived in a squalid, unheated mill house, with the only water provided by a commonly shared pump in the street. His mother and three siblings worked in the mills, where their combined pay was less than $30 a week. It was during Oates's grade school years that he discovered his love of learning. "I had found in school the avenue of my freedom from the grinding poverty, ugliness, filth and brutality I saw happening around me. I sensed that learning words would give me power for the struggle to be free. School—education—would be my avenue to the larger world of mankind where I could meet and learn from all kinds of people."

From these unpromising beginnings as a cotton-mill boy, Oates fashioned, with tenacity, intellect, and an indomitable spirit, a remarkable career as one of America's most influential theologians. He enjoyed an international reputation in the field of the psychology of RELIGION and in the movements of pastoral care and counseling. He is considered the father of pastoral care, a discipline that combines psychotherapy with theological interpretation. He was the author of more than fifty-seven books and also wrote hundreds of articles addressing the relationship between faith and healing. In a 1968 article he coined the expression "workaholic," a word whose use is now ubiquitous, employing an inventive use of the suffix that is now in standard use for describing addictions.

Oates received his education at Mars Hill Junior College, Wake Forest University (B.A., 1940), Duke University, SOUTHERN BAPTIST THEOLOGICAL SEMINARY (B.D., 1945; Th.D., 1947), Union Theological Seminary, and the UNIVERSITY OF LOUISVILLE.

Ordained a Baptist minister in 1940, he served as a pastor of Baptist churches in Nash County, North Carolina (1940-43); Union City, Kentucky (1943-45); and Louisville (1945-48). He was a professor at Southern Baptist Theological Seminary from 1947 to 1974 and again from 1983 to 1992. In 1974 he formally joined the medical school faculty at the University of Louisville, where he became professor of psychiatry and behavioral sciences. He was the first full professor at any U.S. medical school whose only graduate training was from theological institutions.

He married Pauline Rhodes and had two children, William Wayne, who died in May 1999, and Charles Edwin. He is buried in CAVE HILL CEMETERY.

See *Courier-Journal,* Oct. 23, Oct. 24, 1999; Wayne E. Oates, *Introduction to Pastoral Counseling* (Nashville 1954); *Workaholics: Make Laziness Work for You* (Garden City, N.Y., 1978); *The Religious Care of Psychiatric Patients* (Philadelphia 1978); *Struggle to Be Free* (Philadelphia, 1983).

OGDEN, CHARLES FRANKLIN (b Charlestown, Indiana; d Louisville, April 10, 1933). U.S. congressman. Ogden attended public school in Indiana and then graduated from the University of Louisville Law School in 1896. In 1897 he took up practice in Louisville, and in 1898 and 1899 he served as a member of the Kentucky House of Representatives. He served as captain in a volunteer infantry company in the Spanish-American War. He was elected to the Sixty-sixth and Sixty-seventh Congresses as a Republican, where he served from March 4, 1919, until March 3, 1923, when he failed to be renominated. He returned to Louisville and practiced law until his death. He is buried in Resthaven Cemetery.

See *Biographical Directory of the American Congress 1776–1961* (Washington, D.C., 1961).

OGDEN, NEWELL & WELCH. Ogden, Newell & Welch is a Louisville law firm that evolved from the private practice of BERNARD FLEXNER beginning in 1898. Before 1898, Bernard and his brother Washington had a business known as Flexner Brothers that printed stationery, did engraving, and published books. After Bernard became a lawyer, Washington went on to work for the Courier-Journal Job Printing Co. Bernard practiced law alone from the Kentucky Title Building on Fifth St. between Jefferson and Market until 1903, when he joined the firm of Bodley, Baskin & Morancy, which then became Bodley, Baskin & Flexner. In 1905 Flexner left the firm and resumed solo practice. In 1909 he became a partner with J. Wheeler Campbell and, along with Robert S. Gordon, created the firm of Flexner & Campbell. In 1911 Gordon became a partner, and the firm name was changed to Flexner, Campbell & Gordon. Late in 1911 or early in 1912, Campbell left the firm, which then took the name of Flexner & Gordon.

In 1914 Flexner moved to Chicago and became associated with Samuel Insull's utility empire, after which the firm operated under the name of Robert G. Gordon. In 1915 Joseph Scott Laurent, who had moved to Louisville from Nashville, Tennessee, to join the firm in 1913, became a partner in Gordon & Laurent.

On January 1, 1922, the Gordon firm merged with the Louisville firm of Bruce & Bullitt and became Bruce, Bullitt, Gordon & Laurent. On January 1, 1926, Gordon and Laurent left the Bullitt firm along with Squire R. Ogden, who had joined it in the summer of 1923 along with John E. Tarrant, to practice on their own once again. In 1928 Ogden was made a partner of the firm, now named Gordon, Laurent & Ogden. In 1934 Thomas M. Galphin, who had joined Gordon and Laurent in 1926 after they had left the Bullitt firm, was made a partner, and his name was added to the end of the firm's name: Gordon, Laurent, Ogden & Galphin.

On September 28, 1935, Joseph Laurent died. One year later, Daniel L. Street joined the firm. Two years after that, in 1938, Robert Gordon died. In 1940 John E. Tarrant left the Bullitt firm and joined the Ogden firm, now Ogden, Tarrant, Galphin & Street. On October 1, 1947, Percy Brown Jr. joined the Ogden firm, and Daniel Street left to become vice president and later president of Brown-Forman Distillers Corp.

In the summer of 1948, there was a sweeping reshuffling of the law firms in Louisville. At this time Tarrant left the Ogden firm and, along with members of the Bullitt & Middleton firm, formed Bullitt, Dawson & Tarrant. In September 1948 Charles A. Robertson, in November 1951 Malcolm Y. Marshall, and in July 1956 Richard F. Newell joined the Ogden firm. On December 1, 1958, William H. Abell, who had joined the firm in 1945, left to become the president and chief executive officer of Commonwealth Life Insurance Co. The firm name then changed to Ogden, Brown, Robertson & Marshall.

In January 1959 James S. Welch joined the Ogden firm. In 1961 Brown retired from law and died in 1964. The firm was then known as Ogden, Robertson & Marshall. On June 2, 1973, Joseph A. Paradis III joined and in 1977 left the Ogden firm to become executive vice president of Brandeis Machinery and Supply Co.

On December 1, 1973, the firm moved its offices to One RIVERFRONT PLAZA. In December 1984, Robertson retired from the firm. A year and a half later, in 1986, Marshall left the firm to join Barnett & Alagia, and the firm was then called Ogden & Robertson. On January 1, 1989, the Ogden firm merged with the Lexington firm of Sturgill, Turner & Truitt and the Ashland firm of Welch & Purdom and became Ogden, Sturgill & Welch. Three years later, in 1992, the firms split off from each other. The firm name then became Ogden, Newell & Welch. The firm has represented clients in areas of business law. Its most notable clients have been Kentucky Utilities and BROWN-FORMAN CORP.

OGLE, PAUL W. (b Vevay, Indiana, June 18, 1907; d Jeffersonville, Indiana, March 22, 1989). Businessman and philanthropist. Although a native of Vevay, Indiana, Ogle lived in Jeffersonville for more than forty years, where he established himself as a well-respected businessman. Ogle was the founder of Silgas, Inc. in Jeffersonville. His work as a businessman was equaled by his generosity. Ogle was founder and president of the Paul Ogle Foundation, which was formed in 1979 and has continued to contribute money to a number of area causes including education and the restoration of Vevay. Ogle's generosity extended to INDIANA UNIVERSITY SOUTHEAST in NEW ALBANY. In 1996, seven years after his death, the Paul W. Ogle Cultural and Community Center opened its doors on the university campus. Ogle is buried in the Vevay Cemetery.

O'HARA, THEODORE (b Danville, Kentucky, February 11, 1820; d Guerrytown, Alabama, June 6, 1867). Journalist, soldier, and poet. Theodore O'Hara, the son of noted educator Kean O'Hara, graduated from St. Joseph College in Bardstown in 1839. After being admitted to the bar in 1842, he abandoned the legal profession to pursue a career in journalism and went to work for the treasury department in 1845.

Appointed captain and assistant quartermaster at the outbreak of the MEXICAN WAR, O'Hara served on the staff of Gen. Gideon J. Pillow during the American advance on Mexico City. He was breveted major for "gallant and meritorious conduct" on August 20, 1847, and honorably discharged on October 15, 1848.

In 1850 O'Hara, an ardent supporter of American expansionism, joined Gen. Narciso Lopez, who sought to liberate Cuba from Spanish rule. As colonel of Lopez's "Kentucky Regiment," O'Hara was seriously wounded in the battle of Cardenas on May 18, 1850. Contrary to most accounts, which place the event during the Mexican War, O'Hara wrote his famous martial elegy, "The Bivouac of the Dead," during the aftermath of the Cardenas expedition while recovering from his wounds, not during the war with Mexico. In the years following the CIVIL WAR, the second quatrain of the first stanza was adopted as the formal inscription for display in the country's national CEMETERIES.

"On Fame's eternal camping-ground
Their silent tents are spread
And Glory guards with solemn round
The bivouac of the dead."

Lopez's defeat and death in 1851 led O'Hara to return to journalism. In 1852 he helped found the *LOUISVILLE TIMES* (not to be confused with the later newspaper of the same name), a staunch Democratic organ that supported Stephen Douglas for the presidency; denounced the antiforeign, anti-Catholic Know-Nothing Party; and advocated the annexation of Cuba.

The prospect of serving in Gen. John A. Quitman's "filibuster" expedition against Cuba led O'Hara to leave the Times in 1853. When Quitman's expedition was abandoned, O'Hara obtained a commission in the U.S. Army. A captain in the Second U.S. Cavalry, he returned to Louisville in 1855 as a recruiting officer prior to his service against the Indians on the Texas frontier. He was charged with drunkenness by Lt. Col. Robert E. Lee and reluctantly resigned in 1856 to avoid a court-martial.

There is little evidence to support accounts of O'Hara's subsequent service with William Walker's "filibusters" in Nicaragua. After serving on the editorial staff of the *Mobile (Alabama) Register,* O'Hara enlisted in the Confederate Army in 1861. Although he distinguished himself as a staff officer at Shiloh and Stone's River, O'Hara, a bitter critic of Gen. Braxton Bragg and the Jefferson Davis administration, spent the balance of the war in a futile effort to obtain a regimental command.

Settling in Columbus, Georgia, after the war, he later moved to Guerrytown, Alabama. He was buried in Columbus, Georgia and was reinterred in the Frankfort Cemetery on September 15, 1874.

See J. Stoddard Johnston, "Sketch of Theodore O'Hara," *Register of the Kentucky Historical Society* 11 (Sept. 1913): 67–72; Edgar Erskine Hume, "Colonel Theodore O'Hara: Author of the Bivouac of the Dead," *Southern Sketches* 6 (Charlottesville, Va. 1936).

James M. Prichard

OHIO RIVER. The Ohio River Basin comprises a large geographic area of the United States east of the Mississippi River—204,000 square miles. Nearly the size of France, it contains about 25 million people and reaches northeast into New York, west to Illinois, and south through the drainage area of the Tennessee River into Georgia, Alabama, and Mississippi. Through the heart of this vast area, the 981-mile-long Ohio River carries the largest volume of water of all the tributaries of the Mississippi River. The Ohio is formed by the juncture of the Allegheny and Monongahela Rivers at Pittsburgh, Pennsylvania, and empties into the Mississippi at Cairo, Illinois.

Native American cultures used the resources of the Ohio for centuries, drinking its waters, eating its fish, and transporting trade goods. The river was the principal route of transport during the great migration to the trans-Appalachian West in the late eighteenth and early nineteenth centuries. Traveling by flatboat, keelboat, and later by steamboat, these pioneers sought new homes and new lives in the much publicized Kentucky country. In its natural, unimproved state, the Ohio was littered with snags (trees and brush rafts) and strewn with boulders, and its flow was broken by sand and gravel bars, rocks, rapids, and the major impediment to navigation, the Falls at Louisville. Here, within a distance of 21/2 miles, the river dropped 26 feet over a series of rock outcroppings, ledges, and narrow passages. The FALLS OF THE OHIO is the reason the Louisville metropolitan area exists today.

As communities at the Falls grew and as river craft evolved, authorities sought ways to overcome the natural impediments to safe and dependable navigation. Located 600 miles downstream from Pittsburgh, the Falls was the only place on the river where the natural bedrock was exposed. It was navigable for only a brief period each year during high-water season; at seasons of low water, the Falls area was not navigable. At high water, pilots could "shoot the rapids," navigating through narrow, boulder-strewn passages that often caused loss of cargo, craft, and lives.

By 1798, specially licensed pilots were contracted to take boats over the Falls. Later known as the Falls Pilots Association, these public officials were listed in the Louisville city directory until 1901. The hydrographic studies and mapping of the Falls in 1766 by Thomas Hutchins publicized the nature and extent of the barrier, and as early as 1781 THOMAS JEFFERSON speculated on possible improvements. Following years of debate, petitions, and politicking over which side of the river to build a canal on, in 1825 the Kentucky General Assembly chartered the Louisville and PORTLAND Canal Co., a private stock venture, to construct a canal with locks around the Falls; the project was completed in 1830.

After the CIVIL WAR, the movement of coal downriver from Pittsburgh increased greatly, and the size of coal tows grew in length as powerful steam towboats pushed more and more wooden barges. To accommodate the burgeoning coal trade, the Army Corps of Engineers studied means of providing a year-round dependable navigation depth on the Ohio. Following an international investigation of navigation projects, engineer officers concluded that the Ohio could best be improved by constructing a series of locks and dams to create slackwater pools. The first complete lock and dam project built by the corps on the Ohio was at Davis Island, a few miles below Pittsburgh, which was opened to navigation in 1885.

The project proved its worth, and in 1910 Congress passed the Rivers and Harbors Act, authorizing construction of a river-length system of locks and dams that would create a 9-foot navigation depth. When completed in 1929, the canalization project consisted of fifty-one movable dams with wooden wickets and a lock chamber 600 feet long and 110 feet wide. At low-water stage the dams were raised to pool water, and at high-water the wickets were lowered, allowing vessels to avoid the locks, a condition known as "open river" navigation.

River improvements were carried out at Louisville as part of the canalization system, and the structures there became known as Lock and Dam No. 41. A wicket dam was constructed, a standard-sized lock chamber was built, and the canal was widened to 200 feet. This work was completed in 1921. The hydroelectric generating station at the Falls, operated by the Louisville Gas and Electric Co., was built between 1925 and 1927. The original 1830s locks were removed about 1910, and with the work completed in the 1920s there were two operating locks at the Falls, the older lock having been completed ca 1872.

In the 1940s the transition from steam- to diesel-powered towboats enabled tows longer than the 600-foot locks to navigate the river, requiring "double locking": the string of barges had to be locked through in two maneuvers. The corps in the 1950s undertook the Ohio River Navigation Modernization Program to replace the obsolete system of wicket dams. As part of the program each of the new high-lift concrete and steel dams would replace at least two of the old structures; and each would consist of two locks, one 600 x 110 feet, and one 1,200 x 110 feet. The dams are nonnavigable, requiring traffic to use the locks. The eighteen locks and dams serve only navigation purposes; they do not provide FLOOD CONTROL. As part of the continuing modernization program, the facility at the Falls was greatly modified in the 1960s. The canal was widened to 500 feet, the old dam was replaced with a gated dam structure, and the larger 1,200-foot lock chamber was built. The project was renamed McAlpine Locks and Dam in honor of William H. McAlpine, the only civilian to serve as district engineer at Louisville. Locks and Dams 52 and 53, on the lower river, are the last of the old wicket dams and are scheduled for replacement by the Olmsted Locks and Dam project, to be completed in 2008.

In 1996 nearly 57 million tons of cargo moved through McAlpine Locks, a figure projected to triple by the year 2050. In order to accommodate that increase, the Corps of Engineers will build a second 1,200-foot lock chamber, scheduled for completion in 2006.

See Historical Files, Louisville District, U.S. Army Corps of Engineers, Louisville; Leland R. Johnson, *The Falls City Engineers: A History of the Louisville District Corps of Engineers,*

United States Army (Louisville 1974).

Charles E. Parrish

OHIO RIVER ISLANDS. In the Louisville area there are several islands located in the OHIO RIVER. One, whose remains lie beneath the pool formed by McAlpine Dam, is Corn Island, which was near the Kentucky shore out from the end of present-day Twelfth St. Initially dubbed Dunmore's Island (for the royal governor of Virginia) by THOMAS BULLITT's surveying party in 1773, it was on this island that GEORGE ROGERS CLARK camped with his small band of soldiers in 1778 while they were on their way to engage the British and the Indians in the Northwest campaigns of the Revolutionary War. Presumably, the name CORN ISLAND derives from a crop of corn raised there in the summer of 1778. In the nineteenth century, stone was quarried from the island to pave the streets of Louisville.

Moving upstream from Louisville, there are six extant islands. Sand Island, noted on some early maps of the Ohio as Sandy Island, is about 48 acres in size and is located just below Shippingport Island; both are within the boundary of the FALLS OF THE OHIO National Wildlife Conservation Area and are under the jurisdiction of the Army Corps of Engineers. Shippingport Island was formed by the construction of the Louisville and PORTLAND Canal, 1825–30. The FRENCH brothers Tarascon established the town of SHIPPINGPORT in 1806 and developed boat-building and milling operations; part of the mill structure foundation is still visible. When the canal was built, a fine stone-arch bridge at Eighteenth St. provided access from Louisville to Shippingport and ELM TREE GARDEN, a popular entertainment area. The town was subject to frequent flooding, and after each flood fewer people returned. The 1937 flood had devastating effects, washing away many buildings; after that there were only a handful of inhabitants. The last residents left the island in the late 1950s when the federal GOVERNMENT purchased the 250-acre area for the construction of the McAlpine Locks and Dam project. The Louisville Gas and Electric Co. built its hydroelectric generating station on the lower end of the island in the 1920s. Though most of Shippingport Island is not accessible to the public, the corps has a small visitor area near the locks.

Towhead Island is a small, 12-acre area located just upstream of the BIG FOUR BRIDGE and offshore from the Municipal Boat Harbor. A map in *The Western Pilot* (1847) shows a small, unnamed sandbar at the location of the present Towhead Island. According to river lore, this island was formed around a flatboat that sank ca 1822. After the mouth of BEARGRASS CREEK was diverted in 1854 to its present site upriver, detritus from the flow of the creek has increased the size of the island. The island is owned by NUGENT SAND CO., and the river side of the island is used as a fleeting area for barges.

Six Mile Island is located about 6 miles upstream from downtown Louisville; although it was once farmed, it is now uninhabited. The channel between the island and the Indiana bank is a popular boating area. The Clark Maritime Center is located on the Indiana bank at the upstream end of the island. The island is owned by the Kentucky State Nature Preserves Commission.

Twelve Mile Island is approximately 12 miles upstream from Louisville and is about 160 acres in size. This part of the river is a popular sailboating area. The Oldham-Jefferson County line bisects the island, and it is jointly owned by both counties. Eighteen Mile Island is located about 21 miles above Louisville and contains just over 100 acres, all situated in Oldham County. It is separated from the Kentucky bank by a narrow channel. It has been privately owned for many years, with previous owners farming and grazing cattle on part of the island. The present owners also hold title to about 900 adjacent acres in OLDHAM COUNTY, the entire complex once known as Clifton Farm.

See Historical Files, Louisville District, U.S. Army Corps of Engineers, Louisville; R.R. Jones, *The Ohio River* (Washington, D.C., 1929); *Courier-Journal*, Sept. 19, 1992.

Charles E. Parrish

OHIO RIVER RECREATION. The Ohio River forms the entire 37-mile northern and western border of Jefferson County, Kentucky, providing for a variety of interactions between the river and people. Native Americans used the river for travel and commerce; a major north-south trail crossed just above the Falls. Arriving white settlers used the Ohio much as the Native Americans did. Once the river had been made safe from Indian attack, it served as the region's principal source of transportation through the first half of the nineteenth century, bringing settlers, travelers, and traders.

By the second half of the century, as the region's network of RAILROADS began to develop, the Ohio was increasingly seen as an obstacle to be bridged. After the canalization of the river was accomplished in 1830, allowing for the 2-mile navigation around the falls, commercial use of the river began to soar. But it was after the CIVIL WAR, and increasingly throughout the twentieth century, that recreation became an important focus of riverfront activity as well.

There was some early interest in the OHIO RIVER as a scenic attraction, as evidenced by Vaux Hall Garden, a gathering spot at the foot of Fifth St. that had a saloon and an outdoor garden as early as 1832. JOHN JAMES AUDUBON spent many hours sketching BIRDS along the river's banks. However, the real flurry of interest in the river as a destination for scenic viewing and recreation emerged after the CIVIL WAR. This new attitude coincided with a national awakening to the pleasures of outdoor sports and recreational activities as a means to increased physical and mental health. As American cities became larger and more urban and as workers gradually found themselves with more leisure time, the lure of newly developed PARKS, healthful countryside destinations, and outdoor activities became more compelling. Swimming and boating were now being viewed as leisure activities, as was camping. Jefferson County was no exception to this national trend. In the last decades of the nineteenth century, such recreational destinations as parks, boat clubs, beachfront camps, and cabins sprang up along the Ohio; and water sports and excursion boats became popular as well.

Summer Resorts and Amusement Parks

In the 1880s a riverside hotel and restaurant, built by Tony Landenwich at Fontaine's Ferry Landing in west Louisville, became a popular terminating point for carriage, streetcar, and bicycle parties. By the 1890s a world class bicycle-racing track had been constructed there. Then in 1905 this resort became the Fontaine Ferry amusement park, the longest-lasting and most famous park of its kind in Louisville. There pleasure seekers could ride the roller coaster, swim in the pool, or take a turn around the dance hall. The AMUSEMENT PARK closed in 1969, and after several attempts to revive it under new names and themes, the land upon which it had been situated was purchased by the city and cleared. The city maintains the land as a park adjacent to SHAWNEE Park.

Fern Grove, located on the Indiana shore about 14 miles northeast of Louisville, was a picturesque site developed with simple picnic pavilions and later a hotel. It was a popular excursion destination from the last decades of the nineteenth century until the early 1920s, when it was more elaborately recreated as ROSE ISLAND, a summer resort area. Developed by Louisville businessman David B.G. Rose, the resort included rental cabins facing the river, a small zoo, a SWIMMING beach, and rental boats, as well as other attractions. About twenty cabins, which sat in a long line on high ground facing the river, were also constructed at the resort. Rose Island lasted until 1937, when that year's devastating flood caused extensive damage and resulted in its abandonment.

WHITE CITY AMUSEMENT PARK opened in 1907 below the south side of Shawnee Park. The park struggled unsuccessfully to compete with FONTAINE FERRY park and stayed in business for only a few years. In late 1910 White City park was destroyed by a fire that was thought to have been set to collect insurance. Reopened as Riverview Park in 1911, by 1913 the enterprise was no longer listed in the city directory.

Parks

By the 1880s, if not before, the Louisville Water Company's magnificent intake facilities on River Rd., completed in 1860, had become one of the most popular destinations in and around the city for recreational carriage rides.

In August 1896, when over ten thousand members of the American Wheelmen, a national BICYCLING club, descended on Louisville for their annual meeting, one of the planned bicycle runs was out River Rd. to the waterworks. While the women bicyclists relaxed on the water-company grounds, many of the men proceeded farther up River Rd. to a destination along the banks of the river where beer was served.

The flat, flood-prone land along the OHIO RIVER was ideally suited for public PARKLAND. Among the parks was Shawnee Park, opened in 1892 along the river, from BROADWAY to Walnut (Muhammad Ali Blvd.) in the city's West End. Chickasaw Park, also in west Louisville, just south of Shawnee Park, was opened in 1922 for AFRICAN AMERICANS. Thruston Square, a small park on THE POINT, a low-lying and frequently flooded section of land to the west of the BEARGRASS CREEK cutoff, was donated to the city by the Thruston Ballard family in 1919 and expanded several times in the 1920s. By 1955 Thruston Park, as it was then known, had expanded by 35 acres; but in 1995 it closed, and the land was designated for use as part of the Falls Harbor riverfront redevelopment project.

In 1935 an army of WPA workers funded by the federal and the city governments built a municipal harbor on the eastern bank of the Beargrass Creek cutoff. The marina was to benefit local boaters strapped by the economic hard times and was popular from its opening in 1937 until the cost of upkeep proved too much for the city, and it leased the property to a private group of boat owners who operate it to this day. Eva Bandman Park was established nearby in 1955 and expanded until it encompassed more than 50 acres. Farther east, Carrie Gaulbert Cox Park was established by the county in the early 1950s. To the west of downtown, Lannan Park, north of Interstate 64 between Twenty-second and Twenty-sixth Streets, dates originally to 1947; and Riverview Park, located in the southwest part of the county at Lower River Rd. and Greenwood Rd., opened in the late 1960s. RiverWalk, a project of the Louisville Waterfront Development Corp., eventually planned to skirt the Ohio from one end of the county to the other, has been completed along the nearly 7 miles from the downtown Fourth St. wharf to Chickasaw Park.

Although the downtown area has been separated from the river by the building of an elevated interstate highway in the 1960s, beginning with the opening of the new GALT HOUSE hotel at the foot of Fourth St. in 1972, interest was rekindled in riverfront property. The adjoining RIVERFRONT PLAZA/Belvedere brought people to view the river and the Falls Fountain. RESTAURANTS such as Kingfish were built to take advantage of river views. But the most significant new development was the building of WATERFRONT PARK. A master plan for development was drawn up by Hargreaves Associates, a San Francisco landscape ARCHITECTURE firm. It reconnected the city to its river heritage by extending the park under the expressway and into the city grid. What had been a heavily industrial area became a 110-acre public park in the late 1990s.

The driving force behind WATERFRONT PARK has been David Karem, Waterfront Development Corp. president and executive director since 1987. The corporation is responsible for the planning and public-private funding of the park, which celebrated the completion of its first phase with a dedication ceremony and Fourth of July gala in 1999. A member of the Kentucky General Assembly since 1972, Karem served two terms in the House of Representatives before his election to the Senate in 1976. He is the senior member of the Senate and a national leader in public education reform.

Excursions

Trips on the Ohio River also became a popular pastime. The first STEAMBOATS were designed solely to carry freight and passengers from one river town to another; but early on, the attractions of steamboat travel became apparent, and people began to enjoy the ride for its own sake. Impromptu excursions were sometimes arranged when boats were delayed by low water. In addition, charters for private parties, church picnics, and political rallies were common events, as were special trips to transport people to fairs and horse races.

Louisville became a busy embarkation point for Ohio River excursions. The earliest scheduled excursion service at Louisville may have been aboard the *Sunshine,* a ferry owned by the Louisville & Jeffersonville Ferry Co., which in 1888 began making summer runs to Fern Grove. For many years, Louisville and Cincinnati residents were also able to take advantage of a unique Ohio River excursion service known as Meet the Boat, offered by the Louisville & Cincinnati Packet Co. These ten-hour trips involved two regularly scheduled steamers, one traveling from each port to the other, that would meet to exchange passengers about midway between the two cities. Sometimes the transfer of passengers occurred at a river landing, but often, if a river landing was not nearby when the boats passed, the exchange occurred with the two boats tied together in midriver. Each boat would then continue on to its destination, and the passengers would return to their starting point on the other boat.

In 1924 Louisville also had three home port excursion boats with a combined capacity of nearly five thousand. By the early 1920s the *America* had become one of Louisville's principal resident excursion steamers. The *America* was destroyed in 1930, a victim of arson. In 1931 the *Idlewild,* which had previously served on the Mississippi River, was brought to Louisville to replace the *America.* For a time it provided regular service to Rose Island and was used for other excursions as well. After WORLD WAR II, the steamer was renamed the *Avalon* and was based in Cincinnati, but in 1962 it was sold to Jefferson County, refurbished, and renamed the *BELLE OF LOUISVILLE.* Put into service as an excursion boat home-based in Louisville, it continues in that role today, providing both chartered and scheduled river cruises.

Showboats

One other popular and pervasive form of riverfront entertainment was SHOWBOATS, barges fitted up as THEATERS and propelled by small steamboats that stopped for riverside engagements in the towns and cities along its banks. However, most of the showboats of the late nineteenth and early twentieth century tended to bypass the river's largest cities, where citizens were already amply entertained at local theaters, music halls, and opera houses. Thus, because of Louisville's size, the showboat phenomenon did not play a big role in the community's history. Showboats were more likely to tie up at the Indiana towns across from Louisville. Of the very few showboats that did visit the Louisville wharf, the *Hollywood,* which stayed for twenty-one weeks in 1930, and the *Majestic,* which came for engagements in the 1950s, are well documented.

Pleasure Boats

An increasingly popular pastime of Louisvillians in the 1890s was recreational sculling and sailing. Groups of congenial enthusiasts soon formed clubs. Among the oldest is the Louisville Boat Club, founded in 1879 by a group of prominent businessmen and originally located on a wharf boat near the foot of Sixth St. Club members participated in sailboat regattas and held barge parties throughout the summer months. Another of the old clubs is Pastime Boat Club, whose first members often did not own boats but rented them to enjoy the river. The club started in 1892 with a houseboat docked along the wharf as its headquarters. Now members of the Cruising Club of Louisville and the Louisville Sailing Club race on various river courses between the Second St. Bridge and Twelve Mile Island during the summer months.

During the first three decades of the twentieth century, motorboats became a fixture on the Ohio. By the 1920s and possibly even earlier, powerboat regattas were becoming popular. For example, the Mississippi Valley Power Boat Association regatta, a series of hydroplane races, was held at Rose Island over the July Fourth weekend in 1926. The Falls City Regatta was an annual event on the river between the downtown bridges for a number of years in the 1950s and 1960s.

One other type of pleasure boat, the houseboat, has enjoyed great success on the Ohio, particularly in the Louisville area. SHANTYBOATS had been in existence in the area since the nineteenth century; in the 1920s following the gradual canalization of the Ohio and the creation of summer slackwater pools behind the new dams, the first gasoline motors were attached to shantyboats. Then, beginning in the 1930s and accelerating in the 1940s after World War II, custom-built houseboats, fabricated by a variety of local boat-builders, began to proliferate around Louisville.

These early custom-built houseboats ranged from very simple structures similar to their crude shantyboat antecedents to extremely elegant boats commissioned by the wealthy. By the 1950s houseboats were mass-produced. By the 1990s houseboats made up a large portion of the pleasure-boating traffic in the upper pool above Louisville. Since few boat ramps and docking and service facilities are provided on the lower pool below McAlpine Locks and Dam, houseboats and other pleasure craft are limited there. In 1999 eleven marinas served the 17,240 boats licensed in Jefferson County. Many of them use the Ohio's upper pool, where names of marinas such as Rose Island, HARRODS CREEK, and Juniper Beach reflect nearby geographic features found along the river.

Swimming

Swimming had become a popular recreational pastime across America by the 1880s and 1890s, but it was not until 1915 that Louisville's first public swimming pool was built. Certainly by the 1890s, if not before, swimming was becoming an accepted summer activity along the Ohio in Jefferson County, and it continued as such through the 1930s. Though it was likely that swimming was common all along the river wherever gently sloping sandy banks or sandbars were located, there were a number of established "bathing beaches" in the area. For example, there was a swimming beach at Shawnee Park in the West End and others on Towhead Island, just to the east of downtown, and on Sand Island, to the east of the Kentucky and Indiana Railroad Bridge. Fontaine Ferry Park and White City also had bathing beaches.

In 1911 the Louisville Turners, the local chapter of the national physical fitness organization, built Turner Park on the river. During its early years along the river, the club frequently had fifty to a hundred people at its pier and often held swimming matches for its members. In southwestern Jefferson County, which during the 1930s and 1940s was still primarily agricultural, many of the farms had Ohio River frontage. At almost every farm, a simple wooden float was anchored in the river to serve as a focus for swimming activities.

By the 1950s and 1960s, however, two factors combined to reduce swimming in the Ohio. Continued dam improvements and construction in the area and all along the Ohio from the turn of the century through the 1970s permanently raised the summer water level and dramatically altered the character of the river's banks. Most beaches were partially or totally inundated. In addition, the river had become increasingly polluted as more and more industries located along its banks and as more sewage from suburban areas was discharged into its water. Until the practice was forbidden, a large number of Louisville sewer outfalls dumped directly into the river. By the 1960s swimming was being increasingly discouraged by the Jefferson County Health Department. Also by that time, most of the riverside clubs had built swimming pools and had virtually abandoned river swimming.

The problems that discouraged swimming affected fishing as well. It had been both a pastime and a means of surviving, but fishing from boats and the banks diminished in the mid–twentieth century.

Summer Houses

In the GLENVIEW–Harrods Creek area atop the bluffs along Upper River Rd., summer residences, some with spectacular views of the river, followed quickly in the wake of the Louisville, Harrods Creek & Westport Railroad, which was completed as far as PROSPECT in 1877. The Fincastle Club, established on 15 acres of land on the bluffs at Glenview, was organized in the late 1880s as an early country club and summer community. A rustic, chalet-like, three-story clubhouse was built, and on surrounding lots summer cottages were constructed by some of Louisville's most prominent families. By 1900 the club had been dissolved and the clubhouse purchased as a private residence. The cottages and the clubhouse were demolished, and since 1911, Bushy Park–Melcombe, the Charles T. Ballard–ROBERT WORTH BINGHAM estate, has occupied the site.

More definitely documented in Jefferson County was a growing twentieth-century interest in summer riverfront living that resulted in the creation of some unique houses. This summer movement to the river clearly coincided with the coming of the automobile, which made it easier for city dwellers to travel to riverside locations. Beginning around 1910 and rapidly developing through the 1920s and 1930s in the Louisville area, many beachfront communities of small seasonal cabins were built directly along the Ohio River banks on both sides of the river and on some of its islands. Although the areas were prone to flooding, people were willing to risk the hazard for the cool river breezes and direct access to the water. Many houses were constructed on piers to avoid inundation.

Transylvania Beach, the first Jefferson County riverfront community with lots for sale, was platted and developed beginning in 1923 as part of a larger subdivision known as Transylvania. Transylvania was laid out with a 2.3-acre bathing beach and park designed for the communal use of all landowners in the development. The housing on Transylvania Beach was primarily of three types: wood-frame houses used as summer residences only, one-story concrete-block cabins, and larger concrete-and-brick structures designed for year-round living. Transylvania Beach, like many other Jefferson County beachfront communities, has evolved into primarily a neighborhood of substantial year-round homes. Most of the modest cabins from the 1930s through the 1950s have either been torn down or drastically altered through additions.

Juniper Beach was platted in 1925, but by 1930 only five of the original twenty-seven beachfront lots had been sold. Most of the earliest development along this beach occurred in the 1950s, and a number of concrete-block houses from that decade still remain.

Turner Village, on the grounds of the Louisville Turners riverfront property, was likely one of the earliest beaches to lease lots. By 1917 the Turners reported that about twenty-five small cabins had been constructed on the property by members of the club. As of the late 1990s only a few of the original riverfront dwellings remained. Adjacent to the Turners to the northeast was the community of Waldoah, on land purchased by Emil and Minna Waltenberger in 1919. Waldoah had a few lots for lease by the early 1920s. In 1955 the lots were sold off to the fourteen families who owned existing houses at the time.

Less than half of the early cabins remain at Guthrie Beach, to the southwest of Captain's Quarters Restaurant at the mouth of Harrods Creek. Guthrie Beach was developed during the 1930s by the Amelia Guthrie family, which leased lots on which a series of simple, primarily wooden structures were built. Structures at several other upriver beaches have disappeared entirely. Both Shirley Beach, just to the northeast of Transylvania Beach, and Riverside Beach, just to the southwest of Guthrie Beach, had small groups of simple cabins that are now gone. From 1924 until 1937, when the flood damaged the buildings beyond repair, the Young Men's Hebrew Association operated CAMP TAPAWINGO, a summer camp for children, on 12 acres along the river just above Juniper Beach. Sleeping cabins, a dining room, and other facilities were all simple wood-frame structures built up on piers to protect them from frequent flooding.

At the southwest end of Jefferson County, between Dixie Hwy. and the river, three beaches were developed between the 1920s and the 1960s. The earliest of these is now called Kulmer's Beach but was historically known as Howlett's Camps. Small beachfront residences began to appear on the beach in the 1920s. The land, in the Howlett family since the 1870s, was inherited by Mattie Howlett Kulmer, hence the later name. Kulmer's Beach remained in the Kulmer family until 1981, when it was sold to the Kulmer Beach Corp. As of the late 1990s all the cabins had been demolished. Dixie Beach, the easternmost of the three lower beaches, was developed in two stages platted in 1930 and 1938, respectively. Little construction appears to have gone on before the late 1930s, and little of that remains intact. Many of the present houses at Dixie Beach are year-round residences. The last of the three lower beaches to be developed was Abbott's Beach. Concrete cabins began to be constructed there in the late 1940s. Most of the houses were built in the 1960s and later.

Also in the southwestern part of the county was Riverside Gardens, a subdivision at the end of Lee's Ln. off Cane Run Rd. Opened in 1926 as a resort community, it had a clubhouse overlooking the river and a swimming pavilion as well. In the decades to follow, junkyards and a landfill became a blight on the community.

The only other location of riverside camps is at Lake Dreamland, just to the south of the industrial development at RUBBERTOWN. Lake Dreamland was laid out in 1931 by Ed Hartlage on his 65-acre farm. In order to maximize waterfront locations in his development, Hartlage dammed Bramer's Run, a stream that runs through the property, and created the small lake that gave the community its name. Most of Lake Dreamland's small residences are post–World War II structures or radically altered buildings, and many are in a seriously deteriorated condition.

Carolyn Brooks

OKOLONA. Okolona, a suburb in southern Jefferson County, is centered around the intersection of Preston Hwy. and the Outer Loop. The first settlers in the vicinity, primarily farmers from Virginia and Pennsylvania, arrived in the late 1700s. Shortly thereafter the first churches of the area were established, Cooper Memorial United Methodist Church and Pennsylvania Run Presbyterian Church. In the late nineteenth century the name Lone Oak was chosen for the area, most likely in honor of the large oak tree that stood at the corner of Preston Hwy. and Okolona Terrace until lightning destroyed it in the early 1970s. When the post office was established at the beginning of the twentieth century, residents discovered that a town in McCracken County near Paducah was named Lone Oak, so the two words were rearranged to produce Okolona. By the early years of the new century, the small farming community was known for its production of charcoal from the abundant supply of timber in the nearby WET WOODS, a strip of swampy forest to the west of Preston Hwy. that was said to have also harbored dangerous criminals.

The electric interurban line from Louisville reached the Okolona area in 1905. The waiting station for passengers was located near the town's celebrated oak tree. The community did not truly flourish, however, until the 1953 opening of the General Electric Co. Appliance Park to the northeast on Shepherdsville Rd. By the early 1980s, the area's POPULATION had dramatically increased. When the city of Louisville attempted annexation of the growing area, local residents sought incorporation as a fourth-class city. The case went to the state supreme court in 1986 and ended with a ruling against the incorporation efforts, which also compelled city GOVERNMENT to halt annexations until 1998.

Local landmarks include Okolona Park and the Cooper Memorial United Methodist Church, which has housed worshipers since its construction in 1897, though the congregation dates to the early 1800s. There are several shopping complexes in the area, including Jefferson Mall, built in 1978.

See Leslee F. Keys, ed., *Historic Jefferson County* (Louisville 1992); *A Place in Time: The Story of Louisville's Neighborhoods* (Louisville 1989).

OLDHAM, WILLIAM (b Berkeley County, Virginia, June 17, 1753; d Ohio, November 4, 1791). William Oldham's parents were John and Jane (Conway) Oldham. During the Revolutionary War, he served as a captain and was at the battles of Brandywine and Monmouth before he resigned and moved to the FALLS OF THE OHIO in 1779. Oldham was one of the first magistrates, a justice of Jefferson County court, and Jefferson County sheriff. Recorded in his name between 1780 and 1785 were 26,420 acres of land in Jefferson County. While commanding the Kentucky militia in Ohio, he was killed in the famous Indian battle known as St. Clair's Defeat in which 890 enlisted men and 16 officers were killed or wounded. OLDHAM COUNTY, Kentucky, was named in his honor.

Colonel Oldham in 1783 married Penelope Pope (1769–1821), daughter of Col. William (1745–1826) and Penelope (Edwards) Pope (1748–1825). Their children were Judge John Pope Oldham (1785–1858), Maj. Richard A. Oldham (1787–), Abigail Oldham Churchill (1789–1854), and William Oldham (1791–).

See *Early Kentucky Settlers, The Records of Jefferson County, Kentucky* (Baltimore 1988); Willard Rouse Jillson, *Old Kentucky Entries and Deeds* (Baltimore 1987); Lewis Collins and Richard H. Collins, *History of Kentucky,* vol. 2 (Covington, Ky. 1882); Kathleen Jennings, *Louisville's First Families* (Louisville 1920); William Oldham will, Jefferson County, Ky., Will Book.

James Houston Barr III

OLDHAM COUNTY. Oldham, one of Louisville's two fastest-growing suburban counties (along with Bullitt), lies just northeast of Jefferson County. LaGrange, its seat, is only 24 miles from Louisville's main post office (via I-71). The county's 1995 estimated POPULATION of 42,287 was a 27 percent increase over the 33,263 counted in the 1990s census and 55 percent more than the 27,276 enumerated ten years earlier. By 1996 the population had reached 43,248. Much of Oldham's recent growth came from the influx of Louisville-area families; as well as those from outside the region, attracted to the increasingly industrialized eastern Jefferson County job market. The growth was immeasurably enhanced by the completion, in the early 1970s, of I-71 between Cincinnati and Louisville.

Selected Statistics for Oldham County, 1990

Population	33,263
Population per square mile	175
Percent African American	3.6
Percent 0 to 17 years	28.6
Percent 65 years and over	6.8
Percent 25 years and over with a high school degree or equivalency	80.2
Percent 25 years and over with a bachelors degree	22.9
Per capita income in 1989	$42,143
Unemployment rate	3.9%
Married-couple families as a percent of total households	72.9
Median home value	$57,000

Most of Oldham's 190-square-mile area is drained by the OHIO RIVER—its 13-mile-long

Grape packers on the Tyler Farm near Worthington, Oldham County, c. 1909.

northwestern border with Indiana—and by the river's two historically important tributaries, Harrods and Eighteen Mile Creeks and their branches. The county's thickly settled south-central section is drained by FLOYDS FORK and its Curry's Fork, historically significant streams in the Salt River system.

The county's TOPOGRAPHY ranges from fairly level or gently rolling in the west to hilly in the east, where stream erosion has created an appreciable network of hills and valleys. Until the mid–twentieth century, Oldham was primarily agricultural, with corn, hay, and TOBACCO its principal crops; the raising of beef and dairy cattle, hogs, and poultry also contributed substantially to its ECONOMY. AGRICULTURE has been supplemented by only modest industrial and commercial developments. Most of the county's working population commutes to jobs in Jefferson County, in effect making it a bedroom community for its neighbor's workforce.

Of the 10,130 employed Oldham residents in 1995, only 11 percent were in some phase of manufacturing; 25 percent worked in state or local GOVERNMENT (including education), 24 percent were in retail or wholesale trade, 22 percent were in service activities, and 12 percent were in the construction trades.

Kentucky's seventy-fourth county in order of establishment, Oldham was created by legislative act on December 15, 1823, from parts of Jefferson, Henry, and Shelby Counties. It was named for Col. WILLIAM OLDHAM (1753–91), a native of Berkeley County, Virginia, who had settled at the FALLS OF THE OHIO in 1779 and was killed by a confederation of Indians led by the Miami at Arthur St. Clair's defeat on November 4, 1791, approximately 90 miles north of Fort Washington (present-day Cincinnati). In January 1833 the section of Oldham east of Floyds Fork was returned to SHELBY COUNTY, making that stream the dividing line between the two counties. Part of Oldham's northeastern area was lost to the new Trimble County in 1837. Oldham assumed its present boundaries in March 1856.

It took the citizens of Oldham County fourteen years to decide on the location of a permanent seat of government. On June 1, 1824, the committee appointed to find "the most convenient and suitable" place for it recommended the establishment of a town to be called Lynchburg on 50 acres of John Button's farm. This is believed to have been in the vicinity of the future Eighteen Mile Church, just south of U.S. 42 and 4 miles north-northwest of LaGrange. Opposition to Lynchburg by Ohio River residents led to the relocation of the seat to George Varble's home near the already established riverport town of WESTPORT (then West Port). Here the first court session was held. The seat remained at Westport till July 1827 when it was moved to LaGrange. Nine months later it was returned to Westport, where it stayed till 1838, when it was permanently relocated to LaGrange.

Oldham's seven currently incorporated communities are the fourth-class LaGrange, with a 1996 population of 5,040; the fifth-class PEWEE VALLEY with 1,631 residents; and the sixth-class CRESTWOOD and Goshen with populations of 1,841 and 1,155, respectively. Each of these still has its own post office. Three recently established, strictly suburban cities are Orchard Grass Hills, a fifth-class city with 1,354 residents, and the sixth-class cities of River Bluff and Park Lake with 579 and 336 residents.

Oldham's oldest town, Westport, still maintains the county's oldest post office. It was founded in 1797 by Joseph Dupuy and Harmon BOWMAN on the 300-acre Elijah Craig treasury warrant at the mouth of Eighteen Mile Creek. Its name likely reflects early aspirations for the town as a river port for trade with the newly developing Northwest Territory. The local post office was established in 1815 as West Port, but the spelling was changed to Westport by mid-century. By the 1840s the town had become a busy industrial community, steamboat landing, and shipping port, enjoying a modest rivalry with nearby Louisville. Its decline began with the location of the Louisville & Frankfort (later the Louisville & Nashville) Railroad through LaGrange in 1851, which attracted business away from the river.

Two other nineteenth-century towns whose economic futures were thwarted when they were bypassed by the railroad were Floydsburg and Brownsboro. Floydsburg, founded at or near one of the several pioneer stations built in the early 1780s, had its own post office between 1822 and 1861. Brownsboro, which developed around a trading post and Callahan's Tavern at the junction of two pioneer roads, was once the county's main industrial and commercial center. Its name, probably honoring Kentucky's first senator, John Brown, was first applied to the post office in 1824 and then to the town when it was chartered in 1830. In 1838 it was an unsuccessful contender for the transfer of the county seat from Westport. It lost its post office in 1908.

The village of Ballardsville, 4 miles southeast of LaGrange, was also settled early. It was named for the brothers Thomas and Addison Ballard, antebellum county leaders. The Ballardsville post office operated between 1825 and 1903. The community now called Centerfield grew up around the Centreburg post office, which from 1839 to 1845 served an area between Ballardsville and what became Buckner. From 1850–1871 the office operated as Centrefield and from 1883 to 1903 as Worth. The latter name was only applied to the post office established by, and probably named for, local storekeeper Allen Worth Brown.

Several key towns and post offices grew up around stations on the Louisville & Frankfort Railroad. The site of one of these, LaGrange, was acquired and settled by Maj. William Berry Taylor before 1800 and was first called the Cross Roads because it was the junction of early routes connecting Louisville with the Bluegrass Region and Westport with SHELBYVILLE. In 1827 Taylor's offer of the site for the county seat's first relocation was accepted, whereupon the town was created and named by Taylor for the country estate in France of the Marquis de Lafayette, who had recently visited the area. Its post office was also established in 1827, and the town was incorporated in 1840.

The short-lived (October 1851 through 1853) Clores Depot post office, at or near the site of the future Camden, may have served as the first station on the new rail line. Its first postmaster, Richard Clore, had established this office in January 1851 as Hinklesburg, at an as-yet-undetermined site from which it moved to the station.

The first of the county's towns to actually be developed around its rail station was, at its founding in 1852, called Smith's Station. It was probably named for and by its developer, Henry S. Smith, who had acquired much of the site from his father, a pioneer settler. The post office was established in February 1856 as Pewee Valley. The derivation of this name has long fascinated Kentuckians. According to tradition, a less prosaic name than Smith's Station was being sought for the new office when the distinctive call of the eastern wood pewee, a bird common to the area, was heard, and everyone agreed that that would make a good name. But no one seems to know why "Valley" was tacked onto it, since the community lies on an elevation. The town was incorporated in 1870 and by 1900 had become a famous resort with a large hotel and two colleges. Many Louisville residents kept summer homes there, enjoying the cooler temperatures away from the city. Pewee Valley is best known today as the home of ANNIE FELLOWS JOHNSTON and the setting of her famous *Little Colonel* series of children's books.

Just northeast of Pewee Valley is Crestwood. It also grew up around a station with another name, Beard's, on a site donated by Joseph M. Beard, for whom it was named. Its post office, established in July 1857 as Beard's Station, became Beard in 1880, as did the community it served. For a time railroad men called the station "Whiskers." Fearing ridicule, turn-of-the-century newcomers to the community succeeded in changing its name and that of the station and post office to Crestwood, which is most curious because it was not at the crest of anything.

Brownsboro Station, the next rail town to be established, was nearly 3 rail miles north of Crestwood. Its post office, which opened in February 1862, was named for the station serving the town of Brownsboro, 2 miles west. But though the station remained Brownsboro, the post office name was shortly changed to the inexplicable Peru. In 1906 both station and post office became Glenarm, on the suggestion of a local man whose family had come from a town with a similar name in County Antrim, Ireland.

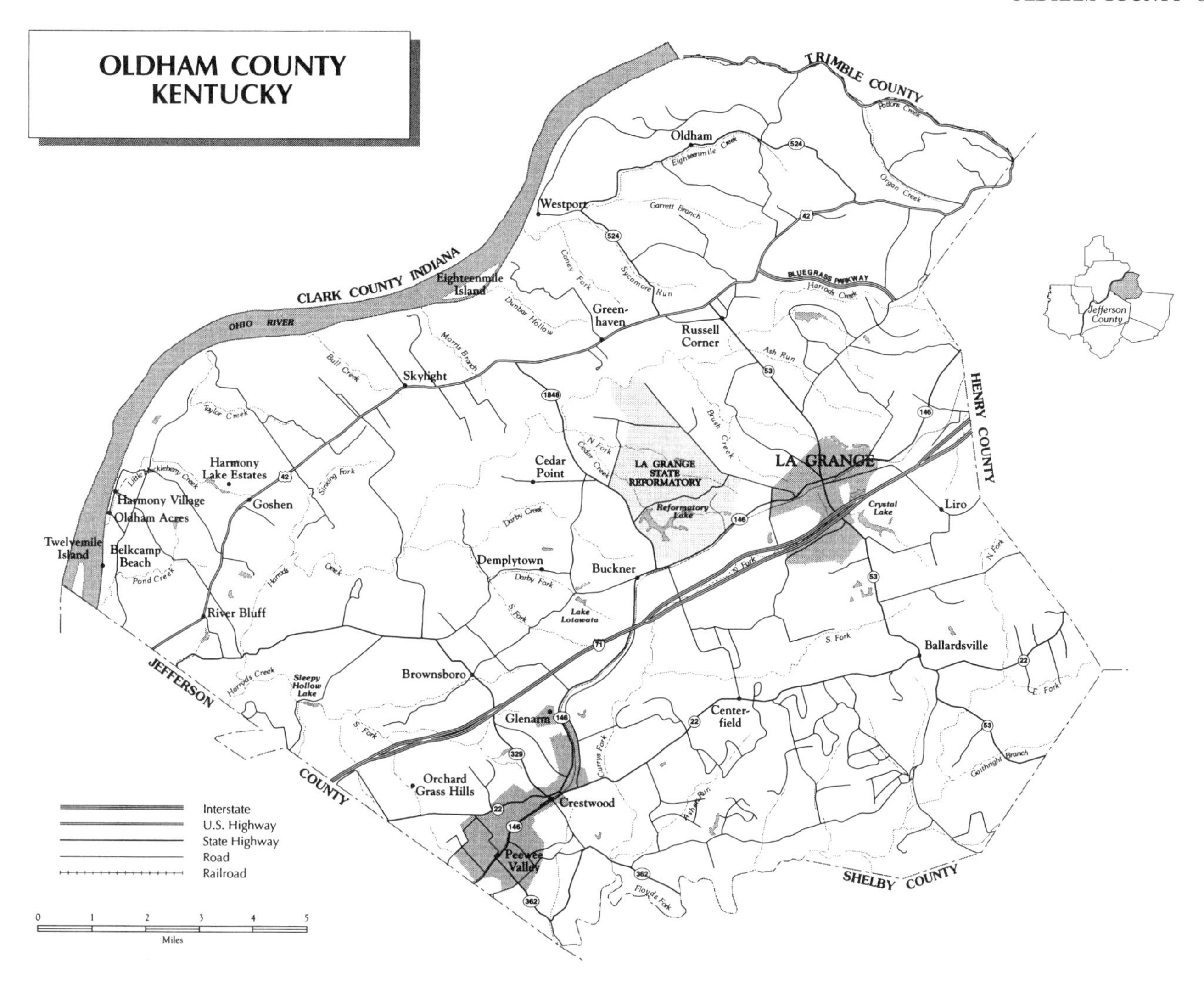

Buckner, which is the site of the county's consolidated high and middle schools and two lumber companies and is near the KENTUCKY STATE REFORMATORY, is 3 rail miles southwest of LaGrange. Its station and post office, near the site of the earlier LaFayetteville post office (1827–29), was established in January 1867 and named for the family of local landowner Coleman Buckner. By 1880 the local community had a sawmill, two distilleries, a wagonworks, a hotel, grain, and livestock dealerships, and several stores and shops.

The last rail station with a post office to be established was Camden, probably named for William Camden Hays, whose father began the post office in his store in 1879.

In the 1790s Thomas and Daniel Trigg arrived by flatboat to settle in the Ohio bottom below the future Westport. To commemorate their relatively harmonious journey down the river from Pennsylvania, they named their new home Harmony Landing. By 1833, when this name was applied to the local post office, it had become a fairly prosperous river port. In early 1851, however, the post office was moved some 2 miles inland to serve the new community of Saltillo. But since the latter name was already in use by a Morgan County post office, the relocated office was called Goshen for the local church, and shortly the community too became Goshen. Harmony Landing continued as a river port well into the twentieth century. In the mid-1960s its area experienced new growth with boat-building and maintenance shops, a Martin-Marietta plant, a sand-and-gravel operation, and several real estate developments such as Harmony Village, named for the landing one-half mile north.

The village of Skylight, 31/2 miles northeast of Goshen, was first called Tippecanoe by veterans of that famous battle in Indiana Territory. In 1854, though, the post office was established as Oldhamburgh and operated till 1870. It was reopened in 1888 as Skylight because, according to local tradition, after a long cloudy spell someone noted the appearance of the sun and remarked, "How light the sky is getting."

Other communities with post offices were Fishers Tanyard, Rowlington, Wheeler's Store, Allan Grove, Kelly's Landing, Belle Rose (at a location on the Ohio called Lynchburg or near the site of Lynchburg), and another area on the Ohio called Oldham's Landing.

In addition to its role as a Louisville-area bedroom community, Oldham County is best noted as the home of the Kentucky State Reformatory just west of LaGrange, the KENTUCKY CORRECTIONAL INSTITUTE FOR WOMEN near Pewee Valley, the 5,100-acre L'Esprit complex for the breeding and raising of Arabian horses near LaGrange, and the state's only official cemetery for Confederate CIVIL WAR veterans in Pewee Valley. The cemetery lies adjacent to the former site of the Confederate Veterans Home. Among notable Oldham County natives were pioneer filmmaker DAVID WARK GRIFFITH, born on a farm near Crestwood but a resident of LaGrange; Adm. William J. Crowe, former chairman of the U.S. Joint Chiefs of Staff; and Rob Morris, the founder of the Order of the Eastern Star.

One Oldham County resident who deserved better recognition than he has been given was its early-twentieth-century historian, Lucien V. Rule. He was the author of several biographies and books of POETRY and a series of sketches on county history, including accounts of its communities and post offices that were serialized in the weekly *Oldham Era* in 1921–22. In the 1920s he moved to Indiana, where, as chaplain of that state's reformatory at Jeffersonville, he pioneered work on prisoner rehabilitation and wrote a history of the Indiana prison system.

See Robert M. Rennick, *Post Offices of Northern Kentucky* (Lake Grove, Ore. 2000); "Lucien V. Rule's Historical Sketches of Oldham County," in *The Oldham Era, March 1921 through October 1922; History and Families of Oldham County, Kentucky (The First Century, 1824–1924)* (Paducah, Ky. 1996).

Robert M. Rennick

OLD HOUSE RESTAURANT. The three-story townhouse at 432 S Fifth St., which became the Old House Restaurant, was built about 1829. An early owner, Dr. William A. McDowell, was known for his study of tuberculosis; he used the quaint treatment of sending his patients to Mammoth Cave to live in a small cabin.

In 1868 the house was acquired by Elizabeth and J.F. Canine and was the home of three generations of dentists. This home was the first in Louisville to be heated by steam and to have electricity. In 1946 Erma Biesel Dick opened a restaurant there that soon became known for its haute cuisine. Celebrities who dined at the Old House Restaurant include Walt Disney; singer Tex Ritter; boxer Rocky Marciano; actors Raymond Burr, Cesar Romero, Van Johnson, and Rod Steiger; and former presidents Gerald Ford and Ronald Reagan. On January 30, 1979, Mrs. Dick closed the restaurant. In February 1980 a group of businessmen bought the restaurant and operated it until 1984. In the fall of 1986, two chefs, Phillip Cooper and Jim Henry, signed a ten-year lease and purchased the assets of the previous owners. By 1995 the restaurant was closed, and the building was put up for sale.

See *Courier-Journal,* Feb. 23, 1947; Sept. 21, 1958; Jan. 7, 1967; Jan. 31, 1979; Feb. 1, 1980; Aug. 25, 1986; David Miller, "The Old House: Landmark of Fine 'Wining and Dining,'" *Louisville Skyline,* Oct. 24, 1984; Erma Dick, *My Old House* (Louisville 1988).

Robert Bruce French

OLD KENTUCKY DISTILLERY CO. With several locations, including 205 W MAIN St. (1892), BROADWAY and Twenty-eighth St. (1895), and 215 W Main St. (1901), the Old Kentucky Distillery Co. was the creation of Dietrich Meschendorf, a highly respected authority on Kentucky bourbon. In 1892 he purchased the Mayflower Distillery, founded about 1880, from H.A. Thierman Sr., renaming it Old Kentucky Distillery Co. Meschendorf operated the distillery until his death on November 11, 1911, serving as both president and distillery manager. From 1912 to 1920, the officers were O.H. Irvine, president; Dan Schlegel, vice president; and J.J. Sass, secretary and treasurer. During PROHIBITION, in 1923, the whiskey was removed from the warehouses and destroyed, and all warehouses were razed. The distillery did not, unlike Brown-Forman Distillers, take advantage of a provision in the Volstead Act that permitted the sale of whiskey that was left on hand for medicinal purposes.

After the repeal of Prohibition in 1933, Col. J.J. Sass took control of the property and erected a modern plant on the site. Brands associated with the distillery over the years were Kentucky Dew, Cherokee Spring, and Old Kentucky. Later additions were Watermill, Normandy Rye, Old Jefferson County, and Dew Drops Malt. Blended whiskeys included Woodbury, Old Stoney Fort, and Royal Velvet. The Sass family sold the distillery to the Brown-Forman Distillers Corp. in 1940, and the name was changed to Early Times.

See "The Old Kentucky," *Spirits,* April 1935, 31–35; William L. Downard, *Dictionary of the History of the American Brewing and Distilling Industries* (Westport, Conn. 1980); H.W. Coyte, unpublished papers, University of Louisville Archives and Records Center.

Al Young
Lindsey Apple

OLD LOUISVILLE. The neighborhood known as Old Louisville, south of the central business district, is not—as the name implies—the oldest part of Louisville. Intensive residential development of the area did not begin until the 1880s, long after such NEIGHBORHOODS as PORTLAND and BUTCHERTOWN had reached maturity. The name Old Louisville was applied in 1961 in connection with a major and largely successful effort to preserve and revitalize the area, once the city's premier residential neighborhood.

Most of the area of Old Louisville was annexed to the city in 1868 as part of a sweeping enlargement of the city's boundaries that also added substantial areas to the east and the west. The southern boundary was moved from Kentucky St. to a line generally along Burnett St., with a long pocket extending farther south to include the HOUSE OF REFUGE grounds (later Belknap Campus of the UNIVERSITY OF LOUISVILLE). Only a year later architect GIDEON SHRYOCK called the annexed area "a growing and beautiful suburban locality."

The principal roadway through what was then referred to as simply the Southern Extension or the southern part of the city was the privately owned Central Plank Rd., which became Third St. Development of the area immediately south of BROADWAY began as early as the 1850s. In 1853 a citizens' petition to the city requested that Fourth St. be paved and graded south of Broadway. The work was carried three blocks south to Kentucky St. In 1858 the Louisville Gas Co. extended a line out Third St. to near Breckinridge St. In 1866 Fourth St. was paved and graded to Oak St., and adjacent parallel streets began a southward advance.

By the early 1870s, real estate agents were listing lots for sale on Brook, First, Second, Third, and FOURTH Streets in what was to become Old Louisville. The *Louisville Commercial* of January 1, 1874, noted that "south of Broadway we have almost a new city. It is within the memory of even our young men . . . when ducks and snipe were hunted along Long Pond, Dutch Ditch, and Thompson's Pond, and game could be found anywhere beyond where College St. [two blocks south of Broadway] has been made." Now, the newspaper added, "magnificent residences" are found there.

But intensive development did not extend beyond Oak St. South of that point, housing was scattered, and large estates were common. In 1871, for instance, a ten-room brick house offered for rent was located on a 5-acre site between First and Second Streets two blocks south of Oak. The property included a vegetable garden, stables, and "all other necessary outbuildings." In 1877 a householder at Third St. and Weissinger Ave. (Park Ave.) advertised for a woman to cook, do general housework, and milk cows.

The SOUTHERN EXPOSITION of 1883–87 seems to have been the catalyst that spurred rapid development south of Oak. The numerous tracts of open land, or commons, began sprouting closely spaced residences in the architectural styles of the time—Queen Anne, Richardsonian Romanesque, Chateauesque, Renaissance Revival, and others—that combine elements of various styles in an eclectic manner. In 1885 alone, 260 homes were built in the area. The most costly and impressive were built along Third St., the first lengthy Louisville thoroughfare to be paved with asphalt. Churches, too, mostly in Gothic Revival style, dotted the area. Many had moved from the downtown area; among them are Calvary Episcopal and First Unitarian.

An unusual urban-planning departure marked St. James and Belgravia Courts, developed in the early 1890s on the site of the Southern Exposition by the Victoria Land Co. St. James Ct., extending one block from Magnolia Ave. (renamed Victoria Place for a few years) to Hill St., boasted a grass mall with a carriageway on either side. On the mall the developers placed an imposing fountain that has become a symbol of Victorian Old Louisville. Legend holds that the fountain came from England, but it was more likely a product of the J.L. Mott Iron Works of New York City. Belgravia Ct., extending two blocks from Fourth to Sixth Streets, was an afterthought but unusual in plan. It was a mall without vehicular access; sidewalks only were provided. The prestige of St James Ct. rivaled that of Third St. By the mid-1920s, however, the neighborhood, though still fashionable, had lost its premier status to the HIGHLANDS, where open tracts still provided space for new residences in the latest styles for the elite. Old Louisville suffered from the automobile's easy mobility and the glamour of the new eastern SUBURBS. Some of the imposing residences were given over to business uses, others to apartments. But it was during WORLD WAR II and the years following that decline accelerated. As Louisville became a major center of war production, housing for the enlarged workforce became a problem. The federal GOVERNMENT actively encouraged the conversion of spacious older residences into multiple-unit dwellings and provided low-interest loans.

Old Louisville, with its hundreds of large houses and good public transit, was a particular target. Most of the work was done shoddily.

At the war's end, with the departure of the wartime labor force, rents were lowered to attract tenants who were far from affluent. The cycle fed on itself, especially on the edges where housing was smaller and plainer. It was this cycle that spurred interest in Old Louisville's architectural treasure trove. A vigorous public education program aroused interest. Actual rehabilitation of ten homes in 1961 by a private group, Restoration Inc., turned the tide just at the time when national interest in HISTORIC PRESERVATION was rising. Area churches also became involved, joining with other groups to form the Neighborhood Development Corp. in 1968. But the real strength came from the new and activist younger residents who rehabilitated the old homes on their own and created a neighborhood cohesiveness—the process dubbed gentrification.

It was primarily the renaissance of Old Louisville that led to the creation by the city of the Historic Landmarks and Preservation Districts Commission in 1973. In June 1974 it designated a portion of Old Louisville as the city's first Historic Preservation District. In February 1975 the neighborhood was listed on the NATIONAL REGISTER OF HISTORIC PLACES. The boundaries of the two designations are identical: an irregular area from Kentucky St. on the north to Cardinal Blvd. on the extreme south, Floyd St. on the east, and generally Sixth St. on the west. In popular usage *Old Louisville* refers to the area from Broadway south to Eastern Pkwy., Seventh St. on the west, and Interstate 65 on the east.

See Carl E. Kramer, *Old Louisville: A Changing View* (Louisville 1982); Samuel W. Thomas and William Morgan, *Old Louisville: The Victorian Era* (Louisville 1975); Theodore Brown and Margaret M. Bridwell, *Old Louisville* (Louisville 1961); Marguerite Gifford, *St. James Court in Retrospect* (Louisville 1966); Barbara Hadley, "New Directions for Old Louisville," *Louisville* 29 (Oct. 1978): 38–45, 75–78; *Courier-Journal,* Dec. 2, 1869; July 13, 1871; *Louisville Democrat,* April 21, 1853.

George H. Yater

OLD STONE INN. Listed on the NATIONAL REGISTER OF HISTORIC PLACES, the Old Stone Inn, a SHELBY COUNTY landmark, is in SIMPSONVILLE on U.S. 60 (old Midland Trail). The construction of the building is believed to have begun in the late 1790s or soon after 1800. Though it was originally intended to be a private home, its first owner, Samuel Mitchell, sold it to Fleming P. Rogers about 1817, and Rogers operated it as a tavern and stagecoach stop until 1827. Erected with stone from a quarry at the rear of the surrounding farm, the Georgian vernacular structure was equipped with chimneys at each end and three front dormers. It has stone walls nearly 2 feet thick and flooring of oak on the first level and poplar on the second. Early descriptions of the inn mention a cupola or belfry on its roof, but no such adornment exists today, and over the years the structure has undergone remodeling.

As stated on its bronze historical marker, the Old Stone Inn is Shelby County's oldest surviving dwelling that is still utilized. As such, it has accommodated a number of owners. Its early owners included Isaac Greathouse, who purchased the inn from Rogers in 1827, and Philip Johnston, who bought it in 1833. Two years later the building was sold to Lindsay W. George, and for decades after that the inn served as a private residence. Then, in the early 1920s, the historic building was again opened to the public as a restaurant and has remained a popular dining spot to the present day.

See J. Winston Coleman, *Historic Kentucky* (Lexington 1967); F. Kevin Simon, ed., *The WPA Guide to Kentucky* (Lexington 1939).

OLMSTED FIRM. The origins of the Olmsted firm of landscape architects date to 1858, when Frederick Law Olmsted, who has been called the father of American landscape ARCHITECTURE, and Calvert Vaux designed New York City's Central Park. Although their partnership was dissolved in 1872, Olmsted continued to lay out other park systems from his New York office and later from Brookline, Massachusetts, where he moved in the early 1880s. Credited with designing the grounds of the Capitol in Washington, D.C., Stanford University, and the Biltmore estate in Asheville, North Carolina, among others, Olmsted and his firm had a part in planning the grounds of nearly 190 Louisville area projects ranging from public PARKS to private residences.

Between 1873 and 1874, Olmsted undertook his first local project when he laid out the grounds surrounding the Jeffersonville QUARTERMASTER DEPOT. Though it would be another seventeen years before he returned to the area, Olmsted's work on the new public park system ensured his local legacy. After receiving a request to discuss his design philosophies before the newly created Board of Park Commissioners, Olmsted, invited by leather merchant and board member ANDREW COWAN, spoke at the PENDENNIS CLUB on the evening of May 20, 1891. Although some proponents desired a local engineer to lay out the PARKLANDS, the nationally recognized Olmsted signed a contract to design the Louisville park system within two days of his arrival. Olmsted's principles, displayed throughout his work locally and nationwide, called for minimal manipulation in order to embrace the existing natural environment of each site and capture its distinctive TOPOGRAPHY and characteristics. In the three large parks to the south, the west, and the east of the city, Olmsted attempted to emphasize the elevated KNOBS of IROQUOIS PARK; the flat, meadowy riverlands of SHAWNEE Park; and the rolling hills of Cherokee Park. The larger landscapes tended to be planned with this ideal, but other and smaller interior spaces, such as Boone Square, were laid out more formally with groomed walks and carefully manicured vegetation. The Olmsted firm's relationship with the park board continued through the 1930s, primarily as a consultant in the later years.

As the firm's reputation grew, local individuals and groups frequently sought the services of the landscape architect and his successors. After laying out ANCHORAGE between 1913 and 1915 (its only local effort at city planning), the firm was solicited by real estate developers, especially in eastern Jefferson County, to plan subdivisions such as Lakeside (1922-23), the Viglini and Fairfield units of CHEROKEE GARDENS (1925), and Indian Hills (1925-26). The rounded intersections, curvilinear drives, and natural terrain found throughout Olmsted-designed NEIGHBORHOODS affected other areas as well. Developers who did not want to pay the Olmsted fees frequently attempted to emulate these ideas as they planned their own communities and used local engineers such as Stonestreet and Ford to accomplish the look. The Olmsted firm also worked with individual property owners on their landscaping. With an emphasis on formality and privacy, the architects planned the grounds for the Norton sisters (GARDENCOURT, 1902-27), William S. Speed (Altagate, 1915-17), and others such as ANDREW COWAN, PETER L. ATHERTON, Frank Fehr, and George G. Brown.

Not confined to landscape planning for residences and parks, the Olmsted firm was contracted to design the grounds of numerous other facilities throughout the area, both public and private. The architects planned the land around Male High School at Brook and Breckinridge Streets (1907-10) and also landscaped the area surrounding the LOUISVILLE FREE PUBLIC LIBRARY at Fourth and YORK Streets (1908-35).

Local country clubs planned by the Olmsted firm included the Louisville Country Club (1925-40) and Big Spring Country Club (1927). Churches, religious organizations, CEM-

ETERIES, and charitable associations also commissioned the firm's services throughout the years, some of the most notable being St. Francis-in-the-Fields Episcopal Church (1946-58), CAVE HILL CEMETERY (1905- 54), SOUTHERN BAPTIST THEOLOGICAL SEMINARY (1921-70), and the Masonic Widows and Orphans Home (1927-28). From the industrial sector, the Brown-Forman Distillers Corp. had the firm landscape their Early Times and Old Forester plants in Shively between 1946-47 and continued to work with the architects on other facilities until 1970.

One of the last great projects in the area undertaken by the firm was Bernheim Forest, a 10,000-acre native woodland located in BULLITT COUNTY near Clermont, donated by Louisville distiller and philanthropist Isaac Wolfe Bernheim in 1929. The Olmsted firm worked on the large conservation and recreation area from 1931 until 1965.

See Carl E. Kramer et al., *Louisville's Olmstedian Legacy: An Interpretive Analysis and Documentary Inventory* (Louisville 1988).

O'NEAL, EMMET (b Louisville, April 14, 1887; d Washington, D.C., July 18, 1967). Congressman. Emmet was the son of Lydia Elizabeth (Wright) and Joseph Thomas O'Neal. His father was a prominent Louisville attorney. Emmet O'Neal had a family active in Democratic politics. His brother, Joseph T. O'Neal Jr., served briefly as mayor of Louisville (June to November 1927). Emmet O'Neal attended Male High School in Louisville. An accomplished athlete, he was captain of the FOOTBALL, BASEBALL, and BASKETBALL teams both there and in college.

In 1907 O'Neal graduated from Centre College in Danville, Kentucky, with a bachelor's degree. The following year he completed a second baccalaureate at Yale University. In 1910 he received his law degree from the UNIVERSITY OF LOUISVILLE and was admitted to the bar.

He practiced law in Louisville until WORLD WAR I, when he entered the army as a private in the Fifth Field Artillery in the First Division. He served in France and was commissioned in 1917 as a lieutenant in the Third Field Artillery in the Twenty-sixth Division. Following the war, he returned to Louisville, where he practiced law and was a partner in the investment securities firm O'Neal, Alden & Co. On July 30, 1921, he married Glessie Morris. They had two daughters, Mary Hamilton and Lydia Wright.

In 1934 O'Neal ran for Congress in the third district. Defeating Frank M. Drake, he was the first Democrat to represent Jefferson County since 1916. O'Neal served in Congress from January 3, 1935, to January 3, 1947. Known as a conservative Democrat, O'Neal opposed several of Pres. Franklin Roosevelt's New Deal plans. During his second term, he voted against funding for the Tennessee Valley Authority, the Wage-Hour Act, and the Anti-lynching Bill. O'Neal served on the House Appropriations Committee and was a strong advocate of a balanced budget. In 1946 O'Neal lost his bid for reelection to Republican THRUSTON BALLARD MORTON. Following the defeat, Pres. Harry Truman appointed him ambassador to the Philippines, a post he held from June 20, 1947, to January 20, 1949, when he retired to practice law in Washington, D.C. From 1953 until his death, O'Neal served as a member and later the chair of the Corregidor-Bataan Memorial Commission, an organization that planned and supervised the construction of a WORLD WAR II memorial on Corregidor Island at the entrance of Manila Bay in the Philippines.

See *Biographical Directory of the American Congress, 1774-1996: The Continental Congress, September 5, 1774, to October 21, 1788, and the Congress of the United States, from the First through the 104th Congress, March 4, 1789, to January 3, 1997* (Alexandria, Va., 1997).

O'NEAL, JOSEPH THOMAS, JR. (b Louisville, August 13, 1881; d Louisville, September 4, 1944). Mayor. Joseph T. O'Neal Jr. was the son of Joseph Thomas and Lydia Elizabeth (Wright) O'Neal. His brother, Emmet, was a congressman from the Louisville area in the 1930s and 1940s. O'Neal's father was a well-known lawyer in Louisville and was associated with several local law firms, including O'Neal, Jackson & Phelps. The elder O'Neal ran for mayor of Louisville in 1905 as a candidate of the Fusionists, a group of prominent Louisville reformers made up of independent Democrats and Republicans. The Fusionists challenged the Whallen brothers' Democratic machine, but O'Neal was defeated by PAUL C. BARTH in a contest marred by rampant election fraud on the part of the Democrats. The elder O'Neal was also a candidate for the Democratic nomination for judge of the Court of Appeals in 1894; he lost the nomination to Judge Sterling B. Toney.

Joseph T. O'Neal Jr. was one of four brothers. After graduating from LOUISVILLE MALE HIGH SCHOOL and from Centre College in Danville, he received his law degree from the UNIVERSITY OF LOUISVILLE in 1903 and began practicing with his father in the law firm of O'Neal & O'Neal.

O'Neal, a Democrat, served as mayor of Louisville from June 25, 1927, through November 22, 1927. He originally ran against Republican Arthur Will in the 1925 election and was defeated. O'Neal had been chosen to run as the Democratic nominee for mayor only days before the election, when it was discovered that Democratic nominee William T. Baker had ties to the Ku Klux Klan. An aide to REPUBLICAN PARTY boss CHESLEY SEARCY discovered in October that Baker had been a member of the Ku Klux Klan as recently as April 1925. Baker ended his candidacy after Louisville's *Herald-Post* reported extensively on that membership. O'Neal stepped in as the Democratic nominee the week before the election but was narrowly defeated at the polls by Will.

The Democrats then alleged voting fraud and corruption on the part of the Republicans. A lawsuit was filed in November 1925, and in June 1927 the Court of Appeals ruled the election invalid. O'Neal was appointed by Gov. William J. Fields to serve out the remainder of the term until a November 7 special election. O'Neal ran in that election against Republican William B. Harrison and was defeated by a narrow margin. O'Neal also served as judge of the Court of Appeals for several months but refused to seek reelection. He married Clara Swift of Louisville on January 30, 1926.

See Mary Young Southard and Ernest C. Miller, eds., *Who's Who in Kentucky: A Biographical Assembly of Notable Kentuckians* (Louisville 1936); J. Stoddard Johnston, ed., *Memorial History of Louisville* (Chicago 1896).

OPERATION BRIGHTSIDE. Established in April 1986 by Mayor Jerry Abramson, Operation Brightside is a public-private partnership funded by public money, private cash contributions, and in-kind gifts and services. Donors help underwrite cleanup, beautification, and environmental education programs. City funds cover maintenance crew overhead, staff salaries, and administrative costs of publicly owned properties. Brightside relies heavily on volunteers from neighborhood associations, businesses, churches, service clubs, civic organizations, and schools to assist with beautification campaigns, recycling projects, litter-free events, and festivals. Administration and leadership are provided by a volunteer board of directors and an executive director and staff, under the supervision of the mayor's office.

Brightsites—small, landscaped street-side PARKS, intersections, and medians adopted and maintained by NEIGHBORHOODS, groups, and businesses—are signature beautification projects; other projects include community gardens, plant donations, and memorial tree-plantings. Cleanup efforts include neighborhood cleanup, block-by-block challenges, and participation in the national Great American Cleanup. Operation Brightside offers consultation, resource materials for teachers and libraries, and classes on the principles of gardening to students in public, private, and parochial schools through its environmental education programs.

See David Block, "Operation Brightside Sets Example for Other Cities," *Business First of Louisville* 11 (Jan. 16, 1995): 30, 32; Jerry Abramson, "Brightside Program Gets Older and Better," *Business First of Louisville* 13 (April 28, 1997): 7; *Courier-Journal*, April 3, 1986.

Glenda S. Neely

ORAL HISTORY. Oral history may be defined as recorded interviews that preserve historically significant memories for future use. Since the establishment of Columbia

University's oral history program in 1948, institutions across the country and throughout the world have created oral history collections to augment archival holdings and to document the lives of persons generally neglected in traditional sources. Independent researchers have also used oral history methods and have collected interviews that are reflected in their publications.

Organized oral history activity in Louisville and Jefferson County dates back to approximately the mid-1960s. Donald Anderson, then director of the University of Louisville's Photographic Archives, began interviewing photographers such as Frank Shook of Caufield & Shook Photographers to supplement the Photographic Archives collections. Prof. Charles Berry of the UNIVERSITY OF LOUISVILLE history department created an Oral History Center in the early 1970s and began a project to document the LOUISVILLE ORCHESTRA. Dr. Carl Ryant succeeded Berry as director of the center, and in 1978 the Oral History Center united with the University Archives and Records Center, which since 1973 had been conducting interviews on the history of the university. Ryant and Dr. Dwayne Cox from the university archives served as codirectors from 1978 to 1986, a period that saw tremendous growth in the collection. Projects on such subjects as the Louisville & Nashville Railroad, the *COURIER-JOURNAL* and the *LOUISVILLE TIMES,* African American and Jewish communities, and the DISTILLING industry in Kentucky established the center as an important oral history repository within the state as well as the nation. As of July 1996, the Oral History Center contained over thirteen hundred interviews on such diverse topics as early women lawyers, school desegregation in Jefferson County, and Actor's Theatre of Louisville. Ryant continued with the center until his death in 1993. Dr. L. Dale Patterson succeeded Cox in 1987 and served as codirector until 1993. In 1995 Dr. Tracy K'Meyer and Mary Margaret Bell were named as new codirectors for the center. Later center focus included efforts to document the CIVIL RIGHTS movement in Louisville and Jefferson County. Also at the University of Louisville, the Health Sciences Library maintains a collection of over seventy interviews, including a project on the Louisville General Hospital School of Nursing, the predecessor of the University of Louisville School of Nursing.

Several other Louisville organizations also maintain oral history collections, including the CABBAGE PATCH Settlement House, the Lou Tate Foundation, the LOUISVILLE VISUAL ART ASSOCIATION, PORTLAND MUSEUM, and the JEWISH COMMUNITY CENTER. The Jefferson County Office of Historic Preservation and Archives has collected more than 125 interviews on NEIGHBORHOODS, social services in the county, and the Louisville–Jefferson County Children's Home. BELLARMINE COLLEGE has amassed a collection through the efforts of students under the direction of Dr. Wade Hall and other professors. Hall has used oral methods in his own research, which has resulted in books on Louisvillians LYMAN JOHNSON, PEE WEE KING, and MAE STREET KIDD.

Authors, artists, political and business leaders, community leaders, and hundreds of others are being interviewed by countless researchers on a regular basis and are adding immeasurably to the historical record of the largest city in Kentucky. Many of these interviews are also located in repositories outside of Jefferson County and have been funded by grants from the Kentucky Oral History Commission, a program of the KENTUCKY HISTORICAL SOCIETY in Frankfort that serves as a clearinghouse for information on collections in the state.

See Cary C. Wilkins, ed., *The Guide to Kentucky Oral History Collections* (Frankfort 1991).

Kim Lady Smith

ORCHESTRAS. Many attempts have been made in the past two hundred years to form a permanent orchestra in Louisville, but it was not until the first quarter of the twentieth century that those efforts succeeded.

It is believed that the St. Cecilia Society, which existed from 1822 to about 1824, was the earliest purely orchestral organization. Printed parts of works by Haydn, Mozart, Pleyel, and Rossini used by this group have survived and are housed in the University of Louisville School of Music Library. Ernst W. Gunter, the organist of ST. PAUL'S EPISCOPAL CHURCH, is credited with the formation of two groups in this early period: the Mozart Society about 1843 and the Musical Fund Society in 1857.

In 1866 the thirty-five instrumentalists of the latter group were joined by members of local choirs to form the Philharmonic Society. After many months of rehearsals at the Masonic Temple at Fourth and Jefferson Streets, the society presented its first concert on December 3. The audience heard for the first time in Louisville the Grand March from Wagner's opera *Tannhäuser.* The *Louisville Daily Courier* reviewer stated that this was music that "has taken by storm the most select salons of the old world and almost crazed the music-mad King Ludwig of Bavaria." During the playing of *Dublin Waltzes* by Labitzky, the audience was "particularly requested not to dance to this beautiful music." LOUIS HENRY HAST, the director, was assisted by Harry Peters and George Zoeller in this historic concert. Within two months, on February 15, 1867, the organization became the first incorporated musical group in Kentucky.

In the summer of 1872, Professor Moebius conducted a forty-piece orchestra in biweekly concerts at Central Park. That fall he presented concerts twice a day for the LOUISVILLE INDUSTRIAL EXPOSITION at Fourth and Chestnut Streets. In 1879 Otto Schuler founded and conducted the Louisville Amateur Orchestra, which gave about twenty concerts over the next three years. A second philharmonic orchestra, led by Theodore Becker, gave two seasons of concerts beginning in 1886.

The Liederkranz, a German singing society, had thirty-five instrumentalists in its organization in 1891, but nine years later the players withdrew to form the Philharmonic Society of Louisville under cellist Karl Schmidt. Another group, the Louisville Symphony Orchestra, was formed in 1908 by R. Gratz Cox, but competition for audiences and finances led to bankruptcy for both groups by 1911.

In 1916 a small group of instrumentalists was assembled at the Young Men's Hebrew Association (YMHA) by Morris Simon, a local businessman. By 1926 the group had grown sufficiently to call itself the YMHA Little Symphony, and in 1929 it became the YMHA Symphony. This ensemble became a part of the Louisville Civic Arts Association in 1931 and changed its name to the Louisville Civic Symphony Orchestra. Joseph Horvath was the conductor, and Simon was the manager. At the same time, the UNIVERSITY OF LOUISVILLE developed an orchestra of seventy-five players.

In 1937 officials of the Louisville Civic Arts Association began to make plans to merge the two groups under a better conductor. Horvath and Simon refused to cooperate and were fired. As a result, the Louisville Civic Symphony Orchestra split, and Horvath and Simon formed a new orchestra at the YMHA with those players who were loyal to them. Later, after the JEWISH COMMUNITY CENTER opened on Dutchmans Ln., the group became the Jewish Community Center Orchestra. Simon died in 1959, and Leon Fuchs, his assistant, became manager.

Over the years there were a number of conductors associated with that organization. Among them were Lawrence Fitzmayer, the first director; Howard Koch; Herbie Koch, who later became well known as the organist on WHAS radio and TELEVISION; Tony Resta; Jay Fay; Vladimir Bakaleinikoff; Paul Held; Jacques Gottlieb; George Maull; Joseph Klan; and Rubin Sher, the present conductor.

At the time of the split in 1937, the Louisville Civic Arts Association, led by Dann C. Byck, appointed a committee to search for a new director. Robert S. Whitney, a pianist, composer, and conductor in Chicago, was selected. The new orchestra, with thirty members, was named the Louisville Civic Orchestra. The first concert, with extra musicians from Cincinnati, was given November 2, 1937, at the Memorial Auditorium at Fourth and Kentucky Streets. In 1942 the group changed its name to the Louisville Philharmonic Orchestra. During the years of WORLD WAR II, the orchestra had a constant deficit, and prospects for its survival beyond 1947 looked dim. Acting on the advice of Mayor CHARLES FARNSLEY, Whitney decided to commission one new composition for each subscription concert, move to Columbia Auditorium (now the University Center Building Auditorium at SPALDING UNIVERSITY), and cut the orchestra to fifty players. The concerts were successful, and articles about the commissioning project appeared in NEWSPAPERS all over the world.

However, by Christmas 1949 the symphony, now called the LOUISVILLE ORCHESTRA, was again in financial trouble and was to be disbanded after the concert on January 5, 1950. The principal work on that program was *Judith,* a choreographic poem by composer William Schuman. Martha Graham, the celebrated modern dancer, performed on the stage in front of the orchestra. Rave reviews followed, and the orchestra was invited to play a program of commissioned works, including *Judith,* in New York's Carnegie Hall on December 29, 1950. The next day the orchestra cut its first commercial disc by recording *Judith* and *Undertow,* two ballet scores by Schuman.

In 1952 Mayor Farnsley persuaded the Rockefeller Foundation to give the orchestra $400,000 over four years, and later another $100,000, to commission forty-six works a year and to issue one record each month. Among the commissioned composers from many countries were Luigi Dallapiccola (Italy), Alberto Ginastera (Argentina), Roy Harris (USA), Paul Hindemith (Germany), Carlos Chavez (Mexico), Darius Milhaud (France), Bernard Reichel (Switzerland), and Hector Villa-Lobos (Brazil). With a grant from Broadcast Music in 1955, the orchestra released the first recording on its own First Edition Records label. By October 1970 one hundred recordings had been issued.

In 1963 the orchestra moved its concerts to the Brown Theatre. Whitney retired in 1967 and was succeeded by Jorge Mester. During the 1960s the orchestra also had several guest conductors such as Igor Stravinsky and Aaron Copland. When Mester's contract was not renewed, Akiro Endo was appointed conductor in 1980. In 1983 the Kentucky Center for the Arts was completed, and the orchestra moved to its new home. Lawrence Leighton Smith, the new music director, was on the podium for the opening of the orchestra's forty-seventh season. Smith resigned in 1995 and was followed by Max Bragado Dorman, who was followed in 1999 by Uriel Segal.

In addition to the orchestras already mentioned, several community and youth groups were organized in the last half of the twentieth century. In 1958 the Louisville Academy of Music sponsored a summer orchestral program led by violinist Rubin Sher. In the fall the group was established on a permanent basis and became the LOUISVILLE YOUTH ORCHESTRA. By 1962 it had grown to over a hundred members, and the leadership decided to divide it into two ensembles. Ten years later a string orchestra for younger players was added.

Sher was hired in 1963 by the NEW ALBANY–Floyd County Consolidated School Corp. to develop a string program. Starting with eight students, he soon had five hundred enrolled, and the foundation was laid for a new youth orchestra. In 1996 Sher and fellow teacher Donald McMahel cofounded the Southern Indiana Orchestra. Its purpose was to provide a cultural outlet for the community and to provide an opportunity for musicians to play. Sponsored by the school system the orchestra and its affiliated group, the Southern Indiana Chorus, combined their talents to present Haydn's *The Seasons,* Handel's *Messiah,* and Bernstein's *Mass.* Instrumental programs included soloists in Gershwin's *Rhapsody in Blue* and Lalo's *Symphonie Espagnole.* The orchestra folded in 1981 after the school district trimmed expenses and could no longer fund it.

Sher and McMahel also organized the Floyd County Youth Symphony in 1975. Beginning with sixty-five students, the orchestra grew rapidly and in December 1977 played at the Midwest National Band and Orchestra Clinic in Chicago. An official of the Friendship Ambassadors Foundation who was present invited them to tour Romania. After raising $109,000, the 103 young musicians left in July 1979 for Europe, where they played eight concerts in three weeks. In 1984 they were invited to participate in the International Music Festival in Toronto, Canada, and again in Montreal in 1986. Sher retired that year. McMahel continued to conduct until 1991 when the orchestra appeared again at the festival. Gold medals were won in 1986 and 1991. The orchestra, continuing its search for gold, traveled to Vienna in 1995 under the leadership of the current conductors, J. Douglas Elmore and Philip Thomas.

See Carole Caudill Birkhead, "The History of the Orchestra in Louisville" (M.A. thesis, University of Louisville, 1977); J. Stoddard Johnston, ed., *Memorial History of Louisville* (Chicago 1896); *Courier-Journal,* March 20, 1973; May 18, Sept. 14, 1986; Herman Landau, *Adath Louisville, the Story of a Jewish Community* (Louisville 1981); Jeanne Marie Belfy, "The Commissioning Project of the Louisville Orchestra 1948–1958: A Study of the History and Music", Ph.D. dissertation, University of Kentucky in conjunction with the University of Louisville, 1986.

Robert Bruce French

ORMSBY, STEPHEN (b County Sligo, Ireland, 1759; d Lyndon, Kentucky, March 4, 1844). U.S. congressman, federal judge, and bank president. Ormsby immigrated to Philadelphia in the 1770s, where he pursued classical studies and law. He was admitted to the bar in 1786 and began to practice in Danville, Kentucky. In 1787 he moved to Louisville and became attorney of Jefferson County. He served in the early Indian wars as a brigadier general under Gen. Josiah Harmar in the disastrous campaign of 1790, in present-day Ohio.

In 1791 Ormsby was appointed district court judge in Jefferson County, and in 1796 he served as a presidential elector. Appointed by Gov. James Garrard to the Louisville Twelfth Circuit Court bench in 1803, he served in that position until 1810. He was elected as a Democrat to the Twelfth U.S. Congress, serving from March 4, 1811, to March 3, 1813, but was defeated in his bid for reelection. However, when his successor and opponent, John Simpson, was killed at the battle of Raisin River in the War of 1812, Ormsby was appointed to fill the vacated seat. Reelected, he served from April 20, 1813, to March 3, 1817, but was again defeated in his bid for the Fifteenth Congress. In 1817 he traveled to Philadelphia to solicit the opening of a branch of the Second Bank of the United States in Louisville. He was successful and served as the branch's first president.

About 1803 Ormsby purchased land on Goose Creek and established his farm, Maghera Glass (Gaelic for "green meadows"), near Lyndon. In 1830 he gave his 800-acre farm to his son, Col. Stephen Ormsby Jr., who built a house and lived there until his death in 1869. On September 5, 1832, writer Washington Irving dined in the house on the farm; in his journal he described the house and the property. When the elder Ormsby died, he was buried in the family burial ground at Ormsby Station, near Lyndon. In 1896 the house and part of the land were purchased by the KENTUCKY MILITARY INSTITUTE, which owned the house and used it as a school until the early 1970s. The house was largely renovated after an arson fire damaged it in 1982. It is now part of the Ten Broeck Hospital.

See *Biographical Directory of the American Congress 1774–1961* (Washington, D.C. 1961); *History of the Ohio Falls Cities and Their Counties,* vol. 2 (Cleveland 1882); Leslee F. Keys, ed., *Historic Jefferson County* (Louisville 1992); John F. McDermott, ed., *The Western Journals of Washington Irving* (Norman, Okla. 1944).

ORMSBY VILLAGE–RIDGEWOOD. Ormsby Village was the popular name given to a residential institution for dependent and delinquent children that was funded jointly by the city of Louisville and Jefferson County between 1920 and 1968. Its official name was the Louisville and Jefferson County Children's Home, and it was authorized and approved by a 1920 ordinance. The home included a residential facility for white children (Ormsby Village) and one for black children (Ridgewood) at the campus in Lyndon, on LaGrange Rd. between Whipps Mill Rd. and Dorsey Ln.; a home for very young dependent children in Jeffersontown called Sunshine Lodge; and the Juvenile Detention Center in downtown Louisville on Chestnut St. across from the old General Hospital. Its staff of social workers also supervised many children in foster homes.

Traditionally, Ormsby Village referred to the main residential campus on LaGrange Rd. This facility had its origins in Progressive Era reforms in the care of children by local government. The county government (JEFFERSON COUNTY FISCAL COURT) purchased the 400-acre Hamilton Ormsby farm near Lyndon for its new child care facility, the Parental Home and School Commission, in 1912. Reformers at the time favored locating facilities for the care of children in the countryside, away from the crowded cities. The construction of the Louisville, Anchorage & Pewee Valley electric railroad (part of the interurban railroad network) a few years earlier helped make the use of a rural site practical by providing a means of easy transportation for the staff and family members of the residents, most of whom still lived in Louisville. In 1920 this agency was merged with the older and much larger city of Louisville Industrial School of Reform to form the Louisville and Jefferson County Children's Home. The bipartisan Board of Managers was appointed jointly by the mayor and the county judge.

By 1923 the former Industrial School property at Third and Shipp Streets was sold to the University of Louisville, and an expanded facility was constructed on the Ormsby land under the leadership of the new superintendent, George Colvin, who later became president of the University of Louisville. Bellevoir, the 1867 Ormsby mansion north of Beargrass Creek, became the residence of the superintendent. The Ormsby Village campus constructed around it included an administration building, a central dining hall and kitchen, a service building, an industrial building, a school, and a hospital. About forty children lived in each of fourteen cottages. The Ridgewood campus, south of Beargrass Creek with access off Dorsey Ln., was similar, although smaller. On the balance of the property were athletic fields, a swimming pool, poultry yards, and a dairy.

According to the ordinance of 1920 establishing the Louisville and Jefferson County Children's Home, commitments of children to the facility were usually made through the Jefferson County Juvenile Court, although occasionally children could be admitted directly by the Board of Managers. For the first three decades of the home's operation, the majority of the children placed there were dependents, children whose parents could no longer care for them. The home also accepted children who were committed for mild forms of delinquency. At its height during the tenure of its third superintendent, Henley V. Bastin (1926–52), the Louisville and Jefferson County Children's Home housed over four hundred children at three facilities and supervised several hundred more in foster homes or other types of supervised care.

After World War II, with improved economic conditions, the dependent population at Ormsby Village declined in comparison to the delinquent population. In the early 1960s the facility was integrated and the school was closed. The Board of Managers was dissolved in 1968 and handed over control of the facility to the Metro Social Services Department, a joint city-county social service agency. The Ridgewood buildings were leased to the state and renamed Lynnwood. The main Ormsby Village campus was used for various treatment programs. Metro Social Services was dissolved in 1979, at which time the county government closed the facility.

During the 1980s the Ormsby Village property was used for various county government programs, most notably a community garden site. The Kentucky Railway Museum was located there for several years also. In 1987 the county government announced that the bulk of the property would be developed as a new office park to be named Hurstbourne Green; and as the office park developed, all of the Ormsby Village and Ridgewood institutional buildings were demolished, with the exception of Bellevoir.

See *Courier-Journal,* April 25, June 22, July 12, Aug. 1, Oct. 10, Nov. 19, 1919; March 7, July 17, 1920; April 1, 1970; Oct. 1, 28, 1979; Oct. 11, 1983; Aug. 13, 1985.

David Morgan

ORPHANAGES. The first colonial orphanage was built in New Orleans by the Ursuline Sisters, a Roman Catholic religious order, in 1739. By the end of that century six more institutions had been established, all by religious organizations. Through most of the eighteenth and nineteenth centuries, the care of orphans—much of it heroic, some of it inept if not criminal—was seen as the province of the religious, or of the philanthropic. Civil authority showed little interest in the matter except insofar as it affected crime or public order.

The oldest orphanage in Louisville, the St. Vincent Orphan Asylum, was established by the Sisters of Charity, another Roman Catholic religious order, in response to a severe cholera epidemic in 1832. Originally the children were boarded in the nuns' small residence next to the St. Louis church (later the site of the Cathedral of the Assumption). By the next year the sisters had twenty-five orphans under their care. Shortly thereafter, about 1835, the Protestant Episcopal Orphan Asylum was begun in a rented house on Market St. between Ninth and Tenth Streets. The first charges there numbered six. William Sale was president of the asylum.

Between 1832 and 1875 there were ten institutions in Louisville specifically designated orphanages. Only two, the Colored Orphan Home, 2236 Eighteenth St., and the Masonic Widows and Orphans Home and Infirmary of Kentucky, on Second St. south of Bloom St., were philanthropies not associated with a specific church; both of them, however, were supported by various church donations.

After the Civil War, Louisville's population increased rapidly. The city, using land originally purchased for use as a cemetery (and which later became the University of Louisville Belknap Campus), made provisions for the House of Refuge, a combination reformatory-orphanage. This was the first civil institution in Louisville to deal with orphans. Children between the ages of seven and sixteen, segregated by race and sex, would be accommodated at the home, in the words of the state legislature, "to prevent our youth from becoming adepts in crime and subjects for the penitentiary."

The first boy was committed to the "refuge" by the city court in July 1865. In eighteen months there were 136 residents. By 1887 the institution had been renamed the Industrial School of Reform. Although admission to the facility was always enacted by a judge, the original act of incorporation did not limit access to the home to those juveniles who were found guilty of crime. The school accepted orphans who could not be admitted to the denominational orphan asylums because of restrictions of race, creed, age, or available space. By 1896, when all arrangements for a segregated popula-

German Protestant Orphans Home, now the site of the Mid-City Mall on Bardstown Road, 1927.

tion had been completed, residents at the industrial school numbered 483.

The first comprehensive effort to care for orphans from all Kentucky counties was initiated in December 1895 by Judge Reginald H. Thompson and twenty prominent citizens. Thompson, who also helped found the Industrial School for Boys and the NEWSBOYS' HOME, was a Louisville Police Court judge. With county judges, he founded the Kentucky Children's Home Society to care for children who formerly would have been consigned to the county almshouses. The society was chartered to act as guardian to orphans and abandoned children. One judge in each county was authorized by statute "to turn over to the society such children as were about to become charges on the county." These children were placed in a receiving home in Louisville until the society could arrange foster-home placement. The children became wards of the state, and the society maintained guardianship over them until a child either reached the age of majority or was adopted. By 1921, when the society relocated to LYNDON, it had placed over five thousand children in Kentucky homes. In September 1936 the home was closed to new commitments, and from 1936 to its closing in 1973, it functioned as a receiving and placement agency for the state Department of Public Welfare.

The COLORED ORPHANS' HOME, the earliest institution in Louisville for African American children, was opened in January 1878 in an abandoned army hospital, rented for $25 per month, in the Taylor Barracks, which stood in the block bounded by Second, Third, Oak, and Ormsby Streets, and incorporated as the Colored Orphans Home Aid Society on April 8, 1878. It moved in May 1879 to a nine-room worn-out brick house on 3 acres of farmland on the corner of Eighteenth and Dumesnil Streets. At a time when public opinion in the South had not yet reached the stage where humanitarian efforts were free from race limitations, the enterprise suffered terribly from lack of funds. The facility cared for children between the ages of three and fifteen, sometimes with their mothers as well. Operating funds were raised from street fairs, and small donations came from churches and friends. Clothes were donated, food was grown on the farm, and the children slept sometimes three to a bed.

Between 1880 and 1919 the home cared for an average of thirty children. Finally, in 1920, after forty-seven years of courage and perseverance in the face of the most severe conditions of poverty, the home came under the protection of the Welfare League. By 1924, as a member of the Community Chest, it ministered to fifty-three children. With improved financial conditions, the dilapidated facility was rebuilt. In 1934 the orphanage and the land were sold to Simmons Bible College.

The All-Prayer Foundling Home was begun in 1905 as a nonsectarian institution for infants up to three years of age, sometimes accompanied by their mothers. Originally on Story Ave., it began with an enrollment of eight children. Founded by Lutheran pastor George C. Cromer and his wife, the foundling home was modeled on a similar institution in Bristol, England, founded by George Mueller. Both Mueller and Cromer committed themselves to supporting their institutions entirely by voluntary contributions in answer to prayer. No solicitations for help were ever made, although Cromer did publish a small quarterly magazine, called the *Helper,* to proselytize his home's work. In 1918 the enterprise relocated to 2305 Sycamore Ave., with twelve mothers and twenty-nine children in its care. In forty-five years of service, the home cared for over a thousand infants and five hundred mothers, with an infant mortality rate of less than 10 percent. In 1947 it became a home for unwed mothers; it closed in 1969.

By the first half of the twentieth century, institutional care for the area's orphans was broad-based and comprehensive. In 1922 there were 2,406 dependent children, all wards of the city, cared for in twenty-three homes and institutions. Louisville ranked first among cities of its size in its number of institutionalized children. Oakland, CALIFORNIA, with about half that number, ranked second. By 1939 there were 892 children in institutions, a huge decrease from 1922 but still enough to make Louisville the leader among seven southern cities of comparable size.

The decline in institutional care for orphans occurred because of many precipitating factors. The orphan population decreased with the lessening of public calamities. Health EPIDEMICS such as cholera (1832), yellow fever (1851), and influenza (1919) were things of the past, and health conditions, public and personal, improved dramatically. Birthing fatalities for women practically disappeared. Mothers dying in childbirth in 1919, for example, numbered about 79.9 in 10,000 births. By 1955 the figure was less than 8 in 10,000 births. Fathers also lived longer, and as their employment became more reliable, the stability of vulnerable families increased.

Another factor was society's acceptance of unwed mothers and their children. Because attitudes became more tolerant, more single mothers kept their children. The isolation and poverty of racial SEGREGATION began to be addressed. Lessons were learned from the massive financial dislocation of the GREAT DEPRESSION. With the formation of the Kentucky Department of Welfare in 1940, public funds eventually became more accessible to the needy and the unemployed of all races. Then, too, the cost of institutional care for orphans became prohibitive. Home counseling designed to keep families together was found to be more effective, and it was cheaper. For instance, in 1955 the per capita cost to maintain a child in an institution was between $2,000 and $3,000 per annum. In March 1955 the state Department of Economic Security paid out $117,444 for the care, either in their own homes or in foster homes, of 4,636 dependent children, including counseling and skilled casework.

Finally, philosophically speaking, the 1895 observation of the Kentucky Children's Home Society that the family home is always the most ideal place for the child found its proper weight. By the 1980s long-term institutional care of orphans had come to an end. Those homes that survived worked with children in dysfunctional and troubled relationships and were aided by state welfare agencies. Boarded care in these facilities, when necessary, averaged months, not years. The primary effort was to reunite families. Orphaned children were placed in foster family care or were adopted, and payment for foster care shifted from voluntary to public auspices.

Religious Orphanages

Roman Catholic

St. Vincent, begun in 1832, was at Wenzel and Jefferson Streets from 1836 to 1891. In 1850 its male population was split off and became St. Thomas Orphanage. In 1874 a foundling home, a separate facility solely for the care of infants, was added. From 1892 to 1901 St. Vincent occupied Preston Park (the present-day site of BELLARMINE COLLEGE). From 1901 to 1955 its residence was 2120 Payne St. It then moved to Ward Ave. near ANCHORAGE. In 1984 the orphanage was closed and the land was sold to a developer.

The orphanage at the Sisters of Good Shepherd Convent (Maryhurst) was established in 1843 at Eighth St. between Walnut (Muhammad Ali Blvd.) and Madison. It was the first of many orphanages established in the United States by the nuns of this FRENCH order. In 1867 a facility was completed on Bank St. to accommodate white female children. By 1940, as noted in Caron's City Directory, it was called Maryhurst. In 1963 the Bank St. facility was combined with the sisters' orphanage for African American girls, forming a new integrated facility with a population of about seventy-five female children.

By the 1950s the sisters had begun to work more with troubled children and less with orphans. In 1976 Maryhurst moved to 1015 Dorsey Ln. and, as a multiservice agency for children, aided more than twenty-five hundred children in twenty-three years. September 15, 1999, marked Maryhurst's 156-year anniversary, making it Kentucky's oldest continuously used children's facility.

St. Joseph Orphans Asylum (ST. JOSEPH CHILDREN'S HOME) was established in 1850 at Eighth St. between Grayson and Walnut by Father Karl Boeswald and the German Roman Catholic churches of St. Boniface and St. Mary. In 1886 the orphanage moved to 32 acres on Frankfort Ave., its present site. Beginning with six boys, by 1865 it housed one hundred children. In 150 years the institution has cared for thousands of children. It has been run by the Ursuline nuns for more than one hundred years and is famous for its yearly fund-raising picnic, a tradition that began with its founding.

St. Thomas Orphanage was constituted in 1850 at St. Thomas Seminary in Nelson County from the male population of St. Vincent Orphanage. In 1889 the facility there was destroyed by fire, and until 1938 the orphanage was located alternately in Nelson County and Preston Park, Louisville. In 1938 the boys were reunited with St. Vincent. St. Thomas closed in 1983.

The Good Shepherd Home for Colored Girls was founded in 1897 at 800 W Walnut St. It cared for African American girls between the ages of six and eighteen and had an average population of fifty children. In 1963 this facility was integrated with Maryhurst.

Our Lady's Home for Infants was established by the Sisters of Charity and the Queen's Daughters, a laywomen's charity, in 1924. First located at the former Cedar Grove Academy, Thirty-fifth St. and Rudd Ave., by 1925 it had relocated to 809 S Brook St. It ministered to infants up to the age of two. The home began with twelve children in 1924 and quickly reached an average enrollment of twenty-five infants. By 1961 it had moved to 523 Park Ave.; it closed in 1990.

The Catholic Orphans Home was a 300-acre facility that opened in Anchorage in 1938 to care for the boys of the burned-out St. Thomas Home. The girls of St. Vincent Home moved to this facility in 1955. It closed in 1984.

Protestant

The Louisville Orphan's Home Society (Louisville Presbyterian Orphanage, 1876; Presbyterian Synodical Orphanage, 1920; Bellewood, 1961) was founded on February 26, 1849, on Plank Rd. (Preston St.) south of Kentucky St. It was the earliest child care facility of the Presbyterian church in the United States. On June 4, 1853, the first orphan was admitted. In 1875 the home relocated to Anchorage on the grounds of Bellewood Woman's Seminary, where, beginning at the turn of the century, its population numbered between 75 and 100 children. By 1984 Bellewood's emphasis had shifted to the residential treatment of adolescents, averaging 80 children a year. In 1999, under chief executive officer Greg Mathews, it marked its 150th year of continuous service to youth.

The German Protestant Orphan Asylum opened in 1851 on Jefferson St. between Nineteenth and Twentieth Streets. The first orphans cared for by the Reverend Louis Daubert were children whose German-immigrant parents had died en route to Louisville during a yellow fever epidemic. By 1902, when it was renamed the Protestant Orphans Home and relocated to 1250 Bardstown Rd. (present-day Mid-City Mall), the home had provided for more than two thousand children. In 1961 it moved to Goldsmith Ln. and became Brooklawn Childrens Home. From 1982 to 1990, as Brooklawn Treatment Center, it worked with the chemically dependent. In 1991 it shifted its focus to troubled boys, ages six to eighteen and by 1999 had accommodations for sixty-seven children.

The Louisville Baptist Orphan's Home, also known as the Home for Helpless Children, was established in 1869 by the Ladies Aid Society of the Walnut Street Baptist Church. In 1870 the society constructed a facility at First and St. Catherine Streets, the first Baptist orphanage in the United States. By 1888, 560 children had been admitted to the home, 200 boys and 360 girls. Roughly half of them were adopted into families. In 1950 the home was renamed Spring Meadows and moved to Middletown, where it became an agency for abused and troubled children. By 1969, its centennial anniversary, an estimated 8,000 youngsters had been cared for by the institution. In 1998 Spring Meadows Children's Home's licensed capacity was 48; and 113 children, ages nine to eighteen, had received care by the year's end.

The Orphanage of the Good Shepherd was founded in 1869 by the Episcopal Diocese of Kentucky as a home for boys. It was built by Miss Sarah Clayland on Crestwood Ave. near Frankfort Ave. In the 1920s the facility was converted to the service of troubled boys referred to it by Louisville and Jefferson County social agencies. In 1938 it was renamed Woodcock Hall to commemorate Bishop Charles Woodcock. It closed in 1955.

The Home of the Innocents was founded in 1879 by the Reverend James T. Helm, M.D., in a rented home on Clay St. Incorporated in 1880 as an Episcopal institution for the care of children up to the age of six, regardless of denomination. Beginning with an enrollment of 8 children, by 1914 it averaged 40. In 1930 it merged with the Episcopal Receiving Home, established in 1835, and moved to 245 E Chestnut St. It remained within this neighborhood, at different addresses, for forty-nine years before moving in 1979 to 485 E Gray St. By this time the home had become a shelter–care facility for abused, abandoned, and neglected children, as well as a provider of long-term care for medically fragile children. Through the 1990s it had cared for about 1,200 children annually. In 1999 the home bought the Bourbon Stock Yards' 20.5 acre site to build a larger facility.

The Christian Church Widows and Orphans Home was opened in May 1884. Its first location was 1013 E Jefferson St.; later it relocated to 809 W Jefferson. By 1895 it was providing for fifty-seven children. From 1905 to 1949 its residence was 225 College St.; in 1949 it moved to Danville, Kentucky.

Jewish

The Jewish Children's Home was established on December 4, 1910, at 223 Jacob St. Miss Anne Nevils, its first director, continued in that position for forty-five years. From 1912 to 1922 the home was at 1233 Garvin Pl.; then it moved to 1135 S First St. In 1933 the facility, as a Community Chest Agency, became a home for convalescent children. It closed in 1975.

Civic, Fraternal, and Philanthropic Orphanages

The House of Refuge (Industrial School of Reform, Ormsby Village) admitted its first child in 1865. An institution of 80 acres, it built separate facilities for girls in 1872, for African American boys in 1877, and for African American girls in 1894. In 1920 the Industrial School of Reform, as it was then called, moved to 400 acres in Lyndon, where it was known as Ormsby Village. In 1974–75 Superintendent David Riffe closed the facility, after it had aided many thousands of children.

The Masonic Widows and Orphans Home was incorporated on January 15, 1867, on Second St. south of Bloom. The first resident was admitted in 1871. In 1927 the home relocated to a 176-acre farm on Frankfort Ave. in St. Matthews. Over the years the home cared for thousands of children. In 1988, 95 acres of the home's farm were sold to a private developer, and in 1997 existing buildings were converted into 103 apartment units for senior citizens.

The Jeffersonville Orphan Asylum in Jeffersonville, Indiana, was built in the fall of 1879 at 823 Meigs Ave. on land donated to the Orphans Home Society by Mrs. Wilhemina Zulauf. The society, established March 23, 1876, had previously maintained an orphanage in a rented house on Front St., caring for 16 children in three years. The new brick building could accommodate 45 children, and by 1909 it sheltered 32. It closed in 1921.

The Cornelia Memorial Orphans Home in New Albany, Indiana, was, in 1883, located on Ekin Ave. above Vincennes. The buildings and grounds were a gift of William S. Culbertson. Previously chartered on September 21, 1877, as a nonsectarian orphanage for children to the age of sixteen, it was first located in a rented building on Main St. It accepted children from Floyd and surrounding counties, with the largest population at any one time being sixty children. It closed in 1943, having provided care and protection for hundreds. In 1953 the real estate was sold to Floyd County and the proceeds donated to the county hospital delivery room.

The Kentucky Children's Home Society was established in 1895. Orphans were sent to the society from throughout Kentucky by county judges. The children became wards of the state, and the society acted as their guardian. Thousands of orphaned children were aided in finding foster-home placement and/or adoption. By 1939 its functions were absorbed by the state Department of Public Welfare, Child Welfare Division.

The All-Prayer Foundling Home was begun

in 1905 as a home for infants. Located at 2305 Sycamore Ave., it was modeled after a famous institution in England. In 1947 it became a home for unwed mothers.

The Holt Masonic Orphans Home was established in 1917 from the proceeds of the estate of businessman James Holt. The bequest was made to Masonic Lodge No. 4, Clark County, for the establishment and maintenance of an orphanage for children with a Masonic affiliation, to the age of eighteen. The home is on the site of the old Jefferson General Hospital, the third-largest hospital in the United States during the Civil War. Although, as of 1999, there were no orphans, the facility still functions; all operating funds continue to be furnished from Mr. Holt's bequest. The facility can accommodate sixteen children.

The Kentucky Home Society for Colored Children was organized in 1908 by Dr. C.H. Parrish and friends. It was the segregated version of the Kentucky Children's Home Society and had offices at 807 S Sixth St. The former Eckstein Norton School buildings, near Lotus, Kentucky, became the first receiving home. The Kentucky legislature made its first appropriation to the society, $5,000, in 1910. Yearly subsidies increased. By 1918, 542 children had been cared for, all of them received by the society on court order. By 1933, with the receiving institution now at 825 S Sixth St., the society had cared for some 1,500 African American children from eighty-one counties in Kentucky. By 1940 the S Sixth St. address was closed, its functions having been absorbed by the state Department of Public Welfare, Child Welfare Division.

The National Home Finding Society for Colored Children was organized and incorporated in 1909 by Rev. Octavius Singleton, who was also its superintendent, and others. Its headquarters were at 1716 W Chestnut St., where, in its first ten years, it cared for about 180 children. All finances for support of the children were raised by Singleton. In 1938 the institution, for black children ages two to twelve, was moved to Irvington in Breckinridge County.

See W.H. Slingerland, *Child Welfare Work in Louisville* (Louisville 1919); *A Directory of Homes for the Aged and Homes and Agencies for the Children of Kentucky* (Frankfort 1940); *Jefferson County's Foster Family Care Service* (Louisville 1967); G.C. Cromer, *Forty Years of Trust* (Louisville 1944); *Courier-Journal,* March 3, 1916; Feb. 4, 1917; Oct. 17, 1920; June 22, Aug. 1, 1922; May 18, 1938; May 27, Dec. 14, 1939; Oct. 6, 1955; *Louisville Herald,* Jan. 11, 1920; *Louisville Times,* April 11, 1921.

OXMOOR. Although mention of the Oxmoor name now conjures visions of a large shopping complex, its origins were first wilderness and then farmland. William Christian, one of the early pioneers of Kentucky, was the original owner of at least half of the land now known as Oxmoor; it was located about 8 miles from Louisville on Beargrass Creek. Christian deeded 1,000 acres from his holdings to his daughter Priscilla and her new husband, Alexander Scott Bullitt, as a wedding present on February 10, 1786, shortly after their marriage.

Bullitt apparently purchased an adjoining 1,000 acres in 1787. Other smaller sections of land were bought and sold, but these two main tracts formed Oxmoor Farm. No one knows who named the land, but it is agreed that it was known by that name as early as 1785 and that it was called Oxmoor from the classic *The Life and Opinions of Tristram Shandy, Gentleman.* The property adjoined A'Sturgus Station, one of the six forts along the Middle Fork of Beargrass Creek, and was near the land of William Christian, who had recently built three log cabins at the nearby fort. Because the Bullitt family owned the farm for the next two centuries, the history of the home and the farm is intertwined with that of its owners.

As was so often the case on Kentucky's frontier, Bullitt first lived in a log cabin while planning and building a more substantial permanent residence. By 1791 the new four-room clapboard house was ready for Bullitt, his wife, and their three children. At a time when most people were living in log cabins or brick houses, the clapboard structure was relatively rare. It incorporated architectural features not previously seen in the area, such as corner fireplaces that joined to form a single chimney at each end of the house, but it also conformed to the frontier style in having no dormer windows. There was no front porch, but there probably was a protective hood over the front door and over the back entrance.

Alexander Scott Bullitt's younger son, William C. Bullitt, inherited Oxmoor from his father in 1816. By the late 1820s, expanding the house to accommodate eight children was a priority for William and his wife, Mildred Ann Fry. A large brick addition was built in 1829 with a passageway to connect it to the original clapboard structure. The addition displayed several features that were characteristic of two other homes in the area—Farmington and Ridgeway—which were owned by Mildred's sister Lucy Speed and William's sister, Helen Massie, respectively. The older wooden building became bedrooms, while the new brick addition consisted of an entrance hall flanked by a parlor and a dining room over a cellar. The new recessed portico entrance was in the Federal style. The expanded home served as the Bullitt residence for thirty-four years.

Three of Bullitt's sons were fighting for the Confederacy and one was a lawyer in Pennsylvania when, in 1863, William C. Bullitt, who by then was seventy years old, decided to close the house at Oxmoor and rent the land. Bullitt concluded that it was neither desirable nor safe to remain on the farm, especially after Lincoln's Emancipation Proclamation, and also after the occupation of the neighborhood by federal troops. He and his wife, Mildred, moved to the home of a daughter, Helen Chenoweth.

Bullitt's children were scattered and disinterested in living in the home, so it stood empty. At the deaths of Bullitt and his wife, in 1877 and 1879 respectively, Oxmoor Farm was divided among their children. The house remained empty and unused except for storage for almost fifty years.

In 1906 Alexander Bullitt's great-grandson, William Marshall Bullitt (son of Thomas Walker Bullitt) bought a considerable portion of the original land, including the residence, from the John C. Bullitt estate. Within the next three years he acquired all of the other children's Oxmoor property. By 1909 he was living in the house and had begun the long process of restoring and refurbishing the old residence so that his father could spend his final years in his childhood home.

A 1916 addition to the west side held a kitchen and servants' quarters. In 1926 a second story was built over the front part of the house for bedrooms. By 1926 architect F. Burrall Hoffman Jr. of New York had been commissioned to design and build a new 60 x 28 foot library, unequaled in Kentucky. It was planned to be both beautiful and functional with room to house William Marshall Bullitt's ninety-five hundred books.

As Oxmoor Farm became part of the eastward development of Louisville, the land served various new uses. In 1970 plans were drawn up and land was sold for the Oxmoor Woods residential development. In 1971 a 34-acre shopping mall, Oxmoor, was built on part of the property. The Oxmoor Steeplechase is held as an annual charity benefit on a course built in 1945.

In 1991 William Marshall Bullitt's son Thomas Walker Bullitt willed the house, the immediate outbuildings, and 70 acres to the Filson Club Historical Society in perpetuity through a conservation easement donated to the Kentucky Heritage Council. Included with the property is a two-story log house located near a fork of Beargrass Creek that is believed to be the home built in the 1780s by William Christian, Alexander Scott Bullitt's father-in-law. Other eighteenth- and nineteenth-century outbuildings on the estate include a stone springhouse and an icehouse, a smokehouse, a kitchen, and slave quarters, all built of brick. Evidence of the original A'Sturgus Station, one of the six original Beargrass forts, is also part of the farm. Early-twentieth-century tenant houses, two-story, gable-roofed, and clapboarded, are also part of the farm complex today.

See *Historic Jefferson County* (Louisville 1992); Samuel W. Thomas, "Oxmoor: The Bullitt House in Jefferson County, Kentucky," *Kentucky Review* 9 (Fall 1989); Thomas W. Bullitt, *My Life at Oxmoor* (Louisville 1911; rev. ed., Chevy Chase, Md. 1995).

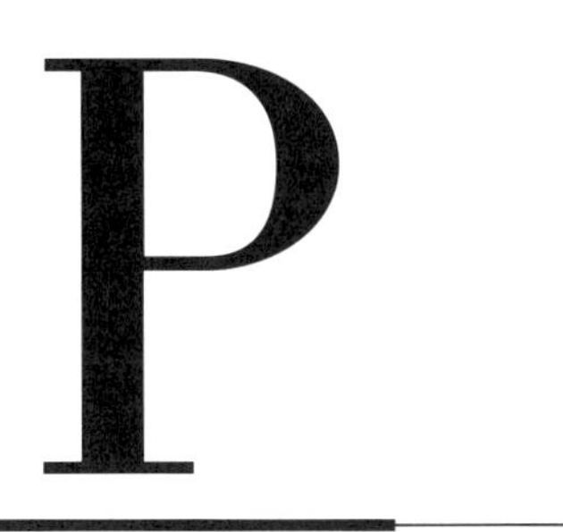

PAGE, GROVER (b Gastonia, North Carolina, November 10, 1892; d Louisville, August 5, 1958). Cartoonist. Page, the son of James E. and Georgia Page, was an editorial cartoonist for the COURIER-JOURNAL for nearly forty years. He decided at age ten to become a cartoonist. For a few months when he was eighteen, he worked in the art department for the *Baltimore Sun,* but he returned to Gastonia to recover from an illness. He attended the Art Institute in Chicago, where some of his contemporaries were Billy DeBeck of "Barney Google" fame and Frank King, creator of "Gasoline Alley." From there, Page went to Atlanta, where he worked on commercial animated cartoons; he was a pioneer in the field. When the company failed, he returned to Gastonia for a brief period and worked for the city's PUBLIC WORKS Department as a draftsman. In 1917 Page accepted a position with the *Nashville Tennessean,* where he began to develop a reputation. Many of his cartoons were reprinted in magazines, books, and other NEWSPAPERS. After two years in Nashville, he came to the *Courier-Journal.*

One of Page's first cartoons for the paper, reprinted in more than 350 magazines and newspapers, portrayed a wolf in sheep's clothing. The wolf represented the adversaries of Pres. Woodrow Wilson, and the sheep's clothing represented the opposition to the League of Nations. Page used forms of media besides the usual pen-and-ink sketches, including wood engraving and linoleum blocks. He was credited with putting more "art" into cartooning—perhaps more than any other cartoonist in the country. Page was a self-styled short-order artist who executed his final sketches in about a half hour. However, they were preceded by endless trial sketches and frequent conferences with *Courier-Journal* editors.

Page was awarded the Edward S. Shorter prize for the best block print in the Southern Art League competition on three occasions. He spoke before civic and school groups and clubs. He was one of twelve cartoonists in the United States selected to go to Japan and Korea in 1953 to entertain wounded men with sketches and caricatures. Page described these few weeks as the most strenuous but most satisfying of his life. An amateur card-trick artist, he was vice president of the Magicians Club of Louisville and was a member of the Southern Printmakers, the Southern States Art League, and the ARTS CLUB OF LOUISVILLE.

Page married Gertrude Boland, with whom he had one son, Grover Page Jr.

See *Courier-Journal,* Aug. 6, 1958.

PAINT AND COATING INDUSTRY. Because of its proximity to raw materials such as oils, lead, and colors; its river and railroad facilities; and its centralized location with respect to the South, the West, and the Northeast; the Louisville area was important in the development of the paint and coatings industry in the mid-nineteenth century. The first paint supply house in town was the H. Marcus Co., founded in 1853 by Herman Marcus on MARKET St. Many of the early firms imported their paint (manufacturing here began a few years after this company was formed) and sold other items such as linseed and lubricating oils, pigments, and glass. Before the end of the century, other companies, such as Peaslee-Gaulbert Co., with its famous Pee-Gee brand label (founded 1867); Blatz Paint Co. (founded 1870); Bridges, Smith & Co. (founded 1889 as Bridges-McDowell Co.); Louisville Varnish Co. (founded 1883 as Louisville Asphalt Mining & Importing Co.); Charles R. Long, Jr., Co. (founded 1897); Lampton, Crane & Ramey Co. (founded 1893, closed 1931), and Kurfees Coatings (founded 1897 as Kurfees Paint Co.) entered the burgeoning business. By 1898 the growing number of production plants and retail shops prompted several local entrepreneurs to form the Louisville Paint, Varnish, and Lacquer Manufacturers Club (the predecessor to the Louisville Paint and Coatings Association) in order to share ideas and assist each other in times of need.

The turn of the century brought three important trends that would characterize the paint industry throughout the century: the strengthening of old firms, the establishment of new ones, and acquisitions. New firms to enter the local market after 1900 included Reliance Universal (founded 1919 as Reliance Varnish Co.), Porter Paint Co. (founded 1921 as Becker-Tabb Paint Co.), DeHart Paint & Varnish Co. (founded 1931), Hy-Klas Paints (founded 1920 as Merchants & Manufacturers Paint Co.), Progress Paint Co., makers of Gray Seal Paint (founded 1912), Kelley Technical Coatings (founded 1949), Jellico Chemical Co. (founded 1954), Schaefer Varnish Co. (founded 1926), and Jones-Dabney Co. (founded 1919).

Among the many purchases by outside companies that have occurred since the turn of the century, the most notable were the 1928 purchase of the Peaslee-Gaulbert Co. and the 1938 purchase of the Jones-Dabney Co., both by Devoe & Raynolds Co. of New York. Devoe & Raynolds, the oldest paint manufacturer in the United States, moved its headquarters to Louisville in 1954, thus bringing substantial attention to the long-thriving industry in town. Ten years later, the entire Devoe business was purchased by the Celanese Corp., which broke the company into several divisions.

Buyouts such as Guardsman Chemical Coating's purchase of the Schaefer Varnish Co. in 1965 and Progress Paint Company's purchase of Blatz Paint in 1981 and Kurfees Paint in 1997 have continued to dominate the local scene. In late 1998, as part of the consolidation of the paint industry, Porter Paint Company's two-hundred-employee plant at 400 S Thirteenth St. was purchased by Pittsburgh-based PPG Industries from Akzo Nobel NV, a Dutch firm. Courtaulds PLC of Britain had acquired the company in 1987 and sold it to Akzo Nobel NV in July 1998. PPG Industries also owned another Louisville plant, at 6804 Enterprise Dr., that employed seventy-five people in the production of stains and deck products under the Olympic brand. Porter Paint's products were sold through retail company stores and independent distributors throughout North America.

Research has always been a significant component of the paint and coatings industry in the city. The Louisville Paint and Varnish Production Club (the predecessor of the Louisville Society for Coatings Technicians) was formed in 1930 to provide educational opportunities for paint production specialists and chemists. While running programs of their own, the club also worked with scientists at the UNIVERSITY OF LOUISVILLE and created a nationally known coatings education center at the school. Many of the paint industry's significant discoveries have occurred in Louisville, including the development of the first alkyd resins and paints, the first epoxy resins and paints, and the first fast-drying railroad car paints.

By 1958 the Louisville area was said to be fifth in national production of paint and coatings. However, within eight years, the city's sixteen companies, employing approximately twenty-three hundred workers, claimed that Louisville had become the nation's largest paint-manufacturing city. By 1997 the industry still maintained a strong presence in Louisville, with eight manufacturing companies and several retailers.

See "Paint and Varnish Now Chemical Coatings," *Louisville Magazine* 17 (Dec. 20, 1966): 12-16; *Courier-Journal,* Dec. 1, 1998.

PAINTING. Louisville artists have created an ongoing tapestry of images, a sense of who Louisvillians are and a sense of place unique to Louisville. Much like Frederick Olmsted's circle of PARKS that spirals the GEOGRAPHY of hills, giving the city dimension and delivering it from flatness, Louisville painters mirror both passing currents and the city's perpetual character, helping to reflect Louisville's pleasing distinction.

The spirited FALLS OF THE OHIO attracted JOHN JAMES AUDUBON (1785–1851), who sketched nearby BIRDS soon after he arrived by riverboat and settled in Louisville in 1807. Using pencil, pastel, and watercolor, Audubon captured the scarlet tanager, the hooded merganser, and the now-extinct passenger pigeon—

all abundant at the Falls. Audubon painted a graceful swallow in flight, and he estimated that nine thousand such birds roosted in the dense sycamore forests near Louisville. Although he initially sketched for pleasure, his 1810 encounter with visiting artist-naturalist Alexander Wilson (1766–1813) caused him to realize that his love of ornithology could have a broader purpose. This idea culminated in the 1838 publication of his magnum opus, *The Birds of America,* which contains 435 engravings portraying a total of 1,065 birds. The scientific and encyclopedic scope of Audubon's project—conceived at the Falls of the Ohio—seems to be an American outgrowth of the Age of Enlightenment as well as the genesis of Louisville painting.

Audubon turned to portraiture to earn a living because portraits were in great demand. Before the introduction of the daguerreotype in the 1840s, portraiture was the only means of recording a likeness. A portrait could connote one's social standing, and more important, portraiture gave people a sense of permanence during an era when sudden illnesses often cut people's lives short.

Famous portraitists coming to Louisville during the city's early years included New York's leading painter, John Wesley Jarvis (1780–1840). In November 1820 Jarvis portrayed Lucy and WILLIAM CROGHAN at their family estate, Locust Grove, where their engrossing portraits remain. Chester Harding (1792–1866), a prominent Boston artist, made frequent visits to depict Louisville citizens during the 1830s and 1840s. Another periodic guest was George Peter Alexander Healy (1813–94), an internationally famous portraitist who had exhibited at the Royal Academy, London, and the Paris Salon. Healy's 1864 *Portrait of the Speed Family* (Filson Club) conveys the character and humanity of his subjects.

Joseph H. Bush (1794–1865), born in Frankfort, Kentucky, was perhaps Louisville's foremost resident painter during the antebellum period. His early talent had been recognized by Henry Clay, who financed Bush's study with noted artist Thomas Sully in Philadelphia between 1814 and 1817. Afterward Bush settled permanently in Louisville—although he, like all early portrait painters, traveled frequently to seek commissions.

Bush's career spanned five decades, and his style evolved brilliantly, meeting the changing tastes of the day. Bush's early style is evident in his portrait of Gen. WILLIAM CLARK, about 1817, who was coleader of the Lewis and Clark expedition to the Pacific coast (Filson Club). Bush establishes a bond between subject and viewer through his masterful rendering of the human face. He used a hard linear technique, characteristic of his early style, to convey the general's uniform; he also tended to stylize features, such as the uniform's epaulets.

By the mid-1830s Bush began to inject romantic elements into such portraits as *General Zachary Taylor,* 1848 (White House). Taylor stands in three-quarter view with a dramatic sunset background—an aged, victorious military hero near the end of his career. In a style typical of his later works, Bush used strong contrast between light and dark colors, emphasized shading, and employed much freer brushstrokes.

Bush's friend Samuel Woodson Price (1828–1918) first studied with Louisville portrait painter William Reading and later with the well-known Lexington painter Oliver Frazer. From 1851 to 1859, Price had a flourishing portrait studio in Louisville. He was highly complimented by former president Millard Fillmore after Price completed Fillmore's portrait in New York in 1856 (Filson Club). Price's heroic life-scale portrait depicted Fillmore during his unsuccessful run for the presidency as the American Party candidate.

Today Price is especially remembered for his book, *Old Masters of the Bluegrass,* published in 1902. Price was blind when he dictated the work, and Filson Club president R.T. Durrett wrote of him in the book's preface, "In thus groping his way through eternal darkness, he rescued his fellow-artists from oblivion." Price knew the artists personally—including Louis Morgan (1814–52), who painted portraits in Louisville in the winter of 1838 or 1839, and MATTHEW HARRIS JOUETT (1788–1827), the Lexington artist who portrayed many distinguished Louisvillians in his short, prolific career.

James Reid Lambdin (1807–89)—like Bush, a student of Thomas Sully—maintained a studio in Louisville from 1832 until 1838. John Peter Frankenstein (1817–81) worked as both portrait painter and sculptor during visits to the city in 1839, 1847, and 1851. William C. Allen opened his studio in Louisville during the 1840s after having established his reputation with the impressive *Daniel Boone,* 1838 (KENTUCKY HISTORICAL SOCIETY). Allen's romantic image of Boone—commissioned by the Kentucky legislature for $250—graced the then-new capitol in Frankfort. Notable antebellum Louisville portraitists also included Clement Reeves Edwards (1820–98) and THOMAS CAMPBELL (1790–1858). Campbell portrayed Abigail and Samuel Churchill in an attractive pair of portraits for their Spring Grove home in Jefferson County (Filson Club).

Although portraiture dominated antebellum painting, interesting activity also occurred in genre art (genre consists of subjects taken from everyday life). Robert Brammer (1811–53) was listed in the 1838–39 Louisville city directory as an artist "of oil paintings and views in the United States." By 1840 Brammer was a partner with German-born Augustus Von Smith (ca. 1811–53), and together they painted the *Oakland House and Race Course,* 1840 (SPEED ART MUSEUM). In that painting, Brammer and Von Smith convey race-day excitement as prosperous Louisvillians on horseback and in carriages approach the track east of Seventh Street Rd. in the area of later Magnolia and Hill Streets.

Whereas *Oakland House* captures the city's love affair with HORSE RACING, competition of another kind—politics—was the subject of an influential work brought to Louisville by America's foremost genre artist, George Caleb Bingham (1811–79). Bingham exhibited his *County Election* for two months in 1853 at Hegan's Picture Store on MAIN St. The *Louisville Daily Times* on April 6, 1853, urged the public, "If you wish to enjoy the most delightful treat you have had for years, go take a look."

In addition to genre, landscape became an increasingly popular subject as the century progressed. Many early visitors to Louisville marveled at the beauty of the sycamore trees that majestically rose along the river's edge. In 1828 writer and artist Capt. Basil Hall (1788–1844) drew a sycamore near Louisville, noting on his sketch that the tree measured "35 feet in circumference at 5 feet from the ground." Hall made additional sketches (Lilly Library, Indiana University, Bloomington) showing sycamore groves and a panoramic view of the Ohio at SHIPPINGPORT for his 1829 publication, *Travels in North America.*

John Banvard (1815–91) began working in Louisville as a portrait painter in 1830, but between 1841 and 1846 he created his grandiose riverscape, *Panorama of the Mississippi* (destroyed). River travel was Louisville's main mode of transportation prior to its first rail connection in 1851. Louisvillians could easily identify with the vicarious river journey Banvard offered them, and people crowded into the Apollo Rooms to watch performances of the painting fifty years before THOMAS EDISON treated Louisville to the first screen projector. Billed as the largest painting in the world, Banvard's four-foot-high masterwork was three miles in length! Viewers might have felt they were aboard a steamboat as the gigantic painting—attached to two upright revolving cylinders—displayed changing river scenes along the journey. After the Louisville debut, Banvard traveled to New York City with his *Panorama* and then to Europe, where his cinematic painting attracted thousands.

Banvard expressed the essence of the city's riverside in his *Panorama,* while other landscapists portrayed the unique character of Kentucky's land. Joseph Rusling Meeker (1827–89) studied at the National Academy of Design in New York City before his arrival in Louisville in 1852. Meeker created landscapes that evoked an Eden of rolling hills and fields. Alexander Helwig Wyant (1836–92), a landscape painter of national prominence, began his career in Frankfort in 1854. Wyant's style was strongly influenced by the Hudson River landscapist George Inness, whom he met in 1858. For a time Wyant operated from his Louisville studio on Main St. between Third and FOURTH Streets, over Hegan's Picture Store. Wyant's impressive *Falls of the Ohio and Louisville,* 1863, depicts the setting where Audubon developed his art more than a half century earlier (Speed Art Museum). The foreground of Wyant's landscape shows the OHIO RIVER shores where people gathered to enjoy nature's beauty. However, a closer look at the city's riverside reveals the radical change since Audubon's days. The distant horizon in Wyant's painting is filled not with the flight of scarlet tanagers and other birds, but with the billowing smoke of factories straining to produce materials for the CIVIL WAR.

Wyant's painting shows that Louisville remained unscathed and even prospered during the Civil War. Nonetheless, the city's North-South border location meant divided alliances and divided artistic perspectives, too. NICOLA MARSCHALL (1829–1917) fought for the South and designed the Confederate flag and uniform. After the war Marschall came to Louisville and ran a studio at Fourth and Green (Liberty) Streets for more than forty-five years, painting portraits of many Confederate notables and many Union leaders, including Abraham Lincoln. Marschall's painting of JOSIAH STODDARD JOHNSTON (1833–1913) (Filson Club) shows portraiture's increasing gravitation toward realism at mid-century as painters must now compete with the photograph.

Thomas Waterman Wood (1823–1903), a Vermont native, studied in Boston with Chester Harding and settled in Louisville in 1863. Inspired by the haunting image of a one-legged African American veteran walking the streets of Louisville with a homemade crutch, Wood began a landmark series titled *War Episodes* (Metropolitan Museum of Art, New York City). The paintings commemorate the plight of black soldiers during the Civil War. Wood's *War Episodes* received much praise when exhibited at the National Academy of Design in New York in 1869 and resulted in his election to the academy.

The POPULATION of Louisville doubled during the last thirty years of the nineteenth century. The era's wealth is revealed in lavish portraits by Benoni Irwin (1840–96), JOHN RAMSIER (1861–1936), and AURELIUS O. REVENAUGH (1840–1908). But the harsher reality of life, experienced by many living in the city, is seen in Revenaugh's *Newsboy,* about 1890 (Speed Art Museum). The newsboy stands on a chilly downtown street in a snowstorm stoically offering an unseen customer a newspaper with his unmittened hands.

Louisville leaders wanted to project to the nation pictures of a dynamic commercial and cultural city. The Industrial Expositions, beginning in 1872, allowed Louisville to promote its products and also to display its sophistication via painting exhibitions. Art was showcased in an even more extraordinary fashion from 1883 to 1887 at the SOUTHERN EXPOSITION of Art, Industry, and Agriculture. Under Charles M. Kurtz, art gallery director, committees were sent to New York City, Boston, and Philadelphia to borrow works valued at more than $1 million from notable collectors such as John Pierpont Morgan, August Belmont, and Gen. U.S. Grant. In addition to paintings by the old masters, the work of virtually every famous contemporary world artist was included in this Louisville exhibit, as well as works by local artists.

For the Southern Exposition, a separate fireproof art gallery housing more than five hundred paintings was built overlooking a lake. The gallery's cross-plan design permitted the 1883 artwork to be divided into four distinct groups: American art by Hudson River School artists such as Frederick Church and Albert Bierstadt; English works, including landscapes by Joseph Turner; works by FRENCH Salon artists, including William Bougereau and Jean Léon Gérômc; and Barbizon School landscapes by François Millet and Camille Corot. The significance of this grand event was summarized in the 1886 catalogue: "As an art exhibition the Southern Exposition has never been excelled in America. The Art Gallery of 1883 was by far the finest collection of paintings ever to that time offered to the public anywhere in this country."

In addition to the special art exhibitions of the Southern Exposition, a permanent gallery of art had been established by the LOUISVILLE FREE PUBLIC LIBRARY. The library was founded in 1871 not only as a book repository but as an art and cultural center as well. Within its Second Empire–style building on Fourth St. between Liberty and Walnut (Muhammad Ali Blvd.), the library offered a scientific museum, a fourteen-hundred-seat musical auditorium, and an art gallery. An 1874 engraving from *Frank Leslie's Illustrated Newspaper* shows the art gallery hung with crystal chandeliers and crowded with patrons admiring its painting-covered walls. The library's art collection continued to grow through the decades, as its 1928 *Catalogue of Art* reveals. By that time nearly every major Louisville artist was represented in the collection, along with world-famous creations.

Undoubtedly inspired by the magnificent art displays at the public library and the expositions, Louisville Tonalism developed during the last quarter of the nineteenth century. Tonalism is the term applied to work in which the artist employs dim lighting and muted colors to elicit an evocative mood. It was initiated by a group of French artists in the village of Barbizon in the 1830s who made drawings and oil sketches directly from nature rather than creating landscapes solely in the studio. Inspired by the beech woods of Louisville's parks as well as the landscapes of the French Barbizon school, local artists of this school created a distinctive style. The most typical Louisville subject was the trees of the area's forests silhouetted against the fading light of dusk. In contrast to their dynamic age, Tonalists' landscapes captured a nostalgic sense of fading beauty, a reminder of life's transience.

Famous Tonalists included CARL BRENNER (1838–88), JOSEPH KREMENTZ (1840–1928), Patty Thum (1853–1926), Clarence Boyd (1855–83), and HARVEY JOINER (1852–1932), but perhaps the most inventive member of the group was John Bartholomew Botto (?-1910), a painter of Italian descent. Botto, a Louisville native, began exhibiting landscapes as early as the 1872 Industrial Exposition. Using aspects of Tonalism, Botto created paintings as allusive as those of James McNeill Whistler. Even a Botto title, such as *Where the Sunbeam Strikes,* conveys the dreamy nature of his transcendental images.

Louisville's best-known Tonalist was Carl C. Brenner. Works by Brenner—such as *A Glimpse of the Ohio* and *Autumn Reverie*—adorned the walls of many Victorian mansions rising along Third St. Patty Thum in an unpublished manuscript in the Speed Art Museum Library describes the heated rivalry between Tonalists Brenner and Botto. Thum recalls that Brenner expressed "contempt for Mr. Botto's paucity of output," and Botto accused Brenner of work that was "machine made." After his death in Europe, Botto's body was brought back to Louisville's St. Louis Cemetery, where his rival Brenner is also buried.

Another artist of Italian ancestry, Guio "Guy" Leber (1857–1927), was nationally known for his large mural paintings, including works in the Library of Congress. An example of Leber's work in situ is his 1899 *Isola Bella* in Louisville's Conrad–Caldwell House Museum. The artist, along with his brother, in 1914 founded the firm of Leber Brothers, specializing in portraits and religious and fresco paintings.

During this flourishing of Louisville art, nineteenth-century women were rarely encouraged to become professional artists. Amateur Magdalen Harvie McDowell (1829–1918) portrayed her young relative, ROGERS CLARK BALLARD THRUSTON, with spirited potential (Filson Club). Regrettably, McDowell had few opportunities as a painter. Patty Thum, who studied with William Merritt Chase in New York City, excelled in creating light-drenched impressionistic subjects as well as book illustrations. Thum became nationally known for her floral still lifes and received honorable mention for her book illustrations at the 1893 Columbian Exposition in Chicago. Two talented portraitists, Cornelia S. Pering (1840–1923) and Xantippe Saunders (1837–1922) (a relative of Mark Twain), operated the Pering and Saunders Art School at 223 W Walnut St. (Muhammad Ali Blvd.) between Second and Third Streets from the 1890s until WORLD WAR I.

About the turn of the century, local painting began to reflect trends of early modernism in Europe: artists began retreating from naturalism and pursued more subjective approaches. Hewitt Green (1865–1901) turned to the forest along BEARGRASS CREEK for his subject in

Autumnal Grove, 1895 (Speed Art Museum). Green chose a purely Tonalist image but translated it into a flattened decorative style inspired by the Japanese print and Post-impressionism. However, this progressive painting presented great difficulties for the artist. Patty Thum notes, "Green felt a lack of congenial atmosphere to such an extent that he was much saddened and discouraged" (unpublished manuscript, "Artists of the Past in Kentucky," Speed Art Museum Library).

By 1909 the art scene in Louisville changed dramatically with the founding of the Louisville Art Association. This new group answered the need for changing art exhibitions in the city and held its first exhibition from June 1 to 19, 1909,in the newly completed Louisville Free Public Library on York St. The impressive show featured work by thirty-five American and European artists, including Mary Cassatt, Jean Baptiste Corot, and Maxfield Parrish.

The Art Association's successful two-week exhibition drew four thousand visitors—but also the ire of some local artists. As a result, the Louisville Artists League was formed in 1910 to encourage local artists by offering them the opportunity to exhibit yearly. An earlier Art League of 1892 was led by Hewitt Green, but after four exhibitions held above a Fourth Ave. store, that league ended in financial ruin. When the first league disbanded, artists were once again forced to limit their exhibitions to their own studios.

The 1910 Artists League exhibition attracted much attention from the public and the local press, including the complaint by several reviewers that Louisville was still the only large city in America without a permanent art gallery or museum. The league's 1910 exhibition included 129 paintings by twenty-four local artists—a virtual ode to the parks and forests of Louisville and southern Indiana. Local newspapers reproduced numerous landscapes from the exhibit, including *The Arched Pathway* by John A. Doll, *"Big Ben" Cherokee Park* by T.E. Grove, *Bright October Day* by J. Krementz, *Big Indian Creek* by John C. Davidson, *Beech Woods* by Herman Schwabacker, and *Sunlight in the Beech Woods* by Harvey Joiner.

Ferdinand Walker (1859–1927), Artists League president from 1910 to 1920, was considered by critics to be the city's most accomplished and versatile contemporary painter. Walker found his subject for *The Blind Violinist* on Fourth Ave., where the mustachioed musician in a dark hat was a familiar sight to passersby. Walker also exhibited impressionistic landscapes, and his brilliance in portraits can be seen in his painting of Carl Baude (1895–1918) (Filson Club). This painting conveys the subject in military uniform in the year of his death. The disturbing expression on Baude's face long remains in the viewer's memory.

Paul Plaschke (1880–1954) and John Bernard Alberts (1886–1931) were also gifted members of the Artists League. Plaschke, best known as a noted Louisville cartoonist between 1899 and 1937, was also a gifted landscapist who studied with the Ashcan school painter George Luks. In *The Mill,* 1910, and *Bathers at Silver Creek,* 1919, Plaschke conjures up idyllic scenes along the stream at the base of New Albany's Silver Hills. Plaschke's flat, decorative designs resemble the dreamlike works of his talented friend Alberts, whose *Pied Piper* appeared in the first Artists League show. Alberts' portrait of local poet Madison Julius Cawein (1865–1919) dates from that year (Filson Club).

The Artists League's exhibition became an annual event, a lasting contribution to the city's art scene. Later called the Kentucky and Southern Indiana Exhibition, its name was again changed in 1954 to Art Center Annual and today continues as the Water Tower Annual.

By the end of World War I, Louisville still lacked an art museum and a professional art school. However, the 1920s was a dynamic decade for art in Louisville. In 1927 Hattie Bishop Speed, a charter member of the Art Association, opened the J.B. Speed Memorial Art Museum. In 1929 the Art Center School was founded at 125 E Jacob St. in the Fine Arts Building of the Conservatory of Music.

The Art Center School's inspirational director from 1929 to 1944 was Fayette Barnum (1870–1960), a native of Louisville who achieved acclaim as a costume and set designer in New York. For five years Barnum was a student of noted educator, author, and artist Arthur Dow of Columbia University. The Louisville Art Center was praised in the August 1933 issue of the *American Magazine of Art* as "outstanding in the United States, due largely to the vision of the director." Barnum expressed the aims of the school: "The philosophy is that mere representation of nature is not art, that experimentation by each individual for himself is the path to creative art, that ability to create in the visual arts is not confined to a specially endowed group of people, that creative desire and ability have a social significance of far-reaching character" (Covi, Hodapp, and Price, *Tapestry of an Art Association,* 16–17).

Barnum encouraged students to explore the fundamental elements of design, form, and color that underlie objects and scenes in the contemporary world. Art Center School student Orville Carroll (1912–86) adopted Barnum's perspective when creating for the public library a series of heroic murals depicting everyday life. Carroll's murals were part of the WPA's Public Works of Art project. Other former Art Center students also received WPA commissions: Paul Childers, Charles Goodwin, Ollie Patton, and Mary Spencer Nay. Orville Carroll long remained popular in Louisville's art scene, including the St. James Art Fair. Even in the 1970s, Carroll's work was consistently sold out within hours of his arrival at the show.

Between the world wars, painting in Louisville was wide-ranging in subject and style. Along with Jane Mengel Allen (1888–1952), among the most active still-life artists was Maud Ainslie (1871–1960), whose delicate compositions were inspired by Cézanne.

Landscape painting remained the most popular venue for many, including Harvey Joiner, Arthur D. Allen (1879–1949), Morris Belknap Jr. (1893–1952), Dorothy Kohlhepp (1908–64), Norman Kohlhepp (1892–1986), Lennox Allen (1914–80), Lucy Diecks (1908–98), and Marion Lee Long (1898–1994). In 1931 the landscapes of Marcia Hite (1876–1946) were described by the *Courier-Journal* as synonymous with the new spirit. Titles such as *May in Kentucky, The Jockey,* and *The Ohio River Towboat* reflect her keen ties to the place that is Louisville.

In 1940 *Louisville: A Guide to the Falls City* designated portraitist Charles Sneed Williams (1882–1964) as the city's best-known painter and Dean Cornwell (1892–1960) as the most internationally famous. Cornwell received his first art training from Paul Plaschke at the YMCA night school, and among his early works are riverboat scenes along the Ohio River. By 1927 Cornwell's riverside scene shifted to the Thames in London, where he worked for three years with British artist Frank Brangwyn (1867–1956), painting six huge historical panels for the House of Lords. Cornwell later became one of the country's most renowned illustrators and muralists, with elaborate murals in more than twenty public buildings, including the Los Angeles City Hall. In an October 31, 1926, *Courier-Journal* interview he candidly stated his belief that modern art "is about ninety percent pure bunk."

During the post–World War II era, Mary Spencer Nay (1913–93) was often described as Louisville's most distinguished artist. Nay's paintings and prints range from realism to abstraction, but their dominant trait is introspection. Nay speculated on the spiritual content of her 1948 painting, *Levitation:* "A totem form represents the previous evolution of man who from this point may possibly attain the fourth state of cosmic consciousness, the highest level of evolution." Nay began her study of art at age ten with Fayette Barnum in the children's free art classes offered by the Louisville Art Association. While an advanced Art Center student in 1934, Nay taught the first art appreciation course at the University of Louisville. After studying with Yasuo Kuniyoshi at the Art Students' League in New York, she returned to Louisville and served as Art Center director from 1944 to 1949. In 1939 the Art Center moved to S First St., a half block north of the University of Louisville Belknap Campus.

In 1946 the Hite family left a bequest of $1 million to found the Allen R. Hite Art Institute at the University of Louisville. The gift allowed for an immediate expansion of the university's art faculty and the hiring of German painter Ulfert Wilke (1907–88). Wilke had studied in his homeland with German Expressionist artist Willy Jaeckel (1888–1944) before emigrating to the United States in 1938 to escape Hitler. From 1948 to 1962 Wilke influenced generations of Louisville artists. His abstractions feature an obsessive repetition of calligraphic notations that create rhythmic fields across the canvas or paper. Unlike his abstract paintings, such works as *Woman Shopping at Scotty's Market,* 1959, reveal Wilke's impressions of his adopted Louisville.

During the 1950s another distinguished Louisville painter was Eugene W. Leake Jr. (1911–). Leake studied at the Art Students' League in New York City during the 1930s with John Steuart Curry (1897–1946), a mural painter of the American Regionalist movement. Leake served as director of the Art Center Association from 1949 to 1959 and taught painting at the University of Louisville. Leake's paintings exhibit an acerbic tension characteristic of Abstract Expressionism, which was given added stature in Louisville with the presence of Carl Holty (1900–1973) as visiting professor at the university from 1962 to 1964.

Leake, Wilke, and Nay were the guiding lights for a constellation of talented Louisville students who later attained careers of national and international reputation. The paintings of abstractionist Sally Hazelet Drummond (1924–) distill the calligraphic strokes of Wilke into canvases of pointillist dots that both hold and fracture light.

Native Louisvillian Mary Ann Currier (1927–), a realist known for her vivid oil pastel still lifes, attended the Chicago Academy of Fine Art from 1945 to 1947 and the LOUISVILLE SCHOOL OF ART from 1958 to 1962, teaching there from 1962 to 1982. On July 2, 1949, she married Lionel F. Currier. After eight years in Florida, Currier returned to Louisville in 1990. Galleries throughout the United States have exhibited her works, and they are a permanent part of the Twentieth Century Collection at the Metropolitan Museum of Art in New York City.

Abstraction was also the dominant mode for an impressive group of African American painters from Louisville's West End who became prominent in Louisville art during the late 1950s and early 1960s and formed Gallery Enterprises. Gallery Enterprises was a black visual artists group that fostered a remarkable generation of Louisville artists, including Greg Ridley, Bob Thompson, Sam Gilliam, Robert Douglas, Kenneth Victor Young, and Houston Conwill.

Bob Thompson (1937–66) initiated Gallery Enterprises and became the first black Louisville painter to receive national recognition. He was noted for his expressionistic fantasies saturated with brilliant hues. Like Thompson, Sam Gilliam (1933–) studied with Nay, Wilke, and Leake. Gilliam received his art education at the University of Louisville with a B.A. degree in 1955 and an M.A. in 1961. Gilliam was born November 30, 1933, in Tupelo, Mississippi, to Sam Sr. and Estery (Cousin) Gilliam but grew up in Louisville. He moved to Washington, D.C., in 1962, where he has since lived and worked. During the 1960s he began his characteristic sculpted paintings by removing the canvas from the frame to stretch or drape the canvas itself on the wall. Later he has wrapped the canvas and also added sculptural elements to his surfaces. This phase was followed by the creation of multimedia installations, which employed brightly stained polypropylene, dozens of layers of painted and printed color, computer-generated images, and handmade paper. His approach requires the viewer to take an active part in seeing his work. Some of his public works can be found in the Philadelphia Veteran's Administration Center, the La Guardia Airport, and the New Orleans Customs House.

Kenneth Young (1933–), a Louisville native, received a B.S. degree in art from the University of Louisville in 1962 and later became a member of the Washington Color Painters. Louisville artist Houston Conwill (1947–) became an apprentice in Sam Gilliam's studio and later produced an extensive commission of stained-glass windows and murals for his hometown church, St. Augustine in Louisville. The tradition that began with Gallery Enterprises continues decades later at the University of Louisville: Prof. Mark Priest, a former Gilliam apprentice and a University of Louisville and Yale graduate, draws on his experiences living and working in Louisville in paintings such as *Bill and John (the Mechanics),* 1997.

The Louisville Public Library's once-remarkable painting collection was dispersed over many years, the last of the lot being sent to auction in New York City. Louisville artists now exhibit at numerous local galleries, among them the B. Deemer Gallery, Galerie Hertz, the Images Friedman Gallery, the Kentucky Art & Craft Gallery, the Swanson Cralle Gallery, and the Zephyr Gallery. In 1984 the Art Center Association changed its name to the Water Tower Art Association, reflecting its new headquarters in the 1860 neoclassic waterworks building. The association continues to serve local artists and provides space for exhibitions. The Speed Art Museum, reopened in 1997 after extensive renovation, was the beneficiary of a $50 million gift from Mrs. Berry V. Stoll, daughter of William S. Speed and granddaughter of JAMES BRECKINRIDGE SPEED. The gift enables the museum to expand its programs and collection well into the twenty-first century.

Bertha Mathilde (Honoré) Palmer (Mrs. Potter Palmer) c. 1895.

See Edna Talbott Whitley, *Kentucky Ante-Bellum Portraiture* (Paris, Ky., 1956); Arthur Jones and Bruce Weber, *The Kentucky Painter* (Lexington 1981); *Kentucky Expatriates: Natives and Notable Visitors* (Owensboro, Ky., 1984); Madeline Covi, Dorothy Hodapp, and Charlotte Price, *Tapestry of an Art Association, 1909–1984* (Louisville 1984); Exhibition catalogs, Allen R. Hite Art Institute (1947 to present); John F. McDermott, *The Lost Panoramas of the Mississippi* (Chicago 1958); Manon Porter, "Ancestor of the Movies," *Courier-Journal Magazine,* Jan. 20, 1957; University of Louisville catalog, "Mary Spencer Nay," 1950.

John Franklin Martin

PALMER, BERTHA MATHILDE (HONORÉ) (b Louisville, May 22, 1849; d Sarasota, Florida, May 5, 1918). Socialite and businesswoman. Bertha was one of six children born to Henry Hamilton and Eliza Dorsey (Carr) Honoré. Her great-great-grandfather, Jean Antoine Honoré (a.k.a. John Anthony Honoré), was among the city's first FRENCH families. He was one of the builders of the first Catholic church in Louisville, at Tenth and MAIN Streets.

In 1855 the family moved to Chicago, where Bertha's father became wealthy through real estate investments. She graduated from the Convent of the Visitation in Washington, D.C., receiving several scholastic honors.

On July 8, 1870, she married Chicago merchant and real estate magnate Potter Palmer, twenty-three years her senior. Palmer made much of his fortune, estimated at $7 million when he married Bertha, selling his successful Chicago department store business to Marshall Field and Levi Leiter. Bertha's sister, Ida, also married well: she and Lt. Col. Frederick Dent Grant, son of Pres. Ulysses S. Grant, were married in December 1874.

According to legend, on October 8, 1871, Mrs. Catherine O'Leary's cow kicked over the kerosene lamp that started one of the worst urban fires in U.S. history. Potter Palmer lost

Palmer House, a mansion built as a wedding gift for his wife; a hotel; and thirty-two new buildings located on State St. Bertha's parents' home was also destroyed in the fire.

For many years Bertha Palmer was a leader in Chicago society and worked for many local and national causes. She served as chairman of the Board of Lady Managers of the 1893 World's Columbian Exposition, and she visited European capitals to encourage participation in the fair. A few years later President McKinley appointed her the only woman member of the national commission representing the United States at the Paris Exposition of 1900; she was awarded the Legion of Honor by the French government for her efforts.

After her husband died in 1902, Palmer helped to expand the family fortune and became internationally known as one of the wealthiest businesswomen in America. Their home on Lake Shore Dr., completed in the 1880s and known as Palmer Castle, was one of the most elegant in Chicago. Later in life she owned and operated a large-scale farm and ranch in Sarasota, Florida. The Palmers had two sons, Honoré and Potter Jr. She is buried in a mausoleum beside her husband at Graceland Cemetery in Chicago.

See Ishbel Ross, *Silhouette in Diamonds: The Life of Mrs. Potter Palmer* (New York 1960).

PAPA JOHN'S INTERNATIONAL INC. In March 1984 John H. Schnatter spent approximately $1,600 converting an old broom closet in a struggling JEFFERSONVILLE, INDIANA, bar (co-owned by his father) into a pizza kitchen. Shortly thereafter, Schnatter was selling three hundred to four hundred pizzas a week to the bar's customers and to neighboring residents.

Schnatter, a native of Jeffersonville, is the son of Mary and Robert Schnatter. He graduated in 1983 from Ball State University with a business administration degree. Having long planned to begin a pizza business and eager to start, he decided to complete his degree by taking all his junior and senior year classes in one year. That same year he entered the restaurant business world as manager of Mick's Lounge, which was in financial difficulty. Schnatter credits his success largely to his two mentors, his late grandfather Louis Ackerson and his late father. Ackerson was a business owner and attorney who included hotelier Al Schneider as one of his clients. Schnatter's father was a Jeffersonville judge, prosecutor, and small business entrepreneur. Schnatter is married to Annette (Cox) Schnatter, and they have two daughters. After achieving considerable business success, Schnatter began making major contributions to local community interests, including SOUTHEAST CHRISTIAN CHURCH.

Schnatter quickly outgrew the tavern's facilities and moved nearby into the first Papa John's restaurant in 1985. Within one year, he had sold his first franchise. The chain continued to grow and opened its 100th store in 1991, its 500th store in 1994, and its 1,000th store in 1996.

Papa John's rapid growth was based on the formula of keeping the process simple and using premium ingredients. In an effort to consistently produce high quality, Schnatter decided from the start to focus his company simply on the delivery and take-out of pizza, bread and cheese sticks, and SOFT DRINKS (no sit-down dining is available in any of the RESTAURANTS). Since Papa John's restaurants purchase all supplies from a company-owned commissary that manufactures and ships dough and sauces twice weekly, each restaurant could produce similar pizzas.

By April 1997 Papa John's operated eight commissaries, which contain their own water-purification systems, and had distribution centers in Louisville; Orlando; Raleigh; Denver; Dallas; Phoenix; Jackson, Mississippi; and Rotterdam, New York.

After opening its 300th store in May 1993, Papa John's made its initial public stock offering on the NASDAQ market (PZZA) and collected a net profit of $18 million. Subsequent stock offerings netted $22.4 million in January 1994, $12.6 million in November 1994, $30 million in August 1995, and $50 million in May 1996. By April 1997 there were 1,250 Papa John's restaurants operating in thirty-five states and Washington, D.C., of which 925 were franchised and 325 were owned by the company. The company celebrated the opening of its 1,500th restaurant in early 1998.

The chain began to receive national attention from various publications after it opened its 600th store, in late 1994. *Forbes* magazine placed Papa John's tenth on its 1995 list of the best two hundred small companies in the country; *Entrepreneur* magazine honored the chain the following year by ranking it number one in the pizza category and thirty-fifth overall on its list of the five hundred best franchise opportunities. By the end of 1996 the pizza had been chosen by various publications, including *LOUISVILLE* MAGAZINE, as "Best Pizza" in more than forty markets. However, the most substantial award was received in early 1997 when *Restaurant and Institutions* magazine declared that Papa John's had unseated Pizza Hut as the best pizza chain in the United States. In 1999 company executives expected to move into third place in overall pizza sales in the nation.

In May 1996 CEO and founder John Schnatter announced his company's pledge of $5 million to complete the funding of the new forty-five-thousand-seat UNIVERSITY OF LOUISVILLE FOOTBALL stadium. Because of this sizable donation, the new structure, opened in 1998, was named Papa John's Cardinal Stadium.

In 1998 Pizza Hut (owned by Louisville-based Tricon Global Restaurants) sued Papa John's, claiming that Papa John's slogan—"Better Ingredients. Better Pizza"—and comparative ads illegally damaged Pizza Hut. A federal jury in Dallas found in favor of Pizza Hut in 1999. In January of 2000 a federal district judge ruled that Papa John's would have to stop using its slogan in ADVERTISING, signs, and paper goods. Papa John's appealed and was granted a stay of the order, allowing it to continue using the slogan during the appeals process.

See *Courier-Journal,* May 21, 1999, November 30, 1999, January 3, 2000.

PARAMOUNT FOODS. Paramount Foods was founded in 1886 as Hirsch Brothers & Co. by David, Louis, Benjamin, and Leon Hirsch. They began squeezing apple cider to use in manufacturing vinegar in a shop on Second St. near Main. The brothers added a sideline, selling cider and fresh fruit. Soon, pickles, sauerkraut, mincemeat, and apple butter were added. Within ten years, they moved into a larger plant at Fourteenth and Cedar Streets. The business remained family-owned for 109 years, with ownership passing to the Hirsch children and grandchildren.

The company continued to expand, manufacturing jelly, ketchup, chili sauce, chili con carne, tamales, and mayonnaise. By 1931 there were over a hundred different products sold under the brand name Paramount. Hirsch Brothers had become the world's second-largest manufacturer of pickles and other food products. There were branch offices in Pittsburgh and Detroit and distribution centers in Chicago, Columbus, Memphis, Atlanta, New Orleans, and Houston. Paramount foods were popular in delicatessens, homes, meat markets, and RESTAURANTS, as well as in the U.S. Army, Navy, Marine Corps, and veterans' HOSPITALS.

In 1959 company president Lewis Hirsch received the National Pickle Packers Association Golden Pickle Award. He was the first person in the industry to be so honored and was recognized for his clever, humorous, and highly successful marketing that benefited other manufacturers as well as his own company by promoting pickles and prepared foods in general. Also in 1959, Hirsch Brothers & Co. completed building a new facility, called Pickledilly Station, on FERN VALLEY RD. The company headquarters was moved there, and the name of the distribution operations was changed to Paramount Foods Co.

In 1992 both Pres. Kenneth L. Hirsch and Chairman of the Board Ronald I. Sternberg died suddenly following heart attacks. In May of that year, F. Miller Owings became president and chief executive officer, the first person unrelated to the Hirsch family ever to run the company. He resigned in July 1994.

In 1995 Paramount Foods was purchased by Louisville automobile dealer Stuart Frankenthal, thus passing out of the founding family. Frankenthal in turn sold Paramount to Dean Foods in December 1995. The Louisville plant was closed in early 1996.

See *Courier-Journal,* July 21, 1931; Jan. 15, May 6, 1992; July 20, 1994; June 23, 1995;

Louisville, May 20, 1956; Jan. 20, 1959; June 20, 1961.

Otis Amanda Dick

PARK DUVALLE. A neighborhood in western Louisville bounded by the Shawnee Expwy. to the west, the Norfolk Southern railroad tracks to the north, Cypress St. to the east, and a combination of Bells Ln. and Algonquin Pkwy. to the south. The neighborhood's name appears to reflect the existence of several parks in the area, such as Algonquin Park, Harris Drive Park, and Russell Lee Park, and also the presence of DuValle Junior High School. The school was moved from downtown to the area in 1956 and was named after Lucie DuValle, an educator and the first female principal of a public high school in Louisville. Today the school is the site of Duvalle Education Center, which offers various learning opportunities to the surrounding community.

Though the area developments began in the late nineteenth century, a majority of the subdivisions were platted after the 1940s. Originally considered part of greater Parkland, the neighborhood included Little Africa, a community that was home to thousands of blacks beginning in the years following the Civil War. With urban renewal and integration, Little Africa with its shanty houses disappeared, to be replaced by Cotter and Lang Homes housing projects.

In the mid-1990s the neighborhood became the focus of a $180 million revitalization effort as the dilapidated Cotter and Lang Homes housing projects were cleared to make way for over twelve hundred new homes and townhouses. The project—under a partnership that included the federal and Louisville city governments, the Housing Authority of Louisville, and the private sector—is expected to be completed by 2007.

See *Courier-Journal,* Dec. 16, 1997; Jan. 18, 1999.

PARK HILL. A neighborhood west of downtown Louisville bounded by the csx railroad tracks to the east, Hill St. to the south, Twenty-sixth St. to the west, and a combination of Virginia Ave. and Oak St. to the north. In earlier times, the southeastern corner of the neighborhood was commonly known as the Cabbage Patch, because of the large number of farmers who grew vegetables, particularly cabbage, in the area. The citizens of the Cabbage Patch inspired Alice Hegan Rice's 1901 popular children's novel, *Mrs. Wiggs of the Cabbage Patch.* In 1910 Louise Marshall established the Cabbage Patch Settlement House on S Ninth St. to aid the area's needy. Another landmark in the neighborhood was Simmons University for African American students. It began as the Kentucky Normal and Theological Institution in 1879, and after 1884 it was known as State University. In 1918 the university was renamed Simmons to honor Rev. William J. Simmons, one of its presidents. Growing financial troubles prompted the institution's trustees to sell the campus property to the University of Louisville in 1930, which transformed it into Louisville Municipal College. The old Saints Mary and Elizabeth Hospital was located between Twelfth and Magnolia Streets before 1958, when its site became a commercial property. The hospital, located in an area of heavy industry, always maintained a close link with Louisville's industrial growth. It admitted many patients injured in railroad shops or other industrial plants. During the 1937 flood, the hospital became one of the city's principal relief stations because it was the only hospital in the city that had electricity and running water. Emergency power was furnished by industries in the neighborhood.

See George H. Yater, *Two Hundred Years at the Falls of the Ohio* (Louisville 1987).

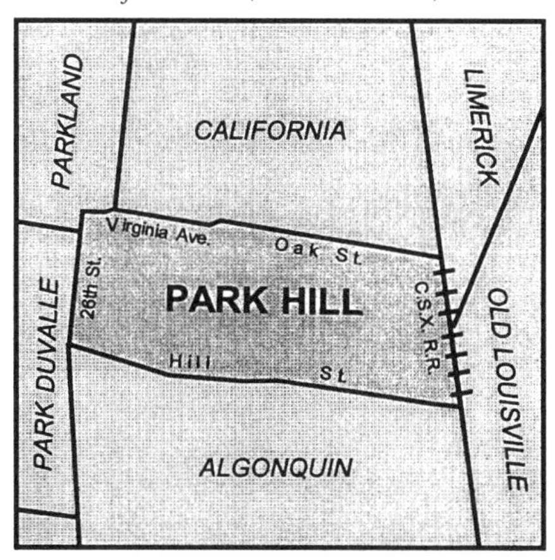

PARKLAND. A primarily residential neighborhood west of downtown Louisville and bounded by Twenty-sixth St. to the east, Broadway to the north, Thirty-fourth St. to the west, and a combination of Woodland and Wilson Avenues and Catalpa St. to the south. In the mid–nineteenth century, the land, designated on some maps as Homestead, was inhabited by sparse settlements of German and African American farmers. Civil War soldiers roamed the area after Union forces constructed Fort Karnasch, located near Wilson Ave. (then Cane Run Rd.) between Twenty-sixth and Twenty-eighth Streets.

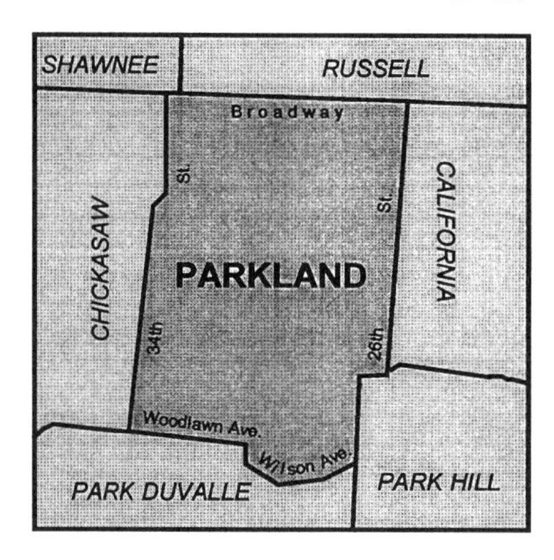

Residential development began in the area in 1871, when the real estate firm of Morris, Southwick & Co. subdivided a 346-acre rural tract into 1,072 lots and auctioned them to the public. Prompted by alluring ads, a speculative fever raced through Louisville, impelling business owners to close on July 10 as approximately two thousand people attended the auction. The developers had ensured transportation to the then-distant community by contracting with the Central Passenger Railway Co. to extend its Walnut St. (Muhammad Ali Blvd.) tracks to Twenty-eighth St. and then southward to Greenwood Ave. In 1874 the town of Parkland was incorporated.

By 1890 Parkland had become a prestigious and fashionable address, as large Victorian, Queen Anne, and Romanesque homes were erected along the tree-lined Dumesnil and Virginia Avenues. Town ordinances prohibited bars, hunting, odor-spewing factories, and other nuisances. However, the prosperity temporarily came to a halt after the tornado of March 27, 1890, touched down just south of Parkland and cut a diagonal path toward the northeast. With a dozen homes destroyed and many others damaged, Parkland never recovered financially and was annexed by Louisville in 1894.

Many of the grand houses were rebuilt and others added, but the area also witnessed a change as working-class people began moving into the community and constructing bungalows and shotgun cottages along Hale and Woodland Avenues. Nearby, a small community of African Americans, known initially as black Parkland and later as Little Africa, developed on swampland southwest of Parkland. Much of the construction in the area was completed by 1915.

In the early decades of the twentieth century, an area centered around Twenty-eighth and Dumesnil Ave. had become a thriving business district. Ultimately, it included establishments such as Schneider's Department Store, office buildings, the Parkland Theatre, the Royal Bank, an A&P grocery store, and a branch of the public library. By the 1950s, however, some white families had started to leave Parkland for the suburbs, a trend that continued well into the 1960s after the desegregation of public

View along 28th Street in Parkland, looking south toward Dumesnil Street and the Parkland Masonic Hall, 1920s.

SCHOOLS. Neighborhood businesses followed this lead after civil unrest erupted at the intersection of Twenty-eighth St. and Greenwood Ave. in May 1968 on the heels of the assassination of Martin Luther King Jr. Following days of looting and random outbursts of violence, many owners closed their shops, leaving the business district virtually deserted. Between 1970 and 1980, Parkland lost roughly 25 percent of its POPULATION.

In 1980 the business district was designated a local preservation district, and the neighborhood was placed on the NATIONAL REGISTER OF HISTORIC PLACES, spurring some revitalization efforts in the area. Further plans to rehabilitate the neighborhood stalled through the 1980s until a feasibility study in 1987 prompted the city to inject millions of dollars into the community. By restoring historic buildings, providing loans to new businesses, erecting new housing, and improving the area's roads, the city hoped to lure residents and businesses back to the area.

See George H. Yater, *Two Hundred Years at the Falls of the Ohio* (Louisville 1987); Ethel I. King, *From Parkland to the River's Edge* (Louisville 1990).

PARKS. Louisville and Jefferson County's park system is one of the nation's oldest and includes 112 parks (more than 11,000 acres of parkland), with 15 miles of historic PARKWAYS. It has the distinction of being one of only five park systems in America to have a system of parks and connecting parkways designed by Frederick Law Olmsted Sr., the "father of American landscape architecture." Olmsted and his firm designed sixteen parks and three parkways for Louisville, which remain some of the best-preserved of his works.

Although several attempts to acquire parklands were made in the nineteenth century, it was 1880 when Mayor John G. Baxter dedicated the first city park, Baxter Square at Eleventh and Jefferson Streets. Col. ANDREW COWAN, a prominent MAIN St. leather merchant and an admirer of other cities' park systems, led the SALMAGUNDI CLUB in proposing, in 1887, the development of three large suburban parks as a spur to economic and population growth. This movement led to the 1890 creation of the Board of Park Commissioners by act of the Kentucky General Assembly. After purchasing land with a $600,000 bond issue, the commissioners—who through the years included prominent Louisvillians such as Gen. John B. Castleman, Louis Seelbach, and Morris BELKNAP—recruited Olmsted, the designer of Central Park in New York City, the Biltmore estate, and the U.S. Capitol grounds, to plan the system.

Olmsted and the park commissioners sited the first three parks—SHAWNEE, Cherokee, and IROQUOIS—to capture the region's three distinct native landscapes. With Shawnee's flat OHIO RIVER terraces, Cherokee's rolling BEARGRASS CREEK valley, and Iroquois's rugged knob of old-growth forest, the trio of landscapes complement each other as components of one great urban park. The parks were designed to offer a complete range of park experiences as defined by Olmsted, from civic gatherings and social interactions to organized athletics and personal recreation. The parks' west, south, and east locations anchor each distinctive region of Louisville, and the tree-lined parkways connect residents throughout the city to the parks.

The Board of Park Commissioners continued to add neighborhood parks, interior squares, and local playgrounds to the system until 1942. Early in that year, the board was dissolved and the Department of Parks and Recreation was created within the city GOVERNMENT. Citing the need to cut costs during the war, Mayor Wilson Wyatt attempted to streamline control of the park and recreation systems, which had been under the control of several administrative bodies such as the Board of Park Commissioners, the BOARD OF EDUCATION, and the Department of Welfare.

In 1944 the Jefferson County Fiscal Court responded by creating a Playground and Recreation Board for the administration of properties outside the city. Under the leadership of Charlie Vettiner, the board cultivated an extensive system of recreation committees as a means of community involvement and cost-sharing. In 1968 the recreation and park management functions for the city and county were merged into one body, the Metropolitan Parks and Recreation Board. This board became an advisory commission in 1986 when the management of the properties was turned over to the newly formed Louisville and Jefferson County Parks Department. With an operating budget of $21 million in 1997, the department employs a year-round staff of three hundred and seasonal employees numbering fifteen hundred.

The metro parks system (as it is commonly known) offers a wide array of facilities. There are seventeen fishing lakes, nine GOLF courses, five bridle trails, two public stables, four archery ranges, seven systems of hiking trails, two team-building courses, two outdoor theaters, and the 5,200-acre JEFFERSON COUNTY MEMORIAL FOREST. Otter Creek Park, located in Meade County along one mile of Ohio River frontage, adds

Iroquois Park as photographed by Will Bowers.

Metro Parks and Playgrounds

Park	*Size (if one acre or more)*	*Location*
Algonquin Park	16 acres	Cypress St. and Burwell Ave.
Auburndale Playground	4 acres	Old Third St. and Palatka Rd.
Ballard Park	1 acre	Caldwell and Hancock Streets
Baxter Square	2 acres	Twelfth and Jefferson Streets
Beechmont Center	1 acre	W Wellington Ave.
Bellevue Park	1 acre	Bellevue Ave.
Ben Washer Park	2 acres	Fifth and Kentucky Streets
Berrytown Park	24 acres	Heafer and Hines Roads
Bingham Park	4 acres	Coral Ave. and Brownsboro Rd.
Black Mudd Park	18 acres	Rangeland and Ridgecrest Roads
Blue Lick Park	26 acres	Mud and Smith Lanes
Boone Square	4 acres	Twentieth and Rowan Streets
Bradley Park		Bradley Ave. and Locust Ln.
Breslin Park	4 acres	Lexington Ave. and Payne St.
Buechel Park	16 acres	Beargrass Ave. and Bardstown Rd.
California Park	7 acres	Sixteenth and St. Catherine Streets
Carrie Gaulbert Cox Park	59 acres	River Rd. and Indian Hills Trail
Castlewood Open Space	1 acre	Castlewood Ave.
Central Park	17 acres	Fourth St. and Park Ave.
Charles Young Park		Lytle and Twenty-seventh Streets
Charlie Vettiner Park	283 acres	Marydell Ln. and Billtown Rd.
Cherokee Park	409 acres	Eastern Pkwy. and Cherokee Rd.
Chickasaw Park	61 acres	South Western Pkwy. and Greenwood Ave.
Churchill Park	7 acres	Boxley Ave. and Crittenden Dr.
Cliff Park		Cliff and Woodlawn Avenues
Clifton Park	1 acre	Arlington Ave. and Charlton St.
Crescent Hill Park	77 acres	Brownsboro Rd. and Zorn Ave.
Crosby Park	20 acres	Cedardale Rd. and Madison Rd.
Des Pres Park	27 acres	Lowe Rd.
Douglass Park	5 acres	Douglass Blvd.
Dumeyer Playground	5 acres	Squires Dr. and Cayuga St.
E. Leland Taylor Park	9 acres	Thirty-fifth and Duncan Streets
E.P. "Tom" Sawyer State Park	377 acres	Freys Hill Rd.
East Louisville Park	5 acres	Liberty and Clay Streets.
Eastwood Park	5 acres	Old Shelbyville Rd.
Elliott Square	3 acres	Twenty-eighth and Magazine Streets
Eva Bandman Park	54 acres	River Rd. and Barbour Ave.
Farman Park	5 acres	South Park Rd. and Farman Ct.
Farnsley Park	5 acres	Crums Ln. and Schaffner Dr.
Fern Creek Park	31 acres	Ferndale and Renate Roads
Fisherman's Park	65 acres	Old Heady and Hopewell Roads
Flaget Field	10 acres	Forty-fifth St. and Greenwood Ave.
Floyd's Fork Park	102 acres	Old Taylorsville and South Pope Lick Roads
G.G. Moore Park		M and Rodman Streets
George Rogers Clark Park	46 acres	Poplar Level Rd. and Thruston
Germantown-Paristown Park		Kentucky St.
Ginny Reichard Park		Wenzel and Franklin Streets
Gnadinger Park		Ellison and Reutlinger Avenues
Hays Kennedy Park	77 acres	Bass Rd. and River Rd.
Highview Park		Briscoe Ln. and Vaughn Mill Rd.
Hounz Lane Park	24 acres	Hounz Ln.
Huston Quin Park	2 acres	First St. and Fairmont Ave.
Irish Hill Park		Lexington Rd. and Cooper St.
Iroquois Park	739 acres	Taylor Blvd. and Southern Pkwy.
Ivy Court Park		Thirty-fourth St. and Larkwood Ave.
Jefferson County Memorial Forest	5,123 acres	Mitchell Hill Rd.
Joe Creason Park	68 acres	Trevilian Way
Kennedy Court		Kennedy Ct. and Frankfort Ave.
Klondike Park	7 acres	Klondike Ln.
Lake Dreamland Park	2 acres	Lake Dreamland Rd.
Lampton Park	2 acres	Lampton and Jackson Streets
Lannan Park	17 acres	Twenty-sixth St. and Ohio River
LaPorte Playground	2 acres	Twenty-fifth and Bank Streets
Liberty Bell Playground		Liberty Bell Way
Lincoln-Preston Park	11 acres	Augustus Ave. and Preston St.
Long Run Park	394 acres	Flat Rock Rd.
Louis B. Israel Park		First St. and Woodlawn Ave.
Magnolia Park		Magnolia Ave. and Second St.
McNeely Park	746 acres	Cooper Chapel and Mount Washington Roads
Medora Park	4 acres	Pendleton Rd. and Bohannon Ave.
Memorial Park		Fourth and Kentucky Streets
Muhammad Ali Park		Nineteenth and Cedar Streets
Nelson Hornbeck Park	18 acres	Fairdale Rd. and Tin Dor Way
Nightingale Park		Nightingale and Poplar Level Roads
Okolona Park	15 acres	Clay and O'Brecht Avenues
Old Walnut (Beecher) Park	4 acres	Wilkins Ave. and Muhammad Ali Blvd.
Otter Creek Park	3,600 acres	Otter Creek Park Rd., near Brandenburg, Ky.
Parkhill Park	4 acres	S Thirteenth St. and Patton Ct.
Patterson Playground		Morton Ave.
Pee Wee Playground	3 acres	Klondike Ln. and Jupiter Rd.
Petersburg Park	28 acres	Ellington Ave. and Petersburg Rd.
Portland Park	4 acres	Montgomery and Twenty-seventh Streets
Riverfields Nature Preserve	31 acres	River Rd.
Riverside Gardens	10 acres	Lees Ln. and Campground Rd.
Riverview Park	37 acres	Greenwood Ave. and Lower River Rd.
Rubel Park	2 acres	Rubel Ave. and Broadway.
Russell Lee Park	18 acres	Southern Ave. and Thirty-fourth St.
St. Louis Park		Twenty-second and St. Louis Streets
Seneca Park	333 acres	Cannons Ln.
Shawnee Park	316 acres	Broadway and South Western Pkwy.
Shelby Park	16 acres	Clay and Shelby Streets
Sheppard Park	2 acres	Seventeenth and Magazine Streets
Slevin Park		Twenty-fifth and Slevin Streets
South Central Park	11 acres	Colorado and Weller Streets
Story Avenue Playground	1 acre	Story Ave. and Washington St.
Sun Valley Park	118 acres	Bethany Ln. and Mill Creek
Sylvania Park	10 acres	Sylvania Rd.
Taylor Memorial Park	11 acres	Poplar Level Rd. and Lee St.
Thirty-Fifth Street Park		Thirty-fifth St. and Doerhoefer Ave.
Toonerville Trolley Park	2 acres	Oak and Brook Streets
Twin Park Open Space	41 acres	River and Mockingbird Valley Roads
Tyler Park	13 acres	Baxter Ave. and Tyler Park Dr.
Victory Park	4 acres	Twenty-second and Kentucky Streets
Watterson Lake Park	11 acres	S Wheatmore Dr.
Waverly Park	300 acres	Arnoldtown Rd.
Wayside Park	2 acres	Southern Pkwy. and Oakdale Ave.
Westonia Park	2 acres	Thirtieth and Rowan Streets
William B. Stansbury Park	7 acres	Third St. and Eastern Pkwy.
William Britt Park		Twenty-eighth and Magazine Streets
William Harrison Park	2 acres	Oleanda and Utah Avenues
Willow Park		Willow Ave. and Cherokee Pkwy.
Wyandotte Park	25 acres	Taylor Blvd. and Beecher St.

Metro Parkways

Algonquin Pkwy.
Cherokee Pkwy.
Douglass Blvd.–Millvale Rd.
Eastern Pkwy.
North Western Pkwy.
Southern Pkwy.
South Western Pkwy.

Members of the Griswold family sit atop Big Rock in Cherokee Park, ca 1896.

3,000 acres to the system. Combining historic sites, campsites, and recreational facilities, Otter Creek was developed by the Civilian Conservation Corps and given to the city of Louisville in 1947 by the federal government to be a public park in perpetuity.

Toward the end of the century, planning efforts for the metropolitan park system were focusing on acquisition and development of adequate open space to meet the needs of the future and on linking the parks with stream corridors and river frontage in a greenways network for recreation and conservation.

When public concern about the deterioration of the Olmsted legacy began in the 1980s, an advocacy and preservation organization was founded with support from the parks department. The Louisville Friends of Olmsted Parks soon recognized that the parks were threatened, and encouraged then-mayor Jerry Abramson to determine that a separate nonprofit organization was needed to help fund renovations in a public-private partnership with the city. In 1989 Mayor Abramson and the Louisville BOARD OF ALDERMEN established the Louisville Olmsted Parks Conservancy to advise the mayor on planning and to raise private funds to carry out recommended projects and programs. The 1994 Master Plan for Louisville's Olmsted Parks and Parkways takes an ecological approach toward restoring these important cultural landscapes, calling for renewed connections between the community and its parks. With joint conservancy-city funding, the first projects were opened to the public in 1996. They included active sports facilities, woodland and savannah restoration, wetland creation, multiuse recreational paths, reconstruction of bridle and hiking trails, and the reinstatement of place names within each park. The conservancy established a volunteer program called Park Champions in 1997 to involve citizens in landscape restoration and as park stewards.

Susan M. Rademacher

Lincoln Park, on Fourth Street between Chestnut and Guthrie, 1954.

PARKWAY FIELD. Parkway Field, home of the semiprofessional LOUISVILLE COLONELS baseball team, was built in 1923 following an off-season fire that destroyed ECLIPSE PARK in November 1922. THE UNIVERSITY OF LOUISVILLE purchased a 39-acre tract from the Louisville and Jefferson County Children's Home (better known as the Industrial School of Reform) in January, which became the school's BELKNAP Campus. Eight acres were sold for $44,500 to the Louisville Base Ball Co. for the new stadium. It was located at Brook St. and Eastern Pkwy., a newly opened thoroughfare that gave the stadium its name.

Colonels owner William Knebelkamp was the principal investor in the new facility. Architect Leslie Abbott was commissioned to design the stadium, which was constructed in sixty-three days at a cost estimated at $250,000. The construction of the stadium forced a partial rerouting of Eastern Pkwy., which originally ran through what became the center-field gate and curved between third base and home plate. The road project was paid for in part by the BASEBALL club.

Abbott was also responsible for a revolutionary patented adjustment to stadium seats. Parkway Field was the first stadium to have seats without legs—which made sweeping up after games easier. The cast-iron seats, which have become standard at all ballparks, folded down like movie THEATER seats. The steel-framed grandstand seated 13,500.

The first game took place May 1, 1923, before an over-capacity crowd of 18,000—the largest in the stadium's history. The Colonels beat the Toledo Mud Hens 5–1; Mayor HUSTON QUIN threw out the first ball, and Kentucky native Earle Combs made the first out, catching a fly in left field.

The field was a structure of considerable proportions: 329 feet down the left-field line; 507 to dead center, and 345 feet down the right-field line. An ongoing debate questioned whether anyone, including Babe Ruth, could ever hit a home run over the center-field wall, a difficult feat because of the unusually long distance.

Many legends of baseball played in Park-

Parkway Field, Eastern Parkway at Brook Street, was the home of the Louisville Colonels from 1923 to 1956.

way Field, including Ruth, who played there three times: in 1924, 1928, and 1932. Lou Gehrig, along with the rest of the New York Yankees, played in a 1932 exhibition game. "Pee Wee" Reese got his start in Parkway Field with the Colonels, and in 1938, nineteen-year-old Ted Williams became the only player to hit two inside-the-park home runs in one game at the stadium. Joe DiMaggio once played in Parkway Field, and Jackie Robinson played there in the 1946 Little World Series.

In 1932 Knebelkamp installed lights at the ballpark, allowing night baseball to be played in Louisville for the first time, and an electric public address system to replace a handheld megaphone. In 1938 the Knebelkamp family sold the stadium and franchaise to the Boston Red Sox, which continued to support the Colonels. In 1948 the new owners added a women's lounge, a ticket lounge, a scoreboard, and concession stands at a cost of $150,000. On December 29, 1953, the university purchased the Red Sox interest in the stadium for $250,000. The Colonels continued to play at Parkway until they moved to the KENTUCKY FAIR AND EXPOSITION CENTER in 1956.

Parkway Field became the permanent home of the University of Louisville baseball team after the university's natural sciences building was constructed in 1951 on the same grounds that housed the "Belknap Campus diamond," where the baseball and track teams had played and practiced. The Cardinals played their first game at Parkway Field on April 26, 1952, before its purchase by the university. In 1961 Parkway Field, in a state of serious disrepair, underwent a major renovation. The grandstands, 80 percent of which were unusable, were removed, and the stadium was refashioned by the summer of 1962 to make room for a new track facility. The Cardinals baseball team continues to play home games at the ball park.

See *University of Louisville Cardinal,* April 9, 1993.

Henry Mayer

PARKWAYS. Louisville's parkways, whose development is linked with the creation of the city's park system, played a central role in residential growth and are still major traffic arteries. Community leaders had suggested the need for a city park system as early as 1824. But the first serious step in that direction occurred in early 1887, when Thomas Speed read a paper on public parks at the SALMAGUNDI CLUB. Businessman Andrew Cowan subsequently addressed the group and suggested the creation of large, picturesque PARKS on the eastern, southern, and western fringes of the city. Although Cowan did not discuss parkways, he did note the need for streetcar access and expressed confidence that establishing parks would stimulate residential construction.

Cowan's speech appeared in the *COURIER-JOURNAL* on June 5, 1887, and three days later a reader endorsed his idea and added the concept of a connecting boulevard system. Cowan quickly agreed, recommending that the parks be connected by a crescent-shaped road that would intersect with every local turnpike. Cowan hoped such a system would be developed according to a careful plan. But others, including Mayor Charles D. Jacob, wanted to move quickly. In the fall of 1888 Jacob purchased Burnt Knob (Iroquois Hill), a 313-acre tract of forest land 4 miles south of the city, with his own funds. He turned the land over to the city and collected a check for $9,800. Jacob then sought donations of land to build the Grand Boulevard, a 150-foot-wide avenue that would extend from Third and Shipp Streets to Burnt Knob. Donations came rapidly for the project—which Jacob prophesied would rival Paris's Champs-Élysées—especially from the perspective of speculators interested in residential development. But many citizens questioned the regularity of Jacob's transaction and the motives of the donors of land for Grand Blvd. In May 1890 Cowan, JOHN MASON BROWN, and other park advocates persuaded the Kentucky General Assembly to create a Louisville Board of Park Commissioners to oversee park development.

A short time later the City Council transferred jurisdiction over all city parkland and parkways to the new board. The following year, the board retained the firm of landscape architect Frederick Law Olmsted to design the city's park system. His plan, submitted in September 1891, called for three large parks, which became IROQUOIS, Cherokee, and SHAWNEE, linked by tree-lined parkways designed to provide access to the entire system.

Though individual sections differed in design, each parkway was intended to carry only low-intensity, park-related traffic, with no access by commercial vehicles. For this reason the Louisville Railway Co. was denied the right in the early 1920s to operate double-deck buses on the thoroughfare. In most cases, rights-of-way were donated by adjoining property owners who realized that homes fronting a parkway could command a premium price. Grand Blvd., which was renamed Southern Pkwy. June 6, 1893, was opened to the public eight days later and became a popular place for carriage drivers and bicyclists. It was followed by Eastern Pkwy., completed in late 1913 between Cherokee Park and Third St. Gen. JOHN BRECKINRIDGE CASTLEMAN, longtime park board president, donated a 1,709-foot section of the 4-mile boulevard between Baxter and Barret Avenues. That section's right-of-way measured 100 feet wide and included a tree-lined median.

Western Pkwy., including what are now South Western and North Western Parkways, brought donations from James and John Whallen, Louisville's Democratic bosses, and several other local businessmen. The entire 26-mile system was completed in the 1930s with the construction of Algonquin Pkwy., linking Western Pkwy. with Southern Pkwy. via Winkler Ave. and Third St. In 1942 the Kentucky General Assembly passed control of the parkways to the city Department of PUBLIC WORKS, and in 1958 the city opened the parkways to all passenger and commercial traffic.

See *Louisville Survey: Central and South Report* (Louisville 1978); *Louisville Survey: East Report* (Louisville 1980); Judith Hart English, "Louisville's Nineteenth Century Suburban Growth: Parkland, Crescent Hill, Cherokee Triangle, Beechmont, and Highland Park", M.A. thesis, University of Louisville, 1972.

Carl E. Kramer

Grand Boulevard, now Southern Parkway, c. 1906.

PAROQUET SPRINGS. One of the largest and most popular of Kentucky's 125 nineteenth-century watering places, PAROQUET SPRINGS was located 18 miles from Louisville on Salt River, within the present city limits of SHEPHERDSVILLE. Paroquet started out as a salt lick, and salt was made there briefly in 1803. It was named for the large flocks of colorful parakeets that frequented the spring in pioneer days. Their feathers were favorite decorations for ladies' hats, and the BIRDS soon became extinct.

In 1807 John McDowell, one of the men who had made salt at Paroquet Springs, purchased the tract. McDowell settled one of his daughters and her husband, R.D.N. Morgan, on the property. Morgan saw the possibilities for converting the lick into a spa. He tried to improve access to the well and to promote use of the water from it. But he was unable to convince his father-in-law of the value of making it into a prosperous watering place. In September 1836 McDowell sold 250 acres of this land to Humphrey Simmons, who in turn sold 150 acres, including the lick, to JAMES GUTHRIE, attorney for John D. Colmesnil, a prominent Louisville merchant.

In 1838 Colmesnil opened the spa to the public with accommodations for 250 people on 20 acres of land. Through the years he expanded the grounds to 100 acres and made additional improvements. Paroquet boasted three medicinal springs, whose waters were advertised to be "rich in the chloride of sodium" (i.e., salt) and also to contain calcium, potassium, magnesium, iron, "appreciable quantities of bromides," and plenty of "sulphureted hydrogen" (hydrogen sulfide gas, which gave the spring its distinctive odor of rotten eggs). The water was declared to be highly effective "in cases of general debility, irregularity of the bowels, nervous diseases, headache, dyspepsia and . . . particularly in diseases of females." It could be drunk (three to four quarts a day were recommended) or taken externally in the form of warm showers or vapor baths.

Paroquet undoubtedly did benefit the health of its customers by providing them a place of refuge to escape cholera, yellow fever, and other EPIDEMICS that made the cities dangerous. After 1851 and the building of the L&N railroad, Louisville was just forty minutes away. But like all fashionable watering places, Paroquet was more a social center than a facility for medical treatment. It offered fine FOODS and beverages, card-playing, dancing, billiards, and a variety of healthful outdoor activities—croquet, horseshoes, tenpins, walking, riding, excellent fishing in Salt River, "gunning," and (in later years) twice-monthly fox hunts.

A visitor in 1840 described Paroquet Springs as "one of the most lovely and attractive summer retreats to be found in the Union." He reported gravel and bark walks laid among natural growths of hickory, cedar, oak, maple, locust, and buckeye. Near the main hotel were bathhouses, a dining hall, and rows of neat family cottages. A large ballroom had just been completed.

In 1871 a group of Louisville businessmen purchased Paroquet Springs, and the Colmesnils returned to Louisville, where John D. Colmesnil died on July 30, one day before his eighty-fifth birthday. The new owners constructed a large two-story hotel, with two wings and a three-story octagon in its center front, all surrounded by verandas on both levels. There was a detached kitchen opposite the center of the main building. This new hotel could accommodate five hundred guests, and its capacity was increased to eight hundred in 1872. The old hotel continued to be used for storage, band rehearsals, and sleeping rooms for servants.

On May 16, 1879, the new hotel burned to the ground. Although Paroquet continued for a number of years, perhaps in the old hotel, it never achieved its former success. According to 1897 issues of the *Salt River Tiger,* the grounds remained popular even at that late date for picnics, camping, political rallies, and other neighborhood activities. Today the Paroquet Springs Shopping Center and access roads to Interstate 65 cover the original site.

See *Charleston (Mo.) Courier,* Sept. 2, 1871; Audrea McDowell, "The Pursuit of Health and Happiness at the Paroquet Springs in Kentucky, 1838 to 1888," *Filson Club History Quarterly* 69 (Oct. 1995): 390–420.

PARRISH, CHARLES HENRY, JR. (b Louisville, January 12, 1899; d Newark, New Jersey, July 15, 1989). Educator. Charles Henry Parrish Jr., the son of Charles Henry Sr. and Mary V. (Cook) Parrish, was educated in the city's black PUBLIC SCHOOLS and graduated in 1916 from Central High School. After earning his bachelor's degree in mathematics from Howard University in 1920 and a master's degree in sociology from Columbia University in 1921, he served on the faculty of SIMMONS UNIVERSITY from 1921 to 1930.

During 1931–50 Parrish was a professor of sociology and education at LOUISVILLE MUNICIPAL COLLEGE, an all-black division of the UNIVERSITY OF LOUISVILLE. He taught during the entire existence of the college and directed at the state level several scholarly studies, including the 1936 WORKS PROGRESS ADMINISTRATION–funded "Study of Negro White Collar Workers." In 1938 he married educator Frances Elizabeth Murrell and in 1944 received his Ph.D. in sociology from the University of Chicago.

When the Municipal College was closed in 1950 and its students matriculated at the University of Louisville's BELKNAP Campus, Parrish became the University of Louisville's first black faculty member. Initially he was assigned to advise black students and teach elective sociology courses. Parrish published nationally recognized scholarly articles on color caste and race relations, was a guest lecturer at colleges and professional organizations across the nation, and served as a resource person on race relations for the Kentucky and Louisville GOVERNMENTS. From 1959 to 1964, he served as chairperson of the university's Department of Sociology, the first black to do so.

Although he retired as professor of sociology at the University of Louisville in 1969, he continued to teach at other universities in the United States and Africa and to serve in numerous Louisville civic and social welfare organizations.

See *Courier-Journal,* July 21, 1989; Charles Henry Parrish Jr. Papers, University of Louisville Archives and Records Center.

John A. Hardin

PARRISH, CHARLES HENRY, SR. (b Lexington, Kentucky, April 18, 1859; d Louisville, April 8, 1931). Educator and Baptist church leader. Parrish was born to Hiram and

Harriet Parrish, who were slaves. After emancipation he attended local segregated schools until 1874, when he temporarily dropped out to help his family. In 1880 at the urging of his pastor, Rev. WILLIAM J. SIMMONS, Parrish enrolled in State University in Louisville. Although he worked his way through college, he excelled. He received one of the first State University bachelor's degrees and was named class valedictorian in 1886.

Parrish was appointed professor of Greek and secretary-treasurer at State (later Simmons) University in 1886, pastored Louisville's Calvary Baptist Church from 1886 to 1931, was selected delegate to the Kentucky Republican state convention, was president of the Executive Board of the General Association of Negro BAPTISTS in Kentucky, and from 1890 to 1912 served as president of ECKSTEIN NORTON INSTITUTE in Cane Springs, Kentucky (1890–1912). He also established the Kentucky Home Society for Colored Children in Louisville (1908), was a member and secretary of the Board of Trustees of Lincoln Institute (1909–19), and served as president of SIMMONS UNIVERSITY in Louisville (1918–31).

Parrish became renowned nationally for his religious activities after serving as a delegate to both Baptist and ecumenical meetings in London, Jamaica, JERUSALEM, Sweden, and New York City. In 1905 he preached in seventeen German towns. He was a founder of the National Baptist Convention and served as its chairman.

In 1898 he married Mary V. Cook of Bowling Green, Kentucky. In the following year, she gave birth to their son, Charles H. Parrish Jr. The elder Parrish is buried in Louisville Cemetery.

See George A. Hampton, *Diamond Jubilee of the General Association of the Colored Baptists in Kentucky* (Louisville 1943); Clement Richardson, *The National Cyclopedia of the Colored Race* (Montgomery, Ala., 1919); William D. Johnson, *Kentucky's Prominent Negro Men and Women* (Lexington 1897).

John A. Hardin

PARRISH, MARY (COOK) (b Bowling Green, Kentucky, April 8, 1863; d Louisville, October 22, 1945). Educator, writer, lecturer, businesswoman, and community activist. Born Mary Virginia Cook, she attended school in Bowling Green following the CIVIL WAR. After receiving a limited education, she was asked to teach AFRICAN AMERICANS at a new local private school. Soon afterward, a group of area Baptist women helped further Parrish's education by sending her first to New England and then to Louisville's State University (later SIMMONS UNIVERSITY) in 1881.

She graduated at the head of her class in the normal department in 1883, completed college courses in 1887, and received an honorary master's degree in 1889. Before completing her college credits, Parrish joined the faculty and quickly became the principal of the normal school department. This allowed her to lecture throughout the South on the importance of a Christian education, while also engaging in fund-raising for Simmons University.

In 1890 Parrish became the educational editor for the African American Baptist magazine *Our Women and Children.* In 1892 she joined her future husband, the Reverend CHARLES HENRY PARRISH Sr., as the secretary for the ECKSTEIN NORTON INSTITUTE in Cane Springs, Kentucky. After marrying early in 1898, she returned to Louisville, where she worked as the financial secretary for her husband's church, Calvary Baptist. In the early 1900s, she accepted many prominent positions: she was president of the King's Daughters Missionary Society, corresponding secretary for the Women's Missionary Convention (she held both of these positions until her death), and treasurer of the National Baptist Convention's auxiliary, the women's convention.

In the 1930s Parrish became more vocal in civic activities, as she organized the first parent-teacher organization in Louisville's African American schools, headed a committee to establish the community's first African American playground, served as the first president of the Colored Republican's Women's Club, cofounded the Phillis Wheatley (West End) YWCA, and sat on the board of the Kentucky Home Society for Colored Children. In 1932 she was an alternate delegate to the national Republican convention in Chicago.

Mary and Charles Parrish had one child, Charles Henry Parrish Jr., who became a well-known sociologist.

See George Wright, *Life Behind a Veil* (Baton Rouge 1985).

PARSONS, EDWARD YOUNG (b Middletown, Kentucky, December 12, 1842; d Washington, D.C., July 8, 1876). U.S. congressman. Parsons was educated in Louisville PUBLIC SCHOOLS until he was twelve years old; he then studied one year at St. Louis High School in St. Louis, Missouri. He graduated from the UNIVERSITY OF LOUISVILLE in 1861 and taught there for three years. In 1865 he received his law degree from the University of Louisville Law School and moved to Henderson, Kentucky, to practice law. He returned to Louisville before being elected to the Forty-fourth Congress as a Democrat, where he served from March 4, 1875, until his death on July 8, 1876. He is buried in CAVE HILL CEMETERY.

See *Biographical Directory of the American Congress 1776–1961* (Washington, D.C., 1961).

PATTEN, BRYCE MCLELLAN (b Topsham, Maine, March 1, 1814; d Farmington, Iowa, March 15, 1891). Educator of the blind. Patten was born to Actor and Ann Wilson Patten. Soon after graduating from Bowdoin College (1837), he moved to Covington, Kentucky, and taught at a school there. He came to Louisville in 1839 and opened the Louisville Collegiate Institute, a school for boys.

Bryce Patten had a visually impaired brother, Otis, who was a student of the pioneer educator of blind children, Dr. Samuel Gridley Howe, at the Massachusetts Institution for the Blind in Boston. It was because of this association that Bryce Patten became interested in setting up a school for blind children in Kentucky. Beginning in 1839, with a group of six blind students, Patten undertook their instruction in addition to teaching his students at the institute. His dedication resulted in the founding of the Kentucky Institution for Education of the Blind in 1842. He was superintendent and a member of the board until his resignation in 1871.

Patten was active with the American Association of Instructors of the Blind and, with the encouragement of this national organization, became a founder of the AMERICAN PRINTING HOUSE FOR THE BLIND in 1858. As the first general manager and secretary, Patten purchased the press and initiated the printing of embossed books.

Patten married Mary Earle in 1851; she died five years later. In 1870 he married Josephine Burns at Chariton, Iowa. In 1871 he resigned his offices in Louisville and moved to Iowa, where he farmed, lectured, and kept a hotel. Bryce and Josephine Patten had four children: Bryce E., Ida, Helena, and Lela. He is buried in Farmington, Iowa.

Carol Brenner Tobe

PATTEN, JAMES (b Augusta County, Virginia, 1748; d Louisville, December 29, 1815). Pioneer and pilot. James Patten (sometimes spelled Patton), was one of the 1778 CORN ISLAND settlers and the first FALLS OF THE OHIO pilot. His parents were John Patten and his first wife, a Miss Rogers, both natives of northern Ireland. Nothing is known of James Patten's early life except that he received 100 acres of land in 1757 by his father's will and that he sold it in 1777, apparently preparing for the move to Kentucky.

He came to Corn Island with his wife, Phoebe (maiden name unknown), and three young daughters, Martha, Peggy, and Mary. It is a deposition made by Patten in a chancery court case that establishes May 27, 1778, as the date when the settlers and Clark's militia arrived at the Falls of the Ohio. When the move from the island to the mainland was made in late summer 1778, Patten seems to have been in charge of building the stockade at the foot of the present Twelfth St. Now referred to as Fort on Shore, it was usually called Patten's Fort at the time. He served as a captain in the Jefferson County militia, accompanied Col. John Bowman's strike against the Indians in Ohio, and was with Clark on his 1780 foray to the same area.

L. D. PEARSON. E. C. PEARSON.
L. D. PEARSON & SON,
ESTABLISHED 1848.
Funeral Directors & Embalmers,
DEALERS IN ALL KINDS OF
METALLIC AND WOODEN BURIAL CASKETS AND CASES.
BURIAL ROBES, LININGS, TRIMMINGS, ETC.
Nos. 220 to 224 WEST JEFFERSON STREET,
BETWEEN SECOND AND THIRD.
TELEPHONE 170, RING 2.
LOUISVILLE, KY.
CARRIAGE STABLES, Nos. 215 AND 217 WEST GREEN ST.
THE VERY BEST OPEN AND CLOSED CARRIAGES FOR HIRE.

L.D. Pearson Funeral Home advertisement from 1893 City Directory.

When the drawing for lots was held in 1779, Patten secured land on the northeast corner of Eighth and Main Streets, where he built a cabin attached to a huge hollow sycamore tree, the hollow serving as a room. Later he erected the town's first stone house on this lot. The stone was secured from the Corn Island shoal, the first stone quarried from this site.

On the roof of his initial cabin home, Patten had erected a kind of cupola with a clear view of the Falls of the Ohio. From the cupola he could watch flatboats and keelboats as they "crossed" the Falls. It might have been from this perch that he noted the proper course to avoid disaster on the rocks. In any event he became an expert pilot to take boats over the Falls, where wrecks were frequent. In 1797 the Jefferson County Court, under the authority of an act of the Kentucky legislature, appointed him the first licensed Falls of the Ohio pilot. His pay was the $2 fee collected from each boat he piloted. Anyone piloting boats over the Falls without a license was fined $10.

Patten's daughter Peggy, on May 17, 1798, married Nathaniel Pryor, one of the Kentuckians who was a member of the Lewis and Clark Expedition to the Pacific coast. She must have died before the expedition departed Louisville in late 1803, because only single men were recruited. Patten was buried in the old Western Cemetery on W Jefferson St. The body may have been later reburied elsewhere.

See William S. Muir, "Captain James Patton of Augusta County, Virginia, and Louisville, Kentucky: Ancestors and Descendants," *Register of the Kentucky Historical Society* 42 (July 1944): 227–54; George H. Yater and Carolyn S. Denton, *Nine Young Men from Kentucky* (Missoula, Mont., 1992).

George H. Yater

PEARSON FUNERAL HOME. L.D. Pearson came to the Louisville area in 1832, making his home in Shelby County, where he became a master at cabinetmaking. In time Pearson, who built more coffins than cabinets, went into the funeral home business with James Coudrey. Their first location was on Main near Second St. next to the Galt House in Louisville. The partnership did not last long, as J.C. King bought Coudrey's share just a year after opening. With King as his new partner, Pearson moved the funeral home to Jefferson St. between Second and Third. In 1848 the name was changed to L.D. Pearson & Son. The funeral home stayed on Jefferson St. until 1898, when it was moved to Third and Chestnut. In 1924 the firm moved again, this time into the Ferguson mansion at 1310 S Third. The business flourished here, and by 1951 a second mortuary had been opened at 149 Breckenridge Ln. in St. Matthews. The S Third St. location was closed in 1977 and became the home of the Filson Club Historical Society. L.D. Pearson & Son added another mortuary in 1993 at 12900 Shelbyville Rd. under the name of Pearson-Ratterman Brothers Funeral Home.

PEDESTRIAN COURTS. When Belgravia Ct., in what later became Old Louisville, was laid out in 1891, it was the precedent for a kind of urban planning that is apparently unique to Louisville. Instead of a street, the two-block-long stretch (originally Belgravia Ave.) was served only by a wide grassed mall with sidewalks on each side. There was no vehicular access. Trees were planted along each sidewalk. Extending from Fourth St. to Sixth and crossing St. James Ct., Belgravia was not in the original planning of the Victoria Land Company's St. James Ct. It was added perhaps to permit more intensive land use by accommodating more residences on smaller lots than those on the stately St. James. The usual street noises would also have been diminished for Belgravia residents.

Whatever the rationale, the concept struck a chord with Louisville developers. Similar pedestrian courts began to appear, first in Old Louisville and later in other neighborhoods. There were at least twenty such pedestrian-only enclaves. The second was Fountain Ct. (1893), extending one block westward from Fourth St. to St. James Ct. at the landmark fountain. Others in Old Louisville include Floral Terrace (in what had been the privately owned Floral Park) from Sixth to Seventh Streets and Ormsby Ct. (off Ormsby Ave.), both begun in 1905; Avery Ct. (1904), off Avery St.; and Ouerbacker Ct. (1911).

Two pedestrian courts in Old Louisville, Kensington (1910) and Reeser (1915) were lined with apartment buildings rather than single dwellings. Keller Ct. (1913) ran east off of Second St. north of Barbee St. Layton Ct. (1908), off Preston St. on the edge of Fort Hill, contained only a bevy of the ubiquitous Louisville shotgun cottages, providing a quiet retreat for lower-income families.

The pedestrian court did not reach the Highlands until 1914, when Ivanhoe Ct., approached from Bardstown Rd. by an impressive flight of stone steps, was laid out. Nearby Maple Pl. followed the next year. In 1916 Edgewood Pl. was created between Alta Ave. and Bonnycastle. Crescent Hill claims only Marion Ct. (1912) off Bayly Ave.

In the South End a block-long pedestrian court, Oakdale Terrace (1904), stretched westward from Oakdale Ave. (then National Turnpike) to the Park Third trolley line. Renamed Terrace Park in 1910, it grew from the original five houses to some twenty-two of the type often dubbed American Foursquare. Residents waiting for the north bound streetcar looked across the tracks to the barns at Churchill Downs. Two other short pedestrian courts were launched in the South End in 1909: Maple and Hilltop off Sixth St. in the Southern Heights neighborhood.

Oddly, the final creation of the pedestrian courts occurred in Old Louisville where they began. The matching and short Rose and Eutropia Courts on opposite sides of Fourth St. north of Bloom, and Hughes Ct. off First St., were begun in 1924. All three were lined with modest, matching homes.

The Great Depression of the 1930s, followed by World War II, brought building and development to a virtual halt for fifteen years. When development resumed in the late 1940s, the automobile changed its pattern; the age of suburbia had arrived. New housing began rising on what had been farmland surrounding Louisville, now easily reached by automobile. The pedestrian court reflected the era of heavy dependence on public transit in the form of the streetcar and the concomitant dense development.

Three of the pedestrian courts have vanished: Avery and Hughes Courts to urban renewal demolition for the expansion of the Belknap Campus of the University of Louisville and Terrace Park to neglect by out-of-town owners, descendants of the original developer. But the others remain, providing quiet retreats from busy city streets. The earlier ones, with large brick homes, are the finest examples of the genre. Belgravia Ct., the first, tops the list.

See George H. Yater, "Court Society," *Louisville,* Oct. 1986, 21–22.

George H. Yater

PENDENNIS CLUB. The Pendennis Club, probably the most widely known social club in Kentucky, was established in Louisville in 1881. It was modeled in part on English gentlemen's clubs. From its inception it has filled the role of a downtown businessmen's social club. The name, which comes from Thackeray's *History of Pendennis,* has a Cornish derivation, meaning "high place."

The first clubhouse, acquired in 1883, was the former BELKNAP mansion, located on Walnut St. between Third and FOURTH Streets. The first great banquet in that clubhouse was given to entertain Pres. Chester A. Arthur on August 1, 1883, when he came to Louisville to inaugurate the SOUTHERN EXPOSITION. Robert Todd Lincoln, the secretary of war, accompanied the president. The NEWSPAPERS omitted no detail in describing the elegant party, even setting forth in full the menu of the feast prepared by the chef, one Monsieur Lecon Gaston, late of the Union League Club in Philadelphia.

In later years ARTHUR KROCK, the Louisville native who was the Washington correspondent of the *New York Times,* stated that "if the term 'gentleman' is held to its proper definition to mean a civilized, educated, well-mannered man, then no club in the United States numbered more such persons proportionate to its size than the Pendennis."

A new clubhouse was built in 1928 on the south side of Walnut (Muhammad Ali Blvd.) at Second St., one block east of the original location. Many generations of debutantes have been introduced to society in the great third-floor ballroom. One of the club's most famous employees was Henry Bain, who served for forty years in the old clubhouse, mostly as headwaiter. African American Henry Bain went to work there as an elevator boy shortly after the club opened. At the time of his death, just weeks before the 1928 Derby, he was a legend, one of the city's most recognized individuals and a man who knew, it was said, the names and pedigrees of everyone in Louisville society. ROLAND HAYES, the great lyric tenor, was his nephew, and Bain arranged for him to make his professional debut at the Pendennis Club in 1910. "Captain Henry" was a commanding presence with a staff of busboys and waiters at his beck and call by the time he created the gourmet sauce that has delighted generations of Louisvillians. Another famous employee, "Captain John" Johnson, was known to generations of Louisville leaders in the last half of the twentieth century for his demeanor in positions from headwaiter to manager.

The club, which once restricted itself to males, was closed through much of its history to minorities and JEWS. In the late twentieth century this policy was dropped. Although its membership is now open to anyone who is approved and there are women, African American, and Jewish members, the image of a closed club has persisted in the minds of some Louisvillians.

See Pendennis Club, *Officers, Members, Articles of Incorporation, By- laws and House Rules of Pendennis Club* (Louisville 1921); *Centennial of the Pendennis Club* (Louisville 1981).

Jo M. Ferguson

PENN, SHADRACK, JR. (b Frederick, Maryland, 1790; d St. Louis, Missouri, June 15, 1846). Journalist. While still young, Penn moved to Kentucky with his parents, Shadrack and Margaret (Holland) Penn. They settled on a farm in Scott County, near Georgetown. When Penn reached his late teens, he began work as an apprentice at a newspaper in Georgetown, learning the printing trade and developing his skills as a writer. He soon took on editorial duties with a political paper in Georgetown before enlisting as a soldier in the War of 1812. After his military service, Penn spent a brief period in the mercantile business before returning to the press. In 1818 he came to Louisville and on June 23 founded the *Louisville Public Advertiser,* a Democratic paper that evolved from a weekly to a semiweekly and finally, on April 4, 1826, to the first daily newspaper in Kentucky. Once described as "an experienced politician, a forcible writer, and a man of extraordinary tact," Penn became the dominant editorial voice in the state. During Kentucky's relief crisis of 1819–23, Penn, an antirelief partisan, denounced the New Court and the idea of a Commonwealth Bank. In 1828 he was offered a cabinet post by Pres. Andrew Jackson but declined, choosing instead to continue making his voice heard through the vehicle of the press. Then in 1830 Penn's paper encountered stiff competition in the form of George D. Prentice, a staunch Whig, and his *LOUISVILLE JOURNAL.* For more than a decade they carried on a celebrated editorial rivalry that was described as "without parallel in the newspaper history of the country." (Towles, 9)

In 1841 Penn bowed out of his battles with Prentice and moved to St. Louis, Missouri, where he began the *Reporter,* another Democratic newspaper. He served as editor of the paper for the next five years and established himself as an important figure in the Missouri political arena. Among the issues to which Penn lent his editorial support were the district plan of election for congressional candidates and limited issue state BANKING, as opposed to a strictly gold and silver currency.

When Penn died, he left behind a large family. He is buried in the family cemetery of Capt. HENRY M. SHREVE in St. Louis.

See *Biographical Cyclopedia of the Commonwealth of Kentucky* (Chicago 1896); Herndon J. Evans, *The Newspaper Press in Kentucky* (Lexington 1976); Donald B. Towles, *The Press of Kentucky, 1787–1994* (Lexington 1994).

PETER, ARTHUR, SR. (b Louisville, January 27, 1872; d Louisville, November 15, 1960). Jefferson County judge. Arthur Peter was the son of Minor Cary and Nellie (Crutcher) Peter. His grandfather, also named Arthur Peter, came to Louisville from England and established Arthur Peter & Co., a wholesale drug firm. His father also went into the retail drug business, operating Peter-Neat-Richardson & Co.

Peter attended Allmond's University School and LOUISVILLE MALE HIGH SCHOOL. He received his law degree from the University of Virginia in 1892 and began practicing law in Louisville that year. He was a member of the law firm of Peter & Newcomb from 1904 to 1907. From 1910 to 1918, he was trust counsel for Fidelity & Columbia Trust Co., a precursor to Citizens Fidelity Bank & Trust Co. (now PNC).

From 1918 to 1921, he was a member of the legal firm of Bingham, Peter, Tabb & Levi, where he was a partner with ROBERT WORTH BINGHAM, owner and publisher of the *COURIER-JOURNAL.* Peter also worked as an attorney for the NEWSPAPERS. From 1920 to 1922 he was with the law firm Peter, Tabb & Levi, from 1922 to 1932 with Peter, Lee, Tabb, Krieger & Heyburn, and from 1932 to 1934 with Peter, Tabb, Heyburn & Marshall. He was also a member of the firm of Peter, Heyburn, Marshall & Wyatt. When Wilson Wyatt was elected mayor in 1941, he left the firm, and it became Peter, Heyburn & Marshall. Peter specialized in corporate and probate law.

Peter, a Republican, was Jefferson County judge from November 14, 1907, until December 31, 1910. He ran for the office in 1906 as a representative of the Fusionists, a mixture of Republicans and reform Democrats who united against the Democratic machine of the Whallen brothers. Peter was defeated in that election by 2,486 votes, but a lawsuit alleging election fraud went to the Kentucky Court of Appeals, which ruled the election invalid and forced the winners from office in 1907. Peter then ran again for county judge and easily defeated the Democratic candidate, Louisville lawyer Marion W. Ripy, by 5,452 votes. The Republicans, led by Mayor JAMES GRINSTEAD, took almost every city and county race in the 1907 special election.

Peter also served as director of the Louisville Gas & Electric Co. and the Liberty National Bank & Trust Co. He served as an officer in many other businesses.

Peter was a member of the Louisville, Kentucky, and American Bar Associations, and he was a member and a president of the Pendennis Club.

Peter married Louise Valadon Cowling of Louisville on November 12, 1895. The couple had two sons, Richard Cowling and Arthur Jr. Peter died at his home, 48 Hill Rd., and is buried in CAVE HILL CEMETERY.

See Mary Young Southard and Ernest C. Miller, eds., *Who's Who in Kentucky: A Biographical Assembly of Notable Kentuckians* (Louisville 1936); *Courier-Journal,* Nov. 17, 1960.

PETER-BURGHARD MARBLE CO. In 1882 Joseph H. Peter and Ernest R. Burghard, a former milliner, worked together in the stone business out of a small shop at 1407 High Ave. in Louisville. One year later, then known as Peter & Burghard Salem Lime & Steam Works, they moved to a 30-foot lot on the corner of Fourteenth and Maple Streets. In 1890 they incorporated as Peter & Burghard Stone Co. Peter was president of the new firm, and Burghard was treasurer, until 1896. Then Peter sold his interest to Burghard and left to open Joseph H. Peter & Co. Monuments at 923 E BROADWAY.

The company kept its original name, and Burghard remained president until his death. During his stewardship the company's facilities expanded several times. By 1908 the Peter & Burghard Stone Co. occupied the entire block of Maple St. between Thirteenth and Fourteenth Streets. It had a marble shop and mill that measured 425 x 60 feet and was furnished with all the latest machinery. It also had a fully equipped cut-stone and granite finishing complex that measured 425 x 80 feet.

By 1908 business was booming. The cut-stone department had furnished the stone for many buildings throughout the United States. Locally, it supplied stone for the construction of the Presbyterian Theological Seminary (now the JEFFERSON COMMUNITY COLLEGE), the WALNUT STREET BAPTIST CHURCH, the J. Ross Todd residence named Rostrevor, and many banks, churches, and private residences. Across the United States the firm provided the stone for the construction of post office buildings in New York, New Jersey, Massachusetts, and Pennsylvania, and the ten-story First National Bank building in Montgomery, Alabama, among many others. The marble branch of the business completed some of the largest interior marble contracts in America, employing more than thirty different varieties of marble, both domestic and foreign. The imported marble came principally from Greece, Italy, and Spain. The firm's work can still be seen in courthouses, banks, RAILROAD STATIONS, and HOTELS from San Francisco to Boston and from Indiana to Texas. The granite branch of the company designed and executed large numbers of monuments, mausoleums, and statuary of every description—many of them in Vermont-quarried stone. For years, in fact, the letterhead of the Peter & Burghard Stone Co. carried a sketch of the monument that the firm had built in CAVE HILL CEMETERY for the HENRY WATTERSON family.

Joseph E. Burghard, the son of Ernest R. Burghard, became head of the firm after his father's death. During his time the company emerged as one of the largest cut-stone and monument plants in the South and one of the best-known organizations of its kind in the country. By 1931, with a workforce of about 150 men, the company had fabricated and shipped its products to practically every state in the Union as well as Tokyo and Havana. In Louisville alone, the J.B. SPEED ART MUSEUM, the HEYBURN BUILDING, the Brown Hotel and Office Building (now the Camberley Brown), the STARKS BUILDING, the Louisville War Memorial (now the LOUISVILLE MEMORIAL AUDITORIUM), and the U.S. Post Office Building (now the Gene Snyder U.S. Courthouse and Customhouse), among other buildings, include the firm's cut-stone and marble work. The *COURIER-JOURNAL* of November 22, 1932, offered the following description of the beauty and craftsmanship of the interior marble work in the Post Office Building:

> The interior of the massive new building is artistically finished in marble of varied composition and pattern. On the second floor a spacious corridor extends around the entire building. The wainscoting of matched Roseale marble blocks were taken from QUARRIES in Tennessee and measure three feet six inches in height and have matched cap and base, the marble border in the floor being of light pink marble.
>
> Impressively rising from the main floor are thirty-two huge fluted columns of light pink marble from quarries in Tennessee, while the floor is patterned in Jersey green and pink Tennessee marbles. Two large entrance lobbies also are done in marble.
>
> The marble stairs from the basement to the fifth floor are of Roseale and gray marbles. There are fifty-eight circle arches of Kasota stone from quarries in Minnesota. Forty-two lavatories also are finished in marble.

Throughout the 1920s and 1930s, the company also designed and executed thousands of cemetery memorials and mausoleums every year. Pres. ZACHARY TAYLOR's mausoleum on Brownsboro Rd., as well as the Art League Memorial at the same site, are examples of the firm's work from this period.

As an industry nonessential to the war effort, Peter & Burghard Stone Co. was dormant during WORLD WAR II. In the spring of 1946, however, it began to rehire workers. With the death of Joseph E. Burghard, J. Tyler Thomas, the grandson of founder E.R. Burghard, became president in 1947. Tyler was the last of the Burghard family to manage the firm. In 1955, though retaining ownership of the factory buildings, he sold the business to Morris Denny of Bedford, Indiana. Although the company never again experienced the glory years of the 1920s and 1930s, still the new company would know some local success using Bedford carvers to produce statuary and bas-relief figures for churches. But increasingly, stone statuary, cut-block stone building materials, and exotic marbles were becoming financially prohibitive in the building industry.

On February 18, 1963, the company suffered a fire, of uncertain origin, that damaged the south wing of the factory. The next morning at 1:50, a three-alarm fire broke out—again, of uncertain origin—and destroyed most of the north wing. The company never fully recovered. After the fire the firm was bought by Oval June Bradshaw, formerly of the American Mosaic and Tile Co. in Louisville. It was called the Peter-Burghard Marble Co., and it contracted marble work until 1990, when Bradshaw sold to the Anderson-Klein Group. The firm is now located on Sanita Rd., off Poplar Level Rd., in a 7,000-square-foot facility.

PETERSON AVENUE HILL. Peterson Avenue Hill, located between Grinstead Dr. and Frankfort Ave. in CRESCENT HILL, is one of Louisville's better-known streets. The street is named for the Joseph Peterson family, which was active in the tobacco business and whose home is nearby. An unusual feature of this hill is its steep fifteen-degree slope. Constructed in 1902, it is one of the few Louisville streets still paved with vitrified bricks; the bricks were originally laid at angles in a sand base. The angling was unusual, not found in any other street surface in Louisville; it helped create traction on the surface in wet WEATHER.

Brick street paving came into vogue with mass brick production in the late nineteenth century. This brick hill is often incorrectly called a cobblestone hill. Oral tradition relates that early automobile buyers would drive their car up the hill in high gear to see if their new purchase could "pull Peterson Hill," thus verifying the vehicle's worthiness.

The Peterson Avenue Hill was designated a local landmark in June 1979 by the Historic Landmarks and Preservation Districts Commission. It was placed on the NATIONAL REGISTER OF HISTORIC PLACES in March 1980.

Allan M. Steinberg

PETERSON-DUMESNIL HOUSE. The Peterson-Dumesnil House, at 301 S Peterson Ave. in the Crescent Hill neighborhood, was built for Joseph Peterson (1812–89) about 1869–70 in the Italian Villa style. Peterson, a TOBACCO wholesaler, came to Louisville from Philadelphia in 1836 and made this residence his country house. He had acquired 31 1/8 acres in 1859 on the Louisville and SHELBYVILLE Pike from J.H. Colston. When Peterson died in 1889, he left the property to his granddaughters, one of whom married Harry Dumesnil, whose ancestors were from France. Members of the Dumesnil family were the last residents of the home. Oral tradition has attributed Peterson's country home to the well-known Louisville architect HENRY WHITESTONE (1819–93). The elegant brick house has a large cupola and Victorian interior details; it is typical of many homes found in CRESCENT HILL.

The Louisville BOARD OF EDUCATION purchased the house in 1948 from the Carrie L. Rowland estate and Elizabeth L. Dumesnil. In 1953 the board leased it to the Louisville Education Association, which used it for meetings. In 1977 it was leased to the Crescent Hill Community Council. The house was declared surplus by the Louisville-Jefferson County Board of Education in 1982, and that year the Peterson-Dumesnil House Foundation was established as a fund-raising organization. In cooperation with the Crescent Hill Community

Opening of Pewee Valley Louisville & Nashville Railroad Station in 1867.

Council, $155,000 was raised to buy the house from the board in 1984.

The house is now maintained by this foundation and utilized for Crescent Hill community events. It is also leased for weddings, receptions, and other activities on a year-round basis. It is the home base of the LOUISVILLE HISTORICAL LEAGUE. This historic house was designated a Louisville landmark in 1976 by the Historic Landmarks and Preservation Districts Commission. It was added to the National Register of Historic Places in 1975.

See Samuel W. Thomas, *Crescent Hill Revisited* (Louisville 1987).

Allan M. Steinberg

PEWEE VALLEY. Fifth-class city located just over the northeastern Jefferson County line in OLDHAM COUNTY, centered around the intersection of LaGrange Rd. and Central and Ash Avenues. Settlers moved into the area during the early 1800s and established a community known as Rollington, which served as a stopping place for people traveling from Louisville to Brownsboro and from MIDDLETOWN to WESTPORT. In 1851 the Louisville & Frankfort Railroad was completed, linking the two cities. Its track was alongside the modern-day LaGrange Rd. A depot was built in 1867. In 1852 the railroad company established a stop nearly 2 miles southwest of Rollington and called it Smith's Station, for Henry S. Smith, who laid out the town in 1856 on land given to him by his father. Residences were built around the new hub of the area, and within three years commuter service into Louisville was begun.

By the mid-1850s, fifteen residences, mainly rural estates constructed by wealthy Louisville citizens who wished to escape the city heat, dotted the area. Soon a post office was established in Smith's Station. As more people moved into the community, organized religious groups, including EPISCOPALIANS, Catholics, and PRESBYTERIANS, established local churches.

With the area's growing population, the state legislature incorporated the town of Pewee Valley in 1870. The name was chosen after several residents of the town, which is actually located on a ridge, heard the distinctive call of the eastern wood pewee bird. By 1874 the city, with a POPULATION of approximately 250 people, three churches, two hotels, four stores and one doctor, had become a popular summer vacation spot. This role was fortified in 1901 as electric interurban rail service into Louisville was introduced at half-hour intervals. A year later, the Villa Ridge Inn, a four-story turreted hotel that had been constructed near the depot in 1889, was converted into a state-supported home for CIVIL WAR Confederate veterans; it was known as the Kentucky CONFEDERATE HOME. Although most of the structure was destroyed by fire in 1920, the home continued to lodge veterans until it closed in 1934.

From its earliest years, Pewee Valley attracted a number of artists and intellectuals, such as grammar textbook author Noble Butler, *COURIER-JOURNAL* founder Walter N. Haldeman, painter CARL BRENNER, poet and journalist William D. Gallagher, and novelist Elisha Warfield. Two of Pewee Valley's most famous residents captured life in the idyllic town at the turn of the century. ANNIE FELLOWS JOHNSTON, who lived there briefly in the 1890s and returned in 1911 after living in Arizona, CALIFORNIA, and Texas, based the fictional hamlet of Lloydsboro Valley on the town in her internationally popular *Little Colonel* series of children's books. In addition to providing illustrations for the *Little Colonel* books, photographer Kate Matthews depicted the people and surroundings of the area in her work, which also appeared in national magazines such as *Cosmopolitan* and *Good Housekeeping*.

By the 1920s, the number of vacationers dwindled as improved modes of transportation linked travelers to other destinations. This trend continued following the GREAT DEPRESSION; the population declined and commuter rail service was terminated. However, the community began to regain its popularity as an automobile suburb when its first large-scale subdivision, Lloydsboro, was platted in 1962.

Located in the area are the Confederate Cemetery, near the site of the old veterans' home; the KENTUCKY CORRECTIONAL INSTITUTE FOR WOMEN, which was established in 1937; and the Little Colonel Playhouse. Originally a Masonic Lodge constructed around 1915, the playhouse was converted into a ninety-seat THEATER for the Little Colonel Players. The troupe was begun in 1956 by the local woman's club as a reading and discussion group and evolved into a community theater that typically performs four plays each summer and conducts several children's workshops.

The population of Pewee Valley in 1970 was 950; in 1980, 982, and in 1990, 1,283. In 1996 the population was 1,631.

See Carolyn Brooks, *Historic Pewee Valley* (Louisville 1991); *A Place in Time: The Story of Louisville's Neighborhoods* (Louisville 1989); Robert M. Rennick, *Kentucky Place Names* (Lexington 1984).

PHARMACY. In Louisville's early days, medicines were dispensed by physicians as part of their practices. This was the norm throughout the United States as well. As the settlement at the Falls of the Ohio began to grow into a city, however, the purveying of MEDICINES became a distinct business. Louisville became the headquarters for the supply of drugs and medicines to the surrounding settlements in Kentucky and Indiana in the early nineteenth century. One of the first suppliers was Dr. Richard W. Ferguson, who began to dispense medications to the public independently of his medical practice. Another significant early figure was Dr. Daniel Wilson, who established a drugstore at Jefferson and Fifth Streets in 1817. Wilson's business evolved to become a wholesale drug supply house and became the foremost company of the kind west of the Appalachian Mountains by the outbreak of the CIVIL WAR, according to C. Lewis Diehl, an early leader in Louisville pharmacy.

By the 1830s physicians had left the business, and pharmacists had emerged to compound and dispense prescriptions. Many then used the titles of chemist and apothecary. Training was received through apprenticeship. Drugstores were principally located on Main and MARKET Streets from the 1830s to the 1850s. By the 1860s Louisville was the home of many retail and wholesale houses; was known for the qualifications, reliability, and integrity of its druggists; and was the regional center for pharmacy in the West. The city's pharmaceutical ranks were influenced by an influx of educated

German pharmacists, who emigrated following the revolutions in Europe in the late 1840s.

In 1856 a pharmaceutical manufacturing concern, the Louisville Chemical Works, was established. Dr. Edward R. Squibb of Brooklyn, New York, who founded the Squibb Corp., was one of the original partners. The Louisville company had a plant on High and Thirteenth Streets, but the firm closed during the Civil War when the principal partner, Dr. J. LAWRENCE SMITH, a Southern sympathizer, went abroad. The company was reestablished briefly under new ownership during the late 1860s, under the directorship of C. Lewis Diehl, but soon closed again.

Local pharmacists, interested in establishing more formal education for their profession, founded the Louisville College of Pharmacy on August 16, 1870, one of the first such institutions in the nation. Diehl became the college's first president. Following the raising of funds, lectures began in September 1871 at Mrs. Mary P. Pope's building on Third St. between Walnut (Muhammad Ali Blvd.) and Guthrie to a class of twenty-six students. Lectures were later held in temporary quarters, first on Jefferson St. and later in the German-English Academy at Second and Gray Streets. The college then purchased a building on Green St. (Liberty) between First and Second Streets in 1879. In 1888 a larger property was purchased, containing two buildings at First and Chestnut Streets.

Area pharmacists were also influential in instituting professional standards at the state level, promoting the passage of one of the pioneer state pharmacy laws in the nation in 1874. The establishment of the Kentucky Pharmacists Association followed three years later.

Women expressed interest in attending the Louisville College of Pharmacy in the 1880s but were not permitted to enroll. A Louisville pharmacist, Joseph P. Barnum, who had encouraged their applying to the college, then organized the Louisville School of Pharmacy for Women in 1883, the only such school in the United States. It was located in Barnum's drugstore on Fourth St. The school presented a small exhibit at the SOUTHERN EXPOSITION held in Louisville the same year. According to the Kentucky Pharmacy Act of 1874, the school's graduates were eligible to become registered pharmacists.

In 1890 the Louisville College of Pharmacy changed its policy and admitted women students on the same terms as men. Alice Churchill became the college's first woman graduate the following year. The admission of women to the larger school, plus a fire and financial reverses at Barnum's store, terminated the women's separate school in 1892. An attempt to revive it at the store of Charles S. Mayer on Fifth St. lasted only a year or two more.

A company of AFRICAN AMERICANS, led by a man named Williams who graduated from the School of Pharmacy at Meharry College, a black institution in Nashville, Tennessee, opened People's Drug Co. in Louisville in 1895. Physician E.D. Whedbee managed the store at Tenth and Madison Streets. By 1909 the city had two drugstores owned by blacks, but they were failing. The *Indianapolis Freeman* charged that black physicians did not encourage their patients to patronize the black pharmacists. The local pharmacy college was not integrated until the 1950s, when William Schulz graduated as a member of the class of 1954.

In 1926 the Louisville College of Pharmacy lengthened its course of study leading to the pharmacy degree to three years. In 1932 the course was extended to four years. The college was being held to increasingly exacting national standards. In this same era, instruction in the business and legal aspects of pharmacy was added to the curriculum.

Practicing pharmacists who were themselves graduates of the college constituted most of the faculty throughout its history. With the raising of academic requirements for graduation, the college added faculty to teach languages, humanities, and similar subjects. Its finances were hard-pressed to meet its needs, despite increasing interest in the study of pharmacy.

The class entering the school in 1946, just after WORLD WAR II, was the largest ever. College leaders began discussions with the UNIVERSITY OF LOUISVILLE and the University of Kentucky about merger. An agreement was reached with the University of Kentucky, and the Louisville College of Pharmacy was succeeded by the University of Kentucky College of Pharmacy on July 1, 1947. For eleven years, entering students attended introductory college classes on the University of Kentucky's main Lexington campus for a year before relocating to the existing college plant in Louisville for the remainder of their studies. In 1958 a new pharmacy building was dedicated in Lexington, ending pharmacy education in Louisville.

By 1950 there were more than two hundred retail drugstores in Louisville, most of them independently owned and operated. Drugstores had become more business-oriented long be-

Zubrod & Co. drug store was at 307 West Market Street in the 1880s.

fore that time. Many featured soda fountains or luncheonettes. In the later part of the twentieth century, however, the practice of pharmacy in Louisville faced considerable change, as it did throughout the United States. Pharmacists encountered new issues in the provision of health care, including the emergence of managed-care insurance plans and government programs such as Medicare and Medicaid. At the same time, pharmacists assumed a greater role in providing patient counseling concerning medication.

These changes in what had become the health industry heightened competition, squeezed profits, and fostered a trend toward consolidation among drugstores. Many independent pharmacies and smaller chains were bought out by national concerns by the century's end, including the Taylor Drug Store chain. Taylor's, founded by T.P. Taylor in Louisville in 1879, operated stores mainly in the Louisville metropolitan area and southern Indiana. It was the oldest drugstore chain in America when it was purchased by the national Rite Aid chain in 1996.

In addition to participating in professional organizations at the state and national level, Louisville area pharmacists also established local associations. The Louisville Retail Druggists Association was founded near the end of the nineteenth century. It merged with the Jefferson County Pharmacists Association, organized in 1957, to create the Jefferson County Academy of Pharmacy in 1962. A local chapter of the Veterans Drug Club was begun in 1937. This chapter's membership was limited to twenty-five Louisville area druggists who possessed twenty-five or more years of experience in the pharmacy field.

See J. Stoddard Johnston, ed., *Memorial History of Louisville* (Chicago 1896); Sylvia Wrobel, *The First Hundred Years of the University of Kentucky College of Pharmacy 1870-1970* (Lexington 1972); Eunice Bonow Bardell, "America's Only School of Pharmacy for Women," *Pharmacy in History* 26 (1984): 127–33; Louisville College of Pharmacy Records, University of Kentucky Margaret I. King Library Department of Special Collections and Archives; *The Kentucky Pharmacist,* (periodical, various issues) Kentucky Pharmacists Association, Frankfort; George C. Wright, *Life Behind a Veil* (Baton Rouge 1985); H.C. Weeden, *Weeden's History of the Colored People of Louisville* (Louisville 1897); *Kentucky Medical History, WPA Research Project Records, 1801–1940* (Louisville 1985), microfilm.

Mary Margaret Bell

PHILIP MORRIS USA. Englishman Philip Morris opened his London TOBACCO store on that city's famed Bond St. in 1847, and by 1854 he was not only a merchant but a manufacturer of cigarettes as well. Morris died in 1873, and around the turn of the century, his heirs sold the firm to William Thomson. Thomson was responsible for introducing the company's cigarettes to the U.S. market in 1902. In 1919 a group of American investors acquired the rights to the company's leading cigarette brands, and the firm now known as Philip Morris Companies was formed.

With its headquarters in New York City, Philip Morris USA, the domestic tobacco subsidiary of Philip Morris Companies, is the largest producer of cigarettes in the United States. It has two manufacturing centers, Richmond, Virginia, and Concord, North Carolina.

Until 2000 there was a third plant located at 1930 Maple St. in Louisville's West End. Philip Morris opened its Louisville manufacturing facility after paying $20 million for the Axton-Fisher Tobacco Company's production plant and stores of tobacco in 1944. Its operations included a five-building production complex, an administrative annex, and more than fifty additional buildings including warehouses, all of which covered approximately 106 acres. The plant, the largest single cigarette-producing plant in Kentucky and one of the world's largest, peaked in the mid-1980s with four thousand employees. Philip Morris was the top buyer of Kentucky burley tobacco, and the Louisville plant produced such cigarette brands as Basic, Benson & Hedges, and Marlboro, the world's top-selling cigarette. Sales of Philip Morris brands accounted for more than half of the U.S. cigarette market in 1997.

Deeply involved in community affairs, the company was generous to various arts groups, especially the Kentucky Center for the Arts endowment fund. It also sponsored KENTUCKY DERBY FESTIVAL events such as the Philip Morris Festival of Stars, a free-admission country music event held each year. It made significant contributions to such Louisville area projects as the historic Riverside, the FARNSLEY-MOREMEN LANDING.

Philip Morris announced on February 24, 1999, that because of declining sales in both its domestic and foreign markets, within two years it would phase out production at its Louisville plant. Production was consolidated in the larger, more modern plants in Virginia and North Carolina.

See Martin E. Biemer, *In Celebration of Louisville* (Northridge, Calif., 1988); Bob Hill and Dan Dry, *Louisville: A River Serenade* (Memphis, Tenn., 1995); Jay P. Pederson, ed., *International Directory of Company Histories,* vol. 18 (Detroit 1997); *Courier-Journal,* Feb. 25, 1999.

PHOENIX HILL. Neighborhood east of downtown Louisville, bounded by MARKET St. to the north, Preston St. to the west, BROADWAY to the south, and the Baxter Ave.-Broadway intersection to the east. The majority of the area consists of what was known as Preston's Enlargement, a part of Col. WILLIAM PRESTON's land grant of 1774. This area was annexed to the city in 1827, and by the time of the CIVIL WAR it had become highly populated. St. Martin of Tours Church was an important place of worship, and some of the BLOODY MONDAY riots occurred in its vicinity. A portion of the PHOENIX HILL neighborhood, however, a triangular area bounded by BEARGRASS CREEK, Baxter Ave., and Broadway, remained largely undeveloped during the antebellum period. This portion did not become a popular recreation site until 1865, after PHOENIX HILL PARK was opened and after Philip Zang, Philip Schillinger, and Gottfried Miller established the PHOENIX HILL BREWERY at 12 Underhill St. Although some families resided in the vicinity of the park, no true residential developments were platted until the 1890s.

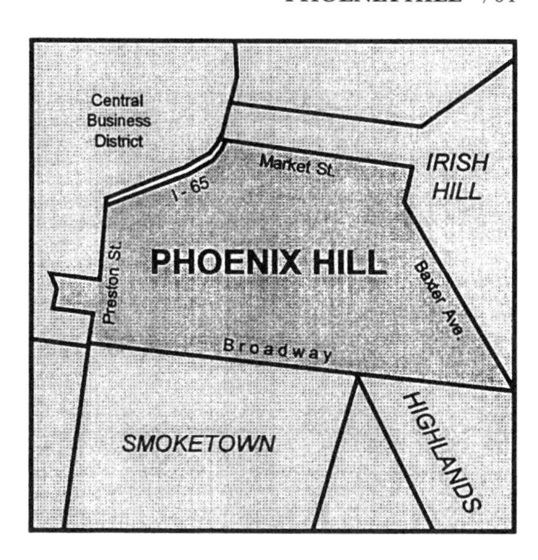

Crowds would flock to the parklike setting on the scenic knoll to play cards, listen to orators such as Theodore Roosevelt and William Jennings Bryan, bowl, dance, and drink Bohemian lagers at the 111-foot-long bar. The community surrounding the park prospered until PROHIBITION forced the brewery, as well as the park (because of a declining number of visitors), to close in 1919.

The buildings were torn down in 1938, although the horse stables and a few of the underground caves that were used for beer storage were left intact. During the FLOOD OF 1937, the eastern terminus of the PONTOON BRIDGE was at Baxter Ave., and thousands of people were brought to dry ground through the neighborhood.

Through the first half of the twentieth century, the predominantly German neighborhood flourished. However, following WORLD WAR II many of the white residents and businesses moved out to the SUBURBS, leaving their homes (many of them SHOTGUN COTTAGES) and other structures to decay. To combat the desolation of their neighborhood, several business leaders and residents banded together in 1975 to create the PHOENIX HILL ASSOCIATION, a group dedicated to the community's rebirth.

They received a substantial boost in 1977 when Mayor Harvey Sloane declared the blighted area a prime revitalization candidate and secured federal funds to rebuild it. Since that time dilapidated houses have been removed, several new housing developments have been constructed, and many businesses have moved back into Phoenix Hill. Popular night spots such as the Phoenix Hill Tavern and the Brewery Co. bring large numbers of people into the area.

See *Louisville Survey: East Report* (Louisville 1980); *A Place in Time: The Story of Louisville's Neighborhoods* (Louisville 1989).

PHOENIX HILL ASSOCIATION. The Phoenix Hill Association, a nonprofit neighborhood association created in 1975, has been a catalyst for revitalization. Membership includes residents and businesses. PHOENIX HILL is bounded by MARKET St. to the north, Preston St. to the west, Broadway to the south, and the Baxter Ave.–BROADWAY intersection to the east.

Beginning in the late 1970s, the association conducted neighborhood surveys, and afterwards devised strategies for revitalization. Then in the early to middle 1980s, two major housing developments were constructed. Phoenix Hill Townhouses is a 45-unit development opened in 1983. Under Section Eight, which was enacted in 1974, low-income people could receive federal subsidies for housing. Phoenix Place Apartments, a 268-unit, market-rate complex, is a complement to the townhouses and the area. A unique development, completed in the late 1980s, is the Cain Center for the Disabled. The center provides accessible, affordable housing for physically handicapped individuals.

In the early 1990s the association renewed surveys and strategies for the continued gentrification of the neighborhood. The result was thirteen single-family, market-rate homes showcased in the first inner-city Homearama in the country. Every home sold in the two-week duration of Homearama, showing that a market did exist for new single-family homes in the downtown area. Invigorated by this success, the association has continued each year to purchase vacant lots and deteriorated houses, replacing them with new homes. The yield from the first three phases has been thirty new market-rate, owner-occupied, single-family homes. This activity also sparked revitalization efforts by others, but perhaps the most inspiring aspect of the Phoenix Hill Association's success is that it has been accomplished by voluntary efforts of concerned residents and businesspeople.

In addition to the new home developments, the association routinely monitors the condition of existing structures and lots to ensure their compliance with local ordinances. The objective is to create a physical environment that is safe.

The people of Phoenix Hill have had an association to turn to with their concerns for over two decades. Community outreach is the most basic and important function of the association. As a result, the voice of one grows into the voice of many thereby increasing the likelihood of accomplishing the desired goal.

See *Courier-Journal,* May 30, 1978.

Michael Stoner Morris

PHOENIX HILL PARK AND BREWERY. Phoenix Hill Park was built in 1865 on the southwest side of Baxter Ave. and is surrounded by Payne, Barret (then Underhill), and Rubel (then Overhill) Streets. It was a popular place to hold picnics and political rallies. John Philip Sousa's band was one of many to entertain the crowds that came to drink Phoenix Bohemian Beer. The politicians who spoke at Phoenix Hill included Theodore Roosevelt, William Howard Taft, Charles Evans Hughes, and William Jennings Bryan. The latter, a "free silver" candidate for president in 1896, attracted a crowd of fifteen thousand people. The first indoor BASEBALL game in Louisville was held on January 18, 1891, in the Phoenix Hill dance hall. In 1897 six-day bicycle races, a popular event at the time, were held in the "bicycle bowl" with women contestants.

In 1865 Philip Zang, Philip Schillinger, and Gottfried Miller opened the Phoenix Hill Brewery on the grounds at 12 Underhill St. The L-shaped site was about 600 feet deep and 480 feet wide. The enlarged brewery and park grounds were designed by Gottfried Miller. Because the hill sloped down toward BEARGRASS CREEK on the northwest, the beer garden was level with the entrance at Baxter Ave. but about 20 feet above Rubel and Barret Avenues at the back corner. The main brewery building was three stories high, and an old illustration shows horse-drawn wagons taking beer out from the lower level onto Barret. On the beer garden level there was a large auditorium. By 1890 there were at least seven buildings on the site, plus a skating rink, a large covered pavilion, and a bandstand. One of the buildings contained a 111-foot-long bar, four bowling alleys, and a card room.

Although one of the most popular places in Louisville, the Phoenix Hill Brewery was closed in 1919 because of PROHIBITION, never to reopen. One by one the buildings were torn down, and the great hall was finally razed in 1938. Much of the dirt was removed for road construction, eliminating the truly spectacular views from the hill. The last remaining building, formerly the stable, is still occupied by a business and sits at 508 Baxter Ave. at Hull St.

See Stratton O. Hammon, "Phoenix Hill Park, Louisville, Kentucky," *Filson Club History Quarterly* 44 (April 1970): 156–63.

Neal O. Hammon

PHOTOGRAPHY. Louisville's first photographer, like most of the early U.S. practitioners, was both an artist and an entrepreneur. John M. Hewitt's lavish advertisement in the city directory for 1850 says that his daguerreotype studio, located on MAIN St. between Third and FOURTH Streets, was founded ten years earlier and for a long time was the only one in the city. During its first ten years of operation, it was affiliated with two national chains operated by John Plumbe Jr. and T.J. Dobyns. Under both affiliations the studio was known as Hewitt's National Daguerreian Gallery and employed several camera operators and finishers.

An 1848 description of Hewitt's studio describes it as one of the most magnificent in the United States, with a reception room 65 by 63 feet, furnished with the most costly furniture, including a "splendid pianoforte" kept for the entertainment of visitors. A separate "ladies' toilet" was similarly furnished. Both of these areas were separate from the room where likenesses were taken, which had a "magnificent light and is equal to the other rooms spoken of." All were ornamented with likenesses "of the most eminent men and the most beautiful ladies in the United States." THE FILSON CLUB HISTORICAL SOCIETY owns a fine set of daguerreotype portraits by Hewitt, and his work is also found in Louisville family collections. The studio does not appear in directories after 1856.

Ben Casseday's 1852 *History of Louisville* states that there were twenty-three people engaged in making daguerreotypes in that year. Since only eight studios are listed in the city directory for 1851–52, each studio must have employed an average of two to three individuals.

During the 1850s several studios were founded that became Louisville's most prominent and lasted until the end of the nineteenth century. Webster & Brother (Edward Z. and Israel B. Webster) was established in about 1851 on the south side of Main between Fourth and Fifth Streets. The Webster studio served as a meeting place for Union sympathizers at the outbreak of the CIVIL WAR, and Israel Webster traveled with Union troops making photographs. Almost no Civil War photographs by Louisville photographers have survived, but an Israel Webster photograph of Ohio troops can be viewed at the Ohio Historical Society.

Theodore Harris, a native of Canada, is said to have made one of the earliest English translations of the original FRENCH instructions for the daguerreotype. He opened a studio in Louisville in about 1855 on Main St. between Fourth and Fifth Streets, which he operated for several years. He later served as president of the Louisville Banking Co. He was the father of Credo Harris, director of WHAS radio station in the 1930s.

Daniel Stuber opened his studio on Market at Preston at about the same time. The studio included Michael Stuber after about 1866 and was variously know as D & M. Stuber and Stuber & Bro. Michael Stuber was the father of WILLIAM G. STUBER, who stated that Michael was "attached to several Union regiments as a sort of official cameraman." Hundreds of Civil War portraits were said to have been lost when William Stuber's studio burned in the 1890s. The Stuber studio was in business until about 1891 when it was sold to Albert Fearnaught. Many examples of Stuber portraits are found in the collections of both the Filson Club and the UNIVERSITY OF LOUISVILLE Photographic

ARCHIVES.

The last of the major studios established in the 1850s was owned by EDWARD KLAUBER, a native of Bohemia who came to the United States at the age of eighteen. His Main Street Studio has been compared to that of Matthew Brady in New York City. Lavishly furnished, it was popular with stage personalities who appeared at MACAULEY'S THEATRE, many of whom are said to have preferred Klauber's portraits to all others. Several excellent Klauber portraits of the actress MARY ANDERSON are owned by the University of Louisville Photographic Archives. The Filson Club has many examples of Klauber's documentary photographs of bridges, locks, and dams. Klauber also did documentary work for the Kentucky Geological Survey, and he made the portraits of prominent Louisvillians that appeared in *Louisville Past and Present* (1875). The studio continued in business until about 1913. Klauber died in 1918 and is buried in the Temple Cemetery.

Other large nineteenth-century Louisville studios were operated by J. HENRY DOERR, Elrod Brothers (John C., Eugene, Arthur, and Walter), and Frank Wybrant. Henry Hesse, photographer and inventor for more than sixty years, opened his first Louisville studio in 1895 on S Third St. The painter JOSEPH KREMENTZ briefly operated an independent PHOTOGRAPHY studio beginning about 1870. After closing the studio, he worked as a retoucher in the Klauber studio for much of the rest of the century.

During the last quarter of the nineteenth century, photography seems to have been one of the few fields in which women could succeed as independent artists and businesswomen.

J. Henry Doerr photography studio, corner Twelfth and Market Streets, c. 1876.

Kate Matthews became well known as a photographic artist and several women operated successful portrait studios in Louisville.

Louis Bergman opened a Louisville photo studio in 1872 on W Market. After 1885, however, Caroline Bergman is listed as the proprietor and photographer, and Louis is listed only as "manager." This very successful studio was in operation until 1896. The Sisters Maltby (Alice, Mary, Ellen, and Julia) operated a photography and PAINTING studio at 216 W Market St. beginning in 1873. Ella M. Crosby was a partner (with George E. Crosby) in the G.E. & E.M. Crosby studio, which opened in 1881 on Center St. (Armory Place) and later moved to W Market.

Sally Garrity opened the Miss Garrity studio on Market St. at Fourth in 1887, employing Thomas W. Garrity and, later, John Garrity as camera operators. Julia Brown began as a retoucher in the Miss Garrity studio in 1888 and was in business as the J.S. Brown & Co. studio in 1889. Lillian Richardson opened a photography studio at 307 Fourth St. in 1891. Many photographs of school classes from the 1880s and 1890s identify "Miss Brobston" as the photographer. Her name does not appear in classified listings of the period, however, indicating that she probably operated under contract to the school system and without a studio address.

Following close on the heels of these nineteenth-century businesswomen was Ethel Standiford, who from 1901 until 1934 had a portrait studio in Louisville on S Fourth St. Standiford also briefly operated a studio in Cleveland, Ohio, and her work is represented in the Standiford Collections at the Cleveland Public Library.

The first AFRICAN AMERICAN photographer to appear in Louisville city directories was W.H. Lawson, whose studio at 319 W Walnut (Muhammad Ali Blvd.) opened in 1879. He operated the studio until 1886, after which he was listed as an artist in city directories through the 1890s. Harvey Husbands, the second African American photographer of whom we have any knowledge, appears in the city directory for 1884 as a porter at the studio of J. Henry Doerr, but he was operating his own studio at 967 W Jefferson in 1886. Unfortunately, no work by either Lawson or Husbands seems to have survived.

The most successful early African American studio was that of Jesse Robert Neighbors, which opened on Walnut between Ninth and Tenth in 1899 as Neighbors & Bros. (with G.W. Neighbors until 1903). The studio was in operation until 1929. Examples of Neighbors's work are found in family collections in Louisville, and a very beautiful group portrait is owned by the Photographic Archives at the University of Louisville.

Arthur P. Evans opened his portrait and commercial studio at 605 S Tenth St. in about 1905. The studio moved in the 1920s to the thriving African American business district west of Fifth St. Its ultimate location at 819 W Chestnut became a landmark. By far the most successful African American photographer, Evans was in business until the 1960s. Although the studio and its negatives were destroyed by vandals after its Chestnut St. building was condemned as part of an URBAN RENEWAL project, many fine examples of Evans's work are contained in both private and public collections.

James Sydnor documented African American social life for the *LOUISVILLE DEFENDER* and as a freelance photographer during the second and third quarters of the twentieth century. Many of his photographs appear in Prof. Bruce Tyler's *African American Life in Louisville* (1998).

Twentieth-century Louisville photography was dominated by large studios founded early in the century. The Royal Photo Co. was founded by Louis Bramson in 1903 and remained in business until 1972. The firm was a portrait and commercial studio until the American entry into WORLD WAR I, when it closed its downtown studio to concentrate on portrait and group photography at CAMP ZACHARY TAYLOR. Reopening in downtown Louisville after the war, the firm prospered in commercial photography. Louis Bramson's son Stern joined the firm in 1930, becoming chief photographer and operating the studio following Louis's death. The studio, on S Jefferson St., was sold in 1972 when STERN BRAMSON retired. The studio's negatives were acquired by the University of Louisville Photographic Archives in 1982. Stern Bramson's work was much admired in artistic circles, resulting in one-man exhibitions at important galleries in both New York and California. His work was also the subject of a one-man exhibition at the Art Institute of Chicago in 1988, shortly before his death.

James M. Caufield and Frank W. Shook founded the Caufield & Shook studio in 1903, later taking as a partner one of their chief photographers, William Bowers. The studio, located at W Market and S FOURTH STREETS, dominated Louisville photography until its closing in 1978. The studio was sold in 1960 to Richard "Dick" Duncan and Ned Tansell. The new owners donated all the studio's negatives (over four hundred thousand items) to the University of Louisville Photographic Archives. The collection is regarded as one of the best documentations of any American city. The firm served as official photographers of the KENTUCKY DERBY and, before 1920, took most of the photographs that appeared in the *COURIER-JOURNAL*, the *LOUISVILLE TIMES*, and the *Louisville Herald*.

John C. Rieger was Louisville's best portrait photographer from 1901 until 1962. His portraits were always made under natural light in his specially built studio at 810 Baxter Ave. He was the first photographer in Louisville to photograph in color, using the Autochrome process shortly after its invention in 1904. Rieger made the portraits of VICTOR MATURE that the actor used to get screen tests in Hollywood. He also made the portraits of Col. HARLAND SANDERS that became the trademark of Kentucky Fried Chicken.

Other significant twentieth-century studios include the portrait studios of John Cusick (1896–1955) on W Market and of Walton Jones Sr. and Walton Jones Jr. (1929–1980s) at Fourth and Chestnut Streets; the commercial studio of Lin Caufield, nephew of James M. Caufield; and the studios of the Kuprion family (Arthur and Doris) on W Market St. Arthur Kuprion was the inventor of a finish-line camera that was used at major race tracks in the United States.

The *Courier-Journal* and other NEWSPAPERS began to make use of news photographs in about 1920. Their earlier use of photographs consisted of feature material photographed for the papers by local studios. By the 1950s the *Courier-Journal* had one of the best photographic staffs of any paper in the United States. Two of its photographers were named photographer of the year by the University of Missouri School of Journalism: Barney Cowherd in 1949 and William "Bill" Strode in 1966. The *Courier-Journal* has also received two PULITZER PRIZES for news photography. The 1976 award was received for feature photography for the coverage of court-ordered BUSING in Louisville. In 1980 the paper received the Pulitzer for international reporting for a series on the Cambodian crisis by reporter Joel Brinkley and photographer Jay Mather.

Louisvillian Sidney W. Park turned a love of flying and a talent for manufacturing aerial cameras into one of Louisville's most successful firms, Park Aerial Survey. Headquartered at LOUISVILLE INTERNATIONAL AIRPORT, it is now the largest aerial photography business in the Midwest and the Southeast and continues to be a leader in high-resolution and digital photogrammetry.

Other Louisvillians have also made significant national contributions to photography. Robert Doherty, professor at the University of Louisville from 1959 until 1972, founded the collections now known as the University of Louisville Photographic Archives. From 1972 until 1979 he served as director of the International Museum of Photography at the George Eastman House, Rochester, New York. He has also written books on social documentary photography. Louisvillian Andrew Eskind has served as assistant to the director of the International Museum of Photography since the 1970s. Charles H. Traub has served as the director of Light Gallery, New York, and as director of photography at the School of the Visual Arts in New York City.

Since its founding in 1962, the University of Louisville Photographic Archives has amassed a collection of over 1.2 million documentary and fine art photographs, making it one of the largest university-based collections in the United States. Researchers from around the world make use of its collections and research facilities. Prints from its collections are exhibited by museums throughout the United States.

The Filson Club Historical Society has a photographic collection of about fifty thousand images, including many historical photographs by nineteenth-century Louisville photographers. The J.B. SPEED ART MUSEUM also owns an excellent collection of works by nineteenth- and twentieth-century photographic artists.

See *Louisville Merchants' Mechanics' and Manufacturers' Business Directory for 1850* (Louisville 1850); Ben Casseday, *History of Louisville* (Louisville 1852); John S. Craig, *Craig's Daguerreian Registry,* 3 vols. (Torrington, Conn., 1994–); *Illustrated Louisville: Kentucky's Metropolis* (Chicago 1891); W.O. Carver, "Louisville Was Picture Minded Early," *Louisville Times,* Jan. 20, 1939; "Edward Klauber Dies" *Courier-Journal,* Jan. 26, 1918.

James C. Anderson

PICKETT, ALICE NEWCOME (b Finchville, Shelby County, Kentucky, 1888; d Louisville, November 17, 1971). Physician. Known affectionately as "Ma Pickett" by her medical students, Pickett received her medical degree from the Women's Medical College in Philadelphia in 1909. After four years of working in various HOSPITALS, she moved back to her native state in 1913 and set up practice in Louisville. During WORLD WAR I she served with the Red Cross as a civilian doctor overseas, where for a time she was the sole physician in a FRENCH town of forty thousand. After the war she returned to Louisville and in 1921 joined the medical faculty of the UNIVERSITY OF LOUISVILLE as the head of the obstetrics department. She held that position for the next twenty-five years. Pickett remained a professor of obstetrics at the university until her retirement on January 1, 1952.

Pickett was also noted for her civic contributions. She served on the board of directors of the Louisville chapter of the Red Cross and sat on the advisory committee of the U.S. Children's Bureau. Pickett was instrumental in establishing Kentucky's first prenatal clinic as well as the Birth Control Clinic of Louisville. In 1957 she was the recipient of the University of Kentucky's Sullivan Medal for Service, and in the 1960s the *COURIER-JOURNAL* and the LOUISVILLE TIMES Foundation recognized Pickett's social service by making a sizable contribution to the Red Cross in her name. In 1962 she also received honors from the local YWCA and the Louisville branch of the National Council of Jewish Women. Pickett was cremated and buried in Grove Hill Cemetery, SHELBYVILLE, Kentucky.

See *Courier-Journal,* Nov. 18, 1971.

PILCHER, WILLIAM STANTON (b Stafford County, Virginia, January 5, 1803; d Louisville, August 14, 1858). Mayor. William Pilcher was the son of Frederick Pilcher, who was born in 1769 and married Margaret Alsop in Spotsylvania County, Virginia, on September 3, 1792. Frederick was a successful manufacturer, employing a large number of laborers. He died in Fredericksburg, Virginia, on December 27, 1827. William came to Louisville in 1833 to study law.

Initially a Jacksonian Democrat, William Pilcher ran for lieutenant governor in 1844 with Col. William O. Butler, who ran for governor. Pilcher lost the race that year to Archibald Dixon, who ran with William Owsley on the Whig ticket.

Pilcher later ran for mayor on the American, or Know-Nothing, Party ticket and was elected on April 4, 1857. He received 1,410 popular votes, and his closest rival received 224. He served until May 13, 1858, when he became too ill to continue his duties as mayor. Thomas Riley, president of the Board of Councilmen, the lower chamber of the city's bicameral legislature, was chosen mayor pro tem by the General Council to fill Pilcher's unexpired term. Pilcher died that August.

He married Dolly Alsop Fisher. He was also a successful lawyer in Louisville and a general of the militia.

See Lewis C. Collins and Richard H. Collins, *History of Kentucky,* 2 vols. (Covington, Kentucky 1874); *Louisville Daily Journal,* April 4, 1857.

PIPE ORGANS. After the CIVIL WAR, Louisville's industrial and commercial enterprises, including organ building, grew dramatically. Henry Pilcher's Sons, a firm that moved to Louisville from Chicago after that city's great fire of 1871, dominated the area's organ business until WORLD WAR II. For 122 years, Henry Pilcher and his descendants built Pilcher pipe organs, first in England and then in the United States. Established in Louisville in 1874, Henry Pilcher's Sons became known for instruments of exceptional quality. The company was named for English organ builder Henry Pilcher (1798–1880), who came to the United States in early 1832 and retired from the trade in 1858. In *Memorial History of Louisville* Henry Pilcher's Sons were praised for giving Louisville more fame at home and abroad than any other instrument maker. It noted that Pilcher's organ at the 1893 Chicago World's Fair Columbian Exposition earned the highest awards for outstanding completeness and modern improvements. The company continued building fine instruments until economic pressures and the war effort forced the business to close on June 30, 1944. It was bought by the M.P. Moller Co. of Hagerstown, Maryland.

Pilcher's largest organ, and one of Louisville's most famous instruments, is the huge organ in LOUISVILLE MEMORIAL AUDITORIUM, formerly known as the War Memorial Auditorium. The 5,288-pipe organ, Pilcher Opus 1454, was constructed and installed in 1929. Approximately two thousand Pilcher pipe organs were built for churches all over the United States. In 1942

Pilcher Organ in the sanctuary of Second Presbyterian Church, Broadway at Second Street, c. 1938.

more than one hundred religious institutions in Louisville used Pilcher organs.

Other notable large pipe organs include the instruments in the North Recital Hall at the University of Louisville School of Music; the Roman Catholic CATHEDRAL OF THE ASSUMPTION; and Caldwell Chapel, Louisville Presbyterian Seminary. These instruments were crafted by the Louisville firm of Steiner-Reck. Founded in 1957 by Phares L. Steiner in Cincinnati, Ohio, the firm moved to Louisville in 1962 and became an incorporated partnership when German-born Gottfried C. Reck joined as equal partner. As Steiner-Reck, the firm continues in business. The University of Louisville School of Music organ, with 3,298 pipes distributed over three manuals (keyboards) plus pedals, is the company's largest instrument.

Louisville's largest pipe organ is located in the Alumni Memorial Chapel of the SOUTHERN BAPTIST THEOLOGICAL SEMINARY. This four-manual organ of 113 ranks (sets of pipes) and over six thousand pipes was built by the Aeolian-Skinner Co., Boston, Massachusetts, as its Opus 1162A. Begun in the early 1950s, the organ was completed in 1963.

In the last quarter of the nineteenth century, the Louisville organ-building firm of August Prante & Sons built a number of exceptionally fine instruments for churches in the OHIO RIVER Valley region. August Frederick Prante (1844–1900) was born in the Westphalia district of Prussia. He first appeared in the Louisville city directory in 1866 as an organ builder working with his father, Joseph. August Prante's Louisville organs include instruments for St. Peter Evangelical Church, St. Joseph Catholic Church, and St. Boniface Catholic Church. Prante was completing the St. Boniface organ when he died on September 8, 1900, from a skull fracture suffered in a buggy accident. Each of these instruments has been subsequently rebuilt, retaining some of Prante's original pipe work. Both the St. Joseph and the St. Peter instruments retain Prante's casework and pipe facade. One of the four extant Prante organs, the organ built for the Catholic Church of St. Philip Neri, Louisville, is one of the area's finest examples of nineteenth-century tracker (mechanical action) organ building. Now relocated to Louisville's Holy Trinity Catholic Church, the instrument is in original condition.

Louisville's other noteworthy nineteenth-century instruments include the 1893 Koehnken & Grimm organ at BELLARMINE COLLEGE, the 1889 Louis Van Dinter organ in St. Frances of Rome Catholic Church, the 1898 J.H. & C.S. Odell & Co. organ in OKOLONA Baptist Church (originally built for the First PRESBYTERIAN CHURCH, NEW ALBANY, Indiana), and the 1867 William Evans organ in the chapel of CHRIST CHURCH UNITED METHODIST.

With its handsome organ case, complete with polychromed pipes and Latin inscriptions, the organ in St. Martin of Tours Catholic Church, Louisville, is the area's largest nineteenth-century pipe organ. The grand instrument was built in 1894 by the Detroit firm of Farrand & Votey as their opus 714. The builders utilized some pipes from previous instruments built for St. Martin's by Cincinnati organ builders Koehnken & Grimm in 1861 and 1876. The organ underwent various repairs and major changes, mainly in the 1940s when the original console was discarded. The instrument was thoroughly renovated and rebuilt, including a new nineteenth-century-style console, by Louisville's Miller Pipe Organ Co. in 1991.

St. Andrew's Episcopal Church, Louisville, houses the famous pipe organ built for the Temple of Religion at the 1939 World's Fair at Flushing, New York. John W. Hausserman Jr. of Briarcliff Manor, New York, persuaded G. Donald Harrison of Boston's Aeolian-Skinner Organ Co.; Walter Holtkamp, founder of Cleveland's Holtkamp Organ Co.; and famed organist Parvin Titus to collaborate on a design for a landmark organ. The organ was built by Aeolian-Skinner, installed at the World's Fair, and then moved to Hausserman's music room at Briarcliff, all at Hausserman's expense. In 1947 the organ was sold to St. Andrew's Episcopal Church, where it was installed by Louisville organ builder Sylvester E. Kohler, a former Pilcher employee who had established his own organ tuning and servicing business.

While Louisville no longer has any remaining THEATER PIPE ORGANS (the last surviving theater organ, a Wurlitzer installed in the FOURTH Street Loew's United Artists Theatre, was removed during renovations in the late 1970s and early 1980s when the theater became the Louisville Palace), one historic theater-style instrument remains. In 1932 the George Kilgen & Son Pipe Organ Co. of St. Louis, Missouri, contracted with WHAS radio to build a theater-style pipe organ for the station's broadcast studio at Third and Liberty Streets. After appointing Herbie Koch as station organist in 1933, WHAS initiated a series of additions to the organ. In July 1947 the organ was fitted with a new, lavishly equipped four-manual console, the largest ever built by Kilgen. The organ was moved to the station's new studios at Sixth and BROADWAY in late 1948 and installed in early 1949. In 1968 the organ was moved to its present location in the GARDENS OF LOUISVILLE. It contains over two thousand pipes in addition to a full complement of theater organ sounds such as harp, xylophone, drums, sleigh bells, orchestra bells, and triangle.

As of 1998 Steiner-Reck was Louisville's only firm engaged solely in the crafting of new pipe organs. The Miller Pipe Organ Co., founded by James E. Miller in 1976, is the area's largest pipe organ service firm, with clients throughout ten states. While serving as area representative for the Schantz Organ Co. of Orrville, Ohio, the company does extensive tuning, rebuilding, and new organ work. Similar organ-building and tuning work is carried out by Webber Pipe Organ Co., founded by Peter B. Webber.

See *Courier-Journal Magazine,* April 2, 1972; J. Stoddard Johnston, ed., *Memorial History of Louisville* (Chicago 1896)

Philip T. Hines Jr.

PIRTLE, ALFRED (b Louisville, March 25, 1837; d Louisville, February 2, 1926). Engineer, author, and historian. Born to Henry and Jane Ann (Rogers) Pirtle, Alfred Pirtle was trained as a civil engineer in local private schools. He left school in 1855 at age eighteen to join the engineering corps of the Lexington & Big Sandy Railroad Co., which was constructing a line between Lexington and Ashland. Within two years Pirtle had returned to Louisville and, after a brief position with the city's engineering department, joined the transportation department of the Louisville & Nashville Railroad Co.

At the outbreak of the CIVIL WAR in 1861, Pirtle joined the Union army. As a private, he took part in the battles of Stone's River, Chickamauga, and Chattanooga. He achieved the rank of first lieutenant by the time he was honorably discharged in 1864 for health reasons.

Pirtle entered the insurance business in Kansas City, Missouri, in 1868. After moving back to Louisville in 1874, he continued to work in the insurance field and was the first insurance agent for Trader's Life Insurance Co. in Louisville. He opened the Alfred Pirtle Fire Insurance Agency, which later became the firm of Pirtle & Weaver. At the time of his death, he was the senior partner at Pirtle, Weaver & Menefee, located on Jefferson between Fifth and Sixth Streets.

Aside from business, Pirtle had a keen interest in the history of Louisville. He wrote more than a dozen papers for the Filson Club, of which he was secretary from 1905 to 1917 and president from 1917 to 1923. He also penned *James Chenoweth* (1921) and *Where Louisville Started* (1921) and coauthored *The Union Regiment of Kentucky* (1897) with Thomas Speed. He was president of the Louisville Board of Fire Underwriters and the Louisville Salvage Corps and president emeritus of the First Unitarian Society of Louisville.

Pirtle married Fannie Alevia Nold; they had three children: Nanny, Henry, and Juliet. He is buried in CAVE HILL CEMETERY.

See J. Stoddard Johnston, ed., *Memorial History of Louisville* (Chicago 1896); Bess A. Ray, ed., *Biographical and Critical Materials Pertaining to Kentucky Authors* (Louisville 1941); *Courier-Journal*, Feb. 3, 1926.

PIRTLE, HENRY (b Washington County, Kentucky, November 5, 1798; d Louisville, March 28, 1880). Lawyer and politician. Born to the Reverend John and Amelia (Fitzpatrick) Pirtle, Henry studied in the local schools and under the tutelage of his father, a Methodist preacher. After Pirtle finished his early education, Judge JOHN ROWAN persuaded him to stay in his Bardstown home, Federal Hill, and study law. In 1819 Pirtle began his own law practice, which was based in Ohio County, Kentucky, but served clients throughout the area. Six years later, he moved to Louisville and opened an office; he was appointed a circuit court judge by Gov. Joseph Desha in 1826.

After resigning from his judgeship in 1832 in order to boost his income, Pirtle resumed his private practice in offices on Jefferson St. Three years later he opened an office on Walnut (Muhammad Ali Blvd.) between Sixth and Seventh Streets, with future U.S. attorney general JAMES SPEED. The long, often interrupted partnership led to a lifelong friendship between the two, and each man named a son after the other. Between 1840 and 1843, Pirtle served in the Kentucky Senate for two terms. In 1850 he was elected chancellor of the Louisville Chancery Court for a six-year term and returned to the position again in 1862.

Upon the formation of the UNIVERSITY OF LOUISVILLE law school in 1846, Pirtle became a professor and taught until 1873, when he was named professor emeritus. He also served as a university trustee for twenty years and as a director for the LOUISVILLE WATER CO.; he was one of the founders of the KENTUCKY HISTORICAL SOCIETY.

Pirtle married Elizabeth Gilbert in 1829. They had five children, although only two, John and Mary, survived. Pirtle is buried in CAVE HILL CEMETERY.

See *History of the Ohio Falls Cities and Their Counties* (Cleveland 1882); J. Stoddard Johnston, ed., *Memorial History of Louisville* (Chicago 1896).

PIRTLE, JAMES SPEED (b Louisville, November 8, 1840; d Louisville, September 25, 1917). Attorney and university president. James Pirtle was the son of William and Jane Ann (Rogers) Pirtle. After graduating from Male High School in 1859, James studied law. He received his degree from the law department of the UNIVERSITY OF LOUISVILLE in 1861 and entered into a partnership with John Speed. In 1873 Pirtle became a professor in the university's law department. He was made a trustee of the University of Louisville in 1880, sat on the board until 1915, and was its secretary for twelve years. From 1886 to 1905 Pirtle served as president of the University of Louisville. During his tenure there was greater attention to academic concerns, especially in the School of Medicine. New facilities were added, and admissions requirements were made more rigorous.

Pirtle, a partner in Pirtle, Trabue, Doolan & Cox and Pirtle & Caruth, sat as a special judge on the chancery court and served as attorney for the ILLINOIS CENTRAL RAILROAD (now Illinois Central Gulf). He was president of the Louisville Bar Association, a founder in 1878 and a charter member of the American Bar Association, and a founder in 1884 and a charter member of the FILSON CLUB HISTORICAL SOCIETY.

Pirtle married Emily Bartley on May 22, 1878; they had four children: Robert, William, Jane, and Emily. Pirtle died after a short illness and is buried in CAVE HILL CEMETERY.

See James S. Pirtle biographical files, University of Louisville; J. Stoddard Johnston, ed., *Memorial History of Louisville* (Chicago 1896).

Margaret L. Merrick

PITT, FELIX NEWTON (b Fairfield, Kentucky, February 18, 1894; d Louisville, March 15, 1971). Cleric and educator. Pitt's youth was spent in Nelson County, Kentucky, with his parents, Henry Washington and Sallie (Bertle) Pitt. As a young man devoted to the Roman Catholic faith, Pitt attended the St. Meinrad Seminary in Indiana from 1911 to 1915. Later he studied at the Catholic University in Washington, D.C., Notre Dame University, and St. Mary's Seminary in Baltimore, Maryland. While at St. Mary's he received an A.B. in 1916 and a master's degree in 1917. On July 17, 1920, Pitt was ordained by Bishop John T. McNicholas, O.P., in the chapel of the Dominican House of Studies in Washington.

During his first four years in the priesthood, Pitt served the rural churches around Bardstown, Finley, and Campbellsville, Kentucky. In December he moved to Louisville to serve as assistant at the CATHEDRAL OF THE ASSUMPTION.

In 1925 Bishop John A. Floersh named Pitt secretary and executive director of the Catholic Diocesan School Board. Over the next several years, he reorganized the board, which had been dormant. He standardized textbooks, set up institutes for the training of teachers, centralized all record-keeping, and instituted a supervisory team to oversee the actions of the board as well as the teachers. In 1927 he organized the League of Catholic Parent-Teacher Associations in Louisville and became its first president.

In September 1931 Pitt traveled to Switzerland, where he studied at the University of Fribourg and received his doctorate in philosophy in 1933. During the mid-1930s he led the Catholic Thought Association of Louisville and was named head of URSULINE COLLEGE's philosophy department in 1934. In the summer of 1936, Pitt took up residence at the Motherhouse and Academy of the Ursuline Sisters of Louisville, 3115 Lexington Rd., and became the institution's senior chaplain.

In 1947 Pitt was elected president of the Superintendents of the National Catholic Education Association. Two years later he was named monsignor and given the title of right reverend. He later became a charter member and a panelist for WHAS's pioneering ecumenical radio program, *The MORAL SIDE OF THE NEWS*, in 1952. Pitt was honored by WHAS radio in 1956 when, as a result of his work toward an integrated parochial school system, he was named Man of the Year. In 1961 he received the first honorary degree ever given by BELLARMINE COLLEGE and another from Ursuline College in 1964.

Pitt was also a civic-minded individual. He did much to help the youth of Louisville by instituting such programs as the Junior Great

Books Program. He was instrumental in the founding of the Ursuline-Pitt school for special needs children in 1949. That school, located at 4605 Poplar Level Rd., changed its name to Pitt Academy in 1993. He also was founder, secretary, and treasurer of Handicapped Children's Inc., and he established the Cerebral Palsy School of Louisville in 1950 with the support of the Louisville chapter of United Cerebral Palsy. He also served as a trustee and vice president of the LOUISVILLE FREE PUBLIC LIBRARY from 1943 until 1964. He wrote several articles and books on topics ranging from the advancement of education to the turmoil surrounding Europe in the early 1930s. Because of his prestigious reputation, Pitt was selected by the U.S. Departments of State and War in August 1946, to travel to Germany in order to evaluate its postwar education system.

Pitt retired in 1967 because of poor health and moved to Christopher East Nursing Home at 4200 Browns Ln., where he died. He is buried in the cemetery of the Sisters of Charity in Nazareth, Kentucky.

See Clyde Crews, *An American Holy Land: A History of the Archdiocese of Louisville* (Louisville 1987); *Courier-Journal,* May 25, 1967; March 17, 1971; *Louisville Times,* March 16, 1971.

PLANNING AND ZONING. During the late nineteenth and early twentieth centuries, many American cities adopted comprehensive land use plans and created regulatory tools such as subdivision control regulations, building restrictions, and zoning districts to implement them. These plans were designed to bring order and beauty to the city, to stabilize property values by preventing inappropriate mixtures of land use, to curb land speculation, and to guide long-term development in a rational, scientific manner.

The urban planning movement in Louisville was spearheaded by architect James C. Murphy, who in 1901 read a paper before the Louisville Engineers and Architects Club calling for a local arts commission. Seven years later he persuaded the club to appoint a city planning committee. Over the next two decades, he led a coalition of business and civic leaders in a campaign to obtain state enabling legislation that would allow Louisville to create a city planning commission and a city plan. In June 1927 Louisville's General Council acted on its own to create a city planning commission and enact a temporary zoning ordinance. The elected plan commission chairman was J.C. Murphy.

In January 1929 the commission hired Harland Bartholomew & Associates of St. Louis to prepare a comprehensive plan for Louisville and a fringe area extending 3 miles into unincorporated Jefferson County. The commission felt it necessary to zone this unincorporated area to facilitate the projected growth of the city's POPULATION and to meet commercial and transportation needs. Meanwhile, Murphy and his allies pursued enabling legislation, which was passed in March 1930. The city planning commission was reorganized under the terms of the new legislation, and again Murphy was elected chairman. Shortly thereafter the planning commission adopted a zoning ordinance that fixed residential, commercial, and industrial districts and established regulations to control the size, type, and height of buildings in each district. After numerous amendments, the BOARD OF ALDERMEN approved the ordinance in July 1931. In October 1930 the aldermen had approved land subdivision regulations. In October 1932, after all components had been completed and reviewed by the plan commission, the Board of Aldermen passed an ordinance adopting the city's first comprehensive plan.

Much of the comprehensive plan, especially the land subdivision regulations, had little immediate impact because at that time the GREAT DEPRESSION was nearly at its worst. From 1931 until mid-1936, virtually no residential subdivision activity occurred in Louisville. However, with the advent of President Roosevelt's New Deal in 1933, the planning commission took on a major role in planning federally financed slum clearance, PUBLIC HOUSING, and major PUBLIC WORKS projects. Home-building improved somewhat as recovery set in during 1936, but the subdivision regulations were poorly enforced. The result was premature speculative development along the edge of the city and its unincorporated fringe, much of which lacked adequate streets, sidewalks, utilities, and drainage. This problem led to a movement to extend planning controls to the county. In November 1942 the Board of Aldermen and the JEFFERSON COUNTY FISCAL COURT enacted legislation to create a Louisville and Jefferson County Planning and Zoning Commission. The following May the new commission adopted a zoning plan that applied to the unincorporated portions of the county.

The establishment of a countywide planning body brought stricter enforcement of subdivision regulations and required developers to be much more careful in their treatment of the landscape. The narrow lots typical of the central city were abandoned for larger lots that accommodated automobile driveways, attached garages, and larger side yard and setback requirements than had existed before. But the new approach did not end development problems. Within months after the new structure's adoption, local industrial leaders began complaining that the existing industrial zones did not provide sufficient land for large, modern industrial plants that required room to expand horizontally. And there was a need for zoning districts in the unincorporated county that would accommodate public land use, for example to build HOSPITALS, playgrounds, churches, and schools. There were intense controversies over requests for zoning changes and special-use permits.

By 1949 the postwar residential building boom produced a battle over subdivision regulations that pitted developers and builders against planners and others who were concerned about drainage, traffic congestion, sewage disposal, and construction quality. Such concerns were compounded by "wildcatting"—the sale of lots without approval of the planning and zoning commission because of a quirk in the wording of the state subdivision regulation law. The incipient urban sprawl contributed to a movement for a new comprehensive plan.

In 1954 the Planning and Zoning Commission again hired Harland Bartholomew & Associates to study long-term planning needs. In 1957 the consultant presented a new comprehensive plan, along with proposed new zoning ordinance and subdivision regulations. Adopted the following year, the new plan for the first time imposed the same set of subdivision design and zoning standards on both Louisville and the unincorporated portions of the county.

The Bartholomew Plan was an important advance, but by the mid-1960s it was clear that the new standards, which fostered low-density growth, had done little to stem the tide of urban sprawl. A planning commission study in 1966 revealed that the amount of land in residential use had more than doubled in the previous decade, jumping from 27,000 acres in 1956 to 57,000 acres in 1966, while population had increased only 17 percent. At the same time, more and more land along major radial streets such as Dixie Hwy., Preston Hwy., and Shelbyville Rd. was being converted to commercial use, particularly strip shopping centers. These concerns led to a movement for a new comprehensive plan, which was adopted in 1970. Prepared primarily by the planning commission staff, with assistance from various consultants, the new plan attempted to focus future development around significant activity centers or "nodes" located at major highway intersections. But the plan's primary feature was a detailed map that attempted to project what the future land use ought to be in any given area. During the 1970s the map often became the center of bitter fights between those who wanted development to follow the map to the most minute degree and those who believed the map should not be adhered to so rigidly that it became a straitjacket, preventing the community from taking advantage of opportunities that could not have been anticipated when the map was drawn up.

As a result of such conflicts, the Comprehensive Guided Growth and Redevelopment Plan for Louisville and Jefferson County was adopted in 1979. Instead of a detailed land-use plan map, its central components were a broad-ranging set of development guidelines and core graphics. The plan was designed to foster sensible, orderly growth while showing concern for older areas, making better use of existing resources, protecting the natural environment, encouraging compatibility among land uses, promoting opportunities for a variety of lifestyles, and balancing competing goals—for example, both improving air and water quality and encouraging economic development. The Guided Growth Plan fostered the flexibility that critics of the prior plan sought. But as the 1980s progressed, a growing number of residents argued that the plan was being interpreted so loosely as to eliminate any certainty in planning commission decisions on zoning, commercial development, and residential subdivision cases.

Dissatisfaction with the Guided Growth Plan culminated in 1993 with Cornerstone 2020, a new plan intended to be "broad enough and flexible enough to guide our development for the next twenty-five years." Funded jointly by city and county government and the Louisville Chamber of Commerce (later Greater Louisville Inc.), the development of Cornerstone 2020 brought together some two hundred citizens from throughout the metropolitan area who developed a vision of what the community should look like in 2020 and participated in committees dealing with livability, mobility, the marketplace, and community form issues. A major innovation from the standpoint of Louisville and Jefferson County's planning history was the replacement of traditional zoning districts with twelve distinct "form districts," each with its own set of guidelines to preserve the district's fundamental character while promoting harmonious growth and safety.

See Carl E. Kramer, "James C. Murphy and the Urban Planning Movement in Louisville," *Filson Club History Quarterly* 64 (July 1990): 317–59; George H. Yater, *Two Hundred Years at the Falls of the Ohio* (Louisville 1987).

Carl E. Kramer

PLASCHKE, PAUL A. (b Berlin, Germany, February 2, 1880; d New Albany, Indiana, February 12, 1954). Cartoonist, artist, and illustrator. Paul Plaschke was the son of Emil J. Plaschke and Augusta (Schnabel) Plaschke. The family came to the United States in 1884 and first settled in Hoboken, New Jersey.

Paul Plaschke studied engineering at the Stevens Institute in Hoboken. He received formal training in drawing at the Cooper Union Art School and the Art Students League in New York City. At the Art Students League, Plaschke studied with George B. Luks, the creator of the pioneer comic strip "The Yellow Kid." In 1898 he began working for the *New York World;* subsequently he moved to Louisville and worked as a cartoonist for the *Louisville Commercial* and the *Evening Post.*

Plaschke began PAINTING landscapes in 1905; he was entirely self-taught as a painter. His painting reflected the ideals of the art colony called the Hoosier School, based in Brown County, Indiana. Plaschke and others of the Hoosier School were heavily influenced by the impressionist movement and outdoor landscape painters of the late nineteenth century. He won awards for his work at the Richmond, Indiana, Art Association show of 1917; the Nashville, Tennessee, Art Association show of 1925; the Hoosier Salon of 1929 and 1934; the Louisville Art Association of 1932; and the Southern States Art League in 1936. His work is included in the collection of the J.B. SPEED ART MUSEUM.

Plaschke's greatest local renown came from the cartoons that he drew for local NEWSPAPERS. He served as cartoonist for Louisville's *Evening Post* and for the *LOUISVILLE TIMES,* the *Chicago Herald Examiner,* and the Sunday *COURIER-JOURNAL* from 1913 to 1949. He worked for the *Herald Examiner* and other Hearst newspapers until his retirement in 1949. Plaschke's most popular creation was a cartoon character named Monk who appeared in many of the artist's illustrations. He illustrated books, contributing to a volume of caricatures titled *Kentuckians as We See Them* (1905). His work was also displayed by the Vanderpoel Art Association of Chicago, an organization founded in 1915 as a memorial to the well-known Chicago artist John H. Vanderpoel. Plaschke's cartoons appeared in *Life, Puck, Judge,* and other magazines.

Plaschke was a member of the Association of Chicago Painters and Sculptors, the Society of Arts and Sciences in New York, the Hoosier Salon Society, and the Southern States Art League. In 1935 he was named outstanding artist of his community by the Society of Arts and Sciences. Plaschke also served on the Board of Governors for the J.B. Speed Art Museum and as a director of the Louisville Art Academy.

Paul Plaschke married Ophelia Bennett in Louisville on September 15, 1899. The couple had three sons: Emil, Harvey, and Albert, and made their home in New Albany. Plaschke is buried in CAVE HILL CEMETERY.

See Peter Hastings Falk, *Who Was Who in American Art* (Madison, Conn., 1985); Bettie M. Henry, *Biographical Extracts Relating to Prominent Artists of Louisville and Kentucky* (Louisville 1939); Mary Young Southard, *Who's Who in Kentucky 1936* (Louisville 1936).

Candace K. Perry

PLATO, SAMUEL M. (b Montgomery County, Alabama, 1882; d Louisville, May 13, 1957). Architect and contractor. Samuel M. Plato, one of the first African American building contractors and architectural designers, was the son of James and Katie (Hendricks) Plato. His father, who passed on his carpentry skills to his son, was a farmer who had apprenticed in carpentry under black artisan Samuel Carter, for whom the younger Plato was named. Samuel Plato as a youngster attended Mt. Meigs Training School near Waugh, Alabama. He spent a year of study in Winston-Salem, North Carolina, then enrolled at SIMMONS UNIVERSITY in Louisville in 1898. Plato took a teachers' training course and liberal arts courses, with plans to study law. While attending Simmons he took correspondence courses in ARCHITECTURE and carpentry from the International Correspondence School.

In 1902 Plato moved to Marion, Indiana, where he lived until sometime between 1919 and 1921. While in Marion, Plato formed a partnership with black building contractor Jasper Burden that lasted about ten years. Plato then moved to Louisville, where he practiced building design both independently and for a time with William L. Evans. At a time when few blacks were practicing architecture, Plato's contract to build a U.S. post office in Decatur, Alabama, was the first such contract awarded to a black. He built more than thirty-nine post offices at various locations throughout the United States. During the era of WORLD WAR II, he was one of the few blacks to be awarded contracts to build defense housing. He designed and built numerous residences, apartment houses, and office buildings, and several banks, as well as schools and churches, in Louisville and in Marion. He served as contractor for Westover, a subdivision developed between 1925 and 1947 in Louisville's West End. Among the buildings Plato is credited with designing are the Classical Revival–style Broadway Temple A.M.E. Church (1915) at Thirteenth and BROADWAY, the Lampton Street Baptist Church, and his own Tudor-style home (ca. 1929) on W Walnut St. (Muhammad Ali Blvd.).

Plato was twice married, first to a Marion native, Nettie Lusby. After her death, he married Elnora Davis Lucas. Plato is buried in the Louisville Cemetery.

See Kathrine Jourdan, "The Architecture of Samuel M. Plato," *Black History News and Notes* 37 (Aug. 1989): 4–7.

Joanne Weeter

PLATO, WILLIAM (b Prussia, 1831; d ?). Brass band leader, music teacher, and composer. Plato came to Louisville around 1852 and joined Sigismund Arbogast's popular Saxhorn Band. In 1854 he took over the band, and it became known as Plato's Saxhorn Band. It was in constant demand for parades, balls, and other events. Its members included CHRISTIAN HAUPT and Andrew Schneider, both of whom later led their own well-known brass bands. After 1858 Plato devoted his time to teaching and composing. His compositions included "Fourteen Years Ago" (1859), "Beautiful Eyes" (1860), "I and Olive Bell" (1860), and "Nannie Vane" (1860). He resided on Breckinridge St. between Floyd and Preston. During the 1870s he continued to teach and was an active participant in the Liederkranz Society. He apparently moved from Louisville in 1879, and his whereabouts after that date are unknown.

Cornelius Bogert

PLEASURE RIDGE PARK. Suburb in southwestern Jefferson County centered on the intersection of U.S. 60-31W (Dixie Hwy.), Greenwood Rd., and St. Andrews Church Rd. As early as 1831, stagecoach passengers traveling from Nashville to Louisville used the area along the old Salt River Turnpike (Dixie Hwy.) as a stopping point on their long journey. By the middle of the nineteenth century, several families had moved into the region to establish dairy farms and lumber production centers. St. Andrew's Church, completed in 1851 by FRENCH and German Catholics, who settled to the east of modern-day Dixie Hwy., was the area's first church. Although the POPULATION still had not grown significantly, an 1858 map branded the intersection of Greenwood Rd. and Dixie Hwy. as Painesville, apparently because of the large amount of land in the area owned by L.M. Paine.

In 1874 the Elizabethtown & Paducah Railroad (now the Paducah & Louisville) built a depot in the budding community. The railroad not only expedited the transportation of goods to Louisville markets but also brought summer visitors hoping to escape the urban heat. Visitors noticed that, after spending a day in the blazing sun, local workers headed to a steep wooded hill, part of the Muldraugh Ridge just east of the depot, for shaded relief. This quickly came to be known as Pleasure Ridge. It became the focal point of the burgeoning resort community, which named itself Pleasure Ridge Park in 1876 when the area's post office was opened. The TOURISM industry continued to flourish in the late 1800s and early 1900s, and the Paine family constructed an eighteen-room resort hotel, a store, and a distillery; in addition a dance hall opened, and an electric interurban line was built through the area from Louisville. By WORLD WAR I the number of vacationers journeying south to Pleasure Ridge Park began to decline.

The most substantial growth in the area occurred in the 1950s and 1960s because of the inexpensive land there, the ease of transportation into downtown via the Dixie Hwy., and the growth of FORT KNOX and Louisville. In 1984 the area successfully fought an annexation attempt by the city of SHIVELY.

An important landmark was the Waverly Hills Tuberculosis Sanitorium, a treatment center that opened in 1911 just south of Pleasure Ridge Park. The hospital opened initially with a capacity for forty bedridden patients; the number was expanded to four hundred in 1924. In 1961 the hospital's name was changed to the Waverly Hills Geriatrics Center, and the remaining tuberculosis patients were relocated to the HAZELWOOD Tuberculosis Sanitarium. The hospital was closed by the state in 1981 because of alleged patient neglect. It sat vacant until Louisville businessman Bob Alberhasky announced plans in 1996 to construct a 155-foot statue of Jesus Christ atop the building, with the possibility of transforming the old hospital into condominiums. His fund-raising attempt was unsuccessful, and the project was abandoned.

See *A Place in Time: The Story of Louisville's Neighborhoods* (Louisville 1989); Robert M. Rennick, *Kentucky Place Names* (Lexington 1984).

PLYMOUTH CONGREGATIONAL UNITED CHURCH OF CHRIST. Formed as a Methodist church in the 1870s, the church became Congregational in the early 1880s when a small group of dissidents with a taste for dignified church services switched their affiliation. The church changed its name from Congregation Methodist Church to Congregation Church and by 1884 to Congregational Plymouth Church. It had moved to its present location in the RUSSELL neighborhood at 1630 W Chestnut St. by 1893, when the Reverend EVERETT G. HARRIS arrived to be its pastor. The church developed a strong influential base during those years and grew to be a small but leading African American congregation dominated by black professionals and college graduates.

The national Congregational church subsidized Harris. A civic-minded man, Harris led the Plymouth Church for more than four decades. In 1910 he began planning the Plymouth Settlement House (later Plymouth Community Renewal Center) as an extension of his ministry. Between 1914 and 1917 he raised enough money from white supporters and the Welfare League to build a $20,000 structure.

During the nineteenth century there were few Congregational churches in the South because that church was associated with the antislavery movement before the CIVIL WAR and the black educational movement afterward. For many years Plymouth was the only Congregational church in the city and had no white members. LYMAN JOHNSON, a leading twentieth-century Louisville CIVIL RIGHTS leader, began attending Plymouth Church shortly after he moved to Louisville in 1930, remaining a member until his death in 1997.

See George C. Wright, *Life Behind a Veil* (Baton Rouge 1985); Wade Hall, *The Rest of the Dream: The Black Odyssey of Lyman Johnson* (Lexington 1988).

PNC. The history of PNC in Louisville is composed of two trails—the bank side and the trust side. On February 17, 1858, the General Assembly of Kentucky chartered the Merchants Deposit Bank, first located at the northeast corner of Bullitt and MAIN Streets. In 1863 its name was changed to Citizens Bank. The first president of Citizens Bank was W.B. Belknap, founder of the BELKNAP Hardware & Manufacturing Co. In 1874 Citizens Bank changed its charter to a national charter and its name to Citizens National Bank, continuing to do business at its original location.

On October 2, 1889, a second parent bank, Union National Bank, obtained a national charter. George W. Swearingen was its first president. Union National was originally located at the southeast corner of Sixth and Main Streets and later moved to Fifth and Jefferson in the Inter-Southern Life Insurance Company's building.

In 1919 Citizens National and Union National joined to become the Citizens Union National Bank. The merger was the result of sixteen years of effort by Gilmer S. Adams of Citizens and WILLIAM MARSHALL BULLITT of Union. Their efforts finally paid off when they discovered and reported that James B. Brown, president of the National Bank of Commerce, was attempting to bring Citizens as a third bank, along with the National Bank of Commerce and the American-Southern National Bank, into Kentucky National Bank. The consolidated Citizens Union National Bank headquarters were at the same location of Union National Bank.

Louisville Safety Vault Co., chartered in 1880, and Fidelity Trust Co., chartered in 1882, consolidated in 1884 and formed the Fidelity Trust & Safety Vault Co. The company's name was changed to Fidelity Trust Co. in 1903. Fidelity Trust was the first trust company west of the Allegheny Mountains. For a corporation such as Fidelity Trust to act as executor, guardian, trustee, or agent was new to the general public of Louisville.

In 1912 Columbia Trust Co. and Fidelity Trust Co. merged, forming the new Fidelity & Columbia Trust Co. Columbia Trust Co. had resulted from the joining of Mechanics Trust Co. (1889) and Columbia Finance & Trust Co. (1890) in 1906.

In 1944 Citizens Union National Bank and Fidelity & Columbia Trust Co. merged and formed Citizens Fidelity Bank & Trust Co. To allow for an even greater expansion of services, Citizens Fidelity reorganized and formed a bank holding company, Citizens Fidelity Corp., in 1974.

Citizens immediately took advantage of a new BANKING law in 1984 that allowed holding companies to expand across county lines and state lines through acquisition. In 1985 acquisitions of American Bank & Trust Co. in Lexington, Central Kentucky Bancorp in Hardin County, and Winchester Bancorp in Winchester were completed. In 1986 Citizens purchased Mercer County National Bank of Harrodsburg; Bank of OLDHAM COUNTY in LaGrange; First Midwest Bancorp in FLOYD COUNTY, INDIANA; and Indiana Southern Financial Corp. in CLARKSVILLE, INDIANA.

In February 1987 the first major takeover of a Louisville bank by an out-of-state group occurred when PNC Financial Corp. purchased Citizens Fidelity Corp. In January 1998 Citizens Fidelity Bank & Trust Co. was renamed PNC BANK NA. In 2000 the name was changed to PNC.

See Bart A. Brown, "Citizens Fidelity Bank and Trust Co.'s Hundredth Anniversary," *Filson Club History Quarterly* 32 (Oct. 1958): 329–35; Kentucky Bankers Association, "1858—Citizens Fidelity Bank and Trust Co., Louisville," *500th Edition of the Kentucky Bankers Magazine*, Feb. 1967.

James R. McCabe

POETRY. When the English poet Lord Byron

was including pioneer Daniel Boone in canto 8 of his epic poem *Don Juan,* the early settlers of Louisville had scant time for reading and little access to books. Poets were slow to grace the banks of the OHIO RIVER even after the founding of Louisville in 1778. Not until 1847, almost twenty years after Louisville was granted city status, did THEODORE O'HARA (1820–67) write "Bivouac of the Dead," a poem that was and still is revered throughout the world and is engraved at the gateway to Arlington National Cemetery.

In the early 1800s, only one other poem with a Louisville association gained notable international response. Written by Young E. Allison (1853–1932), "On Board the Derelict" is an extension of the first few lines of Robert Louis Stevenson's *Treasure Island.*

In contrast to the long-lasting fame of O'Hara and, to a more limited extent, Allison, Louisville's and Kentucky's most famous poet of the time, MADISON CAWEIN (1865–1914), was celebrated only briefly nationally and internationally. Although Cawein was widely applauded for the poems he prolifically composed about nature and imaginary creatures, his writing income was not sufficient to support his lifestyle. Cawein supplemented his funds by investing in the stock market and real estate. After suffering heavy financial losses in a market crash in 1912, Cawein and his family abandoned their home in St. James Ct. It has been pointed out that T.S. Eliot's poem *The Waste Land* is strikingly similar to Cawein's *Waste Land,* which was written eight years before Eliot's well-known poem. Suggestions of plagiarism have been bandied about that would undoubtedly have lightened Cawein's embittered outlook. Born in Louisville and a lifelong resident, Cawein can easily be declared a Louisville poet. A bust of Cawein at the LOUISVILLE FREE PUBLIC LIBRARY testifies to his abilities.

Having moved to Louisville with her parents in 1834, Amelia Coppuck Welby (1819–52) was admired by Edgar Allan Poe and listed in *Female Poets of America* (1856). She was published frequently in George Prentice's *LOUISVILLE JOURNAL.* As a publisher and as a writer of occasional verse, Prentice was a highly regarded leader in literary and intellectual matters. In 1868 his newspaper merged with the *LOUISVILLE COURIER,* which was already established as one of the best outlets for poetry in the West.

FORTUNATUS COSBY JR. (1801–71) served in several government posts while frequently contributing "charming poems and prose" to Louisville NEWSPAPERS. William Wallace Harney, whose native Kentucky parents moved with him to Louisville when he was five, succeeded in a career of education, law, and journalism, also finding time to contribute regularly to several poetry journals. Nelly (Marshall) McAfee, born in Louisville, the daughter of Gen. HUMPHREY MARSHALL, was of the mid-1800s "thee" and "thou" school of passion and pathos. She, too, was a regular contributor to magazines and newspapers that were willing recipients of poetic works.

Agnes Mitchell wrote "When the Cows Come Home," about 1870, not suspecting that her title would become a household phrase. JOSEPH SEAMON COTTER (1861–1949), Kentucky's first acclaimed African American poet, lived a long life in Louisville, where he wrote drama and fiction as well as verse. His career as a teacher and a principal in the Louisville school system spanned fifty years. His son, Joseph Seamon Cotter Jr. (1895–1919), established himself as a poet of promise before his early death.

CALE YOUNG RICE (1872–1943) published twenty-one volumes of verse and ten volumes of verse-drama. His love songs to his wife, the writer Alice (Hegan) Rice, are marked by local color. Among the varied works of Hortense (Flexner) King (1885–1973), there were three collections of verse that were favorably reviewed by such magazines as the *Saturday Review of Literature, Poetry,* and the *New Yorker.*

Among poets who wrote in the latter half of the nineteenth century and the early years of the 1900s, Langdon "Denver" Smith (1858–1908) is fondly remembered by many for his poem "Evolution, a Fantasy," a hauntingly tender poem of marital happiness. It was published among classified ads in a New York newspaper, as contemporary now as it was then, a classic of its genre. Smith began the poem to his wife in 1895 and worked on it for four years, more focused than his rhythmic lines might indicate when he wrote "Mindless we lived and mindless we loved, / And mindless at last we died."

The stream of verse, both good and bad, seems to have dried up in Louisville during the first half of the twentieth century. If there are records of Louisville poets and their work in that period, they have not yet reached the official ARCHIVES. There was a definite lull, a barren stretch such as individual poets occasionally lament in their own creative lives. Perhaps it was due to the GREAT DEPRESSION and anxieties over the approach of WORLD WAR II, which, when it came, took literary historians and poets among its fighting men. Later a few poems were found that had survived the war. Some never came to light. There were no magazines being offered solely for poetry. There were college and UNIVERSITY OF LOUISVILLE publications that solicited poems, short stories, and essays from students, but space was too limited to encourage outside writing.

Despite the lack of publishing outlets, a few poetic voices began to be heard in the 1960s: Leon Driskell (1932–94) professor of creative writing at University of Louisville was a literary leader; Roberta Scott Bunnell worked in BROADCASTING at WAVE and WKLO and wrote poems rivaling those of Dorothy Parker; Cora Lucas, married to a Louisville physician, lent a classicism to the scene; and Lee Pennington (1939–) came from Appalachia to be a Louisville resident of persuasive writing talents.

A journal devoted wholly to Kentucky poetry, the *Kentucky Poetry Review,* came into being in 1964, soon to be followed by other Kentucky poetry magazines in which the names of Louisville poets increasingly appeared. A renaissance had begun. Between 1960 and 2000, many Louisville poets became known for their outstanding poetry both throughout Kentucky and outside its borders. Some of them are Althea Parmenter, Ron Seitz, Ann Jonas, Leonore Wells Thomas, Prentice Baker, Sarah Gorham, Jeffrey Skinner, Dot Gibbs, Wade Hall, Jane Mayhall, Frederick Smock, Patricia Ramsey, Maureen Morehead, Helen Glover, Shirley Sotsky, and Henry Tim Chambers, whose delightful ballad "Where the Bush Is All Berries" was first seen in the anthology *Contemporary Kentucky Poetry 1967.*

See William S. Ward, A *Literary History of Kentucky* (Knoxville, Tenn. 1988); Lewis Collins and Richard H. Collins, *History of Kentucky* (Frankfort 1874, 1966); Sister Mary Carmel Browning, *Kentucky Authors* (Evansville Ind., 1968); Robert Ian Scott, "The *Waste Land* Eliot Didn't Write," *London Times Literary Supplement,* 1995; Judith Egerton, *A Way with Words* (Louisville 1997).

Joy Bale Boone

THE POINT. Former community in eastern Louisville along the OHIO RIVER opposite Towhead Island. Before city engineers rerouted the BEARGRASS CREEK channel in 1854, the creek and the river, which met downtown between Third and FOURTH Streets, formed a nearly two-mile-long, narrow, point-like peninsula, dubbed "The Point." Tradition holds that people began settling the peninsula in the early 1800s. The Beargrass Bridge crossed the creek one block north of MAIN St. at the foot of Second St. and led to both Preston's Landing, the long river shoreline where boats could dock, and to the woodlands, which provided a popular picnic spot. The lower half of the peninsula, which was defined as the area west of Campbell St., also contained coffeehouses, TAVERNS, grocers, and some residences, while shipyards, sawmills, and other businesses were located farther upstream. At the upper end of the peninsula, at least two large, elegant homes, such as the Paget or MANSION HOUSE, were erected. Several New Orleans families, hoping to escape the southern city's summer heat and EPIDEMICS, allegedly built homes on Fulton St., causing the area to be dubbed Frenchman's Row. The influence of the FRENCH visitors was also evidenced by the name of another residence, the French Garden.

After the city cut off Beargrass Creek, some two miles upstream, the lower creek bed was gradually filled in, erasing a recognizable portion of the peninsula. From this time on, the upper part of the peninsula became popularly known as The Point. However, many of the graceful homes in that area were either destroyed or carried away by recurrent flooding and were replaced with shanty boats, SHOTGUN COTTAGES,

Saw Mill on the Point. Drawing by Alexander Van Leshout.

and small industrial operations. After the FLOODS of 1937 and 1945, city officials declared the area unsafe for residential use and built Thruston Park on a portion of the old community. The waterfront was transformed into the Louisville Boat Harbor and an apartment and marina complex.

Aside from the Paget House, another landmark in the area is the HEIGOLD HOUSE facade. The house was originally constructed on Marion St. by German immigrant stonecutter Christian Heigold in the 1850s. The city moved the house's ornamental facade to River Rd. in 1953 after purchasing its former site for the expansion of the dump.

See *Louisville Times*, Oct. 24, 1970.

POISONED WEDDING. In April 1891 Henry M. Goodman, a member of the medical faculty at the University of Louisville School of Medicine, and a team of expert volunteers solved the mystery of several deaths that had occurred soon after the wedding of Fannie Belle Herr and Winfred Snook on April 15. Herr and Snook were married at the farm of her father in LYNDON, Kentucky, in the presence of about seventy-five friends and family members. Soon guests began feeling ill. More than sixty of them were stricken, and within two weeks six had died, including the groom. Panic followed as doctors treating the victims disagreed about the cause. Rumors claimed that the deaths were caused by arsenic poisoning.

A team from the UNIVERSITY OF LOUISVILLE, which included Professors H.A. Cottell, Turner Anderson, William Bailey, and James S. Chenoweth (class of 1889), gathered evidence at the MEDICAL SCHOOL laboratory, conducted autopsies, and tested the suspected food. Over a month later an inquest was held, complete with testimony from some suspected poisoners and several physicians. The unanimous report from the medical team was that the cause of the tragedy was bacterial contamination of the chicken salad, made with meat that had been cooked more than forty-eight hours before the celebration and stored in the broth at room temperature.

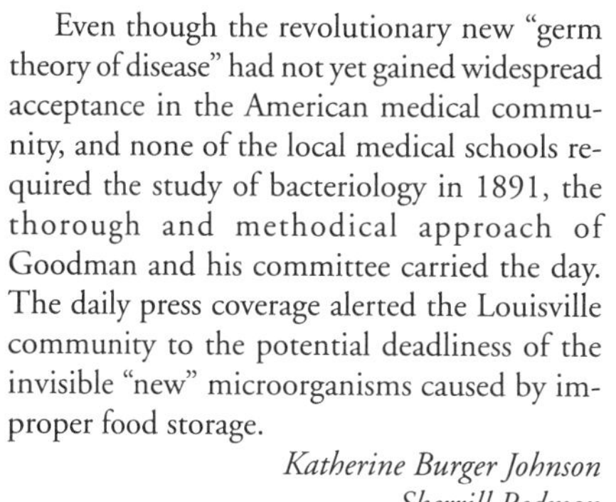

Even though the revolutionary new "germ theory of disease" had not yet gained widespread acceptance in the American medical community, and none of the local medical schools required the study of bacteriology in 1891, the thorough and methodical approach of Goodman and his committee carried the day. The daily press coverage alerted the Louisville community to the potential deadliness of the invisible "new" microorganisms caused by improper food storage.

Katherine Burger Johnson
Sherrill Redmon

PONTOON BRIDGE, FLOOD OF 1937. On January 21, 1937, in the midst of the worst OHIO RIVER flood ever to strike the Louisville metropolitan area, fire department mechanic Jake Britt reportedly proposed the construction of a pontoon bridge to link the dry HIGHLANDS with the city's inundated downtown. City officials initially viewed his suggestion as unnecessary; but as floodwaters continued to rise, two days later the idea was approved.

Placed in charge of the project was William S. Arrasmith, a local architect and a captain in the U.S. Army Reserves. Through the efforts of about three hundred volunteers, a bridge was constructed by laying planks on top of whiskey barrels taken from a local distillery. Cable from the waterlogged warehouses of the Belknap Hardware & Manufacturing Co. held the barrels together and anchored them to TELEPHONE poles. The 2,000-foot bridge was completed on January 26 and spanned BEARGRASS CREEK from Johnson and Jefferson Streets to the foot of Baxter Ave. It was lighted by lamps that were hung every 6 feet. Refugees from Louisville's

Magnolia Stock Farm, scene of a poisoned wedding.

Pontoon Bridge, Jefferson Street at Baxter, looking west during the flood of 1937.

flooded downtown crossed the bridge single file. Hundreds of people were assisted out of boats and onto the bridge and so walked out of the flooded area. After evacuation, they were loaded onto buses and trucks that took them to their destinations. Evacuees were not permitted to return to the downtown area without a military pass. When the water receded, the pontoon bridge was scrapped.

See *Courier-Journal and Louisville Times Flood Edition,* Jan. 27, 1937; *Courier-Journal Magazine,* Jan. 18, 1987.

POPE, HENRY CLAY (b Louisville, November 5, 1808; d Louisville, June 14, 1849). Publisher and soldier. The son of Col. Alexander Pope and Martha Miner "Patsy" Fontaine, Henry was the scion of an old and respected family. His grandfather, WILLIAM POPE, was one of Louisville's earliest settlers, and his father, a leading Louisville attorney, served in the Kentucky legislature. Not surprisingly, young Henry was educated for the legal profession. However, in 1844, he and his friend THEODORE O'HARA established a newspaper, the *Democratic Rally,* in Frankfort. The *Rally* vigorously supported James K. Polk in 1844 for the presidency, and both youthful editors afterward became the recipients of party patronage. Journeying to Washington in 1845, Pope and O'Hara obtained clerical positions in the Treasury Department.

Soon after the outbreak of the MEXICAN WAR, on May 27, 1846, Pope secured a commission as a captain of U.S. regulars. He commanded Company D of the Mounted Rifle Regiment during Gen. Winfield Scott's successful advance on Mexico City. The young Kentuckian later boasted in a letter to his mother, "I begin to think I am immortal, having been in eight severe battles & skirmishes without a scratch." He added sardonically, "I think I have killed 10 [of the enemy]" and now "have blood enough on my hands to satisfy the largest patriotism."

Unfortunately, in the aftermath of the campaign there was a clash with his superiors that ended his military career. Pope's hot temper, hard drinking, and reckless bravery made many enemies in his regiment. Charged with chronic drunkenness, he was tried and acquitted by a court-martial that convened in Mexico City on October 5, 1847. He alleged afterward that the same clique of officers who had engineered his court-martial tricked him into resigning his commission. Claiming that he was temporarily deranged as a result of illness at the time he signed the document, Pope made a desperate but futile attempt to withdraw his resignation. His resignation was accepted on December 31, 1847, and the humiliated Pope returned to Louisville in the spring of 1848 and resumed the practice of law. Pope bombarded Washington with lengthy, unsuccessful appeals for reinstatement to the army throughout the summer of 1848.

In 1849 word spread through the city that Dr. David W. Yandell, a member of the UNIVERSITY OF LOUISVILLE medical faculty, had been challenged to a duel by one Dudley M. Haydon. Pope was no stranger to the code of honor. He had participated in a colorful encounter on the streets of Louisville in 1833 and in the fall of 1848 narrowly avoided a duel with Matt Ward, who afterward gained notoriety for the 1854 slaying of a Louisville schoolteacher. Pope's only brother, William F., had been killed on the "field of honor" in 1831. However, in regard to the Yandell-Haydon dispute, Pope was among several prominent citizens who successfully brought about a reconciliation on June 11.

On the evening of the same day, Pope, his good friend John T. Gray, and two other gentlemen engaged in a friendly game of cards at the GALT HOUSE. Having drunk heavily, Pope exploded in a rage and threatened one of those present with a knife. Fearing for the life of his fellow player, Gray disarmed his friend. However, he soon found himself the target of Pope's loud and vicious personal attacks. When Pope loudly accused Gray of mistreating his own wife, the latter gave him a merciless beating.

Pope refused to overlook the incident when he sobered up the next morning and determined to save face by issuing a challenge. Both parties agreed to meet on Indiana soil on the morning of June 14. Armed with twelve-gauge shotguns, Gray's weapon of choice, the two antagonists fired at twenty paces. Pope fell mortally wounded and died before he reached the Kentucky shore. The stricken man in his last moments forgave his old friend; however, Gray was sharply criticized for his role in the affair and left the state for several years.

The public outcry over Pope's senseless death led many to advocate the inclusion of an antidueling provision during the 1849 state constitutional convention. Although that provision was voted down, those opposed to the code duello were able to obtain a revision of the old 1812 law. The revision required all state officials and attorneys, before taking office, to swear that they had never participated in a duel, and the 1891 Constitution included the provision. Pope's tragic death did much to bring the practice of dueling into disrepute in Kentucky.

See J. Winston Coleman, *Famous Kentucky Duels* (Lexington 1969); Nathaniel C. Hughes Jr. and Thomas C. Ware, *The Bivouac of the Dead: The Ordeal of Theodore O'Hara* (Knoxville 1998); Pope-Humphrey Family Papers, Filson Club Historical Society.

James M. Prichard

POPE, PATRICK HAMILTON (b Louisville, March 17, 1806; d Louisville, May 4, 1841). Lawyer and politician. The eldest son of WORDEN POPE, a prominent lawyer active in Louisville's political life, and his wife Elizabeth, in 1827 Patrick began his own law practice in the city. He soon became a popular and successful attorney. His law office was on the north side of Jefferson St. between Sixth and Seventh Streets, and his residence was on Sixth St. between Green (Liberty) and Walnut (Muhammad Ali Blvd.) Streets.

Pope was a Jacksonian Democrat, as was his father. With the aid of his politically prominent family, Pope mounted a successful campaign for the U.S. House of Representatives in the 1832 election. He defeated the talented Henry Crittenden for the Eighth District congressional seat by a majority of 600 votes. Pope served as the youngest member of the Twenty-third Congress from March 4, 1833, to March 3, 1835. In the 1834 congressional election, he was defeated by anti-Jackson Whig William J.

Graves of New Castle. Still deeply involved in Louisville politics, Pope then ran and was elected in 1836 to the Kentucky House of Representatives representing Jefferson County.

In 1827 he married Sarah L. Brown (1810–80), the daughter of James Brown, a wealthy farmer in Jefferson County, and his wife, Urith. Patrick and Sarah Pope had eight children, twins Elizabeth Thruston and Urith Lawrence, James Brown, Mary Emiline, Ellen E., Worden, Mary Anna, and Alfred Thruston.

Pope was buried in the Brown Cemetery on Browns Ln. in Louisville and reinterred in CAVE HILL CEMETERY on April 20, 1880.

See *History of the Ohio Falls Cities and Their Counties* (Cleveland 1882); *The Biographical Encyclopedia of Kentucky of the Dead and Living Men of the Nineteenth Century* (Cincinnati 1878); *Biographical Directory of the American Congress, 1774–1961* (Washington, D.C. 1961).

Becky Loechle
Rick Loechle

POPE, WILLIAM (b Westmoreland County, Virginia, ca. 1750; d Louisville, 1826). City pioneer and official. William Pope's parents were Worden (1700–1749) and Hester (Netherton) Pope, and he was a third cousin of George Washington. He served as a captain in the Fauquier County, Virginia, militia in 1778. Between 1779-80 Pope and his brother Benjamin and sister, Jane Helm, and their families moved to the FALLS OF THE OHIO. In the lottery of April 24, 1779, Benjamin Pope drew half-acre lot no. 80 on the southwest corner of Main and Ninth Streets. The Pope families went to work at once clearing the lot and built one of the first residences in what is now the city of Louisville.

In 1780 the Virginia legislature and Gov. THOMAS JEFFERSON appointed William Pope as a trustee of the newly formed town of Louisville. He was commissioned lieutenant colonel of the Jefferson County militia in 1781 and resigned as colonel in 1788. In 1783 he surveyed the town, laying out the plan for the streets of Louisville on a tract of 1,000 acres. In 1785 he represented Jefferson County in the Virginia legislature. He was a magistrate, justice of the peace, commissioner of Oyer and Terminer Court, and high sheriff of Jefferson County. Recorded in the name of William Pope from 1783–89 were Virginia land grants of 16,730 acres, and from 1780–99 Kentucky land grants of 33,500 acres.

In 1765 Pope married Penelope Edwards (1748–1825), daughter of Haden (Hayden) (1716–1805) and Penelope (Sanford) Edwards (1723–1808) of Fauquier County. Pope County, Arkansas, was named for their son Gov. John Pope (1770–1845); and Pope County, Illinois, was named for their son U.S. judge Nathaniel Pope (1784–1850). Their other children were Penelope Oldham Churchill (1769–1821), Jane Field (1772–1852), William Junior (1775–1844), Colonel Alexander (1781–1826), Elizabeth Trotter Hall (ca. 1787–1850), and Hester Edwards.

See J. Stoddard Johnston, ed., *Memorial History of Louisville* (Chicago 1896); Judge Charles Kerr, ed., *History of Kentucky* (Chicago 1922); Richard H. Collins, *History of Kentucky* (Covington, Ky. 1882); Will of William Pope, Jefferson Co., Ky., Will Book 2, 340.

James Houston Barr III

POPE, WORDEN (b Pope's Creek, Westmoreland County, Virginia, 1776; d Louisville, April 20, 1838). County clerk and politician. Worden Pope's parents were Benjamin and Behethland (Foote) Pope. The family came to the FALLS OF THE OHIO in 1779 and later settled in SHEPHERDSVILLE. Here Benjamin Pope established a ferry across Salt River, which Worden later operated.

Worden attended Mr. Priestley's school in Bardstown until 1792 and worked as a clerk in Grayson's law office in Bardstown in 1793–94; in 1794 he worked as a clerk in the office of Jefferson County clerk STEPHEN ORMSBY at Captain Breckinridge's on BEARGRASS CREEK, where the office was kept. In 1795 it was moved to Louisville, where Pope lived the rest of his life. According to family tradition, the move to Jefferson County was prompted by Ormsby, who, during his travels on the court circuit, took note of the apt young ferryman and procured the clerk's position for him. Pope also served as Louisville postmaster in 1797–98. In 1796 Pope, a Jeffersonian Republican, was named clerk by members of the county court. Shortly before, he had been awarded the clerkship of the circuit court, with Stephen Ormsby as judge.

Since the COURTS co-opted new members, the majority remained of the Democratic persuasion and kept Pope in the lucrative posts for forty years, even after Louisville and Jefferson County had, by 1830, tended to become Whig strongholds. Pope had become an important figure in local politics by 1815. A strong backer of Andrew Jackson for the presidency in 1828, Pope brought Louisville and Jefferson County into the Jackson camp, winning 60 percent of the vote for him.

Extremely competent in his duties, Pope also saw that relatives were given posts on the court system staff. He had married Elizabeth Thruston in 1804, and they were parents of thirteen children, at least nine of them boys.

The Pope dominance so annoyed George D. Prentice, editor of the Whig *LOUISVILLE JOURNAL*, that the family appeared frequently in his paper in a critical light. Prentice once expressed tongue-in-cheek "regret" that the Popes were "not prolific enough to furnish a great lazy, lubberly boy for every office . . . throughout the state." The Whigs attempted to oust the Popes by trying to make Louisville a separate county in 1835, but the proposal failed in the state legislature. Pope's tenure in the clerk's office is the longest ever in Jefferson County.

Pope resigned the circuit court clerkship in 1834 and was succeeded by a son, Edmund Pendleton Pope, also an attorney, who died after being stricken while arguing a case in court. Another son, Curran, succeeded him as clerk of the county court upon his death. WARDEN POPE was noted for his charities, and his funeral procession was reported by the *Louisville Public Advertiser* to have been nearly a mile long. Even Prentice's *Louisville Journal* called the outpouring a "wonderful and just tribute." Pope was no doubt buried in the old Western Cemetery on Jefferson St., but whether the body was later moved is unknown.

See J. Stoddard Johnston, ed., *Memorial History of Louisville,* vol. 2 (Chicago 1896); *History of the Ohio Falls Cities and Their Counties* (Cleveland 1882); Robert M. Ireland, *The County Courts in Antebellum Kentucky* (Lexington 1972); *William Pope et al. vs Thomas Stansbury et al.,* Bullitt County Circuit Court Records, Robert E. McDowell Collection, vol. 7:417, Filson Club Historical Society; Jefferson County Minute Order Books, vol. 18:15; *Louisville Public Advertiser*, Jan. 13, 1835.

George H. Yater

POPE LICK MONSTER. A half-man, half-goat creature has been rumored to live under the Norfolk Southern Railroad trestle across Pope Lick Creek and S Pope Lick Rd. near FISHERVILLE in eastern Jefferson County. Stories of encounters have abounded for more than three generations and have served as the mood-setter for multiple romantic encounters between teenage boys and girls, many involving alcohol and tests of "bravery" that require climbing onto the trestle. According to the legend, the creature hypnotizes trespassers into venturing out onto the trestle, thus luring them to their death before an oncoming train. Several people have been killed either on the trestle or by falling from it, and many more have been injured.

A 1988 film, *The Legend of the Pope Lick Monster,* by local independent producer Ron Schildknecht visualizes the fictional story of teens who venture into the goat-man's domain. The sixteen-minute film recounts the experience of growing up in 1980s Louisville. In it, three teens—brother and sister Ben and Katie and their friend Clancy—acquire a six-pack of beer and head to Pope Lick Rd. intent on testing their bravery. Ben ventures onto the trestle to drink the ceremonial beer and is hypnotized by the goat-man, only to be shaken sensible by the rumble of an oncoming train. Ben is forced to cling by his fingertips to the edge of the trestle as the train whistles by, then safely climbs back up. The goat-man has struck again.

James D. Kendall

POPLAR LEVEL. Neighborhood in eastern Louisville bounded by Eastern Pkwy. to the north, Poplar Level Rd. to the west, Watterson

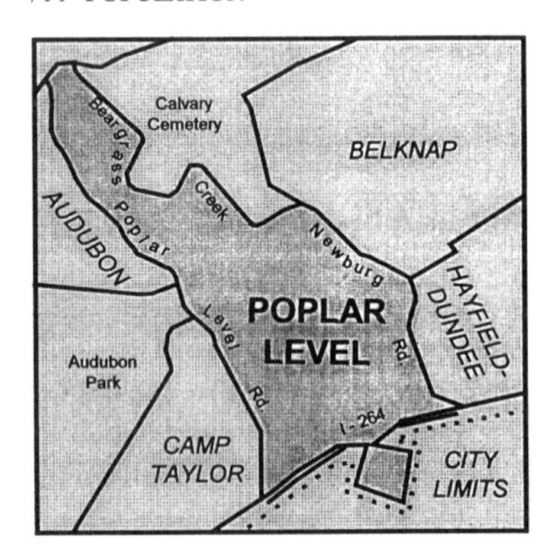

Expwy. to the south, and Newburg Rd. to the east. A mixed residential and commercial neighborhood, the area includes the Louisville Zoological Garden, JOE CREASON Park, the Louisville Tennis Center, the GERMANTOWN BASEBALL field, Norton Audubon Hospital, Calvary Cemetery, Louisville Cemetery, and ST. XAVIER HIGH SCHOOL. It also encompasses the Caritas Peace Center, formerly known as Our Lady of Peace Hospital, a sanitorium founded by the Sisters of Charity of Nazareth in 1913 that moved to its present location in 1951. In 1991 the Little Sisters of the Poor, a Roman Catholic charitable and religious order, opened a new facility for its NURSING home on Audubon Plaza Dr. The monastery of Carmelite Sisters is located on Newburg Rd.

POPULATION. About 1 million people live in the seven-county Louisville METROPOLITAN STATISTICAL AREA (MSA). Estimates for 1998 put the population at 999,000, and forecasts indicate a total of 1,009,000 in 2000. Two in every three residents (672,000, or 67 percent) of the Louisville MSA live in Jefferson County, Kentucky, including 255,000 inhabitants of the city of Louisville. Another 104,000 (10 percent) live in the Kentucky counties of Bullitt and Oldham, with the remainder (223,000, or 22 percent) in the Indiana counties of Clark, Floyd, Harrison, and Scott.

Louisville achieved its current population through a pattern of steady, sometimes rapid, growth (see table 1). With the exception of the 1980s, when the metropolitan population declined by 5,000 (0.5 percent), the number of people enumerated in each census year has been greater, often much greater, than that counted the decade before. The population of the seven-county area grew by 15 percent or more in fifteen of the twenty decades prior to 1990. Current indicators show moderate growth in the 1990s, with gains averaging less than 1 percent per year since 1990.

Overall metropolitan growth has occurred in the Louisville MSA in recent decades despite declines in population within the city of Louisville. The city reached its largest population total, 391,000 residents, in 1960. That number has declined in every subsequent census. By

Population of Counties Included in the Current Louisville Metropolitan Statistical Area (1790–1998)

County	*1790*	*1800*	*1810*	*1820*	*1830*
Kentucky					
Bullitt	-	3,542	4,311	5,831	5,652
Jefferson	4,765	8,754	13,399	20,766	23,979
Oldham	-	-	-	-	9,588
Indiana					
Clark	-	-	5,670	8,709	10,686
Floyd	-	-	-	2,776	6,361
Harrison	-	-	3,595	7,875	10,273
Scott	-	-	-	2,334	3,092

County	*1840*	*1850*	*1860*	*1870*	*1880*
Kentucky					
Bullitt	6,334	6,774	7,289	7,781	8,521
Jefferson	36,346	59,831	89,404	118,953	146,010
Oldham	7,380	7,629	7,283	9,027	7,667
Indiana					
Clark	14,595	15,828	20,502	24,770	28,610
Floyd	9,454	14,875	20,183	23,300	24,590
Harrison	12,459	15,286	18,521	19,913	21,326
Scott	4,242	5,885	7,303	7,873	8,343

County	*1890*	*1900*	*1910*	*1920*	*1930*
Kentucky					
Bullitt	8,291	9,602	9,487	9,328	8,868
Jefferson	188,598	232,549	262,920	286,369	355,350
Oldham	6,754	7,078	7,248	7,689	7,402
Indiana					
Clark	30,259	31,835	30,260	29,381	30,764
Floyd	29,458	30,118	30,293	30,661	34,655
Harrison	20,786	21,702	20,232	18,656	17,254
Scott	7,833	8,307	8,323	7,424	6,664

County	*1940*	*1950*	*1960*	*1970*	*1980*
Kentucky					
Bullitt	9,511	11,349	15,726	26,090	43,346
Jefferson	385,392	484,615	610,947	695,055	685,004
Oldham	10,716	11,018	13,388	14,687	27,795
Indiana					
Clark	31,020	48,330	62,795	75,876	88,838
Floyd	35,061	43,955	51,397	55,622	61,169
Harrison	17,106	17,858	19,207	20,423	27,276
Scott	8,978	11,519	14,643	17,144	20,422

County	*1990*	*1998*
Kentucky		
Bullitt	47,567	59,304
Jefferson	664,937	672,104
Oldham	33,263	44,395
Indiana		
Clark	87,777	93,805
Floyd	64,404	71,990
Harrison	29,890	34,730
Scott	20,991	22,939

Population and rank of the City of Louisville (1790–1998)

Year	*Population*	*Rank*	*Year*	*Population*	*Rank*
1790	200	Fifteenth	1900	204,731	Eighteenth
1800	359	Nineteenth	1910	223,928	Twenty-fourth
1810	1,357	Twenty-fourth	1920	234,891	Twenty-ninth
1820	4,012	Seventeenth	1930	307,745	Twenty-fourth
1830	10,341	Fourteenth	1940	319,077	Twenty-fifth
1840	21,210	Sixteenth	1950	369,129	Thirtieth
1850	43,194	Fourteenth	1960	390,639	Thirty-first
1860	68,033	Twelfth	1970	361,706	Thirty-third
1870	100,753	Fourteenth	1980	298,451	Forty-ninth
1880	123,758	Sixteenth	1990	269,157	Fifty-eighth
1890	161,129	Twentieth	1998	255,045	Sixty-fourth

1998 the city had one-third fewer residents than it had four decades before. But because growth continued in other parts of Jefferson County and the rest of the metropolitan area, the Louisville MSA grew 27 percent between 1960 and 1998.

After World War II, population growth rates were particularly dramatic in many outlying parts of the MSA. From 1960 to 1998, for example, Bullitt County grew by 277 percent, Oldham County by 232 percent, and Harrison County by 81 percent. Within Jefferson County, new cities emerged in previously rural areas (Hurstbourne, developed after 1960, had 4,420 inhabitants by 1990 and 4,715 in 1998), and many older communities expanded rapidly (e.g., Jeffersontown's population increased from 3,431 in 1960 to 25,678 in 1998).

In addition to Louisville and Jeffersontown, other cities in the Louisville MSA with more than 10,000 population are (1998 estimates): St. Matthews (16,583) and Shively (16,608) in Kentucky and Clarksville (19,688), Jeffersonville (26,018), and New Albany (38,265) in Indiana.

Louisville and Jefferson County have the largest populations of any city and county in Kentucky. Overall, 6 percent of the state's population reside in the city of Louisville, 17 percent (including the Louisville population) in Jefferson County. Bullitt, Jefferson, and Oldham Counties together are home to 20 percent of Kentucky's total population of 3.9 million and to more than 40 percent of the commonwealth's metropolitan population of 1.9 million.

Louisville has maintained its position as the largest city in Kentucky since 1830, but its national ranking has declined significantly in the last century and a half. In 1860 Louisville was the twelfth-largest city in the nation; by 1900 it ranked eighteenth in size, and by 1998 sixty-fourth. Among all metropolitan areas, the Louisville MSA ranked forty-eighth nationally in 1997.

Most early residents of Louisville were migrants who had moved westward from more populated areas along the Atlantic coast. In addition, in the decades prior to the Civil War, significant numbers of immigrants from northern and western Europe settled in Louisville. By 1850 17 percent of Louisville's population were natives of German-speaking areas of Europe, and another 7 percent were from Ireland. African Americans, some free (28 percent) but most slave (72 percent), were also a sizable part of pre–Civil War Louisville, totaling more than 6,800, or 10 percent, of the city's population in 1860.

Subsequent immigrant streams to the United States from eastern and southern Europe and, more recently, from Asia and Latin America, have largely bypassed Louisville. The 1990 census found that only about 1 percent of the current metropolitan population is foreign-born. Almost all residents of the Louisville MSA are white, non-Hispanic (85 percent in 1998) or African American (13 percent). Of the remainder, the largest groups are Asian and Pacific Islanders (0.8 percent of the 1998 MSA population) and persons of Hispanic origin (0.8 percent). The black population in the seven-county metropolitan area is disproportionately located in Jefferson County. Of the 128,000 African Americans in the Louisville MSA, 117,000 (92 percent) live in Jefferson County. African Americans comprise around a third of the city of Louisville's population.

Many residents of the Louisville MSA trace their family origins to the British Isles and other parts of northern and western Europe. Among the largest ancestry groups are German, listed in 1990 as over 300,000 inhabitants; Irish, 200,000; English, 140,000; and African American, 125,000. Around 100,000 residents simply listed "United States" or "American" as their sole ancestry in response to the 1990 census question.

Most Louisville residents were either born in the area or moved to it from nearby; in 1990 three-fourths (74 percent) of all residents in the Louisville MSA lived in the same state in which they were born. Among residents five years old and over in 1990, 57 percent resided in the same house or apartment where they had lived five years before, and another 33 percent had switched residences but remained within the Louisville MSA. In short, only 10 percent of the 1990 metropolitan Louisville population age five and older had lived outside the MSA in 1985.

Other characteristics of the metropolitan Louisville population (1990 figures) include more female (52 percent) than male (48 percent) residents; a median age of 33 years (25 percent are age 17 and under; 62 percent are 18–64; and 13 percent are 65 years or older); and an average household size of 2.5 persons. In a recent year (1997), the birth rate was 13.5 per 1,000 population, and the death rate was 9.7 per 1,000.

In the Louisville MSA population age 25 and over in 1990, 7 percent had a professional or graduate degree, 11 percent had a college degree, 24 percent had attended some college, 32 percent had graduated from high school, and 26 percent had completed schooling without receiving a high school diploma. Median household income for 1995 in the Louisville MSA ranged from a high of $52,475 in Oldham County to $29,416 in Scott County. Other values, in descending order, were Bullitt County, $39,618; Floyd County, $36,732; Harrison County, $35,520; Jefferson County, $34,863; and Clark County, $34,049. Poverty rates in 1995 were highest in Jefferson County (14.4 percent of all persons lived in poverty), Scott County (14.0 percent), and Bullitt County (10.1 percent). In the other four counties, the percentage of persons living in poverty was 9.6 in Floyd, 9.5 percent in Clark, 9.0 percent in Harrison, and 5.9 percent in Oldham.

Official projections for Kentucky and Indiana counties forecast moderate population increases for the Louisville MSA in the next few decades. By 2010 the Louisville metropolitan area is expected to have more than 1,039,000 residents, and 1,051,000 residents by 2020.

See U.S. Bureau of the Census, *County and City Data Book 1994* (Washington, D.C., 1995); U.S. Bureau of the Census, *Statistical Abstract of the United States 1998,* 118th ed. (Washington, D.C., 1999); U.S. Bureau of the Census, Internet Web site for population statistics, <www.census.gov>, 1997; George C. Wright, *Life behind a Veil* (Baton Rouge 1985).

John P. Marcum Jr.

PORTER, ARTHUR D. (b Bowling Green, Kentucky, July 4, 1877; d Louisville, February 16, 1942). Funeral director. Porter came to Louisville as a young adult to attend Central High School. Following graduation, he moved to Cincinnati to train as an embalmer. He returned to Louisville and worked for local funeral homes until 1908, when he opened his own business on Fifteenth St. Over time Porter's business grew to be known as one of the best-managed black-owned establishments in the city. Business was not the only area in which he excelled, for Porter was known as an important leader in Louisville's African American community, gaining a reputation as a "race man" who was deeply concerned about the injustices that African Americans suffered and was committed to bringing about change.

He attempted to maintain friendly relations with the city's older black leaders, but he let it be known that they did not speak for him. Porter's status in the black community reached its peak when he became the mayoral candidate for the newly formed Lincoln Independent Party in 1921. Though he received only 274 votes, the campaign was seen as a success. The Independent-Lincoln Party was a sign that change was long past due, and the Republican Party later admitted spending a considerable sum of money to ensure an overwhelming defeat of the newly formed party. W.E.B. Du Bois and the NAACP applauded the campaign and claimed that the 274 votes reported were a mere tenth of the total votes cast for Porter. The rest were allegedly dumped into the Ohio River or simply not counted at the polls. After the election Porter went back to operating his funeral home. He was survived by his wife, Imogene, and four children: Arthur Jr., Woodford R., Ferda Burden, and Clara Porter. He is buried at Louisville Memorial Gardens. A.D. Porter & Sons was still owned and operated by the Porter family in the late 1990s.

See George C. Wright, *Life Behind a Veil* (Baton Rouge 1985).

PORTER, JAMES D. (b Portsmouth, Ohio, 1810; d Shippingport, Kentucky, April 25, 1859). Tavern keeper. Jim Porter, also known as the Kentucky Giant, moved to Shippingport

Portland Department Store.

with his parents in 1811. Considered small for his age as a youth, Porter worked as a jockey at the Elm Tree Garden racetrack. At about the age of seventeen Porter's rapid growth began, and it was said that he once grew an entire inch in one week. By the time he reached his final height, at about the age of thirty, the 300-pound Porter measured 7 feet, 8 inches tall. That, as his grave marker would later note, was an inch shorter than what he claimed. Porter's towering frame led Charles Dickens, who met the "Giant" in 1842, to note that Porter looked like a lighthouse amongst lamp-posts. Porter, who generally shied away from public attention, did tour in 1836–37 with dwarfs in a production based on *Gulliver's Travels*. However, he declined subsequent offers to exhibit himself, even refusing P.T. Barnum, who wished to display Porter in his circus.

As a young man, Porter worked both as a cooper and a hack driver, driving public carriages along the Portland and Louisville Turnpike. In 1836 he opened a tavern in Shippingport near the locks of the Portland Canal. Porter's tavern flourished early on because of the number of river travelers and traders it attracted. In 1848 he was able to open an even larger establishment on Front St. in Shippingport, complete with specially designed furniture built to seat Porter himself comfortably. However, as river navigation began to lose ground to rail transport in the early 1850s, Porter's business declined.

When Porter, who never married, died from heart disease, no coffin could be found large enough to accommodate him, so a special 9-foot-long casket was constructed. He is buried at Cave Hill Cemetery. Among Porter's famous personal belongings were his 4-foot spiral shaped cane, his 8-foot rifle, and a 5-foot sword. In later years a Louisville restaurant bore his name.

See Samuel W. Thomas, ed., *Views of Louisville since 1766* (Louisville 1971); *Cave Hill Cemetery, A Pictorial Guide and Its History* (Louisville 1985); Billy Reed, *Famous Kentuckians: A Collection of Bicentennial Columns from Courier Journal* (Louisville 1977).

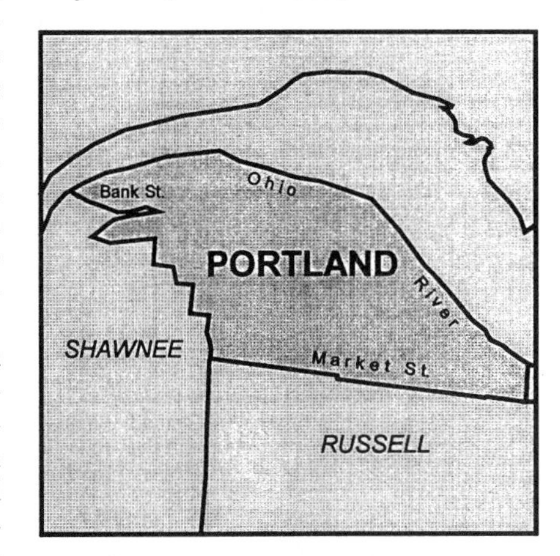

PORTLAND. Now a neighborhood west of downtown Louisville bordered by Tenth St. to the east, the Ohio River to the north, Market St. to the south, and Interstate 264 to the west. Portland developed in the early nineteenth century, along with Louisville and Shippingport to the east. Gen. William Lytle of Cincinnati, surveyor general of the Northwest Territory, sent his agent, Joshua G. Barclay, and a surveyor, Alexander Ralston, to lay out the town of Portland in 1811 on part of 3,000 acres of land that Lytle had bought from Henry Clay and Fortunatus Cosby. The first commercial buildings were built in 1812, and the town soon included a wharf, a warehouse, taverns, foundries, and shipyards at the river's edge. Capt. Henry M. Shreve bought one of the 5-acre lots, called country seats, and took over Lytle's ferry from Portland to New Albany, Indiana.

In 1817 Lytle sold lots in an "enlargement," extending the boundaries of Portland to Thirteenth St. on the east and Fortieth St. on the west. Lytle expected to use the proceeds to further his ambitious dream of building a canal to take river traffic around the Falls of the Ohio, but economic conditions in the panic of 1819 forced him to abandon his plans. He sold out to Judge John Rowan of Bardstown and the Bank of the United States. Starting in 1820, Portland real estate was divided into smaller and smaller lots, making it possible for working-class families to buy homesites.

Many early settlers came to Portland from France soon after the beginning of the nineteenth century. Charles Maquaire arrived in Shippingport about 1835 and later moved to Portland, where he and Paul Villier established the St. Charles Hotel. Father Stephen T. Badin, the first Roman Catholic priest ordained in America, often stayed at the Maquaire home and celebrated Mass there. Portland's most famous personality, Jim Porter, also moved to the town from Shippingport. Porter, known as the Kentucky Giant, ran taverns in both communities and later served as a Louisville councilman representing Portland. Squire Jacob Earick, whose house still stood in 2000, was the town's first magistrate. The town also attracted numerous Irish immigrants in the 1850s who came to the United States as a result of the potato famine. Many of the Irish settlers worked on the canal and the railroads.

When the Louisville and Portland Canal was completed in 1830, there was no longer a need to unload all boats before passing through the Falls. Four years later, the Kentucky legislature chartered the town of Portland. Lexington businessmen, eager for access to a river port below the Falls of the Ohio, planned to lay track for the Lexington & Ohio Railroad (L&O) from Lexington to Portland's wharf. However, Louisville businessmen wanted the railroad to terminate at Louisville in order to retain the profitable transfer business around the Falls. In a compromise, Portland agreed to be annexed in 1837, and Louisville agreed to lay track along Main St. as part of a railroad linking the two towns' wharves. In 1842, angered because the railroad failed to connect directly to either wharf, Portlanders demanded and won independence. Ten years later, however, the citizens voted to become part of Louisville once again. The wharf and warehouses in Portland gradually became empty after the Portland Canal was deepened and widened in 1871 to accommodate larger boats.

Local landmarks include the Notre Dame du Port (Church of Our Lady), completed in 1841 as the city's third Catholic church, and the U.S. Marine Hospital, opened in 1852. The hospital was designed in the office of federal architect Robert Mills, and in 1998, designated as a National Historic Landmark.

Since the day of settlement, FLOODS have been destructive to the area. The 1937 and 1945 floods drove many families from the Portland neighborhood, as the entire area became inundated. A flood wall, which displaced more than 140 homes, was begun in 1948 and completed in 1957, and the building of Interstate 64 pushed Portland away from the riverbank. In 1967 Portland lost its political identity when it was divided among three aldermanic WARDS. The Portland Museum spotlights the waterfront and the neighborhood's tie to the river. Many large historic homes testify to the day when this was an important river port city, though the wharf is now hardly discernible or buried under silt outside the flood wall. Nevertheless, Portland retains much of its nineteenth-century river town heritage.

See Judy Munro-Leighton, Nathalie Andrews, Bill Munroe-Leighton, *Changes at the Falls: Witnesses and Workers* (Louisville 1982); *A Place in Time: The Story of Louisville's Neighborhoods* (Louisville 1989); *Church of Our Lady: Centenary of the Parish* (Louisville 1939).

Nathalie Taft Andrews

PORTLAND MUSEUM. Located at 2308 Portland Ave. in the 1852 mansion of William Skene, the Portland Museum exhibits and collects artifacts relating to the PORTLAND neighborhood and publishes educational materials. Teachers at Theodore Roosevelt Elementary School at 222 N Seventeenth St. founded the Portland Museum in 1978 as a classroom project, using the community as its own resource. The teachers, recognizing the need for local history materials to use in their teaching, created stories, classroom activities, and exhibits based on community resources. Their concept of a museum-in-the-schools won two National Endowment for the Humanities (NEH) elementary education awards.

As the museum developed into a stand-alone, community-based institution, it won additional NEH support for exhibit development. In 1980 the Jefferson County BOARD OF EDUCATION closed Roosevelt School but allowed the Portland Museum to take up residence in a portable classroom outside the empty school. In 1981 the J. Graham Brown School invited the museum to move into the building it shared with Ahrens High School. There the museum stayed until it purchased Beech Grove, the 1852 home of the Skene family. In 1983 the museum installed its core exhibit, "Portland: The Land, the River and the People." In 1995 the museum acquired the Squire Jacob Earick property (ca. 1811) on Thirty-fourth St. from the Portland Development Organization.

Nathalie Taft Andrews

PORTLAND UNITED METHODIST CENTER. The Portland United Methodist Center is at 1831 Baird St., just west of downtown. The United Methodist Church has had a mission in PORTLAND since 1853, but the present one was begun in November 1956 by Richard and Mary Catherine Sluyter and was called the Sunshine Mission. It was at the corner of Eighteenth and Baird Streets. The Sluyters, who established their first mission in the early 1950s in a poverty-ridden area near the OHIO RIVER called THE POINT, moved to Portland and started the Sunshine Mission by preaching outdoors to small groups of neighborhood children.

The atrium of the Post Office and Custom House on Fourth at Chestnut, decorated for the 1900 conclave of the Knights Templar.

In January 1957 the mission moved into a house at 1839 Baird St., holding worship services and Sunday school meetings. In 1958 the SHAWNEE Methodist Church started to provide service workers, and in 1959 the United Methodist Church officially began to support the mission. During the early 1960s it expanded, purchasing the shotgun homes on Baird where it remained until the early 1990s. In 1965 Trinity Temple Methodist Church took over responsibility for operating the mission. Over the years the Sluyters remained active in the mission and the center.

In 1991 the Portland-area service agency changed its name from the Baird Street Mission to the Portland United Methodist Center to reflect the relationship with its primary sponsor. Before the change the Baird Street Mission was primarily a soup kitchen and a provider of youth and religious services. After the name change, the center expanded to include a mission church; a Sunday school; and recreation, counseling, and tutoring for children and families. More than twenty local United Methodist churches sponsored activities and contributed volunteer workers to staff center programs.

During that year efforts began to build a larger facility that could serve the Portland community with a full-time urban ministry with expanded staff and services. A new $900,000 all-purpose facility was dedicated on October 12, 1997; it included a chapel and worship space, an after-school community center, and a recreation area.

See *Courier-Journal*, Nov. 20, 1991; July 1, 1996; Oct. 8, 1997.

POST OFFICES. The study of a state or a county's post offices has long engaged the attention and efforts of postal historians. From lists of offices furnished by the U.S. Postal Service or the National Archives, historians have sought locations, histories, and name derivations. Old maps, county histories, local NEWSPAPERS, land records, and personal interviews have provided most of the necessary data. But the systematic and comprehensive study of an area's post offices is not easy. Aside from the obvious lack of available information on many offices, there is the problem of deciding how to locate particular offices.

The customary practice is to consider a post office as a single place, and that is how it appears on a map or in a gazetteer. But over 80 percent of Kentucky's seventy-eight hundred–plus offices occupied more than one site during their existence. Since placing each site of each office on a map would yield an impossibly congested map, mapmakers have most often settled on one site for each one, usually the office's longest-held or most recent location. Of course, when a site change involved a move of

Highland Park Post Office, on Park Blvd. at Ottawa in 1936.

more than several miles, and especially when there was an interruption in service or a change in name, the office would be shown in more than one place.

Like many other features of American history, post office site changes can be politically explained. Until the middle of the twentieth century, postmasters were generally political appointees whose positions were dependent on their partisan adherences. Thus, after a presidential election, many Kentucky offices would have new postmasters. Since rural offices were then usually in the postmaster's store or home, each change in postmaster would result in a change in location.

Learning the derivation of a post office's name is also a difficult task. Because few of the premier postmasters, who were usually allowed to name their new offices, left written records explaining their choices, it is seldom possible to accurately determine why particular names were given. From examinations of post office names throughout the state, we know that over half of Kentucky's post offices bore the names of local or area people. Others were named for a stream on or near their first location or for some other aspect of the local GEOGRAPHY, for a distant place or a famous nonlocal person of the time, or for the ongoing economic or social activities of the area's residents. But why a particular name was chosen rather than some other name, equally appropriate, may never be known.

Many post office names were not those originally intended for them, and some offices bore a different name from that of the community they served. Postal rules had long proscribed name duplication in a state. By 1900, in Kentucky as elsewhere, all the common names were already taken, so desperate postmasters would accept name proposals from outsiders, who seldom revealed the reasons for, or the meanings of, their suggestions.

Historians have challenged the popular belief that community names, and especially the names of post offices, are fairly permanently fixed. In Kentucky at least one-fourth of all post offices experienced name changes. Some of these were reestablished offices whose original names had been assumed by other offices elsewhere in the state. In other cases, it was because a name was perceived to be inappropriate that it was replaced by another name. The names derived from persons or places known to or admired by the namers but having little to do with the place itself or of no significance to later residents were often changed. So were names associated with abandoned establishments such as stage stops, landings, mills, or RAILROAD STATIONS. Names were also changed in response to alterations in the character or the appearance of the place or to commemorate some important event that had occurred there after the original naming and had given the place a new significance. Some changes were made simply to improve the place's public image.

In addition, several hundred Kentucky post office names had minor, inadvertent spelling changes. Others, following the standards of name simplification prescribed in the 1890s by the U.S. Board on Geographic Names, were divested of superfluous letters or words (a terminal *h* or "City") or had two or more words combined into one.

Nineteen of Jefferson County's sixty-nine independent post offices were within Louisville's city limits as the city expanded. Yet, except for Masonic Home, the county's most recently established office (1934), each was set up to serve an area not yet included in Louisville. At least two-thirds of the county's offices served definable communities with concentrated POPULATIONS and, with a few exceptions, took their names from them. Most of the other offices were established in rural areas around which communities later grew up, adopting the office names. Nearly all of the rural offices were connected with at least a store, a stage stop, a river landing, or, in later years, a railroad station.

Rural Free Delivery, begun in 1896, and the advent of improved roads, which made larger towns and their services more accessible to rural families, led to the closing of many of Jefferson County's smaller post offices within the first two decades of the twentieth century. Nineteen offices were closed in the first decade alone, eleven of them in only two years, 1902 and 1903. Only seven Jefferson County post offices (Louisville, PROSPECT, GLENVIEW, FAIRDALE, HARRODS CREEK, FISHERVILLE, and Eastwood) were still in operation in the late 1990s. A number of county offices—those serving incorporated or relatively large unincorporated communities—were replaced only late in the twentieth century by branches of the Louisville office, and they usually retained the old post office names. A branch or station, however, has generally not been an independent post office. It is established to provide services for a neighborhood or rural area. An example is the Baxter Station located in the HIGHLANDS neighborhood.

Twenty offices were named for local or county residents (Bishop, Bossdale, BUECHEL, Clark, Eastwood, Edwards, Fisherville, Gagel, HIKES POINT, Hoertz, Howesburgh, Keller's Tavern, Malott, Neville, O'Bannon, Routt, (misspelled by post office as Rout) SHIVELY, Thixton, Tucker, and WORTHINGTON). Louisville honored a famous foreigner, King Louis XVI, for aiding the American Revolutionary cause. Nine names had geographical or locational references (BEECHMONT, CRESCENT HILL, Cross Roads, FAIRDALE, Lakeland, Middletown, OKOLONA, PARKLAND, and VALLEY STATION).

Distant places (Saxony and Palatka) gave rise to two post office names; fifteen were given the names of area features (eight streams—Cedar Creek, Falls of Harrod, FERN CREEK, Fish Pools, Floyd's Fork, Goose Creek, Harrods Creek, and Long Run; a city—SOUTH LOUISVILLE; a pioneer station—LYNDON; a farm—Glenview; a street—Prestonia; a church—ST. MATTHEWS; an institution—Masonic Home; and a military base—CAMP TAYLOR.

Economic and social activities contributed to three more office names (PLEASURE RIDGE PARK, Salina, and Shippingport). JEFFERSONTOWN, of course, was named for the county. Two offices (HIGHLAND PARK and KOSMOSDALE) were named for the business firms that had established the communities. One (Newburgh) served a newly founded community. ANCHORAGE's name was symbolic. Three offices had more than one possible name derivation: CLIFTON's name either had a geographic refer-

United States Post Office and Custom House, Fourth and Guthrie Streets, c. 1906.

ence or came from a Jefferson County family, Avoca's name may have had a literary reference or may have come from a place in New York with a literary source, and PROSPECT's name was either descriptive or symbolic.

The origins of nine post office names have never been determined (Albemarle, Fairmount, Lochland, Meadow Lawn, Mechanicsville, Minoma, Orell, Smyrna, and Warwick Villa). Three Jefferson County post offices (Albemarle, Keller's Tavern, and Neville) have never been precisely located. Another unlocated office, which was to be named Mitchell, was authorized in 1899, but its order was rescinded the following year, and it never opened.

The names of ten post offices were not those originally proposed for them. In several cases the preferred names (e.g., Parksville, replaced by Edwards; Minnoma replaced by Prestonia; and Springdale, replaced by Summit) were already in use by other Kentucky post offices.

Following is a list of Louisville and Jefferson County post offices with their dates of establishment and closing, name changes, and the dates some offices became Louisville branches.

Louisville Post Offices (1795–present)
Shippingport, 1819; transferred to Portland in 1839; closed in 1870
Edwards', 1865–72
Fair Grounds, 1877; name changed to Crescent Hill in 1881; became a Louisville branch in 1903
Doup's Point, 1879; name changed to Saxony in 1891; closed in 1896
Hikes Point, 1879; name changed to Hikes in 1895; closed in 1902
Sax, 1883–87; reestablished as South Louisville in 1888; closed in 1894
Minoma, 1886–92
Parkland, 1886–94
Clifton, 1887–97
Palatka, 1888–91
Bossdale, 1891–96
Highland Park, 1891–1913
Albemarle, 1895–95
Beechmont, 1897–1906
Prestonia, 1899–1902
Gagel, 1901–2
Camp Taylor, 1922–46
Masonic Home, 1934

Jefferson County Post Offices
Middletown, before November 1803; became a Louisville branch in 1968
Jeffersontown, 1816; became a Louisville branch in 1966
Long Run, 1828–1931
Currey's, 1833; name changed to Fisherville in 1847; still active
Salina, 1834–65
Neville, 1836–37
Keller's Tavern, 1838–38
Newburgh, 1839–50; reestablished in 1864; closed again in 1878; reestablished as Newburg in 1894; closed in 1902
Snow Hill, 1847; name changed to Hays' Spring in 1850; name changed to Fairmount in 1862; closed in 1902
Lynnford, 1849; name changed to St. Matthews in 1851; became a Louisville branch in 1931
Williamson, 1850; name changed to O'Bannon in 1859; closed in 1964
Cross Roads, 1850–54; reestablished in 1874; closed again in 1879
Lacona, 1850–54; name changed to Pleasure Ridge Park in 1876; closed in 1903; reestablished in 1948; became a Louisville branch in 1964
Fern Creek, 1851; became a Louisville branch in 1966
Grassy Pond, 1854; name changed to River View in 1860; relocated and name changed to Kosmosdale in 1905; became a Louisville branch in 1966
Fish Pools, 1854–56
Cedar Creek, 1856–62
Falls of Harrod, 1856–64
Deposit, 1857; relocated and name changed to South Park in 1889; relocated and name changed to Coral Ridge in 1926; relocated and name changed to Fairdale in 1955; still active
Hobbs Station, 1865; name changed to Anchorage in 1872; became a Louisville branch in 1965
Orell, 1865–1909
Worthington, 1870–1907
Summit, 1870–74; reestablished in 1892 as Goose Creek; closed in 1902
Lyndon, 1871; became a Louisville branch in 1963
Floyd's Fork, 1871–88
Taylor's Station, 1872; name changed to Eastwood in 1881; still active
Eden, 1873; name changed to Avoca in 1896; closed in 1929
Valley Station, 1874; became a Louisville branch in 1967
Lochland, 1874–1903
Harrods Creek, 1875–present
Howesburgh, 1878–88
Smyrna, 1881–1902
Malott, 1882–1907
Buechel, 1883; became a Louisville branch in 1954
Wilhoyte, 1886; name changed to Prospect one month after establishment; still active
Asylum, 1887; name changed to Lakeland in 1888; closed in 1963
Okolona, 1889; became a Louisville branch in 1955
Clark's Station, 1890; name changed to Clark Station in 1892; name changed to Clark in 1894; closed in 1933
Hoertz, 1890–1903
Warwick Villa, 1893–98
Glenview, 1893–present
Meadow Lawn, 1893–1907
Bishop, 1894–1903
Rout, 1895–1907
Shively, 1897; became a Louisville branch in 1949
Tucker, 1897–1907
Thixton, 1900–1902
Mechanicsville, 1901–2
Waverly Hills, 1930–61

See Robert M. Rennick, *Kentucky Place Names* (Lexington 1984); Robert M. Rennick, *Kentucky's Salt River Valley: A Survey of the Post Offices of the Greater Louisville* Area (Lake Grove, Ore., 1997); U.S. Post Office Department, "Site Location Reports—Jefferson County, Kentucky, from 1866 to 1950," Record Group M1126, National Archives, Washington, D.C.

Robert M. Rennick

PRATHER, THOMAS (b Frederick County, Maryland, December 2, 1770; d Louisville, February 3, 1823). Merchant. Born to Thomas Sprigg and Jeanette (Smiley) Prather Jr., young Prather migrated to Louisville and had opened a store on MAIN St. by the mid-1790s. On one of his many purchasing trips to Philadelphia, Prather encountered John J. Jacob of Hampshire County, Virginia, who was on his way west in search of opportunity. Prather invited Jacob to Louisville, and the two became partners in the merchandising firm of Prather & Jacob. Their relationship was further solidified when Jacob married Prather's sister-in-law.

Prather's house, located in the middle of the block encompassed by Third, Fourth, Green (Liberty), and Walnut (Muhammad Ali Blvd.) Streets, was originally owned by Judge FORTUNATUS COSBY. The property contained the Cosby family's cemetery and a large orchard. After becoming one of the state's first millionaires, Prather established Louisville's first incorporated bank, a branch of the BANK OF KENTUCKY, at Fifth and Main Streets on January 1, 1812. He sat as its president until he angrily resigned the post when the directors suspended specie payments during the War of 1812 with Great Britain. Prather was known throughout the city for his charitable and civic endeavors such as the donation of a major part of the land for the City Hospital. In recognition of this and other acts, a major thoroughfare, Dunkirk Road, was renamed Prather St. (BROADWAY).

Prather married Matilda Fontaine, daughter of AARON FONTAINE, on February 12, 1800; they had six children: James Smiley, William, Mary Jane, Matilda, Maria Julia, and Catherine Cornelia. Thomas Prather was buried in the family cemetery in Prather Square, but his body was later moved to CAVE HILL CEMETERY.

See Ernest Jackson Prather, *Thomas Prather, 1604–1666, Descendants and Allied Kin*

(Georgetown, Ky., 1994); J. Stoddard Johnston, ed., *Memorial History of Louisville* (Chicago 1896).

PREHISTORIC EARTHWORKS. Prehistoric earthworks were once common features across the eastern United States. When colonizing Europeans in the sixteenth and seventeenth centuries first encountered the mounds, they believed them to have been constructed by a mysterious race of people they called the Moundbuilders. It was universally believed that the Native American tribes had vanquished the Moundbuilders, because it was not thought possible that the "savage" and "uncivilized" natives were capable of the degree of social organization and creativity required to construct the massive earthworks or make the artifacts contained within them. It has now been demonstrated archeologically that the mounds were indeed built by the ancestors of the American Indians.

Earthen mounds and monumental constructions are attributable to several of the later prehistoric cultures in the eastern United States from approximately 1000 B.C. through a.d. 1700. Early Woodland Period (1000 B.C.– A.D. 200) Adena peoples built conical mounds to house the dead. The succeeding Middle Woodland Period (200–500) Hopewellian culture continued this practice and also built large earthworks in geometric or animal effigy shapes. Although the precise functions of the mounds are not known, they are generally believed to be ceremonial or sociopolitical in nature; others may have served as fortifications. The later Mississippian Period (1000–1700) culture built pyramidal, flat-topped mounds that served as platforms for temples or high-status dwellings.

Numerous mounds within the OHIO RIVER Valley have been professionally investigated and preserved. It has been commonly thought that such earthworks were absent at the FALLS OF THE OHIO RIVER at what is now Louisville. This is because most of the mounds south of the Falls were destroyed early in the history of the city, long before professional interest was stimulated in this area. As elevated and dry features on the landscape, the mounds were leveled during the early nineteenth century to fill in the many ponds and low-lying marshes of the flood plain in downtown Louisville. Fortunately, a few early historical accounts have survived and provide some limited information on the nature and locations of some mounds.

The naturalist Constantine Rafinesque wrote of four ancient earthworks and one monument in Jefferson County on the Ohio near Louisville. Unfortunately, he provided no further information regarding the location or contents of these mounds. Richard H. Collins's 1874 history of the state relates that mounds or "tumuli" around Louisville were fairly numerous. Many were opened by the curious, and the earth was hauled away. In most of these, there were only some human and animal bones. Though some contained but one human skeleton, others held the remains of twenty or more. Collins thought it very probable that the former were designed as the mausoleums of chiefs or distinguished persons and the latter for those of the community.

A few mounds have been recorded in somewhat more detail. J. Stoddard Johnston's 1896 *Memorial History of Louisville* describes a large mound, 60 feet in diameter, that was located at what is now Fifth and Main Streets. The Main St. Mound was excavated by EVAN WILLIAMS in 1802 when Fifth St. was opened from Main to the river. The mound provided fill dirt for the construction. REUBEN DURRETT's 1893 *Centenary of Louisville* reported that this mound was significant in the lot numbering of the young city. The mound, an apparent and easily recognized early landmark, was situated on a tract that became Lot 1.

Durrett also described the Gwathmey, or Grayson, Mound. An early prestigious Louisville landmark, the Gwathmey house was built atop a large prehistoric mound. The earthwork was reportedly 15 feet in height and was located on Sixth St. near Walnut St. (Muhammad Ali Blvd.). This mound was excavated by Frederick W. Grayson, a later owner, to fill the nearby Grayson's Pond in 1821. Artifacts continued to be found by later residents. According to reports, the mound yielded stone axes, arrowheads, pipes, pottery, and "war clubs." A newspaper article from 1926 provides a description of the 5-acre tract of land on which the Gwathmey-Grayson house was built. The tract ran from Cedar to Walnut St. and from Center to Seventh St. The article states that the property included two mounds, both containing human burials. It further relates that "when, in 1821, Mr. Grayson, exercising his prerogative as lord of the manse, began to fill in the lake with earth taken from the mounds, there arose protest, long and loud, but it availed the protestants naught" ("Gwalthmey [*sic*] Home, Over Century Old, Crowns Indian Mound on Sixth Street," *Herald-Post,* May 2, 1926). In 1849 St. Paul's Church was built on Sixth St. near Walnut over a portion of one of the mounds. By 1926 one mound had been completely destroyed, and remnants of the other remained beneath the Grayson house. The location of one other mound is also recorded. On Fifth St., between Walnut and Chestnut Streets, the residence of a Judge Nichols stood on a mound that was reportedly man-made.

Additional mound sites have been identified along the Ohio River flood plain within a 100-mile radius of the Falls. Locally, mounds have been reported from the areas of Hunting Creek and HARRODS CREEK. A massive mound was once present in Meade County, and mounds have been documented along the Salt River in SPENCER COUNTY. Mounds are also known from Floyd and Clark Counties in Indiana, including the large Mississippian-era Prather Mound located in southern Clark County. That is one of the very few mounds in the region that has been professionally examined. The occurrence of mounds was not restricted to the flood plain. A large mound group was reported to exist as late as 1932 near the present site of the city of JEFFERSONTOWN on BEARGRASS CREEK. Another mound is located nearby on Beargrass, in the area of the OXMOOR Farm. Although the age of most of the earthworks around the Falls of the Ohio cannot now be determined, since they have been destroyed, the fact that some were associated with stone-box CEMETERIES suggests that at least several date to the late prehistoric Mississippian culture that flourished in the area from A.D. 1000 to 1450.

See Donald E. Janzen, "Archaeological Investigations in Louisville and Vicinity: A Historical Sketch," *Filson Club History Quarterly* 46 (Oct. 1972): 305–21; James B. Griffin, "Late Prehistory of the Ohio Valley," in *Handbook of North American Indians,* vol. 15 (Washington, D.C., 1978), 547–59; Bennett H. Young, *The Prehistoric Men of Kentucky* (Louisville 1910); *History of the Ohio Falls Cities and Their Counties* (Cleveland 1882); Jon Muller, *Archaeology of the Lower Ohio River Valley* (New York 1986); J. Stoddard Johnston, ed., *Memorial History of Louisville* (Chicago 1896); Reuben T. Durrett, *The Centenary of Louisville* (Louisville 1893); Richard H. Collins, *History of Kentucky* (Frankfort, rev 1966).

Anne Tobbe Bader

PREHISTORIC INHABITANTS. The first people to come to the FALLS OF THE OHIO were nomadic Paleo-Indian hunters who followed herd mammals into Kentucky at the close of the Wisconsin glacial period about 13,000 B.C. Small mobile bands of Paleo-Indians lived in temporary shelters. Their hunting equipment featured a unique fluted form of projectile points and large, keeled scrapers that were thick and resembled the keel of a boat. These Clovis and Cumberland points are found throughout Kentucky. Little is known about the distinction between the peoples who produced these two types of fluted points. They used spears tipped with compound darts to kill the massive herd animals that formed the staple of their diet. They hunted tundra and coniferous forest animals such as mammoths, mastodons, bison, horses (horses were later reintroduced by the Europeans), peccaries, giant ground sloths, and other now-extinct animals. They also hunted elk, white-tailed deer, and beavers. They supplemented their diets by gathering wild plants and nuts. Their clothes were sewn leather.

By 8000 B.C. the region was warming, as the last of the glaciers retreated. With the northward advance of deciduous forests and the extinction of the large postglacial herds, efficient seasonal exploitation of the forest became the means by which people lived. This period, known as the Archaic, is divided into Early Archaic (8000–5000 B.C.), Middle Archaic (5000–

3000 B.C.), and Late Archaic (3000–1000 B.C.).

Site types seasonally occupied by Archaic peoples include rock shelters, cave entrances, open sites, and shell mounds. The Archaic peoples moved in a seasonal cycle, exploiting area resources of deer, fowl, fish, shellfish, and plants through hunting, fishing, and gathering. Late Archaic people began to domesticate local plants. Food was cooked in watertight baskets using heated rocks.

Tools and weapons reflect the diversity of Archaic subsistence and technology. Projectile points, scrapers, and drills are found with ground-stone axes, hammerstones, and spear-thrower weights. The intensive bone industry included making fishhooks, spear-thrower hooks, awls, and engraved pins. Artifacts made of copper, marine shell ornaments, and other items made from nonnative materials indicate an extensive trade network in the Southeast by the Late Archaic Period.

Archaic bands were large, with small groups dispersing to acquire food and chert for arrowheads. The structures they built were not permanent. Burials occurred within the camp by tightly flexing the bodies and placing them in old storage pits, hearths, or refuse heaps (middens). Somewhat inconsistent with this treatment of the dead is the inclusion of grave goods such as bracelets, necklaces, pins, rings, beads, gorgets, and ear plugs, made from exotic materials. Human remains have been found with wounds and with projectiles embedded in the bone. Ceremonialism is also indicated in the burial of dogs in direct association with human burials.

There are numerous archeological sites located in the Louisville area that show evidence of past human activity. One example is the Hornung shell mound in southwest Jefferson County, which contains a Late Archaic component. Inhabitants concentrated on fishing, gathering seeds and nuts, and supplementing their diet with mussels, deer, and aquatic snails.

Several Late Archaic components are known from Jefferson County's central lowlands. The KENTUCKY AIR NATIONAL GUARD (KYANG) site represents a wetland-oriented subsistence. It was characterized by gathering mussels; hunting deer, turkey, and small mammals; and fishing. KYANG burials were in old storage pits and hearths.

The Lone Hill and the Minor's Ln. sites are similar to the KYANG site. Both were located on elevations above wetlands. Lone Hill was a 200-meter-diameter hill above the surrounding wetlands. It was reported by an employee at the Ford plant, which stands on the site now, that a midden, a crematory pit, burials, storage pits, hearths, and Late Archaic artifacts were uncovered during the site's destruction at Minor's Ln. There was a midden over a knoll that contained burials and Late Archaic artifacts.

McNeely Lake Cave in south central Jefferson County was occupied during the Early and Late Archaic as well as the Middle and Late Woodland Periods. An extensive Archaic stone tool inventory was found, along with several hearths and burials. The primary food was deer. The presence of many grinding and processing implements suggests that the diet contained a substantial amount of plant material. Nearby, the Durrett site contained a Late Archaic layer. The diet appears to be have been heavily dependent upon hunting and less dependent upon gathering. Tools from the Durrett site include a high percentage of projectile points and scrapers but only one pestle.

The Adena culture is a specialized form of the Late Archaic and Early Woodland cultures (800 B.C.–A.D. 0) concentrated in central and northern Kentucky, with extensions into the Falls area. Adena is defined primarily by the ceremonialism associated with the dead, ritual items, and burial in conical mounds.

The Adena ECONOMY consisted of horticultural gathering, hunting, and fishing. Seeds, nuts, and squashes were the staples. The people lived in semisedentary villages of round houses, with four center supports holding up conical thatched roofs. The houses were burned and covered with earth after the owner's death, forming the distinctive Adena conical mound.

Death and burial for some people of the Adena were associated with elaborate items and rituals. The dead were placed in log tombs and buried under conical mounds. Ceremonial items included cut animal jaws, mica ornaments, and tubular clay pipes. The bodies were decorated with shell, bone, copper and galena beads, red ochre, earrings, bone combs, bracelets, necklaces, gorgets, and pins. These offerings were made from exotic materials. Mass cremation was the means of disposing of the majority of the individuals in this culture. Mass cremation would occur when many people had died in battle.

Everyday tools included projectiles with rounded bases, celts, drills, scrapers, shell spoons, gourd cups, and Fayette Thick pottery vessels. The art on stone tablets and pottery includes stylized animals and BIRDS.

An Early Woodland component covered the Late Archaic occupation at the Hornung site. A thick, undecorated, grit-tempered pottery (Salt River Plain) related to the Fayette Thick–Adena Plain was found, as well as a piece of charred corn cob. Paleofecal samples from Mammoth and Salts Caves show that squash, chenopod, sunflower, gourds, and maygrass were all dietary items.

The Arrowhead Farm and Spadie sites, located on the second terrace of the Ohio River in southwest Jefferson County, have Early Woodland horizons. This represents the Late Archaic transition to Adena.

Settlement in large villages on first or second terraces of the Ohio River began in the Early Woodland about 1000 B.C. Along Mill Creek, small hunting camps or village dependencies are present.

The Zorn Ave. site, located on the bluffs above the Ohio River, contained an important Adena component. This site was a large village with deep storage pits, hearths, houses, and midden with large quantities of Adena pottery. On a high point above a bend in HARRODS CREEK, the Hunting Creek site had a series of three low mounds at the base of a ridge and an occupation area that contained Adena projectile points and pottery.

The Woodland Period, divided into Early Woodland (1000–300 B.C.), Middle Woodland (300 B.C.–A.D. 300), and Late Woodland (A.D. 300–1200), saw the introduction and use of pottery and an early form of horticulture-agriculture as cultural traits. Cultivated plants included squash, chenopod, sumpweed, ragweed, sunflowers, and maize. Hunting and fishing were also important activities. Deer, fish, and shellfish remained major dietary items. The bow and arrow were used for hunting. During the Late Woodland, flint and shell hoes were used. Structures were constructed of poles forming a framework for woven fabric covering.

The Hopewell Culture (A.D.0–300), centered north of the Ohio River, is considered to be a development from the Adena in Ohio, Indiana, and Illinois. It is characterized by burial mounds, earthen enclosures, and elaborate ritualism. Zone-incised, fingernail-punctated, and stamped ceremonial pottery; heart-shaped cache blades; prismatic flake knives; platform pipes; mica cutouts; copper earspools; and corner-notched projectile points, some of obsidian, are items found distributed outside the Hopewell area in Kentucky. The Zorn Ave. and Hunting Creek sites in Jefferson County have Hopewellian elements.

Several sites near the Ohio River in southwest Jefferson County have shown that a snail found in the estuarial waters of the Gulf of Mexico from Texas to Florida was carried into Kentucky. It was brought along the same route as the concept of intensive agriculture that characterized the Middle and Late Woodland. Crab Orchard CERAMICS from Illinois accompanied this concept into the Ohio River Valley. The most prominent of the sites with these gastropods is Arrowhead Farm, where the Middle Woodland midden yielded pottery related to Crab Orchard types.

The Late Woodland component at Arrowhead Farm contained numerous hearths and storage pits, pottery, and triangular projectiles. A Late Woodland occupation at McNeely Lake Cave extends 60 meters outside the cave entrance. North of McNeely Lake Cave, large villages have been reported with shell-tempered pottery and triangular projectiles.

The Mississippian–Fort Ancient Period (a.d. 1000–1650) appeared as a new form of cultural organization specializing in intensive agriculture in fertile river bottoms. It emerged from the Lower Mississippi area and fully developed in the middle Mississippi River Valley. Large, palisaded ceremonial centers with plazas, temple and burial mounds, and associated smaller satellite communities represent this pattern. It spread to the Ohio, Tennessee, and Cumberland River bottoms in Kentucky. Mississippian traits extend to the Salt River.

Mississippian ornamentation included gorgets, bracelets, necklaces, beads, and pendants. Artificial cranial deformation was practiced. Rectangular houses of wattle and daub construction had thatched roofs. Burials give evidence of social stratification. Grave goods and effigy figurines were included with those of high status, whereas others were interred without goods in shallow stone-box graves or below hearths within houses.

Subsistence was by intensive cultivation of maize, beans, and squash, supplemented by hunting and fishing. The principal weapon was the bow and arrow tipped with small triangular points. Pottery vessels, in many specialized forms, were of a fine, shell-tempered paste. Bottles, dishes, bowls, and cups were decorated by painting, incising, or molding. Elbow pipes were used for smoking tobacco.

The population supported by the economy and organized by the centralization of authority was large. Craft specialization was practiced, as shown by burial caches of tools or effigies of almost identical appearance. These items were made from materials procured from distant sources. A distinction between ceremonial and utilitarian pottery also indicates craft specialization.

The Fort Ancient culture in the upper Ohio Valley of north-central Kentucky is a culmination of a Woodland-Mississippian blend at approximately a.d. 1200. It is equated in its later stages with the Shawnee. Intensive agriculture of maize, beans, and squash was supplemented by hunting and fishing. The cultural inventory is similar to that of the Mississippian peoples. Villages, located near streams, supported smaller populations than those of the Mississippians.

Ceremonialism derived from the Mississippian culture and from southern cultures that participated in the Southern Cult. Incised shell gorgets and other items decorated with buzzard, swastika, kneeling-man, human-face, and weeping-eye motifs demonstrate this association. Temple mounds are rare and small. Ornamentation was dominated by shell and bone beadwork. Burials were in stone slab boxes with placement of pottery vessels near the hips and the head. Cranial deformation was practiced.

Artistic expression was limited to incised decoration of pottery and to some effigy elbow pipes. Trade networks were not widespread, although some intertribal contacts are evident. Southern Cult and European trade goods appear to be the best indications of the exchange network.

Thirty sites in Jefferson County have evidence of Mississippian or Fort Ancient traits. These sites include Riverport Site no. 34, Pryor no. 3, Orange no. 2, the Brown's Ln. site, the Big Spring site, Cannons Ln. no. 5, and the Bardstown Pike site. The Falls lies at the juncture of Mississippian cultural influence from the west and Fort Ancient from the east.

Just prior to the Historic stage (a.d. 1650), the Kentucky populations were in a state of flux. The introduction of European trade goods through tribal middlemen caused economic warfare. Euramerican contacts with the Iroquois, the Shawnee, the Miami, the Potawatomi, and the Cherokee provoked rivalry and trade conflict. The dark and bloody ground legend had its origins in the disruption of indigenous groups, such as the Shawnee, by European expansion beyond the Appalachians. Historic Indian villages were fortified with loopholes to shoot guns, a standard trade item. By 1750 the log cabin was adopted as a house type in most Indian communities. Common trade goods were copper kettles and buckets, Venetian glass beads, brass rings, kaolin pipes, steel knives, tomahawks, scissors, and needles. These completely replaced native tool industries. Indian settlements were virtually indistinct from Euramerican frontier settlements. Native populations rapidly declined through disease, displacement, and warfare.

See Bennett Henderson Young, *The Prehistoric Men of Kentucky* (Louisville 1910); Mary L. Bowman, *Bibliography of Kentucky Archaeology* (Louisville 1973).

Philip DiBlasi

PRENTICE, GEORGE DENNISON (b Preston, Connecticut, December 18, 1802; d Jefferson County, Kentucky, January 22, 1870). Newspaper editor. George Dennison Prentice was the son of Rufus and Sarah (Stanton) Prentice. His father was a farmer educated in New England, and his mother was a highly intelligent teacher-housewife. It was said that George D. Prentice at three and a half years of age could read several chapters of the Bible. He attended the Griswold District School, where he excelled in the classics, arithmetic, and writing. By the time he reached age fourteen, his parents had determined that he should attend college. To pay for college, Prentice taught school for a short time; he proved to be a strict disciplinarian.

Prentice entered Brown University in the fall of 1820 as a sophomore and graduated in 1823. At Brown he had as a tutor Horace Mann, the great disciple of public education. The two remained friends and correspondents throughout their lives. Mann was a guest of the Prentices in Louisville in 1843.

Following graduation from Brown University, Prentice became a contributor to highly literate quarterly reviews. He also studied law in Canterbury, Connecticut, and was admitted to the bar in that state, but his interest was in literature. He gave more time to writing articles and POETRY than to *Chitty on Pleading.* After an exceedingly brief practice of law, Prentice became the successful editor of the newly organized *Hartford New England Review* in 1828. So forceful were his political writings that the local Henry Clay partisans persuaded him to take a leave of absence from the *New England Review* and come to Kentucky to write a campaign biography of Henry Clay; he left behind as substitute editor John Greenleaf Whittier. The Clay biography was first published in Hartford in 1831 and sold more than twenty thousand copies; but because the publisher went bankrupt, Prentice received nothing for his labors.

Following the completion of the Clay book, a young man in Cincinnati suggested that he and Prentice establish a second newspaper in Louisville to rival Shadrack Penn's *Louisville Public Advertiser.* The first issue of the four-page LOUISVILLE JOURNAL appeared on November 24, 1830. The appearance of this paper marked the beginning of a running editorial feud with Penn and his newspaper that continued until 1841, with Prentice usually proving more clever than his adversary. Penn moved to St. Louis in 1841, where he published the *Statesman* until his death in 1846. Both editors engaged in libelous thrusts. Penn threatened a lawsuit until on second thought he realized that he had been equally as libelous.

The *Louisville Journal* quickly gained a reputation for both its new features and George D. Prentice's biting editorial quips. Fortunately, Kentucky, the lower South, and the expanding West opened a market for the *Journal.* Prentice's paragraphs were lifted, praised, and published in much of the American press. An example of his editorial wit and bite was the editor's reply to an angry young woman who said she had thrown the *Journal* on the ground and stomped on it. Prentice replied that she should use modest care because "the paper has a lot of i's." When an eastern editor published in his paper that he would accept rye, corn, potatoes, hoop poles, and ashes in payment, Prentice retorted, "They [ashes] are said to be a very necessary article in a lie factory." An eastern editor noted that "scarcely an exchange is opened, but contains some half dozen of his short, pithy, keen little paragraphs."

At heart George D. Prentice was a dedicated political partisan of strong Whiggish flavor. By 1855 the WHIG PARTY was badly fragmented. There came that dark moment in both national and Kentucky history when, overzealous in expounding the nativist-nationalist cause, he got caught up in the Know-Nothing paranoia and allowed his reputation to become stained. The dual national-sectional issues of slavery and the inrush of foreign immigrants created near hysteria. This fact was reflected in *Journal* editorials. By the advent of the election on August 6, 1855, the bigotry and nationalistic paranoia were out of hand in Louisville. There were the horrendous murders, beatings, and house burnings in the German and Irish areas of the town. "BLOODY MONDAY" was a travesty whose stain was pressed deep upon the history of the city and upon the reputation and character of George D. Prentice. Prentice was conforming

The original Sunday School founded by the Presbyterian Colored Mission (Presbyterian Community Center) 1911.

to an American fashion of the time that demanded virulence in Newspapers. Archbishop John L. Spalding noted that, to his credit, Prentice publicly regretted his role in the riots.

The voice and influence of George D. Prentice and the *Louisville Journal* were strong during the decade 1850–60. Prentice was unwavering in his loyalty to the Union, but he wavered at times with regard to its policies during the Civil War. He was an influential member of that small group of Kentucky leaders who early in 1861 sought to keep Kentucky from seceding, encouraging the state to establish its neutrality instead. During the war Louisville remained Unionist at heart and escaped the ravage of the war. In the postwar years Prentice was a staunch critic of the senseless excesses of radical Reconstruction. The *Journal* was one of the few Southern papers, if not the only one, that had earned the right to speak out critically and fearlessly against federal issues. Possibly no historian can assess fully the influence exerted by the Louisville editor in one of the most troubled eras in American history.

George D. Prentice married Harriett Benham of Louisville in 1833. The couple had four children. Two died in infancy, leaving two sons, William Courtland and Clarence Joseph. Courtland was one of the twenty-one Confederates killed in the battle of Augusta, Kentucky, on September 21, 1862. Harriett Prentice died in 1864, and after that Prentice practically lived in the *Journal's* editorial office. He became a registered member of the Christ Church on March 25, 1845, but was not baptized in that faith until December 7, 1862.

Henry Watterson became editor of the newly consolidated *Louisville Courier* and *Journal* in November 1868. A rumor was set afloat that there was enmity between him and Prentice, a rumor both men denied. In the meantime Prentice went into a physical if not an emotional decline. He allowed his hair to grow long, and his traditionally clean-shaven face grew a bushy gray beard. On Saturday afternoon before Christmas 1869, he set out to visit his son Clarence, who lived south of Louisville near the Salt River Rd. (Dixie Hwy.). When he left the *Courier-Journal* office, he appeared to be in good spirits and in reasonably good health. On the way he contracted influenza, and the ensuing pneumonia proved fatal. His body was returned to Louisville to lie in state in the Masonic Temple. The funeral was conducted by the Reverend Dr. James Craik in Christ Church. Prentice's body was placed in a burial vault at Cave Hill Cemetery. In his extensive eulogistic essay, Henry Watterson wrote, "The man is dead. But Prentice is not dead."

George Prentice continues to be the subject of debate. Objections have been raised several times concerning the white marble statue of him by Louisville sculptor Alex Baily. It originally belonged to the *Courier-Journal* but was given to the library in 1914. The statue stands outside the Louisville Free Public Library. For some it symbolizes Prentice's journalistic ability, and others believe it epitomizes the anti-Catholic and anti-immigrant rhetoric that brought him fame.

See *Louisville Journal,* 1830–68; *Courier-Journal,* 1868–70; July 5, 1998; Henry Watterson, *Memorial Address,* January 1870; George D. Prentice, *Biography of Henry Clay* (Hartford, Conn., 1831); Bess A. Ray, *Louisville Library Collection,* vol. 2 (Louisville 1941); Agnes G. McGann, *Nativism in Kentucky to 1860* (Washington, D.C., 1944); Betty Carolyn Congleton, "George D. Prentice: Nineteenth Century Southern Editor," *Register of the Kentucky Historical Society* 65 (April 1967): 94–119; George D. Prentice, *Prenticeana,* 227 (New York 1860).

Thomas D. Clark

PRESBYTERIAN CHURCH (USA) CENTER. On October 29, 1988, the Presbyterian Center was dedicated in downtown Louisville on a site once owned by the Belknap Hardware Co. The center was created from two turn-of-the-century buildings renovated and linked by a modern atrium to house the national offices of the Presbyterian Church (USA).

The decision to move the church offices from New York City and Atlanta followed the reunion in 1983 of the two major branches of the Presbyterian Church in the United States—the United Presbyterian Church in the USA and the Presbyterian Church in the US. The denomination had separated in 1861 over the issue of slavery.

Louisville was one of forty-seven cities that sought the denominational headquarters. Dr. John M. Mulder, president of the Louisville Presbyterian Theological Seminary, and David A. Jones, chairman of Humana, led the city's effort. Louisville's bid was rejected by a site selection committee, which recommended in January 1987 that the headquarters be located in Kansas City.

That same month Jones, an elder at Louisville's Highland Presbyterian Church, acquired title to the Belknap property. Jones offered to donate space for the headquarters and to help raise $8 million for its renovation. In June 1987, five thousand people turned out for a rally on Main St. inviting the Presbyterians to town. A videotape of the rally was shown later that month in Biloxi, Mississippi, where the church's General Assembly met for a final vote on the location.

Louisville mayor Jerry Abramson led a delegation of community leaders to Biloxi, who appealed to the church's historic commitment to mission and stewardship. They passed out souvenir Louisville Slugger bats and told the assembly that by accepting Louisville's offer, the church would save $21.5 million—the amount it would have cost to buy and renovate the proposed site in Kansas City. The savings, they said, could be used to support the church's work in the United States and around the world. The assembly voted 332–309 to reject Kansas City in favor of Louisville.

Renovation of the Belknap buildings began immediately. Work that would normally have taken up to three years was completed in fifteen months. Witherspoon St. in front of the Presbyterian Center was named for the Reverend John Witherspoon, who became the denomination's first moderator in 1789 and was the only member to sign the Declaration of Independence. The Presbyterian Center was an early part of the renovation of Louisville's historic riverfront.

See *Courier-Journal,* March 25; June 16, 17, 18, 1987.

Gary W. Luhr

PRESBYTERIAN COMMUNITY CENTER. The Presbyterian Community Center, at 760 S Hancock St., began as Louisville's first African American mission Sunday school on February 3, 1898, in an old lottery office on Preston St. in the Uptown neighborhood. Six students from the Louisville Presbyterian Seminary led the popular afternoon Sunday school and evening preaching services, which were expanded to the SMOKETOWN community across BROADWAY in April 1899, with another mission at the corner of Jackson and Lampton Streets (later moved to Roselane and Hancock). The Reverend John Little stayed on as director of the missions after his graduation from the Presbyterian Seminary, continuing until his death in 1949. He created an innovative program of industrial work classes and recreation and opened the first playground for black children in Louisville at the PRESTON STREET Mission in 1904.

Officially incorporated in 1910 with a board of directors from four local presbyteries, the missions also received support from the Welfare League and the Community Chest. In the 1960s federal grant money allowed for the development of new social service programs for preschool children, youths, and senior citizens. In 1971 community leaders formed their own Smoketown Council to organize additional neighborhood services.

The Uptown center closed in 1965 in order to merge both centers in the Hancock St. building, newly named the Presbyterian Community Center founded by John Little. The center will be moved to the corner of Hancock and Finzer Streets when the new facility there is completed late in 2000. Executive directors after 1949 include the Reverend Charles Allen (1949–62); the Reverend Dr. Grayson Tucker (1962–66); the Reverend Irvin Moxley (1966–76); the Reverend Louis Coleman Jr. (1978–88); the Reverend Ted Adams (1989–93); and Edna McDonald (1994–98). Ernest "Camp" Edwards was named interim director in 1998.

See Anne F. Downs, "Service from Sunday School to Social Science: A History of Louisville's Presbyterian Community Center," Louisville Presbyterian Seminary, 1982; E.T. Thompson, *Presbyterian Missions in the Southern United States* (Richmond, Va., 1934); Anne F. Vouga, "Presbyterian Missions and Louisville Blacks: The Early Years, 1898–1910," *Filson Club History Quarterly* 58 (July 1984): 310–35.

Anne Vouga

Warren Memorial Presbyterian Church, southwest corner of Broadway at Fourth Street, 1932.

PRESBYTERIANS. Presbyterianism has had a strong presence in the Louisville area since the late eighteenth century. During the 1790s many Scotch-IRISH and Huguenot Presbyterians moved into Jefferson County. By 1799 they had established churches at MIDDLETOWN and Pennsylvania Run in the eastern part of the county. In January 1816 several prominent Louisville citizens organized a Presbyterian Society led by the Reverend Daniel C. Banks, a Congregational missionary from Connecticut.

He had come to the FALLS OF THE OHIO region in 1815 under the terms of the 1801 Plan of Union between the General Assembly of the Presbyterian Church and the Congregational Association of Connecticut. In 1817 the society formally organized as FIRST PRESBYTERIAN CHURCH and erected a building on the west side of Fourth St. between Jefferson and MARKET Streets. Banks led the congregation for about four years but never was officially recognized by the Presbytery of Louisville (also organized in 1817) because of his Congregational affiliation.

The First Presbyterian Church quickly became a center of frontier Presbyterianism and attracted influential ministers. The Reverend Gideon Blackburn, founder of several Presbyterian churches in Tennessee, served as pastor from 1823 to 1827 before becoming president of Centre College in Danville. The Reverend William Lewis Breckinridge, a prominent antislavery leader, served as pastor from 1836 to 1858.

First Presbyterian also served as the mother church for other congregations. In April 1830 twelve members of the congregation organized the SECOND PRESBYTERIAN CHURCH under the leadership of the Reverend Eli N. Sawtell. In 1832 the new congregation completed a permanent edifice on the east side of Third St. between Green (Liberty) and Walnut (Muhammad Ali Blvd.). Also in 1830 several members of the First Presbyterian Church organized the First Presbyterian Church in JEFFERSONVILLE, INDIANA. The Reverend Michael A. Remley was called as a supply minister of the Jeffersonville church in June. He served until December 1833, when he was succeeded by the Reverend E.P. Humphrey, who later became a prominent Louisville pastor.

In May 1832 the Louisville Presbytery established a commission to organize a new congregation in the eastern part of the city. Known as Third Presbyterian Church, this congregation worshiped for about four years in a building on the east side of Hancock St. between Main and Market. But the members soon became widely scattered, and the congregation dissolved by early 1836. The building served for several years as the site of a mission Sunday school directed by elder W.J. Dinwiddie.

Meanwhile another congregation was organized in 1832 under the leadership of the Reverend John G. Simrall to serve the western part of the city. Initially called Fourth Presbyterian Church, the congregation erected a sanctuary on the east side of Tenth St. between Market and Jefferson. But in April 1836, after the collapse of the Third Presbyterian Church, the Fourth Presbyterian was reorganized as Third Presbyterian Church. By mid-decade Louisville had three Presbyterian congregations with more than six hundred members.

During the 1830s and 1840s, Presbyterianism in Kentucky was disrupted by the Old School–New School controversy, a conflict over differences about church GOVERNMENT, the control of educational and missionary operations, doctrine, revivalism, and slavery. Many of these issues were rooted in conflicting opinion arising out of the 1801 Plan of Union and the Second Great Awakening of the early nineteenth century. Generally speaking, the Old School opposed participation by Congregationalists in Presbyterian church courts, favored control of educational and missionary operations by the General Assembly, advocated orthodox Calvinist doctrine, opposed revivalist innovations in worship and sacrament, and tolerated slavery. The New School favored allowing Congregationalists to sit in Presbyterian church courts, advocated control of missionary and educational operations by volunteer societies, were less rigid on Christian doctrine, were more sympathetic toward revivalism, and tended to oppose slavery.

The First Presbyterian Church showed a general affinity for the Old School, whereas the Second Presbyterian Church tended to favor the New School. The Reverend Dr. Thomas Cleland, leader of the New School faction in Kentucky, organized a short-lived New School church at the home of the Reverend Daniel C. Banks during the early 1840s. There is little indication, however, that the controversy triggered a major division within any individual congregations or within the Presbytery of Louisville.

Despite the relatively benign impact of the Old School–New School controversy, the years between 1836 and the CIVIL WAR were a period of both growth and unrest for Presbyterianism in Louisville. In October 1836 the First Presbyterian Church was destroyed by fire, and a new church was constructed on the south side of Green St. (Liberty) between Center St. (Armory Place) and Sixth St. In 1844 the First Church hosted the General Assembly of the Presbyterian Church, and in 1859 its recently retired pastor, William L. Breckinridge, was elected moderator of the General Assembly.

In the fall of 1848 the Second Presbyterian Church suffered a severe division, which resulted in the withdrawal of the entire governing body and sixty-one other members, who organized the Chestnut Street Presbyterian Church and built an edifice at the corner of Fourth and Chestnut Streets. In the spring of 1858, Second Presbyterian called the Reverend Dr. STUART ROBINSON from his post at Centre College in Danville to serve as pastor. Meanwhile the Third Presbyterian Church had relocated twice, first to the east side of Ninth St. between Jefferson and Green, and then in 1854 to the northeast corner of Walnut and Eleventh Streets, where it became known as the WALNUT STREET PRESBYTERIAN CHURCH. On Sunday, August 27, 1854, while services were in progress, the new church building was demolished by a tornado, and fifteen persons were killed.

A new effort to establish a church in the eastern part of the city began in March 1846 with the organization of the Fourth Presbyterian Church. In August 1847 the Reverend Mason D. Williams became the permanent pastor, and in June 1848 the congregation dedicated a new building on the site of the former Dinwiddie Mission on Hancock St. between Main and Market Streets, which had been destroyed by fire several years earlier. The last new congregation organized in Louisville before the Civil War was the Portland Avenue Presbyterian Church, formed in September 1855 under the supervision of the Presbytery of Louisville.

Louisville and Jefferson County were not the only antebellum strongholds of Presbyterianism in the Falls area. A Presbyterian society was organized in Charlestown, Indiana, in 1812. By 1860 Presbyterian congregations had been established in the Clark County settlements of New Market and Borden as well as in Jeffersonville. In Floyd County in 1816, Joel Scribner, one of the founders of NEW ALBANY, was instrumental in establishing the First Presbyterian Church, a forerunner of the present St. John's Presbyterian Church. It was followed by the Mount Tabor Church in 1830, the Greenville Church in 1843, and the Bethel Church in Scottsville, probably during the 1850s.

Another expression of Presbyterianism in Louisville was the Cumberland Presbyterian Church. This movement was rooted in the evangelism of the Reverend James McGready during the "Great Revival" of 1800–1802. Soon thereafter the Presbyterian Synod of Kentucky created a new Cumberland Presbytery from a portion of the Transylvania Presbytery. But a rift developed between the revival and antirevival parties, and in 1806 the Kentucky Synod dissolved the Cumberland Presbytery. Four years later several revivalists reconstituted it, hoping to rejoin the Synod of Kentucky. Though that effort failed, the new presbytery continued to grow, and in 1813 it organized a new Cumberland Synod with three presbyteries, laying in the process the foundation of a new denomination.

Louisville's first Cumberland Presbyterian congregation was formally established in 1852 under the leadership of the Reverend E.C. Trimble. After meeting for several years in a local school, the congregation dedicated a new brick building at the southwest corner of Floyd and Chestnut Streets in May 1856. The church hosted the General Assembly of the Cumberland Presbyterian Church later in the month. Meanwhile, Louisville had become the headquarters of the denominational printing house.

Slavery was a significant source of controversy within Louisville-area churches during the decades before the Civil War. Slaveholding was common in Louisville, and many Presbyterians were slaveowners. But the antislavery movement also included numerous Presbyterians. The Reverend Dr. William L. Breckinridge, pastor of the First Presbyterian Church, was an organizer of the Kentucky Colonization Society and an outspoken opponent of slavery. The society was an attempt to free slaves and transport them to Africa. Breckinridge was a delegate to a statewide emancipationist convention in Frankfort in 1849. The most prominent proslavery spokesman was the Reverend Dr. Stuart Robinson, pastor of the Second Presbyterian Church. Born in Ireland and reared in Virginia, Robinson became the most outspoken opponent of Breckinridge and his more vocal brother, Lexington pastor Robert J. Breckinridge.

The Civil War profoundly affected Louisville's Presbyterian churches. In addition to drawing members into the armies of both sides, the war highlighted divisions within the larger church. When the Old School General Assembly met in Philadelphia in May 1861, New York minister Gardiner Spring introduced a resolution that called upon ministers and churches to remain loyal to the federal government. Delegates from the Confederate states walked out and ultimately formed the Presbyterian Church of the Confederate States of America. The Synod of Kentucky remained loyal, but many members and pastors of some Louisville churches harbored pro-Confederate sympathies. The most prominent among these was Stuart Robinson, who expressed his sentiments in a journal called the *True Presbyterian.* In 1862, while he was in Canada to visit an invalid brother, federal troops seized copies of his paper, and friends warned that he might be jailed for sedition if he returned to Louisville. So Robinson remained in Canadian exile until 1866, when he returned to the Second Presbyterian Church.

Upon returning to Louisville, Robinson led many local Presbyterian churches into the Southern church, which had since been renamed Presbyterian Church in the United States (PCUS). At least five Louisville churches joined the PCUS, with several experiencing internal divisions that resulted in the formation of new congregations that adhered to the Northern church, the Presbyterian Church in the United States of America (PCUSA). The Chestnut Street Presbyterian Church was the only prewar Presbyterian church that remained undivided and loyal to the PCUSA. Over the next three decades, both the Northern and the Southern Presbyteries of Louisville vigorously pursued the formation of new congregations as Louisville expanded south, east, and west. The new congregations included the Highland (1882), Stuart Robinson (1888), Warren Memorial (1884), and Crescent Hill (1896) Presbyterian Churches.

The late nineteenth and early twentieth centuries were a period of significant institutional development and mission activity. Several of these efforts involved considerable cooperation between the Northern and the Southern churches. In the 1850s Chestnut Street Presbyterian Church had taken the lead in founding the Louisville Orphans' Home Society, located on what is now Kentucky St. After the Presbyterians split, the Southern Presbyterians relocated to ANCHORAGE, where they occupied the former Bellewood Seminary, which had been a finishing school for girls. The facility had been known for many years as Bellewood Presbyterian Home for Children.

The LOUISVILLE PRESBYTERIAN THEOLOGICAL SEMINARY was founded by the synods of Kentucky and Missouri (PCUS) in 1893 as the Louisville Theological Seminary. In 1901 the Danville Theological Seminary, founded in Danville in 1853 and associated with the Northern church, united with the Louisville Seminary to form the Presbyterian Theological Seminary of Kentucky. It became known as Louisville Presbyterian Theological Seminary in 1927. After meeting in temporary quarters for several years, the seminary dedicated a new campus at First St. and E Broadway in 1904, where it remained until moving to a new campus on Alta Vista Rd. in 1963.

The PRESBYTERIAN COMMUNITY CENTER in the Smoketown neighborhood began as an expression of late-nineteenth-century social Gospel theology. In 1897, in response to a call by the Reverend A.L. Philips, secretary of Colored Evangelism in the PCUS, the Reverend John Little and several other members of the Student's Missionary Society of the Louisville Presbyterian Seminary started a Sunday school program for the neighborhood's black residents. In February 1898 Little organized a settlement house known as Hope Mission Station on Hancock St. It was followed in April 1899 by the Grace Mission Station about a mile away at Hancock and Roselane Streets. Both locations provided Sunday school programs—vocational, sewing, canning, and cooking classes—and a variety of recreational activities. Each also gave rise to a church—the Grace Presbyterian Church, supported by the PCUS, and the Hope Presbyterian Church, affiliated with the PCUSA. The two congregations later merged to create the Grace-Hope Presbyterian Church.

Louise Marshall, a member of the Second Presbyterian Church, founded the CABBAGE PATCH Settlement House at 1461 S Ninth St. in 1910. The Presbytery of Louisville adopted the Cabbage Patch in 1924 and changed its name to the Ninth and Hill Settlement. The settlement assumed its original name in 1929 when it moved to larger quarters on Sixth St. It is governed by an independent board of directors and offers a wide variety of programs and services to families in Louisville's inner city. Ventures such as the Louisville Presbyterian Theological Seminary and the Presbyterian Community Center signaled an era of ecumenical cooperation and unifying tendencies that became a hallmark of twentieth-century Presbyterianism both within the denomination and with other faiths. In 1904 the Cumberland Presbyterian Church congregations and the Presbyterian Church in the USA voted to merge. In 1958 the United Presbyterian Church, centered primarily in Pennsylvania and the West, merged with the PCUSA to create the United Presbyterian Church in the USA. The PCUS voted down a merger proposal in 1955, but its Kentucky presbyteries favored merger, and by 1970 union presbyteries had been created across the state. In Louisville and Jefferson County these unifying tendencies were apparent in the cooperation between both Louisville presbyteries in the formation of new congregations during the wave of suburban development following WORLD WAR II.

Since the late 1960s local Presbyterian churches have been widely involved in a variety of ecumenical COMMUNITY MINISTRIES such as the OLD LOUISVILLE Neighborhood Development Corp., Highland Community Ministries, United Crescent Hill Ministries, and ST. MATTHEWS Area Ministries. Presbyterian churches are also involved in shared ministries with each other and with other denominations. HIGHLAND PRESBYTERIAN CHURCH, a largely white congregation, has a cooperative ministry with West Chestnut Street Baptist Church, a predominantly African American congregation.

The post–World War II era also witnessed a broadening role for women in the ministry. Women became ruling elders and joined sessions, a congregations governing body, in both the PCUSA and the PCUS. Women were first ordained as ministers in the PCUSA in 1955 and in the PCUS in 1967. The first woman ordained by the Presbytery of Louisville was Jane Krauss-Jackson, who was installed as pastor of the Portland Avenue Presbyterian Church on November 24, 1974.

The twentieth century's unifying tendencies culminated with the 1983 decision to merge the PCUSA and PCUS to form the Presbyterian Church (USA). Louisville Presbyterians, led by Humana chief executive officer David Jones, a member of the Highland Presbyterian Church, and Louisville Presbyterian Theological Seminary president John M. Mulder, along with Louisville and Jefferson County officials and others, spearheaded a successful community effort to move the headquarters to Louisville. The new headquarters was dedicated on October 28–29, 1988, in two newly restored buildings of the old Belknap Hardware Co. complex, which Jones donated to the denomination. The Presbyterian Church (USA) Foundation also began operations in its new office building in Jeffersonville, Indiana, in September 1988, with dedication of the new facility on October 21.

See Louis B. Weeks, *Kentucky Presbyterian* (Atlanta 1983); J. Stoddard Johnston, ed., *Memorial History of Louisville* (Chicago 1896); George C. Wright, *Life Behind a Veil* (Baton Rouge 1985); *History of the Ohio Falls Cities and Their Counties* (Cleveland 1882); Lewis Collins and Richard H. Collins, *History of Kentucky* (Frankfort 1966).

Mary Kagin Kramer
Carl E. Kramer

PRESENTATION ACADEMY. Founded in 1831, Presentation Academy is the oldest school in continuous operation in Louisville. It was originally in the basement of St. Louis Church on Fifth between Green (Liberty) and Walnut (Muhammad Ali Blvd.) Streets. The school's founder, CATHERINE SPALDING, was superior of the Sisters of Charity of Nazareth, who also founded Louisville's first Catholic orphanage and infirmary, located near the Cathedral.

In 1893 the school's new red brick building was erected on the northeast corner of Fourth and Breckinridge Streets. At first an elementary school, it became a secondary school for girls in 1945. Counted among the school's alumni is the famous actress MARY ANDERSON, "America's Dream Girl," who made her stage debut at MACAULEY'S THEATRE when she was seventeen.

Presentation has a landmark Richardsonian Romanesque tower atop the school building. Other interesting features of the building, designed by noted Louisville architect D.X. Murphy, are the tile mosaic entrance hall and the old fireplaces with colored ceramic tiles. The third floor was originally used as an auditorium and a convent. When a fire destroyed the auditorium in 1938, a gym was added.

In keeping with long-held school traditions, only seniors and visitors are allowed to use the school's front staircase, and generations of students signed their names on the tower walls. When the tower was rebuilt after a 1977 fire, alumni returned to re-sign their names.

Presentation reached a peak enrollment of 800 students in the late 1950s and early 1960s, but a steady decline resulted in an all-time low of 230 in 1993. Enrollment inched upward to 237 by 1995, but the school was $700,000 in debt. Negotiations with next-door neighbor SPALDING UNIVERSITY (named for Presentation's founder) to take over administration of the high school failed. On January 19, 1995, the Sisters of Charity of Nazareth announced that the 164-year-old school would close that May.

Students sparked an outpouring of community support to save their school. The determination of Presentation students and families inspired other contributions from Louisvillians. Within a week of the announcement to close, nearly $760,000 was raised. All debts were paid, and the Sisters of Charity gave control of the school to Spalding University. Presentation and Spalding then instituted a successful program that doubled enrollment by 1997.

See *Courier-Journal,* Nov. 28, 1991; Jan. 19–26, 1995;. Clyde F. Crews, *Spirited City: Essays in Louisville History* (Louisville 1995); Kenny Karem, *Discover Louisville* (Louisville 1988).

Rhonda Abner

PRESERVATION ALLIANCE. The Preservation Alliance of Louisville and Jefferson County was a private, nonprofit coalition made up of civic organizations, neighborhood groups, historical societies, and public agencies. Established in 1972, the group advocated the preservation and continued use of Louisville and Jefferson County's historical and architectural heritage. From 1972 through the early 1990s, Preservation Alliance was an active force in the community, drawing public attention to the cause of historic preservation. During that time, the coalition worked to educate the public by holding walking tours of historic NEIGHBORHOODS and sponsoring a lecture series. From 1974 to 1992, it maintained a bookstore and headquarters on MAIN St. The group also established a now-defunct revolving fund for the purpose of buying, restoring, and selling historic homes. Demonstrations held by members of Preservation Alliance against the demolition of historic buildings were instrumental in the retention and preservation of the UNIVERSITY OF LOUISVILLE'S BELKNAP Playhouse, FORT NELSON Park at Seventh and Main Streets, houses owned by the WOMAN'S CLUB OF LOUISVILLE on Fourth St., and UNION STATION on Broadway. The group played a part in the restoration of the MONSARRAT (Fifth Ward School) at Fifth and YORK Streets, the SEELBACH HILTON HOTEL on Fourth St., and the CAMBERLEY BROWN HOTEL at Fourth St. and BROADWAY. Other group activities included the presentation of preservation awards and the establishment of a "ten endangered buildings" list. As of the mid-1990s, the group's activities were limited to advocacy on an as-needed basis.

See *Courier-Journal,* Aug. 16, 1983; *Louisville Times,* Jan. 16, 1974; May 19, 1978.

Ellen Birckett Morris

PRESTON, WILLIAM (b "Preston Lodge," Jefferson County, Kentucky, October 16, 1816; d Lexington, September 21, 1887). Soldier, politician, and lawyer. William Preston was the son of Maj. William and Caroline (Hancock)

General William Preston, c. 1864.

Preston. The family had moved from Virginia to Jefferson County the year before his birth and settled on extensive property that Major Preston had inherited from his father, Col. William Preston. Young Preston received a good education, acquiring much of it away from home. He attended Augusta College in Augusta, Kentucky, and then St. Joseph's College in Bardstown, Kentucky. He entered Yale University and received a degree in literary studies in 1835. In 1836 he entered Harvard's law school and received his LL.B. in 1838.

Returning to Louisville, he practiced law and devoted much time to the family estate. Allying himself with the WHIG PARTY, Preston became involved in politics. When the MEXICAN WAR began in 1846, he was commander of the Washington Blues, a part of the LOUISVILLE LEGION, and helped the state acquire loans for its war efforts. He was commissioned lieutenant colonel of the Fourth Kentucky Infantry under Gen. William O. Butler on October 4, 1847, and participated in the campaign that resulted in the capture of Mexico City. He was mustered out on July 25, 1848, when the regiment returned to Louisville.

Preston was elected to the 1849 state constitutional convention, the state House of Representatives (1850–51), the state Senate (1851–52), and the U.S. House of Representatives (1852–55). Upon the breakup of the Whig Party, he became a Democrat and actively supported that party. He was a delegate to the 1856 National Democratic Convention and campaigned for James Buchanan. In 1858 he was appointed minister to Spain. When he learned in early 1861 of the secession of South Carolina, Preston submitted his resignation, determined to return to Kentucky and try to persuade his state to join the Confederacy. Because Kentucky remained loyal to the Union, Preston joined Confederate forces under kinsman Albert Sidney Johnston at Bowling Green in September 1861.

Preston served as a colonel on Johnston's staff until Johnston died at Shiloh in April 1862. He then held commands in the western THEATER of the war, and briefly in southwestern Virginia. He rose to the rank of brigadier general and participated in the battles of Corinth, Stone's River, and Chickamauga and other engagements. In January 1864 he was appointed the Confederacy's minister to Mexico, but his mission was unsuccessful. He resigned and then crossed into Texas and joined Edmund Kirby Smith's command in December 1864 and was commissioned a major general.

At the end of the war, he went into exile in England and then Canada. In 1866 he was granted a pardon and returned to Kentucky, settling in Lexington. As a prominent Confederate, Preston was quite popular, and he reluctantly reentered the political arena. His name was circulated as a possible gubernatorial candidate, and he served one term in the state House of Representatives, 1868–69, representing Fayette County. Afterward he declined public office but did serve as a delegate to the 1868 and 1880 Democratic National Conventions. He is buried in CAVE HILL CEMETERY.

Preston married his cousin Margaret Preston Wickliffe (1819–98), daughter of Robert and Mary Preston Howard Wickliffe of Lexington, on December 9, 1840, in Lexington. They had six children: Mary Owen, Caroline Hancock, Margaret Howard, Robert Wickliffe, Susan Christy, and Jesse Fremont.

See Ellis Merton Coulter, "William Preston," *Dictionary of American Biography*

The Hub shoe store, 415 South Preston Street, in 1960.

(New York 1935); John Frederick Dorman, "General William Preston," *Filson Club History Quarterly* 43 (Oct. 1969): 301–8; John Frederick Dorman, *The Prestons of Smithfield and Greenfield in Virginia* (Louisville 1982).

James J. Holmberg

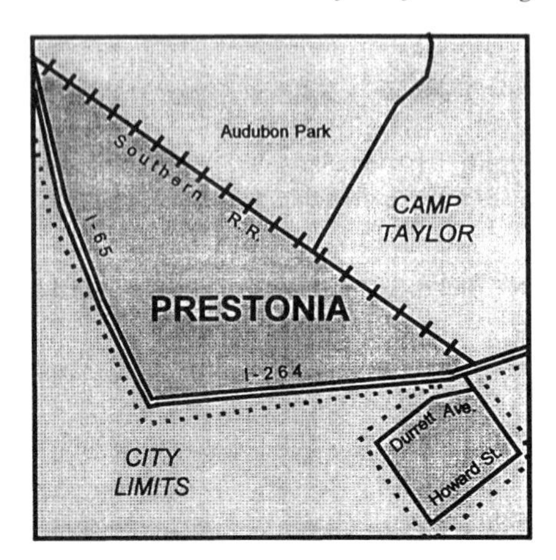

PRESTONIA. This amorphous Louisville neighborhood occupies the area on both sides of Preston Hwy. between Watterson Expwy. and the KENTUCKY FAIR AND EXPOSITION CENTER. The name was probably first applied to a station on the Louisville Southern Railway, where the highway (then PRESTON Street Rd.) crossed the tracks, and then to the post office serving this station from February 23, 1899, to mid-October 1902. Its only postmaster, Henry M. Kleier, had been unsuccessful in calling his new office Minnoma probably referring to the earlier (1886–92) Minoma post office on Preston Street Rd., about a mile north. Prestonia may have been named for the road or for J.T.L. Preston, an early local landowner.

See Robert M. Rennick, *Kentucky's Salt River Valley: A Survey of the Post Offices of the Greater Louisville Area* (Lake Grove, Ore., 1997).

Robert M. Rennick

PRESTON STREET. A major thoroughfare in Louisville, Preston St. begins at the Great Lawn on the OHIO RIVER and runs south to Eastern Pkwy. where it is joined by Shelby St. to become Preston Hwy. (formerly Preston Street Rd.). In the mid–nineteenth century the road was a major route south to SHEPHERDSVILLE and Nashville and was called the Flat Lick or Preston Street Plank Rd. It is named after Col. WILLIAM PRESTON, who was one of the early landholders in the area. Preston held 1,000 acres that became known as Preston's Enlargement in 1827 as the city grew eastward.

Between about 1880 and 1950, the six blocks of Preston St. between Market and BROADWAY housed a polyglot world busy with retailing and commercial traffic. Horse-drawn wagons—later newfangled trucks—used for hauling vied for a passageway while trolley cars clanged slowly through the maelstrom of traffic.

Lining both sides of Preston were small retail stores of every description. One could buy anything there but a horse, although you could outfit your horse at Nold's Harness Shop on the west side near Jefferson. Virtually all of the stores were Jewish-owned. The custom of the day was for the owners to live either behind or above their stores. In the alleys at the rear, in shacks or converted stables, lived AFRICAN AMERICANS. It was always an integrated neighborhood, although, due to the presence of so many immigrant JEWS, one was likely to hear more Yiddish than English spoken on the street. How Preston St. became the artery of Jewish settlement is unknown. In those days a mom and pop store could be opened for as little as $500, although that was a princely sum at the time. The upscale stores on Fourth St., which was then the retailing center of Louisville, gave short shrift to African Americans, so they turned to Preston St. for their shopping. The sidewalks were always crowded. There also was a large white clientele from the heavily populated area east of the downtown business district. The Preston St. retailers knew their customers by name, even in the largest business in the area, Waterman's Department Store, just north of Walnut St. (Muhammad Ali Blvd.).

The concentration of Jewish POPULATION gave the area some of the atmosphere of the European shtetl, the difference being that the shtetl was a ghetto, or self-contained village, and not part of a mixed society. One synagogue, Beth Hamedrash Hagodol, stood at the corner of Preston and Fehr (Liberty) Streets. Three other synagogues, B'nai Jacob, ADATH JESHURUN, and ANSHEI SFARD, were not far away. For several decades, until his death in 1932, Rabbi A.L. Zarchy was the spiritual leader of the entire Orthodox Jewish community. The sage of the area was a black physician, Dr. William Pickett. Black or white, everyone in need of medical attention turned to him.

The combination of URBAN RENEWAL, flight to the SUBURBS, and expressway-building changed the character of the area and wiped out most of the retailing area after WORLD WAR II. One group—the shoe stores—did survive, and until late in 1996 the block between Liberty and Jefferson was known informally as Shoe St. The street became Louisville's sample and used-shoe mecca in 1884. The area declined before World War II but revived during World War II, when ration books were necessary to make shoe purchases, and reached its height in the 1950s. At one time there were twelve stores dealing in shoes, handbags, and accessories. Schlossberg's was at 203 S Preston, Strasberg's at 209, the Boot Shop at 206, Watterson Bootery at 331, Goldstein Brothers at the corner of Jefferson, Mel Golde Men's Shoes at 205, Sam Pozitzer at 201, Travers Shoe Stores at 211, Williams Shoe Center at 220, Goldy's Shoe Mart at 339, Potters at 204, and Sam Wittenbaum at 219. The rise of discount stores wrought havoc with the Preston St. businesses, and one by one they closed. Goldy's, closed in the fall of 1996. The area lying south of BROADWAY is a mixture of residences, light industry, and small businesses. A number of relief agencies are located there, including the Franciscan Shelter House, the ST. VINCENT DE PAUL SOCIETY Store, and the VOLUNTEERS OF AMERICA. The CSX Transportation tracks and Interstate 65 both intersect Preston. St. Stephen's Cemetery is at the corner of Brandeis Ave. In that area Preston is more residential with many smaller businesses.

See *Courier-Journal,* April 3, 1995; Herman Landau, "First-Person History: American Ghetto," *Filson Club History Quarterly* 72 (April 1998): 193–99.

Herman Landau

PRINCE MADOC. The Madoc legend first appeared in print in the 1580s in an English pamphlet promoting British colonization of America. Originally used as "an instrument of imperial conflict" to defend English intrusion into Spanish-controlled North America, the legend is now largely considered a myth by scholars.

According to the legend, America was discovered in the twelfth century by the Welsh prince known as Madoc, the son of Owain Gwyneed, ruler of North Wales. The saga presents an account of the recurring theory that Prince Madoc, tired of the civil wars waged between his brothers, left his homeland to embark on a sea adventure. He supposedly made landfall in 1170 somewhere along the coast of either Mexico, Florida, or Alabama and founded a small colony in America.

The legend follows the migratory trail of Madoc's colony through Alabama, Georgia, and Tennessee, up to the FALLS OF THE OHIO at Louisville, which allegedly become the site of a great prehistoric battle. The battle was fought between a faction of American Indians, led by the IROQUOIS, and the White, or Welsh, Indians, who were a race of half-breeds, led by the descendants of Prince Madoc.

The tradition holds that the followers of Prince Madoc were killed on Sand Island and the battered remnants of the White Tribe fled up the Mississippi to the far reaches of the Missouri River, where they became known as the Mandans. Stories circulated in the nineteenth century that skeletons, each accompanied by a brass breastplate emblazoned with the Welsh coat of arms, had been unearthed near JEFFERSONVILLE, INDIANA, in the 1790s. However, no evidence of this was found, and it is apparently just another facet of the intriguing legend.

See Zella Armstrong, *Who Discovered America?* (Chattanooga, Tenn., 1950); Richard Deacon, *Madoc and the Discovery of America—1170* (New York 1965); Reuben Thomas Durrett, *Traditions of the Earliest Visits of Foreigners to North America, the First Formed and First Uninhabited of the Continents* (Louisville 1908); Gwyn A. Williams, *Madoc* (Oxford 1987).

Dana Olson

PRINTING AND PUBLISHING. Louisville has long been a center of the printing industry in Kentucky and the South. Printing began in Louisville in 1800 when Samuel Vail, from Fairhaven, Vermont, started the city's first newspaper, the *FARMER'S LIBRARY and Ohio Intelligencer.* His shop filled the need for small printing work.

Vail and a partner, Elijah C. Berry, published in 1803 the first book made in Louisville, *An Address to Judge Innes* by Richard Dickinson. It was the community's appetite for NEWSPAPERS that kept the fledgling industry alive as early efforts faded and new entrepreneurs tried their hands at publishing. In the first decade of the nineteenth century, these included Francis Peniston, who published the *Western American* in 1806 and advertised, "All kinds of printing will be executed with neatness and dispatch," and Joseph Charless, who brought out the new *Louisville Gazette* in 1808.

The second decade of that century brought back Elijah Berry, who began the *Louisville Correspondent* in 1810, but changes came frequently for tradesmen in the developing West, and the birds of passage were numerous. During just a few years, that newspaper's proprietors were, in sequence, William Farquhar, Mann Butler, William Wood, James Hughes, and Harlsey Deming.

A newspaper strong enough to survive twenty-five years, the *Public Advertiser* was established in 1818 by SHADRACK PENN JR. Jacob Eliot joined the firm in 1838 and later became its proprietor. From its 1810 POPULATION of about fourteen hundred, Louisville by 1830 had become the largest city in the state with a population of approximately ten thousand. There was a mushrooming need for more newspapers and publications of every kind in addition to the countless industrial, commercial, organizational, social, and personal printing demands of a restless community.

Louisville's population doubled by 1840 and doubled again by 1850, to forty-three thousand. In mid-century the printing and publishing fraternity had expanded greatly. During the years 1830–50, at least sixty-nine newspapers and periodicals came into being, including the *Louisville Democrat,* the *Courier,* and the *Journal,* the three ancestors of the city's longest-running newspaper, the *COURIER-JOURNAL.* The *Courier-Journal* and the *LOUISVILLE TIMES* were two newspapers heavily involved in the job-printing trade. Broadsides, pamphlets, and ADVERTISING made up a great deal of the printing contracts of these businesses.

By the late 1850s the city had a dozen printing establishments. Two of them, Morton & Griswold and John P. Morton & Co., were among the largest textbook publishers in the nation. Newspapers, book printers, job printing, and magazines were a vital part of the Louisville ECONOMY. Other names associated with printing were William Worsley, George D. Prentice, George W. Weissinger, and James Freeman Clarke.

Throughout the last half of the nineteenth century, numerous publishing establishments operated in Louisville. Major publishing houses such as the American Book Co., Collier's, J.B. Lippincott & Co., Standard Publishing Co., and Scribner's had offices in the city. Others included George G. FETTER PRINTING CO., Levering, Hull Brothers, Hurd & Burrows, B.J. Webb, Louisville Lithographic Co., Louisville Steam Lithographing Co., Hanna & Co., Robyn & Co., Bradley & Gilbert, C.T. Dearing Co., Fawcett-Dearing, Gibbs-Inman Printing Co., and Louisville Lithographing Co.

Major religious groups, including BAPTISTS, Catholics, METHODISTS, and Pentecostals, also were prominent in the publishing business. The Baptist Book Concern and the AMERICAN BAPTIST Co. were in Louisville in the 1890s, as was the Religious Fiction Publishing Co. The PROHIBITION News Co. published pamphlets and broadsides attacking the manufacture and use of alcoholic beverages.

Farm and home journals were published in Louisville. The Home and Farm Publishing Co., the Farmers' Home Journal Co., Home & Fireside Co., Inland Farm Publishing Co., Southern Home Co., and the Southern Journal Co. printed many domestic publications. One of the most influential domestic publications was Caron's CITY DIRECTORIES. These informative publications not only listed householders and their addresses but also contained an extensive commercial directory.

Ethnic groups were active in the publishing field. The KENTUCKY IRISH-AMERICAN Print Co. and the *Louisville Anzeiger* (Advertiser), established in 1849, were strongly tied to the Irish and the German communities. Large numbers of Irish and German immigrants poured into the city during the late 1840s and the 1850s, and the ethnic business concerns were important in retaining a sense of identity for the immigrant community.

The heyday of the publishing trade in Louisville lasted from the mid–nineteenth century until the years just before WORLD WAR II. However, publishing remains a part of the city's economy.

See "The Newspaper Press of Louisville," in *Memorial History of Louisville,* ed. J. Stoddard Johnston (Chicago 1896).

Martin F. Schmidt
Ron D. Bryant

PROHIBITION. The United States officially prohibited the manufacture, sale, and transport of most alcoholic beverages when the Eighteenth Amendment to the Constitution was ratified on January 16, 1920. Prohibition hit Kentucky, and especially Louisville, harder than most other areas of the country. The support of the TEMPERANCE movement by the national majority overrode the opposition of many Kentuckians. For many years, Kentucky had been one of the leading producers of whiskey and the traditional supplier of bourbon in the United States.

Louisville, with twelve breweries, thirty or so distilleries, and extensive transportation connections, was at the very heart of the industry. At one time it could boast one thousand licensed SALOONS. As a direct result of Prohibition, Louisville alone lost six thousand to eight thousand jobs in the spirit and related industries, including barrel makers, RAILROADS, and printing plants. Owensboro and Bardstown were also hard hit. Local ethnic communities were vocal in their opposition to Prohibition. In addition to the economic consequences, cultures such as Irish and German, in which alcohol played a historical part, were hampered in maintaining long-held traditions.

Prohibition efforts in Kentucky, prodded by religious fervor and anti-immigrant sentiment, date from the 1840s. The movement gained strength after the CIVIL WAR when unscrupulous politicians continued the old practice of plying prospective voters with liquor in order to get their votes on election day. Violent confrontations between inebriated men punctuated elections, sometimes sparking feuds. The continued prohibition of liquor sales on election days is a reminder of this problem.

In 1898 the Kentucky General Assembly strengthened the laws that supported the dry forces by ordering that parts of any county could remain dry by local option. In 1906 the state again strengthened its local option laws. If the majority of the county electorate voted a county "dry," such a decision would be law for the entire county. If, however, they voted for the county to be "wet," such an election would not affect those jurisdictions of the county that wished to be dry. A majority of Kentucky's counties had already banned liquor. By 1915 only eighteen counties, mostly along the OHIO RIVER and around urban areas such as Louisville, remained wet.

Whenever the issue came up, Louisville voted consistently and strongly against prohibition. An alternative to prohibition—licensing— was offered by Thomas M. Gilmore, publisher of the *Bonfort's Wine and Spirits Circular,* an international trade publication of the liquor industry. The National Model License League was formed in Louisville in October 1907, headquartered in the COLUMBIA BUILDING on Main St. with Gilmore as its president. This national organization of leading brewers, distillers, wholesale liquor dealers, and wine makers advocated licensing as a means of making the saloon a "place of warmth and light, of good fellowship, music, sobriety, and intellectual conversation" for men and women alike. It hoped to turn the tide of prohibition by creating a great national resort, like the BEER GARDENS of Germany and the cafés of France. Claiming thirty-five thousand members, the league caused liquor laws in several states to be changed. It preferred to control alcohol sales by regulation rather than prohibition. But the group was unsuccessful in preventing Prohibition.

Once Prohibition was instituted nationally by amendment, the city flagrantly ignored it. Louisville became the leading source of demand in the state for illegal alcohol. Even though it served as regional enforcement headquarters for the federal forces until 1930, speakeasies and illegal saloons known as "blind tigers" proliferated. Many citizens learned how to make gin in their bathtubs. Hip or leg flasks became common.

CUNNINGHAM'S RESTAURANT at Fifth and Breckinridge Streets—owned by a police captain—had a reputation for being well supplied with liquor. Another was Abe's White Doorknob, on Preston between Walnut (Muhammad Ali Blvd.) and Liberty Streets. At Snyder's Iroquois Garden and the Bide-a-Wee Club in the South End, managers looked the other way as they saw patrons bringing in liquor. Lawbreaking crossed all class boundaries. When federal agents raided the exclusive PENDENNIS CLUB in 1930, they found the place flowing with every conceivable type of liquor.

A thriving underground network was quickly established. By 1926 an estimated 430 gallons of illegal whiskey—not to mention other forms of liquor—were shipped to the city from Chicago every week. Louisville's warehouses, which continued to store whiskey legally, were another source for entrepreneurs. Many eastern Kentucky moonshiners also prospered.

Legal alcohol for scientific, mechanical, sacramental, or medicinal use was still available. A very limited number of special permits, one to Brown-Forman for example, permitted the sale of "whiskey on hand" for medicinal purposes. Kentucky's prohibition laws, closely following those of the Eighteenth Amendment, allowed doctors to prescribe one pint of liquor every ten days to a single individual. Federal regulations allowed one hundred such prescriptions per pharmacist every three months. When their use began to decrease, some believed that Prohibition was finally taking hold. More likely, imbibers were simply finding cheaper outlets, such as soda shacks.

Some distilleries tried to stay open by switching over to the manufacture of industrial alcohol or soda beverages, with little success. Others opened their doors to tourists. Many were torn down. Ouerbacker Ct., in the OLD LOUISVILLE neighborhood, is built on the grounds of one such distillery. Its architecture remains distinctly different from the area's older Victorian homes.

Prohibition created new opportunities for organized crime, and corruption inevitably seeped into the public ranks. In 1925 five Louisville policemen were discharged for mixing up records on alleged liquor violators. Many citizens began losing respect for the law. Louisville did not develop the kind of gang problem that made Chicago notorious during these years, but there were rival factions and occasional unsolved murders. Another problem was the rise in deaths or permanent mental impairment caused by contaminated liquor. Explosions in stills killed many. Arrests for public intoxication increased.

Local enforcement was considered the key to success, but the Kentucky legislature never funded it adequately, if at all. They left it to federal agents, who were spread too thin. Even so, in the first six years of the noble experiment, 1 percent of the state's population had been arrested for bootlegging. In 1929 Kentucky ranked second in the nation in arrests for bootlegging and first in convictions per capita.

Calls for repeal of Prohibition were heard throughout the 1920s. But repeal did not have a chance until after the crash of the New York Stock Exchange in October 1929. As unemployment grew, the public looked to the spirit industry, among others, for jobs and revenue. Before Prohibition, taxes on spirits and fermented liquors had brought a whopping $484 million to the federal coffers. In 1930 the revenue from those taxes was negligible. In Louisville and throughout the state, the cry of states' rights was also raised.

By 1930 Ernest Rowe, in charge of the enforcement district that included Kentucky, conceded, "It seems to be more or less the idea in Kentucky, as elsewhere in the nation, that where a person has a little home-brew cider or wine in his possession, for his own use, he should be left alone." The federal program was beginning to crack. Before a 1931 congressional committee, the head of federal Prohibition efforts suggested tentatively that "home option" brewing be allowed. He also recommended an army of new enforcers, at a time when the federal government could ill afford them. The public had had enough.

In 1930 several prominent Louisville women, led by Mrs. James Todd, formed a chapter of the Women's Organization for National Prohibition Reform. Membership soon thrived statewide, and Todd herself went on to national prominence. The crusade eventually paid off as Congress approved and sent to the states a repeal amendment that was approved in late 1933.

A 1921 federal law had required the maintenance of 2 million gallons of whiskey nationally for emergencies. By 1929 those stocks were becoming depleted. Since it takes four years for whiskey to age properly before use, Glenmore and other distilleries remaining in Kentucky and Pennsylvania convinced the federal government to authorize limited new production in 1929, 1931, and 1932. At repeal, Glenmore was thus well positioned to meet the new demand, while others rushed to establish themselves. Glenmore maintained command of the industry for many years thereafter.

In 1935 whiskey production—with Louisville in the lead—soared to nearly 59 million gallons nationwide, up 22 million gallons from 1934. Federal tax revenues increased accordingly. Louisville was well on its way to returning to leadership in the spirit industry.

See John Kobler, *Ardent Spirits: The Rise and Fall of Prohibition* (New York 1949); Joseph Earl Dabney, *Mountain Spirits: A Chronicle of Corn Whiskey from King James' Ulster Plantation to America's Appalachians and the Moonshine Life* (New York 1974); John Y. Hamilton, "You Had to Know Somebody," *Louisville* 30 (Jan. 1979): 42; George H. Yater, *Flappers, Prohibition and All That Jazz* (Louisville 1984); George H. Yater, *Two Hundred Years at the Falls of the Ohio* (Louisville 1979); T.M. Gilmore, *Bonfort's Wine and Spirits Circular,* Jan. 10, 1910 (New York).

David Williams

PROJECT SAFE PLACE. Launched in 1983 to provide help and protection to troubled children and teens, Project Safe Place is an outgrowth of Louisville's YMCA Shelter House for Runaways. Various public places and businesses, designated by yellow diamond-shaped signs that show arms embracing a child, serve as links to shelters that assist at-risk youngsters. Employees at Safe Place locations in Louisville are instructed to contact the YMCA Shelter House, which then sends a trained volunteer to pick up a child who has come for help. The child is taken to the shelter for counseling and, if needed, a place to stay. The first Safe Place was established at a fire station at Sixth and Hill Streets; by the late 1990s, over three hundred such sites had been designated in Louisville and over two thousand children aided. In 1995 the TRANSIT AUTHORITY OF RIVER CITY announced that its buses would also serve as Safe Places.

In 1986 the program went nationwide and was honored by Pres. Ronald Reagan (1981–89) as one of the nation's thirty most innovative and outstanding privately funded public service programs. Since then, more than a hundred cities throughout the United States have adopted the program, resulting in the establishment of over eight thousand Safe Place sites.

See *Courier-Journal,* May 26, 1995; March 17, 1998.

PROSPECT. Prospect is located in the northeastern tip of Jefferson County and is bordered by the OLDHAM COUNTY line to the northeast, the OHIO RIVER to the northwest, and HARRODS CREEK to the south.

The first settlers came to this region in the late 1700s via flatboats traveling to Harrods Creek. The area started to resemble a town when the narrow-gauge Louisville, Harrods Creek & Westport Railroad was built in the 1870s. It was originally known as Sand Hill because it is part of a sandy stretch of landscape. It is not known who gave it its current name, but the name itself is believed to come from the belief that the area held a "good prospect" for residents.

In the early 1900s, with the transformation of the railroad into an electric interurban line, Prospect began to grow more rapidly. At that time the POPULATION was a mixture of poor farmers, wealthy landowners, and the descendants of slaves.

Prospect had been a rural farm community for much of its history, but with the opening of Hunting Creek in the mid-1960s, the area became home to some of Louisville's most affluent people. Hunting Creek, which boasts its own country club and GOLF course, was one of the first of Prospect's plush suburban subdivisions that have sprung up along Highway 42, the main transportation artery running through prospect

For more than seven decades, the heart of Prospect was the Prospect Store, a general store that stood just north of U.S. 42 and Covered Bridge Rd. The store opened in 1911 and was the main gathering place for area residents until it was replaced by a gas station and food mart.

In the mid-1800s, James Trigg, president of the narrow-gauge railroad, built a twelve-room brick mansion just south of U.S. 42 and Covered Bridge Rd. The elegant mansion (known as the Trigg house) became the home of MARK ETHRIDGE, the general manager and publisher of the *COURIER-JOURNAL* and the *LOUISVILLE TIMES* from 1936 to 1963, and his wife, WILLIE SNOW ETHRIDGE, a writer of several books about family life in Prospect. The Ethridge estate was a cultural center of Louisville's social scene. The family was famous for entertaining many guests at the mansion, including big-band leader Benny Goodman. In 1956, on the day of the KENTUCKY DERBY, the Ethridges were entertaining several guests, one of whom was author John Steinbeck. During the festivities at their home, Steinbeck wrote "Ode to the Kentucky Derby" on a typewriter provided by the Ethridges.

Other notable residents of Prospect include GEORGE GARVIN BROWN, president and chairman of Brown-Forman distilleries, and William F. Knebelkamp, president of the Louisville Baseball Co., which owned the LOUISVILLE COLONELS professional BASEBALL team. The two men and their families occupied the same home at different times on a farm known as Sutherland. In the late 1980s the land was developed into Sutherland Farms, an expensive subdivision.

One of the most unusual attractions during the past two decades has been Henry's Ark, a petting zoo on Rose Island Rd. near Prospect run by Henry Wallace. The 30-acre zoo features animals that eat out of visitors' hands, such as zebras, bison, giraffes, camels, and deer.

Prospect was incorporated as a fourth-class city in 1974. The population was 1,981 in 1980, 2,788 in 1990, and 2,963 in 1996.

See *A Place in Time: The Story of Louisville's Neighborhoods* (Louisville 1989).

James Strohmaier

PROSSER, CHARLES ALLEN (b New Albany, Indiana, September 20, 1871; d Minneapolis, Minnesota, November 26, 1952). Pioneer in American vocational education. Prosser was the son of Reese William and Sarah Emma (Leach) Prosser. He earned a B.A. in 1897 and an M.A. in 1906 from DePauw University, a law degree in 1898 from the UNIVERSITY OF LOUISVILLE, and a Ph.D. from Columbia University in 1915. He married Zerelda A. Huckeby on December 30, 1896, and they had a son, William L. Prosser.

After a stint in elementary and high school teaching, Prosser served as New Albany school superintendent from 1900 to 1908. In 1909 he became the superintendent of the Children's Aid Society of New York and served until 1910, when he was appointed assistant commissioner of education for Massachusetts.

In 1912 he moved to Washington, D.C., as secretary of the National Society for the Promotion of Industrial Education. In this position he was instrumental in drafting the Smith-Hughes Act of 1917, which provided federal grants for vocational education in high schools. He became director of the William Hood Dunwoody Industrial Institute in Minneapolis, Minnesota, in 1915 and held that position until 1945. The Charles Allen Prosser Institute of Technology in NEW ALBANY is named in his honor. He is buried in Minneapolis.

Carl E. Kramer

PROSTITUTION. The exact time prostitution began in Louisville is unknown, but it was unlikely to have occurred in the earliest days when the main concerns were land-clearing, cabin-building, and the threat of Indian raids. However, it was thriving by 1820, when a grand jury was distressed by the many "nurseries of vice and immorality" and "the great and unusual increase of tippling houses and houses of ill-fame." Four years later a public meeting castigated town officials for seeming to ignore the problem.

Ohio and Mississippi River cities were especially prone to the twin evils of GAMBLING and prostitution because of the diverse throng of humanity, including rivermen, passing through during the heyday of steamboat travel. In 1832 Councilman John M. Talbott noted at a City Council meeting that Louisville was "greatly infested at this time with robbers, felons, pickpockets, and swindlers and vagrants" who were also "resorting to houses of prostitution, grog shops, and gambling houses." He wanted the watchmen to "take them to a proper tribunal" (Council minutes, July 16, 1832).

The following year, when James Trotter, editor of Lexington's *Kentucky Gazette,* fired shots on the street in Louisville at rival editor George Prentice of the *LOUISVILLE JOURNAL,* the act for some reason spawned mob violence. The *Louisville Public Advertiser* reported that a dozen houses "occupied by women of ill fame were almost battered to pieces and three days later two more were burned."

Lafayette and Marshall Streets east of the city center seem to have been home to the first red-light districts, or concentrations of brothels, also called bagnios and a variety of other names in the Louisville press. Adopting FRENCH terminology, local NEWSPAPERS referred to Rue de Lafayette, Boulevard de Lafayette, and Faubourg de Marshall by the 1860s. Even earlier, on June 13, 1855, the *Louisville Courier* commented on the *Femmes de Pave* "nightly to be seen on Main and certain of our cross streets."

During the CIVIL WAR, prostitution flourished because of the concentration of troops in the city. The aftermath was described by Mayor John Bunce in 1869 in his annual message to the aldermen and councilmen. "It is a sad and well-known fact to us all," he declared, "that all the legislation and most determined efforts of

12

ELSIE LIVINGSTON,

828 Grayson Street.

While out seeing the sights, boys, do not fail to drop in upon MISS ELSIE at the above number, and you will be royally entertained. Everything and everybody connected with her establishment is first-class. She has the following named ladies to entertain you:

Misses Freddie,
Annie,
Edna,
Alice,
Blanche,
Marie,
Grace.

MISS ELSIE is an Ohio girl and will be pleased to see all visitors from home.

She has a fine line of

Wine and Beer.

13

HALLIE REED,

824 Grayson St.

Visitors to the Encampment and Races will not make their visit complete if they fail to pay Miss HATTIE a visit. She has just opened the above number and has a corps of pretty girls to entertain callers.

She also keeps the choices brands of Wine and Beer.

Georgia Stewart,

830 Grayson Street.

As there are only a few first-class houses upon this street, and as the Guide only contains the names of first-class resorts it will therefore be the duty of the writer to devote a space to the above-named lady. She is a clever and liberal entertainer and has a number of beautiful girls to assist her to entertain her callers.

She also has a fine line of Wine and Beer.

Pages from a "Souvenir Sporting Guide" to Louisville published for the 1895 encampment of the Grand Army of the Republic. (G.A.R.)

the police have utterly failed in this, as in other cities, to suppress these vices, gambling and prostitution." He suggested that because "harlotry has grown to such dimensions as it now assumes in our midst" it be subjected to "such sanitary regulations . . . as will stem the flood of diseases issuing from the brothels of Lafayette, Marshall, and other streets" (*Louisville Municipal Reports for the Year Ending December 31, 1868,* 16–18). Venereal diseases were common, judging from the number of newspaper advertisements offering treatment for "Private diseases."

By the late 1870s and early 1880s, the "disorderly houses" were concentrated in an area called the Chute (the origin of the name is unknown), centered around the intersection of Floyd and Jefferson Streets. The American House at that corner was particularly notorious. In an attempt to discourage patronage of the bagnios, the police began in 1873 keeping a register of all visitors to these establishments. The book was open for public inspection. A citizens' group called the Law and Order League also took a hand and was later credited by the *Louisville Herald* with scattering "the inmates" of the houses in the Chute about 1890.

That was when they moved to Green (Liberty) and Grayson Streets between Sixth and Tenth Streets, according to the *Louisville Post* of June 12, 1893. But "street walkers" were found on Green and also Market and Jefferson Streets between Second and Eighth as early as 1880. "The streets have been crowded every night of late by bands of notorious females who flaunt their brazen charms in the face of every male person who comes their way," the *Commercial* reported.

Some of the bawdy establishments were known as "panel houses," reported the *Commercial.* A precise description of the sliding panels in the walls was given. They were so arranged that the visitor's pockets could be rifled while he was otherwise engaged. Louisville lore holds that the victim always found a nickel remaining in his pocket—streetcar fare home. Some of the madams who operated the brothels were practically public figures, and at their death their funerals were reported in detail by the press. Some were buried in CAVE HILL CEMETERY. A few made successful transitions to other occupations. One Lizzie Manning moved her operations to Chicago in 1886, invested her profits in Florida orange groves, and became wealthy. Another semipublic figure in the twentieth century was Anna S. Haines, who may well have held the record for longevity in her business. Official police records document a career in prostitution-related activities from 1926 to at least 1970, much of it from a house in the 300 block of E Oak St. Louisville's last madam passed away at the age of eighty-five in 1979.

The Green St. concentration was broken up by city authorities in 1917 at the demand of the army shortly after the nation entered WORLD WAR I and CAMP ZACHARY TAYLOR was established. But Green St. (Liberty after 1917), along with Seventh St., continued to have a reputation for vice well into the twentieth century, as did stretches of Market and Eighteenth Streets.

In 1937 a nine-page survey by Louisville GOODWILL INDUSTRIES found 365 women working in eighty-five houses of prostitution in an area bounded roughly by the OHIO RIVER and BROADWAY from Fifth to Twelfth Streets. By 1938 women working in the city's red-light district numbered about 500. The city registered, fingerprinted, and photographed the prostitutes of the district. Health examinations found that an extremely high percentage of the women were infected with syphilis or gonorrhea, or both. In a fifteen-month period, from March 1937 to May 1938, incidents of venereal diseases reported to local clinics jumped from two thousand to almost seven thousand. The situation became so serious that the U.S. Army rented a building in the center of the district, on Seventh St. between Walnut and Cedar, and established a prophylaxis station. On one night alone, in March, 254 soldiers were treated. At that time the MEDICINE cost less than a penny per treatment.

Such was Louisville's contribution to a national epidemic that caused the federal government to appropriate $3 million for one of the most intensive campaigns in U.S. medical history to control the spread of sexually transmitted diseases. By the end of WORLD WAR II, the vice district had shifted to the area surrounding the HAYMARKET, especially along Jefferson St. between Preston and Second. A peaceful market in the daytime became a completely transformed world after dark. A December 1948 grand jury report recommended that the state police be called in to help police in the area if local authorities would not or could not do the job. The commonwealth's attorney, Frank A. Ropke, estimated the area to be responsible for 50 percent of the city's crimes of "prostitution, slugging robberies, and so forth."

In 1969 a three-man team contracted by the federal government to study commercialized prostitution throughout the United States reported that the silk and marble pleasure palaces were dying out, that organized crime was investing in more profitable enterprises, and that, as a result, prostitution was becoming more and more disorganized. Their report, listed under "U.S. Government Procurements," cited Louisville as among the nation's five worst cities for prostitution.

Male prostitution is, of course, as old as female prostitution, but it has a much more subterranean history. Certain public PARKS in the city and the area around Fourth and York Streets have been known sites for sixty years or more. However, the years 1980–85 saw this old form of prostitution brought to a new light of public consciousness. The area around Central Park had developed a reputation for male prostitution. In response to neighborhood complaints, the police, using an officer as a decoy, began to make arrests for criminal solicitation. Many of the male prostitutes working the OLD LOUISVILLE area were runaways, some as young as thirteen. By 1985 city safety director Ernest E. Allen had estimated that the male prostitution problem in Louisville was larger than the female prostitution problem. Others concurred.

The Mayor's Task Force on Neighborhood Prostitution was convened in 1985. After issuing recommendations, it noted that the city spends about $1,000—in court, jail, and public-defender expenses—every time a prostitute is arrested. There are no red-light districts in Louisville today, but prostitution continues. Arrangements are sometimes made by telephone, or perhaps over the Internet, or at massage parlors. Activity waxes and wanes. At Derby time the number of prostitutes working the city increases by about 20 percent, and many come from out of state to make a run for the Rolexes. As the city swells with visitors, streetwalkers can make from $50 to $100 a customer; those working from HOTELS or through taxi drivers can add another zero to the price list.

On some streets ladies of the evening still flash "their brazen charms in the face of every male person who comes their way," today usually in an automobile.

See *Report of the Vice Commission of Louisville, Kentucky* (Louisville 1915); *Courier-Journal,* Oct. 3, 1937; *Advertiser* June 19, 1938; Dec. 15, 1948; Dec. 11, 1969; June 8, 1974; Oct. 23, 1980; May 14, July 22, 1985; *Louisville Public Advertiser,* April 26, 1820; Dec. 22, 1824; *Kentucky Gazette,* Sept. 14, 1839; *Louisville Herald,* April 3, 1903, 12; *Commercial,* May 28, 1880, 4; Sept. 2, 1886.

George H. Yater

PUBLIC HEALTH. Public health has been defined as "the art and science of preventing disease, prolonging life, and promoting physical health and efficiency through organized community effort" (C.E.A. Winslow, quoted in Hanlon, *Principles of Public Health Administration,* 4). Public health focuses on preventing disease and injury in the community as a whole, as opposed to clinical medicine, which treats disease in individuals.

The goal of public health is to promote, protect, and monitor the health of the community. To do this, it performs three core functions: assessment, policy development, and assurance. Assessment is the collection, analysis, and dissemination of information on the health of a community. Policy development uses scientific knowledge and other data gathered through assessment to develop comprehensive plans for the improvement of the community's health. The assurance function of public health requires health departments to make sure that appropriate activities are carried out and services are offered to achieve public health policy goals. Health departments may ensure that public health goals are met by the passage of laws or regulations, by encouraging private entities to engage in certain activities, or by providing services directly.

Public health in Louisville and in the United States grew, in part, out of the Marine Hospital Service that was established to provide basic medical care to merchant seamen. In 1798 Congress established that service and set up a network of health care facilities along waterways such as the OHIO RIVER and in coastal cities. Marine Hospitals were established in Paducah and Louisville. The former Marine Hospital in Louisville, which is now owned by the Louisville and Jefferson County Board of Health, still stands today on the grounds of the Portland Family Health Center and has been designated a National Historic Landmark.

Public health in Louisville is almost as old as the city itself. In 1802 dead animals in the streets were declared a nuisance and ordered removed. Also outlawed was the dumping of slop jars into the streets. The early 1800s saw outbreaks of yellow fever, malaria, smallpox, and cholera in Louisville. Temporary health boards were set up in the city as early as 1822 to deal with numerous outbreaks. The yellow fever outbreak in 1817 led to the establishment of Louisville's City Hospital. A permanent BOARD OF HEALTH was established in Louisville in 1866 with Dr. H.W. Bullitt appointed as health officer. Despite similar claims by the Yakima County Health Department, established in 1911 in the state of Washington, "the nation's and Kentucky's first full-time county health department was established in Jefferson County in 1908" (Ellis, *Medicine in Kentucky,* 74). In 1942 the Louisville and Jefferson County Boards of Health merged under the name the Louisville and Jefferson County Board of Health. This merger created a single health department, the Louisville and Jefferson County Health Department, which became an agency of JEFFERSON COUNTY FISCAL COURT under the Cooperative Compact Act of 1986.

The Louisville and Jefferson County Health Department is operated under the direction of the county judge/executive and Jefferson County Fiscal Court. An eight-member Board of Health appointed by the county judge and the mayor of Louisville oversees the agency, which provides a wide range of services, including communicable disease control, chronic disease prevention and screening, family health services, and environmental services. The department also investigates and tracks the outbreak of infectious diseases and provides health planning and health education services.

The health department maintains its own laboratory, used to perform over 130,000 tests annually to detect such infectious diseases as tuberculosis as well as contamination in food or water supplies. The department immunizes more than twenty-four thousand children and adults each year against deadly diseases. The department has also teamed up with Jewish Hospital and the UNIVERSITY OF LOUISVILLE to open a state-of-the-art clinic that provides vaccinations for travelers to foreign countries.

The health department offers comprehensive care and education to expectant mothers. In 1997 it received an $8 million federal Healthy Start grant to help lower the infant mortality rate in targeted west Louisville NEIGHBORHOODS. The same year the department began the Mommy and Me Program, a parental case-management initiative in which health department nurses visit the homes of expectant mothers both before and after the birth of the baby to ensure a safe pregnancy and a healthy environment for the newborn.

Through nutritional programs such as WIC (Women, Infants, and Children), the department gives nutritional counseling and healthful food to ensure the healthy growth of the community's children. The health department offers well-child assessments each year to children from birth to six years of age.

The Louisville and Jefferson County Health Department was at the forefront of the efforts to eliminate polio when it conducted Salk vaccine field trials in 1956. Outbreaks of new infectious diseases, such as AIDS, and familiar diseases that have become resistant to therapeutic drugs, such as some strains of tuberculosis, pose new challenges to public health. In response to the AIDS problem, the department has established an HIV prevention and testing program. The department also tests for and treats such other sexually transmitted diseases as syphilis, chlamydia, and gonorrhea. In 1997 the department opened the Collaborative Center for AIDS Services, which brings the department's HIV services under one roof with various community AIDS groups. As a component of its HIV prevention strategy, the department has established the Methadone/Opiate Rehabilitation and Education (MORE) Center to treat opiate-addicted intravenous drug users, who may spread disease by sharing infected needles.

The Health Department's Division of Environmental Health and Protection inspects package sewage treatment plants and SWIMMING pools and also certifies lifeguards. Environmentalists perform housing inspections, investigate complaints of mosquitoes and rats, and quarantine animals involved in biting incidents to guard against the spread of rabies. The division inspects Jefferson County's restaurant and grocery facilities as well as all temporary food vendors at major public events like the KENTUCKY DERBY, the KENTUCKY STATE FAIR, and THUNDER OVER LOUISVILLE.

The department also responds to disasters. For example, health department nurses gave over three thousand tetanus immunizations during the flood of 1997; environmentalists, with other Jefferson County government personnel, went door to door in flood-ravaged areas to ensure that public health and safety were maintained.

Services are also augmented through the Neighborhood Place program, which brings together comprehensive health, education, and human services from a variety of organizations. There are currently six Neighborhood Places throughout Jefferson County, each with its own advisory board made up of members drawn from the community it serves. Through the Neighborhood Places, residents may receive health services, mental health services, job counseling, temporary financial assistance, housing assistance, and information about available social programs.

Services offered by the department often go beyond the traditional public-health services. The department has established full-service and specialty centers throughout the community that provide primary health care and dental services to special populations. These services are provided in collaboration with Family Health Centers, the University of Louisville, and the PARK DUVALLE Community Health Center. The department has also established the Office of

Parkway Place homes, 1954.

Minority Health, which removes barriers to good health among minority members of the community. The department's Lead Safe Neighborhood project treats and prevents lead poisoning in children. The National Lead Training and Resource Center, the only trainer of lead-poisoning professionals in the United States today, is located at the Louisville and Jefferson County Health Department.

See Cabinet for Health Services, Department for Public Health, *Kentucky Health Improvement Plan* (Frankfort 1998); Institute of Medicine, *The Future of Public Health* (Washington, D.C., 1988); U.S. Department of Health and Human Services, *For a Healthy Nation* (Washington, D.C., 1995); Virginia D. Durrett and Bruce K. Lane, *A History of Public Health in Louisville and Jefferson County* (Louisville 1997); John H. Ellis, *Medicine in Kentucky* (Lexington 1977); Rice C. Leach, "A General History of Public Health," in *Papers and Proceedings of the Governor's Conference on the Future of Public Health in Kentucky* (Louisville 1997); J.J. Hanlon, *Principles of Public Health Administration* (St. Louis 1969).

David Langdon

PUBLIC HOUSING. Louisville's initial public housing effort focused on slum clearance and low-rent housing for the working poor. The impetus for the initiative evolved from a 1933 survey conducted by Mayor William B. Harrison that illustrated the need for public assistance in housing for city residents. His successor, Neville Miller, actually applied to the Federal Public Works Administration for public housing assistance on February 19, 1934. Several years later, in 1937, the authority for federal housing complexes was transferred from the Public Works Administration to the U.S. Housing Authority.

By 1938 two housing complexes were completed at College Ct. and LaSalle Pl. College Ct., located next to the Louisville Municipal College on the site of the old Eclipse Ball Park, was reserved for African Americans. LaSalle Place, at Dixie Hwy. and Algonquin Pkwy., was for white tenants. In 1940 two more complexes, Clarksdale and Beecher Terrace, were built as urban slum clearance projects. The four complexes were placed under the jurisdiction of the newly created Louisville Municipal Housing Commission, which later became the Housing Authority of Louisville.

During World War II, new construction of public housing was suspended, though two projects, Parkway Place and Sheppard Square, were already under way. They were completed under a provision that earmarked them for emergency housing for war workers. After the war they reverted to public housing for families with very low incomes. In 1946 converted army barracks near Bowman Field Airport were opened to veterans and families of servicemen as public housing units. Bowman Field Homes was turned over to the city in 1950 and was deactivated as public housing in 1963.

Construction on Iroquois Homes, the area's largest public housing project, began in 1951 for low-income white residents. Located at the Watterson Expwy. and Taylor Blvd., the completed complex contained 854 units and was built at a cost of over $9 million. Cotter Homes, a companion project for African Americans on Thirty-fourth St., was financed under a provision of the Housing Act of 1949 and finished a few years later. Nearby Lang homes, for larger families, was completed in 1959.

In 1956 twelve African Americans sued the city's Municipal Housing Commission to gain entrance to traditionally white public housing that had open units, rather than remain on waiting lists for units in the African American complexes. The Lang Homes were the first legally integrated public housing complex. Although the city was compelled to stop assigning units by race, de facto segregation persisted. Iroquois Homes was one of the few public housing operations that became realistically integrated.

In the 1960s the philosophy of public housing assistance underwent a shift. Income requirements for tenants were reduced; so residents often had little or no income, and their rent was subsidized by the U.S. government. Construction of the Village West Apartments began in 1966 to provide badly needed central-city housing. The complex, located on an urban renewal tract of 34 acres, was conceived as a model neighborhood. The financing was from federal sources, but the complex was managed by a private company. The building schedule was often delayed, and it was not until 1970 that the apartments were opened to tenants.

During the 1980s the city was forced to examine the reality of the problems of the aging projects. Extensive renovations were made to a number of the projects, and others were slated for demolition. The Cotter and Lang homes were demolished in 1996 to make room for mixed-income developments, and in 1998 Village West was totally redesigned and renamed City View Park.

See *Courier-Journal,* Sept. 3, 1966; May 14, 1986; Jan. 14, 1996; June 21, March 19, 1997.

Margaret L. Merrick

PUBLIC RELATIONS. On the national scene, the public relations profession came into being just after the turn of the twentieth century in New York City, when Ivy Lee and Edward Bernays began to advise corporate clients. The profession grew slowly until after World War II, when corporate America began to recognize the role of public relations as a management function. It took another few years for Louisville to treat public relations seriously.

In the late 1950s corporate public relations was introduced as an important management function in the Louisville marketplace. The Bluegrass Chapter of the Public Relations Society of America (PRSA) was founded in 1957; and William Wicks, public relations manager of International Harvester, was its first president. The local PRSA chapter continues to be part of a national professional society for public relations professionals.

At the time the PRSA chapter was born, public relations professionals began taking on more responsibilities: no longer were they confined to issuing press releases and handling media calls; public relations professionals expanded into areas such as community relations, crisis communications, government relations, and investor relations.

Rather than reporting to personnel or human resources departments, the public relations official, in many instances, began reporting directly to the chief executive officer. Also, at this time many companies began expanding their public relations presence from one or two people to full-blown departments. William T. Owens of Girdler Co.–Tube Turns and Addison McGhee of Brown-Forman Corp. were among the first public relations practitioners in Louisville.

Beginning in 1961 many Louisville companies began not only to cultivate stronger public relations departments but to diversify the functions of those departments as well. One of the first to do so was Brown & Williamson Tobacco Corp. John Blalock of that firm developed community outreach through corporate sponsorship of the arts and various cultural events throughout the city, in addition to overseeing the company's public relations department. Brown & Williamson sponsored the Louisville Orchestra and the Kentucky Opera and contributed heavily to the Fund for the Arts, continuing these activities as the year 2000 began.

Other early notables in the Louisville public relations scene were Warren McNeill and Charles Castner of the Louisville & Nashville Railroad (L&N). McNeill was the first to head the railroad's public relations department. L&N won the prestigious Golden Freight Car award for excellence in corporate communications under his direction. Castner, meanwhile, focused his attention on a new type of public relations work in the Louisville market, crisis communications. From the late 1970s to the late 1980s, he not only oversaw communications revolving around crisis situations—such as a train derailment—but he also acted as the official spokesperson on behalf of the company.

In 1964 Owens won a coveted Silver Anvil Award from the PRSA for his work. (Since Owens's award, only three other local chapter members have won the Silver Anvil: Al Jolly, Bob Irvine, and Dan Burgess.) Jan Haller became the first woman to be named local PRSA chapter president in 1965. Another individual who made his mark on the corporate public relations landscape was Jack Guthrie, who directed Philip Morris's Louisville community relations department beginning in 1967. Through his direction, Philip Morris became involved in many charitable contributions and company-sponsored cultural and arts events, many of which continue. In 1977 Guthrie founded his own independent public relations practice, Jack Guthrie & Associates, later Guthrie/Mayes & Associates, specializing in areas such as media relations, product and service marketing, crisis management, government relations, and special events.

Gardner DeWitt had the distinction of becoming one of the city's first vice presidents of public relations. DeWitt, who worked for Brown-Forman Corp., was named a vice president in 1978. He focused mainly on developing business-to-business relations with Brown-Forman's distributors and wholesalers while also handling media relations, which, claims DeWitt, was different at that time, because of the media's lack of confidence and familiarity with public relations professionals.

In 1964 the practice of public relations expanded beyond the corporate scene. One of the first such entries into the field came that same year when Ray Simmons relocated from Chicago, making Louisville's second-largest ADVERTISING agency at the time—Doe-Anderson—the first advertising agency in the city to form its own public relations division. Through the years, other ad agencies, such as Creative Alliance and Bandy Carroll Hellige, have followed suit. Simmons later formed his own public relations agency in 1973, Simmons Public Relations.

One of the first purely public relations agencies in Louisville—Amster & Associates—was formed in 1964 by Betty Lou Amster to serve clients such as the Louisville Bar Association, the local American Red Cross chapter, and various owners of horse farms. The firm was sold in 1970 and disappeared shortly thereafter.

The following year, another solely public relations agency, Wenz-Neely Co., was formed by Rod Wenz and Randy Neely, both of whom had experience in the news media and in corporate public relations. Wenz-Neely specialized in financial and investor relations, product promotions, public-issues management, and government relations. In 1989 Wenz-Neely was acquired by Shandwick International, a worldwide public relations company.

The presence of public relations in Louisville at the end of the twentieth century was strong and growing. The local PRSA chapter has grown to include more than two hundred members, two-thirds of whom are women.

Andrew Eggers

PUBLIC SCHOOLS. The first Charter of the City of Louisville was granted by the General Assembly of the Commonwealth of Kentucky on February 13, 1828. The Act gavae the city the authority to establish "free schools." On April 24, 1829, the mayor and the councilmen passed an ordinance to establish the first public schools in each ward of the city and to levy a property tax for school purposes, for all children under sixteen years of age. The first trustees selected under the ordinance were JAMES GUTHRIE, John P. Harrison, William Sale, James Overstreet, FORTUNATUS COSBY JR., and Samuel Dickinson. Dr. Mann Butler was selected as the head of the public school, and on August 17, 1829, a school was opened at the southwest corner of Fifth and Green (Liberty) Streets in the rented upper story of the Baptist Church with an enrollment of 250 pupils. Instruction was confined to the common branches of English studies, with no fee for tuition; thus, it was the first free school established by law in Louisville and in Kentucky. The following year a new schoolhouse was built on the corner of Fifth and Walnut (Muhammad Ali Blvd.) Streets, on a lot on Fifth St. and running through to Centre St. The property was purchased from James Guthrie and Edward Shippen for $2,100.

Although the charter provided for free schools, when the new building was occupied, tuition was charged. The tuition consisted of $1.00 per quarter in the primary grades and $1.50 in other departments. The trustees could waive the fee if, in their judgment, pupils were unable to pay. The students were in school from 8:00 a.m. to 12:00 noon and from 2:00 to 6:00 p.m., from October to April. Holidays were Saturdays and Sundays and one week from Christmas to January 2. The City Council directed that the first school be conducted using the monitorial, or Lancastrian, system of teaching. This system's chief feature was the selection of monitors or subteachers from the more apt scholars, who instructed the other pupils while the principal teacher and assistants supervised and gave special instructions to other monitors. Lessons were studied only at school, not at home, because of the necessity to use candles, grease lamps, and kerosene for home lighting. The fact that the town was small, making the distance from school to home short in the days when Louisville's first school opened, explains the long school day.

Because the city of Louisville had demonstrated its ability to maintain public schools, the state gave half of the JEFFERSON SEMINARY property to Louisville for the purpose of erecting a "High School College," and by 1838 the city had a complete school system under its control. The 1837 report of the trustees of the Louisville public schools noted an enrollment of 716 students. It was not until 1851 that tuition was abolished for all residents of the city of Louisville. The Male High School and Female High School opened in 1856. In the two decades between 1851 and 1871, twenty lots were purchased and seventeen schools built. The enrollment increased from 4,303 in 1851 to 13,503 in 1871, and the number of teachers increased from 43 to 276.

The city charter of 1870 provided that schools for African American children be established, and a committee on schools for African American students was appointed. On October 1, 1870, the first public schools for AFRICAN AMERICANS were opened in Louisville, one in the Center Street African Methodist Church, where Sallie Adams presided as principal, and the other in the Fifth St. African Baptist Church, with Susie Adams as the principal. In 1873 a school building was constructed solely for the purpose of public education for blacks. On October 7, 1873, the school, located at Sixth and Kentucky Streets, was dedicated.

By the end of the 1896–97 school year, the enrollment in the Louisville public schools had increased to 26,242 (20,559 white and 5,683 black). Students attended school for ten months, and the average monthly teacher wage was $51.50. By the 1907–8 school year, attendance had increased to 29,211 (23,458 white and 5,753 black). The Louisville public school district continued to grow and in 1912 began a gradual annexation of property located in Jefferson County, property that had already been annexed by the city of Louisville. Enrollment in the Louisville public school district for grades one through twelve was 45,841 (33,831 white and 12,010 black) in the 1956 school year, the first year the public schools were desegregated. In 1974, the last year that Louisville was a separate district, the enrollment was 40,939 (19,171 white and 21,768 black).

In the early years following statehood, Kentucky had no system of public education. Therefore, in the county, schools were private. Later, "field schools" served many of the communities. The act of the legislature to establish a system of common schools in the state of Kentucky was approved February 16, 1838. In the 1840 *Annual Report of the Superintendent of Public Instruction,* communicated to both branches of the legislature of Kentucky, the common schools of Jefferson County reported that thirty schools were "districted previous to 1840." Those districts adopted the 1838 act of the legislature to establish a system of common schools. In the same report, the "whole POPULATION" of Jefferson County was reported to be 36,310; 5,843 were "children from 5 to 15," and 3,744 were "children from 7 to 17." Of those, 626 children were reported "at school." There were twenty-eight male teachers and three female teachers. The *Legislative Documents* (in "Reports Communicated to Both Branches of the Legislature of Kentucky...1840") listed the Jefferson County commissioners as DAVID MERIWETHER, Alfred N. Luckett, and James Pomeroy. In 1850 Jefferson County again listed 30 districts with 561 children attending six-month schools, and 130 attending three-month schools. Reports made by the commissioner of the Common Schools of Jefferson County to the State Superintendent of Public Instruction for the 1876–77 school year indicated that there were fifty-eight schools for white children and ten for black children in Jefferson County.

In 1884 the state BOARD OF EDUCATION was created, and a county superintendent elected by popular vote replaced the appointed commissioner. The 1920 General Assembly passed the County Administration Law requiring appointment of the county superintendent by the Board of Education.

In 1934 the state legislature completely revised and codified state school laws, and the resulting New School Code reduced to two the number of types of school districts, to be known as county districts and independent districts (Jefferson County was a county district and Louisville an independent district). Enrollment in the Jefferson County schools was 36,308 (34,911 white and 1,397 black) in the 1956 school year. In 1974, the last year in which the Jefferson County School District was a separate district, the enrollment was 89,405 (84,666 white and 4,739 black).

On February 28, 1975, the state Board of Education ordered the merger of the Louisville and Jefferson County school systems effective April 1, 1975. On April 21, 1975, the Supreme Court denied appeals to reverse a Sixth Circuit Court order, and on July 17, 1975, a final order to U.S. District judge James F. Gordon stipulated that a desegregation plan would be implemented at the beginning of the 1975–76 school year, which began on September 4, 1975. Ernest C. Grayson, former Jefferson County public school district deputy superintendent, became the first superintendent of the merged districts.

In 1978 Judge Gordon ended the court's active supervision of the desegregation plan. However, the order was never fully lifted. The Jefferson County public school district continued mandatory BUSING but changed its racial guidelines. In 1984 the desegregation plan for middle and high schools was changed to a system of zones and satellite areas. Mandatory busing was replaced in 1992 by a program designed to integrate elementary schools by giving parents a choice of schools. Racial guidelines were altered with each of the above plans. In 1996 the district approved a new integration plan requiring that all schools maintain racial guidelines of between 15 and 50 percent African American. Six black parents sued in 1998 to eliminate the student assignment plan based on race that limits the number of African Americans who can enroll in Central High School to a maximum of 50 percent.

On June 10, 1999, U.S. District judge John G. Heyburn II ruled that U.S. District judge James F. Gordon did not dissolve his 1975 desegregation decree in 1978. Portions of Judge Gordon's decree remain in effect. Judge Heyburn also ruled that the Jefferson County Board of Education may use racial classifications to prevent the reemergence of racially identifiable schools and gave anyone wanting to see the remaining parts of the 1975 desegregation decree dissolved until July 12, 1999, to file the motion. On June 15, 1999, lawyers for a parents' group filed a motion to dissolve the 1975 decree.

The Kentucky Education Reform Act (KERA) of 1990, and subsequent amendments by the General Assembly, were enacted to improve Kentucky's system of public education. The KERA became law on July 13, 1990. Jefferson County Public Schools, as well as the entire state of Kentucky, began a new era of educational opportunity, designed to improve an efficient system of common schools.

The district offers various instructional programs including the Comprehensive Program, the Advance Program, Exceptional Child Education, the Honors Program, Magnet Career Academies, Magnet Schools, the Montessori Program, Optional Programs, Traditional Programs, the English as a Second Language Program, the Teenage Parent Program, the Homeless Education and Youth Program, the Migrant Education Program, Metropolitan Middle and High Schools, Independent Study, Jefferson County High School, and Liberty High School. Kindergarten is offered in the elementary schools. In addition, early childhood education and child care services are offered, including Cradle School, Head Start, the Parent Child Center, Prekindergarten, Preschool, Jump Start, and child care enrichment programs. Continuing education is also offered, including adult education programs that enable adults to increase their academic and job skills, a GED testing center, work site training programs, the Welfare-to-Work Program, and a career assessment center. Family Education–Even Start programs offer parents and their children the opportunity to attend school together.

In the 1997–98 school year the Jefferson County school district had a student enrollment of 96,993. Of these, 20,852 were enrolled in optional programs and magnet schools, with 6,606 in the Advance Program. There were 5,650 teachers, 82 percent of whom had a master's degree or higher. The student-teacher ratio was seventeen to one. In the 1998–99 school year, the Jefferson County school district had an enrollment of 93,888 (including Preschool, Kindergarten, Exceptional Child Education, and grades one through twelve) in 151 schools and was ranked as the twenty-sixth-largest school district in the United States.

Jefferson County Public Schools (1998–99)

Ahrens Educational Resource Center, 546 S First St.
Ahrens Learning Center, 546-A S First St.
Alex R. Kennedy Metro Middle, 4515 Taylorsville Rd.
Atherton High School, 3000 Dundee Rd.
Atkinson Elementary, 2800 Alford Ave.
Auburndale Elementary, 5749 New Cut Rd.
Audubon Traditional Elementary, 1051 Hess Ln.
Ballard High, 6000 Brownsboro Rd.
Barret Traditional Middle, 2561 Grinstead Dr.
Bates Elementary, 7601 Bardstown Rd.
Bellewood Presbyterian Home for Children, 11103 Park Rd.
Binet School, 3410 Bon Air Ave.
Blake Elementary, 3801 Bonaventure Blvd.
Bloom Elementary, 1627 Lucia Ave.
Blue Lick Elementary, 9801 Blue Lick Rd.
Bowen Elementary, 1601 Roosevelt Ave.
Boys' Haven, 2301 Goldsmith Ln.
Brandeis Elementary, 2817 W Kentucky St.
Breckinridge-Franklin Elementary, 1351 Payne St.
Brooklawn, 2125 Goldsmith Ln.
Brown School (Elementary, Middle, High), 546 S First St.
Buechel Metropolitan High, 1960 Bashford Manor Ln.
Butler Traditional High, 2222 Crums Ln.
Byck Elementary, 2328 Cedar St.
Camp Taylor Elementary, 1446 Belmar Dr.
Cane Run Elementary, 3951 Cane Run Rd.
Cardinal Youth Development Center, 2915 Freys Hill Rd.
CARITAS Peace Academy, 2020 Newburg Rd.
Carrithers Middle, 4320 Billtown Rd.
Carter Traditional Elementary, 3628 Virginia Ave.
Central High School Magnet Career Academy, 1130 W Chestnut St.
Central Kentucky Youth Development Center, 8310 Westport Rd.
Charter School, 1405 Browns Ln.
Chenoweth Elementary, 3622 Brownsboro Rd.
Churchill Park School, 435 Boxley Ave.
Cochrane Elementary, 2511 Tregaron Ave.
Cochran Elementary, 500 W Gaulbert Ave.
Coleridge-Taylor Elementary, 1115 W Chestnut St.
Conway Middle, 6300 Terry Rd.
Coral Ridge Elementary, 10608 National Turnpike
Crosby Middle, 303 Greathouse Ln.
Crums Lane Elementary, 3212 S Crums Ln.
Dixie Elementary, 10201 Casalanda Dr.
Doss High School Magnet Career Academy, 7601 St. Andrews Church Rd.
Dunn Elementary, 2010 Rudy Ln.
du Pont Manual High, 120 W Lee St.
DuValle Education Center, 3500 Bohne Ave.
Eastern High, 12400 Old Shelbyville Rd.
Eisenhower Elementary, 5300 Jessamine Ln.
Engelhard Elementary, 1004 S First St.
Fairdale Elementary, 10104 Mitchell Hill Rd.
Fairdale High School Magnet Career Academy, 1001 Fairdale Rd.
Farnsley Middle, 3400 Lees Ln.
Fern Creek Elementary, 8703 Ferndale Rd.
Fern Creek Traditional High, 9115 Fern Creek Rd.
Field Elementary, 120 Sacred Heart Ln.
Foster Academy, 4020 Garland Ave.
Frayser Elementary, 1230 Larchmont Ave.
Frost Middle, 13700 Sandray Blvd.
Gilmore Lane Elementary, 1281 Gilmore Ln.
Goldsmith Elementary, 3520 Goldsmith Ln.
Greathouse/Shryock Traditional Elementary, 2700 Browns Ln.
Greenwood Elementary, 5801 Greenwood Rd.
Gutermuth Elementary, 1500 Sanders Ln.
Hartstern Elementary, 5200 Morningside Way
Hawthorne Elementary, 2301 Clarendon Ave.
Hazelwood Elementary, 1325 Bluegrass Ave.
Hazelwood Facility School, 1800 Bluegrass Ave.
Highland Middle School, 1700 Norris Pl.
Hite Elementary, 12408 Old Shelbyville Rd.
Indian Trail Elementary, 3709 E Indian Trail
Iroquois High School Magnet Career Academy, 4615 Taylor Blvd.
Iroquois Middle, 5650 Southern Pkwy.
Jacob Elementary, 3701 E Wheatmore Dr.
JCPS/State Agency Children's Program, 8300<1/2> Westport Rd.
Jefferson County High, 900 S Floyd St.
Jefferson County Traditional Middle, 1418 Morton

Ave.
Jeffersontown Elementary, 3610 Cedarwood Way
Jeffersontown High School Magnet Career Academy, 9600 Old Six Mile Ln.
Johnson-Breckinridge, 8711 LaGrange Rd.
Johnson Traditional Middle, 2509 Wilson Ave.
Johnsontown Road Elementary, 7201 Johnsontown Rd.
Kammerer Middle, 7315 Wesboro Rd.
Kennedy Montessori Elementary, 3800 Gibson Ln.
Kenwood Elementary, 7420 Justin Ave.
Kerrick Elementary, 2210 Upper Hunters Trace
King Elementary, 4325 Vermont Ave.
Klondike Lane Elementary, 3807 Klondike Ln.
Knight Middle, 9803 Blue Lick Rd.
Lassiter Middle, 8200 Candleworth Dr.
Laukhuf Elementary, 5100 Capewood Dr.
Layne Elementary, 9831 E Ave.
Liberty High, 911 S Brook St.
Lincoln Elementary, 930 E Main St.
Louisville Day Treatment Center, 8711 LaGrange Rd.
Louisville Male High, 4409 Preston Hwy.
Lowe Elementary, 210 Oxfordshire Ln.
Luhr Elementary, 6900 Fegenbush Ln.
Maryhurst, 1015 Dorsey Ln.
Maupin Elementary, 1312 Catalpa St.
McFerran Preparatory Academy, 1900 S Seventh St.
Medora Elementary, 11801 Deering Rd.
Meyzeek Middle, 828 S Jackson St.
Middletown Elementary, 218 N Madison Ave.
Mill Creek Elementary, 3816 Dixie Hwy.
Minors Lane Elementary, 8510 Minors Ln.
Moore Traditional High, 6415 Outer Loop
Moore Traditional Middle, 6415 Outer Loop
Myers Middle, 3741 Pulliam Dr.
Newburg Middle, 4901 Exeter Ave.
Noe Middle, 121 W Lee St.
Norton Elementary, 8101 Brownsboro Rd.
Okolona Elementary, 7606 Preston Hwy.
Pleasure Ridge Park High School Magnet Career Academy, 5901 Greenwood Rd.
Portland Elementary, 3410 Northwestern Pkwy.
Price Elementary, 5001 Garden Green Way
Rangeland Elementary, 5001 Rangeland Rd.
Rice Audubon, 8711 LaGrange Rd.
Roosevelt-Perry Elementary, 1606 Magazine St.
Rutherford Elementary, 301 Southland Blvd.
St. Joseph Children's Home, 2823 Frankfort Ave.
St. Matthews Elementary, 601 Browns Ln.
Sanders Elementary, 8408 Terry Rd.
Schaffner Traditional Elementary, 2701 Crums Ln.
Semple Elementary, 724 Denmark St.
Seneca High School Magnet Career Academy, 3510 Goldsmith Ln.
Shacklette Elementary, 5310 Mercury Dr.
Shawnee High School Magnet Career Academy, 4018 W Market St.
Shelby Elementary, 930 Mary St.
Slaughter Elementary, 3805 Fern Valley Rd.
Smyrna Elementary, 6401 Outer Loop
Southern High School Magnet Career Academy, 8620 Preston Hwy.
Southern Middle, 4530 Bellevue Ave.
Spring Meadows, 10901 Shelbyville Rd.
Stonestreet Elementary, 10007 Stonestreet Rd.
Stuart Middle School, 4601 Valley Station Rd.
Teenage Parent Program, Georgia Chaffee, South Park, 1010 Neighborhood Pl.
Teenage Parent Program, Georgia Chaffee, Westport, 8800 Westport Rd.
Ten Broeck School, 8521 LaGrange Rd.
Thomas Jefferson Middle, 4401 Rangeland Rd.
Trunnell Elementary, 7609 St. Andrews Church Rd.
Tully Elementary, 3300 College Dr.
Valley High School Magnet Career Academy, 10200 Dixie Hwy.
Waggener Traditional High, 330 S Hubbards Ln.
Waller-Williams Environmental, 2415 Rockford Ln.
Watson Lane Elementary, 7201 Watson Ln.
Watterson Elementary, 3900 Breckenridge Ln.
Wellington Elementary, 4800 Kaufman Ln.
Western Math Science Technology Magnet High School, 2501 Rockford Ln.
Western Middle, 2201 W Main St.
Westport Middle, 8100 Westport Rd.
Wheatley Elementary, 1107 S Seventeenth St.
Wheeler Elementary, 5410 Cynthia Dr.
Wilder Elementary, 1913 Herr Ln.
Wilkerson Elementary, 5601 Johnsontown Rd.
Wilt Elementary, 6700 Price Ln.
Young Elementary, 3526 W Muhammad Ali Blvd.
Youth Performing Arts School, 1517 S Second St.
Zachary Taylor Elementary, 9620 Westport Rd.

Superintendents of the Louisville Public School District

In 1828-29 Trustees managed the schools. Until 1847 an "Agent of the Board" headed the schools. In 1847 the title "Superintendent" came into use.

1828—Trustees: James Guthrie, John P. Harrison, William Sale, James Overstreet, Fortunatus Cosby Jr., and Samuel Dickinson
Mann Butler, principal of first public school in Louisville, 1829
Trustees: Garnett Duncan, Fortunatus Cosby Jr., Jacob Rheinhard, J.P. Dectary, James W. Palmer. Mann Butler, principal Grammar Department, and Alexander Ewell, principal Primary Department, 1830
Samuel Dickinson, "Agent of the Board," 1837
Rev. James F. Clarke and Fortunatus Cosby Jr. 1839
Samuel Dickinson, 1841
James H. Overstreet, 1842
Fortunatus Cosby, 1843
Silas Sisson, 1846 (In 1847 "superintendent")
Fortunatus Cosby Jr. Jan. 1849
C.F. Johnson, June, 1849
James McBurnie, 1852
John P. Smith, 1854
George W. Anderson, 1859
Joseph Gheens, 1862
George H. Tingley Jr., 1863
Edgar H. Mark, 1894
Ernest O. Holland, 1910
O.L. Reid, 1916
Zenos E. Scott, 1920
Byron W. Hartley, 1923
Leslie R. Gregory, 1929
Frederick Archer, 1932
W.T. Rowland Jr., assistant superintendent in charge of secondary education, 1936
C.A. Rubado, assistant superintendent in charge of elementary education, 1936
Zenos E. Scott, 1937
C.A. Rubado and Joseph Kindred Long, acting superintendents, 1944
Omer Carmichael, 1945
Samuel Noe, 1960
Newman Walker, 1969
Milburn T. Maupin, interim superintendent, 1975

Superintendents of the Jefferson County Public Schools

Leonidas Jackson Stivers, 1884–94
Alfred Herr Hite, 1894–98
Rosa Phillips Stonestreet, 1898–1910
Orville Jackson Stivers, 1910–50
Richard VanHoose, 1950–74
Ernest C. Grayson, 1975–80
David DeRuzzo, 1980–81
Donald W. Ingwerson, 1981–93
Booker T. Rice, acting superintendent, 1993
Stephen W. Daeschner, 1993–present

See Marie T. Doyle, "The Public School Merger Issue in Jefferson County, Kentucky", Ph.D. diss., University of Kentucky, 1975; George D. Wilson, *A Century of Negro Education in Louisville, Ky.,* published by Louisville Municipal College as a report on Official Project No. 66543-3-77-2 conducted under the auspices of the Work Projects Administration, 1941; Reports of the Commission of the Common Schools of Jefferson County to the Superintendent of Public Instruction, 1876–77, microfilm; Reports Communicated to Both Branches of the Legislature of Kentucky at the December Session, 1840; *Annual Progress Report, Jefferson County Public Schools, 1974, 1984, 1999; Annual Statistical Report, Jefferson County Public Schools, 1979,* 1979.

Shirley Botkins

PUBLIC WORKS. The original streets and ALLEYS of Louisville were laid out by a board of trustees that governed the city until 1828. The first paved street was MAIN St. between Third and Sixth Streets. It was surfaced with limestone slabs in 1813. In 1828 Louisville was formally incorporated as a city and elected its first mayor, John C. Bucklin. During the nineteenth century, as Louisville grew to become one of the largest cities in the United States, its municipal needs gradually encompassed not only street construction and repair but also traffic control, water supply, sewerage and drainage, natural gas supply, and electrification. THE LOUISVILLE WATER CO. was chartered in 1854, and the Louisville Gas Co. consolidated with the Louisville Electric Light Co. in 1890 to become the forerunner of the Louisville Gas & Electric Co. The COMMISSIONERS OF SEWERAGE was formed in 1906 to manage sewer construction and repair. This agency was replaced in 1946 by the Louisville and Jefferson County Metropolitan Sewer District.

The Board of Public Works was formed in 1893 when the municipal organization of Louisville was changed by a state legislative charter. Under the charter, the Board of Public Works and the Board of Public Safety were the principal executive boards. The first Board of Public Works was composed of three members, with Aaron Kohn as its first chairman. The board oversaw bureaus of engineering, street cleaning, public lighting, public buildings, and street repairing. Charles V. Mehler was the first chief engineer. Prior to the 1893 charter, potholes in the streets, removal of animal wastes from public rights-of-way, and unregulated digging in the streets were prominent issues.

In 1945 the Department of Public Works was formed, with a director as its chief officer. The position of city engineer was changed to an assistant to the director. One of the responsibilities of the department is to supervise the construction and maintenance of streets and sidewalks and to oversee improvements in traffic control. The first one-way streets were introduced in Louisville in 1935, and traffic signals were synchronized on major thoroughfares in 1949. Most brick and cobblestone streets, once commonplace in the city, have been resurfaced with asphalt in the last fifty years. The department also issues permits and approves plans for all construction in public rights-of-way, maintains public buildings, and manages the city's fleet of vehicles.

The department acts as the principal engineering consultant to the city and, as such, has coordinated numerous major construction projects since WORLD WAR II. Examples include the construction of the OHIO RIVER flood wall by the U.S. Army Corps of Engineers; the construction of the Watterson Expwy. and Interstate Highways 71, 65, and 64 through Louisville by the Kentucky Department of Transportation; the siting of the Kennedy Bridge and the Sherman Minton Bridge; the construction of the RIVERFRONT PLAZA; and, more recently, the construction of the LOUISVILLE INTERNATIONAL AIRPORT and the Waterfront Park. The department has both engineering and architectural divisions and employs fifteen full-time engineers and two architects.

See *Annual Report of the Department of Public Works, City of Louisville, Kentucky, for the Fiscal Year 1945–46;* J. Stoddard Johnston, ed., *Memorial History of Louisville* (Chicago 1896); *Louisville Municipal Reports for the Fiscal Year Ending August 31, 1894* (Louisville 1895); R.C. Riebel, *Louisville Panorama: A Visual History of Louisville* (Louisville 1954).

C. Robert Ullrich

PUBLISHERS PRESS. When Nicholas Simon founded Publishers Printing Co., the parent company of Publishers Press, in 1866, his goal was to create the finest possible printing resource for publishers. Four generations later, Publishers Press remains a family-owned business that continues to uphold the goals and ideals set by its founder.

On December 28, 1846, Nicholas Simon arrived in New York City from Albersweiler, Germany. On October 20, 1847, he enlisted in the U.S. Army and saw service in the MEXICAN WAR under Gen. Winfield Scott. Simon was honorably discharged but rejoined at the outbreak of the CIVIL WAR. He was assigned to duty as a drillmaster and as the commander of militia. Simon drafted his own company of men and participated as a guard for Indiana. He was mustered out of the Union army in 1866, purchased an interest in a newly formed German newspaper that may have been the *Katholischer Glaubensbote* (Catholic messenger of faith), and founded his printing company as the Printing Rooms of Nicholas Simon. In 1879 the company began printing the *Record,* the monthly newspaper of the Catholic Archdiocese of Louisville.

In 1880 Nicholas retired, and his sons, John E. and Frank X., operated the business as a partnership until 1885. More business came to the company in 1881 when the *Record* became a weekly publication. In 1885 the *Katholischer Glaubensbote* was incorporated and began printing weekly from the Simon firm. Also in 1885 the brothers incorporated the firm as the Glaubensbote Publishing Co. George D. Deuser was its president, and its offices were located at 371 E MARKET St. In 1892 the firm began printing the *Argus,* a supplement to the *Katholischer Glaubensbote* that carried news from Germany.

In 1910 Frank X. Simon invited his son Alfred J. Simon to join the family company. Alfred was elected a director; his father was secretary and his uncle, John E. Simon, was president. On September 19, 1914, John E. Simon retired from the firm, and Frank X. took over the role of president.

As business increased, in 1922 the firm erected a new building at the corner of Brook and E Chestnut Streets, and Frank X. asked his other son, Frank A. Simon, to join the company after his graduation from the UNIVERSITY OF LOUISVILLE. In April 1922 Alfred advised the board of directors that 75 percent of people could not pronounce, spell, or understand the company's name. In September the board voted to change the name to Publishers Printing Co. In 1923 the *Katholischer Glaubensbote* ceased publication in response to strict sanctions imposed by the federal GOVERNMENT upon all German and German-language publications during and after WORLD WAR I.

In 1925 Frank X. Simon died, and his son Alfred was elected president and general manager. It was Alfred who drew the company's trademark of the father reading the newspaper. In 1927 Frank A. Simon left the company to return to school to study chemistry. He later became a doctor and one of the country's leading allergists. In 1929 Publishers Printing Co. secured a contract for its first nationally distributed publication, the *Market Growers Journal.* The journal was purchased and published by the company until it was sold in 1935. In 1936 the firm acquired the Louisville printing establishment of Brandt & Fowler. Publishers Printing Co. continued printing through the 1937 flood in Louisville by bringing employees to work by boat and using a gasoline engine for power.

In 1946 Frank E. Simon, son of Alfred, joined the family firm as a typesetter, one of only twenty-two employees in the firm. He had to quit the University of Louisville in 1950, six hours short of his degree, because his father fell and broke his leg and Frank had to assume more responsibilities in the company.

Frank E. Simon became president of the firm in 1954. In 1958 the firm had to move from its thirty-four-year home to make way for Interstate 65. Simon decided to move the plant to SHEPHERDSVILLE because the new location was close to Louisville, an available piece of land had access to the railroad, and costs were lower. The company purchased the 5 acres for $7,500. The new plant encompassed 33,000 square feet. In 1965 another 15,000 feet were added to the Shepherdsville plant, and throughout the 1960s and 1970s Frank Simon continued to update and improve technology. In the early 1970s Publishers Printing was one of the first printers to begin to use computers in their prepress facility. By 1977 the company employed 250 workers and had revenues of a little under $2 million. Three years later, revenues had increased to $5 million.

Since 1971 Frank E. Simon had been the sole owner of the company. In September 1981 and October 1982, Nicholas X. and Michael J. Simon, sons of Frank E., joined the firm after completing college. On May 20, 1990, Frank E. Simon died. Nicholas became president and Michael executive vice president. The sons opened a new 120,000-square-foot plant in Lebanon Junction to take pressure off the Shepherdsville plant. By 1994 an additional 120,000 square feet had been added to the Lebanon Junction plant. Publishers Printing is the largest employer in BULLITT COUNTY. In 1999 it printed over six hundred titles spanning a wide variety of subject matter. Included were *Radiologic Technology, Professional Roofing, Sportswear International, The Lane Report,* and *Saratoga.*

PULITZER PRIZES (NEWSPAPERS). Pulitzer Prizes have been awarded each May since 1917 in recognition of outstanding accomplishments in journalism, letters, music, and drama. The prizes are paid from the income of a fund left by Joseph Pulitzer to the trustees of Columbia University, and recipients are chosen on the recommendation of an advisory board comprising journalists and the president of the university, with the dean of the graduate school of journalism as secretary.

Called journalism's most prestigious recognition, fourteen awards of $3,000 each are offered in the areas of general news reporting, investigative reporting, national reporting, international correspondence, editorial writing, editorial cartooning, spot news PHOTOGRAPHY, feature photography, commentary, criticism, feature writing, explanatory journalism, and specialized reporting (sports, business, science, education, or RELIGION). A gold medal is presented for distinguished and meritorious public service in journalism. As of 1997, the *COURIER-JOURNAL* and the *LOUISVILLE TIMES,* sister NEWSPAPERS, had distinguished themselves by receiving nine Pulitzers in journalism:

1918, *Courier-Journal,* for editorial writing; to Henry Watterson, editor, for a series of editorials after the United States entered World War I.

1926, *Courier-Journal,* for news reporting; to William Burke "Skeets" Miller, police reporter, for articles written during the nineteen days Floyd Collins was trapped inside Sand Cave, Edmonson County, Kentucky.

1956, *Louisville Times,* for editorial cartooning; to Robert York for the cartoon "Achilles," showing an overstuffed representation of American prosperity whose ragged shoes were labeled "farm prices."

1967, *Courier-Journal,* for public service; to the news staff for coverage of problems in strip-mining in Kentucky, and in recognition of the campaign for stronger control of strip-mining operations.

1969, *Courier-Journal,* for local general news reporting; to John Fetterman, staff writer for the *Courier-Journal & Times Magazine,* for a picture essay, "Pfc. Gibson Comes Home," a report on the funeral of a Kentucky soldier killed in Vietnam.

1976, *Courier-Journal* and *Louisville Times,* for feature photography; to the photographic staff for coverage of court-ordered busing in Louisville and Jefferson County schools.

1978, *Courier-Journal,* for local general news reporting; to Richard Whitt, reporter, for his coverage of a disastrous fire at the Beverly Hills Supper Club in Southgate, Kentucky, and for his three months of investigation of its aftermath.

1980, *Courier-Journal,* for international reporting; to Joel Brinkley, reporter, and Jay Mather, photographer, for a series of stories on the Cambodian crisis.

1989, *Courier-Journal,* for general news reporting; to the news staff for its coverage of a church bus crash in which twenty-seven people died on Interstate 71 near Carrollton, Kentucky.

Mary Lawrence Young

1887 birds-eye view of the Quartermaster Depot, Jeffersonville, Indiana.

QUARRIES. Quarrying and mining operations in the Louisville area have taken place since the beginning of the nineteenth century and continue today. The extent of the operations has followed both the need and the use of the quarried material, which is mainly limestone, dolomite, and siltstone. The quarried stone has been used as agricultural limestone, rail ballast, road-base coarse material, dimensional cut stone, and aggregate for construction purposes. Quarries differ from mines in that quarries usually involve open surface extraction of stone.

Many of the local quarries were well known for their stone. Limestone from the William F. Woodruff Quarry, through which Interstate 71 now passes near Zorn Ave., was shipped to Pittsburgh, where it was used to make iron. The stone in this quarry was chemically ideal for the iron-making process. The demand for this specific limestone dropped when the iron-making industry discovered that any limestone could be chemically altered, eliminating the need to ship this stone from Louisville. Following this loss and the economic failures of the GREAT DEPRESSION, the quarry went out of business.

Stone from the WORKHOUSE quarry on Payne St. was used in the construction of the workhouse and the old jail at Sixth and LIBERTY Streets. Jefferson County Stone Quarry in Avoca, now owned by the Rogers Group, was once owned by the LOUISVILLE & NASHVILLE RAILROAD. It used the stone for rail ballast in the maintenance of the railroad.

Although there were a few large quarries around Louisville, most operated on a small scale for either farm use or minor commercial concerns. Many quarries came into existence at the end of the nineteenth century to provide stone for the construction of roads and RAILROADS, curbing, and foundations in the Louisville area. With the expanded use of concrete, the demand for local stone diminished, bringing an end to most of the small local quarries. The sites of these quarries have since been used for other purposes.

Although many of the quarries have been abandoned or used for dumping, many have been put to good use. One of the most well-known quarries, formerly the Atkins & Staebler Quarry, is now used by the Lakeside Swim Club on Trevilian Way near Bardstown Rd. The quarrying operation was stopped when water was encountered. Abandoned quarries were sought out during the summer months as places to swim clandestinely. Unfortunately, many drownings occurred until the quarries were either effectively sealed off or developed into safe SWIMMING sites.

Other well-known facilities in former quarries include the Alpine Ice Arena and Lighthouse Park on Gardiner Ln., a swimming club in Cox's Lake, Mockingbird Valley Soccer and Tennis Club on Mellwood Ave., shopping centers on Brownsboro Rd. in the CRESCENT HILL neighborhood, and a shopping center on Poplar Level Rd. near Quarry Rd.

The Louisville Crushed Stone Company's quarry and mine, located by the Watterson Expwy. between Newburg and Poplar Level Roads, which closed in the early 1970s, became the Louisville Underground, an underground storage facility. The constant temperature is beneficial for some storage purposes. For years the city Department of PUBLIC WORKS used the facility to store road salt, and during the Cold War, plans were drawn to use the facility as a civil defense shelter. The facility has up to 4 million square feet of storage space, with ceiling elevations from 22 to 90 feet.

Because of the nature of quarries, there are few left in the Louisville area. Encroaching suburban development and the dust and noise involved in quarrying are incompatible. Most of the major quarries have been closed or abandoned. The only operating mines in 1999 in the Louisville area are the Jefferson County Stone Quarry (formerly the Avoca Quarry), owned by the Rogers Group; the FERN CREEK Stone Quarry; and the Laurel Dolomite. Other operations in the area include BULLITT COUNTY Stone and OLDHAM COUNTY Stone, both owned by the Rogers Group; Quality Stone and Ready Mix in northern Bullitt County; Liters Quarry in Oldham County and its two quarries in SELLERSBURG, Indiana; and the KAT shale quarry in Brooks, Kentucky.

See Mary Lee Turner, "A History of the Quarries of Jefferson County, Kentucky," University of Louisville Archives and Record Center, Student Papers box 12; *Courier-Journal,* April 20, 1999.

QUARTERMASTER DEPOT, JEFFERSONVILLE. JEFFERSONVILLE, INDIANA, became a distributing depot for military and quartermaster supplies during the CIVIL WAR (1861–65). At the end of the war, millions of dollars worth of supplies remained stored in temporary housing. Meanwhile the need for a permanent location was being discussed by the quartermaster general in Washington and Jeffersonville city officials. In January 1870 the city purchased about 19 acres at a cost of $11,000 and donated it to the United States for the purpose of building a permanent depot. Construction began in the spring of 1871 and was completed in 1874. The original storage capacity was 2.7 million cubic feet. Warehouses were added periodically until the complex eventually grew to cover about 200 acres.

The depot was designed by Brevet Maj. Gen. Montgomery C. Meigs, quartermaster general, who was best known for supervising construction of the wings and cast-iron dome of the U.S. Capitol and designing the Pension Building (now a museum of architecture) in Washington, D.C. The completed depot was a beautiful example of utilitarian ARCHITECTURE. To discourage attack, the street sides were solid brick with a built-in pattern of arches. There was an open space in the center of the complex where a two-story building was constructed for the use of the commandant. Atop this building was a 100-foot-high lookout tower. Later the bricks under the arches were removed and glass windows were installed. The tower was torn down in 1902.

The depot functioned as a manufacturer and issuer of army clothing as well as a distributor of quartermaster supplies throughout the United States, the Philippines, Cuba, Puerto Rico, and the Hawaiian Islands. During WORLD WAR I, 9,000 people were employed, some of whom sewed shirts at home. Employment figures were 6,200 during WORLD WAR II and 5,200 during the Korean conflict. In the 1930s the depot also supplied the Civilian Conservation Corps in eight states. But after the army found it less costly to buy from private companies, the Quartermaster Depot was moved in 1955 to Natick, Massachusetts. The land and most of the buildings were sold in 1959 to Joseph Conner. Part of the complex was destroyed by fire in 1992.

In May 1997 the Historic Landmarks Foundation of Indiana listed the Quartermaster Depot in Jeffersonville as one of the ten most-endangered historic places in the state. The Jeffersonville District Review Board proposed that the landmark be placed in a conservation district. Attorneys representing the estate of Joseph Conner, who died in 1995, were in opposition, and the proposal was defeated by the Jeffersonville City Council.

See Louis C. Baird, *Baird's History of Clark County, Indiana* (Indianapolis 1909); William Lee, *1889 History Clark County, Ind.* (Chicago 1889); Margaret Sweeney, *Fact, Fiction and Folklore of Southern Indiana* (New York 1967); *History of the Ohio Falls Cities and Their Counties* (Cleveland 1882); Charlestown Library Folder File, Charlestown, Indiana.

Charline Judd Hall

QUIN, HUSTON (b Anchorage, Kentucky, August 4, 1876; d Louisville, August 14, 1938). Louisville mayor and Kentucky Court of Appeals judge. He was the son of Joseph B. and Matilda (Huston) Quin. Huston Quin's father was born in Louisville in 1857 and was in the drug business and later the insurance business. His mother was born in Louisville in 1858 and died there in 1879 when Huston, her only child, was three years old. Joseph Quin later married Nettie E. Jones of Louisville, and the couple had two children, Clinton Simon and Sherman T. Quin. Clinton Quin became a bishop coadjutor of Texas for the Protestant Episcopal church in 1918. Sherman was in charge of the Louisville & Nashville Railroad creosoting plant at Guthrie, Kentucky.

Huston Quin was educated in the public schools in Louisville and worked as an office boy for the well-known law firm of Helm & Bruce. He received his law degree from the University of Louisville in 1900. From 1900 to 1908 he practiced law with the Helm & Bruce firm. In 1908 he became first assistant city attorney, holding this post until 1912 when he became a member of the law firm of Blakey, Quin & Lewis. In December 1917 he was appointed to a four-year term as city attorney. In November 1918 he ran on the Republican ticket for judge of the Kentucky Court of Appeals and was elected to an eight-year term, serving from January 1, 1919, to March 1921.

Quin was elected mayor of Louisville in 1921 and served from November 22, 1921, until November 17, 1925. During his administration Quin helped to get the Second Street Municipal Bridge project under way. After a Board of Trade Bridge Commission report outlining the viability of a Louisville-to-Jeffersonville bridge was presented to the city on January 1, 1924, Quin and the City Council tried to get the project financed. They proposed building a toll-free bridge to be financed by a bond issue to be paid through taxes, but that proposal was rejected by the electorate in 1926. A revised proposal called for bridge tolls to aid in retiring the bond issue, but it was defeated in 1927. The bridge construction was eventually financed during William B. Harrison's term as mayor.

Quin was the first mayor to appoint African Americans to the city's fire and police departments. He oversaw the installation of the first traffic lights on Louisville's streets and urged the development of an airport to be financed by a bond issue. The bond issue was passed two years after he left office. During his administration Chickasaw Park for African Americans was established, and Thruston Square and George Rogers Clark Park were added to the park system. He was instrumental in removing the Louisville and Jefferson County Children's Home from the present site of the University of Louisville and transferring many of the university's units to that location. Quin led the movement to build Parkway Field for the Louisville Colonels baseball team, to replace the fire-ravaged facility at Seventh and Kentucky Streets.

Quin was a director of the Jefferson Savings & Building Co. and became vice president of the Louisville Trust Co. in December 1924. He was president of the Louisville Title Mortgage Co. and the Title Insurance & Trust Co. from 1932 until his death. He was director of the Louisville Board of Trade at the time of his death. He married Martha B. Rivers, daughter of W.J. and Martha (Bolling) Rivers, on June 9, 1904, in Anchorage, Kentucky. He died of a heart ailment and is buried in Resthaven Memorial Park.

See Edmond Asher Jonas and Thomas R. Underwood, eds., *Kentucky and Its Builders* (n.p., n.d.); Mary Young Southard and Ernest C. Miller, eds. *Who's Who in Kentucky: A Biographical Assembly of Notable Kentuckians* (Louisville 1936).

QUINN CHAPEL AFRICAN AMERICAN METHODIST EPISCOPAL CHURCH. One of Louisville's oldest African American congregations, Quinn Chapel African American Methodist Episcopal Church was established in 1838 as Bethel, House of God, in a room over a public stable at Second and Main Streets. The church is named after the Right Reverend William Paul Quinn, a senior bishop in the A.M.E. church from 1848 to 1873 and the first African American bishop to visit the city. About ten years after its founding, the church relocated to Fourth and Green (Liberty) Streets, where it became known also as the Old Fourth Street Church. With the financial aid of Quaker Friends, Dr. W.R. Revels, pastor, opened the doors of the first school for blacks within the city of Louisville. After another move and a short stay at Ninth and Green Streets, a new brick building was completed and dedicated for the church in 1854 at Ninth and Walnut Streets (Muhammad Ali Blvd.). There the church remained until 1910 when Quinn Chapel moved to its fifth and current location at 912 W Chestnut St. The building was purchased from the Weaver Memorial Baptist Church, a white congregation. This building is noted as a prime example of the Gothic Revival architectural style, and it is listed on the National Register of Historic Places. Carrying on the A.M.E. tradition of resistance to discrimination, Quinn Chapel early became known as the Abolitionist Church, with many slaveholders forbidding their slaves to attend services. Over the years Quinn Chapel has continued to actively protest against discrimination in streetcar access (1870), for open housing (1914), and for access to public accommodations (1961). On May 3, 1967, Quinn Chapel was the starting point for an open-housing march to City Hall and through the downtown area led by Rev. Dr. Martin Luther King Jr. It was his second visit to the city in support of local open-housing efforts.

See H.C. Weeden, *Weeden's History of the Colored People of Louisville* (Louisville 1897); G. Horace Jenkins and J. Bryant Cooper, *One Hundred Years of Celebration of Quinn Chapel AME Church, 1838 to 1938* (Louisville 1938); W.H. Gibson Sr., *History of the United Brothers of Friendship and Sisters of the Mysterious Ten, a Negro Order* (Louisville 1897); Kentucky Commission on Human Rights, *Kentucky's Black Heritage* (Frankfort 1971); Historical marker at the church, 912 W Chestnut St., Louisville, Kentucky; Monica Newton Tate, "Faith in Action: Quinn Chapel to Revisit Its Four Former Homes," *Courier-Journal,* Feb. 22, 1997.

Walter W. Hutchins

QUINN'S ROW. Quinn's Row was a block of houses and apartments just west of Louisville's downtown, occupied by Irish immigrants during the 1850s. It was named for an Irish immigrant, Francis Quinn, who with his brother, John, came to the United States in the 1830s. In Louisville, Francis became a merchant of small commodities. With the support of Francis, John prepared for the priesthood and was ordained in 1839.

Fr. John Quinn, who served St. Louis parish on Fifth St. between Green (Liberty) and Walnut (Muhammad Ali Blvd.), was good at investing money, and many immigrants entrusted him with their savings. So successful was the business that over the years he accumulated a fortune. Upon his death from cholera in 1852, Francis inherited the money and invested it in real estate.

He acquired property and constructed apartments and houses on Main St. near Eleventh Street. He lived in one of the houses. Referred to as Quinn's Row and housing large numbers of Irish people, it had a short history. On election day, August 6, 1855, which became known as "Bloody Monday," a nativist mob attacked both Germans and Irish. In the frenzy, the mob turned its wrath on property and destroyed Quinn's Row. Between seven and eleven o'clock at night, all houses in the block were burned. Several residents were shot as they ran from the flaming buildings. According to newspaper accounts, a number of people died, including Francis.

Like other victims of the tragedy, Quinn's

heirs filed suit for compensation under an 1860 act that authorized the Louisville Council to compensate for property harmed by the Bloody Monday riots. The property owned by Francis Quinn was valued at $34,038 in 1855, and the heirs had sued for $20,000. It is not clear why, but the claim was rejected by the Common Council in 1869.

See Benjamin J. Webb, *A Centenary of Catholicity in Kentucky* (Louisville 1884); Agnes Geraldine McGann, *Nativism in Kentucky to 1860* (Washington D.C., 1944); Stanley Ousley, "The Irish in Louisville" M.A. thesis, University of Louisville, 1969; *Louisville Daily Journal,* Aug. 8, 1855; Emmet V. Mittlebeeler, "The Aftermath of Louisville's Bloody Monday Election Riot of 1855," *Filson Club History Quarterly* 66 (April 1992): 197–219.

RAGTIME. Ragtime is a style of piano music that is characterized by a right- hand syncopated melody, accenting the second and third beats, against a steady bass line. It is generally believed that it developed from late-nineteenth-century attempts to apply the syncopated banjo music of AFRICAN AMERICANS to the piano. Scott Joplin (1868–1917) is considered to be the earliest and most influential ragtime pianist and composer. He developed his style in Sedalia, Missouri, in the early 1890s. Sedalia was the home of many other talented pianists, including Scott Hayden and Arthur Marshall, and it had an abundance of places—SALOONS, clubs, and houses of PROSTITUTION—where they could find employment. In 1893 Joplin played in Chicago during the Columbian Exposition, where he met many other ragtime players, and a few years later he played in Louisville.

Louisville in the 1890s had many similarities, although on a much larger scale, to Sedalia. It was a river port, there was a large pool of talented piano players, saloons dotted the city's street corners, and a red-light district had developed in an area bounded roughly by Grayson (Cedar) and Green (LIBERTY) Streets and stretching from Sixth to Tenth Streets. Pianos had been a fixture in most of the saloons in the area since the 1880s, and pianos, not bands, were the choice of musical entertainment in the city's bordellos. One of the best known of these early pianists was Benjamin "Ben" R. Harney (1871–1938). Harney was born into a prominent family in Middletown, Kentucky, and was playing on Green St. by the early 1890s. In 1895, while he was still playing at Robinson's Music Hall, he published "You've Been a Good Old Wagon, but You've Done Broke Down." He moved to New York City in 1896, published "Mr. Johnson Turn Me Loose," and achieved great popularity. Although these are not ragtime compositions in a strict sense, they do contain elements of ragtime (and BLUES). Other contemporary ragtime players, about whom little is known, include William Rehm, "Plunk" Reeder, and Robert Newsom, who played at Shelly's Saloon on Green St.

By the turn of the century, the most popular Louisville ragtime pianist was an African American named Price Davis, who was born in Cave City, Kentucky, in 1879. In 1900 he was playing at Milton Wiggins's Saloon at Tenth and Green. By 1908 he had moved to Pittsburgh. Davis's protégé, Glover Compton, was born in Harrodsburg, Kentucky, in 1884 and came to Louisville in 1902.

In 1904 Tony Jackson, the famous New Orleans pianist, came to Louisville and played in several clubs with Compton. In 1912 Compton moved to Chicago and enjoyed a successful career that lasted into the 1950s. Another popular pianist, who knew both Compton and Davis, was Mike Jackson (1887–1949). Jackson began as a ragtime pianist in the saloons and THEATERS in Louisville and moved to Chicago in 1912, where he established himself as a successful JAZZ pianist and songwriter.

Ragtime began to decline in popularity during World War I as the red-light districts were closed. The best piano players left town, and Dixieland jazz became popular. By the 1920s ragtime was seldom heard, except in MOVIE THEATERS. In 1974 the movie *The Sting* caused renewed interest in the works of Scott Joplin and ragtime in general.

See Rudi Blesh and Harriet Janis, *They All Played Ragtime* (New York 1950); Edward A. Berlin, *King of Ragtime: Scott Joplin and His Era* (New York 1994); William H. Tallmadge Papers, Kentucky Historical Society, Frankfort.

Cornelius Bogert

RAILROADS. From the 1850s well into the twentieth century, Louisville and Jefferson County depended on railroads, both intercity freight and passenger common carriers and their local switching counterparts, to provide essential freight and passenger transportation services. Indeed, it was the advent of railroads in the middle of the nineteenth century that helped move Louisville into an industrial ECONOMY, enabling local businesses to grow and compete for sectional and, later, national and global markets. By 1900 these railroads and their successors had joined the city and the region to the North American rail network (including Canada and Mexico), with direct service to twenty-eight of the forty-eight states as well as to Boston, New Orleans, and other major Atlantic and Gulf Coast ports.

No fewer than fifteen steam and electric interurban lines, some having merged into larger systems after 1900, used "Louisville" in their corporate titles; and the Louisville & Nashville, enthusiastically backed by the city from its inception, based corporate headquarters and extensive repair shops here. Recognizing the coming rail age, the city in 1855 adopted as its official seal the image of a steam locomotive bearing the name "Progress."

Proposals to build railroads between Louisville and the Falls cities were being discussed as early as the 1830s. An 1835 scheme involving a projected line from Cincinnati to Charleston, South Carolina, generated enough interest locally for Louisvillians to urge that their city also be connected. The national economic decline after 1837, however, precluded the project's ever being carried out. Meanwhile the Lexington & Ohio, Kentucky's first railroad, had commenced operations (in 1834) between Lexington and Frankfort and fully intended to build west to some point on the OHIO RIVER near Louisville. In April 1838 a 3-mile stretch of the L&O even began running from downtown Louisville to PORTLAND. However, after several months, residents objected to the noise and smoke from the line's locomotives. Operations were suspended, to be restored in 1840 with horse-drawn cars.

Because of financial difficulties, the pioneer line was never built west of Frankfort, but in 1847 the LOUISVILLE & FRANKFORT RAILROAD was organized by Louisville businessmen to fill the gap. Utilizing some of the L&O's unfinished roadbed, the L&F completed trackage to Frankfort in 1851 to become Louisville's first intercity railroad. A connection was made in Frankfort for trains to Lexington. Two southern Indiana railroads, meanwhile, were chartered in the late 1840s and began building northward. These were the Jeffersonville (later, Pennsylvania Railroad), which reached Indianapolis in 1852, and the NEW ALBANY & Salem (Monon), running the length of Indiana to Michigan City by 1854.

The success of these pioneer carriers did not go unnoticed. In its zeal to compete for southern markets, and needing better transport than was available, Louisville eagerly supported the formation of the Louisville & Nashville in 1849–50. The city subscribed more than $1 million in stock to help equip the L&N and capitalize its construction in the 1850s to the Tennessee capital. The L&N finished its main line to Nashville in October 1859 and, with two connecting roads in 1861, completed a line to Memphis. Each route offered local shippers and travelers greatly improved train services to the South.

During the CIVIL WAR, area railroads transported troops and matériel, first in support of the Confederacy and then, after 1862, for the Union. The city also become a major federal supply base, with local industries providing foodstuffs, uniforms, and other supplies to the military. The tracks of the Jeffersonville and the L&N, separated by the Ohio River, were connected by a PONTOON BRIDGE. Both lines were part of a strategic Midwest-Southeast route that helped fuel Gen. William T. Sherman's Atlanta campaign in 1863–64.

In the war's aftermath, the network of rail lines ultimately to serve Louisville began to take shape. Endorsement and financial support came from the city and its entrepreneurs. Declared the *Louisville Daily Journal* in April 1867, "We must rely on railroads, more than ever, to develop and restore the country. . . . The iron horse is king" (Share, *Cities in the Commonwealth,* 70). The Louisville & Frankfort built its Louisville-Cincinnati Short Line from LAGRANGE to Covington between 1867 and 1869, and the Elizabethtown & Paducah (later Illinois Central) in 1872 linked its named cities, entering Louisville on its own tracks in 1874. The L&N

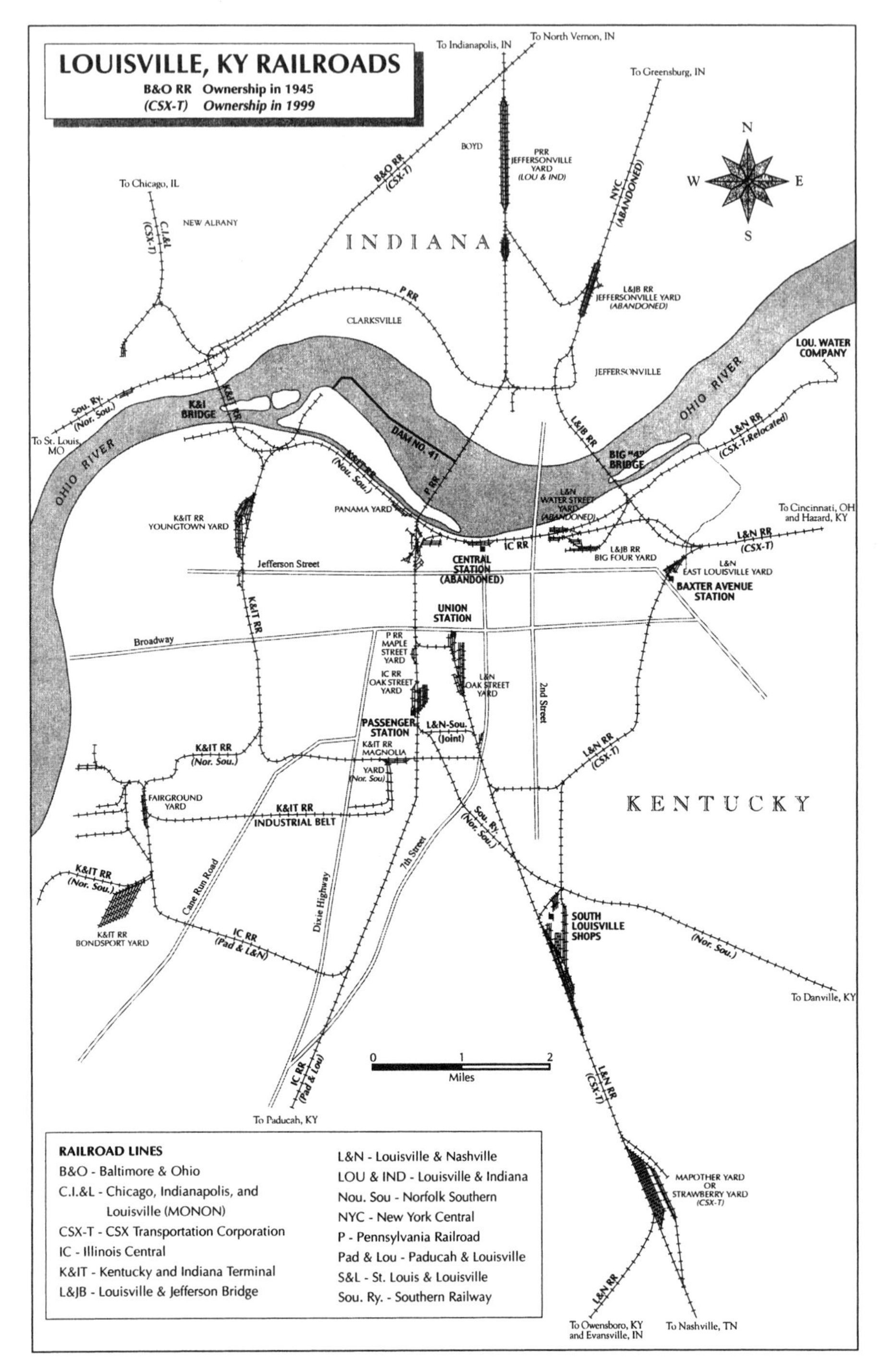

Advertisement for the Louisville and Portland Railroad from an 1858 city directory.

and the Jeffersonville, Madison & Indianapolis (Jeffersonville's successor) backed the construction of an Ohio River bridge, which opened in February 1870 to become the city's first river crossing.

A second route from Cincinnati (via North Vernon, Indiana) was finished by the Ohio & Mississippi Railroad (later the Baltimore & Ohio) to Jeffersonville in 1869, and after 1870 its trains entered Louisville over the new Ohio River bridge. The narrow-gauge Louisville, HARRODS CREEK & Westport, intending to push upriver, built to PROSPECT by 1877. The L&N reached Montgomery in 1872 and the Gulf Coast in 1880; its Lebanon branch was extended to southeastern Kentucky and, via connections, to Knoxville by 1883.

As Louisville's rail network spread, its lines helped local industries market to other regions of the nation, especially the South, prostrated from the war years. Rivals Cincinnati and Evansville competed vigorously for the same southern markets, and each city sponsored its own rail links to the South. The Louisville business community backed its home roads in opposing those competing bids as they came before the Kentucky General Assembly. For a time, city fathers even required new lines entering the area to be of a different track gauge so that freight cargo would have to break bulk for transfer. But in 1880 Louisville lost its monopoly when Cincinnati completed its own line south through central Kentucky to Chattanooga.

Nevertheless, other railroads reached Louisville or were built from the Falls cities during the 1880s and early 1890s, several aided by city funding: the Louisville, New Albany & St. Louis, completed across southern Indiana and Illinois in 1882; the Louisville, St. Louis & Texas, to Owensboro and Henderson with a branch to Hardinsburg (1889); and the Louisville Southern (LS), finishing a route to Lawrenceburg and Harrodsburg (in 1888), to connect near Danville with the Cincinnati-Chattanooga road (an LS branch to Lexington swinging off at Lawrenceburg was finished in 1889).

A Chesapeake & Ohio Railway predecessor also built west from Ashland to Lexington in 1880–81 and arranged for its trains to be conveyed over L&N rails to Louisville from Lexington. It then (1884) built a trestle along the riverfront to connect at Fourteenth and MAIN Streets with the Elizabethtown & Paducah, by then reorganized as the C&O Southwestern and leased by C&O's president Collis P. Huntington. He hoped to shape a transcontinental rail route. The city-organized Central Transfer Railway & Storage Co., meanwhile, put tracks along W Ormsby to improve the interchange of freight between the L&N, the C&OSW, and other lines. The L&N and Southern eventually bought the connection.

A second Ohio River crossing was built between 1883 and 1886, linking the Portland neighborhood with New Albany. Erected by the newly formed Kentucky & Indiana Bridge Co., the structure consummated efforts by the Monon (successor to the New Albany & Salem) and a Southern railway predecessor, the Louisville, Evansville & St. Louis, to obtain their own entries to Louisville. Until 1886 each had used the 1870 (the first) Ohio River bridge at Fourteenth St. With its two roadways straddling a single-track rail line, the K&I bridge provided the first vehicular access between Louisville and southern Indiana. In 1886 the bridge company also commenced a rail commuter service that ran from downtown Louisville to New Albany. In 1899 the K&I Bridge Co. was purchased by its three user railroads, which reorganized it as a local switching railroad and proceeded to build more extensive terminal facilities in Louisville's West End in the next three decades. In 1911–13 the reorganized company also replaced the 1886 Ohio River bridge with a newer double-tracked steel structure, which remains in use today.

A third railroad bridge across the Ohio River was constructed between 1889 and 1895 by the

Louisville & Jeffersonville Bridge & Railroad Co. Its owner, the Cleveland, Cincinnati, Chicago & St. Louis Railroad (Big Four, later New York Central System), had pieced together a previously constructed north-south route through Indiana to reach Louisville. L&JB (Big Four) tracks touched down in Louisville at Preston and Main Streets, where the line built a yard and terminal that it shared for many years with the C&O.

Louisville's two major passenger stations were built during the mid-1880s and early 1890s. First was Union Depot, later called Central Station, at Seventh and River Rd. It opened in 1884 but was replaced after the 1890 tornado by a larger brick station. The L&N completed UNION STATION at Tenth and BROADWAY in September 1891.

Other railroads, especially the L&N, the IC, and Southern, provided commuter service from such outlying communities as ANCHORAGE, CRESCENT HILL, Harrods Creek, JEFFERSONTOWN, Pleasure Ridge, and VALLEY STATION into the city. Just after 1900, several interurban electric railroads were projected through greater Louisville and southern Indiana. One line connected the Falls cities with Indianapolis; other routes radiated from Louisville to Anchorage, Jeffersontown, LaGrange, and SHELBYVILLE, also passing through the city's outlying NEIGHBORHOODS. Providing frequent passenger service as well as handling freight, the INTERURBANS competed vigorously against the steam railroads; with the advent of autos and paved county highways, all were abandoned by 1939.

By the time of WORLD WAR I (1914–18), tracks of the eight line-haul carriers and those of two terminal railroads encircled much of Louisville. Many of the city's industries by then had located in or near those rail corridors. The railroads also built miles of sidings and tracks to directly serve other industries, and several lines, notably the K&I and the L&N, helped create industrial districts. Within the city, all of the railroads also had freight stations to handle less-than-carload shipments, which local drayers conveyed to and from the loading docks of factories not served by rail.

Peak passenger traffic volumes were reached in the 1920s by the city's intercity railroads, exceeded only by WORLD WAR II traffic. Some seventy daily passenger trains were scheduled in and out of Central and Union Stations, offering services to a score or more cities in the East, the Midwest, and the South, many just an overnight journey away. Freight traffic volume also rose in the 1920s; in 1923 the city's railroads conveyed about 1.5 million cars, triple the 431,392 cars moved in 1902, and up from the 719,000 cars (or 14 million tons) moved during 1917. A 1918 newspaper *Louisville Post* story touted the 12,345-car total capacity of the sidings and team tracks serving city industries. Some 11,700 men and women, added the *Post,* worked for the city's railroads, making them collectively the area's top employer. During the period 1910-29, the K&I and the L&N expanded their switching yards, and grade separation projects in the 1920s and 1930s elevated several heavily used IC, K&I, L&N, and Pennsylvania tracks over principal downtown streets.

As more paved intercity highways and secondary roads spread across the nation during the late 1920s and the 1930s, automobile highway travel and competing bus and truck lines began to eat at the rails' share of freight and passenger traffic. Some branchline and local trains running to and from the city were dropped. Nonetheless, area railroads strove to improve their long-distance trains and advertised lower fares, faster schedules, and air-conditioned cars to lure back passengers; in 1940 the city's first streamliner, the Chicago-Florida *South Wind,* was inaugurated, offering twenty-five-hour travel time to Miami. Several railroads, notably the L&N, introduced pickup and delivery of less-than-carload shipments to attract more freight business.

In September 1939, after pressure from CITY HALL and local media, the first diesel-electric switch engines (bought by L&N) went into operation, helping reduce industrial smoke emissions; and in 1942 L&N placed new diesel locomotives in mainline passenger service. The city's other railroads followed during the 1940s and 1950s, replacing line haul and switching steam locomotives with the cleaner, more efficient diesels.

Passenger and freight tonnage peaks were again reached by city railroads during World War II (1941–45). Much of the increased traffic was generated by new wartime industries, including the bag and ammunition plants in Charlestown, Indiana, and Curtiss-Wright aircraft, Naval Ordnance, and the Du Pont and other RUBBERTOWN chemical plants. Commuter trains were operated to Charlestown for workers at the ammo and bag plants, and the FORT KNOX Armored Center, greatly expanded for wartime training, sent heavy troop and tank movements by rail.

The city's railroads also participated in Louisville's post–World War II economic boom, laying tracks to serve new developments such as General Electric's Appliance Park (in 1953), Ford Motor Company's Fern Valley Rd. assembly plant (1955), and Ford's Kentucky truck plant near Anchorage (1968) as well as other area industries that converted to peacetime production. Tracks were also built to the Clark Maritime Center in southern Indiana and the Jefferson County Riverport facilities for transfer of bulk commodities between rail and water carriers. Larger capacity freight cars for specific industry use were introduced by the lines after 1950, along with piggyback service, or truck trailers moving on rail flatcars. Such technical advances as welded rail, computerized car tracing, centralized dispatching, and radio communications also helped modernize the services.

But other modes—air, highway trucking, pipelines, and river barges—began cutting deeply into the traffic once moved by the city's railroads, and by the 1970s the lines handled less than three hundred thousand carloads of freight a year. Jet air service and completion of the interstate highway system all but eliminated a once-flourishing rail passenger business. Central Station was closed in 1963, and in 1971 Amtrak took over the remaining nationwide passenger services. Locally, the L&N, the C&O, and Penn Central made their last passenger runs, leaving the city with only a Chicago-Florida train, which survived until late 1979. In November 1996 Amtrak (with Greyhound) began a direct bus link between Louisville and Union Station in Chicago, the carrier's midwest hub. In December 1999, the bus link was upgraded to a through train service via Indianapolis that terminated in Jeffersonville.

Within the rail industry, mergers and downsizings also affected Louisville's rail scene. Upon L&N's acquisition of Monon's line to Chicago in 1971, a merger condition permitted the Milwaukee Road (then serving the Midwest and the Pacific Northwest) to extend freight service to Louisville from Bedford, Indiana. A decade later (1981), the K&I was acquired by Southern, which then merged with Norfolk & Western to become Norfolk Southern. In 1986 CG&T Industries of Western Kentucky acquired IC's former Kentucky Division to create the Paducah & Louisville. Conrail (successor to Penn Central) in 1994 discarded its Indianapolis-Louisville line. The route and its Fourteenth Street Ohio River bridge were purchased by holding company Anacostia & Pacific and operated as the Louisville & Indiana Railroad.

Over the years, several plans were considered by the city and the railroads to consolidate stations and yards and channel train movements through fewer corridors to reduce delays at grade crossings. Declining rail passenger travel obviated the need for the stations. In the wake of rail mergers, remaining rail freight activity was concentrated at CSX's modern Osborn yard and Norfolk Southern's former K&I yard. Redundant rail rights-of-way were also being considered for light rail transit use. Closer cooperation between modes—rail, highway and water—also altered how freight moved in and out of the area. By the 1990s sizable volumes of coal and grains went by rail to the Riverport in southwestern Jefferson County and southern Indiana's CLARK MARITIME CENTRE for transshipment by river barges, and growing numbers of containers and truck trailers were exchanged between highway carriers and rails. As the century drew to a close, Louisville was served by three major rail systems, CSX Transportation, Norfolk Southern, and Soo-Milwaukee, along with two regional lines, the Louisville & Indiana and the Paducah & Louisville.

Historic Terminal, Trunkline Railroads Serving Louisville and Falls Cities

Auto-Train. Between 1974 and 1976, carrier operated a Louisville–Sanford, Florida, service that handled passengers and their cars; new terminal was built just south of Louisville, and trains ran over the L&N and the Seaboard Coast Line, to Sanford. Combined with Amtrak's Chicago-Florida train in 1976; discontinued in 1977.

Baltimore & Ohio (B&O). Predecessor Ohio & Mississippi, chartered 1848, completed Louisville branch from North Vernon, Indiana, in 1869; O&M acquired by B&O in 1900; B&O merged into CSX in 1986.

Chesapeake & Ohio (C&O). Predecessor Elizabethtown & Big Sandy, chartered 1852, reorganized as Elizabethtown, Lexington & Big Sandy in 1871; completed Ashland-Lexington line in 1881 (cars conveyed to Louisville by L&N until 1896 when C&O gained trackage rights over L&N to the city); L&BS and Elizabethtown & Paducah purchased by Chesapeake, Ohio & Southwestern in 1881; CO&SW built passenger station at Seventh St. and the river, connecting tracks in 1884; CO&SW acquired by C&O in 1892; C&O became Chessie System in 1973; merged into CSX in 1986.

Illinois Central (IC). Predecessor Elizabethtown & Paducah, chartered 1869, finished line between namesake cities in 1872, built its own line to city from Cecilia, Kentucky, in 1874; bought by CO&SW in 1881; acquired by IC in 1896; Kentucky division acquired by Paducah & Louisville in 1986.

Kentucky & Indiana Terminal Railroad Co. (K&IT). Owned by B&O, Monon, and Southern. Bridge company chartered in 1880, completing Ohio River bridge between Louisville and New Albany in 1886; reorganized by owner railroads as K&I Terminal Railroad Co., 1899; Youngtown yard built, 1918–26; acquired by Norfolk Southern System in 1982.

Lexington & Ohio (L&O). Chartered 1830, completing line between Lexington and Frankfort in 1834; short segment opened from Louisville to Portland in 1838. Frankfort-Lexington line acquired by Louisville, Cincinnati & Lexington in 1867; Louisville trackage sold to street railway system in 1842.

Louisville, Cincinnati & Lexington (LC&L). Organized 1869 as successor to Lexington & Ohio and Louisville & Frankfort railroads; built main line from La Grange to Covington, 1869; acquired by L&N 1881 (Shelbyville-Anchorage link built as Shelby Railroad in 1871, acquired by L&N in 1881).

Louisville & Frankfort (L&F). Chartered in 1847, completing Louisville-Frankfort line in 1851, connecting with Lexington & Frankfort (successor to Lexington & Ohio) in Frankfort. Acquired by LC&L in 1869; acquired by L&N in 1881.

Louisville, Harrods Creek & Westport (LHC&W). A narrow-gauge line chartered 1870 and opened to Prospect by 1877; acquired by L&N in 1881; electrified and acquired by Louisville & Interurban in 1904; abandoned 1935.

Louisville & Nashville (L&N). Chartered 1850, Lebanon branch opened 1857; main line to Nashville operating 1859; Memphis branch completed 1861; built Union Station 1891; South Louisville Shops 1905; merged into Seaboard System in 1983; acquired by CSX Transportation in 1986.

Louisville, Henderson & St. Louis (LH&StL). Chartered as Louisville, St. Louis & Texas, 1882; completed line from Henderson to West Point, 1889; reorganized as LH&StL, 1896; West Point–South Louisville completed 1905; acquired by L&N in 1929.

Monon (Mon). Predecessor New Albany & Salem, chartered 1847; main line to Michigan City, Indiana, completed 1854; reorganized as Chicago, Indianapolis & Louisville, 1897; acquired by L&N in 1971.

National Railroad Passenger Corp. (Amtrak). Did not own trackage in Jefferson County but between 1971 and 1979 operated Chicago-Florida daily passenger train through city on L&N and Penn Central tracks; used Union Station, 1971–76, then Auto-Train terminal until 1979. Restored service to metro area (Jeffersonville) in 1999.

New York Central (NYC). Predecessor Vernon, Greensburg & Rushville, incorporated 1879; built line between Rushville and North Vernon in 1881; acquired by Cleveland, Chicago, Cincinnati & St. Louis (Big Four) in 1892; merged into New York City Central System in 1930; Louisville & Jeffersonville Bridge and Railroad Co. organized by Big Four and C&O, 1890; Ohio River Bridge completed 1895; acquired by Penn Central in 1968; operations over Ohio River bridge abandoned 1968.

Pennsylvania (PRR). Predecessor Jeffersonville Railroad, chartered in 1846 and built line to Columbus, Indiana, 1852; continued to Indianapolis in 1853 over Madison & Indianapolis; the two companies merged in 1866 as JM&I; entered Louisville over Ohio River bridge opened in 1870; acquired by Pennsylvania RR in 1921; PRR became Penn Central in 1968 and Conrail in 1976; Indianapolis-Louisville line acquired by to Louisville & Indiana in 1994.

Southern (SouRy). Predecessor Louisville Southern, first chartered as Louisville, Harrodsburg & Virginia, 1868; reorganized as Louisville Southern, 1884; completed line in Kentucky to Lawrenceburg, Harrodsburg, and Burgin in 1888; also Lawrenceburg-Lexington line in 1889; to Southern Railway in 1896; completing line to Danville in 1906; predecessor Louisville, Evansville & St. Louis, chartered in 1870, completed line from New Albany to East St. Louis in 1890; acquired by Southern Railway System in 1900; Southern Railway became Norfolk Southern in 1982.

Soo/Canadian Pacific. Predecessor Southern Indiana Railroad, chartered 1897 and finished line between Terre Haute, Bedford, Seymour, and Westport in 1907; acquired by Chicago, Milwaukee, St. Paul & Pacific (Milwaukee Road) in 1921; Milwaukee Road reached Louisville via L&N (over former Monon) from Bedford, Indiana, in 1973; acquired by Soo in 1986 and Canadian Pacific in 1998.

See Allen J. Share, *Cities in the Commonwealth* (Lexington 1982); George H. Yater, *Two Hundred Years at the Falls of the Ohio* (Louisville 1979); Leonard P. Curry, *Rail Routes South* (Lexington 1969); *A Place in Time: Story of Louisville's Neighborhoods* (Louisville 1989); *Louisville Post,* March 12, 1918; Sept. 13, 1924; *Courier-Journal,* Feb. 23, 1997; R.C. Riebel, *Louisville Panorama* (Louisville 1954); K.A. Herr, *Louisville & Nashville Railroad, 1850–1959* (Louisville 1959); Richard S. Simons and Francis H. Parker, *Railroads of Indiana* (Bloomington, Ind. 1997); Elmer G. Sulzer, *Ghost Railroads of Kentucky* (Indianapolis 1968); Charles W. Turner, *Chessie's Road* (Richmond, Va. 1956).

Charles B. Castner

RAILROAD STATIONS. From the mid-1880s until the 1960s, Louisville was served by two large downtown railroad passenger terminals, Central Station (first named Union Depot) at Seventh and River Rd., and UNION STATION at Tenth and BROADWAY.

The first station to occupy the Seventh and River site was a wood-frame building completed by the Chesapeake & Ohio Railway (C&O) in 1886, adjacent to elevated tracks along the riverfront. The C&O president, Collis P. Huntington, envisioned a transcontinental railroad utilizing lines through Lexington, Louisville, Memphis, and New Orleans to link Virginia with California. Huntington's dream did not come to fruition, and C&O routes east of Louisville remained with the parent, while lines west of Louisville (called C&O Southwestern) went

First Louisville & Nashville freight and passenger station at 9th and Broadway, built in 1856.

to the Illinois Central (IC) in 1890.

The Seventh and River station thus came under IC's ownership and was renamed Central, the name it used until it closed in 1963. A March 1890 tornado destroyed a new brick station under construction. Designed by the Louisville architectural firm McDonald Brothers in the massive Richardsonian Romanesque style, it was rebuilt and reopened in the spring of 1891. That building was badly damaged in a fire in 1909, and the IC, in postfire RECONSTRUCTION, added individual platform sheds in place of the train shed. In 1944 the tower and the third floor were removed as a WORLD WAR II ECONOMY measure.

Ultimately, passenger trains of five railroads—the Baltimore & Ohio, the C&O, the IC, the New York Central, and the Southern—came to use Central Station, and in its peak years (the 1920s) the terminal handled the arrival and departure of forty trains daily. Destinations (via direct service or connecting cars) were Asheville; Baltimore; Charleston, South Carolina; Cincinnati; Detroit; Memphis; New Orleans; New York; Norfolk; Paducah; Pittsburgh; Richmond; St. Louis; and Washington, D.C. OHIO RIVER floodwaters interrupted train service at the station in 1937 and again in 1945. During the latter flood, some trains were shifted to Union Station. For many years Central, like Union Station, handled special trains and extra cars on regular trains each KENTUCKY DERBY weekend.

After World War II's heavy travel demands, Central's use as a rail passenger facility declined. By 1961 the C&O had the last two passenger trains at the station. In June 1963 the C&O shifted those trains to Union Station, and the station was purchased and used by Actors Theatre until the theatrical company moved to Main St. Central was demolished in 1968 to make way for Interstate 64.

From the 1920s on, metro area studies periodically recommended that the city's eight RAILROADS combine their passenger operations at one large modern station, such as was done in Buffalo, Cincinnati, and elsewhere. In 1945 a new station was proposed at a site near the present KENTUCKY FAIR AND EXPOSITION CENTER. Citing the uncertain future of passenger service and the high cost of building such a station, city railroads hedged on launching the project, and the station was never built.

Over the years smaller stations were maintained by the city's railroads at various city and suburban locations. The Louisville & Frankfort's trains first used a depot at Jefferson and Brook Streets, moving in 1881 to a larger facility at First and River. That depot also handled trains to and from PROSPECT and Lexington until about 1910. Before Central and Union Stations opened, several railroads provided passenger accommodations from a station known as the Bridge Depot at Fourteenth and MAIN Streets.

The Louisville & Nashville's original wood-frame station at Baxter Ave. was replaced in 1937 by a concrete building as part of an extensive east downtown grade separation project finished that year. The IC and the Southern, as well as the L&N, also maintained small wood-frame structures at ANCHORAGE, BUECHEL, HIGHLAND PARK, JEFFERSONTOWN, ST. MATTHEWS, and VALLEY STATION, where local passengers commuted to and from the city. There was no station at CRESCENT HILL; some C&O and L&N trains regularly stopped at Crescent Ave. to pick up or discharge passengers. Trains of the B&O, the Monon, the New York Central, the Pennsylvania, and the Southern called at small stations owned by those railroads in Jeffersonville and NEW ALBANY.

The city's two interurban electric railroad systems had terminals in the vicinity of Third and LIBERTY Streets. In May 1974 the Auto-Train Corp. opened a station on National Turnpike in southern Jefferson County to serve as the northern terminus for its triweekly auto carrier train service to and from Sanford, Florida. Autos of passengers were loaded aboard special rail cars for transit. In 1976 that service was combined with Amtrak's daily Chicago-Louisville-Florida train, and in November 1976 Amtrak shifted its train from Union Station to the Auto-Train facility. The auto carrier service was discontinued in 1977, and Amtrak ran its last passenger trains from that station in October 1979.

See George H. Yater, *Two Hundred Years at the Falls of the Ohio* (Louisville 1979); "Planning for the Louisville Area," issue no. 8, Louisville Area Development Association, June 1945; George H. Yater, "Union Station in Transit," *Louisville* 31 (July 1980): 30–35.

Charles B. Castner

RALLY'S HAMBURGERS. In 1985 James Patterson, the founder of Long John Silver's Seafood Shoppes, and several other Louisville investors purchased a fast-food restaurant in Nashville named Rally's. The prototype, containing two buildings with a single drive-through lane between them, was reworked into one small building with lanes on both sides (dubbed the double drive-through) and a walk-up window. The idea was to offer a limited menu and capture the low-priced, quick-service market that other large chains had abandoned as they expanded their choices. In addition, the RESTAURANTS contained no indoor seating and could be operated with minimum real estate and labor costs. The first restaurant opened in Jeffersonville in 1985. By 1988 the chain, still privately owned, had 52 restaurants in 10 states and was starting to gain industry attention.

In 1989 the quickly growing company passed two milestones as it became a public company with 161 stores in 23 states and posted its first profitable year. Soon after the initial public stock offering, a group of investors led by Hollywood producer Burt Sugarman, chairman of the Beverly Hills–based holding company Giant Group LTD, and businessmen William Trotter II and James M. Trotter III wrested control of the company from Patterson during a bitter struggle. Sugarman and his supporters plotted an aggressive course for the chain, which opened its 200th unit in early February 1990. In its annual review that year, *Inc.* magazine named Rally's the fifth-fastest-growing publicly held company in the nation. During the next two years, this growth continued. Rally's purchased a series of chains such as Snapps of Columbus, Ohio; Maxie's of Tallahassee, Florida; and Zipp's of St. Louis, which allowed Rally's to gain a wide market throughout the South and the Midwest. At the end of 1992, the chain had been named third on *Forbes* magazine's best small companies list and operated 430 restaurants in 25 states.

The rapid expansion continued into the next year as the Louisville-based chain opened its 500th restaurant in its hometown in September. However, the aggressive spending, which was funded by an $85 million bond issue in March 1993, and price cutting by the larger chains finally caught up with the company. It reported its first yearly loss of nearly $9 million for 1993. Over the next two years, the chain failed to turn a profit. It lost approximately $19 million in 1994 and $46 million in 1995 before posting a profit of almost $2 million in 1996.

In 1996 California companies CKE Restaurants and Fidelity National Financial gained control of Rally's. In 1997 Rally's began acquiring the stock of Checker's Drive-In Restaurants, a similar double drive-through chain with approximately 480 restaurants, based in Clearwater, Florida. This came after a possible merger with the chain had been called off earlier in the year. In November the two chains attempted to reduce corporate costs by entering into a management services contract that consolidated ACCOUNTING, technology, and other service departments at the Clearwater headquarters. By late 1997 Rally's hamburgers were being served in eighteen states. Rally's had reduced its 480 restaurants, with 252 owned by franchisees and 228 owned by the company. On March 20, 1998, the chain closed its offices on Shelbyville Rd. and moved to Clearwater, Florida, thus ending a fourteen-year history in the Louisville area.

See *Courier-Journal,* March 11, 1990, March 31, 1998.

RALSTON PURINA CO. Founded in 1894 in St. Louis as the Robinson-Danforth Commission, Ralston Purina began as a horse and mule feed business. The company, known for its popular checkerboard logo, changed to its current name in 1902 and spent its early years focusing on agricultural animal feeds and hot breakfast cereals. In the 1920s it began producing commercial pet foods. Ralston Purina's first facility in Louisville opened in 1957. With a capacity of 75,000 tons per year, the livestock feed manufacturing plant was erected on an 8-acre tract on Fern Valley Rd. between Grade Ln. and Preston Hwy. The following year, the company moved into a facility on Floyd St. south of Eastern Pkwy. formerly owned by the Buckeye Cellulose Corp. Ralston Purina processed soybeans in one part of the plant and manufactured polymer coating products in another.

In 1977 Ralston Purina acquired the Bremner Biscuit Co., founded in 1907 as the Grocers Biscuit Co. It moved into an old hangar at STANDIFORD Field (LOUISVILLE INTERNATIONAL AIRPORT) in the early 1960s and became one of the nation's largest producers of private-label crackers and cookies. In 1993 Bremner moved its plant to Princeton, Kentucky, when its site was needed for airport expansion.

In 1981 Ralston Purina exploded onto the local news scene after a series of massive sewer eruptions rocked south-central Louisville just before dawn on February 13. Extending from the UNIVERSITY OF LOUISVILLE west to Twelfth St., damages included nearly 2 miles of collapsed streets and sewers, private property and business losses, public utility outages, and injuries to four persons. Suspicion almost immediately fell upon the Ralston Purina soybean processing plant on Floyd St. after it was discovered that a high concentration of the flammable solvent hexane was present in the sewage (hexane is used to remove oil from soybeans). Although a spill had been reported by Ralston Purina to the Metropolitan Sewer District (MSD), an inspector could find no leaking CHEMICALS. It was later confirmed that 18,000 gallons of hexane had escaped and run into the sewers. Fire marshals suspected that a spark from a passing car had set off the explosions.

Assured of federal disaster aid that paid for 75 percent of the costs, the city started the rebuilding process. Within two months, city officials filed a class-action lawsuit in U.S. District Court for $50 million to cover rebuilding costs and losses by private citizens and businesses; the MSD filed a separate suit for $26.3 million. Although more than a hundred families had settled privately with Ralston Purina by November, many residents ignored the city's lawsuit and joined a class-action suit for $250 million.

By July 1984 many of the claims had been settled out of court: the MSD for $18 million; a total of $4 million to the city, the state, the LOUISVILLE WATER CO., and the University of Louisville; $2 million to residents who settled out of court. At that time the remaining residents and businesses were expected to receive approximately $12 million. The city streets and sewers had been mostly rebuilt by September 1982. However, the MSD did not allow the soybean plant to reopen until the fall of 1983, after Ralston Purina had spent $2.2 million on improvements and repairs.

In the fall of 1984 the soybean processing plant was sold to Cargill, an international processor and marketer of agricultural commodities based in Minneapolis, Minnesota. Two years later, Ralston Purina sold its livestock and poultry feed division to BP Nutrition Ltd., a subsidiary of the British Petroleum Corp. By early 1998, the Fern Valley Rd. plant was owned by Koch Industries and operated under the name of Purina Mills. The Ralston Purina Company's presence in Louisville came to an end in late 1997 when E.I. DU PONT DE NEMOURS & CO. acquired Protein Technologies International, the subsidiary of Ralston Purina that operated the Floyd St. polymer plant.

See *Courier-Journal*, Feb. 14, 1981; Oct. 19, 1984.

RAMEY, C. (CHARLES) DOUGLAS (b East Point, Kentucky, October 4, 1908; d Louisville, October 24, 1979). Actor. A graduate of Chicago's Goodman Theatre, Ramey was active in Louisville area community troupes before and after he started a THEATER workshop in 1949; this grew into a progressive repertory company, the Carriage House Players. In the summer of 1962, the players, with Ramey as director and actor, began Louisville's Shakespeare in Central Park, which became the KENTUCKY SHAKESPEARE FESTIVAL. From 1950 to 1967, the resonant-voiced Ramey also hosted the weekly program *Songs of Faith* on WHAS-TV. Health reasons forced him to stop directing Shakespeare during the 1975 summer season, but he remained as producer until 1979. In 1977 Central Park's amphitheater was named for Ramey. The "Bard of Central Park" is buried in East Point, Kentucky.

See Jane Elizabeth Davis, "A History of Shakespeare in Central Park, Louisville, Ky.", M.A. thesis, University of Kentucky, 1981.

John Spalding Gatton

RAMSIER, JOHN (b Switzerland, 1861; d Louisville, March 30, 1936). Artist. The son of Mr. and Mrs. Johann von Ramseier (who later "Americanized" their name), John Ramsier immigrated to the United States from Switzerland with his family in 1883. They settled in NEW ALBANY, Indiana, and the twenty-two-year-old Ramsier, who had studied PHOTOGRAPHY in his homeland, went to work for the photography firm of C. Heimburger & Sons.

Shortly thereafter he went to Louisville to practice his trade, working as a retoucher, first for photographer EDWARD KLAUBER and then for William Stuber & Brothers. Ramsier worked for Stuber until 1893, when the business failed.

He then developed a brief partnership with W.A. Johnston, but their photography firm, Johnston & Ramsier, did not survive long, because a fire destroyed their studio at 531 S Third St. Afterward, Ramsier began to devote more attention to PAINTING, and by 1897 he was listed in the commercial section of the city directory as an artist. By 1901 he was noted specifically as a painter of miniatures.

From 1901 to 1934 John Ramsier created approximately three thousand miniature paintings in his studio at 2410 W Jefferson St. Though he also did watercolors, India inks, and other works, he was most known for his miniatures, which he sometimes painted from photographs but usually from sittings. He painted miniatures of some of Louisville's most prominent citizens, including HENRY WATTERSON and REUBEN T. DURRETT. He had customers from across the United States as well as France, Canada, and Panama. Ramsier and his wife, Mathilde (Burri) Ramsier, had six children. He is buried in Louisville's St. Louis Cemetery.

See *Courier-Journal Magazine*, Dec. 18, 1955; Arthur F. Jones and Bruce Weber, *The Kentucky Painter from the Frontier Era to the Great War* (Lexington 1981).

RANEY, JAMES ELBERT "JIMMY" (b Louisville, August 20, 1927; d Louisville, May 9, 1995). JAZZ guitarist. Jimmy Raney was the son of Elbert and Pearl Raney. When he was nine, his mother bought him his first guitar. He began taking classical guitar lessons from A.J. Giancola, a teacher at Durlauf's music store in Louisville, and after four years began to study with Durlauf's jazz specialist, Hayden Causey. Causey introduced him to the electric jazz-guitar style of Charlie Christian, a member of Benny Goodman's band. In 1944 Raney got his first break when Causey called and asked if he would take his place for three months with Jerry Wald's band at the Hotel New York in New York City. A significant new influence on Raney in New York City was Charlie Parker, a bebop alto saxophonist. Returning to Louisville for six months, Raney worked to transfer Parker's bebop style to the guitar.

In late 1944 Raney left Louisville for Chicago, where he played with various bands including Lou Levy's. Four years later, he moved to New York City and played with Woody Herman's orchestra (1948); Al Haig, Buddy DeFranco, Artie Shaw, and Terry Gibbs (1949–50); Stan Getz's quintet (1951–53, 1962); Red Norvo and trumpeter Les Elgart (1953–54); and the Jimmy Lyon trio (1955–60). It was during his first tenure with Getz that Raney became known internationally. In 1954 and 1955 he won the International Critics Poll of *Down Beat* magazine in the category of Talent Deserving Wider Recognition. During the mid-1960s, Raney worked as a studio musician in radio and played in orchestra pits.

Following the breakup of his marriage in 1968, Raney returned to Louisville but continued to play both nationally and internationally in Europe and Asia. Raney was a three-time winner of a French national jazz poll, and in 1977 a Netherlands poll ranked him the best non-Dutch jazz guitarist. In 1974 he and Al Haig performed at Carnegie Hall. Two years later he toured Japan with Haig and his son, Doug Raney, also a jazz guitarist. He initially had few places to play in his home city. From

1970 to 1982, he played occasionally at Captain's Quarters and the Water Tower jazz series. At the end of his life, he played regularly on Thursdays at Zena's Café, a blues bar. He taught advanced students at the Music Education Institute and made instructional records with New Albany jazz saxophonist Jimmy Aebersold.

Raney recorded fifty albums during his career, and he played on eighty more. Among his albums were *Jimmy Raney Quintet* (1955), *Duets* (1979) with Doug Raney, and *Special Brew* (1974) with Al Haig. Following his death, Dan Morgenstern, director of the Institute of Jazz Studies at Rutgers University, hailed Raney as "one of the greatest and most original of all jazz guitarists." The *New Grove Dictionary of Jazz* (1988) judged him "one of the true innovators on his instrument."

Raney had two sons, Doug and Jonathan, a pianist. His body was cremated.

See Leonard Feather and Ira Gitler, eds., *The Encyclopedia of Jazz in the Seventies* (New York, 1976); Barry Kernfeld, ed., *The New Grove Directory of Jazz* (New York, 1988); *Courier-Journal Magazine,* Oct. 4, 1987.

RASH, DILLMAN A. (b Earlington, Kentucky, July 1, 1907; d Louisville, September 7, 1998). Philanthropist and investor. Rash was the son of Frank Dillman, a prominent engineer, and Susan Elizabeth (Atkinson) Rash. A graduate of Male High School, Rash went on to graduate from Princeton University and its ROTC program. He was hired as the head of research at Louisville's J.J.B. Hilliard & Son, an investment firm, and became a partner in 1947.

During World War II Rash received the Bronze Star and the French Medaille de Reconnaissance. In 1959 he became the top Army Reserve officer in Kentucky. In 1961 he returned to active duty during the Berlin Crisis. He trained thirty thousand soldiers in one year, a feat that earned him the Legion of Merit and a citation from Pres. John F. Kennedy. He retired from the army in 1964. While serving his country in the military, Rash simultaneously served his city on numerous private and public boards and committees.

He had a particular affection for the arts that dated back to 1949 when he was chairman of the fund drive for the former Louisville Fund and culminated in serving on the J.B. Speed Art Museum's board of governors from 1968-84. As president of the Louisville Chamber of Commerce (greater Louisville, Inc.), he promoted downtown development and planning for urban renewal. In 1962 he became the chairman of the Louisville–Jefferson County Economic Progress Commission, which promoted industry and tourism. His interest in sports and fitness led him to reactivate the Kentucky Sports Hall of Fame. However, Rash believed his greatest civic achievement was his service on the mayor's committee to promote racial integration in downtown Louisville. A strong advocate of integration, he and others helped to persuade HOTELS, MOVIE THEATERS, and RESTAURANTS to integrate voluntarily.

He was married to Nancy Batson and had three daughters: Elizabeth, Marianne, and Nancy. He is buried at CAVE HILL CEMETERY.

See *Courier-Journal,* Sept. 9, 1998.

RAT RACE DANCE. The Rat Race has been a popular, albeit little-known, Louisville dance for at least seventy years. Some say the Rat Race got its start in the PORTLAND area. Although the origin of the name is obscure, old-timers note that rats were once so numerous in Portland that people had to invent innovative ways to exterminate them. At night one could see the rats running everywhere, so residents formed what they called a Rat Chase.

The Rat Race has components of other dances such as the Peabody, the One Step, and the Fox Trot. Rat Racing has sort of a slide and glide step. However, it is a barroom dance as opposed to a ballroom dance. In the 1920s there seemed to be a saloon with a dance floor at every Louisville streetcar stop, where the carefree dance celebrated pre–GREAT DEPRESSION good times.

See Ken Forcht, *Dancin' The Rat Race* (Louisville, 1996); George Yater, *Flappers, Prohibition, and All That Jazz* (Louisville 1984).

Kenneth W. Forcht

RAUCH, JOSEPH (b Podhajoe, Austria, December 25, 1880; d Louisville, February 17, 1957). Rabbi and community leader. As a boy of twelve, Rauch traveled alone to the United States, where he joined his parents, who had settled in Galveston, Texas. Later he moved with his family to Cincinnati; there he attended the University of Cincinnati and was ordained at the Hebrew Union College. Rauch also studied at the University of Chicago, Columbia University, and Cambridge University in England. He earned his doctorate in theology from the SOUTHERN BAPTIST THEOLOGICAL SEMINARY in Louisville and was granted an honorary Ph.D. from Hebrew Union College in 1944.

Rauch came to Louisville in 1912 after having served for seven years as a rabbi in Sioux City, Iowa. On April 12, 1912, he became rabbi of Temple Adath Israel (later Temple Adath Israel–Brith Sholom), Kentucky's oldest known organized Jewish congregation. So beloved was he that in 1942 the members elected Rauch rabbi for life; his tenure there lasted forty-five years.

An internationally recognized spiritual leader, Rauch was active in a number of organizations that reflected both his commitment to the Jewish community and his goodwill toward those of the Christian faith. During his lifetime he was a member of the Young Men's Hebrew Association (later the JEWISH COMMUNITY CENTER), the National Jewish Welfare Board, the Central Conference of American Rabbis, and the National Conference of Christians and JEWS. In 1955 Rauch spoke before the first conference of the World Union for Progressive Judaism in Paris and was named its first honorary lifetime member. He was also a panelist on WHAS's *MORAL SIDE OF THE NEWS* program. Many times he was invited to speak to Protestant congregations.

Rauch was head of the Louisville Chapter of the American Red Cross for four years. From 1933 to 1946, he served on the UNIVERSITY OF LOUISVILLE Board of Trustees, and in 1953 he cochaired the citizens' committee for a six-year school-building program. Rauch was president of the Board of Trustees of the LOUISVILLE FREE PUBLIC LIBRARY for seventeen years. The library ended its racial SEGREGATION policy during his tenure. Rauch was also involved in the Southern Council on International Affairs and the International Prison Congress and was the first chairman of the University of Louisville's International Center. Following WORLD WAR I, he was sent on a fact-finding mission to Eastern Europe by Herbert Hoover, American relief administrator at that time. He also traveled to Israel after WORLD WAR II to investigate conditions there.

Rauch married Etta Rosenfelder on June 17, 1913. He is buried in the Adath Israel Cemetery. In tribute to his memory, a school in NEW ALBANY, Indiana, for mentally handicapped children was named in his honor, as was the University of Louisville's Rauch Memorial Planetarium. The planetarium, located on the BELKNAP Campus, was formally dedicated on April 17, 1962. Financing for the $125,000 building was raised through public donations and a grant from the JEFFERSON COUNTY FISCAL COURT, along with the cooperation of the university and the local BOARD OF EDUCATION. The building was razed in March 1998, and in 2000 a larger planetarium was opened on the campus.

REBEL YELL BOURBON. CHARLES FARNSLEY, later a mayor of Louisville, was the nephew of Alex T. Farnsley, a partner at the STITZEL-WELLER DISTILLERY. Soon after PROHIBITION, he created several brands of whiskey and personally controlled their distribution. These brands were Charlie Farnsley Special Reserve, Lost Cause, and Rebel Yell. The Rebel Yell brand remained in limited distribution until 1962 when the Stitzel-Weller Distillery decided to release the brand to commemorate the centennial of the CIVIL WAR. The brand was sold only below the Mason-Dixon Line from the time that Stitzel-Weller started controlling the marketing until 1984, when new owners decided to distribute Rebel Yell in every bourbon market.

Michael R. Veach

RECONSTRUCTION. Louisville, strictly speaking, was not one of the South's reconstructed cities. Kentucky did not secede from the Union, and Louisville—unlike Atlanta and

Richmond—was not destroyed by warfare. Indeed, as a result of its strategic location at the FALLS OF THE OHIO and as the northern terminus of the LOUISVILLE & NASHVILLE RAILROAD, Louisville profited from the war, becoming a vital wartime jumping-off point for Union troops and supplies during the drive through the lower South. To many Southerners, Louisville was a city in the enemy's camp.

The city continued to prosper during the Reconstruction era (1863–77), when a fundamental shift from a mercantile to an industrial base took place. Factories and industrial workers became commonplace, building upon a start made in this sector before and during the war. After the war, boilers, cast-iron products, cement, furniture, plows, steam engines, and woolen goods flowed from the city to the nation's markets. An influx of laborers, including blacks, increased the POPULATION by almost 50 percent during the 1860s, when the number of industrial workers grew by 31 percent. The growing population caused the city's geographical area to expand by one-third, and mule-drawn STREETCARS allowed its citizens to reach new NEIGHBORHOODS on the outskirts of town. The LOUISVILLE INDUSTRIAL EXPOSITION, which opened during the fall of 1872, displayed the city's industrial products for visiting buyers and quickly became an annual event.

Beneath the surface of industrial prosperity, however, were racial fears and tensions that resembled those throughout the defeated South. Although the CIVIL WAR ended slavery, freedom did not arrive immediately for many AFRICAN AMERICANS. Since Kentucky remained in the Union, the Emancipation Proclamation—issued early in 1863 to liberate only those slaves in the Confederacy—freed no slaves in Louisville or Kentucky. Thus, some sixty-five thousand slaves remained in bondage in the commonwealth after the war ended. Months after Appomattox, the status of the city's African American population remained vague and contested. When Union general John M. Palmer, in charge of the Kentucky Military District, freed a slave from the WORKHOUSE during the summer of 1865, the *Louisville Democrat* called him a "military dictator," expressing an opinion widely shared by slave owners.

Subsequently, Palmer was indicted by a Louisville grand jury in November 1865 for aiding the escape of slaves, largely because he issued passes permitting blacks to cross the OHIO RIVER to Indiana. Some masters simply refused to admit that slavery had ended until Palmer announced in December 1865 that three-fourths of the states had ratified the Thirteenth Amendment. Slavery, declared Palmer, had ceased to exist in Kentucky.

Despite the initial uncertainty regarding the status of slaves in Louisville, it is clear that many rural African Americans considered the city a refuge from their former masters, agricultural work, and terrorist activities by groups like the Ku Klux Klan. By the end of the war, the freedmen were arriving in the city at a rate of about two hundred a week. The number of blacks in Louisville more than doubled during the 1860s, reaching approximately fifteen thousand by the end of the decade. SMOKETOWN, a black neighborhood bounded by E BROADWAY, Floyd, Kentucky, and the L&N tracks, emerged as a symbol of this new migration of freed people from the countryside.

An office of the Freedmen's Bureau, a federal agency, was opened to help blacks make the transition from a slave to a free-labor market, and facilities providing temporary housing and medical care were set up. Blacks founded a newspaper, opened RESTAURANTS and barbershops, and found employment as day laborers and teamsters. Many were successful in their endeavors. The Louisville branch of the Freedmen's Savings & Trust Co. received almost $650,000 in deposits in four years. Moreover, by the mid-1870s, African American schools had been established in the CALIFORNIA and SMOKETOWN neighborhoods.

In addition to the migration of thousands of rural blacks from the countryside, Louisville became the temporary home for federal soldiers waiting to be mustered out. It has been estimated that slightly more than seventy thousand bored, hot, war-weary troops were encamped on the outskirts of town during the summer of 1865, ready to go home. Violence among these soldiers, as well as between them and Louisville's citizens, black and white, became commonplace. Occasionally, the brawls became riots; that was the case in June when eight boatloads of soldiers broke into several SALOONS and helped themselves to cigars and whiskey. All too often, the Union soldiers treated Louisville like an occupied Southern city and its citizens like former rebels.

The unsettled conditions that Louisville experienced immediately after the war were less disruptive than those in the Kentucky countryside, where local law enforcement had broken down and bushwhacking and the vigilante movement sprang up. During the first five years after the war's end, an estimated one hundred African Americans were lynched in Kentucky. It was from Louisville that state militia units were sent out to restore peace in rural communities like Lebanon and Crab Orchard. Citizens often resented interference from troops, especially if their communities had been pro-Confederate in sentiment. The appearance of the Louisville-based units as well as the fact that Louisville prospered while much of the countryside was still struggling to recover from the war may have created some resentment toward the city.

In many respects, Louisville became more Southern in outlook after the war than it had been at any previous time in its history. Many of its citizens, alienated by the policies of General Palmer and other federal officers, the excesses of Union soldiers, and the emancipation of African Americans, felt like conquered Confederates, and in some cases they were. There was also a large military presence in the city because Louisville served as headquarters for the Military Division of the South until the 1870s. The *COURIER-JOURNAL*, the most influential Democratic party newspaper in the state, was edited by Henry Watterson, briefly a wartime aide to Confederate general Nathan Bedford Forrest, and owned by Walter N. Haldeman, whose *Daily Courier* had been seized by Union troops. The *Courier-Journal* became an advocate for the state, the South, and the DEMOCRATIC PARTY, which was increasingly dominated by ex-Confederates. Moreover, as the price of industrialization caught up with the community—overcrowding, pollution, and labor-management problems, which increased after the depression of 1873 and peaked with the riots of 1877—the myths and nostalgia of the plantation era seemed all the more attractive to many whites.

Reconstruction ended with the resolution of the disputed election of Rutherford B. Hayes in 1876. Although Democrat Samuel J. Tilden received a majority of the popular vote, the electoral votes in several Southern states were disputed. An electoral committee awarded them to Hayes, and when the Republicans and Hayes agreed to certain concessions, HENRY WATTERSON, who had been one of Tilden's staunchest supporters, maneuvered to deny Tilden his rightful presidential victory. Republicans had promised certain aid to the South and the withdrawal of the last of the federal army. Although Hayes did not keep all of the promises, the troops were summarily removed in April 1877, and the last Reconstruction governments collapsed. Louisville did not officially undergo federal Reconstruction, but it was during that era that its white citizens, like those in other Southern cities, became susceptible to a Lost Cause mythology.

See George H. Yater, *Two Hundred Years at the Falls of the Ohio* (Louisville 1979); Robert Emmett McDowell, *City of Conflict: Louisville in the Civil War, 1861–1865* (Louisville 1962); Lowell H. Harrison and James C. Klotter, *A New History of Kentucky* (Lexington 1997); Ross A. Webb, *Kentucky in the Reconstruction Era* (Lexington 1979).

Mark V. Wetherington

RED CROSS HOSPITAL. Despite its name, the Red Cross Hospital was never associated with the American Red Cross but rather was established in 1899 by a group of African American physicians led by W.T. Merchant and Ellis D. Whedbee. Because of their color, they were prevented from practicing in local HOSPITALS. Red Cross Hospital was started to provide medical services for the black community and was opened in a rented two-story house on Sixth St. between Walnut (Muhammad Ali Blvd.) and Green (LIBERTY) St. In 1905 the hospital moved to a new, larger facility at 1436 S Shelby St.

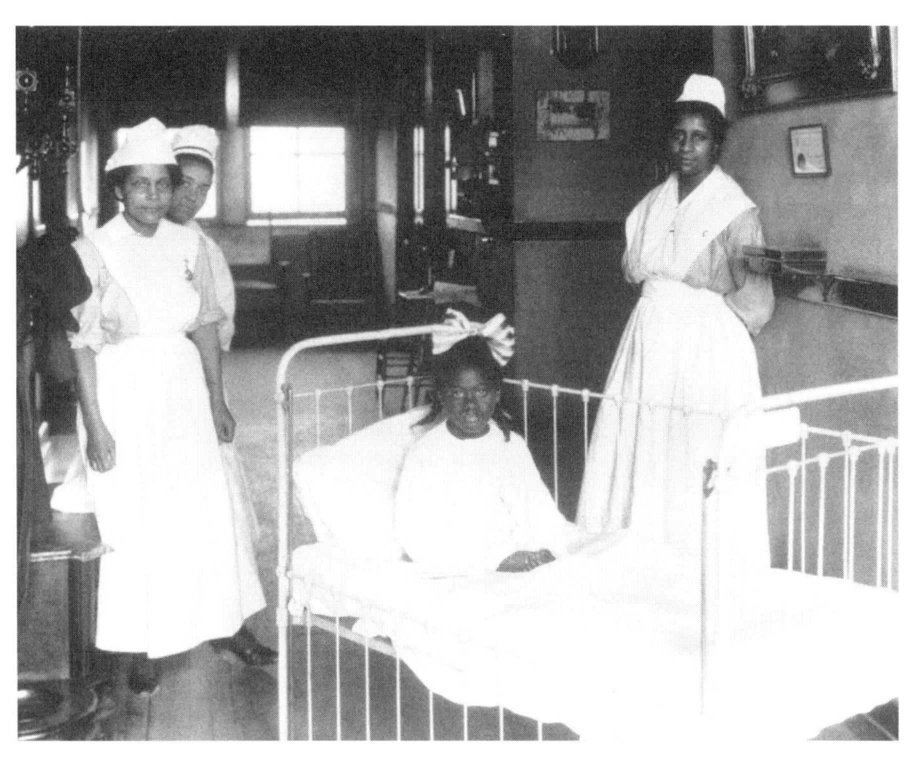

Child patient with nurses at Red Cross Hospital, 1436 South Shelby Street, 1920.

Recognizing that the cost of medical treatment was a serious issue for many poor black families, the hospital offered its services at a fraction of the amount charged by other hospitals; it also offered a free preventive care clinic. Another prominent feature was its nurses' training program. Red Cross was the only Kentucky hospital to admit African American women to a nurses' training program. The program was discontinued in 1937 because of insufficient funds and a loss of certification but was reinstated in 1948. That same year Red Cross Hospital was the country's first private black hospital authorized by the American Cancer Society to operate a small cancer clinic.

Throughout its history, Red Cross Hospital was plagued by financial worries. It depended heavily on support from the white community, specifically from prominent families like the Speeds and the BELKNAPS, who were instrumental in founding the Red Cross Club and the Red Cross advisory board, which, among other things, paid for numerous renovation projects. At different times the hospital also received funds from the state, the Community Chest, and various foundations. Though the hospital struggled through its first three decades hampered by inadequate facilities and substandard equipment, the 1940s and 1950s brought major modernization efforts that briefly improved the hospital's economic status.

However, by the early 1960s the move toward racial integration of Louisville's hospitals and increasing operational costs resulted in the facility's ultimate decline. Many of Red Cross's past patients chose to go to bigger, more technically advanced hospitals. Red Cross, which changed its name to Community Hospital in 1972, continued attempting to upgrade its facilities until 1975, by which time it was in debt, and the lack of patients forced a closure. The last patient was admitted in September 1975. Bankruptcy was declared the following January. In 1978 VOLUNTEERS OF AMERICA purchased the hospital's building, which now houses the organization's Men's Transitional Living Center.

See *Courier-Journal,* Feb. 21, 1988; George C. Wright, *Life Behind a Veil* (Baton Rouge 1985).

REDIN, WILLIAM HENRY (b Suffolk County, England, October 30, 1822; d Bluefield, West Virginia, July 16, 1904). Architect and artist. Redin was a son of William Henry and Martha Eliza (Young) Redin. The family came to the United States after 1826 and was in the Louisville area by 1834. Redin studied at the National Academy of Design in New York City in 1843–44 and is known to have worked as an artist and portrait painter for nearly twenty years. By 1860 he advertised as an architect and artist. It is for his architectural work, particularly his churches, that he is remembered. His known works (all in Louisville unless otherwise noted) include remodeling Christ Church (Episcopal Cathedral) (1858–60), and designing St. James Episcopal Church (PEWEE VALLEY, 1868–71), ANCHORAGE PRESBYTERIAN CHURCH (ANCHORAGE, 1869), the oldest part of Calvary Episcopal Church (1872–89), College Street Presbyterian Church (1873–74, razed 1964), houses for William H. Dillingham and William Cornwall (1877–78, razed), Hobbs Memorial Chapel (Anchorage, 1877, burned 1954), CAVE HILL CEMETERY Entrance and Clock Tower (1880–82), John P. Morton Church Home (1881–84, razed), and St. Anthony's Catholic Church (1884). Redin is buried in OLDHAM COUNTY, Kentucky.

See *Illustrated Louisville, Kentucky's Metropolis,* 1891; Robert R. White and Mary Jean Kinsman, "William Henry Redin: Artist and Architect of Louisville," manuscript in preparation.

Mary Jean Kinsman

REED, PAUL BOOKER (b Frankfort, Kentucky, October 7, 1842; d McLeod, Alberta, Canada, November 9, 1913). Mayor. Paul Booker Reed was the son of William Decatur Reed (d 1858) and Jane Maxwell Sharp (1818–98). He was born at Glen Willis, near Frankfort. His father was a well-known Louisville lawyer and Kentucky statesman. William Decatur Reed served as secretary of state under Gov. William Owsley (1844–48) and was a Kentucky elector for the 1856 Buchanan and Breckinridge presidential ticket. For several years he was the law partner of Charles Morehead, who served as governor of Kentucky from 1855 to 1859.

Jane Maxwell Sharp was also from a well-known Kentucky family. She was the daughter of Solomon P. Sharp, attorney general of the commonwealth from 1821 to 1825 and a member of the U.S. Congress from 1813 to 1817. Solomon Sharp was assassinated in Frankfort in 1825.

Paul Booker Reed studied at Forest Academy in Jefferson County under the Reverend Burr Hamilton McCown and in Louisville under the Reverend STUART ROBINSON and attended Centre College in Danville, Kentucky, before leaving school after the outbreak of the CIVIL WAR. He eventually returned to study MEDICINE and graduated from the medical department of the University of Louisiana at New Orleans. He had additional schooling in Paris and Vienna and in Berlin, Munich, and Wurzburg, Germany.

When the Civil War began, Reed enlisted as a private in the Confederate army and saw four years of active military service in the Ninth Kentucky Infantry, originally a part of the famed Orphan Brigade and later under Gen. John Hunt Morgan's command. He was captured twice but spent only about two months as a prisoner of war. After the war he was abroad for five years and then returned to Louisville to become a successful manufacturer.

In 1880 he was appointed receiver of the Louisville Chancery Court, holding that position until he resigned in 1884 to run successfully for mayor. Reed, a Democrat, defeated John W. McGee on December 2, 1884, by a vote of 11,780 to 3,368. He served a three-year term. A fiscal conservative, he announced that the city GOVERNMENT's expenditures would no longer exceed its revenues. He began reform ing city government by discharging several city employees and cutting the salaries of others, including his own, which he lowered by one-fifth. He also tried to curb corruption in city government by cutting Louisville's awarding of lucrative contracts to favored city businessmen.

While mayor, Reed also attempted to clean up the city's GAMBLING dens and PROSTITUTION houses. He appointed Col. John H. Whallen chief of police, and the two worked together to rid the city of gambling casinos and the red-light district. Whallen, who was the real power behind DEMOCRATIC PARTY politics in Louisville, had helped engineer Reed's election as mayor.

After serving as mayor, Reed was elected to the BOARD OF ALDERMEN as a Republican in 1899, serving until 1900. He was also president of the Republican-controlled board for twelve months during that time. In 1901 Reed ran for the Republican nomination for mayor against JAMES GRINSTEAD but dropped out of the race before the election.

Reed was made chairman of the state Central Committee of the Democratic Party in 1884. He supervised Democrat Grover Cleveland's 1884 successful presidential campaign in Kentucky. Later in life Reed moved out west, settling first in Seattle and later in Canada. Reed married twice—first to Hettie Kamerer and after her death to her sister, Ida B. Kamerer. He had no children with his first wife but had three daughters and one son with his second. He is buried in CAVE HILL CEMETERY.

See Lewis C. Collins and Richard H. Collins, *History of Kentucky,* 2 vols. (1874; reprint, Frankfort 1966); J. Stoddard Johnston, ed., *Memorial History of Louisville,* 2 vols. (Chicago 1896); *Courier-Journal,* Nov. 11, 1913.

REESE, HAROLD HENRY (b Meade County, Kentucky, July 23, 1918; d Louisville, August 14, 1999). BASEBALL player. Harold Henry "Pee Wee" Reese, the son of Carl and Emma Reese, was born on a small farm between Ekron and Brandenburg. When he was a child, the family moved to Louisville, where he got his nickname—not because of his size but because of his prowess at marbles. One year he was the runner-up to the national champion in the *COURIER-JOURNAL* marble tournament. He graduated from DU PONT MANUAL HIGH SCHOOL in 1936.

As a professional baseball player, Reese was first signed by the LOUISVILLE COLONELS of the American Association in 1937. His fielding skill at shortstop attracted the notice of major-league scouts, and in 1939 a group that included Boston Red Sox owner Tom Yawkey purchased the Louisville Colonels baseball club for $195,000, largely because they wanted Reese's contract. Later that year the club sold Reese to the Brooklyn Dodgers for the equivalent of $75,000 ($35,000 in cash and four players). At the time Larry MacPhail, president of the Dodgers, described Reese as the most instinctive base runner he had ever seen.

During his rookie year (1940), the Kentuckian displaced Dodger regular Leo Durocher and thus began a sixteen-year tenure at shortstop that was interrupted only by a three-year stint in the navy (1943–45). During the seasons that Reese played full-time with the Dodgers (1941–42 and 1946–57), his team finished first in the league seven times, second four times, and third twice. He played in seven World Series. Reese was known for his clutch hitting and for big plays in the field. He also led the National League in stolen bases (30 in 1952), in double plays four times (1942 and 1946–48), in runs scored (132 in 1947), and in fielding average (.977 in 1949). He was named to the All-Star Team eight times (1947–54). Reese was such a dominant shortstop that the well-stocked Dodger farm system was unable to produce a player capable of dislodging him. Players who tried (Tommy Brown, Mike Sandlock, Stan Rojek, Eddie Miksis, Chico Carrasquel, Bobby Morgan, Billy Hunter, Don Zimmer, and Chico Fernandez) all ended up playing for other teams. Reese's offensive career totals (126 home runs, 885 runs batted in, and a .269 batting average) do not begin to measure his value to the team. He was the team's captain, and Dodger sportscaster Red Barber described him as the glue that kept his team together.

Reese, instrumental in smoothing Jackie Robinson's entrance into baseball, was called "the catalyst of baseball integration" by author Roger Kahn. In 1947 Robinson broke the color line in major-league baseball by playing second base for the Brooklyn Dodgers. Reese was the team's established shortstop. Before Robinson's call-up from Brooklyn's Montreal farm team, a petition was circulated by several of Reese's teammates threatening a boycott to protest major-league integration. Reese, a southerner, was expected to sign. His quiet refusal doomed the petition. As the 1947 season progressed, depending on the ballpark, racial incidents increased in frequency and intensity, both in the stands and on the field. During the Dodgers' first trip to Cincinnati's Crosley Field, racial taunting was particularly ugly and fierce. The ballpark organist accented the day's mood with a rendition of "Bye Bye Blackbird." In the sixth inning, Reese walked from shortstop to second base and put his hand reassuringly on Robinson's strong shoulder. This simple, understated gesture unplugged the tension and disarmed the hecklers. Reese throughout his life always downplayed the significance of this gesture, saying that he tried to treat others just the way he would want to be treated. But the larger truth is, as Hall-of-Famer Monte Irvin noted, that this simple act "actually made it better for all of us. We're indebted to Jackie for doing a great job of pioneering, but we're also grateful to Pee Wee for that wonderful gesture he made." So, also, is baseball.

After his baseball career, Reese worked as a broadcaster with CBS, NBC, and the Cincinnati Reds. He was elected to Baseball's Hall of Fame in Cooperstown, New York, on August 12, 1984. He was director of the college and professional baseball staff at HILLERICH & BRADSBY, maker of the LOUISVILLE SLUGGER bat. For years he was the chairman of a local annual fund-raiser for the Cystic Fibrosis Foundation. He was also an avid two-handicap golfer. Reese married Dorothy Walton on March 29, 1942; they had two children, Barbara and Mark. He is buried in Resthaven Memorial Park.

See Roger Kahn, *The Boys of Summer* (New York 1972); Gary Luhr, "Dizzy, Jackie and the 'Boys of Summer': Pee Wee Reese Talks about Baseball Then and Now," *Rural Kentuckian* (July 1981); *Courier-Journal,* Aug. 15, 1999.

William Marshall
Kenneth Dennis

REGIONAL AIRPORT AUTHORITY. Following the establishment of BOWMAN FIELD airport in 1919, the state legislature created the Louisville and Jefferson County Air Board in July 1928 to administer the facility as a public airport. Although the first board, comprising three mayor-appointed and three county judge–appointed citizens, acted primarily in an advisory capacity because the park board owned the airport land, the air board's responsibilities grew after it took control of Standiford Field airport in 1946 and Bowman Field a year later. STANDIFORD Field was named for Dr. Elisha Standiford, who owned a portion of the original airport acreage. In 1995 the name of the airport changed to LOUISVILLE INTERNATIONAL AIRPORT to mirror the new objectives and the expansion of its operations.

To reflect the board's goal of branching out to serve the entire region—Louisville, Jefferson County, and southern Indiana—its name was changed in 1980 to the Regional Airport Authority. Six years later, amid criticism of poor marketing and a lack of growth for the airports, the structure of the board was changed to include the mayor and three appointees, the county judge/executive and three appointees, two governor-appointed members, and the state commerce secretary.

In 1988 the Regional Airport Authority began a large-scale, $676 million renovation of Standiford Field, which included a new terminal, a parking garage, and an air-traffic control tower, as well as two parallel runways. The expansion of the airport provoked some controversial reaction from nearby NEIGHBORHOODS, especially from Standiford, PRESTONIA, and HIGHLAND PARK. These neighborhoods were to be acquired under an URBAN RENEWAL plan to make way for the expansion. The neighbors, who were joined by residents who would be affected by greater noise levels because of the new parallel runways for the airport, took the case to court. After three years of dispute, a federal judge ruled against the use of urban renewal powers in the expansion project but allowed the acquisitions and the relocation of neighborhoods to proceed. Since 1988 more than 8,000 people in 2,569 homes and 150 businesses in Standiford, Prestonia, Highland Park, and neighboring areas have been relocated.

As owner and operator of the two airfields, the self-sustaining board, which collects revenue from leases, landing and concession fees, and airfield use, is in charge of maintenance, construction, finance, security, marketing, and day-to-day operations, while acting as a landlord to the airlines, the car rental agencies, and other vendors. The Regional Airport Authority sets policies, approves the budget, and hires the airport's general manager, who reports to the Board of Directors. To accommodate neighbors surrounding the airport, a member of the public was added to the authority in March 1998. The representative was required to be a member of the executive board of the Airport Neighbors Alliance, an organization representing over eighty thousand people living around Louisville International Airport.

See "Regional Airport Authority," Urban and Regional Reference Files, 1992, University of Louisville Archives and Records Center; "Louisville International Airport," Urban and Regional Reference Files, University of Louisville Archives and Records Center.

REGIONAL GOVERNMENT. Regional and transportation planning in the Louisville urban area began with the formal establishment of the Louisville Metropolitan Comprehensive Transportation and Development Program (LMCTDP) on August 27, 1963, to satisfy the requirements of the Federal-Aid Highway Act of 1962. The Technical Advisory Committee (currently the Transportation Technical Coordinating Committee), composed of representatives from local planning commissions, the Louisville and Jefferson County Air Board, and two state highway agencies, was formed to give technical guidance and direction to the LMCTDP. The Transportation Policy Committee, composed of the policymakers represented on the Technical Advisory Committee, was formed to set transportation planning policies for the Louisville urban area.

In order to facilitate and coordinate other necessary urban planning efforts, the FALLS OF THE OHIO Metropolitan Council of Governments (FOMCOG) was formed on September 29, 1966, to cover the urbanized areas of Jefferson County, Kentucky, and Clark and Floyd Counties in Indiana. The council was particularly active in administering the planning programs sponsored by the U.S. Department of Housing and Urban Development.

In October 1971 the Jefferson Area Development District was formed at the insistence of the Kentucky Program Development Office (now the Department for Local GOVERNMENT) to provide regional planning coordination and technical assistance to the member counties. Membership included Jefferson County as well as the six surrounding rural counties—Bullitt, Henry, Oldham, Shelby, Spencer, and Trimble.

In the spring of 1973, negotiations between the Kentucky Department of Transportation and the Council of Governments resulted in a shift of the comprehensive transportation and development program from a state responsibility to a council responsibility. It was agreed by both parties that urban transportation planning was more properly the responsibility of a local planning organization and that close cooperation and coordination were needed between urban transportation planning and other urban planning activities.

Also during the spring of 1973 the U.S. Department of Housing and Urban Development notified both the Council of Governments and the development district that it would not support the duplicate programs of the two agencies with comprehensive planning assistance funds beyond fiscal 1973. As a result the two entities merged as the KENTUCKIANA Regional Planning and Development Agency (KIPDA) on July 11, 1973, with final legal approval granted on November 1, 1973. It consists of seven county governments in Kentucky (Bullitt, Henry, Jefferson, Oldham, Shelby, Spencer, and Trimble) and two in Indiana (Clark and Floyd).

KIPDA obtains its statutory authority from Kentucky Revised Statute 147A.050.120, which established a system of substate districts, and from Indiana Code title 18, article 5, chapter 1 and title 18 article 7, chapter 5.5. Local authorization for KIPDA's planning efforts is based on the KIPDA charter signed by the member jurisdictions and by various interlocal agreements and memoranda of understanding between KIPDA and other planning agencies. On a federal level, the Environmental Protection Agency (EPA) has designated KIPDA as the area EPA-208 planning agency. The U.S. Department of Transportation has certified KIPDA as adequately performing the requirements of a cooperative, continuing, and comprehensive transportation planning program. The Office of Management and Budget recognizes KIPDA as the metropolitan-regional clearinghouse. Finally, the federal Department of Housing and Urban Development recognizes KIPDA as the metropolitan planning agency for the Louisville urbanized area. The states of Kentucky and Indiana have agreed on the designation of KIPDA as the metropolitan planning organization responsible for carrying out, in cooperation with the two states, the provisions of the federal metropolitan planning and transportation codes for the Louisville urbanized area through designation by the governor of Kentucky on March 5, 1974, and by the governor of Indiana on December 26, 1973. These designations have been accepted by the U.S. Department of Transportation. In addition to funds from the above-mentioned agencies, KIPDA receives planning funds from the U.S. Department of Health, Education, and Welfare; the U.S. Department of Labor; the Kentucky Department for Local Government; the Kentucky Department for Human Resources; and the Kentucky Department for Natural Resources and Environmental Protection.

The Board of Directors of KIPDA is composed of the county judge/executive from each county, the county judge/executive's appointee, and a sample of mayors from the various classes of cities. The board and its staff work closely with other local officials and community leaders first to determine and then, in partnership with state and federal agencies, to achieve development goals and objectives by following agreed-upon development.

KIPDA serves as a neutral, areawide forum for local public and private sector leaders to discuss and deal with common problems. The effect has been to greatly lessen provincialism. There is, in effect, a formal linkage between the community leadership within the region and the many state, federal, and private sector service agencies. KIPDA provides professional planning and development services staff for counties, cities, and community-based organizations that individually cannot afford such a staff. Also, KIPDA is part of a statewide system connecting the governor's office, the various cabinets, and the General Assembly for near-instant information dissemination and data collection, community-based strategic development planning, and professional, contract-based service delivery.

This multicounty "area development council" brings community leaders together to deal with common problems and to speak with one voice to state and federal agencies. The economies realized in using a regional partnership approach to public services has become increasingly evident. This approach became a Kentucky recommendation to Presidents Kennedy and Johnson and was written into a number of federal acts, including the Appalachian Development Act and the PUBLIC WORKS and Economic Development Act of 1965. Most recently the regional concept was written into the Intermodal Surface Transportation Efficiency Act of 1991.

KIPDA provides services directly to recipients of social services, such as the elderly in Kentucky. It is designated by the Kentucky State Clearinghouse as the regional review agency for most applications for state and federal funds made by area governments or other organizations. KIPDA also helps to coordinate and supervise transportation planning and programming in the Louisville area, emphasizing highway, public transit, pedestrian, and bicycle modes of transportation. KIPDA encourages cooperative decision making by state and local elected officials on metropolitan transportation issues such as bridge and highway construction. The Public Administration Division strives to bring miscellaneous federal and state grants, such as Community Development Block Grants and Urban Development Action Grants, to the region under a common administrative and planning umbrella. Through the Kentuckiana Ozone Prevention Coalition, KIPDA promotes programs such as carpooling to lessen the impact of ozone emissions on the region.

Robert T. Moore

REID, BENJAMIN LAWRENCE (b Louisville, May 3, 1918; d Holyoke, Massachusetts, November 30, 1990). Educator and author. Ben Reid won the 1969 Pulitzer Prize in biography for *The Man from New York: John Quinn and His Friends* (1968). Another of his books, *The Lives of Roger Casement* (1976), was a finalist for the 1976 National Book Award. Among his other works were books about Gertrude Stein and William Butler Yeats. His last book, *Necessary Lives: Biographical Reflections* (1990), includes essays on John Keats and T.S. Eliot. Reid's narrative of his early years, *First Acts: A Memoir* (1988), is a portrait of Louisville in the 1930s and the struggles of a young man trying to help his family through the GREAT DEPRESSION.

Born to Isaac Errett and Margaret (Lawrence) Reid in 1918, Reid spent much of his youth on the BASEBALL fields of SHAWNEE PARK, to which he walked from his home. He played BASKETBALL at Male High School and at the UNIVERSITY OF LOUISVILLE and graduated in 1943. He received his M.A. degree from Columbia University in 1950 and his Ph.D. from the University of Virginia in 1957. As a conscientious objector during WORLD WAR II, Reid was assigned to build bridges in the Great Smoky Mountains National Park and served as a ward attendant at a mental hospital in Virginia.

He married Jane Coleman Davidson, also a Louisville native, July 15, 1942, and they had one daughter, Jane Lawrence "Laurie" (Mrs. Michael A. McAnulty), and one son, Colin Way. Reid taught at Mount Holyoke College from 1957 until 1983. He was on the faculty at Iowa State College in Ames from 1946 to 1949, Smith College from 1948 to 1951, and Sweet Briar College from 1951 to 1957. He remained active in literary endeavors until his death.

See *Courier-Journal,* Sept. 25, 1988; Dec. 5, 1990; Benjamin L. Reid, *First Acts: A Memoir* (Athens, Ga., 1988).

Bob Edwards

RELIGION. The history of organized religion in Louisville has both obscure and somewhat inglorious roots. The earliest expressions of worship may still lie hidden in the remains of various ancient Indian burial mounds that the founders of Louisville leveled in the late eighteenth and early nineteenth centuries. These founders seemed as unconcerned with preserving Native American sacred soil as they were with establishing their own religious institutions.

Some log chapels were built in the countryside, but church structures of any kind were hardly present in town during Louisville's first thirty years. Before 1810 the few religious services that did take place in Louisville generally were held in private residences. Public meeting spaces occasionally were shared by different religious denominations, but any further effort to organize religion apparently had been eclipsed by what settlers considered to be more pressing political and commercial concerns. Steele's Meeting House on MAIN St. was one location of religious services. Horse-racing and DISTILLING outpaced the business of constructing churches. Several visitors consequently complained about the irreverence of frontier Louisville.

The NEW MADRID EARTHQUAKES of 1811 and 1812 induced some Louisville residents to consider more regular church attendance in order to get right with God. A few years before the earthquakes, in 1809, METHODISTS had erected the first church in the area that is now termed downtown, on the north side of Market between Seventh and Eighth Streets. In 1811 Catholics raised the second, the chapel of St. Louis, which served a mostly FRENCH congregation at Tenth near the river. In 1817 PRESBYTERIANS built the city's third house of worship, the FIRST PRESBYTERIAN CHURCH, on the west side of Fourth between Jefferson and Market. In 1822 fifteen EPISCOPALIANS began preparations for Christ Church, which was completed on Second St. in late 1824. This structure is the oldest church building in Louisville still standing. BAPTISTS did not construct a church until 1826 even though they had been in the area for some time; the First Baptist congregation was organized in a private home eleven years before the first church was built. During this organization of First Baptist, a mission for slaves also was established. Shortly thereafter the mission became the First African Baptist Church. Unitarians organized in Louisville in the late 1820s and built the FIRST UNITARIAN CHURCH at Fifth and Walnut (Muhammad Ali Blvd.) early in the next decade. Organized religion was beginning to have an impact when Louisville became the first Kentucky town to achieve city status in 1828.

Into the 1830s Louisville welcomed waves of German immigrants, most of whom were Roman Catholic. New congregations of this faith formed. As a consequence of the growth in the Catholic POPULATION, and in response to the growing importance of the city of Louisville, the seat of the Kentucky Catholic diocese moved in 1841 from nearby Bardstown to Louisville. The headquarters of the Episcopal church diocese relocated from Lexington to Louisville that same year. By 1852 the Louisville Catholic population nearly equaled the number of all neighboring Protestants combined, even though enough Protestants had been among the new immigrants to precipitate the establishment in Louisville of German Methodist, German Baptist, and German Evangelical churches. The latter served as the forerunner of the United CHURCH OF CHRIST.

Struggles within denominations, especially over the issue of slavery, split many churches, but numerous incidents nevertheless indicate that a generally congenial spirit with good interfaith relations prevailed throughout the 1830s into the early 1850s. For example, Presbyterians hosted Catholics for worship while the new St. Louis Catholic Church was under construction in 1831. Other diverse religious edifices, including a number of African American churches and even a few black schools, also arose during this time with the general support of the wider community. In 1842 the first Jewish congregation, Adath Israel, took up residence on MARKET St. In 1843 Brigham Young, the leader of the then highly controversial Church of Jesus Christ of Latter-Day Saints, or Mormons, came through Louisville but was not harassed as he was in many other towns. In October 1844 the unusual prophet William Miller was enthusiastically received even though his prediction that the world would end that very month did not pan out. In 1848 some Trappist monks (on their way to establish Gethsemani Abbey) were acclaimed at the public landing for their good manner and potential contribution to the community. And after the tornado of August 27, 1854, the entire city seemed to mourn the deaths of fifteen members of the Fourth Presbyterian Church who had lost their lives when the tornado struck the church during worship services.

Though tolerance seemed to rule, Louisville's religious climate turned ugly during a couple of political situations. The continued influx of GERMANS, along with many poor, solidly Catholic IRISH immigrants, fueled nativist prejudice. In 1852 James S. Speed was elected mayor but then was forced from office because he was a Catholic. Next came the rise of the anti-immigrant American, or Know-Nothing, Party. During the elections of August 6, 1855, nativist mobs terrorized immigrants on what henceforth was called BLOODY MONDAY. Catholic bishop MARTIN JOHN SPALDING, along with a handful of Protestant leaders, calmed the rage, but by the end of the riot some twenty-two people had been killed and others died later of wounds. The Know-Nothings meanwhile won the election; yet, once in office, they enacted virtually none of their threatened legislation against Catholics. As a sure sign that Know-Nothingism had been short-lived, a decade after Bloody Monday Louisville elected a German-born mayor.

As would be expected in a border city, some Louisville church members supported the Union during the CIVIL WAR, and others supported the Confederacy. The Unitarians at the First Unitarian Church were somewhat unusual with their consistent advocacy of emancipation. Other denominations generally divided over the issue, sending soldiers both north and south. Most Louisville denominations included both slaveholders and nonslaveholders. There were various religious leaders, sometimes even in the same congregation, defending each side. The more outspoken voices included the Reverend James Craik, the pastor of Christ Church Episcopal, who delivered such a powerful address to the Frankfort legislature that some attributed Kentucky's remaining in the Union to his influence. Representing the other side, Stuart Robinson of Second Presbyterian attacked the Union in his paper, the *True Presbyterian.* Federal troops subsequently seized his press, and he fled to Canada to avoid arrest. In a speech at Louisville after the war, Frederick Douglass captured the diverse stances of Louisville churches when he reminded his audience that, although some churches did awaken the American conscience to the evils of slavery, many did not. In fact, Douglass pointed out that numerous denominations actually had profited from the system. Men and women, he asserted, had been sold to build churches, while the pulpit had been used to defend the system.

Church attendance increased all across the country after the Civil War, with Louisville in particular adding numerous churches, especially along the axis of Fourth St. By the 1870s this downtown area included massive elegant houses of worship whose thriving congregations were led by energetic pastors. By the middle 1880s, Louisville newspapers reported on Sunday sermons from leading downtown preachers. Future religious leaders could henceforth be trained at one of the three new Louisville schools, the Southern Baptist Theological Seminary, which moved to Louisville in 1877; the Kentucky Normal and Theological Institute, which was chartered in 1879 for the segregated professional education of African Americans; and the Presbyterian Theological Seminary, which opened in 1893.

By the late 1880s, Louisville could boast not only of intelligent and articulate religious leaders, but of colorful ones as well. Most notable were Rabbi Adolph Moses of Adath Israel, Prof. John Broadus of Southern Baptist Seminary, Fr. Michael Bouchet of the Catholic Cathedral of the Assumption, Episcopal bishop Thomas Underwood Dudley, Pastor Charles H. Parrish of Calvary Baptist Church, and Pastor Edward L. Powell of First Christian Church.

While these men and their churches grew in prominence, other denominations as well as some diverse religious figures also gained a following in Louisville. Although German Lutheran churches had been present in Louisville since 1850, after several false starts, the First English Lutheran Church (now the First Lutheran Church) was organized on E Broadway in 1872, raising a building two years later. This church would give birth to many other Lutheran congregations. Jehovah's Witnesses (originally known simply as Bible Students) first gathered in Louisville in 1881, renting meeting space for many years. In the mid–twentieth century, they finally built the first of what would later become many Kingdom Halls. In 1888 Elder A. Barry, a licensed African American minister, instructed a small group of believers who two years later organized as the Magazine Street Seventh-day Adventist Church.

Also in 1888 the first Christian Science service was held in Louisville at a private home. Ten years later this group incorporated as First Church of Christ, Scientist. Their first building was on Fourth St. between Chestnut and Broadway, but eventually they built a house of worship at Third and Ormsby. Amid all the denominational growth, Victorian Louisville also welcomed America's premier evangelist, Dwight L. Moody, as well as the nation's most celebrated infidel, Robert G. Ingersoll.

During this Victorian age, women still had not attained the status of clergy, but nonetheless they played increasingly significant roles in church and community life. Some of the more influential local women included Christ Church members Sarah Clayland, who established an orphanage; Mary Louisa Norton, who helped make possible a hospital; and Barbee Castleman, who worked as one of the first suffragists in Kentucky. Methodists Mary Ogilvie and Mrs. George Gaulbert helped found Wesley House for the needy in 1903, and Maggie Judge headed the Catholic Women's Club. An army of Catholic sisters also ran the increasing number of hospitals, social agencies, and schools, including Nazareth College (now Spalding University), which opened in 1920 in the old Tompkins-Buchanan mansion. But the most highly revered of all citizens in Victorian Louisville may have been the invalid Jennie Casseday. Widely acclaimed for her charitable work, each Sunday she used a special telephone hookup in her home to "attend" services at the Warren Memorial Presbyterian Church at Fourth and Broadway.

At the turn of the century, the Social Gospel movement challenged many Louisville churches to confront oppressive social structures. These churches consequently became far more than places of worship and religious education. They now also cared for the sick, the poor, and the homeless. Storefront missions and soup kitchens sprang up. The YMCA and YWCA movements, which had first appeared in Louisville in the 1850s, took on a new social consciousness in the twentieth century. Many ministers had long used their individual pulpits to excoriate such things as gambling, prostitution, and saloons, but amid the rampant political corruption of the early 1900s, some of these same religious leaders now joined forces under the collective name of Fusionists (really a union of Republicans and reform Democrats, but ministers participated). Prominent among these reformers were Episcopal bishop Charles E. Woodcock and Southern Baptist Seminary president Edgar Y. Mullins. In 1910 some of the Fusionist ministers formed the Churchman's Federation (the predecessor of the Louisville Area Council of Churches), which among other things conducted antigambling and prohibitionist campaigns. Just before World War I, Charles Parrish of Calvary Baptist, aided in part by the Quinn Chapel African Methodist Episcopal Church, led a fight against an impending residential segregation ordinance. Although the ordinance was enacted by Louisville officials and supported by the Kentucky Court of Appeals, it was eventually overturned by the Supreme Court in 1917. While this fight was going on, Louisville churches debated whether the United States should enter the war. Once troops had been engaged, however, most churches offered their support.

The postwar years brought new challenges for Louisville churches. As unemployment hit 30 percent during the Great Depression, religious organizations strained their own limited resources to attempt to meet the need. One institution that faced the challenge courageously was the well-known Cabbage Patch Settlement House, which had been founded by sixteen-year-old Louise Marshall of the Second Presbyterian Church in 1910. During the 1937 flood, churches in dry areas often served as refugee, relief, and medical centers. Concordia Lutheran was well positioned for this ministry, with the water stopping but 200 feet from the church. The *Courier-Journal* reported that more than two hundred black men sang spirituals while working around the clock at the Riverside electric plant in a vain attempt to keep the city supplied with power. Throughout the tragedy, as the paper reported, no distinctions based on denomination, creed, color, or class were ever drawn. In response to another kind of emergency, many religious groups of Louisville again came together to assist the American cause during World War II.

The postwar flight to the suburbs caused many denominations to debate whether they should remain downtown to serve their dwindling congregations or follow their membership outside the city limits. Broadway Baptist and Second Presbyterian moved to the suburbs; Walnut Street Baptist, Fourth Avenue Methodist, and Warren Memorial (later Central Presbyterian) remained downtown. Adath Israel and First Christian also moved outward, leaving their excellent downtown buildings to Greater Bethel Temple and Lampton Baptist, respectively. Other religious institutions, including a new wave of hospitals, also arose in the suburbs. During these transitions, additional institutional changes occurred, some of which revolved around the ever-expanding roles for lay people in the church, as well as the eventual ordination of women in some denominations.

In the second half of the twentieth century, Louisville came forward as a national center of interfaith cooperation, spurred on in part by the struggle for human rights. In the 1950s black leaders such as Bishop C. Ewbank Tucker and Pastors W.J. Hodge and A.D. Williams King (brother of Martin Luther King Jr.) challenged Louisville's segregation laws. A number of white clerics, many of whom had already been quietly working for change, now joined the public fight for civil rights. These supporters

Ticker tape parade during campaign visit of Richard Nixon in 1960.

included Catholic bishop Charles Maloney, Episcopal bishop Gresham Marmion, rabbis Joseph Rauch and Herbert Waller, and Quaker Mansir Tydings.

Though not all religious leaders endorsed these and other struggles for justice, significant changes did occur, including the eventual disappearance of color lines in most Louisville religious institutions. In the 1960s the Louisville Council on Religion and Race and the Human Relations Commission at City Hall were organized. Bellarmine College president Msgr. Alfred Horrigan and Rabbi Martin Perley led these organizations. Consistent with this spirit of religious cooperation, local radio station WHAS featured a pioneering interfaith Sunday broadcast called *The Moral Side of the News*. Listeners relished the commentaries of Rabbi Rauch and Msgr. Felix Newton Pitt of the Catholic School Office. From this program the average citizen became aware of new patterns of understanding, toleration, and mutual learning. America had entered an ecumenical age, and the people of Louisville stood at the cutting edge. One sign of their openness to the future came in 1979 when the Catholic Cathedral of the Assumption and Christ Church Episcopal Cathedral formed a covenant in which they agreed to pray for one another, study and pray together, and work together in social service. In 1987 enthusiastic crowds representing diverse denominations welcomed the establishment in Louisville of the national headquarters of the Presbyterian Church (USA).

Organized religion in Louisville has come a long way since frontier days when nary a church existed in the city. By the end of the twentieth century, houses of worship can be found everywhere. Catholics and Baptists currently comprise the largest denominations in Louisville, with Catholics constituting perhaps a quarter (that is, about 175,000) of the total population of Jefferson County. Baptists are harder to count in large part because at least three major, somewhat divergent, groups of Baptists exist in the area: the General Association of Baptists, the Kentucky Baptist Convention, and Independent Baptists. The United Methodist Church boasts nearly 20,000 members in Jefferson County, while Presbyterians, Jews, Episcopalians, and Muslims in the county number probably between 5,000 and 10,000 each. Muslims have been organized since 1974 when they founded the Islamic Cultural Association of Louisville. Buddhist and Hindu congregations have been formed in the Louisville area and, like the Muslims, are growing rapidly at the end of the century. The remaining religious groups in Louisville may be small in number, but they certainly are not insignificant to the life of what clearly is now one of the most ecumenical cities in the world.

See Clyde F. Crews, "Communities of Memory, Communities of Hope—A Brief Narrative of the Religious History of Downtown Louisville," pamphlet prepared for Cathedral of the Assumption, 1992; Clyde F. Crews, *Spirited City: Essays in Louisville History* (Louisville 1995); George H. Yater, *Two Hundred Years at the Falls of the Ohio* (Louisville 1987).

C. Walker Gollar

REPUBLICAN PARTY. The Kentucky Republican Party and its arm in Louisville and Jefferson County have led parallel lives. They each historically do well in presidential and congressional elections, but the Democrats rule when voters choose state and local officials. It is a phenomenon manifested by registration figures in Jefferson County, where Democrats outregister Republicans by about two to one. The GOP controlled City Hall and the courthouse for extended periods only twice in this century. Former court of appeals judge and county attorney Samuel Steinfeld, who became active in local Republican politics about 1928, said, "When the Democrats were fighting among themselves, the Republicans could win. When the Democrats were together, they would win."

The Reconstruction policies of the national Republican Party during and after the Civil War haunted Kentucky Republicans for many years. People resented the state GOP because of its ties to the national party, and Democrats dominated state and local politics for thirty years before William O'Connell Bradley was elected the state's first Republican governor in 1895.

Several weeks later, George D. Todd became Louisville's first Republican mayor following the midterm death of Democrat mayor Henry S. Tyler. But Republican factions were split between Todd and William Johnson to succeed Tyler. The Republican-controlled Common Council chose Todd to fill the unexpired term. The two waged a public dogfight before the Republican-dominated Board of Aldermen and City Council appointed Todd as mayor on January 31, 1896.

At the time, Todd pledged a clean, businesslike administration and predicted, "The Republican party will remain in power for years to come" (*Louisville Times*, Feb. 1, 1896). Todd was overly optimistic. He ran for a full term in 1897 but was plagued by party dissension over jobs and other issues and lost to Democrat Charles Weaver.

The GOP held the mayor's office for only two of the next twenty years. The only exception stemmed from the 1905 elections, when the powerful Democratic machine beat Republican and Democratic reformers known as the Fusion ticket. The Fusion candidates were Joseph T. O'Neal Sr. for mayor and Arthur Peter for county judge. After a campaign of violence and controversy, the Democratic ticket of Paul Barth for mayor and Charles A. Wilson for county judge was the apparent winner. The count showed Barth beating O'Neal by about 3,100 votes and Wilson defeating Peter by nearly 4,100.

Fusionists challenged the results in court, accusing the Democratic machine of stealing the election. Among other things, they said the Democrats hired so-called repeaters to vote more than once. The GOP also accused Democratic-controlled police of seizing ballots and bullying, beating, and arresting Republican voters and election officers. Eighteen months later, the Court of Appeals (then Kentucky's highest court) ruled that the Democrat machine was "guilty of a conspiracy to steal the election by fraud and violence." The high court nullified the election, and Gov. J.C.W. Beckham appointed Democrat Robert Worth Bingham mayor. In 1907 James Grinstead was elected mayor and Arthur Peter county judge, both Republicans.

Voters returned the Democrats to power in 1909 and kept them there until 1917. That is when voters gave the Republicans undisputed control for the first time at City Hall and the

Courthouse. GEORGE WEISSINGER SMITH ran for mayor and WILLIAM KRIEGER for county judge, and each won by more than 2,200 votes. Chairman WILLIAM MARSHALL BULLITT called it "a magnificent victory. The people wanted a change and they got it." Under the leadership of men like Bullitt and organization chairman CHESLEY SEARCY, local Republicans had a heyday between 1917 and 1933.

The only interruption came after the 1925 elections. This time, Republicans felt the wrath of the Court of Appeals. Democrats contested the election of ARTHUR A. WILL as mayor and Henry I. Fox as county judge. They accused the Republicans of fraud and voter intimidation. In June 1927 the high court threw Will, Fox, and others out of office and replaced them with Democrats. The high court blamed the alleged fraud on "an inner circle of practical men." The *Louisville Times,* on June 17, 1927, observed that "if Kentucky history repeats itself, the city and state will show strong Democratic preferences for several years as a result of the court ouster." The prediction was premature. Five months later the Republicans celebrated, electing William B. Harrison as mayor, Fox as county judge, and other GOP candidates. Harrison was a popular mayor and an excellent speaker. In November 1929 he was reelected to a full term. He established a planning commission, started civil service for the police and fire departments, and was instrumental in the building of a new OHIO RIVER bridge (Clark Memorial Bridge) between Louisville and Jeffersonville. He was the unsuccessful Republican candidate for governor in the Depression year 1931.

In 1933 Democrats swept elections from the White House to City Hall. GOP mayoral candidate Dan Carrell lost to Democrat NEVILLE MILLER by 3,000 votes, and Stanley Briel lost to Democrat BENJAMIN EWING in the race for county judge. The party also lost traditionally strong support in the black community because of Pres. Franklin D. Roosevelt and his New Deal policies. Ironically, Republican CHARLES ANDERSON in 1935 became the first black elected to the Kentucky legislature. Otherwise, 1933 began a long drought for local Republicans, broken only by Horace Barker's 584-vote win for county judge in 1945 over Edwin Willis.

Mayoral candidate Roy W. Easley made a strong run against Democrat E. Leland Taylor in 1945. Easley pledged to "remove the seat of GOVERNMENT from Third and LIBERTY [the location of the *COURIER-JOURNAL* and the Louisville Times] and put it back at Sixth and Jefferson where it belongs." He accused the Democratic administration of waste and of lacking "the moral soundness, responsibility and dependability which are the foundations of integrity" (*Louisville Times,* Nov. 4, 1945). Democratic mayor Wilson W. Wyatt accused the Republican Board of Aldermen of obstructionism and penny-pinching politics. Easley lost by only 228 votes. Otherwise, the party survived over the years with the financial support and leadership of such prominent Republicans as Jouett Ross Todd, George W. Norton Jr., S. Tilford Payne, Edwin Middleton, Henry Brooks, and Henry Heyburn. Republicans did hold the Third District congressional seat for twelve years between 1946 and 1958. Thruston B. Morton served three terms before his election to the U.S. Senate in Pres. Dwight D. Eisenhower's landslide of 1956. Morton helped give the Republicans a solid base in the county until his retirement in 1968. John M. Robsion Jr. held the Third District for the Republicans until 1958, when he lost to Democrat Frank W. Burke. The following year, Robsion was the party nominee for governor but lost a lopsided decision to Democrat BERT COMBS.

Between 1952 and 1996, Republicans carried the county in nine out of twelve presidential elections. Local Republicans broke through in 1961, electing a mayor for the first time in twenty-eight years, a county judge for the first time in twelve, a Board of Aldermen, and sweeping races for other countywide offices. In all, the Republicans won forty-two of forty-four races, including circuit judges, magistrates, and constables. Leading the revolution was 39-year-old William O. Cowger, president of a mortgage firm, and 35-year-old Marlow W. Cook, an attorney who had served in the Kentucky House since 1958. Cowger soundly defeated 69-year-old William S. Milburn, president of the Board of Aldermen, by more than 11,000 votes. Cook set an all-time record, trouncing 36-year-old House floor leader Thomas L. Ray by about 20,000 votes.

Cowger ran against Fourth St. Democratic headquarters, calling its leaders "sinister forces" who controlled Milburn and other Democratic candidates. Cook blasted the Democrats for failure to deal with the county's drainage problems and pledged to submit to voters a $7 million bond issue for major improvements. He also called the county police merit system a joke. He said he would improve it and promised that the police department would no longer operate as an arm of the county judge's office. Democratic organization chairman JOHN CRIMMINS said simply, "Evidently the people were ready for a change and the twenty-eight year cycle ran its course and caught me at the end."

But there were other factors at work. Cowger and Cook were a young, progressive, and dynamic team. The Democrats lost the support of such traditional constituencies as organized labor and the black community. Cowger received more than 60 percent of the black vote, which had defected because Milburn and the administration opposed an ordinance banning discrimination by businesses serving the public. Cowger and Cook also used the media effectively, frequently summoning reporters to news conferences to announce a platform plank or bash the Democrats. During his administration, Cowger created a Human Relations Commission and backed the first public accommodations law enacted in any city south of the Mason-Dixon Line. He also started plans for a Louisville zoo.

Cook benefited when a court challenge of the county occupational tax was settled, releasing millions of dollars held in escrow for major projects. He and Democratic members of a split Fiscal Court squabbled over patronage and other issues. Cook and Cowger filed a successful redistricting suit in federal court to force the state Democratic administration to give the county more representation in the Kentucky legislature. They also created an industrial development agency called the Economic Progress Commission. Cook also began acquiring land for a Riverport industrial park and attracted national attention by buying an old steamboat and turning it into a tourist attraction, the *BELLE OF LOUISVILLE.*

The Republican momentum continued in 1962. Boosted by a 23,000-vote majority in Jefferson County, Senator Morton won reelection over Wyatt, who was lieutenant governor at the time. Morton's majority helped magistrate M. Gene Snyder upset incumbent FRANK BURKE in the Third District. Snyder, a self-styled conservative, was ousted by former mayor CHARLES FARNSLEY in the 1964 landslide of Pres. Lyndon Johnson, but that was just a bump in the road for the GOP. In 1963 it elected two more county commissioners after two years of a politically split Fiscal Court. In 1965 Cook led the way as Republicans swept the city and the county again. Judge Cook was reelected and set another record, beating Democratic attorney William Stansbury by more than 54,000 votes, or about 65 per cent of the countywide vote. Cowger could not succeed himself, but fifty-three-year-old Kenneth A. Schmied, president of the Board of Aldermen, was elected mayor. Schmied defeated Marlin Volz, dean of the UNIVERSITY OF LOUISVILLE law school, by about 10,000 votes, including about 52 percent of the black vote. Schmied, a gregarious and plainspoken businessman, was hands-on in the daily operations of city government. He pushed forward with URBAN RENEWAL programs and plans to revitalize downtown Louisville.

In 1966 Cowger was elected Third District congressman. Snyder went after the newly drawn Fourth District, which combined eastern Jefferson County with several northern Kentucky counties. Snyder and businessman James "Buddy" Thompson fought it out in a rare GOP primary. The party backed away from any endorsement, and Snyder won with a strong Jefferson County base. He represented the district for twenty years before retiring in 1986. In 1970 Cowger lost his Third District seat by 211 votes to Democrat Romano Mazzoli. Cowger had his eye on the U.S. Senate in 1968 but dropped the idea after Cook was endorsed by a majority of executive committee members. Cook's massive victory in 1965 had propelled him into the 1967 governor's race, where he lost a bitterly fought primary to former Barren

County judge Louie Nunn. Nunn beat Democrat Henry Ward in the general election but barely carried Jefferson County. At the same time, Republicans lost eleven of twelve seats on the Board of Aldermen despite Schmied's warning that the election of a Democratic board would be "catastrophic." Schmied and the Republican aldermen alienated the black community by refusing to enact an ordinance banning discrimination in housing. The Democrats got about 65 percent of the black vote, enough to make the difference in many aldermanic races that were decided by less than 1,000 votes.

In 1968 Cook was elected to the U.S. Senate, defeating Democrat Katherine Peden for the seat vacated by Morton's retirement. Local Republicans wanted Governor Nunn to name Commonwealth's Attorney Edwin Schroering to succeed Cook as county judge. But hard feelings remained from the 1967 gubernatorial primary, and Nunn instead chose County Attorney Erbon P. "Tom" Sawyer, a longtime friend and ally. In 1969 Sawyer ran for a full term with businessman John Porter Sawyer as his running mate for mayor. Six weeks before the election, Erbon Sawyer was killed in a car crash.

This time, local Republicans snubbed Schroering and chose businessman W. Armin Willig as Sawyer's successor. Circumstances and factionalism weakened the ticket. The Democrats did not play up the housing issue but did not have to. They charged that the Schmied administration was getting nothing done and the community was stagnant. The Democrats made their comeback complete, recapturing City Hall and sweeping most county offices. Among Republicans, only Schroering, the county clerk, and the coroner were reelected. For mayor, John Sawyer lost to former congressman Burke by about 7,500 votes. And twenty-nine-year-old attorney TODD HOLLENBACH beat Willig for county judge by more than 4,000 votes. Burke said, "A lot of Democrats have come back home to their party."

In most cases, Democrats have stayed home since, attracted by candidates with strong personalities and backed by organized labor and black voters. Republicans meantime had increasing difficulty getting a pool of good candidates. That was especially so in the city, with many traditional Republican constituencies having moved to the SUBURBS. Cowger's career was cut short by his death in October 1971. As an aftermath of Watergate, Cook was defeated for reelection to the Senate in 1974 and never ran for public office again.

A major exception to Democratic dominance was thirty-five-year-old attorney MITCH MCCONNELL. After serving as party chairman, McConnell was very much an underdog in 1977 when he challenged Hollenbach's bid for a third term as county judge. But McConnell took the fight to Hollenbach, gained endorsements from county police and organized labor, and used TELEVISION ADVERTISING effectively. One ad ridiculed Hollenbach's truthfulness by portraying a farmer tossing a shovel of manure. McConnell beat Hollenbach by more than 10,000 votes but was the only Republican to be elected.

In 1981 he survived another Democratic sweep and edged County Commissioner Jim Malone by about 6,000 votes. During his tenure at the courthouse, McConnell scrapped with a politically divided Fiscal Court, pushed development of the Riverport industrial park, and was a leader in efforts to help missing and exploited children. He tightened security and reformed management of the county jail, which had acquired the nickname of "FREEDOM HALL" because of frequent escapes. He also joined with Democratic mayor Harvey Sloane to campaign for government merger, but the proposal narrowly lost. In 1984 McConnell became the first Republican to win a statewide race in Kentucky in sixteen years by upsetting Democratic senator Walter "Dee" Huddleston. Pres. Ronald Reagan had long coattails that year, and Huddleston was the only Democratic incumbent senator to lose.

McConnell waged an effective, well-financed campaign, portraying Huddleston as a backbencher and absentee lawmaker. He used a now classic television commercial showing a pack of bloodhounds chasing a Huddleston look-alike who was not tending to business. McConnell, a skilled political fund-raiser, was reelected in 1990 and 1996, establishing himself as a major national figure in the Republican Party. Tilford Payne, a Republican Party leader in Jefferson County, said McConnell had "the shrewdest political mind I've ever seen." It was McConnell's theory that local Republicans can never dominate but can win individual elections by getting strong candidates to target offices that are vulnerable.

Republicans won two major county offices in 1993, electing a sheriff for the first time in twenty-four years and reelecting a county clerk, both by overwhelming majorities. The results raised Republican hopes for future victories, but the Democrats swept all other local races, with their mayoral and county judge candidates facing only token opposition. GOP officials said the election showed that Democrats will vote for Republicans here if they have superior candidates. In 1996 the Republicans won the Third Congressional District seat for the first time in twenty-six years when state representative ANNE MEAGHER NORTHUP won a close victory over one-term incumbent Democrat Mike Ward.

Jefferson County was also the focal point of the controversial 1995 gubernatorial election. Democratic lieutenant governor Paul Patton rolled up a 25,000-vote majority in Louisville and Jefferson County, giving Patton the pad he needed to edge Republican Lawrence E. Forgy by about 21,000 votes statewide. Patton was helped in Louisville by his running mate for lieutenant governor, Steve Henry, a Louisville doctor with political ties to Jefferson County. Forgy and Jefferson County chairman William Stone blamed the defeat on election fraud. Specifically, they charged that the Patton campaign used labor union money to get around campaign spending limits. A special grand jury was impaneled to investigate the charges. Indictments were handed down against several of Patton's campaign supporters in September 1998 but were thrown out in a court case in June 1999.

The local Republican Party is governed by a forty-four-member executive committee. Eighteen members are legislative district chairmen, twenty-two are chosen at large, and four represent major Republican political organizations. Legislative district chairmen name precinct captains. Until the late 1960s, the organization usually selected party nominees without a primary. Or as Malcolm Jewell, a political science professor at the University of Kentucky, wrote, "With a network of capable precinct organizations turning out a good vote for the 'official' party man, the challengers (lone wolves, mavericks or whatever) have a formidable obstacle to overcome." The organization has no such power now. Instead, it is responsible for party structure, recruiting viable candidates and educating them, getting out the vote, manning the polls, and helping candidates by distributing LITERATURE and providing voter lists. At the end of 1997 Democrats out-registered Republicans countywide, 257,743 to 132,918.

See Malcolm Jewell, *Kentucky Politics* (Lexington 1968); John Kleber, ed., *The Kentucky Encyclopedia* (Lexington 1992); Joel Goldstein, ed., *Kentucky Government and Politics* (Bloomington, Ind. 1984); Lowell H. Harrison and James C. Klotter, *New History of Kentucky* (Lexington 1997).

David Nakdimen

RESTAURANTS. The earliest Louisville establishments serving meals were TAVERNS and inns of questionable quality. One visitor in the 1780s described the taverns scattered along MAIN St. and the streets leading down to the wharf as "little better than grog shops." But as the frontier moved westward beyond Louisville and commerce animated the growing town, the situation improved. By 1805 Christy's Inn, at the sign of the Eagle, was ADVERTISING in the town's first newspaper, the *FARMER'S LIBRARY*. Some travelers complained, however, about prices. John S. Wright noted that "the tavern charges, here, are the most extravagant I ever p[aid]. Fifty cents for a common meal, twenty-five for lodging, twenty-five for a gill of spirits, and seventy-five for horse keeping" (*Letters from the West,* 27).

An early example of better accommodations was Washington Hall on the south side of Main St. near Third St. It was opened about 1820 and was described by an English tourist as "a handsome hotel, supplied apparently with the usual luxuries of European inns, except clean floors" (Fordham, *Personal Narratives of Travels . . . in Kentucky,* 36). But the first tavern or inn

Advertisement for Lucas' Saloon from an 1868 city directory.

to live in Louisville memory was John Gwathmey's Indian Queen, built about 1803 on the northeast corner of Fifth and Main Streets and enlarged and renamed Union Hall by 1819. It was here that JOHN JAMES AUDUBON and his bride, Lucy, settled in 1808. By 1823 Gwathmey was operating a tavern-restaurant in New Orleans, but Union Hall continued many years under the ownership of Archibald Allan, who had previously operated Washington Hall. It was Allan who served as host to the Marquis de Lafayette on his Louisville visit in 1825, and it was at Union Hall where the banquet in Lafayette's honor was held.

In the 1830s, when Louisville had achieved city status and a booming ECONOMY, the first "four-star" hotels—the GALT HOUSE and the LOUISVILLE HOTEL—brought top-quality cuisine to the growing metropolis and set the standard for later hostelries. Less formal dining spots outside the hotels also made an appearance, usually calling themselves coffee houses, though the patrons consumed more alcohol than coffee. Possibly the first was Henry Hyman's Western Coffee House on MARKET St. near Fifth St. There he served "pig's feet, pickled tripe, sauced sturgeon, sauced mackerel, &c, &c," as well as "Hot Punch, Lemonade, Hot Toddies, &c, and Fresh Cincinnati Beer" (*Louisville Public Advertiser,* March 26, 1828). Such establishments were for men only.

Other similar male retreats soon followed, the most famous being Walker's Coffee House, opened on Fourth St. near Main in August 1834 by William H. Walker. It quickly became the informal headquarters of the Whig Party in Louisville and the venue where Henry Clay met with local party leaders when he was in the city. By 1845 it was called Walker's Restaurant Hotel and advertised that "all the substantials and delicacies of this and other markets can be had at all hours" (*Louisville Morning Courier and American Democrat,* Feb. 22, 1845). In 1851 the establishment was moved to a newly erected building on Third between Main and Market Streets. Its culinary fame was maintained with "Chesapeake Bay canvas-back ducks, New York oysters in the shell, venison and grouse from the prairies, mutton and beef from Bourbon County, pheasants, quail, woodcock, plover, salmon, bass, etc." (*Louisville Daily Courier,* July 19, 1851). After the move it became Walker's Exchange and continued in business until the early 1890s.

In 1866 a coach stop inn with a general store, a bar, and guest rooms on the Louisville-Brownsboro toll road opened; many years later this establishment was purchased by Min Perryman and became Min's Steakhouse and later Pat's Steakhouse at 2437 Brownsboro Rd.

In 1870, as Louisville's economic interests began to involve more manufacturing, two cornerstone RESTAURANTS were established, Bauer's at 3612 Brownsboro Rd. and Cunningham's at Fifth and Breckinridge Streets. John Bauer opened Bauer's next to his blacksmith shop and wagon manufacturing firm on the toll road, originally serving only beer and sandwiches. His son and grandsons later developed the restaurant with a traditional American menu, which continued until the business was sold in the 1980s. In 1870 Cunningham's was a delicatessen-grocery and horse stable operated by Charles Melton. Dave Oswald bought it in 1871 and later reopened it as a restaurant with a carved wood beer bar and large mirrors. Later owned by JAMES CUNNINGHAM, in 1942 Cunningham's was Louisville's first drive-in restaurant.

In 1874 Louis Seelbach opened Seelbach's Restaurant and Cafe. In 1905 he opened the Seelbach Hotel at Fourth and Walnut (Muhammad Ali Blvd.); its Oak Room later became known for its gourmet regional menu and continental kitchen, extensive wine list, and excellent service. In 1884 Philip Mazzoni opened an oyster bar with beer and free ROLLED OYSTERS; the most famous downtown location on Third St. was removed to Seventh St. because of URBAN RENEWAL, and later to TAYLORSVILLE Rd.

Another cornerstone restaurant, Kunz's, was established when Jacob Kunz in 1892 opened a wholesale wine and liquor business. In 1903 Kunz's became a delicatessen and grocery offering buffet service and private dining rooms. During the following years, KUNZ'S restaurant changed its location several times within the downtown area. In 1987 it moved to Fourth and Market and remained downtown Louisville's oldest continuously family-owned-and-operated restaurant.

In the 1890s and early 1900s, restaurants combined with confectioneries became popular. Examples include Christ Kraemer's Restaurant, Bakery, & Confectionary on Third St.; SOLGER'S CONFECTIONERY Store at Fourth and BROADWAY; and JENNIE BENEDICT'S catering business on Fourth St., which later became Benedict's Confectionary with its popular benedictine sandwiches. While Louisville ladies visited Jennie's, the men patronized Sullivan and Brook's saloon and restaurant and the popular Vienna Restaurant on Fourth St., which opened in 1893. The restaurant closed in 1927, but the ornate, glazed-tile name remained on the original building front until demolition to make way for 1980s redevelopment.

In 1898 the R.W. Miller family began serving meals to their rooming-house students from the UNIVERSITY OF LOUISVILLE medical school. After one hundred years of service to the Louisville area, family members decided to close MILLER'S CAFETERIA on Second St. in 1998. In 1913 Roland White from Cleveland opened the COLONNADE CAFETERIA at 417 S Fourth St., hired Otto Seelbach as manager, and utilized the "free-square style" that allowed customers to go to a certain section and get the desired food, without waiting. When the STARKS BUILDING was erected in 1925–26, the cafeteria moved to its now-familiar spot in the building's basement. In 1934 the first BLUE BOAR CAFETERIA was opened at 410 W Walnut; eventually several were built. In 1974 JAY'S CAFETERIA opened. Black owner Frank Foster stressed friendly service, a product customers liked, and good prices. On the fringes of the city, cafeterias such as Morrison's and Picadilly's became popular.

In 1923 JAMES GRAHAM BROWN opened the Brown Hotel at Fourth and Broadway; later, its English Grill with dark wood paneling decor became famous for its cuisine with a regional menu, diverse influences, outstanding wine list, and excellent service. In 1926 the Mayflower Hotel at 425 W Ormsby Ave. opened as an apartment hotel and restaurant; in later years the restaurant or bistro was called Buck's. HASENOUR'S RESTAURANT & Bar opened in 1952 at the corner of Barret Ave. and Oak St. The restaurant had served the city's area for nearly forty-four years when it closed in 1996.

One of the earliest seafood establishments was MIKE LINNIG'S (1925), a popular restaurant and outdoor beer garden with fish sandwiches and fresh corn grown on his family farm. Other seafood restaurants included the Kingfish restaurants (1948), opened by Russell L. Austin and Harry Burns; the Captain's Quarters (1969), at HARRODS CREEK, which Dottie Mahon opened next to the OHIO RIVER; the New Orleans House (1972), the Fishery (1984), Stan's Fish Sandwich (1987), Rubino's (1988), and Carolina Shrimp and Seafood (1995).

An early bistro-type restaurant and neighborhood bar was Jack Fry's (1933) on Bardstown

Rd. Fry, a colorful host, owned the restaurant for forty-eight years. After his death, the place became an upscale restaurant. Several notable eateries sprang up along Bardstown Rd. in the 1970s, encouraging other culinary development along Frankfort Ave. and other locations. In 1977 Doug Gossman and Tim Martin opened the Bristol Bar and Grille with moderate prices and "bistro comfort food." The Uptown Cafe (1985), KT's (1985), Train Station (1987), Timothy's (1988), Baxter Station (1989), Brasserie Deitrich's (1989), Garrett's (1993), Club Grotto (1993), Bobby J's (1993), Azalea with fusion cuisine (1994), and Zephyr Cove (1996) all followed.

Several barbecue, steak, and otherwise "down home" restaurants opened beginning in the 1930s. Carl and Margaret Kaelin opened KAELIN'S RESTAURANT in 1934, which claims to have originated the cheeseburger and which was one of the first Kentucky Fried Chicken franchises. Other establishments included Masterson's (formerly Hollywood Steak House) (1938), the Dizzy Whizz Drive-In (1947), Check's Café (1948), John E's (formerly Bill Boland's) (1950), the Spencers' Old Walnut Chile Parlor (1960), the Pit Stop Bar-B-Q (1980), W.W. Cousins (1983), Mark's Feed Store (1988), LYNN'S PARADISE CAFE (1991), Dillon's Steakhouse (1992), Vince Staten's Old Time Barbecue (1992), and Jucy's (1996).

The OLD HOUSE RESTAURANT (1946) at 432 S Fifth St. was established in an old house built before the CIVIL WAR; a combination of FRENCH and southern cuisine was served, for which the Old House received many awards and came to be nationally known as the local epitome of sophisticated dining—a must-stop for KENTUCKY DERBY diners. Another elegant restaurant and tearoom was the Orchid Room (1949) in Stewart's department store.

In the 1950s the opening of the expressways resulted in many businesses moving to the SUBURBS. Drive-in restaurants flourished during the fifties, including Hicks' on Dixie Hwy. and Chick's Burger Boy on Taylor Blvd. Restaurant business further increased because of increasing disposable income and because business employees were traveling more by automobile and by air. In 1957 Richard Chin opened Louisville's first CHINESE restaurant, the Lotus Chinese and American Restaurant on Dixie Hwy. In 1962 George and Laura Leong followed with the Hoe Kow, whose name means "something different" in Cantonese. Later came the Oriental House, Jade Palace (1980), the Emperor of China (1985), Sichuan Garden (1989), Sesame Chinese (1989), and New World (1997). Pacific Rim and other Asian restaurants included Sachicoma (1972), Lee's Korean (1980), Cafe Mimosa (1987), Thai-Siam (1990), Vietnam Kitchen (1992), Thai Cafe (1994), Asiatique (1994), Kim's Asia Grill (1995), and Shalimar Indian Restaurant (1995).

In 1959 Albert and Ferd Grisanti opened Casa Grisanti, a northern Italian restaurant at 1000 Fehr Ave. (E LIBERTY St.). It was named to the *Nation's Restaurant News* Fine Dining Hall of Fame and was designated as one of the country's top twenty-five restaurants by *Esquire* magazine; it closed in 1991 because of disagreements between the sons of the founder. Other Italian restaurants included Lentini's (1961) on Bardstown Rd., Ferd Grisanti's (1973) in JEFFERSONTOWN, Rocky's Sub Pub (1977), Porcini's (1992), and Allo Spiedo (1994) on Frankfort Ave.

One of the first Mexican restaurants was the Chili Bowl, opened in 1952 at 616 W Broadway. Beginning in the 1970s, more Mexican and southwestern restaurants opened—Tumbleweed (1975), Chico's (1979), Alameda Bar and Grill (1989), Frontera (1992), Mexico Tipico (1993), Lolita's Tacos (1993), Judge Roy Bean's (1995), and El Mundo (1995).

The 1980s and 1990s have given rise to a citywide variety of ethnic restaurants popping up with many in the Bardstown Rd. and the Frankfort Ave. areas. They included the Rudyard Kipling (1985), Gasthous (1993), Cafe Kilimanjaro (1993), Irish Rover (1993), Grape Leaf (1994), Pita Delights (1994), Pita Pantry (1994), Mo Flav (1994), Ramsi's Café (1995), Cajun Cafe (1995), and Joe's OK Bayou (1995).

Coffee shops and dessert restaurants also became popular around the same time. In 1976 John Conti opened OXMOOR Center Mall's john conti retail store. Sweet Surrender (1987), Twice-Told Coffeehouse (1993), Heine Brothers' Coffee (1994), and Day's Espresso and Coffee Bar (1995) followed.

Also in the 1980s and 1990s, several fine-dining restaurants opened. They included Cafe Metro (1981), 211 Clover Lane (1984), Vincenzo's (1986), Equus (1986), Lilly's (1987), Le Relais (1988), De La Torre's (1988), Inn on Spring (1991) in Jeffersonville, and Shariat's (1993). These restaurants often combined fresh regional ingredients with cross-cultural cuisine, had special appetizers or famous desserts, used decorated plates and edible flowers, or had extensive wine lists. Another unique fine-dining restaurant was Winston's (1996), which opened as part of the culinary arts school at SULLIVAN COLLEGE.

In the 1990s microbrewery pubs came to the Louisville area. Today these include Rich O's (1990) in NEW ALBANY and Bluegrass Brewing Co. (1993) and Hop's (1998) in Louisville.

Throughout the metropolitan area, fast-food and chain restaurants compete with local establishments for the diner's dollar. As always, restaurants continue to come and go, change locations, or undergo frequent name changes. Such is the fluid nature of the business that few restaurants trace their origins back more than fifty years. In general, Louisville has followed the national trend toward an explosion of dining places as busy Americans choose to spend more time and money eating out.

See Marty Godbey, *Dining in Historic Kentucky: A Restaurant Guide with Recipes* (Kuttawa, Ky., 1985); John S. Wright, *Letters from the West; or A Caution to Emigrants* (Salem, N.Y., 1819); E.P. Fordham, *Personal Narratives of Travels . . . in Kentucky* (London, ca. 1825).

Gay Helen Perkins

REVENAUGH, AURELIUS O. (b Zanesville, Ohio, 1840; d Louisville, August 29, 1908). Artist. Aurelius O. Revenaugh was the son of John and Clarinda (Blake) Revenaugh. Upon his graduation from the University of Michigan at Ann Arbor with a degree in MEDICINE, he enlisted in the Signal Corps of the Union army. At the conclusion of the CIVIL WAR, he married Lavina Mason of Elmira, New York, and returned to Ann Arbor, where he pursued an early interest in PAINTING. Except for a brief period of study with John Mix Stanley (1814–72) of Detroit, a painter of portraits and Western scenes, Revenaugh never received instruction.

In 1871 he opened a studio in Jackson, Michigan, where he lived until he moved to Louisville in 1886. His first Louisville studio was in the COURIER-JOURNAL Building. Later he was in the Wilkes block on Fourth St.

Revenaugh gained recognition primarily for his portraits and was commissioned to paint them in Woodford, Fayette, and Madison Counties. One of his best known images, *Newsboy*, is in the collection of Louisville's J.B. SPEED ART MUSEUM. By employing a limited range of color and dim lighting in this painting, Revenaugh exhibited a style akin to the tonalist paintings of HARVEY JOINER and Carl Brenner. In addition to his career as an artist, he was a maker of violins that were considered by many musicians superior to factory-made ones.

Mary Jane Benedict

REYNOLDS, LOUISE ELLIOTT "MATTIE" (b Cornersville, Tennessee, May 4, 1916; d Louisville, March 3, 1995). Politician. Reynolds was brought to Louisville as a child, where she graduated from Louisville Central High School. She attended Louisville Municipal College and the UNIVERSITY OF LOUISVILLE, after it was integrated in 1951. That same year Reynolds went into real estate and was elected president of the Real Estate Brokers Association six years later. Her political career began in 1952 when she became secretary to U.S. Rep. John M. Robsion; she was the first African American woman to be secretary to a Kentucky congressman.

Reynolds became the first black female alderman when she was elected Eleventh Ward alderman in 1961 as a Republican. In 1967, when the party's six-year control of city GOVERNMENT ended with the election of eleven Democratic aldermen, Reynolds was the only Republican survivor. When Mayor William O. Cowger and aldermanic president Kenneth A. Schmied visited out of town for three days in 1965, Reynolds became the first black female to serve as mayor of a southern city. For her accomplishments, she received national publicity and dined at the White House with Pres. Lyndon B. Johnson. Reynolds was later appointed to a national Republican task force on human rights and responsibilities. After leaving elected office, she handled minority affairs for the Small Business Administration's office.

She married James Elwood, and they had one child, Linda. Reynolds died at Brownsboro Hills Nursing Home and is buried at CAVE HILL CEMETERY.

See *Courier-Journal,* March 5, 1995.

REYNOLDS METALS COMPANY. A metal-foil producing plant founded in Louisville in 1919 to manufacture lead and tin foil and currently the second-largest producer of primary aluminum in the United States, Reynolds Metals was founded as the Reynolds Corp. by Richard S., Clarence K., and Abram D. Reynolds, the nephews of tobacco magnate R.J. Reynolds. Richard Reynolds was lured to Louisville by the LOUISVILLE INDUSTRIAL FOUNDATION in 1917 to start a plant producing foils for packaging cigarettes and other TOBACCO products. The plant was at Thirtieth St. and Grand. Business expanded into food packaging in 1924 when the Eskimo Pie Co. became the first company to use a foil wrapper to safeguard its product. In 1926 Reynolds produced its first aluminum foil, the forerunner of the modern Reynolds Wrap.

In 1930 the company's corporate headquarters were moved from Louisville to New York City, and in 1938 they were moved to Richmond, Virginia. In 1959 the company tried on two occasions to build an office–research center and fabricating plant near CENTRAL STATE HOSPITAL and at the east corner of Newburg Rd. and Watterson Expwy. in Louisville. When both sites were opposed because of a desire to keep the areas residential, Reynolds moved its general sales office from Louisville to Richmond, Virginia, and built the office–research center there.

By the beginning of WORLD WAR II, Reynolds Metals was producing 100,000 tons of aluminum a year, much of which went to the national war effort. In 1997 Reynolds sold the aluminum paste and powder plant in Louisville to the German company Eckart Aluminum as part of a financial restructuring. Reynolds continues to own and operate three other Louisville facilities that are located on Hale Ave. and produce plain foil products, laminated products, and consumer products; they have an annual production capacity of about 130 million pounds.

See *Courier-Journal,* Sept. 18, 1957.

RICE, ALICE CALDWELL (HEGAN) (b Shelbyville, Kentucky, January 11, 1870; d Louisville, February 10, 1942). Author. Alice Caldwell Hegan Rice was the daughter of Samuel Watson and Sallie P. (Caldwell) Hegan.

Alice Hegan Rice.

She attended a private school in Shelbyville and Miss Hampton's School for Girls in Louisville, where she began writing. During that time she wrote a parody of *Reveries of a Bachelor* by Ik Marvel, which the COURIER-JOURNAL published. She and several other women in Louisville organized the AUTHORS CLUB of Louisville, where, on Saturday mornings, they discussed writing and read their works aloud.

At a time when reformers and settlement house workers were calling attention to the living conditions of the urban poor, Hegan began volunteer social work in the area south of Oak St. and west of Sixth St. known as the CABBAGE PATCH. There she taught a boys' Sunday school class at a city mission of the FIRST CHRISTIAN CHURCH. Inspired by Mary Bass, a resident of the desperately poor area, Hegan transformed her into the fictional Mrs. Wiggs, a widow with five children who lived in dire poverty and had many misfortunes but who faced life with steadfastness, cheerfulness, and hope. Mrs. Wiggs took in washing, and her children—Jimmy, Billy, Asia, Australia, and Europena—sold kindling to try to prevent the loan shark from foreclosing on the family home.

In 1901 Hegan introduced her novel, *Mrs. Wiggs of the Cabbage Patch,* to the authors' club. That year she submitted her manuscript to a publisher, and within six months of publication, ten thousand copies a month were being printed—later forty thousand copies per month. The novel was a best-seller for two years, with sales in excess of 650,000 copies in one hundred printings. It was translated into French, Spanish, Norwegian, Danish, German, and Japanese and also written in Braille. *Mrs. Wiggs* was such an international success that Louisvillian Anne Crawford Flexner helped adapt the novel for a stage play presented at MACAULEY'S THEATRE in 1903. The *Courier-Journal* proclaimed the play "a distinct success," and it ran for seven years in the United States and two years in England. *Mrs. Wiggs* also spawned four movies. The first two (1919 and 1926) were silents. The 1934 film, featuring W.C. Fields and Zasu Pitts, had its world premiere at the Rialto Theatre on Fourth St. in Louisville. It was proclaimed "the literary event of the season." A fourth film adaptation premiered in December 1942 at the Strand Theater in Louisville, with Louisville actress Fay Bainter portraying Mrs. Wiggs.

On December 18, 1902, Hegan married Cale Young Rice, a poet, playwright, and philosopher from Louisville. Samuel McClure, publisher of *McClure's Magazine,* bought Cale Rice's first book soon after the wedding and invited the Rices to accompany him on a vacation trip to Europe. Alice Rice's novel *Sandy* (1905) was a fictional portrayal of McClure and his career. On the trip, she met and formed a friendship with social reformer and muckraker Ida Tarbell, with whom she shared a zeal for reform.

Alice Rice wrote twenty books, including several sequels to *Mrs. Wiggs,* most notably *Lovey Mary* (1903). Her personal favorite was *Mr. Opp* (1909), in which the title character appeared to be a failure to all outsiders yet saw himself as a success in the world, one who refused to recognize defeat. Mrs. Wiggs's observation at the end of the novel expressed this kind of optimism: "Looks like everything in the world comes right, if we jes' wait long enough!" Rice wrote in her autobiography, *The Inky Way* (1940) that she did not want to record life's tragedy. Rather she wanted her autobiography "to follow, through a long life, the course of an inky way that happened to follow a flowery path." Her posthumously published work, *Happiness Road* (1942), was described by the *New York Herald Tribune* in 1942 as "an exercise in the discipline of happiness."

The Rices built a house in 1910 at 1444 St. James Ct., where for thirty years she played the role of gracious hostess. Throughout her life, Rice was involved in philanthropic work. In 1910 Louise Marshall founded the Cabbage Patch Settlement, first located on Hill St., a settlement house to reach out to the poor families in the urban neighborhood. Rice was a member of its first board. During WORLD WAR I she served as a hospital volunteer at Camp ZACHARY TAYLOR. She used that experience as a source for her 1921 novel, *Quin.* Rice supported PROHIBITION and served on the Kentucky State Committee of Law Enforcement. During the 1920s, Rice collaborated with her husband on two books of short stories. In the 1930s the Rices suffered illness and financial reversals, and her works from that time were written under the burden of financial necessity: *Mr. Pete & Co.* (1933); a picaresque tale of the Louisville waterfront, *Passionate Follies* (1936), written with her husband; and *My Pillow Book* (1937), a volume of devotions and comments on life.

In 1937 she received an honorary doctor of LITERATURE degree from the UNIVERSITY OF LOUISVILLE. Rice is buried in CAVE HILL CEMETERY.

See Mary Boewe, "Back to the Cabbage Patch: The Character of Mrs. Wiggs," *Filson Club History Quarterly* 59 (April 1985): 179–204; William S. Ward, *A Literary History of Kentucky* (Knoxville Tenn., 1988).

Gail Ritchie Henson
James Duane Bolin

RICE, CALE YOUNG (b Dixon, Kentucky, December 7, 1872; d Louisville, January 23 or 24, 1943). Poet, dramatic lyricist, and novelist. Cale Young Rice was the son of Laban M. and Martha (Lacy) Rice. The family moved to Evansville, Indiana, in 1879, where Rice attended public and private schools. From 1889 to 1893 Rice attended Cumberland University in Lebanon, Tennessee; then, following a year of employment as a store clerk, he entered Harvard University. At Harvard, Rice completed requirements for a bachelor of arts degree (1895) and a master's degree (1896).

Rice returned to Cumberland University to teach, but after a year there he gave up teaching to write. His production of POETRY and prose spanned more than four decades. His first book of poems, *From Dusk to Dusk* (1898), was followed by other collections of verse and drama. His *Collected Plays and Poems* was published in 1926. Rice also wrote two novels and an autobiography, *Bridging the Years* (1939), and collaborated with his wife, Alice (Hegan) Rice, on three collections of short stories. Rice's work was more favorably received abroad, especially in England, than in the United States.

Rice settled in Louisville in 1897 and married Alice Caldwell Hegan, the Louisville author of *Mrs. Wiggs of the Cabbage Patch,* on December 18, 1902. Although the couple traveled extensively in Europe and the Far East, Rice desired recognition as a southern poet. He identified closely with his Louisville home, taking an active role in the Louisville arts, literary, and club scenes. He was founder and first president of the Louisville Arts Club, served on the Board of Governors of the J.B. SPEED ART MUSEUM, and belonged to the Big Spring Golf Club. The Rices' home at 1444 St. James Ct. was a gathering place for Louisville's literary and social elite. In 1937 the UNIVERSITY OF LOUISVILLE conferred on both Rices the honorary doctor of LITERATURE degree.

After Alice's death in 1942, Rice sold their St. James Ct. home and moved into the nearby Mayflower Apartments. Despondent over his wife's death, Rice died of a self-inflicted gunshot wound. He is buried in CAVE HILL CEMETERY.

See Cale Young Rice, *Bridging the Years* (New York 1939); Rice Collection, Kentucky Library, Western Kentucky University, Bowling Green, Ky.; Jenny Rose Bere, "Cale Young Rice: A Study of His Life and Works" M.A. thesis, University of Louisville, 1939; William S. Ward, *A Literary History of Kentucky* (Knoxville, Tenn. 1988).

James Duane Bolin

RICE, THOMAS D. (b New York City, May 20, 1808; d New York City, September 19, 1860). Actor. Rice came to Louisville in March 1830 to join SAMUEL DRAKE's stock company at the City Theatre. Supposedly, Rice observed a lame black stable hand named JIM CROW dancing and singing the refrain, "Wheel about, and turn about, and do just so; Every time I wheel about, I jump Jim Crow." Rice was an experienced blackface performer but a mediocre actor, and he decided to copy Jim Crow's dance and song to bolster his routine. Rice first "jumped Jim Crow" on May 21, 1830, at the City Theatre during the melodrama *The Kentucky Rifle.* He was an overnight sensation and soon achieved worldwide fame for his routine. Rice is generally regarded as the father of MINSTRELSY. After the CIVIL WAR the term "Jim Crow" came to refer to segregation.

See Robert C. Toll, *Blacking Up: The Minstrel Show in Nineteenth-Century America* (New York 1974); George Yater, *Two Hundred Years at the Falls of the Ohio* (Louisville 1987).

Cornelius Bogert

RICHIE, CHARLES GRIFFITH (b Louisville, January 18, 1868; d ?). Jefferson County judge. Charles Griffith Richie was the son of Henry Clay Richie of NEW ALBANY, Indiana, and Sophie Spurrier of Sumner County, Tennessee. His father was a well-known Louisville merchant and author who wrote several historical texts, including an economic treatise against the issue of the free coinage of silver during the Bryan-McKinley presidential campaign of 1896. The younger Richie grew up in Louisville and was educated at city schools, graduating from Male High School in 1887. He received his law degree from the UNIVERSITY OF LOUISVILLE law department in 1889 and began working as an associate in the law offices of WALTER EVANS; he stayed in that position for three years. In 1892 he started the firm of Speckert & Richie with his partner, A.J. Speckert, and remained with the firm until he became county judge.

Richie, a Republican, was county judge from January 1, 1895, until December 31, 1897. He was the youngest person ever elected to the office, taking the oath just before his twenty-seventh birthday. He was also the first Republican to fill any judicial position in Jefferson County. He defeated Democratic incumbent WILLIAM HOKE in the November 6, 1894, election by 1,857 votes (18,506–16,649). The Republicans swept most of the city and county elections that year.

Richie ran for reelection in 1897 but was defeated by Democrat James P. Gregory by fewer than 450 votes out of 44,000 cast in the election. He then returned to private practice in Louisville.

On August 29, 1895, Richie married Margaret Pierce of Sumner County, Tennessee. She was the daughter of Lafayette and Nannie (Lyles) Pierce. The couple lived on Brook St., and Ritchie had an office in the Kenyon Building. There is no record of Richie in Louisville after 1904. Several members of his family, including his mother and father, are buried in a family plot at CAVE HILL CEMETERY. His mother died in Louisville in 1912 and his father in 1914.

See J. Stoddard Johnston, ed., *Memorial History of Louisville* (Chicago 1896); John M. Gresham, *Biographical Cyclopedia of the Commonwealth of Kentucky* (Chicago 1896); H. Levin, *The Lawyers and Lawmakers of Kentucky* (Chicago 1897).

RIDGEWAY. Located at 4095 Massie Ave. in ST. MATTHEWS, Ridgeway is considered one of the finest examples of Federal ARCHITECTURE in the state. It is also variously described as Jeffersonian or Early Classical Revival. The house was built during 1816, 1817, and 1818 for Col. Henry Massie, an early Kentucky surveyor, who married Helen Scott Bullitt, daughter of ALEXANDER SCOTT BULLITT, Kentucky's first lieutenant governor.

Ridgeway features the typical Jeffersonian hipped roof, along with two recessed connectors with hipped roofs, false doors, and lunettes. It is strikingly similar to the William Morton House, built in Lexington in 1810, and Homewood, built in 1803 in Baltimore, Maryland. The four-column Roman portico, also typically Jeffersonian, resembles that of nearby OXMOOR—built in 1829 by WILLIAM CHRISTIAN BULLITT, Massie's brother-in-law—as well as that of Farmington. The main entrance, with its fanlight lunette and sidelights, is in the Federal style.

The interior features arched doorways and interior windows that also serve as doors. A transverse passage permits movement to each room without going through another. The rooms, except for the library, have sets of double doors to limit noise. Rarities include closets and large, 20 x 13 inch windowpanes. The woodwork is poplar, and the doors are pine. Along the eastern walls, the fireplaces are flush, whereas those on the west generally protrude into rooms. The doors in the rear rooms of the house's main portion open onto a long porch. A covered passage connects the kitchen building to the rest of the house.

The original 434 acres were divided among family members at Massie's wife's death in 1871. The parcel that included the house was purchased by the Kaelin family and operated as a dairy farm until it was sold to Aubrey and Maud Woodson Cossar, who renovated the house and installed modern conveniences. The house and land were purchased by Judge Churchill Humphrey and his wife Martha in 1931 and by Ben and Carole Birkhead in the 1970s. The Birkheads restored the house in the 1980s.

See Clay Lancaster, *Ante-bellum Architecture of Kentucky* (Lexington 1991); Virginia and Lee McAlester, *A Field Guide to American Houses* (New York 1984); Elizabeth F. Jones and Mary Jean Kinsman, *Jefferson County: Survey of Historic Sites in Kentucky* (Louisville 1981); John J.-G. Blumenson, *Identifying American Architecture: A Pictorial Guide to Styles and Terms, 1600–1945* (New York 1995); John C. Poppeliers, S. Allen Chambers Jr., and Nancy B. Schwartz, *What Style Is It? A Guide to American Architecture* (Washington, D.C. 1983).

Thomas E. Stephens

RIDING CLUBS AND SHOW HORSES. Because of CHURCHILL DOWNS, Louisville is known worldwide as a center of Thoroughbred HORSE RACING. To American Saddlebred horse fanciers, Louisville is known internationally as the site of the ROCK CREEK Riding Club.

The Thoroughbred horse, a high-strung, hot-blooded cross between Arabian stallions and Irish and Scottish mares, originated in England. Colonial plantation owners in Virginia, Maryland, and the Carolinas mated Thoroughbreds with mares of lesser pedigree to produce calm, tractable horses suitable for riding and driving. Early settlers brought these horses to Kentucky. Thus, by 1850 a breed originally known as the Kentucky Saddler emerged from Bluegrass stock farms. Developed from Thoroughbred, Narragansett Pacer, and Morgan bloodlines, the Saddler was a multipurpose family horse, sturdy and surefooted enough to carry a man all day across fields, gentle enough for a woman's sidesaddle perch, yet sufficiently flashy to do a family proud when hitched to a buggy. The American Saddlebred Association, the first such organization for an American breed, was established in Louisville in 1891 under the presidency of Gen. John B. Castleman.

The Saddlebred was prominent Louisville urbanites' pleasure horse of choice. According to an article in the *Evening Post* of March 25, 1895, about the Louisville Riding Club at Fifth and Hill Streets, the facility had an indoor arena where Louisville's fashionable families rode in evening programs that included band music and refreshments. All breeds of horses were represented, but "a mare that ranks as the best saddle mare even in Kentucky" was the cynosure of all attendees. Morris B. Belknap was the board member in charge.

In 1927 a group headed by the Seelbach, Cronan, Belknap, Horner, Ballard, and Weir families rented, then purchased from William S. Speed, 37 acres off Cannons Ln. Mrs. Henning Chambers, the club's first president, named the site Rock Creek, after Washington, D.C.'s Rock Creek Park. It included a Victorian frame house and barn surrounded by potato fields.

Rock Creek held its first horse show, for members only, in 1933. Four years later the show, offering prize money, trophies, and ribbons to competitors, was opened to nonmember exhibitors. Club manager Bayse Howell's daughter, equitation instructor Jane (Howell) Fleming, first organized a program for junior riders there in 1935.

In 1954 the club's board brought professional trainers Charles and Helen Crabtree to Rock Creek. During their four-year tenure, the Crabtrees changed Rock Creek from a social club to a national competition site that first showcased the abilities of outstanding young Louisville riders April Denham and Mary Ann O'Callaghan. The latter, at age fifteen, was named Girl Athlete of the Year by the *COURIER-JOURNAL* and *LOUISVILLE TIMES* sportswriters in 1960.

Trainers Jim B. Robertson (1959–65) and Edward Teater (1966–72) brought Rock Creek to national prominence. During the seven-teen-year presidency of Harold Morgeson, Rock Creek, under trainers Frank and Nancy McConnell (1975–79) and Rob and Sarah Byers (1980–88), was home to more national champion Saddlebreds and riders than any other stable in America. According to Morgeson, "The Rock Creek Horse Show, the Lexington JUNIOR LEAGUE Horse Show and the KENTUCKY STATE FAIR Horse Show have been, to the American Saddlebred, what the Triple Crown is to the Thoroughbred."

On February 16, 1996, eighteen Saddlebreds perished in a fire that left only the Rock Creek pleasure barn standing, but the facility was rebuilt in time to hold the fifty-ninth annual Rock Creek Horse Show there in June 1996.

See the American Saddle Horse Museum, Kentucky Horse Park, Lexington, Ky.

Lynn S. Renau

RIEHM, CHARLES E. "CAL" (b Louisville, January 20, 1912; d Louisville, October 6, 1991). Monument designer-builder and cemetery director. Charles E. Riehm was the son of John L. and Mary Catherine (Phelan) Riehm. He graduated from ST. XAVIER HIGH SCHOOL, attended the UNIVERSITY OF LOUISVILLE, and was married in 1938 to Katherine Grigsby of Bardstown. He began his work with Muldoon Monument Co. in 1932.

His firm, Riehm-Gerlack Memorials, was founded in 1951. It produced notable mausoleums, including those of J. Graham Brown, Ben and Bess Collins, and CHARLES GHEENS in Louisville's CAVE HILL CEMETERY and of Robert Lehman, owner of Derby winner Dust Commander, in Lexington's Calvary Cemetery.

Riehm won a national contest to design the monument for DAVID WARK GRIFFITH, an early innovator in the film industry, in 1950; he also designed the WORLD WAR II Memorial outside the JEFFERSON COUNTY COURTHOUSE. Asked to design the mausoleum for Elvis Presley in Tennessee, he declined because he had "never liked" the famous rock singer. He designed bases for many Louisville SCULPTURES, including *The Bride*, *Louis XVI*, *Daniel Boone*, and *The Thinker* at the UNIVERSITY OF LOUISVILLE.

As director and general manager of Catholic Cemeteries for the Archdiocese of Louisville from the early 1970s to 1991, he renovated Louisville's five Catholic CEMETERIES. His layout and design for Catholic cemeteries in the South and the Midwest influenced other cemetery design nationwide. Riehm is buried in Calvary Cemetery.

Louisa Riehm
Joan Riehm

RILEY, THOMAS W. (b 1804?; d Bullitt County, Kentucky, December 27, 1872). Mayor. Riley, a prominent Louisville lawyer, was a representative in the Kentucky General Assembly from Bullitt County in 1835 and 1836 and from Nelson County in 1849 and 1850. He served as Speaker of the House from December 31, 1849, through November 4, 1850. A Whig, he was an elector in the 1841 presidential election, voting for William Henry Harrison.

About 1849 he formed a law partnership with Peter B. Muir in Bardstown. In January 1852 the firm moved to Louisville. In 1857, when Muir was elected judge of the circuit court for the unexpired term of Judge William F. Bullock, the partnership of Riley and Muir was dissolved. Muir was also on the Louisville City Council and was the first judge of the Jefferson Court of Common Pleas.

Riley was elected to the City Council in 1855 and again in 1857. He was president of the Board of Councilmen in 1855. On May 13, 1858, he was selected by the general council to fill the unexpired term of Mayor William S. Pilcher. After several ballots, Riley was finally chosen mayor pro tem over alderman THOMAS CRAWFORD by a vote of 12 to 9 (two other council votes went to a third candidate). Pilcher died on August 14, 1858, and Riley served until April 2, 1859.

In the mid-1860s, Riley worked in the law firm of Riley & Russell with Samuel Russell. He was in the firm of Thomas W. & W.H. Riley (his only child, William) from 1865 to 1870. His law office was located on W Jefferson St. Riley was married to Kate F. Riley.

See *Biographical Cyclopedia of the Commonwealth of Kentucky* (Chicago 1896); Lewis and Richard H. Collins, *History of Kentucky* (Covington, Ky. 1874; reprint 1966).

RITTER, JOSEPH ELMER (b New Albany, Indiana, July 20, 1892; d St. Louis, Missouri, June 10, 1967). Religious leader. The son of Nicholas and Bertha (Luette) Ritter, Joseph Elmer Ritter began his education at St. Mary's Catholic School, from which he graduated in 1906. In 1907 he entered St. Meinrad Seminary in southern Indiana and on May 30, 1917, was ordained a priest. Ritter was then assigned to Indianapolis, where at first he served as the assistant at St. Patrick's Church and eventually became rector of the Cathedral of Saints Peter and Paul.

His swift rise through the ranks of the Roman Catholic church in Indianapolis resulted in his consecration as bishop on March 28, 1933, at the age of forty-one. In 1944 Ritter became the first archbishop of the city when the Indianapolis see was elevated to an archdiocese. Two years later, he was chosen to succeed John Cardinal Glennon as the archbishop of St. Louis, and on December 10, 1960, he was made a cardinal by Pope John XXIII.

Throughout his career, Cardinal Ritter was well known as a liberal leader within the church, championing such causes as CIVIL RIGHTS and religious freedom. It was under his direction, in both Indianapolis and St. Louis, that parochial schools were desegregated. A strong proponent for progressive change within the church, Ritter made certain that the St. Louis archdiocese was "in the forefront of the movement toward Christian unity and liturgical reform." In fact, the first Mass celebrated in the vernacular in the United States came under his direction in St. Louis in 1965. Ritter took his progressive views to the Second Vatican Council in 1962–65, where he was a prominent figure. Ritter is buried in Calvary Cemetery in St. Louis.

RIVER CITY MALL. The River City Mall, or Fourth St. Mall, was originally part of a large-scale downtown redevelopment project that encompassed almost all of the central business district. In 1960 the first experimental pedestrian mall, known as Guthrie Green, was created on a small stretch of Guthrie St., a cross street running between Fourth and Second Streets. The mall was an early attempt by the LOUISVILLE CENTRAL AREA (LCA), a spin-off of the Louisville Chamber of Commerce's Downtown Committee, to revitalize the downtown area with a pedestrian mall.

The first plan to address DOWNTOWN DEVELOPMENT, the Design for Downtown, was formulated by the LCA in 1962. It proposed FOUNDERS SQUARE and the FOURTH STREET Mall, in addition to Guthrie Green and a Ninth Street Thoroughfare. Downtown development of the center area took off when the Louisville and Jefferson County Planning Commission formalized a comprehensive program in 1968 and adopted it in 1969.

The River City Mall, which got its name from a name-the-mall contest sponsored by the LCA and a local radio station, opened in August 1973. It stretched along Fourth St. from LIBERTY St. to BROADWAY. Traffic was closed on March 3, 1972, and the street was repaved and tree boxes, fountains, and benches were installed. The mall was extended north to Market St. with the opening of the Commonwealth Convention Center in 1977(now KENTUCKY INTERNATIONAL CONVENTION CENTER) and the Hyatt Regency Louisville Hotel (1978).

Although the mall was not successful at revitalizing the downtown retail district, it helped to keep the central business district viable. Projects such as the GALLERIA, the Convention Center, and Theatre Square were made possible in part because of the mall's presence. In 1996 the mall was abandoned when Fourth St. was reopened to traffic from Muhammad Ali Blvd. to Broadway.

See George H. Yater, "It's Louisville to the Core," *Louisville* 24 (Aug. 1973): 39–46; "Fourth Street: A Whole New Mallgame," *Louisville* 23 (Nov. 1972): 30–33.

RIVER FIELDS, INC. Founded in January 1959 by Archibald P. Cochran, a prominent Louisville businessman and civic leader, River Fields is the ninth-oldest river conservation organization in the United States and the largest such group on the OHIO RIVER. Its mission is to protect and preserve the natural, recreational, historical, and cultural resources of the Ohio River around Louisville on both sides of the river.

Early projects undertaken by River Fields included transforming Caperton Swamp (located on Upper River Rd.) from a poorly zoned commercial strip to a wetlands preserve open to the public. River Fields unsuccessfully fought construction of the CLARK MARITIME CENTRE in JEFFERSONVILLE, INDIANA, believing that the riverport facility would be an inappropriate introduction of industry into the river corridor. The organization was pivotal in proving that a coal-pulverizing plant slated for a Zorn Ave.–River Rd. site would have brought heavy industry to the area.

The realization that the ripple effect would have affected the core of the downtown waterfront helped stimulate the move to revitalize the area. River Fields mounted the campaign that persuaded local leaders and politicians to recommit to a people-friendly public access riverfront instead of an expanded industrialization. Its campaign resulted in a study and subsequently the Waterfront Development Plan, which has altered the course of the downtown riverfront for generations to come.

In recent years River Fields has increased its role in advocacy and education on environmental issues, public policy, and appropriate urban development. It initiated and helped to fund the Ohio River Corridor Master Plan adopted as part of Cornerstone 2020, a plan to "reconnect" people to the river and the varied resources of its corridor. River Fields has questioned the construction of an East End bridge across the Ohio River and has supported the building of a new downtown bridge to ease traffic congestion.

River Fields also operates as a land trust. Conservation strategies such as the purchase and donation of land and conservation easements have enabled the organization to preserve riverine land and promote public access to the river. Since 1982 River Fields has acquired nine key parcels of river corridor land totaling 80 acres (some of which include wetlands) at a cost of $1.5 million. The leadership and vision of Laura Lee Brown facilitated the preservation of 46 acres of fertile river bottomland now named GARVIN BROWN PRESERVE and open to the public.

In 1999 Sallie Bingham donated a conservation easement on 412 acres of farmland in eastern Jefferson County to be held jointly by River Fields and the Kentucky Heritage Council. The easement includes the historic WOLF PEN BRANCH MILL.

River Fields is governed by a twenty-six-member board of trustees that represents diverse backgrounds. Its presidents have included Armin S. Willig, MARY CAPERTON BINGHAM, James W. Stites, Christina Lee Brown, James S. Welch Jr., Kenneth W. Moore, and Hunter G. Louis. Lee Cochran became the first executive director in the early 1980s; Meme Sweets Runyon succeeded her in 1986. In the early 1990s River Fields moved into office space at Seventh and MAIN Streets with a full-time professional staff.

From 1994 to 1997, River Fields was given awards by Kentucky's Environmental Quality Commission, the Ohio River Basin Consortium for Research and Education, the Kentucky Waterways Alliance, and the LOUISVILLE HISTORICAL LEAGUE.

Meme Sweets Runyon

RIVERFRONT PLAZA/BELVEDERE. The seed of the idea for extensive riverside development in downtown Louisville was first evidenced in the 1930 plan by the St. Louis city-planning consultation firm of Harland Bartholomew & Associates, who suggested a large, open plaza adjacent to the water between Third and Seventh Streets. Nothing came of this scheme until 1957, when Mayor ANDREW BROADDUS invited New York City developer William Zeckendorf to undertake the project of improving the urban landscape with private business complexes, APARTMENT BUILDINGS, and a large park.

Although Zeckendorf's firm showed interest, the plans went unrealized. In 1960 the REYNOLDS METALS CO. announced its intention to engage Greek architect Constantinos A. Doxiadis, through his office in Washington, D.C., to develop several possibilities for the riverfront project and a year later unveiled a $24 million plan that included four skyscrapers, an auditorium, RESTAURANTS, shops, and a pleasure boat marina. By 1963 the project was quickly moving along as the General Electric Co. joined Reynolds as a coventurer and the federal government agreed to provide URBAN RENEWAL funds for the costs of clearing and preparing the site.

However, early in 1964 officials from LOUISVILLE CENTRAL AREA slowed the activity by announcing its desire to split the proposed Interstate 64 between Third and Fifth Streets, known as Riverside Expwy. at this site, and establish a

The Farnsley-Moremen home in the 1880s.

park. The plan again stalled the following year when city officials relayed their concerns over the cost of the proposed marina and the Corps of Engineers disapproved of the plan because of the danger caused by commercial river traffic entering the canal. The marina concept was abandoned by 1966 when local architects Lawrence P. Melillo and Jasper Ward, with consultation from Doxiadis, released a revised plan.

After losing the support of the Reynolds Metals Co. in 1967, the project regained momentum under the leadership of the Waterfront Commission and the Urban Renewal Agency in 1969. The BOARD OF ALDERMEN approved a $10 million bond issue to aid in the construction of a parking garage. Investors and developers began to show interest in the plaza later in the year when the final plans for the $13.5 million project were released. In December ground was finally broken on the parking garage, and the project was under way. On April 27, 1973, a rejuvenated 7-acre area from Third St. to Sixth St. was dedicated as the Riverfront Plaza/Belvedere, with the Belvedere, a grassy, park-like section, elevated above the then-unfinished Interstate 64 to the west. Riverfront Plaza, an area containing fountains, shelters, an ice-skating rink, and privately funded enterprises such as the GALT HOUSE hotel, the American Life Building, and the One Riverfront Plaza Building, was situated on the eastern half. Three months later, a bronze statue of Gen. GEORGE ROGERS CLARK, by Felix de Weldon (1907–), was stationed on the Belvedere after being donated to the city by the estate of Arthur E. Hopkins. In 1983 the Kentucky Center for the Arts was incorporated into the southern portion of the Belvedere fronting on MAIN St.

The city undertook a $3.8 million renovation of the area in 1996 after numerous garage patrons filed lawsuits asserting that corrosive materials had leaked through the Belvedere's roof onto their cars. In April 1998, the updated eastern half of the park reopened with a waterproof barrier, new shelters, enhanced landscaping with less concrete, improved fountains and seating, a widened path from Fifth St. to the river, and a concert stage. The remodeling of the western half was expected to be completed by 1999 with improved landscaping and new rest rooms.

Over the years the Belvedere and Riverfront Plaza have been the site of summer international festivals bringing together the talents of various ethnic groups living in Louisville. Such multicultural entertainment was first organized in 1974 by the Heritage Corp. of Louisville and Jefferson County. Arab, Greek, Hungarian, Italian, IRISH, Japanese, Latin American, Ukrainian, and other ethnic communities showcase their native music and dance, offer samples of exotic food and beverages, teach special games, and exhibit and sell their arts and crafts. In the late 1980s, some of the ethnic festivals began to take place in different parts of the city. The ethnic festivals, coordinated by the mayor's office, became an important part of the local community to promote greater understanding between all cultures.

See Samuel W. Thomas, *Louisville since the Twenties* (Louisville 1978); *Courier-Journal,* April 27, 1973; April 6, 1998.

RIVERSIDE, THE FARNSLEY-MOREMEN LANDING. Located at 10908 Lower River Rd. at Moorman Rd. in southwestern Jefferson County, the Farnsley-Moremen house was opened to the public as a historic house and farm in October 1993. One of the last remaining nineteenth-century houses in that area, it is a brick Kentucky "I"-house and is the centerpiece of a more-than-300-acre Jefferson County landmark now called Riverside, the Farnsley-Moremen Landing. An "I" house is simply the once-common center-hall house that has a hallway extending from the front door straight through to the rear door, with rooms on either side of the hallway. The rear ell may have been part of the original construction of the house. Built about 1837 by Gabriel Farnsley (1800–1849), the house is located near the 623-mile marker on the OHIO RIVER, 13 miles south of downtown Louisville. Farnsley raised livestock and cultivated a variety of crops including corn, wheat, hay, and rye. He traded goods with passing riverboats at his boat landing, where he also operated a ferry transporting people and goods between Harrison County, Indiana, and Kentucky.

In 1862 the house was purchased by Alanson (1803–90) and Rachel (Stith) Moremen (1811–1900) (sometimes spelled Moreman or Moorman), who eventually increased the farm holdings to more than 1,500 acres. They continued to operate the boat landing. According to Moremen family tradition, the landing became known as Soap Landing because the Moremens sold lye soap and other household products to boats that stopped at the landing. By 1879 the Moremens had named their farm Riverside. The house remained in Moremen family ownership for 126 years.

In 1979 the Farnsley-Moremen house was placed on the NATIONAL REGISTER OF HISTORIC PLACES. In 1988 it was purchased by the JEFFERSON COUNTY FISCAL COURT to be restored and preserved as a testament to the agricultural history and river heritage of the county. Accurate restoration of the house was done, and replicas of outbuildings were completed. A visitors' center housing offices, a gift shop, and a large meeting room was completed in 1993. A dock was constructed for the county-owned *SPIRIT OF JEFFERSON* riverboat, which boards passengers at Riverside for Ohio River cruises. In 1998 an open-air pavilion was built to shelter passengers waiting to board the riverboat and to provide space for outdoor events.

See Patti Linn and Donna M. Neary, *Riverside: The Restoration of a Way of Life, Exploring the History of a Nineteenth Century Farm on the Ohio River* (Louisville 1998).

Patti Linn

RIVERSIDE GARDENS. The Riverside Gardens subdivision, located on the OHIO RIVER between Lees Ln. and Cane Run Rd. was established in 1926. The developers of the subdivision in western Jefferson County had in mind a unique resort community; they built a clubhouse with a view of the river and a bathing pavilion and promised more facilities in the

Entrance to Riverside Gardens, on the Ohio River between Lees Lane and Cane Run Road, 1926.

future, including boating, fishing, and a beach. Early lots sold for $99. In the 1920s one could pay $15 down and $2 a week. The developers offered free bus trips to the tract office located on the site. Following the Great Depression and the flood of 1937, interest in the Riverside Gardens community waned.

The resort feel, which the developers had tried so hard to establish, was all but forgotten by the 1940s as the beautiful original clubhouse became (briefly) a church and then a nightclub. The dilapidation of the area increased: junkyards opened and a landfill operator buried refuse by the river. It was not until the 1970s that residents of Riverside Gardens, with help from county officials, began to reclaim their community. They closed the unseemly businesses and rebuilt their neighborhood. Their efforts were stalled in 1978 when methane gas was discovered leaking from one of the landfills. The ensuing court battle with twenty-three companies ended in 1990 when the companies agreed to pay $2.4 million for the cleanup.

ROBERTSON, ARCHIBALD THOMAS (b near Chatham, Virginia, November 6, 1863; d Louisville, September 23, 1934). Minister and educator. Robertson graduated from Wake Forest College in 1885 and entered the SOUTHERN BAPTIST THEOLOGICAL SEMINARY in Louisville. Following graduation in 1888, he began a long, distinguished career as professor of Greek at the seminary that continued until his death. In 1894 he married Ella Broadus, daughter of John A. Broadus. Their son, Cary, became Sunday editor of the *COURIER-JOURNAL.* In 1897 at Louisville Archibald Robertson helped establish the influential newspaper the *Baptist Argus,* and he was an early advocate of the founding of the Baptist World Alliance. Robertson became an internationally renowned expert in the study of the Greek New Testament, a reputation still intact. Author of forty-five books, his most enduring, and still highly regarded, publication was the exhaustive *Grammar of the Greek New Testament in the Light of Historical Research* (1914).

See Everett Gill, *A.T. Robertson: A Biography* (New York 1943).

Ronald F. Deering

ROBINSON, STUART (b Strabane, County Tyrone, Ireland, November 14, 1814; d Louisville, October 5, 1881). Presbyterian minister. Stuart Robinson was the fifth of seven children born to James and Martha (Porter) Robinson. His family immigrated to the United States and settled near Martinsburg, Berkeley County, Virginia. Stuart's mother died when he was age six or seven, and although he had a partially disabled right hand and arm from a fall in infancy, he was placed with a German farmer almost immediately after her death. The farmer, recognizing the boy's intelligence and the handicap that would preclude his doing farm work, arranged with Rev. James M. Brown, a Presbyterian minister, to take the boy, at age thirteen, into his home and supervise his education.

Robinson taught school to pay his way at Amherst College and graduated with high honors in 1836. He continued to teach during his years at Union Theological College in Virginia and attended Princeton Theological Seminary from 1840 to 1841. In 1841 he entered the Presbyterian ministry and became pastor of a small church in Malden, a salt-manufacturing center near Charlestown, Virginia (now West Virginia). In September of that year, he married Mary Elizabeth Brigham, daughter of Col. and Mrs. William Brigham. He is said to have managed his mother-in-law's business affairs astutely.

In 1846 he filled the pulpit of the Second PRESBYTERIAN CHURCH in Louisville during the nine-month absence of its pastor, Rev. Dr. Edward P. Humphrey. From 1847 to 1854 he was pastor of the Presbyterian Church at Frankfort, Kentucky, and during that time served as president of the female seminary there, of a cotton factory, and of a turnpike road company. He also became a director of the Farmers' Bank of Kentucky. In May 1854 he became pastor of the Duncan Presbyterian Church in Baltimore, Maryland, out of which he built the CENTRAL PRESBYTERIAN CHURCH. In 1855 and 1856 he also edited the *Presbyterian and Critic.*

In 1856 Robinson was elected by the General Assembly of the Presbyterian Church in the USA to the chair of church government and pastoral theology at the Theological Seminary at Danville, Kentucky. In 1858 he returned to Louisville and became the pastor of the SECOND PRESBYTERIAN CHURCH. In 1861 he began to publish a religious weekly, the *True Presbyterian,* in Louisville. The paper was twice suppressed by Union military officials because of its pro-Southern stand.

In 1862 Robinson was arrested for his Confederate sentiments. He was released almost immediately, but a short time later, while in Cincinnati, he received word that another order for his arrest had been issued. He took a train to Canada, where he continued to preach until 1866. A letter he wrote to Pres. ABRAHAM LINCOLN from Canada in 1865 tells of the conduct of Union military men and officers in Louisville: their vandalism and unnecessary destruction of Robinson's crops and property, which included present-day Central Park. Upon his return to Louisville, he resumed his service at Second Presbyterian Church but had some difficulties with a portion of his congregation because of his Confederate sympathies and previous refusal to take the oath of allegiance to the Union.

On September 2, 1871, he sold his home and property to Alfred V. du Pont, and in 1872 he moved with his family into a new brick and stone residence that he built at the northeast corner of Fourth St. and Magnolia Ave., also a part of his property. This home was later known as Landward House. At one time Robinson owned all the land between the present Park Ave. and Magnolia and between Third St. and the alley dividing Sixth and Levering Streets.

Robinson was the pastor of Second Presbyterian Church for twenty-three years and was active on many church councils and organizations until ill health forced him to resign. Only three of the Robinsons' eight children lived to maturity. Of these, the only son, Lawrence, died of consumption in St. Paul, Minnesota, in 1869, barely having reached the age of twenty-one. Robinson's older daughter, Mattie, married Col. Bennett H. Young, and his younger daughter, Lizzie, married Dr. John Giles Cecil.

See *History of the Ohio Falls Cities and Their Counties* (Cleveland 1882); Audrea McDowell, "Landward House," *Filson Club History Quarterly* 44 (April 1970): 117–32.

Audrea McDowell

ROBSION, JOHN MARSHALL, JR. (b Barbourville, Kentucky, August 28, 1904; d Fort Lauderdale, Florida, February 14, 1990). U.S. congressman. John Robsion was the son of John Marshall and Lida Robsion. In 1918 his father, a Barbourville attorney, was elected as a Republican to the U.S. House of Representatives. The senior Robsion served thirteen terms in the House and was appointed to the Senate in January 1930 to fill the vacancy left by the resignation of Frederic M. Sackett.

Young Robsion moved to Washington, D.C., following his graduation in 1919 from Union College Academy in Barbourville. Working as a congressional secretary in his father's office, he continued his studies at George Washington University and at National University. In 1926 he received a law degree from the latter institution. Two years later, he established his home in Louisville. From 1929 to 1935, Robsion worked as the chief of the law division in the U.S. Bureau of Pensions in Washington. He resigned and returned to Louisville, where he practiced law.

During WORLD WAR II, he was an army captain and served in Africa, Italy, and Austria. At the time of his discharge in 1946, he held the rank of major. From 1946 to 1952, he served as a special circuit judge in Kentucky, after being appointed by both political parties. On July 15, 1949, he married Laura S. Drane.

Robsion threw his hat into the political ring in 1952 following the decision of Thruston B. Morton not to seek a fourth term in the U.S. House of Representatives. Running as a Republican, Robsion defeated county judge BOMAN L. SHAMBURGER to win the Third District congressional seat. He served three terms in Congress, from January 3, 1953, until January 3, 1959. During his first term, he was assigned to the Judiciary Committee. In his second campaign, he narrowly defeated his Democratic opponent, Louisville attorney Harrison M. Robertson. A strong supporter of Pres. Dwight Eisenhower, he enjoyed a solid victory in his third campaign, which coincided with Eisenhower's landslide reelection victory.

In 1958 Robsion lost his fourth bid for the House to Frank W. Burke, who was later mayor of Louisville. Following Robsion's defeat, leaders of the Kentucky REPUBLICAN PARTY asked him to enter the state's gubernatorial race. He lost the 1959 election to his Democratic challenger, Bert T. Combs. Even though he did not seek public office again, Robsion continued to be active in Republican politics, attending several Republican National Conventions as a delegate and serving as a member of the Louisville–Jefferson County Republican Executive Committee. He is buried in CAVE HILL CEMETERY in Louisville.

See *Biographical Directory of the American Congress, 1774–1989* (Washington, D.C. 1989).

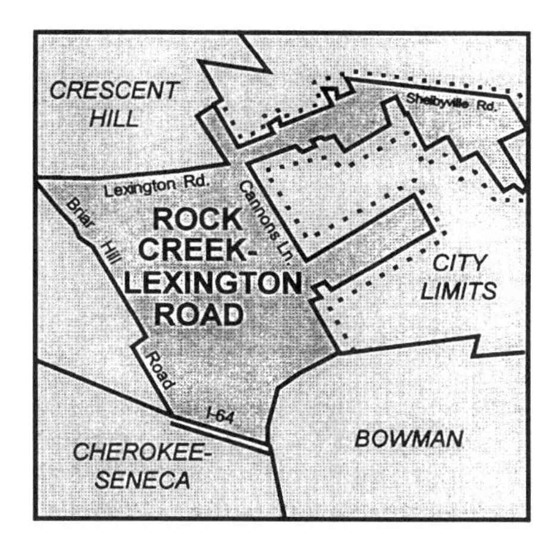

ROCK CREEK–LEXINGTON ROAD. Irregular-shaped neighborhood in eastern Louisville between Seneca Park and Briar Hill Rd. to the west, Cannons Ln. to the east, Interstate 64 to the south, and Lexington Rd. to the north. The community also includes the areas immediately adjoining Shelbyville Rd. from Cannons Ln. to Fairfax Ave. and those along Nanz Ave. from Cannons Ln. to Macon Ave. This was one of the earliest areas to develop after World War II.

The first subdivision was started in 1949 by Martin L. Adams & Sons at Chamberry Dr. and Old Cannons Ln. Located in the neighborhood across from Seneca Park is the ROCK CREEK Riding Club, an organization that reportedly dates from the 1920s when a group of riders managed to rent stables off Cannons Ln. from William S. Speed for $50 per month.

See *Louisville Survey: East Report* (Louisville, 1980).

ROCK MUSIC. Since the late 1970s, rock music in Louisville has crossed the spectrum of bands from heavy metal (Kinghorse) to the singer-songwriter style (the Palace Brothers) to the brash attitude and high energy of punk rock (Squirrel Bait) to the positive hardcore of straightedge (Elliott). An active garage band environment and an early connection with Chicago musicians, particularly because of musician and recording engineer Steve Albini of the band Big Black, were partly responsible for the thriving rock scene. Although no major bands or artists have been headquartered in Louisville, much local activity has achieved national and international notice. Indeed, something that has set the city apart in the volatile and highly energized world of rock music is the confluence of strong, creative ideas among musicians who refuse to be taken on by major recording labels.

The "indie" (independent) rock scene in the city is so strong that, paradoxically, it was the main reason for *Playboy* magazine's identification of the city as one of three (rock) "music meccas" in 1998 (the other two being Austin, Texas, and Bristol, England). Local musicians received the news with some surprise, noting that although there had certainly been this sort of activity at various times in the past decade, by the late 1990s things had changed. Jeffrey Lee Puckett quotes Edenstreet's Screaming John Hawkins as saying, "I haven't really noticed anything different. You hear about it, but you don't see record-label guys driving down the street every day." Two problems may be largely responsible: first, for a variety of reasons including the lack of a number of good places to play, bands have had difficulty building a local audience base; and second (perhaps partly because of the first), bands often do not stay together for more than one or two years.

Two early groups were the Babylon Dance Band and Endtables, both from the late 1970s. Their high energy and rebellious style, reminiscent of MC5 and the Stooges, did much to lay a foundation for Louisville's active punk scene some years later, even though they made no recordings. Further, the Babylon Dance Band launched the career of guitarist Tara Key, who went on to cofound the New York–based Antietam and is today considered one of rock's most influential female artists.

The frequent interchange of band personnel, as well as the influence of Louisville musicians on the rock world in general, can be seen especially in a late-80s band called Slint, consisting at various times of Dave Pajo, Brian McMahon, Britt Walford, Ethan Bucker, and Todd Brashear (some of whom played with the band Squirrel Bait). Although Slint did very little touring and produced only two official albums (plus one album of out-takes), it is still considered to have had the biggest impact on the rock scene of all Louisville bands. Its hypnotic, somewhat cryptic style, which really cannot be classified under any of the conventional categories, was new to the music, not only in Louisville, and the band's sound continues to have an effect even after its breakup in the late 1980s, when each member went on to play with other bands, both local (Evergreen, King Kong) and national (the Breeders, Tortoise, The For Carnation). Other bands such as Kinghorse, Bastro, Crain, and Rodan were active around the same time, representing a cross-section of personnel and styles from the same earlier band.

In the early 1990s an enigmatic musician, Will Oldham, produced a single under the band name the Palace Brothers, with the help of several musicians active in other area bands, including former members of Slint. He has since produced several other projects, all with the name Palace in them in some way, and all by himself. Oldham caught the attention of major labels but, true to the city's tradition, has never signed with one.

Though some local musicians will point out that the *Playboy* spotlight came approximately ten years after the real height of activity in the city, local bands continue to attract national and international attention. The Pennies, for example, played in the Meer dan Woorden Festival (Goes, Holland, 1997), and both Rodan and The Rachels have been invited to appear on the radio show of British mega-rock DJ John Peel.

One apparent exception to Louisville's avoidance of major labels has been a band named Days of the New, which signed with Outpost/Geffen in 1997. However, local musicians will quickly point out that although the band's leader, Travis Meeks, is from the region (Charlestown, Indiana), he is not actually from the city (though the band records in Louisville) and that the band's sound is not representative of Louisville rock music.

Since 1998 a major event in the city has been Krazyfest, a festival aimed at all ages and therefore somewhat limited to straightedge rock (that is, music that avoids themes dwelling on drugs, violence, and sex). This was started by Initial Records, an indie label that moved to Louisville in 1996. After the *Playboy* article, which mentions this festival, city GOVERNMENT stepped forward to find more ways to help promote local music. This resulted in festivals such as Louisville City Stage (summer weekends) and Harvest Showcase (mid-September). More recently (1999) the Louisville Music Industry Alliance was formed to help promote local bands.

Other notable support has come from Marvin Maxwell, owner of Mom's Music (retail sales and, more important, recording studios), as well as radio stations WTTX-FM and NPR affiliate WFPK-FM, which promote local music. Especially noted music venues have included the BUTCHERTOWN Pub, the Toy Tiger, and especially, for about twenty years until closing in the mid-1990s, Tewligan's Tavern—the last two on Bardstown Rd., one of the major creative locations in the city. Also on Bardstown Rd. are Ground Zero, an important outlet for locally produced music; the Guitar Emporium, where locals may encounter artists such as Neil Young and the Rolling Stones shopping for guitars; and Ear X-tacy, famous nationally as a place to obtain otherwise hard-to-find music on independent labels.

See *Slamdek A to Z* (Louisville 1996); Barbara Nellis, "The Buzz," *Playboy,* April 1998; *Courier-Journal,* March 28, 1998.

Jack Ashworth
Jeremy Podgursky

RODES. Rodes, a menswear specialty store, opened in Louisville in 1890 as Crutcher & Starks. It reincorporated in 1915 utilizing the names of its two principal entrepreneurs, John Starks Rodes and William H. Rapier. (Rapier's name was dropped from its advertising after his retirement.) Closely associated with the STARKS BUILDING, in 1921 Rodes-Rapier moved from the northwest to the southwest corner of the structure where it currently resides at Fourth St. and Muhammad Ali Blvd. (formerly Walnut St.)

The business has been owned or operated over the years by Reed Embry, Hanford Smith (Embry's son-in-law) and his descendants, and the Rodes family itself. The family relinquished majority control in 1983. Rodes has maintained a suburban branch at Louisville's OXMOOR Mall. Today, more than half of the company's revenues come from its professional uniforms division.

Though never connected to a larger conglomerate of retail stores and the resultant buying power, Rodes menswear has long been equated with the top of the line in the Louisville market.

Kenneth L. Miller

ROLLED OYSTER. Few things have become more synonymous in Louisville history than the rolled oyster and Mazzoni's Café, where it has been served for more than 115 years. The tradition began in 1884 when three Mazzoni brothers, Charles, Angelo, and Phillip, came to Louisville from Genoa, Italy. Each opened a tavern, serving a free boiled egg, wiener, or rolled oyster with each beer or drink of whiskey. The rolled oyster (three raw oysters rolled in pastinga, a batterlike breading, and deep fried) became a favorite. As the outside of the rolled oyster turned a golden brown, the meat inside became steamed and burst, releasing its flavor into the breading. What was once given away gained such popularity that it was sold as a menu item.

The Mazzoni's Café on the west side of Third between Market and Jefferson Streets was a mainstay in Louisville for ninety years; a streetcar ride downtown to Mazzoni's on Saturday morning became a popular pastime. A fourth-generation Mazzoni's Café is now serving rolled oysters at 2804 Taylorsville Rd. Other area RESTAURANTS serve their own versions of the rolled oyster.

Bob Hill

ROMAN CATHOLICS. The Catholic community of Louisville is distinctive in several ways: Louisville is the historic see city (administrative center) of the oldest inland Catholic diocese in the United States, it is one of the few heavily Catholic urban areas in the American South, and it cherishes the memory of many of its own who rose to national significance. These include Benedict Joseph Flaget, CATHERINE SPALDING, JOHN LANCASTER SPALDING, and THOMAS MERTON.

Only a scattered number of Catholics—mainly FRENCH—were resident in Louisville during the first generation after its settlement. A young priest exile from the French Revolution, Benedict J. Flaget, passed through in the fall of 1792. Not until 1805 did a congregation begin to gather with some regularity. Their priest was Frenchman Stephen Badin, the first priest ordained in the United States. Artist JOHN J. AUDUBON was an early parishioner.

This initial parish of the city (which now continues as the CATHEDRAL OF THE ASSUMPTION) took the name St. Louis and opened its first sanctuary on Christmas Day 1811 near Tenth and MAIN Streets. Significant financial support for its construction came from Protestants in the city. The first resident pastor, Philip Hosten, died on October 30, 1821, a victim of his ministry to those stricken in a typhoid epidemic. The city was not noted for its piety. By 1820 it had only a handful of churches of any denomination, and in that same year Flaget, back for a visit as bishop of Bardstown, declared Louisville to be a place "where dissipation reigns."

The St. Louis parish built a new church on Fifth St. (the site of today's cathedral), which opened in 1831. Cornerstone ceremonies had been held in the nearby Presbyterian church. At St. Louis parish during the 1830s, Mother Catherine Spalding of the Sisters of Charity of Nazareth was instrumental in founding a school (Presentation), an orphanage (St. Vincent's), and an infirmary (St. Joseph's). In 1841 Rome moved the headquarters of the Diocese of Bardstown to the growing city of Louisville. When Benedict Flaget arrived as bishop, he found three Catholic parishes in place: St. Louis for the English-speaking, St. Boniface (opened 1836) for GERMANS, and Our Lady's (Notre Dame du Port) at PORTLAND (opened 1839) for the French.

Meanwhile, Indiana had been designated a separate diocese by Pope Gregory XVI in 1834 with Vincennes as its see city (Indianapolis became the see city in 1898). Kentucky's Bishop Flaget had consecrated Indiana's first bishop, Simon Bruté, and that prelate was to oversee the growth of Catholic churches north of the OHIO RIVER. St. Michael, a parish founded at Dogwood in Harrison County, was the first in that region. It closed in 1928. St. Mary of the KNOBS, established in Floyd County in 1823, remains the oldest extant Catholic parish in metro southern Indiana. Its early members represented many nationalities, including Belgian, French, German, Irish, and Swiss.

Over a dozen antebellum congregations were set up in the region, including Holy Trinity in 1836 and St. Mary (originally primarily for Germans) in 1858, both at NEW ALBANY. The Sisters of Providence arrived to teach in this area in 1857. In Clark County, St. Anthony parish was founded in 1851 but was renamed St. Augustine in 1854 when a move was made to new property. German Catholics of the parish continued to use the old building and assumed the original name of St. Anthony. (The St. Anthony parish moved to Clarksville in 1949.) Monks of the Benedictine order established one of the oldest American monasteries of that tradition in nearby SPENCER COUNTY in

1854. St. Meinrad Seminary continues to educate large numbers of priests, and many of its graduates have served in the Greater Louisville area.

By the 1840s waves of immigrants, mainly Catholic, were coming to Louisville from Germany and Ireland. The *Catholic Advocate* began publication in the city in 1840. In 1842 Jesuits arrived to staff what proved to be short-lived educational ventures. Much more lasting were the works of other groups: the Sisters of the Good Shepherd arrived from France in 1843 to be active in social service, XAVERIAN BROTHERS from Belgium established their first American foundation in 1854 and started St. Xavier's High School (1864), and in 1858 Ursuline Sisters came from Germany as teachers and established Ursuline (1860) and Sacred Heart (1877) Academies.

When the Cathedral of the Assumption opened on October 3, 1852, the new bishop, MARTIN JOHN SPALDING (1810–72), declared the structure a monument to his recently deceased, saintly predecessor, Flaget. That same year, James S. Speed (1811–60) was elected mayor of Louisville but was forced from office when he converted to Catholicism. Anti-immigrant tensions and the rise of the Know-Nothing Party resulted in the BLOODY MONDAY riot of August 6, 1855, in which more than twenty immigrants were killed and churches were threatened. Pacific action by both Bishop Spalding and a group of Protestant ministers helped to quiet the crisis.

During the CIVIL WAR, Louisville Catholics experienced the divisions so common to a border city. An organist at Our Lady's was upbraided by her pastor for weaving "Dixie" into a recessional one Sunday. Strict in his public neutrality, Bishop Spalding hosted memorial services at the Cathedral for the fallen of both the blue and the gray. NURSING sisters from the Bardstown area served bravely as volunteers in Louisville's military HOSPITALS.

The long-lived and controversial postwar bishop of Louisville was William George McCloskey (1823–1909). Over twenty-five parishes were opened in the city during his tenure, including St. Augustine's, the premier African American parish in Louisville. But McCloskey's authoritarian style alienated many of the sisters and priests of the diocese. In 1875 "The Troubles," as they were named at the time, became highly public and sparked pulpit controversies. One talented priest who departed the diocese during these disputes was the renowned John Lancaster Spalding (1840–1916), later called "the Catholic Emerson" for his elegant essays; he was also a founder of the Catholic University of America in Washington, D.C.

German influence remained especially strong in this era, as evidenced in the work of the St. Joseph's Orphans' Society and the publication of the *Glaubensbotte* from 1869 through 1914. After the English-language Catholic *Guardian* ceased publication in 1862 (a victim of the Civil War), the *Catholic Advocate* revived as a Louisville Catholic weekly and was published from 1869 to 1899, although its status as official paper of the diocese was assumed by the *Record,* founded in 1879. Lay organizations took on increased significance during the gaslight era and included the ST. VINCENT DE PAUL Society (founded 1853), the Ancient Order of Hibernians (1874), the Knights of St. John (1889), and later the Queen's Daughters (1914).

The Cathedral played a major role in the life of the community in the years before WORLD WAR I. Long under the pastoral leadership of the beloved and eccentric Fr. Michael Bouchet (1827–1903)—who patented an early version of the adding machine—the Cathedral parish became noted for its liturgy, choirs, concerts, slide shows, free schools, and other services for the urban poor.

As the century turned, lay Catholics were increasingly visible in civic and cultural affairs. Included were the Whallen brothers, John (1850–1913) and James (1851–1930), who began a political dynasty in the local DEMOCRATIC PARTY. MARY ANDERSON (1859–1940), a Presentation graduate, went on to international fame as an actress, and Edward J. McDermott (1852–1926) became lieutenant governor of Kentucky. Industrialist PATRICK HENRY CALLAHAN (1866–1941) became widely known nationally for his efforts in economic justice and racial harmony.

During the first generations of the twentieth century, parishes often tended to be identified with their beloved and long-term pastors, who were also men of deep civic involvement. These included Bernard Boland (1877–1955), John Knue (1878–1945), James McGee (1895–1955), Joseph Newman (1889–1957), Charles Raffo (1859–1938), George Schuhmann (1865–1931), and John Vance (1900–1976). A noted intellectual prominent in national and local educational circles was Msgr. Felix Pitt (1894–1971), who also helped to pioneer the landmark ecumenical program *THE MORAL SIDE OF THE NEWS* in 1952 on WHAS Radio.

Catholic Louisville welcomed as its new bishop in 1924 JOHN ALEXANDER FLOERSH (1886–1968). When the diocese was raised by Pope Pius XI to the status of an archdiocese in 1937, Floersh became Louisville's first archbishop. He was a man noted both for his deep spirituality and his astuteness in real estate. The latter was to prove extremely useful because construction was a constant fact of life as the city and its Catholic community grew, especially with the explosive suburban growth at the end of WORLD WAR II. Over thirty suburban parishes opened between 1945 and 1970, as well as a series of new institutions such as Boy's Haven, founded by Father James Maloney in 1949, and ST. THOMAS SEMINARY (1950–72).

At mid-century, some said the city resembled a little Rome. Recognizing the growth of the Catholic population in the area, Pope Pius XII appointed Louisville native Charles G. Maloney to be the city's first auxiliary bishop in 1955. Meanwhile, scattered around the city were houses of many religious communities. Women's orders so represented included Carmelite, Dominican, Franciscan, Good Shepherd, Mercy, and Ursuline Sisters (both Louisville and Maple Mount Motherhouses) as well as the Sisters of Charity of Nazareth, the Sisters of Loretto, and the LITTLE SISTERS OF THE POOR. Among its religious orders of men were to be found Carmelites, Dominicans, Franciscans, Passionists, Resurrectionists, and Xaverians. All of these groups are represented in the city in the late 1990s, though most of them in diminished numbers.

By 1960 Louisville hosted some eighty Catholic parishes (most with a grade school attached), over a dozen Catholic high schools, four hospitals (St. Anthony's, St. Joseph's, Saints Mary and Elizabeth's, and Our Lady of Peace), three major CEMETERIES (St. Louis, St. Michael, and Calvary), TWO ORPHANAGES, and three colleges. Nazareth College, which opened on Fourth St. in 1920, became SPALDING UNIVERSITY in 1984; BELLARMINE COLLEGE was founded in 1950; and URSULINE COLLEGE (founded 1938) merged with Bellarmine in 1968. Noted Catholic figures (some of them controversial) came increasingly to visit in the city: Dorothy Day, Hans Küng, Bernard Lonergan, Jacques Maritain, Karl Rahner, and Mother Teresa.

The early 1960s marked a time of dramatic change for Catholics in America. The election in 1960 of John F. Kennedy as the nation's first Catholic president removed unofficial political barriers. MARLOW COOK, a Catholic from Louisville, was elected U.S. Senator from Kentucky in 1968. In 1969 Louisvillians elected Catholics to the top two posts in metropolitan government: Frank W. Burke as mayor (the first of his faith to be elected in the twentieth century) and TODD HOLLENBACH III as county judge. The following year, Romano Mazzoli was elected to the U.S. House of Representatives from Louisville, a post he retained for thirteen consecutive terms.

Catholics of this era also became quite vocal in addressing the moral aspects of sometimes divisive civic issues. Louisville's Archbishop THOMAS J. MCDONOUGH (in office 1967–81) and Bishop Charles Maloney—along with significant numbers of local Catholics—were active in the movement for CIVIL RIGHTS of the 1960s and beyond. Local Catholics (mirroring America) found themselves divided on the issue of the war in Vietnam, though some were quite outspoken in their opposition. Greater cohesion was to be found in opposition to abortion after the Roe v. Wade decision of 1973.

The Second Vatican Council, which met in Rome from 1962 to 1965, unleashed many new forces in the ancient faith. Among those who attended the council were the two Louisville bishops; Sr. Mary Luke Tobin of the Kentucky Sisters of Loretto; Msgr. Alfred Horrigan, founding president of Bellarmine College;

Crowd at Rose Island boat landing in 1926.

Passionist Fr. Carroll Stuhlmueller; and Baptist Seminary professor Leo Garrett. Though not present at the council, the internationally renowned Kentucky Trappist monk and writer Thomas Merton reflected its spirit in many of his works. Merton often visited the main Louisville library downtown, and he referred to Louisville as "my city."

As a result of the Vatican Council, Louisville Catholics discovered new energies, new freedoms and tolerations, new ecumenical openings, and deepened spiritual awareness. A host of new commissions and service agencies came into being among Louisville Catholics, such as the Archdiocesan Communications Center, the Center for Family Ministries, the Office for African American Ministries, the Office of Ecumenism, the Office of Evangelization, the Pastoral Council of the Archdiocese, the Peace and Justice Center, the Priests' Council, and the Respect Life Pastoral Plan. The role of the laity in the ministries of the church was expanded and intensified.

But in the intervening years, there have also been painful conflicts, changes, and transitions. The growth of suburban areas often spelled the decline of treasured old inner-city parishes. Some were closed, others consolidated. St. Anthony's and St. Joseph's Hospitals closed, as did such landmark high schools as Flaget, Loretto, and Ursuline. The annual outpouring of some fifty thousand faithful to take part in the Corpus Christi procession at Churchill Downs diminished in size until it was discontinued after 1976.

One of the first acts of Thomas C. Kelly, O.P., when he arrived in Louisville as its new archbishop in 1982, was to begin the work of revitalizing the Cathedral of the Assumption as a model of excellence. It now is a nationally respected center of Catholic roots, interfaith outreach, and community social and cultural service. Catholics in the city welcomed new international groups into their midst, especially the Hispanic and the Vietnamese. The archdiocese also developed under Kelly a mission statement that searched tradition in order to establish planning goals for the future. The core of the mission is threefold: to proclaim the Gospel, to celebrate the liturgy, and to serve human needs. By the end of 1996, in Louisville and Jefferson County, there were 73 Catholic parishes, 42 elementary schools with 14,599 students, and 9 high schools with 5,625 students. Catholics were estimated to constitute between 22 and 25 percent of the population of Jefferson County.

Bishops of the Diocese of Bardstown/Louisville

Benedict Joseph Flaget, 1810–50; assisting Flaget as bishops: John Baptist David, 1819–41; Guy Ignatius Chabrat, 1834–45
Martin John Spalding, 1850–64
Peter Joseph Lavialle, 1865–67
William George McCloskey, 1868–1909
Denis O'Donaghue, 1910–24
John Alexander Floersh, 1924–67
Thomas J. McDonough, 1967–82
Thomas Cajetan Kelly, O.P., 1982–present; assisting Floersh, McDonough, and Kelly as bishop since 1955: Charles Garrett Maloney

See *The 1997 Catholic Directory: Archdiocese of Louisville;* Clyde F. Crews, *An American Holy Land* (Wilmington, Del. 1987); Clyde F. Crews, *The Faithful Image* (Louisville 1986); Ben Webb, *Centenary of Catholicity in Kentucky* (Louisville 1884); Thomas McAvoy, *The Catholic Church in Indiana 1789–1834* (New York 1940).

Clyde F. Crews

ROSE ISLAND. Once the nineteenth-century picnic spot known as Fern Grove, Rose Island in Clark County, Indiana, became a premier family resort in the 1920s and the 1930s. Located at the mouth of Fourteen Mile Creek where it enters the Ohio River, Rose Island was not an island at all: it was bordered by water on only two sides. It was named for its owner and the president of the Rose Island Co., David B.G. Rose.

Rose Island opened in 1924 and at its peak had as many as four thousand visitors daily. The recreation area was equipped with rental cottages, a hotel, a dining hall, a petting zoo, tennis courts, a swimming pool, and a dance pavilion featuring the Rose Island Orchestra. From the Kentucky side, the resort was accessible to Louisville citizens by taking River Rd. to Prospect, Kentucky. From there, Rose Island Rd. led to the Ohio River, where a ferry for Rose Island departed every ten minutes, as advertised to the public. The excursion steamer *America* made regular trips, conveying church, school, and civic groups from Louisville to Rose Island. The resort was popular with patrons until it experienced extensive damage in the great flood of 1937. It did not reopen.

The park land was purchased by the U.S. government in 1941 as part of the large acreage of the Indiana Ordnance plant at Charlestown, Indiana. In 1996 the former site of Rose Island was dedicated as Charlestown State Park by the Indiana Department of Natural Resources. The land is noted for its rugged beauty, including Devil's Backbone, a ridge running above the Ohio River.

See Gerald O. Haffner, *A Brief, Informal History of Clark County Indiana* (New Albany, Ind. 1985); *Louisville Civic Opinion,* May 3, 1924.

Rossmore Apartments (later Berkeley Hotel) 644 South Fourth Street, 1953.

ROSSMORE APARTMENT HOUSE. This long-gone building was hailed by news reports in 1893 as Louisville's "first metropolitan apartment house." Designed by local architects Kenneth McDonald and J.R. Sheblessy in the Richardsonian Romanesque manner, it stood on the west side of Fourth St. just north of BROADWAY in what was redeveloped as Theatre Square. The upper floors were "flats," and the ground floor was commercial. Following the style consistent with the structure's Chicago School precursors, McDonald used long oriel windows to admit maximum light and air. Louisville grocer Alonzo J. Ross developed the five-story building in apparent response to the growing need for APARTMENTS for downtown professionals and others. Expanded in 1899, it ushered in a pre–WORLD WAR I boom of such developments in the Broadway vicinity and south. In 1920 it was called the Raleigh Apartments and renamed the Berkeley Hotel two years later, a name it kept until its demolition in 1981.

Douglas L Stern

ROTHERT, OTTO ARTHUR (b Huntingburg, Indiana, June 21, 1871; d Greenville, Kentucky, March 28, 1956). Historian. Otto Arthur Rothert was the youngest of the five children of Herman Rothert, who came to the United States from Germany in 1844, and Franziska (Weber) Rothert, also born in Germany. The family moved to Louisville in 1889, where Herman Rothert had a TOBACCO exporting business. Otto Rothert graduated from the University of Notre Dame in 1892 with a science major; he had written several articles published in the *Notre Dame Scholastic.* After graduation, Rothert worked for his father and later for his brother John at the Falls City Tobacco Works, then became a clerk at the GALT HOUSE hotel, where his genial nature served well. In 1904 and 1905 he made an extended tour of the western states, Hawaii, and Mexico, sending back descriptive articles to the *Huntingburg Independent.* When he returned, he wrote articles for the *Muhlenberg Sentinel* and the *Greenville Record* on the history of Muhlenberg County, where his family owned 2,600 acres. The result of that work was his classic *History of Muhlenberg County* (1913).

In 1908 Rothert became a member of the Filson Club, where he read several of his papers on historical topics. In 1917 he was elected secretary of the club, serving in that role until his retirement on November 1, 1945. As secretary, Rothert edited books in the Filson Club publication series, arranged the annual lecture series, and, beginning in 1928, edited the *FILSON CLUB HISTORY QUARTERLY.* He set high editorial standards and earned scholarly respect for the journal. His devoted service helped establish the Filson Club as a leader among local history societies in the United States. He gave the club his large library of books and manuscripts.

Rothert's many publications included *The Outlaws of Cave-in-Rock* (1924), *The Story of a Poet: Madison Cawein* (1921), and *The Filson Club and Its Activities, 1884–1922* (1922). He was known as "Uncle Otto" to the emerging historians of Kentucky who profited by his tutelage, among them Holman Hamilton, Hambleton Tapp, Thomas D. Clark, and J. Winston Coleman. He is buried in Huntingburg, Indiana.

See Hambleton Tapp, "Otto Arthur Rothert, 1871–1956," *Filson Club History Quarterly* 61 (Jan. 1987): 54–67.

James R. Bentley

ROUSSEAU, LOVELL HARRISON (b Lincoln County, Kentucky, August 4, 1818; d New Orleans, January 7, 1869). General and congressman. Lovell Harrison Rousseau was one of seven surviving children born to the family of David Rousseau. The young Rousseau was largely self-taught and, following his father's death from cholera, was employed as a turnpike construction laborer. In 1840 Rousseau undertook the study of law and was admitted to practice the following year in Greene County, Indiana. He married Antoinette Dozier, daughter of James J. Dozier of Tennessee. He was elected to the Indiana legislature as a Whig in 1844 and was a captain in the Second Indiana Infantry during the MEXICAN WAR. Captain Rousseau's company was actively engaged in the battle of Buena Vista on February 23, 1847.

After the war, Rousseau was elected to the Indiana Senate, but he resigned and in 1850 relocated to Louisville and opened a law practice with his brother Richard. Lovell was well known as a criminal defense lawyer and was involved in a number of celebrated cases during the ten years preceding the CIVIL WAR. A strong supporter of the WHIG PARTY and of Henry Clay's emancipation program, Rousseau was part of the minority of the party that rejected the principles of the Know-Nothing Party. During the Know-Nothing riots of 1855, Rousseau was shot in the abdomen while attempting to defend the right of a German to vote. Rousseau served as alderman from the Sixth Ward and was elected to the Kentucky Senate in 1859.

During the legislative sessions of 1861, Rousseau was a frequent and outspoken supporter of the Union. As the Civil War approached, he was appointed on April 20, 1861, by Mayor John M. Delph to be brigadier general of the Louisville Guard. In the summer of 1861, Rousseau opened a recruiting camp near JEFFERSONVILLE, INDIANA, named Camp Joe Holt. There the LOUISVILLE LEGION was recruited and Rousseau was appointed colonel in the regular army. On October 1, 1861, he was promoted to brigadier general and assigned to a brigade command. His brigade served with distinction on the second day of the battle of Shiloh and during the siege of Corinth, Mississippi.

In July 1862 Brigadier General Rousseau was given command of the Third Division of the Army of the Ohio. In the bloody battle of Perryville, Rousseau displayed reliable leadership and courage in commanding his battered division. Because of his gallantry at Perryville, he was promoted to major general, and his commission bore the date of the battle. Rousseau's division was heavily engaged in the Battle of Stone's River and participated in the Tullahoma campaign. Rousseau missed the battle of Chickamauga but arrived upon the battlefield in time to help in organizing the defeated Federal forces.

On November 10, 1863, General Rousseau was assigned to command the district of Nashville. In mid-July 1864, he led one of the most successful cavalry raids of the war, riding 400 miles through the state of Alabama before joining William T. Sherman's army outside Atlanta. The raiders severely damaged the Montgomery & West Point Railroad and destroyed extensive Confederate supplies at Opelika, Alabama. During Gen. John Bell Hood's invasion of middle Tennessee, Rousseau successfully defended Fortress Rosecrans at Murfreesboro.

Rousseau resigned his commission in the U.S. Army on November 30, 1865, after being elected as a Republican to represent the Fifth District in the House of Representatives; he served from December 4, 1865, to July 21, 1866. Rousseau's political views immediately moderated because of the punitive RECONSTRUCTION measures in Kentucky. He began to propound Democratic principles and became a supporter of Pres. Andrew Johnson.

As agitation for stricter measures grew among his former Republican colleagues, Rousseau became increasingly at odds with Rep. Josiah B. Grinnell of Iowa. The men had a confrontation in a corridor of the Capitol that resulted in Rousseau's striking Grinnell with his cane. For this action, Rousseau received the censure of the House and resigned his seat in Congress. However, his constituency overwhelmingly reelected him to fill the vacancy, and he served again from December 3, 1866, to March 3, 1867.

On March 28, 1867, he was appointed brigadier general (brevet major general) in the U.S. Army. In that capacity, Rousseau accepted the transfer of Alaska from Russia. General Rousseau testified on behalf of Pres. Andrew Johnson at his impeachment trial. On July 28, 1868, the general was assigned to command the Department of Louisiana and died in that position after a brief illness. Lovell H. Rousseau has a monument in CAVE HILL CEMETERY, but he is buried in Arlington National Cemetery.

See Thomas Speed, *The Union Cause in Kentucky* (New York, 1907); Ezra J. Warner, *Generals in Blue* (Baton Rouge 1964).

David Deatrick Jr.

ROWAN, JOHN (b York, Pennsylvania, July 12, 1773; d Louisville, July 13, 1843). Lawyer, congressman, and U.S. senator. The son of William and Sarah Elizabeth (Cooper) Rowan,

Aerial photograph of the "Rubbertown" area of West Louisville, 1960.

John came to Kentucky with his family in 1783. He spent much of his childhood in the frontier outpost of Fort Vienna, near the long falls of the Green River. In 1790 the family moved to Bardstown, where John began his education at nearby Salem Academy, headed by Dr. James Priestly. In 1793 he went to Lexington, Kentucky, to study law under George Nicholas, Kentucky's first attorney general. He was admitted to the bar in 1795 and set up private practice in Louisville.

Espousing Jeffersonian Republicanism, Rowan, as one of Kentucky's leading defense attorneys, fought for individual liberty and limited government. He represented Nelson County in the second state constitutional convention held in Frankfort on July 22, 1799. Rowan was a strong advocate of legislative supremacy over the executive and judicial branches and of a greater role for the people; the Constitution adopted by the convention on August 17, 1799, called for the direct election of the governor and state senators.

On February 3, 1801, Rowan killed Dr. James Chambers in a duel near Bardstown. Purportedly, the duel was the result of an argument over which of the two men was the better scholar of dead languages. Though Rowan was charged with murder and brought to trial, he was later released on grounds of insufficient evidence. The case was widely reported but did not hamper Rowan's political rise.

Rowan was appointed Kentucky's secretary of state in 1804 by Gov. Christopher Greenup. He served in that capacity until 1806, when he was elected as a Democrat-Republican from Nelson County to the U.S. House of Representatives, serving from March 4, 1807, to March 3, 1809. Rowan was elected to the Kentucky House of Representatives from Nelson County (1813–17) and from Jefferson County (1822–24). Between 1819 and 1821 he served on the Kentucky Court of Appeals, then the state's highest court. In 1824 he was elected to the U.S. Senate, serving from March 4, 1825, to March 3, 1831. Rowan then returned to Kentucky and divided his time between Bardstown and Louisville. In 1838 he became president of the KENTUCKY HISTORICAL SOCIETY in Louisville, a position he held until his death.

Rowan married Ann Lytle on October 29, 1794. They had nine children, three sons and six daughters. About 1795 construction began in Bardstown on Rowan's famed Georgian-style home, Federal Hill, (popularly known as "My Old Kentucky Home")which was completed in 1818. Rowan is buried in the family plot at Federal Hill. Rowan St. in Louisville is named for him.

See Stephen Tackler, "John Rowan and the Demise of Jeffersonian Republicanism in Kentucky, 1819–1831," *Register of the Kentucky Historical Society* 78 (winter 1980): 1–26.

RUBBERTOWN. Industrial complex in western Jefferson County between the SHAWNEE neighborhood to the north, the LAKE DREAMLAND community to the south, the OHIO RIVER to the west, and Cane Run Rd. to the east. Because Japan controlled 95 percent of the world's natural rubber market by the end of 1942, America searched for sites to produce the synthetic rubber needed for WORLD WAR II. The possibility of locating a major production center in Louisville offered many advantages, including numerous local distilleries that could convert their operations to produce the large amount of alcohol necessary for the manufacture of rubber.

The city also had a plentiful labor supply, easy access to many forms of transportation, abundant water from the Ohio River, inexpensive electricity from the Louisville Gas & Electric Co. and the Tennessee Valley Authority, and an inland position comfortably removed from the coasts, yet close to the grain supply of the Midwest.

A year before the attack on Pearl Harbor in 1941, three companies, synthetic rubber producers E.I. DU PONT DE NEMOURS & CO. and the B.F. Goodrich Co. and the chemical-producing National Carbide Corp., had already begun construction of plants near the river. This, along with the near completion of one of the two generators at Louisville Gas & Electric's Paddy's Run generating station, induced the government to purchase the rubber and chemical plants and immediately turn them back over to the original owners for management, while constructing additional rubber and chemical plants nearby.

The five Rubbertown factories cost the government approximately $92.4 million, employed nearly four thousand local workers, and yielded 195,000 tons of synthetic rubber during the wartime peak year of 1944, making Louisville the world's leading supplier of the product. By 1996 the number of major plants in the area had grown to ten.

In addition to the two previously mentioned synthetic rubber companies, which repurchased their plants from the government at the end of the war, the companies included the Carbide/Graphite Group (previously known as the National Carbide Corp.), the Geon Co., Zeon Chemicals Kentucky, the BASF Corp., Rohm & Haas Kentucky, Borden—Chemical Division, the American Synthetic Rubber Corp., and the aluminum powder and pigment division of the REYNOLDS METALS CO.

See *Louisville Survey: Central and South Report* (Louisville 1978); George H. Yater, *Two Hundred Years at the Falls of the Ohio* (Louisville 1987).

RUBY, EARL. (b Louisville, November 3, 1903; d Louisville, May 9, 2000) Sports editor. Earl Ruby's near-seventy-year association with he *COURIER-JOURNAL* began at age thirteen when he went to work for the newspaper as a newsboy. Ruby attended DuPont Manual High School where he was known to be a stand-out athlete. This led to his receiving a football scholarship to the UNIVERSITY OF LOUISVILLE. In the early 1920s, while taking classes at the university, Ruby took a job working as an officeboy for the sports department of the local paper. Ruby began writing for the sports department, and by 1939 he had worked his way up to sports editor, a position he held until his retirement in 1968. Ruby, however, continued to write even after his retirement. His weekly outdoors column in the *Courier-Journal* ran until August 1989.

In addition to writing for the *Courier-Journal,* Ruby worked on several other projects. He was the author of three books: *The Golden Goose*

(1974), a biography of jockey *Roscoe Goose; Red Towel Territory* (1979), a work describing athletics at Western Kentucky University; and *Hunting and Fishing in Kentucky* (1978). Ruby's writings were not limited to topics concerning Kentucky. In 1961 he was commissioned by the United States Information Agency to write a series of articles on BASKETBALL for worldwide distribution. He was also essential to the formation of the "Vietnam Sports Section," a four page weekly published by the *Courier-Journal* and sent to over 3,600 men and women from Kentucky and Indiana serving in the VIETNAM WAR.

In his almost seventy years of working for the paper, Ruby wrote over 10,000 columns. Of these, more than twenty stories were included in the annual anthology "Best Sports Stories." Ruby was also the recipient of the National Headliners Award for best sports column in the country in 1945. Another honor was the League of Kentucky Sportsmen's "Sportsman of the Year" award in 1968. He also received the "Outstanding Kentuckian Award," which was presented to im in 1969 by Governor Louie B. Nunn. In 1975 Ruby was elected to both the Kentucky Athletic Hall of Fame and the Kentucky Journalism Hall of Fame. He also had several horse races named in his honor, including the Earl Ruby Handicap at Ellis Park.

Ruby was one of the "founding fathers" of the KENTUCKY DERBY FESTIVAL. In 1956 Ruby, Addison McGhee, Ray Wimberg, and Basil Caummisar worked together to organize and stage the first Pagasus Parade. In 1999 Ruby was honored for his work by being given the Distinguished Service Award by the Kentucky Derby Festival, only the seventh such award in the festival's history.

Ruby died at age 96, only nine months after his wife of 73 years, Evelyn Ruby, died. He is survived by three children: Joan R. Perry, Margaret R. Smock, and Paul H. Ruby.

See the *Courier-Journal* May 10, 2000.

RUNNING OF THE RODENTS. Louisville's SPALDING UNIVERSITY celebrates final examination week every year with a tradition that began in 1972, the Running of the Rodents. An event that parodies the KENTUCKY DERBY, it began when Sr. Julia Claire Fontaine, a science professor, overheard a student complaining that finals week was like a rat race. Fontaine decided to initiate a program, the Spalding Rat Races, that could relieve stress and help students learn about behavior modification. The races take place about April 21 every year in the Spalding gymnasium. Students and others come to enjoy the festivities.

The celebration begins with a Rat Parade, for which students dress themselves and their vehicles in accordance with the year's theme and the names of their rats. This is followed by seven races with seven rats, the main race being the Spalding Derby. The winner of the Spalding Derby receives a garland of Fruit Loops cereal and has its name placed on the Wall of Champions with past winners. Past winners have included Deep Throat, who holds the record for the fastest time of 1.8 seconds. Mr. Uranus holds the record for the most wins in one year, winning five of the seven races. The rats' names are based on the theme for the given year, such as "Planet of the Rats," the "Olympics," "Watergate," and "Party Like It's 1999."

Sean M. Davis

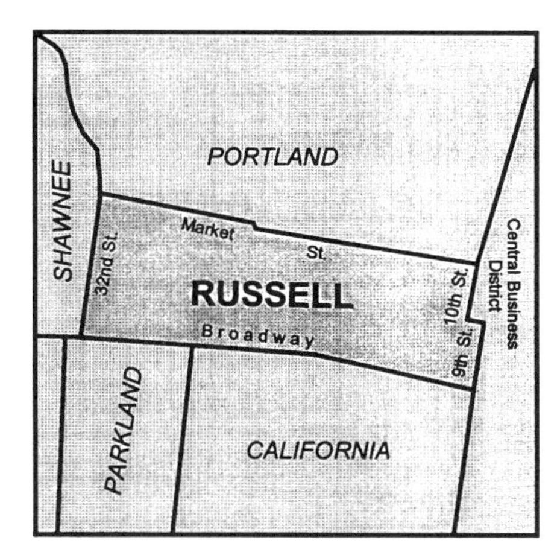

RUSSELL. A primarily residential neighborhood west of downtown Louisville, bounded by MARKET St. to the north, Thirty-second St. to the west, BROADWAY to the south, and Roy Wilkins Ave. to the east. The eastern section of the area was inhabited by numerous free African American families in the years before the CIVIL WAR. The RUSSELL area, named for nationally recognized black educator Harvey C. Russell, attracted substantially more people in the 1870s. At first, into the 1880s, the "suburban" community became a fashionable address for wealthy white families spurred by the crowded downtown conditions, mule-drawn streetcar lines, and the romantic connotations associated with rural living. They were further enticed by developers such as Basil Doerhoefer, who was also president of the American Tobacco Works. Russell was home to architect Max Drach, Falls City Stone Works owner Michael Blatz, and Philip Stitzel of the U.P. STITZEL BROTHERS DISTILLERY. Scattered among the grand Victorian and Italianate homes on Chestnut, Walnut (Muhammad Ali Blvd.), and Jefferson Streets, AFRICAN AMERICANS and working-class whites, some of whom were employed as servants, constructed smaller frame and shotgun-style houses on the minor streets and along back ALLEYS.

With the development of the eastern and southern portions of the city in the 1890s, white residents began leaving the Russell neighborhood. Concentrated primarily in the eastern portion of the community before this time, middle-class African Americans slowly replaced the white families in a westward pattern; professionals purchased the larger homes, and the working-class moved into the more modest dwellings.

The continued settlement of African Americans was affected by the city's Residential Segregation Ordinance in 1914, which was intended to slow housing integration by prohibiting African Americans from moving onto a predominantly white street and vice versa. After the measure was declared unconstitutional by the U.S. Supreme Court in 1917 (*BUCHANAN V. WARLEY*), African Americans continued to migrate into the community and pushed west of Twenty-first St. A substantial concentration of African Americans existed by the 1920s, evidenced by the establishment of the Western Colored Branch Library in 1908 at Tenth and Chestnut Streets and the Plymouth Settlement House in 1917 at Sixteenth and Chestnut Streets.

By the 1940s Russell was the city's premier African American neighborhood. Businesses lined the bustling Walnut St. corridor, and popular night spots such as the Top Hat Club, Charlie Moore's, and Joe's Palm Room dotted the area. However, in the years following WORLD WAR II, many of the wealthier African American residents abandoned the area, an action that increased dramatically during the 1960s as housing became more integrated throughout the city. Many of the abandoned homes were bulldozed during the sixties after heirs frequently refused to claim their relatives' property. URBAN RENEWAL was an important factor of change that leveled old abandoned buildings. Crime, drugs, and poverty became so rampant that the city had difficulty finding people to purchase lots even when they were offered for one dollar in the 1970s and the early 1980s.

The 1980s witnessed the beginning of Russell's rebirth. After years of neglect, the placement of a large section of the neighborhood on the NATIONAL REGISTER OF HISTORIC PLACES in 1980 prompted organizations such as Habitat for Humanity, the Louisville Central Development Corp., and REBOUND (Rebuilding Our Urban Neighborhood Dwellings) to begin rehabilitating and building new houses in the area. The Old Walnut Street Capital Campaign, a $3 million fund-raising drive organized by Louisville Central Community Center, also planned several new facilities, including a neighborhood services center, an entrepreneurial development center, a youth and adult training center, and a child development center. By 1996, 100 new homes and 170 APARTMENTS (such as Hampton Place) had been built in the area and a $33.7 million renovation project was announced for the large Village West (now called City View Park–Walnut) housing development that had been constructed in 1973.

See *Louisville Survey West: Final Report* (Louisville 1977); *A Place in Time: The Story of Louisville's Neighborhoods* (Louisville 1989)

RUSSELL, HARVEY CLARENCE, SR. (b Bloomfield, Kentucky, June 7, 1883; d Louisville, September 21, 1949). Educator. Russell attended Kentucky State Normal School and later earned an A.B. degree from SIMMONS UNIVERSITY in Louisville and an M.A. degree from the University of Cincinnati. In his long and distinguished career, Russell taught in the Bloomfield PUBLIC SCHOOLS and at Frankfort Normal School, Booker T. Washington Elementary School in Louisville, and Louisville Normal School.

He served as dean of Kentucky State College, then as president of Western Kentucky Industrial College (1937–38) and its successor, Western Kentucky Vocational College (1943–47) in Paducah, and from 1939 to 1942 as director of the National Youth Administration. Between 1917 and 1922, Russell was president of the Kentucky Negro Education Association; he was instrumental in establishing African American parent-teacher associations as part of the KNEA and organizing the State High School Athletic Association. Russell was also one of the founders of the Domestic Life Insurance Co., a National Grand Master of the United Brothers of Friendship, an educational columnist for the *LOUISVILLE LEADER,* and a business manager for Simmons University in his later years.

In 1926 Russell and his wife Julia moved from 1029 W Madison St. to 2345 W Chestnut, where he lived until his death. Russell had five children: Harvey Jr., George, Anna, Howard, Bessie and Ronda. Several of them became successful elsewhere, most notably Harvey Junior, who was a vice president of the Pepsi Cola Co. in the 1960s. Because of his many achievements, the Russell Neighborhood in West Louisville came to bear his name, as did the former Madison Street Junior High School, which was rededicated as Harvey C. Russell Junior High School on February 9, 1960.

See Alice A. Dunnigan, *The Fascinating Story of Black Kentuckians: Their Heritage and Traditions* (Washington, D.C., 1982); *Courier-Journal,* Sept. 23, 1949; *Louisville Defender,* Feb. 9, 1960; *Louisville Leader,* Sept. 24, 1949; *Louisville Times,* Sept. 23, 1949.

J. Blaine Hudson

RUSSIANS. There have been three waves of Russian immigrants to Louisville, both predominantly Jewish. The first group came between 1880 and 1920, during the period of the largest overall immigration to America. The second, much smaller, group came after the 1970s. The breakup of the Soviet Union resulted in the third.

Though the first group was classified as Russian, it really was a mixture of many nationalities. There were Lithuanians, Latvians, Hungarians, Poles, and Romanians; the borders of their native countries had changed as they were divided among Russia, Germany, and Austria-Hungary before WORLD WAR I.

There were more than 1,500,000 Easter European Jewish immigrants to the United States between 1880 and 1910, according to the *Encyclopedia Judaica.* The effect of this influx can be seen from POPULATION statistics. In *The Synagogues of Kentucky,* Lee Shai Weisbach states that in 1898 there were 3,600 JEWS in Kentucky. By 1920 the Jewish population of Louisville alone had reached 10,000.

The 1880–1920 arrivals in Louisville were mostly from Russian-occupied Lithuania and were generally known as Litvaks. For the most part they were employed in Louisville's then-burgeoning garment industry. Others became peddlers, concentrated on MARKET St. between Brook and Floyd. There were many nationalities, one newspaper said, but Russian Jews were "largely in the majority and their little junk shops and secondhand stores make up nearly all the business houses on the south side of the street." Strongly traditional in religion, they quickly organized three synagogues—B'nai Jacob in 1877, Beth Hamedrash Hagodol in 1887, and ANSHEI SFARD in 1893. Anshei Sfard still exists, but the others merged to form KENESETH ISRAEL. Immigration laws passed in 1924 put an end to the massive immigration.

The second wave of immigration from the Soviet Union occurred between 1977 and 1979. At this time about two hundred persons settled in Louisville under the auspices of the city's Jewish Federation. Soon, motivated by family connections and the promise of employment, one-half of the original number left to make their homes in other cities and communities in the United States.

Then in 1989, as democratic reforms were taking place in the Soviet Union, the third, more numerous wave of immigration began. This surge of new Americans continues, with more than nine hundred people having already settled in the Louisville area. Perhaps one of the most interesting aspects of this immigration is the sheer diversity of its cultural and ethnic makeup. Although most of the newcomers have come from Russia, Byelorussia, and Ukraine, a substantial number from the Soviet republics of Uzbekistan, Kazakhstan, Lithuania Moldova, and Georgia also have arrived. This rich tapestry of culture and nationality has created a kind of "diversity within diversity."

In addition to several hundred Jews from the Soviet Union, many Catholics have come from Ukraine. Both Jew and Catholic have tended to settle in the HIKES POINT and JEFFERSONTOWN areas.

Although never an official organization advocating Russian concerns, the JEWISH COMMUNITY CENTER (JCC) soon began sponsoring a wide variety of cultural activities and programs. It naturally became a place for education, recreation, and community and cultural exchange for the new Americans. The center provides a library of books, magazines, and NEWSPAPERS in Russian so that the new Americans can keep up with current affairs in the former Soviet Union and read the great classics in their mother tongue.

A separate department of acculturation for the Russian-speaking immigrants was established in 1992, supported in part by public and in part by philanthropic sources. Among many innovative programs, one of the most popular is the "I Love Louisville" program, which are tours given to newcomers to see Louisville's cultural and physical facilities. Other programs in demand by the immigrants are health and wellness activities, the Russian Club for seniors, tours to surrounding cities, and musical concerts featuring Russian entertainers.

In 1993 and 1994 the JCC sponsored the New American Festival. Organized like an old-fashioned country fair, the festival showcased the skills, talents, and culture of Louisville's Russian community. Expressive of the community's diversity, the festival displayed native woodcarving, batik, OIL PAINTINGS, watercolors, handmade stone SCULPTURES, doll collections, postage stamps, and countless objects from the old country.

Russian immigrants have already made their presence felt in Louisville: they have started prosperous businesses, served in various professions, provided skilled labor for the factories, and even offered their considerable linguistic skills to Louisville's International Culture Center and Sister City programs. Two local grocery stores, the International Star and the Golden Key, both owned by new Americans, carry a variety of Russian food and delicacies.

Herman Landau
Bronislava Nedelin

S

SACKETT, FREDERIC MOSELEY, JR. (b Providence, Rhode Island, December 17, 1868; d Baltimore, Maryland, May 18, 1941). Lawyer, United States senator, and diplomat. Frederic Moseley Sackett Jr. was the son of Frederic M. and Emma Louisa (Paine) Sackett. In 1890, he was awarded a baccalaureate degree from Brown University in Providence, R.I.; three years later he graduated from the law school of Harvard University. He worked as an attorney in Columbus (1893–97) and Cincinnati (1897–98) before moving to Louisville, where he established a lucrative practice.

In 1907 Sackett abandoned law to devote his full attention to business and civic interests. From 1907 to 1912, he served as president of the Louisville Gas Co. and the Louisville Lighting Co. He also held directorships in a number of coal and cement enterprises. In 1917 he began a seven-year term as a director of the Louisville branch of the FEDERAL RESERVE BANK OF ST. LOUIS. That same year he was elected president of the Louisville Board of Trade, a position he would again hold in 1922 and 1923. During WORLD WAR I, President Woodrow Wilson appointed Sackett, a Republican, to serve as federal food administrator for Kentucky, in charge of distributing and rationing food throughout the state. Sackett earned widespread recognition for his management of the two-year program, which brought him into frequent contact with Herbert Hoover, who directed the federal conservation effort.

In 1924 state Republican leaders persuaded Sackett to seek his first elected office. Benefiting from the presidential coattails of Calvin Coolidge at the top of the ticket, Sackett defeated the incumbent United States senator, Augustus Owsley Stanley, a former governor and a leader in the DEMOCRATIC PARTY for more than two decades. Sackett's 11,702-vote majority in Jefferson County proved insurmountable, and he captured 51.6 percent of the vote statewide. Sackett took office on March 4, 1925, and although a junior senator, he was given positions of confidence and trust in that body. He devoted particular attention to his work on the Senate Finance Committee and was an ardent proponent of American membership in the Court of International Justice (or World Court). His staunch support of President Coolidge and close friendship with Herbert Hoover, now secretary of commerce, proved invaluable.

In October 1929, Sackett declared his intention to seek a second term. Many state GOP leaders, however, openly questioned whether Sackett—a wealthy Louisvillian with an Ivy League education—would be the strongest Republican candidate in a traditionally Democratic state. The new president, Herbert Hoover, shared their concern. Torn between his friendship with Sackett and his determination to preserve a narrow Republican majority in the Senate, Hoover decided in December to resolve the situation by nominating the Kentuckian to be ambassador to Germany. Sackett, who had had no inkling of the appointment, was delighted. On January 9, 1930, he resigned from the Senate, which had promptly confirmed his nomination.

As ambassador, Sackett worked to bolster the stability of the fledgling Weimar Republic. He considered his principal contribution in Berlin to have occurred during the financial crisis of 1931, when he and President Hoover persuaded the wartime allies to accept a one-year moratorium on the payment of war debts and reparations. In the midst of a worldwide depression, Sackett early on warned the United States secretary of state, Henry Stimson, that the Nazi Party of Adolf Hitler posed a greater threat to the survival of democracy in Germany than did the Communists.

With the election of Franklin D. Roosevelt, a Democrat, to the presidency, Sackett's diplomatic service came to an end. His resignation, tendered March 4, 1933, was accepted two weeks later. He and his wife, Olive (Speed) Sackett, whom he had married on April 12, 1898, returned to Louisville and their home, Edgecomb, near Cherokee Park. They had no children.

Sackett, described by Stimson as "one of the best of our ambassadors," maintained a keen interest in foreign affairs; he made at least one return visit to Germany. He suffered a heart attack and died unexpectedly in Baltimore, Maryland. He is buried in CAVE HILL CEMETERY.

See Bernard V. Burke, "Senator and Diplomat: The Public Career of Frederic M. Sackett," *Filson Club History Quarterly* 61 (April 1987): 185–216; *Courier-Journal*, May 19, 20, 1941; A.H. McDannald, ed., *The Americana Annual* (New York 1942); the Sackett papers, Filson Club Historical Society, Louisville.

Thomas H. Appleton Jr.

ST. AUGUSTINE CATHOLIC CHURCH. St. Augustine Roman Catholic Church, 1310 W BROADWAY in Louisville, was founded February 20, 1870. It is the sixth oldest African American Catholic church in the United States. Louisville's first African American Catholics migrated from Maryland in 1785 but not until 1868 did Bishop William McCloskey appoint Father John L. Spalding to organize an African American parish. St. Augustine was selected as the patron of the congregation. The first parishioners worshiped in the basement of the CATHEDRAL OF THE ASSUMPTION until the first church was built on Broadway between Fourteenth and Fifteenth Streets. On February 20, 1870, seventy-five members marched from the Cathedral's basement to the new site. The facilities included a school on the ground level, a church on the second floor, and a rectory next door. The school opened in 1871 and was operated by Sisters of Charity of Nazareth.

The growing congregation necessitated a new building. The second church building was blessed May 18, 1902, and the first church was remodeled and used for a parish hall. The third and present site of the church was blessed September 10, 1912.

A high school was established in 1921. In 1928, the high school was moved to Eighth and Cedar Streets and was operated by the Archdiocese of Louisville until 1958 under the name of CATHOLIC COLORED HIGH SCHOOL. The cornerstone for the new elementary school was laid in 1961 and was blessed in March 1962 by the Most Reverend Charles G. Maloney. In 1967, three parishes—St. Louis Bertrand, St. Philip Neri, and St. Augustine—consolidated into one school named Pope Paul VI Consolidated School. In 1969, the school merged with Pope John XXIII Consolidated School to become Popes Paul and John Consolidated Schools. It was closed in 1973. Renovation of the church began January 6, 1974, and was completed in early April. Murals and icons were designed by Houston and Kinshasha Conwill. Sculptor Ed Hamilton created a bronze crucifix.

St. Augustine was the first parish in the Archdiocese of Louisville to have the ordination of a deacon, Robert J. Mueller, in 1973. It had the first black permanent deacon, Robert Grundy, in 1977. Father Edward Branch, the first archdiocesan black priest, offered his first Mass at St. Augustine in 1974.

Angela Partee

ST. BONIFACE CATHOLIC CHURCH. Saint Boniface Roman Catholic Church, 531 E LIBERTY, was founded in 1838 as a parish for the rising numbers of German immigrants. By 1830 the German POPULATION of Louisville numbered nearly two thousand. Reverend John Martin Henni, founder of the first German Catholic Church in Cincinnati, had become an occasional visitor to Louisville, attending to the immigrants' spiritual needs in their own language.

The arrival of Reverend Joseph Stahlschmidt in Louisville in November 1836, specifically to pastor to the German community, made clear the need for a German Catholic Church. He soon set about raising the funds to construct a church in a section of town that was still pasture. The sixty-by-two-hundred-foot lot was purchased, and construction began in July 1837. Parish members paid monthly dues of twelve and one-half cents to the building fund, and work on the church became a focal point for the German community, with men volunteering their labor and women working to furnish the church.

Built in the Gothic style, the church was named after the patron saint of Germany. The dedication service was November 1, 1838, All Saints Day, but evidence points to the facility being used for worship even prior to its completion. Stahlschmidt was criticized for his floor plan of the church, but his design later proved visionary, as the church required expansion only twelve years later. In December 1838, less than two months after the church's dedication, Reverend Stahlschmidt disappeared while on a fund-raising mission (in the U.S. and Mexico), and was never seen again.

By 1848 the church had established the first German parochial school in the city and had purchased the adjoining lot for a parsonage. In 1849 the parish was taken over by the Franciscans, and in 1850 the church was expanded. Later that year an orphanage was constructed to fill the needs of the community recently hit with a cholera epidemic. In 1851 the church became the center of a controversy when members of the St. Boniface Benevolent Society purchased a piece of property on S Preston at Rawlings St. to use as a cemetery for Catholics unable to afford the six-dollar interment fee at the German Catholic Cemetery in PORTLAND.

Wishing to be independent of the church, the society refused to surrender the lot's deed to the church. As a result, the priests refused to consecrate the ground of St. Stephen's Cemetery, as it became known. The dispute culminated with a crowd of nearly six hundred gathering outside the church on September 12, 1851, demanding that the cemetery be recognized and consecrated. The Benevolent Society garnered the support of several trustees who were soon deposed by the church and quickly replaced. This only served to heighten tensions. The following Sunday the church became the scene of a scuffle during services. Eventually the society was officially banned and forbidden from holding any meetings on church property, although the cemetery was eventually recognized.

For the next fifty years the church continued to prosper and expand, adding a monastery and building a new church in 1899–1900. It was not until 1925 that all church prayers and records were finally in English. The friary was converted into low-income APARTMENTS in September 1991; the parish school was later converted to Liberty House, a shelter for homeless teens. The church continues to serve several hundred families, many of them descendants of the early German parishioners who founded the church. The Fransciscan fathers left St. Boniface Parish on June 17, 1998.

See Clyde Crews, *An American Holy Land: A History of the Archdiocese of Louisville* (Louisville 1987); Rev. John Wuest, O.F.M., ONE HUNDRED YEARS OF ST. BONIFACE PARISH (Louisville 1937).

ST. BRIGID CATHOLIC CHURCH. St. Brigid Church was established by Bishop William G. McCloskey in September 1873 along with two other new churches, Sacred Heart and St. Cecilia. The first site of the church was on Baxter Ave. between Rogers and Payne Streets with the first small frame building blessed and ready for use on October 19, 1873. In 1874 a school was started in the church building with two Sisters of Charity as teachers. The sanctuary was separated from the school by green curtains, with kneelers and pews serving as desks. In 1890 the spelling was changed from the Church of St. Bridget to the Church of St. Brigid by the Reverend Henry Connelly, who also moved the church to its present location at the corner of Baxter and Hepburn Avenues. Those parishioners who did not wish to move to the new site formed a new parish, St. Aloysius, that built a church on Payne St. The current church building was designed by CORNELIUS A. CURTIN and built in 1912–13 in the mid-nineteenth-century French Renaissance style.

Sister Mary Leander Eiting, who became the principal of St. Brigid School in 1909, led the establishment of the Parent Teacher Association in Louisville with the first meeting held at St. Brigid in October 1917. A new St. Brigid School was built in 1927–28 and blessed in February 1928. For many years St. Brigid School was the model school for young teachers studying at Nazareth College (now SPALDING UNIVERSITY). In the 1950s the number of families with children in the neighborhood declined, causing the school enrollment to drop. The school closed in 1973.

During the Great FLOOD OF 1937, victims were housed in the church and the school. Hot meals were served to these people and others who were being housed in the neighborhood. Food supplies were distributed from St. Brigid to as many as sixteen hundred people a day. The facility also provided space to a Red Cross clinic offering the services of two doctors, nurses, and a dentist as well as immunization against typhoid fever.

St. Brigid is one of the Catholic churches and institutions including a hospital, CEMETERIES, an orphanage, monasteries, and a college along a section of Barret and Baxter Avenues and Newburg Rd. that over the years has been dubbed the Catholic Mile.

Clyde F. Crews, *An American Holy Land: A History of the Archdiocese of Louisville* (Louisville 1987); Sister Marita Riede, S.C.N.-M.A., *A History of St. Brigid Church from 1873 to 1998* (Louisville 1998).

ST. JAMES/BELGRAVIA COURTS. St. James/Belgravia Courts, a residential area bounded on the east and west by Fourth and Sixth and by Magnolia and Hill Streets to the north and south, was the neighborhood of choice for many of the city's literary and political elite. At one time a truck-farming area and by 1875 the location of a BASEBALL park, the ten-acre area was once owned by the Louisville branch of the du Pont family and provided the site for the SOUTHERN EXPOSITION, Louisville's little world's fair. This New South Exposition, which was the idea of Louisville's local Board of Trade and was promoted by HENRY WATTERSON, editor of the COURIER-JOURNAL, was opened and dedicated by President Chester A. Arthur on August 1, 1883. After the closing of the exposition in 1887, the Victoria Land Co., led by William Slaughter, purchased the land and—inspired by residential parks in London, England—developed the tract into "a quiet, secluded, tree-lined, fashionable community" (Ward, A Literary History of Kentucky, 141).

In 1890 Slaughter designed the court to include the central esplanade and installed a cast-iron fountain, reminiscent of the finest residential areas of England. In addition two stone lions were placed at each of the entrances creating one of the city's most fashionable areas of the period. Slaughter had S.J. Hobbs draw a map of sixty-three lots to sell in the court, with lot prices ranging from $450 to $4,173, depending on size and location. Slaughter originally purchased seven lots but continued to acquire as many as he could.

Victoria Place, later renamed Magnolia, bounded the northern entrance of St. James Court, and after 1904 Central Park to the north of Magnolia provided a quiet, restful buffer from the burgeoning city. The southern border, laid out in 1892 as Belgravia Ave. (later Ct.), stretched from Fourth St. to Sixth St. While St. James Ct. was open to traffic, Belgravia Ct. was designed mainly as a pedestrian-only court and served as a prototype for others within the city.

Attracting poets, writers, artists, and politicians, the neighborhood was home at one time to medical education reformer ABRAHAM FLEXNER and his dramatist wife, Anne Crawford Flexner; Alice Hegan Rice, the author of Mrs. Wiggs of the CABBAGE PATCH, and her poet husband, CALE YOUNG RICE; and poet MADISON CAWEIN. Others living in the courts were writers Letitia and Wallace Irvin, Charles Neville Buck, Abbie Carter Goodloe, Elizabeth Robbins, Fannie Macauley, ELEANOR MERCEIN KELLY, Elizabeth Maddox Roberts, and geographer Virginia Cary Hudson. Artists Nelle Peterson, Lennox Allen, Helen Patterson, MARY ALICE HADLEY, and Sarah Lansdell made St. James Ct. their home. The courts also served as the residence for Louisville mayors George D. Todd, CHARLES F. GRAINGER, William B. Harrison, and BRUCE HOBLITZELL. Such an array of talent living in one area prompted W.F. Axton to exclaim that "nothing like it has ever been seen before or since in the history of the Commonwealth" (Axton, "Foreword," in Rice, *Mrs. Wiggs of the Cabbage Patch*, ix). The area is the site of the annual St. James Court Art Show held in early October.

See Marguerite Gifford, St. *James Court in*

Retrospect (Louisville 1966); Melville O. Briney, *Fond Recollection: Sketches of Old Louisville* (Louisville 1955); George H. Yater, *Two Hundred Years at the Falls of the Ohio* (Louisville 1979); *Courier-Journal Magazine*, March 28, 1948; William S. Ward, *A Literary History of Kentucky* (Knoxville, Tenn., 1988); James C. Klotter, *Kentucky: Portrait in Paradox, 1900–1950* (Frankfort 1996).

James Duane Bolin

ST. JAMES COURT ART SHOW. An annual event held in October in the heart of the OLD LOUISVILLE neighborhood. The show began in 1957 as the St. James Court Clothesline Art Show in which local artists hung their work on clotheslines that had been strung from trees. At first sponsored by the St. James Court neighborhood association, it was originally a one-day fund-raiser for neighborhood improvements and renovations. Now the three-day event is one of the country's largest outdoor art fairs, which by the mid-1990s was annually drawing approximately 300,000 visitors to view the works of more than 650 artists from across North and South America.

The show takes place south of Central Park along St. James Ct., Belgravia Ct., Magnolia Ave., and Third and Fourth Sts. The art that is displayed and sold covers a wide range of mediums, including SCULPTURE, PAINTING, pottery, PHOTOGRAPHY, various crafts, and more. Profits from the event go toward art scholarships, community charities, and the continued maintenance of the neighborhood.

As of 1994, a full-time art show director was hired, and a coordinating body for the art show, known as the consortium, was created in an effort to more effectively produce the event. The consortium consists of representatives from the St. James Court Association, Belgravia Court Association, South FOURTH Street Association, Third Street Neighborhood Association, 1300 South Third Street Association, and the West End Baptist Church.

ST. JOHN'S EVANGELICAL CHURCH (UNITED CHURCH OF CHRIST). St. John's Evangelical Church was founded in 1843 by a group of German Protestants who had been meeting irregularly in private homes since 1836. It is the second-oldest church of its denomination in Louisville (St. Paul's preceded it).

The congregation first used the name United German Lutheran Church to reflect the traditions of its members rather than a denomination affiliation when it purchased an old church building near the corner of Fifth and Walnut (Muhammad Ali Blvd.) Streets. Although not associated with the Evangelical Lutheran Synod, it was listed as the Second Lutheran Church for a few years in Louisville directories. In 1848 the congregation moved to the east side of Hancock St. between MARKET and Jefferson, a location closer to the homes of its members. In 1861 land was purchased at the southwest corner of Clay and Market Streets. By 1867 the present Gothic-style building, enhanced with thirteen stained glass windows, had been built there. Later a parsonage (1883) and parish hall (1869 and rebuilt 1906) were added. St. John's sponsored a parochial school for German students that continued for almost forty years between 1849 and 1881.

Scholars believe the first pastor of the fledgling congregation was Josef Anton Fischer, a former priest who renounced Catholicism and became a vigorous advocate of Protestantism while still in Germany. Although his time at St. John's was short, he joined with pastors of four other German churches in southern Ohio and one from NEW ALBANY, Indiana, to form the German United Evangelical Synod of North America, which grew and merged over the years to create the German Evangelical Synod of North America. After subsequent mergers, the denomination in 1957 became the United CHURCH OF CHRIST.

German remained the official language until 1893, when services in English were gradually introduced. This act caused some of the congregation's members to split and form a church that retained the use of German, among them Immanuel United Church of Christ, founded in 1898.

The church houses the archives of the German Heritage Society. Official church records containing baptismal, confirmation, marriage, and death entries date from 1848 and provide some of the best documentation for the early German community in Louisville.

See St. John's Evangelical Church anniversary booklets for the years 1903, 1943, 1973, and 1993; Theodore S. Schlundt Memorial Archives of St. John's Evangelical Church; Anita Boss Weisert and Carl E. Kramer, ed., "German Protestants on the Urban Frontier: The Early History of Louisville's St. John's Evangelical Church," *Filson Club History Quarterly* 72 (Oct. 1998): 379–418.

LaVern S. Rupp

ST. JOSEPH CHILDREN'S HOME. The St. Joseph Catholic Orphans Society was founded on August 5, 1849. A group of men from two German Catholic parishes, St. Boniface and St. Mary's, met to establish a home for the many German Catholic children orphaned by the cholera epidemic of 1849. The Reverend Karl Boeswald was joined by Jacob Pfalzer, Joseph Buckel, Anton Geher, Johann Schulten, and Marin Seng to compose a constitution and by-laws for the new society. Members of the society paid an initiation fee of one dollar, plus twenty-five cents monthly.

The first home was built in 1850 near St. Mary's Church on Eighth St. and Grayson (Cedar). During this time many German immigrants came to Louisville. With many parents not living to see their children grown, the orphan POPULATION increased. In 1854 the society purchased the spacious Jason Rogers home at Jackson St. and Fehr Ave. (LIBERTY). This location was near ST. BONIFACE CHURCH and School, permitting the children to attend the parish school. By 1875 more than one hundred children lived in the home, making expansion necessary. An advertisement in the Record, the diocesan newspaper, read: "Land wanted: St. Joseph Society wishes to purchase a tract of land not to exceed forty acres, near Louisville. The land must be in a high location and in a healthy neighborhood." On July 23, 1883, the society purchased JAMES HARRISON's twenty-two-acre homestead adjoining the old Fair Grounds site

Thanksgiving dinner at St. Joseph Catholic Orphans Home in 1940.

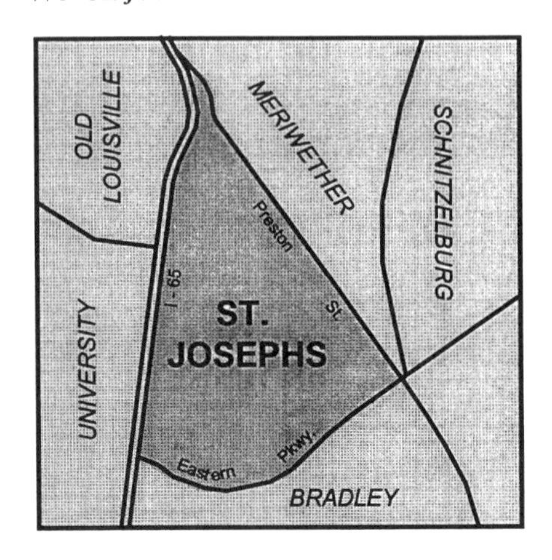

at 2823 Frankfort Ave. The children moved into the new facility on September 16, 1886.

Until the end of World War II the society cared primarily for German Catholic orphan children. At that time most parents lived to see their children grown, but children whose parents deserted or abused them needed care, and the society provided it. Responding to this need, the society developed a special staff to care for children who had suffered sexual and emotional abuse and neglect. A sense of stability and permanency is the goal for the residents who have often been in many foster homes before arriving at St. Joseph's. Children are reunited with their siblings under one roof, often for the first time. The home also offers a foster parent training program to ensure that those children who are placed in foster homes are well treated. The "friendly visitor" program is one of the home's most popular among the children. It provides caring adults who take children for occasional outings and weekend visits. Where dormitories with rows of iron beds once characterized the facility, it is now a series of apartments with kitchens and semi-private bedrooms. In 1999 the home marked its 150th anniversary with a rededication of the Chapel of the Holy Family at the home.

The Ursuline Sisters of the Immaculate Conception staffed the home as teachers and child-care workers until 1972. In 1851 a fair was organized to meet the payments on the society's first home. This annual picnic continues to be a major fund-raiser as well as a community social event.

See Samuel W. Thomas, *Crescent Hill Revisited* (Louisville 1987); Courier-Journal, Feb. 6, 1999.

Herman J. Naber

ST. JOSEPHS. Triangular neighborhood south of downtown Louisville bounded by Preston St. to the east, Eastern Pkwy. to the south, and Interstate 65 to the west. It is one of the three neighborhoods, including Bradley and Meriwether, known as "Greater Schnitzelburg." The area received its name from St. Joseph's Infirmary, which stood at the corner of Preston St. and Eastern Pkwy. Formerly known as St. Vincent's Infirmary and Orphanage, the facility was established by the Sisters of Charity of Nazareth in 1836 at Jefferson St. The facility was moved to Fourth St. in 1852, and its name was changed.

St. Joseph's relocated to the Eastern Pkwy. site in 1926. The hospital was purchased by Humana Inc. in 1970 and ten years later razed. The neighborhood had been developed before the arrival of the hospital and contained a number of German residents. St. Stephen's Cemetery, which was established in 1851, is a landmark in the northern point of the neighborhood.

See Louisville Survey: Central and South Report (Louisville 1978).

ST. LOUIS BERTRAND CATHOLIC CHURCH. St. Louis Bertrand Roman Catholic Church, at Sixth and St. Catherine Streets in the Limerick neighborhood of Louisville, is an example of Gothic Revival architecture. The parish was established in 1866 by the Dominican Order of St. Joseph Province for the growing Irish population. After outgrowing a smaller building on Seventh St., the current church was dedicated in 1873, with seating for one thousand. The exterior is constructed of quarry stone from Oldham County, Kentucky, trimmed with White River limestone from Bowling Green.

The interior has a clerestoried, 125-by-40-foot nave 60 feet in height. The sanctuary features a five-sided apsis. The church's white oak altars, carved by artists in Oberammergau, Germany, were installed in 1947. The main altar reflects the heritage of the Dominican order, with figures of Dominican saints carved into the baldachin. The stations of the cross are also made of hand-carved wood. As a sign of the Dominicans' devotion to the Virgin Mary, the church's stained-glass windows depict each of the fifteen mysteries of the rosary. The church also houses perhaps the oldest grotto shrine (completed in 1887) to Our Lady of Lourdes in the United States.

The church organ is a twenty-two-rank instrument originally constructed by the Hilbourne L. Roosevelt Pipe Organ Co. in 1883 and restored three times since. To reflect the neighborhood's Irish heritage, a mosaic of Our Lady of Limerick was installed above the main entry on the exterior of the church in 1988. The parish operated a parochial school from 1891 to 1971. In recent years the school building has housed an independent Catholic Montessori school.

See Henry C. Mayer, *One Hundred Twenty Five Years of St. Louis Bertrand Parish Louisville, Kentucky 1866–1991* (Louisville 1991); Elva Anne Lyons, ed., *Local History Series: Catholic Schools and Churches*, vol. 27 (Louisville 1940); St. Louis Bertrand Church, unpublished pamphlet, n.d., University Archives ephemera files, University of Louisville.

Mary Margaret Bell

ST. MARTIN OF TOURS CATHOLIC CHURCH. The cornerstone of St. Martin of Tours, Louisville's fourth Catholic church, was laid on October 20, 1853, and the church dedicated on August 20, 1854. It was named for the fourth-century bishop of Tours, France, who was also the patron saint of Martin John Spalding, the bishop of Louisville at the time of the founding of St. Martin's at Shelby and Gray Streets.

Built to accommodate the overflow of German Catholics from St. Boniface, the city's first German Catholic church, St. Martin's rapidly outgrew its original seventy-five-by-fifty-foot brick building. In 1860 parishioners expanded the church to its present cross-shaped size. Measuring 1,851 feet in length, 531 feet wide in the body of the church and 831 feet wide at the transept, it is one of the largest churches in the city.

The church's first five pastors were German-born, and German was the language of sermons, confessions, and newsletters. On the hot summer night of August 6, 1855, a Know-Nothing mob threatened to sack and burn the church during the Bloody Monday election day riots. The nativist Americans accused the Germans of hiding arms in the church. A search by Know-Nothing mayor John Barbee proved there were no weapons on the premises. His pleas prevented the destruction of the building.

Nativism continued to dog the parish, and the German tradition ceased because of strong anti-German sentiment during World War I. Native Louisvillian Reverend Leo Dreckmann became the parish's first American-born pastor in 1939.

The church's notable stained-glass windows were designed and created at the Royal Bavarian Art Glass Institute of Munich, Germany, and installed between 1893 and 1895. A stained glass window in the St. Gregory Chapel and another in the Chapel of Divine Mercy (formerly the St. Cecilia Chapel) were acquired from a seventeenth-century European monastery. The marble Stations of the Cross were fashioned at the Art Shop of Mayer and Co. in Munich and installed in 1895. The church is also home to a century-old pipe organ, some parts of which were installed as early as 1876.

In 1901 the church became the resting place of the remains of two saints, St. Magnus, a Roman centurion, and a Roman virgin, St. Bonosa, who were martyred in the third century. Their full skeletal remains are encased in glass reliquaries at the front of the sanctuary on either side of the main altar.

At the request of St. Martin's first pastor, Reverend Leander Streber, three Ursuline Sisters arrived in Louisville on October 31, 1858, to begin the church's first coeducational school. Later there were separate schools for boys and girls. The last boys' school was located in what is now the rectory, and in 1896 the parish built a three-story brick girl's school on Gray St. across from the church. The schools were combined

St. Martin of Tours, 637 South Shelby Street as photographed by Edward Klauber.

in this building about 1917.

The zenith of St. Martin's occurred in the early twentieth century when the congregation numbered approximately nine hundred families. A change in neighborhood demographics caused a steady decline in membership. The school closed in 1968. By 1978 the church also faced closure. However, under the direction of Reverand Vernon Robertson, who came to St. Martin in 1978 with a strong commitment to those in urban areas, the parish underwent revitalization and regrowth. After years of disrepair, the church building was restored to its former beauty. By the time Robertson retired in 1993, the parish had established a neighborhood outreach program and a restaurant, which Robertson dubbed the Afro-German Tearoom, to reflect the change in the neighborhood's ethnic makeup. Robertson died in 1998 at the age of seventy-five. By 1997 St. Martin's was home to approximately five hundred families.

See *Centenary of the Church of St. Martin of Tours 1853–1953* (Louisville 1953); Deborah Yetter, *The Renaissance of the Church of St. Martin of Tours* (Shepherdsville 1992).

ST. MATTHEWS. Large, irregularly shaped, fourth-class city approximately five miles east of downtown, centered at the intersection of Breckenridge Ln., Chenoweth Ln., Westport Rd., Lexington Rd., and Shelbyville Rd., with the latter bisecting the community. Col. John Floyd established the area's first station in 1779, though he was greeted by eleven squatters when he arrived on his property. Located along the middle fork of Beargrass Creek near the modern-day Jamestown Apartments on Breckenridge Ln., Floyd's Station was constructed as protection from periodic Indian attacks. As the danger subsided near the end of the century, other settlers from Virginia, Pennsylvania, and Maryland descended on the fertile grounds.

Transportation routes, like the Louisville and Lexington Turnpike, Frankfort Ave., and Shelbyville Rd., developed as stagecoach paths connecting the growing downtown area with Lexington and Frankfort. By the time the Louisville and Frankfort Railroad Co. laid tracks through the area in 1849, the region had already become known as Gilman's Point, named after tavern and general store owner Daniel Gilman, and was developing a small business district. When it came time to officially name the area's first post office in 1851, several image-conscious residents decided that a town should not be named after a tavern. It was decided to name the community St. Matthews after the Episcopal church established in 1839 on Westport Rd. near modern-day St. Matthews Ave. The church merged with St. Marks in Crescent Hill in 1910, but a new church named St. Matthews Episcopal was founded in 1948 at the intersection of Hubbards Ln. and Massie Ave.

Although the region continued to attract residents through the last half of the nineteenth century, a majority were farmers. It was not until 1893 that St. Matthews witnessed its first residential development, with the platting of a subdivision off Cannons Ln. and Grandview Ave. In 1901 the interurban was laid to connect St.Matthews and Louisville. By 1906 St. Matthews was prosperous enough to warrant a small bank, appropriately named the Bank of St. Matthews. The interurban and low property taxes helped St. Matthews become known as a growing point between Louisville and Middletown, but at the same time it also gained a reputation as a major center for cockfighting and sported several establishments that housed the contests.

However, the area and its loamy soil gained its greatest renown in the first half of the twentieth century as St. Matthews claimed to be the potato capital of the world. With the establishment of R.W. Hite's St. Matthews Potato Exchange, positioned beside the rail lines near present Clover Ln., the region exported 13 million pounds of potatoes in 1913, making it the second-largest shipper in the country. Many of the large potato-farming families are still remembered in street names such as Monahan, Brown, and Rudy. In the face of rising competition, lowered prices, and hungry land developers, the exchange closed in 1946.

By this time St. Matthews had attracted many new residents, especially during the 1920s, who could shop in the stores along nearby Lexington Rd. An even larger influx followed the 1937 flood, as many families from Louisville's West End preferred to rebuild on St. Matthews's higher ground. As more families moved to the area, the growing population of school children made new and larger facilities on Grandview Ave. essential for Greathouse, the much-loved local elementary school. After World War II, as returning soldiers sought housing, it was estimated that the community contained approximately ten thousand people. While thought to be the largest unincorporated area in the nation, St. Matthews's growth prompted the city of Louisville to institute annexation proceedings in 1946.

After a bitter twelve-year battle, Louisville was able to acquire only the business district center along Lexington and Shelbyville Roads and Frankfort Ave. These annexation attempts prompted St. Matthews to incorporate as a sixth-class city in 1950, with a leap to fourth-class city four years later, and encouraged three other neighborhoods—Springlee, Bellewood, and Norbourne Estates—to incorporate as well. By 1998 twelve sixth-class cities dotted the St. Matthews community. The population of St. Matthews was 15, 691 in 1990, and 16,562 in 1996.

In the three decades between 1940 and 1970, a large business district developed to serve the expanding area suburbs. Along Shelbyville Rd., Lexington Rd. and Frankfort Ave. the casual observer of that time could see Bacon's,

St. Matthews Potato Festival parade, July 1948. University of Louisville Photographic Archives: Lin Caufield Collection.

Kentucky's first suburban department store; Byck's and Maxwell's clothing stores; DOLFINGER'S jewelry store; the Vogue Theatre; Woolworth's five and dime; Chism's Hardware; a Sears department store; an A&P grocery store; Thornbury's toy store; and, farther east on Shelbyville Rd., the East Drive-In Theater.

Like its larger counterparts, the St. Matthews downtown area suffered from deurbanization. One by one the familiar retail establishments have closed and relocated farther east or disappeared, so the downtown is less oriented toward shopping. In 1999 Bacon's home store, once the anchor of the business district, was moved to the Mall St. Matthews after being bought and closed by Dillard's Inc. Gradually new businesses such as the Bluegrass Brewing Co., Rainbow Blossom Natural Foods, Indigo Restaurant, and Paul's Fruit Market have opened.

Area landmarks east of the central area include Trinity High School, Waggener High School, J. Graham Brown Memorial Park, Baptist Hospital East, Norton Suburban Hospital, the Shelbyville Road Plaza (one of the area's first shopping malls), and The Mall St. Matthews and OXMOOR Mall.

See *History of the Ohio Falls Cities and their Counties* (Cleveland 1882); Louisville Survey: East Report (Louisville 1980); *A Place in Time: The Story of Louisville's Neighborhoods* (Louisville 1989); *Courier-Journal,* May 12, 1999; Elva Anne Lyon, ed., *University of Louisville Local History Series,* vol. 15 (Louisville, 1937–42); Samuel W. Thomas, *St. Matthews: The Crossroads of Beargrass* (Louisville 1999).

ST. MICHAEL THE ARCHANGEL EASTERN ORTHODOX CHURCH.

LEBANESE and SYRIAN families came to the new world with hopes and dreams of a better life. The Orthodox faith was a bond to just fifty families in the first few years of the twentieth century. They gathered in area churches and at the NEIGHBORHOOD HOUSE, a settlement house on First St. As their bond strengthened, they wanted their own spiritual home.

The women organized first. They held Bible studies under the leadership of Jaleelah Aboud. Visiting priests to Louisville would hold services in families' homes, where small chapels were formed. But it was not enough. A church in which to raise their families in the Orthodox faith was desperately needed, and this would take funds.

Thus, the women began to meet this need with the tradition of the family dinner. With the permission for use of the Neighborhood House and generous donations from area businesses, they served their first meal and raised five hundred dollars. Together, they used these funds to help in the purchase of a building at 432 E Jefferson St. It was across the street from Louisville's famous HAYMARKET where many Syrian and Lebanese families had opened businesses. Originally the temple of the B'nai Jacob Jewish congregation, the building was dedicated to the protection of Archangel Michael in November 1934.

During the early years of the growing parish, the services of the church were conducted in classical Arabic by such clergy as the Reverend Fathers Thomas Abodeely, Gerasimos Yerrid, George Trad, Michael Deeba, John Hakim, Anthanasious Rihbany, Elias Hajj, Basilios Saffi, Nicholas Husson, Basil Kazan, Elia Abi Karem, and Alexander Atty.

Realizing the needs of youth, a group of theologians was commissioned to translate the Divine Services of the Church into English. With the presence of an English-speaking priest, Rev. Fr. Gregory Reynolds, youngsters began to learn and live their Orthodox faith.

Early in 1962 the parish both recognized the need to expand and experienced the loss of the church on E Jefferson St., demolished to make way for the construction of Interstate 65. Rt. Rev. Michael Howard and the parish council began negotiations for a nine-and-one-quarter acre tract that included two homes. In 1963, under the pastorate of Rev. Fr. George S. Corey and the council leadership of Tommy Thomas, the property at 3024–28 Hikes Ln. was purchased for eighty-five thousand dollars, and the first phase of expansion ended.

The educational building was completed and officially blessed in November 1965. St. Michael Church, which is the only Byzantine structure in the commonwealth of Kentucky, was consecrated on October 8, 1972. The church, designed by local architects H. Carleton Godsey Associates, boasts a gold-plated chandelier made in Greece with over 265 lights, patterned after the chandeliers that hung in the early Orthodox churches in Constantinople. The iconostasis, or icon screen, which separates the inner sanctuary from the main church, includes icons of Christ, the Blessed Mother, and the saints, and is carved with grape leaves, peacocks, and the double-headed eagle, symbolizing the hierarchy of the church. In 1996 St. Michael played host to the *J.B. Speed Art Museum* series on church *architecture*, the first church in the area to hold such an event. St. Michael completely frescoed the interior of the church with Byzantine icons.

Following St. Paul's example that "faith without works is dead," the parishioners of St. Michael feel an obligation to assist the poor. Activities for that purpose include local soup kitchens, Neighborhood House, the Morgan Center, and the Healing Place. Community outreach is done with an Ethnic Fair, held the weekend after Labor Day since the mid-1980s.

In the 1990s the parish has doubled in size, encompassing traditional Orthodox Christians in the community as well as bringing converts from other faiths. Since the fall of communism, the parish has been an outreach to traditional Orthodox Christians from Serbia, Russia, Ukraine, Romania, and Bulgaria, as well as Ethiopian Orthodox who have made Louisville their home. The Epistle and Gospel readings are printed in Russian each Sunday for those parishioners who still have difficulty reading English. A chapel, patterned after St. George Chapel in a monastery on Greece's Mount Athos peninsula, was opened in 1998. It is available for twenty-four-hour worship to members who come from throughout the metropolitan area.

Alexander Atty

ST. PAUL'S EPISCOPAL CHURCH.

Founded in 1834, St. Paul's Episcopal Church is the second-oldest Episcopal church in Louisville, predated only by CHRIST CHURCH CATHEDRAL. Sensing the need to establish a second congregation in Louisville, local Episcopal leaders first organized St. Paul's at a meeting at the LOUISVILLE HOTEL on MAIN St. in 1834. Construction of their first facility, a Gothic structure on Sixth St. between Green (LIBERTY) and Walnut (Muhammad Ali Blvd.), began in 1837 and was completed in 1839. The architect was JOHN STIREWALT. (Two other Episcopal churches named St. Paul's were also established in the metropolitan area about that same time: St. Paul's Episcopal Church in NEW ALBANY, Indiana, also in 1834, and another congregation by the same name in JEFFERSONVILLE, INDIANA, in 1836.)

During the 1870s the Home Mission Society at St. Paul's undertook a project to improve medical care in the city. A local widow made a large contribution to that fund, imposing only the stipulation that the resulting facility be named for her late husband, Rev. John N. Norton. In 1886 the John N. Norton Memorial Infirmary came into being, which would eventually become Norton Hospital.

In 1894, after the church building burned, the congregation moved to a new location on Fourth St. at Magnolia Ave. In 1937, the Diocese of Kentucky merged St. Paul's with two other local Episcopal congregations, Calvary and St. Andrew's, with the name Calvary St. Paul's Episcopal Church. However, the following year the merger was reversed, due largely to fears that the combined congregations would lose their identities. In 1955 the decision was made to sell the property on Fourth St. and move to Lowe Rd. near Taylorsville Rd.

Innovative approaches to ministry have characterized the life of the church during the 1990s. For instance, in 1992 St. Paul's cosponsored a joint worship service and discussion session with the largely African American West End Baptist Church in order to more closely unite Christian worship with the cause of social justice and interracial understanding.

See *Courier-Journal*, March 27, 1988; *Records of St. Paul's Episcopal Church, Louisville, Kentucky, 1834–1978*, University of Louisville Archives and Records Center.

Timothy L. Wood

ST. REGIS PARK. Fourth-class city in eastern Jefferson County with an irregular boundary consisting of Browns Ln., Lowe Rd.,

Brookhaven Ave., Parksdale Ave., and Interstate 64. Until the mid-twentieth century, it was an area of immense potato fields. Farmers hauled their crops to the potato market in ST. MATTHEWS. Following WORLD WAR II, suburban growth propelled people into Louisville's outlying lands along Taylorsville Rd. and Breckenridge Ln. In 1952 Robert Marshall, a developer from St. Matthews, laid out the community of St. Regis Park and named it after the elegant New York hotel. Within a year, the POPULATION had grown enough for St. Regis to be classified as a sixth-class city. Through annexations of nearby communities such as Ashfield Acres the primarily residential community was reclassified as a fifth-class city in 1964 and as a fourth-class city in 1974.

The population of the city in 1980 was 1,735, in 1990 it was 1,725, and in 1996 it was 1,649.

ST. THOMAS ORPHANAGE. St. Thomas Orphanage for boys was founded about 1858 in Nelson County, Kentucky, on the grounds of the ST. THOMAS SEMINARY. For about the first decade of its operation, the home was under the care of the Brothers of Christian Instruction of the Sacred Heart, who were then succeeded by the Sisters of Charity of Nazareth. In 1889 the orphanage buildings were ravaged by fire, resulting in the home's temporary relocation to the Preston Park Seminary grounds in Louisville and then to vacant buildings at St. Joseph's College in Bardstown, where it remained until late 1909. At that time the orphanage returned to the Preston Park property, operating there until 1938. On November 21, 1938, the children were moved to a new facility on Ward Ave. near ANCHORAGE. The home was closed in 1983.

See Ben J. Webb, *The Centenary of Catholicity in Kentucky* (Louisville 1884); Dixie Hibbs, *Nelson County Kentucky: A Pictorial History* (Norfolk, Va., 1989); Clyde F. Crews, An *American Holy Land: A History of the Archdiocese of Louisville* (Louisville 1987).

Herman J. Naber

ST. THOMAS SEMINARY. On September 24, 1952, the Catholic Archdiocese of Louisville opened St. Thomas Seminary at 7101 Brownsboro Rd. Under its supervision, the seminary was operated by priests from the Society of St. Sulpice, the Sulpicians, in Baltimore, Maryland. It consisted of a four-year high school and a two-year junior college that was intended to prepare young men from the Louisville area to serve as archdiocesan priests.

Named after the Old St. Thomas Seminary founded by the Sulpicians in 1811 in the Bardstown area, it was closed at the end of the school year in 1970 because of rising costs and declining enrollment. The highest enrollment at the seminary was in 1961, when it had 240 high-school students and fifty-two seminarians. At the time of its closing, St. Thomas had fifty-six high-school students and twenty-two seminarians. The property was put on the market in 1973 but did not sell until 1985 when it was purchased by Robert J. Thieneman, a real estate developer.

See Clyde F. Crews, *An American Holy Land: A History of the Archdiocese of Louisville* (Louisville 1987).

ST. VINCENT DE PAUL SOCIETY, LOUISVILLE BRANCH. The society was formed in 1833 in Paris by Sorbonne University students led by twenty-year-old Antoine Frederic Ozanam. Today the St. Vincent de Paul Society, named after the seventeenth-century founder of the Congregation of the Priests of the Missions and the Daughters of Charity, is an international organization composed primarily of Catholic laymen volunteers dedicated to serving the poor. The society gives aid and comfort to the poor and stresses the importance of showing respect to those less fortunate.

The first U.S. conference was organized in November 1845 in St. Louis. In Louisville the first conference took place on December 11, 1853, at the CATHEDRAL OF THE ASSUMPTION. Bishop John Spalding came in contact with the society during trips to Europe to recruit teachers for Kentucky's Catholic school system. Reverend John McGill, who established the Catholic Benevolent Society in Louisville in 1841 to work with the needy, was also instrumental in organizing the society. On October 26, 1856, a second conference was organized at St. John's, and a third at St. Patrick's on June 13, 1858. In 1856 the Council of Louisville was established to coordinate and support conferences in the Louisville area.

By 1933 there were conferences in all but four of the parishes in Louisville. By 1945 there were forty conferences with approximately eleven hundred members in the Louisville archdiocese.

In 1983 the society took over the Holy Name Salvage Bureau thrift store. In the fall of 1983 the society inaugurated the Open Hand Kitchen in the basement of St. Paul's Church on S Jackson St. The kitchen, which serves more than one hundred thousand free meals annually to Louisville's homeless or hungry, was moved to the society's new community center in 1997. On February 7, 1983, the Council of Louisville formed the St. Vincent de Paul Center and formally incorporated.

In 1984 the society opened a men's shelter in the former St. Paul's elementary school building. In 1985 the society launched St. Jude House, a halfway house for recovering women alcoholics at Jackson and E St. Catherine Streets in SHELBY PARK. The facility was replaced in 1998 by a new eight-thousand-square-foot building for women recovering from alcohol and DRUG ABUSE. In 1992 Tranquil House opened to provide housing for men and women with mental illness. The growth in activities in the 1980s led to more sophisticated fund-raising efforts such as the Good Samaritan program. In the late 1990s the society had begun several other facilities for homeless individuals or recovering alcoholics.

See Michael P. Murphy, *The Frederic Ozanam Story* (n.p., 1976); *Courier-Journal,* Dec. 3, 1997, Aug. 5, 1998.

ST. VINCENT ORPHANAGE. At a meeting on August 10, 1832, Mother CATHERINE SPALDING, founder of the Sisters of Charity of Nazareth, established the Catholic Orphan Asylum known as St. Vincent to care for English-speaking girls. Originally located at 443 S Fifth St., the home moved to Wenzel and Jefferson Streets on October 6, 1836. From 1892 to 1901 the orphanage was located at what was known as the "Preston Park" property off Newburg Rd., the present site of BELLARMINE COLLEGE. In 1901 it moved to 2120 Payne St. The final move was made in 1955 when it moved to Ward Ave. near Anchorage. The home was closed in 1983.

See Clyde F. Crews, *An American Holy Land: A History of the Archdiocese of Louisville* (Louisville 1987).

Herman J. Naber

ST. XAVIER HIGH SCHOOL. St. Xavier High School was established in Louisville by the XAVERIAN BROTHERS for the moral, intellectual, and physical development of young men. It began in 1863 in a small building next to ST. BONIFACE CHURCH on E Green (LIBERTY) St. under the name St. Aloysius Select School. In 1864 the school moved to Fourth St. near BROADWAY, where it combined with the Cathedral Parish School under the new name of St. Xavier Institute. The students, ranging in age from six to eighteen years, were largely the children or grandchildren of IRISH and German immigrants. In 1872 the Kentucky legislature approved the school's program of studies and authorized the granting of diplomas. In 1890 the General Assembly conferred on the school a new charter, empowering it to confer college degrees and to be known as St. Xavier College. That same year the brothers bought the Newcomb estate at 118 W Broadway. The school moved there the next year, expanding the building in 1901.

After WORLD WAR I the school closed the college and elementary section to concentrate on a college preparatory program. By 1961 the enrollment and program needs led the school to relocate on a twenty-seven-acre campus on Poplar Level Rd. Over time, several buildings have been added.

Saint X (as it is known locally) participates in all the sports sponsored by the Kentucky High School Athletic Association. However, it is proud not only of numerous regional and state trophies but that it dared to break the color line in Kentucky when it competed in FOOTBALL in 1951 with Central High School, then a school for AFRICAN AMERICANS.

Throughout the school's history, adherence to Catholic beliefs and tradition has been en-

St. Xavier High School, south side of Broadway between First and Second Streets, 1921.

couraged through instruction, retreats, liturgies, and service programs.

See Brother Julian Ryan, C.F.X. *Men and Deeds* (New York 1950); Brother John Joseph, C.F.X. *Growing in Excellence: The Story, Spirit and Tradition of Xavier* (Louisville 1989).

Brother John Joseph Sterne

SALMAGUNDI CLUB. Known as "The Salmagundi," this all-male social and literary club was founded January 18, 1879, by what has been described as "some of the city's intellectual and business elite" at the home of Prof. Jason W. Chenault on Third St. in Louisville. In the year of Salmagundi's founding, Louisville's first TELEPHONE exchange was installed and, one year earlier, the first electric arclight was lighted. The city's POPULATION was about 120,000. Salmagundi was defined as a dish (or, later, as a conversation occasion) of pungent mixture and had been named earlier in the Salmagundi Papers, 1807–8, a joint venture of Washington Irving and J.K. Paulding.

The seventeen original members—"well-known gentlemen of the area"—included Gen. BASIL W. DUKE, JOHN MASON BROWN, William R. Belknap, and Richard Jouett Menifee, with such additions soon thereafter as Thomas Speed, HENRY WATTERSON, and Alex P. Humphrey. The total was limited to twenty-four. The first elected chairman was Abram D. Hunt.

The Salmagundi ventured into the public eye in 1887 when, joining with the Commercial Club, it sponsored studies leading to Louisville's first and now-famous system of PARKS and PARKWAYS. First, Capt. Thomas Speed, in a paper to the Salmagundi, proposed a park system for Louisville. It developed that another Salmagundian, ANDREW COWAN, had studied parks elsewhere, as well as locations for a park system around the growing city of Louisville. Cowan's subsequent formal Salmagundi paper, "which was ordered to be printed in the *COURIER-JOURNAL*," aroused wide interest.

The Salmagundi then joined the Commercial Club in sponsoring a Park Act, drafted by Salmagundian John Mason Brown. It was approved by the city, adopted by the General Assembly, signed by the governor, and approved by Louisville voters in a special election August 4, 1890. The new Park Board bought 1,079 acres around Louisville, then contracted with the noted firm of landscape architects, Frederick Law Olmsted and Co. of Brookline, Massachusetts, to produce plans for the new "necklace of parks" and parkways.

Almost a century later, when the now-famous Olmsted parks were being renovated following the 1974 tornado and with support of the new Olmsted Conservancy, the Salmagundi contributed $18,500 to the conservancy to pay for permanent historical markers throughout the parks.

A central feature of Salmagundi monthly dinner meetings at a member's home or club (except in summer) is a formal paper or commentary given by the host, followed by comments from each member. In earlier times, each member was required to give "a five-minute researched rebuttal, or be fined fifty cents." In those days, a menu of oysters as well as a meat dish was specified.

One early tradition has fallen by the wayside: that of automatically extending membership to the presidents of the UNIVERSITY OF LOUISVILLE and of the LOUISVILLE & NASHVILLE RAILROAD. Recent university presidents have gravitated to other venues, while the L&N disappeared into CSX Transportation.

One persisting aspect of the Salmagundi is family continuity: three generations of Kennedy Helms have been members; Henning Hilliard represents the third in family succession since the days of founder A.D. Hunt and his partner J.J.B. Hilliard. Alex P. Humphrey, descended from a founding member, was a member into the 1980s. Membership continues to include many long-term family connections.

Following WORLD WAR II, papers were often given on "My War"—including the experience of several members in invasion forces and/or as prisoners of war. A Salmagundi paper may become the private testing ground or launch pad for a new publication, business venture, or civic enterprise—and on occasion the speaker's authority gives his paper the ring of history-in-the-making.

See J. Stoddard Johnston, ed., *Memorial History of Louisville* (Chicago 1896.)

Grady Clay

SALT LICKS. Pioneer Kentucky abounded in areas where the ground was impregnated with salt water from underground springs. For the enormous herds of bison, elk, and deer that roamed North America—and before them the mammoth and mastodon—salt was a dietary necessity. They made great roads into these regions, licking deep trenches in the salt-impregnated clay. Thus the name "licks."

To the earliest trans-Appalachian settlers, salt was equally essential, both in their diet and as a preservative. Their chief food was meat, and without salt to preserve it they would have starved when game was scarce or Indians hostile. It was impossible to import enough salt from the seaboard, especially since the Revolution had cut off many of the older colonies' own sources.

Most of Kentucky's numerous SALT LICKS could supply a little salt for the pioneers' personal use, but a source of salt large enough to support commercial production became vital once large-scale settlement got under way. It was just south of Louisville that the settlers discovered an area that could produce large amounts of salt.

This area began a little north of FAIRDALE and ran southward along the eastern foot of the KNOBS, crossing Salt River and extending as far as Bardstown Junction in present-day BULLITT COUNTY. Nowhere else was there such a concentration of salt wells and furnaces. Centered on a half dozen major salt licks, Kentucky's first industry employed hundreds of men as woodchoppers and waggoners, kettle tenders and water drawers. It supported many more that worked as hunters, storekeepers, coopers, and carpenters. Merchants, traders, and individual settlers came from all over the wilderness to buy salt. At a time when money was virtually nonexistent in Kentucky, notes for salt circulated the way currency does today.

BULLITT'S LICK, on Salt River near the

present town of SHEPHERDSVILLE, was the site of Kentucky's first commercial saltworks, erected in 1779. Bullitt's Lick was named for THOMAS BULLITT, a Virginia surveyor who illegally led a party into Kentucky in 1773. It is unlikely that Bullitt was the original discoverer; salt licks were widely known to Indian and white hunters because of the game they attracted. But Bullitt was the first to survey it, and there located a thousand acres of land for Col. WILLIAM CHRISTIAN, a veteran of the French and Indian War. The next year, 1774, James Douglas resurveyed Christian's entry, and it was on his survey that Christian's patent was granted.

There is some evidence that salt was being made in small quantities at Bullitt's Lick by 1778. However, SQUIRE BOONE deposed later that he and two friends had killed a couple of buffalo at Bullitt's Lick in the spring of 1779. No large-scale saltworks could have been erected by then, for the big game was soon driven away when a lick was opened for salt-making. But in November of the same year, when Col. William Fleming journeyed from Harrodsburg to the Falls, he found a full-scale saltworks in operation at Bullitt's Lick. He wrote in his journal: "Nov. 3, 1779—Bullitt's Creek, as it is cald is perhaps the best Salt Springs in the country. . . . They have a trough that holds very near 1000 gals. which they empty thrice in the 24 hours. . . . They have 25 kettles belonging to the Commonwealth which they keep constantly boiling and filling them up as the water waistes. . . ." The saltworks must, therefore, have been erected sometime in the summer or fall of 1779.

Col.Christian, the owner of Bullitt's Lick, did not come to Kentucky until 1785 and was killed by Indians the following year. He left "Saltsburg," as Bullitt's Lick had come to be called, to his son, John Henry Christian. Moses Moore had been leasing the entire lick, subletting in turn to half a dozen men who operated furnaces independently. He continued this arrangement with Patrick Henry, young Christian's uncle and guardian, after his mother's death. John Henry Christian died young, and his five sisters inherited Bullitt's Lick. One sister had married ALEXANDER SCOTT BULLITT, and another married John Pope. In the end, WILLIAM POPE Jr., brother of John Pope, controlled three-fifths of Bullitt's Lick and the Bullitt family two-fifths.

Bullitt's Lick was at this time the only saltworks west of the Allegheny Mountains. But within a few years, other licks in the salt-rich area straddling Salt River began to be commercially exploited. On November 11, 1780, Charles Broughton entered a 250-acre warrant on Long Lick Creek, south of Salt River and just west of what is today Bardstown Junction. There, sometime before October 27, 1785 (when he had his entry surveyed), Broughton erected the area's second saltworks.

But many people had claimed land around the Long Lick. Shortly after Broughton erected his saltworks, HENRY CRIST and Solomon Spears acquired the claim of Parmenas Briscoe, a hunter at Brashear's Garrison. Whether Briscoe's claim was superior is still uncertain. But Crist and Spears took over Broughton's saltworks as early as 1787, and the next year a patent was issued on Briscoe's survey in their names.

However, Charles Broughton had made another entry nearby, covering what was known as the Dry Lick. He found excellent water there, sank a well about a mile from the Long Lick, and went back into business. He and his heirs continued to make salt there for many years.

MANN'S LICK was the next to be opened. Second only to Bullitt's Lick in importance, it lay to the north of Bullitt's Lick among the ponds and wetwoods near present-day Fairdale in Jefferson County. Mann's Lick was well known to the earliest settlers. In 1780 John Todd made an entry on a military warrant for two hundred acres, including Mann's Lick. JAMES SPEED entered six hundred acres adjoining Todd's entry the same year. But no settlement was attempted, and the land remained drowned in ponds and swamps until Joseph Brooks entered the scene in 1787.

Brooks, a Pennsylvanian who came to the Falls in the spring of 1780, worked in the saltworks at Bullitt's Lick from 1781 to 1784, and in 1785 opened a tavern on the road between the Falls and the saltworks. He saw the possibilities of Mann's Lick, and in the fall of 1787 approached John Todd's widow and rented the lick from her for six years. However, Mrs. Todd did not have an undisputed title. William Fleming owned a quarter interest, and James Speed claimed a quarter interest in addition to his own adjoining entry. In 1788 Speed rented his part of the lick to George Wilson, who put up a saltworks close to Brooks's furnaces.

Unlike Bullitt's Lick, Mann's Lick was fortified to some extent. In 1788 the danger from Indians was acute. Mann's Lick occupied an exposed situation, with the knobs on one hand and the swampy wetwoods on the other. In winter, wolves came right into the lick and pulled down stock. However, as time went on more wells were sunk, more furnaces built. Wilson bought out Fleming and became one of the proprietors. Brooks acquired part of the land outright. The Speeds, Charles Beeler, Col. James Francis Moore, and William Pope all operated saltworks at Mann's Lick or engaged in the salt trade there. In 1805 a traveler reported that fourteen furnaces were working at Mann's Lick, producing some two hundred bushels of salt a day.

The next lick of significance was not opened until 1798. That year Jonathan Irons, a saltmaker at Bullitt's Lick, found salt water on the south side of Salt River, just a few steps from a buffalo ford below the mouth of Bullitt's Lick Run. The last saltworks to be erected in this historic salt-making area came into being because of an effort (one of many) to corner the market in salt. In 1802 the Bullitts Lick–Mann's Lick Co. was formed to regulate the salt trade. Depositories were built at Shepherdsville and near South Park to store the salt. Independent operators were notified that their current leases would not be renewed. During most of 1802, Bullitt's Lick lay idle. It was the first time such a thing had happened since 1779, when Indians forced the salt-makers to abandon their works. The price of salt shot from a dollar to three dollars a bushel.

About half a mile above Shepherdsville, which had been established in 1793, was a pretty little lick on the north bank of Salt River. It was known variously as McGee's Lick or the Parakeet Lick, from the flocks of these colorful BIRDS that frequented the place. Here James Burks discovered salt water and secured a lease from the McGees.

James Burks formed a partnership with John Dunn, who had plenty of kettles, and in 1803 they began to make salt at the Parakeet Lick. The salt water was never too plentiful at Parakeet Lick nor of a very high grade. However, the machinations of the Bullitt's Lick–Mann's Lick Co. and the resulting scarcity of salt guaranteed the profitability of the new operation.

In the first years of the nineteenth century, Bullitt's Lick and the other saltworks near Louisville continued to flourish, but Kentucky's salt trade soon became a casualty of the steamboat. Salt finally could be imported more cheaply than it could be made by the crude processes in use at the licks. Richer sources of salt and better methods of extracting it were being discovered. In 1830 the fires were allowed to go out under the last kettle at Bullitt's Lick. Elsewhere in Kentucky salt production gradually dwindled. It disappeared entirely by the last quarter of the nineteenth century.

Ironically it was the latest and smallest of the saltworks near Louisville that achieved fame throughout Kentucky and the South. Salt-making at PARAKEET LICK was abandoned soon after Bullitt's Lick started up again. But Parakeet Lick became Paroquet Springs, a fashionable spa of the old South. One of its humble salt wells was the sulfur spring that drew thousands to seek the health-giving waters of Paroquet.

See Robert E. McDowell, "Bullitt's Lick, the Related Salt Works and Settlements," *Filson Club History Quarterly* 30 (July 1956): 241–70.

Audrea McDowell

SALT-MAKING. Due to its necessity for the preservation of food, early settlers erected several saltworks in the Jefferson County area following the establishment of BULLITT'S LICK in 1779.

The first salt wells were dug and shored with timber instead of stone. Later they were deepened by boring with an auger. Sometimes dikes were thrown up around them to keep out floodwater. The furnaces or pits were erected at some distance from the well, close to a good stand of timber, for it was not considered profitable to haul wood much beyond a mile.

If the furnace was close enough to the well, the water was brought to the pit by means of a covered wooden trough or flume. As wood grew scarce about the licks, the furnaces were moved farther and farther off. The water was conveyed to them through wooden pipes made from gum or sassafras logs. These wooden pipes were drilled out by hand, fitted together, and a wooden or iron sleeve fashioned around the joints. Then a trench was dug and the pipes were buried beneath the frost line. Some of these pipes went for miles. One string went from Bullitt's Lick all the way to SHEPHERDSVILLE, crossed Salt River and ended at the furnace a half mile south of the river. Another left Bullitt's Lick and followed the general course of the Pitt's Point road to a furnace located well within the present boundary of the FORT KNOX reservation.

The furnaces themselves were long trenches dug back along the top of a bank and walled with slate or brick about fifteen inches thick, laid with clay mortar. They were fired from the front, the flames and smoke being sucked along under the kettles and out through a stone chimney at the far end of the pit. The kettles held at least twenty-two gallons each and some were much larger. They sat on top of the trench in a row, with as many as fifty in the string. Generally they were protected from the elements by a shed roof supported on poles. It was common for two of the long, narrow furnace pits to be under one roof. A single furnace produced thirty-five or forty bushels of salt each day and consumed two or three cords of wood.

Commercial production of usable salt required three steps. The black, sulfur-laden water that emerged from the salt springs was put into iron kettles or "salt pans" (the latter holding as much as sixteen hundred gallons). As it boiled away, new water was constantly added—a kettle or pan boiled down twelve to fourteen times in twenty-four hours. After that, the brine, which by now had lost most of its blackness, was transferred to a "cooler"—a trough that acted as a settling tank—and left to stand until nearly cold.

The cool brine was then drawn off into another set of kettles or pans and boiled rapidly until it began to grain, i.e., form crystals. Blood, lime, tallow, cornmeal, or the white of an egg was often added to promote the crystallization and to obtain salt of good texture and color. When the salt began to grain, the fires were slackened to a "simmering boil." The salt was dipped out as it crystallized and put into baskets to drain. Historically such baskets were usually cone-shaped. According to Col. William Fleming, three thousand gallons of water boiled down in this way yielded from three to four and a half bushels of salt.

The drippings were caught in pans and returned to the "mother," as the water in the kettles was called. The kettles holding the mother were never allowed to boil dry. When the water got too low, water that had been previously boiled for twenty-four hours was added, and the boiling-down repeated. However, after a certain number of boilings the mother became so charged with impurities that it was necessary to throw it out and start the whole process again.

With the rise of the steamboat, salt could be imported more cheaply than it could be made by the crude processes in use at the licks. In addition, better sources and methods were being discovered, rendering the industry obsolete. Salt was produced for the last time in the area at Bullitt's Lick in 1830.

See Robert E. McDowell, "Bullitt's Lick, the Related Salt Works and Settlements," *Filson Club History Quarterly* 30 (July 1956): 241–70.

Audrea McDowell

SALT RIVER. The Salt River, in north central Kentucky, has a drainage area of more than 2,920 square miles and forms the fifth-largest watershed in the state. The river starts about three miles east-southeast of Danville in Boyle County, flows about fifty miles north toward Lawrenceburg, then turns west toward SHEPHERDSVILLE and flows for about ninety miles to the point where it empties into the OHIO RIVER one mile north of West Point. The river is about twenty-four feet wide at its mouth and flows through Boyle, Mercer, Anderson, Spencer, Hardin, and Bullitt Counties. Its tributaries include the Rolling and Beech Forks and Clear, Guist, Plum, Cox, and Brashears Creeks.

The Salt River flows through some of the most fertile agricultural land in the state: the Inner Bluegrass physiographic region, the Eden Shale Belt in SPENCER COUNTY, and the KNOBS region in BULLITT COUNTY. It is one of the finest wade-fishing and rock bass streams in the state. Cities along the river include Shepherdsville, Bondville, West Point, TAYLORSVILLE, Glensboro, and Vanarsdell.

The river takes its name from the salt-producing operations begun by HENRY CRIST in 1779 near BULLITT'S LICK and present-day Shepherdsville. Salt-making expanded to a major business in the early nineteenth century. In a typical salt pan operation, four hundred gallons of water were evaporated, leaving fifty pounds of salt. The water was drawn from wells sunk about thirty feet deep.

In 1808 Quarry and Tyler established a water mill on the Salt River in Bullitt County to power an iron plant. They built a dam of hewn timber across the river, fastened to the bedrock of the stream by iron bolts. Surveys in 1837 and 1873 to determine whether the river could be improved for navigation by building locks and dams yielded unfavorable reports. The river was prone to flooding, and the problem continued even after a dam was constructed near Taylorsville in 1983, forming Taylorsville Lake in Spencer County, approximately sixty miles above the confluence of the Salt and Ohio Rivers.

In 1832, when Henry Clay was campaigning for the presidency against Andrew Jackson, he boarded a riverboat on Salt River at Pitts Point in Bullitt County for a campaign speech in Louisville. A Jackson supporter is said to have bribed the boat's captain to take Clay up Salt River instead of downriver to the Ohio and on to Louisville. Clay missed the speaking date and lost the national election. While much more than missing that speech explains the outcome, the expression, "up Salt River" does refer to a political defeat. While the story may be untrue, the term continues in use.

See James P. Henley, *The Inventory and Classification of Streams in the Salt River Drainage* (Frankfort 1983); Warren Raymond King, *The Surface Waters of Kentucky* (Frankfort 1924).

Michael E. Walters

SALVATION ARMY, THE. A charitable organization, the Salvation Army is an international movement and an evangelical part of the universal Christian church. The organization's message is based on the Bible, and it attempts to meet human needs without discrimination.

William Booth (1829–1912) formed the organization in England in 1865. His crusade was to win the lost multitudes of London to Christ. Booth abandoned the conventional notion of church and went into the streets to preach the gospel to the homeless, hungry, and destitute. Thieves, prostitutes, gamblers, and drunkards were among Booth's first converts to Christianity. He employed titles and music based upon the British Army to lead his followers to Christ. The Salvation Army bands are still found in England and around the world.

A small corps was set up in Philadelphia in 1879, but the first authorized missionary to the United States was George Scott Railton, who reached New York City in March 1880 with seven women "soldiers."

The JEFFERSON COUNTY COURTHOUSE was the site of the first Salvation Army meeting in Louisville. In 1883 the *COURIER-JOURNAL* announced in a headline: "The Salvation Army pitches its tents in Louisville, and comes to stay as long as there is a sinner unsaved." It noted that "about twenty-five forlorn and shivering men and women gathered about a broken stove and prayed." All the while boys threw snowballs at the door.

In 1895 the first corps was opened at the site of Bowles Market and Hall at 336 E Jefferson St. It was in 1898 that the social work of the Army was begun in earnest. A shelter and a "workingman's hotel" opened in Louisville. In 1916 the Salvation Army purchased property at 216 W Chestnut St. for a new headquarters. On January 27, 1927, Louisville became the headquarters to oversee the work of the Salvation Army in Kentucky and Tennessee.

The Salvation Army became widely respected and known for its efficient administration of many services. It has always been there to assist, especially in wartime when its workers baked doughnuts, wrote letters, sewed, and provided other services for American troops abroad. The tremendous amount of unemployment put a severe strain on the army during the GREAT DEPRESSION, and the organization gradually declined in importance at that time, as its mix of services and evangelizing came to be perceived as outmoded and as the GOVERNMENT assumed a greater role in social welfare. During WORLD WAR II it joined with the Red Cross, the YMCA, the YWCA, and other groups to form the United Service Organizations, which provided personal services to American troops.

The unorthodox style of the first local leaders, Capt. J.W. Blosser, Capt. Lizzie Pellatt, and Lt. Mattie Standevere, coupled with the need for an advocate for outcasts, led to the establishment of a relationship with Louisvillians that continues. In Louisville, the Salvation Army offers a variety of services and programs that focus on providing hope and solutions to individuals in crisis. Corps Community Centers are the fundamental and basic unit through which the Salvation Army carries out its mission. These worship centers offer neighborhood religious services, along with character-building and social service programs. Emergency shelters furnish clean beds, a place to shower, personal counseling, and spiritual guidance for the homeless. The Salvation Army's dining facilities serve hot meals twice a day every day of the year. Transitional housing helps targeted struggling families break the cycle of HOMELESSNESS by offering long-term independent housing, counseling, child care, referrals, and practical training. Long-term living arrangements are also available for single people who are committed to making positive changes in their life. The Center of Hope at 831 S Brook St. is a complex that offers many of these services.

Since 1942 the Salvation Army Boys and Girls Clubs have offered Louisville-area children supportive and supervised places to go for recreation and personal development. For a nominal membership fee, children ages six to eighteen build self-esteem by participating in programs focusing on personal adjustment, leadership development, cultural enrichment, health and physical education, social and recreational activities, and environmental education.

The Adult Rehabilitation Center helps men who are drug and alcohol dependent rebuild their lives. It uses trucks to make pick-ups. Drivers, often men enrolled in the alcohol and drug rehabilitation program, pick up discarded items from donors. Many of the items are rejuvenated by men in the program and then sent to thrift stores for sale. Sales of the items are the sole support of this program. Personal and spiritual counsel are available to the men along with the basic necessities of life—food, clothing, and shelter. Also, victims of disaster can count on having immediate needs met by the Salvation Army.

Each Christmas, the Salvation Army, along with helpers from the community, distributes toys to needy children. Donors also give gifts of new clothing to needy children through the Salvation Army Angel Tree program with WAVE TV-3 and Kroger. Volunteers staff area mall tables where willing donors pick up shopping information. Once the gifts are purchased, they are taken to the mall tables and distributed by volunteers in time for Christmas. The Salvation Army's kettle tradition began in San Francisco in 1891 when Capt. Joseph McFee put a pot on a dock to collect money to feed the needy. It is uncertain when the kettles were first used in Louisville, but it must have been shortly after their use in California. Locally, the Salvation Army has an ensemble made up of band players who are officers assigned to duty in this area. The band plays sporadically and is less significant than in the past in calling attention to the work of the army.

Almost three-quarters of the Salvation Army's operating budget comes from individual donations. The Salvation Army also receives METRO UNITED WAY funding. More than 80 percent of the annual budget goes to services for those in need.

See William Booth, *In Darkest England, and the Way Out* (London 1890); Richard Collier, *The General Next to God* (New York 1965); Allen Satterlee, *Sweeping through the Land, A History of The Salvation Army in the Southern United States* (Atlanta 1989).

Marilyn Markwell

SANATORIUMS. Sanatoriums, also spelled sanitariums, began to grow in popularity in the late nineteenth and early twentieth centuries as an alternative form of residential treatment for chronic diseases and disorders such as tuberculosis and various forms of mental illness. While these HOSPITALS varied in size and services, the larger ones tended to be those that cared for tuberculosis patients. Louisville had two of these institutions. WAVERLY HILLS SANATORIUM, the larger, was located off Dixie Hwy.

With the rise of tuberculosis cases in the early 1900s, the disease was called the great white plague. In 1906 the general assembly created the Board of Tuberculosis Hospital, which operated Waverly Hills. Construction on the facility began in 1908 and was finished in 1911. Although it remained a small facility for many years, its population grew steadily, leading to the construction of a larger building in 1926, at which time there were four hundred patients. The patient POPULATION ranged from infants to adults. The facility was equipped with a playground and library facility and offered a school curriculum to accommodate young patients. The hospital was nationally known for its tuberculosis treatment, but the disease proved less of a health problem when the drug streptomycin became available in the late 1940s. This allowed tuberculosis patients to be treated as outpatients. Waverly Hills closed in 1961, and the remaining patients were sent to Hazelwood Sanatorium in Louisville's South End.

In 1906 the Louisville Anti-tuberculosis Association (later called the Louisville Tuberculosis Association) was created. In 1907 it organized the Hazelwood Sanatorium on Bluegrass Ave. for care of tuberculosis patients. This sanatorium was run by the association for twelve years before it was turned over to the commonwealth of Kentucky in 1919 to be used as a state hospital.

Jefferson County tuberculosis patients were being well cared for by Waverly Hills. Hazelwood went through a number of financial ups and downs. There were financial crises as well as expansions, including a new building erected in 1961 when Waverly Hills was closed. In 1961, the number of patients at Hazelwood increased from 150 to 272. In 1971, Hazelwood was converted into a home for the severely mentally handicapped.

There were other sanatoriums throughout the area that provided a quiet, relaxed atmosphere and medical care for a number of ailments, the most common being nervous and mental diseases. They also treated alcohol and drug addiction. They advertised "high tech" facilities that provided X-ray diagnosis, hydrotherapy, electrotherapy, thermotherapy, and sinusoidal treatments. Many of these institutions were in operation for only a few years, but others operated for a long time. One of the earliest was the Blackburn Sanatarium on Hamilton Ave. near Payne St., run by a former Kentucky governor, Dr. LUKE BLACKBURN. This facility was used by Blackburn for the treatment of nervous and mental disorders from 1884 to 1886. Dr. Barton W. Stone opened Beechhurst Sanitarium by 1900 on Transit Ave. (now Grinstead Dr.) near Dudley. Stone died in 1901, but Beechhurst remained open until 1936, when the building was torn down.

The Pope Sanatorium, established in 1890 by Dr. Curran Pope at 115 W Chestnut St., remained open until 1941. The Louisville Neuropathic Sanatorium, located at 1412 S Sixth St. near Central Park, was in existence from 1916 to 1944. It was run by W.E. Gardner. The Dr. Stokes Sanatorium, on Cherokee Rd., lasted from 1913 to 1949 and was run by Dr. Edgar W. Stokes. The Mount Saint Agnes Sanatorium at 2026 Newburg Rd. was run by the Sisters of Charity from 1915 to 1949.

Sanatoriums that were shorter-lived include the Louisville Sanatorium, the Dale Sanitarium, Dr. F.L. Cenna's Sanatorium, the Russell Sanatorium, the Bush Sanatorium, the Boner Sanatorium, Lynn Holmes Sanatorium, the Red Cross Sanitarium, the Kentucky Baptist Sanitarium, and the Schott Clinic and Sanatorium. Located in ANCHORAGE, Kentucky, in eastern Jefferson County were the Pleasant Grove Hospital and Hord's Sanitarium.

See *A Place in Time: The Story of Louisville's Neighborhoods* (Louisville 1989); *Louisville Times*, Dec. 31, 1909.

SANDERS, HARLAND DAVID (COL.) (b Henryville, Indiana, September 9, 1890; d Louisville, December 16, 1980). Restaurateur. His father, Wilbert, died when Harland was six years old. His mother, Margaret Ann (Dunlevy) Sanders, sharecropped the eighty-acre farm near Henryville. He had two siblings: Clarence, born in 1892, and Catherine, 1895. When he was seven, Harland's mother took a job in a canning factory in Henryville to earn a little extra money. She would stay in town for one or two nights a week with her brother, leaving Harland to care for his younger brother and sister. That was young Harland's first experience in solo cooking.

When he was ten, Harland got his first job, working for farmer Charlie Norris, clearing land for two dollars per month. He found watching squirrels and BIRDS more interesting and ended up getting fired. When he told his mother about it, she gave him "a tongue-lashing," wondering if he'd "ever amount to anything." (Sanders, 16). He resolved that if he ever got a job again, nothing would ever keep him from finishing what he started out to do.

In 1902 his mother married William Broaddus, and the family moved to Greenwood, Indiana. Conflicts arose continually between Harland and his stepfather, who soon kicked him out. Harland went to live with relatives and continued going to school. But when they started teaching algebra, school lost its appeal, and Harland dropped out after completing the sixth grade.

Over the next twenty years, Sanders held a variety of jobs, several of which were in the Louisville metropolitan area—farmhand in Southern Indiana; installing electric track bonds on the new interurban line between Louisville and Seymour, Indiana; streetcar conductor in NEW ALBANY, Indiana; ferryboat entrepreneur (on the Froman M. Coots between JEFFERSONVILLE, INDIANA, and Louisville); and secretary of the Columbus, Indiana, Chamber of Commerce.

Sanders left the Louisville area in the late 1920s, working several other jobs before finally settling in Corbin, Kentucky, in 1930 as operator of a restaurant and service station. Soon he became as famous for his home cooking as for the service at his filling station. Sanders often told of his experimentation with a variety of recipes for his fried chicken, after he moved across the street to a larger restaurant and motor court, until he hit upon the unique combination of eleven herbs and spices that "stand on everybody's shelf." In 1935 Kentucky governor Ruby Laffoon (1931–35) made Sanders a Kentucky Colonel for his contributions to the state's cuisine.

His reputation grew after his establishment was listed in Duncan Hines' Adventures in Good Eating in 1939. In 1952 Colonel Sanders (as he was called by this time) signed up a Salt Lake City restaurant owner, Pete Harman, as the first franchisee for his specialty item,

Col. Harland Sanders.

Original Recipe (Kentucky Fried Chicken). In 1955 Colonel Sanders signed Louisville restaurateur Carl Kaelin as the city's first KFC franchisee. When Kaelin added Original Recipe® to his menu, volume at KAELIN'S RESTAURANT on Newburg Rd. and Speed Ave. took such a sharp upsurge that a new kitchen had to be built.

In 1956 when plans showed that Interstate 75 would bypass Corbin by seven miles, the Colonel realized his restaurant and motel business, which had been rebuilt after a fire in 1939, would be dramatically affected. So he sold his operations, realizing just enough profit to pay off his debts. Using his monthly $105 Social Security check (he was 66 years old) Sanders hit the road, recruiting more restaurant owners to become Kentucky Fried Chicken franchisees. Although initial sales were slow, by the end of the decade more than two hundred KFC outlets existed in the United States and Canada.

In 1960 Colonel Sanders established his new company's headquarters in SHELBYVILLE, Kentucky. He and his wife, Claudia, built the business to six hundred outlets by the time he sold Kentucky Fried Chicken for $2 million to John Y. Brown Jr. and Jack Massey in 1964. Seven years later, Heublein Inc. of Connecticut bought the chain for $285 million. After being sold to the R.J. Reynolds Co. in 1978, PepsiCo Inc. purchased KFC in 1986 for $840 million. In 1997 PepsiCo spun off its restaurant holdings as TRICON GLOBAL RESTAURANTS, INC. Sanders remained active in the company as goodwill ambassador, traveling some 250,000 miles a year until his death.

The Colonel was an avid supporter of the Boy Scouts, Junior Achievement, the SALVATION ARMY (he provided funds for the Sanders Citadel—a church facility at the corner of Payne and Charlton Streets—in Louisville), and the March of Dimes, for which he was national chairperson for several years until his death. He helped build a geriatric wing at Louisville's Jewish Hospital and contributed to small colleges, religious institutions, charities, and medical research (such as the University of Kentucky's Sanders-Brown Institute on Aging).

Harland Sanders married Josephine King in 1908 and was divorced in 1947. They had three children: Margaret, Harland Junior, and Mildred. Sanders married Claudia Leddington Price in 1949.

He is buried in CAVE HILL CEMETERY. The monument at his gravesite is a bust of the Colonel sculpted by daughter Margaret. A yellow line painted on the road into the cemetery from Grinstead Dr. leads to the Colonel's grave. His widow, Claudia, died on December 31, 1996, at her home in Shelbyville and is buried next to her husband.

See "KFC Developments in the Falls Cities Area," Bucket 6 (Sept.–Oct. 1962):1–4, 6; "KFC International Headquarters: Open for Business," Bucket 3 (Sept. 1970): 3–5; "KFC Breaks Ground for New Technical Center," Bucket 26 (Oct.–Dec. 1984): 19; *Colonel Harland Sanders, Life As I Have Known It Has Been 'Finger Lickin' Good* (Carol Stream, Ill., 1974); John Ed Pearce, *The Colonel* (Garden City, N.Y., 1982); *Courier-Journal,* Aug. 1, 1997.

Jeannie Vezeau

SANITATION. Maintaining the health of its citizens is a chief concern for any city. According to an 1868 entry by Louisville's health officer in the annual municipal reports, "The city in which there is neither an avoidable death nor an avoidable case of sickness is the only one which is entitled to claim that she has fully discharged her sanitary duty."

There was little concern for sanitation when Louisville was founded in 1778. The setting was an alluvial flood plain covered with dense virgin forests, next to a clear river teeming with fish. As the settlement grew into a town of several thousand, some of the natural features on the landscape proved to be a threat to health.

Not only was the area prone to frequent flooding, but many natural ponds and swamps dotted the landscape. By the early 1800s, diseases, particularly malaria spread by mosquitoes, were bred in these ponds and from the town waste that fouled them. According to an 1867 municipal report, in the early 1800s "Louisville was looked upon as a very unhealthy point at which to locate, and many emigrants were deterred from settling by the fear of sickness and death. The numerous ponds which covered the level land produced sickness."

In 1805 the state General Assembly gave authorization to town leaders to raise funds to drain the ponds. However, the cost of this activity was deemed too expensive and was subsequently delayed until EPIDEMICS hit Louisville in 1817 (smallpox) and 1822 (yellow fever), prompting town officials finally to act. An 1867 Louisville Municipal Report seems to indicate that the problem was still there. These ponds were systematically filled throughout the nineteenth century with garbage and material from the Indian mounds that dotted the area.

In addition to filling ponds, street drainage was an important sanitary issue in the first half of the nineteenth century, with nearly 4,713 feet of sewers being completed before 1850. The primary goal of these sewers was to prevent streets from flooding and new stagnant ponds from forming. A modest system of sewers was constructed in the following half century, contracted by the city engineering office. By 1860 the underground sewer system was less than two miles long. These actions were solutions only to the obvious problems created by the occupation of an existing environment; little were the citizens of Louisville aware of the future health problems being created by their daily activities and wastes being deposited upon the landscape. The underground sewers led directly to ditches, streams, and ultimately the OHIO RIVER.

Because the engineering office was charged with constructing sewers, it became responsible for overseeing city sanitation. It was not until 1853 that the city's most dangerous sanitary threat was addressed, with the enactment of the first city ordinance concerning sanitation. It concerned the construction of privy vaults, with outhouses located on top of these vaults, and the time of day they could be cleaned out. During much of the nineteenth century, privy vaults were the prevalent method for disposing of human waste in Louisville. Unfortunately, they were prone to leakage, which often contaminated cisterns and wells.

In light of its costs, city dwellers had resisted construction of a water company until the mid-1850s when several fires caused great property damage. The state, with prodding from city leaders, chartered a private corporation in 1854 to raise money for construction of the LOUISVILLE WATER CO. After several false starts, Louisville completed construction of the city waterworks in 1857 and began service to the city in 1860. The city urged residents to give up wells and cisterns and hook up to the waterworks. Although several cities throughout the Midwest suffered through devastating cholera outbreaks due to contaminated water, Louisville was relatively free of epidemics during the mid- to late nineteenth century. A water system was essential for proper sanitation, especially after the invention of the flush toilet.

The engineering office's growing burden of maintaining city sanitation led to the creation of the BOARD OF HEALTH in 1865. The following year, the board was authorized to appoint sanitary inspectors whose first duty was the inspection of privy vaults. Other duties included the inspection of sewers and gutters and the tabulation of mortality reports for the year. However, sanitary inspectors lacked the force to follow up on notices served, and the time-consuming process of responding to public nuisances lessened the ability of the office to have any impact on improving sanitation. When it did attempt to enforce its rules, the board received little support from city leaders or the judicial system. Sanitation violations were thrown out of court, and calls to protect the citizens from invisible disease were ignored. Still, city leaders could not ignore the highly visible problem of garbage collection.

Later in the nineteenth century the cleanliness of the streets became the most important sanitary issue for city leaders and its engineering office. By 1866 the condition of Louisville streets had become unbearable for City Engineer George Steeley. In his 1866 municipal report, Steeley decried "the very objectionable and general practice of depositing all the rubbish, ashes, filth, slops, and other waste matter on their surface or in the gutters." Not only was this practice unsightly, malodorous, and a danger to pedestrians, it damaged the pavement, which was costing his office large sums of money. Although the disposing of garbage into the streets was outlawed, garbage piled up in city streets at an alarming rate. The gross inefficiency of the garbage collection system run by private contractors prompted the city to begin its own garbage collection service, with the creation of the street-cleaning department in 1873.

For the rest of the century, the department and the Board of Health were responsible for the city's sanitation. The street-cleaning department was most concerned about the lack of landfill space, while the Board of Health was most concerned with abolishing the privy vault system. Sanitation remained an unimportant issue to many city leaders. The mayor even cut funding for the street-cleaning department and abolished the Board of Health in 1876. However, the board was reinstated in 1879 and continued the fight against the privy vault system. It urged an end to the privy vault system and the connection of properties to a sanitary sewer, but the expense caused strong resistance to the latter idea. Although the Board of Health gained more power during the 1890s, very little progress was made in abolishing the privy vault system and promoting connection to the sewer system. In 1906 voters approved a $4 million bond issue to build new sewers. Over the next seven years about fifty-four miles of major sewer lines were built. These were combined sewers that carried both wastewater and storm water in the same pipes. Unfortunately during heavy rains the combined sewers became overloaded, and their mixture of waters was poured into streams or backed up into basements. This problem continued into the 1990s and was especially noticeable in the 1997 flood, when more than six hundred miles of combined sewers remained, although no combined lines had been built since the mid-1950s.

By the beginning of the twentieth century, the board had made great strides in sanitation with the implementation of milk, meat, and produce inspections and its insistence that the Louisville Water Co. install a filtration system. However, despite these important advances, the board was still losing its battle to abolish the privy vault system. These efforts were hampered by the rather good health of the city, which had managed to avoid serious epidemics during the late nineteenth century. Unfortunately, the healthy status of the city did not continue into the 1900s. As the Louisville Water Co. began construction of a filtration plant on Frankfort Ave. to ensure a safe supply of water for the city, the cases of typhoid fever increased dramatically. Once the plant began operations in August 1909, however, the number of cases dropped significantly, about 60 percent in the first year.

However, Louisville's sanitary image received a devastating blow in 1909 when a report about the city's tenement houses was released. It revealed the horrors of tenement life and its extremely unsanitary conditions. The report was particularly critical of Louisville's use of the privy-vault system, stating that "Louisville, with a POPULATION of two hundred and fifty thousand ... still tolerates this unclean, indecent, and dangerous method of disposal." Even a 1917 ordinance requiring the elimination of privy vaults where sewers were available and requiring the construction of a sanitary privy where sewers were not available failed to reduce their number significantly.

In 1935 a survey of Louisville's health needs indicated that 25 percent of the dwellings were not connected to a sewer and that more than twelve thousand privies were still in use. It also mentioned that 75 percent of these privies were located on lots where sewer connections were available. This was the case in spite of the many miles of major new sewers that were built in the boom years of the 1920s and with federal money during the GREAT DEPRESSION. This survey found that the $100 to $125 sewer hookup fee probably interfered with the elimination of privies. As late as 1936, people were still getting sick from cistern and well water contaminated by privy vaults. However, when THE FLOOD OF 1937 destroyed most of the privies, they were then replaced with toilets connected to a sewer or a sanitary privy system endorsed by the state Board of Health. In the suburban growth of the 1950s, septic tanks adjoined nearly every house. In the late twentieth century, the Metropolitan Sewer District (MSD) replaced these devices as new sewer lines were built beyond the city limits.

All wastewater and storm water emptied alike into the Ohio River, which had become a large open sewer. Due to its costs, construction of a treatment plant was postponed until 1956. In 1958 MSD's first treatment plant went into operation.

The street-cleaning department also had problems during the early 1900s. For most of the 1800s garbage was used to fill in the ponds that had caused so many sanitary problems early in the city's history. However, once those ponds had been filled, finding a place to dispose of trash became a major problem. During the early 1900s the city experimented with incinerators to burn garbage. However, the incinerator system required that garbage be separated, with only combustible trash being accepted for the incinerators. This experiment only succeeded in creating a more complex garbage collection system that was more expensive.

In 1957 the city opened a garbage incinerator south of SHELBY PARK. The twin two-hundred-foot smokestacks were a landmark of Louisville's skyline for almost forty years. The incinerator ceased operation in 1991 after the city declined to spend the $70 million on improvements needed to comply with the new federal standards of the 1990 Clean Air Act. It was razed in 1995. Eventually, the use of rural landfills became the preferred method of garbage disposal, which prevails to the present day. The nature of these landfills was much improved over the old city dumps, the largest of which was located on River Rd. It frequently caught fire, and the stench permeated a great area along the riverfront.

By the 1940s sanitation became an important issue for city leaders. No longer an issue handled by a couple of underfunded city departments, it became a concern for many city departments and agencies. However, the bulk of sanitary responsibility in Louisville falls upon the Metropolitan Sewer District, the Department of Sanitation, the Board of Health, and the Louisville Water Co. The Metropolitan Sewer district (formed in 1946) is responsible for drainage and wastewater. The Department of Sanitation, which was formed from the street-cleaning department in 1976, collects and disposes of trash in the city.

In the county, private trash collectors are hired to serve the ninety-two incorporated cities and the rural areas. The Board of Health protects the city and county from disease caused by unsanitary conditions. The Water Co. ensures a safe supply of drinking water.

In 1990 city officials contracted with a private waste management company to start a curbside recycling program in five target areas throughout Louisville—HIKES POINT, the HIGHLANDS, OLD LOUISVILLE, SHAWNEE, and IROQUOIS. Waste Management of Kentucky, a private recycling firm, had the first contract with the city. In 1996 Rumpke Recycling took over the operation. By 1996, 66 percent of Louisville households were involved in curbside recycling, and recycling and composting had reduced the size of the city's waste-stream by almost 25 percent.

Louisville's air quality is monitored by the U.S. Environmental Protection Agency out of Atlanta and the Jefferson County Air Pollution Control District. For purposes of ozone control, the Louisville area includes Floyd and Clark Counties in Indiana, all of Jefferson County, and small sections of OLDHAM COUNTY and BULLITT COUNTY.

A number of measures have been used to manage ozone levels, including the introduction of reformulated gasoline, vehicle emissions testing, and controls on industrial pollution. There are also numerous specific controls and regulations on small firms such as auto paint shops and dry cleaners. In 1998 stronger vehicle emissions tests, including the use of a "treadmill" test at VET centers, were introduced in Floyd, Clark and Jefferson Counties in response to the city's smog problem. Since 1996 Louisville has exceeded federally mandated ozone levels on several occasions, leading to the city's reclassification as a problem area. The violations can force stricter controls on businesses and vehicles.

Although Louisville has failed to meet ozone standards, air quality in the city has improved markedly since the 1970 passage of the federal Clean Air Act, which was enhanced in 1977 and again in 1990. Levels of major pollutants such as carbon monoxide, sulfur dioxide, dust, and ozone have declined statewide, but urban areas such as Louisville, while cleaner, still struggle to meet federal levels.

See *City of Louisville Municipal Reports,* University of Louisville Archives; Chadwick Montrie, "A Path to Reform: Confronting the Garbage Crisis in Louisville, 1865–1873," *Filson Club History Quarterly* 70 (Jan. 1996): 27–38; M. Jay Stottman, "Out of Sight, Out of Mind: The Archaeological Analysis of the Perception of Sanitation," M.A. thesis, University of Kentucky, 1996; Paul R. Lederer, "Solid Waste Management in Louisville, Kentucky, 1860–1940," University of Louisville Archives, 1993; George Yater, *Two Hundred Years at the Falls of the Ohio* (Louisville 1987); Martin E. Biemer, *Fifty Years of Service* (Louisville 1998).

M. Jay Stottman

SATELLITES OF MERCURY. The "Satellites of Mercury" was an organization incorporated in 1888 by Louisville businessmen to promote and advertise the city's business and trade. It was, in a sense, the successor to the SOUTHERN EXPOSITION that closed its five-year run in 1887. The Satellites held an annual festival that attracted thousands of participants and visitors. It included a parade of illuminated floats, an elaborate pageant, and a lavish reception and ball. The events were modeled on the New Orleans Mardi Gras carnival, with a king and queen selected to reign over a grand ball that ended the week of festivities. Well-known businessmen from Louisville and other Kentucky towns were members of the court and were given ducal titles. Young women of society and current debutantes (many from surrounding towns) were chosen maids of honor, and one was selected queen of the court. Socially prominent married women were named "chaperones" of the court. The celebration was held each autumn from 1888–93, when it ceased, perhaps a victim of an economic downturn.

See *Louisville Times*, March 3, 1949; *Courier-Journal,* Sept. 21, 1890; George H. Yater, "Hang On! Here Comes the Derby Festival . . . It's the Satellites of Mercury up-to-date" *Louisville* (April 1975): 68–71, 79–85.

Mary Jean Kinsman

SATTERWHITE, PRESTON POPE (b Louisville, September 28, 1867; d Great Neck, New York, December 27, 1948). Physician and art connoisseur. He was the son of Dr. Thomas Palmer and Maria Preston Pope (Rogers) Satterwhite. His ancestors, the Breckinridges and Prestons, were early settlers in Kentucky. Satterwhite's father, who was a graduate of the University of Louisville School of Medicine, provided Louisville's first free medical dispensary, along with Dr. Robert J. Breckinridge.

Satterwhite lived in Louisville until he was twenty-five, when he moved to New York City to complete an internship and residency for his medical degree. He became a successful practicing surgeon and a well-known art collector. In 1908 he married Florence Brokaw Martin of New York, and they became part of the social set in Manhattan and Palm Beach, Florida.

Satterwhite made numerous contributions to the J.B. SPEED ART MUSEUM. His first association with the museum came in 1936 when he contributed a collection of eighteenth-century fans. His first major gift was a group of art objects dating from the Gothic period to the eighteenth century, which became part of the museum's collection in 1940. He was made an honorary member and benefactor in 1941 and elected to the museum's Board of Governors in 1943. In memory of Mrs. Hattie Bishop Speed, founder of the museum, he donated the English Renaissance Room in 1944. This oak-paneled room from the time of King James I (1603–25) of England had been previously owned by newspaper publisher William Randolph Hearst and had been moved in its entirety from the Grange in Broadhembury, Devon, England. It was considered one of the finest examples of carved English interiors of this period.

At his death, Satterwhite bequeathed to the museum the remainder of his collection and ample funds to build a wing to house his gifts. The Satterwhite Wing opened in October 1954. The collection included Oriental CERAMICS and fine carpets from the Near East; Medieval, Renaissance, and baroque decorative art from Europe; Ispahan rugs; and numerous Egyptian bronzes, SCULPTURES, and jade from the late Middle Ages.

Mrs. Satterwhite died in 1927 and is buried in CAVE HILL CEMETERY in one of its most elaborate memorials. Designed by the architect Horace Trumbauer, it was adapted from the Temple of Love created for Marie Antoinette by Richard Mique and built near the Petit Trianon at Versailles. Dr. Satterwhite is buried at the Cave Hill memorial he erected to his wife.

See *Courier-Journal*, Dec. 28, 1948, Oct. 24, 1954; *New York Times*, Dec. 28, 1948.

SAUNDERS, MARY ANN PARMELIA XANTIPPE "TIP" (b Columbia, Kentucky,

January 1, 1838; d Louisville, December 4, 1922). Artist. Her mother, Mary Hancock, was Samuel L. Clemens's aunt and the basis for Aunt Polly in his Adventures of Tom Sawyer (1876). Saunders was known particularly for her portraits. She studied in Louisville at Prof. Cornelius Pering's art school for girls and in New York City. Together with Cornelia Pering, she established Louisville's Pering and Saunders Art School in 1870. Cornelia was the daughter of Cornelius and had studied in Europe with her father. They ran the school for twenty-five years. Saunders was last listed in the American Art Annual in 1901. She was a member of the Louisville Art League. The KENTUCKY HISTORICAL SOCIETY owns her portraits of the Rev. John D. Steele and Simon Kenton, painted in 1873. Saunders lived at 3129 Western Pkwy. in Louisville at the time of her death. She is buried in Cave Hill Cemetery.

Roger H. Futrell

SAWYER, ERBON POWERS "TOM" (b Metcalfe County, Kentucky, 1915; d Louisville, September 23, 1969). Jefferson County judge. He was the son of J.G. Sawyer, a one-time Republican sheriff of Metcalfe County. His father named him Powers after Caleb Powers, a Republican who spent eight years in prison in connection with the assassination of Gov. William Goebel, who was shot on January 30, 1900, and died four days later on February 3. Sawyer grew up on a farm, one of nine children. He attended Lindsey Wilson College in Columbia, Kentucky, where he met his future wife, Jean Dunagan of Wayne County. The couple was married in 1939. He studied at Western Kentucky University to be a teacher. After graduating, he taught high school in Summer Shade, Kentucky, for one year before coming to Louisville. He studied at the UNIVERSITY OF LOUISVILLE and the JEFFERSON SCHOOL OF LAW while working at the Naval Ordnance Station. In 1943 he was admitted to the bar.

In WORLD WAR II, Sawyer enlisted in the navy, serving as a commanding officer of a submarine chaser in the South Pacific. He returned to Louisville in 1946, going into private law practice and then serving as assistant to Commonwealth Attorney Frank A. Ropke from 1947 until 1951, and as county attorney from 1951 until he was named judge.

Sawyer, a Republican, was Jefferson County judge from December 17, 1968, until September 23, 1969. He was appointed by Gov. Louie B. Nunn after County Judge Marlow W. Cook was elected to the United States Senate.

Sawyer was killed in a one-car accident early in the morning on Interstate 64, half a mile east of the WATTERSON EXPRESSWAY. Sawyer was in the middle of a reelection campaign to serve a full four-year term as county judge. In September 1971, Nunn dedicated Jefferson County's first state park, named in honor of the former judge. The four-hundred-acre E.P. "TOM" SAWYER STATE PARK is in eastern Jefferson County on land that was formerly part of the grounds of CENTRAL STATE HOSPITAL.

Sawyer was the father of two daughters, TELEVISION journalist Diane Sawyer and Linda, both former Kentucky Junior Misses. He is buried at Resthaven Memorial Park.

See *Courier-Journal*, Sept. 24, 1969.

SCHENLEY DISTILLERS CORP. In 1923 Louis Rosenstiel created the Schenley Products Co. to sell "medicinal" whiskey during PROHIBITION. The firm had its headquarters in Cincinnati. By the end of Prohibition, Rosenstiel had changed his company's name to the Schenley Distillers Corp. and had acquired four distilleries. In 1937 Schenley acquired the Bernheim Distilling Co. in Louisville, its distillery at Seventeenth and Breckinridge Streets, and all of its brands.

One of the brands acquired was Old Charter. Adam and Ben Chapeze founded a distillery at Chapeze Station in BULLITT COUNTY, Kentucky, in 1867. In 1874 they introduced a premium bourbon called Old Charter. The brand, named for the Charter Oak of Connecticut, honored the centennial of the American Revolution. The brand and distillery were sold to the Louisville firm of Wright and Taylor in 1896. Old Charter was made a bottled-in-bond bourbon in 1901 and was marketed from coast to coast and even in the district of Alaska. During Prohibition it was distributed as a "medicinal" whiskey by W.L. Weller and Sons for Wright and Taylor, but after Prohibition the Old Charter brand was sold to Schenley. After 1937 Schenley made and bottled the bourbon at its Bernheim Distillery in Louisville.

The Bernheim Distillery was the organizational center for Schenley's Western Kentucky region. When Schenley decided to rebuild George A. Dickel's Cascade distillery in Tullahoma, Tennessee, most of the technical expertise came from Louisville and the Bernheim Distillery.

In 1954 Schenley acquired controlling interest in the Park and Tilford Co., giving it a second distillery within the Louisville city limits—located in the PORTLAND area at Thirty-fifth and Parker. This distillery was built by the Bonnie Bros. Distillery Co. before PROHIBITION and was acquired by Park and Tilford in 1938. Schenley closed this distillery in the 1970s.

Schenley also acquired the Louisville Cooperage Co. in 1945 and the Chess and Wymond Cooperage in 1946, merging it into Louisville Cooperage. Louisville Cooperage made barrels until the early 1980s, when it was closed down.

Louis Rosenstiel retired in 1968, and Schenley became part of the Glen Alden Corp. In 1987 Schenley was acquired by Guinness PLC of London, which dissolved in 1992 and divided its brands between United Distillers Glenmore and Schieffelin and Somerset Imports. Schenley's distilleries became part of UNITED DISTILLERS MANUFACTURING Inc.

Michael R. Veach

SCHMIED, KENNETH ALLEN (b Louisville, July 11, 1911; d Louisville, April 5, 1973). Mayor. One of four children, Schmied was the son of a Swiss immigrant who settled in Louisville and went to work selling coffee door to door. Eventually Schmied's father started a furniture store, American Home Supply Co. The younger Schmied and his brothers eventually took over the family business.

Schmied entered politics relatively late in life. Although a lifelong member of the REPUBLICAN PARTY, it was not until J. Leonard Walker, a party leader, called on him in 1960 to help organize a rally for presidential candidate Richard Nixon that he became politically active. His executive ability prompted party officials to tap Schmied for the 1961 race for Third Ward alderman. His work in the primary led to his selection as cochairman of the Republicans' fall election campaign. The Republicans swept the general elections, in part due to Schmied's campaign efforts. William O. Cowger was elected Louisville's first Republican mayor in more than thirty years. Schmied was elected to the BOARD OF ALDERMEN and was chosen to be president of the board.

Schmied was mayor of Louisville from 1965 through 1969. He was Cowger's hand-picked successor and, with the backing of the mayor and MARLOW COOK, then county judge, defeated former sheriff William Cranfill for the Republican nomination. Schmied then went on to defeat Democrat Marlin Volz by 11,511 votes. The Republicans also retained control of the Board of Aldermen.

In 1965 Schmied and the board won voter approval of a $29.8 million bond issue for several PUBLIC WORKS projects, including an addition to the LOUISVILLE FREE PUBLIC LIBRARY, a site for the JEFFERSON COMMUNITY COLLEGE, UNIVERSITY OF LOUISVILLE medical-dental complex and science classrooms, and FOUNDERS SQUARE. Schmied also was instrumental in promoting riverfront development.

Schmied's administration reflected the racial tensions throughout the country. There was a movement by CIVIL RIGHTS activists to pass a city ordinance banning racial discrimination in the sale and rental of housing. The movement for "open housing" gained momentum in the fall of 1966, with more demonstrations in 1967. While Schmied favored fair housing, he opposed the passage of a city ordinance on the grounds that legislating fair housing was unnecessary. The Republican Board of Aldermen also refused to pass any kind of open-housing ordinance. The Democrats were able to rally around the issue in the 1967 city elections and took control of the board, passing an open-housing ordinance shortly thereafter. Schmied neither signed nor vetoed the legislation.

With the Democrats in control of the board, the remainder of Schmied's tenure as mayor was marred by partisan in-fighting. The board passed several ordinances that Schmied vetoed, only to have the board override his actions.

Schmied's administration continued to be plagued by racial strife in May 1968. Civil disorder broke out in Louisville's West End after black leaders accused Schmied of failing to address problems in that part of the city. Black leaders chided Schmied for poor distribution of city services to their neighborhoods. Complaints included inadequate police protection, poor park and recreation facilities, weak enforcement of housing codes against slumlords, and poor garbage collection. The pivotal issue was the charge that Schmied refused even to visit the area to see the problems firsthand or meet with local officials. Schmied said he made quiet trips to the disturbed areas and understood the magnitude of the problems in the West End.

During his mayoral tenure, he was known as "the SCHNITZELBURG Cannonball" because of his heavy-set physique and his connection to the Schnitzelburg neighborhood. After serving as mayor, Schmied went back to the family furniture business.

He was married to Ethel Harlamert. The couple had two sons, Kenneth Allen Jr. and Roger Warren. The family lived at 3004 Colonial Hill Rd. He is buried in CAVE HILL CEMETERY.

See *Louisville Times*, April 6, 1973.

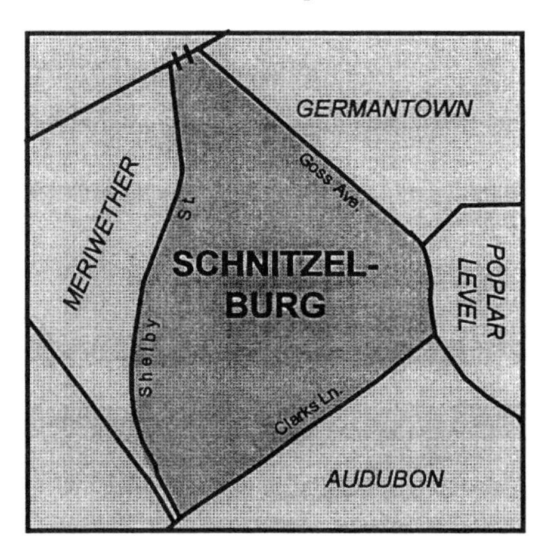

SCHNITZELBURG. Triangular-shaped neighborhood considered part of greater GERMANTOWN to the southeast of downtown Louisville, bounded by Goss Ave., Shelby St., and Clarks Ln. Originally part of Alexander Spottswood's thousand-acre land grant (owned later by Alexander Spottswood Dandridge), the area was first platted by developer D.H. Meriwether in 1866. However, it did not attract many residents until the completion of the Goss Ave.–Texas Ave. streetcar loop in 1891. Although growth resumed shortly thereafter, it slowed during WORLD WAR I, fueled by the animosity directed toward the high concentration of German Americans who settled in the community and the adjacent GERMANTOWN neighborhood.

Once known as Meriwether's Enlargement, the evolution of the area's modern name has several explanations. One story claims that the name was derived from the song, "Schnitzelbank," which was sung loudly in the local TAVERNS on Saturday nights. Other accounts claim that the name evolved from translations of the word "schnitzel," one of which referred to the residents' inclination towards carpentry and woodworking, while another claimed that the word referred to the area's popular fried-beef dish.

A favorite game in the neighborhood is dainty, and beginning in 1971, the community hosted the World Championship DAINTY Contest in its streets. The competition involved placing a small wooden stick on the ground, hitting it with another stick, and then attempting to hit the airborne rod as far as possible.

See Carl E. Kramer, "The City-Building Process: Urbanization in Central and Southern Louisville, 1772–1932," Ph.D. dissertation, University of Toledo, 1980; John C. Rogers, *The Story of Louisville Neighborhoods* (Louisville 1955).

SCHOLTZ, JOSEPH DENUNZIO (b Louisville, January 16, 1890; d Louisville, September 25, 1972). Mayor. The son of Charles and Hermine S. Scholtz, he attended public grade school in Louisville and graduated from du Pont Manual Training High School. He attended Cornell University, graduating in 1912. Returning home, he worked in his family's fruit and produce company, the Joseph Denunzio Fruit Co. His father, who died in 1942, was president of the company, while Joseph became vice president.

Scholtz entered politics when his friend, Richard R. Williams, a civic leader and member of the Louisville Board of Sinking Fund Commissioners, appointed him commissioner of the Sinking Fund. He later served as president of the Board of Park Commissioners from 1933 until 1935. He had the distinction of being the only Democrat to serve in Republican mayor William B. Harrison's administration. He became president of the LOUISVILLE WATER CO. in 1935, serving when the 1937 flood disrupted service.

Scholtz was mayor of Louisville from 1937 through November 1941. During his administration a business license tax was enacted by the city. He also helped with the planning for the building of STANDIFORD Field (now LOUISVILLE INTERNATIONAL AIRPORT). Scholtz helped convince the BOARD OF EDUCATION to increase the pay for black teachers in the city. From 1939 until 1940 he was president of the Kentucky Municipal League.

Scholtz left office one week before the Japanese bombed Pearl Harbor. In 1942 he served as regional director for the Office of Civil Defense based in Omaha, Nebraska, serving a nine-state area. In May 1943 he was commissioned a major in the United States Army. After attending the University of Virginia's military GOVERNMENT school, he was sent to North Africa and later to Italy. While in Italy he was a commissioner for the Allied Military Government. He received the Legion of Merit, the highest noncombat medal awarded, for his service in the war. After the war he worked as Kentucky representative for the Surplus Property Administration. Scholtz had also served in World War I and was stationed at CAMP TAYLOR in Louisville.

In 1947 he was appointed Louisville postmaster, supervising the main post office and seventeen branch offices. He served until January 31, 1960. When Scholtz took over as postmaster, receipts for the Louisville Postal Service were $4.5 million. When he left office in 1960, the receipts, which reflected the city's growth, had increased to $11.5 million.

He married Ann Louise Cassilly of Louisville on October 24, 1914. The couple had three sons: Robert L., Philip H., and Joseph D. Jr., and a daughter, Ann Q. He is buried in CAVE HILL CEMETERY.

SCHOOL OF AIR EVACUATION. The School of Air Evacuation was established as part of the WORLD WAR II expansion at BOWMAN FIELD. During its tenure, it was the only school of air evacuation in the entire Army Air Force.

The school, on the east side of the field, was officially activated on October 6, 1942, as the 349th Air Evacuation Group. It trained surgeons, flight nurses, and medical technicians to airlift patients from combat zones. Because of the urgent need for trained medical evacuation personnel worldwide, early classes were brief and informal. Redesignated the Army Air Force School of Air Evacuation on June 25, 1943, the curriculum had matured into an eight-week course. Training emphasized patient classification, medical treatment, and loading and unloading patients from aircraft. Specialized training was conducted in Louisville HOSPITALS. In addition, instruction in self-defense was provided. Effective October 15, 1944, the school was moved to Randolph Field in San Antonio, Texas.

During World War II, the pioneering effort of the school played a major role in the treatment of the sick and wounded. Between January 1943 and May 1945, over 1 million patients had been air-evacuated by Army Air Forces around the world.

See Evelyn Page, ed., *The Story of Air Evacuation 1942–1989* (Dallas 1989); *Courier-Journal*, Dec. 6, 1942, Feb. 19, 1943, Oct. 4, 1944.

Charles W. Arrington

SCIENCE HILL FEMALE ACADEMY. Science Hill Academy was founded by Virginia-born teacher Julia Ann (Hieronymous) Tevis (1799–1880), wife of John Tevis (1792–1861), a Methodist minister whom she married in 1824. Tevis was originally sent to Louisville to preach but "a spirit of discord had well-nigh ruined the early prospects of Methodism." The Tevises moved to SHELBYVILLE, where John Tevis had family. With support from the Methodist church, Julia Tevis opened her school in 1825.

"A good Protestant school was much needed," John Tevis wrote in his memoirs. "Young ladies of Protestant family, educated in Romanish institutions of learning, returned to their families thoroughly imbued with Romanism." The school was unlike any other girls' academy in Kentucky. Under Julia Tevis's superintendence, students were taught mathematics and chemistry; teachers she hired had to be proficient in languages and classical studies.

Hard times and a cholera epidemic nearly closed the school in the 1830s. In the spring of 1839, Tevis published her first Science Hill Female Academy catalog, not knowing whether the school would reopen or not. By 1857 it boasted 230 students from all over the South, housed in a substantial brick edifice in downtown Shelbyville. John Tevis, a teacher at Science Hall died on the eve of the CIVIL WAR. His widow shocked Shelbyville's Confederate supporters by refusing to pray for the Southern cause or "gallant, misled, erring General Lee." Julia Tevis believed in both emancipation and the United States of America. The academy celebrated its semi-centennial on March 25, 1875, with Julia Tevis as its principal. In 1879 she sold the school to Dr. Wiley Taul Poynter. He and his wife, then their daughters, ran the school until it closed in 1939. The building remains, housing a restaurant and shops.

See Julia Ann Tevis, Sixty Years in a School-Room (Cincinnati 1878); Rachel M. Varble, Julia Ann (New York 1939).

Lynn S. Renau

SCOTT COUNTY, INDIANA. Scott County, with a total area of 193 square miles, is Indiana's fourth-smallest county. Beginning about 1970 the county established a trend of slow but steady POPULATION growth. Between the 1970 and 1980 census counts, Scott County's population jumped from 17,144 to 20,422. Indeed, the county's estimated 1997 population of 22,900 still amounted to a 9.1 percent increase over the 1990 census figure of 20,991.

Despite the county's relatively small size, it displays surprising geographic diversity. While much of Scott County is bottomland that drains into the Muscatatuck River basin, the county also has several hilly, upland regions, rich with deposits of limestone and dolomite. Covering the county's uncultivated land, one finds thick forests of oak and hickory. Ironically, the county's best-known geographic feature is not natural at all. In 1973 the Indiana Department of Natural Resources opened Hardy Lake State Recreation Area, a 1,321-acre park featuring Hardy Lake, a 741-acre man-made reservoir averaging 35 to 40 feet in depth.

It is believed that the earliest inhabitants were of the prehistoric Mound Builder cultures, known for stockade villages and ceremonial mounds, followed by a period of dominance by the Woodland tribes. By historic times, only scattered Delaware Indian settlements remained within the future confines of the county. Instead, members of the SHAWNEE, Delaware, and Potawatomi tribes used the area primarily as a hunting ground.

In 1781, in appreciation for his services during the U.S. Revolution, the state of Virginia issued Gen. GEORGE ROGERS CLARK a large land grant in southern Indiana that extended into the southern part of the future county. In 1805 William Henry Harrison, acting on behalf of the United States government, officially purchased from the Shawnee Indians through the Treaty of Grouseland an area that included the future county.

On a stream now known as Kimberlin Creek, John Kimberlin founded the earliest known settlement in 1805. Another early settlement was that of Pigeon Roost, founded in 1809. Unfortunately, the residents soon found themselves in conflict with the Shawnee. Those strained relations were partially due to the general tension that had existed between Indiana settlers and the Native Americans since the Battle of Tippecanoe in 1811. In addition, the Indians complained that the settlers had stolen a white elk and that they had been deliberately intoxicated before trade negotiations. Thus, on September 3, 1812, a Shawnee war party under the leadership of chief Misselemetaw entered the settlement and killed twenty-four of its inhabitants, effectively dispersing that particular settlement. (In 1904, a monument commemorating the event was erected on the site just off U.S. Hwy. 31.)

The first permanent settlement was Lexington, which was founded in 1810 and named after the city of Lexington, Kentucky, where many of its settlers had originated. Five years later, in 1815, the town of Vienna was established to the west of Lexington. Later, in 1849, the Jeffersonville Railroad to Indianapolis would be routed through Vienna. In 1816 settlers began to cluster in what is now Finley Township. By 1884 that town had come to be known as Leota in honor of the deceased infant daughter of one of its early residents.

In 1820 Scott County was officially established by the state of Indiana. The county was composed of territory previously belonging to Clark, Jefferson, Washington, Jackson, and Jennings Counties. The county was named after Gen. Charles Scott (1739–1813), a veteran of both the French and Indian and the Revolutionary Wars. Scott eventually settled in Kentucky, where he became the state's fourth governor (1808–12). The county's oldest existing settlement, Lexington, was chosen as the first county seat.

After the establishment of Scott County, several new communities came into existence. The year 1837 saw the founding of Albion, located near present-day state highway 256. The following year New Frankfort was established less that a mile away. Also in that same vicinity the community of Wooster was settled in 1847. However, when those three villages were bypassed by the RAILROADS during the 1850s and 1870s (the Jeffersonville Railroad ran six miles to the west, and the Ohio & Mississippi Railroad ran two miles to their east), Albion, New Berlin, and Wooster quickly withered away. In 1850 the town of Centerville began, located just north of Vienna at the present-day site of Scottsburg. In 1853 the town of Austin, north of Centerville, emerged. In 1871 the town of Scottsburg was platted, literally in Centerville's backyard, as a potential location for a new county seat. Eventually, Scottsburg would totally engulf Centerville. (Interestingly, Scottsburg was not named for Charles Scott but for a railroad superintendent named Col. Horace Scott.) The town of Holman (now known as Blocher) was established on the route of the Ohio & Mississippi Railroad in the very northeast corner of the county about 1870.

During the CIVIL WAR Confederate cavalry general John Hunt Morgan and his troops crossed the OHIO RIVER into Indiana in July 1863. The Confederates entered Scott County, pillaged Finley Township, and occupied first Vienna and then Lexington without a shot being fired. Morgan's raid was finally ended later that month with his capture by Union forces in eastern Ohio.

On May 22, 1868, Scott County witnessed the world's second train robbery. It was perpetrated by the notorious Reno brothers. When a late train on the Jeffersonville, Madison, & Indianapolis Railroad stopped at the small railroad depot of Marshfield (located between Scottsburg and Austin) at about 9:30 p.m., the train's crew was attacked, the engine hijacked, and about ninety-six thousand dollars stolen and divided up among the Reno gang. Several members of the gang were eventually captured and imprisoned in Lexington to await trial. However, authorities feared the possibility of mob retribution against the Renos, so they were quietly spirited away to NEW ALBANY on a midnight train. Nevertheless, on December 8, 1868, a band of vigilantes stormed the New Albany jail and imposed their own brand of justice on the Renos, killing all.

In 1874, after a fierce political battle, the county seat was finally moved from Lexington to Scottsburg. In 1907 an interurban electric rail system, connecting Louisville and Indianapolis, was run through the center of the county. That line served local commuters until its demise in 1939. In 1961 Interstate 65 was routed through the county.

The turn of the century saw one of the region's economic backbones, the canning industry, come of age in Scott County with the founding of such enterprises as the Vienna Canning Co. in 1895, the Scottsburg Canning Co. in 1899, and especially the Austin Canning Co. in 1899 by entrepreneur Joseph S. Morgan. Scott County farmers began supplying the canning factories and by 1907 the county had 2,265 acres planted in tomatoes (the most of any county in the state) headed for the can-

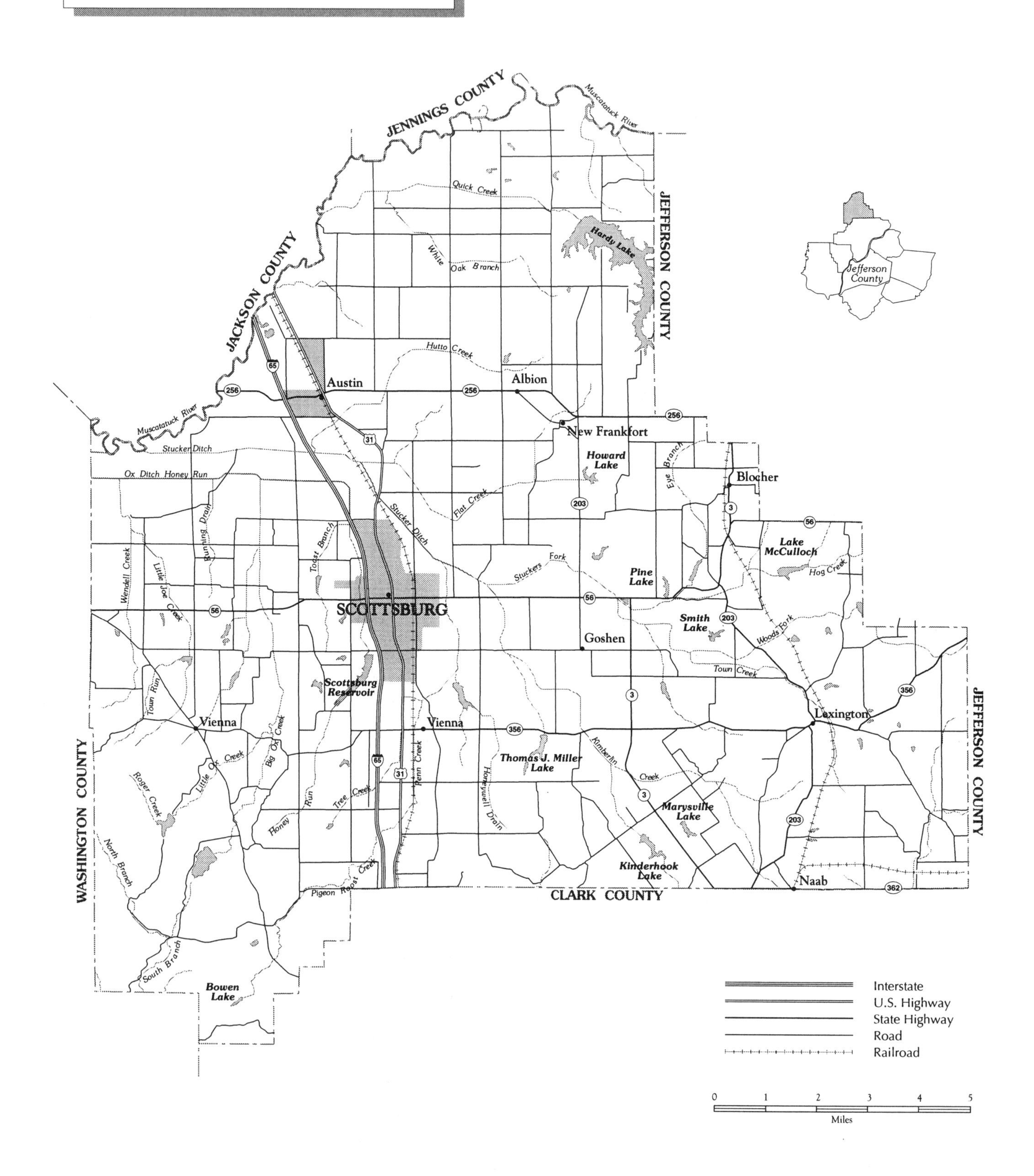
SCOTT COUNTY
INDIANA
JENNINGS COUNTY
JACKSON COUNTY
JEFFERSON COUNTY
WASHINGTON COUNTY
CLARK COUNTY
Jefferson County
Muscatatuck River
Quick Creek
Hardy Lake
White Oak Branch
Hutto Creek
Austin
Albion
New Frankfort
Howard Lake
Blocher
Stucker Ditch
Ox Ditch Honey Run
Flat Creek
Eye Branch
Lake McCulloch
Hog Creek
Wendell Creek
Little Joe Creek
Bunning Drain
Toast Branch
Stuckers Fork
Pine Lake
Smith Lake
SCOTTSBURG
Goshen
Woods Fork
Town Creek
Town Run
Scottsburg Reservoir
Vienna
Lexington
Big Ox Creek
Little Ox Creek
Roger Creek
Thomas J. Miller Lake
Kimberlin Creek
Penn Creek
Honeywell Drain
Honey Run
Tree Creek
Marysville Lake
Kinderhook Lake
North Branch
Pigeon Roost Creek
Naab
South Branch
Bowen Lake
Interstate
U.S. Highway
State Highway
Road
Railroad
0
1
2
3
4
5
Miles

nery. In 1917 the name of Morgan's company was changed to the Morgan Packing Co., and by the 1920s it had bought out most of its competitors and dominated the Scott County food-packing industry. In 1985 the corporation's name was again changed, to Morgan Foods Inc.

Although the county still maintains a rural flavor, many areas, especially along the interstate, are developing an increasingly suburban feel, with the advent of large chain retailers and fast-food RESTAURANTS. According to the 1990 census, only about 3 percent of the county's workforce was involved in farming. Predominant employment continues to be in manufacturing, followed distantly by white-collar workers and retail and service personnel. The estimated 1997 populations of the county's six largest communities were Scottsburg, 5,734; Austin, 4,310; Lexington, 450; Blocher, 200; Vienna, 120; and Leota, 40. The number of people commuting to work in adjacent counties and Louisville brought it into the Louisville METROPOLITAN STATISTICAL AREA after the census of 1990.

See Carl R. Bogardus Sr., *Centennial History of Austin, Scott County, Indiana* (Austin, Ind., 1953); *The Early History of Scott County, Indiana, 1820–1870* (Scottsburg, Ind., 1970); *Scott County, Indiana Celebrating 175 Years: A Pictorial History* (Paducah, Ky., 1995).

SCOTTSBURG, INDIANA. Located approximately thirty miles north of Louisville at the intersection of Highways 56 and 31, Scottsburg is the county seat of SCOTT COUNTY, INDIANA. Although Scottsburg itself was not founded until 1871, a small, struggling community known as Centerville originally occupied part of the site. Founded in 1850, Centerville was eventually swallowed up by its growing neighbor. Centerville's old borders correspond approximately with the boundaries of what is now N Main, Kerton, and Owen Streets in present-day Scottsburg.

Prior to the founding of Scottsburg, a heated battle raged for several years over moving the Scott County seat away from neighboring Lexington. In 1870 three acres of land adjoining Centerville were donated to the county as the site of the new seat. After several years of litigation and political infighting, the seat of government was transferred in 1873. By that time, the new community had come to be known as Scottsburgh, named after Col. Horace Scott, a popular superintendent of the Jeffersonville, Madison, & Indianapolis Railroad, which passed through the town. By 1874, with a new courthouse and jail, Scottsburg officially assumed its function as the county's political capital. However, bitterness on the part of the citizens of Lexington necessitated that the county records be spirited away at night to Scottsburg.

In 1892 the name of the post office, and consequently the community, was revised to its present spelling as Scottsburg, without the last letter "h." In 1906 the first TELEPHONES were installed. The following year an interurban electric rail system connecting Louisville and Indianapolis was run through Scottsburg, where the repair shop and power house were built. The line served local commuters until its demise on October 31, 1939, a victim of paved roads and private automobiles. In 1961 Interstate 65 was routed through Scottsburg, facilitating travel that eventually brought Scottsburg and Scott County into the Louisville METROPOLITAN STATISTICAL AREA. In 1959 the voters approved a referendum to make their community a fifth-class city. In January 1964, Blake Burns became the first mayor of Scottsburg.

Over the past four decades Scottsburg has experienced slow but steady growth, with a 1970 POPULATION of 4,791, a 1980 count of 5,068, then 5,334 in 1990, and 5,734 in 1997. Although the city still remains agriculturally oriented, its proximity to Louisville has increasingly given the community a suburban feel in recent years. Scottsburg High School graduated its first class about the turn of the century. The community also has its own newspaper, the Scott County Journal, established in 1882 and printed in Scottsburg since 1886. Since the coming of the interstate highway in the 1960s, local businesses have experienced some decline due to increased competition from large fast-food chains and retailers such as Wal-Mart, coupled with easier access to the large shopping centers in Clarksville and Louisville. However, in 1997 the county was still able to undertake a $4 million dollar restoration of the city's 125-year-old courthouse. A major industry is American Plastic Molding Corp., making molds for custom injection thermal plastic parts. King Machine Co. designs and manufactures custom machinery.

See Carl R. Bogardus Sr., *Centennial History of Austin, Scott County, Indiana* (Austin, Ind., 1953).

SCULPTURE. At the beginnig of the twenty-first century there were more than one hundred pieces of public outdoor sculpture in Jefferson County, comprising over one-quarter of all outdoor works of art in Kentucky. Historic and contemporary public art is in PARKS, on church and synagogue properties, in schoolyards, outside museums and businesses, in CEMETERIES, and as part of buildings' architectural and decorative elements.

Louisville's sculptural history replicates that of the rest of the United States, with much of the late-nineteenth- and early-twentieth-century work commemorating important persons or events. These realistic figurative works memorialize the history of the city, the state, and the nation. The oldest known outdoor work in Louisville is the marble sculpture of LOUIS XVI, ca. 1816, located in front of the JEFFERSON COUNTY COURTHOUSE. It was a gift from Louisville's sister city, Montpellier, France, in 1966.

Louisville artist ENID YANDELL (1870–1934) created the sculpture of Daniel Boone that

Enid Yandell's statue of Daniel Boone in its original location in Cherokee Park, c. 1907.

stands in Cherokee Park. This work was first created in plaster for the Kentucky Building at the Chicago World's Fair in 1893. Yandell later created the bronze work that was dedicated in 1906. The bronze figure of Pan in Cherokee Park was also sculpted by Yandell.

The Carrara marble piece of George Prentice, founder and editor of the LOUISVILLE JOURNAL, was sculpted by Louis Alexia Achille Bouly (1805–76) and dedicated in 1876. Originally placed above the main entrance of the Courier-Journal building at Fourth and Green (LIBERTY) Streets, the sculpture was donated in 1913 to the main public library on York St. between Third and Fourth Streets. Following an article in the *Courier-Journal Magazine* in 1955 suggesting that Prentice's writing helped incite rioting during BLOODY MONDAY in 1855, the Library Board received letters demanding that the statue be removed. A committee was appointed to investigate, and it was decided that the sculpture would remain at the library.

Louisville sculpture commemorating other noted figures includes *GEN. JOHN BRECKINRIDGE CASTLEMAN* by R. Hinton Perry, created in 1912. This life-size equestrian sculpture at the intersection of Cherokee Rd. and Cherokee Pkwy. was paid for by popular subscription. The bronze figure of THOMAS JEFFERSON by Sir Moses Jacob Ezekiel (1844–1917) was presented to the people of Kentucky by Isaac and Bernhard Bernheim and was unveiled in 1901. The sculpture stands in front of the Jefferson County Courthouse. George Grey Barnard's (1863–1938) bronze figure of ABRAHAM LINCOLN was given to the city of Louisville by Mr. and Mrs. Isaac W. Bernheim. Dedicated in a public ceremony in 1922, the work stands along Fourth St. outside the main public library. The CONFEDERATE MONUMENT containing three bronze cast figures at Third and Brandeis Streets was created in 1895 by Ferdinand Von Miller II (1843–1929) after Enid Yandell's design was withdrawn. Funds for this sculpture were raised by the Kentucky Woman's Confederate Monument Association, which also commissioned the work.

Ten sculptures were installed on the original Louisville WATER TOWER, erected between 1858 and 1860, instead of the ten urns shown in the architectural design. A tornado in 1890 destroyed at least eight of the sculptures, and it is not known what happened to the surviving pieces. The new works chosen to replace the destroyed sculptures were Greek and Roman classical figures, with the exception of an Indian Hunter with Dog. Nine of these pieces were ordered by catalogue from the Fiske Co. of New York. In 1993 the sculptures were removed from the tower, restored, and re-installed.

Later twentieth-century sculptural works were often abstract, noncommemorative sculptures selected for their aesthetic value. While several of Louisville's works were created between 1890 and 1920, the majority of the city's sculpture was created after 1950, again following the national trend.

Contemporary works by well-known local, national, and international artists are located throughout the city. The Kentucky Center for the Arts is home to such works as *Faribolus and Perceval* by Jean Dubuffet (1901–85), fabricated of polyurethane and steel and created between 1973 and 1982; Alexander Calder's (1898–1976) painted steel *Red Feather*, 1975; and the sixty-five-thousand-pound *Gracehoper*, created by Tony Smith (1912–80) of painted steel between 1969 and 1972. *Gracehoper* was moved to the WATERFRONT PARK in 1999. The heroic-size bronze sculpture of GEORGE ROGERS CLARK located on the RIVERFRONT PLAZA/Belvedere was created by artist Felix de Weldon in 1973. In 1973 de Weldon also sculpted the bronze figure of Benjamin Franklin at the main LOUISVILLE FREE PUBLIC LIBRARY. Works by Louisville sculptors BARNEY BRIGHT, Charlotte Price, Ed Hamilton, Bob Lockhart, Tom Butsch, and Paul Fields, among others, are located around the city.

Ed Hamilton's The Spirit of Freedom, a three-thousand-pound bronze memorial sculpture to black soldiers and sailors who fought in the CIVIL WAR, was installed in Washington, D.C., in 1998. Hamilton was born to Amy Jane (Camp) and Edward Norton Hamilton Sr. February 14, 1947, in Louisville. A 1969 graduate of the LOUISVILLE SCHOOL OF ART, he began his career in 1973 by teaching art at IROQUOIS High School. Hamilton originally worked as a painter but moved to sculpture after working with Louisville sculptor Barney Bright. Hamilton's additional national works include *Armistad Memorial or In Memory of Joseph Cinque*, New Haven CITY HALL, Connecticut (1992); *Joe Louis,* Cobo Center, Detroit (1985); and *Booker T. Washington*, Hampton University, Hampton, Virginia (1983). In Louisville Hamilton's works include: *Monorah Tree of Life* with C. Robert Markert at THE TEMPLE (1986) and *Risen Christ* at St. Margaret Mary Catholic Church (1994–95). Hamilton is married to Bernadette Sonya (Chapman) and they have a daughter and a son.

Thomas C. Butsch has numerous local works including the sixty-nine-foot tubular steel steeple (1988) on the FIRST UNITARIAN CHURCH at Fourth and YORK Streets. Balancing the River (1989), a thirty-six-foot brass and steel moving sculpture, is located at the PORTLAND MUSEUM. Night-Lights (1990) is the name bestowed by HUMANA Waterside Building employees on the forty-foot kinetic lobby installation. Butsch was born October 5, 1942, in Schenectady, New York, to Alfred G. and Mary A. (Santor) Butsch. He moved to Louisville when he was twelve years old. Butsch received his B.A. degree from the University of Kentucky in 1968 and his M.A. in fine arts from the University of California, Santa Barbara, in 1970. In 1980 he returned to Louisville to establish himself as a studio artist. Butsch also has work in the permanent collections in museums at the University of California, Santa Barbara; at Indiana University; and on the St. Meinrad campus in Indiana.

Many fine examples of sculpture, both historic and contemporary, are in CAVE HILL CEMETERY. The cemetery served as one of the earliest sources of accessible public art. Works in cemeteries, including those in Louisville, generally remain where they were originally placed, unlike much other public sculpture. Monuments in Cave Hill include works by such famous sculptors as Robert Eberhardt Launitz as well as many noted Louisville artists. Examples of work by MICHAEL MULDOON and Charles Bullet of the Louisville Muldoon Monument Co. are also found throughout the cemetery.

In 1974 the Altrusa Club of Louisville Inc. researched freestanding sculpture available for public viewing. Its findings were documented in the publication *Cut, Cast, Carved: A Catalogue of Free-Standing Sculpture Available for Public Viewing in Louisville and Jefferson County, Kentucky.* Between 1993 and 1996 Louisville sculpture was located and inventoried as part of the Kentucky Save Outdoor Sculpture! project, which documented all of the known outdoor sculpture in the state. This project was part of the national SOS! effort initiated to locate, conduct condition assessments, and document all outdoor sculpture in the nation.

Selective List of Louisville Sculpture

Abraham Lincoln (1922)
George Grey Barnard
Louisville Free Public Library
West lawn
301 W York St.

Ad Astra (To the Stars)
Otello Guarducci
University of Louisville
Health Sciences Mall
500 Preston St.

Aristides
Churchill Downs
700 Central Ave.

Baptismal Font (1975)
Charlotte W. Price
Calvin Presbyterian Church
2501 Rudy Ln.

Bellarmine Knight (1998)
Robert Lockhart Jr.
Bellarmine College
Front of library
2001 Newburg Rd.

Benjamin Franklin (1973)
Felix de Weldon
Louisville Free Public Library
Entrance to new wing
301 W York St.

Big Red (1990)
Tom Lear
University of Louisville
College of Business and Public Administration

Bride (1964)
Reginald Cotterell Butler
Galleria
401 S Fourth Ave.

Burning Bush (1958)
Henry Roth
Adath Jeshurun Synagogue
Front Wall
2401 Woodbourne Ave.

Candelabra (1976)
Don Lanham
First Unitarian Church
322 W York St.

Ceremonial Mace (1967)
John Prangnell
University of Louisville
Used at Graduation Ceremony

Charles Farnsley (1999)
Dawn Yates
Louisville Fund for the Arts
In the front of the building
623 W Main Street

Christ (1880)
Bertel Thorvaldsen
Cave Hill Cemetery
Main Entrance
701 Baxter Ave.

Communications (1961)
John Prangnell
WAVE-TV Studios
In front of building
725 S Floyd St.

Confederate Monument (1895)
Ferdinand von Miller II
Near University of Louisville
Third and Brandeis Streets

Crucified Christ (1974)
Robert Lockhart Jr.
Cathedral of the Assumption
443 S Fifth St.

Crucifix (Processional Cross) (1974)
Edward Hamilton

St. Augustine Church
1340 W Broadway
Daniel Boone (1906)
Enid Yandell
Cherokee Park
Eastern Pkwy. entrance
Effervescence (1999)
David Caudill
University of Louisville
School of Music
Expanding Hemispheres (1992)
Richard Smith
Louisville International Airport
Faribolus and Perceval
Jean Dubuffet
Kentucky Center for the Arts
Front of building
W Main St.
Fountain in Memorial Garden (1970)
Charlotte W. Price
Second Presbyterian Church
Memorial Garden
3701 Old Brownsboro Rd.
General George Rogers Clark (1973)
Felix de Weldon
Belvedere/Riverfront Plaza
General John Breckinridge Castleman (1913)
R. Hinton Perry
Cherokee Triangle Neighborhood
Cherokee Rd. and Cherokee Pkwy.
George Prentice (1876)
Louis Alexia Achille Bouly
Louisville Free Public Library
Front lawn
301 W York St.
Glass Sculpture
Fred diFrenzi
Louisville Water Co.
Front Courtyard
Third and Chestnut
Gracehoper
Tony Smith
Waterfront Park
Overlook
Harmony (1968)
Otello Guarducci
WAVE-TV Studios
Garden
725 S Floyd St.
Henry Clay (1867)
Joel Tanner Hart
Jefferson County Courthouse
Rotunda
J. Graham Brown
Raymond Graf
Camberley Brown Hotel
Fourth and Broadway
Judge Louis D. Brandeis (1942)
Eleanor Platt
University of Louisville
School of Law foyer
La Porta (the Door) (1969)
Arnaldo Pomodoro
Jefferson Community College
NE corner of courtyard
109 E Broadway
Let's Play Ball (1997)
Kim Hillerich and Albert Nelson
Louisville Slugger Museum
Atrium
800 W Main St.
Lions (1880s)
Sculptor unknown
St. James Court
Street end of mall
Louis XVI (ca. 1816)
Achille Joseph Etienne Valois
Jefferson County Courthouse
Front of building
Northeast corner of Sixth and Jefferson
Louisville Clock (1976)
Barney Bright
Currently in storage
Originally on Fourth Street Mall
Louisville–Jefferson County–Shively Firefighters Memorial
Barney Bright
Jefferson Square
Martin Luther (1960)
Frederick A. Soetebier
First Lutheran Church
417 E Broadway
Moon
Louise Nevelson
Kentucky Center for the Arts
Foyer
W Main St.
Pamela Brown (1972)
Barney Bright
Actors Theatre
Lobby
316 W Main St.
Pan (1905)
Enid Yandell
Cherokee Park
Hogan's Fountain
Cherokee Scenic Loop
Pegasus (1985)
Elizabeth Berrian
James Thompson
Louisville International Airport
Personnage
Joan Miro
Kentucky Center for the Arts
Lobby
Prodigal Son (1939)
George Grey Barnard
J.B. Speed Art museum
Front of building
2035 S Third St.
Red Feather (1975)
Alexander Calder
Kentucky Center for the Arts
Front of building
Reminiscence (1952)
Romuald Kraus
University of Louisville
School of Music
River Horse (1973)
Barney Bright
Mazzoli Federal Building
Federal Square Plaza
Sidney Terr Memorial (1961)
John Prangnell
University of Louisville
Ekstrom Library
Smoketown Monument (1991)
Ed Hamilton, Zephra May-Miller
Hancock and Lampton Streets
St. Francis of Assisi
Charlotte W. Price
St. Francis of Assisi Catholic Church
Lawn of church
1960 Bardstown Rd.
St. James Court Fountain (ca. 1895)
St. James Court
The Coloured Gates of Louisville
John Chamberlain
Kentucky Center for the Arts
Bomhard Theater Wall
The Thinker (1904)
Auguste Rodin
University of Louisville
Front of Grawemeyer Hall
Thomas Jefferson (1901)
Sir Moses Jacob Ezekial
Jefferson County Courthouse
Front of building
527 W Jefferson St.
Truth and Justice (1973)
Barney Bright
Legal Arts Building
200 S Seventh St.
Water Tower Sculptures (1858-60)
Louisville Water Co.
On water tower
Zorn Ave. and River Rd.
Wendell Ford (1998)
Daniel Edwards
Louisville International Airport
Zachary Taylor Monument (1883)
Zachary Taylor National Cemetery
4701 Brownsboro Rd.

See Altrusa Club of Louisville Inc., *Cut, Cast, Carved: A Catalogue of Free-Standing Sculpture Available for Public Viewing in Louisville and Jefferson County,* Kentucky (Louisville 1974); *Kentucky Save Outdoor Sculpture*! Surveys, Kentucky Arts Council, 1994-96.

Lori Meadows

SEAGRAM'S CALVERT DISTILLERY. Joseph E. Seagram & Sons Inc. traces its roots to 1857 when William Hespeler built a distillery in Waterloo, Ontario. In 1864 Hespeler hired Joseph Seagram as a bookkeeper and manager for the distillery. In 1883 Seagram bought the distillery from Hespeler and changed the name of the operation to Joseph Seagram Flour Mill and Distillery. In 1911 the company was incorporated under the name Joseph E. Seagram and Sons Ltd. Joseph Seagram died in 1919.

In 1924 Samuel Bronfman acquired Joseph E. Seagram and Sons. When PROHIBITION ended in the United States in 1933, Bronfman legally entered the United States spirit market by acquiring several distilleries. Seagram's came to Louisville in 1937 when it built the Calvert

Distillery on Seventh Street Rd. The building, designed by Joseph and Joseph, is a prime example of Art Deco style with brick warehouses and a tunnel system designed so that barrels were never seen as they were moved from building to building. The Regency Revival office building was the headquarters for Seagram's operations in Kentucky.

In 1943 Seagram acquired the Frankfort Distilleries Inc. and the Four Roses distillery and brand. Seagram operated both distilleries until the early 1960s when it closed down the Four Roses distillery in Shively. Declining bourbon sales caused Seagram to consolidate its brands and close down plants all over the state of Kentucky in the 1970s, and in 1983 it ended its operation in Louisville.

Michael R. Veach

SEALS. Since its incorporation as a city in 1828, Louisville has had four different seals. The seal is stamped on official city documents to certify their authenticity. The official keeper of the seal is the city director of finance. Depicting a steamboat ascending the falls toward a wharf laden with boxes and bales, Louisville's first city seal, adopted in 1828, symbolized the city's prominence as a river town. Engraved with the words "City of Louisville" at the top, the seal bore the motto "Perseverando," meaning "by persevering." Indeed, through perseverance, Louisville soon became one of the chief commercial centers of the upper South.

By mid-century, however, the city was no longer completely dependent on the Ohio River for its commercial success. The introduction of the steam locomotive was opening new opportunities, and as the Louisville & Nashville Railroad continued its advance southward, the city decided to adopt a new official image. The second city seal, approved by the council on May 8, 1861, pictured a steam locomotive with the word "Progress" emblazoned underneath. This seal served the city well for the next forty-nine years, but by 1910 many believed that the steam locomotive was outdated as a symbol of progress.

In 1910 the Louisville Convention and Publicity League held a contest for designs for a new city seal. The award was fifty dollars or an engraved cup, and the winner was John Ray Bauscher, whose entry was adopted by the city on December 21, 1910. The third seal depicted a woman, representing Louisville, holding in one hand a banner inscribed with the word "Progress," and in the other hand an overflowing cornucopia. To her right was a train, to her left a steamboat; behind her stood the towering buildings of the city, and above her was engraved the phrase, "The Nation's Thoroughfare."

In 1953 Mayor Charles P. Farnsley decided that a simpler seal would be better, and on November 25 of that year the city's fourth seal was adopted. It reflected Louisville's beginnings. Included on the seal were the words "City of Louisville" surrounding the city's date of settlement, 1778, as well as thirteen stars representing the original states, and three fleur-de-lis arranged in a triangle. The fleur-de-lis, French for "lily flower," was the symbol of the French King, Louis XVI, after whom Louisville was named.

See Louis V. Hebel, "Louisville's Official Signature," Louisville 17 (Aug. 20, 1966): 14–15.

SEARCY, CHESLEY HUNTER (b Louisville, December 14, 1881; d Louisville, May 9, 1935). Republican Party boss. Searcy, the son of John and Rosa (Colter) Searcy, attended Louisville public grade schools and Male High School and studied at Vanderbilt University in Nashville from 1901 until 1903. He received his law degree from the University of Louisville in 1904 and started practicing in the law offices of William Krieger, a former circuit court judge and later Jefferson County judge. From 1908 until 1910 he was assistant Jefferson County attorney.

Searcy got his start in politics in 1893 at the age of twelve, working in the thirteenth precinct in the Fifth Ward, serving as an office boy to Democratic Party boss John Whallen. In 1896 he was elected a page of the Kentucky House of Representatives. Between 1911 and 1915, Searcy, now a Republican, was helping to build a successful party in Louisville, putting his charm and quick wit to use in the behind-the-scenes organization. He started off as a district campaign manager for Republican gubernatorial candidates Edward C. O'Rear in 1911 and Edwin P. Morrow in 1915, both of whom were defeated. He also was a Republican party candidate for the state senate in 1911 but was defeated by Hite C. Huffaker. Searcy also was the district campaign manager for Charles Evans Hughes's unsuccessful bid for the United States presidency in 1916. Searcy earned national recognition for his supervision of the successful election of Republican Richard P. Ernst over Democratic incumbent J.C.W. Beckham to the United States Senate in 1920.

Searcy's most important contribution to local politics was the creation of the Republican League, a permanent, full-time political organization with paid staff and precinct personnel. The league, which was formally organized in December 1916, managed the party locally well into the 1920s. It was controlled by Searcy and two other party leaders, Robert H. Lucas and J. Matt Chilton, who came to be known as "The Triumvirate" for orchestrating major Republican victories in local and state elections. The group's influence began to wane when Searcy and Chilton refused to support Lucas's bid for the 1927 Republican gubernatorial nomination.

Searcy played a major role in several of the city's most colorful local elections. In 1917 the Republican Party captured the mayor's office by handing the Whallen machine its final defeat, electing the first full-term Republican mayor, George Weissinger Smith, over Sheriff Charles J. Cronan Sr. in an election marred by controversy. In the 1925 election, amid repeated calls by Democrats for an end to Republican bossism, or "Searcyism" as it was called, Searcy took out a full-page ad in a local paper the Sunday before the election announcing that Democratic mayoral candidate William T. Baker had been a member of the Ku Klux Klan. Baker withdrew from the race at the last minute, and Republican Arthur A. Will easily defeated the Democrats' stand-in candidate, Joseph T. O'Neal Jr. But by 1927 Searcy was losing control, especially after the election of Mayor William Harrison, who led a new faction of the party. After the Democrats regained control of city government in 1933 under the leadership of Michael "Mickey" Brennan, that party dominated local politics for nearly thirty years.

Searcy held every major Republican leadership position during his stewardship, serving as the Louisville Republican Committee chairman (1917–18), the Republican State Committee chairman (1919–20), and as a member of the Republican National Committee (1921–24). Searcy was also a member of the Board of Sinking Fund Commissioners from 1918 until his death, serving as president for several years.

Searcy married Mary Lillian Black on February 16, 1906; they had four children: Chilton, Alvin Hert, Lillian Lucas, and Frances Rose. Searcy died of a heart attack at his desk in his office in the Realty Building and is buried in Cave Hill Cemetery.

SEATONVILLE. Located on Floyd's Fork Creek in southeastern Jefferson County about two miles from the Bullitt County line, Seatonville was named for members of the Seaton family, who were among the earliest settlers in Jefferson County. In the early nineteenth century a road from Jeffersontown to Taylorsville ran past Seatonville, and the popular Funk's Mill was located just one-half mile upstream. This late-eighteenth-century mill was built by John Mundell, who sold it to Jonathan Funk in the 1790s. It remained in operation by members of the Funk family until about 1876. The resulting traffic supported several commercial ventures in the little village, which was surrounded by woods and was a full day's wagon journey from Louisville.

In 1900 the town had about seventy-five residents, two stores, several grist and saw mills, and a one-room school. Perhaps most successful was the general merchandising business operated by brothers William C. and Charles A. Seaton, whose store was credited with spurring the town's growth. When a post office was established, postal authorities renamed the village Malott, for postmaster M.A. Malott, believing the name Seatonville was too unwieldy. Although the post office was discontinued about 1908, the village continued to be designated Malott every election day until 1919, when villagers successfully petitioned the county court for a return to the Seatonville name.

Improved transportation and the advent of the automobile proved to be the beginning of the end for Seatonville. As competition from large farming operations put smaller truck farms out of business, the stores and mills in Seatonville slowly disappeared. Today only a few older residences mark the spot where the village once flourished.

See The Jeffersonian, July 24, 1913; *History of the Ohio Falls Cities and Their Counties,* vol. 2 (Cleveland 1882); *Atlas of Jefferson and Oldham Counties* (Philadelphia 1879); Courier-Journal, *June 27, 1919, Sept. 6, 1970.*

Joellen Tyler Johnston

SECOND BAPTIST CHURCH. Founded in 1838, Louisville's Second Baptist Church began when several members of the First Baptist Church withdrew from that body and were seeded as a new Baptist congregation under the leadership of the Reverend Reuben Morey. Little is known about the formation of the Second Baptist Church, because early church minutes and records were not preserved.

The church originally occupied a building on Green (LIBERTY) St. between First and Second Streets, where it soon experienced steady growth. By 1843 membership had reached more than 160, compared to its charter membership of 19 five years earlier. In 1849 Second Church began constructing a new home on the corner of Third and Guthrie Streets.

About the same time the church found its pulpit vacant. It so happened that neighboring First Church was also searching for a new pastor. As chance would have it, in 1849 the members of both the First and Second churches called the same minister, Rev. Thomas Smith Jr., to lead their respective congregations. Smith accepted the pastorate of both churches. However, in order to make such an arrangement work, in the fall of 1849 the two congregations opened negotiations for a possible merger. Finally, on October 12, 1849. the First and Second Baptist Churches of Louisville officially joined together to form a new entity, to be known as the WALNUT STREET BAPTIST CHURCH. The enlarged congregation then moved to the corner of Fourth and Walnut (Muhammad Ali Blvd.) Streets.

See T.T. Eaton, *History of the Walnut Street Baptist Church of Louisville, Kentucky* (Louisville 1937).

SECOND PRESBYTERIAN CHURCH. The church, at 3701 Old Brownsboro Rd., is the second-oldest continuously active Presbyterian congregation in Jefferson County. It has been situated at four different locations, three of them in downtown Louisville. From this church have come clergy, missionaries, and lay leaders dedicated to outreach. Five of its pastors have served as moderators of the denomination's General Assembly.

The first Second Presbyterian Church building, Third Street between Walnut and Chestnut, 1832.

The church was organized on April 17, 1830, when twelve members of Louisville's FIRST PRESBYTERIAN CHURCH withdrew to organize the Second Presbyterian Church. Dr. Eli Sawtell was chosen as the first pastor. By 1832 the congregation, which numbered a hundred, was located in a permanent sanctuary downtown on Third St.

This church's history of mission work began in 1850 with these programs initiated by women members: Bible classes, the city's first free kindergarten, aid to the poor, and work with prospective ministers.

After Dr. STUART ROBINSON arrived as minister in 1858, the church membership grew to fifteen hundred. In 1869, property was acquired at Second St. and Broadway to build a larger facility. The first unit, an educational wing, was followed in 1874 by the main Gothic structure. These buildings served as the church's home until 1956, when the congregation moved to eastern Louisville.

Between 1875 and 1900 the growing congregation helped start seven local Presbyterian churches. Also, two members were responsible for the founding of the PRESBYTERIAN COMMUNITY CENTER in 1898 and the CABBAGE PATCH Settlement House in 1910. The first classes of the LOUISVILLE PRESBYTERIAN THEOLOGICAL SEMINARY, established in 1893, were held at the church.

As the POPULATION shifted outward in the 1950s, Second Church built a chapel on Old Brownsboro Rd. in Rolling Fields subdivision to serve that area. After a fire in February 1956 destroyed the downtown facility, all activities were moved to the Rolling Fields chapel. More recently, the church, although damaged, served as an emergency center in the wake of the April 1974 tornado. Additional classrooms, offices, and a 660-seat sanctuary were built and dedicated April 27, 1980.

See *History of the Second Presbyterian Church of Louisville, Ky.* (Louisville 1930); Charles B. Castner Jr., "A Brief History of the Second Presbyterian Church," Second Presbyterian Church Sesquicentennial. Dedication of New Building 1830–1980, April 1980.

Elsa Taylor Kalmbach

SEELBACH HILTON HOTEL. Located in the center of downtown Louisville, the hotel is known for its turn-of-the-century grandeur. The Seelbach and its rich history were recognized with its listing on the NATIONAL REGISTER OF HISTORIC PLACES. In 1983 it was honored as one of the top forty HOTELS in the world by the Preferred Hotels Association.

Situated on the southwest corner of Fourth and Walnut (Muhammad Ali Blvd.) Streets, the Seelbach was the ambitious concept of two German immigrant brothers, Louis and Otto Seelbach. Though Louis had initially enjoyed success with a restaurant located at Sixth and Main St., he still endeavored to create an establishment of unsurpassed splendor. In 1871 Otto joined him from Germany, and the two formed the Seelbach Hotel Co. In 1903, construction began on a new hotel, situated well out of the hotel district. Designed in the Beaux Arts style by architects W.J. Dodd of Louisville and Frank M. Andrews of Dayton, Ohio, it cost upon completion in 1905 a total of $950,000. The Seelbach was built and furnished with materials from around the globe, including bronze from France, imported marble, IRISH linens, Oriental rugs, and hardwood from the West Indies. Its main lobby displayed large murals, portraying pioneer life in Kentucky, which were completed in 1904 by the renowned painter of Native American art, Arthur Thomas. The hotel also featured Louisville's first roof garden, and a later project resulted in the famed basement Rathskeller, a room of medieval-style ARCHITECTURE that is adorned with Rookwood Pottery tiles from Cincinnati. The Seelbach's Rathskeller, which was closed during PROHIBITION and reopened in 1934, is the only complete Rookwood Pottery room surviving. The opulence of the hotel and how it was viewed by an Appalachian family was described in a humorous short story written by CORDIA GREER-PETRIE: Angeline at the Seelbach (1921). In his novel, *The Great Gatsby* (1925), F. Scott Fitzgerald called the hotel the Muhlbach. As he wrote it, it was there that Tom Buchanan stayed in the summer of 1919 when he came to Louisville to marry Daisy Fay. Tom rented a whole floor of the hotel and brought a hundred friends down from Chicago in four private Pullman cars.

Enjoying years of success, the Seelbach catered to the elite and accommodated a number of famous people, such as Fitzgerald, who enjoyed the hotel so much he passed out drunk on the ballroom floor. The hotel was sold in 1926 to Chicago real estate man Abraham Liebling for $2.5 million, which made it the largest real estate deal in Louisville's history up to that point. The following years saw the Seelbach change hands a number of times until, finally, the financial strain of operating such an establishment resulted in its closing on July 1, 1975. When the hotel sold at auction to a Baltimore man in 1976, the Seelbach's creditors received a mere $245,000.

After an attempt to raise funds for the hotel's renovation failed, it was sold again in 1978 to Louisville native Roger Davis and construction company president Gil Whittenberg for $800,000. With $20 million in financing from the Metropolitan Life Insurance Co., the restoration of the Seelbach to its former glory was begun. Every effort was made to recapture the elegant look and atmosphere of the turn-of-the-century treasure. The process included custom-designed rugs, mahogany four-poster beds and wardrobes in each sleeping room, a complete rewiring and repiping of the ten-story building, and a tenth-floor Georgian-style ballroom featuring Palladian windows and refinished maple flooring. The Seelbach was officially reopened on April 14, 1982.

In 1990 Medallion Hotels, a New York–based company, took over the Seelbach, and in 1994 a major new conference center was added in an attempt to attract more business customers. In 1997 ownership of the hotel was transferred to the CapStar Hotel Co. of Washington, D.C., in association with Hilton Hotels, and the hotel's official name became the Seelbach Hilton.

See Bob Hill and Dan Dry, *Louisville: A River Serenade* (Memphis 1995); *Courier-Journal Magazine*, April 15, 1979.

SEELBACH-PARRISH HOUSE. The Seelbach-Parrish House, located at 926 S Sixth St. in the city's LIMERICK Preservation District, is an example of the picturesque wood-brick-and-stone Queen Anne style. Its architects in 1888 were the local firm of Wehle and Dodd, and its original owner was hotelier Louis Seelbach.

The German-born Seelbach was then just beginning to make his fortune as the proprietor of Seelbach's European Hotel at Sixth and Main. In 1905 he would build the magnificent Seelbach Hotel, at Fourth St. and Walnut (now Muhammad Ali Blvd.). From 1939 to 1969, the house was owned by Dr. Charles Parrish Jr., a noted African American sociologist and member of the faculty at the UNIVERSITY OF LOUISVILLE.

Douglas L Stern

SEGREGATION. Being a border city in a state that permitted slavery, Louisville developed a system of racial segregation in the late 1800s and early 1900s. Kentucky's slaves were not freed by the Emancipation Proclamation but by the Thirteenth Amendment to the Constitution. Although AFRICAN AMERICANS were officially free, the slave-master mentality bred both traditional discrimination and new legal restrictions that reminded blacks that most whites did not acknowledge their status as equals.

After the CIVIL WAR, Louisville was home to a number of ex-Confederates who remained loyal to the Confederate mindset. One of the leading spokesmen of the "New South" was HENRY WATTERSON, editor of the *COURIER-JOURNAL*. Watterson advocated separation of the races and white supremacy. Often referring to African Americans in derogatory terms such as "niggers" and "darkies," he opposed their involvement in politics and was a strong advocate of disenfranchisement, saying that the black vote was "offensive to whites." Although Louisville never legally deprived blacks of their voting rights, what began in the early 1860s as sporadic discrimination developed into a strong legal system of SEGREGATION that was challenged by Louisville's African Americans throughout the late nineteenth and twentieth centuries.

During the 1870s racial discrimination was inconsistent; African Americans were excluded from some areas of society and not from others. They were allowed limited access to public transportation, health and welfare agencies, and some white business establishments, but AMUSEMENT PARKS, RESTAURANTS, and HOTELS often extended them their services. Historian George Wright described Louisville's race relations as "polite racism," where relations were good as long as blacks remained "in their place." Black leaders believed that their situation was better in Louisville than throughout most of the South and so encouraged blacks to avoid white establishments where they were not welcomed because they offended whites and increased racial tension.

One example of the inconsistencies in segregation was the STREETCARS. The city's three streetcar companies made their own policies regarding blacks. All three companies allowed black women to sit in the cars, but men were required either to stand on the outside platform or were excluded altogether. In October 1870 the legality of these restrictions was tested. Three men, Horace Pierce and Robert and Samuel Fox, paid their fare and boarded a streetcar. After the three men were forcibly ejected, they took their case to the federal court, where Judge Bland Ballard decided that a public carrier was obliged to carry customers who paid the same fare under the same circumstances. When the announcement was made public, black men rushed to test its validity, and widespread violence broke out along the city's streetcar lines. City officials met with streetcar company presidents, who capitulated to prevent any further damage to the streetcars. They agreed that all passengers could ride inside the car. Attempts were made in the 1890s to pass a municipal ordinance segregating streetcars, but the attempt failed. Blacks were, however, expected to sit in the backs of the cars.

As early as the 1860s blacks were excluded from THEATERS, the annual fair, and expositions and were, in most cases, denied access to welfare institutions. Blacks also were excluded from any services in private HOSPITALS, and public hospitals refused to increase the beds and rooms available to them. In 1899 a small group of black physicians led by Dr. W.T. Merchant and Dr. Ellis D. Whedbee established the RED CROSS HOSPITAL, and that organization treated blacks until other hospitals were desegregated. During its first years the Red Cross Hospital was supported almost entirely by money raised within the black community. Later, a number of white citizens contributed.

Religious institutions maintained a strong line of segregation. Some white churches refused memberships to blacks and others allowed them to visit but restricted their seating to the back of the church. Blacks founded their own churches, and these organizations also provided social services. By 1900 Louisville had sixty-six black churches, mostly Baptist. The larger ones were often involved in CIVIL RIGHTS initiatives.

The federal Civil Rights Act of 1875 prohibited discrimination in hotels, restaurants, public conveyances, and public amusement parks, but the act was ignored in Louisville as well as elsewhere in the South and was declared unconstitutional by the Supreme Court in 1883. In the 1880s and 1890s steps were taken to eliminate the inconsistencies in segregation. More white establishments began to exclude blacks even though they had been previously admitted.

At the end of the Civil War, Louisville blacks sought to attend PUBLIC SCHOOLS. Between 1865 and 1870 the only schools for blacks were run by the Freedman's Bureau and missionary societies. It was not until 1870 that blacks received their first public school and in 1873 their first school building—CENTRAL COLORED School at Kentucky and Sixth. Black schools were overcrowded and highly inferior to schools for whites. After the 1896 Supreme Court decision *Plessy v. Ferguson,* which gave constitutional support to segregation, a myriad of segregation laws followed. In 1904 the Day Law, named after Kentucky state representative Carl Day, was passed by the General Assembly, making it illegal for black and white students to attend school together, even colleges and nursing schools.

Housing was another area in which segregation intensified over time. In the late 1800s and early 1900s, most African Americans lived in large NEIGHBORHOODS near the center of town. There also were other large concentrations of blacks, including one in the West End running along Walnut (Muhammad Ali Blvd.) and Chestnut Streets. The Petersburg community, located in the WET WOODS near Old SHEPHERDSVILLE and Newburg Roads, was settled by free blacks in the 1850s. After the Civil War, blacks were able to acquire land in the area because its swampy conditions made it undesirable for whites. Having absorbed Petersburg in the late nineteenth century, by 1990 NEWBURG became an unincorporated residential community with a POPULATION of 21,650, most African American. Within Louisville's city limits, blacks who did reside in white areas lived in SHOTGUN COTTAGES along ALLEYS adjacent to white residential streets, in a carryover from antebellum days when free blacks and slaves often lived in close proximity to the whites they served. Throughout the West End blocks were either all black or all white, creating a checkerboard pattern. In the first two decades of the twentieth century, blacks moved into the West End in increasing numbers, which alarmed whites in the area, and induced them to advocate an ordinance segregating housing.

On May 11, 1914, the Louisville BOARD OF ALDERMEN enacted an ordinance that in effect prohibited blacks from moving into blocks that were white and were designated by the city as "white blocks." The law applied equally to whites moving into blocks designated as black. In a test case by the National Association for the Advancement of Colored People (NAACP), Charles Buchanan, a white real estate dealer, sold a plot of land in a white area in PORTLAND to WILLIAM WARLEY, a black man. Buchanan agreed to the terms in the deed that stated that Warley would purchase the land only if he was allowed to reside there. Under the law he would not be able to do so, and Buchanan filed suit in Jefferson County Court to test the validity of the ordinance. The county court and the Kentucky Court of Appeals (then the state's highest tribunal) upheld the constitutionality of the ordinance. But on April 17, 1917, the U.S. Supreme Court, in *Buchanan vs. Warley,* declared the ordinance unconstitutional, on the grounds that it denied members of both races the right to own and dispose of property as they saw fit. The absence of a valid ordinance did not end housing segregation. In restrictive covenants written into deeds, buyers agreed not to sell their property to members of the other race. When in 1968 the Federal Fair Housing Act made such discrimination illegal, it became common practice among realtors to sell or rent to blacks only property in black areas.

Not until after WORLD WAR II did Louisville's African Americans begin to seriously challenge segregation. The separate-but-equal doctrine was attacked on one front after another. At the forefront of the struggle was the NAACP, which led most of the legal battles, and the *LOUISVILLE DEFENDER*, an African American newspaper that urged blacks to protest discrimination. In 1947, with the help of the NAACP, Dr. P.O. Sweeney filed suit against the city for the right to play golf on the municipal golf courses until such times as separate but equal facilities were provided. In 1952, after many court hearings and appeals, a federal court ruled that the city must allow blacks to play on city golf courses until equal facilities were available. The first amendment to the Day Law came in 1948 when black representative Charles A. Anderson placed a bill before the Kentucky General Assembly to permit NURSING schools to accept members of either race. The bill passed with an amendment to include postgraduate courses for doctors that would allow black physicians to take their residencies in white hospitals.

Also in 1948 Central High School teacher Lyman T. Johnson applied to the University of Kentucky to enter the graduate program in history, since Kentucky State University, an all-black state school, offered no such program. Denied admittance because of his race, Johnson filed suit against the university. In March 1949 federal judge H. Church Ford ordered the university to admit blacks to the colleges of law, engineering, PHARMACY, and the graduate school, since Kentucky State did not provide those programs. In March 1950 the Kentucky General Assembly amended the Day Law to permit students of both races to attend the same institutions of higher education, providing that the governing body of that institution approved and that a comparable course was not taught at Kentucky State. Shortly after, BELLARMINE COLLEGE, URSULINE COLLEGE, SOUTHERN BAPTIST THEOLOGICAL SEMINARY, and the Louisville Presbyterian Seminary all desegregated. The UNIVERSITY OF LOUISVILLE attempted to delay desegregating, but with the NAACP prepared to file suit the trustees voted to open professional and graduate schools in the summer of 1950 and the rest of the university in the 1951–52 school year. Consequently, LOUISVILLE MUNICIPAL COLLEGE closed in 1951.

Many other areas were desegregated in the postwar period. The trustees of the LOUISVILLE FREE PUBLIC LIBRARY voted to open all branches to all persons in 1952. In 1955 Mayor ANDREW BROADDUS ordered all city PARKS, SWIMMING pools, and amphitheaters to admit everyone.

In May 1954 the historic *Brown v. Board of Education of Topeka* decision was handed down by the U.S. Supreme Court. Shortly thereafter Louisville school superintendent OMER CARMICHAEL and Kentucky governor Lawrence W. Wetherby announced that the city and the state would do whatever was necessary to comply with the law of the land. These statements had the effect of eliminating school desegregation as a political issue. Thus Louisville avoided anything that resembled the ugly debacle at Little Rock, Arkansas, in 1957. The Louisville plan, implemented in 1956, reorganized the entire Louisville school district to serve all children as conveniently as possible regardless of race. This plan did not cover all of the incorporated city nor any regions beyond it. All parents were allowed to request a transfer to a school in another district, provided that school was not full of students from its own district. In almost all cases, parents were granted the transfer of their first choice. In the end, there was 100 percent integration in principle, but because of the transfers there was very little actual integration. Throughout the sixties and seventies, whites left the city for the suburbs in large numbers, many to escape integration. This made the schools even more segregated. In 1973 a suit was brought against the public schools by a coalition of civil rights groups in an effort to take positive action to integrate schools. The suit was dismissed by federal judge James F. Gordon, but his decision was reversed by the U.S. Circuit Court in the summer of 1975, and the appeals court ordered Gordon to implement a desegregation plan by the fall term. Gordon worked with school officials in merging city and Jefferson County school systems. He imposed a plan that merged all Jefferson County districts except ANCHORAGE Independent, and integrated the public schools through the busing of students. BUSING met enormous resistance, leading to school boycotts and violent demonstrations in the southern and southwestern parts of the county. In the end, school integration prevailed in the merged county schools. Busing no longer exists for the sole purpose of integration.

The attempt to desegregate downtown public facilities began in 1960. With nonviolent demonstrations sweeping the South, Louisville civil rights leaders focused on legislation. Black Louisville alderman William W. Becket introduced a public accommodations ordinance in January. The measure was defeated eleven to one that March. After continued negotiation between civil rights leaders and Mayor BRUCE HOBLITZELL's Committee on Human Relations failed to bring about favorable results with the Democratic aldermen, two tactics were adopted. First, a voter registration drive was begun to add thousands of new black voters to defeat the Democratic administration and replace it with aldermen and a mayor who would pass a public accommodation ordinance. Second, nonviolent demonstrations took place during the late winter and spring of 1961. Large numbers of blacks, mostly youths, and a number of white supporters picketed downtown restaurants, and a number of sit-ins took place. Police arrested demonstrators, charging the youths with delinquency and the adults with disorderly conduct. A boycott of downtown businesses exerted economic pressure to deflate the usual Easter sales boom. The demonstrations resulted in negotiations by the Mayor's Committee on Human Relations with downtown businessmen. By June most downtown businesses agreed to voluntary desegregation.

Meanwhile the voter registration drive was a factor in replacing the mayor and aldermen with a Republican administration. Newly elected mayor William O. Cowger announced the creation of the Louisville Human Relations Commission that worked to draw up a public accommodations ordinance and enlist communitywide support for the measure. On May 14, 1963, the aldermen passed the ordinance that forbade racial discrimination in public businesses and imposed fines up to one hundred dollars for each violation. A two-year drive resulted in a statewide civil rights act passed in 1966 that prohibited discrimination in public accommodations and employment.

The last big struggle for desegregation in Louisville was in housing. After World War II, hundreds of new homes were being built in the suburbs, especially in the South and East Ends. African Americans, for the most part, were excluded from moving into these areas because of unfair practices of real estate agents and lending institutions. Blockbusting by white entrepreneurs in the West End during the 1960s drove whites out in large numbers. Fearing this would create one large ghetto in the West End, concerned citizens, white and black, tried to convince other whites in the area not to move. These efforts failed, and white flight eventually swept the West End. The main housing concern was that African Americans did not have the freedom to live anywhere in the county that they chose.

As early as 1964, the Human Relations Commission worked to get an enforceable housing ordinance passed by the aldermen. When the Republican administration refused to support such a measure, the Committee on Open Housing was formed in October 1966. The committee, a coalition of leaders from several civil rights groups, mostly black, negotiated with city officials throughout the winter of 1966-67. When the negotiations broke down that spring, these groups organized nonviolent demonstrations downtown and in the South End. The South End demonstrations had the expected result of drawing large numbers of South End residents out on the streets to heckle, taunt, and throw objects at the marchers. The demonstrations failed to pressure city officials into voting for the ordinance, and the demonstrations were discontinued in June, when housing supporters changed their strategy to focus on voter registration. These efforts resulted in the replacement of ten of the twelve aldermen in the November election, and an enforceable open-housing ordinance was passed the next month. The ordinance has had a minimal effect, as more sophisticated forms of discrimination were practiced. Although African Americans live in most areas of the county, the West End is now predominantly black, and the East and South Ends are, to a lesser extent, predominantly white. Racial divisions have left a residue of tensions between the races.

See George C. Wright, *Life Behind a Veil* (Baton Rouge 1985); Kentucky Commission on Human Rights, *Kentucky's Black Heritage* (Frankfort 1971); George H. Yater, *Two Hundred Years at the Falls of the Ohio* (Louisville 1978 and 1987), 152–53.

SELLERSBURG. Tribes of Eastern Woodland Indians once inhabited the area where the town of Sellersburg, Indiana, lies. About 1790, frontiersmen hunters traveled north from the OHIO RIVER along a narrow path called Hunters' Trace. Along the path grew ninety-foot-tall hickory trees, oak trees with five-foot diameters, and very large poplars. Once pioneers crossed the Alleghenies into the region to purchase farms from recipients of Clark's Grant land, the trail became a wagon path. The portion of U.S. Hwy. 31 running through Sellersburg follows this same route.

By 1800 settlers from Pennsylvania, Virginia, and North Carolina had established farms near the bottomlands of *Silver Creek* and its tributaries. Their presence soon created a need for grist mills to grind their grain and lumber mills to furnish materials for the ship-building industries in Jeffersonville and NEW ALBANY. There was also a demand for whiskey, and many farmers operated stills.

In 1815 the Clark County commissioners were asked by residents to build a road from New Albany to Charlestown. When finished, it passed through what was to be Sellersburg in the proximity of the present New Albany St. In 1820 the Utica and Salem Rd. was built between Utica and New Providence (Borden). The present Utica St. is located on or near a portion of that road.

In 1846, the Indiana legislature authorized the Jeffersonville Railroad Co. to build a line from Jeffersonville to Columbus, Indiana, to connect with the Madison & Indianapolis Railroad. Completed in late 1851, it was merged with the Madison & Indianapolis line in 1866, creating the Jeffersonville, Madison, & Indianapolis Railroad. The track was near the intersection of the New Albany and Charlestown and Utica and Salem Roads, where Moses W. Sellers and John Hill owned a large tract of land. In 1846 they platted a village that they called Sellarsburgh. It was laid out without right angles and has been described as resembling a box twisted and squeezed together. Sellers became a merchant in the new village and was appointed its first postmaster in 1852. Sellersburg was incorporated as a town on November 10, 1890.

The most significant early industrial enterprise was the manufacture of cement. Layers of limestone and veins of hydraulic lime (natural cement) provided more than adequate raw material. The first cement mill was built in 1866 by the Falls City Cement Co. The Louisville Cement Co., located in the adjacent town of Speed, was by 1900 the largest manufacturer of natural cement in the nation. In the early 1900s a superior product was developed using limestone, shale, and added CHEMICALS. Since there was an abundance of limestone and shale, cement mills switched to the new PORTLAND cement. Louisville Cement was recognized as a leading producer of the new product as early as 1905. Although the proximity of the cement directly affected the ECONOMY of Sellersburg, the town always had its own factories, mills, and other business ventures. The awarding of defense contracts to Louisville Cement and the building of the Indiana Ordnance Works in Charlestown during WORLD WAR II opened thousands of jobs for the people of Sellersburg.

The Sellersburg Stone Co., founded in 1932, supplied stone for the construction of the ordnance works. The work was done by hand and was slow. After the war, the stone company was mechanized in order to meet the demand for stone to be used in road construction and lime dust for agricultural purposes. The company, under new ownership, remains a solid contributor to the economy. Another survivor is Haas Cabinet Co., established in 1938. The company adapted to the demands of World War II by switching to making ammunition boxes and pallets. At the beginning of the postwar building boom, Haas began selling to home builders and later to distributors. Its market now extends from the East Coast to the Rocky Mountains.

Sellersburg's failed attempts to annex Speed and portions of Hamburg have made it more difficult to plan for further growth. Sellersburg is located in SILVER CREEK Township in Clark County, adjacent to Interstate 65. It is served by the Clark County Airport and is the home of Region 13 campus of Indiana Vocational Technical College.

The POPULATION of the city was 3,177 in 1970, 3,211 in 1980, 5,745 in 1990, and 6,039 in 1997.

See Lewis C. Baird, Baird's History of Clark County (Indianapolis 1909); Carl E. Kramer, Sellersburg: A Century of Change (Sellersburg, Ind., 1990); William Lee, History Clark County, Ind., (Chicago 1889); L.A. Williams, History of the Ohio Falls Cities and Their Counties (Cleveland 1882); Sellersburg Library folder files.

Charline Hall

SELLIGER, MAX (b [?] 1852; d Philadelphia, Pennsylvania, April 10, 1938). Distiller. In 1872 Max Selliger started as a bookkeeper for the whiskey house of Barkhouse Bros. & Co. The Barkhouse brothers built a distillery on Story Ave. in 1877 and changed the company's name to Kentucky Distilling Co. Selliger became a salesman for the firm. In 1879 he left the company to form a partnership with Nathan Hofheimer. The new company, Hofheimer and Selliger, was located at 8 MAIN St. below First St. This wholesale liquor company had exclusive control of many of Kentucky's finest bourbons.

In 1881 George H. Moore opened the Belmont Distillery between Seventeenth and Eighteenth Streets on Lexington St. (now Breckinridge) and later built the Astor Distillery at the same location. Selliger became treasurer of the Belmont Distillery Co. but continued his partnership with Hofheimer until 1884, when he left that firm and became a partner in the new firm of Moore and Selliger.

Moore and Selliger had offices at 110 W Main, in the heart of Louisville's "Whiskey Row." In 1897 George Moore died and the company became Max Selliger and Co. It continued to operate the Belmont and Astor Distilleries until 1920 when PROHIBITION shut them down. In 1933 Selliger sold his distilleries and all his brands to Leo Gerngross and Emil Schwarzhaupt, who also bought the Bernheim Distilling Co. in 1933. They combined the two companies and renamed them the Bernheim Distilleries. Eventually Bernheim became a subsidiary of UNITED DISTILLERS MANUFACTURING INC., a subsidiary of Guinness PLC.

Michael R. Veach

SEMONIN, PAUL F., JR. (b Louisville, 1908; d Louisville, March 18, 1993). Realtor. The Semonin family has been part of Louisville's civic and business community for three generations. William J. Semonin, a Louisville native, was actively involved in civic affairs and various small businesses such as the Parkland Swimming Pool on Hazel St. south of Magnolia Ave. He held various posts in county GOVERNMENT including Jefferson County assessor through 1901, Jefferson County court clerk from 1902 to 1906, county magistrate and indexer of public records before his death in 1915. He and his wife Ida (Dietsler) Semonin, had one son, Paul Francois Senior, born in Louisville November 21, 1882.

As a young man, Paul worked with his father in the assessor's office and helped in the family businesses. He graduated from the University of Louisville School of Law in 1906 and was admitted to the bar but practiced only two years. He spent five years in the ADVERTISING department of both the *COURIER-JOURNAL* and the *LOUISVILLE TIMES* but, foreseeing the post–WORLD WAR I residential and commercial growth in Louisville, opened the real estate firm of Semonin-Goodman Co. Semonin was president and Harry W. Goodman vice president of the fledgling company at 207–8 Paul Jones Building. In 1919 Semonin sold his interest in the firm to Goodman and became president of Peerless Manufacturing Co. the next year. In 1921 he was with the Louisville Real Estate and Development Co., and in 1925 he re-entered the real estate business as Paul Semonin Inc. with offices in the Starks Building at Fourth and Walnut (Muhammad Ali Blvd.) Streets.

Paul F. Semonin Sr. married Edith Shallcross, daughter of Marcellus B. Shallcross, June 14, 1905. They had four children: William, Paul F. Junior, Marcellus, and Edith. He died in 1941.

Paul F. Semonin Jr. became the third generation of the Semonin family to be active in Louisville's civic life. He attended Male High School where he was a member of the football team. He also played FOOTBALL for the UNIVERSITY OF LOUISVILLE in the mid-1920s. Semonin is best known for heading the real estate and development firm founded by his father in 1914. Although he had worked in the business since the mid-1930s, he did not become president until his father died in 1941. Under his management Paul Semonin Realtors grew to be the largest real estate firm in Kentucky, with offices in Louisville, Lexington, and southern Indiana.

When Semonin assumed leadership, his first venture in subdivision development was the completion of Indian Hills in eastern Jefferson County, a project his father had begun in 1927 on a five-hundred-acre tract known as the Indian Hill Stock Farm. The Semonin firm became well known for its subsequent developments, both residential and commercial.

Paul Semonin Jr. was active in both local and national trade associations, serving as president of the Louisville Board of Realtors in 1948 and the Kentucky Association of Realtors, and he was named Realtor of the Year by both in 1960. He was also a vice president and director of the National Association of Realtors, which named him Realtor emeritus.

Community service also was important to Semonin. He was appointed a director of the Louisville Chamber of Commerce (GREATER LOUISVILLE INC.), and in 1956 he served as chairman of the URBAN RENEWAL advisory committee for Mayor William O. Cowger and as chairman of a citizens' committee organized to promote the adoption of a proposal to merge Louisville and forty-six square miles of its SUBURBS. His interest in civic affairs earned him the Louisville Board of Realtors' John R. Carpenter Memorial Award for Community Service.

He was married to Virginia Reeves. They had three children: Judith, Paul F. III, and David S. Semonin is buried in CAVE HILL CEMETERY.

In 1986 George Gans III bought controlling interest in the company and also formed Semonin Commercial Group to handle sale and lease of commercial space. Since the commercial division produced only 1.25 percent of the firm's income, Gans decided to close it in 1994. Since then Semonin has concentrated on residential property. In 1999 the Minneapolis-based HomeServices.Com, a subsidiary of MidAmerican Energy Holdings Co. of Des Moines, Iowa, purchased Paul Semonin Realtors, although Gans was kept on as CEO of the local operation. The HomeService company provides national resources such as online services for the local company.

See *History of Kentucky: The Bluegrass State* (Louisville 1928); *Courier-Journal*, March 19, 1993.

SEMPLE, ELLEN CHURCHILL (b Louisville, January 8, 1863; d West Palm Beach, Florida, May 8, 1932). Geographer. Semple was born to hardware wholesaler Alexander Bonner and Emerine (Price) Semple. After attending private schools in Louisville, she went on to Vassar College in New York to receive a B.A. in 1882 and an M.A. in 1891. Semple began studies at the University of Leipzig in Germany in 1891–92 and 1895 with Friedrich Ratzel, who influenced her to study GEOGRAPHY. She lectured at the University of Chicago in anthropo-geography early in the twentieth century, as well as at the Royal Geographic Society in London and the Royal Scottish Geographical Society in Edinburgh.

Semple taught for a number of years at the SEMPLE COLLEGIATE SCHOOL and then did research abroad. The school was located on Fourth St. between St. Catherine and Oak Streets. Semple was a member of a group of scholars who advised President Woodrow Wilson for the Peace Conference of Versailles in 1919. She urged the president to consider the ethnic characteristics of Europe when redrawing its territorial boundaries. In 1921 she joined the staff at Clark University's School of Geography in Worcester, Massachusetts. Semple studied geography when the field was just emerging in the United States, and she was influential in defining it and establishing it as a legitimate academic endeavor here.

In addition, she educated a whole generation of future leaders in the field. She lectured extensively in the United States and Europe and traveled the world doing research for her many publications. Semple often returned to Louisville between traveling and lecturing to write.

Semple's first publications included "The Influence of the Appalachian Barrier upon Colonial History" (1897) and "Louisville, a Study in Economic Geography" (1900), both of which appeared in the *Journal of School Geography.* Her other works include *American History and Its Geographic Conditions* (1903), *Influences of Geographic Environment*, on the basis of Ratzel's system of Anthropo-Geography (1911), and *The Geography of the Mediterranean* (1931). She also published in the *Bulletin of the American Geographical Society* and the *Geographical Journal*, London.

Semple received many awards, including

Ellen Churchill Semple.

alumna membership in Phi Beta Kappa at Vassar in 1899, the American Geographical Society's Cullum Geographical Medal in 1914, and the Geographical Society of Chicago's Helen Culver Medal in 1931. In 1923 she became the first woman to receive an honorary degree from the University of Kentucky. Semple was also a charter member of the Association of American Geographers, of which she was president in 1921. The present-day Ellen Churchill Semple Elementary School, located at 724 Denmark St., was named in her honor after her death in 1932.

Funeral services were held at the Church of the Advent in Louisville and she is buried in CAVE HILL CEMETERY. Semple has been honored annually since 1973 at the University of Kentucky by Ellen Churchill Semple Day, a symposium on geography sponsored by the Department of Geography.

See Preston E. James, Wilford A. Bladen, and Pradyumna P. Karan, "Ellen Churchill Semple and the Development of a Research Paradigm" in *The Evolution of Geographic Thought in America: A Kentucky Root,* ed. Wilford A. Bladen and Pradyumna P. Karan (Dubuque, Iowa 1983); John W. Leonard, ed. *Woman's Who's Who of America* (New York 1914).

Matthew J. Brandon

SEMPLE, PATRICIA BLACKBURN (b Louisville, Kentucky, May 20, 1853; d Louisville, June 4, 1923). Educator and civic leader. Born to Alexander Bonner and Emerine (Price) Semple, Patty Semple had one brother, Frank, and two sisters, Frances and distinguished geographer Ellen Churchill. After attending Vassar College, she married Fred Effinger of Washington, D.C., and resided in that city until their divorce in the mid-1880s.

Semple retook her maiden name and returned to Louisville, where she began teaching at the Hampton College on Walnut St. (Muhammad Ali Blvd.). In 1893 Semple established a girls college preparatory school, first known as the Patty B. Semple School and later the SEMPLE COLLEGIATE SCHOOL, located on Fourth St. In March 1890 Semple was one of thirty-seven prominent women present at Susan Avery's home at Fourth and BROADWAY for the founding of the WOMAN'S CLUB OF LOUISVILLE. The group drafted a constitution on the model of the recently formed Chicago Woman's Club and elected Semple its first president.

The civic-minded Semple was also responsible for founding the Kentucky Women's College Club, the Legal Aid Society, and the GIRL SCOUT COUNCIL of Louisville. She also aided in the drive to establish a city juvenile court. She sat on the board of the Children's Protective Association, and she was the first woman to be named to the board of the LOUISVILLE FREE PUBLIC LIBRARY. During WORLD WAR I, Semple chaired the war work of the Home Department of the Food Administration.

She had one daughter, Bonner, who became a well-known playwright and author. Semple died after a two-year illness and is buried in Cave Hill Cemetery.

See Bess A. Ray, ed., *Dictionary of Prominent Women of Louisville and Kentucky* (Louisville 1940); Mary Adelberg, ed. *The Woman's Club of Louisville, 1890–1990* (Louisville 1990).

SEMPLE COLLEGIATE SCHOOL. Semple Collegiate School, on S Fourth St. between St. Catherine and Oak Streets, was a private school for girls founded by Patty Blackburn Semple along with her sister ELLEN CHURCHILL SEMPLE. The Semple sisters were well-educated, progressive women. Both attended Vassar College, where Patty studied from 1868 to 1871 and Ellen graduated in 1882. In 1891 Ellen received a master's degree by correspondence from Vassar. Both sisters began their teaching careers in Louisville in 1884, Patty at Hampton College and Ellen at the Kentucky School for Girls and the Female Seminary.

Building a solid professional reputation as skilled teachers, the Semple sisters wanted to open a new school where they could implement a more rigorous curriculum for girls. The Semple Collegiate School started in 1893. Four teachers instructed a small group of students ranging in age from six to seventeen. The school was strong in mathematics and science but stressed the humanities. Classical and modern LITERATURE, ancient and modern history, GEOGRAPHY, art, music, foreign languages (German, Latin, and FRENCH), and anthropology were among the subjects offered. It was known as one of the region's best college preparatory schools for women.

Patty Semple ran the school until 1900. At that time, she decided to retire, in part because of health problems but also due to an increasing involvement in different civic activities and because her daughter, who graduated from Semple in 1899, had been a reason for opening the school. Ellen Semple gave up the school because she began to spend more of her time on research, writing books and articles, giving lectures at various universities on subjects of anthropology and geography, and traveling extensively abroad.

In 1900 management of the school was taken over by Annie Moore and Anna J. Hamilton, and the name was changed to Semple Collegiate College and Moore Primary School. The school closed in 1915. That year many of the Semple students transferred to the newly opened Louisville Collegiate School.

Semple Collegiate School was one of the progressive schools in Louisville that addressed the importance of a solid academic education while it emphasized the principles of learning through active participation and thinking rather than memorization.

See Vickey A. Kime, "Semple Collegiate School," unpublished paper, University of Louisville Archives and Records Center, 1987; Florence M. Wolf, "A Study of Girl's Schools in Louisville Prior to 1900," M.A. thesis, University of Louisville, 1951; Elizabeth Booker, *The Girl Graduate, Her Own Book* (memory book of Semple Collegiate and Moore Primary School), Louisville Free Public Library, 1912.

SENG JEWELERS. In 1889 Charles E. Seng, who had worked with Joseph Kern as a watchmaker, and his brother Christopher, who had previously been employed at Buschemeyer and Seng Jewelers, established Seng Brothers jewelry business on MARKET St. Although Christopher soon left the business, Charles continued to offer retail jewelry and watch repair services while also grinding spectacle lenses. After several moves into different structures along Market St., the business was purchased from Seng by Benn B. Davis in 1938. In 1952 Davis moved the business, which hand-crafts pieces on site, into the STARKS BUILDING, with its showroom windows fronting Fourth St. Davis's son Lee joined his father as a partner in the business in 1969.

SENNING'S PARK. Located off New Cut Rd. opposite IROQUOIS PARK, it was opened just after the beginning of the twentieth century by Frederick Carl Senning, who settled in Louisville in 1868 upon his arrival from Germany. In 1877 he married Minnie Goepper, and they opened their first restaurant on MARKET St. In 1883 they built and operated Louisville's first bowling alley at Eighth and MAIN Streets. Later they branched out into a successful hotel business—Senning's Hotel at Second and Jefferson Streets.

In 1902 the Sennings bought two and a half acres of land from the estate of Fredrika Oswald at the corner of New Cut Rd. and Kenwood Dr., south of the Grand Blvd. (Southern Pkwy.) for the park. It was conveniently located just one block from the Fourth St. electric streetcar loop. From the beginning the park became a popular spot for dancing and dining and for large gatherings such as conventions, political rallies, and picnics.

During PROHIBITION the Sennings' son, William, opened a zoo in the park. It was the first in the city and had a large variety of animals including lions, leopards, deer, alligators, and bears. The zoo drew many people, especially children, who were the biggest consumers of SOFT DRINKS and ice cream.

The PARK barely survived the GREAT DEPRESSION. Attendance dropped and it became expensive to keep the zoo, since some animals required special food and care. The Sennings, however, managed to keep the park and the zoo going until 1939 when Frederick died. In 1940 the property was sold for $15,000 to B.A. Watson, who changed the name to Colonial Gardens Restaurant and Grill and closed the zoo.

See Jill Herman, "Senning's Park," unpublished student paper, University of Louisville Archives and Records Center, 1985; *Courier-Journal*, March 5, 1939; *Sentinel-News*, Shelbyville, Ky., May 18, 1988.

Post card advertisement for Sennings Park.

SEPARATE COACH LAW. African American travelers had to endure the humiliations of SEGREGATION on American RAILROADS from the 1830s until the 1960s. Although the CIVIL RIGHTS Act of 1875 assured blacks of "full and equal enjoyment of the accommodations" on railroads, the law did not guarantee compliance. The Supreme Court emasculated the Civil Rights Act in 1883, ruling that, while states could not impose segregation, private individuals (including corporations) were free to do so. By the 1890s the Kentucky General Assembly ignored even that provision when on March 15, 1892, it passed the separate coach law requiring every interstate railroad passenger car (this law did not relate to STREETCARS or INTERURBANS) to be divided by a wooden partition and a door with conspicuous signs denoting each part, which were supposed to be equal, as either "white" or "colored." Several people, including Col. Robert Ingersoll, renowned agnostic and orator, were interviewed by a *COURIER-JOURNAL* reporter in October 1893 and opposed the law, saying a person should be allowed to ride wherever he wished. "As far as I am concerned, I would rather sit by a clean negro than an unclean white man." Others such as Gov. William O. Bradley (1895–99), in his address to the General Assembly in 1898, lamented the law, claiming that "every citizen should be judged according to his conduct, decency, and good citizenship, rather than his color."

However, few in Kentucky agreed. The General Assembly used the criteria of race, even though the railroad companies primarily opposed the JIM CROW law, more often due to the expense incurred in the duplication of equipment than out of any moral sentiment. In the end, they reluctantly complied or faced fifteen-hundred-dollar fines. In the Louisville area, African American leaders joined the statewide anti-separate-coach movement and promoted a boycott of Kentucky railroads.

After more than a year of successful boycotting, the leaders developed a test case for the COURTS by having Evansville, Indiana, minister W.H. Anderson purchase first-class tickets on the LOUISVILLE & NASHVILLE RAILROAD (L&N) for his wife and himself from Evansville to Madisonville, Kentucky. On October 30, 1893, the minister and his wife boarded the train and uneventfully enjoyed their ride to the Kentucky border. However, when the train crossed the OHIO RIVER, the Andersons were asked to move to the "colored" section. After refusing to leave their seats, they were removed from the car. The minister and his wife then purchased two tickets from Henderson, Kentucky, to Madisonville and were again removed from the train after refusing to leave the white compartment.

In the ensuing lawsuit, in which Anderson sued the L&N for $15,000, U.S. District Court judge John W. Barr ruled on June 4, 1894, that, while the right to segregate the coach for intrastate travel rested within the state's powers, the attempt to regulate interstate commerce, an area reserved for the U.S. Congress, was unconstitutional (W.H. Anderson v. Louisville & Nashville Railroad Co.). Although this was not the total victory for which they had hoped (Anderson, in addition, only received a one-cent judgment plus court costs), AFRICAN AMERICANS still held triumphant celebrations in Louisville, Lexington, and Owensboro.

The victory was short-lived, however, because in May 1896, the U.S. Supreme Court decision in Plessy v. Ferguson ruled that state laws requiring segregated railroad cars and all public facilities were indeed constitutional as long as the facilities provided were "separate but equal." While the intrastate portion of the law was again validated in 1900 by the U.S. Supreme Court (Chesapeake and Ohio Railway Co. v. Commonwealth of Kentucky), the interstate ruling in the Anderson case was overturned by the 1920 ruling in South Covington and Cincinnati Street Railway v. Kentucky, which legalized segregation by requiring all Kentucky railroad companies to provide separate coaches for African Americans. In 1955 the Interstate Commerce Commission banned racial discrimination on interstate, but not intrastate, railroad passenger traffic. But Jim Crow persisted due to pressure from state governments determined to prevent desegregation of any public facilities even though railroads wanted to abandon the practice as a burdensome expense. After the civil rights laws passed by Congress with President Lyndon Johnson's encouragement, the Kentucky General Assembly repealed all "dead letter" segregation laws with a sweeping CIVIL RIGHTS bill. Implemented in the summer of 1966, the laws brought the state into compliance with the Federal Civil Rights Act of 1964 and guaranteed every individual the "full and equal enjoyment" of all public accommodations.

See George C. Wright, *A History of Blacks in Kentucky* (Frankfort 1992); George C. Wright, *Life Behind a Veil* (Baton Rouge 1985).

SETTLE, ANNA (HUBBUCH) (b Louisville, July 20, 1887; d Louisville, March 27, 1951). Attorney and civic leader. Anna Hubbuch Settle was the daughter of William Otto and Anna (Schmid) Hubbuch. She graduated from Louisville Girls High School and the Spencerian Commercial School (SPENCERIAN COLLEGE). From 1907 until 1913, she worked as a secretary at the LOUISVILLE FREE PUBLIC LIBRARY where she met, and later married, George Thomas Settle, head of the library.

In 1923 she earned a law degree from the UNIVERSITY OF LOUISVILLE. In addition to her practice, Settle was a temporary judge of the Jefferson County Court on several occasions. She was the first woman to sit as a judge in Jefferson County.

For more than twenty-five years, Settle was active in community, welfare, education, and cultural matters in Louisville and the state. She worked on many important legal cases and helped to draft a number of laws to aid Kentucky's children, the blind, and women.

Settle was involved in local and state politics. In 1929 she served on the mayor's committee to investigate and reorganize the magistrate COURTS. She was also a member of the mayor's committee that drafted a constitutional amendment, never passed, to combine Louisville and Jefferson County. Settle was chair of the women's division of Jefferson County's election organization during Democrat Keen Johnson's successful gubernatorial bid in 1939. Following his election, Johnson called on Settle to handle a legal case to allow Kentucky to give financial aid to the state's dependent children. In 1943 she was chosen by the U.S. Department of Labor to serve as a field representative to coordinate, along with War Manpower Commission officials, the transfer of women from nonessential jobs to war-production employment.

Settle also championed a number of other civic causes. As president of the Consumers' League of Kentucky from 1930 until 1944, she fought against legislation attacking Kentucky's minimum-wage law and frequently spoke out in support of stronger minimum-wage legislation for women. She also fought against loansharking and helped to draft the state's small-loan law.

Settle was part of an organization of business and professional women, the Altrusa Club, and served as national president in 1922. She served as president of the state chapter of the LEAGUE OF WOMEN VOTERS, the Louisville Women's City Club, and the Louisville Chorus.

Settle and her husband, who died in 1930, had no children. She is buried in CAVE HILL CEMETERY.

See *Courier-Journal*, March 28, 1951; *Louisville Times*, March 28, 1951.

SETTLEMENT HOUSE MOVEMENT. As the nineteenth century came to a close, national attention was focusing on social problems in urban areas where immigrants and others were living in overcrowded, unhealthful tenements. Concerned civic leaders and ordinary citizens alike began to realize that GOVERNMENT was not meeting the many needs of inner-city families, particularly children. The settlement house movement was a nationwide response to social ills in the form of urban, neighborhood-based, organizations whose mission was to meet the needs of the poor who lived nearby. Whether church-sponsored or not, settlement houses became thriving social and civic centers that played a vital role in the urban environment and were a practical expression of democratic ideals for their founders. Although their role in the urban community has been fundamentally that of a civic center offering social services, the nature and scope of what settlement houses provide has always varied, modified in response to the specific needs of the people they serve.

The settlement house movement in the United States began with the establishment of Neighborhood Guild, now University Settlement, in New York City in 1886. It was modeled after Toynbee Hall, established in London two years earlier by vicar Barnett of St. Jude's Parish. Among the pioneers of the movement was Jane Addams, cofounder in 1889 of Hull House in Chicago. The movement came to Louisville in 1895. In that year two theology students, Archibald Hill and W.E. Wilkins, invited future Nobel Peace Prize winner Addams and Dr. Graham Taylor of Chicago Commons to visit the Louisville area. Their ideas on social settlements were well received in Louisville amid the growing concern for the welfare of those who lived in the "less favored district of the city." The movement began in earnest with NEIGHBORHOOD HOUSE in 1895 at Preston and Jefferson St. Currently located at 225 N Twenty-Fifth St. in the PORTLAND neighborhood, and grew with the opening of Wesley Settlement House in 1896 at 803 E Washington St.; Presbyterian Colored Mission in 1898 at 760 S Hancock CABBAGE PATCH Settlement House in 1910 at 1413 S Sixth St.; Plymouth Settlement House in 1917 at 1626 W Chestnut St.; and Louisville Central Community Centers in 1948, at 1015 W Chestnut St. and Village West Mall.

In 1911 the National Federation of Settlements and Neighborhood Centers was founded in the United States. Similar federations also exist in Austria, Canada, Denmark, Finland, France, Germany, Great Britain, the Netherlands, Norway, and Sweden. In 1926 the various national federations formally established the International Federation of Settlements, which would later be represented by observers at the United Nations.

Louisville's settlement houses continue to be successful anchors for NEIGHBORHOODS in need as they adapt their services in response to the welfare of those they serve. Representatives from the houses met together in 1991 to discuss the possibility of joining together to meet program and financial challenges facing the individual agencies. In 1992 the Urban Neighborhood Centers Alliance of Louisville (UNCAL) was formed to facilitate collaboration among the organizations. The founding members include Neighborhood House, Wesley Community House, Cabbage Patch Settlement House, and Louisville Central Community Centers. PRESBYTERIAN COMMUNITY CENTER joined the alliance one year later. Each organization maintains its individuality but, on issues common to all, UNCAL speaks with a strong and influential voice in the city.

Neighborhood House (est. 1896), 225 N Twenty-fifth St. Louisville's first settlement house began in one room at Preston and Jefferson Streets with the financial support of Lucy Belnap of the Belnap Hardware family. Several months later it moved to an old saloon building. By 1902, after serveral moves, it relocated at 530 First St. Expansion under the thirty-five-year leadership of Frances Ingram provided bigger facilities and more services. Over the years NEIGHBORHOOD House's mission has remained essentially the same. It continues to be a human service center that enriches the PORTLAND community through flexible and innovative programming. Current Neighborhood House services include summer day camp for children of single working parents, piano lessons, drama, parents day out, after school enrichment, young adolescent program, hot evening meals for children and teens, emergency food assistance, a senior citizen program that features daily nutritious lunches and support groups, social activities for all ages, and a weekly nursing clinic.

PRESBYTERIAN COMMUNITY CENTER (est. 1898), 760 S Hancock St. The Center began as Hope Community Center in a rented building on Preston St. near Pearl St. Soon Grace Mission Station at Jackson and Lampton Streets was started. Both were founded and supported by JOHN LITTLE, a white Presbyterian minister, with the support of students from the Presbyterian Theological Seminary. Their original purpose was to offer Sunday school classes to the predominantly black neighborhood of SMOKETOWN, but the project soon grew to include sewing, cooking, and carpentry classes. Today a wide array of programs is offered: a child development center, sports and recreation, after school programs, senior citizens activities, hot evening meals for area children and teens, drug and alcohol abuse counseling, employment referral, and emergency assistance for food, rent, and MEDICINE.

Wesley Community House (est. 1903), 803 E Washington St. Originally known as Wesley Settlement House and located at 834 E Jefferson, Wesley Community House is unique among Louisville's settlement houses because it still retains residential staff and volunteers to provide support and services. Among the services Wesley House provides the BUTCHERTOWN and PHOENIX HILL neighborhoods are a child-development center, an array of senior services, and job readiness and computer skills training for single female heads of households. In addition, Wesley's Youth Brigade is part of a comprehensive youth program that also includes services to prevent violence among urban youth.

Cabbage Patch Settlement House (est. 1910), 1413 S Sixth St. The Cabbage Patch Settlement House was first located at 1461 S Ninth St. on what was once the back side of the old Oakland Race Course. The house was originally called "the Oakland." Its name was derived from Alice Hegan Rice's novel Mrs. Wiggs of the Cabbage Patch (1901), which was set in the same neighborhood. In 1929 industrial development forced Cabbage Patch to move to its present location. The founder, Louise Marshall, managed the settlement house for almost seven decades until her death in 1981. Under her capable leadership Cabbage Patch racially integrated its programs in the early 1950s, long before school and community athletic leagues, and remained the only settlement house in Louisville to be funded exclusively by private donations. Cabbage Patch currently offers extensive educational and recreational programs for youth, childcare for preschoolers, and numerous support and assistance programs for families.

Plymouth Community Renewal Center Inc. (est. 1917), 1626 W Chestnut St. First known as Plymouth Settlement House, it was organized by the Reverend E.G. Harris to serve as a center of culture, recreation, and practical training for blacks in Louisville's West End. The work began in the PLYMOUTH CONGREGATIONAL UNITED CHURCH OF CHRIST but soon moved to a small three-story structure. The initial program focused on the needs of children and adults in the Russell neighborhood. It soon included among its programs a dormitory for young black women who had recently moved to the city. By 1944 Plymouth had grown from a local church agency to a citywide Community Chest organization with city leaders as members of the board of directors. The current name was adopted in 1980. It is now associated with Plymouth Church and the Council for Health and Human Ministries of the United Church of Christ and still serves the entire West End.

Louisville Central Community Centers (est. 1948), 1015 W Chestnut St. and Village West Mall. Louisville Central Community Centers is the youngest settlement house in Louisville and plays an active and vital role in the RUSSELL neighborhood. Louisville Central first served newcomers to the city from Appalachia but today the agency provides education, day care, and comprehensive social services for inner-city families. The neighborhood is kept updated by Louisville Central's newspaper, *West Downtown*, which lists and describes available services and acts as a forum for community discussion. Every year Louisville Central honors two local individuals—one adult and one youth—for leadership initiative in education and/or race relations with the Lyman T. Johnson Distinguished Leadership Award. The award recognizes the dedication and struggle of its namesake and honors equally committed recipients.

See George H. Yater, *Two Hundred Years at the Falls of the Ohio* (Louisville 1987); Elva Anne Lyon, University of Louisville Local History Series vol. 17 (Louisville 1940).

John Barrow Jr.
Edna McDonald
Fred Mitchell
J. Tracy Holladay
Sam Watkins

743 CLUB. Suite 743 in the Seelbach Hotel was headquarters for Democratic candidates running statewide between 1947 and 1971. During an era when formal political headquarters were deemed essential, the Seelbach name, location in the center of Louisville at Fourth and Walnut Sts. (Muhammad Ali Blvd.), and hostelry refinements provided an ideal address. Small precinct meetings or Grand Ballroom rallies were serviced with style and efficiency. In every sense a nerve center and command post, headquarters devised strategy, generated publicity, raised money, and organized special interest groups.

The 743 saga began with Gov. Earle C. Clements (1947–50) and closed with Gov. Bert T. Combs (1959–63). It included eleven gubernatorial, twelve U.S. Senate, four presidential, and five lieutenant governor campaigns. On August 21, 1982, approximately two hundred staff members celebrated their participation in this epoch of Kentucky's political past. The reunion assured Suite 743 an enduring legacy in DEMOCRATIC PARTY history. Attending were former governors BERT COMBS, Lawrence Wetherby, and Edward Breathitt Jr.; Lieutenant Governor Wilson Wyatt; and incumbent governor John Y. Brown Jr. Clements and Henry Ward, former highway secretary, sent telegrams. Judge James Mulligan's poem, "In Kentucky," calling politics "the damnedest," was read; and the lusty 743 crowd did little to moderate the judge's opinion.

See "Kentucky Politics: 743—The Seelbach Hotel," program booklet for the 743 Club Reunion, Aug. 21, 1982; *Courier-Journal,* July 18, 1982.

Edward A. Farris

SEVENTH-DAY ADVENTISTS. The name Seventh-day Adventist embodies the two major doctrines of this Christian evangelical church: the seventh day Sabbath as a memorial of creation and the nearing advent of Christ. The Seventh-day Adventist yearbook annually states, "We believe in a transcendent, personal, communicating God as revealed in the Father, the Son, and the Holy Spirit, each equally and uniquely divine, personal, and eternal. We believe in creation by divine fiat and recognize the fall of the human race. Humans are by nature mortal, but may receive immortality through divine grace and the redemption offered through the total atoning work of Jesus Christ."

The church's history nationally dates back to the 1840s, a time of spiritual awakening in the United States. In Louisville in 1888 Elder A. Barry, a licensed African American minister, instructed a small group of ten believers. This group organized as a church February 16, 1890. Today this church is the Magazine Street Seventh-day Adventist Church. It is one of the oldest predominantly black Adventist churches in the world.

In 1896 the first predominantly white Adventist church was organized. Soon afterward, the offices for the Kentucky Conference of Seventh-day Adventist were located at Fourth and Jefferson Streets. This center of activity and membership growth brought about the building of a house of worship at Seventeenth and Jefferson. Eventually a new church was built at 1621 S Fourth St. From a membership of 110 in 1923, a steady growth occurred until the mid-1960s. New churches were established in the south and east ends of Louisville. The congregation on Fourth St. became the First Church. Its continued growth culminated in the construction of a new church building and a ten-grade school on Newburg Rd. along BEARGRASS CREEK.

By 1999, there were seven Louisville churches and small groups, including those organized to provide for the special needs of Spanish- and Korean-speaking people.

Christian education has always been important to Adventists. About 1909 the first Seventh-day Adventist church school in Louisville opened at Twenty-sixth and Hale Streets in a storefront. The church on Fourth St. included three schoolrooms with a playground (the latter now occupied by a TELEPHONE building). In 1959 the house next to the church was purchased and became the school's home for nearly ten years. As enrollment increased a larger facility was needed, resulting in a modern ten-grade school on Southland Blvd.

In 1952 the Magazine Church organized the Emma L. Minnis Elementary School. Seventh-day Adventists have a unique system of beliefs, customs, and spiritual standards that justify these special schools. While private, the schools are open to all who wish a Christian elementary education.

The local churches build upon a strong heritage emphasizing evangelism, publication, health and welfare work, and distribution of Christian literature. Life-Talk Radio, 3–ABN (Three Angels Broadcasting Network), and computerized web sites are some recent endeavors to meet community needs.

Clifton Keller

SHAMBURGER, BOMAN L. (b Cuba, Alabama, June 15, 1906; d Louisville, March 8, 1975). Jefferson County judge. He attended Newton High School in Newton, Mississippi, where he was president of his senior class. He then played semipro baseball briefly in Mississippi, Arkansas, and Texas before attending college on an athletic scholarship. He received a law degree from the University of Mississippi. He moved to Louisville in the early 1930s and began practicing law in County Judge Ben F. Ewing's law firm. He also served as probate commissioner under Ewing from 1932 until 1936.

Shamburger, a Democrat, was Jefferson County judge from January 2, 1950, until December 31, 1953. He defeated Republican Miles R. Thacker by 6,251 votes (66,338–60,087) in the 1949 election. Some of the accomplishments of his administration included the institution of a county police merit system to replace the system of political patronage; creation of a volunteer county fire department to replace the permanent, paid department; creation of a county park system; establishment of a county law library; and the beginning of work to establish a county building code.

Shamburger ran for U.S. representative from the Third District in 1952 but was defeated by Republican John M. Robsion by 14,525 votes (93,738–79,213). From 1954 until 1960 he served as probate commissioner under County Judge Bertram C. Van Arsdale. He later was appointed to the city Board of Registration and remained until the board was abolished in 1972. At the time of his death, Shamburger was serving as chief judge in Jefferson County probate court. Shamburger, who was appointed by County Judge Todd Hollenbach in July 1974, was the county's first full-time probate judge.

Shamburger was married to Florence Newton of Campbellsville, Kentucky. The couple had one son, William. Shamburger is entombed in Resthaven Memorial Park.

See *Courier-Journal*, Jan. 3, 1954, March 9, 1975.

SHANNON FUNERAL SERVICES INC. At the end of the twentieth century, Shannon Funeral Services, Inc. of Shelbyville, Kentucky, had been in business for more than 130 years, with a continuous location for the past hundred years at 1124 Main St.

The firm traces its beginnings to the independent efforts of two cousins, John W. and John S. Shannon. In 1865 John W. established an undertaking and cabinet business in LaGrange. After his death in 1893 his son, R. Lee Shannon Sr., took charge of the business, and in the fall of 1899 he moved it to Shelbyville.

Birds of Passage: Shanty Boats on the Ohio. Drawing by Alexander Van Leshout.

In 1884 cousin John S., with partners S.M. Long and Thomas Ellis, established S.M. Long and Co., also in the funeral and furniture business. Between 1884 and 1891 this company went through several metamorphoses, finally to emerge as the firm of Shannon and Reid. Upon the death of Reid in 1899, R. Lee Shannon Sr., formerly of LaGrange, bought out Reid's interest, and the two Shannon families formed the firm of Shannon and Co., engaged in the business of both funeral services and furniture sales.

Shannon and Co. operated until 1908 when John S. Shannon sold his interest to Edgar Sleadd. The Shannon and Sleadd Co. functioned for about a year, until a devastating fire destroyed both the company and a large section of Main St. businesses.

After the 1909 fire, R. Lee Shannon Sr. and family, minus Sleadd, formed the Shannon Undertaking Co., focusing solely on the funeral business. In 1935 they reorganized as Shannon Funeral Service Inc. The company has passed through several generations of family leadership and had been wholly owned by the Shannon family until 1992, when James W. Davis, an employee, purchased a part of the company and became a partner.

SHANTYBOATS. A "shanty" is defined as a small, roughly built shelter or dwelling. When it is made to float, it is known as a "shantyboat." Shantyboats have provided an alternative lifestyle for a very long time. In the United States some of the earliest shantyboat dwellers were loggers in the Northwest. Shacks were constructed on top of large logs lashed together, and they floated on the same waterways used to float the logs to the sawmills. When the logging operations moved, the shantyboats were towed to the new location.

Shantyboats had indefinite early beginnings on the Ohio River, which was one of the few accessible rivers that flowed westward with the current providing propulsion. The river became a pathway for settlers migrating to the Midwest. The boats they used had to provide living quarters and cargo capacity for all of their belongings. Immigrants crossed the Allegheny Mountains by land in the eighteenth and early nineteenth centuries to the area now known as Pittsburgh. At places in that region, such as Liogoner, flatboats were constructed by boat builders using native timber. Boxy, scow bow designs were fashioned from crude local lumber. As with the Conestoga wagons, these flatboats carried settlers and all their possessions for hundreds of miles downriver to places that would become their new homes. They lived aboard until the materials in the boats were used to build homes ashore.

The design of the first shantyboats on the Ohio River followed the features of the flatboats, with more cabin space incorporated. The hull design with the flat bottom and scow bow was used with a rectangular cabin. Relatively small boats that were rarely over thirty-five feet long were the rule. One-room floor plans with a bathroom were usual. Small deck areas fore and aft were like porches. They were often used for fishing and relaxation.

Colonies of boat dwellers sprang up on the

fringes of developing cities. Connecting boardwalks resembled sidewalks. Some even remained on the riverbank above the water level until seasonal high water periods came. These alternative housing communities primarily accommodated poorer persons. Taxes and land rentals were avoided. In some situations a two-boat arrangement was utilized, with the second one used for potted gardens and for livestock such as chickens. Shantyboats were most numerous during the period after the stock market crash of 1929.

In the Louisville area, BEARGRASS CREEK was the most popular shantyboat community location. The site known as THE POINT had a group of shantyboats tied to shore, while HARRODS CREEK and the area of Portland were also used to a lesser extent. During the years leading up to the GREAT DEPRESSION, shantyboats provided an alternate lifestyle. After the economic collapse, more persons sought a boat-based home. Fish caught were commonly bartered for other goods. Odd jobs and tight finances were routine. Shantyboat children usually attended local schools. These shantyboaters did not migrate and follow the vagabond lifestyle that others chose.

The shantyboat lifestyle in Louisville was all but eliminated by the great FLOOD OF 1937, although there were dwellers as late as the 1950s. Damage to the mooring areas was as severe as damage to the vessels. This forced most shantyboaters to find alternatives ashore. The communities disbanded as improving economics and the flood devastation brought an end to the era. A small number of shantyboaters remained in more isolated locations. These people were more likely to be recluses, out of the mainstream of city life.

Harlan and Anna Hubbard built a shantyboat at Fort Thomas, Kentucky, in the 1940s. Harlan's book, *Shantyboat: A River Way of Life* (1977), chronicled their floating migration to the Louisiana bayous. Their travels took them past Louisville. They are no doubt the best known shantyboaters. Harlan was also an artist and frequently made drawings of their shantyboat. The design of their boat has become the stereotype for these boats, since Hubbard's drawings are so well known. The Hubbards' experience was, however, well past the prime period for shantyboats. Their experiences were not typical of the shantyboat dwellers in the Louisville area.

See Harlan Hubbard, *Shantyboat: A River Way of Life* (Lexington 1977); Carl R. Bogardus, *Shantyboat* (Austin, Ind. 1959).

Frederick M. Parkins

SHAWNEE. Neighborhood in western Louisville bounded by Bank St. to the north, the Shawnee Expressway to the east, BROADWAY to the south, and the OHIO RIVER. In the decades prior to the CIVIL WAR, the fertile lands were sparsely inhabited by Irish, GERMAN, and AFRICAN AMERICAN truck farmers. Many of these

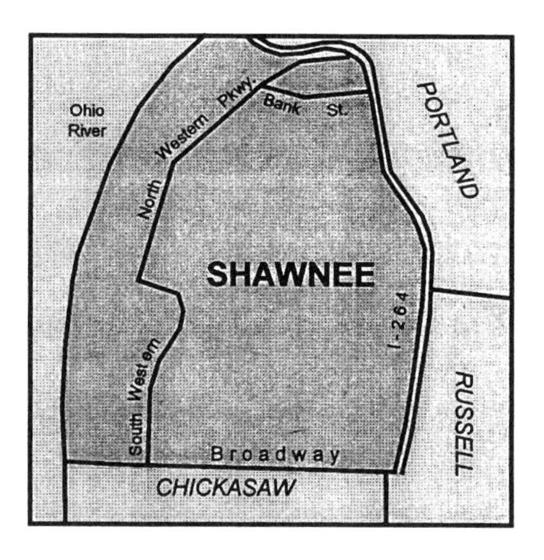

people began to leave the area in the 1870s not only in search of better jobs but also to flee the encroaching POPULATION moving out from the city. By the early 1890s, the region was still used primarily as farm and dairy land. The area began to receive attention from developers and speculators such as Basil Doerhoefer after the 1892 opening of the waterfront Shawnee Park.

In 1895 the city annexed the park along with the surrounding land. This prompted the installation of streetcar lines out to the scenic grounds and induced some affluent families to build homes in western Louisville, which was thought of as more convenient, more economical, and less pretentious than the "snobby" East End. The area continued to gain popularity after the Fontaine Ferry AMUSEMENT PARK opened in 1905 adjacent to SHAWNEE PARK.

The neighborhood was transformed in the decades following WORLD WAR II as white residents moved to the suburbs and sold to African Americans, making the area predominantly black. The mixed residential and commercial community experienced a further change following the desegregation of PUBLIC SCHOOLS as more white families moved to the suburbs and were slowly replaced by African American families in the 1950s and 1960s.

See "Louisville Survey West: Final Report" (Louisville 1977); A Place in Time: The Story of Louisville's Neighborhoods (Louisville 1989).

SHELBY COLLEGE. Shelby College was chartered by the Kentucky General Assembly on December 22, 1798, as Shelby Academy. Along with the charter, the trustees were granted six thousand acres of land south of the Green River. After selling the distant lands to acquire capital, construction began in the SHELBY COUNTY seat of SHELBYVILLE in 1810. Although the academy employed only two teachers by 1816, the school was constantly troubled by financial problems fueled by poor land sales during three subsequent land lotteries, another common method used to secure education funding in the early nineteenth century.

In 1836 the institution was reorganized and rechartered as Shelby College. Continuing financial concerns impelled the trustees to turn the school over in 1841 to the Episcopal Church, which added a theological seminary to the eighteen-acre campus. The school had a preparatory department for ages ten to sixteen and a college that offered a liberal arts curriculum and military instruction.

Aided by an additional land lottery in late 1849, the college expanded to include a scientific school for surveyors, civil engineers, astronomers, pharmacists, and physicians. The school became famous for its astronomical observatory, said to have housed the fourth-largest equatorial telescope in the world, under the guidance of William J. Waller. The school became purely male after 1860, and changed its name to the St. James College following the CIVIL WAR. However, disputes over the use of additional lotteries to provide funding hurt the college, and it closed in 1871.

See Edward D. Shinnick, *Some Old Time History of Shelbyville and Shelby County* (Frankfort 1974).

SHELBY COUNTY. Shelby, the twelfth Kentucky county in order of formation and the third created after Kentucky was admitted into the Union, occupies an area of 383 square miles in north-central Kentucky. It is bounded on the north by Oldham and Henry Counties, on the east by Franklin and Anderson, on the south by Spencer, and on the west by Jefferson. It was created from a portion of Jefferson County on June 23, 1792, and was named in honor of Kentucky's first governor, Isaac Shelby. The county seat is SHELBYVILLE. The 1800 census gave the POPULATION as 8,191; in 1820 the population was 21,047, but by 1870, through emigration to other parts of the West, it had dropped to 15,733, of whom 10,350 were white and 5,383 African American.

Selected Statistics for Shelby County, 1990

Population: 24,824
Population per square mile: 64
Percent African American: 9.9
Percent 0 to 17 years: 25.3
Percent 65 years and over: 13.1
Percent 25 years and over with a high school degree or equivalency: 69.9
Percent 25 years and over with a bachelor's degree: 12.9
Per capita income in 1989: $28,500
Unemployment Rate: 3.3 percent
Married couple families as a percent of total households: 64.2
Median home value: $86,500

The streams of the northeastern part of the county, Benson and Six Mile Creeks, flow into the Kentucky River; the streams of the much larger southern and western watersheds—Clear, Beech, Guist, Brashears, Bull Skin, Fox Run, Plum, Long Run, and FLOYDS FORK—join and flow into the Salt River. The land is gently undulating and in a high state of cultivation. The soil is based upon limestone with red clay foundation and is black, friable, and remarkably fertile. JEPTHA KNOB in eastern Shelby County, named by SQUIRE BOONE, is a unique feature, considered by geologists to be a cryptoexplosion structure or a Silurian-age meteor crater. The sixth-class city of Simpsonville, established in 1816 and named after Capt. John Simpson, is located six miles west of Shelbyville.

Squire Boone, Daniel's younger brother, established the first settlement in Shelby County, the Painted Stone Station, along the banks of Clear Creek, about three miles north of present Shelbyville. In the spring of 1780 he brought thirteen families to this tract. As captain, he organized a small company of militia. The station was abandoned temporarily in September 1781 because of Indian attacks, and the settlers were attacked en route to Linn's Station, twenty-one miles distant, in what has become known as the Long Run Massacre.

Shortly after Squire Boone reestablished his station in the winter of 1783, early Holland Dutch settlers, represented by Abraham Banta, purchased from him 5,610 acres about six miles northeast of the Painted Stone Station on the headwaters of Drennon's and Six Mile Creeks. Here on land that by 1786 included 8,610 acres, they established a Low Dutch Colony. Indian attacks continued to take a toll during the early settlement days in Shelby County.

Harrod's Trace, blazed by James Harrod about 1778 from Harrodsburg to the Falls of the Ohio, passed through Shelby County about two miles south of Shelbyville. The first significant dirt road originated in Maysville and passed through Lexington, Frankfort, and on through Shelbyville to Louisville. In 1825 it became Kentucky's first big macadamized stagecoach road. With the advent of the motor vehicle it was the state's first blacktopped thoroughfare and long the most traveled of any in the state. It was later known as the Midland Trail and subsequently as U.S. Hwy. 60. Cross Keys Tavern, no longer in existence, was built by Adam Middleton about five miles east of Shelbyville in about 1800. It was a popular inn and stagecoach stop located on this historic turnpike. In the early 1970s, as the interstate highway system was expanded, the principal motor route though the county, paralleling the earlier routes, became Interstate 64.

In the 1850s the railroad from Frankfort to Louisville passed through Christiansburg in northeast Shelby County. In 1870 the Shelby Railroad Co. built the line from Anchorage to Shelbyville. Both routes later became part of the Louisville & Nashville Railroad system. An 1895 extension from Shelbyville created a shorter route from Louisville through Shelbyville to Frankfort and points east. With the addition in 1887–88 of the Louisville Southern Railroad route from Louisville to Lexington that passed through Shelbyville, and the construction of interurban lines, Shelby County, by 1910, enjoyed fine transportation facilities for passengers and freight.

Important early settlers included:

Maj. William Shannon (ca. 1740–94), commissary for George Rogers Clark, who became a large landowner in the county and was donor of the land upon which the Shelby County Courthouse was built.

Capt. Bland Ballard (1761–1853) joined the militia upon his arrival in Kentucky in 1779 and was present at the Long Run Massacre in 1781.

Col. John Allen (1771–1813), a successful attorney in Shelby County, who was elected to represent his county in the General Assembly in 1800. He served in the Kentucky house until 1807 and then in the senate until 1812. In December 1806 he and Henry Clay acted as defense attorneys in Aaron Burr's trial in Frankfort. Commanding the First Rifle Regiment of

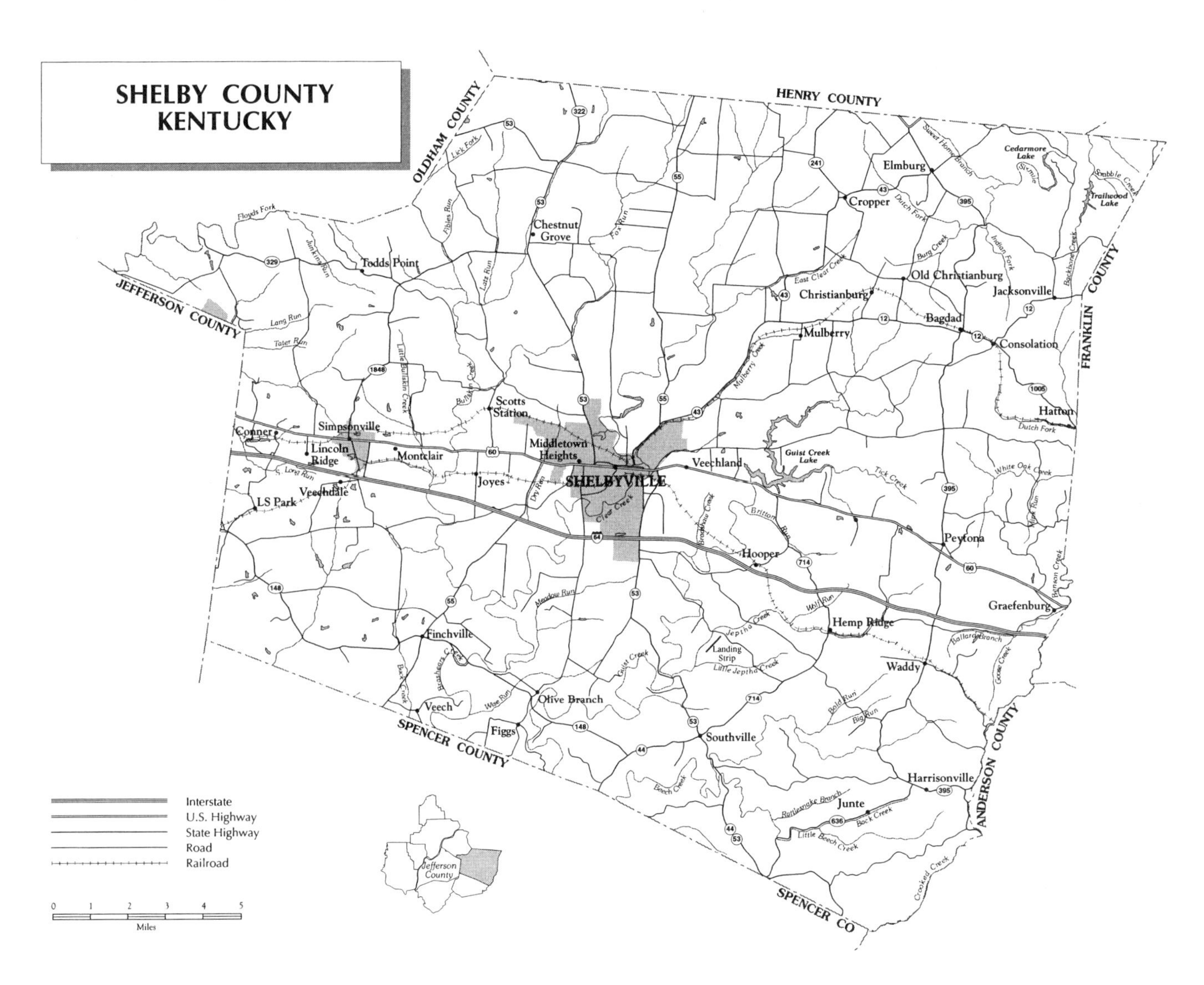

the Kentucky Militia against the British and their Indian allies, Allen was killed on January 22, 1813, while rallying his troops at the Battle of the River Raisin. He was one of more than four hundred Kentuckians to die in that defeat. Three states—Ohio, Indiana, and Kentucky—named counties in Allen's honor.

Col. Abraham Owen (1769–1811), the son of Brackett Owen, who made his home available as the first meeting place of the Shelby County Court at its first term on October 15, 1792. After coming to Kentucky in 1785, Owen became a distinguished military leader and political figure. He served as a lieutenant in Arthur St. Clair's defeat in Ohio in 1791, receiving two wounds in that engagement, and in Gen. Anthony Wayne's successful campaign against the Indians. He was killed on November 7, 1811, while serving as an aide-de-camp to Gen. William Henry Harrison in the Battle of Tippecanoe in Indiana. He served in the state legislature representing Shelby County and shortly before his death was a member of the Kentucky senate. Owen County, Kentucky, established in 1819, was named in his memory.

Dr. John Knight (ca. 1751–1838), who emigrated from Scotland about 1773 and subsequently participated in many engagements of the American Revolution as a surgeon's mate. He joined Col. William Crawford at the Mingo town on the OHIO RIVER in May 1782 and proceeded with the army to the plains of Sandusky, where Crawford's command met a disastrous defeat. He witnessed the agonizing death of Colonel Crawford, who was burned at the stake, but Knight was able to escape before receiving similar treatment. He survived to become one of the original town trustees of Shelbyville and a practicing physician.

Gen. Benjamin Logan (1743–1802), frontiersman, distinguished military leader, and legislator, who participated in the spring of 1775 in establishing the Kentucky settlement called St. Asaph and subsequently in the building of a fort there, often called Logan's Fort. Shortly after coming from Lincoln County to Shelby County in 1795, he was chosen to represent Shelby in the General Assembly. In 1796, as one of three candidates for governor, he received the highest number of electoral votes. However, the electors, believing that a majority was required, called for a second ballot, in which James Garrard was the winner. Logan represented Shelby County during two additional terms in the lower house of the General Assembly and in 1799 was a member of the convention that drafted Kentucky's second constitution.

Prominent residents include Augustus Owsley Stanley (1867-1958). Augustus Owlsey Stanley, governor during 1915-19, was born in Shelby County. In November 1918 he was elected to the U.S. Senate, filling a vacancy caused by the death of Senator Ollie M. James. Resigning the governorship in May 1919, he served in the Senate until March, 1925, losing a bid for reelection.

Major General J. Franklin Bell (1856-1919), a native of Shelby County, was a winner of the Congressional Medal of Honor for his gallantry in action against the Filipino insurgents at Luzon, Philippine Islands on September 9, 1899. In his efforts to raise the professional standards of the army, he established the staff college at Leaveworth, Kansas in 1905. He served as the fourth chief of staff of United States Army (1906-10), but was the first to serve a complete four year term.

The county was the birthplace of Gov. MARTHA LAYNE COLLINS (1936–), Whitney Young Sr. (1897–1975), and Whitney Young Jr. (1921–71), director of the National Urban League. Young Senior was associated with the LINCOLN INSTITUTE, opened in 1912 to educate young AFRICAN AMERICANS. Located on 444 acres near SIMPSONVILLE, the school closed in 1966. The facility is occupied by the Whitney M. Young Jr. Job Corps Center.

AGRICULTURE and livestock were the basis of the county's wealth. Corn, hemp, and wheat were the primary Shelby County crops before the CIVIL WAR. In 1870 the county produced the following crops:

Corn: 1,108,605 bushels (highest in the state)
Hemp: 308,200 pounds
TOBACCO: 239,450 pounds
Wheat: 175,996 bushels
Hay: 4,188 tons
Barley: 1,156 bushels

The livestock inventory in 1870 was:
Hogs: 22,089 (highest in the state)
Cattle: 11,804 (fifth in the state)
Horses: 6,690
Mules: 1,484.

In the early twentieth century, the Jersey Bulletin, noting that there were 450 imported and 1,500 Jersey cattle in the county, including the prize herd at ALLEN DALE FARM, claimed Shelby County to be the Jersey Isle of America.

Tobacco, corn, soybeans, hay, beef, and dairy cattle are now the principal farm products. Shelby County in 1996 was first in the state in the production of burley tobacco and third in the production of dairy products. It is also well known for its alfalfa hay grown in deep, limestone-shale-embedded soil.

Estimated crop production for 1996 was:
Burley tobacco: 9,560,000 pounds
Alfalfa hay: 36,480 tons
All other hay: 92,000 tons
Winter wheat: 210,000 bushels
Soybeans: 533,800 bushels
Corn: 1,530,000 bushels
Estimated livestock data for 1996:
Average number milk cows: 5,500
(Total milk production: 60 million pounds)
All cattle and calves: 49,000
Hogs and pigs: 11,000

In 1992 there were 1,640 farms in Shelby County, with a total acreage of 229,838. In 1995 the county's cash receipts from farm marketing totaled $60,641,000, ninth in the state.

The American Saddlebred is the only horse that Kentucky claims to have originated. The first horse of this breed was registered from Shelby County by the American Saddlebred Horse Association in 1891. The breeding and training of Saddlebred horses has become particularly important in Shelby County since the establishment in 1958 near Simpsonville of a prominent training stable. Based upon the number of Saddlebred horses bred and trained in the county and the success of these horses in international competition, Shelby County claims to be the Saddlebred Capital of the World.

Industrial enterprises are principally near Shelbyville, where fifty manufacturing firms employed 5,648 individuals in 1998. Shelby County's largest employer is the Budd Co., with 675 employees manufacturing metal parts for automobiles. Second is Leggett & Platt in Simpsonville, which employs 424 in the manufacture of swivel chairs, sofa beds, and reclining chair mechanisms. The Purnell Sausage Co., which employs 300, is also located in Simpsonville. Other industries employing more than 100 in Shelby County include Alcoa-Fujikura, Atlantic Envelope, Black & Decker, Curtis Industries, Ichikoh Manufacturing, Johnson Controls, Katayama American, Lawson Mardon Packaging, Ledco, Louise's Fat Free Potato Chips, Ohio Valley Aluminum, Omega Plastics, Owens Corning, Roll Forming, and Shelbyville Mixing Center.

Tourist attractions include the Wakefield-Scearce Galleries, known throughout the country and abroad for its antique English furniture and silver; the OLD STONE INN, once a stagecoach tavern near Simpsonville; Science Hill Inn Dining Room; and Claudia Sanders Dinner House, established by Col. Harlan Sanders, creator of the Kentucky Fried Chicken franchise, and his wife. Thousands each summer attend the Shelbyville Horse Show, which is now considered the prototype for small, county-level HORSE SHOWS.

Clear Creek Park, which includes Lake Shelby, a fishing lake, is an extensive recreational area of about two hundred acres for picnicking and outdoor sports. Fishing, water skiing, and camping are available on the larger Guist Creek Lake. A Clear Creek Trust has been established for the maintenance as a tourist attraction of Clear Creek, which meanders through Shelbyville and Shelby County. TOURISM expenditures in the county totaled over $1.1 million in 1996.

The population of the county has grown from 18,999 in 1970 to 23,328 in 1980, to 24,824 in 1990, and 28,836 in 1997.

See George L. Willis, *History of Shelby County, Kentucky* (Hartford, Ky. 1929); Richard H. Collins, *History of Kentucky* (Frankfort, reprinted 1966); Edward D. Shinnick, *Some Old Time History of Shelbyville and Shelby County* (Frankfort 1974).

R.R. Van Stockum

SHELBY COUNTY TRUST BANK. The Shelby County Trust Bank was founded on April 27, 1887, and was initially called the Shelby County Trust and Banking Co. The original stockholders numbered seven: L.A. Weakley (president), C. Kinkel (vice president), R.A. Smith (treasurer), S. Van Natta, J. Guthrie, J.C. Beckham, and J.A. Middleton.

The bank first took office space in the old Wayne Building on the southeast corner of Fountain Square in Shelbyville. In 1904, however, this building was razed and replaced by a three-story office building of brown glazed brick with stone coping, the design of SHELBYVILLE architect Lynn Gruber. The company occupied a ground-floor office facing Main St. and the Square. In the rear of this property was a city building housing the local police and fire departments. In 1964 this building was torn down to make way for extensive renovations to the bank, which today includes a lobby, office and conference spaces, and drive-through facilities.

In 1999 the Shelby County Trust Bank, including all of its branch offices, employed about seventy people. The bank is now a wholly owned subsidiary of Commonwealth Bancshares Inc., a privately owned company. It has total assets of about $160 million, and, in addition to the original facility at 422 MAIN St., has three other branch banks—in Waddy, which opened in 1955; in SIMPSONVILLE, which opened in 1974; and in West Shelbyville, which opened in 1979.

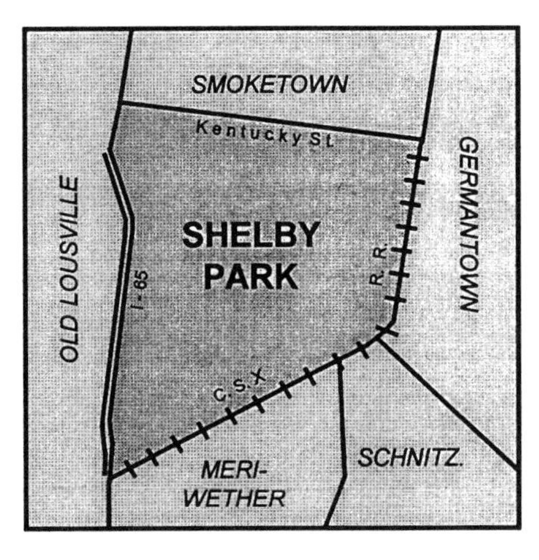

SHELBY PARK. Neighborhood to the southwest of downtown Louisville bounded by Kentucky St. to the north, the CSX railroad tracks to the east and south, and Floyd St. and Interstate 65 to the west. The area developed in three stages at different times. Although the subdivision of the upper third of the neighborhood began in 1847, settlement was slow until 1876. The 1870s witnessed the platting of the lower portion of the neighborhood, while the middle section remained mostly vacant until 1894. Three years earlier, the opening of the Goss Ave.–Texas Ave. streetcar loop and the proximity to the GERMANTOWN and SCHNITZELBURG NEIGHBORHOODS prompted an increasing number of GERMANS to locate in the neighborhood. Local landmarks include the centrally located SHELBY PARK, established in 1908, and the old Shelby Park Library, which was rededicated as a community center in 1994.

See Carl E. Kramer, "The City-Building Process: Urbanization in Central and Southern Louisville, 1772–1932," Ph.D. dissertation, University of Toledo, 1980.

SHELBYVILLE. Shelbyville, named in honor of Kentucky's first governor, Isaac Shelby, is the county seat of Shelby County and a fourth-class city. Shelbyville is governed by a mayor and a board of council consisting of six members elected at large from the city. The town was founded in October 1792 at the first Shelby County Court meeting, when William Shannon offered to lay off fifty acres into town lots and provide the county with an acre of land for public buildings. The town was established on the west side of Clear Creek, opposite the mouth of Mulberry Creek and close to where the road from Louisville to Frankfort crossed Clear Creek.

The legislature appointed trustees in December 1792, and the first lot was sold in March 1793. The town trustees required each lot owner to build at least a one-and-one-half-story hewed log house with a stone chimney, and by 1795 there were some forty of these structures. Soon thereafter, brick buildings were constructed. The second courthouse, completed in 1798, is an early example. The POPULATION in 1800 was 262, and new town lots were platted in 1803, 1815, and again in 1816.

Shelbyville came to be located nearly in the center of Shelby County as the legislature, in the process of creating new counties, reduced Shelby to less than one-half its original size. The town was the principal provider of goods and services to surrounding farms and functioned as a point of sale and distribution for crops and livestock. In the period before the CIVIL WAR there was some local processing of agricultural products, such as flour and corn milling, and, on a smaller scale, rope making, cotton and wool milling, TOBACCO processing, and lumber sawing. The 1850 census reveals a community in which most people were employed in direct or indirect support of the farm ECONOMY. Merchants, saddlers, wagon makers, blacksmiths, carpenters, masons, cabinet and chair makers, tailors, and shoemakers were all represented, as well as physicians, lawyers, teachers, and ministers.

Schools and academies were organized from the earliest times. The Shelbyville Academy, founded in 1798, operated for many years at Eighth and Washington Sts. before moving to College St. In 1836 it became SHELBY COLLEGE. Five years later the Episcopal church took control and, under the presidency of Rev. William I. Waller, constructed several buildings, including a classroom building that had on its roof an astronomical observatory. Prof. Joseph Winlock, who had taught at Shelby College and was a Shelby County native, returned in 1869 along with some of his colleagues from Harvard University to observe the total eclipse of the sun that occurred on August 7. Waller assumed ownership of Shelby College at the end of the Civil War. Under the name St. James College, it continued to operate—primarily as a school for boys—until declining enrollment forced it to close in 1871. The city took control, removed the observatory, and operated a grade school in the building until 1939, when it was replaced by a new structure.

The best known of the Shelbyville schools was SCIENCE HILL FEMALE ACADEMY, founded in 1825 by Julia Ann Tevis. Tevis and her husband, Rev. John Tevis, a Methodist minister, operated Science Hill as a Protestant boarding school for girls between twelve and sixteen years of age. Located on Washington St., it drew pupils from all over Kentucky and the southern states. Day students from the town attended, including boys and girls not old enough to enter the academy. The mission of the school was to "make an elegant, cultivated, refined woman for society, and fit for the higher duties of home life" (Tevis, *Sixty Years in a School Room*, 463).

Discipline was strict and moral, and religious principles were emphasized. In addition to the usual classes in music, composition, orthoepy (the study of correct pronunciation and dictation), elocution, penmanship, and mathematics, Mrs. Tevis, believing that young ladies needed a sound background in the natural sciences, included ASTRONOMY, chemistry, and GEOLOGY in the curriculum. In 1879 Science Hill was taken over by Dr. Wiley T. Poynter, who developed it into a college preparatory school. After his death in 1896 his widow, Clara M. Poynter, became principal and, together with her daughters Harriet and Juliet Poynter, operated the school until her death in 1937. Science Hill School closed in 1939.

Another school, the Shelbyville Female Seminary, was founded in 1839 by Rev. William F. Hill. In 1846 he erected a building at Seventh and Main Streets that would house the boarding school for the next sixty-six years. In 1849 he changed the name to Shelbyville Female Institute. Rev. David T. Stuart purchased the school in 1851, changing the name to Stuart's Female College and operating it under the auspices of the Presbyterian church. After his death in 1868, his son, W.H. Stuart, assumed control and renamed the school Shelbyville Female College. In 1890 it was sold to J.E. Nunn, who, not to be outdone, renamed it Shelbyville College and operated it as a Baptist school until it closed in 1912.

During the Civil War the town was harassed by Confederates. Early on the morning of August 24, 1864, a group of Confederate guerrillas led by Shelby native Capt. Dave Martin attacked the courthouse in an attempt to seize muskets stored there. They were driven off by heavy gunfire from townsmen Thomas C. McGrath, a merchant, and J.H. Masonheimer, a tailor. Three guerrillas were killed, along with a black man by the name of Owen who was on the street at the time of the raid and was ordered by the guerrillas to hold their horses. Martin missed the gunfire because he was at the jail in the rear of the courthouse being upbraided by the jailer's wife, Mrs. Henry Burnett Sr., for endangering the lives of innocent civilians, including his own wife and children, then living in town.

As a result of the raid, the town trustees in January 1865 ordered a log blockhouse, about fourteen feet in diameter, built in front of the courthouse at the intersection of Fifth and Main Sts. Every white male in the town over eighteen years of age was enrolled as a police guard, and a watch was kept, with the blockhouse serving as the headquarters.

On January 25, 1865, in a driving snowstorm, thirty-five Union soldiers herding GOVERNMENT cattle to Louisville were killed in Shelby County just west of Simpsonville by Confederate guerrillas believed to have been led by Dick Taylor. That night the SPENCER COUNTY courthouse burned. About this time, William Clarke Quantrill, the Confederate guerrilla leader who had been operating on the Missouri-Kansas border, moved into Kentucky and began raids in Spencer, Mercer, and Nelson Counties. In an effort to stop Quantrill, Gen. John Palmer, in command of Union forces in Kentucky, placed Capt. Edwin Terrell of the Shelby County Home Guard and thirty of his men on the federal payroll on April 1, 1865. Along with Lt. Harry Thompson, Terrell led his men through Shelby and surrounding counties, hunting down Confederate guerrillas and intimidating Southern sympathizers. He and his men were welcomed in Shelbyville and the town trustees encouraged them to stay by paying their bills at local HOTELS. On May 10, 1865, Terrell and his men caught up with Quantrill's raiders at a barn near Wakefield in Spencer County. In the ensuing fight Quantrill was mortally wounded, and his guerrilla band was broken up. A few days later, Terrell rode into Shelbyville to the cheers of its citizens. The Union army paid off and disbanded Terrell and his men on May 24, 1865, and a month later the trustees of Shelbyville stopped paying for their room and board.

With the war over and the threat of guerrilla attacks ended, the blockhouse was torn down in September 1865 and the police guard removed a few months later. Union military men Ed Terrell and Harry Thompson, however, emerged as troublemakers. On August 25 while in Shelbyville they murdered and robbed William R. Johnson, a stock trader from Illinois. They were arrested and tried for the crime in March of the following year, but the jury could not reach a verdict. Terrell was transferred to the jail in TAYLORSVILLE to await trial there for another killing. He escaped and, with two companions, returned to Shelbyville on the evening of May 26, 1866. While he and his friends were drinking at the Armstrong Hotel, Town Marshal George W. Caplinger organized a posse. When Terrell came out of the hotel, he rode a short distance east and stopped to talk to hotel keeper Merrett Redding. As he turned to leave, a volley of shots rang out. Terrell was wounded in the spine, and his kinsman, John R. Baker, was killed. Merrett Redding was also wounded in the crossfire and died a month later.

Terrell was taken to Louisville but, because of the seriousness of his wound, did not stand trial. He returned to his home in Harrisonville in October, but his health did not improve. He determined to return to Louisville for an operation to remove the bullet from his back. The surgery was not successful, and he died sometime before the end of 1867 at the age of twenty-two. The date and place of his death and the location of his grave are not known. Meanwhile, his friend Harry Thompson escaped from the Shelby County Jail on October 23, 1866. Local tradition says that he went to Texas where he became a prosperous farmer, using the name Henry T. Grazian.

Main Street in Shelbyville around 1876.

The half century between the CIVIL WAR and WORLD WAR I was a period of unprecedented commercial and residential development in Shelbyville. The city limits, little changed since 1816, were expanded to the east and west along Main St. Nearly all the buildings in the central business district between Fourth and Seventh Streets were replaced by larger structures designed in the Italianate and Classical Revival styles popular at the time. Some of the new construction was necessitated by a disastrous fire that struck the business district in 1909. The city expanded its firehouse and CITY HALL on the public square in 1912, and the county completed the present courthouse in 1914. The four oldest banks in Shelby County were all organized at this time, despite the financial panics of 1873, 1893, and 1907. Along west Main St. the town's merchants, bankers, and mill owners built large, two-story brick and frame houses.

In January 1895 a public water system replaced the community wells that had served the town for a hundred years and were the cause of recurring cholera EPIDEMICS. The Shelbyville Water and Light Co. also provided the first electrical light service to the city's streets in December 1884. TELEPHONE service also began in 1895 and a CARNEGIE LIBRARY opened in 1903. The King's Daughters built the city's first hospital on Henry Clay St. in 1906.

The growing prosperity of Shelbyville was directly related to AGRICULTURE, which had evolved from a more or less subsistence level before the Civil War to one of increasing production and surplus. Burley tobacco, the most important cash crop grown in the county, was marketed through warehouses in Shelbyville. Wheat and corn were sold to local flour and meal mills. Hemp continued to be grown, particularly on farms close to the town's supply of day laborers. Purebred beef cattle, mules, and saddlebred horses were raised and sold throughout the nation. The dairy industry, which depended on quick and reliable delivery to the Louisville market, grew to become an important part of the economy.

Improvements in transportation played a major role in the growth of Shelbyville and its commercial development. The Shelby Railroad Co. constructed a line from ANCHORAGE, Kentucky in 1870, thereby joining the town to the main line of the Louisville, Cincinnati & Lexington Railroad, which was later the LOUISVILLE & NASHVILLE RAILROAD and then CSX Transportation. THE LOUISVILLE SOUTHERN RAILROAD, later the Norfolk Southern, built a line through the town in 1887–88. The Cumberland & Ohio Railroad had a section of line from Shelbyville south to Taylorsville, and the Shelby Division of the Louisville & Interurban electric railroad operated in the area between 1910 and 1934. These transportation links, together with the replacement of toll roads with county and state roads, enabled the products of Shelby County farms to be moved quickly to major markets. Shelbyville lay at the center of that network of roads and RAILROADS.

AFRICAN AMERICANS did not participate in the growing prosperity. The population of the town in 1870 was 2,180, with 44 percent blacks, most of whom worked as day laborers in town or on farms in the vicinity. The average wage for African Americans was ten or twelve dollars a month. On January 1 of each year, the anniversary of Lincoln's Emancipation Proclamation, blacks from all over the county would gather in town to celebrate and to hire out for the coming year. Most of the black citizens of Shelbyville lived in a section called Martinsville in rented houses owned by whites. The Ku Klux Klan, centered in the eastern part of the county, created an atmosphere of intimidation, coercion, and occasional violence. In 1901 and again in 1911, white mobs entered the county jail and lynched blacks. These conditions, together with low wages and the lack of real opportunity, led to a decline in the county's black population from 5,383 in 1870 to 3,266 in 1920. The population of Shelbyville in 1920 was 3,760, with 1,224, or 32 percent, being black. Although the number of blacks in the town increased from 1870 to 1920, there was a 12 percent decline in their numbers relative to the white population. In 1990 blacks represented 23 percent of the population of the city.

The period from 1917 to 1945 can be characterized as a time when Shelbyville survived rather than prospered. The two world wars did not generate much economic growth, except for a few industries associated with processing agricultural products. The town participated mainly by providing manpower to the military and by reducing civilian consumption in order to free up supplies for the war effort. The GREAT DEPRESSION had a deep impact. The decline in farm commodity prices, together with the problems imposed by the breakdown of the BANKING system, threatened to lead to the collapse of local lending institutions and retail businesses. Measures taken by the federal government to support farm prices by cutting the production of tobacco and milk, along with loan programs and relief projects, helped stabilize the local economy but did not lead to recovery.

The ten years following WORLD WAR II continued the low rate of growth in the first half of the century. Manufacturing jobs in Shelby County in 1950 numbered only 448. However, by the mid-1950s conditions began to improve. A new county hospital was dedicated in 1954, and in 1957 the Shelby County Industrial and Development Foundation was formed to recruit industry and provide sites. Three years later the interstate highway system arrived with I-64 crossing the county two miles south of the city. A system of good highways and railroads, adequate utilities, suitable plant sites, and a traditionally nonunion workforce drawn from Shelby and surrounding counties set the stage for the movement of industry into the area.

In the years since 1960 more than forty-five companies employing more than five thousand people have established plants in Shelby County. Most of the new plants have been built in three industrial PARKS located on the western edge of Shelbyville. The city built a new fire and police station in 1960 and new administrative offices in 1996.

Residential developments and commercial centers were created both east and west of the city. Many of these areas were incorporated into the city because of the availability of public sewers and the fact that the sale of alcohol was permitted in the city but not the county. Shelbyville grew in size from 1.6 square miles in 1960 to 7.4 square miles in 1997 and, during the same period, from a population of 4,525 to an estimated population of 8,299. Its population was 4,182 in 1970, then 5,329 in 1980, and 6,238 in 1990.

See George L. Willis Sr., *History of Shelby County, Kentucky* (Shelbyville, Ky., 1929); Edward D. Shinnick, *Some Old Time History of Shelbyville and Shelby County* (Shelbyville, Ky., 1974); Thomas Shelby "Bob" Watson, *The Silent Riders* (Louisville 1971); Julia A. Tevis, *Sixty Years in a School-Room* (Cincinnati 1878).

Charles T. Long

SHEPHERDSVILLE. Shepherdsville, the county seat of BULLITT COUNTY, is eighteen miles south of Louisville on Interstate 65. The fourth-class city is named for Adam Shepherd, who owned the land on which the town was established. Shepherd owned six hundred acres on the south side of the Falls of Salt River and nine hundred acres on the north side of the falls, the best place to cross Salt River. The falls are bedrock that continue for about a mile with a drop of about fourteen feet. A "road" that had been created by large herds of buffalo and other wild game crossed at the falls.

Shepherd was a native of Baltimore, Maryland. His father, Peter Shepherd, had emigrated from the Netherlands to America. He was a surveyor who was particularly drawn to the Bullitt County area because of the prospects for salt. According to family tradition, Shepherd bartered a tract of land he owned in SHELBY COUNTY for a salt kettle. He was married to Rachel Drake of Lincoln County, Kentucky, on April 20, 1784. They had six children, all girls. Shepherd never lived in the town proper and represented Bullitt County in the Kentucky General Assembly in 1799, 1800, and 1802. He died in 1818 and is buried near Shepherdsville.

Shepherd petitioned the Kentucky legislature to establish a town bearing his name on fifty acres he had set aside on the north bank of Salt River at the falls. The legislature passed an act creating Shepherdsville on December 11, 1793. At that time Shepherdsville was in Jefferson County. In 1784 Nelson County was created out of Jefferson County. Salt River was the dividing line between the two counties. This division remained until Bullitt County was created in 1796.

The law that established Shepherdsville also named the first trustees of the town: Nacy Brashear, Samuel Crow, Michael Troutman, Fredrick Pennabaker, Benjamin Stansbury, Joseph Brooks, and John Essery. They were responsible for selling the lots that had been laid out, but the money was paid to Shepherd. Lots were sold at auction, the first sale being between 1794 and 1796 and the second in 1797. Owners of lots had seven years in which to build a house or forfeit the lot. Houses could be built of log, brick, or stone with a stone chimney. If the lot was forfeited the trustees could resell it. The original survey shows eighty lots on the fifty acres.

When Bullitt County was formed in 1796, Shepherdsville was the only town in the county, was centrally located, and naturally became the county seat. The county justices created a public square, subject to the owners of lots twelve, thirteen, and twenty giving up a parcel of their lot equal to forty feet square "next to center" and the owner of lot number twenty-one giving up half his lot. All public buildings were to be erected in this square.

According to the census of 1800, Shepherdsville had a population of ninety-six. Of the twenty-nine towns in Kentucky, Shepherdsville was eighteenth largest. The first post office was established in 1806, with Thomas T. Grayson as postmaster. In 1818 a bank was established, one of forty established that year by the Kentucky legislature. Because of poor BANKING practices, the bank lasted only a year or two.

Within a short distance of Shepherdsville a forge, rolling mill, and grist mill were built on Salt River. The complex was started in 1819 by John W. Beckwith. It was incorporated in 1837 as the Shepherdsville Iron Manufacturing Co. Usable iron or "pig" iron came from iron furnaces located elsewhere in Bullitt County. Notable products from the mill were the stoves and arches used at Pleasant Hill (Shakertown). The economic panic of 1837 adversely affected the iron industry and temporarily stopped production.

In 1838 John D. Colmesnil opened nearby PAROQUET SPRINGS, a MINERAL WATER spa, on twenty acres. It accommodated up to 250 guests. Over the years the springs became popular, drawing many people from Louisville and other parts of Kentucky as well as many other southern states. The season ran usually from the last of May through the first of September. At its peak the grounds covered one hundred acres, and eight hundred guests could be cared for. In 1872 one could stay at the springs for three dollars per day, sixteen dollars per week, or sixty dollars per month. Servants and children stayed for half price.

Over the years Shepherdsville prospered and grew. Collins's, History of Kentucky (1847 edition) lists Shepherdsville with twelve mechanical trades, four stores, five doctors, and seven lawyers in addition to its businesses. POPULATION had increased to about four hundred.

A severe outbreak of cholera occurred in Bullitt County in 1854. Nineteen people died, many of them from Shepherdsville. Several of the victims were buried in the Shepherdsville cemetery.

A school had been located in Shepherdsville as early as 1809, with a Mr. Cook as the teacher. The school was located on School House Alley. It most likely was the Bullitt Academy that had been authorized by the Kentucky legislature in 1798. Collins states that the Bullitt Academy was located in the town's Methodist church building.

The LOUISVILLE & NASHVILLE RAILROAD was constructed in the mid-1850s through the town. The railroad bridge was the first across the Salt River at Shepherdsville. The railroad gave Shepherdsville an economic boost when a station was established on the east side of the tracks.

During the CIVIL WAR, Shepherdsville was the site of bustling activity. All troop or supply trains going south passed through the city. Various sites around the town were Union troop encampments. To protect the railroad bridge, a stockade was built, probably on the south side of the bridge. A force of about five hundred Confederate troops successfully attacked the stockade on September 8, 1862, and the bridge was badly damaged. Confederate general Braxton Bragg raced toward Louisville in the latter part of September 1862, but Union general Don C. Buell entered Louisville first and Bragg then went to Bardstown. Buell regrouped and marched toward Bardstown to meet Bragg. The right wing of his army marched out the Shepherdsville Pike and into Shepherdsville. Confederate soldiers who had occupied Shepherdsville fled in the direction of High Grove and then on to Bardstown. In December 1862 Confederate forces under John Hunt Morgan attacked the railroad again during his famous Christmas raid. Morgan's men destroyed the rebuilt bridge.

Another sort of disaster occurred on December 20, 1917. It was one of the worst train accidents on the Louisville & Nashville rail system. A fast train, of nine steel cars bound for New Orleans and trying to make up lost time, plowed into the rear of the Springfield local train of three wooden cars, which had stopped at the station. Fifty-one people were killed.

Periodic flooding plagues Shepherdsville, since it is located astride the Salt River. The worst flooding occurred during the 1937 flood. The entire town was inundated. Water even got into the courthouse. Many residents were housed in the Masonic temple until it, too, was threatened by rising water. All roads into town were covered. The railroad tracks were the only avenue in or out of town. Railroad authorities at one point parked a train on the bridge to keep it from washing away. The extent of the flooding was immense, running from the Gap-in-Knob to Bardstown Junction and beyond. Subsequent large FLOODS have affected smaller parts of the city.

In the late twentieth century the city's largest employers were Publishers Printing Co.; Interlake Inc., which makes conveyors; Monarch Hardware, which makes door and exit hardware; and Standard Publishing, printer of the Pioneer News, a biweekly newspaper. The interchange on Interstate 65 has attracted a large number of fast-food RESTAURANTS and four motels.

The population of Shepherdsville was 2,769 in 1970, 4,454 in 1980, 4,805 in 1990, and 4,667 in 1996.

See Robert M. Rennick, *Kentucky's Salt River Valley: A Survey of the Post Offices of the Greater Louisville Area* (Lake Grove, Ore. 1997); *Louisville Commercial,* Dec. 25, 28, 1917; *Louisville Herald,* Dec. 21, 1917; Audrea McDowell, "The Pursuit of Health and Happiness at the Paroquet Springs in Kentucky," *Filson Club History Quarterly* 69 (Oct. 1995): 390–420.

Tom Pack

SHEPPARD, WILLIAM HENRY (b Waynesboro, Virginia, 1865; d Louisville, November 25, 1927). Presbyterian minister and missionary. The son of William and Fannie S. Sheppard, William H. Sheppard entered the Hampton Institute in 1880. Upon graduation, he attended the Tuscaloosa Theological Institute (now Stillman College) in Alabama, where he received his theological training. After completing his studies, Sheppard served as pastor of a church in Montgomery, Alabama, and in 1887 went to Atlanta as pastor of the Harrison Street Presbyterian Church.

In 1890 the Southern Presbyterian church sent Sheppard as a missionary to the Belgian Congo, where he remained for two decades. After only three years of service, Sheppard was honored as one of the few AFRICAN AMERICANS to be made a fellow of the Royal Geographic Society of London. This was in recognition of his extensive research and explorations in Africa, especially of the xenophobic Kuba people.

During his twenty years in Africa, Sheppard was active in denouncing the oppression induced by Belgian King Leopold II's heavy tributes on ivory and rubber. A highly publicized libel trial against Sheppard and others ended in a surprise acquittal and led the parliament to withdraw Leopold II's direct ownership of the Congo. Upon returning to the United States, Sheppard wrote of his African experiences in *Pioneers in Congo* (1912).

Sheppard came to Louisville in 1912 after accepting the offer of Rev. JOHN LITTLE, the superintendent of Presbyterian colored missions in the city, to become pastor of Grace Presbyterian Church. He was officially installed as the church's minister on September 15, 1912, and remained there until his death. Sheppard's presence as a well-known and respected black minister brought new life to the church, resulting in increased attendance and membership. Under his guidance, the church became a center for black Presbyterian leadership in Kentucky. In addition, Sheppard often spoke at white churches to raise contributions for Presbyterian mission work in the black community. In his honor, the city of Louisville opened the William H. Sheppard Park in 1924 at Seventeenth and Magazine Streets. This provided a playground and SWIMMING pool for the surrounding African American neighborhood.

Sheppard was known for his appreciation of African art. Several of the pieces collected by him are housed in the J.B. SPEED ART MUSEUM and at the Hampton Institute in Hampton, Virginia.

More than a thousand people attended his funeral, and he was eulogized by black and white ministers alike. Sheppard, who was survived by his wife, Lucy (Gantt) Sheppard, is buried in Louisville Cemetery. Fifteen years after his death, on October 30, 1942, the Sheppard Square Housing Project, located in the Smoketown neighborhood, was dedicated by Mayor Wilson W. Wyatt.

See William H. Sheppard, *Pioneers in Congo* (Louisville 1912); Louis B. Weeks, *Kentucky Presbyterians* (Atlanta 1983); George C. Wright, *Life Behind a Veil* (Baton Rouge 1985); William E. Phipps, *The Sheppards and Lapsley: Pioneer Presbyterians in the Congo* (Louisville 1991).

Peter Morrin
Ed Tuttle

SHERLEY, "GEORGE" DOUGLASS (b Louisville, June 27, 1857; d Martinsville, Indiana, December 28, 1917). Journalist and author. The only child of wealthy steamboat captain Zachariah Sherley and his wife Susan (Cromwell) Sherley, he was enrolled at Centre College in Danville, Kentucky, and studied law at the University of Virginia. A bachelor, he lived at Sherley Place, 300 W Chestnut. After 1904 he resided at Sherley Crest, a farm near Lexington. He privately published four short books, including *The Valley of Unrest: A Book without a Woman* (1883), then other occasional pieces. His national reputation resulted in a lecture tour with James Whitcomb Riley beginning on April 11, 1893, in Louisville, and ending March 3, 1894, in New York City, where the two shared a stage with Mark Twain. Sherley is buried in CAVE HILL CEMETERY.

See Mary Boewe, "On Stage and Off with James Whitcomb Riley and Mark Twain," *Traces of Indiana and Midwestern History* 7 (Fall 1996): 16–25; Charles G. Morehead, "Douglass Sherley," M.A. thesis, Duke University, 1931.

Mary Boewe

SHERLEY, JOSEPH SWAGAR (b Louisville, November 28, 1871; d Louisville, February 13, 1941). Attorney and U.S. congressman. Swagar Sherley was the son of Thomas H. and Ella (Swagar) Sherley. Educated in local public schools and at LOUISVILLE MALE HIGH SCHOOL, he later enrolled in the law program of the University of Virginia, where he graduated in 1891. Later that year he was admitted to the Kentucky bar and undertook the practice of law in Louisville. During the next decade his partners included such locally prominent attorneys as L.H. Noble, Joseph T. O'Neal, and Merit O'Neal.

At age twenty-seven, Sherley failed in his bid to be elected commonwealth's attorney. Four years later, in 1902, he won the first of eight consecutive terms in the United States House of Representatives (March 4, 1903–March 3, 1919). An expert in the fields of budget and finance, the youthful Kentuckian emerged as one of the most influential Democrats in Washington. President Woodrow Wilson considered him among his staunchest allies in his campaign to equip the United States militarily for possible entrance into WORLD WAR I. Following the declaration of war on Germany in April 1917, Sherley, as chairman of the House Appropriations Committee, worked closely with Wilson and his assistant secretary of the navy, Franklin D. Roosevelt, particularly on fiscal policy.

Swept out of office in the Republican landslide of November 1918, Sherley resumed the practice of law in Washington but continued to advise Democratic candidates and officeholders. He maintained his close associations with Sam Rayburn, a future speaker of the House, and with Roosevelt. During the presidential campaign of 1932, he was onc of FDR's most trusted advisers on financial matters, especially the budget. Later he advised the president on reorganization of the federal GOVERNMENT.

Sherley met his future wife, Mignon Critten, when, as a congressman, he was touring the Philippines in 1905 with Secretary of War William Howard Taft. The couple married on April 21, 1906, at her home on Staten Island, New York. They were the parents of two sons, Thomas and Swagar Jr., and three daughters, Olive, Mignon, and Marjorie. Although he resided for decades in Washington, D.C., Sherley often boasted of his Kentucky birth. "I don't get back very often, and I have lived in the capital so long I am considered a Washingtonian," he once remarked, "but I am and always have been a Kentuckian and my home is in Louisville." During a visit to his hometown he became ill, was operated on, and subsequently died. Following Episcopal services he was buried in CAVE HILL CEMETERY.

See *Courier-Journal,* February 14, 15, 1941; A.H. McDannald, ed., T*he Americana Annual* (New York 1942).

Thomas H. Appleton Jr.

SHERLEY, ZACHARIAH MADISON "ZACHARY" (b Louisa County, Virginia, May 7, 1811; d Louisville, February 18, 1879). Entrepreneur. He came with his family to Louisville as a child. In time he made his living in transportation along the OHIO RIVER. Sherley became a partner in the Louisville and Cincinnati United States mail line and owned an interest in a line of packets running from Louisville to Evansville and Henderson. He also was co-owner of Sherley, Woolfolk, & Co., a steamboat supply store located on Fourth St.

During the CIVIL WAR, Captain Sherley frequently transported Union troops by steamboat. His STEAMBOATS were instrumental in getting Union general DON CARLOS BUELL and twenty-five thousand troops and supplies downriver from Louisville to the Battle of Shiloh at Tennessee's Pittsburgh Landing on April 6–7, 1862. Although the battle did not produce a decisive victory for either side, Buell arrived on the second day of the battle in time to help Gen. Ulysses S. Grant force the Confederate army to withdraw to Corinth, Mississippi, allowing Grant to regain much of the territory lost the day before.

Sherley also played an important role in one of the most famous Civil War battles that never took place—the Battle of Louisville. In September 1862, when Confederate general Braxton Bragg, in conjunction with Gen. Edmund Kirby Smith, threatened Louisville with invasion, Sherley was commissioned by the Union army to build a PONTOON BRIDGE across the Ohio River just below Towhead Island to assist the arrival of troops and supplies and to provide a means to evacuate the city. Another bridge was later built from the PORTLAND area to NEW ALBANY, Indiana.

On orders from Union general William "Bull" Nelson, commander of the Army of Kentucky, Gen. Jeremiah T. Boyle was instructed to supply Sherley with whatever was needed to build the bridges. Although General Nelson originally issued an order for women, children, and Southern sympathizers to cross the river into southern Indiana, the order was never actually issued, according to a Union major. Still, as the Confererates got closer to the city, many Louisvillians crossed over, seeking safety from an attack that never came. Bragg's advance was redirected when Union general Don Carlos Buell marched into Louisville on September 25. On October 8, the two armies finally met at the Battle of Perryville.

Sherley also supplied boats for relief efforts during the war. The Ladies' Relief Society, one of the most active in Louisville during the war, was aided on several occasions by transportation provided by Sherley's line. After the Battle of Fort Donelson in February 1862 (the first major Union victory of the war), Sherley provided the steamboat Gray Eagle to the relief society to ferry nurses and supplies downriver to Grant's forces in Tennessee. He also was involved in similar relief efforts after Shiloh and was on an organizing committee to coordinate Louisville's relief response to Perryville.

In addition to his business interests, Sherley was a community leader. In 1864 he was involved in one of the earliest attempts to establish a street railway system in the city. With several other prominent Louisvillians, including General Boyle who served as company president, the Louisville City Railway Co. was incorporated to provide a horse-drawn rail system with lines running along MAIN St. and Portland Ave.

Sherley also served as president of the board of directors of the Louisville and Jeffersonville Ferry Co., was a founder of the Citizens National Bank, a trustee of the medical school at the UNIVERSITY OF LOUISVILLE, member of the board of trustees of the Kentucky Institute for the Blind, and a trustee of CAVE HILL CEMETERY.

Sherley married three times—Nanine (Tarascon) Taylor of Louisville, Clara Jewell of Louisiana, and Susan W. Cromwell of Fayette County, Kentucky. He had three sons, one by each wife. Stomach cancer was the cause of his death. He is buried at Cave Hill Cemetery.

See *History of the Ohio Falls Cities and Their Counties* (Cleveland 1882); J. Stoddard Johnston, ed., *Memorial History of Louisville* (Chicago 1896).

SHIPPINGPORT. Lying between Louisville to the east and PORTLAND to the west, Shippingport is little more than a name now, but it was once vital to the settlements at the FALLS OF THE OHIO. Strategically situated on a peninsula of rich alluvial soil with a good natural harbor below the Falls, the site attracted land speculators who changed its name three times in the process of establishing a town. Neither the town nor the land was destined to retain its shape. The LOUISVILLE AND PORTLAND CANAL, begun in 1825, turned the site into an island. Successive enlargements to the canal and the creation of a surge basin devoured much of the land.

Incorporated as Anonymous, having no name, by an act of the Virginia legislature on October 10, 1785, the name changed quickly to Campbell Town in honor of the revolutionary patriot, JOHN CAMPBELL, who owned the land and laid out town lots. His half-brother and heir, Allan Campbell, sold forty-five acres to brothers Jean Antoine and Louis Anastase Tarascon through their partner, James Berthoud, in 1803. This Philadelphia-based partnership of FRENCH expatriates changed the name to Shippingport and began an ambitious development plan that included relocating themselves and their shipyard and establishing

Houses on Canal Street in Shippingport, 1926.

a warehouse, a rope walk, and milling operations to take advantage of the strategic location midway between eastern markets and the Gulf of Mexico. Their automated flour mill, rising 102 feet from the riverbed, was both a landmark and marvel of technology. The Tarascons and Berthoud encouraged other French families to settle in Shippingport and drew intellectuals to their parlors. Constantine Rafinesque, naturalist and philologist, visited and corresponded with Louis Tarascon; Lucy Bakewell AUDUBON and her sons spent extended periods in the Berthoud household, while her husband, John J. Audubon, was on PAINTING and sketching exhibitions. A daughter, Rose Audubon, is buried in an unmarked grave at Shippingport.

The mill and the STEAMBOATS that pulled into three wharves brought Shippingport's POPULATION to six hundred by 1820, but the digging of the canal (1825–30) to allow boats to avoid the falls and bypass Shippingport helped doom the settlement, both economically and physically. For a time the flour mill was used to process cement made from the limestone found when the canal was excavated. Shippingport was cut off from the shore and connected by a bridge across the canal. The man-made island's homes and businesses, including a hotel, were repeatedly inundated by FLOODS in the nineteenth and early twentieth centuries. The landscape was further changed in 1927 when Louisville Gas and Electric Co. built a hydroelectric plant at the tip of the island. In 1958 the federal GOVERNMENT acquired the remaining privately-owned property in order to widen the canal. The human price of that expansion was the eviction of families, many of whom, like the Zurlinden family, had lived in the town for nearly a hundred years.

See Leland R. Johnson, *The Falls City Engineers* (Louisville 1974); Portland Museum, *The Tarascon Mill: Shippingport's Great Mill Reconstructed in Words, Pictures and a Model* (Louisville 1981); Doyce B. Nunis Jr., "Tarascon's Dream of an American Commercial Empire in the West," *Mid-America* 42 (July 1960): 170–84; John J. Crnkovich, "Tarascon Junr., James Berthoud & Co. and the Development of Shippingport, Kentucky," M.A. thesis, University of Louisville, 1955.

Nathalie Taft Andrews

SHIVELY. A third-class city since 1986, Shively is southwest of Louisville and centered at the junction of U.S. 60 and 31W (Dixie Hwy.). Shively began when Christian William Shively and his three brothers settled on one thousand acres at what is now the intersection of Seventh Street Rd. and Dixie Hwy. He constructed a mill nearby on a branch of Mill Creek in 1810. Others followed and large estates developed around the area, which became known as the Shively precinct.

In 1816 Shively donated land for a church. In the early days, both Methodist and Baptist congregations worshiped there. The congregation has survived several moves and name changes, and continues today as Parkview Methodist, Jefferson County's oldest continuous Methodist congregation. The area's first school, Cane Run, was established around 1832. About 1850 the first Mill Creek School was built.

Shortly before the CIVIL WAR, German immigrants, mostly Catholics from the Alsace region, began to settle the area. They bought small tracts of land and developed truck farms, growing mainly vegetables. These farms supplied vegetables to Louisville from the late 1800s into the 1930s, and truck farming was the major business in the area during that time. By 1897 a Catholic priest, John Baptist Peifer, organized St. Helen's Catholic Church and school, which gradually gave its name to the area. Peifer retired in 1938 and was replaced as pastor of St. Helen's by Joseph A. Newman, who served there for nineteen years until his death in 1957. Newman helped to organize the Shively Public Library, negotiated the purchase of the land for Shively Park, and raised money for the building of the shelter house. During his service he doubled the size of the parish school and built a new convent for the sisters who taught there. In recognition of Newman's works Shively dedicated its new civic center to him in 1959.

The area got its first post office in 1902. When it could not be named St. Helen's because there was already a St. Helen's in Lee County, residents chose Shively after the pioneer family.

The interurban electric line began operating between Louisville and Orell in 1904. This permitted the community to accommodate visitors and welcome an increased number of new residents. In 1908 thirty-three area merchants and farmers adopted articles of incorporation for the Bank of St. Helen's. It was located in the "V" formed by Seventh Street Rd. and Eighteenth St. (Dixie Hwy.).

After PROHIBITION ended in 1933, eight distilleries quickly opened in the area, among them Stitzel-Weller, Brown-Forman, Frankfort, National, Yellowstone, Schenley, and Joseph Seagram. At their urging and in order to avoid Louisville annexation and taxation, Shively was incorporated on May 23, 1938, as a one-half-mile-square area centered around the intersection of Seventh Street Rd. and Eighteenth St. Four days later, the town trustees passed an ordinance annexing the distilleries and increased its tax base by $20 million. Into the 1960s, taxes on the distilleries kept Shively's coffers so full that in 1951 city officials boasted that it was the richest town in Kentucky.

Annexations and the post–WORLD WAR II building boom combined to make Shively the state's fastest-growing city during the 1950s. It became a fifth-class city in 1942 and fourth-class in 1952. By 1970 Shively's POPULATION had reached 19,223. In 1980 it was 16,645. Since that time it has continued to decline, and by 1990 it had dropped to 15,535. In 1996 the population was 14,899.

A change in consumer demand and an increase in state whiskey taxes led to the closing of most of the distilleries in the 1960s. These closings, coupled with a loss in revenue sharing in the 1980s, led to budget deficits and curtailment of some city services. In 1984 the city attempted to recover some of the tax losses in a hard-fought yet unsuccessful effort to annex the nearby community of PLEASURE RIDGE PARK. That year Police Chief Michael Donio acknowledged accepting bribes to allow PROSTITUTION and other unlawful activities at the former Red Garter Lounge on Seventh Street Rd.

Beginning in 1994, the city's finances improved. Aging police cars and PUBLIC WORKS and fire department equipment were replaced. In 1994 the city began a recycling program. In 1999 a new police/fire station was constructed. The city has continued to attract new business, and established businesses have expanded. Bearno's Pizza, Applebee's, O'Charley's, and Sue's Touch of Country are among the RESTAURANTS opened in Shively in recent years. Two business schools—SPENCERIAN COLLEGE and Kentucky College of Business—are located in the city.

In 1999 Shively encompassed 21.8 square miles. It was Jefferson County's only third-class city and the only city in Jefferson County other than Louisville with a full-time paid fire department. It owned thirty-acre Shively Park, two-acre Leeds Park, and a nine-hole GOLF course.

See *A Place in Time: The Story of Louisville's Neighborhoods* (Louisville 1989); Rowena Bolin, *From the Wilderness to the Millennium: The History of Shively, Kentucky, from 1780 to 1998* (Louisville 1998); *Courier-Journal,* April 1, 1957.

Rowena E. Bolin

SHOPPING CENTERS AND MALLS.

Shopping centers and malls are the direct outgrowth of the automobile and the suburban sprawl that resulted from it. Various forms of them appeared as early as 1907 in Baltimore. The NATIONAL REGISTER OF HISTORIC PLACES credits Market Square in Lake Forest, Illinois, as "the nation's first planned center in 1916" (Bryson, Made in America, 214). In 1922 the Country Club Plaza opened in Kansas City. This particular development was unique because its construction was directly linked to a newly built residential area five miles south of the city. And by 1931 the HIGHLAND PARK Shopping Center in Dallas, Texas, had taken the unprecedented step of turning its back to the street, signaling "the possibility that the shopping center could create its own special world within itself" (Kowinski, *The Malling of America,* 105).

Automobiles freed Americans from both living and shopping within city boundaries. As people spread farther out from the city core, the shopping experience switched from an almost formal, dress-up event to an informal one in which the success of the venture was measured by how little time it took. Square footage retail space vied with the number of available parking spaces for what attracted both merchants and shoppers.

In Louisville, unplanned string or strip "centers" had evolved along the heavily traveled streets and intersections. These locations were limited in terms of sales volume by the amount of on-street parking that was available. Places such as the ST. MATTHEWS Triangle and Bardstown Rd.'s Douglass Loop and Bonnycastle districts fit this description.

Louisville's first shopping center with off-street parking as a part of its original design was wrapped around the corner created by the junction of Highland and Baxter Avenues, a location where a streetcar barn had once stood. Constructed in 1938 by the leader of the area's shopping center builders, Joe Dahlem (and eventually his son Bernard), the five-store development featured a twenty-foot setback so that autos could pull in and back out conveniently. The Dahlem family, that had begun in storefront construction along Fourth St., went on to build more than thirty centers in Jefferson County and was a charter member of the International Council of Shopping Centers (ICSC) founded in 1957.

In the mid-1940s the Louisville Area Development Association (LADA) endorsed the construction of two limited-access highways. One was to form an arc around the outer fringes of the city from Shelbyville Rd. west to Dixie Hwy. The other was to connect the midpoint of the arc directly to the downtown commercial district. The rationale behind the construction of Louisville's first expressways was that "by providing easy access to the central business district . . . the belt road plus its connecting road to the city's core would discourage commercial development on the fringes" (Yater, *Two Hundred Years at the Falls of the Ohio,* 215). Indeed, just the opposite resulted.

The WATTERSON EXPRESSWAY arc was begun in 1949 and completed in 1958. By 1959 the newly constructed North/South Expressway extended to BROADWAY and, as a result of the federal Interstate Highway System, connected to points far beyond the county's borders. With the appearance in the early 1950s of General Electric's immense Appliance Park and the Ford Motor Assembly plant, both in rural Jefferson County, the stage was set for an explosion in suburban growth. "At the very time that city bus use was declining, vehicle registration in Jefferson County increased by 300 percent. Moreover, though the city's POPULATION peaked in 1960 (391,000) at its highest point ever, the county population (outside of Louisville) in the 1950s decade had increased by nearly 100%" (Yater, *Two Hundred Years at the Falls of the Ohio,* 226). A Louisville magazine 1955 cover story about the "Big Boom in Subdivisions" noted that, since 1953, there were 199 new suburban developments totaling 19,400 lots in various stages of completion. The article went on to note that "building in county areas outside Louisville has passed Louisville home construction by three to one" (Sept. 20, 1955, 9). Within 7 years an additional 408 plats had been recorded and approved by the City-County Zoning Commission.

At first, Louisville's shopping centers appeared piecemeal. Open-spaced gaps that broke the flow of a shared facade waited for the appearance of willing investors. According to a 1955 Louisville Chamber of Commerce classification, an "outlying shopping center" had to have a minimum of ten stores including at least one grocery, one drugstore, three retail, and three service facilities (banks, barbers, etc.). As developers saw the advantages of the commercial chemistry created by a central location tied together by a common parking lot, they began to act as catalysts pulling diverse retailers together. The days of the ninety-nine-year lease gave way to percentage-of-the-profits arrangements as the rental agreement. By 1955 there were twenty-four such centers.

As the strip and string centers evolved, one developer envisioned something much larger and grander at S Third and Southland Blvd. The twelve-store "million dollar" IROQUOIS Manor opened in November 1954. It touted 612 parking spaces on 11 acres. William A. Gardner followed this success a year later with the area's first super center, Dixie Manor. Located on twenty-four acres along Dixie Hwy. in Shively, the center proclaimed "acres and acres" of free customer parking illuminated by ninety-two double standard lights. The *COURIER-JOURNAL* (Nov. 16, 1955) gushed with enthusiasm as it noted that the facility with its New Orleans design motif would "serve as a new downtown" for that area of the county and in fact" had more store frontage in the development than on one side of Fourth St. from Market to Broadway." By the end of the decade Gardner would also open his Algonquin Manor along Cane Run Rd.

In another end of the county, Roy F. McMahan eyed the HIKES POINT area along Taylorsville Rd. for the site of his own McMahan Center. Opened in 1954, this enterprise was soon joined by the Dahlem Co. developments of Gardiner Lane Shopping Center (spring 1954), Shelbyville Road Plaza (fall 1955), and Indian Trail Shopping Center on Preston Hwy. (fall 1957).

Louisville's shopping centers were viewed by most as clear indicators of the community's commercial progress. Indeed, in the winter of 1954 the J.B. SPEED ART MUSEUM featured a "Shopping Centers of the Future" exhibit (*Courier-Journal,* Jan. 10, 1954). On display were the architectural ideas of the nation's shopping center guru, Victor Gruen of California. However, the residents of the BON AIR Estates neighborhood along Goldsmith Ln. struggled to see the beauty in the Austrian-born Gruen's ideas when they learned that the first shopping center not on a main traffic thoroughfare was to appear inside their subdivision. Though a hot zoning debate ensued with the appearance of a neighborhood protective association, Bon Air Manor opened June 3, 1959, to receptive patrons.

Across the river in JEFFERSONVILLE, INDIANA, George Young, a Lexington, Kentucky, native who would eventually dominate shopping center development in that city, opened his Youngstown Center on E Tenth St. in 1956 with the Dahlem Co. handling the construction concerns. However, his efforts to do the same in NEW ALBANY, Indiana, along State St. hit a brick wall of both political and neighborhood opposition that ultimately was resolved by a 1963 Indiana Supreme Court decision. Though Colonial Manor opened along Charlestown Rd. in June 1965 with little fanfare, groundbreaking on the New Albany Plaza did not commence until 1972. Fears that that shopping center would have adverse effects upon the HOOSIER city's downtown merchants were well founded. The commercial vibrancy that was once commonly found downtown nearly disappeared.

As shopping center developers debated the proper ratios of retail space versus parking space and the maximum distance shoppers were willing to travel from their automobiles to entryways, a century-old concept of merchandising design was being reborn. Diverse retail outlets separated by a walkway yet operating under a shared roof had appeared in both London and Milan. The Burlington Arcade and La Galleria were European forerunners of American malls. Indeed, the term itself had a British origin stemming from a croquet type game played along grass fairways referred to as malls. "Long after the game had faded, mall came to mean a specially designed pedestrian environment. Thus, a shopping mall is more precisely a shopping center with a mall in the middle, inside it" (Kowinski, *The Malling of America*, 106).

America's first true enclosed shopping center opened in 1956 in Edina, Minnesota. Designed by none other than Victor Gruen, Southdale Mall exuded all the characteristics of the "shopping towns" (Bryson, *Made in America*, 215) that would soon proliferate across the country. Anchor stores at both ends between which could be found gathering places, fountains, shrubbery, and benches would create consumer environments. Accentuated by controlled climates and almost limitless parking outside, Gruen hoped that communities would work better when people were "together face-to-face, not isolated in cars, housing tracts, and office buildings" (Kowinski, *The Malling of America*, 118). And, as William Kowinski noted, "It was now clear the shopping center was going to be the center of everything for suburbia . . . and, the signature structure of the age" (Kowinski, *The Malling of America*, 122).

In a 1956 Louisville magazine article entitled, "Think Big, Think Ahead, Think Together," (December 6, 1956), William Embry, president of the Chamber of Commerce noted that "our most attractive merchandising tool would be the proposed FOURTH Street Mall." His dream became a reality with a downtown pedestrian (unenclosed) mall in 1973 and an enclosed GALLERIA in 1982. However, downtown retailers had dropped the ball in the fifties. Suburban merchants were now competing for commercial leadership. The decade came to a close with a January 25, 1959, front page *Courier-Journal* story proclaiming a "Roofed Mall Trade Center Planned Here." Located on the west side of the junction formed by Shelbyville Rd. and the Watterson Expressway on what had been the old Arterburn estate, the state's first mall appropriately named the Shelbyville Road Mall (Mall St. Matthews) opened its doors for business in March 1962. Downtown merchants viewed the 67-acre facility surrounded on all sides with parking spaces as a threat not to them, but to suburban shopping centers. It was an immediate retailing success that, though it had an A&P, no longer depended upon grocery stores, drugstores, and banks as anchors. Indeed, it attracted decades-old Louisville retailers, KAUFMAN-STRAUS and Rodes-Rapier (RODES). Though Bardstown Rd.'s Mid-City Mall also opened in the same year not far from where Joe Dahlem's first off-street shopping center had appeared, it was to be the suburban malls along wide highways and expressways and deeply rooted in the subdivision communities around them that were to provide the new competition for the Mall St. Matthews.

In 1968 Greentree Mall opened in CLARKSVILLE, INDIANA. Located along what had been an old country road known as McCulloch Pike, the more accurately described Highway 131 was to serve as a corridor of commercial development. By 1990, less than a half mile from the Greentree entrance, though even closer to Interstate 65, appeared River Falls Mall.

The same pattern of competitive proximity had also appeared along Jefferson County's Shelbyville Rd. Located on the east side of the junction formed by the Watterson Expressway and Shelbyville Rd. was OXMOOR Mall, built in 1971 on a portion of the Bullitt family's Oxmoor estate. Here a particularly significant retail development occurred: the department store leader of the entire metropolitan community, Stewart's Dry Goods, opened its first suburban outlet.

In 1973 BASHFORD MANOR Mall opened in West BUECHEL at the site of an old horse farm, Bashford Manor, where three KENTUCKY DERBY winners had been sired. Situated between Bardstown Rd. and Newburg Rd. and a half mile south of the Watterson Expressway, it became the outer limit of mall success in that area of the county. Indeed three years later and just four miles out the same street, Raceland Mall stumbled to a start, struggled throughout, and ultimately failed.

In western Louisville, Lyles Plaza, a strip center, appeared in 1975. As a result of the success experienced in this location, ten years later Lyles Mall opened at 2600 W Broadway. A product of the community spirit and commercial foresight of its namesake, FOOTBALL great Lenny Lyles, this three-story facility was tailored to the shopping and service needs of its patrons. Though a business in every sense of the word, it also has served the community as a positive symbol of African American entrepreneurial drive and vision.

Jefferson Mall, situated along the county's Outer Loop and one mile east of Interstate 65, threw open its doors in the summer of 1978. Within a year of its opening this center would tout four anchor stores that included Stewart's, Sears, J.C. Penney, and Shillito's (Lazarus).

In 1998 there were approximately 140 shopping centers in Jefferson County. BUSINESS FIRST maintained a top-twenty-eight list based upon gross leasable area of retail/rental space. The Louisville-Jefferson County Planning Commission groups the facilities in categories ranging from neighbor and community sizes to regional and super-regional size customer bases. With the appearance of outlet malls, Wal-Marts, and multi-product warehouse grocery stores, the retail picture continues to evolve and change. No doubt the relationship between consumers, their homes, and the roads and highways that connect them to where they work and shop will continue to influence the shifting patterns of development. Already new malls were moving toward the GENE SNYDER FREEWAY, such as the Springhurst Towne Center that includes the Tinseltown movie complex.

Largest Area Shopping Complexes Gross Leasable Area, 1998

Jefferson Mall (Louisville) (1.1 million sq. ft.)
Mall St. Matthews (Louisville) (1.03 million sq. ft.)
Oxmoor Center (Louisville) (911,000 sq. ft.)
Green Tree Mall (Clarksville, Indiana) (786,073 sq. ft.)
Springhurst Towne Center (Louisville) (781,998 sq. ft.)
River Falls Mall (Clarksville, Indiana) (745,000 sq. ft.)
Bashford Manor Mall (Louisville) (560,000 sq. ft.)
Dixie Manor Shopping Mall (Louisville) (373,100 sq. ft.)
Algonquin Manor (Louisville) (357,319 sq. ft.)
Indian Trail Square (Louisville) (355,306 sq. ft.)
Louisville Galleria (Louisville) (282,000 sq. ft.)
Westport Plaza (Louisville) (258,000 sq. ft.)
Shelbyville Road Plaza (Louisville) (248,000 sq. ft.)
Clarksville Commons (Clarksville, Indiana) (237,032 sq. ft.)
Townfair Center (Louisville) (235,892 sq. ft.)

See William Kowinski, *The Malling of America* (New York 1985); Bill Bryson, *Made in America* (New York 1994); *Business First Book of Lists*, (*Louisville*, Oct. 26, 1998); Helen G. Henry, ed., "Big Boom in Subdivisions," Louisville 9 (Sept. 1955); William C. Embry, "Think Big, Think Ahead, Think Together," *Louisville* 5 (Dec. 1956); *Courier-Journal*, Nov. 16, 1955; Jan. 10, 1945.

Kenneth L. Miller

SHORT, CHARLES W. (b Woodford County, Kentucky, October 6, 1793; d Louisville, March 9, 1863). Physician, botanist, academic. The son of Peyton and Maria (Symmes) Short, he was born at Greenfield, the family estate. He attended Transylvania University, graduating with honors in 1810, and in 1813 went to Philadelphia to study MEDICINE with the renowned Dr. Caspar Wistar. He was granted the M.D. degree in 1815 by the University of Pennsylvania, where he developed his interest in botany through studies with Benjamin Smith Barton.

From 1817 to 1825 he practiced medicine and continued his botanical research in Hopkinsville, Kentucky. In the latter year he was called to Transylvania University as professor of materia medica and medical botany in the medical department, a post he filled with distinction, and in 1827 he became dean of the medical faculty. While in Lexington he was a cofounder of the Transylvania Journal of Medicine and the Associate Sciences, among the earliest journals of its type west of the Appalachians.

In 1838 he left Transylvania to join the faculty (and later became dean) of the new LOUISVILLE MEDICAL INSTITUTE, which in 1846 became the medical department of the UNIVERSITY OF LOUISVILLE. He retired in 1849 after receiving a large bequest in the will of his uncle, William Short, who had served as THOMAS JEFFERSON's private secretary in Paris and held other diplomatic posts. Dr. Short bought George Hancock's estate, Hayfield, south of Louisville off the Bardstown Rd. Here he pursued botanical research and established an herbarium and maintained a lively correspondence with botanists in the United States and overseas. He died of pneumonia and is buried in CAVE HILL CEMETERY. His herbarium of more than fifteen hundred species is at the Academy of Natural Sciences in Philadelphia.

See Dumas Malone, ed., *Dictionary of American Biography* (New York 1964); Deborah Susan Skaggs, "Charles Wilkins Short: Kentucky Botanist and Physician," M.A. thesis, University of Louisville, 1982.

George H. Yater

Shotgun house at 721 West St. Catherine Street, 1921.

SHORT, ROY HUNTER (b Louisville, October 19, 1902; d Nashville, Tennessee, July 2, 1994). Methodist minister and bishop. Short was the son of Minnie Lee (Badders) and Jesse Peters Short, who lived on the north side of Franklin St. near Wenzel. Then he lived in the 800 block of Washington St. (1907–24).

He was educated in the city schools of Louisville and received the following degrees: UNIVERSITY OF LOUISVILLE, A.B., 1924; LOUISVILLE PRESBYTERIAN THEOLOGICAL SEMINARY, B.D., 1927 and Th.M., 1929; Kentucky Wesleyan College, D.D., 1939 and LL.D., 1964; Florida Southern College, LL.D., 1949; Tennessee Wesleyan College, Litt.D., 1957; Emory University, D.D., 1957; Emory and Henry College, D.CnL., 1957; Lycoming College (Williamsport, Pennsylvania), D.D. 1966.

He married Louise Clay Baird of CLARKSVILLE, INDIANA, September 1, 1926. They had three sons, Hunter Baird, Murray Malcolm, and Riley Phillips.

He was ordained to the Methodist ministry in 1921 and admitted to the Louisville Conference of the Methodist Episcopal church, South, serving the following churches in the Louisville area: Those in the Jefferson Circuit (1921–22); Mt. Holly and Mill Creek (1922–26); Oakdale (1926–28); Marcus Lindsey, his home church (1928–30); and St. Paul Methodist Church (1941–44). He was superintendent of the Louisville District from 1937 until 1941. Short served two pastorates outside the Louisville area: Greenville, Kentucky, (1930–35), and the Elizabethtown District (1935–37).

He served the larger church as editor of the Upper Room, a multilingual devotional guide published by the General Board of Evangelism of the Methodist church from 1944 to 1948.

In 1948 he was elected to the episcopacy by the Southeastern Jurisdiction and served the following areas as bishop: the Florida Area (Florida and Cuba) (1948–52); the Nashville area (1952–64); and the Louisville area (1964–72). He served as secretary of the Council of Bishops, the most influential office in United Methodism, from 1956 to 1972. He gave firm and compassionate leadership during one of the most significant eras of the United Methodist Church with a strong focus upon evangelism.

Short wrote ten books including *Evangelistic Preaching: Evangelism through the Local Church* (1956); *Chosen to be Consecrated* (1976); and *Methodism in Kentucky* (1979). He wrote position papers for the general church. In 1989 he published his autobiography for his family, *Recollections of Bishop Roy Hunter Short.* In 1980 the Upper Room published *Builder of Bridges, a Biography of Roy Hunter Short* by Bishop T. Otto Nall.

Bishop Edgar Love, an African American, said, "Some of the bishops talk about race. Bishop Short doesn't talk much about race, rather in his quiet way he does something about it." (Short, *Recollections of Bishop Roy Hunter Short,* 99). He retired in 1972 to Nashville, Tennessee. He is buried in Louisville's CAVE HILL CEMETERY.

See Nolan B. Harmon, ed., *Encyclopedia of World Methodism* (Nashville 1974); Roy Hunter Short, *Recollections of Bishop Roy Hunter Short* (published by author, 1989); T. Otto Nall, *Builder of Bridges: A Biography of Roy Hunter Short* (Nashville 1980).

R. Kenneth Lile

SHOTGUN COTTAGES. The shotgun house, a common residential building type found in many of Louisville's historic working-class NEIGHBORHOODS, can best be described as a modest, rectangular structure that is typically one-story high, one room wide, and three to four rooms deep. It is among the most common late-nineteenth- and early-twentieth-century house types in the urban South. By some estimates shotgun houses comprise 10 percent of Louisville's building stock. The majority of local examples were built between the end of the CIVIL WAR, when the city was experiencing a period of postwar industrial expansion, and 1910.

Particularly strong concentrations of shotgun cottages can be found in the PORTLAND, PHOENIX HILL, SMOKETOWN, BUTCHERTOWN, GERMANTOWN, SCHNITZELBURG, RUSSELL, CALIFORNIA, and the lower HIGHLANDS neighborhoods. Oral tradition attributes its name to the distinct floor plan: the linear alignment of all exterior and interior doors allows a person to stand at the front door of the house, shoot a shotgun, and have its shot pass through each of the building's rooms and out the back door without ricocheting off any interior wall.

Most of Louisville's shotgun houses are constructed of wood or brick (although some stone examples exist) and are topped by a hipped or front-facing gabled roof. Typically the front room serves as the living room with the bedroom(s) in the middle and the kitchen to the rear. Often the side windows face the windowless side of the house next door, adding an unusual element of privacy. To this basic building form a variety of Victorian architectural revival styles are applied: Italianate, Princess Anne, and Classical Revival are among the most common. The exterior of the shotgun houses often features such amenities as partial or full-width front porches, elaborate window and door surrounds, gingerbread trim, and shined or leaded glass windows. Interior features might include hardwood floors, cast-iron fireplace mantels, and built-in cabinetry.

Variations on the shotgun house type include the double shotgun (a single building with one roof over two shotgun-plan living spaces divided by a common wall); the camelback shotgun (three to four rooms deep but with an added room located above the kitchen); and the double camelback shotgun (two camelback shotgun houses sited side-by-side and sharing a common roof). Also typical is the addition of a small side porch that provides access to the bedroom and the kitchen, or a recessed side porch that extends nearly the entire length of the house.

Theories abound as to how the shotgun house type came about. Some speculate that the shotgun house type closely resembles house forms historically found in West Africa and that this distinct vernacular architectural tradition may have traveled with slaves and free blacks to the West Indies and from there to New Orleans. Eventually, vernacular builders brought the house type up the inland waterways to port towns such as St. Louis, Evansville, NEW ALBANY, Jeffersonville, and Louisville. The shotgun house evolved along every step of the way, modified by indigenous cultural, material, and architectural influences. Others speculate that it is essentially a hall/parlor house plan adapted to fit narrow urban city lots, that it evolved from typical nineteenth-century frame office buildings, or that it has Native American antecedents.

Whatever the origin, it is clear that shotgun houses are among Louisville's most abundant house types and are tangible reminders of solidly built, attractive, late-nineteenth- and early-twentieth-century worker housing. They remain one of our most viable and adaptable local house types.

See Preservation Alliance of Louisville and Jefferson County, Inc., *The Shotgun House: Urban Housing Opportunities* (Louisville 1980); John S. Sledge, "Shoulder to Shoulder . . . Mobile's Shotgun Houses," *Gulf Coast Historical Review* 6 (Fall 1990): 57–64; John Vlach, "Shotgun Houses," *Natural History* 86 (Feb. 1977): 51–57; *Courier-Journal*, Aug. 16, 1995; Henry Glassie, *Pattern in the Material Folk Culture of the Eastern United States* (Philadelphia 1968).

Joanne Weeter

SHOWBOATS. Showboats were popular entertainment boats that plied America's rivers from the early 1830s to the late 1950s. More than a hundred showboats were built during that time. They ranged from small primitive SHANTYBOATS to the large elaborate "temples of amusement" with circuses, museums, and especially THEATERS aboard. Generally the showboats had a steam calliope to produce "soul-stirring" music to announce their arrival and attract people to the landing for performances. Among the famous showboats along the OHIO RIVER were *Cotton Blossom, French's Sensation,* and *Floating Palace.*

Showboats preferred to stop at small towns where their shows were sometimes the only source of entertainment. Because of its size and sophistication, Louisville offered a variety of entertainment that precluded the need for showboats. However, some did stop at the city's municipal wharf. Many showboats stopped across the river at the smaller cities of Jeffersonville and NEW ALBANY.

One of the largest showboats to visit was Captain Menke's HOLLYWOOD in 1930. It stopped in Louisville for repairs and decided to give a one-night production of *Tidly Ann* to compensate for the repair costs. To everyone's surprise, Louisvillians were so enthusiastic about the performance that the boat stayed twenty-one more weeks with capacity audiences each night. Productions of melodrama were a reason for the popularity. They expressed the growing sense of nostalgia then in vogue for simple and sentimental representation of life.

In the 1950s Capt. Thomas J. Reynolds's large showboat *Majestic* made frequent stops at Louisville while offering a varied repertoire of performances. In 1959 former mayor CHARLES FARNSLEY was campaigning for the purchase of the boat by the city as an entertainment and tourist attraction. However the project was expensive, and the boat was acquired by Indiana University. The university's theater department performed old-time melodramas for seven summers from 1960 to 1966—the last two at anchor at JEFFERSONVILLE, INDIANA. In 1967 the city of Cincinnati purchased the boat for its Riverfront Park.

While showboats entertained thousands of people in the river towns, these "floating palaces" could not survive the growing competition from other forms of mass culture, particularly motion pictures and TELEVISION.

See Philip Graham, *Showboats: The History of an American Institution* (Austin, Tex., 1951); Betty Bryant. *Here Comes the Showboat* (Lexington 1994); *Courier-Journal*, Oct. 2, 1927, June 26, 1941, Aug. 26, 1948, July 23, 1959.

SHREVE, HENRY M. (b New Jersey, October 21, 1785; d Missouri, March 6, 1851). Steamboat pioneer. After the Revolutionary War, Shreve moved with his family to Pennsylvania, where he knew the hardships of frontier life. As a young man he began trading trips down the Monongahela and OHIO RIVERS by keelboat. His successful fur-trading expedition to St. Louis in 1807 helped begin trade between that city and Philadelphia by way of Pittsburgh. Encouraged by the success of the *New Orleans,* the first steamboat to navigate the Ohio and Mississippi, in 1811, Shreve realized the potential of steam navigation. In 1814 he piloted the steamboat *Enterprise*, laden with munitions for Gen. Andrew Jackson's army, from Pittsburgh to New Orleans, arriving in time to take part in the Battle of New Orleans in January 1815. He brought the *Enterprize* back to Louisville in 1815—the first successful upstream steam voyage from New Orleans to the FALLS OF THE OHIO.

Using his experience and knowledge of steam mechanics, Shreve and some business associates built the boat Washington in 1816 at Wheeling (then in Virginia.) It was the first double-decked steamboat, first to have its cylinders connected by a pitman (drive shaft) to the paddlewheel, and first to have the boilers on the deck rather than below deck—improvements that became basic to steamboat construction on the inland waterways. Captain Shreve piloted the Washington from Pittsburgh to New Orleans and back to Louisville in 1816, and in 1817 made the round-trip between Louisville and New Orleans in the record time of forty-one days. Shreve's successes as steamboat builder, pilot, and merchant brought him into conflict with the powerful business interests of Robert Fulton and associates, to whom monopoly of steam navigation on the lower Mississippi River had earlier been granted by the Louisiana territorial legislature. Shreve was successful in litigation brought against him by the Fulton group. That opened navigation of the Mississippi and its tributaries to competition. Shreve became a highly respected boat captain, and in 1819 historian HENRY MCMURTRIE wrote that "it is to his exertions, his example, his integrity, and principle, that Louisville is indebted for the present flourishing state of its navigation."

In 1826 Shreve was appointed by President John Quincy Adams as superintendent of Western rivers improvements, a position he would hold for the next fifteen years under the administration of the Army Corps of Engineers. In that position he was responsible for continuing the federal project of clearing snags and other obstructions from the rivers, as authorized by Congress in the first Rivers and Harbors Act in 1824. While superintendent, Shreve undertook measures to improve navigation at the Grand Chain of Rocks, a major impediment about two miles long near the mouth of the Ohio.

In 1829–30 he directed removal of tons of rocks and the construction of a wing dam ex-

Simmons University students. Photograph by Harvey Husbands, 1880s.

tending from the Illinois shore to direct more water into the channel. When completed, water depth through the channel was increased to forty-eight inches, where formerly at times of low water only twenty-two inches was available. The Grand Chain project was one of many wing dams or dikes constructed by the Corps in the nineteenth century to enhance navigation conditions.

Shreve is perhaps most remembered as the designer of the steam-powered snag boat in 1827. In 1828, while living in PORTLAND where he operated a warehouse on the wharf, he built a prototype vessel at a NEW ALBANY, Indiana, shipyard. Named the Heliopolis, it and other snag boats built later performed yeoman service in removing great jams (called rafts) of logs and brush on the Ohio, Mississippi, and other rivers. So successful were these operations that the boats became known as "Uncle Sam's Toothpullers." In the Louisville area Shreve and crew removed a two-mile log raft just downstream of the LOUISVILLE AND PORTLAND CANAL in 1830, producing twelve hundred cords. Following his successes on the Ohio and Mississippi Rivers, Shreve went to work removing the "Great Raft" on the Red River in Louisiana. His base of operation at Bennett's Bluff was later incorporated and named Shreveport. Shreve was removed from the superintendent's position by the Tyler administration in 1841 and retired to Missouri, where he died in 1851. An imposing monument marks his burial place in Bellefontaine Cemetery, St. Louis.

See Edith McCall, CONQUERING THE RIVERS: HENRY MILLER SHREVE AND THE NAVIGATION OF AMERICA'S INLAND WATERWAYS (Baton Rouge 1984); Charles E. Parrish, "Henry M. Shreve," *The Falls City Engineer* (Louisville, October 1988).

Charles E. Parrish

SHREVE, LEVEN LAWRENCE (b Maryland, August 27, 1793; d Louisville, April 3, 1864); and **SHREVE, THOMAS TALLIAFERRO** (b Hagerstown, Maryland, February 4, 1796; d Louisville, November 5, 1869). Merchants, manufacturers, and civic leaders. The Shreve brothers' father, Judge William Shreve, moved his family to Nicholasville, Kentucky, about 1800 and settled on a farm. The brothers were each given five thousand dollars by their father and went to Greenupsburg (later Greenup) where they purchased several blast furnaces and established an iron trade business.

In 1832 they came to Louisville and opened a merchant shop with James Hewitt on MAIN St. between Fifth and Sixth Streets. Shortly thereafter the brothers reentered the iron business by opening the Fulton Foundry on Main St. between Ninth and Tenth Streets, with Reddick D. Anderson and John H. Thomas joining the partnership. By 1848 Leven had started a new business on Main St. named L.L. Shreve and Co. This venture in general iron trading eventually branched out to Cincinnati and became one of the leading ironmonger houses in the South.

While Leven made his fortune in the iron business, he also occupied himself with several other ventures. Along with John I. Jacob, James Rudd, and Robert Tyler, Shreve helped found the Louisville Gas and Water Co. and was elected its first president in 1838. He later went on to become a leader in establishing the LOUISVILLE & NASHVILLE RAILROAD and served as its first president, from September 1851 until October 1854. Shreve also was instrumental in the creation of CAVE HILL CEMETERY, was a major stockholder in the LOUISVILLE HOTEL, and sat on the city council in 1834, 1842–46, and 1848–49.

Thomas was known as a shrewd investor who seemed to have the "Midas touch"; he was associated with several BANKING institutions after 1850 such as Shreve, Tucker, and Co.; J.P. Curtis and Co.; and the old BANK OF LOUISVILLE. He also was president of the Hope Insurance Co. in 1864 as well as being a leading investor in the new GALT HOUSE hotel and the Louisville, Cincinnati, & Lexington Railroad Co. In 1833 he was a city council member. His final gesture to the city was the donation of five acres of land to establish the Masonic Widows' and Orphans' Home of Louisville in 1867 on Second St. After laying the cornerstone during a snowstorm on October 24, 1869, Thomas is said to have caught the cold that led to his death almost two weeks later. He is buried in CAVE HILL CEMETERY.

Thomas's first marriage was to Mary Scott of Jessamine County, and they had one child, John William. By his second wife, Eliza A. Rogers of Sharpsburg, Kentucky, he fathered two children, Charles and Mary. The third marriage, to Belle Sheridan of Louisville, resulted in four children, Mattie Belle, Thomas William, Adele Lawrence, and one child who died at birth.

The wealthy brothers, whose complementary business skills are said to have led to their enormous success, were also known for the large house they shared on Walnut St. (Muhammad Ali Blvd.) between Sixth and Centre (Armory Place) Streets. Designed by ELIAS E. WILLIAMS and built in the 1830s, the Shreve mansion gained attention locally after being the first in the city to be lighted by gas. It stood until the late 1800s. The Jefferson County Armory (now the GARDENS OF LOUISVILLE) was constructed on its site in 1905.

Leven Shreve was married twice, to Hannah Andrews of Fleming County and later to Mary Sheppard of Virginia, and had no children. He is buried in Cave Hill Cemetery.

See J. Stoddard Johnston, ed., *Memorial History of Louisville*, vol. 1 (Chicago 1896); George H. Yater, *Two Hundred Years at the Falls of the Ohio* (Louisville 1987).

SHRYOCK, GIDEON (b Lexington November 15, 1802; d Louisville June 19, 1880). Architect. He was Kentucky's first native-born, professionally trained architect. His parents were Mathias and Mary Elizabeth (Gaugh) Shryock, and he was the third of eleven children. Shryock was trained at Mr. Aldridge's Lancastrian Academy for boys in Lexington and apprenticed under his father to learn the principles of design and construction. In October 1823 he traveled to Philadelphia and studied under architect William Strickland, a student of Benjamin Henry Latrobe. Shryock returned to Lexington in 1825 and two years later received his first important commission, to design the second Kentucky State Capitol in Frankfort (the first had burned in 1824). Construction was completed in 1830. It was an early example of Greek Revival ARCHITECTURE in the West. He modeled the design after the temple of Minerva Polis at Priene in Ionia; it featured a curved, freestanding staircase under the dome.

The years between 1827 and 1842 were the most successful in Shryock's career. During these years, his accomplishments included Morrison Hall of Transylvania University (1833); a temple in the Old Episcopal Cemetery in Lexington, which honored his father (1833); Arkansas State Capitol (1833); Franklin County Courthouse in Frankfort (1835); Orlando Brown House in Frankfort (1835); and the LOUISVILLE MEDICAL INSTITUTE (1838). Some of his most noted accomplishments were in Louisville.

In 1835 Shryock moved to Louisville and was appointed the city architect, a position he held until he was dismissed in 1842. The old BANK OF LOUISVILLE (later the Southern Bank of Louisville) on MAIN St. is generally accepted as the first city building on which he supervised the construction. However, the original designs have been credited to James Dakin, even though most sources still cite Shryock as the architect. Arthur Scully, who wrote James Dakin's biography, found original drawings of the Bank of Louisville dating from 1834. There was also written evidence, found in several legal documents, pointing to Dakin as the original architect. Shryock did, however, supervise the building's construction after the death of the original supervisor. Critics such as Rexford Newcomb concluded that the structure was Shryock's reinterpretation of Dakin's design by comparing Dakin's drawings to the finished product. Some of those differences included a greater contrast between verticals and horizontals, almost equal height and width, alteration of the main entrance, a lesser number of steps, and the inclusion of windows. Overall, his alteration of Dakin's design rendered the facade of the bank more visually attractive.

The building later housed ACTORS THEATRE OF LOUISVILLE and is listed on the NATIONAL REGISTER OF HISTORIC PLACES. Shryock showed a talent for modifications of Greek Revival design and treatment. The building combined Ionic columns, palmette motifs, and a portico of battered antae. Inside were Corinthian columns and Dakin's elliptical dome in the ceiling. The work was marked by Shryock's creative use of details, excellent proportions, and a functional approach in planning. The building is an example of "exquisite taste" and overall dignity and simplicity of design.

In 1835 Shryock designed the JEFFERSON COUNTY COURTHOUSE. Work began in 1836. The county's first major public building, it was constructed in the Greek Revival style. It is located on the north side of Jefferson between Fifth and Sixth Streets. Shryock worked on the project until 1842, when he retired due to such problems as defective materials, alterations of plans, and change of responsibility and funding from county to city. Although it opened in 1842, ALBERT FINK, engineer and bridge designer, completed the project between 1858 and 1860.

The final structure was a reduced version of Shryock's original scheme. However, it still reflected his plans of proportion and creativity. It was large, simple, and definite in form, and showed a straightforward use of detail. The courthouse's classical architecture included a tetrastyle portico with Greek Doric columns, rotunda columns, a spiral staircase, and a skylight. This building was sometimes referred to as a "grand Doric temple." Although not completed as Shryock originally envisioned, the Jefferson County Courthouse was considered his principal work in Louisville.

In 1838 Shryock designed the Louisville Medical Institute at Eighth and Chestnut Streets. It was his last completed example of Greek Revival architecture. The building burned in 1856 and was rebuilt under the supervision of Louisville architect HENRY WHITESTONE.

The last known structure designed by Shryock was the Chestnut Street Christian Methodist Episcopal Church, later known as the Brown Memorial Christian Methodist Episcopal Church. It was built between 1863 and 1864 at 800 W Chestnut St. The church was a blend of Greek Revival and Romanesque Revival architectural styles, marked by double stairways, stained-glass windows, and round brick arches.

Shryock's later life was spent in seclusion. He maintained his architectural practice, but it is unknown if he received any more commissions. He did, however, design the house in which he died, at 66 Madison St. between Eighth and Ninth Streets. He married Elizabeth Pendleton Bacon in 1829 and had ten children.

At his death, he was remembered for the introduction of Greek Revival architecture to Kentucky. His public buildings displayed a purity of line, striving after the ideals of Grecian art. It was this notion of classic beauty for which he was known. Gideon Shryock is buried in CAVE HILL CEMETERY.

See Rexford Newcomb, *Architecture in Old Kentucky* (Urbana, Ill., 1953); Arthur Scully Jr., *James Dakin, Architect, His Career in New York and the South* (Baton Rouge 1973); Henry F. Withey and Elsie Rathburn Withey, *Biographical Dictionary of American Architects* (Deceased) (Los Angeles 1956).

Shannon Phlegar

SILLIMAN, BENJAMIN, JR. (b New Haven, Connecticut, December 4, 1816; d New Haven, Connecticut, January 14, 1885). Editor and professor. Silliman, the son of Benjamin and Harriet (Trumbull) Silliman, was greatly influenced by his father, a professor of chemistry and natural history at Yale University and a prominent scientist. Upon graduating from Yale in 1840, the younger Silliman went to work for his father as a teaching assistant and associate editor of the American Journal of Science. In 1845, when his father resigned as chief editor, Silliman took over the duties. In 1846 he was appointed professor of practical chemistry and assisted in establishing the school of applied chemistry. The next year he was made professor of medical chemistry and toxicology at the UNIVERSITY OF LOUISVILLE, where he stayed five years.

He resigned to take his father's chair of chemistry at Yale. Besides teaching classes, Silliman spent most of his time writing. His best-known books were two textbooks, *First Principles of Chemistry* (1847) and *First Principles of Physics* (1859). He was a member of the American Association for the Advancement of Science and an original member of the National Academy of Sciences. Silliman married Susan Huldah Forbes on May 14, 1840. They had seven children. He is buried in New Haven, Connecticut.

See *American Journal of Science* (Feb. 1885).

SILVER CREEK. Rising in the southern part of SCOTT COUNTY, INDIANA, historic Silver Creek, with tributaries Pleasant Run, Muddy Fork, and Sinking Fork, drains 219 square miles of land, dropping 168 feet over 34 miles to its meeting with the OHIO RIVER. The upper stretches include many mud banks and bottoms, but as the stream descends to its mouth, banks lined with sycamores, walnuts, and maples are steeper, almost cliff-like, and the water courses rapidly.

Etching the boundary line between Clark and Floyd Counties, Silver Creek is home to muskrats and wood ducks, bluegill, bass, and garfish; and it is visited by white-tail deer and blue herons. Deposits of shale and limestone are plentiful.

The waterway also is home to many legends, including anecdotal references to Indian silver mines and Indian battles against a "strange" people, purportedly the source of a controversial theory that Welshmen, notably PRINCE MADOC, had settled in the area in prehistoric days.

What is known is that the stream was called Silver Creek as early as the GEORGE ROGERS CLARK grant of land from Virginia. Indians mined for flint along the banks, seeking a superior flint found only where argillaceous, or silvery limestone, is deposited. Clark lived in a log cabin in Clarksville near the mouth of the creek; Clark's brother William joined Meriwether Lewis there on the famous Lewis and Clark Corps of Discovery to the Pacific Coast. Four DUELS were fought at the creek's mouth on long-gone Shirt-tail Bend by Ken-

Glenwood Park, on Silver Creek in New Albany, Indiana, 1907.

tuckians who battled as close as they could to their own state, where dueling was outlawed. The most famous of these was the Henry Clay–Humphrey Marshall affair of honor stemming from a dispute in the Kentucky General Assembly in 1809.

See Historical Series of New Albany III, pamphlet published by Union National Bank, New Albany, Ind., based on material furnished by the Floyd County Historical Society; *History of the Ohio Falls Cities and Their Counties* (Cleveland, Ohio, 1882); *Water and Waterways, Flood Plain Information, Clark County, Indiana* (U.S. Army Corps of Engineers, Louisville District 1973); *Courier-Journal,* July 1, 1990; *Louisville Times,* July 12, 1929.

Betty Lou Amster

SIMMONS, WILLIAM J. (b Charleston, South Carolina, June 29, 1849; d Louisville, October 30, 1890). Minister and educator. Simmons was the son of enslaved Edward and Esther Simmons. While still a child, Simmons, his two sisters, and his mother escaped to Philadelphia, where they lived in bitter poverty with his uncle, who became his protector and first teacher. Simmons was apprenticed to a New Jersey dentist in 1862 but eventually fled and, on September 16, 1864, enlisted in the Union army (Forty-first U.S. Colored Troops). Following the Civil War, he worked as a journeyman for a black Philadelphia dentist in 1866. He was converted to the Baptist faith in 1867, ordained a minister in 1868, and, with assistance from the church, began attending Madison University of New York. Simmons also attended Rochester University and then transferred to Howard University in Washington, D.C., from which he graduated in 1873.

Simmons taught briefly in Arkansas and then returned to Washington. In 1879 he moved to Kentucky to accept the pastorate of the First Baptist Church of Lexington. In September 1880 he was appointed principal, soon changed to president, of the fledgling black-controlled Kentucky Normal and Theological Institute that opened on November 25, 1879, at Seventh and Kentucky Streets in Louisville. At the time of his appointment, Kentucky Normal had only two faculty members, thirteen students, and no funds. Simmons developed a coherent academic program on the secondary and collegiate levels, established graduate/professional courses and/or programs in law, medicine, music, and theology, and devoted considerable effort to fund-raising with the assistance of Kentucky Normal's "jubilee singers." The institute thrived under his leadership. It was renamed State University in 1885 to reflect its comprehensive mission and became Simmons University in 1918 in recognition of his work.

Simmons was moderate, but progressive politically, and challenged the structure of segregation while at the same time working pragmatically within its limitations to serve African Americans. On September 29, 1882, he was elected editor of the American Baptist magazine, and his strong editorials were extensively copied throughout the nation. He delivered major addresses before the American Baptist Home Mission Society in 1882, 1885, 1886, and 1887, and organized the Baptist Women's Educational Convention in 1883. In 1884 Simmons was appointed commissioner for Kentucky's "colored department" of the World's Industrial and Cotton Exposition held in New Orleans. In addition, Simmons chaired the executive committee of the State Convention of Colored Men of Kentucky and, in 1886, was chosen to present the views and grievances of Kentucky African Americans to the Kentucky General Assembly. He also was elected president of the National Colored Press convention in 1886 and, in 1888, began editing *Our Women and Children,* which became Kentucky's leading black magazine. In 1887 he published *Men of Mark: Eminent, Progressive and Rising* to emphasize the notable achievements of individual African Americans.

In 1890 Simmons resigned the presidency of State University and, with financial support from local whites and the assistance of Rev. C.H. Parrish Sr., one of his most gifted students, founded the Eckstein Norton Institute at Cane Springs in Bullitt County. Eckstein Norton was conceived as a normal school, with the vocational orientation of Hampton and Tuskegee Institutes. However, Simmons died suddenly of a heart attack on the threshold of achieving national stature rivaling that of his better-known contemporaries, T. Thomas Fortune, Ida B. Wells, and the then-emerging Booker T. Washington.

Simmons married Josephine Silence of Washington, D.C., on August 25, 1874, and was the father of three children: Josephine, William, and Effie. He lived at 712 W Kentucky St. Simmons is buried in Eastern Cemetery.

See Alice A. Dunnigan, *The Fascinating Story of Black Kentuckians: Their Heritage and Traditions* (Washington, D.C., 1982); Marion B. Lucas, *A History of Blacks in Kentucky: From Slavery to Segregation, 1760–1891* (Frankfort 1992); W.J. Simmons, *Men of Mark: Eminent, Progressive and Rising* (New York 1968); George C. Wright, *Life Behind a Veil: Blacks in Louisville, Kentucky, 1865-1930.* (Baton Rouge 1985).

J. Blaine Hudson

SIMMONS UNIVERSITY. In August 1865 the General Association of Colored Baptists of Kentucky, under the leadership of Rev. Henry Adams of Louisville's Fifth Street Baptist Church, voted to establish a college for Kentucky African Americans. However, translating their intent into a viable school would require sustained commitment over more than a decade amidst the turbulence of Reconstruction in the commonwealth.

In 1869 the General Association applied to the Kentucky General Assembly for a charter and began raising funds with which they purchased the "Old Fort Hill" property in Frankfort as a future site for the college. This property proved unsatisfactory and was soon sold, after which a more suitable site was purchased at Seventh and Kentucky Streets in Louisville. After more years of planning and fund-raising, the Kentucky Normal and Theological Institute opened on November 25, 1879, headed initially by Rev. Elijah P. Marrs. It was the first African American–controlled higher educational institution in Kentucky.

In September 1880 the General Association was fortunate in attracting Rev. William J. Simmons, a former slave and a well-educated young minister beginning to gain a national reputation, to the presidency of the fledgling college. Simmons held B.A. and M.A. degrees from Howard University. Under his leadership the college developed preparatory (elementary), academic (secondary), normal (teacher training) and religious education programs. After a college department was added in 1885, the institute was renamed State University. Simmons acquired financial support from both Northern and Southern BAPTISTS. Simmons resigned in 1890, but the university continued to evolve. By 1893, 159 students had completed the normal school program and 30 had graduated from the college department. By 1900 State University was offering nurses' training programs and professional education in MEDICINE and law through its affiliation with the LOUISVILLE NATIONAL MEDICAL COLLEGE and the Central Law School, respectively.

Nevertheless, State University was a religious institution committed to liberal arts education and, as a result, received neither public funds nor private support from the white philanthropic organizations that sustained "industrial education" schools such as Tuskegee and Hampton Institute. Consequently, despite its achievements, the university was beset constantly by financial troubles that, after 1900, made it difficult to maintain physical facilities and to attract and retain the most qualified faculty.

In 1918 Rev. Charles H. Parrish Sr., a State University graduate, was appointed president. Parrish renamed the school in honor of former president Simmons, his early mentor, and launched a determined campaign to revitalize the school's curriculum and improve its facilities. By 1922 there were 467 students in the college department, 33 theological students, and property valued at $750,000. With an endowment of only $54,000, fund-raising efforts in 1922 and 1925 were moderately successful, and Parrish's tireless labors were repaid when, in March 1930, Simmons University was awarded "B" rating as a senior college by the Committee on Accredited Relations of the University of Kentucky. However, this reversal of fortunes proved short-lived when, with the onset of the GREAT DEPRESSION, Simmons became insolvent.

On August 31, 1930, the UNIVERSITY OF LOUISVILLE purchased the Simmons University property as the future location of LOUISVILLE MUNICIPAL COLLEGE for Negroes—the black branch of the University of Louisville that opened on February 9, 1931, only two months before President Parrish's death on April 8, 1931. Simmons retained the temporary use of one building and agreed to limit its offerings to religious instruction. In 1934 the University of Louisville exercised its option on the remaining Simmons property; and the school, now renamed Simmons Bible College, moved to its present location at Eighteenth and Dumesnil Streets in Louisville.

See Alice A. Dunnigan, *The Fascinating Story of Black Kentuckians: Their Heritage and Traditions* (Washington, D.C., 1982); John A. Hardin, *Fifty Years of Segregation: Black Higher Education in Kentucky, 1904–1954* (Lexington 1997); J. Blaine Hudson, "The Establishment of Louisville Municipal College: A Case Study in Racial Conflict and Compromise," *Journal of Negro Education* 64 (1995): 111–23; "The History of Louisville Municipal College: Events Leading to the Desegregation of the University of Louisville," Ph.D. dissertation, University of Kentucky, 1981; LOUISVILLE LEADER, Aug. 24, 1929, March 15, 1930, Aug. 9, 1930, Aug. 23, 1930, Sept. 6, 1930, Sept. 20, 1930, Feb. 7, 1931, April 11, 1931; Lawrence H. Williams, *Black Higher Education in Kentucky, 1879–1930: The History of Simmons University* (Lewiston, N.Y., 1987); George D. Wilson, *A Century of Negro Education in Louisville, Kentucky* (Louisville 1941).

J. Blaine Hudson

SIMONS, THOMAS C. (b Pasadena, California, November 12, 1928; d Louisville, August 17, 1988). Businessman. Simons's professional life took root in 1950 when he earned a bachelor's degree in economics from Harvard University, married Radcliffe student Joan Gardiner, and began a tour of duty with the U.S. Navy.

In 1953 he took his first step up the corporate ladder with a job selling insurance for Connecticut General Life Insurance Co. in California. He worked twenty-five years for the company, working his way up to executive vice president of individual and group insurance. Simons left California for Louisville in 1978 to take over as chairman, president and chief executive officer of Capital Holding Corp. He embarked on a mission to revitalize its old-line insurance companies. By 1988 he had done just that. Profits had increased substantially, and Simons was credited with turning Capital Holding into a nationally recognized financial services organization. He accomplished this by expanding and redefining the company's traditional home-service focus and pursuing nontraditional marketing avenues and imaginative distribution channels. Despite opposition of others in management, he added national direct-response marketing (telemarketing and direct mailing) to Capital Holding's offerings, thereby including a full range of insurance and financial services.

Simons's desire for growth and change spilled over into his civic involvement. He promoted Louisville's economic development, and he viewed the $120 million Broadway Project as the cornerstone to downtown's URBAN RENEWAL. The project was the umbrella for refurbishing old downtown structures including Capital Holding's corporate headquarters and the Brown Hotel at Fourth and Broadway, creating Theater Square, and providing a trolley-like bus service along Fourth Ave. between Broadway and the river.

Simons was also an adamant supporter of United Way and chaired the organization's fund-raising efforts in Louisville. He served on the boards of Citizens Fidelity Bank and Trust Co., Citizens Fidelity Corp., the B.F. Goodrich Co., Champion International Corp., and PNC Financial Corp. He headed the board of the American Council of Life Insurance from 1984 to 1986 and was a trustee and senior member of the Conference Board. In addition, Simons was a member of the board of trustees of Berea College, a member of the UNIVERSITY OF LOUISVILLE'S Board of Trustees, and vice chairman of the Chamber of Commerce's development finance group. He received the Wall Street Transcript Award and was named Insurance Chief Executive Officer of the Year for 1981, 1982, and 1983. Simons retired from Capital Holding in March 1988, after ten years at the helm. He died five months later and was cremated.

Michele Alford

SIMPSONVILLE. Sixth-class city in SHELBY COUNTY, located on U.S. 60 along the old Midland Trail just north of Interstate 64, six miles west of SHELBYVILLE. Established in October 1816, the small town was granted on motion and application of Isaac Watkins, although it was not incorporated until January 1832. Later that year in November, the small community began attracting new residents and businesses following the county court's approval of the relocation of the road from Shelbyville to Louisville through Simpsonville.

The town was named for a prominent Virginia-born lawyer in Shelby County, Capt. John Simpson. Simpson represented the county in the state legislature from 1806 to 1811 and was elected to the United States Congress early in 1812. Killed at the Battle of Raisin River early in 1813, he did not serve his term.

Local landmarks in the growing mixed-industrial, commercial, and residential city include the Purnell Sausage Co., makers of Old Folks Sausage; the OLD STONE INN, one of the oldest stone structures in Kentucky; and the site of the former LINCOLN INSTITUTE, an African American boarding high school (later integrated) that operated from 1912 until 1970. The area also boasts a number of horse farms and trainers, prompting the city to adopt the nickname of the "Saddlebred Capital of the World."

The POPULATION in 1970 was 628, in 1980 it was 642, and in 1990 it was 907. In 1996 it had increased to 1,042.

See Robert M. Rennick, *Kentucky Place Names* (Lexington 1984); Edward D. Shinnick, *Some Old Time History of Shelbyville and Shelby County* (Frankfort 1974).

SISTER CITIES OF LOUISVILLE. Sister Cities of Louisville Inc. is a nonprofit, volunteer membership organization dedicated to advancing global friendship, multicultural understanding, and economic growth by developing lasting relationships between the Louisville area and sister cities around the world.

Louisville twinned with its first sister city,

Montpellier, France, in 1956. An ongoing exchange program that began in 1951 between the UNIVERSITY OF LOUISVILLE and the Université de Paul Valäéry laid the foundation for this relationship. In 1962 Louisville and Quito, Ecuador, became sister cities. Mainz, Germany, became Louisville's third sister city in 1977. Sister Cities of Louisville was incorporated as a not-for-profit organization in 1978. The following year Louisville and Tamale, Ghana, became sister cities. La Plata, Argentina, and Perm, Russia, both became Louisville sister cities in 1994.

Sister Cities International (SCI) is responsible for most of the partnerships between cities in the United States and foreign cities. Sister Cities International was started in 1967 as an outgrowth of President Eisenhower's People to People program. The organization helps United States cities find partners and develop activities. It sponsors exchange programs and provides funding for special projects. Any city, county, state, or sister city committee can become a member of SCI by paying dues. Sister Cities of Louisville is a member of Sister Cities International. Sister Cities of Louisville has twice hosted the Sister Cities International Conference (1979 and 1994).

Although active participation of a city's mayor is essential for two cities to sign an official sister cities agreement, the programs are created and organized on a community people-to-people level. Generally, a local group initiates the interest in identifying a sister city. Mayors of Louisville and the designated city exchange letters of intent. If the board of directors approves, the cities enter into a "friendship" relationship. At the end of two years, the board and the mayor may confer full sister city status by signing the appropriate documents. The mayor of Louisville acts as the honorary chairman of the board of directors. Likewise, the president of the United States is the honorary chairman of Sister Cities International.

Sister Cities of Louisville has four main goals: to nurture lasting partnerships on all levels between the Louisville community and its designated sister communities around the world; to create, publicize, and promote international programs that will provide aid, comfort, cooperation, education, and mutual understanding; to foster learning about multiple issues of community life through international dialogue (e.g., artistic, athletic, cultural, educational, environmental, medical, municipal, and technical); and to collaborate with other local and international organizations that have compatible visions and goals. It encourages individuals, organizations, and businesses to participate in the many exchanges, events, and membership activities.

See Leslie Burger and Debra L. Rahm, *Sister Cities: In a World of Difference* (Minneapolis 1997).

Tristan G. Pierce

SIX FLAGS KENTUCKY KINGDOM. Kentucky's only full-scale AMUSEMENT PARK is located at the KENTUCKY STATE FAIR and Exposition Center. Originally called Kentucky Kingdom and owned by the Larc Co. of Texas, it opened in 1987 but closed that fall with a debt of nearly $3.6 million. In February of 1988 the company filed for bankruptcy. Louisville investor Edward Hart stated his intention to reopen the park, which he did in 1990 under a new company, 227 Plus One, that included 66 of the 227 suppliers and other firms that had lost money with the first park. This venture was much more successful than its predecessor. Attendance increased every year during the 1990s, climbing from 180,000 in 1990 to 1.1 million in 1997.

A number of factors contributed to the park's success. The park is nearly twice the size of the original, with twice as many rides, including a number of thrill rides that were lacking in the first park. The park also includes Hurricane Bay, a water park with water slides and a wave pool. The park retained several attractions from 1987, including a 1,500-seat amphitheater, an enclosed 225-seat playhouse, and Starchaser, an indoor roller coaster. Starchaser was sold in 1996 as a result of several lawsuits that were filed over two injury accidents that occurred in July 1994.

In late February 1998, Kentucky Kingdom sued WHAS-TV for libel in reports it made in 1996 that Starchaser "malfunctioned," was "dangerous," and that Kentucky Kingdom had "removed key components of the ride." Park officials held that the accidents were due to operator failure and not a "malfunction." Kentucky Kingdom sued WHAS-TV for $7.4 million in damages, including eight hundred thousand dollars in profits it said it lost due to WHAS' reports. A jury found against WHAS-TV and awarded Kentucky Kingdom a libel judgment of nearly $4 million.

Roller coasters have been the park's main attraction for visitors. Two coasters were added in 1990: Thunder Run, a wooden twister, and Vampire, a steel boomerang. Other coasters include the Roller Skater, a steel junior coaster added in 1994, and T2, a suspended looping coaster added in 1995; 1997 saw the emergence of Chang, a steel, standing coaster that broke five world records, including tallest vertical loop.

In November 1997 Kentucky Kingdom was sold to Premier Parks Inc., the second-largest theme PARK company in the world. Premier set out on a three-year growth plan that included a $10 to $13 million expansion of the park. Hurricane Bay was expanded for the first time since 1993 with the addition of Hook's Lagoon, a forty-foot tree house with a variety of water slides. Also added was Twisted Sisters, a double train coaster costing $5 million.

Much of the park's previous expansions had come through additional thrill rides at the expense of smaller rides, RESTAURANTS, and shops. To improve these areas, five smaller rides were added, including three for small children. An additional $2 million was spent on such other amenities as eateries, additional restrooms, and enlarged gift shops. Premier Parks also set out to attract customers from other markets. With the 1997 closing of Opryland Theme Park in Nashville, Tennessee, that area became Kentucky Kingdom's main target for attracting new customers. To elevate the park's stature as a major regional attraction, in June 1998 Kentucky Kingdom was designated a Six Flags amusement park, one of eight so called by Premier Parks. The name was changed to Six Flags Kentucky Kingdom. Six Flags' attendance totaled 25 million visitors in 1997.

See *Courier-Journal*, Feb. 12, 1998, March 3, 1998, April 1, 1998, June 23, 1998.

SIX MILE ISLAND STATE NATURE PRESERVE. Managed by the Kentucky State Nature Preserves Commission, this eighty-one-acre island located in the OHIO RIVER one and a half miles upstream from the Cox Park boat landing on River Rd. was dedicated as a protected natural area in June 1979. Known for its diversity of water BIRDS, the preserve offers excellent opportunities for birdwatching, and fishing is also allowed. Although the island had once been settled and farmed, it is now being returned to its original natural state and is accessible only by boat.

SLAUGHTER, ELVIRA SYDNOR (MILLER) (b Wytheville, Virginia, October 12, 1860; d Louisville, February 28, 1937). Author and journalist. Slaughter came to Louisville at a young age with her parents when they moved to Kentucky to collect an inheritance. Educated at PRESENTATION ACADEMY, she had her first book, *Songs of the Heart,* published in 1885. About that time, she joined the staff of the *LOUISVILLE TIMES* as its first female journalist. After three years as a reporter, Slaughter took over editorship of the paper's daily *Tattler* column, originally created by Will Hull and "devoted to gossip and personal mentions." Fourteen years later she resigned from the paper when she married W.H Slaughter Jr., a coal salesman.

Slaughter's other published works include *The Tiger's Daughter and Other Stories* (1889), *Confessions of a Tattler* (1905), and *Sundown Lane and Other Poems* (1924). Even after leaving the *Louisville Times,* she continued to submit various poems and articles to NEWSPAPERS. She died in a grocery store near her home in the PORTLAND area, the victim of a heart attack. Slaughter is buried in CAVE HILL CEMETERY.

See Elvira Miller Slaughter, *Confessions of a Tattler* (Louisville 1905); *Courier-Journal,* March 1, 1937.

SLAUGHTER, HENRY PROCTOR (b Louisville, September 17, 1871; d Washington, D.C., February 14, 1958). Journalist. The son of Charles Henry and Sarah Jane (Smith) Slaughter, Henry began his involvement with the NEWSPAPER business at an early age. When Slaughter was six, his father died, and he began selling newspapers to help support the family. After graduating as salutatorian of his class at Louisville CENTRAL COLORED High School, he accepted a journalistic apprenticeship as a printer with the Louisville Champion. Slaughter became associate editor of the Lexington Standard in 1894. He studied at Livingstone College in Salisbury, North Carolina, and at the same time served as the manager of that city's AME Zion Publishing House.

In 1896 he was appointed a compositor at the United States Government Printing Office in Washington, D.C., and occupied that position until 1937. Committed to education, Slaughter did not allow his responsibilities at the printing office to interfere with his learning. Although not a practicing attorney, he received a bachelor of law degree (1899) and a master of law (1900) from Howard University in Washington. Slaughter, who was active in such FRATERNAL ORGANIZATIONS as the Masons and Odd Fellows, also edited the Odd Fellows Journal from 1910 to 1937. Although he lived outside Kentucky for most of his life, Slaughter remained in contact with his home state as a correspondent for the Bardstown (Kentucky) Standard. He also served as secretary of the Kentucky Republican Club in Washington, D.C.

In addition to his professional pursuits, Slaughter spent a lifetime collecting materials associated with African American history and culture. His private library had a particular emphasis on the CIVIL WAR and slavery and was estimated to contain upwards of ten thousand volumes. The collection is now at Clark Atlanta University, Atlanta, Georgia.

Slaughter married Ella M. Russell on April 27, 1904; she died on November 2, 1914. On November 24, 1925, he married Alma Level, whom he later divorced. Slaughter, who died in Washington, D.C., was cremated.

See *Louisville Defender*, Feb. 20, 1958.

SLAVERY IN LOUISVILLE 1820–1860.

Since Kentucky was part of Virginia until 1792, many early settlers were slaveholders. The first known slave in Louisville was Cato Watts, owned by settler John Donne. Soon other black slaves were brought to the new settlement. Some were French-speaking blacks owned by Vincennes, Indiana, merchants who came to Louisville. Their labor was important in building the community. By the time of the Missouri Compromise (1820–21)—marking the beginning of what came to be called the antebellum period of the American South—Louisville had already established itself as a slave city. Indeed, the slave proportion of the city's population was at its highest point (nearly 26 percent) in 1820. By 1860 the slave proportion of the city's population had dropped to 7.8 percent, as the following table shows.

1820		
Louisville	White:	2,944
FPC*:		93
Slave:		1,031
Jefferson County	White:	11,004
FPC:		122
Slave:		5,855
1830		
Louisville	White:	7,703
FPC:		223
Slave:		2,406
Jefferson County	White:	8,139
FPC:		68
Slave:		4,387
1840		
Louisville	White:	17,161
FPC:		619
Slave:		3,430
Jefferson County:	White:	26,987
FPC:		823
Slave:		8,596
1850		
Louisville	White:	36,224
FPC:		1,538
Slave:		5,432
Jefferson County:	White:	47,283
FPC:		1,636
Slave:		10,911
1860		
Louisville	White:	61,213
FPC:		1,917
Slave:		4,903
Jefferson County:	White:	77,093
FPC:		2,007
Slave:		10,304

*Denotes a Free Person of Color

A second table, which lists the population broken down by race, condition of servitude, and sex, sheds further light on the composition of the slave group in Louisville during this period.

1820	
Louisville	*Jefferson County*
Whites (Male): 1,882	Whites (Male): 5,911
Whites (Female): 1,062	Whites (Female):5,093
Slave (Male): 495	Slave (Male): 3,135
Slave (Female): 536	Slave (Female): 2,720
FPC (Male): 73	FPC (Male): 50
FPC (Female): 43	FPC (Female): 43
1830	
Louisville	*Jefferson County*
Whites (Male): 4,843	Whites (Male): 4,277
Whites (Female): 2,860	Whites (Female): 3,862
Slave (Male): 1,135	Slave (Male): 2,406
Slave (Female): 1,271	Slave (Female): 1,981
FPC (Male): 108	FPC (Male): 42
FPC (Female): 115	FPC (Female): 26
1840	
Louisville	*Jefferson County*
Whites (Male): 9,272	Whites (Male): 14,604
Whites (Female): 7,889	Whites (Female): 12,383
Slave (Male): 1,383	Slave (Male): 4,164
Slave (Female): 2,047	Slave (Female): 4,432
FPC (Male): 300	FPC (Male): 382
FPC (Female): 319	FPC (Female): 441
1850	
Louisville	*Jefferson County*
Whites (Male): 19,468	Whites (Male): 25,328
Whites (Female): 16,756	Whites (Female): 21,955
Slave (Male): 2,410	Slave (Male): 5,345
Slave (Female): 3,022	Slave (Female):5,566
FPC (Male): 698	FPC (Male): 753
FPC (Female): 840	FPC (Female): 883
1860	
Louisville	*Jefferson County*
Whites (Male): 31,299	Whites (Male): 39,751
Whites (Female): 29,914	Whites (Female): 37,342
Slave (Male): 1,968	Slave (Male): 4,703
Slave (Female): 2,935	Slave (Female): 5,601
FPC (Male): 862	FPC (Male): 904
FPC (Female): 1,055	FPC (Female): 1,103

The slave population throughout the antebellum period was primarily female. Females also dominated the free black population. Among whites, however, men outnumbered women throughout the entire forty-year span.

Louisville's slave population was denser in some areas than others. According to John Jegli, who published several Louisville CITY DIRECTORIES in the 1840s and 1850s and the 1860 slave schedule of the federal census, 81 percent of the city's slaves lived in the Third, Fourth, Fifth, Sixth and Seventh Wards. Likewise, 79 percent of the free blacks lived in the same WARDS. These wards made up an area that was bordered on the north by the OHIO RIVER, on the south by what is now St. Catherine St., on the east by Floyd St., and on the west by Tenth St. The most densely populated areas were north of what is now Liberty St. Jefferson County tax schedules indicate that, at least through 1838, city lots north of Green St. (LIBERTY) were uniformly laid off in half-acre tracts. Lots south of Green were five, ten, or twenty acres each.

Generally, urban slaves' quarters were connected to their owners' property, usually in "servant's rooms." A typical newspaper ad from this period described a brick house for sale as having eleven rooms, two passages, a large kitchen, three servants' rooms, and a washhouse. Sometimes advertisements of this nature made it clear that the servants' rooms were in an outbuilding. In most cases, outbuildings were located behind the main house, on the alley. This is significant when coupled with the fact that most city lots, as evidenced by newspaper ads, were long and narrow. Thus, the white population was housed on the street side while their servants were relegated to the alley side of city lots. This arrangement had the effect of providing whites and blacks their own separate spaces, an important fact to the slaves who welcomed time away from the constant vigilance of whites.

An examination of both newspaper advertisements and foreign travelers' accounts indicate that most slaves who lived with their owners were housed in brick buildings, which had the advantage of being cool in the summer and warm in the winter. As one traveler noted, there were a number of elegant houses, situated in gardens, with living quarters for the slaves behind the main building.

Often slaves were hired out by their owners to someone else. In this event, slaves were usually responsible for finding their own housing. Testimony from local slaves indicated that they much preferred to live away from their owners even if the accommodations they found for themselves weren't as good as those provided by the owner. For instance, Charlotte, a Louisville slave who was hired out by her owner, Thomas Strange, expressed pride in the fact that she was able to pay her own rent and support herself and children without the assistance of her master.

Both slaves living with their owners and those who were hired out probably ate as well as whites. Throughout the antebellum period, food was plentiful and cheap in the South. There does not appear to have been any weekly rationing of food to urban slaves, as was done by rural slave owners. Both slave and white Louisvillians grew a variety of their own vegetables; and pork, a staple food, was only about three cents a pound.

Although Louisville ordinances strictly forbade the practice, the ability of slaves to hire themselves out was an important part of slavery in the city. Louisville slaves worked at a variety of occupations in the broad category of domestic service, mostly as maids, butlers, gardeners, laundresses, nurses, and cooks in private homes, HOTELS, inns, or STEAMBOATS. In December, when the yearly contracts were soon to expire, contemporary NEWSPAPERS were filled with advertisements to hire slaves as domestic servants. By 1860, some 15 percent of the slaves in Louisville were employed in businesses throughout the city. The GALT HOUSE had fifty-one black workers, the LOUISVILLE HOTEL had twenty-three, the National Hotel hired twenty-one, and the United States had fourteen.

Employers regularly advertised to buy, hire, or sell slaves to do such diverse jobs as dray driver and coach (or hack) driver. Slaves also were an integral part of Louisville's industrial workforce in local factories like the William A. Richardson Bagging Factory, where forty slaves worked alongside whites for much lower wages. In the building trade, slaves worked as bricklayers, carpenters, plasterers, and blacksmiths. River traffic, which played such an important role in Louisville's economic growth, also was an important employer, using slaves as musicians, firemen, waiters, roustabouts, and stewards, the most envied position on a steamboat. Late in the Civil War many black men were recruited into the Union army. Two regiments were organized in Louisville in 1865. By that time nearly twelve thousand had already left the state to enlist elsewhere.

Despite continual harassment and brutality by civil authorities and owners, black economic success provided funding for the first black church in the city, Fifth St. Baptist, organized in 1829. Successful blacks also supplied backing for black schools that educated slaves whose owners had given their written permission. Others joined the Independent Sons of Honor, founded in 1848, and a Freemason's society in 1850. White authorities knew of these activities but allowed the limited freedoms except during periods of tension in the city.

Louisville's reputation as a slave city derived from the slave markets that flourished during the antebellum period. As the demand for slaves grew in the Lower South, an increasing number of men in Louisville dealt exclusively in the sale of blacks who could be easily shipped South via the Ohio River. In the 1836 city directory, thirty-eight traders are listed. During the height of the slave trade to the Lower South—1843–44—the number of traders reached the incredible number of eighty-four. On the eve of the Civil War in 1860, fifteen men were engaged in the slave trade. Prominent slave traders included John Clark, William Kelley, William Talbott, Thomas Powell, and the Arterburn brothers, Jordan and Tarlton, who were active in Louisville for more than twenty years. So well known was Louisville for its booming slave market that George Prentice, editor of the Journal newspaper, boasted that blacks were in good supply in his city and anyone wanting one could leave an order in Louisville.

The varied work and lifestyles available to slaves in Louisville did a great deal to loosen the bonds of servitude for individual slaves. They also played a large role in weakening the entire institution of slavery in Kentucky, as rural slaves routinely ran away to the relative freedom of Louisville. The presence of the Ohio River and free states to the north resulted in many slaves escaping, or attempting to. For those who resided in the city, the close physical confines and tradition of hiring-out enabled Louisville slaves to establish their own churches, schools, and community institutions, away from the constant hostile supervision of whites. As a result, freed slaves in Louisville were in a better position to adjust to life after emancipation than were their rural counterparts.

Life in Louisville did not change immediately, however. Confusion about the status of slaves and slavery continued even after the ratification of the Thirteenth Amendment. Just a few months after Lincoln's death in April 1865, many blacks that were still held as slaves were given passes by military authorities to leave the state. It was necessary for a guard to be stationed on Ohio River ferryboats to JEFFERSONVILLE, INDIANA, to ensure the passes were properly honored. At the same time, a General Palmer was indicted by a Louisville grand jury for violation of the law prohibiting the enticement of slaves from the state. By December the indictment was dismissed, the court holding that, before the indictment, the requisite number of states had adopted the Thirteenth Amendment; therefore, all criminal laws of Kentucky pertaining to slavery were null and void.

In the first decade after the Civil War, a nucleus of whites who demanded fair treatment for blacks developed in Louisville; nevertheless, progress continued at an uneven pace in the city. In 1865 a Freedmen's Bureau, a federal organization, began to provide assistance to former slaves in their transition to freedom. It gave most of the humanitarian relief for blacks in the city in the forms of food, clothing, fuel, and health care. The bureau opened Louisville's Refugee's and Freedmen's Hospital at Fifteenth and BROADWAY in 1866. The hospital, experiencing shortages of almost all necessities, managed to serve between 150 and 200 patients a month until it closed in 1869. The Freedmen's Bureau, because it lacked money and leadership, could not reach all indigent, poor, and sick blacks.

Many continued to live in shacks, shanties, and outbuildings in a predominantly black area known as SMOKETOWN. The lack of proper housing, clothing, food, and medical care greatly increased diseases and death among blacks. In February 1866 alone, 135 blacks died in Louisville, a 16 percent per annum death rate. Louisville officials did not want to take responsibility for sick blacks, arguing that they did not control the pauper fund, and private physicians required a two-dollar to five-dollar fee that was impossible for blacks to pay. Exceptions were communicable diseases such as smallpox; in those cases, Louisville authorities isolated blacks in a "pest house" to protect the general public. Some churches and leading citizens established relief organizations by early 1866. FIFTH STREET BAPTIST CHURCH and several other churches opened a hospital for blacks at the corner of Seventh and Broadway.

A measure was introduced in the Kentucky General Assembly in 1866 to charter a bank in Louisville, to be managed by blacks and called the Grand Bank. Although it passed the senate by a three-to-one margin, it failed in the house. Also in 1866 a judge of the city court decided the federal CIVIL RIGHTS bill was incompatible with state law and inoperative in Kentucky, thereby refusing to admit testimony by free blacks in court.

Problems experienced by blacks during the immediate postwar years eased during the 1880s. There was an increasing trend toward stronger nuclear families among blacks. The number of black two-parent families in Louisville increased from 70.8 percent to 75.8 percent in 1880, and the number of orphans declined.

See Ira Berlin, *Slaves without Masters* (New York 1974); John Blassingame, *The Slave Community* (New York 1972); Clement Eaton, *A History of the Old South* (New York 1975); Eugene Genovese, *Roll, Jordan, Roll: The World the Slaves Made* (New York 1972); Herbert Gutman, *The Black Family in Slavery and Freedom* (New York 1976); Richard Wade, *Slavery in the Cities* (New York 1964); Marion B. Lucas, *A History of Blacks in Kentucky*, vol. 1 (Frankfort 1992); *History of the Ohio Falls Cities and Their Counties* (Cleveland 1882); George C. Wright, LIFE BEHIND A VEIL (Baton Rouge 1985).

Mary Lawrence Bickett O'Brien

SLOANE, GEORGE HARVEY INGALLS (b New York, New York, May 11, 1936). Mayor, Jefferson County judge/executive, physician. Sloane was from a prominent family, the son of George Sloane, a New York investment banker, and Katherine Ingalls. His great-grandfather, Melville Ezra Ingalls, was president of the "Big Four" Railroad and once ran for mayor of Cincinnati, but lost. His father retired from investment banking to breed horses and foxhounds at WHITEHALL, a large estate in Warrenton, Virginia, where the younger Sloane grew up.

He attended prep school in Concord, New Hampshire, and received a bachelor of arts degree in American studies from Yale University in 1958. In 1963 he graduated from Cleveland's Western Reserve School of Medicine and served a one-year internship at a Cleveland medical clinic. A surgeon, Sloane worked for the U.S. Public Health Service from 1964 until 1966, serving as a member of a federally sponsored relief team providing medical care to residents of eastern Kentucky.

In 1966 Sloane served as a volunteer physician in Vietnam providing care to South Vietnamese civilians. Between 1966 and 1972, with a $1.4 million grant from the U.S. Office of Economic Opportunity, he initiated and directed the PARK DUVALLE Community Health Center in Louisville's West End. He also developed the city's first comprehensive emergency ambulance service with trained emergency medical technicians.

In 1968 Sloane, a Democrat, founded Action for Clean Air, and the group's lobbying activities got Sloane selected to serve on the county's Air Pollution Control Board. As a spokesman for clean air and health-care issues, Sloane began to expand his political base; and in 1971, with the encouragement of friends, he entertained the idea of running for mayor. In 1973 he ran against Carroll Witten in the Democratic primary. Witten, president of the BOARD OF ALDERMEN, was a favorite of the old-line members of the party organization, but Sloane marshaled considerable financial resources to overcome Witten's early lead in the polls. He won the nomination with a majority in all twelve WARDS.

Sloane was elected mayor in November 1973, defeating Republican C.J. Hyde, a former city police chief, by a margin of more than two-to-one, 69,471 to 31,816. He took office on December 1, 1973, and served until December 1, 1977. In 1981 he was elected to a second term as mayor, receiving more than 102,000 votes to Republican Louie Guenthner's 52,700. A 1980 state law changed the inauguration date from December 1 to January 1, so he served as mayor from 1982 until 1986. Sloane also served a term as Jefferson County judge/executive from January 4, 1986, until January 1, 1990. He defeated Republican George Clark by almost 28,000 votes out of the more than 84,000 cast.

As mayor Sloane presided over some of Louisville's most turbulent crises, including the April 3, 1974, tornado and a garbage strike that same year. A federal court ordered the desegregation of the city's school system through BUSING. Some of his important accomplishments as mayor included a voter-approved occupational tax increase to help fund the city's bus system (TARC), and the creation of the city's Emergency Medical Service. He also championed air pollution controls and other environmental causes in public and private life. In 1975 he and such other city leaders as Wilson Wyatt Jr., were instrumental in reviving the Louisville GALLERIA project.

As successful as Sloane was in local politics, he was unable to win a victory in three tries for state and national office. In 1979 he was narrowly defeated for the Democratic gubernatorial nomination by John Y. Brown Jr. The vote was so close that Sloane did not concede the primary election for two days. In 1983 he again sought the nomination but was defeated by then-lieutenant governor MARTHA LAYNE COLLINS in another close primary. In 1990 he tried again for higher office, running against incumbent Republican MITCH MCCONNELL for the U.S. Senate, but he was defeated in a hotly contested race. Sloane lost by 4.4 percent of the popular vote (about 40,000 votes out of almost 914,000 cast).

In 1991 Sloane and his family moved to Washington, D.C., so he could work as a lobbyist, health-care consultant, and fund-raiser. In 1995 he was named PUBLIC HEALTH commissioner for the District of Columbia by mayor Marion Barry. But in 1997, Sloane's position was terminated after a dispute with Barry. Sloane claimed he was fired because, without notifying the mayor, he issued an order to boil the city's water before using it for drinking and cooking. But Barry stated that Sloane failed to significantly improve health care during his tenure.

Sloane married Kathleen McNalley in 1969. She was a member of a prominent Pittsburgh fabric-importing family. The couple have three children: a daughter, Abigail, and two sons, Patrick and Curtis.

See *Louisville Times*, Nov. 7, 1973; *Courier-Journal*, Nov. 11, 1990; *Washington Post*, June 14, 1998.

SMITH, ARTHUR RAYMOND (b New Albany, Indiana, July 4, 1869; d Louisville, July 20, 1955). Architect. The son of Fidelia (Palmer) and George M. Smith, he lived in NEW ALBANY until 1927, when he moved to Louisville. He trained in the office of Louisville architect MASON MAURY, later Maury and Dodd, from 1885 to 1893. After working briefly in St. Louis in the office of T.C. Link and back in Louisville with D.X. Murphy & Bro. and Dodd & Cobb, Smith established his own office in 1895. From that time until the early 1930s, he was a prolific designer of houses in Louisville for individual clients and for developers such as the Hieatt Brothers.

His residences are scattered throughout CRESCENT HILL and the HIGHLANDS, with particularly high concentrations on Eastover Ct., Windsor Pl., and Spring Dr. His early houses have a strong Prairie and/or Craftsman influence (the Harrison Robertson House at 2542 Ransdell Ave. is the finest example), while the later houses are eclectic, many with distinct English Tudor or FRENCH elements. In the 1930s and 1940s he was associated with the construction of local housing projects and did freelancing for other architects. He surrendered his license in 1947.

Carolyn S. Brooks

SMITH, GEORGE WEISSINGER (b Louisville, October 10, 1864; d Louisville, January 28, 1931). Mayor. He was the son of United States Army captain Thomas Floyd and Blanche (Weissinger) Smith. Smith's mother was the daughter of George Weissinger, publisher of the *LOUISVILLE JOURNAL* during George D. Prentice's tenure as editor.

George Smith attended private school, and in 1883 he was graduated from LOUISVILLE MALE HIGH SCHOOL. He was graduated from the University of Virginia in 1886 and received a law degree from the UNIVERSITY OF LOUISVILLE in 1887. He practiced law in Louisville from 1887 until his death in 1931. His law partners included Charles H. Gibson and Judge Samuel B. Kirby.

Smith entered into politics as a Democrat and was elected to the Kentucky House of Representatives in 1898. In November 1917, Smith was elected mayor on the Republican ticket. He defeated Democrat CHARLES J. CRONAN by a 2,000-vote margin. Smith was mayor of Louisville from November 20, 1917, until November 22, 1921.

In the 1917 election, the Republicans ran against the corruption associated with the Democratic machine headed by the Whallen brothers, John and James. Two of the most prominent targets were the many GAMBLING and PROSTITUTION houses located on what was then Green St. The Republican administration set about closing the brothels along Green, and the city's Herald newspaper responded with a contest to rename the street—an attempt to take the stigma off the thoroughfare. The Republican-led City Council renamed the street "Liberty" on April 5, 1918, an appropriate name during WORLD WAR I.

Smith's administration was instrumental in coordinating Louisville's war efforts. Smith was actively involved in liberty bond drives and other war work. CAMP ZACHARY TAYLOR, one of the largest cantonments in the country for servicemen going overseas, was in operation during his tenure as mayor. Smith's administration also took an active role in PROHIBITION, ordering the police department to assist federal agents in enforcing the law. He also helped to establish the police school. During his administration the city grew by more than 40 percent by the annexation of surrounding lands.

Smith served as president of the LOUISVILLE WATER CO. after his tenure as mayor. He retired from that position in 1926, although the water company's board of directors resisted his resignation. Smith also served as president of the parental and school committee of Jefferson County. From 1908 to 1911 he was a trustee of the Louisville Industrial School. He served as a private in the LOUISVILLE LEGION for three years.

Smith married Ellen Hunt, the daughter of G.R. and Mary (Prather) Hunt, on October 30, 1890. They had four children, three boys and a girl. He lived with his family on Cherokee Rd., where he died of a cerebral hemorrhage. He is buried in CAVE HILL CEMETERY.

See Mary Young Southard and Ernest C. Miller, eds., *Who's Who in Kentucky; A Biographical Assembly of Notable Kentuckians* (Louisville 1936); George Yater, *Two Hundred Years at the Falls of the Ohio* (Louisville 1987).

SMITH, J. LAWRENCE (b near Charleston, South Carolina, December 16, 1818; d Louisville, October 12, 1883). Scientist and businessman. His father, Benjamin Smith, was a well-to-do merchant. A precocious child, he showed a special aptitude for mathematics. He was educated at Charleston College and the University of Virginia, where he graduated belles lettres in 1837. He studied civil engineering, GEOLOGY, and mineralogy. Not finding engineering to his taste, Smith entered the Medical College of South Carolina, graduating in 1840. He continued his medical studies in Europe, adding chemistry, geology, and mineralogy to his schedule.

In 1844 he launched a medical practice in Charleston and co-founded a medical journal. His published research on the marl soils of South Carolina led to his selection in 1850 by James Buchanan, then secretary of state, to respond to a request by the Turkish GOVERNMENT for an adviser on cotton culture. He was soon asked to investigate MINERAL RESOURCES. His discovery of coal, emery, and chrome ore were profitable to Turkey and to Smith, who received annual royalties throughout his life. His observations on the minerals associated with emery, communicated to BENJAMIN SILLIMAN JR., a professor at the UNIVERSITY OF LOUISVILLE, resulted in the discovery of emery deposits in the United States, considerably reducing the cost of emery for grinding and polishing.

Smith returned home in 1850 and in June 1852 married Sarah Julia, daughter of JAMES GUTHRIE, and in that year became professor of chemistry at the University of Virginia. In 1854 he succeeded BENJAMIN SILLIMAN JR. as professor of medical chemistry and toxicology at the University of Louisville, holding this post until 1866. He published frequently in scientific journals in both this country and Europe. In Louisville he also became interested in meteorites. His collection of these celestial objects, one of the finest in the United States, is now at Harvard University.

In addition to his own ongoing scientific research (he spent several hours each day in his private laboratory), Smith became involved in the commercial life of Louisville, serving as president of the Louisville Gas Co. and the Mutual Life Insurance Co. of Kentucky as well as a director of the Galt House Co. and the Western Financial Corp., the latter a potent force in the city's ECONOMY. He was active in charitable work, including the founding and initial endowment of the Baptist Orphans' Home, now Spring Meadows near Middletown.

It is for his far-ranging scientific work that he is remembered, however. He was elected president of the American Association for the Advancement of Science, one of the highest honors American science can bestow on its own, in 1872. Most of his 145 separate papers were published in Louisville in 1873 as *Mineralogy and Chemistry: Original Researches.*

Smith died in October 1883 and is buried in CAVE HILL CEMETERY. Pallbearers were initially selected from students at the Southern Baptist Seminary, but Smith had requested that laboring men be his pallbearers. Nine burly fellows from the Muldoon Marble and Granite Works were chosen.

See Dumas Malone, ed., *Dictionary of American Biography* (New York 1964) 9: 304–5; J. Stoddard Johnston, ed., *Memorial History of Louisville* (Chicago 1896).

George H. Yater

SMITH, JOSEPH BROWN (b Dover, New Hampshire, May 14, 1823; d Louisville, May 6, 1859). Musician and teacher. Smith was the first totally blind person to graduate from a university in the United States. Smith became blind in infancy. He studied at the Massachusetts Institution for the Blind in Boston and entered Harvard in 1840. There he excelled in Latin, Greek, and mathematics and became fluent in FRENCH and German.

His musical genius was early evident when he composed a march at age nine. After graduating from Harvard in 1844, Smith came to Louisville to teach music at the Kentucky Institution for the Education of the Blind. He was also the organist and choir director for the Unitarian Church for thirteen years and taught private pupils. His entire career as a musician and teacher was spent in Louisville.

Married twice, first to Elizabeth Jane Cone and then to Sarah J. Nash, Smith had a son from each marriage—Joseph Haydn and Bryce Patten. He is buried at CAVE HILL CEMETERY.

See John H. Heywood, *Discourse on the Life and Character of Joseph Brown Smith* (Louisville 1859).

Carol Brenner Tobe

SMITH, LUCIUS ERNEST (b Sacramento, McLean County, Kentucky, October 6, 1878; d Louisville, August 31, 1955). Physician. Smith's father, Willis Smith, was a Presbyterian minister. Smith attended the University of Kentucky and in 1915 received an M.D. from Johns Hopkins University. In 1920 Smith married Beulah Grace Lipps of Lexington. For more than a decade he served in Africa as a physician with the Presbyterian Board of Foreign Missions. When his wife's poor health forced their return to the United States, the Smiths settled in Breathitt County, where he battled tuberculosis, the state's number one killer among preventable diseases.

In 1930 Smith moved to Louisville, accepted a position as executive secretary of the Kentucky Tuberculosis Association, and dedicated the remainder of his career to eradicating the disease. Knowing that the malady could be prevented and treated in its early stages, he launched a statewide educational crusade. Showing films, slides, and charts, Smith encouraged Kentuckians to have physical checkups and chest X-rays, and he urged schools to teach courses on personal and public hygiene. He raised hundreds of thousands of dollars through the Christmas Seal program, and he lobbied the legislature for money to build and staff sanitariums. His efforts paid off. When he commenced his work in 1930, Kentucky's death rate from the "white plague" was 94 per 100,000 deaths; 20 years later, the rate had been reduced to 33 per 100,000.

Smith retired in 1951. A stroke and heart disease marred his last few years. He was buried in CAVE HILL CEMETERY.

See Frederick Eberson, *Portraits: Kentucky Pioneers in Community Healthh and Medicine* (Louisville 1968); *Bulletin of the Department of Health* (Louisville 1930-1951).

Nancy D. Baird

SMITH, MILTON HANNIBAL (b Greene County, New York, September 12, 1836; d Louisville, February 22, 1921). Railroad executive. Milton H. Smith was president of the LOUISVILLE & NASHVILLE RAILROAD (L&N) for thirty-three years, the longest of any of L&N's chief executives. Smith, more than any other, influenced the railroad's destiny, shaping it into one of the nation's major rail systems.

Smith grew up near Chautauqua, New York. In l850 his family moved to Shaumburg, Illinois, where he was educated in a one-room school. Smith left home when he was twenty, clerked in a store in western Tennessee, then (in l858) began his long career in transportation as a telegrapher for two RAILROADS in northern Mississippi. During much of the CIVIL WAR, he served the United States Military Railroads in Alabama, Georgia, and Tennessee.

After the war Smith came to Louisville, worked for a short time as a freight manager for a shipping firm, then was hired in l866 by ALBERT FINK, L&N's general superintendent, as a local freight agent. Smith was promoted to general freight agent in l869. During the early

1870s he helped promote L&N's southward expansion through Alabama. That work involved personal solicitation for on-line industries, much of it in the Birmingham area. During the decade, Smith learned much about ratemaking, representing the L&N at several high-level rail industry conferences that addressed the issue. Smith abruptly left the L&N in 1878 after cutting off all northern freight into Montgomery when the city refused to permit trains carrying yellow fever patients to stop at its depot. When the indignant city council dispatched a delegation to protest Smith's edict, the president of the railroad overruled his subordinate, and Smith resigned. Between 1878 and 1882, he served as general freight agent for the Baltimore & Ohio and Pennsylvania Railroads. Returning to the L&N in 1882, he became third vice president and traffic manager and helped restore stability to management in the wake of four short presidencies. In 1884 he was named president, shared leadership of the company with Eckstein Norton between 1886 and 1891, then re-assumed the presidency and served until his death.

During his long tenure, Smith continued L&N's expansion into the South and the Gulf Coast as well as into the eastern Kentucky coalfields after 1900. He also directed systemwide curve and grade-reduction programs as well as motive power and rolling stock modernization to improve operating efficiencies. Hating bureaucracy, he greatly simplified L&N's Louisville management and administrative staff as well as supervision across the road's far-flung system. Sometimes controversial and not always understood by his critics, Smith still was respected by his peers and beloved by employees, his office was always accessible to them.

Smith and his first wife, Eva Jones, had two children. After Eva's death, he married her sister, Annette, who bore him three children, one of whom, Sidney, served in L&N's law department. A grandson, Milton II, also worked as an attorney for the railroad. Smith's Louisville residence was on S Fourth St. He is buried in Cave Hill Cemetery.

See Harry N. Clarke, "M.H." *L&N Employees' Magazine* 12 (Dec. 1936): 3–8; Maury Klein, *History of the Louisville & Nashville Railroad* (New York 1972); Mary K. Bonsteel Tachau, "The Making of a Railroad President: Milton H. Smith and the L&N," *Filson Club History Quarterly* 43 (April 1969): 125–50.

Charles B. Castner

SMITH, ZACHARY F. (b Eminence, Henry County, Kentucky, January 7, 1827; d Louisville, July 4, 1911). Educator, businessman, and historian. Smith was born on the old Dupuy farm (wife's family farm in Henry County). His name also appears as Zachariah, but best evidence indicates that he used Zachary and generally went by Z.F. He was the only child of Zachariah (also listed as Zachary) and Mildred (Dupuy) Smith. His father died before he was born, and he was raised by his mother, who never remarried. Smith was educated in the local schools and at Bacon College in Harrodsburg, Kentucky. Upon graduation from Bacon, Smith returned to Henry County, engaging in farming and stock-raising until about 1860 when he became president of Henry College in New Castle, Henry County. In 1866 he resigned, sold his interest in the school, and moved to Eminence. In 1867 Smith was elected Kentucky's superintendent of public instruction on the Democratic ticket. He achieved a number of reforms during his four-year term. He is credited with designing Kentucky's postbellum school system, significantly improving schools. During this same time, Smith became involved in the railroad business. In 1869 he, along with several others, founded the Cumberland & Ohio Railroad Co., which was intended to connect Nashville and Cincinnati. Only two short sections were constructed. He served as its president until severing his ties with the company in June 1873. He afterwards was involved in railroad companies in Texas and the Southwest. He also served as a manager of one of publisher D. Appleton & Co.'s offices for four years.

In 1884 Smith moved to Louisville, spending the rest of his life there. For the next two years he concentrated on writing *The History of Kentucky* (1886). Three years later he published *A School History of Kentucky* (1889) for use in the schools. Smith wrote other biographical and historical books and spoke a number of times before the Filson Club on various topics. He served as a board member of Kentucky University for some thirty years, beginning in 1858, until it merged with Transylvania University. He then continued on the Transylvania board until 1909. He was an active and influential member of the Christian Church for most of his life, including being the founder and president of the Kentucky Christian Education Society (1857–ca. 1870). At the time of his death he had almost completed a book proposing that Barton Stone, not Alexander Campbell, was the founder of the Christian church in Kentucky.

Smith married Susan Helm (d. 1879) of Shelby County in 1852. They had eight children: Mildred, Zachary F. Junior, Joseph Helm, Winthrop Hopkins, Austin Dupuy, William Helm, Susan Viola, and Virgil Drane. In 1890 he married Anna Asa Pittman of Louisville. Smith is buried in Eminence.

See J. Stoddard Johnston, ed., *Memorial History of Louisville* (Chicago 1896); *The Biographical Encyclopedia of Kentucky* (Cincinnati 1878); Z.F. Smith, *The History of Kentucky* (Louisville 1892); Alwin Seekamp and Roger Burlingame, eds., *Who's Who in Louisville* (Louisville 1912); B.H. Dupuy, *The Huguenot Bartholomew Dupuy and his Descendants* (Louisville 1908).

James J. Holmberg

SMOKE ORDINANCE. Air pollution has been a problem in Louisville since the onslaught of industrialization. With the growth of Population the problem was exacerbated until, in the early 1940s, anyone turning off Baxter Ave. and heading down E Broadway would have viewed the downtown skyline usually obscured by a thick cloud of pollution. Referred to euphemistically as haze, it was soot and smoke from burning coal spewed from industrial plants and thousands of residential and commercial building furnaces. The Louisville Times published in March 1941 a United States Public Health Service Study that estimated that the average city dweller spent about thirty dollars per year for smoke-pollution-related problems such as increased laundry bills, damage to property, corrosion of metals, paint deterioration, and doctors' bills related to throat and lung illnesses. In 1941 Mayor Joseph D. Scholtz established a Smoke Elimination Committee to find a solution to the growing problem.

The committee began its work by evaluating the 1919 smoke ordinance. That ordinance had serious omissions: it failed to include private homes, which were producing about 60 percent of the city's smoke pollution; it omitted factories outside of Jefferson County; and it did not specify the allowable density of smoke produced in the use of household and industrial furnaces.

The committee determined that the major cause of smoke pollution was the lower-grade Kentucky coal that burned slowly, thus producing much smoke. The committee worked on provisions aimed at heavy polluters that required mechanical firing equipment or a better grade of coal. Homeowners, however, were permitted to use a lower grade of coal if the price of a better grade became high. The committee also included a provision that required the inspection of coal grades sold in the Louisville area.

The ordinance issue was widely publicized and gained public support. The League of Women Voters' poll showed that 92 percent of people were in favor and 70 percent were willing to pay more for the better grade of coal to have cleaner air.

The major forces against the ordinance were the Kentucky coal companies and the Louisville & Nashville Railroad, whose shops and locomotives were serious producers of smoke pollution. They stated that the 1919 ordinance was not being fully enforced, and with the new ordinance many jobs and industries would be lost if a better grade of coal were brought in from other states.

Although Mayor Scholtz supported the ordinance, the Board of Aldermen voted 9 to 2 against it. The decision of the board came as a surprise to the public, and there was a widespread belief that it had failed because three of the aldermen worked for the Louisville & Nashville Railroad.

In time the burning of coal diminished as homes converted to heating oil or natural gas and locomotives became diesels. However, a new kind of pollution resulted from an increase in automobile emissions. Air pollution became a concern of state government in the 1950s and the federal GOVERNMENT in the 1960s. In order to deal with the problem, Jefferson County enacted legislation requiring vehicle emissions tests that did improve air quality. Cleaner-burning gasoline was introduced. Air pollution alerts are issued and advisories recommend the curtailment of certain polluting activities such as mowing grass.

See Joe Boone, "Proposed Smoke Ordinance—1941." unpublished student paper, 1982, University of Louisville Archives and Records Center.

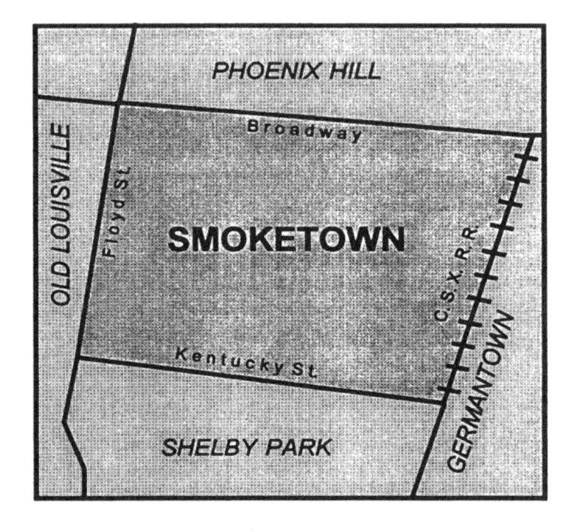

SMOKETOWN. Louisville's Smoketown neighborhood is a compact and cohesive residential, commercial, and industrial enclave. Located just east of Louisville's central business district, it is bounded to the north by BROADWAY, to the south by Kentucky St., to the east by BEARGRASS CREEK and the CSX Railroad, and to the west by Floyd St. It is Louisville's only surviving neighborhood that reflects the continuous presence of AFRICAN AMERICANS before the CIVIL WAR.

The name apparently came from the large number of brick kilns in the area that produced great volumes of smoke. Brick-making started early. An advertisement for the sale of the farm and residence of "the late Mark Lampton" (*Louisville Public Advertiser*, April 16, 1823) noted that included was a brickyard and utensils as well as up to 150,000 bricks. The advertisement also stated that the buyer could hire "Negro men well skilled in the brickmaking business." Lampton St., south of and parallel to Broadway, probably takes its name from Mark Lampton.

In 1841 the City Council adopted a resolution introduced by John J. Jacob that digging in Prather St. (Broadway) west of Preston St. be stopped. The mayor was directed to require those responsible "to restore the street to its original grade" (Council Minutes, March 29, 1841). Caron's Louisville City Directory for 1871 listed nine brickyards concentrated in the Smoketown area out of twenty in the city. The others were scattered in various locations. By 1880 none were left in Smoketown as now defined, although two were nearby in the FORT HILL and GERMANTOWN NEIGHBORHOODS. Apparently the clay that lay under Smoketown was mined out. By that year a portion of Smoketown had acquired the name Frogtown. It was located around Lampton and Jackson Streets and the name may reflect abandoned, water-filled clay pits that attracted frogs (*Courier-Journal*, Jan. 5, 1880, 4).

Field Day, Presbyterian Community Center, 1945. St. Peter Claver Church, 522 Lampton, is in the background.

Some residential development in Smoketown began in the 1850s by whites of German ancestry. By war's end freed slaves settled there, with an African American community firmly established by 1870.

Smoketown developed as a thriving business and industrial center in part because of the opening of a streetcar line on Preston St. to Kentucky St. in 1865. Beargrass Creek, an important water source, also attracted industry. TOBACCO processing plants were major employers. While whites performed skilled labor and held managerial positions, Smoketown's African American residents were employed in low-paying, labor-intensive jobs. An exception to this pattern was a tiny enclave of African American–owned businesses on Preston St. near College St., where two blacksmiths and a wagon maker's shop were located.

Because Smoketown's white residents were more affluent than their black neighbors, they had the means to build and own more substantial brick and frame houses. African Americans by contrast lived in modest rental housing owned by whites and situated in densely settled blocks and minor streets and alleys. For both races the shotgun house was the most prevalent building type.

Because of the economic and social climate in Smoketown during its early years, examples of African American property ownership were rare. There were, however, a few exceptions to the rule. WASHINGTON SPRADLING JR., one of Louisville's most prominent African American citizens, owned a large amount of rental real estate in the area. In another instance, a group of enterprising African Americans built simple shotgun houses on land leased from whites. They later lost ownership when the panic of 1873 wiped out their savings and they were unable to pay their rent.

Smoketown has historically been home to many churches and institutions that have provided important social services in the community for generations. Most notable were the Booker T. Washington School (built in 1874 as the Eastern Colored School and one of Louisville's earliest schools for blacks), the Presbyterian Colored Mission (begun with the founding of Hope Mission in 1898 and Grace Mission in 1899), Eastern Colored Branch Library (a Carnegie-endowed library for African Americans that opened in 1914), and Sheppard Square Housing Project (built in 1942 as segregated war worker housing and named for William Sheppard, the first African American missionary to the Congo).

In time the industrial base left the area.

Housing developments replaced the old single-family units. Smoketown has experienced a renaissance in recent years as neighborhood groups have emerged, businesses have relocated to the area, houses have been built, and older homes have been restored. In 1996 select residential portions of the Smoketown neighborhood most closely associated with African American settlement were listed on the NATIONAL REGISTER OF HISTORIC PLACES for their historic significance.

See *Louisville Survey East Report*, City of Louisville Development Cabinet, 1979; Henry Clay Weeden, *Weeden's History of the Colored People of Louisville* (Louisville 1897); George C. Wright, *Life Behind a Veil* (Baton Rouge 1985); Janet E. Kemp, *Report of the Tenement House Commission of Louisville* (Louisville 1909).

Joanne Weeter

SNOWSTORM OF 1994. On January 16–17, 1994, a devastating snowfall covered the Louisville area, breaking the 1978 record to that time exactly sixteen years before. In a twenty-four-hour period, 15.9 inches of snow blanketed the Falls City, closing highways, businesses, and schools, halting EMS vehicles, stopping mail service, slowing road crews, and resulting in massive power outages.

Because of the hazardous conditions, on January 18, Gov. Brereton Jones ordered that Kentucky's Interstate highways be closed indefinitely. During the next four days temperatures in Louisville plunged as low as minus twenty-two degrees and kept the city at a complete standstill for nearly a week. By Saturday, January 20, roads had reopened and temperatures had returned to above freezing marks. Between February 4 and 6, 1994, a deeper snow of 22.3 inches fell in the area, but warmer temperatures and better prepared road crews kept incidents to a minimum.

See *Courier Journal*, Jan. 18–23, 1994.

Aaron D. Purcell

SNYDER, MARION GENE (b Louisville, January 26, 1928). U.S. congressman. Snyder grew up attending PUBLIC SCHOOLS, graduating from DU PONT MANUAL HIGH SCHOOL. He attended the UNIVERSITY OF LOUISVILLE from 1945 to 1947, then entered the JEFFERSON SCHOOL OF LAW, where he received his LL.B. in 1950. Snyder pursued careers in farming, real estate, and law before entering politics in 1954. From 1954 to 1958, he served as JEFFERSONTOWN city attorney. Snyder left the position after being elected magistrate of the First District of Jefferson County (1958–62) in November 1957. Snyder campaigned as a Republican for a position in the Eighty-eighth Congress as a representative from the Third District of Kentucky. He defeated incumbent FRANK BURKE by 2,565 votes out of more than 184,000 cast and served his first term from January 3, 1963, to January 3, 1965. Snyder was unsuccessful as a candidate for reelection in 1964, when the REPUBLICAN PARTY nominated Barry Goldwater as its candidate for president. The poor showing by Goldwater in the presidential election took its toll on all Republicans running for office, as Snyder was defeated by CHARLES FARNSLEY. Snyder was elected as representative in the newly formed Fourth District in 1966, defeating veteran congressman Frank Chelf, and then was reelected to nine succeeding Congresses (January 3, 1967–January 3, 1987). During his time in Congress, Snyder served on the Merchant Marine, PUBLIC WORKS, and Transportation Committees. In 1986, against the wishes of the Republican Party, Snyder declined to run for Congress. The same year he was honored by having the Jefferson Freeway named in his honor. Snyder had initiated legislation that provided $52 million for the freeway's completion. With the last piece of legislation to be passed by Congress in 1986, the federal courthouse at Sixth St. and BROADWAY was renamed Gene Snyder Courthouse and Customhouse by his peers. Snyder was married to Louise Hodges on March 23, 1951, and they had one son, Mark.

See *Biographical Directory of the United States Congress, 1774–1989* (Washington, D.C., 1989).

SOCIALIST PARTY. The ideas of socialism were popular among many working people in the nineteenth century. Utopian experiments such as Robert Dale Owen's New Harmony in Indiana were usually short-lived and futile efforts that appealed to few. With industrial growth, however, the popularity of Marxist and socialist ideas grew. The Socialist Labor Party, the first socialist party in the United States, was formed in 1877. It appealed particularly to German workers. In Louisville GERMANS had been responsible for the LOUISVILLE PLATFORM of 1854, remarkable for its progressive ideas of equality and freedom.

Many Germans were attracted when the Social DEMOCRATIC PARTY of Louisville, known to its members as the "Local Louisville," was founded in January 1899. Its members were primarily working-class trade unionists, with large contingents of printers and carpenters, although it also counted doctors, teachers, businessmen, and a newspaper editor among its ranks. From its inception, the Local Louisville was the focal point of party activity in Kentucky. It spearheaded the effort to establish a state party in August 1900 and led the state party during its eight-month career as an independent socialist organization in 1901. In August 1901 Local Louisville affiliated with the national Socialist Party of America (SPA), dropped the democratic from its name and became the SOCIALIST PARTY of Louisville. The SPA had been formed in Indianapolis in 1901.

On paper the Local Louisville had only ninety-nine members by 1904, with still fewer members actually active in party business. Despite its small size, however, Local Louisville engaged in a broad range of activities including political campaigns, public lectures, social events, and publication of pamphlets and other materials. It also engaged in a persistent, if cordial, rivalry with the Socialist Labor Party, another Marxist party active in Louisville at the same time.

During the 1890s, that party was led nationally by Daniel DeLeon, who imposed upon it an uncompromising and revolutionary kind of socialism. In the spring of 1904, Local Louisville was bitterly divided by a controversy involving three members accused of violating socialist principles by acting as strikebreakers. This controversy split the party and resulted in its temporary dissolution. By 1906, however, Local Louisville had rebounded well enough to host the first national convention of the Christian Socialists.

During WORLD WAR I Louisville socialists, like socialists all over the country, came under harsh public attack for their opposition to America's involvement in the European conflict. On January 2, 1920, federal justice department agents conducted an armed raid on Local Louisville's headquarters at Karl Marx Hall on Jefferson St. as part of a nationwide crackdown on radicals. Party members were detained and federal agents seized documents allegedly linking the Socialist Party of Kentucky with the German Communist Party and advocating the overthrow of the American GOVERNMENT. Although no arrests were made, the raid effectively crippled the Socialist Party in Louisville as well as the rest of the state.

It was not until the GREAT DEPRESSION that the Local Louisville was revived. In 1933 Arthur S. Kling, who would later become a prominent community activist, ran as the Socialist candidate for mayor on a platform that called for public ownership of Louisville Gas & Electric Co. and full economic and political equality for the city's AFRICAN AMERICANS. Like its predecessor, the party of the 1930s provided much of the leadership for the state organization. It also reached out to new constituencies by establishing a standing women's committee and sponsoring a Young People's Socialist League at the UNIVERSITY OF LOUISVILLE.

Despite these initiatives, Local Louisville found it harder and harder to attract new members or keep the ones it had as depression hardship gave way to New Deal reforms and the full employment of the war boom. In 1941 Local Louisville had only twenty members, and by 1943 the party was entirely inactive. Hopes for a postwar revival never materialized, although Louisville socialists would serve as candidates in sporadic state campaigns throughout the 1940s and early 1950s.

See minute book of the Social Democratic Party of America. Filson Club Historical Society, Special Collections, Louisville, Kentucky; Courier-Journal, 1917–53; Arthur S. Kling papers, University Archives and Records Center, University of Louisville.

James R. Recktenwald

Group at headquarters of Associated Charities of Louisville, 1921.

SOCIAL SERVICES/EDUCATION. The values of a society are reflected in its basic beliefs and the programs of its social welfare system. Helping those in need (mutual aid) was possible with the neighborliness, stability, and solidarity of a rural agricultural society. With the Industrial Revolution simple neighborliness was no longer enough. Due to economics, social changes, and mobility, society's poor and needy were seen as having a moral fault or character deficit, making them lazy, shiftless, intemperate, or less than human.

Throughout the 1800s yellow fever, cholera, floods, tornadoes, and droughts left many people homeless, orphaned, destitute, disabled, displaced, or in need of medical care. Numerous services were established, notably a workhouse for the poor, sick, and petty offenders, Wayfarer's Rest; orphanages for Roman Catholic children and for Baptist, Presbyterian, and other Protestant children (e.g. German Protestant Children's Home, now Brooklawn); House for the Rescue and Care for Outcast Girls and Women; Almshouse for Dependent Children; the House of Refuge/School of Reform for Correction and Instruction for Juvenile Delinquents; Masonic Widows and Orphans Home; Children's Free Hospital; and the Home for the Aged and Infirmed (poor house.)

In a community with a significant Roman Catholic population, there was concern for the spiritual welfare of its dependent and neglected children, thus bringing about the establishment of St. Vincent's Home for Girls (1832); the Convent of the Sisters of Good Shepherd (1843)—later Maryhurst; St. Joseph's Orphans Home (1849); St. Thomas Home for Boys (1850); and Our Lady's Home for Infants (1925), the latter often referred to as a maternity home to provide services for children born out of wedlock and their unwed mothers. Boys Haven came into being in 1950. To coordinate and plan for more efficient and better services, Catholic Charities was created (1939). Rev. J. Lammers, a professionally trained social worker, was appointed its director by Bishop John A. Floersh, a position he held for thirty-six years.

With the growth of many relief-giving societies, there was a concern about duplication and lack of cooperation. The Charity Organization Society (COS) was formed locally (1883) as part of the COS movement—establishing the first private nonsectarian social agency in Louisville. Its goals were coordination with existing services to eliminate duplication, suppression of begging, and provision of work for the employable poor. Adding a Case Committee for individual case review, COS was renamed as Associated Charities (1907) and later as Family Service Organization (1921). Associated Charities, because of increased efficiency and effectiveness in the merger of supporting functions, created the Federation of Social Agencies and Community Council, both in 1907. The Federation was responsible for the "collection and distribution of funds for twenty-five social organizations and the operation of social service exchange, as well as supplying accurate information on welfare needs." In 1919 it was renamed the Welfare League. Community Council was primarily seeking "to establish a complete understanding of welfare needs among the many agencies whose fields of work touch; to further cooperation and to prevent duplication of effort; to serve in an advisory capacity concerning new work to be undertaken; and to increase efficiency of work already done." In 1924 Community Council divided its interest into three organizations: Recreation Council, Health Council, and Family and Child Welfare Council.

During this period children's programs were started under the Children's Protective Association (1917) and the Children's Bureau (1924). Their merger formed the Children's Agency (1931). While services were provided for residents, there was little or no help for those who were passing through. This brought about the founding of the Traveler's Aid Society (1904) for transients. In 1959 the merger of Family Service Organization, Children's Agency, and Traveler's Aid Society established Family and Children's Agency. In 1997 the agency name became Family and Children's Counseling Centers.

The social settlement movement began in the late nineteenth century. Locally there were such agencies as Neighborhood House (1896), Presbyterian Community Center (1897), Wesley Community Center (1903), Cabbage Patch Settlement (1910), Plymouth Settlement (1917), Louisville Central Community Center (1927), and the Educational Alliance (Jewish Settlement House). In 1901 Alice Caldwell Hegan Rice wrote her well-known novel, *Mrs. Wiggs of the Cabbage Patch*, about the area later served by that settlement house. Hull House in Chicago was the model for Neighborhood House, Cabbage Patch Settlement, and Plymouth Settlement. Initially programs focused on immigrants, enabling them to become naturalized citizens and to become acclimated to a new country. Services included English language lessons, parenting classes, well-baby clinics, and whatever was needed to become "an American."

Both movements focused on the giving of service and improving the lives of individuals. COS concentrated on individual changes, while settlements looked to the understanding of and changing of the neighborhood (community).

Along with locally initiated agencies, local branches of national and international organizations were formed. The Salvation Army (1883) developed a shelter and workingman's hotel in 1898. To meet the Salvationist's concern about the temptations faced by young men in the military (World War I), they provided wholesome fellowships with refreshments, recreations, and guest rooms for a visiting family in settings called "huts." This was the forerunner of United Service Organizations (USO) in World War II under governmental and voluntary auspices. Col. Harland Sanders of KFC fame was a longtime friend and a major contributor to the corps' projects.

In 1914 the local Volunteers of America in Kentucky was established. It met a major need by providing affordable housing for low-income families and the elderly. Locally its first homeless shelter helped to keep families intact by providing them with their own living quarters. Previously the missions always separated the father from the mother and children. The

Volunteers own and operate an apartment complex for single men and women with serious mental illness.

A social services exchange or central index was formed in 1914. Its reason for being was the prevalent attitude that "the poor cannot be trusted," and it was formed to avoid duplication of giving to the same person/family and to prevent fraud by those who might shop around.

As more organizations were created, there was a growing concern about the need for community planning and fund-raising for the coordination of social services and for more efficient use of dollars. The answer was the Community Chest in 1923 (fund-raising) and the Council of Social Agencies (planning) movement, now known as the METRO UNITED WAY. The Louisville Federation of Social Agencies was created in 1917; initially, twenty-five agencies provided a variety of services.

The GREAT DEPRESSION revived the argument that poverty might be caused by external forces over which individuals have little control; therefore, social action should be initiated to eliminate poverty. Such arguments ran counter to the prevailing notion of social Darwinism popular in the late-nineteenth century. This placed the blame for poverty on individual failures or inexorable laws of nature that must be recognized and accepted regardless of the suffering. By this theory, the knowledge and fear of poverty motivated people to work, resulting in individual success and the advance of civilization.

Those unable to work felt the brunt of such deterministic thinking. With the new attitude of doing something, it was soon evident that affected voluntary agencies were unable to meet demands for services. During the New Deal the federal government set standards and provided programs for public assistance, employment, health, and related services. These were the alphabet soup programs (CCC, WPA, NRA etc.). The trend toward increased federal funding for human services has continued in view of the diverse and numerous requests, plus the inability of local/state resources to finance and/or reorder priorities. The 1960s brought the "War on Poverty" and in the late 1990s things came full circle—more dollars were returned to the states, which set their own priorities and distribution formulas. To date Louisville has had its share of federal grants. A combined effort of governments on all levels led to a drastic reduction of the social welfare rolls. Recipients were expected to remove themselves from government assistance through job training and work.

For those who provide the social services, education has become increasingly institutionalized and important. In the nineteenth century, there was the "Friendly Visitor," often a well-meaning woman of wealth who brought food and clothing. With time it became apparent that more skill was needed for an unbiased investigation of a request for service. Facilities were developed to prepare trained social workers. Professional training would make a volunteer a paid employee.

Social work education was started as early as 1918 when the Louisville Conference of Social Workers with the Louisville Welfare League, predecessor to Metro United Way, sponsored classes in social work. By 1923 the Louisville School of Social Work was established by the Louisville Welfare League. In 1926 the school was accepted as part of the sociology department at the UNIVERSITY OF LOUISVILLE as an undergraduate program. The school closed the same year, but U of L continued to offer classes in theoretical and practical training in social work. Under Dr. Margaret Strong, the first director of the university's Graduate Division of Social Administration, a solid base for the growth and promotion of social work was established in 1936.

In 1944 the school came into its own as a separate entity and was named the Raymond A. Kent School of Social Work after a University of Louisville president who contributed greatly to securing and insuring professional social work education at the university. Kent School was an autonomous graduate school from 1936 to 1983. For the next fourteen years, due to structural and administrative changes, autonomy was removed. Independent graduate school status was restored in 1997. Through these years Kent developed several alternative on-site programs statewide. Locally, weekend courses for students from outside Louisville were offered beginning in 1988. International student and faculty exchange have existed since 1990; and research, training, and consultation are ongoing commitments. The fall of 1997 produced a joint Ph.D. program with the University of Kentucky. It is the only dual doctoral program in social work in Kentucky. When it began, Kent was one of five graduate social work programs in the South and the only one in Kentucky.

Then in 1984 a second graduate program was established locally with the creation of the CARVER SCHOOL OF CHURCH SOCIAL WORK at the SOUTHERN BAPTIST THEOLOGICAL SEMINARY. It was named for Dr. William Owen Carver, a professor who was committed to providing professional social work training to those working in Baptist settings. Its MSW degree required a certificate in theology upon admission to the regular and or advanced social work program. Nationally this was the only accredited social work degree granted by a seminary. Because of philosophical differences in the professional education of those in theology and in social work, the Carver School was terminated by the seminary July 31, 1997. Prior to becoming an accredited program there was a joint venture between Kent School and the School of Religious Education–Social Work Program offering a dual degree—Master of Social Work (U of L) and Master of Religious Education (SBTS).

CATHERINE SPALDING UNIVERSITY has had an undergraduate degree program in social work—Bachelor of Social Work (BSW)—since 1974. This is the entrance degree into social work. In 1999 Spalding granted its first MSW degree.

Social work has been based on the apprenticeship model. As a practice profession there has been a reliance on agency-based supervision as a means of socialization into the profession. With new knowledge and changing times, there was a move into private practice and consultation. Louisville social workers have kept pace with the trend.

With the realization that the professions needed a united front, seven social work professional organizations merged in 1955, creating the National Association of Social Workers (NASW) with state chapters. In Louisville there is the Jefferson Branch. NASW has founded and administers a national accreditation body—the Academy of Certified Social Workers.

Kentucky social workers were instrumental in the passage of a state social work license law in 1974, with a one-year grace period. Since June 21, 1975, social work professionals must be licensed to practice in Kentucky. Licensure enables social work professionals to receive third-party payments. Licenses are renewable every three years with the requirement for training in HIV and domestic violence cases. With a concentration of professional social workers and social services, Louisville has the largest number of licensed social workers in the state.

Lillian C. Milanof

SOFT DRINKS AND MINERAL WATER. Methods for impregnating water with carbon dioxide were developed in the late eighteenth century, and the manufacture of carbonated water commenced in the United States by 1807. Soda water, carbonated water, and seltzer water all refer to water impregnated with carbon dioxide. Soda waters flavored with fruit or spice flavors and sweetened are generally called soft drinks, or "pop."

Mineral waters from various springs and wells were widely consumed for their reputed therapeutic value. Waters from mineral springs containing various mineral salts were purported to cure or alleviate such ailments as constipation, dyspepsia, rheumatism, gout, kidney disorders, liver disease, diabetes, tuberculosis, syphilis, and nearly every other sort of malady. Three of the major local sources were Blue Lick (Nicholas County, Kentucky), French Lick (Orange County, Indiana), and DuPont Artesian Spring (Louisville Artesian Well). Imitations of famous European waters were also made by adding small quantities of various chloride, carbonate, and sulfate salts of magnesium, sodium, potassium chloride, etc. Mineral water was often artificially carbonated.

The first directory listing for soda and mineral waters in Louisville was Dr. James W. Garrison, a local druggist, in 1838. By 1859 there were five listed in the city directory, but there were probably others, such as DuPont Artesian water, for which 1850s period bottles have been recovered. By 1881 Industries of Louisville listed six mineral water manufacturers with a total capital of $15,200, employing an average workforce of twelve male adults and two children, working ten hours a day, with wages of $1 to $2 per day, and producing $26,693 worth of products. By comparison, the local cooperage industry was listed as having $361,300 in capital with an average workforce of 543 and producing products worth $762,800.

As indicated by the 1881 statistics, most local bottling firms at that time consisted of two or three men, often the partners of the firm, siphon-filling the bottles by hand. Soda bottles were made of very thick glass because of the high level of carbonation. Initially corks, which had to be wired down, were used. Only a few hundred bottles could be filled in a day. With the advent of crown caps and modern bottling line machinery and automatic bottle washers from about 1890 to 1910, large scale production became possible. Better SANITATION and quality standards plus the influence of the TEMPERANCE movement made soft drinks increasingly popular.

Though most nineteenth-century soda manufacturers lasted for only a few years, several local companies continued larger operations well into the twentieth century. In the early 1900s several local beverages were popular, including Teapho, Rivo-Cola, Mel-Ola and Parfay. The firm of Herman Epping, begun in 1863, was continued by his son John G. Epping and was a major local soft drink manufacturer into the 1960s. Products included Seven-Up, Kentucky Club Ginger Ale, Orange Crush, Epps-Cola, Epping's Grape, and Lemon Sour. In the late 1930s the company also operated branch plants in NEW ALBANY, Indiana, and Campbellsville and Lexington, Kentucky, and used a fleet of forty trucks to deliver its products. The plant was purchased by Pepsi-Cola General Bottlers in 1967 for $1.3 million, including franchises for Seven-Up, Orange Crush, and the like. The Pepsi-Cola plant was at the northwest corner of Logan and BROADWAY. The mineral water bottling firm of W. Springer was begun in 1873 and operated until 1939 as Springer Brothers. Joseph Renn of New Albany began bottling in 1870. His son, Joseph Renn Jr., operated a bottling business in New Albany until 1947.

About the beginning of the twentieth century franchised beverages began to be manufactured in Louisville. The local Coca-Cola bottling plant was begun by Fred S. Schmidt in 1901 on W MAIN St. between Tenth and Eleventh. It was the second Coca-Cola franchise, the first one being in Chattanooga, Tennessee. The plant purchased syrup from the parent company, then diluted and bottled it. Coca-Cola distributed syrup for fountain drinks through a separate company, which to some degree competed with the bottled product. The plant was moved to larger quarters at Sixteenth and Bank Streets in 1912, and to a much larger plant at 1661 Hill St. in 1941. Bottling was discontinued in 1991 and moved to Cincinnati, Ohio, where the company had about four hundred employees.

Pepsi-Cola was first bottled in Louisville in 1937 by Pepsi-Cola Louisville Bottlers Inc. The plant at 1500 Algonquin Pkwy., built in 1942, employed a workforce of 130 when it was acquired by Pepsi-Cola General Bottlers Inc. of Chicago in 1956. A new plant was built at 4008 Crittenden Dr. in 1957. Bottling at the Louisville plant was discontinued in 1991, though distribution operations continue in Austin, Indiana.

Dr. Pepper Bottling Co. of Kentucky operated a plant at 2340 Frankfort Ave. from 1937 to 1979. Royal Crown began bottling in Louisville in 1946 and in 1998 was the only bottler remaining in Louisville, at 6207 Strawberry Ln. In 1995 it had about 165 employees and produced 15 million cases of soft drinks. In 1962 Royal Crown introduced Diet Rite, the first nationally distributed diet soft drink. The current trend in the soft drink industry is toward bottling at very large regional plants, with the former bottling plant sites sometimes remaining as distributors.

Following the pattern of breweries in other parts of the United States, the Falls City, Oertel, and Fehr breweries were notable entrants to the field of local soft drink manufacturing during the PROHIBITION period. All enjoyed considerable success in soft drink manufacturing but quickly dropped the products to resume the manufacture of beer after repeal in 1933. One Oertel soft drink, Say Tay, was designed by the brewmaster and contained cinnamon and yerba mate, a South American herb widely used there as a beverage. The Renn family operated a bottling works on State St. in New Albany for seventy-five years, first bottling ale, porter, stock ale, and lager beer, as well as mineral water and soft drinks. There were several other soft drink bottling operations in New Albany.

Peter Richard Guetig
Conrad Selle

Coca-Cola Bottling Company, 1533 Bank Street, 1930.

SOLDIER'S RETREAT. Located at 9300 Seaton Springs Pkwy. in the HURSTBOURNE area east of Louisville, Soldier's Retreat was the nine-hundred-acre farm and home of Col. Richard Clough Anderson (1750–1826), a Virginia native and Revolutionary War veteran who came to Louisville in 1783 as a surveyor. He married Elizabeth Clark, a sister to Gen. GEORGE ROGERS CLARK and Lucy Clark Croghan of Locust Grove. In 1789 Anderson began buying land on BEARGRASS CREEK in Jefferson County and about 1793 built a large, two-story Georgian-style stone house with surrounding stone dependencies. According to family accounts, the house was damaged in the New Madrid earthquake of 1811, partly destroyed by lightning in 1840, and razed several years later. Four of the original stone outbuildings still exist, including two slave houses, a kitchen, and a springhouse.

In the late 1980s a replica of the main house was built on the original site by L. LeRoy Highbaugh Jr., using descriptions in family records to guide the reconstruction. The Anderson family cemetery, where Colonel Anderson, his two wives, and four of his twelve children are buried, is located nearby. Highbaugh died on July 6, 1994, and his heirs sold the house in June 1997 to Brooks H. and Marilyn Bower. The Bowers retain ownership of the house and dependencies, but the cemetery was acquired by the city of Hurstbourne in February 1998. The site, the cemetery, and the original dependencies have been designated a Jefferson County Landmark.

See Kitty Anderson, "Soldiers' Retreat, A Historical House and its Famous People," *Register of the Kentucky State Historical Society* 17 (Sept. 1919): 67–77; George H. Yater, "L.L. Highbaugh Recreates Pioneer Home in Hurstbourne," *Louisville* (Sept. 1982): 32–34.

Mary Jean Kinsman

SOLGER'S CONFECTIONERY. Solger's, Louisville's renowned confectionery and catering service, was on the northeast corner of Broadway and Fourth St. Theodore L. Solger, who was born in New Albany, Indiana, in 1839, learned the catering business as a young man by working for Charles Schultess, Louisville's first well-known caterer. In the early 1870s Solger bought the combination three-story brownstone-front residence and confectionery that faced Broadway at Fourth St. and had been built and operated by an Italian immigrant. His family moved in upstairs, and he began operation of his own confectionery below. A summer garden, located behind the house and surrounded by a brick wall, was open to the public during the warm months.

Whether a customer's taste ran to chicken salad and ice cream sodas or to more exotic delicacies, Solger's guaranteed satisfaction. Solger went abroad each year in search of new recipes. His famous chocolate truffle was made from a recipe discovered in Cologne, Germany. His piece de resistance, however, was the "snow ball," a brandied peach covered with ice cream, rolled in shredded coconut, with egg-nog sauce.

In addition to a perennially brisk local business, Solger's routinely catered parties as far west as Kansas City and as far northeast as New York. Food, waiters (one waiter for every four guests), linen, and silver were all loaded into railroad cars and transported to the parties.

Solger died on January 23, 1911, but his family continued the operation of the business until the building was demolished to make way for the Brown Hotel in 1923.

See Melville O. Briney, *Fond Recollection* (Louisville 1955); William Carnes Kendrick, *Reminiscences of Old Louisville* (Louisville 1937).

Kenneth Dennis

Solger's Confectionery, northeast corner Broadway at Fourth, just before building was razed for construction of the Brown Hotel, 1923.

SONGS/MUSIC. Compositions about Louisville have been written since the earliest days of the city. The first known published work is "Louisville March and Quick Step" (1829) by William Cumming Peters. Some compositions were dedicated to Louisville residents. John Ascher dedicated his "Belle de Nuit" to Oliver Lucas of Louisville, and Will S. Hays's song "We May Never Meet Again" was written for Miss Belle Bridgeford of Louisville.

In the late twentieth century, local collectors who have specialized in Louisville music include Walter Barney and Morgan Jeffries. Barney has many pieces of sheet music, some with beautiful lithographed covers. Jeffries has concentrated on local bands and owns twenty-eight hundred records and tapes, many of which contain songs about Louisville.

Other collections may be found in the Filson Club Historical Society and the University of Louisville School of Music. Former music school librarian Marion Korda has published *Louisville Music Publications of the 19th Century* (1991), which describes 1,450 items of music published in Louisville by Louisville publishers.

The following list of compositions in fifteen categories is a comprehensive catalogue of works inspired by Louisville and its many activities. The listing in each section are from the earliest to the latest date.

Belles

Joseph Messemer. "La Belle de Louisville." Piano. Nineteenth century.

L.V.H. Crosby. "Belle of Louisville." Song. 1851.

Victor W. Smith. The Belle of Louisville. Piano. 1899.

Blues

Bob Ricketts and Mike Jackson. "Louisville Blues. Song." 1922.

"Louisville Bluezees." Song. Recorded by Cora Gray (vocal) and Clifford's Louisville Jug Band. 1925.

Tim Krekel. "Highlands Blues." Song. Written for and recorded by Da Mud Cats Blues Band. 1995.

Edward Edelson. "Derby Blues (Louisville, Kentucky)." Trumpet and trombone duet. 1997.

Dances

William Cumming Peters. "The Louisville Gallopade." Piano. 1830.

William Cumming Peters. "Louisville Quadrilles with Appropriate Figures." Piano. 1839.

William Cumming Peters. "The Louisville Waltz." Piano. 1840.

F.J. Webster. "Canary Bird Waltz." Piano. "For the Ladies of the Louisville Polka and Mazurka Club." 1847.

Louis Wagener. "Falls City Waltz Rondo." Piano. 1853.

Walter Owen. "Galt House Waltz." Piano. Pertains to Louisville's famous hotel on the northeast corner of Second and Main Streets. 1867.

George Jonas. "Owl Polka." Piano. Pertains to the Louisville Owl Club. 1868.

Edward Mahr. "Galt House Gallop." Piano. 1869.

Julia E.L. Sterling. "Louisville Commercial March, New Two-Step." Piano. 1895.

Arizona H. Meyers. "Class of '96 Two-Step." Piano. Pertains to the Louisville Girls High School class of 1896. 1897,

William J. Carkeek. "The Derby Two-Step." Piano. 1898.

J. Blumenberg. "D.H. Baldwin & Co. Two-Step." Piano.

Published by the company store at 529–31 Fourth Ave. to advertise the Baldwin piano. 1899.

R.E. Gutterman. "Beautiful Senning's Park March and Two-Step." Piano. 1914.

"Exposition Waltz." Piano. Advertises the Louisville Conservatory of Music. Title refers to the annual expositions where products are displayed. 1915 or later.

"Louisville Stomp." Instrumental. Recorded by the Dixieland Jug Blowers. 1926.

Jefferson County

Joanne Allen. "It's Jefferson." Song. "The Official Song of Jefferson County." 1947.

Big Bill Johnson. "Jefferson County Jail." Song. Late twentieth century.

Kentucky Derby

William J. Carkeek. "The Derby Two-Step." Piano. 1898.

H.A. Wiedemeier. "On Derby Day." Song. 1947.

Hugh Lyons. "On Derby Day." Song. 1958.

Dan Fogelberg. "Run for the Roses." Song. 1981.

Central Avenue. Recorded by the Love Jones band. Pertains to the party on the street next to Churchill Downs. 1993.

Gary Biel and Tom Campbell. "Lilies for the Fillies." Song. Pertains to the Kentucky Oaks, a race for fillies held at Churchill Downs on the Friday before Derby Day. 1997.

Tim Krekel. "Here Ever After." Song. "They fell in love in the holding tank that first Friday in May. It was their first offense so they got out in time to whoop it up on Derby Day." 1998.

Louisville

"The Louisville Burglar." Folk song.

Ted Snyder and Willie Weston. "My Bill from Louisville." Song. 1911.

Irving Berlin. "When You're Down in Louisville (Call on Me)." Song. 1915.

Ernesto Natiello and Charles Hamilton Musgrove. "We Can, We Will, in Louisville." Song. Written for the Louisville Board of Trade to promote the city. 1916.

Ray Henderson and Lew Brown (real name: Louis Brownstein). "Counterfeit Bill from Louisville." Song. 1923.

Irving Caesar. "Louisville. Instrumental." Recorded by the California Ramblers. 1923.

Milton Ager and Jack Yellen. "Louisville Lou (That Vampin' Lady)." Song. 1923.

Joseph Meyer and B.G. DeSylva (real name: George Gard DeSylva). "Headin' for Louisville." Song. 1925.

"Louisville Special." Instrumental. Recorded by Earl McDonald's original Louisville Jug Band. 1927.

"Take Me Back to Louieville, Louieville, K-Y." Song. Recorded by Ella Fitzgerald. 1930s.

Peter De Rose and Billy Hill (real name: George Brown). "Louisville Lady." Song. 1933.

Bert Myer. "Louisville Louie." Song. 1936.

Sunny Skylar. "Louisville, K-Y." Song. 1940. Copyright 1980.

Louis Marshall "Grandpa" Jones. "Eight More Miles to Louisville." Song. 1941. Copyright 1947.

Jacques Ibert. "Louisville Concerto." Orchestral work commissioned and first performed by the Louisville Orchestra on Feb. 17, 1954. Recorded 1955.

Henk Badings. "The Louisville Symphony (No. 7)." Orchestral work commissioned and first performed by the Louisville Orchestra on Feb. 26, 1955. Recorded 1956.

Hilding Rosenberg. "The Louisville Concerto." Orchestral work commissioned and first performed by the Louisville Orchestra on March 12, 1955. Recorded 1956.

Klaus Egge. "Symphony No. 3 (Louisville Symphony)." Orchestral work commissioned and first performed on March 4, 1959. Recorded 1960.

Chuck Rogers. "Louisville." Country music song recorded by Leroy Van Dyke. 1964.

Winston Hardy. "Goin' Down to Louisville." Song. 1969.

"Follow Me Back to Louisville." Song. Recorded by The Friendly Room band in 1969 and Don Williams in 1976.

Mark Kinnamon. "I Love Louisville." Song. 1978.

"My Old Friends in Louisville." Song. Recorded by Gary "Doc" Dockery. 1980.

Nancy Moser and Joe Brown. "Look What We Can Do, Louisville." Promotional song for the city recorded by Hazel Miller and the Louisville Orchestra. 1982.

Mark Kinnamon. "Louisville, K-Y." Song. Recorded by Louisvillian Rick Bartlett. 1990

"Louisville Our City." Song. Composed and recorded by Chequee, a local rock band. 1993.

Louisville Church of Christ Choir. "We Love It in Louisville." Song. 1994.

John Goodin. "Louisville Suite." Instrumental. 1995.

Gary Biel and Tom Campbell. "Kentucky Blue (Homesick for Louisville)." Song. Recorded 1997.

Marches

William Cumming Peters. "Louisville March and Quick Step." Piano. 1829.

William Cumming Peters. "The Louisville Odd Fellows March." Piano. 1839.

William Cumming Peters. "March of the Louisville Guards." Piano. 1839.

Charles Warren. "Louisville Legion Quick Step." Piano. 1840.

Carl O. Edelman. "Louisville Citizen Guards March." Piano. 1858.

John Mason Strauss. "The Louisville Times March. Piano." 1894.

Carrie Rothschild (Sapinsky). "'95 March." Piano. Pertains to Louisville Girls High School Class of 1895.

Julia E.L. Sterling. "Louisville Commercial March, New Two-Step." Piano. 1895.

Charles Wright. "Baldwin March." Piano. Published by the company store at 529–31 Fourth Ave. to advertise the Baldwin piano. 1899.

Frederick Pfeiffer. "The White and Green—Louisville Training School March." Piano. Nineteenth century.

(Mrs.) Clara MacDonald. "Greater Louisville Exposition March." Piano. 1900.

J.H. Siesennop. "Falls City March." Piano. 1901.

R.E. Gitterman. "Beautiful Senning's Park March and Two-Step." Piano. 1914.

Ernesto Natiello. "Fontaine Ferry Park March." Piano. 1914.

Robert B. Griffith. "Courier-Journal March." Band. 1961.

Miscellaneous

W.G. Hefferman and Rev. Sidney Dyer. "Oh! No, I Am Not Blind!" Song. 1851. Pertains to the Kentucky Institute for the Blind in Louisville.

J.C. Meininger. "The Fairies of St. Matthews.' Song. The cover of the sheet music carries a lithographed view of a girls' school and is "inscribed to the Young Ladies of St. Matthews (vicinity of Louisville), Reverend Carter Page (principal)." 1871.

Clement White. "I'm As Happy As the Day is Long." Voice with chorus, and piano. Song advertising Louisville businesses. 1871.

Morgan C. Kennedy. "Fire Song." 1876. "Oh what a noble call is that/Where life and death might meet/As thro' the crowd rolls madly on/The engine through the streets."

Dr. T.H. Greenhough. "Exposition Romanza." Piano. Pertains to the Louisville Exposition of that year. 1880.

Esther Priest Dietzman. "Down in Old Kentucky." Song. Written for and published by the Louisville Founding Festival. 1953.

Jay Petach. "Come on Back to Beer." Song about persuading young people to discontinue smoking marijuana and taking LSD and return to drinking beer in Louisville. Recorded by The Oxfords band. 1970.

Big Bill Johnson. "Where Were You When the Sewers Blew?" Song about the explosion in the sewer at Twelve and Hill Streets on February 13, 1981.

"Leave." Song about walking on the Belvedere, which overlooks the Ohio River. Recorded by Your Food band. 1983.

Barry Stucker and Chuck Baxter. "Born Joey." Song about the Standard Gravure Co. printing plant and Joseph T. Wesbecker. He was on a long-term disability leave but returned to the plant on September 14, 1989, killed seven people, wounded twelve, and shot himself to death with a 9mm pistol. 1989.

Bryan Hoagland. "Kenny N Tong N Me." Rap song about two young athletes and a girl who are cruising at Fourth and Muhammad Ali Blvd. Police stop them because of a broken turn signal and find that Tony has drugs in his pants pocket. Recorded by This! is? Doris! band. 1989.

"Bardstown Road." Song. Recorded by the Pope Lick band. 1990.

Dan Killian. "Breckenridge Lane." Song. Recorded by The Uglies band. 1992.

Ethan Buckler. "Tornado." Song about the tornado that hit Louisville on April 3, 1974. Recorded by the King Kong band. 1993.

Alan Rhody. "Hangin' Out in the Highlands." Song. Recorded 1995.

Paul Dell Aquila. "Cherokee Park." Song about moving back to Louisville to be near Cherokee Park. Recorded by Another Colour band. 1996 on cassette tape. 1997 on compact disc.

Dan Trisko. "Shakespeare in the Park." Song. Recorded by the Slim Chance band. Pertains to the summer plays in Central Park. 1996.

Tim Krekel. "Kentucky Samba." Song. "Fresh Kentucky oysters, Falls City beer, Purnell's Whole Hog Sausage, y'all come down here."

1998.
Shannon Lawson. "Bardstown Road." Song. Recorded by The Galoots. Late twentieth century.
Steve Ferguson. "Jack Salmon and Derby Sauce." Composer draws on what he sees around him in Louisville. Late twentieth century.
Peter Searcy. Outlook Inn. Song. Recorded by Starbilly band. Pertains to a tavern on Bardstown Rd. Late twentieth century.
Peter Searcy. Slow Town. Song. Recorded by the Big Wheel band. Late twentieth century.

Neighborhoods

Tim Krekel. "West End Song." A song about the composer growing up next to Fontaine Ferry (amusement) Park. 1978.
Chris Gilbert and Lynn Weiss. "East End Boys." "They drive you crazy." Recorded by the Dead Serious band. 1980.
Jim Braun. "Preppy Chics." "Preppy chics make me sick... they date preppy guys with preppy ties, wear plaited skirts with a button-down shirt, live in Indian Hills and take a little yellow pill . . ." Recorded by The Bollocks band. 1982.
Chuck D. "One Million Bottlebags." Song. 1991. A rap song inspired by a walk down Muhammad Ali Blvd. where he was greeted "by churches and liquor stores."
Tim Krekel. "Highlands Blues." Song. Written for and recorded by Da Mud Cat Blues Band. 1995.
Tim Laun. "Highland Nocturne." Instrumental. Recorded by the Chicken Hawk band. 1995.
Alan Rhody. "Hangin' Out in the Highlands." Song. 1995.
The Underground Mafia. "Gangsta Walk." A charming and picturesque look at life in the low income housing projects in the West End of Louisville.

Newspapers

John Mason Strauss. "The Louisville Times March." Piano. 1894.
Julia E.L. Sterling. "Louisville Commercial March, New Two-Step." Piano. 1895.
Eddie Neibaur. "My ABC's Are Puzzling Me." Song. Pertains to The *Louisville Times* $3,000 Alphabet Contest. 1929.
Robert B. Griffith. "Courier-Journal March." Band. 1961.

Ohio River

"Down on the Banks of the Ohio." Folksong.
Mickey Clark. "Shanty Boat Bill." Song about an alcoholic named Bill Carrigan who had been captain of the River Queen. When a storm sent the boat out of control, three crewmen were killed at the Falls of the Ohio. Bill retired to a shanty boat on Harrods Creek but later moved to a room above Cole's Cafe at Third and Jefferson Streets. Recorded 1982.
"Roll on into Louisville." "oh, to be way out on the water (river)." Recorded by the Jefferson Freeway band. 1987.
George Brackens. "Rollin' My Own. " Song about traveling on the river. First line: "I was born in Louisville." 1977.
Ben Daugherty and Chris Hawpe. "Ohio River." Song about having a rock 'n' roll party on the river. Recorded by the Love Jones band. 1993.

Products

Cliff Slider. "Watch the Fords Go By (Louisville Motors Inc.)." Song. Song advertising the Louisville Ford dealer. 1936.
Comtrack Inc. and Hal Kome. "Real Goodness from Kentucky Fried Chicken." Song. 1975.
Stan Tarner and Murray Skurnick. "Ford, It's the Going Thing." Song. Pertains to the automobile that has been built in Louisville since 1916. 1968.

Railroads

George W. Meyer and Sam M. Lewis. "Make That Engine Stop at Louisville." Song. 1914.
"The Old Reliable." Song. Words: G.W. Veech. Music: Tune to "River Shannon." Pertains to the Louisville & Nashville Railroad. 1928.
"The Veteran. Song." Words: G.W. Veech. Music: Tune to "My Old Kentucky Home." Pertains to the Louisville & Nashville Railroad. 1928.
"The L & N Blues." Instrumental. Recorded by Jimmie Gordon and His VIP VOP Band. Pertains to the Louisville & Nashville Railroad.1940.
Jean Ritchie. "The L and N Don't Stop Here Anymore." Song. Recorded by Jean Ritchie, Johnny Cash, and Guy Carawan. About 1958, "Louisville, Nashville, Southbound Train." Song. Recorded by Johnny Duncan. 1970.

Steamboats

"Ballad of the Belle." Song. Recorded by The Indigos, a female trio. 1966.
"Delta Queen." Song. Recorded by Sue Powell. 1981.
Frank French. "The Belle of Louisville." Song. 1995.
Gary Biel and Tom Campbell. "Belle of Louisville." Song. Recorded 1997.

Sports

"Catch the Cardinal Spirit." Song. Pertains to the University of Louisville basketball team. Recorded by Bobby Lanz in 1980 and Mickey Clark in 1983.
"We Love Our Louisville Redbirds.{ Song. Recorded by Guy Shannon. 1983.

Robert Bruce French

SOUTHEAST CHRISTIAN CHURCH. The stated mission of Southeast Christian Church, an independent Christian church not affiliated with DISCIPLES OF CHRIST, is to evangelize the lost, edify the saved, minister to those in need, and be the conscience of the community. It began in 1962 when fifty-five believers founded a new church. The church met in members' homes and at Goldsmith Elementary School until it was able to purchase two and a half acres of land at 2601 Hikes Ln. in 1965. In June 1966 Rev. Bob Russell began his ministry at Southeast. Two months later, the congregation moved into its new building complex, with a 500-seat sanctuary.

Bob Russell was born October 10, 1943, in Conneautville, Pennsylvania, a small farm town, to Charles and Catherine Russell. He originally planned to become a high school BASKETBALL coach. During his senior year in high school, Russell decided to enter the ministry and enrolled in the Cincinnati Bible Seminary, graduating in 1965 with a B.A. He is married to Judy Thomas, and they have two sons.

By 1984, fifteen hundred people were worshiping weekly at Southeast, and the elders of the church and the membership began to consider a relocation project. As a result, a twenty-two-acre site on Hikes Ln. was acquired and plans were developed for a $10 million complex with a twenty-five-hundred-seat sanctuary, classroom facilities, and a family life center. On April 12, 1987, more than two thousand people worshiped in the new sanctuary, and within five years the church outgrew its new facility, with attendance having tripled to seventy-five hundred.

The elders voted unanimously to begin searching for new property. In March 1992, the congregation voted 95 percent in favor of purchasing eighty-eight acres off Interstate 64 on Blankenbaker Rd. A facility was proposed that included a ninety-one-hundred-seat sanctuary, a youth and activities building, and a fellowship hall. The total project would have approximately 650,000 square feet and cost about $78 million. In 1993 a goal was set to raise $26 million to begin construction on the new sanctuary. The congregation moved in December 1998. In a gesture that upheld tradition, two hundred members marched the eight miles from the old church to the new facility. By that time the congregation numbered among the largest in the United States. The old facility was occupied by the HIKES POINT Christian Church.

See *Courier-Journal*, Dec. 20 and 21, 1998.

Rusty Russell

SOUTHERN BAPTIST THEOLOGICAL SEMINARY. The first of six seminaries operated by the Southern Baptist Convention, the Southern Seminary opened in 1859 in Greenville, South Carolina, with four faculty members and twenty-six students. In May 1871 the convention, because of the growing financial crisis at the school following the CIVIL WAR, began to rebuild its endowment, which had been invested in Confederate bonds and currency. Additionally, the convention resolved to receive bids for the school's relocation to escape the war-torn ECONOMY of the Deep South.

At a meeting in Louisville that July, a group of Kentucky BAPTISTS offered to raise three hundred thousand dollars of the proposed five-hundred-thousand-dollar endowment if the remainder was forthcoming from out of state. Louisville beat out cities such as Chattanooga, Nashville, Memphis, Atlanta, and Russellville, Kentucky, when the convention declared a year later

Norton Hall, Southern Baptist Seminary building on Broadway at Fifth Street, 1929.

that the school would be moved to Louisville because of the city's strategic location, its size, and the wealth and generosity of the local Baptists.

By 1877 all but thirty thousand dollars of the money had been raised, and officials approved the relocation for the fall term. In September the seminary opened with four professors and ninety students. Without a campus, the school spent its early years based at the Polytechnic Society Library on Fourth St. between Green (LIBERTY) and Walnut (Muhammad Ali Blvd.), and students boarded at local establishments such as the Elliot, Victoria, and Waverly Hotels.

Through the generosity of such local businessmen as William and George Norton and out-of-state benefactors such as John D. Rockefeller, the seminary began constructing its own buildings in 1888 at the corner of Fifth St. and BROADWAY. By the mid-1890s, the complex consisted of a dormitory, a library, a main building, and a gymnasium. By 1895 enrollment was 316 students.

However, as the downtown corridor grew, the increasing noise coupled with the aging buildings prompted seminary officials in 1910 to consider a move to the SUBURBS. Although a site on Brownsboro Rd. between Birchwood and Zorn Avenues was purchased, this property was sold because of poor transportation links. In 1921 the board purchased a thirty-five-acre tract known as the Beeches (because of the prevalent beech trees in the area) along Lexington Rd. for sixty thousand dollars. Within two years, plans for a $3 million campus had been drawn up by New York architect James Gamble Rogers, in association with local architect ARTHUR LOOMIS and the famous Olmsted Brothers landscape firm. Groundbreaking on the first Georgian Colonial–style building occurred on November 29, 1923. The cornerstone of the seminary was laid on November 5, 1924; and Mullins Hall, the men's dormitory building, was in use by the spring of 1925. Classes began at the new campus in 1926.

In addition to traditional religious education and ministry training, the school added the School of Church Music, the School of Religious Education, the Boyce Bible School, the CARVER SCHOOL OF CHURCH SOCIAL WORK, and the Billy Graham School of Missions, Evangelism, and Church Growth.

Over the years, the seminary has seen a number of controversies, some of which have captured the national spotlight. The first arose in 1869 over interpretations of the Old Testament. In the 1890s president William Whitsitt was forced out when he challenged the popular belief—known as Old Landmarkism—that the Baptist identity could be traced back to the time of Jesus. During the discussions of human evolution in the 1920s, the school was labeled liberal by several Southern BAPTISTS, who threatened to cut off funds unless a more conservative position was taken. A 1958 conflict over decreased faculty input for the direction of the school led to the resignation of thirteen professors.

When a majority of fundamentalists took over the board of trustees in 1990, a new era of controversy erupted as an attempt was made to steer the school away from its moderate position. Paralleling transformations in the Southern Baptist Convention and at the Southwestern Seminary in Fort Worth, Texas, and the new Southeastern Seminary in Wake Forest, North Carolina, the Southern Seminary leadership instituted new guidelines for hiring, tenure, and promotions based on narrowly defined religious and social beliefs, including the inerrancy of, and literal interpretation of, the Bible, as well as conservative social views on abortion, homosexuality, and the role of women.

In 1992 moderate president Roy L. Honeycutt Jr. resigned his post and was succeeded the following year by the Reverend R. Albert Mohler Jr. In his attempts to redefine and reorient the seminary and bring it into line with the Southern Baptist Convention's newly adopted views, Mohler closed the Carver School of Church Social Work, inciting student protests and bomb threats. He also insisted that incoming faculty agree with radically conservative views on biblical inerrancy, abortion, homosexuality, and women in the ministry. Existing faculty members were expected to accept this change of direction. Between 1992 and June 1996, forty full-time professors left the institution. Annual cumulative enrollment also suffered during the realignment period, dropping from 3,285 in 1989–90 to 2,107 in 1996–97. By 1997 the Association of Theological Schools in the United States and Canada found significant improvement from two years earlier in communication and trust between the faculty and the administration.

In 1999 the trustees of Southern Baptist Theological Seminary approved a $70 million construction and renovation plan. A new 1,500-seat performance facility, additional seminar and office space, a library expansion, and more student housing and parking space are to be completed in time for the seminary's 150th anniversary in 2009.

See William A. Mueller, *A History of the Southern Baptist Theological Seminary* (Nashville 1959); *Courier-Journal,* June 29, 1997 and April 21, 1999.

SOUTHERN EXPOSITION. The Southern Exposition, held annually from 1883 through 1887, was Louisville's major bid to enhance its developing manufacturing base in an increasingly competitive ECONOMY that was shifting from a regional to a national basis. Located on forty acres in what was then the city's outskirts, it encompassed today's St. James and Belgravia Courts and Central Park in OLD LOUISVILLE. The main building, a two-story wooden structure (perhaps the largest wooden building ever erected in the United States), covered thirteen acres. Fully half the ground floor was devoted to machinery exhibits, with many of the displays in operation, turning out products ranging from barbed wire and brick to silk fabric.

Publicizing the Exposition before it opened on August 1, 1883, the Exposition Gazetter in June declared, "In the past ten years the growth of the manufacturing interests of Louisville has been extraordinary and this growth continues with increasing rapidity. It is evident that with cheap fuel, cheap lumber, and cheap coal, and unsurpassed transportation facilities, the future of Louisville is assured." The Exposition was

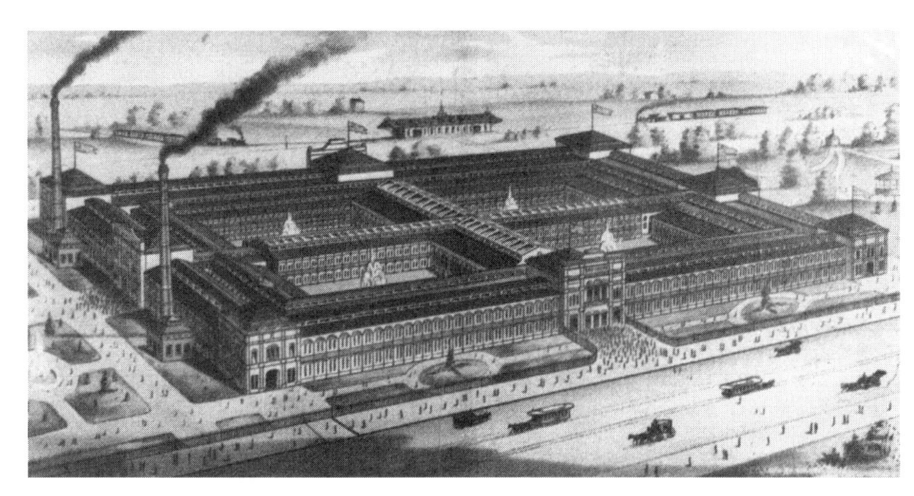

1883 engraving showing the Southern Exposition buildings.

designed to strengthen ties with the South, its largest market, and with the North as a source of capital and new enterprises. President Chester A. Arthur officiated at the opening ceremonies, a political move symbolizing rapprochement between North and South.

In keeping with the theme of progress, the Southern Exposition was the first to be lighted electrically and was the largest installation yet of THOMAS EDISON's newly developed incandescent light—forty-six hundred bulbs. Arc lights were used to illuminate the grounds, and some were installed inside the main building. The eight steam engines and seventeen dynamos that they powered were part of the working exhibits. Electric power also operated the Edison electric railway in Central Park. The exposition boasted the largest single exhibit of agricultural machinery ever, and many types of textile machinery. Of six hundred carloads of machinery from the North for the first year's exhibits, only one hundred were returned. The rest were sold.

Although technology was the main theme, the exposition also included an art gallery with PAINTINGS lent by such wealthy collectors as John Jacob Astor, August Belmont, J. Pierpont Morgan, and Jay Gould. There also were works by local artists. Music by some of the nation's leading symphonic ORCHESTRAS and bands was also a feature. More popular attractions were added from year to year: fireworks displays, a roller coaster (recently invented), and a racetrack where some of Louisville's first bicycle races were held. At the end of the 1887 season it was decided that the Exposition had run its course. It was a remarkable record, since the original intention had been to close at the end of the first season.

The building was still standing in 1888 when it was used for a large Floral Exposition, but in 1889 it was demolished to make way for residential development. Parts of the structure were used to build the Auditorium-Amphitheater at Fourth and Hill Streets.

See William McBride, "The Southern Exposition," A monograph, 1968, at the Filson Club Historical Society; *Great Southern Exposition of Art, Industry and Agriculture* (Louisville 1886).

George H. Yater

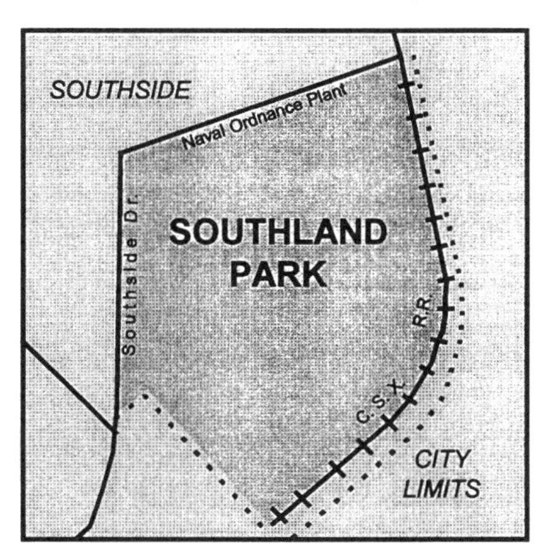

SOUTHLAND PARK. Neighborhood in southern Louisville bounded by Southside Dr. to the west, the Greater Louisville Technology Park (the former United States Naval Ordnance Plant) to the north, the CSX railroad tracks to the east, and the city limits to the south. The neighborhood began to be developed in the late 1940s by Thomas J. Morrison's Iroquois Builders Inc. The growth of this primarily residential community was a result of the increasing industrialization of the area, including the Ordnance Plant, established in 1941 by the United States Navy and privatized in 1996, and the INTERNATIONAL HARVESTER CO., the biggest factory in Kentucky, opened in 1948. International Harvester closed in 1983, and by 1985 its facilities were bought by the Louisville Forge and Gear Works Inc. The plant was moved to Georgetown, Kentucky, in 1997 because its site was purchased for expansion of LOUISVILLE INTERNATIONAL AIRPORT.

SOUTH LOUISVILLE. Neighborhood in southern Louisville bounded by Longfield Ave. to the south, a combination of Taylor Blvd. and

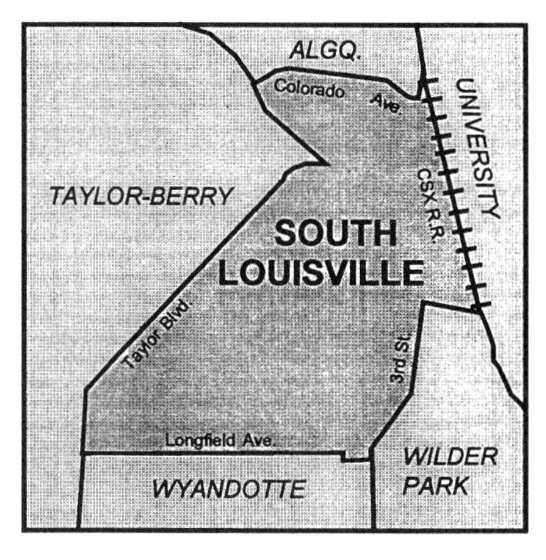

Algonquin Pkwy. to the west, Colorado Ave. to the north, and a combination of the CSX railroad tracks, Third St., and Southern Pkwy. to the east. An early streetcar suburb to the south of the city, the area was farmland owned by the Churchill family until it was platted in 1870. The area grew at a moderate pace until the KENTUCKY WAGON MANUFACTURING CO. moved its operations to the corner of Third St. and Eastern Pkwy. in 1878. The community flourished and received a town charter from the state in 1886. In the early 1890s, developers continued to subdivide the area, and the state granted city status to South Louisville as the Louisville Railway Co. extended its Fourth St. car line along Central Ave. to Taylor Blvd. and IROQUOIS PARK. In 1898 Louisville won a three-year court battle to annex the area. South Louisville continued to grow, however, especially after L&N opened its sixty-eight-acre complex of repair shops in 1905. The shops were closed in 1990 and were cleared for the new UNIVERSITY OF LOUISVILLE FOOTBALL stadium. Included within the neighborhood is CHURCHILL DOWNS, established as the Louisville Jockey Club in 1874.

See Carl E. Kramer, "The City-Building Process: Urbanization in Central and Southern Louisville, 1772–1932," Ph.D. dissertation, University of Toledo, 1980; George H. Yater, *Two Hundred Years at the Falls of the Ohio* (Louisville 1987); "Growing Up with the Downs," *Louisville* 38 (April 1987): 37–39.

SOUTH PARK COUNTRY CLUB. One of the oldest social clubs in Louisville, the South Park Country Club, 915 South Park Rd., was established on land cleared in 1889 by developers working with the LOUISVILLE & NASHVILLE RAILROAD to establish a new suburban residential community between the areas now known as OKOLONA and FAIRDALE. The developers built a ninety-eight-room hotel atop the hill overlooking a lake dug by the railroad company. When the United States experienced an economic depression in 1893, the development plans were halted. Interest in the area was renewed in 1905 when the South Park Fishing Club was founded. Louisville attorney O.H. Harrison sold the land to club incorporators, and he became involved in directing the club.

A log clubhouse was built, lots were sold for cottages, fishing cabins were built by other members, and the hotel was reopened. In 1906 the cost of membership was $150, and annual dues were $5. The club's board of directors tried to limit membership to one hundred members at all times, and the exclusive memberships belonged to some of Louisville's most prominent citizens. The hotel, renamed the Alpine hotel in 1922, was destroyed by fire in 1929. Over the years interest turned from fishing to SWIMMING, boating, and GOLF, and the club was renamed the South Park Country Club in 1969. The original log clubhouse, which still stood at the start of the twenty-first century, has been expanded as the facilities have grown.

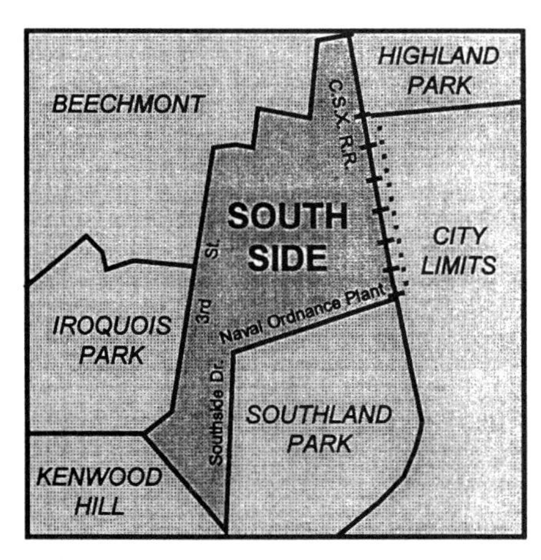

SOUTHSIDE. Neighborhood in southern Louisville bounded by Third St. to the west, a combination of Woodlawn Ave., Allmond Ave., and Hiawatha Ave. to the north, the CSX railroad tracks to the east, and a combination of the southern boundary of the Greater Louisville Technology Park (the former U.S. Naval Ordnance Plant), Southside Dr., and Kenwood Dr. to the south. Similar to the SOUTHLAND PARK neighborhood to the south, this community has developed since the early 1950s as industry has increased. The industry included the ordnance plant established by the U.S. Navy in 1941 (which was privatized in 1996), the old Louisville & Nashville Railroad's Strawberry Yards, and an expanded LOUISVILLE INTERNATIONAL AIRPORT. A local landmark is the all-girl HOLY ROSARY ACADEMY. Established in 1867 by the Dominican Sisters of St. Catherine, Kentucky, the school moved to 4801 Southside Dr. in 1956 from its location at Fourth St. and Park Ave. The neighborhood was the site of the Douglas PARK RACE COURSE, opened in 1895; it ceased to function as a racetrack when it merged with CHURCHILL DOWNS in 1918.

SPALDING, CATHERINE (b Charles County, Maryland, December 23, 1793; d Louisville, March 20, 1858). Religious leader. The cofounder of the Sisters of Charity of Nazareth, Catherine Spalding was the daughter of Edward and Juliet (Boatman) Spalding. The Spaldings moved from Maryland to Nelson County, Kentucky, about 1795. After the death of her parents, Catherine was raised first by Mrs. Thomas Elder, her aunt, and then by Richard and Clementine (Eider) Clark. In January 1813 she joined two other women invited by the Reverend John Baptist David to St. Thomas Farm, near Bardstown, Kentucky, to begin the Roman Catholic Sisters of Charity of Nazareth. Spalding was chosen first superior and whenever eligible was returned to the office by vote, serving a total of twenty-five years.

As "a constructive genius with a natural gift for administration," Spalding made most of the policy decisions affecting the community. In 1814 the first school was opened at St. Thomas; in 1822 it was moved to the site of the present motherhouse near Bardstown. Spalding founded St. Vincent's Academy in Union County (1821) and St. Catherine's Academy in Lexington (1823). In 1831 she came to Louisville to open PRESENTATION ACADEMY, the city's oldest continuous school, next to St. Louis Church on Fifth St. (site of the present cathedral). The following year, Spalding opened St. Vincent's Orphanage in Louisville. In 1836, in a wing of the orphanage, she started an infirmary that would become the core of St. Joseph's Infirmary, which became the largest private hospital in the state. It closed in 1979.

As one of the country's most prominent leaders among Catholic women in the nineteenth century, Spalding inaugurated the programs for which the Sisters of Charity of Nazareth became noted: education, the care of orphans, and health care. Between 1819 and 1856, she was involved in founding academies and parochial schools in Kentucky, Indiana, and Tennessee. In her last term as superior she raised the imposing central building and chapel still standing at the Nazareth motherhouse near Bardstown. In her leadership she deferred to no man, but had consummate tact, great compassion for the disadvantaged, and concern for the members of her order. SPALDING UNIVERSITY in Louisville is named for her.

Spalding died in Louisville in 1858 after having contracted bronchitis on an errand of mercy. She is buried in the Nazareth Community Cemetery near Bardstown.

See Anna Blanche McGill, *The Sisters of Charity of Nazareth, Kentucky* (New York 1917); Agnes Geraldine McGann, *SCNs Serving since 1812* (Nazareth, Ky., 1985); Mary Michael Creamer, "Mother Catherine Spalding–St. Catherine Street, Louisville, Kentucky," *Filson Club History Quarterly* 63 (April 1989): 191–223.

Thomas W. Spalding

SPALDING, JOHN LANCASTER (b Lebanon, Kentucky, June, 2, 1840; d Peoria, Illinois, August 25, 1916). Clergyman. John Lancaster Spalding was the son of Richard Marcus and Mary Jane (Lancaster) Spalding. He studied at St. Mary's College in Marion County and at St. Mary's of the West in Cincinnati. He was ordained a Catholic priest in 1863 at Mechlin, Belgium, and graduated from the University of Louvain in 1864.

Returning to Kentucky after 1865, he served as assistant at the Louisville CATHEDRAL OF THE ASSUMPTION, editor of the *Guardian*, and secretary to two bishops, Peter J. Lavialle and William G. McCloskey. On February 20, 1870, he led seventy-five AFRICAN AMERICANS from the cathedral to the first church for black Catholics in Louisville: St. Augustine, at Fourteenth and Broadway. Spalding served as the church's first pastor.

Largely due to difficulties with McCloskey, Spalding left Louisville in 1872 for New York City, where he wrote *The Life of the Most Rev. M.J. Spalding* (1873), his recently deceased uncle, the former Bishop of Louisville, then Archbishop of Baltimore. He wrote many other collections of addresses, essays, and poems, including ESSAYS AND REVIEWS (1877), *The Religious Mission of the Irish People and Catholic Colonization* (1880), *Lectures and Discourses* (1882), *America, and Other Poems* (1885), *The Poet's Praise* (1887), *Education and the Higher Life* (1890), *Things of the Mind* (1894), *Means and Ends of Education* (1895), *Thoughts and Theories of Life and Education* (1897), *Opportunity* (1900), *Aphorisms and Reflections* (1901), *God and the Soul* (1901), *Religion, Agnosticism, and Education* (1902), *Socialism and Labor* (1902), *Glimpses of Truth* (1903), *and Religion and Art* (1905).

On May 1, 1877, Spalding was consecrated first Bishop of Peoria, Illinois. In 1884 he procured three hundred thousand dollars from Louisville native Mary Gwendolin Caldwell to establish the Catholic University of America in Washington, D.C. Her father, WILLIAM SHAKESPEARE CALDWELL, had suggested this donation in his will. Spalding later was accused of having an affair with Mary Gwendolin, although the allegation was questionable.

Largely due to Spalding's arbitration of the 1902 Pennsylvania coal strike, President Theodore Roosevelt considered him "one of the best men to be found in the entire country." Upon Spalding's retirement in 1908, Pope Pius X granted him the honorary title Archbishop of Scitopolis. On April 30, 1911, Spalding returned to Louisville for the dedication of the third (and present) St. Augustine Church at 310 W Broadway. He is buried in Peoria, Illinois.

See D.F. Sweeney, *John Lancaster Spalding* (Milwaukee 1965); C.W. Gollar, "John Lancaster Spalding's Religious Anthropology," Ph.D. dissertation, University of Saint Michael's College, Toronto, 1995; idem, "The Double Doctrine of the Caldwell Sisters," *Catholic Historical Review* 81 (July 1995): 372–97; idem., "John Lancaster Spalding on Academic Freedom," *Ephermerides Theologicae Lovaniensis* 72 (Nov. 1996): 453–95; C.R. Lee, "The Fundamental Theology of Bishop John Lancaster Spalding," Ph.D. dissertation, Saint Louis University, 1991.

C. Walker Gollar

SPALDING, MARTIN JOHN (b Washington, now Marion County, Kentucky, May 23, 1810; d Baltimore, February 7, 1872). Catholic prelate and writer. Spalding was of Maryland ancestry, the son of Richard and Henrietta (Hamilton) Spalding. He was one of the first two Americans to be educated in the Urban College of the Propaganda in Rome and was ordained a priest there in 1834. After serving as pastor, college president, and vicar general, he was called to Louisville in 1844 to be the vicar general to the aging Bishop BENEDICT JOSEPH FLAGET. On September 10, 1848, he was named coadjutor bishop to Flaget, whom he succeeded as bishop of Louisville upon the latter's death on February 11, 1850.

During the fourteen years Spalding directed the diocese of Louisville (1850–64), its Catholic POPULATION doubled, from thirty-five thousand to seventy thousand, mostly in the city itself and mostly from German and IRISH immigration. For his flock, Spalding created churches, societies, and the parochial school system. For the boys' schools he brought from Europe the XAVERIAN BROTHERS in 1854. In 1849–52 he erected the present CATHEDRAL OF THE ASSUMPTION. In 1855 he had to contend with the anti-Catholic outburst called "BLOODY MONDAY," which slowed considerably Catholic growth in the city. In 1857 he was a founder of the American College of Louvain, Belgium, which provided the diocese with several outstanding priests.

Even before being chosen archbishop of Baltimore in 1864, Spalding was recognized as a legislator, writer, and orator by American Catholics generally. Among his published works are *Sketches of the Early Catholic Missions of Kentucky* (1844), *Life of Bishop Flaget* (1853), Miscellanea (1855), and *History of the Protestant Reformation* (1860). As archbishop of Baltimore, where he was an even more energetic institution builder, he conceived and organized the Second Plenary Council of Baltimore, which provided a code of law for the Catholic Church of the United States. At the First Vatican Council (1869–70) he advanced a compromise definition but ended by strongly supporting the doctrine of papal infallibility. He is buried in the cathedral of Baltimore. He was one of the most effective builders of the American Catholic Church in the nineteenth century.

See Thomas W. Spalding, *Martin John Spalding: American Churchman* (Washington, D.C., 1973); John Lancaster Spalding, *The Life of the Most Rev. M.J. Spalding, D.D., Archbishop of Baltimore* (New York 1873); Clyde F. Crews, *An American Holy Land: A History of the Archdiocese of Louisville* (Wilmington, Del., 1987).

Thomas W. Spalding

Nazareth College (now Spalding University) 851 South Fourth Street.

SPALDING UNIVERSITY. Spalding University is a coeducational, independent, fully accredited liberal arts institution open to all qualified students. Usually classes are small, and students enjoy close, personal attention from their professors. In the late 1990s the average enrollment was fifteen hundred students.

Spalding traces its roots to 1814 when the Sisters of Charity of Nazareth founded Nazareth Academy near Bardstown, Kentucky. It is named for CATHERINE SPALDING, founder of that order. Its missions often focus on education, health care, and social justice. While the degree programs at Spalding today have expanded, a central theme of the university's mission still reflects the sisters' charge to "meet the needs of the times."

Nazareth's academic programs have been well known to many distinguished Kentucky families, including those of ZACHARY TAYLOR, JAMES SPEED, John J. Crittenden, and JOHN ROWAN, whose daughters were enrolled. Like many other nineteenth-century academies for young women, Nazareth conducted not only a standard secondary school curriculum but also college subjects and training to prepare sisters to teach.

The Sisters of Charity purchased the house and grounds of the Tompkins-Buchanan-Rankin mansion at 851 S Fourth St. in 1918. Here in 1920 they opened Nazareth College as Kentucky's first four-year college for women. Still at the core of the campus, the mansion is listed on the NATIONAL REGISTER OF HISTORIC PLACES and is designated a Kentucky Landmark. A year later Nazareth Junior College was formally opened on the original Nazareth Bardstown campus. The two institutions merged between 1940 and 1963 into Nazareth College, maintaining two campuses. In 1963 the name changed to Catherine Spalding College and in 1969 to Spalding College. All instruction was consolidated on the Louisville campus in 1971. Faculty and students have capitalized on the campus location (Fourth St. between YORK and Kentucky) to enhance learning experiences. Proximity to THEATERS, museums, radio and TELEVISION stations, HOSPITALS, businesses, GOVERNMENT, and social service agencies has resulted in a variety of practicum, internship, clinical, and community service opportunities.

In 1973 the college was incorporated as an independent coeducational institution in the Catholic tradition for students of all traditions. To reflect the addition of graduate degrees to the institution's program offerings, the name was changed to Spalding University in 1984.

In 1994 the university's $3.5 million Egan Leadership Center was opened, the first new building in more than twenty-five years. It was named for retiring president EILEEN EGAN, SCN (1925–97), who had served the university for twenty-five years. At present, there are eight buildings on campus.

The university has gained attention as a leader in supporting Catholic secondary education. In January 1995, when the Sisters of Charity announced they could no longer afford to operate PRESENTATION ACADEMY, negotiations resulted in a merger between the two neighboring institutions. Similarly, the Dominican Sisters of St. Catharine, Kentucky, turned over the ownership and operation of Louisville's HOLY ROSARY ACADEMY to Spalding on July 1, 1997.

Campus traditions distinguish student life. Perhaps Spalding's best-known tradition is the RUNNING OF THE RODENTS, which started in

1972. The event, literally a rat race, is a spirited, student-run parody of the Kentucky Derby.

See Bereniece Greenwell, SCN, *Nazareth's Contribution to Education 1812–1933* (New York 1933); Anna Blanche McGill, *The Sisters of Charity of Nazareth, Kentucky* (New York 1917); Agnes Geraldine McGann, SCN, Story of 851, booklet, Spalding University Archives; idem, "Sisters of Charity of Nazareth in the Apostolate from 1812–1976," (Nazareth, Ky, 1976).

Lauren Whelan

SPEED, HARRIETT "HATTIE" BISHOP (b Louisville, February 12, 1858; d Louisville, August 8, 1942). Pianist, philanthropist, and humanitarian. Harriett Theresa Bishop was the youngest of eight children of William and Jane (Fletcher) Bishop. Her father, who died when she was two, had been the proprietor of the Louisville Hotel and coproprietor, with David P. Faulds (later a music publisher), of the first Galt House hotel.

Hattie, as she preferred to be called, was educated in private schools in Louisville and Boston. As a young piano student, she studied with Louis Henry Hast, organist of Christ Church Cathedral, B.W. Foley of Cincinnati, and Benjamin Johnson Lang of Boston. She made her debut at age thirteen, playing Mozart's Piano Concerto No. 20 in D Minor with the Musical Fund Society orchestra, conducted by Hast.

In 1886, at age twenty-eight, she went to Berlin to study with Fritz Schousbe and Karl Klindworth, conductor of the Berlin Philharmonic Orchestra. Moving to Italy, she continued her studies in Rome with Luigi Gulli and Giovanni Sgambati.

She returned to Louisville in 1892 and took up the life of a piano teacher and performer, appearing regularly as soloist, accompanist, and member of the Louisville Quintet Club from 1894 to 1905.

On July 3, 1906, she married James Breckinridge Speed, one of Louisville's most prominent businessmen. At his death on July 7, 1912, she inherited a large estate that included a house at 505 W Ormsby Ave. This building would be a center of music for the next fifty-nine years. In the years following her husband's death, Hattie Speed employed Arthur Loomis to design three buildings: the Music Room behind her residence (1916), the J.B. Speed Memorial Art Museum (1927), and a new Portland Health Center (1930). She also built a second home at 223 Shipp St., near the museum.

In addition, she contributed liberally to two African American institutions: the Red Cross Hospital at 1436 S Shelby St., where she served on the board for many years, and the Plymouth Settlement House at 1626 W Chestnut St. She was especially interested in the Kentucky Humane Society, for which she served seven terms as president.

She died at her home of a heart attack. The body was cremated and the ashes buried next to her parents in Cave Hill Cemetery. Her twenty-one-page handwritten will, which distributed her estate to many organizations and individuals, ended, "I leave the world regretfully, but with a loving & grateful heart, & a bright Hope for the Life more abundant." With her life, she had already fulfilled this hope for others.

See *Courier-Journal*, Dec. 20, 1926, Nov. 21, 1930, Oct. 24, 1937, Feb. 14, 1938, Aug. 10, 1942, Aug. 11, 1942; *Louisville Herald-Post*, May 14, 1932.

Robert Bruce French

SPEED, JAMES (b near Louisville, March 11, 1812; d near Louisville, June 25, 1887). Lawyer, politician, and U.S. attorney general. Speed was born at Farmington, the family estate. He was the son of Judge John Speed and his second wife, Lucy Gilmer Fry. Speed was educated at local schools and graduated from St. Joseph's College in Bardstown, Kentucky, in 1828. After working in the Jefferson County clerk's office in Louisville under the tutelage of longtime county clerk Worden Pope, he entered the law department of Transylvania University. After graduating in 1833, he returned to Louisville and began a successful law practice which he continued, with interruptions for political activities, until shortly before his death.

Speed was an active Whig, involved on the local and state level. In 1847 he was elected to the Kentucky House of Representatives, where he served one session (1847–48). He was a proponent of Kentucky slaves being emancipated and unsuccessfully pushed for such a clause in the commonwealth's 1850 constitution. His emancipationist views were the primary reason he was not chosen as a delegate to the 1849 Kentucky Constitutional Convention.

Locally he served on the Louisville City Council, the University of Louisville law department's board of trustees (1848), and the city's Board of Aldermen from the Sixth Ward (1851–54), including two years as president. In addition to his legal practice and political activities, Speed taught law at the University of Louisville from 1856 to 1858 and from 1872 to 1879.

After the dissolution of the Whig Party in the 1850s, Speed was a man without a party for several years until casting his lot with the new Republican Party. During the crucial period of 1860–61, as the country splintered and Civil War ensued, Speed worked hard to keep Kentucky loyal to the Union. In 1861 he was appointed mustering officer for Kentucky Union volunteers and commander of the Louisville Home Guard. In the Unionist landslide state election of 1861, he was elected to the senate (1861–63). Speed's antislavery stance and association with the Republican Party had limited his political career in Kentucky before the war and in its early years. As the war progressed he became associated with the Radical Republican faction of the party, an unpopular affiliation in the state, and this limited his political career after the war. But in the midst of the war, his politics made him the choice of Abraham Lincoln as his attorney general. Speed's leading role in helping to keep Kentucky in the Union, long association with the Whig Party, and documented stance against slavery stood him in good stead with Lincoln.

To this must be added Speed's personal association with the president. The two men had known each other for many years. Not only were they friends, but Speed's brother, Joshua Fry Speed, was one of Lincoln's closest personal friends. Additionally, Lincoln insisted that a Kentuckian serve in his cabinet, and, therefore, Speed was offered the post in December 1864. He accepted and began his duties that same month. It was during his service as attorney general that Speed increasingly was drawn into the Radical Republican faction. Reflecting the Radicals' differences with President Andrew Johnson, Speed resigned on July 16, 1866.

Speed returned to his Louisville law practice and also worked to further Republican interests on the state and national levels. In September 1866 he served as permanent chairman of the Southern Loyalist Convention in Philadelphia, which opposed President Johnson and his policies. Speed was nominated for the U.S. Senate in 1867 but was not selected. At the 1868 Republican National Convention, the Kentucky delegation nominated Speed as Ulysses S. Grant's vice president, but only they voted for him and his name was withdrawn after the first ballot. He served as a delegate to the 1872 and 1876 Republican National Conventions. An 1870 candidacy for the Kentucky House of Representatives was unsuccessful.

Speed married Jane L. Cochran of Louisville on April 23, 1840. Their children were John, Henry Pirtle, Charles, Breckinridge, James Junior, Joshua Fry, and Edward Shippen. The Speed family was associated with the Unitarian Church, but Speed apparently never officially joined any denomination. He died at his country home, the Poplars, outside Louisville and is buried in Cave Hill Cemetery.

See Thomas Speed, *Records and Memorials of the Speed Family* (Louisville 1892); Ellis Merton Coulter, "James Speed," Dictionary of American Biography (New York 1935); J. Stoddard Johnston, ed., *Memorial History of Louisville* (Chicago 1896); Helen L. Springer, "James Speed, the Attorney General, 1864–1866," *Filson Club History Quarterly* 11 (July 1937): 169–88; Gary Lee Williams, "James and Joshua Speed: Lincoln's Kentucky Friends," Ph.D. dissertation, Duke University, 1971.

James J. Holmberg

SPEED, JAMES BRECKINRIDGE (b near Boonville, Missouri, January 4, 1844; d Rockland, Maine, July 7, 1912). Industrialist

James Breckinridge Speed (standing) and members of his family (from left) Olive Speed, Cora (Coffin) Speed (first wife), William Shallcross Speed, George Coffin.

and businessman. He was the only son of William Pope and Mary Ellen (Shallcross) Speed and the grandson of Judge John Speed, who built the Farmington estate. Speed's mother died when he was an infant. At the age of eleven, he came to Louisville, where he lived with his paternal aunt, Mrs. Lucy Speed Breckinridge. He was educated in the local schools and began his business career as a bank clerk at the age of sixteen. At the outbreak of the CIVIL WAR he enlisted in the First Ohio Battery and became adjutant of the Twenty-seventh Kentucky Regiment. He saw active service under Gen. William T. Sherman, participating in the engagements at Atlanta and Knoxville.

After the war, Speed went to work for the Louisville Hydraulic Cement and Water Power Co., which manufactured cement in the old Tarascon Mill in SHIPPINGPORT. In 1869 the name was changed to Louisville Cement Co., and he became president. In addition, Speed was president of the Louisville Railway Co., the Ohio Valley Telephone Co., the North Jellico Coal Co., the Taylor Coal Co. (later Beaver Dam Coal Co.), and the Louisville Woolen Mills Co.; mainstay and largest shareholder of J.B. Speed & Co., dealers in salt, lime, and coal; and vice president of the Louisville Cotton Mills Co.

Speed traveled widely here and abroad, enjoyed music, gave generously but anonymously to many charities, and collected PAINTINGS and SCULPTURE valued at a hundred thousand dollars.

In 1868 he married Cora A. Coffin of Cincinnati. Three children were born: Olive, William Shallcross, and Douglas Breckinridge, who died in infancy. Following the death of his wife on March 10, 1905, he married forty-eight-year-old Harriett "Hattie" Theresa Bishop, a concert pianist and teacher, on July 3, 1906, at St. Stephen's Episcopal Church in Boston.

In 1909 he developed kidney and heart trouble, and his doctor sent him to Rockland, Maine, for rest in the summers. It was there that he died. He was returned to Louisville where, at the hour of his funeral in the Church of the Messiah (Unitarian), Fourth and YORK, all STREETCARS, wherever they were, were ordered to stop for five minutes. He is buried in CAVE HILL CEMETERY with his first wife.

To perpetuate Speed's memory, the Speed Scientific School at the UNIVERSITY OF LOUISVILLE was established by his two children in 1925, and the J.B. Speed Memorial Art Museum was built by his widow in 1927. It is now simply called the SPEED ART MUSEUM.

See Courier-Journal, July 8, 1912, Feb. 16, 1924, Aug. 24, 1980; Temple Bodley, ed., *History of Kentucky* (Chicago-Louisville 1928); *The Biographical Encyclopedia of Kentucky of the Dead and Living Men of the Nineteenth Century* (Cincinnati 1878); Josiah Stoddard Johnston, ed., *Memorial History of Louisville* (Chicago 1896).

Robert Bruce French

SPEED, JAMES STEPHENS (b near Louisville, 1811; d Chicago, Illinois, 1860). Mayor. Speed was the son of John Speed (b 1773), who had moved to Jefferson County about 1795 from Virginia. James S. Speed was born on his father's farm about nine miles outside Louisville on Salt River Rd. (Dixie Hwy.). When he was seventeen or eighteen he went to the city to work for a Mr. Pickett, a building and railroad contractor. At age twenty-one he was made a partner in the firm of Pickett and Speed.

In 1843 Speed was elected to the state legislature representing Louisville and reelected the following year. In 1849 he was appointed United States marshal for Kentucky by President ZACHARY TAYLOR.

Speed served as mayor of Louisville from April 26, 1852, until April 1855. During Speed's three years as mayor, the question of when the term of office officially ended was never settled. Speed was elected in April 1853 and again in 1854. There was no definitive legal opinion, and neither of the boards of the general council could reach a decision. Although Speed was chosen annually by the voters, he was also never awarded an election certificate.

In 1855 the crisis came to a head. A joint resolution by the general council in February called for another election, although Speed contended that his term of office as mayor did not expire until 1856. He was backed in this by a decision by Judge HENRY PIRTLE of the Louisville Chancery Court.

In the April election, Speed went up against American (Know-Nothing) Party candidate JOHN BARBEE. Speed did not announce his candidacy because of the chancery court's decision and was defeated in the election. Barbee received a majority of the vote and was later recognized as mayor by a council resolution, which was passed over Speed's veto.

The Know-Nothings, led by the editorials of Walter N. Haldeman's *Louisville Daily Courier*, were against Speed, a Whig, because of his Catholicism. Speed was the first Catholic mayor of Louisville. After the election Speed filed a lawsuit in Jefferson Circuit Court challenging the legitimacy of Barbee's victory. Judge William F. Bullock ruled on May 8 that Speed's term of office had not expired. However, the Know-Nothings took the case to the state court of appeals, where Barbee's election as mayor was upheld. In 1856 Speed moved his family to Chicago, where he remained for the rest of his life.

Speed's administration was concerned primarily with PUBLIC WORKS projects. He initiated projects on the Louisville Water Works and was instrumental in getting a number of street construction projects started. A row of city market houses built during his administration was named "Speed Market" after the mayor.

He married Julia Ann Kearney on January 1, 1833. The Kearney family was Catholic, and James S. Speed converted to Catholicism. The couple had ten children: Mary Pickett, Sarah, Julia Ann, William K., Maria Louise, James, Robert Able, Emma, John Kearney, and Blanche. After Speed's death, the family moved from Chicago to Memphis, Tennessee. Julia Speed died in Memphis on June 19, 1892.

See Thomas Speed, *Records and Memorials of the Speed Family* (Louisville 1892); George Yater, *Two Hundred Years at the Falls of the Ohio* (Louisville 1987); Attia Martha Bowmer, "The History of the Government of the City of Louisville," M.A. thesis, University of Louisville, 1948.

SPEED, JOSHUA FRY (b Jefferson County, Kentucky, November 14, 1814; d Louisville, May 29, 1882). Businessman. Speed was born at Farmington, the family estate near Louisville. He was the son of Judge John Speed and his second wife, Lucy Gilmer Fry. Speed was educated locally and at St. Joseph's College in Bardstown, Kentucky. A serious illness forced him to return home before graduating and, once recovered, he decided to pursue a business career rather than return to school.

He spent two or three years as a clerk in the wholesale store of William H. Pope, and in the fall of 1834 visited Springfield, Illinois, contemplating a business career there. In the spring of 1835 he moved to Springfield and spent the next seven years there. He became a partner in the mercantile firm of James Bell and Co. and managed a general store in the town. He also reportedly helped edit a newspaper for a time.

In April 1837 Speed met ABRAHAM LINCOLN,

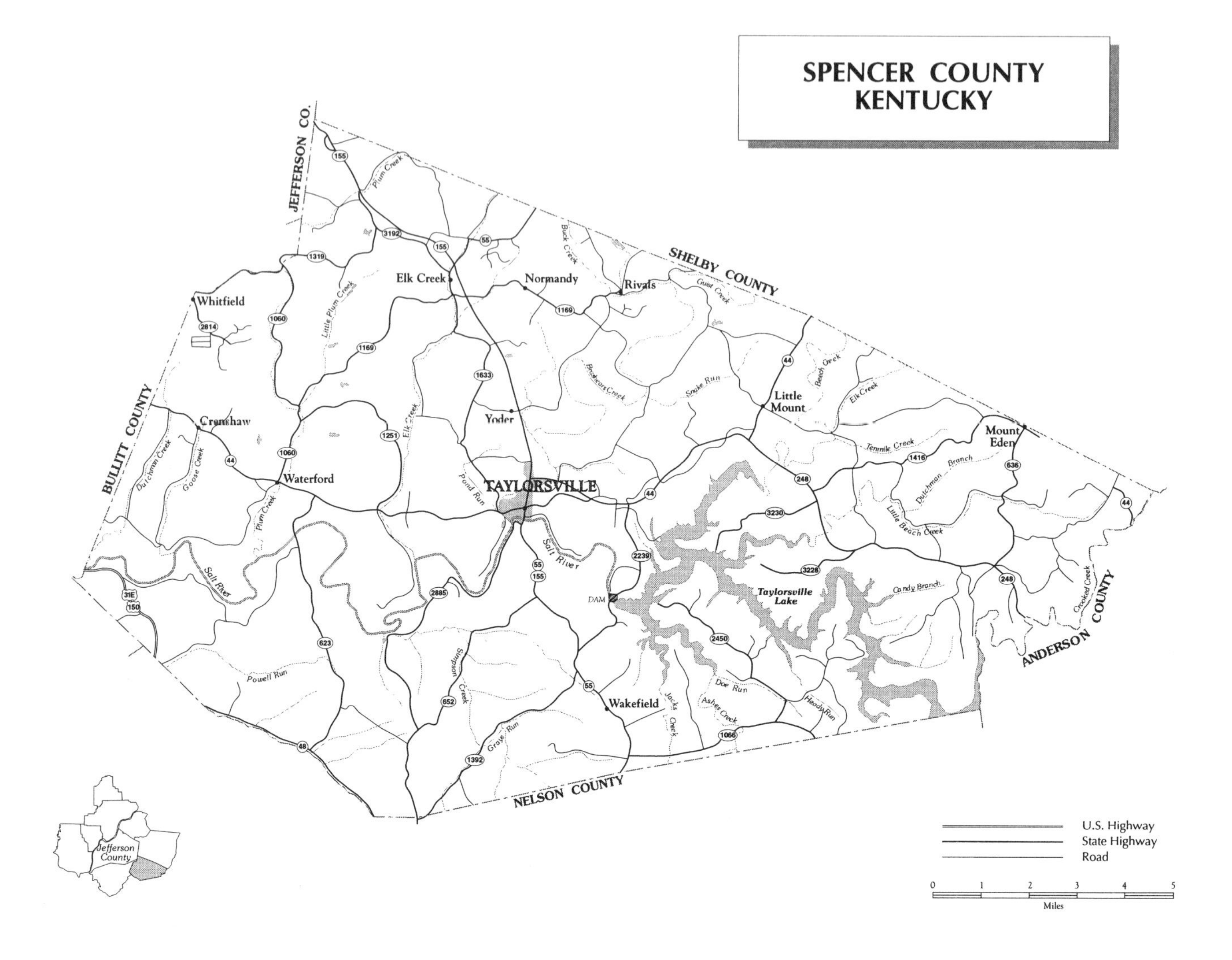

then a young lawyer just arrived in Springfield and in need of a place to stay. Speed's offer to share his room over the store was gratefully accepted. For the next four years they shared quarters, participated in the social and political life of Springfield, and formed a bond so strong that each referred to the other as one of his closest friends for the rest of their lives. Both were associated with the WHIG PARTY at the time but would join different parties—Speed the Democrat and Lincoln the Republican—when the Whigs dissolved in the mid-1850s.

In 1841 Speed returned to Louisville to establish himself as a farmer. That same year Lincoln paid his famous visit to Farmington, staying several weeks with the Speed family. On February 15, 1842, Speed married Fanny Henning, and they resided about thirteen miles south of Louisville in the Pond Settlement area for nine years. He was elected to the state legislature in 1848 as a representative from Jefferson County and served one term. He declined to be nominated again for any political office. In 1851 Speed and his brother-in-law, James W. Henning, formed the successful real estate firm of Henning and Speed, and that same year Joshua and Fanny moved from the country into Louisville. He was very civic-minded and supported projects for Louisville's progress. He served on the boards of a number of companies and was active in developing RAILROADS in the area.

When the CIVIL WAR began, Speed actively supported the Union cause in Kentucky, including intervening personally with now-president Lincoln on behalf of Unionist needs in the state. He reportedly declined Lincoln's offer of a cabinet position, but his brother James served as U.S. attorney general. Speed carried confidential communications between authorities in Kentucky and Washington during the war, and while in Washington conferred with Lincoln—so much so that he was commonly known as the president's agent in Kentucky. In 1867 Speed built a house near Farmington. In 1876 he traveled to California for a visit. He joined the Methodist Church late in life. Speed spent the winter of 1881–82 in Nassau, Bahamas, for his health, but it continued to fail and he died soon after returning home. He is buried in CAVE HILL CEMETERY. He and his wife had no children.

See Robert L. Kincaid, "Joshua Fry Speed: Lincoln's Most Intimate Friend," *Filson Club History Quarterly* 17 (April 1943): 63–121; Thomas Speed, *Records and Memorials of the Speed Family* (Louisville 1892); Joshua F. Speed, *Reminiscences of Abraham Lincoln and Notes of a Visit to California* (Louisville 1884); Gary Lee Williams, "James and Joshua Speed—Lincoln's Kentucky Friends," Ph.D. dissertation, Duke University, 1971.

James J. Holmberg

SPENCER COUNTY. Spencer County, the seventy-seventh in order of formation, is located in western central Kentucky. It is bordered by Bullitt, Jefferson, Nelson, Shelby, and Anderson Counties and contains 193 square miles. The county was formed on January 7, 1824, from parts of Nelson, Shelby, and Bullitt Counties and named for Capt. Spears Spencer. A member of Kentucky's "Corn Stalk Militia" from 1792 to 1801, Spencer formed the Yellow Jackets rifle company in 1809 and joined Gen. William Henry Harrison's command in the Tippecanoe campaign, where he was killed on November 7, 1811. The county seat is TAYLORSVILLE.

The rolling and hilly terrain of the county is intersected by the Salt River and its numerous tributaries, where most of the level land lies. Abundant prehistoric artifacts have been found in the county, particularly near the river and creek valleys. Pioneers utilized the Salt River as a thoroughfare between the settlement at Fort Harrod and saltmaking operations that began at BULLITT'S LICK (in present-day BULLITT COUNTY) in 1779. An Indian attack against Kinchloe's Station (located in nearby Nelson County near the Spencer County line) in the fall of 1782 may have slowed settlement of the area, but by 1790 several homes existed in what would become Taylorsville. In 1798 RICHARD TAYLOR of Fauquier County, Virginia, bought 175 acres in the same area and established the town of Taylorsville the next year.

Primarily an agricultural county from the arrival of the first settlers, Spencer had a slave-based ECONOMY. In 1840 there were 1,911 slaves and 4,650 whites; by 1860 the ratio was 2,205 to 3,974.

The number of slaves in the county led much of the white populace to support the Confederacy in the CIVIL WAR, although numerous men also enlisted in the Union cause. Edward Massie, who served in the Kentucky legislature, was a Unionist and cast one of the votes in 1861 to keep Kentucky in the Union. After Massie returned to his home in Spencer County, he was murdered by a band of guerrillas. Such attacks continued until after the Civil War. In early 1865 a force of Confederate guerrillas, including William C. Quantrill and Marcellus Jerome Clarke ("Sue Mundy"), were chased back and forth across Spencer County. Capt. Edwin Terrill, referred to as a scout but more likely a guerrilla working for both sides, was commissioned by federal authorities to locate Quantrill and his band. Terrill found Quantrill at the farm of James Wakefield in the south-central section of the county on May 10, 1865, and wounded him. Quantrill, who died in a military prison hospital in Louisville on June 6, 1865, had been a house guest of Spencer County judge Jonathan Davis when President ABRAHAM LINCOLN was shot, and had proposed a toast to his death.

With the loss of slave labor, some farms failed after the war, but others flourished. In 1870 the county produced 458,109 bushels of corn, 13,404 head of livestock, and 1,274 tons of hay, along with wheat and barley. The shipping of goods down the Salt River to the Ohio ended when the Louisville, Cincinnati, and Lexington Railroad completed a line from Bloomfield, in Nelson County, through Taylorsville to a main line at SHELBYVILLE in 1881. Soon after its completion, the line was acquired by the LOUISVILLE & NASHVILLE RAILROAD and operated as the "Bloomfield Branch" until its abandonment in 1952.

In 1988 farms occupied 81 percent of the land area, with 62 percent of farmland in cultivation. Crops include TOBACCO, livestock, hay, and vegetables, and in 1997 the county ranked sixty-third in cash receipts from farm marketings. A large number of Spencer County residents are employed outside the county, many in nearby Louisville. During the 1990s the POPULATION grew as people moved in from Jefferson County. Although not included in the Louisville metropolitan area, it is now closely tied to its ECONOMY.

Tourism expenditures brought $4.4 million into the economy in 1988. Taylorsville Lake, impounded on the Salt River in 1982, covers 3,050 acres and offers fishing and boating activities. The Louisville District U.S. Army Corps of Engineers operates a visitors' center at the dam, plus boat ramps, and a marina. More than ten thousand acres surrounding the lake are devoted to wildlife preservation and recreation.

The population of Spencer County was 5,488 in 1970, rose to 5,929 in 1980, to 6,801 in 1990, and to 9,157 in 1997.

Selected Statistics for Spencer County, 1990
Population: 6,801
Population per square mile: 35
Percent African American: 1.7
Percent 0 to 17 years: 26.9
Percent 65 years and over: 12.1
Percent 25 years and over with a high school degree or equivalency: 57.5
Percent 25 years and over with a bachelor's degree 9.9
Per capita income in 1989: $22,680
Unemployment rate: 4.5 percent
Married-couple families as a percent of total households: 69.0
Median home value: $49,300

See Lloyd Lee, *A Brief History of Kentucky* (Berea, Ky., 1981).

SPENCERIAN COLLEGE. Business educator Enos Spencer founded the school bearing his name at Sixth and MAIN Streets in 1892. Spencerian Commercial School, as it was called at the time, was purchased by Alva O. Sullivan in 1926. Roy Whalin bought out Sullivan's interest in February 1962 to become sole owner of what was now Spencerian College, while Sullivan and his son, A.R. Sullivan, founded a new business college, SULLIVAN COLLEGE. The younger Sullivan reacquired the school from Whalin in 1972 and owns it today, along with Sullivan College and Louisville Technical Institute, which, together with Spencerian, form the Sullivan Colleges System. In 1992 Spencerian moved from its sixth downtown location (914 E BROADWAY) to a site at 4627 Dixie Hwy. in SHIVELY.

Throughout most of its history, Spencerian has been dedicated strictly to training office workers. J.W. Drye, president of the college in 1942, declared in a *COURIER-JOURNAL* article that efficient office workers being as necessary to the American war effort as soldiers, Spencerian was instituting intensive courses in dictaphone and mimeograph operation in addition to existing courses in secretarial work, ACCOUNTING, comptometry (adding-machine operation), and stenography (offered in both day and night classes). In the late 1990s Spencerian maintained its emphasis on office work, though its course offerings widened and it added a concentration on allied health. Its School of Business Administration offered programs leading to certificates or diplomas in receptionist work, use of computer software packages, office work, and accounting, along with associate degree programs in accounting and business-office management. The School of Allied Health Sciences offered associate degrees in medical administrative management and diploma programs in practical NURSING and in various medical-office fields.

See *Louisville Times,* Oct. 25, 1982; *Courier-Journal,* Aug. 16, 1942, June 17, 1992.

William Duane Kenney

SPIRIT OF JEFFERSON. *The Spirit of Jefferson* was built in 1963 by the Dubuque (Iowa) Boat and Boiler Co. for Streckfuss Steamers Inc. of St. Louis. Originally named the *Mark Twain*, she operated out of New Orleans as a bayou excursion boat from 1963 to 1970. The *Mark Twain* was then brought to St. Louis and renamed *Huck Finn*. She remained in St. Louis until December 1995 when she was purchased by Jefferson County to operate as an excursion boat on the OHIO RIVER southwest of downtown Louisville.

A community-wide contest was held to rename the boat, and the *Huck Finn* became the *Spirit of Jefferson* in April 1996. The boat is 118 feet long and 30 feet wide and can carry up to 300 passengers. She is powered by two diesel engines and travels at a top speed of fifteen miles per hour. The boat boards passengers at the historic house and farm of Riverside, the Farnsley-Moreman Landing. The *Spirit of Jefferson* is operated, along with the historic steamer Belle of Louisville, by the *BELLE OF LOUISVILLE* operating board, a nonprofit joint city/county agency.

Kadie Engstrom

SPRADLING, WASHINGTON, SR. (b Jefferson County, March 1, 1805; d Louisville, May 13, 1868). Barber, real estate speculator, and legal adviser. He was the son of William Spradling, an overseer, and Maria Dennis, a slave on the Isaac Miller farm. William provided for the emancipation of Maria and their children in his will in 1814. After his emancipation in 1825, Spradling moved to Louisville and established a barbershop, serving mostly wealthy clients. He was a shrewd businessman and soon saved enough money to buy, sell, and lease real estate in Louisville. As Louisville grew, the value of his land appreciated. By building dwellings and subdividing his holdings, Spradling was responsible for establishing an African American presence in the RUSSELL neighborhood by the 1840s. His son Washington Spradling Jr. was responsible for founding the SMOKETOWN neighborhood after the CIVIL WAR on east end property inherited from his father.

By 1860 Spradling's real estate was valued at more than twenty-five thousand dollars, making him one of the wealthiest men in the city. Spradling also gave many African Americans helpful legal advice, and his wealth enabled him to purchase thirty-three slaves in order to give them their freedom. Spradling also was instrumental in founding at least two antebellum African American churches in the area (Centre St. and Jackson St. CME). He married Lucy Ann Jackson in 1828, and their children included William, Will, Washington, Julia, and Martha. Spradling is buried in Eastern Cemetery.

See John W. Blassingame, ed., *Slave Testimony* (Baton Rouge 1977); William H. Gibson Sr., *Sketches of the Colored Race in Louisville* (Louisville 1897).

Pen Bogert

SPRIGG, JAMES CRESAP (b Frostburg, Maryland, 1802; d Shelbyville, Kentucky, October 3, 1852). U.S. congressman. After completing his schooling in Maryland, Sprigg moved to SHELBYVILLE, Kentucky, to study law. After being admitted to the bar and practicing for a time, Sprigg served in several local offices and as a member of the state house of representatives from 1830 to 1834 and from 1837 to 1840. In 1840 he was elected to the Twenty-seventh Congress, where he served from March 4, 1841, to March 3, 1843. He was not reelected to the following session. In 1852 he returned to the state house of representatives and died in Shelbyville. He is buried in Grove Hill Cemetery.

See *Biographical Directory of the American Congress 1776–1961* (Washington, D.C., 1961).

SPRINGFIELDS. Springfields, also known later as Springfield, was the eastern Jefferson County (5608 Apache Rd.) boyhood home of ZACHARY TAYLOR, twelfth president of the United States. Col. RICHARD TAYLOR, his wife, and three children (including eight-month-old Zachary) came to the area from Orange County, Virginia, in 1785 and lived in a log cabin until the two-and-a-half-story Georgian-style brick home was completed in the late 1780s. A two-story brick wing was added to the house sometime between 1810 and 1820. The house, one of the county's earlier brick dwellings, was located on Taylor's four-hundred-acre tract, which eventually was increased to seven hundred acres.

The original part of Springfields has two rooms in the basement, two on the first floor with a wide hall, two rooms and a hall on the second floor, and a loft or attic. The woodwork is stained walnut and poplar. The later wing has the same room arrangement and has painted woodwork with corner blocks. Even in its original form, Springfields was considered a very substantial house by wilderness standards.

Zachary Taylor lived at Springfields until 1808, when he began his military career. He returned on numerous occasions and was buried on the property in 1850 in the family cemetery, now part of the ZACHARY TAYLOR NATIONAL CEMETERY.

Springfields passed out of the Taylor family in 1868 and has had a succession of owners. In the 1950s the property was subdivided, leaving only a small amount of land surrounding the house. On April 3, 1974, a tornado heavily damaged the structure. The home's owner at the time, HUGH HAYNIE, began repairs that evolved into an extensive restoration project, and today the house appears much as it did during the years of Taylor ownership. In 1981 Dr. William Gist and his wife, Elizabeth, purchased the home, becoming its seventeenth owners. It is one of the few presidential homes that remains a private residence, and it has been designated a National Historic Landmark.

See Holman Hamilton, *Zachary Taylor, Soldier of the Republic* (New York 1941).

Kenneth Dennis

SPRINGHOUSES. Part of the Louisville area is underlaid by limestone and dolomite, whose solution by ground water produced karst areas with sinks, caverns, and underground streams. In places the water flowed out of the ground, creating a spring. Springs were an essential source of fresh water for early settlers in the Louisville area, and their presence often constituted the site of settlements. Springhouses, simple stone structures of rectangular or square shape, were built over the natural springs.

All springhouses had a similar type of construction and layout. Stone walls were as much as two feet thick. Doors and windows had wooden frames in post-and-lintel construction. Roofs were made out of wooden shingles of cedar, poplar, or oak. The plan of a springhouse included two sections—one small and one large. The small front section had steps leading down to the source of the spring water. The large back section had a small opening that permitted spring water to flow from the small section into a trench. The trench, which ran the length of the section, usually was one foot wide and eight inches deep.

Springhouses had several purposes. They supplied fresh water for drinking and domestic purposes and also served to refrigerate food. Stone crocks filled with dairy products were stored in the trench. Shallow troughs were placed on one or both sides of the springhouse's trench, where fruits and meat were kept to stay fresh. The temperature of the spring water in the trench was cool enough to preserve perishable FOODS. Springhouses also were used as fortresses against Indian attacks, and they sometimes were called "fort-springhouses." Small windows allowed light to enter and also provided rifle openings. The Chenoweth springhouse is a reminder of the Indian massacre of 1789, when three Chenoweth children and two guards were killed. Mrs. Chenoweth, who was scalped by Indians, was able to survive the attack by finding a safe place in the springhouse. The solid stone walls of the springhouse also were good protection against fire and TORNADOES.

The several surviving springhouses in Jefferson County include those at Soldier's Retreat (1781) on Hurstbourne Pkwy., Chenoweth (1785) on Avoca Rd., Spring Station (ca. 1795) on Trinity Rd., John Herr (1790) on Waterford Rd., Locust Grove (1790) on Blankenbaker Ln., Farmington (ca. 1815) on Bardstown Rd., George Herr (1825) on Rudy Lane, Barnett (ca. 1838) on Hounz Ln., and May Estate (1910) on Owl Creek Ln.

See Christina L. Coke, "The Springhouse in the Louisville Area," unpublished paper, University of Louisville Records and Archives Center, 1978; P.P. Karan and Cotton Mather, *Atlas of Kentucky* (Lexington 1977), 19–24.

Janna Tajibaeva

SQUIRE BOONE'S STATION. Established in early 1780 on the north side of Clear Creek, about two and one-half miles north of present SHELBYVILLE, Kentucky, by SQUIRE BOONE, Daniel's younger brother. It also was known as "The Painted Stone Station" because in 1776, a year after locating it, Boone had picked his name and the date in a stone and painted the letters and figures in red. On November 22, 1779, Boone obtained a certificate from the Commonwealth of Virginia in the name of his brother-in-law Benjamin Van Cleve for the four-hundred-acre settlement tract on which the station was located. Subsequently it was surveyed for Squire Boone, as assignee of Van Cleve, and the patent was issued to Boone.

It was the first station situated near present Shelbyville and for nearly two years was the one station between Harrodsburg and Louisville. Indian threats forced its abandonment in September 1781, when the settlers fled toward Linn's Station, twenty-one miles to the west. They were attacked by Indians and dispersed halfway to their destination in an action that has become known as the Long Run Massacre, but earlier was called the Battle of Long Run.

In the fall of 1783 Squire Boone, with some six or eight families that had decided to resettle the station, found all the old buildings burned down, probably by Indians. In 1784–85 Boone rebuilt his station and subsequently built a grist and saw mill there. He sold his property in early 1786 to Benjamin Roberts, who sold it on January 27, 1787, to NICHOLAS MERIWETHER, early Kentucky land locator and entrepreneur. Meriwether took over operation of the mill, probably improved it, and established a residence that he called Castle Hill, undoubtedly after the renowned residence of Dr. Thomas Walker and his wife, Mildred (Thornton) Meriwether, in Albemarle County, Virginia.

See Willard Rouse Jillson, "Squire Boone," *Filson Club History Quarterly* 16 (July 1942): 141–71; Draper manuscripts, 19C 1–155: interviews with three of Squire Boone's sons; R.R.

Van Stockum, Kentucky and the Bourbons: The Story of Allen Dale Farm (Louisville 1991).

R.R. Van Stockum Sr.

STANDARD GRAVURE. The Standard Gravure Corp. Inc. was established in 1922 by Judge ROBERT WORTH BINGHAM, president and publisher of the *COURIER-JOURNAL* and *LOUISVILLE TIMES,* and David B.G. Rose, president and general manager of Standard Printing Co. It was first located at 220–28 S First St., and Rose served as the firm's first president. Over the next forty years the company saw changes in both its address and its leadership. By 1949 the printing plant was in the new Courier-Journal and Louisville Times building at Sixth and BROADWAY. BARRY BINGHAM Sr. was president and Edwin S. Keller was vice president and operating manager.

Standard Gravure printed the *Courier-Journal Magazine,* locally edited color magazine supplements for a host of NEWSPAPERS across the country, more than a million copies per week of the national Sunday supplement magazine *Parade*, and a variety of commercial catalogues. In the 1940s and 1950s the company was an integral part of a $20 million Louisville printing industry that employed twenty-two hundred people with an annual payroll in excess of $2 million. By 1958 plans were unveiled for a $3.5 million plant expansion. Melzar Lowe, president from 1960 to 1978, noted that at one point Standard Gravure actually brought in more revenue than its parent newspapers and, although the company would never confirm it, it was rumored that Standard Gravure profits helped carry the two newspapers and WHAS Inc. through some financially lean years.

But changing times and an uncanny karma for tragedy profoundly affected the firm's later history. In the 1980s the company faced a shrinking market for magazine printing as the print media came under competition from TELEVISION and computers. In the late 1970s, for example, it printed twenty-five gravure process Sunday newspaper magazines; by 1986 that number had shrunk to five. Competition from a less expensive new printing process called web offset and an expensive workforce cut deeply into profits. In 1982 employees agreed to a wage freeze that was to extend through 1988.

On January 9, 1986, Bingham, in response to family disagreements, announced that all the Bingham communications interests would be sold. When an attempt by the Standard Gravure employees to buy the company failed, Bingham sold it to Michael D. Shea of Atlanta for a sum in excess of $20 million. At the time of the sale, July 30, 1986, the company had 531 employees working in two plants—one downtown on Sixth St., the other in the Jefferson County Riverport industrial park.

The final five years of Standard Gravure history is a tale of tragedy. On November 11, 1988, a chemical explosion and two flash fires ripped through the downtown plant, injuring twenty-one people, eighteen of them firemen. This reduced the workforce to three hundred hourly employees. On November 5, 1990, a second fire—this one arson—caused hundreds of thousands of dollars' damage to executive offices, records, and computers.

Between the dates of the two fires lay a nightmare of pain, confusion, and destruction. On September 14, 1989, Joseph T. Wesbecker, a pressman employed by the company for seventeen years but with a history of mental illness and on disability leave, returned unannounced to his place of employment.

At 8:30 a.m., as the shifts were changing, he methodically stalked the plant with an AK-47 semiautomatic assault rifle. When he had finished firing about forty rounds of ammunition in approximately thirty minutes, nine people lay dead, including Wesbecker himself by suicide. Twelve were wounded, many severely, and an entire city and county were emotionally scarred.

Lawsuits were filed, were eventually consolidated, and finally culminated in a closed secret settlement between Eli Lilly & Co., the manufacturer of Prozac, a medication Wesbecker was taking, and plaintiffs who claimed the antidepressant had triggered Wesbecker's shooting spree. The terms of the settlement, reached just before a jury returned a verdict absolving Lilly of responsibility, were sealed by mutual agreement of the parties concerned. Despite periodic attempts to examine this agreement, it remained secret.

Standard Gravure closed its doors in February 1992, putting 240 people out of work. In October 1992 the building was demolished and the site became a parking lot.

See *Courier-Journal*, Sept. 15, 1989, Sept. 16, 1989, Oct. 29, 1989, Dec. 31, 1989, Sept. 24, 1994; *Louisville* 41 (Jan. 1, 1990).

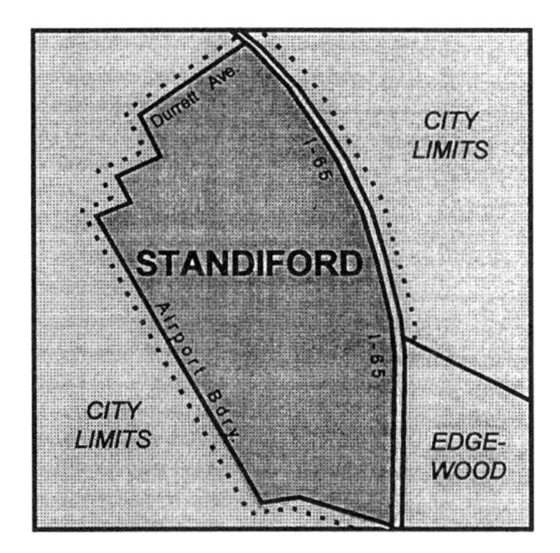

STANDIFORD. Neighborhood in southern Louisville bounded by Interstate 65 to the east and the LOUISVILLE INTERNATIONAL AIRPORT (formerly Standiford Field) boundary to the north, west, and south. Developed on former farm land that was part of the area known as WET WOODS once owned by E.D. Standiford, this community was initially developed in 1946 by George Stettos. As the neighboring airport continued to grow, this residential community increasingly lost land. The remaining residents joined with other communities to fight the proposed expansion of the airport in the late 1980s and early 1990s because of concern over increased noise pollution. After expansion plans were approved, the residents of the community were relocated to other areas, and Standiford ceased to be recognized as a neighborhood.

STANDIFORD, ELISHA D. (b Jefferson County, Kentucky, December 28, 1831; d Louisville, July 26, 1887). Businessman. The man for whom Standiford Field (renamed LOUISVILLE INTERNATIONAL AIRPORT) was named had nothing to do with aviation. He was, however, involved in transportation as president of the LOUISVILLE & NASHVILLE RAILROAD. He was born at the family farm on or near the site that was to become Standiford Field. His parents were Elisha and Nancy (Brooks) Standiford. After graduation from St. Mary's College near Lebanon, Kentucky, he studied at the Kentucky School of Medicine in Louisville and entered practice in the 1850s. This profession did not appeal to him, and he turned to planting, politics, and business.

His farming was on a large scale, mostly on the future airport site. He also was involved in manufacturing, as president of the Louisville Car Wheel Co., producing iron railroad wheels, and of the Red River Iron Works. He became president of the Farmer's and Drover's Bank, Louisville's largest savings bank, in 1870. He entered politics and was elected to the Kentucky senate in 1868 and 1871. In 1872 he was elected to Congress as a representative from the Louisville district but declined renomination in 1874. Though he was a Democrat, the Republican Louisville Commercial (Aug. 14, 1874), commenting on his decision, spoke generally favorably of his term but noted that "it is not too much to say that for some years past the Democratic organization of this city and county has been completely under his control." A major reason for his decision not to run again (he would have been easily reelected) was that he had been named vice president of the L&N in 1873, after several years as a director. In 1875 he became president shortly after the death of Horatio D. Newcomb.

Standiford continued Newcomb's expansionist plans despite the depressed economic conditions that followed the panic of 1873. At the end of his four years in the presidency, the L&N had expanded from 920 miles to 1,150, and the groundwork was in place for the further growth that would extend it from Cincinnati to New Orleans. He also initiated the erection of a large new headquarters building at Second and Main in 1877 to a design by Louisville architect HENRY WHITESTONE. Standiford died at his home on Fourth St. and is buried in CAVE HILL CEMETERY.

See J. Stoddard Johnston, ed., *Memorial*

History of Louisville, vol. 1 (Chicago 1896); Maury Klein, *History of the Louisville & Nashville Railroad* (New York 1977).

George H. Yater

STANLEY, FRANK LESLIE, SR. (b Chicago, Illinois, April 6, 1906; d Louisville, October 19, 1974). Newspaper publisher, political activist, and CIVIL RIGHTS advocate. Stanley's father, Frank Leslie Stanley, was a railroad steward from Moline, Illinois; and his mother, Helen (Cole) Stanley, was a domestic worker from Nashville, Tennessee. In 1912 he moved with his mother to Louisville, where he graduated from Central High School in 1925. He attended Atlanta University, graduated in 1929 with a degree in English and journalism, and afterward taught English at Jackson State College in Jackson, Mississippi. From 1931 to 1933, he taught English and coached FOOTBALL at Central High School in Louisville. In 1933 he joined the staff of the *LOUISVILLE DEFENDER* as a reporter.

In 1936, he married Ione Garrett, a Louisville businesswoman. They had two sons: Frank Jr., who became a noted civil rights activist, and Kenneth, a musician who graduated from the Berklee School (later College) of Music and Boston Conservatory of Music. Also in 1936, he became the editor-general manager of the *Louisville Defender,* founded three years earlier as part of the *Defender* newspaper chain headquartered in Chicago. He sold ads, wrote and edited the news, pasted galleys, and in rapid succession became a board member in 1938, secretary in 1940, secretary/treasurer in 1943, and finally chairman and largest stockholder in 1949, buying out its previous owners.

Under Stanley the *Defender* became Kentucky's top black newspaper, outselling the *LOUISVILLE LEADER,* which stopped publishing in 1950.

He was a crusading editor whose advocacy for racial justice in jobs, schools, housing, public accommodations, and for integrated military units during WORLD WAR II predated the postwar civil rights movement. He was a founder, in 1940, of the National Newspaper Publishers Association, the trade group of America's two hundred black-owned newspapers. In 1946 and 1948 he led delegations appointed by the U.S. State Department to study racial SEGREGATION of American troops in occupied Europe and wrote a report that paved the way for integration of the armed forces.

In Kentucky, with the support of Gov. Earle Clements, Stanley in 1950 wrote Senate Resolution No. 53 that integrated state colleges. In 1960, with support of Gov. BERT COMBS, he drafted the organizational structure of the Kentucky Commission on Human Rights and later served as its vice president. In 1955, as national president of Alpha Phi Alpha, his college fraternity, Stanley won financial support for the Montgomery, Alabama, bus boycott led by fraternity brother Martin Luther King Jr., and he hand-delivered the check.

Stanley divorced in 1960 and in 1961 married Vivian Clarke, a Memphis social scientist educated at Smith College.

He continued to build the circulation and influence of the *Defender*, enhancing his stature as a trusted adviser to civic and GOVERNMENT leaders on the local, state, and national level.

He suffered a heart attack and died at the *Defender*-sponsored Black Expo held at Louisville Gardens. During his life Stanley received numerous honors and awards, including an honorary doctorate of laws from the University of Kentucky. He was posthumously named to the Kentucky Journalism Hall of Fame in 1983, one of the first AFRICAN AMERICANS so honored.

See *Courier-Journal Magazine*, Feb. 6, 1966; *Courier-Journal*, Feb. 23, 1992; *Louisville Defender,* March 24, 1983; *Kentucky's Black Heritage* (Frankfort 1971).

Lawrence Muhammad

STANSBURY, WILLIAM BROWN (b Corydon, Indiana, March 18, 1923; d Louisville, April 4, 1985). Mayor. He was the son of James Bernard and Alliene (Brown) Stansbury. Although born in Indiana, Stansbury grew up in Louisville and attended ST. XAVIER HIGH SCHOOL, graduating as the class salutatorian in 1941. He received a bachelor of arts degree in economics in 1947 and a law degree in 1950, both from the UNIVERSITY OF LOUISVILLE.

Stansbury served in the U.S. Army Air Corps during WORLD WAR II, rising to the rank of captain. He flew fifteen combat missions over Europe and was decorated with the Air Medal with cluster. Stansbury returned to Louisville after the war and started practicing law in 1952. He joined the firm of Mapother, Morgan, & Stansbury, where he worked until 1969.

Stansbury was chosen by the DEMOCRATIC PARTY to run against incumbent Jefferson County judge MARLOW COOK in 1965. He lost by fifty thousand votes. In 1968, Stansbury became chairman of the Jefferson County Democratic Party executive committee, remaining in the post for eight years. He was elected to the BOARD OF ALDERMEN in 1973 and served until 1977. He was president of the board in 1974. Stansbury was mayor of Louisville from 1977 through 1981. He ran against Alderman Creighton Mershon in the Democratic Party primary and defeated him by more than three thousand votes. It was seen as a victory for the more traditional elements of the party. Stansbury easily defeated then Republican Russ Maple in the general election.

Stansbury's administration was embroiled in controversy. When Louisville firefighters went on strike in July 1978, Stansbury claimed he was out of town on business in Atlanta. The *COURIER-JOURNAL* later discovered that Stansbury had been in New Orleans with his administrative assistant, Mary Ellen Farmer, and another couple. The incident prompted the Board of Aldermen to start impeachment proceedings. Months later Stansbury was involved in another controversy concerning campaign fund-raising. Cecil "Randy" Pezzarossi, a city official, pleaded guilty to extorting sixteen thousand dollars from local businessmen. Federal investigators claimed that some of the money had been contributed to Stansbury's mayoral campaign and to Stansbury personally.

Stansbury, called to testify before a federal grand jury, cited the Fifth Amendment against self-incrimination when questioned about the money. He was not charged in the incident, but it only added to the aldermen's quest to impeach him. Many of Stansbury's political foes and supporters, alike, urged him to step down as mayor. The county Democratic Party executive committee, which he had headed, voted to ask him to quit. The aldermen discontinued their impeachment campaign after the state court of appeals denied them the power to subpoena witnesses. Although Stansbury remained in office until the end of his term, he withdrew from public view after the controversies. He granted few interviews, limited his public speaking engagements, and deferred most questions about policy to his aides.

Most of the major accomplishments during Stansbury's tenure as mayor centered on DOWNTOWN DEVELOPMENT. The Louisville GALLERIA, the Broadway Renaissance, the Seelbach Hotel renovation, and the Kentucky Center for the Arts took off during his administration. He also was instrumental in getting a minor-league BASEBALL team, the Louisville Redbirds, to come to Louisville. The team, affiliated with the St. Louis Cardinals, began play in 1982.

Stansbury was a member of the Jefferson County Probate Commission and a probate judge pro tem from 1968 until 1976. He then became a senior partner in the law firm of Wood, Goldberg, Pedley, and Stansbury, where he worked from 1969 to 1977. After leaving the mayor's office, Stansbury returned to private practice in the firm of Mobley, Zoeller, and Celebreeze, where he stayed until his death. He worked as a lobbyist during the 1982 session of the Kentucky General Assembly. He was a member of the American Bar Association and the Kentucky Bar Association. In 1974 he served as president of the Louisville Bar Association.

Stansbury's first marriage ended in divorce in 1980. He married Mary Ellen Farmer in 1983. He had one daughter, Patricia Ann Beckman.

Stansbury was killed in 1985 by a motorist while crossing Bardstown Rd. on his way to church with his wife and mother. Both Stansbury and his mother died at Humana Hospital–University a short time after the accident. Stansbury and his wife were escorting his mother from her home at St. Francis Apartments to the St. Francis of Assisi Catholic Church, 1960 Bardstown Rd. He is buried in Calvary Cemetery.

In 1985, Triangle Park, a seven-acre park

designed by the Frederick Law OLMSTED FIRM in 1900 and located across Third St. from the entrance to the UNIVERSITY OF LOUISVILLE, was renamed Stansbury Park by the Board of Aldermen.

See *Who Was Who in America with World Notables*, vol. 8 (Chicago 1985); *Courier-Journal*, Jan. 2, 1982, April 4, 1985.

STARKS BUILDING. Completed in 1913, this LANDMARK BUILDING is on the northeast corner of Fourth and Muhammad Ali Blvd., on the site of the former FIRST CHRISTIAN CHURCH. It was commissioned by businessman John P. Starks and designed by the prominent Chicago architectural firm of D.H. Burnham and Co., along with the local firm of McDonald and Dodd as associate architects. An example of turn-of-the-century commercial ARCHITECTURE, the fifteen-story office building of cream-colored brick and terra cotta trim reflected the Chicago School tradition with Beaux Arts details. It was adorned with such classical motifs as Greek acanthus leaves, urns, and lions' heads atop medallions. It was originally built in a "U" shape, but a 1926 addition, designed by the Chicago firm of Graham, Anderson, Probst, and White, expanded the north and south wings, enlarged the structure eastward, and enclosed the back side, making it a four-sided building with a central light well.

Over the years, the Starks Building was remodeled several times. A notable addition came in 1953 when a self-park garage, Louisville's first, was opened on an adjacent lot fronting Third St. to accommodate the building's tenants and customers. The interior courtyard was covered by an aluminum and Plexiglas skylight about 1984. In the mid-1980s, the Starks family sold the building and garage to Group Financial Partners Inc., which in turn sold it to out-of-state interests in 1997. The building is home to a mixture of retail and professional interests, including two of its oldest tenants, the COLONNADE CAFETERIA and RODES Men's & Women's Clothing. It is listed on the NATIONAL REGISTER OF HISTORIC PLACES.

See *Courier-Journal*, Nov. 11, 1984, Aug. 17, 1992.

Louisville waterfront with 14th Street Bridge in view, c. 1880. Photo by Joseph Krementz.

STEAMBOATS. Its strategic location on the OHIO RIVER meant that Louisville has always been interested in riverboats. The earliest riverboats at Louisville were canoes and dugouts suitable for carrying Native Americans, a few explorers, or fighting men and their belongings. They were soon augmented by flatboats, crude scows built by settlers to transport their families and belongings to the new lands in the West, at that time the land between the Appalachian Mountains and the Mississippi River. Flatboats were built along every creek and riverbank in western Pennsylvania and Virginia. They ranged from insignificant barges barely more than a foot deep, twenty or so feet long and about ten feet wide, to heavily built hulls three or four feet deep, a hundred feet long, and fifteen to twenty feet wide, with boxy wooden cabins to shelter settlers and their animals. They were frequently dismantled and used for building materials at their destinations.

As the settlers began to produce cash crops, they built flatboats to carry their products to inland markets and to New Orleans for overseas shipment. They floated with the current and were controlled by heavy oars up to forty feet long, called sweeps, located at the forward corners and in the middle of the stern. Because of their boxy shape, they could be propelled or dragged upstream for only very short distances. Their cheapness and shallow draft enabled them to carry freight on most creeks worthy of the name. The produce was loaded while the creeks were more or less dry; then when a freshet occurred they were floated to the nearest river. The Beargrass and HARRODS CREEKS of Jefferson County were used in this way in the very early days. Flatboats were often called "broadhorn boats" because those long oars resembled the horns of cattle. Compared to the work of clearing forests, clearing stumps, and raising log buildings, life was easy on flatboats, lazing along, occasionally rowing across the bends to get in the best currents.

The next development was the keelboat, a finely modeled hull with a keel, substantially built and capable of being pushed or pulled upstream against the current. These were the boats crewed by the renowned "half-horse, half-alligator" men of the ilk of MIKE FINK, who either placed poles to the bottom of the river and walked the length of the deck to push upstream, or went ashore to drag the boats with long rope lines. Cordelling was the process of towing a boat by means of a heavy rope called a cordelle. Bushwhacking was done by grasping limbs that overhung the river and pulling the keelboat along. The work was terribly difficult and only the toughest and strongest men could survive the hardships of dragging a keelboat the fourteen hundred miles from New Orleans to Louisville. Such a voyage could take ninety days or more. Only valuable cargoes could travel in such an expensive way. They included manufactured cloth, buttons, china, wines, coffee and tea, and other products not available in the interior.

Steam navigation arrived on the western rivers in 1811 when Robert Fulton and Livingston's *New Orleans* passed down from Pittsburgh to New Orleans. The boat arrived at Louisville on October 28 and was obliged to wait for enough water depth to pass over the FALLS OF THE OHIO. The next day Nicholas T. Roosevelt, her manager-captain, gave a banquet for Louisville's citizens, who felt the boat could not stem the Ohio's current upstream. They were confounded when the boat made the very first steamboat excursion upriver to Six Mile Island. The boat returned to Cincinnati on November 27, a forty-five-hour trip from Louisville, to run a week of public excursions there.

Three years later the *Enterprise* (Henry Miller Shreve, captain-owner), proved she was powerful enough to climb the four hundred feet from New Orleans to Louisville. She made the trip in a little more than twenty-five days and sounded the death knell of the colorful keelboat.

By 1820 steam packets were making regular trips upstream, but the lowly flatboats continued to compete for downstream movements until the late 1890s. Heavy, imperishable cargoes such as coal, lumber, pig iron, masonry materials, and glassware were delivered in this manner. Flatboats also served as floating photographers' and artists' studios. Many were used by hucksters who sold china and tinware at each landing as they floated down the rivers. Occasionally the flatboats were towed back up the river by steamers. By 1840, steamboats assumed their final form and became the floating palaces so fondly remembered in American lore. They were palaces only when compared with the dwellings and hostelries ashore. They carried huge loads of freight in quantities measured by the bale and the barrel and the packing crate, which were carried aboard on the backs of roustabouts—immigrants only a step above slavery. The fact was that slaves were too valuable to waste in such backbreaking and dangerous work. Black roustabouts replaced immigrants only after emancipation. Trips were slow, punctuated by landings every few miles, where freight was loaded by manual labor.

Those romantic old packets with their elaborate decoration were businesses, run to make money, and the jolly captain and the tap-dancing roustabouts are myths expounded by romantic writers and playwrights. Packets ranged from the mighty *J.M. White* and the racer *Rob't E. Lee,* handsome vessels more than three hundred feet long, to minuscule tubs designed to run on tributaries such as Salt River, where there was a scant foot of water available. One could take packet trips from Louisville to such far-flung places as Terre Haute, Indiana; Pittsburgh; St. Paul; New Orleans; and Fort Benton, Montana. The latter voyage went farther and took longer than a trans-Atlantic crossing. It was also possible to travel by steamboat to Frankfort, Beattyville, and SHEPHERDSVILLE, Kentucky, on the mosquito fleet, so-called because the little boats could float on almost no water at all.

For many years the Ohio River was an almost impenetrable barrier between Louisville and Southern Indiana. Ferry service of a sort between Louisville and Jeffersonville and between PORTLAND and NEW ALBANY commenced with canoes and skiffs soon after the towns were established. The hazardous Falls, which commenced near the north end of the present Clark Memorial Bridge, forced a long upstream pull of a mile before the crossing to Jeffersonville could be safely effected. The skiffs and canoes were soon replaced by horse-powered pulley systems that towed the FERRIES across the river. The earliest known steam ferry service began circa 1827 and ended with the final trip of the Froman Coots on December 31, 1929, forced out of business by the new Second Street (GEORGE ROGERS CLARK) Bridge.

The best and finest boats on the main streams, the Ohio and the Mississippi, were rightly called floating palaces. They were gaudily and elaborately decorated and offered fabulous menus. They ranged from 250 to 325 feet in length and were rated at 2,000 or more admeasured tons. They were fast; many of them could exceed twenty miles per hour in still water. At the opposite end of the scale, the mosquito fleet was plain to the point of pain. Mosquito fleet accommodations ranked from a seat on a bench to vermin-ridden beds that often had to be shared with strangers.

Even for the first-class cabin passengers, life aboard the packets was harsh compared to today's travel. Staterooms were stiflingly hot during summer and bitterly cold in the winter. Those fabulous menus were kinder in print than to the palate. It was said that a good steamboat cook needed only a can of lard and five pounds of sugar to create any dish on the elaborate and fanciful menus. Even the fast boats were dreadfully slow, for they accepted freight at landings only a few miles apart. Each landing represented a delay of a few minutes to many hours, and they significantly added to the length of a trip. Fueling and accidental grounding created long delays as well. Deck passengers were roughly treated. Even in the later days of the nineteenth century, they got cheap transportation and a wooden cot devoid of springs, mattress, or bedding. Some deck passengers paid part of their fare by working as roustabouts.

Steamer *East St. Louis* loading at the Louisville Wharf for a trip to Madison, Indiana, 1920.

Louisvillians not only rode the packets and depended upon them for the amenities of life, but their very livings were based on them. Louisville, owing to the Falls, was the jumping-off place for settlers heading into western Kentucky, Tennessee, and southern Illinois and Indiana. Louisville was the last place where supplies and equipment could be procured. The Falls forced portages during all but a few weeks each year, which made transferring freight and passengers between Louisville and Portland a big business. As Louisville became an important distribution center for the West, vast warehouses were built just above the flood plain along the waterfront in Portland and Louisville. Louisville was known as a city dependent almost solely on merchandising. Manufacturing was a distinctly minor part of its ECONOMY. Louisville's merchants became the civic leaders of the city.

The manufacturing that did develop was primarily devoted to the building, repairing, and equipping of steamboats. The factories were located in a narrow band along the riverbank between Sixth and Twelfth Streets, mostly north of Main. Foundries, machine shops, boiler plants, and planing mills providing the building materials for steamboats were dominant, but finished lumber and stoves were also used for general building purposes.

Two developments of the 1840s foretold the demise of the packets. The first of these was the construction of RAILROADS, which by 1860 were short-hauling the boats over an ever-expanding network of rails. The second began in 1845 when the steamer Walter Forward began towing coal barges downriver from Pittsburgh. By 1860 this new freight system was delivering cargoes of coal, pig iron, grain, and other bulk products that were beyond the abilities and capacities of the packets. Freight was no longer handled by men with wheelbarrows, or no longer "back-and-bellied." Cranes and crude conveyors loaded and emptied the barges. By 1900 the towboats and barges were dominant.

The riverbank above First St. became the terminal for bulk cargoes. Vast piles of sand, gravel, and coal filled the space between River Rd. and the shore below Towhead Island. The Louisville, Cincinnati, and Lexington Railroad (later Louisville & Nashville) had terminal yards on the south side of River Rd., where heavy materials were transshipped to the east and south.

The towboats handled enormous tonnage. In 1904 the steamer *Sprague* moved 57,307 tons of coal from Louisville to Mississippi River ports in a sixty-barge tow. Others did nearly as much. Louisville was an important point in the coal-towing trade owing to the obstructive Falls. Coal boats and barges were tied off on the shores for miles above town, on both the Kentucky and Indiana sides, then moved through the locks in groups of two to four. They were then gathered at New Albany and West Louisville to continue their journeys.

Louisville was both an observer and an agent in all these riverboat affairs. Boatyards were established here long before the first steamboat arrived, and one continues in business today. The biggest, in steamboat days, was the HOWARD SHIPYARD AND DOCK CO., which had yards in SHIPPINGPORT, on THE POINT in Louisville, and in JEFFERSONVILLE, INDIANA. Its successor, JEFFBOAT, continues to build and repair boats and barges. Boat-building was the base of Louisville's first heavy industries, for machinery, boilers, and lumber were all manufactured here. Thousands of workmen were involved in these enterprises, both in and out of the boatyards themselves.

Louisville had as many as twenty-four hundred arrivals and departures of packet boats annually, not counting the ferries that shuttled between Louisville and Indiana. Those boats received and landed passengers, loaded and discharged freight, bought supplies and equipment, and underwent repairs in Louisville to provide employment to several thousand citizens. Draymen transferred freight between Louisville and Portland and also made deliveries to Louisville stores, factories, and HOTELS. The development of steam packets and towboats brought into being a host of other steamboat types. Dredges deepened the channels and excavated sand and gravel for building purposes. Snagboats removed trees, wrecks, and other obstructions from the riverbed. Gunboats fought pitched battles during the CIVIL WAR. Wounded soldiers were treated and transported in hospital boats. SHOWBOATS, THEATERS built on barges, entertained the riparian public. Excursion boats took patrons to AMUSEMENT PARKS or simply for boat rides. Light tenders maintained the navigation beacons. Wharfboats stored and transferred freight between shore and boat.

Dr. Rudolph Diesel changed all this. Diesel invented the internal combustion engine that was patented in 1892. By 1915 gasoline-, diesel-, and distillate-powered towboats began to displace the steamers. The change was complete by 1962. In the 1990s a new Louisville wharf was built to accommodate the river tourists who travel on the Delta Queen Steamboat Co.'s *Delta Queen, Mississippi Queen*, and *American Queen* and the excursionists who ride the *BELLE OF LOUISVILLE*, the *SPIRIT OF JEFFERSON*, and the *Star of Louisville*.

See Leland R. Johnson, *Falls City Engineers* (Louisville 1974); Charles Preston Fishbaugh, *From Paddle Wheels to Propellers* (Indianapolis 1970); Maury Klein, *History of the Louisville and Nashville Railroad* (New York 1972); Kincaid Herr, *Louisville and Nashville Railroad, 1850–1942* (Louisville 1942); *Louisville City Directory, 1867–68*; Leland T. Johnson, *The Ohio River Division* (Cincinnati 1991); Louis C. Hunter, *Steamboats on the Western Rivers* (Cambridge, Mass., 1969); George Yater, *Two Hundred Years at the Falls of the Ohio* (Louisville 1987).

Alan L. Bates

STEWARD, WILLIAM HENRY (b Brandenburg, Kentucky, July 6, 1847; d Louisville, January 3, 1935). CIVIL RIGHTS leader. Steward, a longtime leader of Louisville's African American community, was brought to the city as a child and, although enslaved, was allowed to attend the school operated by Rev. HENRY ADAMS at the First African (now Fifth St.) Baptist Church. As an adult, Steward worked briefly as a teacher in Frankfort and Louisville and as a messenger for the LOUISVILLE & NASHVILLE RAILROAD. In 1876 he became Louisville's first African American postman, which made him an influential liaison between local whites and AFRICAN AMERICANS.

Notwithstanding his moderate political views and his network of relations with local whites, he was a leader in the struggle against racial SEGREGATION. Steward co-founded the AMERICAN BAPTIST newspaper in 1879 and served as its editor for more than fifty years. He was president of the Afro-American Press Association and was active in national REPUBLICAN PARTY politics in the 1890s. In the early 1900s, Steward was among the founders of the Louisville chapter of the National Association for the Advancement of Colored People; served on the Colored Board of Visitors, which advised the BOARD OF EDUCATION; and was chairman of the Board of Trustees of SIMMONS UNIVERSITY. Steward is buried in Eastern Cemetery.

See Alice A. Dunnigan, *The Fascinating Story of Black Kentuckians: Their Heritage and Traditions* (Washington, D.C., 1982); W.J. Simmons, *Men of Mark: Eminent, Progressive and Rising* (New York 1968); George C. Wright, *Life Behind a Veil* (Baton Rouge 1985).

J. Blaine Hudson

STEWART'S DRY GOODS COMPANY. Stewart's appeared initially on MARKET ST. in 1846 under the name Durkee and Heath's New York Store. In 1853 the establishment moved to its first Fourth St. location on the corner of Jefferson St., and, in April, 1907, it occupied its signature building at Fourth and Walnut (Muhammad Ali Blvd.) Sts. Though the business was known until the 1920s as the New York Store, its official name derived from Louis Stewart. It was this Louisvillian who engineered the concern's prominence in the area's commercial retail trade.

Stewart, who began his career as a freight agent for the Louisville & Nashville Railroad, served as the store's president from 1893 to 1900. As a result of his considerable skills, Stewart moved on to head the James McCreery Store in New York City and directed it and his Louisville namesake into the buying group known as Associated Dry Goods. Stewart's remained with Associated until the mid-1980s when Associated was absorbed by the May Co.

Stewart's Dry Goods Co. display window in 1925.

of St. Louis.

At its peak, Stewart's maintained stores in Lexington and Evansville, plus four Louisville-area suburban locations. It dominated Louisville's retail trade from its appearance at 501 S Fourth in 1907 until its absorption by L.S. Ayres in 1985. Indeed, its location defined for many Louisvillians the center city spot known as downtown. With its array of shopping conveniences and promotions ranging from designer windows, Christmas parades, and spring sales to its upscale dining facilities and fashion shows, Stewart's served as both a community and regional role model by which other concerns were measured. The Stewart's Building is listed on the NATIONAL REGISTER OF HISTORIC PLACES. As a result it will continue to serve as the urban anchor for a time period in Louisville's history when going shopping meant far more than a car ride and a parking space. The building is currently being used by Hilliard Lyons Center, Atria Communities, BUSINESS FIRST, NCB, Farm Credit Services, and Trammell Crow Co. (real estate).

See Kenneth L. Miller, *Stewart's: A Louisville Landmark* (Louisville 1991).

Kenneth L. Miller

STIGLITZ CORPORATION. The Stiglitz Corp. is the oldest company in Louisville, tracing its history to 1829. In that year, James Bridgeford founded Bridgeford and Co., a foundry located beside the OHIO RIVER. The company made Ben Franklin stoves. Stiglitz Furnace & Foundry Co. was founded in 1882 by C.G. Stiglitz, forging iron gates and storm drains. In 1932 Stiglitz acquired the Bridgeford foundry. Stiglitz Corp. has been known by its current name since 1945. The family foundry closed in 1948, but the company still made sheet metal parts for its own product line. The company made clothes dryers until 1963 and space heaters, ranges, and ovens until early 1967. Beginning that year, Stiglitz began making sheet metal parts for other manufacturers in the appliance and air conditioning business. Also in November of that year, Stiglitz moved from Twentieth St. and PORTLAND to its current location at 1747 Mellwood Ave. in the BUTCHERTOWN neighborhood. It moved into a forty-four-thousand-square-foot building and has added another forty thousand square feet since then. Today, Stiglitz is a job shop, stamping parts, PAINTING, and providing light assembly. Doug Stiglitz, the company's president and owner, is the fifth-generation president.

Eric Benmour

STIREWALT, JOHN (b Cabarrus County, North Carolina, May 17, 1811; d Louisville, November 20, 1871). Architect. A son of Jacob and Jane (Johnston) Stirewalt, he studied at the University of North Carolina (1828–29) and apprenticed with architects Town and Davis in New York City from 1831 to 1834. He came to Louisville about 1836 with Ithiel Town to work on a bridge spanning the OHIO RIVER. The bridge was not built, but Stirewalt received commissions to design two churches and worked the remainder of his life in Louisville. His important known works include two of the city's earliest Gothic Revival buildings—the FIRST PRESBYTERIAN CHURCH on Green (LIBERTY) St. at Sixth St. (1837–39, razed 1880s); and ST. PAUL'S EPISCOPAL CHURCH on Sixth St. north of Walnut St. (Muhammad Ali Blvd.) (1837–39, razed 1940s); enlarging CHRIST CHURCH CATHEDRAL on Second St. (1840s); Louisville Theatre at Fourth and Green (Liberty) Streets (1842–46, burned 1866); UNIVERSITY OF LOUISVILLE academic building on Chestnut St. at Ninth St. (1846–49, razed 1960s); Egyptian-style receiving vault in Cave Hill Cemetery (1853); College Street Presbyterian Church (1866–67, demolished 1994). Stirewalt, who never married, is buried in CAVE HILL CEMETERY.

See *Louisville Daily Journal*, May 3, 1837, July 20, 1839, Oct. 5, 1839, June 1, 1867; James Craik, *Historical Sketches of Christ Church* (Louisville 1862); Reuben T. Durrett, *Historical Sketch of St. Paul's Church,* Filson Club Publication No. 5 (Louisville 1889).

Mary Jean Kinsman

STITZEL BROTHERS DISTILLERY. In 1872 Philip and Fredrick Stitzel built a distillery in Louisville at W BROADWAY and Twenty-sixth St. The distillery's major brand was "Glencoe." The company of Hollenbach and Vetter purchased the distillery and Glencoe brand in 1877. Frederick Stitzel was an inventor who patented the system of barrel racks first used in warehouses in 1879. Before this barrels were simply stacked atop one another. The "Patent Warehouse" permitted whiskey barrels to be stored with greater air circulation, preventing musty whiskey. A fire destroyed the distillery in 1883, but it was quickly rebuilt at the same site. The Stitzel family continued to operate this distillery for the Glencoe Co. until PROHIBITION closed the distillery.

Michael R. Veach

STITZEL-WELLER DISTILLERY. The Stitzel-Weller Distillery was built at the end of PROHIBITION by JULIAN P. VAN WINKLE, Alex T. Farnsley , and Arthur Philip Stitzel. The distillery opened on Derby Day 1935 with Will McGill as its first master distiller. The owners of this new distillery believed that distilling is an art, not a science. They placed a sign in front of the distillery reading "No Chemist Allowed." The distillery started with two warehouses, each holding 12,600 barrels of whiskey. As the distillery grew, more warehouses were built; there now are eighteen with a capacity of more than three hundred thousand barrels.

The Stitzel-Weller Distillery was the first step to the formal merger of W.L. Weller and Sons with the A. Ph. Stitzel Distillery Co. in 1936. The two had been associated nearly since the opening of the A. Ph. Stitzel Distillery in 1903 at 1033 Story Ave. They had survived Prohibition by selling "medicinal whiskey." In addition, Congress enacted a law creating "consolidation warehouses" where the alcoholic spirits could be stored under government supervision. Distillery president Stitzel was so successful at getting others to store their whiskey in his warehouses that the government issued him a "temporary" consolidation warehouse permit that did not expire during Prohibition. The company's main brand was Old Fitzgerald, and the distillery quickly became popularly known as the Old Fitzgerald Distillery. That brand had been first distilled by John E. Fitzgerald at his distillery in Frankfort, Kentucky. It was made especially for the transportation trade such as railroad diner cars and steamship lines. S.C. Herbst of Milwaukee acquired the distillery and brand in 1901 and sold it worldwide. It was the last pre-Prohibition brand to be made the old-fashioned way in pot stills. During Prohibition it was sold to W.L. Weller and Sons.

Farnsley died in 1941, and Stitzel died in 1947, but Julian Van Winkle lived until 1965. Farnsley had very early joined with Van Winkle to gain controlling interest in the Weller Distillery. The latter, who became known as "Pappy" Van Winkle, was a highly respected member of the liquor industry, and is considered by many to be the last of the "Bourbon Barons." The Van Winkle family continued to operate Stitzel-Weller until it was sold to Norton-Simon in 1972.

Norton-Simon changed the name to the Old Fitzgerald Distillery and made it part of Somerset Imports. In 1984 Somerset Imports was acquired by Distillers Corp. Ltd (D.C.L.). In 1986 D.C.L. was acquired by Guinness P.L.C., which changed the name to United Distillers. The Old Fitzgerald Distillery became part of UNITED DISTILLERS MANUFACTURING Inc., which changed the name of the old Fitzgerald Distillery back to the Stitzel-Weller Distillery in 1993.

Michael R. Veach

STIVERS, ORVILLE JACKSON (b Jefferson County, Kentucky, August 30, 1881; d Louisville, October 8, 1968). Educator and administrator. Orville Jackson Stivers was the son of Leonidas Jackson Stivers, superintendent of the common schools of Jefferson County (1884–94), and Mattie Jackson Stivers, a teacher. Stivers attended school in Jefferson County with his mother as teacher, then went to the University of Kentucky, JEFFERSON SCHOOL OF LAW, and Western Kentucky State College (now Western Kentucky University). He taught in Bullitt and Jefferson Counties and served as superintendent of the Jefferson County PUBLIC SCHOOLS from 1910 until 1950. In 1919 he was elected president of the KENTUCKY EDUCATION ASSOCIATION and in 1952 an elementary school in Jefferson County was named in his honor. Stivers was married to Dorothy Skiles on December 24, 1914; they had a daughter,

Dorothy (Mrs. Hugh B. Standiford). Stivers is buried in Resthaven Memorial Gardens.

Shirley Botkins

STOCKDALE FARM. Stockdale is a Federal-style house located north of SHELBYVILLE, Kentucky, on the Eminence Pike. It was built between 1831 and 1833 for Charles Stewart Todd and his wife, Letitia, on land given Letitia in trust by her father, Gov. Isaac Shelby. Charles was the son of United States Supreme Court Justice Thomas Todd. He studied law after attending the College of William and Mary. His public service included being military aide to Gen. William Henry Harrison in the War of 1812, Kentucky's secretary of state, and United States envoy to Colombia and Russia. He was also a noted farmer and editor.

The five-bay, two-story brick house, with hip roof and interior end chimneys, features six-over-six windows, a pediment over the central bay, detached sidelights similar to Federal Hill, a separate stair hall behind the entry, and blind windows on the chimney ends of the main block. Interior woodwork includes bull's eye corner blocks, sunburst mantels, and paneled cupboards.

Plagued by debt, Todd left Kentucky to seek work on the western frontier. He died in Baton Rouge in 1871. Stockdale was sold by Letitia and her children to Joseph G. Bird in 1858. When he died in 1878 the home was left to his wife, Amantha. To settle their estate, the Bird family sold the property at auction to John Edwin Brown on March 1, 1907, and it remained in his family until purchased in 1984 by Lawrence and Sherry Jelsma. Their renovation of the National Register home received the Ida Lee Willis Preservation Project Award from the Kentucky Heritage Council in 1987.

See George L. Willis Sr., *History of Shelby County, Kentucky* (Louisville 1929); Lewis Collins, *Historical Sketches of Kentucky* (Cincinnati 1847); Sylvia Wrobel and George Grider, *Isaac Shelby, Kentucky's First Governor and Hero of Three Wars* (Danville, Ky. 1974).

John David Myles

STOCK YARDS BANK & TRUST COMPANY. Stock Yards Bank & Trust Co. was founded in 1904 to serve the financial needs of Louisville's growing livestock business. The founders included commission merchants, buyers, and others active in the trade. Its offices were at the corner of E Main and Johnson Streets across from Bourbon Stock Yard. It operated from this site alone until 1985, when it opened a branch in downtown Louisville, and later others in Jefferson County.

For most of its history, Stock Yards Bank functioned mainly as a commercial bank for business customers. In 1972 it established an investment management and trust department and later organized its own mortgage BANKING company. In 1996 the bank initiated private banking services and opened a full-service brokerage department.

During the 1990s, under the leadership of chairman and chief executive officer David Brooks, the bank began expanding, taking advantage of the desire of many consumers to deal with a local bank after the community's largest banks had been purchased by large regional holding companies. By 1996 Stock Yards Bank had nine Kentucky locations, including the main office, and was in the process of transforming the Bourbon Stock Yard Exchange Building into a new operations center. The same year, S.Y. Bancorp Inc., the bank's holding company, expanded into Indiana, purchasing Austin State Bank in Scott County and changing its name to Stock Yards Bank & Trust Co.

In 1997 the main buildings on E MAIN St. underwent work for expansion and rehabilitation. The two buildings were connected by a second-story pedestrian walkway, office space was added, and the original fireplace and the terrazzo floor were restored in the lobby. In 1998 the Stock Yards Bank opened a branch in Clarksville, providing easier access for Southern Indiana.

Carl E. Kramer

STOLL KIDNAPPING CASE. On October 10, 1934, Thomas Henry Robinson Jr. entered the Lime Kiln Ln. home of Berry V. and Alice (Speed) Stoll and kidnapped Mrs. Stoll, the daughter of William S. Speed, president of the Louisville Cement Co. and founder of Louisville Collegiate School, and daughter-in-law of Charles C. Stoll, president of STOLL OIL REFINING CO. Stoll, who was in bed with a cold, put up a brief struggle and attempted to take Robinson's gun. Robinson then hit Stoll over the head with an iron pipe and drove her to Indianapolis. In the wake of the Charles and Anne Lindbergh baby kidnapping, the case aroused national interest as investigators from the FBI and news reporters flocked to the city. The ransom note said that Charles C. Stoll was the intended target and that the abductors wanted fifty thousand dollars delivered within five days to ensure the safe release of Mrs. Stoll.

The money was delivered to Robinson's father, who acted as the intermediary in Nashville, and was then given to Robinson's wife, Frances, who was followed by police as she headed for Indianapolis. While driving Stoll back to Louisville on October 16, Frances Robinson was arrested, as was her father-in-law in Nashville. However, Thomas Robinson had disappeared. Robinson, who had a past record of robberies and stays in mental institutions, had worked at a Stoll service station in Louisville and was described as a shrewd and calculating man who had delusions of grandeur. During his run from the law, Robinson went on several lavish cross-country trips and spent nearly thirty-six thousand dollars of the ransom money in casinos and nightclubs. He was finally tracked down in Glendale, California, in May 1936, after a convenience store worker reportedly spotted the fugitive shopping while dressed in women's clothing.

With fingerprints, writing samples, and several witnesses, including Mrs. Stoll, supporting their case, the police charged Robinson with the kidnapping and released his two accomplices. Robinson immediately pled guilty at trial to avoid the death penalty and within two minutes was sentenced to life in prison, regretting only that he had held the title of the FBI's "Public Enemy Number 1" for such a short time. After spending the next nine years at Alcatraz, Robinson, who had studied law at Vanderbilt and wrote his own appeals, demanded a new trial, claiming temporary insanity and coercion. At the new trial, Robinson was declared sane, convicted of the crime a second time, and sentenced to death.

On June 6, 1945, thirty-three hours before his scheduled execution, Robinson's sentence was commuted to life imprisonment by President Harry S Truman. Robinson was returned to Alcatraz for another nine years before being transferred to a minimum-security prison in Tallahassee. After escaping for a week in 1962, the convict was moved to a Dallas-area prison where again he escaped for a short time three years later. Robinson was finally released from prison in 1970 and died in August 1994 in Nashville. Alice Stoll, who was still living at the time, had no comment on hearing of the death.

See Samuel W. Thomas, *Louisville since the Twenties* (Louisville 1978); *Courier- Journal*, Aug. 27, 1994.

Craig M. Heuser

STOLL OIL REFINING COMPANY. In 1881 the Chess-Carley Co., the agent of Standard Oil in the South, was located in Louisville. Charles C. Stoll was born in Louisville but worked for Standard Oil in Nashville, Tennessee. There he met his future wife, Anne, and they later moved to Louisville, where they reared four sons. When he returned he worked for Chess-Carley and in fifteen years advanced to be assistant to the president. When the company moved to Cincinnati in 1896, however, Stoll remained in Louisville and started his own business. One of the reasons Stoll left Standard Oil was his disgust with the "robber-baron" tactics of John D. Rockefeller's company.

The Charles C. Stoll Co. began as a distribution firm. In 1918 Stoll, with his four sons, changed the name to Stoll Oil Refining Co. and began business at 815 River Rd. Through railroads and pipelines, the company could tap the abundance of natural resources in Kentucky and Indiana.

Crude oil was the foundation of the company, and the Stoll family drilled for oil throughout the state. At first Stoll Oil produced coal oil, axle grease, and steam-cylinder oil. With the growth of the automobile, however, the company began to produce motor oil and gasoline, where it found its biggest market.

In 1924 Stoll Oil had ten gas stations in

Louisville. By 1941 the gas was being sold mainly under the name of Golden Tip, and there were forty-four stations that year. Other stations were found throughout Kentucky, southern Indiana, and Ohio, together with a thousand other outlets where any number of the ninety-six Stoll Oil products could be purchased. That year Charles C. Stoll was the president, Berry V. Stoll and George Stoll were vice presidents, William A. Stoll was a vice president and treasurer, Charles E. Stoll was vice president and secretary, and C.W. Stoll was assistant secretary. Following the death of Charles C. Stoll in 1943, George J. became president. The offices were located at 227 W Main, with the refinery at 815 River Rd.

In 1952 the Stoll family sold the company to Sinclair Oil. Although the purchase price was undisclosed, the company was capitalized at $1,950,000. Sinclair Oil kept the Stoll Oil name on the Louisville-based products until 1956, when Stoll Oil disappeared from the Louisville city directory. By 1998 Sinclair Oil Corp. had twenty-five hundred stations and convenience stores based in the West and Midwest.

See *Courier Journal,* Feb. 1, 1952.

STONESTREET, ROSA ANNA (PHILLIPS) (b Jefferson County, Kentucky, February 18, 1859; d Louisville, April 7, 1936). Educator and school superintendent. The daughter of Murray and America (Shrader) Phillips, she was educated at Nazareth Academy, Nazareth, Kentucky, graduating June 28, 1877. Her career in education began in 1890 when she became a teacher. On November 3, 1897, Stonestreet was elected superintendent of the common schools of Jefferson County by popular vote. She served in this capacity from 1898 until 1910.

Of the ten superintendents who had served the Jefferson County School District and the twenty-seven who had served the Louisville Independent School District by 1997, Stonestreet is the only female. As superintendent, Stonestreet turned her immediate attention to financial problems. In 1898 almost every district in the county was burdened with a large debt and the accumulated interest for four or five years. Her efforts to help liquidate these obligations were successful in many instances. During her service Stonestreet was an outspoken opponent of the trustee system. She was among those who wanted to see Kentucky public education administered by professionals. In 1908 "Educational Legislature" made it possible.

In 1994 the Jefferson County BOARD OF EDUCATION renamed Stonestreet Elementary School "Rosa Phillips Stonestreet Elementary School" in her honor.

Stonestreet was married to Charles Thomas Stonestreet (1854–89) of OLDHAM COUNTY on October 18, 1882, at the Broadway Methodist Episcopal Church on BROADWAY between Brook and Floyd Streets. They had two sons, Robert Ira (1883–1901) and Charles Chester (1886–1927). Stonestreet's husband died in 1889 from tuberculosis. She and her son Charles Chester moved in 1917 to Albuquerque, New Mexico. After Charles Chester's death in 1927, Rosa returned to Louisville. She is buried in CAVE HILL CEMETERY.

Shirley Botkins

STOVALL, THELMA LOYACE (HAWKINS) (b Munfordville, Kentucky, April 1, 1919; d Louisville, February 4, 1994). Lieutenant governor. The first female state representative from Louisville, Thelma Hawkins Stovall also went on to serve as secretary of state and treasurer and was the first female lieutenant governor of Kentucky.

Born to Addie Mae (Goodman) and Samuel Dewey Hawkins, Stovall moved to Louisville when she was eight years old with her mother and younger sister following her parents' divorce. She watched her mother raise two children as a single parent during the GREAT DEPRESSION and accompanied her to work at the local voting precinct. At fifteen, to help with the family finances, Stovall lied about her age to obtain a job sweeping loose TOBACCO at Brown and Williamson Tobacco Co. She graduated from LOUISVILLE GIRLS' HIGH SCHOOL, which had moved in 1934 to Halleck Hall at Second and Lee Streets. In 1936 she married Lonnie Raymond Stovall, whom she had met through their jobs on the cigarette line. She also studied law at LaSalle Extension University in Chicago and attended summer school at the University of Kentucky and Eastern Kentucky University.

Encouraged by friends to run for recording secretary of the Tobacco Workers International Union Local 185, Stovall won and held the position for eleven years. Through her work on the union's League for Political Education and in forming women's auxiliary groups around the state, Stovall became Jefferson County labor's choice to run for the state legislature in 1949 and was elected to the Kentucky house of representatives, serving three consecutive terms. She was a national committee member for the Young Democrats of Kentucky from 1952 to 1956 and served as the organization's first woman president from 1956 to 1958.

In 1955, A.B. "Happy" Chandler, who was running for a second term as governor, tapped Stovall to run for secretary of state because of her strong labor ties. For twenty years Stovall served as either secretary of state (1956–60, 1964–68 and 1972–75) or state treasurer (1960–64 and 1968–72). A fierce defender of equal rights, Stovall collaborated with others in 1968 to establish the Kentucky Commission on Women. In 1975, after defeating ten male opponents in the primary race for lieutenant governor, she went on to serve in the Julian Carroll administration (1974–79).

A passionate supporter of the Equal Rights Amendment (ERA), Stovall gained national attention in 1978 when she assumed the role of governor in Carroll's absence and called a special session of the legislature to veto the rescission of its 1972 ratification of the ERA. In 1979, also as acting governor, she pushed through legislation in a special session that put a ceiling on increases in revenue derived from property taxes.

Stovall ran for governor in 1979 but finished last out of five candidates in the primary that was swept by John Young Brown Jr., who ultimately was elected governor. Her last public office was as labor commissioner during the last year of the Brown administration (1979–83). A plaque honoring her service hangs in the capitol. Stovall suffered a number of strokes, the first in 1971, and was inactive in later years. She was one of only a handful of dignitaries to lie in state in the capitol. She is buried in Resthaven Memorial Park in Louisville.

See LEXINGTON HERALD-LEADER, Feb. 6, 1994; COURIER-JOURNAL, Feb. 6, 1994; FRANKFORT STATE JOURNAL, Dec. 8, 1975.

Lindsay Crawford Campbell

STRAUSS, JOHN MASON (b Louisville, December 8, 1870; d New York City, December 3, 1914). Composer, musician, automobile dealer. The son of Richard and Catherine (Fink) Strauss, John Mason Strauss was born into a musical family. Strauss reflected and occasionally anticipated the musical trends of his time, composing music to be performed in parlors, concert halls, and by bands and touring companies. He wrote at least twenty-four pieces, including the music for ballads, SONGS for a light opera, and a musical show, *The Fortune Hunters.* One of his most popular pieces was "The Louisville Times March," published in 1894.

Strauss was a church organist and choir director for ST. PAUL'S EPISCOPAL CHURCH and for Temple Adath Israel, and a leader of the Louisville Mandolin and Guitar Club. The *LOUISVILLE TIMES* described him as an "organist of unusual merit" and a "composer of ability."

In the early 1900s, Strauss became one of Louisville's first automobile dealers, opening a series of automobile dealerships with various partners. Plagued by lawsuits and, eventually, financial problems, Strauss left the automobile business and moved to New York City around 1912. He died in his studio on Washington Square of a heart ailment just five days short of his forty-fourth birthday.

Strauss is buried in CAVE HILL CEMETERY, where his grave is unmarked.

Linda Raymond
William L. Ellison Jr.

STRAWS, DAVID (b Kentucky, 1799; d Louisville, April 23, 1872). Barber and Methodist church leader. Straws was born into slavery but purchased his freedom and came to Louisville around 1830. He opened a barbershop and in 1848 bought a lot on Sixth St. in the rear of the LOUISVILLE HOTEL. His business prospered and by 1860 his real estate holdings were valued at ten thousand dollars. In 1845 Straws provided many of the funds necessary to purchase a church at Fourth and Green (Liberty) Streets for the use of a black Methodist congregation. The church was organized as Fourth St. Colored Methodist Church, and he was one of the first trustees. In 1848 Straws figured prominently in the successful attempt by the church (now Asbury Chapel) to secede from the white Methodist Episcopal Church South and join with the African Methodist Episcopal Church. He is buried in Eastern Cemetery.

See H.C. Weeden, *Weeden's History of the Colored People of Louisville* (Louisville 1897); William H. Gibson, *History of the United Brothers of Friendship and Sisters of the Mysterious Ten* (Louisville 1897).

Cornelius Bogert

Mule-drawn streetcar in front of Southern Exposition building, 1883.

STREETCARS. The electric streetcar or trolley (so called for the trolley pole that reached to the overhead power wire) provided the first real rapid transit in Louisville. The city's first trolley cars began operation in June 1889, running from Eighteenth St. along Green (Liberty) St. to Baxter Ave. and out Baxter to Highland Ave. This somewhat experimental line soon proved itself a success, and plans were made to convert the dense network of mule-powered streetcar lines to electricity. The electric cars were larger, much faster, far more comfortable, and were lighted by electricity. The last mule car ran in 1901 along Frankfort Ave. to the Crescent Hill Reservoir.

The mule-car era in Louisville had begun in 1844 with the Louisville and Portland Railroad operating rail cars between Twelfth and Main Streets in Louisville alongside the Portland Turnpike (Portland Ave.) to Portland, then a separate municipality. Because of the break in navigation caused by the Falls of the Ohio, there was heavy traffic between the two communities. This pioneer venture (the third street railway in the United States) foundered by 1851 but was revived in 1854 and the track moved to what became Bank St. The line also operated mule-drawn omnibuses along Main St. and carried freight as well as passengers.

Additional street railways were contemplated in the late 1850s, but the Civil War delayed action until 1864 when the Louisville City Railway, founded by Union brigadier general Jeremiah T. Boyle, opened a route on Main St. between Twelfth and Campbell Streets. A third entry, the Central Passenger Railway, built lines on Fourth and on Walnut St. in 1866. This company soon came under the ownership of brothers Alfred V. and A.B. du Pont, major actors in the city's business community. The proliferation of street railways was tied directly to Louisville's development of an industrial economy, which began to overshadow its older mercantile base. The mule car provided the necessary transportation for the blue-collar workers who would have to live on the outskirts where new housing could be built inexpensively; thus the proliferation of the "shotgun" cottage.

With three street railways, competition became intense. In 1872 the Portland Rd., along with a line it sponsored on Market St., were absorbed by the City Railway, leaving two players in the field. Each company tried to outwit the other in reaching new territory. Chicanery and bribery of city councilmen were common to obtain new franchises. The positive result, however, was a system of public transportation that reached every corner of the city. Lines stretched from the Ohio River bank in the far West End to Crescent Hill and out Bardstown Rd. and along Taylorsville Rd. to the future site of Bowman Field and beyond. North-south lines were numerous and many visitors to the first Kentucky Derby in 1875 arrived by mule car.

The switch to electric cars produced a revolution in public transit, however. As the electric lines stretched beyond the limits of the slow-paced mule system (sometimes beyond the city limits, as to Iroquois Park and Fontaine Ferry), areas that were open country became ripe for development. On W Market St., it was noted, "the cars go whizzing past pleasant little farms, with the corn now waving in the breeze, with the cows knee-deep in clover" (*Courier-Journal,* July 27, 1902). Those farms didn't last much longer, however. From the 1890s to the mid-1920s, practically all advertising for new subdivisions stressed the proximity of a streetcar line. Classified advertisements for sale or

Louisville Railway Company trolley delivers passengers to Churchill Downs, 1929.

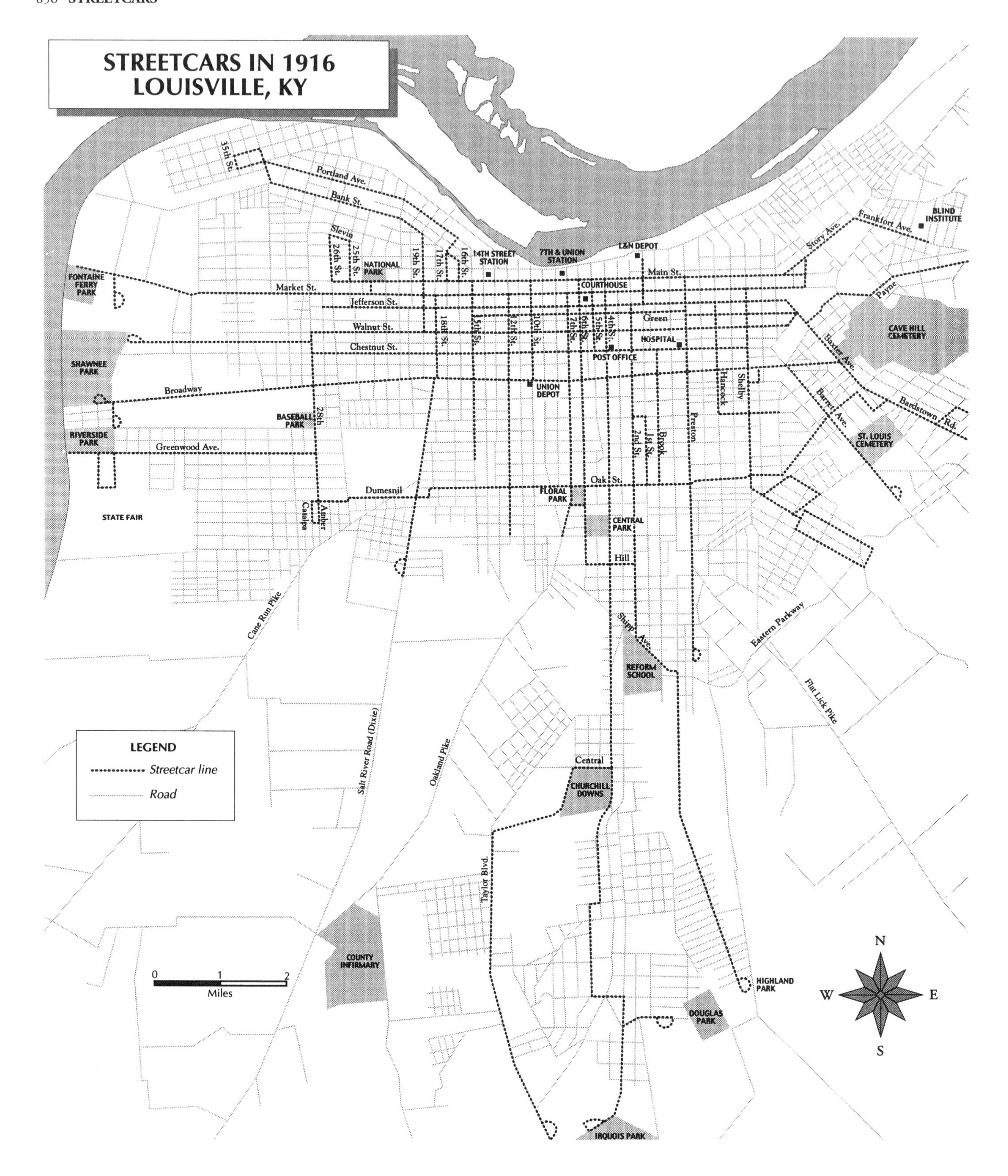
STREETCARS IN 1916
LOUISVILLE, KY
35th St.
Portland Ave.
Bank St.
Slevin
26th St.
25th St.
NATIONAL PARK
19th St.
17th St.
16th St.
14TH STREET STATION
7TH & UNION STATION
L&N DEPOT
Story Ave.
Frankfort Ave.
BLIND INSTITUTE
FONTAINE FERRY PARK
Market St.
Main St.
COURTHOUSE
Jefferson St.
Payne
Walnut St.
18th St.
15th St.
12th St.
10th St.
7th St.
6th St.
5th St.
4th St.
Green
HOSPITAL
CAVE HILL CEMETERY
Chestnut St.
POST OFFICE
Baxter Ave.
SHAWNEE PARK
Broadway
UNION DEPOT
Hancock
Shelby
Bardstown Rd.
Barret Ave.
BASEBALL PARK
28th
Preston
Brook
1st St.
2nd St.
RIVERSIDE PARK
Greenwood Ave.
ST. LOUIS CEMETERY
Oak St.
Dumesnil
FLORAL PARK
Amber
Catalpa
STATE FAIR
CENTRAL PARK
Hill
Cane Run Pike
Shipp Ave.
Eastern Parkway
REFORM SCHOOL
Flat Lick Pike
LEGEND
Streetcar line
Road
Salt River Road (Dixie)
Oakland Pike
Central
CHURCHILL DOWNS
Taylor Blvd.
COUNTY INFIRMARY
0
1
2
Miles
N
W
E
S
HIGHLAND PARK
DOUGLAS PARK
IROQUOIS PARK

rental property carried the tag line "On the car line" as a plus factor.

In the days before widespread automobile ownership, the fixed lines of the streetcar provided controlled mobility that promoted orderly growth as contrasted to the uncontrolled mobility of the automobile and accompanying suburban sprawl. The streetcar operators gained prestige too. The *Louisville Post* noted on June 22, 1891, that the former "mule persuaders" now bore the proud title of "motormen."

The switch to electric operation caused a corporate change as well. The two transit companies were merged in 1890 as the Louisville Railway Co., a move triggered by the high cost of the change to electric operation. With its five hundred cars, power stations, car barns, repair shops, and material yards, the Louisville Railway Co. on the eve of WORLD WAR I was the city's largest taxpayer. But the increase in automobile ownership in the 1920s caused a decline in passengers and earnings, exacerbated by the Depression of the 1930s. Ridership, some 30 million annually by 1900, climbed to 84 million in 1920 and declined to about 55 million by 1940. WORLD WAR II, with restrictions on automobile use, brought a change, and in 1945 the company carried 125 million riders, the peak in transit use.

The Louisville Railway Co. had been utilizing buses since the early 1920s to reach the new suburban developments that had been created by the automobile and lay beyond the streetcar lines. "Feeder" buses carried passengers to the streetcar lines, while others replaced trolleys on short inner-city lines in declining NEIGHBORHOODS. Electrically-powered trolley buses began operating in 1936 on the Walnut St. route, in 1941 on Market St., and in 1948 on Fourth St., but they were supplanted by diesel buses in 1952.

Renewal of the company's franchise in 1940 brought a demand by the city fathers for widespread use of buses, and the trolley began vanishing. However, the change was halted to conserve rubber and gasoline during World War II. With the end of the war, the shift to buses was rapid.

New technologically advanced streetcars were purchased for the Fourth St. line, but they were never used. A change in company management dictated buses for Fourth St. The last streetcars ran on May 1, 1948, carrying crowds to the Kentucky Derby. About 1950 the firm's name was changed to Louisville Transit Co. Continuing decline in ridership forced the company to cease operations in 1974. The public agency, TRANSIT AUTHORITY OF RIVER CITY (TARC), took over the bus system.

See Carlton C. Haydon, "The Street Railway System" in *Memorial History of Louisville*, vol. 1, 326–28 (Chicago 1896); Milo Meadows, "Urban Transportation in Louisville from 1830–1910," M.A. thesis, University of Louisville, 1967.

George H. Yater

STREETS. The first attempt at laying out the streets of Louisville could be said to have occurred in 1773 when THOMAS BULLITT and his surveying party arrived at the FALLS OF THE OHIO. Sent from Virginia to record LAND GRANTS for officers of the French and Indian War, the group laid out a town on the future site of Louisville, but the plan was never adopted because the survey was illegal. An early "street" into town was the Wilderness Rd., cut by Daniel Boone from the Cumberland Gap to Boonesborough. It was later extended to Harrodsburg, to the SALT LICKS in BULLITT COUNTY, and up to FORT NELSON on present Main St. approximately between Sixth and Eighth Streets. The road was later called the Flat Lick Rd. and in Lousville's very early days ran from the courthouse to MT. WASHINGTON in Bullitt County. The road left Broadway near Fifth St. and continued in a southeasterly direction for about two-thirds of a mile and then, near what is now Fourth and St. Catherine, it made a forty-five-degree turn to veer off in a full southeasterly direction until it reached the Shepherdsville Rd. at its present intersection of Preston St. and Burnett Ave.

In 1922, while excavation was underway along Center St. (Armory Pl.), a log was unearthed twelve feet below ground. It was part of the Flat Lick Rd. and demonstrated that it was part of a corduroy road.

Two maps dating from 1779 show the town laid out in a basic grid pattern with half-acre plots from present Main St. between First and Fourteenth Streets. John Corbley's map went down to the river, while WILLIAM POPE's map left room for a wharf. Lots were sold on the basis of Corbley's plan. From the beginning the principal streets were east-west thoroughfares parallel to the river. The cross streets were mere dividers and generally were narrower than those running parallel to the river.

Water St. was the first to be named in 1783. Other street names appeared for the first time on the map of the city drawn by Jared Brooks in 1812. Thirty-foot-wide Water St. ran parallel to the river; the next ones parallel to that were Main, Market, Jefferson, Green (Liberty), Walnut, and South (Chestnut) Streets. Three cross-streets—East, Center, and West—stretched from Green St. to the undeveloped Dunkirk Rd. (Prather, then Broadway), while twelve additional cross-streets (First through Twelfth) ran from Water to Green St. As the city expanded, other early names tended to reflect the activities of certain streets such as Milk St. (part of Oak St.) or Magazine St., named for the powder magazine between Eighth and Ninth Streets. Some streets were named for national leaders such as Washington or Franklin Streets, while others came about because of their proximity to certain features. Walnut St. (Muhammad Ali Blvd.) is said to have bordered a grove of walnut trees between Third and Fourth Streets. Later street names either honored local leaders such as mayors John Baxter and JAMES GRINSTEAD or were named for local developers such as D.H. Meriwether (Meriwether Ave.) or for local landmarks such as Shawnee Park (Shawnee Terrace). In more recent years, names were changed, following petitions to the BOARD OF ALDERMEN, to recognize such local personalities as former heavyweight BOXING champion MUHAMMAD ALI. In recent times, names of newer streets, primarily in the county, have been picked by property developers and approved by the Jefferson County Division of Planning and Development Services.

Early streets were dusty in the summer and virtually impassable during soggy winters. Little was done to improve them other than to fill in mud holes and low places. Sidewalks were placed along the streets using boards from dismantled flatboats.

After the turn of the nineteenth century, the trustees continued to take a role in the construction and maintenance of streets. In 1806 brick-making was prohibited in the streets, as was removal of any sand or dirt for brick manufacture. In that year Capt. John Nelson also started digging wells in order to drain the numerous ponds that blanketed the Louisville area and turned some roads into swamps. In 1811 the state General Assembly passed an act authorizing the trustees to pave streets. Streets were then aligned, curbstones put in place, and limestone or stone taken from the river used as paving on some streets. Limestone was taken from the CORN ISLAND reef, but it did not hold up well. It was too soft and ground to a powder. Still, improvements came slowly. After a writer in the Louisville Public Advertiser claimed in 1822 that "there is not a worse mud-hole within 20 miles of Louisville, than our much admired MAIN STREET," the state legislature offered help with a forty-thousand-dollar lottery designated for drainage projects.

In 1813 the town trustees agreed to pave the intersections of Main St. and the entire street between Third and Sixth. By 1815 town leaders had decided to charge property owners between Third and Sixth Streets for the macadamization (a process of layering increasingly smaller pieces of gravel) and had completed this stretch at a cost of six dollars per square. Three years later First through Twelfth Streets were opened all the way to Broadway (then Dunkirk Rd. and later Prather St.), which then became the southern boundary of development.

The development of Louisville streets was in addition to a number of alleys and routes to other cities. Although HENRY MCMURTRIE claimed in 1819 that the lack of ALLEYS would cause an inconvenience in the future, Louisville had developed alleys within its grid pattern that served the rear of street-fronting properties and became the home to servants and provided access to carriage houses and horse stables.

Many early streets were private toll roads. For example, the City Council approved a resolution in 1870 that the mayor confer with the

Louisville & Shepherdsville Turnpike Co. on immediate removal of their occupancy of Preston St. The Board of Aldermen passed a resolution directing the mayor to purchase from the turnpike company all of Preston St. from Oak south to Meriwether's line. Toll roads to places such as SHELBYVILLE and Bardstown became well-traveled routes and spawned smaller towns such as Middletown, which served as a stopover place on the way east to Lexington. In 1819 the Louisville Turnpike Co. was incorporated and built Bardstown Pike (Baxter Ave. and Bardstown Rd.) between Louisville and Bardstown, setting up toll booths along the way. The first booth was located where present Lexington Rd. crosses Baxter Ave. In 1869 the City Council considered a measure to buy Bardstown Rd. from Beargrass Bridge to the city limits (one mile and present Baxter Ave.) from the turnpike company.

In 1830 the city designated $17,031 of its annual budget of $46,245 for street cleaning and surfacing. Two years later Edward D. Hobbs was named the city's first chief engineer and established the first uniform street grade to simplify construction and drainage. While a substantial amount of cash was appropriated for street cleaning from the 1830s on, it was not until the spring of 1873 that a fear of EPIDEMICS (promoted by the human and animal waste that commonly littered the streets) prompted the establishment of a street-cleaning department. In their inaugural year, the crews maintained approximately 114 miles of paved streets and 22 miles of alleys and removed a total of 25,344 pounds of garbage at a cost of $22,040.

After the CIVIL WAR, the city tested several types of street pavements in order to economically cover the increasing number of routes. In the 1870s private contractors unsuccessfully experimented with a type of street construction using Nicholson wooden blocks. Main St. was paved with granite blocks the following decade, and the city began testing asphalt on certain stretches of roads. A steamroller was first used in 1877 for the paving of Frankfort Ave. Third St. was paved with asphalt as well, since it did not carry wagon traffic. which Second St. did. Asphalt had the advantage of making a smooth surface. This improvement was made possible by the state legislature's 1888 approval of an act allowing Louisville to issue $1.5 million in street improvement bonds. By the close of the century, street construction involved an assortment of materials including crushed boulders, granite blocks (known as Belgian blocks), asphalt, brick, macadam, and gravel. The Peterson Ave. hill is one of the last visible brick streets. Brick became common paving material in the 1890s. It was first used on Second St. from Broadway to Jacob in 1891. It was then adopted as the standard for all new construction. It was reported that in 1895 the total length of paved streets was 151.52 miles and of alleys 49.8 miles.

After the creation of the Board of PUBLIC WORKS in 1893, the street-cleaning department and its budget were absorbed into the new division. Within three years street cleaners swept all asphalt surfaces with hand brooms and all granite and brick surfaces with horse-drawn vehicles employing revolving brushes. In addition to cleaning, the Board of Public Works also inherited the responsibility of building new streets and maintaining existing ones. While cleaning and sprinkling the dusty thoroughfares alone cost more than $80,000 per year, construction and improvements totaled another $250,000. Work continued unabated as the city continued to expand, and by 1916 Louisville had almost 237 miles of paved streets and another 100 miles unpaved. Within four years, street maintenance and construction costs climbed to $1.1 million.

As the city expanded in the late nineteenth and early twentieth centuries, the standard grid pattern started in the central business district tended to slip away either because established streets (such as those in PORTLAND) did not line up, or new developers simply ignored the existing pattern. TOPOGRAPHY was another factor, along with the annexation of county roads by the city. Wilson Rd. north of Algonquin Pkwy. slants northeast until it reaches Dixie Hwy. because it had once been part of Cane Run Rd. With approximately 291 miles of paved streets and 306 miles of unpaved streets within the city limits in the mid-1920s, a comprehensive plan was called for to prepare Louisville for economic and geographic expansion.

Also by the turn of the century traffic congestion and accidents were already becoming problems. In 1902 there were at least twenty or thirty automobiles on the city streets scaring people and horses. By 1909 the busiest corners in the city were on Jefferson St. at Preston and Brook Streets, and at Green and Brook Streets. In 1913 police officers were ordered to report dangerous defects in the public streets and sidewalks that had the potential to cause accidents. They found a total of 1,183. In 1923 all police were instructed not to let anyone skate, coast, or scoot at any time during the day or night in the streets on their beat. In 1924 the first safety islands were built in the center of Broadway to help protect citizens boarding and leaving STREETCARS. On August 13, 1915, the establishment of semaphores at all corners where traffic officers were assigned was considered the greatest stride made in directing traffic and the protection of pedestrians. The semaphores, visual signaling devices with movable arms, were built in the machine shop of the fire department. Police were ordered to "see that all pedestrians obey the new traffic signal." The police chief would later warn that "too many automobiles are not stopping soon enough for the stop sign or are sliding into the intersection."

Speeding had also become a problem even before the introduction of the automobile. The Grand Blvd. (Southern Pkwy.) was a speedway for fast horses. The center part was for carriages and other horse-drawn vehicles. On the east side was a cinder path for bicycles and on the west a bridle path for equestrians. Men driving coal cars, ice wagons, and similar vehicles were often speeding and driving recklessly through town in order to make as many deliveries as possible before sundown. The police used both bicycles and horses to patrol the streets for speeders. The police adopted radar-clocking equipment in 1955. The radar speed calculator was a box on the side of a police car that recorded the speed of passing motorists. The officer in the car would then radio a motorcycle officer the offending motorist's description, speed, and location.

The city adopted a major street plan in 1929 prepared by Harland Bartholomew and Associates, city planners from St. Louis. It proposed the widening of certain streets, the elimination of numerous railroad crossings, and the establishment of more downtown connectors. Unfortunately, money problems delayed the completion of the plan. The GREAT DEPRESSION-era elevation of sections of the Louisville & Nashville and Pennsylvania Railroad tracks did improve traffic flow on such major thoroughfares as Broadway and Baxter Ave. Another plan submitted by the same firm in 1955 called for changes to more than two hundred streets in the Louisville area and received mixed results.

Following WORLD WAR II several changes were instituted to ease traffic problems brought on by increasing use of the automobile. The first one-way streets in downtown Louisville had been established in 1935 when First and Fifth Streets were made one-way northbound between Broadway and Main St., and Third St. was made one-way southbound between Main and Kentucky Streets. This pattern was expanded in 1946 with the addition of Second and Sixth Streets. More one-way streets were added in 1948 and 1950, and by 1956 forty-four streets in the city had been designated one-way. Other additions to the downtown streets included the first parking meters in 1948 and the installation of synchronized traffic lights in the mid-1950s. The first walk/wait signs began operating on October 5, 1954.

A major controversy involved transforming Fourth St. between Liberty and Broadway into a pedestrian mall to increase downtown shopping. Despite criticism from numerous citizens, city leaders closed the thoroughfare, once a popular shopping and THEATER district, to automobiles in 1972 to establish the pedestrians-only RIVER CITY MALL. Although this led to projects such as the GALLERIA and Theater Square, Fourth St. was reopened from Muhammad Ali Blvd. to Broadway in 1996. Because of pressure from the business community, city leaders decided in 1998 to build the Commonwealth Convention Center expansion over Third St., rather than closing the thoroughfare. A plan in 1999 to build a median in the center of Broadway met with much opposition.

By the 1990s an assortment of streets covered the Louisville area ranging from tree-lined

PARKWAYS (Eastern, Southern, North Western) to simple alleys (Billy Goat Strut, Base Ball). While the encircling expressways (the GENE SNYDER FREEWAY and the Watterson Expressway) fostered greater suburbanization, they also led to the widening of major arteries such as Westport Rd. and Hurstbourne Pkwy. because of increased traffic volume. INTERSTATES (I-65, I-64, I-71) handled a huge load of traffic through and within the metropolitan area.

Several major roads into and out of Louisville have been designated as United States highways. These include Bardstown Rd. (U.S. 31E; 150), Brownsboro Rd. (U.S. 42), Dixie Hwy. (U.S. 31W; 60), and Shelbyville Rd. (U.S. 60).

The following is a partial list of streets with their old and revised names. While some through streets bear several names along their length, sometimes only one of the names has been included on this list. Most of the new names were in use by 1895.

Old and New Street Names

Old	New
"A" St.	Gaulbert Ave.
Asylum Ave.	Stoll Ave.
Ashbottom Rd.	Crittenden Dr.
"B" St.	Bloom Ave.
Bardstown Pike	Baxter Ave. and Bardstown Rd.
Beauchamp Rd.	Cannons Ln.
Beargrass St.	Story Ave. (beyond Frankfort Ave.)
Boone St.	Fourteenth St.
Braddock St.	Wenzel St.
Bridge St.	Eighteenth St.
"C" St. (Avery Ave.)	Cardinal Blvd.
Caroline St.	Morton Ave.
Center St.	Armory Pl.
Cherokee Ave.	Seneca Ave.
Cherry St.	Twenty-ninth St.
Clark St.	Fifteenth St.
Clinton St.	Nineteenth St.
Columbia St.	Thirty-first St. and Thirteenth St.
Center St.	Armory Pl.
Commercial St. (Portland)	Thirty-fourth St.
Cromie St.	Twentieth St.
"D" St.	Brandeis Ave.
Daisy Ln.	Transit Ave. (later Grinstead Dr.)
DeWolfe St.	Eighteenth St.
Dunkirk Rd.	Prather St. (later Broadway)
"E" St.	Barbee Ave.
East St.	Brook St.
Eighth Cross St. (Portland)	Twenty-fourth St.
Eleventh Cross St. (Portland)	Twenty-first St.
Elizabeth St.	Sixteenth St.
"F" St.	Atwood Ave.
Falls City Ave.	Forty-third St.
Ferry St. (Portland)	Thirty-sixth St.
Fifth Cross St. (Portland)	Twenty-seventh St.
Finzer Pkwy.	Cherokee Pkwy.
First Cross St. (Portland)	Thirty-first St.
Flat Lick Rd.	Bradley Ave.
Fourth Cross St. (Portland)	Twenty-eighth St.
Front St.	Missouri Ave.
Fulton St. (Portland)	Thirty-third St.
"G" St.	Warnock St.
Green St.	Liberty St.
Grand Blvd.	Southern Pkwy.
Gravier St. (Portland)	Thirty-seventh St.
Grove St. (Portland)	Thirty-fifth St.
"H" St.	Colorado St.
Harney St.	Griffiths Ave.
Howard St.	Breckinridge St.
"J" St.	Creel Ave.
Jessie Ave.	Longview Ave.
"K" St.	Montana Ave.
Kellar St.	Gray St.
Kennedy St.	Thirty-ninth St.
Krupps Ln.	Rufer Ave.
"L" St.	Winkler Ave.
Lock St.	Twenty-sixth St.
Lost Alley	Stoecker Ave.
Maria St.	Seventeenth St.
Mechanic St.	St. Catherine St.
Mercer St.	Twenty-fourth St.
Merry St.	Hoertz Ave.
Midway Ave.	Montgomery St.
Milk St.	Oak St.
Montgomery St.	Twentieth St.
Mott St.	Myrtle St.
Mulberry St.	Sixteenth St.
"N" St.	Iowa Ave.
Ninth Cross St. (Portland)	Twenty-third St.
"O" St.	Heywood Ave.
Orleans St.	Twentieth St.
Overhill St.	Rubel Ave.
"P" St.	Central Ave.
Pipe Line Ln.	Zorn Ave.
Plum St.	Thirtieth St.
Pope St.	Fifth St.
Prather St.	Broadway
Prospect Ave.	Arlington Ave.
"Q" St.	Racine Ave.
"R" St.	Thornberry Ave.
Reservoir Ave.	Mellwood Ave.
Rosenberg Ln.	Beech St.
Rupp St.	Shelby Pkwy.
"S" St.	Thornberry Ave.
Salt River Rd. (or Shippingport Rd.)	Twenty-sixth St.
Sayre St.	Twenty-third St.
Second Cross St. (Portland)	Thirtieth St.
Selby Rd.	Upland Rd.
Seventh Cross St. (Portland)	Twenty-fifth St.
Shelbyville Turnpike	Frankfort Ave.
Slaughter Ave.	Patterson Ave.
South St.	Chestnut St.
Southall St.	Reservoir Ave.
Stonewall St.	Burnett Ave.
Sycamore St.	Thirty-second St. and Seventeenth St.
"T" St.	Calhoun Ave. and Kenton St.
Tenth Cross St. (Portland)	Twenty-second St.
Third Cross St. (Portland)	Twenty-ninth St.
Thompson's Ln.	Thirty-first St.
Todd St.	Lytle St.
Transit Ave.	Grinstead Dr.
Underhill St.	Barret Ave.
Union St.	Twenty-seventh St.
"V" St.	Fairmount Ave.
Vassar Dr.	Overlook Terrace
Victoria Pl.	Magnolia Ave.
Walnut St.	Muhammad Ali Blvd.
Ward St.	Rogers St.
Weissinger St.	Park Ave.
Workhouse Rd.	Lexington Rd.
Zimlich Ave.	Dundee Rd.

In addition to changes of street names, the numbering has also changed. Beginning in October 1908 streets were resurveyed and renumbered. The 1909 Caron's Louisville City Directory gives both the old and new addresses. For example, Frank Schell who had resided at 1021 Wenzel was now at 523 S Wenzel. These changes were formalized in an ordinance approved by the General Councilmen on June 8, 1907. The Board of Public Works was given the responsibility for enforcing the ordinance. Unfortunately, not all streets were marked by name signs on corners, as also required by the law, a situation decried by the publishers of the directory.

See J. Stoddard Johnston, ed., *Memorial History of Louisville* (Chicago 1896); Louisville Municipal Reports, published annually 1869 to 1920, Louiville Free Public Library; Henry McMurtrie, *Sketches of Louisville and Its Environs* (Louisville 1819); Richard C. Wade, *The Urban Frontier: The Rise of Western Cities, 1790–1830* (Cambridge, Mass. 1959).

STRING AND BRASS BANDS. The origins of string and brass bands in Louisville can be traced to at least the early nineteenth century. The development of these bands, which were such an important part of the city's cultural life, directly reflects the growth and diversity of Louisville's ethnic groups and socioeconomic classes. In the 1820s string ensembles were hired by wealthier citizens to play at cotillion parties and balls held at Washington Hall and Woodland Garden, and at the many spas or springs situated throughout rural Kentucky. Much less formal settings were available to the general public, including barbecues and Fourth of July celebrations. At these gatherings fiddlers led string bands and played hornpipes, reels, and other country dances.

One of the earliest bands was organized in 1835 by Henry Williams, a free African American violinist. His band became the most popular in the region, and several band members, including JAMES C. CUNNINGHAM and Samuel Hicks, went on to form their own popular string and brass bands. The growth of trade groups such as carpenters and firemen provided more opportunities for bands to play at balls and parties, and steamboats provided employment for bands all along the Ohio and Mississippi Rivers. By the 1850s brass bands were featured at every conceivable celebration, including parades, balloon ascensions, and the inaugural run of the LOUISVILLE & NASHVILLE RAILROAD in 1859.

The large number of German immigrants to Louisville in the late 1840s included many talented musicians, chief among whom was Sigismund Arbogast. He formed Arbogast's Saxhorn Band in 1851, and his band was popular at military parades and formal dress balls. CHRISTIAN HAUPT and WILLIAM PLATO, both members of this band, later led their own cornet bands. As the older generation of German immigrant musicians passed away, their places were taken by popular bandleaders such as Ehrhardt Eichorn and Andrew J. Seibert.

The end of the CIVIL WAR, with its lifting of restrictions on public gatherings by AFRICAN AMERICANS, brought about a significant increase in opportunities for African American bands. Band leaders such as JAMES R. CUNNINGHAM, Louis Lilly, and WILLIAM COLE were in constant demand at events ranging from formal dances to picnics and barbecues. Cunningham and Seibert were the top band leaders of their day, and they continued performing well into the 1920s. By this time the popularity of string and brass bands had lessened because of changing musical tastes and the advent of the radio, movies, and recorded music.

See Kenneth Kreitner, *Discoursing Sweet Music* (Urbana, Ill. 1990); Margaret Hindle Hazen and Robert M. Hazen, *The Music Men* (Washington, D.C. 1987).

Cornelius Bogert

STRONG, MARGARET KIRKPATRICK (b Hamilton, Ontario, March 8, 1883; d Toronto, April 26, 1971). Social worker, educator, and university administrator. Strong was one of seven children of William and Elizabeth (Main) Strong. She was educated at the University of Toronto, earning a B.A. degree in philosophy in 1905, and received her M.A. in philosophy from Cornell University in 1907. After that she held several teaching positions both in Canada and the United States.

In 1915 she began her career in social work with the Ontario Government Employment Bureau. Strong later attended the University of Chicago, earning a Ph.D. in 1928. After completing her doctorate, she worked for the International Survey of the YMCA and YWCA. In 1930 Dr. Strong was offered a teaching position at the UNIVERSITY OF LOUISVILLE. She worked closely with Raymond A. Kent, the university's president, to establish a degree program in social work that culminated in the establishment of the Division of Social Administration. In time it became the Kent School of Social Work. Strong was named as the division's first director in 1936, holding that position until she left the university in 1941 to return to Canada. Margaret Kirkpatrick Strong is buried in Mount Pleasant Cemetery in Toronto.

See *London Evening Free Press*, London, Ont., April 30, 1971; *Vancouver Sun*, Vancouver, B.C., May 3, 1971.

Margaret Merrick

STUBER, WILLIAM G. (b Louisville, April 9, 1864; d Rochester, New York, June 18, 1959). Photographer, businessman. The son of Michael and Julia Stuber, Stuber's natural inclination toward PHOTOGRAPHY was inherited from his father, who helped in pioneering the art before and after the CIVIL WAR. After his father died, young Stuber continued in his photography business in Louisville. He then spent

1889 advertisement for Stuber & Bro. Photography Studio.

six months in the laboratory of Dr. Hugo Smith in Zurich, Switzerland, and returned to the United States to triumph both in the making of photographic materials and as a master photographer.

Stuber initially went into the manufacture of dry plates, an imaging process that preceded the use of film, in a factory at Thirty-seventh St. and Pflanz Ave., but his downtown gallery, on Fourth St. between Walnut (Muhammad Ali Blvd.) and Green (LIBERTY) Streets, burned, and the factory failed in a money panic in 1893. In 1894 Stuber was invited by photography pioneer George Eastman to go to Rochester, New York, as a sensitized goods expert. The two men had met at a photographic convention, maybe in 1893. Eastman showed interest in Stuber's work on emulsion techniques and connections with the development of a new plate-coating machine in Switzerland. What Stuber did in producing and improving emulsions for various photographic purposes is primarily responsible for the high quality of Eastman film and other Eastman sensitive materials that eventually made possible the high-quality film needed for the filming of motion pictures. Because of his steadfast devotion to the Eastman Kodak Co., Stuber became first vice president. In 1925 Eastman selected Stuber to be the third president of the company. He remained president from 1925 to 1934. Following in Eastman's footsteps, Stuber later resigned the presidency to become chairman of the board.

Stuber's last visit to Louisville was in 1944. At his death, he was a large stockholder of the Eastman Kodak Co. and a multimillionaire.

See *New York Times*, June 19, 1959; *Courier-Journal*, June 19, 1959.

Warder Harrison

SUBURBS. The suburbanization of the Louisville metropolitan area has been a story of POPULATION pressures, improved transportation, booming economic periods, and continued relocation away from the urban core. Although farmers had resided on the fertile county lands since the late eighteenth century, outward movement began in earnest after the 1819 establishment of the Louisville and Lexington Turnpike (Frankfort Ave. and Shelbyville Rd.). As this route facilitated movement into and away from the city to the east, wealthy Louisvillians began to construct country estates as retreats from the bustling center city. Plantations also, with their nearby sharecroppers, squatters, and other poor, contributed to the development of suburbs. Other upper-class residents began to follow this lead after additional links were completed to the east, such as the LOUISVILLE & FRANKFORT RAILROAD in 1851, and others were improved, such as the macadamizing of Bardstown Rd. in 1832. This early retreat to the undeveloped rural areas, while not a large-scale migration, continued at a steady pace until the CIVIL WAR.

Following the end of hostilities in 1865, Louisville, as other urban areas, saw numerous affluent residents settling farther from the city. RAILROADS had a great impact on suburban growth. Commuter travel by steam began in the 1850s. In 1868 EDWARD HOBBS began to develop parts of the suburb later known as ANCHORAGE near the Tywopata Bend of the Louisville & Frankfort Railroad. Nearby, an African American community named BERRYTOWN developed at this time for the domestic helpers of Hobbs's suburb. Farther north, the Louisville, Harrods Creek, & Westport Railroad was completed in 1877 from First St. to Sand Hill (PROSPECT), making the areas later dubbed GLENVIEW and NITTA YUMA accessible. The area west of downtown also welcomed new residents as the growing population spread to the readily available and flat land. As the streetcar lines expanded into the West End following the Civil War, subdivisions such as PARKLAND attracted families who desired the convenient and cheap lands, which were considered less snobby than those to the east. In time, the city limits would expand to incorporate more and more of these suburban areas, turning them into NEIGHBORHOODS.

By 1890 the area south of the city had not seen the widespread development of the west and east. Outside of what later became OLD LOUISVILLE, which became a popular place for wealthy residents after the SOUTHERN EXPOSITION in 1883–87, and LIMERICK, a haven for Irish and African American rail workers at the nearby LOUISVILLE & NASHVILLE RAILROAD (L&N) repair shops and switching yard, not many had moved south of the city because of poor transportation links and bad drainage. With population still on the rise and undivided land becoming more scarce, the movement southward became a necessity.

During the last decade of the nineteenth

century, at which time approximately 15 percent of the population lived outside of the city limits, three major developments sparked a new wave of suburbanization that would last until WORLD WAR I. By 1890 mule-powered streetcar lines laced the city and carried passengers as far south as CHURCHILL DOWNS. During that year the two major railway companies in town, the Louisville City Railway Co. and the Central Passenger Railroad Co., consolidated to create the Louisville Railway Co. With its combined resources and capital, the company continued to extend its reach and carry workers farther from downtown, especially after electric STREETCARS became common later in the decade. Manufacturing, too, was spreading beyond Louisville, especially to HIGHLAND PARK, the incorporated community that stretched along the L&N tracks south of the city. Other unincorporated suburban developments in this area included Oakdale, BEECHMONT, and Jacob's Addition.

Along with the new transportation technology, the establishment of three large rural PARKS drew residents into the suburbs. Starting in 1890 the city developed IROQUOIS PARK in the south, connected to the city via the Grand Blvd. (Southern Pkwy.); Shawnee Park in the west, and Cherokee Park in the east.

The third factor, a result of the previous two, was the desire of more people for a residence outside the city. To the health-conscious of the Gilded Age and later Progressive Era, the country offered the benefits of clean air, cooler temperatures, and a tranquility not found in the bustle of the city. Summer homes sometimes became year-round residences. To meet the demand, in the late nineteenth century there was a substantial rise in the number of real estate agents (twenty-three in 1880 and ninety-five by 1890), subdivision developers, and building and loan associations. These professionals transformed suburbanization by opening up rural living to the middle class. With the development of living areas on smaller lots and more accommodating lending practices, realizing the dream of owning a home was within the reach of many. In addition, electric interurban cars facilitated people traveling to and from suburban homes outside the city. Together these elements led to the establishment of areas such as WILDER PARK in the South End and AUDUBON PARK in 1912 and stimulated the growth of the areas surrounding SHAWNEE and Cherokee Parks.

Still by 1920, only 18 percent of Jefferson County's population lived outside the city limits as movement to the suburbs slowed during the United State's involvement in World War I. Just as migration to areas such as ST. MATTHEWS, Audubon Park, and western Louisville began to return to its prewar pace, spurred by the automobile, improvements to the sewer and water systems, and growth in the area's industrial sector, the GREAT DEPRESSION and World War II halted the plans of many. The great 1937 flood caused many people to move from the West End to the Highlands and East End.

Louisville's city limits moved inexorably to consume new suburbs so that by 1940 the city was still home to 82 percent of the county's population, a figure that was kept high by the bitterly-contested 1922 annexation of the eleven-square-mile area that contained several of the early suburbs, including Oakdale, Highland Park, and HAZELWOOD, and their forty thousand people. However, as the war came to an end, the booming population that had remained bottled up for nearly twenty years of economic depression and war needed room to expand. With the river impeding further growth in the west, developers looked to remaining lands in the east and the south.

Fueled by several factors, suburbanization began an unrelenting rise from the end of WORLD WAR II and continuing into the 1990s. A soaring birthrate coupled with several government programs, including the G.I. Bill, promoted and assisted home ownership for veterans and other middle-class citizens. Utilities began extending services to more distant suburbs following the war. Additionally, downtown workers could live farther from the city because of new highway construction. Automobile ownership ballooned. The number of registered vehicles grew from 64,000 in 1930 to 150,000 in 1950. Starting in 1955, with the construction of the Inner Belt Hwy. (WATTERSON EXPRESSWAY) and followed over the next three decades by the construction of INTERSTATES 65, 64, and 71 and the Outer Belt Hwy. (GENE SNYDER FREEWAY), the metropolitan area built up its freeway and interstate systems, which opened up new regions for development. These were examples of a federal policy that favored private transportation.

Industrial suburbanization also drew people away from the central core as complexes such as RUBBERTOWN in southwestern Jefferson County (World War II), General Electric's Appliance Park (1953), and Ford Motor Co.'s Louisville Assembly Plant (1955) attracted workers and their families to settle nearby. Finally, the 1954 desegregation of PUBLIC SCHOOLS and subsequent forced BUSING caused both blacks and whites to relocate. Coinciding events included what was commonly referred to as "white flight." This came about as AFRICAN AMERICANS moved into the West End as whites relocated to the south and east ends of the county and even across county lines. Several URBAN RENEWAL areas west of Sixth St. and the airport expansion also accelerated "black flight" to the West End, since areas to which African Americans could move were limited.

By 1960 the number of residents living outside the city had risen to approximately 36 percent, up from 24 percent just a decade earlier. Moreover, while the county's population rose approximately 25 percent in the 1940s and 1950s, the city's population rose just under 16 percent in the 1940s and only 5 percent in the 1950s. Housing construction also marked this trend as an average of fifty-four hundred homes was erected outside of the city per year during the 1950s with a peak of eight thousand in 1951. As commercial establishments followed the residents to the outlying districts and established shopping malls, places such as PLEASURE RIDGE PARK, VALLEY STATION, SHIVELY, JEFFERSONTOWN, and St. Matthews witnessed incredible growth. While the developments continued unabated, the county also had to contend with wildcat subdivisions. These small communities arose without the approval and supervision of the PLANNING AND ZONING Commission prior to World War II and continued to plague the county until zoning laws were changed in 1954.

The city attempted to keep pace with the county's growth through annexation and acquired much of the area surrounding the Watterson Expressway between 1956 and 1963 except for St. Matthews. When Louisville attempted to annex the business areas along Lexington and Shelbyville Roads, St. Matthews incorporated as a city in 1950. During this time other smaller communities, fearing annexation and desiring lower taxes, began to incorporate as sixth-class cities. Before 1938 there were only three municipalities in Jefferson County: Louisville (1780), Jeffersontown (1797), and Anchorage (1878). When the city moved to annex Shively, the distillery companies in the area encouraged the community to fight annexation. The community wanted the municipal status to maintain independence. Two months before Shively was incorporated in 1938 the General Assembly passed a bill that prohibited a first-class city from unilaterally annexing smaller cities. The passage of this bill marked a significant change. Before the bill was passed Louisville could annex and then the annexed area could protest. Now Louisville had to get permission of most voters to annex a smaller city.

Numerous other communities followed Shively's example. In the 1950s twenty-nine municipalities incorporated, followed by twenty-two in the 1960s. In 1948 Mayor Charles P. Farnsley, who had sponsored the revision of the annexation procedure in 1938, voiced concern for the governmental fragmentation caused by the incorporation of small cities. Earlier in the year Farnsley pushed for the creation of an occupational license tax. This tax would force suburbanites who worked in the city but lived outside its limits, thus avoiding the city's real-estate taxes, to help shoulder the cost of services. Furthermore, Farnsley pushed for all possible annexation. In 1950 a nine-square-mile area to the southwest was added that included the areas of Standiford Field (LOUISVILLE INTERNATIONAL AIRPORT), the Naval Ordnance Plant, CAMP TAYLOR, and the future sites of the Fair and Exposition Center and the zoo. As a result of this annexation, the small city of Audubon Park was completely surrounded. Even though Farnsley succeeded in annexing this area, the incorporation of small cities continued to grow. By 1999 ninety-three municipalities ranging from sixth-class to third-class cities had incorporated.

The city annexations led to a discussion in the 1950s of merging the city and county governments into one body under what was known as the Mallon Plan. Defeated by county voters who desired autonomy and lower taxes, the plan was resurrected in the 1980s and rejected two additional times. To avoid the constant attempts at annexation and to cooperate to entice companies to the region, the city and county worked out a compact in 1986 in which the city agreed to halt annexations and the county and the city agreed to share its growing occupational tax. However, competition did not subside. The county and the city still vied for jobs, and there was no unified promotion effort to entice new corporations to the area. Despite the shortcomings the compact was renewed in 1998.

While the movement to the suburbs slowed during the 1960s (14 percent growth rate), the city's population dropped over 7 percent, thus increasing the percentage of residents in the county to nearly 50 percent. The gap continued to widen, and by 1980, some 57 percent of the county's residents lived outside of the city. Much of this expansion was in the eastern and southern parts of the county surrounding the newly completed Gene Snyder Freeway.

While the city witnessed a small resurgence following a trend toward moving back to the urban core and to neighborhoods such as BUTCHERTOWN, the outward migration continued into the 1990s (60 percent lived outside of the city limits in 1990) but expanded beyond Jefferson County. From 1990 to 1997 Jefferson County's population only grew .8 percent, while its bordering counties flourished; SHELBY COUNTY grew 16.2 percent, Bullitt County grew 21.9 percent, Oldham County by 30 percent, and Spencer County by 34.6 percent.

Although separated by the Ohio River, a connection has long existed between southern Indiana and Louisville. FERRIES operated between the two regions even after the completion of the first vehicular bridge in 1886. The southern Indiana counties of Clark, Floyd, Harrison, and Scott became a part of the Louisville metropolitan area, and the same growth and development patterns have affected the entire region. Between the end of World War II and 1970 suburban growth was particularly strong in Clark and Floyd Counties. Jeffersonville and its environs experienced heavy residential growth to the east and north along Utica Pike, Middle Rd., Tenth St., Hamburg Pike, and Allison Ln.; and Tenth St. emerged as a major commercial artery. New Albany grew to the west and north in a swath of territory roughly bounded by State Roads 311 and 62 and Interstate 265, with State St., Green Valley and Grant Line Roads, and Klerner Ln. serving as primary spines for development.

As in Louisville, construction of the interstate highway system was a major stimulus of development. Particularly important was Interstate 65, which divides Jeffersonville and Clarksville. Intersecting both Eastern Blvd. and State Rd. 131 in Clarksville, it opened large sections of farmland for residential and commercial development. Since the mid-1960s, Clarksville has become the most rapidly growing municipality in southern Indiana, and SR 131 is now one of the Louisville area's largest regional commercial centers.

Since 1970, growth in Clarksville has remained strong. As a result of new development and aggressive annexation, the town's boundaries now extend to SILVER CREEK Township near SELLERSBURG. Jeffersonville continues to grow in a northeastward direction while New Albany has experienced growth between Interstate 265 and the KNOBS, which extend through western Floyd County and into northwestern Clark County. Significant pockets of suburban development occurred in the Utica and Charlestown townships along SR 62 east and north of JEFFERSONVILLE, in Sellersburg near Interstate 65, and in Monroe Township near Henryville in Clark County. Substantial development in Floyd County has occurred in the Knobs along Interstate 64, US 150, Old Vincennes Rd., and near the towns of Greenville, Georgetown, Galena, and Floyds Knobs. With the completion of Interstate 64 between Louisville and Evansville, Harrison County has become the most rapidly growing county in southern Indiana, with substantial growth in the vicinity of Corydon and Lanesville. Scott County has experienced significant residential and industrial growth in the Scottsburg area since the early 1980s, particularly along SR 50 and its intersections with U.S. 31 and Interstate 65.

Although such towns as Jeffersonville, New Albany, Clarksville, CORYDON, and Scottsburg have strong identities of their own and serve local needs, many of their residents and residents of surrounding counties commute to work in Louisville. In some ways, they are bedroom communities providing labor for the local market. On the other hand, economic growth in these communities has attracted a growing number of workers from Louisville. As a result, commuter traffic in both directions has increased substantially and has created a need for two new bridges. The bridges will mean that, for many, the commute to and from downtown Louisville from southern Indiana will take less time than from the outlying suburbs of Jefferson and surrounding counties. Between 1980 and 2000 the growth of the Indiana counties to some degree reflects the flight to the suburbs that has characterized the area south of the Ohio River. Since land is still readily available and relatively cheap in southern Indiana, it is anticipated that growth there will be significant in the twenty-first century.

See Louisville Survey: Central and South Report (Louisville 1978); Louisville Survey West: Final Report (Louisville 1977); Louisville Survey: East Report (Louisville 1980); George Yater, Two Hundred Years at the Falls of the Ohio (Louisville 1987).

SUGAR GROVE. This once-popular picnic area and campground was in HARRISON COUNTY, INDIANA, on the shore of the OHIO RIVER about thirteen miles below NEW ALBANY at the point where Stewart's Creek flows into the river. Little has been recorded of the history of Sugar Grove, but it was operated by the New Albany and Portland Ferry Co., perhaps as early as 1860. In that year the ferry line used the steamer *Adelaide* as a reserve boat pressed into service when the ferry business was brisk. But it was also used for "pic-nics," perhaps at Sugar Grove. The name of the grounds probably reflected a stand of sugar maple trees at the site.

The recreation spot was definitely in operation by 1878 when the steamer *Frank McHarry* carried an Odd Fellows picnic party to Sugar Grove.

About 1889 the KENTUCKY AND INDIANA BRIDGE CO., which had built a bridge between New Albany and PORTLAND, purchased the ferry company, including Sugar Grove. At that time the steamer MUSIC was used to convey excursionists to the picnic grounds. The *Louisville Post* on April 13, 1891, reported that the bridge company intended to sell Sugar Grove and the *Music*. By 1893 the excursion boats to local riverside recreation areas, including Sugar Grove, were operated by the Louisville and Jeffersonville Ferry Co. The closing date of the recreation spot is unknown, but it was still identified on the 1929 Ohio River Flood Plain Chart 23, issued by the Army Corps of Engineers.

See *Louisville Post*, April 25, 1893.

George H. Yater

SULLIVAN COLLEGE. Sullivan College, originally Sullivan Business College, was founded in 1962 by father and son Alva O. and A.R. Sullivan as a one-year school of business after the Sullivans sold their shares of SPENCERIAN COLLEGE to Roy Whalin, Charles Whalin, and Raymond Jones.

In August 1972 the Kentucky General Assembly, through its state Board of Business Schools, authorized Sullivan and other accredited business schools in Kentucky to grant associate degrees. The following year Bryant and Stratton Business College, founded in Louisville in 1864, (the older Sullivan had been registrar at Bryant and Stratton) merged with Sullivan, with Bryant and Stratton students becoming students at Sullivan College and Sullivan being the surviving institution.

The college made a significant move in 1976, acquiring its own freestanding campus and moving from being accredited as a business school to accreditation as a junior college of business. The name was changed to Sullivan Junior College of Business in 1976, approximately the same time the college moved from the Francis Building on S Fourth St. to its campus at 3101 Bardstown Rd. at the corner of the WATTERSON EXPRESSWAY and Bardstown Rd.

In 1990 the Kentucky Council on Higher Education granted Sullivan approval to award the Bachelor of Science Degree in Business Administration, and the institution received baccalaureate level accreditation from the Southern Association of Colleges and Schools in 1992.

During the period of the early 1980s to the 1990s, Sullivan expanded its program offering beyond the purely business-related programs in ACCOUNTING, management, data processing, and secretarial science to begin a National Center of Hospitality Studies in 1987; it included associate degree programs in culinary arts, baking, and pastry arts, hotel/restaurant management, and travel and TOURISM. In addition, at approximately the same time, Sullivan began to offer associate degree programs in paralegal studies and added a one-year program to train early childhood workers as professional nannies.

In 1997, the college began a graduate school offering a Master in Business Administration (M.B.A.) Degree and the college received accreditation from the Southern Association of Colleges and Schools at the graduate school level. Sullivan College in 1998 became Kentucky's largest private college or university with enrollment of approximately three thousand students at its campuses in Louisville, Lexington, and FORT KNOX.

Sullivan College is a part of the Sullivan Colleges System, which includes Sullivan College, Spencerian College (which the Sullivan family reacquired from the Whalin family in 1972) and the Louisville Technical Institute (which was also acquired in 1972). The Louisville Technical Institute offers programs in mechanical, architectural, and electronic engineering technology, robotics, interior design, marine mechanics, computer-assisted drafting, and computer graphics at both the diploma and associate degree level. Spencerian College, one of the oldest private career schools in the country, was founded in Louisville in 1892 and offers diploma and associate degree programs in NURSING, business, computer science, and medical related fields.

The three colleges comprise the Sullivan College System and provide education and training at seven campus locations in Kentucky. In addition, it offers extended classes at several Kentucky community colleges as well as on several college campuses in Tennessee.

William Duane Kenney

SUMMERS, WILLIAM E., III (b Louisville, October 17, 1917; d Louisville, May 17, 1996). Minister and radio executive. He was the son of Mima (Sweat) and William E. Summers II. Summers started his career in journalism as a writer for the *LOUISVILLE DEFENDER* in 1941. In the late 1940s, he coordinated a talent show for WGRC (which became WAKY) radio. In 1951 he became a part-time sportscaster for WLOU radio, moving into a full-time position. From that position he moved into management of Rounsaville Radio, the company that owned seven radio stations with a black format, including the Louisville-based WLOU. In 1967 he became vice president and general manager of WLOU.

Summers incorporated Summers Broadcasting Inc. and purchased WLOU in 1971 and WNUU FM in 1973 (sold 1976). WLOU was the first Kentucky broadcast property to be owned and operated by a minority group. It was sold in 1982 to Johnson Publishing Co. (Chicago), but Summers remained with WLOU as a consultant until 1988. The Kentucky Broadcasters Association awarded Summers the Golden Mike award for his service to BROADCASTING. He also was inducted into the University of Kentucky Journalism Hall of Fame in 1996 a month before his death.

Summers also served numerous congregations as an African Methodist Episcopal minister, pastoring churches in TAYLORSVILLE, Georgetown, SHELBYVILLE, and Louisville. His longest pastorate was at St. Paul AME Church in Louisville. He served there from 1968 until his retirement in 1988. Active in civic affairs, he was a board member of the LOUISVILLE URBAN LEAGUE, the Boys Clubs of America, the TRANSIT AUTHORITY OF RIVER CITY; board member and ultimately president of the KENTUCKY DERBY FESTIVAL; president of the Food for the Elderly consortium; and a local and national board member of the YMCA. He had marched in Selma, Alabama, in 1965 with Rev. Martin Luther King Jr. For his work, Summers was awarded such honors as the Distinguished Service Award of the Louisville Urban League, the NAACP Educational Award, the Black Achiever of the Year, the City of Louisville's Freedom Award, and the National Association of Christians and Jews Brotherhood Award.

His family included his wife, Feryn (Stigall) Summers; three children: a son, William E. Summers IV, and two daughters, Seretha Summers-Tinsley and Sherryl S. Summers; and seven grandchildren. He is buried in CAVE HILL CEMETERY.

Gail Henson

SUTCLIFFE COMPANY. Founded in 1892 by J.H. Sutcliffe, this sporting goods retail and wholesale firm was originally located on W MAIN St. under the name J.H. Sutcliffe and Co. In its infancy the business primarily retailed knives and firearms and also had a mail order division. A few years after establishing his company, Sutcliffe sold it to Ira Barnett, Dillon Maypother, and Henry Willenbrink. In 1903 the business was taken over and reorganized by George Buechel and H.F. Willenbrink. It was then that Sutcliffe's began to stock a more complete line of sporting goods.

In 1925 Sutcliffe's expanded by adding new product lines, including camera equipment, and moving to a four-story building on Fourth St. between Market and Jefferson Streets. At that time the firm already had two downtown warehouses and a branch store farther down Fourth St. Sutcliffe's wholesale division, through which the firm purchased goods directly from manufacturers and supplied them to various dealers, continued to expand as well. By the late 1960s the wholesale division accounted for about 80 percent of the company's total business, and its service territory included the southeastern and midwestern regions of the United States. For generations of young and old alike, it was a popular shopping place. Its second floor was a wondrous place and had a special allure for children as it housed the toy section. In 1968 a North Carolina wholesale distributor of sporting goods, Davidson Supply Co., purchased the Sutcliffe Co. and maintained it in Louisville as an independent wholesale subsidiary until the early 1970s, when it closed and the building was razed to make way for the Commonwealth Convention Center.

See *Courier-Journal,* Feb. 10, 1943.

SUTTON, CAROL JEAN (b St. Louis, Missouri, June 29, 1934; d Louisville, February 19, 1985). Journalist. Born to Dallas and Marie Sutton, she received her degree from the University of Missouri School of Journalism in 1955 and moved to Louisville. She applied for a reporter's job at the *COURIER-JOURNAL* and *LOUISVILLE TIMES* but was offered a position as a secretary to James S. Pope Sr., the executive editor. Within one year she had been promoted to reporter, where she covered CITY HALL, political candidates, and the 1957 eastern Kentucky flood.

In 1963 Sutton was promoted to editor of the "Woman's World" section, which primarily relayed household tips and society news. She changed its title to "Today's Living," tackling harder issues such as alcoholism, abortion, rural poverty, and migrant labor. She shocked readers when she ran the first installment of a piece on hunger on Thanksgiving Day. In 1971 the section won the J.C. Penney–University of Missouri award for excellence in journalism. Two years later she won the same organization's award for investigative reporting for her piece on the fashion industry and its "freebies" to fashion reporters.

Sutton was named the *Courier-Journal's* managing editor in 1974, the first woman to achieve this position at a major U.S. metropolitan newspaper. Two years later, Sutton, along with eleven other women including First Lady Betty Ford and TENNIS star Billie Jean King, appeared on the cover of *Time* magazine to represent the American woman as the publication's "Man of the Year." That year she moved to a corporate position as the assistant to editor and publisher Barry Bingham Jr. By 1979 she had been made senior editor of both papers and began an aggressive campaign to recruit minority journalists. Because of her efforts, the percentage of African American news and opinion-page writers rose from 3 to 10 percent and led to a story in Time magazine in 1983. Additionally, Sutton became the first non–African American member of the National Association of Black Journalists.

She served as chairperson of the Pulitzer Prize juries in 1975 and 1976, was a member of the selection committee for the Nieman Fellows in Journalism at Harvard in 1976, and edited 40 Years of Aerial Photography over Kentucky (1981), a collection of prints by retired Courier- Journal photographer Billy Davis. She was inducted into the Kentucky Journalism Hall of Fame in 1985 and placed in the "Kentucky Women Remembered" exhibit in the Capitol in Frankfort in 1997.

Sutton married Charles Whaley in 1957 and they had two children, Carrie and Kate. Sutton was cremated.

See Courier-Journal, Feb. 20, 1985.

Swimming pool at Reservoir Park in Crescent Hill, with Louisville Water Company reservoir in background, 1941.

SWIMMING. Swimming, in its many forms, has a very strong presence in Louisville. The Ohio River has always been a challenge to swim in or across. The Louisville Boat Club was a center for this activity when the floating clubhouse was located near the Zorn Ave. pumping station in 1907. In the late 1920s and early 1930s, Ohio River Swims were held. These events began on the Indiana side and, depending on the current, ended near Pastime Club, the American Turners, or present-day Cox Park. All of this was a far cry from the Six Flags Kentucky Kingdom water park that creates artifical waves to delight swimmers.

Today competitive swimming opportunities come in a wide range of disciplines. USA Swimming Inc. (USA) is an age group program that provides competition for its registered swimmers eighteen years old and younger. The senior program provides competition for members who are striving for qualification at national and/or international competition while providing an educational experience and enhancing mental and physical conditioning. Louisville has three USA teams: Lakeside Seahawks, Caritas Poolsharks, and Louisville Tarpons. Louisville is proud of swimmers who participated in Olympic games: Mary Moorman Ryan and Ann Hardin in 1940 and, later, Susie Shields, Camille Wright, Tori Trees, Leigh Ann Fetter, and Mary T. Meagher.

Mary Terstegge Meagher, known as "Mary T.," was an Olympic gold medalist and record-setting butterfly swimmer. In 1980 Meagher qualified for the U.S. Olympic team. When the United States boycotted the 1980 Olympics in Moscow, Meagher returned to Louisville to train with Bill Peak. In August 1981 she won the national championships, establishing two world records—the 100-meter-butterfly (57.9) and 200-meter-butterfly (2:05.9). Her 200-meter mark was the longest-standing record when it was broken in May 2000. Meagher won three gold medals in the 1984 Olympics: the 100- and 200-meter butterfly and the 4x100. She again qualified for the Olympic team in August 1988 and won a bronze medal. Meagher was born October 27, 1965, in Louisville to James L. and Floy (Terstegge) Meagher. Meagher married Michael Plant in 1994; they have two children, Madeline and Andrew.

United States Masters Swimming Inc. offers adults the opportunity to participate in a lifelong fitness and/or competitive swimming program. Louisville boasts three active Masters teams: Crescent Hill Masters, Lakeside Masters, and Louisville Y Masters.

United States Diving Inc. conducts four programs: Junior Olympic for developmental/ physical fitness for youths; Senior to develop national and international divers; International to expose superior divers to the demands of world-class competition; and Masters for physical fitness for those over twenty-one. Louisville has had several national champions, NCAA and Olympic qualifiers from Lakeside Swim Club, Plantation Club, and the University of Louisville.

United States Synchronized Swimming Inc. was represented in past years by programs offered at the Louisville YWCA, Lakeside Swim Club, and E.P. "Tom" Sawyer State Park. The Ladies of Lorelei, of the YMCA of Greater Louisville, are active locally. Masters synchronized swimming is a growing sector of this discipline and an annual national competition is held; it was won by Louisville Synchro Masters in 1983.

United States Water Polo Inc. is not represented in Louisville, but water polo is played by many USA teams and summer leagues as preseason conditioning, along with recreational games.

Louisville also supports three summer leagues: Country Club Swim Association, Louisville Swim Association, and the Kentuckiana Swim Association. Leagues are designed for swimmers wanting to experience a social-team atmosphere, plus competitions, and to give teenagers the opportunity to supplement their high school program.

High school swim programs were formed in Louisville by Brother Fabius, C.F.X., of St. Xavier High School in 1948. The Kentucky High School Athletic Association acknowledged Louisville Male, du Pont Manual, Flaget, and St. Xavier high school swimming and diving teams for boys. In the 1950s girls' teams were formed. In 1998 fourteen high schools in Louisville and Jefferson County had swim teams for boys and girls. During the school year these students participated in local meets and the state swimming and diving championships.

Over the years many pools, public and private, have provided recreational and structured programs, among them Shelby Park, Fontaine Ferry Park, Lighthouse Lake, Tucker's Lake, and the country clubs. Several swimming complexes should be highlighted for their powerful influence on swimming in Louisville.

The YMCA in Louisville has been a vigorous leader of swimming since 1910 when it began the "Learn to Swim" program that provided free lessons to boys ages ten to eighteen. Its new building at Third and Broadway, opened in 1913, included a large indoor pool. Its aquatic program offered monthly swim meets for boys, who were grouped by weight: 60–80 lbs., 81–95 lbs., up to 125 lbs., and unlimited.

Included at these meets were fancy diving and informal water-polo games. Family and friends were invited to swim carnivals that were held to promote swimming, diving, and lifesaving. On March 19, 1922, the first indoor Amateur Athletic Union (AAU)-sanctioned swim meet was held at the Y. By 1929 free Boy Scout swimming classes were held there for second-class scouts to obtain their merit badges in lifesaving and first aid.

The YMCA of Greater Louisville and the three branches, Southwest Y, Southeast Y, and Northeast Y, have many aquatic programs for children and adults. They include Arthritis Aquatics as a joint program with the Arthritis Foundation, aqua fitness, deep-water aerobics, lifeguard certification, Learn to Swim, multiple-sclerosis classes, recreational swims, and lap swimming. U.S. Masters and Kentuckiana Swim Association summer teams cater to the competitive spirits.

On July 29, 1919, the CRESCENT HILL community pool was opened by the LOUISVILLE WATER CO. when a lake, created in a borrow pit, was drained by the water company. The borrow pit was formed when earth was removed to make an earthen berm around the reservoirs across Reservoir Ave. This oval-shaped recreational pool was one of the largest in the region. Exhibition swims were held in the 1930s, where Hall-of-Famer Johnny Weismueller participated. In 1954 the pool was relocated farther up Reservoir Ave., and in 1980 an air structure was erected over it to provide a year-round public pool. Aquatic programs for adults and children were expanded to include aqua exercise, rehabilitation and therapy, swim lessons, lap swimming, recreational swimming, and water polo. Other major users for practices were USA, Masters, and high school swim teams. Many large swim meets were held: high school championships, USA regional, and Masters meets. In 1998 a new state-of-the-art Mary T. Meagher Aquatic Center opened, managed by the Louisville Metro Parks aquatic department. Louisville Metro Parks also operates the Shawnee High School pool year-round for recreational swimmers, lap swimmers, and competitive team practices.

In 1948 the Louisville Metro Parks opened the Wyandotte Park Pool on Taylor Blvd. In 1998 the aquatic department operated eight pools in the city and five in Jefferson County, providing a public swimming opportunity for over ninety-five thousand adults and children each summer.

The American Turners purchased land on the Ohio River in 1911 to provide aquatics for members. Swim lessons were given in the river during the early years; and in the 1940s Joseph Weismueller, cousin to Johnny, who played Tarzan in the movies, was coach and instructor for the river lessons. Turners also sponsored "River Swims" in the 1930s. In 1958 the club's swimming pool was built for recreational and competitive swimmers.

Lakeside Swim Club was incorporated on March 1, 1924, as a private club. At that time it was a murky water-filled quarry where swim carnivals were held along with neighborhood recreational swimming. The first swimming and diving meet held at Lakeside was on September 9, 1928. It became the Ohio Valley Championships and is the oldest swim meet in the nation held at the same pool. In 1938 the AAU's Men's National Championships were held at Lakeside with world backstroke record holder Adolph Kiefer, diver Al Patnik, and Yale University coach Robert Kiputh, who was instrumental in developing competitive swimming in America, in attendance.

By 1998 Lakeside had year-round competitive programs including a three-hundred-member United States Swim Team, open to all the youth of Louisville, and a twenty-five- member United States Diving Team. The teams have included All-American swimmers, national champions, international champions at Pan American Games and the World University Games, and seven Olympians. Lakeside alumni have become university coaches, USA coaches, USMS coaches, and managers of aquatic enterprises across America. The United States Masters team, begun in 1976 by Jack Thompson and Gary Weisenthal, includes world champions and nationally-ranked swimmers.

The University of Louisville men's swim program began in 1948. In 1982 the women's program was inaugurated with men's and women's coach Rick Hill. There have been a number of NCAA national championship qualifiers throughout the years for this Division I team.

The JEWISH COMMUNITY CENTER on Dutchmans Ln. was built in 1954 with indoor and outdoor swimming pools for the health and fitness program. It offers an expanded aquatic program for year-round activities.

Plantation Country Club opened its 50-meter pool on July 22, 1957. Coach Ralph Wright built a strong AAU team. It included international champions at the World Student Games, Pan American Games, and an Olympic bronze medalist. The National AAU Swimming Championships were held at Plantation in 1969 and 1973.

At E.P. "Tom" Sawyer State Park the 50-meter swimming pool with connecting diving well and the recreation building were completed in 1975. Since that time the pool has served an average of twelve hundred people per summer day and over fifty thousand people during the summer months.

The park hosts a triathlon, sanctioned by USA Triathlon Inc., in August of each year. The competitive rules of USA Triathlon Inc. describe its purpose as promoting sportsmanship, equal opportunity, and fair play while protecting the health and safety of participants. The number of entrants from Kentucky and surrounding states has increased from 96 in 1982, the first year, to 168 in 1998. The triathlon consists of a half-mile swim in the fifty-meter pool, a sixteen-mile bike ride, and a five-kilometer run.

Scuba diving has become another exciting and popular area of recreational swimming. Scuba-diving schools in Louisville prepare students to receive certification in open-water diving.

Swimming pool water quality and safety is administered through the Kentucky Department of Health Services, the Louisville and Jefferson County Board of Health, and the American Red Cross. The BOARD OF HEALTH manual includes regulations for pool safety, monthly inspections, weekly water testing, safety equipment required on deck, number of lifeguards based on pool size, and procedures to become a lifeguard in Jefferson County. A lifeguard must complete the following courses to receive a permit: 1) lifeguard training from the American Red Cross, Boy Scouts of America, National Pool and Waterpark Life Guard/CPR Training, or the YMCA; 2) First-aid course; 3) CPR (cardiopulmonary resuscitation) training; and must pass the Jefferson County lifeguard water and written test.

For lifeguard permit renewal, each year the applicant must complete a CPR course and retake the Jefferson County lifeguard water course and the written test for permit. Applicants must still have current certification in a lifeguard and first-aid course. These stringent rules put Jefferson County in the forefront of injury prevention. Swimming in Louisville, and the historically strong presence that continues today, demonstrates that for health, pleasure, or competitive sport, swimming is a lifetime activity.

See Samuel W. Thomas, *Crescent Hill Revisited* (Louisville 1987); Jack Thompson, *The Lakeside Story* (Louisville 1988).

Joanne Gummere Tingley

SWISS PARK. Located on Lynn St. between Shelby and PRESTON Streets, Swiss Park was constructed in 1925 by the Gruelti Helveltica Society, a benevolent association which had been formed in 1850 to lend money to Swiss immigrants new to the Louisville area (this practice was abandoned in the 1950s). A structure dubbed Swiss Hall was erected on the site shortly thereafter and served as a meeting house for the society and the land's two other owners, Swiss Charities Inc. and the Swiss Ladies Club.

The park became a popular summer gathering place for the entire GERMANTOWN community, as it hosted numerous dances, BINGO games, church socials, cookouts, and other lively celebrations. However, by the 1960s attendance had tapered off, and the society stopped providing entertainment in 1971. After that the park was closed except when rented for specific festivities.

In the mid-1980s, the society decided to reopen the park for weekly gatherings and pumped over $110,000 into renovations, which included new picnic tables and benches, a restored snack bar and kitchen, and a new stage and dance floor. However, the refurbished park did not help the group's dwindling membership numbers, which had fallen from 200 to about 110 in the early 1990s. In 1993 the society decided to sell the two-and-one-half-acre site. It was purchased and reopened for summer parties a year later by the Fraternal Order of Police Deputy Sheriff's Lodge 25.

See *Courier-Journal,* July 22, 1992, Aug. 4, 1993.

T

TACHAU, JEAN (BRANDEIS) (b Louisville, August 22, 1894; d Louisville, July 3, 1978). Social reformer. She was the daughter of Alfred and Jennie (Taussig) Brandeis, and the niece of LOUIS BRANDEIS, a United States Supreme Court justice. Her father was a prosperous Louisville grain merchant. After graduating in 1911 from the Kentucky Home School, Tachau attended Bryn Mawr College for one year. She then spent two years in Cambridge, Massachusetts, studying violin.

With the United States' entry into WORLD WAR I in 1917, Tachau joined the war effort through volunteer work with the Red Cross Home Service. The following year, the Children's Protective Association in Louisville hired her as a part-time clerk-typist. However, she soon began to have cases assigned to her, and her duties expanded. She left paid employment following her marriage to Charles G. Tachau on May 11, 1921, but maintained her involvement in social issues through volunteer activities. As chair of the Council of Social Agencies (later the Health and Welfare Council), Tachau worked to get an ordinance passed to require inspection and licensing of all children's boarding homes in Louisville. In 1932 she became president of the Children's Agency. From the early 1930s to WORLD WAR II, she served on the advisory committee of the board of the Louisville and Jefferson County Children's Home. Tachau's involvement in child welfare led her to become an advocate of birth control. In 1933 she and a group of volunteers organized the Kentucky Birth Control League.

Initially, the Kentucky Birth Control League opened a weekly clinic in Norton Infirmary's outpatient department. The infirmary, however, only accepted married, white women for "health reasons." The league then opened clinics in outlying areas, including one for AFRICAN AMERICANS at the Church of Our Merciful Saviour. In 1937 the league decided to establish its own clinic in the 600 block of S Floyd St. to eliminate any restrictions on its clientele. The clinic offered separate days for white and black women and hired both a white and a black physician as well as a part-time social worker. The Louisville group encouraged the formation of a similar organization in Lexington and affiliated with the Mountain Maternal Health League in Berea, Kentucky.

In 1938 the league initiated a program to encourage birth control throughout the state by hiring a part-time field representative to visit doctors in each county seat. During the 1940s, the league shifted its focus from strictly birth control and began to offer family and marriage counseling services with the assistance of Dr. WAYNE E. OATES, a professor of counseling at the SOUTHERN BAPTIST THEOLOGICAL SEMINARY. The clinic, renamed the Family Relations Center, eventually became Planned Parenthood of Louisville.

In 1946 Tachau, as chair of the Child Welfare Division of the Health and Welfare Council in Louisville, worked with Juvenile Commissioner Lawrence W. Wetherby to establish new standards for the juvenile court. When he became governor in 1950, Wetherby appointed Tachau to a legislative advisory committee to study the state's child welfare laws and propose changes. In 1952 the General Assembly passed two important child welfare laws based upon the advisory committee's recommendations. The first law transferred the Division of Child Welfare from the Department of Economic Security to the Welfare Department, a move that consolidated the administration of the state's services and institutions for children. The second act created the Youth Authority to oversee Kentucky's juvenile court system. However, the new child welfare legislation was soon undone by Wetherby's successor, Albert B. Chandler (1955–59). Members of the committee that had recommended the new laws then formed the Kentucky Citizens for Child Welfare, with Tachau as the president. The new organization continued to lobby for stronger child welfare laws and was rewarded for its efforts by the creation of the Kentucky Department of Child Welfare in 1960. Tachau served on the new department's advisory council.

In 1963 Tachau retired as the executive director of the Kentucky Birth Control League, but her work on behalf of children continued. In 1965 she became a member of a committee of the Health and Welfare Council of Jefferson County, and in 1970 she chaired a committee to study and plan for children's institutions and foster home care in Louisville and Jefferson County. During the 1960s Tachau also participated in the open housing demonstrations in Louisville and, on one occasion, put her home up as collateral for the bail bond of a group of African Americans who had been arrested.

Tachau and her husband had three children: Charles, Eric, and Jean. Her ashes are buried in CAVE HILL CEMETERY.

See *Courier-Journal,* July 5, 1978.

TACHAU, MARY KATHERINE (BONSTEEL) (b Cleveland, Ohio, June 8, 1926; d Louisville, October 1, 1990). Educator and activist. An accomplished scholar who also worked tirelessly on behalf of women, Mary K., as she was called, received her undergraduate degree in history from Oberlin College in Ohio in 1948. She met and married in 1947 a fellow classmate, Eric Tachau.

For the next few years she settled into family life but eventually returned to academia, receiving her M.A. degree from the UNIVERSITY OF LOUISVILLE in 1958. At the same time, she became a part-time lecturer at the university. In 1961 she became a full-time member of the history department. In 1972, Tachau earned her Ph.D. from the University of Kentucky; her area of specialization was American constitutional history. Her most distinguished work was *Federal Courts in the Early Republic, Kentucky 1789–1816* (1978).

Tachau was also involved in policymaking at the University of Louisville, especially that which concerned equal opportunity and pay for women. At different times during her tenure, she served as the first female university ombudsman, chair of the Committee on the Status of Women, and, from 1976 to 1977 and 1979 to 1980, she was chair of the university senate. In addition, Tachau was the first woman to serve as chair of the University of Louisville's history department, from 1974 to 1977. In 1988, she was the recipient of the Distinguished Professor Award.

Tachau also gained recognition outside the university. She was a historical adviser to the Senate Watergate Committee and was vice president of the American Historical Association when she died. Her constant agitation for CIVIL RIGHTS led her to serve at various times on the Kentucky State Commission on Civil Rights, the Federal Judicial Selection Commission of Kentucky, the Kentucky Legislative Action for Women Coalition, and the board of the Kentucky American Civil Liberties Union.

Tachau retired from the University of Louisville in July of 1990. She and her husband Eric were the parents of two daughters and a son. After her death, two awards were established in her honor—the Mary K. Bonsteel Tachau Award for Excellence in History, a student award at the University of Louisville, and the Mary K. Bonsteel Tachau Pre-Collegiate Teaching Award, sponsored by the Organization of American Historians.

TARASCON, LOUIS AND JOHN (Louis, b Cabannes, France, February 10, 1759, d New York City, September 1840; John, b Cabannes, April 1, 1765, d Louisville, August 11, 1825). Brothers Louis Anastase Tarascon and Jean Antoine Tarascon, founders of the once-thriving community of SHIPPINGPORT at the lower end of the FALLS OF THE OHIO, came to the United States to escape the French Revolution. They were born in the Tarascon district near Marseilles, sons of Henri and Esprit Gillot Tarascori. After he grew older, Louis moved to Marseilles and established a commercial trading business in that Mediterranean port. His activities likely included shipment of French goods to Philadelphia merchants. When the outbreak of the French Revolution in 1789 led later to the Reign of Terror, Louis fled to Philadelphia, arriving August 25, 1794, on the sloop Birmingham Packet. Also on board were Jacques

Tarascon Mill on Shippingport Island, 1892.

Berthoud (Marquis de Ste. Pierre) and his wife, also escaping the Terror. Louis established an importing business in partnership with Victor Journel, another compatriot on the ocean voyage, and Berthoud evidently became their clerk in the business of importing French silks. Jean Tarascon left France in 1797 to join the prospering business.

The rapidly developing Ohio Valley attracted the Tarascons' attention, and in 1799 Berthoud and a companion were sent on a scouting expedition down the Ohio and Mississippi Rivers to New Orleans to report on the possibility of seagoing sailing vessels descending those streams. Their interest had probably been aroused by the construction as early as 1792 of such vessels in the Pittsburgh area. One was sailing the sea from Philadelphia. In addition, the Spanish had relaxed their stringent regulations at New Orleans in 1798, allowing free trade and eliminating import duties on goods shipped abroad. Based on Berthoud's favorable report, the two brothers and Berthoud bought land at Pittsburgh and planned to carry farm produce of the Ohio Valley directly to Europe. They also operated a general store managed by Berthoud. The merchandise included French silks, an exotic commodity on what had recently been the frontier. The ship *Pittsburgh* was built by Louis in 1802 and, shortly after, the schooner *Amity*. Meanwhile his brother (by then John) and Berthoud built the brig *Nanina* and the ships *Louisiana* and *Western Trader* in 1804. The Tarascon yard was apparently the largest in Pittsburgh at the time.

Seagoing sailing vessels on the Ohio and Mississippi Rivers seem improbable and eventually proved impractical. These ships, although of small tonnage, rode deep in the water and found the Falls of the Ohio impassable except at times of high water. It was often necessary to unload the cargo and wagon it to Shippingport so that the ship would ride higher in the water to pass the Falls. Some had to wait months to pass, and some were wrecked on the rocks. A Tarascon vessel and its cargo were lost on the Falls in 1803, an event that led directly to the founding of Shippingport. John Tarascon declared "We have been convinced by a dear-bought experience that it is below the rapids that vessels fit for the sea must be constructed and laden." (Address to the Citizens of Philadelphia, on the Great Advantages which Arise from the Trade of the Western Country . . . to Philadelphia in Particular [Philadelphia 1806]). In December 1803 they had purchased forty-five acres of what had been JOHN CAMPBELL's land, with Berthoud as the agent in the transaction.

Now they sought Philadelphia capital to carry out their plan to establish a town, a shipyard, a ropewalk, wharves, and warehouses. The Address of 1806 was intended to raise financing and succeeded in its mission. Shippingport began to take shape under John Tarascon's direction, and by 1807 a small mill was in operation to produce the wheat he hoped to ship directly to Europe. Berthoud was a partner in the enterprise, but in 1807 John Tarascon dissolved the partnership because of a rift over the land purchase. Berthoud had reserved some for himself. The breach was never healed. Louis was summoned from Philadelphia to aid in the multitudinous tasks of development. That same year international tensions struck a blow at the Tarascons' hopes. President THOMAS JEFFERSON, seeking to avert American involvement in the mounting dispute between England and Napoleonic France, persuaded Congress to impose an embargo on all American shipping to avoid incidents at sea.

As a result, the planned shipyard was never built and the development of Shippingport slowed but continued. A number of French who had fled the Revolution found their way to the community. The ropewalk, warehouse, and wharf were built, and the POPULATION climbed from 90 in 1810 to 521 in 1820. The greatest achievement was John Tarascon's new water-powered mill of stone and brick that towered six stories from water level. Begun in 1815 and completed about 1819, it utilized the design for automated grain-milling devised by the ingenious Philadelphia mechanic and engineer, Oliver Evans, one of the most important of early American inventors. The mill remained a notable landmark for nearly eighty years. But it was scarcely completed when the Panic of 1819 brought trade almost to a halt.

Philadelphia creditors, mostly French émigrés who had lent some seventy thousand dollars for the development of Shippingport, were feeling the universal distress and were clamoring for repayment. In addition, the new town of Portland, founded in 1814 farther downriver, provided better anchorage for the STEAMBOATS that were making their first appearance. They began to desert the Shippingport wharf and warehouse. By 1825, only six years after the great mill was completed, John Tarascon's financial affairs were so hopeless that he committed suicide, leaving the mill to his four children and naming Louis to operate it in their behalf. But creditors pursued John Tarascon's heirs as relentlessly as they had pursued him. Between 1812 and 1830 there were seventy-nine suits brought in the Jefferson County Chancery Courts in addition to suits filed elsewhere. In 1828 the mill was awarded to local creditors, but the Tarascon heirs regained possession in 1830, only to have a federal court award it to Philadelphia creditors in 1834. Under new ownership the mill continued to grind away. In 1842 it was taken over by John Hulme and Francis McHarry, both connected with the LOUISVILLE AND PORTLAND CANAL that had made Shippingport an island. The canal builders had discovered that the limestone rock surrounding the community was raw material for making natural cement. The new owners put the mill to grinding limestone to make cement. In 1866 a new group took over, forming the Louisville Cement and Water Power Co.—later simply the Louisville Cement Co. Though the company later expanded its operations across the river into Indiana, the old Tarascon mill continued to grind away, turning out as many as a thousand barrels of cement on some days. It gradually came to be seen as a historical landmark. Then on August 29, 1892, a raging fire broke out, leaving only the massive stone foundation and the gaunt brick walls. The last vestiges were removed in the mid-1920s to make way for the Louisville Gas and Electric Co.'s hydroelectric plant, taking its power from the Falls just as the mill did.

Louis Tarascon lived to the ripe old age of eighty, optimistic and committed to democracy and equality to the end of his days, giving free rein to his philosophical and rather impractical ideas. They reflected his devotion to the French philosophes who stressed the application of reason and the perfectibility of man and his endeavors. He issued a number of pamphlets to gain a wide audience for his proposals that included putting the educational theories of the French Enlightenment into practice. Another on the Old Court–New Court controversy that wracked Kentucky in the 1820s favored the debtor class, as might be expected. Ever hopeful, he set forth some of his proposals in letters to Thomas Jefferson, James Madison, and President Andrew Jackson, among others. He moved to New York City about 1837 where he proposed to establish a farm school midway between New York and Philadelphia for the "rational education" of orphan children to promote democracy. He died in New York in September 1840; his burial place is unknown.

See John J. Crnkovich, "Tarascon, Junr., James Berthoud & Co. and the Development of Shippingport," M.A. thesis, University of Louisville, 1959; Leland Baldwin, *The Keelboat Age on the Western Waters* (Pittsburgh 1941); Newman F. McGirr, "Tarascon of Shippingport at the Falls of the Ohio," *West Virginia History Quarterly* (Jan. 1946): 89–100; Doyce B. Nunis Jr., "Tarascon's Dream of an American Commercial Empire in the West," *Mid-America* 42 (Jan. 1960): 170–94; Louis A. Tarascon, *To His Fellow Citizens . . . and . . . His Other Fellow Human Beings on Earth* (New York 1837) reprinted as Extra Number 148 of *Magazine of History* (Tarrytown, N.Y., 1929).

George H. Yater

TAYLOR, EDWARD LELAND (b Knoxville, Tennessee, April 10, 1885; d Louisville, February 16, 1948). Mayor. He was the son of Margaret Jordan and Eugene Augustine Taylor, a Baptist minister. The family came to Louisville when Taylor was thirteen years old. He was educated at LOUISVILLE MALE HIGH SCHOOL and graduated from the University of Virginia, where he was president of his class. In 1912 he received his law degree from Virginia. After law school he practiced in Louisville with the firm of Humphrey & Humphrey, but he eventually left to manage the business interests of his late uncle, Marion E. Taylor, president of the real estate firm of Wright & Taylor. He also served as vice president of Semonin-Goodman, a real estate firm, and was director of the Louisville National Bank and Carter Guaranty Co.

In 1932 Taylor ran for Congress from the Third District. While he won the district nomination by two thousand votes, he was prevented from running by a Kentucky Court of Appeals ruling that the race should be decided by a statewide vote rather than by a count of the voters from the district. The Court of Appeals decision was later reversed, but Taylor did not run for election. Continuing to be interested in politics, Taylor first ran for the Democratic nomination for mayor in 1933 against NEVILLE MILLER in one of the closest primaries in the city's history. After thirteen days of counting ballots, including a recount, Miller edged out Taylor by 651 votes. Miller received 17,707 and Taylor 17,056. Miller went on to win the mayoral election. Taylor was elected mayor in November 1945 and served until his death in office in 1948. Taylor's election victory was also one of the closest in Louisville's history, beating Republican Roy W. Easley by only 221 votes. He had campaigned on a platform of ousting the Republican-dominated BOARD OF ALDERMEN, but, while he won the mayoral race, he was unsuccessful in changing the composition of the board. For the first two years of his tenure as mayor, the board continued to be dominated by Republicans until 1947 when the Democrats took control. Taylor was able to work successfully with the Republicans on such projects as the annexation of more land for the city and the expansion of Louisville's highway system.

Taylor married Edith Somers of Charlottesville, Virginia, on September 19, 1914. The couple had four daughters. He volunteered for WORLD WAR I, serving as a first lieutenant with the field artillery in the United States Army. He is buried in CAVE HILL CEMETERY.

See W.T. Owens, *Who's Who in Louisville; The Gateway to the South* (Louisville 1926); *Courier-Journal*, Feb. 17, 1948.

TAYLOR, RICHARD (b Orange County, Virginia, 1744; d Jefferson County, Kentucky, January 1829). Revolutionary War officer, civic leader, and father of the twelfth president of the United States. The son of Zachary and Elizabeth (Lee) Taylor, Richard was a member of a wealthy and socially established Virginia family. Taylor graduated from the College of William and Mary, and in 1769 the adventurous young man and his older brother, Hancock, set out down the Ohio and Mississippi Rivers from Pittsburgh to New Orleans.

With the coming of the Revolutionary War, Taylor entered into military service and served with different Virginia Continental units, seeing action at the battles of White Plains, Brandywine, Monmouth, and Trenton. By war's end, he had reached the rank of lieutenant-colonel. In 1779, Taylor married Sarah Dabney Strother and began raising a family at his estate, Hare Forest, in his native Orange County, Virginia. His family quickly outgrew the estate's economic resources, and Taylor decided to move to Kentucky. In time, Taylor acquired in excess of eight thousand acres of land in Kentucky, some of it military grants and some purchased. In late 1783, he traveled westward to clear a portion of his land to make it habitable. In 1785, just months after the birth of his third child, future president ZACHARY TAYLOR, Richard and his family settled five miles east of Louisville on a four-hundred-acre farm on BEARGRASS CREEK near what is now U.S. 42. The Taylor home, known as Springfield(s), lay in proximity to the Locust Grove estate of Col. WILLIAM CROGHAN and Richard Clough Anderson's "Soldier's Retreat."

Taylor gained a reputation as an Indian fighter and was wounded in such a skirmish near Eton, Ohio, in 1792. He was also active in the political affairs of Louisville and the infant state of Kentucky. Taylor, as a representative from Jefferson County, played a leading part in the state constitutional conventions of 1792 and 1799. Appointed by President George Washington as Collector of the Port of Louisville, he also sat as a county judge, was a presidential elector for Kentucky in four elections, and served on Louisville's board of trustees. During Kentucky's Old Court–New Court controversy (1819–23), Taylor was a staunch Old Court supporter.

Taylor and his wife, Sarah, were the parents of nine children: Hancock, William, Zachary, George, Elizabeth, Joseph, Sarah, Emily, and a son who died in infancy. Taylor is buried in CAVE HILL CEMETERY.

See K. Jack Bauer, *Zachary Taylor: Soldier, Planter, Statesman of the Old Southwest* (Baton Rouge 1985); Holman Hamilton, *Zachary Taylor: Soldier of the Republic* (New York 1941).

Richard Taylor

TAYLOR, ZACHARY (b Orange County, Virginia, November 24, 1784; d Washington, D.C., July 9, 1850). General and twelfth president of the United States. Taylor was the son of Col. Richard and Sarah (Strother) Taylor. When Taylor was eight months old, the family moved across the Appalachian Mountains, settling on four hundred acres of land in Jefferson County, Virginia (now Kentucky). Here the boy grew up on his father's pioneer plantation called Springfield(s). There being no schools in the area, Taylor received his only formal education from private tutors Kean O'Hara and Elisha Ayer.

Taylor began his military career in 1808, securing a commission as first lieutenant in the Seventh Infantry. While home on leave in the autumn of 1809, he met Margaret Mackall Smith of Calvert County, Maryland, who was visiting her aunt. They were married on June 21, 1810, in a double log house two miles from Harrods Creek Station on the Wolf Pen Rd. The Taylors had six children, two of whom died in childhood.

Distinguishing himself during the War of 1812, Taylor, by then a brevet major, was instrumental in the defense of Fort Harrison in Indiana Territory. In 1814 he purchased a 324-

General Zachary Taylor, 1847 lithograph by Nathaniel Currier.

acre farm on the Muddy Fork of BEARGRASS CREEK from John Veech. Veech had bought the land from RICHARD TAYLOR seven years earlier. Zachary returned to Louisville in 1815 and for a year worked on the farm, living in a cabin and putting in a crop of corn and TOBACCO. Recalled north to active duty, Taylor did not see Louisville again until 1818 when he returned for a year to superintend the recruiting service in the area. It was during this period that President James Monroe, along with Gen. Andrew Jackson, visited Kentucky. Taylor, now a lieutenant colonel, was a member of the party that accompanied them to Frankfort and breakfasted with them at Liberty Hall, the home of former senator John Brown.

After four years on duty in the South, Taylor left Baton Rouge, Louisiana, to become superintendent general of the Western Department's recruiting services, which had offices in Cincinnati and later in Louisville. Leaving Louisville for Washington, D.C., in 1826, he was not to return home for any extended period until 1830, when he received a year's furlough. Occupying a house on the east side of First St. near Jefferson St., Taylor attended to business affairs that included the sale of a portion of his Kentucky property. He had been purchasing land in Louisiana and Mississippi and would subsequently acquire more in those areas.

Taylor took part in the Black Hawk War in 1832 and the Second Seminole War (1835-42), but it was as commander of the Army of the Rio Grande during the MEXICAN WAR (1846–48) that he was propelled to national prominence. Winning victories in the battles of Palo Alto, Resaca de la Palma, Monterrey, and Buena Vista, Gen. Zachary Taylor ("Old Rough and Ready") was acclaimed as a military hero. As a result, he was nominated by the WHIG PARTY as its presidential candidate in 1848. Having no previous political experience, Taylor campaigned on his military record and on his promise of a nonpolitical administration. Although a slave owner, Taylor was committed to the preservation of the Union. He was elected president, defeating Democrat Lewis Cass and Free Soil candidate Martin Van Buren in a very close election. It was as president-elect that Taylor last visited Louisville. On February 14, 1849, he was loudly cheered and lavishly entertained at a banquet as he passed through the city on his way north for his inauguration on March 5, 1849. On July 9, 1850, Taylor died in Washington, D.C., probably from cholera, and was buried in the Congressional Burying Ground. On November 1, 1850, he was re-buried in the Taylor family cemetery, now part of the ZACHARY TAYLOR NATIONAL CEMETERY, at Springfield(s) in Louisville. Following speculation into the cause of Taylor's death, his body was exhumed for examination on June 17, 1991. The results of the pathological tests, however, were inconclusive.

See Holman Hamilton, *Zachary Taylor, Soldier of the Republic* (New York 1941) and *Zachary Taylor, Soldier in the White House* (New York 1951).

Kenneth Dennis

TAYLOR AND WILLIAMS YELLOWSTONE. Located at 3000 S Seventh St., adjacent to the fields where the Union army grazed its horses during the CIVIL WAR, Taylor and Williams Yellowstone was a very brief addition to Louisville's DISTILLING industry. Originally a distributing company, Taylor and Williams was purchased by Joseph Bernard Dant, who in 1865 had built the Cold Spring Distillery at Gethsemani, Kentucky. Known as a first-rate and careful distiller, J.B. Dant is credited with introducing the Yellowstone brand and formula suggested by a salesman, Charles Townsend. Townsend had visited Yellowstone National Park in the 1870s and upon his return convinced associates that it would be a marketable brand name. Dant, Kentucky bourbon's "Grand Old Man," had six sons who were to be affiliated with a number of brands, including Yellowstone, for many years. After assuming full control in 1912, Dant renamed the Gethsemani distillery Taylor and Williams. The company bottled whiskey for medicinal purposes during PROHIBITION (1919–33), then was moved to Louisville. The Seventh St. location had been built in anticipation of repeal. J.B. Dant, along with his sons, ran the firm until his death in 1939 at age eighty-nine. Yellowstone continued to operate under the Dants until 1944 when it was sold along with the Yellowstone brand name to Glenmore Distillers. Since then, the property has gone through a number of owners, including United Distillers. In the early 1990s, the Florida Distillers Co. purchased the property for the purpose of making wine and vinegar for bulk sales.

See William L. Downard, *Dictionary of the History of the American Brewing and Distilling Industries* (Westport, Conn., 1980).

Albert Young
Lindsey Apple

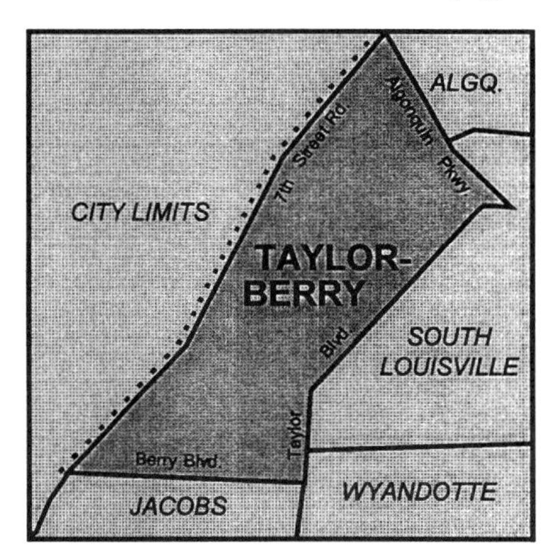

TAYLOR-BERRY. Neighborhood southwest of downtown Louisville bounded by Taylor Blvd. to the east, Berry Blvd. to the south, Seventh Street Rd. to the west, and Algonquin Pkwy. to the north. Development began in the area in the early 1890s by Joseph B. Gathright's Union Land Co. He hoped to build a "streetcar suburb" along the newly built trolley line along Taylor Blvd. to IROQUOIS PARK, known informally for many years as Jacob's Park. It officially became Iroquois Park on August 13, 1891. While most of the land was developed by 1913, additional subdivisions appeared into the 1950s. Local landmarks include South Central Park, William Harrison Park, and Schardein Cemetery.

TAYLOR DRUG STORES. Taylor Drug Stores, established in Louisville in 1879, was one of America's oldest drugstore chains before being sold in 1996. The company was founded by Thomas Pickett Taylor Sr. (1858-1928), a native of Eastwood in far eastern Jefferson County. T.P. Taylor, the son of Edward Gibson Taylor and Mildred (Hord) Taylor, graduated from the Louisville College of Pharmacy at the age of seventeen. He was a druggist in Owensboro for two years, then took a position in a Portland drug store, which he bought in 1879. This store was at Thirty-third St. and Rudd Ave., then the center of steamboat-related traffic. Taylor was able to buy a second store downtown at Third and Jefferson Streets in 1881.

T.P. Taylor continued to purchase stores and incorporated the firm of T.P. Taylor and Co. The firm later became the Taylor-Isaacs Co., reflecting a partnership with Taylor's nephew, E.G. Isaacs. This corporation later dissolved and the T.P. Taylor Co. was constituted, with the principals being T.P. Taylor and his sons, T.P. Jr. and Horace A. Taylor.

By the time of his death in 1928, Taylor's chain numbered eleven drug stores. He had also amassed holdings in Louisville real estate worth $2 million including commercial property on the city's thriving Fourth St. T.P.'s death began a period of uncertainty for the chain, which almost ended the company. The eleven stores were sold to Whelan Drug Co. of New York for $1 million in February 1929. Whelan, affiliated with the United Cigar Stores Co. of New York, operated 184 pharmacies in the East. Whelan agreed to continue to operate the Louisville stores as the T.P. Taylor Co. Whelan, however, began to struggle in the early years of the GREAT DEPRESSION and its Kentucky branch, now holding nine stores, went into receivership in July 1932. Whelan withdrew from Louisville in October 1932. In December 1932 Horace and T.P. Taylor Jr. repurchased their father's four original stores in Louisville and reincorporated the T.P. Taylor Co.

The revived company began to prosper again and could boast that it had filled 4 million prescriptions by 1938, at which time Taylor drug stores had operated for nearly sixty years. By 1952 the chain owned sixteen stores, including outlets in southern Indiana and Elizabethtown, Kentucky. All its stores were air-conditioned and the company made its own ice cream. Following the deaths of Horace Taylor in 1946 and T.P. Jr. in 1953, William H. Harrison, son of a former Louisville mayor and son-in-law of T.P. Jr., became head of the company. The Taylor stores affiliated with Rexall, an organization of seventy-five chain drug companies around the nation. Harrison was elected president of the Rexall Chain Drug Store Association in 1963. In 1983, when Harrison retired in favor of his son, William H. Harrison Jr., the Taylor chain had grown to forty-seven stores, mainly in the Louisville metropolitan area and southern Indiana.

The business environment for drug stores began to change dramatically in the 1980s with the emergence of managed health care. With fewer consumer choices in selecting pharmacies and increased third-party control over prices, profits on each prescription filled decreased and stores were forced to continually cut costs. Locally based chains such as Taylor's found it increasingly difficult to compete. The chain shrank to thirty-four stores by 1996, when it finally was sold to Rite Aid, one of the national corporations consolidating pharmacy ownership across the United States.

Mary Margaret Bell

TAYLORSVILLE. Taylorsville, the county seat of SPENCER COUNTY, is located at the junction of KY 44 and KY 155 just a few miles southeast of Louisville. By 1790 the town had several brick homes. Nine years later it was laid out and named for Richard Taylor, the owner of a gristmill and a large tract of land at the confluence of the Salt River and Brashears Creek. The town was incorporated on January 22, 1829. As early as 1794 Taylorsville had a Baptist church, and in 1808 a Catholic church opened. The Spencer Institute, a private school, started classes in 1846. Four years later the first public school opened in a log building.

In 1833 a covered bridge over Salt River joined Taylorsville with counties to the south. By 1837 a stagecoach route ran from Louisville through Taylorsville to Chaplin in Nelson County. The forty-five-mile trip took nine hours and cost nine dollars. In 1869 the Kentucky General Assembly approved the charter of the Cumberland and Ohio Railroad, which was completed from SHELBYVILLE through Taylorsville to Bloomfield in Nelson County and was 26.7 miles in length. Planned extensions to Nashville, Tennessee, and Madison, Indiana, were never built.

The first courthouse was established in an existing building in 1825. The second courthouse was burned by Confederate guerrillas in 1865, but the county's records were saved and Union troops apprehended the guerrillas at Mount Eden, ten miles from Taylorsville, where one casualty occurred. The next courthouse, an Italianate structure built in 1866, burned in 1914. The present courthouse, of classic Beaux Arts design, was completed in 1915.

Taylorsville's ECONOMY is geared to the county's agricultural products. The 1982 impoundment of the Salt River, creating the 3,050-acre Taylorsville Lake, brought additional revenue to local merchants through increased TOURISM. Louisvillians often visit the lake for recreational purposes, including boating, fishing, camping, hiking, and picnicking. Although it lost POPULATION in the 1980s, Spencer County grew in population in the late 1990s. The population of the sixth-class city was 897 in 1970, 801 in 1980, 774 in 1990, and 1,030 in 1996.

See John E. Kleber, ed., *The Kentucky Encyclopedia* (Lexington 1992).

TELEGRAPH. Not until the mid-1850s was it possible to send messages quickly for any distance. The problem was solved when Samuel F.B. Morse developed the electric telegraph system and an alphabet system called the Morse code. In 1843 Congress appropriated thirty thousand dollars for a test line between Washington, D.C., and Baltimore. The first message was sent May 24, 1844.

The first line to reach Louisville was the Pittsburgh, Cincinnati, and Louisville Telegraph Co., built in 1847 by Henry O'Reilly. From Cincinnati the line came down the Indiana side of the OHIO RIVER through Madison to Jeffersonville. Telegrams and telegraphic news dispatches had to be rowed across the river to Louisville until a wire was stretched across the stream on December 29, 1847. Three tall masts had been erected: one on the Indiana shore, one on Towhead Island, and one on the Kentucky shore. The *Louisville Daily Courier* on the following day noted that "the telegraphic dispatches we publish this morning were received at the office [at Third and Market] in this city, and may therefore be looked upon as the first specimen of Kentucky lightning."

Louisville's first telegrapher was Eugene S. Whitman. He was succeeded by James Leonard, a lad of fourteen years who is generally credited to be the first operator who learned to decode the messages by sound alone. He wrote the message as the telegraph sounder clicked out the dots and dashes of the Morse code. Previously all messages were received on a paper tape imprinted with the dots and dashes. His accomplishment was amazing enough to prompt P.T. Barnum on a visit to Louisville in 1851 to offer to take Leonard on a series of personal appearances through the country. Leonard declined and stayed with his telegraphic career, where he was already known as the fastest writer in the nation.

In 1848 O'Reilly began construction of a line from Louisville to New Orleans, via Memphis, completed in 1849. Louisville stockholders included Horatio D. Newcomb and William B. Belknap. At about the same time Amos Kendall, a Kentucky journalist who had become business agent for Samuel Morse, organized the New Orleans and Ohio Telegraph Co. to build a line between Louisville and New Orleans via Lexington and Nashville. Fierce competition developed between the two companies, leading to the most celebrated telegraphic lawsuit in Kentucky. O'Reilly had contracted to use Morse instruments on all his lines but used the rival Columbian devices on the New Orleans line. Kendall brought suit in federal district court, which ruled against O'Reilly. The latter appealed to the United States Supreme Court, which also ruled against him.

In 1852 Louisvillian Dr. NORVIN GREEN became active in the Morse line to New Orleans and arranged a merger of the rival lines in 1853. In 1860 he became president of merged lines, called the Southwestern Telegraph Co. This was the first move toward creation of the Western Union Telegraph Co. in 1866, which Dr. Green headed from 1878 until his death in 1893.

Other telegraph companies appeared from time to time. The Southern Telegraph Co., chartered in Kentucky in 1866, planned to build from Cincinnati to Louisville, Nashville, Memphis, and New Orleans. The most remarkable thing about this effort was its officers. Former Union general Jeremiah T. Boyle was its first president, while Confederate generals Simon Bolivar Buckner and Edmund Kirby Smith were vice presidents. In 1870 the company was absorbed by Western Union. In 1891 the Postal Telegraph Co., Western Union's only serious rival, opened an office at Third and MAIN Streets, catercornered from Western Union.

The telegraph continued to be an important communications medium well into the twentieth century despite the development of the TELEPHONE in the late 1870s. But later technological advances, including the teletype, facsimile transmission, and electronic mail, cut deeply into the use of the telegraph. By the 1970s the volume was dropping 8 to 10 percent a year. Postal Telegraph closed its office in Louisville about 1945, and Western Union followed in 1985. Yet Western Union still accepts telegram transfers of money-by-wire through a toll-free 800 number or through agencies in many GROCERIES throughout the Louisville metropolitan region.

See John Wilson Townsend, *The Life of James Francis Leonard* (Louisville 1909); J. Stoddard Johnston, *Memorial History of Louisville*, vol. 1. (Chicago 1896); *Lexington Observer and Reporter*, March 1, 1848; *Courier-Journal*, Dec. 20, 1936; *Louisville Times*, Dec. 29, 1955; *Courier-Journal* and *Louisville Times*, April 2, 1972.

Patricia Ayers

TELEPHONE. In 1876, when people first heard about Alexander Graham Bell's invention of the telephone, many ridiculed the idea of transmitting human voices over wires. Some even accused Bell of dealing with the supernatural, saying human speech was sacred and science should not tamper with it. But Bell knew the telephone worked, and to prove it he obtained a one-day exhibitor's pass at the nation's Centennial Exposition in Philadelphia. There, on June 25, 1876, he demonstrated his invention to businessmen, scientists, and judges.

Farsighted businessmen throughout the country were immediately interested in the telephone and knew it could greatly affect trade and commerce. One of those businessmen was James B. Speed from Louisville. He ordered two telephones to connect his office on MAIN St. with his cement mill in PORTLAND. That single line, providing communication between the two points, made Louisville one of the early dots on the nation's telephonic map. It did not take long for that dot to grow. Other local businessmen soon followed Speed's lead. Within a short time hundreds of telephone wires were strung across Louisville's building tops, since few poles were used.

Speed had agreed that if his telephone connection worked under actual business conditions, he would organize a company to promote its use. In February 1879, the first telephone exchange in Louisville went into operation under the direction of the American District Telegraph Co., a Bell-franchised company. It had approximately two hundred subscribers on multiparty lines and was owned by Speed and several associates.

It soon became evident that, if the telephone was to be used for mass intercommunications, a system had to be devised to reduce the number of lines needed for direct connections between subscribers. A solution was found when the first commercial telephone exchange for switched connections opened in New Haven, Connecticut, in January 1878. The first telephone switchboard in Louisville was located on the fourth floor of the Board of Trade building at Third and Main Streets. An 1880 telephone directory listed six hundred subscribers, including nine TOBACCO manufacturers, the Knickerbocker Theater, several undertakers, veterinary surgeons, and a wagon factory—but no phone numbers. You simply gave the operator the name of the party you were calling. By the end of 1882, the company had fourteen hundred subscribers and had been reorganized under the name of the Ohio Valley Telephone Co. Service was growing so fast that overhead wires could not meet the demand. Following the lead of Pittsburgh and Chicago, the company began a system of underground conduit for carrying wire and cables.

In 1884 a building constructed solely to house a telephone exchange was built at 424 W Jefferson St. By the turn of the century, the Ohio Valley Telephone Co., with nearly five thousand phones in service, consolidated with and assumed the name of the Cumberland Telephone & Telegraph Co., which owned other exchanges in the state.

The telephone began to have a real impact on the economic and social structure of the city. It revolutionized business. Citizens could shop by phone and have goods delivered, requiring a greater number of employees to handle the businesses. NEWSPAPERS could receive and print information about important events in a speedier fashion. Telephone service allowed people to move away from the inner cities, and businesses followed. For the first time, people could transact business, summon aid, or socialize across greater distances, without ever leaving their home or business or sending a written message.

Further value was seen when competing companies began providing telephone service. In June 1901, the Louisville Home Telephone Co. opened its doors for business. The Home Co. prospered from the beginning by offering cheaper rates than the Cumberland. Competing companies, however, worked a hardship on both telephone companies as well as the people of Louisville, since there was no interconnection between the two companies. Subscribers from one company could not call subscribers from the other company. Businesses would often subscribe to both companies, getting the same phone number when possible, to stay in touch with all their customers. Although Home's telephone rates were less expensive and it had three times more customers than Cumberland, the new company provided little or no long-distance service. For instance, if a call came in from Chicago for a Home customer, Home would send a messenger on a bicycle to tell the called party to go to a neighbor with a Cumberland phone or come downtown to a telephone booth.

When the situation of competing telephone companies became intolerable, not only in Louisville but in many other cities, federal and state governments intervened, ordering the mergers of telephone companies, saying that, for the benefit of customers and stockholders, only one company should serve an area. On December 29, 1925, the Cumberland Co., which had been absorbed by Southern Bell Telephone & Telegraph Co. in 1912, took over the Home Telephone Co. During the years following the merger, the Southern Bell Telephone & Telegraph Co., which was owned by American Telephone & Telegraph and was part of the Bell System, experienced good growth and prosperity, although, like many other businesses, suffered some setbacks during the GREAT DEPRESSION. At the time of the consolidation, there were eight telephone exchanges in Louisville: Highland, City, East, Main, ST. MATTHEWS, SHAWNEE, South, and Magnolia.

By the end of 1926, Louisville had about 53,000 telephones for a POPULATION of 305,000. The biggest benefit Southern Bell brought to Louisville was the continued expansion and upgrading of service.

In late 1928, Southern Bell asked for an increase in telephone rates. The proposed new rate for a private business line was $10.00; a private residence line was $4.25. At that time, the rate-setting process was an ordinance passed by the Board of Aldermen and signed by both the mayor and officials of the telephone company.

For the next several years, city government and the telephone company were in disagreement over the rates. In May 1935 officials of the Southern Bell Telephone Co. met with the state Public Service Commission, which had been formed by the 1934 Kentucky General Assembly to iron out all possible differences. After the meeting the telephone company recognized the commission as the legal rate-setting power in Kentucky and disregarded the city's right to do this. The city refused to give up the fight. The argument was settled on February 27, 1936, when a circuit court decision ruled that the city had been divested of its rate regulatory power by the Public Service Commission. The Federal Communications Commission was created in 1934 to regulate interstate long-distance rates on a national level. These rate regulatory powers that were established in the 1930s continue to the present time.

Research by Southern Bell predicted that, if growth continued at the present rate, the company would need over four thousand operators to handle the volume of calls, a need that would deplete the city's female labor force. The solution was to install the new automatic dial system. The modern Louisville telephone network began in 1929 when Southern Bell started construction of a new headquarters building at 521 W Chestnut St. This ten-story building, completed in 1930, was configured to accommodate electromechanical switching equipment. In 1932 the first step-by-step switching equipment was activated in the building as the Wabash and Jackson exchanges, replacing the City, Main, and South offices. AT&T Long Lines moved its toll switchboard and carrier equipment from the old Keller Building at Fifth and Main Streets to the new building, allowing it to tie directly into the Louisville network. The process of converting all of Louisville's telephones to dial was a twenty-seven-year effort.

On July 29, 1959, the last manual telephone was converted to dial at the request of Eugene Hill, a director of Southern Bell. He made the last manual call from his residence through the Highland office to Ben Gilmer, president of Southern Bell in Atlanta.

During the Great FLOOD OF 1937, telephone employees fought around the clock sandbagging buildings to keep service working. When the city lost power, workers used welding machines to charge central office batteries. Telephone operators moved in the Chestnut St. building for the duration of the flood. In some local offices they stayed on duty until water got so high that service went out. Louisville always had some service during the disaster and at no time was cut off from the world.

Telephone growth was curtailed during WORLD WAR II because of government restrictions and a lack of raw materials. The government's needs came first, plus many telephone employees answered the call to duty. Before the war the telephone was a luxury, not a necessity. If one or two families on a block had a phone, others were welcome to use it. Following the war, housing starts skyrocketed, and the demand for telephone service was staggering.

The next several decades were marked by growth and technology, requiring millions of dollars in investment every year by the company to keep up with the demand. On August 7, 1960, Louisville was connected to the national Direct Distance dialing network, making it possible for callers to dial direct their own station-to-station calls.

In 1968 the nine-state Southern Bell Co. split into two companies. Five states—Alabama, Kentucky, Mississippi, Louisiana, and Tennessee—formed a new company called South Central Bell, a separate subsidiary of AT&T.

The development of the computer microprocessors changed the basic element of the telephone system, including the way it operated and what it could offer customers. In 1974 the first electronic switching system (ESS) in Louisville began service. With ESS came Touch-Tone® dialing, automatic number identification, and custom calling services such as call waiting, call forwarding, three-way calling, and speed calling. With the conversion of the SHIVELY office in October 1987, Louisville became the first major metropolitan office in the nine-state area to have all electronic switching.

This new computerized technology also brought a host of competitors into the telephone business. Companies could now bypass part of the Bell System. The sixties and seventies are often considered the most dramatic and traumatic in telecommunications history. This period brought increasing competition and numerous antitrust suits, FCC rulings, and legislative activities; and it brought the divestiture of the Bell System, the largest corporate restructuring in the history of American business. In 1982 the Department of Justice dropped its seven-year-old antitrust case against the Bell System after AT&T agreed to divest itself of the local telephone companies. January 1, 1984, marked the first business day for South Central Bell and Southern Bell to operate as subsidiaries of the BellSouth Corp. The two subsidiaries began operating as BellSouth Telecommunications Inc. in the mid-nineties.

The nineties brought even further technological advances in telecommunications. Fiber optic cable, cellular service, voice messaging service, RingMaster®, caller ID, high-speed transmission of data, internet services, and digital services are just some of the information age services available to Louisville customers.

Congress passed the Telecommunications Act of 1996, which ushered in a new era of competition in telecommunications. Local telephone companies would compete in the long-distance market and in CABLE TELEVISION. Long-distance companies and cable companies would enter local telephony. Louisville customers would have an even greater choice of services.

See John Brooks, *Telephone, The First One Hundred Years* (New York 1975); American District Telephone Co. of Louisville, Ky., *1880 Telephone Directory;* South Central Bell fact sheet on Louisville Telephone History; Robert G. Adams, "The Telephone Co. in Louisville (1925–1936)," unpublished paper, University of Louisville.

Patricia Ayers

TELEVISION. Although the technology for television was developed prior to WORLD WAR II, that conflict delayed its commercial development. In the years immediately following the war, only six television stations existed in the nation, none of them in Kentucky. However, two Louisville-area radio station owners were granted permits. On November 24, 1948, WAVE became the first television station to go on the air in Louisville, and the forty-first in the nation. BROADCASTING on Channel 5—although it switched to Channel 3 in 1953—from studios on E BROADWAY at Preston St., the initial program was on a barn-like set and featured music, dancing, comedy, and a ventriloquist. WAVE began its coverage of local sports the following day by televising the Thanksgiving Day Male-Manual FOOTBALL game. This tradition continued into the next year with the first telecast of the KENTUCKY DERBY. An NBC affiliate from its first years, the station expanded its daily scheduling in 1952 to sixteen hours and included public affairs and cultural programs; children's shows such as *Healthy, Wealthy, and Wise* and *Funny Flickers;* and music variety shows such as the *Pee Wee King Show* and *Music Place.* WAVE also had the state's first educational programming when it began carrying English courses for college credit from the UNIVERSITY OF LOUISVILLE in 1950. The station began carrying NBC color programs in 1954 and became the first to broadcast locally in color in 1962, having moved into its new studios at 725 S Floyd three years earlier. In 1968, the Norton family, responsible for WAVE television and radio, formed the Orion Broadcasting Group after purchasing an additional station in Cedar Rapids, Iowa. Twelve years later, the group was sold to Cosmos Broadcasting, a subsidiary of the Greenville, South Carolina–based Liberty Corp.

The second television station to begin broadcasting in the Louisville area was CBS affiliate WHAS. At two o'clock in the afternoon on March 27, 1950, the station transmitted its first signal on Channel 9 from the building at Sixth Street and Broadway that it shared with the COURIER-JOURNAL and WHAS radio. The first day's programming included test patterns, news reels, films, and the *Fred Waring Show,* followed later that night by the station's first newscast. In 1953, the station moved to Channel 11, where it increased in output to 316,000 watts, becoming the first full-powered station in the country. The following year witnessed the station's switch to network color and the first CRUSADE FOR CHILDREN telethon. Using radio personalities such as Jim Walton, Herbie Koch, and Tom Brooks, WHAS developed local programming including *Hi-Varieties* and *What's Your Question,* as well as the children's show *T-Bar-V Ranch.* In 1968, the station moved into its facility on Chestnut St. The Bingham family, who had owned the radio and television stations since their beginnings, sold their holdings to Clear Channel Communications of San Antonio, Texas, in 1986.

By 1952 it is estimated that approximately twenty-five thousand television sets were in use in the Louisville area. Numerous brand sets with either five-inch or seven-inch screens were available locally at stores such as Sun Television on Broadway or Acme Television Appliances on West Market. Ranging between three hundred and five hundred dollars each, the sets could receive all channels on the very-high frequency (VHF) band between 2 and 13. However, when the restrictions ended that year, the FCC opened up the ultra-high frequency (UHF) band to channels 14 to 83 (later reduced to 69). This move instituted the next period for television in Louisville.

Opening a UHF station was considered a risky endeavor for several reasons: the extreme competition from the firmly established VHF channels, the problem of convincing people to purchase a converter for their existing sets, and the limited coverage that the UHF band could reach. However, this did not deter Louisville's third station, WKLO Channel 21, from going on the air on October 18, 1953, from the Henry Clay Hotel on Third St. The station carried programs from the ABC network, which had been split between WAVE and WHAS before that time, as well as the Dumont network and local programming. With few viewers and therefore few interested advertisers, the station suspended operations the following year in April after losing approximately two hundred thousand dollars. After being sold several times and changing its call letters to WEZI in the mid-1960s, the station finally returned to Channel 21 in April 1986 as WBNA. With involvement from several members of the Evangel Tabernacle congregation, the station initially carried primarily religious and family programming. While it added home shopping and movies to its schedule later, the station became the local (Warner Brothers) network affiliate in early 1995.

In January 1953, another channel attempted to establish itself on the UHF band. Claiming to be the first channel in the nation that would specifically target an African American community, Robert W. Rounsaville, the founder of WLOU radio, was granted a permit for Channel 41. However, while the format thrived on the radio, the television station never emerged. After many sales and name changes, the station finally went on the air from a Story Ave. studio as the independent channel WDRB on February 28, 1971. Using a schedule of situation comedy reruns, movies, and sports, WDRB quickly turned a profit and survived. The station endured several changes in the 1980s as it moved into its studios on Muhammad Ali Blvd. in 1980. It was purchased by the Toledo Blade in 1984, and became the local FOX network affiliate in 1986. In March 1994, the station entered into a local marketing agreement with Salem, Indiana's WFTE Channel 58. This station adopted a schedule similar to WDRB in its early years, as WFTE carried syndicated shows, old movies, and sports. WFTE became the local affiliate for the UPN network in January 1995.

With the failure of WKLO, the ABC network was poorly represented in the city before 1961. However, on September 16, WLKY Channel 32 began broadcasting as the local ABC affiliate at two o'clock in the afternoon with the program Kickoff 32. Founded by a group of local businessmen, the channel lobbied with citizens and local television merchants in favor of newer sets with expanded capabilities and for converters that allowed older sets to carry the higher channels. The burgeoning channel received a boost the following year when the FCC required that, beginning in 1964, all new sets would be required to receive every channel on both bands. By 1969, the station, which launched the broadcasting career of Diane Sawyer, moved to its studio on Mellwood Ave. After several ownership transfers, the channel was purchased by Pulitzer Broadcasting in June 1983.

A major reorganization shocked the local industry in 1990 as WHAS ended its forty-year affiliation with CBS and contracted with ABC. WLKY then signed on as the CBS affiliate, while the other local channels maintained their previous associations. Kentucky's first noncommercial educational station, WFPK Channel 15, went on the air in September 1958 with help from the Ford Foundation. While the tower and transmitter were at the downtown library branch, the station's programming was the responsibility of the Jefferson County Board of Education. Initially, the nation's twenty-eighth public station was on the air only during school hours, but the scheduling was expanded into the nighttime hours in 1964 to include documentaries, special features, and programs from the National Education Network (the predecessor of PBS). In 1967, the station's license was transferred to the Jefferson County Board of Education, and the name was changed to WKPC. Supported by auctions, membership drives, show sponsors, and other fund-raising efforts, the channel upgraded its equipment and began broadcasting in color in 1969. The previous year, Kentucky Educational Television (KET), a statewide network based in Lexington, had gone on the air. In 1970, after WKPC refused to join the partnership, WKMJ was established as the city's link to the network on Channel 68. However, WKPC struggled financially and accumulated $4 million in debt by the 1990s. Having no other choice, WKPC decided to sell its equipment and enter the KET network. In July 1997, WKPC became the premier local KET carrier, while WKMJ was renamed KET 2 and continued to broadcast additional educational programming.

The introduction of cable television in the 1970s greatly expanded the number of channels and the variety of television offerings. Louisville channels are subjected to an increasingly competitive market, but they fulfill a need for local news and information.

See Francis M. Nash, *Towers over Kentucky* (Lexington 1995).

TEMPERANCE. Whiskey played an important part in the economic life of Louisville from its earliest days. One of the first distilleries in the state was operated by EVAN WILLIAMS in Louisville in 1783, and in 1816 the HOPE DISTILLERY Co. was chartered in Kentucky with initial capital of one hundred thousand dollars. The Hope Distillery became the largest producer of spirits in the state, and by 1821 its output was claimed to be fifteen hundred gallons a day. Even before the Hope Distillery ceased functioning in 1826, Louisville had become the central port for exporting Kentucky corn, converted into its most economical form—bourbon whiskey.

As Louisville moved into the third decade of the nineteenth century, many of its citizens became concerned over the excessive use of the cheap and readily accessible whiskey. In 1829 alone, the City Council granted 161 licenses to retail alcohol, the majority located along the city's riverfront. This, along with the city's rapid growth and large transient POPULATION, brought to the forefront the social disorder caused by drunkenness. Following the example set by reformers in the northeastern states, a group of Louisvillians formed a temperance society in 1830. By 1832 the society had six hundred members. Led by the upper class and the clergy, these early anti-liquor advocates pledged themselves to abstain from distilled liquors but allowed the moderate drinking of wine and beer. They sought to curb the use of distilled liquors through social pressure and by setting an example through their personal abstinence. In 1832, the society undertook a survey to determine the proportion of crime and disease that could be traced to intemperance. A jurist in Hopkinsville estimated that 99 percent of cases of assault and battery and half of all slander cases in Christian County could be directly attributed to intemperance. A Greenville judge attributed approximately three-fourths of the assault-and-battery actions brought before him to intoxication. The results of this inquiry fueled the fervor of fledgling temperance organizations throughout the state.

When the society did not produce changes in the city's drinking habits, several of the temperance supporters established a total abstinence temperance society. Founded in 1838, the new society believed that drinking any alcoholic beverages eventually leads to intemperance, and its members pledged abstinence from all intoxicating drinks. Gathering support from the middle-class merchants, this society was mainly concerned with limiting the number of liquor licenses in the city, which had increased to 279 by 1838. These abstainers pressured the City Council to enact an ordinance requiring all liquor vendors to collect the signatures of a majority of the persons living or having businesses in the vicinity of the licensed establishment before granting a license.

Louisville's new Medical Institute also joined the temperance cause. Dr. DANIEL DRAKE, professor of pathological anatomy and clinical MEDICINE, organized the Physiological Temperance Society of the Medical Institute in December 1841. The society sought "the suppression of intemperance and the correction of its effects, by an investigation of its causes, consequences, and remedies on physiological and pathological principles." Five years after its founding, 610 current and former students had signed on to study the medical effects of the use of alcohol and to abstain personally from drinking intoxicating liquors for 5 years.

In 1840 several Baltimore artisans had joined together to resist drinking. This fraternal organization, the Washingtonians, had spread to Louisville by November 1841. The Washingtonians were a success as within 2 months of their founding 1,865 people had pledged to stop drinking, including the city's famous editor, George D. Prentice, a pledge that apparently did not last long. The Washingtonians appealed to the working class with their dramatic and emotional meetings. Their influence was limited, however, as many who signed the pledge soon fell back into their former intemperate habits. Although the society existed into 1845, it was replaced in 1846 by a new fraternal organization, the Sons of Temperance, who with their Masonic rituals and ceremonies had a stronger adherence to the pledge. The city's first division of the Sons of Temperance was founded in the spring of 1846, and within a year the city could boast of having twelve divisions. By 1848 Louisville's Sons had 1,304 members, including an all-German division. Another fraternal temperance organization, the Temple of Honor, was also popular, as the city had three temples by the late 1840s.

In the early 1850s the temperance movement became politicized as activists across the nation began to push for statewide laws to prohibit the manufacturing and selling of alcohol except for medical, mechanical, and sacramental uses. Maine was the first state to impose statewide prohibition, and such laws became known as the Maine law. Though Kentuckians were not able to achieve state legislation on the issue, Louisvillians were able to prohibit the selling of alcohol in their city for a short time. Prohibitionists in Louisville allied themselves with the new Know-Nothing Party, which had emerged as a political power in the city during the mid-1850s. This merger was facilitated by the large number of German and IRISH immigrants, the majority of whom were Catholic, who had settled in Louisville in the 1840s and early 1850s. Temperance activists identified these immigrants, especially the Catholics, as the cause of the city's increase in intemperance, crime, and pauperism. The alleged heavy drinking of these immigrants, especially the GERMANS' Sunday drinking and the fact that they operated the majority of the city's drinking establishments, was easily compatible with the Know-Nothings' anti-Catholic and anti-immigrant rhetoric.

The law required all liquor licenses to be renewed each year in either March or September. In 1853 the City Council agreed to submit the question of granting alcohol licenses to the city's voters. That April the prohibitionists' referendum was defeated by 702 votes. In 1855 the city had nearly five hundred liquor retailers when the council again put the issue before the people. By then the anti-license forces had rallied support for their cause, and in the April election they prevailed by nearly 1,000 votes, 3,093 against and 2,131 for licensing. In the same election, the Know-Nothings won nearly all the council seats, and they soon revoked the liquor licenses that had been previously granted in March and refused to grant any new ones. However, a court battle soon emerged over the issue as two of the city's retailers brought the issue up before the Jefferson Circuit Court. Judge William F. Bullock decided in favor of the liquor sellers, pointing out that the council's blanket refusal of all applicants was contrary to state law and the city's charter, which authorized them to grant licenses to all qualified applicants. The judge ordered the council to resume granting licenses. Seven of the councilmen refused and were sent to jail for contempt of court. A few days later they were released as the Kentucky Court of Appeals overturned Judge Bullock's ruling.

Though the council persisted in refusing to grant licenses, many of the city's liquor vendors continued selling without licenses, even after being fined numerous times. However, Gov. Charles S. Morehead, who had the legal authority, later remitted several of these fines. The council again agreed to submit the question to the people in a special election on March 29, 1856. The city's period of prohibition ended as a majority of 1,022 voted for licenses and the council again began granting licenses. After the traumatic "BLOODY MONDAY" election riots of August 6, 1855, and the rise of sectionalism and the slavery issue, the temperance movement in the city soon faded.

Although some of the temperance rhetoric was directed at the use of alcohol by slaves, Louisville's temperance reformers were mainly concerned with the drinking of the free population. Though temperance during the antebellum period was linked with abolition, in Louisville the movement was popular among slaveholders and nonslaveholders alike.

The city's struggle against alcohol in the decades before the CIVIL WAR drew adherents from a diverse portion of the city's population. Louisville's initial temperance impulse was supported by the religious-minded members of the upper class. The working class took up the cause with the growth of fraternal temperance, and the prohibition phase appealed to the city's middle class.

In Louisville, although the anti-drink cause was led and dominated by males, females and youths did participate in the cause. One group, the Independent Order of Good Templars, formed in 1854, did allow women equal participation as members and officers.

After the lapse in temperance reform brought about by the Civil War, it was women who took up the cause in the early 1870s. In the late nineteenth century, the temperance movement intensified on a national level and was ultimately successful because of the work of individuals such as Frances Willard and Carry Nation. The postwar temperance movement in Louisville was slow to gain momentum. Not until 1905 could it find support from a political organization. The Fusionist Party consisted of Democrats and Republicans uniting to right society's wrongs, which they believed stemmed from corrupt politics and law enforcement and the subsequent proliferation of GAMBLING, PROSTITUTION, and SALOONS. The Fusionists caused a stir in the elections of 1905 when they pursued a suit against the city's political machine because of irregular voting procedures. As a result, the Kentucky Court of Appeals (then the highest state court) declared the election invalid. This success encouraged reform-minded Louisvillians. Seeing the tide turn, local brewers attempted to mitigate some of the criticisms by encouraging an ordinance that would close saloons at midnight, under the assumption that most alcohol-related crimes took place after that hour.

In 1891 the new state constitution forbade the General Assembly to interfere in matters of prohibition. By that time fifty-two counties had voted themselves dry. In 1906 the Kentucky General Assembly enacted an amendment to the constitution providing each county with the ability to vote itself dry. In addition, if a county voted dry, every district or city within the county must become dry. On the other hand, if the county voted wet, any precinct within the county could remain dry if it had previously been so voted. This resulted in the illegal shipment of liquor from wet to dry areas, and a number of measures were passed by the General Assembly trying to rectify this problem until the state went dry in 1919. By 1907, with the passage of the refined local option law, 95 of the 119 counties that existed at the time were dry, and by 1915, 102 were dry.

In Louisville, as elsewhere in the nation, temperance supporters rallied under the political banner of the Progressive Party, which lent political power and coordination to the movement. On January 14, 1918, by a vote of 94 to 17, Kentucky became the third state to ratify the Eighteenth Amendment to the federal Constitution, which outlawed the manufacture and sale of alcoholic beverages. In January of the following year, Nebraska ratified, giving it the necessary three-fourths votes.

The prohibition struggle was not finished in Kentucky, however. Prohibition leaders still contended that agreement between the state and federal laws was essential for enforcement. In 1919 a statewide popular vote was taken on a prohibition amendment to the state constitution. After early returns the *Courier-Journal* reported, "Wets Win State Fight, Vote in Cities Indicate." The wet vote took substantial victories in Kenton, Campbell, and especially Jefferson County, where 26,992 of the 36,789 ballots were against prohibition. Two days later the votes from the rural counties had been tallied, and the amendment passed. The law made it "unlawful to manufacture, sell, barter, give away, or keep for sale, or transport spirituous, vinous, malt or intoxicating liquors except for sacramental, medicinal, scientific or mechanical purposes." This made official Louisville's support of the nation's "Noble Experiment."

See Thomas H. Appleton Jr., "'Moral suasion has had its day': From Temperance to Prohibition in Ante-bellum Kentucky," in John David Smith and T.H. Appleton Jr., eds., *A Mythic Land Apart: Reassessing Southerners and Their History* (Westport, Conn., 1997); idem, *Like Banquo's Ghost* (Lexington 1981); *Proceedings of the Physiological Temperance Society of the Medical Institute of Louisville,* 1842 (Louisville 1842); Reuben Anderson, *The Annual Oration of the Physiological Temperance Society of the University of Louisville, Delivered by Appointment February 6th, 1847* (Louisville 1847).

Aaron Hoffman

Streetcars on opening day of Kentucky State Fair 1932 pass Methodist Temple (formerly Temple Adas Israel) on the southeast corner of Broadway at Sixth.

THE TEMPLE (Adath Israel Brith Sholom congregation) was chartered January 13, 1843, as Adas Israel, a traditional synagogue and Louisville's first Jewish congregation. It first met in rented quarters on MAIN St. near Brook. In 1849 it built a two-story building on Fourth St. near Walnut (now Muhammad Ali Blvd.) It was destroyed by fire in 1866. In 1868 it moved to a new temple at the southeast corner of Sixth and BROADWAY and, when it outgrew that, to a Greek Revival building on Third south of YORK. Outward movement of its members led the congregation to purchase land in 1966 at 5101 Brownsboro Rd., which was dedicated in 1980.

In 1976 Adath Israel merged with Temple Brith Sholom, which had been organized in 1880 by families from Germany who wanted services in German. It bought a building at First and Walnut (Muhammad Ali Blvd.). This structure was sold to CONGREGATION ANSHEI SFARD when Brith Sholom moved to a new building at Second and College in 1903. By 1949 another site was needed, and Brith Sholom moved to Cowling and Maryland, a site it occupied until the merger.

After several visits by Dr. Isaac M. Wise of Cincinnati, Adath Israel joined the Reform movement when it was founded in 1873. Among its rabbis who achieved fame after leaving Louisville were Rabbi Emil G. Hirsch and Rabbi H.G. Enelow. Rabbi ADOLPH MOSES came to Louisville from Mobile, Alabama, to be the rabbi of Adath Israel in 1881. He was a medical doctor as well, having graduated from the old Louisville College with high honors. During his tenure, Sunday services were introduced for a time and a Sabbath school was constructed. Moses served the congregation until his death on January 1902. In 1903 the National Council of Jewish Women published a book of Dr. Moses's papers entitled, *Yahvism and Other Discourses*. Dr. JOSEPH RAUCH, a spellbinding orator, came here in 1912. During his forty-five-year tenure he became the unofficial spokesman for Louisville's Jewish community. He also was a leader in civic affairs.

The congregation prides itself on its social-action committee.

Herman Landau

TEMPLE SHALOM. When Temple Adath Israel and Temple Brith Shalom merged in 1976, there were forty-three persons who wanted a smaller and more personal Reform congregation, so they organized Temple Shalom. The new group first held services at the JEWISH COMMUNITY CENTER, then at BELLARMINE COLLEGE. In 1981 Temple Shalom bought a house on Taylorsville Rd. and remodeled it but in a few years had raised enough money to build a temple at 4615 Lowe Rd. For the first few years of its existence Temple Shalom had no rabbi, and services were conducted by laymen or guest speakers. Milton Greenbaum was the first president. Rabbi Stanley Miles came August 1, 1978. The congregation's choir has produced much original liturgical music. Temple Shalom arranged for CAVE HILL CEMETERY to set aside an area for Jewish burials, it being Louisville's only congregation without its own cemetery.

Herman Landau

TENNIS. Newspaper reports credit Thomas Kennedy with setting up the first tennis court in Louisville. He did this in the late 1870s on the circle in front of his home on Kennedy Court in CRESCENT HILL. From then until the turn of the century, brief reports refer to tennis being played on the grounds of the Louisville Tennis Club, Louisville Athletic Club, and Hampton College, which was located at 316 W Walnut St. (Muhammad Ali Blvd.). There were also several private courts at homes owned by various individuals such as Charles Ballard.

The first public park courts were built at Cherokee and SHAWNEE PARKS in 1897. Louisville's top players in 1900 were reported to be A. Lee Robinson, Lewis Hardy, Grinstead Vaughan, Henning Chambers, H. Morton, Joe Eaton, Tom Tuley, Percy Booth, and Russell Houston. Robinson had been playing tennis for a number of years and was often referred to as the "father of tennis in Louisville."

In 1907 the first Falls City Championships were held at Cherokee Park in Louisville. Courts were constructed at three clubs that were soon to become quite prominent in local tennis history—Audubon Country Club (1909), Louisville Country Club (1910), and shortly thereafter the Louisville Boat Club.

The Kentucky Lawn Tennis Association was founded in 1910 and became a part of the Ohio Tennis District. Representing the association, Thomas Tuley of Louisville was successful in bringing the first major tournament to the city. It was known as the Bi-State Tournament (Kentucky and Ohio), and in 1911 it attracted a number of ranking players from across the country. It was played on the six clay courts at AUDUBON. That same year the Louisville Country Club hosted the first Kentucky State Championships to be held in Louisville. The Louisville Country Club, in 1915, became the first state member organization of the KLTA and USLTA.

Louisville's Mary Shreve Lyons won the Southern Women's Championship in 1913. Shelton Arterburn won the third of his four state titles in 1917, but no prizes were given since entry fees were donated to the Red Cross for WORLD WAR I. In 1921, the Kentucky Lawn Tennis Association became affiliated with the Southern Lawn Tennis Association. The first time the Southern Championships were held in Louisville was 1923 at the Audubon Country Club. Hometown player Mary Mason Harding won the women's singles title. By 1924, six of the top-twenty men players in the South were from Louisville. The following year Ed Pfeiffer headed south and captured the men's title.

The West Louisville Tennis Club was organized in the early 1920s at Chickasaw Park, since SEGREGATION prevented AFRICAN AMERICANS from playing on public courts in Shawnee and Central Parks. The club has continued to promote tennis for youths and adults through the years.

Louisville had fifty-five public park courts by 1921, and these facilities continued to host the Falls City Tournament plus many other events. Shawnee Park held the National Public Parks Championships in 1932. Arnold Simons of Louisville won the men's singles and successfully defended his title in New York the next year.

The state championships of the 1920s and 1930s were held at Audubon and the Louisville Boat Club. Local media praised Dr. O.T. Turner and James Means Jr. of Audubon and Ray Jones of the boat club for their work in developing the event. Starting in 1926 the tournament began to attract players of national stature. It was held that year at the boat club.

The Louisville Boat Club hosted the Southern Championships in 1941, 1946, and 1950. The club was the site of Davis Cup Ties in 1951 and 1955. Dick Savitt, Herb Flam, Bill Talbert, and Tony Trabert led the United States to victory over Japan in 1951, while Lew Hoad and Ken Rosewall four years later led Australia's win over Brazil.

After WORLD WAR II, Robert Piatt and O.C. Kelsall were instrumental in bringing first-rate events such as Davis Cup and the Southern Championships to the Louisville Boat Club. In 1952 they founded the Kentucky Junior Invitational, which soon lured such future stars as Billie Jean Moffitt (King), Earl Buchholz, Charles Pasarell, Chuck McKinley, Dennis Ralston, and Harold Solomon.

The Kentucky Tennis Patrons Foundation was founded in 1952, and in 1955 Kentucky officially became a district of the Southern Lawn Tennis Association. Don Kaiser was ranked as high as number twenty-one in U.S. Men's Singles in the 1950s.

In 1955 for the first time, African American tennis players were allowed to play in public PARKS other than Chickasaw. The first African American to play in the Men's State Championships was John McGill. He reached the semifinals in 1961 at Louisville's Central Park.

After twenty-eight years, the National Public Parks Championships returned in 1960 to Shawnee Park. John Evans Jr. won the men's singles, while Rod McNerney and Mickey Schad captured the doubles. All three were from Louisville. The Kentucky Junior Invitational moved to Louisville's Seneca Park in 1966, and the following year that event was renamed the Junior Clay Court National Championships.

The first structure designed for indoor tennis in Kentucky was an air-supported "bubble." It was erected in 1967 over two existing courts at Louisville's Plantation Country Club on Westport Rd. by a private group headed by Sam English Jr.

Pancho Gonzalez, Roy Emerson, Dennis Ralston, and Earl Buchholz helped dedicate the opening of the public Louisville Tennis Center on May 19, 1969. Through the years many of the all-time greats such as Bill Tilden, Don Budge, Jack Kramer, Maureen Connolly, and Arthur Ashe played exhibition matches in Louisville, but in 1970 the first professional tournament was hosted with twenty-five thousand dollars in prize money. Sam English Jr. secured First National Bank of Louisville as the first sponsor, and Rod Laver won the tourney. Through the seventies the crowds grew, and the prize money reached $175,000. National TELEVISION coverage became an annual occurrence, but after 1979 Louisville had to withdraw from the major international circuit because of the lack of adequate sponsor support.

U.S. Open Champion Billie Jean King won a Virginia Slims tournament at the Tennis Center in 1971. Legends Tony Trabert, Frank Sedgman, Frank Parker, Vic Seixas, and others dedicated the new tennis courts at the Plainview Racquet Club in 1974. During the 1980s and 1990s many special events were hosted that included such all-time greats as Chris Evert, Martina Navratilova, Rod Laver, John Newcombe, Fred Stolle, Stan Smith, and Jimmy Connors.

The Kentucky Tennis Hall of Fame was established in 1985 and included distinguished tennis players, organizers, and coaches from the late 1870s to the present. Louisvillians Shelton Arterburn, Jackie Cooper, Sam English Jr., Madelle Lyons Hegeler, Ed Pfeiffer, Robert Piatt, Mickey Schad, Arnold Simons, and Helene Schuhmann Spencer were charter inductees. The Hall of Fame is located in the Bass-Rudd Tennis Center on the UNIVERSITY OF LOUISVILLE campus. Also in 1985, the men's college tennis coaches in the country moved their indoor team championships to the Louisville Tennis Club on Herr Ln. Stanford won the initial tournament, and the event has successfully remained in the city through the present time. The USTA Boys' 18 National Clay Court Championships has continued to be played in Louisville, and 2000 marked the thirty-fourth anniversary. Over the years such greats as Jimmy Connors, John McEnroe, and Pete Sampras participated.

In 1996 the National Public Parks Tennis Championships returned to Louisville for the third time and was played at the newly renovated public Louisville Tennis Center on Trevilian Way. By 2000 there were 173 public park courts in Jefferson County.

Sam O. English Jr.

Tennis at the Louisville Athletic Club, c. 1890s.

TEVIS, ELIZA CURTIS HUNDLEY (b Virginia, ca. 1802; d Jefferson County, 1880s). Landowner and businesswoman. Eliza Curtis Hundley Tevis, one of the most fascinating and imposing women and AFRICAN AMERICANS in Louisville's history, was born enslaved and brought to Kentucky. She was freed in 1833 in recognition of her service to John and, later, Thomas Hundley, owners of the land on which Bashford Manor Mall now stands and from whom she also inherited money and property in Louisville.

On June 17, 1843, she married Henry Tevis (ca. 1804–69), a free man of color, after first formalizing a prenuptial agreement that protected her premarital property from her husband's control. According to oral tradition, Tevis was given enslaved children separated from their families by sale on the Louisville slave market. These she employed or hired out as farm laborers and, consequently, became one of the few African American slaveowners listed in the records of Jefferson County. On February 22, 1851, Tevis and her husband purchased forty acres of land near the Hundley property, constructed a large log house near present-day Newburg Rd. and Indian Trail, and began farming. The Tevis land was subdivided and sold or rented to other African Americans after the CIVIL WAR. Along with an adjacent forty acres purchased by Peter Laws from Col. George Hikes in the 1870s, the entire area evolved into the African American community of Petersburg.

Tevis had a reputation as a healer, was deeply religious, and was instrumental in founding Forest Baptist Church in 1867. She and her husband had no children, although he had five children from a previous union. She was buried, along with family members and other early settlers, in Forest Home Cemetery near her house.

See *Courier-Journal*, Sept. 16, 1979; U.S. Census, 1850, 1860, 1870, 1880.

J. Blaine Hudson

Scenery for outdoor production of *The Pirates of Penzance* in the center of the bicycle track at the Amphitheater Auditorium, Fourth and Hill Streets.

TEVIS, JULIA ANN (HIERONYMOUS) (b Clark County, Kentucky, December 5, 1799; d Shelbyville, Kentucky, April 21, 1880). Educator and author. The daughter of Pendleton and Polly (Bush) Hieronymous, Julia began her education at the early age of four at a country school in her native Clark County. At about age seven, she and her family moved to Virginia, and there she attended a female academy in Winchester. In 1813 her family moved again, to Washington, D.C., and Tevis continued her studies there under private teachers until the age of nineteen.

A year later, she went to work as a teacher in Wytheville, Virginia. She then taught for a time in Abingdon, Virginia, where she married a Methodist preacher from Kentucky, John Tevis, on March 9, 1824. Shortly thereafter, the couple returned to Kentucky and settled in SHELBYVILLE. A year later, Tevis founded the famed SCIENCE HILL FEMALE ACADEMY.

Opened on March 25, 1825, with approximately twenty students, the school was established for white females aged six to twenty-one. As prejudice decreased against women's education, enrollment increased. In time, Science Hill became renowned throughout the country, particularly in the South. Tevis continued to be the chief administrator of the school until shortly before her death in 1880. Tevis's idea of an educational curriculum centered around both moral training for women and instruction in subjects such as mathematics and science. In 1878 she related details of her life and the school's history in her autobiography, *Sixty Years in a School-Room*.

Tevis and her husband were the parents of seven children, one of whom was adopted. She is buried in Grove Hill Cemetery in Shelbyville.

See Julia A. Tevis, *Sixty Years in a School-Room* (Cincinnati 1878).

THATCHER, MAURICE HUDSON (b Chicago, August 15, 1870; d Washington, D.C., January 6, 1973). Congressman. He was the son of John C. and Mary T. (Graves) Thatcher. Early in Thatcher's life, the family relocated to Butler County, Kentucky, where he attended public and private schools. Thatcher graduated from Bryant and Stratton Business College in Louisville. From 1896 to 1898, he studied law at Frankfort, Kentucky, and was admitted to the bar in 1898.

Thatcher began his legal career as an assistant attorney general for Kentucky, a position he held from 1898 to 1900. He then served as the assistant United States attorney general for the Western District of Kentucky from 1900 to 1906. Following this appointment, Thatcher left public office and began to practice law in Louisville. During this period, he also served as the state inspector and examiner for Kentucky. In 1910, President William Howard Taft appointed Thatcher to the Isthmian Canal Commission and as the civil governor of the Panama Canal Zone. These appointments began a lifelong connection between Thatcher and the Canal Zone. For three years, he headed the civil administration, providing for schools, public services, roads, customs, and revenues. In 1913, Thatcher returned to the United States and practiced law in Louisville and Washington, D.C. In 1917, he became a member of the Board of Public Safety in Louisville but resigned two years later when he became the department counsel for the city.

In 1922, Thatcher was elected as a Republican to the United States House of Representatives, where he served from March 4, 1923, to March 3, 1933. During his five terms in the House, Thatcher sponsored legislation to create the Mammoth Cave National Park, provide for permanent maintenance of ABRAHAM LINCOLN's Birthplace Farm, create the ZACHARY TAYLOR NATIONAL CEMETERY, build the Clark Memorial Bridge, establish Fort Knox as a permanent military post, and provide for construction of Louisville's post office, custom, and courthouse building on W BROADWAY. In 1932, Thatcher was nominated for a sixth House term but decided to run for the United States Senate instead. Losing the election to Alben Barkley by a vote of 575,077 to 393,865, Thatcher returned to practicing law in Washington, D.C., and served as general counsel for the Gorgas Memorial Institute of Tropical and Preventive Medicine, an organization he helped establish.

In 1961, Congress honored Thatcher by naming a bridge across the Panama Canal after him. President John F. Kennedy sent Thatcher the pen that he used to sign the act into law. It was the fifteenth pen that Thatcher had received from presidents, from Coolidge to Kennedy, acknowledging his part in legislation affecting the Panama Canal and the Canal Zone.

On May 4, 1910, Thatcher married Anne Bell Chinn. He is buried at the Frankfort Cemetery in Kentucky.

See *Who's Who in America*, vol. 28 (Chicago 1954); *Biographical Directory of the American Congress 1774–1989* (Washington, D.C., 1989).

THEATER. The origins of theater at the FALLS OF THE OHIO belong to the first flowerings of stage activity west of the Appalachian Mountains, which, between 1790 and 1820, saw Lexington, Frankfort, and especially Louisville develop into the principal centers of drama in the region. On April 10, 1790, two years before Kentucky entered the union, students from Lexington's Transylvania Seminary (later University) presented the earliest documented theatrical production in the West. As an alternative to the stages improvised in TAVERNS, HOTELS, and courthouses by amateur and itinerant players, Lexington businessman Luke Usher opened the first permanent western theater on the second floor of his brewery on October 12, 1808.

Also "about the year 1808," according to the Louisville Directory for 1832, the "Dramatic Institution" in that town was formed by "a company of the citizens," and Louisville's first theater building, "a small establishment," was erected on the north side of Jefferson St., approximately midway between Third and FOURTH Streets. "For want of a capable management," however, "it gradually sunk [sic] into nothingness" (Directory, 139).

The first professional acting company in the early West arrived in Kentucky from Canada in 1810, led by James Douglass; he was joined, then succeeded, the following year by Noble Luke Usher, son (not nephew, as he is often identified) of Luke Usher. By 1811 the elder Usher controlled regular playhouses in Lexington and Frankfort, forming the first theatrical circuit in the West. The Douglass-Usher troupe, which had possibly performed in Louisville on unrecorded dates in 1811 or 1812, played there on March 26, 1813, and perhaps for an unadvertised period before the opening of its Lexington season that May.

Noble Luke Usher fulfilled his father's dream of a three-city western circuit when he inaugurated the earliest known season of plays in Louisville in 1814. His company's lengthy engagement at the theater on Jefferson St. ran from February 16 through April 27. As was customary, each performance contained two plays, with such added entertainment as interludes, pantomimes, dances, and recitations. Generally appearing once a week, Usher's repertory troupe offered Louisville twenty-two plays in eleven nights. The actors functioned as a stock company, a permanent troupe headed by an actor-manager regularly attached to one or a group of theaters and performing a number of works in nightly or weekly rotation. The resident company also supported a star traveling alone from town to town playing limited engagements.

Following the death of his son, Luke Usher secured SAMUEL DRAKE, a British-born stage manager in Albany, New York, as general manager of the three-city circuit in Kentucky. Drake and his company—his five children plus five assistants, including Noah Miller Ludlow, a future actor-manager—arrived in Frankfort in November 1815 and traveled to Louisville early the next year. Except for five scattered attractions, the theater there had been closed since late April 1814. "Dark, dingy, and dirty" (Ludlow, *Dramatic Life As I Found It*, 88), the building on Jefferson Street was "but little better than a barn" until Drake had it renovated for his Louisville debut (McMurtrie, *Sketches of Louisville,* 126). Between February 28 and May 14, 1816, he produced twenty-four plays in twelve evenings.

Prior to the 1819 season, Drake purchased the Louisville and Frankfort theaters, but he never owned the Lexington playhouse. Louisville became the base for his theatrical operations in Kentucky and other areas. As early as March 1827, his three-story brick property in Louisville was called the City Theatre. Its auditorium, seating approximately seven hundred, welcomed the Marquis de Lafayette, and its stage was graced by such luminaries as Edwin Forrest, America's first great tragedian; Junius Brutus Booth Sr. (father of actors Edwin and John Wilkes), who died on a steamboat approaching Louisville in 1852; and THOMAS D. RICE, "the father of American MINSTRELSY," who introduced his blackface character "JIM CROW" with his song and dance at the City Theatre in May 1830 (not 1828, as is often given).

Drake retired to his farm in OLDHAM COUNTY, Kentucky, in 1833; he died there in 1854 at age eighty-six. In May 1843, the City Theatre burned down. Since 1814 over a thousand plays had been presented there.

Although Louisville's principal theater, the City was not without competition. Intermittently between 1829 and 1840, a former hippodrome near the corner of Third and Jefferson experienced a succession of managements and architectural transformations to emerge as the Melodramatic Theatre, the Theatre and Circus, the Amphi-theatre, Saubert's Theatre, the American Theatre, Caldwell's, and Cole's Amphitheatre. In its various guises it offered patrons diverse dramatic fare, French dances, equestrian displays, acrobatics, and opera. The building burned in February 1840.

The small Adelphi, on Fifth between Main and Water, generally advertised in the warmer months of 1833–35; its attractions ranged from classical English comedies and melodrama to a man impersonating an orangutan. The Pagoda, on Fifth between Market and Main, opened in July 1837 for a brief, undistinguished career.

When the City Theatre was not promptly replaced, the *Louisville Morning Courier* warned in an editorial on June 13, 1844, that neither travelers nor businessmen would consider investing time or money in a town unable to provide entertainment in "a large and respectable theater." The situation was rectified in Febru-

Shubert Theatre (later The Strand) on Chestnut Street between Third and Fourth, 1921.

ary 1846 with the opening of the Louisville Theatre at the southeast corner of Fourth and Green (now LIBERTY). Illuminated by gas and seating twelve hundred, the city's leading playhouse engaged a resident company as well as such touring stars as William Charles Macready, Edwin Forrest, Charlotte Cushman, Laura Keene, Joseph Jefferson, and the Booths (Junius Brutus Sr., Edwin, and John Wilkes). Burned in 1866, the Louisville Theatre rose from the ashes in March 1867 but was soon renamed the Louisville Opera House. Surpassed by Macauley's (opened October 1873), the theater was demolished to make way for the Courier-Journal building of 1876.

One block north of the Louisville Theatre stood two noteworthy entertainment venues: Mozart Hall and the Masonic Temple Theatre. Soprano JENNY LIND appeared in the recently opened Mozart Hall (northeast corner of Fourth and Jefferson) in April 1851; "the Swedish Nightingale," managed by P.T. Barnum, gave three concerts in its crowded second-floor auditorium. Renovation in 1854 created a regular theater with a permanent stage (presumably replacing a platform), and, in 1858, a resident company was added. As Wood's Theatre (from 1863), the playhouse enjoyed its greatest glory and introduced Louisville audiences to the matinee performance. Among its famous visiting attractions were John Wilkes Booth, Laura Keene, and Lawrence Barrett. Wood's became the Academy of Music in 1866. As the Theatre Comique (1868) and Benson's (1869), its prominence waned, and the hall faded from the scene. Its original identity was recalled by the Mozart Building (or Block) that subsequently occupied the corner.

Diagonally across from Mozart Hall was the Masonic Temple Theatre (southwest corner of Fourth and Jefferson). In the 1850s, it was simply a hall showcasing magicians, minstrels, and exhibits, but in 1870 its second floor was converted into a proper theater. Here appeared dramatic and operatic road companies, Oscar Wilde lecturing on "The Decorative Arts," Charles "Charley" Dickens reading from his father's works, and the Meffert (also Meffert-Eagle) Stock Co. (One of its members in 1897, 1898, and 1899 was the future film director Kentuckian D.W. Griffith, acting under the name "Lawrence Griffith." Louisville native HENRY HULL, later a successful character actor in Hollywood, played child roles for the Meffert Co. When the Masonic Temple burned in November 1903, its theater was known as the Hopkins. A new Masonic Building, on the south side of Chestnut between Third and Fourth, housed the Shubert Masonic Theatre, later the Strand, until it was razed in 1956.

Reflecting Louisville's ethnic composition, German-language theater could be found there as early as 1841, when the New Orleans German Theatre performed at the City Theatre. In the following decade, the second-floor playhouses at Washington Hall (on Fifth between Market and Main), at Mozart Hall, and particularly at Apollo Hall (on Third between Market and Main) offered operettas and serious drama in German with both resident companies and guest artists from Cincinnati, Evansville, and New York. The Know-Nothings' BLOODY MONDAY riots in August 1855 temporarily halted German cultural activities. German plays had returned to Louisville by January 1857 at Histrionic Temple (later Hall), a second-floor auditorium on the south side of Jefferson between Third and Fourth. In the later nineteenth and early twentieth centuries, the Masonic Temple Theatre, Liederkranz Hall (north side of Market between First and Second), Weisiger Hall, and Macauley's featured German-language troupes from Cincinnati and New York as well as stars such as the internationally renowned tragedienne Fanny Janauschek. The Minerva Society, a local amateur group, also gave plays in German.

Weisiger Hall opened in June 1867 on the second floor of the Central Market House, in an impressive three- and four-story, Mansard-roofed pile on the east side of Fourth between Walnut (now Muhammad Ali) and Green (now Liberty). The edifice was purchased in 1872 for the Public Library of Kentucky, and Weisiger Hall became Public Library Hall, managed for a time by prolific songwriter and newspaper columnist William Shakespeare "Will S." Hays. Over the next quarter-century the location was also known as the Louisville Opera House, Harris' Mammoth Museum, Harris' Theatre, and the Bijou. Depending on identity, the building housed drama, opera, concerts, lectures, exhibitions of curiosities, moving pictures, and vaudeville. The structure was razed and replaced in 1903 by the KAUFMAN-STRAUS CO. Harris' Theatre had moved across Fourth from its former address by 1891; as the Avenue (1894–1913), it was Louisville's popular home for melodrama, revivals of New York hits, and summer light opera.

Providing diversions more select in appeal and clientele than other of Louisville's theaters was the Buckingham, a BURLESQUE house owned and managed by brothers James P. and John H. Whallen, powers in the DEMOCRATIC PARTY. The "Buck," on the south side of Jefferson between Third and Fourth, opened in 1880 to replace a similar Whallen establishment, the defunct Metropolitan, successor to the Vaudeville, on Third between Walnut and Green. Early in 1885, the Metropolitan was reborn as the Odeon, ADVERTISING a "first-rate variety show." The Buck changed into the New Grand Theatre in 1885, then into the New Buckingham two years later.

Shifting slightly east, the Buck set up business in 1898 on the north side of Jefferson, between Second and Third, in the Whallens' elegant, two-thousand-seat Grand Opera House (itself preceded at that location by the Tivoli Theatre for variety shows and by the Wonderland Museum, with its curiosities and stage acts). The Grand Opera House had opened in September 1894 for legitimate theater and musical programs suitable for the general public; the management of the renovated and renamed structure now promised refined vaudeville and burlesque for men only. In 1919 the Buck became the Jefferson, which welcomed ladies and children to its touring shows; this inclusive policy continued, but only for a time, in the Savoy (from 1922). In its checkered career, the theater advertised authentic moving pictures from the Spanish-American War in the Philippines, Jimmy Durante, W.C. Fields, the Moulin Rouge Girls, prize fights, and, latterly, adult films. The Savoy, distinguished by its pink façade, was demolished after a fire in 1989; so passed Louisville's longest-operating theater building.

Not all playhouses were situated in Louisville's central theater district, for reasons of size, mobility, or race. Its motto proclaiming "Only For Great Attractions," the Amphitheatre Auditorium entertained audiences from 1889 to 1904 on the southwest corner of Fourth and Hill. Three thousand seats faced an immense stage that accommodated dramatic, operatic, and musical productions, lectures, BOXING matches, and vaudeville. The wooden structure and an adjoining ten-thousand-seat Fireworks Amphitheatre were erected by Capt. William F. Norton Jr., alias "Daniel Quilp." The theater was pulled down a year after Norton's death.

Floating theaters—SHOWBOATS—stopped at Louisville into the twentieth century, usually at the foot of Fourth St., with their repertoires of period melodramas, comedies, thrillers, and vaudeville. Between 1918 and 1942, Billy Bryant's Showboat played the Louisville area—Jeffersonville and NEW ALBANY, Indiana, and SHIVELY, Kentucky. The Hollywood (formerly the American and the Columbia) arrived at Louisville for a lengthy stand in 1930. The Majestic docked in 1949 for a month of performances by Hiram (Ohio) College students; Indiana University Theatre operated the boat from 1960 through 1966, with engagements at Louisville during five summers and at Jeffersonville during two seasons.

During SEGREGATION, theaters on Walnut west of Sixth were for "colored" patrons, according to the CITY DIRECTORIES, earning the street the nickname "Black Broadway." The theater at 1230 W Walnut did business in the 1910s as the Pekin, the Taft, the Olio, and the Pearl. Louisville native John Bubbles (born John William Sublett), half of vaudeville's leading song-and-dance team "Buck and Bubbles," began singing as a boy in an all-black show at the Olio. In his teens, he and Buck (Louisvillian Ford Lee Washington) entertained at parties and worked as ushers at the Mary Anderson Theatre (southwest corner of Fourth and Chestnut). Its manager once asked them to fill in for a weak act. As no black performer had ever appeared there, they had to wear burnt cork and white gloves so the audience would think they were whites in blackface; they were a hit, held over for two weeks.

Eclipsing the fame and prestige of all other Louisville theaters was Macauley's, one of America's premier playhouses for over fifty years. Opened in October 1873 on Walnut just east of Fourth, it welcomed virtually all of that era's famous performers, American and European. MARY ANDERSON, Louisville resident and future international actress, made her stage debut at sixteen at Macauley's, as Juliet, on November 27, 1875; there, too, on December 7, 1883, Helena Modjeska starred in *A Doll's House,* retitled *Thora,* the first professional production in America of Henrik Ibsen's controversial drama. The theater even showed an occasional outstanding film such as *The Birth of a Nation* and *The Ten Commandments.* Bowing to progress, Macauley's was demolished in 1925 for the expansion of the STARKS BUILDING.

The "moving pictures" originally shown as novelties at legitimate theaters in the late 1890s also doomed many such venues. The movies found their first commercial home in Louisville at the Dreamland, opened in 1904 on Market near Fifth. Subsequent theater construction and renovation locally reflected shifting public taste and evolving modes of amusement nationally. Stage plays and vaudeville succumbed to films at such now-vanished playhouses as the Rialto (near the southwest corner of Fourth and Chestnut), the Walnut (later the Drury Lane and the Scoop; south side of Walnut between Fourth and Fifth), and the second Hopkins (formerly Liederkranz, or Music, Hall; north side of Market between First and Second).

To succeed Macauley's as Louisville's legitimate theater, developer J. Graham Brown built the Brown Theatre adjacent to his hotel on the north side of Broadway between Third and Fourth. Seating some fifteen hundred, the Brown opened in October 1925 for stage productions but gave way to films in 1930. The theater reverted to live performances—road shows and local groups—in December 1962, and, in 1972, the renovated Brown was rechristened the Macauley. In 1997 it was renamed the W.L. Lyons Brown Theatre.

With the loss of the Brown's stage for three decades, Memorial Auditorium (1929, northwest corner of Fourth and Kentucky) became the stop for touring musical legends—among them Sigmund Romberg, Rachmaninoff, Marian Anderson, and the Ballet Russe de Monte Carlo—as well as for plays sponsored by New York's Theatre Guild and starring Katharine Hepburn, Alfred Lunt, Lynn Fontanne, and other notables. Traveling companies continue to appear at the Auditorium.

Visiting artists could also be seen at the Iroquois Amphitheatre, opened in 1938 in IROQUOIS PARK for outdoor summer musicals, and, later, the occasional play. More recently, Music Theatre Louisville has entertained audiences there. Tours of Broadway shows and such groups as Stage One: The Louisville Children's Theatre, KENTUCKY OPERA, the Louisville Ballet, and the LOUISVILLE ORCHESTRA regularly use the several theaters in the Kentucky Center for the Arts (1983) at Sixth and Main.

Civic groups in abundance, from amateur to professional, have nurtured and enriched live theater in the area since that "company" of citizens formed Louisville's "Dramatic Institution" about 1808. In the 1800s, plays and dramatic readings were presented, often at the legitimate playhouses, by the likes of the Louisville Dramatic Association, the Pythian Dramatic Society, and the Dickens, Garrick, Falstaff, and Modjeska Clubs.

The national little theater/community theater movement launched in 1911–12 reached Louisville in 1914 when Boyd Martin, a drama and film critic for the *COURIER-JOURNAL* and a speech and theater teacher at the University of Louisville, became director of the U of L Dramatic Club, which evolved into the Little Theatre Co. in 1932, with Martin continuing as director until his retirement in 1955. Five years later, the Little Theatre merged with a U of L student group to create the Belknap Players. In 1925 a former chapel on the campus was converted into the Playhouse, U of L's theater. The nineteenth-century wooden structure was dismantled in 1977 to make way for the William F. Ekstrom Library, then reassembled on a triangular tract bounded by Second, Third, and Avery, and rededicated in 1980.

The Catholic Theatre Guild flourished from 1931 through the early 1970s. In 1996 Stage One: The Louisville Children's Theatre celebrated its fiftieth anniversary, as did Clarksville (Indiana) Little Theatre with its 1996–97 season. The Anchorage Children's Theatre turned fifty in 1998. The Carriage House Players (1949) inaugurated Shakespeare in Central Park in 1962, since 1984 the KENTUCKY SHAKESPEARE FESTIVAL. Theatre One, which described itself as the first all-Negro little-theater company in the South, made its debut in 1953. The Little Colonel Players began in 1956 in PEWEE VALLEY (OLDHAM COUNTY). Of more recent date are Walden Theatre, the Blue Apple Players, Kentucky Contemporary Theatre, Bunbury Theatre, the Not Ready for Shakespeare Players, the Necessary Theatre, Derby Dinner Playhouse (CLARKSVILLE, INDIANA), the Boat House Troupe, Pegasus Rising, and Theatre Workshop of Louisville, among many other groups.

The commonwealth's best-known professional company, and a major American regional theater, is ACTORS THEATRE OF LOUISVILLE (1964), a three-theater complex on the south side of Main between Third and Fourth. Its acclaimed HUMANA Festival of New American Plays had presented some two hundred productions by its twenty-first birthday in 1997. Designated the State Theatre of Kentucky in 1974, ATL received a special Tony Award in 1980 for its contributions to the development of professional theater.

Two centuries on, in settings variously spartan, sylvan, traditional, and ultra-modern, theater thrives at the FALLS OF THE OHIO, bringing the rich diversity of world drama to Louisville while contributing outstanding new plays to the international repertoire.

See West T. Hill Jr., *The Theatre in Early Kentucky: 1790–1820* (Lexington 1971); John J. Weisert, "Beginnings of the Kentucky Theatre Circuit," *Filson Club History Quarterly* 34 (July 1960): 264–85; idem, "The First Decade at Sam Drake's Louisville Theatre," *Filson Club History Quarterly* 39 (Oct. 1965): 287–310; idem, "Golden Days at Drake's City Theatre, 1830–1833," *Filson Club History Quarterly* 43 (July 1969): 255–70; idem, "An End and Several Beginnings: The Passing of Drake's City Theatre," *Filson Club History Quarterly* 50 (Jan. 1976): 5–28; idem, "The Chief Competitor of Drake's City Theatre," *Register of the Kentucky Historical Society* 66 (April 1968): 159–67; idem, "Beginnings of German Theatricals in Louisville," *Filson Club History Quarterly* 26 (Oct. 1952): 347–59; Noah Miller Ludlow, *Dramatic Life As I Found It* (1880; reprinted New York 1966); Henry McMurtrie, *Sketches of Louisville and its Environs* (Louisville 1819; reprinted Louisville 1969); *The Louisville Directory for the Year 1832* (Louisville 1832); Mitzi Friedlander, "History of a Theatre," *Filson Club History Quarterly* 45 (July 1971): 305–14.

John Spalding Gatton

THEODORE ROOSEVELT/WILLIAM H. PERRY SR. ELEMENTARY SCHOOL. The Roosevelt School, at 222 N Seventeenth St. in the PORTLAND neighborhood, is a product of the post-CIVIL WAR "peace dividend" that brought people and prosperity to "neutral" Louisville. The brick-and-stone-trim building was erected (1865-66) as the Eleventh Ward School, part of a citywide expansion program that included this and two other schools (now demolished) designed by the Bradshaw brothers, Louisville architects. The school complex has long been a focus of neighborhood pride and activity. Teachers at the school founded the PORTLAND MUSEUM in 1978 as a classroom project. In 1979 the William H. Perry Elementary School, named for the pioneer African-American educator who was principal of Western Colored School from 1891 to 1927, was combined with the Roosevelt School. The school closed in 1980 and sat vacant for a long time during which it deteriorated badly. Louisville's oldest surviving school building was then renovated by the New Directions Housing Corp. into forty-seven apartment units for low-and moderate-income people, and reopened on June 2, 1998.

See *Courier-Journal,* June 3, 1998.

Douglas L. Stern

THOMAS INDUSTRIES INC. In 1948 Lee B. Thomas and a group of investors acquired a residential lighting fixture company from the Moe family of Fort Atkinson, Wisconsin. In 1949 the company's name was changed from Moe Brothers to Moe Lighting Inc.

The company expanded its lighting production with the 1952 purchase of the Star Lighting Fixture Co. of Los Angeles and the opening of a residential lighting factory in Princeton, Kentucky. A year later the company was merged into the Electric Sprayit Co. of Sheboygan, Wisconsin, a paint sprayer manufacturer, and the name was permanently changed to Thomas Industries Inc.

In 1955 the company moved its headquarters to a building on Third Street in Louisville to more efficiently manage its expanding group of products, which included residential lighting fixtures, portable paint-spraying equipment, reciprocating-blade power saws, and bathroom cabinets. Thomas Industries also went public that year, and sales reached a volume of over $18.5 million. Aside from moving its headquarters to a facility on E BROADWAY in the late fifties, the company acquired the Benjamin Electric Co. and C&M Products of Canada, moving the firm into commercial and industrial lighting.

Throughout the sixties and seventies, Thomas Industries continued to diversify its product lines by acquiring companies that manufactured paint brushes and rollers, specialty tools for the commercial construction industry, grandfather and decorative wall clocks, fireplace screens and accessories, metal chimneys and zero-clearance fireplaces, wallpaper, artificial and preserved floral arrangements, table lamps, and built-in vacuum systems.

In the late 1980s, Thomas Industries realigned its operating divisions and defined a long-range goal concentrating on two core businesses—lighting and compressors/vacuum pumps. In efforts to focus the company, all noncore businesses were sold by 1994, while several acquisitions strengthened the company's position in their core industries. During this time the company also moved its headquarters to an office on Brownsboro Rd. in eastern Jefferson County. By 1998 the company had operations throughout the United States, Canada, Mexico, South America, Europe, and Asia, and sales totaled over a half-billion dollars.

THOMASSON, WILLIAM POINDEXTER (b New Castle, Kentucky, October 8, 1797; d LaGrange, Kentucky, December 29, 1882). U.S. congressman. After serving in Captain Duncan's company in the War of 1812, Thomasson returned home to study law. Before he was twenty-one he was admitted to the bar, and began practicing in CORYDON, Indiana, where he served as a prosecuting attorney for Harrison County. He served in the State house of representatives from 1818 to 1820. In 1841 he moved to Louisville, and was elected to the forty-eighth and forty-ninth Congresses as a Whig candidacy for renomination. Thomasson then moved his law practice to Chicago and then to New York where he served in the New York Volunteer Infantry during the CIVIL WAR. He is buried in CAVE HILL CEMETERY.

See *Biographical Directory of the American Congress 1776-1961* (Washington, D.C. 1961).

THOMPSON, DINNIE D. (b Louisville, January 1857; d Louisville March 7, 1939). Slave. Dinnie D. Thompson was born to Diana (1818–95) and Spencer Thompson (d 1858), enslaved by the family of John and Lucy Fry Speed of Farmington, a Louisville hemp plantation. John Speed died in 1840, and his fifty-seven slaves were parceled out to his wife and eleven children. Diana, Ned Russell, and their children, Lot, Lydia, and Robert Russell, were given to Mary Speed. In 1854 Mary moved her slaves from Farmington to her home on Fifth St. in downtown Louisville. When Ned Russell died Diana married Spencer Thompson, who was enslaved by Peachy Speed Peay at Farmington. Spencer died in 1858, a year after Dinnie's birth.

Diana secreted Dinnie away from Mary Speed's home on several failed attempts to secure passage across the OHIO RIVER to Indiana, but they were always caught and returned. When freed in 1864, Diana and Dinnie traveled to Indianapolis to view President ABRAHAM LINCOLN lying in state. Diana had been Mary Speed's personal slave when Lincoln visited his friend Joshua, John's son, at Fry Speed Farmington in 1841.

In 1870 Dinnie attended a Louisville public school for colored. In 1913 she became the third-floor maid at the NEIGHBORHOOD HOUSE at 428 S First St., a settlement house, where she was employed until her death. While there she befriended a young social worker named Elizabeth A. Wilson, who in 1974, 1978, and 1997 recounted to the *COURIER-JOURNAL* stories that Dinnie had told about her life. For many years Dinnie Thompson was a member of the Sisters of the Mysterious Ten, a benevolent African-American group organized in 1876 by the United Brothers of Friendship. She was an officer in the St. Mary chapter. While hers appears to be an ordinary life, in a larger sense she represented thousands of Kentucky African American women who after slavery persevered and triumphed in spite of horrendous obstacles.

Dinnie never married. She lived fifty-four years in a small cottage at 433 Roselane St. purchased in 1885 by her mother. Dinnie is buried in Louisville's Eastern Cemetery.

See Ann I. Ottesen, "A Reconstruction of the Activities and Outbuildings at Farmington, an Early Nineteenth Century Hemp Farm," *Filson Club History Quarterly* 59 (Oct. 1985): 395–425; *Courier-Journal*, Feb. 21, 1997, May 13, 1997, July 23, 1997.

Juanita White

Dinnie Thompson in her Sisters of the Mysterious Ten uniform, 1920s.

THOMPSON, ROBERT LOUIS (b Louisville, 1937; d Rome, Italy, June 4, 1966). African American artist. The son of Cecil Dewitt and Bessie (Shauntee) Thompson, he revealed his talent for PAINTING at the early age of eight when he began using his mother's window shades as canvases. His family had moved to Elizabethtown, Kentucky, when Thompson was two, but after his father's death in 1950 Thompson was sent to live with an older sister in Louisville. Following graduation from Central High School, he studied pre-MEDICINE at Boston University for one year before returning to study art at the UNIVERSITY OF LOUISVILLE. Thompson left the university after his junior year and in 1959 moved to New York City to pursue a career in painting. There, in 1960, an exhibition of his work was held at the Zabriskie Gallery. Thompson was awarded the Walter Gutman Foundation Grant in 1961 and received the John Hay Whitney Fellowship for 1962–63, both of which allowed him to spend three years studying in Europe. After his return to New York City, Thompson's paintings were shown in the Museum of Modern Art and the Martha Jackson Gallery. In late 1965, Thompson went to Rome to study in the city of the old masters. A few months later, his meteoric career was cut short when he died unexpectedly of a lung hemorrhage following gall bladder surgery. A memorial exhibition of his works, sponsored by the Louisville Art Workshop, was held at the J.B. SPEED ART MUSEUM, February 2–21, 1971.

Thompson's surrealist paintings were characterized by intense colors and were often populated by nudes, giant BIRDS, and demonic figures that cavort and do battle in fantastic landscapes. In 1960 he married Carol Plenda. He is buried at Elizabethtown.

See *Courier-Journal,* Feb. 21, 1971; *Kentucky Expatriates: Natives and Notable Visitors, The Early 1800s to the Present* (Owensboro, Ky., 1984).

THOMPSON BLOCK. The Thompson Block was a small enclave of bohemian culture in downtown Louisville from the late 1930s until the early 1960s. In the 1970s the ragtag structures of turn-of-the-century vintage located on the south side of Jefferson between Third and FOURTH Streets were razed as part of the city's URBAN RENEWAL program for construction of a Hyatt Regency Hotel and its adjoining parking garage.

The block took its name from the prominent, white-tiled Thompson's Restaurant on the south side of Jefferson. A serve-yourself cross between cafeteria and automat, it featured such homestyle dishes as meat loaf and gravy, chicken pot pie, and corned beef and cabbage at low prices without tipping. The format appealed to a wide spectrum of customers, including farmers who trucked their crops twice a week to the nearby HAYMARKET on E Jefferson St. The restaurant also did a brisk trade in quick orders of coffee and pastries. It was a popular meeting place all day long.

The Thompson Block was a unique and lively part of mid-downtown, with busy sidewalks and an ethnically diverse POPULATION and colony of businesses. At various times its roster of enterprises included, in addition to Thompson's, Al Kolb's Oyster & Liquor Bar, Zimmerman's Bookstore, Caufield's Novelties & Decorations, Zena's Cafe, Lococo's Bar & Lounge, the Louisville Transit Co., the Union (Greek) Restaurant, the KENTUCKY IRISH AMERICAN newspaper, and the Rodeo Theater.

The block also was home to one of Louisville's largest concentrations of bookmakers—seven in its heyday, including several that lured bettors with free lunches. Thanks to police protection and a seemingly blind Democratic press, the *COURIER-JOURNAL* and *LOUISVILLE TIMES*, bookies here and hundreds more throughout the city thrived outside the law until Congress passed legislation in 1961 banning the interstate transmission of horse-race results for illegal purposes.

An entity contributing greatly to the Thompson Block's bohemian culture was Zimmerman's used-book store, owned by Phil Zimmerman and his father Abe. Phil's engaging personality and his love for books attracted a large following among students, professors, writers, politicians, and bibliophiles in general—if only for the intellectual stimulation of a far-ranging conversation.

The block also had its own artist-in-residence, Bill Fischer, a former newspaper illustrator who operated a discount shoe store next to Thompson's. In the rear of the store, Fischer maintained a combination office and art studio where he served strong chicory-laced coffee, told bawdy jokes, and showed his latest PAINTINGS to friends and guests.

Lococo's Bar & Lounge and Zena's Cafe on Jefferson St. were the block's favored watering holes. Lococo's had roomy, upholstered booths, a juke box whose muted JAZZ and pop music flowed endlessly, and subdued lighting that provided an appropriate setting day and night for an intimate rendezvous. By contrast, Zena's was a well-lit, noisy, workingman's tavern. Zena's special appeal was the industrious, patriarchal presence of Sam Zena, a LEBANESE immigrant, and his three sons, Henry, Bob, and Eddie. Zena's began as a small restaurant specializing in Lebanese dishes, then gradually expanded its offerings to include beer, hard liquor, card games, and bookmaking.

Another dimension to the block was the close proximity of Gargotto's Pool Room on Jefferson St., a few doors east of Third St. It was a lively emporium that hosted many hotly contested regional tournaments and catered as well to the casual player.

In the decade following WORLD WAR II, a number of returning servicemen, beginning reentry into a peacetime world, discovered the Thompson Block's distinctive off-beat attractions and began gathering at Zimmerman's and Thompson's on a regular basis in search of kindred souls and to bet on the horses and engage in such intellectual pursuits as organizing a local Existentialist society.

Charles H. Thomas

THORNTON OIL CORPORATION. Founded in 1971 by James H. Thornton, the company has held the number-one position in Louisville's "Business First Metro 100" ranking of privately held corporations for six of the ten years the ranking has been compiled. The company experienced meteoric growth during the early and mid-1980s under the leadership of Paul Perconti, who joined the company in 1981 as president and CEO. It was Perconti's decision to embellish the company's existing sites and construct new ones that could offer a full line of convenience products. Thornton Oil also became one of the first convenience retailers to co-brand with selected fast food chains such as Subway and Dunkin' Donuts. Thornton Oil is currently the exclusive Dunkin' Donuts franchisee in Jefferson County. It was also one of the first gasoline retailers to put canopies over its pumps, add automated teller machines to its stores, and provide customers with the ability to pay at the pump using credit cards. Perconti was dismissed from Thornton Oil in the summer of 1998 while being investigated under charges of embezzlement, and Richard Claes was appointed the new president and CEO.

James Hope Thornton was born December 8, 1927, in Lebanon, Kentucky. His family relocated to Louisville in 1933 and later to New Albany, Indiana. While attending NEW ALBANY High School, graduating in 1946, Thornton got his first experience in the gasoline industry working for his stepfather's station. In 1949 he became a real estate broker with Cora Jacobs. At the age of twenty-four in 1951 Thornton became a partner with Gilbert Dance and Alford Mallory in Dixie Dance gas stations. Three years later Thornton opened his first gas station, called Sunny Service, on CORYDON Pike. Not yet thirty years old, Thornton entered a joint venture with ASHLAND INC. in 1955 that eventually resulted in the development of 150 Payless service stations in 22 states. These sites were among the first in the nation to offer self-service gasoline. In 1966 Thornton sold his interest in Payless to Ashland and joined Ashland's board, remaining until late 1970. In 1971 he founded Thornton Oil Corp. and within two years had forty stores. In 1999 Thornton Oil operated over 150 gasoline convenience stores in 6 states. Most are in the Louisville area.

In the late 1980s, Thornton relocated to Georgetown, Kentucky, to his five-hundred-acre Summer Wind Farm, which trains Thoroughbred race horses. Thornton has also been involved in many other ventures outside the gasoline industry. He has been co-owner of Latonia Race Track (now Turfway Park) and has served on the Kentucky State Racing Commission and the boards of METRO UNITED WAY, LOUISVILLE URBAN LEAGUE, SPALDING UNIVERSITY, University of Louisville Athletic Association, Actors Theatre, and the FUND FOR THE ARTS.

Alejandro Magallanez

THRUSTON, ROGERS CLARK BALLARD (b Louisville, November 6, 1858; d Louisville, December 30, 1946). Historian, engineer, and photographer. A son of Andrew Jackson Ballard and Frances Ann (Thruston) Ballard, he adopted his mother's maiden name in 1884. Thruston graduated from Yale University's Sheffield Scientific School in 1880, and in 1882 began work with the Kentucky Geological Survey. He resigned in 1887, founded the Inter-State Investment Co. with his brothers, and for two decades was active in surveying, platting, and buying timber and mineral lands in Kentucky and Virginia. In 1909 he retired to devote his life to historical and genealogical research, to charitable and patriotic organizations, and to the Filson Club, a Louisville historical research institution. He was instrumental in guiding the club through a critical period after the death of its founder, Col. REUBEN T. DURRETT. Serving as president from 1923 to 1946, Thruston provided the impetus for acquiring the club's first headquarters, established an endowment fund, and contributed his research materials, photograph collection, and personal library.

Thruston was an expert on the evolution of the American flag; the genealogies of the signers of the Declaration of Independence; and

George Rogers Clark, a collateral ancestor. His photographs record nineteenth-century mountain life in Kentucky as well as people, places, and events in other states and in foreign countries from 1900 through the 1930s. His meticulous research, his respect for historical accuracy, and his dedication to the preservation of historical materials were his legacy to Kentucky history. He is buried in Cave Hill Cemetery.

See Thomas D. Clark, "Rogers Clark Ballard Thruston, Engineer, Historian, and Benevolent Kentuckian," Filson Club History Quarterly 58 (Oct. 1984): 408–35.

Mary Jean Kinsman

THUM, PATTY PRATHER (b Louisville, October 1, 1853; d Louisville, September 28, 1926). Artist. She was the daughter of Dr. Mandeville and Louisiana (Miller) Thum. As a child she was taught by her mother to draw and later studied art at Vassar College under Henry Van Ingen and at the Art Students' League in New York City with William Merritt Chase. Thum also studied briefly with Thomas Eakins at the Students' Guild of the Brooklyn Art Association in the mid-1880s.

In the mid-1870s Thum returned to Louisville, where she was known primarily as a landscape painter, although she did still-lifes and portraits. She was noted for her paintings of flowers both in vases and in garden settings. Thum used private gardens in Jefferson and Oldham Counties for many of her works. The lily pond in Shawnee Park appeared in several pieces as well. In her landscapes, Thum reproduced Kentucky scenes that highlighted the native beech, tulip poplar, and sycamore trees. For more than thirty-five years she maintained an art studio in Louisville.

She was a member of the Louisville Art Association and the Art Club of Louisville and was art critic for the Louisville Herald. She illustrated the book Robbie and Annie: A Child's Story and in 1893 received honorable mention for book illustrations at the Chicago Columbian Exposition. Her work was exhibited at the New York State Fair in 1898 and at the St. Louis Exposition of 1904. In 1921 she served as art director of the Kentucky State Fair. Thum, who never married, resided with her sister, Adrienne Thum, and is buried in Cave Hill Cemetery.

See Peter Falk Hastings, Who's Who in American Art (Madison, Conn., 1985); Arthur F. Jones, Dreaming over Woods and Hills (Lexington 1992); Bettie M. Henry, Biographical Extracts Relating to Prominent Artists of Louisville and Kentucky (Louisville 1939).

Candace Perry

THUNDER OVER LOUISVILLE. What started as a small outdoor fireworks show and concert has grown into the largest annual fireworks display in North America. The opening ceremonies of the Kentucky Derby Festival began as most Festival events do, with the question of "How can we make this better?"

The Festival leadership wanted to include more people in its 1989 kick-off. Festival Board members Ben Harper of the Kroger Co. and Guy Hempel of WAVE TV proposed staging a lunchtime show at the Waterfront Park Chow Wagon. The show included a concert featuring Suzy Carr, who sang the festival theme song, and a daytime fireworks show. Wayne Hettinger was hired to act as show producer. The production was telecast live and simulcast in the Galt House Grand Ballroom for They're Off Luncheon patrons.

To further increase attendance, the 1990 opening ceremonies became a nighttime event at the Kentucky Fair and Exposition Center and Cardinal Stadium, and the name Thunder Over Louisville was added. More than thirty-five thousand people saw a free concert with Janie Fricke and a fireworks show of four thousand shells. The show's highlight was "Gargantua," a sixteen-inch fireworks shell. The entire event was broadcast live on WLKY-TV. Kroger, UPS, Sam Meyers, and Derby Cone were the event sponsors.

It was apparent that the potential crowd appeal for Thunder Over Louisville was far greater than the Kentucky Fair and Exposition Center could accommodate. Festival president Dan Mangeot wanted to develop a huge fireworks show similar to ones he had seen in Cincinnati over Labor Day weekend. Harper and Mangeot moved the 1991 event back to Louisville's riverfront. Hettinger and Harper brought in Zambelli Internationale Fireworks, and more shells were used in the finale than in the entire first show. To enhance the entertainment value, an air show was added in 1992. The number of food stands increased to more than 130, and the show time was expanded to early afternoon.

By 1996, "Thunder" had grown into one of the most impressive displays in the world. More than thirty thousand shells weighing more than thirty-two tons were shot during a twenty-eight-minute period. There were more fireworks shot off in the first minute than the entire 1990 show. The sound system stretched more than a mile and a half along the Ohio River and had 325 turbo speaker cabinets with a combined power of 425,000 watts.

In 1997, the United States Air Force designated the Derby Festival Opening Ceremonies: Thunder Over Louisville as one of two marquee events for its Fiftieth Anniversary Celebration. More than 125 military aircraft, including the Air Force Thunderbirds, were on display and performed over a 2-day period. This made the event the largest combined fireworks and air show in the United States.

The festival conducted an economic impact survey of Thunder Over Louisville in 1995. It indicated that the free one-day event generated more than $12 million for the local economy. In 1996, that figure had grown to more than $14.3 million. Crowd estimates have exceeded six hundred thousand people.

Clay W. Campbell

TINCHER, HARRY E. (b Hendricks County, Indiana, June 29, 1880; d Louisville, October 16, 1952). Jefferson County judge. Tincher was the son of George Washington and Rhoda (Benbara) Tincher. He was educated at Central Academy in Plainville, Indiana, graduating in 1900, and at Franklin College in Franklin, Indiana, graduating in 1903. Tincher received a law degree from the University of Virginia in 1908 and moved to Louisville to practice law.

Tincher, a Republican, was Jefferson County judge from January 1, 1922, until December 31, 1925. He defeated Democrat James P. Gregory, former county judge from 1898 until 1905, by 5,320 votes. The Republicans won nearly every city and county office, continuing the party's domination of area politics started in 1917. Tincher also served as second assistant city attorney from January 1, 1919, until his election as county judge in 1921. He was appointed city attorney to succeed Huston Quin, who was elected mayor on the same ticket as Tincher in 1921. Tincher was also a fifty-year member of the Phi Delta Theta law fraternity.

He married Katherine McHaffee of Hendricks County, Indiana, on September 4, 1906. He was later married to Alice Johnson. He died at his home at 2080 Ravinia. He is buried in Calvary Cemetery.

See W.T. Owens, *Who's Who in Louisville* (Louisville, 1926); *Courier-Journal,* Oct. 17, 1952.

TOBACCO. Archeological evidence suggests that prehistoric man in Kentucky smoked tobacco in pipes. The first white explorers to Kentucky met Shawnee Indians who grew tobacco for their own use. Settlers in the late eighteenth century, however, brought tobacco seeds with them from Virginia and North Carolina, where tobacco was an established commodity. Along with hemp and wheat, the early settlers planted small patches of tobacco for their own use. The soil and climate produced quality tobacco. It was reported from the Louisville area around 1789 that three times the quantity of tobacco and corn could be raised on an acre than in the seaboard states. An early notion that good tobacco could be raised only on virgin soil contributed to the further development of the crop in frontier areas.

Beginning in 1783 the Virginia Assembly authorized the establishment of tobacco warehouses in Kentucky. A Colonel Campbell reportedly erected one such warehouse in Louisville that year. Officials were appointed to inspect the crop and to order the destruction of inferior-quality leaf. Tobacco was accepted as payment for public debts and taxes at twenty shillings per hundredweight.

At the time, however, Spain controlled New

Orleans and the lower Mississippi River, which was the only viable means of transporting the tobacco crop to the eastern states and European markets. In 1787, James Wilkinson, a brigadier general in the Revolutionary War, set off down the Ohio River with two flatboats loaded with tobacco, bacon, and flour. After his cargo was seized and then released by the Spanish, General Wilkinson negotiated an agreement to become a Spanish agent. Returning to Kentucky, he announced to much public acclaim that he had opened the route to markets in the eastern states and Europe. Soliciting tobacco and other commodities for shipment to New Orleans, Wilkinson began assembling fleets of flatboats that were launched from below the falls at Louisville. One such fleet comprising twenty-five large boats bedecked with flags and armed with three-pound swivel cannons was launched with much fanfare in January 1789. Tobacco that sold for two dollars per hundredweight in Kentucky brought up to ten dollars in Spanish coin at Mississippi ports. Wilkinson soon learned his agency was not exclusive, as Spain began permitting other Americans to ship goods through the Spanish ports. In 1790 Spain began limiting American tobacco purchases to forty thousand pounds annually. It was thought by some that Wilkinson made a fortune by this trade. If so, he soon lost that wealth. In 1791, disgruntled and financially distressed, Wilkinson quit the trade to reenter the United States Army.

While Louisville was the only port on western rivers for a decade after 1789, it was at first a minor concentration point for tobacco compared to Frankfort and Lexington. Continued uncertainty about access to markets for tobacco exports caused Kentucky planters to focus their efforts on wheat and hemp. Between 1815 and 1820, approximately five hundred hogsheads of tobacco were received in Louisville annually. In the 1830s tobacco production in Kentucky underwent its first great expansion. By 1839 the state was producing 53 million pounds, making it second only to Virginia in tobacco production. While Frankfort had been the major market for tobacco in Kentucky, it lost that place to Louisville by the mid-1800s. By 1850 Louisville had eighty-two tobacco and cigar factories that produced approximately $1.4 million in products annually. With the incorporation of the Louisville & Nashville Railroad in 1850, another route for shipping tobacco to the eastern states from Louisville was opened.

Kentucky farmers had traditionally cultivated a dark-fired tobacco cured by hickory smoke in tightly enclosed barns. In 1865 a new type of tobacco was discovered quite by accident when a Kentucky farmer who ran out of seed obtained more seed from Ohio. The Ohio seed unexpectedly produced a lighter-colored leaf that proved to be ideal for heavily sweetened chewing and pipe tobacco. The new variety known as "white Burley" soon spread throughout the Bluegrass, where the soil was especially suited to its cultivation. The new variety could be harvested earlier and easier than the dark-fired version. It was also easier to cure in barns with panels that were opened or closed to control moisture.

Throughout much of this region hemp had been the major cash crop of antebellum farmers. During the Civil War, however, Kentucky's isolation from the South caused a loss of markets for bale rope and bagging made from hemp for southern cotton. Following the war a trend toward jute bagging and iron banding for cotton bales and the replacement of rope rigging with wire on ships further precipitated hemp's decline. Thus, where hemp had been a major crop for many Bluegrass farmers, Kentucky production of hemp declined from nearly forty thousand tons to less than eight thousand within a decade from 1860. This void was filled by tobacco and in particular the new burley variety. During the Civil War and through 1928 Kentucky led the nation in tobacco production, and Louisville edged out New Orleans as the largest tobacco market in the country.

Packing twists of chewing tobacco at the Ryan-Hampton Tobacco Company, 822 South Floyd Street.

A whole culture in Kentucky began to revolve around tobacco-growing, which became the backbone of farming in the region. From early days the raising of tobacco was the most labor-intensive farming enterprise. Tobacco constitutes a nearly yearlong cycle of activity. In early spring seed is put in plant beds or greenhouses and fertilized until the middle of May, when eight-inch-tall plants are transplanted to the field. During the following two months it is cultivated, and additional fertilizer is applied. By the end of July blooms that appear on the four- to five-foot plants must be cut off or "suckered" by hand. A month later the tobacco needs to be cut and hung in large, airy barns for curing. By late October the tobacco is ready for stripping. Stripping is a time-consuming process where the individual leaves are removed from the stalk and sorted according to length and color. The stripped tobacco is placed in a baler that uses compressed air to create ninety-pound bales, which are taken to the warehouses for auction. In Kentucky traditionally the auction market starts around Thanksgiving and ends in February. In early days about three hundred hours were required to raise one acre of tobacco. Today that has probably been reduced by 30 percent due to the changes in technology.

At the beginning tobacco had been packed and sold primarily in large wooden barrels known as hogsheads containing a thousand pounds or more. By 1880 Louisville had become the tobacco manufacturing center of the state and the largest hogshead auction center, selling 175,000 hogsheads of tobacco annually before 1900. Main St. between Eighth and Twelfth Streets was known as the Tobacco District. In 1906, a "loose leaf" auction warehouse opened in Lexington in which tobacco was tied into hands and sold on baskets. This new method, which had long been practiced in Virginia, soon became accepted throughout the state, and Lexington replaced Louisville as the major burley auction market. The last hogshead auction was held for the 1929–30 crop, and after that all sales were loose leaf.

The late 1800s and early 1900s was a time of great economic uncertainty for farmers that gave rise to a number of agrarian societies and movements. Depressed tobacco prices led to a number of attempts to form grower associations in Kentucky to market tobacco cooperatively. In 1904 the Planters Protective Association was

1886 Pickett Tobacco Warehouse advertisement. *The Industries of Louisville and New Albany.*

formed for this purpose by growers in the area of western Kentucky and northern Tennessee known as the "Black Patch," where a darker, flue-cured variety of tobacco was raised. This association was soon assisted in its efforts to pool the tobacco crop for sale by bands of militant farmers known as Night Riders. The Night Riders at first resorted primarily to nocturnal visits designed to encourage recalcitrant neighbors to join the ranks of the PPA. Soon large bands of Night Riders began raiding towns such as Princeton, Hopkinsville, and Russellville to destroy tobacco warehouses. The escalating conflict caused Kentucky's governor to dispatch a company of state militia from Louisville in an attempt to restore order to the region. A similar association was formed in the Burley Belt in the Bluegrass with accompanying, although generally less dramatic or violent, nocturnal activities. These associations were successful in raising prices for a time. After several years the associations succumbed, however, to the dissemination so common to agrarian societies.

Before the cigarette was manufactured, "navy" plug was the most popular form of tobacco. European governments distributed it to their sailors, hence the name "navy." The most famous plug brand of the mid-1800s, "Battle Ax," was made by the Louisville company National Tobacco Works, originally Pfingst, Doerhoefer, and Co. NTW, Weissinger Tobacco Factory (originally Globe Tobacco Works), and Five Brothers Tobacco Works were all prominent plug makers in Louisville.

Five Brothers Tobacco Works (later John Finzer & Co.) was started in 1866 by the five Finzer brothers, John, Benjamin, Frederick, Rudolph, and Nicholas. By 1887 the company was producing 4 million pounds of plug tobacco and 1 million pounds of smoking tobacco, with their most popular brand being "Old Honesty." At the height of productivity they employed more than four hundred people. The building on the corner of Jacob and Jackson Streets was destroyed by fire in 1880, but it was rebuilt on the same spot. The company also published a trade paper, *The Tobacconist*, which had a monthly circulation of thirty-two thousand. In 1904 it became part of the American Tobacco Co. and by 1924 it was out of existence.

Globe Tobacco Works was established in 1869 by Harry Weissinger and Philip B. Bate. In 1887 it was changed to Weissinger Tobacco Works after Weissinger bought out Bate. The plant was originally located on Main near Tenth St., but in 1878 it moved to Floyd St. between Breckinridge and College Streets. Their most popular plug products were "Old Kentucky" and "Hold Fast." The company was in existence until 1903. Although this is not known for a fact, it is highly probable that the company was bought out by a larger company.

NTW began production in Louisville in 1880 and was located at 1806 W Main St. By 1890 NTW was responsible for one-seventh of the total plug production in the United States. In 1891 James Duke, the tobacco magnate from North Carolina, acquired the company, as well as several other tobacco manufacturers, and merged them under the umbrella company of Continental Tobacco Co., later the American Tobacco Co. ATC remained in Louisville until 1970. At that time they employed a thousand people. The factory and stemming plant were located at Seventeenth and Broadway, with a warehouse on Seventh Street Rd. and a leaf-processing operation at 908 S Eighth St. ATC produced such popular brands as "Pall Mall," "Lucky Strike," and "Tareyton." In 1994 it was bought by Brown and Williamson Tobacco Co.

By the late 1800s Louisville was by far the center of the tobacco trade. By 1890 there were fifteen warehouses, sixteen manufacturing plants, and seventy-nine smaller firms that made cigars and snuff. There have been at Louisville ever since its infancy, many cigar manufacturing businesses, of moderate size individually but making in the aggregate an important feature in the business of the city. In 1880, the business reported a capital, real and personal, of $109,027; hands, 368; value of annual product, $354,988. Louisville was the ideal spot for manufacture and trade of tobacco due to the fact that all grades from the finest of white burley to the commonest Regie (low-grade Italian plug tobacco) were available. European contracts could readily be obtained as several countries set up agency houses in the city.

After the turn of the century tobacco manufacturing continued to grow in Louisville, as did the number of people using tobacco. After the first modern blended cigarette was put on the market in 1913 it soon became very popular. Tobacco production increased during World War I because of the cigarette's popularity with soldiers. Increased use meant increased production, and Louisville was at the center of production.

In 1905 Woodford Fitch Axton established the Axton-Fischer Tobacco Co. At first the company was only a regional producer of bagged and chewing tobacco, but in 1926 it became a national producer when they produced the first mentholated cigarette, "Spud." Its ten-cent Depression pack, "Twenty Grand," made the company one of the largest sellers. By 1934 sales reached $28 million, and the plant employed twelve hundred people. The company built its plant at Twentieth and Broadway, and it was turned over to Philip Morris in 1944.

Brown and Williamson Tobacco Co. arrived in Louisville in 1929. The company, started in 1893 by brothers-in-law George Brown and Robert Williamson, has been a subsidiary of the London-based BAT Industries, PLC, since 1927. In 1931 B&W decided to move its headquarters to Louisville. They acquired seventy-two acres at Sixteenth and Hill Streets and constructed seven buildings. Its manufacturing plant was in operation until 1982, and the research and development division until 1994. In 1983 the headquarters moved into the building next to the Galleria on Fourth St. at Liberty. In 1994 B&W purchased the American Tobacco Co. Because of the acquisition B&W was ranked the nation's third-largest manufacturer of cigarettes in 1998. B&W has also contributed to community projects such as the waterfront revitalization, Papa John's Cardinal Stadium, the Fund for the Arts, and Light up Louisville. The company employs five hundred at their headquarters in Louisville and seven thousand nationwide.

Tobacco prices improved during World War I; but the end of the war, coupled with a long rainy season and poor-quality leaf, caused the bottom to drop out of the burley market in 1920. Seeking to aid the farmers and avoid the violent conflicts of the past, Robert W. Bingham, editor and owner of the *Courier-Journal;* Samuel Halley, a noted Lexington planter and warehouseman; and Arthur Krock, the editor of the *Louisville Times*, helped form the Burley Tobacco Growers Cooperative Association, which was effective in increasing tobacco prices for about five years. In 1933 President Roosevelt's New Deal introduced the tobacco support system, which, through production restraints or quotas and price supports, continues to this day to give growers some price protection and relative market stability, although its fate has been the subject of much debate during the last few years of the century.

During the Depression, tobacco production increased as many people used cigarettes as a form of relaxation. In 1932 eleven billion cigarettes were produced in Louisville. Smoking continued to be a popular practice, and thought to be a nonharmful–practice through WORLD WAR II and the 1950s, and Louisville continued to be the center of tobacco manufacturing. ATC's (now B&W's after the buyout in 1994) "Lucky Strike" brand went to war with the country in the 1940s and sponsored the Hit Parade for teenagers in the 1950s.

Philip Morris installed a branch here in 1944, taking over the buildings of Axton-Fischer. By 1960 one-sixth of all cigarettes manufactured in the U.S. were made in Louisville. The city's sixteen plants in 1890 were now only four: B&W, Philip Morris, Lorillard, and ATC. The fifteen warehouses now numbered only one. In 1969 nine thousand Louisvillians were working in the four plants, including a thousand at ATC, a thousand at Lorillard, two thousand at Philip Morris, and five thousand at B&W.

The market floundered in the 1970s and 1980s as news that cigarettes were harmful and addictive became widespread. These growing concerns, coupled with a few bad seasons in the late 1980s and the growing loss of business to South American growers, made the decade a dismal one for farmers. Despite the circumstances, tobacco was still Kentucky's number-one agricultural commodity, with production at 366 million pounds in 1990. In 1993 SHELBY COUNTY led the production of tobacco in the area with 12,035,000 pounds. It was followed by BULLITT COUNTY with a production of 1,418,000 pounds, OLDHAM COUNTY with 1,406,000 pounds, Harrison County with 1,380,000 pounds, Clark County with 1,310,000 pounds, Jefferson County with 595,000 pounds, Scott County with 491,000 pounds, and Floyd County with 293,000 pounds. The labor pool was always located in the rural areas on farms. Beginning in the early twentieth century, many farmers abandoned their land for work in cities such as Louisville, SHELBYVILLE, and SELLERSBURG. Some who left were tenant farmers who took with them the labor that was needed for the growing of tobacco. This and the low wages combined with hard work resulted in the loss of the traditional local labor force. Since 1980 tobacco farmers have relied more on migrant workers from Latin America.

The 1990s were troublesome for the local tobacco business as the tobacco companies were besieged by Congressional investigation, threats of Federal Food and Drug Administration regulation, and numerous lawsuits brought by state's attorney's general, unions, and individuals seeking damages for smoking related illnesses. The lawsuits by the states later resulted in industry settlements totaling $236 billion. A controversy concerning B&W locally exploded in the news media in the early 1990s. When a former company official and researcher, Jeffrey Weigand, went public with allegations that B&W had long known about the addictiveness of nicotine. A movie, *The Insider,* based on Weigand's claims, was filmed in Louisville and released in 1999.

Tobacco was in the spotlight again when, during the political primaries of 1998, Sen. MITCH MCCONNELL announced the decision that the government controls on the production and price of tobacco established during the New Deal would be abandoned. Farmers would be offered a mandatory buyout totaling eighty thousand dollars spread out over three years. Retiring Sen. Wendell Ford's proposal stretched the payments out over ten years, keeping the buyout optional and the coop still operating.

At present there is only one manufacturer left in the city, National Tobacco Co.; and only one warehouse remains, the Lucas-Hussey Tobacco Warehouse at 3611 Seventh Street Rd., although several warehouses operate in Shelbyville. Philip Morris announced on February 24, 1999, that, due to declining sales in both its domestic and foreign markets, within two years it would close the Louisville manufacturer. Its tobacco production will be consolidated in Virginia and North Carolina. National Tobacco Co., which bought out Lorillard's chewing tobacco division, has a production site at 3029 Muhammad Ali Blvd. Lorillard still operates a sales division at 10478 Bluegrass Pkwy., but it is not connected with NTC.

See E. Polk Johnson, *A History of Kentucky and Kentuckians* (Chicago 1912); Charles Kerr, ed., *History of Kentucky* (Chicago and New York 1922); Lowell H. Harrison and James C. Klotter, *A New History of Kentucky* (Lexington 1997); George Yater, *Two Hundred Years at the Falls of the Ohio* (Louisville 1987); Robert K. Heimann, *Tobacco and Americans* (New York 1960); Young E. Allison, *The City of Louisville and a Glimpse of Kentucky* (Louisville 1887); The Tobacco Institute, *Kentucky and Tobacco* (Washington, D.C., 1962); Paul Coomes, *Agribusiness in the Louisville Area Economy* (a report for the Agribusiness Committee, Louisville Area Chamber of Commerce, Louisville 1996); *Courier-Journal,* March 5, 1990, March 15, 1992, May 21, 1994, Oct. 2, 1996, Nov. 19, 1997, May 20, 1998, May 31, 1998, February 25, 1999.

Steven R. Price Sr.

TODD, GEORGE DAVIDSON (b Frankfort, Kentucky, April 19, 1856; d NEW ALBANY, Indiana, November 23, 1929). Mayor. He was a son of one of Kentucky's earliest families. His parents were Harry Innes and Jane (Davidson) Todd. Harry Todd was a two-term sheriff of Franklin County. He was also lessee of the state prison for eight years and then served as warden of the prison for one term. He also served as Franklin County's representative in the state legislature for two terms.

George, the tenth of twelve children, was educated in Frankfort's PUBLIC SCHOOLS. He moved to Louisville in 1874 when he was eighteen and went to work as a bookkeeper for the hardware firm of W.B. Belknap & Co. He started the Todd-Donigan Iron Co. in 1880, serving as vice president of the company. His other business ventures included a tenure as president of the Kentucky Machinery Co. He was also director of Louisville's Board of Trade for several years.

Todd was an active member of the REPUBLICAN PARTY in Kentucky. He served as party treasurer and manager of the state executive committee. Although Republican Robert E. King was the first Republican to serve as pro-tem mayor (for the two weeks preceding Todd's 1896 election), Todd was the first Republican to be elected to the office. He succeeded Democrat Henry S. Tyler, who had died in office. He was chosen mayor by the General Council, which had a Republican majority in both the BOARD OF ALDERMEN and the Board of Councilmen for the first time in the city's history. Todd was sworn in on January 31, 1896.

During Todd's administration, the Republican Party was divided over the appointments of city employees. Moderate Republicans criticized Todd for trying to compromise with the more conservative faction of the party. Republican AFRICAN AMERICANS criticized the low number of blacks Todd appointed to political positions and city jobs. Todd's reform agenda collapsed when he tried to appoint Republicans to the city's Boards of Public Safety and PUBLIC WORKS, which had the effect of dividing the city into warring factions. In November 1897 he ran for re-election against Charles P. Weaver, a Democrat who had the support of the party's political machine. This was the first election to pit a Republican directly against a Democrat. Election fraud, dissension among Republicans, and bad WEATHER all contributed to Todd's defeat, although the margin was only 2,728 votes out of the nearly 40,000 cast.

After the election Todd returned to his iron company. Other of Todd's accomplishments include serving as a delegate from the Fifth District to the convention that nominated William McKinley for president in 1896. He moved to New Albany in the 1920s. He married Laura Chapin Durkee and they had three children, one son and two daughters.

See *Biographical Cyclopedia of the Commonwealth of Kentucky* (Chicago-Philadelphia 1896); George H. Yater, *Two Hundred Years at the Falls of the Ohio* (Louisville 1979).

TODD BUILDING. The Todd Building, also known as the Belleview Building, was constructed at the northeast corner of Fourth and market streets in downtown Louisville in 1902. It was developed by and named for James Ross Todd (1869-1952), and influential Louisville banker, businessman, and REPUBLICAN PARTY official.

The ten-story structure was designed by the partnership of CHARLES JULIAN CLARKE and ARTHUR LOOMIS, one of Louisville's prominent ARCHITECTURAL FIRMS at the beginning of the twentieth century. It was designed in the popular Chicago style, characterized by a steel-frame structure and a minimum of ornamentation, which was integrated directly into the exterior fabric of the building. The Todd Building's first and second stories were sheathed in granite, while the remaining stories were covered with yellow pressed brick. It had a variety of window arrangements, with ornate sandstone and terra cotta trims, and several decorative belt courses. One of the building's most important features was the absence of windows on the north side, symbolizing the fact that by the twentieth century the city had largely turned its back on the OHIO RIVER.

For nearly three decades the Todd Building was one of Louisville's leading office addresses, housing many financial, insurance, real estate, legal, and railroad firms. Occupancy declined during the GREAT DEPRESSION and WORLD WAR II, when its major tenants were New Deal and defense agencies that required inexpensive office space. In 1940, Todd gave the building to Children's hospital, which sold it to the Hoffman Realty Co. of Evansville, Indiana, in 1944. Occupancy continued to decline during the 1960s and 1970s as tenants moved to newer quarters. It was demolished in 1983 to make way for a new state parking garage to support the KENTUCKY INTERNATIONAL CONVENTION CENTER.

Carl E. Kramer

TOMPPERT, PHILIP (b Malmsheim, Würtemberg, Germany, June 21, 1808; d Louisville, October 29, 1873). Mayor. Tomppert immigrated to Wheeling, Virginia, in 1831 and came to Louisville in 1837. He was one of the leaders of Louisville's German community. He was a representative in the state legislature in 1849 and was elected to the City Council in 1861 to fill a vacancy from the Second Ward. He served on the council until 1864.

Tomppert was elected mayor of Louisville on April 1, 1865, defeating Unionist K.P. Thixton for the post. Tomppert was one of the "Peace Democrats" who advocated an end to the CIVIL WAR and a return to the Union "as it was" before the war, with slavery intact. A controversy erupted between Tomppert and the council shortly after he took office. N.S. Glore, a member of the council, had accepted a bribe from Isham Henderson, president of the Louisville & Portland Railroad and a part-owner of the *Louisville Daily Journal.* The five-thousand-dollar bribe was to get Glore to approve a franchise for a street railway to run along MARKET St. The council eventually approved the franchise, but Tomppert refused to sign it into law because of the bribe. The council, with Glore also voting, impeached Tomppert on December 28, 1865, charging neglect of duty. He was voted out by a 10–2 margin. Glore was later impeached and expelled.

Tomppert was replaced by James S. Lithgow on January 2, 1865, after the council unanimously elected him to fill the unexpired term. Lithgow filled the office until February 14, 1867, when he resigned the post after Tomppert was reinstated by the state Court of Appeals. Tomppert served the remainder of the term and was reelected, holding office from 1867 through 1868. He also held other minor offices in the city. Tomppert was also a member of the Union State Central Committee, which decreed on April 18, 1861, that Kentucky would be an independent state during the Civil War. Tomppert's future son-in-law, George Philip Doern, started Louisville's *Anzeiger* newspaper, one of the city's first German NEWSPAPERS, on March 1, 1849. He married Barbara, Tomppert's only daughter, on October 2, 1851.

Tomppert was a freemason, holding the position of master of Mount Zion Lodge, the German Masonic lodge chartered in 1841. Tomppert died of typhoid fever in Louisville. He is in Eastern Cemetery.

See George Yater, *Two Hundred Years at the Falls of the Ohio* (Louisville 1987); Richard H. Collins and Lewis C. Collins, *Historical Sketches of Kentucky,* 2 vols. (Covington, Ky., 1874).

TONINI CHURCH SUPPLY COMPANY. Tonini Church Supply was founded in 1886 by Ferdinand Tonini, a German-speaking Swiss immigrant. Tonini sold religious articles, picture frames, books, and stationery out of a storefront at Shelby and Gray Streets across from St. Martin of Tour's Catholic Church in Louisville. The business eventually expanded to occupy four buildings along Shelby Street. In 1992, the company moved to a new building in the Springs Station Shopping Center at 966 Breckenridge Ln. Using catalog sales to reach a worldwide market, Tonini Church Supply, still owned and operated by the Tonini family, has grown into one of the country's largest church supply houses, carrying more than forty-one thousand items in its inventory.

Charles Thompson

TOONERVILLE TROLLEY. Hilarious Toonerville Trolley cartoons seized the imagination of a nationwide audience in a syndicated series that appeared in more than three hundred metro NEWSPAPERS for forty years. Creator of the popular comic cartoons was Louisville native FONTAINE FOX JR., who was born and reared near the bustling corner of Brook and Oak Streets. The talented young artist rode the Brook Street trolley as a youth and later to work as an editorial cartoonist for a local paper, the *Herald.* The Brook Street trolley became his inspiration. The trolley often was behind schedule because high school pranksters rocked it off its tracks or pulled the trolley pole off the overhead power wire. Fox lampooned its shortcomings in editorial cartoons. Early depictions were refined into the later whimsical trolley illustrations. His memories gave birth to the cartoon series; even the engaging motorman was called the Skipper, as named by schoolboys.

The Toonerville adventure started in 1915 during the romantic era when most city dwellers depended on STREETCARS, and mass transit systems flourished throughout the country. Fans quickly related to the dinky trolley of Toonerville cartoons and developed a fondness for its characters, who became national heroes. It dramatized life in simpler, less hurried times.

"The Toonerville Trolley That Meets All the Trains" (the original title of the cartoon series) was a combination of Louisville's Brook St. trolley and a broken-down country trolley that met all the commuter trains at New Rochelle, New York. Fox rode that car in 1915 after he had moved to New York City. "That night," he recalled, "I thought about the New Rochelle trolley and I remembered the old Brook Street trolley back in Louisville—and that's how the Toonerville Trolley was born." The Brook St. car, of course, never "met all the trains," as its New Rochelle counterpart did. The Brook Street car made its last run in 1935.

Fox's cartoons featured fond remembrances of his youth. Quickly delineated fan favorites were terrible-tempered Mr. Bang, Aunt Eppie Hogg (fattest woman in three counties), Suitcase Simpson (stomped out fires with enormous feet), and Powerful Katrinka (who was able to lift the trolley back on track single-handedly), all patterned after neighborhood acquaintances from childhood remembrances. Katrinka was a family domestic; Fox wrote, "She could lift a potbelly stove with one hand and sweep under it with the other." A larger audience was reached when Toonerville film cartoons were featured in MOVIE THEATERS, entertaining millions of fans, young and old, during the heyday of the popular series. Characters became a part of the everyday language, referred to in COURTS, novels, and news articles due to instant recognition. The legend of tough-guy Mickey McGuire inspired a young actor named Joe Yule (who was advised to change his name to one more imaginative) to adopt McGuire's name. Running afoul of copyright snags, he retained the name Mickey and selected an IRISH last name. Thus, Mickey Rooney's career was launched.

In 1955, Fox retired and denied rights to syndicates who sought to continue the series. The legend and romance of Toonerville is still alive nationwide with collectors of valuable toys and memorabilia. A national Toonerville Trolley Association exists to extend its history.

See *Fontaine Fox's Toonerville Trolley* (New York 1972); *Courier-Journal Magazine,* April 24, 1960; *Courier-Journal,* Nov. 22, 1987.

Louis A. "Lew" Miller

TOPOGRAPHY. The landscape occupied by

Louisville, Jefferson County, and the greater metropolitan area provides a diversity of environments ranging from flood plains indirectly left by the cut and fill of meltwater from retreating glaciers to steep-walled valleys. The Louisville area lies at the boundary between two of Kentucky's major physiographic regions, the Outer Bluegrass and the KNOBS. As a result of this topographic intersection, landscape elements from both regions interact in complex and interesting ways. Topography has always occupied an important place in Louisville's history, and it clearly played the lead role in establishment of initial European (1738) and later American settlement at the FALLS OF THE OHIO, where portage around these rapids encouraged development of accommodations and other industries. Since those early days of settlement, billions of dollars and untold efforts have been invested to overcome the tyranny, at least to movement, of the Louisville area's dissected urban landscape. Topography still influences the arrangement of urban land uses and transportation systems in the metropolitan area.

The Louisville region's landscape evolution began millions of years ago with multiple episodes of massive crustal uplift along an area lying between Cincinnati and Nashville. This area of uplift is a linear geologic structure often referred to as the Cincinnati Arch. There were ancient periods, 600 to 320 million years ago, during which Kentucky and the Louisville area were submerged beneath the sea. During that period of submersion, deposition and lithification of sediments at the ocean floor produced the limestone and shale that characterize the inner and outer Bluegrass regions. The quality of rock materials fromed during these ancient periods depends, at least in part, on the depth of the overlying sea. Since the close of this period of bedrock formation and the later uplift of the Cincinnati Arch, the basic processes shaping the landscape in the area have been erosion and deposition. The uplifted surface of limestone and shale has been eroded primarily by water as it seeks lower areas. Some of the eroded material thus has been redeposited to form younger stone, some of which is quite resistant to further erosion. Some of these older rock materials can be found at the summits of hills in the Louisville area that have survived thousands of years of erosional forces. In some cases, these summits are capped by fossiliferous limestones deposited while Kentucky was submerged beneath the sea. Masses of corals in Silurian (415 million years old) and Devonian (390 million years old) limestones that can be seen in road cuts and rock QUARRIES around Louisville were once the reefs of ancient tropical seas.

The contemporary Louisville landscape might best be described as a set of three divisions, each with relatively distinctive relief and surface drainage. Perhaps the most distinctive landscape elements are the Knobs, which occupy a triangular-shaped area within Jefferson County and then extend southeast through BULLITT COUNTY and beyond as they provide a semicircle bordering the Bluegrass from the west, south, and east. Within Jefferson County, the Knobs extend south from the HAZELWOOD area, southwest toward Medora, and southeast toward South PARK HILL. These hills are conic-shaped erosional remnants of the westward-retreating Mississippian Plateau. They were at one time part of what is now called Muldraugh Hill; i.e., escarpment. They were initially capped with more resistant limestone and siltstone surfaces that have permitted them to survive gradation. Eventually, underlying shale is left to cap the Knobs, and the rate of erosion increases. The Knobs tend to rise 250 to 450 feet above the relatively level areas surrounding their bases. Each of these hills possesses a rough surface from being heavily dissected by small streams and scarred by landslides. Waverly Hills, Red Stone Hill, KENWOOD HILL, Moremens Hill, Dodge Hill, Finley Hill, Miller Hill, Potato Knob, Jefferson Hill, Mitchell Hill, Holsclaw Hill, and South Park Hills are examples. Pond Creek serves as drainage for the central Knobs area within the Louisville region. Those Knobs further south tend to be somewhat higher, with summits between eight hundred and nine hundred feet above sea level. In fact, the highest point in Jefferson County is located in South Park Hills at 902 feet above sea level. The highest Knobs north of Pond Creek are exemplified by Kenwood Hill and Jacobs Park Hill at elevations ranging from 750 to 760 feet above sea level.

Another topographic division is the heavily eroded, dissected upland occupying most of the eastern portion of the Louisville area. It is a landscape division that has presented great challenges to modern residential, commercial, and transportation development. The eastern side of FERN CREEK is an escarpment with a gently sloped flatter area to the west and very rough topography to the east. This eastern portion, especially the landscape paralleling FLOYDS FORK, is heavily dissected with broad ridge lines and varying slopes to valley bottoms. The general elevation of this rough landscape is 700 to 750 feet above sea level. Some of the stream cuts exceed a hundred feet in depth. Floyds Fork in particular provides a broad and level flood plain with steep bluffs at its edges. A similarly rough and dissected landscape parallels the drainage of HARRODS CREEK and its South Fork along the northern boundary of Jefferson County. Again, this area is occupied by steep bluffs that have been cut into some of the highest uplands in the Louisville area. These bluffs often exceed a hundred feet from base to top edge.

Once the Knobs division and the eastern dissected division are accounted for, the remaining landscape division, that of the central and western portions of the Louisville region, are relatively smooth in comparison. However, these landscapes are not flat. In general, the whole region slopes downward from northeast to southwest, with high elevations averaging 700 feet in the northeast and 450 feet in the flat areas to the west of the Knobs. This flat area southwest of Louisville that lies between the OHIO RIVER and the Knobs division extends three to five miles. It was created as a flood plain over thousands of years. This formation includes a mantle of outwash sand, gravel, silt, and clay washed in by meltwater from retreating glaciers to the north and northeast. The narrow strip of flat land paralleling the Ohio River northeast of Louisville also resulted indirectly from glacial activity and has been slowly widened by episodic flooding of the Ohio River.

Surface water from Louisville and the surrounding area is drained by the Ohio River. The Ohio provides a natural boundary between Kentucky and Indiana. It also is the northwest border for Jefferson County. The northwestern portion of the Louisville area drains directly into the Ohio River. From north to south, main streams feeding the Ohio River include Harrods Creek, Little Goose Creek, Goose Creek, North Beargrass, Middle Beargrass, South Beargrass, and Mill Creek. Floyds Fork drains the eastern portion of the Louisville region. Principal tributaries feeding Floyds Fork are Long Run, Brush Run, and Cave Run from the east and Chenoweth Creek and Cedar Creek from the west. Floyds Fork flows in a southerly direction across the extent of Jefferson County. It then flows into the Salt River in northern Bullitt County. The Salt River, in turn, flows into the Ohio River just east of West Point.

The streams of the Louisville region are relatively mature, so they are not steeply graded. Smaller streams that feed into larger streams tend to be more steeply graded than their larger counterparts. Thus in smaller streams, flowing water descends between twenty-five and forty-five feet per mile traveled. Larger streams, like Pond Creek (six feet of descent per mile traveled) and Floyds Fork (nine feet of descent per mile traveled), experience a fall of five to ten feet per mile traveled. Because of this maturity, falls and rapids are very few in the region, although most stream beds are quite rocky.

One set of "falls," the Falls of the Ohio, is actually a set of rapids located on the Ohio River at Louisville. It historically was the only break in navigation on the Ohio/Mississippi system between Pittsburgh and New Orleans and created the initial stimulus for European and later American settlement. The Falls of the Ohio results from the outcrop of more resistant limestone rock, which is rich with fossil remains. The Ohio River falls 26 feet here in a two-mile stretch between Goose Island and Sand Island.

According to the Kentucky Geological Survey (*Topography of Kentucky* by P. McGrain and J.C. Currens), the lowest elevation in Jefferson County is 383 feet above sea level, which is the normal pool for the Ohio River at the mouth of the Salt River. The elevations of other notable landmarks in Louisville include the Courthouse (462 feet), CHURCHILL DOWNS (455 feet), and Standiford Field (475 feet). Other Jefferson County elevations are ANCHORAGE (720 feet), Coral Ridge (490 feet), Eastwood (720 feet), FISHERVILLE (559 feet), JEFFERSONTOWN (711 feet), KOSMOSDALE (449 feet), MIDDLETOWN (721 feet), PROSPECT (460 feet), and VALLEY STATION (452 feet). Surrounding counties have similar elevational norms and extremes. In Bullitt County, the highest elevation is 998 feet, the lowest is 385 feet, and Shepherdsville is at 449 feet. In Oldham County, the highest elevation is 920 feet, the lowest is 420 feet, and LAGRANGE is at 867 feet. In SHELBY COUNTY, the highest elevation is 1188 feet, the lowest is 550 feet, and SHELBYVILLE is at 760 feet. In SPENCER COUNTY the highest elevation is 880 feet, the lowest is 420 feet, and TAYLORSVILLE is at 490 feet.

See Preston McGrain and James C. Currens, *Topography of Kentucky* (Lexington: Kentucky Geological Survey, Special Publication 25, 1978).

Ronald L. Mitchelson

TORBITT AND CASTLEMAN COMPANY. In 1869 the Torbitt and Castleman Co. was founded in Louisville as a wholesale grocery operation, with its first Louisville location on MAIN St. With the OHIO RIVER as its commercial highway, the company sold molasses from Louisiana and corn syrups from Iowa.

At the turn of the century, with the help of railroad lines that accessed new markets, the firm chose to forego the wholesale business in favor of packing syrups for the retail trade. By the 1930s, under the leadership of George Wagner, the company had built the "Bob White" brand into the leading syrup sold in the Kentucky-Tennessee area.

The firm moved to PORTLAND late in the 1800s, and between 1906 and 1975 it was located at Tenth and Magnolia Streets. In 1975 the operation moved to its present address in the OLDHAM COUNTY community of Buckner. In a complex of approximately 220,000 square feet, the company continues in the private-label food industry. Its product lines are marketed both regionally and nationally and include syrups, sauces, and condiments. In addition to the "Bob White" brand, the firm also markets under the "Pennant," "King," and "Dixie Dew" labels but can distribute its goods with any label specified by the purchaser. The company also packs corporate brands for both wholesalers and chain stores.

TORNADOES. Located on the fringes of what WEATHER forecasters dubbed the "Dixie Alley," a stretch running from northern Alabama into western Kentucky whose name alluded to Texas and Oklahoma's famous "Tornado Alley," the Louisville area has witnessed several significant tornadoes, although they are considered a rare occurrence. Kentucky's Ohio River Valley region, nestled between the hills to the east and the Mississippi River, lies along an air corridor where cold air from the North frequently collides with warm, moist air blowing up from the Gulf of Mexico. Generally in early spring, this dangerous combination can result in high winds, hail, severe thunderstorms, and possibly tornadoes.

Notable Louisville area tornadoes:

August 27, 1854

This tornado, which traveled from southwest Jefferson County to the northeast, did its principal damage in the area encompassed by Eighth and Thirteenth Streets, BROADWAY, and the river. Sixteen people were killed when the Third Presbyterian Church, located at Eleventh and Walnut (now Muhammad Ali Blvd.) Streets, was demolished.

May 21, 1860

Moving into the PORTLAND area from NEW ALBANY, this tornado blew the roof off of the UNITED STATES MARINE HOSPITAL and sank twenty-three coal barges in the river before continuing eastward. The twister, responsible for unroofing many homes in the east, continued along the path of the LOUISVILLE & FRANKFORT RAILROAD. No deaths were reported.

November 28, 1879

This small tornado, moving in from the southwest, did minor damage to the Louisville Baseball Park at Fourth and Magnolia Streets (modern-day St. James Court) and moved east to CAVE HILL CEMETERY, where it knocked over numerous tombstones. No deaths were reported.

March 27, 1890

The most deadly tornado in Louisville's history, this storm entered the city in PARKLAND, traveled northeasterly through the downtown business district, jumped the river into Jeffersonville, and recrossed the river to destroy the WATER TOWER. In all, nearly one hundred people were killed, six hundred buildings were destroyed, and property damage was estimated at over $2 million.

March 18, 1925

A wave of storms swept across five Midwest states, spawning several tornadoes and killing over eight hundred people that day. Locally, a twister crossed the river into the LAKE DREAMLAND area, swept northeasterly toward ANCHORAGE, and continued through OLDHAM COUNTY, killing four people in total. In Indiana, another tornado moved through Harrison County, killing three and causing over a hundred thousand dollars in damage.

May 10, 1969

Touching down near SHEPHERDSVILLE in BULLITT COUNTY, this tornado did approximately five hundred thousand dollars' worth of damage, primarily to barns and crops. No deaths were reported.

April 3, 1974

As part of a day of storms that created over 100 tornadoes in 10 states, killed 322 people, and caused a total of over $570 million in damages, 2 tornadoes ripped through the Louisville area in the late afternoon, wreaking havoc. In HARRISON COUNTY, INDIANA, a tornado rampaged through Palmyra and killed one before heading off in a northeasterly direction.

In Louisville, a funnel cloud touched down briefly in KOSMOSDALE, disappeared, and reemerged from the sky at the KENTUCKY FAIR AND EXPOSITION CENTER. After ripping off part of FREEDOM HALL's roof and destroying several horse barns, the twister, which reached speeds of 250 miles per hour and stayed on the ground for approximately 20 minutes, then traveled through AUDUBON PARK, George Rogers Clark Park, up Eastern Pkwy., through Cherokee Park, and along Grinstead Dr. to CRESCENT HILL. Aside from uprooting thousands of trees and flattening or unroofing many of the homes in its path, the tornado also knocked out the transformer at the LOUISVILLE WATER CO. plant on Frankfort Ave., leaving the city with a depleted water supply for the next twenty-four hours.

The tornado continued to cut a swath up Frankfort Ave. and Brownsboro Rd. and out to Oldham County, leaving destruction and desolation in its wake. One of twenty tornadoes in the state that day that amassed damages of over $110 million, the Louisville storm killed two people and caused harm to approximately eighteen hundred homes in the area.

May 28, 1996

Affecting primarily Bullitt and Spencer Counties, violent storms produced a tornado that tore through the communities of Brooks, Pioneer Village, and MT. WASHINGTON. Although no deaths were attributed to the twister, over thirteen hundred homes were damaged, amounting to $75 million worth of property loss.

See April 3, 1974, *Tornado!* (Louisville 1974); J. Stoddard Johnston, ed., *Memorial History of Louisville*, vol. 1 (Chicago 1896).

TORNADO OF 1890. On the evening of Thursday, March 27, 1890, the city of Louisville experienced the most devastating tornado in its history. To those residents reading that morning's WEATHER forecast of fair, with a chance of rain, no indication was given of imminent destruction. However, as the noted Louisville historian J. Stoddard Johnston reported, by early afternoon, the city was receiving weather dispatches via TELEGRAPH from Washington warning of the possibility for "violent atmospheric disturbances" within the next twenty-four hours. Throughout the afternoon, the barometer continued to fall, and by eight o'clock that evening, a thunderstorm with severe lightning had approached. Then, at shortly after eight-thirty, the tornado struck, and, though it took only about five minutes for it to sweep over the city, it left in its wake a three-hundred-yard path of destruction through portions of the city's West End and downtown.

The tornado first entered PARKLAND, which was then a suburb of Louisville. Traveling in a northeasterly direction, it passed up to Eighteenth and Maple Streets, across Broadway near Seventeenth St., and thence to Seventh and River, where it crossed the Ohio River to Jeffersonville, Indiana. In Jeffersonville, it destroyed a number of homes and commercial buildings along Front St. The tornado then crossed the river again and hit the Louisville Water Works, where it demolished the water tower at the pumping station at Zorn Ave. Without the tower, it was impossible to pump water into the reservoir located on Frankfort Ave. Water was rationed as hasty repairs were made.

In all, nearly one hundred people were killed by the storm, and over two hundred were injured, some of whom perished shortly thereafter. Churches were busy with funerals, and due to a shortage of hearses private wagons and even a trolley car were used to take caskets and mourners to Cave Hill Cemetery. Boats in the Ohio River were destroyed. Estimated property damage amounted to $2.15 million, with over six hundred buildings laid to waste. Those structures damaged or destroyed included 5 churches, the Union Railroad depot at Seventh and River, 3 schools, 2 public meeting halls, 32 industrial buildings, 10 tobacco warehouses, and 532 private residences. The hardest hit of the city's business areas was along Main St., below Sixth. There, the *Courier-Journal* reported, large wholesale businesses and tobacco warehouses were "shattered like tinder." One of the sites of the greatest human loss was at Falls City Hall, a public meeting place located at 1126 W Market St. At the time of the tornado's impact, maybe 250 people were gathered on the dance floor on the first floor and in the lodge rooms above. Approximately forty of the casualties of the tornado were pulled from the rubble.

In the aftermath of the storm, the city's streets in the affected areas were so clogged with debris that it took several days to restore traffic. These scenes of devastation attracted hordes of sightseers who came from various parts of Indiana and Kentucky on excursion trains to witness the tornado's wreckage firsthand. Louisvillians proved amazingly resilient in the wake of such a natural disaster. Declining all offers of aid from outside sources, including the federal government and Red Cross, the city was able to raise the necessary funds for relief through private donations and contributions of food, housing, and medical supplies. Within the next year many of the city's storm-ravaged properties had been replaced with new buildings. The disaster remains in the list of city calamities along with the floods of 1937 and 1997, the tornadoes of 1974 and 1996, and the winters of 1978 and 1994.

See J. Stoddard Johnston, *Memorial History of Louisville* (Chicago 1896); R.C. Reibel. Louisville Panorama (Louisville 1954); George Yater, *Two Hundred Years at the Falls of the Ohio* (Louisville 1979); "The Terrible-Tempered Tornado of 1890," *Louisville* 29 (March 1978): 34–36.

TOURISM. Tourism in Louisville is coordinated through the Louisville and Jefferson County Convention and Visitors Bureau, one of the oldest bureaus in the country. It began operating in 1913 and merged with the Louisville Board of Trade, Louisville Area Development Association, and the Retail Merchants Association in 1950 to form the Louisville Chamber of Commerce. In 1968 when a hotel occupancy (bed) tax was enacted, the Louisville and Jefferson County Visitors and Convention Commission was formed, and the bureau split off from the chamber. In 1999 the bureau employed forty full-time staff and dispersed a budget of $5.4 million generated through 3 percent of a 6 percent bed tax. One percent of the tax goes to the Kentucky Center for the Arts for maintenance, while 2 percent is dedicated to partial funding of the expansion and renovation of the downtown Kentucky International Convention Center (formerly the Commonwealth Convention Center).

Today, the tourism industry generates an annual economic impact of more than $1.1 billion, twenty-six thousand jobs, and $220 million in local, state, and federal taxes. It is the third-largest service industry in Jefferson County, which generates the highest economic impact from tourism of any county in the state.

Louisville's early hospitality community developed along the shores of the Ohio River along with its shipping and warehousing businesses. In the late 1700s and early 1800s, travelers to Louisville could oversee the distribution of their goods by way of the mighty Ohio while staying in one of several hotels located along Louisville's Main St., one block south of the river. The Galt House, which bears the name of a Louisville hotel dating back to 1835, is in operation today at Fourth and Main Streets.

By 1875 the Jockey Club, now known as Churchill Downs, introduced an annual horse race that has become Louisville's international signature event. The Kentucky Derby, known as the Run for the Roses, is held the first Saturday in May and attracts as many as a hundred thousand visitors and generates an economic impact in excess of $60 million. It has also provided Louisville with a marketable identity, one that promotes the beauty of its landscapes and the hospitality of its inhabitants. In 1956 "the most exciting two minutes in sports" helped to spawn the Kentucky Derby Festival Inc., a not-for-profit venture that has grown to include seventy events produced over an almost three-week period by more than four thousand volunteers. The festival includes "Thunder Over Louisville," the largest pyrotechnics display in the country; the Great Steamboat Race between the Belle of Louisville and Cincinnati's Delta Queen; the Pegasus Parade, televised nationally; and both a hot-air-balloon race and a mini-marathon. Together, Derby Festival events attract more than a million people to the city each year. The Breeders' Cup has been held at Churchill Downs five times and attracts more than eighty thousand fans. It brings the most serious racing fans to Louisville. Another sporting event that attracts large numbers is the PGA

1890 tornado destruction, northeast corner Eleventh and Market Streets. Photograph by Rueling Studio.

championships. In 1996 and 2000 it was hosted at Valhalla Golf Club.

Churchill Downs continues to be a significant part of Louisville's tourism product, generating the second-highest attendance of all local tourist attractions in 1997, 913,723. Six Flags Kentucky Kingdom occupies first place with an attendance of 1,123,000. The Louisville Zoo is third with 669,808, followed by the Kentucky Center for the Arts with 455,192 and Joe Huber's Family Farm and Restaurant, located across the Ohio in Southern Indiana, with 427,000. Ranking eleventh in attendance is another one of Louisville's signature products, the LOUISVILLE SLUGGER Bat Factory and Museum, with 230,000 attendees. The KENTUCKY DERBY MUSEUM, located on the grounds of Churchill Downs and the only museum in the world dedicated to a single horse race, is ranked fourteenth with an attendance of 166,314.

Louisville's leisure travel product, which includes more than eighty attractions, also features some very significant historic properties, including Locust Grove, the last home of Louisville pioneer and Revolutionary War hero GEORGE ROGERS CLARK. Farmington, an early nineteenth-century hemp plantation, features a c. 1815-16 house built by slaves according to a THOMAS JEFFERSON design that includes two octagonal rooms. Riverside, the FARNSLEY-MOREMEN LANDING, interprets an 1830s farmhouse located right on the river in the southwest part of the county, and the Brennan House is an 1860s urban dwelling with a physician's office attached. The *Belle of Louisville*, which cruises from spring to fall, is the oldest Mississippi-style sternwheeler still plying the water today.

While Louisville has continued to support and develop its leisure tourism component, its greatest strides have been made in positioning itself as a meetings, convention, and trade show destination. Since 1883–1888, when Louisville hosted the first SOUTHERN EXPOSITION on land that is now a historic residential section known as OLD LOUISVILLE, the city has exploited its accessible location, mild climate, and strong sense of service to aggressively promote itself as a site for a wide variety of business- and association-based meetings, conferences, conventions, and exhibitions. And over the years, Louisville's governmental leadership has seen fit to support its position with a series of important infrastructure developments that have allowed Louisville to compete aggressively and successfully. As early as 1893 the city sought and won the reunion of the Grand Army of the Republic, the organization of Union veterans of the CIVIL WAR. In September 1895 an estimated one hundred thousand visitors filled the city, while thirty thousand Union veterans marched in a parade down BROADWAY and later reunited for a campfire at PHOENIX HILL PARK. In 1946 the state legislature voted to fund and build the Kentucky Fair and Exposition Center, opened in 1956. Renovations and expansions in 1976, 1984, 1990, and 1993 have resulted in a facility that boasts more than one million square feet of air-conditioned exhibit space under one roof and on one level. In 1977 the legislature approved what is now the Kentucky International Convention Center in the heart of downtown. A renovation and expansion project undertaken in 1996 resulted in bringing this center to 300,000 square feet of space, including a 150,000-square-foot contiguous, column-free exhibit hall. In 1988 local government joined with federal agencies to clear the way for an expanded airport, which then changed its name from Standiford Field to LOUISVILLE INTERNATIONAL AIRPORT (SDF). This ten-year project created two new parallel runways in order to increase capacity and helped to generate lower-cost commercial carrier air service by spurring competition.

Continuing development of the interstate system put Louisville within a day's drive of more than 60 percent of the nation's POPULATION by putting it at the heart of three major INTERSTATES: I-64, I-65, and I-71. And by 1999 Louisville had more than thirteen thousand hotel rooms. By promoting its accessibility, affordability, and availability of space, Louisville has been able to continuously host four of the Top 25 Trade Shows in the country and six of the Top 200. Louisville is ranked seventh in Trade Show 200 sites, and the Kentucky Fair and Exposition Center is ranked as the tenth-largest facility of its kind in the country. The meetings and convention component generates more than $200 million in economic impact annually and attracts more than seven hundred thousand convention delegates.

Annual trade shows and conventions that call Louisville "home" are the International Lawn, Garden, and Power Equipment Expo; the International Construction Utility Equipment Expo; the Recreation Vehicle Industry Association; the National Street Rod Association Grand Nationals; the National Quartet Convention; Mid America Trucking Show; Equitana USA; and the National FFA (formerly Future Farmers of America) Convention. Each of these conventions attracts more than twenty-five thousand delegates and generates an economic impact in excess of $10 million.

Visitors continue to come to Louisville for a wide variety of reasons. Louisville enjoys a very warm and friendly reputation and delights in being the home of such treats as the cheeseburger, the HOT BROWN, and DERBY PIE®. Louisville has seen its folk arts and crafts market burgeon through the work of the KENTUCKY ART AND CRAFT FOUNDATION and takes pride in its cultural arts community, which boasts its own ballet, orchestra, opera, children's theater, national touring company, and summer outdoor THEATER. Louisville's internationally renowned and Tony Award–winning Actors Theatre hosts its annual HUMANA Festival of New American Plays, which has launched such acclaimed productions as *Agnes of God, Gin Game, Crimes of the Heart, Octette Bridge Club*, and *'Night Mother.*

Louisville has more urban park land per capita than any other city in the country, and a Waterfront Park was dedicated in 1999 that reclaimed much of the industrial-use lands along the Ohio and created a very attractive and welcoming "front door" for the city.

See Amy Board Higgs, "Largest Area Tourist Attractions," Business First (Feb. 23, 1998); Susan McNeese Lynch, Tourism's Economic Impact on Louisville and Jefferson County (Louisville and Jefferson County Convention and Visitors Bureau, 1997); Bill Doolittle, The Kentucky Derby, Run for the Roses (Louisville 1998); Clyde F. Crews, Spirited City: Essays in Louisville History (Louisville 1995).

Susan McNeese Lynch

TOY BOWL. In 1949 the Parochial League of Louisville, now known as the Catholic Schools Athletic Association (CSAA), organized the first annual Toy Bowl. This was to be a single game to decide the city championship of Catholic grade-school FOOTBALL, pitting the best teams from the Big East and Big West Leagues against one another. The idea arose in the late 1940s when karl F. Schmitt, executive director of CSAA, visited Birmingham, Alabama, in order to study a pre-high school championship football game called the Toy Bowl. Back home the concept was well received, and the knights of Columbus offered support through financial sponsorship and with volunteers. The first Toy Bowl was played on December 4, 1949, at Male High School's Maxwell Field on S Brook St. The game was a huge success and nearly seven thousand fans watched St. Agnes defeat St. Elizabeth 13 to 6.

Traditionally, the grade schools take turns hosting the fifth- and sixth-grade game on the first Saturday in November, while the seventh- and eighth-graders play at Trinity High School's Harry Jansen Field on the first Sunday of November. Teams are divided by age, with a fifth- and sixth-grade league and a seventh- and eight-grade league. The teams are further divided into three divisions. The four teams with the best record from season play in each division enter single-elimination playoffs. This playoff system results in a total of six Toy Bowl games per year. By 1998 St. Pius X had won more Toy Bowls than any other school, winning a total of thirteen: seven titles in the seventh and eighth grade division, and six in the fifth and sixth-grade division.

The Toy Bowl continues to be played with few differences. The game is played on fields that are 30 yards shorter and 120 feet narrower than the original 100-yard fields. Weight limits have also been instituted on some offensive positions so that larger boys will not be able to dominate the games.

See the *Record*, November 12, 1998.

TRANSIT AUTHORITY OF RIVER CITY. A public agency best known by its acronym TARC, the transit authority operates Louisville's bus systems including Indiana service to New Albany, Clarksville, and Jeffersonville. TARC was formed in 1971 following state legislative authorization in 1970 for creation of local authorities to operate mass-transit services with local government funding. Transit operators in several Kentucky cities were losing patrons to the automobile at an alarming rate.

In Louisville the transit company posted its first-ever deficit in 1971. The loss followed years of declining ridership (except during WORLD WAR II). In 1972 the company gave notice that it would cease operations on September 1, 1974. Passengers were running about fourteen million annually, not enough to cover costs. In contrast the company in 1920 had carried eighty-four million riders from a smaller POPULATION base, but automobile ownership in 1920 had not yet become widespread.

To shore up the faltering carrier, Louisville and Jefferson County governments in July 1973 began providing a six-month subsidy to enable fares to be lowered. The result was a 9 percent increase in ridership over the same period in 1972, but the deficit remained. That transit service could be lost was demonstrated in 1973 when the Bridge Transit Co., operating between Jeffersonville and Louisville, ceased service before TARC was funded. The funding came in a November 1974 voter-approved transit tax and an $8.8 million federal grant. TARC bought the Louisville Transit Co., purchased new buses, reduced fares, increased service frequency, and extended its service lines.

In 1976 the Blue Motor Coach Lines, serving outlying areas, was acquired; and in 1983 the oddly named Daisy Line between New Albany and Louisville came into the TARC fold. By 1980 TARC ridership increased to 20 million annually. In 1994 TARC was rated third among the top seven transit systems in a study by the University of North Carolina. Passenger loading, however, varies with changes in the ECONOMY, the price of gasoline, and fare levels. It became necessary to raise fares in 1994. Ridership in 1997 was near fifteen million on service provided by 281 buses on fixed routes and 70 special vehicles for the disabled, the latter operated by private operators contracting with TARC.

The transit authority has its administrative and operating headquarters in downtown UNION STATION, an elegant Victorian structure that saw its last train depart in 1976. The following year TARC used a federal grant to purchase the station and sixteen acres of ground to create a base more central to its bus routes. Bus garages and maintenance facilities stand where once was a maze of tracks. TARC is managed by an executive director and an eight-member board of directors, four of whom are appointed by the mayor of Louisville and four by the Jefferson County judge/executive.

See George H. Yater, "End of the Line for Louisville's Bases?" *Louisville* (Feb. 1974); "Union Station in Transit" (July 1980); *PTI Journal* (Nov. 1994).

George H. Yater

TRIAERO. Located at 8310 Johnson School Rd. in Louisville, Triaero, built in 1941 for Irma Bartman, was Jefferson County's first "modern" house. Chicago architect Bruce Goff (1904–82) designed the house and interior furnishings. Goff, who later became nationally prominent, was influenced by Frank Lloyd Wright's work, and this is reflected at Triaero in the triangular plan, central utility core, extensive use of glass, and spreading roof with overhangs of redwood lattice. The house was damaged by fire in 1959, and much of the interior was rebuilt. In the late 1990s the house was restored using Goff's original designs.

See Pauline Saliga and Mary Woolever, eds., *The Architecture of Bruce Goff, 1904–1982: Design for the Continuous Present* (Chicago 1995); Leslee F. Keys and Donna M. Neary, eds., *Historic Jefferson County* (Louisville 1992).

Mary Jean Kinsman

TRICON GLOBAL RESTAURANTS INCORPORATED. Due to sagging sales, PepsiCo Inc. announced its intention to spin off its restaurant division into a separate, publicly traded company in January 1997. The three fast-food chains, Pizza Hut (based in Plano, Texas), Taco Bell (based in Irvine, California), and Kentucky Fried Chicken (based in Louisville), were combined into Tricon Global Restaurants Inc. (Tricon). Owning or franchising nearly thirty thousand units in ninety-five countries, the Tricon restaurants generate over $10 billion in annual revenue and $20 billion in system-wide sales, making it second only to McDonalds in the fast-food industry.

After being offered a $6 million incentive package, the company announced in late July that it had decided to locate its corporate headquarters in Louisville. Citing the quality of life, the workforce, the local schools, and the community's arts and leadership, the Fortune 500 company planned an office complex near the KFC headquarters on Gardiner Ln. In terms of sales, Tricon topped ASHLAND INC. as the largest company in Kentucky by approximately $8 million. Early in 1998, the company announced that it was closing its ACCOUNTING and systems offices in Wichita, Kansas, and dividing the jobs between Louisville and Dallas. The move was expected to bring several hundred additional accounting, finance, and payroll jobs to the area. Through stock option plans and other incentives, Tricon employees owned about 20 percent of the company by 1999.

See *Courier-Journal*, Aug. 1, 1997; May 21, 1999.

TROUT, ALLAN MITCHELL (b Churchton, Tennessee, August 8, 1903; d Frankfort December 8, 1972) Journalist. After attending local PUBLIC SCHOOLS in his hometown, Trout and his family moved to Dyersburg, Tennessee, where he graduated from high school. From 1922 to 1926, he attended Georgetown College in Kentucky, from which he received an A.B. degree. While there, he was a reporter for the Georgetown Times, the Lexington Herald, and the Lexington Leader. After graduating, Trout became the owner and editor of a weekly paper, the Jackson Times, in Jackson, Kentucky. However the paper failed in early 1929.

On February 15, 1929, he began a thirty-eight-year career with the *COURIER-JOURNAL*. Though originally hired as a police reporter, Trout quickly distinguished himself, and in 1932 he received an honorable mention for the Pulitzer Prize for his coverage of a Tennessee BANKING scandal that had repercussions for Kentucky investors. Trout was best known for his daily folk column, "Greetings," a collection of musings on both ordinary events and the outstanding happenings of the day. Many times he would respond to readers' inquiries. For example, a reader from Jamestown, Kentucky, once asked why old hens stop laying eggs in cold WEATHER. Trout responded, "Old hens are smarter than they get credit for. They know the price of eggs go sky high in cold weather. No hen worth her grit wants to see a higher value put on the egg than on herself." Begun in 1939, the column ran 8,998 times, for a total of nearly 5 million words. Collections of Trout's "Greetings" columns were published as *Greetings from Old Kentucky* (vol. 1, 1947; vol. 2, 1959).

In addition to his daily column, Trout, known as the "Sheriff" because of his broad-brimmed hats, also served as the *Courier-Journal*'s senior news reporter for fifteen consecutive regular sessions of the Kentucky General Assembly beginning in 1940. In 1959 and again in 1966, he was awarded the Governor's Medallion for distinguished public service through journalism, and in 1966 he also wrote Your Kentucky Constitution. Trout retired from the paper in 1967 and that year received an honorary doctor of laws degree from the University of Kentucky. He also served as director of company relations for Investor's Heritage Life Insurance Co. of Frankfort, Kentucky.

Trout married Martha Collier in 1934; she died in 1962. He later married Edith Cooper Taylor. Trout lived for a number of years in Frankfort, Kentucky, and is buried in Frankfort Cemetery.

See Mary C. Browning, *Kentucky Authors* (Evansville, Ind., 1968); Kenneth E. Harrell, ed., *The Public Papers of Governor Edward T. Breathitt, 1963–1967* (Lexington 1984).

TUBE TURNS TECHNOLOGIES INC. The Pipe Bending Process Co. Inc. was founded on July 19, 1927. Its four founders were M. Keith Dunham, Charles J. Haines, E.G. Luening, and Walter H. Girdler Sr. The company was founded as a licensee for a German-designed method of making curved pipe fittings, and it was the first producer of forged seamless welding fittings in the United States. In this new process, elbows ("U"-shaped pipe) were formed by forcing short, heated lengths of pipe over a mandrel, producing a seamless pipe product of uniform strength and wall thickness. The company's first plant was a tiny twenty-five- by eighty-foot building on Logan St. On September 24, 1928, it changed its name to Tube Turns Inc.

Co-founder Walter Girdler, born in Louisville in 1887 and a graduate of Manual High School, was an industrial entrepreneur who began his business life as the operator of a general store in Somerset, Kentucky. He soon returned to Louisville, however, and began, with his partners, to develop a business empire. The Girdler Corp. was formed in 1929, and at his death in 1945, he had presided over a multimillion-dollar concern that had employed thousands of workers.

The early years of Tube Turns Inc. saw Dunham as president from 1927 to 1939, followed by Girdler from 1939 to 1945. In May 1938 the firm, with offices at 224 E Broadway, relocated its manufacturing facility to the old circus grounds at Twenty-eighth St. and BROADWAY. Here they erected the first building of a manufacturing complex that would over time become today's six-hundred-thousand-square-foot facility. The company produced industrial-use pipe fittings designed to function under variable conditions of pressure and temperature. Its product line, with variations in size, wall thickness, and alloy composition, would service the expanding technical requirements of pipeline transmission in many industries such as the oil, natural gas, petro-chemical, and food-processing industries. The company has produced pipe fittings from as small as one-half-inch in diameter to as large as a seventy-two-inch diameter "T" fitting for a General Electric generator power station in upstate New York.

During World War II the company, in addition to its regular manufacturing concerns, initiated an Upset forging division. An Upsetter is a horizontal mechanical press. These machines were used to manufacture both artillery shells and airplane parts. Tube Turns made the aluminum cylinder heads for the Pratt-Whitney rotary engine used in military airplanes. In 1942 the employees were awarded both the Maritime "M" Flag and the Army-Navy "E" Award for their outstanding production record during the war. Tube Turns was one of the few firms in the nation to receive both awards. In 1945 George O. Boomer became president of the company and remained so until 1956, when he became president of Tube Turns Plastics Inc.

Tube Turns Plastics Inc., at 2929 Magazine St., pioneered in the U.S. production of injection-molded thermoplastic fittings for the PVC and UPVC pipe industry. Beginning production in 1954, the company by 1960 had installed the largest injection molding press of its kind in the country. The fifteen-hundred-ton press stood three stories high and made the largest pipe fittings and flanges ever molded up to that time from unplasticized polyvinyl chloride. Tube Turns Plastics Inc. was eventually bought by the Cabot Corp. Today, after two more resales, it is Nibco Inc. and is located in Charlestown, Indiana.

In 1956 Tube Turns purchased the adjoining buildings and thirteen acres from the Louisville Transit Co. Under John G. Seiler, president from May 1956 to October 1968, the firm more than doubled the size of its existing plant. Its fittings division manufactured more than four thousand different items, according to its ADVERTISING. Its forgings division produced the first jet engine shafts for the Pratt & Whitney Corp. as well as custom forgings for the aircraft, automobile, and farm implement fields. In the late 1950s the firm made the fittings for the propulsion system of our first nuclear submarine, the Nautilus. In 1967 the navy cited the company for its outstanding work in supplying components for the Polaris nuclear submarine fleet. By the 1970s the company employed about eleven hundred people.

In 1999 Tube Turn Technologies Inc. is a publicly held company owned by Sypris Solutions Inc. Sypris has offices in the STARKS BUILDING. The pipe-fitting division was phased out of production about 1988 because of changes in demand and increased foreign competition. The nuclear fittings work was phased out about 1995. The forged products division does commercial work for such customers as Caterpillar, John Deere, and the Meritor Co., for whom it makes truck axles. It also continues to make jet engine shafts for Pratt & Whitney. The engineered products division, begun in 1959, manufactures fabricated piping components such as quick-opening closures for pipelines and filtration equipment and insulated and transition joints.

See *Courier-Journal,* Aug. 16, 1954, Jan. 8, 1945; George Yater, *Two Hundred Years at the Falls of the Ohio* (Louisville 1987).

TUCKER, AMELIA (MOORE) (b. Alabama, 1908; d Los Angeles, California, February 9, 1987). Legislator. The wife of CIVIL RIGHTS activist Bishop C. Ewbank Tucker, Rev. Amelia M. Tucker was the first African American woman to be elected to the Kentucky state legislature. She was educated at Alabama State Teachers College, Indiana State University, and the UNIVERSITY OF LOUISVILLE. As a Republican representative from the Forty-second District, Tucker served from 1961 to 1963. She worked tirelessly toward the integration of public facilities and supported the Public Accommodations Bill. Though the bill did not pass, the Enabling Act did, and, as a result, second- and third-class cities were granted the ability to pass public accommodation acts of their own. Tucker was also a member of the Jefferson County Republican executive committee in the 1960s and 1970s, and in the early 1970s she sat on President Richard Nixon's advisory council on ethnic groups.

Tucker was a retired minister of the Brown Temple AME Zion Church and was involved with the Interdenominational Ministerial Alliance. She was also an original member of the Interdenominational Ministerial Wives Association and was active in the United Council of Church Women. She and her husband married in 1922 and had two children, Neville and Olivia.

See *Louisville Defender,* Feb. 11, 1971; Louisville Times, Feb. 13, 1987.

TUCKER, CHARLES EWBANK (b Baltimore, Maryland, January 12, 1896; d Louisville, December 25, 1975). Clergyman, lawyer, and CIVIL RIGHTS leader. The son of William A. and Elivia (Clark) Tucker, the Reverend C. Ewbank Tucker was a prominent, and sometimes controversial, figure in the civil rights movement for more than four decades. He began his early education in the British West Indies, finishing at Beckford-Smith College in Spanishtown, Jamaica. He went on to study at Lincoln (1917) and Temple (1919) Universities, both in Pennsylvania. At the Philadelphia-Baltimore conference in 1918, he was ordained into the ministry of the African Methodist Episcopal Zion church. In 1956 he received an honorary divinity degree from Livingston College.

Though Tucker moved to Louisville in 1929 to practice law, he was probably better known for his long career in the ministry. While a pastor in the AME Zion church, he led a number of congregations in various states such as Pennsylvania, Alabama, Mississippi, Georgia, Florida, Indiana, and, lastly, Stoner Memorial Church, 1127 W Oak St., Louisville. In 1956, while serving as a presiding elder of the South Georgia-Kentucky-Indiana conference of the AME church, Tucker was elevated to the bishopric at the AME General Conference. Three years later, he was elected chairman of the national AME church's board of bishops. For eight years he was bishop of the Fifth District, which included Kentucky, Georgia, West Tennessee, and Mississippi. In 1964 Tucker was assigned to the larger Sixth District that encompassed Indiana, Tennessee, Mississippi, Arkansas, and part of West Virginia. He retired as bishop in 1972.

As a civil rights activist, Tucker began agitating for political change in the 1930s. After two years of unheeded protesting to local Republican officials about the lack of black candidates on the party's ticket, Tucker decided to run as an independent candidate from the Fifty-eighth District in 1933. The Democrats, instead of nominating a candidate of their own, announced their support for Tucker. Although Tucker lost to his white Republican opponent, enough blacks voted for the Democrats to ensure their victory over the city administration. The new Democratic city administration recognized the black vote for their margin of victory. In 1935 Tucker, now a Democrat, once again a candidate for the state legislature, was defeated by Republican Charles W. Anderson, who became Kentucky's first black legislator.

Tucker participated in demonstrations in Selma, Alabama, and led a number of sit-in protests against segregated dining and other public facilities in Louisville, such as the bus stations. Some in the civil rights movement saw Tucker as a militant figure, and in 1963 he was criticized by a few of his fellow ministers for advising blacks in the South to arm themselves against threats to their persons, homes, or churches. Tucker believed that Dr. Martin Luther King Jr.'s philosophy of peaceful resistance was ineffective against the occasional violence that civil rights demonstrations encountered.

Despite his early political associations with Democrats, Tucker was a devoted Republican who was one of the few black leaders to support Richard Nixon in the 1968 election. In 1969 he delivered the benediction at President Nixon's inauguration ceremony.

At the time of his death, Tucker was serving as a member of the Louisville–Jefferson County Human Relations Commission. He married Amelia Moore in 1922, with whom he had two children, Olivia and Neville. He was cremated.

See Thomas Yenser, ed., *Who's Who in Colored America*, 5th edition. (New York 1940); George C. Wright, *Life Behind a Veil* (Baton Rouge 1985); *Courier-Journal*, Dec. 26, 1975; *Louisville Defender*, Jan. 1, 1976.

TUMBLEWEED SOUTHWEST MESQUITE GRILL & BAR. The Tumbleweed restaurant chain was started by George R. Keller and his wife, Linda. The first location was a small, twenty-eight-seat southern Indiana eatery with a monthly rent of a hundred dollars located on Vincennes St. across from New Albany High School. It was named after the 1970 Elton John album, "Tumbleweed Connection." The Kellers were married in 1974, and, after a honeymoon trip out west where they ate at a lot of Mexican RESTAURANTS, they decided to give the concept a try in the Louisville area.

In 1978 Linda Keller's parents, owners of the Hillside Manor, the Louisville restaurant and bar located on Mellwood Ave. where George and Linda first met, turned the facility over to Tumbleweed, and it has become the flagship restaurant for the chain. The casual restaurant features spicy Tex-Mex menu items such as burritos and enchiladas and mesquite-grilled fare such as steaks and chicken as its mainstays.

In January 1995 the Kellers sold 90 percent of the business to a group of sixty Louisville-area investors for $9.8 million for the company's assets, plus an additional $1 million in exchange for an agreement not to compete against Tumbleweed's new owners. TW Operations LLC of Louisville purchased the firm to raise money through the sale of stock to finance the company's expansion into Midwest and overseas markets. The buyout deal was led by John A. "Jack" Butorac Jr., a former vice president of Chi-Chi's Inc., who took over as the new president of Tumbleweed, and financial officer Jim Mulrooney.

As of 1998 Tumbleweed has more than thirty restaurants, twenty-two company-owned and the rest franchised, in Kentucky, Ohio, Illinois, Indiana, and Wisconsin. The company plans to open additional U.S. restaurants in 1998, primarily in Tennessee and Kansas, and several in other states. In 1997 the company made a deal with a European licensee to developed Tumbleweed restaurants worldwide. The Belgium-based firm, Tumbleweed International LLC, opened the first overseas Tumbleweed restaurant in October 1997 in Erlangen, Germany. Others are planned in Jedda, Saudi Arabia; Abu Dhabi, United Arab Emirates; and either Amman, Jordan, or Cairo, Egypt. The European firm pays a licensing fee and sales royalties to the Louisville parent. In 1998 the parent company of Tumbleweed announced it would try to raise twelve million by selling shares of common stock directly to the public. Final stock sales in January of 1999 reached 850,000 shares at ten dollars a share to about 1,100 shareholders.

There are several Tumbleweed locations throughout the Greater Louisville area. Including the Louisville restaurant located at 1900 Mellwood Ave., there are also full-service restaurant locations at 3985 Dutchmans Ln., 10000 Linn Station Rd., 4255 Outer Loop, two on Dixie Hwy., and Tumbleweed cafes in Bashford Manor Mall and the Mall St. Matthews.

See *Courier-Journal*, Oct. 14, 1997; *Courier-Journal*, Dec. 29, 1994, June 30, 1998, Jan. 10, 1999.

TURNER, OSCAR JR. (?) (B Woodlands, Kentucky, October 19, 1867; d Louisville, July 17, 1902). U.S. congressman. Attended PUBLIC SCHOOLS in Washington, D.C., and the Louisville Rugby School. He studied law at the UNIVERSITY OF LOUISVILLE before graduating from the University of Virginia in 1886. In 1891 he began his legal career in Louisville. He was elected to the fifty-sixth Congress as a Democrat on March 4, 1899, and served until March 3, 1901, before returning to his law practice. He is buried in CAVE HILL CEMETERY.

See *Biographical Directory of the American Congress 1776-1961* (Washington, D.C. 1961).

TURNERS/TURNVERIENS. The Turner movement was started by a Berlin schoolmaster, Friedrich Ludwig Jahn, who was upset because Napoleon defeated the Prussians at the battle of Jena and occupied their country. The first public Turnplatz was opened by Jahn in the spring of 1811. The boys and young men of Berlin, five hundred strong, responded to his call and followed him to the Hasenheide, an early public park, where they indulged in gymnastic exercises under his direction. After the Napoleonic Wars, Turner organizations developed throughout the German states.

Turnerism in the United States is an offspring of the German Revolution of 1848. When this revolution was crushed, many immigrants settled along the East Coast and in cities along the Ohio and Mississippi Rivers.

Although the Louisville Turners recognize the founding date of September 2, 1850, there is evidence that they were operating earlier. An edition of the *LOUISVILLE ANZEIGER*, a German language newspaper, refers to the activities of the Turners in Louisville in July 1848. They apparently did not get around to formally organizing until 1850.

The first hall established was on MARKET St. between Third and FOURTH Streets in a shed at the rear of a lot on which an inn stood. Mrs. Freihofer, the proprietor of the inn, gave the Turners $149 to equip their gym. It was the first gymnasium in Louisville. In the early days the Turners moved several times. In 1853 the third national athletic meet was hosted by the Louisville Turners.

A critical period for Turners was 1855, when the Know-Nothing Party elected an entire slate. On Monday August 6, Know-Nothing supporters threatened to burn Turner Hall. The Know-Nothings were opposed to newly arrived German and IRISH immigrants.

In 1875 the Turners moved to a permanent location at Preston and Jefferson Streets. The

American Turners group practicing at Churchill Downs for the 1926 National Turnfest, Louisville.

Ladies Auxiliary was started in 1875. In 1911 the Turners purchased the site of Turner Park from the Monongahela Coal and Coke Co. and started a long, successful operation along the Ohio River. When they outgrew their hall, they purchased property at 310 E Broadway that had been the boyhood home of Supreme Court Justice Louis D. Brandeis.

A gymnasium was built on the back of the residence, and the new hall was dedicated in 1917. In 1984 that property was sold, and the operation was moved to Turner Park to operate year-round. The new building and gymnasium were built and dedicated in August 1987 and named Weissmueller Hall in honor of Joseph Weissmueller, who had served as physical instructor for fifty-four years. Local Turners have hosted and participated in several National Turnfests, conventions, and tournaments.

See Henry Metzner, *A Brief History of the North American Gymnastic Union* (1911); Dr. C. Eugene Miller and Forrest F. Steinlage, *Der Turner Soldat* (Louisville 1989)

Forrest F. Steinlage

TYDINGS, JOSEPH MANSIR (b Louisville, November 10, 1905; d Louisville, September 30, 1974). Educator and civil rights leader. Trained as an architect, Tydings designed buildings until the early 1930s. In 1932 he quit that work and became the business manager of Lincoln Institute for African Americans. A white business manager in a black institution was unusual. Tydings stated he wanted no just to build buildings but to build bridges between different people.

In 1944 Governor Simeon Willis appointed him to the Commission on Negro Affairs. The commission was to obtain and study economic, educational, housing, and health conditions of blacks. Possessing a strong feeling for racial justice, Tydings established the Kentucky Council for Interracial Cooperatin in 1945 to promote equality among groups. In 1946 he helped to found the National Association of Intergroup Relations Officials (NAIRO).

From 1947 for almost a quarter of a century, Tydings' life was connected to the Lincoln Foundation where he was the executive director. The Lincoln Foundation grew out of Lincoln Institute and supported human relations and educational programs in the Jefferson County area. The foundation helped students and educators address the challenges of integrated education. On eof the programs was "Youth Speaks, Inc.," a youth citizenship program for high school students. It received national awards and became important for community discussions on questions of advancing educational opportunities for blacks. In 1962 Tydings temporarily left the position to become director of the Louisville Human Relations Commission created by Mayor William O. Cowger to deal with the desegregation of public accommodation. Under Tydings' leadership the commission worked to draw up public accommodations, fair employment, and open housing ordiances.

In the early 1970s Tydings was editor of Journal of Intergroup Relations that considered national issues of human rights and human relations. A Quaker, he was clerk of the Friends Meeting of Louisville. Tydings married Mary Page Gaines and they had two daughter. He is buried at Cave Hill Cemetery.

See *Who is Who in Kentucky* (Hopkinsville, Kentucky 1955); *Courier-Journal* October 1, 1974; J. Griffin Crump. "Mansir Tydings." *Journal of Intergroup Relations* 4, (April 1975): 3-6.

TYLER, EDWARD II (b Queen Anne's Parish, Prince George's Country, Maryland, January 18, 1719; d Jefferson County, Kentucky, 1802). Pioneer. Tyler, the son of Edward and Elizabeth (Duvall) Tyler, migrated to the Virginia frontier in the 1740s. There he worked as a trader. About 1750 he married Nancy (Ann) Langley. In 1780 they came down river with seven of their ten children to the Falls of the Ohio, apparently staying at Linn's Station on Beargrass Creek. By 1782 Tyler purchased 1,00 acres on Chenoweth Run east of present Jeffersontown, where three of his sons and a nephew established homesteads. Tyler and his spouse moved to Louisville an din 1784 began operating a tavern on Main St. near Fort Nelson. They lived there for about five years before retiring to the farm operated by their youngest son. Their children were:

Robert Tyler (1751-1839) came to Kentucky 1783; licensed a distillery in 1798, which was one of the finest legitimate distilleries in Kentucky; established the farm on his father's Chenoweth Run acreage that is today's Blackacre State Nature Preserve.

Delilah Tyler (1754-1798); wife of Captain Charles Polk; came to Kentucky in 1780 with her parents, husband, and several children; settled at Polk's Station in Nelson County; was kidnapped by Indians in 1782; rescued and returned home in December 1783.

William Tyler (Walking Billy) (1755-1836); was a private in George Rogers Clark's Illinois Battalion during Clark's conquest of the Northwest Territory; active in the early exploration and surveying of Jefferson County; seemingly the first of his family to attempt settlement on his father's 1,000 acre tract; was kidnaped by Indians c. 1782; escaped unharmed after about two years.

Elizabeth (Betsy) Tyler (c. 1756-1782); married the Reverend John Corbly c. 1773 in Monogalia County, Virginia; was killed there by Indians in 1782. John Corbly made a survey map of Louisville in 1779.

Nancy Ann Tyler (c. 1763-1838); came to the Falls in 1780; married Capt. Peter A'Sturgus of A'Sturgus Station on Beargrass Creek; became a widow when her husband was killed at Floyd's Defeat in 1781; was kidnapped by Indians c. 1782; returned; married James Denny, sheriff of Jefferson County, 1785; widowed again in 1808; married Michael Humble.

Mary Tyler (born c. 1760); came to the Falls in 1780; married James McHatton in Nelson County, 1787.

Edward Tyler III (1767-1840); immigrated with his parents 1780; lived in Louisville until c. 1788; established a farm on his father's acreage; was father of Levi Tyler, who became a Louisville trustee and prominent businessman; great-grandfather of Henry S. Tyler, mayor of Louisville in the early 1890s.

Priscilla Tyler (1770-1843); married Louisville merchant Abner Martin Dunn, who became the first postmaster of Cincinnati; returned after Dunn's death in 1795 to Chenoweth Run area where she lived until 1815; moved with her married daughter to Clark County, Indiana.

Eleanor (Nelly) Tyler (c. 1773-1800) married William Allison.

In 1986, six hundred acres of the Tyler family's original holdings were designated the Tyler Settlement Rural Historic District. It is the first fully documented rural historic landscape in Kentucky.

See Joellen T. Johnston. "The Tyler Settlement Rural Historic District: Background and Beginning." *The Filson Club History Quarterly* 65 (July 1991): 404-414; Harry Wright Newman, *Mareen Duvall of Middle Plantation* (Washington, D.C. 1952); Joellen T. Johnston. "Captain Robert Langley Tyler of Tyler's Station." *The Filson Club History Quarterly* 67 (July 1993): 387- 402; William J. Tyler. "The Patriarch, Edward Tyler (1719-1802)," Filson Club, Library. Louisville, Kentucky.

Joellen Tyler Johnston

TYLER, HENRY SAMUEL (b Louisville, September 20, 1851; d Louisville, January 14, 1896). Mayor. Tyler was the son of Henry S. and Rebecca (Gwathmey) Tyler and the grandson of Levi Tyler, one of the founders of the city government, serving as chairman of the committee that drafted the original articles of incorporation for Louisville's city status. Levi Tyler was a wealthy Louisville businessman, and his family inherited one of the largest estates in Louisville after his death. Henry Tyler went to public schools in Louisville, then attended Schatlock Hall Military School in Minnesota. He returned to Louisville after his education to become a shipping clerk for the iron merchants George H. Hull & Co. He later worked as a bookkeeper and confidential clerk for the insurance firm of Prather & Shallcross, later becoming employed by another insurance firm, J.L. Danforth & Co. He eventually established his own insurance firm, where he was connected until his death.

Tyler was active in the Democratic Party from an early age. His first candidacy for public office was for the common Council from the Seventh Ward. He was elected and remained a member until he resigned to run for mayor in

1891. He served as president of the Board of Councilmen in 1890. Because of his extensive business interests, he was a powerful voice on the council for industry in the city. Tyler was elected mayor in 1891. In 1893 Tyler was re-elected under the new city charter. Among the many changes in the charter, the mayor was then elected to four-year terms of office, making Tyler the first mayor elected to a four-year term.

Tyler had been instrumental in the drafting of the new city charter during his first two terms of office. He appointed a commission composed of M. Cary Peter, R.W. Knott, and E.J. McDermott to draft the new charter. The charter was passed by the General Assembly. Tyler died in the middle of his four-year term as mayor. Robert E. King, president of the Board of Aldermen, served as mayor pro tem from January 14 until January 31, when the council elected George D. Todd to serve until an open election in November 1896. Tyler's administration had been involved in implementing the reforms laid down by the new city charter.

Tyler married Mary Creel Tyler in 1882. They had three children: Nannie Thompson, John Tip Tyler, and Henry, who died before his father. Tyler was a member of St. Paul's Episcopal Church. He is buried in Cave Hill Cemetery.

See Josiah Stoddard Johnston, ed., Memorial History of Louisville, 2 vols. (Chicago and New York 1896).

Tyler Block, 1946. Razed in 1974.

TYLER BLOCK. Completed in 1874, the Tyler Block was 200-feet-wide, Renaissance Revival-style, limestone-fronted building that sat on the north side of Jefferson St. between Third and FOURTH streets. Designed by local architect Henry Wolters, the building was presumably named for the property's owners, the Tyler Family, who were descendants of Levi Tyler, chairman of the city's 1827 charter convention. Three stories in height and broken into five distinct bays, the structure maintained its architectural integrity except for the first floor, which was midified several times to accommodate up to ten commercial establishments by the mid-twentieth century. The building was demolished in 1974 to make way for the Commonwealth Convention Center, (now KENTUCKY INTERNATIONAL CONVENTION CENTER) despite the attempts of preservationists to incorporate the facade into the new exhibition hall.

See Walter Langsam, *Preservation: Metropolitan Preservation Plan* (Louisville 1973).

TYLER PARK. Neighborhood in eastern Louisville, bounded by Winter Ave. to the north, Bardstown Rd. to the east, Eastern Pkwy. to the south, and Barret Ave. and *BEARGRASS CREEK* to the west. Although part of the area around Bardstown Rd. was originally subdivided in 1873, few showed interest in the plots located on hilly land. Developers had a difficult time finding buyers for another decade. By the end of the century, however, Tyler Park had many incentives that pulled people into the community.

The extension of the streetcar line down Bardstown Rd. to Bonnycastle Ave.; the proximity to Zehnder's Garden, a popular beer garden run by Anton Zehnder until 1903; and the establishment of nearby Cherokee Park produced a flourishing section of town. Developers kept up with demand by platting the lands westward toward Beargrass Creek. The area drew further interest with the establishment of the centrally located Tyler Park in 1910, named for Mayor Henry S. Tyler, who had died during his term in 1896, and the construction of the TYLER PARK BRIDGE on Baxter Ave. by the city's PUBLIC WORKS Department in 1904 (named after the creation of the park). By 1952, much of the mixed residential and commercial neighborhood had been developed. A local landmark is the St. Louis Cemetery, established in 1867.

See Louisville Survey: East Report (Louisville 1980).

TYLER PARK BRIDGE. This massive rusticated Indiana limestone bridge was built by the city's Works Department in 1904 to let Baxter Ave. span a deep valley just north of Eastern Pkwy. and Castlewood Ave. that later became TYLER PARK.

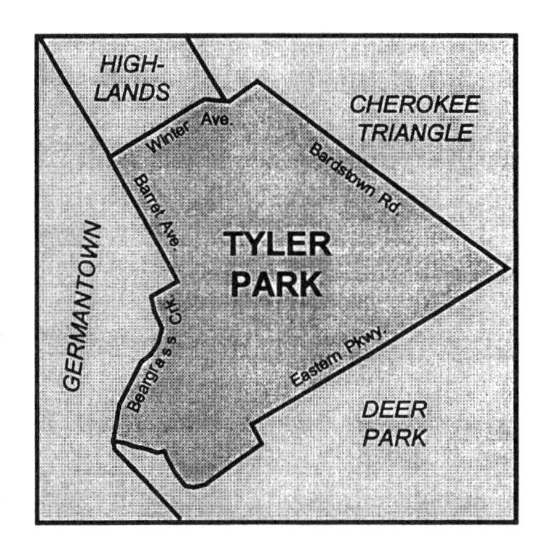

The design of the bridge (attributed to park architect John Olmsted) takes advantage of the site's natural hill and vale TOPOGRAPHY, incorporating a broad, segmental arch seventeen feet high and forty feet wide and, thereby, hastening the development of the park. The opening creates a visual and physical connection that allows pedestrians to move freely from one part of the thirteen-acre park to the other without having to cross the busy street above, a classic Olmsted solution.

The bridge slightly predates the park, the latter having been created in 1910 for residents of fashionable nearby HIGHLANDS-area NEIGHBORHOODS, including one subdivision developed by entrepreneur and park commissioner John B. Castleman.

Douglas L Stern

TYLER SETTLEMENT RURAL HISTORIC DISTRICT. The Tyler family, led by patriarch EDWARD TYLER II, were early farmers who established homesteads on a thousand-acre tract east of JEFFERSONTOWN. Each farm unit had a stone and/or log house, a stone springhouse, one or more log/stone barns, and a variety of utility structures. The Tylers also devised a system of lanes and traces, some of which remain today as landmark features, country lanes, or major paved roads. Because the area has remained essentially rural, many of its fields, pastures, and streams continue to reflect the settlement patterns imposed by the Tyler family so long ago. Today six hundred acres of the family's original property is designated the Tyler Settlement Rural Historic District and is on the National Register.

See Joellen Tyler Johnston, "The Tyler Settlement Rural Historic District: Background and Beginning," FILSON CLUB HISTORY QUARTERLY 65 (July 1991): 404–14.

Joellen Tyler Johnston

UFER, WALTER (b Huckeswagen, Germany, 1876; d Santa Fe, New Mexico, August 2, 1936). Artist. Ufer moved to Louisville with his family. His father, Peter, a craftsman of meerschaum pipes, was an established woodworker and gunsmith in Louisville. Walter received his early art training from his father, who taught him engraving, and from WILLIAM CLARK, a student of Meissonier in Paris who taught Walter to draw with a pen and ink from plaster cast and from nature.

At sixteen, Ufer became an apprentice engraver to Johann Juergens at the Courier-Journal Job Printing Co., one of Louisville's leading lithographing firms. Juergens taught Ufer commercial lithography and design as well as gymnastics at Louisville Turners. In 1893 Ufer went to Hamburg, Germany, to work in Juergens's lithographing firm. In Hamburg, he attended art school in the evenings and learned to design in watercolors and on the lithographic limestone blocks. At nineteen, he attended the prestigious Dresden Royal Academy of Fine Arts.

Upon his return to Louisville in 1898, Ufer was hired by WALTER HALDEMAN, owner of the *COURIER-JOURNAL*, and began working in the art department for the Sunday paper. Ufer went to Chicago in 1900 to work and study, and in 1906 he married artist Mary Monrad Frederiksen (1869–1947) of Copenhagen, Denmark. In 1911–13 he went to Europe and studied in Munich with Walter Thor. In 1914 Ufer first went to Taos, New Mexico, and did PAINTINGS of the Pueblo Indians with his trademark realism and social justice. An early member of the Taos Society of Artists, a group formed on July 15, 1915, to promote their paintings of New Mexico, Ufer was the first artist of the group to receive a prize at the Carnegie International exhibition in Pittsburgh in 1920.

Ufer retained ties with Louisville, and in 1916 he exhibited his paintings from Europe and New Mexico in Louisville in the sixth annual exhibition of the Louisville Artists League in the Art Room of the Carnegie Free Public Library.

His awards were numerous: Martin B. Cahn Prize, 1916; Frank G. Logan Prize, 1917; Thomas B. Clarke Prize from the National Academy of Design, 1918; Associate of the New York National Academy of Design, 1920. His paintings are in private and museum collections: J.B. SPEED ART MUSEUM, Louisville; Phoenix Art Museum; Arizona State University Museum; Anschutz Collection, Denver; Stark Museum of Orange, Texas; Gilcrease Institute of Tulsa; Metropolitan Museum of Art; Art Institute of Chicago; Corcoran Gallery of Art; Los Angeles County Museum of Art; and Pennsylvania Academy of Fine Arts.

See Patricia Janis Broder, *Taos: A Painter's Dream* (Boston 1980); Laura M. Bickerstaff, Pioneer Artist of Taos (Denver 1983); Mary Carroll Nelson, *The Legendary Artists of Taos* (New York 1980).

Carol Bonura

UNDERGROUND RAILROAD. The Underground Railroad has traditionally been seen as an organized network of agents or "conductors," usually white, who crossed into the southern states to guide slaves to freedom. Certainly this did occur, but newspaper and court records show that the majority of runaway slaves from Louisville were aided by other slaves and free blacks who lived in both the city and across the OHIO RIVER in NEW ALBANY and JEFFERSONVILLE, INDIANA. Other slaves struck out on their own without much help at all. Therefore, it is important to distinguish between escape conspiracies organized by Underground Railroad agents such as the Reverend Calvin Fairbank and Levi Coffin and escapes organized in Kentucky with little or no outside assistance.

Louisville's prominence as a major port on the Ohio River and as a terminus for overland routes from the Deep South made it a gateway ot freedom for enslaved AFRICAN AMERICANS escaping from the interior of Kentucky, Alabama, Tennessee, Mississippi, and Louisiana. Twenty-five percent of all runaway slave advertisements which appeared in Louisville NEWSPAPERS between 1820-1860 were placed by slaveowners from the Deep South.

There are several well-known occasions when agents from outside the state were active in Louisville. In 1851 Fairbank was caught trying to aid a runaway slave named Tamar. A free black named JAMES C. CUNNINGHAM had corresponded with Fairbank and was found with Tamar's clothes in his house. Cunningham was not arrested, but Fairbank was convicted and sent to the penitentiary. In 1856 Chapman Harris and the Reverend William Anderson, both well-known African American agents from Madison, Indiana, were suspected of aiding slaves and were arrested on a steamboat. A white man using the alias "Jones" worked closely with Levi Coffin in the late 1850s and helped a number of slaves escape on STEAMBOATS going to Cincinnati. Another white agent was arrested in 1860. He was found to have daguerreotypes of certain slaves he was to find and help escape.

Dozens of free blacks and slaves in Louisville risked their lives to help organize escapes. In 1851 a free boy named Alf Smiley was accused of forging passes for slaves. In 1855 Ralph, a slave of Bishop Martin Spalding, was caught trying to help slaves escape. Other free blacks such as Theodore Sterrett, Alexander Howard, Keziah Carter, Henson McIntosh, John Drummond, and Lydia Williams were also arrested for aiding escaped slaves. White Louisvillians such as Dr. Allen Yocum, William Tatum, John Robinson, and William Lewis were also arrested.

Methods of escape were as varied as one's imagination. In 1823 George Casey, who frequently drove a wagon and team from SHELBY COUNTY to Louisville, did so one day, left them "standing in the STREETS of Louisville," and escaped (*Louisville Public Advertiser*, April 12, 1823). Steamboats were also a favored means of escape. In 1853 an eighty-year-old man tried unsuccessfully to hide in the hold of a steamboat for hours as it sailed up the river to Cincinnati. Many slaves escaped across the river in a skiff, sometimes aided by accomplices from the Indiana side. The Portland Ferry, which ran from PORTLAND to Albany, Indiana was used regularly and escaping slaves often tried to ride the Salem Railroad to Salem, Indiana. There they could link up with agents like Sampson Christie who could get them to Canada. There were a number of blacks in New Albany, including George Carter and William Hardin, who were suspected of aiding runaway slaves. Others escaped from Louisville to Indiana on the Jeffersonville ferry and took the Jeffersonville Railroad to Seymour, Indiana where they could make a connection to Cincinnati via the Ohio & Mississippi Railroad.

Large sums were usually offered for the capture of escaped slaves, and there were cases where persons on the Indiana side of the river, working with cohorts in Louisville, would pretend to hide an escaped slave, wait until a reward was offered, and then bring the slave back to Louisville to collect the reward.

In 1850 the Fugitive Slave Law was passed, and Kentucky adopted a new constitution that increased restrictions on free blacks. Consequently, more slaves attempted to escape during the 1850s, and escape attempts became more sophisticated. During this period over four hundred runaway-slave advertisements were placed in Louisville newspapers alone. The actual number of slaves who successfully escaped may never be known, but the number certainly was high.

See Wilbur H. Siebert, *The Underground Railroad from Slavery to Freedom* (New York 1899); Randolph Paul Runyon, *Delia Webster and the Underground Railroad* (Lexington 1996); Levi Coffin, *Reminiscences of Levi Coffin* (Cincinnati 1876).

Cornelius Bogert

UNION STATION. Dedicated by the LOUISVILLE & NASHVILLE RAILROAD on September 7, 1891, it was the city's largest passenger terminal. At that time, Union was also said to have been the largest station in the South. It replaced a smaller depot at Tenth and Maple Streets, built around 1868–69, and an even older combination freight-passenger station that L&N had opened in 1858. Construction for Union Sta-

Grand lobby of the Louisville and Nashville Railroad's Union Station, 1936.

tion began in 1880 on property purchased at Tenth and BROADWAY, but rising costs suspended work until early 1889.

Union Station was designed by prominent eastern architect F.W. Mowbray, brought in especially for the project. In laying out Union, Mowbray followed the Richardsonian Romanesque style; and barreled vaulting, massive facade, clock tower, turrets, and smaller towers were incorporated in its design. Exterior surfaces were faced with limestone ashlar quarried in Bowling Green, Kentucky. Bedford, Indiana, limestone was used for trim, and the roof, trussed with heavy wood and iron, was covered with slate. Inside, Union's spacious first floor public areas included a central concourse or atrium, dining and women's retiring rooms, and ticket counters. Overlooking the central concourse, an upper balcony (which led to railroad offices) was trimmed with wrought iron. Still higher was the barrel-vaulted ceiling and leaded stained-glass skylight containing eighty-four panels. A rose window, twenty feet in diameter, dominated each end of the atrium and, with the skylight, reflected soft lighting below. Union's interior walls were finished with oak, southern pine, and carved Georgia marble wainscoting, while floors were done in ceramic tile. A covered concourse on the south side of the station led to tracks and platforms for arriving or departing trains. Some tracks were spanned by a protective train shed 450 feet long. A baggage room and separate mail and express buildings as well as the dining car commissary and other passenger service support facilities were located just to the west and south of the station proper. The terminal site, including approach tracks and coach yard, covered some forty acres. Except for the Seth Thomas clock in the corner tower, local contractors and suppliers constructed and outfitted the building, at a total cost of $310,656.47.

Union Station, its elegance matching that of the city's other major buildings, provided an impressive entrance for those arriving in Louisville, whether royalty or commoner. Sarah Bernhardt once performed in Union's lobby, and three United States presidents and their entourages arrived there. A third-floor fire on July 17, 1905, severely damaged interior spaces, and patrons used a temporary structure beside the train shed until the restored station reopened that December. OHIO RIVER floodwaters closed the station for twelve days in January 1937.

As L&N's major Louisville passenger station, Union also served trains of the Louisville, Henderson, & St. Louis (merged with L&N in 1929); Monon; and Pennsylvania RAILROADS and, after 1963, trains of the Chesapeake & Ohio following closing of Central Station. The "depot line" trolleys connected Union with Central on Seventh St. between Main and the river in the early 1900s to facilitate travelers who were changing railroads. Peak usage came in the 1920s when fifty-eight trains arrived and departed daily. Until the mid-1960s, KENTUCKY DERBY weekends brought to the station some twenty or more special trains with racegoers, some staying overnight on the Pullman sleepers and private cars of the specials.

Amtrak used Union Station from May 1971 until October 1976 when it shifted trains to the Auto-Train Terminal on National Turnpike. L&N later sold Union to the TRANSIT AUTHORITY OF RIVER CITY (TARC), which restored it in 1979–80 for $2 million to house administrative offices. A vintage mule car used by the city's street railways before electric STREETCARS is on display in the atrium.

Union Station has been designated a Louisville Landmark and is listed on the NATIONAL REGISTER OF HISTORIC PLACES. Amtrak's revival of train service to the metro area in late 1999 raised the possibility that Union might again host the arrivals and departures of passenger trains.

See Edison H. Thomas, Trains (Milwaukee, Wisc., 1972); "Union Station, An Historic Landmark," Transit Authority of River City, Louisville, ca. 1981 (pamphlet); Janet G. Potter, *Great American Railroad Stations* (New York 1996).

Charles B. Castner

UNITARIAN UNIVERSALISM. This religious movement is a union of two liberal traditions with roots in the Pietist wing of the sixteenth-century Protestant Reformation. Both traditions affirm the freedom of the individual conscience from the constraint of doctrinal authority and assert the ongoing evolution of truth. Resisting many orthodox Protestant tenets, Unitarians-Universalists practice religious tolerance.

The First Unitarian Church of Philadelphia was founded in 1796 by the English-born Joseph Priestly, who argued for the simple humanity of Christ. The American Unitarian Association was born in Boston in May 1825, and congregations already established, many in intentional opposition to the individualist revival spirit of the Great Awakening, began to call themselves Unitarian.

The Universalist Church in America was established in 1779 in Gloucester, Massachusetts, by John Murray. In 1785 the Universalists created a Charter of Compact in Massachusetts, and five years later the Philadelphia Universalists adopted the Philadelphia Articles of Faith. However, it was not until 1942 that the name Universalist Church of America became official. In 1961 the Universalist Church of America and the American Unitarian Association merged to become the Unitarian Universalist Association.

Transylvania University became a mini-center of Unitarianism when Horace Holley became president in 1817. Other Unitarian faculty and graduates traveled to Louisville and were channels through which their liberal religious ideas filtered. The poet FORTUNATUS COSBY, editor of the *Louisville Examiner*, the first Kentucky newspaper dedicated to the emancipation of slaves, and Elisha Bartlett, medical lecturer, poet, musician, and politician, were among Transylvania-educated Unitarians in Louisville.

Although local Unitarians organized in the late 1820s, the FIRST UNITARIAN CHURCH, a Greek Revival structure at Fifth and Walnut (Muhammad Ali Blvd.) Streets, was dedicated in 1832 with the Reverend George Chapman of Massachussetts as its first pastor. The first Universalist congregation of Louisville was formed in the 1840s. A church was erected on MARKET ST. between Eighth and Ninth Streets, and by 1852 the congregation had approximately two hundred members. Even before their merger in 1869, members of First Unitarian Church had reflected their belief in the free agency of human beings by their consistent presence in the forefront of civil rights and other social, political, and cultural concerns including emancipation, housing issues, and full justice for women and homosexuals.

In 1870 the merged congregations completed their new building at Fourth and York Streets, known as the Church of the Messiah, at a cost of about seventy-five thousand dollars and dedicated the structure the following January. It was rebuilt after a fire gutted the interior in 1985. Thomas Jefferson Unitarian Church, on Old Brownsboro Rd., became an autonomous congregation in 1960. Clifton Unitarian Church is on Payne St. in the CLIFTON neighborhood.

See J. Stoddard Johnston, ed., *Memorial History of Louisville* (Chicago 1896); John A. Buehrens and F. Forrester Church, *Our Chosen Faith: An Introduction to Unitarian*-Universalism (Boston 1989); David Robinson, THE UNI-

TARIANS AND THE UNIVERSALISTS (Westport, Conn., 1985); Harry B. Scholefield, *The Unitarians and the Universalist Pocket Guide* (Boston 1991).

Martha S. Gilliss

UNITED CHURCH OF CHRIST. The nineteenth century was not many years old before a host of German immigrants began to arrive in Louisville. Many of these immigrants were deeply religious and gathered regularly in their homes for worship and fellowship. Some of these pious GERMANS brought with them chorales and sermons used in their worship. As their numbers increased, they organized churches and brought pastors to lead the faithful. The first fellowship begun was St. Paul, organized in March 1836. By 1841 a building was erected at Preston and Green (LIBERTY) Streets. Dr. C.L. Daubert, the second pastor, served for thirty years, during which time a large edifice was erected and membership grew.

Early churches experienced growth as immigrants continued to come to Louisville. Other German language churches sprang up, namely one in NEW ALBANY, Indiana, now known as St. Mark; St. John in 1843; St. Peter in 1847; St. Luke in 1856, now merged into St. Stephen; Christ in 1879; St. Matthew in 1889; and Bethlehem in 1891. Some of these new churches took names such as the German Evangelical Lutheran and Reformed Congregation of New Albany; St. John's German Evangelical Church, later affiliated with the Reformed Church in the United States, now known as Lynnhurst; and the German Apostolic Evangelical Church, known today as St. Peter. Zion began as the German Evangelical and Reformed Zion Church.

New church growth continued as St. John members formed Immanuel Church in 1898 and Bethel Church in 1923. Zion nurtured Salem in 1867 and later in a new location merged with Milton Avenue and a mission. Salem founded Sunnydale, now merged into St. Stephen and later Chapel Hill in 1963. Bethlehem helped found St. James, PARKLAND, and Clifton, now a Unitarian church. St. Mathew assisted in the formation of Trinity in 1958. Faith Church in 1984 was begun by members of Christ Church. Other churches had different beginnings. Grace Immanuel was split off the present Third Lutheran Church. St. Paul merged with Bethel in 1995 as Bethel St. Paul United Church of Christ.

Because of the growth and vitality of the Louisville churches, the twentieth General Conference of the German Evangelical Synod of North America met in Louisville in September 1913 in St. Peter Church.

Many early German church members, having experienced the autocratic nature of the church and state in their homeland, resisted "an organization with a president." They and their pastors did fellowship with one another, but any ecclesiastical structure carried very little authority. St. Paul joined the Synod in 1908, St. Mark in 1866, and St. John in 1856. St. Peter, St. Luke, Christ, St. Matthew, and Bethlehem joined immediately.

The early churches provided for the needs of their people by forming the Young People's League, the Churchmen's Brotherhood, and the Women's Guild. In September 1903 at St. Mark, New Albany, the first Indiana District (including Louisville) Young People's League was held. Attendance grew, and soon meetings had to be held at Hanover College.

The first Indiana District's Churchmen's Brotherhood met in St. John Church in 1907. At the 1913 National Synod, an "impressive sight of three hundred men marched from the court house to St. Peter Church for the opening of Synod." The Women's Guild or, in many churches, Die Frauenverein, Missionary Society or Ladies' Aid also grew. In the early years, women's groups worked for Elmhurst College, Eden Seminary, or local charitable institutions. Many local women went to Cincinnati, Ohio, in June 1912 for the formation of the national Evangelical Women's Union.

German piety often took the form of compassionate services to children, the aging, and the ill. Dr. Daubert and the people of St. Paul Church responded to a community need in 1851 by beginning the German Protestant Orphan Asylum at Nineteenth and Jefferson Streets. The home is now known as Brooklawn Youth Services and serves abused and problem children. This was the very first of hundreds of health and human services of the church across the country. Pastor and Mrs. H. Frigge of Christ Church and its members founded the ALTENHEIM, now a multipurpose home for the aging. In 1960 the Evangelical and Reformed churches, along with the Methodist churches, opened a hospital that is now part of NORTON HEALTHCARE. Continuing the community-minded spirit, the congregation of ST. MATTHEWS, on the northeast corner of St. Catherine and Hancock Streets, decided in 1999 to formally dissolve. Instead of selling the property, the members donated the brick church complex to House of Ruth, a local nonprofit agency that helps women and children whose families have been affected by HIV and AIDS.

An organization named Missions Inc. was formed in the 1950s. It was a lay organization with pastoral advisors. The group formed Bethany Church in 1956 and assisted St. Andrew in 1960. These churches today are members of the United Church of Christ (UCC), with a congregational type church government.

The UCC was founded in 1957 as a result of the union of the Congregational Christian churches and the Evangelical and Reformed church. The Evangelical Synod and the Reformed Church in America had united in 1934 and in the 1940s began discussions that resulted in the multichurch merger. Congregational churches known for their New England beginnings merged in 1926 with the General Convention of the Christian Church. The Christian Church had its origins in the South and included many African American congregations.

The one Congregational church in Louisville—Plymouth at Seventeenth and Chestnut Streets—is primarily an African American congregation. It has overseen the Plymouth Urban Center, a neighborhood program providing assistance, tutoring, and recreational programs for residents in the RUSSELL neighborhood.

The Louisville churches today have a partnership with the Christian Church, DISCIPLES OF CHRIST. This partnership functions in worship, study, service, and fellowship.

See *Courier-Journal,* March 9, 1999.

Donald A. Buchhold
William Joseph Schultz

UNITED DISTILLERS MANUFACTURING INC. United Distillers Manufacturing Inc. (UDMI) is a subsidiary of United Distillers, the spirits company of Guinness PLC. In 1986 Guinness acquired the Distillers Corp. Ltd., owners of the STITZEL-WELLER DISTILLERY in SHIVELY. The following year Guinness acquired the Schenley Co. and its Bernheim Distillery in Louisville. In 1991 the Glenmore Distilleries Co. was acquired by Guinness.

United Distillers Manufacturing is the home office for all manufacturing plants owned by Guinness in North America. These plants are the Stitzel-Weller Distillery and the Bernheim Distillery in Louisville; the George Dickel "Cascade" Distillery in Tullahoma, Tennessee; the Gordon's Gin plant in Plainfield, Illinois; and the Valleyfield Distillery in Valleyfield, Quebec.

In 1992 United Distillers rebuilt the Bernheim Distillery into one of the most modern distilleries in the industry. The distillery has both new and old elements in it. The column stills are from the old distillery, but they are controlled by a new state-of-the-art computer system, making the distillery one of the most efficient in the world.

In 1999 United Distillers sold the Bernheim Ditillery to Heaven Hill Distillery. It also sold all of its remaining U.S. marketed bourbons, keeping only I.W. Harper for its sales in Japan, and the George Dickel Tennessee Whiskey

Michael R. Veach

UNITED PARCEL SERVICE (UPS). Founded in Seattle, Washington, in 1907, United Parcel Service (UPS) has had an association with the Louisville area that began with ground service deliveries and pickups in the early 1960s. In the early 1980s, management decided to move the package-sorting station in 1981 from Chicago to Louisville, citing its moderate WEATHER, central location, and the immediate availability of a warehouse site near STANDIFORD FIELD (LOUISVILLE INTERNATIONAL AIRPORT). Approximately one year later, the small regional hub of a hundred employees had become UPS's national air hub, with nearly a thousand employees who sorted not only every regular domestic air package but also those for the new next-day air service.

With the threat of losing the burgeoning express service operations in 1983 to either Smyrna, Tennessee, or Columbus, Ohio, the airport authority allowed UPS to purchase additional land at the airport, including the old Louisville Air Park, clearing the way for a proposed superhub expansion. The city solidified its position as the national air hub for the delivery business two years later when UPS moved its headquarters for the air division from Greenwich, Connecticut, to Louisville and also routed its new letter and small-package service through Louisville.

With the announced intention to create its own plane fleet, control the maintenance operations, and hire its own pilots in 1987 (UPS had contracted earlier through carriers such as Evergreen and Orion Airlines for delivery), the flourishing business needed additional room and runway capacity. To meet this need and many others, the city and the REGIONAL AIRPORT AUTHORITY began an airport improvement project in 1988. After purchasing nearby lands and buying out homeowners in local NEIGHBORHOODS, including PRESTONIA, STANDIFORD, HIGHLAND PARK, and EDGEWOOD, the $600 million expansion was slated to include two longer north-south runways, increased gate capacity, new parking facilities, and additional space for UPS.

Coinciding with the airport construction was UPS's multi-million-dollar hub expansion, which included a new sorting center, a pilot-training center, and a new parts warehouse and hangar. By the end of its construction, UPS held more than three hundred acres of land in the Louisville area and had invested more than $500 million on its facilities. This permitted the package giant to continue increasing its volume and its workforce. Before construction began in 1988, UPS was the second-largest private employer in the city, with approximately fifty-six hundred workers. With the culmination of most of the airport work in 1996, excluding the completion of one of the runways, UPS had become the city and state's largest private employer and its second-largest employer overall. By 1997 UPS had expanded into hundreds of international markets, operated five regional hubs (aside from the Louisville main hub, which sorts international and cross-country deliveries), and maintained approximately two hundred airplanes ranging from DC-8s to 767s. During that same year, the Louisville facility, which had started with only 7 flights per day in 1981, accommodated more than 100 flights per day, sorted 165,000 packages and documents per hour, and employed 14,000 workers (although many of them were part-time package handlers), making it the largest employer in the city.

Since its arrival in the community, UPS has consistently been a top contributor to charitable organizations and causes. In 1996 alone, UPS and its employees gave $3.2 million to such projects as the LOUISVILLE SCIENCE CENTER, the Family Place, the LOUISVILLE ZOO, METRO UNITED WAY, OPERATION BRIGHTSIDE, and the FUND FOR THE ARTS.

In March 1998 UPS officials announced that the delivery company would expand its Louisville operation to create a new mega-sorting center dubbed Hub 2000. With plans to invest $860 million on a new 2.7-million-square-foot building and other improvements, the sorting station, set to be fully operational by 2001, will be able to process three hundred thousand packages an hour. Faced with a local shortage of labor, one of the major concerns for expanding the Louisville hub was the ability to find employees to fill the estimated six thousand new jobs, thirty-nine hundred of which would be part-time. To provide an adequate labor pool, local officials reached into rural counties that had higher jobless rates.

Additionally, the Metropolitan College, an innovative joint venture by the UNIVERSITY OF LOUISVILLE, JEFFERSON COMMUNITY COLLEGE, and the Kentucky Tech Jefferson Campus, features class schedules on a new campus developed to accommodate the late-night hours of package handlers. Aside from the UPS jobs, the expansion was projected to substantially increase state and local tax revenue and to generate an additional eight thousand jobs with new and relocated companies who desired overnight delivery capabilities. However, similar to previous airport construction projects, nearby residents relayed fears of escalating noise pollution levels as the number of flights per day increased.

UNITED STATES ARMY CORPS OF ENGINEERS. The history of the Corps of Engineers can be traced to 1775 when the Second Continental Congress organized an army and appointed Col. Richard Gridley as the first chief engineer. In 1802 Congress established a Corps of Engineers, and it is from that date that the organization's continuous existence dates. Throughout the nineteenth century the corps constructed coastal fortifications and, aided by the Corps of Topographical Engineers, mapped much of the American West. In 1824 legislation authorized the corps to remove snags and sandbars from the Ohio and Mississippi Rivers; thus, both military and civil works construction are ingrained in the corps' heritage.

Corps district offices began to be formed in the 1870s. The Louisville Engineer District was officially established in 1886, and Maj. Amos Stickney was the first officer in charge to have the title of district engineer. The Louisville district is rooted in the role that it has played in the development of navigation projects on the OHIO RIVER, most notably those at the FALLS OF THE OHIO. The presence of army engineers at the Falls can be documented for almost two hundred years. Initially, the engineers assisted local surveyors in mapping the best route for a canal to bypass the treacherous Falls.

Later, as the private company that operated the original LOUISVILLE AND PORTLAND CANAL sought to expand that project, it often turned to the federal engineers. The company sought federal assistance in a major improvement effort in the 1860s and 1870s, and, in fact, army engineers completed that project in 1872, widening the canal and constructing a two-flight lock, the largest in the world at that time. By 1879 the engineers had completed the first movable dam across the river at the Falls. The federal government assumed jurisdiction of the canal in 1874 and soon removed the tolls for lockage that had been charged by the company.

The twentieth-century mission of the corps at the Falls has been the assurance of a safe and efficient navigation infrastructure. In the 1920s the district completed a new movable dam and canal-widening project, built in conjunction with the hydroelectric plant constructed by Louisville Gas and Electric Co. In order to meet projected increases in commercial barge traffic, the corps will construct a second twelve-hundred-foot lock chamber at McAlpine Locks and Dam, scheduled for completion in 2007. The district played a major part in construction of the first canalization project on the entire length of the Ohio, which was completed in 1929, consisting of fifty locks and dams from Pittsburgh to Cairo. In the 1950s the corps began a navigation modernization program, replacing the old wooden wicket dams with high-lift, nonnavigable dams, six of which are in the Louisville district. Locks and Dams 52 and 53 located west of Paducah are the last of the old dams, and they will be replaced by the Olmsted Locks and Dam project, scheduled for completion in 2009. Since the 1880s, locks and dams on the Kentucky and Green Rivers have been under district supervision. Presently, the civil works boundaries of the district include the Ohio River from Meldahl Locks and Dam above Cincinnati, Ohio, to the mouth at Cairo, Illinois, and the tributaries along that stretch of the river, an area encompassing parts of Kentucky, Indiana, Ohio, Illinois, and Tennessee.

Following enactment of the 1936 Flood Control Act, and after record FLOODS in the Ohio Valley in 1936 and 1937, the Corps of Engineers began a national program of comprehensive flood control. In the 1940s the Louisville district began construction of local protection projects—floodwalls and levees—including the protection system at Louisville. Following completion, these projects are operated by local GOVERNMENTS. As part of the comprehensive flood control program, the district has constructed twenty lakes that are part of seventy-eight lakes located throughout the Ohio Valley. Taylorsville Lake, near Louisville, is the most recent lake built by the district, when it impounded the Salt River in 1982.

The military construction mission of the Louisville district began in the WORLD WAR II era when the Corps of Engineers assumed that role from the Quartermaster Corps. During the war the district carried out a diversified program, building complete airfields, barracks for troop housing, mess halls, roads, warehouses, HOSPITALS, utilities systems, and huge munitions production facilities such as the Indiana Ordnance Plant at Charlestown, Indiana. The district's current military program consists of services in master planning, design and construction, and real estate management for the army, air force, and Department of Defense agencies.

The district also responds to national emergencies and disasters, providing assistance in relief and recovery efforts following floods, storms, earthquakes, and drought. The district enforces federal laws to ensure that water resource development is consistent with the needs and welfare of the nation. The corps cleans up hazardous and toxic waste sites, preserves and enhances fish and wildlife resources, preserves and manages cultural resources, and assists the military with closure of installations. The Corps of Engineers is known as the Nation Builders. The corps' motto, "Essayons," is from the French, and translates "let us try."

See *The History of the United States Army Corps of Engineers* (Washington, D.C., 1978); Leland R. Johnson, *The Falls City Engineers: A History of the Louisville District, Corps of Engineers, United States Army,* 2 vols. (Louisville 1975 and 1984); Historical files, Louisville District, United States Army Corps of Engineers, Louisville.

Charles E. Parrish

U.S. Marine Hospital, 1922.

UNITED STATES MARINE HOSPITAL. The old United States Marine Hospital at Louisville is the only surviving structure built by the federal government in the late 1840s for inland sailors. The history of Louisville's three marine HOSPITALS emphasizes the river town's importance as a transportation and commercial center. Early in the town's formative years, residents realized they could not care for the increasing number of river men who, "owing to the fatigue and exposure incident to long voyages," became sick and "languished" in Louisville.

Therefore, in 1817 the Kentucky General Assembly incorporated the Louisville Hospital Co. to create a facility for sick and injured boatmen. The state appropriated $17,500 for its construction, and THOMAS PRATHER and Cuthbert Bullitt donated a seven-acre plot on Chestnut and PRESTON Streets. Opened in 1823, the "commodious and well equipped" three-story Louisville Marine Hospital housed a surgical amphitheater, kitchen, wash house, storerooms, and ward-like facilities outfitted with wooden beds for up to eighty sailors and indigent patients. In the mid-1830s the hospital was remodeled. It received two large additions, and its name was changed to the Louisville City Hospital.

During the mid-1800s the federal government constructed seven marine hospitals along western waterways. A congressional act of March 3, 1837, authorized the secretary of war to appoint a board of medical officers of the army to select and purchase sites for these hospitals. One of those chosen was an eight-acre site overlooking the OHIO RIVER on Louisville's Portland Ave. In 1841 the site was purchased for six thousand dollars. The design for the facility was adapted from a standard plan commissioned in 1837 from architect Robert Mills. Col. Stephen H. Long of the Corps of Engineers supervised the construction, which began in 1845.

The sixty-two-thousand-dollar hospital opened on January 1, 1852, to treat rivermen previously cared for in the Chestnut St. facility at the city's expense and through a fee paid on steamboat tonnage. In 1869 members of the religious community Sisters of Mercy arrived in Louisville from St. Louis to begin NURSING duties at the marine hospital. The Sisters served at the hospital for the next six years. Shortly after the opening of the 1852 structure, the original "marine hospital" became the central portion for Louisville City Hospital; it was razed in 1914 to make way for Louisville General Hospital.

During the CIVIL WAR the federal army used the 1850s structure, but at the conflict's end the hospital returned to caring for inland sailors. It continued to fill this role until the construction of a more modern four-story facility on the hospital's grounds. On the opening of the newer one in the early 1930s, the nearby 1850s building was abandoned. In more recent decades the older structure has housed a heating plant for the 1930s hospital and provides space for the storage of medical records. Purchased by the city of Louisville after WORLD WAR II, the remodeled and refurbished 1930s facility has served as a TB sanitarium and a long-term recovery and rehabilitation center. In 1997 the 145-year-old structure became Louisville's sixth National Historic Landmark.

Nancy D. Baird

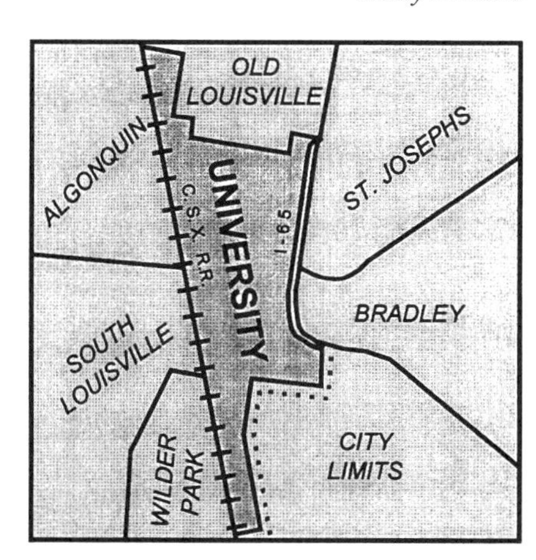

UNIVERSITY. Neighborhood south of downtown Louisville, roughly bounded by the CSX railroad tracks to the west, Dakota Ave. to the south, Interstate 65 to the east, and a combination of Hill St., Avery St., and Bloom Ave. to the north. This primarily residential community developed around the UNIVERSITY OF LOUISVILLE Belknap Campus and the nearby industries, which included the old LOUISVILLE & NASHVILLE RAILROAD yards.

The URBAN RENEWAL projects affected the neighborhood when in late 1960 and during the 1970s many houses around the university area, including a long-standing African American residential section, "The Bottoms," were demolished. This enabled the university to more than double its campus area by expanding north to Avery St. Aside from the university, local landmarks include the J.B. SPEED ART MUSEUM, Stansbury Park, the CONFEDERATE MONUMENT,

Youth Performing Arts School, and DU PONT MANUAL HIGH SCHOOL.

UNIVERSITY OF LOUISVILLE. The University of Louisville is a historic comprehensive public university with a broadly based curriculum at the undergraduate and masters' level and a range of programs at the doctoral level in both professional and arts and sciences areas of research and instruction. Its mission was defined by the commonwealth of Kentucky in 1970 as follows: "It shall serve as Kentucky's urban/metropolitan university. Located in the Commonwealth's largest metropolitan area, it shall serve the specific educational, intellectual, cultural, service and research needs of the greater Louisville region. It has a special obligation to serve the needs of a diverse population, including many ethnic minorities and place-bound, part-time nontraditional students."

The university's history has its roots in the chartering of the JEFFERSON SEMINARY, chartered in 1798, but it was not until 1837 that the City Council created the LOUISVILLE MEDICAL INSTITUTE and the Louisville Collegiate Institute as successor institutions. In 1846 the General Assembly combined the two schools and added a law department to form the University of Louisville. The academic department remained dormant until the twentieth century. For the next sixty years the university was essentially a medical school and a law school reporting directly to the Board of Trustees.

In 1850, meanwhile, opponents of the medical department established a second medical school in the city, the Kentucky School of MEDICINE. This was the first of several local rivals of the medical department of the university. In 1907 the University of Louisville absorbed some of these schools, and the remaining ones closed soon afterward. The medical school mergers coincided with other developments that brought the University of Louisville closer to the twentieth-century model of a university. In 1907 the academic department was activated as the College of Arts and Sciences. Pres. A.Y. Ford (1914–26) directed successful municipal bond issues and increased private donations to the university. In 1923 he oversaw purchase of what became the Belknap Campus, about two miles south of the university's downtown location, at Third St. and Eastern Pkwy.

This campus already had a number of usable structures to which was added Grawemeyer Hall (originally the Administration Building). This structure, modeled on the Georgian style of the University of Virginia, determined the type of ARCHITECTURE on the campus for the next quarter of a century, as buildings were created to accommodate the law school and the new engineering program. The medical school and the more recently established dental school remained downtown.

Pres. GEORGE COLVIN (1926–28) sought to continue the consolidation of central authority initiated by Ford, but his emphasis upon practical instruction and education for citizenship at the expense of creative ideas and dedicated research brought about substantial unrest in the faculty. He was succeeded by Raymond A. Kent (1929–43) a president with a broader academic vision. Under his leadership, programs were added in music and social work, while graduate studies were developed and evening classes were introduced to accommodate part-time working students.

In 1931 an AFRICAN AMERICAN undergraduate division was opened on a separate campus; but after twenty years the legal pressure from blacks, the financial cost of a separate campus, and the support of some influential whites led to the desegregation of the University of Louisville in 1951. Also during this period the university adjusted to the imperatives of WORLD WAR II, and the Belknap Campus became a post for the training of naval personnel. The campus was soon dotted with wooden-frame naval structures that remained a part of its landscape for two or three decades after the war.

Einar W. Jacobsen served as president of the university from 1943 to 1946. It was under Jacobsen's administration that the university's music school was given the Norton family's private residence, GARDENCOURT, on Alta Vista Rd. Mattie Norton left Gardencourt to the school in 1946. It served as the music school until 1969. The house was sold to the LOUISVILLE PRESBYTERIAN THEOLOGICAL SEMINARY in 1987.

The administration of John W. Taylor (1947–50) was a period of substantial growth, as enrollments increased sharply with the influx of World War II veterans. The newly recruited faculty were especially creative but also restive under the pressures of post–World War II conformity. Taylor's leadership was most evident in PUBLIC RELATIONS and intercollegiate sports. During this period the university received national recognition for its developing BASKETBALL program, which later led to NCAA championships in 1980 and 1986.

During the administration of Philip Davidson (1951–68) the university experienced very substantial growth, though it started with a dip in enrollments as the veteran surge receded. Much of the growth occurred in the University College, the name given to a very substantial program in the evening hours. (It had been the Adult Education Division.) Some of this was a duplication of daytime offerings, but there was also a special opportunity for cultural enrichment and career advancement available to thousands who had daytime jobs. The graduate-level programs also expanded as masters' degrees were offered in most departments and doctoral level programs were established in ten or more departments on both the Belknap and medical campuses. At this time the economics department was expanded into the School of Business.

In addition, this was a period in which graduate research institutes were established and special research faculties were hired. During this period extensive construction took place as new buildings rose to accommodate the arts and sciences and engineering programs, along with a new library, student center, and University College building. In addition there was construction of a new gymnasium, and several new dormitories housed an increasing number of students living on the campus. While the university remained essentially a commuter institution (some called it a "STREETCAR college"), it also attracted students from outside the area,

University of Louisville academic building at 119 West Broadway, 1924.

particularly in the professional programs.

On the downtown Health Sciences campus, a whole new complex of buildings, largely federally funded, reflected the expansion of the medical and dental schools and the development of programs in nursing and allied health. The new campus extended eastward along Chestnut and Walnut (Muhammad Ali Blvd.) from Floyd to Hancock Streets. The university had for some time made arrangements with Louisville General Hospital to serve as its teaching hospital.

Davidson succeeded to a considerable extent in centralizing the governance of the university, an important feat in a school whose history had been characterized by semi-autonomous units. The financing of the university presented serious challenges. The tax base of local government did not permit it to expand its support to meet the needs of a developing university, and heavy reliance had to be placed on tuition and private giving for operating budgets. It became obvious that the university could not hope to support expensive professional schools in this manner indefinitely, and conversations began with the commonwealth of Kentucky for support.

In 1966 the General Assembly created a committee to recommend alternatives under which the University of Louisville might enter the state system of higher education. At the end of the Davidson era the university unexpectedly acquired an eastern campus on Shelbyville Rd. as a small Baptist College, Kentucky Southern, was financially unable to continue operation, and the university took over a sizable campus area with a few small buildings, which have since been used primarily for extension classes, conferences, and special programs. The school of music was also located at the newly acquired campus from 1969 to 1980, when it moved to its current location on the Belknap Campus.

Davidson retired in 1968, and the leadership passed to Woodrow Strickler (1968–72), who presided over one of the most difficult and turbulent periods in the university's history. In 1970 the university became a part of the state system of higher education as an independent comprehensive university with all of its programs intact. Over the years, these programs were subject to oversight in Frankfort by the Council on Higher Education; and some of the programs, particularly those at the doctoral level, were modified or eliminated and others were added to assure the accomplishment of the state-defined mission. Not only were there serious problems in adjusting to public university status, but, as enrollments dramatically shot upward, there were daunting space and staffing problems.

The university student enrollment rose from 10,006 in 1969 to 15,188 in 1974–75. In addition there was extensive student unrest reflecting the trauma on the national stage. This resulted in the forceful takeover of buildings in 1969. The problems were resolved without more serious violence. The principal result of this activity was the creation of a Black Student Center and the establishment of a program in Pan-African studies. There were also important community involvements as the university became a cofounder of Jefferson Community College in 1968 and played a leading role in the establishment of the Kentuckiana Metroversity, a consortium of higher education in the Louisville metropolitan area. During this period the schools of education and justice administration, based upon existing programs, came into being.

James Grier Miller (1973–80) devoted himself primarily to a search for the highest possible standards in both faculty and student body. He was also noted for the rapid expansion of the physical plant on both campuses and for his keen interest in the development of information technology. During this period a new library, music hall, chemistry building, and education building arose on Belknap Campus, and a medical complex housing the new University of Louisville Hospital along with an outpatient center opened its doors on the downtown campus.

Miller was succeeded by Donald Swain (1981–95), who began his administration working out a solution to a crisis in the new University Hospital by developing an arrangement with Humana, a private insurance-hospital conglomerate to take over its administration. His major emphasis was on planning and budget, a much-needed control, and community relations, particularly with local business enterprises. As a result of the planning process, he brought about structural changes in the programmatic pattern. During his administration the endowment increased very substantially from about $30 million to over $140 million, which made possible some areas of special excellence. Also in this period, new buildings in both academic and faculty, and student recreational and activities areas were added. Swain near the end of his administration undertook some important revisions in university governance and faculty evaluation.

The administration of John Shumaker (1995–) started out very much like Swain's, with a crisis in the University Hospital. Changes in the corporate structure of the managing business enterprise necessitated a change in the arrangement, which resulted in an affiliation with Alliant Health Systems and Jewish Hospital, both nearby. A new football stadium was built. Led by Shumaker, the three schools—Jefferson Community College, Jefferson Technical College, and University of Louisville—tailored Metropolitan College to the needs of students who work for United Parcel Service. Students could attend classes in the early mornings and evenings and could work overnight shifts at UPS. Shumaker also broadened the scope of university instruction by creating instructional units under its sponsorship in other parts of the world, thus giving it a distinctly international quality.

In 1996–97 the University of Louisville listed twelve schools and colleges: Arts and Sciences, Law, Education, Music, Business and Public Administration, Engineering, Graduate Studies, Social Work, Medicine, Dentistry, Nursing, and Allied Health, with a total enrollment of 21,020, a faculty and staff of 4,613, and more than 87,000 alumni. Its budget in 1996–97 was $243,830,600 in general funds and $356,303,600 in its total operation.

See Dwayne Cox, "A History of the University of Louisville," Ph.D. dissertation, University of Kentucky, 1984; William F. Ekstrom, "Recollection of the University of Louisville," unpublished memoir, 1993, University of Louisville Archives; William Mallalieu, "Origins of the University of Louisville," *Filson Club History Quarterly* 12 (Jan. 1938) 24–41; Kentucky Writers'Project, *A Centennial History of the University of Louisville* (Louisville 1939); Dwayne D. Cox and William J. Morison, *The University of Louisville* (Lexington 1999).

William F. Ekstrom

UNIVERSITY OF LOUISVILLE HEALTH SCIENCES CENTER. The present University of Louisville Health Sciences Center traces its roots to 1823 when the Louisville Hospital Co. was chartered by the Kentucky General Assembly. It built the Louisville Marine Hospital, which was transferred in 1836 to the city of Louisville and became Louisville City Hospital. A new building was erected in 1911 on Chestnut between Brook and PRESTON Streets, and the hospital was renamed Louisville General Hospital in 1942. The large facility was charged with medical care for indigent patients in Louisville and Jefferson County.

The University School of Medicine was founded in 1837 as the LOUISVILLE MEDICAL INSTITUTE. It was located at the corner of Chestnut and Eighth Streets. From the beginning, students from the Louisville Medical Institute and the School of Dentistry (organized 1918) were taught at General Hospital. University medical students also became affiliated with Children's Hospital, Jewish Hospital, Kosair Crippled Children's Hospital, and Norton Memorial Infirmary (now Norton Hospital).

Planning began in the 1960s to build a modern health sciences center downtown that would include the School of Medicine and the teaching hospital. The project was completed in two phases. Phase I was completed in 1970 and cost $26 million. Half the cost came from federal funds and the remainder from state and local funds. Impressive among the four-building complex is the fourteen-story tower housing the School of Medicine on the west side of an inner courtyard between ABRAHAM FLEXNER Way and Muhammad Ali Blvd. On the north side of the courtyard, along Muhammad Ali Blvd., is the Health Sciences Building, housing laboratories where freshmen and sophomore medical students spend the bulk of their time learning the biological and scientific theories of MEDICINE and DENTISTRY. Across the courtyard to the south is the Kornhauser Library and Commons Building. To the east across Preston St. is the School of Dentistry, replacing the old school at the corner of Brook and Broadway.

Because of limited financial resources, a university teaching hospital was not included in Phase I construction. Recognizing the obsolescence of Louisville General Hospital and the need to expand health-care facilities, the citizens of Louisville and Jefferson County voted to support bond issues in 1965 and 1970 to replace General Hospital. In 1971 the university and the Louisville and Jefferson County BOARD OF HEALTH submitted a proposal for federal funds to replace the hospital. The application, along with another one in 1972, was approved but not funded. An appeal for assistance was made to the commonwealth of Kentucky for a university teaching hospital for the care of people of Louisville and western Kentucky. Since the university had entered the state system of higher education in 1970, some felt it was appropriate that funding for the teaching hospital be shifted to the state. Ultimately, two federal grants of $3 million each were obtained, but the bulk of the funding was appropriated by the state legislature.

The hospital complex included the concentrated care building, the ambulatory care building, the parking deck, and the institutional services building, all located at the corner of Jackson and Madison Streets. The concentrated care building was designed as a 380-bed hospital, equipped and staffed as a tertiary-care teaching hospital for the region. It played a leadership role in developing a system of regionalized health-care services, education, and research in the commonwealth. It also contains a trauma center and a helicopter landing site. The ambulatory care building handles patients through a primary care center and dozens of clinics.

Construction on the project, originally estimated to cost $63 million, began in 1976 and was completed in 1982. However, financial problems threatened the future of the hospital before it even opened. Skyrocketing inflation increased the cost of construction to more than $70 million. In 1979 the university took control of General Hospital and named it University of Louisville Hospital. The rising cost of health care caused operating expenses to rise by 61 percent between 1979 and 1982, while GOVERNMENT appropriations rose by only 41 percent.

With potential deficits of $5 million per year, the hospital faced financial disaster. By the end of 1981 the hospital began to turn away indigent patients for a brief period. In July 1982, after exploring all other options, the university issued a request for proposals to operate the hospital. Following seven months of intensive negotiations, the university, state, county, and city governments accepted a proposal by the HUMANA Co. In the agreement signed on January 27, 1983, Humana leased the medical complex for $6.5 million per year for four years with options to renew. Humana assumed complete financial risk, continued to care for the area's indigent patients, and turned over 20 percent of the pre-tax profits to the university. The name was changed to Humana Hospital University, and in the late 1980s to Humana Hospital UNIVERSITY OF LOUISVILLE. Despite predictions that the hospital would lose $10 million in the first year, it made a profit.

In 1993 Humana ended its hospital management and formed a spinoff company called Galen Healthcare Inc. to manage its HOSPITALS. Five months later, this company merged with Columbia Hospital Corp. of America, based in Fort Worth, Texas, to become Columbia Healthcare Corp. One month later, Columbia merged with Hospital Corp. of America, based in Nashville, Tennessee, to form Columbia/HCA. In January 1995 Columbia/HCA moved its headquarters from Louisville to Nashville, breaking a contract clause requiring that it keep its corporate headquarters in Jefferson County.

The university began searching for new management for the hospital, and in October 1995 University Medical Center Inc. was organized. The University Medical Center is a partnership between the University of Louisville, Jewish Hospital Health Care Services Inc., and Alliant Health System Inc. Alliant and Jewish pledged a total of $45 million for training and part of the cost of a planned medical research building. Under the leadership of Chief Executive Officer Pat Davis, the transition took place in February 1996. By July of that year, construction had begun on expanding the emergency department and trauma center. The $13 million plan expanded the emergency department and support services from twenty-one thousand to fifty-six thousand square feet.

Located next to the hospital on Jackson St. is the JAMES GRAHAM BROWN Cancer Center, built in 1981. Since 1973 the University Cancer Center had functioned as a special institute at the university. In 1977 Louisville civic leaders organized a cancer center corporation to construct a facility to expand the program. Funding came from private sources, half of it from the James Graham Brown Foundation. The center is run by the Regional Cancer Center Corp., a combined university-community board. The center pursues all three major areas of cancer activity: patient care, cancer research, and cancer education. The Henry Vogt Cancer Research Institute occupies the top two floors of the building.

The University of Louisville School of Allied Health Sciences, in the K Building, was established in 1977. The school offers undergraduate degrees in cardiopulmonary sciences, clinical laboratories sciences, cytotechnology, nuclear medicine technology, physical therapy, and radiologic technology. Masters programs are offered in expressive therapy and physical therapy. One of the youngest schools at the university is the NURSING school, which achieved full school status in 1979. Originally a division of the School of Medicine, it was housed in a wing of General Hospital. When that institution closed, the nursing program moved to the Carmichael Building. It moved into the K Building in 1996. The school of nursing offers both a bachelor and a master of science in nursing. Both programs are accredited by the National League for Nursing.

Other facilities in the University Medical Center include the Kentucky Lions Eye Center at the corner of Floyd St. and Muhammad Ali Blvd., housing the department of ophthalmology and visual sciences; the Kentucky Lions Eye Research Institute; the Rounsavall Eye Clinic; the Primary Care Eye Clinic; the University of Louisville Lions Eye Bank; and the Kentucky Lions Eye Foundation. Directly across Muhammad Ali Blvd. is the Medical-Dental Research Building, and the Research Resources Center, an animal care facility for research that uses animal models. The kidney disease center, located at the corner of Chestnut and Preston Streets, houses the division of nephrology of the Department of Medicine. These clinics provide treatment for patients with renal disease and hypertension, recipients of kidney transplants, and patients on chronic dialysis.

The Keller Child Psychiatry Center on Jackson St. studies and treats emotional disorders in families and children. At the corner of Floyd St. and Abraham Flexner Way is the Comprehensive Health Care Center for High-Risk Infants and Children, a model for comprehensive health care for children of high-risk mothers and those residing in low socioeconomic areas. The Child Evaluation Center, established in 1965, serves children with developmental disabilities such as mental retardation, learning disorders, birth defects, or genetic disorders. Operating as a nonprofit organization for the School of Medicine, the center's funds are provided by various local, state, and federal sources. Previously at 334 E Broadway, the center moved into its new location at Chestnut and Floyd Streets in 1996. The Irvin and HELEN ABELL Administration Center, located adjacent to the child evaluation center on Chestnut St., houses the administrative offices of the Health Sciences Center. At the corner of Preston and Gray Streets are the Medical-Dental Apartments, providing housing for medical and dental students and their families.

URBAN RENEWAL. The Urban Renewal & Community Development Agency of Louisville is the local public authority designated by the Louisville BOARD OF ALDERMEN to plan and carry out redevelopment projects. Although the agency was created through an ordinance passed by the aldermen, the basic powers and authorities of the agency are derived through an act of the Kentucky General Assembly (KRS 99.330 et seq.).

The agency is governed and guided by the

Urban Renewal Commission. Commission members are appointed from the general public by the mayor, with the consent of the aldermen. Each of the five members of the commission serves a four-year term and may be reappointed. The commissioners elect a chair and vice-chair at their annual meeting in December.

The statute grants numerous powers, authorities, and responsibilities to the urban renewal agency. Certain of these powers are unique to urban renewal and are not available to governmental agencies in general. Chief among these is the power to acquire property and then sell it to private individuals or entities for redevelopment. Traditionally, governments may only acquire property for an express public purpose such as construction of roads, PARKS, or other public facilities. The basic purpose of the agency is to redevelop vacant, abandoned, and blighted property. By doing so, the agency returns those properties to the tax rolls, thereby justifying the public's investment in the redevelopment process. The housing, jobs, and commercial opportunities created within redevelopment areas further add to the benefits derived from such redevelopment. Urban renewal has the power to purchase; lease; or obtain by option, gift, grant, eminent domain (condemnation), or otherwise real and personal property or any interest therein in order to carry out urban renewal redevelopment plans. Redevelopment plan documents must be reviewed and approved by numerous agencies (including the PLANNING AND ZONING Commission, Urban Renewal Commission, and the aldermen) before they take effect. Each redevelopment plan must include a listing of all properties proposed for acquisition in the project area and a description of all uses proposed within the redevelopment area. The redevelopment plan must conform to the master plan of the community, which has been adopted by the Planning and Zoning Commission.

In addition to acquiring property, the agency also has broad powers to sell, exchange, lease, or otherwise dispose of real property acquired for redevelopment purposes. Properties sold for redevelopment in urban renewal areas may be used only for those purposes set out in the redevelopment plan. In approving such transfers, the commission is not bound to sell such properties to the highest bidder nor for an appraised value. Rather, the agency is empowered to make transfers based on its judgment of which proposals provide the highest and best benefit for the community. Should developers fail to comply with the conditions and uses imposed by the commission or fail to meet the time frames fixed by the agency for initiating or completing proposed improvements, the commission has full authority to reclaim ownership of the property.

At its inception in 1959, urban renewal's total budget was 90 percent funded by a direct federal appropriation. The remaining 10 percent came from city matching funds. In 1980 direct federal funding for projects and staff ceased. Currently staffing is provided by the city through the Louisville Development Authority. Urban renewal activities are funded with the approval of the Board of Aldermen as part of the regular annual budgeting process—typically with Community Development Block Grant funds.

The history of urban renewal in Louisville has been marked by two separate and distinct eras: 1959–80 and 1980–present. The eras are distinguished by markedly different funding sources, styles of projects, and impacts.

Urban Renewal 1959–80. In 1957 the voters approved a $5 million bond issue that paved the way for the start of the various urban renewal projects. This era was characterized by large-scale projects, blanket demolition and clearance of the redevelopment areas, and extended periods in which parcels sat vacant. It also dealt with the worst of the blighted and slum conditions, often redeveloping areas that had no streets, no sewers, and no running water.

Southwick Redevelopment Project. Approved in 1960, this project proposed residential and light industrial development for a 149-acre area bounded by Dumesnil, SHAWNEE Park, Thirty-fourth St., and Bohne Ave. Perhaps the worst slum area in Louisville at that time, the area blossomed under a federal grant of some $4.1 million. After redevelopment, the plan ultimately produced parks, schools, hundreds of units of multi- and single-family housing, and a number of light industrial uses.

East Downtown Renewal Area. Approved in 1962, it is bounded by Second, BROADWAY, Jackson, and MARKET Streets. Officially known as the Medical Center, the area includes numerous medical campuses, hospitals, and facilities of the UNIVERSITY OF LOUISVILLE, and motels and office buildings. Federal funds exceeding $16 million made redevelopment of this 215-acre site possible.

West Downtown Renewal Area. Also approved in 1962, this area was known as the Civic Center Project because of numerous public buildings in its 316 acres. Bounded by Broadway, Sixth, Fifteenth, and Market Streets, the project area contained many dilapidated commercial and residential structures. The implementation of the project replaced those structures with city, county, state, and federal office buildings; rebuilt commercial and light industrial sites; and more than fifteen hundred residential units. Unfortunately, the project also demolished the old Walnut district, the main cultural and entertainment district serving Louisville's African American community.

Southwick II: Immediately adjacent to the original Southwick project and approved in 1965, this 38-acre tract is bounded by Thirty-fourth St., railroad tracks, Thirty-second St., and Young Ave. The redeveloped land was used for a parochial school, additional land for an existing church, and new single-family residences.

OLD LOUISVILLE Restoration Area and Old Louisville II: Approved in 1966 and 1968 respectively, these projects enabled the University of Louisville to more than double its campus area by expanding north to Avery St., renamed Cardinal Blvd. Comprising a total of 329 acres bounded by I-65, Eastern Pkwy. Hill St., and the CSX railroad tracks, the area also saw significant housing rehabilitation and industrial expansion and growth.

Riverfront Project. Intended for commercial and public uses, this forty-two-acre site was designated for redevelopment in 1968. Although one of the smallest redevelopment areas, it may be one of the best known, as it is the location of the GALT HOUSE, Galt House East, the Plaza-Belvedere, One RIVERFRONT PLAZA, Kentucky Center for the Arts, National City Tower, Hyatt Regency Hotel, Commonwealth Convention Center, and other buildings.

Watterson Model Town. Granted to urban renewal by the federal GOVERNMENT in 1971, this ninety-eight-acre site of the WORLD WAR I Nichols Army Hospital was cleared and set for residential development. It is now the site of a large park with fishing lake, high-rise elderly housing, and a new single-family housing development. It is at the intersection of Manslick Rd. and March Blvd.

Urban Renewal 1980–Present. Projects in this era are funded by specific appropriations through the Board of Aldermen. While large areas might be encompassed by the redevelopment plan, only a fraction of the properties included would typically be scheduled for acquisition or demolition. Properties that meet current code or support viable businesses would remain; this could best be described as an infill process. Rehabilitation of historically significant properties is a strong priority, particularly in primarily residential projects.

Urban renewal was used by the city in 1989 to acquire STANDIFORD, HIGHLAND PARK, and PRESTONIA NEIGHBORHOODS to expand Standiford Field (LOUISVILLE INTERNATIONAL AIRPORT). The neighborhoods were declared "blighted." When residents contested the term and filed suit, the Kentucky Supreme Court ruled the plan illegal. The lawsuit was settled for $6.2 million, but an agreement permitted the airport's expansion to move forward.

Galleria Project. Approved in late 1980, the GALLERIA was the first Urban Renewal project to include an Urban Development Action Grant (UDAG) in its funding. In addition to the new construction, remodeling of the historic KAUFMAN-STRAUS and Republic Buildings was included.

Station Park. Urban Renewal's first industrial park, this project is bounded by Broadway, Ninth, Fifteenth, and Kentucky Streets. Relocation of the deteriorated residential incursions allowed industry in the area to expand and new industrial users to locate there. Approved in 1981, the project was fully occupied in 1988.

Phoenix Hill. Approved in 1982 and also known as the Park-Clarksdale project, the area is roughly bounded by Muhammad Ali Blvd., Chestnut, Clay, and Baxter. More than three hundred new and renovated housing units were created, including numerous amenities for the residents. A major reconstruction of Chestnut St. routed traffic away from the residential core.
Broadway Area. Phases I-A and II-A of this project include Third St., Broadway, Fifth, and Chestnut Streets. In addition to the construction of Crescent Centre housing, the project resulted in the renovation of the Brown Hotel and the LOUISVILLE PALACE THEATRE.
Medical Center. Passed in 1985, the plan for this two-block area directly east of University Hospital called for the development of facilities to support the medical and PUBLIC HEALTH uses.
Orange Drive. Principally funded by a bond issue from JEFFERSON COUNTY FISCAL COURT, this project was approved in 1987. Bounded by I-65, Fern Valley Rd., and Louisville International Airport, the 170-acre site was developed as an airport-related industrial park. It is now the site of the UPS next-day air and overseas shipment hubs.
200 Block of Fourth Ave.. Covering the west side of Fourth Ave. from Market to Jefferson Streets, this project was a further step in the rejuvenation of Fourth as Louisville's Golden Spine. Approved in 1988, it is the site of the tallest office building in Kentucky, the Aegon Tower. An open space and plaza, along with a parking garage and retail space, complete the project area.
Parkland Business District. Site of civil unrest in the late 1960s, this area along Twenty-eighth St. from Virginia Ave. to Dumesnil St. remained largely vacant until the passage of this plan in 1989. The area now houses the only African American–owned full-service grocery store in Kentucky. In addition, a medical and dental center and more than forty-five new housing units fill once-vacant sites. More than thirteen thousand square feet of retail and commercial use have been attracted to the project.
Russell. This housing infill project was approved in 1990. Bounded by Fifteenth St., Broadway, Twenty-first St., and Congress Alley, the area is ultimately slated for more than nine hundred units of new and remodeled housing. Most will be built on once-vacant and abandoned lots. More than five hundred units had been completed by 1998.
Station Park South. A successor project to Station Park, this redevelopment plan was approved in 1991. Extending from Kentucky to Oak Streets and bounded by Tenth and Thirteenth Streets, the area was fully occupied in 1997. Some sixty-seven families were relocated into decent, safe, and sanitary housing out of the project area. New capital investment in the area exceeded $10 million, and more than four hundred jobs were created.

One of Louisville's most significant urban analysts is Grady Clay, journalist, consultant, author, and lecturer. Since the forties Clay's constructive and provocative urban analysis of Louisville has earned him a reputation as an inspired thinker and gadfly. In a short publication, *Alleys* (1978), Clay characteristically examined origins and new uses of Louisville's hidden resource. Clay proposed visions of *alleys* converted to commons areas or preserved by thorny rose cover to prevent dumping. Among other strategies, he saw alleys as doubling commercial frontages and facilitating rerouted traffic.

Clay arrived in Louisville from New York City in 1939 to report for the *LOUISVILLE TIMES* and later for the *COURIER-JOURNAL* as its real estate editor and subsequently became its first urban affairs editor, a position he held until 1966. In 1961 he also assumed responsibility as editor of the internationally regarded *Landscape Architecture*, moving it from Boston to Louisville. He continued with it until retirement in 1984, when he became a consulting editor specializing in environmental and urban affairs. He is the author of several books including *Close Up: How to Read the American City* (1973), *Right Before Your Eyes: Penetrating the Urban Environment* (1987), and *Real Places: An Unconventional Guide to America's Generic Landscape* (1994). Born November 5, 1916, in Ann Arbor, Mich., to Dr. Grady E. and Eleanor (Solomon) Clay, he grew up in Atlanta and was educated at Emory University and Columbia University, and was a Nieman Fellow at Harvard. Clay and his first wife, Nanine (Hilliard), raised three sons. He and his second wife, Judith McCandless, reside in CRESCENT HILL.

Like Clay, pondering the influence of urban renewal, Dave Nakdimen, writing in *Leo,* said that urban renewal also built streets and sewers in Old Louisville and housing in Newburg and Berrytown. He quotes former Urban Renewal Commission chairman Clark Fenimore, saying urban renewal did a lot of good for downtown Louisville, and he gave it an overall efficiency grade of 70 percent. But he felt 30 percent of the projects should not have been undertaken, including the money spent on Fourth St. But interestingly enough, Nakdimen pondered what happened to his barber's shop on Preston St.

See *Leo*, Oct. 14, 1998.

James Braun

URSULINE ACADEMY OF THE IMMACULATE CONCEPTION. The Ursuline Academy of the Immaculate Conception was founded in Louisville at 806 E Chestnut St. by the Ursuline Sisters in 1858. Sister Mary Salesia Reitmeier, the superior, turned her attention to the principal goal of the school, the Christian education of young girls.

The boarding school first opened in 1859 and the day school in 1860, and both grew rapidly. The CIVIL WAR brought hardships when students were called home, and the sisters suffered from scarcity of food and high prices. It was June 1867 when Miss Anna Kotter finished the twelfth grade and thus became the first graduate of Ursuline Academy.

As enrollment increased over the following decades, the curriculum changed to meet the needs. During the last years of the nineteenth century such skills as knitting, crocheting, and embroidery were taught along with English, French, German, Latin, Spanish, and physical education. By the early years of the twentieth century commercial and music and science classes were added. In the 1950s a five-track curriculum plan was implemented, including

The original Sacred Heart Academy building on Lexington Road.

general foundation, preparation for college, pre-NURSING, courses in the fine arts, and secretarial and clerical training. Enrollment peaked that decade only to begin a decline in the mid-1960s. Reluctantly the Ursuline Sisters made the decision to phase out the academy. The last class graduated in 1972.

See *Annals, Ursuline Sisters 1858–1972;* Helen M. Schweri, *Under His Mighty Power* (Louisville 1983); *1997 All Years Reunion & U.A. Arch Dedication* (Louisville 1997).

M. Concetta Waller

URSULINE COLLEGE. Ursuline College at 3105 Lexington Rd. was an heir of a tradition of more than four hundred years from St. Angela Merici of a system of education centered upon the preservation of the family through the Christian education of girls and young women. It had its beginning in the resident and day school known as Ursuline Academy of the Immaculate Conception founded in 1858. The academy was incorporated by an act of the Kentucky General Assembly on January 12, 1864, as the Ursuline Society and Academy of Education.

The Motherhouse of the Ursuline nuns was at Ursuline Academy on Chestnut St. near Shelby St. until 1877, when it was moved to Lexington Rd. A novitiate for young sisters was established, and Sacred Heart Academy (resident and day school) was opened for other students. The expanding program of education made it increasingly apparent that an institution of higher learning was needed to facilitate the training of members of the Ursuline community.

Mother Mary Theodore Guethoff, builder and educator, began the planning of a junior college. Sacred Heart Junior College and Normal School opened on September 11, 1921. Guethoff had as her guide and coworker Sister Mary Dominica Hettinger, an Ursuline educator who was named the first academic dean of the new college and normal school. In 1938 Ursuline College supplanted and absorbed Sacred Heart Junior College. Miss Gertrude Gilreath and eight Ursuline Sisters received the first baccalaureate degrees from the college the following June. Brescia Hall, a laboratory and classroom building, was constructed in 1940. Later expansions include Marian Hall, opened in 1956, Julianne Hall in 1962, and the administration building in 1963. The education department added training in speech therapy, special education, and Montessori method. The Parents Association was formed with J. Harry Quirico the first chairman. On August 12, 1962, Sister Mary Concetta Waller was named the first president of Ursuline College. The policy was thus discontinued of considering the Superior of the Ursuline community as the automatically appointed president of the college.

In 1963 the Southern Association of Colleges and Schools renewed its accreditation as a four-year liberal arts college. In 1963 the college became a member of the Kentucky Independent College Foundation. After Waller suffered a serious illness, Sister Mary Angelice Seibert was named acting president. She became president on June 1, 1965.

To meet the changing times, Ursuline joined with BELLARMINE COLLEGE for men in 1964 to explore the possibility of inter-institutional cooperation. This four-year period of study and experimentation resulted in a coordination program that ended in the merger of the two colleges as Bellarmine-Ursuline College in 1968 and as Bellarmine College in 1971.

See Helen M. Schweri, *Under His Mighty Power* (Louisville 1983).

M. Concetta Waller

URSULINE MOTHERHOUSE. Ursuline Motherhouse, 3115 Lexington Rd., is "home" to the Ursuline Sisters of the Immaculate Conception of Louisville, whose lives are dedicated to a contemplative love of God and a resulting openness and eagerness to serve the needs of others. This was the charism of the foundress, St. Angela Merici, about 1600 A.D., and is the charism of the Ursuline Sisters today.

The Louisville Ursuline Motherhouse was established by Mother Salesia Reitmeier, with her two companions, Mother Pia Schoenhofer and Sister Maximilian Zwinger, all from Straubing, Germany. They answered the request of Bishop MARTIN JOHN SPALDING for a group of sisters to teach the children of St. Martin's (St. Martin of Tours) School, and in addition they opened URSULINE ACADEMY OF THE IMMACULATE CONCEPTION in 1858. The academy flourished; and in 1877 the boarding school, which had opened in 1859, was moved to an old Italianate red brick house on a small farm on what is now Lexington Rd. and was named Sacred Heart Academy. The first graduate from Sacred Heart Academy was Sabrina Orrick of Canton, Mississippi. On September 1, 1894, the novitiate was moved to this location. A new building was erected in 1903.

On December 8, 1917, a new Motherhouse was dedicated by Rt. Rev. Denis O'Donahue, D.D. on the feast of the Immaculate Conception. The ceremonies were private. The tem perature that day was the lowest and the snow the deepest in Kentucky's history. The administrative activities connected with the Motherhouse were transferred from the Shelby and Chestnut St. building to the new central house on Lexington Rd. Here also postulants and novices were trained. The Motherhouse Chapel became the scene of investitures, professions of vows, retreats, conferences, election of superiors, funerals, and the daily spiritual exercises of the sisters.

On Friday, April 19, 1918, the new Sacred Heart Academy building was reduced to ruins by fire. Parts of the new Motherhouse were converted to the use of the school. A new Sacred Heart Academy was dedicated by the Rt. Rev. Bishop John A. Floersh on May 31, 1926.

Although primarily interested in education, on October 6, 1918, fifteen Sisters went to CAMP ZACHARY TAYLOR on the outskirts of Louisville to serve as nurses during the influenza epidemic of WORLD WAR I, which struck the military camp hard. More and more requests were made for Sisters to teach in the schools. Parallel with these requests were applications of more young women to join the congregation and the need for the preparation of teachers. Campus programs and buildings were upgraded. Since Ursulines are deeply devoted to education, the vacation months were devoted to summer sessions. Sisters attended classes at URSULINE COLLEGE, while other members of the congregation pursued studies toward advanced degrees at universities in both the east and the west. The first Catholic Teachers Institute, Diocese of Louisville, Aug. 27-29, 1925, was conducted by the Rev. George Johnson, Professor of Education at Catholic University. One of the outcomes of the institute was the adoption of uniform diocesan textbooks.

Adversity was not foreign to the peaceful campus, and the members of the congregation suffered the loss of family members during the wars. The buildings were opened to refugees during the 1937 flood. The chapel, campus buildings, and trees were damaged by the April 3, 1974, tornado. On Sunday, January 11, 1976, fire was discovered in the west wing of the Motherhouse. The sisters had just left chapel and gone to the dining room for breakfast. The quick action of the sisters living in the administration building and Sacred Heart Academy Convent helped evacuate the building as the firemen were arriving. Two wings of the building were closed for a year. The Sisters of Charity of Nazareth opened the new wing of Nazareth Home, the Sisters of Mercy; and the Sisters of the Good Shepherd provided care until arrangements could be made for bringing the groups together at Julianne Hall and one wing of Nazareth Home. Times were also given to celebration of jubilees of members and of the congregation. The silver and golden jubilees of the congregation were celebrated at the original Motherhouse. The diamond jubilee, the centenary, and the 125th jubilee celebrations took place at the Lexington Rd. Motherhouse.

In addition, the Ursuline Community celebrated the 400th and the 425th jubilees of the Company of St. Ursula with an elaborate pageant written by Rev. Daniel A. Lord, S.J. The 450th celebration was coordinated worldwide to begin simultaneously by sending a message from time zone to time zone calling members to join a vesper service of thanksgiving.

The Ursuline Sisters have developed a comprehensive plan to reaffirm their mission and to focus on strategic goals for the Ursuline Campus schools, which include Sacred Heart Academy, Sacred Heart Model School, Ursuline Child Development Center, Ursuline Montessori School, and the Ursuline School of Music and Drama. The Ursuline Campus

Schools have been incorporated as Ursuline Campus Schools Inc. Each summer the sisters gather at the Motherhouse for Community Days, which provides time to pray, plan, and celebrate.

The climax of these days is the Missioning Service. Challenged by the Gospel message and the example of St. Angela, their foundress, the Ursuline Sisters are sent to fulfill the call to teach Christian living. They have served in twenty-three states and four foreign countries. In 1996 the Ursulines were teaching in preschool, elementary and secondary schools, and colleges, and are on parish and diocesan staffs in sixteen states and in Peru, South America.

See Martha Buser, *Also in Your Midst* (Green Bay, Wisc., 1990); Helen M. Schweri, *Under His Mighty Power* (Louisville 1983); Mary deLourdes Gohmann, *Chosen Arrows* (New York 1957).

M. Concetta Waller

UTICA, INDIANA. The town of Utica began as a crossing point for ferry boats on the Ohio River. In 1794 James Noble Wood and his wife settled on seven hundred acres of farmland on the OHIO RIVER, about eight miles north of Jeffersonville. There, opposite HARRODS CREEK, Kentucky, Judge Wood established a ferry service. To accommodate livestock he lashed two canoes together and transported the animals with their hind feet in one canoe and their fore feet in another. The dangerous proximity of the Jeffersonville ferry to the FALLS OF THE OHIO gave the future town a commercial advantage.

On August 9, 1816, the town of Utica was platted. The original survey contained 220 lots, each measuring 100 square feet. Five of these lots were set aside for public purposes, namely a public square and a public cemetery. In 1831 the township of Utica was established.

Some of the earliest settlers of the town, among them Judge John Miller, who also was engaged in the ferry business, had emigrated from Utica, New York. They thus named their new Indiana town in commemoration of their earlier home.

In 1833 the Indiana Gazetteer noted that Utica was "a pleasant, thriving post-village in Clark County" with a POPULATION of about two hundred people. By 1854 Utica had grown to over four hundred people, with several stores, a new schoolhouse (the original schoolhouse was built in 1819), several places for religious services of various denominations, and other amenities such as an occasional drinking establishment.

The lime-burning industry flourished in Utica from 1818 through 1907. Burned lime is a principal component of cement, and the various types of limestone belonging to the Niagara epoch were in abundance and readily accessible in and around Utica. The lime industry was the life of Utica for years, and the town was justly famous from Pennsylvania to Louisiana for its product. Although the industry had moved to other areas by 1908, the Utica Lime Co. retained limited operations there until 1928.

More locally, truck gardens also flourished in the area from 1890 to about 1940, supplying Louisville and environs with large quantities of fresh produce. In July 1940 as our nation prepared for WORLD WAR II, large areas of prime farmland became the site of the Indiana Army Ammunition Depot and, as a consequence, commercial AGRICULTURE declined in the Utica area.

In its nearly two-hundred-year history, Utica has been inundated many times by Ohio River FLOODS. Since 1870, when official records were first kept, Utica has suffered thirty-one damaging floods. The U.S. Corps of Engineers calculates floodwater to be damaging to the town of Utica when the Ohio River reaches an elevation of 437 feet above mean sea level at the McAlpine Upper Gauge. In 1937 the Ohio River rose twenty-three feet above that standard; in 1945 it was thirteen; and in the years 1882, 1883, 1884, 1907, 1913, 1933, 1943, 1948, 1962, 1964, and 1997 it rose between three and thirteen feet above this standard.

In 1990 the population was 411 and was 398 in 1996. Since 1928 the population has hovered fairly consistently around the four hundred mark. The town remains vulnerable to flood and faces the prospect of suburban gentrification.

See Lewis C. Baird, *Baird's History of Clark County* (Indianapolis 1909); Henry and Kate Ford, *History of the Falls Cities and Their Counties* (Cleveland 1882); Gerald O. Haffner, *A Brief, Informal History of Clark County, Indiana* (New Albany, Ind., 1985); Margaret Sweeney, *Fact, Fiction and Folklore of Southern Indiana* (New York 1967).

VALLEY OF THE DRUMS. The A.L. Taylor superfund cleanup site, popularly known as the "Valley of the Drums," is in BULLITT COUNTY about fifteen miles south of Louisville. From 1967 to 1978 the hazardous-waste dump, run by Arthur Taylor, became the site of thousands of rusting, bulging, and leaking drums that had been piled into a small hollow just over the Jefferson County line. Taylor also used the site to dump CHEMICALS, clean old drums for reuse, and as a junkyard until his death in 1978. By that time it was one of the most polluted sites in the state. Approximately seventeen thousand drums of hazardous chemicals, including dioxin, volatile organic compounds (VOCs), and polychlorinated biphenyls (PCBs), were found stored underground and on the surface. Of those, four thousand were found to be leaking hazardous waste into Wilson Creek, a tributary of Pond Creek, which feeds into the Salt River. The twenty-three-acre site was listed on the National Priorities List in 1983 and became the top priority in Kentucky for clean-up.

Supervised by the U.S. Environmental Protection Agency, the drums, contaminated surface water, and sludge were removed and a clay cap was installed in the ground to reduce further contamination. Cleanup was completed in 1987, and the site was finally removed from the National Priorities List in 1996, the first completed cleanup in Kentucky under the Superfund Program. Established in 1980, the program locates, investigates, and cleans up the worst hazardous waste sites throughout the United States in an attempt to eliminate health and environmental threats.

See *Courier-Journal*, Nov. 25, 1979, April 23, 1987.

John S. Gillig

VALLEY STATION. Suburb in southwestern Jefferson County centered around the intersection of Valley Station Rd. and U.S. 60/31W (Dixie Hwy.). Few settlers inhabited the area during the frontier era because of swampy conditions, but improved drainage in the nineteenth century prompted establishment of farms. The stagecoach route between Nashville and Louisville brought additional settlement, with the center of town developing near the local tollgate along the old Salt River Turnpike (Dixie Hwy.). Farmers in the area wanting to avoid the twenty-cent toll constructed a bypass that still exists, in a modified version, as Deering Rd.

By 1861 the region was known as the Meadowlawn Precinct. However, the name was changed to Valley Station in 1873 because of the community's position in the valley next to the Muldraugh Ridge and to prepare for the arrival of the Elizabethtown & Paducah Railroad (later the Illinois Central, then Paducah & Louisville) and its station in 1874. While the railroad brought increasing numbers into the area, the extension of the interurban line in 1904 down to Orell advanced the POPULATION further.

The mixed residential and commercial community experienced its largest growth during the 1950s and 1960s because of the relatively inexpensive cost of land and its proximity to both Louisville and FORT KNOX. The population grew at such a rapid pace that local students had to resort to double shifts to attend the undersized Valley High School, which was built in 1937 and had major additions in 1953 and in 1973.

Local landmarks include the National Vietnam Memorial; the Sun Valley Park and Golf Course; the Meadow Lawn Baptist Church; and Riverside, the FARNSLEY-MOREMEN LANDING, a restored house (built in the 1830s) and dock space on the OHIO RIVER.

See *A Place in Time: The Story of Louisville's Neighborhoods* (Louisville 1989).

VAN ARSDALE, BERTRAM CALVIN (b Louisville, March 7, 1908; d Louisville, January 22, 1979). Jefferson County judge. He was the son of Herbert and Sara Belle (Campbell) Van Arsdale. He graduated from LOUISVILLE MALE HIGH SCHOOL in 1925 and attended the University of Louisville for four years before receiving his bachelor's degree from the UNIVERSITY OF KENTUCKY in 1930. In 1941 he began practicing law after graduating *cum laude* from the JEFFERSON SCHOOL OF LAW.

Van Arsdale, who was known as "Pappy," served as secretary to Mayor NEVILLE MILLER in 1936–37. From 1937 until 1942 he was secretary and chief examiner for the Civil Service Board. He was probate commissioner of Jefferson County Court from January 1950 until June 1954, when he was chosen by Gov. Lawrence W. Wetherby to serve as county judge. He was appointed to replace ROBERT T. BURKE Jr. when Burke resigned after less than three months in office. Burke had been appointed by Wetherby to replace newly elected judge George Wetherby, who was killed in an automobile accident. A Democrat, Van Arsdale served from June 15, 1954, until December 31, 1961.

Van Arsdale was elected county judge in November 1957, defeating Republican Freeman L. Robinson, a former state senator and representative, by 18,222 votes (73,269 to 55,047). Van Arsdale was reelected in 1957, defeating Republican Charles F. Gaines by 6,740 votes. Van Arsdale chose not to run again in 1961.

During his administration Van Arsdale was responsible for passage of a county occupational tax, which increased the budget from $8.5 million in the late 1950s to $60 million by the 1980s. He was also involved in an unsuccessful bid by the city to annex developed fringe areas along the city's boundary. Van Arsdale, along with Mayor ANDREW BROADDUS, appointed the seven-member Local Government Improvement Committee that developed the Mallon Plan for extending the city's boundaries to include several of these developed suburban fringe NEIGHBORHOODS. While city residents approved the plan by fourteen thousand votes, the county defeated the measure by a two-to-one margin, and it failed. Van Arsdale also served as the Democratic representative of the two-member Jefferson County Board of Elections from 1961 until one month before his death. He also helped to draw up the legislation for the Jefferson County Police Merit Board and was a member from 1952 to 1953.

Van Arsdale married Elizabeth Dove Attkisson of Louisville on July 18, 1930. The couple, who lived at 211 Chadwick Rd., had two children, Ellen and Herbert Van Arsdale. He is buried in CAVE HILL CEMETERY.

See *Courier-Journal*, Jan. 23, 1979; George H. Yater, *Two Hundred Years at the Falls of the Ohio* (Louisville 1987).

VANCE, WILLIAM RANNELL (b 1806; d 1885). Mayor. Little is known of his early life, although he was a practicing attorney in Louisville. He was elected to the state house of representatives three times—1836, 1840, and 1841—and was a state senator in 1843–44.

Vance, a member of the WHIG PARTY, was mayor of Louisville from May 10, 1847, through May 13, 1850. He defeated two other candidates, garnering 1,053 votes compared to his closest rival, Turner of the Locofoco Party, who received 687 votes.

Vance also served as deputy marshal in 1845. He was elected a justice of the county court of Jefferson County on June 25, 1836, and served until he became mayor. On June 1, 1848, Vance conveyed a tract of land owned by the city on Cave Hill Farm to the Cave Hill Cemetery Co.

He was married to Ella Field, who died in 1869. Vance's children were Samuel D., Hester, Eleanor, Anna, and Abner. He later lived in Columbus, Kentucky.

See Lewis and Richard H. Collins, *History of Kentucky*, 2 vols. (Covington 1874; reprinted, 1966).

VANDERCOOK, MARGARET (WOMACK) (b Louisville, January 12, 1877; d New York City, April 5, 1936). Author. Margaret Vandercook was a daughter of J.M. Womack, who was clerk to Louisville's mayor. She was educated in public and private schools. After graduating from high school, Vandercook worked on the staff of the *Louisville Post*. In her twenties she became a member of the Author's Club, which was known for writers such as Alice

Hegan Rice, George Madden Martin, and Annie Fellows Johnston.

In 1900 she married editor John Vandercook of New York City. Following their marriage the couple spent six years living in London, where John worked as the manager for a press association. After the death of her husband in 1908, Vandercook began writing in New York City, where she spent the rest of her life. She was one of the authors of the Ranch Girls series, *Ranch Girls at Rainbow* (1911) and *Ranch Girls' Pot of Gold* (1912), and other works for girls such as *Girl Scouts* and *Campfire Girls* in the 1910s. Vandercook also published novels including *The Love of Ambrose* (1913) and *The Lady of Desire and Other Imagery Portraits* (1930). Her books and articles were well received but had limited national attention.

See William Ward, *A Literary History of Kentucky* (Knoxville 1988); *Courier-Journal*, Jan. 12, 1920; *Who is Who in America* (Chicago 1920).

VANHOOSE, RICHARD (b Anderson County, Kentucky, July 10, 1910; d Louisville, October 19, 1998). Educator. Upon graduation from Frankfort High School in 1928 VanHoose went to Georgetown College, where he received a bachelor's degree in 1935. In 1939 he earned a master's degree in education administration from the University of Kentucky. In 1955 Georgetown College recognized his contributions to education by conferring upon him an honorary LL.D. degree.

VanHoose began his professional career as a teacher in the Frankfort schools in 1933, where, in 1939, he became principal of the Second Street Elementary School. Moving to Jefferson County, he became superintendent of the Anchorage Independent School District in 1943 and then served as principal of Valley High School in 1946. In the late 1940s VanHoose became assistant superintendent of Jefferson County schools before being named superintendent to replace the retiring Orville J. Stivers in 1950.

VanHoose led the Jefferson County school system for nearly a quarter of a century until his retirement in 1974. During VanHoose's tenure, about 100 new schools were built, and the system expanded from 570 teachers and 16,000 students in 1950 to 4,500 teachers and 90,000 students in 1974. VanHoose developed and broadened special programs including vocational and adult education, advanced-placement honors, and youth development to rehabilitate dropout students.

To let elementary children advance at their own pace, he initiated non-graded classes. Under his leadership the schools implemented the use of educational television and expanded library services. In order to establish better communication links between the schools and the public, VanHoose supported the publication of a monthly bulletin, *Your Jefferson County Schools*. The issues of the merger of Louisville and Jefferson County Schools and desegregation were among the most important topics of education in the 1970s. VanHoose perceived the merger would result in a huge, inflexible system. In 1972 the merger plan failed in the General Assembly, and VanHoose was blamed for lobbying against it. He was concerned that many teachers would be transferred to predominantly black city schools if the plan were adopted. On the question of desegregation, while VanHoose did not oppose it, he opposed cross-district busing to integrate schools. In 1975 the Jefferson County Board of Education voted to name its administrative building at 3332 Newburg Rd. the VanHoose Education Center.

VanHoose is buried in the Frankfort Cemetery. He was survived by his wife, the former Clarice Isaacs; a daughter, Marie V. Sayre; and a son, Warren E. VanHoose.

See *Courier-Journal*, Oct. 20, 1998; *Louisville Times*, Oct. 7, 1972; *Report Card*, Jefferson County Public Schools, vol. 4 (Dec. 1974); clippings from the Jefferson County Public Schools Archives.

VAN WINKLE, JULIAN P., SR. "PAPPY" (b Danville, Kentucky, March 22, 1874; d Louisville, February 16, 1965). Distiller. Van Winkle was the son of John S. and Louisa Thomas (Dillon) Van Winkle. His father once served as Kentucky secretary of state. Pappy, as he was known, graduated from Centre College in 1894 and many years later received its Distinguished Alumnus Award. He was married to Kate Smith. They had two children, Mary Chenault and Julian Proctor.

Van Winkle was best known as cofounder and president of the Stitzel-Weller Distillery. He parlayed slow-cooked mash and a keen promotional sense into a national reputation as a highly successful whiskey maker. Stitzel-Weller was a family firm, which included Pappy's son, Julian Jr., and son-in-law, Charles King McClure.

At the time of his retirement in October 1964, Van Winkle was the oldest active distiller in the nation. He is buried in Cave Hill Cemetery.

Julian P. Van Winkle III

VEECH, ANNIE S. (b Jefferson County, Kentucky, 1871; d Louisville, July 10, 1957). Physician. The youngest child of Richard Snowden and Mary (Nichols) Veech, she graduated from Miss Hampton's School for Girls in Louisville in 1890 and traveled extensively throughout the world for the next fifteen years. In 1905 she entered the Women's Medical College of Pennsylvania and received her M.D. degree in 1909. Dr. Veech then worked at the Women's Hospital in Philadelphia from 1909 to 1911. The following year she became a staff member of the Student Hospital at the State Normal College (now Longwood College) in Farmville, Virginia. Veech returned to Louisville in 1913 and entered private practice. During World War I, she was with the Red Cross as a civilian physician in Blois, France.

Veech then served as public health inspector in the Louisville public schools and helped to organize the state Bureau of Child Hygiene in 1921. In 1922 she became the director of the bureau in Frankfort. Dr. Veech returned to Louisville in 1937 to head the Louisville Department of Health (later Louisville-Jefferson County Health Department), and in 1939, she was a participant in the White House conference on "Children in Democracy."

After the Kentucky Department of Health was reorganized in 1948, Veech was made director of the child hygiene program. At her request, she became associate director and consultant in 1949 and remained as such until her retirement the next year. Even after retiring, she continued the weekly lectures and workshops for mothers that she had begun in 1943. A staunch advocate of breast-feeding for infants, Dr. Veech also emphasized the health benefits of adequate rest for mothers and their young children. She was a member of the American Academy of Pediatrics, the Kentucky State Medical Association, and the American Medical Association. Dr. Veech is buried in Cave Hill Cemetery.

VENCOR INC. National long-term healthcare network based in Louisville. In 1984 Rockcastle County, Kentucky, Hospital board member Bill Bailey and respiratory therapist Michael Barr approached accountant-lawyer William Bruce Lunsford with the idea of dedicating hospitals to the care of patients who required longer stays due to head injuries, cardiopulmonary disorders, spinal-cord damage, or other prolonged difficulties.

Lunsford was born November 11, 1947, in Kenton County, Kentucky, to Amos and Billie Lunsford and grew up on a farm. A 1969 graduate of the University of Kentucky and in 1974 of the Salmon P. Chase School of Law, Lunsford joined the administration of Kentucky governor John Y. Brown in 1979 as deputy commerce secretary, swiftly moving up to become commerce secretary from 1980 to 1983.

He returned to Louisville, researched the idea's practicality, and struck a deal to start Vencare Inc. within ninety days of the first meeting with Bailey and Barr.

The fledgling company was based upon the idea of taking people who required average stays of more than twenty-five days in hospitals' costly intensive care units and placing them in a hospital specifically devoted to this type of patient. By focusing on long-term care, the hospitals were eligible for different funding under Medicare and would receive payments based upon actual cost and not flat fees, which was less profitable.

The investors purchased their first hospital in LaGrange, Indiana, in 1985 and within three months had turned the struggling clinic into a moneymaker. The following year, the company leased twenty-eight beds from the Sandwich Community Hospital near Chicago, which rapidly filled with patients. After these first two successes, the investors decided that not only was there a market but that rapid expansion would help solidify the company's niche in that market. During the next two years, Vencare added hospitals in St. Petersburg, Miami, Tampa, and Fort Lauderdale, Florida. The increased number of beds helped the company weather the Medicare Catastrophic Act, which Congress enacted in late 1988. The act allowed Medicare to pay a greater portion of long-term care charges and thus removed some of the more generous payments from the private insurance companies. Along with the news of the act's repeal, the following year saw the company's name change to Vencor Inc. and its initial public offering on the NASDAQ exchange.

In 1990 the company expanded westward and added hospitals in Fort Worth, Phoenix, and Denver, along with Atlanta. That year also marked the first time Vencor appeared on *Forbes* magazine's "200 Best Small Companies in America" list and on *Inc.* magazine's "Fastest Growing Small Public Companies" list. By 1992 Vencor was no longer thought of as a small regional company, as its operations had expanded to eleven states and included nineteen hospitals that the company owned or leased. By the end of 1992, Vencor had not only joined the New York Stock Exchange but had also become Kentucky's fastest-growing company over the preceding five years, growing an average of 111.6 percent each year. In 1993 the company continued to expand its ownership of hospitals, which totaled twenty-nine in thirteen states by the end of the year. It also entered other fields of the health-care sector by purchasing a minority ownership in Colorado MEDtech Inc., a manufacturer of ventilator filters; by acquiring the Vermont-based company Second Foundation Inc. (Ventech Systems Inc.), whose medical-information software was eventually installed in the hospital's bedside monitors and cut paperwork by 93 percent; and by starting the Vencare contract services program, which supplied assistance to NURSING homes and other clinics. The following year saw the company continue its expansion in the health-care field with the purchase of a subacute service provider and the acquisition of the assets of a respiratory service provider and a management service provider for hospital cardiopulmonary departments.

In 1995 Vencor opened its first hospital in Louisville, which also served as a training facility, on the site of the former St. Anthony Hospital on Barret Ave. It also acquired hospice service providers in Indiana and Ohio, respiratory service providers, and rehabilitation and therapy providers in its continuing effort to corner the long-term health market. However, the most substantial news for Vencor came with the announced merger with the nation's second-largest operator of nursing homes, the Hillhaven Corp. of Tacoma, Washington. This deal, along with the previous acquisitions of service providers, allowed Vencor to extend its spectrum of long-term care by not only managing hospitals and nursing homes but by providing services to other care centers as well through Vencare, which held 2,008 contracts by the end of 1995.

The following year proved to be an equally important year as the company spun off part of its operations to form Atria Communities Inc., a publicly held company that would focus on managing assisted living facilities and retirement housing, many of which came from the Hillhaven merger. In 1996 Vencor, by then a $2.3 billion company, also looked to establish its own headquarters, as it had steadily outgrown its leased office space in the Providian Center. Cincinnati and Ohio, in an attempt to lure the health-care operation to its state, put together a package that reportedly offered incentives worth more than $40 million to move the headquarters.

Kentucky officials offered to float a $3 million bond issue and provide future tax credits of $6.8 million, while Louisville chipped in an additional $1.2 million, bringing the total to $11 million. In May, Chief Executive Officer Lunsford announced that the Vencor headquarters would remain in Louisville.

As of January 1999 Vencor administered 60 long-term hospitals, 292 nursing centers, 34 institutional pharmacies, 23 assisted living communities through Atria; held over 2,000 service contracts through Vencare Health Services; and managed approximately 62,000 employees in 41 states.

In 1998 Vencor received $177.5 million in a sale of most of its stake in Atria to Kapson Senior Quarters Corp. of New York. Vencor retained 12 percent of the shares in Atria and used the money for debt reduction.

In February 1998 Lunsford announced a restructuring of Vencor into a health-care division, which would retain the Vencor name, and a new real estate trust, VenTrust Inc. (later Ventas), which would own or lease all of the Vencor properties.

In June Vencor announced plans to put on hold and later shelved the proposed construction of a signature tower on Louisville's riverfront. Instead the company moved to One Commonwealth Place at Fourth and BROADWAY. Formerly occupied by AEGON USA, the building allowed Vencor to consolidate all of its downtown offices under one roof. Changes in insurance regulations around this time led to financial difficulties for Vencor and Ventas. Lunsford, citing the changing emphasis of his company toward nursing homes as well as its growth, resigned as chairman and chief executive officer on January 22, 1999, and was replaced by Edward L. Kuntz. Lunsford remained chairman of Ventas.

In April 1999 Vencor reported a loss of $651 million for 1998. The company's stock price fell and in June 1999 the New York Stock Exchange dropped Vencor from its listing. Losses for the first half of 1999 were reported to be $64 million. On September 13, 1999, Vencor filed for Chapter 11 bankruptcy protection under the federal bankruptcy law.

See *Courier-Journal,* Feb. 5, 1995, Sept. 10, 1995, Jan. 23, 1999; September 14, 1999.

VERHOEFF, CAROLYN (b Louisville, August 12, 1875; d Louisville, June 27, 1975). Animal rights activist. Verhoeff was one of Louisville's earliest and most successful activists for the humane treatment of animals. She was one of seven children of Mary (Parker) and Herman Verhoeff Jr., a successful grain elevator operator and two-term city councilman. Her grandfather, Herman Verhoeff, served in the Prussian army against Napoleon. She lived almost her entire life in the family's three-story brick-and-stone home at 731 S Second St. that was built by her father in 1879. She graduated from Vassar College in 1897 and did postgraduate work at Radcliffe College.

In the mid-1920s, Verhoeff helped to revive the former Kentucky Animal Rescue League after taking over as the league's president. She approached local officials about the city's treatment of animals after witnessing the "deplorable" conditions at the city pound. In 1924 the city transferred control of the pound to the league.

Shortly thereafter she stipulated that the league provide sheltered animals (primarily dogs) to the University of Louisville School of Medicine for medical experiments. It was required that the animals be treated humanely, including comprehensive guidelines for euthanasia and the inspection of medical school facilities. Still, Verhoeff and the medical school had frequent disagreements.

In 1959 Verhoeff was honored by the National Society for Medical Research for her efforts to promote the humane treatment of animals in medical research. In 1963 the UNIVERSITY OF LOUISVILLE dedicated the Carolyn Verhoeff Animal Care Center in the new Medical-Dental Research Building. The university's medical school was among the first to allow its laboratories to be inspected by representatives of the humane society, and Verhoeff was the first representative to conduct those inspections. The school of MEDICINE also honored Verhoeff in 1957 with a plaque recognizing her "lifetime devotion to the welfare of laboratory animals."

Before her work for the humane treatment of animals, Verhoeff was under contract to run a Cabel St. kindergarten in the BUTCHERTOWN neighborhood for the Louisville BOARD OF EDUCATION. Verhoeff was also the author of three children's books, *All about Johnnie Jones* (1907) and *Four Little Fosters* and *Love Me, Love My Dog*, both published later. Verhoeff never married. After her death, her body was donated to the U of L School of Medicine.

See Jennifer Molloy, "Carolyn Verhoeff and

the Struggle for Satisfactory Treatment of Laboratory Animals," unpublished paper, University of Louisville Records and Archives Center, 1982; *Courier-Journal*, June 28, 1975; Temple Bodley, *History of Kentucky* (Chicago and Louisville 1928).

VERHOEFF, FREDERICK H. (b Louisville, July 9, 1874; d West Hartford, Connecticut, October 22, 1968). Ophthalmologist and academic. He was the son of Herman Henry and Mary Jane (Parker) Verhoeff Jr. Herman Verhoeff's success as a flour and grain merchant, combined with profitable ventures in Louisville grain elevators allowed for the private and individualized education that Frederick received at Marcus Allmond's School, close to the Verhoeff residence on S Second St. The young Verhoeff showed an early aptitude for mathematics. His interest in optics began with experiments on his first camera. Later he earned a Ph.B. degree from the Sheffield Scientific School of Yale University and continued his education at Johns Hopkins Medical School, where he received his M.D. Determined by then to be an ophthalmologist, he spent his first year at the Baltimore Eye, Ear, and Throat Charity Hospital observing the famous Dr. Samuel Theobald. With the help of Dr. William Henry Welch, the distinguished pathologist of Johns Hopkins, Verhoeff assumed the position of pathologist for the Massachusetts Charitable Eye and Ear Infirmary, a post he held for thirty-two years.

In 1903 Verhoeff visited ophthalmologists throughout Europe. When he returned to Boston he designed a new pathology laboratory that facilitated several major discoveries, including finding the filamentous organism, strepthothrix, which he determined to be the cause of Parinaud's conjunctivitis and also of the obstruction of the small tear ducts, the lacrymal canaliculi. He developed his own technique for strengthening the extraocular muscles in strabismus, the Verhoeff posterior sclerotomy, the Verhoeff sliding technique of cataract extraction, the appositionally precise Verhoeff track sutures, a lens expressor, and the Verhoeff needle holder.

In 1913 he was appointed surgeon to the Harvard Infirmary, became assistant professor of ophthalmology at Harvard in 1921, and in 1924 he became a full professor. Verhoeff became director of the Lucien Howe Laboratories of Ophthalmology in 1932. In 1941 he received the honor of emeritus professor from Harvard.

Verhoeff spent most of his service in WORLD WAR I as a major and chief of ophthalmology at Fort Devens, Massachusetts. During his time in the Army Medical Corps he developed his famous Verhoeff capsule forceps to lift the cataractous lens out of the eye in 1916, his electrolytic puncture for retinal detachments in 1917, and began championing applanation measurements of pressure within the eye. He used the simple variable force loader of W.N. Souter pressed against the eye and gauged intraocular pressure from the first distortion of the reflections of a windowpane as seen in the patient's cornea thirty-eight years before a standard for that pressure was developed.

He was elected president of the New England Ophthalmological Society and chair of the American Medical Association section on ophthalmology. Verhoeff was a recipient of the Knapp Medal and Ophthalmic Research Medal of the American Medical Association Section on Ophthalmology, the Howe Medal of the American Ophthalmological Society, the Leslie Dana Medal of the National Association for the Prevention of Blindness, an honorary doctor of letters from Johns Hopkins, and a doctor of science from the UNIVERSITY OF LOUISVILLE.

He married Margaret Frink Lougee of New Hampshire in 1902. They had two daughters, Mary Josephine and Margaret. He is buried in CAVE HILL CEMETERY.

See Arthur H. and Virginia T. Keeney, "Frederick Herman Verhoeff, M.D.," *Filson Club History Quarterly* 55 (April 1981): 202–9.

VIENNA BAKERY AND RESTAURANT. Formerly located at 133–35 S Fourth St., the three-story eatery was founded in 1893 by German immigrant Frank L. Erpeldinger. Notable for its German and Austrian fare, the Vienna was one of Louisville's most popular downtown RESTAURANTS and was a favorite haunt of "the most prominent merchants and professional men."

The first floor was the dining area, furnished with oak tables and chairs imported from Vienna, ceiling fans, and paneled walls. The second story housed the kitchen and bakery, which was famed for its Vienna rolls, while fine pastries were created on the third level. A distinctive feature of the building was its terra cotta facade, created by the Rookwood Pottery of Cincinnati, which included the name "Vienna" spelled out in representations of flowers, leaves, and fruit. From about 1910 to 1926 the establishment was known as the Vienna Model Bakery and Restaurant, but in its last year of operation, the name was changed back to the original.

The Vienna Bakery, 133-135 South Fourth Street, 1926.

Erpeldinger died in 1925, and for the next two years his niece, Ella, ran the Vienna. In 1927 the restaurant closed after being sold to a Chicago firm. In 1951 the building was bought by the Louisville-Jefferson County DEMOCRATIC PARTY for its headquarters. It was renamed the Brennan Building after Michael J. Brennan, a prominent Democrat party leader in the 1930s. In the mid-1980s, the building was torn down to make way for a parking garage.

VIETNAM WAR. Like much of America, Louisville's reaction to the Vietnam War was mixed, producing a divided legacy. Some fought. A few fled. Others remained, expressing heartfelt sentiments either for or against the conflict. Among those who fought, Jefferson County native Fergus Groves, Kentucky's first Vietnam casualty, was killed in early 1962, before Americans were officially serving in combat roles. Over two hundred more Louisville-area men died or were listed as missing in action (MIA) before United States forces departed in 1973. Several soldiers were given medals for heroism. One of the most decorated was Sgt. John J. McGinty. Having fought off communist "human wave" assaults in July 1966, McGinty received America's highest award, the CONGRESSIONAL MEDAL OF HONOR, and South Vietnam's, the Cross of Gallantry.

Of the estimated eighty thousand Americans who sought asylum in Canada, only a small number came from Louisville. By 1971 the expatriates had fashioned a new community at an aged Toronto apartment house called the "Louisville Ghetto." Many of its residents eventually prospered. Sandy Sutton became a Canadian GOVERNMENT clerk, and he and his wife, Geny, purchased a farm 175 miles from Toronto. Another couple, Gil and Anita Steiner, remained in Toronto. A UNIVERSITY OF LOUISVILLE engineering graduate, Gil became a furniture maker in Canada and was working in an antique store in 1977 when President Jimmy Carter pardoned U.S. draft resisters. Asked then if moving to Canada had been the correct choice, the former Louisvillians all agreed that they would not "do anything differently if they had it to do again."

At home the war produced divergent views. In March 1966, one year after U.S. combat forces entered Vietnam, a Louisville sidewalk survey asked seventy-five people their opinion on American involvement. Of those polled, only two asserted that the U.S. should pull "out of the war" immediately. The rest offered strategies for achieving victory ranging from using nuclear weapons to emphasizing negotiation.

One of the first antiwar protests occurred in August, when peace advocates observed the atomic bomb's twenty-first anniversary by picketing the Federal Building, a popular rallying site because it housed Louisville's Selective Service headquarters. Ministers, professors, housewives, students, and children constituted much of the crowd. During the Vietnam era, various antiwar organizations demonstrated, including the Louisville Peace Council, Clergymen and Laymen Concerned about Vietnam, the Kentucky Committee for Negotiation Now, the National Mobilization Committee to End the War, and Students Concerned. World heavyweight BOXING champion MUHAMMAD ALI was Louisville's, and perhaps America's, most-celebrated, controversial "dove." In 1964 he joined the Nation of Islam, changing his name from Cassius Marcellus Clay to Muhammad Ali. Three years later, he refused to enter the United States armed forces because of religious convictions, stating at one point, "I ain't got no quarrel with them Vietcong." Stripped of his title, Ali was banned from boxing until 1970 when a U.S. Supreme Court ruling facilitated a return to the ring.

Louisville also had numerous war supporters. An October 1967 pro-war demonstration produced a seemingly improbable combination: the Concerned Citizens Committee, the Total Effort for America Committee, the Ku Klux Klan, and the Committee for the Continuation of War for the Sake of Love and the Preservation of Peace. Three years later, Father William Zahner watched approximately two hundred parishioners walk out on his antiwar sermon at the CATHEDRAL OF THE ASSUMPTION.

Louisville's national politicians, all Republican, divided on the war. U.S. Senator Thruston Morton, a native of the city, early on advocated American withdrawal from Vietnam. The former mayor of Louisville, U.S. Representative WILLIAM COWGER, severely criticized Morton. Gene Snyder, Jefferson County's other House member, became dovish by 1969, asserting that America "ought to pack up and come home."

As the war dragged on, more individuals agreed with Snyder. Some of Louisville's college campuses (Bellarmine-Ursuline, Jefferson Community, Spalding, and the University of Louisville) participated in the October 1969 Vietnam Moratorium, a national student protest. Professors, ministers, and the families of students also took part. Reportedly, no violence occurred, and each rally was uniquely different. Demonstrators at the University of Louisville planted a "peace tree" on campus, while students at Spalding College sang "We are not afraid" and released a wild dove to symbolize peace. By January 1973 large segments of Louisville were united against the war. A week before President Richard Nixon concluded an agreement for ending American involvement in Vietnam, an estimated crowd of twenty-five hundred, including parents and children, soldiers from nearby FORT KNOX, and the elderly conducted a peace march through downtown in thirty-seven-degree WEATHER. Called "A Walk for Conscience," the procession spanned nearly nine blocks, forcing motorists to wait thirty minutes to cross the busy intersection at Fourth and Market Streets.

In February American prisoners of war began returning home, and a few Louisville families were reunited with loved ones. Air Force lieutenant colonels Robert Purcell and Dewey Lee Smith both received a hero's welcome after extended years of captivity. A small number of Louisville-area men such as Col. Charles Shelton, however, remained unaccounted for during the 1980s. Shelton was the last American categorized as a prisoner of war, and his wife, Marian, worked unceasingly to locate him, even going to Southeast Asia as a POW-MIA activist. In 1990 despair over the inability to find him led her to suicide. Four years later after additional Pentagon efforts uncovered nothing, Colonel Shelton was honored in a memorial service at Arlington National Cemetery. "I think of my mom as a casualty of the Vietnam War," commented a son attending the service.

Postwar readjustment proved difficult for many Vietnam veterans, who complained about a seemingly uncaring country and unresponsive U.S. Veterans Administration. In Louisville, veterans and their relatives often took the initiative to help themselves. To confront unemployment, thousands entered Kentucky colleges using the GI Bill. At the University of Louisville, they formed the Veterans Affairs Group to untangle the "red-tape" associated with VA benefits. Working with the university and the United Presbyterian Church in the early 1970s, one veteran, Tom Williams, established a self-help agency, the Office of Veterans Advocacy at Louisville. By 1976 an estimated five hundred Vietnamese war refugees had settled in Louisville. To acclimate them to American culture, the River Region Crisis and Information Center hired an English-speaking liaison, former South Vietnamese naval officer Tran Khanh Liem.

Over a decade before the Vietnam Memorial was dedicated in Washington, D.C., Louisville established the National Vietnam War Memorial. The fifty-foot-high concrete monument is on the lawn of the Good Shepherd Lutheran Church in VALLEY STATION. Much of the funding, both out-of-state and local, came from individuals who had lost sons in Vietnam.

See *Courier-Journal*, inclusive, March 13, 1966–Sept. 20, 1986; *New York Times*, Oct. 5, 1994; *Register of Vietnam War Casualties from Kentucky* (Frankfort 1988); Elliott J. Gorn, ed., *Muhammad Ali: The People's Champ* (Chicago 1995); Thomas Hauser with Muhammad Ali, *Muhammad Ali: His Life and Times* (New York 1991); James S. Olson, ed., *Dictionary of the Vietnam War* (New York 1988); Clyde F. Crews, "Hallowed Ground: The Cathedral of the Assumption in Louisville History," *Filson Club History Quarterly* 51 (1977): 249–61.

John Ernst

VISITORS. Throughout its history, Louisville has attracted an impressive roster of well-known visitors. Such wayfarers often help to link a city to wider historical and cultural currents, both national and international. They tend to bring with them a deeper (if at times controversial) vision of human experience and possibility. Through their lectures and performances—and sometimes just by the force of their presence—they can leave behind them a community more diverse, challenged, and cosmopolitan.

The listing that follows is, of course, partial and selective. Many more names have been excluded than included. The date given for these figures is a documentable one on which they were in the city and usually one near to a newspaper account of their activities. They may, of course, have remained several days or longer; in many cases there were also multiple visits, though space permits only a single listing here.

All U.S. presidents since Theodore Roosevelt have visited Louisville. Of the twenty-four chief executives before TR, at least fourteen can be documented as having been in the city—a grand total of thirty-one out of forty-one presidents (and most of them visited during their terms of office).

Daniel Boone	May 20, 1784
James Monroe	Jun. 23, 1819
Marquis de Lafayette	May 11, 1825
Andrew Jackson	Jan. 22, 1829
Henry Clay	Jun. 24, 1829
Alexis de Tocqueville	Dec. 9, 1831
Washington Irving	Sept. 4, 1832
Jefferson Davis	Jun. 17, 1835
Daniel Webster	May 30, 1837
Abraham Lincoln	Aug. 18, 1841
Charles Dickens	Apr. 7, 1842
Brigham Young	Jul. 12, 1843
Walt Whitman	Feb. 18, 1848
Ralph Waldo Emerson	Jun. 4, 1850
Jenny Lind	Apr. 7, 1851
Robert E. Lee	Apr. 20, 1855
Oliver W. Holmes Sr.	Sept. 8, 1855
Herman Melville	Jan. 31, 1858
Lola Montez	Mar. 5, 1860
William Tecumseh Sherman	Oct. 22, 1861
Tom Thumb	Jan. 26, 1864
John Wilkes Booth	Jan. 30, 1864
Ulysses S. Grant	Feb. 1, 1864
P.T. Barnum	Oct. 20, 1866
Horace Greeley	Sept. 21, 1872
Elizabeth Cady Stanton	Nov. 19, 1872
Henry Ward Beecher	Feb. 21, 1873
Frederick Douglass	Apr. 21, 1873
Harriet Beecher Stowe	Oct. 13, 1873
Oscar Wilde	Feb. 21, 1882
Charles Stewart Parnell	Feb. 19, 1880
Julia Ward Howe	Oct. 26, 1881
Mark Twain	Jan. 6, 1885
Annie Oakley	Apr. 24, 1885
Buffalo Bill Cody	Apr. 24, 1885
John Philip Sousa	Apr. 28, 1891

Robert G. Ingersoll	Oct. 8, 1893
William Jennings Bryan	Apr. 17, 1897
Sarah Bernhardt	Mar. 18, 1901
Theodore Roosevelt	Apr. 4, 1905
W.C. Fields	Feb. 15, 1906
Ethel Barrymore	Nov. 4, 1907
George M.Cohan	Nov. 30, 1908
Ty Cobb	Apr. 4, 1914
Harry Houdini	Mar. 21, 1915
Woodrow Wilson	Sept. 4, 1916
F. Scott Fitzgerald	Apr. 1, 1918
Jane Addams	Apr. 17, 1919
Eamon De Valera	Oct. 10, 1919
John J. Pershing	Dec. 14, 1919
Isadora Duncan	Nov. 24, 1922
Rudolph Valentino	Apr. 1, 1923
David Lloyd George	Oct., 20, 1923
Bertrand Russell	Apr. 14, 1924
Edna St. Vincent Millay	Jan. 18, 1924
Marie, Queen of Romania	Nov. 18, 1926
Charles A. Lindbergh	Aug. 8, 1927
Clarence Darrow	Feb. 12, 1928
Will Rogers	Apr. 7, 1928
Babe Ruth	Oct. 24, 1928
Thornton Wilder	Apr. 4, 1929
Sergei Rachmaninoff	Nov. 16, 1931
Ignance Paderewski	Mar. 3, 1933
Helen Keller	Apr. 19, 1933
George Gershwin	Feb. 2, 1934
Amelia Earhart	Feb. 14, 1935
Tommy Dorsey	Feb. 16, 1938
Benny Goodman	Apr. 18, 1939
Robert Frost	Oct. 14, 1939
Franklin D. Roosevelt	Jul. 8, 1938
Marian Anderson	Dec. 9, 1939
Glenn Miller	Aug. 3, 1940
Joe Louis	May 3, 1941
Reinhold Niebuhr	Nov. 14, 1944
Joe DiMaggio	Apr. 8, 1946
Jackie Robinson	Sept. 28, 1946
Artur Rubinstein	Feb. 19, 1948
Frank Lloyd Wright	May 28, 1948
Harry Truman	Sept. 30, 1948
Walt Disney	Jan. 21, 1949
Eleanor Roosevelt	Mar. 15, 1950
Mae West	Jan. 30, 1951
Langston Hughes	Feb. 18, 1951
John Foster Dulles	Apr. 11, 1952
Dwight D. Eisenhower	Sept. 22, 1952
George C. Marshall	May 13, 1953
Edward R. Murrow	Jan. 22, 1954
Alexander Fleming	Apr. 13, 1954
Moshe Dayan	Jul. 31, 1954
Carl Sandburg	Jan. 17, 1955
William Faulkner	May 7, 1955
John Steinbeck	May 5, 1956
Adlai Stevenson	Oct. 19, 1956
Elvis Presley	Nov. 25, 1956
Arnold Toynbee	May 7, 1958
Joan Crawford	May 19, 1959
Martin Luther King Jr.	Apr. 19, 1961
John F. Kennedy	Oct. 13, 1962
Billy Graham	Nov. 13, 1964
Duke Ellington	Dec. 15, 1965
Igor Stravinsky	Sept. 17, 1966
Hans Kung	Mar. 5, 1968
Robert F. Kennedy	May 5, 1968
Aaron Copland	Sept. 20, 1969
Richard Nixon	Jul. 14, 1970
Elie Wiesel	Nov. 28, 1973
Margaret Mead	May 8, 1976
B.F. Skinner	May 14, 1977
Karl Rahner	Apr. 2, 1979
Elizabeth Taylor	Apr. 7, 1979
Kurt Vonnegut	Nov. 18, 1979
Andy Warhol	Nov. 2, 1981
Mother Teresa	Jun. 22, 1982
Norman Vincent Peale	Oct. 11, 1982
Carl Sagan	Oct. 30, 1984
Luciano Pavarotti	Jan. 30, 1986
Desmond Tutu	Mar. 12, 1987
Norman Mailer	Sept. 17, 1989
Joyce Carol Oates	Oct. 22, 1990
Louis Farrakhan	Dec. 15, 1990
Leontyne Price	Mar. 24, 1991
Allen Ginsberg	Oct. 1, 1992
Gloria Steinem	Jan. 26, 1993
Mikhail Baryshnikov	Feb. 14, 1993
Bob Dylan	Apr. 12, 1993
Maya Angelou	Jun. 3, 1993
Seamus Heaney	Jan. 27, 1994
Mikhail Gorbachev	Oct. 5, 1995
John Updike	Feb. 25, 1997
Margaret Thatcher	Oct. 19, 1998

See Clyde F. Crews, "Personages: Eminent Visitors in 20th Century Louisville," *Filson Club History Quarterly* 54 (Oct. 1980): 346-359; "The Political Gateway to the South," *Filson Club History Quarterly* 56 (Apr. 1982): 181-200; "Roots of a Renaissance: Cultural Visitors in 19th and Early 20th Century Louisville," *Filson Club History Quarterly* 69 (Jul. 1995): 275-92.

Clyde F. Crews

VOICE-TRIBUNE. The *Voice-Tribune* has long been known as a community newspaper, and when it was first published on July 14, 1949, it was named *St. Matthews, Your Community Newspaper*. It grew into a larger tabloid size and then into a full broadsheet within three years. For years its motto has been "Community News with a Difference," and it has tried to fill its niche as a "hometown" community newspaper for the rapidly growing East End. Originally a ST. MATTHEWS-only paper, the *Voice-Tribune* now covers several other fourth-class cities and East End communities, including Middletown, LYNDON, JEFFERSONTOWN, PROSPECT, HURSTBOURNE, ANCHORAGE, and HIKES POINT.

The paper began as a small, tabloid-size, eight-page paper and was published by James K. Van Arsdale III. Slater & Gilroy Inc. printed the paper, with the distribution handled by Up To Date Distributing Co., which was owned by Van Arsdale's father.

A contest was held to name it, and four-year-old Martha May won the hundred-dollar prize with an entry of the Voice of St. Matthews. Later, when May was in high school, she was a columnist for the paper.

The *Voice-Tribune* provided a forum for its readers about Louisville's attempt to annex St. Matthews in the early 1950s. This issue enabled the paper to build a strong foundation that has helped it thrive through the years. The paper has changed and grown and has had several owners and publishers. Some modified the paper's name and its look, but its focus of serving the community has continued.

Al Shansberg bought the paper in 1952 and was the publisher through the early 1970s. During his ownership, he bought the *Jeffersonian*, the Jeffersontown-based newspaper that began on June 13, 1907. After two years of publishing two papers, he merged them in January 1966 as the *Voice-Jeffersonian.* He sold it in May 1971 to Bruce Van Dusen, who sold it in 1979 to giant newspaper chain Scripps-Howard, which owned several local papers under the *Voice* umbrella. Besides the *Voice*, the *Highland Herald*, *Middletown Mirror* (earlier *Suburban Mirror*), *Jefferson Reporter*, *Okolona Observer*, *Southwest News*, the *Jeffersonian* and *Prospect News* also were published.

Scripps's plan to develop a strong network of papers around the community lasted only a few years, partially because the COURIER-JOURNAL, the metro area's daily newspaper, started its own neighborhood editions.

In July 1981 William Matthews bought the *Voice* from Scripps. He sold to John Waits in 1982, who ran it until the paper ceased publication in September 1986.

Southern Publishing Inc., which now owns the paper, bought the name and assets in 1987 and started publishing again on April 1 of that year. When Southern took over, the weekly had a circulation list of about eighteen hundred. Almost immediately the new owners changed the name to the *New Voice* to let readers know of the new management.

Since then the paper has grown and become the state's largest paid weekly, with a circulation in the late 1990s of about fourteen thousand and a readership of about sixty thousand. On its seven-year anniversary under Southern, the paper took on a new name, the *Voice-Tribune*, to give it more of a classic newspaper name and eliminate the misunderstandings some had of the *New Voice* name.

The *Voice-Tribune*, with its office at 3818 Shelbyville Rd., focuses on local events, people, and businesses. Besides its local news and feature stories, the paper's appeal has been its popular columns on sports, society news, gardening and food advice, as well as wedding announcements and obituaries.

Steven Rush

VOLUNTEER FIREFIGHTERS. Although Louisville had a firefighting bucket brigade and a small hand-pumped fire engine by 1780, there was limited interest in fire protection by the citizenry. The first record of money spent by Louisville for firefighting equipment was in 1807. At that time, an elephant on tour was brought by its handlers into town. The town trustees decided to levy a ten-dollar tax each time the animal was exhibited, with the income committed to buy fire ladders for the community.

By 1821 Louisville had been divided into three WARDS, each having a fire engine manned by forty men. While there is no written description of these engines, it can be assumed that they were hand-pulled, of the four-wheel type, and had a gooseneck nozzle that protruded from the top of the machine. End levers were used in an up-and-down motion to operate pistons that forced water through the nozzle. This style of pumper was incapable of taking suction from a water supply; hence it had to be filled by a bucket brigade. Also, the machine had to be lifted around corners since it had no movable axle. Its effectiveness was further limited since it had to be placed quite close to a fire when in use.

Louisville became a city in 1828, receiving its charter from the Kentucky General Assembly. In this document the mayor and city councilmen were given the authority to organize a fire department, provide fire engines, and appoint able-bodied men as firemen, not to exceed twenty per engine. Such "volunteers" would be exempt from serving on juries and from military duty in peacetime. They would receive no pay.

Property values continued to increase in the congested commercial district of Louisville, but very little was done to improve firefighting. In 1832, there were five volunteer fire companies. The city GOVERNMENT by this time had begun the practice of giving fixed annual contributions of money to each fire company for maintenance of their city-owned firefighting equipment. Also in 1832, copper-riveted leather hose was in use, allowing the hand pumpers to be placed at a safer distance from the fire. Another improvement in firefighting occurred in 1844 when all of the Louisville fire engines were of the type that could take suction from available water supplies. This capability caused the demise of the inefficient citizen bucket brigade.

In 1845 the volunteer companies, then grown to seven, developed their own separate organization of officers. A typical chain of command within a company would be a president, vice president, treasurer, chief director, assistant director, assistant chief, three engine directors, two line directors, three trustees, and two pipe directors. With such an internal structure for each company, an overall command of all the volunteers was not possible because of monumental egos and an unwillingness to forgo intercompany competition.

This lack of control concerned the citizens of Louisville, particularly after a school fire at Fifth and YORK Streets in the spring of 1855. The volunteers responded quickly enough but were soon involved in physical disputes over which company had the right to use what cistern and who had the honor of placing the first hose stream on the fire. The school building, newly completed at public expense, was a total loss as a result of this brawl. Such activities hastened the demise of the volunteers. In 1856, Louisville voters approved bonds for the construction of a municipal water system that was completed in 1860, too late to be of value to the volunteer firemen.

With the advent of 1858, eight volunteer fire companies and one hook-and-ladder company were in service in Louisville:

Fire Company	*Members*
Mechanic No. 1	102
Union No. 2	57
Relief No. 3	114
Hope No. 4	303
Kentucky No. 5	75
Washington No. 7	101
Lafayette No. 8	Unknown
Rescue No. 9	50
Falls City H&L	23

(There was never a No. 6 fire company; two groups got into a squabble over that number, and the issue was resolved by no one using it.)

While it was true that the majority of the volunteers were dedicated and enthusiastic firefighters, it was obvious that they could not meet the needs of the growing city. Hand-pumped engines simply could not suppress fires in large, multistory buildings.

Louisville's burning rate continued to climb in the 1850s. Upriver at Cincinnati, Ohio, the Latta brothers developed in 1853 a steam-powered fire engine capable of outpumping and outlasting the strongest of the volunteers. This event did not escape the attention of a number of concerned citizens of Louisville.

On June 1, 1858, Louisville inaugurated its municipally owned fire department, which had one chief in command and included a Latta steam fire engine. All of the Louisville volunteer companies were disbanded that same date. Louisville, after Cincinnati and St. Louis, became the third city in the United States to have a municipally owned steam fire department.

Today the combination of volunteer and paid firefighters serve smaller cities outside of Louisville. The major firefighter protection departments are in LYNDON, Middletown, ST. MATTHEWS, JEFFERSONTOWN, HARRODS CREEK, and WORTHINGTON and have a full-time paid staff along with volunteers on call.

See David Winges, *Volunteer Firefighters of Louisville, Kentucky* (Louisville 1992).

David Winges

VOLUNTEERS OF AMERICA OF KENTUCKY. Gen. and Mrs. Ballington Booth established the national nonprofit organization in New York City (1896) with local affiliates called "posts." Its mission is dedicated to Christian principles and to creating human service programs to reach and uplift needy people, regardless of religious affiliation.

The Louisville post was founded in 1896. It started as a lodge for transients and continues in that vein today. The 1937 flood found the agency maintaining three refugee distribution centers providing clothes and blankets.

HOMELESSNESS is the agency's main focus. A Family Emergency Shelter was started in 1984. It was the first to allow families to remain together. Formerly, husbands were separated from the wives and children. Today, after a maximum of six months, families move into transitional housing, where they may stay for one year. Then it is into permanent housing with family follow-up for one year with counseling, job training, and placement.

Services/housing for homeless women, indigent families, and ex-convicts is offered. Earlier programs provided shelter for recovering alcoholics at a Men's Rehabilitation Center. Federal s provide work training for the homeless, jobless, and recovering substance abusers to become independent and self-supporting. Religious services are provided at the Jefferson County jail and the women's prison. Services to the middle class include the Kids Korner, child care for the children of NORTON HEALTHCARE and Jewish Hospital Health Care Services employees.

See Jesse Bradley and Stacey Fox, "A Century of Miracles," *Volunteers of America, Kentucky* (Louisville 1996).

Lillian C. Milanof

Volunteers of America, 1930s.

WADE-BRADEN AFFAIR. Just past midnight on June 27, 1954, a time of high racial tensions, an explosion ripped through the Louisville home of black electrician Andrew Wade IV. Since the late 1940s, Louisville had integrated its LIBRARIES, city GOLF courses, amphitheaters, medical and bar associations, civil service, police department, and university. However, rigid SEGREGATION still characterized the city's housing patterns.

Wade, a WORLD WAR II veteran, wanted to move his family out of the JIM CROW urban area to a suburb but was unable to get anyone to sell him a house. He sought the help of two white acquaintances, Carl and Anne Braden. CARL BRADEN, a copyeditor for the *COURIER-JOURNAL,* was an avowed socialist and trade unionist. Anne Braden was a writer, journalist, and civil rights activist who returned to her native Louisville from Birmingham, Alabama, to work as a reporter for the *LOUISVILLE TIMES* in 1947. Being both native southerners and committed integrationists, the Bradens purchased a house on Rone Court (later Clyde Drive) in a previously all-white neighborhood just west of SHIVELY and transferred the title to Wade.

When the Wades moved into the house in May, they immediately became, as they had expected, the victims of fierce harassment. This included gunfire, burning crosses, and broken windows. On May 18, the day after the U.S. Supreme Court declared school SEGREGATION unconstitutional with *Brown v. Topeka Board of Education,* the *Courier-Journal* ran one editorial endorsing the Court's decision and another castigating the Bradens and their attempts to "force the issue" of residential desegregation.

After the bombing of the Wades' house, the commonwealth's attorney, A. Scott Hamilton, developed a theory that the incident was part of a Communist plot hatched by the Bradens to arouse racial strife within the city. Nationally the recent Army-McCarthy hearings had undercut the credibility of unbridled anti-Communist emotions, but challenges to segregation gave anti-communism a new life in the South. The Louisville case electrified the city, as the Bradens, along with five others—Vernon Brown, I.O. Ford, Louise Gilbert, Lew Lubka, and Larue Spiker—were indicted for "criminal syndicalism and sedition" against the governments of the United States and the commonwealth of Kentucky.

Carl Braden was the only "conspirator" brought to trial as a test case for the state, which claimed that his Communist activities dated to early in 1947. No evidence was presented that linked Braden to the bombing. But surprise testimony by a supposed undercover FBI plant, a former family friend who could produce no proof of her employment by the government, told of Carl Braden's alleged Communist connections. The state also claimed that Braden had been involved with at least twenty-seven Communist groups. The jury convicted Braden under a never-before-used 1920 Kentucky sedition law and sentenced him to serve fifteen years in prison and pay a five-thousand-dollar fine.

After serving seven months in the LaGrange State Reformatory, Braden was released on bond. The Kentucky Court of Appeals overturned his conviction on June 22, 1956. The appeals court followed the U.S. Supreme Court precedent of *Pennsylvania v. Nelson,* noting the state did not have the right to prosecute a sedition case against the United States but could retry him for sedition against the commonwealth. In August a judge dismissed the case against Braden. Three months later all charges were dropped against everyone involved in the case.

A second sedition charge came in 1967 when the Southern Conference Education Fund, an interracial South-wide organization seeking to bring white people into active participation in the civil rights movement, was helping people in Appalachia organize against strip-mining. The Bradens won that case and were later successful in getting the Kentucky sedition law declared unconstitutional.

Andrew and Charlotte Wade and their children, however, were never able to return to their house due to financial losses and lingering neighborhood hostility. The actual bombers were never brought to justice.

See Anne Braden, *The Wall Between* (New York 1958); Samuel W. Thomas, *Louisville since the Twenties* (Louisville, 1978); *Courier-Journal,* Dec. 11, 1954.

WALDEN THEATRE. Founded in 1976 by Nancy Niles Sexton, Walden Theatre is located at 1129 Payne St. It offers young people ages eight to eighteen the opportunity for the serious and professional study of THEATER. Over the years, thousands of young people have joined the Walden Theatre Co. to study acting, voice, technical studies, stage movement, and playwriting.

Walden Theatre's Young Playwrights Festival, begun in 1982, has produced seven scripts published by Prestigious Dramatic Publishing Co. These plays have been performed all over the English-speaking world. Further studies are offered in writing and production for media. Students who are members of Walden Theatre Co. attend various public, private, and parochial schools. Classes and rehearsals at Walden Theatre are held after school Tuesday through Friday and on Saturdays.

Walden Theatre offers young people production opportunities in plays written by such playwrights as William Shakespeare, Arthur Miller, Tennessee Williams, and Oscar Wilde. Performance venues include the Kentucky Center for the Arts and ACTORS THEATRE OF LOUISVILLE.

Walden Theatre believes in the enrichment of travel for its students. Trips to the Edinburgh Festival in Edinburgh, Scotland, and the Stratford Shakespeare Festival in Canada are periodically offered. Local and statewide excursions are arranged for students to research various roles for Walden Theatre productions. A member agency of the FUND FOR THE ARTS, Walden Theatre is also part of the Youth Arts Council.

Nancy Sexton

WALKER, FERDINAND GRAHAM (b Mitchell, Indiana, February 16, 1859; d New Albany, Indiana, June 11, 1927). Artist. He was one of nine children born to the Reverend Francis and Mary Elizabeth (Graham) Walker. His father was a Methodist minister and prohibitionist propagandist. At the age of fifteen Ferdinand entered Depauw College in Greenwood, Indiana, where he was instructed by S.W. Price, a noted Louisville artist. He opened an art studio in NEW ALBANY in 1883. He studied in France on two occasions, the first from 1885 to 1887. His picture of a street scene in Rouen, France, in 1886 is well known. Upon his return to the United States, he began PAINTING portraits of prominent politicians, a practice he continued.

In 1902 he returned to France for additional instruction under Jacques Blanche (1861–1942), Bascat Dagnan-Bouveret (1852–1929), and Luc Olive Merson (1846–1920). While in France he served as president of the American Society of Artists in Paris. When he returned to the United States in 1906, Walker opened a studio in Louisville in the Commercial Building at Fourth and MAIN Streets. The studio remained open until 1925. After that his studio was in his residence at 324 E Thirteenth St. in New Albany. The *COURIER-JOURNAL* commissioned him to do a portrait of the newspaper's late editor, HENRY WATTERSON. It depicts Watterson in his office producing one of his noted editorials. When it was done, it was so highly appreciated by the company that Walker was commissioned to paint a portrait of the late WALTER HALDEMAN, founder and publisher of the *Courier-Journal,* which was commissioned for the Jefferson Davis Memorial in Fairview, Kentucky. He also painted a portrait of Sen. A.O. Stanley and portraits of several Kentucky governors.

Walker was also known for his landscape paintings. Among his best are two views of Silver Hills, near New Albany. Some of Walker's paintings were sent to national exhibits, and he was a winner of many prizes. In a 1924 exhibit of work of Kentucky artists in Nashville, Tennessee, Walker was awarded first prize.

Walker married Mary Watkins. They had one son, Stanley Ward. He is buried in Fairview Cemetery in New Albany.

See *Louisville Herald,* Dec. 24, 1922; *Herald Post* June 12, 1927.

WALKER, MARY EDWARDS (b Oswego Town, New York, November 26, 1832; d Bunker Hill, New York, February 21, 1919). Army surgeon. The daughter of Alvah and Veste (Whitcomb) Walker, Mary graduated from Syracuse Medical College in 1855. In 1861, following the outbreak of the CIVIL WAR, she traveled to Washington, D.C., where she attempted to enlist as an army surgeon but was rebuffed by Union officials. She was often the object of ridicule and scorn for her tendency to wear men's clothing. She later gained a position as a civilian contract surgeon and saw service at the first battle of Manassas Junction (Bull Run), Chickamauga, and the battle of Atlanta. She was captured by a Confederate sentry on April 10, 1864, while riding deep behind Confederate lines and charged with spying. She was sent to prison in Richmond, Virginia, where she was held for four months and then released in a prisoner exchange.

Following her release, she was appointed superintendent of the Female Military Prison in the Croghan House, a hotel in Louisville at Jefferson and Center (Armory Place) Streets, by Gen. William T. Sherman. He, like many in the Union army, had initially opposed Walker's service but was swayed by her devotion to the Union cause. Walker's time in Louisville increased male animosity toward a woman who dared supersede their authority with her position. However, she improved the lives and conditions for inmates at the prison, who were women held for spying, sedition, and other anti-Union crimes. She ended fraternization between male guards and their female charges, improved sanitary conditions, and helped win the release of many prisoners who were incarcerated with their infant children. At the time of her appointment, the prison's commander, J.H. Hammond, described conditions at the facility as "no better than a brothel," and upon her departure he credited her with having vastly improved conditions. In March 1865 she applied for a transfer to the front lines but was instead sent to Clarksville, Tennessee, to oversee an orphans' home, where she served out the remainder of the war.

In November 1865 President Andrew Johnson signed a bill awarding her the CONGRESSIONAL MEDAL OF HONOR for meritorious service, making her the first woman ever to receive the award. A change in criterion for the medal in 1918 resulted in the revocation of the award, but it was later reinstated under President Woodrow Wilson.

After the war Walker moved to Washington, D.C., where she worked until an accident left her debilitated. She returned to her native upstate New York, where she died.

See Mary Elizabeth Massey, *Bonnet Brigades* (New York 1966); Charles McCool Snyder, *Dr. Mary Walker: The Little Lady in Pants* (New York 1962); Agatha Young, *The Women and the Crisis: Women of the North in the Civil War* (New York 1959).

Melinda Dorris

WALLACE, TOM (b Hurricane, Crittenden County, Kentucky, November 26, 1874; d Prospect, Kentucky, June 5, 1961). Journalist and conservationist. The son of Tom and Mary Stuart (Dade) Wallace, he was known for his distinguished sixty-year career as a newspaperman. His passionate devotion to the preservation of the environment and the betterment of United States–Latin American relations brought him numerous honors. In his early years, he received his education mainly from tutors, and later at Sampson's Academy in SHELBYVILLE, Kentucky. He also attended Weaver's Business College in Louisville and Randolph-Macon College in Ashland, Virginia.

He then held a succession of brief jobs, first as a bookkeeper in Richmond, Virginia, then at a Shelbyville ice company, and at a tooth powder factory in New York City. Finding the business world distasteful, the twenty-six-year-old Wallace accepted an unpaid position on the staff of the *LOUISVILLE TIMES* as a police reporter. Six weeks later, he went to work for the *Louisville Dispatch,* this time for a salary. Over the next few years, Wallace wrote for a number of papers, including the *Louisville Herald,* the *St. Louis Republic,* and again for the *Louisville Times* as its Washington, D.C., and Frankfort, Kentucky, correspondent. Then in 1905, at the behest of HENRY WATTERSON, he joined the *COURIER-JOURNAL* editorial staff, becoming its youngest member. He remained as an associate editor at the paper until 1923, when he became the head of the *Louisville Times*' editorial page. In 1930 he became editor of the *Times.*

Wallace's editorial style was bold and straightforward, reflecting his opinion that "an editorial page without spunk is bunk" (*Courier-Journal,* June 6, 1961). Though he officially retired from the paper in 1948, at which time he was named editor emeritus, Wallace continued his commentaries on current events in a thrice-weekly column until 1959. During his lengthy career, Wallace received a number of professional honors, including serving as president of the American Society of Newspaper Editors (1940–41) and president of the Inter-American Press Association, which later made him its honorary lifetime president in 1951.

In addition to his professional concerns, Wallace was actively involved in environmental issues. As a conservationist, he lobbied for the protection of streams, forests, and wildlife and was awarded the American Scenic and Historical Preservation Society's Pugsley Silver Medal in recognition of his triumphant campaign against the conversion of Kentucky's Cumberland Falls into a power dam. Wallace was the founder of the Ohio Valley Regional Conference on State Parks and at various times served as vice president of the American Forestry Association, director of the Izaak Walton League, and an adviser to the National Park Service. In 1956 the Tom Wallace chair of conservation was established in the UNIVERSITY OF LOUISVILLE's biology department. Also named in his honor are the Tom Wallace Lake in JEFFERSON COUNTY MEMORIAL FOREST and the Tom Wallace Chapter of the Izaak Walton League.

Wallace married Augusta Graham French on February 23, 1910, an heiress of the Smith, Kline, French (now SmithKline Beecham) Pharmaceutical fortune. They had two children, Henry and Augusta. Wallace is buried in Grove Hill Cemetery, Shelbyville, Kentucky.

Henry French Wallace was born June 12, 1915, in Louisville. The former correspondent was an early rebel expelled from the KENTUCKY MILITARY INSTITUTE for drinking while at winter quarters in Venice, Florida. Instead of using his ticket home, Wallace took to the road, riding in empty railway cars during the GREAT DEPRESSION. Along the way, he was arrested for vagrancy and spent thirty days on an Alabama chain gang. After returning home he enrolled at the University of Kentucky and studied journalism. Wallace worked a few years as a newspaper reporter, followed by work in radio intelligence during WORLD WAR II and three years in the U.S. Merchant Marine (1942–45). In 1946 he moved to Cuba and during six years in Havana was a correspondent for *Time* and *Life* magazines, where he interviewed Ernest Hemingway. Wallace moved on to report in Europe and North Africa, meeting his future first wife, Sonja de Vries. They married in Beirut in 1952, returning to Cuba in 1955 where they developed an admiration for the revolutionary Fidel Castro. In 1957 the couple settled on the PROSPECT farm where Wallace had grown up. His wife's discontent there led them to buy a part-time residence in Amsterdam, her hometown. In 1978 the couple divorced, and Sonja remained in Amsterdam. In later years Wallace developed on his six-hundred-acre farm a nonprofit, open-to-the-public zoo called Henry's Ark, which included exotic animals.

Two of Henry and Sonja Wallace's six children publicly continued family activism and literary contributions. Carla Wallace coordinated the Fairness Campaign, and two of Naomi Wallace's plays have been produced by the HUMANA Festival of New Plays.

Wallace's second wife was Peggy Willet Weir. His third wife is Candice Starr Wallace, a native of Westchester County, New York and a 1982 graduate of Smith College. She manages the Wallace Farm Partnership horse operation on the family farm.

See *Courier-Journal,* June 6, 1961; *Louisville Times,* June 6, 1961.

WALLER, HERBERT S. (b Memphis, Tennessee, October 23, 1914; d Louisville, February 17, 1994). Religious and civic leader. Waller was the son of Jacob and Helen Waller. After graduating from the Memphis PUBLIC SCHOOLS at age fifteen, he attended Southwestern University and the University of Cincinnati, where he earned two degrees. He earned two more degrees from Hebrew Union College in Cincinnati and also had the distinction of earning the highest grades in the seminary's history. Ordained in 1939, Waller spent the next eight years serving as rabbi at Temple Israel in Columbus, Georgia.

Waller moved to Louisville and earned a doctor of theology degree from SOUTHERN BAPTIST THEOLOGICAL SEMINARY in 1949. Waller became an assistant to Rabbi JOSEPH RAUCH at Temple Adath-Israel in 1947. The two became co-rabbis in 1955. Waller led the congregation for over thirty-three years, overseeing its merger with Brith-Sholom, changing its name to the TEMPLE, and its relocation to U.S. Hwy. 42.

Waller was also known outside the Jewish community for his commitment to interfaith cooperation, social justice, and public education. In the 1960s he served on the Louisville BOARD OF EDUCATION, the executive committee of Children's Hospital, the Mayor's Advisory Committee, and the clergy committee of the METRO UNITED WAY. To help bridge the gap between black and white students, Waller organized Louisville Youth Speaks, which provides a forum for high school seniors to discuss current topics. To foster cooperation and coordination among area rabbis, he organized the Louisville Board of Rabbis. Not only did he organize cooperation organizations among students and fellow rabbis,he also saw the need for Christians and JEWS to cooperate. He helped organize the Louisville Area Council on Religion and Peacemaking in 1980. Its coalition of blacks, whites, Christians, and Jews met to discuss peace issues and the threat of nuclear war. This led to the Kentuckiana Interfaith Community, which brings together Christians and Jews in sponsoring COMMUNITY MINISTRIES. He served as an adjunct professor of theology at BELLARMINE COLLEGE for some fifteen years. Waller also served as a moderator on an interfaith panel discussion that aired on the local TELEVISION station, WLKY. *The Pastor's Study* was the first religious television program in the city. In 1973 he became a panelist on the WHAS television show, *THE MORAL SIDE OF THE NEWS*. He remained on the show until December 1993. He remained actively engaged in projects until his death.

Waller married Sylvia Steinberg, and they had one son, David. He is buried in the Temple Cemetery.

See Herman Landau, *Adath Louisville: The Story of a Jewish Community* (Louisville 1981); *Courier-Journal*, Feb. 18, 1994.

WALLING, WILLIAM ENGLISH (b Louisville, March 14, 1877; d Amsterdam, Netherlands, September 12, 1936). Social reformer, author. He was the son of physician Willoughby Walling, who practiced for a time out of an office on Walnut St. (now Muhammad Ali Blvd.), and Rosalind (English) Walling. Walling attended Louisville's private schools and schools in Edinburgh, Scotland, where his father served as U.S. consul. Walling earned a bachelor's degree from the University of Chicago in 1897, took law courses at Harvard, and did graduate work in sociology and economics at Chicago until 1900.

Independently wealthy, Walling made social reform activism his life's work. His notable contacts in this field included J.G. Phelps Stokes, Samuel Gompers, Maxim Gorky, V.I. Lenin, Mary O'Sullivan, and Jane Addams. At the American Federation of Labor's 1903 convention, Walling joined with Addams and others to form the National Women's Trade Union League.

Following the bloody 1908 race riots in Springfield, Illinois, Walling, Mary White Ovington, Oswald Garrison Villard, and others joined with Doctor W.E.B. DuBois and members of the Niagara Movement and organized to fight racism. By l910 the group had incorporated the National Association for the Advancement of Colored People (NAACP), with Walling as its first board chairman. Walling also wrote works that challenged socialist orthodoxy. Among these works are *Socialism As It Is* (1912), *The Larger Aspects of Socialism* (1913), *Progressivism—And After* (1914), *Whitman and Traubel* (1916), *Out of Their Own Mouths* with Samuel Gompers (1921), *American Labor and American Democracy* (1926), and *The Mexican Question* (1927).

During WORLD WAR I, he broke with other Socialists and defended President Woodrow Wilson's war policies. In 1917 Walling resigned from the SOCIALIST PARTY. A critic of the Bolsheviks in the 1920s and the Nazis in the 1930s, he supported international trade union movements. Domestically, he shifted his affiliation to the DEMOCRATIC PARTY and in 1924 made an unsuccessful bid for public office when he ran as a Progressive Democrat from Connecticut's fourth district.

In 1906 he married Anna Strunsky, another socialist writer. They had four children: Rosamond, Anna Strunsky, Georgia, and William Hayden.

His public activities affected his health. While attending a meeting with anti-Nazi GERMANS in Amsterdam, Netherlands, in 1936, he experienced pneumonia and endocarditis complicated by a previous heart attack, and soon died. His ashes are buried in Laurel Hill Cemetery, Indianapolis, Indiana.

See Robert L. Schuyler, ed., *Dictionary of American Biography* (New York 1958); Alden Whitman, ed., *American Reformers* (New York 1985); *New York Times,* Sept. 13, 1936; William McGuire and Leslie Wheeler, *American Social Leaders* (Santa Barbara, Calif., 1993).

John A. Hardin

WALNUT STREET AFRICAN AMERICAN BUSINESSES. "Old Walnut Street" has been described by locals as "a celebrated, colorful street," "a teeming avenue of commerce," "the heart and soul of the black community," and "a bustling microcosm of city life for blacks in a segregated society." This Walnut St. of legend extended westward from Sixth St. to approximately Thirteenth St. and included spillover developments along intersecting side streets. Its heyday was from the 1930s to the 1950s.

The roots of "Old Walnut Street" are found in three slavery-time practices that gained prominence between 1830 and 1860 in most developing southern cities. The first practice was "hiring out." This was the device of permitting excess slave labor to hire themselves to perform work for a fee wherever needed. As it became more common, soon the practice of "living out"—whereby slaves did not have to return to their compound or enclosure each night—was found to be economically profitable by slave owners. The burden of finding shelter was placed on the slave. Finally came "board money," whereby slave owners actually made "payment to slaves of small sums in lieu of food and shelter" (Wade, *Slavery in the Cities*, 71). These situations amounted to a quasi freedom for many and, along with other factors, led to a nearly disintegrated system of slavery in southern cities by 1860.

Market forces soon began meeting the needs this created. First came rooms to rent and rooming houses, then boarding houses, and eventually "eat" shops, sandwich shops, RESTAURANTS, cafes, and SALOONS. As slaves and free blacks

African-American businesses on West Walnut Street, 1946.

intermingled and gradually became participants in the "money" ECONOMY, entrepreneurs, both white and black, took advantage of these business opportunities. Since strict SEGREGATION was the law, merchants and vendors catering nearly exclusively to "colored trade" began to appear. Although this activity was concentrated on urban perimeters, physical segregation was not the issue. Local authorities realized the importance of maintaining a residential racial mixture so as to prevent the buildup of a "cohesive" Negro society.

The first Louisville city directory, published in 1832, was organized alphabetically by last name and showed no racial designations for residents or businesses. In the 1841 city directory, the abbreviation "of col" was used to indicate businesses catering to AFRICAN AMERICANS. There were forty-one businesses so listed out of a total of approximately forty-eight hundred businesses. These business people were distributed throughout the growing city, with no concentration in any one area.

Perhaps the first black business in the Walnut St. area was a boardinghouse in the 900 block operated by Martha A. Cozzens, who was described as an "fwc" (free woman of color) in the 1860 city directory. In 1861 there was a colored barber at Tenth and Walnut Streets, plus four other colored barbers in locations other than Walnut St.

In 1884 the first street listing was published. This allows a more precise analysis of Walnut St. from Sixth St. to Thirteenth St. It showed 51 colored residents interspersed among a total of approximately 254 residents/business owners. Under the colored designation for businesses, there was a church, a restaurant, two barbers, and a confectioner.

By 1900 the Walnut St. colored residents were showing a near dominance in the blocks under review. There were twenty-four colored businesses in the area including three each barbers, restaurants, teamsters, and furnished rooming houses, plus another dozen assorted endeavors.

In the next thirty years, the number of colored businesses increased sixfold to reach 154 listings in the 1932 city directory. Notable during that time period was the appearance of four insurance companies, three THEATERS, and two NEWSPAPERS, along with a proliferation of doctors, dentists, and lawyers—all concentrated in the Walnut St. area.

Significantly the 1932 city directory was the last directory that contained a code to identify colored residents or businesses. The Walnut St. area survived the GREAT DEPRESSION and continued its growth during the early post–WORLD WAR II years. Those years have been described as the "glory" years of old Walnut St. The variety of businesses increased. Important in the life of the street were the nightclubs, such as Top Hat Tavern, which attracted nationally known musical entertainers, especially JAZZ performers. Young whites enjoyed hearing a type of music not presented in other parts of the city. And revelers came from across the nation, especially during KENTUCKY DERBY time, to experience the Tip Top's exciting atmosphere and clientele.

In the 1950s three significant events marked the beginning of the end for old Walnut St. First, the desegregation of stores, restaurants, theaters, and accommodations provided opportunities for colored citizens to spend their money in places where they previously could not. Second, the "white flight" to new suburban housing developments and shopping malls began to decimate the former downtown area. Third, URBAN RENEWAL actions in the late 1960s demolished almost all buildings on Walnut St. between Sixth St. and Thirteenth St. and effectively eliminated the old Walnut St. area. In addition, the street has been renamed Muhammad Ali Blvd. Today, there are only two remaining structures from the old Walnut St. era: the MAMMOTH LIFE AND ACCIDENT INSURANCE CO. building at Sixth St. and the Church of Our Merciful Saviour at Eleventh St.

There have been efforts to preserve the memory of old Walnut St. In 1984 the LOUISVILLE FREE PUBLIC LIBRARY presented a multimedia show that took a nostalgic look back at that vanished part of Louisville. Since 1985 the Kentucky Center for the Arts has produced an annual "Midnite Ramble" series—a recreation of the revues that had added to the fame of old Walnut St. In 1997 a town square renovation project was launched by a local civic organization to "rekindle that spirit of pride and entrepreneurship and . . . attract and redirect capital and business activity and disposable income back into the historic old Walnut St. area and western Louisville" (Louisville Central Community Centers Inc., *Vital Link*,[Summer 1997]: 2).

See Richard C. Wade, *Slavery in the Cities: The South 1820–1860* (New York 1964); J. Winston Coleman Jr., *Slavery Times in Kentucky* (Chapel Hill 1940); H.C. Weeden, *Weeden's History of the Colored People of Louisville* (Louisville 1897); James Mellon, ed., *Bullwhip Days: The Slaves Remember* (New York 1988); Bruce M. Tyler, *African-American Life in Louisville* (Charleston, S.C., 1998).

Walter W. Hutchins

WALNUT STREET BAPTIST CHURCH. In 1849 the First Baptist Church merged with the SECOND BAPTIST CHURCH. A lot 100 x 164 feet on the northwest corner of Fourth and Walnut (Muhammad Ali Blvd.) Streets was purchased, and work on a Gothic-style building started. The congregation voted to name it Walnut Street Baptist Church. The new building was dedicated on January 22, 1854.

By the end of the century the church had no room to expand. A search committee was formed, and the congregation voted to accept the recommendation that they purchase a lot

Walnut Street Baptist Church building on the northwest corner of Fourth and Walnut streets, 1870s.

110 x 180 feet on the southeast corner of Third and St. Catherine Streets. Louisville architect Kenneth McDonald (1852–1940) designed a Gothic-style building. This building has large stained-glass windows on three sides, a tower chime of ten bells, and a three-manual pipe organ. The new building was dedicated November 16, 1902.

Through the years, Walnut Street Baptist Church has expanded greatly, adding an educational building, a children's building, and a complete recreation center. A large off-street parking facility offers its members and visitors easy access to this downtown church complex.

See B.T. Kimbrough, *The History of the Walnut Street Baptist Church* (Louisville 1949).

James Burnley Calvert

WALNUT STREET PRESBYTERIAN CHURCH. The Walnut Street Presbyterian Church (also known as the Third Presbyterian Church) was founded in 1832 and initially located on Hancock St. The church's development came slowly, and the congregation's very survival seemed in doubt during most of the mid-1830s because of low attendance and rapid turnover among the membership. However, with the organizational assistance and support of Louisville's FIRST PRESBYTERIAN CHURCH, membership soon picked up.

After several moves, the church in 1853 finally settled on a site on the corner of Walnut (Muhammad Ali Blvd.) and Eleventh Streets. It was here the congregation first acquired the name Walnut Street Presbyterian Church. However, even at its new location, the church faced more than its share of difficulties. On August 27, 1854, a tornado razed the still-unfinished building during Sunday services, killing fifteen worshipers and injuring nearly two dozen more.

Over a decade later, in 1866, in the aftermath of the CIVIL WAR, the congregation suffered a bitter split over the members' political and geographic loyalty. The controversy was ignited when the pro-southern lay officers of the church attempted to retain the pastoral services of Rev. William T. McElroy, a southern sympathizer, over the objections of the predominantly Unionist congregation. Ignoring the congregation's vote dismissing McElroy, the elders and trustees of the church proceeded to rehire McElroy, prompting outrage in the congregation. In order to rectify the situation the congregation met and elected several additional elders and trustees who reflected their pro-northern sentiments. However, the previous lay officers refused to recognize their new colleagues and denied them access to church facilities. The litigation surrounding that crisis eventually found its way to the Kentucky Court of Appeals (then the highest state court). In *Watson v. Avery*, the court handed down a series of decisions (1867–68) rejecting the claims of the Unionists to be duly elected officers of the church because of several procedural irregularities that violated the constitution of the Presbyterian church.

Undeterred, the Unionist faction launched a second lawsuit in the federal COURTS. After finally arriving on the docket of the United States Supreme Court, that bench ruled in *Watson v. Jones* (1871) that the pro- northern party held rightful control of the church because the southern faction had violated the implied trust of the Presbyterian church's hierarchy by defecting into the southern branch of Presbyterianism. Consequently, the Unionist congregation, affiliated with the northern Presbyterian church, retained control of the Walnut Street Church. Meanwhile, the pro-southern group revived the name Third Presbyterian Church, joined the southern Presbyterian church in the United States, and eventually purchased property on the corner of Sixteenth and Chestnut Streets.

Finally, in 1891, the distinct history of the Walnut Street Presbyterian Church came to an end when it merged with the Jefferson Street Presbyterian Church to form the new Covenant Presbyterian Church at 1901 W Jefferson St.

See Edward L. Warren, *The Presbyterian Church in Louisville: from its Organization in 1816 to the Year 1896* (Chicago 1896); Louis Weeks and James C. Hickey, "'Implied Trust' for Connectional Churches: *Watson v. Jones* Revisited," *Journal of Presbyterian History* 54 (Winter 1976): 459–70.

WALTON, MATTHEW (b ?; d Springfield, Kentucky, January 18, 1819). U.S. congressman. Walton was an early settler of Kentucky and worked for its legal separation from Virginia. In that capacity he was a member of the Danville conventions of 1785 and 1787. He served in the first state constitutional convention in 1792. He was a member of the state house of representatives that year, as well as 1795 and 1808. He was elected to the eighth and ninth congresses and served from March 4, 1803, to March 3, 1807. He returned to Springfield in 1807 and remained there until his death. He is buried in the Springfield Cemetery, Springfield, Kentucky.

See *Biographical Directory of the American Congress 1776–1961* (Washington, D.C., 1961).

WARD, CHARLES L. (b Wheeling, Virginia [now West Virginia], February 27, 1838; d Louisville April 21, 1874). Songwriter. His father, William Ward, a dentist, was a talented musician, and Charles showed musical talent at an early age. The Ward family moved to Pittsburgh in 1840, and when Charles was seven he joined the choir of the Presbyterian Church of Pittsburgh, under the direction of the Stone family. When the Stones decided to move to Louisville in the 1840s, they asked that Ward, who had a beautiful alto voice, be allowed to join them. The boy's parents at first refused, but, when they sent their son to visit the Stones in 1850, he stayed on, singing in a choir and working for the music establishment of Brainerd and Stone. It was there that Ward wrote the first of his nearly two hundred SONGS, *The Old Play Ground* (1855). He also wrote a number of songs published by the Louisville firms of D P. Faulds & Co. and Tripp & Cragg.

When the CIVIL WAR began, Ward joined the Confederate army and played the A-flat alto saxhorn in the band of Gen. Simon Bolivar Buckner's troops. During the war, Ward wrote one of his best-known songs, *Old Town Pump* (1861). At war's end, he wrote a series of songs in tribute to the fallen Confederacy, including *Conquered Flag*, where the Confederate flag was a symbol of all the grief and hopelessness of the struggle. *The Faded Gray Jacket* was about a boy's parents who had only his soiled and battered gray jacket for a memory. *We Know That We Are Rebels*, said that they were indeed rebels but felt no remorse about the blood they shed for a cause in which they believed. Ward wrote a number of polkas, including *Leander Polka* (1855), *Douglas Polka*, and *John Bell Polka* (1860). It was said about Ward that had his ambition equaled his natural talent, he would have been a world-famous songwriter. Ward married Kate Miller in 1865. They had two daughters, Margaret and Ermine. Ward died after a long illness; he is buried in Eastern Cemetery in Louisville.

See Willard A. and Porter W. Heaps, *The Singing Sixties: The Spirit of Civil War Days Drawn from the Music of the Times* (Norman, Okla., 1960); Marion Korda, *Louisville Music Publications of the 19th Century* (Louisville 1991).

WARD, MATTHEWS, TRIAL. The trial of Matthews Flournoy Ward for the murder of William H.G. Butler in April 1854 grew out of a notorious affair of honor in Louisville on November 2, 1853. Ward, the son of a wealthy and prominent Louisville cotton merchant, together with his brother Robert Jr., went to the Louisville High School to demand an apology from its principal, William Butler, who had on the day before whipped Ward's brother William for allegedly telling a lie.

After Butler refused to apologize or explain the whipping before the student body, a scuffle ensued. Matthews Ward shot Butler at close range with one of his two concealed weapons. Butler died, and a Jefferson County grand jury indicted the Wards for murder. Lawyers secured a change of venue to Elizabethtown, where Matthews Ward was tried in April 1854. To defend his son, Ward's father secured the services of some of the finest lawyers in Louisville and elsewhere in Kentucky, including United States senator John J. Crittenden. Students who had witnessed the shooting testified that Matthews Ward assaulted Butler, who only responded in self-defense. Robert Jr.'s contradictory testimony, plus Crittenden's brilliant, albeit controversial, summary, persuaded the jury to acquit Ward.

In Louisville, a mob of nearly twelve thousand residents, convinced of Ward's guilt, endorsed a series of popular resolutions calling for the banishment of Matthews Ward from the city and the resignation of Crittenden from the Senate. Part of the mob did considerable damage to the Ward mansion at Second and Walnut (now Muhammad Ali Blvd.) Streets.

Popular indignation against Ward persisted, causing him and his wife to establish permanent residence at the Ward plantation in Arkansas. He was killed in September 1862 by a Confederate soldier who mistook Ward, attired in blue, for a Union soldier. Crittenden survived the widespread disapproval of his part in the Ward trial and continued his distinguished career as a national political leader.

See Robert M. Ireland, "Acquitted Yet Scorned: The Ward Trial and the Traditions of Ante-bellum Kentucky Criminal Justice," *Register of the Kentucky Historical Society* 84 (Spring 1986): 107–45.

Robert M. Ireland

WARD, MICHAEL D. (b White Plains, New York, January 7, 1951). U.S. congressman. Mike Ward is the son of Jasper Dudley Ward III and Lucretia "Lukey"(Baldwin) Ward. His family lived in Scarsdale, New York, until 1956, when his father, an architect, began work on homes of the future at General Electric Co.'s Appliance Park in Louisville. He has maintained an architectural practice since 1958.

Ward attended Ballard Elementary School and Wilder Elementary School and graduated from Atherton High School in 1969. Ward received a B.S. degree in commerce from the UNIVERSITY OF LOUISVILLE in 1974. During college he worked as the overnight Police Court clerk, writing arrest warrants and bail bonds.

On July 18, 1975, Ward married attorney

Christina Heavrin. They lived in OLD LOUISVILLE and later in CRESCENT HILL before going to Gambia, West Africa, as Peace Corps volunteers in 1978, where they served for one year, he as an advisor to small businesses and she as an advisor to the Gambia Supreme Court. They have two sons: Jasper Dudley Ward IV (1979) and Kevin Michael Ward (1983).

Ward was elected to the Kentucky House of Representatives from the Thirty-fourth District in 1988 and reelected in 1990 and 1992. There he authored the "No Pass-No Drive law," requiring students to stay in school and pass four courses to get and keep a driver's license. He served on the House Education Committee, which voted out favorably the Kentucky Education Reform Act (KERA) and on the Appropriations Committee, as well as the Cities and the Health and Welfare Committees. He sponsored a mandatory seat belt bill, getting it through the house for the first time, but losing on a tie vote in the senate. It passed in the 1994 session.

In the November 8, 1994, election for the Third Congressional District, Ward defeated Republican Susan Stokes in a very close election. Stokes initiated a lawsuit seeking a recount after a recanvass failed to change the outcome. Initial results showed Ward won by 425 votes. Following the recount, a judge ruled in December 1994 that Ward had actually won by 473 votes.

Ward's service in the 104th Congress from January 4, 1995, to January 7, 1997, coincided with the election of the first Republican majority in the U.S. House of Representatives in over fifty years, elevating Newt Gingrich to the office of speaker. Ward opposed the Republicans' efforts to cap social spending. He worked successfully to provide federal funding for the Waterfront Development Project and to save funding for the Louisville-based AMERICAN PRINTING HOUSE FOR THE BLIND. For the Louisville Naval Ordnance Station, slated for closure, Ward supported efforts to allow the workers to move from the Navy payroll to private companies doing essentially the same work maintaining weapons systems. He served on the National Security and the Science Committees.

On November 5, 1996, in a bid for reelection, Ward was defeated by his Republican opponent, Anne Northup, 126,625 to 125,326. The Board of Elections recount requested by Ward confirmed his 1,299-vote loss. After leaving Congress, Ward was appointed by President Bill Clinton as associate director of the Peace Corps.

See *Facts on File*, Jan. 1–5,1995; *Courier-Journal*, Dec. 29, 1994.

Teka Ward

WARD, SALLIE (b Louisville, September 29, 1827; d Louisville, July 7, 1896). Socialite. Sallie Ward (Lawrence, Hunt, Armstrong, Downs) was the daughter of the wealthy merchant Robert J. and Emily (Flourney) Ward. She grew to maturity in her family's mansion at the corner of Second and Walnut (Muhammad Ali Blvd.) Streets in Louisville. Ward attended a French finishing school in Philadelphia and completed her education there in 1844.

In Louisville, Sallie Ward Downs was a social grand dame. She had a passion for music and for art. She spoke French and made a fetish of jewels, white satins, and silks. Ward set the social standards that people striving for status imitated in the way she entertained, in the way she dressed, and even in the way she walked. It was said that in Louisville society her name was attached to articles of clothing such as gloves, shoes, and slippers. There was even a style of walking known as the "Sallie Ward Walk." She sponsored perhaps the first fancy dress ball in Kentucky, set a trend in using cosmetics to enhance her beauty, and introduced opera glasses to the commonwealth. Her frequent benefit balls for the poor contributed to her status as one of Louisville's best-loved residents. No social affair of top-line importance occurred in Louisville without the solicitation of her presence. No debutante was assured of social position unless she was chaperoned by Sallie Ward Downs.

Her numerous marriages made sensational news. Her first was to Bigelow Lawrence of Boston. This wedding took place in the elaborate Ward mansion on Walnut St. (Muhammad Ali Blvd.) in Louisville. This perhaps was, to that date, the most extravagant wedding in Kentucky history. But the impetuous Sallie Ward was not temperamentally adaptable to the sedate mode of life of the proper Bostonians, and she quickly returned to Louisville and the Walnut St. Ward mansion, where she could be free of most social conventions.

After a highly publicized divorce from Lawrence, Ward married Dr. Robert Hunt, "one of the most elegant and polished gentleman of the day." When Dr. Hunt's family raised prenuptial objections to the marriage, he responded that he would rather go to hell with Sallie Ward than go to heaven without her. The couple moved to New Orleans and had three children: Robert Junior (who died in infancy), Emily (who died at age nine), and John Wesley. A supporter of ABRAHAM LINCOLN, Ward returned to Louisville when the CIVIL WAR started, but her husband joined the Confederate army. Hunt died immediately after the Civil War. Sallie Ward then married Vene P. Armstrong, a wealthy Louisville meatpacker. Vene lived only a short time after the marriage.

Ward married George P. Downs in 1885. He also was a wealthy retired merchant. Never lacking for funds, Ward traveled widely. In England she was presented at court, and in Paris she was entertained in the most exclusive social circles. In Paris, George Peter Alexander Healy painted her portrait, which he is said to have exhibited alongside those of other celebrities.

At the time of her death Sallie Ward Downs was a resident in the GALT HOUSE hotel. The attending physician reported that the cause of death was "rupture of an internal abscess," a ruptured stomach ulcer. Two years before, Sallie Ward Downs had outlined careful plans for her funeral. She obtained a white satin shroud and instructed that her head be draped in rare family heirloom lace. She requested that the undertaker supply a lavender casket draped in white satin.

At her funeral on July 8, 1896, an illustrious company of regular and honorary pallbearers assembled in the chapel of St. Mary of Magadalene Church at Brook and College Streets. Her confidante, Father Louis Deppen, delivered the funeral oratory. Sallie Ward Downs's remains were borne with pomp to the grave in CAVE HILL CEMETERY. By that date she had become a Louisville legend of social punctiliousness who seems to have been entirely oblivious to the crass workaday world. Nevertheless, she contributed a verve to this aspect of the commercial city.

Because of Sallie Ward's penchant for gathering in rich husbands and outliving them, Kentucky humorist Irvin Cobb suggested that a fitting tombstone inscription would be, "At Last She Sleeps Alone."

See *Courier-Journal,* July 8, 1896; Thomas D. Clark, *Kentucky* (Lexington 1992); Elizabeth Fries Ellet, *The Queens of American Society* (New York 1873).

Thomas D. Clark

WARD, WILLIAM H. (b Virginia, ?; d Louisville, October 1918). Civil servant. Ward settled in Louisville in 1855. Known primarily for his more than thirty years of service as the chief custodian of City Hall, Ward was also active in the Republican Party. His work meant that he was known to many political leaders. This might have generated his interest in politics. He was the first African American member of the Louisville and Jefferson County Republican Committee. At the local Republican Party convention of 1870, he was among those nominated to run for the position of jailer but was defeated by John Mehringer. Ward made another unsuccessful bid for public office in 1878 when he ran for marshal of the city court. In 1890 he accompanied former mayor Charles D. Jacob on a trip around the world.

See H.C. Weeden, *Weeden's History of the Colored People of Louisville* (Louisville 1897).

WARLEY, WILLIAM (b Louisville, January 6, 1884; d Louisville, April 2, 1946). Editor and civil rights activist. After graduating from Central High School in 1902 and attending State (Simmons) University Law School, he established in 1912 a weekly newspaper, the *Louisville News*. As advocates of racial justice, Warley, who was African American, and white Louisvillian Charles Buchanan, a real estate agent, set the stage for an overturn of the city's residential racial SEGREGATION law. The ordinance, passed in 1914, was designed to stop "the gradual influx of the negro into blocks or squares where none but whites reside." It forbade African Americans from occupying housing in any predominantly white block. Warley purchased from Buchanan a lot in Portland with the stated purpose of erecting a house in a predominantly white block. Buchanan then filed suit in Jefferson Circuit Court, charging that Warley had violated the law. The legislation was upheld by both the Jefferson Circuit Court (December 24, 1914) and the Kentucky Court of Appeals (June 18, 1915). The case was taken by the NAACP to the United States Supreme Court. In a unanimous decision, the Supreme Court declared the ordinance unconstitutional because it interfered with property rights. However, racially restrictive covenants were placed in deeds, thus keeping residential segregation.

In 1926 Warley was fined $250 for editorial criticism of a Madisonville judge during the trial of two blacks for rape. For his activism, Warley lost his post office job and encountered other harassment.

Three weeks after surgery for an undisclosed illness, Warley died at Louisville General Hospital. He is buried in the Louisville Cemetery.

See *Louisville Leader*, April 6, 1946; *Courier-Journal*, Sept. 25, 1961; George C. Wright. *Life Behind a Veil* (Baton Rouge 1985).

John A. Hardin

WARDS. The ward system in Louisville was established by the first city charter in 1828. There were five wards running east to west on a north-south axis. Two representatives from each ward were elected to the City Council by ward residents. After the state ratified a new constitution in 1850, a city charter convention was held, and each ward sent four delegates to the convention. A new charter that was approved by the General Assembly in 1851 created a General Council, a bicameral legislative body composed of a Board of Common Councilmen and a Board of Aldermen.

The city was divided into eight wards, each electing two councilmen to one-year terms (two-year terms after 1865) and one alderman for a two-year term. In 1891 a new state constitution scrapped the old city charter system and in place created a system dividing Kentucky cities into six classes according to population. Louisville's new city charter, approved in 1893, expanded to twelve the number of wards, each represented by two councilmen and one alderman. A 1929 amendment to the charter canceled the Board of Common Council and made the Board of Aldermen the city's sole legislative body.

During the era of machine politics in the late nineteenth and early twentieth centuries, wards were controlled by ward bosses, or ward heelers, who handled problems, gave out patronage positions, helped get out the vote, and often provided charity. The ward bosses also relied on precinct captains to poll the area and to control voting stations, sometimes employing intimidation tactics with the help of polling station personnel and local police to pressure voters.

Although some ward bosses were powerful, the primary power in the city remained with the machine bosses, especially Democrats such as the Whallen brothers in the late 1800s, Mickey Brennan in the early 1900s, and Lennie McLaughlin in the 1940s and 1950s, the last of the Democratic Party bosses. The influence of ward bosses declined after political reforms such as the welfare programs of Franklin Roosevelt's New Deal legislation increasingly limited the control of political machines.

Wards often reflected the ethnic or racial areas of the city, with large pockets of Irish in the Portland area and Germans living east of the central city. Today, some of the ward boundaries tend to reflect racial boundaries, with Louisville's African American communities located in the city's western wards.

As the city expanded south, many of the twelve wards became long and thin, with boundaries running from the river on the north to the southern city limits, no more than a few city blocks in width. In 1961 ward boundaries were fundamentally redrawn to better reflect neighborhood boundaries. The wards were reconstituted so that they no longer ran contiguously from east to west in numerical order. After each census, ward boundaries are redrawn by precinct to be roughly equal in population.

The city-county area is subdivided along legislative districts, each made up of about twenty precincts. In 1999 there were 201 precincts in the city and 485 in Jefferson County. A precinct is a defined geographic area with a polling station for resident voters. Precinct captains are chosen by registered party members of each party to supervise the polling station activities during primaries and general elections.

Aldermen are elected in at-large elections, in accordance with the state constitution. Until the early 1980s party candidates were chosen in citywide primaries, but a problem arose in which some aldermen were getting elected to the board in general elections without winning their wards. In 1981 a state law changed the primary system so that candidates would be nominated by eligible ward voters instead of in citywide races. At-large elections have been credited to a degree for the strength of the Democratic Party on the board. The last Republican to be elected was Louise Reynolds in 1967.

See Attia Bowmer, "A History of the Government of the City of Louisville," M.A. thesis, University of Louisville, 1948; *Your Government at Your Fingertips* (Louisville 1994).

WATERFRONT PARK. Waterfront Park, along the Ohio River in downtown Louisville, is the result of a partnership between the Commonwealth of Kentucky, Jefferson County, and Louisville. The Louisville Waterfront Development Corp. was created in 1986 to oversee redevelopment of Louisville's riverfront and to allow public access along the river. The corporation began to acquire and reclaim riverfront land for public use and to rezone the waterfront area for parkland, housing, and river-oriented commercial use.

Public forums provided input for waterfront programming, and an international search for a master planner resulted in selection of Hargreaves Associates, a San Francisco landscape architecture firm, to develop the Louisville Waterfront Master Plan and park design.

Over the years, many plans had been drafted for the riverfront, including serious proposals for hotels and "skyscraper" apartments. The proliferation of industry and the construction of the Riverside Expressway (I-64) in the 1960s effectively cut off the river from the city. That and the inability to extend planning beyond the term of any one political administration effectively shelved such proposals. Establishing an oversight entity, with the support of city, county, and state governments but independent from any one administration, provided the tool necessary to plan and implement redevelopment efforts. Hargreaves's master plan in the late 1980s was the first to overcome the limitations of the site. The plan offered a solution for reconnecting the city to its river heritage by extending the park under the expressway and into the city grid.

The master plan resulted in the transformation of what was historically a heavy industrial area of sand, gravel, scrap, and petroleum operations into a 110-acre Waterfront District that includes almost 90 acres of parkland. The 55-acre first phase, completed and dedicated on July 4, 1999, includes an extended wharf area, waterfront restaurants, a festival plaza, a water feature, the twelve-acre Great Lawn, a harbor, and the Linear Park. The wharf includes docking space for visiting riverboats and an area of festival seating for concerts and other events. The festival plaza is a four-acre area built specifically to host festivals, concerts, arts and crafts fairs, and other events.

The Great Lawn also hosts concerts and offers a green space for picnics, kite-flying, or watching the river and its marine traffic. The nine-hundred-foot-long water feature is a series of pools and waterfalls that step down to the river from the southern edge of the park. The harbor houses a river patrol and other professionally piloted vessels. The Linear Park is a natural park area in the tradition of landscape architect Frederick Law Olmsted, with tree groves, river inlets, hills, meadows, several miles of walking paths, and a children's play area.

Other redevelopment includes a revitalized commercial district adjacent to the park that has boosted employment in the waterfront area from a few hundred to more than 4,000, the preservation of a river-oriented industrial area, the Romano L. Mazzoli Belvedere Connector, improvements to the original wharf, a trolley

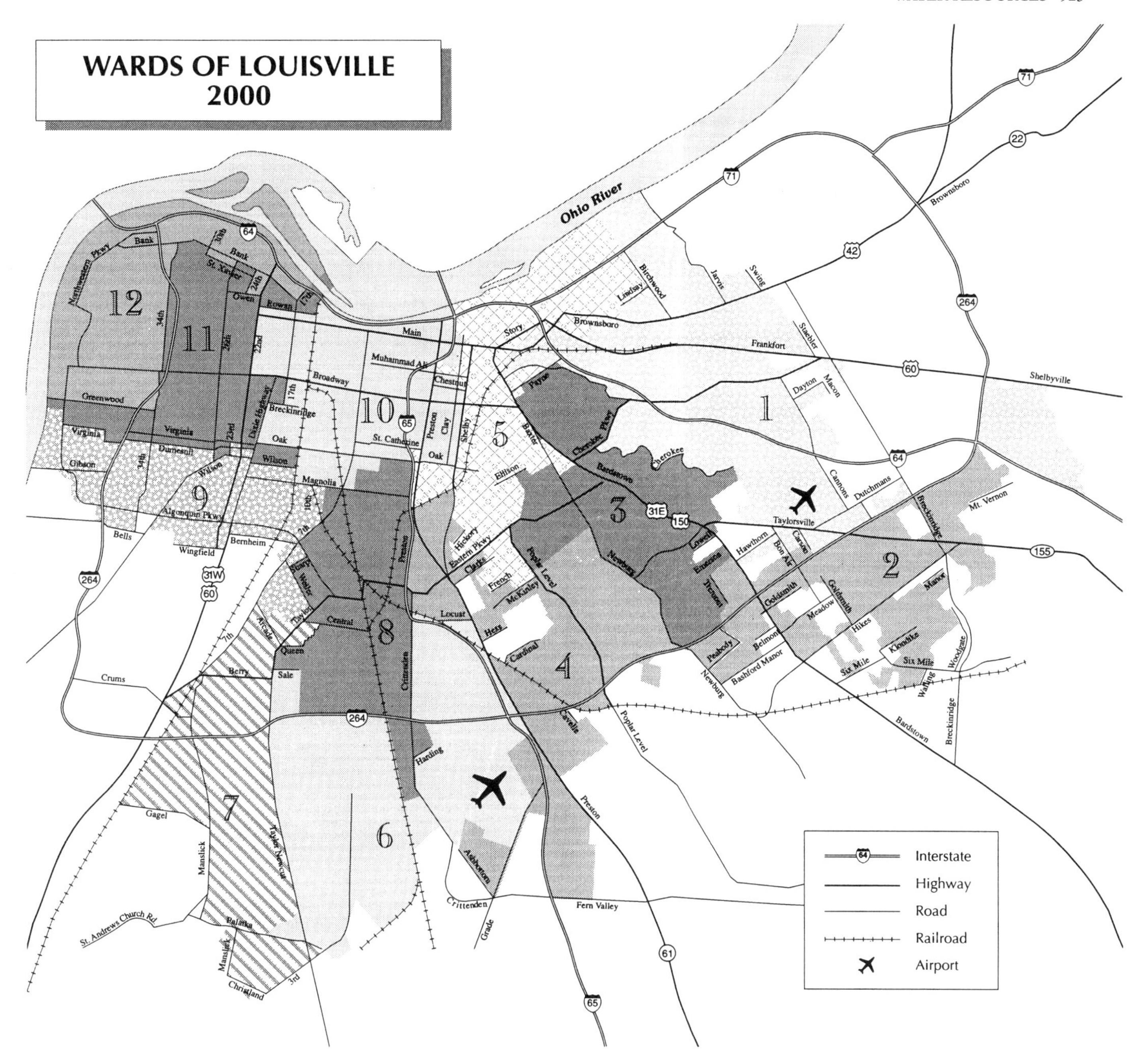

turnaround, and a riverwalk along the full length of the city that terminates in the Olmsted parks in the West End.

Plans for the second phase of park development, an additional thirty-four acres of Linear Park north of River Rd. and east of the Kennedy Bridge, were developed in spring 1999. This section of park includes a link to southern Indiana by way of a pedestrian/bicycle connection to the abandoned Big Four railroad bridge, significantly more recreational space for children, an informal amphitheater, rowing facilities, Towhead Island as a nature preserve, walking paths, picnic areas, and a widening of River Rd. into a parkway between downtown and Zorn Ave.

See *Courier-Journal*, April 16, 1999.

David K. Karem

WATER RESOURCES. The most important sources of water for the Louisville metropolitan area are the Ohio River and groundwater wells. The local hydrologic system at Louisville is dominated by the Ohio River and the glacial-outwash deposits beneath its flood plain, composed of approximately a hundred feet of permeable sand and gravel deposits. The average daily discharge at Louisville for the Ohio River during the 1996 water year (October 1995 through September 1996) was 162,900 cubic feet per second (cfs), or approximately 105 billion gallons per day (gpd). The groundwater reservoir has the potential to contribute an additional 450 million gallons per day (Mgd). These large quantities of water that flow in the Ohio River and move through the alluvial deposits continue to provide readily available sources of adequate public and industrial water supplies.

Essentially the source of all water is precipitation. The normal annual precipitation at Louisville is 44.51 inches for the period 1931–96. The total precipitation for 1996 was 52.04 inches, resulting in a departure from normal of 7.53 inches. Precipitation for 1997 was nearer the norm at 49.71 inches, 5.20 inches above normal. A portion of the local precipitation is taken up by evaporation, transpiration, and soil moisture. This accounts for approximately 53 percent of the annual precipitation. Runoff, generated by rainfall exceeding the infiltration rates of the soils or by falling on impervious areas such as rooftops and pavement and eventually draining to surface streams, claims about 35 percent of the annual precipitation. The portion of precipitation that does not become surface runoff or is evaporated, transpired, or used to replenish the soil moisture seeps farther downward to the zone of saturation and recharges the groundwater system. This recharge to groundwater accounts for the remaining 12 percent of the annual precipitation. The total contribution of precipitation to the water resources of the Louisville area amounted to less than one-half of 1 percent of the average amount of water the Ohio River brought in from outside the area each day for 1996.

The dominant surface-water body in the Louisville metropolitan area is the Ohio River. At Louisville, the Ohio River drains an area of approximately 91,170 square miles. The average daily discharge for 1996 was 162,900 cfs, or approximately 105 billion gpd. The highest daily mean was 573,000 cfs (370 billion gpd) on January 26, 1996, and the lowest daily mean occurred on September 4, 1996, at 11,700 cfs (7.56 billion gpd). The smaller streams, which flow directly or indirectly into the Ohio River, are relatively unimportant as sources of water because their flows in dry years become very low or cease entirely.

The Ohio River contributes valuable services to Louisville and the surrounding area. The river continues to provide the municipal water supply and most water for all other uses, including industrial supplies, fire protection, navigation, hydroelectric power generation, and recreation; and it serves as a medium for sewage and waste disposal. Conversely, the Ohio River has been a destructive force during periods of extreme and severe flooding, and the polluted condition of the river has caused other serious problems in the past.

Treatment is required to make the water from the Ohio River suitable for human consumption and for some industrial uses. The amount and type of treatment required varies with the amount of river discharge and the change in volume of waste entering the river locally. During a May 1995 sampling by the Ohio River Valley Water Sanitation Commission (ORSANCO), the water of the Ohio River at Louisville had a hardness of 120 parts per million (ppm) and total suspended solids of 120 ppm. Other parameters of the May 1995 sampling are summarized in the following table:

Parameter	Value
Sulfate (SO4)	47 mg/L
Total Phosphorus	<0.1 mg/L
Ammonia-N	<0.03 mg/L
Nitrate/Nitrite	0.86 mg/L
Chlorides	13 mg/L
Cyanide	9.0 mg/L
Magnesium	<0.5 mg/L
Cadium	16 &g/L
Copper	5000 &g/L
Iron	5 &g/L
Lead	10 &g/L
Manganese	<0.2 &g/L
Mercury	59 &g/L
Zinc	<4 &g/L

(mg=milligram; &g=microgram; L=liter)

Major floods on the Ohio River at Louisville usually occur during January through April. Ohio River floods typically rise and recede slowly, remaining at or near the crest stage for several days. The flood of January 1937 is the flood of record for the Ohio River at Louisville. It was the highest and most destructive flood in the history of the area. With a crest of 460.15 feet above mean sea level, it was approximately 40 feet above the current-day normal pool stage of 420 feet above mean sea level for the upper gauge.

An average of fifteen inches of annual precipitation in the Louisville area becomes runoff drained by area streams, namely, Harrods Creek, Beargrass Creek, Pond Creek, Floyds Fork, and Silver Creek. These streams contribute flow to the Ohio and Salt Rivers, provide recreational areas, and furnish water for irrigation and avenues for waste disposal; but their flows are typically not adequate for dependable supplies. Flows during the summer months often drop very low, even going dry for a few days to several weeks during extended periods of drought.

In the Louisville area, the principal water-bearing formation is the Ohio River Valley alluvium. The alluvium consists of glacial outwash sands and gravels ranging in thickness from 10 to 150 feet. The alluvium is underlain by bedrock formations of shales and limestones; a blanket of silt and clay, ranging from five to forty feet thick, covers the sand and gravel deposits.

Groundwater has been used in the Louisville area for many purposes over the years: drinking-water supplies, industrial processes, and heating and cooling of downtown buildings. Groundwater use peaked in 1943, when approximately 107 Mgd were being withdrawn for various uses, mainly industrial activities in support of the war effort. A critical groundwater shortage developed as a result of the pumpage in the industrial areas exceeding the natural recharge of the groundwater system by an estimated 20 Mgd. Numerous conservation measures, including artificial recharge, reuse of water, and supplemental use of city water for the processes, lessened the demand on groundwater and the natural recharge was able to replenish supplies over time. Since then, groundwater use has dropped as industry demands changed and heating and cooling systems were replaced with more standard systems. This was spurred by the adoption of a sewer-use tax by the Sewer Commission in 1947. Prior to the tax, groundwater systems for heating and cooling and some industrial processes provided significant cost savings. The tax, which was assessed on the amount of groundwater used, was intended to offset the cost of treating the groundwater that was discharged to the sewers. The cost savings of using the groundwater were soon negated by the tax; thus groundwater was no longer an attractive alternative, and use declined. The total permitted use of groundwater in 1995 for the Louisville area was 28.7 Mgd.

Recharge to the groundwater system in the area comes from infiltration of Ohio River water through the river's bed and banks, discharge from the bedrock to the sands and gravels, and precipitation infiltrating downward through the clay and silt layers to the alluvium. Discharges from the sands and gravels include natural flow to the Ohio River and pumpage from groundwater withdrawal wells.

Rates of recharge to the system and discharge from withdrawal wells can be influenced by the placement of withdrawal wells near the Ohio River. Close proximity to the river allows the inducement of river water to the well, thus increasing the recharge to the alluvium from the river and increasing the amount of discharge available to the well. This assumes a good hydraulic connection exists between the alluvium and the Ohio River. In 1998 the Louisville Water Co. was investigating the feasibility of using this technique (induced riverbank infiltration of Ohio River water) to meet its projected demand of 240 Mgd for public water supply. Previous investigations by the U.S. Geological Survey have estimated that approximately 450 Mgd are available from the groundwater reservoir through the proper design, placement, and operation of a groundwater withdrawal well network.

See M.I. Rorabaugh, F.F. Schrader, and L.B. Laird, *Water Resources of the Louisville Area, Kentucky and Indiana* (U.S. Geological Survey Circular 276, 1953); Edwin A. Bell, *Summary of Hydrologic Conditions of the Louisville Area Kentucky* (U.S. Geological Survey Water-Supply Paper 1819-C, 1966); Mark A. Lyverse, J. Jeffrey Starn, and Michael D. Unthank, *Hydrogeology and simulation of ground-water flow in the alluvial aquifer at Louisville, Kentucky* (U.S. Geological Survey Water Resources Investigations Report 91- 4035, 1996); D.L. McClain, F.D. Byrd, and A.C. Brown, *Water Resources Data Kentucky, Water Year 1996* (U.S. Geological Survey Water-Data Report KY-96-1, 1996); *The World Almanac and Book of Facts 1999* (New Jersey 1998).

Michael D. Unthank

WATER TOWER. The Water Tower is part of the Louisville Water Co.'s Pumping Station #1, at 3005 River Rd. Louisville's pumping station is the only surviving one of four in the United States designed by engineer Theodore R. Scowden. Construction began in 1857, and operation began in 1860. Prior to this time, Louisville was dependent on private and public wells and cisterns, and water was hauled in barrels on water wagons. The 169-foot standpipe tower of Louisville's first waterworks, in the words of Scowden, "is not designed to accord with any architectural order, but to be symmetrical and tasteful in appearance as well as useful."

The adjacent brick building, which housed the pumps, is "in full Corinthian style of architecture." It resembles a Greek temple, with its tall columns. The building has cast-iron and terra-cotta ornamentation. Coal-fired boilers provided the steam to Cornish engines that pumped the water to the tower to equalize the pressure and then to a reservoir where the Veterans Hospital now stands along Zorn Ave. These structures were designated a National Historic Landmark in 1971. Then–Secretary of the Interior Rogers Morton cited it as "the finest example in the country of the symbolic and monumental function of industrial architecture." Engineer CHARLES HERMANY was building Pumping Station #2 when the TORNADO OF 1890 toppled the standpipe tower and demolished most of the zinc statues. Hermany succeeded in improvising a way to pump water until the new pumping station could be finished. The tower was rebuilt and the demolished statues replaced. Pumping Station #1 was thereafter used once a year until 1909, when it was permanently retired. Hermany built Pumping Station #3 around 1917.

In 1977 proposals were invited for the adaptive reuse of the structures. The Art Center Association, a community arts organization dating to 1909, has made its home there since 1980, after successfully raising more than $1 million to renovate both structures and preserve their architectural integrity. The Art Association later changed its name to the LOUISVILLE VISUAL ART ASSOCIATION. The Louisville Water Co. owns the property and has continued to preserve the water tower. In 1996 work began on the exterior of the pump house to restore the facade, columns, and steps to their original design.

Charlotte Williams Price

WATTERSON, HENRY (b Washington, D.C., February 16, 1840; d Jacksonville, Florida, December 22, 1921). Newspaper editor. Henry Watterson was the son of Harvey and Talitha (Black) Watterson. His father represented the Ninth Congressional District of Tennessee as a Democrat. Watterson's childhood was split between the politically vibrant national capital and Maury County, Tennessee.

At a young age Watterson contracted a severe case of scarlet fever that dimmed his eyesight until he was almost blind. Reading was all but impossible for him, but his mother guided his studies, both academically and musically, aiding his conquest of the impairment. After 1843, his father edited the *Washington Union*, a newspaper loyal to the DEMOCRATIC PARTY. It is likely that the younger Watterson learned the art of publishing and printing a newspaper during this time.

He attended school for the first time in 1852 when he enrolled in the Academy of the Protestant Episcopal Church in Philadelphia, headed by George Emlen Hare. Watterson could not participate in athletics, so he started writing for the school newspaper, the *Ciceronian*, of which he was quickly made editor. He remained editor for four years despite a rule restricting editors to one-year terms.

After graduation, he returned to McMinnville, Tennessee, in 1856 to live with his parents. There he published a two-page paper called the *New Era*, in which he reported on local news and guests at the nearby Beersheba Springs Resort. The first editorial he wrote for the paper urged the Democrats to support James Buchanan for the presidency and attacked the Republicans as a threat to the unity of the nation. The *Nashville American* reprinted the editorial, and it was published in the *Washington Union*. With the publication of his editorial, Watterson's talents were nationally recognized. Over the next two years these talents carried him to New York and Washington to work for various NEWSPAPERS in a variety of capacities.

The onset of the CIVIL WAR brought Watterson back to his parents in Tennessee, where, at first, he intended to isolate himself on the sidelines of the war, neutral to both sides. On a trip to Nashville to seek a position on a newspaper, the twenty-year-old Watterson became caught up in the atmosphere of a city charged for war. He joined the Confederate army. Initially, he served on Gen. Leonidas Polk's staff during his occupation of Columbus, Kentucky, but he soon returned home because of illness. After a period of convalescence, Watterson joined Nathan Bedford Forrest's cavalry and participated in several raids made by the daring Confederate general.

Watterson, however, was unsuited for the rigorous life of a mounted raider, so when an opportunity arose in 1862 to publish a newspaper in Chattanooga, he took advantage of it. He called it the *Rebel*. Within its pages he leveled attacks on ABRAHAM LINCOLN and lauded Southern nationalism. After Braxton Bragg's poor showing during the invasion of Kentucky and his equally poor performance at Stone's River, Watterson became highly critical of the unpopular Confederate commander. The *Rebel* became a favorite among Bragg's soldiers. While the paper was based in Chattanooga, Tennessee, Watterson met Walter N. Haldeman, editor of the *LOUISVILLE COURIER*, who was later to become his partner.

After the federal forces occupied Chattanooga, publication of the *Rebel* was done on the run; Watterson eventually returned to military service on Polk's staff and then later on John B. Hood's staff. Hood's misguided campaign into Tennessee in 1864 proved too much for an editor-at-heart, so Watterson accepted a position as an editor for the *Montgomery Mail*. With the Southern cause lost, he made his way to Cincinnati even before the war was over. There he quickly rose to editor-in-chief of Calvin W. Starbuck's Republican paper, the *Evening Times*.

With the conclusion of the war in 1865, Watterson returned to Nashville to edit and help revive the *Republican Banner*. There he married Rebecca Ewing, the daughter of his father's friend Andrew Ewing, on December 20, 1865.

In 1868 publisher Isham Henderson invited Watterson to Louisville to succeed the aged George D. Prentice as editor of the nationally recognized *Journal*. He assumed leadership of a paper competing against Walter N. Haldeman's *Courier* and John Harney's *Democrat*. In a few months he turned the fortunes of the *Journal* around and was able to compete with Haldeman's paper. In October of that year Watterson approached Haldeman, who once before had rejected the idea of combining the two papers, about the *Courier* purchasing Henderson's paper. Watterson saw beyond Louisville and suggested that his editing talents combined with Haldeman's abilities as a publisher would allow them to compete with papers in Cincinnati, St. Louis, and Nashville. Haldeman agreed and bought the *Journal*, along with Harney's *Democrat*. The combination of the three papers became the *COURIER-JOURNAL*, which first appeared on November 8, 1868.

The Liberal Republicans' 1872 convention in Cincinnati provided the springboard for Watterson's first significant role in national politics, where he backed Charles Francis Adams. Although Horace Greeley won the nomination, Watterson supported Adams through the columns of the *Courier-Journal*. In 1876 he became a political advisor to Democrat Samuel J. Tilden. Having achieved what he considered a victory for Tilden, Watterson went to the U.S. Congress in December 1876 to fill out the unexpired congressional term of E.Y. Parson. Watterson was thus on the scene to witness and try to block Tilden's popular vote victory from being turned into defeat by the electoral commission that had been established to settle the disputed election of 1876. Watterson's brief tenure in Congress lasted from August 12, 1876, to March 3, 1877. It was the only political position he ever held. Watterson also helped to put together the political compromise that made Republican Rutherford B. Hayes president.

Over the next several decades Watterson was often criticized for what appeared to be vacillations on Democratic issues. Prominent Democrats such as Grover Cleveland, William Jennings Bryan, and Woodrow Wilson often found themselves being attacked rather than supported by the fickle editor in Louisville. Watterson claimed, however, that he was consistently a Jeffersonian Democrat, believing in individual freedom, free trade, isolationism, and nationalism. In foreign policy, he stood for nationalism, isolationism, and pacifism. Basically a conservative, Watterson nevertheless supported much of the Progressive program of the early twentieth century, breaking with the Progressives only on the issues of PROHIBITION, women's suffrage, and the League of Nations. In 1917 he won the Pulitzer Prize for his prowar editorials.

Despite Watterson's oscillations on prominent issues, the *Courier-Journal* increased its circulation. Its editorials were widely quoted, and its editor became a national figure, watched to see how he would break on an issue. He be-

Henry Watterson, photographed by Richard J. Steffins Studio, c. 1915.

came a dean of American journalism, known simply as Marse Henry, a name he despised.

During WORLD WAR I Watterson, through his editorials, attacked Germany. Louisville's German POPULATION was outraged, and many withdrew ADVERTISING from the newspaper. BRUCE HALDEMAN, who assumed leadership of the paper after the death of his father, Walter Haldeman, in 1902, attempted to control the aging editor. Watterson rebelled and aligned himself with William B. Haldeman to wrest control of the company from the younger Haldeman.

Watterson's inability as a publisher eventually led to the sale of the *Courier-Journal* and *LOUISVILLE TIMES* to ROBERT WORTH BINGHAM in 1918. Watterson continued as editor emeritus for another year, but his disagreement with the *Courier-Journal*'s support of the League of Nations led to his resignation on April 2, 1919.

Watterson spent much of his time in Florida before and after his retirement. He had five children: Ewing, Henry, Harvey, Milbrey, and Ethel. He is buried in CAVE HILL CEMETERY.

See Joseph F. Wall, *Henry Watterson: Reconstructed Rebel* (New York 1956); Henry Watterson, *Marse Henry: An Autobiography* (New York 1919); Donald Ritchie, *American Journalists* (New York 1997).

James T. Kirkwood

WATTERSON EXPRESSWAY. Although first mentioned in the 1920s, the idea of a highway ringing the outskirts of Louisville was not seriously considered until the late 1940s. In early 1949 construction of the first leg of the highway, known as the Inner-Belt, was begun, with a plan to eventually extend the route 12.8 miles from Shelbyville Rd. to Dixie Hwy. With federal assistance funding the early roadwork, the first 2.4-mile stretch opened between Bardstown Rd. and Breckenridge Ln. later in the year.

The road was initially intended simply as a limited-access road, but planners projected that by 1970 the road would carry twenty thousand vehicles per day. However, as more connections opened in the 1950s, some stretches were conveying 23,500 vehicles per day. It became obvious that the two-lane highway, complete with interchanges at grade and accompanying sidewalks, was inadequate.

In 1952 the route was officially renamed the Henry Watterson Expressway in honor of the former editor of *the Courier-Journal.* In 1958 it was designated Interstate 264 in order to receive federal funds for an expansion to create a superhighway. The federal funds were used to construct a four-lane highway with under- and overpasses and to complete the Watterson from Shelbyville Rd. to Dixie Hwy. In 1968 the expressway was extended north to Brownsboro Rd. and Interstate 71. A $400 million widening project was completed in 1995 after eleven years of work, and in 1997 the $25 million reconstruction of the Westport Rd. interchange began. In 1995 the expressway carried approximately 117,000 vehicles per day. This was expected to rise to 135,000 by 2005.

See George H. Yater, *Two Hundred Years at the Falls of the Ohio* (Louisville 1987).

WATTS, CATO. Cato Watts, traditionally Louisville's first African American resident, may have been with the group of first settlers who arrived with GEORGE ROGERS CLARK on May 27, 1778. Said to have been the slave of John Donne Sr., he would be unknown except for the fact that he was accused of murdering his master. Other slaves may have accompanied their owners, but there is no way to tell. AFRICAN AMERICANS, as property, are all but invisible in early public records and private letters and journals. They appear only in wills, appraisals of estates, occasionally in letters, and in rare court appearances when they are accused of serious crimes.

The Jefferson County Court on July 26, 1786, examined Watts, who "pleaded that he had knocked Donne down, but not with the intention of killing him." Two witnesses, Benjamin Reeder and Thomas A. Winn, also appeared, but their testimony was not recorded, as was usual. Perhaps unsure of Watts's degree of guilt or of its jurisdiction, the local court decided that he should be held without bail for trial before the higher court of Oyer and Terminer in Danville in September. The prisoner was taken to Danville by guard George Dament. For this service he was paid three hundred pounds of TOBACCO, a frequent medium of exchange in early Kentucky.

There the paper trail ends. The records of the Danville court, which was discontinued when Kentucky was separated from Virginia in 1792, have vanished. Watts's fate is unknown. A mythical tale, often repeated, holds that he was hanged in Louisville on the south side of Jefferson St. between Sixth and Seventh. This would have been the first hanging in Louisville and should have persisted in local lore, but it appears in no recollections of early settlers or in print until 1880. The same tale makes Watts the hero of the first Christmas in 1778 when

Watterson Expressway at Breckinridge Ln. under construction in 1964. Aerial photograph by Billy Davis.

he played his fiddle for the reels and jigs of the celebration. As with the hanging, there is no basis for this fanciful story. An unanswered question is why Watts had a last name, unusual among slaves. Did he take the name of a previous owner, or was he possibly a free man?

See Jefferson County Court Order Book 2, p. 20; Order Book 3, p. 85; *Courier-Journal*, May l, 1880.

George H. Yater

WAVE. Louisville's second radio station (after WHAS), went on the air December 30, 1933, at 940 kHz (AM), with 1,000 watts of power. The studios were on the fifteenth floor of the Brown Hotel, with a 239-foot tower on the roof. The inaugural program was aired nationwide on NBC, of which WAVE was a continuous affiliate until 1982.

WAVE's early programming, in addition to NBC, had many local originations: the bands of Clayton "Pappy" McMitchen and Pee Wee King, pianist Cliff Shaw, Foster Brooks, sportscaster Don Hill, and *Man on the Street*, with George Patterson and Burt Blackwell. WAVE played a major role during the 1937 flood, sending out appeals for assistance. When electricity failed, the staff got a 100-watt generator and worked around the clock for ten days.

In 1940 WAVE moved to its own building on E Broadway at Preston. The frequency was changed to 970 kHz, the power was increased to 5,000 watts, and a new transmitter and tower were built near Jeffersonville, Indiana. World War II saw the upsurge of radio news on both NBC and WAVE. George Norton, owner of the station, went overseas as an Army Air Corps intelligence officer, and his wife, Jane Norton, joined Nathan Lord to run the station, which then had its first female announcers.

Postwar programming featured WAVE's "Fabulous Five"—announcers Livingston Gilbert, Bob Kay, Bill Gladden, Ryan Halloran, and Ed Kallay—on both radio and television. From 1947 to 1952 WAVE also operated WRXW-FM, at 95.1 mHz, programming mostly classical music. Ahead of its time, its equipment was donated in 1952 to the Louisville Free Public Library, where it has since operated as WFPK-FM.

By the 1960s NBC programming had shrunk to hourly newscasts and the weekend program, so WAVE went to a format of local news and sports, adult music, and personalities, including Pat Murphy and Joe Fletcher. It put up Louisville's first traffic helicopter, which, in April 1974, tracked the Louisville tornado.

WAVE television went on the air November 24, 1948—Kentucky's first television station, and the nation's forty-first. Its founder and owner was George W. Norton Jr., a lawyer and financier. Nathan Lord was vice president and general manager. WAVE-TV's original power was 24,100 watts on Channel 5, with studios, transmitter, and tower at Preston and E Broadway. WAVE-TV has been an affiliate of the National Broadcasting Co. (NBC) ever since its inaugural program. In May 1949 WAVE-TV locally originated the first telecast of a Kentucky Derby.

The national coaxial cable reached Louisville in 1950. Prior to that, NBC programs were shown on film, as was national and foreign news. Local news was done live with Livingston Gilbert; he anchored WAVE-TV and radio news for thirty-nine years.

In 1953 WAVE-TV switched to its present Channel 3, at 100,000 watts, with a new transmitter and 600-foot tower atop a 925-foot (above sea level) knob near New Albany, Indiana. This increased WAVE-TV's coverage by 66 percent. NBC color came in 1954, and WAVE-TV was the first Kentucky station to transmit local color, starting in 1962. In 1958 Norton established the WAVE Foundation, which donates to Louisville educational, medical, charitable, and cultural groups. In 1981 it became the Norton Foundation.

During 1958–59 WAVE-TV produced in its studios educational programs for Jefferson County schools—the forerunner of WFPK-TV, Channel 15. From 1954 to 1962 WAVE-TV also produced, in its studio, *Tomorrow's Champions*, a police- sponsored program for young amateur boxers. Muhammad Ali (then Cassius Clay) got his start there.

In July 1959 WAVE-TV and Radio moved into a new specially designed building on Floyd St. between Broadway and Jacob. It was dedicated with a commissioned opera, *Beatrice*, by Lee Hoiby. Jane Norton, an accomplished artist herself, also commissioned original paintings for the building and statues for the WAVE garden. The garden, facing Broadway, is a small park with water and greenery, now dedicated to the late George Norton.

For the Norton family, 1964 was a pivotal year. In February, George Norton died following an auto crash on the island of Jamaica, and that May his only son, George Norton IV, was killed in a car wreck in Jefferson County. Jane Norton became group chairman and brought in her nephew, T. Ballard Morton, as president. Ralph Jackson was made executive vice president of WAVE-TV. He was also president of the other stations WAVE had acquired through the years, including WFIE-TV in Evansville, Indiana, and stations in Michigan, Wisconsin, and Iowa. The Nortons' daughter, Mary Shands, headed the foundation, and was later board chairman. Nathan Lord retired due to poor health and died in 1967. Lee Browning became station manager of WAVE-TV, and James Caldwell was named general manager of WAVE Radio; in 1979 they became corporate vice presidents.

In 1969 the Norton Group name was changed to Orion Broadcasting after the prominent star constellation. The next year WJMN-TV (Mrs. Norton's initials) was put on the air in Escanaba, Michigan. Orion then greatly expanded its news, weather, editorials, agricultural programs, and documentaries. News bureaus were set up in Frankfort, Kentucky, and Washington, D.C. As a result, WAVE-TV-AM won a number of national awards, including a Peabody.

In 1980, due to the long-range inheritance situation, negotiations were begun to sell the Orion stations for $110 million to Cosmos Broadcasting, a subsidiary of the Greenville, South Carolina, Liberty Corp.. The turnover was made in early 1982, and WAVE-TV and WAVE Radio were split. In the sale, WAVE's call letters were changed to WAVG, and it was sold to Henson Broadcasting of Louisville. In 1988 Henson sold it to Radio One, owned by Tony Brooks, and in 1991 WAVG was bought by Jeffersonville, Indiana's Charles Jenkins, who also operated WXVW. In 1997 Jenkins sold WAVG for $1.8 million to Pulitzer Broadcasting of St. Louis. On June 16, 1997, it took the air as WLKY-AM, an all-news station operating jointly with Pulitzer's WLKY-TV in Louisville. In May 1998 Pulitzer sold their radio and television operations to Hearst-Argyle Television Inc., in a $1.85 billion deal. Hearst-Argyle acquired WLKY-TV and twenty-three other stations.

In 1990 WAVE-TV completed a new 1,712-foot tower in Oldham County, further increasing its coverage. James Keelor, who had become manager of WAVE-TV in 1979, later was made president of Cosmos, and Guy Hempel was named president and general manager of WAVE-TV. Hempel left for a corporate post in late 1998 and was replaced by Steve Langford. News was further expanded, with anchor Jackie Hays and meteorologists Tom Wills and John Belski.

See *WAVE History 1933–1981,* published by the station; Raymond J. Randles, *A Biography of the Norton Family*, M.A. thesis, University of Louisville, 1961; *Courier-Journal*, June 7, 1980, Jan. 9, 1997.

James M. Caldwell

WAVERLY HILLS SANATORIUM. Waverly Hills Sanatorium operated as a tuberculosis hospital for fifty years in the hills off Dixie Hwy. in southwest Jefferson County. At the beginning of the twentieth century, an increase in tuberculosis cases in Louisville and Jefferson County created the need for a facility to treat patients with the disease.

In 1906 the Anti-Tuberculosis Association was organized, with Judge Robert Worth Bingham as chairperson of the first meeting. This organization, whose board members included Bernard Flexner, Temple Bodley, Louis Dittmer, Charles H. Bohmer, H.C. Rieger, Wallace T. Hughes, and Drs. J.H. Baker, George S. Coon, E.Y. Johnson, and Sidney J. Meyer, incorporated as the Louisville Tuberculosis Association.

The association promoted the construction of a tuberculosis treatment center, and the 1906 General Assembly created the board of tuber-

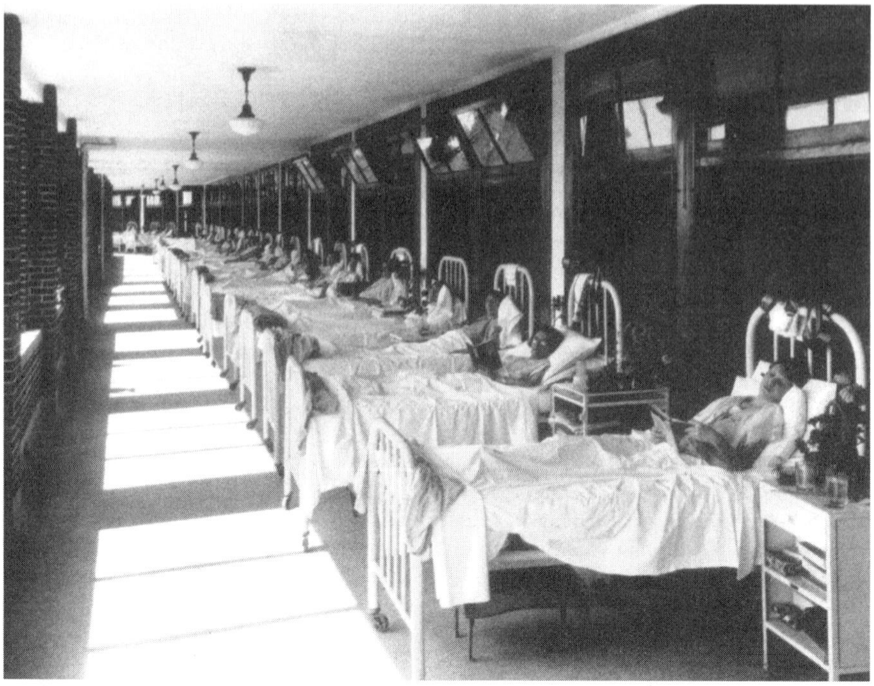

Women's ward of the Waverly Hills Sanitorium in 1926.

culosis hospital. A city/county tax levy was passed by voters, and by 1908 a site was selected for the hospital on the property of Thomas H. Hays, a state senator and vice president of the Pullman Palace Sleeping Car Co. Construction began that year ,and, at its opening in 1911, eight patients were housed in the facility. The patient POPULATION grew steadily, and in 1924–26, a building project was launched to expand the facilities. By that time, Waverly Hills had four hundred resident patients, from infants to adults. Playground facilities and library and school curricula were put in place to accommodate the young patients.

The sanatorium was a community as well as a medical facility. Employees, doctors, nurses, and their families lived on the premises. Both Catholic and Protestant church services were available. A farm for raising crops and a grocery for the residents were also parts of the complex, making it a self-sufficient community. Patient and staff newsletters, such as the *Waverly Chronicle*, the *Bulletin*, and the *Waverly Herald*, were published and noted the many social activities that took place within the complex.

African American patients were treated at the Waverly Hills Sanatorium in a separate wing beginning in the 1920s. Dr. Jesse Bell was one of the first African American physicians at the hospital.

Waverly Hills was nationally recognized for its tuberculosis treatment. The hospital was featured in *On the Firing Line*, a film that documented advances in tuberculosis treatment. Tuberculosis proved less of a PUBLIC HEALTH threat when the drug streptomycin became available. The drug allowed tuberculosis sufferers to be treated as outpatients. Waverly Hills hospital closed in 1961, and the remaining patients were sent to Hazelwood Hospital in southern Louisville.

The medical directors of Waverly Hills were Dr. A.M. Forster (1910), Dr. Dunning S. Wilson (1910–17), Dr. John B. Floyd (1917–18), Dr. E.L. Pirkey (acting director, 1918), Dr. Oscar Miller (1918–30), Dr. B.L. Brock (1930–45), and Dr. Alvin B. Mullen (1945–61.)

Waverly Hills underwent other transformations during the 1960s. The hospital building was renovated into a NURSING home and a mental retardation facility. Both centers later closed, with the nursing home transferring the last patients in 1980. A county park and a nine-hole golf course were developed on land originally part of the hospital property. Since that time, the remaining grounds have been bought by developers. In 1986 the landowners sold three parcels of land to other developers. In 1996 plans for a religious complex with a 155-foot statue of Jesus Christ were developed for one section of Waverly Hills. Fundraising was unsuccessful and the project was abandoned. See *A Place in Time: The Story of Louisville's Neighborhoods* (Louisville 1989).

Margaret Merrick

W.D. GATCHEL AND SONS INC.

Founded by Welcome Darling Gatchel as a photographic supply house in 1862, Gatchel's was originally based in Cincinnati. In the early 1870s, the business expanded to Louisville with a store on Jefferson St. near Third St. By 1880 the company, then known as Gatchel, Hyatt, and Co., established a franchise in St. Louis as well. However, within eight years the partnership between Gatchel and Henry A. Hyatt ended, and the company reverted to its original name, with branch stores in Louisville and Birmingham, Alabama.

Following the panic of 1890, Gatchel's lost twenty thousand dollars it had deposited in the failed National Bank of Cincinnati, forcing the closure of the Cincinnati store. The Birmingham store was closed in 1912 after the death of A.D. Gatchel, one of W.D.'s sons. His other son, Frank, continued to run the Louisville store, which had moved to the Republic Building on Walnut St. (Muhammad Ali Blvd.) near the corner of Fifth St. by 1916. When Frank died in 1942, he was succeeded by his son, William, who increased the company's net worth more than tenfold in eleven years by expanding the business's scope.

After William's untimely death in 1953 his son, Frank Gatchel II, directed the company and moved it to E MARKET St. In 1976 his brother, J. Cleve Gatchel, purchased Frank's interest in the business. By 1997 Gatchel's had a strong regional position in the field of graphic arts, servicing Kentucky, Indiana, Ohio, Illinois, West Virginia, and Tennessee.

WEATHER. Louisville has a continental climate with only occasional interruptions of strong maritime influence. A continental climate is marked by large temperature differences between warm and cold seasons. The transition seasons of spring and fall show large short-term variations as warm and cold weather patterns move across the area frequently. The greatly diminished solar heating patterns of winter create average temperatures in the lower thirties, while the summer months are about forty-five to fifty degrees warmer.

The lower Ohio River Valley has an influence on weather patterns. Winter storms often travel northeastward through the valley. This pushes most potentially major snowfall events northward into Indiana. The valley also acts to guide many thunderstorms along the river into the Louisville area. The range of low hills in southern Indiana, commonly referred to as the KNOBS, also plays a subtle influence on Louisville's weather. Cold air pushing southward is partially blocked by these hills. This effect is most common in the warmer months of the year.

Eastern Jefferson County features rolling hills and numerous creeks. The western area, including most of the city of Louisville, is flatter and has an elevation about one hundred feet lower. This area lies in the flood plain of the Ohio River and is also more prone to flash-flooding from heavy thunderstorms with high rainfall intensities.

Temperatures

Yearly temperatures show a wide range. Table 1 shows the average annual monthly high, low, and mean temperatures for Louisville. January's mean temperature is the coldest of the year, while July normally produces our warmest temperatures. Average temperatures, however, can be very deceiving, especially in the winter months. In fact, most winter months vary considerably from their quoted normals. The long-term averaging of individual extremes hides the distinguishing characteristics of each winter. For instance, January's average of just under 32 degrees hides the fact that winters can have a major warm or cold bias. The city's coldest month was January 1977 with an average temperature of 18.6 degrees. That contrasts sharply from January 1880, which had an average temperature of 50.0 degrees. The other winter months, December and February, also have large differences historically.

During the spring months of March through May, the average temperatures warm rapidly, with each month warming about ten degrees from its predecessor. The warm or cold bias often shown by winter weather still exists but has much less variation.

Louisville summer temperatures are very warm. The difference between the hottest and coolest summer months is less than half of winter's extremes. Although an average of eighty degrees is very high for a summer month here, June, July, and August have all managed to reach that figure at least once. The hottest summer month recorded was an average of 84.2 degrees in July 1901.

The autumn months feature average temperatures falling faster than the spring rate of rise. And the warm and cold bias of monthly extreme temperatures also starts to rise.

Precipitation

Louisville has year-round precipitation. The autumn months tend to be the driest, while the spring months are the wettest. Precipitation is frequent. Measurable precipitation falls on 124 days in an average year. Total precipitation averages over forty-four inches per year. Table 1 lists monthly precipitation and snowfall averages. Snowfall in melted form is included in the precipitation figures.

Heavy rains of short duration are common during spring and summer thunderstorms. Occasionally, heavy rains persist for longer times. These often lead to flooding of the OHIO RIVER at Louisville. The city's wettest month, January 1937, helped produce Louisville's greatest flood. That month, 19.17 inches of rain fell. March 1997 (17.52 inches), July 1875 (16.46 inches), March 1964 (14.91 inches), and January 1907 (12.11 inches) have been the only other months with rainfall totals above 12 inches. All of the above dates except July 1875 have contributed to major Ohio River flooding here. The wettest year has been 1996, with a total of 63.76 inches.

Dry months, and years, also show up in our weather records. The records for each calendar month show at least two years with rainfall totals below one inch. Eight calendar months have at least five years with less than one inch of precipitation. October 1908 was the driest month, with just 0.07 inches of rain. Louisville's driest year was 1930. Only 23.88 inches of rain fell that year. The second-driest year produced 28.12 inches (1934). Every other year of record has produced at least 65 percent of the long-term average precipitation. This consistency of yearly precipitation has been depended upon by area agricultural interests during most of Jefferson County's history. Drought years have been about as common as FLOOD years, but their economic impact to the Louisville area has changed. Floods have become more damaging because of increasing property values in the flood plain, while droughts have a smaller economic impact because of loss of local farmland as the POPULATION expands outward.

During the colder months, rain remains Louisville's dominant precipitation form. Snow, however, has fallen every winter. Snowfall shows the greatest variation of all the yearly weather events in Louisville. At least some snow is likely to fall every month from November until March. Some winters, such as 1988–89 with .9 of an inch, have no snow of any consequence. Colder winters have produced as much as 50.2 inches of snow (1917–18).

Measurable snow has occurred as early as October 19 (1.4 inches, 1989) and as late as May 6 (1.0 inches, 1898). Flurries (or sleet) have been observed as early as October 3 (1989) and as late as May 20 (1894).

Deep snowfalls are very rare. Official weather records began in Louisville in 1872. Since that time, only ten snowstorms have accumulated to as much as ten inches. Six of the seven deepest snows have occurred since 1966.

Winter

Louisville's winters are cold and cloudy. Temperatures fall to 22 degrees or colder eighty-nine days during an average winter. And temperatures never rise above freezing on twenty of those days. Temperatures as cold as zero degrees or lower are rare. Many winters escape zero-degree weather entirely. Only twice in an average winter will temperatures drop to zero. The city's coldest temperature of record is minus 32 degrees on January 19, 1994.

Sunshine is rare during Louisville winters. December, January, and February all produce less than 50 percent of the possible hours of sunshine. December averages only 40 percent of possible sunshine.

Snowfall usually occurs as a series of light snows scattered through the winter. Average snow for the cold season is eighteen inches. Normally, five snows will reach one inch or greater each winter. Louisville's deepest snowstorms were February 4–6, 1998 (22.3 inches), January 16–17, 1994 (15.9 inches), January 16–17, 1978 (15.7 inches), December 7–8, 1917 (15 inches), and November 2–3, 1966 (13.1 inches).

The winter of 1917–18 is noteworthy in that two snows of more than ten inches fell, the only winter to have more than one. Total for the winter was 50.2 inches, the most ever for a winter season here.

Spring

As temperatures warm from March through May, sunshine becomes more likely. Percentage of possible sunshine rises from 51 percent in March to 61 percent during May. The last freezing temperature of the spring usually occurs by mid-April, although it has happened as late as May 10 (1966).

As temperatures warm, our air is able to hold more water vapor. The still-active weather patterns produced by the colder weather interact with this increasing water supply to make spring by far the wettest three-month period of the year.

Along with the increased rainfall comes an increase in thunderstorms. Although thunderstorms occur year-round, they show a major increase starting in March. Louisville averages forty-six days with thunderstorms each year; forty occur between March and September. Spring thunderstorms can be the most dangerous of the year, since the threat of severe weather is greater. Wind damage is the most frequent problem from spring storms. Hail large enough to be damaging is rare. Even rarer are tornadoes. In Louisville's history, four major, severely damaging TORNADOES have struck. The first was a very rare late-summer tornado on August 27, 1854. The other three have been early spring storms—March 27, 1890, March 18, 1925, and April 3, 1974. The 1890 tornado has been our deadliest, with nearly a hundred deaths attributed to it. Other devastating tornadoes have hit the broader metropolitan area.

Summer

The hottest months of the year show the least weather variety of any season. Weather patterns show little day-to-day change during the summer. Thus, every summer is warm and humid. In spite of the generally stable weather, some summers have much more heat and humidity than others. Occasional thunderstorms offer temporary relief from the heat and humidity. Even the number and intensity of thunderstorms diminishes as the summer wears on.

The longest days of the year coincide with the time of greatest percentage of possible sunshine. Each month averages at least 67 percent of possible sunshine. A standard for hot weather is 90 degrees. A typical summer has twenty-nine days when temperatures reach or exceed 90 degrees. Once, in August 1900, Louisville had twenty-nine days of 90 degree temperatures in a single month. The decade of the 1950s was an especially hot time here. A record eighty-one times the temperature reached at least 90 degrees during 1954. Three other years in the 1950s produced seventy or more days of 90-degree temperatures. At the other extreme, the summer of 1974 was able to reach 90 degrees only three times.

Although temperatures in the nineties are

common, 100-degree temperatures are rare. Louisville reaches that mark only about once every two summers. The all-time hottest temperature ever recorded at Louisville is 107 degrees. We have reached that mark three times: July 24, 1901, July 28, 1930, and July 14, 1936.

Summer rainfall has shown wide variability over the years. In general, the hottest summers tend to be the driest. Our two driest summers produced less than 4.5 inches and occurred during the Dust Bowl era of the 1930s. Our driest summer was in 1930, when just 3.22 inches fell. The combination of summer's heat and lack of rainfall have led to the worst cases of short-term drought.

Autumn

Weather patterns begin to resume greater variability by early autumn. The active precipitation cycle of the spring, however, is not repeated. Weather systems are weaker and precipitation is lower until November. Fall rainfall averages less than two-thirds of the spring total.

October has produced the two driest months ever. Only 0.07 of an inch of rain fell during that month in 1908. The 0.10 of an inch recorded in October 1924 was not far behind.

Temperatures fall rapidly. The rate of decrease is even greater than spring's rise. The average daily high temperature falls almost forty degrees during autumn. Fall's first 32-degree temperature is usually seen by late October but has occurred as late as December 5 (1885). October 3, 1974, was the date of our earliest fall freeze.

As the days grow shorter, percentage of possible sunshine drops to 65 percent in September and 61 percent in October. Then, a big drop to 46 percent occurs in November.

Average Annual Totals

High Temperature:	
January:	40 degrees
February:	45 degrees
March:	56 degrees
April:	67 degrees
May:	76 degrees
June:	84 degrees
July:	87 degrees
August:	86 degrees
September:	80 degrees
October:	69 degrees
November:	57 degrees
December:	45 degrees
Year:	66 degrees
Low Temperature:	
January:	23 degrees
February:	27 degrees
March:	36 degrees
April:	45 degrees
May:	55 degrees
June:	63 degrees
July:	57 degrees
August:	66 degrees
September:	59 degrees
October:	46 degrees
November:	37 degrees
December:	28 degrees
Year:	46 degrees
Average Temperature:	
January:	32 degrees
February:	36 degrees
March:	46 degrees
April:	56 degrees
May:	65 degrees
June:	73 degrees
July:	77 degrees
August:	76 degrees
September:	70 degrees
October:	58 degrees
November:	47 degrees
December:	37 degrees
Year:	56 degrees
Average Precipitation:	
January:	2.86 inches
February:	3.3 inches
March:	4.66 inches
April:	4.23 inches
May:	4.63 inches
June:	3.46 inches
July:	4.51 inches
August:	3.54 inches
September:	3.16 inches
October:	2.71 inches
November:	3.7 inches
December:	3.6 inches
Year:	44.35 inches
Average Snowfall:	
January:	5.2 inches
February:	4.7 inches
March:	3.9 inches
April:	0.2 inches
May:	-
June:	-
July:	-
August:	-
September:	-
October:	Trace
November:	1.5 inches
December:	2.6 inches
Year:	18.1 inches

Note: Normal temperatures are calculated from data from 1961 to 1990. About the second year of each decade the normals are recalculated, leaving off the oldest decade and replacing with data from the recently completed decade.

Tom G. Wills

WEAVER, CHARLES PARSONS (b Louisville, March 14, 1851; d Louisville, November 21, 1932). Mayor. The son of William Thomas and Emily Tryphosa (Parsons) Weaver, he was educated at PUBLIC SCHOOLS in Louisville and attended the Bryant & Stratton Commercial College.

Weaver was elected to the BOARD OF ALDERMEN in 1888 from the Twelfth Ward and served until 1894. He served as assistant postmaster before he was appointed postmaster in 1894 by President Grover Cleveland. In 1897 he resigned as postmaster to accept the Democratic nomination for mayor.

Weaver served as mayor from November 16, 1897, until November 19, 1901. He ran against incumbent mayor George D. Todd, who was the first Republican elected by the council to serve as mayor. That mayoral race was the first to pit a Democrat directly against a Republican. Weaver, the candidate of the Whallen political machine, defeated Todd by 2,728 votes out of the 40,000 cast. The election was marred by voter fraud, the most egregious case being the dramatic drop in black voter turnout allegedly caused by strong-arm tactics of the DEMOCRATIC PARTY faithful.

During his tenure as mayor, Weaver was instrumental in the passage of a $500,000 bond issue, $275,000 of which went for the purchase of DuPont Square (Central Park) and the rest for refurbishing the city's sewer system. The bond issue for the park went unused until the du Pont heirs decided to sell the land to the Board of Parks Commissioners in 1904.

Weaver also opposed the sale of the city's stock in the Louisville Gas Co. He fought against a dual TELEPHONE system in Louisville, although a franchise was granted to Home Telephone Co. by the council over his veto. He secured passage of a five-year tax exemption law for new manufacturers.

Weaver served as secretary and treasurer of the Kentucky & Indiana Bridge Co. from 1889 to 1894. He was also secretary and treasurer of the city's COMMISSIONERS OF SEWERAGE. In 1920 he was appointed head of Kentucky Houses of Reform at Greendale, Kentucky. After two years he retired from this position to return to Louisville. He also served as director of the KENTUCKY SCHOOL FOR THE BLIND. He was a member of the Democratic State Central Committee and was also a member of Louisville's Board of Trade for many years.

Weaver married Anna Mary Sewell of Louisville on November 17, 1886. The couple had a son, William Gaulbert, and two daughters, Jesse and Effie. Weaver died of pneumonia at his home at 125 W Ormsby Ave. after an extended illness. He is buried in CAVE HILL CEMETERY.

WEAVER, SYLVESTER (b Louisville, July 25, 1896; d Louisville, April 4, 1960). BLUES guitarist and gospel singer. Weaver was born in the SMOKETOWN neighborhood to Walter Weaver and Maria Cottrell. His recording career began in 1923 when he became the first blues guitarists to record. From 1923 to 1927 he made blues and gospel records and served as a talent scout, bringing singer HELEN HUMES and guitarist Walter Beasley to the attention of OKeh Records. His best-known recording is *Guitar Rag*, which was made famous by Bob Wills and His Texas Playboys as *Steel Guitar Rag*. Around 1928 he became the chauffeur for the family of Gertrude Lemon. He is buried in Louisville Cemetery.

See Sheldon Harris, *Blues Who's Who* (New York 1979); Paul Garon and Jim O'Neal, "Kentucky Blues: Part Two." *Living Blues* 52 (Spring 1982): 15–20.

Brenda K. Bogert

WEBB, BENEDICT JOSEPH (b Bardstown, Kentucky, February 25, 1814; d Louisville, August 2, 1897). Legislator and author. The son of Nehemiah and Clotilda (Edelin) Webb, Benedict was educated at St. Joseph's College in Bardstown. He took a position in 1832 as press-man with the LOUISVILLE JOURNAL. In 1836 he became editor of the *Catholic Advocate* and after 1847 was a partner in the piano manufacturing firm of Peters, Webb in Louisville.

A Whig in politics and a Catholic in faith, Webb turned Democrat when many in the WHIG PARTY moved toward the anti-Catholic Know-Nothing (American Party) persuasion in the 1850s. In 1867 he was elected state senator, a post he held for eight years. Webb produced a well-known anti-Know-Nothing pamphlet, *Religion in Politics*, but is most remembered for his massive history, *The Centenary of Catholicity in Kentucky* (1884). He received an honorary doctorate from the University of Notre Dame in 1885.

Webb married Sarah Ann McGill on January 23, 1839, and ten children were born of the union. At the time of his death the widower Webb was survived by only three of his children. He is buried in St. Louis Cemetery in Louisville.

See J. Stoddard Johnston, "Benedict Webb: Kentucky Historian," *Filson Club History Quarterly* 6 (April 1932): 205–7.

Clyde F. Crews

WEBSTER, BRADFORD (b Waterbury, Connecticut, February 18, 1881; d ?). Inventor. Webster received his early education in Waterbury, Connecticut. He attended college at Yale, where he was the school champion of whist, a card game similar to bridge. He also served as captain of the Yale whist and checkers teams. He graduated in 1903 with an A.B. degree. He arrived in Louisville in 1904, accepting the position of professor in history, mathematics, and civil GOVERNMENT at the University School located at 1047 S Second St. As a result of his love for sports, Webster was also named the school's athletic director. Webster left the University School in 1906 after graduating with L.L. and L.B. degrees from the UNIVERSITY OF LOUISVILLE. In 1907 he graduated from the Washington School of Patent Law.

In 1910 Webster assisted in the publication of *Seymour's Annotations to the Kentucky Constitution*. In the years following, he edited and compiled the second and third editions of the work. He also published works of his own such as his "Essay on Adam Smith and the Wealth of Nations," "Essay on the Nature of Invention," and the "Short Treatise on Hydraulics, Hydrostatics and Heat."

In 1911 Webster began his own company, the Webster Loose-leaf Filing Co. His offices and plant were in the Snead Building at 817 W MARKET St. In addition to running the company, Webster also acted as a patent lawyer and inventor. He made improvements to the valve, oratoriphone (a device that amplified the voice of public speakers), loose-leaf binders, paper punches, and several other innovations such as a self-reversing motor and "knock-down" bookcases and filing cabinets. Webster held patents on these and other products, not only in the U.S. but also in Canada and most of Western Europe. Webster is found in the Louisville city directory for the last time in 1914. It is therefore assumed that he left Louisville before his death.

See Alwin Seekamp and Roger Burlingame, *Who's Who in Louisville* (Louisville 1912).

WEEDEN, HENRY CLAY (b LaGrange, Kentucky, 1862; d Louisville, October 8, 1937). Author, educator, preacher, publisher, editor. Weeden was born into slavery and later educated at LAGRANGE PUBLIC SCHOOLS and in Louisville, as well as at New Castle, Kentucky, under the Reverend ELIJAH P. MARRS. He worked and studied in Louisville under Dr. STUART ROBINSON and Col. Bennett Young. Weeden became sub-editor of the *Christian Index* and in 1881 became editor of *Zion's Banner*, a black religious newspaper. His editorials from the *Banner* were reprinted in the *New York Independent*. During the 1895 GRAND ARMY OF THE REPUBLIC ENCAMPMENT in Louisville, Weeden served as a special correspondent to the city's dailies. He was permitted access to all encampments and activities, both black and white.

A staunch Republican, Weeden was a member of the National Republican League of the United States. During the administration of President Benjamin Harrison (1889–93), he held a high position in the postal service, the highest office of any black man in his district. He served as a delegate to the Republican National Convention for ten years and was a member of the city and county committee for eight years. In 1892 he was elected secretary of the Fifth-District Republican convention, being the first African American to hold the position.

In 1897 *Weeden's History of the Colored People of Louisville* appeared, giving recognition to many black ministers, educators, and political activists who had gone unrecognized for their work in improving the lives of the city's people of color, and the institutions that were important in their lives. He noted in his introduction that he hoped the pages would "inspire us that we may have a greater ambition to become more useful citizens." Weeden received praise for arousing the interest and pride of the colored people by such Louisville notables as Mayor George D. Todd. Although the material was sometimes sketchy and the facts often ambiguous, Weeden's book is a milestone in preserving local history of AFRICAN AMERICANS.

Weeden was socially active. He served as secretary of the Louisville Cemetery Association, which organized the Louisville Cemetery, a cemetery on Poplar Level Rd. for African Americans. He earned a law degree later in life and was a trustee of Atkinson College in Madisonville, Kentucky, and a thirty-second-degree Mason. He was cofounder and served as president of the Mendelssohn Singing Association, which was formed in 1892 and filled many singing engagements. As a church worker, he was musical director and superintendent of the Sabbath schools of the Zion Church for twelve years.

In 1901 he married Anna Marshall Smith, a black Canadian whose grandparents had been active in the UNDERGROUND RAILROAD in Ontario. Following her death, she was recognized as a prominent black poet. They had three children and lived at 816 S Hancock St. Weeden is buried in the Louisville Cemetery.

See George C. Wright, "Blacks in Louisville 1890–1930," Ph.D. thesis, Duke University, 1977; Alice Dunnigan, *The Fascinating Story of Black Kentuckians: Their Heritage and Traditions* (Washington, D.C. 1982).

WEILLER, LOUISE (PENNINGTON) (b New Albany, Indiana, September 12, 1904; d Louisville, October 22, 1996). Radio personality and columnist. She was born Margaret Louise to Chester A. and Eva (Hudgins) Pennington. Her family moved to Louisville shortly after Louise's birth. After graduating from LOUISVILLE GIRLS' HIGH SCHOOL in 1920, she entered the UNIVERSITY OF LOUISVILLE and became the first editor of the newly established yearbook known as *The Thoroughbred*.

Following graduation Louise taught in the Indiana public school system for a year. On June 21, 1926, she married Charles Robert Weiller, and the couple moved to St. Louis. They had a daughter, Constance Pennington, before moving back to Louisville in the early 1940s.

In 1945 Weiller began work on a temporary basis with WINN radio, the local ABC affiliate. By 1950 the station had switched to a pop-music format, and Weiller had her own program, known as *Lookout Lady*, which presented discussions on buying and swapping items. She moved to WHAS radio after a few years for a show relating to new inventions for housewives and children. After a brief hiatus due to the death of her daughter, Weiller returned to radio in 1956 and joined WAVE for a segment discussing home tips, fashions, and arts entitled, *A Woman's Way*. Weiller also wrote a column for the ST. MATTHEWS- based *Voice-Tribune*.

Weiller is buried in CAVE HILL CEMETERY.

WEISSINGER, MUIR (b Louisville, 1870; d Larchmont, New York, August 1, 1952). Jefferson County judge. Weissinger was born into a prominent Louisville family, the son of Col. Harry and Belle (Muir) Weissinger. His father was one of Louisville's most successful TOBACCO manufacturers at the turn of the century. Harry Weissinger was also president of the Louisville BOARD OF ALDERMEN from 1901 to 1902. His grandfather, George W. Weissinger, was owner and publisher, along with George D. Prentice, of the *LOUISVILLE JOURNAL* from 1835 until his death in 1851. His mother's father was prominent Louisville attorney Peter B. Muir, who was also a Kentucky legislator, circuit judge, and member of the Louisville City Council.

Weissinger, a Democrat, was Jefferson County judge from January 1, 1910, until December 31, 1913. He was swept into power along with the rest of the Whallen machine, led by Mayor-elect WILLIAM O. HEAD. Weissinger beat incumbent county judge ARTHUR PETER (27,500 to 25,978), a Republican who had run as a Fusionist candidate in the 1907 special election, and Charles Wilson, a former county judge. Weissinger also served as judge of the Fiscal Court, Quarterly Court, and Juvenile Court.

He was known for his work with dependent and delinquent children. He helped to secure passage of a bill authorizing the placement of delinquent children in private homes rather than reform school. Weissinger was also instrumental in getting the county to purchase the Ormsby estate, which later became ORMSBY VILLAGE, a residential institution for dependent and delinquent children in eastern Jefferson County.

In 1927 he was married to English actress Florence Bond in England. The couple had two children—Muir Jr. and Delphine. The family lived in England from 1927 until they returned to New York during WORLD WAR II. Weissinger died at his home and was buried in Larchmont, New York.

See Alwin Seekamp and Roger Burlingame, eds., *Who's Who in Louisville* (Louisville 1912); *Courier-Journal*, Aug. 2, 1952.

WELBY, AMELIA BALL (COPPUCK) (b St. Michael's, Maryland, February 3, 1819; d Louisville, May 3, 1852). Poet. She was the daughter of William and Mary (Shields) Coppuck, who, shortly after Amelia's birth, moved the family to Baltimore, where Amelia received a minimal education. In 1833 the family moved to Lexington, Kentucky, and to Louisville the following year. Amelia's POETRY began to be published in the *LOUISVILLE JOURNAL* in 1837, and under the tutelage of the paper's editor, George D. Prentice, her popularity grew. In 1845 *Poems by Amelia* was published, and by 1860 it reached its seventeenth edition. This collection touches on a variety of subjects: love, death, children, nature, RELIGION, and brides.

Her best-known poem, "The Rainbow," was reprinted in a popular Southern school book, *Holme's Fifth Reader*. Her verse was described as being "bright and true to nature," and she received praise from such literary greats as Edgar Allan Poe, who reportedly said, "None equal her in the riches and positive merits of rhythmical variety, conception, and invention." In June 1838 Amelia Coppuck married George Welby, a Louisville businessman, and in March 1852, she gave birth to a son. She died two months later and is buried in CAVE HILL CEMETERY.

See J. Stoddard Johnston, ed., *Memorial History of Louisville* (Chicago 1896); William Ward, *A Literary History of Kentucky* (Knoxville, Tenn., 1988); *The National Cyclopedia of American Biography* (New York 1896).

WELLER, WILLIAM LARUE (b Hardin County, Kentucky, July 26, 1825; d Ocala, Florida, March 24, 1899). Distiller. He was the eldest son of Samuel Weller by his second wife, Phebe (LaRue). He grew up on the family farm. In 1844 William left to live in Louisville. After arriving in the city, he joined the LOUISVILLE LEGION and served in the MEXICAN WAR. He returned to Louisville in 1849. That same year he and his brother Charles David Weller (1835–62) started W.L. Weller and Bro., Wholesale Merchants in Foreign and Domestic Liquors.

The business was located on MAIN St. between Sixth and Seventh, opposite the LOUISVILLE HOTEL. The brothers may have been selling the whiskey made by their father in Larue County. The company prospered, with William manning the office and Charles traveling as salesman. Tragedy struck when in 1854 a typhoid epidemic killed Samuel and most of the family in Larue County.

William married Sarah B. Pence in 1850. They had four sons and three daughters. The Wellers were members of the WALNUT STREET BAPTIST CHURCH, and William was one of the founders of the Louisville Baptist Orphans' Home in 1869. William's interest in creating an orphans' home probably resulted from the loss of his parents and several of his brothers and sisters in the typhoid epidemic.

During the CIVIL WAR Weller's brother John and eldest son George joined the Confederate army. His brother Charles was robbed and murdered while collecting bills in Clarksville, Tennessee, on July 1, 1862. Weller found a new partner, James P. Buckner, and his company became W.L. Weller and Buckner. This partnership lasted until Weller's son George returned from the war and joined the company. By 1870 Buckner had left the company, and the firm was renamed W.L. Weller and Sons.

By 1880 the company was selling bourbon as far west as Reno, Nevada. The South and West were major markets for the firm. The company changed locations several times before the end of the century but always remained on Main St. In 1896 William retired, leaving the business to his sons George P. and John C. Weller. William suffered from asthma, and the profits from this business allowed him to spend his winters in Ocala, Florida. He is buried in CAVE HILL CEMETERY.

Michael R. Veach

WESTERN RECORDER. The *Western Recorder* is the weekly newspaper of the Kentucky Baptist Convention, the organization of Southern Baptist churches in the state. First published in 1834 as the *Baptist Banner* in SHELBYVILLE, Kentucky, it moved permanently to Louisville in 1836. In 1839 its circulation rose to about 5,000 when it united with the *Western Pioneer* of Alton, Illinois, and the *Baptist* of Nashville, Tennessee, to become *the Baptist Banner and Western Pioneer.* In 1851 it became the *Western Recorder*. The paper significantly shaped Kentucky Baptist identity, fostering theological consensus and cooperation in missionary and benevolent efforts.

Nineteenth-century editors pledged their columns to "combat error" and to "support and enforce" the "doctrines and practices" of the Baptists (Jan. 14, 1841). They commended a Calvinist revivalism, creeds, closed communion, and believer's baptism by immersion. They opposed the anti-creedal Arminianism of Alexander Campbell, who founded the DISCIPLES OF CHRIST, and the anti-missionary Primitive BAPTISTS. From the CIVIL WAR to WORLD WAR I, editors also advanced the causes of a literally true Bible and Landmark theology—the idea that Baptists have the only true churches and trace their origin to the apostles.

After World War I editors generally supported missionary cooperation and eschewed doctrinal controversies when possible because theological strife diminished contributions to missionary efforts. In 1919 the state convention purchased the paper for the purpose of effectively promoting a southwide campaign to raise $75 million for Southern Baptist missionary and benevolent organizations. The paper saw its primary task as promoting denominational enterprises. When conservative Southern Baptists campaigned to take over the national and state organizations in order to enforce stricter standards of orthodoxy beginning in 1979, the paper opposed them.

Circulation grew rapidly in this period, rising from ten thousand in 1919 to a peak of seventy-one thousand in 1962, an era of strong Southern Baptist growth. Circulation declined thereafter, to forty-six thousand in 1996. Revenues in 1996 were $956,000, one-third of which was given by the Kentucky Baptist Convention. Prominent editors included John L. Waller (1835–41, 1850–54), T.T. Eaton (1887–1907), J.W. Porter (1909–21), V.I. Masters (1921–42), and C.R. Daley (1957–84).

Gregory A. Wills

WESTPORT. This small community on the OHIO RIVER is in northern OLDHAM COUNTY astride State Highway 524. Nestled along Eighteen Mile Creek, Westport was initially part of Elijah Craig's 1780 land grant and became part of SHELBY COUNTY when the state of Kentucky was created twelve years later. In 1796 Joseph Dupuy and Harman Bowman purchased Craig's land and began selling lots for a town dubbed Liberty. Within ten years, the town's name had changed to Westport, reportedly to reflect the desire of the citizens to be a major port on the western waters. By 1800 warehouses lined the riverbanks in the burgeoning town, ready to store flour, hemp, TOBACCO, and other products that were to be carried down to Louisville, St. Louis, or New Orleans. In December 1831 Alexis de Tocqueville, the famed FRENCH commentator on American democracy, passed through Westport during his 1831–32 tour of the United States. Headed toward Louisville, the steamboat on which de Tocqueville was a passenger was hindered by the buildup of ice on the OHIO RIVER and forced to set ashore upriver at Westport. Unable to find a carriage or horses, de Tocqueville and his traveling companion had to traverse the rest of the way to Louisville on foot.

When the General Assembly created Oldham County in December 1823, the thriving trade center was designated as the county seat. After a popular vote in 1827, county residents moved the seat to LaGrange because of its central location. However, political pressures impelled the legislature to return the seat to Westport the following year, and after 1831 the Westport Methodist Church housed the county offices. Following an 1838 referendum, the citizens again voted, by a tally of 655 to 198, to return the county seat to LaGrange. Completely dependent upon the river for its livelihood, the town's POPULATION of nearly 500 people in 1860 had dropped to about 220 twenty years later because of declining steamboat traffic and the increased use of RAILROADS. Since that time, population figures have remained steady.

See *A Place in Time: The Story of Louisville's Neighborhoods* (Louisville 1989); Helen Fairleigh Giltner, *Westport* (Westport, Ky., 1947); George Wilson Pierson, *Tocqueville and Beaumont in America* (New York 1938).

WETHERBY, GEORGE S. (b Middletown, Kentucky, September 5, 1905; d Eastwood, Kentucky, March 19, 1954). Jefferson County judge. He was the son of Dr. Samuel D. and Fannie (Yenowine) Wetherby and the brother of Gov. Lawrence W. Wetherby. George Wetherby attended the University of Kentucky and Western Kentucky University. He received a degree from the JEFFERSON SCHOOL OF LAW in 1933 and went into general practice in Louisville with the firm of Tilford, Wetherby, Dobbins, & Boone from 1933 until he became county judge. From 1937 until 1940, Wetherby served as state highway commissioner for the Third District. He was director of the Kentucky Athletic Board of Control from 1948 to 1952.

Wetherby was Jefferson County judge from January 4, 1954, until March 19, 1954, having defeated Republican Richard P. Watts in the November 1953 election by 75,392 to 64,437 votes. Democrats won all but one of the city and county legislative races in the election.

Wetherby's tenure as county judge was cut short by an auto accident that took his life after less than three months in office. Wetherby, County Attorney Lawrence G. Duncan, and his driver, county policeman Henry St. Clair, were killed in a traffic accident on Shelbyville Rd. near Eastwood, about fifteen miles east of Louisville. Wetherby's county-owned Cadillac hit a westbound truck, driven by William T. Goodlett, at Long Run Hill. Goodlett lost control of the truck when he tried to avoid a car stopped on the downhill lane of a two-lane road. His truck struck the car and then jackknifed into the path of the oncoming car. The county executives had been traveling to Frankfort to meet with Governor Wetherby to save three legislative bills concerning local sewers.

Goodlett was charged with manslaughter and reckless driving, but the manslaughter charges were dropped when the widows of the three killed made a request to the court. Goodlett was convicted of the reckless driving charge and sentenced to a fine of one hundred dollars. Wetherby's brother Alfred and his father, Samuel, were also killed in traffic accidents.

During his brief tenure in office, Wetherby worked with Mayor ANDREW BROADDUS to consolidate some Jefferson County and City of Louisville governmental agencies and functions. He sponsored legislation to separate the enforcement of county alcohol-beverage-control regulations from county police, making it the responsibility of the Alcohol Beverage Control Board. He was also vocal in his support for consolidating the city and county school systems.

Wetherby married Virginia McCullough on May 22, 1930. At the time of his death he lived in ANCHORAGE and was married to Dorothy O'Neill Chapman of Uniontown, Kentucky. He had a son, George Wetherby Jr., and a foster son, Russell Still. He is buried in Middletown Cemetery.

See George Lee Willis Sr., *A History of Kentucky Democracy*, 3 vols. (Louisville 1935); "Wetherby Accomplished a Lot in Short Time in Office," *Courier-Journal*, March 20, 1954; "Crash Kills County Judge and Attorney: Wetherby Dies in Car, Duncan at Hospital," *Courier-Journal*, March 20, 1954.

WETHERBY, LAWRENCE WINCHESTER (b Middletown, Kentucky, January 8, 1908; d Frankfort, March 27, 1994). Governor. The only Kentucky governor who was a Jefferson County native, he was the son of physician Samuel David and Fanny (Yenowine) Wetherby. After graduating from Anchorage High School, Wetherby entered the UNIVERSITY OF LOUISVILLE and graduated from the law school in 1929. He was employed by Judge Henry Tilford, with whom he worked until 1947.

A New Deal Democrat, Wetherby was a part-time attorney for the Jefferson County Juvenile Court in 1933–37 and again in 1942. In March 1943 he was appointed first trial commissioner of the Juvenile Court. Encouraged by the Louisville Democratic machine, he resigned in 1947 to run for and win the post of lieutenant governor, defeating Republican Orville M. Howard by a vote of 367,836 to 271,893. Gov. Earle Clements (1947–50) delegated several functions to Wetherby, including presiding over the Legislative Research Commission. Wetherby became governor on November 27, 1950, after Clements won election to the United States Senate. In a March 1951 special session, Wetherby had a $10 million budget surplus distributed among teachers, old-age recipients, and needy children.

Wetherby was elected governor in 1951 over Republican Eugene Siler by 346,345 votes to 288,014. He actively sought industry for the state, but in 1954 he favored Kentucky's first anti-strip-mining legislation, and he vetoed a right-to-work bill opposed by organized labor. He encouraged improvements of airports and rivers, and he established an agricultural council to coordinate agricultural efforts. Federal FLOOD CONTROL programs were secured for several rivers, a state fairgrounds was built in Louisville, and TOURISM was encouraged. Toll roads, including one from Louisville to Elizabethtown, improved the state's highways.

Wetherby emphasized education. Funding was increased, and he urged the development of educational TELEVISION and increased use of bookmobiles. The Minimum Foundation Act of 1954 provided more equal funding for school districts, and after the 1954 Supreme Court decision Wetherby appointed an advisory council to help schools integrate. Two of his proudest achievements were the creation of a Department of Mental Health and a Youth Authority. Several county HOSPITALS and health centers were built, and changes were made in voter registration, the parole and probation system, and the jury selection process. Despite his opposition, the voting age was lowered to eighteen. He used state police to attack crime and to curb labor unrest in some areas.

Wetherby found more revenue by putting the income tax on a pay-as-you-go basis and by getting higher "sin taxes" on tobacco products, alcohol beverages, and pari-mutuel betting. In 1955 he favored BERT COMBS as his successor and gave only mild support to A.B. Chandler, who won the nomination and election. In 1956 Chandler refused to support Wetherby and Clements in their bids for United States Senate seats, and they lost to Republicans John Sherman Cooper and Thruston Morton.

After leaving office on December 13, 1955, Wetherby returned to Louisville but later moved to Franklin County, where he practiced law and was a consultant to the Brighton Engineering Co. A member of the state Constitutional Assembly in 1964–66, he served in the state senate in 1966 and 1968. He held no public office after 1969 but was active in civic affairs. He married Helen Dwyer of Louisville in 1930. They had three children: Lawrence Jr. (1931), Suzanne (1932), and Barbara Juel (1945).

Wetherby is buried in Frankfort Cemetery.

See: Lowell H. Harrison, ed., *Kentucky's Governors* (Lexington 1985); John E. Kleber, ed., *The Public Papers of Governor Lawrence W. Wetherby, 1950–1955* (Lexington 1983).

Lowell H. Harrison

WET WOODS. A large section of south-central Jefferson County clearly seen on old maps, extending from the present-day GENERAL ELECTRIC APPLIANCE PARK where Newburg and Shepherdsville Roads meet and stretching west to an area near Third Street Rd., southeast of IROQUOIS PARK. From there, it extends northward, east of the park, and eastward, clipping the southern edge of LOUISVILLE INTERNATIONAL AIRPORT. The CSX Transportation's main line railroad tracks to the south divide it nearly in half.

Formed by the retreat of a Devonian-period glacier, the Wet Woods is positioned on a large deposit of NEW ALBANY shale, a highly erodible and impervious material that creates a watertight seal when it weathers. The waters from FERN CREEK and its tributaries, draining from the central part of the county, discharged into the Wet Woods and accumulated there until it rose high enough to spill over in a broad sheet to find its way westward by way of several tributaries into the OHIO RIVER. The buildup and stagnation of water in the Wet Woods area produced the Big Pond, or Oldham's Pond, which in wet weather encompassed most of the Wet Woods. At such times, when the overflow from the Wet Woods met the backwaters from the river, thousands of big fish would come exploring upstream into the swamps, only to be trapped when the waters receded. They would fall prey to farmers armed with pitchforks and to the herds of wild hogs that came down from the ebb of the water.

Until modern times, the land was an impediment to travel. Preston Hwy., which parallels the historic Wilderness Road, was originally a log or plank road through the swamp. It and the more westerly Central Plank Rd., later Third Street Rd., were in constant danger of sinking. Wild hogs, escapees from nearby farms, wandered the swamp and were considered fair game for anyone brave enough to venture there. The poor natural drainage of the area provided a breeding ground for mosquitoes. The area was generally thought by early residents to be an unhealthy or insalubrious source of a number of human ailments, known collectively as consumptive diseases. The area was also the home of thieves and bandits. Farmers suffered heavily from the disappearances of horses, cattle, and now and then a valued slave. The thefts were blamed on a supposed gang of cutthroats with hideouts in the woods. In October 1873, about eight hundred dollars' worth of goods were stolen from a store four miles from the old railroad depot at South Park. The following January, James Danall and West Watson were arrested when the stolen goods as well as other stolen articles were found in their cabin, one mile and a half from the depot.

For many years the area was perceived as a no-man's land, devoid of development. The only prominent establishments were Blackjack Tavern, located south of the present JACOBS neighborhood and Iroquois Park, and Robb's Hotel on Preston Street Rd.

An account of the territory's early ownership reveals that a large section of the Wet Woods was promised to a slave woman named Eliza Curtis. Curtis was freed in 1833 in recognition of her service to John and, later, Thomas Hundley, owners of the land on which BASHFORD MANOR Mall now stands and from whom she also inherited money and property in Louisville. On June 17, 1843, she married Henry Tevis (ca. 1804–69), a free man of color, with whom she purchased forty acres of land near the Hundley property. They constructed a large log house near present-day Newburg Rd. and Indian Trail and began farming. The Tevis land was later subdivided and sold or rented to other AFRICAN AMERICANS after the CIVIL WAR. Along with an adjacent forty acres purchased by Peter Laws from Col. George Hikes in the 1870s, the entire area evolved into the African American community of Petersburg.

After 1900 drainage ditches and systematic filling permitted truck farms and the construction of homes in large parts of the Wet Woods. By 1923 a *COURIER-JOURNAL* article claimed that thousands of acres had been reclaimed and transformed into productive farmland. While the land previously sold for five dollars an acre, the fertile acreage, according to the article, could not be purchased now for less than three hundred dollars per acre. Most of the land was reclaimed for scattered residences and AGRICULTURE by 1941, and what was once estimated at twenty thousand acres of forests was reduced to just a few scattered hundred-acre patches of cut-over timber. By the 1950s, large-scale subdivisions in the OKOLONA and FAIRDALE areas had begun in the Wet Woods area.

During the first week of March 1997, following a downpour of more than twelve inches of rain in a twenty-four hour period, Oldham's Pond reappeared. Communities built in the Wet Woods—Okolona, Fairdale, and much of southern Louisville—were inundated by flood waters. The residential suffering was the result of unregulated wildcat development of the region in the 1950s and 1960s. In light of the devastation, both city and county governments reviewed their policy on the granting of construction permits in flood-prone areas. As has happened so often, the Wet Woods then disappeared awaiting the next big rain to be seen again.

See *Changes at the Falls: Witnesses and Workers* (Louisville 1982); C. Thomas Hardin, ed., *Rain and Ruin* (Louisville 1997); *Courier-Journal*, June 8, 1941, Aug. 5, 1923, Feb. 16, 1919.

James D. Kendall

WGRC. WGRC Radio went on the air in 1936 and became greater Louisville's third radio station, BROADCASTING on 1370 kHz. Its call letters stood for GEORGE ROGERS CLARK, the founder of the city. Owned by Arthur L. Harris and his son Charles L. Harris as Northside Broadcasting, they began operation in NEW ALBANY, Indiana, with a studio in Louisville.

The flood of the OHIO RIVER in 1937 caused heavy damage to the Indiana facility, and the station struggled financially. The following year stockholders hired Steve Cisler from Hot Springs, Arkansas, as president, and J. Porter Smith of Atlanta as general manager. The two bought a financial interest in the station. They recalled that on their arrival they found that a number of the employees were working without pay. Extensive flood damage to the Indiana studios necessitated a move to Louisville to the Kentucky Home Life Building at Fifth and Jefferson Streets.

In 1940 the station joined the Mutual Network, which was to become the largest national network in number of affiliates. WGRC provided two programs that the network featured nationally. Their "singing fireman" Benny Reid was heard weekly. "Biff Baker," a science fiction youth adventure written daily by W.S. Luckenbill, featured local actors and was heard on 190 stations. Kathryn Riddick, an early local announcer, was one of the area's first female radio personalities. An African American gospel singer, Geneva Cooper, performed and delivered a spiritual message on her three-times-weekly program.

In 1943 the station moved its transmitter to JEFFERSONTOWN, Kentucky, but continued its coverage of southern Indiana affairs with the broadcast of "Tri-City Forums," a discussion program of issues of importance both there and in Louisville.

In 1947 J. Porter Smith and Charles Harris put WBOX-FM on the air on 100.7 MHz. Initially it featured music and sports. In 1950 it changed its format and became the "Voice of Religion." In a unique arrangement and with the cooperation of the Louisville Council of Churches, it contracted with some thirty participating churches to give them reduced broadcasting rates. The rates were to cover minimally the high cost of separate FM programming, while allowing some money to be returned to the churches. The innovative approach was not successful, and in 1951 WGRC joined other Louisville FM stations in leaving the airwaves. Many of the religious programs continued on WGRC-AM. Texan Gordon McLendon purchased WGRC from Harris and Smith for $720,000 in 1958. At that time the station became WAKY, an early rock station.

See Francis M. Nash, *Towers over Kentucky: A History of Radio and Television in the Bluegrass State* (Lexington 1995); *Courier Journal*, March 11, 1942, Sept. 25, 1954.

Bettie Shadburne

WHALLEN, JAMES "JIM" PATRICK

(b Maysville, Kentucky, December 4, 1856; d Louisville, March 15, 1930). THEATER manager and politician. He was the son of Patrick and Bridget (Burke) Whallen. Soon after his birth the family moved to Cincinnati. In the late 1870s Jim joined that city's police force; after recovering from a near-fatal wound suffered in the line of duty, he moved to Louisville in 1880 to become a partner with his older brother John in the Buckingham (BURLESQUE) Theater.

Throughout his career, Whallen's fortunes were inextricably linked to those of his older brother, and it was widely considered that, while John was the popular "Buckingham Boss" and affable front-man of the Democratic political organization and burlesque theater, Jim Whallen was the organizational genius behind the scenes. He analyzed political statistics and quietly expanded various Whallen brothers' enterprises, among which were The Fair, the city's first mall, comprised of fifty retail stores, and the Wonderland Museum, complete with bearded lady and a wild man from Borneo. With the passage of the Volstead Amendment, Whallen recognized the disastrous effects PROHIBITION would have on the burlesque and saloon business, and in 1919 he closed the Buckingham Theater. In addition to managing the theater, Whallen engineered the acquisition of extensive real estate holdings, including the Buckingham Theater Building (211 W Jefferson St.) and the Whallen Office Building (322–26 W Jefferson) and was a major investor in the Spring Bank, Lithia Water Co., Whallen and Martel Amusement Co., Empire Circuit Co., Louisville Transfer Co., Ohio Land and Improvement Co., the *Louisville Dispatch*, and Consolidated Bill Posting Co., as well as being a charter member of the Kentucky Colonels.

Although Jim Whallen lacked the charisma of his brother, he continued to control the Democrat Party machine after John's death in 1913 and was credited with maintaining the organization that gave rise to Michael "Mickey" Brennan, John "Johnny" Whallen Crimmins, Lennie McLaughlin, and CHESLEY SEARCY. Searcy came up through the Democratic ranks before switching to the REPUBLICAN PARTY.

James Whallen married Susannah McDermott in 1875. The couple was childless; however, James was guardian of John's surviving children, daughters Ella and Nora. James is entombed in St. Louis Cemetery in the Whallen mausoleum. Following Susannah's death in 1940, the Whallen home at 4420 River Park Dr. was sold to the Archdiocese of Louisville and became FLAGET HIGH SCHOOL.

Sarah R. Yates
Karen R. Gray

WHALLEN, JOHN HENRY (b New Orleans, May 1850; d Louisville, December 3, 1913). Democratic political boss. He was a son of Patrick and Bridget (Burke) Whallen. The family moved upriver, settling in Maysville, Kentucky, and later in Cincinnati. In 1862 Whallen joined Schoolfield's Battery (Confederate States of America) as powder monkey (a boy who carried gunpowder from the magazine to the guns) and scout, and later served as courier for Gen. John Hunt Morgan. In the late 1870s, Whallen moved to Louisville and soon became co-manager of the Metropolitan (formerly Vaudeville) Theater. Early in his career, Whallen attempted to legitimize his business by producing popular melodrama and family fare, including forming a traveling circus in 1878; however, his bid for middle-class respectability failed.

In 1880 Whallen, in partnership with his younger brother, James Patrick, opened the Buckingham (BURLESQUE) Theater, on W Jefferson between Third and FOURTH Streets. There he created a venue for productions that appealed to male patrons from all levels of society, especially the IRISH and GERMAN immigrant laborers. Despite a brief return to legitimate THEATER with the opening of the opulent Grand Opera (1894) at 211 W Jefferson St. in the mid-1890s, Whallen, who was known as the Colonel, continued to exploit the steady profits of burlesque. He expanded his business interests to include ownership of two Brooklyn theaters, the Empire and Casino, and a lavish road show, *The South before the War*, whose cast became one of the most successful touring companies of that era. In this venture Whallen turned author, writing a burlesque called "Brookenbridge," a parody on the breach-of-promise trial of Col. W.C.P. Breckinridge, a well-known Kentucky politician and journalist. In 1897, to safeguard his business interests and to streamline scheduling, Whallen and other theater owners founded the Empire Circuit, the first burlesque syndicate.

Throughout his career, Whallen found it profitable, and at times necessary, to merge business and political interests in order to protect his theater from citizens' groups that periodically formed to protest the bawdiness of burlesque and its associated vices of alcohol, PROSTITUTION, and GAMBLING. This necessity drove him to become active in state and national politics; however, his greatest triumphs came in orchestrating Louisville city elections.

His emergence in local politics came in 1879 when he served as Sixth Ward delegate to the state Democratic convention; however, Whallen's primary political interests lay in serving as power broker, both locally and statewide. In 1885, from the Green Room in the Buckingham Theater, the alleged hub of local Democrat politics, Whallen engineered Booker Reed's mayoral campaign and was rewarded by appointment as chief of police. Whallen, dubbed the "Buckingham Boss," was a force to be reckoned with in every city and state election for the rest of his life, including the 1905 city election, the most fraudulent in Louisville history. His political machinations even implicated him in the alleged conspiracy to assassinate Gov. William Goebel in 1900. Whallen was under scrutiny because weeks before the assassination he had attempted to bribe a Kentucky senator to oppose Goebel's contest for the governorship. Whallen's last major campaign was the 1909 mayoral election of W.O. Head, made into a theatrical political spectacle.

Despite the antipathy Whallen aroused in some citizens, he was immensely popular among Catholics, immigrants, and blue-collar workers, to whom he gave a voice in the political process. An essential component of his popularity was Whallen's generosity, marked by his frequent use of the Buckingham Theater as a community center from which he distributed fuel, food, and aid during natural disasters, labor unrest, and economic hard times.

John Whallen married three times. With Marian Hickey he had three children, Ella, Nora, and Orrie. There is no record of children from his second marriage to a woman known only as Sarah Jane. He later married Grace Edwards Goodrich and adopted her daughter, Grace. Whallen is entombed in the family mausoleum at St. Louis Cemetery. Following his death, his Spring Bank Park estate became Chickasaw Park.

See Karen R. Gray and Sarah R. Yates, "Boss John Whallen: The Early Louisville Years (1876–1883)," *Journal of Kentucky Studies* 1 (July 1984): 171–86; Urey Woodson, *The First New Dealer: William Goebel* (Louisville 1939).

Karen R. Gray
Sarah R. Yates

WHAS. It was the first licensed station in Kentucky when it went on the air on July 18, 1922. When WHAS signed on in Louisville it marked the end of Kentucky's place as one of only seven states that did not have a radio station. Originally operating with 500 watts of power, during the next six years the station's power was increased to 5,000 watts on 820 kHz, then to 25,000 watts in 1931 when a new transmitter was built. In 1933 the station was granted an increase to the maximum power of 50,000 watts. It was then able to reach all of Kentucky and large areas of the United States.

Reaching all of Kentucky's people was an early goal of the station's owner, ROBERT WORTH BINGHAM, who also owned the *Courier-Journal* and *LOUISVILLE TIMES*. A fellow journalist, Credo Fitch Harris, with his precise enunciation, was not only the manager but the announcer as well. In 1929 the station joined with the University of Kentucky in a broadcast from the university at noon each weekday. "Listening Centers" were established throughout eastern Kentucky. Programs were educational and included music and agricultural news. The centers, with donated battery-powered radios, enabled citizens of remote areas to receive radio service.

Early programming included sports scores, 1922 accounts of the World Series, and 1925 details of the KENTUCKY DERBY. Initially there were no news broadcasts because news coverage was left to the owner's NEWSPAPERS. From its beginning, WHAS aired political speeches, special events, and WEATHER reports. The potential of live coverage of news events was discovered in 1925 when a *Courier-Journal* reporter, William "Skeets" Miller, broadcast the story of Floyd Collins, who was trapped in a cave in Sand Hill in Edmonson County. His accounts were fed to other national radio stations.

In 1927 the station joined the national trend toward chain radiocasting when Credo Harris helped to start the southern network of NBC Radio. In 1932 WHAS switched to CBS to avoid duplication of neighboring NBC stations. This affiliation provided listeners with national news and entertainment. New station regulations came about in 1934 when the Federal Communications Commission Act was enacted. It spelled out rules that governed operation of stations, because the decade of the 1930s brought a great increase in the number of stations.

By 1937, when BARRY BINGHAM Sr. had succeeded his father as head of WHAS, the power of radio as a provider of public service was recognized. The station's coverage of the 1937 flood of the OHIO RIVER was credited with minimizing loss of life. The station issued early flood warnings, and as the water rose announcers used shortwave radio to relay messages from the street to be broadcast. People from all over the country listened in as the station broadcast more than 115,000 messages for aid. Announcer Pete Monroe became a national hero. Bingham worked on the street with his reporters. Commercials were eliminated during the 187 hours of uninterrupted service. The station received the Columbia Award for Distinguished Contribution and a special citation from Congress for its reporting. Since the time of its reports of the 1937 flood, news had been the cornerstone of WHAS programming. One of the nation's first ecumenical broadcasts, *THE MORAL SIDE OF THE NEWS,* first aired on WHAS in 1952. The station's commitment to news and public service was still apparent in 1974 when violent TORNADOES touched down in Louisville. WHAS helicopter pilot Dick Gilbert followed their course from the air and gave advance warnings that were credited with saving lives.

The station carried President Franklin D. Roosevelt's Fireside Chats and the news from the various fronts of WORLD WAR II. At war's end the emergence of television stations and the introduction of FM radio stations made the airwaves market more competitive. In 1945 WHAS-FM went on the air. By 1950 the cost of operating the station and the scarcity of listeners willing to purchase FM receivers caused the station to join numerous other stations in closing its FM operations. In 1966 WHAS-FM returned at 97.5 on the dial, featuring classical music that failed to gain an audience. Next was an unsuccessful all-news format in 1975. Finally in 1977 the station, renamed WAMZ-FM, introduced top country music, which gained listeners immediately. WAMZ-FM eventually replaced WHAS-AM as the market's number-one station. In 1949, faced with the enormous cost of constructing a TELEVISION station, its owners considered selling the radio station to the Crosley Corp. in Cincinnati for $1.9 million dollars. That sale was rejected by the Federal Communications Commission because of Louisville's proximity to Crosley's WLW radio station in Cincinnati, and late in 1949 the station was withdrawn from sale.

Becoming the second television station after WAVE-TV to begin BROADCASTING in the Louisville area, WHAS-TV went on the air as a CBS affiliate for the first time at two o'clock in the afternoon on March 27, 1950. Broadcasting on Channel 9 from a building at Sixth St. and Broadway, it shared space with the *Courier-Journal* and WHAS radio. The first day's programming included test programs, newsreels, films, and the *Fred Waring Show,* followed later that night by the station's first newscast. In 1953 the station changed to Channel 11, where it increased its output to 316,000 watts. The station switched to network color in 1954. Using radio personalities such as Jim Walton, Herbie Koch, and Tom Brooks, WHAS-TV developed local programming, including *Hi-Varieties* and *What's Your Question,* as well as the children's show, *T-Bar-V Ranch.*

Contributing to the station's identity as a vital and familiar part of the community has been its development of on-air personalities. Listeners have come to feel that they are friends. Early news reporters and performers were joined by musicians Herbie Koch and Randy Atcher. Jim Walton emceed early studio programs featuring local talent. Farm director Barney Arnold presented agricultural news, and Cawood Ledford became the voice of University of Kentucky sports during his long association as director of sports. Van Vance joined the sports staff in 1957 and in 1981 took over play-by-play broadcasts of the UNIVERSITY OF LOUISVILLE BASKETBALL and FOOTBALL games. From the early 1970s until his death in 1998, FRED WICHE presented farm and garden news.

A radio personality who brought national attention to the station was Milton Metz, who joined in 1946. In July of 1993 Milton Metz signed off the air after completing the thirty-four-year run of his "Metz Here," an evening radio call-in show that began in 1959 with the name "Juniper 5–2385." When phone numbers went to all digits, the name changed to "Metz Here." The show influenced many decisions in city and state politics for more than three decades. This call-in show was one of the earliest programs of its kind and was heard in more than forty states. In the 1990s as the number of radio talk-shows grew and became popular, often with ideologically driven and opinionated hosts, Metz continued his talk show as a good forum for discussion with a variety of guests and topics while maintaining his position as a neutral moderator. He continued to do occasional broadcasts after 1993. Metz is a native of Cleveland, Ohio, and is married to Mirian Metz.

Wayne Perkey went on the air in 1970 with his early morning program. He was the dominating personality in the 5 to 9 a.m. time slot, with a cabinet full of trophies and awards to demonstrate his influence and appeal. Among his recognitions is a 1995 citation for having the eighth-highest rating in the nation for morning drive-time listening. Perkey was also affectionately known as Mr. Crusade, having served as host of the annual WHAS CRUSADE FOR CHILDREN since 1980 and having worked with the Crusade since 1970. Perkey saw Louisville as an early town with a lot of get-up-early country culture, a characteristic that was reinforced when the school district began BUSING in 1975 and youngsters started waiting for buses as early as six in the morning. Perkey retired in June 1999 and was followed by Bob Sokoler, who had been the cohost of WHAS television's *Louisville Tonight* since 1994. Terry Meiners joined the station in 1985 and took over the three-hour afternoon program. The popularity of Meiners and Perkey contributed to the station's high ratings.

Since 1954 the annual *Crusade for Children* on WHAS radio and television has raised millions of dollars for special-needs children of Kentucky and southern Indiana. Its first director and emcee was Jim Walton. Bud Harbsmeier took over as director in 1982,; he retired in 2000. It is the longest-running locally produced fund-raiser in the nation.

In 1968 the studios and offices were moved to a combination radio and television building at Sixth and Chestnut Streets. In 1986, when all of the Binghams' communication properties were sold, WHAS and its FM affiliate, WAMZ, were purchased by Clear Channel Communications of San Antonio, Texas, for $20 million. WHAS-TV was sold the same year to the Providence Journal Corp. of Rhode Island. In 1997 the television station was sold to A.H. Belo Corp. of Dallas. In 1990 WHAS-TV ended its forty-year affiliation with CBS and contracted with ABC, resulting in WLKY-TV becoming the local CBS affiliate. In 1998 WHAS radio moved its studios and offices from the WHAS building on Chestnut St. to a new location on Bishop Ln.

See Francis M. Nash, *Towers over Kentucky: A History of Radio and Television in the Bluegrass State* (Lexington 1995); Terry L. Birdwhistell, "WHAS Radio and the Development of Broadcasting in Kentucky, 1922–1942," *Register of the Kentucky Historical Society* 79 (Autumn 1981): 333–53; Josephine H. MacLatchy, "Education on the Air," *Fifth Yearbook of the Institute for Education by Radio* (Columbus, Ohio, 1934).

Bettie Shadburne

WHIG PARTY. During its lifetime in Kentucky, the Whig Party of Henry Clay dominated elections; generally, the same trend held true in Louisville. In the two decades after 1832, Whigs won five of the six presidential contests in Louisville and Jefferson County, averaging some 56 percent of the vote. During the same period, they carried the county in five of the six gubernatorial races, losing the other one by under 1 percent. Overall, the party dominated city contests on a regular basis as well, with the Democratic plurality win in the 1841 mayoral race a rare exception. In short, for a quarter-century, Whigs were the majority party.

Who were those who voted Whig? Historian Leonard Curry has done some excellent work to date on that subject, and the field remains a fertile one for further investigation. Generally, in antebellum America, Whigs controlled most city governments, where the urban voters were more conservative. As was true elsewhere, the party in Louisville received its greatest support from the central, most affluent WARDS of the city, while Democrats had their strongest base of votes in the western and eastern sections (the latter the pork packinghouse areas). The emphasis of the party of Clay on internal improvements, the river interests, and a strong central bank apparently appealed to the Louisville voters. The fact that one of the leading Whig NEWSPAPERS nationally was located in Louisville also gave the party a strong force among the populace throughout the period. The establishment of the *Louisville Daily Journal* in 1830, and the important editorials of its editor George Prentice after that, meant that the Whig voice would be heard and respected.

Whig successes did not come overnight, nor were they without challenge. For the first two decades of the century, the Jeffersonian Republicans (Democrats) had virtually no opposition to their rule. A two-party system emerged only in the 1820s and—as was true of the party's origins overall in Kentucky—Louisville Whigs rose out of the divisive Old Court-New Court struggles. With people in need, a relief-oriented group sought support that other groups found unwise at best, unconstitutional at worst. Statewide, two separate COURTS were set up, each claiming legitimacy.

Very generally, forces that would evolve into the Whigs tended to go with the anti-relief, Old Court group, while Democrats took the opposite path. In Louisville, the evolution was not so clear-cut, as Old Court forces won in the 1824 city and governor's races and swept the legislative contests in 1825. A year later the New Court forces succeeded, and the city also went for the party of Andrew Jackson in the 1828 governor's race and in the 1830 local elections.

But by 1831 the groups that would be the Whigs had risen to gain the populace's support in a rapidly growing urban area. In 1834 the party garnered all the legislative seats, and Whig William J. Graves of New Castle took the congressional district that Louisville was in. (Graves would not seek renomination in 1840, after he killed fellow congressman Jonathan Cilley in a duel.) Whigs continued to win that seat and were represented by Louisvillians William P. Thomasson (1841–47), W. GARNETT DUNCAN (1847–49), and WILLIAM PRESTON (1851–55)—later a Democrat—as well as others outside Jefferson County.

However, changing times and issues rang the death knell of the Whig Party more loudly with each passing year. Whig stands in partial opposition to the MEXICAN WAR (1846–48) hurt some, party divisions between those who supported Clay or former Louisvillian ZACHARY TAYLOR as the 1848 Whig presidential candidate created deep rifts, the group's perceived opposition to a new state constitutional convention effort caused some to attack it as antidemocratic, and the slavery and sectional issue brought forth questions to which few political groups could offer satisfactory answers. Many of those questions came together in 1849 when Kentuckians elected delegates to a convention to form a new constitution. An emancipation ticket put forth a slate, while a fusion group of both Whigs and Democrats stood in opposition. Indicative of how difficult it is to characterize exactly the makeup of the parties, in that election, won with 54 percent of the vote by the fusion, proslavery group, two of the three fusion candidates were Whig. Yet an analysis of the emancipation ticket vote suggests that it was supported by some one-fifth of the Democrats but two-fifths of the Whigs. Breaking apart—like the nation—on slavery and other issues, the party's symbolic death came when Clay passed away on June 29, 1852.

Yet, in many ways, elements of the party continued. The growth of the American or Know-Nothing Party filled the Whig void, as that group included many ex-Whigs in its ranks. The *Louisville Daily Democrat* of February 23, 1855, even called the Know-Nothings "an old party in a new dress." With most of Louisville's large number of GERMAN and IRISH immigrants in the Democratic ranks, the new party's anti-immigrant rhetoric fit nicely with long-standing Whig opposition to the Democrats generally. In a sense, Know-Nothing victories with almost two-thirds of the vote in Jefferson County in the 1855 governor's race and the 1856 presidential race (with an ex-Whig candidate) showed that the party survived in a mutated form.

Still, "BLOODY MONDAY" riots and the Know-Nothings' inherent weaknesses as a party meant that on the eve of the CIVIL WAR those who had called themselves Whigs increasingly faced a future with confusing political options. In the 1859 gubernatorial campaign, resistance to the Democrats coalesced around an awkward group known simply as "the Opposition." Their strength reflected the lingering Whig ties, while Kentuckians' antagonism to the growing northern Republican movement was shown in Jefferson County's small support for the party of Lincoln. As the Civil War opened and progressed, memories of the Whig legacy of a strong urban economic dynamism grew dimmer.

The question of where those who had supported the Whigs before the Civil War went politically after the conflict has not been answered well enough for definitive conclusions to be drawn. However, fragmentary evidence suggests that they divided to go into both of the two major parties. Some, like prewar Whig William Preston, became Democratic leaders; others, such as new Louisvillian Benjamin Helm Bristow, took up the Republican leadership reins. One wing of the Democrats and the Republicans both incorporated elements of the Whig philosophy in their now-modified organizations. In that sense, a part of the spirit of the party lived on.

While a strong, vibrant group, the Whig Party had controlled Louisville during a period of great growth. They tied city government closely to mercantile and business interests at a time when population increased from 10,000 in 1830 to 68,000 thirty years later. They faded when they could not overcome a series of issues that almost destroyed the nation as well, then came back in various guises—Know-Nothings, and "the Opposition"—but in the end, flickered away and died as a major party in Louisville.

See Leonard P. Curry, *The Corporate City: The American City as a Political Entity, 1800–1850* (Westport, Conn., 1997); George Yater, *Two Hundred Years at the Falls of the Ohio* (Louisville 1979); John Coffin, "The Whig Party in Kentucky" (typescript, University of Kentucky Library).

James C. Klotter

WHITAKER, JOHN (b Maryland, 1722; d Louisville, 1798) Minister. John Whitaker migrated from Maryland to Pennsylvania with his wife and children in about 1771. There he became an ordained minister in the Baptist church. In 1780 he came to Kentucky, settling first at Brashear's Station near present SHEPHERDSVILLE. Later he moved east of Louisville and about 1783 began organizing Bear Grass Baptist Church, today Beargrass Christian, the first and for several years the only church in present Jefferson County. Many couples were married by Reverend Whitaker, whose baptism of Mrs. RICHARD CHENOWETH, ca. 1783, was one of Kentucky's first. Before his death Reverend Whitaker helped establish most of the Baptist churches constituted within fifty miles of Louisville.

See *Baptist Banner & Western Pioneer*, July 21, 1842, microfilm copy, Southern Baptist Theological Seminary; J.H. Spencer, *A History of Kentucky Baptists,* vol. 1 (Cincinnati 1886); George L. Willis Sr., *History of Shelby County, Kentucky* (Louisville 1929); Beaumont W. Whitaker, *John Whitaker, Kentucky's Pioneer Baptist Preacher*, privately printed manuscript, 1983, Filson Club Historical Society.

Joellen Tyler Johnston

Postcard advertisement for White City amusement park, at the foot of Greenwood Avenue, north of Chickasaw Park, c. 1905

WHITE CITY AMUSEMENT PARK. Located at the foot of Greenwood Ave. north of Chickasaw Park on the bank of the OHIO RIVER, WHITE CITY AMUSEMENT PARK opened on April 27, 1907. Billed as "The Coney Island of the South," the property's ornate, white-painted structures were illuminated at night by 250,000 electric lights—a commercially successful marvel of the era. Attractions included the Canals of Venice boats, the steeply sloped Chutes water ride, a scenic railway, skating rink, vaudeville THEATER, dance pavilion, boardwalk, and bathing beach. The park's various entrance gates offered convenient access via the frequent service of the Greenwood Ave. and a lengthy spur of the Broadway streetcar lines, and by the steamboat *Hiawatha*, which was chartered to transport patrons from NEW ALBANY and JEFFERSONVILLE, INDIANA.

White City was encompassed within a tract of open park land established about 1881 as Riverview Park, sometimes referred to as Riverside or Greenwood Park. Following its fourth summer season in 1910, White City suffered extensive fire damage. After rebuilding, it reopened in 1911 as Riverview Park. Facing stiff competition from the larger FONTAINE FERRY PARK nearby, Riverview Park Co.'s Lum Simons announced that Riverview Park would not open for the 1913 season. Simons's entire tract of Riverview Park land remained intact until 1922, when tracts began to be sold to developers for riverside residential properties.

See Samuel W. Thomas, *Views of Louisville since 1766* (Louisville 1971); Eugene Blasi, *Postcard Views of Louisville* (Louisville 1994); U.S. Army Corps of Engineers, "Ohio River: Pittsburgh, Pa. to Mouth," Chart 169, 1912 Survey, District Engineer Office, Louisville; Louisville Title Co. Property Map, 1913–Louisville; *Louisville Herald*, June 17, 1907.

Jerry L. Rice

WHITEHALL. Whitehall, at 3110 Lexington Rd. in Louisville's East End, was built in the Italianate style popular prior to the CIVIL WAR. It has been much altered through the years. The land on which Whitehall sits was originally part of the Spring Station tract owned by Samuel and Norborne Beall. Beals Branch, a tributary of BEARGRASS CREEK, ran through the property. The house was most likely built by John C. Marshall about 1856. He sold the house to Richard Isaacs in 1860.

Blood-stained sheets marked "Hospital Department C.S.A" (Confederate States of America) found in the attic may have come into Union hands at the Battle of Perryville. After the Battle of Perryville the house may have served as a hospital for both Union and Confederate soldiers.

John C. Middleton bought the house in 1909 and added both the east and west wings as well as the portico with six Corinthian columns. The Middletons are thought to have first painted the structure white; thus the name Whitehall.

The last private owner, WILLIAM HUME LOGAN Jr., purchased the home from his father's estate in 1952. It was during his ownership that the antebellum-style furniture was collected that is on display today. The Middletons' gardens were expanded and enhanced. Hume Logan Jr. bequeathed Whitehall with all its furnishings and a cash endowment to the Historic Homes Foundation upon his death July 25, 1992. His total gift, including the home and furniture, exceeded $1.7 million.

Zack H. Logan

WHITE MILLS DISTILLERY. The White Mills Distillery, at Eighteenth and Howard Streets in Louisville, was created in the 1890s when the Hoffheimer Brothers of Cincinnati purchased the Wallwork and Harris Distillery and renamed it White Mills. Hoffheimer Brothers was a wholesale firm that also controlled the output of the T.B. Ripy plants in Anderson County. Nathan Hoffheimer served as president, and S.A. Hoffheimer was superintendent.

Several years later, the size of the operation was increased by the addition of the adjacent Lynndale Distillery property. The White Mills Distillery was first listed in the Louisville city directory in 1895. Whiskeys produced at the distillery included Hoffheimer Brothers' Pure Rye, Lynndale, and White Mills Bourbon. In 1919 the Hoffheimers sold the property to the G. Lee Redmon Co. for use as a concentration warehouse and bottling plant for such distilleries as Taylor and Williams (Yellowstone), MAX SELLIGER and Co. (Belmont), Friedman, Keiler & Co. (Brookhill), and Brown-Forman Distillery Co. (now BROWN-FORMAN CORP.).

This relationship exemplifies the interrelated nature of the Kentucky bourbon industry. In 1924 Brown-Forman purchased the property and remaining whiskey but not the brand names. Throughout PROHIBITION (1920–33) Brown-Forman sold whiskey for medicinal purposes. In 1933, anticipating the end of Prohibition, Brown-Forman built the six-thousand-bushel distillery that forms the center of the firm's present-day operations.

See H.W. Coyte, unpublished papers, University of Louisville Archives and Records Center; *Sanborn Insurance Maps*, 1894, University of Kentucky Map Room.

Albert Young
Lindsey Apple

WHITESTONE, HENRY (b County Clare, Ireland, July 1819; d Louisville, July 6, 1893). Architect. Whitestone emigrated to the United States in 1852 after working as an architect in Ennis, Ireland, where he designed the Ennis Courthouse, which is extant. He had apprenticed with James Paine (1779–1877) in Limerick, Ireland. He began working with Isaiah Rogers (1800–69) on the Capital Hotel in Frankfort, Kentucky, and then came to Louisville in 1853 to work on the enlargement of the first GALT HOUSE hotel at Second and MAIN Streets. Rogers and Whitestone were partners until 1857. Whitestone had married Henrietta Sautelle Baker in Ireland and they had two daughters, Austine Ford and Henrietta.

Whitestone was acclaimed for the fashionable residences he designed on BROADWAY and nearby streets in downtown Louisville. These included residences for James C. Ford, Horatio D. Newcomb, Joseph Tompkins, Silas Miller, Rev. STUART ROBINSON, THOMAS HUNT, Gustave Baurman, Thomas White, James Irvin, Edward Wilder, H. Victor Newcomb, and E.D. Standiford. The Tompkins house stands behind the addition to SPALDING UNIVERSITY on Fourth St.

His country residences included BASHFORD MANOR for James Wilder and Ivywood for William Allen Richardson. All of these except the Baurman house, 1518 W Market St.; the Irvin house at 2910 Northwestern Pkwy.; and the Robinson house, 1387 S Fourth St. have been demolished. He also designed cemetery vaults at Cave Hill for his clients; the two best-known are the Tompkins and Irvin vaults.

The single most important building that Whitestone designed was the Galt House, completed in 1869, at First and Main Streets. It replaced the one at Second and Main that had burned in 1865. The new, imposing five-story Renaissance Revival–style hotel had all of the latest features in hotels, including a lavish interior. A supplement to the *Courier-Journal* in 1869 described the hotel in great detail. Whitestone designed numerous "commercial palaces" on Main St. such as the building at 600 W. main St., and other downtown streets using cast iron, limestone, and other building materials. His commercial buildings included commissions for residential clients such as a store for Joseph Tompkins and a warehouse for Gustave Baurman. Whitestone designed the now-demolished Board of Trade building at Third and Main Streets and the Louisville & Nashville Railroad office building at Second and Main.

Whitestone's public and institutional buildings included the City Hall tower after a fire destroyed the original; work on the steeple of the Cathedral of the Assumption; the Louisville Medical Institute after a fire in 1856 destroyed the original Gideon Shryock building; the House of Refuge; and the Monsarrat School with Rogers. He preferred the Italianate and Renaissance Revival modes. His extensive work made him Louisville's preeminent architect during the second half of the nineteenth century.

Whitestone's firm was taken over about 1881 by D.X. Murphy, whom he had hired as a draftsman.

See Elizabeth Fitzpatrick Jones, "Henry Whitestone: Nineteenth-Century Louisville Architect," M.A. thesis, University of Louisville, 1974; Henry Whitestone Papers, (uncatalogued) Filson Club Historical Society; *Courier-Journal*, March 21–22, 1869, July 7, 1893.

Elizabeth Fitzpatrick "Penny" Jones

Ford Mansion, southwest corner, Broadway at Second, c. 1965. Henry Whitestone, architect.

WHITNEY, ROBERT SUTTON (b Newcastle-upon-Tyne, England, July 9, 1904; d Louisville, November 22, 1986. Musician and conductor. Robert Sutton Whitney was born in England while his American father, Robert Paul Whitney, was a touring tuba player with the Buffalo Bill Wild West Show. In England, the elder Whitney had met and married an English musician and actress, Edith Ogilvie Stewart. Robert was still an infant when the couple moved to Chicago. Four sisters followed, all of whom became professional musicians, and the family of performers became prominent in concert halls in the eastern United States, as well as on early radio. The family's musical talents were broadcast on Chicago's WMAQ, where eighteen-year-old Whitney became the chief announcer in 1922.

Whitney, an accomplished pianist, studied composition at the American Conservatory of Music. At twenty-eight, he made his conducting debut with the Chicago Civic Orchestra, and two years later the Chicago Symphony Orchestra under Frederick Stock premiered his first major work, "Concerto Grosso."

In early 1937, the Louisville Civic Arts Association engaged Whitney to establish the city's first professional orchestra. The Louisville Civic Orchestra played its first performance under Whitney on November 2, 1937, and was given "a cordial reception," according to a contemporary review.

Beginning with fifty-four salaried, part-time musicians, Whitney gradually assembled an experienced, full-sized ensemble that performed with some of the foremost concert soloists of the time. In those early years, Whitney displayed the important outreach missions that would later distinguish the orchestra, with statewide tours and radio broadcasts that brought classical music to rural areas and underserved audiences. Yet, by the close of the tenth season, the orchestra had built a forty-thousand-dollar deficit.

In early 1948, Whitney and Louisville mayor Charles P. Farnsley, who was a former president of the orchestra board, developed what would be called the "Louisville Project," an elaborate plan to save the orchestra by commissioning new works by living composers rather than hiring expensive soloists. Farnsley knew the stakes riding on the project. "There will be lots of criticism and there will be no turning back," Farnsley told Whitney.

Whitney began searching for the first six commissioned works, and on November 9, 1948, the first Louisville world premiere, "Quatro Madrigales Amatorios," by Spanish composer Joaquin Rodrigo, was performed in Columbia Auditorium. The commissioning project evoked positive attention from the national press, but the orchestra's bold experiment provoked dissension among the orchestra's board and audiences and did not relieve the orchestra's financial difficulties.

Whitney continued the commissioning project into the 1949–50 season, but during a December 23, 1949, meeting with board members Whitney was told that the orchestra's finances had reached a breaking point: after the next concert, he was ordered to pay off the musicians and liquidate the organization. Luckily, the next concert was special, the world premiere of "Judith, A Choreographic Poem," which was written by William Schuman and was to be danced by Martha Graham, the famous modern dancer. The performance validated the commissioning project and transformed the orchestra's future. The applause lasted for fifteen minutes, and Schuman and Graham urged Whitney and the Louisville Orchestra to perform the work in Carnegie Hall, which they did on December 29, 1950.

Farnsley soon developed a plan to convert the artistic triumph into financial help for the orchestra. On April 7, 1953, Farnsley announced that the Rockefeller Foundation had awarded the Louisville Orchestra a four-hundred-thousand-dollar grant (with another hundred thousand dollars added later) for the performance, recording, and distribution of musi-

Robert Whitney conducting members of the woodwinds section of the Louisville Orchestra, 1950s.

cal works by living composers. Each year, the grant funded forty-six new works, which were performed in special Saturday afternoon concerts called "readings."

The Louisville Project, and the new recording that emerged each month under the orchestra's First Edition Records label, validated Farnsley's prediction that the Louisville Orchestra would become famous as the champion of twentieth-century music. *Time* magazine referred to the Louisville Orchestra as "the world's busiest performer of new music." By the time Whitney retired, he and his musicians had made eighty recordings of 184 symphonic works by 131 composers.

The 1966–67 orchestra season, Whitney's thirtieth at the helm, was his last as music director. However, he had been named dean of the University of Louisville's School of Music in 1956, and he retained that post after stepping down from the orchestra, building the school's choral and orchestral programs. His attention to education, which spawned the Louisville Orchestra's "Making Music" concerts for schoolchildren, continued at the music school. He brought the Shinichi Suzuki Method of teaching violin to very young children to Louisville, and he initiated Suzuki programs in the city's disadvantaged NEIGHBORHOODS with outstanding success. Following his retirement from the UNIVERSITY OF LOUISVILLE in 1971, he was a full-time music consultant for the Louisville Public Schools for four years.

The music world honored Whitney's work. The twenty-four-hundred-seat auditorium at the Kentucky Center for the Arts bears his name. He received the American Composers Alliance Laurel Leaf, the Ditson Award, the first Giovanni Martini Award from BELLARMINE COLLEGE, "Man of the Year" from WHAS radio, and honorary degrees from the University of Louisville, University of Kentucky, and Hanover College. In 1986 Gov. MARTHA LAYNE COLLINS honored him posthumously with Kentucky's award for outstanding contributions to the arts.

Whitney, who was married to Margaret Gilbert from 1936 until her death in 1965, had two daughters, Martha and Margaret. In 1966, he married Clarita Baumgarten. His body was donated to medical research.

See Robert Whitney Papers, University of Louisville Archives and Records Center; Louisville Orchestra Records, University of Louisville Archives and Records Center; H. Stoddard, Robert Whitney, *Symphony Conductors of the U.S.A.* (New York 1957); D. Hall, "Louisville Harvest," *HiFi Review*, June 1959.

Clarita Whitney

WHITSITT, WILLIAM HETH (b Nashville, Tennessee, November 25, 1841; d Richmond, Virginia, January 20, 1911). Seminary president. He was the son of Rubin Ewing and Dicey (McFarland) Whitsitt. After he graduated from Union University in Jackson, Tennessee, in 1861, he enlisted in the Confederate army as a scout and then as a chaplain for the Fourth Tennessee Cavalry.

At the conclusion of the war Whitsitt continued his education at the University of Virginia (1866); Southern Baptist Theological Seminary in Greenville, South Carolina (1866–68); and spent two years studying in Germany at the University of Leipzig and the University of Berlin. When he returned to the United States he spent a short time as pastor of a Baptist church in Albany, Georgia. In 1872 he was elected chair of ecclesiastical history at the SOUTHERN BAPTIST THEOLOGICAL SEMINARY. In 1895, following the death of John Albert Broadus, Whitsitt was elected president of the seminary, which had moved to Louisville in 1877. His tenure was to be short because of an article published in *Johnson's Universal Cyclopaedia* in 1893 stating that "believer's baptism," or adult baptism, had been restored by English BAPTISTS in 1641. This angered Southern Baptists, who believed that an unbroken succession of Baptist churches could be traced from John the Baptist and the apostolic era. It triggered what became known as the "Whitsitt Controversy." The seminary and Whitsitt were attacked in the religious press. Whitsitt resigned in 1899 with the controversy still raging and was succeeded by J.P. Greene. Whitsitt became a professor of philosophy at Richmond College, Richmond, Virginia, where he taught until his death.

See *Encyclopedia of Southern Baptists* (Nashville, Tenn., 1958); J.H. Spencer, *A History of Kentucky Baptists* (Gallatin, Tenn., 1984).

WICHE, FRED (b La Grange, Illinois, November 11, 1931; d Simpsonville, Kentucky, June 15, 1998). Journalist and gardener. The "Weekend Gardener," as he was known across Kentucky, was the son of Fredric Earl and Helen (Ekdaho) Wiche. He graduated from Kalamazoo (Michigan) College in 1954. Wiche planned to enter the field of marine biology, but he changed his mind after he served in the military in Korea, where he was a newscaster for the Armed Forces Radio. He received a master's degree from the Medill School of Journalism at Northwestern University.

Wiche came to Louisville in 1956 to work at WKLO radio. He joined WHAS radio as a reporter in 1958 and soon became a reporter and news anchor for WHAS-TV. He anchored the station's first hour-long TELEVISION newscast. However, it was his work as the "Weekend Gardener" that made him one of the best-known figures in Louisville BROADCASTING history. With an interest in gardening, he began to do weekend reports in 1974 while anchoring Channel 11's newsroom and covering local and state political news.

As a knowledgeable gardener, Wiche would answer the telephoned questions of home viewers. It was in that capacity that he became well known across the viewing area. What began as a hobby became a profession in 1979 when he succeeded Barney Arnold as farm and garden director of WHAS radio and television. Wiche became an expert on AGRICULTURE and horticulture. His column was syndicated in seventeen weekly NEWSPAPERS. The year 1990 marked the beginning of the Fred Wiche Lawn and Garden Expo, a yearly February showcase that drew large crowds. Wiche was also a partner in Green Thumb Publishing, which printed his locally top-selling books and calendars. *Fred Wiche's Gardening Almanac*, published in 1988, quickly sold all thirty thousand printed copies, becoming one of the best-selling local books and one of the biggest hits ever published in Kentucky. The *Weekend Gardener Calendar* sold well yearly. Wiche made over 150 public appearances a year, speaking before gardening clubs and botanical organizations. He was known as a gentle and kind person who always took the time to answer questions. In October 1997 a garden, sidewalk, and gazebo were added in his honor at the Simpsonville Community Center. Also in 1997 he was inducted into the Kentucky Journalism Hall of Fame, and a section of WATERFRONT PARK in downtown Louisville was named the Fred Wiche Grove of Trees.

Although diagnosed with cancer in 1996 he continued his broadcast, often in pain, until he died at home. He married Jenny Lashley in 1962. They had two daughters, Teal and Jeneen. Wiche was cremated.

See Bruce Allar, "The Gardener of Eden" *Louisville* 43 (March 1992): 28–33; *Courier-Journal*, June 16 1998.

WICKLIFFE, CHARLES ANDERSON (b near Springfield, Kentucky, June 8, 1788; d near Ilchester, Maryland, October 31, 1869). Governor and United States representative. Charles Anderson Wickliffe was born in Kentucky four years after his parents, Charles and Lydia (Hardin) Wickliffe, moved there from Virginia. He read law in Bardstown with his cousin Martin D. Hardin and in 1809 he was admitted to the bar. Wickliffe married Margaret Cripps, and they built Wickland ("Home of Three Governors") in Bardstown. The couple had eight children. After service as a commonwealth's attorney, Wickliffe supported the War of 1812 in the Kentucky House of Representatives (1812–14) and in active duty on the western Canadian front. Elected a state representative again in 1820 and 1821, he then spent a decade (March 4, 1823, to March 3, 1833) in the U.S. House of Representatives.

Politically independent, Wickliffe was a Whig who disagreed with several of Henry Clay's positions. Despite such differences the Whigs selected him to be James Clark's gubernatorial running mate in 1836, and both were elected. Clark died in 1839, and Wickliffe served the last year of the term (September 27, 1839, to September, 2, 1840).

Much of Wickliffe's year in office was dominated by the panic of 1837, which had swept the nation. The state had been operating at a deficit that reached forty-two thousand dollars in 1839, and Wickliffe called for higher property taxes and ECONOMY in GOVERNMENT to restore fiscal soundness. He asked for increased expenditures in only three areas: improvement of river navigation, preservation of state ARCHIVES, and public education. The legislative response was to borrow money to meet current expenses, but Wickliffe was able to maintain the state's credit rating by paying all the interest due on state securities. Much of his time was spent dealing with endless requests for pardons, patronage positions, and special exemptions that have plagued most governors.

A friend of President John Tyler, Wickliffe was appointed U.S. postmaster general during 1841–45. His support for the annexation of Texas, plus a secret mission to Texas that he undertook for President James K. Polk, undermined Whig confidence in Wickliffe. He served in Kentucky's 1849 constitutional convention, and during the sectional crisis that led to the CIVIL WAR he was active in various unsuccessful peace conferences. Elected to the U.S. House as a Unionist, Wickliffe was crippled in a carriage accident the next year, and his service was cut short; he served from March 4, 1861, to March 3, 1863. Kentucky's Peace Democrats ran him for governor in 1863, but he was considered subversive by military authorities, who helped ensure his defeat by regular Democrat THOMAS ELLIOT BRAMLETTE, 68,422 to 17,503. He is buried in the Bardstown Cemetery.

See Jennie C. Morton, "Governor Charles A. Wickliffe," *Register of the Kentucky Historical Society* 2 (Sept. 1904): 7–21; Lowell H. Harrison, *Kentucky's Governors: 1792–1985* (Lexington 1985).

Lowell H. Harrison

WICKLIFFE, JOHN H. (b Kentucky, 1882; d Louisville). Musician. John H. Wickliffe, drummer and early JAZZ band leader, came to Louisville in the 1890s and worked as a porter while studying at the LOUISVILLE CONSERVATORY OF MUSIC at 824 W Walnut St. (Muhammad Ali Blvd.). By 1911 he was working full-time as a musician, and he formed his first band in 1913. In 1916 he left for Chicago and became popular in the early jazz clubs there. Returning to Louisville in 1926, he formed a band made up of top local musicians, including Sylvester Perdue (piano), George Allen (saxophone), and Luke Stewart (guitar). Wickliffe and other members of his band all began their careers with Louisville brass bands. His early group is important in Louisville jazz history because it bridges the gap between brass bands and jazz bands.

Cornelius Bogert

WILDERNESS ROAD. The original Wilderness Road started in Virginia, crossed into Kentucky at Cumberland Gap, and wound its way through Kentucky to Harrodsburg. In 1778, when GEORGE ROGERS CLARK established his headquarters for the conquest of the Illinois country at the FALLS OF THE OHIO, the road was pushed out from Harrodsburg to the Falls. Near Louisville it followed an ancient buffalo trace that meandered southward from the Falls to BULLITT'S LICK near Salt River. This western extension of the Wilderness Road was a part of the lifeline of General Clark's little army and later the main route for anyone traveling between the Falls and settlements in the Bluegrass.

The Wilderness Road began in Louisville at FORT NELSON, built by RICHARD CHENOWETH in 1781 on the banks of the Ohio near what is today Seventh and MAIN Streets. It went east on Main St. and turned south along Sixth. Near Jefferson St. the old trail angled across today's courthouse square to Armory Pl., which it followed as far south as BROADWAY, skirting the ponds that at one time covered much of Louisville. Parts of Armory Pl., formerly Center St., and Fifth St. between St. Catherine and York Streets are some of the last remnants of the Wilderness Road within the city. Part of the road within the city was "corduroyed" with logs laid crosswise across the road. The logs were discovered when Armory Pl. was being repaved in 1922.

The trail continued across Broadway between Fifth and Sixth, then slanted a little southeast to the neighborhood of Fourth and St. Catherine. From there it turned more sharply southeast, cutting diagonally across the present grid of streets until it ran into Preston near Burnett and I-65. From that point today's Preston St. and the Preston Hwy. follow the old route of the Wilderness Road all the way to Bullitt County. The pioneer trail passed by the POPLAR LEVEL, a flat, rich tract timbered with tulip poplar trees located near present AUDUBON PARK, then descended gradually into the Wet Woods, a great dark swamp south of Louisville. The trail forged straight through the eastern reaches of the WET WOODS, treacherous and impassable during high waters, until it was corduroyed early in the nineteenth century.

From here the road ran on to FERN CREEK, which it forded about where Preston Hwy. crosses the Northern Ditch. It joined the Blue Lick Rd. less than a mile beyond the Bullitt County line, passed through the Blue Lick Gap in the KNOBS, then turned almost due west and followed the base of the knobs to Bullitt's Lick. From the saltworks the old trail turned east toward Harrodsburg, almost doubling back on itself.

See Robert Emmett McDowell, "The Wilderness Road in Jefferson County," *Louisville* 18 (June 20, 1967): 7–15; *Courier-Journal*, Nov. 26, 1922; Robert Emmett McDowell, "The Wilderness Road's Louisville End," *Courier-Journal Magazine*, March 4, 1962.

Audrea McDowell

WILDER PARK. This neighborhood in southern Louisville is bounded by Central Ave. to the north, the CSX Railroad tracks to the east, the WATTERSON EXPRESSWAY to the south, and a combination of Third St. and Southern Pkwy. to the west. Before being subdivided it was the site of Greenland racecourse, opened about 1866. When it closed, the area became Wilder Park (middle 1880s), and the clubhouse was used as a park pavilion. It was a favorite place

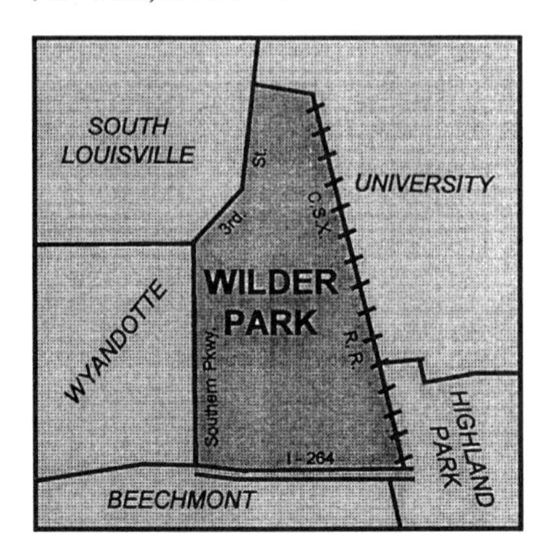

for bicyclists in the 1890s. In 1891 Mrs. Wilder Collins and Bennett H. Young, the president of the Kentucky State Agricultural, Mechanical, Zoological, and Botanical Association, platted land near the Grand Blvd. (Southern Pkwy.) for the purpose of creating a subdivision. Still primarily vacant four years later, the area hosted a day-long picnic featuring a barbecue of a hundred cattle, three hundred sheep, two hundred pigs, and seventy-five gallons of burgoo for approximately a hundred thousand visitors during the last day of the Grand Army of the Republic's annual national convention. The convention, perhaps the largest in Louisville's history, attracted veterans of the Union Army and their families.

Few lots were sold until Collins and Young redivided the land in 1901 and enlisted the help of real estate agent Angus Allmond, who boasted that the subdivision was the most beautiful in the city and offered free transportation to anyone who wished to inspect it. Second St. contains a lovely divided median. With the building of new streetcar lines to IROQUOIS PARK (fare, five cents) and the construction just to the east of new shops by the LOUISVILLE & NASHVILLE RAILROAD, the community began to flourish. Allmond publicized that it offered country living with city services. One could purchase a lot for six to twenty-five dollars per front foot. After another replatting in 1904 to create additional lots, the area became part of the fifth-class city of Oakdale until the entire region was annexed by the city of Louisville in 1922.

See "Louisville Survey: Central and South Report," (Louisville 1978); *A Place in Time: The Story of Louisville's Neighborhoods* (Louisville 1989).

WILL, ARTHUR A. (b Louisville, May 22, 1871; d Pewee Valley, Kentucky, October 8, 1940). Mayor. He was the son of Charles C. and Catherine (Kuebler) Will and one of six children. His father was a well-known building contractor who erected many of Louisville's substantial buildings. Will was born in the PORTLAND neighborhood and educated at PUBLIC SCHOOLS. He left school at sixteen to become a carpenter's apprentice at the John Fichtner Planing Mill Co. He apprenticed there for some time, eventually getting into the lumber business and finally into building and contracting. At twenty he and James Davis started their own construction business. In 1909 he continued the business independently. He built numerous homes in Portland.

Will first entered public life as a member of the City Council during the Grinstead administration. From 1907 to 1909 he served on the Board of Councilmen. He was elected to the BOARD OF ALDERMEN in 1917 to fill the vacancy caused by the resignation of Judge Eugene Dailey. He was twice elected president of the board, in 1921 and 1923. A Republican, he served as mayor from November 17, 1925, until June 1927. He was removed from office when the Kentucky Court of Appeals upheld a lower court's verdict supporting a Democratic lawsuit contesting the 1925 election.

After his term he became chairman of the Board of Public Safety during Mayor William B. Harrison's administration. In 1930 the new city charter consolidated the Board of Aldermen, Board of Councilmen, and the Boards of Public Safety and PUBLIC WORKS into a single legislative body. Will became the first director of the new Department of Works. He held the post until 1933, when Harrison left the mayor's office.

Will was president of the Portland Federal Savings and Loan Association, a director of the Morris Plan Bank, a member of the board of trustees of the Louisville Community Hospital Service, and he was active in Louisville's Community Chest charity. He was also president of the Rose Island Excursion Co.

He married Cora L. Goss of Louisville on November 13, 1901. She was the daughter of Theodore T. Goss, lockmaster for the LOUISVILLE AND PORTLAND CANAL for many years. Will and his wife had two children, Catherine Page and Charles Christian. He was a deacon of the Grace Lutheran Church, a Mason in the Lewis Lodge, a member of the Kosair Temple, and a member of the Improved Order of Red Men. He died of pneumonia. He is buried in CAVE HILL CEMETERY.

See Temple Bodley and Samuel M. Wilson, *History of Kentucky; The Blue Grass State: Biographical vol. 3* (Chicago and Louisville 1928); *Courier-Journal*, Oct. 9, 1940.

WILLARD, ASHBEL P. (b Vernon, New York, October 31, 1820; d St. Paul, Minnesota, October 4, 1860). Indiana governor. Born to Col. Erastus and Sarah (Parsons) Willard, he grew up in the town of Vernon, where his father had served as sheriff. Willard was educated at Hamilton College in Clinton, New York. He graduated in 1842 and practiced law in his home county. Willard moved frequently as a young adult until he settled in Louisville, where he taught school. In 1844 Willard campaigned for James K. Polk's presidential bid, which included a lecture in NEW ALBANY, Indiana. He so impressed the local citizens that he was asked to move there, which he did in 1845. He began to practice law and in 1850 won a position in the Indiana House of Representatives.

The Democrats nominated him for lieutenant governor in 1852, and he defeated William Williams, Whig, and James Miliken, Free Soil, and served from 1853 to 1857. In 1856 the party nominated Willard for governor. Willard defeated Oliver P. Morton, Republican, winning by less than five thousand votes. Willard's administration faced a legislature that preferred to debate national issues rather than making appropriations for state expenses. To secure the state's credit, Willard had to borrow funds to pay the interest on the debt. Late in his term his health began to fail, and in 1860 Willard, who drank heavily, went to Minnesota to recu-

Pavilion in Wilder Park, 1890s.

perate but never regained his health.

Willard married Caroline C. Cook of Vernon, New York, on May 31, 1847; they had two children, James H., and Caroline C. Willard is buried in Fairview Memorial Cemetery in New Albany, Indiana.

See William Woollen, *Biographical and Historical Sketches of Early Indiana* (Indianapolis 1883).

WILLIAMS, CHARLES B., SR. (b Philadelphia, June 7, 1829; d Louisville, August 17, 1915). Actor. The son of Samuel and Celeste (Jouette) Williams, he moved to Louisville at age twenty-one. He began his theatrical career in Philadelphia as a pantomimist and was associated with such stars of the day as Charlotte Cushman and Joseph Jefferson, both of whom were his close friends. Upon Williams's arrival in Louisville, he obtained a position at the old Mozart Hall, later known as Wood's Theater. Later he began appearing at the Louisville Theatre, located at the southeast corner of Fourth and Green (LIBERTY) Streets.

As a member of the stock company, Williams soon acquired a reputation as a star performer in *Humpty Dumpty*, a popular pantomime play at that time. When not on stage, Williams worked as a property man, as many actors did in those days. For a time, Williams also worked an act with his older sister, Mary, and was a member of the famous Martinelli troupe. When the Louisville Theatre burned in 1866, all of Williams's costumes and props were destroyed. Another THEATER was soon completed, at the cost of seventy-five thousand dollars, by Col. Marc Munday, and named the Louisville Opera House. Here Williams once again found himself as part of the stock company and working as a property man.

On March 23, 1853, Williams married Jane Godfried in Louisville, and by 1877 their ninth child, Clarence, had been born. Succumbing to the infirmities of old age, he was buried in CAVE HILL CEMETERY in an unmarked grave.

Warder Harrison

WILLIAMS, CHARLES SNEED (b Evansville, Indiana, May 24, 1882; d London, England, October 17, 1964). Artist. The son of Bailey Peyton and Virginia (Sneed) Williams. In 1912 he married Elsie Luke. They had two children, William and Virginia. Williams studied at Allan Fraser Art College in Arbroath, Scotland. He painted and exhibited commissioned portraits in Louisville, Chicago, Nashville, Great Britain, and France. His prominent Louisville sitters included ROBERT WORTH BINGHAM, Rogers Morton as a child, and Bishop Charles Woodcock. He demonstrated a wide-ranging ability when he painted murals at St. Andrews Church in Louisville. He was a founding member and first vice president of Louisville's Arts Club (1942–45), and the organizer of the Anglo-American Brain Trust under the auspices of the British Army and Navy Education Department. In WORLD WAR II, Williams served as an air-raid warden in London. His works are represented in the United States Capitol, the Confederate Museum in Richmond, the KENTUCKY HISTORICAL SOCIETY in Frankfort, and the J.B. SPEED ART MUSEUM in Louisville.

Charlotte Williams Price

WILLIAMS, ELIAS E. (b near Shepherdstown, Virginia [now West Virginia], November 22, 1791; d Louisville, June 20, 1880). Architect and builder. One of Louisville's leading architects by the late 1840s, Williams came to the city in early 1838 and placed an advertisement in the *Louisville Public Advertiser* that ran from March 22 of that year to midsummer. He announced that he had "located himself permanently in this city and intends to follow his occupation as an architect and housebuilder." He noted that he had "more than twenty years experience in some of the principal cities of the United States," although he did not name them. He did, however, list some well-known local names as references, indicating that he had probably worked in Louisville earlier. He may well have provided architectural services for these references: GARNETT DUNCAN, attorney; George C. Gwathmey, an officer of the BANK OF KENTUCKY; John P. Bull, druggist, who later became one of Louisville's wealthiest men through sales of Bull's Sarsaparilla tonic; and J.C. Buckles, merchant and owner of a steamboat warehouse on the wharf. Like many other architects of his time Williams probably learned his profession as a builder's apprentice and through the study of architectural handbooks.

His first major commission was likely the stately, twenty-two-room Benjamin Smith residence on the south side of Jefferson St. between First and Brook Streets, built about 1841. It was basically a square Italianate house with a columned portico. The interior boasted a handsome spiral staircase to the upper two floors. Other work through that decade is unrecorded but may well have included some of the imposing residences rising on Walnut (Muhammad Ali Blvd.) and Chestnut Streets.

In any event, by 1850 his reputation was secure and his commissions included the Kentucky Institution for the Education of the Blind (1855) in a then-rural setting on the Shelbyville Turnpike (Frankfort Ave.), the massive Masonic Temple (1857) at Fourth and Jefferson Streets, and the United States Post Office and Custom House (1858) at Third and Green (LIBERTY) Streets.

Williams's commissions seem to have slacked off in the 1860s, perhaps because of the CIVIL WAR plus the rising number of younger architects such as HENRY WHITESTONE. Williams is last listed as an architect in the CITY DIRECTORIES in 1865–66 when he was age seventy-five.

By 1870 he was operating a wholesale liquor business on Second St. between MAIN ST. and the river, which he continued to do until his death in 1880. An auction of his effects listed liquors, fishing rods, two violins, and much more. Especially interesting was a separate auction of five hundred books, including "many old and rare volumes." (*Louisville Commercial*, July 4, 1880, 4)

Elias E. Williams. A daguerreotype portrait by John M. Hewitt, c. 1852.

Only the former Custom House and Post Office survives of Williams's buildings. After a new federal building at Fourth and Chestnut was completed in 1892, the 1858 structure became a warehouse and, in 1912, home of the *COURIER-JOURNAL* and *LOUISVILLE TIMES*. It was later converted to offices and since 1996 has been named the LANDMARK BUILDING. The Masonic Temple, which included a large auditorium that was transformed into a THEATER in 1878, was destroyed by fire on July 7, 1902. The school for the blind, with its massive dome and columned portico—a landmark in the CLIFTON neighborhood—was demolished in 1966. The Benjamin Smith mansion was razed about 1966 to make way for an exit from Interstate 65 to Jefferson St. In its later years it had served a variety of purposes, including the Union Gospel Mission. It was here that PATTY HILL set up one of the early kindergartens in the United States.

Williams is buried in CAVE HILL CEMETERY beside his English-born wife, Sarah, who died October 7, 1863. They were parents of a daughter, Virginia, named perhaps for the architect's native state. She married John B. Lewis, an iron merchant. They are buried on the same Cave Hill lot.

See *Courier-Journal*, March 25, 1913; Louisville city directories 1855 to 1879; burial records, Cave Hill Cemetery; National Archives, Washington., D.C., Record Group 121, various items of correspondence.

George H. Yater

WILLIAMS, EVAN (b Pwllheli, Wales, August 10, 1755; d Louisville, October 15, 1810).

Distiller. Williams came by steerage to Philadelphia in 1784 aboard the *Piqoe*. He soon settled in Louisville, where he established a distillery on Fifth St. near the OHIO RIVER. Col. REUBEN T. DURRETT (1824–1913), an early Louisville historian, credits Williams as being Kentucky's first distiller, but this fact would be hard to substantiate. Williams's distillery was listed in the Jefferson County tax returns in 1789. He was issued a whiskey license in 1801 by the United States for three stills, with capacities of 141, 130, and 93 gallons.

Williams was twice elected to Louisville's Board of Trustees and is reported to have brought a jug of his whiskey to meetings, perhaps to lubricate the wheels of GOVERNMENT. He also served as harbor master for the Port of Louisville.

In 1803 Williams was contractor for a five-room, two-story stone jail, which was built on the northwest corner of Sixth and Jefferson Streets. Two years later, he finished building the county clerk's office on the Public Square.

He married Hannah Phillips (1775–1854) on February 18, 1796. They had three sons and two daughters. Williams's grave site is unknown.

See Samuel W. Thomas, "An Inventory of Jefferson County Records," *Filson Club History Quarterly* 44 (Oct. 1970): 321–55; J. Stoddard Johnston, ed., *Memorial History of Louisville* (Chicago 1896).

Blaine A. Guthrie Jr.

WILLIAMS, HENRY H. (b near Lexington, Kentucky, 1790s (?); d Louisville, February 14, 1850). Musician and dancing teacher. Williams was a free African American and a pioneer in many respects in Louisville's musical history. It is unknown how or when he arrived in Louisville, but in 1834 he opened a dancing school at Edward Lynch's Assembly Room on MAIN St. Williams was the first African American and one of the most popular dancing teachers in Louisville and often advertised his services in local NEWSPAPERS. In 1835 he announced the formation of a cotillion band, the earliest African American–led band in the region, which would be "the very best in the country." (*Louisville Public Advertiser*, Oct. 14, 1835). It included other free AFRICAN AMERICANS, slaves, and German immigrants. He chose exceptional musicians and several African American members, including JAMES C. CUNNINGHAM and Samuel Hicks, who later formed their own successful STRING AND BRASS BANDS. By the late 1830s the band was the most popular in the region, playing not only in Louisville but from Cincinnati to New Orleans. In 1839 Williams played at the OAKLAND RACE COURSE during the famous race between Grey Eagle and Wagner. His band was in constant demand on STEAMBOATS and at Kentucky's spas and resorts during the summers, particularly at PAROQUET SPRINGS and Drennon Springs.

He was a talented violinist and was capable of performing whatever type of music the situation required, from marches, waltzes, and polkas at cotillions and fancy balls to Virginia reels and breakdowns at country dances and barbecues.

Louisville newspapers often commented favorably on his musical and teaching talents, and a benefit was given for him at William C. Peters's Apollo Rooms on Main St. in 1848. Despite his popularity, however, he was never included in the formal concerts given by white musical associations such as the St. Cecilia Society, the Louisville Musical Association, or the Louisville Mozart Society.

See *Louisville Morning Courier*, Sept. 18, 1846, March 3, 1848.

Cornelius Bogert

WILLIAM STOCKHOFF & SONS INC. In 1863 John Stockhoff established a hardware and cutlery store on E MARKET St. According to Stockhoff's will, dated February 4, 1887, he was by then in partnership with his sons, Carl, William, and Henry. When John Stockhoff died in December 1892 he left the business to them.

Carl William Stockhoff (b 1860) ran the store, renaming it Wm. Stockhoff & Son sometime after his son, William Fred Stockhoff (1891–1965), came into the hardware business with him. William Fred Stockhoff had three daughters, one of whom married James B. Hayden (1922–). James worked for his father-in-law and bought the business in 1964. In 1966 he moved it to 919 E Jefferson St. His son, Allen Lee Hayden (1951–), bought the business from his father and moved it in 1984 to 6549 W Hwy. 22 in CRESTWOOD, east of Louisville. Hayden refocused the business, eliminating hardware and carrying only horseshoes and farrier's supplies. In 1990 the business relocated to 5907 W Hwy. 22 in Crestwood.

Lynn S. Renau

WILLIG, W. ARMIN (b Louisville, October 19, 1912; d Fort Myers, Florida, December 5, 1992). Jefferson County judge. Willig graduated from LOUISVILLE MALE HIGH SCHOOL in 1930 and earned the B.A. degree from the UNIVERSITY OF LOUISVILLE in 1934. At the university he was president of the Student Council and lettered in BASKETBALL all four years.

Willig, a Republican, was Jefferson County judge from September 29, 1969, until January 4, 1970. He was appointed by Gov. Louie B. Nunn to the post after incumbent county judge E.P. "Tom" Sawyer was killed in an automobile accident while in office. Willig, who was not an attorney, was one of the few county judges who did not have a legal background. He was apolitical unknown when he was recommended by the Louisville-Jefferson County Republican executive committee for the position. In fact he had been a registered Democrat as late as 1964 and had been appointed to the city park board by a Democratic administration.

Willig was hand-picked for the post the night before the executive committee endorsement when the governor met with local representatives of the GOP, including U.S. representative William O. Cowger, Mayor Kenneth A. Schmied, and the GOP nominee for mayor, John Porter Sawyer. In the November election Willig was easily defeated by Democrat Louis J. "Todd" Hollenbach III by 8,574 votes (49,184–40,610). The Democrats were swept back into power during one of the lowest voter turnouts in Jefferson County history.

Willig was a prominent businessman, serving as chairman of the board of the Time Finance Co., Leisure Industries Inc., Dixie Beer Distributors, and Interconnect Communications Systems; president of Ohio Falls Textile Dyers Inc., Harvest Towing Co., Southland Towing Co., and M&M Realty Co.; and vice president of American Barge Line Co.

Willig married Mona-Tate Russell on July 10, 1937, and the couple had two children, Mona-Tate and Caldwell R. At the time of his death he had been remarried to JoAnn Mason. He is buried in CAVE HILL CEMETERY.

See *Courier-Journal*, Sept. 27, 1969, Dec. 7, 1992.

WILLIS, ALBERT SHELBY (b Shelbyville, Kentucky, January 22, 1843; d Honolulu, Hawaii, January 6, 1897). U.S. congressman, minister to Hawaii. Willis was one of three children of Dr. Shelby Willis and Harriet Button. Shelby Willis died in 1846, and the family moved to Louisville in 1850. In 1852 his mother married prominent Louisville attorney J.L. Clemmons. Willis graduated from LOUISVILLE MALE HIGH SCHOOL in 1860 and taught school in the city for four years before graduating from the University of Louisville School of Law in 1866. After being admitted to the bar he practiced law with his stepfather on and off for most of his life.

Willis, a Democrat, served as prosecuting attorney for Jefferson County from 1874 to 1877. He also served as the Democratic presidential elector for the district in the 1872 election, canvassing in Louisville and southern Indiana for the Horace Greeley presidential ticket.

Willis was elected to the U.S. House of Representatives in 1876, serving from March 4, 1877, until March 3, 1887. In his first election he defeated Republican nominee WALTER EVANS, former commissioner of internal revenue. He was finally defeated in the 1886 Democratic primary when he ran for renomination against Asher G. Caruth.

While serving in Congress as chairman of the House River and Harbor Committee, Willis was instrumental in getting the federal GOVERNMENT to remove tolls from the Louisville and PORTLAND CANAL. He also helped to get a bill passed for an endowment for the AMERICAN PRINTING HOUSE FOR THE BLIND. The bill, signed into law on March 3, 1879, called for the purchase of $250,000 worth of U.S. Treasury bonds, the interest from which was to be used to print embossed books for use by schools for the blind throughout the country. After leaving office, Willis founded and was president of the Sun Life Insurance Co. in Louisville.

In 1893 Willis was appointed minister to Hawaii by President Grover Cleveland and served in that capacity until his death. Willis's tenure came at a turbulent time in U.S.-Hawaiian relations. In January 1893 American and European businessmen, led by pro-annexation interests including pineapple tycoon Sanford Dole, instituted a successful coup d'état against Hawaiian Queen Lili'uokalani with the help of a contingent of U.S. Marines. Only days before, the queen had attempted to submit an updated constitution expanding her power and the rights of native Hawaiians. Dole, with the approval of U.S. minister John Stevens, an annexation supporter, was installed as president of the provincial government.

President Cleveland, who took office that March, initially denounced the coup and sent Willis in as the new minister to negotiate a return of Queen Lili'uokalani to the throne. Willis, following the instructions of Cleveland, met with the queen on November 13 to discuss the conditions for her reinstatement as sovereign. Eventually, she capitulated to all of Cleveland's demands and vowed to grant full amnesty to those who had led the insurrection.

Willis then went to Dole to inform him of both the president's support for the queen and her acceptance of the condition of amnesty. After rejecting Cleveland's offer, the provisional government began to prepare for a possible U.S. invasion to restore the queen, but Congress never authorized the use of force. In 1894 the provisional government, still waiting for annexation, declared Hawaii a republic, and in 1898 the islands were finally annexed.

Willis married Florence Dulaney, daughter of a prominent Louisville family, on November 20, 1878. The couple had one son, Albert Jr. President Cleveland was said to have been deeply affected by Willis's untimely death. He is buried in Cave Hill Cemetery.

See J. Stoddard Johnston, ed., *Memorial History of Louisville* (Chicago 1896); John McAfee, *Kentucky Politicians: Sketches of Representative Corn-Crackers and Other Miscellany* (Louisville 1886); *Courier-Journal*, Jan. 16, 1897; *Biographical Directory of the American Congress 1774–1971* (Washington, D.C., 1971); Merze Tate, *The United States and the Hawaiian Kingdom: A Political History* (New Haven and London, 1965).

WILLOUGHBY, LIVELY BURGESS (b Bowling Green, Kentucky, September 2, 1883; d Louisville, January 13, 1971). Entrepreneur. During the 1920s, Willoughby and his wife began to develop containers for ready-to-bake, refrigerated biscuits in an effort to save time for busy housewives. After losing his wholesale bakery business in Bowling Green at the onset of the Great Depression, Willoughby moved to Louisville in the early 1930s where he continued to experiment with the product in a rented building at the corner of Thirty-fourth and Magazine Streets.

Ballard's Mills purchased canned biscuit process from L.B. Willoughby. South side of Broadway west of Beargrass Creek, c. 1918.

With the development of the still-used tubular can, many of the preservation problems were solved and Willoughby began to manufacture them under the label Olde Kentuckie Buttermilk Biscuits. Their initial popularity in local stores attracted attention from several large food companies. In 1931 Willoughby merged his Old Kentuckie Products Co. with a local company, Ballard Flour Mills, which led to the creation of the Oven-Ready Biscuits brand name. The Pillsbury Co. acquired Ballard in 1949.

Willoughby married Eliza Hall Smith. They had three children: Mary Beth, Paul, and R. Eliot. Willoughby is buried in Resthaven Memorial Park.

See *Courier-Journal*, Jan. 14, 1971.

WILLSON, AUGUSTUS EVERETT (b Maysville, Kentucky, October 13, 1846; d Louisville, August 24, 1931). Kentucky governor. Willson's parents, Hiram and Ann Colvin (Ennis) Willson, had moved from New York to Kentucky in the early 1840s. Hiram, a lumber man and mill operator, relocated his family to Covington and then to New Albany, Indiana, before 1852. After being orphaned when he was twelve, young Gus and two of his siblings lived with a grandmother in New York state. They then moved to Cambridge, Massachusetts, to live with their older brother Forceythe, who was a well-known poet.

Willson graduated from Harvard in 1869 and studied law for several months before returning to New Albany in 1870 to live briefly with Congressman Michael C. Kerr. Kerr's recommendation helped Willson secure a position at the Louisville law firm of Harlan, Newman, and Bristow. The firm included notable attorneys Benjamin H. Bristow, who became the United States Secretary of the Treasury in 1874, and future supreme court justice John Marshall Harlan. The latter's ardent support of the Republican Party propelled Willson into the field of partisan politics.

Although well-respected throughout the state, Willson, nicknamed "Hummy" because of his habit of humming to himself, was handicapped by Kentucky's strong allegiance to the Democratic Party in the years after the Civil War. He lost elections for the Kentucky Senate in 1879 and the United States House of Representatives in 1884, 1886, 1888, and 1892. He had never been appointed or elected to a major office when nominated in 1907 to face state auditor Samuel Wilbur Hager for the governor's seat. The bitter campaign focused on the emotional issue of temperance and the adoption of a uniform local option law. The Democrats, controlled by the Beckham-Haly faction, attacked the alleged misconduct during the administration of Republican governor William O'Connell Bradley (1895–99), while the Republicans charged outgoing Democratic governor J.C.W. Beckham with corruption and bossism. With more than 410,000 votes cast, Willson defeated Hager by 18,053, with almost half of the margin (8,970) coming from Louisville and Jefferson County ballots. Willson won on the strength of a unified Republican Party and the fact that many "drys" stayed home, while "wets" considered him more to their liking on the liquor question than Hager.

During his term, Governor Willson declared

martial law and used the State Guard in western Kentucky to curb the Black Patch War, which involved intimidation tactics by night riders to force TOBACCO farmers to join a cooperative that could set the price of their product. Additionally, he pardoned several men who had been implicated in Gov. William Goebel's assassination, set up a bipartisan board to run state institutions, established the Bureau of Vital Statistics, mandated motor vehicle registration, and supported an act to furnish the new state capitol building. However, with the Democrats controlling the General Assembly, many of his attempts to secure legislation were blocked, and critical issues remained unresolved; and the legislative sessions of 1908 and 1910 were among the least productive in the history of the legislature.

At the end of his term in December 1911, Willson returned to his legal practice in the LOUISVILLE TRUST CO. BUILDING at Market and Fifth Streets. Defeated for a United States Senate seat in 1914 by former governor Beckham, Willson did not seek public office again. He was active in civic affairs, and he served on the Harvard Board of Overseers from 1910 to 1918.

He died of pneumonia at his S Fourth St. home and is buried in CAVE HILL CEMETERY. He was survived by his wife of fifty-four years, Mary Elizabeth (Ekin) Willson. Their only son had died in infancy.

See Lowell Harrison, ed., *Kentucky's Governors, 1792–1985* (Lexington 1985); James C. Klotter, *Kentucky: Portrait in Paradox, 1900–1950* (Lexington 1996); Christopher R. Waldrep, "Augustus E. Willson and the Night Riders," *Filson Club History Quarterly* 58 (April 1984): 237–53.

Lowell H. Harrison

WILSON, CHARLES ALEXANDER (b Louisville, 1857; d Louisville, March 3, 1947). Jefferson County judge. He was the son of David W. and Elizabeth Wilson. Wilson, a Democrat, was Jefferson County judge from January 1, 1906, until June 29, 1907, when he was removed from office along with other city and county officers. Wilson defeated ARTHUR PETER, a Fusionist candidate, in 1905. The Fusionists were a mixture of Republicans and reform Democrats who united against the Whallen brothers' Democratic machine. Wilson won by 2,486 out of the more than 40,000 votes cast in the election, but the Fusionists filed a lawsuit alleging election improprieties on the part of the Democrats. WILLIAM MARSHALL BULLITT, HELM BRUCE, and Alexander G. Barret, Fusionist attorneys and prominent Louisville citizens, accused the Democrats of stuffing ballot boxes and employing city police and fire department personnel to intimidate voters at polling stations.

Shackelford Miller and Samuel Kirby, chancellors of the Jefferson Circuit Court, upheld the election results, but the Kentucky Court of Appeals eventually ruled the election invalid in May 1907. All Democratic officials elected in 1905 in Louisville and Jefferson County were thrown out of office, including Judge Wilson. Gov. J.C.W. Beckham appointed Walter P. Lincoln, a Democrat, to serve as county judge until the November 1907 special election, when Arthur Peter was elected.

Wilson also served one term from 1892 through 1893 on the Louisville BOARD OF ALDERMEN, where he was elected president. He was also the first judge of the juvenile court, established in 1904. He was Police Court judge from 1895 until 1901, a member of the first Louisville Board of Public Safety, and an attorney for the Sinking Fund.

Wilson rose to national prominence through his work with juveniles. He helped to organize the Third Street Newsboys Home, a residence house for newspaper boys who sold on downtown street corners. He also served as president of the home. Wilson was also secretary of the board of directors of the Kosair Crippled Children Hospital. He served as legal advisor to FONTAINE FERRY PARK Enterprises for several years and then served as manager of the organization from 1917 to 1932. Wilson was married to Laura A. Pirtle. The couple had two children, Annie J. and Laura E. Wilson. His body was cremated.

See Alwin Seekamp and Roger Burlingame, eds., *Who's Who in Louisville* (Louisville 1912); *Courier-Journal*, March 4, 1947.

WILSON, EDITH GOODALL (b Louisville, September 6, 1896; d Chicago, Illinois, March 31, 1981). BLUES and JAZZ singer. The daughter of William Goodall and Susan Jones, she began her singing career in 1908 performing on the stage at the WHITE CITY AMUSEMENT PARK, which was located on the bank of the Ohio River in western Louisville. After WORLD WAR I, Wilson was discovered by vaudevillians Lena and Danny Wilson and accompanied them to Chicago. During 1921–30 she made dozens of records and appeared in many stage revues. After 1930 she toured the country with the Lucky Millinder Band, Cab Calloway, and others. From 1947 to 1965 she appeared as Aunt Jemima in ads for the Quaker Oats Co. The African American performer drew criticism from CIVIL RIGHTS groups but considered her role as a performance and not a statement. She made a successful comeback in 1972, recording with Eubie Blake and singing at jazz festivals.

See Daphne Duval Harrison, *Black Pearls: Blues Queens of the 1920s* (New Brunswick 1988); Sheldon Harris, *Blues Who's Who* (New Rochelle, N.Y., 1979).

Brenda K. Bogert

WINCHESTER, BOYD (b Ascension Parish, Louisiana, September 23, 1836; d Louisville, May 18, 1923). Lawyer and statesman. Having moved to Louisville with his parents as a child, Winchester received his early education in the city's PUBLIC SCHOOLS. He later attended Centre College in Danville, Kentucky, and, for a time, the University of Virginia. After earning his law degree from the UNIVERSITY OF LOUISVILLE in 1857, Winchester opened his own law office in Louisville on Jefferson St. between Fourth and Fifth Streets.

Winchester entered the political arena in 1867 when he was elected to the Kentucky state senate. After serving only one term there he won a seat as a Democrat in the United States House of Representatives, serving two terms from March 4, 1869, to March 3, 1873. He then returned to Louisville, where he resumed his law practice and, from 1875 to 1877, served as president of the Farmers' and Drovers' Insurance Co. In 1884 Winchester was president of the Democratic state convention as well as a presidential elector. The following year, Pres. Grover Cleveland appointed him minister resident and consul general to Switzerland, a position he held until 1889.

Though retired from public life, Winchester contributed a number of historical and political articles to magazines and the *COURIER-JOURNAL*. In 1891 he wrote a political treatise entitled *The Swiss Republic*, and for many years he traveled the lecture circuit, speaking at colleges and lyceums throughout the southern and western states.

Winchester was married twice, first to Alice Peck and then to Lillian Bowles, who died in 1873. He is buried in CAVE HILL CEMETERY and was survived by a daughter.

See *Courier-Journal*, May 19, 1923; *The Biographical Directory of the United States Congress, 1774–1989* (Washington, D.C., 1989)

WINN, MARTIN J. (b Louisville, June 30, 1860; d Louisville, October 6, 1949). Thoroughbred HORSE RACING executive. "Col. Matt" Winn was the son of west Louisville grocery store owner Patrick Winn and his wife, Julia Flaherty (Hession) Winn. After graduation from Bryant and Stratton Business School, Winn traveled throughout Kentucky, wholesaling staples and procuring produce for Louisville retailers. In 1887 Winn's tailor offered him a partnership. As the firm's sales representative, Winn traveled the southwest circuit from New Orleans to Los Angeles, taking orders for custom-made suits.

In 1888 Winn married Mary Doyle. By 1899, he was a well-known local figure—the first Grand Knight of the first Knights of Columbus Council established south of the OHIO RIVER–and the father of a growing family. A son, Robert, and two daughters, Ethel and Martin, died in childhood. Seven daughters—Ann, Mary, Olive, Elizabeth, Clara, Julia, and Helen—lived to adulthood.

Winn was fourteen when he attended the inaugural 1875 running of the KENTUCKY DERBY. That race became his passion, one to which he devoted half his life. In 1902 he was named vice president of the New Louisville

Jockey Club (CHURCHILL DOWNS), which had fallen on hard times after a decade-long period of poor management. Winn, along with Mayor CHARLES F. GRAINGER, brewing company president Frank Fehr, and hotelman Louis Seelbach, made the most of the initial forty thousand dollar investment necessary to rescue the operation from bankruptcy.

At the insistence of business associates and stockholders, Winn became the track's general manager late in 1903. In 1905 he founded the American Turf Association and served as the organization's president. By 1907, he was general manager of six American tracks. Governor Cripps Beckham honored Winn with a colonelcy in Kentucky's honorary militia for saving Kentucky's signature sport. In 1908 Winn successfully rebuffed Protestant reformers' efforts to close Churchill Downs by reintroducing pari-mutuel machine wagering and buying newspaper advertising space to teach track patrons how to figure odds and payouts. Under this system, the track's oddsmaker set odds, which then fluctuated as bettors put money on favorites or long shots. Within a decade pari-mutuel wagering had become the accepted way to bet on virtually all legally sanctioned North American thoroughbred racing.

When anti-GAMBLING forces closed tracks throughout the East, Winn kept the southern circuit open by operating a racetrack in Juarez, Mexico, from 1909 to 1917. His fund-raising efforts on behalf of the American Red Cross made Churchill Downs a bastion of patriotism during WORLD WAR I. Having gained considerable national clout, he shepherded an alliance of Kentucky racetracks through a second church-led anti-gambling crusade in the 1920s, then Depression-era economics forced him to shut down racing at both the Kentucky Association track in Lexington and Latonia near Cincinnati.

In 1938, as president and executive manager of the newly incorporated Churchill Downs Inc., Winn began a hundred-thousand-dollar expansion program, completing it just before the outbreak of WORLD WAR II. By February 1943, gas rationing and government-mandated shutdown of nonessential recreational facilities threatened the sixty-ninth Derby. Winn wrote wealthy out-of-town box holders, asking them to donate their deluxe Derby Day accommodations to armed forces personnel. Churchill Downs was the only major track not closed by the United States Office of Defense Transportation from 1942 to 1945. The wartime derbies came to be known as "street car derbys," since automobiles were not allowed within a mile of the track, a symbolic gesture that reinforced governmental efforts to conserve gasoline and rubber.

During Winn's long association with Churchill Downs, he built it into the premier track in the country, making the Kentucky Derby the most widely publicized and highly regarded thoroughbred horse racing event of the spring. Five months before his death in 1949, Winn capped his success with the seventy-fifth Diamond Jubilee Derby. That year, television viewers watching some 300 sets around Louisville, and viewers as far away as Lexington and Paducah, saw WAVE newsman George Patterson interview Matt Winn on-site at Churchill Downs.

Winn died following two rounds of surgery at St. Joseph's Infirmary. He is buried in St. Louis Cemetery. Eulogizing Winn, former Kentucky governor Ruby Laffoon (1931–35) said that the tall, soft-spoken, blue-eyed Irishman had "done more than any other man to make Kentucky a household word in the nation." A blanket of roses, a duplicate of the ones placed across the withers of Derby winning horses, adorned his casket at the cathedral.

See Thomas D. Clark, *Helm Bruce, Public Defender, Breaking Louisville's Gothic Politcal Ring, 1905* (Louisville, 1973); Frank G. Menke, *Down the Stretch: The Story of Col. Matt J. Winn* (Louisville 1945); Lynn S. Renau, *Racing around Kentucky* (Louisville 1995) and *Jockeys, Belles and Bluegrass Kings* (Louisville 1996); *Courier-Journal*, October 9, 1949.

Lynn S. Renau

W.K. STEWART BOOKSTORE. William Kerfoot Stewart graduated from Yale University in 1899 and returned to his hometown of Indianapolis to go into the book-selling business. In 1915 he relocated to Louisville and purchased the Dearing Bookstore at 536 S Fourth St., along with Dearing's nearby home at 532. Stewart consolidated the two and opened W.K. Stewart's Bookstore. The store was originally located on Fourth St. between LIBERTY and Walnut (Muhammad Ali Blvd.), moving to its final location at 550 S Fourth St. in 1917. The store quickly earned a loyal clientele due largely to Stewart's love for books and art and his willingness to display his private collection of rare books and documents within the store.

W.K. Stewart bookstore, east side of Fourth Street next to Kaufman-Straus in 1927.

In 1931, Stewart acquired the original charter of the city of Louisville, which had been signed by THOMAS JEFFERSON and had been missing for over seventy-five years. He also was instrumental in bringing many noteworthy art collections and exhibits to Louisville to be displayed and sold in his store, including works by Durer, Rembrandt, and Whistler and first-edition AUDUBON bird prints. The public was invited to attend these free displays just as they were welcome to browse the dark, seemingly endless rows of shelves rising from floor to ceiling and filled with books of all kinds. Shoppers were not only encouraged but also guided through the stacks by Stewart himself and by generations of eager assistants who earned local acclaim for their willingness to find the perfect book for each customer.

When Stewart died in 1959, his wife and then his daughter, Mrs. J.T. Mengel, took over the store until 1965. After donating the rare book collection to the LOUISVILLE FREE PUBLIC LIBRARY and the University of Tennessee, Mengel sold W.K. Stewart's to Martin Brown, who had managed the store under Stewart and who ran the store until it went out of business in 1975. During that time, Brown opened a branch store in the Holiday Manor Shopping Center on U.S. Hwy. 42. In 1977 Donald Roth acquired the branch store opened by Brown and was proprietor until 1982, when Barbara Hendricks purchased it. Hendricks ran the store until it closed in 1999.

The name W.K. Stewart's is likely to stir fond memories for those who can remember stopping by W.K.'s after school or on their lunch hour to browse, read, and discuss books and art with Mr. Stewart, Bess LaCoste, Josef Dignan, Arthur Bensinger, and countless other book lovers who worked in the treasured store.

See *Courier-Journal,* March 3, 1959.

Kyle Yochum

WLOU. WLOU (1350 kHz) was the sixth radio station on the air in Louisville when it signed on in 1948. Called "the station known as Lou," its first owner was Mrs. John Messervy. Station and tower were located on S Third St. between Montana and Winkler. In its bid to be a local station (it had no network affiliation), it featured talent and talk shows and round-table discussions. A morning music show featured an early female disc jockey, Christy Clark.

In October 1951, new owner Robert Rounsaville changed the format of the station to one programmed completely for AFRICAN AMERICANS. The sale had been approved by the Federal Communications Commission, which had eased its policy of not granting licenses to stations that programmed to a specific segment of the community. WLOU became one of the first stations in the country to program exclusively for a minority audience. It featured African American deejays and performers and presented BLUES and spirituals. Early African American personalities included Tobe Howard, Dorothy Howard, Cliff Butler, and Jimmy Rucker.

William Summers III, an ordained African Methodist Episcopal church minister, began working at the station in the early 1950s as a gospel music announcer. He later became the station's general manager. He made appointments that were Louisville radio firsts. He hired a husband-and-wife team, Jimmy and Kathy Curry Carter. In 1969, when he named Betty Rowan to head its news department, she became Louisville's first minority woman news director. Her duties included both gathering and editing news. In that year an article in the *COURIER-JOURNAL* noted, "Black awareness is WLOU's biggest product in the Negro community."

An on-air personality from 1955 to 1965 was Cara Lewis. She appeared first on "Cara's Corner," a five-minute program of fashions and women's news. Her later *Louise Jefferson Show* was thirty minutes long and added helpful hints and interviews to the program. In addition to her programming duties, Lewis did live, on-air commercials. She was required to obtain a third-class radio operator's license because of her on-air duties. Lewis moved to WAVE-TV in 1965.

In 1972 Bill Summers purchased the station from Rounsaville. He was active in both civic and BROADCASTING affairs. When he was elected president of the Kentucky Broadcaster's Association in 1978, he became the first member of a minority group to head the association and first minority president of any state association.

In 1982 a national publishing firm, Johnson Communications of Chicago, purchased the station. John H. Johnson became president, and Summers worked as a consultant. In November 1995 the station was sold to Mortenson Broadcasting of Lexington, Kentucky.

See Francis M. Nash, *Towers over Kentucky: A History of Radio and Television in the Bluegrass State* (Lexington 1995); *Courier-Journal*, Feb. 21, 1969, Nov. 2, 1969.

Bettie Shadburne

WOLFE, NATHANIEL (b Richmond, Virginia, October 29, 1810; d Louisville, July 3, 1865). Lawyer. The son of Benjamin and Sophia Wolfe, Nathaniel graduated from the University of Virginia's law school about 1829 and later moved to Louisville, where he started his law practice. A highly regarded criminal lawyer, he was involved in several of the well-known cases tried in the Louisville and Kentucky COURTS during his time. For example, while a Kentucky state senator in 1854, Wolfe served as a member of the defense counsel for Matthews Ward, son of the wealthy and politically powerful Robert J. Ward Sr., during his celebrated trial. Young Ward was charged with murdering the principal of the Louisville High School by shooting him at point-blank range during an altercation. He was acquitted on the grounds of self-defense.

In a distinguished career in the public sector, Wolfe, a Democrat, was commonwealth's attorney for Jefferson County (1839–52) and a member of the Kentucky Senate (1853–55) and the Kentucky House (1859–63). A committed Unionist, Wolfe was a strong voice in the legislature for Kentucky neutrality in the Civil War. When Wolfe County was formed in 1860, it was named in his honor. Wolfe married Mary Vernon on October 3, 1838; they had ten children. He is buried in Cave Hill Cemetery.

See E. Polk Johnson, *A History of Kentucky and Kentuckians* (Chicago 1912).

WOLF PEN BRANCH MILL. Located in northeastern Jefferson County at 8117 Wolf Pen Branch Rd., the mill is considered to be the oldest remaining industrial building in the county. It is the subject of a famous photo by James Archambeault. Though old deeds to the property refer to an aging mill in disrepair on the site as early as 1844, the present stone, water-powered mill was built around 1875 by Herman Miller, whose family ran the mill until the early 1900s.

In 1925 Eva Lee Cooper (Mrs. Robin Cooper) purchased the Wolf Pen Branch Mill and the surrounding wooded acres from the heirs of Herman Miller. Though the mill had been dormant for years, Cooper quickly brought it into working order and for the next eighteen years operated it for commercial purposes. One important customer was the LOUISVILLE & NASHVILLE RAILROAD, which used the cornmeal for the cornbread served in its dining cars. After WORLD WAR II Cooper continued to run it on a limited basis, grinding cornmeal for her own personal use and for gift giving.

The mill itself is in the center of a farm along HARRODS CREEK. The structure is constructed of rough-hewn limestone blocks, fitted together without mortar. Built into the slope of a ten-foot waterfall, the mill has an overshot wheel by which the water that operates it flows over the top of the wheel. Also standing on the site is Herman Miller's log home from the nineteenth century.

In the 1980s author and media heiress Sallie Bingham bought the 412 acres to preserve it from encroaching development. As a schoolgirl she had ridden horses on the property. "It was always clear to me that the place had to continue as it was whether I was living there or not," she said. In the spring of 1999 Bingham established a conservation easement and donated it to River Fields and the Kentucky Heritage Council. It is thought to be the largest easement donation in Kentucky. Bingham gave $130,000 along with the easement for its supervision and defense. Bingham and her heirs will continue to own and maintain the property, although the property will be preserved for the enjoyment of generations to come.

See Leslee F. Keys, ed., *Historic Jefferson County* (Louisville 1992); *Courier-Journal*, May 14, 1999.

WOMAN'S CLUB OF LOUISVILLE, THE. On March 1, 1890, Susan Avery invited thirty-seven women to her home at Fourth and BROADWAY. What Avery had in mind was the formation of the Woman's Club of Louisville. These were women of vision who had enjoyed excellent educations and the advantages of travel, which had broadened their views.

The Woman's Club was conceived when the modern era began at the end of the nineteenth century. New technological advances freed women from the daily details of the home, and they began to look outward into the world about them.

An old newspaper clipping informs us that "A history of The Woman's Club is almost of necessity a history of Louisville, and particularly of the growth of feminine influence in the city." The chief concern of the Woman's Club has always been civic improvement. Unsafe tenements; impure milk; and the old, unwieldy school board were all condemned.

Physical culture in the schools, truant officers, the Tenement House Commission, a jail library, and a children's room at the Main Library were all fruits of the endeavors of the Woman's Club. Cleanliness, health, education, and the needs of women who work and the unfortunate caught the club's attention and aroused its best efforts. Aside from these practical concerns, the club has maintained a keen interest in the fine arts. It has brought hundreds of lecturers to Louisville to speak on a wide variety of topics.

As various committees of the Woman's Club began to study the problems of this community, their efforts and thrusts became many-faceted. To better the health of children, their nutrition and housing had to improve. There was a need for playgrounds to get the children out into the fresh air and sunshine. Empty lots were hunted out and, at the club's expense, equipped as playgrounds. Thus, the Woman's Club spearheaded the playground concept. The playground project was eventually taken over by the city GOVERNMENT.

There was no idea in 1890 that the Woman's Club would have to enter politics, but this was necessitated by the plight of women in society. The Woman's Club sponsored the Equal Rights Property Bill, which was passed by the Kentucky General Assembly in 1894. Under that law, women would be permitted to handle their own property, collect their own rents, and control their money.

In 1945 Mrs. Spencer Tracy gave a program for the Woman's Club. Her son had been born deaf in 1942, and she and Spencer Tracy had sponsored a clinic to teach deaf children to speak and to lip-read. Because of this presentation, the Kiwanis Club of Louisville and the Woman's Club decided later in the year to sponsor a special school for hearing-impaired children. Every Saturday morning, three little deaf boys arrived for their class, which was held in the basement of the clubhouse. The Louisville Deaf Oral School developed out of this beginning.

Since 1890, The Woman's Club has resided in a number of places. During the early years, the women met in the homes of members such as Susan Avery. As membership grew, other facilities were needed, and events and regular meetings were held at places such as the gymnasium of Hampton College in the old George Keats home on Walnut St. between Third and Fourth Streets, Elk's Hall on Walnut St. (Muhammad Ali Blvd.)between Third and Fourth Streets, and the College Street Presbyterian Church at the corner of Second and College Streets. In 1902 the club obtained its first permanent site after purchasing a home on Fourth St. between Oak St. and Ormsby Ave. When this clubhouse burned down in 1917, Mrs. Morris Belknap offered her home on Fourth St. between Ormsby Ave. and Park Ave. for the under-market price of fifteen thousand dollars. This facility was outgrown again, and a larger building was built on the adjacent garden in 1923. This facility is still used into the 1990s.

See Mary Adelberg, ed., *The Woman's Club of Louisville, 1890–1990* (Louisville 1990).

Mary Milner Adelberg

WOMAN SUFFRAGE. The city of Louisville played a unique role in the woman suffrage campaign, affecting suffrage politics within both the Kentucky and national movements in ways that helped win women's enfranchisement. There were two distinct periods of woman suffrage activity in the city. The first phase, from the 1850s to 1909, was marked by a general public awareness of the woman suffrage debate but limited and sporadic organization of suffragists. Beginning in 1909 Louisville suffragists vastly increased their ranks and undertook a wider range of political actions to win votes for women. In addition, Louisville suffragists wielded greater influence over the strategy and tactics of the Kentucky Equal Rights Association, which up to 1909 was dominated by its founding members from Lexington, Richmond, Newport, and Covington.

The first public discussion of woman suffrage in Louisville seems to have occurred in 1853 when New England abolitionist and woman's rights advocate Lucy Stone delivered three lectures in the city. The close association between the abolitionists and woman's rights causes, plus disruptions from the Civil War and Reconstruction, delayed the start of an organized woman suffrage movement in the South. Nevertheless, by the late 1870s, the *Courier-Journal* kept its readers supplied with a steady stream of information from across the nation about the "woman question," including the issue of female suffrage. Some of these newspaper reports were serious and respectful accounts of the cause's progress, while other references to woman's rights were sarcastic and hostile.

In 1881 Louisville hosted the annual convention of the American Woman Suffrage Association. At its conclusion, a call was issued for the creation of a state organization, and the Kentucky Woman Suffrage Association was formed. Julia Ward Howe, who wrote the "Battle Hymn of the Republic," was in attendance. This organization remained essentially nominal, though Louisvillian John H. Ward, who was elected as its vice president, joined with several other members to lobby the Kentucky legislature in 1882 for women's rights, including the right to municipal and residential suffrage.

It was the Clay sisters of Madison County who did the most in the late nineteenth century to launch and nourish a viable state woman suffrage organization in Kentucky. Mary Barr Clay and Sallie Clay Bennett brought Susan B. Anthony to Kentucky in 1879, and, after Anthony's visit, local suffrage organizations formed in Richmond and Lexington became a small but permanent foundation for the Kentucky movement. In 1888 a third Clay sister, Laura, revamped the Lexington local and used it as a base to establish a new state organization, the Kentucky Equal Rights Association, replacing the defunct Kentucky Woman Suffrage Association. During the early years of the KERA, Louisville's presence was not much in evidence. It appears that Susan B. Anthony bypassed the city on her 1879 tour, and, despite the national suffrage convention and the birth of the first state association in Louisville in 1881, organizational activity was minimal and inconsistent in the 1880s and 1890s. Louisville suffragists hosted the 1891 convention of the KERA, but eighteen years passed before they did so again. Of the twenty-seven yearly conventions of the state association held between 1888 and 1919, the Louisville local failed five times to send in a report of its activity, four of those gaps occurring before 1909. Richmond and Lexington, which were much smaller cities than Louisville, listed 273 and 190 members respectively in their locals in 1909, while the Louisville Woman Suffrage Association could claim only twenty-nine members that year.

Despite the absence in Louisville of a strong organizational base for suffrage activity before the 1910s, there was a small band of committed suffragists who kept the issue alive from the start. Margaret Watts, Caroline Leech, and Susan Look Avery made noteworthy contributions to the Louisville movement during its early years. Watts helped organize the Louisville local on March 1, 1889, served as an officer several times during its first decade, and extended the invitation to the state association to meet in Louisville in 1891. Leech provided the Louisville movement with the most continuity. She was the local's first vice president in 1889, and nearly thirty years later she was still a viable presence, serving as one of the state association's vice presidents from 1916 through 1919. Active in the Kentucky Prohibition party and the Woman's Club of Louisville, Leech was a key liaison between the suffrage, temperance, and club movements. Susan Look Avery, the founder of the Woman's Club of Louisville, also served as an officer in the suffrage local, helped lobby for woman's rights bills in the legislature, and worked to convert more club women to the suffrage cause.

The suffrage work conducted in Louisville before 1909 resembled suffrage activity in the smaller towns of Kentucky. Suffrage education and organizing was carried out on a small scale,

Women voters at the polls in 1920.

with house-to-house visitations, parlor meetings, and personal appeals to prominent individuals, especially ministers, newspaper editors, politicians, and businessmen. Occasionally, noted suffragists were engaged for public lectures, as on January 12, 1895, when the Louisville local hosted Susan B. Anthony and Carrie Chapman Catt, both of whom spoke to a large audience at the Unitarian church at Fourth and YORK Streets.

From 1902 to 1912, the KENTUCKY FEDERATION OF WOMEN'S CLUBS made significant contributions to the campaign to win the school ballot for all literate Kentucky women. Louisville suffragists in the KFWC established a lecture department for school suffrage, mailed out thousands of pieces of suffrage LITERATURE, and lobbied the legislature for a school suffrage bill, which it passed in 1912. Madeline McDowell Breckinridge, a Lexington member of both the KERA and the KFWC, reporting to the latter's convention in 1908 on the progress of the school suffrage bill, observed, "Interest was warmest, I believe, in Louisville" (*Reports of KFWC*, 1908). The bill qualified and enabled women to vote for the election of school trustees and other school officials chosen by the people.

In 1909 the Louisville suffrage local began to eclipse Richmond's and Lexington's domination of the Kentucky movement. Hosting only its second KERA convention in 1909, Louisville was the site of four more, including the last one in 1919. In addition, more Louisville women served as state officers in the last eight years of the movement than in its first twenty. In 1919 five of the KERA's eleven officers were from Louisville.

By the 1910s the Progressive movement and its focus on national solutions to social problems provided a broader context and new impetus for the campaign for the Nineteenth Amendment. The Louisville local, spurred on by the leadership of Virginia Robinson from 1909 to 1911, began to use the more effective mass tactics favored by Progressive reformers to reach the public. Louisville suffragists set up a tent at the state fairs, held street rallies, and entered floats in parades. Between 1909 and 1915, the Louisville suffrage association increased its membership from twenty-nine to four thousand.

Most important for the Kentucky woman suffrage movement was the strong support within the Louisville ranks for the Nineteenth Amendment. Concern for state's rights and efforts to win enfranchisement through a state amendment had long been a part of the KERA's approach, but Louisville suffragists, especially those on the board, increasingly influenced the state association to conform to national strategy begun under Carrie Chapman Catt's leadership in 1916 to make the federal amendment for woman suffrage the first priority. Four years later they were successful when the Nineteenth Amendment was declared ratified, giving women the right to vote.

See Laura Clay Papers, M.I. King Library, Special Collections, Lexington, Ky.; *Kentucky Equal Rights Association Reports of Annual Conventions*, 1889–1919; *Yearbook of The Kentucky Federation of Women's Clubs*, 1897–1915; Elizabeth Cady Stanton, Susan B. Anthony, Matilda Joslyn Gage, Ida Husted Harper, eds., *History of Woman Suffrage* (New York and Rochester 1881–1922); Paul E. Fuller, *Laura Clay and the Woman's Rights Movement* (Lexington 1975); Carol Guethlein, "Women in Louisville: Moving Toward Equal Rights," *Filson Club History Quarterly* 55 (April 1981): 151–78.

Claudia Knott

WOODLAND GARDEN. Operating as a place of amusement in nineteenth-century Louisville, Woodland Garden opened in the late 1820s with William Pickett as its proprietor. Advertised as "the nearest retreat from the city," the public garden was at the east end of MARKET St. between Wenzel and Johnson Streets (near the present STOCK YARDS BANK AND TRUST CO.) and catered to the German immigrant families that moved into the area in the 1830s. A few years after the garden opened, the 1834 Bourbon House (which became the BOURBON STOCK YARDS) was built nearby, catering to livestock drovers. BUTCHERTOWN soon flourished, as distillers, butchers, tanners, and candle makers arrived and made it their home.

In a time before the development of Louisville's park system, these gardens provided a variety of entertainment, which at Woodland included everything from horse- and foot-racing to target-shooting and "rough and tumble" fighting. Because it was a favorite retreat for German immigrants, Woodland featured ethnic SONGS and dances. Later it also housed bowling alleys, a merry-go-round, a shooting gallery, and swings. Its most popular forms of amusement, however, were drinking lager beer or wine; smoking cigars; eating sausage, cheese, and pretzels; and listening to music.

Many Louisvillians experienced their first train ride at Woodland Garden. In 1827 Thomas H. Barlow of Lexington, builder of a small steam locomotive, brought his locomotive to the garden. A car was attached to it, allowing spectators to ride.

In the 1850s the Garden became a target of local nativist organizations. Because the Garden served beer, sold cigars, and played music on Sunday afternoons, local members of the American Party, or Know-Nothings, pointed to it as the means that GERMANS used to defile the Sabbath. But HENRY WATTERSON, editor of the *COURIER-JOURNAL*, saw it differently. Speaking in the 1870s he recalled, "In those days popular music here was known only among the Germans and those few Americans who loved music enough to seek it in the open air. The two public gardens, Woodland . . . and the Lion (at Preston and Kentucky) were . . . as typical gardens as any to be found in the Fatherland . . . simple, peaceful, virtuous Sunday afternoons under the trees, with good music and good beer and good sausage and good cheese and a pretzel."

During the late 1880s gardens began to be replaced by THEATERS and public PARKS as the preferred choice of amusement. Woodland was the last remaining garden in the area, not ceasing operation until 1888. Its lot remained vacant until 1902, when residences were built on the property.

See George Yater, *Two Hundred Years at the Falls of the Ohio* (Louisville 1987); Kentucky Writers' Project, *Louisville: A Guide to the Falls City* (New York 1940); *A Place in Time: The Story of Louisville's Neighborhoods* (Louisville 1989); *Caron Directory* 1832, 1858, 1888, 1902; *History of the Ohio Falls Cities and their Counties* (Cleveland, Ohio, 1882); *Louisville Anzeiger*, March 1, 1898.

Shirley M. Harmon

WOODLAWN RACE COURSE. In June 1858 Bluegrass horsemen met with Louisville businessmen at the GALT HOUSE to raise fifty thousand dollars to construct a race course near the city. Woodlawn was to replace the defunct Oakland course near the present Seventh and Hill Streets. Not until 1860 did the project move forward under the aegis of the Louisville Association for the Improvement of the Breed of Horses. The association purchased 150 acres east of ST. MATTHEWS and between Westport Rd. and the Louisville and Frankfort Railroad. It had been owned by George E.H. Gray, who called the tract Woodlawn.

The track opened May 21, 1860. The *Louisville Daily Courier* described the occasion "with early trains crowded, attendance very large. . . the course in splendid condition and $23,000 sold in pools while thousands were planked up by habitues of the track in the old Kentucky style of betting when pools were unknown." Woodlawn was built with two courses, one for trotters and one for Thoroughbred runners. It had two grandstands (one for women), eight stables, and a clubhouse.

On opening day a tornado struck Louisville, causing some deaths and much damage, but only a torrential downpour at Woodlawn. Nevertheless, it was an omen of the bad luck that would dog the race course. Scarcely had the track opened when the outbreak of the CIVIL WAR put a damper on racing, although some meets were held despite the conflict. After the war, the spring meeting of 1866 proved disappointing, with many horses breaking down. Attendance dropped and the *Turf, Field and Farm* (Oct. 27, 1866) commented, "The people take no interest in racing, and it is thought that the beautiful Woodlawn will have to be abandoned." The distance from Louisville may also have been a factor, but *Turf, Field and Farm* (Aug. 20, 1869) charged "lack of enterprise and a want of tact" in management.

Lexington turfman Robert A. Alexander had

been instrumental in keeping Woodlawn open against the odds, but with his death in December 1867 the track was doomed. The property was sold in parcels in 1872, although the trotting track was in use until at least 1876.

One memento of the ill-fated track still survives, however. The elaborate Woodlawn Vase, crafted by Tiffany and Co. in 1860 and designed to be presented to the owner of the horse winning a four-mile dash in the spring and fall, is now at Pimlico Race Course at Baltimore. A replica of the vase is presented to the owner of the horse winning the annual Preakness Stakes. Two replicas are at the KENTUCKY DERBY MUSEUM at CHURCHILL DOWNS.

See Jane Meyer, "Saratoga of the West," *Courier-Journal Magazine* (May 7, 1961): 22–24; Samuel W. Thomas, *Churchill Downs: A Documentary History of America's Most Legendary Race Track* (Louisville 1995); Lynn S. Renau, *Racing around Kentucky* (Louisville 1995).

Lynn S. Renau

WOOD-MOSAIC CORPORATION.

The Wood-Mosaic Corp. was founded in Rochester, New York, in 1883, a joint venture of Dr. C.F. Rider and William A. MacLean. The name Wood-Mosaic was descriptive of the original product: elegant hardwood parquetry flooring created from the best domestic hardwoods available, as well as many exotic imported species.

The company enjoyed a prosperous existence for over a century. For eighty-six years the firm was directed by a member of the MacLean family, first by William A., then, successively, by Angus D. and Paul R. MacLean. The final sixteen years saw the company with three new owners. In 1969 Wood-Mosaic became a division of Olinkraft Inc. In 1979 Olinkraft sold it to Katz Werke AG. Finally, at the time of its closing in 1985, the company was owned by a corporation formed by Larry Richardson and Wayne Bryant.

William A. MacLean was born in Thurso, Quebec, and arrived in Rochester, New York, before the turn of the twentieth century to work for his brother at the Hugh MacLean Lumber Co. He became president of Wood-Mosaic after he had bought out his partner, Dr. Rider. Shortly thereafter he moved the operation to NEW ALBANY, Indiana. By 1902 Wood-Mosaic Flooring Co. Inc., on E St. near Market, was in business. In addition to a saw mill and the flooring plant in New Albany, MacLean branched out into other aspects of production and sales of hardwood products, including sliced decorative veneers, sawn veneer, and lumber core used in the production of hardwood plywood. Walnut gun stocks and walnut lumber stock for aircraft propellers were produced for the United States and British governments prior to WORLD WAR I.

In early 1922 all of the New Albany operations were moved to the HIGHLAND PARK area of Louisville. A new sawmill was built. It was said to be the first in the state of Kentucky to be constructed of concrete and steel. The main office was located in Highland Park, while the flooring office remained in New Albany.

Customers, by this time, included a broad base of furniture manufacturers, radio cabinet manufacturers, architectural and door manufacturers, and piano makers. The company enjoyed a vast market overseas for its products, both in the United Kingdom and Europe. Wood-Mosaic Lion Brand white oak lumber was respected the world over.

By the mid-1930s manufacturing capabilities were expanded to include two slicing veneer mills, two flooring factories, eight hardwood sawmills, and a veneer slicing factory and sawmill in Woodstock, Ontario. Wood-Mosaic was again producing walnut gun stocks for the British GOVERNMENT, completing an order on December 24, 1940, for over one million Enfield rifle stocks. During WORLD WAR II Wood-Mosaic, which was also producing veneers for aircraft plywood, was awarded the Army-Navy E for efficiency. This marked the first time that the award was given to a hardwood products company in the United States. The company was to be awarded seven more.

At the conclusion of the war, peacetime production resumed with the manufacture of fine face veneer. Wood-Mosiac became the largest producer of fine face veneer in the United States. At this time it also completed a joint venture in the Philippines, building another veneer mill and a sawmill. It added an import/export lumberyard and dry kilns in New Orleans, and it converted the Huntington, West Virginia, mill to a slicing facility. It imported millions of feet of plywood from the Far East for resale, principally to the furniture industry.

During this time Wood-Mosaic employed over eight hundred persons, including four sons of William A. MacLean, and later three of his grandsons. The company came to be known as "the College" because so many young men were trained there, both from America and from several foreign countries.

Perhaps the most notable aspects of Wood-Mosaic included its wide diversity of hardwood products unmatched by any other United States company and its insistence on superior quality.

See John C. Callahan, *The Fine Hardwood Veneer Industry in the United States: 1828–1990.*

Donald MacLean Bell

WORKHOUSE.

The idea for a city workhouse began in the late 1820s when Mayor John Bucklin and the City Council contemplated what to do about the rise of crime in Jefferson County and the cost of keeping prisoners in the county jail. A public notice from the *Louisville Public Advertiser* dated April 15, 1830, stated, "Mayor John Bucklin and Council, by ordinance determined to establish a poor and workhouse and hospital and being desirous to obtain a steward affixed the salary at $400 per annum." Thus, Louisville's first city workhouse, erected on Chestnut St. between Eighth and Ninth Streets, was established.

City Workhouse, Payne Street at Lexington Road, c. 1890s.

At first, all misdemeanor offenders were sent to the workhouse, but later the Police Court judge could, at his discretion, send prisoners in misdemeanor cases to either the workhouse or to jail. All felons were sent to jail. The workhouse building also accommodated the poor and the sick. One wing was used to confine those who did not pay fines inflicted at the mayor's court while they paid off the fines through their labor. These inmates worked at a rate of fifty cents a day until they discharged their penalties. The facility was governed by a superintendent who was answerable to the City Council.

In 1835 the city of Louisville purchased one hundred acres, known as the "Cave Spring tract," from Joseph Chamberlain at one hundred dollars an acre. City officials bought the land to establish a graveyard, a poor house, and a workhouse. Also on this property the City Pest House, which housed those with infectious diseases, was built. While most of the land became CAVE HILL CEMETERY in 1848, a tract at the corner of Payne St. and Lexington Rd., with an adjoining quarry, was reserved for the workhouse. The city established a brickyard at the quarry, where white and African American men and women convicted of misdemeanors could work off their debt to society by producing bricks. Inmates worked from sunup to sundown, paying for their room and board by breaking rocks and gardening (for many years the garden provided vegetables for other area institutions). Some years the workhouse actually secured a profit. The total receipts of the workhouse for 1866, including rock on hand for delivery, product of the workhouse grounds, new wagons, and repair, amounted to $84,916. Expenditures amounted to an additional $22,652. The workhouse, however, managed to maintain a positive balance of $12,263 at year's end.

An ordinance in 1851 sanctioned the construction of the facility's first cellblock, which remained part of the workhouse until its final days. An 1866 report noted that the occupants of the workhouse consisted of 721 white males, 190 white females, 215 African American males, and 200 African American females. From time to time female prisoners were sentenced to hard labor, breaking rock for city streets. During 1866 the female facilities became so overcrowded that a few of the less troublesome prisoners were sent to the Sisters of Charity. In 1867 Mayor Philip Tomppert expressed the opinion that female prisoners should be given an occupation "more suitable" to their sex. In 1868 the task for females of breaking quarry rock was discontinued. They were kept busy washing, cooking, cleaning, mending, and making clothes for prisoners, along with working in the vegetable garden and fields during the summer.

By the 1860s deteriorating conditions caused grand juries and mayors alike to condemn the crowded lockup, which housed petty thieves, intoxicated persons, vagrants, prostitutes, and other offenders. Little relief was offered until the late 1870s when Mayor Charles D. Jacob diverted funds from the city budget for the structure's renovation, the addition of three new wings housing four tiers of cells, and the building of a superintendent's residence. The improved facility, located off Payne St. and Lexington Rd., was completed in 1879.

The end of the 1870s also saw the closing of the brickyard after pressure by private brick companies. A big problem in 1873 was to find another job that would help rehabilitate criminals while making money for the city. The city solved this problem by instituting quarry and rock-breaking operations. Male prisoners mined the city's main quarry at Cave Hill for stone, which was sold to the city as well as to private parties. Eventually, however, the city QUARRIES became depleted of resources, and rock from outside sources, such as PEWEE VALLEY, was unsuitable for breaking. Therefore another rock quarry, which would become Breslin Pond, was created. Quarry labor and rock-breaking allowed the workhouse to support itself for a number of years thereafter.

In June 1890, able-bodied females were once again ordered to work on the rock pile at the workhouse quarry, breaking macadam stone for street covering. An average of a dozen or more women were breaking rock six days a week. It was hoped that their hard labor on rock would disuade other women from committing crimes. An issue of the *Louisville Commercial* on January 1, 1890, also showed the workhouse's value as a criminal deterrent as it stated, "[Police] Chief [Thomas A.] Taylor's order regarding tramps and loafers is already proving beneficial; seven young men applied to Captain Black yesterday for assistance in securing employment. They were all loafers scared into activity by fear of a workhouse sentence. The order is to be vigorously enforced."

Several improvements were made to the workhouse in 1892, including new bunks and night buckets. In 1898 workhouse wages were doubled. An ordinance fixing the wages of those who satisfied, by compulsory work, the fines assessed against them was approved in the police court August 15, 1898.

In the 1940s and 1950s the facility was modernized with central heating, recreational facilities, and the installation of a workshop. Prisoners, who were no longer forced to quarry stone, repaired furniture for city offices and worked on children's toys during the holidays. In addition, the lawbreakers labored on the city farm in SHIVELY, maintained the PORTLAND and Western CEMETERIES, and helped clean the U.S. Marine Hospital in Portland.

Although the improvements temporarily remedied the superficial problems of the aging workhouse, grand juries continually attacked the structure and called for its closure. It was often labeled a dungeon because of its medieval appearance, complete with turrets. For years the workhouse had also been criticized as being everything from an obsolete institution to a fire hazard. In January 1952 Jefferson County authorities proposed that the city abolish its workhouse and lodge all prisoners in its jail. The jail had room for 700 inmates and was averaging between 340 and 350 per day. The workhouse, with room for 250 inmates, had an average of 150. After a federal inspector's critical report was released later in 1952, preliminary plans were launched for the abandonment of the buildings. On July 31, 1954, the last fifteen prisoners were transferred to the county jail, and the workhouse was closed. In 1957 the city utilized the lot to administer driving tests for license applicants. The following year the structure, including the old cells, was used as the city-county dog pound. In 1966 the dog pound was moved to a new site, and the city announced plans to raze the structure. However, shortly after midnight on April 30, 1968, a three-alarm fire destroyed the workhouse. A street maintenance garage and Breslin Park were constructed on the site.

See Samuel W. Thomas, *Cave Hill Cemetery: A Pictorial Guide and Its History* (Louisville 1985); *Louisville since the Twenties* (Louisville 1978).

Morton O. Childress

WORKS PROGRESS ADMINISTRATION. Created by executive order of President Franklin D. Roosevelt on May 6, 1935, the Works Progress Administration (WPA) functioned as a federal work relief agency, offering relief for scores of Americans during the GREAT DEPRESSION. Under the Reorganization Act of 1939, the program was renamed the Works Projects Administration and transferred to the newly formed Federal Works Agency. From 1935 until its demise in 1943, the WPA expended over $11 billion and employed approximately eight million people. In the Bluegrass State, the height of the WPA came between 1936 and 1938, when it employed approximately seventy-three thousand people on various projects.

The projects included construction and improvement of public buildings, roads, PARKS, and utility plants, as well as recreational, educational, and health-service facilities. In addition, professionals were employed under the aegis of the WPA in the Federal Writers', Music, Art, and THEATER Projects. Writers for the WPA were put to work on state guides and ORAL HISTORY projects, among others. *Kentucky, A Guide to the Bluegrass State* and *A Centennial History of the University of Louisville*, both published in 1939, were two such books compiled and written through the Federal Writers' Project in Kentucky.

By 1940 the WPA had been credited with paving about 348 miles of roads and sidewalks and constructing or working on 62 bridges, 18 LIBRARIES, 94 schools, and 103 recreational buildings in Jefferson County. The WPA contributed over $241,000 toward the creation of a concrete runway at BOWMAN FIELD and was also responsible for the construction of the Iroquois Park amphitheater in 1938. Louisville and the surrounding area benefited from a wealth of cultural programs sponsored by the WPA, as well as educational services such as the Adult Education High School sponsored by the WPA at the MONSARRAT School at Fifth and YORK Streets, WPA lunchroom aid, and the operation of WPA nursery schools.

Another prominent project of the WPA was sponsored by the LOUISVILLE FREE PUBLIC LIBRARY. Beginning in 1935, workers for the WPA, utilizing library resources, began to research, compile, and write the first volume in a series of books for the Louisville Library Collections. Consisting of three different series (history, institutions, and biography), the titles included *History of Louisville* (1935), *Institutions of Louisville* (1935), *Artists of Louisville and Kentucky* (1939), *Kentucky Authors* (1940), *Prominent Women of Louisville and Kentucky* (1940), and *Kentucky Statesmen* (1940).

See James S. Olson, ed., *Historical Dictionary of the New Deal* (Westport, Conn., 1985); *Courier-Journal*, Dec. 1, 1937, April 19, 1938, July 9, 1940, Dec. 5, 1942.

WORLD'S CHAMPIONSHIP HORSE SHOW. The World's Championship Horse Show is held annually at Freedom Hall during the KENTUCKY STATE FAIR in Louisville. It is an outgrowth of the first ten-thousand-dollar stake for five-gaited horses held in 1917.

When the governor of Missouri rejected an offer from Curtis P. "Jumps" Cauthorn to hold a ten-thousand-dollar five-gaited world's championship, he made the proposal to Kentucky governor Augustus O. Stanley and Commissioner of Agriculture Mat S. Cohen. Cauthorn, who wanted a show that would determine a true world champion for the first time, had raised five thousand dollars in donations to be matched by whichever state hosted the competition. The Kentucky officials immediately accepted and merged the new contest with the fair's existing horse show.

In the first contest the prize money was divided, with $2,500 awarded to each of the winners of the stallion, mare, and gelding preliminaries, and $2,500 to the grand champion. The first five-gaited world's grand champion was Easter Cloud, owned by Longview Farm, Lee's Summit, Missouri, and shown by John T. Hook. Other classes were added the following year, bringing the total number of events to twenty-four.

By 1998 the World's Championship Horse Show had grown to huge proportions, with approximately 1,650 horses shown from 38 states, Canada, and South Africa. Cash awards totaled over $1 million for the 225 different class competitions. According to an economic study by the University of Louisville in 1985, the show had an impact of $8.9 million, well over half the total for the entire Kentucky State Fair. The report stated, "The impact of the World's Championship Horse Show goes beyond the six days of the show. Its broader impact is on the expansion of the Saddle Horse industry in Kentucky, which in turn provides jobs and tax revenues throughout the commonwealth." A survey in 1997 indicated the economic impact of the show had increased to nearly $15 million.

See Jack Harrison, *Famous Saddle Horses and Distinguished Horsemen* (Columbia, Mo., 1933).

Lynn Weatherman

An Armistice Day parade passing the Jefferson County Court House, 1918.

WORLD WAR I. When the war in Europe erupted in August 1914, the strife and destruction that occurred on the European continent seemed far removed from daily life in Louisville. Though most Louisvillians favored the isolationist stance of the United States, opinions were quickly formed, although sides were not necessarily taken. The Imperial German Consul in Cincinnati ordered all German nationals in Louisville home for war duty. The French Consulate on Fourth St. countered with a summons to Louisville's FRENCH nationals. It was a mini-demonstration of the kind of mobilization leap-frogging that had led to the hostilities across the Atlantic.

The city's main NEWSPAPERS clearly represented the sides that were taking shape in Louisville. The aging but still editorially powerful HENRY WATTERSON of the *COURIER-JOURNAL* put aside his early, unusually passive stance to begin a near daily diatribe assailing the Central Powers led by Germany and Austria-Hungary. The large Louisville German-American community generally sympathized with the country of their forebears and hung on every word of the *LOUISVILLE ANZEIGER* that editorially supported Germany. The Irish-American community, strongly anti-English more than pro-GERMAN, also expressed opposition to Watterson's staunch opinions.

When the sinking of the *Lusitania* on May 7, 1915, by a German U-boat nearly cost the lives of several southern Indiana residents, anti-German feelings intensified, egged on by Watterson's intense writings. The slings and arrows of editorial opinion continued for months. Americans tired of Germany's unrestricted submarine warfare on what they considered the neutral high seas. Public opinion slowly shifted in favor of the Allies. Though most Americans wanted no physical participation in the hostilities, hopes of remaining neutral were fading. The war was a financial boon for the United States and Louisville. Many of Louisville's factories produced war goods for export to both sides.

In the presidential election of 1916, Woodrow Wilson, clinging to an isolationism campaign theme, carried Louisville and Jefferson County by a mere 454 votes. The Socialist Labor Party, vehemently opposed to the war as a capitalist plot, garnered nearly 1,200 votes.

Less than a month after his second inauguration in 1917, Wilson reluctantly asked Congress for a declaration of war against the Central Powers. Lacking tangible evidence that the conflict threatened America, the war became a moral issue. Louisville was caught up in a sea of patriotic fervor. On the day of declaration, April 6, 1917, the *Courier-Journal*, reporting on ninety male volunteers at a patriotic meeting in the gym of the Louisville Boys (Male) High School, took note of the many speakers who insisted "the country was about to take up the gage of battle, not for conquest or commercialism or indemnities, but for principle" (Thomas, 22). The war struck home in May 1917 when a German submarine torpedoed a sailing vessel owned by the Louisville wood-products firm of C.C. Mengel and Bro. as the ship was on its way to Africa for a cargo of hardwood timber. Recruiting stations in Louisville were overwhelmed with enlistees—many of them of German and Irish extraction. Hardly a band in the city played anything but patriotic airs. There were marches and parades. Female volunteers flocked to the Red Cross.

Changes emerged in the German communities. The *Louisville Anzeiger* declared its devotion to "American ideals" (Crews, 36). "German" was dropped from the name of the German Security Bank and was replaced by "Liberty" in the titles of the German Insurance Bank and the German Insurance Co. At ST. MARTIN OF TOURS CATHOLIC CHURCH, English replaced German as the language of the sermons and newsletters. Still, Henry Watterson and the *Courier-Journal* questioned the loyalty of Louisville's German-Americans with references to possible "Kaiserists" lurking about.

To add to the local connection, there was land along Taylorsville Rd. owned by Baron Konrad von Zedtwitz, an officer of the Kaiser's Imperial forces. The young baron, who had never stepped foot on his six hundred acres of Kentucky farmland, inherited the property from his late mother, Kentuckian Mary Breckinridge Caldwell, who by marriage was the Baroness von Zedtwitz. When the United States entered the war, the Alien Property Office seized the land that would eventually become Seneca Park and BOWMAN FIELD.

Louisville headlines brought welcome news in June 1917 when the GOVERNMENT announced Louisville as the site of one of its army training camps, setting off another round of wild celebration. Patriotic zeal intensified. On Registration Day, June 5, 1917, 23,653 Louisville men enrolled for the draft.

The location chosen for CAMP ZACHARY TAY-

LOR was a stretch of farmland about three miles out, just south of AUDUBON PARK in an area between Preston Street Rd. (Hwy.) and Poplar Level Rd. The camp proved a boon to the local ECONOMY and a great source of pride for the community's some 235,000 residents. Within three months of the announcement, nearly ten thousand workmen used just over 45 million feet of lumber to construct one of the largest training camps in the nation. It cost approximately $8 million to build and at its zenith housed about fifty thousand troops at a time in barracks and tents. In its two-year existence, nearly 150,000 doughboys trained there. Almost all of the inductees were from Kentucky, Illinois, and Indiana. Approximately a thousand recruits took the oath of citizenship under a huge American elm tree that stood at the corner of the camp's Lee and Grove Streets. Known as the "Naturalization Tree," the American Forestry Association chose it as one of seven historic American trees, and a picture of it hung in the Tree Hall of Fame in Washington, D.C.

About thirty miles outside Louisville was the smaller Camp Henry Knox that would eventually become FORT KNOX. Louisville teemed with servicemen from the camps. In the city they could find entertainment at many THEATERS such as the Gayety for BURLESQUE or the Strand for movies. They danced at J. Graham Brown's HA-WI-AN GARDENS at Fourth and Broadway and relaxed at the Soldier's Club at 619 S Fourth St. The club operated under the auspices of the War Camp Community Service. Half of the funds to operate came from contributions nationwide, and the rest was given by generous Louisvillians. Wrote one well-traveled doughboy about the Soldier's Club, "Yours is the best. Though the others are kind and thoughtful, nowhere do we receive quite the same treatment as in Louisville" (*Courier-Journal,* Sept. 29, 1918). In one month alone, August 1918, 38,925 soldiers enjoyed the club's billiard and game rooms, cafeteria, dormitory, shoe-shine parlor, canteen, and reading room. Volunteers dispensed nearly fifty thousand sheets of stationery that month in the upstairs writing room. One part of Louisville where soldiers were not to be found was along the stretch of W Green St. (renamed LIBERTY St. during the war) that was the city's traditional "red light" district of brothels. The city had to agree to close down establishments of ill repute before the government would build Camp Zachary Taylor.

Homefront conditions in Louisville were the same as most cities across the nation. The city and county took part in wartime programs of meatless, wheatless, and sugarless days. "Food Will Win the War" was a popular slogan that inspired sacrifice as a citizen's patriotic duty. Housewives replaced meat with eggs, beans, and fish. Syrup was in, sugar was out, and corn took the place of wheat. By late 1918 sugar was restricted to two pounds per month per person, and white bread could hardly be found. Eating out became a lesson in restriction. RESTAURANTS could not serve bread until after the first course, and no sugar bowls were allowed on tables. Entrees offered only one kind of meat, and diners were allotted one-half ounce of butter per person. Automobiles stood idle on "gas-less" Sundays, and, like the rest of the nation, Louisvillians observed "light-less" Monday and Tuesday nights. In March 1918 federal law dictated the start of daylight saving time.

Louisvillians also opened wide their pocketbooks, raising $38,743,886 in Liberty Bonds, War Saving Stamps, and general contributions. Each of the four Liberty Bond drives surpassed original goals, the last one netting nearly $17 million. War relief contributions were distributed to the Red Cross, YMCA, Knights of Columbus War Service Fund, Belgian relief, and the funds for French Wounded, Armenians, and others.

As the tide of war shifted slowly in favor of the Allies by late summer 1918, disaster lurked on the home front. For Louisville and Jefferson County the first signs appeared at CAMP TAYLOR. Hastily built, the camp was not the epitome of sanitary conditions. Often an overflow of soldiers lived in tents. Though primarily a training center, veterans returning from Europe demobilized there. These returning veterans were believed to be the carriers of the virulent "Spanish Influenza" that swept the war-torn nations in 1918 and would eventually strike nearly 20 percent of the American POPULATION. The ailment first appeared in the spring of 1918 and swept the Iberian Peninsula, striking Spain's King Alphonso XIII, who survived the deadly virus. Camp Taylor was one of the hardest hit of the nation's thirty military camps. By early October 1918 fifteen barracks served as HOSPITALS for the approximately eleven thousand ill. The death toll reached nearly 40 a day at the worst, and the final tally numbered 824 dead. The virus spread outside the confines of the camp. Of the 6,415 reported cases of flu in Jefferson County, 879 civilians died. The epidemic exhausted the area coffin supply, and city and county authorities discouraged social gatherings of any kind.

Within a month, the epidemic eased, and caution was completely forgotten on November 7, 1918, when rumors of the German surrender gave way to a wild celebration. With anticipation of victory rampant, citizens mistook the ringing of a city fire station bell as a signal, and the elation of a "false Armistice" was under way. This victory dance was a preview of what came four days later.

At 1:50 a.m. James Carter, the night TELEGRAPH operator at the *Courier-Journal*, was the first to see the message that signaled the Armistice signing. Within minutes factory whistles and church bells aroused the sleeping residents, and Louisvillians again took to the streets. Daylight found the streets packed with cheering, flag-waving revelers who were joined by farm families pouring into town to join the celebration. Many wrapped American flags around themselves and sang patriotic SONGS while "Kaiser Bill" hung in effigy from the Courier-Journal and Louisville Times building at Third and Liberty Streets. Fourth Street was soon packed with joyful citizens who, like others in thousands of cities across the nation, enjoyed confetti, parades, rousing bands, patriotic speeches, and happy turmoil. Citizens spilled out from the center of the city in parades through Louisville's NEIGHBORHOODS well into the night. Two weeks later tens of thousands witnessed the "greatest parade in the history of the city" as ten thousand soldiers from Camp Taylor marched along Broadway and then south on Fourth St. to Central Park. On November 23, a service of Thanksgiving was held with speeches by Henry Watterson and Mayor GEORGE WEISSINGER SMITH. It was a solemn occasion with thoughts of the honored dead.

The death tally for Louisville and Jefferson County numbered 350 military dead, most of whom are buried in Cave Hill and Zachary Taylor National Cemeteries. The war also claimed the lives of three area nurses and Henry Watterson's grandson. Of the 10,000 local soldiers sent overseas, 453 were wounded. Many of the veterans were buried in the ZACHARY TAYLOR NATIONAL CEMETERY, which was dedicated seven years after the end of the Great War.

In 1929 Louisville dedicated the War Memorial Auditorium at Fourth and Kentucky Streets. Memorial Auditorium, home to a large collection of World War I Allied Flags, stands as a lasting shrine to those Louisvillians who sacrificed their lives "over there."

See Clyde F. Crews, *Spirited City: Essays in Louisville History* (Louisville 1995); George H. Yater, *Two Hundred Years at the Falls of the Ohio* (Louisville 1987); Samuel W. Thomas, *Louisville since the Twenties* (Louisville 1978); Gregory K. Culver, "The Sick and the Dead: Self-Dosage, Medical Treatment and Burial during the 1918 Spanish Influenza Epidemic in the Jackson Purchase," *Filson Club History Quarterly* 68 (Jan. 1994): 66–82; *A Place in Time: The Story of Louisville's Neighborhoods* (Louisville 1989); *Louisville Times*, May 1, 1934, Nov. 5, 1933; *Courier-Journal*, Sept. 29, 1918.

Rhonda Abner

WORLD WAR II. When war broke out in Europe in September 1939 the United States was still recovering from a depression and was not prepared for war. The nation, Louisville included, was able to use the war effort to not only pull out of the depression but also to reconstruct its ECONOMY. Louisville became the eighteenth-largest defense supplier in the country. Approximately 306,715 Kentuckians served in the war. From Jefferson County, 1,450 men lost their lives, the highest figure for any county in the state.

The initiatives taken by the federal government to prepare for war opened the floodgates to economic development in Louisville. In 1932 unemployment in Jefferson County was 23.5

Women training as machinists during WWII, du pont Manual High School, 1942.

percent for whites and 37.2 percent for AFRICAN AMERICANS. By 1940 the unemployment rate was down to 11.5 percent. Part of Bowman Field became an Army Air Corps training base. Sharing the airport with commercial flights, an additional field was sought by the city and county air board. Five hundred seventy-one acres near Preston St. and AUDUBON PARK was designated as Municipal Airport Number Two. Constructed in 1941, it was used for military aircraft. The Du Pont Co. opened a $30 million plant in Charlestown, Indiana, in July 1940 to produce smokeless powder for artillery. The plant, owned by the federal government but operated by Du Pont, tripled America's smokeless gunpowder output. In late 1940 the metropolitan area was selected as the site for a naval gun plant for preparing powder charges for artillery. The "bag plant" (or HOOSIER Ordnance Works) located adjacent to the Du Pont plant, was a federal project turned over to Goodyear Tire and Rubber Co. for operation. The Naval Ordnance Plant was a $26 million project that eventually employed four thousand persons. It was located adjacent to the LOUISVILLE & NASHVILLE RAILROAD Strawberry Yards.

In March 1941 Louisville was on its way to becoming the world's largest producer of synthetic rubber after the city was selected for a synthetic- rubber plant operated by the Du Pont company. The plant produced its own formula of neoprene, of which acetylene was an essential ingredient. Two months later it was announced that B.F. Goodrich Co. would establish a synthetic-rubber plant in that area. In September news came of a third plant, this time one for the National Synthetic Rubber Co. The name Rubbertown was coined for the area where the three plants were located on Bells Ln. in western Jefferson County. Synthetic rubber was the only non-metal placed on the United States government's vital materials list. During the peak production year of 1944, RUBBERTOWN plants produced 195,000 tons.

Events in Europe also affected military activity in the area. On July 13, 1940, news came from Washington that fifty thousand national guardsmen would be called up to serve a year of intensive training. Louisville's 149th Infantry departed for its tour of duty six months later. Within days after the fall of France, the War Department announced that Fort Knox military base would become the nation's Army Armor Center. FORT KNOX had served as an artillery range for soldiers from Louisville's WORLD WAR I CAMP ZACHARY TAYLOR, which had closed in 1920. Gold reserves from Europe were sent to the fort for safekeeping along with hundreds of historical documents including the Magna Carta. By early 1942 the armor school was capable of graduating 22,000 enlisted men and 1,440 officers annually. By mid-1942 the graduation rate was almost tripled to sixty-four thousand enlisted men per year.

The intensification of the war effort brought thousands of new workers from rural Kentucky and Indiana into the city. In April the army announced the establishment of the $38 million Nichols General Hospital to be erected on a 120 acre site on Berry Blvd. near Manslick Rd. The thousand-bed hospital was at the time Louisville's largest. The army also built the Louisville Medical Depot on a 575-acre site south of the city along the L&N Railroad and National Turnpike. The navy purchased the Howard Shipyards in JEFFERSONVILLE, INDIANA, in early 1942. The navy also contracted operation of the adjoining Jeffersonville Boat and Machine Co., which was already building submarine chasers. The combined companies built scores of submarine chasers and landing craft used in the D-Day invasion of Normandy as well as in operations in the Pacific Ocean. Standiford Field (LOUISVILLE INTERNATIONAL AIRPORT) was chosen as a site to produce army cargo planes of wood because of the established woodworking industry in the city. A plant, operated by the Curtiss-Wright Corp., began production of the new C-76 Caravans. The plane was a failure, so the plant switched to the conventional C-46 models with components from Reynolds Metals and American Air Filter. Construction of glider planes was undertaken at BOWMAN FIELD, which was also the site of the nation's first glider pilot combat-training center.

In addition, a number of private companies contributed to the war effort. The Ford Motor Co. in Louisville switched to production of military jeeps, building over a hundred thousand by war's end. HILLERICH AND BRADSBY CO. switched from making BASEBALL bats to gunstocks of M-1 carbines. Louisville's distilleries turned to wartime production of industrial alcohol, an essential raw material for butadiene, which in turn was used for the type of synthetic rubber produced by Goodrich and National Synthetic Rubber. Tube Turns and HENRY VOGT MACHINE CO. made artillery shell parts, and most of the city's woodworking industries produced glider parts.

Increased employment created housing shortages. Two housing projects were built for defense workers, one located at Sheppard Square along Preston St., south of BROADWAY in the SMOKETOWN NEIGHBORHOOD, and Parkway Place at Eleventh and Hill Streets. Most housing was absorbed into older housing that was turned into multiple-unit dwellings with the assistance of federal low- interest loans. The Federal Housing Administration encouraged this practice as a contribution to winning the war, and OLD LOUISVILLE was particularly affected when hundreds of large nineteenth-century dwellings were converted. Segregated housing confined African Americans to three small areas in the city and county along with numerous small pockets in the West End. Three to four families often occupied small houses made for a single family.

Employment opportunities were increased for both white and black women. Women worked in jobs traditionally held by men, including industrial defense work. There were also increased opportunities for African American men in higher-paying jobs, though most served in the military. THE LOUISVILLE URBAN LEAGUE described race relations at defense plants as excellent but noticed that many AFRICAN AMERICANS did not possess the skills for many of the new jobs. SEGREGATION was as entrenched as

ever during the war. While German prisoners being escorted to and from Fort Knox were allowed to eat in white establishments, their black guards could not.

The first eleven months of 1941 turned Louisville into a hustle-bustle boomtown, rife with money and plenty of places to spend it. The "invasion" of out-of-towners was a major adjustment for a municipality that, only four years earlier, had been dubbed "the city of let-well-enough-alone" by George R. Leighton in a sketch on Louisville he wrote for *Harper's Magazine.* Dine-and-dance establishments were frequented by soldiers from Fort Knox and workers as the big band dance craze swept the country. Most went in and out of business relatively quickly. Some, along with the more established clubs such as the Iroquois Gardens, the Gypsy Village at FONTAINE FERRY PARK, and the Red Tavern on Bardstown Rd., thrived. For good entertainment, there was always the United Service Organization (USO) located in the Columbia Auditorium on S Fourth St. Its main form of entertainment was dances. Just as the military was segregated, so was the USO. African Americans were provided with a facility at 920 W Chestnut St., in the Colored Branch of the YMCA. Dance clubs along W Walnut St. (Muhammad Ali Blvd.) provided entertainment for black soldiers. Their symphony orchestra performed at Bowman Field, Fort Knox, Nichols General Hospital, and practically all military post and service clubs in the Louisville area. The Louisville Servicemen's Center was USO's counterpart for African Americans. In 1965 these two organizations merged to form the Louisville Service Center Inc. This merged with the Greater Louisville USO in 1966 to form the USO-Louisville Service Club Inc.

While a number of colleges suspended their sports programs during the war, the KENTUCKY DERBY was still held each year. Entertainment for soldiers with less-refined tastes could be found in the city's seamier side. Soldiers could find plenty of mischief among more than a dozen brothels on S Seventh St. between Market St. and Broadway, an area known as "the line." PROSTITUTION became a particular problem. Louisville police began taking prostitutes to the hospital after they were arrested to try to control venereal disease, particularly among soldiers. GAMBLING was also readily available in back rooms of BARS, especially along Jefferson St., and bookmakers had direct news-service lines to the tracks.

When the Japanese attacked Pearl Harbor on December 7, 1941, seven Louisvillians were killed. Japanese hatred ran high in Louisville, though the 1940 census showed that no Japanese were living in the city. The SOUTHERN BAPTIST THEOLOGICAL SEMINARY usually had several Japanese students, but there were not any in December of 1941. Because Louisville's German POPULATION was a large and well-entrenched part of the community, they were not the victims of anti-German sentiment. GERMANS made up 31.5 percent of only 6,201 foreign-born residents in the city.

German and Italian prisoners of war were held at Fort Knox as well as several locations in the Louisville area. In mid-February 1944, Italian prisoners who had been held in the United States since the summer of 1943 arrived at Fort Knox. The Italian prisoners were treated differently from the German prisoners. They were considered more cooperative than the Germans, and many even supported the American war effort. Several volunteered to fight with the United States Army. Soon after they arrived at Fort Knox, they were classified as parolees and worked without armed guards. The ITALIANS and Germans were kept separate from each other, for by that time they shared a mutual hatred. In May 1944 the first German POWs arrived at Fort Knox. Prisoners performed work previously done by United States soldiers, including mess duty, housekeeping, laundry, and all sorts of outside manual labor such as road building. They also worked at Bowman Field, the Jeffersonville QUARTERMASTER DEPOT, and the Louisville Medical Depot, thus freeing up army personnel to concentrate on military duties. In September 1944, 560 Germans were used to harvest burley TOBACCO in Fayette and 9 other counties. This saved the season's crops from frost damage that would have occurred because of the labor shortage. Labor was voluntary, and prisoners who worked were paid eighty cents a day in addition to the regular prisoner-of-war pay of ten cents a day set by the Geneva Convention. At war's end, there were about four thousand prisoners at Fort Knox.

Six days before the Japanese attacked Pearl Harbor, Mayor Wilson W. Wyatt took office. Within a week after Pearl Harbor, Wyatt called for five hundred people to serve as auxiliary police, five hundred people to serve as auxiliary firemen, and a hundred to serve as air raid wardens. Over ten thousand Louisvillians signed up, and the Louisville Metropolitan Defense Council was soon up and running.

Louisville's men and women served in every branch of the armed services. Among the most distinguished was Philip Pendleton Ardery, a lawyer and author from Bourbon County. Serving as a pilot with the U.S. Army Air Corps, he was awarded the Silver Star, Distinguished Flying Cross (twice), Air Medal (four times), and the French Croix de Guerre with palm. Ardery was born March 6, 1914, the third son of William Breckenridge and Julia (Spencer) Ardery. He grew up near Paris, Kentucky. Ardery was a 1935 graduate of the University of Kentucky with a B.A. degree. He was two years out of Harvard Law School and a twenty-six-year-old practicing lawyer in Frankfort when he was called up in 1940. He served until July 1944, flying many missions over enemy territory, including bombing raids on the Ploiesti oil refineries in southern Romania. He married Anne Tweedy on December 6, 1941. They had four children: Peter, Philip Jr., Joseph, and Julia.

In 1945 he returned to practicing law, eventually becoming a partner in the firm of Brown, Todd, and Heyburn in Louisville. Ardery is the author of two books: *Bomber Pilot: A Memoir of World War II* (1978) and *Heroes and Horses: Tales of the Bluegrass* (1996).

Louis Adam "Lew" Miller, another World War II hero of note, received a battlefield promotion for front-line leadership, a Presidential Citation, two Purple Hearts, Four Bronze Stars, five Battle Campaigns, as well as a DAV award

Employees of the Mengel Co. burning Nazi flag in a July 4th celebration in 1944.

(Hero of the Month) for recovery and rehabilitation from serious war injuries. Miller was wounded and badly injured by machine-gun fire near Remagen, Germany, in 1945. Twice hit in the head, he returned to normal life after three years of intensive rehabilitation. He is the son of Charlotte (Hoeferle) and Edward M. Miller Sr. and was born April 4, 1917, in Louisville. Miller attended the UNIVERSITY OF LOUISVILLE and was a General Electric marketing executive for twenty-eight years working in national ADVERTISING. He married Jean Culberson July 12, 1952; they have four children: Mark Louis, Douglas Edward, Gregory Owen, and Rebecca Ann.

See George H. Yater, *Two Hundred Years at the Falls of the Ohio* (Louisville 1987); Richard G. Stone, *Kentucky's Fighting Men 1851–1945* (Lexington 1982); Eric George, "Day of Infamy," *Louisville* 42 (Dec. 1991): 37–43.

Richard R. Bernier

WORTHINGTON. Worthington is a small community in eastern Jefferson County on Old Brownsboro Rd. (KY 22) between Chamberlain Ln. and Ballardsville Rd. Early settlers of the fertile farming land included the Barbour, Dorsey, and Chamberlain families, and Dabney Taylor, brother of ZACHARY TAYLOR. In addition there were African American families among the settlers of the area. In the 1870s the Louisville and Brownsboro Turnpike Rd. (KY 22) was paved with stones, and a toll gate was built at the intersection of Brownsboro and Ballardsville Roads.

POPULATION increase boosted traffic and created the need for a post office. When the post office was established in the 1870s, the local residents decided to name the community for one of its prominent citizens, Guy Worthington Dorsey. Soon after, the Pendleton brothers replaced the old Tarleton general store across the street from the toll house with a two-story brick building. The new structure housed a saloon and a grocery on the first floor and a community hall on the second floor. With a number of different proprietors over the years, Worthington Grocery kept its doors open into the 1960s.

In the early 1900s a drugstore and barbershop were also located near this intersection. The local blacksmith shop, which was established around 1840 by William Henry Harrison Chamberlain, was relocated to the northeast corner of Brownsboro Rd. and Chamberlain Ln. in 1870. The Chamberlain family turned the establishment into an automotive garage and ran the business until 1969 when the building was razed. Carl Chamberlain, proprietor of the garage, was also the first fire chief of the Worthington Volunteer Fire Department, organized in 1943.

The Worthington School was built in 1915 (and razed in 1968) to replace the Rock Bridge School (later Worthington Colored School) on Ballardsville Rd. Henry Frank, a MIDDLETOWN builder, constructed the building on land donated by John W. Netherton. Stone for the building was quarried and hauled by farmers in the community. The opening was marked by a procession of students from the old Rock Bridge School to the new school.

After the turn of the century, WORTHINGTON became a prime potato-growing area. About 1920, at the peak of the county's potato production, the Worthington Potato Growers Cooperative built a shed for processing the local farmers' abundant crop. After farmers dropped off their harvest, the potatoes were shipped to markets in St. Matthews, Cincinnati, or Indianapolis. As prices declined in the 1940s the potato industry faded. During this time wealthy individuals began building large homes on surrounding land. Residential developments continued to arise through the years, encouraged particularly after the opening of Interstate 71 in 1969, the completion of a nearby stretch of Interstate 265 in 1968, and the construction of the Ford truck plant. Outside of the Worthington Cemetery, few remnants of the once-thriving community survive.

See G.T. Bergmann, *Map of Jefferson County Kentucky* (Louisville 1858); *History of the Ohio Falls Cities and Their Counties* (Cleveland 1882); *Louisville Times*, Nov. 12, 1965; *Courier-Journal*, April 20, 1941, April 14, 1969.

Carol Brenner Tobe

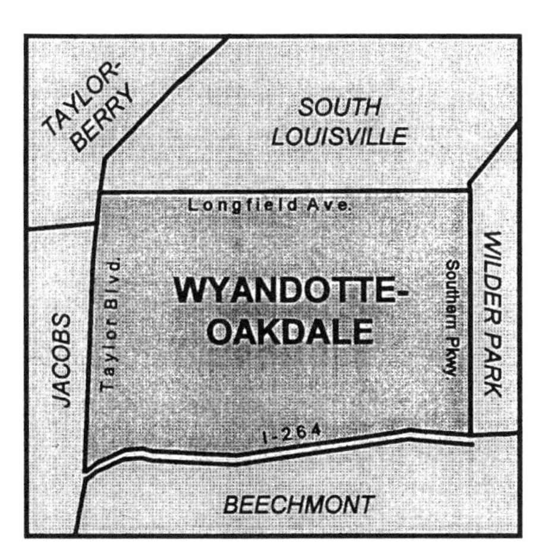

WYANDOTTE/OAKDALE. Neighborhood south of CHURCHILL DOWNS bounded in modern times by Longfield Ave. to the north, Taylor Blvd. to the west, the WATTERSON EXPRESSWAY to the south, and Southern Pkwy. to the east. The creation of IROQUOIS PARK south of Louisville and the construction of Grand Blvd. (later Southern Pkwy.) and two electric streetcar lines to the park in the early 1890s opened a vast expanse of countryside to suburban development south of Louisville. The Coleman-Bush Development Co., anticipating these changes, began ADVERTISING lots for sale in the fall of 1890 in the subdivision it called Oakdale. The name was likely inspired by the abundance of oak trees in the area.

The outward migration of the middle class from the city, made possible by the electric streetcar, soon resulted in sizable new communities; and Oakdale was no exception. In 1904 the area was incorporated as the sixth-class city of Oakdale and soon began expanding its boundaries. Churchill Downs was annexed, as well as part of WILDER PARK east of Third St. By 1908 the POPULATION increase allowed Oakdale to become a fifth-class city with a mayor and council. But in 1916 the Louisville City Council adopted a sweeping annexation ordinance that included Oakdale, among many other areas. A series of court battles followed, initiated by opponents of annexation, including Oakdale. After losing in local COURTS, the plaintiffs appealed to the United States Supreme Court in 1921. The suit was dismissed because it did not involve a question of federal law. In 1922 Oakdale became a part of Louisville.

In 1935 a Louisville city park, named Wyandotte in the local tradition of naming PARKS for American Indian tribes, was opened along Taylor Blvd. in the western section of Oakdale. In the mid-1970s, when federal URBAN RENEWAL grants were replaced by community development block grants, it was necessary to set definite boundaries for NEIGHBORHOODS to be eligible for grants. Because of the park, Wyandotte was chosen as the name and is so shown on the official city neighborhood map. Nevertheless, residents continue to call it Oakdale.

See Barbara N. Bishop, *Oakdale: An Early Twentieth Century Suburb* (Louisville 1989); Carl E. Kramer, "The City-Building Process: Urbanization in Central and Southern Louisville, 1772–1932," Ph.D. dissertation, University of Toledo, 1980.

George H. Yater

WYATT, WILSON WATKINS, SR. (b Louisville, November 21, 1905; d Louisville, June 11, 1996). Louisville mayor and lieutenant governor. Born to Richard H. and Mary (Watkins) Wyatt, he graduated from LOUISVILLE MALE HIGH SCHOOL and attended the UNIVERSITY OF LOUISVILLE for one year. Following graduation from Louisville's JEFFERSON SCHOOL OF LAW, Wyatt was admitted to the Kentucky bar in 1927. On June 14, 1930, he married Anne Kinnaird Duncan. They had three children: Mary Anne, Nancy, and Wilson Junior.

After establishing a law practice in Louisville he served as secretary of the Kentucky Bar Association from 1930 to 1934. In 1935 Wyatt joined the law firm of Peter, Heyburn, Marshall, and Wyatt, where he became principal counsel for ROBERT WORTH BINGHAM'S *COURIER-JOURNAL* and *LOUISVILLE TIMES*, as well as for the other Bingham family enterprises, including WHAS radio and TELEVISION stations.

Elected mayor of Louisville in 1941, Wyatt took office on December 1, only days before the Japaneese attack on Pearl Harbor. With the outbreak of WORLD WAR II the new mayor immediately undertook regional civil defense plans. During the war the home front needed attention, and Wyatt worked for legislation in

Wilson Wyatt with President John F. Kennedy, 1962.

the Kentucky General Assembly to modernize and streamline the Louisville city GOVERNMENT. He took several city-county consolidation steps, one of which was the creation of Louisville–Jefferson County PLANNING AND ZONING Commission.

As Louisville's young, wartime mayor, Wyatt garnered national attention. He became a leading spokesperson for many national civic and public service organizations, including the American Society of Planning Officials and the National Municipal League. Numerous newspaper and magazine articles detailed his ideas concerning governmental and municipal planning, which attracted the attention of the White House. In the spring of 1943 President Franklin D. Roosevelt chose Wyatt to head a Board of Economic Welfare mission to North Africa to formulate plans for coordination of economic development in that region to aid in the war effort.

When his term as mayor ended in 1945, Wyatt's participation in national affairs expanded in January 1946 when President Harry S Truman made him housing expediter in the Office of War Mobilization and Reconversion. Wyatt's New Deal philosophy and approach to dealing with the problems of affordable housing for the returning veterans soon came under fire from the Republican-controlled Congress. When he failed to receive needed support from the White House for his efforts, Wyatt resigned as housing expediter in December 1946.

Returning to Louisville, Wyatt founded the law firm of Wyatt and Grafton. While rebuilding a successful and lucrative law practice, Wyatt maintained his active involvement in politics and public affairs both locally and nationally. He played a key role in the formation of the Americans for Democratic Action, a liberal political action group, and served as the organization's first chairman in 1947. In 1952 he managed nationally the unsuccessful presidential campaign of Adlai Stevenson. He also played a prominent role in Stevenson's 1956 presidential campaign.

In 1958 Wyatt announced his candidacy for governor of Kentucky. Prior to the primary election, however, he withdrew as a gubernatorial candidate and endorsed Bert T. Combs's candidacy, running for lieutenant governor on a united ticket with Combs. In the Democratic primary election, the Combs-Wyatt ticket defeated Harry Lee Waterfield, the candidate of the Chandler faction of the DEMOCRATIC PARTY. Following a victory in the general election in November, Combs and Wyatt took office in December 1959.

As lieutenant governor, Wyatt worked to make the position an active and effective part of the administration. In addition to presiding over the state senate during its biennial sessions, he served as chairman of the newly created Kentucky Economic Development Commission. Wyatt was also the leading proponent for the establishment of the Spindletop Research Center, an early attempt to unite the University of Kentucky's research program with economic development in Kentucky businesses and industry.

In 1962 Wyatt announced his candidacy for the U.S. Senate, running in the general election against the incumbent, Sen. Thruston B. Morton, a fellow Louisvillian. In a hard-fought and often bitter campaign, Wyatt lost to Morton by a narrow margin. However, Wyatt's participation in national affairs continued in 1963 when President John F. Kennedy sent him to Indonesia to mediate a dispute between U.S. oil companies and Indonesian president Sukarno. Sukarno had threatened to nationalize foreign oil operations, but Wyatt was successful in negotiating an agreement that averted an international crisis.

In December 1963 Wyatt established the Louisville law firm Wyatt, Tarrant, and Combs, but his role in national politics continued. Hubert H. Humphrey asked Wyatt to play an important role at the 1968 national Democratic nominating convention by negotiating a compromise agreement in the party's platform regarding the VIETNAM WAR. Never again holding public office, Wyatt served in a wide variety of civic activities both in Louisville and throughout Kentucky.

With Thruston Morton, he drew up a plan for consolidating the Louisville and Jefferson County governments. He was an adviser to mayors, county judge/executives, and governors, and, on occasion, to the editorial board of the *Courier-Journal.* In his later years, he devoted his attention to training a new generation of leaders by co-founding Leadership Louisville. One of his final efforts was to reform Kentucky's tax structure. Wyatt was chairman of the University of Louisville Board of trustees from 1951 to 1955 and the BELLARMINE COLLEGE board from 1981 to 1982. In 1994 Wyatt and his wife, Anne, gave five hundred thousand dollars to the University of Louisville School of Law to help it attract nationally known speakers and to improve teaching. The Wyatts gave the same amount of money to Jefferson County Public Schools to provide scholarships for high school debaters. In 1995 the School of Law building at the University of Louisville was named Wilson W. Wyatt Hall. He is buried in CAVE HILL CEMETERY.

See John Ed Pearce, *Divide and Dissent: Kentucky Politics, 1930–1963* (Lexington 1987); Wilson W. Wyatt Sr., *Whistle Stops: Adventures in Public Life* (Lexington 1985); Wade Hall, *Complete Conviction: The Private Life of Wilson W. Wyatt, Sr.* (Louisville 1997).

Terry L. Birdwhistell

XAVERIAN BROTHERS. This Roman Catholic religious order was founded by Theodore James Ryken in Bruges, Belgium, in 1839. Committed to evangelism, the brothers have taken their mission around the world, primarily by providing education. Outside of Belgium, the brothers have served in the United States, England, Lithuania, Bolivia, Haiti, Kenya, Zaire, and Sudan.

Fifteen years after the order was founded, the Xaverian Brothers began their first missionary work in Louisville. Since then they have played an important role in the education of the area's Catholics.

The Catholic population in Louisville was increasing in the mid-1800s because of GERMAN and IRISH immigration, and it was the desire of the church hierarchy to provide a religious education for every Catholic child in the city. During a trip to Belgium in 1853, Louisville Bishop MARTIN SPALDING (1850-64) met with Brother Ryken, requesting that he bring a group of his teaching brothers to Louisville the following year. Spalding had met Ryken during the latter's visit to Bardstown in 1837.

On August 11, 1854, Ryken and six other brothers arrived in Louisville. With few financial resources, the brothers received nothing more than a blessing from the bishop, who suggested that they temporarily live with private families. They found a home in a building at Thirteenth and MARKET Streets that housed the chapel of St. Patrick's, a new Catholic parish. There they established St. Patrick's School on the middle floor of the building. This occurred in the midst of strong anti-Catholic sentiment in the city. During the "BLOODY MONDAY" riots in August 1855, when more than twenty immigrant Catholics were killed, the brothers were said to be storing ammunition and training young Catholic men for a "bloody war on Protestantism." It was alleged that during the riots they hid their valuables in St. John's Cemetery in PORTLAND. Brother Ryken took no immediate action on withdrawing the brothers from Louisville, but considering the events of "Bloody Monday" and their lack of financial support from Bishop Spalding, he sent three of the brothers to England to strengthen the congregation there. Because of a shortage of teachers, St. Patrick's did not hold classes for the 1859-60 school year.

Xaverian numbers grew in 1860 with the arrival of new brothers from Europe, and they reopened St. Patrick's School, where they taught until 1911. They also established a school known as Immaculate Conception on Eighth St., and took on teaching jobs at St. Boniface School, St. John's School, and the Cathedral School. In 1863 the brothers opened St. Aloysius Select School on E Green (LIBERTY) St. In 1864 this school moved to FOURTH St. near BROADWAY, where it combined with the Cathedral Parish School under the new name of St. Xavier's Institute. Students ranged in age from six to eighteen.

In 1890 the Kentucky General Assembly conferred on the school a new charter, empowering it to award college degrees and to be known as St. Xavier College. In 1891 it moved to 118 W Broadway. After WORLD WAR I the college and elementary sections of the school were closed in order to concentrate on a college preparatory program. The school moved to Poplar Level Rd. in 1961. St. Xavier was the only Catholic male high school in the city until the opening of FLAGET HIGH SCHOOL in 1942. It is the oldest of eight high schools run by the brothers in the United States.

Flaget High School, named after Louisville's first Catholic bishop, Benedict Joseph Flaget, was at Forty-fourth St. and River Park Dr. in the West End. The all-male high school was established and run by the Archdiocese of Louisville, but was partially staffed by the Xaverian Brothers. Because of "white flight" out of the West End in the 1960s, Flaget experienced financial difficulties as enrollment declined to several hundred students, forcing the school to close in 1974.

Today there are between 300 and 400 Xaverian Brothers in the world. The largest concentration in the United States lies in the Northeast. In Louisville the numbers have become very small because few young men are entering the brotherhood. Their only current school is St. Xavier, but the brothers constitute only a handful of the school's faculty. Also located on St. Xavier's property is the Ryken House, one of two retirement homes for the brothers in the United States.

See Brother John Joseph Sterne, C.F.X. *Growing in Excellence: The Story and Tradition of Saint Xavier* (Louisville 1989); *Courier-Journal,* April 18, 1954; J. Devadder, C.F.X. *Rooted in History: The Life and Times of T.J. Ryken Founder of the Xaverian Brothers* (Brugge, Belgium 1986).

Y

YANDELL, DAVID WENDEL (b near Murfreesboro, Tennessee, September 4, 1826; d Louisville, May 3, 1898). Surgeon and medical professor. David was the oldest child of Lunsford Pitts Yandell, physician, and Susan (Wendel) Yandell. He spent his youth in Lexington and Louisville, and, shortly after his 1846 graduation from the LOUISVILLE MEDICAL INSTITUTE, he completed two additional years of studies in French and British HOSPITALS. Because many of his letters from Europe appeared in the *LOUISVILLE JOURNAL* and *Western Journal of Medicine and Surgery*, he quickly gained a reputation for excellence. He joined the medical faculty of the UNIVERSITY OF LOUISVILLE in 1859 but resigned in the summer of 1861 to enlist in the Confederate Medical Department.

As medical director for the armies of (and personal physician to) generals Albert Sidney Johnston, William J. Hardee, Braxton Bragg, Joseph E. Johnston, and Edmund Kirby-Smith, he witnessed the shocking consequences of the ineptitude and inadequate education of his medical colleagues. He also won friends and admirers in both Confederate and Union camps and made contacts that proved important during his postwar career.

Returning to Louisville at the war's end, Yandell reestablished his medical practice, opened a small dispensary for indigents, and in 1867 rejoined the University of Louisville medical faculty as professor of clinical MEDICINE. Two years later he became professor of clinical surgery and in 1871 professor of surgery. His students found him a superb teacher and deft surgeon, but his colleagues criticized his egotistical and overbearing manner. They resented his badgering them to establish teaching clinics, upgrade admission requirements, expand the curriculum, and provide internships for the school's graduates. Each time they protested that another change would force a tuition increase and result in a declining enrollment, Yandell threatened to resign. Because he was the school's most prestigious faculty member, his colleagues acceded to his demands, and one by one the demands became realities.

Yandell also stressed the need for continuing education. He founded and for twenty years co-edited and wrote for the *American Practitioner* (which merged with *Louisville Medical News* to become the *American Practitioner and News*). An active proponent of professional societies, he served as president of the American Medical Association (1872) and of the American Surgical Association (1890). He chaired the surgery section of the 1881 International Medical Congress in London and received honorary membership in the London Surgery Society (1883) and the College of Physicians and Surgeons of Philadelphia (1887). In 1890 he founded the Louisville Surgical Society. Yandell's successors at the University of Louisville honor his memory with an annual guest lectureship.

In addition to his medical activities Yandell was a member of the Louisville school board and belonged to the Filson Club, Salmagundi Literary Club, and PENDENNIS CLUB; and he founded the Louisville Kennel Club (1894). A man of great wit and charm, he served on the committees that arranged for and entertained the Grand Duke Alexis of Russia (1872), Emperor Dom Pedro of Brazil (1876), and presidents Ulysses S. Grant (1879), Rutherford B. Hayes (1877), and Chester A. Arthur (1883) during their visits to Louisville.

Yandell married Frances Jane Crutcher of Nashville in 1851. Two of their three children survived to adulthood. Yandell died May 3, 1898, and is buried in CAVE HILL CEMETERY.

See Yandell Family Papers, Filson Club Historical Society, Louisville; Nancy Disher Baird, *David Wendel Yandell: Physician of Old Louisville* (Lexington 1978).

Nancy D. Baird

YANDELL, ENID (b Louisville, October 6, 1869; d Boston, June 13, 1934). Sculptor. Enid was the daughter of LUNSFORD PITTS YANDELL Jr., a physician and medical professor, and Louise (Elliston) Yandell. She attended Hampton College and in 1889 graduated from the Cincinnati Academy of Art. Two years later she was hired to help prepare SCULPTURE for the World's Columbian Exposition at Chicago. She also designed the caryatids for the roof garden of the fair's Women's Building, for which she won a gold Designer's Medal. In addition, she modeled a seven-foot statue of Daniel Boone at the request of Louisville's Filson Club. The plaster image of the frontiersman stood on the Chicago fairgrounds and at the 1897 Tennessee Centennial Exposition. In 1906 Louisville cigar manufacturer C.C. Bickel underwrote the cost of having the statue cast in bronze, and it was placed in Cherokee Park.

Following her Chicago successes, which included a book written with her roommates about their adventures in Chicago, Yandell established a studio in New York City and served as Karl Bitter's assistant. In the winter of 1894 she journeyed to Paris for further studies. In her left-bank studio she created a twenty-five-foot plaster copy of the Louvre's Athena, which would serve as the focal point for Tennessee's centennial celebration. Unfortunately the statue was not bronzed, and eventually the WEATHER destroyed it. A decade later, however, she accepted a commission for the statue of John Thomas, president of the centennial's board of directors. The twelve-foot bronze statue of Thomas stands in Nashville's Centennial Park.

Enid Yandell in her studio, 1902.

In 1899 Yandell designed the Carrie Brown Memorial Fountain for Providence, Rhode Island, which was placed near the city's railroad station. The bronze fountain generated considerable publicity and undoubtedly won for her numerous other contracts, including a fountain for Louisville's Cherokee Park. Unveiled in 1905, HOGAN'S FOUNTAIN features a mythological Pan dancing and playing his flute for four terrapins. Yandell also collaborated with George Grey Bernard to prepare sculpture for the facade of a New York theater; modeled hundreds of busts, bas reliefs, and miniature portrait figurines; and periodically visited Paris "for inspiration." During a 1913 visit she created her last piece of public statuary, the kneeling figure of Chief Ninigret that graces the harbor of Watch Hill, Rhode Island.

Caught in France at the outbreak of WORLD WAR I, Yandell ran soup kitchens for hungry artists, cared for orphaned and abandoned children, and on her return to the United States raised thousands of dollars for the children of France. She also worked with the American Red Cross in New York (where she had lived since the late 1890s), operated a summer art school at Martha's Vineyard, actively supported the women's suffrage movement, and campaigned for President Calvin Coolidge. Yandell made few public comments about the difficulties of succeeding in a man's field; however, to a New York reporter she proclaimed that sculpture was a "lovely occupation for women." She also advised a group of Louisville women to "get married. Success in other lines is hard won."

A member of the National Sculpture Society, National Art Society and French Academy, Yandell exhibited her work in at least twenty-seven major shows, including international expositions at Chicago (1893), Boston (1901), and St. Louis (1904). Her best-known works—

the Boone, Thomas, and Chief Ninigret statues and Hogan and Brown fountains—stand in public PARKS. Smaller pieces belong to public and private repositories from Maine to Missouri, including busts of John B. Castleman (LOUISVILLE FREE PUBLIC LIBRARY), REUBEN T. DURRETT and ALFRED VICTOR DU PONT (Filson Club), Prof. James J. Rucker (Georgetown College), and William Goebel (KENTUCKY HISTORICAL SOCIETY). The J.B. SPEED ART MUSEUM owns about twenty pieces of her artworks, numerous awards and medals, and a scrapbook of newspaper clippings. She is buried in CAVE HILL CEMETERY.

See Enid Yandell papers, Filson Club Historical Society, Louisville; Enid Yandell, Jean Loughborough, and Laura Hayes, *Three Girls in a Flat* (Chicago 1892); Nancy Disher Baird, "Enid Yandell: Kentucky Sculptor," *Filson Club History Quarterly* 62 (Jan. 1988): 5–31.

Nancy D. Baird

YANDELL, LUNSFORD PITTS, JR. (b Tennessee, June 6, 1837; d Louisville, March 12, 1884). Physician. Lunsford Pitts Yandell Jr. was the son of Lunsford and Susan (Wendel) Yandell. He attended Louisville schools, received a medical degree from the UNIVERSITY OF LOUISVILLE, and in 1858 moved to Memphis, where he practiced MEDICINE and taught materia medica and therapeutics at the Memphis Medical Institute. Caught up in the excitement of the secession agitation, he enlisted in May 1861 as a private in the Fourth Tennessee, explaining to his family that he was anxious to "win glory." However, because of the Confederate army's need for physicians, he switched to the medical corps; and on his first taste of battle Yandell realized that war involved much more bloodshed than glory. He served as brigade surgeon and medical inspector and at the war's end was medical director and personal physician to Gen. William J. Hardee.

Returning to Louisville at the war's end he practiced medicine with his father and brother David, spent a year in Europe studying and traveling, and in 1869 joined the medical faculty at the University of Louisville. During his career he taught materia medica, clinical medicine, theory and practice of medicine, and diseases of the skin. At the time of his death he had begun to attract recognition in the new field of dermatology. As did other members of his family, Yandell developed an engaging writing style. Many of the letters he wrote from Memphis and London and during the war found their way into Louisville papers and medical journals. In the postwar years he published a number of articles for medical journals and edited the *Louisville Medical News*. Yandell is buried in CAVE HILL CEMETERY.

In December 1867 he married Louise Elliston of Nashville. They had four children. Enid, the oldest, became an internationally known sculptor.

Nancy Disher Baird, "A Kentucky Physician Examines Memphis," *Tennessee Historical Quarterly* 37 (Summer 1978): 190–202; "There Is No Sunday in the Army: The Civil War Letters of Lunsford Yandell Jr.," *Filson Club History Quarterly* 53 (Oct. 1979): 317–27; *Courier-Journal*, March 13, 1884.

Nancy D. Baird

YANDELL, LUNSFORD PITTS, SR. (b Sumner County, Tennessee, July 4, 1805; d Louisville, February 3, 1878). Physician, teacher, and minister. Lunsford was the son of Wilson and Elizabeth (Pitts) Yandell. He earned a medical degree from the University of Maryland in 1825, practiced MEDICINE in Murfreesboro and Nashville, and in 1831 joined the faculty of Lexington's Transylvania University as professor of chemistry. Four years later he and several colleagues founded the LOUISVILLE MEDICAL INSTITUTE (which became the Medical Department of the UNIVERSITY OF LOUISVILLE in 1846), where he taught chemistry, materia medica, and physiology. Proud of the institution he helped create, Yandell once wrote that when he felt "low spirited," he found "confidence and hope" by surveying the "grand dimensions [and] splendid proportions" of the structure that housed the institute.

In 1859 Yandell accepted a position at the Memphis Medical Institute, whose faculty hoped his reputation could rescue the financially failing school. Despite his efforts, the outbreak of war in the spring of 1861 forced the school's closing. Yandell supervised a Confederate hospital in Memphis and after the town's fall to federal forces moved to his wife's family plantation near Daceyville, Tennessee. There he took up farming and provided medical and ministerial care for area residents. He was ordained as a Presbyterian minister in 1864.

Yandell returned to Louisville in 1867 but refused to rejoin the medical school faculty, pleading disgust with their continual feuding. He resumed his medical practice, preached occasionally at Louisville churches, and wrote about medicine and natural sciences. In 1872 he was elected president of the Louisville College of Physicians and Surgeons and served in 1878 as president of the State Medical Society (Kentucky Medical Association), an organization he had helped found twenty-six years earlier. He also belonged to Boston's Academy of Sciences and the Philadelphia Academy of Natural Sciences.

Because his scientific interests included GEOLOGY and paleontology, Yandell enjoyed exploring areas around the FALLS OF THE OHIO and BEARGRASS CREEK. He amassed an extensive collection of fossils and wrote of his findings for the *Proceedings of the American Association for the Advancement of Science* (1851), *American Journal of Science and Arts* (1855), and a Geological Society of France journal (1848). In 1847 he and Benjamin Schumard published *Contributions to the Geology of Kentucky*. During the 1870s he also contributed articles about fossils to Louisville's *Home and School*. Paleontologists have saluted Yandell's contributions by naming six fossils after him.

A prolific writer, Yandell edited the *Transylvania Journal of Medicine* (1832–36), co-edited the *Western Journal of Medicine and Science* (1840–55), and wrote more than a hundred treatises on a wide variety of topics, including cholera, old age, the medicinal value of Kentucky's mineral springs, biographical sketches of medical colleagues, and histories of the MEDICAL SCHOOLS at Transylvania and the University of Louisville.

Yandell married Susan Juliet Wendel in October 1825. Four of their thirteen children survived to adulthood. David and Lunsford Jr. practiced medicine and taught at the University of Louisville; William, also a physician, won acclaim as a PUBLIC HEALTH official in San Angelo and El Paso, Texas. After the death of his first wife in 1860, Yandell married Eliza Bland in August 1861; they had no children. Yandell is buried in CAVE HILL CEMETERY.

See Yandell Family Papers, Filson Club Historical Society, Louisville; V.F. Payne, "Lunsford Pitts Yandell (1805–1878)," *Filson Club History Quarterly* 30 (July 1957): 232–39.

Nancy D. Baird

YELLOW CAB TAXIS. Yellow Cab of Louisville traces its origins to 1861 when the Louisville Transfer Co., a rental carriage company, started providing "tally-hos" to city residents. This early taxi service was eventually merged with the Louisville Carriage Co., a similar company founded in the late 1880s by George Lindenberger. John E. Roche, a successful producer of shirts and men's furnishings, became president of the company in the early 1890s. Roche was Louisville's first resident owner of an automobile, a steam-powered machine.

In 1912 the Louisville Carriage Co., located at 421 S Third St., changed its name to the Louisville Carriage and Taxicab Co. In 1918 Lee L. Miles, an early automobile dealer, acquired the company and became president and general manager. *COURIER-JOURNAL* owner and publisher ROBERT WORTH BINGHAM became vice president of the company, serving for several years. In 1919 the Louisville Carriage and Taxicab Co. bought the Louisville Transfer Co. and became the Louisville Taxicab and Transfer Co.

Miles, who was the first to bring the Yellow Cab system to Louisville, helped to organize the company by switching from horse-drawn hacks to motorized vehicles. He was one of the first taxicab operators to use the yellow cabs in place of the larger "custom-made" coaches. Brown cabs were originally used before the company switched to the new style of specially painted standard-brand taxicabs.

In 1942, because many male drivers had left to serve in the armed forces in WORLD WAR II, the company hired the first women replacements as taxi drivers. In 1946 Louisville Taxicab became the first in the city to install two-way radio systems for dispatching cabs to locations. For years taxi drivers had to be certified by the Board of Public Safety and issued permits to operate.

In the late 1960s the company moved from the corner of Ninth and LIBERTY to 1601 S Preston St. In 1967 the company changed its name to the Yellow Cab Co. of Louisville. Yellow Cab of Louisville is part of Louisville Transportation Inc., which includes Yellow Courier and Care-A-Van Wheelchair Transportation and Yellow Limousine Service and Ambulance service. Louisville Transportation Inc., is a part of Interlock Industries, a private, family-owned parent company. As of 1998 Yellow Cab had a fleet of some 250 cabs operating in Greater Louisville, making it the largest taxi cab company in the area.

See *Courier-Journal*, Jan. 21, 1948.

YMCA (YOUNG MEN'S CHRISTIAN ASSOCIATION). This international, interdenominational Christian organization was formed as a prayer group in London in 1844 by George Williams and dedicated to evangelism and the moral and intellectual development of young men. The first branch in the United States was opened in Boston in 1851. A YMCA reading room was set up in New York City in 1852.

The first YMCA movement began in Louisville the next year by ministers in the German Evangelical church and local businessmen concerned about the moral turpitude of the youth in the Protestant German community. The first program, a religious school, was established in late 1854 at the German Methodist church. Initially the focus was on lectures, daily prayers, and missionary work, although the business element promoted programs to encourage the Americanization of immigrants. Throughout the 1860s the YMCA was plagued by internal struggles over programs to establish worship and funding relief for the poor.

In 1862 the association was forced to merge with the United States Christian Commission because of diminishing revenue and membership. The focus was the same, with energies largely devoted to work in CIVIL WAR HOSPITALS and barracks. In 1866 the YMCA was reorganized by five prominent local ministers and numerous leaders from the business community. By 1871 membership and community support had all but disappeared. Between 1871 and 1876 the YMCA was reduced to only a small presence in the German community.

On April 3, 1878, the YMCA Inc. secured a charter by a special act of the General Assembly. One of the earliest branches was the CHESTNUT STREET YMCA, organized in 1883 on W Walnut St. (Muhammad Ali Blvd.) for AFRICAN AMERICANS. It moved to the former John P. Byrne residence in 1906 on W Chestnut St. It was closed in 1932 during the GREAT DEPRESSION but was reorganized and reopened in 1946.

Prior to 1913 the YMCA had several different downtown locations. After a successful campaign to raise $350,000, a new central building was opened at the northeast corner of Third and BROADWAY in 1913. The YMCA remained at this location until 1985 when a new central building was constructed at 501 S Second St.

In 1950 the organization was renamed the YMCA of Greater Louisville and Jefferson County, Kentucky, reflecting the area's growing suburbanization. The YMCA was reorganized into a metropolitan association under the auspices of a Metropolitan Board of Directors in charge of all area branches. In 1967 the YMCA became the YMCA of Greater Louisville to reflect its programs and facilities in southern Indiana and counties outside of Jefferson.

In the late 1990s the YMCA offers educational classes, religious services, sports, child care, and international programs; and it operates gymnasiums and some residential facilities. The YMCA maintains branches on Chestnut St., S Second St., Mill Brook Rd., Six Mile Ln., Fordhaven Rd., and S First St. and in OLDHAM COUNTY, BULLITT COUNTY, and Camp Piomingo near Otter Creek Park. The YMCA also has branches on Short St. in Charlestown, Indiana, and on Hamburg Pkwy. in JEFFERSONVILLE, INDIANA.

See Lawrence W. Fielding and Clark F. Wood, "The Social Control of Indolence and Irreligion: Louisville's First YMCA Movement, 1853–1871," *Filson Club History Quarterly* 58 (April 1984): 219–36.

YORK. York was a member of the LEWIS AND CLARK Expedition (1803–6), accompanying the Corps of Discovery in its epic journey to the Pacific and back as the slave of WILLIAM CLARK. He was the first African American to cross the present United States and the North American continent north of Mexico from coast to coast. He probably was born between 1770 and 1775, most likely in Caroline County, Virginia, where the Clark family lived during that period. It is believed that he was the son of Old York, a Clark family slave, and grew up as the companion and body servant to William Clark. He moved with the Clarks to Jefferson County, Kentucky, in 1785, living at the family plantation, MULBERRY HILL, in what is now George Rogers Clark Park, along Poplar Level Rd. near the AUDUBON PARK community.

During William Clark's military service in the Kentucky militia and the regular army and during his extensive business travels, it is likely that York accompanied him at times. In October 1803 when Lewis and Clark and the nucleus of the Corps of Discovery left the FALLS OF THE OHIO, York was with the explorers. The luxury of having strictly a body servant on such a rigorous and dangerous undertaking could not be enjoyed, and York soon became a valued and equal member of the party. He was particularly valuable regarding diplomatic relations with the various Native American tribes encountered. Many of them had never seen a black man, and he was believed to have great spiritual power. This, together with his large size, strength, and agility, greatly impressed the Indians, and the expedition's leaders used this to their advantage.

He was allowed to vote along with the other men concerning expedition decisions, and he might have been the first slave to actually exercise this right in United States history. Contrary to popular belief he was not freed by Clark immediately following the expedition. It was at least ten years after the expedition before York was finally granted his freedom. In June 1808 Clark moved permanently to St. Louis, which precipitated a severe falling-out between the two lifelong companions. The cause was one of the cruel realities of slavery—York and his wife, who was owned by someone else, were separated. York wanted to remain in Louisville, but Clark insisted he come with him to St. Louis. York's behavior and attitude after this forced move away from his wife became objectionable to Clark; and the relationship between the two men worsened, so much so that Clark considered selling his longtime manservant. In the end York was allowed to live in the Louisville area and either worked for the Clark family or was hired out. In November 1815 York was still a slave, driving a wagon for a Louisville drayage business in which Clark was a partner. Sometime between this date and 1832 Clark manumitted York. He told writer Washington Irving in 1832 that he had freed York after the expedition and had set him up in a drayage business hauling freight between Richmond, Kentucky, and Nashville, Tennessee, but said that York was a poor businessman. He lost the business and, while attempting to return to Clark in St. Louis, died of cholera in Tennessee. The date and exact place of York's death remain unknown. A happier ending for York is a legend, generally discredited by historians, that recounts York was freed and returned to the Rocky Mountains where he became a chief among the Crow Indians. The former fate is much more likely, but regardless of his fate, this enslaved African American, who called Louisville home from 1785 to at least 1816, significantly contributed to what many historians still consider the most famous exploring venture in the history of the United States.

See Robert Betts, *In Search of York* (Boulder, Colo., 1985); James J. Holmberg, "I Wish You to See & Know All," *We Proceeded On* 18 (Nov. 1992): 4–12; George H. Yater, "Nine Young Men from Kentucky," supplement to *We Proceeded On* (May 1992): 12–19.

James J. Holmberg

YOUNG, BENNETT HENDERSON (b Nicholasville, Kentucky, May 25, 1843; d Louisville, February 23, 1919). Attorney, civic leader, and soldier. The son of Robert and Josephine (Henderson) Young, he received his early education at Bethel Academy in

Nicholasville and spent two years at Centre College, Danville, Kentucky, before leaving to join the Confederate army. Young enlisted in Gen. John Hunt Morgan's cavalry, was captured following raids across Indiana and Ohio, and was imprisoned with Morgan in the Ohio State Penitentiary.

He escaped and made his way to Canada in 1864. On October 19, 1864, Young, along with nineteen other men, launched the famous raid on St. Albans, Vermont, seizing gold and currency for the Confederacy. This was the northernmost invasion by Confederate troops during the CIVIL WAR. Escaping back to Canada, Young was the object of a bitter extradition battle. Going into voluntary exile, he studied law at Queen's College in Belfast, Ireland, and took lecture courses at the University of Edinburgh in Scotland.

Finally allowed to return to the United States, Young settled in Louisville in 1868 and began the practice of law, soon becoming one of the city's most highly regarded trial attorneys. He was involved in the reorganization of the Louisville, NEW ALBANY, and Chicago Railroad (later known as the MONON RAILROAD) was its general counsel and, for a short time, its president (1883–84). Young served as president of the SOUTHERN EXPOSITION in 1884. From 1885 to 1886 he was president of the KENTUCKY AND INDIANA BRIDGE CO., which constructed the cantilever bridge over the OHIO RIVER between Louisville and New Albany. It was also at this time that Young was instrumental in organizing the LOUISVILLE SOUTHERN RAILROAD that ran between Louisville and Danville with a branch to Lexington. In 1890 he was named a member of the state constitutional convention.

Civic affairs were also important to Young. He was president of the KENTUCKY SCHOOL FOR THE BLIND and was involved in the activities of Confederate veterans. After holding several positions of leadership in the United Confederate Veterans, Young was named commander-in-chief of the organization in 1913 and honorary commander-in-chief for life in 1916.

Young was long active in the affairs of the Presbyterian church. His mother's experiences as an orphan made him aware of the plight of girls without homes or education and led Young to endow Bellewood Seminary and Kentucky Presbyterian Normal School, located in ANCHORAGE. Together they comprised the largest boarding school for girls in Kentucky.

Writing on a variety of subjects, he was the author of such books as *History and Texts of the Three Constitutions of Kentucky* (1890), *History of the Division of the Presbyterian Church in Kentucky (1898),* and *Confederate Wizards of the Saddle* (1914). His literary interests spurred him to head a fund-raising campaign to revive the city's debt-ridden public library in 1872.

Young's first wife was Mattie R. Robinson, whom he married in 1866. She died in 1891 leaving two sons and two daughters. On June 29, 1895 Young married Eliza S. Sharp. They had two children, a son and a daughter. Young is buried in CAVE HILL CEMETERY.

See Oscar A. Kinchen, *General Bennett H. Young: Confederate Raider and a Man of Many Adventures* (West Hanover, Mass., 1981); Bess A. Ray, ed., *Louisville Library Collections Biography Series,* vol. 2 (Louisville 1941); John M. Gresham, pub., *Biographical Cyclopedia of the Commonwealth of Kentucky* (Chicago 1896).

Kenneth Dennis

YOUNG, WHITNEY MOORE, JR. (b Simpsonville, Kentucky, July 31, 1921; d Lagos, Nigeria, March 11, 1971). Social worker and CIVIL RIGHTS leader. Young was the son of Laura (Ray) and Whitney M. Young. His father was an instructor at and later president of LINCOLN INSTITUTE, and his mother was one of the first African American postmistresses in Kentucky, holding that post in SHELBY COUNTY. Young graduated from Lincoln Institute as valedictorian in 1936 at age fourteen. In 1940 he received a premedical degree from Kentucky State College (now Kentucky State University), graduating at the head of his class. Young then taught mathematics and coached at Rosenwald High School in Madisonville, Kentucky. In July 1942 he enlisted in the army, serving as first sergeant in the 369th Regiment Anti-Aircraft Artillery Group. While in this all-black unit under white officers, Young decided to make race relations his life's work.

During the war Young studied engineering at the Massachusetts Institute of Technology. He attended the University of Minnesota from 1944 to 1947 and helped organize a chapter of the Congress of Racial Equality. After he received a master's degree in social work, he went to work for the Urban League chapter in St. Paul, Minnesota, as director of industrial relations. He was promoted to president of the chapter in Omaha, Nebraska, in 1950 and served until 1953. In January 1954 he moved to Atlanta University to become the dean of the School of Social Work, a position he held until he became executive director of the National Urban League on August 1, 1961.

As director, Young guided the Urban League away from traditional social work and into more progressive programs. He expanded the league by opening new chapters, enlarging the staff, and increasing funding. He walked a tightrope between black activists, who saw him as an accommodationist, and the white power brokers who controlled the jobs, money, and political process and viewed Young's actions and words as threatening. Young's approach was to attack the root causes of inequality, particularly inadequate education and economic discrimination. An advocate of equal employment opportunity, improved housing, and education as the means for social and economic equality for blacks, Young drew upon corporate, government, and foundation support to advance the league's programs. His goal was economically strong black communities that would be integrated into the general society through nonviolent direct action and political lobbying. Under his leadership the league cosponsored the March on Washington in 1963, and Young participated in the Selma, Alabama, march in 1965.

During the 1960s, Young emerged as a national leader of the civil rights movement. His "Marshall Plan" for AFRICAN AMERICANS included the civil rights legislation of the 1960s, especially programs against poverty. He served on seven presidential commissions during the Kennedy and Johnson administrations (1961–69) and was president of both the National Conference on Social Welfare and the National Association of Social Workers. He also wrote a syndicated weekly newspaper column. His book *To Be Equal* (1964) called for a "domestic Marshall Plan" to deal with black poverty, and in *Beyond Racism: Building an Open Society* (1969) Young outlined sweeping programs to create an egalitarian society. He started the "New Thrust" program of the Urban League in 1968 to move into ghettos to attack the causes of minority deprivation, inadequate housing, poor health, and educational disadvantage. He did not want to focus on the symptomatic statistics of joblessness. Young was awarded the Medal of Freedom, the nation's highest civilian award, in 1969 by President Lyndon B. Johnson.

Young married Margaret Buckner of Campbellsville, Kentucky, on January 2, 1944. She became a teacher and an author of children's books about black history and civil rights. They had two children, Marcia and Lauren. Young died in a SWIMMING accident while attending a conference in Lagos, Nigeria, to increase understanding between races. He was buried in Lexington's Greenwood Cemetery, where President Richard Nixon gave a eulogy; later the body was reinterred in New Rochelle, New York.

See Alice A. Dunnigan, *The Fascinating Story of Black Kentuckians: Their Heritage and Traditions* (Washington, D.C., 1982); Nancy Weiss, *Whitney M. Young, Jr. and the Struggle for Civil Rights* (Princeton, N.J., 1989).

John Klee

YOUNG, WHITNEY MOORE, SR. (b Midway, Kentucky, September 26, 1897; d Louisville, August 18, 1975). Educator. Young was born to Taylor and Annie Young. He attended Zion Hill Public School in Scott County, Mayo Underwood School in Frankfort, and the Chandler Normal School in Lexington. He was among the first entrants when Lincoln Ridge (later Institute) opened in SHELBY COUNTY in 1912. He graduated in 1916 and moved to Detroit to work for the Ford Motor Co.

During WORLD WAR I he served in the U.S. Army in France. After the war Moore returned to Ford to work as an electrical engineer. When Pres. A. Eugene Thomas of LINCOLN INSTITUTE offered Young a job in 1920, he left his higher-paying position at Ford and accepted sixty-eight dollars per month to become head of the engineering department. He was promoted to dean of the institute and in 1935 became education director, the first African American to head Lincoln Institute.

With the school ten thousand dollars in debt and on the verge of closing, Young, the faculty, the staff, and the students rallied together and initiated successful fund-raising and student-recruiting campaigns. Under his leadership, Lincoln Institute became the leading black college preparatory school in Kentucky. When the school closed in 1966, Young retired and moved to Louisville.

Young continued his own education while heading the school. In 1938 he graduated from LOUISVILLE MUNICIPAL COLLEGE and in 1944 received an M.A. from Fisk University in Nashville. An honorary doctor of education degree was awarded in 1955 by Monrovia College in Liberia. Young served twice as president of Kentucky's Negro Education Association during the 1950s. In 1964 he served on President Lyndon B. Johnson's committee to implement the new civil rights laws. Young likewise held positions on the Kentucky Commission on Human Rights, the Black History Committee, the Kentucky Chief Justice's Housing Commission, and the state Vocational Advisory Board.

In 1918 Young married Laura Ray of Lebanon, Kentucky. They had three children: Eleanor, who became a professor at the UNIVERSITY OF LOUISVILLE and was one of its first black deans; Whitney Jr., the well-known civil rights leader; and Anita, a professor at the University of Chicago who was also active in social work. Young died on August 18, 1975, and is buried in Lexington's Greenwood Cemetery.

See Alice A. Dunnigan, *The Fascinating Story of Black Kentuckians* (Washington, D.C., 1982); George C. Wright, *A History of Blacks in Kentucky* (Frankfort 1992); Russell L. Adams, *Great Negroes Past and Present* (Chicago 1969).

George T. Vaughn

YWCA (YOUNG WOMEN'S CHRISTIAN ASSOCIATION). The YWCA is a national organization that had its origins in several independent local associations of the late nineteenth century. Formed in various American cities, these associations were intended to meet the physical, intellectual, and spiritual needs of young women. On February 13, 1912, three hundred interested citizens gathered at the SECOND PRESBYTERIAN CHURCH at 128 W BROADWAY to found a YWCA in Louisville. The association was incorporated on March 27, 1912. After formal incorporation the YWCA moved to its first home at 229 S Fourth Ave., occupying the top three floors above the Cohen Shoe Co.

The location was perfect for the newly formed organization. Offices, a gymnasium, and Louisville's first cafeteria were a few of the accommodations provided to members. After eight months the organization boasted a paid membership of 2,445. The first annual report noted that the Louisville Association had set the record for most work accomplished by any city association in the first year of its history.

The report listed two goals: a summer camp and a residence. The following year the first of the goals was accomplished when the association opened its summer camp to women who worked industry. In 1914, after a campaign to raise three hundred thousand dollars was successful, the YWCA purchased the James C. Ford Mansion on Broadway at Second St. The association remained there for the next fifty years while expanding its programs.

The association organized educational and recreational classes, provided a residence for single women, opened the Phyllis (Phillis)Wheatley branch for AFRICAN AMERICANS in the early 1920s, and provided many more services. The association aided families of soldiers at Camp Taylor during WORLD WAR I, held dances and parties for servicemen during WORLD WAR II, helped flood victims in 1937, and provided job training for unemployed women in the 1930s and after. It also provided SWIMMING programs for poor and handicapped children, as well as other recreational activities for teenagers.

In 1964 the association moved to 604 S Third St., the former Henry Clay Hotel. The building was constructed in 1924 as an Elks Athletic Club. Designed by the architectural firm of Joseph & Joseph, the building is an outstanding example of the neo-classical revival.

During the 1970s the YWCA made some of its most social issue–minded advances, establishing a clinic for teenage parents, a rape relief center in 1975, and a spouse abuse center. In 1988 the YWCA moved to Third and Breckinridge Streets. On November 20, 1989, the YWCA of Louisville and Jefferson County voted to end its affiliation with the national YWCA and became the Center for Women and Families. The center canceled the affiliation because the name Young Women's Christian Association did not describe the services and programs that were offered, the cost of affiliation outweighed the benefits, and the center wanted to promote equality by opening membership to both women and men. The center has branches in Shively and at 4303 W Broadway.

See *Courier-Journal*, Dec. 28, 1924, May 16, 1976, Sept. 7, 1962, April 13, 1995.

Z

ZACHARY TAYLOR NATIONAL CEMETERY. This is one of 112 national CEMETERIES in the United States and one of seven located in Kentucky. The others are Mill Springs in Nancy, Lebanon National Cemetery in Lebanon, Camp Nelson in Jessamine County, Danville National Cemetery in Danville, a section in CAVE HILL CEMETERY in Louisville, and a section in the Lexington Cemetery in Lexington. Establishing national cemeteries began during the CIVIL WAR. Although they were intended originally for battlefield dead, these gravesites are now available to honorably discharged veterans who served during either war or peacetime and to their spouses and dependent children. Veterans representing six wars—the Spanish-American War, World Wars I and II, KOREAN WAR, VIETNAM WAR, and the Persian Gulf War—are buried in Zachary Taylor National Cemetery.

An act creating Zachary Taylor National Cemetery was signed by President Calvin Coolidge on February 19, 1925. The cemetery is located at 4701 Brownsboro Rd. in Jefferson County and contains the grave of the nation's twelfth president, ZACHARY TAYLOR (1784–1850). Rep. Maurice H. Thatcher of Louisville proposed the bill that created the cemetery because of the deplorable condition of Taylor's tomb. Taylor died in office on July 9, 1850. He was first interred in Washington, D.C., but was later moved to the family farm on the outskirts of Louisville.

The act creating the cemetery also provided for the construction of a new mausoleum to hold the remains of Taylor and his wife, Margaret. Built by the War Department at a cost of ten thousand dollars, the tomb is constructed of Indiana (Bedford) limestone with a granite base. Inside, marble sarcophagi contain the remains of Taylor and his wife. The mausoleum stands beside a memorial shaft that the state of Kentucky erected in Taylor's honor in 1883. Initially the cemetery consisted of only the Taylor family burial grounds. In 1927 the state donated five acres to the federal government for the cemetery and made a second donation the following year, bringing the size of the grounds to sixteen and one-half acres. In 1928 it was officially named the Zachary Taylor National Cemetery.

By the end of 1938 the cemetery had only 286 interments. During WORLD WAR II and the Korean War, burials at the cemetery increased as deceased soldiers were returned to the United States. Many of these individuals could not be identified and are buried in common graves. In 1997 the cemetery had 621 graves of this type, holding the remains of 1,588 individuals.

In 1951 the U.S. Army Quartermaster Corps proposed to enlarge the cemetery by a hundred acres, an expansion that was opposed by the directors of the Louisville Chamber of Commerce and local developers. In 1960 two members of Kentucky's congressional delegation, Rep. Frank W. Burke and Sen. John Sherman Cooper, made a second unsuccessful attempt to augment the cemetery's holdings. Burke's and Cooper's action followed the filling of the last unreserved grave in January 1960. In 1961 interments, except for the spouses of those already buried, were halted at the cemetery. Following the removal of a road and the relocation of a utility line in 1985, new burials were resumed for four years but were halted in March 1989 when the additional gravesites were filled. The cemetery was reopened briefly for new burials from December 1991 to August 1992. The grounds hold the remains of 12,900 individuals, including two recipients of the CONGRESSIONAL MEDAL OF HONOR, Sgt. Willie Sandlin of Hyden, Kentucky, and Sgt. John C. Squires of Louisville.

In 1991 the cemetery received unusual media attention when the county coroner exhumed President Taylor's remains to test the theory of Clara Rising, a former University of Florida humanities professor, that his death resulted from arsenic poisoning. Tests determined that Taylor died from natural causes, as had been believed in 1850, and not from foul play.

ZION UNITED CHURCH OF CHRIST. The church, located at 1310 E Burnett Ave., was founded in 1849 as the German Reformed Zion's Church. The original church held services in members' homes until 1851 when a building was constructed on Green (LIBERTY) between Clay and Shelby Streets. The church moved into larger quarters on Hancock St. in 1863. In 1899 the church moved to Hancock and BROADWAY and in 1950 to Burnett Ave. near Eastern Pkwy.

The church's affiliation and name have changed several times. In its earliest period it was listed as a Lutheran church, later appearing as a German Evangelical church of the reformed tradition. The "German" designation was dropped in 1867, although sermons continued to be in German into the early 1900s. Zion became an Evangelical and Reformed church in 1934 when the two branches merged. In 1957 when the Evangelical and Reformed churches merged with the Congregational Christian churches, Zion took its current name.

ZORN, SEBASTIAN (b Louisville, June 4, 1853; d Louisville, December 15, 1919). Grain dealer and twice president of the LOUISVILLE WATER CO. The son of Catherine P. and Jacob P. Zorn, a saloon-keeper, young Sebastian became an agent of the merchant-milling establishment of Ferguson Smith on MARKET St. near Jackson St. In 1879 he founded his own grain business, S. Zorn and Co., which became one of the leading firms in Louisville's grain trade. He gained a reputation as an energetic, hard-driving executive.

In 1906 the management structure of the Louisville Water Co. was reorganized by the Kentucky legislature to better define the relationship between the private company and its de facto owner, the city of Louisville. A new Board of Water Works, named by the mayor, replaced the former board of directors. One of the four members appointed by Mayor Paul Barth was Sebastian Zorn, with the obvious intention that Zorn would become the company's president. The new board, required by law to choose the chief officer from its own ranks, named Zorn president on April 3, 1907. He succeeded Charles Long, who had held the post for thirty-two years. Rightly or wrongly, the glacial pace of completing the CRESCENT HILL Filtration Plant was blamed on Long.

Like the new broom that sweeps clean, Zorn began a transformation of the utility's operations. He found too many employees and inflated wages (the result of political favoritism), records in poor shape, and lack of competitive bidding on equipment and supplies. His three years in office produced lower operating costs and better service. He noted as early as 1908 in the company's annual report that "if the Company is run strictly on business principles and kept out of politics you will find the same good results will continue." He stepped down in 1910 (he had a grain business to manage) but not before the company's new office at 435 S Third St. was completed that year.

In 1918 Zorn retired from his grain business, and Mayor George W. Smith reappointed him to the Board of Water Works, which promptly elected him president. He is the only person who served in the office twice. His tenure was short, however. In December 1918 he died unexpectedly of a heart attack. The *COURIER-JOURNAL* in an editorial declared, "He transformed that institution from a political hospital to one of the most efficient public utilities in America." The Board of Water Works, casting about for a fitting memorial, changed the name of Pipe Line Ave. to Zorn Ave.

See George H. Yater, *Water Works: A History of the Louisville Water Company* (Louisville 1996); Alwin Seekamp and Roger Burlingame, eds., *Who's Who in Louisville* (Louisville 1912), 253; *Courier-Journal*, Dec. 16, 1919.

George H. Yater

Bibliographic Essay

The encyclopedia represents the work of more than five hundred authors who relied on primary and secondary source materials. The available sources vary in both quality and quantity depending upon topic and era.

The Louisville area has several repositories of primary research material. Foremost, is The Filson Club Historical Society. Since its founding in 1884 the Club has made a determined effort to identify and acquire manuscripts relating to the city. It possesses the finest collection of pioneer, antebellum, and Civil War manuscripts in Kentucky. In addition, excellent collections containing information on women's studies, African Americans, and Louisville journalism are available to the research community. Other archival and manuscript repositories consulted were: Archdiocese of Louisville Archives; Bellarmine College; Cave Hill Cemetery; City of Louisville Archives; Clark County Public Library; Courier-Journal Photo Services; Episcopal Diocese of Kentucky; J.B. Speed Art Museum; Jefferson County Office of Historic Preservation and Archives (Department of Public History); Jefferson County Public School Archives and Records Retention Center; Jewish Community Center Library; Kentucky Derby Museum; Kentucky Historical Society; Kentucky Department for Libraries and Archives; Louisville Academy of Music; Louisville Free Public Library; Louisville Free Public Library Western Branch; Louisville Presbyterian Theological Seminary; New Albany-Floyd County Public Library; Southern Baptist Theological Seminary; Spalding University; University of Louisville Archives and Records Center; University of Louisville Margaret M. Bridwell Art Library; University of Louisville Dwight Anderson Memorial Music Library Archives; University of Louisville School of Medicine Kornhauser Health Sciences Library Historical Collections; University of Louisville Photographic Archives; University of Louisville Ekstrom Library Rare Books and Special Collections; Ursuline Sisters of the Immaculate Conception. The reader may learn more about these individual holdings by referring to *The Guide to Kentucky Archival and Manuscript Repositories* (1986).

There are relatively few overview histories of Louisville. They are Dr. Henry McMurtrie, *Sketches of Louisville and its (sic) Environs* (1819); Ben Casseday, *History of Louisville* (1852); *History of the Ohio Falls Cities and Their Counties* (1882); Reuben T. Durrett, *The Centenary of Louisville* (1893); J. Stoddard Johnston, ed., *Memorial History of Louisville* (1896); *Louisville Panorama* (1954); Samuel Thomas, *Views of Louisville Since 1766* (1971); George H. Yater, *Two Hundred Years at the Falls of the Ohio: A History of Louisville and Jefferson County* (1987). There are studies of select aspects of Louisville's history too numerous to mention.

Several metropolitan counties have histories. Among the best in Kentucky: (Jefferson) George H. Yater *Two Hundred Years at the Falls of the Ohio: A History of Louisville and Jefferson County* (1987); (Oldham) *History and Families of Oldham County, Kentucky (The First Century, 1824-1924)* (1996); (Shelby) George L. Willis, *History of Shelby County, Kentucky* (1929); Edward D. Shinnick, *Some Old Times in Shelbyville and Shelby County* (1974). In Indiana they are: (Clark) Lewis C. Baird, *Baird's History of Clark County* (1909); Gerald O. Haffner, *A Brief, Informal History of Clark County* (1985); (Floyd) Betty Lou Amster, *New Albany on the Ohio: Historical Review, 1813-1963* (1963); (Harrison) Frederick P. Griffin, *Harrison County's Earliest Years* (1984); (Scott) *Scott County, Indiana, Celebrating 175 Years: A Pictorial History* (1995).

There are many secondary sources that constitute bits and pieces of the Louisville mosaic. Once again, much credit must go to The Filson Club Historical Society for its publications. Since 1926 *The Filson Club History Quarterly* has published papers and book reviews on a vast spectrum of Kentucky history and the Ohio River Valley. In 1884 the Club began a series of publications of historical monographs, the first dealing with John Filson. Before the series ended in 1938, thirty-six volumes appeared, a few of them on Louisville area topics. A second series, beginning in 1964, continues and has published five volumes, the last one dealing with local land records. All volumes were printed for the purpose of making more easily available the material gathered by the members who did the research work and prepared the manuscripts.

Many former students at the University of Louisville were provided the opportunity to research and write on local topics. Under the direction of several instructors, their work has been saved and can be found in the University of Louisville Archives and Records Center. Elva Anne Lyon, director of composition at the University of Louisville, had the foresight to collect and preserve the research and writing projects in her freshman composition class between 1938 and 1942. Bound in thirty-five volumes, students wrote about organizations, places in Louisville, and hometowns. In a similar vein, there are twelve boxes of student research papers (numbering 116), mainly written under the auspices of history professors between the years 1978 and 1982, that cover myriad topics from Charles W. Anderson Jr. to Zachary Taylor Cemetery.

The University of Louisville's Ekstrom Library and the Louisville Free Public Library have tremendous clipping files. These were especially helpful in looking up obituaries. Both libraries contain every copy of the city directories going back to 1832. One cannot underestimate the value of these primary sources in placing individuals, businesses, and structures in their historic context and locations. They contain copies of major city newspapers, the most important being *The Courier-Journal, The Louisville Times*, and the *Louisville Commercial*. The *Courier-Journal* index is helpful.

Photographs

The selection of photographs was made with the idea in mind to include those that have not been widely reproduced in other books.

Given the thousands of photographs at the University of Louisville and The Filson Club, this was not difficult to do. While most archives contain some photographs, the most extensive collections are held by the University of Louisville, The Filson Club Historical Society, and *The Courier-Journal*. Unfortunately, the Great Flood of 1937 destroyed many photographs. In some cases we were able to augment the loss by using vintage illustrations, many of them in the possession of Martin Schmidt of Louisville and some of which can be found in his book, *Kentucky Illustrated: The First Hundred Years* (1992).

Photography Credits

ACTORS THEATRE: Actors Theatre of Louisville. Photograph by Richard Trigg. ADATH JESHURUN: University of Louisville Photographic Archives: Caufield & Shook Collection CS 37570. AFRICAN-AMERICAN BASEBALL: University of Louisville Photographic Archives: James Sydnor Collection 94.27.51. AFRICAN-AMERICAN EDUCATION: University of Louisville Photographic Archives: Caufield & Shook Collection CS 38594. ALI, MUHAMMAD: University of Louisville Photographic Archives: Lin Caufield Collection. ALLEYS: University of Louisville Photographic Archives: Caufield & Shook Collection CS 34615. AMERICAN CAR AND FOUNDRY COMPANY: University of Louisville Photographic Archives: Caufield & Shook Collection CS 259695. AMERICAN PRINTING HOUSE FOR THE BLIND: University of Louisville Photographic Archives: Caufield & Shook Collection CS-O 041098. AMERICAN STANDARD: University of Louisville Photographic Archives: R.G. Potter Collection P 3958. AMPHITHEATER AUDITORIUM: University of Louisville Photographic Archives: R. G. Potter Collection P1172. ANDERSON, MARY: University of Louisville Photographic Archives: Antique Media Collection 79.27.4. ANDERSON, ROBERT: Filson Club Historical Society: People File. ANDREW BROADDUS WHARF BOAT/LOUISVILLE LIFE SAVING Station: University of Louisville Photographic Archives: Caufield & Shook Collection CS-O 37339. APARTMENT BUILDINGS: Filson Club Historical Society: Richard L. Pilling Collection 994PC7. ARCHITECTURE: Historic American Buildings Survey. ARCHITECTURE: University of Louisville Photographic Archives: Caufield & Shook Collection 083861. ARRASMITH, WILLIAM STRUDWICK: University of Louisville Photographic Archives: Caufield & Shook Collection CS 155550. AUDUBON PARK: Filson Club Historical Society: Louisville Railway Co. Collection. AUTOMOBILE MANUFACTURERS: University of Louisville Photographic Archives: Caufield & Shook Collection CS 28786.

BANKING: University of Louisville Photographic Archives: Caufield & Shook Collection CS-O 76034. BARS, TAVERNS AND SALOONS: University of Louisville Photographic Archives: Caufield & Shook Collection CS 132620. BASEBALL, PROFESSIONAL: *The Industries of Louisville and New Albany.* Louisville: J.M. Elstner & Co., 1886. Loaned by Martin Schmidt. BASEBALL, PROFESSIONAL: University of Louisville Photographic Archives: Sutcliffe Sporting Goods Collection 91.25.4233. BASEBALL, PROFESSIONAL: Filson Club Historical Society: SPR-BB-21. BEARGRASS CREEK: Filson Club Historical Society: 989PC11.3. BEECHMONT: University of Louisville Photographic Archives: R.G. Potter Collection P 882. BEER GARDENS: University of Louisville Photographic Archives: Anne Karem Gift 86.37. BELKNAP, INC.: University of Louisville Photographic Archives: Caufield & Shook Collection CS 73707. BELLE OF LOUISVILLE: University of Louisville Photographic Archives: Caufield & Shook Collection CS 133150. BENEDICT, JENNIE CARTER: University of Louisville Photographic Archives: Caufield & Shook Collection CS 40833. BICYCLING: University of Louisville Photographic Archives: R.G. Potter Collection. BIG FOUR BRIDGE: University of Louisville Photographic Archives: Photo by G.W. Finley, Jeffersonville, IN, 96.18.01. BILLY GOAT HILL: Filson Club Historical Society: Print Collection 995PR1. BINGHAM, GEORGE BARRY SR.: *The Courier-Journal* (Louisville) Photograph by Pam Spaulding. BLUE, THOMAS FOUNTAIN: University of Louisville Photographic Archives: Caufield & Shook Collection CS 79246. BOAT BUILDING: University of Louisville Photographic Archives: Howard Steamboat Museum Collection HSM 4. BONNYCASTLE: University of Louisville Photographic Archives: Herald-Post Collection 94.18.1074. BOURBON STOCK YARDS: University of Louisville Photographic Archives: Caufield & Shook Collection CS-O 50433. BOWMAN FIELD: University of Louisville Photographic Archives: Caufield & Shook Collection CS 106268. BOWMAN, ABRAM HITE: University of Louisville Photographic Archives: Herald-Post Collection 97.18.0136. BRENNAN HOUSE: Filson Club Historical Society: Brennan House Album. BREWING INDUSTRY: Filson Club Historical Society: Satellites of Mercury program, 1889. BRIDGES, AUTOMOBILE: University of Louisville Photographic Archives: Caufield & Shook Collection CS-O 119187. BRINLY-HARDY: University of Louisville Photographic Archives: Caufield & Shook Collection CS-O 7075. BROADWAY: University of Louisville Photographic Archives: Caufield & Shook Collection CS 112658. BROOKS, WILLIAM THOMAS: University of Louisville Photographic Archives: Royal Photo Collection R 12941. BROWNING, LOUIS ROGERS "PETE": University of Louisville Photographic Archives: R.G. Potter Collection P 1086. BUECHEL: Filson Club Historical Society: Post Card Collection. BURLESQUE: University of Louisville Photographic Archives: Royal Photo Studio Collection R 5809. BUTCHERTOWN: University of Louisville Photographic Archives: R.G. Potter Collection P 3541.

CABBAGE PATCH: University of Louisville Photographic Archives: Caufield & Shook Collection CS 224576. CAMP ZACHARY TAYLOR: University of Louisville Photographic Archives: Caufield & Shook Collection CS 29938. CARNEGIE LIBRARIES: University of Louisville Photographic Archives: Caufield & Shook Collection CS 79245. CARTER DRY GOODS CO.: University of Louisville Photographic Archives: Caufield & Shook Collection CS-O 43348. CAST-IRON ARCHITECTURE: Filson Club Historical Society: *Louisville Illustrated.* H.R. Page & Co., 1889. CATHEDRAL OF THE ASSUMPTION: Filson Club Historical Society: *Louisville Illustrated.* H.R. Page & Co., 1889. CAVE HILL CEMETERY: University of Louisville Photographic Archives: 85.32.08. CEDAR GROVE ACADEMY: University of Louisville Photographic Archives: Caufield & Shook Collection CS 71239. CEMENT INDUSTRY: Filson Club Historical Society: IDS-52. CENTRAL COLORED/MARY D. HILL SCHOOL: University of Louisville Photographic Archives: Herald-Post Collection 94.18.1013. CENTRAL HIGH SCHOOL: University of Louisville Photographic Archives: Caufield & Shook Collection CS 31943. CENTRAL STATE HOSPITAL: Filson Club Historical Society: 1889 Annual Report of the Central Kentucky Lunatic Asylum. CHECK'S CAFÉ: University of Louisville Photographic Archives: Caufield & Shook Collection CS 267880. CHENOWETH MASSACRE: Filson Club Historical Society: R.C. Ballard Thruston Collection TC-80. CHEROKEE-SENECA: University of Louisville Photographic Archives: R.G. Potter Collection P 1881. CHURCHILL DOWNS: Filson Club Historical Society: Stereo Card Collection 991PC57.6. CITY CHARTERS: Filson Club Historical Society: Oversize Photos. CITY HALL: Filson Club Historical Society: Louisville: Louisville Abstract and Loan Association, 1876. PBL-11. CIVIL WAR: *Sketches of Camp Boone.* C. Alfred Garrett and George H. Nickerson, Louisville: G.T. Shaw, 1860. Loaned by Dr. Ernest M. Ellison. CIVIL WAR FORTIFICATIONS: Filson Club Historical Society: Map Collection: Small map 976.9911/S613s. CLARK, GEORGE ROGERS: Filson Club Historical Society. CLIFTON: University of Louisville Photographic Archives: 95.16.01. COAL HOLE COVERS: University of Louisville Photographic Archives: Bill McBride Collection. COLUMBIA BUILD-

ING: University of Louisville Photographic Archives: Herald-Post Collection 94.18.0180. CONFEDERATE HOME: Filson Club Historical Society: Frederick Verhoeff Collection FHV119. CORN ISLAND: Filson Club Historical Society: R.C. Ballard Thruston Collection TC-558. COTTER, JOSEPH SEAMON: Western Branch, Louisville Free Public Library: Joseph Seamon Cotter Papers. COURIER-JOURNAL: Filson Club Historical Society. COURIER-JOURNAL BUILDING: Filson Club Historical Society: OCB-21. CREASON, JOE CROSS: *The Courier-Journal* (Louisville) Photograph by Bill Strode. CRESCENT HILL: University of Louisville Photographic Archives: Caufield & Shook Collection CS 37437.

DAIRIES: University of Louisville Photographic Archives: Oscar Ewing Dairy Collection 81.08.5. DAVIS, BRINTON BEAUREGARD: University of Louisville Photographic Archives: Brinton B. Davis Collection 91.40.20. DEMOCRATIC PARTY: University of Louisville Photographic Archives: Caufield & Shook Collection CS 38569. DEPARTMENT STORES: University of Louisville Photographic Archives: Caufield & Shook Collection 106252. DISTILLING: University of Louisville Photographic Archives: Caufield & Shook Collection CS 155589. DISTILLING: University of Louisville Photographic Archives: R.G. Potter Collection P 439. DOERR, J. HENRY: University of Louisville Photographic Archives: Gene Hilliard gift 86.11.01. DOUGLAS PARK RACE COURSE: University of Louisville Photographic Archives: R.G. Potter Collection P 6017. DU PONT MANUAL HIGH SCHOOL: Jefferson County Board of Education Archives.

ECLIPSE PARK: University of Louisville Photographic Archives: R.G. Potter Collection P 1609. EDISON, THOMAS ALVA: Filson Club Historical Society: R.C. Ballard Thruston Collection 196F. EPIDEMICS: University of Louisville Photographic Archives: Caufield & Shook Collection CS 24322. ETHRIDGE, WILLIE (SNOW): *The Courier-Journal* (Louisville).

FALLS OF THE OHIO: University of Louisville Photographic Archives: Caufield & Shook Collection CS 44302. FALLS OF THE OHIO: Filson Club Historical Society: Small Map collection 976.9911/F624. FARNSLEY, CHARLES: University of Louisville Photographic Archives: Lin Caufield Studio Collection 9/30/1948. FERRIES: University of Louisville Photographic Archives: Simmons Album 98.11.059. FIRST CHRISTIAN CHURCH: University of Louisville Photographic Archives: Caufield & Shook Collection CS 150107. FLOOD OF 1937: University of Louisville Photographic Archives: Caufield & Shook Collection CS 149479. FONTAINE FERRY PARK: University of Louisville Photographic Archives: R.G. Potter Collection P 3797.1. FORD MOTOR COMPANY: University of Louisville Photographic Archives: Caufield & Shook Collection CS 68174. FOSSILS: Dr. Ernest M. Ellison. FOSSILS AT THE FALLS OF THE OHIO: Dr. Ernest M. Ellison. FOURTEENTH STREET BRIDGE: Filson Club Historical Society: Photograph Collection. FOURTH STREET: University of Louisville Photographic Archives: Caufield & Shook Collection CS-O 8269. FRATERNAL ORGANIZATIONS: University of Louisville Photographic Archives: Brenner Albums 84.31.108. FURNITURE FACTORIES: *Edward's Fourth Annual Directory of the City of Louisville, 1868-1869.* Louisville: Southern Printing Co., 1868.

GALT HOUSE: *Art Work of Louisville.* Louisville, Charles Madison Co., 1897. GARDENS OF LOUISVILLE: Margaret Bridwell Art Library, University of Louisville: Brinton B. Davis Collection. GAST, ROBERT H.: Filson Club Historical Society: Robert H. Gast Collection 996PC21. GERMAN INSURANCE BANK: University of Louisville Photographic Archives: Caufield & Shook Collection CS 32174. GLASS INDUSTRY: *The Industries of Louisville and New Albany.* Louisville: J.M. Elstner & Co., 1886. Loaned by Martin Schmidt. GOLF: Filson Club Historical Society: R. C. Ballard Thruston Collection TC-510. GRACE HOPE PRESBYTERIAN CHURCH: University of Louisville Photographic Archives: Caufield & Shook Collection CS 70779. GRAND ARMY OF THE REPUBLIC ENCAMPMENT: Filson Club Historical Society: *Souvenir Sporting Guide.* Wentworth Publishing House, Printers, 1895. GRAND ARMY OF THE REPUBLIC ENCAMPMENT: University of Louisville Photographic Archives: Gift of Robin Cooper 77.13.118. GREAT DEPRESSION: Margaret Bourke-White/LIFE Magazine, copyright Time Inc. GREEKS: University of Louisville Photographic Archives: Caufield & Shook Collection CS 72509. GREGG, MARY HANSON "CISSY": *The Courier-Journal* (Louisville). GUTHRIE, JAMES: Filson Club Historical Society: 996PC29.

HA-WI-AN GARDENS: University of Louisville Photographic Archives: Caufield Shook Collection CS 62405. HADLEY, MARY ALICE HALE: *The Courier-Journal* [Louisville] Photograph by Cort Best. HALDEMAN, WALTER N.: Filson Club Historical Society: People File. HARRODS CREEK: University of Louisville Photographic Archives: Gift of Mrs. H.C. Riedling 82.35.3. HAYMARKET: University of Louisville Photographic Archives: *Herald-Post* Collection 94.18.1085. HENNING, SUE THORNTON: *The Courier-Journal.* (Louisville) Loaned by Ronald Van Stockum. HENRY VOGT MANUFACTURING COMPANY: University of Louisville Photographic Archives: R.G. Potter Collection P 2967. HIGHLAND PARK: University of Louisville Photographic Archives: Caufield & Shook Collection 46292. HILL, PATTY SMITH: Filson Club Historical Society: People File. HILLERICH & BRADSBY COMPANY: University of Louisville Photographic Archives: Hillerich & Bradsby Collection H&B 428. HOBBS, EDWARD DORSEY: Ekstrom Library Rare Books, University of Louisville: Nanine Hilliard Greene Collection, Album 2, plate 1. HOSPITALS: University of Louisville Photographic Archives: R.G. Potter Collection P 565. HOTELS: University of Louisville Photographic Archives: Caufield & Shook Collection CS-O 59629. HOTELS: University of Louisville Photographic Archives: Caufield & Shook Collection CS-O 152190. HOUSE OF REFUGE: Filson Club Historical Society: Louisville House of Refuge Annual Report for 1875. HOWARD SHIPYARDS AND DOCK COMPANY: University of Louisville Photographic Archives: Howard Steamboat Museum Collection HSM 184.

ICE COMPANIES: University of Louisville Photographic Archives: John Kleber Gift 89.36.3. ILLINOIS CENTRAL RAILROAD: University of Louisville Photographic Archives: Caufield & Shook Collection CS 38482. INDIANA ARMY AMMUNITION PLANT: University of Louisville Photographic Archives: Caufield & Shook Collection CS 239466. INTERSTATES AND EXPRESSWAYS: University of Louisville Photographic Archives: Struck Construction Co. Collection SCC 2083 (photo by *The Courier-Journal.*) INTERURBAN: University of Louisville Photographic Archives: James Calvert Collection 87.71.2. IRON FOUNDRIES: *Smith's Illustrated Business Directory of Louisville New Albany and Jeffersonville.* Louisville: Courier-Journal Job Printing, 1899. Loaned by Martin Schmidt. ITALIANS: University of Louisville Photographic Archives: Caufield & Shook Collection CS 70896.

JACOB, CHARLES D.: Filson Club Historical Society: 986PC32. JEFFERSONVILLE: University of Louisville Photographic Archives: R.G. Potter Collection P6035. JEWS: University of Louisville Photographic Archives: Jewish Hospital Collection 81.45.2. JOHNSON, LYMAN TEFFT: University of Louisville Photographic Archives: *Louisville Defender* Collection LD 3087. JOHNSTON, ANNIE FELLOWS: University of Louisville Photographic Archives: Kate Matthews Collection 80.24.38. JUG BANDS: University of Louisville Photographic Archives: Caufield & Shook Collection CS 139669.

KAUFMAN-STRAUS: University of Louisville Photographic Archives: Gift of Louisville Chamber of Commerce 82.15.131. KENTUCKY AND INDIANA BRIDGE: Filson Club Historical Society: BCO-39. KENTUCKY DERBY: University of Louisville Photographic Archives: Caufield & Shook Collection 187187. KENTUCKY SCHOOL FOR THE BLIND: University of Louisville Photographic Archives: Caufield & Shook Collection CS 41100. KENTUCKY STATE FAIR: University of Louisville Photographic Archives: Caufield & Shook Collection CS 51281. KING, ALFRED DANIEL WILLIAMS: University of Louisville Photographic Archives: *Louisville Defender* Collection 85.26.486. Photograph by *The Courier-Journal.*

L G & E ENERGY: University of Louisville Photographic Archives: *Herald-Post* Collection 94.18.0132. LABOR: University of Louisville

Photographic Archives: Caufield & Shook Collection CS 73856. LAKE LOUISVILLA: University of Louisville Photographic Archives: CS-O 74861. LEBANESE AND SYRIANS: Senator David Karem. LEVY BROTHERS: University of Louisville Photographic Archives: Royal Photo Studio Collection R 50876. LEWIS AND CLARK EXPEDITION: Filson Club Historical Society. LIEDERKRANZ SOCIETY: Filson Club Historical Society: Print Collection PR830.0002. LONG RUN BAPTIST CHURCH: Filson Club Historical Society: R.C. Ballard Thruston Collection TC553. LOUISVILLE & NASHVILLE RAILROAD COMPANY: University of Louisville Photographic Archives: Caufield & Shook Collection, CS 127935. LOUISVILLE AND NASHVILLE RAILROAD: University of Louisville Archives and Records Center: Louisville & Nashville Railroad Records #8326. LOUISVILLE AND PORTLAND CANAL: Filson Club Historical Society: 987PC35.8. LOUISVILLE ATHLETIC CLUB: Filson Club Historical Society: Frederick Verhoeff Collection FHV-114. LOUISVILLE BOARD OF TRADE: University of Louisville Photographic Archives: Caufield & Shook Collection CS-O 7015. LOUISVILLE COLONELS: University of Louisville Photographic Archives: R. G. Potter Collection P 81.5.5616. LOUISVILLE FIRE DEPARTMENT: University of Louisville Photographic Archives: Royal Photo Studio Collection R 50377. LOUISVILLE FREE PUBLIC LIBRARY: University of Louisville Photographic Archives: Louisville Free Public Library Collection 92.18.162. LOUISVILLE GIRLS' HIGH SCHOOL: University of Louisville Photographic Archives: Caufield & Shook Collection CS 6978-A. LOUISVILLE HOTEL: Filson Club Historical Society: Print Collection PR750.0057. LOUISVILLE INDUSTRIAL EXPOSITION: Filson Club Historical Society: Print Collection: PR400.0027. LOUISVILLE INTERNATIONAL AIRPORT: University of Louisville Photographic Archives: Lin Caufield Collection. LOUISVILLE MUNICIPAL COLLEGE: University of Louisville Photographic Archives: 79.59.25. LOUISVILLE POLICE DEPARTMENT: Loaned by Morton Childress. LOUISVILLE POLICE DEPARTMENT: University of Louisville Photographic Archives: R.G. Potter Collection P 709. LOUISVILLE SERVICE CLUB: Filson Club Historical Society: Louisville Service Club Collection 993PC45.42. LOUISVILLE SLUGGER: University of Louisville Photographic Archives: Royal Studio/Stern Bramson Collection R7222. LOUISVILLE WATER COMPANY: University of Louisville Photographic Archives: Jean Cody Collection 87.14.61.

MACAULEY'S THEATRE: University of Louisville Photographic Archives: Caufield & Shook Collection CS-O 250559. MADRID BALLROOM: University of Louisville Photographic Archives: Caufield & Shook Collection CS-O 109424. MAIN STREET: Filson Club Historical Society: Cased Images Collection AMB015. MALE-MANUAL HIGH SCHOOLS FOOTBALL RIVALRY: University of Louisville Photographic Archives: Sutcliffe Sporting Goods Collection. MAMMOTH LIFE AND ACCIDENT INSURANCE CO.: University of Louisville Archives and Records Center: Smith-McGill Family Papers. MANDOLIN ORCHESTRAS: Filson Club Historical Society: MSC-15. MAPS: Filson Club Historical Society: 917.3/H974. MARKET STREET: University of Louisville Photographic Archives: Caufield & Shook Collection CS-O 37630. MASONIC HOMES OF KENTUCKY: University of Louisville Photographic Archives: Caufield & Shook Collection CS 13885. MATTHEWS, KATE: University of Louisville Photographic Archives: Kate Matthews Collection 80.24.26. MAYOR, OFFICE OF: University of Louisville Photographic Archives: R.G. Potter Collection P 656. MCALPINE DAM AND LOCKS: University of Louisville Photographic Archives: Rick Simmons Album 98.11.055. MCHARRY, FRANCIS A. (FRANK): University of Louisville Photographic Archives: Estate of Bruce Mann 82.11.17. MEAT PACKING: Filson Club Historical Society: Print Collection PR010.0025. MENGEL COMPANY: Filson Club Historical Society: Satellites of Mercury program, 1889. METHODISTS: University of Louisville Photographic Archives: Caufield & Shook Collection CS 249505. MODJESKAS: University of Louisville Photographic Archives: R.G. Potter Collection P 3458. MOVIE THEATERS: University of Louisville Archives and Records Center: Smith-McGill Family Papers. MOVIE THEATERS: University of Louisville Photographic Archives: Royal Photo Studio Collection R 5196.07. MOVIE THEATERS: University of Louisville Photographic Archives: Caufield & Shook Collection CS 31965. MOVIE THEATERS: University of Louisville Photographic Archives: Caufield & Shook Collection CS 33416. MULBERRY HILL: Filson Club Historical Society: R.C. Ballard Thruston Collection. MUSIC: University of Louisville Photographic Archives: Royal Photo/Stern Bramson Collection 7070. MUSIC: University of Louisville Photographic Archives: R.G. Potter Collection 81.5.5291. MUSIC PUBLISHING: Filson Club Historical Society: Sheet Music Collection.

NEIGHBORHOOD HOUSE: University of Louisville Photographic Archives: Caufield & Shook Collection CS 39597. NEW ALBANY: University of Louisville Photographic Archives: Caufield & Shook Collection CS 44555. NEWCOMB, HORATIO DALTON: Filson Club Historical Society: Print Collection PR570.0015. NURSING: University of Louisville Photographic Archives: Caufield & Shook Collection CS 35051.

OLDHAM COUNTY: Filson Club Historical Society: Carolus Brenner Album 991PC10X. ORPHANAGES: University of Louisville Photographic Archives: Caufield & Shook Collection CS 83303. OVERVIEW *History of the Ohio Falls Cities and their Counties*. Cleveland: L.A. Williams, 1882. OVERVIEW: *History of the Ohio Falls Cities and their Counties*. Cleveland: L.A. Williams, 1882.

PALMER, BERTHA MATHILDE: Filson Club Historical Society: People File. PARKLAND: University of Louisville Photographic Archives: R.G. Potter Collection P 2407. PARKS: University of Louisville Photographic Archives: Will Bowers Collection 90.6.65. PARKS: University of Louisville Photographic Archives: H.C. Griswold Collection 79.26.98. PARKS: University of Louisville Photographic Archives: Caufield & Shook Collection CS-O 283799. PARKWAY FIELD: University of Louisville Photographic Archives: R.G. Potter Collection P 1339. PARKWAYS: University of Louisville Photographic Archives: Caufield & Shook Collection CS-O 4493. PEARSON'S FUNERAL HOME: Filson Club Historical Society: Print Collection PR10.0011. PEWEE VALLEY: University of Louisville Photographic Archives: Louisville & Nashville Railroad Collection 96.20.152. PHARMACY: University of Louisville Photographic Archives: Keiley Collection 90.15.01. PHOTOGRAPHY: Filson Club Historical Society: 994PC29. PIPE ORGANS: University of Louisville Photographic Archives: Caufield & Shook Collection CS 153593. POISONED WEDDING: *History of the Ohio Falls Cities and their Counties*. Cleveland: L.A. Williams, 1882. PONTOON BRIDGE: University of Louisville Photographic Archives: Caufield & Shook Collection CS-O 149543.5. PORTLAND: University of Louisville Photographic Archives: R.G. Potter Collection P 1528. POST OFFICES: University of Louisville Photographic Archives: *Herald-Post* Collection 94.18.0164. POST OFFICES: University of Louisville Photographic Archives: Caufield & Shook Collection CS 144420. POST OFFICES: University of Louisville Photographic Archives: Caufield & Shook Collection CS-O 6059. PRESBYTERIAN COMMUNITY CENTER: University of Louisville Archives and Records Center: Presbyterian Community Center Records. PRESBYTERIANS: University of Louisville Photographic Archives: Caufield & Shook Collection CS 123852. PRESTON STREET: University of Louisville Photographic Archives: Urban Renewal Commission Collection. PRESTON, WILLIAM: Filson Club Historical Society: 987PC8.4. PUBLIC HOUSING: University of Louisville Photographic Archives: Caufield & Shook Collection CS 283797.

QUARTERMASTER DEPOT: *The City of Louisville and Glimpse of Kentucky*. Louisville: Committee of Industrial and Commercial Improvement, 1887. Loaned by Martin Schmidt.

RAILROAD STATIONS: University of Louisville Photographic Archives: Caufield & Shook Collection CS-O 7010. RAILROAD STATIONS: University of Louisville Photographic Archives: Louisville & Nashville Railroad Collection 96.20.523. RAILROADS: *Louisville City Directory and Business Mirror*, 1858-59. Louisville: Hurd & Burrows, 1858. RED CROSS

HOSPITAL: University of Louisville Photographic Archives: Caufield & Shook Collection CS 29973. REPUBLICAN PARTY: University of Louisville Photographic Archives: James N. Keen Collection. RESTAURANTS: *Edward's Fourth Annual Directory of the City of Louisville, 1868-1869*. Louisville: Southern Printing Co., 1868. RICE, ALICE HEGAN: Filson Club Historical Society: People File. RIVERSIDE GARDENS: University of Louisville Photographic Archives: Caufield & Shook Collection CS 73001. RIVERSIDE, THE FARNSLEY-MOREMEN LANDING: Riverside, The Farnsley-Moremen Landing. ROSE ISLAND: University of Louisville Photographic Archives: Caufield & Shook Collection CS 73913. ROSSMORE APARTMENTS: University of Louisville Photographic Archives: Caufield & Shook Collection CS 278152. RUBBERTOWN: University of Louisville Archives and Records Center: Louisville Chamber of Commerce Records.

SANDERS, COL. HARLAND: KFC Corporation. SCULPTURE: Filson Club Historical Society: Robert Campbell Collection 990PC38.4. SECOND PRESBYTERIAN CHURCH: Second Presbyterian Church. SEMPLE, ELLEN CHURCHILL: Filson Club Historical Society: People File. SENNINGS PARK: University of Louisville Photographic Archives: R.G. Potter Collection P 5209. SHANTY-BOATS: Filson Club Historical Society: Print Collection 995PR1. SHELBYVILLE: Filson Club Historical Society: Otho Williams Collection 994PC17. SHIPPINGPORT: University of Louisville Photographic Archives: Caufield & Shook Collection CS 69941. SHOTGUN COTTAGES: University of Louisville Photographic Archives: Caufield & Shook Collection CS 39101. SILVER CREEK: University of Louisville Photographic Archives: Terhune Collection. SIMMONS UNIVERSITY: University of Louisville Archives and Records Center: Simmons College Records. SMOKETOWN: University of Louisville Photographic Archives: Caufield & Shook Collection CS 209916. SOCIAL SERVICES: University of Louisville Photographic Archives: Caufield & Shook Collection CS 36913. SOFT DRINKS AND MINERAL WATERS: University of Louisville Photographic Archives: Caufield & Shook Collection CS 112736. SOLGER'S CONFECTIONERY: University of Louisville Photographic Archives: R.G. Potter Collection P 4955. SOUTHERN BAPTIST THEOLOGICAL SEMINARY: University of Louisville Photographic Archives: R.G. Potter Collection 2832. SOUTHERN EXPOSITION: Filson Club Historical Society: Print Collection PR400.0026. SPALDING UNIVERSITY: Spalding University. SPEED, JAMES BRECKINRIDGE: Filson Club Historical Society: 990PC54. ST. JOSEPH'S CHILDREN'S HOME: University of Louisville Photographic Archives: Caufield & Shook Collection CS 176943. ST. MARTIN OF TOURS CATHOLIC CHURCH: University of Louisville Photographic Archives: R.G. Potter Collection P 339. ST. MATTHEWS: University of Louisville Photographic Archives: Lin Caufield Collection. ST. XAVIER HIGH SCHOOL: University of Louisville Photographic Archives: Caufield & Shook Collection CS-O 37430. STEAMBOATS: University of Louisville Photographic Archives: Joseph Krementz Collection 78.5.5B. STEAMBOATS: University of Louisville Photographic Archives: Caufield & Shook Collection CS 32638. STEWARTS DRY GOODS COMPANY: University of Louisville Photographic Archives: Caufield & Shook Collection CS 67820. STREETCARS: University of Louisville Photographic Archives: SG 81.27.3. STREETCARS: University of Louisville Photographic Archives: Caufield & Shook Collection CS 103250. STUBER, WILLIAM: *Smith's Illustrated Business Directory of Louisville, New Albany and Jeffersonville*. 1889-1890. Courier-Journal Job Printing and S.C. Smith, 1889. SWIMMING: University of Louisville Photographic Archives: Caufield & Shook Collection CS 181839.

TARASCON, LOUIS AND JOHN: University of Louisville Photographic Archives: Caufield & Shook Collection CS 73764. TAYLOR DRUG STORES: University of Louisville Photographic Archives: Caufield & Shook Collection CS 69760. TAYLOR, ZACHARY: Filson Club Historical Society: Print Collection PR 675.0392. TENNIS: Filson Club Historical Society: Vaughan Albums 986PC2. THE POINT: Filson Club Historical Society: Print Collection 995PR1. THE TEMPLE: University of Louisville Photographic Archives: Caufield & Shook Collection CS 125021. THEATER: University of Louisville Photographic Archives: Caufield & Shook Collection CS 40153. THEATER: University of Louisville Photographic Archives: Amphitheater Auditorium Collection 83.14.04. THOMPSON, DINNIE: Filson Club Historical Society: People File. TOBACCO: Filson Club Historical Society: Ryan-Hampton Collection 990PC32. TOBACCO: *The Industries of Louisville and New Albany*. Louisville: J.M. Elstner & Co., 1886. Loaned by Martin Schmidt. TORNADO OF 1890: University of Louisville Photographic Archives: Gift of Leonard Brecher 77.12.2. TURNERS/TURNVEREINS: University of Louisville Photographic Archives: R.G. Potter Collection P 81.5.5646. TYLER BLOCK: University of Louisville Photographic Archives: Caufield & Shook Collection CS 219767.

UNION STATION: University of Louisville Photographic Archives: Caufield & Shook Collection CS 145566. UNITED STATES MARINE HOSPITAL: University of Louisville Photographic Archives: Caufield & Shook Collection CS 42128. UNIVERSITY OF LOUISVILLE: University of Louisville Photographic Archives: Caufield & Shook Collection CS-O 52665. URSULINE ACADEMY OF THE IMMACULATE CONCEPTION: Ursuline Archives.

VIENNA BAKERY: University of Louisville Photographic Archives: R.G. Potter Collection P 3121. VOLUNTEERS OF AMERICA: University of Louisville Photographic Archives: R.G. Potter Collection P2431.

W.K. STEWART BOOKSTORE: University of Louisville Photographic Archives: Caufield & Shook Collection CS 79079. WALNUT STREET AFRICAN-AMERICAN BUSINESSES: University of Louisville Photographic Archives: Caufield & Shook Collection CS 217678. WALNUT STREET BAPTIST CHURCH: Loaned by James Calvert. WATTERSON EXPRESSWAY: University of Louisville Photographic Archives: Billy Davis Aerials Collection. WATTERSON, HENRY: University of Louisville Photographic Archives: SG 81.30.5. WAVERLY HILLS SANATORIUM: University of Louisville Photographic Archives: Caufield & Shook Collection CS 76031. WHITE CITY: University of Louisville Photographic Archives: R.G. Potter Collection P 5985. WHITESTONE, HENRY: University of Louisville Photographic Archives: Theodore Brown/Robert Doherty Collection 80.03.0025. WHITNEY, ROBERT SUTTON: University of Louisville Photographic Archives: Louisville Free Public Library Collection 92.18.371. Photograph by *The Courier-Journal*. WILDER PARK: Filson Club Historical Society PKL-1. WILLIAMS, ELIAS E.: Filson Club Historical Society: Cased Images Collection. WILLOUGHBY, LIVELY BURGESS: University of Louisville Photographic Archives: 92.29. WOMAN SUFFRAGE: University of Louisville Photographic Archives: Caufield & Shook Collection CS 33312B. WORKHOUSE: Filson Club Historical Society: Stereo Card Collection 991PC57.23. WORLD WAR I: University of Louisville Photographic Archives: 31:02. WORLD WAR II: University of Louisville Photographic Archives: Caufield & Shook Collection CS 188467. WORLD WAR II: University of Louisville Photographic Archives: Caufield & Shook Collection CS 201684. WYATT, WILSON: University of Louisville Photographic Archives: Robert Doherty Collection 81.19.4.

YANDELL, ENID: Filson Club Historical Society: Enid Yandell Collection 987PC57X.168.

Index

Note: Page numbers in boldface refer to main encyclopedia entries. Page numbers in italics refer to illustrations (but illustrations with articles are not indexed separately).